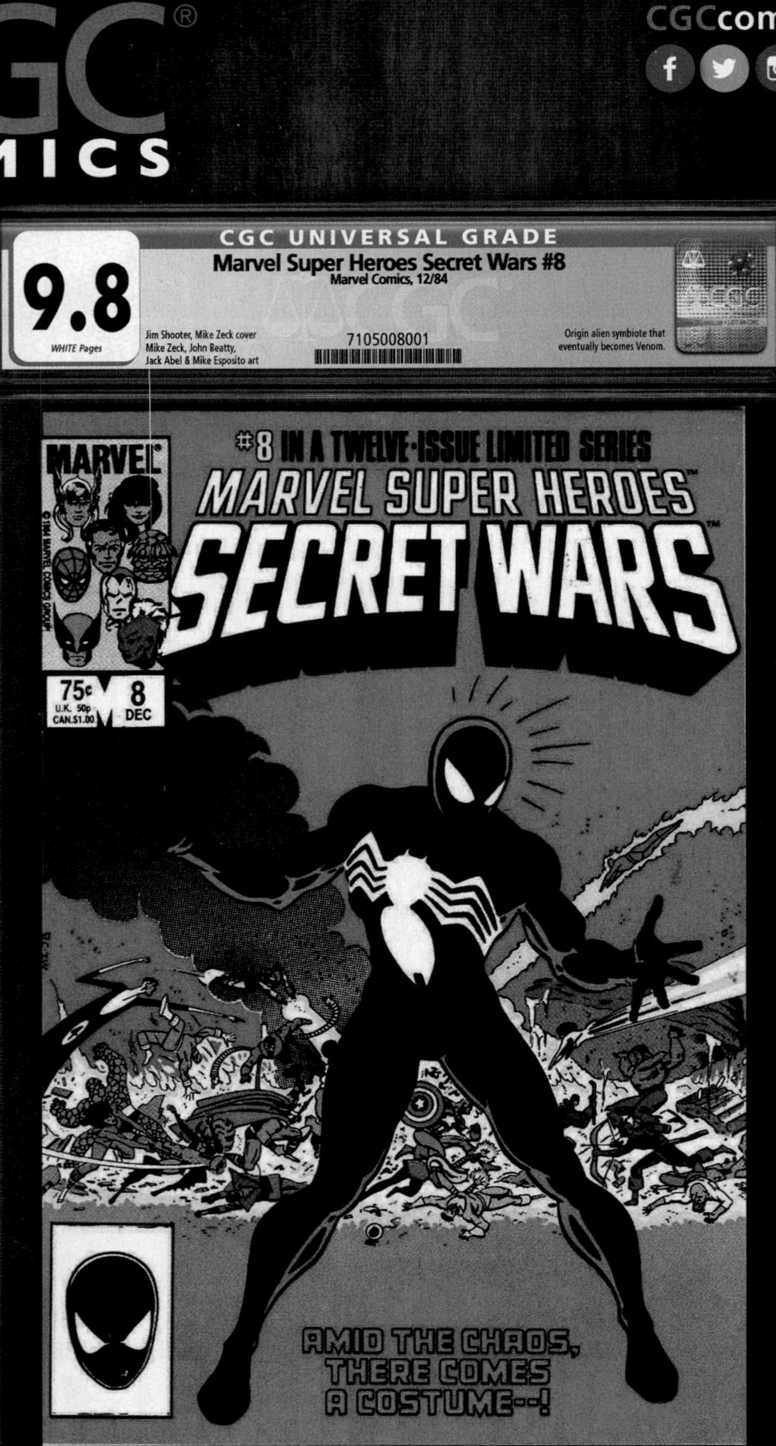

GC®
MICS

CGCcom

CGC UNIVERSAL GRADE

9.8

WHITE Pages

Marvel Super Heroes Secret Wars #8
Marvel Comics, 12/84

Jim Shooter, Mike Zeck cover
Mike Zeck, John Beatty,
Jack Abel & Mike Esposito art

7105008001

Origin alien symbiote that eventually becomes Venom.

#8 IN A TWELVE-ISSUE LIMITED SERIES

MARVEL®

MARVEL SUPER HEROES™

SECRET WARS™

© 1984 MARVEL COMICS GROUP

75¢ U.K. 50p CAN.$1.00 M 8 DEC

AMID THE CHAOS,
THERE COMES
A COSTUME--!

47TH EDITION

COMICS FROM THE 1500s–PRESENT INCLUDED
FULLY ILLUSTRATED CATALOGUE
& EVALUATION GUIDE

by ROBERT M. OVERSTREET

GEMSTONE PUBLISHING

Stephen A. Geppi, President & Chief Executive Officer
J.C. Vaughn, Vice-President of Publishing
Mark Huesman, Creative Director
Amanda Sheriff, Associate Editor
Carrie Wood, Assistant Editor
Braelynn Bowersox, Staff Writer
Mike Wilbur, Warehouse Operations • **Heather Winter**, Office Manager
Tom Garey, Kathy Weaver, Brett Canby, Angela Phillips-Mills, Accounting Services

SPECIAL CONTRIBUTORS TO THIS EDITION

Robert L. Beerbohm • Dr. Arnold T. Blumberg • Braelynn Bowersox • Ed Catto • Gene Gonzales • Jon McClure
Richard D. Olson, Ph.D. • Hans K. Pedersen • Amanda Sheriff • J.C. Vaughn • Mark Wheatley • Carrie Wood

SPECIAL ADVISORS TO THIS EDITION

Darren Adams • Grant Adey • Bill Alexander • David T. Alexander • Tyler Alexander • Lon Allen • Dave Anderson
David J. Anderson, DDS • Matt Ballesteros • L.E. Becker • Robert L. Beerbohm • Jim Berry • Tim Bildhauser
Peter Bilelis • Steve Borock • Scott Braden • Richard M. Brown • Shawn Caffrey • Brett Carreras • Charles Cerrito
Jeff Carreto • Paul Clairmont • Art Cloos • Bill Cole • Ashley Cotter-Cairns • Jesse James Criscione • Frank Cwiklik
Brock Dickinson • Gary Dolgoff • John Dolmayan • Ken Dyber • Daniel Ertle • D'Arcy Farrell • Bill Fidyk
Paul M. Figura • Joseph Fiore • Stephen Fishler • Dan Fogel • John Foster • Dan Gallo • Steve Geppi • Douglas Gillock
Dawn Gomez • Sean Goodrich • Tom Gordon III • Andy Greenham • Eric J. Groves • Terry Hoknes • Greg Holland
Steven Houston • Jeff Itkin • Nick Katradis • Ivan Kocmarek • Robert Krause • Ben Labonog • Ben Lichtenstein
Stephen Lipson • Paul Litch • Doug Mabry • Jon McClure • Todd McDevitt • Mike McKenzie • Steve Mortensen
Marc Nathan • Josh Nathanson • Tom Nelson • Jamie Newbold • Terry O'Neill • Michael Pavlic • Bill Ponseti
Mick Rabin • Jeff Rader • Yolanda Ramirez • Alex Reece • Greg Reece • Rob Reynolds • Stephen Ritter
Barry Sandoval • Matt Schiffman • Dylan Schwartz • Alika Seki • Todd Sheffer • Frank Simmons • Marc Sims
Lauren Sisselman • Tony Starks• West Stephan • Al Stoltz • Doug Sulipa • Maggie Thompson • Michael Tierney
Ted VanLiew • Jason Versaggi • Frank Verzyl • John Verzyl • Rose Verzyl • Mike Wilbur • Harley Yee • Vincent Zurzolo, Jr.

See a full list of Overstreet Advisors on pages 1216-1220

NOTICE: Values for items pictured in this book are based on author's experience, consultations with a network of advisors including collectors specializing in various categories, and actual prices realized for specific items sold through private sales and auctions. The values offered in this book are approximations influenced by many factors including condition, rarity and demand, and they should serve as only guidelines, presenting an average range of what one might expect to pay for the items. In the marketplace, knowledge and opinions held by both sellers and buyers determine prices asked and prices paid. This is not a price list of items for sale or items wanted by the author or publisher. The author and the publisher shall not be held responsible for losses that may occur in the purchase, sale or other transaction of property because of information contained herein. Efforts have been made to present accurate information, but the possibility of error exists. Readers who believe that have discovered an error are invited to mail corrective information to the author, Robert M. Overstreet, at Gemstone Publishing, 1940 Greenspring Dr., Suite I, Timonium, MD 21093. Verified corrections will be incorporated into future editions of this book.

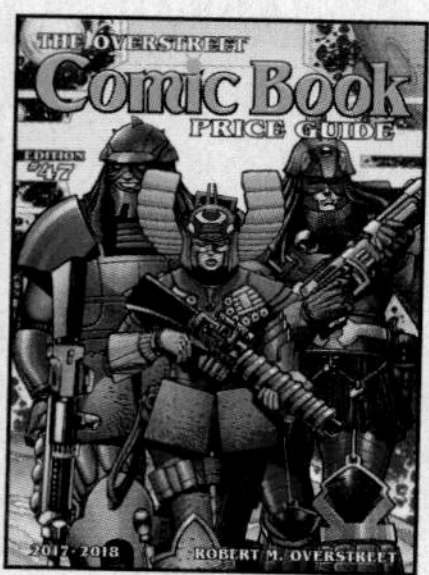

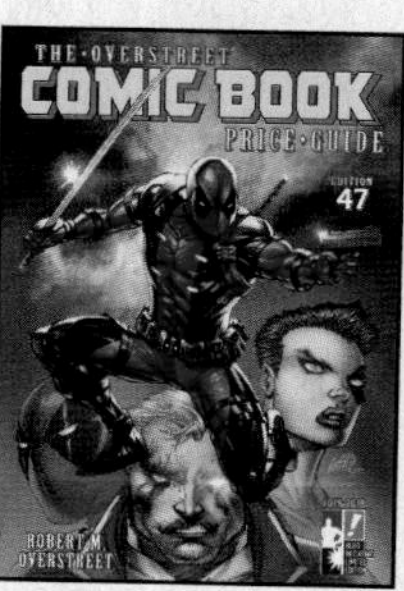

Batman: Art and colors by Jim Steranko. Batman TM & ©2017 DC Comics. Used by permission. All rights reserved.

Rom: Art and colors by Gabriel Rodríguez. HASBRO and its logo and ROM are trademarks of Hasbro and are used with permission. ©2017 Hasbro. All Rights Reserved.

Star Slammers: Art by Walt Simonson and colors by Len O'Grady. Star Slammers and related characters ©2017 Walt Simonson. Used by permission. All rights reserved.

Hero Initiative: Art by Rob Liefeld and colors by Ivan Nunes. Deadpool, Cable and Domino ©2017 MARVEL.

Overstreet® is a Registered Trademark of Gemstone Publishing, Inc.

Batman Hardcover Edition ISBN: 978-1-60360-208-2
Batman Soft Cover Edition ISBN: 978-1-60360-209-9

Rom Hardcover Edition ISBN: 978-1-60360-210-5
Rom Soft Cover Edition ISBN: 978-1-60360-211-2

Star Slammers Hardcover Edition ISBN: 978-1-60360-212-9
Star Slammers Soft Cover Edition ISBN: 978-1-60360-213-6

Deadpool - Hero Initiative Hardcover Edition ISBN: 978-1-60360-215-0

Printed in the United States of America

10 9 8 7 6 5 4 3 2 1

Forty-Seventh Edition: July 2017

TABLE OF CONTENTS

ACKNOWLEDGEMENTS

It's another superb, eclectic year for our covers! The legendary Jim Steranko provided our great Batman piece and we're very pleased to add him to our roster. Likewise, *Locke & Key*'s Gabriel Rodriguez outdid himself on our ROM cover. Walter Simonson (with colorist Len O'Grady) provided our second Hall of Fame cover featuring his Star Slammers. The Hero Initiative cover features Deadpool (with Cable and Domino) by creator Rob Liefeld (with colorist Ivan Nunes), and the Big, Big edition features Billy Tucci's take on The Tick, inspired by Normal Rockwell no less, and colored by Brian Miller of Hi-Fi.

Special thanks to Gemstone's own Mark Huesman, J.C. Vaughn, Amanda Sheriff, Mike Wilbur, Carrie Wood and Braelynn Bowersox.

Special Thanks to the Overstreet Advisors who contributed to this edition, including Darren Adams, Grant Adey, Bill Alexander, David T. Alexander, Tyler Alexander, Lon Allen, Dave Anderson, David J. Anderson, DDS, Matt Ballesteros, L.E. Becker, Robert L. Beerbohm, Jim Berry, Tim Bildhauser, Peter Bilelis, Dr. Arnold T. Blumberg, Steve Borock, Scott Braden, Richard M. Brown, Shawn Caffrey, Mike Carbonaro, Brett Carreras, Charles & Jeff Cerrito, Paul Clairmont, Art Cloos, Bill Cole, Ashley Cotter-Cairns, Jesse James Criscione, Frank Cwiklik, Brock Dickinson, Gary Dolgoff, John Dolmayan, Ken Dyber, Daniel Ertle, D'Arcy Farrell, Bill Fidyk, Paul M. Figura, Joseph Fiore, Stephen Fishler, Dan Fogel, John Foster, Dan Gallo, Steve Geppi, Douglas Gillock, Dawn Gomez, Sean Goodrich, Tom Gordon III, Andy Greenham, Eric J. Groves, Jim Halperin, Rick Hirsch, Terry Hoknes, Greg Holland, Steven Houston, Jeff Itkin, Nick Katradis, Ivan Kocmarek, Robert Krause, Ben Labonog, Ben Lichtenstein, Stephen Lipson, Paul Litch, Doug Mabry, Jon McClure, Todd McDevitt, Mike McKenzie, Steve Mortensen, Marc Nathan, Josh Nathanson, Tom Nelson, Jamie Newbold, Terry O'Neill, Michael Pavlic, Bill Ponseti, Mick Rabin, Jeff Rader, Yolanda Ramirez, Alex Reece, Greg Reece, Rob Reynolds, Stephen & Sharon Ritter, Barry Sandoval, Matt Schiffman, Dylan Schwartz, Alika Seki, Todd Sheffer, Frank Simmons, Marc Sims, Lauren Sisselman, Tony Starks, West Stephan, Al Stoltz, Doug Sulipa, Maggie Thompson, Michael Tierney, Ted VanLiew, Jason Versaggi, Frank Verzyl, John Verzyl, Rose Verzyl, Eddie Wendt, Mike Wilbur, Harley Yee, Vincent Zurzolo, Jr., as well as to our additional contributors, including Stephen Baer, Jonathan Bennett, Mike Bromberg, Dr. Jonathan Calure, Paul Howley, Roger Kevan, Jason Lohr, Rod Matlack, Bill Parker, and Kevin Poling. Without their active participation, this project would not have been possible.

Additionally, I would like to personally extend my thanks to all of those who encouraged and supported first the creation of and then subsequently the expansion of the Guide over the past four decades. While it's impossible in this brief space to individually acknowledge every individual, mention is certainly due to Lon Allen (Golden Age data), Mark Arnold (Harvey data), Larry Bigman (Frazetta-Williamson data), Bill Blackbeard (Platinum Age cover photos), Steve Borock and Mark Haspel (Grading), Glenn Bray (Kurtzman data), Gary M. Carter (DC data), J. B. Clifford Jr. (EC data), Gary Coddington (Superman data), Gary Colabuono (Golden Age ashcan data), Wilt Conine (Fawcett data), Chris Cormier (Miracleman data), Dr. S. M. Davidson (Cupples & Leon data), Al Dellinges (Kubert data), Stephen Fishler (10-Point Grading system), Chris Friesen (Glossary additions), David Gerstein (Walt Disney Comics data), Kevin Hancer (Tarzan data), Charles Heffelfinger and Jim Ivey (March of Comics listing), R. C. Holland and Ron Pussell (*Seduction* and *Parade of Pleasure* data), Grant Irwin (Quality data), Richard Kravitz (Kelly data), Phil Levine (giveaway data), Paul Litch (Copper & Modern Age data), Dan Malan & Charles Heffelfinger (Classic Comics data), Jon McClure (Whitman data), Fred Nardelli (Frazetta data), Michelle Nolan (Love comics), Mike Nolan (MLJ, Timely, Nedor data), George Olshevsky (Timely data), Dr. Richard Olson (Grading and Yellow Kid info), Chris Pedrin (DC War data), Scott Pell ('50s data), Greg Robertson (National data), Don Rosa (Late 1940s to 1950s data), Matt Schiffman (Bronze Age data), Frank Scigliano (Little Lulu data), Gene Seger (Buck Rogers data), Rick Sloane (Archie data), David R. Smith, Archivist, Walt Disney Productions (Disney data), Bill Spicer and Zetta DeVoe (Western Publishing Co. data), Tony Starks (Silver and Bronze Age data), Al Stoltz (Golden Age & Promo data), Doug Sulipa (Bronze Age data), Don and Maggie Thompson (Four Color listing), Mike Tiefenbacher & Jerry Sinkovec (Atlas and National data), Raymond True & Philip J. Gaudino (Classic Comics data), Jim Vadeboncoeur Jr. (Williamson and Atlas data), Richard Samuel West (Victorian Age and Platinum Age data), Kim Weston (Disney and Barks data), Cat Yronwode (Spirit data), Andrew Zerbe and Gary Behymer (M. E. data).

A special thanks, as always, to my wife Caroline, for her encouragement and support on such a tremendous project, and to all who placed ads in this edition.

CGC
Comics Registry
This award is presented to
Doug Schmell
Achievement in
Comics Collecting 2006
Captain Tripps

CGC
Comics Guaranty, LLC
Charter Member Dealer

Sales Reporting Partner
GPAnalysis

EXPERIENCE THE WORLD OF
RIVERDALE®
Pop's
CHOCK'LIT SHOPPE

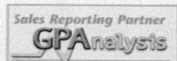

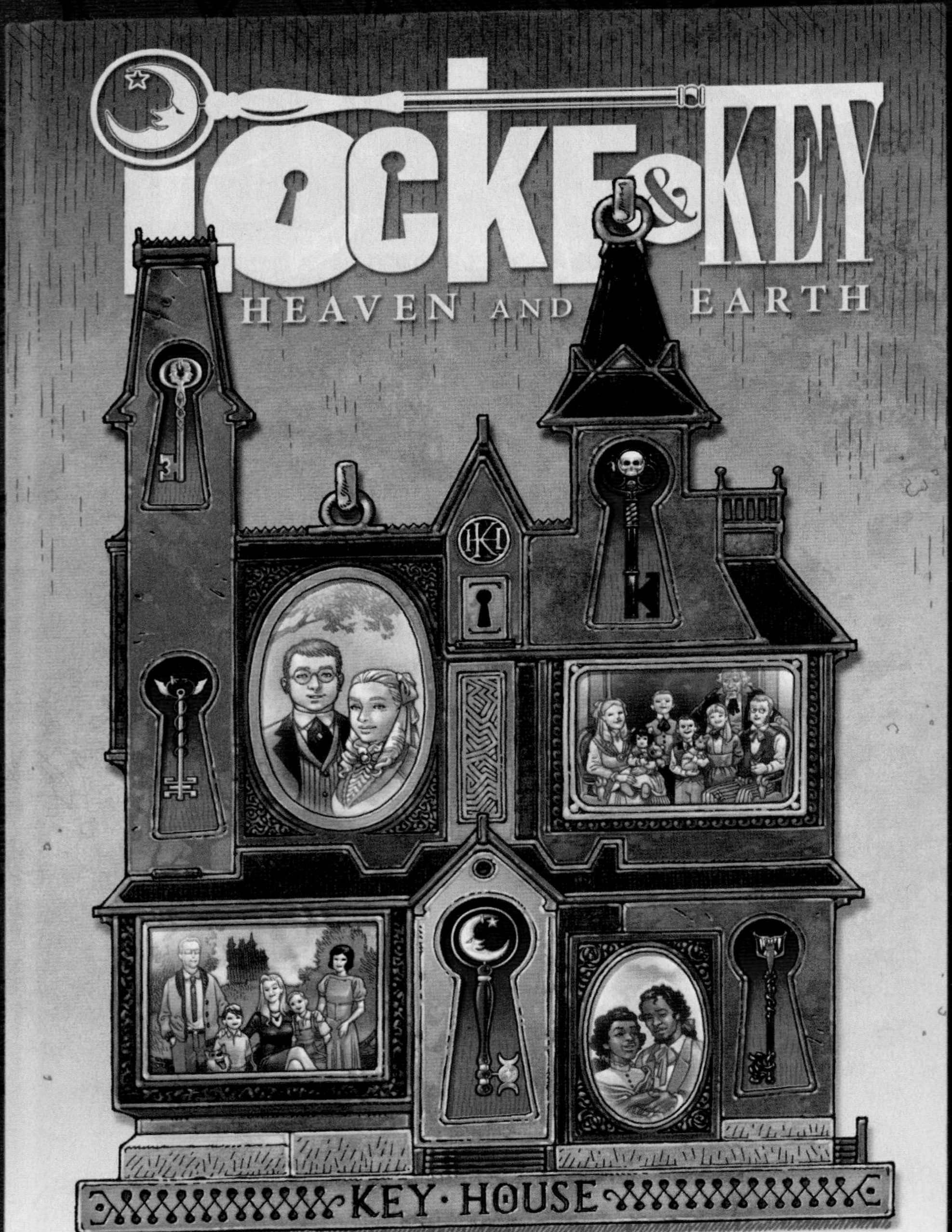

LOCKE & KEY

HEAVEN AND EARTH

KEY · HOUSE

JOE HILL • GABRIEL RODRIGUEZ

A SPECIAL DELUXE COLLECTION FEATURING THE LONG-SOLD-OUT ONE-SHOTS "OPEN THE MOON," AND "GRINDHOUSE," PLUS THE HARD-TO-FIND IDW 10TH ANNIVERSARY "IN THE CAN!" TALE, AND MORE!

JULY 2017
JOE HILL (W) • GABRIEL RODRIGUEZ (A & C)
FULL COLOR • 72 PAGES • $14.99 • ISBN: 978-1-68405-181-6

WWW.IDWPUBLISHING.COM

CBCScomics.com

727-803-6822

Startling Comics #49

Off-White/White

17-0A38DDC-007

Nedor, 1/1948

Cover: Alex Schomburg

Art: Hal Sherman & Ken Battefield

Story: Joe Greene

Classic robot cover.

Featuring LANCE LEWIS, Space Detective

ANC

STARTLING COMICS

10¢

JAN

No. 49

XELA

The choice is *Crystal Clear!*

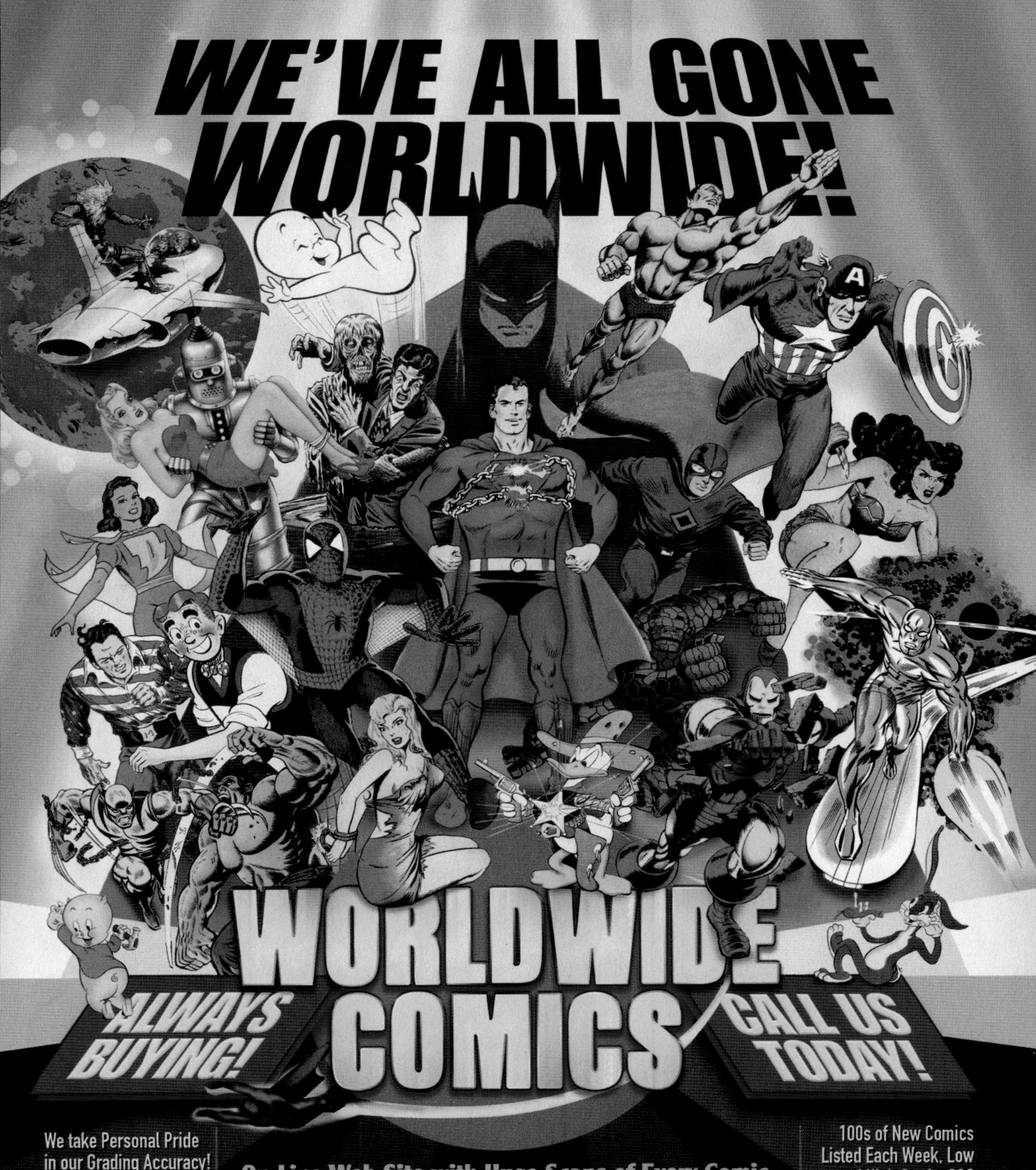

WE'VE ALL GONE WORLDWIDE!
WORLDWIDE COMICS
ALWAYS BUYING!
CALL US TODAY!

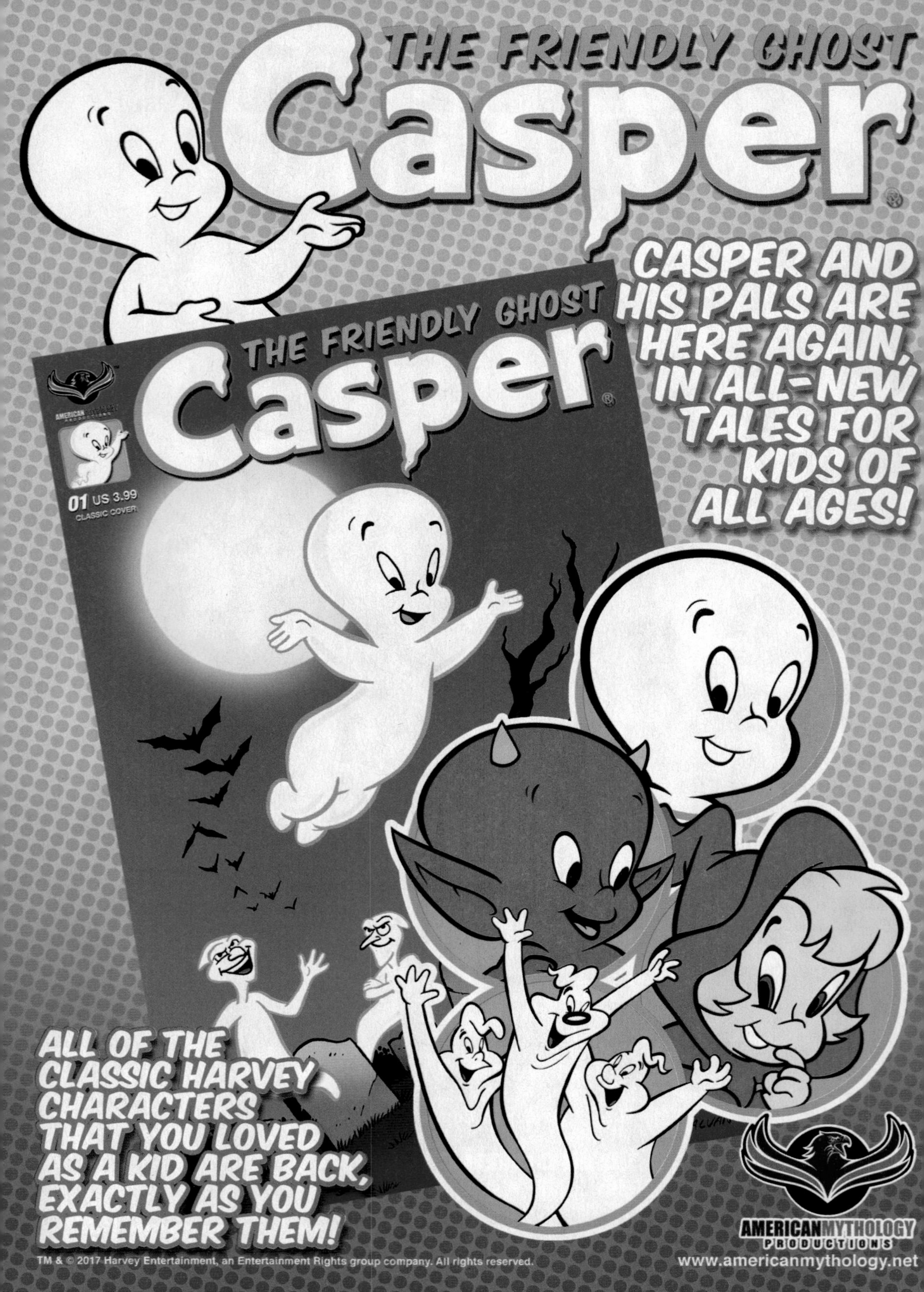
THE FRIENDLY GHOST
Casper
CASPER AND HIS PALS ARE HERE AGAIN, IN ALL-NEW TALES FOR KIDS OF ALL AGES!
THE FRIENDLY GHOST
Casper
01 US 3.99
CLASSIC COVER
ALL OF THE CLASSIC HARVEY CHARACTERS THAT YOU LOVED AS A KID ARE BACK, EXACTLY AS YOU REMEMBER THEM!
AMERICAN MYTHOLOGY
PRODUCTIONS
www.americanmythology.net

The Apex
of Elegance
and Class
ALEX RAYMOND

THE INCREDIBLE HULK
AT LAST! DOCTOR DOOM!
BATMAN
TEEN TITANS
NO ONE LAYS A HAND ON MY SON WHILE I LIVE!
PUNISH NOT MY EVIL SON!

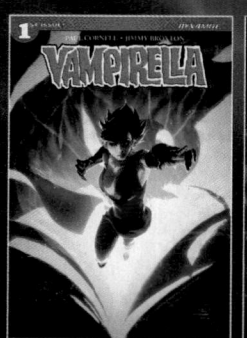

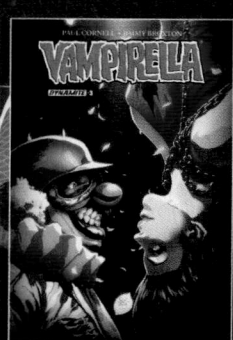

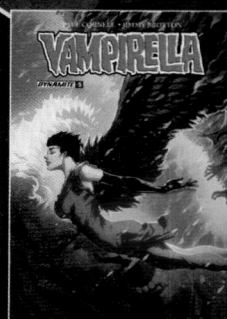

EsquireComics.com™

SPECIALIZING IN BUYING/SELLING
HIGH GRADE AND KEY ISSUES OF
PLATINUM, GOLDEN & SILVER AGE
BOOKS FROM 1930-1963

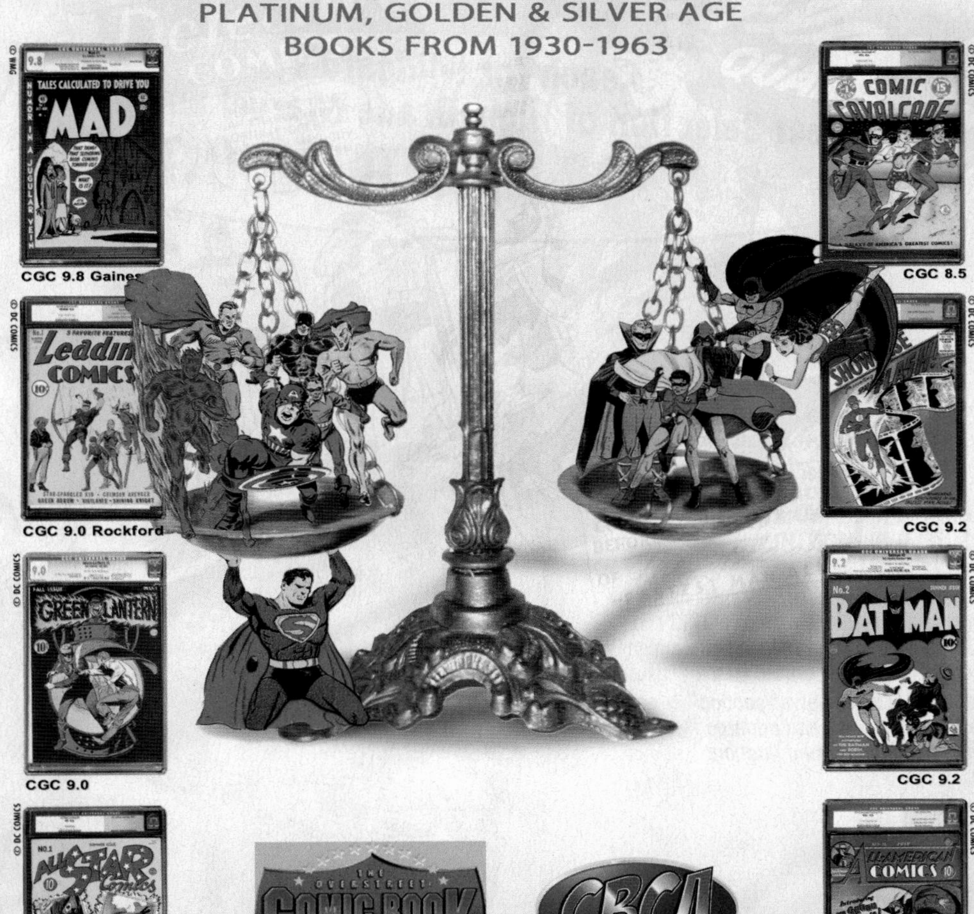

CGC 8.0

CGC 4.5

THE OVERSTREET COMIC BOOK ADVISOR

CBCA ComicCollecting.org

*All books displayed are part of past or current inventory

MARK S. ZAID, ESQ. • ESQUIRECOMICS.COM
P.O. BOX 342-492 • BETHESDA, MARYLAND 20827-2492 • (202) 498-0011
ESQUIRECOMICS@AOL.COM • WWW.ESQUIRECOMICS.COM

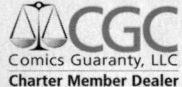

COMING THIS JULY FROM NEW YORK TIMES BEST-SELLING AUTHOR MICKY NEILSON AND ARTIST JASON JOHNSON

A - Blu Ray Homage
by Yvel Guichet/Carlos Eduardo
Standard Intermixed 1:1

B - Movie Poster Homage
by Anton Kokorev
Standard Intermixed 1:1

C - Painted Werewolf Queen
by Yvel Guichet
Retailer Incentive 1:5

D - Wolf by
BILL SIENKIEWICZ
Ultra-Rare 1:20
Retailer Incentive

PASSION for COLLECTING...

When it comes to passion for collecting, dedication to the hobby, and amassing high-grade, award winning runs... few measure up to Pedigree Comics' CEO and President, Doug Schmell, who sold his personal collection of Silver Age Marvels in 2012 for over 3.94 Million Dollars (a record price for a comic book collection).

So, who is best qualified to help you build your collection and find you the books and upgrades you need?

Over the past 20 plus years, I have amassed over fifteen thousand Marvel comic books, most of which are in very high grade condition. When CGC was in the process of forming in March, 1999, I was one of a handful of collectors asked to attend their start-up meeting and provide input to the creation of this third party grading service. When the CGC commenced operations later that year and began encapsulating and grading comic books for the public, I began submitting my runs of Marvel titles. Now, known as "Captain Tripps" on the CGC Registry and chat boards, I have come to be recognized as one of the leading collectors of Marvel Silver and Bronze Age comics, with many of my books being the highest graded copies in existence. In fact, I received the coveted Achievement in Comics Collecting 2006, awarded by the CGC Comics Registry, in honor of the outstanding runs of Marvel comics I had registered since November, 2003, including the highest graded set of virtually every Marvel Silver Age and Bronze Age title.

Although I sold the majority of my Bronze Age titles when I moved to Florida in 2004, I kept and continued to add to my Silver Age sets, looking for upgrades on any individual issue whenever possible. The formation of this collection, which has been painstakingly pared down to around 700 books, took an incredible amount of effort, time, expense, and patience. The stories I could tell of meeting at diners, post offices in Northern New Jersey, law offices, street corners in New York City, dealers' tables, and comic stores around the country in order to obtain that missing issue or coveted upgrade, would blow your mind. My decision to sell the collection was based on my feeling that I had reached a sort of collector's Nirvana, that I had finally obtained every sought after pedigreed issue or top of the CGC census book I could possibly find. The long journey has taken me to this point in time and I couldn't be any happier.

Let me help you find the same fulfillment I have!
Email me at dougschmell@pedigreecomics.com
or call me today at 1-561-422-1120.

PedigreeComics.com

MOUNTAIN MAN
COMICS
WE PAY CA$H FOR COMIC$
BUY, SELL AND CONSIGN COMICS SINCE 1990
WE SPECIALIZE IN GETTING YOU TOP DOLLAR FOR YOUR COLLECTION
1000's OF RAW AND SLABBED COMICS, ORIGINAL ART, TOYS AND STATUES
MONTHLY SUBSCRIPTION SERVICES
WHERE ARE WE LOCATED?
Between Atlanta and Chattanooga
771-B East Main Street, Blue Ridge, GA 30513
CALL US NOW!
706-946-4400
MOUNTAINMANCOMICS.COM
info@mountainmancomics.com

PROTECT YOUR COMICS
MARVEL COMICS GROUP
THE AMAZING SPIDER-MAN
THE PUNISHER!
BATMAN MAGAZINE
MARVEL COMICS GROUP
THE INCREDIBLE HULK
AND NOW THE WOLVERINE!
FANTASTIC FOUR
THE COMING OF GALACTUS!
THE PHANTOM
BOOM-BOOM
PHANTOM CALLS... WATCH FOR TROUBLE...
100 EXTRA CLEAR COMIC BAGS

FIRST COMICS NEWS

FROM THE WORLD'S GREATEST SUPERHEROES

TO THE MOST PITIFUL

WE COVER ALL THE SECRETS WITH AN INDEPENDENT SPIRIT

MAN, I LOVE ALL COMICS!...
& ORIGINAL COMIC ART TOO!
The 'DOLGOFF-WAREHOUSE'... 800,000+ COMICS IN STOCK!
...and GROWING!
SUPERMAN
CAPTAIN AMERICA
HULK
AVENGERS
GREEN LANTERN
Fantastic Four
THE NEW MUTANTS

HAS THERE EVER BEEN A BETTER TIME TO BE A *COMIC BOOK FAN?*
WITH COMIC BOOK-INSPIRED MOVIES, TV SHOWS AND VIDEO GAMES, MORE PEOPLE THAN EVER ARE *DISCOVERING* THE CHARACTERS AND STORIES WE LOVE!

THAT'S *COOL* BECAUSE AS *GREAT* AS MANY OF THE OTHER INCARNATIONS HAVE BEEN, COMICS STILL DO IT *BEST*!

"BUT CHANCES ARE THAT IF YOU'RE READING *THIS* BOOK, YOU ALREADY *LOVE* COMICS OR KNOW SOMEONE WHO DOES."

"IN JUST A MOMENT, WE'LL GET DOWN TO *BASICS*..."

WE HOPE YOU'LL FIND THIS BOOK TO BE A SUPERB REFERENCE, NO MATTER WHAT TYPE OF COMICS YOU LIKE.

OUR *MARKET REPORTS* START ON PAGE 89, AND THEY OFFER THE INSIGHT OF THE *OVERSTREET ADVISORS* ABOUT BACK ISSUE SALES...
AND WE HAVE TONS OF PRICING DATA, TOP COMICS, GRADING TIPS, AND MORE!

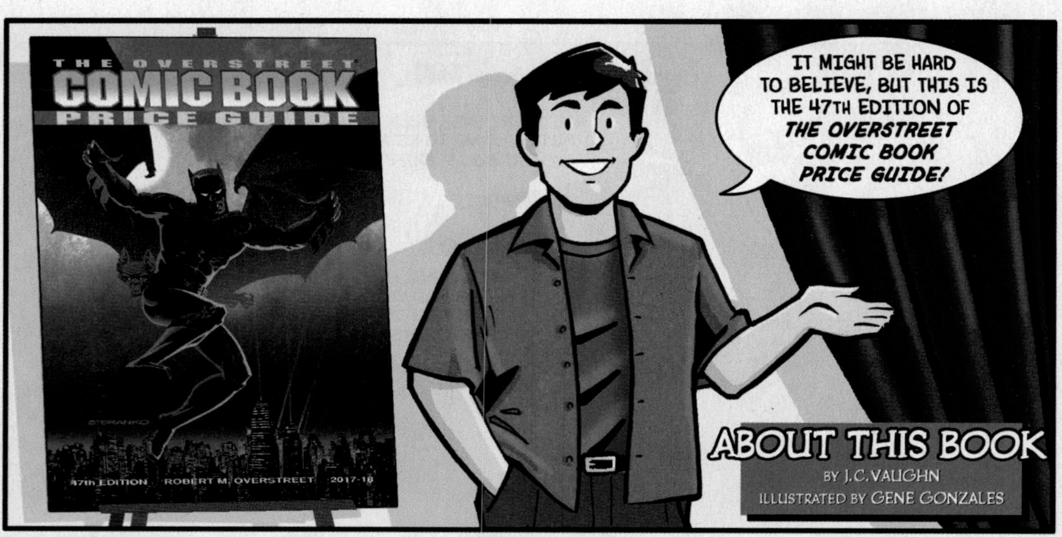
THE OVERSTREET COMIC BOOK PRICE GUIDE
47th EDITION ROBERT M. OVERSTREET 2017-18
IT MIGHT BE HARD TO BELIEVE, BUT THIS IS THE 47TH EDITION OF *THE OVERSTREET COMIC BOOK PRICE GUIDE!*
ABOUT THIS BOOK
BY J.C. VAUGHN
ILLUSTRATED BY GENE GONZALES

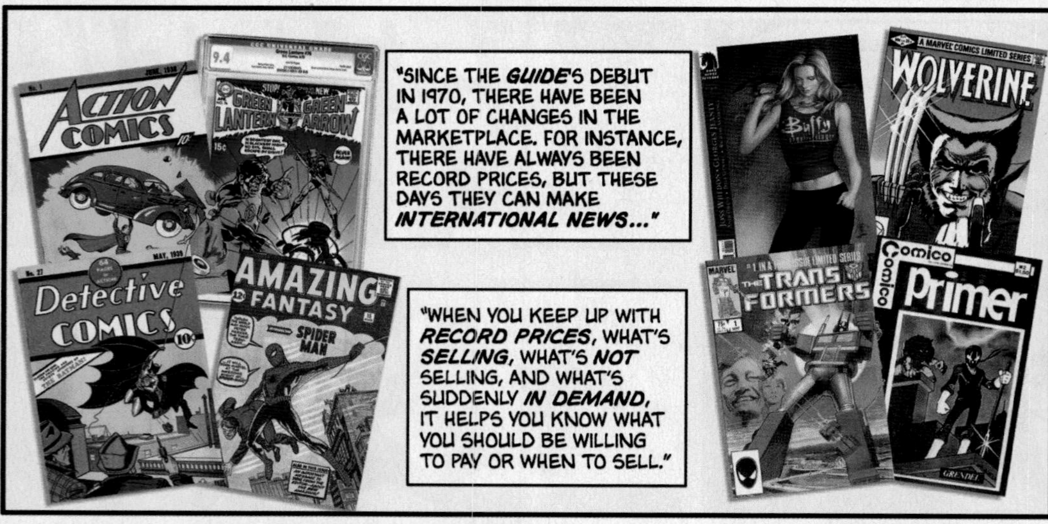
"SINCE THE *GUIDE*'S DEBUT IN 1970, THERE HAVE BEEN A LOT OF CHANGES IN THE MARKETPLACE. FOR INSTANCE, THERE HAVE ALWAYS BEEN RECORD PRICES, BUT THESE DAYS THEY CAN MAKE *INTERNATIONAL NEWS...*"
"WHEN YOU KEEP UP WITH *RECORD PRICES*, WHAT'S *SELLING*, WHAT'S *NOT* SELLING, AND WHAT'S SUDDENLY *IN DEMAND*, IT HELPS YOU KNOW WHAT YOU SHOULD BE WILLING TO PAY OR WHEN TO SELL."
ACTION COMICS
GREEN LANTERN GREEN ARROW
Detective COMICS
AMAZING FANTASY
SPIDER MAN
Buffy
WOLVERINE
THE TRANSFORMERS
Comico
Primer

AND THERE HAVE BEEN LOTS OF OTHER CHANGES, TOO. WE'VE BEEN STUDYING THIS FOR *FOUR DECADES* NOW AND ONE THING IS REALLY CLEAR...

THE MORE YOU *KNOW* ABOUT COMICS, THE MORE YOU *WANT* TO KNOW. AND WE'VE BEEN HAPPY TO HELP PEOPLE LEARN FOR *47 YEARS*.

ONE OF THE COOL THINGS ABOUT COMIC BOOKS IS THAT THERE ARE LOTS OF NEW ONES TO DISCOVER...

AND THERE ARE LITERALLY HUNDREDS OF THOUSANDS OF DIFFERENT BACK ISSUES, TOO!

BACK ISSUE COMICS RANGE FROM LESS THAN COVER PRICE TO **$3,207,852.**
A COMIC BOOK FOR ***$3.2 MILLION?*** HARD TO BELIEVE, HUH?

THE FIRST COMIC TO HIT $1 MILLION WAS ***ACTION COMICS*** #1, THE FIRST APPEARANCE OF ***SUPERMAN***.
THE SECOND, JUST A FEW DAYS LATER, WAS ***DETECTIVE COMICS*** #27, THE FIRST APPEARANCE OF ***BATMAN***.
ANOTHER ACTION #1 SOLD FOR ***$1.5 MILLION*** JUST A SHORT WHILE AFTER THAT.

MANY OTHERS HAVE SOLD FOR RECORD PRICES IN THE LAST FEW YEARS, EVEN WITH THE TOUGH ECONOMY NATIONALLY.

THE GRADE AND SCARCITY OF THE ISSUES HAVE A LOT TO DO WITH THAT. WE'LL GET INTO THAT IN JUST A BIT...

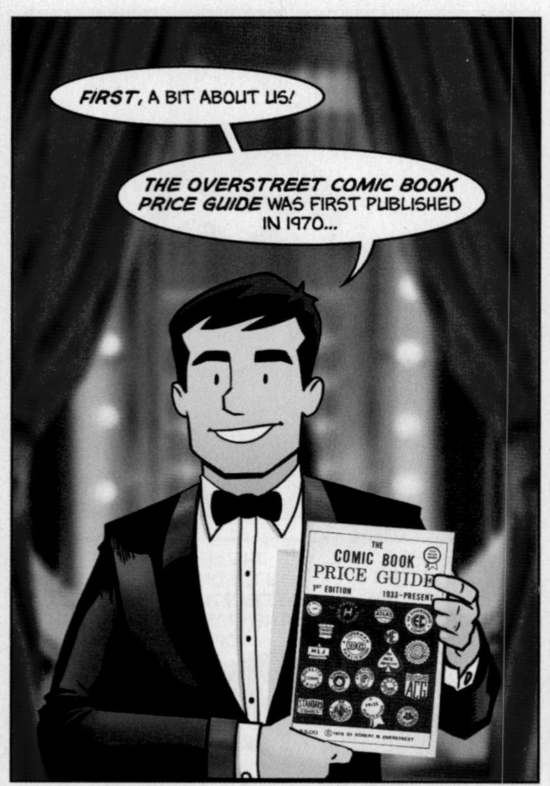

FIRST, A BIT ABOUT US!
THE OVERSTREET COMIC BOOK PRICE GUIDE WAS FIRST PUBLISHED IN 1970...
THE COMIC BOOK PRICE GUIDE
1ST EDITION
1933-PRESENT

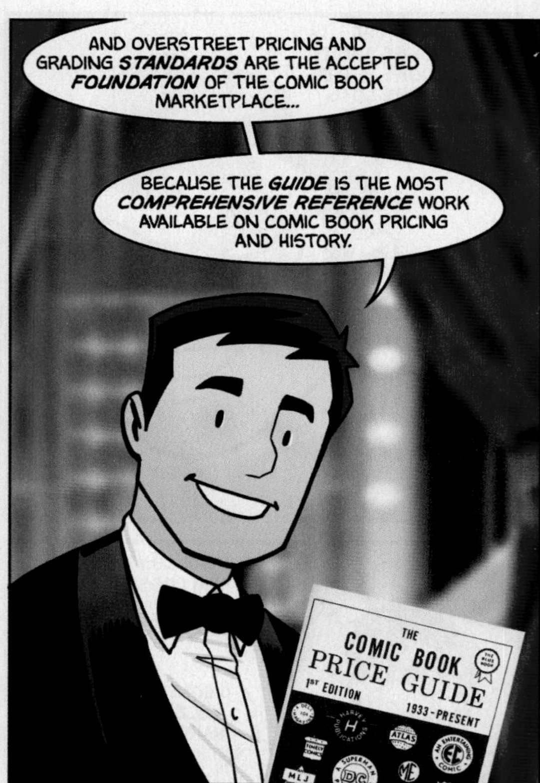

AND OVERSTREET PRICING AND GRADING *STANDARDS* ARE THE ACCEPTED *FOUNDATION* OF THE COMIC BOOK MARKETPLACE...
BECAUSE THE *GUIDE* IS THE MOST *COMPREHENSIVE REFERENCE* WORK AVAILABLE ON COMIC BOOK PRICING AND HISTORY.
THE COMIC BOOK PRICE GUIDE
1ST EDITION
1933-PRESENT

COMICS ARE LISTED *ALPHABETICALLY BY TITLE*, REGARDLESS OF PUBLISHER...

THE MAIN PRICING SECTION FEATURES COMICS FROM 1934 TO PRESENT.

THIS BOOK ALSO INCLUDES...

Big Little Books
Promotional Comics
Pioneer Age Comics
Victorian Age Comics
Platinum Age Comics

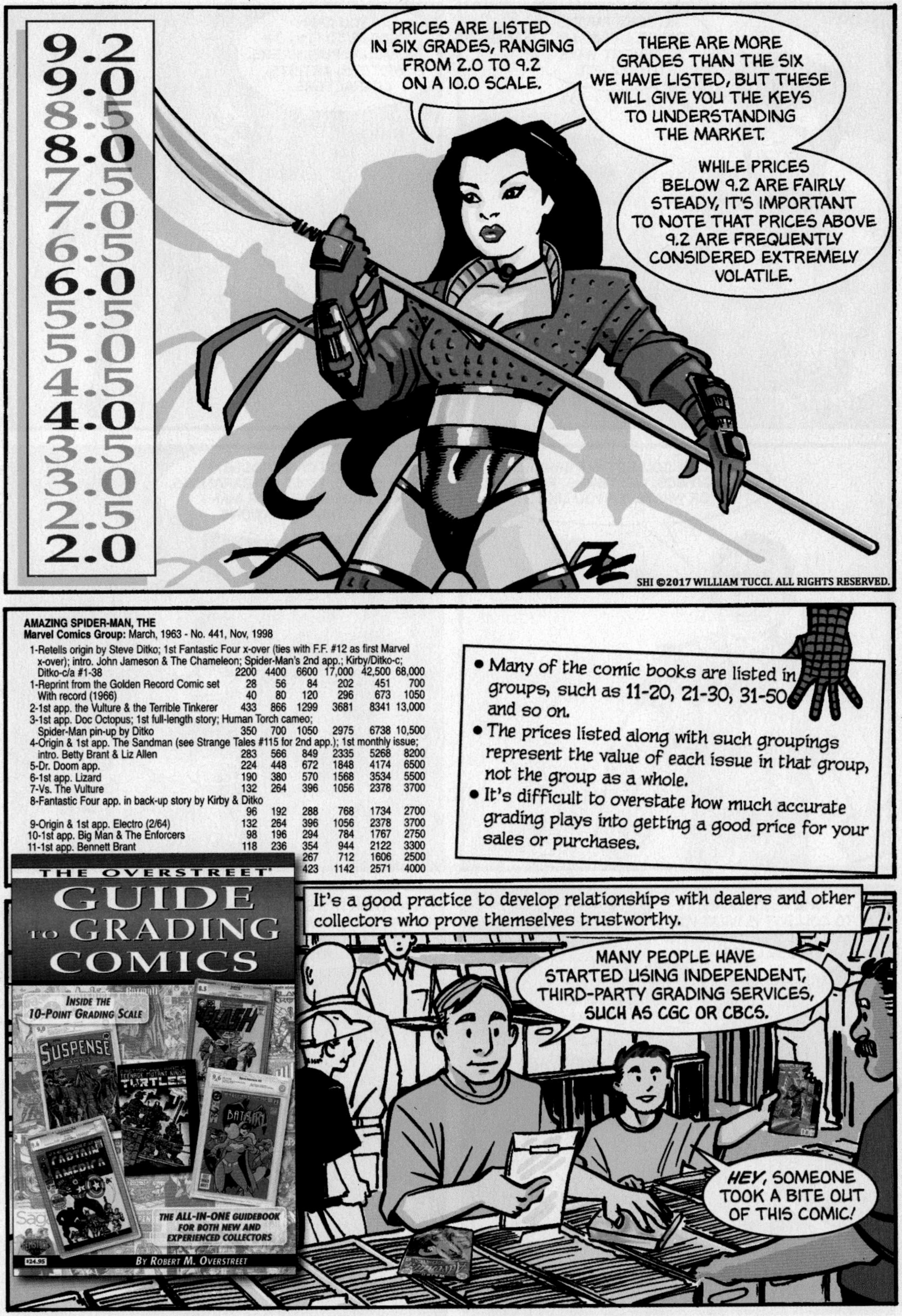

9.2
9.0
8.5
8.0
7.5
7.0
6.5
6.0
5.5
5.0
4.5
4.0
3.5
3.0
2.5
2.0

PRICES ARE LISTED IN SIX GRADES, RANGING FROM 2.0 TO 9.2 ON A 10.0 SCALE.

THERE ARE MORE GRADES THAN THE SIX WE HAVE LISTED, BUT THESE WILL GIVE YOU THE KEYS TO UNDERSTANDING THE MARKET.

WHILE PRICES BELOW 9.2 ARE FAIRLY STEADY, IT'S IMPORTANT TO NOTE THAT PRICES ABOVE 9.2 ARE FREQUENTLY CONSIDERED EXTREMELY VOLATILE.

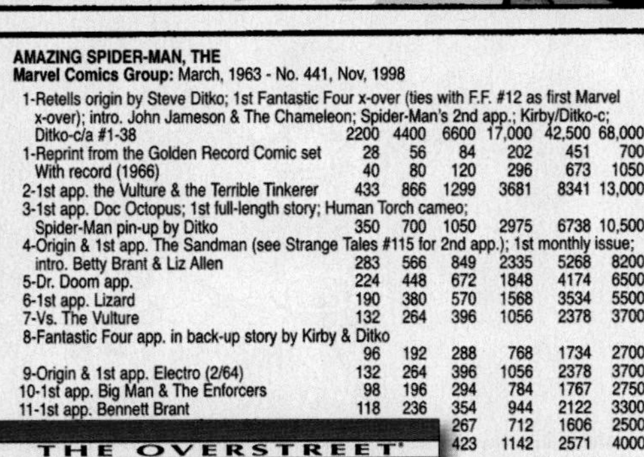

AMAZING SPIDER-MAN, THE
Marvel Comics Group: March, 1963 - No. 441, Nov, 1998

1-Retells origin by Steve Ditko; 1st Fantastic Four x-over (ties with F.F. #12 as first Marvel x-over); intro. John Jameson & The Chameleon; Spider-Man's 2nd app.; Kirby/Ditko-c; Ditko-c/a #1-38	2200	4400	6600	17,000	42,500	68,000
1-Reprint from the Golden Record Comic set	28	56	84	202	451	700
With record (1966)	40	80	120	296	673	1050
2-1st app. the Vulture & the Terrible Tinkerer	433	866	1299	3681	8341	13,000
3-1st app. Doc Octopus; 1st full-length story; Human Torch cameo; Spider-Man pin-up by Ditko	350	700	1050	2975	6738	10,500
4-Origin & 1st app. The Sandman (see Strange Tales #115 for 2nd app.); 1st monthly issue; intro. Betty Brant & Liz Allen	283	566	849	2335	5268	8200
5-Dr. Doom app.	224	448	672	1848	4174	6500
6-1st app. Lizard	190	380	570	1568	3534	5500
7-Vs. The Vulture	132	264	396	1056	2378	3700
8-Fantastic Four app. in back-up story by Kirby & Ditko	96	192	288	768	1734	2700
9-Origin & 1st app. Electro (2/64)	132	264	396	1056	2378	3700
10-1st app. Big Man & The Enforcers	98	196	294	784	1767	2750
11-1st app. Bennett Brant	118	236	354	944	2122	3300
			267	712	1606	2500
			423	1142	2571	4000

- Many of the comic books are listed in groups, such as 11-20, 21-30, 31-50 and so on.
- The prices listed along with such groupings represent the value of each issue in that group, not the group as a whole.
- It's difficult to overstate how much accurate grading plays into getting a good price for your sales or purchases.

THE BEST PART IS THERE ARE MANY DIFFERENT WAYS TO COLLECT.

YOU CAN CHOOSE TO FOLLOW INDIVIDUAL PUBLISHERS, WRITERS, ARTISTS, CHARACTERS...

YOU CAN COLLECT SUPERHEROES, WAR COMICS, WESTERNS, ROMANCE OR WHATEVER YOU LIKE...

YOU CAN CHOOSE #1 ISSUES, FIRST APPEARANCES, CROSSOVERS, OR MANY OTHER VARIATIONS.

THE BEST THING TO COLLECT IS WHAT YOU LIKE, NOT WHAT SOMEONE ELSE LIKES.

WHETHER IT'S SPIDER-MAN OR EVERY COMIC THAT CAME OUT THE MONTH YOU WERE BORN, IT'S BEST TO DO IT WITH A PLAN.

THE BEST WAY TO HAVE A GOOD PLAN IS TO FIRST GET INFORMED.

THE BEST WAY TO GET INFORMED IS TO GO TO THE EXPERTS!
CAN'T I SAY "OR ELSE!" AFTER THAT?

LEARN THE INS AND OUTS OF COLLECTING, INCLUDING HOW TO TAKE CARE OF YOUR COLLECTION!

Learn how to grade your comics and why the grades make a difference!_

LEARN WHAT TO EXPECT AT CONVENTIONS OR WHEN BUYING AND SELLING COMICS.
AND MAYBE HOW TO FIGHT ZOMBIES...

IT'S ALSO IMPORTANT TO REMEMBER THAT THIS BOOK IS A GUIDE, NOT A DEALER'S PRICE LIST. THE MARKET SETS THE PRICES.

WITH INPUT FROM A NETWORK OF EXPERIENCED ADVISORS INCLUDING WELL ESTABLISHED COLLECTORS, DEALERS AND HISTORIANS OF POPULAR CULTURE, WE HAVE UNDERTAKEN SIGNIFICANT EFFORT TO ASSEMBLE THIS PRICING INFORMATION.

THE RESULTING LISTINGS COME THROUGH THE OBSERVATION AND DOCUMENTATION OF PRICES REALIZED THROUGH HOBBY AND TRADE SHOWS, CATALOG SALES, RETAIL SALES, AND INTERNET, LIVE AND MAIL-IN AUCTIONS. DOCUMENTED PERSONAL SALES MAY ALSO BE INCLUDED.

WE HAVE EARNED OUR REPUTATION FOR OUR CAUTIOUS, CONSERVATIVE APPROACH TO PRICING.

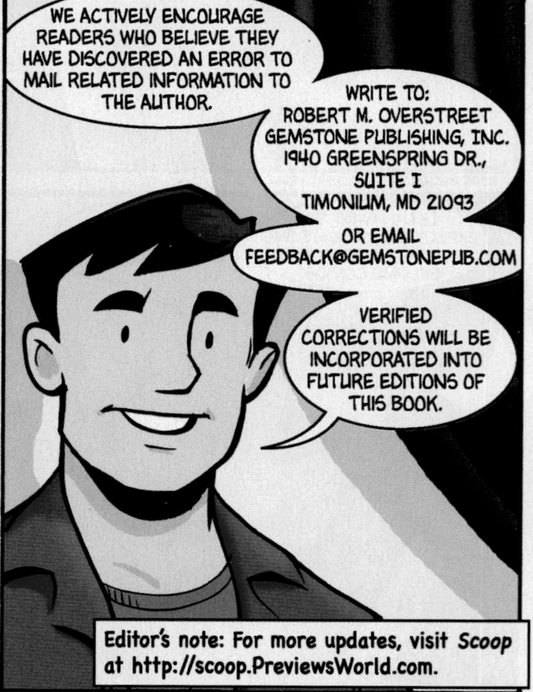
WE ACTIVELY ENCOURAGE READERS WHO BELIEVE THEY HAVE DISCOVERED AN ERROR TO MAIL RELATED INFORMATION TO THE AUTHOR.
WRITE TO: ROBERT M. OVERSTREET GEMSTONE PUBLISHING, INC. 1940 GREENSPRING DR., SUITE I TIMONIUM, MD 21093 OR EMAIL FEEDBACK@GEMSTONEPUB.COM
VERIFIED CORRECTIONS WILL BE INCORPORATED INTO FUTURE EDITIONS OF THIS BOOK.
Editor's note: For more updates, visit *Scoop* at http://scoop.PreviewsWorld.com.

OVERSTREET MARKET REPORT 2017

2016 SAW RECORD PRICES FOR GOLD AND SILVER AGE BOOKS IN ALL GRADES

by Robert M. Overstreet

A few noteworthy sales: ***Detective Comics*** *#33, CGC 1.5 for $15,535,* ***Marvel Comics*** *#1 in CGC 3.0 for $77,675.* ***Superman*** *#1 in CGC 0.5 for $57,360, and* ***Whiz Comics*** *#2 (#1) in CGC 0.5 for $15,535.*

Again, last year, key books in the lower grades continued to be in high demand as evidenced by the few examples shown above. As the top keys continue to skyrocket to higher levels, collectors are adjusting their sights to lower grading tiers.

Golden Age: Robert Krause (Primo Comics) agreed, "We believe that it is only a matter of time before the confluence of an ever increasing collector base demanding vintage books and the scarcity of high grade books manifests itself in a move down to the next desirable tier, mid to lower grade books. This will cause an inevitable increase in prices for these mid to lower grade respective books."

As Eric Groves pointed out, "The market is strong with an influx of new, mostly younger, collectors. Some of the collectors are not accumulating runs of specific titles but seek out only key issues."

Josh Nathanson of Comic Link agreed, "The extreme rarity of the early issues of *Action Comics* and *Detective Comics,* coupled with the popularity of the characters, has driven up prices on all of the late 1930s issues to a high degree. These books are in high demand in any grade--even coverless."

Since the advent of professional certification of comic books in early 2000, hundreds of thousands of issues have been encapsulated. This has made cover themes more important than ever, since books are sealed and covers are all that can be viewed.

As Brock Dickinson stated, "With the advent of 3rd party grading (from CGC, CBCS and others) and encapsulation, the content of a comic book becomes inaccessible, leaving the cover image as the distinguishing feature. This has increased the importance of the cover from a collecting perspective." Josh Nathanson agreed, "The Golden Age market is also extremely cover driven right now and even at the lower end of the pricing spectrum a book with a stand-out cover can blow the doors off *Guide* prices when properly promoted.

Ted VanLiew (Superworld Comics) followed up, "Many collectors are looking for either classic covers, covers by certain noteworthy artists, or just lesser known great covers.

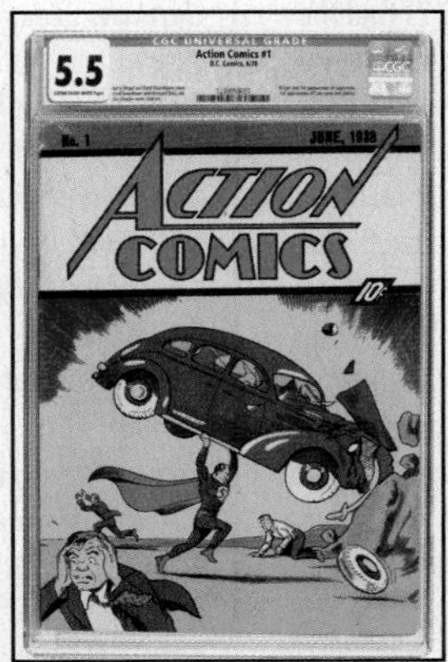

Action Comics *#1 in CGC 5.5 sold for a record $956,000!!*

West Stephan (CBCS) agreed, "We have also noticed a large increase in "Classic Covers" submissions. Books like *Phantom Lady* #17, *Suspense Comics* #3, *Marvel Mystery* #40, #44 & #46 & other classic covers are always in huge demand, and thus, are always the first books to be submitted when a collection containing them is bought. World War II covers are also very coveted & show no signs of slowing down."

"In fact, *Overstreet* may have to start breaking out more WWII covers as they always sell for more than the issues surrounding them that do not have a war cover. Most of the time, the market is more cover driven than anything else at this point. It's the cover that sells the comic, unfortunately the interior stories seem to be of secondary importance."

With cover collecting becoming more widespread, even though everyone wants the highest grade that they can afford, grade has become less important just as long as the cover image has good eye-appeal with defects that do not detract too much.

Ben Labonog reported, "The rarity of Golden Age comics should never be underestimated. The market continues to be healthy with the strongest demand being for 1st appearances and classic, unique covers. There are not many unrestored copies of pre-1945 books left, so it is quite a treat to be able to find them in their original condition."

Heritage Auctions reported sales of nearly $43 million in total revenue for comics, comic art and animation art for the year 2016, the highest ever, breaking the previous record high of $37.8 million spent in 2012.

They feel that high sales were based in part on movie releases with comic-themed plots. Among the items in highest demand during 2016 was an *Action Comics* #1 in FN- 5.5 that brought a record price of $956,000. This was the highest, un-restored copy ever auctioned by Heritage. They also reported a CGC 9.4 copy of *Amazing Fantasy* #15 (Spider-Man's very first app.) sold for $454,100 and a *Superman* #1 in VG+ 4.5 realized $358,500. A *Batman* #1 in CGC FN- 5.5 brought $239,000.

ComicLink reports, "To date, over 300,000 vintage comic books have transacted between ComicLink buyers and sellers. 2016 was the biggest year we've ever seen! Aggressive buyers scooped up many thousands of certified comic books and original artwork to enhance their collections. Strength was exhibited across virtually every collecting genre, from Golden Age rarities of the 1930s and early 1950s to Silver and Bronze Age keys and high-grades of the late 1950s through the '70s and right through Copper and Modern Age era. We see this growth trend continuing for years to come."

Vincent Zurzolo, Frank Cwiklik & Rob Reynolds (Comic Connect) reported, "The past year has been very strong. Big keys are selling very well, private sales and auctions are both doing incredibly well. Convention sales have picked up."

Conventions: Charles & Jeff Cerrito reported: "I find the Pop Culture conventions are gathering more and more steam with every year. Cosplayers make up a lot of the attendee base which makes for crowded conventions. About 15 years ago, the national day conventions usually drew about 20,000-30,000 and that was considered to be a huge massive crowd. Today these same conventions are drawing way over 100,000. For example, we know San Diego draws a max crowd of 126,000. This year's New York Comic Con drew a record crowd of 180,000 and it's still growing." Frank Cwiklik (Metropolis Comics) agreed, "The New York ComicCon is now the biggest comic convention in the world, both in terms of attendance and floor space. Both Chicago cons seemed to enjoy about the same attendance."

Golden Age Sales:

Action Comics #1, CGC 5.5 $956,000, no cover $65,725, no cover, missing 1st wrap $37,666, #4, CBCS 1.8 $3,465, #7 CGC 7.0 cons. $40,500, CGC 6.0 $175,000, CGC 2.0 $71,000, CGC 1.8 $50,000, #10 CGC 0.5 $9,600, #12 CBCS 5.0 R $4,063, #13 CGC 6.5 $70,777, PR, no back-c $14,340, #15 CBCS 7.0 $14,340, #17 CBCS 6.5 $6,572, CGC 6.0 $11,518, #23 CGC 6.5 $28,052, #24 CBCS 5.0 $15,535, #52, CGC 9.4 $31,070

Adventure Comics #40, CGC 4.0 $11,950, #46 CGC 1.0 $1,000, #60 CGC 8.0 $3,577, #72 CGC 8.5 $7,500

All-American Comics #17 CGC 7.5 $6,871, #19 CGC 5.0 $4,063

All-Select Comics #1 CGC 9.2 $45,410

All Star Comics #3 CGC 7.0 $69,000, CGC 1.0 $6,000, no cover $854, #4 CGC 9.4 $21,275, #8 CGC 9.0 $411,000. CGC 5.5 $69,001, CGC 4.5 $54,555, CGC 4.0 $31,070, CGC 2.0 $32,000

All Winners Comics #12 CGC 8.0 $7,700, #19 CGC 7.0 $6,350

Amazing Man Comics #5 CGC 6.0(Larson) $10,501, #13 CGC 8.0 Mile High $2,700, #26 CGC 3.0 $7,060

America's Best Comics #7 CGC 6.5 $2,358

Archie Comics #1 CBCS 4.0 $19,120, CGC 3.0 $29,388, #50 CGC 8.0 $4,600

Archie's Girls #1 CGC 9.0 $5,497

Batman #1 CGC 8.0 $390,000, CBCS 7.5 Mod. R $29,975, CGC 6.5 $180,000, FN R $25,000, CGC 5.5 $239,000, CGC 4.5 $129,000, CGC 2.5 $64,000, #3 CGC 6.0 $3,634, $6 CGC 8.5 $5,600, #9 CBCS 8.0 $5,497, CGC 6.0 $3,650, #11, CGC 9.4 $65,725, CGC 8.5 $22,705, CGC 7.0 $11,352, #15 CGC 9.0 $9,000, #16 CBCS 8.0 $5,975, #44, CGC 8.0 $11,687, #121 CGC 4.0 $850

Black Cat Mystery #50 CGC 8.5 $9,867

Blue Bolt Weird Tales #116 VF $800

Blue Ribbon Comics #9 CGC 1.5 $657, #10 VG- $454

Bold Stories #1 CGC 9.2 $5,258

Captain America Comics #1 CBCS 9.4 R $34,000, CBCS 8.5 Mod. R $47,800, CGC 8.0 $288,000, CGC 2.0 $45,000, no cover $10,755, #2 CGC 7.0 R $14,340, CBCS 5.5 $8,100, CBCS 1.8 $4,780, #6 CGC 8.5 $13,249, #13, CGC 9.0 $33,460, #18 CGC 9.6 $32,000, #23, CGC 9.4 $31,070, nn CGC 2.5 $9,560

Captain Marvel Adventures #1, CGC 5.0 $38,240, CGC 4.5 $33,460

Captain Marvel Jr. #1 CGC 7.0 $1,998

Catman #20 CBCS 9.0 $19,120, #24 CGC 2.5 $1,195

Challengers of the Unknown #1 CGC 6.5 $1,044

Chamber of Chills #19 CGC 9.0 $4,600

Cindy Comics #37 CGC 4.5 $1,500

City of the Living Dead nn CGC 6.5 $1,233

Comic Calvacade #1, CBCS 6.0 $3,943, #16 CGC 9.4 $1,911, #21 CGC 9.4 $1,917

Comics #1 ('37) CGC 9.8 $10,250

Crime Does Not Pay #33 CGC 5.0 $850

Crypt of Terror #17 CGC 9.8 $12,806, VF- $2,300

Daredevil Battles Hitler #1 CGC 8.5 $8950

All Star Comics *#8* in CBCS 1.8 sold for $27,485

Daring Mystery Comics #1 CGC 5.5 $10,157, CGC 1.0 $1,299
Detective Comics #9 CGC 4.5 $4,063, #16 CGC 4.5 $4,000, #22, CGC 7.0 $5,019, #28, CGC 8.5 $64,000, CBCS 4.0 Mod R $5,497, CGC 2.0 $16,730, #29 CGC 3.5 $40,500, CGC 1.8 staples added $22,107, CGC 1.5 $30,029, #30 CGC 7.0 $8,900, #31 CGC 6.0 Mod R $27,617, CGC 4.5 $96,000, CGC 4.0 $90,000, CGC 2.0 $17,299, CGC 1.0 $43,505, #33 CGC 6.5 $51,133, #35 CGC 5.5 $34,333, CGC 3.5 $33,460, CGC 3.0 $23,500, FR $6,453, PR $7,170, CBCS 1.8 trimmed $5,733, #36 CGC 5.0 $21,000, CGC 4.5 $17,977, #37 CGC 7.0 (Larson) $23,792, CGC 6.0 $21,000, #38 CGC 4.0 $35,000, #40, CGC 8.5 $27,500, #54 CGC 9.4 $15,250, #66, CBCS 6.5 $6,800, #71 CGC 7.5 $11,600, #120 CGC 9.6 $10,450, #121 CGC 9.8 $7,100, #168 CGC 7.5 $18,265, CGC 4.5 $8,365
Donald Duck Four Color #4 CGC 7.5 $23,900
Double Action #2 & #1 ashcan pair $80,000
Eerie Comics #1 CGC 8.5 $9,560
Exciting Comics #39 CBCS 5.0 $4,063
Famous Funnies #211 CGC 9.2 $2,550
Feature Book #39 CGC 9.4 $6,350
Fight Against Crime #20 CGC 7.0 $6,233
Flash Comics #1 CGC 6.5 $107,550, #54 CGC 9.6 Mile High $4,600, #86 CGC 4.5 $7,200
Green Hornet #1 CGC 8.5 $7,211, #15 CGC 9.6 Mile High $3,811
Green Lantern #1 CGC 4.0 $5,128, #8 FN/VF $175
Guns Against Gangsters #6 CGC 9.2 $3,300
Hangman #5 CGC 9.2 $6,800
Haunt of Fear #15(#1) CGC 9.8 $13,145, CGC 9.6 $9,877
Hit Comics #5 CGC 5.0 $2,908, #25 CGC 9.2 $4,780
Human Torch #3(#2) CGC 9.0 $6,701, #4 (#3) $5,000, #7, CGC 9.4 $12,750, #8 CGC 8.0 $7,422, #20 CGC 9.2 $3,363
Joe Palooka #1 FN $160
Land of the Lost #1 CGC 9.8 $3,533
Lone Ranger #1 CGC 9.8 $10,755
Looney Tunes #1 CGC 2.0 $2,778, #23 PGX 8.0 $1,830
March of Comics #4 CGC 8.5 $6,572
Marvel Comics #1 CGC 3.0 $77,675
Marvel Mystery Comics #4 GD $2130, #9 CBCS 5.5 Mod R $6,274, #11 CGC 9.2 $15,678, #19, CBCS 9.0 $4,780, #27 CGC 9.4 $11,251, #44 CBCS 4.5 cons. $2,629, 132pg. CGC 6.5 $25,018
Marvel Tales #119 CGC 9.4 $1,800
Mary Marvel #1 CGC 9.0 $1,788
Master Comics #1 VF $4,541
Mickey Mouse Magazine #1 FN- $5,270
More Fun Comics #14 6.0 $5,000, #21 8.0 $3,400, #46 CGC 9.6 Mile High $10,000, #52 CGC 3.0 $39,500, #54 CGC 8.5 $22,100, CBCS 5.5 brittle $4,780, CBCS 3.5 $5,377, #73 CGC 8.0 $104,562, CBCS 6.5 trimmed $16,730, #101 CGC 8.5 $14,294
Motion Picture Funnies Weekly #1 VGF $15,800
Mystery Men Comics #1 CGC 9.2 $39,435
Negro Romance #4 CGC 7.0 $6,572
New Adventure Comics #26 CGC 3.0 $6,109
New York World's Fair 1939 CBCS 6.0 $5,019, VG+ $4,000, 1940 CGC 8.5 $14,583
Pep Comics #2 CGC 9.8 Mile High $33,460, #17 CGC 9.6 Mile High $46,605, #20 CGC 9.2 Mile High $38,240, #22 CBCS 7.0 R $20,250, CBCS 5.0 $73,000, CBCS 2.0 $31,249, #34 CGC 9.2 $57,360, CGC 6.0 $15,251, #35 CGC 9.2 Rockford $17,767
Phantom Lady #14, CGC 9.4 $7,767, #16 CGC 9.4 Mile High $13,145, #17 CGC 8.0 $15,535, CGC 7.5 $14,340,
Plastic Man #1 CGC 9.2 $13,000
Rangers Comics #1 CGC 8.0 $3,550
Red Ryder Comics #1 CGC 9.0 $3,451
Science Comics #1 CGC 8.0 $6,572
Seduction of the Innocent w/dj $3060
Sensation Comics #1 CBCS 5.5 $35,000, CGC 5.0 $31,555, CGC 3.0 $18,606, #6 CGC 5.0 $7,600, #60 CGC 9.4 Mile High $3,653
Seven Seas #4 6.5 $6,094, $4,000
Shadow Comics V2#10 CGC 9.4 $2,988
Spirit #7 (Quality) CGC 9.2 $1,359, #22, CGC 9.2 $10,157, CGC 8.5 $7,170
Spitfire Comics #133 CG 9.8 $15,200
Star Spangled #7 CGC 9.0 $6,450
Startling Comics #10 6.5 $4,200, #49 CGC 9.6 $101,575
Sub-Mariner Comics #1 CBCS 8.5 $5,497, CGC 6.0 $11,000, #6 CBCS 8.5 $9,308, #17 CGC 9.2 $5,988, #19 CGC 9.2 $5,600, #22 CGC 9.4 $5,700, #32 CGC 8.5 MIle HIgh $23,250
Superboy #1 CGC 8.0 $7,767
Superman #1 CGC 4.5 $358,500, CGC 4.0 $295,000, VG+ R $35,000, CGC 1.5 $85,000, CGC .5 no back-c $57,360, #2 CGC 6.5 $16,730, CGC 4.5 $6,274, CGC 2.0 $3,360, #14 CGC 9.2 $45,000, #17 CGC 9.4 $50,000
Suspense Comics #3 CBCS 4.0 $15,535, #11 CGC 9.0 $4,541
Tales From the Crypt #20 CGC 9.8 Gaines $6,107, #33 CGC 9.8 $6,600
Teen-Age Romances #21 GD- $48.00, #37 CGC 6.0 $695
Terrific Comics #5 8.0 $16,000
Tomahawk #1 CGC 9.6 Mile High $7,767
Tomb of Terror #15 CGC 9.2 $5,019
Uncle Sam #1 CGC 9.6 $16,977
USA Comics #1 CGC 7.0 $3,400, #6 CGC 1.5 $1,472, #10 CGC 2
Vault of Horror #14 CGC 9.8 $6,136, #17 CGC 9.8 $5,975
V-Comics #2 CBCS 7.0 $4,541
Walt Disney's Comics & Stories #1 CGC 4.5 $4,302
Wanamaker's CGC 3.0 $5,258
Wanted #52 CGC 8.0 $1,755
War #11 Atlas CGC 5.5 $1,758
Weird Fantasy #13(#1) CGC 9.6 Gaines $7,950, #14 (#2) CGC 9.8 $6,100, #11 CGC 9.8 $3500
Weird Mysteries #12 CGC 7.0 $4,210
Weird Science #12(#1) CGC 9.6 $12,258, #13 CGC 9.6 $2,987
Whiz Comics #1 CGC .5 brittle $15,535, CGC 1.0 $27,055, No Cover $5,075, #2 CGC 5.0 $4,100, #18VG+ $500
Wonder Comics #1 Fox CGC 9.4 $54,970
Wonder Comics #15 Nedor CGC 7.5 $1,666
Wonder Woman #1 CGC 9.0 $291,000, CGC 5.0 $40,500, CGC 4.5 $28,027, #6 CBCS 8.5 $7,766, #7 CGC 6.5 $5,699
Zip Comics #8 CGC 9.4 $6,050

Wonder Comics #1, CGC 9.4 sold for $54,970.

Silver Age: The Silver Age is now over 60 years old and the vast majority of books bought and sold are from this period. Key books continue to set records, even in the lower grades.

Dave Alexander, DDS reported, "Silver Age books are common in grades below fine, but sell readily nonetheless due to huge demand. These books in true Near Mint to Mint condition are very rare and command prices well over *Guide* values."

Paul Clairmont (PNJ Comics) agreed, "We prefer to deal with high grade books and it is particularly difficult finding Silver Age books in true high grade of Very Fine+ (8.5) or better."

Eric Groves pointed out, "Early Silver Age comics, for the most part, deserve the value attributed to them. They constitute a significant milestone in the evolution of comics. The publishers and artists who produced these books are rightly revered. Issues such as *Showcase* #4, *Amazing Fantasy* #15, *Hulk* #1, *Amazing Spider-Man* #1 and *Fantastic Four* #1 are established icons now. We have sold these books many times over. They move out in all grades."

Frank Simmons (Coast to Coast Comics) reported, "Just about every major Silver Age key across the board experienced strong 20% price increases with little or no resistance from customers in the market place. In particular, low grade copies in the 1.0, 1.5, 1.8 & 2.0 range had a tremendous surge in pricing, the demand which by far exceeded the available supply for more affordable copies was in fact the culprit.

Josh Nathanson reported, "Demand for Silver Age comics is as strong as it has ever been. As usual, major Marvel and DC keys led the way in 2016 with exceptional results for several premiere and 1st app. issues achieved. The traditional keys sold for record amounts induding *X-Men* #1 CGC 9.6 for $350,000, *Incredible Hulk* #1 CGC 9.0 for $275,000 and *Tales to Astonish* #27 CGC 9.4 for $205,501."

Steven Houston agreed, "As usual it's all about the keys! Keys, keys and yet more keys. Regardless of movie connections, Marvel's Silver Age product is still the most sought after, with low grade key issues selling for 2 to 5 times *Guide* prices.

Silver Age through Modern Age Sales:

Action Comics #242 PGX 4.0 $1,550, #252 CGC 8.0 $15,300 #253 CGC 3.0 $1,075, #254 CGC 9.2 $1,750

Adventure Comics #247 CGC 6.0 $6,212, #269 CGC 6.5 $250, #335, CGC 9.8 $2,066

Albedo #2 CGC 9.6 $2,556, CGC 8.5 $1,000

All Star Comics #58 CGC 9.8 $2,000, CGC 9.6 $500, NM+ $600, CGC 9.2 $260

Amazing Fantasy #15 CGC 9.2 $460,000, CGC 6.5 $51,070, $50,190, CGC 7.0 $65,000, CGC 3.0 $18,000

Amazing Spider-Man #1 CGC 9.6 $262,900, CGC 9.2 $75,000, CGC 4.5 $6,325, #2 CGC 9.0 $8,400, #3, CGC 9.0 $7,100, CBCS 4.5 $1,399, #6, CGC 9.4 $7,864, CGC 7.0 $950, #16, CGC 9.8 $17,750, CBCS 8.5 $1,100, CGC 8.0 $750, #23, CGC 9.4 $11,111, #39 CGC 9.4 $2,660, #50 CGC 9.2 $2,657, CGC 7.5 $525, #71 CGC 9.8 $1,977, #80 CGC 9.8 $2,577, #86 CGC 9.8 $3,800, #94 CGC 9.8 $2,275, #100 CGC 9.8 $2,601, #101 CGC 9.6 $2,851, #121 CGC 9.8 $4,544, CGC 9.4 $1,250, CGC 4.0 $175, #122 CGC 9.8 $3,000, CGC 9.4 $800, #129 CGC 9.8 $10,600, $8,900, CGC 9.6 $3,450, CBCS 9.0 $1,600, CGC 7.5 $725, VF $700, CGC 5.0 $425, #399 CGC 9.8 $1,600

Aquaman #1 CGC 9.4 $14,001, CGC 4.5 $425, #35 CGC 9.0 $1,601

Avengers #4 CGC 9.0 $7,300, #53 CGC 9.8 $1,351, #55 CGC 9.8 $5,950, #57 CGC 9.4 $2,012, #112 CGC 9.8 $2,333

Batman #181 CGC 7.5 $700, #189 CGC 9.6 $2,400, CGC 8.5 $425, #227 CGC 8.0 $400, #232 CGC 8,5 $550, #357 CGC 9.8 $1300, #232 CGC 9.6 $2,257, #234 CGC 9.8 $4,350, #244 CGC 9.8 $3,350, #251 CGC 9.6 $1,955, #357 CGC 9.8 $1,300

Batman Adventures #12 CGC 9.8 $2,156, CGC 9.6 $885, CGC 9.4 $850, CGC 9.2 $600, VF+ $600, CGC 7.5 $400

Brave and the Bold #25 CGC 8.5 $6,125, #28 CGC 8.0 $16,730, CGC 7.5 $13,350, #93 CGC 9.8 $2,100

Captain America #100 CGC 9.9 $63,500, FN- $200, #110 CGC 9.8 $1,777, #138 CGC 9.8 $900, #217 CGC 9.8 $900

Captain Marvel #1 CGC 9.8 $4,100, #17 CGC 9.8 $1,877, #26 CGC 9.8 $2,111, #33 CGC 9.8 $2,179

Chamber of Darkness #4 CGC 9.8 $875

Chew #1 CGC 9.9 $1,400

Conan the Barbarian #1 CGC 9.8 $5,265, #23 CGC 9.8 $1,257

Daredevil #1 CGC 9.6 $35,850, CGC 9.4 $18,000, CGC 9.2 $10,277, CGC 4.0 $1,150, GD/VG $750, #2 CGC 9.8 $30,400, CGC 9.2 $1,925, #168 CGC 9.8 $1,728, CGC 9.4 $285, CGC 9.2 $235, CGC 9.0 $200

Defenders #1 VG $40

Detective Comics #225 CBCS 8.5 $14,340, CGC 4.5 $3,707, CGC 1.0 $1,050, #226 CBCS 9.0 $4,541, #359 CGC 9.4 $13,380, CGC

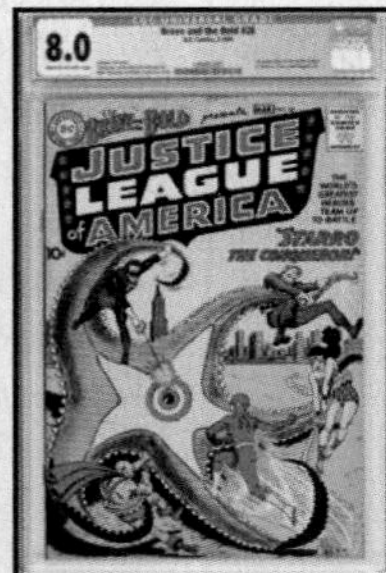

Amazing Fantasy *#15 CGC 9.2 sold for $460,000,* ***Amazing Spider-Man*** *#1 in CGC 9.6 went for $262,900,* ***Brave and the Bold*** *#28 in CGC 8.0 sold for $16,730,* ***Detective Comics*** *#225 in CBCS 8.5 sold for $14,340,* ***Showcase*** *#4 in CGC 1.8 sold for $6,100*

6.5 $595, #400 CGC 9.6 $1,875, #405 CGC 9.6 $1,300, #411 CGC 8.0 $285, #444 CC 9.8 $740

Doctor Solar #1 CGC 8.0 $300

Doctor Strange #1 CGC 9.8 $950

Doom Patrol #99 CGC 6.0 $270

Fantastic Four #1 CGC 9.0 $132,000, CGC 8.5 $65,000, CGC 7.0 $23,859, $20,250, CGC 5.0 $7,500, #5 CGC 9.4 $45,000, #48 CGC 9.0 $1,430, #49 CGC 8.5 $500, #52 CGC 9.8 $90,000, CGC 9.6 $16,750, CGC 8.5 $2,500, $2,150, CGC 8,0 $2,200, CGC 7.0 $725, CGC 5.0 $600, #103 CGC 9.8 $1,177, #112 CGC 9.6 $3,322

Fear #19 CGC 9.8 $1,300

Flash #110 CGC 5.5 $650, #123 CGC 9.4 $21,050, #131 CGC 9.6 $1,987, #135 CGC 9.2 $2,890, #139 CGC 8.5 $2,789, CG 7.0 $800, CGC 5.0 $385, #144 CGC 9.6 $4,450, #147 CGC 9.6 $1,499

Forever People #1 CGC 9.8 $3,600, CGC 9.0 $325

Ghost Rider #1 CGC 9.8 $3,255, CGC 9.6 $2,151

Giant-Size Creatures #1 CGC 9.8 $1,241,

Giant-Size Daredevil #1 CGC 9.8 $919,

Giant-Size Spider-Man #3 CGC 9.8 $1,178,

Giant-Size X-Men #1 CGC 9.8 $7,101, CGC 9.6 $3,211, CGC 9.2 $1.800, CGC 8.5 $1,145, F/VF $530, CGC 6.0 $550

Green Lantern #1 VF- $2,850, G/VG $800, #16 CGC 8.0 $500, #76 CGC 7.0 $425, $2,470, #87 CGC 9.8 $2,600

Harbinger #1 CGC 9.8 $1,000, MT $150

Hero for Hire #1 CGC 9.8 $24,000, CGC 9.0 $1,250

House of Mystery #182 CGC 9.6 $1,399

House of Secrets #88 CGC 9.6 $1,700, #92 CGC 9.6 $9,199, CGC 9.4 $4,700, VF $820, VG $180, #94 CGC 9.6 $1,216, #105 CGC 9.8 $1,200

Howard the Duck #1 CGC 9.8 $1,139, CGC 9.6 $190

Incredible Hulk #1 CGC 9.0 $275,000, CGC 8.5 $132,000, CGC 7.5 (Pence) $40,157, CGC 7.0 $40,000, CGC 6.0 $20,872, $18,411, CGC 5.5 $16,200, #2 CGC 9.2 $16,850, CGC 5.0 $1,250, #3, CGC 9.4 $17,237, #6 CGC 9.6 $25,000, #162 CGC 9.8 $1,251, #180 CGC 9.8 $4,988, #181 CGC 9.8 $115,000, CGC 9.6 $8,025, CGC 8.0 $2,000, CGC 5.0 $1,300, CGC 4.0 $1,100

Invaders #20 (35¢) CGC 9.6 $1,500

Iron Fist #15 CGC 9.8 $900

Iron Man #1 CGC 9.8 $9,051, CGC 8.0 $650, CGC 5.5 $500, FN- $350, VG $200, #7 CGC 9.8 $7,500, #15 CGC 9.8 $15,000, #55 FN+ $400, VF $600, CGC 9.8 $6,877, CGC 9.6 $2,800, FVF $850

Journey Into Mystery #1 CGC 2.0 $2,200, #83 CGC 9.4 $210,000, CGC 3.0 $2,893, #84 GVG $420

Justice League of America #1 6.5 $3,400, #19 CGC 9.4 $4,100, #21 CGC 9.4 $3,322, #39 CBCS 9.6 $3,100

Magnus Robot Fighter #1 CGC 7.0 $350

Marvel Feature #1 CGC 9.8 $8,101, CGC 9.6 $1,877, #3 CGC 9.8 $920, #12 CGC 9.8 $1,025

Marvel Premiere #1 CGC 9.6 $1,621, #4 CGC 9.8 $938, #15 CGC 9.8 $5,350, CGC 9.6 $2,511, $1,200

Marvel Preview #1 CGC 9.6 $1,100, #7 CGC 9.4 $1,667

Marvel Spotlight #5 CGC 9.8 $48,500, CGC 9.6 $4,600, CGC 9.4 $3,322, #32 CGC 9.8 $1,060

Marvel Super Heroes #13 CGC 9.4 $2,751, 9.2 $2,000, #15 CGC 9.8 $2,400

Metal Men #1 CGC 9.4 $3,163

New Mutants #87 CGC 9.8 $550, CGC 9.6 $240, #98 CGC 9.9 $9,201, CGC 9.8 $800, CGC 9.4 $325

New Teen Titans #2 CGC 9.8 $910, CGC 9.6 $275, CGC 9.4 $215. CGC 9.2 $185, CGC 9.0 $150

Nick Fury Agent of SHIELD #4 CGC 9.8 $1,499

Night Nurse #1 CGC 9.8 $7,700, CGC 9.6 $2,001, CGC 8.5 $250

Our Army at War #108, CGC 9.0 $2,777

Primer #2 CGC 9.8 $1,500

Savage Tales #1 CGC 9.8 $2,200

Scooby Doo #1 CGC 8.5 $1,055, VG- $250

Sgt. Fury #1 9.2 $9,000, GD+ $600, #13 CGC 9.4 $3,113, NM $1,750

Shazam! #1 CGC 9.9 $9,900

Showcase #4 CGC 4.5 $19,500, CGC 7.5 R $13,001, CGC 3.5 $13,145, GVG $12,000, CGC 1.8 $6,100 #6, FN/VF $2,600, CGC 2.0 $250, #13, CGC 8.5 $6,850, #22 VG $ 2,300, #30 CGC 8.0 $2,300, #31 CGC 9.2 $1,271, #55 CGC 9.6 $4,200

Spawn #1 CGC 9.9 $3,100

Special Marvel Edition #15 CGC 9.8 $1,857

Star Wars #1 CGC 9.8 $5,400, CGC 9.6 $375, CGC 9.2 $175, 35¢ CGC 9.4 $26,290, CGC 6.5 $3,824

Strange Tales #89 CGC 8.0 $4,888, CGC 7.5 $4,099, #101 GD- $150, #110 CGC 8.5 $9,500, $1,355

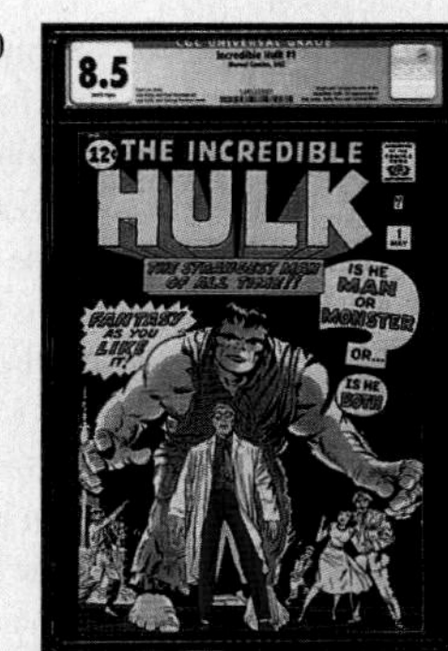

Incredible Hulk #1, CGC 8.5 sold for $132,000.

Suicide Squad #1 VG+ $30

Superman #134 CGC 9.6 $3,400

Swamp Thing #1 CGC 9.8 $3,001

Tales of Suspense #4 CGC 6.0 $425, #39 CGC 9.4 $96,000, CGC 8.5 $25,000, CGC 6.5 $5,860, 5.0 $5,100, #41 CGC 9.4 $5,911, #44, CGC 9.0 $2,177, #48 CGC 9.4 $3,600, #57 CGC 9.4 $5,250

Tales to Astonish #3 CGC 9.4 $51,000, #13, CGC 7.0 $3,450, #27 CGC 9.4 $205,501, CGC 8.5 (Stan Lee sig.) $24,500, #35 CGC 9.2 $28,400, #40 CGC 9.6 $6,433, #44 8.0 $3,500

Teenage Mutant Ninja Turtles #1 CGC 9.6 $15,000

Teen Titans #1 NM $2,400

Thor #176 CGC 9.8 $1,200

THUNDER Agents #1 CGC 9.4 $650

Tomb of Dracula #10 CGC 9.8 $5,002, CGC 9.4 $750, CGC 9.2 $550

Walking Dead #1 CGC 9.8 $3,500, CGC 9.0 $1,650,

Werewolf by Night #15 CGC 9.8 $680.00, #32 CGC 9.6 $8,700, FN $462, #33 CGC 9.8 $3,100

Wolverine #1 CGC 10.0 $17,644

Wonder Woman #199, CGC 9.8 $1,600, #200 FN/VF $70

X-Men #1 CGC 9.6 $350,000, CGC 9.2 $50,500, CGC 8.5 $20,151, FN $7,500, CGC 4.0 $2,520, #4, CGC 9.4 $13,500, CGC 6.0 $800, CGC 5.0 $550, #5 CGC 9.2 $2,255, #66 CGC 9.8 $2,299, #76 CGC 9.6 $3,400, #94 CGC 9.8 $15,535, FN/VF $300, #95 CGC 9.8 $1,631, #101 CGC 8.5 $230, #181 CGC 9.8 $15,000

Bronze Age: Paul Clairmont reported, "It seems there is a resurgence of collectors looking for high grade examples of their favorite 1970s books. There is so much going on during this era when it comes to undervalued and overlooked keys." Josh Nathanson writes, "It was not many years ago that there were only a handful of valuable comics from 1970 and beyond that would sell for $1,000 or more. In recent years that number has increased exponentially thanks to the impact of Hollywood and the realization that books from this era, the oldest of which will be 50 years old in a few years, are not as plentiful in high grade as once thought."

Copper Age: Paul Clairmont wrote, "Certainly, the earlier hot selling books from 2012-2014 leveled off but gave new opportunity for other books to surge in price and once again reaffirm that Copper Age is a lucrative genre with plenty of staying power."

Modern Age: Paul Clairmont reported, "The juggernaut known as *The Walking Dead* has certainly cemented itself as the king of the Modern Age. Copies of issue #1 and #2 continue to soar in price. Not even breaks between the seasons of the TV show seem to slow the increase for long. Now that the show has one of the best modern villains to come along in a while with Negan, I'm seeing prices climb on all issues of the series." Matt Schffman reported, "Still this is a very fun era to find new keys, hidden appearances, resurrected characters, and the new found love for old classics. Condition is everything."

Original Comic Art: The upswing in demand for original comic art (both covers and interior pages) continued to set record prices throughout last year. More and more collectors are buying displayable original art to enhance their comic book collections. There was hundreds of documented sales last year. Here are but a few examples: The cover to *All American Men of War* #101 ('64) by Russ Heath sold for $25,995. A few John Romita Sr. covers sold: *Amazing Spider-Man* #62 went for $179,250, #151 cover ('75) sold for $155,350, *Amazing Spider-Man Special* #6 ('69) brought $143,400, and *The Defenders* #10 cover ('73) sold for $77,675. The cover to *Avengers* #63 ('69) by Gene Colan & George Klein sold for $89,625. *Daredevil* #9 cover ('65) by Wally Wood went for $149,375. A Steve Ditko splash page from *Amazing Spider-Man* #27 brought $139,000. A *Flash Gordon* Sunday (8/14/38) by Alex Raymond went for $95,600 and another Raymond *Flash Gordon* Sunday (4/21/35) sold for $131,450. A *Frankenstein* pg. 154 ('76) by Bernie Wrightson brought $95,600. A Frank Frazetta paperback cover *At the Earth's Core* ('74) went for $1,075,500. Also his painting *The Norseman* sold for $454,100. *Harvey Comics Library* #1 cover by Marvin Bradley & Frank Edgington sold for $46,605. A Graham Ingels 7 pg. story "A Biting Finish" from *Haunt of Fear* #5 sold for $28,688. A Neal Adams cover to *Justice League of America* #66 ('68) went for $41,825. A 6 pg. story "Casey At The Bat" by Jack Davis from *Mad* #6 brought $77,675. The cover to *Silver Surfer* #13 ('70) by John Buscema sold for $68,712. Dan Adkins cover to *Strange Tales* #164 ('68) went for $71,700. The Bernie Wrightson cover to *Swamp Thing* #1('72) sold for $191,200. The Jack Davis cover to *Tales From the Crypt* #40 ('54) brought $71,700. A *Tarzan* Sunday page by Hogarth dated 9/11/49 went for $26,290. Page 1 of *Thunda* #1 ('52) by Frazetta sold for $31,070. The cover to *Weird Science* #8 ('51) by Al Feldstein sold for $33,450. John Byrne's cover to *Wolverine* #17 ('89) brought $33,460 and the cover to *X-Men* #95 ('75) by Dave Cockrum brought $155,350.

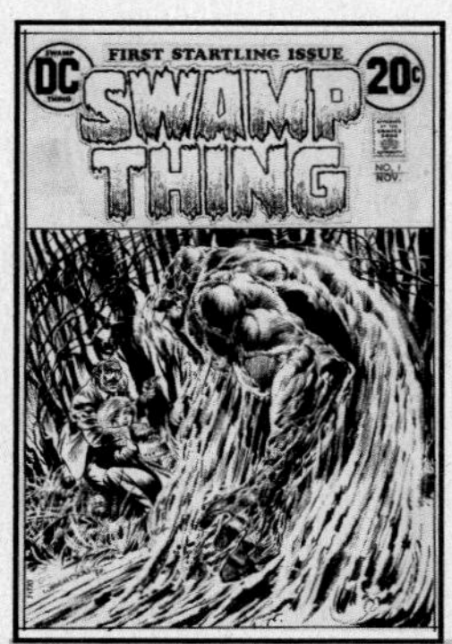

Swamp Thing *#1 cover art by the legendary Bernie Wrightson sold for $191,200.*

Comic Conventions: As Frank Cwiklik (Metropolis Comics) reported, "Even more people crowded into convention halls this year than the year before, with the most notable being the upsurge at the London Supercon (so much so, that they've expanded to a 3-day show this year), and the rather startling fact that the New York ComicCon is now the biggest comic convention in the world both in terms of attendance and floor space. Charles & Jeff Cerrito (Hot Flips) reported, "More and more conventions are being created each month and it seems like there is always a comic book convention to go to every weekend. Whether it is a three or four day convention or just a small local one day show, either way, collectors and dealers are showing up in record numbers. About 15 years ago, you would have a crowd at a small local one day show that would draw 30-50 people, but now it is about 500, with some shows in the thousands. The national day conventions usually drew about 20,000-30,000 and that was considered to be a huge massive crowd. Today these same conventions are drawing way over 100,000. For example, we know San Diego draws a max crowd of 126,000. This year's New York Comic Con drew a record crowd of 180,000 and it's still growing."

Pedigree Collections 2016: Books from top Pedigree collections appeared sporadically in all the top auctions held last year. Mile High (Edgar Church), Larson, Pennsylvania, White Mountain, Gaines file copies, Northford, and others were represented selling to eager buyers.

In Summary: The comic book market is very healthy with hundreds of thousands of comic books sold off web sites, from mailing lists, at conventions, at the major auction houses, and at comic book stores. Prices realized were again mixed depending on rarity, character and grade.

The following market reports were submitted from some of our many advisors and are published here for your information. The opinions in these reports belong to each contributor and do not necessarily reflect the views of the publisher or the staff of *The Overstreet Comic Book Price Guide* or Gemstone Publishing.

They will provide important insights into the thinking of many key players in the marketplace.

See you next year!

Bob

Robert M. Overstreet

COMIC DETECTIVES

MULTIPLE PRINTINGS OF SUPERMAN #1?

The answer is Yes. What it means is still up in the air.

With the record prices commanded over the past few years by *Action Comics* #1 and *Superman* #1, any news about those issues is precisely that: news. So, it made for compelling reading earlier this year when longtime Overstreet Advisor, comic book historian, and veteran dealer Robert Beerbohm posted a discussion topic of Facebook about the first issue of Superman's self-titled series.

"*Superman* #1 (1939) had three distinct print runs of 1) 500,000, 2) 250,000 and 3) 150,000, virtually selling out 900,000 in a bit over a month. The print runs were pretty much right on top of each other," Beerbohm wrote.

That said, he pointed out that no one seemed to have figured out how to distinguish between the printings of these critical key issues, or at the very least no one had communicated such a method to tell them apart to *The Overstreet Comic Book Price Guide*.

Now, he wrote, there is such a way to tell a first printing from the others.

Earlier that day, Beerbohm had posted of the late Fred Guardineer at Wondercon 1999. That in turn led to an exchange which saw Matthew DiMasi post a *Superman* #1 interior page advertisement for *Action Comics* #14.

DiMasi posted "... you can tell by this ad if the *Superman* #1 is a first print or second print. First says 'On Sale June 2' and second print says 'On Sale Now!'"

That's startling enough, but there's more.

Comic book scribe, Batman film producer, and historian Michael Uslan posted a very understandable follow-up: "...Incredible sleuthing! Now... is there any slight difference between the second printing and the third printing?"

Overstreet Advisor and longtime dealer Rick Whitelock pointed out that this topic had been discussed previously on the CGC chat boards but had perhaps remained largely unknown since it never got traction beyond that arena.

As it always has, the position of *The Overstreet Comic Book Price Guide* remains that the marketplace will ascribe any differences in demand, prices realized or esteem attached to any of the three printings of *Superman* #1.

However, we would like to openly request any additional information on these issues. As always, all enlightened opinions are eagerly welcomed, but we are particularly interested in any factual data, including prices realized, regarding this issue.

Additionally, any similar information about other issues would be welcome as well.

- RMO

OVERSTREET COVER SUBJECTS
FIRST APPEARANCES

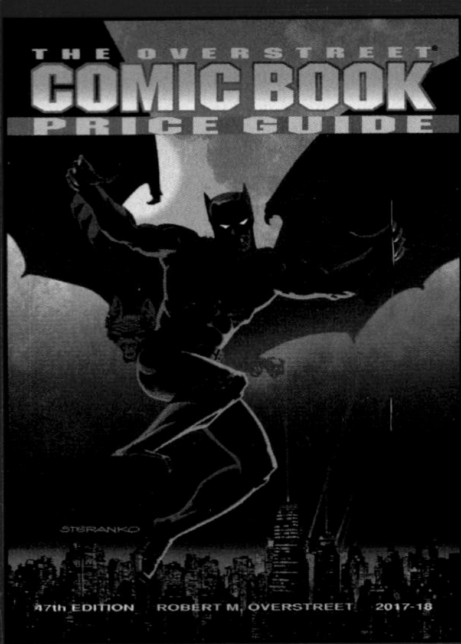

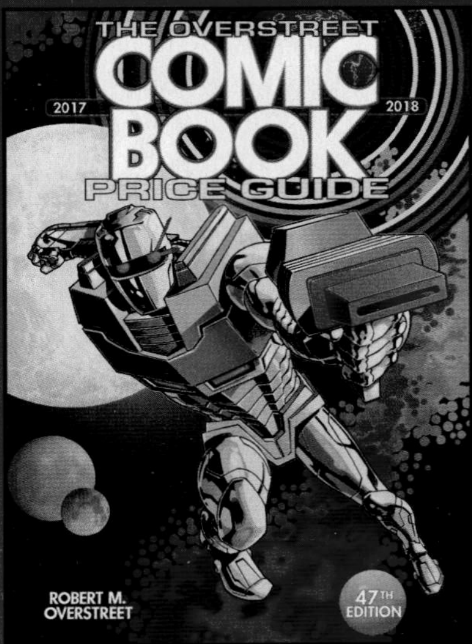

BATMAN
Detective Comics #27
May 1939
2017 NM- PRICE: $2,200,000

ROM, SPACEKNIGHT
Rom #1
December 1979
2017 NM- PRICE: $75

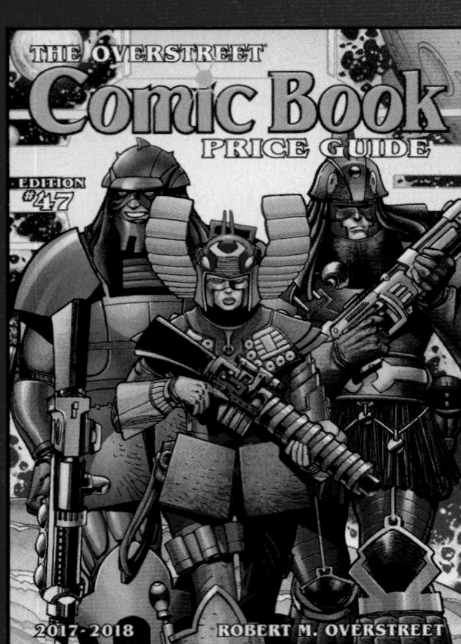

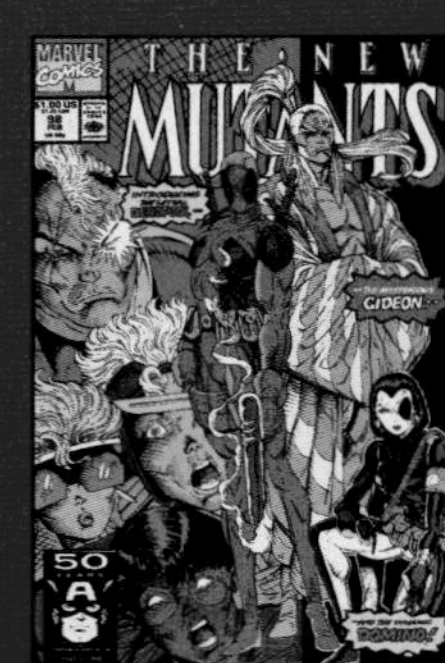

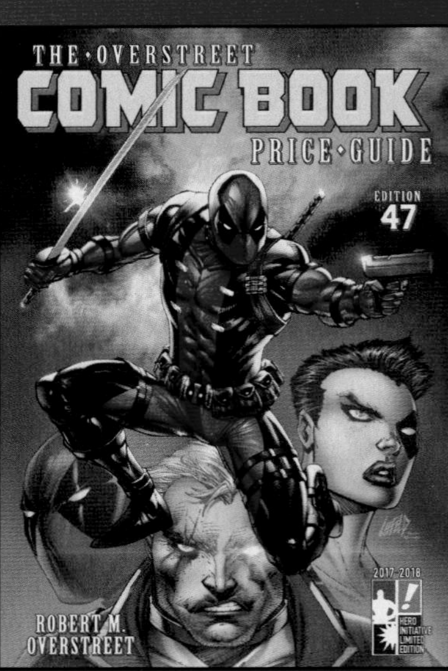

STAR SLAMMERS
Marvel Graphic Novel #6
1983
2017 NM- PRICE: $12

DEADPOOL
New Mutants #98
February 1991
2017 NM- PRICE: $310

Hello,
My name is Darren Adams, owner of West Coast Sports Cards and PristineComics.com. Some of you may know me as the guy from Seattle who sold the THREE MILLION DOLLAR COMIC BOOK. *(see left)*
This sale was viewed by over one million people, marking it as the most watched comic sale in history.
This comic book was originally offered to other dealers prior to myself. Yet in the end, only one company stepped up to meet the demands of the seller... And that was PristineComics.com.
You don't need to have the world's most valuable comic book to sell to us.
We are also one of the largest Buyers of *Magic the Gathering Cards*.

WE ARE ALSO INTERESTED IN:

Comic Books
Magazines
Original Comic Art
Entertainment Items such as
Autographs, Movie Props etc.
Magic The Gathering
Sports Card & Memorabilia

BEFORE SELLING ANYTHING, PLEASE CONSIDER THESE ATTRIBUTES THAT WE GENUINELY OFFER:

DISCRETION: 100% CONFIDENTIAL

We have non-disclosure forms available for those who prefer discretion. We have made other significant purchases that you with not read nor hear about. Quite often for any number of reasons, a seller will prefer discretion.

AN HONEST APPRAISAL:

We know what your comics are truly worth and so will you. Anyone can estimate a value of what a collection might sell for at auction. The fact remains that this is a guess with no guarantees, other than a guarantee only to themselves. They take 10-20+ % of your money regardless of what your comics sell for. YOU pay all shipping costs, have to accept returns in the events a bidder does not pay, take 100% of the risk of getting lower prices than originally estimated, and them have them wait for bidders to pay them, then wait for the auction house to deduct ALL of their fees and send you a check. Sound like fun? Just like in Vegas, the house always wins. Why shouldn't you? After all, it is your collection.
We provide you with a valuation of what your collection is truly worth in today's market and make an offer to purchase your entire collection. If you prefer to sell only certain books with in the collection, we can make offers on those as well. We can also provide you with other favorable suggestions after evaluating your collection.

CONVENIENCE:

We can discuss this by telephone, email and in person.

100% PAYMENT IN FULL NOW:

We pay you 100% in full when purchasing your collection. Period. For those clients who prefer to be paid over time for reasons of their own, we have contracts available.
Consignment centers make you wait until after your items are sold and they have been paid.
Auction houses make you wait until after the auction ends, and after the bidder's funds clear their bank, which oddly enough can take several weeks.

YOUR CHOICE OF PAYMENTS:

We can pay by bank wire, cashier's check or CASH. For those who prefer, we also trade.

QUIT WASTING YOUR TIME !

Confused trying to price your own books?
Do yourself a favor. Drop the guide and let us do the work!

253-941-1986

Paying $250,000+

1986/87 FLEER BASKETBALL FACTORY CASE
The Holy Grail Of Modern Day Basketball
Contains Michael Jordan's Rookie Card and is
The Most Valuable Sports Card
Product of the Last 40 Years.

BGS GRADED "10" BETA BLACK LOTUS
The Highest and Only
BGS 10 Beta Black Lotus
The Holy Grail of Magic The Gathering

PAYING $700,00+
in NM+ condition.
Also buying this book
in ANY condition.

STAN LEE SIGNATURE SERIES

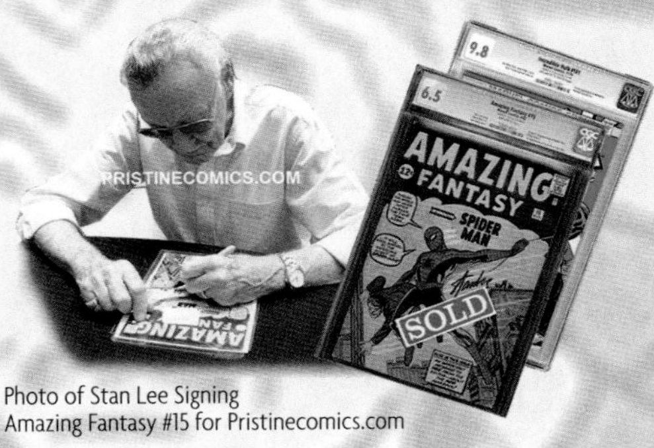

Photo of Stan Lee Signing
Amazing Fantasy #15 for Pristinecomics.com

BUYING SEALED MAGIC THE GATHERING PRODUCTS
Alpha $100,000 a box
Beta/Unlimited/Arabians CALL

- Buying all WOTC MTG produced 1992-2015
- Boxes • Cases • Singles • MOL Sets • Uncut Sheets • Original Art
- Our Largest Deal to Date: 21,000 boxes! No Deal is Too Large!

OUR RETAIL SHOWROOM IS OPEN 7 DAYS A WEEK

WEST COAST SPORTSCARDS
2008 South 314th Street. Federal Way, WA 98003
Located just minutes from Seattle & Tacoma
CALL: 253-941-1986

Darren Adams
Pristine Comics

Greetings comic connoisseurs from the Pristine Comics located in the Pacific Northwest near Seattle!

Golden Age keys such as *Batman* #1 continue selling for high altitude levels and set records. For *Batman* #1, success is not only due to it being *Batman* #1 but also due to the introduction of the Catwoman AND the Joker. The Bat is always hot, meanwhile 1st appearances and 1st cover appearances of key Bat-villains are white hot! Whether it's Joker, Penguin, Riddler, or any of the others, people want them!

Comic fandom as a whole continues its white hot ride. *The Big Bang Theory*, a show about comic geeks is TV's #1 comedy completing its 10th season, with a 2 year renewal in the works as I write this and there are 10 comic related shows on the small screen with half of them superhero related. Then there are the movies, OMG how many are there this year? Some are anticipated, others catch us by surprise, and some are MUCH anticipated!! The list goes on and on. It has truly never been a better time to be a comic fan.

Naturally, this exposure trickles down to back issue sales. Books such as *Amazing Spider-Man* #46 jumped in price when it was announced that the Shocker would be the secondary villain in the new Spidey movie.... what about the Vulture?

2016 featured yet another year of industry growth, comic finds, as well as an INCREDIBLE amount of Hollywood backing in the form of new movies, and an untold number of TV series in the works by all the major networks, along with Netflix and Amazon. The result is equivalent to what would normally amount to a decade worth of media coverage, all of which basically results in a massive ad campaign for the industry, funneled down into a single 12 month period. That alone is phenomenal, but on the heels of well over 5 consecutive years with each year exceeding the other.... WOW!! Stoking the fires and desires of existing and former collectors alike, while also captivating new blood and money into the hobby, you begin to sense existing vintage supply dwindling when compared to demand. All resulting in record prices across the board. A decade's worth of price increases in a single year in many cases. Unlike a stock market bubble however, there IS substance in this equation. First, factor in comics finally getting their due in terms of their rightful place in Americana history and Pop Culture. Then, add the historical significance of character origin and 1st appearances as the point of emphasis in every movie produced. Finally, multiply the number of buyers against a somewhat finite number of vintage books that exist, there is only one way in which the price can go: UP! And the fact is, unlike a bubble, there is rationale to the prices at these levels. Therefore, in my humble opinion, I feel one day in the not to distant future, prices on key Golden Age books in particular will be viewed as ridiculously inexpensive, akin to stepping back in time 10, even 20 years ago and looking to now.

Coins, paintings, vases, even automobiles, these are just a few of the many collectables that have attained single item pricing in the tens of millions and above, and in many cases, even surpassing one hundred million dollar levels. Comics have become respected mainstream pop culture with crossover markets whose demographic reach is as broad as if not broader than the aforementioned categories. I can see no reason to think that these thresholds will also be surpassed with the sale of individual comic books and one day be viewed as expectation rather than surprise. We are just around the corner before the $5 MILLION mark is cracked and certainly the $10 million threshold will be breached at a significantly faster pace.

In terms of Silver Age, record prices occur on a regular basis, and soon enough it will not be uncommon for high calibre books of this era to join *Amazing Fantasy* #15 in surpassing the one million dollar mark. Bronze Age books continue to make shocking headlines as well with record prices being eclipsed on a regular basis. There are, however, exceptions that took place that truly defy logic, and one day perhaps I will understand why a copy of a *Fantastic Four* #52 CGC 9.8 sold for a stunning $90,000. I cannot believe I just wrote that, yet a subsequent copy sold for nearly the same amount just months later. I doubt anyone one saw that coming and if you were lucky enough to be holding one of the other 9.8s that exist at that time, it was a great day for you. That sale still baffles me. I believe the odds in Vegas were significantly higher against *Fantastic Four* #52 hitting 90k than the UFC's Ronda Rousey being defeated!

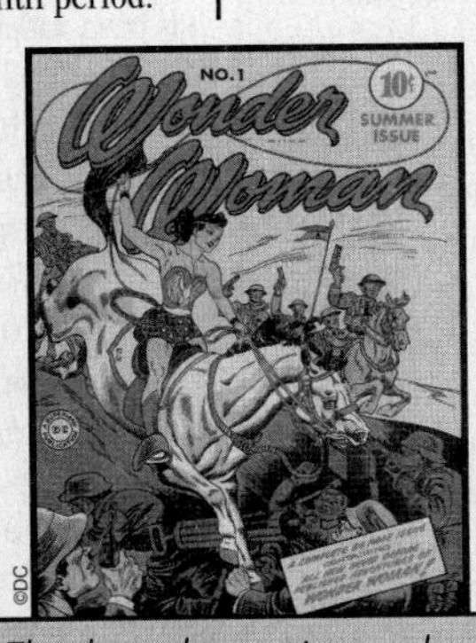

Thanks to the movies, early Wonder Woman issues like ***Wonder Woman #1*** *are shattering records.*

That aside, you cannot go wrong with the blue chips of the industry. 2016 was another great year in the industry and 2017 certainly appears to be even better. The much anticipated *Wonder Woman* movie is upon us and will have already hit the silver screen by the time you recieve this copy of the *Overstreet*! Without doubt, Wonder Woman was the breakout character of 2016's *Batman v Superman*. Audiences could not get enough of Gal Gadot's performance as the Amazing Amazon! With the solo *Wonder Woman* movie coming out this year, *All Star Comics* #8, *Sensation Comics* #1, and *Wonder Woman* #1 are almost guaranteed to continue shattering previous records.

A few months after a copy of *All Star Comics* #8 CGC 9.0 sold for a record price of $411,001, a copy of *Wonder Woman* #1 CGC 9.0 (same grade) sold for nearly $300,000, thus making the *All Star* #8 CGC 9.0 appear like a serious bargain! With her upcoming movie appearances and the surge of female readership and participation, and the magnitude of female characters being created and given their own titles, it stands to reason that it is time for the original Superheroine that started it all to be the first female character in breaking the Million Dollar barrier and join her rightful place in history alongside Batman and Superman!!

As finding original vintage collections gets more difficult, the appreciation for them when you do find them becomes that much more satisfying. Treat people well and good things will happen to you. We feel blessed to be doing something we truly enjoy!! Buy what you enjoy, and invest wisely. In this hobby you get the joy of doing both.

From the Pacific Northwest, Pristine Comics wishes everyone the best for 2017, and remember, we are always looking for quality comics and original comic art and can buy it all! No collection or find is too large. Feel free to call us for free appraisals.

GRANT ADEY
HALO CERTIFICATION PTY LTD. - AUSTRALIA

Conventions: The 2016 convention season kicked in very strong for Halo attending 5 of the major shows. Comic collecting is stronger than I have seen it in the last 12 years, with dealers showcasing their graded comics like never before in this country. All the grading companies, Halo, CGC, CBCS, were represented strongly. On site preliminary grading was working well for both dealers and collectors, with no one on their high horse. Dealers were allowing customers to get a free preliminary check before buying. Collectors were carrying their *Overstreet Price Guide* and their *Grading Guide*. I explain that these two books are field manuals, guide being the operative word. Grading is an art form, not everyone will come to the same conclusion with books 8.5 or less. As I note, certain defects are allowed if other defects are not present.

Supanova conventions continue to attract big crowds of 40,000 people per day, with Sydney and Brisbane being the big two. This year, Halo was invited to Armageddon convention in New Zealand. Those Kiwis have a world class show. I have sold comics worldwide at many conventions in different countries, and Armageddon is world class. Halo was treated to a very attractive offer to make the trip, and success for all was the outcome. The Kiwis are very industrious people, hard working and very quick to learn. I bumped into Harley Yee at Armageddon. I've known Harley for nearly 20 years, and he's always the gentleman. Harley had a very good show and we went out to dinner that Saturday night. Norm Bardell (Fats Comics) joined us chewing over different industry subjects. So for comic sales at these cons, it was all the usuals, Marvel keys, DC books '56 to '60 that have attracted collectors appetites. From what I saw, comics are moving ahead and cosplay is going to the back of the bus.

The Zick Collection: Some of the things a grading company encounters are calls from families who have inherited comic collections. People are wise to the fact these days that comic grades relate to value. A call from the Zick family saw me on a plane for a day's grading and what I saw was unbelievable. Never in my 14 years in the industry here in Oz have I seen anything like this collection. A genuine one owner collection of American comics from the Golden Age. There were 1176 books, all the juicy scarce books from publishers like Ajax, Avon, Hillman, Fox, EC, and pre-Code books galore. Details of the David Zick collection are on the Halo certification website. Since that plane ride in August, another spectacular collection has come to light. A wealthy man had the foresight to buy keys and Golden Age CGCs during those crazy days of "chuck 'em out eBay" in the early 2000s. Presently we are reslabbing his time lapsed CGCs. They are all old label, beautiful books.

New Stuff: Halo recently took the step into the unknown releasing the "flip" or "2up" slab. 2 books inside the one case. This new innovation has been driven by collectors who want to mostly slab long runs of books, late model or new. Collectors can now get two books done for the price of one. Each comic is in its own mylar slip. Two slips, labels on both sides, with a piece of interleafing paper between the two mylar slips to separate the two, so there is no confusion when looking at the book. Each case has a side A and a side B. For lesser grades, defects on the back cover will appear on the label, the same as if there was a torn page, or a page with writing. It's a hidden defects notation. It cuts costs in half, and allows more volume for collectors taking up less space, and also halves the shipping costs. For example, the *Wolverine* #1 to #4 mini series only needs two slabs not four, increasing your margin. Two variants, two autographed issues, linked keys, a 12-part mini series needing only six slabs not twelve, the even number combinations are almost endless. It's a bold move, and though in the early stages, it has been widely accepted by collectors.

Comic Shop Sales Reviews: Comic shops generally are taking more interest in back issues, since grading became readily available. Speaking with an avid collector, I was pleasantly surprised when told a small suburban shop had a couple of *Overstreet* grading guides on the shelf. I work closely with Norm's Fats Comics in Brisbane. Traditionally a back issues only store, it is now expanding into the Diamond weekly comics. Another smart move, Norm has mastered the vintage books department, with his shop holding quarter of a million in stock at any given time. *AF* #15, *ASM* #1's, *FF* #1's, *Hulk* #181, *FF* #48-50, and very strong in Silver and Bronze keys. From my own research, I find books from DC on the break between Golden/Silver Age increasing. *Wonder Woman* #98 kicking her heals up big time. Another interesting fact Golden Age horror and sci-fi getting a giddy up. *Captain Flight* #3, L.B. Cole cover is selling for 6 times *Guide*. Well well well.

International sales: Halo has seen interest in our foreign language labels moving ahead slowly. French and Italian collectors are working with us. The Arabic labels look really cool, but we've only done a few. Australian sales are strong, and meeting the demand has been a challenge. New Zealand is coming on gangbusters. I think we are very close to opening their own facility. USA, boy you guys are tough. It's a hard market, and we continue to probe into the market testing different avenues. Del Stewart, my company man in Tampa, is doing a really good job, and he's working for it, every inch. That's good, as it tells me your grading companies are doing a good job, and the market is tight. Where's the fun if the chicken falls over with its legs in the air. The US market has two heavy weights going toe to toe. It's only Round 3, and on points, there's nothing in it. I run a small grading company and I know a little something and spent 6 years as a professional sportsman. Both these companies are gonna go the 15 rounds. It truly is masterful stuff.

In closing: It's been a great year for Halo. We developed some new products, and opened new offices, both international and domestic. What I find exciting is developing what we have and exploring new possibilities. Thank you to my 2IC Tony Nasser and all the Halo staff and dealers. This is Slim signing off from the furthermost outpost.

Bill Alexander
Collector

Hi everyone and greetings from central California. The comic book market seems to be getting stronger and stronger every day and record high end sales continue to occur with comics from all Ages.

I first off would like to mention that U.S. published comics imported into a foreign country are "U.S. Editions" and they always have been. It appears the hobby is realizing this more and more each day. Many out there wrongly believed that U.S. published comics imported into the U.K., Canada, and Australia were foreign editions even though it never stated anywhere on the books "foreign edition" or a foreign publisher's name. Even today, some comic book grading companies are still misidentifying and mislabeling U.S. published comic books as foreign editions. Change is usually always met with resistance and a well needed change can only help the hobby, not hurt it in any way.. Comic books that are misidentified for what they truly are directly effects their true value in the hobby. These are Type 1a U.S. published first print Edition Marvel U.K. pence cover price variants published in the '60s, '70s and '80s as well as U.S. published first print edition type 1a DC Canadian cover price variants and type 1a Marvel Canadian cover price variants and also Archie type 1a Canadian cover price variants for Archie regular series comics and Archie Adventure Series comics. All are U.S. Editions and were printed with very small print runs. (Type 1a cover price variant) definition can be found in the Overstreet Annual Price Guide #40 on page #1012, where it states "Type 1a Variants: Cover Price Variants intended for foreign distribution with limited regional distribution, published simultaneously with standard or "regular" editions."

Let me move on here and mention a key book from the late Bronze Age which is *Batman* #357 (1st appearance of Jason Todd). The book sold at an online auction house for an amazing $1,300 in CGC 9.8 grade and the book was a Direct Market Edition copy. I wonder what the scarce Type 1a 75 cent Canadian cover price variant of that book would go for in a certified 9.8 grade? *Batman* #357-402 were at the lowest print runs in the history of the title, 75,303-97,941 per month according to *Overstreet* advisor Doug Sulipa. Speaking of Batman, I feel many think that *Batman* #358 4/83 is the 1st full appearance of Batman villain Killer Croc, but it truly is not. Killer Croc's TRUE 1st full appearance is *Detective Comics* #524 3/83 where Killer Croc's face is seen for the first time ever in 3 panels and he appears on 7 story pages in 23 story panels. With *Detective Comics* #524 being his first full appearance in comics, do not expect the book to remain at a very low price in the *Guide*. *Detective Comics* #524 pre-dates *Batman* #358 and was released about 2 weeks earlier than *Batman* #358. Also other Batman books from that era that are really starting to soar in prices realized such as *Batman* #359(first Killer Croc cover with face shown), *Batman* #368, *Batman* #386(1st appearance of the Black Mask). A Modern Age Batman book that is on fire right now I have noticed is *Batman* #635 (first appearance of Jason Todd as the Red Hood). Certified 9.8 graded copies are selling in the $200- $300 range on eBay for that book.

Archie Type1 15-cent cover price variants are up to 90 of 112 confirmed to exist. I believe they are all out there.

The U.S. published first print edition type 1a Marvel Australian cover price variants 1990-1994,1996 that appeared to be off the radar back then to most everyone are becoming more and more known to collectors and are growing in popularity. *New Mutants* #98 is the #1 mega key book of the Marvel Australian cover price variants. One might note that the type 1a Marvel Australian cover price variants 1990-1994 issues are (cover price/month variants) and that the 1996 ones are not cover price/month variants. They are merely cover price variants. I hope 2016 was a good year for everyone and may 2017 be even a better one.

David T. Alexander, Tyler Alexander and Eddie Wendt
DTAcollectibles.com
Culture and Thrills, Inc.

Another amazing comic book year is the best way to describe the activity in 2016. Collecting awareness is at an all-time high among members of the general public. In the past, collectors were often considered to be a little strange or somewhat eccentric. That may still be true but the media exposure to comic books and the entertainment and fun they provide has brought this hobby to the attention of non-collectors worldwide. All the comic character films and TV programs have put the hobby in the face of mainstream society and it has been well received and has come to be respected. The comic book movies are mostly excellent entertainment and it is easy to see how non-collectors are becoming interested in the hobby. Isn't it interesting to see how second level characters like Iron Man and Guardians of the Galaxy are now favorites of people who were barely aware of the existence of comic books a few years ago?

Conventions: Do you remember the early 2000s when the internet was a new phenomenon and was taking control of the comic book hobby and everything else? The convention scene was slowly strangled because collectors could sit at home and buy comics off the web. This was new and convenient and you didn't even have to get dressed to add books to your collection. Convention activity declined for about a decade. Many local and regional shows died. The thing that the internet cannot provide is in-person human interaction and evidently collectors wanted more of it as witnessed by the huge increase in conventions in the last couple of years. Lots of local and regional shows have made a comeback but most of the national publicity is generated by the large multi-media events. Most of these events focus on movie and TV stars and have pushed comics to the background. They might not be the most cost-effective place to buy or sell old comic books, but they do increase awareness of the hobby.

In the past I had attended up to 40 comic shows a year but the internet put an end to that schedule for over a decade. This year I decided to hit a lot more shows around the country and took a 10,000 mile cross country drive starting in Florida and hitting New York and New England before traveling to Chicago to get on Route 66. I went the 2,000 mile distance to Los Angeles and got there in time to make it south to the San Diego Comic Con. I had a dealers table at the first San Diego event in 1970 and attended all of them until 5 years ago when I was firmly based and overly busy in Florida. On this lengthy road trip I was able to check in at many shows around the US and bought tons of books. My car is small so I had to ship boxes almost daily. The Post Office loved me.

This trip had to end as I was setting up at the Tampa Bay Comic Con in early August. Let me take this opportunity to say this. If you have not attended events in Florida you need to consider these: The Tampa Bay Comic Con is considered a regional event but it draws around 60,000 people. There are loads of comics bought and sold at this event. If you come to this one, bring your comics, I would love to take a look at them. It is held at the Tampa Convention Center which is located at the intersection of Tampa Bay and the Hillsborough River and is a very scenic area. Bring along your family, they will have fun.

The other two "can't miss" events in Florida are the Daytona Comic Con and the Deland Toy and Comic show. The Deland event is always early in January and has many buyers and lots of material available. If you are coming from the north in the winter bring some books and set up at this show. The Daytona event takes place twice a year and it is one of the best in Florida for Golden and Silver Age comics. I have nothing to do with any of these shows but just want to share some hidden gems.

New Arrivals: As usual, people are contacting us constantly with material for sale. I cannot remember all the collections that we received in the past year, but there were many as evidenced by our three full 40 foot shipping containers outside the warehouse. I do know there was lots of Golden and Silver Age books, both graded and raw. We did receive a couple of original owner collections that were gobbled up quickly once they were offered for sale.

Comic Sales: What were our top selling books? Marvel and DC Silver Age books were at the top of the list. DC and Timely Golden Age titles were in high demand. I am sure this is not news to anyone. Pre-Code horror and all Romance titles were very popular.

CGC & CBCS graded books sell quickly. Western comics had an uptick. Fawcett superhero comics had increased demand due to rumors of an upcoming film. High grade Bronze Age books sell well. Oddball comics of all types are quick sellers.

Lon Allen and Barry Sandoval Heritage Auctions

As something different for this year's Market Report, we'd like to break down what happened through 2016 from our perspective, i.e. what we sold at auction. This should show what some of the big highlights were throughout the year, and how hot the market has been in general for quality material.

Starting with our Feb. 18-20, 2016 Auction: $5.7 Million total sold of comics and comic art. A CGC 9.4 copy of *Amazing Fantasy* #15, the 1962 first appearance of Spider-Man, sold for $454,100, a record price at public auction for the comic. This copy was not known to the collecting hobby before this auction, as the owner kept it almost perfectly preserved in a safe deposit box for 35 years. Another Spider-Man comic from this collection drew serious attention, selling for $110,537.

A copy of *Detective Comics* #27 shocked the auction room floor when it hammered for $167,300, despite its 4.5 CBCS grade and extensive restoration. A Near Mint 9.4 CGC copy of *Avengers* #1 sold for $98,587. Perhaps foreshadowing the success of his big screen debut in *Captain America: Civil War*, a 9.8 CGC copy of *Fantastic Four* #52, famous for the first appearance of the Black Panther, saw intense bidder interest as it sold for $83,650. *Tales of Suspense* #57, introducing fellow film star and Avenger Hawkeye, sold for $47,800.

The auction included classics of original comic book art, including John Romita Sr.'s original cover art for *Amazing Spider-Man* #62. The 1968 cover, depicting a battle between Spidey and Medusa of the Inhumans, resulted in a war between 26 different bidders that pushed the rarity to $179,250.

The original cover art for *Daredevil* #9, by fan favorite Wally Wood, sold for $149,375. Todd McFarlane's original cover art to *Amazing Spider-Man* #309, a classic 1988 cover featuring four characters, sold for $54,970, and the original art from page 15 from *Amazing Spider-Man* #49 ended at $53,775.

A few more comic book highlights worth mentioning are: *Superman* #1 CGC GD 2.0 $83,650, *Fantastic Four* #49 CGC NM/MT 9.8 $44,215, *Incredible Hulk* #1 CGC VF- 7.5 $43,020, *Tales of Suspense* #39 CBCS NM- 9.2 $43,020, *Fantastic Four* #45 CGC NM/MT 9.8 $35,850 and *Fantastic Four* #50 CGC NM/MT 9.8 $35,850.

May 13-14, 2016 New York auction: $6.55 Million comics and comic art. No piece in the auction garnered more attention than Frank Frazetta's original art for *The Norseman* (1972), which soared amidst spirited bidding to bring a $454,100 final price realized, a record price at auction for the legendary artist.

Original X-Men art is always highly sought-after in Heritage comics events, but Gil Kane and Dave Cockrum's *X-Men* #95 original cover art proved especially popular as it brought home an impressive $155,350 final price. Jack Kirby and Joe Sinnott's *Fantastic Four* #52 unused first Black Panther cover original art saw its historical significance – the first rendition of a black superhero for the cover of a major mainstream comic book (a different version was ultimately used) – drive its final price to an impressive $131,450, the highest price ever achieved for an unpublished piece of original comic art, while Bernie Wrightson's creepy and amazing Page 154 illustration original art from *Frankenstein* (1976) brought a notable $95,600 final price.

All different genres of comics have proven to be strong sellers in this market as proven by these results: *Pep Comics* #34 San Francisco Pedigree CGC NM- 9.2, with a classic Nazi/bondage/hypodermic needle/skull cover by Bob Fujitani, plus a "bullet-in-the-head" panel and an Archie story inside. This copy realized $57,360.

Superman #1 Incomplete CGC PR 0.5: From the front, this looks like a mid-grade copy, but the missing back cover makes this a Poor condition comic book. The final price realized, however, is a first for the hobby for a comic in this modest grade. It realized $57,360.

Richie Rich #1 File Copy (Harvey, 1960) CGC NM+ 9.6: One of the most desirable copies of any Harvey comic in existence. The final price on this comic is a record price by more than $20,000. It realized $48,995.

Captain Marvel Adventures nn (#1) CGC VG/FN 5.0: This is currently tied for the highest-grade of any unrestored copy of the book, illustrating the validity of *Overstreet*'s assertion that the book is "rarely found in Fine or Mint condition," due to being printed on unstable paper stock. One of *Overstreet*'s Top 100 Golden Age Comics, it realized $38,240.

This CGC 9.6 File Copy of **Richie Rich #1** is one of the most desirable Harvey comics in existence.

August 4-6, 2016 Dallas auction: $7.4 Million comics and comic art. *At The Earth's Core*, a 1974 masterpiece by Frank Frazetta, sold for $1,075,500 – setting a world auction record for the hugely popular artist. Records across the board shattered as bidders stepped up to own rare original cover art and a copy of *Action Comics* #1 for $956,000. The sale set a house record for the most valuable copy of *Action Comics* ever sold by Heritage.

The auction's selection of original art sparked intense interest as 23 bids pushed Bernie Wrightson's original cover art for 1972's *Swamp Thing* #1 to $191,200. An iconic 1935 Sunday *Flash Gordon* comic strip original art by Alex Raymond brought $131,450. The artwork, featuring the first appearance of The Witch Queen of Mongo, was executed during the years fans consider the peak of Raymond's artistic achievement.

Making a rare auction appearance, the original comic strip art from Bill Watterson's beloved *Calvin & Hobbes*, dated Jan. 6, 1987, sold for $74,687, and Dan Adkins' 1968 cover art of *Strange Tales* #164 – depicting the mystical Doctor Strange – tied Heritage Auctions' Doctor Strange cover art record at $71,700.

Collectors seeking high-grade comics found plenty to choose, such as the Mile High Pedigree copy of *Startling Comics* #49, 9.6 CGC. The classic cover of a robot kidnapping a damsel in distress vaporized its $50,000 pre-auction estimate to hammer for $101,575. An 8.5 CBCS-graded copy of *Amazing Fantasy* #15 sold for $77,675. An exceptional copy of *Batman* #11, 9.4 CGC, ended at $65,725. A high-grade copy of *Captain America Comics* #1, 8.5 CBCS Restored realized $47,800.

An unbelievable cap to an amazing year was our nearly $10 Million auction held November 17-19 at our Beverly Hills office. Original Underground Comix art and key books from the Golden Age and Silver Age helped push the total value of this auction to nearly $10 million, the second-highest total ever for a comic auction. The #1 Comics auction record ($10,389,821) was set by Heritage in July 2012. The top lot was a rare unrestored copy of *Superman* #1 CGC VG+ 4.5 CGC which sold for $358,500.

One of the auction's highlights was a 9.6 CGC NM+ issue of *Amazing Spider-Man* #1 Curator Pedigree, which is one of the top Silver Age comics Heritage has sold in 15 years of auctions. The book sold for $262,900.

An FN- 5.5 CGC copy of *Batman* #1 was another exceptionally popular Golden Age lot that sold for $239,000. Steve Ditko's *Amazing Spider-Man* #27 Splash Page 1 Original Art hauled in $239,000. The page features Spider-Man and his greatest villain, The Green Goblin.

A *Flash Comics* #1 FN+ 6.5 CGC pulled in $107,550 and *More Fun Comics* #73 VF 8.0 CGC, another coveted issue, went for $104,562.50. In particularly high demand because it includes the origin and first appearance of Aquaman and Green Arrow, its NM- value jumped 43 percent from 2015 to 2016 – the largest jump of any book on *Overstreet*'s Top 100 Golden Age Comics list.

Other top results include, but are not limited to: an Alex Raymond *Flash Gordon* Sunday Comic Strip Original Art dated 8-14-38 (King Features Syndicate) sold for $95,600; a Robert Crumb *Le Monde Selon Crumb* [The World According To Crumb] Promotion Poster Original Art soared to $77,675; a Bill Watterson *Calvin and Hobbes* Daily Comic Strip Original Art dated 4-21-86 achieved $77,675; and *Marvel Comics* #1 GD/VG 3.0 CGC rocketed to $77,675.

If there's something we at Heritage can help you with, you'll find our contact information in our many ads in this book. We look forward to helping more collectors maximize the value of their four-color treasures in the coming year.

Dave Anderson, DDS
Collector

My observations of the comic market over the last year:

1) Prices on any and every key comic or key first appearance of a hero or villain continue to rise almost exponentially. Since it is so costly to assemble runs of titles these days, collectors and investors are buying the key issues.

2) New collectors and investors are entering the marketplace at a healthy and steady pace, and this continues to deplete the availability of desirable comics.

3) Auctions dominate the sales of vintage comic books followed by sales on eBay, and there is much crossover in that a comic can be bought in a Heritage auction (as an example) and immediately be listed on eBay and vice versa. Many times a higher sale results so it appears that buyers don't look at every auction or site, but frequent their favorites.

4) Silver Age books are common in grades below Fine, but sell readily nonetheless due to huge demand. These books in true Near Mint to Mint condition are very rare and command prices well over *Guide* values.

5) Any comic with an unusual or high impact cover will sell immediately at over *Guide*.

6) Any comic that infrequently turns up will sell immediately at over *Guide*.

7) The comic book marketplace continues to be very healthy, and barring a major economic collapse, will continue to be so. Many prices that seem expensive now will look cheap in a short period of time.

Lauren Becker
Comic*Pop Collectibles

A breaking point is coming. The comic market is, at this moment, at its peak. Movies and TV shows have been the reason why the comic market has been soaring to heights of popularity that could never have been imagined. Everyday people, those not associated with the hobby, now want to be "in". How soon until everyday people want "out?"

I am personally seeing a reduction in what people are buying. Yes, numbers are still impressive for print in THIS era...*Black Panther* had a print run of 300,000+, but how many are contributed to retailers speculating on back issue prices (speculators STILL do exist), much less retailer exclusives that were commissioned? How many Avengers and Doctor Strange and Iron Man and Captain America and Inhuman titles ACTUALLY need to be published. There is an over-saturation of titles by the big two at the moment. DC and Marvel trying to outdo the other with relaunches (Marvel NOW vs DC Rebirth) just adds to the ever increasing weight of unsold product that the retailer has to burden himself with, and in this day and age, one massive mis-order could spell doom for the average mom and pop store.

On the flip side, the over-saturation is also affecting secondary market prices. A comic that is under-ordered has a tendency to shoot up very quickly, especially one NOT associated to the big two. Case in point, the new Valiant title *Savage* (#1) has a 1:50 variant. The comic was so under-ordered that an eBay auction for this variant has hit a high of almost $1000. This for a book that was barely two weeks old at time of auction!

So what does this mean? I am seeing declines in the readership of comic purchasing. It's not a doom and gloom observation however. It just means that the wave of popularity is declining where people are not buying "everything". The collecting aspect however, the "I want this because it's valuable" side is still going strong. But how long until the money aspect becomes rocky? These insane, record high prices can't continue...can they?

Everyone laughed when top analysts said that the housing market bubble would burst. When it did, the economic fall out hurt everyone whether they were upside down in their mortgage or not. Property values plummeted, and it would take awhile before the market stabilized. Is the comic market ready for that to happen? Will it?

This past year's sales show no signs of a slow down YET. Prices realized on some graded items that we sold are as follows:

Fantastic Four #52 CGC 8.5...$2500
Ms. Marvel #1 (1977) CGC 9.2...$150
Preacher #1 CGC 9.8...$800
Walking Dead #1 CGC 9.8...$2500
My Greatest Adventures #80 CGC 3.0...$300
Strange Adventures #205 CGC 8.5...$775
Omega Men #3 CGC 9.8...$180
Tomb of Dracula #1 CGC 9.0...$245
Incredible Hulk #181 CGC 8.5...$2200

Prices realized on raw (non-graded) items:

X-Men #1 (gd/vg)...$2800
House of Secrets #92 (FN)...$600
Captain Atom #83 (3 copies in FN)...$120-$150 each
Fantastic Four #3 (GD/GD-)...$250
Batman Adventures #12 (VF newsstand variant) ...$600
Batman #1 (DC 52 NM/MT)...$150

Ultimate Fall Out #4 1:25 variant (NM/MT)...$160

2012 *Captain Marvel* #1 1:25 variant (NM/MT)...$150

This shows that even though (in my opinion) that the readership might be declining, prices on keys and variants are rising, keeping the market afloat based on value of back issues. The other faction that is showing a rise outside of comic books themselves, is in comic related merchandise such as original art and vintage memorabilia/paraphernalia. Some examples:

House of Secrets #3 page by Bernie Wrightson (3 panels...the largest one being all stat)...$1000

Whiz Comics #130 pg 25 ...$300

Marvel Super Hero Club buttons (1966)...$300-$500 ea.

1971 Dr. Strange black light poster...$400

Boxed 1968 Marx Thor Tricycle...$900

The comic related merchandise is starting to be taken a look at a little more (almost as a substitution to comic books themselves). These are unique items that can be "name your own price" pieces, as there is no guide prices. There is a LOT of research that has to be done on items such as these.

It's going to be interesting where the next couple of years are going to take us in this hobby/industry. The ride is going to be wild.

Jim Berry
Collector

Hello. I am a collector and (very) part-time eBay dealer based in Portland, Oregon. I specialize in Golden and Silver Age gems with a particular fondness for pre-Code Horror comics, Science Fiction, Crime, WWII era comics, double covers, anything old, unusual, rare or featuring art/covers by L.B. Cole, Steve Ditko, Jack Kamen, Bernard Baily, Matt Fox, Basil Wolverton, and many more. I also collect and read new stuff by the great creators of today, Warren Ellis, Daniel Clowes, Garth Ennis, Alan Moore, Jeff Lemire, anything Jodorowsky and Moebius.

This year I've moved away from pursuing old comics as I have in the past. Since the early 1990s, I've advertised in the classified section of local papers with great success. I've lived in various cities in that time and there were periods where I'd come home from school or work and have multiple messages (on my analog answering machine) featuring serious inquiries from original owners interested in selling their old comics or, sometimes, just talking about their old comics.

This year has been slow for me. Clearly, with the pop-zeitgeist focused so intensely on Marvel and DC heroes in film and TV coupled with the internet's immediate access to information regarding prices, my model of comic collecting is pretty much dead. Everyone you meet is a potential comic book dealer. A funny story to illustrate:

This past February, I got a call from an elderly couple wanting to sell their comic collection. They lived out on the coast of Oregon in an old, weather-beaten home, and I drove out on a clear, cold day, a two-hour drive. There were around 1000 comics from the 1940s and early '50s, collected and kept by the husband who kept telling his wife, "Just get them out of here!" Their banter was priceless, "You've kept them for 70 years, another few minutes isn't going to kill you!" "Oh, yeah? It might if you keep it up." He was reading the newspaper for most of the time but would chime in when I'd find a cool book. There was a *Batman* #20 in tatters, and I mentioned that it was the first Batmobile cover and his eyes lit up and he said, "My older brother gave me that."

I spent hours going through them. Most of the books were extremely low grade and most were misc. War, Western, and Dell but there were some great books, including a *Mister Mystery* #12 that took my breath away. They were thrilled with my offer, expecting it would be in the hundreds, not the thousands of dollars. And then the phone rang. It was their daughter who, upon hearing of my offer, immediately shut the deal down saying that their grandson (the daughter's son) could sell them on eBay and get more. I was exhausted, hungry, and utterly dejected as I prepared to leave. Seeing this, the old man said, "Why don't you pick out a few and make me an offer on those." So the *Mister Mystery* came home with me after all but just by the skin of my teeth.

One collection I loved finding this year was a complete DC Vertigo collection from the 1990s and 2000s. I read, for the first time, complete runs of *Hellblazer*, *Lucifer*, *Preacher* and many others, some fun, some not so fun. But it reminded me that comic collecting used to be about reading! Sadly, it seems that comic collecting as it exists now is more about speculating on movie and TV characters, flipping books, and going for keys exclusively.

I am encouraged by what has happened in the world of original comic art. Though there is no price guide and little in the way of a metric to predict the value of original comic art, prices continue to push on and up. If you love comics, you owe it to yourself to try and track down the original art to a meaningful comic book page . . . something you loved as a kid, something that speaks to you. Once you see the actual ink the artist placed on the page, you will be hooked. Check out comicartfans.com if you have any interest in comic art.

I went to a few shows this year, all in the Northwest and enjoyed them for what they are, costume parties and a chance for kids to meet their screen stars. To one, The Rose City Show, I brought my daughter and her two friends and we walked around and shot pictures with cosplayers, bought a couple of Lego minifigs. We had a fun time.

Read those comics, people!

My best memories with comics this year are reading them with my daughter, Willa. Our favorites are *Lumberjanes*, *My Little Pony*, *Star Wars*, and *Mouse Guard*. I highly recommend these titles, especially if you have an eight-year-old daughter.

My retailer of the year is John Hill at Hills Of Comes in Auburn, Washington. John is the king and his shop is a palace filled with treasure. It is the most amazing comic shop in the Northwest, 7200 square feet of nothing but comic books. John is also a great guy to deal with if you have an old collection of books.

Thank you to Mr. Overstreet and the crew at Gemstone for their efforts and for the honor of being included in this book.

Good wishes and happy collecting to you in 2017.

Tim Bildhauser
CBCS - Foreign Comic Specialist

It's hard to believe that another year has passed by so quickly, and what a year it's been. Over the course of 2016, CBCS has continued to grow in the industry and submissions don't show any sign of slowing down. This year we attended even more conventions than in 2015 and the crowds appear to be getting bigger year after year.

We took our first shot at on-site grading this year at the Tampa Bay Comic Con in August. I was very pleased overall with how it went and want to thank everyone at the office for the roles they played and for showing what we're capable of accomplishing as a team.

The U.S. market for foreign books has continued to grow steadily this past year. We saw close to three times the number of foreign books submitted for grading this year. Books continue to sell at steadily increasing prices as demand increases. I worked the booth at close to a dozen conventions in the last 12 months and at every single one was asked by at least one person about foreign comics. I also did panels on foreign comics at the Indiana, Denver & Tampa Bay Comic Cons. They were well received by the people that attended and I'm looking forward to, possibly, doing some more next year.

2016 also heralded in CBCS's first foray into international comic shows. We set up at Toronto Comic Con, Fan Expo Toronto & Fan Expo Vancouver. We're definitely looking forward to continuing on that path in 2017.

One of the topics I was asked about most frequently this year was the Canadian editions of some of the 1950s DC books. Some of you, I'm sure, may have seen a few of these over the years. One collector inquired about the difference between the Canadian and U.S. editions. I informed him that, with every example I've seen first hand, the main story based on the cover feature is intact, however, one of the back up stories will be missing. I'm not sure if this was done as a means of reducing production costs or some other reason. I simply haven't been able to examine enough issues from a given title to determine if it's the same back up character left out from month to month or if it was randomly selected features. Time will tell and when it does, I'll keep you posted.

As far as foreign comics in general, there have been a few interesting developments. Everyone in the hobby knows that Harley Quinn is one of the hottest properties out there. What most people don't know is that there are 15 confirmed foreign editions of *Batman Adventures* #12 that exist. Sales on the copies that have hit the American market have been strong and I suspect that trend will continue.

La Prensa and Novaro (Mexico) key issues still lead the pack as far as demand goes but I'm seeing more and more collectors branching out and taking notice of books beyond their initial collecting focus, including original material published in other countries.

There wasn't a month that went by in 2016 that didn't bring the discovery of something new with it. I keep telling people that this is a market in its infancy and the potential it holds is enormous. As more collectors start to look for these international gems, more are discovered. Collections from both Australia and South Africa surfaced and were very quickly swallowed up by those on the lookout. In this corner of the hobby, you have to keep your eyes peeled and act quickly because, plain and simple, if you hesitate when you see a book come up for sale and someone else buys it, you may not get another chance at a copy for years.

The biggest discovery in foreign comics this year is, probably, from the Philippines though. A copy of *All-Star Western* #11 (2nd appearance of Jonah Hex) from National Bookstore surfaced. It gives a solid indication that #10 may possibly exist as well which would be, to date, the most significant key Bronze Age issue of the bookstore editions to surface. We'll just have to wait and see.

In closing I'd like to say that 2016 was a good year for the hobby, CBCS, FCC and myself. Just remember that as a collector, buy what you like and you won't regret buying it but most of all... enjoy it. If you're not having fun collecting comics, you're doing it wrong.

Peter Bilelis, Esq.
Collector

Once upon a time, a vintage comic book got to be worth a lot of money because it was popular and important, and scarce in the marketplace. Today, there are increasing examples of vintage books that were never very popular, that are quite plentiful (even in very high-grade), and yet are going from the $1 long boxes (slight exaggeration) to astronomically priced "wall books." The game has definitely changed and continues to evolve. For instance, it wasn't that long ago that *Werewolf by Night* #32 (1st Moon Knight, a book that is far from scarce) in very nice shape sat in very many "long boxes" and was priced at around $25. Now, this book is on every seller's wall, is in-demand and a high-grade copy could run you $1k or more. It's the same with books like *Avengers* #57, *Hero for Hire* #1 and *Captain America* #117. Snails until very recently. This phenomenon has even affected Golden Age and early Silver Age books. For eons, books like *Tales to Astonish* #27 sat unnoticed, and books like *All Star Comics* #8 and *Marvel Family* #1 were considered dogs. Not anymore. Frankly, I was always amazed that such great books sat in relative obscurity. But they did. As did many others - until Hollywood, Netflix and TV decided to introduce a host of lesser-known or currently less popular characters to the screen, and a mainstream audience.

In 2016, this trend continued. The big and small screen continue to unnaturally influence appeal and back issue market prices. By "unnaturally influence," I mean a B-level or C-level book that was never very popular suddenly blows up in popularity and pricing - not because of, say, a new and exciting storyline, or the early issues now appealing to a new audience, but because of a film or TV series featuring the book's character. Often, even if the character debuted in a book that had a print-run of say 100,000 copies, was known to have been stock-piled and is plentiful today in very high grade, that character's first appearance book will still skyrocket in demand and price with the announcement of an upcoming screen appearance.

In general, I think the "Hollywood factor" is good for the hobby, in that it's helping superheroes become more and more a part of pop culture and, as such, more relevant. I just question whether current value for a lot of this "unnaturally influenced" material is sustainable, given its vast availability (even in very high-grade) and the uncertainty of how popular the character will remain after the film sequels or the TV series ends.

2016 also saw the Platinum Age and Golden Age, and some Silver Age market sectors, continue down the bifurcated path discussed in several of my prior Market Reports. On the one hand, it was clear that: (a) blue chip books, such as *Action*, *Superman*, *Detective*, *Batman*, *Sensation*, *Wonder Woman*, *All Star* (esp. #8 and on), *Captain America Comics*; *Pep* (as of issue #22); *Amazing Fantasy* #15, *Amazing Spider-Man*; *Uncanny X-Men*, etc.; (b) cult status books, such as *New Adventure* #26; *Pep* #22, 34; *More Fun* #14, *Detective* #2, 8; *Marvel Mystery* #9; *Suspense* #3; *National* #7, *Crime Does Not Pay* #24; *True Crime Comics* #2-3; *Green Lantern* #76; *Hulk* #181; *Giant-Size X-Men* #1, etc.; and (c) classic covers, such as *Detective* #31, 35; *Superman* #14; *Adventure* #73, 79; *Master* #27, 32 - 34, 40; *More Fun* #54, 65; *Phantom Lady* #17, 23; *Mask Comics* #1; *Pep* #20; *JLA* #21, 22; *Batman* #227, 234; *Avengers* #4, etc., all have a large and growing audience, with prices continuing to escalate, and some examples reported to have sold for record high prices. And, with respect to blue chip titles, this isn't relegated to key issues - just look at how *Detective Comics* issues featuring Joker cover appearances (e.g. #62, 69, 71, 76) have exploded!

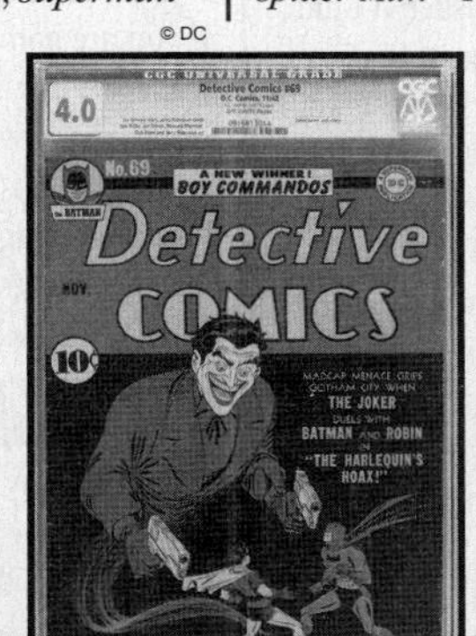

Detective Comics *issues featuring Joker cover appearances (like #69) have exploded.*

Record and very high reported sale prices continue to suggest growing confidence in comic books as a sort of investment. But it also means more of this material is becoming out of reach to most hobbyists. I heard people at a few shows this year refer to uber-expensive books as "one percent" books, meaning only 1% of the hobby could afford to buy them. In my last Market Report I discussed the "drafting effect" which, in essence, means a record sale of one book has the effect of pulling up with it the value of the same book in lower grades, other books in the same title and other similar books. I wonder if one reason books like the Joker cover *Detective*s mentioned above are exploding in value is because the classic Joker cover (*Batman* #11) is now, in high grade, virtually out of reach to most collectors? It's also important to note that reported record sales of many of these 1% books, and probably 2-5% books, are actually between dealers, or to dealers at auctions, rather than from dealers to anyone else in the hobby. For the collector, it's important to recognize that this, in a sense, incestuous dealer-to-dealer "sale" dynamic, also unnaturally influences market perception of value. So, what would be the market value of these über-expensive books without this skewing dynamic? Unknown. But it's important to remember dealer-to-dealer sales, which can take many forms and aren't necessarily cash, or all-cash, deals, are very different than traditional sales to hobbyists, and are not necessarily the best indicator or a true reflection of market value.

And, on the other hand, it's also true that interest in many forgotten characters continues to wane. Because of this, a growing conversation is whether Platinum Age and Golden Age are in a bubble. From what I've seen, the answer is a definite "no." Many cornerstones of fandom stem from this era, with many heroes celebrating 75th birthdays. And, as discussed above, many reported record sale prices are for GA books. In a sense, all this means is that the hobbyist needs to be informed and selective. My approach is to buy the best copies I can afford of the tier 1 titles I collect (blue chips, etc.), and for those "more tenuous" titles I collect, I usually opt for the $250 Fine copy over the $3k Near Mint copy.

In terms of Silver Age, an increasing number of mainstream key books (*AF*#15, *TTA*#27, *Avengers* #4, *Amazing Spider-Man* #1, *B&B* #28, *JLA* #21-22, *JIM* #83, *Hulk* #1 and *Action* #252 to name a few) and their respective titles continued to increase in popularity and price. I also noticed that, due to the enormous number of available copies of these books, collectors were often quite picky, preferring to pass on, say, a CGC 5.5 with a certain type of offensive defect or lesser page quality, knowing there are many other copies in this grade without that particular defect and with preferable page quality. It's also true that, despite best efforts by the poor souls chained to desks grading these books, it's common knowledge that a 5.0 could come up for sale that looks superior in grade to a 5.5, causing hobbyists to be even more judicious in expensive buying decisions. This mid-grade material was also an area where prices were often very negotiable, even on many keys, and I saw several of those mentioned above (in CGC 5.0 - 7.5) sell for 25-40% less than asking price. I used very picky criteria and was still able to score a few of the keys. It was a weird experience, given I primarily collect Golden Age and you're often lucky to just find a copy - in any grade.

Finally, on a "non-market" note (or rant, maybe) I am a huge fan of superheroes on the big screen - especially when the films are great. For this reason, I wish the DC filmmakers would benchmark with either the DC TV folks or the Marvel film folks and start making films with more "real" stories and more relatable characters. I think most DC films feature dark, overly serious and often one-dimensional characters, with film success relying extensively on the hero involved in non-stop action sequences. Compare that to what the DC TV folks are doing with a show like *Gotham*. No superhero, no non-stop action, and yet this show is killing it with both great character development and well-developed, and more intellectual, stories! Marvel films also don't rely on a hero and non-stop action. Just look at what Marvel did with *Thor* and *Ant-Man*. In *Thor*, they took an eternal B character, a thunder god (?) with a truly make-believe backstory and turned him into a flesh-and-blood, believable and relatable hero, accomplishing this through a love story with the hero decked out in …. jeans and a t-shirt. If I were to run into the film version of *Ant-Man*'s Scott Lang or even *Thor* in a coffee shop, I feel like I would know them enough to chat. Because of all the character development, Marvel sequels feel like a soap opera's next episode. My vote is for DC to loan their TV folks to DC film, or just start poaching Marvel talent. To quote, "'nuff said."

Good luck hunting in 2017…

Steve Borock
CBCS
President and Primary Grader

As always, it would be a shame and an injustice if I did not mention that we are all reading this because of the hard work and professionalism that J.C. Vaughn, Mark Huesman, their team and, most importantly, Bob Overstreet has put into this 47th edition of the *Guide*. Without this *Guide* coming out 47 years ago, changing the landscape of our hobby, I truly believe that, not only would our market not be as healthy as it is today, but our sense of community would not be as enjoyable. The friends I have made just by reaching out to people in this *Guide* over the many years has just been incredible! That includes Bob Overstreet, who I not only consider a great friend, but a mentor as well!

I would also be remiss if I did not say "Thank you!" to Steve Geppi and his family for keeping the *Guide* going.

For those of you who do not know, since I am the President and Primary Grader at CBCS, I must stay impartial and stay away from "pricing". This "market report" will only focus on what is being submitted and my take on the "health" of the hobby.

Based on the amount of submissions we are getting, too many to stop us working 24/7, I would say the market is doing great!

What I am seeing submitted is an overabundance of books that you will be reading about in other reports here. That said, every time a new movie or TV show based on a comic is announced, we seem to get inundated with that title or 1st appearances of a certain character or team. Speculation runs rampant. That said, we at CBCS are also seeing a huge amount of vintage books that have nothing to do with movies or TV. Not only are we seeing the "blue chip" comics like *Batman*, *Superman*, *Amazing Spider-Man*, early Marvel, Timely, and DC superheroes, but we are starting to see so many cool esoteric books as well. WWII covers, Good Girl covers, and classic covers are still very being submitted in droves. As for Modern comics, a day does not go by where we do not see a copy of *Batman Adventures* #12 (1st Harley Quinn) or *New Mutants* #98 (1st Deadpool). Those two seem to be the king and queen of Moderns!

Just like last year, restored and conserved comics seem to be gaining more respect, as it's easier and more affordable to get them. I also feel that the quality of work has really improved over the past few years and the books no longer look like "patchwork quilts."

As always, I would like to give a "shout out" to our hobby's greatest charity, the Hero Initiative. Hero gives back to those in need who created the wonderful characters we all enjoy. Please check them out at www.heroinitiative.org. This marks the 8th year that there is a Hero Initiative special limited edition of *The Overstreet Comic Book Price Guide* where the proceeds go directly to the charity! I hope this is the one you are reading right now.

I will end my report the same way I do every year. This is for the newer collectors in our great hobby, as I hope that the more seasoned collectors already know this. Even though I believe in this hobby, the market and its future, and been in it since I was a kid, there is no such thing as a "free lunch." If you are going to invest in comic books, you had better love what you buy. If the economy ever goes "really bad," just like with stocks, precious metal, real estate, or anything else considered an "investment," you will not be able to sell them for a really high price very quickly and you can certainly not use comics to feed, house or feed your family in times of need. The best advice I can give, and I have been saying this for a long, long time is "Buy what you love and can afford." It really is that simple.

Just enjoy collecting and reading comic books, enjoy the friendships we make in this wonderful hobby, look around and enjoy all the cool stuff our hobby has to offer from original art and comic books, to the movies and TV shows based on the characters we love so much, to comic memorabilia and it will all seem worth it in the end.

I hope to see and talk with many of you reading this at the conventions that I and CBCS will be attending this coming year! Thank you for taking the time to read this and, as always, HAPPY COLLECTING!

Richard M. Brown
Collector

I'm getting *Flash* again. So many characters are complicated, and I think the fanboys will drive *Showcase* #4 and early Captain Cold apps. in *Showcase* #8 and *Flash* #106 with Grodd and Pied Piper origins. These have potential (and the TV show certainly helps.)

Disney has a history of famous talking animals like Donald Duck and Mickey Mouse, and I can see further promotion of Rocket Raccoon and Groot now. *Guardians* is fun and the freshness of the characters gives the writers tremendous flexibility with where to go next. And my beloved Howard the Duck is finally popular again, due to the *Guardians* cameo. Howard met KISS, ran for President, and perhaps someday he will meet Donald Duck in the cartoons.

Prices on the Rise: I'll start with Black Adam's only Golden Age appearance in *Marvel Family* #1. Early Justice League like *Brave and the Bold* #28 and *J.L.A.* #1. *New Mutants* #98 and early Harley Quinn appearances. I think DC teased us and the Joker will be permanent in future movies. Offbeat characters like Rocket and Groot will continue to flourish. And finally, *More Fun* #73 and other early Green Arrow appearances.

Prices on the Decline: Green Lantern - at least for now. Buy *Showcase* #22 and *Green Lantern* #1 right now! DC will eventually find its voice and Green Lantern will find its niche. So far, another "ring" character (The Mandarin) is very poorly portrayed in the *Iron Man* movie-verse.

Brett Carreras
VA Comicon

Greetings, fellow Comic Fans! What an incredible year I've had in comics! I moved full-time to Richmond, VA from San Francisco and have completely stepped back into this crazy world. While many of you know me as the director of the VA Comicon (vacomicon.com), in 2016 I spent almost every second diving into this medium from ALL angles... licensing and promoting...operations and exhibiting...even creating and storytelling!

In addition to running the VA Comicon series of shows in 2016, I also took on the daunting role of managing the Going-Out-of-Business Sale of the legendary Dave's Comics retail mega-store in Richmond (remember their ½ page "missed an issue?" ads during the '90s?) following the passing of my longtime friend, David Luebke. Subsequent to the closure of the retail store in July, I have assumed leadership of their massive 750,000 unit warehouse. It has been a lot of work, but I am VERY proud of what we have been able to accomplish these last 8 months. All of this, of course, got me BACK into old funny books, and BACK out on the road. Now I can honestly say: The state of the convention market is STRONG!

My first stop on the convention trail this year was HeroesCon in Charlotte, where I quietly sold an important Golden Age collection before the event even started. It was an amazing show, with total sales approaching six figures for us. Several people were stunned to see me "back on the road", but it is ALWAYS fun when you have exciting inventory!

The other "BIG SHOW" I exhibited at in 2016 was San Diego on behalf of the VA Comicon. This was a marketing show for me, where we have a booth promoting both my show, and Awesome-Con (Washington, DC's largest pop-culture event), a show I am proud to be on the Event Staff for (you will find me wandering around Artist Alley). I brought copies of our *Back to the Future* #1 exclusive to SDCC, and sold out by Saturday. We also participated in the return of *Rom* by debuting our Ltd 500 Silver Foil variant of #1 on launch day, and had a signing with the creative team on Saturday. What a cool experience to have at a comic show! And speaking of comic shows, without further ado, I present to you my first ever...

VA Comicon Convention Market Report: Here goes! For my own show, the VA Comicon, I am really jazzed to say 2016 was our most amazing year EVER! Not only did we celebrate our 30th year (!!!), but we also experienced unprecedented growth, while delivering a family friendly and budget-minded event to both retailers and attendees. (Adult tickets start at just $10!)

When I took over promotion of the show in 2005, we were located in a 2,000 sq. ft. ballroom (more on this later), catering to approximately 150 die-hard comic fans several times a year. In 2016, all three of our VA Comicon events were in a massive 36,000 square foot space, featuring over a hundred 10x10 booths of the neatest stuff, and the greatest comics around!!!

I am VERY happy to say our attendance skyrocketed this year with hallways packed with both customers and some of the coolest collectibles. The fact that THOUSANDS of people come to our shows (Richmond has a population of less than 250,000 people), still blows my mind...especially with how really, really crowded the convention market has become! When I took over promoting the VA Comicon 11 years ago, the only other comic shows I knew of were a firehouse show near DC (with horrible traffic), and Roger Mannon's awesome Vintage Collectibles show once a year in Roanoke...a 4 hour drive from us in Richmond. Today it's crazy. In addition to Wizard World Richmond (5 miles from us), we now we have the NOVA series of comic shows (2 times a year), Shoff Promotions (8 times a year), The Tidewater Comic-Con events (2 times a year), The Roanoke Valley Comicon (2 times a year), and Awesome-Con DC, plus of course, Roger's show. That's 17 other shows (PLUS my shows!) in a state that only takes 4 hours to drive through on I-95.

Thankfully, I am happy to say I know most of these show promoters personally, and am PROUD to call them my friends. The best thing about the Virginia / DC area is that EVERYONE loves comics, and we have ALL experienced awesome growth.

For my show, our first 1-day event of the year (in February) was also one of the most successful for my exhibitors, and was also our best attended 1-day show EVER! We decided to add a Summer event in 2016, which was met with equal success, followed by our gala 2-day event on Halloweekend. All shows were packed with fans, cosplayers and collectors. Many of my traveling exhibitors remarked to me on our growth, and the robust spending of my fans, something I am quite proud of.

As I just mentioned, our Fall event was on Halloweekend. I really wanted 30th anniversary show to be something special for the fans. We pulled out all of the stops, and welcomed Tom King (the #1 writer of *Batman*), Howard Chaykin, Joe Staton, Mark Waid, Larry Stroman, Dan Parent, Fernando Ruiz, Billy Tucci and almost 100 other artists to Richmond, and the fans LOVED it, making it our biggest 2-day showing in our history. And you wouldn't believe the costumes!

Speaking of costumes, I want to speak my piece on the matter of Cosplay, and expound on a few very keen solutions we have discovered which can temper most emotions when it comes to the Cosplay aspect of shows...especially as the market continues to grow. Here goes:

1) I LOVE cosplay. I think it is the coolest thing ever to be able to buy a Batman comic while standing beside Batman! In fact *The Overstreet Guide to Cosplay* debuted at our show back in 2015 and features guests from our show on the cover. Order it today!

2) Approximately 50% of attendees at my show arrive in full costume, with a significant majority of those costumes being hand-made.

3) The huge number of ticket sales to cosplayers is what keeps our admission prices so low.

4) We continued to offer a full hour of early-bird time, limited to only 100 special tickets per show. This program has been a complete treat and gives my vendors time to interact one-on-one with some of their best clients.

5) Finally, I introduced the RVA Comic Collector's Con in December.

The RVA Collector's Con was a response to something I have been feeling in the pit of my stomach for a VERY long time. Do you know what I missed? I missed that old 2,000 square foot ballroom I mentioned earlier. I missed running a show that cost practically nothing to get into, and was just loaded with the best comics and sweetest deals around. So I did something about it. I gathered up my longest running comic vendors, plus reached out to a handful of friends we haven't had at the show in a long time. We rented that VERY SAME 2,000 sq. ft. old ballroom we were in when I began with the VA Comicon, and we had ourselves an event. It was a pure comic show! Twelve of the finest comic vendors on the planet got to spend 6 hours laughing and trading and talking comics with some of the greatest collectors from near and far. I even debuted a double-collection of high-grade Bronze I had the opportunity to invest in with my roommates (I haven't actively exhibited for myself in about 5 years). And y'know what? It was all amazing.

So, looking back on 2016, I realized I promoted an astounding TEN different comic book events (including the INSANE "going out of business" events for Dave's), I helped exhibit at my 2 favorite shows on the planet, San Diego and Heroes-Con, I was on Event Staff at the national-level pop culture show Awesome-Con in DC run by one of my best friends, and I helped to shut down one of the coolest retail stores in the country, while working to develop their packed warehouse into something profitable. In my free time I was lucky enough to take a "Creating Comics" class at the Visual Arts Center co-taught by Scott Wegener (Atomic Robo!!!) as well as a super-cool screen printing class. I also studied several weeks to learn the subtle art of comic book cleaning and pressing. In December I shared a table at the Star Wars Days festival, and gave away free sketches all day long, offering to draw practically anything the children wanted. As far as printed material, I licensed the best looking Rom comic EVER (Silver Foil cover by Kevin Roberts!), printed a series of collectible cosplay trading cards, and published 3 books on Amazon.

For 2017, in addition to running the VA Comicon, I have been tapped to take on promotion of the world-famous Collectibles Expo (collectiblesexpo.com). I will continue to develop the core inventory for Dave's Comics (I can't wait to show people what we are working on with CBCS), while aggressively liquidating some of the bulk of this inventory. For example, we have over 20,000 uncirculated G.I. Joe comics from the 1980s in Mint condition. As of this writing, I am about to announce 3 different Ltd. 100 Wonder Woman exclusives I have been working on for a few months, which we will launch at the "Awesome Convention Exclusives" booth in San Diego, coming out the SAME DAY as this *Overstreet* you are holding right now!

In closing, I wanted to say thank you. Thank you, exhibitors and fans for helping me to break ALL of our records in 2016. Thank you, Sheryl and Marlon for the opportunity to work with you and the Dave's Comics crew. Thank you, people of Richmond, for naming me in *Style Weekly*'s Top 40 under 40, and finally, thank you to the approximately 150 people close enough to make it on my Facebook friends list. The list consists of my VERY closest buddies, confidants, business partners, artists and teachers. I love each and every one of you.

Charles and Jeff Cerrito
Hot Flips

Another year has gone by in the comic book industry. More and more conventions are being created each month and it seems like there is always a comic book convention to go to every weekend. Whether it is a three or four day convention or just a small local one day show, either way, no matter where you attend, collectors and dealers are showing up in record numbers. About 15 years ago, you would have a crowd at a small local 1 day show that would draw 30-50 people, but now it is about 500, with some shows in the thousands. The national day conventions usually drew about 20,000-30,000 and that was considered to be a huge massive crowd. Today these same conventions are drawing way over 100,000. For example, we know San Diego draws a max crowd of 126,000. This year's New York Comic Con drew a record crowd of 180,000 and it's still growing. The comic book convention is not just a pop culture event, it is now a way of life.

As collectors go into these conventions, everyone has a want list. There are people of all ages, men and women, young boys and girls, always looking for that something special. In our experiences at most conventions around the country, kids to young adults plan to look for variant issues as well as comics from the late 1980s and 1990s. I find it amazing that we could not give this stuff away 15 years ago due to the fact it was overproduced. After thinking about that, there are so many more collectors out there than in the last 15 years.

With more and more collectors out there from the 1980s and 1990s, there is more of a demand because the back issues from those years are more affordable, with some exceptions of course. Everyone wants the hottest super hero out there from Deadpool to Harley Quinn, Batman, Avengers, Spider-Man, Why is that? I guess all the movies that are coming out every year. It seems like there are 3 or 4 super hero movies every year. Also a *Star Wars* movie every December, and it helps the comic book industry or we as collectors and dealers help the movie industry produce what we want to see. It might have started as a fad. It is so much more. Who knows when this will end?

We are seeing the most oddball comics spiking in the last few years. It seems like any comic with a first appearance of someone is a key issue. *Ms Marvel* #1, *Strange Tales* #169 (1st appearance of Brother Voodoo) and #180 (1st appearance of Gamora from Guardians of the Galaxy) and *Preacher* #1, to name a few. These comics were once in a dollar bin. You now rarely see $1.00 comics from the 1980s and 1990s at conventions anymore. Some of us dealers don't seem to want to give anything away anymore. A few years ago, I had a full box of *Omega Men* #3 (1st appearance of Lobo). All of these comics wouldn't sell at $1.00, and now all are going for more than that.

As far as the supply business goes, since there are more collectors out there, the bags and backing boards along with storage boxes are selling faster than before. Everyone is always going to need a bag, a backing board and a box to put them in. We can't even hold on to them. By the time we have our shipment in, we are ready to produce more and it is never enough. An average customer who usually buys 1 pack of comic book bags with backing boards (there is 100 total) is now increasing their purchases to 3 packs. A small time dealer usually buying 1 full case of bags with backing boards (1,000 in a case) is now buying between 3-5 cases at a time. A lot of stores who carry our stuff are always selling out. It is a great time to be in the business and as a collector.

©MAR

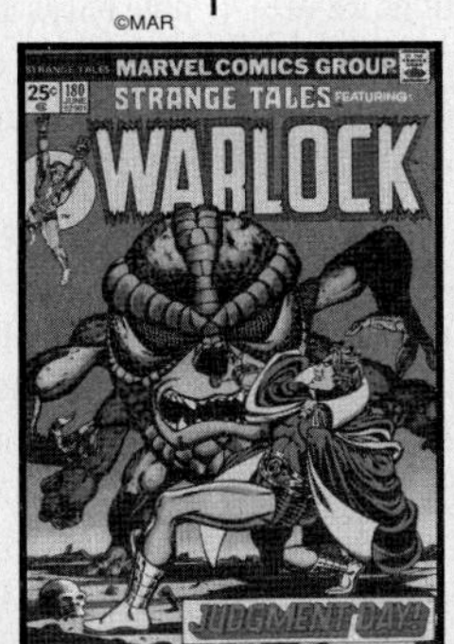

It seems that every comic with a first app. (Gamora) like ***Strange Tales*** *#180 can be a key.*

With all that being said, I find the "Pop Culture" conventions are gathering more and more steam with every year. Cosplayers make up a lot of the attendee base which makes for crowded conventions. I personally think it is great for the hobby. A lot of cosplayers I know do buy comics as well. As they get older, maybe as with any young collector right now, they start buying key issues and so on and so forth. The flip side is right now, there are not many who are going to spend serious money with vintage comic dealers, so for those dealers, they take up aisle space. The only downside for me personally is that, well, Halloween just isn't that cool of a holiday anymore because every weekend is Halloween on the convention circuit. Whether you collect comic books, enjoy dressing up in cosplay, or whatever your reason is for going to a convention, there is new blood at the shows and that's all we as dealers can ask for.

So while I think the comic market is strong right now, everything has a bubble. When will it burst? Who knows? I think it's up to the major companies to keep things fresh and have new ideas to keep things going. Judging by the past 15 years, I say they are doing a great job. I just hope they keep trying new, innovative things to keep it going.

Until next year!!

Paul Clairmont
PNJ Comics

Overview of the Market: It's hard to believe that we are approaching 2017 in just a few short weeks. Here at PNJ Comics we saw the market beginning to settle slightly compared to the fast-paced rise of the last four years but nonetheless, still trending upward. The demand is still very strong for quality books of all eras and books for investors to speculate on. I decided to try and maintain a balance between business and personal life but found that no matter how much I wanted to stop and smell the roses, the demand for great material continued to keep me busier than I have ever been since starting business in 2012.

Completing the 4th full year of operations in 2016, we find ourselves overwhelmed with many projects entering the 1st quarter of our 5th year. Mostly trying to process collections acquired throughout 2016. It was another phenomenal year for PNJ Comics. There was no shortage of finding quality material and growing the inventory of hard-to-find and high grade books that separate us from other comic book dealers. The difficult part is getting the goods listed on our site and eBay store.

Our inventory levels of quality books have grown so much from year to year that we decided to sell knowing we do not need to set record prices on each book, even if it is a key. We have seen too often a book climbing in price as the frenzy of collectors and/or speculators hunt for them only to see the book plummet once the supply has filled the initial demand. With the onslaught of new shows and movies continuing to grow, it has created a smaller window of time for the related comic books to stay hot and therefore capitalize on them.

We are pleased to see a significant increase in business on our website as it shows us that we are gaining more awareness in the industry and making an impact in the marketplace. We continue to have an eBay store to complement our website as it is the #1 source to drive traffic to our site and still continues to provide us with our best exposure. Having an eBay store is essentially a way to advertise your business. Timing is everything! Last year I mentioned in my market report that we would "let the chips fall where they may" and hold an auction on eBay for a near complete run of high grade *Star Wars* comics to coincide with the release of the new *Star Wars* movie in late 2015. This goes against conventional wisdom as we have always advocated that Buy it Now and Best Offers work better in our business model than a no reserve auction. However, because of the timing, it proved very successful and brought record prices on many books. If we tried that now, nearing the end of 2016, we believe that same auction would prove to be a disaster. Hard to believe that *Star Wars* comics were the hot item for a few years. CGC graded copies of issue #1 were bringing unimaginable prices and like most movie-hyped material, have dropped like a lead balloon.

In 2016, the entertainment world continued to roll out the TV shows and movies. One that we thought was particularly interesting was the excellent modern comic book series, *Preacher*. Copies of #1 would barely stick around in our shop before being sold within a day or week. Both 3rd party graded and raw were bringing strong premiums prior to the series start with CGC 9.8 collecting four figures. Just recently we decided to sell off our last CGC 9.8 copy at only $500.00 USD. We know it's in between seasons but as we've always advocated, no profit is too small and we still were happy with 50% profit margin rather than hoping season #2 increases. To compare, the pre-show hype was building fast in the beginning of 2016 and in February we sold a CGC 9.6 for $405.00. If need be, there are always more raw copies sitting in the inventory that we can grade if it spikes again. We wanted to share this example to help illustrate the ebb and flow of speculation. Other new series such as *Luke Cage* on Netflix also experienced the same early hype and leveling off after the series premiered. The one thing I don't like with Netflix is that they release the entire series on one day and there is no anticipation to wait a week to see what happens the next episode and it quickly kills the excitement of the show.

As I look back on the year, not a lot has changed from the trends we talked about last year. Female and visible minority characters are still highly popular and widely sought after. The trend I did see people fall back to was collecting favorite artists. Todd McFarlane is always one of those that fall into that category. I always wondered why his *Amazing Spider-Man* title of the '80s was so highly in demand yet his new material covers of *Marvel Tales* of the same era never took off. Another artist that is red hot is Gabrielle Del'Otto. It seems everything this guy does turns to gold, for the long run or not, that is a question to ask yourself whether you collect for pure enjoyment or buy in hope that your investment was worthwhile.

I use the term "quality books" often in my writing. These are often books that seem to be overlooked in the current marketplace. I'm not sure if it's a generational phenomenon. In my opinion, these are tough to find in high grade books such as 15¢ and 20¢ cover price comics from the late '60s and early '70s. I challenge any collector to find these books in true 9.2 or higher condition, and that means don't count on the grading you see advertised on eBay, but really find this stuff compared to the numerous copies of *New Mutants* #98 or *Batman Adventures* #12 in high grade. I would rather have a copy of *House of Mystery* #174 in 9.2 or better in my inventory than another copy of *New Mutants* #98.

Another area to focus on that is easily overlooked are independent comics. Some of the most recognizable are *Teenage Mutant Ninja Turtles*, *Cerebus* and *Love and Rockets* to name a few but there are many overlooked and undervalued books in this genre. Although some titles have been around since the late '60s, independent books took on a mainstream quality as the books grew in popularity during the '80s thanks in part to titles like *Teenage Mutant Ninja Turtles*. These were cheaply produced black and white books that competed for a share of the market against mainstream publishing. What makes these books unique are the low print runs and very cheap production values as publishers looked to compete on a shoe-string budget making them hard to find in high grade. There are some extremely valuable books due to some of these factors.

A keen collector would start doing research in this area and scoop up this material while it's relatively low in the price guides and most dealers' stock. There are some well written books such as *Elf Lord* and *The Adventurers*. The cost is so low at the moment that it would be a small risk to begin filling long boxes of this stuff.

I've been observing an alarming new trend developing within the hobby with regards to 3rd party graded comic books and/or magazines this past year. We've been selling both uncertified raw comics and 3rd party graded comics for almost 5 years. In that period of time we are proud to say that we have had only 2 returns for an order of uncertified books graded by ourselves from hundreds and hundreds of orders. We understand grading is subjective so we have a no hassle, full refund, return policy on all orders. What is alarming, we are finding more and more people are wanting to return 3rd party graded comics because of the production of the plastic cases. The issue isn't actually with the comic but the person doesn't like the way the book looks in the case. They are unhappy with flaws caused during the production or with flaws that are based on quality such as not being perfectly straight in the plastic well or having an "oily" appearance due to the inner wells pushing on certain areas of the comic only giving an illusion that there is a liquid substance inside. My personal favorite was a buyer who didn't like the way the plastic case had a rough edge from where the cases are separated during manufacturing and wanted to return the perfectly fine comic. It's easier to accept a return no matter what issue the person has with the product but it leaves us laughing and scratching our heads. People have lost sight of what 3rd party grading was created for. To help remind some folks who might not remember; it is to help eliminate a disagreement for 2 parties negotiating a sale, the buyer and the seller, so there are no questions about the grade of the book or whether it has restoration. Some people seem to believe the case has become an extension of the book itself.

Notable Sales of Uncertified copies: *Marvel Premiere* #15 VF+ = $325.00, *Marvel Treasury Edition* #12 NM/MT = $175.00, *DC Limited Collector's Edition* C-36 NM/MT = $150.00, *Uncanny X-Men* #510 Campbell Variant Cover NM+ = $269.00, *Giant-Size X-Men* #1 FN/VF = $530.00, 3 copies of *Amazing Spider-Man* #654 (2nd Printing) VF/NM = $220.00, *Detective Comics* #411 VF/NM = $430.00, *Detective Comics* #411 FN+ = $170.00, *Justice League of America* #179 *June 1980 DC/Whitman Variant* GD+ = $120.00, *New Teen Titans* #2 NM = $245.00, *Werewolf by Night* #32 G/VG = $185.00, *The Tick* #1 NM =$220.00, *Black Lightning* #1 NM = $120.00, *Hero for Hire* #1 VF- = $305.00, *Venus* #2 GD = $220.00, and *Strange Tales* #135 VF- = $135.00.

Notable Sales of Certified (CGC) copies:

Captain Marvel #17 2nd Print (2012 Series) CGC 9.8 = $670.00, *Incredible Hulk* #250 CGC 9.8 = $195.00 *Edge of Spider-Verse* #2 (Land Variant) CGC 9.8 = $430.00, *What If Venom/Deadpool* #1 CGC 9.8 = $315.00, *Harbinger* #1 CGC 9.8 = $630.00, *Daredevil* #181 CGC 9.8 = $200.00, *Preacher* #1 CGC 9.6 = $405.00, *X-Force* #2 CGC 9.8 = $115.00, *Hero for Hire* #1 CGC 8.0 = $615.00, *Marvel Premiere* #24 CGC 9.8 = $230.00, *Werewolf by Night* #33 CGC 9.6 = $830.00, *Special Marvel Edition* #15 CGC 9.6 = $430.00, *Brave and the Bold* #191 CGC 9.8 = $130.00, *Batman* #251 CGC 9.0 = $665.00, *Silver Surfer* #4 CGC 8.0 = $530.00, *Marvel Spotlight* #32 CGC 9.4 = $150.00, *Aquaman* #35 CGC 4.0 = $270.00, *Howard the Duck* #1 CGC 9.6 = $190.00, *Tomb of Dracula* #10 CGC 9.4 = $750.00, *Fantastic Four* #211 CGC 9.8 = $260.00, *Shazam* #28 CGC 9.2 = $327.00, *Marvel Tales* #98 CGC 9.6 = $160.00, *Marvel Tales* #99 CGC 9.8 = $180.00, *Marvel Tales* #106 CGC 9.8 = $170.00, *Batman* #635 CGC 9.6 = $189.00, 3 copies of *Walking Dead* #100 (2nd Print) CGC 9.8 = $225.00 each, *Archie's Pals n' Gals* #23 (35¢ Price Variant) CGC 3.5 = $580.00, *Spectacular Spider-Man* #64 CGC 9.6 = $259.00, *Preacher* #13 CGC 9.6 = $145.00, *Ghost in the Shell* #1 CGC 9.8 = $355.00, *Silver Surfer* #1 CGC 7.5 = $605.00, *Runaways* #1 CGC 9.8 = $380.00, *New Mutants* #98 CGC 8.5 = $270.00, *Ms. Marvel* #20 CGC 9.8 = $280.00, *X-Men* #1 CGC 4.0 = $2,520.00, *X-Men* #221 (So Much Fun Variant) CGC 9.6 = $455.00, *Marvel Super Special* #40 CGC 9.8 = $305.00, *Strange Tales* #89 CGC 2.0 = $465.00, *Fantastic Four* #48 CGC 9.0 = $1,430.00, *Captain America* #275 (Canadian Price Variant) CGC 9.8 = $275.00, *Werewolf by Night* #15 CGC 9.8 = $680.00, *Avengers* #260 (Double Cover – Canadian Price Variant) CGC 9.8 = $200.00, *Micronauts* #1 CGC 9.8 = $170.00, *Giant-Size Defenders* #3 CGC 9.2 = $230.00, *Marvel Team-Up* #3 CGC 9.6 = $230.00, *All Star Comics* #58 CGC 9.2 = $260.00, *Mighty World of Marvel* #198 CGC 9.0 = $330.00, *Detective Comics* #523 CGC 9.8 = $300.00, *Legion of Super-Heroes* #298 CGC 9.8 = $212.00, *Power-Man* #24 CGC 9.6 = $330.00, *Birds of Prey* #8 CGC 9.4 = $120.00, *Strange Tales* #169 CGC 9.6 = $980.00, *Daredevil* #102 CGC 9.8 = $765.00, *X-Men* #89 CGC 9.8 = $510.00, *NYX* #3 CGC 9.2 = $365.00, *Wolverine* #66 (1:50 Turner Variant) = $620.00, *New Mutants* #87 CGC 9.8 = $515.00, *New Mutants* #98 CGC 9.8 = $650.00, *Machine Man* #19 CGC 9.8 = $165.00 and *Marvel Premiere* #57 CGC 9.2 = $105.00

Silver Age: In 2016, we didn't see a lot of Silver Age books surface in collections that we acquired. I think collectors are realizing how tough it can be to replace these books if they trade or sell them from their collections to leverage other purchases. We also didn't sell a lot of Silver Age books in 2016. That is partially due to the fact that we prefer to deal with high grade books and it is particularly difficult finding Silver Age books in true high grade of Very Fine+ (8.5) or better. We sold a nice run of *Silver Surfer* #1 to #5 in varying grades of 7.5 to 9.0 for multiples of *Guide*, but our focus was concentrated in mainly Bronze Age, Copper Age and the Modern Age. We also sold a very rare 35¢ Canadian Price Variant of *Archie's Pal n' Gals* #23 featuring the 1st appearance of Josie in CGC 3.5 for $580.00 USD which is about 500% higher than it is priced in the *Overstreet Guide*.

Bronze Age: Our favorite era of books and our top selling genre of books for 2016. It seems there is a resurgence of collectors looking for high grade examples of their favorite 1970s books. There is so much going on during this era when it comes to undervalued and overlooked keys. Bronze Age books can be a complex and up for debate as to what justifies a character's first appearance. The best example I can use to illustrate this point is the argument collectors have over what Wolverine's 1st appearance is. In *Incredible Hulk* #180 he is clearly introduced on a full page and announces himself as "the Wolverine" to the Hulk and Wendigo but yet #181 gets the glory of 1st appearance. It can be confusing as another resurging character such as Darkseid appears less than Wolverine did in *Hulk* #180 when he first appears in *Superman's Pal, Jimmy Olsen* #134 yet it is designated as Darkseid's 1st appearance. Ultimately, the market has spoken and the prices on these issues are the true indicator where people believe the 1st appearances are, but it begs for consistency and maybe even a change in some of the old way of thinking. I can imagine the deadlock arguments as collectors and dealers try to protect their interests or stake in a particular book.

The Bronze Age isn't immune to the effects of speculation. Early in 2016, a rumor quickly circulated on the internet that Shang-Chi would be appearing on the Netflix show, *Iron Fist*, which still wouldn't be released for over a year or so. Within hours of this rumor surfacing, we were sold out of our high grade copies of *Special Marvel Edition* #15 which features Shang-Chi's 1st appearance and is a very tough book to find in high grade because of the black cover. Before we could adjust to the spike in prices, our two CGC 9.6 copies sold for over $400.00 USD each. We always believed this book was very undervalued and no one paid any attention to it as it sat for years in our inventory. Speculators were fooled and the rumor was unfounded and Shang-Chi was not going to be on the *Iron Fist* TV show. Sadly, this book should sell on its own merit and without the need of rumors. I wanted to illustrate that speculators rarely win, especially if they are trying to pick up the book after the rumor has hit. They are usually buying the sought after book on the upswing while they should have been proactively researching material to find character 1st appearances or key events before any rumors are released. It seems there were more false rumors in 2016 than there were valid ones.

©DC

Speculators are buying up **Black Lightning #1**, with hopes he's the next big TV hero.

There is a lot of movement once again for ethnic super-heroes in this genre. Black Lightning started to get some attention and copies of *Black Lightning* #1 jumped in value as speculation of his own TV show was rumored. Raw NM- (9.2) copies were easily selling for $100.00 USD. *Power Man* #24 is another book that is difficult to obtain in high grade. We had a CGC 9.6 copy that sold for $330.00 USD. This book boasts the 1st appearance of Black Goliath. *Hero for Hire* still continues to climb in price. Selling CGC 8.0 for $600.00 to raw 7.0 for $300.00 of issue #1. The title has so many other keys such as issue #5, 1st appearance of Black Mariah and issue #19 with the 1st appearance of Cotton Mouth. The Netflix show was received to mixed reviews and isn't for everyone, but once again, Marvel and Netflix teamed up to bring another small screen hit that is helping introduce the character to a new group of fans that weren't collectors of the comic book. We sold a CGC 9.6 copy of *Strange Tales* #169 for $950.00 USD, featuring the 1st appearance of Brother Voodoo. Not an easy book to acquire in high grade, nor are the other *Strange Tales* issues featuring Brother Voodoo from #170 to #172. Horror books in this era still remained slow sellers for us, but we believe everything is cyclical and these books will make a return one day.

We were fortunate to come across a very nice high grade collection of Bronze Age from New York and still continue to process the books. The problem with finding such nice, high grade examples of my favorite era of books is that I'm never too particularly rushed to put them up for sale. I guess there still remains a little bit of the collector in me when it comes to great books.

One thing about this era that I find strange is the lack of appreciation for the magazines. A lot of the stories were written for a more mature audience and often the stories are very graphic compared to their comic book cousins. I don't know if it's the size dimensions and storage issues but there isn't a big calling for this stuff lately. Heck, you can find some real gems in these books such as very early solo Moon Knight stories in *Rampaging Hulk* magazine beginning with issue #11 but as hot as Moon Knight seems to be, collectors simply overlook these books and they could be sleepers in the future. There are other great titles such as *Monsters Unleashed*, *Vampire Tales* which actually boasts a few keys. *Deadly Hands of Kung-Fu* can't be ignored with some great early Iron Fist stories along with Bruce Lee material.

Copper Age: Last year I mentioned that prices were beginning to stabilize on a lot of the keys. What I neglected was the never-ending number of new keys and semi-keys that keep popping up on the radar. Certainly, the earlier hot selling books from 2012-2014 leveled off but gave new opportunity for other books to surge in price and once again reaffirm that Copper Age is a lucrative genre with plenty of staying power. While we saw a slow down with interest in books such as *X-Factor* #5 and #6 and an inevitable leveling or drop in prices, it opened doors for other keys that were sleeping giants. Suddenly *Spectacular Spider-Man* #64 shot to the moon with prices for CGC 9.8 clearing $500.00 USD consistently. We sold a copy ourselves for $800.00 USD prior to the rumors of Cloak and Dagger receiving a new TV show.

Honestly, I've lost track of the number of characters that are receiving rumored shows. The safe bet for speculators might just be to assume every character will show up on some form of entertainment and to start buying every 1st appearance. I'm not a fan of people speculating on preview books such as the title, *Marvel Age*. This is where the lines are blurred with crazy speculators and I have to question if they are true comic book collectors.

Needless to say, there are some fantastic and low priced books. I've always been partial to Batman growing up and think some of the best stuff during the Copper Age came from these books. Batman: Year One in *Batman* #404 to #407 by Frank Miller is a classic. Death in the Family was another winner. Zeck's work in Knights of the Beast is fantastic too! I'm surprised that his run with *Captain America* doesn't receive more attention. It seems *Daredevil* #227 is garnering some renewed attention with the "Born Again" story, along with the other issues in the entire storyline. I wonder if we'll see a resurgence for the Death of Kraven storyline. Once again, Mike Zeck was brilliant on that story and it is another classic brought to you by the '80s. I think one of the most undervalued and best books of the era was *Superman* #423 written by Alan Moore. Another spectacular book is *Superman Annual* #11 by Alan Moore as well. A lot of nice mini-series are surprisingly tough to find these days in decent condition. Take the *Hawkeye* mini-series, *Nightcrawler*, *Cloak & Dagger* and *Longshot*.

These are books that were given the typical 25¢ bin treatment and are not easy to find in high grades. Marvel/ Star Comics such as *Ewoks* and *Droids* are not easy to find in high grade. In fact, any Star Comic title eludes collectors in high grade as they were targeted to a younger audience. Death of Supergirl and death of Flash in the *Crisis on Infinite Earths* mini-series are popular key books. Although demand isn't what it used to be for *Watchmen*, it remains a classic mini-series as well but unfortunately, its hype from years past brought many high grade copies to the market place and the supply outweighs the demand. O'Barr's *The Crow* #1 to #4 should be on collector's lists along with *Primer* #2 featuring the 1st Grendel. These are classic books that are not easy to find in grades that appeal to collectors.

Modern Age: The juggernaut known as "*The Walking Dead*" has certainly cemented itself as the king of the Modern Age. Copies of issue #1 and #2 continue to soar in price. Not even breaks between the seasons of the TV show seem to slow the increase for long. Now that the show has one of the best modern villains to come along in a while with Negan, I'm seeing prices climb on all issues of the series. The title is currently up to issue #160 as of this writing, and Negan has been in the series since issue #100. We saw people scramble to find copies of issue #100 2nd printing with its unforgiving black cover and 1st Negan cover appearance. We began selling raw copies for as much as $200 USD and recently sold 3 CGC 9.8 copies for a total of $695.00 USD. The only question I have about this series is how much higher can issue #1 climb?

Last year, female characters like Gwenpool made people start to look for more untapped potential. It appears 2016 was the year for Laura Kinney (X-23), Wolverine's clone daughter who became the all new Wolverine. Her 1st, 2nd and 3rd appearances in the *NYX* series from 2003 are sky-rocketing. It doesn't hurt that she is speculated to be in the final Wolverine movie soon to be released.

Variants are still rolling off the presses and become a lucrative marketing tool for publishers and a nightmare for completionists. I couldn't imagine trying to fill in the gaps to a series with all the 1:10 up to 1:1000 incentive variant covers for a series. I still believe it's a big risk for speculators to get involved in this area. Variants have a very small success rate to increase dramatically. The formula for a successful variant appears to be one that has no intention of being successful. Take *Amazing Spider-Man* #667 Del'Otto variant. People are paying insane amounts of money for a copy because it's an oddly numbered issue that had a variant edition but wasn't on anyone's radar. It was created to sell more issues for the publisher but wasn't meant so much as a hyped marketing tool. In my opinion, this stuff is over-priced due to supply and demand but will drop as more copies surface and the small pool of people that want these books has been filled. It reminds me of the 1st sale of a CGC 9.9 copy of *New Mutants* #98. You will be hard pressed to find anyone that would pay over $12,000 for a copy now.

For my money, my favorite series is *Afterlife with Archie*. In 2016, we were treated to 2 issues. At this semi-annual release rate it should reach issue #20 by 2021. It's too bad that a well written and drawn book like this is overshadowed by the myriad of gimmicky books and "hope it sticks" releases of issue #1s.

I hope this year I didn't sound too cynical because I am still very passionate about this hobby and the comic industry. I may not be emotionally attached to comics as I once was. A pitfall I think many people face when they cross that boundary from being a collector while growing up to being a comic book dealer. It's easy to criticize the changing landscape of the market as more speculation is done over comic books but I still do remember what excites me about comics and it's that connection to those childhood memories that are quickly conjured up when I see a collection that reminds me of the day I bought a lot of these books fresh from the racks with my father. I remind myself to keep it simple and appreciate that I get to do the best job in the world with something I love.

There you have it! We look forward to a promising 2017 and are excited to complete a few more goals and projects. As always, I send my love, gratitude and appreciation to my wife and son, Nicole and Jack. To my father, without you there would never be the memories of collecting comics that I cherish. I would especially like to say a big thanks to my close friends, Doug & Cathy. Your friendship, mentorship and long chats over dinners, games and coffee has helped to make it sane in a sometimes insane market.

Art Cloos
Collector

For me December 1, 2016 closes the reporting year for Advisor reports so with that date having arrived here we go with this year's report from me. When I wrote my market report in the 2016 *Comic Book Marketplace* in July 2016 I wanted to focus on the new collector who might want some guidance on how to approach buying comics as an investment and not just for reading pleasure and I want to follow up with that discussion here. From here in the northeast the comic collector market has not changed much since the summer when I wrote that report and most of the recommendations I made then to those new collectors still hold. Comics continue to be an asset class and as with any asset class prices rise, fall and also remain the same. If you buy for investment purposes then looking for trends is one way to approach it. I have been watching the coming of age of movies, TV shows, and cartoons dedicated to characters from the world of comics and been advocating taking notice of this for investment buying for years now. I had said in *CBM* that I am not pulling back on this recommendation but I was suggesting that it might time to be a bit more careful in approaching comic collecting using this approach and again nothing has changed with that recommendation. I used a mantra traditional to the stock market, "don't buy to chase yield". I said this because while Marvel continued to perform well in movies in 2016, DC's *Batman v Superman*, despite a healthy box office take but one that did not reach the levels expected, received a mediocre reception by the critics. In fact this morning on CNBC, two separate reporters commented on the movie basically being unwatchable. I was taken aback at this and that kind of sentiment does not bode well for the future if it continues. This can be coupled with the release of *Suicide Squad* by DC on August 5th which received very poor critical ratings despite a good overall box office. I personally did not feel that those reviews were especially fair by the way, but those poor reviews, as does the negative commentary of the CNBC reporters, reflect as much as anything the problem for DC and perhaps for investing in comics with a movie tie in. So the question I asked was, "Does this double whammy for DC mean it is advisable to begin look for *superhero fatigue* among movie goers as the line of DC Universe movies has not performed up to the critical standards that its fans demand?" I said back in July that the answer to the question was that it remains to be seen. Let's see if that is still the answer.

To begin, the Marvel *Doctor Strange* movie which opened November 4th received excellent reviews and a *Rotten Tomatoes* score of 91%. It did live up to expectations and perhaps exceeded them. Now in my *CBM* report, I focused on some specific books that I have seen bought or bought myself from January to July to look at what they could tell potential buyers about what's going on in the market. I want to continue that here and look at those same books. I started with Marvel and specifically *Strange Tales* #110 which ties in perfectly my *Doctor Strange* movie comment above. In anyone's book, #110 is a key issue with the first appearance of Doctor Strange. Before the movie announcement, it showed up fairly often at many of the shows that we go to and it was a book that could be bought for very reasonable prices including on eBay. Then the *Doctor Strange* movie went into production and I wrote in *CBM* that the price of the book exploded about 3 years ago. High grade copies began to be offered by sellers as high as in the mid $40 thousand range if not more, lower grades stepped up in price. Then the books disappeared off the racks and there were relatively few copies in any grade available at shows for sale for the last 2 years that we observed. Where did they go I asked? One place (but not the only one) was on eBay and in July I counted 32 copies, slabbed and unslabbed with different pricing within the same grade levels and with books that have been up there for a while and almost all of them were listed as "Buy It Now."

So did the good Doctor's movie move the needle for his book? Well today I counted 56 copies almost all "Buy It Now" with the high price being a 9.2 at $44000.92 with some of the same books for sale now as was in July. I said then and say it now that it is a fair assumption to make that many of these books were bought on speculation and are being offered at higher prices than the market wants to pay and it still seems that demand has softened on it with prices remaining flat and sellers not wishing to back down. Of course some of these sellers could be collectors looking to cash out and take their profit and run. What this suggested in July and still does now is having patience might just get one a better deal than perhaps a year ago depending how stubborn the sellers are and how much they have into their copies.

Next I looked at a *Journey Into Mystery* #83, the first appearance of Thor. This is another example of a book benefiting from a successful movie the result of which was, as with *Strange Tales* #110, we observed that for many years a book that used to be on a not small amount of dealers displays now seldom shows up at the same shows today. After doing my eBay search back in July, I found there were 42 copies slabbed and unslabbed and again with different pricing within the same grade and yes most were "Buy It Now." Today it was 51 not including a whole bunch of Golden Record reprints that had very high asking prices for a reprint book and everyone of them, reprint or not, was "Buy It Now." I had noted that the first Thor appearance had a reputation of being a somewhat scarcer book overall but I was not seeing that then and I sure don't see it now. To me this was and is another example of speculators hoarding copies and also collectors deciding to cash in. I noted that it would seem that this too is a book that with patience a potential buyer can do better on than when the first *Thor* movie came out, but having said that for July and in repeating it now, sellers also seem to hold firm on their prices.

Now switching over to DC, I want to look at *Showcase* #22, a personal favorite of mine and one of the earliest keys I ever owned (and still do today though a better copy than my original). It is another book that used to show up a fair amount at shows we go to but not recently at all and in July on eBay there were only 10 copies, 9 with "Buy It Now" and with one set of #22 to #24 as a bidding auction. Oddly though I have been told by dealers it is a book that does not last long when it does show up on their sales rack at a show. Today on eBay there were 13 copies, only 3 more than in July and with prices above and below *Guide* depending on the grade. I said then and I will say now that if you want one then don't hesitate when you find one because they either are not being offered due to scarcity or due to a perceived lack of buyer interest. This is despite the fact that since the Ryan Reynolds *Green Lantern* movie was released back on June 16, 2011 a significant drop in sales for any of the early Green Lantern Silver Age books occurred. I should add that as with *Suicide Squad* I felt the reviews on that movie were not fair and I actually liked it a fair amount, but my opinion does not translate to box office success. What this does mean is you can pick up many early Silver Age GL keys in the run for decent prices but if you want the mega key, *Showcase* #22, right now you are not necessarily going to get a bargain. I noted in July that a lot will depend on how the next announced Lantern movie featuring the GL corps will do, so if you like the character, now might be the time to dabble in some non-origin Green Lantern keys, or not as the case may be.

Now if you have read any of my reports over the last 2 years you know that I said to keep an eye on *Action* #252, the first Supergirl appearance given the news about her getting her own TV show. It was a book that would show up often at local shows as a dealer wall key with relatively cheap asking prices and yes as the show was announced and hit the airwaves prices on it took off and again is a book that no longer appears very much at local comic shows. In July on eBay there were 23 copies with all but 2 being "Buy It Now" and those 2 had no bids with their auctions ending within 7 hours of when I went through the listings. The highest price book up was one with an asking price on a 7.0 of $6,500. With 23 copies, some of which have been up for a while it seemed demand had cooled on the title. At NYCC in October there were exactly 3 copies that I saw for sale and I bought one of them because it was an absolutely killer copy and for a very fair price. Today there were 47 copies on eBay all with "Buy It Now" and not one regular auction. This should warn the collector looking to add this early Silver Age key to his/her collection to do his or her homework and not jump at the first book they come across. I will say that if the show has a long run on TV will that might well affect prices of the # 252 positively. If the show does not get past its second season, prices might well drop. Only time will tell. Keep an eye too on *Action* #285 the revealing of Supergirl to the world issue, it's a minor key but one affordable even in high grade and a book that might be worth picking up.

Next I want to look at a title featuring my favorite character Batman. He has been pretty much immune to good versus bad movie appearances and that includes this year's *Dawn of Justice* and the prices on his titles simply do not go down in any grade because sellers can get the prices they ask for them. In July I wanted to look here at one issue in particular, specifically *Detective Comics* #184. It is a first appearance of the Firefly and as such a key first appearance, though granted not a major one but a key still and one would think more would show up somewhere. I noted that this was an issue that seldom shows up on eBay and even less on dealer's racks. Checking eBay in July, there were no issues listed and this had been the norm for most of the year with only 1 issue that I could find and that one went considerably over *Guide* in its auction. Today there were zero copies for sale. I decided to add one other key to this which is *Detective* #168. With a 7.0 selling for $17,000 plus this year there were 2 copies on eBay today. As I said in July in the case of Batman, the movies don't seem to mean much in terms of affecting the value of his books and there is absolutely no doubt that vintage *Detective* and *Batman* titles continue to sell well with high grade Silver Age moving very well as does his high grade Golden Age and Atomic Age issues. Since writing my report in July I have seen many early Silver Age *Detectives* and *Batman* title books sell quite strongly and honestly I don't see that changing very much. I said in July that I have tracked these books over the years and know quite well that there are issues of both *Batman* and *Detective* that show up often (some issues a lot and in all grades) and others that seldom do and this does not seem to have anything to do with speculators or hoarding, rather it seems to be more a matter of scarcity and actual copies available and this is something I have observed for years.

When a scarce issue number does show up, it is almost always in low grade. One example is *Detective* #216. In July, there were 12 issues on eBay, a very high number for a book in this issue range, but today, as I type this there were 7 and all the same ones as in July. None were above a VG then and none are now and most did not or do not appear to be as good as the described grade and with the given that one does not grade a book just by the cover or a scanned picture. This is not a book that shows up much in higher than a VG anywhere. The point here is that you have to do your homework when buying the vintage Batman books. If you are buying for investment then go for the books that seldom show up for sale, if you can find them. I could go on, for example do you collect *Comic Cavalcade*? Well finding certain issues in the run can be very difficult in any grade and here the focus is on #19. None were listed in July and none are listed now and one low grade copy last showed up several months ago. With a new *Wonder Woman* movie coming in 2017, is this a sleeper title for collectors to consider investing in? Only time and collector interest will tell and that is really still the answer today to when or if the multi-media world beyond comics will continue to influence sales and prices

I said in July that I did not make a laundry list of the books that I have been watching to put into my *CBM* report and I am not doing that now either because you have to do it for yourself with the books you are interested in. Experienced collectors know all this already and as I said then and I am repeating now this is all for the new or relatively new collector looking for guidance who might not know where to start. Also in both reports I only used eBay and show attendance as markers to keep it relatively simple. Other sources like auction house results and market tracking services such as GPA can be used as well. I try to stress in every report that the major shows will draw a much more diverse group of attendees who will have a far more diverse collecting interest and this will affect what sellers bring (if they have the books) for sale but it is different in local regional shows. Every part of the county (and indeed the world) has a different take on what sells there and one should always keep in mind that regionalism can dictate what is or is not available and or generating interest by collectors. Go back and look at market reports in the *Guide* over the years and see how a report from one part of the country will totally contradict a report from another part when talking about the same issues, titles or genres or collector interest. What is hot in one place may not necessarily be so in another. Scarcity in one area might not be the same in another. So when you are looking to add to your collection, take your time, do your homework. First and foremost decide what you are interested in to read and collect. Compare prices both for different grades and within the same grades. Find out what is really hot and really is not and most importantly buy what you like even if you are doing it for investment too and don't forget to read some. There are plenty of reprints out there both in print and online that can be used instead of trying to read a high grade purchase. After all ultimately the whole idea of comics is to have fun and to enjoy them. See you in 2018.

Ashley Cotter-Cairns & Sean Goodrich SellMyComicBooks.com

Hello comic collectors, investors and fellow professionals! It's an honor for Sean and me to be asked to become *Overstreet* advisors for the first time. As we're new to market reports, a very brief background. I began SellMyComicBooks.com in October 2011 after a decade of eBay trading left me frustrated by the difficulties of sourcing inventory. Sean, who was formerly an auction co-ordinator at ComicLink, joined me as a full-time partner in September 2015. We now have offices in Maine and Montreal.

In late 2015, we unearthed new-to-market Golden Age keys found in Quebec, Canada. They were all low-grade copies formerly bound into a volume (most had binding tape on their edges and some, including *Action Comics* #13, were trimmed), and included a run of *Action* from #2, early Spectre *Adventure*, and an incomplete *All-American* #16. The highlight was *Action Comics* #7 CGC 2.0, which sold for $71,000 at Comiclink in February. Not a bad way to begin a year!

I want to use this report to give some insights into trending books. I think you'll get more from a report with useful data, and maybe a few more books to add to your watch list.

Ten Books to Watch in 2017:

NYX #3: First X-23. The new hottest Modern book. Still not the most expensive (won't be challenging *Walking Dead* #1 or *Batman Adventures* #12 on price – yet). By the time you read this, it will be a four-figure book in CGC 9.8.

Action Comics #242: 1st Brainiac. Much scarcer than #252 (1st Supergirl), almost always missing from collections, even those which contain #252. An untapped villain movie-wise. A no-brainer (see what I did there?) long-term hold.

Marvel Premiere #15: 1st Iron Fist. Netflix has done wonders for many of the Marvel characters. This is the latest key issue to get a boost. All grades above 9.0 are red-hot. Breached the $5k barrier in 9.8.

Incredible Hulk #1: 1st Hulk. I've been tipping this book for years now. It's always been under-valued. Has doubled in value in many grades since 2014 and shows no signs of slowing down, largely thanks to Hulk's starring role in most Avengers-related MCU movies. Entry level is now north of $3,500 for a ragged CGC 0.5!

Wonder Woman #98: New origin story begins. If you're priced out of mega-keys like *All Star* #8, *Sensation* #1, and *Wonder Woman* #1, then this is the book for you. Most books from this run are pretty quiet, but you won't find a copy of #98 in a CGC holder for less than $500, and VG examples are well over $2k now.

Linda Carter, Student Nurse #1: 1st true appearance of Linda Carter, aka Night Nurse. While *Night Nurse* #1 (undoubtedly a cooler book!) is getting all the glory of Linda's Netflix appearances, this overlooked key from 1961 should be on your want list. Unfortunately, it's extremely rare – perhaps the rarest 1960s key issue? There are only 13 copies certified by CGC.

Teenage Mutant Ninja Turtles #1: 1st Turtles. The book to own from the 1980s. A CGC 9.8 broke the $25,000 barrier in April 2016. Strong sales in all grades show the importance of this book, and Turtles movies are still being made.

The book of the '80s, ***Teenage Mutant Ninja Turtles*** *#1, still shows strong sales in all grades.*

Amazing Spider-Man #46: 1st Shocker. Hotly fancied to be among the next big-screen Spidey villains in *Spider-Man: Homecoming*. We have seen strong sales of raw examples, including 6.5 for $112 and 5.5 for $90 — both higher than GP averages at the time of sale.

Ms. Marvel #1 (1977): 1st solo book. This one has followed an interesting trajectory. Smoking hot a couple of years ago, when it touched a record high of $2,200 in CGC 9.8, it cooled off (plenty of supply in the market), but has started to pick up again in high grades. *Marvel Super-Heroes* #13 is much harder to find in high grade and worth much more, but you'll have a better chance of acquiring this book.

Showcase #6: 1st Challengers of the Unknown. Sean's tip for a future movie treatment, and seldom offered. Vastly under-priced. When it does come to market, tends to under-perform other books from this run. I love *Showcase*: I think there are a dozen or more books from this title that are solid long-term bets, aside from #4 and #22. Prices on many *Showcase* issues are setting records, and there is more to come for sure.

No *Walking Dead* issues above?! This title continues to

sell strongly, raw or certified, as more and more seasons of the TV series are signed.

Notable Sales in 2016: *All Star Comics* #35 CGC 7.5, $493, *Amazing Fantasy* #15 CGC 1.5 UK edition, $3,900, *Amazing Spider-Man* #2 CGC 3.5, $795, *Amazing Spider-Man* #50 CGC 7.5, $585, *Batman* #49 CGC 1.8, $450, *Batman* #227 CGC 8.0, $390, *Batman Adventures* #12 CGC 6.5, $223, *Captain America Comics* #29 CGC 2.5, $546, *Crime Does Not Pay* #33 CGC 7.0, $1,103, *Flash* #139 CGC 8.0, $1,005, *Incredible Hulk* #181 CGC 9.0 qualified, missing MVS, $1,025, *Marvel Graphic Novel* #4 CGC 9.8, $671, *Marvel Premiere* #15 CGC 9.2, $635, *Our Army at War* #81 CGC 7.0, $2,027, *Showcase* #6 CGC 5.0, $900, *Showcase* #30 CGC 6.5, $1,212, *Star-Spangled War Stories* #84 CGC 6.5, $1,301 (record sale in any grade,) *Star-Spangled War Stories* #89 CGC 6.0, $386 (Mademoiselle Marie cover; also record sale in any grade,) *Star Wars* #3 CGC 7.0 35c price variant, $750, *Tales of Suspense* #39 CGC 5.5 UK edition, $3,700, *Uncanny X-Men* #266, CGC 9.8 SS Stan Lee, $447 and *X-Men* #1 CGC 1.8, $1,186.

SellMyComicBooks.com specializes in offering tips and investment ideas on the website (sign up by clicking JOIN US). We publish a 100 Hot Comics list every year. The second list is already live on the site as you read this. A great source of books to buy and hold for future gains. We welcome feedback and messages from all other industry professionals. Please reach out anytime. Looking forward to serving you soon!

Jesse James Criscione
Jesse James Comics

In 2016, we saw a year that was about Social impact. Social Media owned the whole year. More news came from media sources, rather than the publishers' web pages. This opened the door for a large amount of speculators, that we hadn't seen since the '90s. This also allowed smaller publishers to be more relevant, almost from their first launch date.

We saw creators impact their book sales at the highest levels. *Harley Quinn* and *Deadpool* were pushed by Jimmy Palmiotti and Rob Liefeld not because they banged out the product to the fans. It was because they showed they cared everyday on Facebook and Twitter about their fans in more of a personal way. A vast amount of creators continue to be more open to discuss their lives and make their fans part of it, than we have ever seen in the past.

Movie impact this year to the local comic book store was next to nothing. There was a small impact on opening days and then dropping off by the end of the opening weekend. The movie companies continue to not show any interest in teaming up with the stores on their movies. The stores in return have started dropping their purchases related to up coming movies almost in half or no increase in orders at all. This is a major fail, until the movie industry opens their coffers to the LCS, the divide will become wider over time. Deadpool, Harley Quinn and TV's *Walking Dead* being the exceptions.

Wholesale numbers versus real sales numbers seemed to become a major issue in 2016. Less stores started relying on warehouse orders and started to rely on in store sales to determine what they were going to carry. This allowed the publishers, not in the big three, to not only increase their sales numbers but get their brand out there more. We also found that wholesale numbers were inflating actual sales and started to create a decline in sales for the big two as the year came to close.

Millennials, as talked about in 2015, have really helped the industry in bringing out more P/C characters and have filled in dead genres with a new life and strong hope for the future. We saw titles like *Invader Zim*, *Rick and Morty*, *Bob's Burgers*, and *Power Rangers* take the market by storm. This group continues to want to explore the culture of comics as well. Back issues continue to grow in this age bracket at a fast pace.

Online sales for us increased over 341% in 2016. "Buy online then pick up at the store" has increased and continues to evolve in a very promising way. Service has out weighted lowest price and continues to make sellers work harder for every sale. Dealers have dropped in big numbers online in 2016. The remaining seem to be very strong, business-minded and committed owners.

We've seen the decline of comic book conventions as there are just too many conventions out there. Publishers are being split in every direction. Creators are getting burnt out by mid season. Retailers are at the brink of overload. There were more bad cons in 2016 than 2015. In fact it wasn't even close. In 2017 expect a lot of cons to close up or not even announce they are doing another year. However, expect new cons to start with more customer orientated themes and genres in the future. Dealers, publishers and creators have had lackluster events all year. Those that had a great year offer the best service and more relevant product than ever. Until fake product can be eliminated from cons this will continue to happen. Con owners need to start vetting vendors and not just sell anybody a table.

In 5 years we have done over 140 store exclusives. In 2016 we dropped most our projects. There are just too many stores that are doing these nowadays. Now, Variants, as well, are out of control. Publishers like Marvel that have set Variant quota's so high, they are just killing the retailer. The market has really become over saturated with variants and most likely a back lass will occur in 2017 with a lot of retailers just saying "NO".

Finally, the overall customer has changed, spending more time in the store. They are looking to be pampered and inspired to buy more books. Just opening up your doors doesn't work anymore. Store owners are now either rewarding customers with point programs or other gimmicks to get one more sale.

Overall, 2017 looks strong for the LCS, but only for those that will fight for every sale, and those who educate, inform and inspire customers to support their store and the comic book industry. But more importantly, it will be strong for those who expand their brand and maintain the tradtion of our industry on the front lines.

Brock Dickinson
Collector

Once again, let me begin by thanking the folks at Overstreet for the opportunity to share my Market Report with the broader community. As always, my report will (primarily) focus on comics from the late Bronze Age to the present. While the Golden and Silver Age books get the biggest share of press – and often the biggest dollars – it's the more modern eras of our hobby that have the biggest number of collectors.

Impacts of the Current Release Market: A lot of the activity in the Bronze, Copper and Modern eras of comic collecting is driven by what's actually going on today. What new issues are doing well on the shelf, and how is that translating into demand for back issues? What movies or TV shows are driving interest in specific characters? What artist or writer is getting hot, with their past work being more frequently sought out?

Over the course of 2016, one of the biggest surprises has been the hugely successful launch of the DC Rebirth line, which reportedly propelled DC's market share past Marvel's for the first time in many years. As the year progressed, interest seemed to be rising in DC's comics, while Marvel was seen to be struggling, caught between the need to identify new markets and the demands of its traditional audiences. And while a Market Report is not necessarily a place for exploring the impact of new issue releases, it's clear that DC's success with Rebirth had an impact on the back issue market.

© Remender & Opena

Seven to Eternity #1
is a surprise hit from Image.

From a short-term perspective, a number of Rebirth releases were rapid sellouts, and quickly commanded a premium on the back market. By year's end, most of these prices had retreated, but rising interest in DC's new titles soon began to spill over into affordable runs of longstanding DC characters. Titles like *Justice League of America*, *Flash*, *New Teen Titans* and *Supergirl* all benefited from renewed interest, particularly with regard to Copper Age and early modern issues. This trend was less pronounced with Marvel books, though stalwarts like *Amazing Spider-Man* continued to do well, and a few titles (including *New Mutants*) seemed to pick up some steam through the year.

There may be a couple of reasons for this activity. With both Marvel and DC engaged in frequent reboots and renumberings of key titles, collectors are becoming less conditioned to focus on a particular series, and more open to buying solid stories from any era. Secondly, with new comics often cover-priced at $4 or $5 each, many back issues are starting to look like bargains. This can be particularly attractive with Copper Age books, which are about 30 years old at this point, and can seem to many current collectors to be books out of ancient history.

Marvel and DC are not the only modern publishers, of course. Image seemed to rebound a bit in interest this year. After the massive hits and rising prices of titles including *Walking Dead*, *Chew* and *Saga*, many Image titles were heavily speculated upon, with the result that supply often outweighed long-term demand, and back market prices never rose. Over the past year, this hyper-speculation seems to have corrected itself, with the result that a few surprise hits from Image did start to rise in the market. Key examples here include *Deadly Class* (#1 at $20), *Monstress* (#1 at $40) and *Seven to Eternity* (#1 at $40).

Other, smaller publishers also continued to produce breakout hits from time to time. The rise of self-publishing tools and online funding technologies and platforms such as Kickstarter has opened doors to many new projects. Some catch on with a wider audience, and the miniscule supplies of early issues are unable to meet market demand. The poster child for this in 2016 was *Henchgirl* from Scout Comics (#1 at $60, #2 at $40), though somewhat more mainstream titles including Eric Powell's *Hillbilly* and BOOM's *Lumberjanes* also rode this wave.

Television and Movie Impacts: For the past few years, movies have been a key driver of the back issue market in the Bronze, Copper and Modern eras. Certainly, 2016 began by following this path – excitement was high for films including *Captain America: Civil War*, *Batman v Superman*, and *Suicide Squad*. Each of these drove back issue prices early in the year, impacting character appearances by key figures including Black Panther, Doomsday and Deathstroke. However, prices generally retreated rapidly after the release of the movies, and releases later in the year (such as Marvel's *Dr. Strange*) had minimal back issue impacts. Looking forward, the hype around back issues linked to *Guardians of the Galaxy 2* is much more muted that the excitement was before the first film came out.

This is not to say that all movie-related increases are gone, as some books did show significant price jumps in 2016 because of film connections. These include *New Gods* #7 (1st appearance of Steppenwolf at $200), *Superman's Pal Jimmy Olsen* #134 (1st appearance of Darkseid at $800) and the "Old Man Logan" run of *Wolverine* Vol. 3 (#66 to 72, with individual issues in the $20-$50 range). It seems, however, that while movies can still have an impact on back issue prices, the heady days of the massive price jumps we saw for characters like Star-Lord, Rocket Raccoon and Groot may be behind us.

While the impact of movies may have retreated, the

impact of television production seems to be rising. Both Marvel and DC had numerous TV series on air in 2016, and in most cases, this led to a steady increase in back issue attention for the characters involved. Overall, the television boost to back issue prices was often smaller than we have been used to from movie-related bumps, but it appears to be more sustained as well. DC characters benefiting from this increased interest in 2016 included Supergirl, Flash, and some of the Vertigo properties such as *Preacher*. Over at Marvel, there was increased interest in Jessica Jones, Luke Cage (Power Man), Iron Fist and the Punisher. The Punisher's appearance on the *Daredevil* TV series from Netflix seemed to have a particularly strong impact on back issues, perhaps because Punisher prices have been low for a prolonged period of time.

Historically, *The Walking Dead* TV series has been a primary driver of the back issue comic market. However, over the past season or two, viewership appears to have declined, and while the launch of each new season still seems to spur interest in *Walking Dead* back issues, the bump was noticeably smaller this year. While *Walking Dead* prices certainly aren't falling, they are also not seeing the aggressive increases of previous years. It will be important to watch this trend closely, as some prices may be due for a correction in coming years.

Key Issues: One of the stories that's emerging from the hobby is about the change from "run collectors" who focused on certain titles, to "key issue" collectors, who speculate on highly desirable single issues featuring first appearances or some other element of significance. While this may be an over-simplified take on things, there's no question that the hottest element of the market is key issues.

The 2016 marketplace seemed to be particularly driven by the first appearances of secondary characters and concepts, perhaps because keys related to first-tier characters have already taken such substantial jumps in recent years. Issues like *Marvel Team-Up* #65 (1st U.S. appearance of Captain Britain) and #95 (1st appearance of Mockingbird), and *Spectacular Spider-Man* #64 (1st appearance of Cloak and Dagger) received significant attention. To some degree, this process appeared to be spilling backward into the Silver Age, as well. The first appearances of the Teen Titans in *The Brave and the Bold* #54 and #60, and even the first appearance of the modern Blue Beetle in *Captain Atom* #83, for example, are substantially underpriced in the *Guide*, as demand outpaces supply.

This search for new keys has also begun to lead many collectors farther afield, and outside of the traditional focus on collecting superheroes. Early appearances of war-related characters are in high demand, but the first appearances of Archie-related characters have seen particularly substantial price increases. Past readers of my Market Reports will know that I've been pointing out the rising values of early Cheryl Blossom appearances for a number of years, but there was huge interest this year in a host of other first appearances, including *Archie's Pals & Gals* #23 (1st appearance of Josie) and *Josie* #45 (1st appearance of Josie and the Pussycats). On the Cheryl Blossom issues, prices seem to have stabilized for her first two or three appearances, but as other early stories come to light, there are issues that continue to increase. One example this past year has been *Everything's Archie* #104, which has jumped into the $60 range.

One interesting trend emerging from the focus on keys is the rise in popularity of the traditionally under-collected anthology and try-out titles. Silver Age collectors have long seen DC's *Showcase* comics as a treasure trove of first appearances, but the Bronze and Copper equivalents of *Showcase* were often regarded as second-tier titles. This isn't the case any more, and the combination of first appearances in "under-collected" quantities is causing high levels of interest in titles including *Marvel Premiere*, *Marvel Spotlight* (volumes 1 and 2), *Marvel Super-Heroes* (volumes 1 and 2), and *Strange Tales*. This has particularly affected Marvel books, but DCs are starting to follow, led by the 1970s revival of *Showcase* (Power Girl issues in particular) and *Strange Adventures* (especially Deadman issues). The trend is even starting to generate renewed interest in the *Marvel Graphic Novel* series, and in many of the over-sized treasury editions.

Copper Age Keys: The Copper Age continues to emerge as a market force, with interest in and knowledge about the period growing every year. Over the past few years and Market Reports, I've launched a new "crowd-sourced" list of the Top 50 Copper Age Keys. This has developed (and argued!) with the many knowledgeable members of the Copper Age Forum on the CGC Collector's Society message boards. As always, I provide some "editorial influence" to whittle things down to a final list. Based on this year's discussions, the Top 50 Copper Keys for 2016 include the following books:

* *Albedo* #2
* *Amazing Spider-Man* #238, #252, #298, #300, #361
* *Archie's Girls Betty and Veronica* #320
* *Batman* #357, #404, #428
* *Batman: The Dark Knight Returns* #1
* *Batman: The Killing Joke*
* *Bone* #1
* *Caliber Presents* #1
* *Crisis on Infinite Earths* #7
* *Daredevil* #181
* *DC Comics Presents* #47
* *G.I. Joe: A Real American Hero* #1
* *Gobbledygook* #1
* *Harbinger* #1
* *Incredible Hulk* #271, #340
* *Iron Man* #282
* *Legends* #3
* *Macross* #1
* *Marvel Graphic Novel* #4
* *Marvel Super Heroes Secret Wars* #8
* *Miracleman* #15
* *New Mutants* #87, #98

* *Omega Men* #3
* *Punisher* (limited series) #1
* *Sandman* #1, #8
* *Silver Surfer* #44
* *Spawn* #1
* *Spectacular Spider-Man* #64
* *Superman* #75
* *Swamp Thing* #21, #37
* *Tales of the New Teen Titans* #44
* *Thor* #337
* *Tick Special Edition* #1
* *Transformers* #1
* *Teenage Mutant Ninja Turtles* #1
* *Uncanny X-Men* #266
* *Warrior* (UK Magazine) #1
* *Watchmen* #1
* *Wolverine* (limited series) #1
* *X-Factor* #6

New entries this year include *Gobbledygook* #1 (1st appearance of the Teenage Mutant Ninja Turtles), *Punisher* #1, and *Silver Surfer* #44 (1st appearance of the Infinity Gauntlet), as well as the return of *Omega Men* #3 (1st appearance of Lobo). Pushed off the list were *Suicide Squad* #1, and a few X-Men and Spider-Man books, as well as indie keys *Crow* #1, *Evil Ernie* #1, and *Starslayer* #2. While these exiting books remain important, they just didn't have as much "heat" this year as in the past.

The Rise (or Return?) of Cover Collectors: In past market reports, I've written about the increasing importance of comic book covers as a driver of value. In some ways, this is a new phenomenon. With the advent of 3rd party grading (from CGC, CBCS and others) and encapsulation, the content of a comic book becomes inaccessible, leaving the cover image as the distinguishing feature. This has increased the importance of the cover from a collecting perspective. While some purists may deride this, it is perhaps leading the hobby back to its roots. In the early days of fandom, popular artists (like Schomburg or Baker) and "classic covers" often drove value, and there were "theme cover" collectors who tracked down books with Christmas covers, atomic bomb covers, or infinity covers. Now, this trend seems to be re-emerging.

Themed covers have caught on strong in 2016, with a particular focus on connecting covers (where multiple covers combine to form a single larger image), cover swipes (where a classic comic cover is emulated on a new comic; *Amazing Spider-Man* #300 was a popular swipe focus this year), and action figure covers (for which the covers are designed to look like a toy action figure hanging on a store shelf).

For all the activity with theme covers, however, it's the rise in desirability – and price – of the works of certain artists that is most noticeable. In the modern market, there is a strong and growing interest in covers produced by artists including J. Scott Campbell, Gabriele Dell'Otto, Frank Cho, Stanley Lau (AKA Artgerm) and Jock, among others. Pushing further back into the Copper and Bronze eras, covers by artists including Neal Adams, Brian Bolland, Michael Kaluta, Jim Steranko, Dave Stevens and Bernie Wrightson can often have a positive impact on prices.

However, the breakout star in this field in 2016 was undoubtedly Adam Hughes. All Hughes-covered books from all eras (he began drawing for small press titles in the 1980s) are in high demand. Given that much of his work had been found on lower circulation titles such as *Wonder Woman*, *Catwoman*, *Tomb Raider* or *Zatanna*, interest has very rapidly outpaced supply, and prices are jumping through the roof. There is a "top tier" of Hughes covers including *Harley Quinn* #0, *Spider-Gwen* #1, and *Supergirl and the Legion of Super-Heroes* #23 that routinely sell for $300 to $600, and substantially higher when graded and slabbed by a third party. A second tier of books – including *Catwoman* (2002 series) #51 ($100), #70 ($60) and #74 ($50), *Wonder Woman* #184 ($100), and *Zatanna* #16 ($40) – is coming up behind with rapid price increases.

Hot Characters: In recent years, a continued focus on the core titles of Batman and Amazing Spider-Man, and a rabid interest in appearances of DC's Harley Quinn and Marvel's Deadpool have been key features of the marketplace. In general terms, this remains true, though the trend was less pronounced in 2016. For Deadpool in particular, there seems to have been a slight ebbing in back issue popularity and prices (though his first appearance in *New Mutants* #98 remains very strong). Overall, these stalwarts remain strong, and many of the market's most desirable issues can be connected to these four characters.

However, there continues to be a rising tide of female-centred books, with back issue prices being pulled up in their wake. Harley Quinn is the obvious leader of the pack, but over the past year there has been growing interest in titles and appearances including Black Widow, Captain Marvel, Ms. Marvel, Power Girl, Psylocke, Wonder Woman, and Zatanna. The breakout character in this area has been X-23, the clone/daughter of Wolverine. Her first appearance in *NYX* #3 now routinely fetches $400, and all of her appearances have been rising in price this year.

2016 also saw a number of established characters begin to rise in popularity again. Both the Punisher and Lobo were attracting higher levels of interest, for example. It was a number of toy tie-ins that saw the biggest revival in interest, though. This was perhaps led by ROM, the spaceknight character published by Marvel beginning in 1979, and revived in 2016 by IDW. Original Marvel issues were in demand, though a similar revival of the Micronauts spurred more muted back issue activity. However, an announcement by Paramount Pictures early in the year suggested that it would be combining multiple properties from toymaker Hasbro into a single "Hasbroverse" with multiple upcoming films has spurred some interesting back issue activity. The deal would involve Hasbro's uber-popular G.I. Joe and Transformers properties, as well as the aforementioned ROM and Micronauts. However, it was suggested that two other properties, MASK and Visionaries, would also be art of the deal. MASK comics were published by DC, and Visionaries by Marvel, both in the 1980s, and there has been rising speculative interest in these books over the year. Price gains so far have been modest, but these books are generally in short supply, and substantial future increases are possible.

A number of characters from independent publishers were hot this year. This group was led by the Teenage Mutant Ninja Turtles, whose early appearances command some of the highest prices in the Bronze Age market. A late-year announcement regarding a possible Bone movie spurred renewed interest in *Bone* #1, which surged past $1,000. There was also heightened interest in the early appearances of The Tick, driven in part by plans for a television production. Finally, there was a great deal of activity around specific issues from Valiant Comics. Valiant collectors are among the most loyal and dedciated fans in the hobby, and there seemed to be a growing base of these collectors in 2016. Demand was definitely rising, but there tended to be substantial variation in prices for key books. It will be interesting to see if this consolidates into more activity over the next year or two.

At the Edges: There were a couple of final trends worth noting in 2016. First, and perhaps somewhat morbidly, celebrity deaths appeared to drive the market. Key examples in 2016 included music superstars Prince and David Bowie, whose deaths spurred massive online interest in their comic book appearances including DC's *Prince: Alter Ego* and Marvel's *Labyrinth*. Prices took big jumps before falling to more sustainable levels, but the process illustrates the celebrity-obsessed nature of our current culture, and flags the potential for gains on other obscure books in the future.

Finally, the debate continues to rage about the pricing and impact of variant covers in the industry. There are now a number of variant books from the recent past that seem to routinely command prices exceeding $1,000 – and sometimes multiples of that figure. It is certainly impossible for a price guide to accurately reflect all of this highly volatile activity, particularly on issues where only a few hundred copies may exist. There is also a substantial concern in some circles that this collector interest and sales activity is unsustainable in the long run, a problem exacerbated by the secretive printing and distribution practices of most publishers, which makes it difficult to assess actual supply. There is no doubt that there are big dollars at play in this portion of the market, and that substantial price jumps are possible. However, it would also be wise to exercise extreme caution when looking at a portion of the market that is ill-defined, highly volatile, and not yet fully mature. There is a growing consensus among collectors that it may be wiser and safer to direct large dollar purchases towards Gold, Silver or Bronze Age keys, rather than gambling on continued interest in the modern variant market.

In Conclusion: That's it for 2016… I hope that you've found some interesting tidbits in the mix of ideas in my report, and – as always – I love getting feedback and suggestions for the future! Thanks as well to all the other Overstreet Advisors for their contributions… Year after year, the Market Reports remain one of my favourite sections of the *Guide*!

GARY DOLGOFF
GARY DOLGOFF COMICS

"Grass roots" collecting is still in! There has been much talk lately in the industry about investing in comics. While that is always a worthy thing, it is the backbone of the comics industry, the collectors, who enjoy the books and collect the books! There are quite a number of them. As a result, I have been happier than ever that I have my inventory/collection of 800,000+ comics and magazines that feed and fuel the collectors' buying hearts with "whatever they want."

If someone wants a run of *Fantastic Four*, *Amazing Spider-Man*, *Flash*, *Justice League*, or whatever (whether 1960s, 1970s, or 1980s through 2000s) or more obscure titles such as *Gasp!* (Charlton), *Peacemaker* (also Charlton), or *Winnie The Pooh* (Gold Key), I like to be able to supply these title affectionados with whatever they collect. That's why I do pride myself on purchasing collections of all kinds in all kinds of conditions (poor to mint, and everything in between.) And I'm also happy that I have a quite capable staff that knows how to grade "the GDC way" so that customers are consistently pleased.

I've also been paying increasing amounts and percentages for those very popular keys, and more expensive books. Last year for instance, I paid close to retail for two *Amazing Fantasy* #15's in CGC 5.0 and CGC 7.0 copies of *Brave and the Bold* #28, *Amazing Spider-Man* #1 and *Fantastic Four* #1. The seller was happy enough. He got 85% of *Guide* due to the popularity of those keys, and those "nice enough" grades, which meant he didn't have to deal with auctioneers' commissions, waiting times, and whatever "ups and downs" of the market that it might experience on a given week.

I've also been lucky enough to get in some original art in the last few months. I've found pages of Jack Kirby Silver and Bronze Age *Fantastic Four*, *Jimmy Olsen*, *Thor*, as well as *Juliet Jones* and *Winnie Winkle* daily and Sunday comic strip art. My favorite piece of the year was an early original *Krazy Kat* daily.

Many of the collections I get in each year contain a goodly amount of Silver and Bronze comics. The Bronze Age, by itself, has been worthy of increased attention, more and more as 1970s comics in general sell well enough (some of them sell great!) and the number of Bronze keys have ever been on the increase over the last couple of years or so.

Collection Report

Hartford, Connecticut area collection: The fellow simply called me up and offered me this core collection. It contained a restored *Captain America* #1, a low-grade, somewhat brittle *Batman* #1, *Silver Streak* #6 (the premiere app. of The Claw!), *Sub-Mariner* #1 (1941, original series), plus a couple dozen exciting Timely comics. He also had a lower-grade restored *Amazing Fantasy* #15, *Fantastic Four*

#1, *Amazing Spider-Man* #1 and a number of other early Marvel keys. Additionally, the collection contained a bunch of 1960s Marvel & DC comics. What made the seller happiest is that (of course) I let him know when any of the above comics was worth over *Guide.* I also kept most of the Timely issues for myself, which made me able to pay somewhat more for them. I love those books! When I bought the books, he said (no kidding) that I paid him, "Better than he expected."

The Central NJ Collection: This fellow had a small core group of a few expensive keys including *Amazing Fantasy* #15's in CGC 5.0 and CGC 7.0 copies of *Brave and the Bold* #28, *Amazing Spider-Man* #1 and *Fantastic Four* #1. So, for this group, I paid him 85% of value (they were worth $125,000 retail and I paid him $105,000 for those. Thus, he got about what he would get on auction, or better because auction results can and do vary, depending upon who's paying attention that week or during the auction time-period.

For the rest of his books (Silver Age consisting of everything from *Amazing Spider-Man* and *Fantastic Four*, to *Justice League* and *Jimmy Olsen*) I paid him close to half-*Guide*, with me and my able assistants grading them (as a lot of comics are, frankly, not worth CGC-ing, as they are either not valuable enough to warrant the CGC fees, or they can be books that if CGC'ed, may then sell for a decent deal under Guide. My calculation was based on paying somewhat over half-*Guide* for the *Amazing Spider-Man* and *Fantastic Four* issues and less than half-*Guide* for the *JLA*s and *Jimmy Olsens*, which I find must be discounted most of the time to move them out and make way for the next arrivals.

U.S.A. Comics *with Captain America and great Schomburg covers are a pleasure to own. (#10 shown)*

Dracut, MA $71,000 Marvel Collection: So, I went with my able assistant Patrick and we spent the better part of 2 days reviewing his collection of 28,000 comics. Much of the quantity of the deal was 1980s to 2000s. Many of my fellow dealers may not have the space, "people-power" or patience to deal with these newer books. I, however, put them up as runs, usually at 50 cents to a dollar a comic. Plus, there are the highlight books which we take into account.

However, he had "one, to a few of each" of most of the '60s & '70s Marvels. Unfortunately, he was missing the early '60s #1s, and some of the really early issues of *Fantastic Four*, *Amazing Spider-Man*, etc., with the notable exceptions of *Amazing Fantasy* #15, *Amazing Spider-Man* #1, and *Fantastic Four* #1, all three being COVERLESS! Otherwise, they were nice. He often had one really nice copy, one in Good to Very Good shape, and then one low-grade copy. Yes, he truly read and also collected, but his other half proclaimed, "It is time for the comics to go." I gave him a price that was fair and bought the books. I must say I really enjoyed getting the collection, as I already have customers for all books in all grades.

In addition to these larger value deals, we happily buy a number of smaller ones, including some Golden Age purchases. We bought a small Golden Age collection that was a study in contrasts grade-wise. There were some mid-1940s Batman issues in sharp shape, and then other Golden Age such as *Master* #11, *Punch* #1, some 1940s *Shadow Comics*, etc. that were in Fair to Poor shape.

We also bought a run of *Mad* comics and magazines. Issues #1 through 23 were comic books, then with #24, they switched to magazine format. Although they don't "fly" from our boxes, we like having them and whatever else comes our way.

We also bought a nice E.C. Collection (*Weird Fantasy/ Science*, *Vault of Horror*, *Crime Suspense*, etc. Most of the books were in Fair to Very Good shape, which is fine by me. E.C.s often come tattered, between the paper quality of them, and the fact that we all love to read them, plus ogle at the art, it's a small wonder.

Golden Age: As the years fly by, these oldies are still worth having, and most Superhero Golden Age comics sell quite well. Timelys are in demand (who can discount the coolness of these awesome prototype Marvels and more?) I myself collect them, and now proudly have over 20 different 1940s *Captain America* issues, including #1. I also have a brilliant 1941 *Sub-Mariner* #1. Though it's only VG or so, the yellow background cover dazzles! Also I am happy to own a couple of early 1940s *Mystic Comics* with the Destroyer and three issues of *U.S.A.* with Captain America (great Schomburg covers!)

DCs sell well in general. Some of my favorites are the early *Action* and *Detective Comics,* many of which are worth wayyy- over *Guide*. Wonder Woman comics sell well, and I have a great collection of those. Of note, issue #7 with the "Wonder Woman for President" cover typically goes for around 5x *Guide*. Some of the best DC Golden Age sellers are the "big logo" earlier issues, especially *Detective*, *Action*, and *More Fun.* Very "majestic" books, indeed!

With Fawcett comics (Captain Marvel, etc.) many of my fellow comic dealers largely discount the "coolness" of these books. Although most of them don't fly off the shelves like their Timely and DC counterparts, I say that they are worth having. Captain Marvel is a mainstay character. Of this, there is no doubt. Those *Master Comics* with the great Mac Raboy covers are a joy to own, and are worth over-*Guide*.

Some Disneys have been still picking up in sales. From other Golden Age companies, later 1930s and early 1940s superhero issue often go for over *Guide*, even in low, low grade.Pre-Code Horror comics sell well, and some of those truly horrific covers can go well over *Guide*. E.C. Horror (*Haunt of Fear*, *Tales From The Crypt*, *Vault of Horror*, and *Crime Suspense*) typically sell for 20% over *Guide.* Science

Fiction issues go for *Guide*. *Two Fisted Tales* and *Frontline Combat* go for *Guide* slowly. To sell them better, many of them sell for a bit under *Guide*.

Silver Age (later 1950s; 1960s-1971): Marvels, these "core" comics, are in general, great sellers, and show no signs of slacking off. I find myself paying premium for Marvel collections in ALL grades. The early 1960s #1s and first appearances (*Amazing Spider-Man* #1, *FF* #1, *DD* #1, *JIM* #83, *TOS* #39, *TTA* #27; *ST* #110, *Incredible Hulk* #1 and of course, the leader of the pack, *Amazing Fantasy* #15) mostly go for over *Guide*, in all grades. So, I find myself paying accordingly. I don't need much markup for these "best of show" babies.

The 1968 #1s (especially *Iron Man*'s first issue) also go for over *Guide*, for the most part. More recently, the premiere issue of *Dr. Strange* (#169) has gone up quite a bit due to that great movie of his. For 1964 to 1971 Marvels, I get *Guide* for them in general, or very close (again, in all grades.)

The most commanding Silver Age DC is *Showcase* #4. I find myself getting well over *Guide* for this book, while paying 70-80% of value on it. *Brave and the Bold* #28 (1st app. JLA) is another Silver Age DC that seems to have a bright future in all grades, especially 5.0 and better, I would say.

Batman sells great and there are now a number of special issues that are worth well over-*Guide*. I sold a *Batman* #232 (1st Ra's al Ghul) in CGC 9.4 for $990. Batman #181, 227, and 251 are three other "well over-*Guide*" issues. *Flash* and *Green Lantern* sell okay to solidly at around *Guide*, especially those great Green Lantern/Green Arrow #76-89 issues. What great stories & art. Silver Age Superman titles sell slowly, and to move them at all, I charge 70-80% of *Guide*. I like having them to make up sets when needed, but "they don't exactly fly."

I have been having my crew put together a number of non-DC/non-Marvel runs lately (everything from *Thunder Agents* and *Captain Atom*, to *Donald Duck* and *Herbie*). I find that there is a market for these runs. They don't fly, but they walk, which is why I enjoy getting them in. The more, the merrier.

Bronze Age (1970's-'81) 20-cents to 50-cents cover price: Comics from this era have taken a place in the comics market as "significant contenders" and are "on fire." It seems funny that I have over 100,000 comics from this era (some I've owned for decades) and finally, at long last, the books are being scooped up with appreciation.

A number of Bronze Age books that are known as movie tie-ins have been getting, in some cases, amazing prices, especially in high grades. *Shazam* #1 CGC 9.6 $175, *Nova* #1 CGC 9.6 $150 & up, and *Ms. Marvel* #1 CGC 9.6 $150 & up. *Hero For Hire* #1 sells for hundreds of dollars, in 3.0 to 5.0. Luke Cage is at last getting the recognition that he deserves. Even issue #48 (the 1st with Iron Fist, who remained with Cage for the rest of the series) in 9.6 is selling repeatedly for $190, and in 9.8 is fetching $590 a few times. There is one thing that I must caution those who own these comics and aspire to receive great values for their collections. The values of most copies of these issues are worth a fraction of these sums unless they are truly a worthy 9.4 or better. As soon as they have a couple of flaws, they are not uniquely "sharp." How many times does one hear a hopeful seller say, "I saw it online for ---?"

Amazing Spider-Man (especially #'s 101 through 150) and *X-Men* up to #143, sell great for me at *Guide* for the non-special issues, and over *Guide* for the special ones. *Incredible Hulk* #181 (1st app. of Wolverine) continues to soar in value, even though they are not especially rare. *Amazing Spider-Man* #129 (1st app Punisher) is continuing its upward trend. I've kept several nicer copies for myself, as an investment. *Hero For Hire* (Luke Cage) #1 sells for hundreds of dollars or more in CGC 3.0 and above. I sold *X-Men* #101 (1st app. Phoenix) in CGC 9.8, for $1500! Yes, you read that right... 1500 bucks!

Most titles that began in the 1970s (*Ms. Marvel*, *Man-Thing*, *Nova*, *Peter Parker Spectacular Spider-Man*, etc.) sell moderately well, with the #1s of all those titles selling real well. What I like doing best, when possible, is selling these 1970s series as "Sets for sale." They are mostly shorter-run sets and affordable for a wider range of potential buyers.

As with the 1960s, the best DC sellers by far are the Batman comics, especially the issues from #251 and earlier! A few Bronze DCs command premium prices over *Guide* such as *Shazam* #1- but also (even moreso) *Shazam* #28, the 1st 1970s app. of Black Adam.

Most Bronze DCs don't sell nearly as well as their Marvel Comics brethren, but they do okay. The 1st ten issues of *Swamp Thing* by Wrightson do well, as do Bronze Age *Detective Comics*.

Modern Comics (later 1980s through the 2000s): I have more appreciation for comics from this era than I used to. I sell sets/runs of Modern-era comics mostly at 55 to 90 cents per issue, with varying success. I of course charge more, and pay more, for better material from this era, such as *Amazing Spider-Man* (especially the McFarlane issues, #298-328), and for stuff such as earlier *Wolverine*, *Suicide Squad*, *Swamp Thing* #20-40 *Dark Knight* #1-4, and better *X-Men* of the period. I like to buy boxes of runs from the Modern era because of our Sets for Sale, which we do quite a bit. And there are quite a few "enhanced value" comics from this era, especially if they're in sharp shape.

Some of the primary examples are *Batman Adventures* #12 (1st app. Harley Quinn) 9.8 issues sell close to $200, *New Mutants* #98 (a CGC 9.8 can sell for $750 and up), *Amazing Spider-Man* #300 (sells for $100 to many hundreds, in most grades), *Swamp Thing* #37 (1st app. Hellblazer), *MSH Secret Wars* #8 (1st black Spidey costume) and much more. When I look at a collection, I always enjoy when these books are present (in singles, or in multiples.)

Original Art: I buy it whenever I'm offered collections of it (or even, individual pieces) for anything resembling a decent price. Art is truly the "Wild West" of our industry pricewise. Some stuff goes up all the time, some stuff doesn't.

So I say to all, keep on enjoying our hobby, and "to all, a good night (and day)."

Ken Dyber
Cloud 9 Comics

Hello friends, readers and collectors. I'm co-owner and founder of Cloud 9 Comics. Cloud 9 Comics has a brick & mortar store in Portland, OR which is open 7 days a week from 11am – 7pm, a website (www.cloudninecomics.com) with thousands of vintage comics for sale, an eBay store (cloudninecomics), as well as a presence at some of the conventions around the country. We sell Golden – Copper Age comic back issues, specializing in key issues/1st appearances, as well as the occasional slab or two (although most of our sales are raw comics).

The conventions we did in 2016 were: San Diego, Portland (Wizard & Rose City), Emerald City, Denver, New York, Tacoma, Southern California, and Baltimore. Our two staff members at the store both entered their 2nd year with the company, so a big thank you to both Moises Rios & Scott Roller.

Convention sales this year were down across the entire board for us, other than Denver, which was slightly up from the previous year with a couple being close to flat. San Diego, Portland's Wizard show, Emerald City and NY were all considerably down from the previous year sales wise. This year in particular, I thought the overall customer foot traffic at San Diego and Emerald City were considerably down from last year. I remember vividly Saturday afternoon at the Seattle Emerald show seeing hardly any people on the convention floor. It was only around 3 years ago, that this show was so crowded on Saturday afternoon, that it was hard to go to the bathroom. Yet… this show is supposedly Sold Out!? So, where are the people? I can only guess that they are off playing games, or doing yoga, or signing up to be in the armed services!? I'm not at all being "That jaded grumpy comic book guy" here either. The entire convention show floor on Saturday afternoon for the toy dealers, comic dealers, t-shirt folks, disco ball racecar drivers, etc… No people, yet they were Sold Out?? Many of us convention dealers have stated repeatedly how conventions are becoming less about comic books, but this once great show (my 2nd favorite after San Diego), seems to have lost its way (Funny that Reed coincidentally took it over last year).

Sure, it could be coincidence, or just our poor luck, as things do go in cycles, but last year seemed quite off for us at conventions. At one point I had for sale 3 *Amazing Fantasy* #15's, a CBCS 1.0, CGC 4.0 & CGC 5.5 at several of the major conventions, and didn't sell one of them. My prices were not that aggressive, really, within market via comparable previous sales, yet there was little to no interest, other than "that guy" who just wanted to hold it. Sorry, but, why would I let a complete stranger hold a $20K comic book where they have no intentions whatsoever in not only purchasing it, but purchasing any comic books I'm selling at my booth. The strangest thing is, that these people then get mad at me for not letting them hold my most expensive comic book in my booth (like it's their right or I'm there to entertain them). Ah yes, there's that older jaded grumpy comic book guy!

Amazing Fantasy #15s a few years ago used to fly out the door as the #1 Silver Age book. Yes, they are not uncommon, they are just awesome, and expensive, but most major dealers usually have access to them or one for sale. I feel the last year or so there's been more of a trend away from Silver Age blue chips into either the much more affordable Bronze Age market, or to more obscure Golden Age books. Books like *Amazing Spider-Man* #1, *TTA* #27, *TOS* #39, *Amazing Fantasy* #15, *Adventure* #247, etc… used to fly of my wall at cons at market, where after I did a major convention, I then had this worrisome fear that I had to immediately work on restocking my inventory for the next con, or else I wouldn't have a very good looking set up. This past year, this just wasn't the case, as I saw many of these usual regular sellers being passed up for rare Golden Age classic covers, or Bronze Age speculator type books like *Hero For Hire* #1, *Marvel Premiere* #15, *Tomb of Dracula* #10, etc.

Copper Age key issues like *New Teen Titans* #2 are also doing quite well, and are almost impossible to keep in stock. Other blue chips like *New Mutants* #98 and *Batman Adventures* #12 have also cooled off considerably appreciation wise, as well as demand wise. This though I think was to be expected given their appearances in movies in 2016, so the excitement has only temporarily died off on these 2 books, as both are A-list characters at this point in time.

Running a comic book store is completely different than selling through the web or setting up at conventions. In many aspects, it's like an entirely different business that has nothing to do with convention sales or customer demands. I've had just over a year learning about Diamond and what to order or not order, and what is or is not selling relating to new comics. My suggestion to any new store owner, is do not order heavily on new comics until you have a customer base, and start ordering titles you know will sell off either at in store sales or at conventions, as there are so many titles being published now that it's very difficult to sell any reasonable quantities of anything unless you're the only game in town, have a huge box customer base, or are located in a market like NY or something. Portland, OR has probably more comic book stores per capita than any other city in the U.S. I would imagine. Heck, this past September, Image Comics moved here! So for a city of like a half million (excluding suburbs), we have Image, Dark Horse & Oni publishing, which are #3 and #4 respectively behind Marvel & DC, and I'm not sure where Oni fits in, but I know they're killing it with *Rick & Morty*, so I'm guessing they're top 10. We also have a ton of creators that live here, so if you like comics, and want to live somewhere where it seems there are comics everywhere, this is the place. For a mid-sized market, we also have 2 successful weekend shows (Wizard's in Feb. & Rose City in Sept.), and the Frankenstein Comic Book swap, which is a small 1 day show that happens around 3 times a year. That is an awesome 1 day "old school" comic book show.

Speaking of "old school" comic book shows, Terry O'Neill's 1 day Southern Cal. Comic show at the end of January is a must if you live in that area. Many of the best/ largest comic dealers set up there as well as many smaller "garage dealers". No toys, gaming, panels, etc... just comic books with a couple of highlight creators. Also, on a larger scale, I have to say the Baltimore show pretty much kicks ass when it comes to being an old school comic show. Yes, they do have some of the other stuff, but for the most part, it's comics. Probably the most comic oriented weekend show of that size going, and definitely worth attending for the serious collector/investor at some point, if not this show, then the Chicago Wizard show in August is probably on par with the same amount of great books there, but that show does have quite a bit more other "stuff."

The new comic market seems to be changing quite a bit just in the little time I've been involved with it from a store standpoint. Trade sales are continuing to increase rapidly, with new comic sales slowing down significantly. I'm not sure if there are too many titles, too many bi-monthly titles, too many price increases (most books are $4 now, with quite a few annuals or #1's at $5!! I mean, $5 for 1 new comic book just seems nuts to me, especially when so little of it is even story. I can read a new comic in a matter of minutes, where ones from the Silver Age take maybe 20 minutes. More people are just waiting for the trade to come out to read it. Publishers (as if any of them read these!)... What the hell is wrong with charging $4.25 for an annual? Why do you have to go right to $5?? Remember when it was $.50, then $.60, then $.65, then $.75, etc? You want to sell more comics, reduce your prices or stop raising them so aggressively.

As for back issue sales of note, I just don't have the time currently to go as in depth as previous market reports to list tons of GPA, auction or eBay sales figures as I did before having a brick & mortar store. Luke Cage and Iron Fist were two of the hottest characters in 2016, not just their first appearances, but any titles/series. *Hero for Hire* #1s in 9.2 are going for around $1500 and *Marvel Premiere* #15s are going for around $500, but I'm sure the later will increase a bunch as we get closer to the new Netflix show. *Champions* and *Defenders* (the later in particular) are really selling well (finally!). *Avengers* sales have really cooled down other than #1,4,57 & 196. *Amazing Spider-Man* and *Batman* still outsell all other characters by a ton. *Jessica Jones* is selling really well too. I almost feel the Netflix shows are being more impactful in sales than the movies these days, as they're taking characters that are much less known or not at all by the general public, and doing great shows with characters people can get excited about. The only movie I think that really impacted books in value at a major level was *Guardians of the Galaxy*, but that would only back up more aforementioned point, as most of those characters were barely known by the public. Hum... seems like an equation here... take a less or unknown character and put them in a movie or TV show, and bam, you've got a hot book going up in price (often a lot in a short amount of time). Spider-Man reboot - not affecting *Amazing Fantasy* #15 sales at all, but the 1st appearance of Mantis, well, there's a book that went from $30 with no demand, to selling for $200-$300 for nice raw copies.

©MAR

Netflix shows like **Jessica Jones** can be more impactful on sales than the movies. (**Alias** #1 shown)

One thing I did want people to think about moving forward is the slabbed 0.5 market. CGC and CBCS grade books that are incomplete at 0.5. Think about that... all books regardless of their overall shape, at 0.5. This makes NO SENSE to me. I saw Metropolis selling a *Superman* #1 CGC 0.5 at San Diego this year for around $75K, and this was a gorgeous book! I mean, the front cover looked 8.0-ish or better, however it was missing the entire back cover. *Superman* #1 which came out in 1939 is a 68 page comic cover to cover, yet if it's missing the back cover, which counts as 2 pages (front & back sides), regardless of what the shape of the rest of the book is in, it's technically a 0.5. So, you could have a *Superman* #1 that structurally looks like a GD+ 2.5 and this one they were selling that looked like the nicest copy out there (very tough book in unrestored condition in nice shape), both without their back covers, both with the same grade. Now, would both sell for the same price, no, of course not, however, when one looks at GPA sales for 0.5 incompletes (we're talking incompletes only here), prices could vary wildly for books like *Superman* #1. Figuring out what a fair price to charge or pay could be crazy, especially for rare books. I was able to sell a *Batman* #1 0.5 incomplete no back cover for $19K in 2015, and for most people that was a crazy asking that price, and yet I was able to sell that book very quickly to a collector (who has since purchased a back cover for it). With the crazy prices *Batman* #1s are going for, that now to me seems like a good buy price even for a dealer to resell, let alone a collector who will keep it for 20 years or more. I also talked with CBCS at San Diego about their view point on 0.5s, and they said that an *Amazing Spider-Man* #238 which initially came out with a "tattoo", would grade at their company as a 0.5 if it was missing the tattoo, as they view that comic as incomplete. We're able to sell copies of that book without tattoos for $50-$100 depending condition regularly, yet a 0.5 in *Guide* is like $3. I disagree with their stance here, as I do not consider a tattoo part of a comic book, yes, it was presented with the book when it originally issued, but this just doesn't sit with me. Regardless, the two companies have different viewpoints on this, so, if you have this book, and it's missing the tattoo, you may want to think twice as to which company you submit it to, cause your grade will dramatically be different via this one attribute alone. I'm not trying to find fault with this grading company, as they have every right to their viewpoints, I'm more so trying to get people thinking about the complexities of the 0.5 market, and huge possibilities for gains or losses on these books.

Lastly, as with previous market reports, I provide for you my top 25 Copper/Modern/Renaissance Age books. For those of you that read my market report last year, I think we have long moved beyond the Modern Age of comics, and are now firmly into the Renaissance Age with the triggering event being the issue of *Walking Dead* #1, which firmly moved people into the non-superhero Marvel/DC controlled world. I hope *Overstreet* will begin publishing this section in the beginning of their price guide with the Top Golden Age, Silver Age & other top books, and this is by far the largest time period being bought, sold, read and collected, and for whatever reason is not represented in the front of our guide. I've only included variants/other printings of things that have very proven sales history as there are so many of them. If I've neglected any obvious books for this list, please contact me directly so I may make the needed changes. Hopefully *Overstreet* will begin publishing this section in the front of the *Guide* sooner than later. Prices are my suggested NM-/9.2 listings for this year's current guide.

1. *Gobbledygook* #1: $6800
2. *Teenage Mutant Ninja Turtles* #1: $5000
3. *Gobbledygook* #2: $4000
4. *Miracleman* #1 Gold Edition: $1200
5. *Walking Dead* #1: $1400
6. *Albedo* #2: $1100
7. *Bone* #1: $750
8. *Batman Adventures* #12: $600
9. *Miracleman* #1 Blue Edition: $600
10. *Vampirella* #113: $500
11. *Batman* #608 Retailer Incentive Edition: $400
12. *Venom Lethal Protector* #1 Black Cover Printing Error $400
13. *Walking Dead* #2: $375
14. *New Mutants* #98: $325
15. *Amazing Spider-Man* #300: $275
16. *Chew* #1: $250
17. *Walking Dead* #19: $225
18. *Y The Last Man* #1: $225
19. *Walking Dead* #3: $225
20. *Knights of the Dinner Table* #1: $200
20. *Walking Dead* #27: $200
20. *Spawn* #1 Black and White Edition $200
23. *Primer* #2: $170
24. *Grendel* #1: $160
25. *Saga* #1 $150
25. *Cry For Dawn* #1 $150
25. *Invincible* #1 $150

Thanks to everyone who came to our booth at a con, our new store in Portland, as well as our website.

Daniel Ertle
CBCS - Modern Expert

Another year has passed in which I can reflect on the books that come across my desk working as a modern expert at CBCS. As I said last year, working at CBCS affords me a unique perspective and insight into our hobby. I will utilize that knowledge in helping understand how this year progressed in terms of trends in modern comics. Certain trends this year have not been too surprising, sticking with marking directions that were reported last year. Movies still appear to be the key motivating factor in modern books being sent in for grading. Reboots, like DC's Rebirth, continue to add interest in books as well. As for some Indie titles, they get hot seemingly out of nowhere and stay popular for a short time. That being said, there are a few changes noticed from the previous year. Certain reprints have come into fashion where maybe reprints were looked down upon before. There have also been some books that I didn't think would be dropping off in submission numbers that have in fact started to slow down.

As mentioned, movies are are still the biggest factor for increasing the submission of modern books and also keeping the same popular titles going strong. With *Batman v Superman* released this year, we saw a lot of variants related to the movie come in for grading. Other modern books featuring the world's finest, such as individual issues of *Superman/Batman* or the second printings of *Batman* #608 and *Superman* #204, remained at their normal level of submission and didn't experience the same boost from the movie release. *Captain America: Civil War* seemed to influence people to send in more *Black Panther* #1s, while also helping to keep the rate of Winter Soldier related books consistent. With this particular movie release, the *Civil War* series itself got the biggest push of all.

Suicide Squad also helped keep the rate of that title coming in relatively high, but that may also be attributed to the fact that Harley Quinn is in it. Last year I reported that Harley and Deadpool were the winners of the year. Harley is keeping that going while Deadpool has slowed down quite a bit. The drop off of *New Mutants* #98 has been a surprise this year with how successful the *Deadpool* movie was. This is not to say that it is a rare occasion that it comes across my desk. *New Mutants* #98 is still more popular than most, just not as much as it was in the past. The most recent movie to come out, *Doctor Strange*, has honestly not made that much of an impact on books being sent in under the Modern tier. As for future movies, the previews can obviously still have an effect on comics being sent in. As I write this, a new trailer for the upcoming *Spider-Man* movie has dropped and Marvel is rolling out additional trailers and information for the new *Guardians of the Galaxy* as well. I am not sure how many more Spider-Man books can be sent in, nor can I guess what characters are going to debut in *Guardians*. However I can be sure that we will starting seeing the effects of these upcoming movies soon.

Reboots are something that seem to happen fairly often these days and it can help boost sales for a company and bring in new readers. Both DC and Marvel have recently gone through reboots, Marvel being more of a soft reset than DC's Rebirth. Between these two companies, DC seems to be winning for most submissions surrounding their respective reboots. At the outset of the event, the Rebirth issues themselves were popular in their own rights and we got a wide variety of titles for those few issues. It wasn't until the series proper began did submissions seem to follow their expected trends. Batman and Harley Quinn related issues are leading as the top for books being sent in. Of course *Dark Knight III* is still a very popular book even though it's not related to the reboot, with Superman and the others following behind. As for Marvel, most issue #1s get sent in but the drop off rates seemed to be much higher. However a trend unique to Marvel are submissions of many random issues being sent in because of their gimmick variants. Things like their Hip Hop variants or 50th anniversary covers, for example, seem to be doing very well. Hopefully I won't have to talk about major companies rebooting next year.

The rest of books that get sent in are in kind of a catch-all category because it's hard to spend a significant amount of time with any one topic. When combined, variants, indie books, and reprints are all things that we see in the office in almost an equal amount to Marvel and DC books. Variants are probably the biggest factor to this, but many times these subjects overlap. For example, Zenescope is an indie publisher but they also have many variants for every convention. These variants are incredibly popular and are sent in for grading frequently. Furthermore, in extreme cases like Dead Pooh/Do You Pooh/Walking Dead Pooh, you have books that are indie, have a staggering amount of variants, and are all mostly reprints. And those books still get sent in at an incredible rate with their schtick being to do cover swipes of famous covers with the Dead Pooh character. Then there are some books that seem to come out of nowhere and get hot fast. These are books like *Animosity* or *Hillbilly*, that many people apparently overlooked but were then quick to realize its popularity and smaller print runs. When this happens, we usually get a good couple of months where these books are sent in frequently and then drop off after that.

One of the most popular books that we have been receiving as of late are the Fan Expo reprints of *Batman Adventures* #12. These have all new covers and some of the variants are foil covers on top of that. The combination of new covers, the fact that it reprints the first appearance of Harley Quinn, and that they are limited spelled the recipe for a hit in this regard. This has also been going on for a while with Wizard World *Walking Dead* #1 reprints, so I suppose this popularity could a be trend going forward.

This year was all-in-all a good year for comics in my opinion. Sales seem to be strong and books are continuing to come in to CBCS at a fast rate. I look forward to seeing what next year brings us. More movies for sure starting with *Rogue One* and then *Guardians of the Galaxy*. I also expect more crazy variants and books that come at us out of nowhere, maybe even more reprints of popular books. As mentioned earlier, I hope there are no reboots for the big two anytime soon. I wish everyone in the hobby a good 2017 and I look forward to reporting on the state of the hobby next year.

D'Arcy Farrell
Pendragon Comics

Modern Back Issue Sales: Now here it comes. Sales for 1980s and up watch out. Those great best stories of the decades most recent past, are getting scooped up. Any key of the past 30 years is in high demand. Best sales of this era for me are as follows: TMNT any issue, *Batman: Dark Knight Returns*, Infinity Gauntlet, Death of Superman, original Valiant titles especially *X-O Manowar* and *Rai*, Thanos appearances especially in *Silver Surfer*, many important Batman stories like Death in the Family, *Venom* minis of 1990s and McFarlane Spideys. There are many numerous single issues of importance like first appearances of Harley or Deadpool, but I'm seeing that many smaller unknown gems are finding their way into the marketplace top demand. Such as early modern *Zatanna*s, or *Tales of Teen Titans* Cyborg, *Captain America* #241, *Wolverine* #10, *Ultimate Fallout* #4 (1st Miles), *Punisher* mini of 1980s, and practically any DC-Vertigo title ever made. So for you investors, recap what was hot back then, and you will see potential in the future to invest. The 1980s-current have many many hot then, but still key and pertinent stories.

Bronze-Copper Age Sales: DC low run titles are still tops in sales and it's expected for years to come. DC has been undervalued forever. Marvel of course sells well in this era, runs like Miller's *Daredevil*, or Byrne's *X-Men*. *X-Men* at that time had probably the finest stories in comics, but the print run was also high, so they are readily available. What I'm suggesting is going after the lower run getting hot items. That means DC like *Wonder Woman*, *Flash*, and *Green Lantern*. Batman never ended and never had low print runs, though he is the top character in our industry as well. So buying Batman anything is never bad.

Silver Age Sales: Just like last year, *JLA* is highest in demand for runs. It would top sales, but there just aren't enough runs available to sell. *Batman* leads the pack overall with *Spider-Man* close behind. Last year I had nice *Showcase*s and *Brave and Bold*s to sell, but this year I just couldn't replace what I sold in 2015. But if I had the issues, they would have sold instantly. Instead I was blessed with many Marvels, especially *Spider-Man* and *Fantastic Four*. *FF* is a bit slower due to Marvel not publishing anything for years on the new market, but *FF* #12,25,46-50 are always top sellers and high demand books. I still consider *FF* #25 a great investment since it is the FIRST Thing vs. Hulk and 2nd

Silver Age Captain America app. Another top seller is *Tales To Astonish* #93(1st full Surfer x-over).

New Comic Releases of 2016: This was definitely the year of DC. DC brought its successful N52 to a close with Rebirth. Rebirth tethered the pre-N52, N52, and new lines of Rebirth all together successfully. All titles are reasonable at $2.99, and even the giant sized one-shot that started it all, was as well. Only *All-Star Batman* is higher. Sales were decent, stories the same. What is exciting is within the one-shot that started it all. Without ruining a story, the thought that the Watchmen will eventually find its way into mainstream DC is awesome. Best titles for sales would be anything Batman, *Harley Quinn*, *Hal Jordan*, *Wonder Woman* and *Superman*. Fans like the super sons angle as well. I'd say *All-Star Batman* was the top seller.

As per DC movies, I liked *Batman v Superman,* and *Suicide Squad*, though it was not a great story, was a hoot to watch.

Marvel was still doing ok with movies. *Deadpool* was probably the most fun to watch. *Doctor Strange* had mixed reviews for my customers.

Unfortunately, Marvel's comics, just like the owners Disney, keep recycling the same typical storyline month after month. Obviously the formula of *Star Wars* and Disney fits well with Marvel books. Quantity over quality. I am yet again seeing a rash of Marvel titles litter the stands. Heroes or villains with multiple titles and reincarnations or variations that hardly deserve a title, just keep coming. Peter Parker is rich, and *Amazing Spider-Man*, the top hero of Marvel, have flat boring stories. Thats actually old news.

The best thing Marvel did was hire Jeff Lemire, probably the best writer in the industry, or at least the hottest. His *Old Man Logan* and *Moon Knight* were great sellers in 2016. I hope his *IVX* crossover of Inhumans vs. X-Men is just as good. I guess Marvel is using the same old tactic from 20 years ago again, when it tried to squash Image with excessive titles on the stands. DC, with its much fewer titles, does so much better in sales. Of course, a few years later, Marvel nearly went broke. Bendis then saved the day. Can Lemire do it again? I don't think he can as Marvel continues to insult long time fans while attempting to woo fickle new film fans. Marvel had a "universe changing" story line that turned everything on its head. And to what benefit? Marvel listened to a pitch from Jonathan Hickman a few years ago and in 2015 birthed "Secret Wars", an unnecessary destruction and reimaging of the Marvel titles, merging the Ultimate and regular title lines (along with some ancillary characters from other alternate universe story lines) and the result was an even bigger mess than before. *Amazing Spider-Man*, once the flagship title, is now little more than *Iron Man* 2.0. But, of course, it isn't just Peter Parker as Spider-Man. We've still got Miles Morales. And alternate Gwen Stacy. And apparently Alternate MC2 Spider-Man with "Mayday" May Parker and even Mary Jane Parker suiting up. *Civil War 2* in 2016 was another disaster. At least the storyline in the core mini-series was somewhat coherent this time. Although Marvel has apparently killed off Bruce Banner and powered down Jennifer in an attempt to reign in the Rampaging Hulks issue from a few years ago.

When Disney first bought out Marvel, the concern was that the story lines would revert to "Mickey Mouse" type situations. Happily, that really hasn't happened (ignoring *Squirrel Girl* and *Slapstick*). However, as Disney continues to score hit after hit at the box office, they've shifted the focus to the characters that they control at the cost of the characters they only control in comics. Fantastic Four, X-Men, Spider-Man have suffered because of it (although it will be interesting to see what becomes of Spider-Man now with the deal with Sony Pictures).

Independents: The last year has seen everyone looking for the next *Walking Dead* mega-hit. It has turned into the equivalent of the stock market. Titles are released and sold on rumour: "this title is in development or has been optioned to XYZ ." *Briggs Land* is an example. In *Previews*, for issue one there was a prominent annotation "In development for an AMC television show". I have started to see more shops add a label "soon to be TV show" on some of the back issues.

Customers are enjoying titles from Image like **Paper Girls**. (#1 shown)

Granted I can see the merit in the attaching a popular show to the comic (*Jessica Jones/Daredevil* spring to mind) but in some cases it has that boiler room mentally. The titles being pushed are initally hot but later the back issues and trades sit on the shelf because most speculators have moved on to the next best and brightest and that $40 book is now back down to a more reasonable price which is good for the customer who just wants a good story.

On a more optimistic note, there has been some really excellent work put out over the last year. Image continues to challenge with the shear volume and quality it issues. If you haven't yet, take a read of *Paper Girls*, *The Wicked and The Divine*, *Citizen Jack*, *Descender*, *Huck*, *PencilHead* (actually, anything McKeever does), *Plutona*, *The Violent*, *Roche Limit*, *Faster Than Light*, *Moonshine* or *The One%*. That was just a partial list based on customers comments.

Image continues put out interesting stories but struggles to grow their fanbase for long term story lines. Other than *The Walking Dead* and *Saga*, I can't think of any Image title that has maintained any interest to our customers. BOOM!, Dynamite, Dark Horse and other independent publishers are also struggling to bring readers in. On the plus side, they will provide a lot of new writers and artists an opportunity to showcase their talents, with many gems being published. Horror, Sci-Fi, Fantasy, Noir stories find their way to dedicated fans to be enjoyed on a regular basis.

BOOM! has put out a few interesting titles (*Kennel Block Blues*, *Last Contract*, *Wild's End*, *The Woods* to name a few), but its market share is slipping.

Dark Horse and Avatar have the best horror ongoing series in *Harrow County* and *Providence* respectively. Both have great art and stories but *Providence* has the edge as it goes into much darker material and it reminds one very much of classic horror. Unfortunately, for Avatar, they hired the once great Alan Moore and sales plummeted. All year fans asked for *Über* as well, Avatar's best title. Lets hope *Über: Invasion* makes the fans happy again.

Dark Horse had other good stories in *The Paybacks*, *Leaving Megalopolis*, *House of Penance*, *Dept. H* and *Lady Killer*. Of course, the *Dark Horse Presents* anthology continues to have some very good stories mixed with with some not so much but that is the nature of the beast. And *Hellboy* and related stories continue to roll along.

Garth Ennis continued to produced very interesting War themed stories for several different publishers (Titan/Avatar /Dark Horse/Aftershock). Customers tend to follow him around. Their allegience is to the writer, not the company. The same goes for Warren Ellis. Regulars will always give a title with his name a chance for a few issues.

Valiant continues its strong efforts with *Faith* and *Divinity*. Of course *Ninjak* and *Bloodshot* are still good although the numbers aren't high. It's a shame this fine company cannot grab onto a regular fanbase like its glory days in the 1990s. The forthcoming movies may give it the notice it needs and deserves.

Titan and Aftershock are both fantastic. Many Horror, Sci-fi, TV/Movie related titles that the big guns do not do. These companies are on the move up. Worth watching and checking out.

BILL FIDYK
COLLECTOR

2016 was another great year of steady appreciation for magazine keys. While there will always be collectors looking to fill holes in their runs of magazine titles, I've noticed that almost all non-key magazines sold very quickly if priced below *Guide*. It didn't matter if it was a high grade issue or a low grade reader - if it was priced with a significant discount below *Guide,* buyers scooped them up. Key magazines, however, sold well regardless with some magazines reaching multiples of *Guide*.

Marvel/Curtis: Easily the front runner in magazine collecting popularity. It seems that the hottest magazine key from Marvel that sells very quickly when it hits the market is *Savage Tales* #1. Not only does this issue predate *Savage Sword of Conan* for the second title featuring Conan, but it also has the first appearance and origin of the Man-Thing. Raw and slabbed copies sell very well with 9.2 and higher grade copies selling multiples of *Guide*. Second in line would be *Marvel Preview* #2 (origin of the Punisher). I think this character will always be popular but the Netflix *Daredevil* series definitely sparked renewed interest in the character. Two honorable mentions as Marvel magazine keys are *Marvel Preview* #4 and 7. These issues have cooled off a bit in 2016 but I expect a small (but not extremely noticeable) uptick in sales when the *Guardians of the Galaxy* sequel is released. The horror titles (*Dracula Lives!*, *Tales of the Zombie*, *Monsters Unleashed*, *Vampire Tales* and *Haunt of Horror*) all sell extremely well if at or below *Guide,* but moving high grade copies for multiples of *Guide* is tough.

Warren: *Vampirella* #1 leads the pack when it comes to key issues from this publisher. Any graded copy sells well with 9.0 and higher selling at multiples of *Guide*. *Creepy* #1 as well as any issue with a Frazetta cover are steady sellers at or above *Guide*. Any issue with a Frazetta signature series sells for large premiums over *Guide* largely due to the fact that there are not many examples that exist. It seems that many of the Warren collectors I talk to fall into two camps: the collector who wants the entire run of the given title or the collector who is an artist collector (like Adams, Wrightson, Frazetta, Corben) who scoops up high grade copies of the issues that contain a story or cover by the artist. Authentic copies of *Eerie* #1 are also very valuable but rarely come up for sale. I would say that this is the second "big" Warren key to have. I have seen just three copies surface for sale (and these seemed to be legit) and sold for multiples of *Guide*. The last copy I ever saw for sale was in 2013.

Skywald: Sells well in any grade at *Guide* prices. High grade examples rarely come up for sale and there are only a few slabbed copies of each Skywald title on the census. So many great artists got their start here. The easy fan favorite and true key issues from Skywald are *Nightmare* #20 (first John Byrne published artwork) and *Psycho* #24 (first published Dave Sim story).

Eerie Publications: No real key issues here but the gorier covers are targeted by collectors. It seems that the gorier (any meat grinder or decapitation covers), the better when it comes to desirability and these are quick sellers.

PAUL FIGURA
CBCS - QUALITY CONTROL
SPECIALIST

Things just keep moving forward here in sunny Florida as I spent my time between Quality Control and grading this year! The amount of books that are coming into our more than capable receiving department is phenomenal. Each month thousands of new submissions are amassed and processed by them, how they keep up is nothing short of miraculous! But with the knowledgeable and professional management that we have steering this ship I can see just how well they execute their plans to keep things streaming through our facility. I also want to thank all of you collectors/

hobbyists that continue to support us and send in your submissions. We couldn't be here doing what we love without you! Now enough of this, onward to what you came here for!

There are enough Modern books out there dominating the hobby. Blank sketch covers, by all the big publishing companies, are huge in popularity right now. More and more sketch covers and autographed books are being submitted, and they show no sign of slowing down. Sketches on blank covers as well as the small quick sketches on the regular or variant covers are becoming phenomenally popular. The hundreds of beautiful sketches, by the industry's top professionals that have crossed my desk this year, as well as the autographed books indicate a monumental increase in this area of collecting. I have checked with a few local retailers, and found that most are reasonably priced for the secondary market. So if you enjoy art by your favorite artists, and can't afford the actual page art or a consignment piece, this would be the way to go. Or, did you find a book that already had an autograph on it? A Jack Kirby, Frank Frazetta or a Jerry Robinson? Is that really a Jerry Siegel and Joe Shuster autograph? That is a real find! But you're not really sure if the signature is authentic. Bob Kane and Stan Lee's signatures have been duplicated over and over. Well CBCS has the answer to that. The VSP program allows signatures to be verified as to their authenticity! Or in some cases not. If it is? Then "Face it Tiger, you just hit the Jackpot"! To compliment the VSP program, CBCS has the ASP program, where authorized witnesses will have your books signed, or accompany you to the signing, so there is no question as to its authenticity.

Some of the usual keys that commonly move through here that one can count on seeing with a bit of regularity are, *Amazing Spider-Man* #50, the 1st appearance of Wilson Fisk. The always popular *Amazing Spider-Man* #129 the 1st appearance of the Punisher. These next two usually show up in tandem, *Amazing Spider-Man* #121 and #122, featuring the deaths of Gwen Stacy and the Green Goblin. In our all about the costume category, *Amazing Spider-Man* #252, *Spectacular Spider-Man* #90, and *Marvel Team-Up* #141 all headlining the first appearance of the black costume. There is some credit as well to *Marvel Age* #12 which came out two months before the above mentioned books, as well as *Marvel Super-Heroes Secret Wars* #8. Which actually came out 9 months later. Bringing up the rear of our Spider-Man list is *Amazing Spider-Man* #300, #344 and #361. Issue #300 features the often-copied Todd McFarlane cover, as well as the first full appearance of Venom. The next two #344 and #361 bring to the Marvel universe the 1st appearance of Cletus Kasady and the 1st appearance of Carnage.

Venturing over to the mutant front, *New Mutants* #98, the first appearance of Deadpool and Domino, *New Mutants* #87, the first appearance of Cable, *X-Force* #2, the second appearance of Deadpool. On a much lesser scale *X-Force* #11 where Domino is revealed to be Copycat aka Vanessa Carlysle. The real Domino, Neena Thurman does makes her appearance in that issue. Another top mutant title that is a constant top key is *Uncanny X-Men* #266, the first appearance in continuity of Gambit. His actual first appearance was in *X-Men Annual* #14. With the *Deadpool* movie being so well received and the indication that Cable will be in the second installment, I see the popularity of these books continuing to increase. So keep a definite eye on those.

Without a doubt though, I would have to say the overall best mutant first appearance still seems to be in *Incredible Hulk* #181, the first full appearance of Wolverine. There seems to be no end to the popularity of this book, as well as the Frank Miller 1982 *Wolverine* four issue miniseries. Those books are a daily sight around here. Speaking of Wolverine, the first and second appearance of his biggest antagonist, Sabretooth was actually in *Iron Fist* #14 and *Power Man and Iron Fist* #66, and is a must have for those mutant fans out there.

Now with the popularity of the Marvel characters on Netflix, are you thinking of grabbing a hold of some Frank Miller *Daredevil*? That would not be a bad stratagem. With the popularity of the show's first two seasons, I can only guess where they will take him in season three. Following closely behind *Daredevil* are the regular and miniseries #1s of The Punisher (remember the popularity of *Amazing Spider-Man* #129!). As the debut of his series draws closer, I am only guessing how many more of those that we will see. *Marvel Premiere* numbers 15 and 16 showcase the talents of Danny Rand, aka Iron Fist, whom we spoke of earlier. His erstwhile partner, Luke Cage, Power Man, made his popular first appearance in *Hero for Hire* #1. As long as I mentioned Netflix, *Marvel Feature* #1, the first appearance of the Defenders, which is supposed to be just around the viewing corner. That book has always had a steady presence at our work stations. Continuing on with our heroes appearances first in comics and onto the big screen let's take a look at the Black Panther, first appearing in the *Fantastic Four* #52, then getting his origin updated in *Avengers* #87, as well as taking the lead in Marvel's *Jungle Action* with issue #5. Some real history here with the Black Panther was the start of self-contained, multi arc story entitled "Panther's Rage". It ran in *Jungle Action* #6 through #18 and is considered to be the first comic that was created as a complete 200 page novel. Finding it shouldn't be hard as it was reprinted in *The Essential Black Panther*, and numerous other Marvel publications.

Having a need to get your Falcon fix? *Captain America* #117 is the place to find it, the first appearance of Sam Wilson as our first African-American Super-Hero, the Falcon. Mr. Wilson is now currently enjoying his time serving as our newest Captain America, taking the reins, or shield as it were in *The All-New Captain America* #1. A fan of the mystical? *Strange Tales* #110, the 1st appearance of Doctor Strange, is no stranger to my desk.

On the DC side of things, we saw a quick increase in *Superman* #123, which was a Supergirl try-out issue. The sudden surge that book saw, with the first season of the *Supergirl* TV show declined just as quickly, but *Action Comics* #252, the first appearance of Supergirl, does make steady appearances. *Adventure Comics* #381, where the Maid of Might began her solo run in that title also makes frequent appearances upon my desk. On a lesser note, her first solo comic in 1972 does show up, but rather infrequently. The top heroine first appearance honors still have to go to *Detective Comics* #359, "The Million Dollar Debut of Batgirl!" aka Barbara Gordon. That book is always turning up around here, and rightly so. Batgirl has been a very beloved addition to the Bat-family, and I see no reason this should stop.

On the more recent side of things the convention exclusive Chrome Foil covers of *Superman*, *Batman* and *Wonder Woman Rebirth* #1, usually autographed, seem to be immensely popular, and we see quite a bit of them. Speaking of Rebirth, it looks as though DC has finally hit a home run with this relaunch and enough of the Rebirth titles are making their way through our system. Keep a watch for those to spike a bit more in popularity. Moving along with the popular DC books. The *Batman: Dark Knight Returns*, and *The Killing Joke* are two of the old prestige format books that although were always fan favorites and usually turning up here frequently, they seem to be picking up a bit of steam, and are continuing to move along as trendy DC titles.

Slipping now to the DC movies side of things, with the use of Parademons and the announcement of Steppenwolf appearing in the *Justice League* movie, can Darkseid be far behind? If so, follow the crowd and grab a copy of *Jimmy Olsen* #134 for his 1st appearance in cameo, and *Forever People* #1 for the first full appearance of the evil god. While you're at it, grabbing a copy of *New Teen Titans* #2 which showcases the talents of Deathstroke might not be a bad idea. Especially with the announcement of him appearing in the new Batman movie. That book being an already popular title should get even a bigger boost with the movie.

Have you heard enough about the newer books? Do you want to see what is cooking on the vintage market? More than enough vintage books come through here every day, those Golden and Silver Age greats that I see cannot compare with the newer books. We recently got in a great collection that featured many key Golden Age issues, all with bright, vibrant colors that would make you drool. Once again, the movies play a role here as well, as *All Star Comics* #8, the first appearance of Wonder Woman has been seen a bit. Also seen were *Wonder Woman* #1 and *Sensation Comics* #1, which continues her origin from *All Star* #8. I don't think I need to speak much more of which issues are gaining in popularity, just mention Golden Age and you grab people's attention. In recent months though, there have been a few that caught my eye, a couple of *More Fun* Spectre appearances and a *Leading Comics* #1. One can never see enough of those! *Flash Comics* #86, with the 1st appearance of the Black Canary has shown up around here a few times, along with *Adventure Comics* #209 and #262, the 1st appearance of Speedy and the retelling of his origin. Those are just some samples of lesser known Hero books that don't see a lot of mention in print, but are still showing up and seem to be on a few want lists.

Slipping over to the Silver Age, and you find the early appearances of the main Spider-Man villains that pop up rather frequently, the Vulture in #2, the Sandman #4, Mysterio in #13, Green Goblin in #14, Kraven the Hunter in #15. Or how about some other fan favorite villains? Doctor Doom in *Fantastic Four* #5, or the very first appearance of an Inhuman in comics, Medusa in the *Fantastic Four* #36, the rest of the Inhumans were quick to follow in issues 44 through 47. On the heels of those great books comes the first appearance of the Silver Surfer and Galactus….no rest for the wicked I guess as these books seem to be staples in the collector world. Other regular Silver Age heroes that always brighten my day, and show up routinely are found within the pages of *Brave and the Bold*. Issues #25 through #30 with first appearances of the Suicide Squad, and the Justice League of America. *Brave and the Bold* #34 the first Silver Age appearance of Hawkman and Hawkgirl. Also this year I have seen my share of *Showcase* #17 the 1st appearance of Adam Strange, and #19 the first Adam Strange cover title. Charlton Comics, a company that had so many great characters and titles, books I see here that I wish I had kept in my collection. I've seen more than a few issues of *Space Adventures* #33, the 1st appearance of Captain Atom, drawn by the legendary Steve Ditko. His adventures ran in *Space Adventures* in issues #33 to #40, and #42. He then reappeared in *Strange Suspense Stories* #75, which became *Captain Atom* with issue #78.

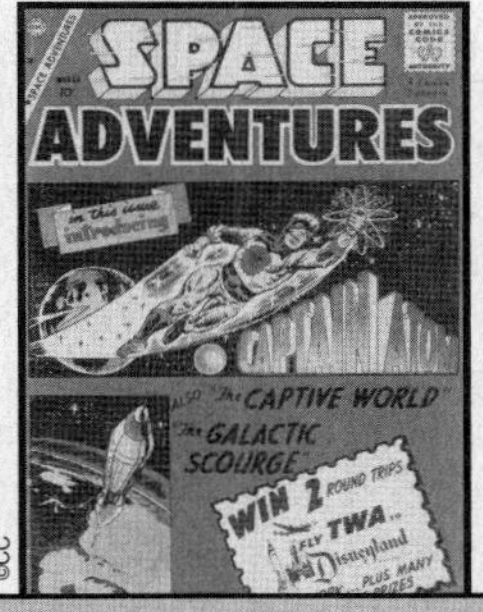

©CC

Space Adventures #33, with the 1st app. of Captain Atom and art by Steve Ditko is popular with collectors.

So there you have it, another year of collecting and enjoying our hobby under our belts, some books moving up the ladder of popularity, some slipping down a few notches. Where your favorite books and heroes end up, who knows, but honestly does it really matter? As long has you are enjoying the search, treasuring the finds, THAT is what really matters. Until next year, happy hunting!

Joseph Fiore
ComicWiz.com

If you had asked me earlier in the year what I was planning to cover in my market report, I'd probably talk about the sustained interest in comics reflected by retailer purchases being the highest since the late '90s. I'd sprinkle in a dash of how movies continued to inject a sustained relevance into mainstream culture, expanding audiences to include more females and younger readers. Even in social media, there hasn't been a month that hasn't passed where a friend or fellow collector has decided to open up their own collectibles shop, signaling a very impressive statistic of new brick-and-mortar shops opening up. These are all amazing signals that the hobby is alive and well!

In fact, a lot of these talking points could probably related back into a topic of conversation that arose casually with this summer's Kempenfest show. For new readers, this is an annual show where I exhibit, and which has traditionally been a successful one for me. It's an "antiques" venue that has allowed me to set-up as the "comic guy" and it's a great way to interface with local collectors who have either been at collecting for years, or are just starting out. Anyhow, back to the conversation - which sort of touches on the rising interest in comics, as well as the subject of literacy. More specifically the question asked what makes comics interesting to people of the new generation?

One of the talking points that seemed to emerge is that comics can be seen as a different sort of literacy because it's primarily visual, and one of the theories put forward that day is that it's been successful because the Internet works in a very similar way. As an example, memes use small amounts of text alongside images, and can sometimes gain as much attention if not more than a well composed post. Social media too continues to trend toward limiting the amount of characters we use in writing posts, and some of the most consumed content in social media are shares of images and video. I thought about this, and became more conscious of my younger customers, and interestingly I found that almost every youngster I asked was far more interested in reading the comics because of the art, and turned to reading to learn more about how their favourite superheroes or characters in the movies or cartoons first made their mark in comics.

Interestingly, this discussion allowed itself to morph into holding a real life experiment to test this theory when our cities local library decided to hold its first ever Comic Con. I had committed to the show before Kempenfest four day show happened in late July/August, and didn't know what to expect. Surprisingly, the show was well attended, by a demographic that went beyond the typical adult male collector, and again included many females, as well as younger and older readers. Many of the adult females were cosplaying along with their children, and sometimes the Dad would show up in costume too, and that family atmosphere made me feel like I was witnessing a real life interpretation of Disney's *The Incredibles* movie.

I did well at both shows with comics priced from $1-$5, but also sold a number of higher value books to both casual collectors and those whose interests in collecting piqued from a string of superhero movies they had enjoyed, and the surprise by a longshot were the ones now asking about a character anticipated to appear in the coming months - Doctor Strange. Comics I couldn't sell if my life depended on it in past years were selling faster than I could pull them out of longboxes, and the grin I wore was wider than any of Benedict Cumberbatch's smiling headshots. Doctor Strange comics, whether they were '80s, '90s, in his own title, *What If*'s, or in team-ups, were my best sellers by a longshot.

However, I have to emphasize it wasn't just the sales that made the shows successful - it was refreshing to hear younger readers who were actually diving into reading the comics they were buying, and interacting with one another about story lines they read. And not just new comic content, but diving into old stories being reimagined for the screen that were referenced from a graphic novel, omnibus, Marvel Milestone or reprinted comic. Those stories and conversations made me feel like an old trivia geek with unusable *Jeopardy* trivia knowledge could now relate again with an audience half my age and sometimes younger.

At the mid-year point, I had made the difficult decision to refocus my collecting interests. An accident in the late winter months made me realize I just wasn't able to divide my time in collecting comics, toys and original comic art anymore. I sold approximately 16,000 comics from my personal collection to fellow Overstreet advisor Marc Sims of Big B Comics. Marc made the whole process very smooth and I couldn't have asked for a better outcome as the comics are now slowly being absorbed in the local collector market.

I had also found a buyer in Texas to acquire a large fragment of my vintage Kenner *Star Wars* toy collection. That too went super smooth, into the hands of a collector who I greatly respect, and I've since began organizing the remaining fragments of my comics and toys, and enjoying the basement space I freed up! I hope to use this coming year as the year I recommence scanning and cataloguing my original comic art collection, and I've already begun the cataloguing part by registering and uploading art to my CAF profile.

Social media continues to be a platform of interest to monitor when it comes to the movement of comics and other items I collect. Facebook groups continue to be a frequent venue for the movement of comics, and the groups see a great number of items being sold and being diverted from sites like eBay. In my opinion however its greatest feature is found with how it continues to serve as a barometer for activity which could help explain patterns and trends. As an example for instance, the situation I'm about to describe takes us to the month of June when CGC had made an announcement it was rehauling its slab design.

Posts began appearing in Facebook groups with complaints on a number of issues, the more serious having to do with books actually being damaged in the new slab. This precipitated panic and outright boycotts of the new case until CGC corrected the issues. The negative trickle effect went beyond that of a reputational nature with numerous examples of certified examples that could be identified as being in the new slab actually dropping in value during this time period. Sadly, this was also met with the vetting of any posts identifying these issues on the CGC forums. The vetting ranged from posts being deleted right through to entire threads and their comments disappearing. There's an old saying that it's better to keep the conversation at your own house than let it spread elsewhere. This is exactly what happens in social media, except by sending collectors away angrier, you can be certain they aren't going to keep the problem to themselves.

CGC forum member Ditch Fahrenheit published several videos on YouTube which do a great job of chronicling the issues and damage caused by the CGC's case, and could be found using a Google keyword search "creep engine cgc." Facebook continued to be the place where the conversation continued and the reason why I think it's important to mention this point is that it gave context to a situation that might have only been seen as an unexplained market correction rather than an issue with a certification company on the ropes of a crisis trying desperately to sweep the issues with their new cases under the rug.

My hottest books pairing sales from the two shows I did with online sales were *New Mutants* #98, *Batman Adventures* #12, *Fantastic Four* #52, and *Incredible Hulk* #181. The hottest Canadian Price Variants activity without a doubt revolves around *Batman* or *Detective Comics* issues, and the speculation for the *Spider-Man: Homecoming* movie saw a frenzy of activity with early appearances of Scorpion, the Vulture, and *Amazing Spider-Man Annual* #1 featuring the first appearance of Sinister Six being a very popular issue. The one comic that I had been tracking closely with the lead up to *Rogue One* in December 2016 is Marvel's *Star Wars* #1, and regrettably prices on 9.4s and up had dropped at about half the value they were selling for a year prior.

So in conclusion, local selling venues have continued to prove to be most successful this past year. Setting up at shows will continue to be my sales approach of choice in the coming year. Even local classified listings have proven to be far more logistically practical to complete a deal, both for selling and buying. Facebook groups have kept a decent level of pace in terms of social media platforms where items continue to pop-up for sale, but haven't been as effective in terms of selling in my own personal experience. Two new buying channels have emerged for me - one is dealing with two different owners of storage facilities who have turned to me a handful of times already to sell collections of toys and comics. In fact, I am processing a 2,000 book collection, and a 200 book collection from two different self-storage facility owners, with both deals happening earlier in the day of me writing this report.

The other channel that has quickly emerged since becoming an accredited appraiser is the estate appraisals business, which has continued to be a great way to remain dialed-in to values for things I have a passion in collecting myself, while allowing me to get a foot in the door for any estates which are looking to be matched-up to a buyer. At the time of this writing, I am handling three assignments, with one looking to have me assist in selling the entire contents of the estate. This has meant reinforcing strong relationships with a network of buyers, and fostering new ones during the period estates are downsized and sold off.

This past year has brought many new interactions and great meeting experiences. It has also meant coming to a realization that we sometimes need to return to our collecting roots to enrich our journey and experience. One of the observations I noted from this experience is a pace, mood and feeling seeming more rushed, maybe a little panicked or even discouraged with a deal slipping through collectors fingers. These could all have something to do with numerous hobbies experiencing significant value gains and people feeling like they are being priced out of their respective hobbies. One thing I personally want to try to work towards in the coming year as a goal is trying to return to some of the basics, revolving around collecting being something meant to be fun and enjoyable, and I encourage readers of this great guide to try to do the same - before you stress about adding more, enjoy what you already have and focus your pursuits on the things that make you most happy. Happy collecting everyone!

JOHN FOSTER
SOUTH PHILLY COMICS

Greetings, everyone, this is John Foster reporting again from sunny South Philadelphia at our friendly neighborhood shop, South Philly Comics! It's been a reasonably interesting and exciting year for comics and for the people who read them. Our monthly comic sales remain strong and are the bulk of our business, with trade paperbacks next in line, and back issue sales being the icing on the cake!

Let's start this report with Modern comic sales and begin by talking about DC Comics' Rebirth, easily the biggest thing to happen this year as far as Modern comics go. The $2.99, 80 page *DC Universe Rebirth* one-shot sold extremely well and set the stage for the first wave of DC Rebirth one-shots to completely sell out in no time. *Batman* pre- and post-Rebirth is still the top DC Comics seller for us, with no other title even coming close. *All-Star Batman*, *Detective Comics*, and *Wonder Woman* are the next tier of leaders. *Omega Men* was critically acclaimed but failed to move at our shop. This year DC also launched a new imprint in the vein of Vertigo called Young Animal, under the guidance of musician/comic writer Gerard Way. Since its debut not too long ago, we have had major success with all of their titles, but especially with *Doom Patrol*.

At Marvel, *Ms. Marvel*, *Karnak*, *Darth Vader*, and *Vision* were our most popular Marvel titles this year. *Unbeatable Squirrel Girl* was also a big seller for us, and I attribute its success to the fact that both kids and adults are interested and never miss an issue. Despite our success with these titles, I have noticed a lot of people jumping ship due to the never ending train of "major" comic crossover events as well as release delays and high prices. Speaking of Marvel's trouble keeping their fans happy, it's also worth mentioning the constant griping I hear from some fans of the "Big 2" about anything and everything. It seems that no matter what, Marvel and DC are damned if they do and damned if they don't. A particular complaint is that Marvel seems to put out a decent amount of books that are obvious, shameless money grabs, like overpriced Annuals which are not even done by the book's main creative team, or event tie-ins that have little to nothing to do with the event.

Image Comics, on the other hand, seems to be able to do no wrong - the only complaint we hear is that they put out too many interesting and good-looking comics and the customers don't always have the bank account to support them all! *East of West*, *Wicked and the Divine*, *Paper Girls*, *Outcast*, *Rumble*, and *Walking Dead* are big sellers, but *Saga* is still king. We probably also sell the most trade paperbacks overall from Image Comics, with their low-to-reasonable prices and timely release dates.

We've seen moderate success with Dark Horse Comics this year. *Black Hammer*, *Harrow County*, Mignola-verse titles, and the occasional Richard Corben horror mini-series or one-shots are popular titles.

Boom Entertainment's *Lumberjanes* has dropped a little in numbers, but is still passionately loved by its readers. I can't seem to be able to order enough *Hillbilly* from the newly resurrected publisher, Albatross Funny Books, which is nice to see since I'm personally a big fan of Eric Powell's work.

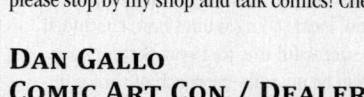

Hillbilly *#1 is a treat for fans of writer/artist Eric Powell.*

Now, onto Back Issue sales! Golden Age comic sales were few and far between for us this year, but we did pick up a few ok c opies of Jungle Tales and Authentic Police Cases, nothing crazy, but they eventually sold. Silver Age books were an entirely different story, though, as we were able to pick-up lots of these wonderful books and sell them pretty quickly. We purchased and immediately flipped a Batman #18 1 (1st app Poison Ivy), a nice looking F antastic Four #25 (2nd SA Captain America app, 1st Hulk/Thing fight, AND the 1st mention of Ben Grimm's sweet old aunt Petunia!), and Adventure Comics #256 (Green Arrow origin story by Jack Kirby). During the *Batman v Superman* movie hype, we did well moving our collection of *World's Finest* issues featuring Batman fighting Superman covers. We also acquired a massive amount of Silver Age Dell, Harvey, Gold Key, and ACG comics and I was astonished at how quickly we moved them. The gem from that haul was Gold Key's *Space Ghost* #1, which flew out of here once posted on social media (which I've found is a great way to drum up interest in our little neighborhood comic shop).

As far as Bronze and Copper Age comics go, we had some great luck finding and selling some "key" issues. *Heroes for Hire* #1 (1st app Luke Cage) sold well over *Guide* price with the popularity of the Netflix show. We also did very well buying and selling back issues of Marvel's first go around with *Star Wars* especially issues #42 & #68 (Boba Fett issues). This year we got a great deal and bought a huge collection of '70s and '80s underground comix and were blown away with how well they sold. I noticed people were quite interested to see books that they never saw before and don't generally see anywhere else, making us a destination for discovering new old books.

This year we were also fortunate enough to grab some nice copies of *Peter Parker, Spectacular Spider-Man* #64 (1st app Cloak & Dagger) and *New Teen Titans* #2 (1st app. Deathstroke). We plan to sit on them until TV/Movie news develops. With comics bombarding TV, Netflix, and the big screen, I've noticed it really only affects these "key" issues, with little to no interest paid to the surrounding issues of the run (outside of longtime collectors filling in gaps of their collections). For instance, I can sell any and all 1st and/or early appearances of Deadpool, but his monthly title is one of our lowest selling titles, despite the huge success of the movie.

With comic fandom rapidly growing and showing no signs of slowing down, we can only fear oversaturation in mass media, but I feel we are still a while away from that. I would like to thank J.C. Vaughn, Mark Huesman, and the rest of the Overstreet gang for putting together this wonderful book and letting me get a word in. I would also like to thank all of you who took the time to read my thoughts on comics this year. If you are ever in the Philadelphia area, please stop by my shop and talk comics! Cheers!

DAN GALLO
COMIC ART CON / DEALER

There is not enough good stuff to go around. The supply is limited while the demand is not. And that's where I come in. I specialize in graded key issues and original comic book art. I don't deal in bulk or miscellaneous issues; only books with significance. I like to say I have the meat but no potatoes. The challenge I have today is the same as I have every year; I just can't acquire material fast enough. I have money I can't spend. That is how strong the hobby is.

Let's talk books. There is nothing more boring than reading pages upon pages of outdated sales data. Really, I would rather shoot myself. Rather than subject you to that, I prefer to write a short, concise report offering some market insight focused more on the future instead of the past. Here we go:

Golden Age: Two words: buy Gold! I like to refer to the top 25 or so books listed in *Overstreet*'s Top 100 GA Books as "Big Gold," (plus *More Fun* #73, *Wonder Woman* #1 and *Sensation* #1 which inexplicitly haven't yet cracked the list). For those monster books it is the Wild West and nearly impossible to pin down a price and get ahead of the curve. It has gotten to a point where only a handful of collectors can play in that pool leaving the rest of the hobby to either settle for restored copies or look downstream for books that haven't popped yet, (much like DC SA keys just a few years ago). Already sought after but less expensive than the books in the top 25 are *Detective* #58, the 1st Penguin, *Detective* #66, the

1st Two Face, *Detective* #140, the 1st Riddler, and *Detective* #168, the origin of the Joker. Also worthwhile are *Wonder Woman* #6, the 1st Cheetah, and *Sensation* #6, the 1st magic lasso. There is also *Superboy* #10, the 1st Lana Lang, and *Superman* #30, the 1st Mr. Mxyztplk. Keep an eye out for classic covers or covers featuring villains such as the Joker and Catwoman. Lastly, I am a big fan of any GA Captain America, (as long as they present well!). In short, even if you are priced out of the "Big Gold" market there are still plenty of good books out there. Now go find them…

Silver Age: *Fantastic Four* #4, which contains the first SA appearance of Namor, has finally begun to move. I have written about it in every market report I have submitted, (this being my fourth), and I am still bullish on it. He is the biggest Marvel character by far yet to have his day on the big screen. His time will come and when you first hear of it, it will already be too late. It is undervalued and I would recommend picking up the highest grade you could afford, (and do it quickly). Still, another favorite of mine is *Tales to Astonish* #13, the first appearance of Groot. There is so much potential for Disney using this character in every way imaginable. How long before we see Groot walking around the Magic Kingdom? Now for an obvious one, *Amazing Spider-Man* #1. With *Amazing Fantasy* #15 prices practically out of reach for many collectors, I can see eyes turning towards *Amazing Spider-Man* #1, for the first time, as a first option. Look for the gap in prices between the two to narrow. It is also a good time to look into *Journey into Mystery* #83, the 1st Thor. The book has been flat the past few years and I look for that to change with his new movie due out in November.

Bronze Age: I am a little down on BA books. I think the sheer quantities available have kept many books flat or trending down. Before you rush to dump, there are exceptions though. *Hulk* #181 and *ASM* #129 are both stronger than ever. *Werewolf by Night* #32 has had a good year, (but I see it topping off already). *Tomb of Dracula* #10, *Marvel Premiere* #15 and *Marvel Spotlight* #5 I still like a lot. Also, when buying BA books it is even more important to get the highest grade possible even if you have to buy fewer books to do so.

Modern Age: *Punisher* Limited Series #1: still a big fan. I love the *Venom* #1 black error edition. They just don't come up often. I also have a soft spot for *Spider-Man* #1 platinum edition. With MA books I would shoot for the 9.8s because they are just too common and I think over time we will see a widening of the gap between the 9.8s and the 9.6s, (although with *Venom* black being so scarce a lower grade would suffice).

Original Comic Book Art: The only thing wilder than the Wild West is original comic book art! As co-promoter of Comic Art Con I have seen the insanity up close. But don't let that scare you. Get your feet wet at a comfortable price point, ease your way in and build from there. You will be glad you did.

Conclusion: My report has tilted towards the investment side as opposed to a pure collector's side. You don't need me or anyone else to tell you how to collect. You buy what you like and follow your gut. If you have your eye on the investment side, then to me it is simple; buy the very best and at the highest grade you can afford. Don't get bogged down with the small stuff. Less is more. I would rather have one big book as opposed to two smaller ones or one even bigger one instead of five others. It helps to have someone who will offer you time payments so that bigger purchases are more easily digestible. Also, when you find yourself with a bunch of really good books consider packaging them all up for one monster book. Let all previous purchases be a down payment on a future grail. Stair step your way to the top, (because that is where you want to be), and remember, the absolute best material is super scarce, (and that is what you want to have).

Eric J. Groves
The Comic Art Foundation

Greetings from the windswept plains of Oklahoma! Herewith we submit our commentary on the market for comic books during this last year. We are pleased to report that in our view, the market is strong with an influx of new, mostly younger, collectors. We temper this view with the observation that some of these collectors are not accumulating runs of specific titles but seek out only key issues, preferably in high grade. This trend reflects a speculative attitude which we think does not serve the best interest of the collecting community as a whole. Time will tell.

We are a boutique operation centered on Golden Age, Atomic Age and early Silver Age comic books. Our focus is largely a function of this advisor's age, which is, shall we say, pre-Code. We fell in love with the comics we read in our youth and spent our years acquiring the issues we were unable to find back in the day. This quest was quite challenging before the organization of comic fandom in the 1960s. But now we have them all!

To some extent, we specialize in acquiring Atomic Age comics. They are of interest because from 1946 to 1954, there was a proliferation of titles embracing subject matter never addressed before. This included crime, horror, romance, war, science fiction, westerns, humor and tie-ins to radio, movies and television. Many of these comics are desirable because they featured the early work of prominent artists like Matt Baker, Wally Wood, Frank Frazetta, Harvey Kurtzman and many others. We delight in turning up offbeat titles like *Uncle Milty*, *Cryin' Lion*, *Sparkie*, *Radio Pixie* and the like. They were emblematic of their time. They were precursors. One era makes the next one possible.

Golden Age: Timely comics continue to rule. When we can find them, they sell the same day we offer them! Nuff said. With DC comics, it all depends on the character. Fair to say that *Batman* is the preeminent title, along with *Detective*, especially lower numbers. *Superman* does well, not so much for *Action*, unless it is early on. Close behind are excellent titles like *Flash*, *All-American*, *Green Lantern*, *All Star*, *More Fun*, *Star Spangled* and *Adventure*. Especially in demand are the scarcer numbers of these titles, some of which flow over into the Atomic Age, such as later issues of *Flash* and *Green Lantern*. *Wonder Woman* and *Sensation* deserve special mention because, at long last, the Amazon princess has been recognized for her remarkable stories and artwork. It is noteworthy that even younger collectors are hunting these titles, many of which are generation-skipping.

The other major publishers are still of interest to serious collectors, but do not enjoy the same level of demand enjoyed by DC. For example, Quality had several superlative titles, like *Plastic Man* by Jack Cole, and *Police*, yet these books do not move as they should. The exception is *Military*, especially with Eisner art, and *Blackhawk* with Reed Crandall.

Fawcett comics were extremely popular in their day, but do not draw collectors as they once did. However, early *Master Comics*, and *Capt. Marvel, Jr.*, are sought after for Mac Raboy art. World War II covers increase desirability. Early *Whiz* numbers fare well; some are relatively scarce. *Mary Marvel* has a following, too. MLJ, before giving way to Archie Andrews, produced some fine comics, particularly those with wartime covers. They sell steadily. Fiction House, the home of scantily clad ladies, are of limited interest, except for *Planet*, always a winner, and low numbers of *Jumbo*, with the oversized ones difficult to find.

Atomic Age: This era fascinates not only collectors of esoterica, but comic historians and scholars, such as Michelle Nolan, author of the master treatise on romance comics. We especially appreciate the period for the courage demonstrated by the publishers of that time, which in some cases were prosecuted for their art during the congressional inquiries of the 1950s. Comics caused juvenile delinquency, certain experts said. The end result was the Comics Code Authority.

A sampler of some of the non-superhero Atomic Age titles we sold this year would include *Frankenstein*, *Fritzie Ritz*, *Joker*, *Mighty Mouse*, *Miss America*, *Paul Terry's Comics*, *Sea Hound*, *Terry-Toons* and *Sparkler*. We also moved a lot of love comics ranging from *High School Confidential Diary* to *True Bride-To-Be Romances*. What great titles. The books most in demand from this period, aside from superheros, are late 1940s Timelys and their successor, Atlas. All Atlas titles sell, even the war comics, which have traditionally been somewhat slow. These are not necessarily high dollar books but they do have an audience.

DC continued putting out its well-established superhero titles during the Atomic Age. However, many issues of DC comics like *Batman*, *Superman*, *World's Finest*, *Wonder Woman* and others may not have been widely distributed, or saved, because they are very hard to find. Also, they were not well made and often have condition problems. Notably, DC also engaged in publishing somewhat experimental titles, often tied in to movies or television. Examples include *Adventures of Alan Ladd*, *Bob Hope*, *Ozzie and Harriet*, *Dale Evans*, *Dean Martin* and *Jerry Lewis* and others. The early issues of these titles presented photo covers, which are very attractive and good sellers. Beyond this, these comics are slow movers, at least for the time being.

A few words about E.C. comics, also published during the Atomic Age. "Pre-trend" titles like *Moon Girl* and *Land of the Lost* (based on a radio show) are in demand, and do well. The "Trend" period, 1950-1954, of course, produced the most desirable comics, with horror titles leading the way. The crime suspense titles are next, followed by the science fiction genre and finally, the war comics. The final E.C. period, "New Direction", actually produced some superlative work from the all-time best stable, such as *Impact*, *Piracy* and *Valor*. E.C. comics from this time frame are bargains. *Mad* is a slow mover, which is hard to figure because it was so brilliantly conceived and executed. Yes, all this E.C. comic art has been reprinted, but nothing beats the experience of holding and reading the original. Like fine wine, the bouquet of an old comic book is unmistakable. Basement or attic? Basement, I think.

Silver Age: Early Silver Age comics, for the most part, deserve the value attributed to them. They constitute a significant milestone in the evolution of comics. As we say, one era makes the next one possible. The publishers and artists who produced these books are rightly revered. Issues such as *Showcase* #4, *Amazing Fantasy* #15, *Hulk* #1, *Amazing Spider-Man* #1 and *Fantastic Four* #1 are established icons now. We have sold these books many times over. They move out in all grades. There seems no end to the demand for low number *Spidey*s and key issues of that title. They are beautiful books, lots of eye appeal. Early *Tales of Suspense* and *Tales to Astonish*, likewise. *Daredevil* and *X-Men* are steady.

As to DC comics: Batman is the character most in demand, especially the hard-to-find issues, *Batman* #80 to 100. Superman is a reliable seller, too. Not much to say about *Superboy*, *Lois Lane* and *Jimmy Olson* except that the lower numbers are on want lists. Key issues of *Showcase* and *Brave and the Bold* continue to do well. Early *Strange Adventures* are marketable, not so much *House of Secrets* and *House of Mystery*. It appears DC television shows (*Arrow*, *The Flash*, *Gotham* and *Supergirl*) have had an impact on the characters portrayed. This can be difficult to gauge. Many late Silver Age comics are not all that difficult to find, so condition can be an important factor in pricing.

Bringing it all Back Home: We do not traffic much in Bronze Age comics, but are in touch with colleagues who do. Much speculation persists here, maybe too much. We continue to advise fans to buy comics they like, not solely for investment purposes. One of the criteria for judging the artistic worth of a comic is the test of time. A truly memorable comic is one that can be read more than once and which evokes a new reaction a year or two later. Some comic art is eternal. If you doubt this, go back and read Carl Barks' *Donald Duck Four Colors*, or Will Eisner's *Spirit* or even the Frank Miller *Daredevil* stories. You may see things you did not see the first time. Comics with inherent artistic merit usually hold their value over time. So buy what you love.

Two other matters: First, if we strive to be precise in establishing *Guide* values, we should look at the prices achieved by the major auction houses, ComicConnect and Heritage. Both auctions regularly present highly graded books, usually including major keys and scarcer items. Thanks to the internet, the comic market is global in scope. Winning bids from everywhere should be taken into account when determining values.

Second, as many other advisors have reported, the major comic conventions have devolved into mere celebrations of popular culture, mostly movies. Comics are no longer the central focus of these enterprises. For example, the 2016 Wizard World ComicCon in Tulsa, we are told, presented only three (3) serious comic book dealers. For serious collectors and dealers, we recommend smaller conventions genuinely devoted to comics and related materials. One such gathering, we shamelessly endorse, is OAF Con, staged annually every fall in Norman, Oklahoma, under the superb guidance of long time collector Bart Bush. Real people and lots of old funny books. If you show up, you won't be disappointed. Until then, we wish every reader of this commentary the best of luck in finding the books you seek. Dicta et picta; comics abide.

TERRY HOKNES
HOKNES COMICS

"Playing catch up" - this is a term I use to explain the larger than normal growth that some books make usually after years of being stagnant. The majority of vintage comics have slow but steady growth which keep the comic market consistent on an upward growth in price. However some books are "discovered" to be undervalued due to either modern movie hype or in comparison to similar type books whether based on age, importance or rarity. This can cause some books to have massive jumps in a short period of time. Some recent books that have seen massive growth in the past couple years include: *Wonder Woman* #98, *Tales To Astonish* #13, *Peanuts* #1, *More Fun Comics* #73. These are examples of books that have taken off for various reasons - but they all played "catch up". One of the fun aspects of the collecting world is for those who study their comic book history to actually learn more about vintage comics and discover gems that perhaps have gone ignored for a long period of time. *Suspense Comics* #3 is a perfect example of a book that two decades ago was a fairly cheap unimportant issue but now with constant growing attention has risen from $6.00 in the first *Overstreet Price Guide* to an incredible $100,000.00 in the last *Guide*.

Younger collectors seem to be primarily interested in superheroes that they can relate to. Unfortunately a huge chunk of comic book history is slowly becoming ignored as many newer collectors are not aware of the thousands of other cool comics that can be collected. Books that are historically important, in many cases much rarer (especially in high grade), and much more affordable. It's a win-win to hunt out treasures. One of the most shocking trends these days is that many collectors have no problem spending $500.00 for a brand new release variant flavour of the week book but don't realize they could be buying 80 year old vintage comics for less than $100.00.

I look for trends in collecting to see what is changing. The current comic book publishers put out so many rare limited variant covers now that almost the only new comics that are heating up in price are "ratio variants". This market has been growing now for the past 10 years and there are now many comics from the past decade that are now more valuable than Golden Age comics.

To help educate a new generation of collectors I have started the massive research project of the History of Comic Books starting with 1933 and looking at every single comic book issue from every publisher in my in-depth video documentary series which can be seen online at www.HoknesComics.com or at www.YouTube.com by searching for Comic Book History 1933.

My true love is for Golden Age and Silver Age comics and their amazing history. For over 20 years I have been researching and compiling data on the growth of comic books and self publish a series of books called "Investing In Comic Books". The purpose of this series is to help collectors/investors make smarter decisions about investing while learning the history of these books. My main resource is the annual *Overstreet Price Guide* which has documented the entire growth of this industry over the past 47 years. Record prices continue to be hit in all era's and genres. More info at www.HoknesComics.com.

Tips On Investing: Here are some of the things you need to know about before you start investing and spending big money on comic books. Bob Overstreet began publishing his Comic Book Price Guide Annual in 1970 and now 47 years later has helped establish the comics collectible market as one of the most consistent, trustworthy and safe investments. Overstreet's pricing information from the past 47 years is used to analyze the growth of each book in all conditions in my book series "Investing In Comic Books". To find out how strong the market is for a book you should do year to year price guide comparisons and then compare them to the highest dollar sales on Heritage or any other auction site to find out if people really are paying high prices to keep driving the price up on a particular comic book. Finally compare the book to other books of similar importance, year, genre and find out if the book is overpriced, under priced or on par with similar books.

Split Between Grades / Prices: Note that sometimes the NM copy might be going up in value but the lower grade copies might at the same time be dropping in value. Over the years the spread between low and high grade copies has been stretching. Back in 1970, a Mint comic was worth 4x that of a Good 2.0 copy. Now when it comes to key issues the

*AfterShock Comics' **Animosity** was one of 2016's books of the year. (#1 shown)*

split is usually around the 20x difference between NM 9.2 and GD 2.0. Also keep in mind that copies of key issues above 9.2 will sell for even more, creating sometimes a spread of 100x difference - meaning a book that sells for $2000 in GD might sell for $100,000 in NM 9.6. Therefore it's easy to see why most collectors prefer to go for the highest end copies as they drive the market and help push prices up each year. Beware that the majority of comic books graded FN 6.0 or less sell for less than the *Guide* price. Usually only rare or key issues sell above *Guide* in lower grades. eBay is the largest market for comic book sales and therefore due to shipping costs and bad grading most buyers seek out deals and do not want to pay *Guide* prices.

I personally believe that vintage comics value should be based a lot on its rarity and one of the best benefits of the CGC Census is we now get an idea of the quantity of comics that exist. Of course not every comic book has been "slabbed" but we get a quick idea which books are truly scarce and which books are getting attention and which are not. There are still some DC superhero comics from the 1940s that have less than 5 copies graded by CGC so even with the high price *Guide* values these books simply do not exist. Now that we have been grading books for 17 years, it's easy to get a picture of the true scarcity of thousands of Golden Age comics.

Researching Comic Books: The internet has made comic book collecting and archiving an amazing tool with the world at your fingertips. Some absolutely amazing websites exist with more data than you can imagine. Some of the best include:

Grand Comics Database - over 500,000 comic book covers from around the world and writer/artist/index info for most http://www.comics.org/

Comic Book DB - Info, checklists and chronologies of superheroes for DC and Marvel comicbookdb.com

Mike's DC Index - amazing site with index of every comic ever from every major publisher - sort able by dates, titles, etc. http://www.dcindexes.com/

Hot New Comics: I write over 200 columns a year reporting on the state of current popular back issues, hot books, speculated books and print runs of new books. Some of the best online websites for articles on investing in modern new comics can be found at comicsheatingup.net, investcomics.com, bleedingcool.com, comicbookspeculation.blogspot.com, comicbookscalping.com, hoknescomics.com.

Investing in new comics is a different game than vintage comics. It's mostly about buying, flipping and selling at just the right time. It's all about supply and demand. Many books each year can jump 1000% in value in only a month but this isn't a guarantee that the prices are going up and up. In fact most modern books peak after their initial big jump, settle and then fall back down if demand is not continual.

Hot Back Issues and the Speculator Market of 2016: Some extraordinary record prices hit on modern books that I have documented. Here are some of the fads that hit 2016: *Animosity* #1 (AfterShock Comics), *Invincible Iron Man* #7 and #9 (1st appearance of Riri Williams), *The Vision* #1-5 (Marvel Comics), *Captain America Steve Rogers* #1, *NYX* #3 (1st X-23), *Spider-Man/Deadpool* #1-3, and *Seven To Eternity* #1 (Image Comics).

Thanks for letting me contribute to the *Overstreet Price Guide* and a happy 47th anniversary to Bob!

GREG HOLLAND
COLLECTOR

Disclaimer: Because I am a collector and have not spent even one day as a retailer, I have the honor of both not knowing what I'm talking about and writing this market report anyway. Now that my ignorance is declared, let's get started.

Comic Books: This report on the comic book market begins by ignoring comic books. It's far more important to write first about…

Movies and Television Series: The impact of recent comic-based movies and television series to the comic market is undeniable. Some say all these movies aren't bringing enough readers to the new comic market, and we're not seeing enough new faces buying back issues. I say we just need to relax. Christopher Reeve defined Superman for generations with just one movie in 1978. The impact of that one movie has continued for almost another 40 years because Cavill's Superman is compared to Reeve's Superman. I was two years old in 1978 and I determined to be Superman when I grew up because of that one movie, but it would be more than 12 years later before I even owned a Superman comic. It was nearly 30 years before I spent more than $100 on a Superman book, but I've spent 100 times that amount by now. The impact of today's movies and television series will grow for decades, with future collectors also wanting to own pieces of the history and origins of their favorite characters from childhood. All it took to make a lifelong impact for me was one two-hour movie when I was two years old. There are now hundreds of hours of comic-based movies and television series and millions of future collectors watching. We have to wait for the seeds to grow and not expect every two-to-twenty year old to start spending money on comics on the way home from the theater.

Sudden Key Issues: Who is Professor Zoom? What does the Black Mercy do? Is Harley Quinn more than just a pretty face? Why was Deadpool mad at Francis? Why would anyone trust an ex-convict like Luke Cage? Is that a walking tree and talking raccoon? Despite these stories happening up to 60 years ago in comic books, it is only in the last 5 years that millions of people found out the answers. The first appearance of a talking animal might be under $5 for thirty years straight, but in year 31 it could be $200 thanks to movies or television. While there is usually a drop in market prices a year after a movie, I'm not sure a single movie-driven instant key has returned to the lower prices seen before any pre-production was announced. Let's see what happens in a few decades when the nostalgia grows from the fans with their own growing up to do.

Variety of Variants: The comic book market has always had variant covers. *Marvel Comics (#1)* from 1939 exists with a cover that says "OCT" and variant that says "NOV". It was a second printing in November. That might not qualify as a variant for some collectors, but the marvel.com website notes them as variants. *Superman #1* from 1939 had three printings, but there doesn't seem to be any way to tell them apart. You can be assured that *Superman #1* will be discussed by its variants when we know which is which. Nothing has changed about these 1939 books, but the industry has changed the meaning of 'variant'. There is now a veritable variety of variant variations. Second printings, cover price changes, foreign editions, title color changes, anniversary reprints, foil, prism, chromium, alternate art, alternate contents, ratio incentives, convention exclusives, retailer exclusives, and even barcode lengths are all now regularly called variants. It's even possible to mix-and-match these descriptors to talk about the regular edition of "*Vexing Variant-Man* #1 and the chromium alternate art reprint from 5 years later with the extra pages of story exclusive to Foreign Land Comic Shop at the Other-Side-Of-The-World Con". Even as you read this sentence, you know which variant of the *Overstreet Guide* you're holding.

By Design or By Chance: The market is still adjusting to the number of variants available today. Books which were once unloved reprints, because they were the cheap substitute for a first printing might become highly-valued variants decades later. The final printings of *Superman: The Man of Steel* #18 regularly sell for more than the first printing, but the *Superman* #75 Platinum variant is the most valuable of all the Death, Funeral, and Return of Superman storylines. *Superman* #75 Platinum has been a coveted book since the day it was released as a planned limited edition variant. *Superman: The Man of Steel* #18 fourth and fifth printings weren't even listed in the *Overstreet Guide* until recently. *Superman* #75 Platinum is valuable by design, but *Superman: The Man of Steel* #18 fourth and fifth printings are valuable by chance. Some final printings for the Superman Death, Funeral, and Return storylines are only now being documented as existing. I don't believe more collectors want a later printing of a comic book than the first printing, but I do believe that the supply of later printings can be low enough to make them more valuable. If the number of copies in each book printing were the same, I have a feeling the first printing would win every time.

What I find myself asking about variants is what the journey for the books has been. Was a variant coveted from the day it was released? Then it has often had a smooth ride, being well-protected and prized by collectors. In the case of *Superman* #75 Platinum, it was limited and historic, and prized for being both from the first day. In the case of *Superman: The Man of Steel* #18 fourth and fifth printings, they were ignored for almost 20 years and are like recently-classified endangered species where we can only estimate the number remaining and we don't really know where to look to find them. These are very different journeys to value, and represent the two most common scenarios for higher variant values in the comic book market, planned editions and chance accidents.

The Journey To Today's Market: We see that variants do not currently make any significant impact on the Golden Age market because the journeys to survival for all Golden Age books were similar and driven mostly by chance. Silver Age variants are beginning to be discussed more often in terms of foreign editions, with U.K. pence copies being U.S. creations destined for the U.K. market. Does the fact that they're U.S. creations and scarcer make them candidates for premium value, or does the fact that they depict U.S. superheroes from U.S. publishers in a clearly non-U.S. packaging keep them discounted as they have been for fifty years? The Silver Age U.K. edition debate appears to be heating up. Bronze Age variants are focused primarily on the 30-cent and 35-cent variants of Marvel issues. Because significant quantities of these variants have not been found, it would appear that the endangered species description applies with few believed to be in existence mainly in a few particular geographies. Chance drove the 40-year journeys for Bronze Age variants, with no intentional value being designed into the variants themselves. Add the movie and television series to the discussion and the *Star Wars* #1 35-cent variant sits high above the market. There is also a growing realization that *Star Wars* #2 holds the first comic book appearances of Obi-Wan Kenobi, Han Solo, Chewbacca, and the Millenium Falcon, bringing the *Star Wars* #2 35-cent variant more attention as a result of the latest movies.

Variants for the 1980s and 1990s include later printings for many popular books and collectors are now beginning to notice the differences between direct editions and newsstand editions, with a side task of identifying Canadian editions with price variations. Thinking about the journeys of each type of book, the direct editions mainly took direct paths into caring collections, while newsstand editions often got mangled by the public before being tossed aside or returned unsold for refunds. When the newsstand market was larger than the direct market in the early 1980s, the two types of books may have survived in similar numbers. The direct market grew and later 1980s and 1990s newsstand editions are just beginning to be recognized for the tougher journeys they faced to survive in high grade conditions today. The

1990s explode with the first widely-known planned incentive variants specifically intended to create more initial and secondary market value. Designed retailer incentives dominate the comic market for 1990s and 2000s with newsstand editions and later printings in an early stage of being evaluated. While a barcode on the cover indicated a newsstand in the 1980s, the barcodes on direct editions in the 1990s may be confusing identities today. The difference is actually simple. Both barcodes have 12 numbers on the bottom. Ignore the 12 numbers under a barcode and see how many numbers are on the top right: newsstand editions have 2, direct editions have 5. You can even see the difference in a tiny photo because 2 numbers are skinnier bars than 5 numbers. If there's a diagonal line over a newsstand edition barcode, it's actually an early direct edition. The available supply for newsstand is likely to be the key factor in future value, with the survival in high grade condition being a reflection of chance over two decades rather than intentional protection from the first day of release like most prized retailer incentive variants.

For comics from 2000 to present, the whole market is heavily dominated by ratio incentives for retailers which required the purchase of 20, 50, 100, or any other specific number of regular editions to qualify for one copy of the variant. Ratio incentives are now being driven into the extreme with 1:1000 or higher variants becoming more common and selling for very high prices before they're even printed. Do new comics belong at the same prices as vintage key issues? Retailer exclusive variants are another type of planned variants which are hard to predict. They may be the most limited variant for some comics, but the journey for most copies is almost completely planned in advance. Local shop customers and online buyers usually obtain their copies with ease, even if they pay significantly more than cover price. For other collectors, a retailer exclusive can be like a souvenir from a place they've never visited. Picture someone actively collecting different Las Vegas casino poker chips but never actually leaving Ohio. It's hard to imagine wide demand for retailer and convention exclusives when most collectors have never been there. If the artwork catches the imagination of the speculator, however, retailer exclusive values can skyrocket immediately. Time will tell if those variants can sustain their altitude after the speculators move on to other gambles.

Current newsstand editions are actually scarcer now than any time in the past, but the market has not given them much attention. Many collectors don't see any difference between newsstand and direct editions because they often have the same artwork. Newsstands are still unlikely to survive the general public handling and returnable journey as often as direct editions exclusively sold in comic shops. Combine the journey with the lower number printed, and there are reasons to believe newsstands from the late 1980s to present are a class of variant on the cusp of breaking out. Other unexpected value in the future of the market is likely already with us but may be impossible to separate from the current fog of retailer incentives. If I had to throw out a guess about which unintentional variants today may have value tomorrow, I'd say first editions of trade paperbacks may be as overlooked today as the later printings of 1990s comics were 20 years ago.

Arguing... With Myself: I've purposefully ignored the story and interior page contents of the books in most of this variant discussion because ignoring the pages inside appears to be what the market is doing. How else could books from recent years sell repeatedly for thousands of dollars? I honestly don't know whether I should argue that extremely high variant prices belong at the same level as vintage key issues because current demand exceeds the variant supply, or if I should argue that the prices are ridiculous because planned exclusive incentive variant covers are usually wrapped around contents which aren't discussed at all. Have we decided the pages inside don't matter anymore? I honestly don't know whether I should argue that a list of the most valuable comic books of all time should have thousands of vintage issues above comics from recent years or if I should argue that the market decides value and the market has some new books selling above many of the classics. I don't know if I should argue that significant numbers of retailer incentive variants have been known to surface years later making heavy investment in recent variants based on low supply extremely dangerous, or if the risk of future discoveries is lower than the reward of having so few known copies today.

Conclusion: I don't know if these arguments will ever be settled. That leads us back to the disclaimer on this report, about how I'm just one collector who doesn't know much anyway, but I do appreciate the time you've taken to read all my ignorance.

Steven Houston & John Dolmayan Torpedo Comics

Steven Houston

The rumors are true! Torpedo Comics has finally opened up its first traditional comic store in Las Vegas, located at 8775 Lindell Rd, unit 150, Las Vegas, Nevada, 89139. The store went 'live' at 10am on Wednesday, August 24th, after ten days of Facebook announcements. The store represents a bold experiment for our company, as both John and I were determined to open a traditional comic store, devoid of gaming with all of its paraphernalia and customer base. There are about ten serious comic stores in Las Vegas, with most offering gaming products, with some having gaming and various role-playing games as their main focus. It was not our intent to compete with other stores within the gaming arena and as such, we stocked our store with 30,000 back issues (1980-2016) on the main floor with a special vintage room containing another 8,000 books (1955-79) as well as a healthy compliment of high-end CGC books. We received some well-meaning advice regarding the amount of space we allocated to back issues, with the main thrust of comments being that stores don't need that many back-issues anymore, due to the vast selection of trade paperbacks and hardcovers available to readers. With a full understanding of the advice, we proceeded with our large back-issue selection format anyway, trying to create a niche for ourselves here in Las Vegas, where there are currently no stores that feature back-issues as a specialty. I will have an update on the success/failure of this retail technique next year – watch this space!

As I write this report, Torpedo Comics is one day removed from its grand opening (December 3rd), an event, which in my humble opinion exceeded all expectations. For the entire month preceding the big day, we used both Facebook and digital billboards around town to advertise the event. We also created special access passes for those that wanted them, with seventeen lucky fans getting the chance to have lunch with Jim Lee, before heading to the store for the actual signing. We had close to five-hundred people for the signing, which took place from 2-6pm, without a hitch, a testament to our organization and pre-planning – not bad for our first signing! Now that the Jim Lee signing is behind us, we will be having many more signings in the months to come, hopefully making Torpedo Comics in Las Vegas the place to be for comic fans.

On a personal front, with the opening of the store, I had to step back into the contemporary world of new issues, with all the resulting ramifications (dealing with Diamond Comics) of running a comic store. We hired a store manager, but the ordering and basic functions of the store are my responsibility, something I had not done since the year 2000. Suddenly I found myself back in the world of new issues, having to research a multitude of publishers and having to gauge how many issues of each title we should order, without driving the store into the red. The main advantage of this situation for me was once again having my 'finger on the pulse' of new issues and once again joining the fast moving world of contemporary publishing.

New Issue Sales: I won't be going into much detail here, since we have only been open since August, but what I have discovered is extremely enlightening, but also alarming. As a fan of Marvel since the early 1980s, I've seen the Marvel Universe go through change after change, all in an effort to increase sales and up until a few years ago I was able to follow my favorite characters. That all changed within the last two-years, as formally favorite characters have undergone drastic changes – the result: Simple, as a fan I simply dropped whatever book I no longer found interesting. Fast-forward to today and it's my job to order product for the store – the result: It seems like I'm not alone in dropping titles. Our Marvel sales have been dismal, so low that I actually spoke to other dealers to see if it was just our area. If the low sales in our store are any indication of a nationwide trend, then Marvel is in trouble, but before they can 'fix' the problem, they will have to acknowledge that they actually have one.

Here's my brief theory as to why Marvel sales have dropped so much: Too much change too quickly. Let me explain further: Take a look at the drastic changes certain Marvel characters have undergone in the past few years – Thor is a woman, the Hulk is a Korean boy, Iron Man is a sixteen-year old girl and the Fantastic Four are no more and that's just the icon characters. When one takes the Marvel Universe as a whole, there seems to be an attempt in 2015-2016 to revamp their characters giving them a younger appeal, the business model is obvious to see – now is the time to bring in the next generation of Marvel fans. What seems odd to many is that Marvel did not have to look too far to get an example of trying to push your audience too far too fast, yes! - I'm talking about the now failed New 52 DC Universe. Sales had drifted so low that DC initiated yet another reboot, the so-called DC Rebirth, bringing back many elements of the pre-New 52 Universe, apparently to fans satisfaction as sales have increased. We can confirm the good reception for 'rebirth' material, as our sales keep going up week after week, while over on the Marvel titles, all I seem to do is drop order numbers, or even more drastic, drop entire titles from our Diamond Comics order. Next year I will be able to give a much more thorough accounting of new issue sales and trends, I just hope Marvel has come to its senses by then.

Silver Age Sales: Selected recent sales: *Tales to Astonish* #27 CGC 5.0, *Fantastic Four* #52 CGC 9.0 and *Iron Man* #1 CGC 9.0 for $8500 (convention sale), *Fantastic Four* #52 CGC 4.0 $500, *Eternals* #1 CGC 9.8 $300, *Amazing Spider-Man* #121 CGC 9.4 $1250, *Amazing Spider-Man* #122 CGC 9.4 $800, *Showcase* #30 CGC 8.0 $2300, *Strange Tales* #128 CGC 9.0 $200 (all store sales) Raw sales in store: *Amazing Spider-Man* #5 GD- $200, #8 GD $150, #9 GD/VG $300, #14 VG $450, #59 VF- $80, *Avengers* #7 VG+ $100, *Batman* #173 VF+ $115, *Captain America* #100 FN- $200, *Daredevil* #1 GD/VG $750, #16 FN/VF $100, *Fantastic Four* #4 VG- $1400, #12 FN- $1000, #36 VG/FN $125, #49 VG+ $160, *Flash* #145 FN/VF $60, #185 VF+ $50, *Iron Man* #1 FN- $350, *Justice League of America* #32 FN+ $50, *Marvel Super-Heroes* #12 VF $250, *Strange Tales* #108 VG $65, #118 VG+ $40, #128 VG+ $50, #161 VF- $48, #163 VF- $52, *Thor* #147 VF- $50, #164 VF+ $100, #167 VF- $35, #170 VF+ $80, *X-Men* #1 FR (cover detached) $700, #21 VF+ $150.

For the last five months we have noticed a downward trend in sales of our higher price CGC eBay books, not for lack of trying on the customers' part, as I have personally turned down countless low-ball offers on many of our books.

Silver Age Report: As usual it's all about the keys! Keys, keys and yet more keys. *Amazing Fantasy* #15 has surged back again, after a period of about a year when everyone seemed to go *Incredible Hulk* #1 crazy. Interestingly, a month before this report was written, the *Dr. Strange* movie was released to both fan and critical acclaim, while down here – in comic land, sales of the Doctor's first appearance in *Strange Tales* #110 have been relatively calm, with the major heat on this issue being two years ago. One book that seems to disappear as soon as it surfaces these days is *Journey Into Mystery* #103 – the first appearance of the Enchantress, a character rumored to make an appearance in the next Thor movie *Ragnarok*, slated for release in November 2017. We have not had a copy, even in low grade, for more than two years. Another character who is rumored to appear in the next Thor movie is the Grandmaster, however his first appearance in *Avengers* #69 has not exploded in demand and price yet, still holding close to the $200 mark for a NM- copy. Regardless of movie connections, Marvel's Silver Age product is still the most sought after, with low grade key issues selling for 2 to 5 times *Guide* prices – I dare you to price a good condition copy of *Amazing Fantasy* #15 for *Guide* price at your next show ($5500), the book will be purchased by another dealer so fast, it will make your head spin. Then the book would be sent in for pressing and grading, hoping for a 2.5, maybe 3.0 or if the stars have aligned, maybe a 3.5, then that book will be priced at between $17,000 and $20,000! That's the current state of key issue collecting in today's world, so if you do have un-pressed, unrestored keys, get to work, your books will be much in demand.

Over to DC Comics for a moment, their next movie blockbusters will be both *Wonder Woman* and *Justice League*. Wonder Woman's Silver Age sales have remained calm as always, as the real hot books for the Amazonian are from the Golden Age, however the Justice League's first appearance in *Brave and the Bold* #28 has not exploded as one would think. The fact that not many of these issues are coming out of the woodwork maybe hurting upward sales momentum, as anything above VF seems to be impossible – a thing of myth! Prices are going up for lower grades, from GD- through VG, which seems to be the only conditions available to collectors at this time. *Showcase* #4 (the first Silver Age Flash) seems to be in the same situation as *Brave and the Bold* #28, with a few sales in the lower grades, but even with a successful television series, this book is so scarce and expensive that 99.9% of all Flash fans have already taken that book out of their collecting equation. In terms of collector heat, for me, Silver Age product has lost a little steam for the regular collector, who seem to have absconded to the Bronze Age of comics.

Bronze Age Sales: Selected Raw sales: *Action Comics* #266 VG- $55, #304 FN/VF $45, *Avengers* #112 VG- $45, #118 VF $60, Annual #7 VF- $50, *Batman* #234 VG- $50, *Batman Family* #6 VG $40, #9 VF/NM $80, *Captain Marvel* #52 NM- $30, #62 NM- $20, *Conan* #8 VF+ $65, #25 NM $50, *Daredevil* #111 VF- $45, *Defenders* #1 VG $40, *Fantastic Four* #122 VF+ $40, *Flash* #202 NM $40, #208 VF+ $45, #211 VF- $40, #215 VF $45, #219 VF+ $50, *Godzilla* #1 VF-20, #18 VF+ $20, *Iron Fist* #10 VF/NM $40, *Marvel Spotlight* #7 VF $60, *Star Wars* #1 VG $30, *Superman's Girlfriend Lois Lane* #118 VF/NM $40, #137 VF- $25, *Thor* #174 VF/NM $70, #220 VF/NM $40, *Wonder Woman* #200 FN/VF $70, *X-Men* #94 FN- $275, #103 VF- $85, #104 VF/NM $100, #108 VF- $60, #112 VF/NM $90, #121 FN/VF $50, #125 VF- $40. CGC sales: *Avengers* #196 9.8 $450, 9.6 $150 (x2), *Daredevil* #158 9.4 $150, *Ghost Rider* #1 6.5 $175, Nova #1 9.0 $100, *Superman's Pal Jimmy Olsen* #135 9.4 $350, *Giant-Size X-Men* #1 9.4 $2000.

Bronze Age Report: The Bronze Age market just keeps growing and growing, not only for the obvious keys, but regular issues as well. For many years, books published within the 1976-79 era were easily available, often being found in bulk amounts in various warehouses across the United States. For Marvel, issues such as *Black Panther* #1 (1977), *Devil Dinosaur* #1 (1978), *Eternals* #1 (1976), *Human Fly* #1 (1977), *John Carter Warlord of Mars* #1 (1977), *Machine Man* #1 (1978), *Micronauts* #1 (1979), *Ms. Marvel* #1 (1977), *Nova* #1 (1976), *Omega the Unknown* #1 (1976), *Peter Parker* #1 (1976), *Rom* #1 (1979), *Spider-Woman* #1 (1978), *Shogun Warriors* #1 (1979), *Star Wars* #1, *Tarzan* #1, *2001: A Space Odyssey* #1 (1976) and *What If* #1 (1977) were easy to find and extremely affordable. From the aforementioned list, six titles have yet to catch on: *Human Fly*, *John Carter*, *Omega the Unknown*, *Shogun Warriors*, *Tarzan* and 2001: *A Space Odyssey*, while *Peter Parker* #1 can still be found in unopened cases. The hottest title out of the bunch has to be *Ms. Marvel*, with high-grade #1's (9.8) selling easily for over $1000! One also has to note that this book has been hot for THREE YEARS and shows little evidence of slowing down. Also astonishing is the fact that the entire 23-issue run is hot, with sales at every show – basically we are unable to keep this book in stock. Marvel has been pushing the Carol Danvers character within the contemporary Marvel Universe (see *Civil War II*), while Academy Award winner, Brie Larson has been chosen to play Captain Marvel in a 2019 blockbuster.

© MAR

***Ms. Marvel* #1 has been hot for 3 years and isn't slowing down with a movie on the way.**

One of the stars of *Captain America: Civil War*, the Black Panther is also hot, with issue #1 selling raw (NM-) for $150, with CGC 9.8 copies selling for close to $600. A signature series signed by Stan Lee broke the $1000 barrier in October of this year. For those of us who have been around awhile, its pretty ironic that issue #1 has become popular in recent years, as it was much maligned in its day, with fans swearing allegiance to the Don McGregor version seen in *Jungle Action* (#6-24) and loudly swearing off the Kirby version seen in *Black Panther* #1. The *Black Panther* title sells well throughout the entire run (#1-15), especially in the higher grades. We sell issue

#15 (last issue) for $45 in NM-, while issues #2-13 move well at $25 in VF/NM, with NM- copies getting $35 each. Talking of Kirby, his other oddball titles, such as *Devil Dinosaur*, *Eternals* and *Machine Man* issue #1s are beginning to pick up, while the first appearance of Machine Man in *2001: A Space Odyssey* #8 is close to being a $100 book these days. *Star Wars* has roared back to collecting life this past two years, with issue #1 still a hot commodity with true NM- 9.2 copies selling for $300 ($100 over *Guide*) at this time. This book, along with *Ms. Marvel* #1 are instantly picked up in NM- condition by dealers and collectors for pressing, making the 9.2 condition hotter than a 9.8 condition book (with both *Ms. Marvel* #1 and *Star Wars* #1 selling for just over $1000 in 9.8 condition). The first six issues of *Star Wars* sell extremely well at over *Guide* for NM- 9.2 condition copies, yet another modern day collecting aberration, as back in the day, stores and conventions were 'swimming' in these issues, while collectors/readers were purchasing copies in multiples off the rack.

While collectors snatch up as many copies of *Ms. Marvel* as they can find, they seem to have lost patience with *Nova*, as 9.8 copies of issue #1, have dropped from a high of $900 in 2014, down to $400 today, with other issues of the run (#2-25) not moving nearly as fast as a *Ms. Marvel* back-issue. The second *Guardians of the Galaxy* movie is coming out in summer 2017, maybe there will be a slight Nova appearance in the movie, or a brief appearance in *Avengers: Infinity War*, causing collectors to look at this book again, but as for right now, *Nova* has cooled off considerably. As for the three 'toy' titles, *Micronauts*, *Rom* and *Shogun Warriors*, *Rom* #1 seems to be the book most in demand. Currently the *Guide* lists NM- copies at $65, however we price them at $100, with CGC 9.8 copies going for over $300. We price NM- copies of *Micronauts* #1 at $30 and *Shogun Warriors* #1 at $20, although to be honest demand for *Shogun Warriors* is rather lackluster.

As for DC, Batman holds sway over the entire DC Comics output from the mid-to-late Bronze Age period, in fact, one can say that perhaps in no other era, does Batman have such dominance over the rest of 'his' fellow DC titles. Without being too controversial, one can say that DC's output from 1976 through 1979 was rather uninspired, as evidenced by a lack of collector activity for anything other than Batman. Regarding new titles collectors have *All-Star Comics* (1976), *Batman Family* (late 1975), *Blackhawk* (#244, 1976), *Black Lightning* (1977), *DC Comics Presents* (1978), *DC Special Series* (1977), *DC Super-Stars* (1976), *Firestorm* (1978), *Freedom Fighters* (1976), *Jonah Hex* (1977), *Karate Kid* (1976), *Kobra* (1976), *Men of War* (1977), *Secret Society of Super-Villains* (1976), *Starfire* (1976), *Star Hunters* (1977), *Super Friends* (1976) and *Warlord* (1976). From the aforementioned list, the only issues that really had any collector appeal, or were even requested on occasion, were *Batman Family* #6 (first Joker's daughter, August 1976) and issue #9, which features a wonderful Batgirl vs. the Joker's daughter cover. We sold a VG+ copy of issue #6 for $40 and a nice VF/NM copy of issue #9 for $80! (Note the current NM- *Guide* price is $65).

The other DC book that we get asked for from this time period is *DC Super-Stars* #17 (November 1977), the first appearance of the Earth-2 Huntress. This is one of those issues were condition is everything, as due to the size of the issue (52 pages), the spine loves to turn, making true NM- copies harder to find than one thinks. We sold a VF+ copy for $100, not bad when one considers that the current *Guide* price for a VF is $54! The sad thing is that both aforementioned issues are related to Batman – the only character that fans seem interested to collect within the mid-to-late Bronze Age of the DC Universe.

Moving into the earlier Bronze Age period (1970-75), this is where collectors and speculators are pouring hundreds and thousands of dollars into the hobby, mainly purchasing Marvel keys. Yes, once again, Marvel is the king of this era, but DC does have some more than just key *Batman* and *Detective* issues to locate, including genres other than super-heroes, such as war, western and horror. Before I delve into DC, lets get back to Marvel for the moment and talk about the top three books of the 1970-75 era: *Incredible Hulk* #181 (first full Wolverine), *Giant-Size X-Men* #1 (first New X-Men) and *Iron Man* #55 (first Thanos). Demand for *Hulk* #181s has not abated, in fact, sales of mid-grade copies are now outstripping the higher grades due to the massive price differential. Forget about keeping raw copies in stock, in any grade, they sell – immediately. We sell GD (2.0) copies for $500 and unless the actual copy is beyond ugly, a dealer will purchase the book for $500. In fact, all grades except 9.8 are still on the upward swing, with 9.6 copies getting the most heat. This is due to pressing of course, as dealers, collectors, speculators and investors are all seeking out that perfect 9.6 copy – by 'perfect', I'm referring to a book that has the potential to be a 9.8. The demand for 9.6 copies is reaching critical mass, as CGC copies are cracked, sent in and pressed and then, if need be cracked again and again and again. The winner in all of this? CGC and CBCS of course, the loser (long term) are the collectors who may be destroying high grade copies as time passes by with all the incessant pressing (and other currently legal restorations). In my humble opinion, the CGC census may already be irrelevant, as countless 9.6 copies are turned into 9.8s.

Giant-Size X-Men #1 and *Iron Man* #1 are still hot, while *Hero For Hire* #1 (1972) is blazing hot, with a sale recently of a 9.8 copy for the ridiculous sum of $24,000! (Note – this book guides at $900 in NM- 9.2) I would have to say that at this moment, the demand for *Hero For Hire* #1s outstrips the demand for *Incredible Hulk* #181s, something that becomes quite obvious when one compares CGC census totals between the two issues. To date, *Incredible Hulk* #181 has 98 certified 9.8 copies, while *Hero For Hire* #1, has only 11 copies graded at 9.8. *Hero For Hire* #1 has become one of those "perfect storm" books, meaning that: (1) After a long period of time, collectors have suddenly decided that they NEED this issue, (2) Collectors have discovered that high-grade copies of this book are akin to "hens teeth" with that dark cover seemingly begging to crease and (3) Popularity has exploded further, due to a critically acclaimed television series which has driven demand to almost hysterical levels. We did not see a high-grade copy of this book all year, instead having to make do with a FN- copy, which I priced at $200. The book *Guides* at $108 in FN, but that did not matter, at the first show we showcased the book it was the first book to sell off our wall.

As for other keys published in this era, the sheer amount of quality material is enough to boggle the mind, the following books are what we at Torpedo put on our Bronze Age wall: (Marvel) *Amazing Adventures* #11 (first new Beast), *Amazing Spider-Man* #96-98 (drug issues), #100 (anniversary issue), #101 (first Morbius), 119-120 (Hulk issues), #121 (death Gwen Stacy), #122 (death Green Goblin), #129 (first Punisher), #136 (first Harry Osborn Goblin), #149 (first Clone), *Astonishing Tales* #25 (first Deathlok), *Avengers* #83 (first Lady Liberators – HOT), #93 (Giant Kree/Skull War), #100 (Barry Smith), #112 (first Mantis – HOT), #116-118 (Avengers/Defenders), #125 (Thanos), *Captain Marvel* #25 (Starlin), #28 (Thanos cover – HOT), #33 (Thanos war conclusion), *Champions* #1, *Conan* #1, *Daredevil* #131 (first Bullseye), *Defenders* #1, #10 (Thor vs. Hulk), *Dr. Strange* #1 (1974), *Fantastic Four* #100 (anniversary issue), #112 (Hulk vs. Thing), *Fear* #10 (Man-Thing), #20 (Morbius), *Frankenstein* #1, *Ghost Rider* #1, *Incredible Hulk* #141 (first Doc Samson), #180-182 (Wolverine appearances), Annual #5 (Groot appearance), *Inhumans* #1 (1975), *Invaders* #1, *Iron Fist* #1, *Iron Man* #55, *Jungle Action* #6 (Black Panther), *Man-Thing* #1, *Marvel Super Special* #1, 5 (Kiss), *Marvel Feature* #1 (first Defenders), #4 (Ant-Man), *Marvel Premiere* #1 (Warlock), #3 (Dr. Strange – HOT), #15 (first Iron Fist – HOT), *Marvel Preview* #2 (Punisher), #4 (Starlord), #7 (Rocket Raccoon), *Marvel Spotlight* #2 (first Werewolf), #5 (first Ghost Rider), *Marvel Team-Up* #1 (HOT in high grade), *Marvel Two-in-One* #1, *Savage Sword of Conan* #1, *Savage Tales* #1 (first Man-Thing), *Special Marvel Edition* #15 (first Master of Kung-Fu), *Strange Tales* #169 (first Brother Voodoo – HOT in high-grade), #178 (Warlock), #180 (first Gamora), *Sub-Mariner* #34, 35 (Defenders), *Supernatural Thrillers* #5 (first Living Mummy), *Tomb of Dracula* #1, #10 (first Blade), *Warlock* #1, *Werewolf by Night* #1, #32 (first Moon Knight – HOT), *X-Men* #94, 95, 97. We have had nearly all of these books in the last year, with the hottest books being either *Hero For Hire* #1, or *Werewolf by Night* #32. We sold a VG- copy of *Werewolf by Night* #32 for $150 – no questions (or discounts asked). Television exposure has increased interest in Iron Fist's first appearance in *Marvel Premiere* #15, while the hit *Dr. Strange* movie has increased demand for nice copies of *Marvel Premiere* #3 and *Dr. Strange* #1. As of writing the second movie preview from *Guardians of the Galaxy 2* has hit social media, increasing interest in *Avengers* #112 – the first appearance of Mantis, while Valkyrie's appearance in *Avengers* #83 momentarily shot up in price as rumors to her role in the *Thor: Ragnarok* movie swept through the internet.

DC's comic universe of the early to mid 1970s contains less key issues, but some of the issues are in extreme high demand: *All-Star Western* #10 (first Jonah Hex), *Batman* #227 (cover swipe of *Detective* #31 – HOT), #232 (first Ra's al Ghul), #234 (first modern Two-Face), #251 (classic Joker issue), *Demon* #1, *Detective Comics* #400 (first Man-Bat), #411 (first Talia), *Forever People* #1 (first full Darkseid), *Ghosts* #1, *Green Lantern* #76 (Neal Adams), #85 (drug issue), *House of Secrets* #92 (first Swamp Thing), *Joker* #1, *Kamandi* #1, *Mister Miracle* #1, *New Gods* #1, *Shazam* #1, *Supergirl* #1, *Superman* #233 (classic Neal Adams cover), *Superman's Girlfriend Lois Lane* #106 (Black Lois Lane), *Superman's Pal Jimmy Olsen* #134 (first Darkseid), *Swamp Thing* #1, *Weird War Tales* #1 and *Wonder Woman* #199,200 (Jeff Jones covers). The upcoming *Justice League* movie is sparking interest in Darkseid's appearances, as well as sparking some interest in Jack Kirby's 'Fourth World' stories, but as usual in this era, Batman is king. Those trying to put together high-grade runs of early 1970s *Batman* and *Detective* had better get used to paying over *Guide*, sometimes, way over *Guide* to complete such a task – especially when one is talking about the Neal Adams' issues, which show no signs of slowing down at this time.

1980s to Current Sales: *Amazing Spider-Man* #252 NM- $90, 298 VF/NM $40, #300 FN/VF $140, #500 NM- $25, *Annihilation Conquest* #6 NM+ $50, *Batman* #359 NM- $35, #429 NM- $25, #612 NM- $30, *Black Panther* #23 (2000) NM- $35, *Catwoman* #51 NM- $40, #89 NM- $15, *Daredevil* #174 VF/NM $30, #254 NM- $30, *Deadpool: Circle Chase* #1 NM- $50, *Crisis on Infinite Earths* #7 NM- $30, #8 VF/NM $20, *Firestorm* #1 (1982) NM- $30, #23 NM- $35, *Flash* #331 NM+ $20, #336 NM+ $20, 344 NM+ $20, 346 NM+ $20, 349 NM+ $20, #350 NM- $25, *Lone Wolf & Cub* #1 NM- $15, *Marc Spector Moon Knight* #55 NM- $45, #57 $35, *New Teen Titans* #1 VF/NM $25, *Punisher kills the Marvel Universe* #1 (2nd) NM+ $50, *Sandman* #4 NM- $30, #5 NM- $30, *Silver Surfer* #44 NM- $150, *Star Wars* #52 NM- $20, #87 NM- $25, #92 NM- $40, *Suicide Squad* #1 (1987) VF+ $30, #23 NM- $25, *Superman Man of Steel* #18 NM- $30, *Umbrella Academy* #1 NM- $20, *Walking Dead* #9 VF/NM $60, #28 NM- $25, #48 NM- $40, *X-Factor* #6 VF/NM $50, *X-Force* #11 NM- $12, *X-Men* #135 NM $100, #135 VF+ $50, #136 NM $100.

CGC sales: *Batman Adventures* #12 9.4 $850, *Booster Gold* #1 9.4 $200, *DC Comics Presents* #41 9.6 $80, *Iron Man* #174 9.8 $60, *New Teen Titans* #2 9.8 $650, #2 9.6 $300, *Spider-Man* #1 Gold 9.8 (1990) $125, *Star Wars: Return of the Jedi* #4 9.6 $125, *Thanos Quest* #1 NM $60, *Thanos Quest* #2 NM $60, *TMNT* #1 (4th) VF/NM- $40, *Transformers* #1 (1984) NM- $60, and *Walking Dead* #17 9.8 $200, #19 CGC 9.0 $200.

This modern section has proven very successful, with

most sales coming from our new store. Books that do not get a second look at shows are moving successfully at the store, a testament to our faith in back issue sales at Torpedo Comics.

1980s Back Issue Report: If you've read through my reports regarding the 1990s and up, you may have noticed no mention regarding condition, with customers expecting NM- 9.2 copies at the very least, something that is easily achievable, even the most cost-conscious collector. However, comics published during the 1980s are no longer easily available in higher conditions, especially if you collect issues between 1980-84. Now to be clear, I'm not saying most 1980s comics are scarce in high grade, far from it, as evidenced by dollar bin sales at conventions where tens of thousands of comics published during the 1980s are still readily available. At the Wizard World Chicago two years ago, I was astonished to see a "big-time" dealer, actually picking up handfuls of 1980s comics from another dealer who was selling comics for a dollar. I quickly noticed that the issues were clean, as if they had been printed yesterday and began to pick up piles of the books for Torpedo. Within minutes I saw other "big-time" dealers and speculators pulling issues out of the boxes, each glaring at the issues, obviously seeking out potential 9.8 copies. How things have changed, as I know that just a few years ago, those same dealers would have scoffed at the dollar books and walked by, with a stack of Gold, Silver or Bronze Age keys under their arms.

What I found fascinating were what titles and more specifically, the era of those titles that were being pulled. Within thirty minutes, nearly every book from 1980-1983 was gone, except for the *Action Comics*, *Alpha Flight*, *Fantastic Four*, *Superman*, *Warlord* and *World's Finest*. I scooped up nice runs of *Avengers*, *Doctor Strange*, *Flash*, *Marvel Team-Up*, *Marvel Two-in-One*, *Micronauts* and *New Mutants*. The above scenario seemingly proves a theory of mine, a theory developed over years of purchasing bulk books from store closeouts, storage locations and even warehouse purchases. In terms of obscene amounts of bulk copies (300-1000 copies), I rarely see those numbers for comics published pre-1984. I've had the odd single issue such as 300 copies of *Moon Knight* #1 (1980), but when it comes to issue after issue of large bulk numbers, I've discovered that after 1984 and especially by 1986, many issues can still be found in huge amounts. The only problem is that many of the issues are not NM- 9.2 copies anymore, more like VF/NM or VF+ copies, after years of being stored in less than satisfactory conditions. In fact, 90% of our higher-grade 1980s issues are not from warehouse or store stock, but private collections.

Okay, with that said, what's actually selling? For DC, its obvious – Batman and Batman, followed by more Batman. We price 9.2 copies of *Batman* (non-key issues) at $25 ranging from issue #319-350, which is a full $10 over *Guide*. Batman collectors with an eye for quality have no problem paying over *Guide* for clean copies and pay way over *Guide* for the 1980s *Batman* keys: #357 (first Jason Todd) an easy sale at $250 in NM- shape, #366 (Jason Todd as Robin, Joker appearance) $50, #368 (first new Robin in costume) $45, #386 (first Black Mask) $100, #400 (Anniversary issue, 1986) $50, #404 (first Miller Year One) $45, #426 (Death in the Family) $35, #428 ('Death' of Robin) $60, #442 (first Timothy Drake as Robin, 1989) $15. Also still hot is the *Dark Knight*, with issue #1 an easy $150 in NM-, while issue #4, featuring the classic red Superman cover has now eclipsed issue #2-3, with NM- copies selling for $45. *Batman: The Killing Joke* (first print, 1988) sells easily for $100 in raw NM- 9.2 condition, while CGC 9.2 copies are a tougher sale, with collectors seeking out the higher grades, which speaks to another facet of 1980s comic collecting – pressing. *The Killing Joke* is a great example of how things have turned 180 degrees regarding high grades, potential for higher grades and locked in grades. Once the grade has been locked in, say 9.8, I'm seeing resistance from many collectors/speculators/amateur dealers, while a 9.6 has 'potential' to be improved upon. A true NM- copy of *The Killing Joke* is almost impossible for speculators to resist, as the difference between a 9.2 and a 9.8 is significant, while a 9.9 grade will garner a huge financial windfall. Thus, a potential purchaser will give a raw copy a full review, seeking out any minor flaw that can be removed by pressing. As soon as the collector spies a potential 'fatal flaw' – or a flaw that locks the book in at 9.2, they will put the book back, realizing there is nothing to be gained from that copy. This technique holds true for CGC copies as well, with 9.8s sitting on wall displays, gathering dust, while other dealers and convention attendees check 9.6 copies again and again, using their little hand-lights to pour over the books flaws, hoping that there's a chance for improvement via pressing. If the person succeeds in pressing the book from a 9.6 to a 9.8, then that book is placed on eBay, where collectors, who are unable to travel to well-stocked shows, or stores, will jump on the chance to purchase a 9.8 copy of what they are looking for. This financial gain on each book after successful grading and pressing can be immense, creating a modern day 'gold rush', as skilled graders pour over CGCs looking for that great deal, either to turn via eBay, or on the rare occasion, to upgrade their own copy.

Returning once again to what collectors are looking for in 1980s comics, as I've stated before, DC has Batman, but little else. *Watchmen* has gained further attention after dropping off the dizzy heights of 2008-09, when the movie sent collectors into a frenzy. For those that know, DC's most recent re-boot, 'Rebirth' has significant ties to the Watchmen universe, although as of this writing, DC editorial is cleverly revealing small parts of an ongoing mystery that will one day reveal the connection. As of now, the *Watchmen* twelve-issue mini-series may not be the purely self-contained universe within the comic industry, as it has been since it was originally published in 1986-87, but rather a series that features key moments in the current DC Universe – watch this space! On a dourer note, the 1980s DC Universe contains whole swaths of back-issues that simply sit, slowly being covered with dust, even when discounted. All Superman titles, *Brave and the Bold*, *Legion of Super-Heroes*, most non-Alan Moore issues of *Swamp Thing*, *Hawkman* and most *Justice League of America* issues (after 1984) are seemingly invisible to collectors. *Flash* sales have improved due to the exposure of the successful television show, especially on issues #324-350 (1983-85), particularly issues #324-325 (Reverse Flash appearances). *New Teen Titans* #2 (first Deathstroke) is still hot, with CGC 9.8 copies hovering around the $600 price, however, more importantly, collectors seem to be purchasing other copies of the 1980-84 run, dare I say it – putting the run together! Clean copies is the name of the game here, as there are hundreds of thousands of these issues in circulation, as it was one of the most heavily ordered titles of the entire 1980s, so if you have FN/VF copies you are out of luck, NM and above are required for this series. I sell raw issue #1 NM- copies for $80, issues #3-9 for $20 each, issue #10 (second Deathstroke) for $30. Issues #11 up are extremely common, so unless the issue is NM- 9.2 or above, I don't sell them. *Suicide Squad* #1 (1987) has dropped in price, with 9.8 copies selling for $120, down from a high of high of $550 in 2015. The surprise for me this year has been the lack of interest regarding Wonder Woman, quite astonishing when one considers that she appeared in the *Batman v Superman* movie and her own project has already excited fans with what looks like a quality preview.

Marvel's output from the 1980s fares a lot better than DC at this time, with a much more diverse series of titles that actually sell. As for the classic runs of books, *Amazing Spider-Man* is still king, while *X-Men* seems to have slipped in recent years, possibly the result of less than stellar sales on current day *X-Men* issues? Much the same as DC's 1980s output, Marvel's comics from 1980-83 are getting harder to find in true NM- 9.2 conditions, unless the collection is purchased from a private collector. Good examples of runs that are getting harder to replace in high grade are: *Avengers* #191-230, *Captain America* #241-283, *Incredible Hulk* #243-279, *Iron Man* #130-169 and *Thor* #291-336. If we do get nice NM- copies of the aforementioned issues I price the books over *Guide*, with 9.4 copies at 3 times *Guide* and 9.6 or above singled out for CGC. Let's be clear here, none of the aforementioned runs are rare, in fact, they are extremely common in lower grades (VF- and below) with many copies in FN being seen in dollar bins at shows, but with trade paperbacks replacing 'reading copies' of these books, collectors who are putting these runs together want clean NM- 9.2 or higher conditions.

Other titles that seem to be picking up (if the books are nice) are: *Power Man and Iron Fist*, *Rom*, *Star Wars* and *Transformers*. With the latter two titles, it's not hard to see why sales would be good, however *Rom* is a true collecting anomaly. This book was found in huge amounts for years with cases of each issue found in warehouse and store backrooms around the country for years. Over the last five years, collectors have been putting runs together, forced to purchase the originals, due to the fact that no trade paperbacks are currently available for the run. Once again, thousands of mid-grade copies of *Rom* still fill discount bins across the United States, but those clean 9.2 or 9.4 issues are not so common anymore. While searching eBay over the course of a year, I saw a range of prices for the set #1-75 plus the four annuals, but never a set advertised as NM. Most of the sets were VF, or FN to VF, with prices of $200 through $300 for the set! Yes, we are talking about *Rom* here – not *X-Men*, or *Amazing Spider-Man*, but *Rom*, a book that was thought of as a joke for years. *Doctor Strange* issues have bumped a little in sales, especially issues #39-62, with *Guide* prices ranging from $6 to $4 each, these issues are a steal right now. I fully expect the price to go up with the next *Guide*, as I am already pricing NM- 9.2 copies of #39-49 at $10 each with issue #60 (Dracula & Scarlet Witch cover) priced at $15 in NM- 9.2. Compared to DC's output in the 1980s, Marvel's product sells over a much more diverse series of titles, from Star Comics *Ewoks* to *Rocket Raccoon*, all the usual icon super-hero titles and the licensed hits such as *Star Wars*. 1980s Marvel is indeed thriving, as long as the book is high grade!

1990s Back Issue Report: What a strange era for comics, on one hand we have super-hot comics like *New Mutants* #98 (first Deadpool, 1991) and *Batman Adventures* #12 (first Harley Quinn, 1993), we have critically acclaimed series like *Sandman*, *Starman* and *Bone*, while on the other hand, we have warehouses (and storage locations) full of *X-Men* #1 (1991) and *Turok* #1 (1993). Something strange has been happening this last year, mainly on eBay, which directly affects 1990s comics – that being the rise in cost (or minimum bid) on multiple titles that were once worthless. The best example of this must be the *Guardians of the Galaxy* series from 1990-1995, a series that has constantly been way above my purchasing price for the last two years. The series began as a hot book in 1990, but by 1992, this book was considered a second-tier title, if that, the proof being in the late 1990s when I was dealing with bulk comics, I found tens of thousands of *Guardians* issues. What I realized later, was that I was finding the same issues, again and again, usually issues #6-46. Here we are in 2016 and collectors have been trying to put this run together and have found the last twelve issues are not as easily found as the rest, thus when 'full runs' are put up on eBay, it's usually #1-45, not #1-62 and the four annuals. To some this may sound preposterous, but I had a customer ask me a year ago to get him a full set of clean NM issues, his budget being $100. I found a few sets, but he had to pay more, almost $200 for a true NM set! Regarding the usual 1990s collectible or at least desirable issues, *Amazing Spider-Man* #361 (first full Carnage, 1992) is a $100 in NM- raw condition, *X-Men* #366 (first Gambit, 1990), is a $200 in NM- raw condition, *Preacher* #1 has cooled in recent months, with NM copies (raw) getting $200, while 9.8 copies now range in at the $500 mark, way down from last year. Once again, collectors and speculators need to know that when it comes to a modern book, the price will explode for a few months and then as soon as more high grade copies come out of the woodwork, the price will fall – every time!

As for the mainline Marvel titles, runs of *Captain America*, *Daredevil*, *Fantastic Four*, *Incredible Hulk*, *Iron Man*, *Spider-Man*, *Thor* and the *X-Men* have to be discounted heavily to move, with a few issues being considered good enough to "collect", such as *Captain America* #360 (first Crossbones) and *Iron Man* #282 (first War Machine). DC has Batman, but not the mainline title, which was produced in huge amounts, but rather titles such as *Batman Adventures* (1992-1995), which collectors have discovered, were not printed in such large amounts. Annual #1 from 1994 is an easy sell for $45 in NM shape, while *Batman Adventures: Mad Love* is still a hot issue, with the first print easily being $100 in NM-, even the prestige format version, which used to be seen everywhere now sells for $30 or more. *Batman and Robin Adventures* (1995-1997) sells well, especially issue #8, which features Poison Ivy and Harley ($25 in NM-). *Batman Beyond* #1 (1999) has become a hot book in recent years, with issue #1 selling for $30 or more in NM- condition. One title that has increased in value recently is *Deathstroke the Terminator* (1991-1996), especially if one wants to purchase an entire set. Similar to what I already mentioned about the 1990s *Guardians of the Galaxy* title, the *Deathstroke* run is garnering extremely high "buy-it-now" prices. Another tough run to put together from DC's 1990's era, is *Lobo* – the series that ran from 1993 to 1999 (#1-64). At the moment, the *Overstreet Guide* lists many of the issues at $3 each, this has to change, as many of the issues, especially from issue 50 on are not that easy to locate.

Although when many collectors talk about G.I Joe or Transformers, most think of the classic 1980s era, but for those seeking full sets, collectors have to extend those runs into the 1990s, only to discover that the later issues are harder to find than the earlier issues. *G.I. Joe* issue #96 is dated January 1990, with *Transformers* hitting the 1990s with issue #62, which leaves a further 59 issues of *G.I. Joe* and 18 issues of *Transformers*. Another thing that collectors discover with these issues is the horrible rippled-look of many of the issues, the product of an overzealous printing process, which overcooked the issues. Many collectors/speculators are now pressing these issues, to get clean copies, something that was near impossible ten years ago. We are currently pricing *Transformers* at $10 for most issues in NM between #96-138, while pricing issue #139 (*Transformers* cover) at $25. From issue #145 through #155 is where most of the collector heat is, as those wanting full sets looking for clean issues will pay over *Guide* every day. We price #146-149 at $15 each, with #150, being $25. #151 and #152 in NM- are $30, #153 is $45, #154 is $80 and the last issue, #155 is $125. As for the *Transformers*, the demand is even higher, with issues #62-80 going for way over *Guide* in NM-/NM conditions. We price issues #62-69 at $25 for NM- and send higher grades off to CGC immediately. Issue #70 ($30), #71-76 ($45), #77-79 ($60), #80 ($100).

Later issues of **Transformers** are bringing higher prices than earlier '80s issues. (#74 shown)

One of the longest running titles to end in the 1990s was *Conan the Barbarian*, concluding with issue #275 (1993), which we currently price at $75 in NM-. Interestingly, when our store opened its doors in August, this was one of the wall-books that sold right away. Other hot (or at least in higher demand) 1990s books (in NM- condition) include *Adventures of Superman* #500 Platinum Edition $50, *Akira* #38 (last issue) $150, *Alf* #48 (controversial rape cover) $125, *Batman Adventures* #12 (1993, first Harley Quinn) $700, *Birds of Prey* #8 (Nightwing appearance, 1999) $75, *Bloodshot* #0 Gold Edition $50, #51 (last issue) $100, *Bone* #1 (1991, first print) $1000, *Deadpool* #1 (1997) $80, *Elseworlds 80-page Giant* (1999), $200, *Evil Ernie* #1 (Eternity, 1991, first Lady Death), *Flash* #92 (1994, first Impulse) $60, *Ghost in the Shell* #1 (1995) $200, *Gold Digger* #1 (1992) $100, *Harbinger* #0 (Pink edition, 1993) $60, *Harbinger* #1 (1992) $80, *Incredible Hulk* #377 (1991, Third Print) $200, *Iron Man* #282 (1992, first War Machine) $35, *Johnny the Homicidal Maniac* #1 (1995) $150, *Lady Death* #1 (1994) $40, *Liberty Meadows* #1 (1999) $35, *Lobo* #64 (1999, last issue) $30, *Lone Wolf and Cub* #45 (1991, last issue) $30, *Marvel Super-Heroes* #8 (1991, first Squirrel Girl – I'm not kidding!!) $75, *Milk & Cheese* #1 (1991) $150, *Miracleman* #24 (1993, last issue) $40, *New Mutants* #98 (1991, first Deadpool) $250, *Next Men* #21 (1993, first full comic book appearance of Hellboy) $90, *100 Bullets* #1 (1999) $45, *Preacher* #1 (1995) $200, *Savage Sword of Conan* #235 (1995, last issue) $60, *Silver Surfer* #44 (first Infinity Gauntlet) $75, *Solar Man of the Atom* #10 (1992 – no fingerprints please!) $45, *Spider-Man* #1 (1990, Platinum Edition) $250, *Spider-Man* #1 (Gold second print w/UPC code) $225, *Strangers in Paradise* #1 (1993) $250, *Tank Girl* #1 (1991) $45 – okay, this price needs to be changed in the guide, *Transmetropolitan* #1 (1997) $50, *Venom: Lethal Protector* #1 (Gold) $75, (Black Cover/printing error edition) $600, *What If?* #105 (1998, first Spider-Girl) $30, *Wolverine* #145 (1999, Nabisco variant) $250, *Wonder Woman* #72 (1993, classic Brian Bolland cover) $25 – price change, price change!!

I would be remiss if I did not mention Marvel's 1990s cosmic era – specifically, those issues featuring the mad Titan, Thanos who will be seen on tens of thousands of big screens around the world within a few years. Speculation is still running rampant, not only within the comic reading community, but across entertainment outlets worldwide, as to what movies will feature a Thanos appearance, cameo or scene. Speculation explodes to new levels when one talks about the individual Infinity Gems or the actual Infinity Gauntlet and where or how it will be utilized within Marvel's cinematic universe, however, within the world of comics, such appearances are already set in stone. The amazing thing about the actual gauntlet's first appearance, in *Silver Surfer* #44 (1990) is that it was not until last year's *Overstreet* (volume #46) that it was actually annotated. Only a few years ago this issue was listed in $5 in the *Guide*, with only the headline "Thanos cover" but what a difference a few years make. Currently, a CGC 9.8 sells constantly for around $300, while speculators and pressing aficionado are scooping up any nice looking raw copies for between $75 and $100. *Infinity Gauntlet* #1-6 still sell very well, above *Guide* in fact, an amazing thing when one considers the massive print-run each issue had. The *Guide* lists issue #1 at $35 in NM-, however, for us a price of $45 is more reasonable, due to the fact that if we price the book lower, it's purchased by other dealers right away. The *Guide* lists issues #2-6 at $15, however, we always price issue #6 higher, from $20 to $25 depending on the quality of the issue. Sales of *Infinity War* initially went through the roof a year ago, however prices have stabilized in recent months, as news concerning the actual *Infinity War* movie seem to point to a decidedly different story. Issues #1-4 (#1 $8, #2-4 $5) are plentiful, with issue #1 available in obscene amounts, however issues #5-6 (#5 $10, #6 $12) were not ordered as heavily and as such, we price them higher that #1-4. The same scenario holds for *Infinity Crusade*, with issues #1-4 easily available (#1 $6, #2-4 $5 each), while issues #5 and #6 seem to have been ordered less. We price issue #5 at $7 and issue #6 at $10.

In conclusion, the 1990s era has certainly made a comeback in recent years, with collectors and speculators taking a serious look at 1990s product, comics that were once universally hailed as "junk" are now getting some time back in the limelight. Many collectors are beginning to discover the 1990s have two distinct mini-eras, 1990-1994 and 1995-1999. The first era coincides with the speculation boom, and record breaking print runs, while from 1994, print runs begin to drop as the industry slid into recession as collectors left the market, leaving only hardcore readers. I can't tell you how many times I've purchased collections from the 1990s, nearly all stocked heavily with multiples from 1990-1994, however from my own personal experience many of the 1990s collectors had stopped collecting by 1996 and this may explain why sellers on eBay are getting more bang for their buck selling full, complete runs of 1990s material.

In Conclusion: With all the super-hero product currently available via television and movies, we within the comic business are still experiencing a "Golden Age" of wider pop culture exposure, with everyone seemingly wanting to be involved in super-hero movies, television, or at least be seen at Comic con. For me, I see signs of future problems, mostly with the current direction of creativity and marketing within current new issue product (from Marvel and DC), but one has to understand – right now, more "civilians" are being exposed to our hobby everyday, we need to make sure they have a great time in our world and make it easy for them to hang around.

John Dolmayan - Torpedo Comics

The Year Of Living Dangerously: 2016 has been a difficult year for trade paperback convention sales, as we saw a major drop at almost every convention with the exception of C2E2 where we saw a 20% increase. With convention prices rising almost yearly we will most likely scale back on our booth space and build a more streamlined booth configuration.

Torpedo's first time displaying at the Amazing Comic Con Hawaii will most likely be its last, with lackluster sales on both trade paperbacks and our high-end Silver/Bronze booths. The show would have been a complete loss if not for major slashing of trade paperback prices that seemed to motivate buyers to open their wallets. The almost non-existent high-end sales coupled with the massive costs associated with transporting to Hawaii essentially assured Torpedo could not take a risk on the show in the foreseeable future.

C2E2 (Chicago): This show continues to outperform nearly every other show in regards to trade paperback sales nearly surpassing San Diego Comic-Con and certainly surpassing SDCC as far as profitability. The convention center is centrally located and well organized bringing in tens of thousands of customers who actually are interested in comics. We are building trust and a reputation for spot on tight grading with the local collectors of Silver-Bronze and high-end investment level CGC/CBCS books increasing sales gradually every year. There is great competition from nearly all high-end Midwest dealers and exceptional buying and trading opportunities all across the board and we enjoy that aspect of this convention as well as the competition to win new clients business.

Emerald City (Seattle): After hearing about this show being the greatest show for back issue sales and high end books flying off the shelves I was shocked to have just an okay show sales wise. The nightmare started when I was informed days before the show that we would be charged drayage by the local mafia otherwise known as either GES or Freeman. For anyone unfamiliar with this, drayage is a charge (by weight) to take your goods from the loading dock of the convention center to your booth. Some conventions work out a deal to spare us those costs and some don't (we usually pass on the ones that don't). This is the reason you haven't seen us at the NYCC and probably never will. After I was informed that we would be given a special discounted rate of $15,000 instead of $30,000 to take our product the nearly 100 feet to our booth (you read that correctly, not around the world, just 100 feet or so to our booth space just inside of the loading docks) we started thinking about canceling the show for the second time in two years. We were informed that at this late hour we would not receive a refund on our booth space so after calming down and evaluating the situation and rather then pay the ridiculous fee I made some calls and arranged an offsite warehouse to transfer everything out of the semi truck and into two Ryder trucks. This was arduous and unnecessary work as well as dangerous as we have large cases that are designed to be forklifted, someone could easily have been injured in the process and we will not undertake it again. At the end of the very slow show we then repeated the process to get our product home. Thankfully we did not pay the extortion and figured a way to navigate around it. In 2017 we are taking a minimal set up that can go in one Ryder truck. Let's hope we do better this time.

Wizard World (Chicago): Our second slowest show of the year and getting worse every year. The local union couldn't be nicer and more helpful showing that unions meant to protect the working man can still benefit the community and companies they provide service to. A well organized convention but our customers spend far to much time waiting in lines for autographs and not enough time walking the floor, giving us a chance to show them our products. We are taking a smaller more streamlined booth configuration in hopes that the organizers can figure something out to get more people on the show floor and out of all day lines. We had some small sales and the trade paperbacks did just okay, but I was able to broker a big deal at the end of the show to a client from the west coast to make the show a break even. Overall very dissatisfied and disappointed in the lack of empathy towards the exhibitors.

Silicon Valley Comic Con (San Jose): Silicon Valley, home of big brains, big bucks, and mediocre sales. Deep in the recesses of the show hidden between two toy dealers at a location Indiana jones couldn't find was the Torpedo Comics booth. With over 2 million dollars of stock you'd think we would have hit it out of the park at this San Francisco adjacent (one of the best comic book markets) comic con. Unfortunately we had a terrible location, fortunately we found some customers and were able to do just enough business to make a small profit. Steve Wyatt is doing a great job on this growing convention, hope next year goes better.

San Diego Comic Con (San Diego): The best show in the world keeps getting more expensive and we keep making less sales. Trade paperbacks took a massive 30% drop in sales, this is up from the 10% drop of the last three years. There are less people looking for comics or who even know what comics are. Thankfully they rarely venture into the Gold and Silver pavilion where sales have improved every year. With about 50% of our sales to dealers as opposed to 60% of previous years we've seen a steady growth of customer acquisition and a consistent return of customers from previous conventions. We are building our brand and the public's faith in our grading and quality is translating into sales and more sales. San Diego Comic-Con is by far the best organized and most enjoyable convention, but wow, are the booth spaces expensive and getting more so. I'm surprised some exhibitors can afford to do the show and sad to see many old timers have stopped attending altogether. Is it possible to keep a show based on comics that has outgrown the comic industry and become a pop culture monster still comic-centric? Or do we face the inevitable truth that the convention everyone based their conventions on is no longer ours, has transcended our hobby, and is bigger than comics. It will be interesting to see how it evolves and what our place will be in its evolution or possibly devolution.

We are proud to be a part of this industry, and we love comics and the altruistic nature of the heroes portrayed in them. Come share our passion for them at our new store in Las Vegas, Nevada. You won't be disappointed.

JEFF ITKIN
ELITE COMIC SOURCE

Hello to everybody reading this, thank you for taking the time. There have been some big changes on my end, but before I get into all that I would like to thank Bob Overstreet and his team, they work so hard to put this guide together every year and we are lucky to have them. Now, back to those changes. The biggest was in the start of this year, where I have branched off on my own again with a new identity in the Comic Marketplace. In the beginning of January 2015 I merged my then existing comic company "Pow Crunch Bang Comics" with a good friend of mine (Ken Dyber of Cloud 9 Comics), and have been half owner of Cloud 9 Comics since. The last couple of years have been a whirlwind, with many great memories and moments, but something was missing. I pulled away from some of the things I really wanted to bring to comic collectors and fans, outside of just great comics. These last 2 years we have been so bogged down with opening a store that the time I could have to put towards the fun of being innovative and creative was lost. Therefore, I have started 2 different websites. The first is www.elitecomicssource.com, which will slowly roll out through 2017 as a "Source" for comics and comic art. The second will be www.thecomicsurge.com, which will provide multimedia (podcasts, trailers and more) related information. I hope for it to be informative and interesting, but still a fun and a playful site to visit.

Then and Now: I will just jump right in and say it, no sugar coating here. "Last year was one of the weakest years for back issues and Key sales I have seen in the last 5 years." Of course there were new benchmark prices and gains for some books, as there are every year, but the market overall felt stagnant. This was evident in all genres except early Atomic Age and Golden Age; which makes sense as the ratio of demand for those books is higher than supply. There was a clear and evident push back of demand and pricing in 2016, especially with Keys of all degree, whether it was 1st to 3rd tier. I believe this push back comes from the large base of buyers that entered the market with the comic movie craze. I feel they have begun to educate themselves more and the consumer that sellers have been so accustomed to having the past few years has changed. This group of buyers no longer seems to impulse buy as they have in the past. They have come to the realization that Silver to Modern Age comics are not rare and can be found at any large convention in multiples of multiples. This new thought process stems from their already brief experiences or observations that the Comic Market can have major fluctuations. That it's more difficult for a comic to retain its newly appointed/hyped value than originally expected, especially when driven by a fleeting or trending event such as a TV show or movie.

Though sales were down in 2016, I do think that 2017 will have a resurgence in buyers. Especially with DC's commitment to their cinematic universe with the arrival of long-awaited characters and teams to make their modern movie debuts. It will be a better year, a more diverse (not just Marvel Keys) year in the collectibles market, with more energy at conventions and anticipation and excitement that should carry through for the next few years.

Movies/TV/Cartoons: Last year we saw some big movies hit the theater screen, but 2017 will be one to really set the tone for comic collecting the next 3 years. The introduction and push of DC's characters onto the Silver Screen will be one that all comic fans are eager to see. With the *Wonder Woman* trailers and quasi-success of *Suicide Squad* and *Batman v Superman* it seems like DC is finally figuring out how to make an appealing movie. There is still room for growth on their end if you ask me, as neither *Suicide Squad* nor *Bats v. Sups* was outstanding. As expected, Marvel continues to succeed in growing their Universe and pushing their Infinity War story line. Golf clap and kudos to them to constantly keeping us entertained and surprising us with successful interpretations of comic books characters in film.

Current/Modern Age(2003-Now): Going to just touch on this briefly. This span of comics like every new era is an exciting, innovative and fun time for comics. They offer great art, outstanding story lines, and interesting, relatable and lovable characters. It's comforting to see some good things continuing to be published as it's very important to keep readership interest so we can continue to create a future of collectors. DC relaunched their Universe in 2016. It was well received by fans so if you are looking to get back into comics, it may be a great time to start up again.

Most of our strongest sales this last year for the shop were in graphic novels and TPBs. This was consistent with the previous year and a trend I don't see slowing down. A large group of readers can't and don't visit their comic shop every week to pick up their new comics. Instead, most of what we see is a customer coming in once or maybe twice a month to pick up a new trade they either heard about, ones they are currently reading and or ones they would like to try. This is still a great way to keep up to date on what's occurring in the comic world and really the only way I can stay somewhat current of what's happening in the industry. Also, it's a great way to interact with your customers and maybe open their eyes to some new titles.

As far as current comics go, it is the toughest of all time frames to speculate on. With the large number of new comics released every week, a lot of it will come in hot and fast, run its course and burn out quickly. An example of the difficulty of speculating in the market are that the highest grossing sales come from variant covers. When I use the term Variant Cover that is a loaded term as I can't even imagine how many Variant Covers are out there. For the sake of this article, I will say there are 10,000 in the Current Age with more published every week. Some of the top Variants are listed here have very impressive prices: *Batman* #608 RRP Variant Cover CGC 9.8 $4,050, *Ms. Marvel* #2 1:50 Molina 2014 Variant CGC 9.8 $2,200, *Saga* #1 Diamond Retailer Variant CGC 9.8 $1,700, X-23 #1 Variant Dell'otto CGC 9.8 $1,200, and *The Dark Knight Returns: The Last Crusade* Jim Lee 1:500 CGC 9.8 $1,025 etc. One of the biggest books as well was a more common variant, *Captain Marvel* #17 2nd print with Kamala Khan on the cover, this is her first appearance and one of the hotter books this past year with pricing around $200-$800 for NM- to NM+. Search eBay finished auction listings for "Variant" and it goes on and on with books you had no idea existed. You can then throw in sketch covers and signatures and it is just too wacky for me to keep up with.

Chrome Age/Steel Age(1992-2003): This is what I am naming it now. I'm tired of over thinking it and waiting for someone to come up with some magical name. It's been almost 25 years since the end of the Copper Age. It's time for a new designation, as far too much has occurred in the comic industry to not create a new divide. From the variety of dynamic covers such as die cut, fold outs and Chrome covers (Chrome Age) to the Death of the Man of Steel (Steel Age). It was a great time frame for innovation of new heroes and a new generation of artist and their styles. It brought us successful publishers such as Image and Valiant and the long line of characters that drove a generation of readers and collectors. Not much going on here that isn't also occurring in the Current/Modern Age. Some of the hotter books that were non-Variant covers in high demand were *NYX* #3 and *Batman Adventures* #12 (slowed down a bit from its epic interest in 2015), all *Amazing Spider-Man*, all *Spawn* and Valiant back issues.

***NYX** #3, the debut of X-23, is a high demand book from what could be called the Chrome Age.*

Bronze and Copper Age: They continue to be the two strongest selling time frames. We can monitor this by the quantity of back issues sold in a convention environment for us. This is no surprise with the quality and amount of so many great heroes to come from these eras. With the success of movies and TV shows continuing to integrate characters from these Ages, it helps keep characters and interest relevant and current. Don't get me wrong, we do have to sell the comics at half *Guide*, unless they are extremely high grade or Key issues, but this has been a standard practice for us and many others for a decade now. Another draw of the BA and CA of comics was the wonderful cover and interior art, especially in the Bronze Age. There was a new level of dynamic and exciting art brought to paper. Some of the hottest books of last year that still have room for growth are *House of Secrets* #92 in all grades as well *Tomb of Dracula* #10, *Batman* #251, *Superman's Pal Jimmy Olsen* #134 and *Amazing Spider-Man* #129. Top sales for 2016 were *Marvel Spotlight* #5 CGC 9.8 $48,500, *Star Wars* #1 35 cent Price Variant CGC 9.4 $26,290, *Hero for Hire* #1 CGC 9.8 $24,000, *X-Men* #94 CGC 9.8 $15,535, *Incredible Hulk* #181 CGC 9.8 CGC 9.8 $15,000, *Amazing Spider-Man* #129 CGC 9.8 $10,600 and one of the more interesting sales was a *Night Nurse* #1 CGC 9.8 for $7,700. The books most in demand for us in the Copper Age were *New Mutants* #87 and 98, *Amazing Spider-Man* #238, 252, 300, and *Teenage Mutant Ninja Turtles* #1.

Silver Age: Keys, keys and more keys. Marvel plays its usual role as the gale wind that blows all other publishers aside. It continues to drive the industry and interest level of collectors and investors. No big surprises here, just people keeping it simple and looking for key books. The most well-known and recoginzed comics for a majority of collectors come from this era, but despite that, it was still a soft year for Silver Age. I don't know if there will be a bounce back this year for Marvel Keys, but I do see DC Keys having a very strong year and the start of their long-awaited growth to comic relevancy congruent with Marvels.

This is a huge movie year for DC and a chance to grow its brand to new fans and expose their world of characters. Key books for purchase that are currently undervalued are *Fantastic Four* #1, 5 and 48, *X-Men* #1, *Brave and the Bold* #28 and 54, *Avengers* #1 and 4, *Amazing Spider-Man* #1, 3, 14, *Justice League* #1, *Aquaman* #1, *Showcase* #34, *Journey Into Mystery* #83, *Showcase* #22, *Green Lantern* #1, *Tales to Astonish* #27 and *Adventure Comics* #247. Some of the blockbuster prices of last year were *Aquaman* #1 CGC 9.4 $14,000, *Detective Comics* #359 CGC 9.4 $13,300, *Amazing Fantasy* #15 CGC 9.4 $454,100, *Showcase* #4 8.0 $84,000 and *Incredible Hulk* #1 9.2 $375,000.

Golden Age: Last year I ranted and raved about this being the most fulfilling genre to collect and how exciting acquiring these books can be. Well let me reiterate that nothing has changed and the Marketplace continues to agree. Unrestored GA Blue Chip books in this time frame of superhero keys continue to be the most consistent in gained values, have the most interest and are the easiest to sell. Really cool right, but you may be reading this and think, "Whoop de freaking do for you if you can afford to buy those!" Which I totally understand, but here is where the mind-blowing begins, "The restored and conserved market is making a push." Yes, I said it out loud. This trend was always looming in the background, but I feel in 2016 it really started to build into something bigger and by the end of the year its interest level has hit an all-time high with new gains to be had in 2017 and no end in sight.

"Our collectible has gotten to that point!" As the comic market continues to grow exponentially every year, a larger group of books enters the realm of unobtainability for collectors. Those Mega Keys in the lowest end of grading can still cost you $30K-$150K, which obviously is a lot of money for 90% of collectors. This realization has led to people succumbing to the feeling and notion that the need and void in their collection can only be filled with a restored or conserved copy. If a place can be found for these books amongst investors and collectors in our market (which I believe has already begun) then it will give new hope and drive for many old and new collectors. Of the many years I have been in this industry, I have spoken to countless people who have either given up on obtaining certain books or just left the collectibles completely for that same reason. This avenue would revitalize those groups of people and new collectors as well. The two things that need to occur for this transition to grow exponentially is their own comfort level to invest (make no doubt about it, comics at this point are an investment) and trust in what they are putting their hard-earned money into. Luckily with sites such as GPA or search engines for Auction Houses past sale history, we have been able to truly monitor and verify growth and trends from actual sales data.

Here are some of my observations for the hottest comics and trends of 2016 that will also continue into 2017, outside of the usual Mega Key suspects that we all know about. All *Captain America Comics* were extremely popular, especially in low grade, as it seems that everyone wants to get them any way they can and there appears to be this stigma that your collection isn't a collection without having at least one GA *Captain America* in it. I think the Golden Age *Caps* are always a smart buy and still far undervalued in mid to high grade. Also in extremely high demand and probably the hottest of books were all Joker covers in *Detective Comics* and *Batman*. As if the Clown Prince needed more attention already, some of these books are having huge gains from already strong 2015 sales, with some numbers doubling what they sold for just a year prior. My prediction for those books in 2017 is that there is still demand and interest but prices have reached a peak until 2018. All things Wonder Woman were extremely strong, especially her first appearance in *All Star* #8 which hit a record numbers all year including a CGC 9.0 sale for $411,000. Her 2nd and 3rd appearance have also been in extremely high demand with a *Wonder Woman* #1 CGC 9.0 selling for $290,000. I see strong growth in her first 3 appearances continuing through 2017 and forward.

As it goes for non-Super Hero comics, there was a huge demand for Horror titles this year, as well as everything Matt Baker. Most of the interest was for EC titles, but just about all Horror was relevant and seemed to be appealing to collectors last year and I am sure it will continue into this year. Matt Baker is already a prevalent name in the community, but his demand was an all-time high this year, and any Baker Romance was near impossible to keep in stock. Good Girl Art and Science Fiction titles were second for demand and Crime took a distant third this year. This information does not affect my feelings towards these genres from the late '40s to early '50s as it is probably the most undervalued and appreciated time frame. I think it has the most potential, undiscovered growth in collectability and value. It should be on everyone's radar for investing and collecting. I will buy most any high grade and reasonably priced Romance, Horror, Sci-Fi, Super Hero, Good Girl Art and or Crime in this time frame.

Other impressive numbers that were reached in 2016 were: *Action Comics* #1 CGC 5.5 $956,000, *Action Comics* #242 CGC 8.0 $34,000, *Action Comics* #252 CGC 8.0 $15,300, *Batman* #1 CGC 8.0 $390,000, *Batman* #15 CGC 9.0 $9,000, *Captain America Comics* #1 CGC 8.0 $288,000, *Captain America Comics* nn CGC 2.5 $9,500, *Detective Comics* #37 CGC 6.0 $21,000, *Detective Comics* #40 8.5 $27,500, *Detective Comics* #69 CGC 5.5 $10,900, *Detective Comics* #71 CGC 7.5 $11,600, *Detective Comics* #168 CGC $18,000, *More Fun* #52 CGC 3.0 $39,000 and *Superman* #1 CGC 4.0 $295,000.

Wrapping it up, I am starting two new sites, *elitecomicsource* and *thecomicsurge* this year, so keep your eyes open and have a little patience as I am still fleshing them out. Last year was a slow year for comics and I did not see much or any growth in any era except Golden Age. I imagine the planned movies for this year will push a different group of super heroes that are not as mainstream as Marvel's characters. This should create a new spark for comic enthusiast, as a new Universe can now be collected. The GA was strong last year and will continue as the demand increases and supply doesn't. Restored and conserved Mega Keys are becoming a viable way for a collector and/or investor to acquire the comic they can no longer can afford, but still provide a solid investment. Remember, collecting is supposed to be fun and if you're not having fun, you are doing something wrong. Thanks for everyone who read this and I'll leave you with one final note and my mantra for those investing in comics, "Buy smart, sell smarter.

Nick Katradis
Comic & Comic Art Collector

2016 was another banner year for comics and original comic art. As a comic fan of over 45 years, I am reveling in this newly created familiarity by mainstream America of the beloved comic book characters that we collectors grew up with.

It seems like only yesterday when comic collectors had to keep their passion for comics to themselves. I remember as an 11 year old in the early 1970s, only my two closest friends knew that I read and collected comics. And they swore secrecy to the outside world or my "image" in school would have been tarnished. These days, I can bring up any comic character from the big screen at a house party and most people are aware of them and/or are collectors themselves. One recent example of this was a few months ago when I changed dentists. When I mentioned comics to my new local dentist on my first visit, he said "Oh, I still have my comic book collection from childhood, too!"

As more and more superhero movies are produced by Marvel and DC, mainstream America is getting quite familiar with comic book characters that were once only known to comic book fans.

As I write this report, *Doctor Strange* has crossed over $653 million in global box office receipts. This is astounding because Dr. Strange is a character that up until a few months ago was one only known to comic geeks. These days, it seems Marvel can do no wrong with its movies. And DC's upcoming movies also seem to be generating the similar levels of anticipation.

Overview: I have been a comic book collector since 1972. I also started collecting comic art in 2002, driven mostly by nostalgia in seeing the original art to the comics I read as a youngster, mostly Bronze Age art.

In 2014, not too long after I became an Overstreet Advisor, I started to certify many comics from my personal collection. I did this for two main reasons:

First, like most collectors that are 50 years old or older, I have become more aware of my own mortality, and I have to take steps to arrange for an orderly succession to my wife and kids of my comics and my original comic art collection. Nothing is more sobering for any collector in any hobby than to come to the realization that our children just do not have the same passion that we have for our hobby. So slabbing my top books was necessary to prevent damage to them and make them much easier to appraise to determine their value once they are certified.

Second, our hobby of collecting comics, fueled by the movies about comic characters, has become big business. Unfortunately, it seems that comics have become a commodity, similar to buying a TV or refrigerator. All you need to do today to own a comic is to simply have the funds to purchase it. You then search for it on eBay, or on a comic dealer's website, or simply search for it on the seemingly endless and weekly auctions conducted by the major Comic auction houses, and simply buy it. For decades, comic collectors searched for months and quite often for years for a specific comic. Without the power of the internet our options were limited, though perhaps more rewarding when we finally found a comic we needed. The same applied when we decided to sell.

Grading services like CGC and CBCS have helped to create a boom in the price structure of many comics.

A "raw" book has its advantages, but these days if it is not certified, most frequently you cannot get a multiple of *Guide* price if you decide to sell it. To their credit, grading services have filled a huge need in the hobby, by doing all the heavy lifting for us collectors. In the old days, when we found a Gold, Silver, or Bronze Age comic, we had to use our own expertise to make sure it was not trimmed, color touched, no glue on the spine, loose staples, pieces missing, etc. And we had to, of course, determine a grade for the book so we could figure out what we would consider paying for it or what to sell it for. But all that expertise is not required these days. All you have to do is buy a slabbed book instead of taking the risk of buying a raw book. It usually costs more but there is little anxiety about other factors.

CGC and CBCS grade the book, which is usually the toughest thing to do correctly. But they also help determine if the book has been restored, which would render its value to only a fraction of what an unrestored copy is worth. As collectors, once we know the grade of the book, and can ascertain that it was not restored, then we can more determine a price for it.

eBay on any given day has over 110,000 CGC comics for sale. Raw comic listings on eBay are in the millions. In addition, comic dealers have increased in numbers once again. Most dealers are online these days but there are still a lot of brick and mortar stores around the country.

Estate Planning: As comics and comic art have skyrocketed in value, and some have become more valuable than many people's homes, all collectors should spend the time to develop a detailed plan of succession, basically what to do with their collections after they are gone.

In the past few years, I have asked many fellow collectors about what would happen to their collections of comics and comic art after they are gone, and I have been stunned that many large collectors have hardly ever thought about it, and many have not put a plan in place.

This implies to me that many collectors today have not devoted the necessary time to create instructions for the future of their treasures. So what would happen upon their untimely demise and/or if a tragic event occurs, which will instantly place their family in the daunting position of deciding what to do with their collections.

It's so important that we all allocate the time and energy to create a plan so our family would know exactly how to prepare to manage an orderly and meaningful disbursement of our collections. All collectors should maintain a detailed inventory of their comics and comic art. They should document what they paid for each comic and/or art and properly document what the market value of each item is. And these values should be updated at least once a year.

More important is for the collector to leave detailed instructions to their family of what to sell and what not to sell. Every collector should have detailed lists of what items are to be kept in the family and distributed to each family member, and what items should be prepared for sale.

In addition, each collector should have one or more trusted individuals that are collectors and directly involved in the hobby that can advise and that can help the family with organizing and determining a plan for the portion of the collection that is to be sold. These individuals should be named in the will or an outside document that provides details as to their respective participation in the process.

I would also recommend that the decision of who should be placed in this advisory role should be done very carefully, and thoroughly researched. Any advisor should be someone who the collector feels will not place their personal interests over those of the family, and be someone who will not compromise the family's best course of action. Any advisor should also be compensated so he is motivated to benefit the family's interests. The collector should also document his wishes to the family on how the individual would be paid and how much.

As morbid as all of this may sound, it is imperative that every collector leaves detailed directions to his or her family as to how he or she would want his collection to be treated. Each collector should make their wishes clearly known to their family members, and in writing. This way the family will make the right decisions with regard to their collections and prevent arguments and squabbling, and minimize any family stress about what to do.

Original Comic Art: As more and more collectors of comics migrate to collecting comic art, I have noticed a few trends occurring, some of which are positive and some which are not.

First, new collectors that enter comic art have no price guide to give them specific pricing on what comic art is worth. Back in 1992, Jerry Weist did publish *Original Comic Art: Identification and Price Guide*, which tried to cover prices for comic book art, newspaper strips, and pulp art. But it fell short since it did not include mainstream artists who are very popular today and whose art has exploded in value. In 2000, and updated edition was published called *The Comic Art Price Guide*, but that also fell short as tracking and recording sales of original art is far more difficult than collecting comic books. However, this *Guide* can be used as a tool for novices in the hobby to get familiar with many artists that are not currently discussed and/or remembered by the collecting community.

Buying or selling a comic has become easier because services like CGC, CBCS, GPA, and *The Overstreet Comic Book Price Guide*, have created a "market price" for every comic ever printed. But when collecting original comic art, new collectors usually lack the knowledge and a clear grasp on what a piece of art should sell for. A little homework will go a long way. New collectors should join Comic Art Fans (www.comicartfans.com), and search the huge site for comic art they may want to own. They can also look at historical actual auction sales on Heritage Auctions archives, which provide for free all of their actual auction sales going back to 2001. Lastly, they can search comic art dealer sites, which usually give specific pricing on comic art.

Prices of original comic art can have a great range, even between pages from the same issue, because comic art pricing is based on content. So if a page has the hero fighting the villain in every panel, the pricing will be far greater than a plain page with no hero or villain on the page. Pricing is also greatly dependent on the historical significance of the comic. So the storyline and its substance plays a big role in the value of the art. Most importantly, comic art values reflect the popularity of the artist and/or inker. Even an average page from an average title drawn by Jack Kirby will be much more desirable than a lot of the more visually appealing pages by less popular and less revered artists. And comic art is basically character driven. So a Batman page is usually more desirable than any other DC character, just as a Spider-Man page is usually more desirable than any other Marvel character.

And lastly, the value of the art depends on whether it is from a primary title as opposed to a secondary title the character appeared in. Example: obtaining a page of art from *Amazing Spider-Man* is typically more desirable and much more valuable than obtaining a page of art from *Spectacular Spider-Man* or *Web of Spider-Man*, which were titles that featured the same character but they came out decades after the primary title. The primary title pages are older and much more difficult to obtain and usually much more expensive. And the primary title pages are usually from the creator of the character so the price of the art reflects it.

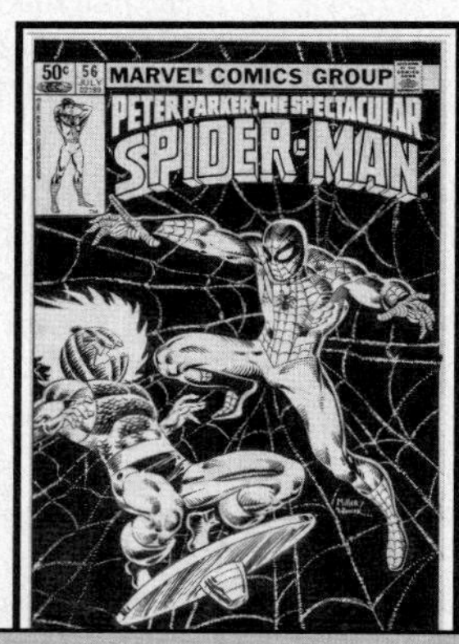

Vintage art, like this Frank Miller cover for ***Spectacular Spider-Man*** *#56 is a solid investment.*

All this criteria will help determine what price that original comic art will sell for. Today, there is the additional factor of comic art done digitally on a computer by the artist and the inker basically inking a copy of the original. This is called "blue line art" and many older and more seasoned collectors avoid it as it does not have the original pencils of the artist underneath the finished art. The penciled and inked art exist separately or the penciled art may not even exist outside of the artist's computer.

Fans of original comic art have grown exponentially the past 10 years as more and more comic fans have become aware of the existence of the original art of their favorite artist. Modern art is very popular today as new and younger collectors enter the hobby. Since modern art reflects what the younger collector is currently reading, it may be more desirable than an older page drawn by someone many years ago. But that's where some pitfalls of collecting may lie.

Even though Modern art today can be usually purchased cheaper than comic art published decades ago, it may not be cheap at all. A lot of modern art drawn today may not hold its value down the road, since the artists are usually less known and the title they are working on may not be around for long. If the story in the comic in uneventful, its desirability in the future will fade quickly. As a result, Modern art can be a more risky "investment" of a collector's time, energy, and money than an older or more vintage piece of art, since it has not yet established a collector base. Many of the characters being published today, even if they are existing characters, may not be desirable to collectors in the near future if the comic is cancelled and /or the storyline does not resonate with collectors in the future.

Vintage art – basically art from the 1960s to the 1990s – may on the other hand be more expensive to purchase but it may hold its value better and appreciate more than the newer art since the character and/or storyline has been around much longer and have already established a track record and fans over the years.

As a lifelong comic fan, and a collector of comic art for over 15 years, I want to give some advice to younger collectors that do not yet have the focus or the scope of what they should collect and how.

First and foremost, limit yourself to an era that resonates with you on a personal level. I collect mostly Bronze Age comic art, since I first read comics as a teen in the early 1970s. When I first started collecting comic art I was buying comic art from the '60s, '70s, and '90s. I was all over the map in buying. Back then most comic art was cheap, so I got away with it. At today's astronomical prices, I would not have lasted long. So after a few years, I gravitated to collecting mostly 1970s art and I learned not to waste my bullets because in comic art opportunities arise to buy when you are least prepared.

Also, by collecting comic art from a period that I have read first hand almost every comic that was being published at the time, I actually have an advantage over the next guy in finding undervalued art because I may remember the storyline and its importance more than the next guy. Knowledge is power, and this hobby is no exception. Also by limiting my collecting focus, I don't fall into the pitfall as a collector of buying "eye candy" art that catches my eye but ages bad very quickly and does not retain its value over time.

I collect mostly based on two criteria: artistic merit of the art and nostalgia. Both are prerequisites to building a quality collection of comic art. But comic art is a hobby based primarily on nostalgia. How else can most of us that have spent absurd amounts of money on a piece of comic art rationally convince ourselves that it was worth it. Vintage comic art commands such high prices these days, that without the personal connection to the piece, a collector will tend to sell it before long as his taste will change or his pocket book will tell him it has. I have kept hundreds of pieces in my collection for 15 years or so because they are part of my well being and selling is just not an option. And time is the best friend of any collecting. If you hold anything over time, you will usually do better than something you owned for a very short time.

Another important piece to collecting is you have to decide early on who your favorite artists are and start to buy quality examples of their work, based on your pocket. Slowly you will learn to gravitate to better and better examples of their work. And you will not be tempted to buy anything that comes along. If you have a good eye for art, you should chose to collect the work of great artists, without losing the conviction and start to second guess yourself. Other collectors may try to sway you away from the artists you collect. But if you do your homework and can see quality in the work in your favorite artists, history will reward you when the collective wisdom of the other collectors finally see what you see. "Never run with the herd," I always say.

While collecting your favorite artists is great, don't be blind to what art is available at any given time. Always "buy the best piece of art you can afford at the time". So if a great page is offered for sale, by a great artist, at a fair price, you grab it if you can. Don't walk away because it's not one of your favorite artists. Opportunity only knocks a few times and you have to know to answer the door. Quality comic art stays buried in collections for decades so if you get a chance to buy an extraordinary page, go for it.

Another piece of advice is that comic art is like real estate. You prefer that you buy the ugliest house in the best neighborhood than the nicest house in the worse neighborhood. So if you have a choice to buy a Spider-Man cover by a lesser artist or a great Flintstones cover, buy the Spider-man cover. If you have a choice of a Batman cover or a lesser DC character, buy the Batman cover, even by a lesser artist. Because in comic art, the popularity of the character on the page greatly determines and defines its resale value in the future.

I want to end my market report with saying that as a collector of both comics and comic art, I am truly astounded by the popularity both hobbies have achieved over the past 5-10 years. I feel the comic industry is currently at its zenith in recognition and awareness by the general public, but it is also at this time that I think it is most vulnerable.

As most collectors know, collecting comics and/or comic art has become increasingly challenging and most difficult for the average collector to afford. It seems that the prices have skyrocketed too far and too fast. The health of any industry is measured by how many people participate in it, and it's the collectors in the middle that are getting shut out. The past few years, I have met a lot of collectors that are either half way out of the hobby or are contemplating getting out. The reason they give is they cannot afford to buy much of what they used to collect. So many of them are cashing out and moving on. Is the hobby poised for a steep correction? Who knows. But as more and more collectors are aging, they are slowly selling their collections to fund retirement and/or fund other purchases in their lives. So the question is, will the music stop any time soon, and if it stops, who can guarantee they will have a chair to sit on.

IVAN KOCMAREK
COLLECTOR

Well, the Bells are ringing, and it's not just because it's the holiday season.

This year saw the largest lot of Canadian war-time comics (WECA Comics—see my article in *Overstreet* #44) that has ever come onto the market and almost all appeared on ComicLink. A huge collection of couple hundred of these books was sent into the auction site at the end of last year or early this year (the collector insisted on remaining anonymous but they were most probably Canadian). They slabbed them and then gently released them in focused auctions throughout the year.

Back in late 2013 when I started writing about these old Canadian books, a bunch of us hoped that collections would start coming out of the woodwork but in three years they have only trickled out into the market and collectors have been starved for them. In the last two years, we have seen two significant collections go into university archives. One at Ryerson in Toronto and the other at Western in London, Ontario. Collectors and the marketplace lament this but researchers laude it.

To have a large collection like this feed the market for just about the entire year has been a luxury. These old Canadian comics are many times scarcer (think Gerber 7s for most as a starting point) than most American Golden Age books and there was no Silver Age in Canada through the '60s to shore up a collecting culture for them. Five to ten years ago, these books were neglected throwaways with dealers knowing almost nothing about them and the great portion of them could be had for under $100 a copy. Strangely, they still don't merit any real place in this guide you've got in your hands and the dozen or so that have found their way into the listings are, for the most part, listed erroneously with unrealistic price points.

A group of us north of the border have managed to put together the first solid, comprehensive checklist and price guide done for these 760 or so Canadian war time comics and look for it out in 2017, Canada's Sesquicentennial.

But let's look at where we're at this year with all these ComicLink auction results. Here are the winning bids for about the top third of the 160 books or so that were auctioned on ComicLink this year:

	Issue	Grade	Sale Price
1	Nelvana 1945 Comp.	5.0	$14,750
2	Nelvana 1945 Comp.	6.5	$11,750
3	Triumph #7	2.0	$9,000
4	Dime Comics #1	3.5	$5,800
5	Colossal (Sub Cover)	2.5	$4,200
6	Triumph-Adventure #5	3.0	$3,655
7	Triumph #12	6.0	$3,600
8	Wow #18	2.5	$3,600
9	Triumph #30	7.5	$3,400
10	Joke #3	1.5	$3,400
11	Robin Hood V1 #1	3.0	$3,339

12	Dime #6	3.0	$3,300
13	Dime #14	4.0	$3,200
14	Wow #16	4.0	$3,100
15	Lucky V1 #1	3.0	$3,090
16	Commando #1	0.5	$3,000
17	Active #18	4.0	$2,900
18	Wow Comics #15	6.0	$2,800
19	Active #27	4.5	$2,800
20	Triumph #9	4.0	$2,600
21	Triumph #28	2.5	$2,600
22	Triumph-Adv. #4	0.5	$2,600
23	Joke #1	2.5	$2,600
24	Active #13	4.0	$2,500
25	Dime #24	4.0	$2,400
26	Wow #17	2.5	$2,400
27	Rocket V5 #4	4.5	$2,400
28	Triumph #26	6.0	$2,400
29	Speed Savage nn	6.0	$2,300
30	Active #14	3.0	$2,300
31	Dime #27	5.0	$2,300
32	Triumph #19	7.0 R	$2,300
33	Wow #25	6.0	$2,300
34	Three Aces V1 #1	3.0	$2,222
35	Triumph #22	1.8	$2,200
36	Triumph #21	7.5	$2,100
37	Wow #29	6.0	$2,100
38	Commando #4	9.2	$2,000
39	Lucky V2 #7	1.8	$2,000
40	Commando #22	7.5	$2,000
41	Dime #24	6.0	$2,000
42	Commando #10	3.5	$1,900
43	Triumph #15	6.0	$1,850
44	Wow Comics #2	7.0	$1,825
45	Dime Comics #2	5.0	$1,800
46	Triumph #29	7.0	$1,800
47	Robin Hood V1 #5	5.5	$1,799
48	Active #3	7.5	$1,714
49	Commando #13	3.0	$1,700
50	Wow Comics #1	5.0	$1,625

Now what can we take away from these results?

First, Bell Features books seem to have solidified in the market as the most desirable of all the Canadian war time books (also known as Canadian Whites and WECA books). Out of these top 50 results, 44 are Bells. They have essentially become the template for what a Canadian Golden Age comic is, namely, American looking on the outside and chewy Canadian maple on the inside. The other publishers never got it quite right the way that Bell did. Vancouver's Maple Leaf Publications, though they have Brok Windsor, Sgt. Canuck, and Cosmo and are the rarest to find, were too staid and steeped in the culture of wholesome literature adventure of the old British annuals. Toronto's other big publisher, Anglo-American, seems to be unable to escape the taint of those cheap looking two-colour newsprint covers they sported for the first four years and the stigma of being mostly a vehicle for Fawcett script redraws until eventually creating its own heroes. However, their main character, Freelance, always lends them some buoyancy and will do more so with Chapterhouse's reboot of the character in 2017. Montreal's Canadian Heroes, never got past looking like a Canadian counterpart of American *True Comics* or *Real Life Comics* though they are passionately collected by those with a wider interest in Canadiana. So with Bell books it looks like the cream has risen to the top.

As with all comics, values are character driven. The top 3 books feature Nelvana as do 6 out of the top 10 books, in fact, about a third of all the books on this list of results are there because they contain a Nelvana cover or story. To a lesser extent, other main Bell characters that prop up values are Johnny Canuck, The Penguin, and Speed Savage. This same effect is found in the other main publishers as well. Brok Windsor covers and appearances boost the values of Maple Leaf books, Freelance does this for Anglo-American books, and Canada Jack does the same for the Montreal books.

Another thing that you'll notice is that grade doesn't seem to be as attached to price point in the consistent gradient way we find it is with Golden Age or Silver Age American books. Take a look at the two *Nelvanas* that top of the list, or the three *Triumphs* at Nos. 20-22, or the two *Triumphs* at Nos. 35-36, and *Triumph* #21 is even a Nelvana cover. This is because of the scarcity of supply with these books. Many of these books, once ComicLink had them slabbed, were the only copies on the census. Even the most common books have only 4 or 5 copies slabbed. This means that collectors will often snap these books up regardless of grade because they might not see another copy come up for a long time, if ever. My fellow advisor and collector Walter Durajlija calls this factor "utility of ownership." Think about grabbing it while you see it or you might regret it.

This brings me to a little beef with CGC and why they continue to put "Canadian Edition" on the info strips at the top of the slabbed books. This is an unwitting condescension that implies that these comics are only later or foreign editions of American books, which can't be farther from the truth. OK, I can see you stamping this on slabbed copies of the Canadian reprint books that came out 1947-56, but not on these. For these books, it should simple read something like "Canadian Comic" period.

What 2016 has showed us concerning Canadian war time comics, is that they have become highly desirable books and that there is a solid market out there for them. Their value profile has higher peaks on it than have ever been reached before and we're still in the early stages of this market. As more is known and understood about them, I only see an upside.

Robert Krause
Primo Comics

Greetings from Primo Comics! We operate an online comic book store at primocomics.com as well as an eBay store at primo comics1. Visit our online stores for great deals on desirable comics. 2016 has been a very strong year for comic book sales from the Golden Age to Copper Age. As comic book related movies continue to popularize the genre globally, the respective characters and the related comic books become more in demand. This is ever-important to the long-term success and demand in the vintage comic book market. For there to be a sustained long-term collector market, the medium needs to attract new collectors, not just fans of the movies. We have been witnessing this trend which is very heartening to us as well as encouraging to the success of the market.

Mid to Lower Grade Comics: High grade, key and non-key comics continue to be in perpetual demand. The demand is so strong that it has become quite difficult to replace these issues once sold. These issues are being purchased by collectors as core holdings in their collections. This then takes these books off the market to an indeterminant amount of time, perhaps for many years. This has the impact of creating perceived scarcity in the marketplace for a particular issue, further driving prices higher. This has also created what we see as an opportunity in the mid to lower grade market for both key and non-key vintage comics. The prices of these mid-grade books are still very reasonable with there being no real competition to acquire these books. This is particularly true for mid and lower grade Silver Age books from Marvel and DC.

We believe that it is only a matter of time before the confluence of an ever increasing collector base demanding vintage books and the scarcity of high grade books manifests itself in a move down to the next desirable tier, mid to lower grade books. This will cause an inevitable increase in prices for these mid to lower grade respective books. The only real demand that collectors appear to have it that the book is complete. Even in lower grades, collectors want to ensure the book is structurally sound. They accept writing in or on the book, loss of gloss and even staple pops. Many of these Silver Age books are 50 years or older and collectors realize that having a copy of a book they want, even in lower grade, is better than never owning a copy at all.

Foreign Comics: This area of collecting is the undiscovered country and the wild west. The foreign comics market is very fractured and no one truly knows what is out there. I am speaking here of the Marvel and DC equivalents outside the United States. These books are basically black and white reprints of comics printed in the United States with many times new and interesting covers and at times oversized as well. I mention this area of collecting since it is tremendously under-collected by fans in the United States and can still be purchased for little money. The United Kingdom editions in the 1970s are oversized and offer great collector eye appeal both inside and outside of the book with new or varied covers of their USA counterparts. You can also find key books printed in various languages for a fraction of the USA equivalents. There is true scarcity here particularly in higher grade. These foreign editions are notoriously in lower grades and true high grades are very difficult to find. A collector does not have the real ability to be choosy though since the offered example of a comic might be the only one you find for quite some time. Buy these books when you see them since you may not see another.

Ben Labonog
Collector

Overview of the Market: "Considering print errors like miscut covers, bad registration, books with no staple holes, blank inside covers, double covers etc...it's really funny that people make such a stink about grade. Books were not intended to be mint." – Anonymous

That was a quote a dear friend emailed me recently and I thought it was on point with regards to comics. Sure, that number in the upper left hand corner of the slab can translate into a nice vacation, retirement funds, college tuition, a new home, or pay off debt. But once you have a complete and presentable copy, it doesn't matter if it's a GD/VG or a FN+ unless one is upgrading to get rid of a major eyesore of a defect such as a spine roll, Marvel chipping, piece out of FC, or faded colors. With these astronomical price points (we all witnessed a $10 Million dollar auction at the end of 2016), save some money and enjoy a lower grade book that still looks great in a Mylar or a slab. As I mentioned in last year's report, I think it's prudent to downgrade those expensive keys and get the same book in lower grade plus cash to buy other books you want. Another friend of mine told me he was recently offered about $1 million dollars for a book in his collection. I advised him to try and downgrade the book and cash the rest out for more books. Or simply keep the book unless he needed the money for something important. There's no sense chopping down a money tree!

I was looking at CGC census numbers that I had printed out in 2006 and compared them to some current numbers for 2016. Here is a sampling of what I found:

Action Comics # 1 2006 (33 total copies), 2016 (65 total copies)

Action Comics # 7 2006 (15 total copies), 2016 (42 total copies)

All-American Comics #16 2006 (17 total copies), 2016 (47 total copies)

Batman #1 2006 (98 total copies), 2016 (231 total copies)

Captain America Comics #1 2006 (67 total copies), 2016 (151 total copies)

Detective Comics #27 2006 (31 total copies), 2016 (64 total copies)

Detective Comics #29 2006 (20 total copies), 2016 (56 total copies)

Detective Comics #31 2006 (32 total copies), 2016 (81 total copies)

Marvel Comics #1 2006 (37 total copies), 2016 (59 total copies)

Marvel Mystery #9 2006 (20 total copies), 2016 (45 total copies)

Superman #1 2006 (60 total copies), 2016 (124 total copies)
Suspense #3 2006 (10 total copies), 2016 (32 total copies)

It took ten years for these books to double or triple in census numbers. When comparing SA/BA census numbers in the same time span, the SA/BA census numbers reflect a tripling/quadrupling or close to fivefold (*Avengers* #1- the Avengers films undoubtedly created a spike in submissions.) increase over the same ten years.

Fantastic Four #1 2006 (574 total copies), 2016 (1802 total copies)
Incredible Hulk #1 2006 (450 total copies), 2016 (1343 total copies)
Amazing Fantasy #15 2006 (844 total copies), 2016 (2609 total copies)
Amazing Spider-Man #1 2006 (1196 total copies), 2016 (3073 total copies)
X-Men #1 2006 (1088 total copies), 2016 (3544 total copies)
Avengers #1 2006 (629 total copies), 2016 (3034 total copies)
Incredible Hulk #181 2006 (3177 total copies), 2016 (8907 total copies)

There could be some statistical errors in the CGC census if the same copies were re-graded and counted more than once on the census, but overall it shows reasonable empirical data that show GA comics are much scarcer than SA/BA comics. Supply and demand create a market, but add rarity into the mix and you have the unique Golden Age comic realm. Gerber's scarcity ratings in his 1989 *Photo Journals* were somewhat accurate in the pre-internet days. I would not expect the census numbers to double or triple in another ten years. We would be lucky to see a 10-20% increase.

As I suggested to Bob Overstreet last year regarding some additions to a few listings (*Action Comics* #7 – 1st time the word Superman printed on a cover, *Captain America Comics* #2 – 1st app. round shield), here are a few more books that I believe should be considered to be broken out (or adjusted) in the guide listings and have the following notes added to them:

Adventure Comics #46 (rare; 16 copies on CGC census) – Classic Sandman cover by Flessel
Detective Comics #13 (rare; 17 copies on CGC census) – Classic Speed Saunders cover by Flessel
Detective Comics #18 – Classic Fu Manchu cover by Flessel
More Fun Comics #32 – contains ad for *Action Comics* #1
USA Comics #8 (rare; 16 copies on CGC census)- Classic Schomburg Japanese plane cover; bondage-c

Golden Age: Ok, let's talk about Timelys! *Captain America Comics* #3 has been skyrocketing in demand the past several years now. I remember winning a VG copy from the Dentist off eBay in 2000 for $2,715. That copy is sitting in someone's vault right now, and is quickly approaching $20k in value. With all of Stan Lee's comic convention signature events and movie cameos, it's not a secret why *Cap* #3 is a hot book since it was his 1st work for Timely (Marvel) in 1941. In addition, it features a classic Schomburg Red Skull bondage cover, a rare yellow cover in the run, and Simon & Kirby interior art. I don't believe it is rare by GA standards (86 total copies on the CGC census), but I haven't seen many unrestored copies on the open market lately. Collectors and dealers have become bullish on prices and reluctant to sell. Stan Lee was fortunate to land his first work in a landmark title/character.

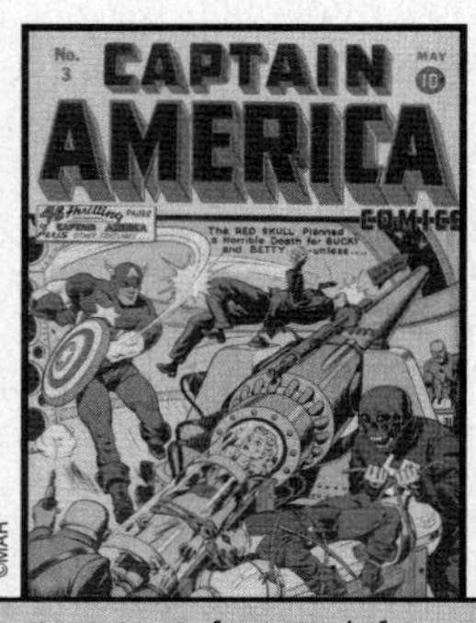

Stan Lee's first work for Timely (Marvel) makes ***Captain America Comics #3*** *quite an object of desire.*

Conversely, Jack Kirby's 1st signed work for Timely was a one shot book called *Red Raven Comics* #1 (August 1940). *RR* #1 certainly deserves more respect and demand, but it is sadly buried in other non-mainstream hero comics that don't have a Hollywood script. Joe Simon had just recruited a young Kirby from Fox to work with him and Martin Goodman. It is a tough book (41 total copies on the CGC census) and sports a fantastic cover by Kirby and two interior stories (Mercury and Comet Pierce) drawn and inked by the King himself. Goodman was doing so much cross marketing in 1940 to compete with other publishers, that he even included a few interior panels advertising the ground breaking battle between the Human Torch and Sub-Mariner (*Marvel Mystery Comics* #9, July 1940) that was currently on sale at the time. *RR* #1 is a must have for the Timely enthusiast or the Kirby fan.

Earlier in 2016, a friend sent me a listing on eBay for a low grade *Marvel Mystery Comics* #4. The book was from an original owner found in an Eastern Pennsylvania estate. The owner was selling his parents' home, and he found the book stashed away in a cupboard along with a few of his Archie comics. The *Marvel Mystery* #4 was the only superhero comic in the pile. I thought it was a cool story. I have not seen an unrestored, CGC *Marvel Mystery* #4 offered in the open market for quite some time. It's a wild, Goodman Timely featuring the 1st Sub-Mariner cover (by Schomburg) as he is attacking Nazi sailors with a metal wrench while saving a girl in bondage. This is also the 1st Nazi Timely cover presented in a pulp-like fashion, green colored sea, and a ship with a pink colored mast. However, without a Hollywood script, Sub-Mariner has lost appeal with the general masses. Only the true Timely fans can still appreciate the original mutant!

The rarity of Golden Age comics should never be underestimated. The market continues to be healthy with the strongest demand being for 1st appearances and classic, unique covers. There are not many unrestored copies of pre-1945 books left, so it is quite a treat to be able to find them in their original condition. Even if you can't afford or don't want to spend five figures on a *Cap* #1, *Superman* #1, or *Batman* #1, there are many other comics that are more affordable and could provide healthy returns such as: *Superman* #3, *Batman* #11,47, *Detective* #156, *Cap* #2,33, *Marvel Mystery* #15, and *Whiz* #18 (great train cover!).

If you are a new collector out there and aren't sure what GA to collect, I would highly recommend the 1989 *Gerber Photo Journal Guide to Comic Books* (Vol. 1 & 2). You can peruse over 20,000 cover images of GA comic covers that will grab your attention. This was the resource that *Suspense Comics* #3 was first given widespread exposure. In addition, if you want to study up on Timely Comics, I would point out George Olshevsky's 1979 article "The Origin of Marvel Comics" that was published in the 10th *Overstreet Price Guide*. The Olshevsky article has some valuable information and perspective on all the early Timely titles and points out the unique color and printing challenges Goodman had with *Marvel Comics* #1.

Silver Age: The *Doctor Strange* movie was surprisingly great! In fact, the following week I picked up a copy of *Strange Tales* #115 at Marc Newman's (House of Comics) Berkeley Con (great little show!) just so I could read the origin. It's a good thing Doctor Strange's origin is not in *Strange Tales* #110, because the #115 is still an affordable bargain and the origin is pretty close to the actual movie. Great movie and great read! The demand for *ST* #110 has been pretty consistent. I just wish Doctor Strange had a clean, full cover in the early *Strange Tales* run, but since he was a minor character at the time, he always shared a split cover with the Torch or Thing.

I'm a big fan of the early, 12-cent bubble Marvels… especially *FF*s. For the new SA collectors out there or for the seasoned dealers who have forgotten, there are many hidden gems (pin up pages and cool ads) in the early Marvels. Take a look and make sure to count those pages on raw books: *FF* #2 - Thing pin up; *FF* #3 - Torch pin up; *FF* #4 - Mr. Fantastic pin up; *FF* #5 - House ad for *Hulk* #1; *FF* #8 - Torch facts page; *FF* #9 - How the Torch flies page; *FF* #10 - Invisible Girl pin up; *FF* #11 - Subby pin up; *FF* #13 - House ad for *TOS* #39 & *ASM* #1; *Hulk* #2 - House ad for FF #5.

SA Marvels have the best stories and the keys can be quite liquid, but, truthfully, it is a bit tiring to see multiple copies of them in every auction and convention. Every 1st appearance of any character is now hoarded and placed in the spec box in anticipation of a future Hollywood movie. It is great to see books like *TTA* #13 out of the $1.00 bin and now on dealers' walls. But I am a firm believer that a bad movie should not decrease the value or demand of a popular character's 1st appearance or title. It will be interesting to see how the market continues to respond in 2017 to movies such as *Logan* (*Hulk* #181), *Guardians of the Galaxy* (*MSH* #18), *Wonder Woman* (*All Star* #8), *Spider-Man: Homecoming* (*AF* #15), and *Justice League* (*B&B* #28). My guess is that the blue chip keys will continue to be solid investments. If you are looking for a *Tales of Suspense* #39, try to get a copy that doesn't have the right edge quotation marks cut off. It's somewhat of a challenge to get a copy of that book with both sets of quotation marks clearly present. Also, finding a copy with more blue space under the table at the bottom left front cover can also be a challenge to find. Perhaps the greatest story of the Marvel Silver Age is the Galactus/Silver Surfer trilogy done by Lee & Kirby in *Fantastic Four* #48-50. Low grade copies are still cheap and readily available. Every comic fan should read that saga.

On the DC Silver front, *Detective Comics* #225 (1st Martian Manhunter) has cooled off a bit after some big sales in late 2015 and early 2016. *Action Comics* #252 (1st Supergirl) seems to have cooled significantly as well. *Adventure Comics* #210 (1st Krypto, the Superdog) still grabs me for some reason; maybe because it was released during the first month of the CCA code and is still one of the scarcer DC Silver keys. I still think *Showcase* #6 (1st Challengers) is an under-valued key as it is a pre-FF Kirby creation. The art on a *Showcase* #6 reminds me of Kirby FF panels for sure. *Green Lantern* #8 (1961) features a fantastic grey tone cover and one of the best SA DC stories I have read. I highly recommend grabbing that book while it is still affordable.

Lastly, I have noticed that some newer collectors are attempting to collect runs of Silver Age titles, and they avoid paying the big money for the keys (i.e. AF #15 and ASM #1) and go for the #2 - #300. Then they complain that they can never afford the big keys. Sometimes one has to complete runs to experience that quantity is not always satisfying. I would recommend that one should go for the big books first and then fill in their runs with popular covers or favorite villain appearances next. The good thing with Silver Age is that they are plentiful and they will always be available, so sell off those runs and focus on obtaining the key books first. You may be much happier owning 2 small boxes of quality key material instead of 12 boxes of semi complete runs with less key books.

Golden Age Sales and Purchases: *Adventure Comics* #46 CGC 1.0 $1,000; *Captain America Comics* #3 CGC 3.0 $11,995; *Daring Mystery Comics* #1 CGC 1.0 $1,200; *Daring Mystery Comics* #4 FR/GD $495; *Marvel Mystery Comics* #4 GD $2,130; *Marvel Mystery Comics* #5 (complete front and back covers only) $563; *More Fun Comics* #32 FAIR $250; *Mystic Comics* #5 FAIR (missing page) $300; *Red Raven Comics* #1 App GD+ (missing BC) $1,100; *USA Comics* #6 CGC 1.5 $1,472; *USA Comics* #10 CGC 2.5 $935; *USA Comics* #10 CGC 2.5 (restored) $675 and *Whiz Comics* #18 VG+ $500.

Silver Age Sales and Purchases: *Action Comics* #242 PGX 4.0 $1,550; *Adventure Comics* #210 CGC 3.5 $1,550; *Adventure Comics* #210 FAIR $340; *Adventure Comics* #247 CGC 2.0 $875; *Batman* #121 CGC 4.0 $850; *Detective Comics* #226 GD/VG $250; *Green Lantern* #8 FN/VF $175; *Incredible Hulk* #2 CGC 5.0 $1,250; *Showcase* #6 CGC 2.0 $250; *Showcase* #30 CGC 1.8 $170; *Strange Tales* #115 GD $35; *X-Men* #4 CGC 5.0 $550.

Bronze Age Sales and Purchases: *Amazing Spider-Man*

#121 CGC 4.0 $175; *Marvel Super Special* #16 CGC 9.0 $66; *Sgt. Rock* #329 (Whitman) FN/VF $110; *X-Men* #94 VG $150; *X-Men* #94 FN/VF $300.

Copper-Modern Age Sales and Purchases: *Harbinger* #1 NM $150; *X-Factor* #24 VG $8.

Which prices should come up: *Captain America Comics* #3 should be ranked higher than *Captain America Comics* #2 based on past and current price point sales. *Cap* 3s are selling for about $4k/point. Suggested listing in the *Guide* for GD2.0 should be $8,000 and VG4.0 $16,000. *Red Raven Comics* #1 - Since Stan Lee's 1st work for Timely (*Cap* 3) experiences a lot of demand and record sales, it's time Jack Kirby's 1st signed work for Timely get some much deserved recognition. My suggestion for listing in the *Guide* for GD2.0 should be $3000 and VG4.0 $6000. *USA Comics* #7 - I've seen incomplete copies sell for close to $1500. I witnessed an apparent GD/VG (amateur resto) copy sell at SDCC 2016 for close to $2,000. In the past I have sold a CGC 2.5 for $2,750 and purchased a raw copy in FR/GD for $1,500. My suggestion for listing in the *Guide* is GD2.0 $2,000 and VG4.0 $4,000. *USA Comics* #8 - in 25 years of collecting Gold, it is by far the rarest of the *USA* Cap covers. I think this issue should be broken out in the *Guide* listing as (scarce) and "a Classic Schomburg bondage Japanese plane cover." A CGC 2.5 brittle sold for $1700+, and I sold that same copy four years ago for $2,500. My suggestion for listing in the *Guide* is GD2.0 $1500 and VG4.0 $3,000.

Which prices should come down: *All-American Comics* #16 - should not be ranked higher than *Marvel Comics* #1, *Batman* #1, or *Captain America Comics* #1; *All-American Comics* #16 should still be in the top 10, but not the top 5 Golden Age books.

BEN LICHTENSTEIN
ZAPP COMICS

Greetings from the Garden State! The comic book biz continues to steam along and we're happy to contribute another market report. After 23 years in business, I look forward to my "job" every day!

Our 2 brick and mortar shops in Wayne and Manalapan continue to thrive, as back issue sales remain strong. I've stopped trying to predict a peak in sales, as the past 6 or 7 years have continued to post gains. We are focused on comics books, but also sell gaming cards, trading cards, action figures (new and vintage) and all things related. We enjoy buying and selling secondary market stuff, like back issues, single cards, vintage toys, etc.

On the new issue front, DC made a big splash with the Rebirth line, which rebooted their entire line-up. DC continues to be very retailer-friendly, with a cover price of $2.99 across the boards and also returnability for retailers. This allowed us to order very heavily with confidence.

Customer response was positive and we sold very high numbers of the first issues. Sales have continued as readers are enjoying the writing. Marvel continues to disappoint, with a disjointed editorial plan and high cover prices. There are lots of wonderful independent titles coming out, some showing legs, such as *Saga*, *Outcast*, *Southern Bastards*, and some fizzling out. Back issues of independents continue to be very hard to manage, with extreme volatility and short supply when a title takes off. *Walking Dead* has not slowed down at all. Sales are very strong on new and back issues.

Free Comic Book Day continues to be a winner, with big crowds enjoying our hobby and supporting us. As the online market continues to expand, customers are showing us that they still value getting out of the house and shopping in-person at their friendly neighborhood comic shop.

Local Comic Book Shop Day is a new event to promote brick and mortar shops. 2016 is the second year for this event and I'm hopeful that it gathers more steam.

Social media continues to be instrumental in communicating with our customers and marketing our shop. Without exaggeration, it is essential to our business.

My partner Corry Brown, with a help from the highly amusing Dave Potosnak, connects to our customers in real time with all the different digital platforms. Please check out Corry and Dave's Zapp Talk videos, Zapp Podcast and general Facebook mayhem-I promise you will be at least mildly amused.

Back Issues - Some trends we're noting: There is white-hot demand for Golden Age books, including the usual Batmans and Timelys, as well as the more obscure stuff. We're seeing much more demand now for these books, as many collectors have finished their Silver Age runs and are chasing the much rarer Golden Age stuff. Atomic Age also showed lots more interest.

Early *Action*s and *Detective*s, any Batman key, Joker covers, etc. all show amazing demand and price jumps. This has also pulled along prices and interest in lesser titles, as some of these books get out of range and buyers look at more affordable options. Many, many books are selling at multiples of *Guide*.

The stigma of restoration on Golden Age books is not nearly as important as Silver Age. A sizable Golden Age collection surfaced in my area and was pieced out to many dealers, including myself. It included nearly every major title from 1940s to 1950s. The owner of the collection had applied lots of unnecessary "conservation" including tape, glue, color, etc. Otherwise the books had beautiful eye appeal. We had many happy customers who are not bothered at all by the restoration and are happy to get scarce Golden Age books at a reasonable price. Sales were brisk, as we discounted from 30% to 60% off of unrestored prices. I sold nearly 100% of it in less than a month. Wish I had bought even more (sigh)....

In contrast, restoration on Silver Age, depending on type, has a large negative impact. For example, we bought a beautiful *Hulk* #1, which graded 8.0 trimmed from CGC. Unrestored: $70K. Trimmed top edge: $8,000 book. When I purchased it, I had to give the seller the bad news on an otherwise gorgeous book. The price hit is not at great for slight color touch but the general good supply of Silver Age means a buyer can afford to be picky.

I was happy to pick up many 1950s collections of DCs and sales were very strong. Copies with strong color strike and eye appeal sell very easily, with *Flash*, *Showcase*, *Wonder Woman* and *Batman* in particular selling the best. We're also seeing increased demand for the DC Sci-Fi stuff from the 1950s, which have often some cool covers, and are not easy to find in better than VG.

Pre-Hero Marvel continue to sell, but I am seeing some softening of demand if it's not a prototype book. I personally love these books, but it appears buyers are focusing on other areas this years.

Archies have picked up nicely, with new issues doing a little better and vintage books (especially pre-1960) really hot!

Silver Age and Bronze Age continue to sell, with prices on most books stabilizing.Not much new to report there. However, I am seeing prices increasing on most 1962/1963 Marvels. In particular, the first 10 issues of all major Marvel titles are showing even stronger pricing and demand, with no end in sight.

As usual, we're seeing the typical spikes in demand for first appearances of characters that are mentioned or introduced in movie and TV. The Netflix Marvel series have been very well received, with *Luke Cage*, *Daredevil*, *Jessica Jones* getting lots of heat. DC is really killing it with their TV series doing great, such as *Gotham*, *Arrow*, *Flash*, etc.

Batman v Superman and *Suicide Squad* were fun, but didn't have the same Marvel movie cohesiveness and continuity. As of this writing, *Doctor Strange* was just released and I thought it was very well done. *Doctor Strange* back issues have been selling steadily, whereas up to 2 years ago, they were near-unsalable.

Our business model is to offer fair, competitive pricing every day rather than price high and then run sales or specials. But, once a year, we hold our legendary pre-Black Friday sale, with big discounts on all back issues, TPBs and toys. This year was our best ever, as customers bought stacks and stacks of back issues. This shows a healthy interest in the hobby beyond just the usual eBay/Facebook flippers. We're very active buyers of collections and selling those non-key books is a must if we want to keep buying collections. Dealing only in keys is a tough gig, as buying individual key issues with even a small margin is tough to do consistently. It would be very difficult to restock our higher end stuff if I didn't purchase entire collections, so we really love it when the "bin" books move.

We attended several conventions this year. We're doing well at most conventions, with plenty of demand at all price levels. Lots of readers are filling in their runs of cheap stuff, and lots of middle buyers are digging in the bargain books for cheap Silver/Bronze, and there are the usual hordes of key issue buyers.

New York Comic Con is our biggest sales event. It continues to grow, with sales very solid on both the bin stock and the wall books.

A sampling of key books we moved this year: *Action* #252 $2,800; *Adventure Comics* #247 $3,000; *Batman* #227,232,244,251; *Brave & the Bold* #28 $2750; *Detective* #359,395,400,411,474; *Showcase* #7,9,13,14,20,22 and more. *Hulk* #181 (about 20 copies from 2.0 to 9.6) still my number one requested book.*Amazing Spider-Man* #1-101,121,122, 129 (about a dozen copies from 2.0 up to 9.8). *Tomb of Dracula* #10; *Werewolf By Night* #32 (multiple copies, could have sold many more). *X-Men* #1-14,94-142; and *Giant-Size X-Men* #1 (probably as hot as *Hulk* #181 right now, just not as expensive).

Other random observations: At the risk of repeating myself, *Batman* would easily be my best selling back issue if I could only find enough of the pre-1980 stuff.

Flash has heated up, with very high interest in both the new Rebirth title and vintage back issues. I could sell tons more *Flash* Silver and Bronze Age back issues if there was ample supply. It's one of my most requested titles right now.

Superman and related titles, in particular from 1962 to present are still very slow. I'm able to sell the Superman Family titles only at a steep discount, usually 60% to 75% below *Guide*. Pre-1960, though, sales are very strong, particularly if they ae 6.0 or higher.

1950s DCs are definitely hard to find above 4.0, so we have lots of buyers for even the weaker titles.

Amazing Spider-Man #252 and *Secret Wars* #8 have moved up in price and demand.

New Mutants #87 exploded, about doubling in value after Cable movie news hit.

New Mutants #98 peaked at $1,000 in 9.8, and as ample supply hits, has stabilized at $650. Raw copies sell quickly for $200 to $300.

Wonder Woman of all eras continue to sell very well, and the upcoming movie has only stoked the fires. This tied in with the increased interest in female characters in general. I can't get enough *Wonder Woman* before 1980!

While non-key issues of Bronze/Copper/Modern are abundant, we are seeing brisk sales when priced accordingly. "Box stock" does move well, but does need to be heavily discounted if in low to mid-grade, usually 40% to 70% off of *Overstreet*. Copies in 8.0 to 9.4, with nice eye appeal, which sell quickly at *Guide* or close to it. We believe in turning over our inventory and don't wish to run a museum. I'm known as a tight grader who prices realistically. This helps us sell more of the non-key issues as well as keys.

On the buying front, we've been busy. It is as competitive as ever, with more and more dealers entering the market and competing for collections. We were able to buy as much as last year, but it didn't come easily.

After some spirited bidding, we purchased a high-grade collection of late Silver to Bronze Age books. These were handpicked by a finicky buyer. Average condition 9.4 to 9.6

and many achieved 9.8, such as *Amazing Spider-Man* #129 and *Batman* #251 in 9.8. Several dealers remarked that this collection was of pedigree quality. Sales have been strong so far, showing plenty of interest in books with exceptional structure and eye appeal.

Pressing continues to grow, as it's no longer the trade secret that it once was. It seems everyone's pressing their own books, with mixed results. I do not do my own pressing, as I would prefer to pay others for the service. It has become a necessary part of the business but I'm judicious in what I choose to press. I often will sell a book un-pressed and leave a little money on the table if I don't think it's a sizable enough improvement.

Overall, sales in 2016 were up very nicely over 2015 and I would like to thank everyone who has bought from, or sold to us this year. I also want to thank my staff at Zapp, which I believe is the best team I've ever had the pleasure of working with.

Stephen Lipson
Collector

Not many people are aware that Canada published their own comics during the Golden Age. These wartime era comics hosted a stable of superheroes that where both analogous and indigenous to Canada. Such iconic heroes as Nelvana of the Northern Lights and her brethren spoke to Canada's role on both the Home front and smashing the Axis abroad.

These comics were published primarily from 1941-1946, as a result of the implementation of the War Exchange Conservation Act, wherein non-essential items were prohibited for import into Canada, including pulp literature. As a result, Canada started its own fledgling comic book industry.

These comics were essentially published with colour covers, with interiors that were published in black and white, in order to defray costly publishing expenses. Hence, these comics are now referred to as "Canadian Whites" by both collectors and historians alike. That said, the very early issues of *Wow Comics* published by Bell Features and the very early issues of *Better Comics* published by Maple Leaf sport colour interiors.

The first publisher was Maple Leaf Publishing books out of Vancouver, BC such as *Better Comics*, *Rocket Comics*, *Bing Bang Comics* and *Lucky Comics*. The aforementioned Maple Leaf comics introduced the first Canadian superhero in *Better Comics* #1 in March of 1941 (The Iron Man). Maple Leaf comics are deemed to be the scarcest and command a premium when changing hands. Anglo American (Double "A") Publishing in Toronto introduced Freelance and a host of Fawcett derived characters to Canada, including Captain Marvel and Spy Smasher. The next publisher was Bell Features in Toronto with Johnny Canuck, Nelvana, the Penguin and Thunderfist, etc. in such flagship titles as *Dime Comics*, *Triumph Comics*, *Active Comics*, and *Commando Comics.* Finally, Educational Projects out of Montreal, Quebec introduced Canada Jack in its flagship title, *Canadian Heroes*.

It is important to note that these vestiges of Canadian Pop Culture helped create a Canadian identity within their pages. Canada Jack was an athlete that battled the 5th column saboteurs on the Canadian home front in *Canadian Heroes* comic books. While he was not larger than life and not endowed with super powers, the Canadian youth of the Second World War at home could emulate and subsequently identify with Canada Jack. This sort of homegrown sentiment could also be likened to Johnny Canuck, who while also was not larger than life, helped smash the Axis abroad, including Hitler.

Nelvana was the first superhero with a Canadian national identity, and graced the pages of *Triumph Comics*. In fact, Nelvana pre-dated Wonder Woman by almost four months! She came to aid of the indigenous peoples of the North West Territories in her early appearances, and could fly along the Aurora Borealis.

Sadly, the War Exchange Conservation Act was repealed in 1946, and subsequently American comic books were allowed to be imported into Canada. Hence, Captain America and Superman and their brethren replaced their Canadian counterparts in full colour for only a dime. This ushered in the demise of the "Canadian Whites", as the floundering industry could no longer complete. The last ditch efforts to produce Canadian homegrown comics in full color just did not stand up against their American predecessors Subsequently, many of the publishing houses in Canada folded, including Anglo-American publishing, Maple Leaf Publishing, and eventually Bell Features.

2016 was a pivotal year for Canadian Golden Age comic books (AKA: Canadian Whites) in terms of not only prices realized at auction, but new unseen rarities coming to light.

One such remarkable discovery was an obscure comic/pulp was published in Toronto by Victory Publishing entitled *Victory* in May 1941. On its cover is a rather crude rendering of an unknown Canadian costumed superhero named Rock Thunder by none other than Ted Steele. Ted was a prolific artist in the Bell Features publishing stable in Toronto during the war years. He contributed such characters such as Speed Savage (the White Mask) for *Triumph Comics.* Rock Thunder currently remains an enigma. However, some information has come to light regarding this elusive book and I would suggest that albeit a pulp, it is significantly historic in the realm of Canadian Golden Age pop culture for a few reasons:

ROCK THUNDER....1st Canadian costumed superhero rendered by Ted Steele after Wolf Savage in April 1941. Rock appeared a scant two months after Canada's first superhero appeared in *Better Comics* # 1 in March of 1941 named Iron Man by Vern Miller.

This hero preceeded Nelvana, Johnny Canuck, Freelance, Thunderfist, et al. In fact, Rock Thunder may have been a crude prototype of the White Mask, (AKA Speed Savage).

The book screams Canadian, right down to the Maple Leaf on Rock Thunder's Chest. The costume with the boots, gloves, and the two guns are similar to that of the later costume donned by Speed Savage. The title is emblazoned with the colors of the Union Jack, that was contemporaneously Great Britain's flag. Remember, Canada was a British commonwealth nation in 1941.

The tome is both fascinating and über-rare, with only one other known copy in existence in a private collection. *Victory* is an esoteric book that is now only coming to light as a hidden gem in the arena of the Canadian Golden Age of comics.

The Canadian Golden Age **Victory #1** in CGC 5.0 sold for $2175.

In Spring of 2016, Comiclink accepted a consignment of roughly 300 Canadian Whites by an anonymous consignor that are being auctioned off over several auctions into 2017. Some of the prices realized have been stunning. The highlights speak volumes (pun intended)

Notable 2016 Canadian Golden Age Comic Sales Via Auction: *Robin Hood* #1 Uncertified $3399.00; *Victory* #1 CGC 5.0 $2175.00; *Nelvana* NN CGC 5.0 $14750.00; *Triumph Comics* #7 CGC 2.0 $9000.00; *Dime Comics* #1 CGC 3.5 $5800.00; *Commando Comics* #1 CGC 0.5 wrong back cover $3000.00; *Triumph-Adventure Comics* #4 CGC 0.5 3.0 $2600.00; and *Wow Comics* #18 CGC 2.5 $3600.00

Notable 2016 Personal Sales: *Marvel Mystery* 128 Page Timely Annual Uncertified Extensive professional Restoration $7800.00; *Jewish War Heroes* # 2 Uncertified $2700.00 and *Weird Suspenstories* # 1 CGC 6.5 $3500.00

Based on the aforementioned auction results and personal sales, it looks like prices are strong across the board and show no signs of slowing down. Scarcity and Demand are the driving factors. It should be interesting to see if the prices come out of the stratosphere in 2017.

DOUG MABRY
THE GREAT ESCAPE

Greetings once again from Tennessee and Kentucky! The comic market continues to plug along pushed forward by other media. But how long can that last? At some point, TV and movies will have mined every minor character ever created, and first appearances seem to be what's driving the market right now. In fact, the back issue market seems to consist in the largest part of people trying to find first appearances no matter how obscure. Except for Batman, X-Men, and Spider-Man, this year has been slow for people putting together runs. But the comic market is nothing if not cyclical, and who knows what next year will bring?

While back issue sales have been steady in terms of dollars, if not units moved, the new comic market has slowed a bit this year. DC's Rebirth reboot has not caught the public's imagination like the New 52 did. In fact, it seemed to be a great jumping off point for many of our customers. It could be that people find themselves disenfranchised after investing so much energy in the books for them to be rebooted so often, it could be that the stories just don't appeal to them as much, or it could be some other factor like the economy. Whatever the case, Rebirth has not achieved like the New 52.

Marvel, however, continues to move along at a pretty consistent pace. In particular, the Netflix series seem to have translated into sales of those characters more than even the movies have. The consistent quality of the Marvel Cinematic Universe has kept their comics as relevant as ever. Now let's talk about some specifics.

Golden Age: This has been a pretty strong area for us this year. We've gotten in more Golden Age than we have since the Great Recession in 2008-2010. And the prices on the more sought after books have really increased in the last year. I monitor prices in this area pretty closely, and I've seen substantial increases in demand and price on things like the Better/Standard/Nedor line. In particular, the esoteric super-hero comics are bringing way over *Guide* in many cases. MLJ books have always been tough to find and pricey, but low grade copies are through the roof. Also hot are the Ace comics like *Super-Mystery*, *Prize Comics*, and Harvey's *Speed Comics*. On the other hand, I've seen a bit of a softening for pre-Code horror this year. I was able to purchase a couple of the most sought after horror covers for substantially less than in the past few years, and we've had a few that have sat on the walls here for a few months before selling. Of course, the pre-Code horror market seems to go through these swings every few years, so it's really nothing new.

Silver Age: Silver Age books, on the other hand, have been disappearing into collections and not coming back out. While we've managed to acquire a good bit, including lots of keys, we just aren't seeing the quantities that we used to see, much less any big runs. On the other hand, some of the DC Silver Age that we have haven't been moving much, so we still have a lot of it in stock. At least in our area, titles like *Action*, *Adventure*, *Metal Men*, *Mystery In Space*, *House Of Mystery*, *World's Finest*, *Lois Lane*, *Superboy*, and *Jimmy Olsen* are much slower sellers.

Bronze Age: This seems to be the hottest and most volatile market at the moment. There are still enough books out there to be had, but few enough to cause lots of demand. And everyone is looking for the first appearances of overlooked characters that are plentiful in these books.

Modern Age: The '90s are finally back! We can't keep back issues of *Spawn* in stock! It's now been twenty-six years since 1990, and for lots of the current collectors, that was the stuff they grew up with. We've started selling lots of 1980s and '90s titles that we had even quit stocking for awhile. I can't keep any of the first series of *Suicide Squad* in stock, and when I do find them they're usually rough from being thrown into quarter boxes for years. But I've even had people putting together runs of *Firestorm* and *New Mutants*.

Well, that's to overview. And now on to some sales of note:

Platinum Age: *Little Orphan Annie* #1, VG, $100, #2, VG, $75.00, #3, VG, $75.00, #4, VG+, $80.00, #5, Fine, $90.00, *Smitty* #1, VG, $100.00, #4, GD, $45.00, *Smokey Stover* #1, Fine, $150.00.

Golden Age: *Action* #114, FR, $30.00, #176, GD, $75.00, *Adventure* #121, FR, $30.00, *All-New Comics* #5, GD, $150.00, *America's Best Comics* #9, VG, $210.00, #19, GD/VG, $100, *Batman* #24, FN-, $500.00, #46, GD, $100, #69, GD, $175.00, *Captain Marvel Adventures* #33, FN, $155.00, *Detective* #59, VG, $500.00, *Doll Man* #38, GD, $40.00, #37, VG, $110.00, *Exciting Comics* #63, GD, $80.00, *Hand Of Fate* #18, GD-, $25.00, *Haunted Thrills* #11, GD, $45.00, *House Of Mystery* #1, FR, $100.00, *Joe Palooka* #1, FN, $160.00, *Power Comics* #4, GD-, $140.00, *Superman* #23, GD, $325.00, #65, FN, $325.00, *Suspense* #12, VG+, $75.00, *Tarzan* #1, FN, $350.00, *Teen-Age Romances* # 21, GD-, $48.00, *True Crime* #3, VG, $300.00, *Vic Torry and His Flying Saucer* #1, $100.00, *Wonder Woman* #49, FR, $75.00, #75, GD+, $100.00, #91, VG, $130.00, *World's Finest* #71, PR/FR, $202.00, and we had a nice run of *Wings* from #60-64 and a #94, VG, $136.00.

Silver Age: *Amazing Adult Fantasy* #9, VG, $88.00, 14, VG, $100.00, *Amazing Spider-Man* #6, CGC 2.5, $210.00, #13, VG+, $300.00, #15, VG, $200.00, #19, VG, $75.00, #21, VG+, $100.00, #25, VG-, $70.00, #26, VG/FN, $100.00, *Avengers* #5, GD, $50.00, *Captain America* #117, VF $225.00, *Fantastic Four* #4, GD, $400.00, #5, VG, $1000.00, #7, GD-, $125.00, #16, GD, $70.00, #18, GD, $55.00, #18, VG, $90.00, #20, GD, $54.00, #48, GD, $167.00, #50, VG, $100.00, #52, GD, $89.00, *House Of Secrets* #92, VG, $180.00, *Iron Man* #1, VG, $200.00, *Journey Into Mystery* #86, VG, $200.00, *Marvel Super-Heroes* #12, VG, $100.00, *Sgt. Fury* #1, GD+, $600.00, *Silver Surfer* #1, VG, $109.00, *Strange Tales* #101, GD-, $150.00, #101, GD, $175.00, #103, VG, $75.00, *Uncanny X-Men* #3, GD, $130.00.

Bronze Age: *Amazing Spider-Man* #129, VF $700.00, *Ghost Rider* #1, VG, $73.00, *Giant-Size X-Men* #1, GD-, $125.00, #1, FN, $450.00, *Iron Man* #55, FN+, $400.00, #55, VF, $600.00, #55, FN+, $450.00, *Werewolf By Night* #32, FN, $462.00.

Modern Age: *Amazing Spider-Man* #601, Near Mint, $50.00, #606, NM, $40.00, #607, NM, $50.00, #300, FN, $125.00, #300, FN+, $147.00, *Batman Adventures* #12, VG, $60.00, *Batman* V2 #1, NM, $100.00, #1 (Variant), NM, $100.00, *Batman: Mad Love* #1, NM, $70.00, *Deadpool* V2 #1, NM, $70.00, *Evil Ernie* #1, VF/NM, $85.00, *Grimm Fairy Tales* #1 (Philly Variant), NM, $90.00, *New Mutants* #98, FN/VF, $133.00, *Revival* #1, CGC 9.8, $50.00, *Marvel Super Hero Secret Wars* #8, NM, $65.00, *Sons Of Anarchy* #1, CGC 9.8. $40.00, *Walking Dead* #1, NM, $1500.00, #2, NM $400.00, #2 (signed), NM, $400.00, #3, NM, $200.00, #19, NM, $280.00, #27, NM, $120.00, #100, NM, $30.00, *Wolverine* V.2 #1, NM, $55.00, *X-Factor* #6, NM, $100.00.

We also acquired several pages of Gene Colan original art from the first issue of the *Howard The Duck* magazine that sold from $450.00 to $725.00.

That's it for this year! If you're in the area, stop in and see us!

Jon McClure
Collector

Greetings from Portland, Oregon! Sales this year on eBay were slow at times, but sales from Black Friday to December 5th include *Batman* #96 VG- (minor restoration) for $80 , #109 VG $95, #153 VF- $149, #157 FN+ $110, #357 NM for $140, #181 FN $295, *Daredevil* #3-5 set in GD for $149, *Detective* #198 VG- $175, #216 GD/VG *Justice League of America* #9 VG $110, *Marvel Premiere* #15 (Marvel value stamp out) G/VG for $45, *Speed Carter Spaceman* #2-5 GD/VG set $275, *Tales of Suspense* #4 GD for $75, *World's Finest* #80 (minor amateur restoration) $70, #94 VG $150, *X-Men* #3 VG- $175, #12 VG- (minor tape) $99, and #13 F+ $149.

Low to mid-grade Marvels of any kind starting at $5 sold in antique malls at 135% *Guide* or higher. Double *Guide* was not uncommon to receive from speculators and collectors looking for undervalued and overlooked titles. Comics sometimes sell in person that just won't move online, even at a fraction of the cost, and reminding buyers that such books are forty years old can help close a deal. *Walking Dead* has slowed a bit since season seven's "head smashing" episode as it turned off many longtime readers and watchers. Can't say I disagree as Glenn's death, in my view, was unnecessary and inappropriate, and he was a highly relatable character going back to season one. Most customers watch as well as collect, so when one goes, the other feels it. I'm a small sampling so others may have had a very different retail response.

DCs were slow to move this year in general except for key issues. Archies sold well overall. I sold less low grade Dells this year except for Western titles in the $5 to $15 range at an average of 100% *Guide*, with Westerns bringing about 60-75% *Guide*. Charlton Romance sales slowed this year, with low to mid-grade copies selling in the $5 to $15 range, although with no resistance to $20 and up on VF or better copies. Comic sales in general were slightly up (regardless of publisher) from last year, with TV and movie tie-ins keys impossible to keep in stock.

Marvel Type 1 test market cover price variants continue to break record sales results that are well above the listed values of easy to find Bronze Age key books such as *Incredible Hulk* #181(11/74) listed in *OPG* #46 at $3000 in raw 9.2 NM- . The highest recorded sale for a 9.4 *Star Wars* #1 35 cent variant is currently $26,290! Type 1 variants lead the herd in demand due to scarcity because such variants were not created to be collectible. Publisher experiments in the 20th century repeatedly birthed Type 1 cover price variants immediately before universal price hikes, such as the shift from 10 to 12 cents per copy that occurred in January 1962, and the 25 cent to 30 cent shift famously embodied by the Marvel variants cover dated 4-8/1976 and from 30 to 35 cents for variants cover dated 6-10/1977. Despite much heckling back in the day from fellow advisors and critics, when I discovered and publicized the existence of the Marvel cover price variants in August 1997, such comics have soared in popularity and value. For a history of comic book variants from the Golden Age to the present, as well as a list of known variants and a lexicon of variant types, with examples that continue to evolve and expand, refer to my article from 2010 in the *Overstreet Comic Book Price Guide* #40, "A History of Publisher Experimentation and Variant Comic Books," pages #1010-1038.

Marvel Type 1 test market cover price variants are absolutely the hottest Bronze Age books pursued by collectors and speculators, with some comics realizing prices of 40 or more times than the same non-variant issues, and often double digit multiples of listed *Guide* values! Auction results on Marvel test market variants can fluctuate wildly. Key books listed by the *Guide* in the top 10 Gold, Silver and Bronze Age categories are there due to consistent sales and demand, and two of the top Bronze Age comics are 35 cent variants. With the *Iron Fist* Netflix show coming out in March 2017, the already hot *Iron Fist* #14 35 cent variant should get a bump.

The ratio of regular 30 cent copies of *Star Wars* #1 in CGC 9.4 NM to 9.8 NM/M (there are over 2000) to the 35 cent variant of #1 is 200 to 1, according to the CGC census. Roughly twenty certified 35 cent copies exist in NM 9.4 or better, of which two certified copies exist in CGC 9.6 NM+ condition to date. One CGC 9.6 NM+ 35 cent variant sold in June 2015 on ComicLink for $36,500! The highest graded examples of Marvel variants are bringing truly astronomical prices at auction.

Archie 15 cent Type 1 cover price variants now have over 80% confirmed to exist, so I feel confident that all 112 issues will eventually surface. Doug Sulipa and I estimate that such 15 cent variants are about 500 times or scarcer than their 12 cent counterparts. In 2015 the few 15 cent variants that changed hands went for only about 2-3 times *Guide* of 12 cent editions when they changed hands at all. In 2015, the sci/fi and monster 1961-1962 regular 12 cent issues sold for about 3-5 times *Guide*, so the 15 cent variants of these books should logically be higher in value. It's difficult to nail down actual worth when such items are rarely change hands, and the listings do not appear in the *Guide* yet, although collectors and dealers are well aware. I believe all 15 cent Archie Type 1 cover price variants have enormous investment potential, especially the three super-keys: *Archie's Madhouse* #22(10/62), *Archie's Girls Betty and Veronica* #75(3/62) and *Josie* #1(2/63).

Sixteen different Type 1 Charlton 15 cent test market cover price variants from March 1962 may be out there, but currently *Space War* #15(3/62) and *Texas Rangers* #32(3/62) are the only two examples confirmed to exist. Such 15 cent variants are so scarce and unknown to collectors that no sales have ever been reported, and only four total copies are confirmed to exist(three #32s and one #15). No additional 15 cent variants surfaced in the last year, and real value is difficult to judge without any money changing hands. I find such cusp era variants interesting and hope collectors will share acquisitions with me and/or the *Guide* so I can disseminate the information.

U.S. published Type 1a cover price variants simultaneously published for foreign distribution are increasing in demand according to Doug Sulipa. Bronze and Copper Age Marvel and to a lesser extent DC Type 1a Canadian cover price variants are now routinely selling for 150-400% *Guide*, and select CGC high grade key issues of popular characters have been bringing 400-2000% of *Guide*; such books are at least 10 times scarcer due to low print runs. Canada's population is about 10% of the US population, thus about 10% of all Print Runs are Canadian copies, however roughly 80% of the surviving copies are Direct Editions, bought in comic shops and saved by collectors. Most of the Newsstand editions were bought by non-collecting readers, with a much lower survival rate, and most are well read FR/GD to FN/VF copies. Most VF/NM or better Type 1a Canadian Newsstand Cover Price Variants are 50 to 300 times scarcer than their US Direct Market counterparts in high grade; randomly checking the CGC census will substantiate this for most items. High grade examples from the Silver and Bronze age of Type 1a variants are scarcer still, largely due to damages that occurred in transit, and in particular water damage found on pence editions shipped overseas. Such difficulties predate contemporary standard procedures like simultaneous off-site printing, a reality that renders the concept of origination meaningless, at least for modern books. Marvel collectors dominate about 75% of the Type 1a Canadian cover price and British pence variant market, while DC and the others split the remaining 25%, with non-DC books accounting for less than 10% of total sales, a ratio that steepens when you hit the 1990s, when Type 1a cover price variants that don't say Marvel or at least DC have yet to show any real pulse outside of key issues.

Interest is increasing in the five DC pence issues that exist from the early Bronze Age: *Action* #402(7/71), *Adventure* #408(7/71), *Detective* #413(7/71), *Flash* #208(8/71), and *Superman's Pal Jimmy Olsen* #139(7/71). *Action* #402, *Detective* #413, and *Flash* #208 have Neal Adams covers, and the *Flash* issue is a 52 page Giant, so such books have attractive qualities beyond just being Type 1a variants, and can bring 300-400% *Guide* or more than cents editions. Interest is also increasing in DC pence editions published from March 1978 to September 1981, and such books often bring double *Guide* or more.

Dell Canadian and U.K. Type 1a cover price editions are being collected more, and currently sell at at a modest premium of 125-150% of standard cents editions. Western Publishing's Type 1a Canadian 75 cent cover price variants of 60 cent Whitmans from 1984 sell briskly at 300-400% *Guide* due to extremely low print runs, according to Doug Sulipa, who states that he has a waiting list for any copies in Fine Plus or better condition. It should be noted that alleged copies of 1983 Type 1a 75 cent Whitman variants do not exist. Whitman pre-pack comics dated 8-12/1980 are red hot sellers due to scarcity and bring $100-$500 or more in Very Fine or better condition. Some dealers have been trying to sell GD/VG copies of the 8-12/1980 Gold Key comics with asking prices of $500 to $1000, which is too much for the market to bear and discourages some collectors from pursuing such scarce books at all as they cannot afford to collect them or complete sets, and also collectors can get more bang for their buck elsewhere. That said, consider a different and more sensible sale, such as the ultra-scarce *Black Hole* #4(9/80), the highest graded copy, selling in CGC 9.8 for a stunning $6250 on 2/21/2014! Refer to my article, "The Whitman Mystery," in *Comic Book Marketplace* magazine #85-86(9-10/01) for the strange story behind what caused the scarcity of Gold Key/Whitman comics dated 1980-1984 and their untimely demise!

Early Marvel Direct Sale Editions are scarcer and sell for an average of 200-300% of regular newsstand editions according to Doug Sulipa; such books were sometimes erroneously referred to as "Marvel Whitmans" due to their simultaneous distribution in department and drug stores in Whitman bags. Early Marvel Direct Market Editions have a duality of purpose, and thus have the unique honor of being "special market editions" that required a secondary market to help justify the cost of their existence in smaller print runs. The Direct Sales market was in its infancy, and Marvel wanted to monitor retailers' return credits, hence the confusion surrounding the odd but necessary difference in appearance between such books and their newsstand counterparts. Short gaps in production occurred from 2/1977 to 5/1979, as it cost less for Marvel to roll the dice against bogus returns than over-produce books erratically purchased by chain retailers. All early Direct Market Editions were produced except for the cover dates 1-3/1978, 7/1978, and 3-4/1979, and such comics are sought after largely by hardcore Marvel collectors and completists.

Collectibles have long been a hedge against inflation. Thoughtful buyers and speculative investors of comic books usually enjoy a faster, higher return than slower liquid investments. Sell your books while they are hot!

TODD MCDEVITT
NEW DIMENSION COMICS

First a little background on me to support why the folks at Overstreet deem my ranting worthy of some space in *The Guide*. I just celebrated my 30th year of opening my 1st store. I've been dealing in comics for over half my life. Now, I'm up to 6 store locations in the Pittsburgh, PA region. I also attend a lot conventions in the northeast especially. If I can drive there, I get there! Where I'm a bit weaker in online. I don't sell much there because I don't need to. All the great collections I buy get gobbled up by my store customers, and I take highlights on the road to the conventions. In fact, I'm very often pursuing collections while I travel. I've been accused of being the Amercan Pickers of comics especially when I roll up in my similar looking cargo van. The difference is that I don't usually "pick" because I want to buy it all!

This past year has been filled with pregnant pauses. Comics have spiraled upwards again. But when will the bubble burst? Record prices continue to be set. I've even had folks offer me big collections at a pricey premium saying that "these are going to be worth more soon". They might be right, but that's not how this works. While most comics are trending up, some have faltered. *Thor* #344 was a solid $25 book for a good while, and while it's the 1st Malekith, a big part of me saw this jump in price and said "who cares?". Plus, this is deep enough into the popular Walt Simonson run that orders would have increased, so there are plenty out there. I may be a prophet since I priced 2 this week at $12. The dips seem to come when the speculation doesn't pay off. By the time this sees ink, Moon Knight may or may not be a Netflix hit. Today, I priced a #1 at $25. This was a $3 book a year ago. I sold a *Werewolf By Night* #32 (FN/VF) for $500 recently as well. Good luck, Moon Knight!!

Bulk buying: I had a guy call me this week with an unopened CASE of *Daredevil* #181 for sale. I just bought a collection with 3 of this book this week. I keep pricing it at $25 and it keeps moving, but it is not something I really need 200 copies of.

Folks are reaching that age where they want to simplify their lives and cash in their collections. I almost prefer dealing with them. Guys that have been collecting for years get how the process works. They understand the market, the hobby, and my role in it. Often, they are very reasonable about what price to sell their collection for. Sure, they can do it the hard way and likely make more, but that takes time, effort, and a giant learning curve. And they know that and are happy to part with them into my fold. I'm at a point in my career that guys I have been selling to for decades are now ready to sell them and I'm flattered they think highly enough of me to continue supporting New Dimension Comics.

This past year I attended more comicons (apparently this is now a real word) than ever. It's always great to hit the road, enjoy a new town, buy some collections, and meet with friends and peers. Plus, it's been interesting to watch this scene evolve in recent years. Cons used to be a meeting of fans and collectors seeking to immerse themselves even deeper into the hobby. They are still there, but so are new factions. Families, cosplayers, celebrity autograph hounds. But, these are not folks looking to dig for an obscure back issue. So, I often have a choice when I vend at these. Do I just bring a traditional selection of long boxes of comics and a display wall of vintage goodies? Or, do I bring items with popular appeal for the masses? Sometimes I do both. This new breed of con attendee is browsing. They will stroll the aisles to see what comicon is all about. So, if you can catch their eye with a popular thing, you can make a few bucks. "Few" is they key word. They may already be down on funds from admission costs or autograph fees. My best seller last year? Pokémon comics for $3-6. At one show, I made about $1000 on these while my *Hulk* #181 sat on my display rack unloved.

Cosplay may be creating the collectors of the future. Many veteran dealers are annoyed by these folks. They clutter up the aisles and don't spend money on traditional comics much. The joke is that they don't have pockets, so they don't have anywhere to carry money. But, they are there. They are dipping into the hobby. It's a new way to turn kids onto comics. They may just be gathering in hallways and taking selfies for now, but some them will embrace comics all the way. Ten years from now, they will be out of college and starting career jobs, so they will have money rolling in. Some small percentage of cosplayers will become collectors. A guy who dressed up as Deadpool might become nostalgic for that *New Mutants* #98 that they could not afford when he was younger and chase one down. I had a gal dressed as a Vulcan buy a Gold Key *Star Trek* from me that she planned to frame.

Steve Mortensen
Miracle Comics

2016 was another great year for comics in all genres. I was surprised to see the surge in post-2000, "Millennial Age," comics. Led by issues like *Walking Dead* #1 and *Saga* #1 as well as Copper/Modern Age stalwarts like *New Mutants* #98, *Batman Adventures* #12, *New Teen Titans* #2, and *Teenage Mutant Ninja Turtles* #1, the high-end (9.8+) market has exploded. *New Mutants* #98 sells for $600 in 9.8 and $7,500 in 9.9; *Batman Adventures* #12 sells for $2,000 in 9.8; *New Teen Titans* #2 sells for $600 in 9.8; *Teenage Mutant Ninja Turtles* #1 (1st Print) sells for $27,000 in 9.8. *Walking Dead* #1 has been selling for $3,000 in 9.8 and $14,000 in 9.9. *Saga* #1 has shown great potential and had a big surge in 2016. It sells for $400 in 9.8 and the variant edition sells for $1,500 in 9.8.

Wonder Woman's first appearance in *All Star Comics* #8 has been very strong. The first appearances of the triad of Batman, Superman, and Wonder Woman are seeing their prices rise with the impact of the movies (*Batman v Superman*, *Wonder Woman* - 2017). *All Star Comics* #8 (December 1941) sold for $411,000 in 9.0 in April 2015. This issue came out the same month as the Pearl Harbor bombing that brought the country into World War II. This past December 7 marked the 75th anniversary of Pearl Harbor, which also launched an explosion of comics that were popular with the troops. During the war, comics served a dual role of providing entertainment to the troops and spreading war-related messages like "The Red Cross Needs Your Support." *Action Comics* #1 (June 1938) sold for $3.2 million in the same grade in 2014 and *Detective Comics* #27 (May 1939) sold for $1 million in 2010 in 8.0. There is still a wide gap in prices, however *All Star Comics* #8 has seen a 35% gain in 5.5 since 2014 ($45,000 in 2014 to $65,000 in 2016).

Luke Cage *Hero for Hire* and *Marvel Spotlight* #5 (1st Ghost Rider) have seen some incredible numbers in 9.8 condition. In February of 2016, Luke Cage *Hero for Hire* #1 sold for $24,000 in 9.8. It last sold in 2014 for $6,102 in 9.8 – a 293% increase in price. Luke Cage has been a highly popular character recently, partly due to the new TV show. *Marvel Spotlight* #5 in 9.8 last sold for $48,500 in October of 2016. The previous sale was in 2013 when the book sold for $13,145. In 2016, Luke Cage *Hero for Hire* #1 had a NM- 9.2 *Guide* value of $900 and *Marvel Spotlight* #5 had a NM- 9.2 *Guide* value of $950. This shows the incredible power of third-party grading on high-end comics.

Suicide Squad was a popular movie this year. Its Silver Age first appearance in *Brave and the Bold* #25 has shot up in value since the movie was announced. In 2015, a copy in 9.2 sold for $25,000. Low grade Good copies sold in the $700 range in 2016.

Speaking of *Suicide Squad*, one of my and my daughter's favorite characters is Killer Croc. We like to buy toys and comics of him and it has become a bonding experience for us. His physical characteristics have morphed over the years. He first took the form of a WWE wrester that had the skin of a lizard (1983). Newer versions of the character make him more alligator-like with the form of a massive, man-eating monster. There are several issues that claim the first appearance of Killer Croc. *Detective Comics* #523 is the earliest with a cameo appearance (February 1983). That issue sells in 9.8 for $100. *Batman* #357 is next, also with a cameo appearance (March 1983). That issue sells in 9.8 for $500. It is also the first appearance of Jason Todd. *Batman* #358 is considered Croc's first full appearance (April 1983) and it sells in 9.8 for $300. Croc's first cover appearance is *Detective Comics* #525 (April 1983) and it sells in 9.8 for $100. This cover shows him from the back arising out of the sewers. His first cover appearance in *Batman* is issue #359 (May 1983) and it sells in 9.8 for $165. That is the first time we see him from the front on a comic book cover with an array of villains around him. This is the iconic cover that fans associate with his first appearance.

An early Killer Croc cameo and Jason Todd's debut make **Batman** #357 a strong seller.

In closing, a note about buying and selling: I purchased several collections this year and passed on many others. I've found the adage of "buy what you know" also applies to "sell what you know." Recently, a friend of mine gave me a referral for a collection. The owner purchased storage lockers and was looking to offload a collection he found in a locker he bought. He had no idea what he was selling and unknowledgeable on the prices of comics. In addition, he did not understand condition. To the novice eye, a Fine comic looks like a Near Mint comic under the presentation of a bag and board. As mentioned above, the prices are far apart. I wasn't expecting a Near Mint collection, however, I buy in bulk and sometimes take my chances on what will pass a 9.8 pre-screen. I specialize in 1980s-current comics, which are best purchased in larger quantities. I made him a fair offer but he refused, thinking that he had something of great value. I've found some of my best deals over the years have come from fellow dealers who understand condition and prices.

The excitement is all in the hunt. This hobby has given me great satisfaction over my 30+ years of collecting. The community that exists in the hobby is very supportive and passionate about collecting. I'm looking forward to 2017 and what lies ahead for the comic market.

Marc Nathan
Cards, Comics and Collectibles
Baltimore Comic-Con

This hasn't been an easy year for new comics, but some Gold, Silver and Bronze Age titles have thrived.

New Comics: It was a tough year for new books based on missed opportunities from publishers, but DC Comics came through in the middle of the year with Rebirth. Rebirth sold very well – while Marvel Comics titles currently this year did not sell that well for lots of reasons. Some of that was due to late shipping, with delayed roll outs of new number ones. Marvel did have some hits this year; Black Panther was certainly a hit. It was easy to see that was going to happen. Here we are, though, on Thanksgiving weekend and the *Civil War II* event has not even come close to an ending. That was a summer event – *Civil War II* #1 came out in May. It seems like the number of titles coming out of the event; the future of the Marvel Universe, people are tired of already. It's dragged on too long.

It seems that Marvel is starting their titles over regardless of what title it is because of new creative teams and story arcs. If you look at older volumes of trade paperbacks, say *Daredevil* for instance, and you look at the numbering for the Brian Bendis run and the Ed Brubaker run, they were sequential issues of the comics, but they were volumes #1 #2, #3, and #4. So, I think publishers are treating the monthlies the same way they are treating the trades by publishing the comics (via) different volumes – which is that a new creative team gets a new number one and a new direction. It seems like that's how they are doing it.

From this time last year, one new publisher that shows it's achieving above the rest is Aftershock. And, it's still growing. Every title that they release should be here for the long haul because Aftershock is making some very good comics, with a couple of breakaway hits. The whole line should be looked at. They are a very good publisher, and I hope they are around forever.

BOOM! Studios has been producing quality comics this year like *Strange Fruit*, *Klaus*, *Skybourne*, *The Woods* and *Goldie Vance* – all of which are great four-color hits that sell very well to readers. Valiant Entertainment also makes some very good, underrated books.

Image Comics chugs along with something new every month, and they certainly have a lot of followers. Image is probably one of the most diverse of today's comic book publishers because there is no house style. Plus it's not a superhero line like it was 20 years ago. It's what each creator brings to the table – and what they bring to the table are usually fresh ideas. There can be a Western, there can be a fantasy, there can be a comedy and there could be a drama. The bottom line: Image Comics publishes creator-driven stories.

Golden Age: In Golden Age, what issues are hot are not necessarily the keys unless it's *Batman* and *Detective Comics*. They are head and shoulders the best-selling of the Golden Age DC titles – especially when you have a Joker cover. *Superman* and *Action Comics* sell extremely well if they have a World War II cover. Almost all *Action* issues are hot.

With Timely Comics, as soon I get them they leave, so they don't matter. And, at good conventions, everything esoteric can sell, such as '50s Horror and Sci-Fi comics which sell great, especially if they have a strange looking cover like you've never seen before.

EC sell great, while Dells also sell very well. Dells are very underrated with how well they sell. At a convention, I would recommend putting photo covers on the wall. You'd be surprised how well they sell – especially John Wayne and *I Love Lucy* covers. Anything you have in inventory; you'd be surprised.

At the same time, a couple of the publishers are difficult to sell. Like Lev Gleason titles, which are very slow. Everything Fiction House is hit or miss. Some Quality Comics are still selling very well, while others are still sitting – even if they are great comics.

Silver Age: Marvel Silver Age has been selling as well as it ever has, if not better – probably based on movies, TV, and interest. Any first appearance of any Marvel character could be listed as hot; I don't care which character it is. Any speculation at all is driving all of them.

Likewise, in some cases, the same is going on with DC Silver Age first appearances, but not like Marvel where it's across the board. Although, some DC first appearances get hot, too.

So, everything Marvel sells, as well as DC keys. Comic books runs are slow, except for, again, *Batman* and *Detective*. *Batman* Silver Age books outsell the *Detectives*, except for the Neal Adams books. Everything Neal Adams is selling above board. Get every Neal Adams title that you can get your hands on. Partially, the high success rate of his books is because Neal has been to so many conventions this year – he's out of the house, so he's around. And he's doing new books for DC Comics like *Superman: The Coming of the Supermen*.

Bronze Age: Everything that's Bronze Age from Marvel is selling well. Even titles low on the list like *Strange Tales: Brother Voodoo* sell great. Things like that – it's everything across the board.

Bronze is even hotter than Silver Age books now because everybody can buy it – not just a select few.

And all retailers and collectors can continue to enjoy the hobby because of that one unbeatable principle: comics are for everyone. Whether it is reading the books, adding them to your collections, or just pulling off that one fantastic sale that's going to lead to many more on the horizon, comic books have had a long, glorious history, and look forward to an even brighter future. In other words, comics stand the test of time.

Josh Nathanson, Douglas Gillock & Rick Hirsch ComicLink

ComicLink.com has been serving the comic book collecting community for 22 years now as a consignment-based firm. Between our Featured and Focused Auctions and The Exchange, we have leveraged the power of the Internet since 1996 as a primary conduit between buyers and sellers transacting in the sale of valuable vintage comic books and related original art online. To date, over 300,000 vintage comic books have transacted between ComicLink buyers and sellers. We are pleased to report that 2016 was the biggest year we've ever seen for our auction division. Aggressive buyers scooped up many thousands of certified comic books and original artwork to enhance their collections, setting hundreds (if not thousands) of sales records for the hobby. We saw a continuation of the trend of the past couple of years, where strength was exhibited across virtually every collecting genre. From Golden Age rarities of the 1930s and early '50s to the Silver and Bronze Age keys and high-grades of the late 1950s through the '70s, and right up through Copper and Modern Age era, the bar was raised on record sales this year. We see this growth trend continuing for years to come. Superhero movies are now the #1 most popular form of entertainment in the world with the build up and release of each film capturing massive attention from millions of fans. 2017 will be the biggest year yet for Hollywood movies and TV shows devoted to our beloved characters and the attention from the mainstream world will continue to create new collectors for decades to come who will be interested in the vintage appearances of their favorites.

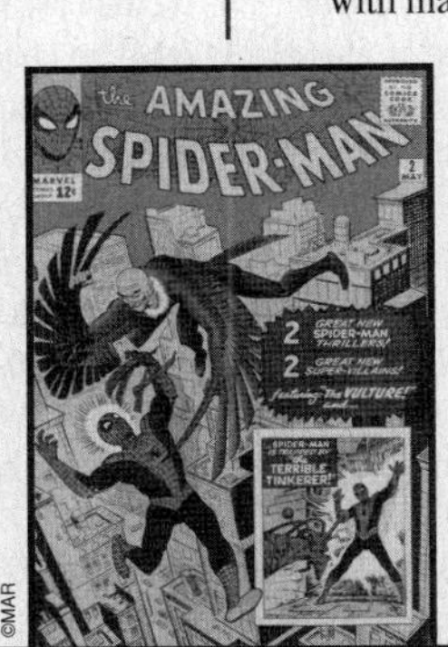

Amazing Spider-Man #2, with the debut of The Vulture, was one of the exceptional sales of the year.

Silver Age: Demand for Silver Age comics is as strong as it has ever been. As usual, major Marvel and DC keys led the way in 2016 with exceptional results for several premiere and "1st app" issues achieved. The traditional keys sold for record amounts including *X-Men* #1 CGC 9.6 for $350,000, *Incredible Hulk* #1 CCG 9.0 for $275,000 and *Tales to Astonish* #27 CGC 9.4 for $205,501. Later Silver Age keys have started seeing some amazing prices including *Fantastic Four* #52 (1st Black Panther) CGC 9.8 Curator pedigree for $90,000, *Superman* #199 (1st Superman/Flash race) CGC 9.6 for $19,750 and *Detective Comics* #359 (1st Batgirl) CGC 9.4 Pacific Coast pedigree for $13,380. In addition to the usual list of valuable books that most collectors are very familiar with, we saw some exceptional prices paid for books that don't immediately come to mind when you think "valuable Silver Age comics". For example, *X-Men* #28 (1st Banshee) CGC 9.8 sold for $9,901, *Iron Man* #7 CGC 9.8 from the Rocky Mountain collection sold for $7,500, *The Flash* #144 CGC 9.6 sold for $4,450, *Justice League of America* #19 CGC 9.4 sold for $4,100, and *Marvel Super-Heroes* #15 (the Medusa issue) in CGC 9.8 went for $2,400! There were hundreds of similar examples of books with prices that would shock collectors who have not been paying close attention to the market in recent years. The Bronze and Modern report below shows this trend continues into the 1970s and beyond.

With many thousands of transactions throughout the year, there are way too many examples on ComicLink.com to list all of the exceptional results here, but here are some representative Silver Age examples: *Action Comics* #252 (1st Supergirl) CGC 8.0 for $15,300, #254 (1st adult Bizarro) CGC 9.2 for $1,750, *Adventure Comics* #247 (1st Legion of Superheroes) CGC 6.0 for $6,212, #335 CGC 9.8 for $2,066, *Amazing Spider-Man* #1 (2nd appearance, series begins) CGC 9.2 for $75,000, #2 (1st Vulture) CGC 9.0 for $8,400, #3 (1st Doctor Octopus) CGC 9.0 for $7,100, #6 (1st Lizard) CGC 9.4 for $7,864, #16 (1st crossover with Daredevil) CGC 9.8 for $17,750, #22 CGC 9.8 for $15,500, #23 (early Green Goblin) CGC 9.6 for $11,111, #39 (1st Romita art, Green Goblin revealed as Norman Osborn) CGC 9.4 for $2,660, #50 (1st Kingpin) CGC 9.2 for $2,657, #71 (Quicksilver appearance) CGC 9.8 for $1,977, *Aquaman* #1 CGC 9.4 for $14,001, #35 (1st Black Manta) CGC 9.0 for $1,601, *Avengers* #4 (1st SA Captain America) CGC 9.0 for $7,300, #53 (X-Men crossover) CGC 9.8 for $1,351, #55 (1st full Ultron) CGC 9.8 for $5,950, #57 (1st Vision) CGC 9.4 for $2,012, *Batman* #189 (1st SA Scarecrow) CGC 9.6 for $2,400, *Brave and the Bold* #25 (1st Suicide Squad) CGC 8.5 for $6,125, #28 (1st Justice League) CGC 7.5 for $13,350, *Captain America* #100 (SA series begins) CGC 9.9 for $63,500, #110 (classic Steranko Hulk cover) CGC 9.8 for $1,777, *Captain Marvel* #1 (series begins) CGC 9.8 for $4,100, #17 CGC 9.8 for $1,877, #18 (Carol Danvers receives her powers) CGC 9.8 for $2,100, *Daredevil* #1 (1st Daredevil) CGC 9.2 for $10,277, #2 (2nd Daredevil) CGC 9.8 Pacific Coast pedigree for $30,400 and CGC 9.2 for $1,925, *Detective Comics* #359 (1st Batgirl/Barbara Gordon) CGC 9.4 Pacific Coast pedigree for $13,380, *Fantastic Four* #1 (1st FF, Marvel Age begins) CGC 7.0 for $20,250, #52 (1st Black Panther) CGC 9.8 Curator pedigree for $90,000 and CGC 9.6 for $16,750, #67 (1st Him/Warlock) CGC 9.6 for $2,995, *Fantastic Four Annual* #4 (1st GA Human Torch in SA) CGC 9.8 for $2,300, *Flash* #123 (Flash of Two Worlds) CGC 9.4 for $21,050, #131 (Green Lantern crossover) CGC 9.6 for $1,987, #135 (1st yellow costume for Kid Flash) CGC 9.2 for $2,890, #139 (1st Reverse Flash) CGC 8.5 for $2,789, #144 CGC 9.6 for $4,450, #147 (2nd Reverse Flash) CGC 9.6 for $1,499, #155 (Rogues Gallery cover) CGC 9.8 for $2,200, *Green Lantern* #40 (1st GA GL in title, origin of Crisis on Infinite Earths) CGC 9.6 for $2,470, *House of Mystery* #182 CGC 9.6 for $1,300, *Incredible Hulk* #1 (1st Hulk) CGC 9.0 for $275,000, #2 (first green Hulk) CGC 9.2 for $16,850, #3 CGC 9.4 for $17,237, #6 (Ditko art, final issue of initial run) CGC 9.6 for $25,000, *Incredible Hulk Annual* #1 CGC 9.8 for $2,099, *Iron Man* #3 CGC 9.8 for $4,200, #6 CGC 9.8 Rocky Mountain pedigree for $2,500, #7 CGC 9.8 Rocky Mountain pedigree for $7,500, *Justice League of America* #19 CGC 9.4 for $4,100, #21 (classic 1st JLA/JSA team-up) CGC 9.4 for $3,322, #39 (1st 80-page giant in series) CBCS 9.6 for $3,100, *Marvel Super Heroes* #13 (1st Carol Danvers who later becomes Ms. Marvel and the current Captain Marvel) CGC 9.4 for $2,751 and 9.2 for $2,000, #15 (Medusa solo story) CGC 9.8 for $2,400, *Nick Fury Agent of SHIELD* #4 CGC 9.8 for $1,300, *Out of This World* #11 CGC 9.0 for $1,423, *Our Army at War* #108 CGC 9.0 for $2,777, *Sgt. Fury* #13 (Captain America crossover) CGC 9.4 for $3,113, *Showcase* #4 CGC 7.5 Slight (B-1) for $13,001, #13 (3rd Flash) CGC 8.5 for $6,850, #55 CGC 9.6 (1st SA Solomon Grundy, classic cover) CGC 9.6 for $4,200, #58 (Enemy Ace) CGC 9.8 Boston pedigree for $2,100, *Strange Tales* #89 (1st Fin Fang Foom) CGC 8.0 for $4,888 and CGC 7.5 for $4,099, *Strange Tales* #110 (1st Doctor Strange) CGC 8.5 for $9,500, #115 (origin of Doctor Strange) CGC 9.4 Don & Maggie Thompson collection for $6,600, #151 (1st Steranko Nick Fury) CGC 9.8 for $3,220, *Superman* #175 CGC 9.8 for $1,878, #187 (80-page giant) CGC 9.8 for $3,600, #199 (1st Superman/Flash race) CGC 9.6 for $19,750, *Superman's Pal Jimmy Olsen* #19 CGC 9.6 for $3,211, *Tales of Suspense* #39 (1st Iron Man) CGC 9.4 for $96,000, #41 (3rd Iron Man) CGC 9.4 for $5,911, #44 CGC 9.0 for $2,177, #46 CGC 9.4 #48 CGC 9.4 for $3,600, #57 (1st Hawkeye) CGC 9.4 for $5,250, #59 (1st SA Captain America series begins) CGC 9.6 for $3,100, #76 CGC 9.8 for $2,200, #98 CGC 9.8SS for $3,100, *Tales to Astonish* #13 (1st Groot) CGC 7.0 for $3,450, #27 (1st Hank Pym who becomes Ant-Man) CGC 9.4 for $205,501, #40 (early Ant-Man) CGC 9.6 for $6,433, #57 (Spider-Man crossover) CGC 9.6 for $3,744, *Thor* #130 CGC 9.8 for $3,100, #165 (1st full Him who becomes Warlock) CGC 9.4 for $2,103, #168 (origin of Galactus) CGC 9.8 for $5,222, *X-Men* #1 (1st X-Men and Magneto) CGC 9.6 for $350,000, #4 (1st Quicksilver & Scarlet Witch) CGC 9.4 for $13,500, #5 CGC 9.2 for $2,255, #6 CGC 9.0 for $1,800, #28 (1st Banshee) CGC 9.8 for $9,901, and #45 (Avengers crossover) CGC 9.8 for $1,800.

Golden Age: Golden Age continued to be a key focus for many of ComicLink's buyers in 2016 and we were excited to offer the largest selection of quality Golden Age books at auction that we've ever provided to our buyers, including hundreds of certified examples from key pedigrees including Mile High, San Francisco, Big Apple, Larson and many more. Early appearances of DC's "Trinity" of Superman, Batman and Wonder Woman saw many record prices across grades this year. The extreme rarity of the early issues of *Action Comics* and *Detective Comics* coupled with the popularity of the characters has driven up prices on all of the late 1930s issues to a high degree. These books are in high demand in any grade--even coverless. Wonder Woman's successful introduction into DC's cinematic universe has collectors paying big prices for her colorful Golden Age adventures. Covers from throughout the Golden Age featuring Batman villains including Joker, Penguin, Catwoman, Two-Face, Riddler and Scarecrow were in especially high demand. Classic covers including the World War II Timely/Marvel era work of Alex Schomburg and the more memorable pre-Code horror classics of the early 1950s continued to explode in value as well. We were excited to auction a large collection of extremely rare Canadian Whites that sold at high prices even in very low grade. In many cases with this collection, these are the only examples that have ever surfaced!

Just a small sampling of top 2016 Golden Age sales includes *Action Comics* #7 (2nd Superman cover) CGC 6.0 for $175,000 and CGC 2.0 for $71,000, #10 (3rd Superman cover) CGC 0.5 for $9,600, #13 (4th Superman cover) CGC 6.5 for $70,777, #17 CGC 6.0 for $11,518, #19 CGC 6.5 for $7,877, #23 (1st Luthor) CGC 6.5 for $28,052, #96 CGC 9.6 for $3,350, *Adventure Comics* #60 (last Sandman in gas mask cover) CGC 8.0 for $3,577, #72 (1st Simon & Kirby DC art) CGC 8.5 for $7,500, *All Star Comics* #8 (1st Wonder Woman) CGC 2.0 for $32,000, *All Winners Comics* #12 CGC 8.0 for $7,700, #19 (1st Marvel team comic ever--the All Winners Squad) CGC 7.0 for $6,350, *Amazing-Man Comics* #5 (1st issue) CGC 6.0 Larson pedigree for $10,501, #13 CGC 8.0 Mile High pedigree for $2,700, #26 CGC 3.0 for $7,060, *America's Best Comics* #7 CGC 6.5 for $2,358, *Archie Comics* #50 (classic Betty "headlights" cover) CGC 8.0 for $4,600, *Batman* #1 (1st Joker & 1st Catwoman) CGC 2.5 for $64,000, #3 (1st Catwoman in costume) CGC 6.0 for $3,634, #6 CGC 8.5 for $5,600, #63 (1st Killer Moth) CGC 7.0 for $1,479, *Black Cat Mystery* #50 (classic horror face melting cover) CGC 8.5 for $9,867, *Blue Beetle* #32 CGC 9.4 Mile High pedigree for $6,000, *Captain America Comics* #1 (1st Captain America, Bucky and Red Skull) CGC 2.0 for $45,000, #2 (2nd Captain America and Bucky) CBCS 5.5 for $8,100, #6 CGC 8.5 for $13,249, #18 CGC 9.6 for $32,000, #49 CGC 9.6 for $9,976, *Captain America Comics* #NN (rare 132 page "Annual" from 1942) CGC 2.5 for $9,560,

Captain Marvel Jr. #1 CGC 7.0 for $1,998, *Chamber of Chills* #19 (classic horror cover) CGC 9.0 for $4,600, *Cindy Comics* #37 (classic Timely cheesecake cover) CGC 4.5 for $1,500, *City of the Living Dead* #NN CGC 6.5 for $1,233, *Comics* #1 (1937, 1st Tom Mix in comics) CGC 8.5 for $2,000, *Comic Cavalcade* #16 CGC 9.4 Ohio pedigree for $1,911, #21 CGC 9.4 for $1,917, *Commando Comics* #1 (Canadian White) CGC 0.5 for $3,000, #22 CGC 7.5 for $2,000, *Crime Patrol* #15 (1st Crypt Keeper) CGC 9.8 for $10,250, *Crypt of Terror* #17 (1st issue) CGC 9.8 for $12,806, *Daredevil Battles Hitler* #1 CGC 8.5 for $8,950, *Detective Comics* #16 CGC 4.5 for $4,000, #31 (classic 3rd Batman cover) CGC 6.0 Mod A-3 for $27,617, #33 (1st origin of Batman, 4th Batman cover) CGC 6.5 for $51,133, #35 (5th Batman cover) CGC 3.5 for $34,333, #37 (last pre-Robin cover) CGC 7.0 Larson pedigree for $23,792, #40 (1st Joker cover) CGC 8.0 for $8,655, #53 CGC 9.0 for $2,800, #54 CGC 9.4 for $15,250, #58 (1st Penguin) CGC 3.0 for $5,052, #71 (classic Joker cover) CGC 7.5 for $11,600, #91 (Joker cover) CGC 9.0 for $4,100, #120 (classic Penguin in bird cage cover) CGC 9.6 for $10,450, #121 CGC 9.8 for $7,100, #140 (1st Riddler) CGC 6.0 for $7,200, #168 (Joker origin/Red Hood) CGC 3.0 for $4,600, #175 CGC 9.4 for $3,101, #180 CGC 8.5 for $4,000, #225 (1st Martian Manhunter) CGC 4.5 for $3,707, *Dime Comics* #1 (Canadian White) CGC 3.5 for $5,800, #24 CGC 6.0 for $2,000, *Famous Funnies* #211 (Frazetta Buck Rogers) CGC 9.2 for $2,550, *Feature Book* #39 (early Phantom) CGC 9.4 for $6,350, *Fight Against Crime* #20 (classic decapitation cover) CGC 7.0 for $6,233, *Flash Comics* #54 CGC 9.6 Mile High pedigree for $4,600, #78 CGC 9.6 Mile High pedigree for $3,950, #86 (1st Black Canary) CGC 4.5 for $7,200, *Green Hornet Comics* #14 CGC 9.6 Mile High pedigree for $3,811, *Guns Against Gangsters* #6 (classic L.B. Cole cover) CGC 9.2 File copy for $3,300, *Hangman Comics* #5 (classic cover) CGC 9.2 for $6,800, *Haunt of Fear* #15 (#1) CGC 9.6 for $9,877, *Hit Comics* #5 (classic Lou Fine cover) CGC 5.0 for $2,908, *Human Torch Comics* #7 CGC 9.4 for $12,750, *Joke Comics* #1 (Canadian White) CGC 2.5 for $2,600, *Journey Into Unknown Worlds* #18 CBCS 9.0 for $3,255, *Jumbo Comics* #1 5.0 for $6,223, *Land of the Lost Comics* #1 (early EC) CGC 9.8 for $3,533, *Marvel Mystery Comics* #11 CGC 9.2 for $15,678, #27 CGC 9.4 for $11,251, #52 CGC 9.2 for $7,990, *Marvel Tales* #119 (Atlas horror) CGC 9.4 for $1,800, *More Fun Comics* #46 CGC 9.6 Mile High for $10,000, #52 (1st Spectre) CGC 3.0 for $39,500, #54 (classic Spectre cover) CGC 8.5 for $22,100, #62 (Spectre cover) CGC 9.2 Detroit Trolley collection for $9,000, #101 (1st Superboy) CGC 8.5 for $14,294, *Nelvana* (key Canadian White) #NN CGC 5.0 for $14,750, *New Adventure Comics* #26 (extremely rare early DC featuring full page interior cover ad for *Action Comics* #1 CGC 3.0 for $6,109, *New York World's Fair* #1940 CGC 8.5 for $14,583, *Pep Comics* #22 (1st Archie, Betty and Jughead) CBCS 2.0 for $31,249, #34 (classic WWII cover) CGC 6.0 for $15,251, *Peter Panda* #5 (classic cover) CGC 8.5 for $2,200, *Phantom Lady* #23 (classic headlights cover) CGC 6.5 for $4,958, *Plastic Man* #1 (solo series begins) CGC 9.2 for $13,000, *Red Ryder Comics* #1 CGC 9.0 for $3,451, *Robin Hood* #1 (Tied for 1st Canadian White) 3.0 for $3,399, *Roy Rogers Annual* #NN (Canadian) CGC 8.0 for $2,433, *Sensation Comics* #1 (2nd Wonder Woman appearance & 1st cover) CBCS 5.5 for $35,0000 and CGC 5.0 for $31,555, #6 CGC 5.0 for $7,600, #14 CGC 9.2 for $5,655, #53 CGC 9.8 Pennsylvania pedigree for $4,823, #60 CGC 9.4 Mile High pedigree for $3,653, #72 CGC 9.4 Mile High pedigree for $3,433, *Shadow Comics* V2 #10 CGC 9.4 for $2,988, *Spirit* (Quality) #7 CGC 9.2 for $1,359, *Star Comics* #3 (1937 "classic" cover) CGC 5.5 for $2,111, *Star Spangled Comics* #7 (1st Guardian and the Newsboy Legion) CGC 9.0 Rockford pedigree for $6,450, *Sub-Mariner Comics* #1 (solo series begins) CGC 6.0 for $11,000, #6 CBCS 8.5 for $9,308, #12 CGC 8.0 for $3,700, #17 CGC 9.2 for $5,988, #19 CGC 9.2 for $5,600, #22 CGC 9.4 for $5,700, #23 CGC 9.2 for $5,888, #32 (origin retold) CGC 8.5 Mile High pedigree for $23,250, #39 CGC 8.5 for $2,750, *Superman* #14 (classic patriotic cover) CGC 9.2 for $45,000, *Tales From the Crypt* #20 CGC 9.8 Gaines File copy for $6,107, #33 CGC 9.8 for $6,600, *Triumph-Adventure Comics* #6 (Canadian White) CGC 3.0 for $3,655, *Triumph Comics* #7 (Canadian White) CGC 2.0 for $9,000, *Vault of Horror* #14 CGC 9.8 for $6,136, *Wambi Jungle Boy* #3 CGC 9.6 MIle High pedigree for $2,000, *Wanted* #52 CGC 8.0 for $1,755, *War* #11 (Atlas) CGC 5.5 for $1,758, *Weird Fantasy* #13 (#1) CGC 9.6 Gaines File for $7,950, *Weird Mysteries* #12 CGC 7.0 for $4,210, *Weird Science* #12 (#1) CGC 9.6 for $12,258, *Whiz Comics* #2 CGC 5.0 for $4,100, *Wings Comics* #84 CGC 9.4 for $1,877, #102 CGC 9.6 Mile High pedigree for $1,544, *Witchcraft* #2 CGC 5.5 for $1,450, *Wonder Comics* #15 CGC 7.5 for $1,666, *Wonder Woman* #1 (solo series begins, origin retold) CGC 4.5 for $28,027, #6 (1st Cheetah) CBCS 8.5 for $7,766, #7 (Wonder Woman for President cover) CGC 6.5 for $5,699, *Wonderworld Comics #7 CGC 4.5 for $8,377*, *Wow Comics* (Canadian White) #18 CGC 2.5 for $3,600, *Zip Comics* #8 CGC 9.4 for $6,050.

Scarcity and particularly scarcity in grade are key factors here with buyers extremely educated on the availability of these items and stepping up aggressively when they did come to market. The Golden Age market is also extremely cover driven right now and even at the lower end of the pricing spectrum a book with a stand-out cover can blow the doors off *Guide* prices when properly promoted.

Bronze Age and Modern Age: It was not that many years ago that there were only a handful of valuable comics from 1970 and beyond that would sell for $1,000 or more. In recent years that number has increased exponentially thanks to the impact of Hollywood and the realization that books from these eras, the oldest of which will be 50 years old in a few years, are not as plentiful in high grade as once thought. While the strong prices for first appearances is not surprising, perhaps even more impressive is seeing prices of $1,000, $2000 and up for non-key "run" books from the early '70s on titles such as *Iron Man*, *Captain America* and *Thor* and *X-Men*. Check out the prices at the end of this section for the

X-Men reprint era issues for an example of how books once thought to have little value are now seen as highly collectible with large price tags that once only applied to Golden Age and Silver Age keys. Scarcity in high grade has led to books like *X-Men* #76 selling for $3,400 in CGC 9.6, higher than the much more famous *X-Men* #94 in the same grade! When a book like *Night Nurse* #1 in CGC 9.8 sells for $7,700 like it did in December of 2016, you know the Bronze Age has started to truly earn its name! With dozens of movies and TV shows now featuring characters of this era, with many more to come, there seems to be no end to the potential for these great comics. The 1980s right now are like the 1970s of 10 or 15 years ago, with only a handful of books selling for big bucks. While '80s books exist in high grade in greater supply than '70s books, it would not surprise us to see an explosion of interest in early '80s books over the next few years, along with corresponding price increases. When the *Power Pack* and *New Warriors* movies are inevitably announced, don't say we didn't warn you!

Some standout sales from the Bronze and Modern eras included *Albedo* #2 (1st Usagi Yojimbo) CGC 9.6 for $2,556, *All-Star Comics* #58 (1st Power Girl) CGC 9.8 for $2,000, *Amazing Spider-Man* #80 CGC 9.8 for $2,577, #86 (1st revamped Black Widow) CGC 9.8 for $3,800, #94 (origin retold) CGC 9.8 for $2,275, #96 (Goblin/Harry on drugs) CGC 9.8 for $2,375, #100 CGC 9.8 for $2,601, #101 (1st Morbius) CGC 9.6 for $2,851, #109 CGC 9.8 for $2,377, #121 (death of Gwen Stacy) CGC 9.8 for $4,544, #122 (death of Green Goblin) CGC 9.8 for $3,000, #129 (1st Punisher) CGC 9.8 for $8,900, #194 (1st Black Cat) CGC 9.8 for $955, #238 (1st Hobgoblin) CGC 9.8SS for $1,200, #300 (1st full Venom) CGC 9.8 for $1,600, *Avengers* #83 (1st Valkyrie and the Liberators) CGC 9.8 for $1,877, #112 (1st Mantis) CGC 9.8 for $2,333, *Batman* #232 (1st Ra's al Ghul) CGC 9.6 for $2,257, #234 (1st Modern Two-Face) CGC 9.8 for $4,350, #244 (Adams Ra's al Ghul Battle cover) CGC 9.8 for $3,350, #251 (classic Adams Joker cover/story) CGC 9.6 for $1,955, #357 (1st Jason Todd and Killer Croc) CGC 9.8 for $1,300, *Batman Adventures* #12 (1st Harley Quinn in comics) CGC 9.8 for $2,156, *Batman: The Dark Knight Returns* #1 (1st Carrie Kelly Robin) CGC 9.8 SS for $1,600, *Batman: Vengeance of Bane Special* CGC 9.9 for $2,388, *Brave and the Bold* #93 (Adams cover and art) CGC 9.8 for $2,100, *Captain America* #138 CGC 9.8 for $900, #217 (1st Quasar) CGC 9.8 for $900, *Captain Marvel* #26 (1st Thanos cover) CGC 9.8 for $2,111, #33 (classic Thanos cover) CGC 9.8 for $2,179, *Chamber of Darkness* #4 CGC 9.8 for $875, *Chew* #1 (1st Tony Chu) CGC 9.9 for $1,400, *Conan the Barbarian* #1 (1st Conan in comics) CGC 9.8 for $5,265, #23 (1st Red Sonja) CGC 9.8 for $1,257, #75 CGC 9.8 Price Variant for $1867, *Daredevil* #168 (1st Elektra) CGC 9.8 SS for $1,728, *Detective Comics* #400 (1st Man-Bat) CGC 9.6 for $1,875, #405 (1st League of Assassins) CGC 9.6 for $1,300, #411 (1st Talia) CGC 9.8 for $8,007, #437 (Simonson's Manhunter begins) CGC 9.8 for $1,111, #444 (100-pager) CGC 9.8 for $740, *Doctor Strange* #1 (1974) CGC 9.8 for $950, *Fantastic Four* #103 CGC 9.8 for $1,177, #112 (classic Thing/Hulk battle cover) CGC 9.6 for $3,322, *Fear* #19 (1st Howard the Duck) CGC 9.8 for $1,300, *Forever People* #1 (1st full Darkseid) CGC 9.8 for $3,600, *Ghost Rider* #1 (1st Daimon Hellstrom) CGC 9.8 for $3,255 and CGC 9.6 for $2,151, *Giant-Size Creatures* #1 (1st Tigra) CGC 9.8 for $1,241, *Giant-Size Daredevil* #1 CGC 9.8 for $919, *Giant-Size Spider-Man* #3 CGC 9.8 for $1,178, *Giant-Size X-Men* #1 (1st Storm, Colossus, Nightcrawler and 2nd full Wolverine) CGC 9.8 for $7,101 and CGC 9.6 for $3,211, *Green Lantern* #77 (2nd Adams Green Lantern/Green Arrow) CGC 9.8 for $1,499, #87 (1st John Stewart GL) CGC 9.8 for $2,600, *Harbinger* #1 CGC 9.8 for $1,000, *House of Secrets* #88 CGC 9.6 for $1,700, #92 (1st Swamp Thing) CGC 9.6 for $9,199 and CGC 9.4 for $4,700, #94 CGC 9.6 for $1,216, #105 CGC 9.8 for $1,200, *Howard the Duck* #1 CGC 9.8 for $1,139, *Incredible Hulk* #125 CGC 9.8 for $1,156, #137 CGC 9.8 for $2,120, #162 (1st Wendigo) CGC 9.8 for $1,251, #180 (1st Wolverine cameo) CGC 9.8 for $4,988, #181 (1st full Wolverine) CGC 9.8 for $15,000, *Invaders* #20 (35 cent variant) CGC 9.6 for $1,500, *Iron Fist* #15 (X-Men crossover by Byrne) CGC 9.8 for $900, *Iron Man* #22 CGC 9.8 for $2,600, #34 CGC 9.8 for $2,975, #36 CGC 9.8 for $2,400, #40 CGC 9.8 for $1,700, #42 CGC 9.8 for $1,600, #43 CGC 9.8 for $1,301, #54 (1st Moondragon) CGC 9.8 $2,055, #55 (1st Thanos and Drax) CGC 9.8 for $6,877 and CGC 9.6 for $2,800, *Iron Man Annual* #1 CGC 9.8 for $1,699, *Marvel Feature* #1 (1st Defenders) CGC 9.8 for $8,101 and CGC 9.6 for $1,877, #3 (third Defenders) CGC 9.8 for $920, #12 (Starlin Hulk/Thing battle cover) CGC 9.8 for $1,025, *Marvel Premiere* #1 (Him becomes Warlock) CGC 9.6 for $1,621, #4 (Doctor Strange) CGC 9.8 for $938, #15 (1st Iron Fist) CGC 9.8 for $5,350 and CGC 9.6 for $2,511, *Marvel Preview* #4 (1st Star-Lord) CGC 9.6 for $1,100, #7 (1st Rocket Racoon) CGC 9.4 for $1,667, *Marvel Spotlight* (1st Ghost Rider) CGC 9.6 for $4,600 and CGC 9.4 Suscha pedigree for $3,322, #32 (1st Spider-Woman) CGC 9.8 for $1,060, *Marvel Team-up* #95 (Bobbi Morse becomes Mockingbird) CGC 9.8 SS for $658, *New Mutants* #87 (1st Cable) CGC 9.8 for $550, #98 (1st Deadpool) CGC 9.9 for $9,201, *New Mutants Annual* #2 (1st Psylocke in U.S. comic) CGC 9.8 for $475, *New Teen Titans* #2 (1st Deathstroke) CGC 9.8 for $910, *Night Nurse* #1 CGC 9.8 for $7,700 and CGC 9.6 for $2,001, *Our Love Story* #4 CGC 9.8 for $650, *Primer* #2 (1st Grendel) CGC 9.8 for $1,500, *Savage Tales* #1 (1st Man-thing) CGC 9.8 for $2,200, *Scooby Doo* #1 (Gold Key) CGC 8.5 for $1,055, *Shazam!* #1 (1st return of the original Captain Marvel since the Golden Age) CGC 9.9 for $9,900, *Spawn*

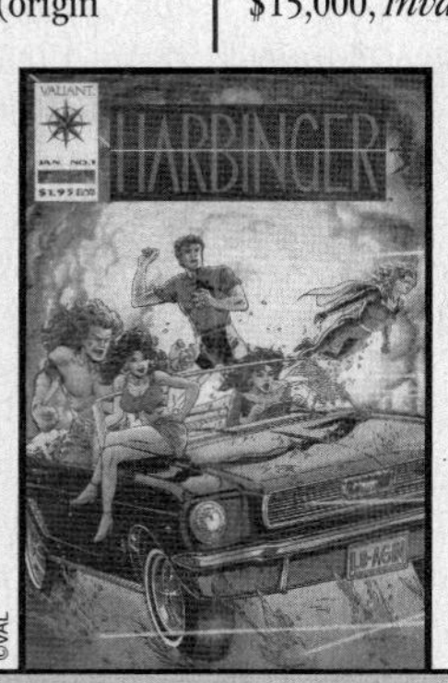

***Harbinger** #1 was one of the standout sales for the year.*

#1 (1st Spawn) CGC 9.9 for $3,100, *Special Marvel Edition* #15 (1st Master of Kung-Fu) CGC 9.8 for $1,857, *Star Wars* #1 Regular Edition CGC 9.8 SS for $5,400, #4 CGC 9.9 for $4,100, #42 (1st Boba Fett and Yoda in comics) CGC 9.9 for $6,600, *Strange Tales* #169 (1st Brother Voodoo) CGC 9.6 for $1,355, #178 (Starlin's Warlock begins) CGC 9.8 for $1,551, *Superman's Pal Jimmy Olsen* #134 (1st Darkseid) CGC 9.6 for $3,400, *Swamp Thing* #1 (1st Alec Holland Swamp Thing) CGC 9.8 for $3,001, *Teenage Mutant Ninja Turtles* #1 CGC 9.6 for $15,000, *Thor* #176 CGC 9.8 for $1,200, #200 CGC 9.8 for $1,000, #264 35 cent variant CGC 9.6 for $1,611, *Tomb of Dracula* #10 (1st Blade) CGC 9.8 for $5,002, *Vampirella* #19 CGC 9.9 for $2,300, *Venom: Lethal Protector* #1 (White Cover Printing Error) CGC 9.8 for $4,655, *Walking Dead* #1 (1st Rick Grimes) CGC 9.8 for $3,500, *Werewolf By Night* #32 (1st Moon Knight) CGC 9.6 for $8,700, #33 (2nd Moon Knight) CGC 9.8 for $3,100, *Wonder Woman* #199 (Jeff Jones bondage cover) CGC 9.8 for $1,600, *X-Men* #66 (last new original X-Men issue) CGC 9.8 for $2,299, #70 CGC 9.8 for $2,350, #71 CGC 9.8 for $3,451, #76 CGC 9.6 for $3,400, #82 CGC 9.8 for $2,277, #95 (death of Thunderbird) CGC 9.8 for $1,631, #99 CGC 9.8 for $2,055, #114 CGC 9.8 for $1,600, #129 (1st Kitty Pryde and Emma Frost) CGC 9.8 for $805, and more.

Original Art: Original Comic Art continues to draw the attention of more and more collectors and this segment of ComicLink's business has been incredibly dynamic in the past few years. Just a few standout 2016 art sales include Steve Ditko panel page from *Amazing Spider-Man* #10 for $68,000, Dick Sprang WWII themed cover for *Batman* #30 for $60,000, John Romita Jr. *Uncanny X-Men* #211 cover from the "Mutant Massacre" event for $51,001, Gil Kane *Giant-Size X-Men* #2 cover for $47,000, Jack Kirby *Fantastic Four Annual* #1 panel page for $42,000, John Romita *Amazing Spider-Man* #50 panel page for $37,000 and his *Amazing Spider-Man* #164 cover for $36,556, Steve Ditko Mr. A *Graphic Illusion* title splash for $36,500, Dave Gibbons *Watchmen* #8 cover for $36,001, John Romita *Captain America* #171 cover for $33,000, Jack Kirby *Black Panther* #6 cover for $32,500, Barry Windsor-Smith *Conan Saga* #5 cover from $32,000, Gene Colan *Doctor Strange* #172 cover for $31,177 and his *Iron Man* #1 title splash for $31,500, John Byrne *X-Men* #141 "Days of Future Past" half splash from $31,000 and a *X-Men* #139 panel page for $30,000, Dave Cockrum *Iron Fist* #12 cover for $28,000, Jack Kirby *Avengers* #3 panel page for $26,475, Frank Miller *Absolute Dark Knight* cover from $26,199, Todd McFarlane *Incredible Hulk* #343 cover for $23,075, Michael Golden *Savage She-Hulk* #8 cover for $19,350, Frank Thorne *Red Sonja* #5 cover for $19,251, Frank Brunner *Fear* #16 cover for $19,250, Gil Kane *Captain America* #189 cover for $18,250, Murphy Anderson and Carmine Infantino *The Flash* #176 cover for $17,805, John Byrne *Marvel Team-up* #72 cover for $17,801, John Buscema *Thor* #194 cover for $17,750, Dan Jurgens *Superman* #74 panel page from the "Death of Superman" saga for $17,150, Tony Moore panel page from *The Walking Dead* #1 for $17,015, Alex Ross painted Galactus and the Silver Surfer splash from *Marvels* #3 for $16,902, Gil Kane *Daredevil* #125 cover for $16,251, Jim Starlin *Captain Marvel* #29 page 1 title splash for $15,570, Don Heck *Tales of Suspense* #52 panel page for $15,438, George Tuska *Iron Man* #8 title splash for $15,251 and so much more.

2017 seems poised to be filled with many more record-breakers on ComicLink.com. With over two decades online serving buyers and sellers in the collecting community, ComicLink is the longest running and most established consignment service in the hobby. If you have material like some of the books or artwork described above and you would like to achieve the types of prices described, come to the web site, view our auction schedule, and give us a call and we will work hand-in-hand with you to optimize the value of your collection. Not only do we sell original art and certified comic books, but we also help owners of collections of every experience level to maximize the value of their collections. We assist owners with everything from evaluating their comic books for third party grading certification with CGC and CBCS to processing, marketing and selling them. We do all this work, and offer upfront cash advances, for a very minimal commission rate, with the focus being a high level of service for each of our sellers.

Tom Nelson
Top Notch Comics

Another year is in the books here in early December 2016 for my 2016 market recap and report for the 2017 *Overstreet Comic Book Price Guide*.

We as a business sell back issues 100% online from the Golden Age to just a few years ago. We do not sell new comics or have a Diamond account. I tend to stay away from current hot moderns and specialize in collectable comics that have gained collector status.

We did sell thousands of Gold and Silver Age comics through a number of online brokers this year and sales were very strong. I want to concentrate my market report this year on books from 1970-1999 and break them up into three eras: 1970-1979, 1980-1989, and 1990 to 1999. I'm going to put together my top 10 from each of these eras and concentrate on comics that had decent distribution to the entire United States. That means I'm not going to include price variants, errors, recalled, pre-packs, convention exclusives, mail away comics and other books that had very spotty distribution. I realize they are valuable and collectable, but tracking sales is difficult as some do not trade on the open market. My goal with these lists is to hit the comic collecting community square. My requirement to qualify for my top ten lists is the book is sold online at least monthly in any type of grade, not necessary high grade, and is available at most major conventions.

Here we go with the 1970 - 1979 listing the 9.2 value:

1) *Incredible Hulk* #181 - $3,500

2) *Cerebus* #1 - $3,000

3) *House of Secrets* #92 - $2,500
4) *Scooby Doo* #1 - $2,500
5) *Green Lantern* #76 - $1,800
6) *Hero for Hire* #1 - $1,500
7) *Amazing Spider-Man* #129 - $1,500
8) *Giant-Size X-Men* #1 - $1,500
9) *Iron Man* #55 - $1,400
10) *Werewolf By Night* #32 - $1,300

The undisputed king of the Bronze Age is the first appearance of Wolverine in *Incredible Hulk* #181. The second position goes to an independent comic book that is scarce in high grade *Cerebus* #1 from 1977. A book who has climbed the charts in the past few years is from the DC Horror line *House of Secrets* #92 the first appearance of Swamp Thing. Number four is a Gold Key comic book *Scooby Doo* #1 from 1970, which is the first comic adaptation of this classic Saturday morning cartoon. A book that has been sliding down the charts the past few years is *Green Lantern* #76. An emerging book on the charts inspired by Netflix is *Hero For Hire* #1, the first appearance of Luke Cage at #6. The very popular *Amazing Spider-Man* #129 with the first appearance of Punisher has seen big increases this year and gets the #7 spot. Number #8 is taken by *Giant-Size X-Men* #1 which brings us the new X-Men team in 1975. Another book that has risen dramatically in recent years is *Iron Man* #55 the first appearance of Thanos in the ninth spot. The final spot for this year's top ten is *Werewolf By Night* #32 the first appearance of Moon Knight. Books that are knocking at the door for breaking into the top ten are *Marvel Spotlight* #5 and *X-Men* #94.

Here are the top ten from 1980-1989:

1) *Teenage Mutant Ninja Turtles* #1 - $4,000
2) *Albedo* #2 - $1,200
3) *Teenage Mutant Ninja Turtles* #1 2nd print - $600
4) *Archie's Girls, Betty and Veronica* #320 - $300
5) *Daredevil* #168 - $250
6) *Crow* #1 - $250
7) *Amazing Spider-Man* #300 - $250
8) *Primer* #2 - $195
9) *New Teen Titans* #2 - $185
10) *Batman* #357 - $185

The big book from the 1980s is *Teenage Mutant Ninja Turtles* #1 and there is no dispute about this book being King. Second goes to an Independent *Albedo* #2 with the first Usagi Yojimbo. Third is the second printing of *Turtles* #1 which had a print run of 6,000 copies. Fourth is *Archie's Girls, Betty and Veronica* #320 first Cheryl Blossom. *Daredevil* #168 has had a strong year with Frank Miller's first Elektra. A surprise book that has been moving up is *Crow* #1, not his first appearance but a desirable cover on a #1. The popular *Amazing Spider-Man* #300 first Venom is at #7. At #8 is *Primer* #2 is the first appearance of Grendel. *New Teen Titans* #2 is the first appearance of Deathstroke. The final book in our top ten is Batman #357 the first Killer Croc and Jason Todd. The list is dominated by 5 Independents, two Marvel and two DC. The print runs on the Marvel and DC are so much higher than the Independents. The demand for *Turtles* #1 first printing of 3000 is so high that it has pulled up the original second printing. Books on the edge of breaking the top ten *Incredible Hulk* #271, and *Batman Dark Knight Returns* #1.

The top ten from 1990-1999:

1) *Bone* #1 - $1,000
2) *Batman Adventures* #12 - $500
3) *Marvel Collectible Classics: Spider-Man* #1 - $350
4) *The Goon* #1 - $250
5) *New Mutants* #98 - $250
6) *Incredible Hulk* #377 3rd printing - $250
7) *Spawn* #1 Black & White edition - $200
8) *Preacher* #1 - $175
9) *Spider-Man* #1 Platinum - $175
10) *Marvel Collectible Classics: Spider-Man* #2 - $175

Bone #1 is an independent comic book that leads the way in the 1990s decade as the most valuable comic book. A strong second place is *Batman Adventures* #12 being the first appearance of Harley Quinn. There is strong demand for her first appearance as she was cast in the *Suicide Squad* movie. *Marvel Collectible Classics Spider-Man* #1 lands at the #3 spot and is the Chrome version of *Amazing Spider-Man* #300 printed in 1998. #4 is *The Goon* #1 by Avatar printed in 1999. *New Mutants* #98 is the first appearance of Deadpool and is at the #5 position, with the strong supply of copies on the market the price of this book dropped from early 2016 when the movie was released. The *Incredible Hulk* #377 3rd printing has strong sales and demand on eBay and gets the 6th spot. Spot #7 is *Spawn* #1 Black and White printed in 1997. *Preacher* #1 saw strong price swings when the TV show aired in May and the price was dropping each month after the show aired but it finished up the year selling for around $175.00. At #9 is *Spider-Man* #1 Platinum edition printed in 1990. The final slot at #10 is the second of the *Marvel Collectible Classics Spider-Man* #2 1998 which is the Chrome version of 1990 *Spider-Man* #1. So out of my top ten there are 5 comics which are first full appearances of characters and the other five comics are reprints that are limited compared to the originals, but have desirable cover art. Books hovering just outside my list are *Evil Ernie* #1 and *Strangers in Paradise* #1.

Some of the best Modern books from 2000-2014 are *Walking Dead* #1 which is the King. Some other books which have been climbing in price and are turning into solid keys: *NYX* #3 the first appearance of X-23, *Saga* #1, *Invincible* #1, and *Y the Last Man* #1.

Some sales this year all in CGC certified grades: *Adventure* #269 6.5 $249.95, *Adventure* #346 8.0 $139.95, *Albedo* #2 8.5 $1,000.00, *All Star Comics* #58 9.6 $499.95, *Amazing Spider-Man* #6 7.0 $949.95, *Amazing Spider-Man* #16 8.0 $749.95, *Amazing Spider-Man* #50 7.5 $525.00, *Amazing Spider-Man* #129 9.6 $3449.95, 7.5 $725.00, 5.0 $425.00, *Amazing Spider-Man* #300 9.8 $1075.00, 9.6

$399.95 (3) copies, *Aquaman* #1 4.5 $425.00, *Avengers* #196 9.4 $149.95, *Avenging Spider-Man* #9 9.8 $300.00, *Batman* #181 7.5 $699.95, *Batman* #189 8.5 $425.00, *Batman* #227 8.0 $400.00, *Batman* #232 8.5 $549.95, *Batman Adventures* #12 9.6 $885.00, 9.2 $599.95, 7.5 $399.95, *Batman Dark Knight Returns* #1 9.4 $199.95, *Batman: The Killing Joke* 9.8 $225.00 (9) copies, *Black Panther* #1 9.8 $600.00, *Crow* #1 9.8 $1025.00, 9.6 $500.00, *Daredevil* #1 4.0 $1150.00, *Daredevil* #168 9.4 $285.00, 9.2 $235.00, 9.0 $200.00, *Detective* #225 1.0 $1050.00, *Detective* #359 6.5 $595.00, *Detective* #411 8.0 $285.00, *Doctor Solar* #1 Gold Key 8.0 $300.00, *Doom Patrol* #99 6.0 $270.00, *Ewoks* #10 9.8 $150.00, *Fantastic Four* #49 8.5 $500.00, *Fantastic Four* #52 8.5 $2,150.00, 7.0 $725.00, *Flash* #110 5.5 $650.00, *Flash* #139 7.0 $800.00, 5.0 $385.00, 3.5 $215.00 *Foom* #10 9.4 $500.00, *Forever People* #1 9.0 $325.00, *Giant-Size X-Men* #1 8.5 $1145.00, 6.0 $550.00, *Green Lantern* #16 8.0 $499.95, *Green Lantern* #76 7.0 $425.00, *Heathcliff* #12 9.8 $150.00, *House of Mystery* #90 9.8 $500.00, *Iron Man* #1 8.0 $650.00, *Iron Man* #128 9.8 $300.00, *Jungle Action* #5 7.5 $175.00, *Longshot* #1 9.8 $125.00, *Magnus Robot Fighter* #1 Gold Key 7.0 $350.00, *Malibu Sun* #13 error 9.2 $550.00, *Marvel Premiere* #15 9.6 $1200.00, *Marvel Premiere* #47 9.8 $600.00, *Marvel Super Heroes Secret Wars* #8 9.8 $175.00, 9.6 $100.00, *Moon Knight* #1 1980 9.8 $175.00, 9.6 $65.00, *New Mutants* #26 9.8 $200.00 9.6 $80.00, *New Mutants* #87 9.8 $500.00, 9.6 $240.00, *New Mutants* #98 9.8 $800.00 9.4 $325.00, *New Teen Titans* #2 9.6 $275.00, 9.4 $215.00, 9.2 $185.00, 9.0 $150.00, *Night Nurse* #1 8.5 $250.00, *NYX* #3 9.8 $825.00, 9.2 $365.00, *Omega Men* #3 9.8 $165.00, 9.6 $85.00, *Rom* #1 9.8 $325.00, 9.6 $85.00, *Sandman* #1 1989 9.8 $300.00 (6) copies, *Star Wars* #1 9.8 $1000.00, 9.6 $375.00, 9.4 $225.00, 9.2 $175.00, *Strangers in Paradise* #1 9.4 $153.00, *Superman's Girlfriend Lois Lane* #70 7.0$200.00, #106 9.0 $300.00, *Jimmy Olsen* #134 7.0 $285.00, *Superman* #128 8.5 $550.00, *Superman's Adventure* #5 9.8 $150.00 (5) copies, *Tales of Suspense* #4 6.0 $425.00, *Teen-Age Romance* #37 6.0 $695.00, *Tomb of Dracula* #10 9.2 $549.95, *X-Men* #4 6.0 $800.00, 6 8.0 $400.00, 28 9.6 $1850.00, 95 9.6 $425.00, #101 8.5 $220.00, X-Men #266 9.8 $350.00, 9.6 $175.00, 9.4 $150.00, 9.2 $115.00, *Walking Dead* #1 9.0 $1650.00, *Watchmen* #1 9.8 $300.00, 9.6 $115.00, *Web of Spider-Man* #1 9.8 $85.00, *Wonderworld Comics* #18 3.0 $700.00, and *Y the Last Man* #1 9.8 $575.00.

Jamie Newbold
Southern California Comics

Welcome to our 2017 market article submission. We would have been Texas-sized toast with nothing to write about for this article had it not been for the surprising number of Golden Age collections we purchased this year. The largest GA collection we purchased consisted of mostly DCs and was the most significant collection we've ever been offered. The collection included *Batman* #1 on, *Superman* #1 on, *Action* and *Detective* from the 1930s on and more. It was our most expensive purchase to date, but worth the effort as we sold a considerable number of books within the first 30 days. We debuted the collection at the shop to a mob of anxious locals, but quite a few buyers excitedly called in and emailed us to purchase and have us ship to them.

Shipping becomes its own negotiated factor but it is often unnecessarily expensive. Roughly ten years ago we invested in collectibles insurance to protect store inventory and cover lost or damaged items for outbound packages. We went 12-plus years without incident (with the exception of items we received). This year we experienced an interesting battle with the USPS over their insurance claim process when a book we shipped to CGC for one of our customers was damaged.

We routinely submit comics to CGC on behalf of our customers or for our own inventory. In July 2016, a long-time customer of ours had decided to submit an issue of *X-23* #1 to CGC to get graded. She had purchased the comic new in 2010, but the comic had since increased substantially in value. When we prepare to submit a comic on behalf of a customer, we council them through the process and give them a preliminary grade so that they have an idea of what to expect back from CGC. Sometimes it's worth the investment for them and other times it's not. In this case, we had estimated the grade to be a 9.6 with a fair market value of $300.

We securely packed the comic up and sent it to Florida through USPS with insurance. When the comic arrived at CGC, we received an email notification that the comic had sustained damage evident by a color-breaking crease over one inch in size located parallel to the top edge of the front cover. This defect was not present when we sent the comic off, and the damage was significant enough to render the comic essentially worthless. CGC offered us two options: they could charge us to press the comic and then grade it, or they could send it back to us as is without grading it so that we could file a claim with the USPS since the package was insured. We spoke with the customer to see what she wanted to do and explained to her that pressing the comic wouldn't be worth the extra cost since pressing won't eliminate the color-breaking crease. The customer opted to file a claim, and the comic was returned.

The insurance claim was an online process; we submitted photos of the damage and a screen shot of the GPAnalysis breakdown displaying the value of *X-23* #1 after CGC completed its grading process (what we expected the comic to be worth after grading).

The claim was immediately denied because the proof of value was insufficient according to the USPS claim guidelines. The second appeal was submitted by the customer and was denied again for the same reason. The denial letter outlined that a completion of payment for the insured amount must be submitted in order for them to pay the $300 insured amount. We had one last chance to get the claim approved with a third and final appeal. Before we submitted any more documents or appeals, we gave the USPS a call to see what information we could use to try to win the case.

I spoke with a supervisor for the USPS domestic claims department and explained the claim was denied due to contention over the item's value. She explained the process of appeal, and why the claim was twice denied. I asked her how someone goes about guaranteeing a collectible will be covered for the full insured value if it is lost or damaged. I offered this example to the supervisor: someone purchases a comic in 1950 for 10 cents, which has since accrued value in the comic market, and they decide to send it to the third-party grader for authentication. An original purchase receipt does not exist for this item, but we have determined the item to be worth $1,000. If this item gets lost or damaged during shipping, how are we to prove the item's value? When posed with this question, the supervisor said that she didn't know; she was as perplexed as I was. Either it was of no consequence to her and I only held onto half of her attention, or she genuinely had no knowledge of the workings of the system she supervised. In any case, if the post office requires the proof of value, why then do they not validate the value prior to selling the insurance? I offered her one final question: why should I bother buying insurance at all? She still had no answer.

For years we operated with the thought that USPS insurance was beyond reproach. Through this ordeal we've learned that collectibles are a grey area. I was curious to see if anyone else had insurance horror stories so I took the time to search for websites and even spoke with my customers to see what other people had gone through. There were many frustrated people with stories to tell, although few pertained to comic book insurance claims. There were not enough examples to quell my concerns that insured packages of comic collectibles would be covered without argument. Three people (me, my store manager Sam, and my employee Rob) spent days digging for answers pertaining to shipping insurance. What we learned was disheartening as we found compelling reasons not to trust postal insurance.

The post office will argue with claimants over the values of collectibles. Claimants get three chances to pursue a claim and there are no appeals after the third try. We won our claim on the third try, but one of my customers (an attorney) filed a claim that was denied all three times. He went a step further and wrote a letter to his congressman. The letter found its way through the government system and at some point he received confirmation that his letter was being forwarded to the Postmaster General for further investigation. Shortly after that, he received a check in the mail covering the amount for his claim. That was it; all over. There wasn't even an accompanying letter of explanation with the check.

Every search I did for alternative insurance covering shipping ended with uncertainty. Fed Ex and UPS cover damages or losses to a limited degree. Neither are interested in fussing with expensive collectibles. At least the post office has registered/insured mail holding every handler in their system accountable for the package, and that shipping tier insures up to $50,000.

So, maybe your package won't get lost. Shippers better pack like their life depends on it. Damage is one thing a shipper can control, the package can be built with as much packaging material and reinforcement as a shipper would like; or not. We all want to save a buck and packaging material can be expensive. I'd feel bad if I packed with a weak hand and the recipient was angered by my lack of effort. The loss of a package carries equal consternation.

USPS tracks packages, but you have to pay for that extra service for basic mail-outs. Fed Ex and UPS track packages every step, yet packages do go missing. Just because a package flows through their system doesn't guarantee it's where their tracking system says it is. For example: packages sent through UPS from Diamond. The package tracks to a certain point then momentarily disappears. The system can't work efficiently enough against the high volume of packages. It takes time to play catch-up. On rare occasions the package was generated at Diamond with a tracking number, but never arrived. We call those packages "ghost" boxes. Neither Diamond nor UPS ever finds proof of their existence; only a tracking number that led nowhere. Thus, insurance against loss is a must since the shipping systems are not 100% safe.

The strongest alternative to risking a shipping entity's insurance coverage suggests buying a policy with a private insurer. That's one way to protect mailed packages from theft, flood, fire and the other fears, especially at store locations. Our collectible comics are fragile and imperiled by roaming thieves. Most traditional insurance companies avoid offering policies for collectibles. If they do cover them the costs are high, often too high to make sense for many collectors. That's especially true if the collector's goal is geared specifically toward insuring shipping.

Within the world of insurance there exist insurance entities that offer insurance for specific collectibles. There are companies that insure classic cars and boats, there are companies that concentrate on jewelry policies and there are companies to insure comic books. Their goals are to write policies for people that maintain and/or ship valuable comic books. At last count with Google-search, there at least four companies vying to write policies for comic book owners and shippers.

Several of us searched the web for stories reviewing policy claims with these companies. We found few examples of claims going public. The claims that were posted on the internet included examples of domestic and international shipping insurance issues. I found several specific stories where claimants complained that their policies were cancelled right after successfully filing claims for either lost or damaged packages. These policy holders posted that they were led to believe their shipments were inarguably covered against loss or damage; fully covered. The truth makes it uncomfortable for me to buy a policy with them.

In 2006 I held a policy with one of those companies. I

have no interest in stating the name of the company here. Our store was covered against flood, fire, theft and the like. Unfortunately we suffered a flood in 2007 and suffered about $12,000 in damages to boxes of modern comic books and some shelving. The policy carrier argued with us about value, set unrealistic terms to maintain the water-damaged comic books for a lengthy period of time and stalled on making payment. We fought back but could only argue them into paying about 85% of the value.

I dwelled on canceling the policy. I reasoned that I would need them to at least protect my outgoing shipments. I decided to reread my policy about coverage during the claim negotiation and skipped over shipping coverage. I went back and reviewed that page and was flabbergasted to learn that shipping protection was not 100% guaranteed. Nor was I likely to get full coverage if I didn't offer independent proof of the value of shipped comic books. All the fine print amounted to "why am I with these guys?"

I canceled my policy.

My exhaustive search for any reputable insurer that would handle shipped comic book coverage ended as this article ends; empty-handed. Comic book insurer policies have hoops to jump through to guarantee coverage of shipped comics. That's some fine print/required reading before anyone commits to a policy.

I'm tired of paying in to the USPS Insurance Slush Fund. I don't want to go on a letter-writing campaign to our government for a logical change at the USPS level. I'm wary of buying an expensive policy with a national insurer. There's no other alternative except to avoid shipping. That's not going to happen.

Calculating my own experiences covering 17 years of shipping, I've dealt with less than six episodes of shipping malfeasance. Out of those examples I've only dealt with one missing package issue; an eBay buyer in Japan claimed it never arrived. I had no way to counter his claim because protection really stops at the U.S. border. He got his way and I covered the cost. I think we are all caught up in a classic "Catch-22" scenario: I need to insure the package to protect myself, but if I insure it and something happens I may not be protected. Ugh!

2016 was the year of DC Rebirth. Similarly, Marvel Now became Now Marvel. Outside of the most extreme variants neither company's changes have registered successful as sales figures go. The initial surge with #1s reduced down to pre-2015 sales numbers. DC's $2.99 twice-monthly titles read well and I found them fun. Some of my customers, however, aren't willing to pay more than $2.99 a month for one title, so the $5.98 (minus store discount) simply provided fence-sitters with jumping-off points. I like much of the comics DC is putting out, so this isn't a grievance directed at them as much as an observation that affects my business the wrong direction. Then there is 2016's DC Comics' heavily-awaited story of the year, *Dark Knight: Master Race*; late, over-priced and pointless to what was happening in the DC Universe. We lost money on over-orders of variants and fewer than expected read the short-run title.

Marvel is a different story. I find their stuff often cumbersome to read. This is a first for me because Marvel comics have been my target reads since the mid-1960s. Their variant and restart madness has confused my customers lost in translating a Marvel Now #1 with a Now Marvel #1. It all appears designed to sell in short-term gains without the predictability of long-running titles. Rampant speculation is still the order of the day. Look at *Invincible Iron Man*: one permutation of the title's #1 hit the stands with a release date of October 2015 with a whopping 279,000 copies. November 2015 the sales for that title dropped to just under 60,000. In December the recorded sales figure is just under 50,000. That's Iron Man, a core character!

Is it the art? My customers don't like all of Marvel's art, so that distaste affects their purchases. Is it the story? I'm afraid it might be. Is it the fence-sitters waiting for jumping-off points? Nowadays that seems to be the norm. Too many titles seemed irrelevant to the requests of Marvel readers and to the Marvel Universe in general. Forgettable titles added prominence to characters no reader was asking for. There's complicating a universe with a huge array of second- and third-tier characters, and then there's over-complication. How about *Civil War II*? My employees found it boring and redundant. The constant shipping delays were maddening to our customers. The other tie-ins moved on without the *Civil War II* mini-series. We already knew how it was going to end before the last issue of *Civil War II* shipped. The drop-off in sales for everything *Civil War II* was a business-killer.

We center our sales on back issues, buffering sales against the unpredicted declination of new comic book sales. Back-issue sales are strong for us through the store, web site and on the road. We had our most profitable Comic-Con International in 2015, bolstering our opinion that if geared-up right a dealer should continue to do well at that show. Our store plunged into hundreds of collections over the past year, many of them exactly what we wanted, on different levels. On some levels the sales of those collections have supplanted the sales of new comics. The back-issue sales are more lucrative than our new comics. This is my theory: the back-issue people want to read the stories, invest in a key or flip the books quickly for profit. If you believe they like the stories then you can understand why our customers don't like today's comic book stories. Some stories are convoluted, some stories work their way through a title of negligible popularity. If the book is failing then the company drops the title. My readers know this and are hesitant to get started on something that may end abruptly or rarely even be published (*Karnak*, *Hawkeye*). The stories appear tedious, over-wrought and they go on so long they seem to be going nowhere.

It's easy enough for me to make comparisons. I still read new comics; 60-80 titles monthly, and I've read most of the DCs and Marvels of the Silver and Bronze Ages. I guess that makes me a legacy reader. Perhaps that also means Marvel and DC (mostly Marvel) do not regard me as a viable target for their current comics. I say perhaps because I feel Marvel doesn't get how many of us were happy with tales as they were scripted even as recently as 15 years ago. DC made a point of addressing legacy readers with Rebirth, asking us to enjoy the attempt to reach out to older readers that may have quit on them during New 52. I am more comfortable with their titles, but I didn't necessarily want DC to try and tie them into their TV universe. That's not seducing enough readers to significantly increase my sales.

Overall, our interpretation of the back issue market seems a lot like last year; another year where we replaced variant cover sales with greater emphasis on old comics. We're not making claims that we're "killing it" with variant sales while playing down the vast quantity of unsold comics we could never profit from. Clichés noted, here's why the trend at our store is consistently reversed from other stores (select one or more; use pen):

- We targeted specific comic book collections to appeal to our customers.
- Most stores thrive on a diversity of gaming, toys, modern comics and other ephemera; not old back-issues.
- Lack of unnecessary clutter burdening the customers.
- A healthy respect for the windfall in business comic book conventions can generate.
- We have a chip reader.
- The consistent acquisition of highly-prized individual back issues, selling at competitive prices.
- We work through our lunch hour.
- We label our grade-worthy comics with grades; the price gun sticker on a $2,000 book without a grade is ludicrous.
- Everything is organized. Not only can we find things in our store, so can the customers.
- Nobody reads these things anyway.

Our web site is the repository for our significant back issue sales. The sold listings on our site post the prices we got, not the prices we listed the comic at. Over time we've posted enough sales to prove that we get prices for comics that are higher than GPA's recorded sales prices.

We use Facebook, Twitter and Instagram to promote new collections, which attracts the locals.

CGC vs. CBCS: either is fine with us, we are not conflicted. Our customers seem less conflicted than even a year ago.

This book will become available during the week of Comic-Con International 2017. At the rate we are going we will have more, new collections to showcase, so come visit us at booth #1115!

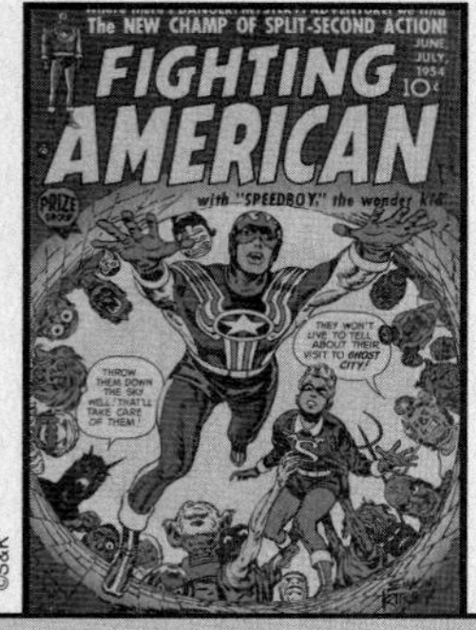

***Fighting American** is a popular Atom Age title despite running only 7 issues. (#2 shown)*

Terry O'Neill
Terry's Comics/CalComicCon/ Nationwide Comics

This report focuses on conventions and mail order aspects of comic collecting. Sales from 2015 to 2016 have been very strong.

Golden Age (1938-1945): The Golden Age market is doing quite well. Fawcett and Dell titles have been moving again. They have great stories and are very affordable. People looking to expand their collecting habits are starting to look at these rare gems of comic history as a great and somewhat affordable (compared to availability) area to collect. Many people are starting to look at the more obscure titles from the Golden Age as it gives them a challenge to complete runs or sections of runs. Certain titles published by Ace, Fox, MLJ, Centaur and Chesler are low in *Guide,* but try finding them. One of our long time customers has just completed an entire run of *Looney Tunes*, not an easy task. Some sales of note: *Silver Streak* #6 GD- $1,350, *Superman* #1 CGC VG+ Resto $35,000, #2 CGC GD $3,360, *Fight Comics* #31 CGC VG $1,600, *Circus the Comic Riot* #1 VG- $1,020, *Looney Tunes* #1 CGC GD $2,778, #2 PGX VF $1830, *Mickey Mouse Magazine* V1#1 FN- $5270, and *Crime Does Not Pay* #33 CGC VG/FN $850.

Atom Age (1946-1955): With lower print runs and poor quality paper, as well as so many publishers, this era is still a largely un-explored collecting frontier. The following genres were selling well: War, Humor and Teen Humor titles like *Battle*, *Blondie*, *Looney Tunes* and *Kilroys*. A title to mention would be *Space Western* as it is a unique cross-over between Western and Sci-Fi. *Fighting American*, while only running seven issues, was being requested often. Other short runs are being sought after, like *Black Knight*, *Yellow Claw*, *Dizzy Dames*, *Hillbillies* and *G.I. Jane*. This era is a great place to start a new run for your collection just for the challenge. Some sales of note: *Casper the Friendly Ghost* # 1 VG- $1,150, *Journey into Mystery* #1 CGC GD $2,200, *Willie Comics* #16 CGC FN $250, *Annie Oakley* #1 CGC VG/FN $475, *Marines in Action* #3 CGC VF $200, *Tell it to the Marines* #2 CGC VF- (double cover) $350, and *Thing* #12 VG/FN $500.

Silver Age (1956-1970): Silver Age prices are currently stable and interest is as strong as ever. High grade DC keys may have the most potential. That said, *Fantastic Four* #48 and #52 are hard to keep in stock. Two of the most affordable early Silver Age Marvels are *Daredevil* #1 and *Sgt. Fury* #1, if you don't currently own a copy, better get one soon as the prices are headed up. As always, *Silver Surfer* #1 and 4 sell very well, usually above *Guide* prices. Also *Strange Tales* #110 and #135 are quite often sought after. Some sales of note: *Amazing Fantasy* #15 NC $2500,

Blue Beetle Charlton 1964 V1#1 CGC NM+ $2400, *Daredevil* #2 CGC NM $3,600, *Showcase* #4 GD/VG $12,000, #6 FN/VF $2,600, #22 VG $2,200, *Strange Tales* #133 NM/MT $2,800, *Tales of Suspense* #57 NM $5000, *Green Lantern* #1 VF- $2,850, *Sgt. Fury* #13 CGC NM $1750, *Teen Titans* #1 CGC NM $2400, *Thunder Agents* #1 CGC NM $650, and *Dynamo* #1 CGC NM/MT $495

Bronze Age (1971-1985): *Tomb of Dracula* #10 and *Werewolf By Night* #32 are two of the most asked for issues. A close third is *House of Secrets* #92, still affordable and with the beautiful Bernie Wrightson cover. *Hero for Hire* and *Power Man* saw a lot of interest due to the *Luke Cage* Netflix series. Titles like *Marvel Feature*, *Defenders* #1, and *Iron Fist* #14 have been selling well with the speculation about a show being made. The Legion of Monsters is also seeing interest in with Ghost Rider (*Marvel Spotlight* #5 and *Ghost Rider* #1) and Moon Knight out there. It's only a matter of time before the rest of the Marvel Monsters make their appearances in TV or movies. Some sales of note: *Incredible Hulk* #181 CGC VF $2,000, *Giant-Size X-Men* #1 CGC NM- $1800, *House of Secrets* #92 CGC VF $820, and *All Star* #58 CGC NM+ $600,

Magazines: Sales of magazines have been limited this past year. We bring only one or two boxes of high grade or key magazines to shows. All other sales are from the catalog. There are lots of hidden gems in those black and white magazines. Some of the best artists of the era made their debuts in Warren and Marvel magazines. Some sales of note: *Savage Sword of Conan* #20 CGC NM/MT $150, #28 CGC NM/MT $150, *Vampirella* #112 CGC VF/NM $200, *Savage Tales* #1 VF $135, and *Creepy* #63 NM- $95.

Modern Age & Independents(1986-Now): *Preacher* was in demand for some time. All *Marvel Super Heroes Secret Wars* were excellent sellers at many conventions. The early 1980s re-peaked my interest in comic books because of the great stories and artwork in PC, Eclipse, First and other independent companies, producing high quality, more adult storylines. Keep a watch on *Fantasy Quarterly: Elfquest*, while from the '70s, it is truly independent and has a lot of potential. Some sales of note: *G.I. Joe* #26 PGX NM/MT $150, *NYX* #3 CGC NM/MT $900, *Omega Men* #3 PGX NM/MT $160, *Savage She-Hulk* #1 PGX NM/MT $190, *Amazing Spider-Man* #361 CBCS NM+ $100, *Batman: Harley Quinn* nn PGX NM/MT $400, and *Watchmen* #1 PGX NM/MT $200.

Graded books: We offer all our third party graded comics in our eBay store. Sales are constant throughout the year. Most of the comics we grade are keys or very high grade expensive books. We try to only submit comics that are worth at least $75 as the time and effort to get them graded adds considerable costs to the product. We buy many comics already graded for what we normally pay for the un-graded versions, so don't add the cost to yourself unless you are sure they have more value than the cost of grading them. Selling graded comics has produced a steady income stream throughout the year, especially when there are few or no comic conventions going on.

Internet Sales: We sell comics from our website by phone or e-mail request as we do too many conventions to have an accurate listing. We still get a lot of requests for scans but we cannot accommodate all the requests and get anything else done. We will send scans for items over $100 and always offer a 30-day unconditional return on all sales. After we have comics for a few years with no interest, we often will send them to the auction houses for sale as they have clients we don't. That said, remember: Whenever you consign comics to auctions with no reserve, you are rolling the dice that two or more people are looking at that auction during the particular window of time your item is offered. Most of our entire inventory is at www.terryscomics.com.

In summary, there was no shortage of demand for the high grade comic books that give the owner a better return than most other forms of investment. I did not start selling comics as a dealer but just as a guy that wanted money to buy more comics to read, so don't forget the original purpose of the hobby.

Michael Pavlic
Purple Gorilla Comics

Holy Moley am I glad 2016 is now in the rear view mirror. My little corner of the world has been dealing with the worst recession in 30 years, tens of thousands of people lost their (generally well paying) jobs. Countless businesses have closed. The loyalty of my customers is much more of a factor in my continued existence than any cost cutting measures I've taken. There are now signs that the economy is slowly starting to revive and the worst is over. I hope so, as I don't think there are too many jobs available for 50 year old comic book sellers out there!!

Now, I know you aren't reading my report to find out the state of Alberta's economy. Any business that lasts long enough will experience hardships, moments of terror and existential crisis. There ain't no guarantees in business or in life.

So let's focus on the positive shall we? Even in a recession, key books from any era still sell and sell quickly at *Guide* price at least. Anything Deadpool sells, as demand still outstrips supply by a wide margin. I've mentioned this in a few reports now, but *Deadpool: Circle Chase* #1 is still a $100 book here, and *X-Force* #2 $45. Harley Quinn is just as popular and supplies are even more scarce. Carnage is now the most popular comic character not associated with movies or TV and I still get $150 for an *Amazing Spider-Man* #361 (1st print). Anything with this guy in it starts at $10. Anything.

For the Silver and Bronze Age comics, any *Amazing Spider-Man* moves briskly, at any grade, for at least 1.25x *Guide*. *Fantastic Four* will sell almost as quickly, but much closer to *Guide*. Of course *Doctor Strange* moves fast, but since it was a weaker selling title back in the day, it's much harder to replace than the old Web-Head. *X-Men* (up to about #143) also have traction. I now consider anything by Neal Adams as "key", can't keep anything in. Even *Jerry Lewis*. Getting that way with Kirby books too, both Marvel and DC, especially the Fourth World issues. *Captain America*, *Thor*, early *Defenders*, all Marvel horror from the 1970s, *Flash*, *Green Lantern*, *Superman*, *Wonder Woman* all sell reasonably well. Silver Age *Batman*, once an easy sell, now languish on my walls, unloved, except for keys and anything by Adams. I am puzzled as to why this is happening.

For the Copper Age, in general, Marvel outsells every other publisher combined by a huge margin. *Amazing Spider-Man*, *Avengers*, *Captain America*, *Punisher*, *Transformers* and *Iron Man* lead the way, with *Hulk* and *Wolverine* not too far behind. McFarlane *Hulk* never lasts. Not much is selling DC wise. *Wonder Woman* does reasonably well as does *Flash*, but *Batman* especially has fallen off the map (again, except keys). Just like *Uncanny X-Men*, the biggest selling titles of the 1980s and 1990s have lost a lot of popularity, at *Guide* price. I had a Black Friday sale where I priced many of my back issues at $2 each and the biggest sellers were, you guessed it, *X-Men* and *Batman*. So there is a demand, but the price point might be too high, especially for the over-printed 1990s books. For the independent titles, the consistent sellers were *Aliens*, *Predator*, Dark Horse *Star Wars* and *Spawn*. Anything horror related, be they EC reprints, *Twisted Tales* and the other PC titles by Bruce Jones, movie adaptations or tie-ins, Clive Barker, *The Crow*, Mr. Monster Super-Duper Specials (and any other pre-code reprint comics) all sell quickly at at least $10 and are hard to replace. Romance comics do reasonably well too, especially if the cover is unintentionally hilarious (and trust me, that's a big number!). Toy tie-ins like Masters of the Universe and video game comics (especially the old Valiants) are always in demand.

I move plenty of comics that are more "off the beaten path", things like *Savage Sword of Conan*, Undergrounds (especially Crumb, Corben and Freak Bros.), Westerns (Dell photo covers) and kids comics. These folks are readers, as opposed to collectors. They don't really care what their collection is worth, they just enjoy the hobby. Lower grade copies can sell just as fast, if not faster than high grades.

It's important to me and my business that I get younger readers into comics. I go out of my way to stock old, kid friendly comics and I keep the price low ($2-$4) to let the parents know that these comics are meant to be read and enjoyed and to not worry about the "value". I've sold long boxes work in a few short months. We, as an industry, must work hard to attract a new generation of comic readers/collectors, otherwise, as the years move on and those of us who've been comic collecting or selling for decades shed our mortal coils and join the Uni-Mind, who's going to replace us? Who's gonna buy your comics? I don't know what the percentage of us that will be hitting or passing retirement age in 25 years, but I'll bet it isn't insignificant.

Everyone who reads these columns and uses this price guide should know by now that the supply of comics, especially key ones, are now stable. There will not be a sudden drop in the supply of *Incredible Hulk* #181 because thousands were destroyed in a mysterious fire. There will probably not be a "warehouse find" of cases of it either. No, the amount of *Incredible Hulk* #181 that exist today, will exist 25 years from now. What can change is the demand for *Incredible Hulk* #181. Will there be the same demand for it 25 years from now? We all hope so, after all, it's gone up steadily now for 40 years. The best way to ensure this is to have a new generation of collectors who desperately want to pay any price for that *Hulk* book. The older generations of collectors who wanted a copy will have gotten their one by then. I wanna be selling comics to people 25 years from now, therefore, I sell kids comics today.

Despite the economy hardships we Albertans have faced and my lingering concerns about the future of comic collecting, I am still thrilled after all these years that I'm able to make a living doing what I LOVE. I'd like to thank a few people who always have my back: Dave at Amazing Fantasy in Red Deer, Ben, Martin and Trevor at Phoenix Comics, Sgt. Erock, Steph and Dom. I'd like to especially thank my loyal customers, for with out them, I'm just a guy who has 45,000 comics jammed in his one bedroom apartment. And finally, I'd like to blame Doyle, 'cos it's still all his fault!

Bill Ponseti
Fantastic Worlds Comics

Greetings Comic Lovers.

2016 has been a very interesting year for me and the hobby as a whole. I pretty much liquidated my entire Golden and Silver Age collection from 2014-16 and found ready buyers for just about everything. The back issue market could not be stronger. Just sit through a Sunday Heritage internet auction and watch everything sell at or above *Guide*, or even at or above GPA. Even the raw lower grade lots sell for more than a dealer would pay, as his/her margin would be non-existent.

After a 20 year absence, and probably after taking leave of my senses, I decided to return to owning a comic book shop. I sold my shops in New Orleans back in 1996, and now have another brick and mortar store in Scottsdale, AZ. Missing 20 years of new comic continuity has me at a disadvantage, but I'm doing my best to catch up as best as I can.

What I have been happy to observe is that there are MANY more youngsters coming in and buying comics than there were in 1996. And they aren't just buying new comics, but back issues as well. Both boys and girls from 10-16 make up a large percentage of our customer base.

We sell Silver and Bronze Age keys as quickly as we can get them in, but our replacement cost on this has gotten higher and higher, and there is beginning to be price resistance in the hobby to the new normal.

The DC Rebirth was a big success for us and still sells well as new collectors want to have all the issues they missed when they first came out. *Civil War II* started off with a bang then kind of fizzled out.

My initial hope was that there would be some collections surfacing and that they would come into the store. My hopes were exceeded. In the first few months we had several very nice Silver Age collections come in and one collection of original owner Golden Age with many rare books in it. That set lasted about 24 hours.

I think the motion picture industry continues to drive new collectors into the hobby as well as bringing old collectors that had left the hobby back in.

The future looks very bright for our hobby for both the new and back issue segments. We attended several west coast conventions this year and noted that business was very brisk with the dealers in attendance. I expect more of the same in 2017.

The original art market continues to spiral upward, and trying to figure it out is an enigma wrapped in a riddle. There are too few folks that control the pricing, and that makes it hard for new entrants into this wonderful area of collecting. But if you set your budget realistically, there is lots of amazing material out there to be had.

My next market report will have more detailed information as we will have been open over a year by then.

So, until next time. Warmest regards from sunny Scottsdale.

JEFF RADER
OFFBEAT ARCHIVES

We do not have anything current this year to report in the way of sales, but hopefully you find something else that piques your interest. Other than poking around looking for books to fill friends' want lists, along with filling gaps in my own collection, I have gone back to my first loves in comicdom; reading, and research (thanks for that, Jerry Bails!) It has been fruitful and added to the volumes of new data that I already have piled around me in notebooks. Hopefully next year I will have completed a volume full of much of the esoteric, unknown, unlisted, obscure tidbits like I usually put in my reports. The gents at *Overstreet* will also be getting files as I work my way through it all to add to the *Guide*. Research has always been my primary focus, and even when listing books to sell, I often run across unnoticed things worthy of mention; unlisted artists, character appearances, cameos, esoteric covers and stories, good girl art, drugs, and other things that would either have Fredric Wertham spinning in his grave and/or send a book right on to somebody's must-have list. Often when doing a page count I am pretty much incapable of not stopping to read anything that I have never read before. I have so much accumulated that it will probably take me years to get everything down but that's not a complaint. The fun is in reading comics to find the unmined items. If you are tired of chasing books that are temporarily affected by movie and TV bubbles, have watched your main want list books climb out of your price range, or just want books in your collection that will make it stand out from the rest, then keep reading.

Something that is still overlooked by much of the comic book collecting community is rarity. I am not talking about high grade books in census but rather books that can only be owned by a few in any grade. Many other collecting arenas are very rarity-driven. In coins the 1913 Liberty nickel is just one of the many coveted rarities that have collectors foaming at the mouth. Stamps? Mention the Inverted Jenny to any philatelist and watch their eyes pop. Just the name Honus Wagner will get any baseball card collector in a frenzy, yet in comics it is primarily high-dollar books that get all of the attention, rarity or scarcity aside. Even a younger set of collectors, those who thrive on Pokémon cards, have a holy grail. Ask any of them about the 1993 Black Lotus and you might just set off a stampede. "Rare in Grade" seems to be about the closest that many take notice of. Yeah, I do know that *Incredible Hulk* #1, and *Fantastic Four* #12, are real beasts to get in high grade, but if you are willing to settle for a nice looking lesser grade copy it can be done pretty much instantaneously. Yet even if/when low grade examples of the non-comic mentions I made above came to market they would set off epic bidding wars and make headlines worldwide. Not so in comics. Given enough funds one could go out and buy a complete set of Marvels, even in high grade, in a short time. I regularly see currently-hot books that I could nab as many copies a day as I wished, while there are others that I can (and have) spend years looking for no matter how much I would be willing to spend on them. No matter how much money a collector has, if they are looking for the coveted *Amazing Man* #26, then they can expect to wait forever for when, IF, a copy shows up, then be prepared to dig deep in the pockets because this book will fly regardless of condition. You Centaur fiends know what I'm talking about.

Another lesser-known rarity is *Adventure Comics* #26 (what is it with these #26s?) This book was one of the final books on the list of DC completionist, Ian Levine, when he was wrapping up his ages-long quest for everything DC. It proved extremely elusive even with much of the community scouring the world for a copy. And he is not the only one that was/is seeking a copy of this one. It is also one of the final pre-hero books and has an ad for *Action Comics* #1 with an early appearance of what was to come when Superman changed everything. Those are only two examples that will be mentioned with reverence once more comic collectors start focusing on rarity. Copies of these books, and so many others, are firmly entrenched in collections of those that know that they will never find another if they let go of theirs. The hunt for hens' teeth also makes for a fun time, as long as you are in no hurry.

While those two are already relatively known, and already go for multiples of *Guide*, in any grade, I have lists of countless examples of books just as near-impossible, and some moreso, to find that are within the budget of any collector. Years ago I saw the ad on the back cover of *Key Comics* #5 that showed a copy of *Masterpieces Illustrated* #1.

It stuck in my head forever. I had been told, and do believe now, that no public copies ever made it to the newsstand. But that insatiable need to keep looking never let up. I regularly kept up the hunt, just in case, and nearly made a mess in my chair when I saw a copy for sale online. It was not a copy of the actual book that some kid nabbed off of the stands but the ashcan that Lloyd Jacquet put together, with all new artwork, in an attempt to nab a share of the *Classics Comics* market after he left Gilberton. It never came to fruition but it made for a heck of a great book, with gorgeous artwork, some of which did see print in other titles. There's one that only one lucky collector can own, but there are so many others that can be had by a few if you dig deep enough.

Another that flew under the radar for decades was *Super Duper Comics* #3 (the only issue published and, though published in Canada, also distributed in the U.S.) It was pretty much an overlooked "Who cares?" book in the *Guide*, and ignored by collectors for decades. This book was the 1st appearance of Mr. Monster, and his only Golden Age appearance. It also has a Nelvana story that Canadians will trample anyone else at auction to get ahold of! When Michael T. Gilbert breathed new life into Mr. Monster decades later this book still laid dormant. I had been on the hunt for a copy for decades with no luck. Fortunately a fellow collector passed his copy on to me. After enjoying that for a few years I had to let it go. It was not a high grade copy, but presented nicely. That book that, in that grade, was listed for around $35 and went into a market that had then woken up as to its significance, and its rarity. It went for over $800, and soon after that sale a friend let his similar copy go for over $900! I doubt I will ever be lucky enough to have another but the hunt is what can make things so fun. You do not need to be Scrooge McDuck to enjoy our hobby. On that note; want a nice key book for a bargain? Go nab a *Four Color* #178 – the 1st appearance of Uncle Scrooge (and compare that to *Uncle Scrooge* #1 (*FC* #386 that came out 5 years later).

Since most key appearances, semi-keys, wannabe-keys, z-list characters, and the like have been "outed" and speculated on, with prices rising, and falling, faster than the tide it may seem as if there may not be much left to dig up. One fun affordable area that still has not been hit too hard with the speculation bit yet are prototypes. Well, other than *Superman* #123 that used to be a fairly well kept secret. Now that Supergirl has soared to new heights that book has found a new fan base and she's flown to heights unattainable for many. Add to that the fact that this book comes from an era in which DCs are not easy to find, especially in grade. While many books listed as being prototypes are really a stretch of the imagination some are actually pretty good scores. If you are a Hulk maniac check out *Journey Into Mystery* #62, 66, and 70, with Xemnu. They have already gotten some attention but are still relatively affordable and pretty cool in seeing how they might have led to the creation of The Hulk. Also check out the reverse Spider-Man prototype in #73 in which a spider gets irradiated and gets the powers of a human, while retaining the power to shoot webs. Fun stuff that will not break your bank. There are countless prototypes out there all the way from the dawn of the Golden Age and are a great niche to focus on. You can probably cross the Dr. Occult appearances off that list unless you are already well into early DCs as they are near impossible, and do not trade hands too often, but Dr. Occult is an interesting way to look at how Siegel and Shuster ran some parallels that led up to the introduction of Superman in *Action Comics* #1. They are already pricey, and many Very Rare, but having even a low grade example of a pre-Superman belongs on every collector's must-have bucket list.

For those that enjoy the hunt looking for rarities there is still so much to be looked for out there. Go out and try to find a copy of *Kokonut Komics* from 1949. It is not yet in the *Guide*, but listed in *The Photo-Journal Guide to Comic Books* with a Scarcity Index rating of 9, meaning that, in his long travels, Ernie Gerber then figured that up to 10 copies existed. I think that the internet has shaken a few more out of the trees but it is still RARE. I have been on the prowl for over 30 years and only managed to lay my hands on two copies. The cool thing about this comic is that, despite its rarity, it can also be seen as a Foreign/non-U.S. comic as it was published in Hawaii before they became a state. Another one I have long been tracking is Fox's *Zoot Comics* #2. This one is listed as being an 8 on the Scarcity Index and while they do occasionally pop up it is far from often. I have nabbed some over the years and my quirk about reading paid off as I found a then-unnoticed superhero story featuring the 1st (only?) appearance of The Jaguar. They are out there but I doubt that we will be flooded with too many new copies anytime in the future. While on the subject of rarity, "Scarce/Rare/Very Rare in *Overstreet*", and Gerber's Scarcity Index, it is due time that hundreds of books gets reassessed and that is part of what I have been spending much of my time on. There are some that are generally thought of as near impossible to find that I almost trip over regularly. Avon's *The Funnies Annual*, from 1959, is a perfect example. A friend and I used to laugh about his growing pile of them that was more than 25 copies deep. Conversely, there are books listed low on the Scarcity Index that I have yet to find in my searching. Hopefully soon I will have all in order and get a revised, updated list of my observations out there.

While there is much speculation going on, books rising out of nowhere to wildly-priced heights, then plummeting back to where they were, or close, to fade back into obscurity, I am banking on Rarity being the final frontier of comic collecting. Yep, we will all always drool over those sweet Marvel keys, *Action Comics* #1, *Detective Comics* #27, and all the rest that make the mainstream news, but there are already different groups of collectors that appreciate just how near-impossible, and even impossible, it is to add certain books to their collections. Variant collectors know exactly what I am talking about, so do the rabid seekers of Canadian Whites, and those that seek out foreign copies of their favorite comic. Since I am already rambling between subjects; how many know about the variants, and different printings, that exist of *Superman* #1, *Batman* #1, *Marvel Comics* #1, and others back in the day? Not that there are but a few collectors that could ever consider completing a collection of those but it is still fun to look into. I am sure that there are more there that will show up in time when collectors compare like issues and find discrepancies. Another relatively new group of collectors that has come to know how much the thrill of the hunt is are the Modern collectors that seek out later printings of certain books. I am not much of a Modern guy but even that is a bit intriguing to me.

Thanks to all of the comic related media being done, our once-geeky, "shh, don't tell anybody!", hobby has gone mainstream and brought in thousands of new collectors. I am amazed at some of the emails I have gotten asking about comics and, believe it or not, we actually have gotten more female readers and collectors than I ever could have imagined. Hopefully many of this new influx of new collectors stick around and take a look into the many areas of collecting that might just set the hook in them.

We happen to have one of the few hobbies left in which there are goldmines of overlooked and neglected areas that are ripe for research. The only thing about that is that you have to actually want to open a book up and read it to see what is hidden inside. In doing that I have found reams of unlisted, overlooked goodies such as unlisted Ditko, and Matt Baker (among others) stories, mind-blowing Good Girl Art in places that you would never expect to find it, character appearances that have eluded notice for decades, atomic bomb stories and panels, hidden (and not so hidden) innuendoes, and so much more that I'll be expanding on as fast as I can. Discoveries in earlier books also tend to make a lasting impact as opposed to the newer up and down bit. Take a gander at *Cindy* #37 from Marvel in 1949. NO, I really mean it, go take a look at that cover! That book sat unnoticed by all but a few for over 60 years. Once word got out that it was a 5-star GGA cover, done in gorgeous greytone to boot, it went wild. If you do manage to find a copy that somebody is willing to let go of you can be assured that you will be paying multiples of *Guide*. The same thing happened with the great sweater girl Betty GGA cover on *Archie Comics* #50 a few years back. Even after a few years it is still highly sought after and another that refuses to be found for *Guide*. Neither of those will ever be had for a bargain again. These are among the type of books still out there that, when discovered, and brought to light, you can pretty much name your price.

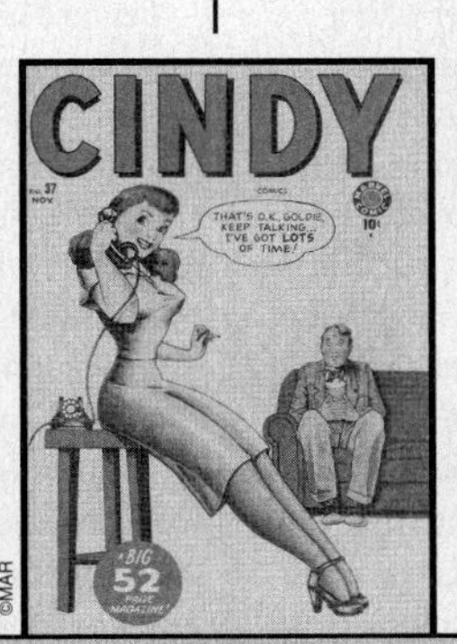

A Good Girl Art cover (and greytone as well) makes ***Cindy*** *#37 one to watch.*

Take a look at Sabrina the Teen-age Witch appearances in *Archie's Madhouse*. It was not so long ago that those books were unexplored territory, lumped in with the rest of the non-Sabrina books, and considered slag. Even now issue #32 is still listed with a "?" signifying that it is unknown if Sabrina appears in that issue. Well, yep, Sabrina does appear in that issue so expect that one to jump up to be on a par with the rest when it becomes common knowledge. Dig deep because there are who-knows-how-many *Cindy* #37s just waiting to be pulled out of obscurity. Much of where I find the unheralded stuff is in the eras that predate organized fandom and all of the early fandom guys and gals started indexing all they could find. If you do find something noteworthy, then drop all of your preconceived notions about high grades. You may just never find another.

I am not so much into the movie/TV bump stuff so I will leave that to those that have it down to an art. But, one example that was interesting was *Tales to Astonish* #13, with the 1st innocuous appearance of Groot. For ages this book has been just one of the many Marvel pre-hero books that were collected primarily by those that loved the Kirby and Ditko work that makes these books such great reading. Now? Due to the *Guardians of the Galaxy* movie this book went out of the range of many pre-hero collectors and into the realm of "Hot" books. The same thing happened to *Marvel Preview* #7 which used to be a cult classic among old Marvel magazine lovers for the great Larkin cover, and Satana story. Now? Satana has been relegated to a minor cover mention and the book is sought after by everybody that wants that 1st appearance of Rocky/Rocket Raccoon. I'll just wait for the heat to die down before nabbing a copy myself.

I am also a bit confused by the crazy jump on *Marvel Super-Heroes* #18, 1st appearance of Guardians of the Galaxy. I have always been a fan of that book, and it has its merits, but am a bit curious as to if I am the only one that has noticed that the line-up in the original Guardians seems to be just a bit more than a little off that what showed up by the time it became a newly-hot property. (I also wonder how long movie-bump books like *Marvel Preview* #4 - 1st Star-Lord, and #7 can be valued more than #2 which contains the first telling of the origin of one of the most well-established, popular, characters ever, The Punisher.) Go figger. I understand that ours is a media-driven hobby in which prices will always be affected by movies, television, etc. but only those with the most finely-tuned foresight that get in to buy first, and sell at the right moment, are the ones making the big bucks. Any seekers after that usually end up paying an (often temporary) inflated price. With the advent of the internet our once-mail-order hobby has gotten to where prices can chance drastically seemingly daily and what is considered Hot can go frigid at any minute. I love it just as much as any other old-school dealer seeing some old book that we once had wasting space in our old quarter boxes all of a sudden become "hot", but that can not last forever. For every one of the newly-outed books that may retain their value there will be countless more that sink as soon as the fad passes, or a movie flops, or fades into obscurity. If you are buying comics in hope of financing that mansion in the sky then this is the wrong hobby in which to do it. There are far safer methods of investing money if your first love is not in the comics themselves.

While the fads come and go there will always be our old standbys to keep us going. I also firmly believe that in this hobby we will soon start to recognize that rarities will become more and more sought after. There is something special about holding a book that only a handful can own. Someday I think that true comic rarities will be among some of those grabbing the attention of the public, just as a 1933 Double Eagle does.

Some overlooked, underappreciated, undervalued books that I have put on my watch list, some due to collectors sending me their updated want lists, others just from watching the marketplace, are:

Giant-Size Invaders #1, which is dated June 1975 while *Invaders* #1 hit the stands 2 months later yet gets all the glory. Hmmm...

Moon Knight seems to be a stable character with a decent following. I think that he has that staying power that the fads, and C-list characters, do not. I have been getting quite a few requests for his early solo stories in the *Hulk* magazine. *Hulk* #13 even has the first work by Bill Sienkiewicz on Moon Knight. We all know what stunning work he did on the Moon Knight series and his art was much of why that series became such a success. Remember what happened when Frank Miller took on *Daredevil* with #158? Earlier this year they could be had for a song but I have watched the prices steadily rise a bit as more catch on. While you're at it, nab a copy of *Rampaging Hulk* magazine #9. With a classic Avengers painted cover like that, plus a great Thor vs. Hulk battle, you can not go wrong. Just do it before that one gets too much attention.

There is gold to be found in those Curtis/Marvel magazines. Some collectors seem to ignore them due to the fact that they are not actual comic books but some great stuff is buried in them. *Savage Tales* is a great one, and #1 also has the oft-overlooked 1st appearance of The Man-Thing. *Deadly Hands of Kung Fu* is bulging at the seams with appearances from everybody from Bruce Lee and Iron Fist, to Captain America, and lots more. *Marvel Preview/Bizarre Adventures* is a killer run even if only for the great reading they tucked in there. *Dracula Lives!* is a must for any collector of Marvel monsters and Tomb of Dracula. If you're a *Mad* or *Cracked* magazine nut, then don't neglect *Crazy* just because it was not one of the top two. This mag is packed with great hilarious covers, artwork by just about anybody you could imagine, plus parodies of pretty much every pop culture phenomenon from the '70s through the '80s. Go nab some and you'll be hooked. The *Planet of the Apes* magazine run contains stories that never appeared in the comic book run so unless you grab those...your collection is not complete, Chim Chim. *Marvel Comics Super Special* already has some high-profile, high-demand, issues but there are still some affordable goodies left in there as well. If some of the stories that appeared in these magazines had been in regular comic books they would now cost you multiples of what you can get them for in the mags sitting as neglected bargains.

DC and Marvel treasury editions are still bargains. Due to their cumbersome size they have never really caught on with the mainstream. Their size also makes them hell to find in high grade as well. As prices of ultra-key books soar into the 7-figure range, the *Famous First Editions* are the absolute best way to read these classic books without having to spend a fortune. The first five issues even had a glossy inner cover that makes them even cooler to have. DC's *Limited Collectors' Edition*, including the *Famous First Editions*, ran for 59 issues and, while full of some of the best reprint stories imaginable, they also slipped in some previously unpublished material in issues as well. Marvel did the same with *Marvel Treasury Edition*, and a few other treasury titles. All of Marvel's then-most-popular characters ended up in there somewhere and some of the most significant Marvel tales, and origins, are in there as well. Don't scoff at them because they are not exactly the current trend, you might just miss out on some great buys. But best of luck trying to find the magazines, and to a much harder extent, the treasuries, in Near Mint. These books were just not cared for in the way that comic books were early on. While I am rambling about over-sized comics, go and nab a copy of *Wham-O Giant Comics* while you are at it. This crazy gigantic comic from 1967 measures out at 21" tall by 14" wide! As if that was not reason enough to snag one it also has artwork by Wallace Wood, Lou Fine, and countless others.

Titles such as *Marvel Collectors' Item Classics/Marvel's Greatest Comics*, *Marvel Comics Presents*, *Marvel Tales*, and other reprint titles are perfect ways for the beginner, or nostalgic old-timer, to read the best of the best Marvel stories without having to spend much more than they would going out to a nice dinner. Me? I'll take the comics over food any day! Many of these reprints were also published very near the time of the actual stories and as close as you can get in time to reading some of the otherwise unaffordable issues.

Whitman variant collectors have been fastidious in seeking out all of the possible Whitman/Gold Key and Whitman/DC poly-bag variants out there but I have recently had a couple inquiries about the rest of the Whitman/Gold Key books that have been considered reprints and/or junk for years. I have no idea just how many Gold Key comics exist with the Whitman logo, going back for ages, but they are numerous. Not too many are really paying much attention yet but the Whitman copies' print runs were a fraction of the Gold Key issues so maybe interest will start kicking in sometime soon. As for now, they can be picked up all over the place for pennies on the dollar in lots. Who knows? Maybe they will remain cheap books, which makes for great, cheap reading, or maybe they will catch the interest of some collectors that love research, and variants, and end up a nice commodity. (The Star Trek collectors, however, are already on top of this one. Nice job, Trekkers!)

Archie comics have finally blown up and attained wild prices, with no sign of slowing down. There are far more seekers of early issues than copies exist so the prices will likely be keeping on the rise for ages. There is a way of living vicariously on a budget though. Archie-type comics flooded the stands just as soon as other publishers saw what a hit MLJ had with the teens. Many Archie-swipe knockoffs, and teenage titles are similar, yet are very affordable, many being downright cheap, and others not so much. Check out *Jonesy*, *A Date With Judy*, *Buzzy*, *Millie the Model*, *Cookie*, *Wilbur*, *Bunny*, *Tippy Teen*, and a plethora of others over the ages. Many of these runs are relatively uncharted territory so if you do grab, and read, some you might just stumble across that next *Archie Comics* #50.

While not bargains, I have a friend shooting for a run of *Sensation Comics* #107-109, and *Sensation Mystery* #110-#116. That is definitely not an easy, nor cheap, chore but if you do not want to have to chase long runs that would take forever, and $$$$$$, then short runs can be a lot of fun. *Congo Bill* is another that is a mean challenge but you will have something to show off to the rest when you pull that one off. For you Marvel Maniacs give *Venus* a go. It only ran 19 issues but that short run somehow managed to bounce through just about every genre imaginable at the time. I'm not forgetting you EC Ghoulunatics. Give *Moon Girl* a look. She danced through titles, and title changes, just as well as she did genres. She came out the gate in *Happy Houlihans* #1 and *Moon Girl and the Prince* #1 (both on the stands at the same time), continued in *Moon Girl* for 5 issues, became *Moon Girl Fights Crime* in #7 and #8, then jumped over to *A Moon, A Girl...Romance* in issue #9 for one last hoorah and then disappeared to leave the last three issues of the series to go on without her. Yikes! If you are really up for a challenge that few dare even ponder go for the the 4-issue run of DC's *It's Gametime*. Yeah, I know, 4 issues sounds like a breeze, huh? Well go give it a shot and when you pull that one off I will be saluting you! If you manage that with copies that managed to escape the pencil, pen, or crayon of some happy kid then I'll be on a flight to see them ASAP. These titles are among what makes our hobby so rewarding.

I have got to wrap this at some point or I will just end up typing beyond the deadline, and into next year. But, before I finally pull the plug on this thing, there are another couple things to mention. Keep an eye on the activity on Canadian Whites. These books have finally come of age and are no longer a niche genre. Whereas it once was primarily proud Canucks, and a couple of us a bit further south, that loved them they have been kicked right into the mainstream. The Canadian Crew has been hard at work researching, compiling, and making discoveries galore (you guys know who you are, Walt, Tony, Scott, Ivan, Mike, Kevin, and all the rest, and I tip my trapper hat to all of you!) They have some indispensable info already out there but the best is on its way. Great work, guys!

Foreign comics (non-U.S., and non-Canadian) have also really jumped into the spotlight thanks to the insanely researched work by Tim Bildhauser and the crew at Foreign Comic Collector. They have really opened up the comic collecting community literally worldwide. It is fun seeing how your favorite comic looked when it was published in Italy, Turkey, Brazil, almost everywhere. Some of the original work in these foreign books is fascinating as well. You do know that Mexico beat Marvel to the punch by years in publishing Conan comics, don't you? This area has some of the rarest comics that exist, many being unique, and countless other presumed to have been lost to time. But do not stop looking. There is still gold to be found!

If you have made it this far, thank you! At the risk of RE-repetition, buy what you love, and read what you buy. If your comics ever end up monetarily just being stacks of pretty colored paper at least you have something that you have enjoyed collecting that you can always read.

GREG REECE & ALEX REECE
REECE'S RARE COMICS

GREG REECE - 2016 was another banner year for vintage comic books. We were able to pick up more Golden Age than any other year we've been in business and it sold briskly. We now have 4,000+ CGC/CBCS certified books on the website and another 4400+ raws. By the time you read this that number will have grown as having Austin join Alex has allowed us to catch up on getting inventory uploaded to the site (reececomics.com) A noticeable trend that developed in 2016 was absolute astronomical prices for key villain appearances, especially Joker covers. Books like *Detective Comics* #69, *Detective Comics* #71 just exploded. I believe as collectors are priced out of the super keys (*Action Comics* #1, *Batman* #1, *Detective Comics* #27, *Superman* #1, etc), they are moving onto the next best thing. There will be plenty of reports about what else was hot so I will move on to my investment picks for 2017, easily the most popular part of my report each year.

***Fantastic Four* #1:** It's hard to say exactly when this blue chip will start moving but it's when, not if. The deplorable stand-alone movies and Marvel seemingly undermining the current storyline are factors that could lead to this venerable franchise landing back in the Marvel Universe. If that happens you will be saying "I would have/should have/could have." Don't make that mistake. If you don't have a *FF* #1 in your collection, now is the time.

***Action Comics* #242:** This book has had a cultish following for what seems forever. I mean that purple cover, who can resist that? If DC could ever make a great Superman movie, and Brainiac was featured, it would result in a stratospheric spike. With just 75 copies grading 5.0 or better (at the time of this writing) and still affordable (relative to other Silver Age keys), there is a lot more upside than downside on this book.

***Daredevil* #1:** Yes, this book was on my list last year, and yes it appreciated. But I think there is still more room to run. A very iconic image (I fondly remember buying my 1st #1 in 1975 for $20. It was in the FN+ range). Netflix finished their second season and just knocked it out of the park. The only amendment I'd make is to now focus on 7.0+ copies as the low grades appreciated at the same rate as better copies, but are much, much more plentiful. So for those reasons I don't think the lower grade copies will perform as well.

***Brave And The Bold* #28:** This book took a breather in 2016 falling about 10% in most grades. With the *Justice League* movie right around the corner I'd anticipate renewed interest in *Brave and The Bold* #28.

***Showcase* #22:** After falling for 2-3 years after the not-well-received *Green Lantern* movie, this book is ready for a comeback. Copies were plentiful a couple of years ago and we just don't see this anymore. Reminds me very much of *Incredible Hulk* #1 from a few years back. The supply was dry for about a year, and then prices went insane.

***Tales of Suspense* #39:** This book has been flat for 3 years. I don't see it continuing. History has taught us to buy when books are out of favor. This is a blue chip classic.

***Marvel Super-Heroes* #18:** The *Guardians of the Galaxy* sequel is on the way and with fans just devouring the 1st movie, it seems #2 is already a guaranteed blockbuster. Fans who only own 1 Guardians book will own this one. Being a square bound I'd concentrate on 9.0 (these can be had for $700 right now. Ridiculously cheap), and higher grades.

***Showcase* #37:** One of my more speculative picks, this is all about whether a Metal Men movie ever gets made. With just 25 copies grading higher than 8.0, if it happens, the sky is the limit. If not, you still own a great looking book!

©DC

***Showcase* #37** *is a great-looking book to have, even if a Metal Men movie never happens.*

***House of Secrets* #92:** This book is not cheap but I think it has room to grow. "I gotta' get one of those one day". We hear at virtually every con. I wouldn't wait for this Wrightson signature work to fall anytime soon.

Show Reports

Wizard, New Orleans: We love doing this show for all of the reasons stated in previous years. It is scheduled perfectly, allowing us, and many others, a break from the cold. It is also a time to showcase and buy new material as most dealers haven't set up at a major show since the October NY show.

MegaCon, Orlando: Have to give the show organizers (Fan Expo) a pass since it was their first year running the show. But that said, load in was a nightmare. We couldn't have been stationed further from our booth for load in. And the now seemingly permanent change to Memorial day weekend is a disappointment. Sales were noticeably slower than in previous years. This show is now on our watch list.

C2E2, Chicago: Chicago is blessed to have 2 quality shows a year to choose from an astounding display of vintage comic books. And to the fans credit, they support both shows whole heartedly. If you haven't been, add it your show list.

Wizard, Chicago: Again, a show you must attend if you are a vintage collector. We were stationed again right beside the CGC booth and the amount of material being on site graded is incredible. It is easily the show we spend the most $$ at. There is literally not enough time to go through all of the booths.

Baltimore Comic Con: One of the last large scale shows owned by an independent operator. I hope Marc doesn't sell it anytime soon as the vibe of the show has been consistent from day 1. Comics, comics and more comics. Again, you could dig for 3 straight days and not get through all of the material for sale.

New York Comic Con: The show with the most pressure from a dealer standpoint (costs are @$10,000 to set up booth rental/hotel/food etc for the team) delivered yet again. Outside of San Diego (where we continue to languish on the waiting list), there is simply no show with the number of deep pocketed, hungry for the best material, customers.

My wish for everyone is world peace, health to your families and much happiness. Thanks for your support of our business over the years and I hope to see many of you on the trade show circuit in 2017.

Alex Reece - Reece's Rare Comics

Hello all! It is hard to believe that another year is closing, and thus another market report is upon us. 2016 was another great year for Reece's Rare Comics. Sales have continued to grow year over year, and to that end we hired Austin (Greg's other son, my younger brother) in June in order to keep up with the growth of our company. His first official show was Wizard World Philadelphia, and he did about five more after that. Stop by the booth sometime in 2016 and introduce yourself if you have not met him yet!

Speaking of shows, we did 14 in 2016. A big hand goes out to ReedPOP for putting on awesome Chicago and New York shows again, and Wizard World deserves recognition for their Chicago show that they have built; all three of these were monster successes for our team. There were several other shows that were great, but did not quite make the top tier status from a sales perspective. Marc Nathan's Baltimore show was very good again. Wizard World Philly, while having a dearth of dealers, was a great show for the dealers that did set up. Heroes was a great comic book show, with almost every booth occupied by actual comic book dealers (a refreshing sight, to be sure). We also did Wonder Con and Emerald City, and got to bring our full show stock to the West Coast for the first time in 4 years. Then there were the more regional shows. Motor City was decent from a sales perspective, while Wizard World Portland was flat out dismal. MegaCon suffered because of the move to Memorial Day Weekend, partially due to the fact that a number of buyers had holiday plans. Furthermore, the buyers from up North who used to fly down to escape the cold weather for a weekend were much more reluctant to come down when the temperatures were in the upper 90s for the entirety of the four day affair. Hopefully MegaCon takes a page from Wizard World's New Orleans show and moves it back to a non-holiday weekend in the colder months.

As far as what I noticed about sales at these shows, it will likely be in line with what many dealers are saying. High grade and key books sold extremely well. There was one particular show last year where we came in with four *Daredevil* #1s, CGC graded from 5.0-9.0, and we left the show having sold all of them. The same thing happened multiple times with *Amazing Spider-Man* #129s, *Hero for Hire* #1s, and many other key issues. All in all, the wall books sold exceedingly well, with the next biggest seller being high grade raws. Unfortunately, the trend of slow sales has continued on more run of the mill raw issues. Even when priced significantly under *Guide*, they are notably sluggish turns.

For investing, a popular question I am asked all the time is, "What do you see moving up in the near future?" I still think Gold and Silver keys are the best place to put your money from an investment standpoint. For instance, from 2015 to 2016, the value of an *Amazing Fantasy* #15 increased 40% in CGC 1.5, 37% in CGC 5.0, and in higher grades the jump is even more pronounced. A CGC 9.2 that sold for $192,000 in 2009 sold for $392,000 this past year. Obviously with a single sale in seven years, this data point is much harder to quantify, but the point is this: the value of the book is moving up all across the board, in any given grade. A Bronze Age book doing this similarly is *Incredible Hulk* #181, a book which continually defies gravity, even when many thought it had peaked a few years ago. There are innumerable examples of these types of books, but I will leave you with this: high grade, first appearances of major characters such as Spider-Man and Wolverine will hold their value and increase even as others fall away. The demand for first appearances of these characters extends beyond the comic book collecting community, and as such there is increased demand over other books.

With that said, however, let's delve into something a little more fun, namely, what is a book I see rising significantly in 2017? My pick is *Amazing Spider-Man* #300. This book sports perhaps the most iconic Copper Age cover (seriously, how many times has this cover been swiped?) and the first appearance of an already extremely popular villain who is ripe for an appearance in a MCU Movie or TV show. Though Venom was portrayed in a previous Spider-Man movie, the execution of his portrayal was so poor that although the book initially surged in price, it quickly fell back down to pre-movie levels. I think once Venom gets announced in the new Marvel Universe, it is only a matter of time before this book sees a dramatic increase, as the character will be entering a well done, established universe, which is very different than the standalone series he was in before. The book has been inching up over the past five years, but I believe it is poised to make another jump in the near future.

Overall I believe the market is healthy. It is still easier to sell books than it is to buy them, which is a very good sign. We will be attending fourteen trade shows this year, so make sure and stop by and say hello. You can find our full schedule on our website (www.reececomics.com), and as always, feel free to reach out to Greg, myself, or Austin if you have any questions about buying, selling, or anything in between. I hope your 2016 was great, and here's to a great 2017!

Stephen & Sharon Ritter
WorldWide Comics

2016 was a solid year for comic sales, but not a banner year. For those not familiar with us and to better understand our view point in this report, WorldWide Comics is primarily an internet site selling vintage comics where we cater to both high and low end collectors, offering comics from the Golden Age to the Copper Age (but little with current comic lines). We currently have over 10,000 3rd Party (CGC and CBCS) graded comics for sale on our website and over 30,000 non-3rd party graded comics. We also set up at most major comic conventions around the country and participate (buying with some selling) in all major auction houses around the country. So you can see that this market report focuses on the vintage comics and is not limited to one part of the country.

Now, on to 2016, sales were good most of the year but not exceptional as the previous two years had been. The internet part of our business turned nine years old in 2016 and up until now, sales in each year have exceeded the previous, however, 2016 was equivalent to 2015 but not better. Although our monthly internet sales were consistent, this year we lacked the large surges we generally see several times a year. Convention selling was also down for us as we set up at fewer cons now (the comic con's focus on multi-media celebrities and such has resulted in a dramatic reduction in comic buyers attending convention shows today). Overall, though, we saw a strong comic market on both the buying and selling side.

Hollywood Impact: The greatest impact to the comic book market has been the huge influx of movies and TV shows produced from comics. Ten years ago we in this business were contemplating who we were going to be selling comics to in 20 years? We all felt we were facing a dying industry as our current customer base was aging and (hate to say it) dying off. There were very few young collectors surfacing as the Millennium Generation grew up with video instead of comics so they had little if any knowledge of comics or comic characters. Then came the success of the first few Spider-Man and X-Men movies. Marvel kept improving the special effects needed in a comic superhero movie, but more importantly they drastically improved the plots to capture those movie goers that never had an interest in superheroes. With the Iron Man, Avengers and even Superman movies, the foundation has now been poured for the future of this hobby. Younger collectors are entering the market so there is a better chance there will be comic collectors around for the next few decades.

Hot Market Trends: A fairly new trend we have been witnessing for the past few years is the sudden rise of a particular comic due to a new movie or TV show using that plot or character introduced. Even before a public release of this information, we would suddenly sell out of every copy on our site in one day. This began most notably in April of 2012 when we sold out of every *Iron Man* #55 we had on our site to collectors in Europe. It became clear why when a month later the Avengers movie came out in the states (it first debuted in Europe) and Thanos showed up at the very end of the movie to be the main villain behind everything. Since then, collectors have been trying to stay tuned to every bit of news on ideas brewing in Hollywood. They are now even speculating more by buying up first appearances on the chance that a character may appear in a future Hollywood release. Some notable examples we saw recently include:

Avengers #62 - 1st Man-Ape (Black Panther villain)

Captain America #168 - 1st Baron Helmut Zemo

Daredevil #4 – 1st Purple Man (Zebediah Killgrave – Netflix TV Series).

Epic Illustrated #3 – 1st Vanth Dreadstar

Eternals #2 (1st Celestials – Part of the Marvel Infinity Gem movie line)

Forever People #1 – 1st Full Darkseid Appearance

Marvel Premiere #19 & #21 – 1st Colleen Wing & Misty Knight (Netflix)

Marvel Two-In-One Annual #7 – 1st Champion (Infinity Gem Owner)

New Gods #7 – Mister Miracle Origin

Power Man #24 & 25 – 1st Black Goliath

Tales of Suspense #94 – 1st MODOK

Thor #132 – 1st Ego

Wonder Woman #6 – 1st Cheetah

World's Finest Comics #252 – New Poison Ivy Origin

The key with these types of comics is to either buy them before the climb in interest and therefore value, or to wait until after the sudden boost occurs (which generally lasts between 6 to 12 months). The chart below shows the typical rise in value of such an issue. After the sudden flash, you can see the cooling period, but the good thing is that every time, the comic will settle at a value higher than before the release. Downtrends seem to especially happen at the eventual release of the movie or TV series that caused the upward spiral. Only exception to that appears to have been the *Guardians of the Galaxy* movie, those comics spurred on by that movie (*Marvel Super-Heroes* #18, *Strange Tales* #180, *Avengers* #259, *Fantastic Four* #65) seemed to sustain its peak values for almost a year after the movie came out. This may have been due to its surprising success at the box office and the coming of a second movie.

Comic Keys: We have a collector friend that made a comment to us about 10 years ago that is turning out to make him appear to be a genius. He said that everyone should be investing in true keys and only the keys. That would be the best investment you could make into comics. And if you look at the market in the past 10 years, you would think he predicted the future. Of course, you don't want to be buying keys when they get hot only to see them cool after your purchase, but in the long run, keys do seem to keep their value and tend to continuously increase over time. Keys that seem to keep exploding in 2016 (not in any particular order):

Adventure Comics #247 – (Waiting for a Legion of Super-Heroes movie or TV series from DC)

All Star Comics #8 – (Resulting from Wonder Woman's new movie debut)

Amazing Fantasy #15 – (1st Spidey is still the #1 Silver Age comic)

Batman #59 – (1st Deadshot, still hot after *Suicide Squad* movie)

Batman #121 – (1st Mr. Freeze, not a main villain, but still tough to find)

Brave and the Bold #25 – (*Suicide Squad* movie has debuted, but true scarcity of this issue keeps it hot)

Captain America Comics #1 – (Cap movies are strong)

House of Secrets #92 – (1st Swamp Thing has exploded in the past 2 years)

Incredible Hulk #181 – (1st Wolverine had crashed in higher grades, but now trending up again)

Sensation Comics #1 – (Resulting from Wonder Woman's new movie debut)

Showcase #4 – (*Flash* TV show started buzz, but true scarcity makes it the fastest climber)

Werewolf by Night #32 – (1st Moon Knight, confusing how popular this book continues to be)

Keys that seem to be cooling or have been cold in 2016:

Action Comics #252 – (*Supergirl* TV series made this explode in 2015, but we now see a slowdown)

Avengers #4 – (Has slowed since first Captain America movie came out)

Fantastic Four #1 – (Movie problems seem to have caused this, though now is a great time to invest in it)

Incredible Hulk #1 – (Not really cooling, but first time we see it no longer climbing in value)

Strange Tales #110 – (Release of the *Doctor Strange* movie downtrend)

Publisher & Era Market Report: For vintage comics, Silver Age is still the best selling material around, Marvel titles still sell better than DC, but all other publishers are a distant third. Bronze Age comics are something we stock heavily on our site as there appear to be more Bronze Age collectors today than Silver Age, likely due to the cheaper costs and more familiarity with the issues from that era due to the ages of most collectors. Charltons have surprisingly been very good sellers at conventions and on our site. Dell/Gold Key seems to remain slow but with many exceptions. The warehouse copies available in the market are still plentiful for most Dells and Gold Keys making the supply greater than the demand for many titles. This is especially the case with Harvey comics, the earlier 1950s issues sell very well due to lack of quantities, but the Harvey warehouse collection has been deluging the marketplace for over 8 years now, making them too plentiful. However, we are told that that warehouse should be emptied before 2017 ends.

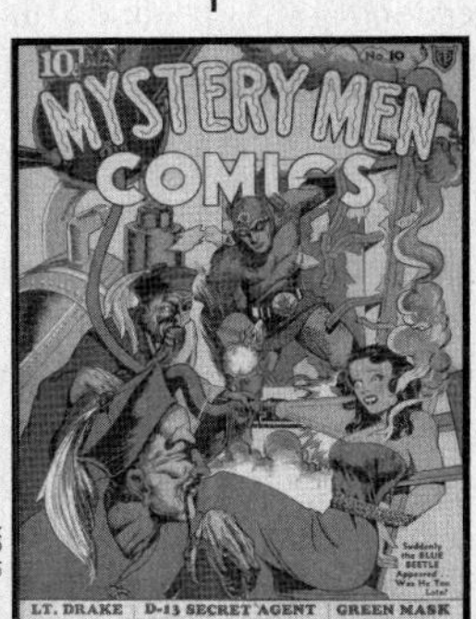

Superhero titles from Fox, Nedor, Ace and Centaur are some of the hottest Golden Age titles. **(*Mystery Men Comics* #10 shown)**

We see the widest fluctuation in sales surprisingly in Golden Age comics. Because this era is collected by so few compared to the total number of comic collectors out there, sales on them are up and down. Timelys, which still sell well, have slowed considerably in past years. In the past, they used to sell as fast as we could get them, not so any more. DC titles sell steadily in all grades as their characters are still mostly all being published today. Higher *Guide* prices than other companies make it a bit more difficult to get full *Guide* sometimes though. The same brilliant friend who said to buy keys 10 years ago, said then to stay away from characters who are not published today. This advice has taken a hit lately as some of the hottest Golden Age titles out there come from Fox, Nedor, Ace and Centaur. Superhero titles like *Exciting*, *Fantastic*, *Four Favorites*, *Mystery Men*, *Speed*, *Startling*, *Super-Mystery* and *Wonder Comics* have been selling for multiples of *Guide* in all grades. Atomic Age (1950s) comics are often some of the rarest to find in grade and can sell for well above *Guide* in higher grades. Superhero and horror genre seem to be the best sellers from this era.

We are looking forward to 2017 and expect the comic market to continue on with the same strong results we have seen in the past five years. However, we need to cultivate a new generation of comic collectors to assure our hobby survives for decades more. Good hunting!!

MATT SCHIFFMAN
COLLECTOR

Platinum Age: This era continues to be a curiosity for most in our hobby, and almost seems to be more vibrant for those collecting rare books. Copies are starting to be featured by those traditional rare books collectors in the UK, Germany and here in the US. There seems to be very low interest for them on eBay and sales results are often well below traditional *Guide* levels.

Big Little Books: Another segment of collectibles that seem to be falling to the wayside for traditional comic book collectors. Even though they feature familiar characters to our hobby, very few of them are prized or valued in the marketplace when featured in traditional comic book auctions. Disney characters have fallen in value and few increases can be found. Green Hornet in high grade has shown to have a vibrant market, but few others do well.

Golden Age: 2016 saw a large price leap in all grades and it was nice to see newfound support for books in the lower to mid-grades. I had been very hard on non-Timely books in that GD to FN+ range in comparison to *Guide* prices, but they have finally begun to rise as well. We've all seen the record setting prices in the headlines of the *Wall Street Journal* and *New York Times* for high grade Gold, but we've known this all along. It really are those mid-grade DC books that have increased in value and that are welcome news for our hobby. Second tier publishers are doing quite well, with Fox titles increasing the most.

Atomic Age: It certainly is no surprise that Good Girl books continue to lead the way and *Phantom Lady* issues set more records this year. A couple of great collections featuring Fox Good Girl came to the market and those high estimates were rewarded. Atlas War books have also jumped in value across the board as issues in VF and above are very hard to find.

Silver Age: I can only imagine that all the market reports in this issue will sound like a broken record – for those of us that remember what that sounds like. Higher prices, minor keys being elevated to major keys with corresponding prices, and movie appearance issues begin sought after. The underlying factor to really study is the prices on grades from GD to VF-. Even with blazing hot keys bringing record prices, those same books in these lower grades are still not being pulled upward to corresponding levels. Yes, they do move up in price, but the spreads are wider than ever. Just because a *Fantastic Four* #52 stuns with a huge price, that same issue in VG increases in value, but nowhere near the same spread. Collectors certainly snap up those issues, but keep an eye on that underlying support. Chasing lower grade keys is a risky business.

Bronze Age: With fewer newer keys being elevated this past year, the focus has been turning back to those traditional key books. A pullback definitively occurred around the start of 2016, but then prices pushed upward again in the Spring and moved to record levels in late summer. *Hero For Hire* #1 continues to have strong support as that cover is very difficult to find in 9.6 or higher. *Amazing Adventures* #11 shares that same cover condition issue, and also *Marvel Feature* #4. *Ghost Rider* #1 and *Marvel Spotlight* #5 moved higher on rumors that something better might be coming from the movie studios. *Fantastic Four* #90 - #140 showed new interest, as well as *Amazing Spider-Man* #103 - #140. *Batman* and *Detective* from 1969 to 1972 moved to new highs in 9.4 and better. DC War from 1969 to 1974 in 9.4 or better is probably one of the hottest markets right now, but not gaining much notoriety. Again, be very aware of the price spreads and how the market is looking at them right now. There are very few keys that can support standard price spreads in the lower grades – *Hulk* #181, *Amazing Spider-Man* #129, *Star Wars* #1 35¢ variant and *X-Men* #94.

Modern Age: Still, this is a very fun era to find new keys, hidden appearances, resurrected characters, and new found love for old classics. Condition is everything. EVERYTHING. Leading the way – early appearances from The Crow, Grendel, Valiant keys, and those key Movie and TV characters buried in *Action*, *Adventure*, *Marvel Team-Up*, *Brave and the Bold*, etc. Collectors still find huge rewards in those small, tiny, obscure, and almost non-distributed titles and last issues in a run. You have to just love those creators that took their books to some out of the loop printer that had no idea what format in which to print a modern comic and they often made it too tall or too wide. Carnage ensued from those books being put upright in boxes and then having weight stacked on top of them. Countless 9.8 books from the bottom edge to ½ inch from the top edge - and then you get a VG crushed top. Built in attrition.

Dylan Schwartz
Collector

It is well known within the market that when television shows, movies and video games about a certain character and / or story-line are made, the market demand increases for products licensed for that character. The same is true with comics that are subject to speculation for a specific character in a movie, as to whether or not the movie will be produced. When a movie or television show comes to fruition and then it is revealed that there is no show or movie, the value for comics showcasing that character drops like a penny off the Empire State Building, declining faster and faster, except the value doesn't go all the way down to zero. This decline does not necessarily negatively impact the market. These books that were yesterday's hot books are not completely worthless however. They are just worth much less than they were during the hype. They were worth money before the hype, so they will be after. For example, *Fantastic Four* #45, which is the first appearance of the Inhumans, saw a significant drop after it was announced that the Inhumans movie was being pulled off the schedule for Marvel's upcoming movies. This book went from hot, to not. These past hot books are then bought by collectors after the price drop which helps fuel the market once again. Collectors and investors fuel the market. Collectors and their interest in this market help keep it strong. Through all the conventions where I have exhibited, I have been a witness to many dealers taking part in large deals with other dealers at somewhat of a discount for hot or key books. This is more evidence that the market is ever changing and fresh-to-market comics are readily being discovered. The demand is also increasing because of the new movies and television shows. This media creates more interest in the hobby, whether the hype is real or artificial.

It is apparent to me that Golden Age has made a large jump in value compared to last year. New books are being discovered. Interest is rising. The comic market is getting better and better. Similar to other hobbies, the oldest and scarcest comics seem to gain the most value over time. With *Action Comics* #1, the most valuable comic book in the world to this day, with a record sale of $3.2 million in 2014. My claim is without a doubt correct. That the oldest and scarcest books gain the most value compared to other books. Collectors and dealers buying comics from one another is also extremely important to the marketplace because they are a source of recorded sales. These records are crucial because they help eliminate some of the guesswork involved in pricing. When there is not enough sales data to comprehend the market, because there are few to no examples for comparison, a blank emerges and only time will tell. When there is only one of a comic available in a certain grade available, the owner sets the price and sets a new market and a new value for that book. Whether through witness of a sale to another customer, or an online auction or sale, the market will be strong for a long time and a comic book will only be worth what someone is willing to pay.

Alika Seki
Maui Comics & Collectibles

Aloha from Maui! We're half way through our second year and what a year it has been! We are still working through DC's Rebirth and the aftermath of Marvel's *Civil War II*. The strongest showings, though, for new comics continue to be *Saga* and *The Walking Dead* on the Image imprint.

This year has brought Maui Comics many collections, mostly small and in the Copper to Modern range. One collection stands out among them – the Uehara Store collection. This collection came to us a few boxes at a time by James and Jean who were hired by the Uehara family to clean out and sell a home for the former store owners. Uehara Store was a small convenience store that sold comics on their magazine rack in the '70s and '80s. Mr. Uehara would select his favorite titles and store them in a box with no bags. These boxes were kept outside on a lanai, and by some miracle over the decades did not get wet at all. Highlights of this collection and their sale prices include: *Giant-Size X-Men* #1 in Very Fine condition (sold for $700), *X-Men* #94 in Fine/Very Fine condition (sold for $350), *House of Secrets* #92 in Very Fine minus condition (sold for $400). Of course the collection was littered with other keys in similar condition from the era (some of which are still available in our store) such as: *Iron Fist* #14, *DC Comics Presents* #26, *Marvel Feature* #1 (sold for $150), *Detective Comics* #400, *Star Wars* #1 (sold for $100), *Marvel Premiere* #47, and more. The Uehara Store collection embodies everything we here at Maui Comics love about collecting. It was carefully selected over time, off-the-rack, by a local business owner who had a great appreciation of the medium.

Maui Comics and Collectibles also worked to bring the first ever comic convention to the island – Maui Comic Con (www.mauicomiccon.com)! Maui Comic Con was founded by Ken Gardner and myself, Alika Seki. The very first Maui Comic Con was free to the public with special guests Steve Leialoha, Trina Robbins, and the creative team of Darkwing Duck; Aaron Sparrow (writer), James Silvani (artist) and Tad Stones (creator). We were honored to be a part of such a big community event that brought out local vendors like Miyako Sushi (owner Mike specializes in collectibles of all kinds), Requests Music (owner Joe used to own one of Maui's earlier comic stores in the '90s), House of Blus, the Rave Corner and Howard Rockman's Rare Comics! Some of you may remember Howard as owner of Over The Rainbow Comics in ABQ, and contemporary of my late mentor, Bruce Ellsworth. We also had many local and Hawaiian artists and creators who were able to bring their projects to the public. The cosplay contest was managed by local Maui girl and cosplay sensation, Night Darling. And of course the NERDWatch podcast handled all the panels and stage show during the two-day event.

Over these past two years our store has grown and I want to thank everyone who has had a part in that, including the podcast that records here every week – the NERDWatch with host Greg "G-Money" Turner, Professor Barry Wurst, Gannon, Jason "Phormat" David, Todd Bernardy, Swan "the comic henchman" Kaho'okele, Bruce Hennesey, Charles "Big C" Yale-Tang and the rotating crew of nerds! And as always I have to give thanks to the guys who helped build this store into the community institution it is becoming. Thanks to Kaleo Kaina, Travis Shultz, Swan Kaho'okele, Ryan Balberdi and Nick Hopkins! And last and most of all I would like to thank Bruce Ellsworth, my late mentor, without whom none of this would be possible. Here's to many more years and many more collections!

Todd Sheffer
Hake's Americana

2016 continued the momentum of last year with the comic book and art markets showing strong results, as collectors and investors add to their collectible investment portfolios. High grade key books continue to fetch record prices, and the demand for mid-grade key books keeps increasing, showing record prices for these issues as well. Certified books have become the standard for many collectors. The strong demand for high grade Gold, Silver and Bronze age key books shows no slowing down at this point, again commanding record prices at auction. Most buyers are committed to paying whatever it takes to own the coveted 9.6 to 9.8 (or higher in rare instances) graded books and are confident in the grades assigned by CGC and CBCS.

Golden Age superhero titles continue to be sought after and even uncertified copies command big prices for even some of the more obscure titles. Once again even lower grade books bring premium prices due to scarcity.

Silver Age Marvel titles are at the top of most buyer's lists. It's been a speculators dream ever since comic sales have been driven by the movie franchises and TV series that are being routinely optioned. Buyers are clamoring to find the next break-out title or character and those are the ones that become red hot. Even the demand and sales of uncertified books is steady. Silver and Bronze first appearances of Groot, Hellcat, Darkseid, TMNT, Moon Knight, Rocket Raccoon, Power Man and Iron Fist will continue to bring in premium prices over the next few years as TV series continue on.

The modern books are no longer being overlooked as first appearances of Deadpool, Cable, Jessica Jones, Harley Quinn, Spider-Gwen and *The Walking Dead* continue to climb in value. Variant covers have skyrocketed to record sales also as more limited printings and cover art variations propel brand new books off the rack to epic high prices.

Comic art prices continue to rise with each unique page or specialty piece that comes to market. Covers and pages that are coming to market from collectors who have had them stored away for years, are making headlines as they also command record prices at auction. Each year we continue to lose some of the classic artists of the past and their art becomes more sought after and sadly we've also lost a few modern artists as well. Look for modern art to keep rising steadily as some artists start to convert over to digital only formatting. Even color guides and preliminary artwork are becoming desired collectibles. Covers and key appearance pages are always the most coveted but art value continues to be driven by the creative team of the piece.

Hake's Americana Comic Sales: *All Star Comics* #4 (9.4) $21,275, *Incredible Hulk* #1 (6.0) $20,873, *Journey Into Mystery* #83 (3.0) $2,893. *Amazing Spider-Man* #1 (4.5) $6,325, *Fantastic Four* #1 (5.0) $7,500, *Metal Men* #1 (9.4) $3,163.

Art Sales: *Master Comics* #21 Cover Recreation by Murphy Anderson $3,813, "Conan The Champion" Paperback Book Cover Painting by Ken Kelly $5,750, *Fantasia*-Night On Bald Mountain Concept Art $11,638.

Merchandise Sales: 1966 Batman Sunglasses Unused Display $3,163, 1941 Captain America Sentinels Of Liberty Club Postcard $4,902, Mego Aquaman 1979 Purple Card $6,591, Kenner Superpowers Hall Of Justice Proof $2,680, 1941 *Sensation Comics* Promotional Postcard $6,958.

Frank Simmons
Coast to Coast Comics

Copper/Modern: There are a host of comics in this area that continue to jump in value. I can't cover them all here but would like to list a half dozen or so that seem to be out performing the rest of the pack. *Batman Adventures* #12, first appearance Harley Quinn, and New *Mutants* #98, the first appearance of Deadpool, just as last year continue to lead the pack and have maintained strong prices realized with only minor drops in value. Many times issues like these peak only to tumble hard in value, but these two are both excellent long term investments in my opinion. Coast To Coast Comics has sold at least a dozen copies of *New Mutants* #98 this year priced at between $400-$600. With all copies being "raw" these are perfect examples of the strength of this issue in particular. Although graded copies of this issue have somewhat stabilized at around $650, this is only down slightly from last year's average around $800 for purchases last year. I expect both raw and slabbed copies to re-coup this dip in value and rise again with the future Deadpool movies to come in the future. In 2017 "graded"-copies should surpass their old mark of $800 or so and go as high as $1000 dollars a copy for CGC or CBCS graded 9.8 copies.

Following a much more aggressive trend *Batman Adventures* #12 has also doubled in value since 2014. Two years ago "graded" 9.8 copies were selling in the $800 range, in 2016 these same books are bringing in a whopping $1700 on average! One reason for this is the #12's scarcity, as it is a lot harder to find in high grade than many other keys of this era. Harley Quinn's first appearance in this comic makes this comic book a must have for Batman and Harley fans alike.

Although not with the strength of the 2015 market, other titles continued to rise in popularity due to the influence of Hollywood like *The Infinity Gauntlet*, *The Walking Dead*, *Uncanny X-Men*, *Deadpool*, *Batman* The New 52, *Saga*, *Danger Girl*, *NYX*, *Edge Of Spider-Verse* and many, many, many more! Within these titles variants continue to dominate the highest price points, many into the thousands of dollars range. The sky is the limit in this area of the market. Have fun, however also make certain to do your research before dropping huge dollars on books in this genre because as I previously mentioned "the skies are the limit," just don't forget that in many cases, the basement on values isn't far below.

Bronze Age/Silver Age/Golden Age: Silver Age once again continued to be one of the most dominant areas in comics for the year 2016. Major key issues, 1st appearances, origin issues, any and all comics with significance continue to be eagerly snapped up with no end in sight. DC keys continue to appreciate in price and value this year just like they did last year. We don't see this ending anytime soon! Marvel Keys like *Amazing Spider-Man* #1, *X-Men* #1, *Fantastic Four* #1, *Journey Into Mystery* #83, *Tales Of Suspense* #39, *Amazing Fantasy* #15 and so on continued to sell extremely fast especially in lower grades and of course when priced correctly. In 2015 we saw *FF* #1 almost double in value, and in 2016 it continued to go up in value but at a more steadied percentage of roughly 20%.

This year's breakout comic in terms of price jump has to be *Amazing Spider-Man* #1. This year it has done what *FF* #1 did the year before meaning almost doubling in value, again most notably in the lower to mid-grade copies. I would like to mention one comic that has become a "sleeper" on the "most wanted" list among collectors, *House Of Secrets* #92. This awesome key 1st appearance of Swamp Thing is illustrated by none other than the Master Of Macabre himself, Mr. Bernie Wrightson! In the year 2016 we followed this comic closely and viewed with great interest the price of high grade copies increases up to and well over $200 a point! In NM 9.4 there was an increase to over $500 per point, this of course will level out however with the print run of this Silver/Bronze mega key being reported as low as 20,000 copies who knows how high prices will be in the next few years?

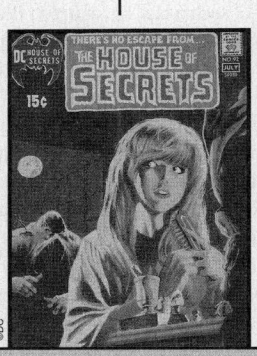

***House of Secrets** #92, the 1st app. of Swamp Thing, crept onto the "most wanted" lists of many collectors.*

Just about every major Silver Age key across the board experienced strong 20% price increases with little or no resistance from customers in the market place. Just like 2015 there is an almost inability to completely quench the collecting public's appetite for these investment comics and childhood treasures. Again as in 2015 there is an obvious sense of urgency for many in the hobby to obtain their childhood dream titles, in particular meaning key #1s and first appearances. I spoke with collectors and dealers alike that all agreed there is a heavy imbalance in availability of these gems which continues to drive prices that many feel will reach an amount that is putting these must-have keys out of the financial grasp of many collectors. In particular, low grade copies in the 1.0, 1.5, 1.8 & 2.0 range had a tremendous surge in pricing, the demand which by far exceeded the available supply for more affordable copies was in fact the culprit.

The Golden Age market, just like the Silver Age market, continues to be very strong with all titles selling strongly again when priced right. We noticed that even some of the more obscure and esoteric titles made a comeback this year, and with a strong comic market economy, the theme was once again (as in 2015) "price it right and it will sell quickly"! Unlike 2015, the influence of the Hollywood movie set was not nearly as strong. Of course we can't say there wasn't any comic market influence from Hollywood, for example *Doctor Strange* #169, 1st appearance and origin re-told, saw a big jump in value as did *Doctor Strange* #1 from 1974.

This year 2016 just like 2015, Coast To Coast Comics, like most dealers across the country was unable to meet 100% of the demand from our customer base. 2017 promises to be an amazing year for everyone involved in this great hobby of ours! Dealers will continue be in hot pursuit of comics and original art to meet the ever-growing demand of their collector customer base. Coast To Coast Comics would like to thank you personally for reading our market input. We also would like to wish all of you in the comic galaxy a healthy and prosperous 2017 in this amazing hobby that we all enjoy, love and even in many cases obsess over! Please look for our auctions on eBay, we are proudly celebrating our 18th year selling on this great venue!

MARC SIMS
BIG B COMICS - BARRIE

Hello *Overstreet* readers! Throughout much of this year, whenever someone has asked me how I am doing, my most common response has been "living the dream!" Today I want to share with all of you just what that has meant for me and my humble comic store, Big B Comics Barrie.

2016 has been a year of challenges, change, and overwhelming positivity for me and my business in Barrie, Ontario, Canada. If you read my report last year, you'll know I set out to grow the back issue comic market in my area by offering a wide range of affordable, mid range material that appeals to buyers young and old. Results have been extremely positive. I built it and they came! It gives me great confidence in the market knowing that there are buyers all over Ontario longing for a reliable and trustworthy source to find new treasures for their collections. Whether they are hard core collectors trying to complete their runs or casual dealers looking to flip for a quick buck, I have met all kinds of new people this year who love comics just as much as I do. It's awesome.

Since I'll be closer to the back of this section you'll probably already have read this a few dozen times, but I will say it again. The market continues to be dominated by keys, keys, and more keys. Comics have gone so mainstream, and collecting "stuff" in general has become so normal, that we have seen a gigantic influx of casual collectors in the market. The one thing that unites nearly all casual collectors is their overwhelming preference to get just one or two really cool back issues for their collection. They don't care about making runs. They want something to put in a frame on their wall. Combine this with the trend amongst even more serious collectors to focus solely on keys, and we get a market that has really become hyper-focused.

The offshoot of this trend among buyers is a whole new subset of nouveau dealers: the flippers, the crack-press-resubmit crowd, the "I maybe have twenty books in my inventory" kinds of guys. These are the guys who usually work full time jobs but buy and sell a little on the side to finance their own collecting or generate some extra cash. When the market is so hyper-focused on a handful of books that everyone wants, it becomes pretty easy to make a few bucks here and there. You don't have to carry a lot of inventory so your risk is minimal, and you learn pretty fast that buying and selling comics can be pretty fun! I love that these guys exist in the market. One, they are some of my best customers. I'm never too concerned about squeezing every last penny out of a sale so they can make some money off of me and therefore they keep coming back. Two, it points to a very active and healthy market where there is plenty of opportunity. I've always said that the more buying and selling that there is going on the better.

Now, there is a downside to all this of course and I feel I must talk about it a bit. First up, if you are a buyer of old comic books and you are about to pull the trigger on a significant purchase, it is incumbent on you to educate yourself a bit to protect yourself. One thing we unfortunately get with a lot of new blood in the market is a little bit of a Wild West approach to grading and pricing. Do simple things like open a book and count the pages. I know lots of "dealers" who don't. Sometimes they come up to me trying to sell me a book that is incomplete and they didn't even know it. These are books that were sitting on their walls for sale priced as though they were complete! I can't imagine how many are sitting in people's collections and they don't even know it. Let's please not get to a point where we don't care anymore that a comic is missing a coupon, has a loose centerfold, is missing an ad page, has easy to spot restoration, or any number of other flaws that you'll never see if you never take the comic out of the bag. These things matter; they should matter to every buyer, and they should especially matter to every dealer.

If you want to educate yourself, there are oodles of handy resources online to learn about comics. Comics.org is an extensive resource that can help you with page counts and story contents so you know if your comic is complete (in addition to just being an overall excellent site). The same folks who produce this price guide publish a very handy grading guide that will help you learn about the different defects that go with every grade. I could go on. Point is, if you don't want to get burned, buy from dealers you know you can trust or take the time to learn for yourself. Or just buy slabs I guess, though that's not nearly as fun. But even then learn to buy the book, not the label. Not all graded comics are created equal.

The other point of caution for me regarding this ever changing market is the fear that the bottom could fall out at any minute. I know, I've just been saying how healthy and positive the market is, so why the doom and gloom? Well, call me cautiously optimistic but also realistic. In any market that could be described as over-heated, it is prudent to know your risks. We have part-time dealers operating on razor thin (sometimes I have to think non-existent) margins, movie-hype books that we all know eventually crash yet we still bid them up, and chasing for the highest grade syndrome that has historically been proven to be a bad bet more often than not.

In addition, collecting comics has become about more than just buying comics. Now we pay to slab them, press them, clean them, restore them, unrestore them, slab them again, and who knows what else. A lot of money is being spent and I fear not all of it for the good. Added costs bring added risk and oftentimes with no intrinsic value being added. In short, lots of people are positioned to lose significant sums of money if there is a modest market correction. What happens then would be interesting.

So, what do you do if you are just someone who loves comics and loves collecting? Buy what you enjoy. Buy things that will make you happy. Buy with an eye towards value but don't expect to get rich overnight. Most Golden and Silver Age comics have historically proven to be very sound long term investments. I don't see that changing anytime soon. But don't re-mortgage your house or cash out your retirement savings to buy comics. Never assume risk that you cannot afford to take.

Let's talk about some of the specific activity I've seen in my little corner of the market for 2016. First up, what I bought. I was fortunate enough to come in to a good number of large collections this year and dozens more smaller 'walk-in' collections. That would be the stuff that I see at my store on a weekly basis and typically consists of moderns or the occasional small batch of Silver/Bronze. Every once in a while someone brings in some Golden Age. For the bigger buys, I started with a near complete Silver Age Marvel run in February 2016. This was deep runs from #1 up of all the major hero titles, all in mid-grade. This positioned me nicely for a good part of the year for all of my bin divers and collectors filling in their runs. Getting nearly all the keys didn't hurt either. The collection was complete but for *Hulk* #1, *FF* #1, *ASM* #1, and *AF* #15. The four best ones I know, but a great collection nonetheless.

In the spring I purchased the entire inventory of a local part-time dealer, roughly 20,000 items. It was primarily comics but also Treasuries, bound editions, digests, magazines, and all sorts of other oddities. The collection ran the whole gamut from Golden Age to Undergrounds to Marvel licensing samples from 1992. Half of these items I liquidated immediately at $54/long box. I don't have the space, time or patience to try to squeeze out $1 each on junk from the '80s and '90s. The rest primarily filled my $2 and $5 bins at the store, where they sold briskly. I also did really well with the Treasury Editions. There were many high grade examples that fetched a significant premium and sold immediately.

Throughout the summer I bought an original owner collection of DCs from about 1967-1972, totaling about 800 comics. These were all bought fresh off the stands locally and then stored perfectly and undisturbed for 40 years. The collection was notable for the high gloss and stunning page quality. Sales have been brisk on issue of *Batman* and *Detective* especially, but also *Lois Lane*, *Brave and the Bold*, *Wonder Woman*, and *Adventure*. I don't care what the titles are, when you have DCs at VF/NM and up, collectors snatch them up fast. They are so much rarer than the Marvels from the same time period.

In the fall I purchased another original owner collection consisting of Marvels from about 1965-1980. These weren't stored quite as nicely so the average grade was lower, but good titles were well represented. It's telling though that many of the books were already my 3rd or 4th copies in inventory.

On to the sales! Here are some noteworthy sales in my store for the year. In all cases, prices are Canadian dollars and were for face to face, local transactions. I do very little in online sales, choosing to focus on the local market. *Amazing Fantasy* #15 CGC 3.0 $18,000, *Amazing Spider-Man* #3 CBCS 4.5 $1300, *Amazing Spider-Man* #5 G/VG $450, *Amazing Spider-Man* #6 VG $500, *Amazing Spider-Man* #9 VG/F $500, *Amazing Spider-Man* #14 GD $490, *Amazing Spider-Man* #16 CBCS 8.5 $1100, *Amazing Spider-Man* #19 CBCS 9.4 $1350, *Amazing Spider-Man* #20 CBCS 8.5 $1000, *Amazing Spider-Man* #41 VF+ $620, *Amazing Spider-Man* #129 CBCS 9.0 $1600, *Amazing Spider-Man* #129 FN- $500 x2, *Amazing Spider-Man* #129 VG $550, *Aquaman* #1 VG- $425, *Avengers* #1 UK Edition CGC 3.5 $1325, *Avengers* #2 VG/FN $440, *Avengers* #4 GD+ $800, *Batman* #5 CGC 3.5 $1300, *Batman* #9 CGC 6.0 $3650, *Batman Adventures* #12 NM $800 x2, *Batman Adventures* #12 VF+ $600, *Blue Bolt Weird Tales* #116, LB Cole VF $800, *Brave and the Bold* #34 VG/FN $400, *Daredevil* #1 VG- $1400, *Detective Comics* #142 Fair, Canadian Edition missing centerfold $300, *Fantastic Four* #2 GD- $400, *Fantastic Four* #4 GD/VG $700, *Fantastic Four* #5 VG- $1275, *Fantastic Four* #45 VG+ $400, *Fantastic Four* #52 CGC 8.0 $2200, *Fantastic Four* #52 CGC 5.0 $600, *Giant-Size X-Men* #1 VG/FN $575, *Giant-Size X-Men* #1 VG+ $525, *Giant-Size X-Men* #1 GD+ $350, *Green Lantern* #1 GD/VG $800, *Hero for Hire* #1 CGC 9.0 $1250, *Hero for Hire* #1 CGC 8.0 $800, *Incredible Hulk* #2 CBCS 3.0 $1100, *Incredible Hulk* #181 CGC 5.0 $1300, *Incredible Hulk* #181 CGC 4.5 (AR) $700, *Incredible Hulk* #181 CGC 4.0 $1100, *Iron Man* #1 CGC 5.5 $500, *Iron Man* #55 FN/VF $850, *Journey into Mystery* #84 GD/VG $420, *Journey into Mystery* #85 VG- $665, *New Mutants* #98 NM+ $500 x3, *Scooby Doo* Gold Key #1 VG- $250, *Showcase* #30 VG/FN $575, *Silver Surfer* #4 CGC 8.0 $600, *Strange Tales* #110 VG- $2100, Superman vs Muhammad Ali Treasury Edition Whitman variant NM+ $250, Superman vs Muhammad Ali Treasury Edition NM- $180, *Suspense* #8 GD- $600, *Tales of Suspense* #40 VG/FN $700, *Tales of Suspense* #52 FN- $550, *Tales of Suspense* #52 CGC 5.0 $500, *Tales of Suspense* #57 VF+ $1300, *Tales of Suspense* #58 CBCS 8.5 $975, *Tales to Astonish* #35 GD/VG $525, *Tales to Astonish* #44 VG- $500, *Vampirella* #1 FN/VF $350, *Wonder Woman* #105 CBCS 2.0 $600 and *X-Men* #1 FN $7500.

This is just a small snapshot of course, and not really indicative of my market. My bread and butter sales still come from $20-$100 comics. I also sell $5 and $2 comics by the boatload. Value priced books at $5 have been some of my best movers. That's where we put all sorts of books that may *Guide* at $10-15 but realistically in this market sell for well below that. I've been writing about this for years in the pages of this book. The majority of mid-grade run books don't realize *Guide* prices, but people are happy to snatch them up at a cheap price. I have found $5 to be pretty much the perfect price point for that.

Still on the subject of sales, I'd like to talk about what has been happening in the world of new comics this year. The big story of the year has to be the DC Rebirth line-wide relaunch in the spring. This was a monumental success and the perfect example of how to do a relaunch right. Kudos to DC. Every issue was 100% returnable, meaning I was able to order way more than I thought I could ever sell and find the ceiling on DC's dime. I still sold out of many first wave titles, largely I think because word spread pretty fast that I was the only store around that still had copies in stock and at cover price no less. I had people driving in from Toronto every week, a city an hour away with probably 30 comic stores, because they just couldn't find the stuff. Crazy.

As an added bonus, the stories and art have been well received and sales continue to be strong 6 months in. Double shipping issues has caused my customers to be more cautious with what they pick up, so the second and third wave of titles have been fairly disappointing sales-wise. But then again, I never expected a whole lot from *Cyborg* or *Blue Beetle* anyways.

Across the aisle at Marvel, we continue to get more of the same old, same old and sales are showing it. People are confused by the characters and teams, consecutive numbering seems to be a thing of the past, and there are just way too many interchangeable titles. Constant relaunches and rebranding force collectors to break the habit, taking a lot of the fun out of collecting. For the first time in a long time, I have been ordering 0 copies of some brand new Marvel titles. No one seems to have noticed that I don't have *Slapstick* #1 on the stands. I wish I had ordered 0 on *Solo* #1 because that's what I have sold. I don't know who is making the decisions to greenlight these series, but I just shake my head at the whole thing.

Our top 10 sellers for the year in new comics tell the story nicely:

1) *DC Universe: Rebirth* #1
2) *Batman* #1
3) *Batman* #2
4) *Batman: Rebirth* #1
5) *Civil War II: Choosing Sides* #5 Perez var (gimmick Justin Trudeau cover)
6) *Batman* #3
7) *Batman* #4
8) *Batman* #5
9) *Civil War II* #1
10) *Justice League: Rebirth* #1

Graphic novels make up the bulk of our sales for other publishers, with Image by far being our biggest seller. We find we get some initial traction with new non super-hero series as single comics, but most people eventually just switch over to the trades. My staff have plenty of go-to recommendations for new readers coming in, and the large majority of them are Image. These are my top 20 best sellers for the year in Graphic Novels:

Walking Dead Vol. 25 TPB No Turning Back
Saga TPB Vol. 6
Paper Girls Vol. 1 TPB
Walking Dead Vol. 26 TPB Call to Arms
Civil War TPB
Batman the Killing Joke Special Ed. HC
Saga TPB Vol. 1
Marvel Universe Deadpool and Wolverine (the only kid-friendly Deadpool book there is)
Suicide Squad TPB Vol. 1 Kicked in the Teeth
Deadly Class TPB Vol. 1 Reagan Youth
Preacher TPB Vol. 1
Wytches TPB Vol. 1
Deadpool Kills the Marvel Universe TPB
Flash TPB Vol. 1 Move Forward
Monstress TPB Vol. 1
DC Super Hero Girls TPB Vol. 1 Finals Crisis
I Hate Fairyland TPB Vol. 1 Madly Ever After
Wolverine Old Man Logan TPB
Color Your Own Deadpool TPB
Preacher TPB Vol. 2

I want to thank everyone that has been involved with Big B Comics Barrie this year and helped make 2016 the year of living the dream. Extra special thanks go out to my staff, without whom I wouldn't even be writing this report. Alice-ann Pilon, Jeremy Moore, and Marshall Geddes – you guys are the best.

A final shout out has to go to Bob Overstreet, Mark Huesman, my fellow advisors, and all the lovely people responsible for the creation of this book you hold in your hands. The *Overstreet Price Guide* is the foundation on which so much of our hobby is built. I use it nearly every day and will for as long as I draw breath. Until next year!

Lauren Sisselman
Comics Journalist

2016 was a great year for signature series collectors. Actors, hard to get creators, and everyone in between was jumping onto the signature series bandwagon. Tough sigs such as Frank Miller became an easy ticket, Doug Moench saw a rise in sig series books, and even the cast and creative team of *Back to the Future* was popular.

I work with a dealer who specializes in Signature Series books. He facilitates getting signatures for clients, and travels extensively throughout the world to do so. I go with him for many of these quests, and have done some on my own as well. The common trend is for Moderns and some Silver Age to get signed, with very few Golden Age books in the mix. Photo covers of comics are always well received, as well are variants and blank covers.

Easily the two most popular Sig Series books this past

year were *Harley Quinn* #1 and *Batman: Rebirth* #1. Gabrielle Dell'Otto covers were also a big hit this year, with graders seeing them come across their desk often. On the Indy comics side, *Henchgirl* from Scout Comics, and *4 Kids Walk Into A Bank* were wildly popular. On the Marvel side, *Punisher* and *Daredevil* were surprise hits, but many fans can thank the Netflix show for the surge in popularity. *Black Panther* #1 was also a very popular SS book this year, if not thanks to the latest *Captain America* movie. *Power Rangers* from BOOM! has also seen a resurgence in popularity, as #0 copies are one of most seen Sig Series books. Even Archie had a rise in SS popularity thanks to the multitude of variants and convention exclusives they release.

Price wise, the Signature Series can vary. For the most part, a signature added to most books will bring the book some value. Other times it can be detrimental. In the Fall of 2015, Frank Miller signed books were going for $600+, but Fall of 2016 prices dropped to $100+ per book, due to the saturation of his signature in the market. Stan Lee's signature, while possibly the most common signature out there, still commands high dollar amounts. An *Amazing Fantasy* #15 in CGC 4.5 with his sig went for $24,950, while a copy without his signature typically goes for under $20,000. A CBCS 0.1 coverless *Batman* #1 signed by Jerry Robinson recently sold for $6K, which is average for a similar copy of that book without a signature. Many Modern books in the 9.4-9.6 range fall between $50-$100, but 9.8s still command the most money.

*Signature Series books signed by Stan Lee still command high dollar amounts. (**Thor** #133 shown)*

Another trend in the signature series side of collecting is creators charging money to people who may be getting their books graded by either CGC or CBCS. Most of the time writers and artists have a donation bucket for the CBLDF, which is a fantastic cause. But more and more are charging $10 if not more for their own personal gain. While this certainly hasn't stopped people from getting books signed and graded, it's still disheartening to see this practice being done. Celebrities such as Gal Gadot or Chris Evans almost always charge for an autograph regardless of the item. There's no escaping that unless you personally know them. But even some of their prices are a little shock inducing, which should make you stop and ask if they really are receiving all of that money, or if someone behind the scenes is. When it comes to paying for a signature, regardless of who's signing, always be sure you're comfortable and OK with paying that price.

Over the next year, signature series will undoubtedly grow in popularity. If you're thinking of jumping into this side of the hobby, seek out a reputable dealer or facilitator to help you get started. It's a rapidly growing hobby, and as with any side of collecting, ever changing too. Happy collecting!

TONY STARKS
COMICS INA FLASH

Another year... and the back issue market continues along similar paths that it has followed the past several years. More blockbuster movies, more Netflix superhero series, more TV superhero series. For the most part, more interest in those characters first and key appearances.

Look at *Superboy* #68 - the first appearance of Bizarro. A great character - a childhood favorite of mine - one that has been good for a lot of sight gags and humor. My favorite gag is Bizarro rubbing two Boy Scouts together to make start a fire. It has always been a sought after issue. When a "Bizarro" Supergirl appeared in February in the popular *Supergirl* TV series, the book jumped another 25%. People only had to talk about the possibility of She-Hulk entering the Marvel cinematic universe (a great idea I think - make her an Avenger) to make *Savage She-Hulk* #1 take off.

Daredevil Season 2 finally did the character of the Punisher justice. So *Amazing Spider-Man* #129 has popped. And keeps going up. *Jessica Jones* (*Alias*) was great and the villain Killgrave the Purple Man stole the movie. His first appearance in *Daredevil* #4 went from minor villain first appearance to must-have on a lot of collectors' lists. Patsy Walker (Jessica's sister) has spiked demand for *Avengers* #144 (Patsy Walker as Hellcat) What to say about Luke Cage?? *Hero for Hire* #1 was already a sought after book. With lots of new fans looking for a copy, those new fans discovered just how hard the book is to find in high grade. And prices have moved up accordingly.

While movies and TV seem to drive first issues and first appearances, year after year we sell lots of average condition run issues of Silver and Bronze Age books. After years of being depressed, the market on this type of material stabilized a couple of years ago. Probably because the huge oversupply of such books has subsided. Half a dozen years ago, collectors were glutting the market by selling these run books trying to raise money for high grade keys. Many have given up - the really big books in high grade are simply too expensive for the vast majority of collectors. They would have to sell their house and kids - not their comics - to purchase a NM *Avengers* #1 ($100,000+). So many have decided to keep their collections (and house and kids) and buy a VG *Avengers* #1 ($2,000) instead. Plus, with all the movies and TV shows, one never knows when some minor character's first appearance in a "run" of issues becomes the next must have book.

Just a few examples of sales of average books: *Avengers* #61, 62, 63 & 64 FN @ $10.00 ea., *Avengers Annual* #2 VF $35.00, *Batman* #183 VG $27.00, *Bullwinkle* #4 NM $10.00 (Ronald Reagan cover), *Daredevil* #7 VG+ $125.00, *Fantastic Four* #36 VG $36.00, *Justice League* #9 FN $100.00, *Mystery In Space* #80 FN/VF $30.00, *Phantom*

Stranger #13 VF $14.00, *Power Man* #19 NM $12.00, *Thor* #127 VG $16.00, *Tomb of Dracula* #13 FN $20.00, *Wonder Woman* #181 VF/NM $42.00, #184, 186 VF @ $22.00 ea., and #200 VF/NM $80.00. Taken over a year, sales like this add up.

But it's not all inexpensive stuff here at Comics Ina Flash! We have some high end and better sales as well, often times professionally graded: *Aquaman* #35 CBCS 6.0 $325.00, *Blackhawk* #133 CBCS 3.0 $450.00 (1958 1st Lady Blackhawk, now part of popular Birds of Prey team), *Captain America* #100 CGC 5.0 $150.00, #109 CGC 9.6 $525.00, 9.2 $200.00, *Defenders* #1 CGC 9.4 $350.00, *Dr. Strange* #1 CGC 9.6 $348.00, *Giant-Size Iron Man* #1 PGX 9.8 (double cover) $358.00, *Incredible Hulk* #102 VF $150.00, #181 PGX 7.5 $1400.00, *New Mutants* #1 CGC 9.8 $100.00, *Star Wars* #1 CBCS 9.8 $860.00, *Superman* #233 CGC 9.0 $223.00, *Tales to Astonish* #57 FN/VF $135.00, *Tales of Suspense* #50 CGC 7.0 $300.00 and *Thor* #193 NM- $140.00.

A few books that a lot of collectors are seeking that might not be ones "everyone" knows: *Blue Beetle* #1 (1967) - first appearance of The Question, *Blackhawk* #133 - first Lady Blackhawk (Birds of Prey) and *House of Secrets* #61 - 1st Eclipso.

EC comics seem to be on a lot more collectors' want lists than they were a few years ago. Any issue that we get in quickly sells. Golden Age as well continues to show renewed interest. Several collectors have remarked to us that Golden Age comics are now more affordable than a lot of Silver Age issues that they want.

Overall, the market's health seems to continue to improve. It is still very driven by movies and TV, but you see solid interest and sales in other genres as well.

WEST STEPHAN CBCS

2016 certainly has been a busy year for CBCS. We just hired 2 more graders and quite a few other employees that work here behind the scenes. There is no slow down on submissions! We've seen many Golden Age and Silver Age original owner collections this year, as well as some collections that were bought second hand in the '70s & '80s that are just now coming back into the market. One such collection was bought in the late '70s - early '80s comprised of only 2 dozen issues, but boy did he pick some winners! Some of those include: *Detective Comics* #27, *Batman* #1-4, #6, *Captain America Comics* #1, *Police Comics* #1, *Action Comics* #3, *Flash Comics* #1, *World's Best Comics* #1 (Larson Copy!), *Fantastic Four* #1, *X-Men* #1 (CBCS 9.4!). Another original owner Golden Age collection that was submitted had a *Marvel Comics* #1 (CBCS 7.5 White Pages), many pre-hero *Detective Comics* and early Fox books. In fact, books from that collection keep arriving as the submitter gets books from the collection in hand-fulls every few months. There's no telling what is left to be found or how many books are still in that collection. What's amazing though is that every single book from that collection has perfect White Pages! Most of the books so far that have been submitted are from 1938-1941 with a few as late as 1946. Another old time collector that has submitted some amazing books recently submitted a *Young Men* #27 (CBCS 8.5 White Pages!). Now there's a book you rarely see in high grade and never see with White Pages! It's the best copy I've seen in my 32 years of collecting!

We have also noticed a large increase in "Classic Covers" submissions. Books like *Phantom Lady* #17, *Suspense Comics* #3, *Marvel Mystery Comics* #40, #44 & #46 and other classic covers are always in huge demand, and thus, are always the first books to be submitted when a collection containing them is bought. World War II covers are also very coveted and show no signs of slowing down. In fact, *Overstreet* may have to start breaking out more WWII covers as they always sell for more than the issues surrounding them that do not have a war cover. Most of the time, the market is more cover driven than anything else at this point. It's the cover that sells the comic, unfortunately the interior stories seem to be of secondary importance at this point.

Speaking of "Classic Covers", we uncovered an error that was made a while back. A 9.4 White copy of *Terrific Comics* #5 was submitted to CBCS as the Crowley Copy. The Edgar Church/Mile High copy has been lost for decades, no one knew where the book had vanished to back in the '70s. It was on the original list of Mile Highs as a NM+ and could have been bought for only $8.00, that was the catalog list price! No wonder no one knew where the book was, in 1977 the book had minimal value. Well, the owner thought that this book might be that lost Edgar Church/Mile High Copy. The previous owner of the book (a very renowned expert on Edgar Church/Mile Highs) also felt that the book was from the Mile High collection. The current owner was told the only way we could be certain if the book was a Mile High would be to crack the book open and inspect the book internally. We had to smell the book (yes, smell the book, as Mile Highs give off a distinct scent that no other comic does) and we had to access the "Whiteness" of the pages and interior cover. Also we needed to look at the cover in hand and not through plastic to see if the book had the "raised" colors and ink reflectivity that Mile Highs typically exhibit. This copy passed every test! After looking at the book for quite a while and contacting other Mile High experts who also agreed with us, the unanimous consensus was that this was that "lost" Mile High! We at CBCS have discovered dozens of books that have been submitted as non-pedigrees were actually from different pedigrees, including the *World's Best Comics* #1 Larson Copy that was mentioned earlier, a copy of *All Select Comics* #8 that we discovered was that Big Apple Copy and the *Suspense Comics* #3 that was submitted to CBCS the previous year that was actually the Pennsylvania Copy!

As we look forward to 2017, I do not expect many changes. The comic book hobby will continue to thrive, movies and TV shows will keep the public interested in comic characters, CBCS will be continue its growth, and in

July, we will all be clamoring to see the newest *Overstreet Comic Book Price Guide*! Thank you Mr. Bob Overstreet, J.C. Vaughn, Mark Huesman and all the others who make this guide a success year after year!

AL STOLTZ
BASEMENT COMICS

What is selling at shows and online? I ask this question of every dealer I know and as usual and for the 100th time as usual it's Keys, rare comics, High grade of some issues of comics or select series. I know, I know that I have said this over and over in my reports for many years and sure enough it is the most common answer I get from other sellers. What about the other 90% or so of remaining items? Well, it looks like half off or more or breaking comics that are slow sellers into price point bins works the best when trying to thin these items out of inventory. We were selling last few years of comics bagged and in order for $2.00 each at a few shows but that model has seemed to have slowed a good bit. We moved to thinning out our warehouse of unwanted older issues like Good to Very Good and at times Fine or better of overstocked stuff from Bronze Age to later Silver Age comics into $3.00 each or "Four comics for $10.00" model. Shows that had large buyers looking to fill up collections like Charlotte Comic Con or New York Comic Con saw the maximum sell through of these priced issues. It was gratifying to see guys happily buy Gold Key *Korak* or *Tarzan* issues along with beat up *WDC&S* issues or even lower grade *Tales of Suspense* or *Avengers*. While $3.00 or even $2.50 each is at times below listed value, I feel this is now the true selling value for many of these titles. We now just adjust our buy price for this material as we know its ultimate destination is bagged and blown out in bargain boxes. Nothing wrong with that and I feel in the end I see that maybe somebody is actually reading these again and not just looking for the Hot books of the week that need to be slabbed and sold for short term money. WE NEED READERS AND COLLECTORS !!! If we end up with a room full of investors, the love for the hobby and for the art form will just be dead.

We published a Fanzine with a print run of 500 copies this year. Fantastic cover by Mark Wheatley and articles about the hobby and fandom and collecting by many including my youngest son Alex (28 yrs old) who seemed to have the crowd favorite story printed in this issue. My hope and attempt was to try and collect stories about comics, convention experiences or items that the people collect and had an interest in and pass them on like the original comic lovers of days long gone by. We will attempt to get a few issues out a year and any serious collectors or dealers that want to contribute 600-700 words are more than welcome to send it along to us and join in this experiment. The history of comic dealers and early pioneers of comic fandom needs to be preserved and hopefully read by those chasing this medium in the future.

Conventions during the year were mostly positive and paid off for the investment into them. I do have to say that after recovering from a badly broken leg the year before and now aged 54, doing these shows is really getting tough! Charlotte and New York Comic Con were perhaps our best shows for the year but Chicago Comic Con, Awesome Con, Mega Con and Baltimore were not too bad and were well worth the effort to set up and display. As suspected we sold lots of Key issues including *Hulk* #181, *Giant-Size X-Men* #1, *Batman Adventures* #12, *Amazing Spider-Man* #129 and Marvel and DC key 1st appearances along the way. Almost all of them third party graded and ready to be added to a comic portfolio of sorts from investor buyers. Art and odd ball items we tend to carry were eagerly bought up and given new homes. We like to carry a wide variety of price point and collectible items at our booths at major shows these days. Like we stated early in this report, the bargain of "four comics for ten dollars" approach seemed to be very well received at NYCC and readers who usually never find *Bugs Bunny* or low grade *Our Army At War* seemed delighted. If this model holds we will try it again next season. I like to keep it interesting and the customers seem to be looking for a wide range of things that can be collected or even used as decorative items in an office or home.

eBay has seemed to be in its death spiral for a year and a half now and selling anything on there is more work than one can tolerate. A platform that I felt single handedly saved back issues sales a bunch of years ago has greatly slowed. Is it because the buyers who loved it 18 years ago are out of the hobby or have filled their lists? Or as many have felt, eBay has restructured who gets more traffic and chances to sell, more of a Big Box sellers versus small individual sellers. Loads of theories abound on chat boards on and off eBay these days and eBay itself offers little sympathy when we call and ask them to allow us to sell something. We have been selling on eBay for over 18 years now and while we do manage to sell a good bit of product, you can easily see that the glory days are fading and it's time to do something else.

Something else for us will be VintagebasementComics.com. As of this writing in December we were waiting for our Beta Version to play with and once we get our hands on it we will work to fill it up with tens of thousands of items that we have held back in our warehouse and better material that will only be available on our webpage. At that time, eBay will begin its role later as just our liquidation system. The comic industry has changed drastically since I started being in it in 1975, and where and how to sell and even what to charge constantly is bouncing all over the place. Hopefully we can promote the website enough to make it a great place for collectors to buy with confidence and enjoy seeing the strange and rare items that we like to post. Along with the website we are working towards our third year of doing pressing comics for ourselves and customers. Basement Comics pressing has been steadily growing and has at this point taken over most of my time at the office. We have cleaned and pressed everything from every Marvel Key to plenty of rare and wonderful Golden Age Comics including a few Mile High copies. What started out as just a means to better my own material has blossomed and now we make a decent living out of offering this service.

I guess this will be a short entry from me this year for the *Overstreet Guide* but I would like to just say that this hobby has provided me with a living for a very long time and we will hit our official 25th year as Basement Comics this coming August. Unofficially I have been walking the aisles of comic shows and flea markets much longer. The hobby changes and so do we as age and time catches up to us. Is it our duty to try and guide young and new buyers to genres of comics that are falling in value and desirability? No, I think that buyers will find what interests them and comics like Tarzan and Westerns and even goofy Golden Age titles will find a buyer somewhere. A different market where things sell but sell for less than they used to a decade ago is here and settled in and that is fine. You buy cheaper and sell cheaper and spread the fun of comics at local and large shows. Somebody always seems to enjoy them for different reasons only they can define. Just keep them reading them...

Doug Sulipa
Doug Sulipa's Comic World

I became obsessed with comics at a young age, due to my love of the 1966 *Batman* TV series, *Superman* TV reruns, Sci-Fi shows, cartoons of the era, TV and the movies. As a child my father took me to second hand bookstores, where I could buy used comics for a nickel, but they also traded 2-for-1, a lesson I fast learned. 2017 is the 50th Anniversary of the year 1967, when I started my Two for One Comic Trading Enterprise out of the basement of my parents house in Winnipeg as a young 11 year old kid. I mainly started it to grow my small collection. It did not take long before I started getting a lot of duplicates. For kids in the neighbourhood with nothing to trade, I would also accept cash for comics for 5 to 10 cents each, so it was literally a "Nickel & Dime" business. The pricey 10¢ comics I sold back then were ironically anything with a 10¢ cover price, which my young mind considered old and rare. With my allowance and nickels and dimes, my mini-enterprise grew my collection to about 5000 comics by 1971, when I started my ads in *RBCC* and my Back Issue catalogues. I owe eternal thanks for my parents Olly and Walter Sulipa for allowing me to continue my obsession, and for all their help and assistance through the decades. They even supported my decision to drop out of University after only 2 of the 4 years that were required to finish.

Naturally in the early 1970s, the comic business seemed ludicrous and laughable to almost anyone I met, but I was always undeterred and only looked forward, because I had already met and dealt with thousands of people worldwide who respected what I did. Fast forward 50 years to the present, I now realize I have sold about 5-10 million comics over the last half century, and still have a hefty current inventory of 1.3 million comics. My wife Cathy Sulipa has been my true inspiration since we met in 1988, and it is amazing all the things we have done together in the last 29 years. I could not have done it without her enormous help, understanding and faith in me. Thanks also to my good buddy Paul Clairmont of PNJ Comics, our visits, friendship, talks and brainstorming sessions have made us both better people.

In the Modern Age, comics, graphic novels, Sci-fi, cartoons/Anime, gaming and all the related fields are now at the cusp and cutting edge of Pop Culture. We now have blockbuster movies that routinely make $250 million to $1 Billion. We also have dozens of conventions that take over entire cities with crowds of 50,000 to 100,000 or more, filled with movie, TV, comic, other stars, celebrities and companies. The San Diego Comic-Con had 167,000 people attend in 2015. Although some print media is down, our Industry is THRIVING in all other media, and comics are now established as worldwide elite collectibles, yet are still accessible to everyone – Ya Gotta Love It !!!.

2016 was another blockbuster year for us, similar to 2015. The meteoric rise in sales has leveled off, but sales are still going strong. After several years of blazing hot comics related to all the movie and television shows, the marketplace frenzy is now somewhat diluted, including all the re-boots, Horror, Sci-fi, toy/action figure, cartoon, Anime and other movie and televison shows, thus buyers have become more selective.

Dozens of people contacted me to thank me for the massive list of items to look for, the list I created for fans, investors and dealers alike, as published in *Overstreet* #46 on pages 178-198. If you missed it, be sure to go back and check it out. Buyers have re-directed some of the attention to the "All-Time Best Lists" and are now buying up many of the overlooked and undervalued Key and minor Key issues of the Silver, Bronze andCopper Ages. Many items have seen 25%-500% price increases over the last four years. A few lists to look up include: IGN's Top 100 Comic Book Villains Of All-Time, Top 100 Comic Book Heroes Of All-Time, Top 50 Avengers, Top 100 Animated Series, and *Comics Buyer's Guide*'s 100 Sexiest Women in Comics List, Top 10 1970s Marvels by the *Comics Bulletin*; various Newsarama Top 10 Lists (Top Super-Teams, Top Archenemies, etc) and more. If you have a hero of interest, find out who their archenemy is and buy the Key issues, including the first appearance (from Golden, Silver, Bronze, Copper and Modern Ages - where applicable), their origin, death and other related issues. Controversial storylines such as: the unwilling pregnancy of Carol Danvers aka Ms. Marvel in *Avengers* #200; *Amazing Adventures* #31 (the first dramatic interracial kiss in AAmerican color comic books history); *Marvel Team-Up* #64 (Misty Knight and Iron Fist become the comics first inter-racial super-hero couple.)

Demand for first appearances of all the major villians (especially the arch enemies) for all the major heroes of Marvel and DC is often higher than demand for the first appearance of the hero, often due to price of the heroes first appearance.

The hunt continues for hundreds of under-valued minor and hidden Key issues of the future: early female characters, early Black, Native/Indian, Chinese and Asian, Mexican, Puerto Rican, Muslim, Half-Breed, interracial, Alien, Gay and more. Collecting more affordable vintage reprints of major key issues is now an established trend, as more and more buyers look for CGC high graded copies (*Marvel Milestone*, *Famous First Edition*, Millennium editions, *Limited Collector's Edition* Treasuries, Promo giveaway reprints, *Marvel Tales* #98,99,106,137,158, *Marvel Super Action* #18, *Sgt. Fury* #167 etc) and many of these are now selling at 200-400% *Guide*. DC purchased the Charlton heroes in the mid 1980s and most of them entered the DC universe through *Crisis* in 1985 through to 1990 or so. Those DC key issues are now up in demand, and the demand is also up for all the Charlton original key issues, especially *Captain Atom* #83. Most fans overlook non-superhero comics and non Marvel and DC comics, but smart buyers are now looking at all the other genres too. Just a few comics that are up in demand, and now command decent CGC prices include: *Back to the Future* (Harvey), *Beetlejuice* (Harvey), *Earthworm Jim* (Marvel), *Gargoyles* (Marvel), *Ghost in the Shell*, *Labyrinth* (David Bowie – Marvel), *Masters of the Universe* (Marvel and DC), *Scooby-Doo* (all publishers), *Thundercats* (Marvel), *Transformers* (Marvel), and *Voltron*. We sold *True Comics* #48 (4/46; the true story of Desmond Doss, the basis for the recent *Hacksaw Ridge* movie in Good+ for $75.

Last issues in the series (especially series with 25 or more issues, ending from 1980 through to 2000) are perhaps among the most over-looked and under-valued Key issues. Most issue #1s from 1975 to date had the higher print runs. Most series get cancelled due to low sales, thus most last issues had low print runs. Many last issues from the 1980-2000 era have *Guide* values of $3.00 to $10.00, yet are routinely in such short supply, that many bring $10, $20 to $50 each and more (300% to 1000% current *Guide* prices.) Just a few hot "last issues" include: Archie Publ. (most last issues), *Brave and the Bold* #200, Charlton (most last issues), *Conan* #275, *Dark Horse Presents* #157, *Deadpool* #69, *Elvira's House Of Mystery* #11, *Gargoyles* #11, *Ghost Rider* V1 #81(1983), *Ghost Rider* V2 #93(1998), *G.I. Joe* #155, *Groo* #120, Harvey Publ. (most last issues), *Howard the Duck* #33, *Jonah Hex* #92, *Marvel Comics Presents* #175, Marvel's "New Universe" title last issues, *Master of Kung Fu* #125, *Masters Of The Universe* #12-13, *Moon Knight* #38, *New Titans* #130, *Planet of the Apes* magazine #29, *Rom* #75, *Savage Sword* #235, *Spider-Man The Manga* #31 (Direct only with Diamond pre-orders of only 2776 copies printed), *Punisher* #104, *Ronin* #6, *Sgt. Rock* #422, *Sick* #134, *Spider-Woman* #50, *Star Wars* #107, *Suicide Squad* #66, *Superman* #423, *Unknown Soldier* #268, Valiant Publ. (most last issues), Warren Publ. (most last issues), *Wonder Woman* #329, *World's Finest* #323, *X-Men The Manga* #26 (Direct only with Diamond pre-orders of only 2616 copies printed.)

Rom *#75 is one of those hot "last issues" that is in short supply.*

Fans have also gone back to trying to complete many of the comic crossover event issues, such as: Amalgam Comics, *Batman vs. Hulk*, *Blackest Night*, *Civil War*, *Crisis on Infinite Earths*, Darkseid Saga, Death of Superman, *Flashpoint*, Great Darkness Saga, *Identity Crisis*, *Infinity Gauntlet-War*, Kree/Skrull War, *Maximum Carnage*, Mutant Massacre, *Secret Wars*, Superman vs. Muhammad Ali, *Superman vs. Spider-Man*, and Thanos Saga.

The super-hero comics of Marvel and DC are by far the most collected of all comics, seizing the majority of the attention and dollars spent on back issues, but there is so very much more for the true comics lover to discover. Circa 1985, I recall setting up a table at the Minneapolis Comic Con with 100 comics worth over $250,000 (*Detective* #27, *Marvel Mystery* #2-10, *Red Raven* #1, *Superman* #1, *Whiz* #2 and more)and it got a lot of media attention at the time, and I eventually sold them all over a few years. At about that point, I made the decision to further my earlier 1978 plan to try to stock at least one copy each of everything printed in comics and many related items too in the affordable price range of $100 or less, but always with a decent selection of $100 to $1000 items. Big ticket items over $1000 still get most of the attention, yet remain unaffordable to 99% of comic collectors, I thus dropped them from being my main focus. So for over 40 years I bought comic collections with all genres of comics by alternative publishers, Archie, Atlas, Atlas Seaboard, Canadian Comics, Charlton, Classics, *Cracked*, Dell, Digests, Eerie pub, Fanzines, Fawcett, Gold Key, Harvey, IW, King, *Mad*, Magazines, Millar, Personality, Petersen, *Sick*, Skywald, Stanley, Super Pub, Tower, Treasuries, Underground, Warren, Whitman and all the other publishers.

There is an amazing overlooked appetite, and tens of thousands of people who love and collect all the other genres of comics including: Action/adventure, Adult, Archie and related, Cartoons, Children, Crime, Fantasy, Funny Animals, History, Horror, Hot-Rod, Hot-Rod and Car Cartoon mags, Humor, Jungle, Licensed Characters, Love/Romance, Manga, Martial Arts, Movie, Mythology, Mystery, Newspaper Comic Strip, Parody/Spoof, Pirates, Pop Music Stars, Radio, Rock, Sci-Fi, Soap Opera, Sports, Sword and Sorcery, Teen, TV, Underground, War, Western, and more. Because I have a huge selection of all these other genres, I have had many years where non-Superhero comics easily outsold Superhero comics. It is mainly the Superhero, and Marvel/DC collectors who are obsessed with getting high grade copies and actually prefer to pay what it takes to get them. I have sold millions of back issues to these collectors, and have loved doing it, and yes indeed the *Guide* is correct in the wide price spreads for GD to FN and VF through NM-.

The majority of the thousands of Oddball comic buyers (non-Superhero comics) are just happy to find what they need at all, so condition has never been a big issue, with most only having to decide between middle grade decent presentable copies, or lower grade more affordable reading copies. I have been very successful in helping fill in gaps in collections for thousands of often very grateful collectors around the World. Oddball comic collectors are usually the most overlooked and forgotten ones by most other sellers. I don't think the *Guide* is correct in the too wide Price Spreads for GD to FN and VF through NM- for Oddball comics. Take Dell Comics for example. 95% of our buyers want GD to FN copies and we sell them at 110-150% *Guide* depending on difficulty of restocking and demand, but VF through NM- copies are in low demand and can often only be sold if discounted below *Guide*. Many Oddball comics are so undervalued in the *Guide*, that all dealers worldwide are always sold out (or do not bother to stock them), and there are only occasional appearances on eBay. For example, attempting to put complete sets in GD through FN of most 1950 through 1970 titles by Archie, Charlton, and Harvey titles can actually be very tough, even though they have low *Guide* values in the $3 to $10 each price range. I have been looking for COMPLETE copies of *Katy Keene Fashion Book* #17 and #19 for a client for five years. I found them 3 times, but all 3 copies had pages missing, so I would be happy to pay $75 for a complete copy in GD ($19 *Guide* value.) Many fans are looking to buy *Millie The Model* #18-93 the Dan DeCarlo issues. If you can find them at all, these routinely sell for 200%-600% *Guide* in low grade. Over half of the 300+ IW and Super comics have absurdly low *Guide* values in the $12-$20 range for NM-.

For comics that are 55-65 years old, only the most common low grade copies are available in the Marketplace, making gathering a complete set a near impossible task. For most pre-1970 Oddball comics, Grade to Price spreads need to be narrowed, raising the prices on the lower graded copies, so that the VF through NM- copies are more desirable, and scarcer undervalued tough-to-find comics come out of the collections for sale. Yes, there are some more common titles that are slower sellers, but as is the tradition, those can go in Bargain Bins or go into Clearance Sale, as dealers have always done.

Once again the big money maker for us this year was high grade Key issue comics graded by CGC. The demand is huge and seems never-ending, so we keep sending in hundreds more, and they keep selling. As with the last few years, most are TV and movie related, but other items have begun to pick up in demand. Below is a sample of some of the more notable CGC Sales we made in 2016:

Action Force #1 G.I. Joe European Missions 1987 UK Marvel Magazine Destro CGC = $249

Afterlife With Archie #4 ComicsPRO Variant Cover Francavilla Zombies CGC 9.8 = $219

All Star Comics #58, CGC 9.4 = $299

All-Star Squadron #25 1st Infinity Inc. Nuklon Atom Smasher CW TV *Flash* CGC 9.8 = $119 (3 copies)

Amazing Spider-Man #50 1st Kingpin CGC 8.0 = $800

Amazing Spider-Man #252 CGC NM/MT 9.8 = $329 (3 Copies)

Amazing Spider-Man #654 1st Flash Thompson as Agent Venom CGC 9.8 = $139

Amazing Spider-Man Annual #16 Origin 1st Black female Captain Marvel 1982 CGC 9.8 = $225

Astonishing Tales #6 1st Bobbi Morse/Mockingbird, Most Wanted SHIELD CGC NM- 9.2 = $265

Avengers #62 Black Panther solo tryout 1969, reprinted in *Jungle Action* #5 (CGC; 8.5=$179; 8.0=$159)

Avengers #223 Classic Hawkeye, Scott Lang Ant-Man 1982 3rd Taskmaster CGC 9.8 = $139

Avengers Annual #7 CGC 9.8 = $469

Batman #307 first Lucius Fox 1979 CGC 9.8=$139; 9.6=$89

Back To The Future #1 Harvey comic 1st Marty McFly & Doc Brown 1991 Gil Kane CGC 9.8 = $159

Beep Beep The Road Runner #93 Whitman Multi-Pack only, 10/1980 Rare CGC 9.4 = $249

Beetlejuice #1 1991 Harvey CGC 9.8 = $119

Birds Of Prey #76 1st Black Alice CGC 9.8 $120

Black Hole #4 (CGC; 9.6=$1799; 9.4=$800; 8.0=$339)

Black Lightning #1 origin/1st Jefferson Pierce 1977 Outsiders JLA CGC NM 9.8 = $499

Black Panther (1977) #1 CGC Copies; 9.8 = $630 (3), 9.6 = $249 (6), 9.4 = $149 (5)

Black Panther #2 1st Shuri, sister of T'Challa CGC 9.8 = $125

Captain America #241 vs. Punisher 1980 Frank Miller CGC 9.8 = $329

Captain America #282 1st Jack Monroe as Nomad 1983 CGC 9.8 = $139

Captain Atom #83 1st Print Ted Cord Blue Beetle 1966 CGC FN- 5.5 = $299

Captain Britain #1 Origin 1st app. UK Marvel 1976 rare bonus mask (CGC 9.8=$849; 9.4=$399 = 4 copies)

Cerebus The Aardvark #11 (1st Cockroach = Tick Prototype? CGC 9.6 $139), 31(1st Full Moon Roach CGC 9.8 $149)

Chip N Dale #68 (10/1980) CGC 9.6 = $449

Daffy Duck #129 CGC NM+ 9.6 = $399

Daredevil #62 origin early Nighthawk, Squadron Sinister, Defenders 1970 CGC 9.4 = $149

Daredevil #197 Bullseye 1st Yuriko Oyama, Lady Deathstrike CGC 9.8 = $149

Daredevil V2 #58 1st Night Nurse CGC NM+ 9.6 = $109

DC Comics Presents #26 1st New Teen Titans CGC 9.8 = $649

DC Super-Stars #17 Origin 1st Huntress 1977 CGC NM 9.4 = $239 (2)

Deadly Hands Of Kung Fu #1(9.6 $399); #8,21,26(CGC 9.8 $229 each); #9,12,16,18,20(9.8 $219 each)

Deadly Hands of Kung Fu #19 1st Puerto Rican White Tiger 1975 (CGC 9.4=$349; 9.2=$249)

Detective Comics #608 1st Anarky 1989, CW TV *Arrow* Season 4, CGC NM/MT 9.8 = $135

Devil Dinosaur #1 1978 CGC 9.8 = $184

Doctor Strange #169 1968 CGC 7.5 = $289

Doctor Strange #1 1974 (CGC 9.8 = $889 = 2 copies) (CGC 9.8 = $849 = 2 copies) (CGC 9.8 = $799 = 2 copies)

Fantastic Four #46 CGC 7.5 = $389

Fantastic Four #168 Luke Cage Power Man Joins 1976 CGC 9.8 $189

Fantasy Quarterly #1 1st Elfquest CGC 9.8 = $499 (2)

Fear #19 1st Howard the Duck CGC NM+ 9.6 = $599

Firestorm #1 1978 CGC 9.8 = $450 (2 copies)

FOOM #15 Howard the Duck 9/1976 1st. app Ms. Marvel, Captain Britain, Star Wars, CGC 9.8 = $499

Ghost Rider #1 1973 CGC NM- 9.2 = $450

Giant-Size Kid Colt #2 Battle at Blood Creek, Gil Kane Low Print 1975 CGC NM 9.4 = $249

Guardians Of Knowhere #1 Guillory Variant 1st Gwenom CGC 9.8 = $99

Haunt of Horror (Marvel Mag.) #2 (CGC 9.8 $209); #4(CGC 9.8 $219); # 5 (CGC 9.8 $229)

Hawaiian Dick #1 Johnny Knoxville 2002 Image UTV NBC TV Series CGC 9.8 (3)

Hawkeye #1 origin Hawkeye, Mockingbird begins 1983 TV Agents of SHIELD CGC 9.8 $139

Incredible Hulk #228 1st Moonstone CGC 9.6 = $169 (2)

Invincible Iron Man #7 1st cameo Riri Williams CGC 9.8 = $99

Iron Man #17 1st Whitney Frost as Madame Masque 1969 *Agent Carter* TV CGC VF/NM 9.0 = $169

Iron Man #128 CGC 9.8 = $333

Kick-Ass #3 1st Hit-Girl CGC 9.8 = $149

Joker #1 1975 CGC 9.8 = $499

Joker #4,8,9 1975 Series CGC 9.8 = $199 each

Legend Of Bruce Lee #1 Photo cover 1983 B&W Nostalgia Comic Magazine CGC 9.6 = $129

Little Lulu #261 Whitman Multi-Pack CGC 9.4 = $249

Looney Tunes #33 and #35 (1980) CGC 9.6 = $499 each

Lumberjanes #1 Virgin Collector's Paradise BOOM! 2014 CGC 9.8 = $119

Marvel Super Special #7 French Sgt. Pepper 1978 Pérez-a, Beatles, Aerosmith Rare CGC VF 8.0 = $249

Marvel Graphic Novel #4 1st New Mutants 1982 Canadian Variant CGC 9.6 = $359 (2)

Marvel Mangaverse #3 1st T'Channa Shuri Sister 2002 CGC 9.8 = $125

Marvel Premiere #1 origin Warlock 1st solo series 1972 CGC NM 9.4 = $619

Marvel Premiere #57 1st USA Doctor Who CGC 9.8 = $219

Marvel Preview #4 CGC 9.6 = $799

Marvel Spotlight #29 CGC 9.8 = $249

Marvel Super-Hero Contest Of Champions #1 CGC 9.8 = $129

Marvel Super-Heroes Volume 2 #8 Winter Special 1991 1st Squirrel Girl CGC 9.8 = $329

Marvel Tails #1 first Peter Porker Spectacular Spider-Ham 1983 CGC 9.8 $159

Marvel Team-Up #103 2nd Full Taskmaster 1981 Scott Lang Ant-Man CGC 9.8 = $139

Marvel Two In One Annual # 2 CGC 9.8 = $399

Marvel Tales #98 (r/*Amazing Spider-Man* #121) CGC 9.8 = $199

Masters of the Universe #1 DC Comics 1982 He-Man Sony Movie Reboot CGC 9.8 = $149

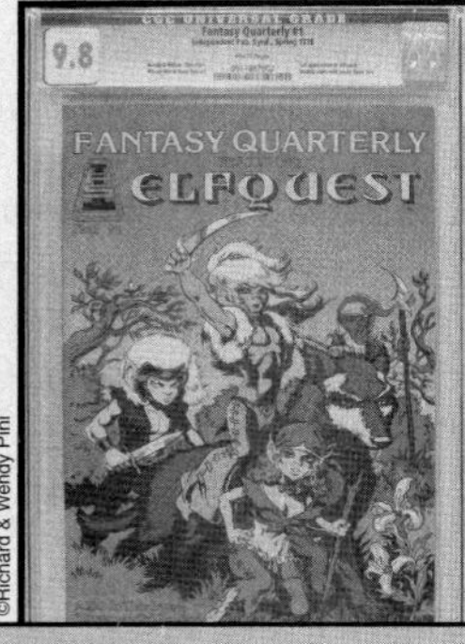

***Fantasy Quarterly** #1 in CGC 9.8 for $499 was a notable sale for 2016.*

Micronauts #1 1979 CGC 9.8 = $149 (5)

Micronauts #8 Golden-a 1st Captain Universe CGC 9.8 = $179

Mighty World Of Marvel #220 Sgt. Fury #1 1976 Luke Cage, Hulk, Daredevil, CGC 9.8 = $149

Ms. Marvel #1 Carol Danvers 1977 (Multiple CGC copies; 9.8=$1100; 9.6=$399; 9.4=$225; 9.2=$169; 9.0=$125)

New Mutants #26 1st Full Legion 1985 CGC 9.8 = $199 (4)

New Teen Titans #2 1st Deathstroke Terminator, *Arrow* TV Series CGC NMMT 9.8 = $599

Our Fighting Forces #151 Losers by Jack Kirby begins 1974 CGC NM/MT 9.8 = $239

Photo News Features #1 Marvel Mag 1974 Hitler CGC 9.8 = $740

Primer #2 Comico 1st Grendel 1982 (CGC; 9.6=$425; 9.4=$339);

Punisher Limited Series #1 Zeck 1986 CGC 9.8 = $499

Punisher #104 vs. Bullseye 1995 Kingpin, scarce last issue CGC 9.6 = $99

Ragman #1 1976 CGC 9.8 = $239

Rom Spaceknight #1 origin, 1st Dire Wraiths, Brandy Clark 1979 CGC 9.8 = $299

Savage Action 1 UK Marvel 1980 Punisher Dominic Fortune, Moon Knight CGC NM/MT 9.8 = $199

Savage She-Hulk #1 1980 CGC 9.8 = $249 (5)

Scooby-Doo (1977-1979; Marvel); #2(CGC 9.6 $139); #3(CGC 9.6 $139); #7(CGC 9.6 $149)

Shogun Warriors #1 First Raydeen Combatra Dangard Ace 1979 Marvel CGC 9.8 = $159

Showcase #30 S.A. Origin Aquaman 1961 Ramona Fradon CGC VGFN 5.0 = $799

Six Million Dollar Man #1 Charlton Mag (9.8 = $399; CGC 9.4 = $175)

Space 1999 #1 Charlton B&W Magazine 1975 TV Gray Morrow, Landau, Bain CGC 9.8 = $249

Special Marvel Edition #15 1st Shang-Chi CGC 9.8 = $1200

Spectacular Spider-Man #90 1st Black Venom Costume 1984 Black Cat CGC 9.8 = $165

Spider-Man and His Amazing Friends #1 Iceman, Firestar, Green Goblin CGC 9.8 = $179

Spider-Woman #1 Jessica Drew, new origin 1978 CGC 9.8 = $129 (5)

Spidey Super Stories #32 2nd cameo Sabretooth 3/1978 3rd Captain Britain CGC 9.4 = $149

Strange Tales #169 first Brother Voodoo, 1973 Avengers, Black Hero CGC 9.0 = $315

Star Wars #68 Re-intro Boba Fett classic cover/story 1983 CGC 9.8 = $249

Star Wars Weekly #1 UK British Marvel Comic 1977-1978 w/rare bonus, CGC NM/MT 9.8 = $699

Steel the Indestructible Man #1 DC 1978 CGC 9.8 = $130

Swamp Thing #49 1st Justice League Dark CGC 9.8 = $189

Tales of The Zombie # 1 CGC 9.6 = $399

Thor #300 CGC 9.8 = $149

Thundercats #1 1985 CGC 9.8 = $149 (2 copies)

The Tick #1 NEC 1988 (CGC 9.4 = $189 = 3 copies; 9.4 = $225; 9.2=$175)

Transformers #80 Scarce last issue 1991 Optimus Prime Marvel Comics CGC 9.8 = $300

Tweety & Sylvester #106 (10/1980) CGC 9.6 = $449

Ultimate Fallout #4 1st Miles Morales, new Spider-Man 2011 1st print CGC NM+ 9.6 = $99

Unknown Worlds Of Science Fiction #1 Bradbury Adams, Kaluta, Brunner CGC NMMT 9.8 = $249

Vampirella #113 1st Harris 1987 Pantha bondage, Low Print 1987 Canadian Variant CGC VF+ 8.5 = $359

Voltron Defender of the Universe #1 Modern Comics 1985 CGC 9.8 = $119

Western Gunfighters #1 Ghost Rider, Gunhawk Marvel 1970 Sutton, Kirby CGC 9.8 = $625

What If? #10 1st Jane Foster as female Thor CGC 9.8 = $299

What If? Planet Hulk #1 First Skarr, Son of Hulk 2007 CGC 9.6 = $99

Wolverine #66 1st Old Man Logan and arc begins 2008 CGC 9.6 = $99

Wynonna Earp #1 1st Appearance SyFy TV 1996 Image IDW Jim Lee, Low Print CGC 9.8 $119

You Don't Say! (More) #2 Stan Lee 1963 Marvel Magazine Highest Graded CGC VF 8.0 = $149

X-Men #4 1st Scarlet Witch, Quicksilver and Toad, 2nd Magneto, 1964 Kirby CGC VG 4.0 = $495.

Maggie Thompson
Collector

My buddy Brent Frankenhoff (who works with me on buying, selling, and collecting) and I have concluded that the pricing bar was on the rise for both buyers and sellers of back issues in 2016. There's plenty of collector traffic out there for comics that are reasonably priced, but both groups have adjusted their price points higher in the past year. Where a collector used to be able to fill holes for 50¢ each for most comics published in the past 20 to 30 years, that's changed. Many of those issues cost 75¢ or $1 now, whereas many of the $2-$3 comics have moved up to the $5-$6 range. Hot keys from the same period – *Walking Dead* #1, for example – still command crazy price bumps. Both key and non-key issues are continuing to sell, as new collectors come into the market looking for popular media characters in their original appearances.

This is also the case with Gold, Silver, and Bronze Age items. Where it was once possible to buy many non-key examples of mid-to-lower-grade comics for $2-$5, that $5 now seems to be the starting point for Gold and Silver in Good-Very Good. Mid-grade Bronze Age comics can be found for $2-$3, but such deals are more readily made when buying in quantity. (Conventions can provide bargains for buyers looking for a quantity of Good items in general genres, rather than for specific issues to fill holes.)

As the collecting base ages, more and more collectors who bought their first comics in the late 1980s and early 1990s have more disposable income and are looking to fill the holes in those runs. (Yes, just the way earlier generations of collectors sought to fill holes in their runs from the late 1960s through the early 1980s. Mind you, there are enough 1980s and 1990s comics that prices aren't stellar for small-press-run non-keys, but there is still money to be made. Moreover, prices may go up, as collectors are willing to part with more of their disposable income to acquire a last missing item in a given run.

As the general public gets more savvy about what older comics are worth, prices that buyers have to offer to acquire Gold, Silver, and Bronze Age comics are also on the rise. Many owners now want higher and higher prices for those comics, because they can do their homework and see what those issues bring online in auctions. On the other hand, a buyer's patience can pay off, as a seller sees that what seemed to be a seller's market may not be quite as lucrative as he or she originally thought.

While *Captain America: Civil War* and *Doctor Strange* didn't produce massive price spikes for their connected comics, there was a price bump for almost anything Harley Quinn related, especially her first comic-book appearance in *Batman Adventures* #12. Whereas so far, at least, her fellow Suicide Squad members did not see similar increases in their key appearances, that may change.

Michael Tierney Collector's Edition & The Comic Book Store

DC Comics might have finally learned the lesson that a satisfied customer buys more than a frustrated one. The Rebirth reboot where DC went back to their roots was a huge success, but because of poor promotional efforts, it initially had the look of a mega bomb.

DC Comics made their own catalog, which had few illustrations and contained only the titles and the names of the creators -- plus the first partial shipment didn't arrive until two weeks before the final ordering deadline. DC also skipped providing a teaser during Free Comic Book Day the month before. The reaction? No interest at all from fans. Not even the crickets were chirping.

DC's fiasco called *Convergence* the year before had enjoyed an avalanche of anticipation when compared to Rebirth, and *Convergence* was an abject sales disaster. So it's no wonder that retailers across the country ordered light, despite an offer of returnability several months later. I know that my wariness of bombs was the same as if I'd heard multiple air raid sirens.

Then the books came out to good reviews, but there were none available for reorder. DC apparently had less faith in their books than I. But expecting retailers to carry all of the burden for their gamble wasn't the worst of it.

The sellout *DC Rebirth* #1 that launched the event immediately went back to a second printing, and retailers had but a single hour in which to order copies. I was reading through my email at the exact moment when the solicitation arrived and immediately placed what I felt were healthy orders for both of my locations. While I was at the very front of the line -- DC decided not to ship even a single copy to either store. I was told that other accounts had placed orders in the 1,000s and all copies went to them on an allocation system that only -- special emphasis here on the ONLY -- DC uses.

The exact same thing happened the first time DC did a month of holographic covers. I had placed realistic initial orders, but received only a tiny fraction because of DC's allocation system. Didn't get enough to even satisfy my reserve accounts for customers who bought the titles on a regular basis. The result? When DC repeated the event the next year, it was a fiasco. I once again ordered realistically am still stuck today with piles of unsold copies. Frustrated customers don't buy more. They buy less.

DC quickly did a third printing of *DC Rebirth* #1 and this time gave everybody plenty of time to order. The result? Once again certain accounts ordered copies in the 1,000s and once again DC's allocation system kicked in. One of my stores received only 3 copies.

It certainly makes it hard to support an event when you can't get the materials to work with. A tilted playing field makes things exponentially more difficult.

Fortunately, after a stumbling and bumbling launch worthy of a follies highlight reel, DC managed to maintain their bi-weekly scheduling and kept the quality of the content up. Despite the stunted initial launch, sales grew with each subsequent issue along an incline that headed steadily upwards for several months before plateauing. The result was that even when sales began to drop across most of the line, for several months DC outsold Marvel Comics with a consistency that I've never seen before in my 36 years as a comics specialty retailer.

This was a case of higher issue numbers on a series selling better than the early issues, as DC quickly rolled up the issue count meter thanks to their bi-weekly schedule. A return to the original three-digit numbering on *Detective Comics* and *Action Comics* was particularly well received, selling much better than they did as part of the New 52, and holding their sales levels even after the rest of the line began to drop.

The DC Rebirth return of **Action Comics** and **Detective Comics** to their original numbering was well received.

Lower print runs for the earliest issues of Rebirth quickly led to increased values.

DC improved their shipping reliability, but they weren't perfect. *Dark Knight III: Master Race* often had long gaps between issues. But that series was outside normal continuity, unlike Marvel's major crossover event for 2016.

Marvel had major problems getting *Civil War II* to market, which fit their pattern of stellar starts which fizzle at the finish.

The fact that the effectiveness of major crossover events have run their course was clearly illustrated in 2016 by the way that DC solidly outsold Marvel during *Civil War II*'s limp into a finale. Sales did hold steady throughout the core series' sporadic run, but all of the spin-offs sold in paltry numbers and the crossovers caused no bump in sales. The books that suffered the most were the relaunches.

The same as they did with *Secret Wars* in 2015, Marvel did not delay titles intended to follow the events in *Civil War II* and shipped them out of sequence. Confusion once again killed enthusiasm, continuing Marvel's pattern of doing reboots where the sales levels soon drop lower than that of the previous series.

As they do every year -- what new titles sell best new on store shelves influences what sells out of the back issue bins, with added fuel from the fires of desire kindled by movies and television.

Our top dollar book of the year was the 1st appearance of Thor in *Journey Into Mystery* #83 in good for $1300. The movie *X-Men: Apocalypse* certainly influenced the sale of

Strange Tales (v1) #128 featuring Quicksilver and Scarlet Witch in VF+ for $195. The first movie appearance of the Black Panther in the *Captain America: Civil War* movie caused a run on his back issues. The Black Panther's first appearance in *Fantastic Four* #52 sold 2 copies in VG+ for $175 each, and another in FN- for $225. Other key *Fantastic Four* sales featured the origin and 1st appearance of the Inhumans in issue #45 for $250 in VG+, and the origin and 1st appearances of Galactus and the Silver Surfer in #48 for $175 in FN-. The very first series of *Doctor Strange*, which picked up the numbering from *Strange Tales*, was hot. Issues #170 through #181 all sold in ranges from VG+ to FN+ for prices between $16 and $19 each.

Sgt. Fury #13, featuring an appearance by Captain America and Bucky, sold in FN- for $110. *Tales to Astonish* (v1) #49, featuring the 1st appearance of Giant Man, sold for $80 in VG-. The villain connecting many of the Marvel movies is Thanos, whose first appearance in *Iron Man* (v1) #55 sold in Fair condition for $55. The 1st appearance of Deadpool in *New Mutants* #98 sold in VF+ for $140. Anticipation of Legion's upcoming TV appearance sold multiple copies of *New Mutants* #26 in VF+ for $18 each. Marvel's *Star Wars* from the '70s were especially hot at values between $10 and $26. We also sold typically large numbers of mid-range *Amazing Spider-Man* and *X-Men* comics.

While the *Suicide Squad* movie outperformed *Batman V. Superman* in theaters, all of these characters' comics were hot. A variant of the first series of *Suicide Squad* #1 sold in VF/NM for $125, while 3 different copies of the New 52 *Suicide Squad* sold in VG/NM for prices ranging from $75 upward to $125. A double-covered copy of *Superman* (v1) #61 in FN, with the outer cover signed by Shuster, sold for $542. *Batman* (v1) #17 sold in VG+ for $600, while the more modern *Batman Adventures* #12, with the first appearance of Harley Quinn, sold in VG+ for $187. The New 52 *Batman* #1 sold in VG- for $75. Sold a large number of Silver Age *Batman*, with the top sellers being issue #145 with a Joker cover and story in FN for $85, and issue #232 featuring Neal Adams' debut of Ra's al Ghul for $54 in VG+. *Aquaman* (v1) #1 sold in VG+ for $300. *Justice League of America* (v1) #1 sold in Fair condition for $230. The origin of the JLA in issue #9 sold in VG+ for $120. The Golden Age *All Star Comics* #33, with a Solomon Grundy appearance, sold in GD- for $100.

The television show *DC's Legends of Tomorrow* influenced the sales of *Atom* #1 in VG+ for $216, the 3rd appearance of the Atom in *Showcase* #36 in VG+ for $95, and *Hawkman* (v1) #1 with the origin and 1st appearance of Zatanna in VG for $150. The 2nd appearance of Supergirl in *Action Comics* #253 sold in GD- for $45.

The popularity of the TV series *The Walking Dead* has kept back issue sales of the comic series brisk. The problem is that everyone is buying and no one is selling, making older inventory scarce. Our top dollar sale was the 1st appearance of Jesus in #92 in NM for $65. I've seen this pattern before, where collectors hoard their copies in expectation of an eternal upward rise in value. What happens is once demand slows everyone starts selling at once and the values crash. But right now, while the show is still airing, demand is strong.

Of course, not all back issues sales were media influenced. We sold many comics to readers simply looking to recapture the good fun that they once enjoyed. *Marge's Little Lulu & Tubby at Summer Camp* #1 sold in VF- for $175. We sold a bunch of mid-range *Marge's Little Lulu* in prices ranging from $12 to $34 each. The first appearance of Bozo the Clown in *Four Color* #285 sold in VG for $90. The scarce *Conan the Barbarian* (v1) #3 sold in VF+ for $95. The 2nd appearance of Judy of the Jungle in *Exciting Comics* #56 sold for $100 in VG. Marvel's Golden Age *Human Torch* #32, which includes appearances by Sungirl and Namora, sold in VG for $300. *Metal Men* (v1) #1 sold in VG+ for $90. *Ozzie & Harriet* #1 sold in FN for $140. Printing enhancements were done on this photo cover, with bright blue dots added to their eyes that made the actors look slightly freakish. Looking at this cover closely, you could almost hear the musical rift from the shower scene in the movie *Psycho*.

We sold a run of the Golden Age era *Picture News*, with #1 going in FN+ for $140, and issues #2, #3, #6, and #7 all going for $100 each in FN+. This interesting series featured a number of illustrated news stories ranging from the future Queen of England working as an auto mechanic during WWII to Joe Lewis' battle for boxing supremacy and a youthful Frank Sinata's public exploits. *Planet Comics* #42 sold in VG+ for $125. *Reptilicus* #2 sold in FN+ for $40. *X-Mas Comics* #7, a very early example of cover enhancements with a green felt stocking printed on the cover, sold in VG- for $140.

Ted VanLiew
Superworld Comics

Comic books still seem to be regarded as the coolest collectible these days. Remember when we were an underground secret society? And it was our badge of shame. Ha Ha. Now we've taken over popular culture. Who could have known?

There's something about comic books that stir a true enduring passion in the hearts of bibliophiles and folks with the collector gene, more so than most other collectibles. We're even getting flocks of women of all ages involved in the hobby, be it Cosplay, Collecting, or Creating. I remember when I couldn't think of a single female at my school who had any known interest in comics or fantasy, or would admit to it, at least. Now, it seems to be *de riguer* to be at least aware of the field, which is great!

The success and high profile of the comic related movies continues to help raise the profile of the hobby, and helps make the mainstream aware of our little slice of the world.

It seems to me that the current market can be divided into 5 main segments:

1) The high end, big ticket, scarce, and hard to find high grade goodies, which appeal to the investors, most of whom are pretty knowledgeable about the comic market, but also many who are looking for a fun and very profitable place to park their disposable income. The returns on the high end stuff have been pretty sensational for quite a few years now, even resisting the enormous economic downturn that began in '08.

2) The Collector/Investor stratus, who I would consider "mid-level." They like to find either semi-affordable key books or high grade copies of good titles. They might not be able to reach for an *Incredible Hulk* #1 in 8.0 or *Captain America Comics* #6 in 8.5 or the like, but will snag an *Avengers* #3 in 8.5, *Fantastic Four* #52 9.0, or *Batman* #23 in 8.0, to pick a few random examples.

3) The Collectors, who want to have nice quality books, but will settle for the ones that don't get into the stratosphere pricewise. For example, maybe *Flash* #123 VG/FN, or *Amazing Spider-Man* #20 in VF, *Weird Tales of the Future* #2 in Good+, or something like that.

4) The Collector/Readers, who just want to get cool vintage books at a good price or a great deal. They'll build runs, which seems to be a bit of a lost art in the investor quarters, and will buy lower to mid-grade copies, which can often be had at really favorable prices. For example, they might build a run of a long running title in Good to Fine condition, depending on what they find.

5) Folks who just want cheap books to read or collect. These collectors will be seen at a show digging through dollar boxes, or maybe deep discount boxes, or maybe collect modern era books (1980s to present) that are very inexpensive.

It seems that there are more cover chasers than ever, especially in the vintage market. Now that we can see what almost any book looks like on the internet with great sites like Grand Comics Database, we can see which covers are outstanding.

I've noticed that especially with Golden Age books, if you look at two consecutive issues, one will be in much higher demand because of how striking the cover is. Take, for example, *Journey into Unknown Worlds* from Atlas, issue #12 & 13. Issue #12 sells ok, but #13 sells instantly for a higher price since it has a striking Bill Everett cover. Not that there's anything wrong with that!

Platinum Age: Platinum Age books are a bit of a minefield, as most are genuinely scarce to rare, but some are high demand, but many tend to get overlooked because they predate Superheroes, Horror, and Science Fiction in comics.

For example, *New Fun Comics* are very rare, the first DC title, and are very sought after. Ditto for early Chesler/Centaur comics. On the other hand, a lot of the humor strip titles have fallen on harder times, such as *Tip Top*, *King Comics*, and so forth. We have seen a bit of a resurgence in interest in these if they turn up in decent shape, probably because they're so hard to find, and are famous titles.

Golden Age: There is a core of super popular items in the Golden Age, along with reams of books that are good, but not as well known or loved.

The mainstream and secondary Timely and DC titles can always be counted on to sell well, along with various rarities with great covers. Better/Nedors are good, along with Centaurs, Fox, some Ace, some early Quality, and some other publishers who are a bit lesser known. On the other hand, Fawcetts, with some exceptions, get no respect. Neither do Quality titles after a certain early period. Both publishers' books often had better art within the books than Timely or Nedor, but the covers are bland by comparison. Prize Pubs, Speed, Harvey, MLJ all are in high demand, while Dells and Classics are pretty croaked off. Again, there are some exceptions. Some *Walt Disney Comics and Stories*, *Famous Funnies*, and *Four Colors* are good, but the majority are slow in the market.

One of the fun aspects of searching out Golden Age comics is that there are SO many rarities or lesser known books that are amazingly cool, such as *Flying Jenny* #2, which sports a great Matt Baker cover and an unusual color scheme. There are hundreds more like that. My advice is to dig, dig, dig, and lots of these books are relative bargains. *Front Page Comic Book*, which is a one shot from 1944, has the first (unacknowledged) horror cover, to the best of my knowledge. So, while the first acknowledged horror comic, *Eerie* #1 from 1947, is a very (deservedly) pricey book, you can find a copy of *FPCB* for a fraction of the price.

Many collectors are looking for either classic covers, covers by certain noteworthy artists, or just lesser known great covers. Schomburg, LB Cole, Kirby, Simon, Lou Fine, Eisner, and Everett are a few of the consistently great artists of the Golden Age. There are many, many great covers by these artists, such as *Terrific* #5 by Schomburg, which we were fortunate to find a nice copy of. That reminds me of another trend that is enduringly popular: Bondage covers, especially with women in distress. I think this appeals to both our prurient interest and subconscious desire to rescue a damsel. *Daredevil Comics* #11 is one of my favorites in this category. Artist Charlie Biro adds a touch of humor to the situation, as you see a woman in the foreground whose feet are being tickled by a feather held by a repulsive deformed hunchbacked monster. The expression on her face is perfectly drawn to show the combination of tickle and pain in her facial expression. It's almost an afterthought that DD is approaching from the back of the dungeon to rescue her.

WW2 covers can also be counted on to be of primary interest to collectors. Some are better in concept and rendering than others, but the good ones can be dazzling and very exciting. It's widely accepted that they depict attitudes that were prevalent during the last 'good' war, and depicted scenarios from the first war that we were involved in while comics existed.

Atomic Age: Often, we tend to categorize this era (late '40s to mid '50s) as part of the Golden Age still, but I will say a few words about it. There are a lot of especially tough to find books in this time period, probably because print runs were down, and the pogrom against comic books occurred during this time. Marvel/Atlas nearly went under because of declining readership, and many other publishers didn't make it.

The more extreme Horror or far out and stylish Science Fiction titles lead the way. Titles like Gilmore's *Weird Mysteries*, many Atlas titles, *Weird Tales of the Future*, and many Avon titles are always sought after. Avon One Shots have all but evaporated, especially in solid grades. ECs, which were the leading lights of the era, are more plentiful, probably since there was such a focused fan base, and Publisher William Gaines was terrific at figuring out what the youngsters would like. They also paid better than the others, and attracted the top talent. They've also been reprinted many times. Consequently, they're a bit slower to sell, since they're more available.

DC Superhero titles from this period are pursued avidly, and finding them in superior grades is really tough! Atlas' short lived Superhero revival issues are also very popular, as they only lasted a few months, and are in short supply.

Silver Age: Well, still the core of the collecting/investing industry. The Baby Boomers came of age during this era, so we are very attached to these books and stories and characters. While there were many talented and productive writers and artists who were in peak form during this period, I believe it was the singular genius of Jack 'King' Kirby that is most responsible for the explosive interest in this period. So many of the characters who emerged, and the stories, and even the style of the storytelling, were the product of Kirby's fevered imagination. And, never has there been a more prolific artist in comics. If you look at the movies that have become a multi-billion dollar industry, the majority of the characters were created by this one man, and fleshed out with the help of Stan Lee.

The Marvels continue to be the flagship titles of the era, while the DC titles seem to wax and wane in popularity. The other publishers of the era, while collectible, recede into the background somewhat.

DC came first though, as they are credited with resurrecting the superhero genre in 1956 with the advent of the Flash in *Showcase* #4, then others, culminating in the excitement generated by the first major Silver Age superhero team, the Justice League in 1960. So, many earlier SA DCs are very collectible. Marvel didn't even get back into the superhero game until late in 1961.

In DC World, issues from the 1950s through 1961 or so, are pretty scarce, and very tough to locate in higher grade.

In Marvel World, issues from *Fantastic Four* #1 in 10/61 up into 1964 are a lot scarcer than the ones after that, esp. in higher grades.

For example, *Batman* #121 is almost impossible to find in anything above VG+, while Batman issues in the #180s are not so hard to find in VF or better, and *Hulk* #2 is a toughie, while *Hulk* #102 is not so tough.

Whenever we get any Marvel in genuinely high grade from the Pre-Hero issues throughout the 1960's, they are quick to sell, but anything from 1964 and earlier in high grade, guys are climbing over each other to get to.

With DC, it's a bit hit or miss, although they're much scarcer than the Marvels. Any good key book in high grade is a goner in record time, as are the earlier era books.

Bronze Age: Bronze era books (1970 to 1980ish) are a growth segment, and are still plentiful, since print runs were increased, and many more titles hit the market. Collectors and speculators were sometimes saving multiple copies and storing the books to keep them in top shape. Of course, there's a steady supply of well read mid to lower grade copies as well.

Most major titles continued their runs in the 1970s, and zillions of new titles were launched, either in their own titles or in anthology titles, such as *Marvel Spotlight*, *DC Comics Presents*, and many, many other Marvel "So and So" and DC "So and So" titles.

Some of the books that are always going to sell quickly when we get them in almost any grade are: *Hulk* #181, *Amazing Spider-Man* #129, *Marvel Spotlight* #5, *Marvel Premiere* #15, *Hero For Hire* #1, *Iron Man* #55, *Iron Fist* #14, *G-S X-Men* #1, *Werewolf by Night* #32, *Green Lantern* #76, 85,87, *Batman* #222,227,232,251, *Detective* #400,411, and almost any issue by Neal Adams from the era.

The early 1970s is when Marvel and DC began launching more Black and female primary characters, and with demographic changes in the country and the comic industry over the years, these are increasing in popularity.

The early appearances of any character who's appearing in a movie or TV show will take off like a rocket, as the speculation impulse ramps up into gear. Some of them will settle down after a while, but some remain firecracker hot!

It seems the line of demarcation for any scarcity is sometime in 1974 or so. Books published after that seem to be extremely plentiful, and we're constantly offered collections that begin in that era.

However, there is increasing demand for many books from the later '70s and into the early '80s, which is great. It's nice to see appreciation for many of these books that have lain dormant for years.

Modern/Copper Age: Well, for most of the time we've been in business, we pretty much ignored books from the '80s onward, except for reading material. But, to our surprise, there's growth in this era as well, especially in books related to movies and TV shows. That's not the whole story though, as even books that aren't necessarily all that expensive are in increasing demand. Who'da thunk it?

There are a small amount of scarce books, since this was the time of the indie explosion. These indies had lower print runs in early issues, as the creators didn't know if they'd find an audience yet. Books like *Teenage Mutant Ninja Turtles* #1,2,3 (1st Print – important), *Cerebus* #1, *Albedo* #2 (first Usagi Yojimbo), and a few others are in very short supply.

Others have taken on unanticipated value, led by *Batman Adventures* #12 (1st Harley Quinn) and *Walking Dead* #1, which can get into the hundreds, or even thousands, of dollars in highest grades. *New Mutants* #87 (1st Cable), #98 (1st Deadpool), *Marvel Superheroes Winter Special* #8 (1st Squirrel Girl), *NYX* #3, *X-23* #1 (both X-23, Wolverine's daughter), *Amazing Spider-Man* #300 (enduringly popular), *X-Men* #266 (1st Gambit), and many others, too numerous to mention.

There's plenty we haven't touched on, but don't want to be long winded, and will fill you all in next time out. Happy Collecting, Ted VL.

Harley Yee
Harley Yee Rare Comics

The 2016 market had one of the best years in the industry. With the announcements of a big slate of DC movies, the DC Silver and Bronze Age markets were energized to heights not seen in many years. This has also brought more attention to the DC Golden Age markets for titles such as *All Star*, *Sensation* and *Wonder Woman*. With the always popular Marvel Silver and Bronze Age, this combination is moving the market to new heights.

In the Golden Age market, new players that before had maybe tended to only collect Marvel or DC have started to hone in on this market going into the Timely, Atlas, Good Girl, Horror, early Fox and MLJs. This trend should continue with the CGC and CBCS forums allowing collectors to post their new gems and getting others excited to post their own new gems.

The 2017 market should continue these trends. The increasingly important foreign market should see to that with an almost unlimited growth potential at this time.

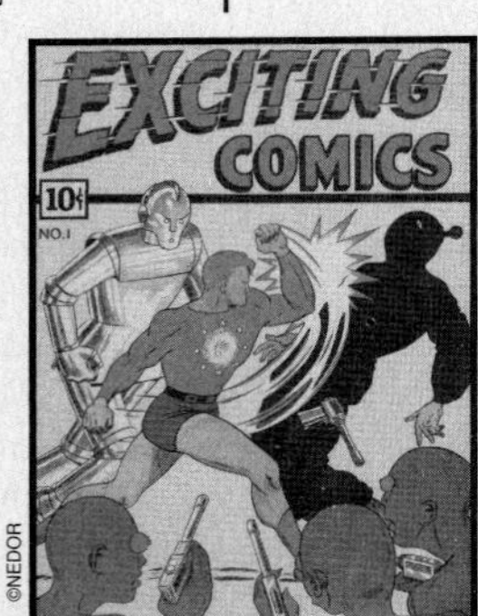

Rare and esoteric titles like **Exciting Comics** (#1 shown) are getting stronger in the market.

Vincent Zurzolo, Frank Cwiklik & Rob Reynolds
Metropolis Collectibles
ComicConnect.com

Vincent Zurzolo - Metropolis Collectibles and ComicConnect.com

It's that time of year again. Simply amazing. Where did the time go? I have vivid recollections of writing my first market report. I think it was 23 years ago. I was so excited I didn't know what to write about first. The market has grown beyond my wildest dreams. Not only in terms of dollar figures but in terms of the acceptance of comic books as a respected art form. I believe there is still plenty of growth ahead of us.

Thinking back about how much has changed in the comic market and for Metropolis and ComicConnect over that period of time is profound. The last 23 years have seen some major changes. The comic implosion, the advent of the Internet, cell phones, eBay, the Vincent's Collectibles (my original company) and Metropolis Collectibles merger, the beginning of CGC, the start of ComicConnect, the beginning of the Marvel Movie Explosion, the first million-dollar comic sale and the half dozen or so other seven-figure sales we've made since then. One can easily see how the vintage comic collecting and investing market has evolved.

The past year has been very strong. Big keys are selling very well. Private sales and auctions are both doing incredibly well. Convention sales have picked up. Gallery sales are strong. If I had to point to one thing I've noticed getting stronger it would be the rare and esoteric vintage comic market. I am referring to titles like *Amazing Man*, *Bouncer*, *Champ*, *Crime Mysteries*, *Exciting*, *Fantastic*, *Feature*, *Funny Pages*, *Future*, *Ghost*, *Lucky*, *Prize*, *Startling*, *True to Life Romances*, *Wonder*, *Wonderworld*, and *Zip*. As the prices of keys like *Action* #1, *Detective* #27 as well as *Superman* #1, *Batman* #1, *Marvel* #1 and *Captain America* #1 continue to soar, more affordable "secondary keys" are looking very appealing. *All Star* #3, *More Fun* #52, *Sub-Mariner* #1, and *Human Torch* #2 (1) are all starting to tick up. If you are thinking about buying a key Golden Age comic, buy it now before the price goes up. Golden Age sales of note include *Captain America Comics* #1 CGC 8.0 $288,000, *Detective* #31 CGC 4.0 $90,000, *Superman* #1 CGC 1.5 $85,000, and *Batman* #1 2.5 $64,000.

Sales of *Hulk* #1 CGC 9.2 $375,000 (record), *Amazing Fantasy* #15 9.0 $237,000, *Journey into Mystery* #83 CGC 9.4 $210,000 and *Fantastic Four* #1 CGC 8.5 $65,000 show that the Silver Age market is still robust with tremendous interest.

Bronze Age keys like *Hulk* #181, *Giant-Size X-Men* #1, *House of Secrets* #92, and *Green Lantern* #76 are still being scooped up as fast as we can get them in. Copper Age and Modern Age comics are as well. The market is humming.

I expect this trend to continue throughout 2017. The new crop of superhero movies and TV shows will help propel characters' first appearances to higher levels as well.

My best advice is to put your want list together and focus on it. Don't get distracted. Focus and have fun!

Frank Cwiklik - Metropolis Collectibles

You know, I hate using the term "think outside the box," as it's become such a cliché. Unfortunately, I have no other way to describe how comic dealers and collectors must think in this brave new world of vintage comic collecting and selling – you gotta think outside the box.

First, let's define "the box": the old methods, the

tried and true, convention deals and phone call sales and occasional big sales online or to clients you may have met through a guy who knows a guy who knows a guy. Trucking boxes of stuff across state lines to swap meets and little sci-fi cons. This has been the nature of the business for nearly four decades, and, no getting around it, it worked for a very long time, and still works today to some extent.

But the rapidly changing face of the average con-goer, the radical shift in how the internet is used by everyday buyers and casual collectors alike, and the increasing demand for the high-octane auction model in nearly every facet of the comic business has necessitated a sea change in how we view our business, and the future of the business in general. Some of this means, sadly, letting go of old ways of doing things, some of this means exciting new fields and opportunities, and all of it is thanks to the continued, seemingly unstoppable growth of this business.

Conventions: On the plus side, even more people crowded into convention halls this year than the year before, with the most notable being the upsurge at the London SuperCon (so much so, in fact, that they've expanded to a 3-day show this year – well done, guys!), and the rather startling fact that the New York ComicCon is now the biggest comic convention in the world, both in terms of attendance and floor space. We did notice a drop in floor traffic at the gold standard, the San Diego ComicCon, but that's likely to do with their adoption of the tap in tap out door policy, which put the kibosh on badge swapping and door cheats. Both Chicago cons seemed to enjoy about the same attendance, which is nothing to sniff at, as both shows do very, very well.

But – and this is a big but – once again, the actual sales on the floor were erratic, hard-fought, and sometimes flat-out dismal. Most show dealers have cheap box stock to fall back on, and many of our colleagues I spoke to admitted that most of their sales were in less expensive inventory and blow-out books. Without those books crowding the tables, I don't know how much money actually would have changed hands at these shows, and even the bigger-ticket sales from our booth and others were often pre-arranged deals, books brought by request, or pieces that were going to sell easily either at the show or after it. I really believe the days when a whale would come in and drop money on a *Batman* #1 or *Captain America Comics* #46 out of the clear blue sky are kinda done.

Another but! That doesn't mean the business is drying up at all – there are two factors at play here. One, the conventions are no longer marketed to deep-pocket buyers, hardcore collectors, or vintage enthusiasts. They're the new shopping malls, with crowds of teens and college-age kids, families out for a day of excitement, older folks reminiscing – in short, not a lot of deep pockets. These folks are delighted with a chance to meet Norman Reedus, take a selfie with the Batmobile, and meet cosplayers; in short, not exactly our clientele. The other factor at play is one that should actually make anyone in this business light up a cigar and smile: we've graduated. A couple of years ago, a *Batman* #1 was a gateway key, relatively inexpensive and easy to find. Now, it's a new grail book, out of reach of most of the folks who crawl the expo halls taking photos of guys dressed as Wolverine.

We've boldly redesigned our booth at the two big shows to reflect this, and have created a kind of museum of comics, with gleaming display cases and a wide-open exhibition-style area. This has worked wonders, generating much attention, and attracting those potential clients to our area with its professionalism, dynamic look, and open spaces. It was a gamble, but we've racked up some impressive numbers at the past few bigger shows as a result. As we're not really show dealers, and therefore don't really have the resources to prep hundreds of boxes of cheap moderns and cut-price Bronze comics, we rely on those dozen or so serious sales to get our numbers up. In addition, cons have become like PR machines for us, or trend-setters. We've actually met several clients over the past few years who came to the booth with stars in their eyes looking at the sparkly museum layout, unable to buy, but then calling us after time passed and money came in, ready to start their journey into Golden Age classics or high-grade Silver keys.

The Web and Social Media: Saying "I don't go online" in 2016 is like someone saying "I don't have a telephone" in the 1980s. The web dominates every aspect of our lives, for better or worse. The most encouraging aspect of social media and the internet in recent years has been the ability of every collector, seasoned or novice, to have the entire knowledge of the comic-collecting market and the history of the medium at their fingertips in seconds. New buyers come into this hobby armed with knowledge and confidence, which sounds intimidating for a dealer, but is a real blessing. Folks know exactly what they want, are smart and precise about their purchases, and need far less handholding and hard-sells than they used to. I am personally delighted by this, as it makes it far easier for us to know what to buy, what to market, and what our client base wants and needs, rather than guessing at trends or throwing out the same half-dozen keys and hoping they'll sell. Conversely, it's a little harder to convince collectors of the real worth of their comics. Too often, I have folks coming to our offices with stacks of mid-grade Bronze filler thinking they've struck it rich because they saw an eBay listing for a 9.8 Spider-Man key for thousands of dollars, and then assume their off-grade off-keys are worth at least half that much. It's tough talking people down from that, and we sometimes have to temper the expectations of consignors who might have outsized predictions for their comics, but the upside is that folks are doing their research and, as a result, rarer and more unusual comics that might have been neglected are now selling very well to buyers who are wisely boning up on census notes and other factoids and cannily plotting out their buying habits. There's a store that was open for decades here in NYC that had the motto "An educated consumer is our best customer", and we've been finding that to be true!

However, the scattershot approach that most social media affords, and the brutally short attention span of most people in the Twitter age, offers a challenge for our business.

We have still to work out how to reach our very specific customer base – not the folks who are already buying, but the new collectors, the next generation of vintage buyers, rather than spamming Facebook accounts with covers and trivia.

Brandon Peck, our Sales Executive, has been doing heroic work trying to navigate our social media account, which he's been updating with info on new collections and gallery openings. I don't pretend to know how this will factor in for our sales in future, as the nature of life on the web changes almost daily, but it's a very important tool and we've been wracking our brains trying to work out exactly how to make it fit with our insanely specific subset of a very specialized business. In addition, we've been hard at work for over a year on a complete and exhaustive overhaul of both our websites, and even our inventory software, to allow for greater flexibility for us and greater search options and customization for our buyers. I think if even half the blue-sky ideas we've been developing come to fruition, all our buyers and sellers will be blown away by the new sites and will be delighted by the change. I know it's been some time in coming, but it will be very much worth the wait, I can guarantee it.

Galleries: Our move to our Herald Square location has been one of the best things we've done for the business in years, allowing us double the space for our ever-growing stock and ever-expanding staff, and also allowing us to create every comic nerd's dream, a beautiful gallery dedicated solely to the comic art form. Our initial experiments with the gallery were all roaring successes, with exhibitions of work from Frank Frazetta, the Brothers Hildebrandt, the art of *Star Wars*, and others, with visits from illustrious artists and legends such as Neal Adams, Frank Miller, Mike Kaluta, Joe Giella, John Cassaday, and even R2-D2! (Seriously, we have photos, it was awesome.) We couldn't be happier with the caliber of artists we've had the honor of working with, and have been delighted to share both their work, and the permanent Metropolis art collection, with the comic collecting community as a whole. The only downside was the immense difficulty in scheduling regular shows for the gallery, as juggling artists' schedules, the availability of art, conventions, etc, made for gaps in our calendar that couldn't be helped, but were nevertheless frustrating.

Luckily, this year will see the installation of a new, permanent gallery of comic art for sale, with a standing exhibit of our top 100 or so pages and covers on display year round, open to the general public, when our special Event Exhibits are not scheduled. Having a permanent gallery available to the public should encourage repeat attendance and generate a new clientele for both comic art and vintage comics, as well as allow New Yorkers and tourists alike the chance to see classic comic art pages they may have otherwise never have been able to see in person. I, personally, am truly excited for this next step in our ongoing evolution and think it will be an enormous boon not just for us but for the industry as a whole, and I invite you all, when in NYC, to stop by the Metropolis Gallery at 36 West 37th St, 6th Floor, to experience the art of comics for yourself. The gallery is open to the public Tuesday through Friday from 10:30 AM to 5 PM, and special exhibits will be listed on the metropolisgallerynyc.com website.

This is the kind of – sorry – "outside the box" thinking that truly excites us. So much of the growth of the comic business has been as a result of these bold new ideas, that weren't even on anyone's radar as recently as 10 years ago (social media, curating con booths as museums, gallery spaces), or that were niche sectors of the market rather than driving forces (the auction model, internet sales, online price guides and research tools). It's the crazy ideas, the risky ventures, keeping an eye on tomorrow, that will propel this business further. 2016 was the strongest year we've yet had, and you'll note I haven't gone into dry recitations of sales and trivia – that's because so much of what made our year great was the people, the enthusiasm, the passion, the drive of not just our team but the collecting community as a whole. If the million-dollar comic book sales were our coming out party, this is our mature period, our chance to shine, to lead, to move forward. I foresee very big things for the vintage comic market, regardless of how well hero movies or conventions may do. All of the growth will now result from us, and our efforts, and our ability to grow our business beyond the convention halls and swap meets, and into a wider, better, stronger world. The sky is the limit, and it's my hope that our efforts will grow the market not just for us, but for all the fine folks who toil away in this demanding but rewarding business, and all the old hands and newcomers falling in love with this uniquely American art form.

Rob Reynolds - ComicConnect.com

We've never had to work this hard before. I'm not complaining. It's a sobering fact but it's also the reason why ComicConnect is so successful, Guinness World Record successful. Brokering the world's most-valuable comic books and comic book art should be hard work, and I work harder than anyone. Funny books are a very serious business, and it's a difficult chore turning over stone after stone (after stone) until you finally get the call or email you've been waiting for and your next auction is set. I've handled thousands of client phone calls, and I've sent over a million emails since the last market report was published. With four multi-million dollar auctions on the schedule every year, the hours are long and the grind is daily. I love it so damn much.

While the good old days weren't always good, you were at least able to pay thirty-five cents on the dollar on a deal and everyone walked away satisfied. Now, more than ever, convention dealers and comic shop owners alike lament that "everybody's a dealer." Comic sellers are asking retail while buyers are asking for huge discounts. Nearly every seller's phone call comes with the caveat that they want to make as much as they possibly can from the sale of their comics. The best part is, I want the same thing too, and ComicConnect was created to bring everyone together. As the Director of Consignments, I create thousands of short and long-term partnerships with clients from around the world and my only job is to sell their comic books for as much as I am able. It's a true pleasure to get to know my clients, often personally, either via convention trips or through client visits to our gallery in midtown Manhattan.

With geek chic at its peak, the ignorant comic book seller is now extinct. Folks now know what their comics are worth and they simply won't settle for less than maximum value. ComicConnect was created to help sellers achieve just that goal. It's a thrill to get the chance to add a rare or one-of-a-kind comic to an auction and watch bidders with means and determination fight it out until the hammer drops. I'm proud to represent the best comics to the best buyers in the business.

In December of 2016, ComicConnect auctioned the collection of Marc Lasry, hedge fund billionaire and co-owner of the NBA's Milwaukee Bucks. Highlights of the collection included the Larson Copy of *Batman* #1 CGC 8.0, a run of early *Action Comics*, and a near complete run of *Superboy*. The highest-graded copies of *Wonder Woman* #1 CGC 9.0 and *Wonder Woman* #2 CGC 9.4 were some of the coolest comics we've ever sold, the pair were auctioned with an extremely rare collection of original promotional documents sent with *Wonder Woman* #1 to *Harper's Magazine*, including: the cover letter to *Harper's* editorial staff signed by associate editor Alice Marble; a copy of the original press release promoting the Amazon Princess' first solo issue; a copy of Wonder Woman creator William Moulton Marston's *Women: Servants For Civilization*; and a press-ready photo of Marble perusing the first issue of *Wonder Woman*, along with a sample Business Reply Card used for readers to suggest Wonder Women of History for the title's text section.

©DC

Pre-Robin issues of **Detective Comics** (#35 shown) are the caviar books for Batman collectors

The Marc Lasry Collection reaped a number of new record sales from its 1,251 lots and was instrumental in crafting the largest auction in ComicConnect's ten-year history. Pre-Robin *Detective*s and Joker covers are the caviar books for Batman collectors, Church copy prices from all publishers remain strong, while Schomburg Hitler covers are the primary drivers of Timely sales and prices.

Top Golden Age and rarity sales this year: A coverless *Action Comics* #1 missing the first wrap sold for $37,666, *Action Comics* #7 CGC 1.8 $50,000, *All Star Comics* #8 CGC 5.5 $69,001, *Batman* #1 CGC 4.5 $129,000, two restored copies of *Batman* #1 in FN condition averaged $25,000, *Captain America Comics* #1 CBCS 9.4 R $34,000, *Detective Comics* #1 CGC 4.5 $26,000, *Detective Comics* #29 CGC 1.5 $30,029, *Detective Comics* #31 CGC 1.0 $43,505, *Human Torch* #12 CGC 8.5 $14,823, *Pep Comics* #22 CBCS 5.0 $72,000, *Spitfire Comics* #133 CGC 9.8 $15,200 (50X Guide), *Superman* #17 CGC 9.4 $50,000, and *Uncle Sam* #1 CGC 9.6 $16,977.

Top 2016 Silver, Bronze, and Modern Sales: *Amazing Fantasy* #15 CGC 6.5 $51,070, *Amazing Fantasy* #15 CGC 7.0 $65,000, *Daredevil* #1 CGC 9.4 $18,000, *Fantastic Four* #1 CGC 9.0 $132,000, *Fantastic Four* #1 CGC 8.5 $65,000, *Fantastic Four* #5 CGC 9.4 $45,000, *Incredible Hulk* #1 CGC 7.5 (Pence) $40, 157, *Journey into Mystery* #83 CGC 9.4 $210,000, *Showcase* #4 CGC 4.5 $19,500, *Tales of Suspense* #39 CGC 9.4 $95,000, *Tales to Astonish* #27 CGC 8.5 Stan Lee Signature Series $24,500, *Tales to Astonish* #35 CGC 9.2 $28,400, *Wolverine* #1 CGC 10.0 $17,644, and *X-Men* #1 CGC 8.5 $20,151.

Our original art market is thriving and some of that success is owed directly to the introduction of our Metropolis Gallery. As new art buyers get acquainted to us through our Manhattan gallery, they often translate into new bidders in our auctions and buyers in our fixed-price marketplace. ComicConnect brokered the sale of Frank Frazetta's Spiderman painting for over a quarter-million dollars. Shortly after, we sold the ultra-patriotic Fred Ray cover to *Superman* #12 for $100,000 which depicts the Man of Steel marching off to war with a pair of real-life superheroes. For zombie fans, Tony Moore's page 2 from *Walking Dead* #2 sold for $14,050. Artists interested in adding pieces to our gallery or to present an entire show simply need to contact Vincent Zurzolo at our office. You can find our ads and contact information throughout the *Price Guide*.

For the investment comic market, you need to buy as many copies of *Amazing Fantasy* #15 as you can get your hands on, and hang on to them. There's thousands of them out there and millions of buyers are clamoring for them. *Batman* #1 and *Superman* #1 have become some of the most-desirable comics on the planet as *Detective Comics* #27 and *Action Comics* #1 have come to market with increasingly less frequency, thereby driving their prices past the reach of even many of our well-heeled collectors. On that note, pick up *Amazing Spider-Man* #1 too as they are still relatively cheap and I expect the book to trend upward similarly as *Amazing Fantasy* #15s get priced up in the marketplace.

The impact of even minor comic book characters' TV and movie appearances is still dominating auction headlines in regards to the speculation market's prices. Netflix is single-handedly driving Marvel back-issue prices to record highs. On the DC side, Wonder Woman is still under-valued but that won't be the case for very long. There's still a short time left to snatch up runs of *Sensation* and *Wonder Woman* before their prices catch up with *Action* and *Detective*.

I'm here to work hard for you, and it's always my pleasure to assist buyers and sellers with some of the world's most-valuable collectibles. Please don't hesitate to find one of our ads and put us to work. We love taking on challenging projects so give us a call and find out how we can help you.

THE WAR REPORT

by Matt Ballesteros & the War Correspondents
(Andy Greenham and Mick Rabin)

This is the ninth iteration of an independently developed report on war comics by avid aficionados of the genre. Through the *Overstreet* vehicle we share (for both our own indulgence and for the enjoyment of the general collecting hobby) our thoughts and conjecture on the war comic segment. For more information on how we came to be and what methodologies we apply to our findings and conclusions, pick up any of the last eight issues of *Overstreet*.

Regrettably, this year's report will be a bit shorter than usual, as our various personal careers have delayed our forward progress in 2017 (e.g. see dreadnought.com). Nevertheless, we intend to reinforce our efforts for the 10th anniversary to make up for this truncated submission. That said, we provide here a brief assessment of the market, a short finding or two, and the Top War comic rankings for each of the main comic ages.

News from the Front

Field Report

Steady as she goes! The latter half of 2016 and first half of 2017 saw war comics holding at relatively the same forward line established in the last couple of years. Consequently, it also experienced nearly the same amount of action. High-grade war from any publisher is snapped up almost immediately, commanding gradually better and better prices. Low to mid-grade war comics (those at 4.0 or less in grade) are being purchased, but at the same modest prices set in the last three to four years. No surprise there, but worth noting. As we have suggested in the most recent reports, this is a good time to get your hands on great swaths of low-grade war, particularly if you are looking to complete collections or trying your hand at the genre as those are readily available in abundance. Low-grade or not, a cornucopia of great stories and amazing art exists within war comics published for you to enjoy, especially between 1956 and 1971. Go get 'em!

On the high-grade side, there are few sales to speak of given that most high-grade war books are tucked away in private collections and rarely see the light of day. This, coupled with the fact that very, very few high-grade war comics exist in the first instance means that rarity is a driving factor in the engagement of war comic collecting. With scant high-grade copies available, the demand is high and the acquisition is low., Attainment of said specimens is thus a true achievement in the war comic segment—garnering both praise and envy amongst the avid war collecting community. Here are some highlights of the 2016-2017 year.

Golden Age War continues to grow in popularity. Existing Fiction House collectors, the heady growth of Don Winslow interest, and collectors attempting to complete a *Wings* run are all collectively placing lesser known Golden Age titles in the spotlight. Good examples of this are *Bill Barnes*, *Boy Commandos*, *Contact Comics*, *U.S. Marines* (and so on), which all continue to sell regardless of issue number. The market price on these is rather friendly by the way, as most available are in less than a 4.0 grade. **Key sales:** *Bill Barnes* #1 CGC 7.0 (1st issue of Air Ace title) – over $550. *Contact Comics* #2 CGC 6.5 – over $450.

Don Winslow is not losing any nautical speed, as he's seeing action throughout any title that he's appearing in. For those of you who haven't read our reports in the past, Don Winslow represents what we believe is the first contiguous war comic character in the hobby (albeit classified as a war "adventure" character), his first appearance in *Popular Comics* #1 dates back, even before Superman, to 1936. **Key sales:** *Don Winslow of the Navy* #1 CGC 7.0 (1937, 1st solo book) – over $1300. *Don Winslow of the Navy* #3 (1943) in CGC 9.2 (Mile High) – over $1600.

Wings remains aloft across its entire 124 issue run. Issues in mid or low-grade are downright attainable. You may, however, have to engage in a skirmish with your Fiction House completists, so, be prepared to pay a little more for *Wings Comics* (and *Fight Comics*) that present well in lower grades. **Key sales:** *Wings* #1 CGC 7.5 – over $1350. *Wings* #3 CGC 7.0 – over $350.

EC War's singular titles *Two Fisted Tales* and *Frontline Combat* continue to command attention across the line. While EC war seems to sell in any grade, the high-grade Gaines File copies are getting the most action of course. **Key sales:** *Two-Fisted Tales* #19 CGC 9.8 (Gaines) – approx. $2400. *Two-Fisted Tales* #19 CGC 9.6 (Gaines) – $2200.

Sgt. Fury is slowly advancing again. Last year we reported a small downturn (issue #1 in particular), most likely due to abundance and some market correction. Importantly, we pointed out that given this momentary stall, it would be a good time to get yourself a copy of this coveted Marvel gem. We hope you have, as it looks like this comic and the ensuing super high-grade copies of the title are all starting to rise in value. There isn't a significant bump in worth yet, but we again recommend that this would be the time to get your hands on this newly Disney-owned IP. **Key sales:** *Sgt. Fury* #1 CGC 7.0 – $3100 to $3600. *Sgt. Fury* #5 CGC 9.8 – approx. $4800.

DC War continues to maintain its preeminent status in the Atomic and Silver Age war genre, particularly because of its "Big Five" titles (*AAMOW, GIC, OAAW, OFF* and *SSWS*). Their importance to the prosperity of the war genre over the last 50 years cannot be understated. That said, no extraordinary sales occurred in the last year, other than the expected general and gradual growth of this entire line. **Key sales:** *GIC* #87 CGC 8.0 (1st app. of Haunted Tank) – approx. $2500. *GIC* #114 CGC 9.4 (Origin Haunted Tank) – over $1300.

Our Army at War's key Sgt. Rock issues continue to garner much of the market's attention. Despite that, ***OAAW* #81**, which was once considered Sgt. Rock's 1st appearance, has softened a bit for the middle- and lower-grade specimens. An understandable market correction given #81 has been recently re-categorized as a Sgt. Rock prototype issue instead. We don't anticipate the book to fall too hard in those lower grades, and we expect market growth in grades 6.0 and above because it is still a pivotal prototype comic, very difficult to acquire, and rare in grades 7.0 and above because of its purple cover. This is the time to snap up a copy folks! We are, however, scratching our heads a bit, because of the lack of sales to report on ***Our Army at War* #82**, and because of the value fluctuations on those actual few sales these last several years. Not a completely surprising development though, as the recent reclassification of #82 (from what would have been Sgt. Rock's 2nd appearance into a prototype) has both collectors and speculators potentially puzzled. Nevertheless, this would still make *OAAW* #82 the seminal final Sgt. Rock prototype. It is the first comic that specifically refers to "a Sgt. Rock" (not "Jimmy" in *GIC* #68 or "Sgt. Rocky" in *OAAW* #81). If there is any Sgt. Rock prototype worth owning, it's this comic! The fact that the market doesn't know what to do with it is in your benefit. Snap it up now! (That is, if you can find a copy.) ***Our Army at War* #83**, of course, continues to demonstrate marked growth, showing no sign of waning. For example, #83s in a 4.0 grade seven years ago were averaging just under $400, now each command nearly $3000 apiece. We see no slowing on this title in any grade, and with approximately less than 150 "known" copies currently (in all grades combined), you're going to have to fight to get a copy of what is considered the *Action* #1 and/or *Detective* #27 of war comics. **Key sales:** *OAAW* #81 CGC 7.0 (key Sgt. Rock prototype) – over $2000. *OAAW* #82 CGC 7.0 (last Sgt. Rock prototype) – over $850. *OAAW* #83 CGC 4.0 (1st true Sgt. Rock) – over $2500.

Intel From the War Correspondents
Dispatch From the Trenches (By Andy Greenham)

As a buyer and seller of books, I set up and sell at about eight shows a year, and I have found that there seems to be a fair amount of continued interest in war books. The most common request that I've had is for *OAAW* #83 (Sgt. Rock), then *GIC* #87 (Haunted Tank), then *SSWS* #84 (Mlle. Marie). After that, it's *SSWS* #151 for people searching out the Unknown Soldier. Interestingly, there seems to be a bit of a pullback in interest for the Sgt. Rock prototype books, even though they're extremely important in the lineage of DC War comics. This past year, I sold two copies of *GIC* #87, one copy of *SSWS* #84, and one copy of *SSWS* #151. If I had any *OAAW* #83s, I could have easily sold them, even at aggressive prices. Folks are just trying to get their copies whenever they pop up. A decent number of customers who are filling in their runs, are just looking for any lower-grade copy.

On a side note, I wanted to touch on going to comic conventions. I can't recommend it enough. Not only is it potentially good for the comic book dealer by getting your business, it's good for yourself by being able to add to your collection. Let's not stop there. At a show, you have the chance to meet many different artists and writers. These are the folks behind bringing us these books (and characters) that we love so much! Life is short, people. We won't be around forever, and neither will these creators. Let's do our best to meet our heroes while we still can. I think back to whom I've met in person before, people involved with the DC war books, and the list is sadly very short. I am fortunate enough to say that I've met the wonderful and extremely talented Neal Adams, the amazing in so many ways, Russ Heath, and the ultimate legend, Joe Kubert. RIP, Joe.

I encourage you to pick your faves and do your best to meet them. Talk to them, ask them to sign some books or maybe even draw something for you. Let's continue to show our support and admiration for these truly wonderful people that have brought us so much joy.

Many thanks to all the *Overstreet* readers. Without you guys, there would be no point to any of this. Andy Greenham, over and out.

War on an Open Field (By Mick Rabin)

A few *OPG*s ago, I wrote an article about the interior stories of DC war comics moving from an eight-page story format to a twelve-page format thus laying the groundwork for the classic character-driven material (i.e. Sgt. Rock) that Kanigher and company are legendary for. I could never quite put my finger on why those issues immediately preceding Rock were better than the earlier stuff, but it was right in front of me the entire time. Apparently, those 4 extra pages to "spread their wings" and take some poetic and artistic license made all the difference.

For this installment, I have a new epiphany that might be a bit less concrete, but bear with me. The focus of comics collecting has—for better or worse—shifted further away from interior stories and more towards covers in the past decade or so. It probably has a lot to do with widespread use of slabs and chat forums where collectors discuss their acquisitions and the thing getting displayed most often is the cover itself.

I picture myself as a bit of an old-school collector in that the interiors are every bit as compelling—if not more so—as the covers themselves. Nonetheless, you'd be hard-pressed to find a DC war comics collector without a "Top-10 Covers" list. I have multiple Top-10 covers lists (favorite Grandenetti covers, favorite wash-tone covers, favorite frogman covers, favorite talking helmet covers; it never ends). Washtone covers, especially the "Perty Thirty" (*GIC* #75 through #104), seem to receive quite a bit of love from seasoned and newbie collectors alike. But there's something else compelling that I recognized about those Perty Thirty that wasn't apparent before. It's not so much about what IS on the covers as what is NOT on the covers.

One of the things that truly screamed out to me when I saw *GI Combat* #75 for the first time on the back wall of a local store was that it was just so diametrically opposed in style and format to any DC books that I was already familiar with. I truly love the Superman titles where Lois, Luthor, and Superman are talking and thinking on the cover. There's a beautiful charm about those books that is uniquely their own. But the time that it takes to process what they're saying is at least as long as it takes to read those thought and word balloons—which for an adult—is a couple seconds, but for a kid, could be considerably more.

GIC #75 is a whole different beast. It's not just the tour-de-force Grandenetti washtone with the greys, blacks, and blues. It's that there ARE NO WORDS ON THE COVER AT ALL (except for that singularly cool *G.I. Combat* title logo). Count Basie would have been proud. The high impact of art, music, and literature is often-times a product of the dynamics between what is rendered, played, and written and what is not. The economy of words, the rests between the notes, the depiction of empty space on a canvas. The masters of each form understand how much is too much and when to hold off.

At some point, Kanigher, Jack Adler, and the war comics crew began piloting the idea of "word-economy." At first, DC war covers started out with chapter titles and wordy descriptions of some of those chapters, but along the way, they began to experiment with fewer words. An early example is *SSWS* #39 from November 1955. It has ZERO captions, chapter titles, or word balloons. Slightly later, *AAMOW* #35 (July '56), the second wash-tone war cover, has NO text box, but just two words in the lower right—"Battle Call." That's it. Short and sweet!

There are other later standouts like *AAMOW* #62 (Oct. '58) with two words—"No Cover" (again NOT contained in a text box). It's definitely one of the best Big-5 covers ever. *SSWS* #74 (Oct. '58) has ZERO text and the silence of the cover poetically parallels the terror and urgency of the frogmen's silent underwater struggle. Feb. 1959 has the next wordless cover with *GIC* #69—the "one-off" before the deluge of the Perty Thirty starting with *GIC* #75. Even I was a bit dumbfounded by the revelation that all but two of the Perty Thirty were wordless (later ones had "Featuring the Haunted Tank" in a thin banner ABOVE the *GI Combat* title logo, but the art below the title remained uncluttered by pointless captions).

The upshot of this is that the Big-5 creators clearly knew what they were doing—go for MAXIMUM IMPACT. Case in point – *OFF* #71. Get the attention of the casual browsing customer. Don't make 'em think for too long. Economize the words, and let the art speak for itself. And did it ever! Chalk it up to another factor that makes DC war books so truly staggering!

GAINING RANK

Nearly a decade ago my colleagues and I embarked on a long-term mission to assemble the most complete list and ranking system for all comic books with a war theme. Each comic book's position in the ranking was based on criteria such as who was on the creative team, key storylines, art, first appearances, popularity, market value, scarcity, etc. From this we developed what we believe is a fairly accurate representation of the top war comics of the genre.

TOP 50 ATOM / SILVER / BRONZE AGE WAR COMICS OF 2017

ISSUE	2017 RANK	2016 RANK	MERIT
Our Army at War #83	1	1	1st true app. of Sgt. Rock (Kanigher/Kubert Master Sgt.)
Sgt. Fury #1	2	2	1st app. of Sgt. Fury
G.I. Combat #87	3	3	1st app. of Haunted Tank
Our Army at War #81	4	4	Sgt. Rock prototype (Non Kanigher/Kubert "Sgt. Rocky")
Our Army at War #82	4-t	5	Sgt. Rock prototype (Non Kanigher/Kubert 4th grade rate Sgt.)
G.I. Combat #68	6	6	Sgt. Rock prototype (Kanigher/Kubert "The Rock" story
Our Army at War #1	7	7	1st issue of Big Five war title
Two-Fisted Tales #18	7-t	8	1st issue to start EC War run
Frontline Combat #1	9	9	1st issue of EC all war title
Our Army at War #90	10	10	How Sgt. Rock got his stripes
Star Spangled War Stories #84	11	12-t	1st app. of Mademoiselle Marie
G.I. Combat #44	12	11	1st DC issue of Big Five war Title, early washtone
Our Fighting Forces #1	13	12-t	1st issue of Big Five war title
Our Army at War #88	14	14	1st Sgt. Rock cover (Kubert)
Our Army at War #84	15	15	2nd app. of Sgt Rock
Our Army at War #85	16	16-t	1st app. of Ice Cream Soldier and 2nd Kubert Sgt. Rock
Star Spangled War Stories #131	17	16-t	1st issue of Big Five war title
Star Spangled War Stories #90	18	19	1st Dinosaur "War That Time Forgot" ish
All American Men of War #127	19	18	1st issue of Big Five war title
Our Fighting Forces #45	20	20	Gunner & Sarge run begins (Kanigher/Grandenetti, predates OAAW #83)
Our Army at War #112	21	22	Classic roster ("Brady Bunch") cover
Our Army at War #91	22	21	1st all Sgt. Rock issue
Our Army at War #151	23	23	1st app. of Enemy Ace
G.I. Combat #1	24	24	1st issue of Quality Comics title
All American Men of War #67	24-t	25	1st app. of Gunner & Sarge (predates OAAW #83, not Grandenetti)
G.I. Combat #91	26	26-t	1st Haunted Tank Cover (washtone)
Battle #1	27	26-t	1st issue of Atlas war title
G.I. Combat #75	28	28	1st in "Perty Thirty" washtone run
Combat #1	29	30-t	1st issue of Atlas War title (black cover)
Blazing Combat #1	30	30-t	1st issue of Warren war Magazine
All American Men of War #28	31	29	1st Sgt. Rock prototype (Kubert art)
Our Army at War #100	32	30-t	Scarce Kubert (black cover)
Star Spangled War Stories #151	33	34-t	1st solo app of Unknown Soldier
Two-Fisted Tales Annual #1	34	34-t	Early 132 pg EC war annual
Our Army at War #86	35	33	Early Sgt. Rock
Foxhole #1	36	37	1st ish Mainline title (classic Kirby cover)
Fightin' Marines 15 (#1)	37	36	1st issue of St. John war Title (Baker art)
G.I. Combat #80	38	38-t	Classic washtone cover

Interesting Facts

OAAW #81's stall and #82's illuminations have these two seminal prototypes tied for the very first time in the nine years of our rankings.

Two-Fisted Tales #18 continues to ascend and is now tied for 7th.

Sgt. Fury #13 (2nd solo Cap) and *GI Combat* #114 (origin Haunted Tank) both make our top 50 for the 1st time!

G.I. Combat #69	39	38-t	1st in Grandenetti washtone trifecta (GIC #83 and OFF #71 are the others)
Our Army at War #168	40	43-t	1st app. of the Unknown Soldier (2nd of Grandenetti washtone trifecta covers)
Our Army at War #128	41	40	Training & origin of Sgt. Rock
All American Men of War #82	42-t	41	1st app. of Johnny Cloud
Our Fighting Forces #49	42-t	42	1st app. of Pooch
Our Army at War #196	44	46	Key transitional comic (classic Kubert cover)
Our Army at War #95	45	43-t	1st app. of Bulldozer
G.I. Combat #83	46	43-t	1st Big Al, Little Al & Charlie
All American Men of War #89	47	47	Historic issue influenced Lichtenstein pop art paintings
Sgt. Fury #13	48	-	2nd Silver Age solo app. of Captain America
Sgt Rock #302	49	50	1st issue of seminal Bronze Age war title
Weird War Tales #1	50-t	48	1st issue in DC War & Fantasy title
G.I. Combat #114	50-t	-	Origin of Haunted Tank

TOP 15 GOLDEN AGE WAR COMICS OF 2017

ISSUE	2017 RANK	2016 RANK	MERIT
Wings #1	1	1	1st issue in long running air war title
War Comics #1	2	2	1st comic completely devoted to war
Don Winslow #1 (1937)	3	4	Very early war adventure title
Real Life #3	4	3	Hitler Cover (early 1942 WWII)
Contact Comics #1	5	5	1st issue of air battles title
Don Winslow #1 (1939)	6	7	Rare Four Color issue (#2)
Real Life Comics #1	7	6	1st issue of adventure title
Rangers Comics #8	8	8	US Rangers begin
Wings Comics #2	9	9	2nd issue of key air war title
US Marines #2	10	10	Classic Cover (Bailey art)
Bill Barnes Comics #1	11	11	1st issue of Air Ace title
Don Winslow of the Navy #1 ('43)	12	12-t	1st comic of 73 issue series (Captain Marvel on cover)
Remember Pearl Harbor (nn)	13	12-t	1942 illustrated story of the battle
Rangers Comics #26	14	14	Classic cover
American Library nn (#1)	15	15	"Thirty Seconds Over Tokyo" (movie)

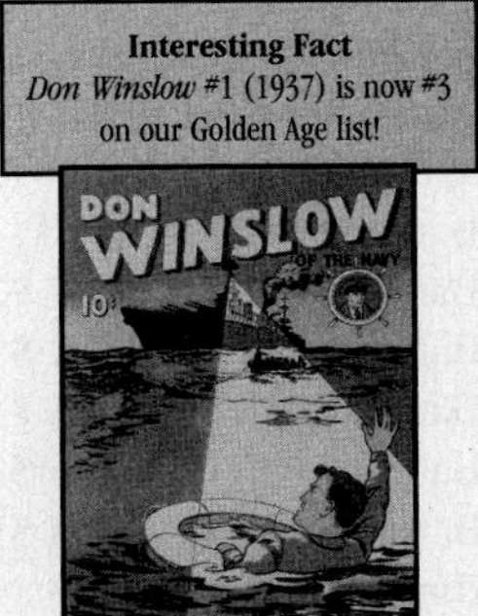

Interesting Fact
Don Winslow #1 (1937) is now #3 on our Golden Age list!

TOP 5 ATLAS WAR COMICS OF 2017

ISSUE	2017 RANK	2016 RANK	MERIT
Battle #1	1	1	1st issue of Atlas war title
Combat #1	2	2	1st issue of Atlas War title (black cover)
War Comics #1	3	3	1st issue of Atlas War title
War Action #1	4	4	1st issue of Atlas War title
War Comics #11	5	5	Classic flamethrower cover

Attack #54

TOP 5 CHARLTON WAR COMICS OF 2017

ISSUE	2017 RANK	2016 RANK	MERIT
Fightin' Marines 15 (#1)	1	1	1st issue in St. John war title (Baker art)
Attack #54	2	2	1st issue in short war title (100 pgs)
Soldier & Marine #11	3	3	1st ish in short war title (Bob Powell art)
US Air Force #1	4	4	1st issue of Charlton war title
Fightin' Navy #74	5	5	1st issue of Charlton war title (formerly Don Winslow)

We hope you enjoyed this year's War Report, albeit in its short form. As always, we truly appreciate the support and encouragement we get from each of you in the hobby and look forward to connecting with you at comic cons, on the threads, or elsewhere. Also, a big thanks to the fine staff at Overstreet. We salute you once again Bob Overstreet, J.C. Vaughn, and Mark Huesman.

This field report would be utterly wanting, were it not for the selfless contributions from my colleagues, friends and contributors Mick Rabin and Andy Greenham. They bring an expertise straight from the field that is nearly unmatched in the genre. You can get more of their know-how on the CGC Boards where they are practically on sentry in the Silver Age War Comic thread.

KEY SALES FROM 2016-2017

The following lists of sales were reported to Gemstone during the year and represent only a small portion of the total amount of important books that have sold. For other sales information, please see the Overstreet Market Report starting on page 89.

GOLDEN AGE - SALES OF CERTIFIED COMICS

Action Comics #1 CGC 5.5 $956,000
Action Comics #36 CGC 8.0 $2200
Action Comics #51 CGC 8.0 $5,497
Action Comics #96 CGC 7.5 $343
Action Comics #151 CGC 7.0 $555
Action Comics #153 CGC 4.5 $187
Action Comics #162 CGC 5.0 $195
Action Comics #173 CGC 4.0 $101
Action Comics #180 CGC 4.5 $175
All Winners Comics #19 CGC 7.0 $5000
Archie Comics #50 CGC 9.0 $12,000
Archie's Pals n Gals #1 CGC 5.0 $196
Batman #1 CGC 3.5 $143,400
Batman #1 CBCS 2.5 $71,700
Batman #11 CGC 7.0 $9,261.25
Batman #11 CGC 5.5 $4,500
Batman #37 CGC 6.5 $1,200
Batman #37 CGC 8.5 $3,500
Batman #55 CGC 4.0 $525
Batman #59 CGC 5.0 $801
Batman #66 CGC 7.0 $858
Blue Ribbon Comics #1 CGC 9.6 $13,145 (Mile High)
Blue Ribbon Comics #9 CGC 9.4 $16,730 (Mile High)
Captain Aero Comics #3 CGC 9.4 $4,000 (Mile High)
Captain America Comics #1 CGC 6.0 $32,000 (restored)
Captain America Comics #2 CGC 7.5 $14,000
Captain America Comics #3 CGC 3.0 $11,995
Captain America Comics #6 CGC 8.5 $15,500
Captain America Comics #7 CGC 8.0 $7,000
Captain America Comics #42 CGC 4.0 $625
Captain America Comics #45 CGC 4.5 $760
Captain America Comics #58 CGC 7.0 $900
Captain America Comics #67 CGC 6.0 $777
Crypt of Terror #17 CGC 7.5 $2,300
Daredevil Comics #1 CGC 8.5 $8,950
Daring Mystery Comics #1 CGC 1.0 $1,200
Detective Comics #8 CGC 2.5 $4,000
Detective Comics #29 CGC 1.8 $20,315
Detective Comics #32 CGC 9.6 $71,700
Detective Comics #33 CGC 1.8 $25,095
Detective Comics #35 CGC 7.5 $119,500
Detective Comics #102 CGC 6.0 $800
Detective Comics #109 CGC 8.0 $1,501
Detective Comics #114 CGC 4.5 $545
Detective Comics #124 CGC 4.0 $385
Detective Comics #124 CGC 8.0 $1,400
Detective Comics #137 CGC 3.5 $550
Detective Comics #140 CGC 4.5 $5,975
Fighting Yank #2 CGC 9.4 $4,780 (Pennsylvania)
Flash Comics #49 CGC 9.0 $902
Flash Comics #51 CGC 9.4 $1,809
Flash Comics #55 CGC 9.2 $1,608
Flash Comics #71 CGC 9.4 $3,101
Flash Comics #79 CGC 9.4 $2,600
Flash Comics #86 CGC 1.5 $1,600
Four Color #108 CGC 9.2 $5,497
Hit Comics #1 CGC 9.0 $19,120 (Mile High)
Hit Comics #5 CGC 9.6 $59,750 (Mile High)
Hit Comics #11 CGC 9.6 $20,315 (Mile High)
Hit Comics #17 CGC 9.4 $21,510 (Mile High)
Human Torch #2 CGC 4.0 $1,637
Human Torch #12 CGC 6.5 $5,000
Marvel Family #1 CGC 4.0 $2,629
Marvel Mystery Comics #15 CGC 5.5 $1,489
Marvel Mystery Comics #20 CGC 9.2 $19,120 (Chicago)
Marvel Mystery Comics #64 CGC 8.5 $2,544
Marvel Mystery Comics #74 CGC 7.0 $661
More Fun Comics #46 CGC 5.5 $550
Mystic #8 CGC 8.5 $10,000
National Comics #6 CGC 9.4 $5,975 (Mile High)
New Comics #9 CGC 3.0 $425
Pep Comics #23 CGC 2.0 $3,585
Phantom Lady #17 CGC 7.5 $12,000
Phantom Lady #23 CGC 6.5 $4,500
Reform School Girl nn CGC 8.0 $16,730

Seven Seas Comics #4 CGC 8.5 $14,340
Shock SuspenStories #8 CGC 9.8 $8,962.50 (Gaines File)
Startling Comics #49 CGC 6.0 $5,258
Superman #1 CGC 4.5 $36,000 (restored)
Superman #1 CGC 1.5 $38,000 (restored)
Superman #3 CGC 8.0 $11,352.50
Superman #17 CGC 9.0 $31,070
Superman #17 CGC 8.5 $17,925
Superman #23 CGC 5.0 $725
Superman #76 CGC 4.0 $875
Superman #76 CGC 5.0 $1,125
Superman #78 CGC 4.5 $122
Suspense Comics #3 CBCS 0.5 $5,520.90
USA Comics #9 CGC 6.5 $6,572.50
USA Comics #11 CGC 8.0 $8,365
Weird Fantasy #13 (#1) CGC 9.4 $4,302
Wonder Woman #6 CGC 8.5 $10,000
World's Finest Comics #71 CGC 3.5 $1,350
World's Finest Comics #71 CGC 4.0 $438

SILVER AGE - SALES OF CERTIFIED COMICS

Action Comics #242 CGC 2.0 $561
Action Comics #242 CGC 6.5 $7,500
Action Comics #252 CGC 6.0 $3,107
Action Comics #252 CGC 6.5 $4,780
Action Comics #252 CGC 7.5 $8,000
Adventure Comics #210 CGC 3.5 $1,550
Adventure Comics #247 CGC 2.0 $875
Amazing Fantasy #15 CGC 8.5 $155,350
Amazing Fantasy #15 CGC 5.5 $25,000
Amazing Fantasy #15 CGC 4.0 $14,000
Amazing Fantasy #15 CGC 3.5 $12,547.50
Amazing Spider-Man #1 CGC 9.0 $62,000
Amazing Spider-Man #1 CGC 9.0 $45,000
Amazing Spider-Man #1 CGC 5.5 $10,755
Amazing Spider-Man #1 CGC 4.0 $4,750
Amazing Spider-Man #5 CGC 8.5 $2,390
Amazing Spider-Man #14 CGC 9.6 $15,535
Amazing Spider-Man #15 CGC 8.5 $3,300
Amazing Spider-Man #27 CGC 9.4 $1,883
Aquaman #35 CGC 4.0 $270
Aquaman #40 CGC 9.8 $657.25
Archie Giant Series Mag. #3 CGC 7.5 $525.80
Avengers #4 CGC 8.0 $3,000
Avengers #6 CGC 9.4 $1,374.25
Avengers #57 CGC 9.6 $3,346
Brave and the Bold #28 CGC 5.5 $7,000
Brave and the Bold #54 CGC 9.2 $1,750
Bullwinkle nn CGC 9.6 $836
Captain America #100 CGC 9.8 $4,302
Daredevil #1 CGC 9.0 $8,066.25
Daredevil #2 CGC 6.0 $250
Doctor Strange #169 CGC 9.8 $8,365
Fantastic Four #1 CGC 7.0 $15,535
Fantastic Four #1 CGC 6.5 $15,500
Fantastic Four #1 CGC 4.0 $5,377.50
Fantastic Four #3 CGC 6.0 $773
Fantastic Four #4 CGC 7.0 $2,270.50
Fantastic Four #5 CGC 7.0 $4,302
Fantastic Four #48 CGC 9.8 $15,535
Fantastic Four #48 CGC 9.0 $1,430
Fantastic Four #52 CGC 9.8 $65,725
Fantastic Four #52 CGC 4.0 $500
Flash #123 CGC 9.2 $12,000
Green Lantern #71 CGC 9.8 $573.60
House of Mystery #174 CGC 9.4 $776.75
House of Secrets #1 CGC 8.5 $4,063
Incredible Hulk #1 CGC 5.0 $13,145
Journey into Mystery #83 CGC 6.5 $8,900
Journey into Mystery #83 CGC 4.5 $4,050
Journey Into Mystery #86 CGC 9.2 $3,107
Justice League of America #1 CGC 1.8 $685
Our Army at War #112 CGC 7.5 $454.10
Showcase #4 CGC 8.0 $84,000
Showcase #13 CGC 4.5 $726
Showcase #14 CGC 4.5 $626
Showcase #17 CGC 7.0 $3,585
Showcase #30 CGC 8.0 $2,300
Silver Surfer #1 CGC 7.5 $605
Silver Surfer #4 CGC 8.0 $530
Strange Tales #89 CGC 2.0 $465
Strange Tales #110 CGC 9.0 $15,535
Strange Tales #111 CGC 9.8 $20,315
Strange Tales #128 CGC 9.0 $200
Superboy #68 CGC 8.5 $6,000
Tales of Suspense #59 CGC 9.4 $1,314.50
Tales to Astonish #35 CGC 6.0 $1,000
Tales to Astonish #37 CGC 6.5 $175
Tales To Astonish #44 CGC 9.6 $26,290
Thor #165 CGC 9.4 $1,792.50
World's Finest Comics #173 CGC 9.8 $627.38
X-Men #1 CGC 7.5 $10,157.50
X-Men #1 CGC 4.0 $2,520
X-Men #1 CGC 3.5 $2,210
X-Men #89 CGC 9.8 $510

BRONZE AGE - SALES OF CERTIFIED COMICS

Action Comics #399 CGC 9.8 $478
All-Star Comics #58 CGC 9.2 $260
Amazing Spider-Man #121 CGC 9.6 $1,580
Amazing Spider-Man #121 CGC 9.4 $1,250
Amazing Spider-Man #122 CGC 9.6 $896.25
Amazing Spider-Man #122 CGC 9.4 $800
Amazing Spider-Man #129 CGC 9.4 $2,151
Archie's Pals n' Gals #23 CGC 3.5 $580 (35¢ price var.)
Avengers #92 CGC 9.8 $1,852.25
Batman #251 CGC 9.0 $665
Brave and the Bold #191 CGC 9.8 $130
Captain America #275 CGC 9.8 $275 (Canadian Var)
Daredevil #102 CGC 9.8 $765
Daredevil #158 CBCS 9.8 $501.90
Daredevil #181 CGC 9.8 $200
Eternals #1 CGC 9.8 $300
Fantastic Four #211 CGC 9.8 $260
Giant-Size Defenders #3 CGC 9.2 $230
Giant-Size X-Men #1 CGC 9.8 $5,497
Giant-Size X-Men #1 CGC 9.4 $2000
Green Lantern #82 CBCS 9.8 $928.52
Hero for Hire #1 CGC 8.0 $615
House of Secrets #92 CGC 9.0 $2,031.50
Howard the Duck #1 CGC 9.6 $190
Incredible Hulk #181 CGC 9.6 $7,300
Incredible Hulk #181 CGC 9.6 $7,170
Incredible Hulk #250 CGC 9.8 $195
Machine Man #19 CGC 9.8 $165
Marvel Premiere #24 CGC 9.8 $230
Marvel Premiere #57 CGC 9.2 $105
Marvel Spotlight #32 CGC 9.4 $150
Marvel Tales #98 CGC 9.6 $160
Marvel Tales #99 CGC 9.8 $180
Marvel Tales #106 CGC 9.8 $170
Marvel Team-Up #3 CGC 9.6 $230
Micronauts #1 CGC 9.8 $170
Ms. Marvel #20 CGC 9.8 $280
New Teen Titans #2 CGC 9.8 $650
New Teen Titans #2 CGC 9.8 $478
Nova #1 CGC 9.0 $100
Power Man #24 CGC 9.6 $330
Shazam! #28 CGC 9.2 $327
Special Marvel Edition #15 CGC 9.6 $430
Spectacular Spider-Man #64 CGC 9.6 $259
Star Wars #1 CBCS 9.8 $956
Star Wars (35¢-) #1 CGC 7.5 $5,019
Star Wars (35¢-c) #2 CGC 7.5 $1,015.75
Strange Tales #169 CGC 9.6 $980
Superman's Pal Jimmy Olsen #135 CGC 9.4 $350
Tomb of Dracula #10 CGC 9.4 $750
Werewolf by Night #15 CGC 9.8 $680
Werewolf by Night #33 CGC 9.6 $830

COPPER - MODERN AGE - SALES OF CERTIFIED COMICS

Batman #635 CGC 9.6 $189
Batman Adventures #12 CGC 9.8 $1,970
Batman Adventures #12 CGC 9.6 $795
Batman Adventures #12 CGC 9.0 $355
Birds of Prey #8 CGC 9.4 $120
Captain Marvel (2012 Series) #17 CGC 9.8 $670 (2nd Print)
DC Comics Presents #41 CGC 9.6 $80
Detective Comics #523 CGC 9.8 $300
Edge of Spider-Verse #2 CGC 9.8 $430 (Land Variant)
Ghost in the Shell #1 CGC 9.8 $355
Harbinger #1 CGC 9.8 $630
Harley Quinn (2011) #1 Hughes var. CGC 9.8 $749.99
Legion of Super-Heroes #298 CGC 9.8 $212
Marvel Comics Super Special #40 CGC 9.8 $305
New Mutants #87 CGC 9.8 $515
New Mutants #98 CGC 9.8 $650
New Mutants #98 CGC 8.5 $270
NYX #3 CGC 9.2 $365
Preacher #1 CGC 9.6 $405
Preacher #13 CGC 9.6 $145
Preacher Preview nn CGC 9.8 $507.88
Revival #1 CGC 9.8 $50
Runaways #1 CGC 9.8 $380
Simpsons #1 CGC 9.8 $90
Sons Of Anarchy #1 CGC 9.8 $40
Teenage Mutant Ninja Turtles #1 CGC 7.0 $2,868
Walking Dead #17 CGC 9.8 $200
Walking Dead #19 CGC 9.8 $597.50
Walking Dead #19 CGC 9.0 $200
Walking Dead #100 CGC 9.8 $225 (2nd Print)
What If Venom/Deadpool #1 CGC 9.8 $315
X-Force #2 CGC 9.8 $115
X-Men #221 CGC 9.6 $455 (So Much Fun var.)

GOLDEN AGE - ATOM AGE SALES

America's Best Comics #9 VG $210
Archie's Rival Reggie #1 FN+ $350
Batman #24 FN- $500
Big Shot Comics #25 FN+ $195
Captain Marvel Adventures #33 FN $155
Daring Mystery Comics #4 FR/GD $495
Detective Comics #59 VG $500
House Of Mystery #1 FR $100
Headline Comics #8 GD $2,000
Junior Comics #15 FN+ $4,000
Marvel Mystery Comics #4 GD $2,130
More Fun Comics #14 FN $5,000
More Fun Comics #32 FR $250
Mystic Comics #5 FAIR (missing page) $300
NY World's Fair 1939 VG+ $4,000
Red Raven Comics #1 App GD+ (missing BC) $1,100
Sunny #11 VG $1,000
Superman #23 GD $325
Tales From the Crypt #23 FN $457
Tarzan #1 FN $350
True Crime #3 VG $300
Venus #2 GD $220
Vic Torry and His Flying Saucer #1 $100
Whiz Comics #18 VG+ $500
World's Finest Comics #71 PR/FR $202

SILVER AGE SALES

Action Comics #242 VG/FN $1,900
Adventure Comics #210 FR $340
Amazing Spider-Man #5 GD- $200
Amazing Spider-Man #13 VG+ $300
Amazing Spider-Man #50 NM- $2,450
Captain America #100 FN- $200
Captain America #117 VF $225
Daredevil #1 GD/VG $750
Detective Comics #226 GD/VG $250
Fantastic Four #1 VG- $3,800
Fantastic Four #4 GD $400
Fantastic Four #5 VG $1,000
Fantastic Four #49 VG+ $160
Green Lantern #8 FN/VF $175
Iron Man #1 FN- $350
Iron Man #1 VG $200
Journey Into Mystery #86 VG $200
Marvel Super-Heroes #12 VG $100
Sgt. Fury #1 VF/NM $9,000
Sgt. Fury #1 GD+ $600
Silver Surfer #1 VG $109
Strange Tales #110 FN+ $3,300
Strange Tales #115 GD $35
Strange Tales #135 VF- $135

BRONZE AGE TO MODERN AGE SALES

Action Comics #362 FN/VF $14
Amazing Spider-Man #129, VF $700.00
Amazing Spider-Man #654 VF/NM $220
Annihilation Conquest #6 NM+ $50
Batman (New 52) #1 NM $100
Batman Adventures #12 VG $60
Batman: Mad Love #1 NM $70
Black Lightning #1 NM $120
DC Limited Collector's Ed. C-36 NM/MT $150
Detective Comics #411 FN+ $170
Detective Comics #411 VF/NM $430
Evil Ernie #1 VF/NM $85
Giant-Size X-Men #1 FN/VF $530
Harbinger #1 NM $150
Hero for Hire #1 VF- $305
House of Secrets #92 VG $180
Incredible Hulk #271 VG $20
Iron Man #55 FN+ $400
Justice League of America #179 GD+ $120 (Whitman Variant)
Marvel Premiere #15 VF+ $325
Marvel Super Hero Secret Wars #8 NM $65
Marvel Treasury Edition #12 NM/MT $175
New Mutants #98 FN/VF $133
New Teen Titans #1 VF/NM $25
New Teen Titans #2 NM $245
Suicide Squad (1987) #1 VF+ $30
The Tick #1 NM $220
Uncanny X-Men #510 NM+ $269
Walking Dead #1 NM $1,500
Walking Dead #19 NM $280
Werewolf By Night #32 FN $462
Werewolf by Night #32 GD/VG $185
X-Men #94 FN/VF $300

TOP COMICS

The following tables denote the rate of appreciation of the top Golden Age, Platinum Age, Silver Age and Bronze Age comics, as well as selected genres over the past year. The retail value for a Near Mint- copy of each comic (or VF where a Near Mint- copy is not known to exist) in 2017 is compared to its Near Mint- value in 2016. The rate of return for 2017 over 2016 is given. The place in rank is given for each comic by year, with its corresponding value in highest known grade. These tables can be very useful in forecasting trends in the market place. For instance, the investor might want to know which book is yielding the best dividend from one year to the next, or one might just be interested in seeing how the popularity of books changes from year to year. For instance, *All Star Comics* #8 was in 15th place in 2016 and has increased to 12th place in 2017. Premium books are also included in these tables and are denoted with an asterisk(*).

The following tables are meant as a guide to the investor. However, it should be pointed out that trends may change at anytime and that some books can meet market resistance with a slowdown in price increases, while others can develop into real comers from a presently dormant state. In the long run, if the investor sticks to the books that are appreciating steadily each year, he shouldn't go very far wrong.

TOP 100 GOLDEN AGE COMICS

TITLE/ISSUE#	2017 RANK	2017 NM- PRICE	2016 RANK	2016 NM- PRICE	$ INCR.	% INCR.
Action Comics #1	1	$3,200,000	1	$2,800,000	$400,000	14%
Detective Comics #27	2	$2,200,000	2	$2,000,000	$200,000	10%
Superman #1	3	$1,200,000	3	$1,100,000	$100,000	9%
All-American Comics #16	4	$750,000	4	$700,000	$50,000	7%
Batman #1	5	$650,000	6	$550,000	$100,000	18%
Marvel Comics #1	6	$625,000	5	$575,000	$50,000	9%
Action Comics #7	7	$420,000	8	$340,000	$80,000	24%
Captain America Comics #1	8	$400,000	7	$365,000	$35,000	10%
Pep Comics #22	9	$320,000	9	$280,000	$40,000	14%
Action Comics #10	10	$280,000	11	$225,000	$55,000	24%
Detective Comics #31	11	$270,000	10	$240,000	$30,000	13%
All Star Comics #8	12	$260,000	15	$175,000	$85,000	49%
Whiz Comics #2 (#1)	13	$240,000	12	$210,000	$30,000	14%
Detective Comics #29	14	$220,000	14	$185,000	$35,000	19%
Flash Comics #1	15	$210,000	13	$195,000	$15,000	8%
Action Comics #2	16	$190,000	15	$175,000	$15,000	9%
Detective Comics #33	16	$190,000	19	$165,000	$25,000	15%
Archie Comics #1	18	$185,000	15	$175,000	$10,000	6%
More Fun Comics #52	19	$180,000	18	$170,000	$10,000	6%
Detective Comics #35	20	$170,000	21	$130,000	$40,000	31%
Action Comics #13	21	$160,000	22	$125,000	$35,000	28%
Adventure Comics #40	21	$160,000	20	$145,000	$15,000	10%
Action Comics #3	23	$135,000	23	$120,000	$15,000	13%
All Star Comics #3	23	$135,000	25	$115,000	$20,000	17%
Detective Comics #38	23	$135,000	23	$120,000	$15,000	13%
Wonder Woman #1	26	$125,000	32	$85,000	$40,000	47%
More Fun Comics #73	27	$115,000	26	$100,000	$15,000	15%
Suspense Comics #3	28	$110,000	26	$100,000	$10,000	10%
Marvel Mystery Comics #9	29	$105,000	26	$100,000	$5,000	5%
Detective Comics #1	30	VF $100,000	29	VF $98,000	$2,000	2%
Detective Comics #28	30	$100,000	30	$90,000	$10,000	11%
Sensation Comics #1	30	$100,000	34	$80,000	$20,000	25%
Marvel Mystery Comics #2	33	$95,000	30	$90,000	$5,000	6%
More Fun Comics #53	34	$84,000	33	$84,000	$0	0%
Captain Marvel Adventures #1	35	$80,000	38	$68,000	$12,000	18%
Detective Comics #36	35	$80,000	46	$55,000	$25,000	45%
Marvel Mystery Comics #5	35	$80,000	36	$75,000	$5,000	7%
Sub-Mariner Comics #1	35	$80,000	35	$77,000	$3,000	4%
Green Lantern #1	39	$72,000	37	$70,000	$2,000	3%
Human Torch #2 (#1)	40	$70,000	38	$68,000	$2,000	3%

TITLE/ISSUE#	2017 RANK	2017 NM- PRICE	2016 RANK	2016 NM- PRICE	$ INCR.	% INCR.
Superman #2	41	$67,000	40	$62,000	$5,000	8%
Detective Comics #37	42	$65,000	55	$45,000	$20,000	44%
Action Comics #4	43	$62,000	42	$58,000	$4,000	7%
Action Comics #5	43	$62,000	42	$58,000	$4,000	7%
Action Comics #6	43	$62,000	42	$58,000	$4,000	7%
Adventure Comics #48	43	$62,000	41	$59,000	$3,000	5%
Marvel Mystery Comics #4	47	$60,000	48	$50,000	$10,000	20%
Captain America Comics #2	48	$58,000	47	$54,000	$4,000	7%
New Fun Comics #1	48	VF $58,000	45	VF $57,000	$1,000	2%
Action Comics #23	50	$56,000	59	$42,000	$14,000	33%
All-American Comics #19	50	$56,000	50	$48,000	$8,000	17%
Marvel Mystery Comics #3	52	$55,000	48	$50,000	$5,000	10%
Captain America Comics #3	53	$52,000	53	$46,000	$6,000	13%
Batman #2	54	$50,000	53	$46,000	$4,000	9%
Daring Mystery Comics #1	54	$50,000	52	$47,000	$3,000	6%
Walt Disney's Comics & Stories #1	54	$50,000	50	$48,000	$2,000	4%
Action Comics #8	57	$47,000	57	$43,000	$4,000	9%
Action Comics #9	57	$47,000	57	$43,000	$4,000	9%
Action Comics #15	59	$45,000	61	$40,000	$5,000	13%
Action Comics #12	60	$44,000	66	$36,000	$8,000	22%
Marvel Mystery Comics 132 pg.	61	VF $43,500	56	VF $43,500	$0	0%
Famous Funnies-Series 1	62	VF $43,000	59	VF $42,000	$1,000	2%
Wonder Comics #1	63	$42,000	61	$40,000	$2,000	5%
Amazing Man Comics #5	64	$40,000	64	$38,000	$2,000	5%
Four Color Series 1 (Donald Duck) #4	64	$40,000	66	$36,000	$4,000	11%
More Fun Comics #54	64	$40,000	63	$39,000	$1,000	3%
Detective Comics #2	67	VF $39,000	71	VF $35,000	$4,000	11%
All-Select Comics #1	68	$38,000	71	$35,000	$3,000	9%
More Fun Comics #55	68	$38,000	66	$36,000	$2,000	6%
Motion Picture Funnies Wkly #1	68	$38,000	71	$35,000	$3,000	9%
Mystic Comics #1	68	$38,000	66	$36,000	$2,000	6%
Red Raven Comics #1	68	$38,000	66	$36,000	$2,000	6%
Captain America Comics 132 pg.	73	VF $37,000	65	VF $37,000	$0	0%
All Winners Comics #1	74	$36,000	71	$35,000	$1,000	3%
Silver Streak Comics #6	74	$36,000	75	$33,000	$3,000	9%
Superman #3	74	$36,000	75	$33,000	$3,000	9%
Fantastic Comics #3	74	$36,000	82	$28,000	$8,000	29%
Marvel Mystery Comics #8	78	$35,000	75	$33,000	$2,000	6%
Captain America Comics #74	79	$33,000	82	$28,000	$5,000	18%
Terrific Comics #5	79	$33,000	78	$30,000	$3,000	10%
Detective Comics #30	81	$32,000	82	$28,000	$4,000	14%
Double Action Comics #2	81	$32,000	82	$28,000	$4,000	14%
Jackpot Comics #4	81	$32,000	82	$28,000	$4,000	14%
Action Comics #17	84	$30,000	82	$28,000	$2,000	7%
All-American Comics #17	84	$30,000	80	$29,000	$1,000	3%
Detective Comics #40	84	$30,000	120	$21,000	$9,000	43%
Jumbo Comics #1	84	VF $30,000	82	VF $28,000	$2,000	7%
Marvel Mystery Comics #10	84	$30,000	82	$28,000	$2,000	7%
New Book of Comics #1	84	VF $30,000	78	VF $30,000	$0	0%
New York World's Fair 1939	84	VFNM $30,000	80	VFNM $29,000	$1,000	3%
Action Comics #19	91	$29,000	93	$27,000	$2,000	7%
All-American Comics #18	91	$29,000	82	$28,000	$1,000	4%
Archie Comics #2	91	$29,000	82	$28,000	$1,000	4%
Green Giant Comics #1	91	$29,000	82	$28,000	$1,000	4%
New Fun Comics #6	91	VF $29,000	82	VF $28,000	$1,000	4%
Action Comics #20	96	$28,000	97	$26,000	$2,000	8%
All-American Comics #25	96	$28,000	93	$27,000	$1,000	4%
Detective Comics #32	96	$28,000	97	$26,000	$2,000	8%
Exciting Comics #9	96	$28,000	97	$26,000	$2,000	8%
Punch Comics #12	96	$28,000	-	$22,000	$6,000	27%

TOP 50 SILVER AGE COMICS

TITLE/ISSUE#	2017 RANK	2017 NM- PRICE	2016 RANK	2016 NM- PRICE	$ INCR.	% INCR.
Amazing Fantasy #15	1	$350,000	1	$260,000	$90,000	35%
Incredible Hulk #1	2	$240,000	2	$180,000	$60,000	33%
Fantastic Four #1	3	$140,000	3	$135,000	$5,000	4%
Showcase #4 (The Flash)	4	$130,000	4	$100,000	$30,000	30%
Brave and the Bold #28 (Justice League)	5	$80,000	5	$72,000	$8,000	11%
Journey Into Mystery #83 (Thor)	6	$75,000	6	$66,000	$9,000	14%
Amazing Spider-Man #1	7	$68,000	7	$62,000	$6,000	10%
Tales of Suspense #39 (Iron Man)	8	$48,000	9	$45,000	$3,000	7%
X-Men #1	8	$48,000	8	$46,000	$2,000	4%
Tales to Astonish #27 (Ant-Man)	10	$45,000	10	$42,000	$3,000	7%
Avengers #1	11	$40,000	11	$36,000	$4,000	11%
Showcase #22 (Green Lantern)	12	$38,000	11	$36,000	$2,000	6%
Flash #105	13	$26,000	13	$24,000	$2,000	8%
Justice League of America #1	13	$26,000	13	$24,000	$2,000	8%
Adventure Comics #247 (Legion)	15	$24,000	16	$20,000	$4,000	20%
Our Army at War #83 (Sgt. Rock)	15	$24,000	15	$22,000	$2,000	9%
Action Comics #252	17	$22,000	19	$17,000	$5,000	29%
Showcase #8	18	$21,000	16	$20,000	$1,000	5%
Action Comics #242	19	$20,000	22	$14,000	$6,000	43%
Fantastic Four #5	19	$20,000	18	$19,000	$1,000	5%
Strange Tales #110 (Dr. Strange)	21	$18,000	19	$17,000	$1,000	6%
Green Lantern #1	22	$17,000	21	$16,500	$500	3%
Fantastic Four #2	23	$14,000	24	$13,500	$500	4%
Fantastic Four #4	23	$14,000	24	$13,500	$500	4%
Showcase #9	23	$14,000	22	$14,000	$0	0%
Amazing Spider-Man #2	26	$13,000	28	$12,400	$600	5%
Fantastic Four #3	26	$13,000	26	$12,500	$500	4%
Fantastic Four #12	26	$13,000	26	$12,500	$500	4%
Sgt. Fury #1	29	$12,500	29	$12,000	$500	4%
Superman's Girlfriend Lois Lane #1	29	$12,500	29	$12,000	$500	4%
Incredible Hulk #2	31	$11,500	31	$10,500	$1,000	10%
Showcase #14	32	$10,800	31	$10,500	$300	3%
Amazing Spider-Man #3	33	$10,500	35	$9,800	$700	7%
Daredevil #1	33	$10,500	33	$10,000	$500	5%
Showcase #13	35	$10,300	33	$10,000	$300	3%
Our Army at War #81	36	$10,000	36	$9,500	$500	5%
Showcase #6	36	$10,000	36	$9,500	$500	5%
Tales to Astonish #35	36	$10,000	38	$9,000	$1,000	11%
Showcase #17	39	$9,500	41	$8,000	$1,500	19%
Richie Rich #1	40	$9,000	39	$8,500	$500	6%
Amazing Spider-Man #4	41	$8,200	40	$8,100	$100	1%
Brave and the Bold #25	42	$8,000	42	$7,000	$1,000	14%
Tales to Astonish #13	42	$8,000	53	$5,600	$2,400	43%
Avengers #4	44	$7,500	44	$6,800	$300	5%
Journey Into Mystery #84	44	$7,500	42	$7,000	$500	7%
Journey Into Mystery #85	46	$7,300	47	$6,500	$800	12%
Flash #106	47	$7,000	47	$6,500	$500	8%
Incredible Hulk #3	47	$7,000	45	$6,700	$300	4%
Brave and the Bold #29	49	$6,800	46	$6,600	$200	3%
Fantastic Four #6	49	$6,800	47	$6,500	$300	5%

TOP 10 BRONZE AGE COMICS

TITLE/ISSUE#	2017 RANK	2017 NM- PRICE	2016 RANK	2016 NM- PRICE	$ INCR.	% INCR.
Star Wars #1 (35¢ price variant)	1	$10,000	1	$7,500	$2,500	33%
Iron Fist #14 (35¢ price variant)	2	$4,000	2	$3,500	$500	14%
Incredible Hulk #181	3	$3,500	3	$3,000	$500	17%
Cerebus #1	4	$2,800	5	$2,600	$200	8%
Green Lantern #76	5	$2,700	4	$2,700	$0	0%
House of Secrets #92	6	$1,800	6	$1,500	$300	20%
Giant-Size X-Men #1	7	$1,600	6	$1,500	$100	7%
Uncle Scrooge #179 (Whitman)	7	$1,600	6	$1,500	$100	7%
Amazing Spider-Man #129	9	$1,500	11	$1,200	$300	25%
Star Wars #2-4 (35¢ price variants)	9	$1,500	13	$1,000	$50	50%

TOP 10 COPPER AGE COMICS

TITLE/ISSUE#	2017 RANK	2017 NM- PRICE	2016 RANK	2016 NM- PRICE	$ INCR.	% INCR.
Gobbledygook #1	1	$6,000	1	$6,000	$0	0%
Teenage Mutant Ninja Turtles #1	2	$4,500	2	$4,000	$500	13%
Gobbledygook #2	3	$2,300	3	$2,300	$0	0%
Miracleman #1 Gold Edition	4	$1,500	4	$1,500	$0	0%
Albedo #2	5	$1,400	5	$1,000	$400	40%
Miracleman #1 Blue Edition	6	$850	6	$850	$0	0%
Vampirella #113	7	$550	7	$550	$0	0%
Spider-Man #1 (2nd pr. w/Gold UPC)	8	$210	8	$200	$10	5%
Grendel #1	9	$190	9	$190	$0	0%
Primer #2	9	$190	10	$170	$20	12%

TOP 10 PLATINUM AGE COMICS

TITLE/ISSUE#	2017 RANK	2017 PRICE	2016 RANK	2016 PRICE	$ INCR.	% INCR.
Yellow Kid in McFadden Flats	1	FN $14,500	1	FN $14,500	$0	0%
Mickey Mouse Book (2nd printing)-variant	2	FN $8,000	2	FN $8,000	$0	0%
Little Sammy Sneeze	3	FN $7,000	3	FN $7,000	$0	0%
Little Nemo 1906	4	FN $5,500	4	FN $5,500	$0	0%
Mickey Mouse Book (1st printing)	5	VF $5,300	5	VF $5,300	$0	0%
Little Nemo 1909	6	FN $4,000	6	FN $4,000	$0	0%
Pore Li'l Mose	6	FN $4,000	6	FN $4,000	$0	0%
Yellow Kid #1	8	FN $3,800	8	FN $3,800	$0	0%
Buster Brown and His Resolutions 1903	9	FN $3,400	9	FN $3,400	$0	0%
Happy Hooligan Book 1	10	VF $3,300	10	VF $3,300	$0	0%
Mickey Mouse Book (2nd printing)	10	VF $3,300	10	VF $3,300	$0	0%

TOP 10 CRIME COMICS

TITLE/ISSUE#	2017 RANK	2017 NM- PRICE	2016 RANK	2016 NM- PRICE	$ INCR.	% INCR.
Crime Does Not Pay #22	1	$12,000	1	$11,500	$500	4%
Crime Does Not Pay #24	2	$11,500	2	$10,500	$1,000	10%
Crime Does Not Pay #23	3	$5,500	3	$5,200	$300	6%
True Crime Comics #2	4	$3,600	4	$3,500	$100	3%
Crime Does Not Pay #33	5	$3,200	5	$2,800	$400	14%
True Crime Comics #3	6	$2,500	6	$2,400	$100	4%
The Killers #1	7	$2,300	7	$2,300	$0	0%
Crimes By Women #1	8	$2,000	8	$2,000	$0	0%
The Killers #2	9	$1,900	9	$1,900	$0	0%
Crime Does Not Pay, Best of ('44)	10	$1,750	10	$1,725	$25	1%

TOP 10 HORROR COMICS

TITLE/ISSUE#	2017 RANK	2017 NM- PRICE	2016 RANK	2016 NM- PRICE	$ INCR.	% INCR.
Journey into Mystery #1	1	$14,000	1	$11,000	$3,000	27%
Eerie #1	1	$12,000	1	$11,000	$1,000	9%
Strange Tales #1	4	$11,000	4	$9,500	$1,500	16%
Tales to Astonish #1	6	$11,000	6	$8,500	$2,500	29%
Tales of Terror Annual #1	3	VF $10,400	3	VF $9,600	$800	8%
Vault of Horror #12	4	$10,000	4	$9,500	$500	5%
Crypt of Terror #17	7	$6,000	7	$5,700	$300	5%
Haunt of Fear #15	8	$5,600	8	$5,500	$100	2%
Crime Patrol #15	9	$4,800	9	$4,700	$100	2%
House of Mystery #1	10	$4,400	10	$4,300	$100	2%

TOP 10 ROMANCE COMICS

TITLE/ISSUE#	2017 RANK	2017 NM- PRICE	2016 RANK	2016 NM- PRICE	$ INCR.	% INCR.
Giant Comics Edition #12	1	$12,000	1	$9,000	$3,000	33%
Daring Love #1	2	$4,000	3	$3,000	$1,000	33%
Negro Romance #1	3	$3,400	2	$3,200	$200	6%
Intimate Confessions #1	4	$3,000	6	$2,500	$500	20%
Giant Comics Edition #15	5	$2,800	7	$2,400	$400	17%
Negro Romance #2	5	$2,800	4	$2,600	$200	8%
Negro Romance #3	5	$2,800	4	$2,600	$200	8%
Giant Comics Edition #9	8	$2,500	8	$2,100	$400	19%
Forbidden Love #1	9	$1,900	9	$1,800	$100	6%
Modern Love #1	10	$1,600	10	$1,550	$50	3%

TOP 10 SCI-FI COMICS

TITLE/ISSUE#	2017 RANK	2017 NM- PRICE	2016 RANK	2016 NM- PRICE	$ INCR.	% INCR.
Showcase #17 (Adam Strange)	1	$9,500	1	$8,000	$1,500	19%
Mystery In Space #1	2	$7,200	2	$7,000	$200	3%
Strange Adventures #1	3	$5,200	3	$5,000	$200	4%
Journey Into Unknown Worlds #36	4	$4,800	4	$4,800	$0	0%
Showcase #15 (Space Ranger)	4	$4,800	5	$4,700	$100	2%
Weird Science-Fantasy Annual 1952	6	$4,700	6	$4,600	$100	2%
Mystery in Space #53	7	$4,500	7	$4,500	$0	0%
Weird Fantasy #13 (#1)	8	$4,000	8	$3,900	$100	3%
Weird Science #12 (#1)	8	$4,000	8	$3,900	$100	3%
Fawcett Movie #15 (Man From Planet X)	10	$3,800	10	$3,800	$0	0%

TOP 10 WESTERN COMICS

TITLE/ISSUE#	2017 RANK	2017 NM- PRICE	2016 RANK	2016 NM- PRICE	$ INCR.	% INCR.
Gene Autry Comics #1	1	$7,500	1	$7,500	$0	0%
*Lone Ranger Ice Cream 1939 2nd	2	VF $4,500	2	VF $4,500	$0	0%
Hopalong Cassidy #1	2	$4,500	2	$4,500	$0	0%
Roy Rogers Four Color #38	4	$4,400	4	$4,400	$0	0%
John Wayne Adventure Comics #1	5	$3,900	5	$3,800	$100	3%
*Lone Ranger Ice Cream 1939	6	VF $3,800	5	VF $3,800	$0	0%
Red Ryder Comics #1	6	$3,800	5	$3,800	$0	0%
Western Picture Stories #1	8	$3,700	8	$3,600	$100	3%
*Tom Mix Ralston #1	9	$3,600	8	$3,600	$0	0%
*Red Ryder Victory Patrol '42	10	$1,300	10	$1,400	-$100	-7%

GRADING DEFINITIONS

When grading a comic book, common sense must be employed. The overall eye appeal and beauty of the comic book must be taken into account along with its technical flaws to arrive at the appropriate grade.

10.0 GEM MINT (GM): This is an exceptional example of a given book - the best ever seen. The slightest bindery defects and/or printing flaws may be seen only upon very close inspection. The overall look is "as if it has never been handled or released for purchase." Only the slightest bindery or printing defects are allowed, and these would be imperceptible on first viewing. No bindery tears. Cover is flat with no surface wear. Inks are bright with high reflectivity. Well centered and firmly secured to interior pages. Corners are cut square and sharp. No creases. No dates or stamped markings allowed. No soiling, staining or other discoloration. Spine is tight and flat. No spine roll or split allowed. Staples must be original, centered and clean with no rust. No staple tears or stress lines. Paper is white, supple and fresh. No hint of acidity in the odor of the newsprint. No interior autographs or owner signatures. Centerfold is firmly secure. No interior tears.

9.9 MINT (MT): Near perfect in every way. Only subtle bindery or printing defects are allowed. No bindery tears. Cover is flat with no surface wear. Inks are bright with high reflectivity. Generally well centered and firmly secured to interior pages. Corners are cut square and sharp. No creases. Small, inconspicuous, lightly penciled, stamped or inked arrival dates are acceptable as long as they are in an unobtrusive location. No soiling, staining or other discoloration. Spine is tight and flat. No spine roll or split allowed. Staples must be original, generally centered and clean with no rust. No staple tears or stress lines. Paper is white, supple and fresh. No hint of acidity in the odor of the newsprint. Centerfold is firmly secure. No interior tears.

9.8 NEAR MINT/MINT (NM/MT): Nearly perfect in every way with only minor imperfections that keep it from the next higher grade. Only subtle bindery or printing defects are allowed. No bindery tears. Cover is flat with no surface wear. Inks are bright with high reflectivity. Generally well centered and firmly secured to interior pages. Corners are cut square and sharp. No creases. Small, inconspicuous, lightly penciled, stamped or inked arrival dates are acceptable as long as they are in an unobtrusive location. No soiling, staining or other discoloration. Spine is tight and flat. No spine roll or split allowed. Staples must be original, generally centered and clean with no rust. No staple tears or stress lines. Paper is off-white to white, supple and fresh. No hint of acidity in the odor of the newsprint. Centerfold is firmly secure. Only the slightest interior tears are allowed.

9.6 NEAR MINT+ (NM+): Nearly perfect with a minor additional virtue or virtues that raise it from Near Mint. The overall look is "as if it was just purchased and read once or twice." Only subtle bindery or printing defects are allowed. No bindery tears are allowed, although on Golden Age books bindery tears of up to 1/8" have been noted. Cover is flat with no surface wear. Inks are bright with high reflectivity. Well centered and firmly secured to interior pages. One corner may be almost imperceptibly blunted, but still almost sharp and cut square. Almost imperceptible indentations are permissible, but no creases, bends, or color break. Small, inconspicuous, lightly penciled, stamped or inked arrival dates are acceptable as long as they are in an unobtrusive location. No soiling, staining or other discoloration. Spine is tight and flat. No spine roll or split allowed. Staples must be original, generally centered, with only the slightest discoloration. No staple tears, stress lines, or rust migration. Paper is off-white, supple and fresh. No hint of acidity in the odor of the newsprint. Centerfold is firmly secure. Only the slightest interior tears are allowed.

9.4 NEAR MINT (NM): Nearly perfect with only minor imperfections that keep it from the next higher grade. Minor feathering that does not distract from the overall beauty of an otherwise higher grade copy is acceptable for this grade. The overall look is "as if it was just purchased and read once or twice." Subtle bindery defects are allowed. Bindery tears must be less than 1/16" on Silver Age and later books, although on Golden Age books bindery tears of up to 1/4" have been noted. Cover is flat with no surface wear. Inks are bright with high reflectivity. Generally well centered and secured to interior pages. Corners are cut square and sharp with ever-so-slight blunting permitted. A 1/16" bend is permitted with no color break. No creases. Small, inconspicuous, lightly penciled, stamped or inked arrival dates are acceptable as long as they are in an unobtrusive location. No soiling, staining or other discoloration apart from slight foxing. Spine is tight and flat. No spine roll or split allowed. Staples are generally centered; may have slight discoloration. No staple tears are allowed; almost no stress lines. No rust migration. In rare cases, a comic was not stapled at the bindery and therefore has a missing staple; this is not considered a defect. Any staple can be replaced on books up to Fine, but only vintage staples can be used on books from Very Fine to Near Mint. Mint books must have original staples. Paper is cream to off-white, supple and fresh. No hint of acidity in the odor of the newsprint. Centerfold is secure. Slight interior tears are allowed.

9.2 NEAR MINT– (NM–): Nearly perfect with only a minor additional defect or defects that keep it from Near Mint. A limited number of minor bindery defects are allowed. A light, barely noticeable water stain or minor foxing that does not distract from the beauty of the book is acceptable for this grade. Cover is flat with no surface wear. Inks are bright with only the slightest dimming of reflectivity. Generally well centered and secured to interior pages. Corners are cut square and sharp with ever-so-slight blunting permitted. A 1/16"-1/8" bend is permitted with no color break. No creases. Small, inconspicuous, lightly penciled, stamped or inked arrival dates are acceptable as long as they are in an unobtrusive location. No soiling, staining or other discoloration apart from slight foxing. Spine is tight and flat. No spine roll or split allowed. Staples may show some discoloration. No staple tears are allowed; almost no stress lines. No rust migration. In rare cases, a comic was not stapled at the bindery and therefore has a missing staple; this is not considered a defect. Any staple can be replaced on books up to Fine, but only vintage staples can be used on books from Very Fine to Near Mint. Mint books must have original staples. Paper is cream to off-white, supple and fresh. No hint of acidity in the odor of the newsprint. Centerfold is secure. Slight interior tears are allowed.

9.0 VERY FINE/NEAR MINT (VF/NM): Nearly perfect with outstanding eye appeal. A limited number of bindery defects are allowed. Almost flat cover with almost imperceptible wear. Inks are bright with slightly diminished reflectivity. An 1/8" bend is allowed if color is not broken. Corners are cut square and sharp with ever-so-slight blunting permitted but no creases. Several lightly penciled, stamped or inked arrival dates are acceptable. No obvious soiling, staining or other discoloration, except for very minor foxing. Spine is tight and flat. No spine roll or split allowed. Staples may show some discoloration. Only the slightest staple tears are allowed. A very minor accumulation of stress lines may be present if they are nearly imperceptible. No rust migration. In rare cases, a comic was not stapled at the bindery and therefore has a missing staple; this is not considered a defect. Any staple can be replaced on books up to Fine, but only vintage staples can be used on books from Very Fine to Near Mint. Mint books must have original staples. Paper is cream to off-white and supple. No hint of acidity in the odor of the newsprint. Centerfold is secure. Very minor interior tears may be present.

8.5 VERY FINE+ (VF+): Fits the criteria for Very Fine but with an additional virtue or small accumulation of virtues that improves the book's appearance by a perceptible amount.

8.0 VERY FINE (VF): An excellent copy with outstanding eye appeal. Sharp, bright and clean with supple pages. A comic book in this grade has the appearance of having been carefully handled. A limited accumulation of minor bindery defects is allowed. Cover is relatively flat with minimal surface wear beginning to show, possibly including some minute wear at corners. Inks are generally bright with moderate to high reflectivity. A 1/4" crease is acceptable if color is not broken. Stamped or inked arrival dates may be present. No obvious soiling, staining or other discoloration, except for minor foxing. Spine is almost flat with no roll. Possible minor color break allowed. Staples may show some discoloration. Very slight staple tears and a few almost very minor to minor stress lines may be present. No rust migration. In rare cases, a comic was not stapled at the bindery and therefore has a missing staple; this is not considered a defect. Any staple can be replaced on books up to Fine, but only vintage staples can be used on books from Very Fine to Near Mint. Mint books must have original staples. Paper is tan to cream and supple. No hint of acidity in the odor of the newsprint. Centerfold is mostly secure. Minor interior tears at the margin may be present.

7.5 VERY FINE– (VF–): Fits the criteria for Very Fine but with an additional defect or small accumulation of defects that detracts from the book's appearance by a perceptible amount.

7.0 FINE/VERY FINE (FN/VF): An above-average copy that shows minor wear but is still relatively flat and clean with outstanding eye appeal. A small accumulation of minor bindery defects is allowed. Minor cover wear beginning to show with interior yellowing or tanning allowed, possibly including minor creases. Corners may be blunted or abraded. Inks are generally bright with a moderate reduction in reflectivity. Stamped or inked arrival dates may be present. No obvious soiling, staining or other discoloration, except for minor foxing. The slightest spine roll may be present, as well as a possible moderate color break. Staples may show some discoloration. Slight staple tears and a slight accumulation of light stress lines may be present. Slight rust migration. In rare cases, a comic was not stapled at the bindery and therefore has a missing staple; this is not considered a defect. Any staple can be replaced on books up to Fine, but only vintage staples can be used on books from Very Fine to Near Mint. Mint books must have original staples. Paper is tan to cream, but not brown. No hint of acidity in the odor of the newsprint. Centerfold is mostly secure. Minor interior tears at the margin may be present.

6.5 FINE+ (FN+): Fits the criteria for Fine but with an additional virtue or small accumulation of virtues that improves the book's appearance by a perceptible amount.

6.0 FINE (FN): An above-average copy that shows minor wear but is still relatively flat and clean with no significant creasing or other serious defects. Eye appeal is somewhat reduced because of slight surface wear and the accumulation of small defects, especially on the spine and edges. A FINE condition comic book appears to have been read a few times and has been handled with moderate care. Some accumulation of minor bindery defects is allowed. Minor cover wear apparent, with minor to moderate creases. Inks show a major reduction in reflectivity. Blunted or abraded corners are more common, as is minor staining, soiling, discoloration, and/or foxing. Stamped or inked arrival dates may be present. A minor spine roll is allowed. There can also be a 1/4" spine split or severe color break. Staples show minor discoloration. Minor staple tears and an accumulation of stress lines may be present, as well as minor rust migration. In rare cases, a comic was not stapled at the bindery and therefore has a missing staple; this is not considered a defect. Any staple can be replaced on books up to Fine, but only vintage staples can be used on books from Very Fine to Near Mint. Mint books must have original staples. Paper is brown to tan and fairly supple with no signs of brittleness. No hint of acidity in the odor of the newsprint. Minor interior tears at the margin may be present. Centerfold may be loose but not detached.

5.5 FINE– (FN–): Fits the criteria for Fine but with an additional defect or small accumulation of defects that detracts from the book's appearance by a perceptible amount.

5.0 VERY GOOD/FINE (VG/FN): An above-average but well-used comic book. A comic in this grade shows some moderate wear; eye appeal is somewhat reduced because of the accumulation of defects. Still a desirable copy that has been handled with some care. An accumulation of bindery defects is allowed. Minor to moderate cover wear apparent, with minor to moderate creases and/or dimples. Inks have major to extreme reduction in reflectivity. Blunted or abraded corners are increasingly common, as is minor to moderate staining, discoloration, and/or foxing. Stamped or inked arrival dates may be present. A minor to moderate spine roll is allowed. A spine split of up to 1/2" may be present. Staples show minor discoloration. A slight accumulation of minor staple tears and an accumulation of minor stress lines may also be present, as well as minor rust migration. In rare cases, a comic was not stapled at the bindery and therefore has a missing staple; this is not considered a defect. Any staple can be replaced on books up to Fine, but only vintage staples can be used on books from Very Fine to Near Mint. Mint books must have original staples. Paper is brown to tan with no signs of brittleness. May have the faintest trace of an acidic odor. Centerfold may be loose but not detached. Minor tears may also be present.

4.5 VERY GOOD+ (VG+): Fits the criteria for Very Good but with an additional virtue or small accumulation of virtues that improves the book's appearance by a perceptible amount.

4.0 VERY GOOD (VG): The average used comic book. A comic in this grade shows some significant moderate wear, but still has not accumulated enough total defects to reduce eye appeal to the point that it is not a desirable copy. Cover shows moderate to significant wear, and may be loose but not completely detached. Moderate to extreme reduction in reflectivity. Can have an accumulation of creases or dimples. Corners may be blunted or abraded. Store stamps, name stamps, arrival dates, initials, etc. have no effect on this grade. Some discoloration, fading, foxing, and even minor soiling is allowed. As much as a 1/4" triangle can be missing out of the corner or edge; a missing 1/8" square is also acceptable. Only minor unobtrusive tape and other amateur repair allowed on otherwise high grade copies. Moderate spine roll may be present and/or a 1" spine split. Staples discolored. Minor to moderate staple tears and stress lines may be present, as well as some rust migration. Paper is brown but not brittle. A minor acidic odor can be detectable. Minor to moderate tears may be present. Centerfold may be loose or detached at one staple.

3.5 VERY GOOD– (VG–): Fits the criteria for Very Good but with an additional defect or small accumulation of defects that detracts from the book's appearance by a perceptible amount.

3.0 GOOD/VERY GOOD (GD/VG): A used comic book showing some substantial wear. Cover shows significant wear, and may be loose or even detached at one staple. Cover reflectivity is very low. Can have a book-length crease and/or dimples. Corners may be blunted or even rounded. Discoloration, fading, foxing, and even minor to moderate soiling is allowed. A triangle from 1/4" to 1/2" can be missing out of the corner or edge; a missing 1/8" to 1/4" square is also acceptable. Tape and other amateur repair may be present. Moderate spine roll likely. May have a spine split of anywhere from 1" to 1-1/2". Staples may be rusted or replaced. Minor to moderate staple tears and moderate stress lines may be present, as well as some rust migration. Paper is brown but not brittle. Centerfold may be loose or detached at one staple. Minor to moderate interior tears may be present.

2.5 GOOD+ (GD+): Fits the criteria for Good but with an additional virtue or small accumulation of virtues that improves the book's appearance by a perceptible amount.

2.0 GOOD (GD): Shows substantial wear; often considered a "reading copy." Cover shows significant wear and may even be detached. Cover reflectivity is low and in some cases completely absent. Book-length creases and dimples may be present. Rounded corners are more common. Moderate soiling, staining, discoloration and foxing may be present. The largest piece allowed missing from the front or back cover is usually a 1/2" triangle or a 1/4" square, although some Silver Age books such as 1960s Marvels have had the price corner box clipped from the top left front cover and may be considered Good if they would otherwise have graded higher. Tape and other forms of amateur repair are common in Silver Age and older books. Spine roll is likely. May have up to a 2" spine split. Staples may be degraded, replaced or missing. Moderate staple tears and stress lines may be present, as well as rust migration. Paper is brown but not brittle. Centerfold may be loose or detached. Moderate interior tears may be present.

1.8 GOOD– (GD–): Fits the criteria for Good but with an additional defect or small accumulation of defects that detracts from the book's appearance by a perceptible amount.

1.5 FAIR/GOOD (FR/GD): A comic showing substantial to heavy wear. A copy in this grade still has all pages and covers, although there may be pieces missing up to and including missing coupons and/or Marvel Value Stamps that do not impact the story. Books in this grade are commonly creased, scuffed, abraded, soiled, and possibly unattractive, but still generally readable. Cover shows considerable wear and may be detached. Nearly no reflectivity to no reflectivity remaining. Store stamp, name stamp, arrival date and initials are permitted. Book-length creases, tears and folds may be present. Rounded corners are increasingly common. Soiling, staining, discoloration and foxing is generally present. Up to 1/10 of the back cover may be missing. Tape and other forms of amateur repair are increasingly common in Silver Age and older books. Spine roll is common. May have a spine split between 2" and 2/3 the length of the book. Staples may be degraded, replaced or missing. Staple tears and stress lines are common, as well as rust migration. Paper is brown and may show brittleness around the edges. Acidic odor may be present. Centerfold may be loose or detached. Interior tears are common.

1.0 FAIR (FR): A copy in this grade shows heavy wear. Some collectors consider this the lowest collectible grade because comic books in lesser condition are usually incomplete and/or brittle. Comics in this grade are usually soiled, faded, ragged and possibly unattractive. This is the last grade in which a comic remains generally readable. Cover may be detached, and inks have lost all reflectivity. Creases, tears and/or folds are prevalent. Corners are commonly rounded or absent. Soiling and staining is present. Books in this condition generally have all pages and most of the covers, although there may be up to 1/4 of the front cover missing or no back cover, but not both. Tape and other forms of amateur repair are more common. Spine roll is more common; spine split can extend up to 2/3 the length of the book. Staples may be missing or show rust and discoloration. An accumulation of staple tears and stress lines may be present, as well as rust migration. Paper is brown and may show brittleness around the edges but not in the central portion of the pages. Acidic odor may be present. Accumulation of interior tears. Chunks may be missing. The centerfold may be missing if readability is generally preserved (although there may be difficulty). Coupons may be cut.

0.5 POOR (PR): Most comic books in this grade have been sufficiently degraded to the point where there is little or no collector value; they are easily identified by a complete absence of eye appeal. Comics in this grade are brittle almost to the point of turning to dust with a touch, and are usually incomplete. Extreme cover fading may render the cover almost indiscernible. May have extremely severe stains, mildew or heavy cover abrasion to the point that some cover inks are indistinct/absent. Covers may be detached with large chunks missing. Can have extremely ragged edges and extensive creasing. Corners are rounded or virtually absent. Covers may have been defaced with paints, varnishes, glues, oil, indelible markers or dyes, and may have suffered heavy water damage. Can also have extensive amateur repairs such as laminated covers. Extreme spine roll present; can have extremely ragged spines or a complete, book-length split. Staples can be missing or show extreme rust and discoloration. Extensive staple tears and stress lines may be present, as well as extreme rust migration. Paper exhibits moderate to severe brittleness (where the comic book literally falls apart when examined). Extreme acidic odor may be present. Extensive interior tears. Multiple pages, including the centerfold, may be missing that affect readability. Coupons may be cut.

0.3 INCOMPLETE (INC): Books that are coverless, but are otherwise complete, or covers missing their interiors.

0.1 INCOMPLETE (INC): Coverless copies that have incomplete interiors, wraps or single pages will receive a grade of .1 as will just front covers or just back covers.

PUBLISHERS' CODES

The following abbreviations are used with cover reproductions throughout the book for copyright purposes:

ABC-America's Best Comics
AC-AC Comics
ACE-Ace Periodicals
ACG-American Comics Group
AJAX-Ajax-Farrell
ACP-Archie Comic Publications
BP-Better Publications
C & L-Cupples & Leon
CC-Charlton Comics
CEN-Centaur Publications
CCG-Columbia Comics Group
CG-Catechetical Guild
CHES-Harry 'A' Chesler
CM-Comics Magazine
CN-Cartoon Network
CPI-Conan Properties Inc.
DC-DC Comics, Inc.
DELL-Dell Publishing Co.
DH-Dark Horse
DIS-Disney Enterprises, Inc.
DMP-David McKay Publishing
DYN-Dynamite Entertainment
DS-D. S. Publishing Co.
EAS-Eastern Color Printing Co.
EC-E. C. Comics
ECL-Eclipse Comics
ENWIL-Enwil Associates
EP-Elliott Publications
ERB-Edgar Rice Burroughs
FAW-Fawcett Publications
FC-First Comics
FF-Famous Funnies
FH-Fiction House Magazines
FOX-Fox Features Syndicate
GIL-Gilberton
GK-Gold Key
GP-Great Publications
HARV-Harvey Publications
H-B-Hanna-Barbera
HILL-Hillman Periodicals
HOKE-Holyoke Publishing Co.
IM-Image Comics
KING-King Features Syndicate
LEV-Lev Gleason Publications
MAL-Malibu Comics
MAR-Marvel Characters, Inc.
ME-Magazine Enterprises
MLJ-MLJ Magazines
MS-Mirage Studios
NOVP-Novelty Press
NYNS-New York News Syndicate
PG-Premier Group
PINE-Pines
PMI-Parents' Magazine Institute
PRIZE-Prize Publications
QUA-Quality Comics Group
REAL-Realistic Comics
RH-Rural Home
S & S-Street and Smith Publishers
SKY-Skywald Publications
STAR-Star Publications
STD-Standard Comics
STJ-St. John Publishing Co.
SUPR-Superior Comics
TC-Tower Comics
TM-Trojan Magazines
TMP-Todd McFarlane Prods.
TOBY-Toby Press
TOPS-Tops Comics
UFS-United Features Syndicate
VAL-Valiant
VITL-Vital Publications
WB-Warner Brothers.
WEST-Western Publishing Co.
WHIT-Whitman Publishing Co.
WHW-William H. Wise
WMG-William M. Gaines (E. C.)
WP-Warren Publishing Co.
YM-Youthful Magazines
Z-D-Ziff-Davis Publishing Co.

OVERSTREET ADVISORS

Even before the first edition of *The Overstreet Comic Book Price Guide* was printed, author Robert M. Overstreet solicited pricing data, historical notations, and general information from a variety of sources. What was initially an informal group offering input quickly became an organized field of comic book collectors, dealers and historians whose opinions are actively solicited in advance of each edition of this book. Some of these Overstreet Advisors are specialists who deal in particular niches within the comic book world, while others are generalists who are interested in commenting on the broader marketplace. Each advisor provides information from their respective areas of interest and expertise, spanning the history of American comics.

While some choose to offer pricing and historical information in the form of annotated sales catalogs, auction catalogs, or documented private sales, assistance from others comes in the form of the market reports such as those beginning on page 97 in this book. In addition to those who have served as Overstreet Advisors almost since *The Guide*'s inception, each year new contributors are sought.

With that in mind, we are pleased to present our newest Overstreet Advisors:

THE CLASS OF 2017

ASHLEY COTTER-CAIRNS
SellMyComicBooks.com
Montreal, Canada

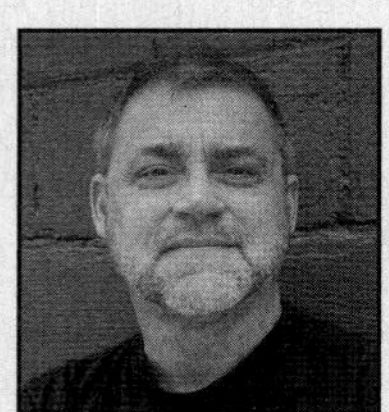

SHELTON DRUM
Heroes Aren't Hard to Find
Charlotte, NC

SEAN GOODRICH
SellMyComicBooks.com
Maine, USA

KEITH GOSS
Collector
Staten Island, NY

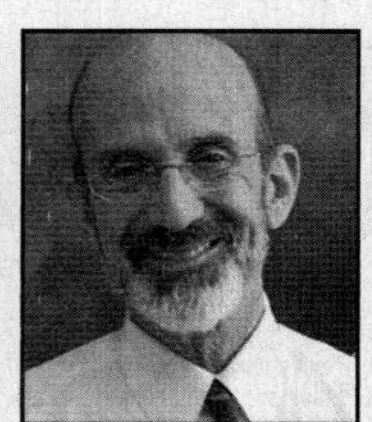

DR. STEVEN KAHN
Inner Child Comics
& Collectibles
Kenosha, WI

DYLAN SCHWARTZ
DylanUniverseComics.com
Great Neck, NY

BIGGER AND BETTER 52 PAGES 25¢ COMICS INA FLASH! 52 PAGES 25¢

COMICS INA FLASH!

Giant-Size X-Men #1 © MCG

House of Secrets #92 © DC

We are the **KING** of **Bronze Age** books!

Detective Comics #225 © DC

Yes, we have plenty of **Silver Age** books too!

Showcase #4 © DC

BUY-SELL & TRADE COMICS 1956-1980

CONTACT US!! We'll send you our free photo packed catalogue which lists 1000's of comics with prices starting under $1.00!!

Tony Starks
COMICS INA FLASH®℠
PO Box 3611
Evansville, IN 47735-3611
Phone/FAX 812-401-6127
Outside USA 812-401-6127

NOW OFFERING:
Fast, Affordable & Professional comic book pressing service.

See our website for full details.

www.comicsinaflash.com
email: comicflash@aol.com

Comics Ina Flash! is a registered service mark of Tony Starks

DAVID T. ALEXANDER COLLECTIBLES
WE'RE ALWAYS BUYING!
CELEBRATING 48 YEARS OF
FUN IN THE COMIC BOOK BIZ
WE NEED YOUR COLLECTION!
Visit our website
dtacollectibles.com
for details
PROFESSIONAL PRICES PAID!
ebay
Seller ID: DTACOLL

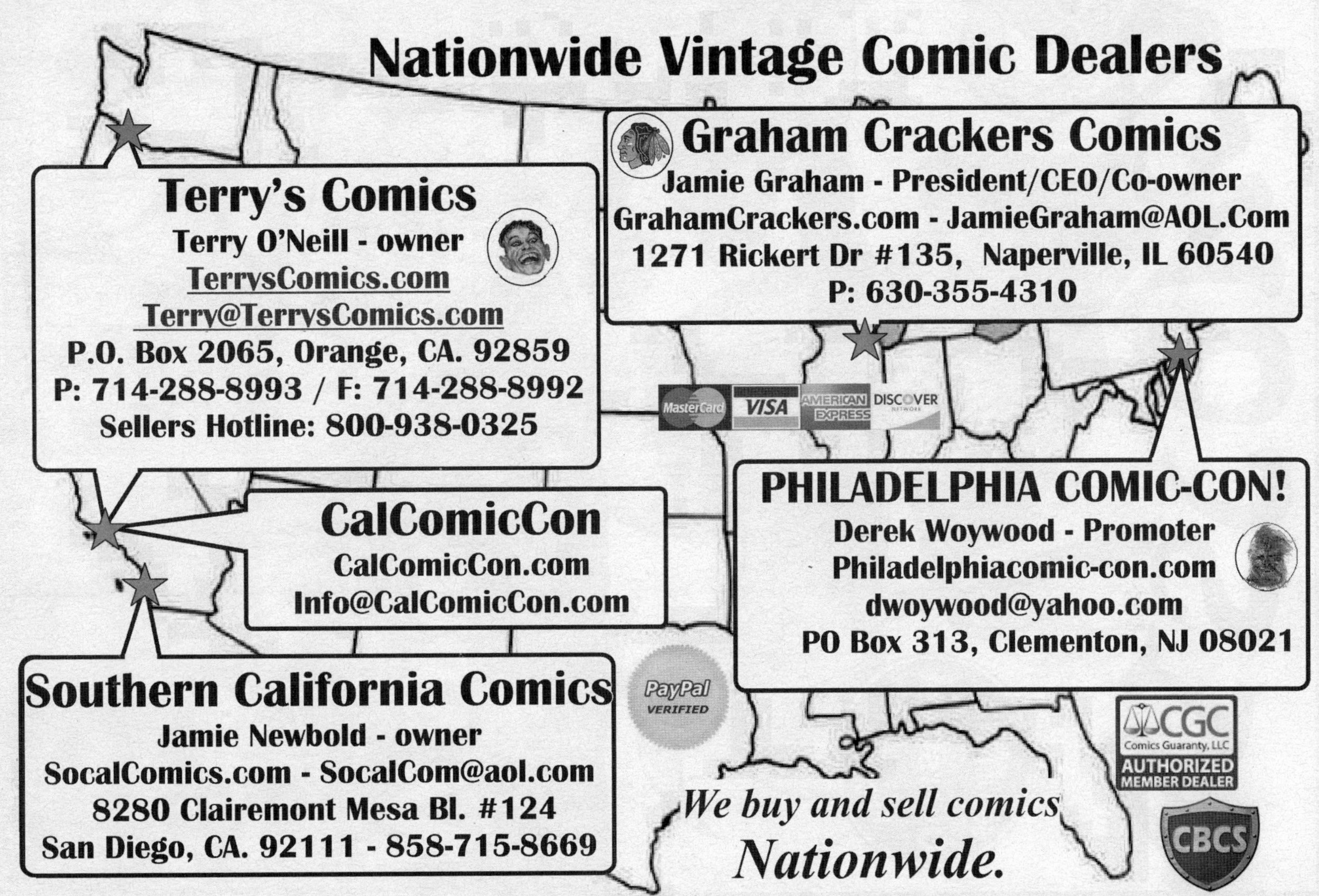

Nationwide Vintage Comic Dealers
Terry's Comics
Terry O'Neill - owner
TerrysComics.com
Terry@TerrysComics.com
P.O. Box 2065, Orange, CA. 92859
P: 714-288-8993 / F: 714-288-8992
Sellers Hotline: 800-938-0325
Graham Crackers Comics
Jamie Graham - President/CEO/Co-owner
GrahamCrackers.com - JamieGraham@AOL.Com
1271 Rickert Dr #135, Naperville, IL 60540
P: 630-355-4310
MasterCard
VISA
AMERICAN EXPRESS
DISCOVER
CalComicCon
CalComicCon.com
Info@CalComicCon.com
PHILADELPHIA COMIC-CON!
Derek Woywood - Promoter
Philadelphiacomic-con.com
dwoywood@yahoo.com
PO Box 313, Clementon, NJ 08021
Southern California Comics
Jamie Newbold - owner
SocalComics.com - SocalCom@aol.com
8280 Clairemont Mesa Bl. #124
San Diego, CA. 92111 - 858-715-8669
PayPal VERIFIED
CGC
Comics Guaranty, LLC
AUTHORIZED MEMBER DEALER
CBCS
We buy and sell comics
Nationwide.

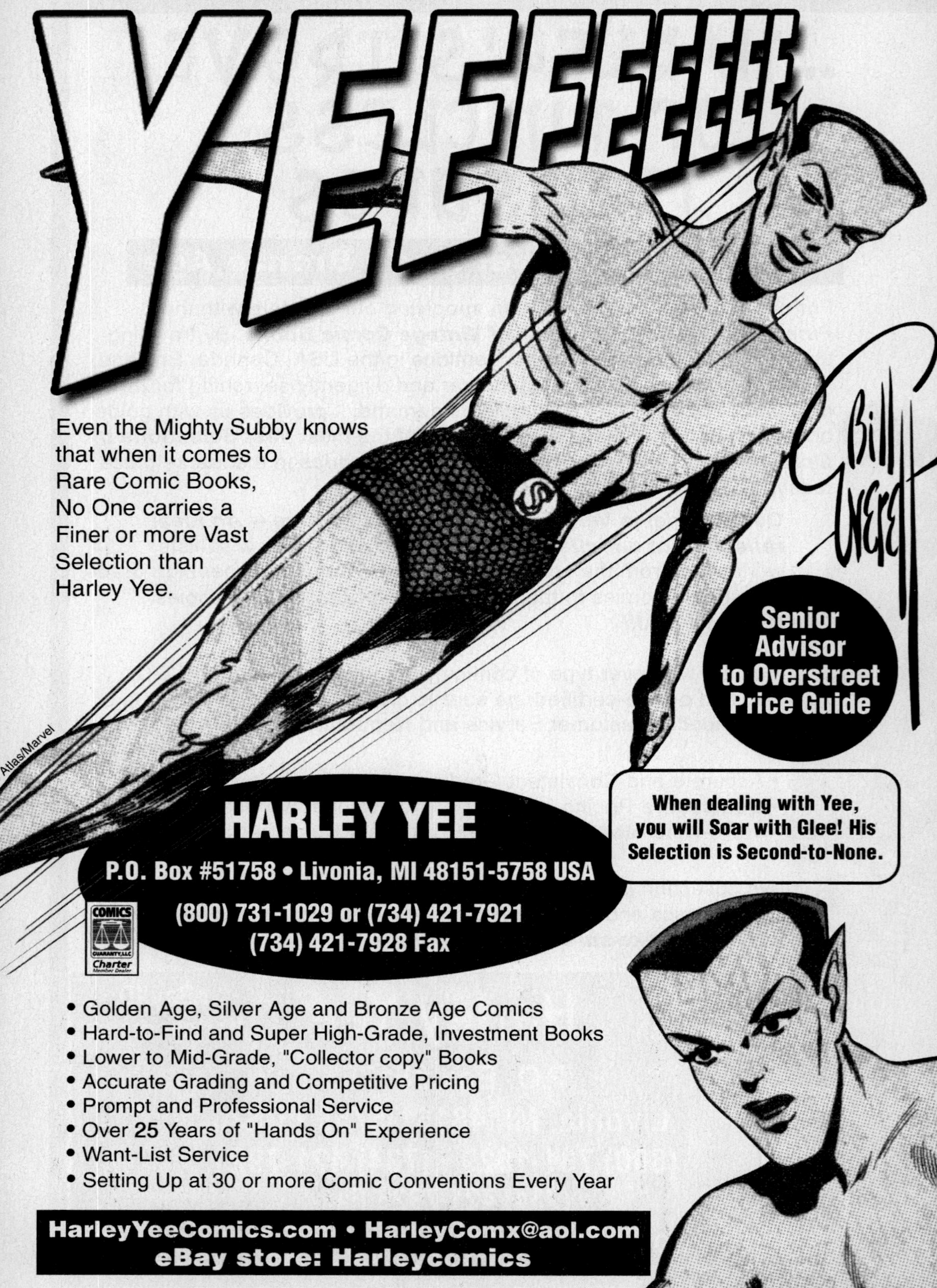
YEEEEEEEE
Even the Mighty Subby knows that when it comes to Rare Comic Books, No One carries a Finer or more Vast Selection than Harley Yee.
Bill Everett
Senior Advisor to Overstreet Price Guide
When dealing with Yee, you will Soar with Glee! His Selection is Second-to-None.
© Atlas/Marvel
HARLEY YEE
P.O. Box #51758 • Livonia, MI 48151-5758 USA
(800) 731-1029 or (734) 421-7921
(734) 421-7928 Fax
COMICS GUARANTY, LLC Charter Member Dealer
• Golden Age, Silver Age and Bronze Age Comics
• Hard-to-Find and Super High-Grade, Investment Books
• Lower to Mid-Grade, "Collector copy" Books
• Accurate Grading and Competitive Pricing
• Prompt and Professional Service
• Over 25 Years of "Hands On" Experience
• Want-List Service
• Setting Up at 30 or more Comic Conventions Every Year
HarleyYeeComics.com • HarleyComx@aol.com
eBay store: Harleycomics

We are paying 65% of Guide for the following:

Action 16-200
Adventure 32–100
All American
All Flash
All Top 8–18
Blonde Phantom
Blue Beetle 47–57
Brenda Starr 1–12
Crash
Daring Mystery
Fantastic
Flash (1st)
Hit 1–20
John Wayne
JO-JO 7–29
Kid Komics
Miss Fury
More Fun 52–107
Mysterious Adventure
Mystic (1st)
National 1–23
New Book of Comics
Pep 1–21
Phantom Lady
Phantom Stranger
Rangers 1-20
Rulah
Science (Fox)
Sensation
Silver Streak 1-17
Smash
Speed 1-20
Strange Tales 1–100
U.S.A. 1-5
Weird Comics
Zoot 7–16

We are paying 60% of Guide for the following:

Adventure 101–200
Adv. of Bob Hope 1–50
Adv. of Jerry Lewis 1-50
Adv. of Ozzie & Harriet
Air Fighters
All Star
Amazing Spiderman 3–10
America's Greatest
Batman 2-100
Blue Ribbon 2-20
Brave & the Bold 1–20
Bulletman
Captain Marvel
Captain Marvel Jr.
Captain Midnight
Challengers 1–10
Comic Cavalcade 1–29
Daredevil 1st 1–20
Detective 28-100
Dollman
Fantastic Four 3–10
Fight 1–30
Frontier Fighters
Green Hornet 1–20
Green Lantern (1st)
House of Mystery 1–50
House of Secrets 1–25
Ibis
Journey Into Mystery 1–115
Jumbo 11–50
Jungle 1–50
Lash Larue 1–46
Leading 1–14
Legend of D. Boone
Marvel Family
Mary Marvel
Master
Military
Modern
Movie Comics (D.C.)
My Greatest Adv. 1–50
Mystery in Space 1–50
Nickel
Planet
Police 1–20
Red Ryder 1-100
Saint
Shadow (1st)
Showcase 1–3, 5-20
Shield Wizard
Spy Smasher
Star Spangled
Superman 2–125
Superman's Pal 2–30
Strange Adventure 1–120
Superboy 1–50
Top-Notch
W.D. Comics & Stories 1–40
Whiz
World's Finest 1–110
Zip 1–39

We are also paying 50-100% of Guide for many other titles. Comics must be properly graded and complete. Please send your listing of comics for sale or a list of comics you wish to purchase. We are dealing in Marvels, D.C.'s, Timelys, Nedors, Western, Funny Material and much more! Please check our web site or send for our 100-page catalog. We will travel for large collections or, if you're passing through the area, call for an appointment.

JAMES PAYETTE
Rare Books & Comics
P.O. Box 750 • Bethlehem, NH 03574
Tel (603) 869-2097 • Fax (603) 869-3475
www.jamespayettecomics.com
jimpayette@msn.com

CREDENTIALS

Special Advisor to Overstreet Guide	1985–present
Member AACBC	1990–present
Sotheby's Authenticating, Certification, and Grading committee	1991–2002
Experience as a Dealer/Collector	since 1975
CBG Customer Service Award Winner for many years	

PLEASE SEE OUR OTHER ADS FOR FURTHER REFERENCE

GRADING COMICS

Over even short amounts of time within the world of comic book collecting, there are many, frequent changes. Collectors, dealers, and even publishers can come and go. Events or particular issues can be hyped and be written, wiped out, and written again.

However, in the world of comic book grading, things tend to change more slowly. But over time, they can and do sometimes change.

First came the acknowledgement that comic books in different conditions would be worth differing amounts of money. Then came recognition that even with a specific grade, there could be determining factors that gave one comic more appeal than another.

As prices in our market began to climb, the demand for more and more detail in grading and greater consistency increased. The grading scale evolved, was refined, and finally took on the form of the 10.0 scale we use today.

The addition of third party, independent grading to the mix was a major development. It's hard to argue against the notion that it helped to increase the liquidity in the marketplace, and that in turn spurred prices even higher.

It is those higher prices and our old friends, supply and demand, that have helped to bring us to another change in comic book grading with our most recent edition. It's not a huge one since it occurs in the lowest grades, but it is nonetheless significant because it is definitely market-driven.

Accurate grading of comic books has never been more important because the stakes have never been higher. While you probably won't look into the extreme realm of purchasing a CGC-certified 9.0 copy of *Action Comics* #1 for $3.2 million, it's safe to say that every collector wants the best possible copy of their favorite comic. Knowing that condition is of the highest importance, learning how grades are determined is the next step. And if you grade your own comics, you need to know what you're doing!

JUL161642 $24.95 SC

Hardcore comic book collectors will get a lot out of this book simply because it contains some of the most hardcore comic collecting information – the breakdown of grades and the imperfections on a book that would cause it to fall into that grade. But even the more casual collectors who may not care too terribly much about having all of their books slabbed would want to pick this one up as well simply because of how valuable the information inside is. Everyone stands to learn something new from *The Overstreet Guide to Grading Comics*. The newest edition includes not just the 10-point grading system (including the new 0.1 and 0.3 grades) but exhaustive descriptions of Primary and Split Grades and a ton of examples of each grade.

Available at your local comic shop or directly from

www.gemstonepub.com

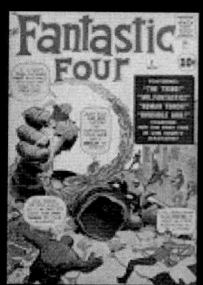

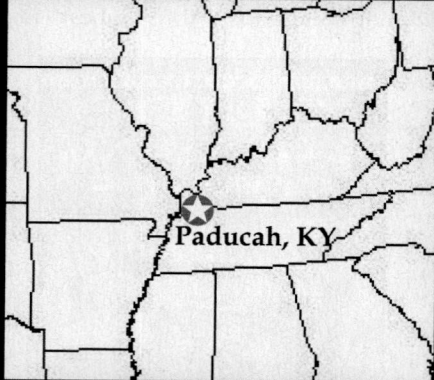

Geppi's
ENTERTAINMENT
MUSEUM
POP CULTURE WITH CHARACTER
LE OF THE
DEAD
APPALLING!
pop culture with character
GEPPI'S
entertainment
MUSEUM

ZAPP BUYS COMICS!

Selling your comic books? Zapp! Comics is buying now!

What are we buying? CGC graded comics, vintage comics, entire collections. Dealer inventories and warehouse stocks always wanted. Graphic Novels, Action Figures, Statues, Original Art, and Video Games.

Why sell to us? Friendly, professional transactions, every time. No consignment or auction fees, just a fast response and immediate payment. Unlimited funds available at all times. We have buyers for every level of comic book, from Golden Age Keys to last week's issue and everything in-between!

We are very competitive and do not cherry-pick! Over the past few years, we've bought millions of comic books from all over the Northeast. Call us first or get some other offers and call us last, it doesn't matter. Our goal is a fair, professional transaction every time.

• Authorized CGC Dealer • Overstreet Advisor
• Over 30 years buying and selling comic books!

Call or e-mail Ben now!
973-727-6171 • ben@zappcomics.com
ZappBuysComics.com

When in New Jersey, visit our Zapp! Comics locations!

574 Valley Road
Wayne, NJ 07470

700 Tennent Road
Manalapan, NJ 07726

Ebay ID: zappcomicsnj • ZappComics.com

Find us on f YouTube

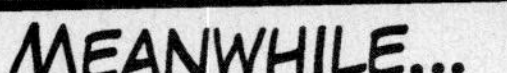

ORIGINAL COMIC ART

How would you like to own an original Jack Kirby cover from *Fantastic Four*, an original *Peanuts* Sunday page by Charles Schulz, or an actual cel from Disney's *Snow White And The Seven Dwarves?* Collecting original comic book, original comic strip, and animation art can be a very rewarding experience!

Like comic books themselves, original comic art has a lot to offer the collector. Great characters, wonderful stories, and an incredible cool factor.

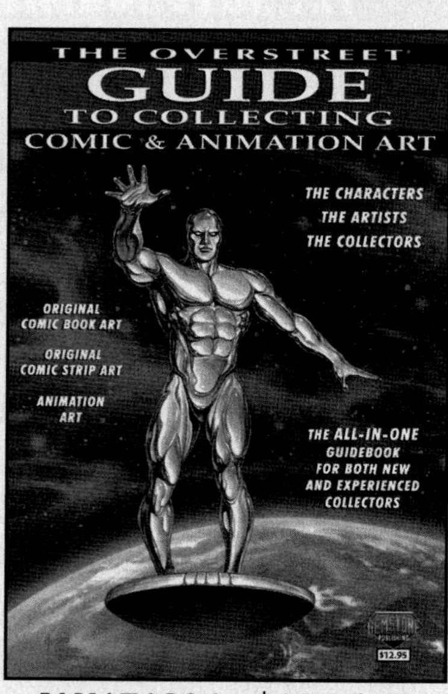

JAN171806 $12.95 SC

There are many ways to collect original comic book, comic strip and animation art, and while these fields may be under-documented compared to comic books themselves, the original art market now commands a tremendous amount of attention.

The first thing we always say though, whether in art or comic books or any other specialty, is collect what you love. Whether you're spending tens of dollars or $10,000, don't let anyone talk you into anything you wouldn't want to keep in your collection. While the market for original comic book art is very liquid at the moment, the best bet to a path with as few regrets as possible is to collect what you love.

And as you'll always hear us say in each of our publications, get informed.

Don't be afraid of diverse and sometimes conflicting opinions. Eventually you'll have to sort things out for yourself, but the key to understanding any field of endeavor is to get informed.

Another important element to understand is that while there are many record prices being paid, there are many pieces in each of these niches that are priced so that even the most unseasoned beginner can pick up some truly enjoyable pages, strips or cels. Again, when you start with something you love, it's hard to go wrong.

In recent years we've seen many additional record prices. But there are still thousands upon thousands of reasonably priced pages. In fact, it's safe to say that the majority of original comic book pages and original comic strips are reasonably priced.

Even with the majority of comic art priced in much more accessible fashion, the original comic book art market continues to be intriguing to observe. We now have conventions dedicated specifically to original art – Comic Art Con is the first, but we doubt it will be the last of its kind – and the market seems to be thriving.

Animation art is also a very interesting market. From Bugs Bunny to the classic Disney material, and from Hanna-Barbera to Terry Toons, there is just as much or more to learn about this part of the market.

The Overstreet Guide To Collecting Comic & Animation Art can be your guide to learning about the market or simply to thinking about it in new ways.

Available at your local comic shop or directly from

www.gemstonepub.com

MOVIE POSTERS

From *Casablanca* to *Vertigo*, from *Chinatown* to *Apocalypse Now*, from *Blade Runner* to *Scarface*, and from *Snow White* to *Frankenstein*, the best movie posters have almost always had the ability to project us into the world that the movie depicts before we actually see the film.

Sometimes they carve out brief, pivotal moments in the story, ones that compel us to see the movie or get us even more excited about a film we already planned to attend. At other times they capture more of the feeling or the tone of a movie rather than a specific element. And in yet other instances they focus on the stars or the characters…

Like so many great collectibles, there is no *one* answer about what makes movie posters iconic, but perhaps there is a way to describe their effect.

Writing on the Creative Bloq website in 2013, Cavan Scott said, "An iconic movie poster is one that has been burned onto the public consciousness, something that has become so recognizable that you feel that you've always known it. It should spring to mind as soon as you hear the film's name, be easily described and trigger excitement and intrigue, no matter how many times you see it."

JAN171807 $15.00 SC

Take a moment to consider the posters you love. Once we get beyond nostalgia – always a powerful force – it frequently boils down to the images that grab us and hold our attention, sometimes even if the film itself isn't all that good.

Take a look at what Amanda Sheriff and our team of writers have done in *The Overstreet Guide to Collecting Movie Posters*.

It provides film lovers and collectors a look inside the Silver Screen. There are profiles on directors, film stars, and movie poster artists. It includes in-depth features on movie genres and franchises, such as Star Wars, musicals, superheroes, James Bond, film noir, Blaxploitation, and Tarzan.

There are interviews with collectors and dealers who share their experiences, thoughts on elements of the hobby, and provide suggestions on collecting. Poster care is covered with articles on framing, storage, linen-backing, and poster autographs.

If you want to know how to grade a poster, that's in the book as well.

Whether you're looking at U.S. half-sheets, one-sheets, three-sheets, six-sheets, or lobby cards, or the great posters offered from a variety of nations around the world, if you like movies, there's a poster for you. And that's great, because as we say in every collecting category, you should collect what you love.

Amanda Sheriff and the contributors to this book love movies and movie posters and it shows. From silent films to the most recent CGI-filled mega-fest, spanning just about every genre you can think of, this book can be your gateway.

Available at your local comic shop or directly from

www.gemstonepub.com

CONCERT POSTERS

Music inspires us and affects our emotions. It can be upbeat and poppy, have a rock attitude, be soulful, loud and teeth rattling, or soft and sweet. Whatever the style or tempo, music can energize, be a salve to wounded spirits, or bring us closer to one another.

Concert posters are a visual representation of the music we love. They are advertisements that go beyond providing event details to entice and mesmerize audiences with a taste of the musical style. They can help people recall the memories of the best shows, and in many cases, youthful days gone by.

They're also highly collectible.

There are several ways to approach a concert poster collection. For many it starts with the musician, artist, or poster style. Collecting by musician is probably the easiest route; just determine which musician you either enjoy, that is affordable, or that appreciates in pricing, and start buying.

Another solid option is to collect by the artist who created the poster. The artists whose work adorns great concert posters are incredibly talented people. They are able to capture the style and attitude of the musicians in the art, making it very clear that it was made for one, specific group. The artists live the music, transferring it from auditory to visual, crafting impressive advertisements for the musicians.

The market for concert posters is strong and steady. Prices typically range from $50 to $1,000, putting them in a solidly affordable price range for most collectors. Posters for modern musicians, some boxing style examples, and some from popular 1960s series can be purchased for $20 to $100. More valuable posters include acts like The Grateful Dead, Jimi Hendrix, Jefferson Airplane, artists like Rick Griffin, and Bill Graham or Family Dog series posters, ranging in price from a few hundred to $10,000.

Like other areas of collecting, concert poster collectors are a community. People can connect with each other and the musicians they admire. It's a hobby where music lovers and art lovers come together to recall, with nostalgic joy, great pop culture history.

DEC161709 $15.00 SC

The Overstreet Guide to Collecting Concert Posters is a guide for both beginners and experienced collectors. There are features on popular musicians within concert poster collecting, profiles on artists who created posters, and histories of concert promoters and venues.

Industry experts and collectors share their expertice on buying and selling posters, restoration, collecting suggestions, and advice to collectors. A poster artist and a musician provide a look into their creative worlds.

It contains suggestions and advice on poster care, current prices on notable posters, and explores collecting other music memorabilia. Grading definitions and grading factors, plus top poster sales are presented with participation by auction houses.

Whether our book is your introduction to this world or you find it as an already experienced collector, it will offer you a gateway to seeing concert posters in a whole new light!

Available at your local comic shop or directly from

www.gemstonepub.com

VIDEO GAMES

If you're a longtime Overstreet fan, *The Overstreet Guide To Collecting Video Games* might not be the first thing that would pop into your mind. That could well change after you read this book. The market for collectible vintage video games may only be in its infancy, but it's growing rapidly, is getting organized, and has many passionate, devoted, serious fans.

There are still many to whom collecting video games might seem odd, but for the most part they just haven't stopped to consider how long video games have been around. Not only have the games and game systems themselves become highly sought after, but so have various related items as well.

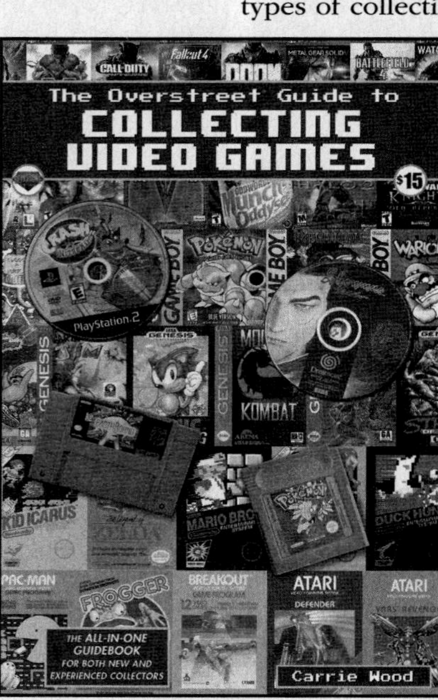

SEP161712 $15.00 SC

As it has been in just about every field, nostalgia may be the first impulse that makes older material collectible, but markets rarely develop solely from nostalgia. Our old friends supply and demand seem to always get into the mix as well. We've had video games for decades now. It's really only natural that things have evolved to the point where this book was a must.

Video games and their related merchandise are as collectible as comic books, movie memorabilia or sports collectibles. And the people who do so are just as passionate about their collections as anyone else in any other collecting hobby. Though video games are relatively young compared to comic books or the sort, that fact alone doesn't make gaming collections any less legitimate.

This book examines not just the history of video games, but also three major types of collecting in this hobby: by franchise, by console, and by developer.

So whether you're interested in literally catching 'em all in the *Pokémon* franchise or racing your way through the *Sonic the Hedgehog* series, we've got you covered. If you're loyal to either Nintendo, Microsoft or Sony, you'll find plenty of representation from your chosen console, too. And from Activision to Valve and nearly everyone in between, there's plenty of developer representation from throughout video game history.

We also have some wildly informative interviews on arcade cabinets and pinball machines, and on game-related merchandise and how to avoid fakes. On top of that, we've got a really great report on some of the most valuable games on the market right now. This is a book that will aid even the most seasoned, veteran collectors as well as it will help the newcomers to the hobby.

Available at your local comic shop or directly from

www.gemstonepub.com

THESE DIDN'T HAPPEN WITHOUT YOUR HELP.

The Overstreet Comic Book Price Guide doesn't happen by magic. A network of advisors – made up of experienced dealers, collectors and comics historians – gives us input for every edition we publish. If you spot an error or omission in this edition or any of our publications, let us know!

Write to us at
Gemstone Publishing Inc.,
1940 Greenspring Dr., Suite I-L,
Timonium, MD 21093.
Or e-mail **feedback@gemstonepub.com**.

We want your help!

BIG LITTLE BOOKS

INTRODUCTION

In 1932, at the depths of the Great Depression, comic books were not selling despite their successes in the previous two decades. Desperate publishers had already reduced prices to 25¢, but this was still too much for many people to spend on entertainment.

Comic books quickly evolved into two newer formats, the comics magazine and the Big Little Book. Both types retailed for 10¢.

Big Little Books began by reprinting the art (and adapting the stories) from newspaper comics. As their success grew and publishers began commissioning original material, movie adaptations and other entertainment-derived stories became commonplace.

GRADING

Before a Big Little Book's value can be assessed, its condition or state of preservation must be determined. A book in **Near Mint** condition will bring many times the price of the same book in **Poor** condition. Many variables influence the grading of a Big Little Book and all must be considered in the final evaluation. Due to the way they are constructed, damage occurs with very little use - usually to the spine, book edges and binding. More important defects that affect grading are: Split spines, pages missing, page browning or brittleness, writing, crayoning, loose pages, color fading, chunks missing, and rolling or out of square. The following grading guide is given to aid the novice:

9.4 Near Mint: The overall look is as if it was just purchased and maybe opened once; only subtle defects are allowed; paper is cream to off-white, supple and fresh; cover is flat with no surface wear or creases; inks and colors are bright; small penciled or inked arrival dates are acceptable; very slight blunting of corners at top and bottom of spine are common; outside corners are cut square and sharp. Books in this grade could bring prices of guide and a half or more.

9.0 Very Fine/Near Mint: Limited number of defects; full cover gloss with only very slight wear on book corners and edges; very minor foxing; very minor tears allowed, binding still square and tight with no pages missing; paper quality still fresh from cream to off-white. Dates, stamps or initials allowed on cover or inside.

8.0 Very Fine: Most of the cover gloss retained with minor wear appearing at corners and around edges; spine tight with no pages missing; cream/tan paper allowed if still supple; up to 1/4" bend allowed on covers with no color break; cover relatively flat; minor tears allowed.

6.0 Fine: Slight wear beginning to show; cover gloss reduced but still clean, pages tan/brown but still supple (not brittle); up to 1/4" split or color break allowed; minor discoloration and/or foxing allowed.

4.0 Very Good: Obviously a read copy with original printing luster almost gone; some fading and discoloration, but not soiled; some signs of wear such as corner splits and spine rolling; paper can be brown but not brittle; a few pages can be loose but not missing; no chunks missing; blunted corners acceptable.

2.0 Good: An average used copy complete with only minor pieces missing from the spine, which may be partially split; slightly soiled or marked with spine rolling; color flaking and wear around edges, but perfectly sound and legible; could have minor tape repairs but otherwise complete.

1.0 Fair: Very heavily read and soiled with small chunks missing from cover; most or all of spine could be missing; multiple splits in spine and loose pages, but still sound and legible, bringing 50 to 70 percent of good price.

0.5 Poor: Damaged, heavily weathered, soiled or otherwise unsuited for collecting purposes.

IMPORTANT

Most BLBs on the market today will fall in the **Good** to **Fine** grade category. When **Very Fine** to **Near Mint** BLBs are offered for sale, they usually bring premium prices.

A WORD ON PRICING

The prices are given for **Good**, **Fine** and **Very Fine/ Near Mint** condition. A book in **Fair** would be 50-70% of the **Good** price. **Very Good** would be halfway between the **Good** and **Fine** price, and **Very Fine** would be halfway between the **Fine** and **Very Fine/ Near**

Mint price. The prices listed were averaged from convention sales, dealers' lists, adzines, auctions, and by special contact with dealers and collectors from coast to coast. The prices and the spreads were determined from sales of copies in available condition or the highest grade known. Since most available copies are in the **Good** to **Fine** range, neither dealers nor collectors should let the **Very Fine/Near Mint** column influence the prices they are willing to charge or pay for books in less than near perfect condition.

The prices listed reflect a six times spread from **Good** to **Very Fine/ Near Mint** (1 - 3 - 6). We feel this spread accurately reflects the current market, especially when you consider the scarcity of books in **Very Fine/Near Mint** condition. When one or both end sheets are missing, the book's value would drop about a half grade.

Books with movie scenes are of double importance due to the high crossover demand by movie collectors.

Abbreviations: a-art; c-cover; nn-no number; p-pages; r-reprint.

Publisher Codes: BRP-Blue Ribbon Press; **ERB**-Edgar Rice Burroughs; **EVW**-Engel van Wiseman; **FAW**-Fawcett Publishing Co.; **Gold**-Goldsmith Publishing Co.; **Lynn**-Lynn Publishing Co.; **McKay**-David McKay Co.; **Whit**-Whitman Publishing Co.; **World**-World Syndicate Publishing Co.

Terminology: *All Pictures Comics*-no text, all drawings; *Fast-Action*-A special series of Dell books highly collected; *Flip Pictures*-upper right corner of interior pages contain drawings that are put into motion when rifled; *Movie Scenes*-book illustrated with scenes from the movie. *Soft Cover*-A thin single sheet of cardboard used in binding most of the giveaway versions.

"Big Little Book" and "Better Little Book" are registered trademarks of Whitman Publishing Co. "Little Big Book" is a registered trademark of the Saalfield Publishing Co.

"Pop-Up" is a registered trademark of Blue Ribbon Press. "Little Big Book" is a registered trademark of the Saalfield Co.

Top 20 Big Little Books and related size books*

Issue#	Rank	Title	Price
731	1	Mickey Mouse the Mail Pilot (variant version of Mickey Mouse #717) (A VG copy sold at auction for $7,170)	
nn	2	Mickey Mouse and Minnie Mouse at Macy's	$2,700
nn	3	Mickey Mouse and Minnie March to Macy's	$2,200
717	4	Mickey Mouse (skinny Mickey on-c)	$2,000
W-707	5	Dick Tracy The Detective	$1,500
725	6	Big Little Mother Goose HC	$1,300
717	7	Mickey Mouse (reg. Mickey on-c)	$1,200
nn	8	Mickey Mouse Silly Symphonies	$1,100
721	9	Big Little Paint Book (336 pg.)	$1,000
nn	10	Mickey Mouse Mail Pilot (Great Big Midget Book)	$925
725	11	Big Little Mother Goose SC	$900
nn	11	Mickey Mouse (Great Big Midget Book)	$900
nn	11	Mickey Mouse and the Magic Carpet	$900
721	14	Big Little Paint Book (320 pg.)	$800
nn	14	Mickey Mouse Sails For Treasure Island (Great Big Midget Book)	$800
4063	16	Popeye Thimble Theater Starring... (2nd printing)	$700
1126	17	Laughing Dragon of Oz	$650
4063	18	Popeye Thimble Theater Starring... (1st printing)	$600
nn	18	Buck Rogers	$600
nn	18	Buck Rogers in the City of Floating Globes	$600

*Includes only the various sized BLBs; no premiums, giveaways or other divergent forms are included..

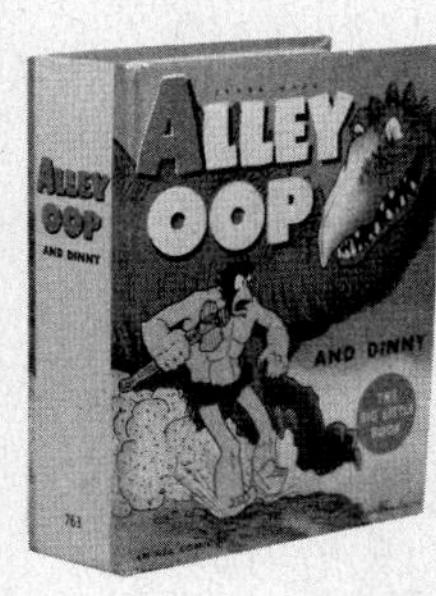

763 - Alley Oop and Dinny © WHIT

1083 - Barney Google © Saalfield

1432 - Big Chief Wahoo and the Lost Pioneers © WHIT

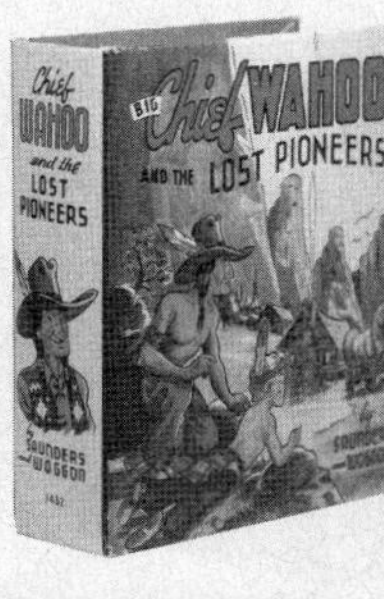

GD FN VF/NM

1175-0- Abbie an' Slats, 1940, Saalfield, 400 pgs. 11.00 27.50 70.00
1182- Abbie an' Slats-and Becky, 1940, Saalfield, 400 pgs. 11.00 27.50 70.00
nn- ABC's To Draw and Color, The, 1930s, Whitman, 4" x 5 1/4" x 1 1/12" deep, cardboard box contains 320 double-sided sheets to color and a box of crayons 29.00 73.00 200.00
1177- Ace Drummond, 1935, Whitman, 432 pgs. 11.00 27.50 70.00
Admiral Byrd (See Paramount Newsreel ...)
nn- Adventures of Charlie McCarthy and Edgar Bergen, The, 1938, Dell, 194 pgs., Fast-Action Story, soft-c 20.00 50.00 140.00
1422- Adventures of Huckleberry Finn, The, 1939, Whitman, 432 pgs., Henry E. Vallely-a 10.00 25.00 65.00
1648- Adventures of Jim Bowie (TV Series), 1958, Whitman, 280 pgs. 4.00 10.00 26.00
1056- Adventures of Krazy Kat and Ignatz Mouse in Koko Land, 1934, Saalfield, 160 pgs., oblong size, hard-c, Herriman-c/a 57.00 143.00 400.00
1306- Adventures of Krazy Kat and Ignatz Mouse in Koko Land, 1934, Saalfield, 164 pgs., oblong size, soft-c, Herriman-c/a 64.00 160.00 450.00
1082- Adventures of Pete the Tramp, The, 1935, Saalfield, hard-c, by C. D. Russell 10.00 25.00 65.00
1312- Adventures of Pete the Tramp, The, 1935, Saalfield, soft-c, by C. D. Russell 10.00 25.00 65.00
1053- Adventures of Tim Tyler, 1934, Saalfield, hard-c, oblong size, by Lyman Young 20.00 50.00 140.00
1303- Adventures of Tim Tyler, 1934, Saalfield, soft-c, oblong size, by Lyman Young 20.00 50.00 140.00
1058- Adventures of Tom Sawyer, The, 1934, Saalfield, 160 pgs., hard-c, Park Sumner-a 10.00 25.00 65.00
1308- Adventures of Tom Sawyer, The, 1934, Saalfield, 160 pgs., soft-c, Park Sumner-a 10.00 25.00 65.00
1448- Air Fighters of America, 1941, Whitman, 432 pgs., flip picture 11.00 27.50 70.00
Alexander Smart, ESQ. (See Top Line Comics)
759- Alice in Wonderland, 1933, Whitman, 160 pgs., hard-c, photo-c, movie scenes 36.00 90.00 250.00
1481- Allen Pike of the Parachute Squad U.S.A., 1941, Whitman, 432 pgs. 12.00 30.00 75.00
763- Alley Oop and Dinny, 1935, Whitman, 384 pgs., V. T. Hamlin-a 17.00 42.50 120.00
1473- Alley Oop and Dinny in the Jungles of Moo, 1938, Whitman, 432 pgs., V. T. Hamlin-a 17.00 42.50 120.00
nn- Alley Oop and the Missing King of Moo, 1938, Whitman, 36 pgs., 2 1/2" x 3 1/2", Penny Book 10.00 25.00 60.00
nn- Alley Oop in the Kingdom of Foo, 1938, Whitman, 68 pgs., 3 1/4" x 3 1/2", Pan-Am premium 23.00 57.50 160.00
nn- Alley Oop Taming a Dinosaur, 1938, Whitman, 68 pgs., 3 1/2" x 3 3/4", Pan-Am premium 23.00 57.50 160.00
nn- "Alley Oop the Invasion of Moo," 1935, Whitman, 260 pgs., Cocomalt premium, soft-c; V. T. Hamlin-a 18.00 45.00 125.00
Andy Burnette (See Walt Disney's...)
Andy Panda (Also see Walter Lantz ...)
531- Andy Panda, 1943, Whitman, 3 3/4x8 3/4", Tall Comic Book, All Pictures Comics 14.00 35.00 100.00
1425- Andy Panda and Tiny Tom, 1944, Whitman, All Pictures Comics 10.00 25.00 65.00
1431- Andy Panda and the Mad Dog Mystery, 1947, Whitman, 288 pgs., by Walter Lantz 10.00 25.00 65.00
1441- Andy Panda in the City of Ice, 1948, Whitman, All Picture Comics, by Walter Lantz 10.00 25.00 65.00
1459- Andy Panda and the Pirate Ghosts, 1949, Whitman, 88 pgs., by Walter Lantz 10.00 25.00 65.00
1485- Andy Panda's Vacation, 1946, Whitman, All Pictures Comics, by Walter Lantz 10.00 25.00 65.00
15- Andy Panda (The Adventures of), 1942, Dell, Fast-Action Story 14.00 35.00 100.00
707-10 - Andy Panda and Presto the Pup, 1949, Whitman 10.00 25.00 65.00
1130- Apple Mary and Dennie Foil the Swindlers, 1936, Whitman, 432 pgs. (Forerunner to Mary Worth) 10.00 25.00 65.00
1403- Apple Mary and Dennie's Lucky Apples, 1939, Whitman, 432 pgs. 10.00 25.00 65.00
2017- (#17)-Aquaman-Scourge of the Sea, 1968, Whitman, 260 pgs., 39 cents, hard-c, color illos 4.00 10.00 27.00
1192- Arizona Kid on the Bandit Trail, The, 1936, Whitman, 432 pgs. 10.00 25.00 60.00
1469- Bambi (Walt Disney's), 1942, Whitman, 432 pgs. 18.00 45.00 125.00
1497- Bambi's Children (Disney), 1943, Whitman, 432 pgs., Disney Studios-a 18.00 45.00 125.00
1138- Bandits at Bay, 1938, Saalfield, 400 pgs. 8.00 20.00 50.00
1459- Barney Baxter in the Air with the Eagle Squadron, 1938, Whitman, 432 pgs. 10.00 25.00 65.00
1083- Barney Google, 1935, Saalfield, hard-c 16.00 40.00 115.00
1313- Barney Google, 1935, Saalfield, soft-c 16.00 40.00 115.00
2031-(#31)- Batman and Robin in the Cheetah Caper, 1969, Whitman, 258 pgs. 4.00 10.00 27.00
5771- Batman and Robin in the Cheetah Caper, 1974, Whitman, 258 pgs., 49 cents 2.00 5.00 12.00
5771-1- Batman and Robin in the Cheetah Caper, 1974, Whitman, 258 pgs., 69 cents 2.00 5.00 12.00
5771-2- Batman and Robin in the Cheetah Caper, 1975?, Whitman, 258 pgs. 2.00 5.00 12.00
nn- Beauty and the Beast, nd (1930s), np (Whitman), 36 pgs., 3" x 3 1/2" Penny Book 4.00 10.00 22.00
Beep Beep The Road Runner (See Road Runner)
760- Believe It or Not!, 1933, Whitman, 160 pgs., by Ripley (c. 1931) 10.00 25.00 60.00
Betty Bear's Lesson (See Wee Little Books)
1119- Betty Boop in Snow White, 1934, Whitman, 240 pgs., hard-c; adapted from Max Fleischer Paramount Talkartoon 46.00 115.00 325.00
1119- Betty Boop in Snow White, 1934, Whitman, 240 pgs., soft-c; same contents as hard-c (Rare) 64.00 160.00 450.00
1158- Betty Boop in "Miss Gullivers Travels," 1935, Whitman, 288 pgs., hard-c (Scarce) 57.00 143.00 400.00
2070- Big Big Paint Book, 1936, Whitman, 432 pgs., 8 1/2" x 11 3/8", B&W pages to color 21.00 52.50 150.00
1432- Big Chief Wahoo and the Lost Pioneers, 1942, Whitman, 432 pgs., Elmer Woggon-a 11.00 27.50 70.00
1443- Big Chief Wahoo and the Great Gusto, 1938, Whitman, 432 pgs., Elmer Woggon-a 11.00 27.50 70.00
1483- Big Chief Wahoo and the Magic Lamp, 1940, Whitman, 432 pgs., flip pictures, Woggon-c/a 11.00 27.50 70.00
725- Big Little Mother Goose, The, 1934, Whitman, 580 pgs. (Rare) Hardcover 163.00 408.00 1300.00
725- Big Little Mother Goose, The, 1934, Whitman, 580 pgs. (Rare) Softcover 123.00 308.00 900.00
1005- Big Little Nickel Book, 1935, Whitman, 144 pgs., Blackie Bear stories and Donna the Donkey 8.00 20.00 50.00
1006- Big Little Nickel Book, 1935, Whitman, 144 pgs., Blackie Bear stories, folk tales in primer style 8.00 20.00 50.00
1007- Big Little Nickel Book, 1935, Whitman, 144 pgs., Peter Rabbit, etc. 8.00 20.00 50.00
1008- Big Little Nickel Book, 1935, Whitman, 144 pgs., Wee Wee Woman, etc. 8.00 20.00 50.00
721- Big Little Paint Book, The, 1933, Whitman, 320 pgs., 3 3/4" x 8 1/2", for crayoning; first printing has green page ends; second printing has purple page ends (both are rare) 114.00 285.00 800.00
721- Big Little Paint Book, The, 1933, Whitman, 336 pgs., 3 3/4" x 8 1/2", for crayoning; first printing has green page ends; second printing has purple page ends (both are rare) 125.00 313.00 1000.00
1178- Billy of Bar-Zero, 1940, Saalfield, 400 pgs. 10.00 25.00 60.00
773- Billy the Kid, 1935, Whitman, 432 pgs., Hal Arbo-a 10.00 25.00 65.00
1159- Billy the Kid on Tall Butte, 1939, Saalfield, 400 pgs. 9.00 22.50 60.00
1174- Billy the Kid's Pledge, 1940, Saalfield, 400 pgs. 9.00 22.50 60.00
nn- Billy the Kid, Western Outlaw, 1935, Whitman, 260 pgs.,

1432 - Bob Stone the Young Detective © WHIT

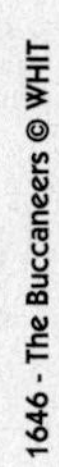
1646 - The Buccaneers © WHIT

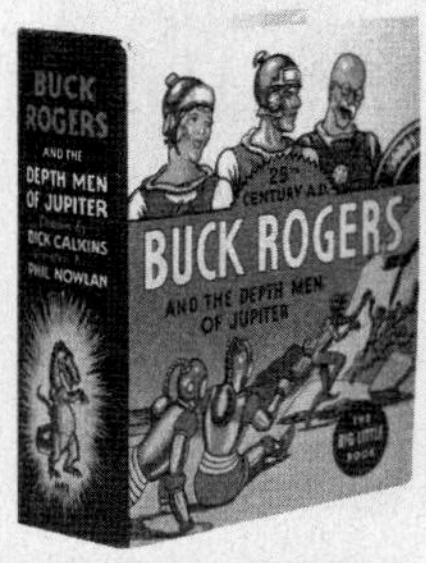

1169 - Buck Rogers and the Depth Men of Jupiter © KING

	GD	FN	VF/NM
Cocomalt premium, Hal Arbo-a, soft-c	12.00	30.00	85.00
1057- **Black Beauty**, 1934, Saalfield, hard-c	8.00	20.00	50.00
1307- **Black Beauty**, 1934, Saalfield, soft-c	8.00	20.00	50.00
1414- **Black Silver and His Pirate Crew**, 1937, Whitman, 300 pgs.	10.00	25.00	65.00
1447- **Blaze Brandon with the Foreign Legion**, 1938, Whitman, 432 pgs.	10.00	25.00	65.00
1410- **Blondie and Dagwood in Hot Water**, 1946, Whitman, 352 pgs., by Chic Young	10.00	25.00	60.00
1415- **Blondie and Baby Dumpling**, 1937, Whitman, 432 pgs., by Chic Young	10.00	25.00	65.00
1419- **Oh, Blondie the Bumsteads Carry On**, 1941, Whitman, 432 pgs., flip pictures, by Chic Young	10.00	25.00	65.00
1423- **Blondie Who's Boss?**, 1942, Whitman, 432 pgs., flip pictures, by Chic Young	10.00	25.00	65.00
1429- **Blondie with Baby Dumpling and Daisy**, 1939, Whitman, 432 pgs., by Chic Young	10.00	25.00	65.00
1430- **Blondie Count Cookie in Too!**, 1947, Whitman, 288 pgs., by Chic Young	10.00	25.00	60.00
1438- **Blondie and Dagwood Everybody's Happy**, 1948, Whitman, 288 pgs., by Chic Young	10.00	25.00	60.00
1450- **Blondie No Dull Moments**, 1948, Whitman, 288 pgs., by Chic Young	10.00	25.00	60.00
1463- **Blondie Fun For All**, 1949, Whitman, 288 pgs., by Chic Young	10.00	25.00	60.00
1466- **Blondie or Life Among the Bumsteads**, 1944, Whitman, 352 pgs., by Chic Young	10.00	25.00	65.00
1476- **Blondie and Bouncing Baby Dumpling**, 1940, Whitman, 432 pgs., by Chic Young	10.00	25.00	65.00
1487- **Blondie Baby Dumpling and All!**, 1941, Whitman, 432 pgs. flip pictures, by Chic Young	10.00	25.00	65.00
1490- **Blondie Papa Knows Best**, 1945, Whitman, 352 pgs., by Chic Young	10.00	25.00	60.00
1491- **Blondie-Cookie and Daisy's Pups**, 1943, Whitman, 1st printing, 432 pgs.	10.00	25.00	65.00
1491- **Blondie-Cookie and Daisy's Pups**, 1943, Whitman,. 2nd printing with different back-c & 352 pgs.	9.00	22.50	55.00
703-10- **Blondie and Dagwood Some Fun!**, 1949, Whitman, by Chic Young	8.00	20.00	48.00
21- **Blondie and Dagwood**, 1936, Lynn, by Chic Young	16.00	40.00	115.00
1108- **Bobby Benson on the H-Bar-O Ranch**, 1934, Whitman, 300 pgs., based on radio serial	12.00	30.00	75.00
Bobby Thatcher and the Samarang Emerald (See Top-Line Comics)			
1432- **Bob Stone the Young Detective**, 1937, Whitman, 240 pgs., movie scenes	11.00	27.50	70.00
2002- **(#2)-Bonanza-The Bubble Gum Kid**, 1967, Whitman, 260 pgs., 39 cents, hard-c, color illos	4.00	10.00	27.00
1139- **Border Eagle, The**, 1938, Saalfield, 400 pgs.	8.00	20.00	50.00
1153- **Boss of the Chisholm Trail**, 1939, Saalfield, 400 pgs.	8.00	20.00	50.00
1425- **Brad Turner in Transatlantic Flight**, 1939, Whitman, 432 pgs.	10.00	25.00	60.00
1058- **Brave Little Tailor, The** (Disney), 1939, Whitman, 5" x 5 1/2", 68 pgs., hard-c (Mickey Mouse)	12.00	30.00	85.00
1427- **Brenda Starr and the Masked Impostor**, 1943, Whitman, 352 pgs., Dale Messick-a	12.00	30.00	80.00
1426- **Brer Rabbit** (Walt Disney's ...), 1947, Whitman, All Picture Comics, from "Song Of The South" movie	18.00	45.00	125.00
704-10- **Brer Rabbit**, 1949, Whitman	14.00	35.00	100.00
1059- **Brick Bradford in the City Beneath the Sea**, 1934, Saalfield, hard-c, by William Ritt & Clarence Gray	13.00	32.50	90.00
1309- **Brick Bradford in the City Beneath the Sea**, 1934, Saalfield, soft-c, by Ritt & Gray	13.00	32.50	90.00
1468- **Brick Bradford with Brocco the Modern Buccaneer**, 1938, Whitman, 432 pgs., by Wrn. Ritt & Clarence Gray	10.00	25.00	60.00
1133- **Bringing Up Father**, 1936, Whitman, 432 pgs., by George McManus	12.00	30.00	85.00
1100- **Broadway Bill**, 1935, Saalfield, photo-c, 4 1/2" x 5 1/4", movie scenes (Columbia Pictures, horse racing)	11.00	27.50	70.00
1580- **Broadway Bill**, 1935, Saalfield, soft-c, photo-c, movie scenes	11.00	27.50	70.00
1181- **Broncho Bill**, 1940, Saalfield, 400 pgs.	10.00	25.00	60.00
nn- **Broncho Bill**, 1935, Whitman, 148 pgs., 3 1/2" x 4", Tarzan Ice Cream cup lid premium	25.00	62.50	175.00
nn- **Broncho Bill in Suicide Canyon** (See Top-Line Comics)			
1417- **Bronc Peeler the Lone Cowboy**, 1937, Whitman, 432 pgs., by Fred Harman, forerunner of Red Ryder (also see Red Death on the Range)	10.00	25.00	60.00
nn- **Brownies' Merry Adventures, The**, 1993, Barefoot Books, 202 pgs., reprints from Palmer Cox's late 1800s books	3.00	7.50	18.00
1470- **Buccaneer, The**, 1938, Whitman, 240 pgs., photo-c, movie scenes	12.00	30.00	75.00
1646- **Buccaneers, The** (TV Series), 1958, Whitman, 4 1/2" x 5 1/4", 280 pgs., Russ Manning-a	4.00	10.00	25.00
1104- **Buck Jones in the Fighting Code**, 1934, Whitman, 160 pgs., hard-c, movie scenes	14.00	35.00	95.00
1116- **Buck Jones in Ride 'Em Cowboy** (Universal Presents), 1935, Whitman, 240 pgs., photo-c, movie scenes	14.00	35.00	95.00
1174- **Buck Jones in the Roaring West** (Universal Presents), 1935, Whitman, 240 pgs., movie scenes	14.00	35.00	95.00
1188- **Buck Jones in the Fighting Rangers** (Universal Presents), 1936, Whitman, 240 pgs., photo-c, movie scenes	14.00	35.00	95.00
1404- **Buck Jones and the Two-Gun Kid**, 1937, Whitman, 432 pgs.	10.00	25.00	65.00
1451- **Buck Jones and the Killers of Crooked Butte**, 1940, Whitman, 432 pgs.	10.00	25.00	65.00
1461- **Buck Jones and the Rock Creek Cattle War**, 1938, Whitman, 432 pgs.	10.00	25.00	65.00
1486- **Buck Jones and the Rough Riders in Forbidden Trails**, 1943, Whitman, flip pictures, based on movie; Tim McCoy app.	12.00	30.00	80.00
3- **Buck Jones in the Red Rider**, 1934, EVW, 160 pgs., movie scenes	21.00	52.50	150.00
8- **Buck Jones Cowboy Masquerade**, 1938, Whitman, 132 pgs., soft-c, 3 3/4" x 3 1/2", Buddy Book premium	24.00	60.00	170.00
15- **Buck Jones in Rocky Rhodes**, 1935, EVW, 160 pgs., photo-c, movie scenes	29.00	73.00	200.00
4069- **Buck Jones and the Night Riders**, 1937, Whitman, 7" x 9", 320 pgs., Big Big Book	39.00	98.00	275.00
nn- **Buck Jones on the Six-Gun Trail**, 1939, Whitman, 36 pgs., 2 1/2" x 3 1/2", Penny Book	10.00	25.00	60.00
nn- **Buck Jones Big Thrill Chewing Gum**, 1934, Whitman, 8 pgs., 2 1/2" x 3 1/2" (6 diff.) each...	14.00	35.00	100.00
742- **Buck Rogers in the 25th Century A.D.**, 1933, Whitman, 320 pgs., Dick Calkins-a	43.00	108.00	300.00
nn- **Buck Rogers in the 25th Century A.D.**, 1933, Whitman, 204 pgs.,Cocomalt premium, Calkins-a	29.00	73.00	200.00
765- **Buck Rogers in the City Below the Sea**, 1934, Whitman, 320 pgs., Dick Calkins-a	32.00	80.00	225.00
765- **Buck Rogers in the City Below the Sea**, 1934, Whitman, 324 pgs., soft-c, Dick Calkins-c/a (Rare)	57.00	143.00	400.00
1143- **Buck Rogers on the Moons of Saturn**, 1934, Whitman, 320 pgs., Dick Calkins-a	32.00	80.00	225.00
nn- **Buck Rogers on the Moons of Saturn**, 1934, Whitman, 324 pgs., premium w/no ads, soft 3-color-c, Dick Calkins-a	50.00	125.00	350.00
1169- **Buck Rogers and the Depth Men of Jupiter**, 1935, Whitman, 432 pgs., Calkins-a	34.00	85.00	240.00
1178- **Buck Rogers and the Doom Comet**, 1935, Whitman, 432 pgs., Calkins-a	31.00	78.00	220.00
1197- **Buck Rogers and the Planetoid Plot**, 1936, Whitman, 432 pgs., Calkins-a	31.00	78.00	220.00
1409- **Buck Rogers Vs. the Fiend of Space**, 1940, Whitman, 432 pgs., Calkins-a	40.00	100.00	280.00
1437- **Buck Rogers in the War with the Planet Venus**, 1938, Whitman, 432 pgs., Calkins-a	31.00	78.00	220.00
1474- **Buck Rogers and the Overturned World**, 1941, Whitman, 432 pgs., flip pictures, Calkins-a	33.00	83.00	230.00

1465 - Bugs Bunny
The Masked Marvel © WB

1142 - Bullets Across the Border
© Saalfield

734 - Chester Gump at
Silver Creek Ranch © WHIT

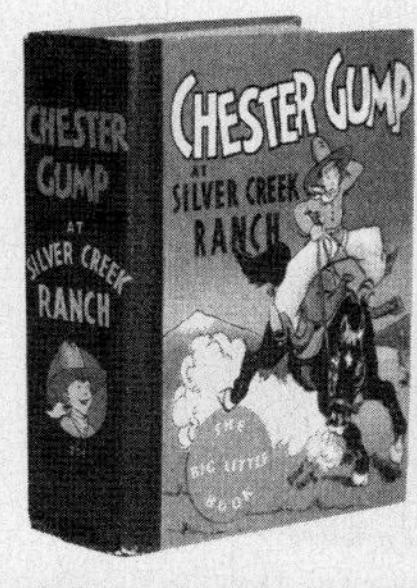

GD FN VF/NM

1490- Buck Rogers and the Super-Dwarf of Space, 1943, Whitman, 11 Pictures Comics, Calkins-a 31.00 78.00 220.00

4057- Buck Rogers, The Adventures of, 1934, Whitman, 7" x 9 1/2", 320 pgs., Big Big Book, "The Story of Buck Rogers on the Planet Eros," Calkins-c/a 71.00 178.00 500.00

nn- Buck Rogers, 1935, Whitman, 4" x 3 1/2", Tarzan Ice Cream cup premium (Rare) 86.00 215.00 600.00

nn- Buck Rogers in the City of Floating Globes, 1935, Whitman, 258 pgs., Cocomalt premium, soft-c, Dick Calkins-a 86.00 215.00 600.00

nn- Buck Rogers Big Thrill Chewing Gum, 1934, Whitman, 8 pgs., 2 1/2" x 3 " (6 diff.) each... 21.00 52.50 150.00

1135- Buckskin and Bullets, 1938, Saalfield, 400 pgs. 8.00 20.00 50.00

Buffalo Bill (See Wild West Adventures of ...)

nn- Buffalo Bill, 1934, World Syndicate, All pictures, by J. Carroll Mansfield 10.00 25.00 60.00

713- Buffalo Bill and the Pony Express, 1934, Whitman, hard-c, 384 pgs., Hal Arbo-a 11.00 27.50 70.00

nn- Buffalo Bill and the Pony Express, 1934, Whitman, soft-c, 384 pgs., Hal Arbo-a; three-color premium (Rare) 43.00 108.00 300.00

1194- Buffalo Bill Plays a Lone Hand, 1936, Whitman, 432 pgs., Hal Arbo-a 10.00 25.00 60.00

530- Bugs Bunny, 1943, Whitman, All Pictures Comics, Tall Comic Book, 3 1/4" x 8 1/4", reprints/Looney Tunes 1 & 5 17.00 42.50 120.00

1403- Bugs Bunny and the Pirate Loot, 1947, Whitman, All Pictures Comics 11.00 27.50 70.00

1435- Bugs Bunny, 1944, Whitman, All Pictures Comics 12.00 30.00 75.00

1440- Bugs Bunny in Risky Business, 1948, Whitman, All Pictures & Comics 11.00 27.50 70.00

1455- Bugs Bunny and Klondike Gold, 1948, Whitman, 288 pgs. 11.00 27.50 70.00

1465- Bugs Bunny The Masked Marvel, 1949, Whitman, 288 pgs. 11.00 27.50 70.00

1496- Bugs Bunny and His Pals, 1945, Whitman, All Pictures Comics; r/Four Color Comics #33 11.00 27.50 70.00

13- Bugs Bunny and the Secret of Storm Island, 1942, Dell,194 pgs., Fast-Action Story 27.00 68.00 190.00

706-10- Bugs Bunny and the Giant Brothers, 1949, Whitman 10.00 25.00 60.00

2007- (#7)-Bugs Bunny-Double Trouble on Diamond Island, 1967, Whitman, 260 pgs., 39 cents, hard-c, color illos 5.00 12.50 33.00

2029-(#29)- Bugs Bunny, Accidental Adventure, 1969, Whitman, 256 pgs., hard-c, color illos. 4.00 10.00 22.00

2952- Bugs Bunny's Mistake, 1949, Whitman, 3 1/4" x 4", 24 pgs., Tiny Tales, full color (5 cents) (1030-5 on back-c) 10.00 25.00 60.00

5757-2- Bugs Bunny in Double Trouble on Diamond Island,1967, (1980-reprints #2007), Whitman, 260 pgs., soft-c, 79 cents, B&W 2.00 5.00 14.00

5758- Bugs Bunny, Accidental Adventure, 1973, Whitman, 256 pgs., soft-c, B&W illos. 2.00 5.00 14.00

5758-1- Bugs Bunny, Accidental Adventure, 1973, Whitman, 256 pgs., soft-c, B&W illos. 2.00 5.00 14.00

5772- Bugs Bunny the Last Crusader, 1975, Whitman, 49 cents, flip-it book 2.00 5.00 14.00

5772-2- Bugs Bunny the Last Crusader, 1975, Whitman, $1.50, flip-it book 1.00 2.50 6.00

1169- Bullet Benton, 1939, Saalfield, 400 pgs. 10.00 25.00 60.00

nn- Bulletman and the Return of Mr. Murder, 1941, Fawcett, 196 pgs., Dime Action Book 39.00 98.00 275.00

1142- Bullets Across the Border (A Billy The Kid story), 1938, Saalfield, 400 pgs. 10.00 25.00 60.00

Bunky (See Top-Line Comics)

837- Bunty (Punch and Judy), 1935, Whitman, 28 pgs., Magic-Action with 3 pop-ups 12.00 30.00 80.00

1091- Burn 'Em Up Barnes, 1935, Saalfield, hard-c, movie scenes 10.00 25.00 60.00

1321- Burn 'Em Up Barnes, 1935, Saalfield, soft-c, movie scenes 10.00 25.00 60.00

GD FN VF/NM

1415- Buz Sawyer and Bomber 13,1946, Whitman, 352 pgs., Roy Crane-a 10.00 25.00 60.00

1412- Calling W-1-X-Y-Z, Jimmy Kean and the Radio Spies, 1939, Whitman, 300 pgs. 11.00 27.50 70.00

Call of the Wild (See Jack London's...)

1107- Camels are Coming, 1935, Saalfield, movie scenes 10.00 25.00 60.00

1587- Camels are Coming, 1935, Saalfield, movie scenes 10.00 25.00 60.00

nn- Captain and the Kids, Boys Vill Be Boys, The, 1938, 68 pgs., Pan-Am Oil premium, soft-c 12.00 30.00 85.00

1128- Captain Easy Soldier of Fortune, 1934, Whitman, 432 pgs., Roy Crane-a 11.00 27.50 70.00

nn- Captain Easy Soldier of Fortune, 1934, Whitman, 436 pgs., Premium, no ads, soft 3-color-c, Roy Crane-a 20.00 50.00 140.00

1474- Captain Easy Behind Enemy Lines, 1943, Whitman, 352 pgs., Roy Crane-a 11.00 27.50 70.00

nn- Captain Easy and Wash Tubbs, 1935, 260 pgs., Cocomalt premium, Roy Crane-a 11.00 27.50 70.00

1444- Captain Frank Hawks Air Ace and the League of Twelve, 1938, Whitman, 432 pgs. 11.00 27.50 70.00

nn- Captain Marvel, 1941, Fawcett, 196 pgs., Dime Action Book 50.00 125.00 350.00

1402- Captain Midnight and Sheik Jomak Khan, 1946, Whitman, 352 pgs. 16.00 40.00 115.00

1452- Captain Midnight and the Moon Woman, 1943, Whitman, 352 pgs. 18.00 45.00 125.00

1458- Captain Midnight Vs. The Terror of the Orient, 1942, Whitman, 432 pgs., flip pictures, Hess-a 18.00 45.00 125.00

1488- Captain Midnight and the Secret Squadron, 1941, Whitman, 432 pgs. 18.00 45.00 125.00

Captain Robb of.. (See Dirigible ZR90 ...)

nn- Cauliflower Catnip Pearls of Peril, 1981, Teacup Tales, 290 pgs., Joe Wehrle Jr.-s/a; deliberately printed on aged-looking paper to look like an old BLB 4.00 10.00 27.00

20- Ceiling Zero, 1936, Lynn, 128 pgs., 7 1/2" x 5", hard-c, James Cagney, Pat O'Brien photos on-c, movie scenes, Warner Bros. Pictures 11.00 27.50 70.00

1093- Chandu the Magician, 1935, Saalfield, 5" x 5 1/4", 160 pgs., hard-c, Bela Lugosi photo-c, movie scenes 13.00 32.50 90.00

1323- Chandu the Magician, 1935, Saalfield, 5" x 5 1/4", 160 pgs., soft-c, Bela Lugosi photo-c 14.00 35.00 100.00

Charlie Chan (See Inspector ...)

1459- Charlie Chan Solves a New Mystery (See Inspector..), 1940, Whitman, 432 pgs., Alfred Andriola-a 12.00 30.00 85.00

1478- Charlie Chan of the Honolulu Police, Inspector, 1939, Whitman, 432 pgs., Andriola-a 12.00 30.00 85.00

Charlie McCarthy (See Story Of ...)

734- Chester Gump at Silver Creek Ranch, 1933, Whitman, 320 pgs., Sidney Smith-a 13.00 32.50 90.00

nn- Chester Gump at Silver Creek Ranch, 1933, Whitman, 204 pgs., Cocomalt premium, soft-c, Sidney Smith-a 14.00 35.00 100.00

nn- Chester Gump at Silver Creek Ranch, 1933, Whitman, 52 pgs., 4" x 5 1/2", premium-no ads, soft-c, Sidney Smith-a 21.00 52.50 150.00

766- Chester Gump Finds the Hidden Treasure, 1934, Whitman, 320 pgs., Sidney Smith-a 12.00 30.00 85.00

nn- Chester Gump Finds the Hidden Treasure, 1934, Whitman, 52 pgs., 3 1/2" x 5 3/4", premium-no ads, soft-c, Sidney Smith-a 21.00 52.50 150.00

nn- Chester Gump Finds the Hidden Treasure, 1934, Whitman, 52 pgs., 4" x 5 1/2", premium-no ads, Sidney Smith-a 21.00 52.50 150.00

1146- Chester Gump in the City Of Gold, 1935, Whitman, 432 pgs., Sidney Smith-a 12.00 30.00 85.00

nn- Chester Gump in the City Of Gold, 1935, Whitman, 436 pgs., premium-no ads, 3-color, soft-c, Sidney Smith-a 24.00 60.00 165.00

1402- Chester Gump in the Pole to Pole Flight, 1937, Whitman,

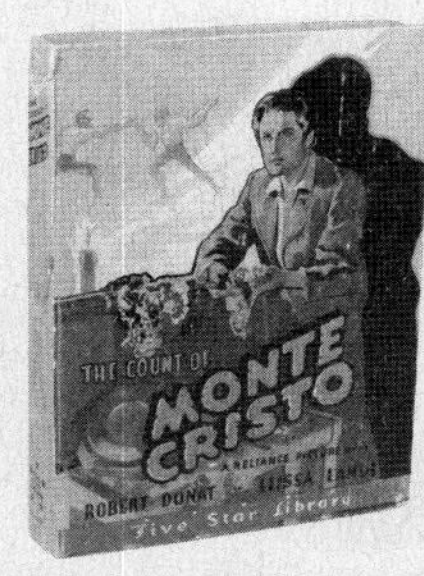
1 - Count of Monte Cristo © EVW

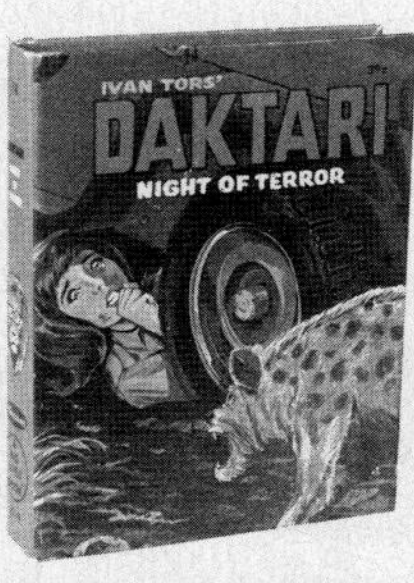
2018 - Daktari - Night of Terror © WHIT

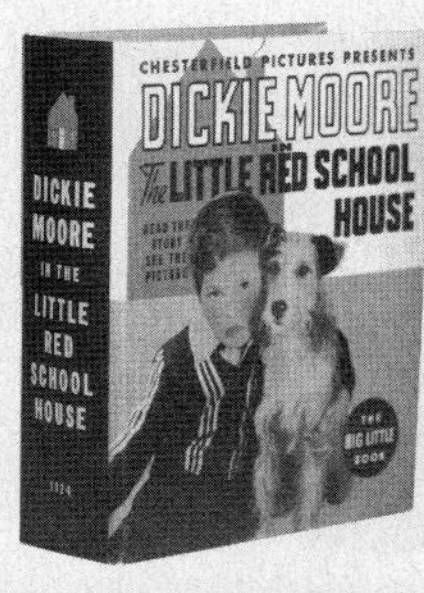
1124 - Dickie Moore in the Little Red School House © WHIT

GD FN VF/NM

432 pgs. 12.00 30.00 75.00

5- Chester Gump and His Friends, 1934, Whitman, 132 pgs., 3 1/2" x 3 1/2", soft-c, Tarzan Ice Cream cup lid premium
23.00 57.50 160.00

nn- Chester Gump at the North Pole, 1938, Whitman, 68 pgs. soft-c, 3 3/4" x 3 1/2", Pan-Am giveaway 23.00 57.50 160.00

nn- Chicken Greedy, nd(1930s), np (Whitman), 36 pgs., 3" x 2 1/2", Penny Book 4.00 10.00 22.00

nn- Chicken Licken, nd (1930s), np (Whitman), 36 pgs., 3" x 2 1/2", Penny Book 4.00 10.00 22.00

1101- Chief of the Rangers, 1935, Saalfield, hard-c, Tom Mix photo-c, movie scenes from "The Miracle Rider" 13.00 32.50 90.00

1581- Chief of the Rangers, 1935, Saalfield, soft-c, Tom Mix photo-c, movie scenes 13.00 32.50 90.00

Child's Garden of Verses (See Wee Little Books)

L14- Chip Collins' Adventures on Bat Island, 1935, Lynn, 192 pgs.
11.00 27.50 70.00

2025- Chitty Chitty Bang Bang, 1968, Whitman, movie photos
4.00 10.00 27.00

Chubby Little Books, 1935, Whitman, 3" x 2 1/2", 200 pgs.

W803- Golden Hours Story Book, The 5.00 12.50 30.00

W803- Story Hours Story Book, The 5.00 12.50 30.00

W804- Gay Book of Little Stories, The 5.00 12.50 30.00

W804- Glad Book of Little Stories, The 5.00 12.50 30.00

W804- Joy Book of Little Stories, The 5.00 12.50 30.00

W804- Sunny Book of Little Stories, The 5.00 12.50 30.00

1453- Chuck Malloy Railroad Detective on the Streamliner,1938, Whitman, 300 pgs. 8.00 20.00 50.00

Cinderella (See Walt Disney's...)

Clyde Beatty (See The Steel Arena)

1410- Clyde Beatty Daredevil Lion and Tiger Tamer, 1939, Whitman, 300 pgs. 12.00 30.00 80.00

1480- Coach Bernie Bierman's Brick Barton and the Winning Eleven, 1938, 300 pgs. 10.00 25.00 60.00

1446- Convoy Patrol (A Thrilling U.S. Navy Story), 1942, Whitman, 432 pgs., flip pictures 10.00 25.00 60.00

1127- Corley of the Wilderness Trail, 1937, Saalfield, hard-c
10.00 25.00 60.00

1607- Corley of the Wilderness Trail, 1937, Saalfield, soft-c
10.00 25.00 60.00

1- Count of Monte Cristo, 1934, EVW, 160 pgs., (Five Star Library), movie scenes, hard-c (Rare) 20.00 50.00 140.00

1457- Cowboy Lingo Boys' Book of Western Facts, 1938, Whitman, 300 pgs., Fred Harman-a 8.00 20.00 50.00

1171- Cowboy Malloy, 1940, Saalfield, 400 pgs. 7.00 17.50 40.00

1106- Cowboy Millionaire, 1935, Saalfield, movie scenes with George O'Brien, photo-c, hard-c 12.00 30.00 80.00

1586- Cowboy Millionaire, 1935, Saalfield, movie scenes with George O'Brien, photo-c, soft-c 12.00 30.00 80.00

724- Cowboy Stories, 1933, Whitman, 300 pgs., Hal Arbo-a
10.00 25.00 65.00

nn- Cowboy Stories, 1933, Whitman, 52 pgs., soft-c, premium-no ads, 4" x 5 1/2" Hal Arbo-a 12.00 30.00 80.00

1161- Crimson Cloak, The, 1939, Saalfield, 400 pgs.
10.00 25.00 60.00

L19- Curley Harper at Lakespur, 1935, Lynn, 192 pgs.
10.00 25.00 60.00

5785-2- Daffy Duck in Twice the Trouble, 1980, Whitman, 260 pgs., 79 cents soft-c 1.00 2.50 6.00

2018-(#18)-Daktari-Night of Terror, 1968, Whitman, 260 pgs., 39 cents, hard-c, color illos 4.00 10.00 27.00

1010- Dan Dunn And The Gangsters' Frame-Up, 1937, Whitman, 7 1/4" x 5 1/2", 64 pgs., Nickel Book 29.00 73.00 200.00

1116- Dan Dunn "Crime Never Pays," 1934, Whitman, 320 pgs., by Norman Marsh 8.00 20.00 50.00

1125- Dan Dunn on the Trail of the Counterfeiters, 1936, Whitman, 432 pgs., by Norman Marsh 8.00 20.00 50.00

1171- Dan Dunn and the Crime Master, 1937, Whitman, 432 pgs., by Norman Marsh 8.00 20.00 50.00

1417- Dan Dunn and the Underworld Gorillas, 1941, Whitman, All Pictures Comics, flip pictures, by Norman Marsh
8.00 20.00 50.00

1454- Dan Dunn on the Trail of Wu Fang, 1938, Whitman, 432 pgs., by Norman Marsh 10.00 25.00 65.00

1481- Dan Dunn and the Border Smugglers, 1938, Whitman, 432 pgs., by Norman Marsh 7.00 17.50 45.00

1492- Dan Dunn and the Dope Ring, 1940, Whitman, 432 pgs., by Norman Marsh 7.00 17.50 45.00

nn- Dan Dunn and the Bank Hold-Up, 1938, Whitman, 36 pgs., 2 1/2" x 3 1/2", Penny Book 8.00 20.00 50.00

nn- Dan Dunn and the Zeppelin Of Doom, 1938, Dell, 196 pgs., Fast-Action Story, soft-c 18.00 45.00 125.00

nn- Dan Dunn Meets Chang Loo, 1938, Whitman, 66 pgs., Pan-Am premium, by Norman Marsh 23.00 57.50 160.00

nn- Dan Dunn Plays a Lone Hand, 1938, Whitman, 36 pgs.,
2 1/2" x 3 1/2", Penny Book 8.00 20.00 50.00
3 3/4" x 3 1/2", Buddy book 24.00 60.00 170.00

6- Dan Dunn Secret Operative 48 and the Counterfeiter Ring, 1938, Whitman, 132 pgs., soft-c, 3 3/4" x 3 1/2", Buddy Book premium
24.00 60.00 170.00

9- Dan Dunn's Mysterious Ruse, 1936, Whitman, 132 pgs., soft-c, 3 1/2" x 3 1/2", Tarzan Ice Cream cup lid premium
24.00 60.00 170.00

1177- Danger Trail North, 1940, Saalfield, 400 pgs. 10.00 25.00 60.00

1151- Danger Trails in Africa, 1935, Whitman, 432 pgs.
12.00 30.00 80.00

nn- Daniel Boone, 1934, World Syndicate, High Lights of History Series, hard-c, All in Pictures 10.00 25.00 60.00

1160- Dan of the Lazy L, 1939, Saalfield, 400 pgs. 10.00 25.00 60.00

1148- David Copperfield, 1934, Whitman, hard-c, 160 pgs., photo-c, movie scenes (W. C. Fields) 12.00 30.00 80.00

nn- David Copperfield, 1934, Whitman, soft-c, 164 pgs., movie scenes
12.00 30.00 80.00

1151- Death by Short Wave, 1938, Saalfield 10.00 25.00 65.00

1156- Denny the Ace Detective, 1938, Saalfield, 400 pgs.
10.00 25.00 60.00

1431- Desert Eagle and the Hidden Fortress, The, 1941, Whitman, 432 pgs., flip pictures 10.00 25.00 65.00

1458- Desert Eagle Rides Again, The, 1939, Whitman, 300 pgs.
10.00 25.00 65.00

1136- Desert Justice, 1938, Saalfield, 400 pgs. 10.00 25.00 60.00

1484- Detective Higgins of the Racket Squad, 1938, Whitman, 432 pgs. 10.00 25.00 65.00

1124- Dickie Moore in the Little Red School House, 1936, Whitman, 240 pgs., photo-c, movie scenes (Chesterfield Motion Picts. Corp)
12.00 30.00 80.00

W-707- Dick Tracy the Detective, The Adventures of, 1933, Whitman, 320 pgs. (The 1st Big Little Book), by Chester Gould (Scarce) 188.00 470.00 1500.00

nn- Dick Tracy Detective, The Adventures of, 1933, Whitman, 52 pgs., 4" x 5 1/2", premium-no ads, soft-c, by Chester Gould
79.00 198.00 550.00

nn- Dick Tracy Detective, The Adventures of, 1933, Whitman, 52 pgs., 4" x 5 1/2", inside back-c & back-c ads for Sundial Shoes, soft-c, by Chester Gould 82.00 205.00 575.00

710- Dick Tracy and Dick Tracy, Jr. (The Advs. of ...), 1933, Whitman, 320 pgs., by Chester Gould 57.00 143.00 400.00

nn- Dick Tracy and Dick Tracy, Jr. (The Advs. of ...), 1933, Whitman, 52 pgs., premium-no ads, soft-c, 4" x 5 1/2", by Chester Gould
57.00 143.00 400.00

nn- Dick Tracy the Detective and Dick Tracy, Jr., 1933, Whitman, 52 pgs., premium-no ads, 3 1/2"x 5 1/4", soft-c, by Chester Gould
57.00 143.00 400.00

723- Dick Tracy Out West, 1933, Whitman, 300 pgs., by Chester Gould
26.00 65.00 185.00

749- Dick Tracy from Colorado to Nova Scotia, 1933, Whitman, 320 pgs., by Chester Gould 24.00 60.00 170.00

nn- Dick Tracy from Colorado to Nova Scotia, 1933, Whitman, 204 pgs., premium-no ads, soft-c, by Chester Gould 26.00 65.00 185.00

1105- Dick Tracy and the Stolen Bonds, 1934, Whitman, 320 pgs.,

1436 - Dick Tracy and the Mad Killer © NYNS

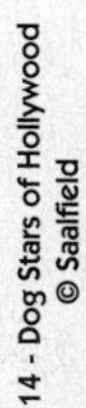

1114 - Dog Stars of Hollywood © Saalfield

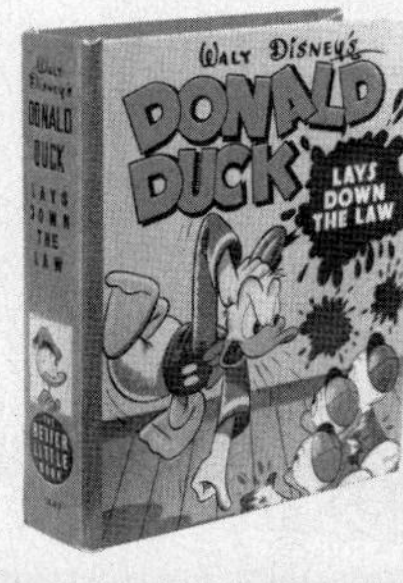

1449 - Donald Duck Lays Down the Law © DIS

GD FN VF/NM

by Chester Gould 14.00 35.00 100.00

1112- Dick Tracy and the Racketeer Gang, 1936, Whitman, 432 pgs., by Chester Gould 14.00 35.00 95.00

1137- Dick Tracy Solves the Penfield Mystery, 1934, Whitman, 320 pgs., by Chester Gould 14.00 35.00 100.00

nn- Dick Tracy Solves the Penfield Mystery, 1934, Whitman, 324 pgs., premium-no ads, 3-color, soft-c, by Chester Gould 36.00 90.00 250.00

1163- Dick Tracy and the Boris Arson Gang, 1935, Whitman, 432 pgs., by Chester Gould 15.00 37.50 105.00

1170- Dick Tracy on the Trail of Larceny Lu, 1935, Whitman, 432 pgs., by Chester Gould 14.00 35.00 95.00

1185- Dick Tracy in Chains of Crime, 1936, Whitman, 432 pgs., by Chester Gould 15.00 37.50 105.00

1412- Dick Tracy and Yogee Yamma, 1946, Whitman, 352 pgs., by Chester Gould 14.00 35.00 95.00

1420- Dick Tracy and the Hotel Murders, 1937, Whitman, 432 pgs., by Chester Gould 15.00 37.50 105.00

1434- Dick Tracy and the Phantom Ship, 1940, Whitman, 432 pgs., by Chester Gould 15.00 37.50 105.00

1436- Dick Tracy and the Mad Killer, 1947, Whitman, 288 pgs., by Chester Gould 13.00 32.50 90.00

1439- Dick Tracy and His G-Men, 1941, Whitman, 432 pgs., flip pictures, by Chester Gould 15.00 37.50 105.00

1445- Dick Tracy and the Bicycle Gang, 1948, Whitman, 288 pgs., by Chester Gould 13.00 32.50 90.00

1446- Detective Dick Tracy and the Spider Gang, 1937, Whitman, 240 pgs., scenes from "Adventures of Dick Tracy" serial 19.00 47.50 130.00

1449- Dick Tracy Special F.B.I. Operative, 1943, Whitman, 432 pgs. by Chester Gould 15.00 37.50 105.00

1454- Dick Tracy on the High Seas, 1939, Whitman, 432 pgs., by Chester Gould 15.00 37.50 105.00

1460- Dick Tracy and the Tiger Lilly Gang, 1949, Whitman, 288 pgs., by Chester Gould 13.00 32.50 90.00

1478- Dick Tracy on Voodoo Island, 1944, Whitman, 352 pgs., by Chester Gould 13.00 32.50 90.00

1479- Detective Dick Tracy Vs. Crooks in Disguise, 1939, Whitman, 432 pgs., flip pictures, by Chester Gould 15.00 37.50 105.00

1482- Dick Tracy and the Wreath Kidnapping Case, 1945, Whitman, 352 pgs. 14.00 35.00 95.00

1488- Dick Tracy the Super-Detective, 1939, Whitman, 432 pgs., by Chester Gould 15.00 37.50 105.00

1491- Dick Tracy the Man with No Face, 1938, Whitman, 432 pgs. 15.00 37.50 105.00

1495- Dick Tracy Returns, 1939, Whitman, 432 pgs., based on Republic Motion Picture serial, Chester Gould-a 15.00 37.50 105.00

2001- (#1)-Dick Tracy-Encounters Facey, 1967, Whitman, 260 pgs., 39 cents, hard-c, color illos 4.00 10.00 27.00

3912- Dick Tracy Big Little Book Picture Puzzles, 1938, Whitman, 7 1/2" x 10 1/4" box with 2 jigsaw puzzles 50.00 125.00 350.00
Variant set, same cover w/2 puzzles showing Dick Tracy & Jr. in crime lab & Dick Tracy patting down a gangster 50.00 125.00 350.00

4055- Dick Tracy, The Adventures of, 1934, Whitman, 7" x 9 1/2", 320 pgs., Big Big Book, by Chester Gould 57.00 143.00 400.00

4071- Dick Tracy and the Mystery of the Purple Cross, 1938, 7" x 9 1/2", 320 pgs., Big Big Book, by Chester Gould (Scarce) 50.00 125.00 350.00

nn- Dick Tracy and the Invisible Man, 1939, Whitman, 3 1/4" x 3 3/4", 132 pgs., stapled, soft-c, Quaker Oats premium; NBC radio play script, Chester Gould-a 37.00 93.00 260.00

Vol. 2- Dick Tracy's Ghost Ship, 1939, Whitman, 3 1/2" x 3 1/2", 132 pgs., soft-c, stapled, Quaker Oats premium; NBC radio play script episode from actual radio show; Gould-a 37.00 93.00 260.00

3- Dick Tracy Meets a New Gang, 1934, Whitman, 3" x 3 1/2", 132 pgs., soft-c, Tarzan Ice Cream cup lid premium 36.00 90.00 250.00

11- Dick Tracy in Smashing the Famon Racket, 1938, Whitman, 3 3/4" x 3 1/2", Buddy Book-ice cream premium, by Chester Gould 36.00 90.00 250.00

nn- Dick Tracy Gets His Man, 1938, Whitman, 36 pgs., 2 1/2" x 3 1/2", Penny Book 8.00 20.00 50.00

GD FN VF/NM

nn- Dick Tracy the Detective, 1938, Whitman, 36 pgs., 2 1/2" x 3 1/2", Penny Book 8.00 20.00 50.00

9- Dick Tracy and the Frozen Bullet Murders, 1941, Dell, 196 pgs., Fast-Action Story, soft-c, by Gould 37.00 93.00 260.00

6833- Dick Tracy Detective and Federal Agent, 1936, Dell, 244 pgs., Cartoon Story Books, hard-c, by Gould 39.00 98.00 275.00

nn- Dick Tracy Detective and Federal Agent, 1936, Dell, 244 pgs., Fast-Action Story, soft-c, by Gould 34.00 85.00 240.00

nn- Dick Tracy and the Blackmailers, 1939, Dell, 196 pgs., Fast-Action Story, soft-c, by Gould 34.00 85.00 240.00

nn- Dick Tracy and the Chain of Evidence, Detective, 1938, Dell, 196 pgs., Fast-Action Story, soft-c, by Chester Gould 34.00 85.00 240.00

nn- Dick Tracy and the Crook Without a Face, 1938, Whitman, 68 pgs., 3 1/4" x 3 1/2", Pan-Am giveaway, Gould-c/a 29.00 73.00 200.00

nn- Dick Tracy and the Maroon Mask Gang, 1938, Dell, 196 pgs., Fast-Action Story, soft-c, by Gould 34.00 85.00 240.00

nn- Dick Tracy Cross-Country Race, 1934, Whitman, 8 pgs., 2 1/2" x 3", Big Thrill chewing gum premium (6 diff.) 12.00 30.00 85.00

nn- Dick Whittington and his Cat, nd(1930s), np(Whitman), 36 pgs., Penny Book 3.00 7.50 20.00

Dinglehoofer und His Dog Adolph (See Top-Line Comics)

Dinky (See Jackie Cooper in ...)

1464- Dirigible ZR90 and the Disappearing Zeppelin (Captain Robb of ...), 1941, Whitman, 300 pgs., Al Lewin-a 14.00 35.00 100.00

1167- Dixie Dugan Among the Cowboys, 1939, Saalfield, 400 pgs. 10.00 25.00 65.00

1188- Dixie Dugan and Cuddles, 1940, Saalfield, 400 pgs., by Striebel & McEvoy 10.00 25.00 65.00

Doctor Doom (See Foreign Spies... & International Spy...)

Dog of Flanders, A (See Frankie Thomas in ...)

1114- Dog Stars of Hollywood, 1936, Saalfield, photo-c, photo-illos 12.00 30.00 75.00

1594- Dog Stars of Hollywood, 1936, Saalfield, photo-c, soft-c, photo-illos 12.00 30.00 75.00

nn- Dolls and Dresses Big Little Set, 1930s, Whitman, box contains 20 dolls on paper, 128 sheets of clothing to color & cut out, includes crayons 36.00 90.00 250.00

Donald Duck (See Silly Symphony... & Walt Disney's ...)

800- Donald Duck in Bringing Up the Boys, 1948, Whitman, hard-c, Story Hour series 10.00 25.00 65.00

1404- Donald Duck (Says Such a Life) (Disney), 1939, Whitman, 432 pgs., Taliaferro-a 19.00 47.50 130.00

1411- Donald Duck and Ghost Morgan's Treasure (Disney), 1946, Whitman, All Pictures Comics, Barks-a; reprints FC #9 24.00 60.00 165.00

1422- Donald Duck Sees Stars (Disney), 1941, Whitman, 432 pgs., flip pictures, Taliaferro-a 18.00 45.00 125.00

1424- Donald Duck Says Such Luck (Disney), 1941, Whitman, 432 pgs., flip pictures, Taliaferro-a 18.00 45.00 125.00

1430- Donald Duck Headed For Trouble (Disney), 1942, Whitman, 432 pgs., flip pictures, Taliaferro-a 18.00 45.00 125.00

1432- Donald Duck and the Green Serpent (Disney), 1947, Whitman, All Pictures Comics, Barks-a; reprints FC #108 20.00 50.00 140.00

1434- Donald Duck Forgets To Duck (Disney), 1939, Whitman, 432 pgs., Taliaferro-a 18.00 45.00 125.00

1438- Donald Duck Off the Beam (Disney), 1943, Whitman, 352 pgs., flip pictures, Taliaferro-a 18.00 45.00 125.00

1438- Donald Duck Off the Beam (Disney), 1943, Whitman, 432 pgs., flip pictures, Taliaferro-a 18.00 45.00 125.00

1449- Donald Duck Lays Down the Law, 1948, Whitman, 288 pgs., Barks-a 18.00 45.00 125.00

1457- Donald Duck in Volcano Valley (Disney), 1949, Whitman, 288 pgs., Barks-a 18.00 45.00 125.00

1462- Donald Duck Gets Fed Up (Disney), 1940, Whitman, 432 pgs.,Taliaferro-a 18.00 45.00 125.00

1478- Donald Duck-Hunting For Trouble (Disney), 1938, Whitman, 432 pgs., Taliaferro-a 18.00 45.00 125.00

1484- Donald Duck is Here Again!, 1944, Whitman, All Pictures Comics, Taliaferro-a 18.00 45.00 125.00

1486- Donald Duck Up in the Air (Disney), 1945, Whitman, 352 pgs., Barks-a 20.00 50.00 140.00

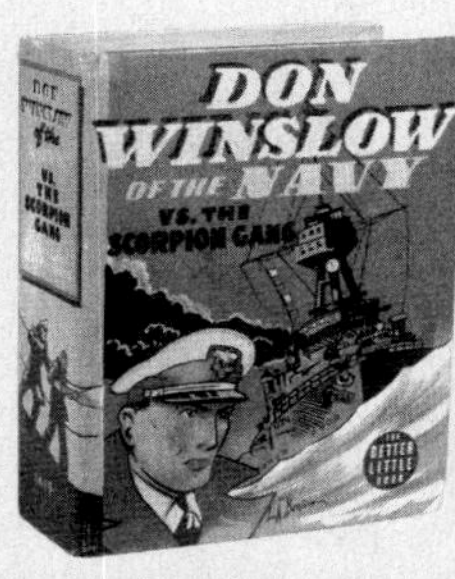

1419 - Don Winslow of the Navy Vs. the Scorpion Gang © WHIT

Ella Cinders Solves a Mystery © WHIT

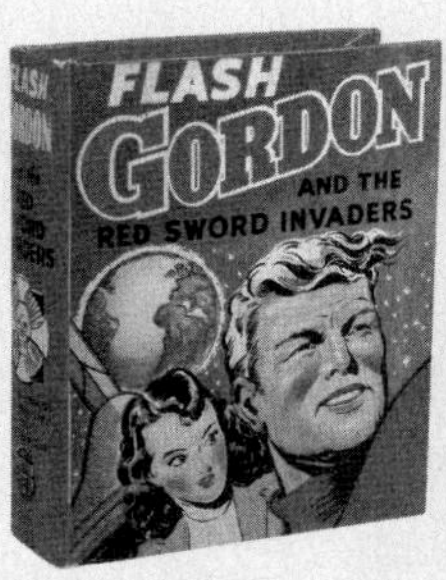

1479 - Flash Gordon and the Red Sword Invaders © KING

GD FN VF/NM

705-10- Donald Duck and the Mystery of the Double X, (Disney), 1949, Whitman, Barks-a 12.00 30.00 80.00
2033-(#33)- Donald Duck, Luck of the Ducks, 1969, Whitman, 256 pgs., hard-c, 39 cents, color illos. 4.00 10.00 22.00
2009-(#9)-Donald Duck-The Fabulous Diamond Fountain, (Walt Disney), 1967, Whitman, 260 pgs., 39 cents, hard-c, color illos 4.00 10.00 27.00
5756- Donald Duck-The Fabulous Diamond Fountain, (Walt Disney), 1973, Whitman, 260 pgs., 79 cents, soft-c, color illos 3.00 7.50 20.00
5756-1- Donald Duck-The Fabulous Diamond Fountain, (Walt Disney), 1973, Whitman, 260 pgs., 79 cents, soft-c, color illos 3.00 7.50 20.00
5756-2- Donald Duck-The Fabulous Diamond Fountain, (Walt Disney), 1973, Whitman, 260 pgs., 79 cents, soft-c, color illos 3.00 7.50 20.00
5760- Donald Duck in Volcano Valley (Disney), 1973, Whitman, 39 cents, flip-it book 3.00 7.50 20.00
5760-2- Donald Duck in Volcano Valley (Disney), 1973, Whitman, 79 cents, flip-it book 2.00 5.00 14.00
5764- Donald Duck, Luck of the Ducks, 1969, Whitman, 256 pgs., soft-c, 49 cents, color illos. 3.00 7.50 20.00
5773- Donald Duck - The Lost Jungle City, 1975, Whitman, 49 cents, flip-it book; 6 printings through 1980 2.00 5.00 14.00
nn- Donald Duck and the Ducklings, 1938, Dell, 194 pgs., Fast-Action Story, soft-c, Taliaferro-a 36.00 90.00 250.00
nn- Donald Duck Out of Luck (Disney), 1940, Dell, 196 pgs., Fast-Action Story, has Four Color #4 on back-c, Taliaferro-a 36.00 90.00 250.00
8- Donald Duck Takes It on the Chin (Disney), 1941, Dell, 196 pgs., Fast-Action Story, soft-c, Taliaferro-a 36.00 90.00 250.00
L13- Donnie and the Pirates, 1935, Lynn, 192 pgs. 10.00 25.00 60.00
1438- Don O'Dare Finds War, 1940, Whitman, 432 pgs. 10.00 25.00 60.00
1107- Don Winslow, U.S.N., 1935, Whitman, 432 pgs. 16.00 40.00 110.00
nn- Don Winslow, U.S.N., 1935, Whitman, 436 pgs., premium-no ads, 3-color, soft-c 19.00 47.50 130.00
1408- Don Winslow and the Giant Girl Spy, 1946, Whitman, 352 pgs. 12.00 30.00 75.00
1418- Don Winslow Navy Intelligence Ace, 1942, Whitman, 432 pgs., flip pictures 14.00 35.00 100.00
1419- Don Winslow of the Navy Vs. the Scorpion Gang, 1938, Whitman, 432 pgs. 14.00 35.00 100.00
1453- Don Winslow of the Navy and the Secret Enemy Base, 1943, Whitman, 352 pgs. 14.00 35.00 100.00
1489- Don Winslow of the Navy and the Great War Plot, 1940, Whitman, 432 pgs. 14.00 35.00 100.00
nn- Don Winslow U.S. Navy and the Missing Admiral, 1938, Whitman, 36 pgs., 2 1/2" x 3 1/2", Penny Book 7.00 17.50 40.00
1137- Doomed To Die, 1938, Saalfield, 400 pgs. 10.00 25.00 60.00
1140- Down Cartridge Creek, 1938, Saalfield, 400 pgs. 10.00 25.00 60.00
1416- Draftie of the U.S. Army, 1943, Whitman, All Pictures Comics 10.00 25.00 65.00
1100B- Dreams (Your dreams & what they mean), 1938, Whitman, 36 pgs., 2 1/2" x 3 1/2", Penny Book 3.00 7.50 20.00
24- Dumb Dora and Bing Brown, 1936, Lynn 11.00 27.50 70.00
1400- Dumbo, of the Circus - Only His Ears Grew! (Disney), 1941, Whitman, 432 pgs., based on Disney movie 18.00 45.00 125.00
10- Dumbo the Flying Elephant (Disney), 1944, Dell, 194 pgs., Fast-Action Story, soft-c 29.00 73.00 200.00
nn- East O' the Sun and West O' the Moon, nd (1930s), np (Whitman), 36 pgs., 3" x 2 1/2", Penny Book 3.00 7.50 20.00
774- Eddie Cantor in An Hour with You, 1934, Whitman, 154 pgs., 4 1/4" x 5 1/4", photo-c, movie scenes 12.00 30.00 85.00
nn- Eddie Cantor in Laughland, 1934, Goldsmith, 132 pgs., soft-c, photo-c, Vallely-a 12.00 30.00 85.00
1106- Ella Cinders and the Mysterious House, 1934, Whitman, 432 pgs. 12.00 30.00 75.00
nn- Ella Cinders and the Mysterious House, 1934, Whitman, 52 pgs., premium-no ads, soft-c, 3 1/2" x 5 3/4" 14.00 35.00 100.00
nn- Ella Cinders and the Mysterious House, 1934, Whitman, 52 pgs., Lemix Korlix desserts ad by Perkins Products Co. on back-c, soft-c, 3 1/2" x 5 3/4" 18.00 45.00 125.00
nn- Ella Cinders, 1935, Whitman, 148 pgs., 3 1/4" x 4", Tarzan Ice Cream cup lid premium 24.00 60.00 165.00
nn- Ella Cinders Plays Duchess, 1938, Whitman, 68 pgs., 3 3/4" x 3 1/2", Pan-Am Oil premium 16.00 40.00 115.00
nn- Ella Cinders Solves a Mystery, 1938, Whitman, 68 pgs., Pan-Am Oil premium, soft-c 16.00 40.00 115.00
11- Ella Cinders' Exciting Experience, 1934, Whitman, 3 1/2" x 3 1/2", 132 pgs., Tarzan Ice Cream cup lid giveaway 24.00 60.00 165.00
1406- Ellery Queen the Adventure of the Last Man Club, 1940, Whitman, 432 pgs. 12.00 30.00 80.00
1472- Ellery Queen the Master Detective, 1942, Whitman, 432 pgs., flip pictures 12.00 30.00 80.00
1081- Elmer and his Dog Spot, 1935, Saalfield, hard-c 8.00 20.00 50.00
1311- Elmer and his Dog Spot, 1935, Saalfield, soft-c 8.00 20.00 50.00
722- Erik Noble and the Forty-Niners, 1934, Whitman, 384 pgs. 8.00 20.00 50.00
nn- Erik Noble and the Forty-Niners, 1934, Whitman, 386 pgs., 3-color, soft-c (Rare) 36.00 90.00 250.00
684- Famous Comics (in open box), 1934, Whitman, 48 pgs., 3 3/4" x 8 1/2", (3 books in set): Book 1 - Katzenjammer Kids, Barney Google, & Little Jimmy
Book 2 - Polly and Her Pals, Little Jimmy, & Katzenjammer Kids
Book 3 - Little Annie Rooney, Katzenjammer Kids, & Polly and Her Pals
Complete set 50.00 125.00 350.00
2019-(#19)- Fantastic Four in the House of Horrors, 1968, Whitman, 256 pgs., hard-c, color illos. 4.00 10.00 27.00
5775 - Fantastic Four in the House of Horrors, 1976, Whitman, 256 pgs., soft-c, color illos. 3.00 7.50 20.00
5775-1 - Fantastic Four in the House of Horrors, 1976, Whitman, 256 pgs., soft-c, color illos. 3.00 7.50 20.00
1058- Farmyard Symphony, The (Disney), 1939, 5" X 5 1/2", 68 pgs., hard-c 11.00 27.50 70.00
1129- Felix the Cat, 1936, Whitman, 432 pgs., Messmer-a 24.00 60.00 170.00
1439- Felix the Cat, 1943, Whitman, All Pictures Comics, Messmer-a 21.00 52.50 150.00
1465- Felix the Cat, 1945, Whitman, All Pictures Comics, Messmer-a 18.00 45.00 125.00
nn- Felix (Flip book), 1967, World Retrospective of Animation Cinema, 188 pgs., 2 1/2" x 4" by Otto Messmer 4.00 10.00 27.00
nn- Fighting Cowboy of Nugget Gulch, The, 1939, Whitman, 2 1/2" x 3 1/2", Penny Book 4.00 10.00 25.00
1401- Fighting Heroes Battle for Freedom, 1943, Whitman, All Pictures Comics, from "Heroes of Democracy" strip, by Stookie Allen 8.00 20.00 50.00
6- Fighting President, The, 1934, EVW (Five Star Library), 160 pgs., photo-c, photo ill., F. D. Roosevelt 10.00 25.00 60.00
nn- Fire Chief Ed Wynn and "His Old Fire Horse," 1934, Goldsmith, 132 pgs., H. Vallely-a, photo, soft-c 10.00 25.00 60.00
1464- Flame Boy and the Indians' Secret, 1938, Whitman, 300 pgs., Sekakuku-a (Hopi Indian) 8.00 20.00 50.00
22- Flaming Guns, 1935, EVW, with Tom Mix, movie scenes
Hardcover 43.00 108.00 300.00
(Scarce) Softcover 50.00 125.00 350.00
1110- Flash Gordon on the Planet Mongo, 1934, Whitman, 320 pgs., by Alex Raymond 39.00 98.00 275.00
1166- Flash Gordon and the Monsters of Mongo, 1935, Whitman, 432 pgs., by Alex Raymond 37.00 93.00 260.00
nn- Flash Gordon and the Monsters of Mongo, 1935, Whitman, 436 pgs., premium-no ads, 3-color, soft-c, by Raymond 61.00 153.00 430.00
1171- Flash Gordon and the Tournaments of Mongo, 1935, Whitman, 432 pgs., by Alex Raymond 36.00 90.00 250.00
1190- Flash Gordon and the Witch Queen of Mongo, 1936,

1467 - Flint Roper and the Six-Gun Showdown © WHIT

1164 - Freckles and the Lost Diamond Mine © WHIT

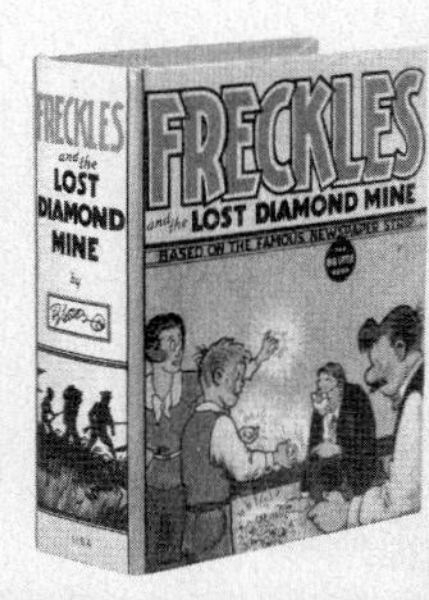

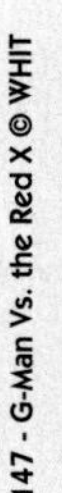
1147 - G-Man Vs. the Red X © WHIT

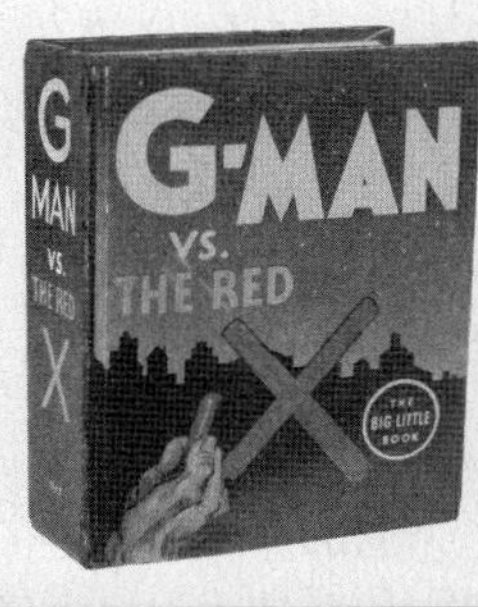

GD FN VF/NM

Whitman, 432 pgs., by Alex Raymond 36.00 90.00 250.00

1407- Flash Gordon in the Water World of Mongo, 1937, Whitman, 432 pgs., by Alex Raymond 31.00 78.00 215.00

1423- Flash Gordon and the Perils of Mongo, 1940, Whitman, 432 pgs., by Alex Raymond 29.00 73.00 200.00

1424- Flash Gordon in the Jungles of Mongo, 1947, Whitman, 352 pgs., by Alex Raymond 23.00 57.50 160.00

1443- Flash Gordon in the Ice World of Mongo, 1942, Whitman, 432 pgs., flip pictures, by Alex Raymond 30.00 75.00 210.00

1447- Flash Gordon and the Fiery Desert of Mongo, 1948, Whitman, 288 pgs., Raymond-a 23.00 57.50 160.00

1469- Flash Gordon and the Power Men of Mongo, 1943, Whitman, 352 pgs., by Alex Raymond 31.00 78.00 220.00

1479- Flash Gordon and the Red Sword Invaders, 1945, Whitman, 352 pgs., by Alex Raymond 29.00 73.00 200.00

1484- Flash Gordon and the Tyrant of Mongo, 1941, Whitman, 432 pgs., flip pictures, by Alex Raymond 31.00 78.00 220.00

1492- Flash Gordon in the Forest Kingdom of Mongo, 1938, Whitman, 432 pgs., by Alex Raymond 39.00 98.00 270.00

12- Flash Gordon and the Ape Men of Mor, 1942, Dell, 196 pgs., Fast-Action Story, by Alex Raymond 36.00 90.00 250.00

6833- Flash Gordon Vs. the Emperor of Mongo, 1936, Dell, 244 pgs., Cartoon Story Books, hard-c, Raymond-c/a 43.00 108.00 300.00

nn- Flash Gordon Vs. the Emperor of Mongo, 1936, Dell, 244 pgs., Fast-Action Story, soft-c, Alex Raymond-c/a 36.00 90.00 250.00

1467- Flint Roper and the Six-Gun Showdown, 1941, Whitman, 300 pgs. 10.00 25.00 60.00

2014-(#14)- Flintstones-The Case of the Many Missing Things, 1968, Whitman, 260 pgs., 39 cents, hard-c, color illos 4.00 10.00 27.00

nn- Flintstones: A Friend From the Past, 1977, Modern Promotions, 244 pgs., 49 cents, soft-c, flip pictures 2.00 5.00 11.00

nn- Flintstones: It's About Time, 1977, Modern Promotions, 244 pgs., 49 cents, soft-c, flip pictures 2.00 5.00 11.00

nn- Flintstones: Pebbles & Bamm-Bamm Meet Santa Claus, 1977, Modern Promotions, 244 pgs., 49 cents, soft-c, flip pictures 2.00 5.00 11.00

nn- Flintstones: The Great Balloon Race, 1977, Modern Promotions, 244 pgs., 49 cents, soft-c, flip pictures 2.00 5.00 11.00

nn- Flintstones: The Mystery of the Many Missing Things, 1977, Modern Promotions, 244 pgs., 49 cents, soft-c, flip pictures 2.00 5.00 11.00

2003-(#3)- Flipper-Killer Whale Trouble, 1967, Whitman, 260 pgs., hard-c, 39 cents, color illos 3.00 7.50 20.00

2032-(#32)- Flipper, Deep-Sea Photographer, 1969, Whitman, 256 pgs., hard-c, color illos. 3.00 7.50 20.00

1108- Flying the Sky Clipper with Winsie Atkins, 1936, Whitman, 432 pgs. 10.00 25.00 60.00

1460- Foreign Spies Doctor Doom and the Ghost Submarine, 1939, Whitman, 432 pgs., Al McWilliams-a 12.00 30.00 75.00

1100B- Fortune Teller, 1938, Whitman, 36 pgs., 2 1/2" x 3 1/2", Penny Book 3.00 7.50 20.00

1175- Frank Buck Presents Ted Towers Animal Master, 1935, Whitman, 432 pgs. 11.00 27.50 70.00

2015-(#15)-Frankenstein, Jr. - The Menace of the Heartless Monster, 1968, Whitman, 260 pgs., 39 cents, hard-c, color illos. 4.00 10.00 27.00

16- Frankie Thomas in A Dog of Flanders, 1935, EVW, movie scenes 12.00 30.00 75.00

1121- Frank Merriwell at Yale, 1935, 432 pgs. 10.00 25.00 60.00

Freckles and His Friends in the North Woods (See Top-Line Comics)

nn- Freckles and His Friends Stage a Play, 1938, Whitman, 36 pgs., 2 1/2" x 3 1/2", Penny Book 10.00 25.00 60.00

1164- Freckles and the Lost Diamond Mine, 1937, Whitman, 432 pgs., Merrill Blosser-a 11.00 27.50 70.00

nn- Freckles and the Mystery Ship, 1935, Whitman, 66 pgs., Pan-Am premium 12.00 30.00 75.00

1100B- Fun, Puzzles, Riddles, 1938, Whitman, 36 pgs., 2 1/2" x 3 1/2", Penny Book 3.00 7.50 20.00

1433- Gang Busters Step In, 1939, Whitman, 432 pgs., Henry E. Vallely-a 11.00 27.50 70.00

1437- Gang Busters Smash Through, 1942, Whitman, 432 pgs. 11.00 27.50 70.00

1451- Gang Busters in Action!, 1938, Whitman, 432 pgs. 11.00 27.50 70.00

nn- Gang Busters and Guns of the Law, 1940, Dell, 4" x 5", 194 pgs., Fast-Action Story, soft-c 27.00 68.00 190.00

nn- Gang Busters and the Radio Clues, 1938, Whitman, 36 pgs., 2 1/2" x 3 1/2", Penny Book 8.00 20.00 50.00

1409- Gene Autry and Raiders of the Range, 1946, Whitman, 352 pgs. 12.00 30.00 80.00

1425- Gene Autry and the Mystery of Paint Rock Canyon, 1947, Whitman, 288 pgs. 12.00 30.00 80.00

1428- Gene Autry Special Ranger, 1941, Whitman, 432 pgs., Erwin Hess-a 16.00 40.00 115.00

1433- Gene Autry in Public Cowboy No. 1, 1938, Whitman, 240 pgs., photo-c, movie scenes (1st Autry BLB) 29.00 73.00 200.00

1434- Gene Autry and the Gun-Smoke Reckoning, 1943, Whitman, 352 pgs. 16.00 40.00 110.00

1439- Gene Autry and the Land Grab Mystery, 1948, Whitman, 290 pgs. 12.00 30.00 75.00

1456- Gene Autry in Special Ranger Rule, 1945, Whitman, 352 pgs., Henry E. Vallely-a 16.00 40.00 110.00

1461- Gene Autry and the Red Bandit's Ghost, 1949, Whitman, 288 pgs. 11.00 27.50 70.00

1483- Gene Autry in Law of the Range, 1939, Whitman, 432 pgs. 16.00 40.00 110.00

1493- Gene Autry and the Hawk of the Hills, 1942, Whitman, 428 pgs., flip pictures, Vallely-a 16.00 40.00 110.00

1494- Gene Autry Cowboy Detective, 1940, Whitman, 432 pgs., Erwin Hess-a 16.00 40.00 110.00

700-10- Gene Autry and the Bandits of Silver Tip, 1949, Whitman 11.00 27.50 70.00

714-10- Gene Autry and the Range War, 1950, Whitman 11.00 27.50 70.00

nn- Gene Autry in Gun-Smoke, 1938, Dell, 196 pgs., Fast-Action story, soft-c 27.00 68.00 190.00

2035-(#35)- Gentle Ben, Mystery of the Everglades, 1969, Whitman, 256 pgs., hard-c, color illos. 3.00 7.50 20.00

1176- Gentleman Joe Palooka, 1940, Saalfield, 400 pgs. 10.00 25.00 60.00

George O'Brien (See The Cowboy Millionaire)

1101- George O'Brien and the Arizona Badman, 1936?, Whitman 10.00 25.00 60.00

1418- George O'Brien in Gun Law, 1938, Whitman, 240 pgs., photo-c, movie scenes, RKO Radio Pictures 10.00 25.00 60.00

1457- George O'Brien and the Hooded Riders, 1940, Whitman, 432 pgs., Erwin Hess-a 8.00 20.00 50.00

nn- George O'Brien and the Arizona Bad Man, 1939, Whitman, 36 pgs., 2 1/2" x 3 1/2", Penny Book 8.00 20.00 50.00

1462- Ghost Avenger, 1943, Whitman, 432 pgs., flip pictures, Henry Vallely-a 10.00 25.00 60.00

nn- Ghost Gun Gang Meet Their Match, The, 1939. Whitman, 2 1/2" x 3 1/2", Penny Book 8.00 20.00 50.00

nn- Gingerbread Boy, The, nd(1930s), np(Whitman), 36 pgs., Penny Book 2.00 5.00 15.00

1118- G-Man on the Crime Trail, 1936, Whitman, 432 pgs. 11.00 27.50 70.00

1147- G-Man Vs. the Red X, 1936, Whitman, 432 pgs. 12.00 30.00 80.00

1162- G-Man Allen, 1939, Saalfield, 400 pgs. 11.00 27.50 70.00

1173- G-Man in Action, A, 1940, Saalfield, 400 pgs., J.R. White-a 11.00 27.50 70.00

1434- G-Man and the Radio Bank Robberies, 1937, Whitman, 432 pgs. 12.00 30.00 80.00

1469- G-Man and the Gun Runners, The, 1940, Whitman, 432 pgs. 12.00 30.00 80.00

1470- G-Man vs. the Fifth Column, 1941, Whitman, 432 pgs., flip pictures 12.00 30.00 80.00

1493- G-Man Breaking the Gambling Ring, 1938, Whitman, 432 pgs., James Gary-a 12.00 30.00 80.00

nn- G-Man on Lightning Island, 1936, Dell, 244 pgs., Fast-Action Story,

8 - Great Expectations © EVW

17 - The Hoosier Schoolmaster © EVW

1435 - Jack Armstrong and the Ivory Treasure © WHIT

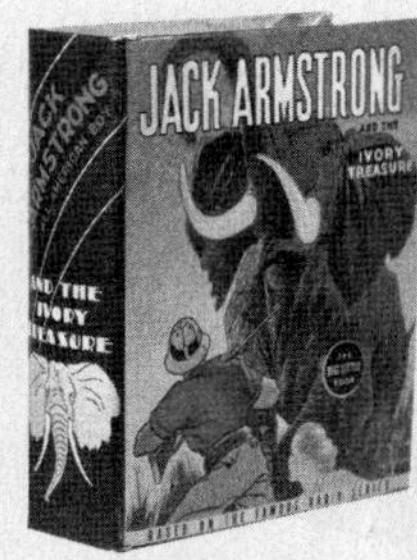

	GD	FN	VF/NM
soft-c, Henry E. Vallely-a	24.00	60.00	170.00
nn- G-Man, Underworld Chief, 1938, Whitman, Buddy Book premium,	29.00	73.00	200.00
6833- G-Man on Lightning Island, 1936, Dell, 244 pgs., Cartoon Story Book, hard-c, Henry E. Vallely-a	18.00	45.00	125.00
4- G-Men Foil the Kidnappers, 1936, Whitman, 132 pgs., 3 1/2" x 3 1/2", soft-c, Tarzan Ice Cream cup lid premium	24.00	60.00	165.00
1157- G-Men on the Trail, 1938, Saalfield, 400 pgs.	10.00	25.00	60.00
1168- G Men on the Job, 1935, Whitman, 432 pgs.	12.00	30.00	75.00
nn- G-Men on the Job Again, 1938, Whitman, 36 pgs., 2 1/2" x 3 1/2", Penny Book	10.00	25.00	60.00
nn- G-Men and Kidnap Justice, 1938, Whitman, 68 pgs., Pan-Am premium, soft-c	12.00	30.00	75.00
nn- G-Men and the Missing Clues, 1938, Whitman, 36 pgs., 2 1/2"x 3 1/2", Penny Book	10.00	25.00	60.00
1097- Go Into Your Dance, 1935, Saalfield, 160 pgs.. photo-c, movie scenes with Al Jolson & Ruby Keeler	13.00	32.50	90.00
1577- Go Into Your Dance, 1935, Saalfield, 160 pgs., photo-c, movie scenes, soft-c	13.00	32.50	90.00
2021- Goofy in Giant Trouble (Walt Disney's ...), 1968, Whitman, hard-c, 260 pgs., 39 cents, color illos.	3.00	7.50	20.00
5751- Goofy in Giant Trouble (Walt Disney's ...), 1968, Whitman, soft-c, 260 pgs., 39 cents, color illos.	3.00	7.50	20.00
5751-2- Goofy in Giant Trouble, 1968 (1980-reprint of '67 version), Whitman, soft-c, 260 pgs., 79 cents, B&W	1.00	2.50	8.00
8- Great Expectations, 1934, EVW, (Five Star Library), 160 pgs., photo-c, movie scenes	14.00	35.00	100.00
1453- Green Hornet Strikes!, The, 1940, Whitman, 432 pgs., Robert Weisman-a	34.00	85.00	240.00
1480- Green Hornet Cracks Down, The, 1942, Whitman, 432 pgs., flip pictures, Henry Vallely-a	31.00	78.00	220.00
1496- Green Hornet Returns, The, 1941, Whitman, 432 pgs., flip pictures	34.00	85.00	240.00
5778- Grimm's Ghost Stories, 1976, Whitman, 256 pgs., Laura French-s adapted from fairy tales; blue spine & back-c	2.00	5.00	13.00
5778-1- Grimm's Ghost Stories, 1976, Whitman, 256 pgs., reprint of #5778; yellow spine & back-c	2.00	5.00	13.00
1172- Gullivers' Travels, 1939, Saalfield, 320 pgs., adapted from Paramount Pict. Cartoons (Rare) Hardcover	26.00	65.00	180.00
(Scarce) Softcover	29.00	73.00	205.00
nn- Gumps In Radio Land, The (Andy Gump and the Chest of Gold), 1937, Lehn & Fink Prod. Corp., 100 pgs., 3 1/4" x 5 1/2", Pebeco Tooth Paste giveaway, by Gus Edson	20.00	50.00	140.00
nn- Gunmen of Rustlers' Gulch, The, 1939, Whitman, 36 pgs., 2 1/2" x 3 1/2", Penny Book	7.00	17.50	40.00
1426- Guns in the Roaring West, 1937, Whitman, 300 pgs.	7.00	17.50	40.00
1647- Gunsmoke (TV Series), 1958, Whitman, 280 pgs., 4 1/2" x 5 3/4"	5.00	12.50	30.00
1101- Hairbreath Harry in Department QT, 1935, Whitman, 384 pgs., by J. M. Alexander	10.00	25.00	65.00
1413- Hal Hardy in the Lost Land of Giants, 1938, Whitman, 300 pgs., "The World 1,000,000 Years Ago"	10.00	25.00	65.00
1159- Hall of Fame of the Air, 1936, Whitman, 432 pgs., by Capt. Eddie Rickenbacker	8.00	20.00	50.00
nn- Hansel and Grethel, The Story of, nd (1930s), no publ., 36 pgs., Penny Book	2.00	5.00	15.00
1145- Hap Lee's Selection of Movie Gags, 1935, Whitman, 160 pgs., photos of stars	13.00	32.50	90.00
Happy Prince, The (See Wee Little Books)			
1111- Hard Rock Harrigan-A Story of Boulder Dam, 1935, Saalfield, hard-c, photo-c, photo illos.	10.00	25.00	60.00
1591- Hard Rock Harrigan-A Story of Boulder Dam, 1935, Saalfield, soft-c, photo-c, photo illos.	10.00	25.00	60.00
1418- Harold Teen Swinging at the Sugar Bowl, 1939, Whitman, 432 pgs., by Carl Ed	10.00	25.00	60.00
nn- Hercules - The Legendary Journeys, 1998, Chronicle Books, 310 pgs., based on TV series, 1-color (brown) illos	1.00	2.50	9.00
1100B- Hobbies, 1938, Whitman, 36 pgs., 2 1/2" x 3 1/2", Penny Book	2.00	5.00	15.00

	GD	FN	VF/NM
1125- Hockey Spare, The, 1937, Saalfield, sports book	7.00	17.50	40.00
1605- Hockey Spare, The, 1937, Saalfield, soft-c	7.00	17.50	40.00
728- Homeless Homer, 1934, Whitman, by Dee Dobbin, for young kids	4.00	10.00	25.00
17- Hoosier Schoolmaster, The, 1935, EVW, movie scenes	13.00	32.50	90.00
715- Houdini's Big Little Book of Magic, 1927 (1933), 300 pgs.	14.00	35.00	95.00
nn- Houdini's Big Little Book of Magic, 1927 (1933), 196 pgs., American Oil Co. premium, soft-c	14.00	35.00	95.00
nn- Houdini's Big Little Book of Magic, 1927 (1933), 204 pgs., Cocomalt premium, soft-c	14.00	35.00	95.00
Huckleberry Finn (See The Adventures of...)			
nn- Huckleberry Hound Newspaper Reporter, 1977, Modern Promotions, 244 pgs., 49 cents, soft-c, flip pictures	2.00	5.00	13.00
1644- Hugh O'Brian TV's Wyatt Earp (TV Series), 1958, Whitman, 280 pgs.	5.00	12.50	30.00
5782-2- Incredible Hulk Lost in Time, 1980, 260 pgs., 79¢-c, soft-c, B&W	2.00	5.00	10.00
1424- Inspector Charlie Chan Villainy on the High Seas, 1942, Whitman, 432 pgs., flip pictures	14.00	35.00	95.00
1186- Inspector Wade of Scotland Yard, 1940, Saalfield, 400 pgs.	10.00	25.00	60.00
1194- Inspector Wade and The Feathered Serpent, 1939, Saalfield, 400 pgs.	10.00	25.00	60.00
1448- Inspector Wade Solves the Mystery of the Red Aces, 1937, Whitman, 432 pgs.	10.00	25.00	60.00
1148- International Spy Doctor Doom Faces Death at Dawn, 1937, Whitman, 432 pgs., Arbo-a	12.00	30.00	75.00
1155- In the Name of the Law, 1937, Whitman, 432 pgs., Henry E. Vallely-a	10.00	25.00	60.00
2012-(#12)-Invaders, The-Alien Missile Threat (TV Series), 1967, Whitman, 260 pgs., hard-c, 39 cents, color illos.	4.00	10.00	27.00
1403- Invisible Scarlet O'Neil, 1942, Whitman, All Pictures Comics, flip pictures	12.00	30.00	75.00
1406- Invisible Scarlet O'Neil Versus the King of the Slums, 1946, Whitman, 352 pgs.	10.00	25.00	60.00
1098- It Happened One Night, 1935, Saalfield, 160 pgs., Little Big Book, Clark Gable, Claudette Colbert photo-c, movie scenes from Academy Award winner	14.00	35.00	100.00
1578- It Happened One Night, 1935, Saalfield, 160 pgs., soft-c	14.00	35.00	100.00
Jack and Jill (See Wee Little Books)			
1432- Jack Armstrong and the Mystery of the Iron Key, 1939, Whitman, 432 pgs., Henry E. Vallely-a	12.00	30.00	85.00
1435- Jack Armstrong and the Ivory Treasure, 1937, Whitman, 432 pgs., Henry Vallely-a	12.00	30.00	85.00
Jackie Cooper (See Story Of..)			
1084- Jackie Cooper in Peck's Bad Boy, 1934, Saalfield, 160 pgs., hard, photo-c, movie scenes	15.00	37.50	105.00
1314- Jackie Cooper in Peck's Bad Boy, 1934, Saalfield, 160 pgs., soft, photo-c, movie scenes	15.00	37.50	105.00
1402- Jackie Cooper in "Gangster's Boy," 1939, Whitman, 240 pgs., photo-c, movie scenes	15.00	37.50	105.00
13- Jackie Cooper in Dinky, 1935, EVW, 160 pgs., movie scenes	15.00	37.50	105.00
nn- Jack King of the Secret Service and the Counterfeiters, 1939, Whitman, 36 pgs., 2 1/2" x 3 1/2", Penny Book, by John G. Gray	10.00	25.00	60.00
L11- Jack London's Call of the Wild, 1935, Lynn, 20th Cent. Pic., movie scenes with Clark Gable	12.00	30.00	80.00
nn- Jack Pearl as Detective Baron Munchausen, 1934, Goldsmith, 132 pgs., soft-c	12.00	30.00	85.00
1102- Jack Swift and His Rocket Ship, 1934, Whitman, 320 pgs.	16.00	40.00	110.00
1498- Jane Arden the Vanished Princess, Whitman, 300 pgs.	10.00	25.00	60.00
1179- Jane Withers in This is the Life (20th Century-Fox Presents...), 1935, Whitman, 240 pgs., photo-c, movie scenes	12.00	30.00	80.00

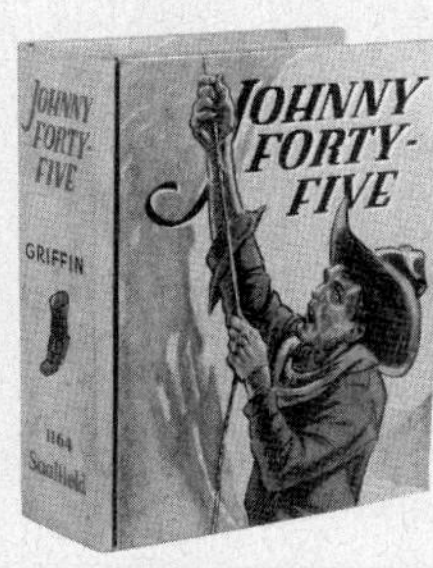

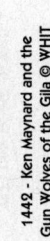

1164 - Johnny Forty-Five © Saalfield

1442 - Ken Maynard and the Gun Wolves of the Gila © WHIT

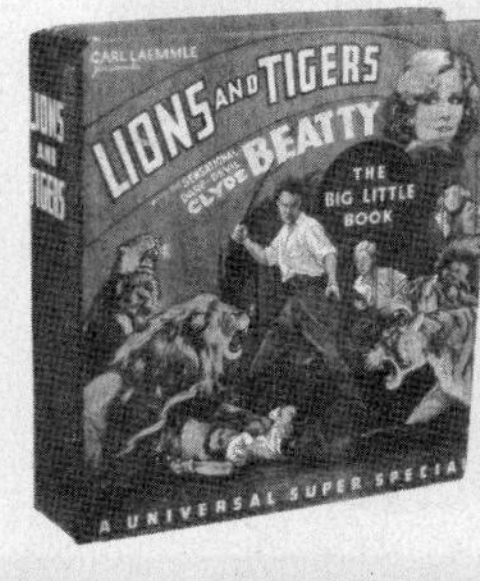

653 - Lions and Tigers (With Clyde Beatty) © WHIT

GD FN VF/NM

1463- Jane Withers in Keep Smiling, 1938, Whitman, 240 pgs., photo-c, movie scenes 12.00 30.00 80.00

Jaragu of the Jungle (See Rex Beach's ...)

1447- Jerry Parker Police Reporter and the Candid Camera Clue, 1941, Whitman, 300 pgs. 10.00 25.00 60.00

Jim Bowie (See Adventures of ...)

nn- Jim Brant of the Highway Patrol and the Mysterious Accident, 1939, Whitman, 36 pgs., 2 1/2" x 3 1/2", Penny Book 9.00 22.50 55.00

1466- Jim Craig State Trooper and the Kidnapped Governor, 1938, Whitman, 432 pgs. 10.00 25.00 60.00

nn- Jim Doyle Private Detective and the Train Hold-Up, 1939, Whitman, 36 pgs., 2 1/2" x 3 1/2", Penny Book 10.00 25.00 65.00

1180- Jim Hardy Ace Reporter, 1940, Saalfield, 400 pgs., Dick Moores-a 10.00 25.00 65.00

1143- Jimmy Allen in the Air Mail Robbery, 1936, Whitman, 432 pgs. 10.00 25.00 65.00

27- Jimmy Allen in The Sky Parade, 1936, Lynn, 130 pgs., 5 x 7 1/2", Paramount Pictures, movie scenes 12.00 30.00 75.00

L15- Jimmy and the Tiger, 1935, Lynn, 192 pgs. 10.00 25.00 65.00

1428- Jim Starr of the Border Patrol, 1937, Whitman, 432 pgs. 10.00 25.00 65.00

Joan of Arc (See Wee Little Books)

1105- Joe Louis the Brown Bomber, 1936, Whitman, 240 pgs., photo-c, photo-illos. 20.00 50.00 140.00

Joe Palooka (See Gentleman ...)

1123- Joe Palooka the Heavyweight Boxing Champ, 1934, Whitman, 320 pgs., Ham Fisher-a 18.00 45.00 125.00

1168- Joe Palooka's Great Adventure, 1939, Saalfield 14.00 35.00 100.00

nn- Joe Penner's Duck Farm, 1935, Goldsmith, Henry Vallely-a 11.00 27.50 70.00

1402- John Carter of Mars, 1940, Whitman, 432 pgs., John Coleman Burroughs-a 50.00 125.00 350.00

nn- John Carter of Mars, 1940, Dell, 194 pgs., Fast-Action Story, soft-c 64.00 160.00 450.00

1164- Johnny Forty Five, 1938, Saalfield, 400 pgs. 10.00 25.00 60.00

John Wayne (See Westward Ho!)

1100B- Jokes (A book of laughs galore), 1938, Whitman, 36 pgs., 2 1/2" x 3 1/2", Penny Book, laughing guy-c 2.00 5.00 15.00

1100B- Jokes (A book of side-splitting funny stories), 1938, Whitman, 36 pgs., 2 1/2" x 3 1/2", Penny Book, clowns on-c 2.00 5.00 15.00

2026-(#26)- Journey to the Center of the Earth, The Fiery Foe, 1968, Whitman 4.00 10.00 27.00

Jungle Jim (See Top-Line Comics)

1138- Jungle Jim, 1936, Whitman, 432 pgs., Alex Raymond-a 20.00 50.00 140.00

1139- Jungle Jim and the Vampire Woman, 1937, Whitman, 432 pgs., Alex Raymond-a 20.00 50.00 140.00

1442- Junior G-Men, 1937, Whitman, 432 pgs., Henry E. Vallely-a 11.00 27.50 70.00

nn- Junior G-Men Solve a Crime, 1939, Whitman, 36 pgs., 2 1/2" x 3 1/2", Penny Book 11.00 27.50 70.00

1422- Junior Nebb on the Diamond Bar Ranch, 1938, Whitman, 300 pgs., by Sol Hess 11.00 27.50 70.00

1470- Junior Nebb Joins the Circus, 1939, Whitman, 300 pgs. by Sol Hess 11.00 27.50 70.00

nn- Junior Nebb Elephant Trainer, 1939, Whitman, 68 pgs., Pan-Am Oil premium, soft-c 13.00 32.50 90.00

1052- "Just Kids" (Adventures of ...), 1934, Saalfield, oblong size, by Ad Carter 18.00 45.00 125.00

1094- Just Kids and the Mysterious Stranger, 1935, Saalfield, 160 pgs., by Ad Carter 13.00 32.50 90.00

1184- Just Kids and Deep-Sea Dan, 1940, Saalfield, 400 pgs., by Ad Carter 12.00 30.00 75.00

1302- Just Kids, The Adventures of, 1934, Saalfield, oblong size, soft-c, by Ad Carter 20.00 50.00 140.00

1324- Just Kids and the Mysterious Stranger, 1935, Saalfield, 160 pgs., soft-c, by Ad Carter , 13.00 32.50 90.00

1401- Just Kids, 1937, Whitman, 432 pgs., by Ad Carter 13.00 32.50 90.00

1055- Katzenjammer Kids in the Mountains, 1934, Saalfield, hard-c, oblong, H. H. Knerr-a 16.00 40.00 115.00

1305- Katzenjammer Kids in the Mountains, 1934, Saalfield, soft-c, oblong, H. H. Knerr-a 16.00 40.00 115.00

14- Katzenjammer Kids, The, 1942, Dell, 194 pgs., Fast-Action Story, H. H. Knerr-a 18.00 45.00 125.00

1411- Kay Darcy and the Mystery Hideout, 1937, Whitman, 300 pgs., Charles Mueller-a 12.00 30.00 80.00

1180- Kayo in the Land of Sunshine (With Moon Mullins), 1937, Whitman, 432 pgs., by Willard 13.00 32.50 90.00

1415- Kayo and Moon Mullins and the One Man Gang, 1939, Whitman, 432 pgs., by Frank Willard 11.00 27.50 70.00

7- Kayo and Moon Mullins 'Way Down South, 1938, Whitman, 132 pgs., 3 1/2" x 3 1/2", Buddy Book 21.00 52.50 150.00

1105- Kazan in Revenge of the North (James Oliver Curwood's...), 1937, Whitman, 432 pgs., Henry E. Vallely-a 11.00 25.00 60.00

1471- Kazan, King of the Pack (James Oliver Curwood's...), 1940, Whitman, 432 pgs. 9.00 22.50 55.00

1420- Keep 'Em Flying! U.S.A. for America's Defense, 1943, Whitman, 432 pgs., Henry E. Vallely-a, flip pictures 10.00 25.00 60.00

1133- Kelly King at Yale Hall, 1937, Saalfield 9.00 22.50 55.00

Ken Maynard (See Strawberry Roan & Western Frontier)

5- Ken Maynard in "Wheels of Destiny," 1934, EVW, 160 pgs., movie scenes (scarce) 20.00 50.00 140.00

776- Ken Maynard in "Gun Justice," 1934, Whitman, 160 pgs., hard-c, movie scenes (Universal Pic.) 14.00 35.00 95.00

776- Ken Maynard in "Gun Justice," 1934, Whitman, 160 pgs., soft-c, movie scenes (Universal Pic.) 14.00 35.00 95.00

1430- Ken Maynard in Western Justice, 1938, Whitman, 432 pgs., Irwin Myers-a 11.00 27.50 70.00

1442- Ken Maynard and the Gun Wolves of the Gila, 1939, Whitman, 432 pgs. 11.00 27.50 70.00

nn- Ken Maynard in Six-Gun Law, 1938, Whitman, 36 pgs., 2 1/2" x 3 1/2", Penny Book 9.00 22.50 55.00

1134- King of Crime, 1938, Saalfield, 400 pgs. 10.00 25.00 60.00

King of the Royal Mounted (See Zane Grey)

nn- Kit Carson, 1933, World Syndicate, by J. Carroll Mansfield, High Lights Of History Series, hard-c 10.00 25.00 60.00

nn- Kit Carson, 1933, World Syndicate, same as hard-c above but with a black cloth-c 10.00 25.00 60.00

1105- Kit Carson and the Mystery Riders, 1935, Saalfield, hard-c, Johnny Mack Brown photo-c, movie scenes 13.00 32.50 90.00

1585- Kit Carson and the Mystery Riders, 1935, Saalfield, soft-c, Johnny Mack Brown photo-c, movie scenes 13.00 32.50 90.00

Krazy Kat (See Adventures of...)

2004- (#4)-Lassie-Adventure in Alaska (TV Series), 1967, Whitman, hard-c, 260 pgs., 39 cents, color illos 4.00 10.00 27.00

5754- Lassie-Adventure in Alaska (TV Series), 1973, Whitman, soft-c, 260 pgs., 49 cents, color illos 2.00 5.00 15.00

2027- Lassie and the Shabby Sheik (TV Series), 1968, Whitman, hard-c, 260 pgs., 39 cents 4.00 10.00 25.00

5762- Lassie and the Shabby Sheik (TV Series), 1972, Whitman, soft-c, 260 pgs., 39 cents 2.00 5.00 15.00

5769- Lassie, Old One-Eye (TV Series), 1975, Whitman, soft-c, 260 pgs., 49 cents, three printings 2.00 5.00 15.00

1132- Last Days of Pompeii, The, 1935, Whitman, 5 1/4" x 6 1/4", 260 pgs., photo-c, movie scenes 12.00 30.00 85.00

1128- Last Man Out (Baseball), 1937, Saalfield, hard-c 10.00 25.00 60.00

L30- Last of the Mohicans, The, 1936, Lynn, 192 pgs., movie scenes with Randolph Scott, United Artists Pictures 12.00 30.00 80.00

1126- Laughing Dragon of Oz, The, 1934, Whitman 432 pgs., by Frank Baum (scarce) 86.00 215.00 600.00

1086- Laurel and Hardy, 1934, Saalfield, 160 pgs., hard-c, photo-c, movie scenes 21.00 52.50 145.00

1316- Laurel and Hardy, 1934, Saalfield, 160 pgs. soft-c, photo-c, movie scenes 21.00 52.50 145.00

1092- Law of the Wild, The, 1935, Saalfield, 160 pgs., photo-c, movie scenes of Rex, The Wild Horse & Rin-Tin-Tin Jr. 11.00 27.50 70.00

1120 - Little Miss Muffet © WHIT

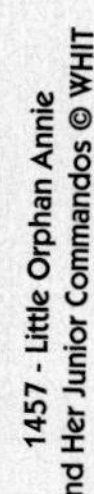
1457 - Little Orphan Annie and Her Junior Commandos © WHIT

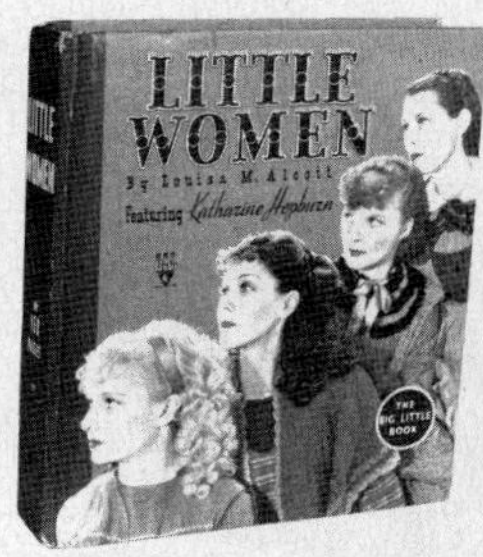
757 - Little Women © WHIT

GD FN VF/NM

1322- Law of the Wild, The, 1935, Saalfield, 160 pgs., photo-c, movie scenes, soft-c 11.00 27.50 70.00

1100B- Learn to be a Ventriloquist, 1938, Whitman, 36 pgs. 2 1/2" x 3 1/2", Penny Book 2.00 5.00 15.00

1149- Lee Brady Range Detective, 1938, Saalfield, 400 pgs. 9.00 22.50 55.00

L10- Les Miserables (Victor Hugo's ...), 1935, Lynn, 192 pgs., movie scenes 12.00 30.00 80.00

1441- Lightning Jim U.S. Marshal Brings Law to the West, 1940, Whitman, 432 pgs., based on radio program 10.00 25.00 65.00

nn- Lightning Jim Whipple U.S. Marshal in Indian Territory, 1939, Whitman, 36 pgs., 2 1/2" x 3 1/2", Penny Book 8.00 20.00 50.00

653- Lions and Tigers (With Clyde Beatty), 1934, Whitman, 160 pgs., photo-c movie scenes 12.00 30.00 85.00

1187- Li'l Abner and the Ratfields, 1940, Saalfield, 400 pgs., by Al Capp 14.00 35.00 95.00

1193- Li'l Abner and Sadie Hawkins Day, 1940, Saalfield, 400 pgs., by Al Capp 14.00 35.00 95.00

1198- Li'l Abner in New York, 1936, Whitman, 432 pgs., by Al Capp 15.00 37.50 105.00

1401- Li'l Abner Among the Millionaires, 1939, Whitman, 432 pgs., by Al Capp 15.00 37.50 105.00

1054- Little Annie Rooney, 1934, Saalfield, oblong - 4" x 8", All Pictures Comics, hard-c 14.00 35.00 100.00

1304- Little Annie Rooney, 1934, Saalfield, oblong - 4" x 8", All Pictures, soft-c 14.00 35.00 100.00

1117- Little Annie Rooney and the Orphan House, 1936, Whitman, 432 pgs. 11.00 27.50 70.00

1406- Little Annie Rooney on the Highway to Adventure, 1938, Whitman, 432 pgs. 11.00 27.50 70.00

1149- Little Big Shot (With Sybil Jason), 1935, Whitman, 240 pgs., photo-c, movie scenes 12.00 30.00 85.00

nn- Little Black Sambo, nd (1930s), np (Whitman), 36 pgs., 3" x 2 1/2", Penny Book 12.00 30.00 75.00

Little Bo-Peep (See Wee Little Books)

Little Colonel, The (See Shirley Temple)

1148- Little Green Door, The, 1938, Saalfield, 400 pgs. 10.00 25.00 60.00

1112- Little Hollywood Stars, 1935, Saalfield, movie scenes (Little Rascals, etc.), hard-c 12.00 30.00 85.00

1592- Little Hollywood Stars, 1935, Saalfield, movie scenes, soft-c 12.00 30.00 85.00

1087- Little Jimmy's Gold Hunt, 1935, Saalfield, 160 pgs., hard-c, Little Big Book, by Swinnerton 16.00 40.00 110.00

1317- Little Jimmy's Gold Hunt, 1935, Saalfield, 160 pgs., 4 1/4" x 5 3/4", soft-c, by Swinnerton 16.00 40.00 110.00

Little Joe and the City Gangsters (See Top-Line Comics)

Little Joe Otter's Slide (See Wee Little Books)

1118- Little Lord Fauntleroy, 1936, Saalfield, movie scenes, photo-c, 4 1/2" x 5 1/4", starring Mickey Rooney & Freddie Bartholomew, hard-c 10.00 25.00 60.00

1598- Little Lord Fauntleroy, 1936, Saalfield, photo-c, movie scenes, soft-c 10.00 25.00 60.00

1192- Little Mary Mixup and the Grocery Robberies, 1940, Saalfield 10.00 25.00 60.00

8- Little Mary Mixup Wins A Prize, 1936, Whitman, 132 pgs., 3 1/2" x 3 1/2", soft-c, Tarzan Ice Cream cup lid premium 24.00 60.00 165.00

1150- Little Men, 1934, Whitman, 4 3/4" x 5 1/4", movie scenes (Mascot Prod.), photo-c, hard-c 10.00 25.00 65.00

9- Little Minister, The,-Katharine Hepburn, 1935, 160 pgs., 4 1/4" x 5 1/2", EVW (Five Star Library), movie scenes (RKO) 14.00 35.00 100.00

1120- Little Miss Muffet, 1936, Whitman, 432 pgs., by Fanny Y. Cory 11.00 27.50 70.00

708- Little Orphan Annie, 1933, Whitman, 320 pgs., by Harold Gray, the 2nd Big Little Book 43.00 108.00 300.00

nn- Little Orphan Annie, 1928('33), Whitman, 52 pgs., 4" x 5 1/2", premium-no ads, soft-c, by Harold Gray 29.00 73.00 200.00

716- Little Orphan Annie and Sandy, 1933, Whitman, 320 pgs., by Harold Gray 24.00 60.00 170.00

GD FN VF/NM

716- Little Orphan Annie and Sandy, 1933, Whitman, 300 pgs., by Harold Gray 20.00 50.00 140.00

nn- Little Orphan Annie and Sandy, 1933, Whitman, 52 pgs., premium, no ads, 4" x 5 1/2", soft-c by Harold Gray 29.00 73.00 200.00

748- Little Orphan Annie and Chizzler, 1933, Whitman, 320 pgs., by Harold Gray 14.00 35.00 100.00

1010- Little Orphan Annie and the Big Town Gunmen, 1937, 7 1/4" x 5 1/2", 64 pgs., Nickel Book 12.00 30.00 85.00

nn- Little Orphan Annie with the Circus, 1934, Whitman, 320 pgs., same cover as L.O.A. 708 but with blue background, Ovaltine giveaway stamp inside front-c, by Harold Gray 36.00 90.00 250.00

1103- Little Orphan Annie with the Circus, 1934, Whitman, 320 pgs. 14.00 35.00 100.00

1140- Little Orphan Annie and the Big Train Robbery, 1934, Whitman, 300 pgs., by Gray 14.00 35.00 100.00

1140- Little Orphan Annie and the Big Train Robbery, 1934, Whitman, 300 pgs., premium-no ads, soft-c, by Harold Gray 26.00 65.00 180.00

1154- Little Orphan Annie and the Ghost Gang, 1935, Whitman, 432 pgs. by Harold Gray 14.00 35.00 100.00

nn- Little Orphan Annie and the Ghost Gang, 1935, Whitman, 436 pgs., premium-no ads, 3-color, soft-c, by Harold Gray 26.00 65.00 180.00

1162- Little Orphan Annie and Punjab the Wizard, 1935, Whitman, 432 pgs., by Harold Gray 14.00 35.00 100.00

1186- Little Orphan Annie and the $1,000,000 Formula, 1936, Whitman, 432 pgs., by Gray 13.00 32.50 90.00

1414- Little Orphan Annie and the Ancient Treasure of Am, 1939, Whitman, 432 pgs., by Gray 12.00 30.00 80.00

1416- Little Orphan Annie in the Movies, 1937, Whitman, 432 pgs., by Harold Gray 12.00 30.00 80.00

1417- Little Orphan Annie and the Secret of the Well, 1947, Whitman, 352 pgs., by Gray 11.00 27.50 70.00

1435- Little Orphan Annie and the Gooneyville Mystery, 1947, Whitman, 288 pgs., by Gray 12.00 30.00 75.00

1446- Little Orphan Annie in the Thieves' Den, 1949, Whitman, 288 pgs., by Harold Gray 12.00 30.00 75.00

1449- Little Orphan Annie and the Mysterious Shoemaker, 1938, Whitman, 432 pgs., by Harold Gray 12.00 30.00 85.00

1457- Little Orphan Annie and Her Junior Commandos, 1943, Whitman, 352 pgs., by H. Gray 10.00 25.00 60.00

1461- Little Orphan Annie and the Underground Hide-Out, 1945, Whitman, 352 pgs., by Gray 10.00 25.00 60.00

1468- Little Orphan Annie and the Ancient Treasure of Am, 1949 (Misdated 1939), 288 pgs., by Gray 10.00 25.00 60.00

1482- Little Orphan Annie and the Haunted Mansion, 1941, Whitman, 432 pgs., flip pictures, by Harold Gray 12.00 30.00 80.00

3048- Little Orphan Annie and Her Big Little Kit, 1937, Whitman, 384 pgs., 4 1/2" x 6 1/2" box, includes miniature box of 4 crayons-red, yellow, blue and green 64.00 160.00 450.00

4054- Little Orphan Annie, The Story of, 1934, Whitman, 7" x 9 1/2", 320 pgs., Big Big Book, Harold Gray-c/a 30.00 75.00 210.00

nn- Little Orphan Annie Gets into Trouble, 1938, Whitman, 36 pgs., 2 1/2" x 3 1/2", Penny Book 9.00 22.50 55.00

nn- Little Orphan Annie in Hollywood, 1937, Whitman, 3 1/2" x 3 1/4", Pan-Am premium, soft-c 23.00 57.50 160.00

nn- Little Orphan Annie in Rags to Riches, 1939, Dell, 194 pgs., Fast-Action Story, soft-c 26.00 65.00 180.00

nn- Little Orphan Annie Saves Sandy, 1938, Whitman, 36 pgs., 2 1/2" x 3 1/2", Penny Book 10.00 25.00 60.00

nn- Little Orphan Annie Under the Big Top, 1938, Dell, 194 pgs., Fast-Action Story, soft-c 25.00 62.50 175.00

nn- Little Orphan Annie Wee Little Books (In open box) nn, 1934, Whitman, 44 pgs., by H. Gray

	GD	FN	VF/NM
L.O.A. And Daddy Warbucks	9.00	22.50	55.00
L.O.A. And Her Dog Sandy	9.00	22.50	55.00
L.O.A. And The Lucky Knife	9.00	22.50	55.00
L.O.A. And The Pinch-Pennys	9.00	22.50	55.00
L.O.A. At Happy Home	9.00	22.50	55.00
L.O.A. Finds Mickey	9.00	22.50	55.00
Complete set with box	57.00	143.00	400.00

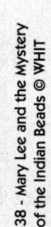

5774 - The Lone Ranger Outwits Crazy Cougar © Lone Ranger Inc.

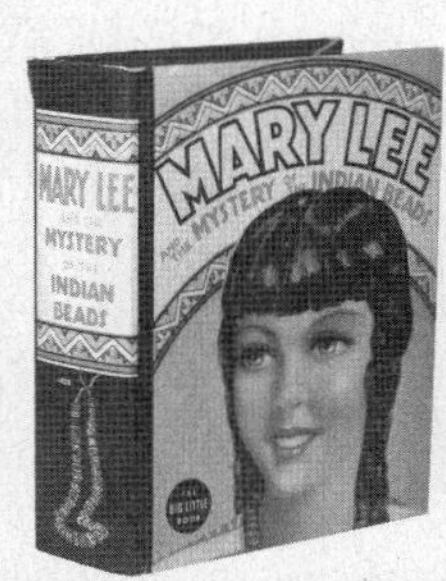

1438 - Mary Lee and the Mystery of the Indian Beads © WHIT

1187 - Mickey Mouse and the Sacred Jewel © DIS

GD FN VF/NM

nn- Little Polly Flinders, The Story of, nd (1930s), no publ., 36 pgs., 2 1/2" x 3", Penny Book 2.00 5.00 15.00

nn- Little Red Hen, The, nd(1930s), np(Whitman), 36 pgs., Penny Book 2.00 5.00 15.00

nn- Little Red Riding Hood, nd(1930s), np(Whitman), 36 pgs., 3" x 2 1/2", Penny Book 2.00 5.00 15.00

nn- Little Red Riding Hood and the Big Bad Wolf (Disney), 1934, McKay, 36 pgs., stiff-c, Disney Studio-a
Sized (7 3/4" x 10") 24.00 60.00 170.00
Different version (6 1/4" x 8 1/2") blue spine 16.00 40.00 115.00

757- Little Women, 1934, Whitman, 4 3/4" x 5 1/4", 160 pgs., photo-c, movie scenes, starring Katharine Hepburn 14.00 35.00 100.00

Littlest Rebel, The (See Shirley Temple)

1181- Lone Ranger and his Horse Silver, 1935, Whitman, 432 pgs., Hal Arbo-a 20.00 50.00 140.00

1196- Lone Ranger and the Vanishing Herd, 1936, Whitman, 432 pgs. 16.00 40.00 110.00

1407- Lone Ranger and Dead Men's Mine, The, 1939, Whitman, 432 pgs. 14.00 35.00 100.00

1421- Lone Ranger on the Barbary Coast, The, 1944, Whitman, 352 pgs., Henry Vallely-a 12.00 30.00 80.00

1428- Lone Ranger and the Secret Weapon, The, 1943, Whitman, 12.00 30.00 80.00

1431- Lone Ranger and the Secret Killer, The, 1937, Whitman 432 pgs., H. Anderson-a 16.00 40.00 110.00

1450- Lone Ranger and the Black Shirt Highwayman, The, 1939, Whitman, 432 pgs. 14.00 35.00 100.00

1465- Lone Ranger and the Menace of Murder Valley, The, 1938, Whitman, 432 pgs., Robert Wiseman-a 13.00 32.50 90.00

1468- Lone Ranger Follows Through, The, 1941, Whitman, 432 pgs., H.E. Vallely-a 13.00 32.50 90.00

1477- Lone Ranger and the Great Western Span, The, 1942, Whitman, 424 pgs., H. E. Vallely-a 12.00 30.00 80.00

1489- Lone Ranger and the Red Renegades, The, 1939, Whitman, 432 pgs. 16.00 40.00 110.00

1498- Lone Ranger and the Silver Bullets, 1946, Whitman, 352 pgs., Henry E. Vallely-a 12.00 30.00 80.00

712-10- Lone Ranger and the Secret of Somber Cavern, The, 1950, Whitman 10.00 25.00 65.00

2013- (#13)-Lone Ranger Outwits Crazy Cougar, The, 1968, Whitman, 260 pgs., 39 cents, hard-c, color illos 4.00 10.00 27.00

5774- Lone Ranger Outwits Crazy Cougar, The, 1976, Whitman, 260 pgs., 49 cents, soft-c, color illos 4.00 10.00 22.00

5774-1- Lone Ranger Outwits Crazy Cougar, The, 1979, Whitman, 260 pgs., 69 cents, soft-c, color illos 4.00 10.00 22.00

nn- Lone Ranger and the Lost Valley, The, 1938, Dell, 196 pgs., Fast-Action Story, soft-c 26.00 65.00 180.00

1405- Lone Star Martin of the Texas Rangers, 1939, Whitman, 432 pgs. 12.00 30.00 85.00

19- Lost City, The, 1935, EVW, movie scenes 12.00 30.00 80.00

1103- Lost Jungle, The (With Clyde Beatty), 1936, Saalfield, movie scenes, hard-c 12.00 30.00 80.00

1583- Lost Jungle, The (With Clyde Beatty), 1936, Saalfield, movie scenes, soft -c 11.00 27.50 70.00

753- Lost Patrol, The, 1934, Whitman, 160 pgs., photo-c, movie scenes with Boris Karloff 12.00 30.00 75.00

nn- Lost World, The - Jurassic Park 2, 1997, Chronicle Books, 312 pgs., adapts movie, 1-color (green) illos 3.00 7.50 20.00

1189- Mac of the Marines in Africa, 1936, Whitman, 432 pgs. 10.00 25.00 60.00

1400- Mac of the Marines in China, 1938, Whitman, 432 pgs. 10.00 25.00 60.00

1100B- Magic Tricks (With explanations), 1938, Whitman, 36 pgs., 2 1/2" x 3 1/2", Penny Book, rabbit in hat-c 2.00 5.00 15.00

1100B- Magic Tricks (How to do them), 1938, Whitman, 36 pgs., 2 1/2" x 3 1/2", Penny Book, genie-c 2.00 5.00 15.00

Major Hoople (See Our Boarding House)

2022-(#22)- Major Matt Mason, Moon Mission, 1968, Whitman, 256 pgs., hard-c, color illos. 4.00 10.00 27.00

1167- Mandrake the Magician, 1935, Whitman, 432 pgs., by Lee Falk & Phil Davis 16.00 40.00 110.00

GD FN VF/NM

1418- Mandrake the Magician and the Flame Pearls, 1946, Whitman, 352 pgs., by Lee Falk & Phil Davis 12.00 30.00 85.00

1431- Mandrake the Magician and the Midnight Monster, 1939, Whitman, 432 pgs., by Lee Falk & Phil Davis 14.00 35.00 95.00

1454- Mandrake the Magician Mighty Solver of Mysteries, 1941, Whitman, 432 pgs., by Lee Falk & Phil Davis, flip pictures 14.00 35.00 95.00

2011-(#11)-Man From U.N.C.L.E., The-The Calcutta Affair (TV Series), 1967, Whitman, 260 pgs., 39¢, hard-c, color illos 4.00 10.00 27.00

1429- Marge's Little Lulu Alvin and Tubby, 1947, Whitman, All Pictures Comics, Stanley-a 27.00 68.00 190.00

1438- Mary Lee and the Mystery of the Indian Beads, 1937, Whitman, 300 pgs. 10.00 25.00 60.00

1165- Masked Man of the Mesa, The, 1939, Saalfield, 400 pgs. 9.00 22.50 55.00

nn- Mask of Zorro, The, 1998, Chronicle Books, 312 pgs., adapts movie, 1-color (yellow-green) illos 1.00 2.50 9.00

1436- Maximo the Amazing Superman, 1940, Whitman, 432 pgs., Henry E. Vallely-a 12.00 30.00 80.00

1444- Maximo the Amazing Superman and the Crystals of Doom, 1941, Whitman,432 pgs., Henry E. Vallely-a 12.00 30.00 80.00

1445- Maximo the Amazing Superman and the Supermachine, 1941, Whitman, 432 pgs. 12.00 30.00 80.00

755- Men of the Mounted, 1934, Whitman, 320 pgs. 12.00 30.00 80.00

nn- Men of the Mounted, 1933, Whitman, 52 pgs., 3 1/2" x 5 3/4", premium-no ads; other versions with Poll Parrot & Perkins ad; soft-c 14.00 35.00 100.00

nn- Men of the Mounted, 1934, Whitman, Cocomalt premium, soft-c, by Ted McCall 10.00 25.00 60.00

1475- Men With Wings, 1938, Whitman, 240 pgs., photo-c, movie scenes (Paramount Pics.) 12.00 30.00 85.00

1170- Mickey Finn, 1940, Saalfield, 400 pgs., by Frank Leonard 10.00 25.00 865.00

717- Mickey Mouse (Disney), (1st printing) 1933, Whitman, 320 pgs., Gottfredson-a, skinny Mickey on cover 235.00 588.00 2000.00

717- Mickey Mouse (Disney), (2nd printing)1933, Whitman, 320 pgs., Gottfredson-a, regular Mickey on cover 150.00 375.00 1200.00

nn- Mickey Mouse (Disney), 1933, Dean & Son, Great Big Midget Book, 320 pgs. 123.00 308.00 900.00

731- Mickey Mouse the Mail Pilot (Disney), 1933, Whitman, (This is the same book as the 1st Mickey Mouse BLB #717(2nd printing) but with "The Mail Pilot" printed on the front. Lower left of back cover has a small box printed over the existing "No. 717." "No. 731" is printed next to it.) (Sold at auction in 2014 in VG+ condition for $7170, and in FR/GD condition for $2,500)

726- Mickey Mouse in Blaggard Castle (Disney), 1934, Whitman, 320 pgs., Gottfredson-a 30.00 75.00 210.00

731- Mickey Mouse the Mail Pilot (Disney), 1933, Whitman, 300 pgs., Gottfredson-a 30.00 75.00 210.00

731- Mickey Mouse the Mail Pilot (Disney), 1933, Whitman, 300 pgs., soft cover; Gottfredson-a (Rare) 64.00 160.00 450.00

nn- Mickey Mouse the Mail Pilot (Disney), 1933, Whitman, 292 pgs., American Oil Co. premium, soft-c, Gottfredson-a; another version 3 1/2" x 4 3/4" 30.00 75.00 210.00

nn- Mickey Mouse the Mail Pilot (Disney), 1933, Dean & Son, Great Big Midget Book (Rare) 124.00 310.00 925.00

750- Mickey Mouse Sails for Treasure Island (Disney), 1933, Whitman, 320 pgs., Gottfredson-a 30.00 75.00 210.00

nn- Mickey Mouse Sails for Treasure Island (Disney), 1935, Whitman, 196 pgs., premium-no ads, soft-c, Gottfredson-a (Scarce) 36.00 90.00 250.00

nn- Mickey Mouse Sails for Treasure Island (Disney), 1935, Whitman, 196 pgs., Kolynos Dental Cream premium (Scarce) 36.00 90.00 250.00

nn- Mickey Mouse Sails for Treasure Island (Disney), 1933, Dean & Son, Great Big Midget Book, 320 pgs. 114.00 285.00 800.00

756- Mickey Mouse Presents a Walt Disney Silly Symphony (Disney), 1934, Whitman, 240 pgs., Bucky Bug app. 29.00 73.00 200.00

801- Mickey Mouse's Summer Vacation, 1948, Whitman, hard-c, Story Hour series 12.00 30.00 85.00

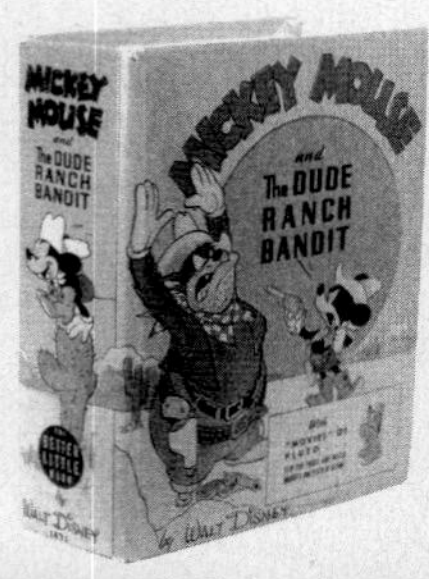
1471 - Mickey Mouse and the Dude Ranch Bandit © DIS

1058 - Mother Pluto © DIS

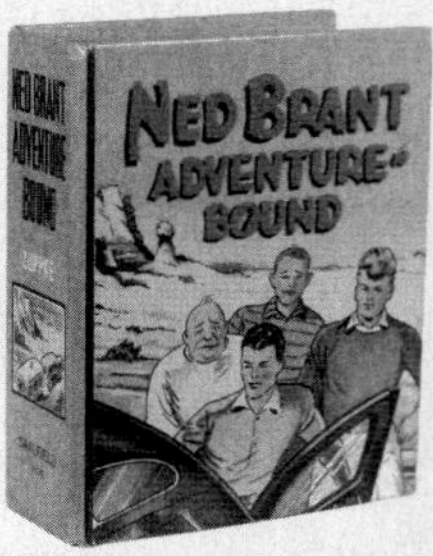
1179 - Ned Brant Adventure Bound © Saalfield

GD FN VF/NM

1058- Mickey Mouse Box, The (Disney), 1939, Whitman, 10" x 11 1/2" x 1", (set includes 6 books from the 1058 series, all 5" x 5 1/2", 68 pgs. Lid features Mickey & Minnie, Donald Duck, Goofy and Clarabelle Cow. The six books are: The Brave Little Tailor, Mother Pluto, The Ugly Ducklings, The Practical Pig, Timid Elmer, and The Farmyard Symphony (a VF set sold for $5175 in Nov, 2014)

1111- Mickey Mouse Presents Walt Disney's Silly Symphonies Stories, 1936, Whitman, 432 pgs., Donald Duck app. 29.00 73.00 200.00

1128- Mickey Mouse and Pluto the Racer (Disney), 1936, Whitman, 432 pgs., Gottfredson-a 24.00 60.00 170.00

1139- Mickey Mouse the Detective (Disney), 1934, Whitman, 300 pgs., Gottfredson-a 29.00 73.00 200.00

1139- Mickey Mouse the Detective (Disney), 1934, Whitman, 304 pgs., premium-no ads, soft-c, Gottfredson-a (Scarce) 43.00 108.00 300.00

1153- Mickey Mouse and the Bat Bandit (Disney), 1935, Whitman, 432 pgs., Gottfredson-a 26.00 65.00 180.00

nn- Mickey Mouse and the Bat Bandit (Disney), 1935, Whitman, 436 pgs., premium-no ads, 3-color, soft-c, Gottfredson-a (Scarce) 43.00 108.00 300.00

1160- Mickey Mouse and Bobo the Elephant (Disney), 1935, Whitman, 432 pgs., Gottfredson-a 26.00 65.00 180.00

1187- Mickey Mouse and the Sacred Jewel (Disney), 1936, Whitman, 432 pgs., Gottfredson-a 24.00 60.00 170.00

1401- Mickey Mouse in the Treasure Hunt (Disney), 1941, Whitman, 430 pgs., flip pictures of Pluto, Gottfredson-a 22.00 52.50 155.00

1409- Mickey Mouse Runs His Own Newspaper (Disney), 1937, Whitman, 432 pgs., Gottfredson-a 22.00 52.50 155.00

1413- Mickey Mouse and the 'Lectro Box (Disney), 1946, Whitman, 352 pgs., Gottfredson-a 16.00 40.00 115.00

1417- Mickey Mouse on Sky Island (Disney), 1941, Whitman, 432 pgs., flip pictures, Gottfredson-a; considered by Gottfredson to be his best Mickey story 22.00 52.50 155.00

1428- Mickey Mouse in the Foreign Legion (Disney), 1940, Whitman, 432 pgs., Gottfredson-a 22.00 52.50 155.00

1429- Mickey Mouse and the Magic Lamp (Disney), 1942, Whitman, 432 pgs., flip pictures 22.00 52.50 155.00

1433- Mickey Mouse and the Lazy Daisy Mystery (Disney), 1947, Whitman, 288 pgs. 16.00 40.00 115.00

1444- Mickey Mouse in the World of Tomorrow (Disney), 1948, Whitman, 288 pgs., Gottfredson-a 24.00 60.00 170.00

1451- Mickey Mouse and the Desert Palace (Disney), 1948, Whitman, 288 pgs. 16.00 40.00 115.00

1463- Mickey Mouse and the Pirate Submarine (Disney), 1939, Whitman, 432 pgs., Gottfredson-a 22.00 52.50 155.00

1464- Mickey Mouse and the Stolen Jewels (Disney), 1949, Whitman, 288 pgs. 21.00 52.50 145.00

1471- Mickey Mouse and the Dude Ranch Bandit (Disney), 1943, Whitman, 432 pgs., flip pictures 22.00 52.50 155.00

1475- Mickey Mouse and the 7 Ghosts (Disney), 1940, Whitman, 432 pgs., Gottfredson-a 22.00 52.50 155.00

1476- Mickey Mouse in the Race for Riches (Disney), 1938, Whitman, 432 pgs., Gottfredson-a 22.00 52.50 155.00

1483- Mickey Mouse Bell Boy Detective (Disney), 1945, Whitman, 352 pgs. 21.00 52.50 145.00

1499- Mickey Mouse on the Cave-Man Island (Disney), 1944, Whitman, 352 pgs. 21.00 52.50 145.00

2004- Mickey Mouse With This Big Big Color Set, Here Comes (Disney), 1936, Whitman, (Very Rare), 224 pgs., 12" x 8 1/4" box, with red, yellow and blue crayons, contains 224 loose pages to color, reprinted from early Mickey Mouse related movie and strip reprints. Attached to center of lid is a 5" tall separate die-cut cardboard Mickey Mouse figure (a VF/NM set sold for $1701 in July 2014) 235.00 588.00 2000.00

2020-(#20)- Mickey Mouse, Adventure in Outer Space, 1968, Whitman, 256 pgs.,hard-c, color illos. 4.00 10.00 27.00

3059- Mickey Mouse Big Little Set (Disney), 1936, Whitman, 8 1/4" x 8 1/2", with crayons, box contains a 4" x 5 1/4" soft-c book with 160 pgs. of Mickey to color, reprinted from early Mickey Mouse BLBs, (Rare) (a copy in NM sold for $1897 in Nov, 2011, a VF copy sold for $1147 in 2013)

5750- Mickey Mouse, Adventure in Outer Space, 1973, Whitman, 256 pgs.,soft-c, 39 cents, color illos. 2.00 5.00 15.00

3049- Mickey Mouse and His Big Little Kit (Disney), 1937, Whitman, 384 pgs., 4 1/2" x 6 1/2" box, includes miniature box of 4 crayons-red, yellow, blue and green (a copy in VF/NM sold for $335 in 2015)

3061- Mickey Mouse to Draw and Color (The Big Little Set), nd (early 1930s), Whitman, with crayons; box contains 320 loose pages to color, reprinted from early Mickey Mouse BLBs 123.00 308.00 880.00

4062- Mickey Mouse, The Story Of, 1935, Whitman, 7" x 9 1/2", 320 pgs., Big Big Book, Gottfredson-a 82.00 205.00 575.00

4062- Mickey Mouse and the Smugglers, The Story Of, 1935, Whitman, (Scarce), 7" x 9 1/2", 320 pgs., Big Big Book, same contents as above version; Gottfredson-a 82.00 205.00 575.00

708-10- Mickey Mouse on the Haunted Island (Disney), 1950, Whitman, Gottfredson-a 12.00 30.00 80.00

nn- Mickey Mouse and Minnie at Macy's, 1934 Whitman, 148 pgs., 3 1/4" x 3 1/2", soft-c, R. H. Macy & Co. Christmas giveaway (Rare, less than 20 known copies) 300.00 750.00 2700.00

nn- Mickey Mouse and Minnie March to Macy's, 1935, Whitman, 148 pgs., 3 1/2" x 3 1/2", soft-c, R. H. Macy & Co. Christmas giveaway (scarce) 259.00 648.00 2200.00

nn- Mickey Mouse and the Magic Carpet, 1935, Whitman, 148 pgs., 3 1/2"x 4", soft-c, giveaway, Gottfredson-a, Donald Duck app. 123.00 308.00 900.00

nn- Mickey Mouse Silly Symphonies, 1934, Dean & Son, Ltd (England), 48 pgs., with 4 pop-ups, Babes In The Woods, King Neptune

	GD	FN	VF/NM
With dust jacket	138.00	345.00	1100.00
Without dust jacket	100.00	250.00	700.00

nn- Mickey Mouse the Sheriff of Nugget Gulch (Disney) 1938, Dell, 196 pgs., Fast-Action Story, soft-c, Gottfredson-a 36.00 90.00 250.00

nn- Mickey Mouse Waddle Book, 1934, BRP, 20 pgs., 7 1/2" x 10", forerunner of the Blue Ribbon Pop-Up books; with 4 removable articulated cardboard characters Book Only 100.00 200.00 500.00
(A complete copy in VG/FN w/VF dustjacket sold for $5676 in 2010)
(A complete copy in VF with dustjacket ramp & band sold for $573 in 2014)

nn- Mickey Mouse with Goofy and Mickey's Nephews, 1938, Dell, Fast-Action Story, Gottfredson-a 36.00 90.00 250.00

16- Mickey Mouse and Pluto (Disney), 1942, Dell, 196 pgs., Fast-Action story 36.00 90.00 250.00

512- Mickey Mouse Wee Little Books (In open box), nn, 1934, Whitman, 44 pgs., small size, soft-c

	GD	FN	VF/NM
Mickey Mouse and Tanglefoot	13.00	32.50	90.00
Mickey Mouse at the Carnival	13.00	32.50	90.00
Mickey Mouse Will Not Quit!	13.00	32.50	90.00
Mickey Mouse Wins the Race!	13.00	32.50	90.00
Mickey Mouse's Misfortune	13.00	32.50	90.00
Mickey Mouse's Uphill Fight	13.00	32.50	90.00
Complete set with box	96.00	240.00	675.00

1493- Mickey Rooney and Judy Garland and How They Got into the Movies, 1941, Whitman, 432 pgs., photo-c 12.00 30.00 75.00

1427- Mickey Rooney Himself, 1939, Whitman, 240 pgs., photo-c, movie scenes, life story 12.00 30.00 75.00

532- Mickey's Dog Pluto (Disney), 1943, Whitman, All Picture Comics, A Tall Comic Book , 3 3/4" x 8 3/4" 20.00 50.00 140.00

284- Midget Jumbo Coloring Book, 1935, Saalfield 43.00 108.00 300.00

2113- Midget Jumbo Coloring Book, 1935, Saalfield, 240 pgs. 43.00 108.00 300.00

21- Midsummer Night's Dream, 1935, EVW, movie scenes 12.00 30.00 85.00

nn- Minute-Man (Mystery of the Spy Ring), 1941, Fawcett, Dime Action Book 36.00 90.00 250.00

710- Moby Dick the Great White Whale, The Story of, 1934, Whitman, 160 pgs., photo-c, movie scenes from "The Sea Beast" 12.00 30.00 85.00

746- Moon Mullins and Kayo (Kayo and Moon Mullins-inside), 1933, Whitman, 320 pgs., Frank Willard-c/a 12.00 30.00 75.00

nn- Moon Mullins and Kayo, 1933, Whitman, Cocomalt premium, soft-c, by Willard 12.00 30.00 75.00

1134- Moon Mullins and the Plushbottom Twins, 1935, Whitman, 432 pgs., Willard-c/a 12.00 30.00 75.00

nn- Moon Mullins and the Plushbottom Twins, 1935, Whitman, 436 pgs., premium-no ads, 3-color, soft-c, by Willard 18.00 45.00 125.00

1058- Mother Pluto (Disney), 1939, Whitman, 68 pgs., hard-c

1403 - Oswald Rabbit Plays G-Man © DIS

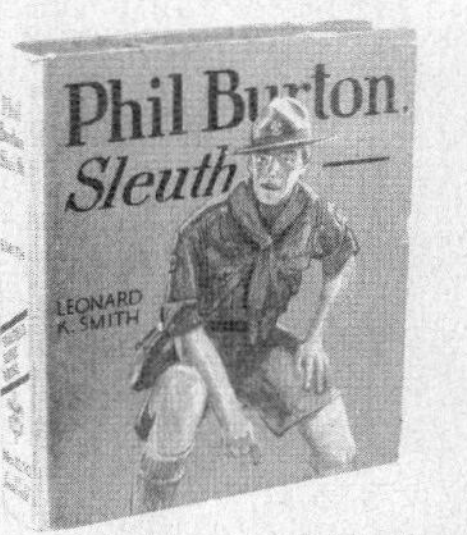

1130 - Phil Burton, Sleuth © Saalfield

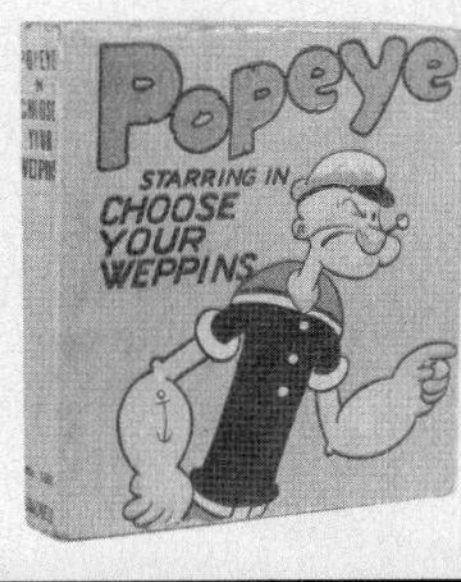

1593 - Popeye Starring in Choose Your Weppins © KING

	GD	FN	VF/NM

11.00 27.50 70.00

1100B- Movie Jokes (From the talkies), 1938, Whitman, 36 pgs., 2 1/2" x 3 1/2", Penny Book 2.00 5.00 15.00

1408- Mr. District Attorney on the Job, 1941, Whitman, 432 pgs., flip pictures 10.00 25.00 65.00

nn- Musicians of Bremen, The, nd (1930s), np (Whitman), 36 pgs., 3" x 2 1/2", Penny Book 2.00 5.00 15.00

1113- Mutt and Jeff, 1936, Whitman, 300 pgs., by Bud Fisher 26.00 65.00 180.00

1116- My Life and Times (By Shirley Temple), 1936, Saalfield, Little Big Book, hard-c, photo-c/illos 12.00 30.00 85.00

1596- My Life and Times (By Shirley Temple), 1936, Saalfield, Little Big Book, soft-c, photo-c/illos 12.00 30.00 85.00

1497- Myra North Special Nurse and Foreign Spies, 1938, Whitman, 432 pgs. 11.00 27.50 70.00

1400- Nancy and Sluggo, 1946, Whitman, All Pictures Comics, Ernie Bushmiller-a 12.00 30.00 75.00

1487- Nancy Has Fun, 1946, Whitman, All Pictures Comics 12.00 30.00 75.00

1150- Napoleon and Uncle Elby, 1938, Saalfield, 400 pgs., by Clifford McBride 11.00 27.50 70.00

1166- Napoleon Uncle Elby And Little Mary, 1939, Saalfield, 400 pgs., by Clifford McBride 11.00 27.50 70.00

1179- Ned Brant Adventure Bound, 1940, Saalfield, 400 pgs. 10.00 25.00 60.00

1146- Nevada Rides The Danger Trail, 1938, Saalfield, 400 pgs., J.R. White-a 10.00 25.00 60.00

1147- Nevada Whalen, Avenger, 1938, Saalfield, 400 pgs. 10.00 25.00 60.00

Nicodemus O'Malley (See Top-Line Comics)

1115- Og Son of Fire, 1936, Whitman, 432 pgs. 12.00 30.00 85.00

1419- Oh, Blondie the Bumsteads (See Blondie)

11- Oliver Twist, 1935, EVW (Five Star Library), movie scenes, starring Dickie Moore (Monogram Pictures) 12.00 30.00 80.00

718- Once Upon a Time, 1933, Whitman, 364 pgs., soft-c 12.00 30.00 80.00

712- 100 Fairy Tales for Children, The, 1933, Whitman, 288 pgs., Circle Library 10.00 25.00 60.00

1099- One Night of Love, 1935, Saalfield, 160 pgs., hard-c, photo-c, movie scenes, Columbia Pictures, starring Grace Moore 12.00 30.00 85.00

1579- One Night of Love, 1935, Sat, 160 pgs., soft-c, photo-c, movie scenes, Columbia Pictures, starring Grace Moore 12.00 30.00 85.00

1155- $1000 Reward, 1938, Saalfield, 400 pgs. 10.00 25.00 60.00

Orphan Annie (See Little Orphan ...)

L17- O'Shaughnessy's Boy, 1935, Lynn, 192 pgs., movie scenes, w/Wallace Beery & Jackie Cooper (Metro-Goldwyn-Mayer) 11.00 27.50 70.00

1109- Oswald the Lucky Rabbit, 1934, Whitman, 288 pgs. 16.00 40.00 115.00

1403- Oswald Rabbit Plays G-Man, 1937, Whitman, 240 pgs., movie scenes by Walter Lantz 18.00 45.00 125.00

1190- Our Boarding House, Major Hoople and his Horse, 1940, Saalfield, 400 pgs. 11.00 27.50 70.00

1085- Our Gang, 1934, Saalfield, 160 pgs., photo-c, movie scenes, hard-c 15.00 37.50 105.00

1315- Our Gang, 1934, Saalfield, 160 pgs., photo-c, movie scenes, soft-c 15.00 37.50 105.00

1451- "Our Gang" on the March, 1942, Whitman, 432 pgs., flip pictures, Vallely-a 15.00 37.50 105.00

1456- Our Gang Adventures, 1948, Whitman, 288 pgs. 12.00 30.00 85.00

nn- Paramount Newsreel Men with Admiral Byrd in Little America, 1934, Whitman, 96 pgs., 6 1/4" x 6 1/4", photo-c, photo ill. 14.00 35.00 100.00

nn- Patch, nd (1930s), np (Whitman), 36 pgs., 3" x 2 1/2", Penny Book 2.00 5.00 15.00

1445- Pat Nelson Ace of Test Pilots, 1937, Whitman, 432 pgs. 10.00 25.00 60.00

1411- Peggy Brown and the Mystery Basket, 1941, Whitman, 432 pgs., flip pictures, Henry E. Vallely-a 10.00 25.00 65.00

1423- Peggy Brown and the Secret Treasure, 1947, Whitman, 288 pgs., Henry E. Vallely-a 10.00 25.00 65.00

1427- Peggy Brown and the Runaway Auto Trailer, 1937, Whitman, 300 pgs., Henry E. Vallely-a 10.00 25.00 65.00

1463- Peggy Brown and the Jewel of Fire, 1943, Whitman, 352 pgs., Henry E. Vallely-a 10.00 25.00 65.00

1491- Peggy Brown in the Big Haunted House, 1940, Whitman, 432 pgs., Vallely-a 10.00 25.00 65.00

1143- Peril Afloat, 1938, Saalfield, 400 pgs. 10.00 25.00 60.00

1199- Perry Winkle and the Rinkeydinks, 1937, Whitman, 432 pgs., by Martin Branner 14.00 35.00 95.00

1487- Perry Winkle and the Rinkeydinks get a Horse, 1938, Whitman, 432 pgs., by Martin Branner 14.00 35.00 95.00

Peter Pan (See Wee Little Books)

nn- Peter Rabbit, nd(1930s), np(Whitman), 36 pgs., Penny Book, 3" x 2 1/2" 5.00 12.50 33.00

Peter Rabbit's Carrots (See Wee Little Books)

1100- Phantom, The, 1936, Whitman, 432 pgs., by Lee Falk & Ray Moore 27.00 68.00 190.00

1416- Phantom and the Girl of Mystery, The, 1947, Whitman, 352 pgs. by Falk & Moore 12.00 30.00 80.00

1421- Phantom and Desert Justice, The, 1941, Whitman, 432 pgs., flip pictures, by Falk & Moore 14.00 35.00 100.00

1468- Phantom and the Sky Pirates, The, 1945, Whitman, 352 pgs., by Falk & Moore 13.00 32.50 90.00

1474- Phantom and the Sign of the Skull, The, 1939, Whitman, 432 pgs., by Falk & Moore 16.00 40.00 110.00

1489- Phantom, Return of the..., 1942, Whitman, 432 pgs., flip pictures, by Falk & Moore 14.00 35.00 100.00

1130- Phil Burton, Sleuth (Scout Book), 1937, Saalfield, hard-c 7.00 17.50 40.00

Pied Piper of Hamlin (See Wee Little Books)

1466- Pilot Pete Dive Bomber, 1941, Whitman, 432 pgs., flip pictures 10.00 25.00 60.00

5776- Pink Panther Adventures in Z-Land, The, 1976, Whitman, 260 pgs., soft-c, 49 cents, B&W 1.00 2.50 8.00

5776-2- Pink Panther Adventures in Z-Land, The, 1980, Whitman, 260 pgs., soft-c, 79 cents, B&W 1.00 2.50 8.00

5783-2- Pink Panther at Castle Kreep, The, 1980, Whitman, 260 pgs., soft-c, 79 cents, B&W 1.00 2.50 8.00

Pinocchio and Jiminy Cricket (See Walt Disney's ...)

nn- Pioneers of the Wild West (Blue-c), 1933, World Syndicate, High Lights of History Series 7.00 17.50 40.00
With dustjacket 29.00 73.00 200.00

nn- Pioneers of the Wild West (Red-c), 1933, World Syndicate, High Lights of History Series 7.00 17.50 40.00

1123- Plainsman, The, 1936, Whitman, 240 pgs., photo-c, movie scenes with Gary Cooper (Paramount Pics.) 14.00 35.00 100.00

Pluto (See Mickey's Dog ... & Walt Disney's ...)

2114- Pocket Coloring Book, 1935, Saalfield 27.00 68.00 190.00

1060- Polly and Her Pals on the Farm, 1934, Saalfield, 164 pgs., hard-c, by Cliff Sterrett 12.00 30.00 80.00

1310- Polly and Her Pals on the Farm, 1934, Saalfield, soft-c 12.00 30.00 80.00

1051- Popeye, Adventures of..., 1934, Saalfield, oblong-size, E.C. Segar-a, hard-c 43.00 108.00 300.00

1088- Popeye in Puddleburg, 1934, Saalfield, 160 pgs., hard-c, E. C. Segar-a 18.00 45.00 125.00

1113- Popeye Starring in Choose Your Weppins, 1936, Saalfield, 160 pgs., hard-c, Segar-a 36.00 90.00 250.00

1117- Popeye's Ark, 1936, Saalfield, 4 1/2" x 5 1/2", hard-c, Segar-a 19.00 47.50 135.00

1163- Popeye Sees the Sea, 1936, Whitman, 432 pgs., Segar-a 20.00 50.00 140.00

1301- Popeye, Adventures of..., 1934, Saalfield, oblong-size, Segar-a 43.00 108.00 300.00

1318- Popeye in Puddleburg, 1934, Saalfield, 160 pgs., soft-c, Segar-a 19.00 47.50 135.00

1405- Popeye and the Jeep, 1937, Whitman, 432 pgs., Segar-a 20.00 50.00 140.00

1406- Popeye the Super-Fighter, 1939, Whitman, All Pictures Comics,

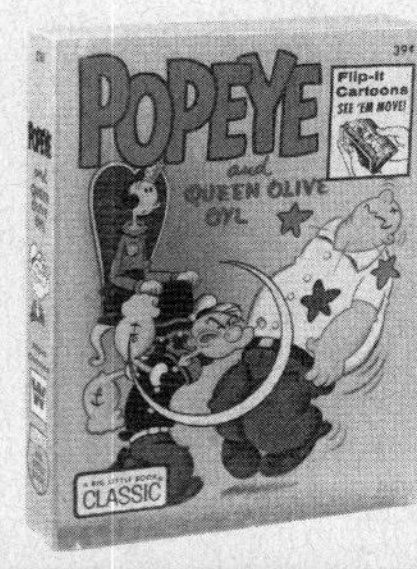

5761 - Popeye and Queen Olive Oyl © KING

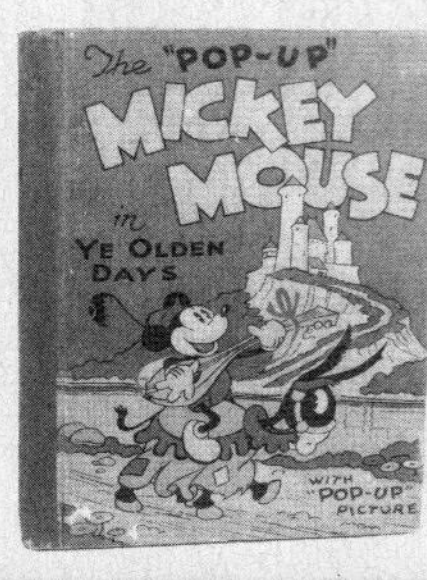

101 - "Pop-Up" Mickey Mouse in "Ye Olden Days" © DIS

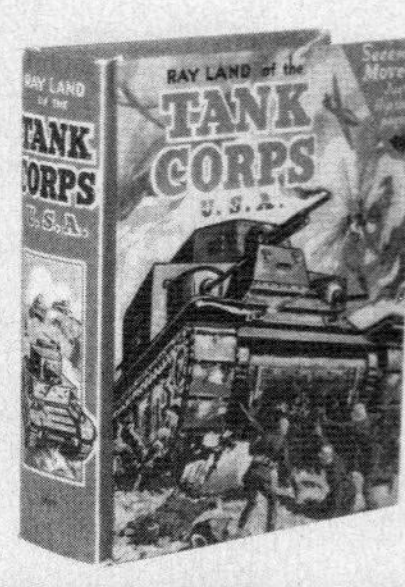

1447 - Ray Land of the Tank Corps, U.S.A. © WHIT

GD FN VF/NM

flip pictures, Segar-a 19.00 47.50 135.00

1422- **Popeye the Sailor Man**, 1947, Whitman, All Pictures Comics
12.00 30.00 85.00

1450- **Popeye in Quest of His Poopdeck Pappy**, 1937, Whitman,
432 pgs., Segar-c/a 14.00 35.00 100.00

1458- **Popeye and Queen Olive Oyl**, 1949, Whitman, 288 pgs.,
Sagendorf-a 12.00 30.00 85.00

1459- **Popeye and the Quest for the Rainbird**, 1943, Whitman,
Winner & Zaboly-a 14.00 35.00 95.00

1480- **Popeye the Spinach Eater**, 1945, Whitman, All Pictures Comics
12.00 30.00 85.00

1485- **Popeye in a Sock for Susan's Sake**, 1940, Whitman,
432 pgs., flip pictures 14.00 35.00 95.00

1497- **Popeye and Caster Oyl the Detective**, 1941, Whitman,
432 pgs. flip pictures, Segar-a 16.00 40.00 115.00

1499- **Popeye and the Deep Sea Mystery**, 1939, Whitman, 432 pgs.,
Segar-c/a 16.00 40.00 115.00

1593- **Popeye Starring in Choose Your Weppins**, 1936,
Saalfield, 160 pgs., soft-c, Segar-a 16.00 40.00 115.00

1597- **Popeye's Ark**, 1936, Saalfield, 4 1/2" x 5 1/2", soft-c, Segar-a
16.00 40.00 115.00

2008-(#8)- **Popeye-Ghost Ship to Treasure Island**, 1967, Whitman,
260 pgs., 39 cents, hard-c, color illos 4.00 10.00 27.00

5755- **Popeye-Ghost Ship to Treasure Island**, 1973, Whitman,
260 pgs., soft-c, color illos 2.00 5.00 15.00

2034-(#34)- **Popeye, Danger Ahoy!**, 1969, Whitman, 256 pgs.,
hard-c, color illos. 4.00 10.00 25.00

5768- **Popeye, Danger Ahoy!**, 1975, Whitman, 256 pgs.,
soft-c, color illos. 2.00 5.00 15.00

4063- **Popeye, Thimble Theatre Starring**, 1935, Whitman, 7" x 9 1/2",
320 pgs., Big Big Book, Segar-c/a; (Cactus cover w/yellow logo)
86.00 215.00 600.00

4063- **Popeye, Thimble Theatre Starring**, 1935, Whitman, 7" x 9 1/2",
320 pgs., Big Big Book, Segar-c/a; (Big Balloon-c with red logo),
(2nd printing w/same contents as above) 100.00 250.00 700.00

5761- **Popeye and Queen Olive Oyl**, 1973,
260 pgs., B&W, soft-c 4.00 10.00 27.00

5761-2- **Popeye and Queen Olive Oyl**, 1973 (1980-reprint of 1973 version),
260 pgs., 79 cents, B&W, soft-c 2.00 5.00 15.00

103- **"Pop-Up" Buck Rogers in the Dangerous Mission**
(with Pop-Up picture), 1934, BRP, 62 pgs., The Midget Pop-Up Book
w/Pop-Up in center of book, Calkins-a 121.00 303.00 850.00

206- **"Pop-Up" Buck Rogers - Strange Adventures in the Spider Ship, The**,
1935, BRP, 24 pgs., 8" x 9", 3 Pop-Ups, hard-c,
by Dick Calkins 121.00 303.00 850.00

nn- **"Pop-Up" Cinderella**, 1933, BRP, 7 1/2" x 9 3/4", 4 Pop-Ups, hard-c
With dustjacket ($2.00) 68.00 170.00 475.00
Without dustjacket 57.00 143.00 400.00

207- **"Pop-Up" Dick Tracy-Capture of Boris Arson**, 1935, BRP, 24 pgs.,
8" x 9", 3 Pop-Ups, hard-c, by Gould 68.00 170.00 475.00

210- **"Pop-Up" Flash Gordon Tournament of Death, The**,
1935, BRP, 24 pgs., 8" x 9", 3 Pop-Ups, hard-c, by Alex Raymond
114.00 285.00 800.00

202- **"Pop-Up" Goldilocks and the Three Bears, The**, 1934, BRP,
24 pgs., 8" x 9", 3 Pop-Ups, hard-c 36.00 90.00 250.00

nn- **"Pop-Up" Jack and the Beanstalk**, 1933, BRP, hard-c
(50 cents), 1 Pop-Up 36.00 90.00 250.00

nn- **"Pop-Up" Jack the Giant Killer**, 1933, BRP, hard-c
(50 cents), 1 Pop-Up 36.00 90.00 250.00

nn- **"Pop-Up" Jack the Giant Killer**, 1933, BRP, 4 Pop-Ups, hard-c
With dustjacket ($2.00) 68.00 170.00 475.00
Without dust jacket 57.00 143.00 400.00

105- **"Pop-Up" Little Black Sambo**, (with Pop-Up picture), 1934, BRP,
62 pgs., The Midget Pop-Up Book, one Pop-Up in center of book
43.00 108.00 325.00

208- **"Pop-Up" Little Orphan Annie and Jumbo the Circus Elephant**,
1935, BRP, 24 pgs., 8" x 9 1/2", 3 Pop-Ups, hard-c, by H. Gray
68.00 170.00 475.00

nn- **"Pop-Up" Little Red Ridinghood**, 1933, BRP, hard-c
(50 cents), 1 Pop-Up 43.00 108.00 300.00

nn- **"Pop-Up" Mickey Mouse, The**, 1933, BRP, 34 pgs., 6 1/2" x 9",
3 Pop-Ups, hard-c, Gottfredson-a (75 cents) 54.00 135.00 375.00

nn- **"Pop-Up" Mickey Mouse in King Arthur's Court, The**, 1933, BRP,
56 pgs., 7 1/2" x 9 1/4", 4 Pop-Ups, hard-c, Gottfredson-a
With dust jacket ($2.00) 123.00 308.00 900.00
Without dustjacket 93.00 233.00 650.00

101- **"Pop-Up" Mickey Mouse in "Ye Olden Days"** (with Pop-Up picture),
1934, 62 pgs., BRP, The Midget Pop-Up Book, one Pop-Up
in center of book, Gottfredson-a 107.00 268.00 750.00

nn- **"Pop-Up" Minnie Mouse, The**, 1933, BRP, 36 pgs., 6 1/2" x 9",
3 Pop-Ups, hard-c (75 cents), Gottfredson-a 50.00 125.00 350.00

203- **"Pop-Up" Mother Goose, The**, 1934, BRP, 24 pgs.,
8" x 9 1/4", 3 Pop-Ups, hard-c 43.00 108.00 300.00

nn- **"Pop-Up" Mother Goose Rhymes, The**, 1933, BRP, 96 pgs.,
7 1/2" x 9 1/4", 4 Pop-Ups, hard-c
With dustjacket ($2.00) 46.00 115.00 325.00
Without dustjacket 43.00 108.00 300.00

209- **"Pop-Up" New Adventures of Tarzan**, 1935, BRP,
24 pgs., 8" x 9", 3 Pop-Ups, hard-c 107.00 268.00 750.00

104- **"Pop-Up" Peter Rabbit, The** (with Pop-Up picture), 1934, BRP,
62 pgs., The Midget Pop-Up Book, one Pop-Up in center of book
50.00 125.00 350.00

nn- **"Pop-Up" Pinocchio**, 1933, BRP, 7 1/2" x 9 3/4", 4 Pop-Ups, hard-c
With dustjacket ($2.00) 61.00 153.00 425.00
Without dust jacket 54.00 135.00 375.00

102- **"Pop-Up" Popeye among the White Savages** (with Pop-Up picture),
1934, BRP, 62 pgs., The Midget Pop-Up Book, one Pop-Up in center
of book, E. C. Segar-a 61.00 153.00 425.00

205- **"Pop-Up" Popeye with the Hag of the Seven Seas, The**, 1935, BRP,
24 pgs., 8" x 9", 3 Pop-Ups, hard-c, Segar-a 68.00 170.00 475.00

201- **"Pop-Up" Puss In Boots, The**, 1934, BRP, 24 pgs., 3 Pop-Ups,
hard-c 37.00 93.00 260.00

nn- **"Pop-Up" Silly Symphonies, The** (Mickey Mouse Presents His ...),
1933, BRP, 56 pgs., 9 3/4" x 7 1/2", 4 Pop-Ups, hard-c
With dust jacket ($2.00) 107.00 268.00 750.00
Without dust jacket 71.00 178.00 500.00

nn- **"Pop-Up" Sleeping Beauty**, 1933, BRP, hard-c, (50 cents),
1 Pop-up 41.00 103.00 290.00

212- **"Pop-Up" Terry and the Pirates in Shipwrecked, The**, 1935, BRP,
24 pgs., 8" x 9", 3 Pop-Ups, hard-c 71.00 178.00 500.00

211- **"Pop-Up" Tim Tyler in the Jungle, The**, 1935, BRP,
24 pgs., 8" x 9", 3 Pop-Ups, hard-c 46.00 115.00 325.00

1404- **Porky Pig and His Gang**, 1946, Whitman, All Pictures Comics,
Barks-a, reprints Four Color #48 20.00 50.00 140.00

1408- **Porky Pig and Petunia**, 1942, Whitman, All Pictures Comics,
flip pictures, reprints Four Color #16 & Famous Gang Book of Comics
12.00 30.00 85.00

1176- **Powder Smoke Range**, 1935, Whitman, 240 pgs., photo-c,
movie scenes, Hoot Gibson, Harey Carey app. (RKO Radio Pict.)
11.00 27.50 70.00

1058- **Practical Pig!, The** (Disney), 1939, Whitman, 68 pgs.,
5" x 5 1/2", hard-c 11.00 27.50 70.00

758- **Prairie Bill and the Covered Wagon**, 1934, Whitman,
384 pgs., Hal Arbo-a 10.00 25.00 60.00

nn- **Prairie Bill and the Covered Wagon**, 1934, Whitman, 390 pgs.,
premium-no ads, 3-color, soft-c, Hal Arbo-a 12.00 30.00 85.00

1440- **Punch Davis of the U.S. Aircraft Carrier**, 1945, Whitman,
352 pgs. 9.00 22.50 55.00

nn- **Puss in Boots**, nd(1930s), np(Whitman), 36 pgs., Penny Book
2.00 5.00 15.00

1100B- **Puzzle Book**, 1938, Whitman, 36 pgs., 2 1/2" x 3 1/2", Penny Book
3.00 7.50 20.00

1100B- **Puzzles**, 1938, Whitman, 36 pgs., 2 1/2" x 3 1/2", Penny Book
3.00 7.50 20.00

1100B- **Quiz Book, The**, 1938, Whitman, 36 pgs., 2 1/2" x 3 1/2", Penny Book
3.00 7.50 20.00

1142- **Radio Patrol**, 1935, Whitman, 432 pgs., by Eddie Sullivan &
Charlie Schmidt (#1) 12.00 30.00 75.00

1173- **Radio Patrol Trailing the Safeblowers**, 1937, Whitman,
432 pgs. 10.00 25.00 60.00

1496- **Radio Patrol Outwitting the Gang Chief**, 1939, Whitman,
432 pgs. 10.00 25.00 60.00

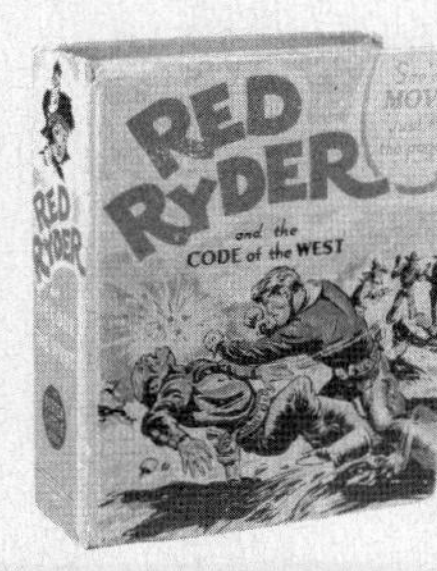

1427 - Red Ryder and the Code of the West © WHIT

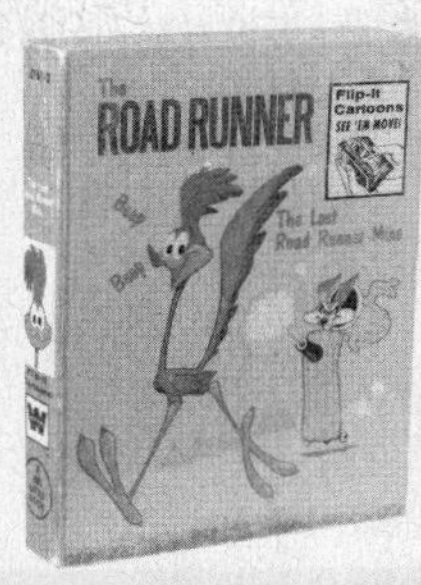

5767-2 - Road Runner, The Lost Road Runner Mine © WB

715-10 - Roy Rogers Range Detective © Roy Rogers

GD FN VF/NM

1498- Radio Patrol and Big Dan's Mobsters, 1937, Whitman, 432 pgs. 10.00 25.00 60.00
nn- Raiders of the Lost Ark, 1998, Chronicle Books, 304 pgs., adapts movie, 1-color (green) illos 4.00 10.00 22.00
1441- Range Busters, The, 1942, Whitman, 432 pgs., Henry E. Vallely-a 10.00 25.00 60.00
1163- Ranger and the Cowboy, The, 1939, Saalfield, 400 pgs. 10.00 25.00 60.00
1154- Rangers on the Rio Grande, 1938, Saalfield, 400 pgs. 10.00 25.00 60.00
1447- Ray Land of the Tank Corps, U.S.A., 1942, Whitman, 432 pgs., flip pictures, Hess-a 10.00 25.00 60.00
1157- Red Barry Ace-Detective, 1935, Whitman, 432 pgs., by Will Gould 12.00 30.00 85.00
1426- Red Barry Undercover Man, 1939, Whitman, 432 pgs., by Will Gould 12.00 30.00 75.00
20- Red Davis, 1935, EVW, 160 pgs. 11.00 27.50 70.00
1449- Red Death on the Range, The, 1940, Whitman, 432 pgs., Fred Harman-a (Bronc Peeler) 11.00 27.50 70.00
nn- Red Falcon Adventures, The, 1937, Seal Right Ice Cream, 8 pgs., set of 50 books, circular in shape
Issue #1 64.00 160.00 450.00
Issue #2-5 43.00 108.00 300.00
Issue #6-10 36.00 90.00 250.00
Issue #11-50 21.00 52.50 150.00
nn- Red Hen and the Fox, The, nd(1930s), np(Whitman), 36 pgs., 3" x 2 1/2", Penny Book 3.00 7.50 18.00
1145- Red-Hot Holsters, 1938, Saalfield, 400 pgs. 10.00 25.00 60.00
1400- Red Ryder and Little Beaver on Hoofs of Thunder, 1939, Whitman, 432 pgs., Harman-c/a 13.00 32.50 90.00
1414- Red Ryder and the Squaw-Tooth Rustlers, 1946, Whitman, 352 pgs., Fred Harman-a 12.00 30.00 75.00
1427- Red Ryder and the Code of the West, 1941, Whitman, 432 pgs., flip pictures, by Harman 12.00 30.00 80.00
1440- Red Ryder the Fighting Westerner, 1940, Whitman, Harman-a 12.00 30.00 80.00
1443- Red Ryder and the Rimrock Killer, 1948, Whitman, 288 pgs., Harman-a 11.00 27.50 70.00
1450- Red Ryder and Western Border Guns, 1942, Whitman, 432 pgs., flip pictures, by Harman 12.00 30.00 80.00
1454- Red Ryder and the Secret Canyon, 1948, Whitman, 288 pgs., Harman-a 11.00 27.50 70.00
1466- Red Ryder and Circus Luck, 1947, Whitman, 288 pgs., by Fred Harman 11.00 27.50 70.00
1473- Red Ryder in War on the Range, 1945, Whitman, 352 pgs., by Fred Harman 12.00 30.00 75.00
1475- Red Ryder and the Outlaw of Painted Valley, 1943, Whitman, 352 pgs., by Harman 11.00 27.50 70.00
702-10- Red Ryder Acting Sheriff, 1949, Whitman, by Fred Hannan 10.00 25.00 65.00
nn- Red Ryder Brings Law to Devil's Hole, 1939, Dell, 196 pgs., Fast-Action Story, Harman-c/a 29.00 73.00 200.00
nn- Red Ryder and the Highway Robbers, 1938, Whitman, 36 pgs., 2 1/2" x 3 1/2", Penny Book 10.00 25.00 65.00
754- Reg'lar Fellers, 1933, Whitman, 320 pgs., by Gene Byrnes 11.00 27.50 70.00
nn- Reg'lar Fellers, 1933, Whitman, 202 pgs., Cocomalt premium, by Gene Byrnes 11.00 27.50 70.00
1424- Rex Beach's Jaragu of the Jungle, 1937, Whitman, 432 pgs. 9.00 22.50 55.00
12- Rex, King of Wild Horses in "Stampede," 1935, EVW, 160 pgs., movie scenes, Columbia Pictures 10.00 25.00 60.00
1100B- Riddles for Fun, 1938, Whitman, 36 pgs., 2 1/2" x 3 1/2", Penny Book 3.00 7.50 20.00
1100B- Riddles to Guess, 1938, Whitman, 36 pgs., 2 1/2" x 3 1/2", Penny Book 3.00 7.50 20.00
1425- Riders of Lone Trails, 1937, Whitman, 300 pgs. 10.00 25.00 65.00
1141- Rio Raiders (A Billy The Kid Story), 1938, Saalfield, 400 pgs. 10.00 25.00 65.00
2023-(#23)- The Road Runner, The Super Beep Catcher, 1968, Whitman, 256 pgs., hard-c, color illos. 1.00 2.50 9.00
5759- The Road Runner, The Super Beep Catcher, 1973, Whitman, 256 pgs., soft-c, 39 cents, B&W illos., and flip pictures 2.00 5.00 12.00
5767-2- Road Runner, The Lost Road Runner Mine, The, 1974 (1980), 260 pgs., 79 cents, B&W, soft-c 2.00 5.00 12.00
5784- The Road Runner and the Unidentified Coyote, 1974, Whitman, 260 pgs., soft-c, flip pictures 2.00 5.00 12.00
5784-2- The Road Runner and the Unidentified Coyote, 1980, Whitman, 260 pgs., soft-c, flip pictures 2.00 5.00 12.00
nn- Road To Perdition, 2002, Dreamworks, screenplay from movie, hard-c (Dreamworks and 20th Century Fox) 1.00 2.50 9.00
Robin Hood (See Wee Little Books)
10- Robin Hood, 1935, EVW, 160 pgs., movie scenes w/Douglas Fairbanks (United Artists), hard-c 14.00 35.00 100.00
719- Robinson Crusoe (The Story of...), nd (1933), Whitman, 364 pgs., soft-c 12.00 30.00 75.00
1421- Roy Rogers and the Dwarf-Cattle Ranch, 1947, Whitman, 352 pgs., Henry E. Vallely-a 12.00 30.00 75.00
1437- Roy Rogers and the Deadly Treasure, 1947, Whitman, 288 pgs. 12.00 30.00 75.00
1448- Roy Rogers and the Mystery of the Howling Mesa, 1948, Whitman, 288 pgs. 12.00 30.00 75.00
1452- Roy Rogers in Robbers' Roost, 1948, Whitman, 288 pgs. 12.00 30.00 75.00
1460- Roy Rogers Robinhood of the Range, 1942, Whitman, 432 pgs., Hess-a (1st) 14.00 35.00 100.00
1462- Roy Rogers and the Mystery of the Lazy M, 1949, Whitman 10.00 25.00 65.00
1476- Roy Rogers King of the Cowboys, 1943, Whitman, 352 pgs., Irwin Myers-a, based on movie 16.00 40.00 110.00
1494- Roy Rogers at Crossed Feathers Ranch, 1945, Whitman, 320 pgs., Erwin Hess-a , 3 1/4" x 5 1/2" 12.00 30.00 75.00
701-10- Roy Rogers and the Snowbound Outlaws, 1949, 3 1/4" x 5 1/2" 10.00 25.00 60.00
715-10- Roy Rogers Range Detective, 1950, Whitman, 2 1/2" x 5" 10.00 25.00 60.00
nn- Sandy Gregg Federal Agent on Special Assignment, 1939, Whitman, 36 pgs., 2 1/2" x 3 1/2", Penny Book 9.00 22.50 55.00
Sappo (See Top-Line Comics)
1122- Scrappy, 1934, Whitman, 288 pgs. 12.00 30.00 75.00
L12- Scrappy (The Adventures of...), 1935, Lynn, 192 pgs., movie scenes 12.00 30.00 75.00
1191- Secret Agent K-7,1940, Saalfield, 400 pgs., based on radio show 9.00 22.50 55.00
1144- Secret Agent X-9, 1936, Whitman, 432 pgs., Charles Flanders-a 15.00 37.50 105.00
1472- Secret Agent X-9 and the Mad Assassin, 1938, Whitman, 432 pgs., Charles Flanders-a 15.00 37.50 105.00
1161- Sequoia, 1935, Whitman, 160 pgs., photo-c, movie scenes 12.00 30.00 75.00
1430- Shadow and the Living Death, The, 1940, Whitman, 432 pgs., Erwin Hess-a 39.00 98.00 275.00
1443- Shadow and the Master of Evil, The, 1941, Whitman, 432 pgs., flip pictures, Hess-a 39.00 98.00 275.00
1495- Shadow and the Ghost Makers, The, 1942, Whitman, 432 pgs., John Coleman Burroughs-c 39.00 98.00 275.00
2024- Shazzan, The Glass Princess, 1968, Whitman, Hanna-Barbera 3.00 7.50 20.00
Shirley Temple (See My Life and Times & Story of..)
1095- Shirley Temple and Lionel Barrymore Starring In "The Little Colonel," 1935, Saalfield, photo hard-c, movie scenes 18.00 45.00 125.00
1115- Shirley Temple in "The Littlest Rebel," 1935, Saalfield, photo-c, movie scenes, hard-c 18.00 45.00 125.00
1575- Shirley Temple and Lionel Barrymore Starring In "The Little Colonel," 1935, Saalfield, photo soft-c, movie scenes 18.00 45.00 125.00
1595- Shirley Temple in "The Littlest Rebel," 1935, Saalfield, photo-c, movie scenes, soft-c 18.00 45.00 125.00
1195- Shooting Sheriffs of the Wild West, 1936, Whitman, 432 pgs. 8.00 20.00 50.00
1169- Silly Symphony Featuring Donald Duck (Disney), 1937, Whitman, 432 pgs., Taliaferro-a 25.00 62.50 175.00

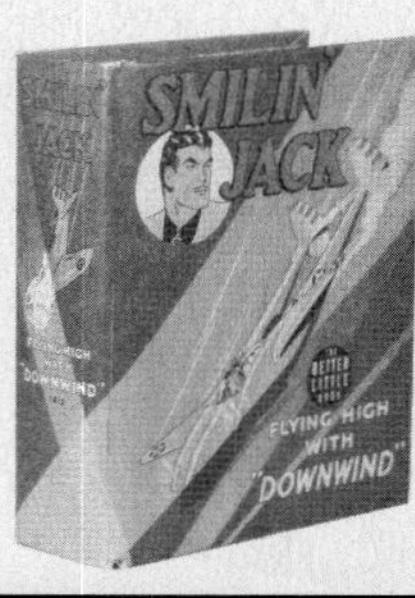

1412 - Smilin' Jack Flying High with "Downwind" © WHIT

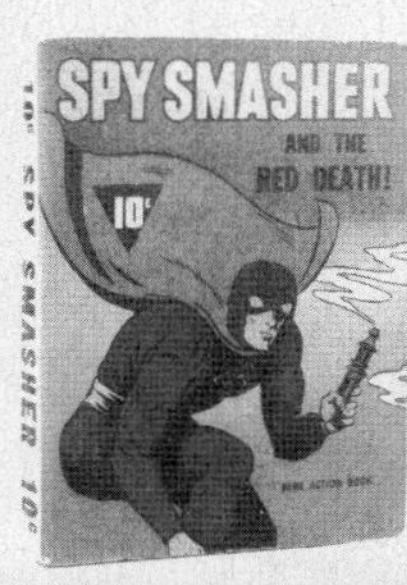

Spy Smasher and the Red Death © FAW

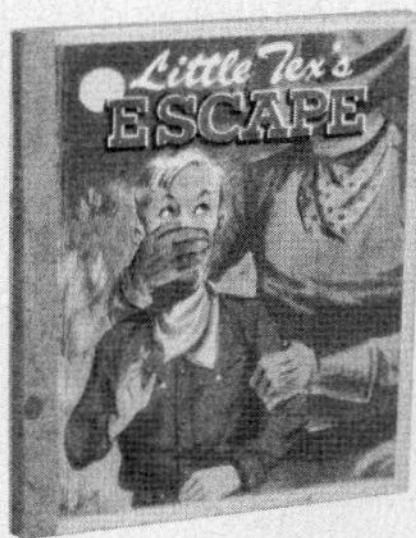

582 - "Swap It" Book Little Tex in the Midst of Trouble © Samuel Lowe Co.

GD FN VF/NM

1441- Silly Symphony Featuring Donald Duck and His (MIS) Adventures (Disney), 1937, Whitman, 432 pgs., Taliaferro-a 25.00 62.50 175.00

1155- Silver Streak, The, 1935, Whitman, 160 pgs., photo-c, movie scenes (RKO Radio Pict.) 10.00 25.00 65.00

Simple Simon (See Wee Little Books)

1649- Sir Lancelot (TV Series), 1958, Whitman, 280 pgs. 6.00 18.00 35.00

1112- Skeezix in Africa, 1934, Whitman, 300 pgs., Frank King-a 8.00 20.00 50.00

1408- Skeezix at the Military Academy, 1938, Whitman, 432 pgs., Frank King-a 8.00 20.00 50.00

1414- Skeezix Goes to War, 1944, Whitman, 352 pgs., Frank King-a 8.00 20.00 50.00

1419- Skeezix on His Own in the Big City, 1941, Whitman, All Pictures Comics, flip pictures, Frank King-a 8.00 20.00 50.00

761- Skippy, 1934, Whitman, 320 pgs., by Percy Crosby 8.00 20.00 50.00

4056- Skippy, The Story of, 1934, Whitman, 320 pgs., 7" x 9 1/2", Big Big Book, Percy Crosby-a 23.00 57.50 160.00

nn- Skippy, The Story of, 1934, Whitman, Phillips Dental Magnesia premium, soft-c, by Percy Crosby 8.00 20.00 50.00

1127- Skyroads (Hurricane Hawk's name not on cover), 1936, Whitman, 432 pgs., by Lt. Dick Calkins, Russell Keaton-a 11.00 27.50 70.00

1439- Skyroads with Clipper Williams of the Flying Legion, 1938, Whitman, 432 pgs., by Lt. Dick Calkins, Keaton-a 11.00 27.50 70.00

1127- Skyroads with Hurricane Hawk, 1936, Whitman, 432 pgs., by Lt. Dick Calkins, Russell Keaton-a 10.00 25.00 65.00

Smilin' Jack and his Flivver Plane (See Top-Line Comics)

1152- Smilin' Jack and the Stratosphere Ascent, 1937, Whitman, 432 pgs., Zack Mosley-a 12.00 30.00 85.00

1412- Smilin' Jack Flying High with "Downwind," 1942, Whitman, 432 pgs., Zack Mosley-a 12.00 30.00 80.00

1416- Smilin' Jack in Wings over the Pacific, 1939, Whitman, 432 pgs., Zack Mosley-a 12.00 30.00 80.00

1419- Smilin' Jack and the Jungle Pipe Line, 1947, Whitman, 352 pgs., Zack Mosley-a 12.00 30.00 75.00

1445- Smilin' Jack and the Escape from Death Rock, 1943, Whitman, 352 pgs., Mosley-a 12.00 30.00 75.00

1464- Smilin' Jack and the Coral Princess, 1945, Whitman, 352 pgs., Zack Mosley-a 12.00 30.00 75.00

1473- Smilin' Jack Speed Pilot, 1941, Whitman, 432 pgs., Zack Mosley-a 12.00 30.00 80.00

2- Smilin' Jack and his Stratosphere Plane, 1938, Whitman, 132 pgs., Buddy Book, soft-c, Zack Mosley-a 27.00 68.00 190.00

nn- Smilin' Jack Grounded on a Tropical Shore, 1938, Whitman, 36 pgs., 2 1/2" x 3 1/2", Penny Book 1000 25.00 60.00

11- Smilin' Jack and the Border Bandits, 1941, Dell, 196 pgs., Fast-Action Story, soft-c, Zack Mosley-a 24.00 60.00 170.00

745- Smitty Golden Gloves Tournament, 1934, Whitman, 320 pgs., Walter Berndt-a 12.00 30.00 75.00

nn- Smitty Golden Gloves Tournament, 1934, Whitman, 204 pgs., Cocomalt premium, soft-c, Walter Berndt-a 12.00 30.00 85.00

1404- Smitty and Herby Lost Among the Indians, 1941, Whitman, All Pictures Comics 10.00 25.00 60.00

1477- Smitty in Going Native, 1938, Whitman, 300 pgs., Walter Berndt-a 10.00 25.00 60.00

2- Smitty and Herby, 1936, Whitman, 132 pgs., 3 1/2" x 3 1/2", soft-c, Tarzan Ice Cream cup lid premium 24.00 60.00 170.00

9- Smitty's Brother Herby and the Police Horse, 1938, Whitman, 132 pgs., 3 1/4" x 3 1/2", Buddy Book-ice cream premium, by Walter Berndt 24.00 60.00 170.00

1010- Smokey Stover Firefighter of Foo, 1937, Whitman, 7 1/4" x 5 1/2", 64 pgs., Nickel Book, Bill Holman-a 12.00 30.00 85.00

1413- Smokey Stover, 1942, Whitman, All Pictures Comics, flip pictures, Bill Holman-a 12.00 30.00 85.00

1421- Smokey Stover the Foo Fighter, 1938, Whitman, 432 pgs., Bill Holman-a 12.00 30.00 85.00

1481- Smokey Stover the Foolish Foo Fighter, 1942, Whitman, All Pictures Comics 12.00 30.00 85.00

1- Smokey Stover the Fireman of Foo, 1938, Whitman, 3 3/4" x 3 1/2", 132 pgs., Buddy Book-ice cream premium, by Bill Holman 27.00 68.00 190.00

1100A- Smokey Stover, 1938, Whitman, 36 pgs., 2 1/2" x 3 1/2", Penny Book 10.00 25.00 65.00

nn- Smokey Stover and the Fire Chief of Foo, 1938, Whitman, 36 pgs., 2 1/2" x 3 1/2", Penny Book, yellow shirt on-c 10.00 25.00 65.00

nn- Smokey Stover and the Fire Chief of Foo, 1938, Whitman, 36 pgs., Penny Book, green shirt on-c 10.00 25.00 65.00

1460- Snow White and the Seven Dwarfs (The Story of Walt Disney's ...), 1938, Whitman, 288 pgs. 18.00 45.00 125.00

1136- Sombrero Pete, 1936, Whitman, 432 pgs. 10.00 25.00 60.00

1152- Son of Mystery, 1939, Saalfield, 400 pgs. 10.00 25.00 60.00

1191- SOS Coast Guard, 1936, Whitman, 432 pgs., Henry E. Vallely-a 10.00 25.00 65.00

2016-(#16)-Space Ghost-The Sorceress of Cyba-3 (TV Cartoon), 1968, Whitman, 260 pgs., 39¢-c, hard-c, color illos 10.00 25.00 60.00

1455- Speed Douglas and the Mole Gang-The Great Sabotage Plot, 1941, Whitman, 432 pgs., flip pictures 10.00 25.00 60.00

5779- Spider-Man Zaps Mr. Zodiac, 1976, 260 pgs., soft-c, B&W 1.00 2.50 9.00

5779-2- Spider-Man Zaps Mr. Zodiac, 1980, 260 pgs., 79¢-c, soft-c, B&W 1.00 2.50 6.00

1467- Spike Kelly of the Commandos, 1943, Whitman, 352 pgs. 10.00 25.00 60.00

1144- Spook Riders on the Overland, 1938, Saalfield, 400 pgs. 10.00 25.00 60.00

768- Spy, The, 1936, Whitman, 300 pgs. 12.00 30.00 75.00

nn- Spy Smasher and the Red Death, 1941, Fawcett, 4" x 5 1/2", Dime Action Book 43.00 108.00 300.00

1120- Stan Kent Freshman Fullback, 1936, Saalfield, 148 pgs., hard-c 8.00 20.00 50.00

1132- Stan Kent, Captain, 1937, Saalfield 8.00 20.00 50.00

1600- Stan Kent Freshman Fullback, 1936, Saalfield, 148 pgs., soft-c 8.00 20.00 50.00

1123- Stan Kent Varsity Man, 1936, Saalfield, 160 pgs., hard-c 8.00 20.00 50.00

1603- Stan Kent Varsity Man, 1936, Saalfield, 160 pgs., soft-c 8.00 20.00 50.00

nn- Star Wars - A New Hope, 1997, Chronicle Books, 320 pgs., adapts movie, 1-color (blue) illos 3.00 7.50 20.00

nn- Star Wars - Empire Strikes Back, The, 1997, Chronicle Books, 296 pgs., adapts movie, 1-color (blue) illos 3.00 7.50 20.00

nn- Star Wars - Episode 1 - The Phantom Menace, 1999, Chronicle Books, 344 pgs., adapts movie, 1-color (blue) illos 1.00 2.50 9.00

nn- Star Wars - Episode 2 - Attack of the Clones, 2002, Chronicle Books, 340 pgs., adapts movie, 1-color (blue) illos 1.00 2.50 9.00

nn- Star Wars - Return of the Jedi, 1997, Chronicle Books, 312 pgs., adapts movie, 1-color (blue) illos 3.00 7.50 20.00

1104- Steel Arena, The (With Clyde Beatty), 1936, Saalfield, hard-c, movie scenes adapted from "The Lost Jungle" 12.00 30.00 75.00

1584- Steel Arena, The (With Clyde Beatty), 1936, Saalfield, soft-c, movie scenes 12.00 30.00 75.00

1426- Steve Hunter of the U.S. Coast Guard Under Secret Orders, 1942, Whitman, 432 pgs. 10.00 25.00 60.00

1456- Story of Charlie McCarthy and Edgar Bergen, The, 1938, Whitman, 288 pgs. 10.00 25.00 60.00

Story of Daniel, The (See Wee Little Books)

Story of David, The (See Wee Little Books)

1110- Story of Freddie Bartholomew, The, 1935, Saalfield, 4 1/2" x 5 1/4", hard-c, movie scenes (MGM) 10.00 25.00 60.00

1590- Story of Freddie Bartholomew, The, 1935, Saalfield, 4 1/2" x 5 1/4", soft-c, movie scenes (MGM) 10.00 25.00 60.00

Story of Gideon, The (See Wee Little Books)

W714- Story of Jackie Cooper, The, 1933, Whitman, 240 pgs., photo-c, movie scenes, "Skippy" & "Sooky" movie 12.00 30.00 80.00

Story of Joseph, The (See Wee Little Books)

Story of Moses, The (See Wee Little Books)

Story of Ruth and Naomi (See Wee Little Books)

1089- Story of Shirley Temple, The, 1934, Saalfield, 160 pgs., hard-c, photo-c, movie scenes 11.00 27.50 70.00

1319- Story of Shirley Temple, The, 1934, Saalfield, 160 pgs., soft-c, photo-c, movie scenes 11.00 27.50 70.00

1090- Strawberry-Roan, 1934, Saalfield, 160 pgs., hard-c, Ken Maynard

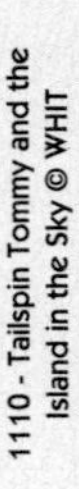
1110 - Tailspin Tommy and the Island in the Sky © WHIT

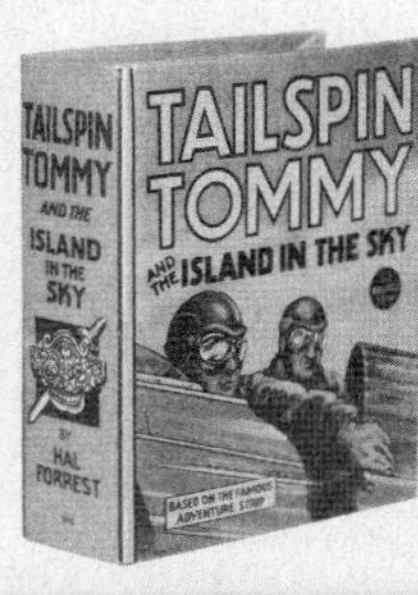

1452 - Tarzan the Untamed © ERB

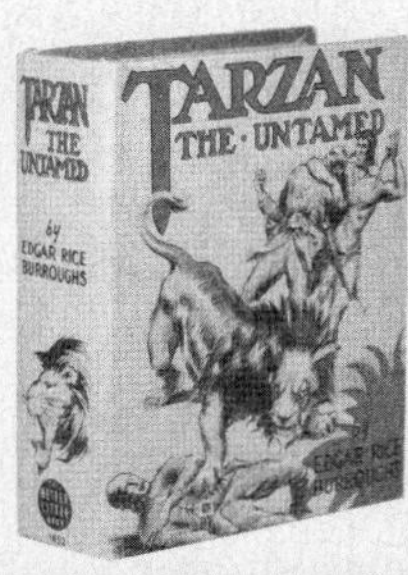

1420 - Terry and War in the Jungle © WHIT

GD FN VF/NM

photo-c, movie scenes 11.00 27.50 70.00

1320- Strawberry-Roan, 1934, Saalfield, 160 pgs., soft-c, Ken Maynard photo-c, movie scenes 11.00 27.50 70.00

Streaky and the Football Signals (See Top-Line Comics)

5780-2- Superman in the Phantom Zone Connection, 1980, 260 pgs., 79¢-c, soft-c, B&W 1.00 2.50 9.00

582- "Swap It" Book, The, 1949, Samuel Lowe Co., 260 pgs., 3 1/2" x 4 1/2"
1. Little Tex in the Midst of Trouble 5.00 12.50 30.00
2. Little Tex's Escape 5.00 12.50 30.00
3. Little Tex Comes to the XY Ranch 5.00 12.50 30.00
4. Get Them Cowboy 5.00 12.50 30.00
5. The Mail Must Go Through! A Story of the Pony Express 5.00 12.50 30.00
6. Nevada Jones, Trouble Shooter 5.00 12.50 30.00
7. Danny Meets the Cowboys 5.00 12.50 30.00
8. Flint Adams and the Stage Coach 5.00 12.50 30.00
9. Bud Shinners and the Oregon Trail 5.00 12.50 30.00
10. The Outlaws' Last Ride 5.00 12.50 30.00

Sybil Jason (See Little Big Shot)

747- Tailspin Tommy in the Famous Pay-Roll Mystery, 1933, Whitman, hard-c, 320 pgs., Hal Forrest-a (# 1) 12.00 30.00 85.00

747- Tailspin Tommy in the Famous Pay-Roll Mystery, 1933, Whitman, soft-c, 320 pgs., Hal Forrest-a (# 1) 12.00 30.00 85.00

nn- Tailspin Tommy the Pay-Roll Mystery, 1934, Whitman, 52 pgs., 3 1/2" x 5 1/4", premium-no ads, soft-c; another version with Perkins ad, Hal Forrest-a 18.00 45.00 125.00

1110- Tailspin Tommy and the Island in the Sky, 1936, Whitman, 432 pgs., Hal Forrest-a 11.00 27.50 70.00

1124- Tailspin Tommy the Dirigible Flight to the North Pole, 1934, Whitman, 432 pgs., H. Forrest-a 12.00 30.00 85.00

nn- Tailspin Tommy the Dirigible Flight to the North Pole, 1934, Whitman, 436 pgs., 3-color, soft-c, premium-no ads, Hal Forrest-a 29.00 73.00 200.00

1172- Tailspin Tommy Hunting for Pirate Gold, 1935, Whitman, 432 pgs., Hal Forrest-a 11.00 27.50 70.00

1183- Tailspin Tommy Air Racer, 1940, Saalfield, 400 pgs., hard-c 11.00 27.50 70.00

1184- Tailspin Tommy in the Great Air Mystery, 1936, Whitman, 240 pgs., photo-c, movie scenes 12.00 30.00 85.00

1410- Tailspin Tommy the Weasel and His "Skywaymen," 1941, Whitman, All Pictures Comics, flip pictures 10.00 25.00 65.00

1413- Tailspin Tommy and the Lost Transport, 1940, Whitman, 432 pgs., Hal Forrest-a 10.00 25.00 65.00

1423- Tailspin Tommy and the Hooded Flyer, 1937, Whitman, 432 pgs., Hal Forrest-a 11.00 27.50 70.00

1494- Tailspin Tommy and the Sky Bandits, 1938, Whitman 432 pgs., Hal Forrest-a 11.00 27.50 70.00

nn- Tailspin Tommy and the Airliner Mystery, 1938, Dell, 196 pgs., Fast-Action Story, soft-c, Hal Forrest-a 43.00 108.00 300.00

nn- Tailspin Tommy in Flying Aces, 1938, Dell, 196 pgs., Fast-Action Story, soft-c, Hal Forrest-a 43.00 108.00 300.00

nn- Tailspin Tommy in Wings Over the Arctic, 1934, Whitman, Cocomalt premium, Forrest-a 14.00 35.00 100.00

nn- Tailspin Tommy Big Thrill Chewing Gum, 1934, Whitman, 8 pgs., 2 1/2" x 3 " (6 diff.) each.. 11.00 27.50 70.00

3- Tailspin Tommy on the Mountain of Human Sacrifice, 1938, Whitman, soft-c, Buddy Book 29.00 73.00 200.00

7- Tailspin Tommy's Perilous Adventure, 1934, Whitman, 132 pgs., 3 1/2" x 3 1/2" soft-c, Tarzan Ice Cream cup premium 29.00 73.00 200.00

nn- Tailspin Tommy, 1935, Whitman, 148 pgs., 3 1/2" x 4", Tarzan Ice Cream cup premium 32.00 80.00 225.00

L16- Tale of Two Cities, A, 1935, Lynn, movie scenes 12.00 30.00 85.00

744- Tarzan of the Apes, 1933, Whitman, 320 pgs., by Edgar Rice Burroughs (1st) 43.00 108.00 300.00

nn- Tarzan of the Apes, 1935, Whitman, 52 pgs., 3 1/2" x 5 1/4", soft-c, stapled, premium, no ad; another version with a Perkins ad; reprints panels from Hal Foster's newspaper adaptation 54.00 135.00 375.00

769- Tarzan the Fearless, 1934, Whitman, 240 pgs., Buster Crabbe photo-c, movie scenes, ERB 29.00 73.00 200.00

770- Tarzan Twins, The, 1934, Whitman, 432 pgs., ERB 82.00 205.00 575.00

770- Tarzan Twins, The, 1935, Whitman, 432 pgs., ERB 54.00 135.00 375.00

nn- Tarzan Twins, The, 1935, Whitman, 52 pgs., 3 1/2" x 5 3/4", premium-with & without ads, soft-c, ERB 68.00 170.00 475.00

nn- Tarzan Twins, The, 1935, Whitman, 436 pgs., 3-color, soft-c, premium-no ads, ERB 71.00 178.00 500.00

778- Tarzan of the Screen (The Story of Johnny Weissmuller), 1934, Whitman, 240 pgs., photo-c, movie scenes, ERB 29.00 73.00 200.00

1102- Tarzan, The Return of, 1936, Whitman, 432 pgs., Edgar Rice Burroughs 21.00 52.50 150.00

1180- Tarzan, The New Adventures of, 1935, Whitman, 160 pgs., Herman Brix photo-c, movie scenes, ERB 24.00 60.00 165.00

1182- Tarzan Escapes, 1936, Whitman, 240 pgs., Johnny Weissmuller photo-c, movie scenes, ERB 29.00 73.00 200.00

1407- Tarzan Lord of the Jungle, 1946, Whitman, 352 pgs., ERB 14.00 35.00 100.00

1410- Tarzan, The Beasts of, 1937, Whitman, 432 pgs., Edgar Rice Burroughs 21.00 52.50 145.00

1442- Tarzan and the Lost Empire, 1948, Whitman, 288 pgs., ERB 14.00 35.00 100.00

1444- Tarzan and the Ant Men, 1945, Whitman, 352 pgs., ERB 14.00 35.00 100.00

1448- Tarzan and the Golden Lion, 1943, Whitman, 432 pgs., ERB 20.00 50.00 140.00

1452- Tarzan the Untamed, 1941, Whitman, 432 pgs., flip pictures, ERB 20.00 50.00 140.00

1453- Tarzan the Terrible, 1942, Whitman, 432 pgs., flip pictures, ERB 20.00 50.00 140.00

1467- Tarzan in the Land of the Giant Apes, 1949, Whitman, ERB 14.00 35.00 100.00

1477- Tarzan, The Son of, 1939, Whitman, 432 pgs., ERB 20.00 50.00 140.00

1488- Tarzan's Revenge, 1938, Whitman, 432 pgs., ERB 20.00 50.00 140.00

1495- Tarzan and the Jewels of Opar, 1940, Whitman, 432 pgs. 20.00 50.00 140.00

4056- Tarzan and the Tarzan Twins with Jad-Bal-Ja the Golden Lion, 1936, Whitman, 7" x 9 1/2", 320 pgs., Big Big Book 60.00 150.00 470.00

709-10- Tarzan and the Journey of Terror, 1950, Whitman, 2 1/2" x 5", ERB, Marsh-a 10.00 25.00 65.00

2005- (#5)-Tarzan: The Mark of the Red Hyena, 1967, Whitman, 260 pgs., 39 cents, hard-c, color illos 4.00 10.00 27.00

nn- Tarzan, 1935, Whitman, 148 pgs., soft-c, 3 1/2" x 4", Tarzan Ice Cream cup premium, ERB (scarce) 86.00 215.00 600.00

nn- Tarzan and a Daring Rescue, 1938, Whitman, 68 pgs., Pan-Am premium, soft-c, ERB (blank back-c version also exists) 50.00 125.00 350.00

nn- Tarzan and his Jungle Friends, 1936, Whitman, 132 pgs., soft-c, 3 1/2" x 3 1/2", Tarzan Ice Cream cup premium, ERB (scarce) 86.00 215.00 600.00

nn- Tarzan in the Golden City, 1938, Whitman, 68 pgs., Pan-Am premium, soft-c, 3 1/2" x 3 3/4", ERB 50.00 125.00 350.00

nn- Tarzan The Avenger, 1939, Dell, 194 pgs., Fast-Action Story, ERB, soft-c 36.00 90.00 250.00

nn- Tarzan with the Tarzan Twins in the Jungle, 1938, Dell, 194 pgs., Fast-Action Story, ERB 36.00 90.00 250.00

1100B- Tell Your Fortune, 1938, Whitman, 36 pgs., 2 1/2" x 3 1/2", Penny Book 4.00 10.00 24.00

nn- Terminator 2: Judgment Day, 1998, Chronicle Books, 310 pgs., adapts movie, 1-color (blue-gray) illos 1.00 2.50 9.00

1156- Terry and the Pirates, 1935, Whitman, 432 pgs., Milton Caniff-a (#1) 14.00 35.00 100.00

nn- Terry and the Pirates, 1935, Whitman, 52 pgs., 3 1/2" x 5 1/4", soft-c, premium, Milton Caniff-a; 3 versions: No ad, Sears ad & Perkins ad 29.00 73.00 200.00

1412- Terry and the Pirates Shipwrecked on a Desert Island, 1938, Whitman, 432 pgs., Milton Caniff-a 12.00 30.00 85.00

1420- Terry and War in the Jungle, 1946, Whitman, 352 pgs., Milton Caniff-a 12.00 30.00 80.00

1058 - "Timid Elmer" © DIS

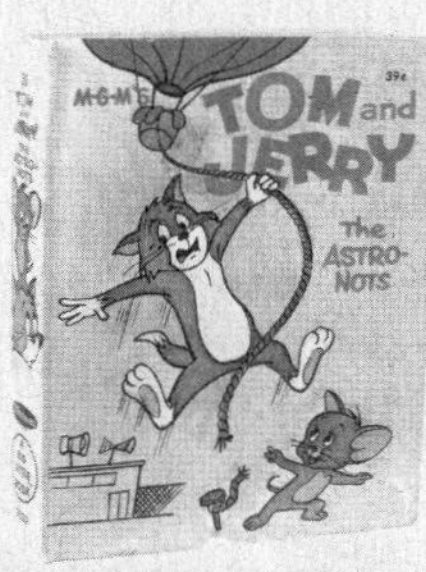

2030 - Tom and Jerry, The Astro-Nots © MGM

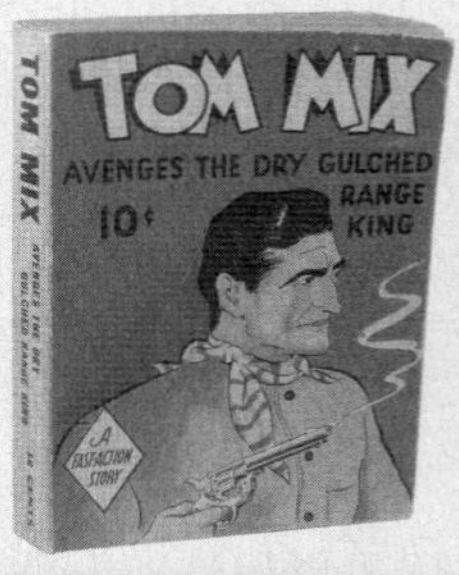

Tom Mix Avenges the Dry Gulched Range King © DELL

GD FN VF/NM

1436- Terry and the Pirates The Plantation Mystery, 1942, Whitman, 432 pgs., flip pictures, Milton Caniff-a 12.00 30.00 85.00

1446- Terry and the Pirates and the Giant's Vengeance, 1939, Whitman, 432 pgs., Caniff-a 12.00 30.00 85.00

1499- Terry and the Pirates in the Mountain Stronghold, 1941, Whitman, 432 pgs., Caniff-a 12.00 30.00 85.00

4073- Terry and the Pirates, The Adventures of, 1938, Whitman, 7" x 9 1/2", 320 pgs., Big Big Book, Milton Caniff-a 39.00 98.00 275.00

4- Terry and the Pirates Ashore in Singapore, 1938, Whitman, 132 pgs., 3 1/2" x 3 3/4", soft-c, Buddy Book premium 27.00 68.00 190.00

10- Terry and the Pirates Meet Again, 1936, Whitman, 132 pgs., 3 1/2" x 3 1/2", soft-c, Tarzan Ice Cream cup lid premium 39.00 98.00 275.00

nn- Terry and the Pirates, Adventures of, 1938, 36 pgs., 2 1/2" x 3 1/2", Penny Book, Caniff-a 10.00 25.00 60.00

nn- Terry and the Pirates and the Island Rescue, 1938, Whitman, 68 pgs., 3 1/4" x 3 1/2", Pan-Am premium 21.00 52.50 150.00

nn- Terry and the Pirates on Their Travels, 1938, 36 pgs., 2 1/2" x 3 1/2", Penny Book, Caniff-a 10.00 25.00 60.00

nn- Terry and the Pirates and the Mystery Ship, 1938, Dell, 194 pgs., Fast-Action Story, soft-c 29.00 73.00 200.00

1492- Terry Lee Flight Officer U.S.A., 1944, Whitman, 352 pgs., Milton Caniff-a 12.00 30.00 75.00

7- Texas Bad Man, The (Tom Mix), 1934, EVW, 160 pgs., (Five Star Library), movie scenes 18.00 45.00 125.00

1429- Texas Kid, The, 1937, Whitman, 432 pgs. 8.00 20.00 50.00

1135- Texas Ranger, The, 1936, Whitman, 432 pgs., Hal Arbo-a 8.00 20.00 50.00

nn- Texas Ranger, The, 1935, Whitman, 260 pgs., Cocomalt premium, soft-c, Hal Arbo-a 12.00 30.00 75.00

nn- Texas Ranger and the Rustler Gang, The, 1936, Whitman, Pan-Am giveaway 21.00 52.50 150.00

nn- Texas Ranger in the West, The, 1938, Whitman, 36 pgs., 2 1/2" x 3 1/2", Penny Book 8.00 20.00 50.00

nn- Texas Ranger to the Rescue, The, 1938, Whitman, 36 pgs., 2 1/2" x 3 1/2", Penny Book 8.00 20.00 50.00

12- Texas Ranger in Rustler Strategy, The, 1936, Whitman, 132 pgs., 3 1/2" x 3 1/2", soft-c, Tarzan Ice Cream cup lid premium 26.00 65.00 180.00

Tex Thorne (See Zane Grey)

Thimble Theatre (See Popeye)

26- 13 Hours By Air, 1936, Lynn, 128 pgs., 5" x 7 1/2", photo-c, movie scenes (Paramount Pictures) 12.00 30.00 75.00

nn- Three Bears, The, nd (1930s), np (Whitman), 36 pgs., 3" x 2 1/2", Penny Book 3.00 7.50 20.00

1129- Three Finger Joe (Baseball), 1937, Saalfield, Robert A. Graef-a 8.00 20.00 50.00

nn- Three Little Pigs, The, nd (1930s), np (Whitman), 36 pgs., 3" x 2 1/2", Penny Book 3.00 7.50 20.00

1131- Three Musketeers, 1935, Whitman, 182 pgs., 5 1/4" x 6 1/4", photo-c, movie scenes 14.00 35.00 100.00

1409- Thumper and the Seven Dwarfs (Disney), 1944, Whitman, All Pictures Comics 21.00 52.50 150.00

1108- Tiger Lady, The (The life of Mabel Stark, animal trainer), 1935, Saalfield, photo-c, movie scenes, hard-c 10.00 25.00 60.00

1588- Tiger Lady, The, 1935, Saalfield, photo-c, movie scenes, soft-c 10.00 25.00 60.00

1442- Tillie the Toiler and the Wild Man of Desert Island, 1941, Whitman, 432 pgs., Russ Westover-a 11.00 27.50 70.00

1058- "Timid Elmer" (Disney), 1939, Whitman, 5" x 5 1/2", 68 pgs., hard-c 11.00 27.50 70.00

1152- Tim McCoy in the Prescott Kid, 1935, Whitman, 160 pgs., hard-c, photo-c, movie scenes 18.00 45.00 125.00

1193- Tim McCoy in the Westerner, 1936, Whitman, 240 pgs., photo-c, movie scenes 1400 35.00 100.00

1436- Tim McCoy on the Tomahawk Trail, 1937, Whitman, 432 pgs., Robert Weisman-a 12.00 30.00 75.00

1490- Tim McCoy and the Sandy Gulch Stampede, 1939, Whitman, 424 pgs. 10.00 25.00 65.00

2- Tim McCoy in Beyond the Law, 1934, EVW, Five Star Library, photo-c, movie scenes (Columbia Pict.) Hardcover 14.00 35.00 100.00
(Rare) Softcover 36.00 90.00 250.00

GD FN VF/NM

10- Tim McCoy in Fighting the Redskins, 1938, Whitman, 130 pgs., Buddy Book, soft-c 27.00 68.00 190.00

14- Tim McCoy in Speedwings, 1935, EVW, Five Star Library, 160 pgs., photo-c, movie scenes (Columbia Pictures) 1900 47.50 135.00

nn- Tim the Builder, nd (1930s), np (Whitman), 36 pgs., 3" x 2 1/2", Penny Book 3.00 7.50 20.00

Tim Tyler (Also see Adventures of ...)

1140- Tim Tyler's Luck Adventures in the Ivory Patrol, 1937, Whitman, 432 pgs., by Lyman Young 10.00 25.00 65.00

1479- Tim Tyler's Luck and the Plot of the Exiled King, 1939, Whitman, 432 pgs., by Lyman Young 10.00 25.00 60.00

767- Tiny Tim, The Adventures of, 1935, Whitman, 384 pgs., by Stanley Link 12.00 30.00 85.00

1172- Tiny Tim and the Mechanical Men, 1937, Whitman, 432 pgs., by Stanley Link 12.00 30.00 75.00

1472- Tiny Tim in the Big, Big World, 1945, Whitman, 352 pgs., by Stanley Link 12.00 30.00 75.00

2006- (#6)-Tom and Jerry Meet Mr. Fingers, 1967, Whitman, 39¢-c 260 pgs., hard-c, color illos. 4.00 10.00 27.00

5752- Tom and Jerry Meet Mr. Fingers, 1973, Whitman, 39¢-c 260 pgs., soft-c, color illos., 5 printings 2.00 5.00 15.00

2030-(#30)- Tom and Jerry, The Astro-Nots, 1969, Whitman, 256 pgs., hard-c, color illos. 3.00 7.50 20.00

5765- Tom and Jerry, The Astro-Nots, 1974, Whitman, 256 pgs., soft-c, color illos. 2.00 5.00 15.00

5787-2- Tom and Jerry Under the Big Top, 1980, Whitman, 79¢-c, 260 pgs., soft-c, B&W 2.00 5.00 15.00

723- Tom Beatty Ace of the Service, 1934, Whitman, 256 pgs., George Taylor-a 12.00 30.00 75.00

nn- Tom Beatty Ace of the Service, 1934, Whitman, 260 pgs., soft-c 12.00 30.00 75.00

1165- Tom Beatty Ace of the Service Scores Again, 1937, Whitman, 432 pgs., Weisman-a 11.00 27.50 70.00

1420- Tom Beatty Ace of the Service and the Big Brain Gang, 1939, Whitman, 432 pgs. 11.00 27.50 70.00

nn- Tom Beatty Ace Detective and the Gorgon Gang, 1938?, Whitman, 36 pgs., 2 1/2" x 3 1/2", Penny Book 10.00 25.00 60.00

nn- Tom Beatty Ace of the Service and the Kidnapers, 1938?, Whitman, 36 pgs., 2 1/2" x 3 1/2", Penny Book 10.00 25.00 60.00

1102- Tom Mason on Top, 1935, Saalfield, 160 pgs., Tom Mix photo-c, from Mascot serial "The Miracle Rider," movie scenes, hard-c 18.00 45.00 125.00

1582- Tom Mason on Top, 1935, Saalfield, 160 pgs., Tom Mix photo-c, movie scenes, soft-c 18.00 45.00 125.00

Tom Mix (See Chief of the Rangers, Flaming Guns & Texas Bad Man)

762- Tom Mix and Tony Jr. in "Terror Trail," 1934, Whitman, 160 pgs., movie scenes 18.00 45.00 125.00

1144- Tom Mix in the Fighting Cowboy, 1935, Whitman, 432 pgs., Hal Arbo-a 12.00 30.00 85.00

nn- Tom Mix in the Fighting Cowboy, 1935, Whitman, 436 pgs., premium-no ads, 3 color, soft-c, Hal Arbo-a 21.00 52.50 150.00

1166- Tom Mix in the Range War, 1937, Whitman, 432 pgs., Hal Arbo-a 10.00 25.00 65.00

1173- Tom Mix Plays a Lone Hand, 1935, Whitman, 288 pgs., hard-c, Hal Arbo-a 10.00 25.00 65.00

1183- Tom Mix and the Stranger from the South, 1936, Whitman, 432 pgs. 10.00 25.00 65.00

1462- Tom Mix and the Hoard of Montezuma, 1937, Whitman, H. E. Vallely-a 10.00 25.00 65.00

1482- Tom Mix and His Circus on the Barbary Coast, 1940, Whitman, 432 pgs., James Gary-a 10.00 25.00 65.00

3047- Tom Mix and His Big Little Kit, 1937, Whitman, 384 pgs., 4 1/2" x 6 1/2" box, includes miniature box of 4 crayons-red, yellow, blue and green 71.00 178.00 500.00

4068- Tom Mix and the Scourge of Paradise Valley, 1937, Whitman, 7" x 9 1/2", 320 pgs., Big Big Book, Vallely-a 29.00 73.00 200.00

6833- Tom Mix in the Riding Avenger, 1936, Dell, 244 pgs., Cartoon Story Book, hard-c 19.00 47.50 130.00

nn- Tom Mix Rides to the Rescue, 1939, 36 pgs., 2 1/2" x 3", Penny Book 10.00 25.00 60.00

nn- Tom Mix Avenges the Dry Gulched Range King, 1939, Dell, 196 pgs., Fast-Action Story, soft-c 20.00 50.00 140.00

540 - Top-Line Comics
Broncho Bill in Suicide Canyon © WHIT

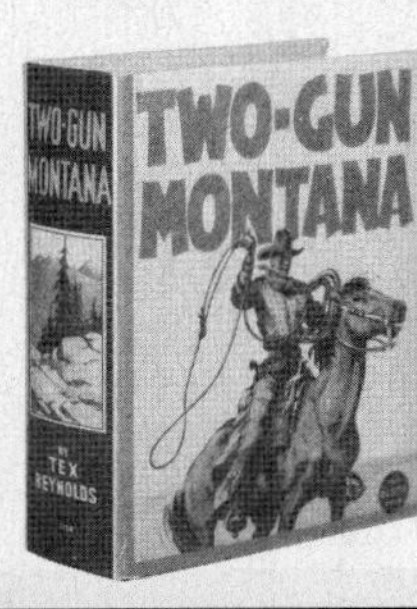

1104 - Two-Gun Montana © WHIT

1066 - Walt Disney's Story of
Pluto the Pup © DIS

GD FN VF/NM

nn- Tom Mix in the Riding Avenger, 1936, Dell, 244 pgs.,
Fast-Action Story 20.00 50.00 140.00
nn- Tom Mix the Trail of the Terrible 6, 1935, Ralston Purina Co.,
84 pgs., 3" x 3 1/2", premium 18.00 45.00 125.00
4- Tom Mix and Tony in the Rider of Death Valley,
1934, EVW, Five Star Library, 160 pgs., movie scenes
(Universal Pictures), hard-c 17.00 42.50 120.00
4- Tom Mix and Tony in the Rider of Death Valley,
1934, EVW, Five Star Library, 160 pgs., movie scenes
(Universal Pictures), soft-c (Rare) 36.00 90.00 250.00
7- Tom Mix in the Texas Bad Man, 1934, EVW, Five Star Library,
160 pgs., movie scenes, hard-c 18.00 45.00 125.00
7- Tom Mix in the Texas Bad Man, 1934, EVW, Five Star Library,
160 pgs., movie scenes; soft-c (Rare) 36.00 90.00 250.00
10- Tom Mix in the Tepee Ranch Mystery, 1938, Whitman,
132 pgs., Buddy Book, soft-c 21.00 52.50 150.00
1126- Tommy of Troop Six (Scout Book), 1937, Saalfield, hard-c
9.00 22.50 55.00
1606- Tommy of Troop Six (Scout Book), 1937, Saalfield, soft-c
9.00 22.50 55.00
Tom Sawyer (See Adventures of ...)
1437- Tom Swift and His Magnetic Silencer, 1941, Whitman,
432 pgs., flip pictures 29.00 73.00 200.00
1485- Tom Swift and His Giant Telescope, 1939, Whitman,
432 pgs., James Gary-a 21.00 52.50 150.00
540- Top-Line Comics (In Open Box), 1935, Whitman, 164 pgs.,
3 1/2" x 3 1/2", 3 books in set, all soft-c:
Bobby Thatcher and the Samarang Emerald 16.00 40.00 110.00
Broncho Bill in Suicide Canyon 16.00 40.00 110.00
Freckles and His Friends in the North Woods 16.00 40.00 110.00
Complete set with box 50.00 125.00 350.00
541- Top-Line Comics (In Open Box), 1935, Whitman, 164 pgs.,
3 1/2" x 3 1/2", 3 books in set; all soft-c:
Little Joe and the City Gangsters 16.00 40.00 110.00
Smilin' Jack and His Flivver Plane 16.00 40.00 110.00
Streaky and the Football Signals 16.00 40.00 110.00
Complete set with box 50.00 125.00 350.00
542- Top-Line Comics (In Open Box), 1935, Whitman, 164 pgs.,
3 1/2" x 3 1/2", 3 books in set; all soft-c:
Dinglehoofer Und His Dog Adolph by Knerr 16.00 40.00 110.00
Jungle Jim by Alex Raymond 18.00 45.00 125.00
Sappo by Segar 18.00 45.00 125.00
Complete set with box 64.00 160.00 450.00
543- Top-Line Comics (In Open Box), 1935, Whitman, 164 pgs.,
3 1/2" x 3 1/2", 3 books in set; all soft-c:
Alexander Smart, ESQ by Winner 16.00 40.00 110.00
Bunky by Billy de Beck 16.00 40.00 110.00
Nicodemus O'Malley by Carter 16.00 40.00 110.00
Complete set with box 50.00 125.00 350.00
1158- Tracked by a G-Man, 1939, Saalfield, 400 pgs.
9.00 22.50 55.00
25- Trail of the Lonesome Pine, The, 1936, Lynn, movie scenes
12.00 30.00 85.00
nn- Trail of the Terrible 6 (See Tom Mix ...)
1185- Trail to Squaw Gulch, The, 1940, Saalfield, 400 pgs.
10.00 25.00 60.00
720- Treasure Island, 1933, Whitman, 362 pgs. 12.00 30.00 85.00
1141- Treasure Island, 1934, Whitman, 164 pgs., hard-c, 4 1/4" x 5 1/4",
Jackie Cooper photo-c, movie scenes 12.00 30.00 85.00
1141- Treasure Island, 1934, Whitman, 164 pgs., soft-c, 4 1/4" x 5 1/4",
Jackie Cooper photo-c, movie scenes 12.00 30.00 85.00
1018- Trick and Puzzle Book, 1939, Whitman, 100 pgs.,
soft-c 3.00 7.50 20.00
1100B- Tricks Easy to Do (Slight of hand & magic), 1938, Whitman,
36 pgs., 2 1/2" x 3 1/2", Penny Book 3.00 7.50 20.00
1100B- Tricks You Can Do, 1938, Whitman, 36 pgs., 2 1/2" x 3 1/2",
Penny Book 3.00 7.50 20.00
5777- Tweety and Sylvester, The Magic Voice, 1976, Whitman, 260 pgs.,
soft-c, flip-it feature; 5 printings 2.00 5.00 11.00
1104- Two-Gun Montana, 1936, Whitman, 432 pgs., Henry E. Vallely-a
10.00 25.00 60.00
nn- Two-Gun Montana Shoots it Out, 1939, Whitman, 36 pgs.,
2 1/2" x 3 1/2", Penny Book 10.00 25.00 60.00
1058- Ugly Duckling, The (Disney), 1939, Whitman, 68 pgs.,
5" x 5 1/2", hard-c 14.00 35.00 95.00
nn- Ugly Duckling, The, nd (1930s), np (Whitman), 36 pgs.,
3" x 2 1/2", Penny Book 4.00 10.00 22.00
Unc' Billy Gets Even (See Wee Little Books)
1114- Uncle Don's Strange Adventures, 1935, Whitman, 300 pgs.,
radio star-Uncle Don Carney 10.00 25.00 65.00
722- Uncle Ray's Story of the United States, 1934, Whitman,
300 pgs. 10.00 25.00 65.00
1461- Uncle Sam's Sky Defenders, 1941, Whitman, 432 pgs., flip pictures
10.00 25.00 60.00
1405- Uncle Wiggily's Adventures, 1946, Whitman, All Pictures Comics
12.00 30.00 85.00
1411- Union Pacific, 1939, Whitman, 240 pgs., photo-c, movie scenes
11.00 27.50 70.00
With Union Pacific letter 36.00 90.00 250.00
1189- Up Dead Horse Canyon, 1940, Saalfield, 400 pgs.
9.00 22.50 55.00
1455- Vic Sands of the U.S. Flying Fortress Bomber Squadron,
1944, Whitman, 352 pgs. 11.00 27.50 70.00
nn- Visit to Santa Claus, 1938?, Whitman, Pan Am premium by
Snow Plane; soft-c (Rare) 29.00 73.00 200.00
1645- Walt Disney's Andy Burnett on the Trail (TV Series),
1958, Whitman, 280 pgs. 4.00 10.00 27.00
803- Walt Disney's Bongo, 1948, Whitman,
hard-c, Story Hour Series 12.00 30.00 75.00
711-10-Walt Disney's Cinderella and the Magic Wand, 1950, Whitman,
2 1/2" x 5", based on Disney movie 10.00 25.00 65.00
845- Walt Disney's Donald Duck and his Cat Troubles (Disney), 1948,
Whitman, 100 pgs., 5" x 5 1/2", hard-c 12.00 30.00 75.00
845- Walt Disney's Donald Duck and the Boys, 1948, Whitman, 100 pgs.,
5" x 5 1/2", hard-c, Barks-a 21.00 52.50 150.00
2952- Walt Disney's Donald Duck in the Great Kite Maker,
1949, Whitman, 24 pgs., 3 1/4" x 4", Tiny Tales, full color (5 cents)
10.00 25.00 60.00
804- Walt Disney's Mickey and the Beanstalk, 1948, Whitman,
hard-c, Story Hour Series 12.00 30.00 75.00
845- Walt Disney's Mickey Mouse and the Boy Thursday,
194 pgs., Whitman, 5" x 5 1/2", 100 pgs. 12.00 30.00 75.00
845- Walt Disney's Mickey Mouse the Miracle Maker,
1948, Whitman, 5" x 5 1/2", 100 pgs. 12.00 30.00 75.00
2952- Walt Disney's Mickey Mouse and the Night Prowlers, Whitman, 1949,
24 pgs., 3 1/4" x 4", Tiny Tales, full color (5 ¢) 10.00 25.00 60.00
5770- Walt Disney's Mickey Mouse - Mystery at Disneyland, Whitman, 1975,
260 pgs., four printings 2.00 5.00 13.00
5781-2- Walt Disney's Mickey Mouse - Mystery at Dead Man's Cove, Whitman,
1980, 260 pgs., two printings 2.00 5.00 11.00
845- Walt Disney's Minnie Mouse and the Antique Chair,
1948, Whitman, 5" x 5 1/2", 100 pgs. 12.00 30.00 75.00
1435- Walt Disney's Pinocchio and Jiminy Cricket, 1940,
Whitman, 432 pgs. 25.00 62.50 175.00
nn- Walt Disney's Pinocchio and Jiminy Cricket, Fast Action Story,
1940, Dell, 432 pgs. 36.00 90.00 250.00
845- Walt Disney's Poor Pluto, 1948, Whitman, 5" x 5 1/2",
100 pgs., hard-c 12.00 30.00 75.00
1467- Walt Disney's Pluto the Pup (Disney), 1938, Whitman,
432 pgs., Gottfredson-a 16.00 40.00 110.00
1066- Walt Disney's Story of Clarabelle Cow (Disney),
1938, Whitman, 100 pgs. 12.00 30.00 75.00
66- Walt Disney's Story of Dippy the Goof (Disney),
1938, Whitman, 100 pgs. 12.00 30.00 75.00
1066- Walt Disney's Story of Donald Duck (Disney), 1938,
Whitman, 100 pgs., hard-c, Taliaferro-a 12.00 30.00 75.00
1066- Walt Disney's Story of Goofy (Disney), 1938, Whitman, 100 pgs.,
hard-c 12.00 30.00 75.00
1066- Walt Disney's Story of Mickey Mouse (Disney), 1938, Whitman, 100
pgs., hard-c, Gottfredson-a, Donald Duck app. 12.00 30.00 75.00
1066- Walt Disney's Story of Minnie Mouse (Disney),
1938, Whitman, 100 pgs., hard-c 12.00 30.00 75.00
1066- Walt Disney's Story of Pluto the Pup, (Disney),
1938, Whitman, 100 pgs., hard-c 12.00 30.00 75.00

518 - Wee Little Books © WHIT

1458 - Wimpy the Hamburger Eater © KING

5 - Zane Grey's King of the Royal Mounted in the Far North © WHIT

	GD	FN	VF/NM
2952- **Walter Lantz Presents Andy Panda's Rescue**, 1949, Whitman, Tiny Tales, full color (5 cents) (1030-5 on back-c)	10.00	25.00	60.00
751- **Wash Tubbs in Pandemonia**, 1934, Whitman, 320 pgs., Roy Crane-a	12.00	30.00	75.00
nn- **Wash Tubbs in Pandemonia**, 1934, Whitman, 52 pgs., 4" x 5 1/2", premium-no ads, soft-c, Roy Crane-a	20.00	50.00	140.00
1455- **Wash Tubbs and Captain Easy Hunting For Whales**, 1938, Whitman, 432 pgs., Roy Crane-a	12.00	30.00	75.00
6- **Wash Tubbs in Foreign Travel**, 1934, Whitman, soft-c, 3 1/2" x 3 1/2", Tarzan Ice Cream cup premium	29.00	73.00	200.00
513- **Wee Little Books** (In Open Box), 1934, Whitman, 44 pgs., small size, 6 books in set (children's classics) (Both Red box and Green box editions exist)			
Child's Garden of Verses	5.00	12.50	30.00
The Happy Prince (The Story of)	5.00	12.50	30.00
Joan of Arc (The Story of)	5.00	12.50	30.00
Peter Pan (The Story of)	5.00	12.50	30.00
Pied Piper Of Hamlin	5.00	12.50	30.00
Robin Hood (A Story of...)	5.00	12.50	30.00
Complete set with box	31.00	78.00	220.00
514- **Wee Little Books** (In Open Box), 1934, Whitman, 44 pgs., small size, 6 books in set			
Jack And Jill	5.00	12.50	30.00
Little Bo-Peep	5.00	12.50	30.00
Little Tommy Tucker	5.00	12.50	30.00
Mother Goose	5.00	12.50	30.00
Old King Cole	5.00	12.50	30.00
Simple Simon	5.00	12.50	30.00
Complete set with box	33.00	83.00	230.00
518- **Wee Little Books** (In Open Box), 1933, Whitman, 44 pgs., small size, 6 books in set, written by Thornton Burgess			
Betty Bear's Lesson-1930	5.00	12.50	30.00
Jimmy Skunk's Justice-1933	5.00	12.50	30.00
Little Joe Otter's Slide-1929	5.00	12.50	30.00
Peter Rabbit's Carrots-1933	5.00	12.50	30.00
Unc' Billy Gets Even-1930	5.00	12.50	30.00
Whitefoot's Secret-1933	5.00	12.50	30.00
Complete set with box	33.00	83.00	230.00
519- **Wee Little Books** (In Open Box) (Bible Stories), 1934, Whitman, 44 pgs., small size, 6 books in set, Helen Janes-a			
The Story of David	5.00	12.50	30.00
The Story of Gideon	5.00	12.50	30.00
The Story of Daniel	5.00	12.50	30.00
The Story of Joseph	5.00	12.50	30.00
The Story of Ruth and Naomi	5.00	12.50	30.00
The Story of Moses	5.00	12.50	30.00
Complete set with box	33.00	83.00	230.00
1471- **Wells Fargo**, 1938, Whitman, 240 pgs., photo-c, movie scenes	12.00	30.00	80.00
L18- **Western Frontier**, 1935, Lynn, 192 pgs., starring Ken Maynard, movie scenes	14.00	35.00	100.00
1121- **West Pointers on the Gridiron**, 1936, Saalfield, 148 pgs., hard-c, sports book	7.00	17.50	45.00
1601- **West Pointers on the Gridiron**, 1936, Saalfield, 148 pgs., soft-c, sports book	7.00	17.50	45.00
1124- **West Point Five, The**, 1937, Saalfield, 4 3/4" x 5 1/4", sports book, hard-c	7.00	17.50	45.00
1604- **West Point Five, The**, 1937, Saalfield, 4 1/4" x 5 1/4", sports book, soft-c	7.00	17.50	45.00
1164- **West Point of the Air**, 1935, Whitman, 160 pgs., photo-c, movie scenes	12.00	30.00	75.00
18- **Westward Ho!**, 1935, EVW, 160 pgs., movie scenes, starring John Wayne (Scarce)	57.00	143.00	400.00
1109- **We Three**, 1935, Saalfield, 160 pgs., photo-c, movie scenes, by John Barrymore, hard-c	10.00	25.00	60.00
1589- **We Three**, 1935, Saalfield, 160 pgs., photo-c, movie scenes, by John Barrymore, soft-c	10.00	25.00	60.00
Whitefoot's Secret (See Wee Little Books)			
nn- **Who's Afraid of the Big Bad Wolf**, "Three Little Pigs" (Disney), 1933, McKay, 36 pgs., 6" x 8 1/2", stiff-c, Disney studio-a	27.00	68.00	190.00
nn- **Wild West Adventures of Buffalo Bill**, 1935, Whitman, 260 pgs., Cocomalt premium, soft-c, Hal Arbo-a	12.00	30.00	80.00

	GD	FN	VF/NM
1096- **Will Rogers, The Story of**, 1935, Saalfield, photo-hard-c	8.00	20.00	50.00
1576- **Will Rogers, The Story of**, 1935, Saalfield, photo-soft-c	8.00	20.00	50.00
1458- **Wimpy the Hamburger Eater**, 1938, Whitman, 432 pgs., E.C. Segar-a	14.00	35.00	100.00
1433- **Windy Wayne and His Flying Wing**, 1942, Whitman, 432 pgs., flip pictures	10.00	25.00	60.00
1131- **Winged Four, The**, 1937, Saalfield, sports book, hard-c	10.00	25.00	60.00
1407- **Wings of the U.S.A.**, 1940, Whitman, 432 pgs., Thomas Hickey-a	10.00	25.00	60.00
nn- **Winning of the Old Northwest, The**, 1934, World Syndicate, High Lights of History Series, full color-c	10.00	25.00	60.00
nn- **Winning of the Old Northwest, The**, 1934, World Syndicate, High Lights of History Series; red & silver-c	10.00	25.00	60.00
1122- **Winning Point, The**, 1936, Saalfield, (Football), hard-c	7.00	17.50	40.00
1602- **Winning Point, The**, 1936, Saalfield, soft-c	7.00	17.50	40.00
nn- **Wizard of Oz Waddle Book**, 1934, BRP, 20 pgs., 7 1/2" x 10", forerunner of the Blue Ribbon Pop-Up books; with 6 removable articulated cardboard characters. Book only	54.00	135.00	375.00
Dust jacket only	61.00	153.00	490.00
Near Mint Complete - $12,500			
710-10- **Woody Woodpecker Big Game Hunter**, 1950, Whitman, by Walter Lantz	9.00	22.50	55.00
2010-(#10)- **Woody Woodpecker-The Meteor Menace**, 1967, Whitman, 260 pgs., 39¢-c, hard-c, color illos.	4.00	10.00	27.00
5753- **Woody Woodpecker-The Meteor Menace**, 1973, Whitman, 260 pgs., no price, soft-c, color illos.	1.00	2.50	6.00
2028- **Woody Woodpecker-The Sinister Signal**, 1969, Whitman	4.00	10.00	22.00
5763- **Woody Woodpecker-The Sinister Signal**, 1974, Whitman, 1st printing-no price; 2nd printing-39¢-c	1.00	2.50	6.00
23- **World of Monsters, The**, 1935, EVW, Five Star Library, movie scenes	12.00	30.00	85.00
779- **World War in Photographs, The**, 1934, Whitman, photo-c, photo illus.	9.00	22.50	55.00
Wyatt Earp (See Hugh O'Brian ...)			
nn- **Xena - Warrior Princess**, 1998, Chronicle Books, 310 pgs., based on TV series, 1-color (purple) illos	1.00	2.50	9.00
nn- **Yogi Bear Goes Country & Western**, 1977, Modern Promotions, 244 pgs., 49 cents, soft-c, flip pictures	2.00	5.00	13.00
nn- **Yogi Bear Saves Jellystone Park**, 1977, Modern Promotions, 244 pgs., 49 cents, soft-c, flip pictures	2.00	5.00	13.00
nn- **Zane Grey's Cowboys of the West**, 1935, Whitman, 148 pgs., 3 3/4" x 4", Tarzan Ice Cream Cup premium, soft-c, Arbo-a	29.00	73.00	200.00
Zane Grey's King of the Royal Mounted (See Men of the Mounted)			
1010- **Zane Grey's King of the Royal Mounted in Arctic Law**, 1937, Whitman, 7 1/4" x 5 1/2", 64 pgs., Nickel Book	12.00	30.00	75.00
1103- **Zane Grey's King of the Royal Mounted,** 1936, Whitman, 432 pgs.	10.00	25.00	65.00
nn- **Zane Grey's King of the Royal Mounted**, 1935, Whitman, 260 pgs., Cocomalt premium, soft-c	12.00	30.00	85.00
1179- **Zane Grey's King of the Royal Mounted and the Northern Treasure**, 1937, Whitman, 432 pgs.	10.00	25.00	60.00
1405- **Zane Grey's King of the Royal Mounted the Long Arm of the Law**, 1942, Whitman, All Pictures Comics	10.00	25.00	60.00
1452- **Zane Grey's King of the Royal Mounted Gets His Man**, 1938, Whitman, 432 pgs.	10.00	25.00	60.00
1486- **Zane Grey's King of the Royal Mounted and the Great Jewel Mystery**, 1939, Whitman, 432 pgs.	10.00	25.00	60.00
5- **Zane Grey's King of the Royal Mounted in the Far North**, 1938, Whitman, 132 pgs., Buddy Book, soft-c (Rare)	36.00	90.00	250.00
nn- **Zane Grey's King of the Royal Mounted in Law of the North**, 1939, Whitman, 36 pgs., 2 1/2" x 3 1/2", Penny Book	7.00	17.50	45.00
nn- **Zane Grey's King of the Royal Mounted Policing the Frozen North**, 1938, Dell, 196 pgs., Fast-Action Story, soft-c	18.00	45.00	125.00
1440- **Zane Grey's Tex Thorne Comes Out of the West**, 1937, Whitman, 432 pgs.	10.00	25.00	60.00
1465- **Zip Saunders King of the Speedway**, 1939, 432 pgs., Weisman-a	10.00	25.00	60.00

THE MARKETING OF A MEDIUM

by Dr. Arnold T. Blumberg, DCD

with new material and additional research by Sol M. Davidson, PhD, and Robert L. Beerbohm

Everyone wants something for free. It's in our nature to look for the quick fix, the good deal, the complimentary gift. We long to hit the lottery and quit our job, to win the trip around the world, or find that pot of gold at the end of the proverbial rainbow. Collectors in particular are certainly built to appreciate the notion of the "free gift," since it not only means a new item to collect and enjoy, but no risk or obligation in order to acquire it.

Ah, but there's the rub. Because things are not always what they seem, and "free gifts" usually come with a price. As the saying goes, "there's no such thing as a free lunch," so if it seems too good to be true, it probably is. This is the case even in the world of comics, where premiums and giveaways have a familiar agenda hidden behind the bright colors and fanciful stories. But where did it all begin?

Some of the earliest characters that were used as successful tools in promotional comics were Palmer Cox's creation "The Brownies." The illustration shown here showcases them drinking and endorsing Seal Brand Coffee.

EXTRA EXTRA

As we learn more about the early history of the comic book industry through continual investigation and the publishing of articles like those regularly featured in this book, we gain a much greater understanding of the financial and creative forces at work in shaping the medium, but perhaps one of the most intriguing and least recognized factors that influenced the dawn of comics is the concept of the premium or giveaway. (Note: Some of the historical information referenced in this article is derived from material also presented in Robert L. Beerbohm's introductory article to the Platinum Age section.)

The birth of the comic book as we know it today is intimately connected with the development of the comic strip in American newspapers and their use as an advertising and marketing tool for staple products such as bread, milk, and cereal. From the very beginning, comic characters have played several roles in pop culture, entertaining the youth of the country while also (sometimes none too subtly) acting as hucksters for whatever corporation foots the bill. From important staples to frivolous material produced simply to make a buck, these products have utilized the comics medium to sell, sell, sell. And what better way to hook a prospective customer than to give them "something for nothing?"

Starting in the 1850s, comics were being used in free almanacs such as **Elton's**, **Hostetter's** and **Wright's** to lure readers for the little booklets to sell patent medicine, farm products, tobacco, shoe polish, etc. Most of these are exceedingly rare today, hence it is difficult to compile an accurate history. More mention of these early precursors can be found in the Victorian Comics Era essay following this one. But although comic characters themselves were already being aggressively merchandised all around the world by the mid-1890s--as with, for example, Palmer Cox's **The Brownies**--the real starting point for the success of comics as a giveaway marketing mechanism can be traced to the introduction of **The Yellow Kid**, Richard Outcault's now legendary newspaper strip.

Newspaper publishers had already recognized that comic strips could boost circulation as well as please sponsors and advertisers by drawing more eyes to the page, so Sunday "supplements" were introduced to entice fans. Outcault's creation cemented the theory with proof of comic characters' marketing and merchandising power.

This unused cover was designed as the second cover for "Motion Picture Funnies Weekly." While the concept for this promotional comic title never caught on, the inaugural issue did feature the origin and first printed appearance of the Sub-Mariner.

Soon after, Outcault (who had most likely been inspired by Cox's merchandising success with **The Brownies** in the first place) caught lightning in a bottle once more with **Buster Brown**, who has the distinction of being America's first nationally licensed comic strip character. Soon, comic strips proliferated throughout the nation's newspapers as tycoons like Hearst and Pulitzer recognized the drawing power of the new medium and fought circulation wars to capture the pennies of the nouveau readership. They paid exorbitant salaries to comic strip artists such as Rudolph Dirks (**Katzenjammer Kids**), and used the funnies as newspaper supplements and as premiums to attract readers. Corporations soon had the chance to license recognizable personas as their own personal pitchmen (or women or animals...). Comic character merchandise wasn't far behind, resulting in a boom of future collectibles now catalogued in volumes like **Hake's Price Guide to Character Toys**.

TWO BIRTHS FOR THE PRICE OF ONE

Comic books themselves were at the heart of this movement, and giveaway and premium collections of comic strips not only appealed to children and adults alike, but provided the impetus for the birth of the modern comic book format itself. It could be said that without the concept of the giveaway comic or the marketing push behind it, there would be no comic book industry as we have it today. Well-known now is the story of how in spring 1933 Harry Wildenberg of Eastern Color Printing Company convinced Proctor & Gamble to sponsor the first modern comic book, **Funnies on Parade**, as a premium. Its success led to the first continuing comic book, **Famous Funnies**, and the rest, as they say, is history.

In 1935, while working on the printing presses of Eastern Color developing how modern comic books get printed, Juliun J. Proskauer came up with an idea for printing "Comic-Books-For-Industry." In July 1936 he made his first sale through his newly formed William C. Popper & Co. to David M. Davies, then advertising manager for Seagram's Distillers Corp. for three million copies of **Seagram's Merrymakers** in time for the 1936-37 Christmas season. "Thus was a new industry born," wrote **Printing News** in August 1945.

Even a casual perusal of the listings in this section of the Guide will dazzle the reader with the endless variety of purposes that this medium has served. Yes, promos have been used to hawk products from athletic equipment to zithers and zip codes, but comics are too versatile an art form to be confined to a few uses. They've swayed elections in cities (**The O'Dwyer Story**, 1949), in states (**Giant for a Day**: Jacob Javits, 1946) and nationwide (**The Story of Harry Truman**, 1948); solicited for charities (**Donald Duck and the Red Feather**, 1948); addressed health issues (**Blondie**, 1949, mental hygiene); discouraged kids from smoking (**Captain America Meets the Asthma Monster**, 1987); coached youngsters in sports skills (**Circling the Bases**, 1947, A.G. Spaulding); explained scientific complexities (**Adventures in Science**, 1946-61, GE); pleaded for social justice (**Consumer Comics**, 1975); espoused religious causes (**Oral Roberts' True Stories**, 1950s); protected the environment (**Our Spaceship Earth**, 1947); encouraged tourism (**Wyoming, The Cowboy State**, 1954); conveyed a sense of history (**Louisiana Purchase**, 1953); taught about computers (**Superman Radio Shack Giveaway**, 1980); trained employees (**Dial Finance Dialogues**, 1961-70) and executives (**Beneficial Finance System, Managing New Employees**, 1950s); cautioned safety (**Willy Wing Flap**, 1944(?)); announced corporate annual results (**Motorola Annual Report**, 1952); defended free enterprise (**Steve Merritt**, 1949); hammered communism (**How Stalin Hopes to Destroy America**, 1951); fought discrimination (**Mammy Yokum & the Great Dogpatch Mystery**, 1956, B'nai Brith); aided young workers in job-hunting (**The Job Scene**, 1969); battled the scourge of sickle cell anemia (**Where's Herbie**, 1972, U.S. H.E.W.); inspired the overcoming of adversity (**Al Capp by Li'l Abner**, 1946); fostered reading (**Linus Gets a Library Card**, 1960); recruited for the armed forces (**Li'l Abner Joins the Navy**, 1950); beguiled readers into learning languages (**Blondie**, 1949, Philadelphia public schools); and even instructed in such delicate matters as birth control

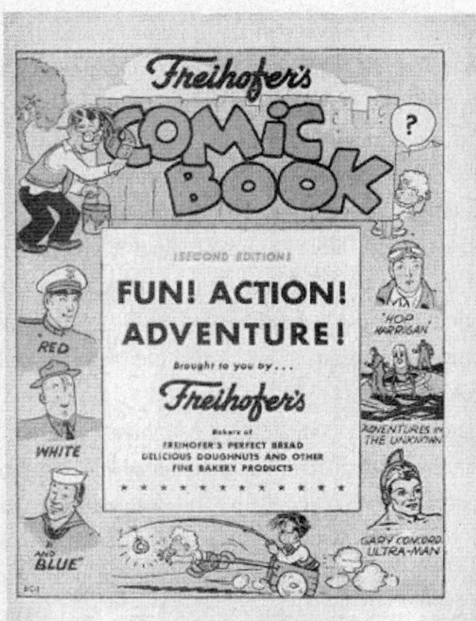

Every market and product has been on the promotional comic book bandwagon. Freihofer's Baking Company distributed a comic in the 1940s that featured reprinted pages from "All-American Comics."

(**Escape from Fear**, 1950 (revised 1959, etc.), for Planned Parenthood).

READ ALL ABOUT IT

The impact of this new approach to advertising was not lost on the business world. Contrary to modern belief, comic books were hardly discounted by the adults of the time...at least not those who had the marketing savvy to recognize an opportunity - or a threat - when they saw one. In the April 1933 issue of **Fortune** magazine, an article titled "The Funny Papers" trumpeted the arrival of comics as a force to be reckoned with in the world of advertising and business, and what's more, a force to fear as well. At first providing a brief survey of the newspaper comic strip business (which for many of the magazine's readers must have seemed a foreign topic for serious discussion), the article goes on to examine the incredible financial draw of comics and their characters:

"Between 70 and 75 per cent {sic} of the readers of any newspaper follow its comic sections regularly...Even the advertiser has succumbed to the comic, and in 1932 spent well over $1,000,000 for comic-paper space."

"**Comic Weekly** is the comic section of seventeen Hearst Sunday papers...Advertisers who market their wares through balloon-speaking manikins {sic} may enjoy the proximity of Jiggs, Maggie, Barney Google, and other funny Hearst headliners."

Although the article continues to cast the notion of relying on comic strip material to sell product in a negative light, actually suggesting that advertisers who utilize comics are violating unspoken rules of "advertising decorum" and bringing themselves "down to the level" of comics (and since when have advertisers been stalwart preservers of good taste and high moral standards), there is no doubt that they are viewing comics in a new light. The comic characters have arrived by 1933...and they're ready to help sell your merchandise too.

Fortune wasn't the only one to take notice as World War II came and went. In 1948, Louis P. Birk, the head of Brevity, Inc., an important promotional comics publisher said, "Comics are serious business." In an article in **Printers' Ink** magazine, he estimated that more than 80 different "comic booklets" had been produced and more than 45,000,000 million copies distributed in the five years before 1948. But of course, comics were serious business long before businessman/historian Birk noted the fact for posterity.

THE MARCH OF WAR AND BEYOND

Through the relentless currents of time, comic strips, books, and the characters that starred in them became more and more an intrinsic part of American culture. During the turmoil of the Great Depression and World War II, comic characters in print and celluloid form entertained while informing and selling at the same time, and premium and giveaway comics came well and truly into their own, pushing everything from loaves of bread to war bonds.

In the 1950s and '60s, there was a shift in focus as the power of giveaway and premium comics was applied to more altruistic endeavors than simply selling something. Comic book format pamphlets, fully illustrated and often inventively written, taught children about banking, money, the dangers of poison and other household products, and even chronicled moments in American history. The comic book as giveaway was now not only a marketing gimmick--it was a tool for educating as well.

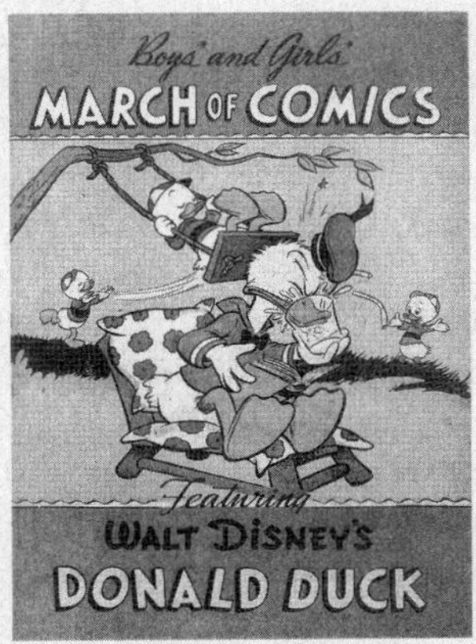

The promotional title "March of Comics" was a prolific comic that ran for 36 years and 488 issues featuring a variety of subjects and characters. (#20 shown)

The 1970s and '80s saw another boom in premium and giveaway comics. Every product imaginable seemed to have a licensing deal with a comic book character, usually one of the prominent flag bearers of the Big Two, Marvel or DC. Spider-Man fought bravely against the Beetle for the benefit of All Detergent; Captain America allied himself with the Campbell Kids; and Superman helped a class of computer students beat a disaster-conjuring foe at his own game with the help of Radio Shack Tandy computers.

Newspapers rediscovered the power of comics, not just with enlarged strip supplements but with actual comic books. Spider-Man, the Hulk, and others turned up as giveaway comic extras in various American newspapers (including Chicago and Dallas publications), while a whole series of public information comics like those produced decades earlier used superheroes to caution children about the dangers of smoking, drugs, and child abuse.

Comics also turned up in a plethora of other toy products as the 1980s introduced kids to the joy of electronic games and action figures. Supplementary comics provided "free" with action figure and video game packages told the backstory about the product, adding depth to the play experience while providing an extra incentive to buy. Comics became an intrinsic part of the Atari line of video cartridges, for example, eventually spawning its own full-blown newsstand series as well.

As the twentieth century gave way to the twenty-first, giveaway comics were still being produced for inclusion in action figure and video game packages, as well as in conjunction with countless consumer items and corporations. It seems that the medium still has a lot to offer for all those companies desperate to make the most of their market share.

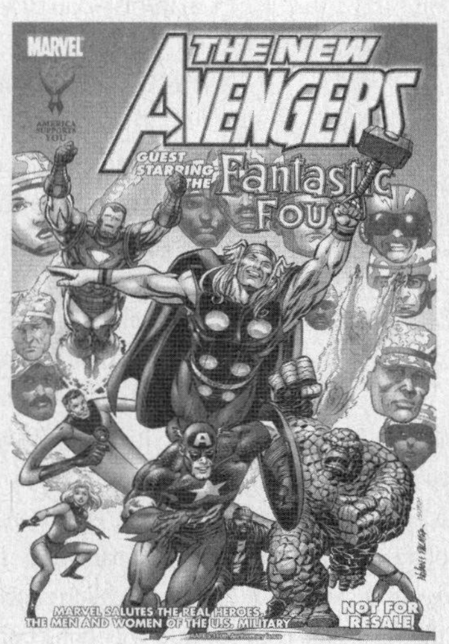

Today, promotional comics continue to be used as a marketing tool to reach both children and adults alike. This 2005 comic was produced by Marvel Comics as a salute to the men and women of the armed forces.

A COMIC BY ANY OTHER NAME

One of the earliest names for promotional comics was "special purpose comics." In their pursuit of superheroes, collectors have allowed promotional comics to lie fallow - under-appreciated and uncollected. Without a legitimate name, these products were given sundry other appellations - industrial comics, promos, giveaways, premiums, promics - each accurate but only for a small segment of the unorganized but lusty and lively medium. Perhaps no one name can cover all the variations and purposes of this branch of comic art, but for practical reasons if we accept the general premise that these comics were created to promote an idea, a product or a person, then "Promotional Comics" is probably as convenient a catch-all title as we can come up with.

We used the phrase "for practical reasons" because the word "practical" goes to the heart of promotional comics more than it does for any other comics product. What greater testimony is there to the medium's impact on American culture than to note their use by hard-headed, profit-minded business people and corporations? They invest their money and they expect results.

Today, premium comics continue to thrive and are still utilized as a valuable marketing and promotional tool. "Free" comics are still packaged with action figures and video games, and offered as mail-away premiums from a variety of product manufacturers. The comic industry itself has expanded its use of giveaway comics to self-promote as well, with "ash-can" and other giveaway editions turning up at conventions and comic shops to advertise upcoming series and special events. Many of these function as old-fashioned premiums, with a coupon or other response required from the reader to receive the comic.

As for the supplements and giveaways printed all those years ago, they have spawned a collectible fervor all their own, thanks to their atypical distribution and frequent rarity. For that and the desire to delve deeper into comics history, we hope that by focusing more directly on this genre, we can enhance our understanding of this vital component in the development and history of the modern comic book.

Whether you're a collector or not, we're all motivated by that desire to get something for nothing. For as long as consumers are enticed by the notion of the "free gift," promotional comics will remain a vital marketing component in many business models, but they will also continue to fight the stigma that has long been associated with the industry as a whole. "Respectable" sources like **Fortune** may have taken notice of the power of comic-related advertising 71 years ago, but after all this time comics still fight an uphill battle to establish some measure of dignity for the medium. Perhaps the higher visibility of promotional comics will eventually prove to be a deciding factor in that intellectual war.

See ya in the funny papers.

Action Zone #1 © CBS

Adventures of Big Boy #4 © Timely

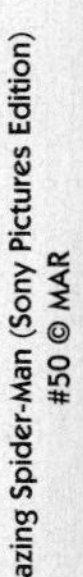
Amazing Spider-Man (Sony Pictures Edition) #50 © MAR

ACTION COMICS
DC Comics: 1947 - 1998 (Giveaway)

	GD 2.0	VG 4.0	FN 6.0	VF 8.0	VF/NM 9.0	NM- 9.2
1 (1976) paper cover w/10¢ price, 16 pgs. in color; reprints complete Superman story from #1 ('38)	4	8	12	25	40	55
1 (1976) Safeguard Giveaway; paper cover w/"free", 16 pgs. in color; reprints complete Superman story from #1 ('38)	4	8	12	25	40	55
1 (1983) paper cover w/10¢ price, 16 pgs. in color; reprints complete Superman story from #1 ('38)	3	6	9	15	22	28
1 (1987 Nestle Quik; 1988, 50¢)	2	4	6	8	10	12
1 (1992)-Came w/Reign of Superman packs						4.00
1 (1998 U.S. Postal Service, $7.95) Reprints entire issue; extra outer half-cover contains First Day Issuance of 32¢ Superman stamp with Sept. 10, 1998 Cleveland, OH postmark	1	2	3	5	6	8
Theater (1947, 32 pgs., 5" x 7", nn)-Vigilante story based on Columbia Vigilante serial; no Superman-c or story	65	130	195	416	708	1000

ACTION ZONE
CBS Television: 1994 (Promotes CBS Saturday morning cartoons)

	GD 2.0	VG 4.0	FN 6.0	VF 8.0	VF/NM 9.0	NM- 9.2
1-WildC.A.T.s, T.M.N.Turtles, Skeleton Warriors stories; Jim Lee-c						4.00

ADVENTURE COMICS
IGA: No date (early 1940s) (Paper-c, 32 pgs.)

	GD 2.0	VG 4.0	FN 6.0	VF 8.0	VF/NM 9.0	NM- 9.2
Two diff. issues; Super-Mystery-r from 1941	20	40	60	120	195	270

ADVENTURE IN DISNEYLAND
Walt Disney Productions (Dist. by Richfield Oil): May, 1955 (Giveaway, soft-c., 16 pgs)

	GD 2.0	VG 4.0	FN 6.0	VF 8.0	VF/NM 9.0	NM- 9.2
nn	11	22	33	60	83	105

ADVENTURES @ EBAY
eBay: 2000 (6 3/4" x 4 1/2", 16 pgs.)

	GD 2.0	VG 4.0	FN 6.0	VF 8.0	VF/NM 9.0	NM- 9.2
1-Judd Winick-a/Rucka & Van Meter-s; intro to eBay comic buying						2.50

ADVENTURES IN JET POWER
General Electric: 1950

	GD 2.0	VG 4.0	FN 6.0	VF 8.0	VF/NM 9.0	NM- 9.2
nn	8	16	24	40	50	60

ADVENTURES OF BIG BOY (Also titled Adventures of the Big Boy)
Timely Comics/Webs Adv. Corp./Illus. Features: 1956 - Present (Giveaway) (East & West editions of early issues)

	GD 2.0	VG 4.0	FN 6.0	VF 8.0	VF/NM 9.0	NM- 9.2
1-Everett-c/a	110	220	330	704	1202	1700
2-Everett-c/a	43	86	129	271	461	650
3-5: 4-Robot-c	20	40	60	114	182	250
6-10: 6-Sci/fic issue	9	18	27	52	126	190
11-20: 11,13-DeCarlo-a	7	14	21	44	72	100
21-30	4	8	12	25	40	55
31-50	3	6	9	16	24	32
51-100	2	4	6	9	13	16
101-150	2	4	6	8	10	12
151-240: 239-Wizard of Oz parody-c	1	2	3	5	7	9
241-265,267-269,271-300:						6.00
266-Superman x-over	3	6	9	17	26	35
270-TV's Buck Rogers-c/s	3	6	9	14	20	25
301-400						4.00
401-500						3.00
1-(2nd series - '76-'84,Paragon Prod.) (...Shoney's Big Boy)	1	3	4	6	8	10
2-20						5.00
21-50						3.00
Summer, 1959 issue, large size	6	12	18	42	79	115

ADVENTURES OF G. I. JOE
1969 (3-1/4x7") (20 & 16 pgs.)

First Series: 1-Danger of the Depths. 2-Perilous Rescue. 3-Secret Mission to Spy Island. 4-Mysterious Explosion. 5-Fantastic Free Fall. 6-Eight Ropes of Danger. 7-Mouth of Doom. 8-Hidden Missile Discovery. 9-Space Walk Mystery. 10-Fight for Survival. 11-The Shark's Surprise.
Second Series: 2-Flying Space Adventure. 4-White Tiger Hunt. 7-Capture of the Pygmy Gorilla. 12-Secret of the Mummy's Tomb.
Third Series: Reprinted surviving titles of First Series. **Fourth Series:** 13-Adventure Team Headquarters. 14-Search For the Stolen Idol.

	GD 2.0	VG 4.0	FN 6.0	VF 8.0	VF/NM 9.0	NM- 9.2
each....	3	6	9	17	26	35

ADVENTURES OF JELL-O MAN AND WOBBLY, THE
Welsh Publishing Group: 1991 ($1.25)

	GD 2.0	VG 4.0	FN 6.0	VF 8.0	VF/NM 9.0	NM- 9.2
1						4.00

ADVENTURES OF KOOL-AID MAN
Marvel Comics: 1983 - No. 3, 1985 (Mail order giveaway)
Archie Comics: No. 4, 1987 - No. 8, 1989

	GD 2.0	VG 4.0	FN 6.0	VF 8.0	VF/NM 9.0	NM- 9.2
1-8: 4-8-Dan DeCarlo-a/c	1	2	3	5	7	9

ADVENTURES OF MARGARET O'BRIEN, THE
Bambury Fashions (Clothes): 1947 (20 pgs. in color, slick-c, regular size) (Premium)

	GD 2.0	VG 4.0	FN 6.0	VF 8.0	VF/NM 9.0	NM- 9.2
In "The Big City" movie adaptation (scarce)	20	40	60	120	195	270

ADVENTURES OF QUIK BUNNY
Nestle's Quik: 1984 (Giveaway, 32 pgs.)

	GD 2.0	VG 4.0	FN 6.0	VF 8.0	VF/NM 9.0	NM- 9.2
nn-Spider-Man app.	2	4	6	9	13	16

ADVENTURES OF STUBBY, SANTA'S SMALLEST REINDEER, THE
W. T. Grant Co.: nd (early 1940s) (Giveaway, 12 pgs.)

	GD 2.0	VG 4.0	FN 6.0	VF 8.0	VF/NM 9.0	NM- 9.2
nn	8	16	24	40	50	60

ADVENTURES OF VOTEMAN, THE
Foundation For Citizen Education Inc.: 1968

	GD 2.0	VG 4.0	FN 6.0	VF 8.0	VF/NM 9.0	NM- 9.2
nn	4	8	12	27	44	60

ADVENTURES WITH SANTA CLAUS
Promotional Publ. Co. (Murphy's Store): No date (early 50's) (9-3/4x 6-3/4", 24 pgs., giveaway, paper-c)

	GD 2.0	VG 4.0	FN 6.0	VF 8.0	VF/NM 9.0	NM- 9.2
nn-Contains 8 pgs. ads	6	12	18	31	38	45
16 pg. version	7	14	21	35	43	50

AIR POWER (CBS TV & the U.S. Air Force Presents)
Prudential Insurance Co.: 1956 (5-1/4x7-1/4", 32 pgs., giveaway, soft-c)

	GD 2.0	VG 4.0	FN 6.0	VF 8.0	VF/NM 9.0	NM- 9.2
nn-Toth-a? Based on 'You Are There' TV program by Walter Cronkite	10	20	30	56	76	95

ALASKA BUSH PILOT
Jan Enterprises: 1959 (Paper cover, 10¢)

1-Promotes Bush Pilot Club (A 9.4 sold for $62 in 2014)
NOTE: *A CGC certified 9.9 Mint sold for $632.50 in 2005.*

ALICE IN BLUNDERLAND
Industrial Services: 1952 (Paper cover, 16 pgs. in color)

	GD 2.0	VG 4.0	FN 6.0	VF 8.0	VF/NM 9.0	NM- 9.2
nn-Facts about government waste and inefficiency	15	30	45	86	133	180

ALICE IN WONDERLAND
Western Printing Company/Whitman Publ. Co.: 1965; 1969; 1982

	GD 2.0	VG 4.0	FN 6.0	VF 8.0	VF/NM 9.0	NM- 9.2
Meets Santa Claus(1950s), nd, 16 pgs.	6	12	18	28	34	40
Rexall Giveaway(1965, 16 pgs., 5x7-1/4) Western Printing (TV, Hanna-Barbera)	3	6	9	16	23	30
Wonder Bakery Giveaway(1969, 16 pgs, color, nn, nd) (Continental Baking Company)	3	6	9	15	22	28

ALICE IN WONDERLAND MEETS SANTA
No publisher: nd (6-5/8x9-11/16", 16 pgs., giveaway, paper-c)

	GD 2.0	VG 4.0	FN 6.0	VF 8.0	VF/NM 9.0	NM- 9.2
nn	9	18	27	50	65	80

ALL ABOARD, MR. LINCOLN
Assoc. of American Railroads: Jan, 1959 (16 pgs.)

	GD 2.0	VG 4.0	FN 6.0	VF 8.0	VF/NM 9.0	NM- 9.2
nn-Abraham Lincoln and the Railroads	6	12	18	28	34	40

ALL NEW COMICS
Harvey Comics: Oct, 1993 (Giveaway, no cover price, 16 pgs.)(Hanna-Barbera)

	GD 2.0	VG 4.0	FN 6.0	VF 8.0	VF/NM 9.0	NM- 9.2
1-Flintstones, Scooby Doo, Jetsons, Yogi Bear & Wacky Races previews for upcoming Harvey's new Hanna-Barbera line-up	1	2	3	4	5	7

NOTE: *Material previewed in Harvey giveaway was eventually published by Archie.*

AMAZING SPIDER-MAN, THE
Marvel Comics Group

	GD 2.0	VG 4.0	FN 6.0	VF 8.0	VF/NM 9.0	NM- 9.2
Acme & Dingo Children's Boots (1980)-Spider-Woman app.	2	4	6	11	16	20
Adventures in Reading Starring... (1990,1991) Bogdanove & Romita-c/a						5.00
Aim Toothpaste Giveaway (36 pgs., reg. size)-1 pg. origin recap; Green Goblin-c/story	2	4	6	10	14	18
Aim Toothpaste Giveaway (16 pgs., reg. size)-Dr. Octopus app.	2	4	6	10	14	18
All Detergent Giveaway (1979, 36 pgs.), nn-Origin-r	2	4	6	10	14	18
Amazing Fantasy #15 (8/02) reprint included in Spider-Man DVD Collector's Gift Set						5.00
Amazing Fantasy #15 (2006) News America Marketing newspaper giveaway						4.00
Amazing Spider-Man nn (1990, 6-1/8x9", 28 pgs.)-Shan-Lon giveaway; retells origin of Spider-Man; Bagley-a/Saviuk-c	2	4	6	8	10	12
Amazing Spider-Man nn (1990, 6-1/8x9", 28 pgs.)-Shan-Lon giveaway; reprints Amazing Spider-Man #303 w/McFarlane-c/a	2	4	6	8	10	12

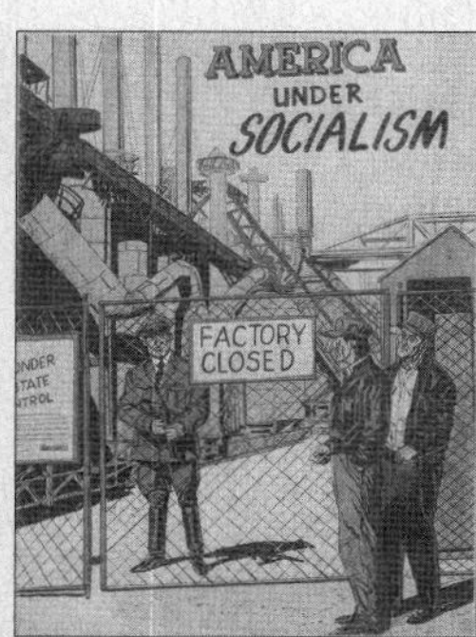

America Under Socialism nn © NRB

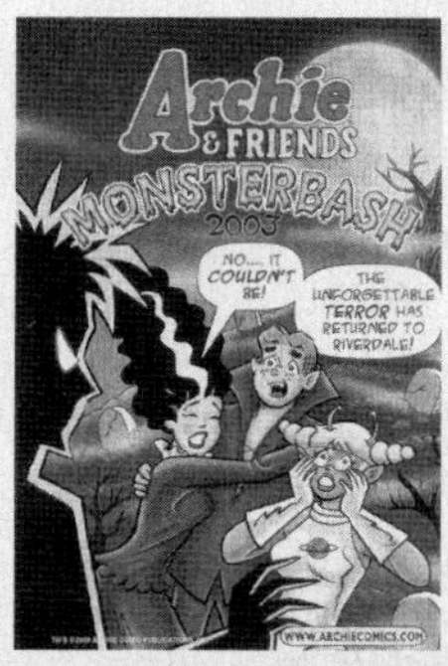

Archie and Friends Monster Bash 2003 © AP

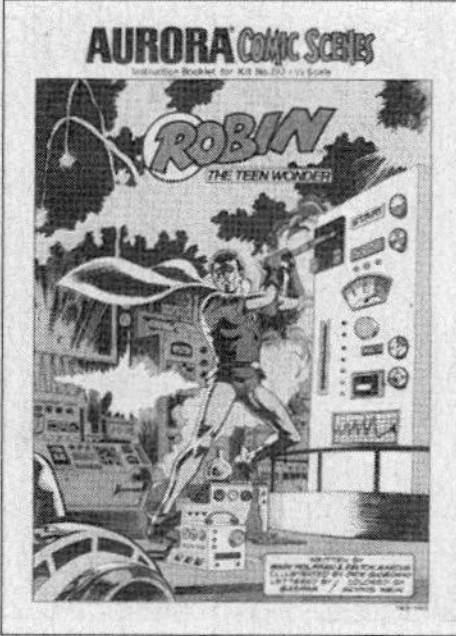

Aurora Comic Scenes Instruction Booklet - Robin © DC

	GD	VG	FN	VF	VF/NM	NM-
	2.0	4.0	6.0	8.0	9.0	9.2

Amazing Spider-Man #1 Reprint (1990, 4-1/4x6-1/4", 28 pgs.)-Packaged with the book "Start Collecting Comic Books" from Running Press 4.00
Amazing Spider-Man #3 Reprint (2004)-Best Buy/Sony giveaway 2.50
Amazing Spider-Man #50 (Sony Pictures Edition) (8/04)-mini-comic included in Spider-Man 2 movie DVD Collector's Gift Set; r/#50 & various ASM covers with Dr. Octopus 2.50
Amazing Spider-Man #129 (Lion Gate Films) (6/04)-promotional comic given away at movie theaters on opening night for The Punisher 2.50
...& Power Pack (1984, nn)(Nat'l Committee for Prevention of Child Abuse) (two versions, mail offer & store giveaway)-Mooney-a; Byrne-c
Mail offer 2 4 6 9 11 14
Store giveaway 5.00
...& The Hulk (Special Edition)(6/8/80; 20 pgs.)-Supplement to Chicago Tribune .2 4 6 10 14 18
...& The Incredible Hulk (1981, 1982; 36 pgs.)-Sanger Harris or May D&F supplement to Dallas Times, Dallas Herald, Denver Post, Kansas City Star, Tulsa World; Foley's supplement to Houston Chronicle (1982, 16 pgs.)- "Great Rodeo Robbery"; The Jones Store-giveaway (1983, 16 pgs.) 2 4 6 13 18 22
...and the New Mutants Featuring Skids nn (National Committee for Prevention of Child Abuse/K-Mart giveaway)-Williams-c(i) 5.00
... Battles Ignorance (1992)(Sylvan Learning Systems) giveaway; Mad Thinker app. Kupperberg-a 1 2 3 5 7 9
...Captain America, The Incredible Hulk, & Spider-Woman (1981) (7-11 Stores giveaway; 36 pgs.) 2 4 6 11 16 20
...: Christmas in Dallas (1983) (Supplement to Dallas Times Herald) giveaway 2 4 6 11 16 20
...: Danger in Dallas (1983) (Supplement to Dallas Times Herald) giveaway 2 4 6 11 16 20
...: Danger in Denver (1983) (Supplement to Denver Post) giveaway for May D&F stores 2 4 6 11 16 20
..., Fire-Star, And Ice-Man at the Dallas Ballet Nutcracker (1983; supplement to Dallas Times Herald)-Mooney-p 2 4 6 11 16 20
Giveaway-Esquire Magazine (2/69)-Miniature-Still attached (scarce) 12 24 36 83 182 280
Giveaway-Eye Magazine (2/69)-Miniature-Still attached 9 18 27 60 120 180
...: Riot at Robotworld (1991; 16 pgs.)(National Action Council for Minorities in Engineering, Inc.) giveaway; Saviuk-c 1 2 3 5 6 8
..., Storm & Powerman (1982; 20 pgs.)(American Cancer Society) giveaway; also a 1991 2nd printing and a 1994 printing 1 2 3 5 6 8
...Vs. The Hulk (Special Edition; 1979, 20 pgs.)(Supplement to Columbus Dispatch) 2 4 6 13 18 22
...Vs. The Prodigy (Giveaway, 16 pgs. in color (1976, 5x6-1/2")-Sex education; (1 million printed; 35-50¢) 2 4 6 8 10 12
Spidey & The Mini-Marvels Halloween 2003 Ashcan (12/03, 8 1/2"x 5 1/2") Giarusso-s/a; Venom and Green Goblin app. 2.00

AMERICA MENACED!
Vital Publications: 1950 (Paper-c)
nn-Anti-communism 39 78 117 236 388 540

AMERICAN COMICS
Theatre Giveaways (Liberty Theatre, Grand Rapids, Mich. known): 1940's
Many possible combinations. "Golden Age" superhero comics with new cover added and given away at theaters. Following known: Superman #59, Capt. Marvel #20, 21, Capt. Marvel Jr. #5, Action #33, Classics Comics #8, Whiz #39. Value would vary with book and should be 70-80 percent of the original.

AMERICA UNDER SOCIALISM
National Research Bureau: 1950 (Paper-c)
nn-Anti-communism; 16 pages (a VG copy sold for $806 in 2016)

ANDY HARDY COMICS
Western Printing Co.:
...& the New Automatic Gas Clothes Dryer (1952, 5x7-1/4", 16 pgs.) Bendix Giveaway (soft-c) 6 12 18 31 38 45

ANIMANIACS EMERGENCY WORLD
DC Comics: 1995
nn-American Red Cross 5.00

APACHE HUNTER
Creative Pictorials: 1954 (18 pgs. in color) (promo copy) (saddle stitched)
nn-Severin, Heath stories 15 30 45 85 130 175

AQUATEERS MEET THE SUPER FRIENDS
DC Comics: 1979
nn 2 4 6 11 16 20

ARCHIE AND HIS GANG (Zeta Beta Tau Presents...)
Archie Publications: Dec. 1950 (St. Louis National Convention giveaway)
nn-Contains new cover stapled over Archie Comics #47 (11-12/50) on inside; produced for Zeta Beta Tau 25 50 75 150 245 340

ARCHIE COMICS (Also see Sabrina)
Archie Publications
... And Friends and the Shield (10/02, 8 1/2"x 5 1/2") Diamond Comic Dist. 4.00
... And Friends - A Halloween Tale (10/98, 8 1/2"x 5 1/2") Diamond Comic Dist.; Sabrina and Sonic app.; Dan DeCarlo-a 4.00
... And Friends - A Timely Tale (10/01, 8 1/2"x 5 1/2") Diamond Comic Dist. 4.00
... And Friends Monster Bash 2003 (8 1/2"x 5 1/2") Diamond Comic Dist. Halloween 4.00
...And His Friends Help Raise Literacy Awareness In Mississippi nn (3/94) 1 2 3 5 6 8
...And His Friends Vs. The Household Toxic Wastes nn (1993, 16 pgs.) produced for the San Diego Regional Household Hazardous Materials Program 1 2 3 5 6 8
...And His Pals in the Peer Helping Program nn (2/91, 7"x4 1/2") produced by the FBI 1 2 3 5 6 8
...And the History of Electronics nn (5/90, 36 pgs.)-Radio Shack giveaway; Bender-c/a 1 2 3 5 6 8
Fairmont Potato Chips Giveaway-Mini comics 1970 (6 issues-nn's.,6 7/8" x 2 1/4", 8 pgs. each) 3 6 9 18 28 38
Fairmont Potato Chips Giveaway-Mini comics 1971 (4 issues-nn's.,6 7/8" x 5", 8 pgs. each) 3 6 9 18 28 38
Little Archie, The House That Wouldn't Move ('07, 8-1/2" x 5-3/8" Halloween mini-comic) 2.00
...'s Ham Radio Adventure (1997) Morse code instruction; Goldberg-a 6.00
...'s Weird Mysteries (9/99, 8 1/2"x 5 1/2") Diamond Comic Dist. Halloween giveaway 3.00
Tales From Riverdale (2006, 8 1/2"x 5 1/2") Diamond Comic Dist. Halloween giveaway 3.00
...: The Dawn of Time ('10, 8-1/2" x 5-3/8" Halloween mini-comic) 3.00
...: The Mystery of the Museum Sleep-In ('08, 8-1/2" x 5-3/8" Halloween mini-comic) 3.00
... Your Official Store Club Magazine nn (10/48, 9-1/2x6-1/2, 16 pgs.)- "Wolf Whistle" Archie on front-c; B. R. Baker Co. ad on back-c (a CGC 7.5 copy sold for $1912 in Feb. 2013)

ARCHIE SHOE-STORE GIVEAWAY
Archie Publications: 1944-50 (12-15 pgs. of games, puzzles, stories like Superman-Tim books, No nos. - came out monthly)

Issue	GD 2.0	VG 4.0	FN 6.0	VF 8.0	VF/NM 9.0	NM- 9.2
(1944-47)-issues	22	44	66	132	216	300
2/48-Peggy Lee photo-c	22	44	66	132	216	300
3/48-Marylee Robb photo-c	20	40	60	114	182	250
4/48-Gloria De Haven photo-c	22	44	66	132	216	300
5/48, 6/48, 7/48, 10/48	20	40	60	114	182	250
8/48-Story on Shirley Temple	24	48	72	140	230	320
5/49-Kathleen Hughes photo-c	19	38	57	111	176	240
6/49, 7/49, 9/49	17	34	51	98	154	210
8/49-Archie photo-c from radio show	28	56	84	165	270	375
10/49-Gloria Mann photo-c from radio show	21	42	63	122	199	275
11/49, 12/49, 2/50, 3/50	19	38	57	112	179	245

ARCHIE'S JOKE BOOK MAGAZINE (See Joke Book ...)
Archie Publications
Drug Store Giveaway (No. 39 w/new-c) 8 16 24 40 50 60

ARCHIE'S TEN ISSUE COLLECTOR'S SET (Title inside of cover only)
Archie Publications: June, 1997 - No. 10, June, 1997 ($1.50, 20 pgs.)
1-10: 1,7-Archie. 2,8-Betty & Veronica. 3,9-Veronica. 4-Betty. 5-World of Archie. 6-Jughead. 10-Archie and Friends each... 5.00

ASTRO COMICS
American Airlines (Harvey): 1968 - 1979 (Giveaway)(Reprints of Harvey comics)
1968-Richie Rich, Hot Stuff, Casper, Wendy on-c only; Spooky and Nightmare app. inside 3 6 9 19 30 40
1970-Casper, Spooky, Hot Stuff, Stumbo the Giant, Little Audrey, Little Lotta, & Richie Rich reprints. Five different versions 3 6 9 16 23 30
1973,1975,1976: 1973-Three different versions 2 4 6 9 12 15
1977-r/Richie Rich & Casper #20. 1978-r/Richie Rich & Casper #25. 1979-r/Richie Rich & Casper #30 (scarce) 2 4 6 8 10 12

ATARI FORCE (Given away with Atari games)
DC Comics: 1982 - No. 5, 1983
1-3 (1982, 5X7", 52 pgs.) 1 2 3 5 6 8
4,5 (1982-1983, 52 pgs.)(scarcer) 2 4 6 9 12 15

AURORA COMIC SCENES INSTRUCTION BOOKLET (Included with superhero model kits)
Aurora Plastics Co.: 1974 (6-1/4x9-3/4," 8 pgs., slick paper)
181-140-Tarzan; Neal Adams-a 3 6 9 18 27 38
182-140-Spider-Man. 4 8 12 23 37 50
183-140-Tonto(Gil Kane art). 184-140-Hulk. 185-140-Superman. 186-140-Superboy.

Bionicle #9 © LEGO

Blind Justice © DC

Blood is the Harvest © CG

	GD 2.0	VG 4.0	FN 6.0	VF 8.0	VF/NM 9.0	NM- 9.2

187-140-Batman. 188-140-The Lone Ranger(1974-by Gil Kane). 192-140-Captain America(1975). 193-140-Robin 3 6 9 16 23 30

BACK TO THE FUTURE
Harvey Comics
Special nn (1991, 20 pgs.)-Brunner-c; given away at Universal Studios in Florida 6.00

BALTIMORE COLTS
American Visuals Corp.: 1950 (Giveaway)
nn-Eisner-c 43 86 129 271 461 650

BAMBI (Disney)
K. K. Publications (Giveaways): 1941, 1942
1941-Horlick's Malted Milk & various toy stores; text & pictures; most copies mailed out with store stickers on-c 43 86 129 271 461 650
1942-Same as 4-Color #12, but no price (Same as '41 issue?) (Scarce) 97 194 291 621 1061 1500

BATMAN
DC Comics: 1966 - Present
Act II Popcorn mini-comic(1998) 5.00
Batman #121 Toys R Us edition (1997) r/1st Mr. Freeze 5.00
Batman #279 Mini-comic with Monogram Model kit (1995) 5.00
Batman #362 Mervyn's edition (1989) 5.00
Batman #608 New York Post edition (2002) 5.00
Batman Adventures #25 Best Western edition (1997) 5.00
Batman and Other DC Classics 1 (1989, giveaway)-DC Comics/Diamond Comic Distributors; Batman origin-r/Batman #47, Camelot 3000-r, Justice League-r('87), New Teen Titans-r 5.00
Batman and Robin movie preview (1997, 8 pgs.) Kellogg's Cereal promo 3.00
Batman Beyond Six Flags edition 1 2 3 5 6 8
Batman: Canadian Multiculturalism Custom (1992) 5.00
Batman Claritan edition (1999) 3.00
Kellogg's Poptarts comics (1966, Set of 6, 16 pgs.); All were folded and placed in Poptarts boxes. Infantino art on Catwoman and Joker issues.
"The Man in the Iron Mask", "The Penguin's Fowl Play", "The Joker's Happy Victims", "The Catwoman's Catnapping Caper", "The Mad Hatter's Hat Crimes", "The Case of the Batman II"
each.... 5 10 15 30 50 70
Mask of the Phantasm (1993) Mini-comic released w/video 1 2 3 5 7 9
Onstar - Auto Show Special Edition (OnStar Corp., 2001, 8 pgs.) Riddler app. 3.00
Pizza Hut giveaway (12/77)-exact-r of #122,123; Joker-c/story 2 4 6 9 12 15
Prell Shampoo giveaway (1966, 16 pgs.)- "The Joker's Practical Jokes" (6-7/8x3-3/8") 10 20 30 64 132 200
Revell in pack (1995) 4.00
...: The 10-Cent Adventure (3/02, 10¢) intro. to the "Bruce Wayne: Murderer" x-over; Rucka-s/ Burchett & Janson-a/Dave Johnson-c; these are alternate copies with special outer half-covers (at least 10 different) promoting comics, toys and games shops 3.00

BATMAN RECORD COMIC
National Periodical Publications: 1966 (one-shot)
1-With record (still sealed) 12 24 36 79 170 260
Comic only 7 14 21 49 92 135

BEETLE BAILEY
Charlton Comics: 1969-1970 (Giveaways)
Armed Forces ('69)-same as regular issue (#68) 2 4 6 10 14 18
Armed Forces ('70) 2 4 6 10 14 18
Bold Detergent ('69)-same as regular issue (#67) 2 4 6 10 14 18
Cerebral Palsy Assn. V2#71('69) - V2#73(#1,1/70) 2.00
Red Cross (1969, 5x7", 16 pgs., paper-c) 2 4 6 10 14 18

BELLAIRE BICYCLE CO.
Bellaire Bicycle Co.: 1940 (promotional comic)(64 pgs.)
nn-Contains Wonderworld #12 w/new-c. Contents can vary w/diff. 1940's books 39 78 117 231 378 525

BEST WESTERN GIVEAWAY
DC Comics: 1999
nn-Best Western hotels 2.50

BETTER LIFE FOR YOU, A
Harvey Publications Inc.: (16 pgs., paper cover)
nn-Better living through higher productivity 3 6 9 15 22 28

BEWARE THE BOOBY TRAP
Malcolm Alter: 1970 (5" x 7")
nn-Deals with drug abuse 4 8 12 23 37 50

B-FORCE (Milwaukee Brewers and Wisconsin Dental Asso.)
Dark Horse Comics: 2001 (School and stadium giveaway)
nn-Brewers players combat the evils of smokeless tobacco 3.00

BIG BOY (see Adventures of...)

BIG JIM'S P.A.C.K.
Mattel, Inc. (Marvel Comics): No date (1975) (16 pgs.)
nn-Giveaway with Big Jim doll; Buscema/Sinnott-c/a 4 8 12 23 37 50

"BILL AND TED'S EXCELLENT ADVENTURE" MOVIE ADAPTATION
DC Comics: 1989 (No cover price)
nn-Torres-a 4.00

BIONICLE (LEGO robot toys)
DC Comics: Jun, 2001 - No. 27, Nov, 2005 ($2.25/$3.25, 16 pages, available to LEGO club members)
1 1 2 3 5 6 8
2-5 6.00
6-13 4.00
14-27 3.00
The Legend of Bionicle (McDonald's Mini-comic, 4-1/4 x 7") 4.00
Special Edition #0 (Six Heroes...One Destiny) '03 San Diego Comic Con; Ashley Wood-c 6.00

BLACK GOLD
Esso Service Station (Giveaway): 1945? (8 pgs. in color)
nn-Reprints from True Comics 6 12 18 28 34 40

BLADE SINS OF THE FATHER
Marvel Comics: Aug, 1996 (24 pgs. with paper cover)
1-Theatrical preview; possibly limited to 2000 copies (Value will be based on sale)

BLAZING FOREST, THE (See Forest Fire and Smokey Bear)
Western Printing: 1962 (20 pgs., 5x7", slick-c)
nn-Smokey The Bear fire prevention 3 6 9 14 20 26

BLESSED PIUS X
Catechetical Guild (Giveaway): No date (Text/comics, 32 pgs., paper-c)
nn 8 16 24 40 50 60

BLIND JUSTICE (Also see Batman: Blind Justice)
DC Comics/Diamond Comic Distributors: 1989 (Giveaway, squarebound)
nn-Contains Detective #598-600 by Batman movie writer Sam Hamm, w/covers; published same time as originals? 6.00

BLONDIE COMICS
Harvey Publications: 1950-1964
1950 Giveaway 8 16 24 40 50 60
1962,1964 Giveaway 3 6 9 16 23 30
N. Y. State Dept. of Mental Hygiene Giveaway-(1950) Regular size; 16 pgs.; no # 4 8 12 23 37 50
N. Y. State Dept. of Mental Hygiene Giveaway-(1956) Regular size; 16 pgs.; no # 3 6 9 16 24 32
N. Y. State Dept. of Mental Hygiene Giveaway-(1961) Regular size; 16 pgs.; no # 3 6 9 15 22 28

BLOOD IS THE HARVEST
Catechetical Guild: 1950 (32 pgs., paper-c)
(Scarce)-Anti-communism (21 known copies) 245 490 735 1568 2684 3800
Black & white version (5 known copies), saddle stitched 107 214 321 680 1165 1650
Untrimmed version (only one known copy); estimated value - $1000
NOTE: *In 1979 nine copies of the color version surfaced from the old Guild's files plus the five black & white copies.*

BLUE BIRD CHILDREN'S MAGAZINE, THE
Graphic Information Service: V1#2, 1957 - No. 10 1958 (16 pgs., soft-c, regular size)
V1#2-10: Pat, Pete & Blue Bird app. 2 4 6 8 11 14

BLUE BIRD COMICS
Various Shoe Stores: 1947 - 1950 (Giveaway, 36 pgs.)
Charlton Comics: 1959 - 1964 (Giveaway)
nn-(1947-50, not Charlton)(36 pgs.)-Several issues; Human Torch, Sub-Mariner app. in some 18 36 54 105 165 225
1959-(Charlton) Lil Genius, Wild Bill Hickok, Black Fury, Masked Raider, Timmy The Timid Ghost, Freddy (All #1) 3 6 9 14 20 26
1959-(Charlton, same 6 titles; all #2-5) except (#5) Masked Raider #21 3 6 9 14 20 25
1959-(#5) Masked Raider #21 3 6 9 15 22 28
1960-(6 titles, all #6-9) Black Fury, Masked Raider, Freddy, Timmy the Timid Ghost,

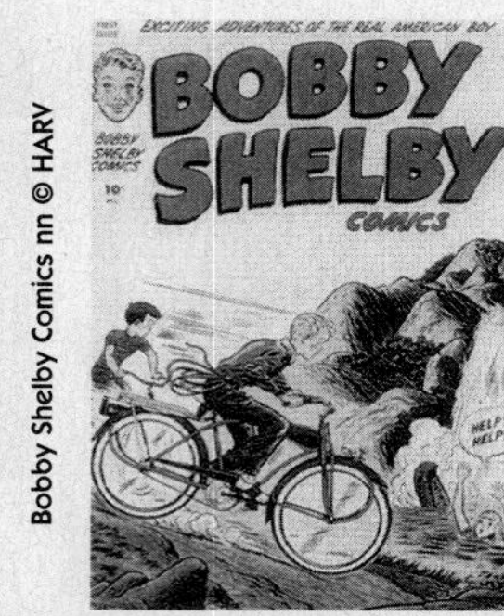

Bobby Shelby Comics nn © HARV

Buster Brown Comics #8 © Brown Shoe Co.

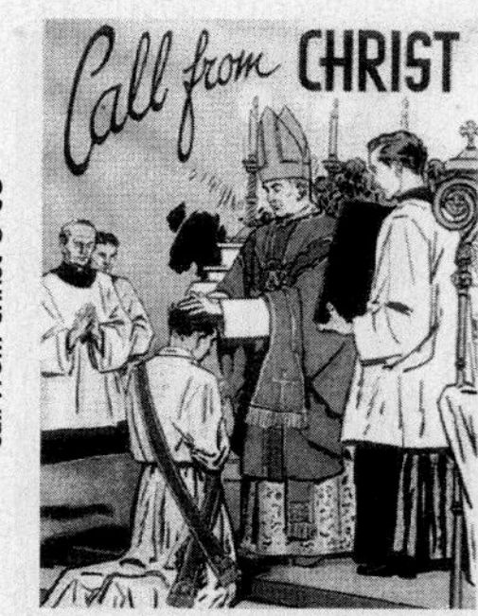

Call From Christ © CG

	GD	VG	FN	VF	VF/NM	NM-
	2.0	4.0	6.0	8.0	9.0	9.2

Li'l Genius, Six Gun Heroes 3 6 9 14 19 24
1961-(All #10's) Black Fury, Masked Raider, Freddy, Timmy the Timid Ghost,
Li'l Genius, Six Gun Heroes (Charlton) 2 4 6 13 18 22
1961-(All #11-13) Lil Genius, Wyatt Earp, Black Fury, Timmy the Timid Ghost, Atomic Mouse,
Freddy 2 4 6 13 18 22
1962-(All #14) Lil Genius, Wyatt Earp, Black Fury, Timmy the Timid Ghost, Atomic Mouse,
Freddy 2 4 6 13 18 22
1962-(6 titles, all #15) Lil Genius, Six Gun Heroes, Black Fury, Timmy the Timid Ghost,
Texas Rangers, Freddy 2 4 6 13 18 22
1962-(7 titles, all #16) Lil Genius, Six Gun Heroes, Black Fury, Timmy the Timid Ghost,
Texas Rangers, Wyatt Earp, Atomic Mouse 2 4 6 13 18 22
1963-(All #17) My Little Margie, Lil Genius, Timmy the Timid Ghost, Texas Rangers (Charlton)
2 4 6 9 13 16
1964-(All #18) Mysteries of Unexplored Worlds, Teenage Hotrodders, War Heroes, Wyatt Earp
(Charlton) 2 4 6 9 13 16

NOTE: *Reprints comics of regular issue, with Blue Bird shoe promo on back cover, with upper front cover imprint of various shoe retailers. Printed from 1959 to 1962, with issues 1 thru 16. The 8 different front cover imprints for issues 1 thru 16 are, 1) Blue Bird Shoes, 2) Schiff's Shoes, 3) Big Shoe Store, 4) E.D. Edwards Shoe Store, 5) R & S Shoe store, 6) Federal Shoe Store, 7) Kirby's Shoes, 8) Gallenkamps.*

BOB & BETTY & SANTA'S WISHING WHISTLE (Also see A Christmas Carol, Merry Christmas From Sears Toyland, and Santa's Christmas Comic Variety Show)
Sears Roebuck & Co.: 1941 (Christmas giveaway, 12 pgs., oblong)
nn 21 42 63 122 199 275

BOBBY BENSON'S B-BAR-B RIDERS (Radio)
Magazine Enterprises/AC Comics
...in the Tunnel of Gold-(1936, 5-1/4x8"; 100 pgs.) Radio giveaway by Hecker-H.O. Company (H.O. Oats); contains 22 color pgs. of comics, rest in novel form
11 22 33 64 90 115
...And The Lost Herd-same as above 11 22 33 64 90 115

BOBBY SHELBY COMICS
Shelby Cycle Co./Harvey Publications: 1949
nn 5 10 14 20 24 28

BONE
Cartoon Books: Halloween, 2008 (8-1/2" x 5-3/8" mini-comic giveaway)
nn-Jeff Smith-s/a 2.00

BOY SCOUT ADVENTURE
Boy Scouts of America: 1954 (16 pgs., paper cover)
nn 5 10 15 22 26 30

BOYS' RANCH
Harvey Publications: 1951
Shoe Store Giveaway #5,6 (Identical to regular issues except Simon & Kirby centerfold replaced with ad) 14 28 42 76 108 140

BOZO THE CLOWN (TV)
Dell Publishing Co.: 1961
Giveaway-1961, 16 pgs., 3-1/2x7-1/4", Apsco Products
5 10 15 30 50 70

BRER RABBIT IN "ICE CREAM FOR THE PARTY"
American Dairy Association: 1955 (5x7-1/4", 16 pgs., soft-c) (Walt Disney) (Premium)
nn-(Scarce) 39 78 117 231 378 525

BUCK ROGERS (In the 25th Century)
Kelloggs Corn Flakes Giveaway: 1933 (6x8", 36 pgs)
370A-By Phil Nowlan & Dick Calkins; 1st Buck Rogers radio premium & 1st app. in comics (tells origin) (Reissued in 1995) 54 108 162 400 - -
with envelope 74 148 222 550 - -

BUGS BUNNY (Puffed Rice Giveaway)
Quaker Cereals: 1949 (32 pgs. each, 3-1/8x6-7/8")
A1-Traps the Counterfeiters, A2-Aboard Mystery Submarine, A3- Rocket to the Moon, A4-Lion Tamer, A5-Rescues the Beautiful Princess, B1-Buried Treasure, B2-Outwits the Smugglers, B3-Joins the Marines, B4-Meets the Dwarf Ghost, B5-Finds Aladdin's Lamp, C1-Lost in the Frozen North, C2-Secret Agent, C3-Captured by Cannibals, C4-Fights the Man from Mars, C5-And the Haunted Cave
each.... 8 16 24 40 50 60
Mailing Envelope (has illo of Bugs on front)(Each envelope designates what set it contains, A,B or C on front) 8 16 24 40 50 60

BUGS BUNNY (3-D)
Cheerios Giveaway: 1953 (Pocket size) (15 titles)
each.... 10 20 30 58 79 100
Mailing Envelope (has Bugs drawn on front) 10 20 30 58 79 100

BUGS BUNNY
DC Comics: May, 1997 ($4.95, 24 pgs., comic-sized)
1-Numbered ed. of 100,000; "1st Day of Issue" stamp cancellation on-c 6.00

BUGS BUNNY POSTAL COMIC
DC Comics: 1997 (64 pgs., 7.5" x 5")
nn -Mail Fan; Daffy Duck app. 4.50

BULLETMAN
Fawcett Publications
Well Known Comics (1942)-Paper-c, glued binding; printed in red (Bestmaid/Samuel Lowe giveaway) 15 30 45 85 130 175

BULLS-EYE (Cody of The Pony Express No. 8 on)
Charlton: 1955 (Great Scott Shoe Store giveaway)
Reprints #2 with new cover 18 36 54 103 162 220

BUSTER BROWN COMICS (Radio)(Also see My Dog Tige in Promotional sec.)
Brown Shoe Co.: 1945 - No. 43, 1959 (No. 5: paper-c)
nn, nd (#1,scarce)-Featuring Smilin' Ed McConnell & the Buster Brown gang "Midnight" the cat, "Squeaky" the mouse & "Froggy" the Gremlin; covers mention diff. shoe stores.
Contains adventure stories 61 122 183 390 670 950
2 19 38 57 112 179 245
3,5-10 13 26 39 74 105 135
4 (Rare)-Low print run due to paper shortage 18 36 54 103 162 220
11-20 9 18 27 47 61 75
21-24,26-28 6 12 18 31 38 45
25,33-37,40,41-Crandall-a in all 10 20 30 56 76 95
29-32-"Interplanetary Police Vs. the Space Siren" by Crandall (pencils only #29)
10 20 30 58 79 100
38,39,42,43 6 12 18 31 38 45

BUSTER BROWN COMICS (Radio)
Brown Shoe Co: 1950s
...Goes to Mars (2/58-Western Printing), slick-c, 20 pgs., reg. size
14 28 42 78 112 145
...In "Buster Makes the Team!" (1959-Custom Comics)
8 16 24 44 57 70
...In The Jet Age (`50s), slick-c, 20 pgs., 5x7-1/4" 10 20 30 58 79 100
...Of the Safety Patrol ('60-Custom Comics) 3 6 9 17 26 35
...Out of This World ('59-Custom Comics) 7 14 21 35 43 50
...Safety Coloring Book ('58, 16 pgs.)-Slick paper 7 14 21 35 43 50

CALL FROM CHRIST
Catechetical Educational Society: 1952 (Giveaway, 36 pgs.)
nn 7 14 21 35 43 50

CANCELLED COMIC CAVALCADE
DC Comics, Inc.: Summer, 1978 - No. 2, Fall, 1978 (8-1/2x11", B&W)
(Xeroxed pgs. on one side only w/blue cover and taped spine)(Only 35 sets produced)
1-(412 pgs.) Contains xeroxed copies of art for: Black Lightning #12, cover to #13; Claw #13,14; The Deserter #1; Doorway to Nightmare #6; Firestorm #6; The Green Team #2,3.
2-(532 pgs.) Contains xeroxed copies of art for: Kamandi #60 (including Omac), #61; Prez #5; Shade #9 (including The Odd Man); Showcase #105 (Deadman), 106 (The Creeper); Secret Society of Super Villains #16 & 17; The Vixen #1; and covers to Army at War #2, Battle Classics #3, Demand Classics #1 & 2, Dynamic Classics #3, Mr. Miracle #26, Ragman #6, Weird Mystery #25 & 26, & Western Classics #1 & 2.
(A FN set of Number 1 & 2 was sold in 2005 for $3680; a VG set sold in 2007 for $2629)

NOTE: *In June, 1978, DC cancelled several of their titles. For copyright purposes, the unpublished original art for these titles was xeroxed, bound in the above books, published and distributed. Only 35 copies were made. Beware of bootleg copies.*

CAP'N CRUNCH COMICS (See Quaker Oats)
Quaker Oats Co.: 1963; 1965 (16 pgs.; miniature giveaways; 2-1/2x6-1/2")
(1963 titles)- "The Picture Pirates", "The Fountain of Youth", "I'm Dreaming of a Wide Isthmus".
(1965 titles)- "Bewitched, Betwitched, & Betweaked", "Seadog Meets the Witch Doctor", "A Witch in Time" 5 10 15 31 53 75

CAPTAIN ACTION (Toy)
National Periodical Publications
...& Action Boy('67)-Ideal Toy Co. giveaway (1st app. Captain Action)
10 20 30 68 144 220

CAPTAIN AMERICA
Marvel Comics Group
...& The Campbell Kids (1980, 36pg. giveaway, Campbell's Soup/U.S. Dept. of Energy)
2 4 6 9 13 16
...Goes To War Against Drugs(1990, no #, giveaway)-Distributed to direct sales shops; 2nd printing exists 1 2 3 5 6 8

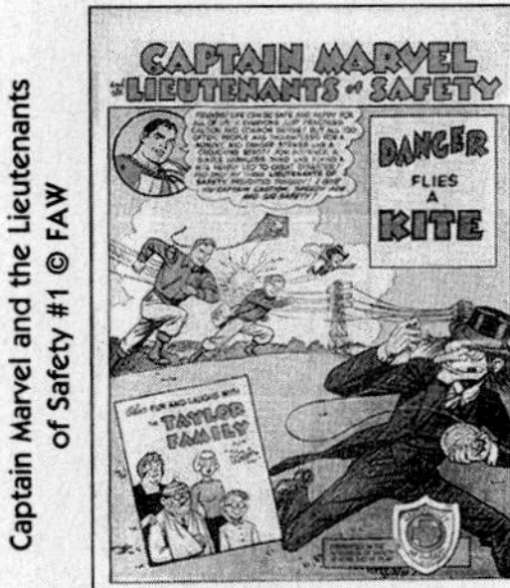

Captain Marvel and the Lieutenants of Safety #1 © FAW

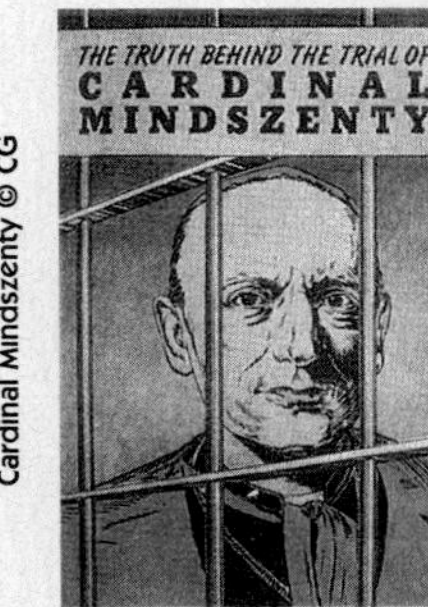

Cardinal Mindszenty © CG

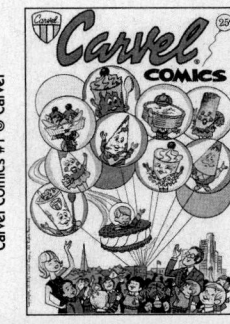

Carvel Comics #1 © Carvel

	GD 2.0	VG 4.0	FN 6.0	VF 8.0	VF/NM 9.0	NM- 9.2
...Meets The Asthma Monster (1987, no #, giveaway, Your Physician and Glaxo, Inc.)	1	2	3	5	6	8
Return of The Asthma Monster Vol. 1 #2 (1992, giveaway, Your Physician & Allen & Hanbury's)	1	2	3	5	6	8
...Vs. Asthma Monster (1990, no #, giveaway, Your Physician & Allen & Hanbury's)	1	2	3	5	6	8

CAPTAIN AMERICA COMICS
Timely/Marvel Comics: 1954

Shoestore Giveaway #77	161	322	483	1030	1765	2500

CAPTAIN ATOM
Nationwide Publishers

...- Secret of the Columbian Jungle (16 pgs. in color, paper-c, 3-3/4x5-1/8")-Fireside Marshmallow giveaway	6	12	18	28	34	40

CAPTAIN BEN DIX
Bendix Aviation Corporation: 1943 (Small size)

nn	8	16	24	44	57	70

CAPTAIN BEN DIX IN ACTION WITH THE INVISIBLE CREW
Bendix Aviation Corp.: 1940s (nd), (20 pgs, 8-1/4"x11", heavy paper)

nn-WWII bomber-c; Japanese app.	7	14	21	37	46	55

CAPTAIN BEN DIX IN SECRETS OF THE INVISIBLE CREW
Bendix Aviation Corp.: 1940s (nd), (32 pgs, soft-c)

nn	7	14	21	35	43	50

CAPTAIN FORTUNE PRESENTS
Vital Publications: 1955 - 1959 (Giveaway, 3-1/4x6-7/8", 16 pgs.)

"Davy Crockett in Episodes of the Creek War", "Davy Crockett at the Alamo", "In Sherwood Forest Tells Strange Tales of Robin Hood" ('57), "Meets Bolivar the Liberator" ('59), "Tells How Buffalo Bill Fights the Dog Soldiers" ('57), "Young Davy Crockett"	4	7	9	14	17	20

CAPTAIN GALLANT (...of the Foreign Legion) (TV)
Charlton Comics

Heinz Foods Premium (#1?)(1955; regular size)-U.S. Pictorial; contains Buster Crabbe photos; Don Heck-a	1	3	4	6	8	10
Mailing Envelope						20.00

CAPTAIN JOLLY ADVENTURES
Johnston and Cushing: 1950's, nd (Post Corn Fetti cereal giveaway) (5-1/4" x 4-1/2")

1-3: 1-Captain Jolly Advs. 2-Captain Jolly and His Pirate Crew in Off To Treasure Island. 3-C.J. & His Pirate Crew in The Terror Of The Deep	2	4	5	7	8	10

CAPTAIN MARVEL ADVENTURES
Fawcett Publications

Bond Bread Giveaways-(24 pgs.; pocket size-7-1/4x3-1/2"; paper cover): "...& the Stolen City" ('48), "The Boy Who Never Heard of Capt. Marvel", "Meets the Weatherman" (1950) (reprint) each....	22	44	66	128	209	290
...Well Known Comics (1944; 12 pgs.; 8-1/2x10-1/2")-printed in red & in blue; soft-c; glued binding - (Bestmaid/Samuel Lowe Co. giveaway)	15	30	45	94	147	200

CAPTAIN MARVEL ADVENTURES (Also see Flash and Funny Stuff)
Fawcett Publications (Wheaties Giveaway): 1945 (6x8", full color, paper-c)

nn- "Captain Marvel & the Threads of Life" plus 2 other stories (32 pgs.)	65	130	325	650	-	-

NOTE: *All copies were taped at each corner to a box of Wheaties and are never found in Fine or Mint condition. Prices listed for each grade include tape. File copy stamped "June 21, 1947".*

CAPTAIN MARVEL AND THE LTS. OF SAFETY
Ebasco Services/Fawcett Publications: 1950 - 1951 (3 issues - no No.'s)

nn (#1) "Danger Flies a Kite" ('50, scarce),	41	82	123	256	428	600
nn (#2)"Danger Takes to Climbing" ('50),	30	60	90	177	289	400
nn (#3)"Danger Smashes Street Lights" ('51)	30	60	90	177	289	400

CAPTAIN MARVEL, JR.
Fawcett Publications: (1944; 12 pgs.; 8-1/2x10-1/2")

...Well Known Comics (Printed in blue; paper-c, glued binding)-Bestmaid/Samuel Lowe Co. giveaway	14	28	42	76	108	140

CARDINAL MINDSZENTY (The Truth Behind the Trial of...)
Catechetical Guild Education Society: 1949 (24 pgs., paper cover)

nn-Anti-communism	12	24	36	67	94	120
Press Proof-(Very Rare)-(Full color, 7-1/2x11-3/4", untrimmed) Only two known copies						300.00
Preview Copy (B&W, stapled), 18 pgs.; contains first 13 pgs. of Cardinal Mindszenty and was sent out as an advance promotion. Only one known copy						300.00 - 400.00

NOTE: *Regular edition also printed in French. There was also a movie released in 1949 called "Guilty of Treason" which is a fact-based account of the trial and imprisonment of Cardinal Mindszenty by the Communist regime in Hungary.*

CARNIVAL OF COMICS
Fleet-Air Shoes: 1954 (Giveaway)

nn-Contains a comic bound with new cover; several combinations possible; Charlton's Eh! known	5	10	15	24	30	35

CARTOON NETWORK
DC Comics: 1997 (Giveaway)

nn-reprints Cow and Chicken, Scooby-Doo, & Flintstones stories						4.00

CARVEL COMICS (Amazing Advs. of Capt. Carvel)
Carvel Corp. (Ice Cream): 1975 - No. 5, 1976 (25¢; #3-5: 35¢) (#4,5: 3-1/4x5")

1-3	1	2	3	5	6	8
4,5(1976)-Baseball theme	2	4	6	8	10	12

CASE OF THE WASTED WATER, THE
Rheem Water Heating: 1972? (Giveaway)

nn-Neal Adams-a	4	8	12	27	44	60

CASPER SPECIAL
Target Stores (Harvey): nd (Dec, 1990) (Giveaway with $1.00 cover)

Three issues-Given away with Casper video						6.00

CASPER, THE FRIENDLY GHOST (Paramount Picture Star...)(2nd Series)
Harvey Publications

American Dental Association (Giveaways):						
...'s Dental Health Activity Book-1977	2	4	6	8	11	14
...Presents Space Age Dentistry-1972	2	4	6	9	13	16
..., His Den, & Their Dentist Fight the Tooth Demons-1974	2	4	6	9	13	16
Casper Rides the School Bus (1960, 7x3.5", 16 pgs.)	2	4	6	9	13	16

CELEBRATE THE CENTURY SUPERHEROES STAMP ALBUM
DC Comics: 1998 - No. 5, 2000 (32 pgs.)

1-5: Historical stories hosted by DC heroes						4.00

CENTIPEDE
DC Comics: 1983

1-Based on Atari video game	2	4	6	9	13	16

CENTURY OF COMICS
Eastern Color Printing Co.: 1933 (100 pgs.)
Bought by Wheatena, Malt-O-Milk, John Wanamaker, Kinney Shoe Stores, & others to be used as premiums and radio giveaways. No publisher listed.

nn-Mutt & Jeff, Joe Palooka, etc. reprints	1974	3948	5922	15,000	-	-

CHEERIOS PREMIUMS (Disney)
Walt Disney Productions: 1947 (16 titles, pocket size, 32 pgs.)

Mailing Envelope for each set "W,X,Y & Z" (has Mickey illo on front)(each envelope designates the set it contains on the front)	9	18	27	47	61	75
Set "W"						
W1-Donald Duck & the Pirates	9	18	27	47	61	75
W2-Bucky Bug & the Cannibal King	5	10	15	24	30	35
W3-Pluto Joins the F.B.I.	5	10	15	24	30	35
W4-Mickey Mouse & the Haunted House	6	12	18	28	34	40
Set "X"						
X1-Donald Duck, Counter Spy	9	18	27	47	61	75
X2-Goofy Lost in the Desert	5	10	15	24	30	35
X3-Br'er Rabbit Outwits Br'er Fox	5	10	15	24	30	35
X4-Mickey Mouse at the Rodeo	6	12	18	31	38	45
Set "Y"						
Y1-Donald Duck's Atom Bomb by Carl Barks. Disney has banned reprinting this book	76	152	228	470	810	1175
Y2-Br'er Rabbit's Secret	5	10	15	24	30	35
Y3-Dumbo & the Circus Mystery	5	10	15	24	30	35
Y4-Mickey Mouse Meets the Wizard	6	12	18	31	38	45
Set "Z"						
Z1-Donald Duck Pilots a Jet Plane (not by Barks)	9	18	27	47	61	75
Z2-Pluto Turns Sleuth Hound	5	10	15	24	30	35
Z3-The Seven Dwarfs & the Enchanted Mtn.	6	12	18	31	38	45
Z4-Mickey Mouse's Secret Room	6	12	18	31	38	45

CHEERIOS 3-D GIVEAWAYS (Disney)
Walt Disney Productions: 1954 (24 titles, pocket size) (Glasses came in envelopes)

Glasses only...	4	7	10	14	17	20
Mailing Envelope (no art on front)	6	12	18	28	34	40

Cheerios 3-D Giveaways - Mickey Mouse, Phantom Sheriff © DIS

Christmas is Coming

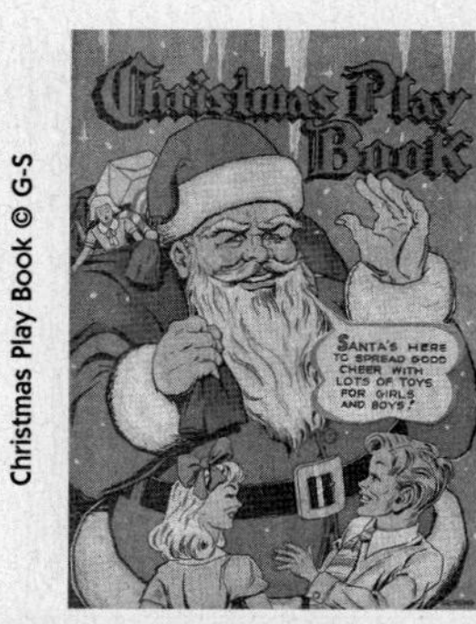

Christmas Play Book © G-S

	GD 2.0	VG 4.0	FN 6.0	VF 8.0	VF/NM 9.0	NM- 9.2
(Set 1)						
1-Donald Duck & Uncle Scrooge, the Firefighters	7	14	21	35	43	50
2-Mickey Mouse & Goofy, Pirate Plunder	6	12	18	28	34	40
3-Donald Duck's Nephews, the Fabulous Inventors	7	14	21	37	46	55
4-Mickey Mouse, Secret of the Ming Vase	6	12	18	28	34	40
5-Donald Duck with Huey, Dewey, & Louie; ...the Seafarers (title on 2nd page)	7	14	21	35	43	50
6-Mickey Mouse, Moaning Mountain	6	12	18	28	34	40
7-Donald Duck, Apache Gold	7	14	21	35	43	50
8-Mickey Mouse, Flight to Nowhere	6	12	18	28	34	40
(Set 2)						
1-Donald Duck, Treasure of Timbuktu	7	14	21	35	43	50
2-Mickey Mouse & Pluto, Operation China	6	12	18	28	34	40
3-Donald Duck and the Magic Cows	7	14	21	35	43	50
4-Mickey Mouse & Goofy, Kid Kokonut	6	12	18	28	34	40
5-Donald Duck, Mystery Ship	7	14	21	35	43	50
6-Mickey Mouse, Phantom Sheriff	6	12	18	28	34	40
7-Donald Duck, Circus Adventures	7	14	21	35	43	50
8-Mickey Mouse, Arctic Explorers	6	12	18	28	34	40
(Set 3)						
1-Donald Duck & Witch Hazel	7	14	21	35	43	50
2-Mickey Mouse in Darkest Africa	6	12	18	28	34	40
3-Donald Duck & Uncle Scrooge, Timber Trouble	7	14	21	35	43	50
4-Mickey Mouse, Rajah's Rescue	6	12	18	28	34	40
5-Donald Duck in Robot Reporter	7	14	21	35	43	50
6-Mickey Mouse, Slumbering Sleuth	6	12	18	28	34	40
7-Donald Duck in the Foreign Legion	7	14	21	35	43	50
8-Mickey Mouse, Airwalking Wonder	6	12	18	28	34	40
CHESTY AND COPTIE (Disney)						
Los Angeles Community Chest: 1946 (Giveaway, 4pgs.)						
nn-(One known copy) by Floyd Gottfredson (a GD copy sold for $371.65 on 2/12/17)						
CHESTY AND HIS HELPERS (Disney)						
Los Angeles War Chest: 1943 (Giveaway, 12 pgs., 5-1/2x7-1/4")						
nn-Chesty & Coptie	50	100	150	315	533	750
CHOCOLATE THE FLAVOR OF FRIENDSHIP AROUND THE WORLD						
The Nestle Company: 1955						
nn	6	12	18	28	34	40
CHRISTMAS ADVENTURE, THE						
S. Rose (H. L. Green Giveaway): 1963 (16 pgs.)						
nn	2	4	6	10	14	18
CHRISTMAS ADVENTURES WITH ELMER THE ELF						
1949 (paper-c)						
nn	4	7	10	14	17	20
CHRISTMAS AT THE ROTUNDA (Titled Ford Rotunda Christmas Book 1957 on) (Regular size)						
Ford Motor Co. (Western Printing): 1954 - 1961 (Given away every Christmas at one location)						
1954-56 issues (nn's)	8	16	24	42	54	65
1957-61 issues (nn's)	7	14	21	37	46	55
CHRISTMAS CAROL, A						
Sears Roebuck & Co.: No date (1942-43) (Giveaway, 32 pgs., 8-1/4x10-3/4", paper cover)						
nn-Comics & coloring book	22	44	66	128	209	290
CHRISTMAS CAROL, A (Also see Bob & Santa's Wishing Whistle, Merry Christmas From Sears Toyland, and Santa's Christmas Comic Variety Show)						
Sears Roebuck & Co.: 1940s? (Christmas giveaway, 20 pgs.)						
nn-Comic book & animated coloring book	20	40	60	120	195	270
CHRISTMAS CAROLS						
Hot Shoppes Giveaway: 1959? (16 pgs.)						
nn	4	8	11	16	19	22
CHRISTMAS COLORING FUN						
H. Burnside: 1964 (20 pgs., slick-c, B&W)						
nn	2	4	6	11	16	20
CHRISTMAS DREAM, A						
Promotional Publishing Co.: 1950 (Kinney Shoe Store Giveaway, 16 pgs.)						
nn	5	10	15	23	28	32
CHRISTMAS DREAM, A						
J. J. Newberry Co.: 1952? (Giveaway, paper cover, 16 pgs.)						
nn	5	10	14	20	24	28

	GD 2.0	VG 4.0	FN 6.0	VF 8.0	VF/NM 9.0	NM- 9.2
CHRISTMAS DREAM, A						
Promotional Publ. Co.: 1952 (Giveaway, 16 pgs., paper cover)						
nn	5	10	14	20	24	28
CHRISTMAS FUN AROUND THE WORLD						
No publisher: No date (early 50's) (16 pgs., paper cover)						
nn	5	10	15	23	28	32
CHRISTMAS FUN BOOK						
G. C. Murphy Co.: 1950 (Giveaway, paper cover)						
nn-Contains paper dolls	6	12	18	29	36	42
CHRISTMAS IS COMING!						
No publisher: No date (early 50's?) (Store giveaway, 16 pgs.)						
nn-Santa cover	6	12	18	29	36	42
CHRISTMAS JOURNEY THROUGH SPACE						
Promotional Publishing Co.: 1960						
nn-Reprints 1954 issue Jolly Christmas Book with new slick cover	3	6	9	16	23	30
CHRISTMAS ON THE MOON						
W. T. Grant Co.: 1958 (Giveaway, 20 pgs., slick cover)						
nn	9	18	27	47	61	75
CHRISTMAS PLAY BOOK						
Gould-Stoner Co.: 1946 (Giveaway, 16 pgs., paper cover)						
nn	9	18	27	47	61	75
CHRISTMAS ROUNDUP						
Promotional Publishing Co.: 1960						
nn-Marv Levy-c/a	2	4	6	9	13	16
CHRISTMAS STORY CUT-OUT BOOK, THE						
Catechetical Guild: No. 393, 1951 (15¢, 36 pgs.)						
393-Half text & half comics	8	16	24	42	54	65
CHRISTMAS USA (Through 300 Years) (Also see Uncle Sam's...)						
Promotional Publ. Co.: 1956 (Giveaway)						
nn-Marv Levy-c/a	4	7	9	14	16	18
CHRISTMAS WITH SNOW WHITE AND THE SEVEN DWARFS						
Kobackers Giftstore of Buffalo, N.Y.: 1953 (16 pgs., paper-c)						
nn	8	16	24	42	54	65
CHRISTOPHERS, THE						
Catechetical Guild: 1951 (Giveaway, 36 pgs.) (Some copies have 15¢ sticker)						
nn-Stalin as Satan in Hell; Hitler & Lincoln app.	25	50	75	150	245	340
CHUCKY JACK'S A-COMIN'						
Great Smoky Mountains Historical Assn., Gatlinburg, TN: 1956 (Reg. size)						
nn-Life of John Sevier, founder of Tennessee	8	16	24	42	54	65
CINDERELLA IN "FAIREST OF THE FAIR" (Walt Disney)						
American Dairy Association (Premium): 1955 (5x7-1/4", 16 pgs., soft-c)						
nn	10	20	30	56	76	95
CINEMA COMICS HERALD						
Paramount Pictures/Universal/RKO/20th Century Fox/Republic:						
1941 - 1943 (4-pg. movie "trailers", paper-c, 7-1/2x10-1/2")(Giveaway)						
"Mr. Bug Goes to Town" (1941)	15	30	45	90	140	190
"Bedtime Story"	11	22	33	64	90	115
"Lady For A Night", John Wayne, Joan Blondell ('42)	19	38	57	111	176	240
"Reap The Wild Wind" (1942)	12	24	36	69	97	125
"Thunder Birds" (1942)	11	22	33	64	90	115
"They All Kissed the Bride"	11	22	33	64	90	115
"Arabian Nights" (nd)	12	24	36	69	97	125
"Bombardie" (1943)	11	22	33	64	90	115
"Crash Dive" (1943)-Tyrone Power	12	24	36	69	97	125
NOTE: *The 1941-42 issues contain line art with color photos. 1943 issues are line art.*						
CLASSICS GIVEAWAYS (Classic Comics reprints)						
12/41–Walter Theatre Enterprises (Huntington, WV) giveaway containing #2 (orig.) w/new generic-c (only 1 known copy)	90	180	270	576	988	1400
1942–Double Comics containing CC#1 (orig.) (diff. cover) (not actually a giveaway) (very rare) (also see Double Comics) (only one known copy)	155	310	465	992	1696	2400
12/42–Saks 34th St. Giveaway containing CC#7 (orig.) (diff. cover) (very rare; only 6 known copies)	331	662	993	2317	4059	5800
2/43–American Comics containing CC#8 (orig.) (Liberty Theatre giveaway) (different cover)						

Comic Book Confidential #1 © Sphinx

Comic Books - The Green Jet © MPC

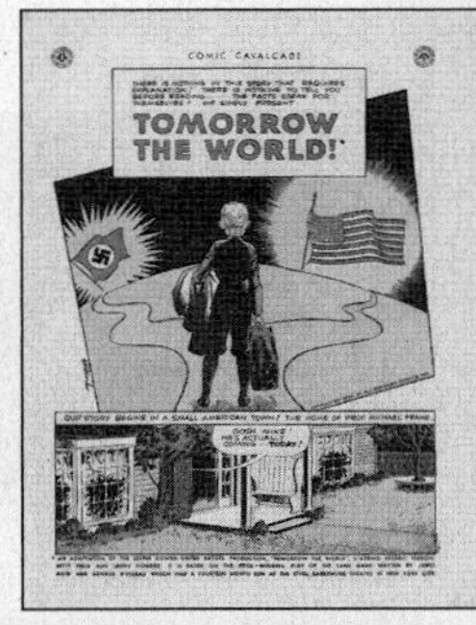

Comic Cavalcade - Tomorrow the World! © DC

GD 2.0 | VG 4.0 | FN 6.0 | VF 8.0 | VF/NM 9.0 | NM- 9.2

(only one known copy) (see American Comics) 116 232 348 742 1271 1800
12/44–Robin Hood Flour Co. Giveaway - #7-CC(R) (diff. cover) (rare)
(edition probably 5 [22]) 187 374 561 1197 2049 2900
NOTE: How are above editions determined without CC covers? 1942 is dated 1942, and CC#1-first reprint did not come out until 5/43. 12/42 and 2/43 are determined by blue note at bottom of first text page only in original edition. 12/44 is estimated from page width each reprint edition had progressively slightly smaller page width.

1951–Shelter Thru the Ages (C.I. Educational Series) (actually Giveaway by the Ruberoid Co.) (16 pgs.) (contains original artwork by H. C. Kiefer) (there are 5 diff. back cover ad variations: "Ranch" house ad, "Igloo" ad, "Doll House" ad, "Tree House" ad & blank)
(scarce) 61 122 183 390 670 950
1952–George Daynor Biography Giveaway (CC logo) (partly comic book/pictures/newspaper articles) (story of man who built Palace Depression out of junkyard swamp in NJ) (64 pgs.) (very rare; only 3 known copies, one missing back-c)
377 754 1131 2639 4620 6600
1953–Westinghouse/Dreams of a Man (C.I. Educational Series) (Westinghousebio./ Westinghouse Co. giveaway) (contains original artwork by H. C. Kiefer) (16 pgs.) (also French/Spanish/Italian versions) (scarce) 50 100 150 315 533 750
NOTE: Reproductions of 1951, 1952, and 1953 exist with color photocopy covers and black & white photocopy interior ("W.C.N. Reprint") 2 4 5 7 8 10
1951-53–Coward Shoe Giveaways (all editions very rare); 2 variations of back-c ad exist:
With back-c photo ad: 5 (87), 12 (89), 22 (85), 32 (85), 49 (85), 69 (87), 72 (no HRN), 80 (0), 91 (0), 92 (0), 96 (0), 98 (0), 100 (0), 101 (0), 103-105 (all Os)
30 60 90 177 289 400
With back-c cartoon ad: 106-109 (all 0s), 110 (111), 112 (0)
31 62 93 186 303 420
1956–Ben Franklin 5-10 Store Giveaway (#65-PC with back cover ad)
(scarce) 24 48 72 142 234 325
1956–Ben Franklin Insurance Co. Giveaway (#65-PC with diff. back cover ad)
(very rare) 48 96 144 302 514 725
11/56–Sealtest Co. Edition - #4 (135) (identical to regular edition except for Sealtest logo printed, not stamped, on front cover) (only two copies known to exist)
28 56 84 165 270 375
1958–Get-Well Giveaway containing #15-CI (new cartoon-type cover) (Pressman Pharmacy)
(only one copy known to exist) 28 56 84 165 270 375
1967-68–Twin Circle Giveaway Editions - all HRN 166, with back cover ad for National Catholic Press.
2(R68), 4(R67), 10(R68), 13(R68) 3 6 9 21 32 42
48(R67), 128(R68), 535(576-R68) 4 8 12 22 34 45
16(R68), 68(R67) 5 10 15 30 48 65
12/69–Christmas Giveaway ("A Christmas Adventure") (reprints Picture Parade #4-1953, new cover) (4 ad variations)
Stacey's Dept. Store 3 6 9 20 31 42
Anne & Hope Store 5 10 15 30 50 70
Gibson's Dept. Store (rare) 5 10 15 30 50 70
"Merry Christmas" & blank ad space 3 6 9 20 31 42

CLEAR THE TRACK!
Association of American Railroads: 1954 (paper-c, 16 pgs.)
nn 5 10 15 24 30 35

CLIFF MERRITT SETS THE RECORD STRAIGHT
Brotherhood of Railroad Trainsmen: Giveaway (2 different issues)
...and the Very Candid Candidate by Al Williamson 1 3 4 6 8 10
...Sets the Record Straight by Al Williamson (2 different-c: one by Williamson, the other by McWilliams) 1 3 4 6 8 10

CLYDE BEATTY COMICS (Also see Crackajack Funnies)
Commodore Productions & Artists, Inc.
...African Jungle Book('56)-Richfield Oil Co. 16 pg. giveaway, soft-c
11 22 33 62 86 110

C-M-O COMICS
Chicago Mail Order Co.(Centaur): 1942 - No. 2, 1942 (68 pgs., full color)
1-Invisible Terror, Super Ann, & Plymo the Rubber Man app. (all Centaur costume heroes)
116 232 348 742 1271 1800
2-Invisible Terror, Super Ann app. 77 154 231 493 847 1200

COCOMALT BIG BOOK OF COMICS
Harry 'A' Chesler (Cocomalt Premium): 1938 (Reg. size, full color, 52 pgs.)
1-(Scarce)-Biro-c/a; Little Nemo by Winsor McCay Jr., Dan Hastings; Jack Cole, Guardineer, Gustavson, Bob Wood-a 226 452 678 1446 2473 3500

COLONEL OF TWO WORLDS, THE
DC Comics: 2015 (Kentucky Fried Chicken promotion, no price)
1-Flash, Green Lantern and Colonel Sanders vs. the evil Colonel of Earth-3; Derenick-a 3.00

COMIC BOOK (Also see Comics From Weatherbird)
American Juniors Shoe: 1954 (Giveaway)
Contains a comic rebound with new cover. Several combinations possible. Contents determine price.

COMIC BOOK CONFIDENTIAL
Sphinx Productions: 1988 (Givewaway, 16 pgs.)
1-Tie-in to a documentary about comic creators; creator biographies; Chester Brown-c 5.00

COMIC BOOK MAGAZINE
Chicago Tribune & other newspapers: 1940 - 1943 (Similar to Spirit sections) (7-3/4x10-3/4"; full color; 16-24 pgs. ea.)
1940 issues 7 14 21 37 46 55
1941, 1942 issues 6 12 18 28 34 40
1943 issues 5 10 15 24 30 35
NOTE: *Published weekly. Texas Slim, Kit Carson, Spooky, Josie, Nuts & Jolts, Lew Loyal, Brenda Starr, Daniel Boone, Captain Storm, Rocky, Smokey Stover, Tiny Tim, Little Joe, Fu Manchu appear among others. Early issues had photo stories with pictures from the movies; later issues had comic art.*

COMIC BOOKS (Series 1)
Metropolitan Printing Co. (Giveaway): 1950 (16 pgs.; 5-1/4x8-1/2"; full color; bound at top; paper cover)
1-Boots and Saddles; intro The Masked Marshal 6 12 18 28 34 40
1-The Green Jet; Green Lama by Raboy 20 40 60 117 189 260
1-My Pal Dizzy (Teen-age) 4 8 12 18 22 25
1-New World; origin Atomaster (costumed hero) 9 18 27 52 69 85
1-Talullah (Teen-age) 4 8 12 18 22 25

COMIC CAVALCADE
All-American/National Periodical Publications
Giveaway (1944, 8 pgs., paper-c, in color)-One Hundred Years of Co-operation-r/Comic Cavalcade #9 43 86 129 271 461 650
Giveaway (1945, 16 pgs., paper-c, in color)-Movie "Tomorrow The World" (Nazi theme); r/Comic Cavalcade #10 58 116 174 371 636 900
Giveaway (c. 1944-45; 8 pgs, paper-c, in color)-The Twain Shall Meet-r/Comic Cavalcade #8
43 86 129 271 461 650

COMIC SELECTIONS (Shoe store giveaway)
Parents' Magazine Press: 1944-46 (Reprints from Calling All Girls, True Comics, True Aviation, & Real Heroes)
1 5 10 15 22 26 30
2-6 4 8 11 16 19 22

COMICS FROM WEATHER BIRD (Also see Comic Book, Edward's Shoes, Free Comics to You & Weather Bird)
Weather Bird Shoes: 1954 - 1957 (Giveaway)
Contains a comic bound with new cover. Many combinations possible. Contents would determine price. Some issues do not contain complete comics, but only parts of comics. Value equals 40 to 60 percent of contents.

COMICS READING LIBRARIES (Educational Series)
King Features (Charlton Publ.): 1973, 1977, 1979 (36 pgs. in color) (Giveaways)
R-01-Tiger, Quincy 2 4 6 8 11 14
R-02-Beetle Bailey, Blondie & Popeye 2 4 6 10 14 18
R-03-Blondie, Beetle Bailey 2 4 6 8 11 14
R-04-Tim Tyler's Luck, Felix the Cat 3 6 9 16 23 30
R-05-Quincy, Henry 2 4 6 8 11 14
R-06-The Phantom, Mandrake 3 6 9 16 23 30
1977 reprint(R-04) 2 4 6 9 13 16
R-07-Popeye, Little King 2 4 6 13 18 22
R-08-Prince Valiant (Foster), Flash Gordon 3 6 9 18 27 36
1977 reprint 2 4 6 11 16 20
R-09-Hagar the Horrible, Boner's Ark 2 4 6 10 14 18
R-10-Redeye, Tiger 2 4 6 8 11 14
R-11-Blondie, Hi & Lois 2 4 6 8 11 14
R-12-Popeye-Swee'pea, Brutus 2 4 6 13 18 22
R-13-Beetle Bailey, Little King 2 4 6 8 11 14
R-14-Quincy-Hamlet 2 4 6 8 11 14
R-15-The Phantom, The Genius 2 4 6 13 18 22
R-16-Flash Gordon, Mandrake 3 6 9 18 27 36
1977 reprint 2 4 6 10 14 18
Other 1977 editions.... 2 4 6 8 10 12
1979 editions (68 pgs.) 2 4 6 8 10 12
NOTE: *Above giveaways available with purchase of $45.00 in merchandise. Used as a reading skills aid for small children.*

COMMANDMENTS OF GOD
Catechetical Guild: 1954, 1958
300-Same contents in both editions; diff-c 5 10 15 24 29 34

COMPLIMENTARY COMICS
Sales Promotion Publ.: No date (1950's) (Giveaway)
1-Strongman by Powell, 3 stories 8 16 24 40 50 60

Davy Crockett In the Raid at Piney Creek © WDC

DC Spotlight #1 © DC

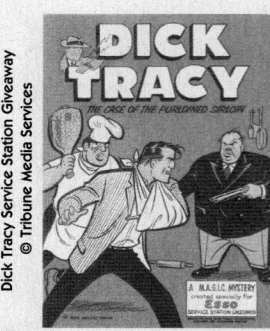

Dick Tracy Service Station Giveaway © Tribune Media Services

GD VG FN VF VF/NM NM-
2.0 4.0 6.0 8.0 9.0 9.2

COPPER - THE OLDEST AND NEWEST METAL
Commercial Comics: 1959
nn 3 6 9 14 20 25

CRACKAJACK FUNNIES (Giveaway)
Malto-Meal: 1937 (Full size, soft-c, full color, 32 pgs.)(Before No. 1?)
nn-Features Dan Dunn, G-Man, Speed Bolton, Buck Jones, The Nebbs, Clyde Beatty, Freckles, Major Hoople, Wash Tubbs 90 180 270 576 988 1400

CRAFTSMAN BOLT-ON SYSTEMS SAVE THE JUSTICE LEAGUE
DC Comics: 2012 (Giveaway promo for Craftsman Bolt-On Tool System)
1-Christian Duce-a/c; New-52 Justice League, The Key and Royal Flush Gang app. 3.00

CRISIS AT THE CARSONS
Pictorial Media: 1958 (Reg. size)
nn 5 10 15 24 30 35

CROSLEY'S HOUSE OF FUN (Also see Tee and Vee Crosley...)
Crosley Div. AVCO Mfg. Corp.: 1950 (Giveaway, paper cover, 32 pgs.)
nn-Strips revolve around Crosley appliances 5 10 15 22 26 30

DAGWOOD SPLITS THE ATOM (Also see Topix V8#4)
King Features Syndicate: 1949 (Science comic with King Features characters) (Giveaway)
nn-Half comic, half text; Popeye, Olive Oyl, Henry, Mandrake, Little King, Katzenjammer Kids app. 7 14 21 35 43 50

DAISY COMICS (Daisy Air Rifles)
Eastern Color Printing Co.: Dec, 1936 (5-1/4x7-1/2")
nn-Joe Palooka, Buck Rogers (2 pgs. from Famous Funnies No. 18, 1st full cover app.), Napoleon Flying to Fame, Butty & Fally 34 68 102 204 332 460

DAISY LOW OF THE GIRL SCOUTS
Girl Scouts of America: 1954, 1965 (16 pgs., paper-c)
1954-Story of Juliette Gordon Low 5 10 15 22 26 30
1965 2 4 6 9 12 15

DAN CURTIS GIVEAWAYS
Western Publishing Co.:1974 (3x6", 24 pgs., reprints)
1-Dark Shadows 2 4 6 11 16 20
2,6-Star Trek 2 4 6 11 16 20
3,4,7-9: 3-The Twilight Zone. 4-Ripley's Believe It or Not! 7-The Occult Files of Dr. Spektor. 8-Dagar the Invincible. 9-Grimm's Ghost Stories 2 4 6 9 12 15
5-Turok, Son of Stone (partial-r/Turok #78) 2 4 6 11 16 20

DANNY AND THE DEMOXICYCLE
Virginia Highway Safety Division: 1970s (Reg. size, slick-c)
nn 3 6 9 19 30 40

DANNY KAYE'S BAND FUN BOOK
H & A Selmer: 1959 (Giveaway)
nn 7 14 21 35 43 50

DAREDEVIL
Marvel Comics Group: 1993
...Vs. Vapora 1 (Engineering Show Giveaway, 16 pg.) - Intro Vapora 6.00

DAVY CROCKETT (TV)
Dell Publishing Co.
...Christmas Book (no date, 16 pgs., paper-c)-Sears giveaway 6 12 18 31 38 45
...Safety Trails (1955, 16pgs, 3-1/4x7")-Cities Service giveaway 8 16 24 40 50 60

DAVY CROCKETT
Charlton Comics
Hunting With... nn ('55, 16 pgs.)-Ben Franklin Store giveaway (Publ.-S. Rose) 5 10 15 24 30 35

DAVY CROCKETT
Walt Disney Prod.: (1955, 16 pgs., 5x7-1/4", slick, photo-c)
...In the Raid at Piney Creek-American Motors giveaway 8 16 24 40 50 60

DC SAMPLER
DC Comics: nn (#1) 1983 - No. 3, 1984 (36 pgs.; 6 1/2" x 10", giveaway)
nn(#1) -3: nn-Wraparound-c, previews upcoming issues. 3-Kirby-a 1 2 3 4 5 7

DC SPOTLIGHT
DC Comics: 1985 (50th anniversary special) (giveaway)
1-Includes profiles on Batman: The Dark Knight & Watchmen 6.00

DEATH JR. HALLOWEEN SPECIAL
Image Comics: Oct, 2006 (8-1/2"x 5-1/2", Halloween giveaway)
nn-Guy Davis-a/Joe Morrisey-s; wraparound-c 2.50

DENNIS THE MENACE
Hallden (Fawcett)
...& Dirt ('59)-Soil Conservation giveaway; r-# 36; Wiseman-c/a 3 6 9 14 20 26
...& Dirt ('68)-reprints '59 edition 2 4 6 8 11 14
...Away We Go('70)-Caladryl giveaway 2 4 6 8 10 12
...Coping with Family Stress-giveaway 2 4 6 8 10 12
...Takes a Poke at Poison('61)-Food & Drug Admin. giveaway; Wiseman-c/a 2 4 6 8 10 12
...Takes a Poke at Poison-Revised 1/66, 11/70 1 2 3 5 6 8
...Takes a Poke at Poison-Revised 1972, 1974, 1977, 1981 1 2 3 4 5 7

DESERT DAWN
E.C./American Museum of Natural History: 1935 (paper-c)
nn-Johnny Jackrabbit stars. Three known copies: A Fair copy (brittle) sold for $657 in 2007. A GD+ copy (brittle) sold for $2300 in 2005. Another Fair copy (brittle) sold for $690 in 2004

DETECTIVE COMICS (Also see other Batman titles)
National Periodical Publications/DC Comics
27 (1984)-Oreo Cookies giveaway (32 pgs., paper-c) r-/Det. #27,#38 & Batman #1 (1st Joker) 4 8 12 27 44 60
38 (1995) Blockbuster Video edition; reprints 1st Robin app. 3.00
38 (1997) Toys R Us edition 3.00
359 (1997) Toys R Us edition; reprints 1st Batgirl app. 3.00
373 (1997, 6 1/4" x 4") Warner Brothers Home Video 3.00

DICK TRACY GIVEAWAYS
1939 - 1958; 1990
Buster Brown Shoes Giveaway (1940s?, 36 pgs. in color); 1938-39-r by Gould 21 42 63 126 206 285
Gillmore Giveaway (See Superbook)
...Hatful of Fun (No date, 1950-52, 32pgs.; 8-1/2x10")-Dick Tracy hat promotion; Dick Tracy games, magic tricks. Miller Bros. premium 15 30 45 90 140 190
Motorola Giveaway (1953)-Reprints Harvey Comics Library #2; "The Case of the Sparkle Plenty TV Mystery" 6 12 18 31 38 45
Original Dick Tracy by Chester Gould, The (Aug, 1990, 16 pgs., 5-1/2x8-1/2")-Gladstone Publ.; Bread Giveaway 1 3 4 6 8 10
Popped Wheat Giveaway (1947, 16 pgs. in color)-1940-r; Sig Feuchtwanger Publ.; Gould-a 4 8 12 18 22 25
...Presents the Family Fun Book; Tip Top Bread Giveaway, no date or number (1940, Fawcett Publ., 16 pgs. in color)-Spy Smasher, Ibis, Lance O'Casey app. 30 60 90 177 289 400
Same as above but without app. of heroes & Dick Tracy on cover only 14 28 42 82 121 160
Service Station Giveaway (1958, 16 pgs. in color)(regular size, slick cover)-Harvey Info. Press 5 10 14 20 24 28
Shoe Store Giveaway (Weatherbird and Triangle Stores)(1939, 16 pgs.)-Gould-a 14 28 42 80 115 150

DICK TRACY SHEDS LIGHT ON THE MOLE
Western Printing Co.: 1949 (16 pgs.) (Ray-O-Vac Flashlights giveaway)
nn-Not by Gould 8 16 24 42 54 65

DICK WINGATE OF THE U.S. NAVY
Superior Publ./Toby Press: 1951; 1953 (no month)
nn-U.S. Navy giveaway 5 10 15 24 30 35
1(1953, Toby)-Reprints nn issue? (same-c) 5 10 14 20 24 28

DIG 'EM
Kellogg's Sugar Smacks Giveaway: 1973 (2-3/8x6", 16 pgs.)
nn-4 different issues 1 3 4 6 8 10

DISNEY MAGAZINE
Procter and Gamble giveaway: nn (#1), Sept, 1976 - nn (#4), Jan, 1977
nn-All have an original Mickey story in color, 12-13 pgs. ea. and info/articles on Disney movies, cartoons. All have partial photo covers of a movie star with 1-2 pg. story. Covers: 1-Bob Hope, 2-Debbie Reynolds, 3-Groucho Marx, 4-Rock Hudson. 2 4 6 10 14 18

DOC CARTER VD COMICS
Health Publications Institute, Raleigh, N. C. (Giveaway): 1949 (16 pgs. in color) (Paper-c)

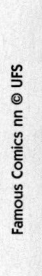

Donald Duck in "The Litterbug" © WDC

Famous Comics nn © UFS

Favorite Comics #3

	GD 2.0	VG 4.0	FN 6.0	VF 8.0	VF/NM 9.0	NM- 9.2
nn	21	42	63	122	199	275

DONALD AND MICKEY MERRY CHRISTMAS (Formerly Famous Gang Book Of Comics)
K. K. Publ./Firestone Tire & Rubber Co.: 1943 - 1949 (Giveaway, 20 pgs.)
Put out each Christmas; 1943 issue titled "Firestone Presents Comics" (Disney)

	GD	VG	FN	VF	VF/NM	NM-
1943-Donald Duck-r/WDC&S #32 by Carl Barks	77	154	231	493	847	1200
1944-Donald Duck-r/WDC&S #35 by Barks	74	148	222	470	810	1150
1945- "Donald Duck's Best Christmas", 8 pgs. Carl Barks; intro. & 1st app. Grandma Duck in comic books	107	214	321	680	1165	1650
1946-Donald Duck in "Santa's Stormy Visit", 8 pgs. Carl Barks	65	130	195	416	708	1000
1947-Donald Duck in "Three Good Little Ducks", 8 pgs. Carl Barks	65	130	195	416	708	1000
1948-Donald Duck in "Toyland", 8 pgs. Carl Barks	65	130	195	416	708	1000
1949-Donald Duck in "New Toys", 8 pgs. Barks	61	122	183	390	670	950

DONALD DUCK
K. K. Publications: 1944 (Christmas giveaway, paper-c, 16 pgs.)(2 versions)

	GD	VG	FN	VF	VF/NM	NM-
nn-Kelly cover reprint	107	214	321	680	1165	1650

DONALD DUCK AND THE RED FEATHER
Red Feather Giveaway: 1948 (8-1/2x11", 4 pgs., B&W)

	GD	VG	FN	VF	VF/NM	NM-
nn	20	40	60	120	195	270

DONALD DUCK IN "THE LITTERBUG"
Keep America Beautiful: 1963 (5x7-1/4", 16 pgs., soft-c) (Disney giveaway)

	GD	VG	FN	VF	VF/NM	NM-
nn	5	10	15	33	57	80

DONALD DUCK "PLOTTING PICNICKERS" (See Frito-Lay Giveaway)

DONALD DUCK'S SURPRISE PARTY
Walt Disney Productions: 1948 (16 pgs.) (Giveaway for Icy Frost Twins Ice Cream Bars)

	GD	VG	FN	VF	VF/NM	NM-
nn-(Rare)-Kelly-c/a	219	438	657	1402	2401	3400

DOT AND DASH AND THE LUCKY JINGLE PIGGIE
Sears Roebuck Co.: 1942 (Christmas giveaway, 12 pgs.)

	GD	VG	FN	VF	VF/NM	NM-
nn-Contains a war stamp album and a punch out Jingle Piggie bank	12	24	36	69	97	125

DOUBLE TALK (Also see Two-Faces)
Feature Publications: No date (1962?) (32 pgs., full color, slick-c)
Christian Anti-Communism Crusade (Giveaway)

	GD	VG	FN	VF	VF/NM	NM-
nn-Sickle with blood-c	18	36	54	105	165	225

DRUMMER BOY AT GETTYSBURG
Eastern National Park & Monument Association: 1976

	GD	VG	FN	VF	VF/NM	NM-
nn-Fred Ray-a	3	6	9	15	22	28

DUMBO (Walt Disney's..., The Flying Elephant)
Weatherbird Shoes/Ernest Kern Co.(Detroit)/ Wieboldt's (Chicago): 1941
(K.K. Publ. Giveaway)

	GD	VG	FN	VF	VF/NM	NM-
nn-16 pgs., 9x10" (Rare)	43	86	129	269	455	640
nn-52 pgs., 5-1/2x8-1/2", slick cover in color; B&W interior; half text, half reprints 4-Color No. 17 (Dept. store)	22	44	66	131	216	300

DUMBO WEEKLY
Walt Disney Prod.: 1942 (Premium supplied by Diamond D-X Gas Stations)(4 pgs. each)

	GD	VG	FN	VF	VF/NM	NM-
1	34	68	102	199	325	450
2-16	13	26	39	72	101	130
Binder only (linen-like stock)						160

NOTE: *A cover and binder came separate at gas stations. Came with membership card.*

EAT RIGHT TO WORK AND WIN
Swift & Company: 1942 (16 pgs.) (Giveaway)
Blondie, Henry, Flash Gordon by Alex Raymond, Toots & Casper, Thimble Theatre(Popeye), Tillie the Toiler, The Phantom, The Little King, & Bringing up Father - original strips just for this book -(in daily strip form which shows what foods we should eat and why)

	GD	VG	FN	VF	VF/NM	NM-
	27	54	81	158	259	360

EDWARD'S SHOES GIVEAWAY
Edward's Shoe Store: 1954 (Has clown on cover)
Contains comic with new cover. Many combinations possible. Contents determines price, 50-60 percent of original. (Similar to Comics From Weatherbird & Free Comics to You)

ELSIE THE COW
D. S. Publishing Co.

	GD	VG	FN	VF	VF/NM	NM-
Borden's cheese comic picture bk ('40, giveaway)	20	40	60	114	182	250
Borden Milk Giveaway-(16 pgs., nn) (3 ishs, "A Trip Through Space" and 2 others, 1957)	14	28	42	81	118	155
Elsie's Fun Book(1950; Borden Milk)	14	28	42	81	118	155
Everyday Birthday Fun With... (1957; 20 pgs.)(100th Anniversary); Kubert-a	14	28	42	81	118	155

ESCAPE FROM FEAR
Planned Parenthood of America: 1956, 1962, 1969 (Giveaway, 8 pgs., color) (On birth control)

	GD	VG	FN	VF	VF/NM	NM-
1956 edition	11	22	33	62	86	110
1962 edition	4	8	12	27	44	60
1969 edition	3	6	9	17	26	35

EVEL KNIEVEL
Marvel Comics Group (Ideal Toy Corp.): 1974 (Giveaway, 20 pgs.)

	GD	VG	FN	VF	VF/NM	NM-
nn-Contains photo on inside back-c	4	8	12	27	44	60

FAMOUS COMICS (Also see Favorite Comics)
Zain-Eppy/United Features Syndicate: No date; Mid 1930's (24 pgs., paper-c)

	GD	VG	FN	VF	VF/NM	NM-
nn-Reprinted from 1933 & 1934 newspaper strips in color; Joe Palooka, Hairbreadth Harry, Napoleon, The Nebbs, etc. (Many different versions known)	63	126	189	403	689	975

FAMOUS FAIRY TALES
K. K. Publ. Co.: 1942; 1943 (32 pgs.); 1944 (16 pgs.) (Giveaway, soft-c)

	GD	VG	FN	VF	VF/NM	NM-
1942-Kelly-a	39	78	117	240	395	550
1943-r-/Fairy Tale Parade No. 2,3; Kelly-a	26	52	78	154	252	350
1944-Kelly-a	23	46	69	136	223	310

FAMOUS FUNNIES - A CARNIVAL OF COMICS
Eastern Color: 1933
36 pgs., no date given, no publisher, no number; contains strip reprints of The Bungle Family, Dixie Dugan, Hairbreadth Harry, Joe Palooka, Keeping Up With the Jones, Mutt & Jeff, Reg'lar Fellers, S'Matter Pop, Strange As It Seems, and others. This book was sold by M. C. Gaines to Wheatena, Malt-O-Milk, John Wanamaker, Kinney Shoe Stores, & others to be given away as premiums and radio giveaways (1933). Originally came with a mailing envelope.

	GD	VG	FN	VF	VF/NM	NM-
	530	1060	1590	3869	6835	9800

FAMOUS GANG BOOK OF COMICS (Becomes Donald & Mickey Merry Christmas 1943 on)
Firestone Tire & Rubber Co.: Dec, 1942 (Christmas giveaway, 32 pgs., paper-c)

	GD	VG	FN	VF	VF/NM	NM-
nn-(Rare)-Porky Pig, Bugs Bunny, Mary Jane & Sniffles, Elmer Fudd; r/Looney Tunes	68	136	204	435	743	1050

FANTASTIC FOUR
Marvel Comics

	GD	VG	FN	VF	VF/NM	NM-
nn (1981, 32 pgs.) Young Model Builders Club	2	4	6	9	13	16
Vol. 3 #60 Baltimore Comic Book Show (10/02, newspaper supplement) 200,000 copies were distributed to Baltimore Sun home subscribers to promote Baltimore Comic Con						4.00

FATHER OF CHARITY
Catechetical Guild Giveaway: No date (32 pgs.; paper cover)

	GD	VG	FN	VF	VF/NM	NM-
nn	5	10	15	25	31	36

FAVORITE COMICS (Also see Famous Comics)
Grocery Store Giveaway (Diff. Corp.) (detergent): 1934 (36 pgs.)

	GD	VG	FN	VF	VF/NM	NM-
Book 1-The Nebbs, Strange As It Seems, Napoleon, Joe Palooka, Dixie Dugan, S'Matter Pop, Hairbreadth Harry, etc. reprints	103	206	309	659	1130	1600
Book 2,3	61	122	183	390	670	950

FAWCETT MINIATURES (See Mighty Midget)
Fawcett Publications: 1946 (3-3/4x5", 12-24 pgs.) (Wheaties giveaways)

	GD	VG	FN	VF	VF/NM	NM-
Captain Marvel "And the Horn of Plenty"; Bulletman story	14	28	42	80	115	150
Captain Marvel "& the Raiders From Space"; Golden Arrow story	14	28	42	80	115	150
Captain Marvel Jr. "The Case of the Poison Press!" Bulletman story	14	28	42	80	115	150
Delecta of the Planets; C. C. Beck art; B&W inside; 12 pgs.; 3 printing variations (coloring) exist	20	40	60	114	182	250

FEARLESS FOSDICK
Capp Enterprises Inc.: 1951

	GD	VG	FN	VF	VF/NM	NM-
...& The Case of The Red Feather	6	12	18	28	34	40

FIFTY WHO MADE DC GREAT
DC Comics: 1985 (Reg. size, slick-c)

	GD	VG	FN	VF	VF/NM	NM-
nn	1	3	4	6	8	10

FIGHT FOR FREEDOM
National Assoc. of Mfgrs./General Comics: 1949, 1951 (Giveaway, 16 pgs.)

	GD	VG	FN	VF	VF/NM	NM-
nn-Dan Barry-c/a; used in **POP**, pg. 102	6	12	18	33	41	48

FIRE AND BLAST
National Fire Protection Assoc.: 1952 (Giveaway, 16 pgs., paper-c)

	GD	VG	FN	VF	VF/NM	NM-
nn-Mart Baily A-Bomb-c; about fire prevention	16	32	48	94	147	200

FIRE CHIEF AND THE SAFE OL' FIREFLY, THE

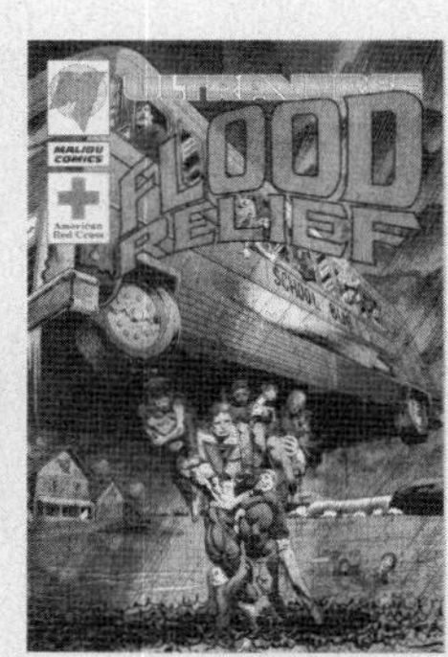

Flood Relief #1 © MAL

Funnies on Parade © EAS

G.I. Comics #28 © various

	GD	VG	FN	VF	VF/NM	NM-
	2.0	4.0	6.0	8.0	9.0	9.2

National Board of Fire Underwriters: 1952 (16 pgs.) (Safety brochure given away at schools) (produced by American Visuals Corp.)(Eisner)
nn-(Rare) Eisner-c/a 41 82 123 263 442 620

FLASH, THE
DC Comics
nn-(1990) Brochure for CBS TV series 4.00
The Flash Comes to a Standstill (1981, General Foods giveaway, 8 pages, 3-1/2 x 6-3/4", oblong) 2 4 6 11 16 20

FLASH COMICS (Also see Captain Marvel and Funny Stuff)
National Periodical Publications: 1946 (6-1/2x8-1/4", 32 pgs.)(Wheaties Giveaway)
nn-Johnny Thunder, Ghost Patrol, The Flash & Kubert Hawkman app.; Irwin Hasen-c/a 100 200 700 1000 - -
NOTE: *All known copies were taped to Wheaties boxes and are never found in mint condition. Copies with light tape residue bring the listed prices in all grades*

FLASH FORCE 2000
DC Comics: 1984
1-5 6.00

FLASH GORDON
Dell Publishing Co.: 1943 (20 pgs.)
Macy's Giveaway-(Rare); not by Raymond 58 116 174 371 636 900

FLASH GORDON
Harvey Comics: 1951 (16 pgs. in color, regular size, paper-c) (Gordon Bread giveaway)
1,2: 1-r/strips 10/24/37 - 2/6/38. 2-r/strips 7/14/40 - 10/6/40; Reprints by Raymond each.... 2 4 6 9 12 15
NOTE: *Most copies have brittle edges.*

FLINTSTONES FUN BOOK, THE
Denny's giveaway: 1990
1-20 1 2 3 5 6 8

FLOOD RELIEF
Malibu Comics (Ultraverse): Jan, 1994 (36 pgs.)(Ordered thru mail w/$5.00 to Red Cross)
1-Hardcase, Prime & Prototype app. 6.00

FOREST FIRE (Also see The Blazing Forest and Smokey Bear)
American Forestry Assn.(Commerical Comics): 1949 (dated-1950) (16 pgs., paper-c)
nn-Intro/1st app. Smokey The Forest Fire Preventing Bear; created by Rudy Wendelein; Wendelein/Sparling-a; 'Carter Oil Co.' on back-c of original 19 38 57 111 176 240

FOREST RANGER HANDBOOK
Wrather Corp.: 1967 (5x7", 20 pgs., slick-c)
nn-WIth Corey Stuart & Lassie photo-c 2 4 6 13 18 22

FORGOTTEN STORY BEHIND NORTH BEACH, THE
Catechetical Guild: No date (8 pgs., paper-c)
nn 5 10 15 24 30 35

FORK IN THE ROAD
U.S. Army Recruiting Service: 1961 (16 pgs., paper-c)
nn 2 4 6 11 16 20

48 FAMOUS AMERICANS
J. C. Penney Co. (Cpr. Edwin H. Stroh): 1947 (Giveaway) (Half-size in color)
nn - Simon & Kirby-a 11 22 33 64 90 115

FOXHOLE ON YOUR LAWN
No Publisher: No date
nn-Charles Biro art 4 7 10 14 17 20

FRANKIE LUER'S SPACE ADVENTURES
Luer Packing Co.: 1955 (5x7", 36 pgs., slick-c)
nn - With Davey Rocket 4 8 12 17 21 24

FREDDY
Charlton Comics
Schiff's Shoes Presents... #1 (1959)-Giveaway 4 8 11 16 19 22

FREE COMIC BOOK DAY EDITIONS (Now listed in the regular section)

FREE COMICS TO YOU FROM... (name of shoe store) (Has clown on cover & another with a rabbit) (Like comics from Weather Bird & Edward's Shoes)
Shoe Store Giveaway: Circa 1956, 1960-61
Contains a comic bound with new cover - several combinations possible; some Harvey titles known. Contents determine price.

FREEDOM TRAIN
Street & Smith Publications: 1948 (Giveaway)
nn-Powell-c w/mailer 16 32 48 94 147 200

	GD	VG	FN	VF	VF/NM	NM-
	2.0	4.0	6.0	8.0	9.0	9.2

FREIHOFER'S COMIC BOOK
All-American Comics: 1940s (7 1/2 x 10 1/4")(Freihofer's Donuts promotional)
2nd edition-(Scarce) Cover features All-American Comics characters Ultra-Man, Hop Harrigan, Red, White and Blue, Scribbly and others (A CGC 4.0 copy sold for $836.50 in May, 2012)

FRIENDLY GHOST, CASPER, THE
Harvey Publications: 1967 (16 pgs.)
American Dental Assoc. giveaway-Small size 3 6 9 17 25 32

FRITO-LAY GIVEAWAY
Frito-Lay: 1962 (3-1/4x7", soft-c, 16 pgs.) (Disney)
nn-Donald Duck "Plotting Picnickers" 5 10 15 30 50 70
nn-Ludwig Von Drake "Fish Stampede" 3 6 9 19 30 40
nn- Mickey Mouse & Goofy "Bicep Bungle" 3 6 9 21 33 45

FROM GOODWILL INDUSTRIES, A GOOD LIFE
Goodwill Industries: 1950s (regular size)
1 8 16 24 40 50 60

FRONTIER DAYS
Robin Hood Shoe Store (Brown Shoe): 1956 (Giveaway)
1 4 7 10 14 17 20

FRONTIERS OF FREEDOM
Institute of Life Insurance: 1950 (Giveaway, paper cover)
nn-Dan Barry-a 8 16 24 44 57 70

FUNNIES ON PARADE (Premium)(See Toy World Funnies)
Eastern Color Printing Co.: 1933 (36 pgs., slick cover)
No date or publisher listed
nn-Contains Sunday page reprints of Mutt & Jeff, Joe Palooka, Hairbreadth Harry, Reg'lar Fellers, Skippy, & others (10,000 print run). This book was printed for Proctor & Gamble to be given away & came out before Famous Funnies or Century of Comics. 975 1950 2919 7100 12,550 18,000

FUNNY PICTURE STORIES
Comics Magazine Co./Centaur Publications: 1930s (Giveaway, 16-20 pgs., slick-c)
Promotes diff. laundries; has box on cover where "your Laundry Name" is printed 34 68 102 199 325 450

FUNNY STUFF (Also see Captain Marvel & Flash Comics)
National Periodical Publications (Wheaties Giveaway): 1946 (6-1/2x8-1/4")
nn-(Scarce)-Dodo & the Frog, Three Mouseketeers, etc.; came taped to Wheaties box; never found in better than fine 50 100 350 500 – –

FUTURE COP: L.A.P.D. (Electronic Arts video game)
DC Comics (WildStorm): 1998
nn-Ron Lim-a/Dave Johnson-c 3.00

GABBY HAYES WESTERN (Movie star)
Fawcett Publications
Quaker Oats Giveaway nn's(#1-5, 1951, 2-1/2x7") (Kagran Corp.)-...In Tracks of Guilt, ...In the Fence Post Mystery, ...In the Accidental Sherlock, ...In the Frame-Up, ...In the Double Cross Brand known 10 20 30 54 72 90
Mailing Envelope (has illo of Gabby on front) 10 20 30 54 72 90

GARY GIBSON COMICS (Donut club membership)
National Dunking Association: 1950 (Included in donut box with pin and card)
1-Western soft-c, 16 pgs.; folded into the box 5 10 14 20 24 28

GENE AUTRY COMICS
Dell Publishing Co.
...Adventure Comics And Play-Fun Book ('47)-32 pgs., 8x6-1/2"; games, comics, magic (Pillsbury premium) 22 44 66 132 216 300
Quaker Oats Giveaway(1950)-2-1/2x6-3/4"; 5 different versions; "Death Card Gang", "Phantoms of the Cave", "Riddle of Laughing Mtn.", "Secret of Lost Valley", "Bond of the Broken Arrow" (came in wrapper) each... 10 20 30 58 79 100
Mailing Envelope (has illo. of Gene on front) 10 20 30 58 79 100
3-D Giveaway(1953)-Pocket-size; 5 different 10 20 30 58 79 100
Mailing Envelope (no art on front) 8 16 24 44 57 70

GENE AUTRY TIM (Formerly Tim) (Becomes Tim in Space)
Tim Stores: 1950 (Half-size) (B&W Giveaway)
nn-Several issues (All Scarce) 19 38 57 109 172 235

GENERAL FOODS SUPER-HEROES
DC Comics: 1979, 1980
1-4 (1979), 1-4 (1980) each... 12.00

Gulf Funny Weekly #375 © Gulf

Hopalong Cassidy Grape Nuts Flakes © FAW

How Stalin Hopes We Will Destroy America © PM

GD 2.0 | VG 4.0 | FN 6.0 | VF 8.0 | VF/NM 9.0 | NM- 9.2

GD 2.0 | VG 4.0 | FN 6.0 | VF 8.0 | VF/NM 9.0 | NM- 9.2

G. I. COMICS (Also see Jeep & Overseas Comics)
Giveaways: 1945 - No. 73?, 1946 (Distributed to U. S. Armed Forces)
1-73-Contains Prince Valiant by Foster, Blondie, Smilin' Jack, Mickey Finn, Terry & the Pirates, Donald Duck, Alley Oop, Moon Mullins & Capt. Easy strip reprints (at least 73 issues known to exist) 8 16 24 42 54 65

GODZILLA VS. MEGALON
Cinema Shares Int.: 1976 (4 pgs. on newsprint) (Movie theater giveaway)
nn-1st. comic app. Godzilla in U.S. 4 8 12 17 21 24

GOLDEN ARROW
Fawcett Publications
...Well Known Comics (1944; 12 pgs.; 8-1/2x10-1/2"; paper-c; glued binding)- Bestmaid/ Samuel Lowe giveaway; printed in green 10 20 30 54 72 90

GOLDILOCKS & THE THREE BEARS
K. K. Publications: 1943 (Giveaway)
nn 13 26 39 74 105 135

GREAT PEOPLE OF GENESIS, THE
David C. Cook Publ. Co.: No date (Religious giveaway, 64 pgs.)
nn-Reprint/Sunday Pix Weekly 5 10 15 23 28 32

GREAT SACRAMENT, THE
Catechetical Guild: 1953 (Giveaway, 36 pgs.)
nn 5 10 15 22 26 30

GREEN JET COMICS, THE (See Comic Books, Series 1)

GRENADA
Commercial Comics Co.: 1983 (Giveaway produced by the CIA)
1-Air dropped over Grenada during the 1983 invasion 40.00

GRIT (YOU'VE GOT TO HAVE...)
GRIT Publishing Co.: 1959
nn-GRIT newspaper sales recruitment comic; Schaffenberger-a. Later version has altered artwork 5 10 15 22 26 30

GROWING UP WITH JUDY
1952
nn-General Electric giveaway 4 8 12 18 22 25

GULF FUNNY WEEKLY (Gulf Comic Weekly No. 1-4)(See Standard Oil Comics)
Gulf Oil Company (Giveaway): 1933 - No. 422, 5/23/41 (in full color; 4 pgs.; tabloid size to 2/3/39; 2/10/39 on, regular comic book size)(early issues undated)

	GD	VG	FN	VF	VF/NM	NM-
1	68	134	204	435	743	1050
2-5	31	62	93	184	300	415
6-30	20	40	60	117	189	260
31-100	14	28	42	82	121	160
101-196	10	20	30	58	79	100
197-Wings Winfair begins(1/29/37); by Fred Meagher beginning in 1938	23	46	69	136	223	310
198-300 (Last tabloid size)	14	28	42	82	121	160
301-350 (Regular size)	9	18	27	52	69	85
351-422	8	16	24	42	54	65

GULLIVER'S TRAVELS
Macy's Department Store: 1939, small size
nn-Christmas giveaway 14 28 42 82 121 160

GUN THAT WON THE WEST, THE
Winchester-Western Division & Olin Mathieson Chemical Corp.: 1956 (Giveaway, 24 pgs.)
nn-Painted-c 5 10 15 24 30 35

HAPPINESS AND HEALING FOR YOU (Also see Oral Roberts'...)
Commercial Comics: 1955 (36 pgs., slick cover) (Oral Roberts Giveaway)
nn 9 18 27 52 69 85
NOTE: *The success of this book prompted Oral Roberts to go into the publishing business himself to produce his own material.*

HAPPI TIME FUN BOOK
Sears, Roebuck & Co.: 1940s - 1950s (32 pgs., soft-c)
nn-Comics, games, puzzles, & magic tricks cut -outs 4 7 10 14 17 20

HAPPY CHAMP, THE (The Story of Joker Osborn)
Western Publ.: 1965
nn-About water-skiing 3 6 9 19 30 40

HAPPY TOOTH
DC Comics: 1996
1 3.00

HARLEM YOUTH REPORT (Also see All-Negro Comics and Negro Romances)
Custom Comics, Inc.: 1964 (Giveaway)(No #1-4)
5-"Youth in the Ghetto" and "The Blueprint For Change"; distr. in Harlem only; has map of central Harlem on back-c (scarce) 57 114 171 456 1028 1600

HAWKMAN - THE SKY'S THE LIMIT
DC Comics: 1981 (General Foods giveaway, 8 pages, 3-1/2 x 6-3/4", oblong)
nn 2 4 6 10 14 18

HAWTHORN-MELODY FARMS DAIRY COMICS
Everybody's Publishing Co.: No date (1950's) (Giveaway)
nn-Cheerie Chick, Tuffy Turtle, Robin Koo Koo, Donald & Longhorn Legends 2 4 6 8 11 14

HENRY ALDRICH COMICS (TV)
Dell Publishing Co.: 1951 (16 pgs., soft-c)
Giveaway - Capehart radio 3 6 9 19 30 40

HERE IS SANTA CLAUS
Goldsmith Publ. Co. (Kann's in Washington, D.C.): 1930s (16 pgs., 8 in color) (stiff paper covers)
nn 14 28 42 80 115 150

HERE'S HOW AMERICA'S CARTOONISTS HELP TO SELL U.S. SAVINGS BONDS
Harvey Comics: 1950? (16 pgs., giveaway, paper cover)
Contains: Joe Palooka, Donald Duck, Archie, Kerry Drake, Red Ryder, Blondie & Steve Canyon 20 40 60 114 182 250

HISTORY OF GAS
American Gas Assoc.: Mar, 1947 (Giveaway, 16 pgs., soft-c)
nn-Miss Flame narrates 9 18 27 50 65 80

HOME DEPOT, SAFETY HEROES
Marvel Comics.: Oct, 2005 (Giveaway)
nn-Spider-Man and the Fantastic Four on the cover; Olliffe-a/c; Roseman-s 2.50

HONEYBEE BIRDWHISTLE AND HER PET PEPI (Introducing...)
Newspaper Enterprise Assoc.: 1969 (Giveaway, 24 pgs., B&W, slick cover)
nn-Contains Freckles newspaper strips with a short biography of Henry Fornhals (artist) & Fred Fox (writer) of the strip 4 8 12 28 47 65

HOODS UP
Fram Corp.: 1953 (15¢, distributed to service station owners, 16 pgs.)
1-(Very Rare; only 2 known); Eisner-c/a in all (a CGC 9.0 copy sold for $1840 in 2006)
2-6-(Very Rare; only 1 known of #3, 2 known of #2,4) 48 96 144 302 514 725
NOTE: *Convertible Connie gives tips for service stations, selling Fram oil filters.*

HOOKED (Anti-drug comic distributed at NYC methadone clinics)
U.S. Dept. of Health: 1966 (giveaway, oblong)
nn-Distributed between May and July, 1966 3 6 9 21 33 45

HOPALONG CASSIDY
Fawcett Publications
Grape Nuts Flakes giveaway (1950,9x6") 14 28 42 78 112 145
...& the Mad Barber (1951 Bond Bread giveaway)-7x5"; used in **SOTI**, pgs. 308,309 18 36 54 103 162 220
...Meets the Brend Brothers Bandits (1951 Bond Bread giveaway, color, paper-c, 16 pgs., 3-1/2x7")- Fawcett Publ. 9 18 27 47 61 75
...Strange Legacy (1951 Bond Bread giveaway) 9 18 27 47 61 75
White Tower Giveaway (1946, 16pgs., paper-c) 9 18 27 52 69 85

HOPPY THE MARVEL BUNNY (WELL KNOWN COMICS)
Fawcett Publications: 1944 (8-1/2x10-1/2", paper-c)
Bestmaid/Samuel Lowe (printed in red or blue) 10 20 30 56 76 95

HOT STUFF, THE LITTLE DEVIL
Harvey Publications (Illustrated Humor):1963
Shoestore Giveaway 3 6 9 21 33 45

HOW KIDS ENJOY NEW YORK
American Airlines: 1966 (Giveaway, 40 pgs., 4x9")
nn-Includes 8 color pages by Bob Kane featuring a tour of New York and his studio (a VG copy sold for $180 and a FN+ sold for $250 in 2004)

HOW STALIN HOPES WE WILL DESTROY AMERICA
Joe Lowe Co. (Pictorial Media): 1951 (Giveaway, 16 pgs.)
nn 39 78 117 240 395 550

HURRICANE KIDS, THE (Also See Magic Morro, The Owl, Popular Comics #45)
R.S. Callender: 1941 (Giveaway, 7-1/2x5-1/4", soft-c)

Is This Tomorrow? © CG

Jo-Joy 1948 © W.T. Grant

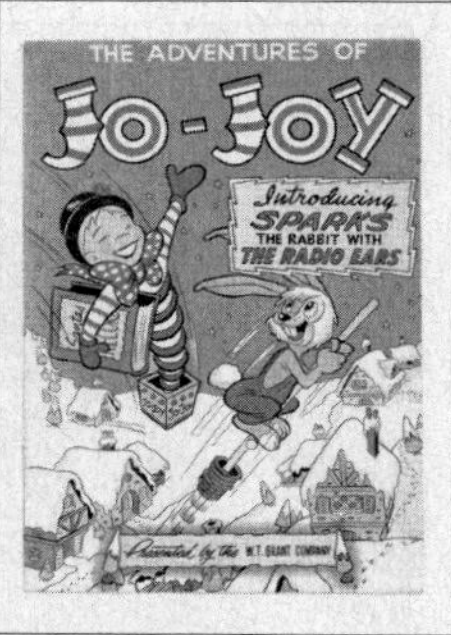

Kasco Komics #2 © Kasko

GD VG FN VF VF/NM NM-
2.0 4.0 6.0 8.0 9.0 9.2

nn-Will Ely-a. 8 16 24 44 57 70

IF THE DEVIL WOULD TALK
Roman Catholic Catechetical Guild/Impact Publ.: 1950; 1958 (32 pgs.; paper cover; in full color)

nn-(Scarce)-About secularism (20-30 copies known to exist); very low distribution 116 232 348 742 1271 1800
1958 Edition-(Impact Publ.); art & script changed to meet church criticism of earlier edition; 80 plus copies known to exist 33 66 99 194 317 440
Black & White version of nn edition; small size; only 4 known copies exist 36 72 108 211 343 475

NOTE: *The original edition of this book was printed and killed by the Guild's board of directors. It is believed that a very limited number of copies were distributed. The 1958 version was a complete bomb with very limited, if any, circulation. In 1979, 11 original, 4 1958 reprints, and 4 B&W's surfaced from the Guild's old files in St. Paul, Minnesota.*

IN LOVE WITH JESUS
Catechetical Educational Society: 1952 (Giveaway, 36 pgs.)

nn 7 14 21 37 46 55

INTERSTATE THEATRES' FUN CLUB COMICS
Interstate Theatres: Mid 1940's (10¢ on cover) (B&W cover) (Premium)

Cover features MLJ characters looking at a copy of Top-Notch Comics, but contains an early Detective Comic on inside; many combinations 13 26 39 74 105 135

IN THE GOOD HANDS OF THE ROCKEFELLER TEAM
Country Art Studios: No date (paper cover, 8 pgs.)

nn-Joe Simon-a 8 16 24 42 54 65

IRON GIANT
DC Comics: 1999 (4 pages, theater giveaway)

1-Previews movie 3.00

IRON HORSE GOES TO WAR, THE
Association of American Railroads: 1960 (Giveaway, 16 pgs.)

nn-Civil War & railroads 3 6 9 16 23 30

IS THIS TOMORROW?
Catechetical Guild: 1947 (One Shot) (3 editions) (52 pgs.)

1-Theme of communists taking over the USA; (no price on cover) Used in **POP**, pg. 102 32 64 96 188 307 425
1-(10¢ on cover)(Red price on yellow circle) 32 64 96 188 307 425
1-(10¢ on cover)(Yellow price on circle) 32 64 96 188 307 425
1-(10¢ on cover)(Yellow price on black circle) 36 72 108 211 343 475
1-Has blank circle with no price on cover 36 72 108 211 343 475
Black & White advance copy titled "Confidential" (52 pgs.)-Contains script and art edited out of the color edition, including one page of extreme violence showing mob nailing a Cardinal to a door; (only two known copies). A VF+ sold in 2/08 for $3346. A NM 9.6 sold in 1/07 for $5975

NOTE: *The original color version first sold for 10 cents. Since sales were good, it was later printed as a giveaway. Approximately four million in total were printed. The two black and white copies listed plus two other versions as well as a full color untrimmed version surfaced in 1979 from the Guild's old files in St. Paul, Minnesota.*

IT'S FUN TO STAY ALIVE
National Automobile Dealers Association: 1948 (Giveaway, 16 pgs., heavy stock paper)

Featuring: Bugs Bunny, The Berrys, Dixie Dugan, Elmer, Henry, Tim Tyler, Bruce Gentry, Abbie & Slats, Joe Jinks, The Toodles, & Cokey; all art copyright 1946-48 drawn especially for this book 15 30 45 84 127 170

IT'S TIME FOR REASON - NOT TREASON
Liberty Lobby: 1967 (Reg. size, soft-c) (Anti-communist)

nn 6 12 18 41 76 110

JACK AND CHUCK LEARN THE HARD WAY
Commercia Comics/Wagner Electric Co.: 1950s (Reg. size, soft-c)

nn-Automotive giveaway 9 18 27 47 61 75

JACK & JILL VISIT TOYTOWN WITH ELMER THE ELF
Butler Brothers (Toytown Stores): 1949 (Giveaway, 16 pgs., paper cover)

nn 5 10 15 22 26 30

JACK ARMSTRONG (Radio)(See True Comics)
Parents' Institute: 1949

12-Premium version (distr. in Chicago only); Free printed on upper right-c; no price (Rare) 18 36 54 107 169 230

JACKIE JOYNER KERSEE IN HIGH HURDLES (Kellogg's Tony's Sports Comics)
DC Comics: 1992 (Sports Illustrated)

nn 5.00

JACKPOT OF FUN COMIC BOOK
DCA Food Ind.: 1957, giveaway (paper cover, regular size)

GD VG FN VF VF/NM NM-
2.0 4.0 6.0 8.0 9.0 9.2

nn-Features Howdy Doody 12 24 36 67 94 120

JEDLICKA SHOES
DC Comics: 1961 (Funny animal-c)

nn-Contains Superman #142 9 18 27 58 114 170

JEEP COMICS
R. B. Leffingwell & Co.: 1945 - 1946 (16 pgs.)(King Features Syndicate)

1-46 (Giveaways)-Strip reprints in all; Tarzan, Flash Gordon, Blondie, The Nebbs, Little Iodine, Red Ryder, Don Winslow, The Phantom, Johnny Hazard, Katzenjammer Kids; distr. to U.S. Armed Forces from 1945-1946 6 12 18 31 38 45

JINGLE BELLS CHRISTMAS BOOK
Montgomery Ward (Giveaway): 1971 (20 pgs., B&W inside, slick-c)

nn 6.00

JOAN OF ARC
Catechetical Guild (Topix) (Giveaway): No date (28 pgs., blank back-c)

nn-Ingrid Bergman photo-c; Addison Burbank-a 13 26 39 72 101 130

NOTE: *Unpublished version exists which came from the Guild's files.*

JOE PALOOKA (2nd Series)
Harvey Publications

...Body Building Instruction Book (1958 B&M Sports Toy giveaway, 16 pgs., 5-1/4x7")-Origin 8 16 24 42 54 65
...Fights His Way Back (1945 Giveaway, 24 pgs.) Family Comics 11 22 33 62 86 110
...in Hi There! (1949 Red Cross giveaway, 12 pgs., 4-3/4x6") 7 14 21 37 46 55
...in It's All in the Family (1945 Red Cross giveaway, 16 pgs., regular size) 8 16 24 40 50 60

JOE THE GENIE OF STEEL (Also see "Return of...")
U.S. Steel Corp., Pittsburgh, PA: 1950 (16 pgs, reg size)

nn-Joe Magarac, the Paul Bunyan of steel 9 18 27 50 65 80

JOHNNY GETS THE WORD
Dept. of Health of New York City: 1963 (small size)

nn - Prevention of venereal diseases 4 8 12 27 44 60

NOTE: *A CGC 9.6 copy sold in 2016 for $263.*

JOHNNY JINGLE'S LUCKY DAY
American Dairy Assoc.: 1956 (16 pgs.; 7-1/4x5-1/8") (Giveaway) (Disney)

nn 5 10 15 24 30 35

JOHNSON MAKES THE TEAM
B.F. Goodrich: 1950 (Reg. size) (Football giveaway)

nn 6 12 18 31 38 45

JO-JOY (The Adventures of...)
W. T. Grant Dept. Stores: 1945 - 1953 (Christmas gift comic, 16 pgs., 7-1/16x10-1/4")

1945-53 issues 7 14 21 37 46 55

JOLLY CHRISTMAS BOOK (See Christmas Journey Through Space)
Promotional Publ. Co.: 1951; 1954; 1955 (36 pgs.; 24 pgs.)

1951-(Woolworth giveaway)-slightly oversized; no slick cover; Marv Levy-c/a 7 14 21 37 46 55
1954-(Hot Shoppes giveaway)-regular size-reprints 1951 issue; slick cover added; 24 pgs.; no ads 6 12 18 31 38 45
1955-(J. M. McDonald Co. giveaway)-reg. size 6 12 18 28 34 40

JOURNEY OF DISCOVERY WITH MARK STEEL (See Mark Steel)

JUMPING JACKS PRESENTS THE WHIZ KIDS
Jumping Jacks Stores giveaway: 1978 (In 3-D) with glasses (4 pgs.)

nn 6.00

JUNGLE BOOK FUN BOOK, THE (Disney)
Baskin Robbins: 1978

nn-Ice Cream giveaway 2 4 6 9 12 15

JUSTICE LEAGUE OF AMERICA
DC Comics: 1999 (included in Justice League of America Monopoly game)

nn - Reprints 1st app. in Brave and the Bold #28 2.50

KASCO KOMICS
Kasko Grainfeed (Giveaway): 1945; No. 2, 1949 (Regular size, paper-c)

1(1945)-Similar to Katy Keene; Bill Woggon-a; 28 pgs.; 6-7/8x9-7/8" 20 40 60 120 195 270
2(1949)-Woggon-c/a 15 30 45 84 127 170

KATY AND KEN VISIT SANTA WITH MISTER WISH

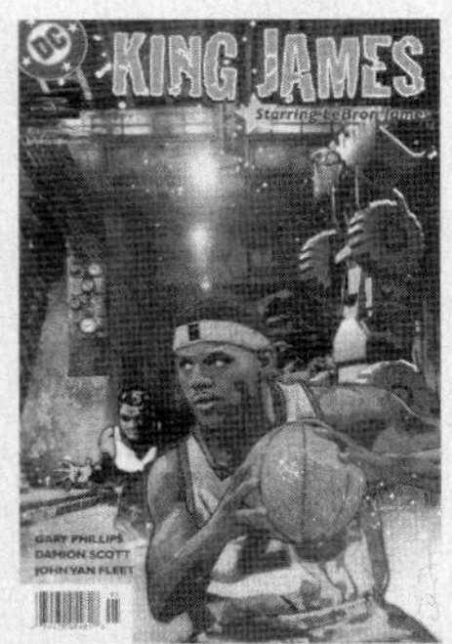

King James © DC

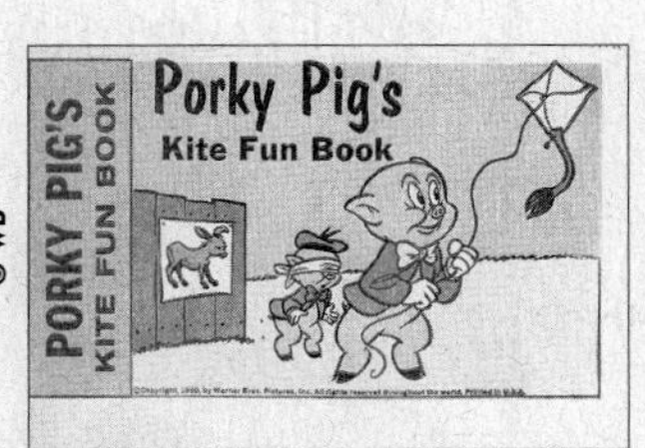

Kite Fun Book 1960 - Porky Pig © WB

The Life of the Blessed Virgin © CG

	GD 2.0	VG 4.0	FN 6.0	VF 8.0	VF/NM 9.0	NM- 9.2
S. S. Kresge Co. : 1948 (Giveaway, 16 pgs., paper-c)						
nn	6	12	18	29	36	42
KELLOGG'S CINNAMON MINI-BUNS SUPER-HEROES						
DC Comics: 1993 (4 1/4" x 2 3/4")						
4 editions: Flash, Justice League America, Superman, Wonder Woman and the Star Riders each.....						4.00
KERRY DRAKE DETECTIVE CASES						
Publisher's Syndicate						
...in the Case of the Sleeping City-(1951)-16 pg. giveaway for armed forces; paper cover	7	14	21	35	43	50
KEY COMICS						
Key Clothing Co./Peterson Clothing: 1951 - 1956 (32 pgs.) (Giveaway)						
Contains a comic from different publishers bound with new cover. Cover changed each year. Many combinations possible. Distributed in Nebraska, Iowa, & Kansas. Contents would determine price, 40-60 percent of original.						
KING JAMES "THE KING OF BASKETBALL"						
DC Comics: 2004 (Promo comic for LeBron James and Powerade Flava23 sports drink)						
nn - Ten different covers by various artists; 4 covers for retail, 4 for mail-in, 1 for military commissaries, and 1 general market; Damion Scott-a/Gary Phillips-s						2.50
KIRBY'S SHOES COMICS						
Kirby's Shoes: 1959 - 1961 (8 pgs., soft-c)						
nn-Features Kirby the Golden Bear	3	5	7	10	12	14
KITE FUN BOOK						
Pacific, Gas & Electric/Sou. California Edison/Florida Power & Light/ Missouri Public Service Co.: 1952 - 1998 (16 pgs, 5x7-1/4", soft-c)						
1952-Having Fun With Kites (P.G.&E.)	10	20	30	58	79	100
1953-Pinocchio Learns About Kites (Disney)	39	78	117	240	395	550
1954-Donald Duck Tells About Kites-Fla. Power, S.C.E. & version with label issues -Barks pencils-8 pgs.; inks-7 pgs. (Rare)	226	452	678	1446	2473	3500
1954-Donald Duck Tells About Kites-P.G.&E. issue -7th page redrawn changing middle 3 panels to show P.G.&E. in story line; (All Barks-a) Scarce	194	388	582	1242	2121	3000
1955-Brer Rabbit in "A Kite Tail" (Disney)	25	50	75	150	245	340
1956-Woody Woodpecker (Lantz)	13	26	39	72	101	130
1957-Ruff and Reddy (exist?)						
1958-Tom And Jerry (M.G.M.)	9	18	27	52	69	85
1959-Bugs Bunny (Warner Bros.)	4	8	12	27	44	60
1960-Porky Pig (Warner Bros.)	4	8	12	28	47	65
1960-Bugs Bunny (Warner Bros.)	4	8	12	28	47	65
1961-Huckleberry Hound (Hanna-Barbera)	5	10	15	31	53	75
1962-Yogi Bear (Hanna-Barbera)	4	8	12	25	40	55
1963-Rocky and Bullwinkle (TV)(Jay Ward)	5	10	15	35	63	90
1963-Top Cat (TV)(Hanna-Barbera)	3	6	9	19	30	40
1964-Magilla Gorilla (TV)(Hanna-Barbera)	3	6	9	17	26	35
1965-Jinks, Pixie and Dixie (TV)(Hanna-Barbera)	3	6	9	15	22	28
1965-Tweety and Sylvester (Warner); S.C.E. version with Reddy Kilowatt app.	2	4	6	9	13	16
1966-Secret Squirrel (Hanna-Barbera); S.C.E. version with Reddy Kilowatt app.	5	10	15	30	50	70
1967-Beep! Beep! The Road Runner (TV)(Warner)	2	4	6	11	16	20
1968-Bugs Bunny (Warner Bros.)	2	4	6	13	18	22
1969-Dastardly and Muttley (TV)(Hanna-Barbera)	3	6	9	19	30	40
1970-Rocky and Bullwinkle (TV)(Jay Ward)	4	8	12	27	44	60
1971-Beep! Beep! The Road Runner (TV)(Warner)	2	4	6	11	16	20
1972-The Pink Panther (TV)	2	4	6	10	14	18
1973-Lassie (TV)	3	6	9	15	22	28
1974-Underdog (TV)	2	4	6	11	16	20
1975-Ben Franklin	2	4	6	8	10	12
1976-The Brady Bunch (TV)	3	6	9	16	23	30
1977-Ben Franklin (exist?)	2	4	6	8	10	12
1977-Popeye	2	4	6	9	13	16
1978-Happy Days (TV)	2	4	6	11	16	20
1979-Eight is Enough (TV)	2	4	6	9	13	16
1980-The Waltons (TV, released in 1981)	2	4	6	9	13	16
1982-Tweety and Sylvester	2	4	6	8	11	14
1984-Smokey Bear	1	3	4	6	8	10
1986-Road Runner	1	2	3	5	6	8
1997-Thomas Edison						4.00
1998-Edison Field (Anaheim Stadium)						3.00
KNOWING'S NOT ENOUGH						
Commercial Comics: 1956 (Reg. size, paper-c) (United States Steel safety giveaway)						

	GD 2.0	VG 4.0	FN 6.0	VF 8.0	VF/NM 9.0	NM- 9.2
nn	7	14	21	35	43	50
KNOW YOUR MASS						
Catechetical Guild: No. 303, 1958 (35¢, 100 Pg. Giant) (Square binding)						
303-In color	7	14	21	35	43	50
KOLYNOS PRESENTS THE WHITE GUARD						
Whitehall Pharmacal Co.: 1949 (paper cover, 8 pgs.)						
nn	6	12	18	31	38	45
KOLYNOS PRESENTS THE WICKED WITCH						
Whitehall Pharmacal Co.: 1951 (paper cover, 8 pgs.)						
nn-Anti-tooth decay	4	7	10	14	17	20
K. O. PUNCH, THE (Also see Lucky Fights It Through & Sidewalk Romance)						
E. C. Comics: 1948 (VD Educational giveaway)						
nn-Feldstein-splash; Kamen-a	110	220	330	704	1202	1700
KOREA MY HOME (Also see Yalta to Korea)						
Johnstone and Cushing: nd (1950s, slick-c, regular size)						
nn-Anti-communist; Korean War	23	46	69	136	223	310
KRIM-KO KOMICS						
Krim-ko Chocolate Drink: 5/18/35 - No. 6, 6/22/35; 1936 - 1939 (weekly)						
1-(16 pgs., soft-c, Dairy giveaways)-Tom, Mary & Sparky Advs. by Russell Keaton, Jim Hawkins by Dick Moores, Mystery Island! by Rick Yager begin	14	28	42	78	112	145
2-6 (6/22/35)	10	20	30	58	79	100
Lola, Secret Agent; 184 issues, 4 pg. giveaways - all original stories each....	8	16	24	40	50	60
LABOR IS A PARTNER						
Catechetical Guild Educational Society: 1949 (32 pgs., paper-c)						
nn-Anti-communism	37	74	111	222	361	500
Confidential Preview-(8-1/2x11", B&W, saddle stitched)-only one known copy; text varies from color version, advertises next book on secularism (If the Devil Would Talk) (A VF- copy sold for $2629 in 11/2016)						
LADIES - WOULDN'T IT BE BETTER TO KNOW						
American Cancer Society: 1969 (Reg. size)						
nn	4	8	12	22	35	48
LADY AND THE TRAMP IN "BUTTER LATE THAN NEVER"						
American Dairy Assoc. (Premium): 1955 (16 pgs., 5x7-1/4", soft-c) (Disney)						
nn	9	18	27	47	61	75
LASSIE (TV)						
Dell Publ. Co						
The Adventures of... nn-(Red Heart Dog Food giveaway, 1949)-16 pgs, soft-c; 1st app. Lassie in comics	36	72	108	216	351	485
LIFE OF THE BLESSED VIRGIN						
Catechetical Guild (Giveaway): 1950 (68pgs.) (square binding)						
nn-Contains "The Woman of the Promise" & "Mother of Us All" rebound	8	16	24	40	50	60
LIGHTNING RACERS						
DC Comics: 1989						
1						4.50
LI'L ABNER (Al Capp's) (Also see Natural Disasters!)						
Harvey Publ./Toby Press						
...& the Creatures from Drop-Outer Space-nn (Job Corps giveaway; 36 pgs., in color) (entire book by Frank Frazetta)	21	42	63	124	202	280
...Joins the Navy (1950) (Toby Press Premium)	11	22	33	62	86	110
Al Capp by Li'l Abner (Circa 1946, nd, giveaway) Al Capp bio and his life as an amputee	11	22	33	62	86	110
LITTLE ALONZO						
Macy's Dept. Store: 1938 (B&W, 5-1/2x8-1/2")(Christmas giveaway)						
nn-By Ferdinand the Bull's Munro Leaf	9	18	27	50	65	80
LITTLE ARCHIE (See Archie Comics)						
LITTLE DOT						
Harvey Publications						
Shoe store giveaway 2	4	8	12	27	44	60
LITTLE FIR TREE, THE						
W. T. Grant Co. : nd (1942) (8-1/2x11") (12 pgs. with cover, color & B&W, heavy paper) (Christmas giveaway)						

How the Lone Ranger Captured Silver © Lone Ranger Inc.

The Man Who Wouldn't Quit © HARV

March of Comics #4 © WDC

GD VG FN VF VF/NM NM-
2.0 4.0 6.0 8.0 9.0 9.2

GD VG FN VF VF/NM NM-
2.0 4.0 6.0 8.0 9.0 9.2

nn-Story by Hans Christian Anderson; 8 pg. Kelly-r/Santa Claus Funnies (not signed); X-Mas-c 94 188 282 597 1024 1450

LITTLE KLINKER
Little Klinker Ventures: Nov, 1960 (20 pgs.) (slick cover) (Montgomery Ward Giveaway)

nn - Christmas; Santa-c 3 6 9 14 20 25

LITTLE MISS SUNBEAM COMICS
Magazine Enterprises/Quality Bakers of America

Bread Giveaway 1-4(Quality Bakers, 1949-50)-14 pgs. each 6 12 18 31 38 45
Bread Giveaway (1957,61; 16pgs, reg. size) 5 10 15 24 30 35

LITTLE ORPHAN ANNIE
David McKay Publ./Dell Publishing Co.

Junior Commandos Giveaway (same-c as 4-Color #18, K.K. Publ.)(Big Shoe Store); same back cover as '47 Popped Wheat giveaway; 16 pgs; flag-c; r/strips 9/7/42-10/10/42 26 52 78 154 252 350
Popped Wheat Giveaway ('47)-16 pgs. full color; reprints strips from 5/3/40 to 6/20/40 4 8 12 18 22 25
Quaker Sparkies Giveaway (1940) 18 36 54 103 162 220
Quaker Sparkies Giveaway (1941, full color, 20 pgs.); "LOA and the Rescue"; r/strips 4/13/39-6/21/39 & 7/6/39-7/17/39. "LOA and the Kidnappers"; r/strips 11/28/38-1/28/39 15 30 45 94 147 200
Quaker Sparkies Giveaway (1942, full color, 20 pgs.); "LOA and Mr. Gudge"; r/strips 2/13/38-3/21/38 & 4/18/37-5/30/37. "LOA and the Great Am" 15 30 45 88 137 185

LITTLE TREE THAT WASN'T WANTED, THE
W. T. Grant Co. (Giveaway): 1960, (Color, 28 pgs.)

nn-Christmas story, puzzles and games 3 6 9 21 33 45

LOADED (Also see Re-Loaded)
DC Comics: 1995 (Interplay Productions)

1-Garth Ennis-s; promotes video game 4.00

LONE RANGER, THE
Dell Publishing Co.

Cheerios Giveaways (1954, 16 pgs., 2-1/2x7", soft-c) #1- "The Lone Ranger, His Mask & How He Met Tonto". #2- "The Lone Ranger & the Story of Silver" each.... 12 24 36 69 97 125
Doll Giveaways (Gabriel Ind.)(1973, 3-1/4x5")- "The Story of The Lone Ranger," "The Carson City Bank Robbery" & "The Apache Buffalo Hunt" 2 4 6 12 16 20
How the Lone Ranger Captured Silver Book(1936)-Silvercup Bread giveaway 55 110 165 352 601 850
...In Milk for Big Mike (1955, Dairy Association giveaway), soft-c; 5x7-1/4", 16 pgs. 10 20 30 58 79 100
Legend of The Lone Ranger (1969, 16 pgs., giveaway)-Origin The Lone Ranger 4 8 12 21 33 45
Merita Bread giveaway (1954, 16 pgs., 5x7-1/4")- "How to Be a Lone Ranger Health & Safety Scout" 14 28 42 80 115 150
Merita Bread giveaway (1955, 16 pgs., 5x7-1/4")- "Official Lone Ranger and Tonto Coloring Book" 12 24 36 69 97 125
Merita Bread giveaway (1956, 16 pgs., 5x7-1/4")- "Tells the Story of Branding" 12 24 36 69 97 125

LONE RANGER COMICS, THE
Lone Ranger, Inc.: Book 1, 1939(inside) (shows 1938 on-c) (52 pgs. in color; regular size) (Ice cream mail order)

Book 1-(Scarce)-The first western comic devoted to a single character; not by Vallely 543 1086 1629 3800 - -
2nd version w/large full color promo poster pasted over centerfold & a smaller poster pasted over back cover; includes new additional premiums not originally offered (Rare) 643 1286 1929 4500 - -

LOONEY TUNES
DC Comics: 1991, 1998

Claritin promotional issue (1998); Colgate mini-comic (1998) 3.00
Tyson's 1-10 (1991) 4.00

LUCKY FIGHTS IT THROUGH (Also see The K. O. Punch & Sidewalk Romance)
Educational Comics: 1949 (Giveaway, 16 pgs. in color, paper-c)

nn-(Very Rare)-1st Kurtzman work for E.C.; V.D. prevention 168 336 504 1075 1838 2600
nn-Reprint in color (1977) 7.00
NOTE: *Subtitled "The Story of That Ignorant, Ignorant Cowboy". Prepared for Communications Materials Center, Columbia University.*

LUDWIG VON DRAKE (See Frito-Lay Giveaway)

MACO TOYS COMIC
Maco Toys/Charlton Comics: 1959 (Giveaway, 36 pgs.)

1-All military stories featuring Maco Toys 3 6 9 14 19 24

MAD MAGAZINE
DC Comics: 1997, 1999, 2008

Special Edition (1997, Tang giveaway) 3.00
Stocking Stuffer (1999) 3.00
San Diego Comic-Con Edition (2008) Watchmen parody with Fabry-a; Aragonés cartoons 3.00

MAGAZINELAND USA
DC Comics: 1977

nn-Kubert-c/a 3 6 9 16 22 28

MAGIC MORRO (Also see Super Comics #21, The Owl, & The Hurricane Kids)
K. K. Publications: 1941 (7-1/2 x 5-1/4", giveaway, soft-c)

nn-Ken Ernst-a. 10 20 30 54 72 90

MAGIC OF CHRISTMAS AT NEWBERRYS, THE
E. S. London: 1967 (Giveaway) (B&W, slick-c, 20 pgs.)

nn 1 3 4 6 8 10

MAGIC SHOE ADVENTURE BOOK
Western Publications: 1962 - No. 3, 1963 (Shoe store giveaway, Reg. size)

nn-(1962) 5 10 15 34 60 85
1 (1963)-And the Flaming Threat 4 8 12 28 47 65
2 (1963)-And the Winning Run 4 8 12 28 47 65
3 (1963)-And the Missing Masterpiece Mystery 4 8 12 28 47 65

MAJOR INAPAK THE SPACE ACE
Magazine Enterprises (Inapac Foods): 1951 (20 pgs.) (Giveaway)

1-Bob Powell-c/a 5.00
NOTE: *Many warehouse copies surfaced in 1973.*

MAMMY YOKUM & THE GREAT DOGPATCH MYSTERY
Toby Press: 1951 (Giveaway)

nn-Li'l Abner 15 30 45 88 137 185
nn-Reprint (1956) 5 10 15 22 26 30

MAN NAMED STEVENSON, A
Democratic National Committee: 1952 (20 pgs., 5 1/4 x 7")

nn 9 18 27 47 61 75

MAN OF PEACE, POPE PIUS XII
Catechetical Guild: 1950 (See Pope Pius XII... & To V2#8)

nn-All Powell-a 7 14 21 35 43 50

MAN OF STEEL BEST WESTERN
DC Comics: 1997 (Best Western hotels promo)

3-Reprints Superman's first post-Crisis meeting with Batman 4.00

MAN WHO RUNS INTERFERENCE
General Comics, Inc./Institute of Life Insurance: 1946 (Paper-c)

nn-Football premium 5 10 15 22 26 30

MAN WHO WOULDN'T QUIT, THE
Harvey Publications Inc.: 1952 (16 pgs., paper cover)

nn-The value of voting 4 8 12 18 22 25

MARCH OF COMICS (Boys' and Girls'...#3-353)
K. K. Publications/Western Publishing Co.: 1946 - No. 488, April, 1982 (#1-4 are not numbered) (K.K. Giveaway) (Founded by Sig Feuchtwanger)

Early issues were full size, 32 pages, and were printed with and without an extra cover of slick stock, just for the advertiser. The binding was stapled if the slick cover was added; otherwise, the pages were glued together at the spine. Most 1948 - 1951 issues were full size,24 pages, pulp covers. Starting in 1952 they were half-size (with a few exceptions) and 32 pages with slick covers.1959 and later issues had only 16 pages plus covers. 1952 -1959 issues read oblong; 1960 and later issues read upright. All have new stories except where noted.

nn (#1, 1946)-Goldilocks; Kelly back-c (16 pgs., stapled) 47 94 141 296 498 700
nn (#2, 1946)-How Santa Got His Red Suit; Kelly-a (11 pgs., r/4-Color #61 from 1944) (16pgs., stapled) 30 60 90 177 289 400
nn (#3, 1947)-Our Gang (Walt Kelly) 36 72 108 211 343 475
nn (#4)-Donald Duck by Carl Barks, "Maharajah Donald", 28 pgs.; Kelly-c? (Disney) 757 1514 2271 5526 9763 14,000
5-Andy Panda (Walter Lantz) 18 36 54 107 169 230
6-Popular Fairy Tales; Kelly-c; Noonan-a(2) 20 40 60 117 189 260
7-Oswald the Rabbit 19 38 57 111 176 240
8-Mickey Mouse, 32 pgs. (Disney) 41 82 123 256 428 600

March of Comics #72 © KING

March of Comics #104 © Gene Autry

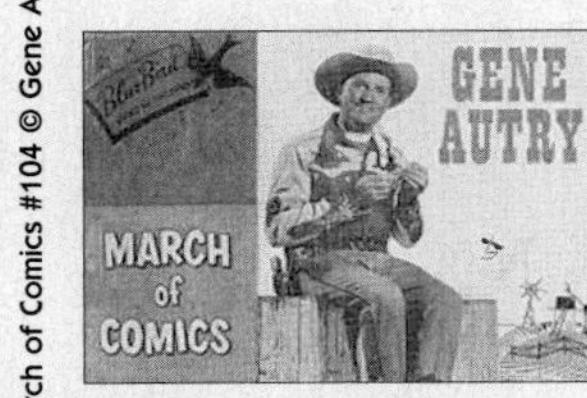

March of Comics #125 © ERB

	GD 2.0	VG 4.0	FN 6.0	VF 8.0	VF/NM 9.0	NM- 9.2
9(nn)-The Story of the Gloomy Bunny	12	24	36	69	97	125
10-Out of Santa's Bag	11	22	33	64	90	115
11-Fun With Santa Claus	10	20	30	58	79	100
12-Santa's Toys	10	20	30	58	79	100
13-Santa's Surprise	10	20	30	58	79	100
14-Santa's Candy Kitchen	10	20	30	58	79	100
15-Hip-It-Ty Hop & the Big Bass Viol	10	20	30	56	76	95
16-Woody Woodpecker (1947)(Walter Lantz)	14	28	42	78	112	145
17-Roy Rogers (1948)	20	40	60	120	195	270
18-Popular Fairy Tales	12	24	36	67	94	120
19-Uncle Wiggily	10	20	30	58	79	100
20-Donald Duck by Carl Barks, "Darkest Africa", 22 pgs.; Kelly-c (Disney)	271	542	813	1734	2967	4200
21-Tom and Jerry	11	22	33	62	86	110
22-Andy Panda (Lantz)	11	22	33	62	86	110
23-Raggedy Ann & Andy; Kerr-a	13	26	39	72	101	130
24-Felix the Cat, 1932 daily strip reprints by Otto Messmer	18	36	54	103	162	220
25-Gene Autry	17	34	51	100	158	215
26-Our Gang; Walt Kelly	16	32	48	96	151	205
27-Mickey Mouse; r/in M. M. #240 (Disney)	29	58	87	172	281	390
28-Gene Autry	17	34	51	98	154	210
29-Easter Bonnet Shop	9	18	27	47	61	75
30-Here Comes Santa	8	16	24	44	57	70
31-Santa's Busy Corner	8	16	24	44	57	70
32-No book produced						
33-A Christmas Carol (12/48)	9	18	27	47	61	75
34-Woody Woodpecker	11	22	33	62	86	110
35-Roy Rogers (1948)	19	38	57	112	179	245
36-Felix the Cat(1949); by Messmer; '34 strip-r	15	30	45	84	127	170
37-Popeye	14	28	42	78	112	145
38-Oswald the Rabbit	8	16	24	44	57	70
39-Gene Autry	16	32	48	94	147	200
40-Andy and Woody	8	16	24	44	57	70
41-Donald Duck by Carl Barks, "Race to the South Seas", 22 pgs.; Kelly-c	245	490	735	1568	2684	3800
42-Porky Pig	9	18	27	47	61	75
43-Henry	8	16	24	42	54	65
44-Bugs Bunny	9	18	27	52	69	85
45-Mickey Mouse (Disney)	20	40	60	120	195	270
46-Tom and Jerry	9	18	27	52	69	85
47-Roy Rogers	15	30	45	90	140	190
48-Greetings from Santa	6	12	18	31	38	45
49-Santa Is Here	6	12	18	31	38	45
50-Santa Claus' Workshop (1949)	6	12	18	31	38	45
51-Felix the Cat (1950) by Messmer	14	28	42	82	121	160
52-Popeye	11	22	33	62	86	110
53-Oswald the Rabbit	8	16	24	40	50	60
54-Gene Autry	15	30	45	84	127	170
55-Andy and Woody	8	16	24	40	50	60
56-Donald Duck; not by Barks; Barks art on back-c (Disney)	21	42	63	124	202	280
57-Porky Pig	8	16	24	40	50	60
58-Henry	7	14	21	35	43	50
59-Bugs Bunny	8	16	24	44	57	70
60-Mickey Mouse (Disney)	20	40	60	120	195	270
61-Tom and Jerry	8	16	24	40	50	60
62-Roy Rogers	15	30	45	90	140	190
63-Welcome Santa (1/2-size, oblong)	6	12	18	31	38	45
64(nn)-Santa's Helpers (1/2-size, oblong)	6	12	18	31	38	45
65(nn)-Jingle Bells (1950) (1/2-size, oblong)	6	12	18	31	38	45
66-Popeye (1951)	10	20	30	58	79	100
67-Oswald the Rabbit	8	16	24	40	50	60
68-Roy Rogers	15	30	45	86	133	180
69-Donald Duck; Barks-a on back-c (Disney)	20	40	60	114	182	250
70-Tom and Jerry	8	16	24	40	50	60
71-Porky Pig	8	16	24	42	54	65
72-Krazy Kat	9	18	27	47	61	75
73-Roy Rogers	14	28	42	82	121	160
74-Mickey Mouse (1951)(Disney)	19	38	57	111	176	246
75-Bugs Bunny	8	16	24	42	54	65
76-Andy and Woody	8	16	24	40	50	60
77-Roy Rogers	14	28	42	82	121	160
78-Gene Autry (1951); last regular size issue	14	28	42	80	115	150

Note: All pre #79 issues came with or without a slick protective wrap-around cover over the regular cover which advertised Poll Parrot Shoes, Sears, etc. This outer cover protects the inside pages making them in nicer condition.
Issues with the outer cover are worth 15-25% more

	GD 2.0	VG 4.0	FN 6.0	VF 8.0	VF/NM 9.0	NM- 9.2
79-Andy Panda (1952, 5x7" size)	7	14	21	35	43	50
80-Popeye	8	16	24	40	50	60
81-Oswald the Rabbit	6	12	18	29	36	42
82-Tarzan; Lex Barker photo-c	15	30	45	84	127	170
83-Bugs Bunny	7	14	21	37	46	55
84-Henry	6	12	18	29	36	42
85-Woody Woodpecker	6	12	18	29	36	42
86-Roy Rogers	11	22	33	62	86	110
87-Krazy Kat	8	16	24	44	57	70
88-Tom and Jerry	6	12	18	31	38	45
89-Porky Pig	6	12	18	29	36	42
90-Gene Autry	11	22	33	62	86	110
91-Roy Rogers & Santa	11	22	33	62	86	110
92-Christmas with Santa	5	10	15	24	30	35
93-Woody Woodpecker (1953)	5	10	15	23	28	32
94-Indian Chief	10	20	30	54	72	90
95-Oswald the Rabbit	5	10	15	23	28	32
96-Popeye	10	20	30	54	72	90
97-Bugs Bunny	7	14	21	35	43	50
98-Tarzan; Lex Barker photo-c	14	28	42	82	121	160
99-Porky Pig	5	10	15	23	28	32
100-Roy Rogers	10	20	30	58	79	100
101-Henry	5	10	15	22	26	30
102-Tom Corbett (TV)('53, early app).; painted-c	12	24	36	67	94	120
103-Tom and Jerry	5	10	15	23	28	32
104-Gene Autry	10	20	30	56	76	95
105-Roy Rogers	10	20	30	56	76	95
106-Santa's Helpers	5	10	15	24	30	35
107-Santa's Christmas Book - not published						
108-Fun with Santa (1953)	5	10	15	24	30	35
109-Woody Woodpecker (1954)	5	10	15	24	30	35
110-Indian Chief	6	12	18	31	38	45
111-Oswald the Rabbit	5	10	15	22	26	30
112-Henry	4	9	13	18	22	26
113-Porky Pig	5	10	15	22	26	30
114-Tarzan; Russ Manning-a	14	28	42	82	121	160
115-Bugs Bunny	6	12	18	27	33	38
116-Roy Rogers	10	20	30	56	76	95
117-Popeye	10	20	30	54	72	90
118-Flash Gordon; painted-c	10	20	30	58	79	100
119-Tom and Jerry	5	10	15	22	26	30
120-Gene Autry	10	20	30	58	76	95
121-Roy Rogers	10	20	30	58	76	95
122-Santa's Surprise (1954)	5	10	15	22	26	30
123-Santa's Christmas Book	5	10	15	22	26	30
124-Woody Woodpecker (1955)	4	9	13	18	22	26
125-Tarzan; Lex Barker photo-c	14	28	42	78	112	145
126-Oswald the Rabbit	4	9	13	18	22	26
127-Indian Chief	7	14	21	35	43	50
128-Tom and Jerry	4	9	13	18	22	26
129-Henry	4	8	12	17	21	24
130-Porky Pig	4	9	13	18	22	26
131-Roy Rogers	10	20	30	56	76	95
132-Bugs Bunny	5	10	15	23	28	32
133-Flash Gordon; painted-c	10	20	30	58	76	95
134-Popeye	8	16	24	42	54	65
135-Gene Autry	10	20	30	56	76	95
136-Roy Rogers	10	20	30	56	76	95
137-Gifts from Santa	4	7	10	14	17	20
138-Fun at Christmas (1955)	4	7	10	14	17	20
139-Woody Woodpecker (1956)	4	9	13	18	22	26
140-Indian Chief	7	14	21	35	43	50
141-Oswald the Rabbit	4	9	13	18	22	26
142-Flash Gordon	10	20	30	56	76	95
143-Porky Pig	4	9	13	18	22	26
144-Tarzan; Russ Manning-a; painted-c	13	26	39	72	101	130
145-Tom and Jerry	4	9	13	18	22	26
146-Roy Rogers; photo-c	10	20	30	56	76	95
147-Henry	4	8	11	16	19	22
148-Popeye	8	16	24	42	54	65
149-Bugs Bunny	5	10	15	22	26	30
150-Gene Autry	10	20	30	56	76	95

March of Comics #208 © Lone Ranger Inc.

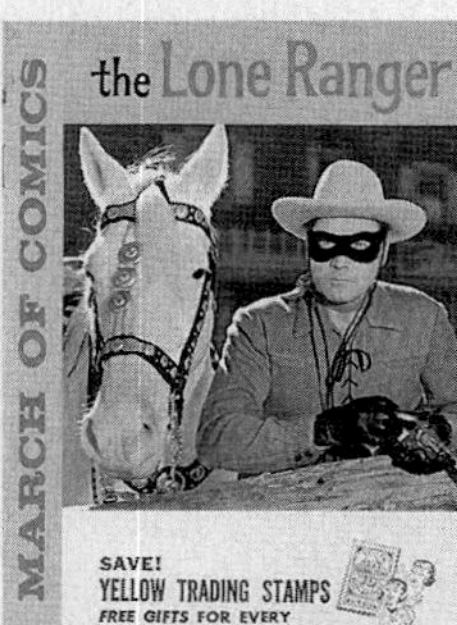

March of Comics #243 © H-B

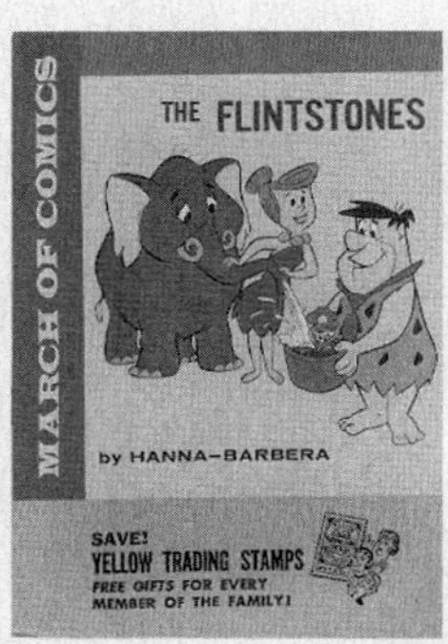

March of Comics #290 © WEST

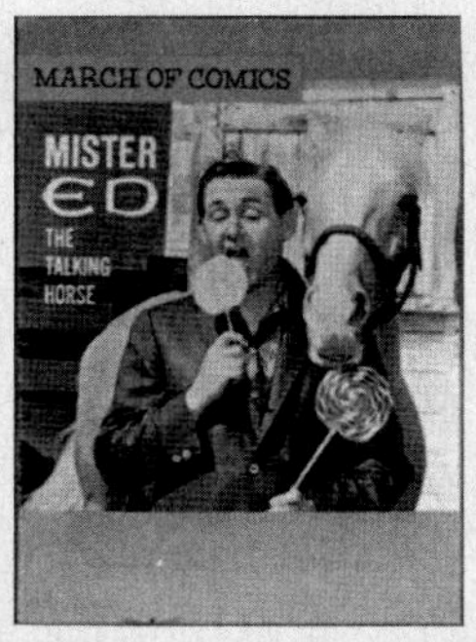

	GD 2.0	VG 4.0	FN 6.0	VF 8.0	VF/NM 9.0	NM- 9.2
151-Roy Rogers	10	20	30	56	76	95
152-The Night Before Christmas	4	8	11	16	19	22
153-Merry Christmas (1956)	4	9	13	18	22	26
154-Tom and Jerry (1957)	4	9	13	18	22	26
155-Tarzan; photo-c	12	24	36	69	97	125
156-Oswald the Rabbit	4	9	13	18	22	26
157-Popeye	7	14	21	35	43	50
158-Woody Woodpecker	4	9	13	18	22	26
159-Indian Chief	7	14	21	35	43	50
160-Bugs Bunny	5	10	15	22	26	30
161-Roy Rogers	9	18	27	52	69	85
162-Henry	4	8	11	16	19	22
163-Rin Tin Tin (TV)	8	16	24	42	54	65
164-Porky Pig	4	9	13	18	22	26
165-The Lone Ranger	10	20	30	54	72	90
166-Santa and His Reindeer	4	7	10	14	17	20
167-Roy Rogers and Santa	9	18	27	52	69	85
168-Santa Claus' Workshop (1957, full size)	4	8	11	16	19	22
169-Popeye (1958)	7	14	21	35	43	50
170-Indian Chief	7	14	21	35	43	50
171-Oswald the Rabbit	4	8	12	17	21	24
172-Tarzan	11	22	33	60	83	105
173-Tom and Jerry	4	8	12	17	21	24
174-The Lone Ranger	10	20	30	54	72	90
175-Porky Pig	4	8	12	17	21	24
176-Roy Rogers	9	18	27	47	61	75
177-Woody Woodpecker	4	8	12	17	21	24
178-Henry	4	8	11	16	19	22
179-Bugs Bunny	4	8	12	17	21	24
180-Rin Tin Tin (TV)	7	14	21	37	46	55
181-Happy Holiday	4	7	9	14	16	18
182-Happi Tim	4	8	11	16	19	22
183-Welcome Santa (1958, full size)	4	7	9	14	16	18
184-Woody Woodpecker (1959)	4	8	11	16	19	22
185-Tarzan; photo-c	10	20	30	58	79	100
186-Oswald the Rabbit	4	8	11	16	19	22
187-Indian Chief	6	12	18	28	34	40
188-Bugs Bunny	4	8	11	16	19	22
189-Henry	4	7	10	14	17	20
190-Tom and Jerry	4	8	11	16	19	22
191-Roy Rogers	8	16	24	44	57	70
192-Porky Pig	4	8	11	16	19	22
193-The Lone Ranger	9	18	27	52	69	85
194-Popeye	6	12	18	31	38	45
195-Rin Tin Tin (TV)	7	14	21	35	43	50
196-Sears Special - not published						
197-Santa Is Coming	4	7	10	14	17	20
198-Santa's Helpers (1959)	4	7	10	14	17	20
199-Huckleberry Hound (TV)(1960, early app.)	8	16	24	42	54	65
200-Fury (TV)	6	12	18	28	34	40
201-Bugs Bunny	4	8	11	16	19	22
202-Space Explorer	8	16	24	42	54	65
203-Woody Woodpecker	4	7	10	14	17	20
204-Tarzan	9	18	27	52	69	85
205-Mighty Mouse	6	12	18	33	41	48
206-Roy Rogers; photo-c	8	16	24	42	54	65
207-Tom and Jerry	4	7	10	14	17	20
208-The Lone Ranger; Clayton Moore photo-c	10	20	30	58	79	100
209-Porky Pig	4	7	10	14	17	20
210-Lassie (TV)	6	12	18	33	41	48
211-Sears Special - not published						
212-Christmas Eve	4	7	10	14	17	20
213-Here Comes Santa (1960)	4	7	10	14	17	20
214-Huckleberry Hound (TV)(1961)	7	14	21	35	43	50
215-Hi Yo Silver	8	16	24	40	50	60
216-Rocky & His Friends (TV)(1961); predates Rocky and His Fiendish Friends #1 (see Four Color #1128)	9	18	27	52	69	85
217-Lassie (TV)	6	12	18	31	38	45
218-Porky Pig	4	7	10	14	17	20
219-Journey to the Sun	5	10	15	24	30	35
220-Bugs Bunny	4	8	11	16	19	22
221-Roy and Dale; photo-c	8	16	24	42	54	65
222-Woody Woodpecker	4	7	10	14	17	20
223-Tarzan	9	18	27	50	65	80
224-Tom and Jerry	4	7	10	14	17	20
225-The Lone Ranger	8	16	24	40	50	60
226-Christmas Treasury (1961)	4	7	10	14	17	20
227-Letters to Santa (1961)	4	7	10	14	17	20
228-Sears Special - not published?						
229-The Flintstones (TV)(1962); early app.; predates 1st Flintstones Gold Key issue (#7)	10	20	30	54	72	90
230-Lassie (TV)	6	12	18	27	33	38
231-Bugs Bunny	4	8	11	16	19	22
232-The Three Stooges	9	18	27	52	69	85
233-Bullwinkle (TV) (1962, very early app.)	9	18	27	52	69	85
234-Smokey the Bear	5	10	15	23	28	32
235-Huckleberry Hound (TV)	7	14	21	35	43	50
236-Roy and Dale	7	14	21	35	43	50
237-Mighty Mouse	6	12	18	27	33	38
238-The Lone Ranger	8	16	24	40	50	60
239-Woody Woodpecker	4	7	10	14	17	20
240-Tarzan	8	16	24	44	57	70
241-Santa Claus Around the World	4	7	9	14	16	18
242-Santa's Toyland (1962)	4	7	9	14	16	18
243-The Flintstones (TV)(1963)	8	16	24	44	57	70
244-Mister Ed (TV); early app.; photo-c	7	14	21	35	43	50
245-Bugs Bunny	4	8	11	16	19	22
246-Popeye	6	12	18	27	33	38
247-Mighty Mouse	6	12	18	27	33	38
248-The Three Stooges	10	20	30	54	72	90
249-Woody Woodpecker	4	7	10	14	17	20
250-Roy and Dale	7	14	21	35	43	50
251-Little Lulu & Witch Hazel	11	22	33	60	83	105
252-Tarzan; painted-c	8	16	24	42	54	65
253-Yogi Bear (TV)	8	16	24	40	50	60
254-Lassie (TV)	6	12	18	27	33	38
255-Santa's Christmas List	4	7	10	14	17	20
256-Christmas Party (1963)	4	7	10	14	17	20
257-Mighty Mouse	6	12	18	27	33	38
258-The Sword in the Stone (Disney)	8	16	24	42	54	65
259-Bugs Bunny	4	8	11	16	19	22
260-Mister Ed (TV)	6	12	18	31	38	45
261-Woody Woodpecker	4	7	10	14	17	20
262-Tarzan	8	16	24	40	50	60
263-Donald Duck; not by Barks (Disney)	9	18	27	52	69	85
264-Popeye	6	12	18	27	33	38
265-Yogi Bear (TV)	6	12	18	31	38	45
266-Lassie (TV)	5	10	15	23	28	32
267-Little Lulu; Irving Tripp-a	10	20	30	56	76	95
268-The Three Stooges	9	18	27	47	61	75
269-A Jolly Christmas	3	6	8	12	14	16
270-Santa's Little Helpers	3	6	8	12	14	16
271-The Flintstones (TV)(1965)	8	16	24	44	57	70
272-Tarzan	8	16	24	40	50	60
273-Bugs Bunny	4	8	11	16	19	22
274-Popeye	6	12	18	27	33	38
275-Little Lulu; Irving Tripp-a	9	18	27	50	65	80
276-The Jetsons (TV)	12	24	36	67	94	120
277-Daffy Duck	4	8	11	16	19	22
278-Lassie (TV)	5	10	15	23	28	32
279-Yogi Bear (TV)	6	12	18	31	38	45
280-The Three Stooges; photo-c	9	18	27	47	61	75
281-Tom and Jerry	4	7	9	14	16	18
282-Mister Ed (TV)	6	12	18	31	38	45
283-Santa's Visit	4	7	9	14	16	18
284-Christmas Parade (1965)	4	7	9	14	16	18
285-Astro Boy (TV); 2nd app. Astro Boy	26	52	78	154	252	350
286-Tarzan	7	14	21	37	46	55
287-Bugs Bunny	4	8	11	16	19	22
288-Daffy Duck	4	7	10	14	17	20
289-The Flintstones (TV)	8	16	24	44	57	70
290-Mister Ed (TV); photo-c	5	10	15	24	30	35
291-Yogi Bear (TV)	6	12	18	27	33	38
292-The Three Stooges; photo-c	9	18	27	47	61	75
293-Little Lulu; Irving Tripp-a	8	16	24	42	54	65
294-Popeye	5	10	15	24	30	35
295-Tom and Jerry	4	7	9	14	16	18
296-Lassie (TV); photo-c	5	10	15	22	26	30
297-Christmas Bells	3	6	8	12	14	16
298-Santa's Sleigh (1966)	3	6	8	12	14	16

March of Comics #362 © Smokey Bear

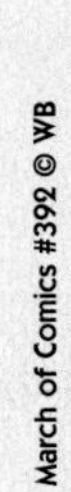
March of Comics #392 © WB

March of Comics #435 © Terrytoons

	GD 2.0	VG 4.0	FN 6.0	VF 8.0	VF/NM 9.0	NM- 9.2
299-The Flintstones (TV)(1967)	8	16	24	44	57	70
300-Tarzan	7	14	21	37	46	55
301-Bugs Bunny	4	7	10	14	17	20
302-Laurel and Hardy (TV); photo-c	6	12	18	28	34	40
303-Daffy Duck	3	6	8	12	14	16
304-The Three Stooges; photo-c	8	16	24	44	57	70
305-Tom and Jerry	3	6	8	12	14	16
306-Daniel Boone (TV); Fess Parker photo-c	7	14	21	35	43	50
307-Little Lulu; Irving Tripp-a	7	14	21	37	46	55
308-Lassie (TV); photo-c	5	10	15	22	26	30
309-Yogi Bear (TV)	5	10	15	24	30	35
310-The Lone Ranger; Clayton Moore photo-c	10	20	30	58	79	100
311-Santa's Show	4	7	9	14	16	18
312-Christmas Album (1967)	4	7	9	14	16	18
313-Daffy Duck (1968)	3	6	8	12	14	16
314-Laurel and Hardy (TV)	6	12	18	27	33	38
315-Bugs Bunny	4	7	10	14	17	20
316-The Three Stooges	8	16	24	40	50	60
317-The Flintstones (TV)	8	16	24	42	54	65
318-Tarzan	7	14	21	35	43	50
319-Yogi Bear (TV)	5	10	15	24	30	35
320-Space Family Robinson (TV); Spiegle-a	11	22	33	62	86	110
321-Tom and Jerry	3	6	8	12	14	16
322-The Lone Ranger	7	14	21	37	46	55
323-Little Lulu; not by Stanley	5	10	15	24	30	35
324-Lassie (TV); photo-c	5	10	15	22	26	30
325-Fun with Santa	4	7	9	14	16	18
326-Christmas Story (1968)	4	7	9	14	16	18
327-The Flintstones (TV)(1969)	8	16	24	42	54	65
328-Space Family Robinson (TV); Spiegle-a	11	22	33	62	86	110
329-Bugs Bunny	4	7	10	14	17	20
330-The Jetsons (TV)	10	20	30	56	76	95
331-Daffy Duck	3	6	8	12	14	16
332-Tarzan	6	12	18	28	34	40
333-Tom and Jerry	3	6	8	12	14	16
334-Lassie (TV)	4	9	13	18	22	26
335-Little Lulu	5	10	15	24	30	35
336-The Three Stooges	8	16	24	40	50	60
337-Yogi Bear (TV)	5	10	15	24	30	35
338-The Lone Ranger	7	14	21	37	46	55
339-(Was not published)						
340-Here Comes Santa (1969)	3	6	8	12	14	16
341-The Flintstones (TV)	8	16	24	42	54	65
342-Tarzan	3	6	9	19	30	40
343-Bugs Bunny	2	4	6	10	14	18
344-Yogi Bear (TV)	3	6	9	16	23	30
345-Tom and Jerry	2	4	6	9	13	16
346-Lassie (TV)	3	6	9	15	21	26
347-Daffy Duck	2	4	6	9	13	16
348-The Jetsons (TV)	5	10	15	34	60	85
349-Little Lulu; not by Stanley	3	6	9	16	23	30
350-The Lone Ranger	3	6	9	17	26	35
351-Beep-Beep, the Road Runner (TV)	2	4	6	11	16	20
352-Space Family Robinson (TV); Spiegle-a	6	12	18	41	76	110
353-Beep-Beep, the Road Runner (1971) (TV)	2	4	6	11	16	20
354-Tarzan (1971)	3	6	9	17	26	35
355-Little Lulu; not by Stanley	3	6	9	16	23	30
356-Scooby Doo, Where Are You? (TV)	6	12	18	37	66	95
357-Daffy Duck & Porky Pig	2	4	6	8	11	14
358-Lassie (TV)	3	6	9	14	19	24
359-Baby Snoots	2	4	6	10	14	18
360-H. R. Pufnstuf (TV); photo-c	6	12	18	37	66	95
361-Tom and Jerry	2	4	6	8	11	14
362-Smokey Bear (TV)	2	4	6	8	11	14
363-Bugs Bunny & Yosemite Sam	2	4	6	9	13	16
364-The Banana Splits (TV); photo-c	5	10	15	33	57	80
365-Tom and Jerry (1972)	2	4	6	8	11	14
366-Tarzan	3	6	9	17	26	35
367-Bugs Bunny & Porky Pig	2	4	6	9	13	16
368-Scooby Doo (TV)(4/72)	5	10	15	33	57	80
369-Little Lulu; not by Stanley	3	6	9	14	19	24
370-Lassie (TV); photo-c	3	6	9	14	19	24
371-Baby Snoots	2	4	6	9	13	16
372-Smokey the Bear (TV)	2	4	6	8	11	14
373-The Three Stooges	4	8	12	23	37	50

	GD 2.0	VG 4.0	FN 6.0	VF 8.0	VF/NM 9.0	NM- 9.2
374-Wacky Witch	2	4	6	8	11	14
375-Beep-Beep & Daffy Duck (TV)	2	4	6	8	11	14
376-The Pink Panther (1972) (TV)	2	4	6	10	14	18
377-Baby Snoots (1973)	2	4	6	9	13	16
378-Turok, Son of Stone; new-a	6	12	18	42	79	115
379-Heckle & Jeckle New Terrytoons (TV)	2	4	6	8	11	14
380-Bugs Bunny & Yosemite Sam	2	4	6	8	11	14
381-Lassie (TV)	2	4	6	11	16	20
382-Scooby Doo, Where Are You? (TV)	5	10	15	30	50	70
383-Smokey the Bear (TV)	2	4	6	8	11	14
384-Pink Panther (TV)	2	4	6	8	11	14
385-Little Lulu	2	4	6	13	18	22
386-Wacky Witch	2	4	6	8	11	14
387-Beep-Beep & Daffy Duck (TV)	2	4	6	8	11	14
388-Tom and Jerry (1973)	2	4	6	8	11	14
389-Little Lulu; not by Stanley	2	4	6	13	18	22
390-Pink Panther (TV)	2	4	6	8	11	14
391-Scooby Doo (TV)	4	8	12	25	40	55
392-Bugs Bunny & Yosemite Sam	2	4	6	8	10	12
393-New Terrytoons (Heckle & Jeckle) (TV)	2	4	6	8	10	12
394-Lassie (TV)	2	4	6	9	13	16
395-Woodsy Owl	2	4	6	8	10	12
396-Baby Snoots	2	4	6	8	11	14
397-Beep-Beep & Daffy Duck (TV)	2	4	6	8	10	12
398-Wacky Witch	2	4	6	8	10	12
399-Turok, Son of Stone; new-a	6	12	18	40	73	105
400-Tom and Jerry	2	4	6	8	10	12
401-Baby Snoots (1975) (r/#371)	2	4	6	8	11	14
402-Daffy Duck (r/#313)	1	3	4	6	8	10
403-Bugs Bunny (r/#343)	2	4	6	8	10	12
404-Space Family Robinson (TV)(r/#328)	5	10	15	35	63	90
405-Cracky	1	3	4	6	8	10
406-Little Lulu (r/#355)	2	4	6	10	14	18
407-Smokey the Bear (TV)(r/#362)	2	4	6	8	10	12
408-Turok, Son of Stone; c-r/Turok #20 w/changes; new-a	5	10	15	34	60	85
409-Pink Panther (TV)	1	3	4	6	8	10
410-Wacky Witch	1	2	3	5	6	8
411-Lassie (TV)(r/#324)	2	4	6	9	13	16
412-New Terrytoons (1975) (TV)	1	2	3	5	6	8
413-Daffy Duck (1976)(r/#331)	1	2	3	5	6	8
414-Space Family Robinson (r/#328)	5	10	15	34	60	85
415-Bugs Bunny (r/#329)	1	2	3	5	6	8
416-Beep-Beep, the Road Runner (r/#353)(TV)	1	2	3	5	6	8
417-Little Lulu (r/#323)	2	4	6	10	14	18
418-Pink Panther (r/#384) (TV)	1	2	3	5	6	8
419-Baby Snoots (r/#377)	1	3	4	6	8	10
420-Woody Woodpecker	1	2	3	5	6	8
421-Tweety & Sylvester	1	2	3	5	6	8
422-Wacky Witch (r/#386)	1	2	3	5	6	8
423-Little Monsters	1	3	4	6	8	10
424-Cracky (12/76)	1	2	3	5	6	8
425-Daffy Duck	1	2	3	5	6	8
426-Underdog (TV)	3	6	9	21	33	45
427-Little Lulu (r/#335)	2	4	6	8	11	14
428-Bugs Bunny	1	2	3	4	5	7
429-The Pink Panther (TV)	1	2	3	4	5	7
430-Beep-Beep, the Road Runner (TV)	1	2	3	4	5	7
431-Baby Snoots	1	2	3	5	6	8
432-Lassie (TV)	2	4	6	8	10	12
433-437: 433-Tweety & Sylvester. 434-Wacky Witch. 435-New Terrytoons (TV). 436-Wacky Advs. of Cracky. 437-Daffy Duck	1	2	3	4	5	7
438-Underdog (TV)	3	6	9	19	30	40
439-Little Lulu (r/#349)	2	4	6	8	11	14
440-442,444-446: 440-Bugs Bunny. 441-The Pink Panther (TV). 442-Beep-Beep, the Road Runner (TV). 444-Tom and Jerry. 445-Tweety and Sylvester. 446-Wacky Witch	1	2	3	5	6	8
443-Baby Snoots	1	2	3	5	6	8
447-Mighty Mouse	2	4	6	8	10	12
448-455,457,458: 448-Cracky. 449-Pink Panther (TV). 450-Baby Snoots. 451-Tom and Jerry. 452-Bugs Bunny. 453-Popeye. 454-Woody Woodpecker. 455-Beep-Beep, the Road Runner (TV). 457-Tweety & Sylvester. 458-Wacky Witch	1	2	3	5	6	8
456-Little Lulu (r/#369)	2	4	6	8	10	12
459-Mighty Mouse	2	4	6	8	10	12
460-466: 460-Daffy Duck. 461-The Pink Panther (TV). 462-Baby Snoots. 463-Tom and Jerry.						

March of Comics #487 © WB

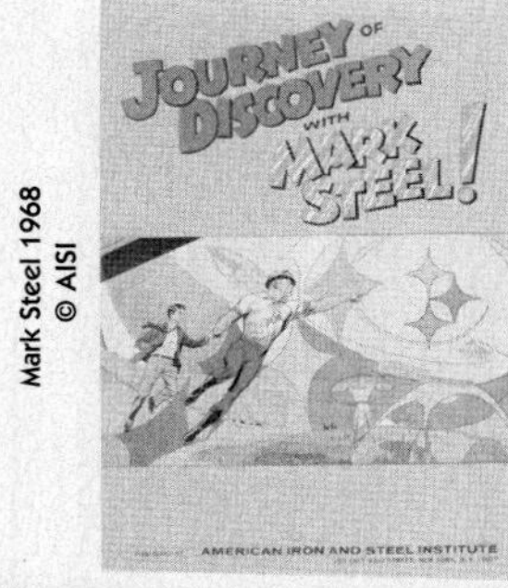

Mark Steel 1968 © AISI

Meet the New Post-Gazette Sunday Funnies © NYNS

	GD 2.0	VG 4.0	FN 6.0	VF 8.0	VF/NM 9.0	NM- 9.2
464-Bugs Bunny. 465-Popeye. 466-Woody Woodpecker	1	2	3	5	6	8
467-Underdog (TV)	3	6	9	17	26	35
468-Little Lulu (r/#385)	1	2	3	5	6	8
469-Tweety & Sylvester	1	2	3	5	6	8
470-Wacky Witch	1	2	3	5	6	8
471-Mighty Mouse	1	3	4	6	8	10
472-474,476-478: 472-Heckle & Jeckle(12/80). 473-Pink Panther(1/81)(TV). 474-Baby Snoots. 476-Bugs Bunny. 477-Popeye. 478-Woody Woodpecker	1	2	3	5	6	8
475-Little Lulu (r/#323)	1	3	4	6	8	10
479-Underdog (TV)	3	6	9	16	23	30
480-482: 480-Tom and Jerry. 481-Tweety and Sylvester. 482-Wacky Witch	1	2	3	4	5	8
483-Mighty Mouse	1	3	4	6	8	10
484-487: 484-Heckle & Jeckle. 485-Baby Snoots. 486-The Pink Panther (TV). 487-Bugs Bunny	1	2	3	4	5	8
488-Little Lulu (4/82) (r/#335) (Last issue)	2	4	6	10	14	18

MARCH TO MARKET, THE
Swift & Co.: 1950 (Giveaway)

nn-The story of meat	4	7	9	14	16	18

MARGARET O'BRIEN (See The Adventures of...)

MARK STEEL
American Iron & Steel Institute: 1967, 1968, 1972 (Giveaway) (24 pgs.)

1967,1968- "Journey of Discovery with..."; Neal Adams art	4	8	12	27	44	60
1972- "...Fights Pollution"; N. Adams-a	2	4	6	9	13	15

MARTIN LUTHER KING AND THE MONTGOMERY STORY
Fellowship Reconciliation: 1957 (Giveaway, 16 pgs.) (A Spanish edition also exists)

nn-In color with paper-c (a CGC 9.2 copy sold for $350 and a FN+ sold for $200 in 2004)

MARTIN LUTHER KING AND THE MONTGOMERY STORY
Top Shelf/Fellowship Reconciliation: 2011, 2013 ($5.00, newsprint-c, 16 pgs.)

nn-(2011) Reprint of the 1957 giveaway published by Fellowship Reconciliation; stapled	10.00
nn-(2013) Reprint has glued binding unlike the stapled 2011 version	10.00

MARVEL COLLECTOR'S EDITION: X-MEN
Marvel Comics: 1993 (3-3/4x6-1/2")

1-4-Pizza Hut giveaways	5.00

MARVEL COMICS PRESENTS
Marvel Comics: 1987, 1988 (4 1/4 x 6 1/4, 20 pgs.)
...Mini Comic Giveaway

nn-(1988) Alf	1	2	3	5	6	8
nn-(1987) Captain America r/ #250	1	2	3	4	5	7
nn-(1987) Care Bears (Star Comics...)	1	2	3	4	5	7
nn-(1988) Flintstone Kids	1	2	3	5	6	8
nn-(1987) Heathcliffe (Star Comics...)	1	2	3	4	5	7
nn-(1987) Spider-Man-r/Spect. Spider-Man #21	1	2	3	4	5	7
nn-(1988) Spider-Man-r/Amazing Spider-Man #1	1	2	3	4	5	7
nn-(1988) X-Men-reprints X-Men #53; B. Smith-a	1	2	3	4	5	7

MARVEL GUIDE TO COLLECTING COMICS, THE
Marvel Comics: 1982 (16 pgs., newsprint pages and cover)

1-Simonson-c	1	2	3	4	5	7

MARVEL MINI-BOOKS
Marvel Comics Group: 1966 (50 pgs., B&W; 5/8x7/8") (6 different issues) (Smallest comics ever published) (Marvel Mania Giveaways)

Captain America, Millie the Model, Sgt. Fury, Hulk, Thor each...	2	4	6	11	16	20
Spider-Man	3	6	9	14	20	25

NOTE: *Each came from gum machines in six different color covers, usually one color: Pink, yellow, green, etc.*

MARVEL SUPER-HERO ISLAND ADVENTURES
Marvel Comics: 1999 (Sold at the park polybagged with Captain America V3 #19, one other comic, 5 trading cards and a cloisonne pin)

1-Promotes Universal Studios Islands of Adventures theme park	4.00

MARY'S GREATEST APOSTLE (St. Louis Grignion de Montfort)
Catechetical Guild (Topix) (Giveaway): No date (16 pgs.; paper cover)

nn	5	10	15	23	28	32

MASK
DC Comics: 1985

1-3	6.00

MASKED PILOT, THE (See Popular Comics #43)
R.S. Callender: 1939 (7-1/2x5-1/4", 16 pgs., premium, non-slick-c)

nn-Bob Jenney-a	8	16	24	44	57	70

MASTERS OF THE UNIVERSE (He-Man)
DC Comics: 1982 (giveaways with action figures, at least 35 different issues, unnumbered)

nn	2	4	6	8	10	12

MATRIX, THE (1999 movie)
Warner Brothers: 1999 (Recalled by Warner Bros. over questionable content)

nn-Paul Chadwick-s/a (16 pgs.); Geof Darrow-c	1	2	3	5	6	8

McCRORY'S CHRISTMAS BOOK
Western Printing Co: 1955 (36 pgs., slick-c) (McCrory Stores Corp. giveaway)

nn-Painted-c	5	10	15	22	26	30

McCRORY'S TOYLAND BRINGS YOU SANTA'S PRIVATE EYES
Promotional Publ. Co.: 1956 (16 pgs.) (Giveaway)

nn-Has 9 pg. story plus 7 pgs. toy ads	4	8	11	16	19	22

McCRORY'S WONDERFUL CHRISTMAS
Promotional Publ. Co.: 1954 (20 pgs., slick-c) (Giveaway)

nn	4	8	12	18	22	25

McDONALDS COMMANDRONS
DC Comics: 1985

nn-Four editions	5.00

MEDAL FOR BOWZER, A (Giveaway)
American Visuals Corp.: 1966 (8 pgs.)

nn-Eisner-c/script; Bowzer (a dog) survives untried pneumonia cure and earns his medal; (medical experimentation on animals)	15	30	45	105	233	360

MEET HIYA A FRIEND OF SANTA CLAUS
Julian J. Proskauer/Sundial Shoe Stores, etc.: 1949 (18 pgs.?, paper-c)(Giveaway)

nn	6	12	18	33	41	48

MEET THE NEW POST-GAZETTE SUNDAY FUNNIES
Pittsburgh Post Gazette: 3/12/49 (7-1/4x10-1/4", 16 pgs., paper-c)
Commercial Comics (insert in newspaper) (Rare)

Dick Tracy by Gould, Gasoline Alley, Terry & the Pirates, Brenda Starr, Buck Rogers by Yager, The Gumps, Peter Rabbit by Fago, Superman, Funnyman by Siegel & Shuster, The Saint, Archie, & others done especially for this book. A fine copy sold at auction in 1985 for $276.00.

	260	520	780	1700	-	-

MEN OF COURAGE
Catechetical Guild: 1949

Bound Topix comics-V7#2,4,6,8,10,16,18,20	6	12	18	33	41	48

MEN WHO MOVE THE NATION
Publisher unknown: (Giveaway) (B&W)

nn-Neal Adams-a	6	12	18	33	41	48

MERRY CHRISTMAS, A
K. K. Publications (Child Life Shoes): 1948 (Giveaway)

nn-Santa cover	8	16	24	44	57	70

MERRY CHRISTMAS
K. K. Publications (Blue Bird Shoes Giveaway): 1956 (7-1/4x5-1/4")

nn-Santa cover	4	8	12	18	22	25

MERRY CHRISTMAS FROM MICKEY MOUSE
K. K. Publications: 1939 (16 pgs.) (Color & B&W) (Shoe store giveaway)

nn-Donald Duck & Pluto app.; text with art (Rare); c-reprint/Mickey Mouse Mag. V3#3 (12/37)(Rare)	245	490	735	1568	2684	3800

MERRY CHRISTMAS FROM SEARS TOYLAND (See Santa's Christmas Comic, Bob & Betty & Santa's Wishing Whistle, and A Christmas Carol)
Sears Roebuck Giveaway: 1939 (16 pgs.) (Color)(Die-cut)

nn-Dick Tracy, Little Orphan Annie, The Gumps, Terry & the Pirates	103	206	309	659	1130	1600

MICKEY MOUSE (Also see Frito-Lay Giveaway)
Dell Publ. Co

...& Goofy Explore Business(1978)	2	4	6	8	10	12
...& Goofy Explore Energy(1976-1978, 36 pgs.); Exxon giveaway in color; regular size	2	4	6	8	10	12
...& Goofy Explore Energy Conservation(1976-1978)-Exxon	2	4	6	8	10	12
...& Goofy Explore The Universe of Energy(1985, 20 pgs.); Exxon giveaway in color; regular size	1	2	3	5	7	9

Mr. Peanut (The Personal Story Of...) © Planters

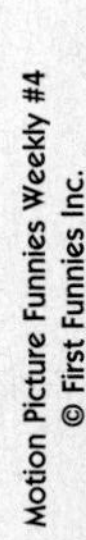

Motion Picture Funnies Weekly #4 © First Funnies Inc.

On the Air nn © NBC

	GD 2.0	VG 4.0	FN 6.0	VF 8.0	VF/NM 9.0	NM- 9.2
The Perils of Mickey nn (1993, 5-1/4x7-1/4", 16 pgs.)-Nabisco giveaway w/ games, Nabisco coupons & 6 pgs. of stories; Phantom Blot app.						6.00

MICKEY MOUSE MAGAZINE
Walt Disney Productions: V1#1, Jan, 1933 - V1#9, Sept, 1933 (5-1/4x7-1/4")
No. 1-3 published by Kamen-Blair (Kay Kamen, Inc.)
(Scarce)-Distributed by dairies and leading stores through their local theatres.
First few issues had 5¢ listed on cover, later ones had no price.

	GD	VG	FN	VF	VF/NM	NM-
V1#1	417	834	1668	5000	-	-
2-4	150	300	600	1200	-	-
5-9	100	200	400	800	-	-

MICKEY MOUSE MAGAZINE
Walt Disney Productions: V1#1, 11/33 - V2#12, 10/35 (Mills giveaways issued by different dairies)

	GD	VG	FN	VF	VF/NM	NM-
V1#1	129	258	387	826	1413	2000
2-12: 2-X-Mas issue	45	90	135	284	480	675
V2#1 (11/34) Donald Duck in sailor suit pg. 6 (cameo)	37	74	111	222	361	500
V2#2-4,6-12: 2-X-Mas issue. 4-St. Valentine-c	36	72	108	211	343	475
V2#5 (3/35) 1st app. Donald Duck in sailor outfit on-c	94	188	282	597	1024	1450

MICKEY MOUSE MAGAZINE
K.K. Publications: V4#1, Oct, 1938 (Giveaway)

	GD	VG	FN	VF	VF/NM	NM-
V4#1	41	82	123	256	428	600

MIGHTY ATOM, THE
Whitman

	GD	VG	FN	VF	VF/NM	NM-
Giveaway (1959, '63, Whitman)-Evans-a	3	6	9	16	23	30
Giveaway ('64r, '65r, '66r, '67r, '68r)-Evans-r?	2	4	6	10	14	18
Giveaway ('73r, '76r)	2	4	6	8	11	14

MILES THE MONSTER (Initially sold only at the Dover Speedway track)
Dover International Speedway, Inc.: 2006 ($3.00)

	GD	VG	FN	VF	VF/NM	NM-
1,2-Allan Gross & Mark Wheatley-s/Wheatley-a						3.00

MILITARY COURTESY
Harvey Publications: (16 pgs.)

	GD	VG	FN	VF	VF/NM	NM-
nn-Regulations and saluting instructions	5	10	14	20	24	28

MINUTE MAN
Sovereign Service Station giveaway: No date (16 pgs., B&W, paper-c blue & red)

	GD	VG	FN	VF	VF/NM	NM-
nn-American history	4	7	9	14	16	18

MINUTE MAN ANSWERS THE CALL, THE
By M. C. Gaines: 1942,1943,1944,1945 (4 pgs.) (Giveaway inserted in Jr. JSA Membership Kit)

	GD	VG	FN	VF	VF/NM	NM-
nn-Sheldon Moldoff-a	22	44	66	132	216	300

MIRACLE ON BROADWAY
Broadway Comics: Dec, 1995 (Giveaway)

	GD	VG	FN	VF	VF/NM	NM-
1-Ernie Colon-c/a; Jim Shooter & Co. story; 1st known digitally printed comic book; 1st app. Spire & Knights on Broadway (1150 print run)						20.00

NOTE: *Miracle on Broadway was a limited edition comic given to 1100 VIPs in the entertainment industry for the 1995 Holiday Season.*

MISS SUNBEAM (See Little Miss Sunbeam Comics)

MR. BUG GOES TO TOWN (See Cinema Comics Herald)
K.K. Publications: 1941 (Giveaway, 52 pgs.)

	GD	VG	FN	VF	VF/NM	NM-
nn-Cartoon movie (scarce)	68	136	204	435	743	1050

MR. PEANUT, THE PERSONAL STORY OF
Planters Nut & Chocolate Co.: 1956

	GD	VG	FN	VF	VF/NM	NM-
nn	4	8	12	22	35	48

MOTHER OF US ALL
Catechetical Guild Giveaway: 1950? (32 pgs.)

	GD	VG	FN	VF	VF/NM	NM-
nn	5	10	15	23	28	32

MOTION PICTURE FUNNIES WEEKLY (Amazing Man #5 on?)
First Funnies, Inc.: 1939 (Giveaway)(B&W, 36 pgs.) No month given; last panel in Sub-Mariner story dated 4/39 (Also see Colossus, Green Giant & Invaders No. 20)

	GD	VG	FN	VF	VF/NM	NM-
1-Origin & 1st printed app. Sub-Mariner by Bill Everett (8 pgs.); Fred Schwab-c; reprinted in Marvel Mystery #1 with color added over the craft tint which was used to shade the black & white version; Spy Ring, American Ace (reprinted in Marvel Mystery #3) app. (Rare)-only eight known copies, one near mint with white pages, the rest with brown pages.	5429	10,858	16,287	27,144	38,000	-
Covers only to #2-4 (set)						800

NOTE: Eight copies (plus one coverless) were discovered in 1974 in the estate of the deceased publisher. Covers only to issues No. 2-4 were also found which evidently were printed in advance along with #1. #1 was to be distributed only through motion picture movie houses. However, it is believed that only advanced copies were sent out and the motion picture houses not going for the idea. Possible distribution at local theaters in Boston suspected. The "pay" copy (graded at 9.0) was discovered after 1974, bringing the total known to nine. The last panel of Sub-Mariner contains a rectangular box with "Continued Next Week" printed in it. When reprinted in Marvel Mystery, the box was left in with lettering omitted.

MY DOG TIGE (Buster Brown's Dog)
Buster Brown Shoes: 1957 (Giveaway)

	GD	VG	FN	VF	VF/NM	NM-
nn	5	10	15	24	30	35

MY GREATEST THRILLS IN BASEBALL
Mission of California: Date? (16 pg. Giveaway)

	GD	VG	FN	VF	VF/NM	NM-
nn-By Mickey Mantle	54	108	162	343	574	825

MYSTERIOUS ADVENTURES WITH SANTA CLAUS
Lansburgh's: 1948 (paper cover)

	GD	VG	FN	VF	VF/NM	NM-
nn	13	26	39	72	101	130

NAKED FORCE!
Commercial Comics: 1958 (Small size)

	GD	VG	FN	VF	VF/NM	NM-
nn	3	6	8	11	13	15

NATURAL DISASTERS!
Graphic Information Service/ Civil Defense: 1956 (16 pgs., soft-c)

	GD	VG	FN	VF	VF/NM	NM-
nn-Al Capp Li'l Abner-c; Li'l Abner cameo (1 panel); narrated by Mr. Civil Defense	10	20	30	56	76	95

NAVY: HISTORY & TRADITION
Stokes Walesby Co./Dept. of Navy: 1958 - 1961 (nn) (Giveaway)

	GD	VG	FN	VF	VF/NM	NM-
1772-1778, 1778-1782, 1782-1817, 1817-1865, 1865-1936, 1940-1945: 1772-1778-16 pg. in color	5	10	15	22	26	30
1861: Naval Actions of the Civil War: 1865-36 pg. in color; flag-c	5	10	15	22	26	30

NEW ADVENTURE OF WALT DISNEY'S SNOW WHITE AND THE SEVEN DWARFS, A
(See Snow White Bendix Giveaway)

NEW ADVENTURES OF PETER PAN (Disney)
Western Publishing Co.: 1953 (5x7-1/4", 36 pgs.) (Admiral giveaway)

	GD	VG	FN	VF	VF/NM	NM-
nn	13	26	39	72	101	130

NEW AVENGERS... (Giveaway for U.S Military personnel)
Marvel Comics: 2005 - Present (Distributed by Army & Air Force Exchange Service)

	GD	VG	FN	VF	VF/NM	NM-
... Guest Starring the Fantastic Four (4/05) Bendis-s/Jurgens-a/c						5.00
...: Pot of Gold (AAFES 110th Anniversary Issue) (10/05) Jenkins-s/Nolan-a/c						5.00
(#3) ...: Avengers & X-Men Time Trouble (4/06) Kirkman-s						5.00
(#4) ...: Letters Home (12/06) Capt. America, Punisher, Silver Surfer, Ghost Rider on-c						5.00
5-The Spirit of America (10/05) Captain America app.						5.00
6-Fireline (8/08) Spider-Man, Iron Man & Hulk app. Richards-a/Dave Ross-c						5.00
7-An Army of One (2009) Frank Cho pin-up on back-c						5.00
8-The Promise (12/09) Captain America (Bucky) app.						5.00

NEW FRONTIERS
Harvey Information Press (United States Steel Corp.) : 1958 (16 pgs., paper-c)

	GD	VG	FN	VF	VF/NM	NM-
nn-History of barbed wire	4	8	12	18	22	25

NEW TEEN TITANS, THE
DC Comics: Nov. 1983

	GD	VG	FN	VF	VF/NM	NM-
nn(11/83-Keebler Co. Giveaway)-In cooperation with "The President's Drug Awareness Campaign"; came in Presidential envelope w/letter from White House (Nancy Reagan)	1	2	3	5	6	8
nn-(re-issue of above on Mando paper for direct sales market); American Soft Drink Industry version; I.B.M. Corp. version						5.00

NEW USES FOR GOOD EARTH
Mined Land Conservation: 1960 (paper-c)

	GD	VG	FN	VF	VF/NM	NM-
nn	3	6	9	19	30	40

NOLAN RYAN IN THE WINNING PITCH (Kellogg's Tony's Sports Comics)
DC Comics: 1992 (Sports Illustrated)

	GD	VG	FN	VF	VF/NM	NM-
nn						5.00

OLD GLORY COMICS
Chesapeake & Ohio Railway: 1944 (Giveaway)

	GD	VG	FN	VF	VF/NM	NM-
nn-Capt. Fearless reprint	8	16	24	40	50	60

ON THE AIR
NBC Network Comic: 1947 (Giveaway, paper-c, regular size)

	GD	VG	FN	VF	VF/NM	NM-
nn-(Rare)	18	36	54	107	169	230

OPERATION SURVIVAL!
Graphic Information Service/ Civil Defense: 1957 (16 pgs., soft-c)
nn-Al Capp Li'l Abner-c; Li'l Abner cameo (1 panel); narrated by Mr. Civil Defense

Oxydol-Dreft #2 © TOBY

Poll Parrot #1 © K.K. Pub

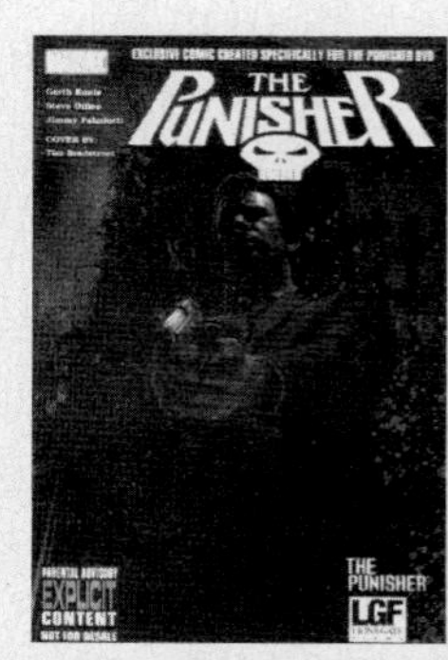

Punisher: Countdown © MAR

GD VG FN VF VF/NM NM-
2.0 4.0 6.0 8.0 9.0 9.2

GD VG FN VF VF/NM NM-
2.0 4.0 6.0 8.0 9.0 9.2

10 20 30 56 76 95

OUT OF THE PAST A CLUE TO THE FUTURE
E. C. Comics (Public Affairs Comm.): 1946? (16 pgs.) (paper cover)
nn-Based on public affairs pamphlet "What Foreign Trade Means to You"
20 40 60 120 195 270

OUTSTANDING AMERICAN WAR HEROES
The Parents' Institute: 1944 (16 pgs., paper-c)
nn-Reprints from True Comics 5 10 15 22 26 30

OVERSEAS COMICS (Also see G.I. Comics & Jeep Comics)
Giveaway (Distributed to U.S. Armed Forces): 1944 - No. 105?, 1946 (7-1/4x10-1/4"; 16 pgs. in color)
23-105-Bringing Up Father (by McManus), Popeye, Joe Palooka, Dick Tracy, Superman, Gasoline Alley, Buz Sawyer, Li'l Abner, Blondie, Terry & the Pirates, Out Our Way
7 14 21 35 43 50

OWL, THE (See Crackajack Funnies #25 & Popular Comics #72)(Also see The Hurricane Kids & Magic Morro
Western Pub. Co./R.S. Callender: 1940 (Giveaway)(7-1/2x5-1/4")(Soft-c, color)
nn-Frank Thomas-a 15 30 45 86 133 180

OXYDOL-DREFT
Toby Press:1950 (Set of 6 pocket-size giveaways; distributed through the mail as a set) (Scarce)
1-3: 1-Li'l Abner. 2-Daisy Mae. 3-Shmoo 9 18 27 47 61 75
4-John Wayne; Williamson/Frazetta-c from John Wayne #3
12 24 36 67 94 120
5-Archie 11 22 33 62 86 110
6-Terrytoons Mighty Mouse 9 18 27 47 61 75
Mailing Envelope (has All Capp's Shmoo on front) 9 18 27 52 69 85

OZZIE SMITH IN THE KID WHO COULD (Kellogg's Tony's Sports Comics)
DC Comics: 1992 (Sports Illustrated)
nn-Ozzie Smith app. 5.00

PADRE OF THE POOR
Catechetical Guild: nd (Giveaway) (16 pgs., paper-c)
nn 6 12 18 27 33 38

PAUL TERRY'S HOW TO DRAW FUNNY CARTOONS
Terrytoons, Inc. (Giveaway): 1940's (14 pgs.) (Black & White)
nn-Heckle & Jeckle, Mighty Mouse, etc. 13 26 39 72 101 130

PETER PAN (See New Adventures of Peter Pan)

PETER PENNY AND HIS MAGIC DOLLAR
American Bankers Association, N. Y. (Giveaway): 1947 (16 pgs.; paper-c; regular size)
nn-(Scarce)-Used in **SOTI**, pg. 310, 311 15 30 45 88 137 185
Diff. version (7-1/4x11")-redrawn, 16 pgs., paper-c 10 20 30 56 76 95

PETER WHEAT (The Adventures of...)
Bakers Associates Giveaway: 1948 - 1957? (16 pgs. in color) (paper covers)
nn(No.1)-States on last page, end of 1st Adventure of...; Kelly-a
26 52 78 154 252 350
nn(4 issues)-Kelly-a 14 28 42 82 121 160
6-10-All Kelly-a 10 20 30 54 72 90
11-20-All Kelly-a 9 18 27 50 65 80
21-35-All Kelly-a 8 16 24 40 50 60
36-66 6 12 18 28 34 40
...Artist's Workbook ('54, digest size) 6 12 18 28 34 40
...Four-In-One Fun Pack (Vol. 2, '54), oblong, comics w/puzzles
7 14 21 35 43 50
...Fun Book ('52, 32 pgs., paper-c, B&W & color, 8-1/2x10-3/4")-Contains cut-outs, puzzles, games, magic & pages to color 8 16 24 44 57 70
NOTE: ***Al Hubbard** art #36 on; written by Del Connell.*

PETER WHEAT NEWS
Bakers Associates: 1948 - No. 30, 1950 (4 pgs. in color)
Vol. 1-All have 2 pgs. Peter Wheat by Kelly 21 42 63 126 206 285
2-10 13 26 39 72 101 130
11-20 8 16 24 40 50 60
21-30 6 12 18 28 34 40
NOTE: *Early issues have no date & **Kelly** art.*

PINOCCHIO
Cocomalt/Montgomery Ward Co.: 1940 (10 pgs.; giveaway, linen-like paper)
nn-Cocomalt edition 43 86 129 271 456 640
nn-store edition 36 72 108 215 350 485

PIUS XII MAN OF PEACE
Catechetical Guild: No date (12 pgs.; 5-1/2x8-1/2") (B&W)
nn-Catechetical Guild Giveaway 6 12 18 33 41 48

PLOT TO STEAL THE WORLD, THE
Work & Unity Group: 1948, 16pgs., paper-c
nn-Anti commumism 18 36 54 105 165 225

POCAHONTAS
Pocahontas Fuel Company (Coal): 1941 - No. 2, 1942
nn(#1), 2-Feat. life story of Indian princess Pocahontas & facts about Pocahontas coal, Pocahontas, VA. 15 30 45 86 133 180

POLL PARROT
Poll Parrot Shoe Store/International Shoe
K. K. Publications (Giveaway): 1950 - No. 4, 1951; No. 2, 1959 - No. 16, 1962
1 ('50)-Howdy Doody; small size 18 36 54 107 169 230
2-4('51)-Howdy Doody 15 30 45 88 137 185
2('59)-16('62): 2-The Secret of Crumbley Castle. 5-Bandit Busters. 6-Fortune Finders. 7-The Make-Believe Mummy. 8-Mixed Up Mission('60). 10-The Frightful Flight. 11-Showdown at Sunup. 12-Maniac at Mubu Island. 13-...and the Runaway Genie. 14-Bully for You. 15-Trapped In Tall Timber. 16-...& the Rajah's Ruby('62) 2 4 6 11 16 20

POPEYE
Whitman
Bold Detergent giveaway (Same as regular issue #94) 2 4 6 9 13 16
Quaker Cereal premium (1989, 16pp, small size,4 diff.)(Popeye & the Time Machine, --On Safari, --& Big Foot, --vs. Bluto) 2 4 6 8 10 12

POPEYE
Charlton (King Features) (Giveaway): 1972 - 1974 (36 pgs. in color)
E-1 to E-15 (Educational comics) 2 4 6 9 13 16
nn-Popeye Gettin' Better Grades-4 pgs. used as intro. to above giveaways (in color) 2 4 6 9 13 16

POPSICLE PETE FUN BOOK (See All-American Comics #6)
Joe Lowe Corp.: 1947, 1948
nn-36 pgs. in color; Sammy 'n' Claras, The King Who Couldn't Sleep & Popsicle Pete stories, games, cut-outs 10 20 30 58 79 100
Adventure Book ('48)-Has Classics ad with checklist to HRN #343 (Great Expectations #43)
9 18 27 52 69 85

PORKY'S BOOK OF TRICKS
K. K. Publications (Giveaway): 1942 (8-1/2x5-1/2", 48 pgs.)
nn-7 pg. comic story, text stories, plus games & puzzles
55 110 165 352 601 850

POST GAZETTE (See Meet the New...)

PUNISHER: COUNTDOWN (Movie)
Marvel Comics: 2004 (7 1/4" X 4 3/4" mini-comic packaged with Punisher DVD)
nn-Prequel to 2004 movie; Ennis-s/Dillon-a/Bradstreet-c 2.50

PURE OIL COMICS (Also see Salerno Carnival of Comics, 24 Pages of Comics, & Vicks Comics)
Pure Oil Giveaway: Late 1930's (24 pgs., regular size, paper-c)
nn-Contains 1-2 pg. strips; i.e., Hairbreadth Harry, Skyroads, Buck Rogers by Calkins & Yager, Olly of the Movies, Napoleon, S'Matter Pop, etc. Also a 16 pg. 1938 giveaway with Buck Rogers 35 70 105 208 339 470

QUAKER OATS (Also see Cap'n Crunch)
Quaker Oats Co.: 1965 (Giveaway) (2-1/2x5-1/2") (16 pgs.)
"Plenty of Glutton", starring Quake & Quisp; 3 6 9 14 19 24
"Lava Come-Back", "Kite Tale" 1 3 4 6 8 10

RAILROADS DELIVER THE GOODS!
Assoc. of American Railroads: Dec, 1954; Sept, 1957 (16 pgs., paper-c)
nn-The story of railway freight 6 12 18 28 34 40

RAILS ACROSS AMERICA!
Assoc. of American Railroads: nd (16 pgs.)
nn 6 12 18 28 34 40

READY THEN, READY NOW
Western Publications: 1966 (National Guard military giveaway, regular size)
nn 5 10 15 33 57 80

REAL FUN OF DRIVING!!, THE
Chrysler Corp.: 1965, 1966, 1967 (Regular size, 16 pgs.)
nn-Schaffenberger-a (12 pgs.) 1 2 3 5 6 8

Reddy Kilowatt nn © EC

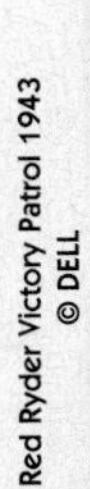

Red Ryder Victory Patrol 1943 © DELL

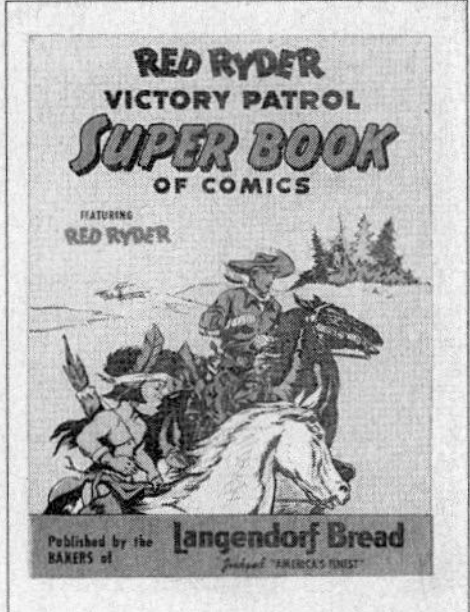

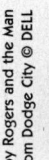

Roy Rogers and the Man From Dodge City © DELL

	GD 2.0	VG 4.0	FN 6.0	VF 8.0	VF/NM 9.0	NM- 9.2

REAL HIT
Fox Features Publications: 1944 (Savings Bond premium)

1-Blue Beetle-r; Blue Beetle on-c 16 32 48 94 147 200

NOTE: *Two versions exist, with and without covers. The coverless version has the title, No. 1 and price printed at top of splash page.*

RED BALL COMIC BOOK
Parents' Magazine Institute: 1947 (Red Ball Shoes giveaway)

nn-Reprints from True Comics 4 8 12 17 21 24

REDDY GOOSE
International Shoe Co. (Western Printing): No number, 1958?; No. 2, Jan, 1959 - No. 16, July, 1962 (Giveaway)

nn (#1) 4 8 12 23 37 50
2-16 3 6 9 14 20 25

REDDY KILOWATT (5¢) (Also see Story of Edison)
Educational Comics (E. C.): 1946 - No. 2, 1947; 1956 - 1965 (no month) (16 pgs., paper-c)

nn-A Visit With Reddy (1948-1954?) 9 18 27 52 69 85
nn-Reddy Made Magic (1946, 5¢) 13 26 39 74 105 135
nn-Reddy Made Magic (1958) 9 18 27 52 69 85
2-Edison, the Man Who Changed the World (3/4" smaller than #1) (1947, 5¢) 13 26 39 74 105 135
...Comic Book 2 (1954)- "Light's Diamond Jubilee" 10 20 30 56 76 95
...Comic Book 2 (1956, 16 pgs.)- "Wizard of Light" 9 18 27 52 69 85
...Comic Book 2 (1958, 16 pgs.)- "Wizard of Light" 9 18 27 50 65 78
...Comic Book 2 (1965, 16 pgs.)- "Wizard of Light" 4 8 12 28 44 60
...Comic Book 3 (1956, 8 pgs.)- "The Space Kite"; Orlando story; regular size 9 18 27 47 61 75
...Comic Book 3 (1960, 8 pgs.)- "The Space Kite"; Orlando story; regular size 4 8 12 28 44 60

NOTE: *Several copies surfaced in 1979.*

REDDY MADE MAGIC
Educational Comics (E. C.): 1956, 1958 (16 pgs., paper-c)

1-Reddy Kilowatt-r (splash panel changed) 11 22 33 60 83 105
1 (1958 edition) 6 12 18 31 38 45

RED ICEBERG, THE
Impact Publ. (Catechetical Guild): 1960 (10¢, 16 pgs., Communist propaganda)

nn-(Rare)- "We The People" back-c 30 60 90 216 483 750
2nd version- "Impact Press" back-c 23 46 69 161 356 550
3rd version- "Explains comic" back-c 23 46 69 161 356 550
4th version- "Impact Press w/World Wide Secret Heart Program ad" 23 46 69 161 356 550
5th version- "Chicago Inter-Student Catholic Action" back-c 23 46 69 161 356 550

NOTE: *This book was the Guild's last anti-communist propaganda book and had very limited circulation. 3 - 4 copies surfaced in 1979 from the defunct publisher's files. Other copies do turn up.*

RED RYDER COMICS
Dell Publ. Co.

Buster Brown Shoes Giveaway (1941, color, soft-c, 32 pgs.) 16 32 48 94 147 200
Red Ryder Super Book of Comics (1944, paper-c, 32 pgs.; blank back-c) Magic Morro app. 18 36 54 105 165 225
Red Ryder Victory Patrol-nn(1942, 32 pgs.)(Langendorf bread; includes cut-out membership card and certificate, order blank and "Slide-Up" decoder, and a Super Book of Comics in color (same content as Super Book #4 w/diff. cover (Pan-Am)) (Rare) 84 168 252 538 919 1300
Red Ryder Victory Patrol-nn(1943, 32 pgs.)(Langendorf bread; includes cut-out "Rodeomatic" radio decoder, order coupon for "Magic V-Badge", cut-out membership card and certificate and a full color Super Book of comics comic book) (Rare) 58 116 174 371 636 900
Red Ryder Victory Patrol-nn(1944, 32 pgs.)-r-/#43,44; comic has a paper-c & is stapled inside a triple cardboard fold-out-c; contains membership card, decoder, map of R.R. home range, etc. Herky app. (Langendorf Bread giveaway; sub-titled 'Super Book of Comics') (Rare) 58 116 174 371 636 900
Wells Lamont Corp. giveaway (1950)-16 pgs. in color; regular size; paper-c; 1941-r 14 28 42 82 121 160

RETURN OF JOE THE GENIE OF STEEL (Also see Joe The Genie of Steel)
U. S. Steel Corp., Pittsburgh, PA/Commercial Comics: 1951 (U. S. Steel Corp. giveaway)

nn-Joe Magarac, the Paul Bunyan of steel 4 8 12 28 47 65

REX MORGAN M.D. TALKS ABOUT YOUR UNBORN CHILD
(No publisher) Fetal Alcohol, Tobacco & Firearms giveaway, 1980 (Reg. size, paper-c)

nn 3 6 9 19 30 40

RICHIE RICH, CASPER & WENDY NATIONAL LEAGUE
Harvey Publications: June, 1976 (52 pgs.) (newsstand edition also exists)

1 (Released-3/76 with 6/76 date) 3 6 9 15 22 28
1 (6/76)-2nd version w/San Francisco Giants & KTVU 2 logos; has "Compliments of Giants and Straw Hat Pizza" on-c 3 6 9 15 22 28
1-Variants for other 11 NL teams, similar to Giants version but with different ad on inside front-c 3 6 9 15 22 28

RIDE THE HIGH IRON!
Assoc. of American Railroads: Jan, 1957 (16 pgs.)

nn-The Story of modern passenger trains 5 10 15 24 30 35

RIPLEY'S BELIEVE IT OR NOT!
Harvey Publications

J. C. Penney giveaway (1948) 9 18 27 50 65 80

ROBIN HOOD (New Adventures of...)
Walt Disney Productions: 1952 (Flour giveaways, 5x7-1/4", 36 pgs.)

"New Adventures of Robin Hood", "Ghosts of Waylea Castle", & "The Miller's Ransom" each.... 4 7 10 14 17 20

ROBIN HOOD'S FRONTIER DAYS (...Western Tales, Adventures of... #1)
Shoe Store Giveaway (Robin Hood Stores): 1956 (20 pgs., slick-c)(7 issues?)

nn 6 12 18 31 38 45
nn-Issues with Crandall-a 8 16 24 42 54 65

ROCKETS AND RANGE RIDERS
Richfield Oil Corp.: May, 1957 (Giveaway, 16 pgs., soft-c)

nn-Toth-a 16 32 48 92 144 195

ROUND THE WORLD GIFT
National War Fund (Giveaway): No date (mid 1940's) (4 pgs.)

nn 12 24 36 67 94 120

ROY ROGERS COMICS
Dell Publishing Co.

...& the Man From Dodge City (Dodge giveaway, 16 pgs., 1954)-Frontier, Inc. (5x7-1/4") 12 24 36 69 97 125
Official Roy Rogers Riders Club Comics (1952; 16 pgs., reg. size, paper-c) 15 30 45 90 140 190

RUDOLPH, THE RED-NOSED REINDEER
Montgomery Ward: 1939 (2,400,000 copies printed); Dec, 1951 (Giveaway)

Paper cover-1st app. in print; written by Robert May; ill. by Denver Gillen 15 30 45 83 124 165
Hardcover version 19 38 57 109 172 235
1951 Edition (Has 1939 date)-36 pgs., slick-c printed in red & brown; pulp interior printed in four mixed-ink colors: red, green, blue & brown 11 22 33 62 86 110
1951 Edition with red-spiral promotional booklet printed on high quality stock, 8-1/2"x11", in red & brown, 25 pages composed of 4 fold outs, single sheets and the Rudolph comic book inserted (rare) 47 94 141 296 498 700

SABRINA THE TEENAGE WITCH
Archie Comic Publications: (8 1/2"x 5 1/2", Diamond Comic Dist. Halloween giveaway)

... And The Archies (2004)-Tania Del Rio-s/a; manga-style; Josie and the Pussycats app. 2.50

SABRINA THE TEENAGE WITCH AND HER BOOK OF MAGIC
Archie Comic Publications: 1970 (small size giveaway)

2 - (A graded 9.4 copy sold for $121 in 2014)

SAD CASE OF WAITING ROOM WILLIE, THE
American Visuals Corp. (For Baltimore Medical Society): (nd, 1950?) (14 pgs. in color; paper covers; regular size)

nn-By Will Eisner (Rare) 45 90 135 282 476 670

SAD SACK COMICS
Harvey Publications: 1957-1962

Armed Forces Complimentary copies, HD #1-40 (1957-1962) 3 6 9 15 22 28

SALERNO CARNIVAL OF COMICS (Also see Pure Oil Comics, 24 Pages of Comics, & Vicks Comics)
Salerno Cookie Co.: Late 1930s (Giveaway, 16 pgs, paper-c)

nn-Color reprints of Calkins' Buck Rogers & Skyroads, plus other strips from Famous Funnies 42 84 126 265 445 625

SALUTE TO THE BOY SCOUTS
Association of American Railroads: 1960 (16 pgs., paper-c, regular size)

nn-History of scouting and the railroad 3 6 9 16 23 30

Santa's Christmas Comic Variety Show © Sears

Santa's Toytown Fun Book © KK

Sergeant Preston of the Yukon © DELL

	GD 2.0	VG 4.0	FN 6.0	VF 8.0	VF/NM 9.0	NM- 9.2

SANTA AND POLLYANNA PLAY THE GLAD GAME
Western Publ.: Aug, 1960 (16 pgs.) (Disney giveaway)
nn 3 6 9 14 20 25

SANTA & THE BUCCANEERS
Promotional Publ. Co.: 1959 (Giveaway, paper-c)
nn-Reprints 1952 Santa & the Pirates 2 4 6 11 16 20

SANTA & THE CHRISTMAS CHICKADEE
Murphy's: 1974 (Giveaway, 20 pgs.)
nn 2 4 6 8 10 12

SANTA & THE PIRATES
Promotional Publ. Co.: 1952 (Giveaway)
nn-Marv Levy-c/a 4 8 12 17 21 24

SANTA CLAUS FUNNIES (Also see The Little Fir Tree)
W. T. Grant Co./Whitman Publishing: nd; 1940 (Giveaway, 8x10"; 12 pgs., color & B&W, heavy paper)
nn-(2 versions- no date and 1940) 14 28 42 82 121 160

SANTA IS HERE!
Western Publ. (Giveaway): 1949 (oblong, slick-c)
nn 6 12 18 33 38 45

SANTA ON THE JOLLY ROGER
Promotional Publ. Co. (Giveaway): 1965
nn-Marv Levy-c/a 2 4 6 8 10 12

SANTA! SANTA!
R. Jackson: 1974 (20 pgs.) (Montgomery Ward giveaway)
nn 1 3 4 6 8 10

SANTA'S BUNDLE OF FUN
Gimbels: 1969 (Giveaway, B&W, 20 pgs.)
nn-Coloring book & games 2 4 6 8 10 12

SANTA'S CHRISTMAS COMIC VARIETY SHOW (See Merry Christmas From Sears Toyland, Bob & Betty & Santa's Wishing Whistle, and A Christmas Carol)
Sears Roebuck & Co.: 1943 (24 pgs.)
Contains puzzles & new comics of Dick Tracy, Little Orphan Annie, Moon Mullins, Terry & the Pirates, etc. 54 108 162 343 574 825

SANTA'S CHRISTMAS TIME STORIES
Premium Sales, Inc.: nd (Late 1940s) (16 pgs., paper-c) (Giveaway)
nn 6 12 18 33 41 48

SANTA'S CIRCUS
Promotional Publ. Co.: 1964 (Giveaway, half-size)
nn-Marv Levy-c/a 2 4 6 9 12 15

SANTA'S FUN BOOK
Promotional Publ. Co.: 1951, 1952 (Regular size, 16 pgs., paper-c) (Murphy's giveaway)
nn 6 12 18 27 33 38

SANTA'S GIFT BOOK
No Publisher: No date (16 pgs.)
nn-Puzzles, games only 4 8 12 17 21 24

SANTA'S NEW STORY BOOK
Wallace Hamilton Campbell: 1949 (16 pgs., paper-c) (Giveaway)
nn 6 12 18 33 41 48

SANTA'S REAL STORY BOOK
Wallace Hamilton Campbell/W. W. Orris: 1948, 1952 (Giveaway, 16 pgs.)
nn 6 12 18 33 41 48

SANTA'S RIDE
W. T. Grant Co.: 1959 (Giveaway)
nn 3 6 9 14 19 24

SANTA'S RODEO
Promotional Publ. Co.: 1964 (Giveaway, half-size)
nn-Marv Levy-a 2 4 6 9 12 15

SANTA'S SECRET CAVE
W.T. Grant Co.: 1960 (Giveaway, half-size)
nn 2 4 6 11 16 20

SANTA'S SECRETS
Sam B. Anson Christmas giveaway: 1951, 1952? (16 pgs., paper-c)
nn-Has games, stories & pictures to color 4 8 12 18 22 25

SANTA'S STORIES
K. K. Publications (Klines Dept. Store): 1953 (Regular size, paper-c)
nn-Kelly-a 15 30 45 90 140 190
nn-Another version (1953, glossy-c, half-size, 7-1/4x5-1/4")-Kelly-a 11 22 33 64 90 115

SANTA'S SURPRISE
K. K. Publications: 1947 (Giveaway, 36 pgs., slick-c)
nn 8 16 24 42 54 65

SANTA'S TOYTOWN FUN BOOK
Promotional Publ. Co.: 1953 (Giveaway)
nn-Marv Levy-c 4 8 11 16 19 22

SANTA TAKES A TRIP TO MARS
Bradshaw-Diehl Co., Huntington, W.VA.: 1950s (nd) (Giveaway, 16 pgs.)
nn 4 8 11 16 19 22

SCHWINN BIKE THRILLS
Schwinn Bicycle Co.: 1959 (Reg. size)
nn 8 16 24 40 50 60

SCIENCE FAIR STORY OF ELECTRONICS
Radio Shack/Tandy Corp.: 1975 - 1987 (Giveaway)
11 different issues (approx. 1 per year) each.... 3.00

SECRETS BEHIND THE COMICS
Famous Enterprises, Inc.: 1947 (Small size; advertised in Timely comics)
nn - By Stan Lee; profile of Syd Shores (w/4 pgs. of his Blonde Phantom), Mike Sekowsky, Basil Wolverton, Al Jaffee & Martin Goodman; description of Captain America's creation with images (A CGC 6.5 copy sold for $502 in 2016)

SEEING WASHINGTON
Commercial Comics: 1957 (also sold at 25¢)(Slick-c, reg. size)
nn 6 12 18 28 34 40

SERGEANT PRESTON OF THE YUKON
Quaker Cereals: 1956 (4 comic booklets) (Soft-c, 16 pgs., 7x2-1/2" & 5x2-1/2") Giveaways
"How He Found Yukon King", "The Case That Made Him A Sergeant", "How Yukon King Saved Him From The Wolves", "How He Became A Mountie" each... 9 18 27 47 61 75

SHAZAM! (Visits Portland Oregon in 1943)
DC Comics: 1989 (69¢ cover)
nn-Promotes Super-Heroes exhibit at Oregon Museum of Science and Industry; reprints Golden Age Captain Marvel story 2 4 6 9 12 15

SHERIFF OF COCHISE, THE (TV)
Mobil: 1957 (16 pgs.) Giveaway
nn-Schaffenberger-a 4 9 13 18 22 26

SIDEWALK ROMANCE (Also see The K. O. Punch & Lucky Fights It Through)
Health Publications: 1950
nn-VD educational giveaway 43 86 129 271 461 650

SILLY PUTTY MAN
DC Comics: 1978
1 2 4 6 11 16 20

SKATING SKILLS
Custom Comics, Inc./Chicago Roller Skates: 1957 (36 & 12 pgs.; 5x7", two versions) (10¢)
nn-Resembles old ACG cover plus interior art 4 7 10 14 17 20

SKIPPY'S OWN BOOK OF COMICS (See Popular Comics)
No publisher listed: 1934 (Giveaway, 52 pgs., strip reprints)
nn-(Scarce)-By Percy Crosby 377 754 1131 2639 4620 6600
Published by Max C. Gaines for Phillip's Dental Magnesia to be advertised on the Skippy Radio Show and given away with the purchase of a tube of Phillip's Tooth Paste. This is the first four-color comic book of reprints about one character.

SKY KING "RUNAWAY TRAIN" (TV)
National Biscuit Co.: 1964 (Regular size, 16 pgs.)
nn 5 10 15 35 63 90

SLAM BANG COMICS
Post Cereal Giveaway: No. 9, No date
9-Dynamic Man, Echo, Mr. E, Yankee Boy app. 9 18 27 50 65 80

SMILIN' JACK

Snow White and the Seven Dwarfs © WDC

Space Ghost Coast to Coast © Cartoon Network

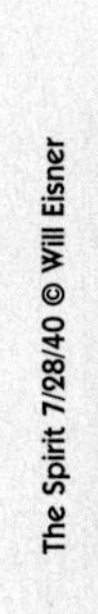
The Spirit 7/28/40 © Will Eisner

GD VG FN VF VF/NM NM-
2.0 4.0 6.0 8.0 9.0 9.2

Dell Publishing Co.
Popped Wheat Giveaway (1947)-1938 strip reprints; 16 pgs. in full color 2 4 6 8 11 14
Shoe Store Giveaway-1938 strip reprints; 16 pgs. 5 10 15 24 30 35
Sparked Wheat Giveaway (1942)-16 pgs. in full color 5 10 15 24 30 35

SMOKEY BEAR (See Forest Fire for 1st app.)
Dell Publ. Co.: 1959,1960
True Story of..., The -U.S. Forest Service giveaway-Publ. by Western Printing Co.; reprints 1st 16 pgs. of Four Color #932. Inside front-c differs slightly in 1959 & 1960 editions 6 12 18 28 34 40
1964,1969 reprints 3 6 9 14 19 24

SMOKEY STOVER
Dell Publishing Co.
General Motors giveaway (1953) 8 16 24 42 54 65
National Fire Protection giveaway(1953 & 1954)-16 pgs., paper-c 8 16 24 42 54 65

SNOW FOR CHRISTMAS
W. T. Grant Co.: 1957 (16 pgs.) (Giveaway)
nn 4 8 12 18 22 25

SNOW WHITE AND THE SEVEN DWARFS
Bendix Washing Machines: 1952 (32 pgs., 5x7-1/4", soft-c) (Disney)
nn 11 22 33 62 86 110

SNOW WHITE AND THE SEVEN DWARFS
Promotional Publ. Co.: 1957 (Small size)
nn 6 12 18 28 34 40

SNOW WHITE AND THE SEVEN DWARFS
Western Printing Co.: 1958 (16 pgs, 5x7-1/4", soft-c) (Disney premium)
nn- "Mystery of the Missing Magic" 6 12 18 31 38 45

SNOW WHITE AND THE 7 DWARFS IN "MILKY WAY"
American Dairy Assoc.: 1955 (16 pgs., soft-c, 5x7-1/4") (Disney premium)
nn 7 14 21 35 43 50

SOLDIER OF GOD
Conventual Franciscans of Marytown: 1982 ($1.00)
nn-Story of Father Maximilian Kobe, priest in WWII Poland; Ray Chatton-a 5.00

SPACE GHOST COAST TO COAST
Cartoon Network: Apr, 1994 (giveaway to Turner Broadcasting employees)
1-(8 pgs.); origin of Space Ghost 6.00

SPACE PATROL (TV)
Ziff-Davis Publishing Co. (Approved Comics)
...'s Special Mission (8 pgs., B&W, Giveaway) 45 90 135 284 480 675

SPARKY
Fire Protection Association: 1961 (Reg. size, paper-c)
nn 3 6 9 16 24 32

SPECIAL AGENT
Assoc. of American Railroads: Oct, 1959 (16 pgs.)
nn-The Story of the railroad police 6 12 18 28 34 40

SPECIAL DELIVERY
Post Hall Synd.: 1951 (32 pgs.; B&W) (Giveaway)
nn-Origin of Pogo, Swamp, etc.; 2 pg. biog. on Walt Kelly (One copy sold in 1980 for $150.00)

SPECIAL EDITION (U. S. Navy Giveaways)
National Periodical Publs.: 1944 - 1945 (Reg. comic format with wording simplified, 52 pgs.)
1-Action (1944)-Reprints Action #80 58 116 174 371 636 900
2-Action (1944)-Reprints Action #81 58 116 174 371 636 900
3-Superman (1944)-Reprints Superman #33 58 116 174 371 636 900
4-Detective (1944)-Reprints Detective #97 58 116 174 371 636 900
5-Superman (1945)-Reprints Superman #34 58 116 174 371 636 900
6-Action (1945)-Reprints Action #84 58 116 174 371 636 900
NOTE: ***Wayne Boring** c-1, 2, 6. **Dick Sprang** c-4.*

SPIDER-MAN (See Amazing Spider-Man, The)

SPIRIT, THE (Weekly Comic Book)(Distributed through various newspapers & other sources)
Will Eisner: 6/2/40 - 10/5/52 (16 pgs.; 8 pgs.) (no cover) (in color)
NOTE: **Eisner** script, pencils/inks for the most part from 6/2/40-4/26/42; a few stories assisted by Jack Cole, Fine, Powell and Kotsky.
6/2/40(#1)-Origin/1st app. The Spirit; reprinted in Police #11; Lady Luck (Brenda Banks) (1st app.) by Chuck Mazoujian & Mr. Mystic (1st. app.) by S. R. (Bob) Powell begin (rare) 371 742 1113 2600 4550 6500
6/9/40(#2) 65 130 195 416 708 1000
6/16/40(#3)-Black Queen app. in Spirit 39 78 117 236 388 540
6/23/40(#4)-Mr. Mystic receives magical necklace 30 60 90 177 289 400
6/30/40(#5) 30 60 90 177 289 400
7/7/40(#6)-1st app. Spirit carplane; Black Queen app. in Spirit 32 64 96 188 307 425
7/14/40(#7)-8/4/40(#10): 7/21/40-Spirit becomes fugitive wanted for murder 26 52 78 154 252 350
8/11/40-9/22/40: 9/15/40-Racist-c 24 48 72 142 234 325
9/29/40-Ellen drops engagement with Homer Creep 21 42 63 122 199 275
10/6/40-11/3/40 21 42 63 122 199 275
11/10/40-The Black Queen app. 21 42 63 122 199 275
11/17/40, 11/24/40 21 42 63 122 199 275
12/1/40-Ellen spanking by Spirit on cover & inside; Eisner-1st 3 pgs., J. Cole rest 24 48 72 142 234 325
12/8/40-3/9/41 16 32 48 94 147 200
3/16/41-Intro. & 1st app. Silk Satin 20 40 60 118 192 265
3/23/41-6/1/41: 5/11/41-Last Lady Luck by Mazoujian. 5/18/41-Lady Luck by Nick Viscardi begins, ends 2/22/42 15 30 45 90 140 190
6/8/41-2nd app. Satin; Spirit learns Satin is also a British agent 18 36 54 103 162 220
6/15/41-1st app. Twilight 17 34 51 98 154 210
6/22/41-Hitler app. in Spirit 16 32 48 94 147 200
6/29/41-1/25/42,2/8/42 14 28 42 81 118 155
2/1/42-1st app. Duchess 16 32 48 94 147 200
2/15/42-4/26/42-Lady Luck by Klaus Nordling begins 3/1/42 15 30 45 84 127 170
5/3/42-8/16/42-Eisner/Fine/Quality staff assists on Spirit 12 24 36 69 97 125
8/23/42-Satin cover splash; Spirit by Eisner/Fine although signed by Fine 17 34 51 98 154 210
8/30/42,9/27/42-10/11/42,10/25/42-11/8/42-Eisner/Fine/Quality staff assists on Spirit 12 24 36 67 94 120
9/6/42-9/20/42,10/18/42-Fine/Belfi art on Spirit; scripts by Manly Wade Wellman 9 18 27 50 65 80
11/15/42-12/6/42,12/20/42,12/27/42,1/17/43-4/18/43,5/9/43-8/8/43-Wellman/Woolfolk scripts, Fine pencils, Quality staff inks 9 18 27 50 65 80
12/13/42,1/3/43,1/10/43,4/25/43,5/2/43-Eisner scripts/layouts; Fine pencils, Quality staff inks 10 20 30 54 72 90
8/15/43-Eisner script/layout; pencils/inks by Quality staff; Jack Cole-a 8 16 24 44 57 70
8/22/43-12/12/43-Wellman/Woolfolk scripts, Fine pencils, Quality staff inks; Mr. Mystic by Guardineer-10/10/43-10/24/43 8 16 24 44 57 70
12/19/43-8/13/44-Wellman/Woolfolk/Jack Cole scripts; Cole, Fine & Robin King-a; Last Mr. Mystic-5/14/44 8 16 24 42 54 65
8/20/44-12/16/45-Wellman/Woolfolk scripts; Fine art with unknown staff assists 8 16 24 42 54 65
NOTE: *Scripts/layouts by Eisner, or Eisner/Nordling, Eisner/Mercer or Spranger/Eisner; inks by Eisner or Eisner/Spranger in issues 12/23/45-2/2/47.*
12/23/45-1/6/46: 12/23/45-Christmas-c 9 18 27 52 69 85
1/13/46-Origin Spirit retold 13 26 39 72 101 130
1/20/46-1st postwar Satin app. 11 22 33 64 90 115
1/27/46-3/10/46: 3/3/46-Last Lady Luck by Nordling 9 18 27 52 69 85
3/17/46-Intro. & 1st app. Nylon 11 22 33 64 90 115
3/24/46,3/31/46,4/14/46 9 18 27 52 69 85
4/7/46-2nd app. Nylon 10 20 30 56 76 95
4/21/46-Intro. & 1st app. Mr. Carrion & His Pet Buzzard Julia 13 26 39 72 101 130
4/28/46-5/12/46,5/26/46-6/30/46: Lady Luck by Fred Schwab in issues 5/5/46-11/3/46 9 18 27 52 69 85
5/19/46-2nd app. Mr. Carrion 10 20 30 56 76 95
7/7/46-Intro. & 1st app. Dulcet Tone & Skinny 11 22 33 64 90 115
7/14/46-9/29/46 9 18 27 52 69 85
10/6/46-Intro. & 1st app. P'Gell 13 26 39 74 105 135
10/13/46-11/3/46,11/16/46-11/24/46 9 18 27 52 69 85
11/10/46-2nd app. P'Gell 11 22 33 62 86 110
12/1/46-3rd app. P'Gell 10 20 30 54 72 90
12/8/46-2/2/47 9 18 27 50 65 80
NOTE: *Scripts, pencils/inks by Eisner except where noted in issues 2/9/47-12/19/48.*
2/9/47-7/6/47: 6/8/47-Eisner self satire 9 18 27 50 65 80
7/13/47- "Hansel & Gretel" fairy tales 11 22 33 64 90 115
7/20/47-Li'L Abner, Daddy Warbucks, Dick Tracy, Fearless Fosdick parody; A-Bomb blast-c 13 26 39 72 101 130
7/27/47-9/14/47 9 18 27 50 65 80

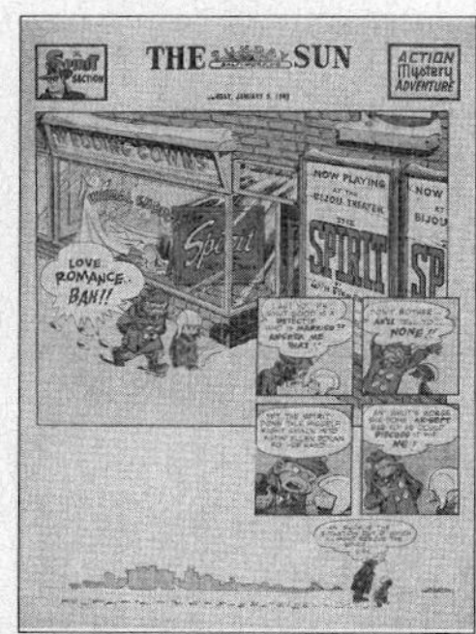

The Spirit 1/09/49 © Will Eisner

The Spirit 3/12/50 © Will Eisner

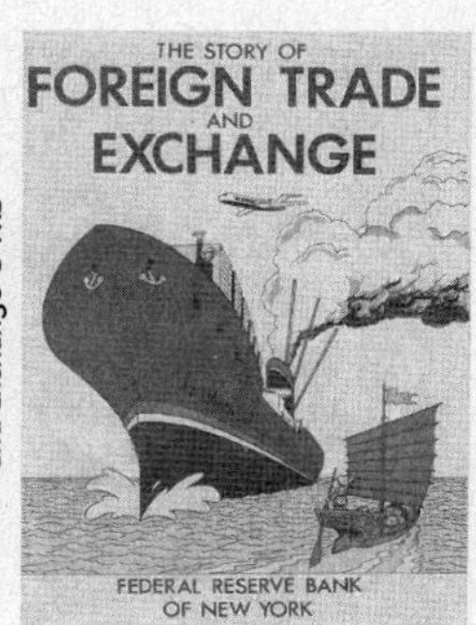

The Story of Foreign Trade and Exchange © FRB

	GD 2.0	VG 4.0	FN 6.0	VF 8.0	VF/NM 9.0	NM- 9.2
9/21/47-Pearl Harbor flashback	10	20	30	56	76	95
9/28/47-1st mention of Flying Saucers in comics-3 months after 1st sighting in Idaho on 6/25/47	18	36	54	103	162	220
10/5/47- "Cinderella" fairy tales	11	22	33	64	90	115
10/12/47-11/30/47	9	18	27	50	65	80
12/7/47-Intro. & 1st app. Powder Pouf	13	26	39	72	101	130
12/14/47-12/28/47	9	18	27	50	65	80
1/4/48-2nd app. Powder Pouf	10	20	30	54	72	90
1/11/48-1st app. Sparrow Fallon; Powder Pouf app.	10	20	30	54	72	90
1/18/48-He-Man ad cover; satire issue	10	20	30	54	72	90
1/25/48-Intro. & 1st app. Castanet	13	26	39	72	101	130
2/1/48-2nd app. Castanet	9	18	27	52	69	85
2/8/48-3/7/48	9	18	27	50	65	80
3/14/48-Only app. Kretchma	9	18	27	52	69	85
3/21/48,3/28/48,4/11/48-4/25/48	9	18	27	50	65	80
4/4/48-Only app. Wild Rice	9	18	27	52	69	85
5/2/48-2nd app. Sparrow	9	18	27	50	65	80
5/9/48-6/27/48,7/11/48,7/18/48: 6/13/48-TV issue	9	18	27	50	65	80
7/4/48-Spirit by Andre Le Blanc	8	16	24	42	54	65
7/25/48-Ambrose Bierce's "The Thing" adaptation classic by Eisner/Grandenetti	15	30	45	90	140	190
8/1/48-8/15/48,8/29/48-9/12/48	9	18	27	50	65	80
8/22/48-Poe's "Fall of the House of Usher" classic by Eisner/Grandenetti	15	30	45	90	140	190
9/19/48-Only app. Lorelei	10	20	30	54	72	90
9/26/48-10/31/48	9	18	27	50	65	80
11/7/48-Only app. Plaster of Paris	11	22	33	64	90	115
11/14/48-12/19/48	9	18	27	50	65	80

NOTE: *Scripts by Eisner or Feiffer or Eisner/Feiffer or Nordling. Art by Eisner with backgrounds by Eisner, Grandenetti, Le Blanc, Stallman, Nordling, Dixon and/or others in issues 12/26/48-4/1/51 except where noted.*

	GD 2.0	VG 4.0	FN 6.0	VF 8.0	VF/NM 9.0	NM- 9.2
12/26/48-Reprints some covers of 1948 with flashbacks	9	18	27	50	65	80
1/2/49-1/16/49	9	18	27	50	65	80
1/23/49,1/30/49-1st & 2nd app. Thorne	10	20	30	54	72	90
2/6/49-8/14/49	9	18	27	50	65	80
8/21/49,8/28/49-1st & 2nd app. Monica Veto	10	20	30	54	72	90
9/4/49,9/11/49	9	18	27	50	65	80
9/18/49-Love comic cover; has gag love comic ads on inside	10	20	30	54	72	90
9/25/49-Only app. Ice	9	18	27	52	69	85
10/2/49,10/9/49-Autumn News appears & dies in 10/9 issue	9	18	27	52	69	85
10/16/49-11/27/49,12/18/49,12/25/49	9	18	27	50	65	80
12/4/49,12/11/49-1st & 2nd app. Flaxen	9	18	27	52	69	85
1/1/50-Flashbacks to all of the Spirit girls-Thorne, Ellen, Satin, & Monica	14	28	42	76	108	140
1/8/50-Intro. & 1st app. Sand Saref	15	30	45	86	133	180
1/15/50-2nd app. Saref	13	26	39	72	101	130
1/22/50-2/5/50	9	18	27	50	65	80
2/12/50-Roller Derby issue	10	20	30	54	72	90
2/19/50-Half Dead Mr. Lox - Classic horror	11	22	33	64	90	115
2/26/50-4/23/50,5/14/50,5/28/50,7/23/50-9/3/50	9	18	27	50	65	80
4/30/50-Script/art by Le Blanc with Eisner framing	8	16	24	40	50	60
5/7/50,6/4/50-7/16/50-Abe Kanegson-a	8	16	24	40	50	60
5/21/50-Script by Feiffer/Eisner, art by Blaisdell, Eisner framing	8	16	24	40	50	60
9/10/50-P'Gell returns	10	20	30	54	72	90
9/17/50-1/7/51	9	18	27	50	65	80
1/14/51-Life Magazine cover; brief biography of Comm. Dolan, Sand Saref, Silk Satin, P'Gell, Sammy & Willum, Darling O'Shea, & Mr. Carrion & His Pet Buzzard Julia, with pin-ups by Eisner	11	22	33	64	90	115
1/21/51,2/4/51-4/1/51	9	18	27	50	65	80
1/28/51- "The Meanest Man in the World" by Eisner	11	22	33	64	90	115
4/8/51-7/29/51,8/12/51-Last Eisner issue	9	18	27	50	65	80
8/5/51,8/19/51-7/20/52-Not Eisner	8	16	24	40	50	60
7/27/52-(Rare)-Denny Colt in Outer Space by Wally Wood; 7 pg. S/F story of E.C. vintage	47	94	141	296	498	700
8/3/52-(Rare)- "Mission...The Moon" by Wood	47	94	141	296	498	700
8/10/52-(Rare)- "A DP On The Moon" by Wood	47	94	141	296	498	700
8/17/52-(Rare)- "Heart" by Wood/Eisner	43	86	129	271	461	650
8/24/52-(Rare)- "Rescue" by Wood	47	94	141	296	498	700
8/31/52-(Rare)- "The Last Man" by Wood	47	94	141	296	498	700
9/7/52-(Rare)- "The Man in The Moon" by Wood	47	94	141	296	498	700
9/14/52-(Rare)-Eisner/Wenzel-a	30	60	90	177	289	400
9/21/52-(Rare)- "Denny Colt, Alias The Spirit/Space Report" by Eisner/Wenzel	31	62	93	186	303	420
9/28/52-(Rare)- "Return From The Moon" by Wood	44	88	132	277	469	660
10/5/52-(Rare)- "The Last Story" by Eisner	26	52	78	154	252	350

Large Tabloid pages from 1946 on (Eisner) - Price 200 percent over listed prices.

NOTE: *Spirit sections came out in both large and small format. Some newspapers went to the 8-pg. format months before others. Some printed the pages so they cannot be folded into a small comic book section; these are worth less. (Also see Three Comics & Spiritman).*

SPY SMASHER
Fawcett Publications

	GD 2.0	VG 4.0	FN 6.0	VF 8.0	VF/NM 9.0	NM- 9.2
Well Known Comics (1944, 12 pgs., 8-1/2x10-1/2"), paper-c, glued binding, printed in green; Bestmaid/Samuel Lowe giveaway	15	30	45	83	124	165

STANDARD OIL COMICS (Also see Gulf Funny Weekly)
Standard Oil Co.: 1932-1934 (Giveaway, tabloid size, 4 pgs. in color)

	GD 2.0	VG 4.0	FN 6.0	VF 8.0	VF/NM 9.0	NM- 9.2
nn (Dec. 1932)	54	108	162	343	574	825
1-Series has original art	45	90	135	284	480	675
2-5	20	40	60	118	192	265
6-14: 14-Fred Opper strip, 1 pg.	14	28	42	76	108	140
1A (Jan 1933)	47	94	141	296	498	700
2A-14A (1933)	30	60	90	177	289	400
1B (1934)	37	74	111	222	361	500
2B-?B (1934)	30	60	90	177	289	400

NOTE: *Series A contains Frederick Opper's Si & Mirandi; Series B contains Goofus: He's From The Big City; McVittie by Walter O'Ehrle; interior strips include Pesty And His Pop & Smiling Slim by Sid Hicks.*

STAR TEAM
Marvel Comics Group: 1977 (6-1/2x5", 20 pgs.) (Ideal Toy Giveaway)

	GD 2.0	VG 4.0	FN 6.0	VF 8.0	VF/NM 9.0	NM- 9.2
nn	3	6	9	14	19	24

STEVE CANYON COMICS
Harvey Publications

	GD 2.0	VG 4.0	FN 6.0	VF 8.0	VF/NM 9.0	NM- 9.2
Dept. Store giveaway #3(6/48, 36pp)	10	20	30	54	72	90
...'s Secret Mission (1951, 16 pgs., Armed Forces giveaway); Caniff-a	9	18	27	47	61	75
Strictly for the Smart Birds (1951, 16 pgs.)-Information Comics Div. (Harvey) Premium	8	16	24	40	50	60

STORIES OF CHRISTMAS
K. K. Publications: 1942 (Giveaway, 32 pgs., paper cover)

	GD 2.0	VG 4.0	FN 6.0	VF 8.0	VF/NM 9.0	NM- 9.2
nn-Adaptation of "A Christmas Carol"; Kelly story "The Fir Tree"; Infinity-c	30	60	90	177	289	400

STORY HOUR SERIES (Disney)
Whitman Publ. Co.: 1948, 1949; 1951-1953 (36 pgs., paper-c) (4-3/4x6-1/2")
Given away with subscription to Walt Disney's Comics & Stories

	GD 2.0	VG 4.0	FN 6.0	VF 8.0	VF/NM 9.0	NM- 9.2
nn(1948)-Mickey Mouse and the Boy Thursday	12	24	36	67	94	120
nn(1948)-Mickey Mouse the Miracle Master	12	24	36	67	94	120
nn(1948)-Minnie Mouse and Antique Chair	12	24	36	67	94	120
nn(1949)-The Three Orphan Kittens(B&W & color)	9	18	27	47	61	75
nn(1949)-Danny-The Little Black Lamb	9	18	27	47	61	75
800(1948)-Donald Duck in "Bringing Up the Boys"	15	30	45	88	137	185
1953 edition	11	22	33	64	90	115
801(1948)-Mickey Mouse's Summer Vacation	10	20	30	56	76	95
1951, 1952 editions	7	14	21	35	43	50
802(1948)-Bugs Bunny's Adventures	9	18	27	50	65	80
803(1948)-Bongo	8	16	24	40	50	60
804(1948)-Mickey and the Beanstalk	9	18	27	47	61	75
805-15(1949)-Andy Panda and His Friends	8	16	24	40	50	60
806-15(1949)-Tom and Jerry	8	16	24	44	57	70
808-15(1949)-Johnny Appleseed	8	16	24	40	50	60

1948, 1949 Hard Cover Edition of each....30% - 40% more.

STOP AND GO, THE SAFETY TWINS
J.C. Penney: no date (giveaway)

	GD 2.0	VG 4.0	FN 6.0	VF 8.0	VF/NM 9.0	NM- 9.2
nn	5	10	15	24	30	35

STORY OF CHECKS THE
Federal Reserve Bank: 1979 (Reg. size)

	GD 2.0	VG 4.0	FN 6.0	VF 8.0	VF/NM 9.0	NM- 9.2
nn	1	3	4	6	8	10

STORY OF CHECKS AND ELECTRONIC PAYMENTS
Federal Reserve Bank: 1983 (Reg size)

	GD 2.0	VG 4.0	FN 6.0	VF 8.0	VF/NM 9.0	NM- 9.2
nn	1	2	3	5	6	8

STORY OF CONSUMER CREDIT
Federal Reserve Bank: 1980 (Reg. size)

	GD 2.0	VG 4.0	FN 6.0	VF 8.0	VF/NM 9.0	NM- 9.2
nn	1	2	3	5	6	8

STORY OF EDISON, THE

Super Book of Comics #4 © WEST

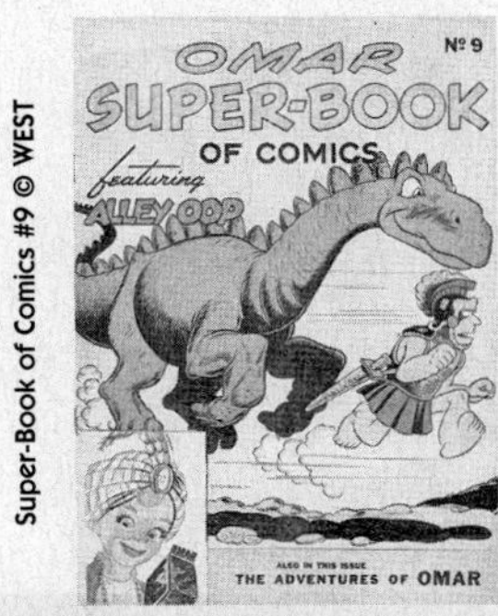

Super-Book of Comics #9 © WEST

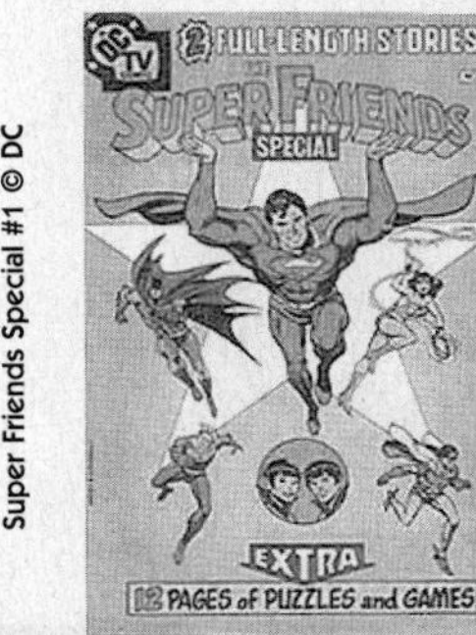

Super Friends Special #1 © DC

	GD 2.0	VG 4.0	FN 6.0	VF 8.0	VF/NM 9.0	NM- 9.2
Educational Comics: 1956 (16 pgs.) (Reddy Killowatt)						
nn-Reprint of Reddy Kilowatt #2(1947)	7	14	21	37	46	55
STORY OF FOREIGN TRADE AND EXCHANGE						
Federal Reserve Bank: 1985 (Reg. size)						
nn	1	2	3	5	6	8
STORY OF HARRY S. TRUMAN, THE						
Democratic National Committee: 1948 (Giveaway, regular size, soft-c, 16 pg.)						
nn-Gives biography on career of Truman; used in **SOTI**, pg. 311	14	28	42	76	108	140
STORY OF INFLATION, THE						
Federal Reserve Bank: 1980s (Reg size)						
nn	1	3	4	6	8	10
STORY OF MONEY						
Federral Reserve Bank: 1984 (Reg. size)						
nn	1	3	4	6	8	10
STORY OF THE BALLET, THE						
Selva and Sons, Inc.: 1954 (16 pgs., paper cover)						
nn	4	8	11	16	19	22
STRANGE AS IT SEEMS						
McNaught Syndicate: 1936 (B&W, 5" x 7", 24 pgs.)						
nn-Ex-Lax giveaway	8	16	24	44	57	70
SUGAR BEAR						
Post Cereal Giveaway: No date, circa 1975? (2 1/2" x 4 1/2", 16 pgs.)						
"The Almost Take Over of the Post Office", "The Race Across the Atlantic", "The Zoo Goes Wild" each...	1	2	3	5	6	8
SUNDAY WORLD'S EASTER EGG FULL OF EASTER MEAT FOR LITTLE PEOPLE						
Supplement to the New York World: 3/27/1898 (soft-c, 16pg, 4"x8" approx., opens at top, color & B&W)(Giveaway)(shaped like an Easter egg)						
nn-By R.F. Outcault	18	36	54	107	169	230
SUPER BOOK OF COMICS						
Western Publ. Co.: nd (1942-1943?) (Soft-c, 32 pgs.) (Pan-Am/Gilmore Oil/Kelloggs premiums)						
nn-Dick Tracy (Gilmore)-Magic Morro app. (2 versions: Dick Tracy Jr. on cover and a filing cabinet cover)	33	66	99	194	317	440
1-Dick Tracy & The Smuggling Ring; Stratosphere Jim app. (Rare) (Pan-Am)	33	66	99	194	317	440
1-Smilin' Jack, Magic Morro (Pan-Am)	14	28	42	76	108	140
2-Smilin' Jack, Stratosphere Jim (Pan-Am)	14	28	42	76	108	140
2-Smitty, Magic Morro (Pan-Am)	14	28	42	76	108	140
3-Captain Midnight, Magic Morro (Pan-Am)	22	44	66	131	216	300
3-Moon Mullins?	13	26	39	74	105	135
4-Red Ryder, Magic Morro (Pan-Am). Same content as Red Ryder Victory Patrol comic w/diff. cover	15	30	45	85	130	175
4-Smitty, Stratosphere Jim (Pan-Am)	13	26	39	74	105	135
5-Don Winslow, Magic Morro (Gilmore)	15	30	45	85	130	175
5-Don Winslow, Stratosphere Jim (Pan-Am)	15	30	45	85	130	175
5-Terry & the Pirates	17	34	51	98	154	210
6-Don Winslow, Stratosphere Jim (Pan-Am)-McWilliams-a	15	30	45	85	130	175
6-King of the Royal Mounted, Magic Morro (Pan-Am)	15	30	45	85	130	175
7-Dick Tracy, Magic Morro (Pan-Am)	19	38	57	112	179	245
7-Little Orphan Annie	11	22	33	64	90	115
8-Dick Tracy, Stratosphere Jim (Pan-Am)	17	34	51	98	154	210
8-Dan Dunn, Magic Morro (Pan-Am)	11	22	33	64	90	115
9-Terry & the Pirates, Magic Morro (Pan-Am)	17	34	51	98	154	210
10-Red Ryder, Magic Morro (Pan-Am)	15	30	45	85	130	175
SUPER-BOOK OF COMICS						
Western Publishing Co.: (Omar Bread & Hancock Oil Co. giveaways) 1944 - No. 30, 1947 (Omar); 1947 - 1948 (Hancock) (16 pgs.)						
NOTE: The Hancock issues are all exact reprints of the earlier Omar issues. The issue numbers were removed in some of the reprints.						
1-Dick Tracy (Omar, 1944)	15	30	45	94	147	200
1-Dick Tracy (Hancock, 1947)	14	28	42	78	112	145
2-Bugs Bunny (Omar, 1944)	8	16	24	40	50	60
2-Bugs Bunny (Hancock, 1947)	6	12	18	32	39	46
3-Terry & the Pirates (Omar, 1944)	11	22	33	60	83	105
3-Terry & the Pirates (Hancock, 1947)	10	20	30	54	72	90
4-Andy Panda (Omar, 1944)	8	16	24	40	50	60
4-Andy Panda (Hancock, 1947)	6	12	18	32	39	46
5-Smokey Stover (Omar, 1945)	6	12	18	32	39	46
5-Smokey Stover (Hancock, 1947)	5	10	15	24	30	35
6-Porky Pig (Omar, 1945)	8	16	24	40	50	60
6-Porky Pig (Hancock, 1947)	6	12	18	32	39	46
7-Smilin' Jack (Omar, 1945)	8	16	24	40	50	60
7-Smilin' Jack (Hancock, 1947)	6	12	18	32	39	46
8-Oswald the Rabbit (Omar, 1945)	6	12	18	32	39	46
8-Oswald the Rabbit (Hancock, 1947)	5	10	15	24	30	35
9-Alley Oop (Omar, 1945)	11	22	33	64	90	115
9-Alley Oop (Hancock, 1947)	11	22	33	60	83	105
10-Elmer Fudd (Omar, 1945)	6	12	18	32	39	46
10-Elmer Fudd (Hancock, 1947)	5	10	15	24	30	35
11-Little Orphan Annie (Omar, 1945)	8	16	24	42	53	64
11-Little Orphan Annie (Hancock, 1947)	7	14	21	36	45	54
12-Woody Woodpecker (Omar, 1945)	6	12	18	32	39	46
12-Woody Woodpecker (Hancock, 1947)	5	10	15	24	30	35
13-Dick Tracy (Omar, 1945)	11	22	33	64	90	115
13-Dick Tracy (Hancock, 1947)	11	22	33	60	83	105
14-Bugs Bunny (Omar, 1945)	6	12	18	32	39	46
14-Bugs Bunny (Hancock, 1947)	5	10	15	24	30	35
15-Andy Panda (Omar, 1945)	6	12	18	28	34	40
15-Andy Panda (Hancock, 1947)	5	10	15	24	30	35
16-Terry & the Pirates (Omar, 1945)	11	22	33	60	83	105
16-Terry & the Pirates (Hancock, 1947)	9	18	27	47	61	75
17-Smokey Stover (Omar, 1946)	6	12	18	32	39	46
17-Smokey Stover (Hancock, 1948?)	5	10	15	24	30	35
18-Porky Pig (Omar, 1946)	6	12	18	28	34	40
18-Porky Pig (Hancock, 1948?)	5	10	15	24	30	35
19-Smilin' Jack (Omar, 1946)	6	12	18	32	39	46
nn-Smilin' Jack (Hancock, 1948)	5	10	15	24	30	35
20-Oswald the Rabbit (Omar, 1946)	6	12	18	28	34	40
nn-Oswald the Rabbit (Hancock, 1948)	5	10	15	24	30	35
21-Gasoline Alley (Omar, 1946)	8	16	24	42	53	64
nn-Gasoline Alley (Hancock, 1948)	7	14	21	36	45	54
22-Elmer Fudd (Omar, 1946)	6	12	18	28	34	40
nn-Elmer Fudd (Hancock, 1948)	5	10	15	24	30	35
23-Little Orphan Annie (Omar, 1946)	8	16	24	40	50	60
nn-Little Orphan Annie (Hancock, 1948)	6	12	18	32	39	46
24-Woody Woodpecker (Omar, 1946)	6	12	18	28	34	40
nn-Woody Woodpecker (Hancock, 1948)	5	10	15	24	30	35
25-Dick Tracy (Omar, 1946)	11	22	33	60	83	105
nn-Dick Tracy (Hancock, 1948)	9	18	27	50	65	80
26-Bugs Bunny (Omar, 1946))	6	12	18	28	34	40
nn-Bugs Bunny (Hancock, 1948)	5	10	15	24	30	35
27-Andy Panda (Omar, 1946)	6	12	18	28	34	40
27-Andy Panda (Hancock, 1948)	5	10	15	24	30	35
28-Terry & the Pirates (Omar, 1946)	11	22	33	60	83	105
28-Terry & the Pirates (Hancock, 1948)	9	18	27	47	61	75
29-Smokey Stover (Omar, 1947)	6	12	18	28	34	40
29-Smokey Stover (Hancock, 1948)	5	10	15	24	30	35
30-Porky Pig (Omar, 1947)	6	12	18	28	34	40
30-Porky Pig (Hancock, 1948)	5	10	15	24	30	35
nn-Bugs Bunny (Hancock, 1948)-Does not match any Omar book	6	12	18	28	34	40
SUPER CIRCUS (TV)						
Cross Publishing Co.						
1-(1951, Weather Bird Shoes giveaway)	8	16	24	40	50	60
SUPER FRIENDS						
DC Comics: 1981 (Giveaway, no ads, no code or price)						
...Special 1 -r/Super Friends #19 & 36	2	4	6	9	13	16
SUPERGEAR COMICS						
Jacobs Corp.: 1976 (Giveaway, 4 pgs. in color, slick paper)						
nn-(Rare)-Superman, Lois Lane; Steve Lombard app. (500 copies printed, over half destroyed?)	18	36	54	126	281	435
SUPERGIRL						
DC Comics: 1984, 1986 (Giveaway, Baxter paper)						
nn-(American Honda/U.S. Dept. Transportation) Torres-c/a	2	4	6	8	11	14
SUPER HEROES PUZZLES AND GAMES						
General Mills Giveaway (Marvel Comics Group): 1979 (32 pgs., regular size)						
nn-Four 2-pg. origin stories of Spider-Man, Captain America, The Hulk, & Spider-Woman						

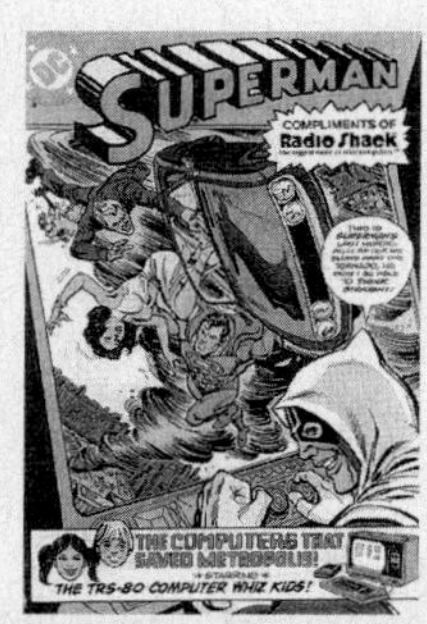

Superman - Radio Shack (7/80) © DC

Superman's Christmas Adventure © DC

Swamp Fox © DIS

	GD 2.0	VG 4.0	FN 6.0	VF 8.0	VF/NM 9.0	NM- 9.2
	3	6	9	14	20	26

SUPERMAN
National Periodical Publ./DC Comics

72-Giveaway(9-10/51)-(Rare)-Price blackened out; came with banner wrapped around book; without banner — 74 148 222 470 810 1150
72-Giveaway with banner — 119 238 357 762 1306 1850
Bradman birthday custom (1988)(extremely limited distribution) - a CGC 9.6 copy sold for $2600, a NM copy sold for $1125, and a FN/VF copy sold for $800 in 2011-2012, plus a CGC 9.0 sold for $421 in 12/12 and a CGC 9.6 copy sold for $1314 in 8/15
... For the Animals (2000, Doris Day Animal Foundation, 30 pgs.) polybagged with Gotham Adventures #22, Hourman #12, Impulse #58, Looney Tunes #62, Stars and S.T.R.I.P.E. #8 and Superman Adventures #41 — 2.50
Kelloggs Giveaway-(2/3 normal size, 1954)-r-two stories/Superman #55 — 29 58 87 170 278 385
Kenner: Man of Steel (Doomsday is Coming) (1995, 16 pgs.) packaged with set of Superman and Doomsday action figures — 4.00
...Meets the Quik Bunny (1987, Nestles Quik premium, 36 pgs.) — 1 2 3 5 7 9
Pizza Hut Premiums (12/77)-Exact reprints of 1950s comics except for paid ads (set of 6 exist?); Vol. 1-r#97 (#113-r also known) — 2 4 6 8 10 12
Radio Shack Giveaway-36 pgs. (7/80) "The Computers That Saved Metropolis", Starlin/Giordano-a; advertising insert in Action #509, New Advs. of Superboy #7, Legion of Super-Heroes #265, & House of Mystery #282. (All comics were 68 pgs.) Cover of inserts printed on newsprint. Giveaway contains 4 extra pgs. of Radio Shack advertising that inserts do not have — 1 2 3 5 7 9
Radio Shack Giveaway-(7/81) "Victory by Computer" — 1 2 3 5 7 9
Radio Shack Giveaway-(7/82) "Computer Masters of Metropolis" — 1 2 3 5 7 9

SUPERMAN ADVENTURES, THE (TV)
DC Comics: 1996 (Based on animated series)

1-(1996) Preview issue distributed at Warner Bros. stores — 4.00
Titus Game Edition (1998) — 2.50

SUPERMAN AND THE GREAT CLEVELAND FIRE
National Periodical Publ.: 1948 (Giveaway, 4 pgs., no cover) (Hospital Fund)

nn-In full color — 68 136 204 435 743 1050

SUPERMAN AT THE GILBERT HALL OF SCIENCE
National Periodical Publ.: 1948 (Giveaway) (Gilbert Chemistry Sets / A.C. Gilbert Co.)

nn-(8 1/2" x 5 1/2") — 39 78 117 231 378 525

SUPERMAN (Miniature)
National Periodical Publ.: 1942; 1955 - 1956 (3 issues, no #'s, 32 pgs.)
The pages are numbered in the 1st issue: 1-32; 2nd: 1A-32A, and 3rd: 1B-32B

No date-Py-Co-Pay Tooth Powder giveaway (8 pgs.; circa 1942)(The Adventures of...) Japanese air battle — 39 78 117 240 395 550
1-The Superman Time Capsule (Kellogg's Sugar Smacks)(1955) — 21 42 63 122 199 275
1A-Duel in Space (1955) — 20 40 60 114 182 250
1B-The Super Show of Metropolis (also #1-32, no B)(1955) — 20 40 60 114 182 250

NOTE: *Numbering variations exist. Each title could have any combination-#1, 1A, or 1B.*

SUPERMAN RECORD COMIC
National Periodical Publications: 1966 (Golden Records)

(With record)-Record reads origin of Superman from comic; came with iron-on patch, decoder, membership card & button; comic-r/Superman #125,146 — 10 20 30 64 132 200
Comic only — 5 10 15 30 50 70

SUPERMAN'S BUDDY (Costume Comic)
National Periodical Publs.: 1954 (4 pgs., slick paper-c; one-shot) (Came in box w/costume)

1-With box & costume — 123 246 369 787 1344 1900
Comic only — 55 110 165 352 601 850
1-(1958 edition)-Printed in 2 colors — 17 34 51 98 154 210

SUPERMAN'S CHRISTMAS ADVENTURE
National Periodical Publications: 1940, 1944 (Giveaway, 16 pgs.)
Distributed by Nehi drinks, Bailey Store, Ivey-Keith Co., Kennedy's Boys Shop, Macy's Store, Boston Store

1(1940)-Burnley-a; F. Ray-c/r from Superman #6 (Scarce)-Superman saves Santa Claus. Santa makes real Superman Toys offered in 1940. 1st merchandising story; versions with Royal Crown Cola ad on front-c & Boston Store ad on front-c; cover art on each has the same layout but different art — 366 732 1098 2562 4481 6400
nn(1944) w/Santa Claus & X-mas tree-c — 100 200 300 635 1093 1550
nn(1944) w/Candy cane & Superman-c — 100 200 300 635 1093 1550
nn(1944) w/1940-c (Santa over chimney); Superman image (from Superman #6) on back-c — 100 200 300 635 1093 1550

SUPERMAN-TIM (Becomes Tim)
Superman-Tim Stores/National Periodical Publ.: Aug, 1942 - May, 1950 (Half size) (B&W Giveaway w/2 color covers) (Publ. monthly 2/43 on)(All have Superman illos)

8/42 (#1)- 2 pg. Superman story — 129 258 387 826 1413 2000
9/42 (#2) Superman/Uncle Sam flag-c — 53 106 159 334 567 800
12/42-Christmas-c — 42 84 126 265 445 625
1/43 — 41 82 123 256 428 600
2/43, 3/43 — 40 80 120 246 411 575
4/43, 5/43, 6/43, 7/43, 8/43 — 37 74 111 222 361 500
9/43, 10/43, 11/43, 12/43 — 30 60 90 177 289 400
1/44-12/44 — 24 48 72 140 230 320
1/45-5/45, 8/45, 10-12/45, 1/46-8/46 — 22 44 66 128 209 290
6/45-Classic Superman-c — 23 46 69 138 227 315
7/45-Classic Superman flag-c — 23 46 69 138 227 315
9/45-1st stamp album issue — 48 96 114 302 509 715
9/46-2nd stamp album issue — 41 82 123 256 428 600
10/46-1st Superman story — 29 58 87 170 278 385
11/46, 12/46, 1/47-8/47 issues-Superman story in each; 2/47-Infinity-c. All 36 pgs. — 29 58 87 170 278 385
9/47-Stamp album issue & Superman story — 40 80 120 246 411 575
10/47, 11/47, 12/47-Superman stories (24 pgs.) — 29 58 87 170 278 385
1/48-7/48,10/48, 11/48, 12/48, 2/49, 4/49-11/49 — 23 46 69 138 227 315
8/48-Contains full page ad for Superman-Tim watch giveaway — 23 46 69 138 227 315
9/48-Stamp album issue — 32 64 96 188 307 425
1/49-Full page Superman bank cut-out — 23 46 69 138 227 315
3/49-Full page Superman boxing game cut-out — 23 46 69 138 227 315
12/49-3/50, 5/50-Superman stories — 25 50 75 150 245 340
4/50-Superman story, baseball stories; photo-c without Superman — 29 58 87 170 278 385

NOTE: *All issues have Superman illustrations throughout. The page count varies depending on whether a Superman-Tim comic story is inserted. If it is, the page count is either 36 or 24 pages. Otherwise all issues are 16 pages. Each issue has a special place for inserting a full color Superman stamp. The stamp album issues had spaces for the stamps given away the past year. The books were mailed as a subscription premium. The stamps were given away free (or when you made a purchase) only when you physically came into the store.*

SUPER SEAMAN SLOPPY
Allied Pristine Union Council, Buffalo, NY: 1940s, 8pg., reg. size (Soft-c)

nn — 4 8 12 18 22 25

SURVEY
Marvel Comics Group: 1948 (Readership survey for advertisers, reg. size)

nn-Harvey Kurtzman-c/a — 81 162 243 518 884 1250

SWAMP FOX, THE
Walt Disney Productions: 1960 (14 pgs, small size) (Canada Dry Premiums)

Titles: (A)-Tory Masquerade, (B)-Turnabout Tactics, (C)-Rindau Rampage; each came in paper sleeve, books 1,2 & 3; Set with sleeves — 5 10 15 31 53 75
Comic only — 2 4 6 13 18 22

SWORDQUEST
DC Comics/Atari Pub.: 1982, 52pg., 5"x7" (Giveaway with video games)

1,2-Roy Thomas & Gerry Conway-s; George Pérez & Dick Giordano-c/a in all — 2 4 6 10 14 18
3-Low print — 3 6 9 15 22 28

SYNDICATE FEATURES (Sci/fi)
Harry A. Chesler Syndicate: V1#3, 11/15/37; V1#5, 12/15/37 (Tabloid size, 3 colors, 4 pgs.) (Editors premium) (Came folded)

V1#3,5-Dan Hastings daily strips-Guardineer-a — 155 310 465 992 1696 2400

TAKING A CHANCE
American Cancer Society: no date (giveaway)

nn-Anti-smoking — 2 4 6 11 16 20

TASTEE-FREEZ COMICS (Also see Harvey Hits and Richie Rich)
Harvey Comics: 1957 (10¢, 36 pgs.)(6 different issues given away)

1-Little Dot on cover; Richie Rich "Ride 'Em Cowboy" story published one year prior to being printed in Harvey Hits #9. — 8 16 24 54 102 150
2,4,5: 2-Rags Rabbit. 4-Sad Sack. 5-Mazie — 2 4 6 9 12 15
3-Casper — 3 6 9 14 20 25
6-Dick Tracy — 3 6 9 14 20 25
nn-Brings You Space Facts and Fun Book — 1 3 4 6 8 10

TAYLOR'S CHRISTMAS TABLOID
Dept. Store Giveaway: Mid 1930s, Cleveland, Ohio (Tabloid size; in color)

nn-(Very Rare)-Among the earliest pro work of Siegel & Shuster; one full color page called

Titans Beat #1 © DC

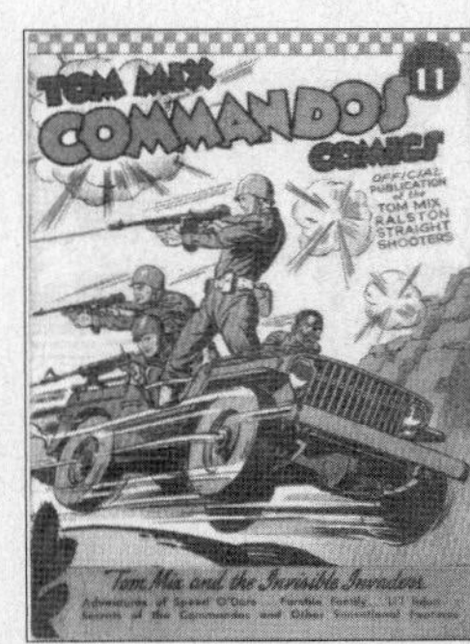

Tom Mix Commandos Comics #11 © FAW

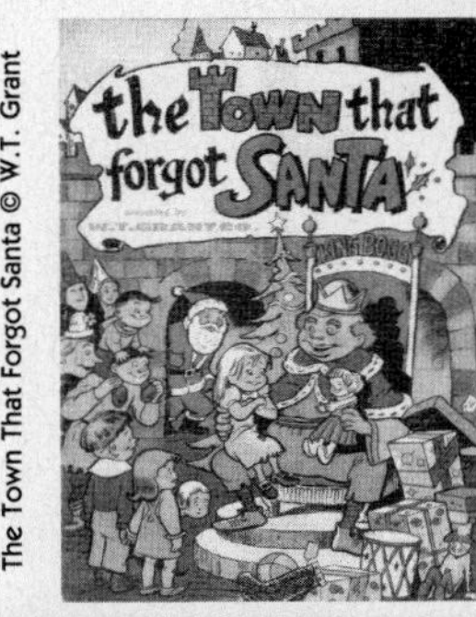

The Town That Forgot Santa © W.T. Grant

	GD 2.0	VG 4.0	FN 6.0	VF 8.0	VF/NM 9.0	NM- 9.2

"The Battle in the Stratosphere", with a pre-Superman look; Shuster art thoughout. (Only 1 known copy) Estimated value... 4000.00

TAZ'S 40TH BIRTHDAY BLOWOUT
DC Comics: 1994 (K-Mart giveaway, 16 pgs.)
nn-Six pg. story, games and puzzles 4.00

TEE AND VEE CROSLEY IN TELEVISION LAND COMICS (Also see Crosley's House of Fun)
Crosley Division, Avco Mfg. Corp. : 1951 (52 pgs.; 8x11"; paper cover; in color) (Giveaway)
Many stories, puzzles, cut-outs, games, etc. 7 14 21 35 43 50

TEEN-AGE BOOBY TRAP
Commercial Comics: 1970 (Small size)
nn 4 7 10 14 17 20

TENNESSEE JED (Radio)
Fox Syndicate? (Wm. C. Popper & Co.): nd (1945) (16 pgs.; paper-c; reg. size; giveaway)
nn 20 40 60 117 189 260

TENNIS (...For Speed, Stamina, Strength, Skill)
Tennis Educational Foundation: 1956 (16 pgs.; soft cover; 10¢)
Book 1-Endorsed by Gene Tunney, Ralph Kiner, etc. showing how tennis has helped them 6 12 18 28 34 40

TERRY AND THE PIRATES
Dell Publishing Co.: 1939 - 1953 (By Milton Caniff)
Buster Brown Shoes giveaway(1938)-32 pgs.; in color 20 40 60 114 182 250
Canada Dry Premiums-Books #1-3(1953, 36 pgs.; 2x5")-Harvey; #1-Hot Shot Charlie Flies Again; 2-In Forced Landing; 3-Dragon Lady in Distress) 14 28 42 78 112 145
Gambles Giveaway (1938, 16 pgs.) 9 18 27 50 65 80
Gillmore Giveaway (1938, 24 pgs.) 9 18 27 52 69 85
Popped Wheat Giveaway(1938)-Strip reprints in full color; Caniff-a 2 4 6 8 10 12
Shoe Store giveaway (Weatherbird & Poll-Parrot)(1938, 16 pgs., soft-c)(2-diff.) 9 18 27 52 69 85
Sparked Wheat Giveaway(1942, 16 pgs.)-In color 9 18 27 52 69 85

TERRY AND THE PIRATES
Libby's Radio Premium: 1941 (16 pgs.; reg. size)(shipped folded in the mail)
"Adventure of the Ruby of Genghis Khan" - Each pg. is a puzzle that must be completed to read the story 400 800 1200 2600 - -

THAT THE WORLD MAY BELIEVE
Catechetical Guild Giveaway: No date (16 pgs.) (Graymoor Friars distr.)
nn 5 10 14 20 24 28

THREAT TO FREEDOM
1965 (Small size)
nn - Anti-communism pamphlet; hammer & sickle-c 6 12 18 38 69 100

3-D COLOR CLASSICS (Wendy's Kid's Club)
Wendy's Int'l Inc.: 1995 (5 1/2" x 8", comes with 3-D glasses)
The Elephant's Child, Gulliver's Travels, Peter Pan, The Time Machine, 20,000 Leagues Under the Sea: Neal Adams-a in all each.... 3.50

350 YEARS OF AMERICAN DAIRY FOODS
American Dairy Assoc.: 1957 (5x7", 16 pgs.)
nn-History of milk 3 6 8 12 14 16

THUMPER (Disney)
Grosset & Dunlap: 1942 (50¢, 32pgs., hardcover book, 7"x8-1/2" w/dust jacket)
nn-Given away (along with a copy of Bambi) for a $2.00, 2-year subscription to WDC&S in 1942. (Xmas offer). Book only 15 30 45 90 140 190
Dust jacket only 10 20 30 56 76 95

TILLY AND TED-TINKERTOTLAND
W. T. Grant Co.: 1945 (Giveaway, 20 pgs.)
nn-Christmas comic 7 14 21 37 46 55

TIM (Formerly Superman-Tim; becomes Gene Autry-Tim)
Tim Stores: June, 1950 - Oct, 1950 (B&W, half-size)
4 issues; 6/50, 9/50, 10/50 known 17 34 51 98 154 210

TIM AND SALLY'S ADVENTURES AT MARINELAND
Marineland Restaurant & Bar, Marineland, CA: 1957 (5x7", 16 pgs., soft-c)
nn-copyright Oceanarium, Inc. 2 4 6 8 11 14

TIME OF DECISION
Harvey Publications Inc.: (16 pgs., paper cover)
nn-ROTC recruitment 4 7 10 14 17 20

TIM IN SPACE (Formerly Gene Autry Tim; becomes Tim Tomorrow)
Tim Stores: 1950 (1/2 size giveaway) (B&W)
nn 14 28 42 80 115 150

TIM TOMORROW (Formerly Tim In Space)
Tim Stores: 8/51, 9/51, 10/51, Christmas, 1951 (5x7-3/4")
nn-Prof. Fumble & Captain Kit Comet in all 14 28 42 80 115 150

TIM TYLER'S LUCK
Standard Comics (King Feat. Syndicate): 1950s (Reg. size, slick-c)
nn-Felix the at app. 4 7 10 14 17 20

TITANS BEAT (Teen Titans)
DC Comics: Aug, 1996 (16 pgs., paper-c)
1-Intro./preview new Teen Titans members; Pérez-a 4.00

TOM MIX (...Commandos Comics #10-12)
Ralston-Purina Co.: Sept, 1940 - No. 12, Nov, 1942 (36 pgs.); 1983 (one-shot)
Given away for two Ralston box-tops; 1983 came in cereal box
1-Origin (life) Tom Mix; Fred Meagher-a 232 464 696 1485 2543 3600
2 53 106 159 334 567 800
3-9 41 82 123 256 428 600
10-12: 10-Origin Tom Mix Commando Unit; Speed O'Dare begins; Japanese sub-c. 12-Sci/fi-c 37 74 111 222 361 500
1983- "Taking of Grizzly Grebb", Toth-a; 16 pg. miniature 2 4 6 9 12 15

TOM SAWYER COMICS
Giveaway: 1951? (Paper cover)
nn-Contains a coverless Hopalong Cassidy from 1951; other combinations known 3 6 9 14 20 25

TOO MUCH, TOO LITTLE
Federal Reserve Bank: 1989 (Reg. size)
9-13 1 3 4 6 8 10

TOP-NOTCH COMICS
MLJ Magazines/Rex Theater: 1940s (theater giveaway, sepia-c)
1-Black Hood-c; content & covers can vary 55 110 165 352 601 850

TOWN THAT FORGOT SANTA, THE
W. T. Grant Co.: 1961 (Giveaway, 24 pgs.)
nn 3 6 9 16 23 30

TOY LAND FUNNIES (See Funnies On Parade)
Eastern Color Printing Co.: 1934 (32 pgs., Hecht Co. store giveaway)
nn-Reprints Buck Rogers Sunday pages #199-201 from Famous Funnies #5. A rare variation of Funnies On Parade; same format, similar contents, same cover except for large Santa placed in center (value will be based on sale)

TOY WORLD FUNNIES (See Funnies On Parade)
Eastern Color Printing Co.: 1933 (36 pgs., slick cover, Golden Eagle and Wanamaker giveaway)
nn-Contains contents from Funnies On Parade/Century Of Comics. A rare variation of Funnies On Parade; same format, similar contents, same cover except for large Santa placed in center. A GD/VG 3.0 copy sold for $5258 in May 2016.

TRAPPED
Harvey Publications (Columbia Univ. Press): 1951 (Giveaway, soft-c, 16 pgs)
nn-Drug education comic (30,000 printed?) distributed to schools.; mentioned in **SOTI**, pgs. 256,350 2 4 6 8 10 12
NOTE: *Many copies surfaced in 1979 causing a setback in price; beware of trimmed edges, because many copies have a brittle edge.*

TRIPLE-A BASEBALL HEROES
Marvel Comics: 2007 (Minor league baseball stadium giveaway)
1-Special John Watson painted-c for Memphis, Durham and Buffalo; generic cover with team logos for each of the other 27 teams; Spider-Man, Iron Man, FF app. 3.00

TRIP TO OUTER SPACE WITH SANTA
Sales Promotions, Inc/Peoria Dry Goods: 1950s (paper-c)
nn-Comics, games & puzzles 5 10 15 22 26 30

TRIP WITH SANTA ON CHRISTMAS EVE, A
Rockford Dry Goods Co.: No date (Early 1950s) (Giveaway, 16 pgs., paper-c)
nn 5 10 15 22 26 30

TRUTH BEHIND THE TRIAL OF CARDINAL MINDSZENTY, THE (See Cardinal Mindszenty)

24 PAGES OF COMICS (No title) (Also see Pure Oil Comics, Salerno Carnival of Comics, & Vicks Comics)
Giveaway by various outlets including Sears: Late 1930s
nn-Contains strip reprints-Buck Rogers, Napoleon, Sky Roads, War on Crime

Two Faces of Communism © CACC

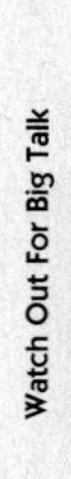
Watch Out For Big Talk

Wheaties B-1 © DIS

	GD 2.0	VG 4.0	FN 6.0	VF 8.0	VF/NM 9.0	NM- 9.2
	31	62	93	186	303	420

TWO FACES OF COMMUNISM (Also see Double Talk)
Christian Anti-Communism Crusade, Houston, Texas: 1961 (Giveaway, paper-c, 36 pgs.)
nn 20 40 60 114 182 250

2001, A SPACE ODYSSEY (Movie)
Marvel Comics Group
Howard Johnson giveaway (1968, 8pp); 6 pg. movie adaptation, 2 pg. games, puzzles; McWilliams-a 2 4 6 9 12 15

UNCLE SAM'S CHRISTMAS STORY
Promotional Publ. Co.: 1958 (Giveaway)
nn-Reprints 1956 Christmas USA 2 4 6 10 13 16

UNCLE WIGGILY COMICS
Herberger's Clothing Store: 1942 (32 pgs., paper cover)
nn-Comic panels with 6 pages of puzzles 14 28 42 80 115 150

UNKEPT PROMISE
Legion of Truth: 1949 (Giveaway, 24 pgs.)
nn-Anti-alcohol 10 20 30 58 79 100

UNTOLD LEGEND OF THE BATMAN, THE
DC Comics: 1989 (28 pgs., 6X9", limited series of cereal premiums)
1-1st & 2nd printings known; Byrne-a 2 4 6 8 10 12
2,3: 1st & 2nd printings known 1 2 3 5 7 9

UNTOUCHABLES, THE (TV)
Leaf Brands, Inc.
Topps Bubblegum premiums produced by Leaf Brands, Inc.-2-1/2x4-1/2", 8 pgs. (3 diff. issues) "The Organization, Jamaica Ginger, The Otto Frick Story (drug), 3000 Suspects, The Antidote, Mexican Stakeout, Little Egypt, Purple Gang, Bugs Moran Story, & Lily Dallas Story" 3 6 9 16 23 30

VICKS COMICS (See Pure Oil Comics, Salerno Carnival of Comics & 24 Pages of Comics)
Eastern Color Printing Co. (Vicks Chemical Co.): nd (circa 1938) (Giveaway, 68 pgs. in color)
nn-Famous Funnies-r (before #40); contains 5 pgs. Buck Rogers (4 pgs. from F.F. #15, & 1 pg. from #16) Joe Palooka, Napoleon, etc. app. 54 108 162 343 592 840
nn-16 loose, untrimmed page giveaway; paper-c; r/Famous Funnies #14; Buck Rogers, Joe Palooka app. Has either "Vicks Comics" printed on cover or only a local store name as the logo. 22 44 66 131 216 300

WALT DISNEY'S COMICS & STORIES
K.K. Publications: 1942-1963 known (7-1/3"x10-1/4", 4 pgs. in color, slick paper) (folded horizontally once or twice as mailers) (Xmas subscription offer)
1942 mailer-r/Kelly cover to WDC&S 25; 2-year subscription + two Grosset & Dunlap hardcover books (32-pages each), of Bambi and of Thumper, offered for $2.00; came in an illustrated C&S envelope with an enclosed postage paid envelope
(Rare) Mailer only 22 44 66 130 213 295
with envelopes 27 54 81 162 266 370
1947,1948 mailer 18 36 54 103 162 220
1949 mailer-A rare Barks item: Same WDC&S cover as 1942 mailer, but with art changed so that nephew is handing teacher Donald a comic book rather than an apple, as originally drawn by Kelly. The tiny, 7/8"x1-1/4" cover shown was a rejected cover by Barks that was intended for C&S 110, but was redrawn by Kelly for C&S 111. The original art has been lost and this is its only app. (Rare) 39 78 117 234 382 530
1950 mailer-P.1 r/Kelly cover to Dell Xmas Parade 1 (without title); p.2 r/Kelly cover to C&S 101 (w/o title), but with the art altered to show Donald reading C&S 122 (by Kelly); hardcover book, "Donald Duck in Bringing Up the Boys" given with a $1.00 one-year subscription; P.4 r/full Kelly Xmas cover to C&S 99 (Rare) 17 34 51 100 158 215
1952 mailer-P1 r/cover WDC&S #88 14 28 42 82 121 160
1953 mailer-P.1 r/cover Dell Xmas Parade 4 (w/o title); insides offer "Donald Duck Full Speed Ahead," a 28-page, color, 5-5/8"x6-5/8" book, not of the Story Hour series; P.4 r/full Barks C&S 148 cover (Rare) 14 28 42 82 121 160
1963 mailer-Pgs. 1,2 & 4 r/GK Xmas art; P.3 r/a 1963 C&S cover (Scarce) 6 12 18 41 76 110
NOTE: *It is assumed a different mailer was printed each Xmas for at least twenty years.*

WALT DISNEY'S COMICS & STORIES
Walt Disney Productions: 1943 (36 pgs.) (Dept. store Xmas giveaway)
nn-X-Mas-c with Donald & the Boys; Donald Duck by Jack Hannah; Thumper by Ken Hultgren 45 90 135 284 480 675

WALT DISNEY'S DONALD DUCK
Gemstone Publishing: 2006
nn-(8-1/2"x 5-1/2", Halloween giveaway) r/"A Prank Above" -Barks-s/a; Rosa-s/a 2.50
nn-(2008, 8-1/2"x 5-1/2", Halloween giveaway) "The Halloween Huckster"; Rota-s/a 2.50

WARLORD
DC Comics: (Remco Toy giveaway, 2-3/4x4")
nn 5.00

WATCH OUT FOR BIG TALK
Giveaway: 1950
nn-Dan Barry-a; about crooked politicians 7 14 21 37 46 55

WEATHER-BIRD (See Comics From..., Dick Tracy, Free Comics to You..., Super Circus & Terry and the Pirates)
International Shoe Co./Western Printing Co.: 1958 - No. 16, July, 1962 (Shoe store giveaway)
1 4 8 12 24 38 52
2-16 3 6 9 14 19 24
NOTE: *The numbers are located in the lower bottom panel, pg. 1. All feature a character called Weather-Bird.*

WEATHER BIRD COMICS (See Comics From Weather Bird)
Weather Bird Shoes: 1955 - 1958 (Giveaway)
nn-Contains a comic bound with new cover. Several combinations possible; contents determine price (40 - 60 percent of contents).

WEEKLY COMIC MAGAZINE
Fox Publications: May 12, 1940 (16 pgs.) (Others exist w/o super-heroes)
(1st Version)-8 pg. Blue Beetle story, 7 pg. Patty O'Day story; two copies known to exist. (a VF copy sold in 5/07 for $1553)
(2nd Version)-7 two-pg. adventures of Blue Beetle, Patty O'Day, Yarko, Dr. Fung, Green Mask, Spark Stevens, & Rex Dexter (two known copies, a FN sold in 2007 for $1912, other is GD)
(3rd version)-Captain Valor (only one known copy, in VG+; it sold in 2005 for $480) -
Discovered with business papers, letters and exploitation material promoting **Weekly Comic Magazine** for use by newspapers in the same manner of **The Spirit** weeklies. Interesting note: these are dated three weeks before the first Spirit comic. Letters indicate that samples may have been sent to a few newspapers. These sections were actually 15-1/2x22" pages which will fold down to an approximate 8x10" comic booklet. Other various comic sections were found with the above, but were more like the Sunday comic sections in format.

WE HIT THE JACKPOT
General Comics, Inc./American Affairs: 1947 (Promotional comic)(Paper-c)
nn 6 12 18 31 38 45

WHAT DO YOU KNOW ABOUT THIS COMICS SEAL OF APPROVAL?
No publisher listed (DC Comics Giveaway): nd (1955) (4 pgs., slick paper-c)
nn-(Rare) 103 206 309 659 1130 1600

WHAT IF THEY CALL ME "CHICKEN"?
Kiwanis International: 1970 (giveaway)
nn-Educational anti-marijuana comic 4 8 12 23 37 50

WHAT'S BEHIND THESE HEADLINES
William C. Popper Co.: 1948 (16 pgs.)
nn-Comic insert "The Plot to Steal the World" 6 12 18 31 38 45

WHAT'S IN IT FOR YOU?
Harvey Publications Inc.: (16 pgs., paper cover)
nn-National Guard recruitment 4 7 10 14 17 20

WHEATIES (Premiums)
Walt Disney Productions: 1950 & 1951 (32 titles, pocket-size, 32 pgs.)
Mailing Envelope (no art on front)(Designates sets A,B,C or D on front) 7 14 21 37 46 55

(Set A-1 to A-8, 1950)
A-1-Mickey Mouse & the Disappearing Island, A-5-Mickey Mouse, Roving Reporter each... 6 12 18 28 34 40
A-2-Grandma Duck, Homespun Detective, A-6-Li'l Bad Wolf, Forest Ranger, A-7-Goofy, Tightrope Acrobat, A-8-Pluto & the Bogus Money each... 5 10 15 24 30 35
A-3-Donald Duck & the Haunted Jewels, A-4-Donald Duck & the Giant Ape each... 8 16 24 42 54 65

(Set B-1 to B-8, 1950)
B-1-Mickey Mouse & the Pharoah's Curse, B-4-Mickey Mouse & the Mystery Sea Monster each... 6 12 18 31 38 45
B-2-Pluto, Canine Cowpoke, B-5-Li'l Bad Wolf in the Hollow Tree Hideout, B-7-Goofy & the Gangsters each... 5 10 15 24 30 35
B-3-Donald Duck & the Buccaneers, B-6-Donald Duck,Trail Blazer, B-8 Donald Duck, Klondike Kid each... 8 16 24 42 54 65

(Set C-1 to C-8, 1951)
C-1-Donald Duck & the Inca Idol, C-5-Donald Duck in the Lost Lakes, C-8-Donald Duck Deep-Sea Diver each... 8 16 24 42 54 65
C-2-Mickey Mouse & the Magic Mountain, C-6-Mickey Mouse & the Stagecoach Bandits each... 6 12 18 31 38 45
C-3-Li'l Bad Wolf, Fire Fighter, C-4-Gus & Jaq Save the Ship, C-7-Goofy, Big Game Hunter each... 5 10 15 24 30 35

(Set D-1 to D-8, 1951)
D-1-Donald Duck in Indian Country, D-5-Donald Duck, Mighty Mystic each... 8 16 24 42 54 65

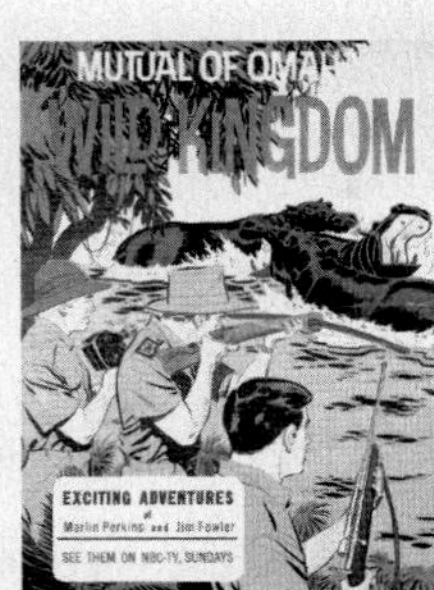
Wild Kingdom nn © WEST

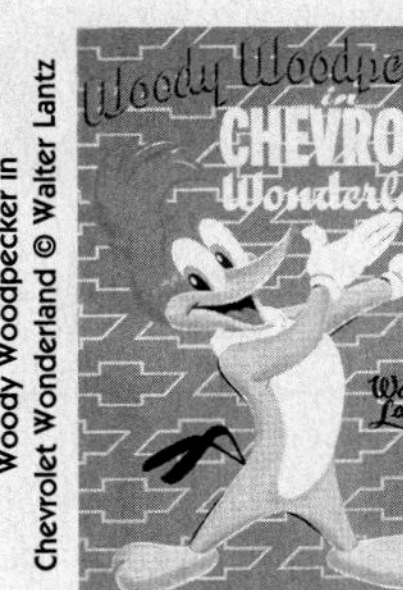
Woody Woodpecker in Chevrolet Wonderland © Walter Lantz

X2 Presents The Ultimate X-Men #2 © MAR

	GD 2.0	VG 4.0	FN 6.0	VF 8.0	VF/NM 9.0	NM- 9.2
D-2-Mickey Mouse and the Abandoned Mine, D-6-Mickey Mouse & the Medicine Man each...	6	12	18	31	38	45
D-3-Pluto & the Mysterious Package, D-4-Bre'r Rabbit's Sunken Treasure, D-7-Li'l Bad Wolf and the Secret of the Woods, D-8-Minnie Mouse, Girl Explorer each...	5	10	15	24	30	35

NOTE: *Some copies lack the Wheaties ad.*

WHEEL OF PROGRESS, THE
Assoc. of American Railroads: Oct, 1957 (16 pgs.)

	GD 2.0	VG 4.0	FN 6.0	VF 8.0	VF/NM 9.0	NM- 9.2
nn-Bill Bunce	6	12	18	28	34	40

WHIZ COMICS (Formerly Flash Comics & Thrill Comics #1)
Fawcett Publications

	GD 2.0	VG 4.0	FN 6.0	VF 8.0	VF/NM 9.0	NM- 9.2
Wheaties Giveaway(1946, Miniature, 6-1/2x8-1/4", 32 pgs.); all copies were taped at each corner to a box of Wheaties and are never found in very fine or mint condition; "Capt. Marvel & the Water Thieves", plus Golden Arrow, Ibis, Crime Smasher stories	80	160	400	–	–	–

WILD KINGDOM (TV) (Mutual of Omaha's...)
Western Printing Co.: 1965, 1966 (Giveaway, regular size, slick-c, 16 pgs.)

	GD 2.0	VG 4.0	FN 6.0	VF 8.0	VF/NM 9.0	NM- 9.2
nn-Front & back-c are different on 1966 edition	2	4	6	9	12	15

WISCO/KLARER COMIC BOOK (Miniature)
Marvel Comics/Vital Publ./Fawcett Publ.: 1948 - 1964 (3-1/2x6-3/4", 24 pgs.)
Given away by Wisco "99" Service Stations, Carnation Malted Milk, Klarer Health Wieners, Fleers Dubble Bubble Gum, Rodeo All-Meat Wieners, Perfect Potato Chips, & others; see ad in Tom Mix #21

	GD 2.0	VG 4.0	FN 6.0	VF 8.0	VF/NM 9.0	NM- 9.2
Blackstone & the Gold Medal Mystery (1948)	8	16	24	42	54	65
Blackstone "Solves the Sealed Vault Mystery" (1950)	8	16	24	42	54	65
Blaze Carson in "The Sheriff Shoots It Out" (1950)	8	16	24	42	54	65
Captain Marvel & Billy's Big Game (r/Capt. Marvel Adv. #76)	24	48	72	144	237	330
(Prices vary widely on this book)						
China Boy in "A Trip to the Zoo" #10 (1948)	5	10	15	24	30	35
Indoors-Outdoors Game Book	4	7	10	14	17	20
Jim Solar Space Sheriff in "Battle for Mars", "Between Two Worlds", "Conquers Outer Space", "The Creatures on the Comet", "Defeats the Moon Missile Men", "Encounter Creatures on Comet", "Meet the Jupiter Jumpers", "Meets the Man From Mars", "On Traffic Duty", "Outlaws of the Spaceways", "Pirates of the Planet X", "Protects Space Lanes", "Raiders From the Sun", "Ring Around Saturn", "Robots of Rhea", "The Sky Ruby", "Spacetts of the Sky", "Spidermen of Venus", "Trouble on Mercury"	7	14	21	35	43	50
Johnny Starboard & the Underseas Pirates (1948)	5	10	15	22	26	30
Kid Colt in "He Lived by His Guns" (1950)	8	16	24	44	57	70
Little Aspirin as the "Crook Catcher" #2 (1950)	4	7	10	14	17	20
Little Aspirin in "Naughty But Nice" #6 (1950)	4	7	10	14	17	20
Return of the Black Phantom (not M.E. character)(Roy Dare)(1948)	6	12	18	28	34	40
Secrets of Magic	4	8	11	16	19	22
Slim Morgan "Brings Justice to Mesa City" #3	4	8	11	16	19	22
Super Rabbit(1950)-Cuts Red Tape, Stops Crime Wave!	9	18	27	50	65	80
Tex Farnum, Frontiersman (1948)	5	10	15	22	26	30
Tex Taylor in "Draw or Die, Cowpoke!" (1950)	7	14	21	35	43	50
Tex Taylor in "An Exciting Adventure at the Gold Mine" (1950)	6	12	18	31	38	45
Wacky Quacky in "All-Aboard"	3	6	8	12	14	16
When School Is Out	3	6	8	12	14	16
Willie in a "Comic-Comic Book Fall" #1	4	8	11	16	19	22
Wonder Duck "An Adventure at the Rodeo of the Fearless Quacker!" (1950)	9	18	27	47	61	75

Rare uncut version of three; includes Capt. Marvel, Tex Farnum, Black Phantom (A VG copy sold in Sept. 2015 for $147)
Rare uncut version of three; includes China Boy, Blackstone, Johnny Starboard & the Underseas Pirates (A FN/VF copy sold in Sept. 2015 for $137)
Rare uncut version of three; all Jim Solar (A VG copy sold in Sept. 2015 for $79)
Rare uncut version of three; includes Willie in a "Comic-Comic Book Fall", Little Aspirin #2, Slim Morgan Brings Justice to Mesa City (a VF/FN copy sold for $54 in Nov. 2007)

WIZARD OF OZ
MGM: 1967 (small size)

	GD 2.0	VG 4.0	FN 6.0	VF 8.0	VF/NM 9.0	NM- 9.2
"Dorothy and Friends Visit Oz", "Dorothy Meets the Wizard", "The Tin Woodsman Saves Dorothy" each...	2	4	6	8	10	12

WOLVERINE
Marvel Comics

	GD 2.0	VG 4.0	FN 6.0	VF 8.0	VF/NM 9.0	NM- 9.2
145-(1999 Nabisco mail-in offer) Sienkiewicz-c	10	20	30	64	132	200
...Son of Canada (4/01, ed. of 65,000) Spider-Man & The Hulk app.; Lim-a						3.00

WOMAN OF THE PROMISE, THE
Catechetical Guild: 1950 (General Distr.) (Paper cover, 32 pgs.)

	GD 2.0	VG 4.0	FN 6.0	VF 8.0	VF/NM 9.0	NM- 9.2
nn	6	12	18	28	34	40

WONDER BOOK OF RUBBER
B.F. Goodrich: 1947 (Promo giveaway

	GD 2.0	VG 4.0	FN 6.0	VF 8.0	VF/NM 9.0	NM- 9.2
nn	4	8	12	18	22	25

WONDERFUL WORLD OF DUCKS (See Golden Picture Story Book)
Colgate Palmolive Co.: 1975

	GD 2.0	VG 4.0	FN 6.0	VF 8.0	VF/NM 9.0	NM- 9.2
1-Mostly-r	1	3	4	6	8	10

WONDER WOMAN
DC Comics: 1977

	GD 2.0	VG 4.0	FN 6.0	VF 8.0	VF/NM 9.0	NM- 9.2
Pizza Hut Giveaways (12/77)-Reprints #60,62	2	4	6	9	13	16
... - The Minotaur (1981, General Foods giveaway, 8 pages, 3-1/2 x 6-3/4", oblong)	2	4	6	13	18	22

WONDER WORKER OF PERU
Catechetical Guild: No date (5x7", 16 pgs., B&W, giveaway)

	GD 2.0	VG 4.0	FN 6.0	VF 8.0	VF/NM 9.0	NM- 9.2
nn	6	12	18	28	34	40

WOODY WOODPECKER
Dell Publishing Co.

	GD 2.0	VG 4.0	FN 6.0	VF 8.0	VF/NM 9.0	NM- 9.2
Clover Stamp-Newspaper Boy Contest('56)-9 pg. story-(Giveaway)	8	16	24	40	50	60
In Chevrolet Wonderland(1954-Giveaway)(Western Publ.)-20 pgs., full story line; Chilly Willy app.	18	36	54	105	165	225
...Meets Scotty MacTape(1953-Scotch Tape giveaway)-16 pgs., full size	18	36	54	105	165	225

WOOLWORTH'S CHRISTMAS STORY BOOK
Promotional Publ. Co.(Western Printing Co.): 1952 - 1954 (16 pgs., paper-c) (See Jolly Christmas Book)

	GD 2.0	VG 4.0	FN 6.0	VF 8.0	VF/NM 9.0	NM- 9.2
nn: 1952 issue-Marv Levy c/a	7	14	21	35	43	50

WOOLWORTH'S HAPPY TIME CHRISTMAS BOOK
F. W. Woolworth Co. (Western Printing Co.): 1952 (Christmas giveaway)

	GD 2.0	VG 4.0	FN 6.0	VF 8.0	VF/NM 9.0	NM- 9.2
nn-36 pgs.	6	12	18	31	38	45

WORLD'S FINEST COMICS
National Periodical Publ./DC Comics

	GD 2.0	VG 4.0	FN 6.0	VF 8.0	VF/NM 9.0	NM- 9.2
Giveaway (c. 1944-45, 8 pgs., in color, paper-c)-Johnny Everyman-r/World's Finest	21	42	63	124	202	280
Giveaway (c. 1949, 8 pgs., in color, paper-c)- "Make Way For Youth" r/World's Finest; based on film of same name	19	38	57	111	176	240
#176, #179- Best Western reprint edition (1997)						3.00

WORLD'S GREATEST SUPER HEROES
DC Comics (Nutra Comics) (Child Vitamins, Inc.): 1977 (Giveaway, 3-3/4x3-3/4", 24 pgs.)

	GD 2.0	VG 4.0	FN 6.0	VF 8.0	VF/NM 9.0	NM- 9.2
nn-Batman & Robin app.; health tips	2	4	6	10	14	18

WYOMING THE COWBOY STATE
1954 (Giveaway, slick-c)

	GD 2.0	VG 4.0	FN 6.0	VF 8.0	VF/NM 9.0	NM- 9.2
nn	5	10	15	22	26	30

XMAS FUNNIES
Kinney Shoes: No date (Giveaway, paper cover, 36 pgs.?)

	GD 2.0	VG 4.0	FN 6.0	VF 8.0	VF/NM 9.0	NM- 9.2
Contains 1933 color strip-r; Mutt & Jeff, etc.	30	60	90	177	289	400

X-MEN THE MOVIE
Marvel Comics/Toys R' Us: 2000

	GD 2.0	VG 4.0	FN 6.0	VF 8.0	VF/NM 9.0	NM- 9.2
Special Movie Prequel Edition						5.00

X2 PRESENTS THE ULTIMATE X-MEN #2
Marvel Comics/New York Post: July, 2003

	GD 2.0	VG 4.0	FN 6.0	VF 8.0	VF/NM 9.0	NM- 9.2
Reprint distributed inside issue of the New York Post						2.50

YALTA TO KOREA (Also see Korea My Home)
M. Phillip Corp. (Republican National Committee): 1952 (Giveaway, paper-c)

	GD 2.0	VG 4.0	FN 6.0	VF 8.0	VF/NM 9.0	NM- 9.2
nn-(8 pgs.)-Anti-communist propaganda book	18	36	54	105	165	225

YOGI BEAR (TV)
Dell Publishing Co.

	GD 2.0	VG 4.0	FN 6.0	VF 8.0	VF/NM 9.0	NM- 9.2
Giveaway ('84, '86)-City of Los Angeles, "Creative First Aid" & "Earthquake Preparedness for Children"	1	2	3	4	5	7

YOUR TRIP TO NEWSPAPERLAND
Philadelphia Evening Bulletin (Printed by Harvey Press): June, 1955 (14x11-1/2", 12 pgs.)

	GD 2.0	VG 4.0	FN 6.0	VF 8.0	VF/NM 9.0	NM- 9.2
nn-Joe Palooka takes kids on newspaper tour	6	12	18	27	33	38

YOUR VOTE IS VITAL!
Harvey Publications Inc.: 1952 (5" x 7", 16 pgs., paper cover)

	GD 2.0	VG 4.0	FN 6.0	VF 8.0	VF/NM 9.0	NM- 9.2
nn-The importance of voting	5	10	14	20	24	28

THE PIONEER AGE

The American Comic Book: 1500s-1828

For the last few years, we have featured a tremendous article by noted historian and collector Eric C. Caren on the foundations of what we now call "The Pioneer Age" of comics. We look forward to a new article on this significant topic in a future edition of *The Overstreet Comic Book Price Guide*. In the meantime, should you need it, Caren's article may be found in the 35th through 39th editions.

That said, even with the space constraints in this edition of the *Guide*, we could not possibly exclude reference to these incredible, formative works.

German broadsheet, dated 1569.

Why are these illustrations and sequences of illustrations important to the comic books of today?

The Murder of King Henry III (1589).

Quite frankly, because we can see in them the very building blocks of the comic art form.

The shooting of the Italian Concini (1617).

Over the course of just a few hundred years, we the evolution of narration, word balloons, panel-to-panel progression of story, and so much more. If these stories aren't developed first, how would be every have reached the point that that *The Adventures of Mr. Obadiah Oldbuck* could have come along in 1842?

As the investigation of comic book history has blown away the notion that comic books were a 20 century invention, it hasn't been easy to convince some, even with the clear, linear progression of the artful melding of illustration and words.

"Want to avoid an argument in social discourse? Steer clear of politics and religion. In the latter category, the most controversial subject is human evolution. Collectors can become just as squeamish when you start messing with the evolution of a particular collectible," Eric Caren wrote in his article. "In most cases, the origin of a particular comic character will be universally agreed upon, but try tackling the origin of printed comics and you are asking for trouble."

"The Bubblers Medley" (1720).

"Join, or Die" from the Pennsylvania Gazette*, May 9, 1754.*

"Amusement for John Bull..." from The European Magazine *(1783).*

But the evidence is there for any who choose to look. Before the original comics of the Golden Age, there were comic strip reprints collected in comic book form. The practice dated back decades earlier, of course, but coalesced into the current form when the realities of the Great Depression spawned the modern incarnation of the comic book and its immediate cousin, the Big Little Book.

Everything that came later, though, did so because the acceptance of the visual language had already been worked out. Before Spider-Man and the Hulk, before Superman and Batman, before the Yellow Kid, Little Nemo, and the Brownies, cartoonists and editorial illustrators were working out how to tell a story or simply convey their ideas in this new artform.

Without this sort of work, without these pioneers, we simply wouldn't be where we are today.

CONNECTICUT MIRROR.

Cartoons satirizing Napoleon on the front page of the Connecticut Mirror*, dated January 7, 1811.*

Another Napoleon cartoon, this time dubbing him "The Corsican Munchausen," from the London Strand*, December 4, 1813.*

"A Consultation at the Medical Board" from The Pasquin or General Satirist *(1821)*.

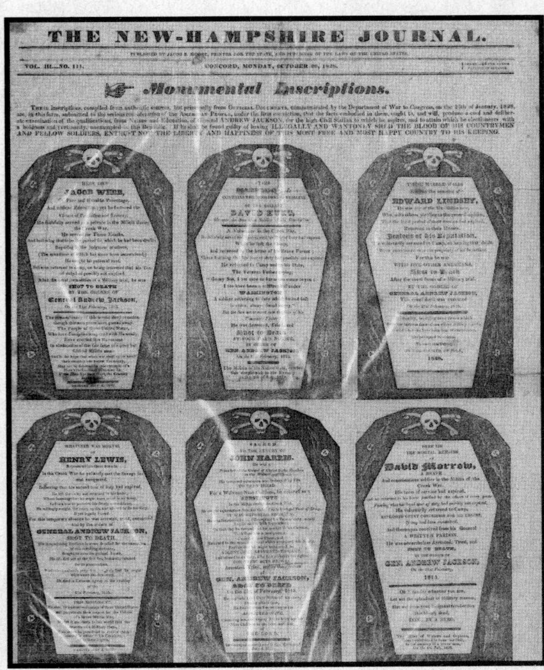

THE NEW-HAMPSHIRE JOURNAL.

CONCORD, MONDAY, OCTOBER 20, 1828.

Monumental Inscriptions.

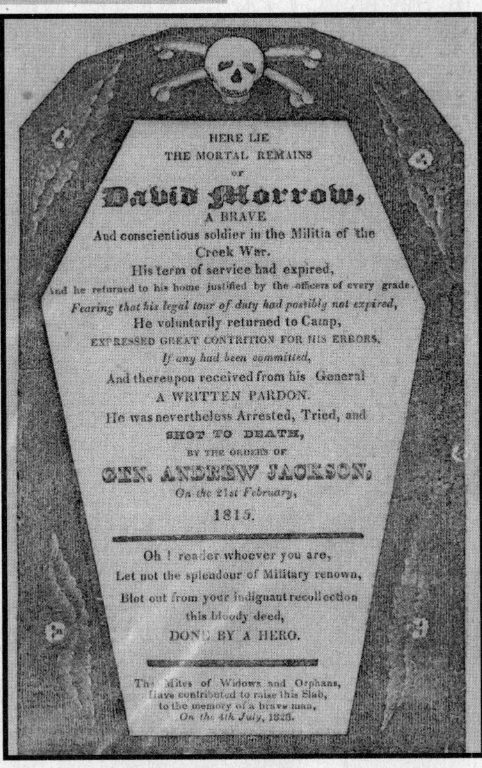

HERE LIE
THE MORTAL REMAINS
OF
David Morrow,
A BRAVE
And conscientious soldier in the Militia of the
Creek War.
His term of service had expired,
and he returned to his home justified by the officers of every grade.
Fearing that his legal tour of duty had possibly not expired,
He voluntarily returned to Camp,
EXPRESSED GREAT CONTRITION FOR HIS ERRORS,
If any had been committed,
And thereupon received from his General
A WRITTEN PARDON.
He was nevertheless Arrested, Tried, and
SHOT TO DEATH,
BY THE ORDERS OF
GEN. ANDREW JACKSON,
On the 21st February,
1815.

Oh! reader whoever you are,
Let not the splendour of Military renown,
Blot out from your indignant recollection
this bloody deed,
DONE BY A HERO.

The Mites of Widows and Orphans,
Have contributed to raise this Slab,
to the memory of a brave man,
On the 4th July, 1828.

Above left, the front page of The New Hampshire Journal, *dated October 20, 1828, with multiple tombstone "panels." To the right is a detail of the bottom right tombstone.*

THE VICTORIAN AGE

Comic Strips and Books: 1646-1900

A Concise History & Price Index Of The Field As Of 2017

ORIGINS OF EARLY AMERICAN COMIC STRIPS BEFORE THE YELLOW KID

by Robert Lee Beerbohm, Richard Samuel West & Richard D. Olson, PhD ©2017

(This article was originally created by Doug Wheeler, Robert Beerbohm and Richard D. Olson, PhD for CBPG #32 and continues to be revised annually by the current authors.) We welcome any and all corrections and additions. Special Thanks This Installment To Leonardo De Sa, Terrence Keegen, Gabriel Laderman and Joe Rainone.

Left: "The Burning of Mr. John Rogers," 1646 is the earliest-known North American cartoon printed on paper printed in the earliest children's primer in America.

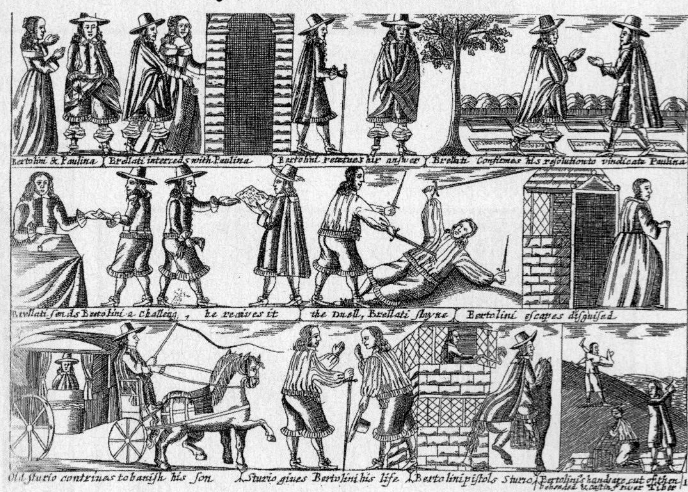

"God's Revenge For Murder" By John Reynolds, unknown artist, 1656. Earliest-known sequential comic "panel" strip created in the English language.

Left: From his pamphlet Plain Truth 1747 containing Ben Franklin's earliest-known cartoon titled "Heaven Helps Only Those Who Help Themselves" depicting ancient "super hero" Hercules in the upper right corner. Middle: "A Warm Place - Hell", one of two images definitely known to be drawn and engraved by Paul Revere, 1768. Word balloons had wide-spread usage in many cartoons in the 1700s. Right: The Tables Turned by James Gillray, 1797 commenting on an "invasion" of England by 1400 French convicts. The use of word balloons was wide spread in many parts of the world long before the Yellow Kid's parrot uttered a few words in 1896.

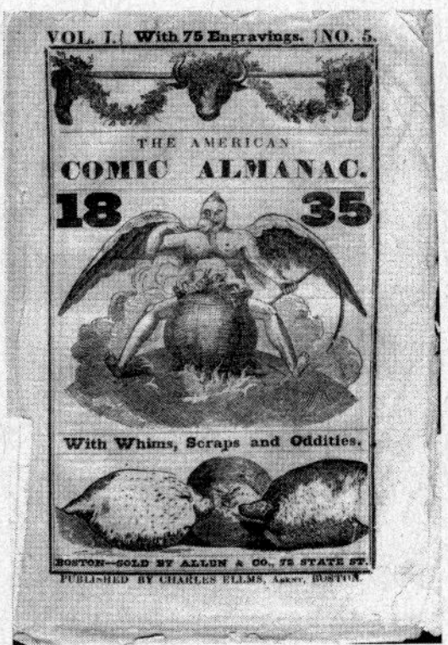

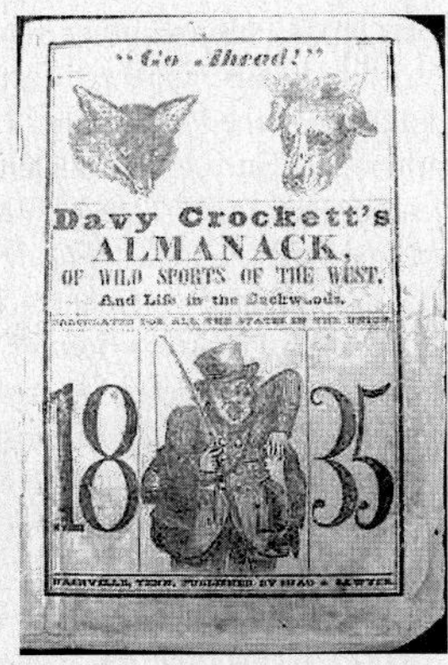

The Comic Almanac(k) debuted in America in 1831 with the earliest-known titles starting heavy with humor and sporting crude woodcut single panel cartoons. Ellm's American Comic Almanac was one of the first. By 1835 Davy Crockett, one of the nation's earliest national folk heroes, began issuing his own version. In the late 1840s the Comic Almanac(k)s began to offer tall-tale sequential comic strips which became somewhat commonplace in the 1850s, fueled by the advent of the California Gold Rush. They were instrumental in the development of the American comic strip and we will be reporting more new finds after further research into American folklore.

We have a lot of new discoveries to share with you again this year as amply evident in the price index which follows this year's history lesson. A quantum leap has finally been achieved in the area of introducing the comic book collecting world to *American Comic Almanac(k)s* as well as a huge multitude of American humor periodicals, many of which contained sequential comic strips.

This Victorian Era section is devoted to comic strips and books published during the years the United States expanded across the North American continent, fought a Civil War, shifted from an agrarian to an industrial society, "welcomed" waves of immigrants, and struggled over race, class, religion, temperance, and suffrage - and all of it depicted and satirized by generations of mostly now long-forgotten cartoonists. The social attitudes, beliefs, and conventions of 19th century America, the good as well as the bad, are to be found in abundance. Perhaps the first question to pop into most readers' minds will be, "What, beyond the happenstance of publication date, are Victorian Era comics?"

There has been a long slow-motion evolution of the comic strip which was not invented in America, contrary to many previous history books on the subject. One must examine many aspects of concurrent popular culture. The main aspect that we believe most distinguishes Victorian Era comic strips from those of later eras was the extremely rare use of word balloons within sequential (multi-picture) comic stories. When word balloons were used, it was nearly always within single-panel cartoons. On the occasions when they appeared inside a strip, with very few exceptions, the ballooned dialogue was inconsequential. Nineteenth-century comics tended to place both narration and dialogue beneath comic panels rather than within the panel's borders as they were thought by many to interfere with the art. Many of these comics are to the word balloon-strewn post-Yellow Kid comics of the 20th Century as silent movies are to the later "talkies." Just as sound changed how stories were structured on film, so too did comic strips change when the words were moved from beneath panels to inside them, and dialogue rather than narration drove the story in conjunction with the pictures.

The Victorian Era of actual comic strip books began on different dates in different nations, depending on when the first publication of a sequential comic book on their soil is known to have occurred. For the U.S. this happened when the American literary periodical *Brother Jonathan* printed the 40-page, 195-panel graphic novel *The Adventures of Mr. Obadiah Oldbuck* as a special extra dated September 14, 1842. Almost six decades later, America's Victorian comics came to their end, replaced by the onslaught of Platinum Age books reprinting newspaper strips from Bennett, Hearst, and Pulitzer Sunday comic sections, among many others.

There is considerable overlap between Victorian Era and Platinum Age comic books and strips. Those publications that continued from one century into the next, such as *Puck*, *Judge*, and *Life*, have their pre-1900 issues listed within the Victorian Age section, while their post-1899 issues can be found inside the Platinum Age. Some non-sequential (i.e., single-panel) American comic items existing prior to 1842 are also listed herein, going back to 1795. These belong to what could tentatively be called the Age of Caricature (1770s through 1830s). This was a fertile period for the art in England, when Gillray and Rowlandson, and, later, Cruikshank, Heath, and Seymour were that nation's top cartoonists. During the same period in the U.S., there were no artists who made their living as caricaturists, though William Charles, printer and engraver, did produce about two dozen spirited cartoon broadsides from 1805 to 1820, the most important ones concerning events of the War of 1812.

In addition, one can trace origins of American comic books to the humorous Comic Almanacs which began in earnest in the early 1830s.

The earliest known cartoon-like woodcut printed on paper in North America was in a Puritan children's book first published in 1646. Titled simply *The Burning of Mr. John Rogers*, it showed in flaming graphic detail what happens to those who stray from the flock and have to be burned at the stake. Dr. Wertham would have had a field day with that one!

Cartoon broadsides and other single panel images, often using word balloons, appeared from pre-Revolution days through the end of the 19th Century. The earliest known attributed cartoon, designed by the ubiquitous Benjamin Franklin, was "Heaven Helps Only Those Who Help Themselves," which first appeared in his pamphlet *Plain Truth* in 1747.

The most popularly remembered 18th-Century American cartoons are likely Franklin's *"Join or Die"* in 1754, representing the American Colonies as severed snake parts, and *"The Bloody Massacre Perpetrated in King Street"* -- Paul Revere's 1770 depiction of the Boston Massacre, which he pirated from the earlier Henry Pelham broadsheet cartoon *"The Fruits of Arbitrary Power."*

In September 1826, John Warner Barber, New Haven, Ct. (1798-1885) designed and self-published the broadside *The Drunkard's Progress, Or The Direct Road to Poverty, Wretchedness and Ruin* showing in four stages sequentially "The Morning Dram" which is "The Beginning of Sorrow, " "The Grog Shop" with its "Bad Company," "The Confirmed Drunkard" in a state of "Beastly Intoxication," and the "Concluding Scene" with the family being driven off to the alms house. It is an interesting set of cuts, faintly reminiscent of Hogarth. Barber began his career in 1819, age 21, engraving on wood. He devoted most of his career to the multitude of art chores associated with book production. As late as 1870 he was issuing *Barber's Temperance Tracts,* which built upon his 1826 original plus four panels showing the positive effects of living without alcohol.

The first American whose fame was based primarily on his cartoons appears to be David Claypoole Johnston (1798-1865). Johnston provided illustrations for various almanacs, books, and periodicals, including the masthead for *Brother Jonathans*. Most notable of Johnston's comics work was his nine-issue series *Scraps*, which he self-published from 1828 to 1849. This series was highly influenced by George Cruikshank's series *Scraps and Sketches*, which first appeared in 1827. Because of the resemblance, Johnston became known in his day as "the American Cruikshank." Each issue of Johnston's *Scraps* consists of four large folio-sized pages, printed on one side, with nine to twelve single-panel cartoons per page, and each page often organized around a theme. Also popular was his comic album Outlines Illustrative of the Journal of F****** A*** K***** (1835), which parodied passages from the journal of recently published observations on America by British actress Fanny Kemble.

Johnston, himself a failed actor, had an interest in the theater his entire career. In addition to producing a number of prints depicting American actors in famous roles, he collaborated with actor Henry J. Finn to produce the 1831 *(American) Comic Annual*, with Finn as Editor and Johnston as artist, published by Richardson, Lord and Holbrook, Boston. It featured almost 30 full-page Johnston-designed copper engravings and woodcuts. Also that year, Finn solo produced *Finn's Comic Sketch Book*, a twelve-page album similar to Johnston's *Scraps* with upwards of half a dozen single-panel cartoons per page. It was published by Peabody and Co, of New York in business from 1831-1843. (Finn died tragically in a steamboat accident Jan. 13, 1840.)

Perhaps Johnston's most interesting contribution to the history of the comic strip in American came in 1837, when he produced the sequential comic broadside, *Illustrations of the Adventures & Achievements of the Renowned Don Quixote & his Doughty Squire Sancho Panza* (27.4 x 30.4 cm). This blank-reverse engraved print was an elaborate twelve-panel satire of the Andrew Jackson-Van Buren administration. It likely sold for 25 cents, seeing distribution in Boston, New York and Philadelphia. Much later, in 1863, Johnston drew another sequential comic broadside, *The House the Jeff Built* (27.5 x 36.7 cm), a bitter indictment of Jefferson Davis and the Southern slavocracy.

In July 1839, Wilson and Company, a newly formed New York printing firm, began publishing a mammoth newspaper by the name of *Brother Jonathan*. The publisher, J. Gregg Wilson had employed the newspaper format for *Brother Jonathan* to circumvent the higher postage rates imposed on magazines, but *Brother Jonathan* was a newspaper in format only -- it contained not a shred of news, instead specializing in serialized fiction, some of it written by Americans but most of it pirated from foreign sources. Despite the cost savings, the mammoth format had its limitations; when opened it measured a whopping three feet by four feet. So, once *Brother Jonathan* was an established success, Wilson and Day began in January 1841 the simultaneous publication of a magazine-sized quarto edition of *Brother Jonathan* that reprinted the contents of the mammoth edition.

Later that same year, to capitalize on the name recognition of their successful twin publications, Wilson and Company started issuing book-length *Brother Jonathan Extras* in the same format as the quarto magazine. These reprints are counted among the earliest paperback books in America. Most of the *Extra* numbers were pirated European novels. For example their eighth extra was the first American printing of a Charles Dickens novel. But for their ninth *Extra*, they did something no American publisher had ever done before -- they pirated a graphic novel, Rodolphe Töpffer's *The Adventures of Mr. Obadiah Oldbuck*. By reformatting *Oldbuck* from its original small oblong strip design to fit *Brother Jonathan's* standard quarto format Wilson and Company inadvertently made this edition (alone) of *Obadiah Oldbuck* resemble a modern comic book. *Oldbuck's* arrival on the shores of the New World would directly inspire a wave of American imitators. [*This first Wilson printing of Oldbuck from 1842 was reprinted in same-size limited edition facsimile by the Naples Comicon in 2003. An English translation by Leonardo De Sá of Töpffer's original draft is at leonardo desa.interdinamica. net/comics/lds/*]

Even though in 1904 (in its September 3 edition), *The New York Times* accurately identified the *Brother Jonathan Extra* as the first American comic book as well as Wilson & Co. utilizing Tilt & Bougue's original printing plates as well as still being in print for sale in New York at such a late date, Töpffer has already been largely forgotten in the New World. It is high time Töpffer received credit long overdue as the inventor of the modern comic strip, laying previously long-held myths to rest.

Töpffer (1799-1846) was a playwright, novelist, artist, and teacher from Geneva, Switzerland, who in 1827 had begun producing what he called "picture novels," sharing them with his friends and students. His earliest editions were self-published via lithography on transfer paper as they use the word "autographie" in their imprints. The earliest printers were J. Freydig, Frutiger (1830s) and Schmidt (1840s). These first sequential comic books, scripted in Töpffer's native French language, found their way to Paris and became an instant hit. According to Gombrich in *Art and Illusion* (1960), "Töpffer recognized that he could rely on the reader to supplement from their own lives what was omitted between the panels. This is crucial in the development of the sequential comic strip."

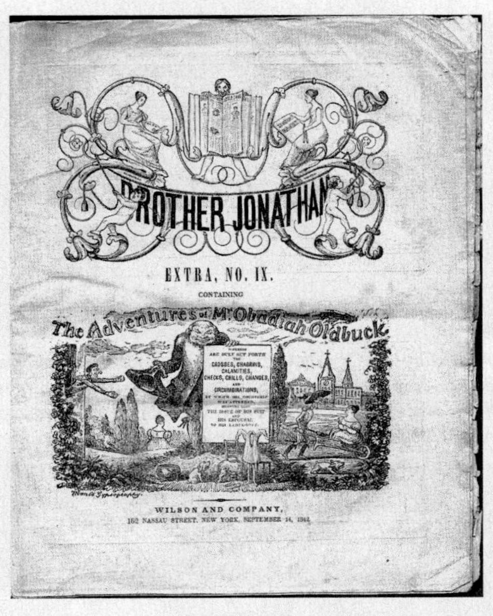

Cover to the subscriber version of the earliest-known sequential comic book published in America, The Adventures of Mr. Obadiah Oldbuck, Sept. 1842, Wilson & Co. New York, originally conceived in 1828 in Geneva Switzerland by creator Rodolphe Töpffer.

The demand for his comic books soon outstripped the supply, and pirated editions, redrawn by others, were created by Parisian publisher Aubert to capitalize on this. In a world where international copyright conventions did not exist, this was perfectly legal, if morally questionable. Thus, in 1841, London publisher Tilt and Bogue commissioned George Cruikshank to create an English version of Töpffer's *Les Amours de M. Vieux Bois* by pirating Aubert's pirated edition of the Geneva original.

This English translation, co-financed by George Cruikshank himself, sported a new cover page by George's brother Robert, based on a montage of Töpffer's scenes. Confirmation of this fact came when George Cruikshank's personal copy surfaced in auction recently with the inscription "Copied from a French book by my Brother Robert" above the title page with the same scene. This is the translation that was reprinted by America's Wilson and Company as *The Adventures of Mr. Obadiah Oldbuck* utilizing the original Tilt and Bogue printing plates.

Tilt and Bogue followed up their success by translating into English two additional stories of Töpffer's seven published graphic novels: *Beau Ogleby*, circa 1843 (originally Histoire de M. Jabot), and *Bachelor Butterfly* two years later (from *Histoire de M. Cryptogame)*. David Bogue also published picture-story strip books by John Leighton using the pseudonym Luke Limner. He wrote and drew beautiful comic books titled *London Out of Town or The Adventures of the Browns At The Seaside; Comic Art-Manufactures; and The Ancient Story of the Old Dame and Her Pig* starting in 1847, but none of these seem to have ever been republished in America. They follow a definite Töpffer influence. This growing body of comic book production was made easier by the spreading understanding of transfer paper lithography, otherwise the panels would have had to have been drawn and lettered mirror reverse. Gombrich referred to Töpffer's comic books as "the innocent ancestors of today's manufactured dreams... everywhere in these countless episodes of almost surrealist inconsequence we find a mastery of physiognomic characterization which sets the standard for such influential humorous draftsmen in the 19th century as Wilhelm Busch in Germany."

A Register of The New York City Book Trades 1821-1842 by Sidney F. & Elizabeth Stege12, Huttner (The Bibliographical Society of America, NYC, 1993) mentions Benjamin H. Day bought into *Brother Jonathan*'s publisher, Wilson and Company, in this year, becoming at some point an equal partner with owner J. Gregg Wilson. The Register lists them both as publishers of *Brother Jonathan* at the same address of 162 Nassau Street. Other historical artifacts state Day eventually became sole-owner and publisher. Exactly when has not yet been determined, though we have figured out with certainly before 1850 .

This is the same Benjamin H. Day who started the first successful penny newspaper in 1833, *The (New York) Sun*, transforming it in four short years into the largest circulation daily in the world at that time. He sold out his ownership of the Sun to his brother-in-law during the financial "panic" of 1837, a mistake he regretted the rest of his life. He re-emerged heavily involved in *Brother Jonathan* definitely by 1840 and as a partner by 1841. *Brother Jonathan's* offices were right next door to Tamany Hall. (See the first 20 minutes of the 2002 movie *Gangs of New York* to visualize the period atmosphere and their customer base.) According to *The Brothers Harper* by Eugene Exmen (Harper & Row, 1965), on page 125, "*Brother Jonathan...* offered in its weekly edition and also in special supplements very cheap reprints of English novels. In effect, it began a price-cutting war against the older established 'pirates' among the book publishers..." Day, it appears, had found the perfect project on which to build a new empire.

Desirous of repeating the success they had with *Obadiah Oldbuck*, Wilson and Company published the first American edition of *Bachelor Butterfly* in 1846. Three years later, they reformatted *Obadiah Oldbuck* back into its original British shape using lithography, dropping a handful of comic panels and altering the text to hide these deletions. Soon thereafter, they published other comic books for a steadily growing market that they had helped to stimulate. In recognition of their significant role in the dissemination of sequential comics, Wilson and Company deserve to be remembered as the first comic book publisher in America.

The Adventures of Obadiah Oldbuck, rare newly discovered 4th edition from mid 1850s. Says now "Published at Brother Jonathan Offices." Art & Story now accredited to the pseudonym "Timothy Crayon" - see Peter Piper ad previous page.

***The Strange and Wonderful Adventures of Bachelor Butterfly** by Rodolphe Töpffer (New York, 1846) was America's 3rd comic book; Wilson & Company's second comic book, this time out staying with the original European format.*

Back in Europe, perhaps inspired by his involvement with Töpffer's *Obadiah Oldbuck*, George Cruikshank soon created several sequential comic books of his own. These too found their way to America. *The Bachelor's Own Book*, published first in Britain in 1844, became the second known U.S. published sequential comic book when it was reprinted by Burgess, Stringer and Company the following year. Next was Cruikshank's masterpiece *The Bottle*, the Hogarthian-style tale of a man whose addiction to alcohol brings himself and his family to ruin. After debuting in London in 1847, it was reprinted the same year in a British-American co-publication between David Bogue and Americans Wiley and Putnam. Both printings were in huge folio form, available in either black and white or professionally hand-tinted versions. In 1848, the story saw American print again, this time in smaller form, placed at the front of the otherwise prose volume *Temperance Tales; Or, Six Nights with the Washing-tonians*. It continued to be reprinted by a variety of publishers into the early 20th Century. *The Bottle* was even reproduced onto painted glass slides and then projected by magic lantern onto a screen for the moral edification of temperance audiences. *The Drunkard's Children, Cruikshank's sequel to The Bottle*, was issued July 1, 1848 as a British-American-Australian co-publishing venture, but was less successful, and had not nearly as many reprints.

The most clearly sequential, as well as fun, of George Cruikshank's comic books was *The Tooth-Ache*, first issued in London in 1849. It was reprinted in America later that same year by Philadelphia map maker J.L. Smith. An additional concurrent version was also issued from Boston.

When closed, this booklet appears an unassuming 5-1/4 inches tall by 3-1/4 inches wide. Its striking feature is that the book folds open accordion style, stretching the entire 43-panel story along one single strip of paper, which when fully extended is seven feet, three inches long! *The Tooth-Ache* was issued in both black and white and professionally hand-colored editions. Abridged editions of the story, printed in black and white and with a "normal" page-turning rather than foldout presentation, appeared inside promotional giveaway comics issued by American companies in the 1880s.

Thanks to Töpffer, Cruikshank, and a handful of enterprising American publishers, the 1840s should be remembered as the decade when America first fell in love with the comics. It had seen the U.S. publication of six sequential comic books, as well as the importation of other comics with foreign imprints. America's growing interest in graphic humor was further stimulated by the growth of two other fields: the cartoon broadside and the humor magazine.

As mentioned before, the cartoon broadside had been a part of the American scene since pre-Revolution days, but it did not flourish until stone lithography (introduced in 1818 and in wide use by the 1830s) made the reproduction of images relatively fast and cheap. From the early 1830s into the mid 1840s, the leading producer of cartoon broadsides in America was New York printer H. R. Robinson, who either drew his own cartoons or employed others, especially E. W. Clay, to do it. Clay is notable for having produced the first sequential comic broadside in America. Published in 1834 and entitled, "This Is the House that Jack Built" (50 x 32 cm), the nine-panel parody of the classic nursery rhyme was an attack on the Jackson Administration. The dominant theme of American cartoon broadsides was political, as befitted a nation where politics was the leading spectator sport. As the American electorate grew increasingly educated and prosperous, the demand for cartoon broadside also increased. During the 1840s, lithographers in New York, Boston, and Philadelphia, entered the field to satisfy that demand. The best known of these, Nathaniel Currier, later Currier and Ives, joined the fray in 1848. The firm employed many artists, but its chief political cartoonist was Louis Maurer and its chief comic artist was Thomas Worth.

Except for the three previously cited sequential cartoon broadsides, nearly all of the cartoon broadsides published in America from 1832 to 1876, its dominant era, were single panels. From the 1860s onward, broadside series on a single comic theme became common, the most famous being Thomas Worth's *Darktown* series. These can be loosely categorized as sequential comics since they employed the same characters and formed a story of sorts when hung together on a wall, as was the publisher's expectation. Sequential art or not, the cartoon broadsides nearly always employed the speech balloons that later became one of the defining characteristic of the American comic strip.

During the same decade that sequential comics and cartoon broadsides were growing in popularity, the illustrated American humor magazine made its debut. The British comic weekly *Punch*, founded in 1841, was an immediate success, both in England and the United States. It was a handsomely printed quarto, initially twelve pages and later sixteen, with a repeating cover design, backed by a page of small advertisements, humorous text interspersed with comic spot art, and a single panel full-page cartoon. A significant subset of *Punch*'s subscriber base was located in the U.S., to which thousands of copies were exported on an ongoing trans-Atlantic basis. Inevitably, enterprising American publishers attempted to repulse this invader with a home-grown comic weekly. The first, *Yankee Doodle*, came to town (New York, that is) on October 10, 1846, for one year. *Judy* (November 28, 1846 to February 20, 1847), *The John-Donkey* (January 1 to October 21, 1848), and *The Elephant* (January 22 to February 19, 1848) soon followed. None of them was successful, but all of them continued to feed the growing American interest in comic art.

By the late 1840s, comic art was flourishing in America. The conditions were right for the production of the earliest known American-created sequential comic book. Brothers James and Donald Read, who had worked for a time as cartoonists on *Yankee Doodle*, were the creators of *Journey to the Gold Diggins by Jeremiah Saddlebags*. This spirited send-up of the California gold rush craze was published in June 1849 by Stringer and Townsend, the late publishers of *Judy*, and, soon after, by U. P. James of Cincinnati. This Töpffer-influenced comic book chronicles the adventures of its hero *Jeremiah Saddlebags* in his get-rich-quick quest for gold in California. It is highly sought by collectors of Western Americana. Interestingly, the back cover of the Stringer and Townsend edition carries an advertisement for *Rose and Gertrude* - a Genevese Story, one of Rodolphe Töpffer's non-comics prose novels.

Stringer and Townsend was making something of a name for itself as a publisher of comic art. It will be remembered that it was one of the 1845 participants in the American publication of *The Bachelor's Own Book*. And, then, in 1846-47, it published *Judy*. Its decision to issue *Jeremiah Saddlebags* was all in due course.

The Gold Rush proved to be a gold mine for American comic artists. Aside from being a featured topic in the 1849 edition of David Claypool Johnston's *Scraps*, in comic almanacs, and in Currier cartoon prints, it was the subject of several other significant sequential series. The first, *The Adventures of Mr. Tom Plump* (a fat man who nearly starves to death in his failed attempt at California Gold riches), saw print in 1850. The second, *The Adventures of Jeremiah Old-Pot* (a twelve-part burlesque narrative of a New York businessman who attempts to get rich selling tin in price-inflated California), ran throughout 1852 in *Yankee Notions*. Though the narrative was distinctly American in its humor, the artwork was probably German in origin. *Yankee Notions*' Publisher, T. W. Strong, built his business on recycling old woodcuts with new captions attached. It should be noted that the *Old-Pot* series, borrowed or otherwise, was the first sequential art to appear in an American humor magazine. *Yankee Notions*, published from 1852 to 1875, also has the distinction of being the first comic monthly published in America.

"Moses Keyser the Bowery Bully's Trip to the California Gold Mines," was a 13-page comic story that appeared in *Elton's Californian Comic All-My-Nack* for 1850. It was reprinted at least twice in the circa 1850-51 booklet *The Clown, Or The Banquet of Wit* and later again in *Sam Slick's Comic Almanac* in 1857. *The Clown* is also notable as the earliest known anthology of sequential comics, with the bonus that each multi-panel story is by a different artist. Many of the artists are as yet unidentified, and how much of it is original American material versus that reprinted from Europe is presently unknown. But verified are cartoons by George Cruikshank, Elton (American), the Read brothers, Grandville (French), and Richard Doyle (British). The Doyle contribution reprints the comics story "Brown, Jones and Robinson and How They Went to a Ball," which originally saw print in the August 24, 1850 issue of *Punch*. This is the first known American appearance of these Doyle characters, and was almost certainly pirated.

Richard Doyle's *The Foreign Tour of Messrs. Brown, Jones, and Robinson* is basically a travelogue in illustrated form, told via humorous episodes, part sequential cartoon sequences, and part snapshots of moments jumping forward in time. This halfway sequential format was ideal for most 19th Century cartoonists, who, with rare exception, had not quite grasped how to maintain a single sequential story for much longer than two dozen successive panels. Doyle had simplified Töpffer's formula in a manner most artists could attempt to emulate. Episodes of "*Brown, Jones, and Robinson*" originally appeared in *Punch* in 1850, until a dispute between the Roman Catholic Doyle and Punch's editors over an anti-Papal joke ended with Doyle's resignation. Doyle redrew and expanded the story into a single album, first seeing print in 1854 from British publisher Bradbury and Evans.

New York Publisher D. Appleton brought the album to America, reprinting it in 1860, 1871, and 1877. Next, Dick and Fitzgerald of New York pirated Doyle's story sometime in the early 1870s. Doyle's format from *Foreign Tour* was emulated again and again. Examples include: the 1857 *Mr. Hardy Lee, His Yacht*, by Charles Stedman; the 1860s- 1870s G. W. Carleton-published *Our Artist In...* series, set in various Latin American countries; the Augustus Hoppin 1870s sketch novels *On the Nile, Crossing the Atlantic*, and *Ups and Downs on Land and Water*; and *Life* founder John Ames Mitchell's 1881 (pre-Life) *The Summer School of Philosophy at Mt. Desert*. D. Appleton, the official, authorized American publisher of *Foreign Tour*, even commissioned an American artist - Toby - to create a sequel comic album involving Doyle's characters visiting the U.S. and Canada, published in 1872 as *The American Tour of Messrs Brown, Jones and Robinson*. In terms of influencing the development of mid-19th Century American comics, Doyle's *Foreign Tour* ranks with the works of Töpffer, Cruikshank, and Busch.

Doyle was also the author of an equally popular earlier cartoon series for Punch, titled, *In Manners and Customs of Ye Englyshe, Mr. Pips Hys Diary*, which was reprinted in 1849. In this work, Doyle told his story using a deliberately primitive almost stick-figure art style, combined with the Hogarthian structure of large single panel cartoons leaping forward in time with each picture.

Manners and Customs of Ye Harvard Studente, which ran in the first year of the *Harvard Lampoon* (1876-current), shows the clearest influence. The series by then student Francis Gilbert Attwood was collected in 1877 by Houghton Mifflin. Attwood followed it up with *Manners and Customs of Ye Bostonians*, again in the pages of the *Harvard Lampoon*, but it is unknown whether that series was ever reprinted in book form. Attwood later became one of the regular artists in *Life*.

The Extraordinary and Mirth-provoking Adventures by Sea and Land of Oscar Shanghai, inspired by Bachelor Butterfly, was issued May 1855 by Garrett and Company, Publishers, No. 18 Ann Street, New York. Oscar Shanghai has many misadventures including being swallowed by a whale, making a trip in a flying machine to Africa, where he is shot out of a huge bow by a "Black Prince" for refusing to marry a local princess of color. After more adventures, he makes it back home.

Oscar Shanghai's first publisher was confirmed in 2002 with the discovery of a very rare 36-page catalog from 1856 of books, pamphlets and prints handled by B.H. Day (successor to Wilson and Company) who was by this time publishing *Brother Jonathan* as a twice-a-year holiday pictorial only. The catalog has a few crossover advertisement pages from an associate publisher, Garrett and Company. This rediscovered treasure, which sold for $750 in 2002, contains within a sequential strip of one panel per page over 32 of those pages titled *"Peter Piper in Bengal,"* by John Tenniel, reprinted from four 1853 issues of *Punch*. In the narrative, Peter Piper tries his hand hunting all different kinds of wild game with many misadventures.

Amongst the many varied types of "Cheap Books" for sale in this rare catalog are the comic books *The Adventures of Obadiah Oldbuck, Bachelor Butterfly's Queer Love Adventures and Misfortunes*, and *The Fortunes of Ferdinand Flipper*, plus the aforementioned *Oscar Shanghai*. All were priced at "25¢ per copy, postage free, refunds paid out in stamps." There is also an advertisement for a comic book entitled *A Day's Sport - Or, Hunting Adventures of S. Winks Wattles, a Shopkeeper, Thomas Titt, a "legal gent," and Major Nicholas Noggin, a Jolly Good Fellow Generally* by Henry L. Stephens (1824-1882) of Philadelphia.

Stephens, later the political cartoonist for *Vanity Fair* (New York, 1859-1863) and a leading children's book illustrator, produced his first work, *Illustrations of the Poets: From Passages in the Life of Little Billy Vidkins*, a small wrappered album of 32 comic woodcuts, in 1849. It was first published by S. Robinson, of Philadelphia, and reprinted with variant titles several times in the 1850s including *Yankee Notions*. It is likely that Little *Billy Vidkins* was printed before *Jeremiah Saddlebags*, though more research is needed before making this claim.

Garrett and Company was also responsible for the 1856 publication of *The Sad Tale of the Courtship of Chevalier Slyfox-Wikof, Showing His Heart-Rending Astounding and Most Wonderful Love Adventures with Fanny Elssler and Miss Gambol*. This book parodied the very public relationship between the then-famous wealthy American aristocrat Henry Wikoff, and the even more famous European actress/ dancer Fanny Elssler. It is dated thusly because Wikoff's memoir is pictured in the comic book.

Apparently in late 1854 Garrett and Company formed a brief two-year partnership with Dick and Fitzgerald, officially becoming Garrett, Dick and Fitzgerald in November 1856, while continuing to operate out of the same 18 Ann Street address in New York. One month later they issued Richard Doyle's British published graphic novel *The Foreign Tour of Messrs. Brown, Jones, and Robinson,* reformatting it into the same oblong shape as Garrett's two prior comic books (which in turn were formatted in imitation of Töpffer's albums). This information came to light just this year. The interested scholar is encouraged to check out the new listings for Garrett's The Home Circle in the index.

In 1858, Garrett appears to have dropped out, leaving Dick and Fitzgerald alone with the former's book stock, his place of business, and most importantly, the printing plates for his comic books. For reasons unknown, Dick and Fitzgerald steered away from reprinting Garrett's comic books for more than a decade. But in the 1870s they resumed publication - not only of the three albums published by Garrett, but also of *Obadiah Oldbuck and Bachelor Butterfly* from Wilson and Company, and *Ferdinand Flipper* from *Brother Jonathan* - all of them also making use of the original printing plates. The inclusion of books from *Brother Jonathan*, Wilson and Company, and Garrett and Company all within the same promotional Peter Piper catalog from B.H. Day suggests that these early publishers of comic books had many over-lapping fields of interest,, and that Dick and Fitzgerald became the inheritor/acquirer of all of it. Dick and Fitzgerald also reprinted in the 1870s the earlier William T. Peter published *Ichabod Academicus* (how that title might have connected, if at all, with B.H. Day's business remains unclear). We can now say, though, that an evolving group of a handful of publishers was responsible, over a span of 46 years, beginning with the very first graphic novel published in America in 1842, for keeping in print in America a cluster of slightly over half a dozen graphic novels.

Tebbel's *History of Book Publishing* in the US (vol. 1, pages 351-2) states that Burgess and Stringer was dissolved in late 1840s and became two firms, Stringer and Townsend, and Burgess and Garrett. Burgess retired in 1850 and his nephew William Brisbane Dick stepped into the partnership, whereupon the new company was renamed Garrett, Dick and Fitzgerald. Garrett retired in 1851 and the firm became Dick and Fitzgerald. The firm persisted under that name until 1917.

Collections reprinting cartoons from Punch saw print in the U.S., such as *Merry Pictures by the Comic Hands*, imported for the 1859 Christmas Season, plus various John Leech, George Du Maurier, and Phil May books which appeared from the 1850s through 1910s. Finally, many American weekly newspapers and weekly and monthly magazines, humorous and non-humorous, reprinted cartoons from Punch. Such inclusions often became a prelude to switching to original material by American artists, if that publication find's cartoon section find American cartoonists of sufficient talent.

Harper's Monthly, the leading American monthly, was a prime example. Soon after it commenced publication in November 1850, it began to carry a few pages of single panel cartoons reprinted from *Punch* at the rear of each issue. This evolved into reprinting sequential comic pages from the British periodical *Town Talk*, and then, starting December 1853, original sequential comics by the great Frank Bellew.

Bellew (1828-1888) should be regarded as the "Father of American Sequential Comics." Born in India, educated in France and England, he emigrated to America in 1850. His earliest work shows an influence from Doyle, but he rapidly developed his own unique art style. Bellew's comics, both sequential and single panel, graced nearly every American comic periodical published from the 1850s into the 1870s.

Journey to the Gold Diggins By Jeremiah Saddlebags, June 1849, so far the earliest known sequential comic book by American creators, J.A. and D.F. Read. Above: a couple sample pages. Note similarity to Töpffer's comics especially **Bachelor Butterfly**

A month after the publication of the anonymous first installment of *Jeremiah Old-Pot* in *Yankee Notions*, Bellew began contributing his six-part, 18-panel comic series, *"Mr. Blobb in Search of a Physician"* to *The Lantern*, a New York comic weekly published from January 10, 1852 to July 2, 1853. The series ran in six of the nine issues published from January 31 through March 27, 1852. This was followed in April and May by the 16-panel, three-issue comic sequence *"Mr. Bulbear's Dream"*, which concluded with the main character awakened from his dream by falling out of bed, exactly like *Little Nemo* would do five decades later.

These two series were just the beginning for Bellew, who contributed a voluminous amount of work to the *New York Picayune* (1850-1860) (which he also edited for a time in 1857-58), *The Comic Monthly* (1859-1881), *Momus*, an 1860 comic daily, *The Phunniest of Awl* (1864-1867) (which he also edited), *Punchinello* (1870), and *Wild Oats* (1870-1881), to name the most prominent.

The Comic Monthly deserves special mention. Started in March 1859 and published by J. C. Haney and Company, of 119 Nassau Street, New York, *The Comic Monthly* was a profusely illustrated 16-page folio, the same size as *Harper's Weekly*. It focused its graphic satire on politics, the theater, and the comedy of everyday life. A preponderance of the purely comic satire took the form of sequential art. Here are random samplings of highlights from issues from 1860:

- February: "A Day of Humiliation, Fasting, Supplica-tion, and Prayer (four panels, unsigned), "New Year Calls under the Influence of Hard Times" (twelve panels, unsigned), "Young Trouble-some; or, Master Jacky's Holidays" (nineteen panels covering three and half pages, unsigned);
- April: "Four Years After Marriage" (sixteen panels, unsigned), "Our Masked Ball" (twelve panel centerspread, Bellew), "Trials of a Witness" (eight panels, Bellew);
- May: "Precocities of Young Springles" (seven panels, unsigned), "The Fight for the Championship" (twenty-four panel centerspread, Bellew), "Steam Applied to Music" (three panels, unsigned), "The Course of True Love" (four panels, Bellew);
- June: "Further Particulars of the Fight" (nine panel cover, Bellew), "The Man Who Went to See the Fight" (twelve panels, unsigned);
- July: "Explaining American Politics to an Intelligent Foreigner" (twelve panels, unsigned), "The Meerschaum Mania" (two panels, Bellew), "The Art of Stump Speaking" (ten panels, unsigned), "Our Little Friend, Tom Noddy" (three panels, unsigned); "The Japanese in New York" (twelve panel centerspread, Bellew), "The Observant Child" (three panels, unsigned), "Mr. Dibbs Goes to Pike's Peak and Comes Back Again" (fourteen panel back cover, unsigned);
- September: "The Zouave Fever" (four panel cover, unsigned), "Mr. Lupell" (two panels, Bellew), "The Prince of Wales in America" (twenty-four panel centerspread, J. H. Howard), "D'ye Think It's True?" (three panels, Bellew);
- October: "The Duties of the Wide Awake" (four panels, Bellew), "Our Charley (two panels, unsigned), "The Three Young Friends" (eighteen panel back cover, unsigned);
- November: "The Hanlon's (sic) At Home" (nine panel back cover, unsigned);
- December: "The Target Excursion" (seventeen panel centerspread, signed with an unidentifiable monogram); "The Sporting Critic" two panels, Bellew).

The Comic Monthly also published many multi-panel cartoons grouped under a single heading, which were not strictly sequential in nature. Bellew was the monthly's chief artist, assisted by Thomas Nast, A. R Waud, and others. Some of the unsigned art was certainly by Bellew, some by journeymen artists, and some of it pirated from European journals.

The Comic Monthly was not the first folio-sized humor magazine. Those laurels go to *The New York Picayune,* which began as a newspaper, switched to a folio in 1856, adopted *Punch's* format for thirty-five issues in 1857-58, and returned to a folio for the remainder of its run.

Frank Leslie's *Budget of Fun*, the greatest of the folio monthlies, began in January 1859 and was published until June 1878. Its star cartoonist during the sixties was William Newman (c. 1817-1870), one of the founding artists of Punch. As we have noted, *The Comic Monthly* began two months later.

Frank Leslie was born Henry Cart in Ipswich, England in 1821. He became a very skilled engraver before coming over to

Yankee Notions #1, January, 1852. This title began the first sequential comic strips in an American humor magazine, The Adventures of Jerimiah Old-Pot.

America in 1948. He first worked as manager for P.T. Barnum's *New York Illustrated News* for several years. in 1850 he legally had his name changed to Frank Leslie. He died in 1880 and his wife continued the numerous publications he was publishing. Many of Frank Leslie's periodicals had a lot of sequental comic art.

Quarto-sized monthlies to compete with the successful *Yankee Notions* were also proliferating. *Nick-Nax* was the first (May 1856 to December 1875), followed by *Phunny Phellow* (October 1859- 1876) and *Merryman's Comic Monthly* (January 1863 to December 1875), to name the most prominent.

Enterprising publishers continued to attempt an American comic weekly in the style of *Punch*. The most notable efforts, *Vanity Fair* (1859-1863), *Mrs. Grundy* (1865), and *Punchinello* (1870), were distinguished but unsuccessful.

Nearly all of them, weeklies and monthlies, to varying degrees, featured sequential comic art. By the time of the American Civil War, sequential comic art was a part of the American graphic landscape.

While Bellew stood out for his sequential comics, Thomas Nast (1840-1902) brought a new style to American political cartoons, of which he is regarded the father. Even though he created several sequential strips early in his career (especially for Nick-Nax in 1859), Nast made his name in the pages of the national news periodical, *Harper's Weekly*, for which he worked from 1862 until 1886. Nast was influenced more by the dark wood engravings of Franco-German illustrator Gustave Dore than by the cartoonists of *Punch*. His somber cartoons were a novelty in American cartooning. Nast in the pages of *Harper's Weekly* (and Newman in the pages of the *Budget of Fun*) popularized the extravagant double-page folio-sized cartoon, which had no precedent in European or American cartooning, save for the separately published cartoon broadsides. This format would come to full maturity after 1876 in the pages of *Puck* (1876-1918) and then *Judge* (1881-1947).

As Nast grew in prominence and success, American cartoonists increasingly emulated him. U.S. humor publications evolved towards an amalgamation of Nast and Punch, rather than sheer imitation of the latter. After the War, with Nast's style of cartoons more entrenched in American readers' minds, efforts to launch *Punch*-like American periodicals floundered quickly. *Mrs. Grundy*, ironically most famous for its cover design by Nast, died after a mere twelve issues (running July 8 to September 23, 1865). *Punchinello* (April 2 to December 24, 1870) struggled nine months before its backers gave up. *Punchinello* had been financed by Tammany Hall politicians Tweed and Sweeney, as counter-propaganda against Nast's ongoing assault upon their corruption. They attempted to buy and threaten Nast into silence, to no avail.

American comics continued their pull away from Anglo-Franco imitation with the infusion of a third major European influence – the German humor magazine. The German-American community swelled significantly after the failed revolution of 1848. These émigrés brought with them a culture of humor, expressed most flamboyantly in their native humor magazines, the most famous being *Kladderadatsch, Fliegende Blätter*, and *Münchener Bilderbogen*. As high in quality, as were the graphic artists who contributed to them, one German comic artist in particular excelled beyond the rest, his stories breaking out and crossing over into English language translations, the demand for which resulted in numerous printings. This artist, of course, was Heinrich Christian Wilhelm Busch (1832-1908).

Busch's work appeared in English in the 1860s in both British and American periodicals, often uncredited. For example, four of Busch's strips appeared in English in the pages of *Merryman's Monthly* in 1864, while in 1879 his graphic story "Fipps der Affe" was serialized across a 10-issue run of Puck as "Troddledums the Simian." The earliest known English language appearance of Busch in book form was *The Flying Dutchman, or The Wrath of Herr von Stoppelnoze*, in 1862, from New York publisher G. W. Carleton. Carleton not only pirated Busch's strip, but went so far as to credit the entire story to American poet John G. Saxe, with Busch's cartoons mere illustrations accompanying Saxe's prose!

The next known English language Busch book was *A Bushel of Merry Thoughts*, an 1868 London-published anthology collecting various Busch strips. Some of these same stories later appeared in the U.S.-published *The Mischief Book* (1880), newly translated and with a few more Busch tales added. One of these additions was "Hans Huckebein," a tale of a mischievous pet raven who in the end gets drunk and accidentally hangs himself. It became, at least in the States, Busch's second most popular sequential comic story. The unrepentant bird was promoted to title character in two later collections: the rare *Hookeybeak the Raven and Other Tales* in 1878 and *Jack Huckaback, the Scapegrace Raven*, circa 1888. There were also at least three trade card series in the 1870s and 1880s that reprinted the ending sequence, as *Fritz Spindle-Shanks, The Raven Black*.

The most popular Busch tale, though, was easily Max und Moritz, which in the U.S. saw print as *Max and Maurice - A Juvenile History in Seven Tricks*. Published in Boston in 1871, this English language version saw at minimum of 60 reprintings by the century's end, plus countless more printings thereafter. A separate British translation debuted in 1874, under the title *Max and Moritz*. It is well known that the later Rudolph Dirks comic strip series, Katzenjammer Kids, beginning in late

1897, was based on *Max und Moritz*.

According to documents found by comics historian Alfredo Castelli, *Katzenjammer Kids* may not have been pirated as has been assumed but was licensed by William Randolph Hearst instead. Hearst's *New York Journal* was published in different language editions for New York City's immigrant communities. In the German edition, the strip was published under its original name, *Max und Moritz*. Numerous other translations of Busch were published in America - too many to name in this article. Several can be found in the Victorian Age Price Index.

The most significant humor magazine of the 1870s, prior to the founding of the German-language *Puck* in 1876, was *Wild Oats* (1870-1881), which for part of its run also published a German-language edition, *Schnedereddeng*. In terms of the quality of its cartoons and comics, this New York City publication was in 1872 at an artistic level *Puck* would not achieve until 1880. Published by Winchell and Small (later Collin and Small) and distributed through the New York News Company, *Wild Oats* carried a cross-section of old and new generation comic artists, from the more established W. M. Avery, Frank Beard, Frank Bellew, E.S. Bisbee, Michael Angelo Woolf, and Thomas Worth, to up-and-comers such as Livingston Hopkins, Frederick Burr Opper, Palmer Cox, and James A. Wales.

Wild Oats began carrying sequential comic strips as early as #26, dated March 14, 1872, with the Livingston Hopkins strip pictured on the next page (we do not know anything yet about the first 25 issues). The very next issue has a Worth double-page spread titled "The Political Humpty Dumpty... Horace Greeley" told in eleven panels plus the sequential fictional "Graphic Account of the Assassination of Queen Victoria" and "Love As the Angels Love." "The Doings of the Japanese Embassy At Washington" related in twelve panels by W. M. Avery follows up in #28 April 11, 1872. An unknown hand drew "The Physiology of Moving" in six panels in #30. Hopkins returns with a beautiful intense 28-panel double-page spread in #31 May 23. Hopkins and Worth alternated for many issues with sequential comic strips on baseball, horse racing and other pertinent subjects of the day. In #45 December 5, 1872, E.S. Bisbee contributed his first sequential in seventeen panels and Worth showed up in "Humor and Pathos of a New England Thanksgiving" in eleven panels. Issue 47 expands the concept with a twelve-panel job by Bisbee, twenty-panel effort on one page by Hopkins and a three-panel effort by Worth. And on it goes through 1873 as well - comic strip after comic strip. Issue 58 June 5, 1873, includes a particularly humorous nineteen-panel double-pager drawn by someone still unknown titled "The Terrible Adventures of Messrs. Buster and Stumps, with the Indians" which begins with two white men heading out west in an effort to exterminate Indians - and their misadventures of not quite getting the job done. It reads across both pages in a unique evolution similar to Popeye #2052 (found in the Platinum listings). Issue 65 contains two nine-panel Thomas Worth strips "Only a Mad Dog Scare - Another Lesson For Nervous People" and "Only a Cholera Scare - Something For Nervous People to Read and Ponder Over." Issue 66 Sept 18, 1873, has the very funny Hopkins twelve-panel strip as well as two more ten-panel Worth strips on the delights of Hunting and Fishing plus one by Hopkins titled "The Adventures of Mr Old Party with Jersey Mosquitoes" in twelve-panels. All told, four comic strips in this issue. They obviously liked what they were doing, judging from the exuberance of the work.

The next issue has Worth's nine-panel report on "The Adventures of Young Muttonhead among the Free Lovers" which was all about the "free sex" convention recently held in Chicago. Issue 68 has a nine-panel "An Adventure with a New Jersey Mosquito" which smacks of Winsor McCay in subject and even art style. Maybe McCay was inspired by this for his later animated cartoon as well as earlier Rarebit Fiend. We'll never know for sure. On through 1875, *Wild Oats* presented sequential comic strips issue after issue. With #148, October 27, 1875, Frederick Opper contributes his very first Wild Oats cover, a political cartoon on inflation then rampant in the US. He does covers through at least #161 before a short break and then comes back with many more. In #158, January 5, 1876, Palmer Cox - some five years before inventing The Brownies - begins a wonderful series of 24-panel double page spread comic strips, with a couple sample titles being "The Adventures of Mr. and Mrs. Sprowl And Their Christmas Turkey-A Crashing Chasing Tearful Tragedy But Happily Ending Well" and "Bachelor Broke and Widow Snuggi: A Pictorial Account of Their Sleigh Ride and What Became of It."

Even though he had been contributing many covers and interior single panel jobs to *Wild Oats* for years, Frank Bellew does not show up with his first comic strip until #190, August 16, 1876, with a nine-panel effort he titled, "Rodger's Patent Mosquito Armour." By this time America's "Father of the sequential comic strip" had inspired many other cartoonists to try their hand telling stories with words and pictures.

Another highly desirable American graphic novel, sought especially by collectors of Western lore, is *Quiddities of an Alaskan Trip* by William H. Bell which debuted in 1873. Bell was Timothy O'Sullivan's assistant photographer on the 1871-74 expeditions of Lt. George Wheeler, surveying and mapping the western territories for the U.S. government. The story panels are laid out within ornate frames like those of stereograph cards, such as Bell was involved in creating on the expedition. It involves a parody of a trip from Washington, D.C., to survey the newly purchased territory of Alaska, which at the time was derisively referred to as "Seward's Folly." Bell published *Quiddities* in Portland, Oregon, in 1873, meaning that he drew it while he was on just such an expedition.

The seemingly disparate influences of Thomas Nast and German comics came together in the work of Austrian immigrant Joseph Keppler (1838-1894). Like many cartoonists in America, Keppler desired to rival Nast. Unlike most, he possessed the talent and drive to accomplish it. Keppler, trained as an artist but working as an actor, began contributing comic art to *Kikeriki* (1861-1923) in his native Vienna. He emigrated to St. Louis in 1868, where he took his first stab at starting a comic weekly, the German language *Die Vehme* (Aug 28, 1869 - Aug. 20, 1870). Seven months later, still in St. Louis, he tried again, launching another German language humor periodical, titled *Puck*. This German *Puck* began on March 18, 1871, joined by an English language version one year later, but both ended on Aug. 24, 1872.

Keppler moved to New York City and began working for Frank Leslie. His cartoons appeared in *Frank Leslie's Illustrated Newspaper*, Frank Leslie's *Budget of Fun*, and the Leslie-owned *Jolly Joker* and *Day's Doings*. (To capitalize on the 1876 Centennial Exposition in Philadelphia, Leslie published in that year a paperback collection of Centennial-related humor, *Centennial Fun*, most of which was Keppler's work.) Four years after the first *Puck* died, Keppler was ready to try again. He re-launched the German language edition of *Puck* in New York City on September 27, 1876.

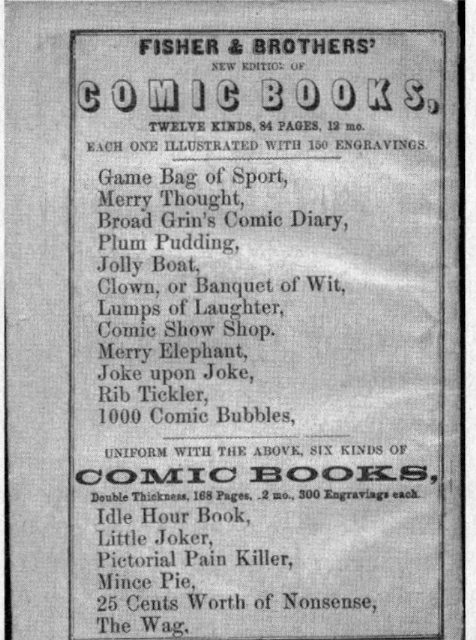

FISHER & BROTHERS'
NEW EDITION OF
COMIC BOOKS,
TWELVE KINDS, 84 PAGES, 12 mo.
EACH ONE ILLUSTRATED WITH 150 ENGRAVINGS.
Game Bag of Sport,
Merry Thought,
Broad Grin's Comic Diary,
Plum Pudding,
Jolly Boat,
Clown, or Banquet of Wit,
Lumps of Laughter,
Comic Show Shop.
Merry Elephant,
Joke upon Joke,
Rib Tickler,
1000 Comic Bubbles,
UNIFORM WITH THE ABOVE, SIX KINDS OF
COMIC BOOKS,
Double Thickness, 168 Pages, .2 mo., 300 Engravings each.
Idle Hour Book,
Little Joker,
Pictorial Pain Killer,
Mince Pie,
25 Cents Worth of Nonsense,
The Wag,

Earliest-known use of the description COMIC BOOKS dates from the early 1850s.

This *Puck* was both familiar and exotic. Its format of an extravagant centerspread cartoon sandwiched between front and back cover cartoons had by this time become something of a comic periodical standard, certainly for the monthlies. But *Puck* was different from what had come before. The cartoons were lithographed, not engraved, which lent to them a softer, more pleasing quality, and they were in color, something virtually without precedent in American comic periodical literature.

Initially, the magazine's cartoons were tinted in just one color, but *Puck* appeared, ambitiously, every week, and the coloring set it apart from anything else on American stands. The parallel English language edition of *Puck* was launched six months after the German version, on March 14, 1877. This English edition of *Puck* was a money-loser for several years, kept afloat by the German edition's profits and the determination of the English edition's literary editor, H.C. Bunner, not to give up. By 1880, *Puck* was a huge success. It became the new model for American humor publications. In time, Keppler hired other artists, most notably Frederick Burr Opper, Eugene Zimmerman ("Zim") and F. M. Howarth, and added black and white sequential comics to the magazine's interior and then, with increasing frequency in the early 1890s to the magazine's back cover. *Funny Folks* by F. M. Howarth, 1899, collected many early sequential comics from *Puck;* one of the titles many consider bridges the Victorian and Platinum Ages of comics. *Puck* was the model that inspired William Randolph Hearst to add a color comics section to his Sunday Journal in 1895.

With the first issue dated October 29, 1881, *Puck's* chief rival, *Judge*, was born. Founded by *Puck* artist James A. Wales, it also featured the work of Thomas Worth and Livingston Hopkins. *Judge* made several forays into *Puck*'s talent pool over the years. Its best capture was Eugene Zimmerman ("Zim"), who became for Judge the star artist that Frederick Burr Opper was for Puck.

Judge struggled financially for several years, and likely would have ceased publication had it not been for Puck's powerful performance during the 1884 election. *Puck*'s success galvanized Republican powerbrokers into recognizing the importance of the political cartoon weekly. They financed newspaperman W. J. Arkell's purchase of *Judge* in 1886 to turn it into a reliable Republican house organ.

Also worthy of mention is the New York City newspaper *The Daily Graphic* (March 4, 1873 to Sept 23, 1889), which claims the distinction of being the first regularly illustrated daily newspaper in the world, published every day except Sundays and holidays. The majority of its illustrations were portraits or depictions of news events, but nearly every issue contained some comic drawing, many of them gracing the front cover.

With so many pages to fill on a daily basis, *The Daily Graphic* became a rotating door for many young American cartoonists in the early stages of their careers (making one suspect that it was not the best paying gig in town). Within its pages, like needles to be found in the haystack of its more than 4800 issues, is early work by Livingston Hopkins (who mysteriously appears, vanishes, reappears, etc., for months to whole years at a time, right up to his 1884 departure to Australia), pre-*Life* work by Kemble, pre-*Harper*'s appearances by A.B. Frost and W.A. Rogers, pre-Puck and Judge Opper, C.J. Taylor, Hamilton, and Gillam. Old hats, too, appear at times, such as Michael Woolf and Frank Bellew, Sr.

Further, *The Daily Graphic* regularly plundered British periodicals for its back and sometimes center pages, not only perpetrating the usual swipes of single-panel *Punch* cartoons, but also stealing sequential strips from Punch's two main rival publications, *Judy* and *Fun*. This included occasionally reprinting (albeit at random) episodes of continuing British strips "The British Workman" by James Sullivan, and "McNab of that Ilk" by James Brown, though, strangely enough, not Marie Duval's *Ally Sloper*, despite the fact that *The Daily Graphic* did reprint some of Duval's non-"Sloper" strips. ("Ally Sloper" was a continuing sequential strip character who debuted in 1867, lasting into the 1920s, and had very successful solo British book collections of his strip appearances published as early as 1873, more than two decades prior to *Yellow Kid in McFadden*'s Flats).

Livingston Hopkins, whose art style changed like a chameleon from one year to the next, exhibited a definite Duval influence in his work within a year following the publication of the first *Ally Sloper* collection. Given that Hopkins worked for *The Daily Graphic* during the same period in which this newspaper was stealing cartoons from *Sloper*'s home publication, *Judy*, this can hardly be considered coincidental. Hopkins contributed a daily comic strip to *The Daily Graphic* in 1874-75, complete with word balloons. By the time Hopkins was preparing to emigrate to Australia to become lead cartoonist for the Sydney Bulletin, his art style was an imitation of Kemble's, who was also working at *The Daily Graphic.*

Life debuted on January 4, 1883, founded by J.A. Mitchell, and modeled after the Harvard Lampoon. It quickly rose to become the third main pillar of late 1800s American humor periodicals. Smaller in size, black and white, and priced the same as *Puck* and *Judge*, it nevertheless succeeded by appealing to a more genteel audience. Its earliest artists included Kemble and Palmer Cox, but its foremost artist was Charles Dana Gibson, becoming world renowned as the hand behind the graceful, aristocratic "Gibson Girls."

Unlike *Judge*, which had to become a low-brow imitation of *Life* to survive in the next century, and *Puck*, which attempted but failed to become an American version of the highbrow European humor magazines, Life transitioned into the 20th century virtually unaltered, and thrived. By the mid-1880s, with *Puck, Judge*, and *Life* all solidly in place, American comics and cartoon humor had come very much into their own, no longer looking first at Europe to take their cues.

Almanacs began to appear in America starting in 1639. Humor was introduced as early as 1647 by Samuel Danforth. A very important one was *Leed Almanac* beginning in 1687. John Tulley produced the first humorous almanac in 1688. James Franklin, brother of Ben, began the *Rhode Island Almanac* in 1728 using the name "Poor Robin" and his younger brother began *Poor Richard's Almanac* in 1732. Farmer's Almanac began in 1792 and used some humor.

The first comic almanac totally devoted to humor was published by Charles Ellm in Boston in 1831 and featured the artwork of D.C. Johnston. Perhaps the most famous comic almanacs (certainly the most valuable) are the *Davy Crockett* series (1835-1856) which began in Nashville, Tennessee. The comic periodicals all ended up issuing comic almanacs beginning with *Yankee Notions* in 1856 and continuing into the 1890s with a one-shot comic almanac published by *Judge* for the year 1894.

Beginning in the 1850s, a new breed of almanacs appeared. Usually created by medicine and farm product companies, they were distributed for free to promote the company's product. Competition amongst companies, whose goal was to get customers to read the almanacs and the advertisements contained therein again and again, meant that attention-getting humorous cartoons soon found their way back into these giveaway pamphlets. Initially their cartoons were done cheap, either poorly drawn or pirated from elsewhere, such as those found in the Hostetter's and Wright's almanac series. More elaborate promotional almanacs eventually did evolve, though, and amongst the best of these was *Barker's Illustrated Almanac*, first produced for the year 1878, and annually into the 1930s. Each *Barker's Almanac* contained ten to twelve full page cartoons, wonderful and bizarre in design, frequently racist, but also comically manic and crammed with details in a manner similar to Outcault's much later *Yellow Kid* pages. The cartoons in *Barker's Almanac* were so popular that in 1892, The Barker, Moore, and Mein Medicine Company published their first edition of *Barker's Komic Picture Souvenir*, reprinting nearly 150 pages of cartoons from their almanacs.

This first *Barker's Souvenir* features a wraparound color cover depicting people headed towards the Columbian World's Fair Exposition, which was to be held in Chicago the next year. It is the earliest confirmed "premium" comic book, sent to customers who mailed in a box label and outside wrapper from two different Barker's products. The *Souvenir* album was *Barker's* most in-demand premium. It was reprinted as a thick unnumbered booklet three more times in the 1890s, with the contents reorganized each time. Later, between 1901 and 1903, *Barker's* broke the album into three separate "Parts," each of which required still more box labels and wrappers to obtain. The 3-part series of reprint albums expanded to four parts circa 1906 or 1907. Both the 3 and 4-part album series had multiple printings.

Also very American in character were the country's promotional comics, which flourished throughout the latter half of the 19th century. They trace their beginnings to Comic Almanacs, which flourished in England and the United States since they first appeared in the 1830s. The first promotional comics which did not double as almanacs began to appear in the 1870s. They included the aforementioned reprints of Cruikshank and Busch strips, reprints of strips lifted from American sources (A.B. Frost's strip "The Bull Calf" was a particular favorite), and original material placing the product being promoted as the focus of the story. These original short cartoon dramas were in many ways similar in storyline to those found in modern television advertisements, except that the clothing is Victorian, and the claims, pre-F.D.A. and F.C.C., were unabashedly wild, over-the-top, and blunt. Chewing tobacco and snuff saved romances, calmed crying babies, and made the sick well. Stove polish that propelled you to wealth and power. Corsets that brought you a husband. The objective, of course, in an era before TV or radio, was to make each comic handout so entertaining that customers would want to keep and read the advertisement again and again.

The more wonderful graphics and outrageous claims tended to come from tobacco companies, who were using comic books and strips to sell their products more than a century before cries against "Joe Camel." The most elaborate of these were printed full color, and unfolded into a single long strip, just like Cruikshank's *The Tooth-Ache* from the 1840s, though usually limited to just the cover plus seven panels.

The earliest known anthology devoted to collecting the comic strips of a single American artist was A.B. Frost's *Stuff and Nonsense* in 1884. The next known American collection came in 1888, the very rare Frederick Burr Opper anthology, *Puck's Opper Book*. Both proved popular, so more Frost and Opper collections followed, to be joined within a few years by reprints collecting the cartoons and strips of Keppler, Kemble, Zim, Gibson, Mayer, Taylor, Frank Bellew's son "Chip," Howarth, Woolf, etc.

Puck, Judge, and *Texas Siftings* all began monthly Library series - 8-1/2" x 11" magazines, mostly black and white, which organized previously published material around one theme or one artist. For example, the first *Puck's Library* (July 1887) was titled "The National Game," and gathered beneath one cover *Puck* material poking fun at the game of baseball. The third (March 1888) and ninth (November 1889) issues of *Judge's Serial (later named Judge's Library)* were devoted entirely to the work of Zim.

Life tended more towards hardcover collections, such as its annual ten-issue series *The Good Things of Life* (1884-1893), which included cartoons and strips by Palmer Cox, T.S. Sullivant, Hy Mayer, and others. *The Good Things of Life* was published initially by the firm of White, Stokes, and Allen, but which by the fourth book, had become simply Frederick A. Stokes. Stokes published a number of other cartoon books in the 1880s and 1890s, the majority of them reprint collections. The experience he gained at this time with these reprint albums placed Stokes in the perfect position to pick up the wealth of material about to be created for the comics supplements of William R. Hearst's newspapers, making Stokes the first major publisher of the coming Platinum Age.

In 1892, Charles Scribner's Sons published A. B. Frost's *Bull Calf and Other Tales*. It contains sequential comic strip art on quite a few pages as well as single panel cartoons. By 1898, Charles Scribner's Sons also issued Kemble's *The Billy Goat and Other Comicalities* as a 112-page hardcover, which also has sequential comic strips.

In the early 1890s, the slum children cartoons of artist Michael Woolf (many of which were reprinted in the 1896 collection *99 Woolfs from Truth* and in the posthumous 1899 collection *Sketches of Lowly Life in a Great City*) were popular. *Truth* magazine, which followed Puck's format of color front cover, back cover and centerspread cartoons, but in style was more akin to the aristocratic Life, was initially unable to secure Woolf's services, creating an opportunity for the young cartoonist Richard F. Outcault, who desired to break into one of the weekly comic periodicals.

It was in his Woolf-inspired slum children cartoons for *Truth* that Outcault's prototype of the *Yellow Kid* first emerged. The bald, sack-clothed youngster made four appearances in *Truth*, starting with #372 on June 2, 1894, prior to his newspaper debut.

During the rise of Yellow Kid's popularity, he appeared in American comic magazines in parodies drawn by others, with politicians, even Hearst and Pulitzer, dressed up as the *Yellow Kid*. Such cartoons are known to have appeared in *Judge, Life, The Bee*, and *Vim* plus various newspapers across the country. More about the *Yellow Kid's* importance can be found in the Platinum Age section of this book.

While comics definitely have their roots in Europe, and the earliest American comic books either reprinted or emulated those of Europe, the direction of influence was by no means one way. By at least the 1870s, American cartoons were being published and seen in the Old World, as evidenced by the arrest in Spain of the on-the-lamb corrupt Tammany Hall politician Boss Tweed by Spanish police who recognized Tweed from a Nast cartoon.

European piracy of American cartoons was just as lucrative as the American piracy of Europeans. In the 1880s and '90s, the comics of Zim, Chip Bellew, and Charles Dana Gibson all saw reprint in Europe. In April 1899, *Pictorial Comedy*, a monthly magazine destined for a ten-year run, commenced publication in London. It was made up entirely of cartoons reprinted with permission from *Puck* and *Life*. F.M. Howarth's domestic comedies from *Puck* were favorites in France. American Hy Mayer was commissioned to create original comics work for *Black and White* (Britain), *Le Rire* (France), and *Fliegende Blätter*. Michael Woolf's slum children cartoons saw print in the British periodical *Pick-Me-Up*, during the same years that top British artist Phil May's first published work debuted in that publication. May later became famous for his Woolf-inspired street children cartoons as well as his influence on the development of comics in Australia.

As the 19th Century ended, American comics were coming to the fore worldwide, soon to explode into a position of dominance with the Platinum Age revolution brought about by the emergence of the color comic supplement in America's newspapers and the arrival of Richard F. Outcault's *Yellow Kid*.

END NOTE: Victorian Era comics were issued in many relatively obscure formats compared to what most of us are used to today. The Victorian Era section can only grow as there are many more heretofore undiscovered comics from the 1800s which have fallen off the radar of history. Some may wonder why some of the earlier items listed contain as of yet no prices. The reason is simple. These books are part of a relatively "new" market which is still establishing itself.

High-grade copies are almost unheard of in almost all instances. Some books may truly have only a handful left in existence. We are sure there are some known to have been published which no (as of yet) known copies have survived the ravages of time and neglect.

Each year expect another quantum leap in our ever-expanding knowledge of the fascinating earliest origins of the comic strip as it relates to North America. Your input in helping this section of the Guide grow and mature is most welcome!

Robert Lee Beerbohm first sold comics through the legendary RBCC beginning in 1966, set up at his first comicon in 1967, helped found the northern California Comics & Comix chain of stores in August 1972, co-hosted Berkeleycon 1973, the first UG creator-owned comix con and operated comic book stores from 1972-1994. He now owns Robert Beerbohm Comic Art that specializes in buying and selling scarce comics and related material from the 1840s-1980s. He has been compiling a detailed history book of the business of the American comic book for some time now and hopes to complete it soon.

Contact Robert directly at www.BLBComics.com

Richard Olson is an Research Professor Emeritus at the University of New Orleans. He published the Richard Outcault Collector for years. Reach Richard directly at: rolsonredoak@bellsouth.net

Richard Samuel West is the author of Satire on Stone: The Political Cartoons of Joseph Keppler (University of Illinois, 1988) and The San Francisco Wasp: An Illustrate History (Periodyssey Press, 2004) and editor of several cartoon collections. He is the owner of Periodyssey, a business that specializes in buying and selling significant and unusual American magazines. Richard can be reached at: www.oldmagazines.com

All three are life-long collectors and students of all forms of the comics who welcome corrections and additions to this concise compilation of our earliest American comics heritage dating back almost two centuries. Happy Hunting!

The American Comic Almanac #11
1835 © Charles Ellms, NYC

The Strange and Wonderful Adventures
of Bachelor Butterfly by Rodolphe Töpffer
1870s © Dick & Fitzgerald, NYC

Barker's "Komic" Picture Souvenir, 3rd Edition
1894 © Barker, Moore & Klein Medicine Co.

COLLECTOR'S NOTE: Most of the books listed in this section were published well over a century before organized comics fandom began archiving and helping to preserve these fragile popular culture artifacts. With some of these comics now over 160 years old, they almost never surface in Fine+ or better shape. Be happy when you simply find a copy.

This year has seen price growth in quite a few comic books in this era. Since this section began growing almost a decade now, comic books from Wilson, Brother Jonathan, Huestis & Cozans, Garrett, Dick & Fitzgerald, Frank Leslie, Street & Smith and others continue to be recognized by the more savvy in this fine hobby as legitimate comic book collectors' items. We had been more concerned with simply establishing what is known to exist. For the most part, that work is now a *fait accompli* in this section compiled, revised, and expanded by Robert Beerbohm with special thanks this year to Terrance Keegan plus acknowledgment to Bill Blackbeard, Chris Brown, Alfredo Castelli, Darrell Coons, Leonardo De Sá, Scott Deschaine, Joe Evans, Ron Friggle, Tom Gordon III, Michel Kempeneers, Andy Konkykru, Don Kurtz, Richard Olson, Robert Quesinberry, Joseph Rainone, Steve Rowe, Randy Scott, John Snyder, Art Spiegelman, Steve Thompson, Richard Samuel West, Doug Wheeler and Richard Wright. Special kudos to long-time collector and scholar Gabriel Laderman.

The prices given for Fair, Good and Fine categories are for strictly graded editions. If you need help grading your item, we refer you to the grading section in this book or contact the authors of this essay. Items marked Scarce, Rare or Very Rare we are still trying to figure out how many copies might still be in existence. We welcome additions and corrections from any interested collectors and scholars at robert@BLBcomics.com

For ease ascertaining the contents of each item of this listing and the Platinum index list, we offer the following list of categories found immediately following most of the titles:
E - EUROPEAN ORIGINAL COMICS MATERIAL; Printed in Europe or reprinted in USA
G - GRAPHIC NOVEL (LONGER FORMAT COMIC TELLING A SINGLE STORY)
H - "HOW TO DRAW CARTOONS" BOOKS
I - ILLUSTRATED BOOKS NOTABLE FOR THE ARTIST, BUT NOT A COMIC.
M - MAGAZINE / PERIODICAL COMICS MATERIAL REPRINTS
N - NEWSPAPER COMICS MATERIAL REPRINTS
O - ORIGINAL COMIC MATERIAL NOT REPRINTED FROM ANOTHER SOURCE
P - PROMOTIONAL COMIC, EITHER GIVEN AWAY FOR FREE, OR A PREMIUM GIVEN IN CONJUNCTION WITH THE PURCHASE OF A PRODUCT.
S - SINGLE PANEL / NON-SEQUENTIAL CARTOONS

Measurements are in inches. The first dimension given is Height and the second is Width. Some original British editions are included in the section, so as to better explain and differentiate their American counterparts.

ACROBATIC ANIMALS
R.H. Russell: 1899 (9x11-7/8", 72 pgs, B&W, hard-c)
nn (Scarce) 175.00 325.00 675.00
NOTE: *Animal strips by Gustave Verbeck, presented 1 panel per page.*

ALMY'S SANTA CLAUS (P,E)
Edward C. Almy & Co., Providence, R.I.: nd (1880's) (5-3/4x4-5/8", 20 pgs, B&W, paper-c
nn - (Rare) 12.50 40.00 85.00
NOTE: *Department store Christmas giveaway containing an abbreviated 28-panel reprinting of George Cruikshank's* ***The Tooth-ache****. Santa Claus cover.*

AMERICAN COMIC ALMANAC, THE (OLD AMERICAN COMIC ALMANAC 1839-1846)
Charles Ellms: 1831-1846 (5x8, 52 pgs, B&W)
1-First American comic almanac ever prrinted 650.00 1300.00 2600.00
2-16 125.00 210.00 450.00
NOTE:#1 from 1831 is the First American Comic Almanac

AMERICAN PUNCH
American Punch Publishing Co: Jan 1879-March 1881, J.A. Cummings Engraving Co (last 3 issues) (Quarto Monthly)
Most issues 25.00 50.00 175.00

THE AMERICAN WIT
Richardson & Collins, NY: 1867-68 (18-1/2x13. 8 pgs, B&W)
2/3 Frank Bellew single panels 50.00 100.00 250.00

AMERICAN WIT AND HUMOR
Harper & Bros, NY: 1859 (
nn - numerous McLenan sequential comic strips 130.00 260.00 525.00

ATTWOOD'S PICTURES - AN ARTIST'S HISTORY OF THE LAST TEN YEARS OF THE NINETEENTH CENTURY (M,S)
Life Publishing Company, New York: 1900 (11-1/4x9-1/8", 156 pgs, B&W, gilted blue hard-c)
nn - By Attwood 50.00 100.00 185.00
NOTE: *Reprints monthly calendar cartoons which appeared in* ***LIFE****, for 1887 through 1899.*

BACHELOR BUTTERFLY, THE VERITABLE HISTORY OF MR. (E,G)
D. Bogue, London: 1845 (5-1/2x10-1/4", 74 pgs, B&W, gilted hardcover)
nn - By Rodolphe Töpffer (Scarce) 500.00 1250.00 3000.00
nn - Hand colored edition (Very Rare) (no known sales)
NOTE: *This is the British Edition, translated from the re-engraved by Cham serialization found in* ***L'Illustration*** *- a periodical from Paris publisher Dubochet. Predates the first French collected edition. Third Töpffer comic book published in English. The first story page is numbered Page 3. Page 17 shows Bachelor Butterfly being swallowed by a whale.*

BACHELOR BUTTERFLY, THE STRANGE ADVENTURES OF (E,G)
Wilson & Co., New York: 1846 (5-3/8x10-1/8", 68 pgs, B&W, soft-c)

nn - By Rodolphe Töpffer (Very Rare) 600.00 1500.00 3300.00
nn - At least one hand colored copy exists (Very Rare) (no known sales)
NOTE: *2nd Töpffer comic book printed in the U.S., 3rd earliest known sequential comic book in the USA. Reprinted from the British D. Bogue 1845 edition, itself from the earlier French language* ***Histoire de Mr. Cryptogame****. Released the same year as the French Dubochet edition. Two variations known, the earlier printing with Page number 17 placed on the inside (left) bottom corner in error, with slightly later printings corrected to place page number 17 on the outside (right) bottom corner of that page. Another first printing indicator is pages 17 and 20 are printed on the wrong side of the page. For both printings: the first story page is numbered 2. Page 17 shows Bachelor Butterfly already in the whale. In most panels with 3 lines of text, the third line is indented further than the second, which is in turn indented further than the first.*

BACHELOR BUTTERFLY, THE STRANGE ADVENTURES
Brother Jonathan Press, NY: 1854 (5-1/2x10-5/8", 68 pgs, paper-c, B&W) (Very Rare)
nn - By Rodolphe Töpffer 250.00 500.00 1300.00

BACHELOR BUTTERFLY,THE STRANGE & WONDERFUL ADVENTURES OF
Dick & Fitzgerald, New York: 1870s-1888 (various printings 30 Cent cover price, 68 pgs, B&W, paper cover) (all versions Rare) (E,G)
nn - Black print on blue cover (5-1/2x10-1/2"); string bound 125.00 250.00 550.00
nn - Black print on green cover (5-1/2x10-1/2"); string bound 100.00 200.00 440.00
NOTE: *Reprints the earlier Wilson & Co. edition. Page 2 is the first story page. Page 17 shows Bachelor Butterfly already in the whale. In most panels with 3 lines of text, the second and third lines are equally indented in from the first. Unknown which cover (blue or green) is earlier.*

BACHELOR'S OWN BOOK. BEING THE PROGRESS OF MR. LAMBKIN, (GENT.) IN THE PURSUIT OF PLEASURE AND AMUSEMENT (E,O,G)
(See also PROGRESS OF MR. LAMBKIN)
D. Bogue, London: August 1, 1844 (5x8-1/4", 28 pgs printed one side only, cardboard cover & interior) (all versions Rare)
nn - First printing hand colored 200.00 400.00 900.00
nn - First printing black & white 200.00 400.00 900.00
NOTE: *First printing has misspellings in the title. "PURSUIT" is spelled "PERSUIT", and "AMUSEMENT" is spelled "AMUSEMEMT".*
nn - Second printing hand colored 200.00 400.00 900.00
nn - Second printing black & white 200.00 400.00 900.00
NOTE: Second printing. The misspelling of "PURSUIT" has been corrected, but "AMUSEMEMT" error is still present.
nn - Third printing hand colored No misspellings 200.00 400.00 900.00
nn - Third printing black & white 200.00 400.00 900.00
NOTE: *By George Cruikshank. This is the British Edition. Issued both in black & white, and professionally hand-colored editions. Hand-colored editions have survived in higher quantities than uncolored. Originally made with thin paper sheets covering the plates.*

BACHELOR'S OWN BOOK; OR, THE PROGRESS OF MR. LAMBKIN, (GENT.), IN THE PURSUIT OF PLEASURE AND AMUSEMENT, AND ALSO IN SEARCH OF HEALTH AND HAPPINESS, THE (E,O,G)
David Bryce & Son: Glasgow: 1884 (one shilling; 7-5/8 x5-7/8", 62 pgs printed one side only, illustrated hardcover, page edges guilt
nn - Reprints the 1844 edition with altered title 25.00 50.00 125.00
nn - soft cover edition exists 20.00 35.00 70.00

BACHELOR'S OWN BOOK. BEIN-G TWENTY-FOUR PASSAGES IN THE LIFE OF MR. LAMBKIN, GENT. (E,G)
Burgess, Stringer & Co., New York on cover; Carey & Hart, Philadelphia on title page: 1845 (31-1/4 cents, 7-1/2x4-5/8", 52 pgs, B&W, paper cover)
nn - By George Cruikshank (Very Rare) (no known sales)
NOTE: *This is the second known sequential comic book story published in America. Reprints the earlier British edition. Pages printed on one side only. New cover art by an unknown artist.*

BAD BOY'S FIRST READER (O,S)
G.W. Carleton & Co.: 1881 (5-3/4 x 4-1/8", 44 pgs, B&W, paper cover)
nn - By Frank Bellew (Senior) 60.00 125.00 275.00
NOTE: *Parody of a children's ABC primer, one cartoon illustration plus text per page. Includes one panel of Boss Tweed. Frank Bellew is considered the "Father of the American Sequential Comics."*

BALL OF YARN OR, QUEER, QUIANT & QUIZZICAL STORIES, UNRAVELED WITH NEARLY 200 COMIC ENGRAVINGS OF FREAKS, FOLLIES & FOIBLES OF QUEER FOLKS BY THAT PRINCE OF COMICS, ELTON, THE (M)
Philip. J. Cozans, 116 Nassau St, NY: early 1850s (7-1/4x3-1/2", 76 pgs, yellow-wraps)
nn - sequential comic strips plus singles (no known sales)
NOTE: Mose Keyser-r, Jones, Smith & Robinson Goes To A Ball-r; The Adventures of Mr Goliah Starvemouse-r are all sequential comic strips printed in a number of sources

BARKER'S ILLUSTRATED ALMANAC (O,P,S)
Barker, Moore & Mein Medicine Co: 1878-1932+ (36 pgs, B&W, color paper-cr)
1878-1879 (Rare) 60.00 125.00 275.00
NOTE: *Not known yet what the cover art is.*
1880 Farmer Plowing Field-c 50.00 100.00 220.00
1881-1883 (Scarce,7-3/4x6-1/8") *4-mast ships & lighthouse-c* 50.00 100.00 220.00
1884-1889 (8x6-1/4") *Horse & Rider jumping picket fence-c* 50.00 100.00 220.00
1890-1897 (8-1/8x6-1/4") 50.00 100.00 220.00
1898-1899 (7-3/8x5-7/8") 50.00 100.00 220.00
1900+: see the Platinum Age Comics section (7x5-7/8")
NOTE: *Barker's Almanacs were actually issued in November of the year preceding the year which appears on the almanac. For example, the 1878 dated almanac was issued November 1877. They were given away to retailers of Barker's farm animal medicinal products, to in turn be given away to customers. Each Barker's Almanac contains 10 full page cartoons. These frequently included racist stereotypes of blacks. Each cartoon*

The Comical Adventures of Beau Ogleby
1843 © Tilt & Bogue, London

The Bottle by George Cruikshank
1871 © Geo. Gebbie

Buzz A Buzz Or The Bees By Wilhelm Busch
1873 © Henry Holt And Company, New York

contained advertisements for Barker's products. It is unknown whether the cartoons appeared only in the almanacs, or if they also ran as newspaper ads or flyers. Originally issued with a metal hook attached in the upper left hand corner, which could be used to hang the almanac.

BARKER'S "KOMIC" PICTURE SOUVENIR (P,S)
Barker, Moore & Mein Medicine Co: nd (1892-94) (color cardboard cover, B&W interior) (all unnumbered editions Very Rare)

nn - (1892) (1st edition, 6-7/8x10-1/2, 150 pgs) wraparound cover showing people headed towards Chicago for the 1893 World's Fair 250.00 600.00 1200.00
nn - (1893) (2nd edition, ??? pgs) same cover as 1st edition 250.00 600.00 1200.00
nn - (1894) (3rd edition, 180 pgs, 6-3/4x10-3/8") 250.00 600.00 1200.00
NOTE: *New cover art showing crowd of people laughing with a copy of Barker's Almanac.The crowd picture is flanked on both sides by picture of a tall thin person.*
nn - (1894) (4th edition, 124 pgs, 6-3/8x9-3/8") same-c as 3rd edition 250.00 400.00 1000.00
NOTE: *Essentially same-c as 3rd edition, except flanking picture on left edge is now gone. The 2nd through 4th editions state their printing on the first interior page, in the paragraph beneath the picture of the Barker's Building. These have been confirmed as premium comic books, predating the Buster Brown premiums. They reprint advertising cartoons from Barker's Illustrated Almanac. For the 50 page booklets by this same name, numbered as "Part"s, see the PLATINUM AGE SECTION. All "Editions in Parts", without exception, were published after 1900.*

BEAU OGLEBY, THE COMICAL ADVENTURES OF (E,G)
Tilt & Bogue: nd (c1843) (5-7/8x9-1/8", 72 pgs, printed one side only, green gilted hard-c, B&W)

nn - By Rodolphe Töpffer (Rare) 500.00 1000.00 2300.00
nn - Hand coloured edition (Very Rare) (no known sales)
NOTE: *British Edition; no known American Edition. 2nd Töpffer comic book published in English. Translated from Paris publisher Aubert's unauthorized redrawn 1839 bootleg edition of Töpffer's* ***Histoire de Mr. Jabot****. The back most interior page is an advertisement for* ***Obadiah Oldbuck****, showing its comic book cover*

BEE, THE
Bee Publishing Co: May 16 1898-Aug 2 1898 (Chromolithographic Weekly)

most issues 50.00 100.00 200.00
8 June Yellow Kid Hearst cover issue 175.00 350.00 750.00

BEFORE AND AFTER. A LOCOFOCO CHRISTMAS PRESENT. (O, C)
D.C. Johnston, Boston: 1837 (4-3/4x3", 1 page, hand colored cardboard)

nn - (Very Rare) by David Claypoole Johnston (sold at auction for $400 in GD)
NOTE: *Pull-tab cartoon envelope, parodying the 1836 New York City mayoral election, picturing the candidate of the Locofoco Party smiling "Before the N.York election", then, when the tab is pulled, picturing him with an angry sneer "After the N.York election".*

BILLY GOAT AND OTHER COMICALITIES, THE (M)
Charles Scribner's Sons: 1898 (6-3/4x8-1/2", 116 pgs., B&W, Hardcover)

nn - By E. W. Kemble 125.00 250.00 600.00

BLACKBERRIES, THE (N,S) (see Coontown's 400)
R. H. Russell: 1897 (9"x12", 76 pgs, hard-c, every other page in color, every other page in one color sepia tone)

nn - By E. W. Kemble 200.00 400.00 1800.00
NOTE: *Tastefully done comics about Black Americana during the USA's Jim Crow days.*

BOOK OF BUBBLES, YE (S)
Endicott & Co., New York: March 1864 (6-1/4 x 9-7/8",160 pgs, guilt-illus. hard-c, B&W

nn - By unknown 150.00 300.00 600.00
NOTE: *Subtitle: A contribution to the New York Fair in aid of the Sanitary Commission; 68 single-sided pages of B&W cartoons, each with an accompanying limerick. A few are sequential.*

BOOK OF DRAWINGS BY FRED RICHARDSON (N,S)
Lakeside Press, Chicago: 1899 (13-5/8x10-1/2", 116 pgs, B&W, hard-c)

nn - 80.00 160.00 350.00
NOTE: *Reprinted from the* ***Chicago Daily News****. Mostly single panel. Includes one* ***Yellow Kid*** *parody, some Spanish-American War cartoons.*

BOTTLE, THE (E,O) (see also THE DRUNKARD'S CHILDREN, and TEA GARDEN TO TEA POT, and TEMPERANCE TALES; OR, SIX NIGHTS WITH THE WASHINGTONIANS)
D. Bogue, London, with others in later editions: nd (1846) (16-1/2x11-1/2", 16 pgs, printed one side only, paper cover)

D. Bogue, London (nd; 1846): first edition:
nn - Black & white (Scarce) 250.00 450.00 1200.00
nn - Hand colored (Rare) (no known sales)
D. Bogue, London, and Wiley and Putnam, New York (nd; 1847) : second edition, misspells American publisher "Putnam" as "Putman":
nn - Black & white (Scarce) 150.00 300.00 725.00
nn - Hand colored (Rare) (no known sales)
D. Bogue, London, and Wiley and Putnam, New York (nd; 1847) : third edition has "Putnam" spelled correctly.
nn - Black & white (Scarce) 150.00 300.00 725.00
nn - Hand colored (Rare) (no known sales)
D. Bogue, London, Wiley and Putnam, New York, and J. Sands, Sydney, New South Wales: (nd; 1847) : fourth edition with no misspellings
nn - Black & white (Scarce) 150.00 300.00 725.00
nn - Hand colored (Rare) (no known sales)
NOTE: *By George Cruikshank. Temperance/anti-alcohol story. All editions are in precisely identical format. The only difference is to be found on the cover, where it lists who published it. Cover is text only - no cover art.*

BOTTLE, THE HISTORY OF THE
J.C. Becket, 22 Grea St James St, Montreal, Canada: 1851 (9-1/8x6", B&W)

nn - From Engravings by Cruikshank 175.00 325.00 725.00
NOTE: *As published in The Canada Temperance Advocate.*

BOTTLE, THE (E)
W. Tweedie, London: nd (1862) (11-1/2x17-1/3", 16 pgs, printed one side only, paper cover)

nn - Black & white; By George Cruikshank (Scarce) 100.00 200.00 420.00
nn - Hand colored (Scarce) (no known sales)

BOTTLE, THE (E)
Geo. Gebbie, Philadelphia: nd (c.1871) (11-3/8x17-1/8", 42 pgs, tinted interior, hard-c)

nn - By George Cruikshank 100.00 200.00 420.00
NOTE: *New cover art (cover not by Cruikshank).*

BOTTLE, THE (E)
National Temperance, London: nd (1881) (11-1/2x16-1/2", 16 pgs, printed one side only, paper-c, color)

nn - By George Cruikshank 100.00 200.00 420.00
NOTE: *See Platinum Age section for 1900s printings.*

BOTTLE, THE (E)
Marques, Pittsburgh, PA: 1884/85 (6x8", 8 plates, full color, illustrated envelope)
nn - art not by Cruickshank; New Art 75.00 125.00 250.00
NOTE: Says Presented by J.M. Gusky, Dealer in Boots and Shoes

BROAD GRINS OF THE LAUGHING PHILOSOPHER
Dick & Fitzgerald,NY: 1870s
nn - (4) panel sequential strip 25.00 50.00 150.00

BROTHER JONATHAN
Wilson & Co/Benj H Day, 48 Beekman, NYC: 1839-???

July 4 1846 - ads for Obadiah & Butterfly 50.00 100.00 225.00
July 4 1856 catalog list - front cover comic strip 100.00 200.00 400.00
Xmas/New Years 1856 75.00 150.00 300.00
average large size issues 25.00 50.00 100.00
NOTE: has full page advert for Fredinand Flipper comic book116

BULL CALF, THE (P,M)
Various: nd (c1890's) (3-7/8x4-1/8", 16 pgs, B&W, paper-c)

nn - By A.B. Frost Creme Oatmeal Toilet Soap 50.00 75.00 200.00
nn - By A.B. Frost Thompson & Taylor Spice Co, Chicago 50.00 75.00 200.00
NOTE: *Reprints the popular strip story by Frost, with the art modified to place a sign for Creme Oatmeal Soap within each panel. The back cover advertises the specific merchant who gave this booklet away - multiple variations exist.*

BULL CALF AND OTHER TALES, THE (M)
Charles Scribner's Sons: 1892 (120 pgs., 6-3/4x8-7/8", B&W, illus. hard cover)

nn - By Arthur Burdett Frost 50.00 150.00 500.00
NOTE: *Blue, grey, tan hard covers known to exist.*

BULL CALF, THE STORY OF THE MAN OF HUMANITY AND THE (P,M)
C.H. Fargo & Co.: 1890 (5-1/4x6-1/4", 24 pgs, B&W, color paper-c)

nn - By A.B. Frost 50.00 100.00 200.00
NOTE: *Fargo shoe company giveaway; pages alternate between shoe advertisements and the strip story.*

BUSHEL OF MERRY THOUGHTS, A (see Mischief Book, The) (E)
Sampson Low Son & Marsten: 1868 (68 pgs, handcolored hardcover, B&W)

nn - (6-1/4 x 9-7/8", 138 pgs) red binding, publisher's name on title page only 250.00 500.00 1000.00
nn - (6-1/2 x 10", 134 pgs) green binding, publisher's name on cover & title page 250.00 500.00 1000.00
NOTE: *Cover plus story title pages designed by Leighton Brothers, based on Busch art. Translated by Harry Rogers (who is credited instead of Busch). This is a British publication, notable as the earliest known English language anthology collection of Wilhelm Busch comic strips. Page 13 of second story missing from all editions (panel dropped). Unknown which of the two editions was published first. A modern reprint, by Dover in 1971.*

BUTTON BURSTER, THE (M) (says on cover "ten cents hard cash")
M.J. Ivers & Co., 86 Nassau St., New York: 1873 (11x8-1/8", soft paper, B&W)

By various cartoonists (Very Rare) 150.00 300.00 600.00
NOTE: *Reprints from various 1873 issues of Wild Oats; has (5) different sequential comic strips: (3) by Livingston Hopkins, (1) by Thomas Worth, other one creator presently unknown; Bellew, Sr. single panel cartoons.*

BUZZ A BUZZ OR THE BEES (E)
Griffith & Farran, London: September 1872 (8-1/2x5-1/2", 168 pgs, printed one side only, orange, black & white hardcover, B&W interior)

nn - By Wilhelm Busch (Scarce) 112.00 225.00 500.00
NOTE: *Reprint published by Phillipson & Golder, Chester; text written by English to accompany Busch art.*

BUZZ A BUZZ OR THE BEES (E)
Henry Holt & Company, New York: 1873 (9x6", 96 pgs, gilted hardcover, hand colored)

nn - By Wilhelm Busch (Scarce) 125.00 250.00 500.00
NOTE: *Completely different translation than the Griffith & Farran version. Also, contains 28 additional illustrations by Park Benjamin. The lower page count is because the Henry Holt edition prints on both sides of each page, and the Griffith & Farran edition is printed one side only.*

CALENDAR FOR THE MONTH; YE PICTORIAL LYSTE OF YE MATTERS OF

The Carpet Bag #14
1851 © Snow & Wilder

Centennial Fun (Keppler cover)
July 1876 © Frank Leslie

Comic Monthly v6 #8
March 1865 © J.C.Haney, NY

FR1.0 GD2.0 FN6.0

INTEREST FOR SUMMER READING (P,M)
S.E. Bridgman & Company, Northampton, Mass: nd (c. late 1880's-1890's) (5-5/8x7-1/4", 64 pgs, paper-c, B&W)
nn - (Very Rare) T.S. Sullivant-c/a 125.00 250.00 500.00
NOTE: Book seller's catalog, with every other page reprinting cartoons and strips (from Life??). Art by: Chips Bellew, Gibson, Howarth, Kemble, Sullivant, Townsend, Woolf.

CARICATURE AND OTHER COMIC ART
Harper & Brothers, NY: 1877 (9-5/16x7-1/8", 360 pgs, B&W, green hard-c)
nn - By James Parton (over 200 illustrations) 30.00 60.00 250.00
*NOTE: This is the earliest known serious history of comics & related genre from around the world produced by an American. Parton was a cousin of Thomas Nast's wife Sarah. A large portion of this book was first serialized in **Harper's Monthly** in 1875.*

CARPET BAG, THE
Snow & Wilder, later Wilder & Pickard, Boston: March 21 1851-March 26 1853
Each average issue 25.00 50.00 100.00
Samuel "Mark Twain" Clemmons issues (first app in print) 800.00 1500.00 3000.00
NOTE: Many issues contain cartoons by DC Johnston, Frank Bellew, others; literature includes Artemus Ward's Miss Partington who had a mischevious little Katzenjammer Kids-like brat. Carpet Bag was not considered derogatory pre-Civil War.

CARROT-POMADE (O,G)
James G. Gregory, Publisher, New York: 1864 (9x6-7/8", 36 pgs, B&W)
nn - By Augustus Hoppin 75.00 150.00 300.00
NOTE: The story of a quack remedy for baldness, sequentially told in the format parodying ABC primers. Has protective tissue pages (not part of page count).

CARTOONS BY HOMER C. DAVENPORT (M,N,S)
De Witt Publishing House: 1898 (16-1/8x12", 102 pgs, hard-c, B&W)
nn 100.00 200.00 400.00
NOTE: Reprinted from Harper's Weekly and the New York Journal. Includes cartoons about the Spanish-American War. Title page reads "Davenport's Cartoons".

CARTOONS BY WILL E. CHAPIN (P,N,S)
The Times-Mirror Printing and Binding House, Los Angeles: 1899 (15-1/4x12", 98 pgs, hard-c, B&W)
nn - scarce 100.00 200.00 400.00
NOTE: Premium item for subscribing to the Los-Angeles Times-Mirror newspaper, from which these cartoons were reprinted. Includes cartoons about the Spanish-American War.

CARTOONS OF OUR WAR WITH SPAIN (N,S)
Frederick A. Stokes Company: 1898 (11-1/2x10", 72 pgs, hardcover, B&W)
nn - By Charles Nelan (r-New York Herald) 40.00 100.00 200.00
nn - 2nd printing noted on copy right page 30.00 60.00 120.00

CARTOONS OF THE WAR OF 1898 (E,M,N,S)
Belford, Middlebrook & Co., Chicago: 1898 (7x10-3/8",190 pgs, B&W, hard-c)
nn 50.00 100.00 200.00
NOTE: Reprints single panel editorial cartoons on the Spanish-American War, from American, Spanish, Latino, and European newspapers and magazines, at rate of 2 to 6 cartoons per page. Art by Bart, Berryman, Bowman, Bradley, Chapin, Gillam, Nelan, Tenniel, others.

CENTENNIAL FUN (O,S) (Rare)
Frank Leslie, Philadelphia: (July) 1876 (25¢, 11x8", 32 pgs, paper cover, B&W)
nn - By Joseph Keppler-c/a;Thomas Worth-a 175.00 350.00 700.00
NOTE: Issued for the 1876 Centennial Exposition in Philadelphia. Exists with both black & white, and orange, black & white covers. One copy of the latter had an embossed newstand label from Partland, Maine, implying that the orange cover version, at least, was distributed and sold outside of Philadelphia.

CHAMPAIGNE
Frank Leslie: June-Dec 1871
1-7 scarce 150.00 225.00 400.00

CHIC
Chic Publishing Co: 1880-81 (Chromolithographic Weekly)
1-38 Livingston Hopkins, Charles Kendrick, CW Weldon 75.00 150.00 325.00

CHILDREN'S CHRISTMAS BOOK, THE
The New York Sunday World: 1897 (10-1/4x8-3/4", 16 pgs, full color)
Dec 12, 1897 - By George Luks, G.H. Grant, Will Crawford, others) (Rare) 75.00 125.00 300.00

CHIP'S DOGS (M)
R.H. Russell and Son Publishers: 1895 hardcover, B&W)
nn - By Frank P. W. "Chip" Bellew 25.00 50.00 100.00
Early printing 80 pgs, 8-7/8x11-7/8"; dark green border of hardcover surrounds all four sides of pasted on cover image; pages arranged in error -- see NOTE below. (more scarce)
nn - By Frank P. W. "Chip" Bellew 12.50 25.00 50.00
Later printing 72 pgs, 8-7/8x11-3/4";green border only on the binding side (one side) of the cover image.
*NOTE: Both are strip reprints from **LIFE**. The difference in page count is due to more blank pages in the first printing -- all printings have the same comics contents, but with the pages in the first printing arranged differently. This is noticeable particularly in the 2-page strip "Getting a Pointer", which appears on the 2nd & 3rd to last pages of the later printings, but in the early printing the first half of this strip is near the middle of the book, while the last half appears on the 2nd to last story page.*

CHIP'S OLD WOOD CUTS (M,S)
R.H. Russell & Son: 1895 (8-7/8x11-3/4", 72 pgs, hardcover, B&W)
nn - By Frank P. W. ("Chip") Bellew 25.00 50.00 100.00
nn - 1897 reprint 15.00 30.00 60.00

CHIP'S UN-NATURAL HISTORY (O,S)
Frederick A. Stokes & Brother: 1888 (7x5-1/4", 64 pgs, hardcover, B&W)
nn - By Frank P. W. ("Chip") Bellew 12.50 25.00 50.00
NOTE: Title page lists publisher as "Successors to White, Stokes & Allen."

CLOWN, OR THE BANQUET OF WIT, THE (E,M,O)
Fisher & Brother, Philadelphia, Baltimore, New York, Boston: nd (c.1851) (7-3/8x4-1/2", 88 pgs, paper cover, B&W)
nn - (Very Rare; 3 known copies) 600.00 1200.00 2400.00
NOTE: Earliest known multi-artist anthology of sequential comics; contains multiple sequential comics, plus numerous single panel cartoons. A mixture of reprinted and original material, involving both European and American artists. "Jones, Smith, and Robinson Goes to a Ball" by Richard Doyle (1st app. of Doyle's "Foreign Tour" in America, reprinted from PUNCH, August 24, 1850); "Moses Keyser The Bowery Bully's Trip to the Californian Gold Mines", by John H. Manning; "The Adventures of Mr. Gulp" (by the Read brothers?); more comics by artists unknown; cartoons by George Cruikshank, Grandville, Elton.

COLD CUTS AND PICKLED EELS' FEET; DONE BROWN BY JOHN BROWN
P.J. Cozans, New York: nd (c1855-60) (B&W)
nn - (Very Rare) 100.00 200.00 300.00
NOTE: Mostly a children's book. But, pages 87 to 110, and 111 to 122, contain narrative sequential stories.

COLLEGE SCENES (O,G)
N. Hayward, Boston: 1850 (5x6-3/4", 72 pgs, printed one side only, B&W lithography)
nn - (Rare) by Nathan Hayward 200.00 400.00 700.00
NOTE: This is the 2nd such production for an American University; the first issued at Yale circa 1845, decent funny art of story about life of a Harvard student from his entrance thru graduation entirely in caricature. Has art on back cover as well.

COLLEGE CUTS Chosen From The Columbia Spectator 1880-81-82 (S)
White & Stokes, NY: 1882 (8x9-5/8", 92 pgs, B&W)
By F. Benedict Herzog, H. McVickar, W. Bard McVickar, others 20.00 40.00 100.00
nn - 2nd edition reprint (1888) (8-1/4x10-3/8) 10.00 20.00 50.00

COMICAL COONS (M)
R.H. Russell: 1898 (8-7/8 x 11-7/8", 68 pgs, hardcover, B&W)
nn - By E. W. Kemble 350.00 700.00 1500.00
NOTE: Black Americana collection of 2-panel stories.

COMICAL ALMANAC
Anton Bicker, Cinncinati, OH: 1885 (9x6, 260 pgs, B&W, illustrated-c)
nn - two (12) page sequential Busch comic strips 50.00 100.00 250.00

COMIC ALMANAC, THE
John Berger. Baltimore: 1854-? (7-1/2x6-1/4, 36 pgs, B&W)
nn - 65.00 125.00 275.00

COMIC ANNUAL, AMERICAN (O,I)
Richardson, Lord, & Holbrook, Boston: 1831 (6-7/8x4-3/8", 268 pgs, B&W, hard-c)
nn - (Scarce) 150.00 300.00 620.00
NOTE: Mostly text; front & back cover illustrations, 13 full page, and scattered smaller illustrations by David Claypoole Johnston; edited by Henry J. Finn.

COMIC HISTORY OF THE UNITED STATES, (I)
Carleton & Co., NY: 1876 (6-7/8x5-1/8", 336 pgs, hardcover, B&W)
nn - By Livingston Hopkins. 20.00 40.00 80.00
2nd printing: Cassell, Petter, Galpin & Co.: 1880 (6-7/8x5-1/8", 336 pgs, hardcover, B&W)
nn - By Livingston Hopkins. 20.00 40.00 80.00
*NOTE: Text with many B&W illustrations; some are multi-panel comics. Not to beconfused with **Bill Nye's Comic History Of The U.S.** which contains Frederick Opper illustrations.*

COMIC MONTHLY, THE
J.C. Haney, N.Y.: March 1859-1880 (16 x 11-1/2", 30 pgs average, B&W)
Certain average issues with sequential comics 50.00 100.00 200.00
11 (Jan 1860) Bellew-c 25.00 50.00 100.00
v2#2 (Apr 1860) Bellew-c 25.00 50.00 100.00
v2#3 (May 1860) Bellew-c 25.00 50.00 100.00
v2#4 (June 1860) Comic Strip Cover 50.00 100.00 200.00
v2#5 (July 1860) Bellew-c; (12) panel Explaining American Politics To An Intelligent Foreigner; (10) panel The Art of Stump Speaking; (15) panel Mr. Dibbs Goes to Pike's Peak and Comes Back Again 125.00 250.00 525.00
v2#7 (Sept 1860) Comic Strip Cover; (24) panel double page spread The Prince of Wales In America 50.00 100.00 200.00
v2#8 (18) panel The Three Young Friends Sillouette Strip 25.00 50.00 100.00
v2#9 (Nov 1860) (9) panel sequential 25.00 50.00 100.00
v2#10 11 not indexed 25.00 50.00 100.00
v2#12 (Jan 1861) (12) panel double page spread 25.00 50.00 100.00

COMIC TOKEN FOR 1836, A COMPANION TO THE COMIC ALMANAC, THE
Charles Ellms, Boston: 1836 (8x5', 48 pgs, B&W)
nn - 50.00 100.00 200.00

COMIC WEEKLY, THE
???, NYC: 1881-???
issues with comic strips (Chips, etc) 60.00 125.00 250.00

Comics From Scribner's Magazine
1891 © Scribner's

The Daily Graphic #158
Sept. 4, 1873 © The Graphic Company, NY

Elton's Californian Comic All-My-Nack #17
1850 © Elton's, NY

COMIC WORLD
???: 1876-1879 (Quarto Monthly)
issues with comic strips 37.50 75.00 150.00

COMICS FROM SCRIBNER'S MAGAZINE (M)
Scribner's: nd (1891) (10 cents, 9-1/2x6-5/8", 24 pgs, paper cover, side stapled, B&W)
nn - (Rare) F.M.Howarth C&A 175.00 350.00 700.00
NOTE: *Advertised in SCRIBNER'S MAGAZINE in the June 1891 issue, page 793, as available by mail order for 10 cents. Collects together comics material which ran in the back pages of Scribner's Magazine. Art by Attwood, "Chip" Bellew, Dōes, Frost, Gibson, Zim.*

COMUS OFFERING CONTAINING HUMOROUS SCRAPS OF DIVERTING COMICALITIES, THE (O, S)
B. Franklin Edmands, 25 Court St, Boston: c1830-31 (8-7/8x10-3/4", 16 pgs, thin brown paper-c, blank on backs,
nn - (William F Straton, Engraver, 15 Water St, Boston) (no known sales)
NOTE: All hand-colored single panel cartoons format definitely inspired by D.C. Johnston's Scraps with every panel character using well-defined word balloons. Might become a seminal step in the evolution of the American comic book. More research is needed.

CONTRASTS AND CONCEITS FOR CONTEMPLATION BY LUKE LIMNER (O)
Ackerman & Co, 96 Strand, London: c1848 (9-3/4x6-1/4, 48 pgs, B&W)
nn - By John Leighton 50.00 100.00 200.00

COONTOWN'S 400 (M) (see **Blackberries**) (M)
The Life (Magazine) Co.: 1899 (10-15/16x8-7/8, 68 pgs, cloth light-brown hard-c, B&W
nn - By E.W. Kemble (scarce) 325.00 600.00 1900.00
NOTE: *Tastefully drawn depictions of Black Americana over one hundred years ago during Jim Crow days.*

CROSSING THE ATLANTIC (O,G)
James R. Osgood & Co., Boston: 1872 (10-7/8x16", 68 pgs, hardcover, B&W);
Houghton, Osgood & Co., Boston: 1880
1st printing - by Augustus Hoppin 50.00 100.00 200.00
2nd printing (1880; 66 pgs; 8-1/8x11-1/8") 32.50 65.00 150.00

C.R. PITT'S COMIC ALMANAC
C.R. Pitt: 1880 (7-1/2x4-5/8", 28 pgs)
nn - contains (8) panel sequential 50.00 100.00 200.00

CRUIKSHANK'S OMNIBUS: A VEHICLE FOR FUN AND FROLIC (E,S)
E. Ferrett & Co., Philadelphia: 1845 (25 cents, 7-1/2" x 4-5/8", 96 pgs, B&W, paper-c)
nn - By George Cruikshank c/a (Very Rare) 150.00 300.00 750.00
NOTE: *Mostly prose, with 10 plates of cartoons printed on one-side (about half the plates with multiple cartoons), plus illustrated cover, all by George Cruikshank. First (perhaps only) American printing of Cruikshank's Omnibus, which was published first in Britain. It is only a partial reprinting.*

CYCLISTS' DICTIONARY (S)
Morgan & Wright, Chicago: 1894 (5 x3-3/4, 80 pgs, soft-c, B&W
nn - By Unknown 37.50 75.00 150.00

THE DAILY GRAPHIC
The Graphic Company, 39 Park Place, NY: 1873-Sept 23, 1889 (14x20-1/2, 8 pgs, B&W)
Average issues with comic strips 15.00 20.00 40.00
Average issues without comic strips 10.00 15.00 30.00
NOTE:

DAVY CROCKETT'S COMIC ALMANACK
???, Nashville, TN, then elsewhere: 1835-end (32 pages plus wraps)
1 550.00 1100.00 2200.00
2-13 15 end 275.00 550.00 1100.00
14 contains (17) panel Crocket comic strip bio 1848 1050.00 1600.00 3200.00

DAY'S DOINGS (was The Last Sensation) (Becomes New York Illustrated Times)
James Watts, NYC: #1 June 6 1868-early 1876 (11x16, 16 pgs, B&W)
average issue with comic strips 10.00 15.00 25.00
Paul Pry & Alley Sloper character issues 25.00 50.00 100.00
Aug 19 1871 - First Alley Sloper in America?? 50.00 100.00 200.00
NOTE: *James Watts was a shadow company for Frank Leslie; outright sold to Frank Leslie in 1873. There are a lot of issues with comic strips from 1868 up.*

DAY'S SPORT - OR, HUNTING ADVENTURES OF S. WINKS WATTLES, A SHOPKEEPER, THOMAS TITT, A "LEGAL GENT," AND MAJOR NICHOLAS NOGGIN, A JOLLY GOOD FELLOW GENERALLY, A (O)
Brother Jonathan, NY: c1850s (5-7/8x8-1/4, 44 pgs)
nn - By Henry L. Stephens, Philadelphia (Very Rare) (no known sales)

DEVIL'S COMICAL OLDMANICK WITH COMIC ENGRAVINGS OF THE PRINCIPAL EVENTS OF TEXAS, THE
Turner & Fisher, NY & Philadelphia: 1837 (7-7/8x5", 24 pgs)
nn - many single panel cartoons 125.00 250.00 550.00

DIE VEHME, ILLUSTRIRTES WOCHENBLATT FUR SCHERZ UND ERNEST (M,O)
Heinrich Binder, St. Louis: No.1 Aug 28, 1869 - No.?? Aug 20, 1870 (10 cents, 8 pgs, B&W, paper-c) (see also PUCK)
1-?? (Very Rare) by Joseph Keppler 100.00 200.00 400.00
NOTE: *Joseph Keppler's first attempt at a weekly American humor periodical. Entirely in German. The title translates into: **"The Star Chamber: An Illustrated Weekly Paper in Fun and Ernest"**.*

DOMESTIC MANNERS OF THE AMERICANS
The Imprint Society, Barre, Mass: 1969 (9-3/4 x 7-1/4", 390 pgs, hard-c in slipcase, B&W)
nn - 15.00 25.00 60.00
NOTE: *Reprints the 1832 edition of this book by Mrs. Trollope with an added insert. The 28-page insert is what is of primary interest to us -- it reproduces SCRAPS No. 4 (1833) by D.C. Johnston.*

DRUNKARD'S CHILDREN, THE (see also THE BOTTLE) (E,O)
David Bogue, London; John Wiley and G.P. Putnam, New York; J. Sands, Sydney, New South Wales: July 1, 1848 (16x11", 16 pgs, printed on one side only, paper-c)
nn - Black & white edition (Scarce) 400.00 800.00 1200.00
nn - Hand colored edition (Rare) (no known sales)
NOTE: *Sequel story to THE BOTTLE, by George Cruikshank. Temperance/anti-alcohol story. British-American-Australian co-publication. Cover is text only - no cover art.*

DRUNKARD'S PROGRESS, OR THE DIRECT ROAD TO POVERTY, WRETCHEDNESS & RUIN, THE
J. W. Barber, New Haven, Conn.: Sept 1826 (single sheet)
nn - By John Warner Barber (Very Rare) (no known sales)
NOTE: *Broadside designed and printed by barber contains four large wood engravings showing "The Morning Dram" which is "The Beginning of Sorrow"; "The Grog Shop" with its "Bad Company"; "The Confirmed Drunkard" in a state of "Beastly Intoxication"; and the "Concluding Scene" with the family being drive off to the alms house. It is an interesting set of cuts, faintly reminiscent of Hogarth. Many modern reprints exist.*

DUEL FOR LOVE, A (O,P)
E.C. DeWitt & Co., Chicago: nd (c1880's) (3-3/8" x 2-5/8", 12 pgs, B&W, paper-c)
nn - Art by F.M. Howarth (Rare) 25.00 50.00 125.00
NOTE: *Advertising giveaway for DeWitt's Little Early Risers, featuring an 8-panel strip story, spread out 1 panel per page.*

DURHAM WHIFFS (O, P)
Blackwells Durham Tobacco Co: Jan 8 1878 (9x6.5", 8 pgs, color-c, B&W)
v1 #1 w/Trade Card Insert 37.50 75.00 200.00
NOTE: Sold in 2008 CGC 9.4 $1250

DYNALENE LAFLETS (P)
The Dynalene Company: nd (3 x 3-1/2", 16 pgs, B&W, paper cover)
nn - Dynalene Dyes promo (9) panel comic strip 25.00 50.00 75.00

ELEPHANT, THE
William H Graham, Tribune Building, NYC: Jan 22 1848-Feb 19 1848 (11x8.5", B&W)
1-5 Rare - single panel cartoons 175.00 325.00 650.00

ELTON'S COMIC ALL-MY-NACK (E,O.S)
Elton, Publisher, 18 Division & 98 Nassau St, NY: 1833-1852 (7-1/2x4-1/2", 36pgs, B&W
1-5 99% single panel cartoons 100.00 200.00 400.00
6 (1839) 100.00 200.00 400.00
NOTE: Two different covers & different interiors exist for this title and number
7-15 - 99% single panel cartoons 100.00 200.00 400.00
16 - contains 6 panel "A Tales of A Tayl-or" 1848-49 200.00 400.00 650.00
17 - contains "Moses Keyser, The Bowery Bully's Trip To the California Gold Mines" 1850 By John H. Manning, early comics creator, told in 15 panels 200.00 400.00 650.00
18-19 presently unknown contents 100.00 200.00 400.00
NOTE: *Contains both original American, and pirated European, cartoons. All single panel material, except where noted. Almanacs are published near the end of the year prior to that for which they are printed -- like calendars today. Thus, the 1833 No. 1 issue was really published in the last months of 1832. #17 has Elton's Californian Comic-All-My-Nack on the cover.*

ELTON'S COMIC ALMANAC (Publsiher change)
GW Cottrell & Co, Publishers & C Cornhill, Boston, Mass: 1853 (7-7/8x4-5/8,36pgs,B&W
20 - (2) sequential comic strips (9) panel "Jones, Smith and Robinson Goes To A Ball; (21) panel "The Adventures of Mr. Gulp" Rare 350.00 750.00 1500.00
NOTE: *Both strips appear in* The Clown, Or The Banquet of Wit

ELTON'S FUNNY ALMANACK (title change to Almanac)
Elton Publisher and Engraver, New York: 1846 (8x6-1/2", 36 pgs)
1 1846 50.00 100.00 225.00

ELTON'S FUNNY ALMANAC (#1 titled Almanack)
Elton & Co, New York: 1847-1853 (8x6-1/4, 36 pgs, B&W)
2 (1847) #3 (1848) 50.00 100.00 225.00
nn 1853 (8-1/8x4-7/8"; (5) panel comic strip "The Adventures of Mr. Goliah Starvemouse"

ELTON'S RIPSNORTER COMIC ALMANAC
Elton, 90 Nassau St, NY: 1850 (8x5, 24 pgs, B&W, paper-c)
nn - scarce 50.00 100.00 225.00

ENGLISH SOCIETY (S)
Harper & Brothers, Publishers, New York: 1897 (9-5/8x12-1/4", 206 pgs, B&W)
nn - by George Du Maurier 50.00 75.00 110.00

ENGLISH SOCIETY AT HOME (S)
James R. Osgood and Company: 1881 (10-7/8x8-5/8, 182 pgss, protective sheets on some pages - not included in pages count, hard-c, B&W 50.00 75.00 110.00
nn - by George Du Maurier

ENTER: THE COMICS (E,G)
University of Nebraska Press: 1965 (6-7/8x9-1/4", 120 pgs, hard-c)

The Evolution Of A Democrat
1888 © Paquet & Co, NY

Flying Leaves
1880s © E.R. Herrick & Company, New York

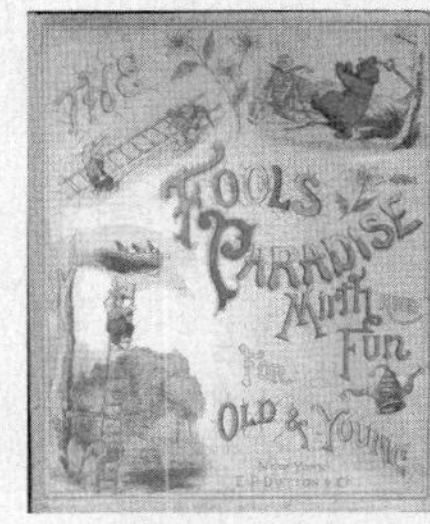

The Fools Paradise Mirth and Fun
For Old and Young
1883 © E.P. Dutton & Co, NYC

FR1.0 GD2.0 FN6.0

nn - By Ellen Weisse 25.00 50.00 100.00
NOTE: *Contains overview of Töpffer's life and career plus only published English translation of Töpffer's Monsieur Crepin (1837); appears to have been re-drawn by Weisse in the days before xerox machines.*

ESQUIRE BROWN AND HIS MULE, STORY OF
A.C. Meyer, Baltimore, Maryland: 1880s (5x3/7/8", 28 pgs, B&W)
Booklet (9 panel story plus cough remedies catalog) 35.00 70.00 150.00
Fold-Out of Booklet (9 panel version) 35.00 70.00 150.00

"EVENTS OF THE WEEK" REPRINTED FROM THE CHICAGO TRIBUNE
Henry O. Shepard Co, Chicago: 1894 (5-3/8x15-7/8", 110 pg, B&W, hard-c)
First Series, Second Series - By HR Heaton 37.50 75.00 150.00

EVERYBODY'S COMICK ALMANACK
Turner & Fisher, NY & Philadelphia: 1837 (7-7/8x5", 36 pgs, B&W)
nn 50.00 100.00 200.00

EVOLUTION OF A DEMOCRAT - A DARWINIAN TALE, THE (O,G)
Paquet & Co., New York: 1888 (25 cents, 7-7/8x5-1/2", 100 pgs, printed one side only, orange paper cover, B&W) (Very Rare)
nn - Written by Henry Liddell, art by G. Roberty 375.00 700.00 1500.00
NOTE: *Political parody about the rise of an Irishman through Tammany Hall. Grover Cleveland appears as linked with Tammany. Ireland becomes the next state in the USA.*

FABLES FOR THE TIMES (S, I)
R.H. Russell & Son, New York: 1896 (9-1/8x12-1/8", 52 pgs, yellow hard-c)
nn - By H.W. Phillips and T.S. Sullivant Scarce 75.00 150.00 300.00

FERDINAND FLIPPER, ESQ., THE FORTUNES OF (O,G)
Brother Jonathan, Publisher, NY: nd (1851) (5-3/4 x 9-3/8", 84 pgs, B&W, printed both sides)
nn - By Various (Very Rare) 700.00 1200.00 3200.00
NOTE: *Extended title: "...Commencing With A Period of Four Months And Anterior To His Birth Going Thru The Various Stages of His Infancy, Childhood, Verdant Years, Manhood, Middle Life, and Green and Ripe Old Age, And Ending A Short Time Subsequent to His Sudden Decease With His Final Exit, Funeral And Burial." Extremely unique comic book, put together by gathering 145 independent single illustrations and cartoons, by various artists, and stringing them together into a sequential story. The majority of panels are by Grandville. Also included are at least 19 scarce signed Charles Martin, reprinted from 1847 issues of Yankee Doodle, 5 panels from D.C. Johnston, plus other panels by F.O.C. Darley, T.H. Matheson, and others. The story also contains several panels of Gold Rush content . Printed by E.A. Alverds. The 1851 date is derived from an advertisement found in the Oct-Dec 1851 issue of the Brother Jonathan newspaper. It isposible, however, that it actually came out even earlier.*

FERDINAND FLIPPER, ESQ., THE FORTUNES OF (G)
Dick & Fitzgerald, New York: nd (1870's to 1888) (30 Cents, 84 pgs, B&W, paper cover)
nn - (Very Rare reprint - several editions possible) 375.00 750.00 1700.00

FINN'S COMIC ALMANAC
Marsh, Capen, & Lyon; Boston: 1835-??? (4.5x7.5, 36 pgs, B&W)
nn 100.00 200.00 400.00

FINN'S COMIC SKETCHBOOK (S)
Peabody & Co., 223 Broadway, NY: 1831 (10-1/2x16", 12 pgs, B&W)
nn - By Henry J. Finn (Very Rare) (no known sales)
NOTE: *Designs on copper plates; etched by J. Harris, NY; should have tissue paper in front of each plate.*

50 GREAT CARTOONS (M,P,S)
Ram's Horn Press: 1899 (14x10-3/4, 112 pgs, hard-c)
nn - By Frank Beard 30.00 60.00 125.00
NOTE: *Premium in return for a subscription to **The Ram's Horn** magazine.*

FISHER'S COMIC ALMANAC
Ames Fisher and Brother, No 12 North Sixth St, Philadelphia , Charles Small in NYC, Also in Boston: 1841-1868 (4-1/2 x 7-1/4, 36 pgs, B&W)
1-7 (1841-1847) 100.00 200.00 440.00
12 reprints mermaid-c with word balloon (1868) 100.00 200.00 440.00

F**** A*** K*****, OUTLINES ILLUSTRATIVE OF THE JOURNAL OF** (O,S)
D.C. Johnston, Boston: 1835 (9-5/16 x 6", 12 pgs, printed one side only, blue paper cover, B&W interior) (see also **SCRAPS**)
nn - by David Claypoole Johnston (Scarce) 650.00 1100.00 1750.00
NOTE: *This is a series of 8 plates parodying passages from the Journal of Fanny (Frances) A. Kemble, a British woman who wrote a highly negative book about American Culture after returning from the U.S. Though remembered now for her campaign against slavery, she was prejudiced against most everything American culture, thus inspiring Johnston's satire. Contains 4 protective sheets (not part of page count.)*

FLYING DUTCHMAN; OR, THE WRATH OF HERR VONSTOPPELNOZE, THE (E)
Carleton Publishing, New York: 1862 (7-5/8x5-1/4", 84 pgs, printed on one side only, gilted hardcover, B&W)
nn - By Wilhelm Busch (Scarce) 35.00 70.00 160.00
nn - 1975 Scarce 100 copy-r 74 pgs Visual Studies Workshop 5.00 10.00 20.00
NOTE: *This is the earliest known English language book publication of a Wilhelm Busch work. The story is plagiarized by American poet John G. Saxe, who is credited with the text, while the uncredited Busch cartoons are described merely as accompanying illustrations.*

FLYING LEAVES (E)
E.R. Herrick & Company, New York: nd (c1889/1890's) (8-1/4" x 11-1/2", 76 pgs, B&W interior, orange, b&w hard-c)
nn- (Scarce) 85.00 175.00 260.00

FR1.0 GD2.0 FN6.0

NOTE: *Reprints strips and single panel cartoons from 1888 Fliegende Blatter issues, translated into English. Various artists, including Bechstein, Adolf Hengeler, Lothar Meggendorfer, Emil Reinicke.*

FOOLS PARADISE WITH THE MANY ADVENTURES THERE AS SEEN IN THE STRANGE SURPRISING PEEP SHOW OF PROFESSOR WOLLEY COBBLE, THE (E)
(see also THE COMICAL PEEP SHOW)
John Camden Hotten, London: Nov 1871 (1 crown, 9-7/8x7-3/8", 172 pgs, printed one side only, gilted green hardcover, hand colored interior)
nn - By Wilhelm Busch (Rare) 500.00 1000.00 2000.00
NOTE: *Title on cover is: **WALK IN! WALK IN!! JUST ABOUT TO BEGIN!!! the FOOLS PARADISE**; below the above title page. Anthology of Wilhelm Busch comics, translated into English.*

FOOLS PARADISE WITH THE MANY WONDERFUL SIGHTS AS SEEN IN THE STRANGE SURPRISING PEEP SHOW OF PROFESSOR WOLLEY COBBLE, FURTHER ADVENTURES IN (E)
Chatto & Windus, London: 1873 (10x7-3/8", 128 pgs, printed one side only, brown hardcover, hand colored interior)
nn - By Wilhelm Busch (Rare) 400.00 800.00 1600.00
NOTE: *Sequel to the 1871 **FOOLS PARADISE**, containing a completely different set of Busch stories, translated into English.*

FOOLS PARADISE MIRTH AND FUN FOR THE OLD & YOUNG (E)
Griffith & Farran, London: May 1883 (9-3/4x7-5/8", 78 pgs, color cover, color interior)
nn - By Wilhelm Busch (Rare) 100.00 200.00 425.00
NOTE: *Collection of selected stories reprinted from both the 1871 & 1873 **FOOLS PARADISE**.*

FOOLS PARADISE - MIRTH AND FUN FOR THE OLD & YOUNG (E)
E.P. Dutton and Co., NY: May 1883 (9-3/4x7-5/8", 78 pgs, color cover, color interior)
nn - By Wilhelm Busch (Rare) 100.00 200.00 425.00
NOTE: *Collection of selected stories reprinted from both the 1871 & 1873 **FOOLS PARADISE**.*

FOREIGN TOUR OF MESSRS. BROWN, JONES, AND ROBINSON, THE (see Messrs....)

FRANK LESLIE'S BOYS AND GIRLS
Frank Leslie, NYC: Oct 13 1866-#905 Feb 9 1884
average issue with comic strip 20.00 30.00 50.00

FRANK LESLIE'S BUDGET OF FUN
Frank Leslie, Ross & Tousey, 121 Nassau St, NYC: Jan 1859-1878 (newspaper size)
1-5 no comic strips 50.00 100.00 250.00
6 June 1859 (9) panel "The Wonderful Hunting Tour of Mr Borridge After the Deer" 75.00 150.00 440.00
7-9 no comic strips 25.00 50.00 130.00
10 Sept 1859 sequential comic strip 50.00 100.00 250.00
11 (8) panel sequential "Apropos of the Great Eastern" 50.00 100.00 250.00
12-14 25.00 50.00 130.00
15 Feb 1860 (12) panel "The Ballet Girl" strip 50.00 100.00 240.00
16-18 25.00 50.00 130.00
19 June 1860 comic strip front cover 100.00 200.00 400.00
NOTE: Cover is (11) panel "The Very Latest Fashionable Amusement..."; Back cover comic strip "Mr Jogg's Reasons For Preferring to Board to Keeping House" (7) panels using word balloons. Plus centerfold double page (18) panel spread "The New York May, Moving in General, and Mrs. Grundy's In Particular."
20 24 25 no comic strips 25.00 50.00 130.00
21 (7/15/60) (8) panel Mr Septimus Verdilater Visits the Baltimore Convention" 50.00 100.00 260.00
22 (8/1/60) (3) panel 25.00 50.00 130.00
23 (8/15/60) (12) panel "Superb Scheme For Perfecting of Dramatic Entertainment" 50.00 100.00 260.00
25 (9/15/60 (9) panel sequential 25.00 50.00 130.00
27 AbrahamLincoln Word Balloon cover 50.00 100.00 260.00
28 Wilhelm Busch sequential strip-r begin 50.00 100.00 260.00
29, 31-51 25.00 50.00 130.00
30 (12/15/60) (3) panel sequential strip 25.00 50.00 130.00
31 (Jan 1861) (12) panel The Boarding School Miss 25.00 50.00 130.00
32 (Feb 1861) (10) panel Telegraphic Horrors; Or, Mr Buchanan Undergoing A Series of Electric Shocks 50.00 100.00 260.00
35 (4/1/61) Abraham Lincoln Word Balloon cover 50.00 100.00 260.00
43 44 no sequential comic strips 25.00 50.00 130.00
45 (Nov 1861) (6) panel sequential; (11) panel The Budget Army and Infantry Tactics; First Bellew here? - Many Bellew full pagers begin 50.00 100.00 260.00
48 (Feb 1862) Bellew-c; (2) panel Bellew strip plus singles 50.00 100.00 260.00
49 (Mar 1862) Bellew-c; (16) panel Wilhelm Busch "The Fly Or The Disturbed Dutchman A Story without Words" 50.00 100.00 260.00
50 (April 1862) Bellew-c "Succession Bath" plus singles 25.00 50.00 130.00
51 (May 1862) Bellew-c; (25) panel Busch The Toothache (6) panel Definitions of the Day 50.00 100.00 260.00
52 (June 1862) Bellew-c; (9) panel A Cock & A Bull Expedition; (6) panel Bellew The First Campaign of the Home Guard 50.00 100.00 260.00
NOTE: Johnny Bull & Louis Napolean with Brother Jonathan
53-67 To Be Indexed in the Future 25.00 50.00 130.00
68 (11/18///63) (6) panel Bellew strip "Cuts On Cowards" 25.00 50.00 130.00
NOTE: contains (1) panel William Newman 1817-1870, mentor to Thomas Nast
71 (Feb 1864) Word Balloon Jefferson Davis-c 25.00 50.00 130.00
72 (Mar 1864) Word Balloon-c 25.00 50.00 130.00
73 (April 1864) Word Balloon-c in (6) panels 25.00 50.00 130.00

Frank Tousey's Illustrated New York Monthly #9
June 1882 © Frank Tousey

The Funnyest Of Awl And The Funniest Sort Of Phun v4#4
1865 © A.T. Bellew Word Balloon Cover

Funny Folk by F.M. Howarth
1899© E.P. Dutton

FR1.0 GD2.0 FN6.0

74 (May 1864) Newman Word Balloon-c 25.00 50.00 130.00
75 77 78 no sequentials 25.00 50.00 130.00
76 (July 1864) Newman Word Balloon-c 25.00 50.00 130.00
79 (Oct 1864) Word Balloon-c 25.00 50.00 130.00
80 (Nov 1864) Robt E Lee & Jeff Davis-c; no sequentials 25.00 50.00 130.00
81 (Dec 1864) Word Balloon "Abyss of War"-c 25.00 50.00 130.00
83 (2/18/65) Back-c (6) panel "Petroleum" 25.00 50.00 130.00
84 (Mar 1865) (6) panel sequential 25.00 50.00 130.00
85 (Apr 1865) Word Balloon-c 25.00 50.00 130.00
86 89 90 92 no sequentials 25.00 50.00 130.00
88 (7/6/65) (6) panel "Marriage" 25.00 50.00 130.00
91 (Oct 1865) (6) panel "Brief Confab At The Corner 25.00 50.00 130.00
93-98 yet to be indexed 25.00 50.00 130.00
99 (June 1866) (18) panel Mr Paul Peters Adventures
While Trout-Fishing In The Adirondacks 50.00 100.00 260.00
100 (July 1866) (4) panel sequential comic strip 25.00 50.00 130.00
102 (Sept 1866) (6) panel sequential comic strip 25.00 50.00 130.00
103 (Oct 1866) (9) panel strip; (12) pane;l back cover
Adventures of McTiffin At Long Branch 50.00 100.00 260.00
104 (Nov 1866) (4) panel; (23) panel "The Budget Rebuses; (2) panel
Glut On Treason Market;back-c; (6) sequential strip 25.00 50.00 130.00
105 (12/18/66) Word Balloon-c; (20) panel sequential back-c 37.50 65.00 156.00
NOTE: Artists include William Newman (1863-1868), William Henry Shelton, Joseph Keppler (1873-1876), James A. Wales (1876-1878), Frederick Burr Opper (1878)

FRANK LESLIE'S LADY'S MAGAZINE
Frank Leslie, NYC: Feb 1863-Dec 1882 (8.5x12", typically 152 pgs)
issues with comic strips 20.00 40.00 60.00

FRANK LESLIE'S PICTORIAL WEEKLY
Frank Leslie, Ross & Tousey, 121 Nassau St, NYC:
average issue (Very Rare) 50.00 100.00 210.00

FRANK TOUSEY'S NEW YORK COMIC MONTHLY
Frank Tousey, NYC: (no known sales)

FREAKS
???, Philadelphia: Jan 8, 1881-April? 1881 (Chromolithographic Weekly)
(Very Rare) 125.00 250.00 500.00

FREELANCE, THE
A.M. Soteldo Jr, Edito, 292 Broadway, NYC: 1874-75 (Folio Weekly)
(Rare) 25.00 50.00 100.00

FREE MASONRY EXPOSED
Winchell & Small, 113 Fulton, NY: 1871 (7-5/8x10-1/2", 36pgs, blue paper-c, B&W)
nn- Thomas Worth Scarce 100.00 200.00 450.00
NOTE: Scathing satircal look at Free Masons thru many cartoons, their power waning by the 1870s

FREETHINKERS' PICTORIAL TEXT-BOOK, THE (S,O)
The Truth Seeker Company, New York: 1890, 1896, 1898 (9x12, hard-c, B&W)
1 (1890 edition) - Scarce 382 pgs By Watson Heston 225.00 450.00 900.00
1 (1896 edition) - Scarce 378 pgs By Watson Heston (1890-r)100.00 200.00 500.00
2 (1898 edition) - Scarce 408 pgs By Watson Heston 125.00 250.00 500.00
NOTE: *Sought after by collectors of Freethought/Atheism material. There is also 200 copy Modern Reprint.*

FRITZ SPINDLE-SHANKS, THE RAVEN BLACK
Cosack & C o, Buffalo, NY: 1870/80s (4-3/8x2-3/4", color)
(10) card comic strip set by Wilhelm Busch 25.00 50.00 100.00

FUN BY RALL
Unknown: circa 1865 (11x7-7/8", 68 pgs, soft-c, B&W)
nn - By presently unknown (Very Rare) 125.00 250.00 475.00
NOTE: *Wraparound soft cover like modern comic book; yellow paper cover with red & black ink.*

FUN FOR THE FAMILY IN PICTURES
D. Lothrop and Company: 1886 (4 x 7", 48 pgs, Silver & Red stiff-c; interior pages have various single color inks)
nn - By unknown hand 75.00 125.00 250.00
NOTE: *Single panel cartoons and sequential stories.*

FUN FROM LIFE
Frederick A Stokes & Brother, New York: 1889 (9 1/8 by 7 1/8, 72 pages, hard-c)
nn - Mostly by Frank "Chips" Bellew Jr 62.50 125.00 250.00
NOTE: *Contains both single panel and many sequential comics reprints from Life.*

FUNNYEST OF AWL AND THE FUNNIEST SORT OF PHUN, THE
AT Bellew Or W. Jennings Demorest, 121 Nassau St, NY : 1865-67 (30 issues, 16x11 tabloid 16 pgs B&W Monthly, 1-8 © American News; 9-on © A.T. Bellews)
1 (April 1864) Bellew-c 50.00 100.00 225.00
4 (1865) Bellew-c 50.00 100.00 225.00
5 (1865) Busch (20) panel comic srtip The Toothache 75.00 150.00 350.00
7 (1865) Bellew-c 50.00 100.00 225.00
8 (1865) Special Petroleum oil issue - much cartoon art 100.00 200.00 450.00
9 (July 1865) Bellew Bullfrog-c; centerfold double page spread hanging
many Confederates; (6) panel strip hanging Jeff Davis 100.00 200.00 450.00

FR1.0 GD2.0 FN6.0

10 (Aug 1865) Bellew-c (13) panel Busch strip with two ducks, a frog
and a butcher who gets the ducks in the end 100.00 200.00 450.00
11 (Sept 1865) Bellew Bull Frog Anti-French-c 50.00 100.00 225.00
13 14 15 (12/65-1/66) Bellew-c no sequential comic strips 50.00 100.00 225.00
16 (March 1866) address change to 39 Park Ave 50.00 100.00 225.00
22 (Sept 1866) 133 Nassau St 50.00 100.00 225.00
34 (Oct 1867) 133 Nassau St (7) panel Baseball comic strip;
Last Known Issue - were there more? 100.00 200.00 450.00
NOTE: *Radical Republican politics distributed by Great American News Company; owned by Frank Bellew's wife as a front for her husband. When the Civil War ended, the brutal anti-Confederate comic strips and jokes switched to frogs and began attacking France. Funny thing, history says without France's help in the 1700s, there just might not have been a United States.*

FUNNY ALMANAC
Elton & Co., NY: 1853 (8-1/8x4-7/8, 36 pgs)
nn - sequential comic strip 50.00 100.00 200.00
NOTE: (5) panel strip "The Adventures of Mr. Goliah Starvemouse"

FUNNY FELLOWS OWN BOOK, A COMPANION FOR THE LOVERS OF FROLIC AND GLEE, THE (M,N)
Philip. J. Cozans, 116 Nassau ST, NY: 1852 (4-1/2x7-1/2", 196 pgs, burnt orange paper-c)
nn - contains many sequential comic strips (Very Rare) (no known sales)
NOTE: Collected from many different Comic Alamac(k)s including Mose Keyser (Calif Gold Rush); Jones, Smith and Robinson Goes To A Ball; Adventures of Mr. Gulp, Or the Effects of A Dinner Party; The Bowery Bully's Trip To The California Gold Mines plus lots more. This one is a sleeper so far.

FUNNY FOLK (M)
E. P. Dutton: 1899 (12x16-1/2", 90 pgs,14 strips in color-rest in b&w, hard-c)
nn - By Franklin Morris Howarth 200.00 425.00 1800.00
nn - London: J.M. Dent, 1899 embossed-c; same interior 250.00 500.00 1100.00
NOTE: *Reprints many sequential strips & single panel cartoons from **Puck**. This is considered by many to be yet another "missing link" between Victorian & Platinum Age comic books. Most comic books 1900-1917 re-printing Sunday newspaper comic strips follow this size format, except using cardboard-c rather than hard-c.*

FUNNY SKETCHES...Also Embracing Comic Illustrations
Frank Harrison, New York: 1881 (6-5/8x5", 68 pgs, B&W, Color-c)
nn - contains (3) sequential comic strips; one strip is (6) pages long;
plus one (3) pages; one more (2) pager 75.00 150.00 350.00

GIBSON BOOK, THE (M,S)
Charles Scribner's Sons & R.H. Russell, New York: 1906 (11-3/8x17-5/8", gilted red hard-c, B&W)
Book I 50.00 100.00 200.00
NOTE: *Reprints in whole the books: Drawings, Pictures of People, London,Sketches and Cartoons, Education of Mr. Pipp, Americans. 414 pgs. 1907 2nd editions exist same value.*
Book II 50.00 100.00 200.00
NOTE: *Reprints in whole the books: A Widow and Her Friends, The Weaker Sex, Everyday People, Our Neighbors. 314 pgs 1907 second edition for both also exists. Same value.*

GIBSON'S PUBLISHED DRAWINGS, MR. (M,S) (see Plat index for later issues post 1900)
R.H. Russell, New York: No.1 1894 - No. 9 1904 (11x17-3/4", hard-c, B&W)
nn (No.1; 1894) Drawings 96 pgs 30.00 60.00 125.00
nn (No.2; 1896) Pictures of People 92 pgs 30.00 60.00 125.00
nn (No.3; 1898) Sketches and Cartoons 94 pgs 30.00 60.00 125.00
nn (No.4; 1899) The Education of Mr. Pipp 88 pgs 30.00 60.00 125.00
nn (No.5; 1900) Americans 30.00 60.00 125.00
NOTE: *By Charles Dana Gibson cartoons, reprinted from magazines, primarily **LIFE**. The Education of Mr. Pipp tells a story. Series continues how long after 1904? Each of these books originally came in a boxx and are worth more with the box.*

GIRL WHO WOULDN'T MIND GETTING MARRIED, THE (O)
Frederick Warne & Co., London & New York: nd (c1870's) (9-1/2x11-1/2", 28 pgs, printed 1 side, paper-c, B&W)
nn - By Harry Parkes 75.00 150.00 300.00
NOTE: *Published simultaneously with its companion volume, **The Man Who Would Like to Marry**.*

GOBLIN SNOB, THE (O)
DeWitt & Davenport, New York: nd (c1853-56) (24 x 17 cm, 96 pgs, B&W, color hard-c)
nn - (Rare) by H.L. Stephens 350.00 600.00 1250.00

GOLDEN ARGOSY
Frank A. Munsey, 81 Warren St, NYC: 1880s (10-1/2x12, 16 pgs, B&W)
issues with full page comic strips by Chips and Bisbee 20.00 40.00 60.00

GOLDEN DAYS, THE
James Elverson, Publisher, NYC: March 6 1880-May 11 1907 weekly, 16 pgs
issues with comic strips 4.00 7.50 15.00
Horatio Alger issues 10.00 20.00 40.00
v10 #49-v11#1 1889 first Stratemeyer story 25.00 50.00 100.00

GOLDEN WEEKLY, THE
Frank Tousey, NYC: #1 Sept 25 1889-#145 Aug 18 1892 (10-3/4x14-1/2, 16 pgs, B&W)
average issue with comic striips 15.00 25.00 50.00

GREAT LOCOFOCO JUGGERNAUT, THE (S)
publisher unknown: Fall/Winter 1837 (7-5/8x3-1/4, handbill single page)
nn - By David Claypoole Johnston (a VG copy sold for $2000 in 2005)

The Story of Han's The Swapper Cover & First Two Panels
1865 © L. Pranc & Co, Boston

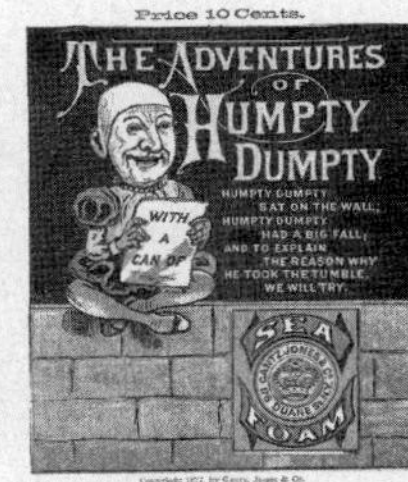

Humpty Dumpty, The Adventures of...
© Gantz, Jones and Co.

Imagerie d'Epinal
1888 © Mumoristic Publishing Co.

nn - **Imprint Society:** 1971 (reprint) 6.00 12.00 25.00

HALF A CENTURY OF ENGLISH HISTORY (S. M)
G.P. Putnam's Sons - The Knickerbocker Press, New York and London: 1884 (7-3/4 x 5-3/4", 316 pgs., illustrated hard-c)

nn - By Various 50.00 75.00 200.00
NOTE: *Subtitle: Pictorially Presented in a Series of Cartoons from the Collection of Mr. Punch. Comprising 150 plates by Doyle, Leech, Tenniel, and others, in which are portrayed the political careers of Peel, Palmerston, Russell, Cobden, Bright, Beaconsfield, Derby, Salisbury, Gladstone and other English statesmen.*

HAIL COLUMBIA! HISTORICAL, COMICAL, AND CENTENNIAL (O,S)
The Graphic Co., New York & Walter F. Brown, Providence, RI: 1876 (10x11-3/8", 60 pgs, red gilted hard-c, B&W)

nn - by Walter F. Brown (Scarce) 125.00 250.00 500.00

HANS HUCKEBEIN'S BATCH OF ODD STORIES ODDLY ILLUSTRATEDED
McLoughlin Bros., New York: 1880s (9-3/4x7-3/8, 36?? pg?

nn - By Wilhelm Busch (Rare) 75.00 150.00 300.00

HANS THE SWAPPER, THE STORY OF (O)
L. Pranc & Co., 159 Washington St, Boston: 1865 (33 inch long fold out in colors)

nn - unique fold out comic book on one long piece of paper 75.00 150.00 300.00

HARPER'S NEW MONTHLY MAGAZINE
Harper & Brothers, Franklin Square, NY: 1850-1870s (6-3/4x10, 140 pgs, paper-c, B&W)
1850s issues with comic strips in back advert section 20.00 30.00 75.00

HEALTH GUYED (I)
Frederick A. Stokes Company: 1890 (5-3/8 x 8-3/8, 56 pgs, hardcover, B&W)

nn - By Frank P.W. ("Chip") Bellew (Junior) 50.00 75.00 200.00
NOTE: *Text & cartoon illustration parody of a health guide.*

HEATHEN CHINEE, THE (O)
Western News Co.: 1870 (5-1/32x7-1/4, B&W, paper)
nn - 10 sheets printed on one side came in envelope 75.00 150.00 320.00

HITS AT POLITICS (M,S)
R.H. Russell, New York: 1899 (15" x 12", 156 pgs, B&W, hard-c)

nn - W.A. Rogers c/a 100.00 200.00 300.00
NOTE: *Collection of W.A. Rogers cartoons, all reprinted from Harper's Weekly. Includes Spanish-American War cartoons.*

THE HOME CIRCLE
Garrett & Co, NY: 1854-56 (26x19", 4 pgs, B&W)

1 (1/54) beautiful ad of Garrett Building 100.00 200.00 425.00
2/4 (4/66) Cover ad for Yale College Scraps 100.00 200.00 425.00
2/5 (5/55) First ad for Oscas Shanghai 75.00 150.00 310.00
2/6 (6/55) another ad forOscas Snanghai 75.00 150.00 310.00
2/8 (#20) (8/55) Oscar Shanghai comic book cover repro 200.00 400.00 1000.00
3/1 (#25) (1/56) 200.00 400.00 1000.00
NOTE: Garrett's 2nd comic book Courtship of Chavalier Slyfox-Wikoff
3/8 (#32) (8/56) 50.00 100.00 210.00
NOTE: First print ad for Foreign Tour of Messrs. Brown, Jones, and Robinson
35 (11/56) first official Garrett, Dick & Fitzgerald issue 50.00 100.00 210.00
37 (1/57) 100.00 200.00 425.00
NOTE: Front page comic strip repro ad for Messrs. Brown, Jones, and Robinson's Foreign Tour; Back cover full of short sequentials, singles panel

HOME MADE HAPPY. A ROMANCE FOR MARRIED MEN IN SEVEN CHAPTERS (O,P)
Genuine Durham Smoking Tobacco & The Graphic Co.: nd (c1870's) (5-1/4 tall x 3-3/8" wide folded, 27" wide unfolded, color cardboard)

nn - With all 8 panels attached (Scarce) 30.00 60.00 200.00
nn - Individual panels/cards 5.00 10.00 25.00
NOTE: *Consists of 8 attached cards, printed on one side, which unfold into a strip story of title card & 7 panels. Scrapbook hobbyists in the 19th Century tended to pull the panels apart to paste into their scrapbooks, making copies with all panels still attached scarce.*

HOME PICTURE BOOK FOR LITTLE CHILDREN (E,P)
Home Insurance Company, New York: July 1887 (8 x 6-1/8", 36 pgs, b&w, color paper-c)

nn (Scarce) 50.00 100.00 180.00
NOTE: *Contains an abbreviated 32-panel reprinting of "The Toothache" by George Cruikshank. Remainder of booklet does not contain comics. Some copies known to exist do not contain The Toothache - buyer beware!*

HOOD'S COMICALITIES. COMICAL PICTURES FROM HIS WORKS (E,S)
Porter & Coates: 1880 (8-1/2x10-3/8", 104 pgs, printed one side, hard-c, B&W)

nn 30.00 50.00 100.00
NOTE: *Reprints 4 cartoon illustrations per page from the British Hood's Comic Annuals, which were poetry books by Thomas Hood.*

HOOKEYBEAK THE RAVEN, AND OTHER TALES (see also JACK HUCKABACK, THE SCAPEGRACE RAVEN) (E)
George Routledge and Sons, London & New York: nd (1878) (7-1/4x5-5/8", 104 pgs, hardcover, B&W)

nn - By Wilhelm Busch (Rare) 100.00 200.00 450.00

HOW ADOLPHUS SLIM-JIM USED JACKSON'S BEST, AND WAS HAPPY. A LENGTHY TALE IN 7 ACTS. (O,P)
Jackson's Best Chewing Tobacco & Donaldson Brothers: nd(c1870's) (5-1/8 tall x 3-3/8" wide folded, 27" wide unfolded, color cardboard)

nn - With all 8 panels attached (Scarce) 30.00 60.00 250.00
nn - Individual panels/cards 10.00 15.00 30.00
NOTE: *Consists of 8 attached cards, printed on one side, which unfold into a strip story of title card & 7 panels. Scrapbook hobbyists in the 19th Century tended to pull the panels apart topaste into their scrapbooks, making copies with all panels still attached scarce.*

HOW DAYS' DURHAM STANDARD OF THE WORLD SMOKING TOBACCO MADE TWO PAIRS OF TWINS HAPPY (O,P)
J.R. Day & Bro. Standard Durham Smoking Tobacco, Durham, NC: nd (c late 1870's/early 1880's) (3-5/8" x 5-1/2", folded, 21-3/4" tall unfolded, color cardboard)

nn- With all 6 panels attached (Scarce) 150.00 300.00 600.00
nn- Individual panels/cards 20.00 40.00 60.00
NOTE: *Highly sought by both Black Americana and Tobacciana collectors. Recurring mid-19th Century story about two African-American twin brothers who romance and marry a pair of African-American twin sisters. Although the text is racist at points, the art is not. Consists of 6 attached cards, printed on one side, which unfold downwards into a strip story of title card & 5 panels. Scrapbook hobbyists in the 19th Century tended to pull the panels apart and paste into their scrapbooks, making copies with all panels attached scarce. Note, there are numerous cartoon tellings of this same story, including several card series versions (with different art, and story variations, each time). But, the above is the only version which unfolds as a strip of attached cards. The cards from all the unattached versions are smaller sized, and thus distinguishable.*

HUGGINIANA; OR, HUGGINS' FANTASY, BEING A COLLECTION OF THE MOST ESTEEMED MODERN LITERARY PRODUCTIONS (I,S,P)
H.C. Southwick, New York: 1808 (296 pgs, printed one side, B&W, hard-c)

nn - (Very Rare)) (no known sales)
NOTE: *The earliest known surviving collected promotional cartoons in America. This is a booklet collecting 7 folded plus 1 full page flyer advertisements for barber John Richard Desborus Huggins, who hired American artists Elkanah Tisdale and William S. Leney to modify previously published illustrations into cartoons referring to his barber shop.*

HUMOROUS MASTERPIECES - PICTURES BY JOHN LEECH (E,M)
Frederick A. Stokes: nd (late 1900's - early 1910's) No.1-2 (5-5/8x3-7/8", 68 pgs, cardboard covers, B&W)

1- John Leech (single panel cartoon-r from **Punch**) 25.00 50.00 110.00
2- John Leech (single panel cartoon-r from **Punch**) 25.00 50.00 110.00

HUMOURIST, THE (E,I,S)
C.V. Nickerson and Lucas and Deaver, Baltimore: No.1 Jan 1829 - No.12 Dec 1829 (5-3/4x3-1/2", B&W text w/hand colored cartoon pg.)

Bound volume No.1-12 (Very Rare; copies in libraries 270 pgs) (no known sales)
NOTE: *Earliest known American published periodical to contain a cartoon every issue. Surviving individual issues currently unknown -- all information comes from 1 surviving bound volume. Each issue is mostly text, with one full page hand-colored cartoon. Bound volume contains an additional hand-colored cartoons at front of each six month set (total of 14 cartoons in volume). Cartoons appear to be of British origin, possibly by George Cruikshank.*

HUMPTY DUMPTY, ADVENTURES OF...(I,P)
1877 (Promotional 4x3-1/2", 12 page chapbook from Gantz, Jones & Co, 10¢-c.)

nn-Promotes Gantz Sea Foam Baking Powder; early app. of a costumed character, dressed as Humpty Dumpty 125.00 150.00 600.00

HUSBAND AND WIFE, OR THE STORY OF A HAIR. (O,P)
Garland Stoves and Ranges, Michigan Stove Co.: 1883 (4-3/16 tall x 2-11/16" wide folded, 16" wide unfolded, color cardboard)

nn - With all 6 panels attached (Scarce) 50.00 75.00 150.00
nn - Individual panels/cards 5.00 10.00 25.00
NOTE: *Consists of 6 attached cards, printed on one side, which unfold into a strip story of title card & 5 panels. Scrapbook hobbyists in the 19th Century tended to pull the panels apart topaste into their scrapbooks, making copies with all panels still attached scarce.*

ICHABOD ACADEMICUS, THE COLLEGE EXPERIENCES OF (O,G)
William T. Peters, New Haven, CT: 1850 (5-1/2x9-3/4",108 pgs, B&W)

nn - By William T. Peters (Rare) 1000.00 2000.00 4300.00
NOTE: *Pages are not uniform in size. Also, a copy showed up on eBay with misspelled Academicus. Has "n" instead of "m" - not known yet which printing is earliest version.*

ICHABOD ACADEMICUS, THE COLLEGE EXPERIENCES OF (O,G)
Dick & Fitzgerald, New York: nd (1870s-1888) (paper-c, B&W)

nn - By William T. Peters (Very Rare) 275.00 550.00 1100.00
NOTE: *Pages are uniform in size.*

ILLUSTRATED SCRAP-BOOK OF HUMOR AND INTELLIGENCE (M)
John J. Dyer & Co.: nd (c1859-1860)

nn - Very Rare 225.00 450.00 900.00
NOTE: *A "printed scrapbook" of images culled from some unidentified periodical. About half of it is illustrations that would have accompanied prose pieces. There are pages of single panel cartoons (multiple per page). And there are roughly 8 to 12 pages of sequential comics (all different stories, but appears to all be by the same presently unidentified artist).*

ILLUSTRATED WEEKLY, THE
Chars C Lucas & Co, 11 Dey St, NY: 1876 (15x18", 8pgs, 8¢ per issue)

2/8 (2/19/76) back-c all sequential comic strips 100.00 200.00 400.00
2/12 (3/18/76) full page of British-r sequentials 100.00 200.00 400.00
2/14 (4/1/76) April Fool Issue - (6) panel center; plus more 100.00 200.00 400.00
2/15 (4/8/76) (6) panel sequential 100.00 200.00 400.00
issues without comic strips 12.50 25.00 50.00

Jingo No. 3, Sept 24
1884 © Art Newspaper Co, Boston & NYC

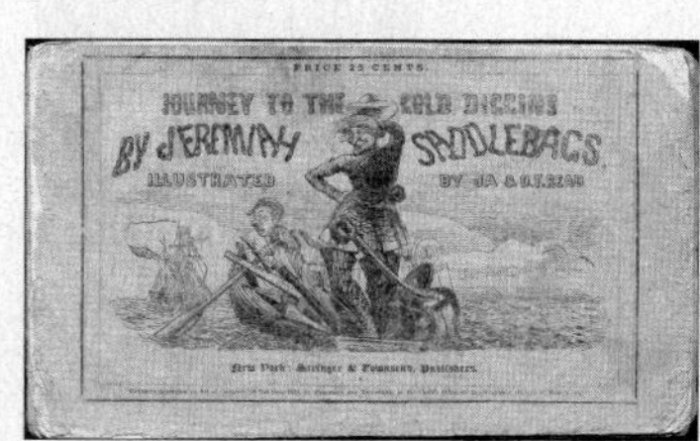

Journey To The Gold Diggings By Jeremiah Saddlebags
1849 © Various - First Original USA Comic Book

The Lantern Dec 18
1852 © Stringer & Townsend

FR1.0 GD2.0 FN6.0

ILLUSTRATIONS OF THE POETS: FROM PASSAGES IN THE LIFE OF LITTLE BILLY VIDKINS (See A Day's Sport...)
S. Robinson, Philadelphia: May 1849 (14.7 cm x 11.3 cm, 32 pgs, B&W)

nn - by Henry Stephens (very rare) (no known sales)
NOTE: *Predates Journey to the Gold Diggins By Jeremiah Saddlebags by a few months and is an original American proto-comic strip book. More research needs to be done. A later edition brought $800 in G/VG 2007*

IMAGERIE d'EPINAL (untrimmed individual sheets) (E)
Pellerin for Humoristic Publishing Co, Kansas City, Mo.: nd (1888) No.1-60 (15-7/8x11-3/4",single sheets, hand colored) (All are Rare)

1-14, 21, 22, 25-46, 49-60 - in the Album d'Images 17.50 35.00 70.00
15-20, 23,24, 47, 48 - not in the Album d'Images 30.00 60.00 125.00
NOTE: *Printed and hand colored in France expressly for the Humoristic Publishing Company . Printed on one side only. These are single sheets, sold separately. Reprints and translates the sheets from their original French.*

IMAGERIE d'EPINAL ALBUM d'IMAGES (E)
Pellerin for Humoristic Publishing Co., Kansas City. Mo: nd (1888) (15-1/2x11-1/2",108 pgs plus full color hard-c, hand colored interior)

nn - Various French artists (Rare) 500.00 1000.00 2200.00
NOTE: *Printed and hand colored in France expressly for the Humoristic Publishing Company . Printed on one side only. This is supposedly a collection of sixty broadsheets, originally sold separately. All copies known only have fifty of the sixty known of these broadsheets (slightly bigger, before binding, trimming the margins in the process, down to 15-1/4x11-3/8".). Three slightly different covers known to exist, with or without the indication in French "Textes en Anglais" ("Texts in Englishi), with or without the general title "Contes de FEes" ("Fairy Tales"). All known copies were collected with sheets 15-20, 23,24, 47, and 48 missing.*

IN LAUGHLAND (M)
R.H. Russell, New York: 1899 (14-9/16x12", 72 pgs, hard-c)

nn - By Henry "Hy" Mayer (scarce) 150.00 300.00 600.00
NOTE: *Mostly strips plus single panel cartoon-r from various magazines. The majority are reprinted from Life, with the rest from: Truth, Dramatic Mirror, Black and White, Figaro Illustre, Le Rire, and Fliegende Blatter.*

IN THE "400" AND OUT (M,S) (see also **THE TAILOR-MADE GIRL**)
Keppler & Schwarzmann, New York: 1888 (8-1/4x12", 64 pgs, hardc, B&W)

nn - By C.J. Taylor 42.50 85.00 200.00
NOTE: *Cartoons reprinted from **Puck**. The "400" is a reference to New York City's aristocratic elite.*

IN VANITY FAIR (M,S)
R.H.Russell & Son, New York: 1896 (11-7/8x17-7/8", 80 pgs, hard-c, B&W)

nn - By A.B.Wenzell, r-LIFE and HARPER'S 50.00 100.00 200.00

JACK HUCKABACK, THE SCAPEGRACE RAVEN (see also HOOKEYBEAK THE RAVEN) (E)
Stroefer & Kirchner, New York: nd (c1877) (9-3/8x6-3/8", 56 pgs, printed one side only, hand colored hardcover, B&W interior)

nn - By Wilhelm Busch (Rare) 100.00 200.00 400.00
NOTE: *The 1877 date is derived from a gift signature on one known copy. The publication date might in truth be earlier. There are also professionally hand colored copies known to exist which would be worth more.*

JEFF PETTICOATS
American News Company, NY: July 1865 (23 inches folded out; 6-1/4x8 folded,, B&W)
nn - Very Rare Frank Bellew (6) panel sequential foldout (10¢) (no known sales)
NOTE: printed also in **FUNNYEST OF AWL AND THE FUNNIEST SORT OF PHUN** #9 (July 1865) (6) panel strip hanging Jeff Davis; This sold hundreds of thousand of copies in its day

JINGO (M,O)
Art Newspaper Co., Boston & New York: No.1 Sept 10, 1884 - No.11 Nov 19, 1884 (10 cents, 13-7/8" x 10-1/4",16 pgs, color front/back-c and center, remainder B&W, paper-c)

1-11(Rare) 50.00 100.00 225.00
NOTE: *Satirical Republican propaganda magazine, modeled after **Puck** and **Judge**, which was published during the last couple months of the 1884 Presidential Election campaign. The Republicans lost, **Jingo** ceased publication, and Republican backers soon after purchased **Judge** magazine.*

JOHN-DONKEY, THE (O, S)
George Dexter, Burgess, Stringer & Co., NYC: 1848 (10x7.5",16 pgs,B&W, 6¢

1 Jan 1 1848 75.00 150.00 300.00
2-end (last issue Aug 12 1848) 50.00 100.00 200.00

JOLLY JOKER
Frank Leslie, NY: 1862-1878 (B&W, 10¢)

20/6 (July 1877) (Bellew Opper cover & single panels 150.00 300.00 600.00

JOLLY JOKER, OR LAUGH ALL-ROUND
Dick & Fitzgerald, NY: 1870s? (8-1/4x4-7/8", 148, B&W, illustrated green cover)

nn - cartoons on every page 100.00 200.00 400.00

JONATHAN'S WHITTLINGS OF THE WAR (O, S)
T.W. Strong, 98 Nassau St, NYC: April 1854-July 8 1854 (11.5x8.5", 16 pgs, B&W)

1 April 1854 100.00 200.00 400.00
NOTE: *Begins Frank Bellew's sequential comic strip "Mr. Hookemcumsnivey, A Russian Gentleman, Hears That His Country Is In A State of War"*
2-12 (July 8 1854) Many Bellew & Hopkins 100.00 200.00 400.00

JOURNAL CARRIER'S GREETING
???, Minn, Minn: 1897-98? (giveaway promo, 10-1/8x8-1/4, 36, B&W, paper-c)
nn - rare 50.00 100.00 200.00

JOURNEY TO THE GOLD DIGGINS BY JEREMIAH SADDLEBAGS (O,G)

FR1.0 GD2.0 FN6.0

Various publishers: 1849 (25 cents, 5-5/8 x 8-3/4", 68 pgs, green & black paper cover, B&W interior)

nn -- New York edition, Stringer & Townsend, Publishers
(Very Rare) By J.A. and D.F. Read. 5500.00 8800.00 12,000.00
nn -- Cincinnati, Ohio edition, published by U.P. James
(Very Rare) By J.A. and D.F. Read. 5500.00 8800.00 12,000.00
nn -- 1950 reprint, with introduction, published by William P. Wreden, Burlingame, California: 1950 (5-7/8 x 9", 92 pgs, hardcover, color interior)
(390 copies printed) By J.A. and D.F. Read. 67.50 125.00 275.00
NOTE: *Earliest known original sequential comic book by an American creator; directly inspired by Töpffer's **Obadiah Oldbuck** and **Bachelor Butterfly** The New York and Cincinnati editions were both published in 1849, one soon after the other. Antiquarian Book sources have traditionally cited that the Cincinnati edition preceded the New York, but without referencing their evidence. Conflicting with this, the Cincinnati edition lists the New York publishers' 1849 copyright, while the New York edition makes no reference to the Cincinnati publishers. Such would indicate that the New York edition was first. Both are very rare, and until resolved both will be regarded as published simultaneously. A New York copy with missing back cover, detached front cover, and G/VG interior sold for $2000 in 2000. Two copies sold at auction in 2006 for $11,500 and 12,000. (Prices vary widely.)*

JUDGE (M,O)
Judge Publishing, New York: No.1 Oct 29, 1881 - No. 950, Dec ??, 1899 (10 cents, color front/back c and centerspread, remainder B&W, paper-c)

1 (Scarce) (no known sales)
2-26 (Volume 1; Scarce) 30.00 55.00 110.00
27-790,792-950 12.50 25.00 50.00
791 (12/12/1896; Vol.31) - classic satirical-c depicting Tammany Hall politicians as the Yellow Kid & Cox's Brownies 100.00 250.00 500.00
Bound Volumes (six month, 26 issue run each):
Vol. 1 (Scarce) (no known sales)
Vol. 2-30,32-37 140.00 280.00 600.00
Vol. 31 - includes issue 791 **YK/Brownies** parody 200.00 300.00 850.00
NOTE: *Rival publication to Puck. Purchased by Republican Party backers, following their loss in the 1884 Presidential Election, to become a Republican propaganda satire magazine.*

JUDGE, GOOD THINGS FROM
Judge Publishing Co., NY: 1887 (13-3/4x10.5", 68 pgs, color paper-c)

1 first printing 50.00 100.00 200.00
NOTE: Zimmerman, Hamilton, Victor, Woolf, Beard, Ehrhart, De Meza, Howarth, Smith, Alfred Mitchell

JUDGE'S LIBRARY (M)
Judge Publishing, New York: No.1, April 1890 - No. 141, Dec 1899 (10 cents, 11x8-1/8", 36 pgs, color paper-c, B&W)

1 15.00 30.00 60.00
2-141 15.00 30.00 60.00
151-??? (post-1900 issues; see Platinum Age section)
NOTE: ***Judge's Library** was a monthly magazine reprinting cartoons & prose from **Judge**, with each issue's material organized around the same subject. The cover art was often original. All issues were kept in print for the duration of the series, so later issues are more scarce than earlier ones.*

JUDGE'S QUARTERLY (M)
Judge Publishing Company/Arkell Publishing Company, New York: No.1 April 1892 - 31 Oct 1899 (25¢, 13-3/4x10-1/4", 64 pgs, color paper-c, B&W)

1-11 13-31 contents presently unknown to us 15.00 30.00 60.00
12 ZIM Sketches From Judge Jan 1895 100.00 200.00 425.00
NOTE: *Similar to **Judge's Library**, except larger in size, and issued quarterly. All reprint material, except for the cover art.*

JUDGE'S SERIALS (M,S)
Judge Publishing, New York: March 1888 (10x7.5", 36 pgs)

#3 - Eugene Zimmerman 100.00 200.00 400.00
NOTE: *A bit of sequential comic strips; mostly single panel cartoons. This series runs to at least #8.*

JUDY
Burgess, Stringer & Co., 17 Ann St, NYC: Nov 28 1846-Feb 20 47 (11x8.5",12 pgs,B&W)

1 Nov 28 1846 67.50 125.00 250.00
2-13 50.00 100.00 200.00

JUVENILE GEM, THE (see also THE ADVENTURES OF MR. TOM PLUMP, and OLD MOTHER MITTEN) (O,I)
Huestis & Cozans: nd (1850-1852) (6x3-7/8", 64 pgs, hand colored paper-c, B&W) (all versions Very Rare)

nn - First printing(s) publisher's address is 104 Nassau Street (1850-1851)
(1 copy sold for $800.00 in Fair)
nn - 2nd printing(s) publisher's address is 116 Nassau Street (1851-1852) (no known sales)
nn - 3rd printing(s) publisher's address is 107 Nassau Street (1852+) (no known sales)
NOTE: *The JUVENILE GEM is a gathering of multiple booklets under a single, hand colored cover (none of the interior booklets have the covers which they were given when sold separately). The publisher appears to have gathered whichever printings of each booklet were available when copies of THE JUVENILE GEM was assembled, so that the booklets within, and the conglomerate cover, may be from a mixture of printings. Contains two sequential comic booklets: THE ADVENTURES OF MR. TOM PLUMP, and OLD MOTHER MITTEN AND HER FUNNY KITTEN, plus five heavily illustrated children's booklets - **The Pretty Primer**, **The Funny Book**, **The Picture Book**, **The Two Sisters**, and **Story Of The Little Drummer**. Six of these -- including the two comic books -- were reprinted in the 1960's by Americana Review as a set of individual booklets, and included in a folder collectively titled "Six Children's Books of the 1850's".*

LANTERN, THE
Stringer & Townsend:1852-1853 (11x8-3/8", 12 pgs, soft paper, 6 ¢)

Leslie's Young America #1
1881 © Leslie & Company, NYC

Life Jan 3
1884 © J.A. Mitchell

Life's Book of Animals
1888 © Doubleday & McClure Co.

	FR1.0	GD2.0	FN6.0
1 Jan 10, 1852	37.50	75.00	175.00
2	25.00	50.00	110.00
3 First Frank Bellew cartoons onwards each issue	37.50	75.00	175.00
4 Bellew 's Mr Blobb begins 1/31/52	50.00	100.00	250.00

NOTE: *Bellew serial sequential comic strip "Mr Blobb In Search Of A Physician" becomes 2nd earliest known recurring character in American comic strips plus full page single panel Bellew cartoon "The Modern Frankenstein" take-off on Shelly's story.*

	FR1.0	GD2.0	FN6.0
5 Hunsdale 2-panel "The Horrors of Slavery"; Mr Blobb	50.00	100.00	230.00
6 DF Read 15 panel "A Volley of Valentines"; Mr Blobb	50.00	100.00	230.00
7-8 10 Bellew's Mr Blobb continues	25.00	50.00	110.00
9 (4) panel "The Perils of Leap Year" MrBlobb	50.00	100.00	230.00
11 no Mr Blobb	20.00	40.00	100.00
12 Bellew's Mr Blobb continues 3/27/52	50.00	100.00	230.00
13 Bellew (10) panel sequential "Stump Speaking Studied"	50.00	100.00	230.00
14 no comic strips	20.00	40.00	100.00
15 Bellew's Mr Blobb ends (5) panel 4/17/52	50.00	100.00	230.00
16 Bellew begins new comic strip serial, "Mr. Bulbear, A Stockbroker, After having Supped at Delmonicos, Has A Dream", Part One, (6) panels	50.00	100.00	230.00
17 Bellew's Mr Bulbear continues	25.00	50.00	110.00
18 Bellew (8) panel "Trials of a Witness"	50.00	100.00	230.00
19 Bellew's Mr Bulbear's Dream continues	25.00	50.00	110.00
20-23 no comic strips	20.00	40.00	100.00
24 Bellew "Trials of a Publisher" (6) panel	50.00	100.00	230.00
25 comic strip "Travels of Jonathan Verdant"recurring character	25.00	50.00	110.00
26-49 contents to be indexed soon			
50 (12/18/52) (2) panel Impertinent Smile	25.00	50.00	110.00
58 (2/12/53) (6) panel Trip to California	25.00	50.00	110.00
66 (4/9/53) (3) panel sequential strip	25.00	50.00	110.00

LAST SENSATION, THE (Becomes Day's Doings)
James Watts, NYC: Dec 27 1867-May 30 1868 (11x16 folio-size, 16 pgs, B&W)

	FR1.0	GD2.0	FN6.0
issues with comic strips	50.00	100.00	200.00

LAUGH AND GROW FAT COMIC ALMANAC
Fisher & Brother, Philadelphia, New York & Boston: 1860-? (36 pgs)

	FR1.0	GD2.0	FN6.0
nn	60.00	120.00	250.00

LEGEND OF SAM'L OF POSEN (O)
M.B. Curtis Company: 1884-85 (8x3-3/8", 44 pgs, Color-c, B&W interior)

	FR1.0	GD2.0	FN6.0
nn - By M.B. Curtis	50.00	100.00	200.00

NOTE: Cover blurb says: From Early Days in Fatherland to affluence And Success in the Land of His Adoption, America

LESLIE'S YOUNG AMERICA (O. S)
Leslie & Co, 98 Chamber St, NY: 1881-82 (11-1/2x8", 5¢, B&W)

	FR1.0	GD2.0	FN6.0
1 (7/9/81) back cover (6) panel strip	150.00	300.00	630.00
2 (7/16/81) back cover (9) panel strip	50.00	100.00	250.00
3 (7/23/81) back cover (16) panel Busch strip	67.50	125.00	275.00
9 (9/3/81) sequentials; Hopkins singles	50.00	100.00	250.00
15 (10/15/81) Zim or Frost? (6) panel strip	50.00	100.00	250.00
19 (11/12/81) (9) panel back-c strip	50.00	100.00	250.00
24 (4) panel strip 25 (2) panel back-c strip	50.00	100.00	250.00
26 27 (6) panel back-c strip	50.00	100.00	250.00
29 31 (12) panel strip	50.00	100.00	250.00
32 (2/11/82) (8) panel strip	50.00	100.00	250.00
issues without comic strips or Jules Verne	25.00	50.00	125.00

NOTE: Jules Verne stories begin with #1 and run thru at least #42

LIFE (M,O) (continues with Vol.35 No. 894+ in the Platinum Age section)
J.A.Mitchell: Vol.1 No.1 Jan. 4, 1883 - Vol.1 No.26 June 29, 1883 (10-1/4x8", 16 pgs, B&W, paper cover); J.A. Mitchell: Vol. 2 No. 27, July 5, 1883 - Vol. 6 No.148, Oct 29, 1885 (10-1/4x8-1/4", 16 pgs., B&W, paper cover); Mitchell & Miller: Vol.6 No.149, Nov. 5, 1885 - Vol. 31, No. 796, March 17, 1898 (10-3/8x8-3/8", 16 pgs., B&W, paper cover); Life Publishing Company: Vol. 31 No. 797, March 24, 1898 - Vol. 34 No. 893, Dec 28, 1899 (10-3/8 x 8-1/2", 20 pgs., B&W, paper cover)

	FR1.0	GD2.0	FN6.0
1-26 (Scarce)		(no known sales)	
27-799	5.00	10.00	20.00
800 (4/7/1898) parody Yellow Kid / Spanish-American War cover (not by Outcault)	67.50	125.00	275.00
801-893	5.00	10.00	20.00

NOTE: *All covers for issues 1 - 26 are identical, apart from issue number & date.*

Hard bound collected volumes:

	FR1.0	GD2.0	FN6.0
V. 1 (No.1-26) (Scarce)	67.50	125.00	250.00
V. 2-34	45.00	90.00	180.00
V. 31 YK #800 parody-c not by RFO	70.00	140.00	300.00

NOTE: *Because the covers of all issues in Volume 1 are identical, it was common practice to remove the covers before binding the issues together. This is not true of later volumes, though, in all volumes it was common to drop the advertising pages which appeared at the rear of each issue. Information on many more individual issues will expand next Guide.*

LIFE AND ADVENTURES OF JEFF DAVIS (I)
J.C. Haney & Co., NY: 1865 (10 cents, 7-1/2" x 4", 36 pgs, B&W, paper-c)

	FR1.0	GD2.0	FN6.0
nn - By McArone (Scarce)	175.00	350.00	750.00
nn - 1974 Reprint (350) copies 6-3/4x4-3/8	50.00	10.00	20.00
nn - 1997 Reprint (7th Fla. Sutler, Clearwater, 6-3/4x4-1/4")	–	–	2.00

NOTE: *Humorous telling of the capture of Confederate President Jeff Davis in women's clothing, from the publisher of Merryman's Monthly. It contains an ad page for that publication; the material is perhaps reprinted from it. J.C. Haney licensed it to local printers, and so various publishers are found -- all printings currently regarded as simultaneous. (The Geo. H. Hees printing, Oswego, NY, contains an ad for the upcoming October 1865 issue of Merryman's Monthly, thus placing that printing in September 1865). Modern facsimile editions have been produced.*

LIFE IN PHILADELPHIA
W. Simpson, 66 Chestnut, Philadelphia; Siltart, No. 65 South Third St, Philadelphia: 1830 (7-3/4x6-7/8", 15 loose plates, hand colored copies exist, maybe B&W also)

	FR1.0	GD2.0	FN6.0
nn - By Edward Williams Clay (1799-1857) (Very Rare)		(no known sales)	

NOTE: *First 13 plates etched, with many word balloons; scenes of exaggerated Black Americana in Philadelphia viewed one by one as broadsides. Had several publishers over the years. Was also eventually collected into a book of same name but only with the first 13 plates used; the last two not used in book. Collected book not yet viewed to share info.*

LIFE'S BOOK OF ANIMALS (M,S)
Doubleday & McClure Co.: 1898 (7-1/4x10-1/8", 88 pgs, color hardcover, B&W)

	FR1.0	GD2.0	FN6.0
nn	30.00	55.00	110.00

NOTE: *Reprints funny animal single panel and strip cartoons reprinted from LIFE. Art by Blaisdell, Chip Bellew, Kemble, Hy Mayer, Sullivant, Woolf.*

LIFE'S COMEDY (M,S)
Charles Scribner's Sons: Series 1 1897 - Series 3 1898 (12x9-3/8", hardcover, B&W)

	FR1.0	GD2.0	FN6.0
1 (142 pgs). 2, 3 (138 pgs)	60.00	120.00	250.00

NOTE: *Gibson a-1-3; c-3. Hy Mayer a-1-3. Rose O'Neill a-2-3. Stanlaws a-2-3. Sullivant a-1-2. Verbeek a-2. Wenzell a-1-3; c(painted)-2.*

LIFE, THE GOOD THINGS OF (M,S)
White, Stokes, & Allen, NY: 1884 - No.3 1886 ; Frederick A. Stokes, NY: No.4 1887; Frederick Stokes & Brother, NY: No.5 1888 - No.6 1889; Frederick A. Stokes Company, NY: No. 7 1890 - No.10 1893 (8-3/8x10-1/2", 74 pgs, gilted hardcover, B&W)

	FR1.0	GD2.0	FN6.0
nn - 1884 (most common issue)	35.00	75.00	160.00
2 - 1885	35.00	75.00	160.00
3 - 1886 (76 pgs)	35.00	75.00	160.00
4 - 1887 (76 pgs)	35.00	75.00	160.00
5 - 1888	35.00	75.00	160.00
6 - 1889	35.00	75.00	160.00
7 - 1890	35.00	75.00	160.00
8 - 1891 (scarce)	75.00	150.00	300.00
9 - 1892	35.00	75.00	160.00
10 - 1893	35.00	75.00	160.00

NOTE: *Contains mostly single panel, and some sequential, comics reprinted from LIFE. Attwood a-1-4,10. Roswell Bacon a-5. Chip Bellew a-4-6. Frank Bellew a-4,6. Palmer Cox a-1. H. E. Dey a-5. C. D. Gibson a-4-10. F.M. Howarth a-5-6. Kemble a-1-3. Klapp a-5. Walt McDougall a-1-2. H. McVickar a-5; J. A. Mitchell a-5. Peter Newell a-2-3. Gray Parker a-4-5,7. J. Smith a-5. Albert E. Steiner a-5; T. S. Sullivant a-7-9. Wenzell a-8-10. Wilder a-3. Woolf a-3-6.*)

LIFE, THE SPICE OF (E,M,)
White and Allen: NY & London: 1888 (8-3/8x10-1/2",76 pgs, hard-c, B&W)

	FR1.0	GD2.0	FN6.0
nn	50.00	100.00	225.00

NOTE: *Resembles **THE GOOD THINGS OF LIFE** in layout and format, and appears to be an attempt to compete with their former partner Frederick A. Stokes. However, the material is not from **LIFE**, but rather is reprinted and translated German sequential and single panel comics.*

LIFE'S PICTURE GALLERY (becomes LIFE'S PRINTS) (M,S,P)
Life Publishing Company, New York: nd (1898-1899) (paper cover, B&W) (all are scarce)

	FR1.0	GD2.0	FN6.0
nn - (nd; 1898, 100 pgs, 5-1/4x8-1/2") Gibson-c of a woman with closed umbrella; 1st interior page announcing that after January 1, 1899 Gibson will draw exclusively for LIFE; the word "SPECIMEN" is printed in red, diagonally, across every print; a-Gibson, Rose O'Neill, Sullivant	37.50	75.00	150.00
nn - (nd; 1899, 128 pgs, 4-7/8x7-3/8") Gibson-c of a woman golfer; 1st interior page announcing that Gibson & Hanna, Jr. draw exclusively for LIFE; the word "SPECIMEN" is printed in red, horizontally, across every print. Includes prints from Gibson's **THE EDUCATION OF MR. PIPP**; a-Gibson, Sullivant	37.50	75.00	150.00

NOTE: *Catalog of prints reprinted from **LIFE** covers & centerspreads. The first catalog was given away free to anyone requesting it, but after many people got the catalog without ordering anything, subsequent catalogs were sold at 10 cents.*

LIGHT AND SHADE
William Drey Doppel Soap: 1892 (3-3/4x5-3/8", 20 pgs, B&W, color cover)

	FR1.0	GD2.0	FN6.0
nn - By J.C.	50.00	100.00	200.00

NOTE: Contains (8) panel comic strip of black boy whose skin turns white using this soap.

LITTLE SICK BEAR, THE
Edwin W. Joy Co, San Francisco, CA: 1897 (6-1/4x5", 20 pgs, B&W, Scarce)

	FR1.0	GD2.0	FN6.0
nn - By James Swinnerton one long sequential comic strip	200.00	400.00	850.00

LONDON OUT OF TOWN, OR THE ADVENTURES OF THE BROWNS AT THE SEA SIDE BY LUKE LIMNER, ESQ. (O)
David Bogue, 86 Fleet St, London: c1847 (5-1/2x4-1/4, 32 pgs, yellow paper hard-c, B&W

	FR1.0	GD2.0	FN6.0
nn - By John Leighton	150.00	350.00	725.00

NOTE: one long sequential comic strip multiple-panel per page story; each page crammed with panels inspired by the Töpffer comic books Bogue began several years earlier.

LORGNETTE, THE (S)

Merryman's Monthly v3#5 with Bellew strip
May 1865 © J. C. Haney & Co., New York

Minneapolis Journal Cartoons Second Series
1895 © Minneapolis Journal

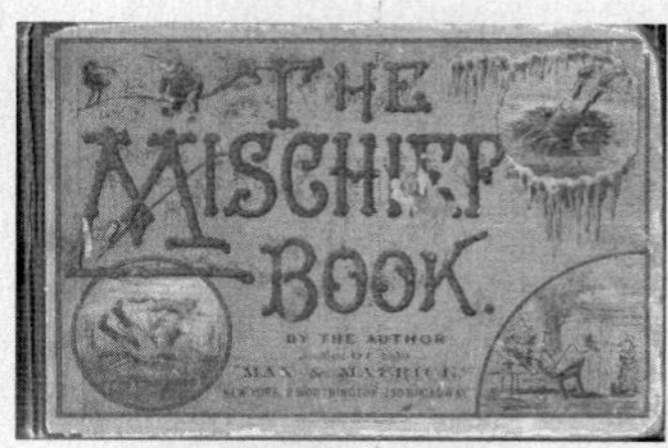

The Mischief Book by Wilhelm Busch
color cover art variation
1880 © R. Worthington, New York

George J Coombes, New York: 1886 (6-1/2x8-3/4, 38 pgs, hard-c, B&W)
nn - By J.K. Bangs 50.00 100.00 200.00

LOVING BALLAD OF LORD BATEMAN, THE (E,I)
G.W. Carleton & Co., Publishers, Madison Square, NY: 1871 (9x5-7/8",16 pgs, soft-c, 6¢)
nn - By George Cruikshank 50.00 100.00 200.00

MADISON'S EXPOSITION OF THE AWFUL & TERRIFYING CEREMONIES OF THE ODD FELLOWS
T.E. Peterson & Brothers, 306 Chestnut St, Phila: 1870s? (5-3/4x9-1/4, 68 pgs, B&W)
nn - single panel cartoons 50.00 100.00 200.00

MANNERS AND CUSTOMS OF YE HARVARD STUDENTE (M,S)
Houghton Mifflin & Co., Boston & Moses King, Cambridge: 1877 (7-7/8x11", 72 pgs, printed one side, hardc, B&W)
nn - by F.G. Attwood 100.00 225.00 450.00
NOTE: *Collection of cartoons originally serialized in the **Harvard Lampoon**. Attwood later became a major cartoonist for **Life**.*

MAN WHO WOULD LIKE TO MARRY, THE (O)
Frederick Warne & Co., London & New York: nd (c 1880's) (9-1/2x11-1/2", 28 pgs, printed 1 side, paper-c, B&W)
nn - By Harry Parkes 62.50 125.00 275.00
NOTE: *Published simultaneously with its companion volume, **The Girl Who Wouldn't Mind Getting Married**.*

MAX AND MAURICE: A JUVENILE HISTORY IN SEVEN TRICKS (E)
(see also Teasing Tom and Naughty Ned)
Roberts Brothers, Boston: 1871 first edition (8-1/8 x 5-1/2", 76 pgs, hard & soft-c B&W)
nn - By Wilhelm Busch (green or brown cloth hardbound) 285.00 560.00 1150.00
nn - exactly the same, but soft paper cover 175.00 350.00 700.00
NOTE: *Page count includes 56 pgs of art, two blank endpapers at the front (one colored), 8 pgs of ads at the back, two blank endpapers at the end (one colored), and the covers. Green or brown illustrated hardcover. The name of the author is given on the title page as "William Busch." We assume this to be the 1st edition. Back side of title page states: Entered according to Act of Congress, in the year 1870, by Roberts Brothers, In the office of the Librarian of Congress at Washington.*
nn - By Wilhelm Busch (1872 edition) 250.00 500.00 1150.00
nn - 1875 reprint 100.00 200.00 450.00
nn - 1882 reprint (76 pgs, hand colored- c/a, 75¢) 100.00 200.00 400.00
nn- 1889 reprint with new art on cover printed in full color 100.00 200.00 400.00
NOTE: *Each of the above contains 56 pages of art and text in a transitional format between a regular children's book and a comic book (the page count difference is ad pages in back). Seminal inspiration for William Randolph Hearst to acquire as a "new comic" (following the wild success of Outcault's Yellow Kid) to license M&M from Busch and hire Rudolph Dirks in late 1897 to create a New York American newspaper incarnation. In Hearst's English language newspapers it was called The Katzenjammer Kids and in his German language NYC newspaper it was titled Max & Moritz, Busch's original title. At least 50 other reprints versions are reputed to exist printed thru 1900. Translated from the 1865 German original. We are still sorting out the edition confusion.*

MAX AND MAURICE: A JUVENILE HISTORY IN SEVEN TRICKS (E)
(see also Teasing Tom and Naughty Ned)
Little, Brown, and Company, Boston: 1898-1902 (8-1/8 x 5-3/4", 72 pgs, hardcover, black ink on orange paper) (various early reprints)
nn - 1898 , 1899 By Wilhelm Busch 50.00 100.00 250.00
nn - 1902 (64 pages, B&W) 20.00 35.00 100.00

MERRY MAPLE LEAVES Or A Summer In The Country (S)
E.P. Dutton And Company, New York: 1872 (9-3/8x7-3/8", 90 and 86 pgs pgs, hard-c)
nn - By Abner Perk 25.00 50.00 150.00
NOTE: *Each drawing contained in a maple leaf motif by Livingston Hopkins and others.*

MERRYMAN'S MONTHLY A COMIC MAGAZINE FOR THE FAMILY (M,O,E)
J.C. Haney & Co, NY: 1863-1875 (10-7/8x7-13/16", 30 pgs average, B&W)
Certain issues with sequential comics 100.00 200.00 425.00
NOTE: *Sequential strips by Frank Bellew Sr, Wilhelm Busch found so far; others?*

MERRYTHOUGHT, OR LAUGHTER FROM YEAR TO YEAR, THE
Fisher & Brother, Phila, Baltimore: early 1850s (4-1/2x7", B&W)
nn - many singles, some sequential (Very Rare) (no known sales)
NOTE: *See Vict article for back cover pic which is earliest known use of the term Comic Book*

MESSRS. BROWN, JONES, AND ROBINSON, THE FOREIGN TOUR OF
(see also **THE CLOWN, OR THE BANQUET OF WIT**) (E,M,O,G)
Bradbury & Evans, London: 1854 (11-5/8x9-1/2", 196 pgs, gilted hard-c, B&W)
nn - By Richard Doyle 35.00 70.00 225.00
nn - Bradbury & Evans 1900 reprint 25.00 50.00 100.00
NOTE: *Protective sheets between each page (not part of page count). Expanded and redrawn sequential comics story from the serialized episodes originally published in PUNCH. Also comes in a 174 pg 8-3/4x11" version.*

MESSRS. BROWN, JONES, AND ROBINSON, THE LAUGHABLE ADVENTURES OF (E,M,G)
Garrett, Dick & Fitzgerald, NY: nd (1856 or 1857) (5-3/4x9-1/4", 100 pgs, printed one side only, paper-c, B&W)
nn - (Very Rare) by Richard Doyle c/a 325.00 550.00 1275.00
NOTE: *1st American reprinting of the "Foreign Tour"; reformatted into a small oblong format. Links the earlier Garrett & Co. to the later Dick & Fitzgerald. Back cover reprints full size the Garrett & Co. version cover for Oscar Shanghai. Interior front cover reprints full size the Garrett & Co. version cover for Slyfox-Wikof. Issued without a title page.*

MESSRS. BROWN, JONES, AND ROBINSON, THE FOREIGN TOUR OF (E,M,G)
D. Appleton & Co., New York: 1860 & 1877 (11-5/8x9-1/2", 196 pgs, gilted hard-c, B&W)
nn - (1860 printing) by Richard Doyle 30.00 60.00 220.00
nn - (1871 printing) by Richard Doyle 30.00 60.00 150.00
nn - (1877 printing) by Richard Doyle 30.00 60.00 150.00
NOTE: *Protective sheets between each page (not part of page count). Reprints the Bradbury & Evans edition.*

MESSRS BROWN JONES AND ROBINSON, THE AMERICAN TOUR OF (O,G)
D. Appleton & Co., New York: 1872 (11-5/8x9-1/2", 158 pgs, printed one side only, B&W, green gilted hard-c)
nn - By Toby 100.00 200.00 550.00
NOTE: *Original American graphic novel sequel to Richard Doyle's Foreign Tour of Brown, Jones, and Robinson, with the same characters visiting New York, Canada, and Cuba. Protective sheets between each page (not part of page count).*

MESSRS. BROWN, JONES, AND ROBINSON, THE LAUGHABLE ADVEN. OF (E,M,G)
Dick & Fitzgerald, NY: nd (late 1870's - 1888) (5-3/4x9-1/4", 100 pgs, printed one side only, green paper-c, B&W)
nn - (Scarce) by Richard Doyle 110.00 210.00 475.00
NOTE: *Reprints the Garrett, Dick & Fitzgerald printing, with the following changes: Takes what had been page 12 in the Garrett, D&F printing (art by M.H. Henry), and makes it a title page, which is numbered page 1. The first story page, "Go to the Races", is numbered 2 (whereas it is numbered 1 in the Garrett, Dick & Fitzgerald version). Numbering stays ahead of the G,D&F edition by 1 page up through page 12, after which the page numbering becomes identical.*

MINNEAPOLIS JOURNAL CARTOONS (N,S)
Minneapolis Journal: nn 1894 - No.2 1895 (7-3/4" x 10-7/8", 76 pgs, B&W, paper-c)
nn (1894) (Rare) 50.00 100.00 210.00
Second Series (1895) (Rare) 50.00 100.00 210.00
nn- "War Cartoons" Jan 1899 (9x8", 160 pgs, paperback, punched & string bound) (Scarce) 25.00 100.00 180.00
NOTE: *Reprints single panel cartoons from the prior year, by Charles "Bart" L. Bartholomew.*

MISCHIEF BOOK, THE (E)
R. Worthington, New York: 1880 (7-1/8 x 10-3/4", 176 pgs, hard-c, B&W)
nn - Green cloth binding; green on brown cover; cover art by R. Lewis based on Busch art by Wilhelm Busch 200.00 400.00 800.00
nn - Blue cloth binding; hand colored cover; completely different cover art based on Busch by Wilhelm Busch 200.00 400.00 800.00
NOTE: *Translated by Abby Langdon Alger. American published anthology collection of Wilhelm Busch comic strips. Includes two of the strips found in the British "Bushel of Merry-Thoughts" collection, translated better, and with the dropped panel restored. Unknown which cover version was first.*

MISSES BROWN, JONES AND ROBINSON, THE FOREIGN TOUR OF THE (E,O,G)
Bickers & Sons, London: nd (c1850's) (12-1/4" x 9-7/8", 108 pgs, printed on one side, B&W, hard-c)
nn- "by Miss Brown" (Rare) 100.00 200.00 410.00
NOTE: *A female take on Doyle's Foreign Tour, by an unknown woman artist, using the pseudonym "Miss Brown."*

MISS MILLY MILLEFLEUR'S CAREER (S)
Sheldon & Co., NY: 1869 (10-3/4x9-7/8", 74 pgs, purple hard-c)
nn - Artist unknown (Rare) 75.00 150.00 300.00

MR PODGER AT COUP'S GREATEST SHOW ON EARTH HIS HAPS AND MISHAPS, THE ADVENTURES OF (O,S)
W.C. Coup, New York: 1884 (5-5/8x4-1/4", 20 pgs, color-c, B&W)
nn - Circus Themes; Similar to Barker's Comic Almanacs 30.00 60.00 110.00

MR. TOODLES' GREAT ELEPHANT HUNT (See Peter Piper in Bengal)
Brother Jonathan, NYC: 1850s (4-1/4x7-7/8", page count presently unknown)
nn - catalog contains comic strip (Very Rare) (no known sales)

MR. TOODLES' TERRIFIC ELEPHANT HUNT
Dick & Fitzgerald, NYC: 1860s (5-3/4x9-1/4", 32 pgs, paper-c, B&W) (Very Rare)
nn - catalog reprint contains 28 panel comic strip 150.00 300.00 650.00

MRS GRUNDY
Mrs Grundy Publishing Co, NYC: July 8 1865-Sept 30 1865 (weekly)
1-13 Thomas Nast, Hoppin, Stephens, 50.00 100.00 200.00

MUSEUM OF WONDERS, A (O,I)
Routledge & Sons: 1894 (13x10", 64 pgs, color-c, color thru out)
nn - By Frederick Opper 125.00 250.00 520.00

MY FRIEND WRIGGLES, A (Laughter) Moving Panorama, of His Fortunes And Misfortunes, Illustrated With Over 200 Engravings, of Most Comic Catastrophes And Side-Splitting Merriment) (O,G)
Stearn & Co, 202 Williams St, NY: 1850s (5-7/8x9-3/4", 100 pgs, B&W)
nn - By S. P. Avery (also the engraver) (Very Rare) 225.00 450.00 900.00

MY SKETCHBOOK (E,S)
Dana Estes & Charles E. Lauriat, Boston; J. Sabins & Sons, New York: circa 1880s (9-3/8x12", brown hard-c)
nn - By George Cruikshank 25.00 50.00 150.00
NOTE: *Reprints British editions 1834-36; extensive usage of word balloons.*

Nasby's Life Of Andy Jonson
1866 © Jesse Haney Company

99 "Woolf's" from Truth
1896 © Truth Company

The Adventures of Obadiah Oldbuck 4th printing
mid-1850s © Brother Jonathan Offices, NY

NASBY'S LIFE OF ANDY JONSON (O, M)
Jesse Haney Co., Publishers No. 119 Nassau St, NY: 1866 (4-1/2x7-1/2, 48 pgs, B&W)
nn - President Andrew Johnson satire 125.00 250.00 500.00
NOTE: Blurb further reads: With a True Pictorial History of His STumping Tour Out West By Petroleum V. Nasby, A Dimmicrat of Thirty Years Standing, And Who Allus Tuk His Licker Straight. Front of book has long sequential comic strip satire on President Andrew Johnson, misspelling his name on the cover on purpose.

NAST'S ILLUSTRATED ALMANAC
Harper & Brothers, Franklin Square, NYC: 1872-1874 (8x5.5", 80 pgs, B&W, 35¢)
nn 65.00 125.00 250.00

NAST'S WEEKLY (O,S)
???: 1892-93 (Quarto Weekly)
all issues scarce 50.00 100.00 200.00

NATIONAL COMIC ALMANAC
An Association of Gentlemen, Boston: 1838-?? (8.25x4.75", 34 pgs, B&W)
nn 60.00 120.00 250.00

NEW AMERICAN COMIC ALL-IMAKE (ELTON'S BASKET OF COMICAL SCRAPS), THE
Elton, Publisher, New York: 1839 (7-1/2x4-5/8, 24 pgs)
1 100.00 200.00 400.00

NEW BOOK OF NONSENSE, THE: A Contribution To The Great Central Fair In Aid of the Sanitary Commission (O,S)
Ashmead & Evans, No. 724 Chestnut St, Philadelphia: June 1864 (red hard-c)
nn - Artists unknown (Scarce) 50.00 150.00 300.00

NEW YORK ILLUSTRATED NEWS
Frank Leslie, NYC: 10/14/76-June 1884
average issues with comic strips 25.00 50.00 100.00

NEW YORK PICAYUNE (see PHUN FOTOCRAFT)
Woodward & Hutchings: 1850-1855 newspaper-size weekly; 1856-1857 Folio Monthly 16x10.5; 1857-1858 Quarto Weekly; 1858-1860 Quarto Weekly
Average Issue With Comic Strips 50.00 100.00 200.00
Issues with Full Front Page Comic Strip 100.00 200.00 400.00
NOTE: *Many issues contain Frank Bellew sequential comic strips & single panel cartoons. Later issues published by Woodward, Levison & Robert Gun (1853-1857) ; Levison & Thompson (1857-1860)*

NICK-NAX
Levison & Haney, NY: 1857-1858? (11x7-3/4", 32 pgs, B&W, paper-c)
v2 #10 Feb 1858 has many single panel cartoons 50.00 100.00 200.00

99 "WOOLFS" FROM TRUTH (see Sketches of Lowly Life in a Great City, Truth)
Truth Company, NY: 1896 (9x5-1/2", 72 pgs, varnished paper-like cloth hard-c, 25 cents)
nn - By Michael Angelo Woolf (Rare) 150.00 300.00 600.00
NOTE: *Woolf's cartoons are regarded as a primary influence on R.F. Outcault in the later development of The Yellow Kid newspaper strip. Copy sold in 2002 on eBay for $800.00.*

NONSENSE OR, THE TREASURE BOX OF UNCONSIDERED TRIFLES
Fisher & Brother, 12 North Sixth St, Phila, PA, 64 Baltimore St, Baltimore, MD: early 1850s (4-1/2x7", 128 pgs, B&W)
nn - much Davy Crocket sequential story-telling comic strips 300.00 600.00 1200.00

OBADIAH OLDBUCK, THE ADVENTURES OF MR. (E,G)
Tilt & Bogue, London: nd (1840-41) (5-15/16x9-3/16", 176 pgs,B&W, gilted hard-c)
nn - By Rodolphe Töpffer 800.00 1300.00 3000.00
nn - Hand coloured edition (Very Rare) (no known sales)
NOTE: *This is the British edition, translating the unauthorized redrawn 1839 edition from Parisian publisher Aubert, adapted from Töpffer's "Les Amours de Mr. Vieux Bois" (aka "Histoire de Mr. Vieux Bois"), originally published in French in Switzerland, in 1837 (2nd ed. 1839). Early 19th century books are often found rebound, with original cover and/or title page gone. To distinguish editions having no cover or title page: the British oblong editions (published by Tilt & Bogue) use Roman Numerals to number pages. American oblong shaped editions use Arabic Numerals. British are printed on one side only. This is the earliest known English language sequential comic book. Has a new title page with art by Robert Cruikshank.*

OBADIAH OLDBUCK, THE ADVENTURES OF MR. (E,G)
Wilson and Company, New York: September 14, 1842 (11-3/4x9", 44 pgs, B&W, yellow paper-c on bookstand editions, hemp paper interior)
Brother Jonathan Extra No. IX - Rare bookstand edition 2200.00 5000.00 10,000.00
Brother Jonathan Extra No. IX Very Rare subscriber/mailorder 2200.00 5000.00 10,000.00
NOTE: *By Rodolphe Töpffer. Earliest known sequential American comic book, reprinting the 1841 British edition. Pages are numbered via Roman numerals. States "BROTHER JONATHAN EXTRA - ADVENTURES OF MR. OBADIAH OLDBUCK." at the top of each page. Prints 2 to 3 tiers of panels on both sides of each page. Copies could be had for ten cents according to adverts in* ***Brother Jonathan.*** *By Rodolphe Töpffer with cover masthead design by David Claypool Johnston, and cover art beneath the masthead reprinting Robert Cruikshank's title page art from the Tilt & Bogue edition. A special, additional cover was added for copies sold on stands (it was not issued with mail order or subscriber copies). Only 1 known copy possesses (partially) this very thin outer yellow cover. A decent (subscriber) copy sold on eBay in later October 2002 for over $3500.00. In 2005, a G/VG for $20,000; and a VG for $20,000. An apparent GD copy sold in auction in 2007 for $9560. A FA/GD copy sold in 2008 for $4182.50. A bound edition sold in 2010 for $2270.50. (Prices vary widely.)*

OBADIAH OLDBUCK, THE ADVENTURES OF MR. (E,G)
Wilson & Co, New York: nd (1849) (5-11/16x8-3/8", 84 pgs, B&W,paper-c)
nn - by Rodolphe Töpffer; title page by Robert Cruikshank (Very Rare) 500.00 1200.00 4100.00
NOTE: *2nd Wilson & Co printing, reformatted into a small oblong format, with nine panels edited out, and text modified to smooth out this removal. Results in four less printed tiers/strips. Pages are numbered via Arabic numerals. Every panel on Pages 11, 14, 19, 21, 24, 34, 35 has one line of text. Reformatted to conform with British first edition.*

OBADIAH OLDBUCK, THE ADVENTURES OF MR. (E,G)
Wilson & Co, 162 Nassau, NY: nd (early-1850s) (5-11/16x8-3/8", 84 pgs, B&W, yellow-c
nn - 3rd USA Printing by Rodolphe Töpffer; title page by Robert Cruikshank (Very Rare) Says By Timothy Crayon, an obvious pseudonym 800.00 1600.00 4100.00
NOTE: Front cover banner the giant is holding says "Done With Drawings By Timothy Crayon, Gypsographer, 188 Comic Etchings On Antimony" Title page changes address to No. 15 Spruce-Street. (Late 162 Nassau Street.)

OBADIAH OLDBUCK, THE ADVENTURES OF MR..
Brother Jonathan Offices: ND (mid-1850s) (5-11/16x8-3/8", 84 pages, B&W, oblong)
nn - 4th printing; Originally by Rodolphe Töpffer (Very Rare) 500.00 1200.00 4100.00
NOTE: *Cover States: "New York: Published at the Brother Jonathan Office". Front cover banner the giant is holding says "Done With Drawings By Timothy Crayon, Gypsographer, 188 Comic Designs On Antimony."*

OBADIAH OLDBUCK, THE ADVENTURES OF MR. (E,G)
Dick & Fitzgerald, New York: nd (various printings; est. 1870s to 1888) (Thirty Cents, 84 pgs, B&W, paper-c) (all versions scarce)
nn - Black print on green cover(5-11/16x8-15/16"); string bound 200.00 400.00 1000.00
nn - Black print on blue cover; same format as green-c 200.00 400.00 1000.00
nn - Black print on white cover(5-13/16x9-3/16"); staple bound beneath cover); this is a later printing than the blue or green-c 200.00 400.00 1000.00
NOTE: *Reprints the abbreviated 1849 Wilson & Co. 2nd printing. Pages are numbered via Arabic numerals. Many of the panels on Pages 11, 14, 19, 21, 24, 34, 35 take two lines to print the same words found in the Wilson & Co version, which used only one text line for the same panels. Unknown whether the blue or green cover is earlier. White cover version has "thirty cents" line blackened out on the two copies known to exist. Robert Cruikshank's title page has been made the cover in the D&F editions.*

OLD FOGY'S COMIC ALMANAC
Philip J. Cozans, NY: 1858 (4-7/8x7-1/4, 48 pgs)
nn - sequential comic strip told one panel per page 50.00 100.00 220.00
NOTE: Contains (12) panel "Fourth of July in New York" sequential

OLD MOTHER MITTEN AND HER FUNNY KITTEN (see also **The Juvenile Gem**) (O)
Huestis & Cozans: nd(1850-1852) (6x3-7/8"12pgs, hand colored paper-c, B&W)
nn - first printing(s) publisher's address is 104 Nassau Street (1850-1851) (Very Rare) (no known sales)
NOTE: *A hand colored outer cover is highly rare, with only 1 recorded copy possessing it. Front cover image and text is repeated precisely on page 3 (albeit b&w), and only interior pages are numbered, together leading owners of coverless copies to believe they have the cover. The true back cover has ads for the publisher. Cover was issued only with copies which were sold separately - books which were bound together as part of THE JUVENILE GEM never had such covers.*

OLD MOTHER MITTEN AND HER FUNNY KITTEN (see JUVENILE GEM) (O)
Philip J. Cozans: nd (1850-1852) (6x3-7/8",12 pgs, hand colored paper-c, B&W)
nn - Second printing(s) publisher's address is 116 Nassau Street (1851-1852) (Very Rare) (no known sales)
nn - Third printing(s) publisher's address is 107 Nassau Street (1852+) (Very Rare) (no known sales)

OLD MOTHER MITTEN AND HER FUNNY KITTEN
Americana Review, Scotia, NY: nd (1960's) (6-1/4x4-1/8", 8 pgs, side-stapled, cardboard, B&W)
nn - Modern reprint 5.00 10.00 15.00
NOTE: *Issued within a folder titled SIX CHILDREN'S BOOKS OF THE 1850'S. States "Reprinted by American Review" at bottom of front cover. Reprints the 104 Nassau Street address.*

ON THE NILE (O,G)
James R. Osgood & Co., Boston: 1874 ; **Houghton, Osgood & Co., Boston:** 1880 (112 pgs, gilted green hardcover, B&W)
1st printing (1874; 10-3/4x16") - by Augustus Hoppin 50.00 100.00 200.00
2nd printing (1880; smaller sized) 32.50 65.00 130.00

OSCAR SHANGHAI, THE EXTRAORDINARY AND MIRTH-PROVKING ADVENTURES BY SEA & LAND OF (O, G)
Garrett & Co., Publishers, No. 18 Ann Street, New York: May 1855 (5-3/4x9-1/4", 100 pgs, printed one side only, paper-c, 25¢, B&W)
nn - Samuel Avery-c; interior by ALC Very Rare) 1000.00 2000.00 4000.00
NOTE: *Not much is known of this first edition as the data comes from a recently rediscovered* ***Brother Jonathan*** *catalog issued circa 1853-55. No original known yet to exist.*

OSCAR SHANGHAI, THE WONDERFUL AND AMUSING DOINGS BY SEA AND LAND OF (G)
Dick & Fitzgerald, 10 Ann St, NY: nd (1870s-1888) (25 ¢, 5-3/4x9-1/4", 100 pgs, printed one side only, green paper c, B&W)
nn - Cover by Samuel Avery; interior by ALC (Rare) 300.00 500.00 1100.00
NOTE: *Exact reprint of Garrett & Co original.*

OUR ARTIST IN CUBA (O)
Carleton, New York: 1865 (6-5/8x4-3/8", 120 pgs, printed one side only, gilted hard-c, B&W)
nn - By Geo. W. Carleton 50.00 100.00 200.00

OUR ARTIST IN CUBA, PERU, SPAIN, AND ALGIERS (O)
Carleton: 1877 (6-1/2x5-1/8", 156 pgs, hard-c, B&W)
nn - By Geo. W. Carleton 50.00 100.00 200.00
nn - By Geo. W. Carleton (wraps paper cover) (Rare) 45.00 90.00 180.00

The Wonderful and Amusing Doings by Sea & Land of Oscar Shanghai
1870s © Dick & Fitzgerald, New York

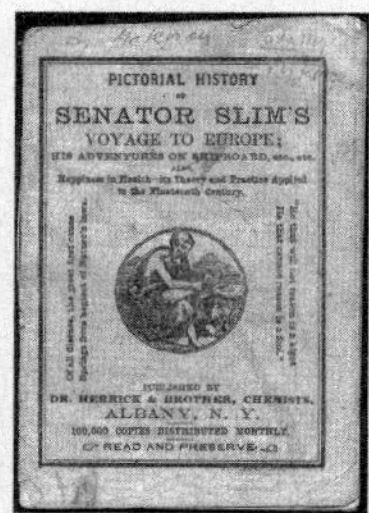

Pictorial History of Senator Slim's Voyage To Europe
1860 © Dr. Herrick & Brother, Albany, NY

Puck #1
1877 © Keppler & Schwarzman, NY

FR1.0 GD2.0 FN6.0

NOTE: *Reprints OUR ARTIST IN CUBA and OUR ARTIST IN PERU, then adds new section on Spain and Algiers.*

OUR ARTIST IN PERU (O)
Carleton, New York: 1866 (7-3/4x5-7/8", 68 pgs, gilted hardcover, B&W)
nn- By Geo. W. Carleton 37.50 75.00 150.00
NOTE: *Contains advertisement for the upcoming books **OUR ARTIST IN ITALY** and **OUR ARTIST IN FRANCE**, but no such publications have been found to date.*

PARSON SOURBALL'S EUROPEAN TOUR (O)
Duff and Ashmead: 1867 (6x7-1/2", 76 pgs, blue embossed title hard-c)
nn - By Horace Cope 100.00 200.00 400.00
NOTE: see **REV. MR. SOURBALL'S EUROPEAN TOUR, THE** for the soft paper cover version

PEN AND INK SKETCHES OF YALE NOTABLES (O,S)
Soule, Thomas and Winsor, St. Louis: 1872 (12-1/4x9-3/4", B&W)
By Squills 25.00 50.00 110.00
NOTE: *Printed by Steamlith Press, The R.P. Studley Company, St Louis.*

PETER PIPER IN BENGAL
Bengamin H Day.Publisher, Brother Jonathan Cheap Book Establishment, 48 Beekman, NY: 1953-55 (6-5/8x4-1/4, 36 pgs, yellow paper-c, B&W, 3 cents - two dollars per hundred) (Very Rare)
nn - By John Tenniel - 32 panel comic strip Punch-r 500.00 1000.00 2300.00
NOTE: *Actually also a catalog of inexpensive books, prints, maps and half a dozen comic books for sale on separate pages from publishers Day and Garrett - see full story of this brand new find in the Victorian Era essay. A complete copy with split spine sold in November 2002 for $750.00. Published date most likely 1855.*

THE PHILADELPHIA COMIC ALMANAC (S)
G. Strong, 44 Strawberry St, NYC: 1835 (8-1/2x5", 36 pgs)
nn - 100.00 200.00 600.00
NOTE: 77 engravings full of recurring cartoon characters but not sequential; early use of recurring characters.

PHIL MAY'S SKETCH BOOK (E,S,M)
R.H. Russell, New York: 1899 (14-5/8x10", 64 pgs, brown hard-c, B&W)
nn - By Phil May 35.00 70.00 140.00
NOTE: *American reprint of the British edition.*

PHUNNY PHELLOW, THE
Oakie, Dayton & Jones: Oct 1859-1876; **Street & Smith** 1876: (Folio Monthly)
average issue with Thomas Nast 50.00 100.00 200.00

PHUN FOTOCRAFT, KEWREUS KONSEETS KOMICALLY ILLUSTRATED BY A KWEER FELLER (N) (see **NEW YORK PICAYUNE)**
The New York Picayune, NY: 1850s (104 pgs)
nn - Mostly Frank Bellew, some John Leach 250.00 550.00 1100.00
NOTE: Many sequential comic strips as well as single cartoons all collected from The New York Picayune. Ross & Tousey, Agents, 121 Nassau St, NY. The Picayune ran many sequential comic strips in its decade.

PICTORIAL HISTORY OF SENATOR SLIM'S VOYAGE TO EUROPE
Dr. Herrick & Brother, Chemists, Albany, NY: 1860 (3-1/4x4-3/4", 32 pgs, B&W)
nn - By John McLenan Very Rare 150.00 300.00 600.00

PICTURES OF ENGLISH SOCIETY (Parchment-Paper Series, No.4) (M,S,E)
D. Appleton & Co., New York: 1884 (5-5/8x4-3/8", 108 pgs, paper-c, B&W)
4 - By George du Maurier; Punch-r 30.00 60.00 125.00
NOTE: *Every other page is a full page cartoon, with the opposite page containing the cartoon's caption.*

PICTURES OF LIFE AND CHARACTER (M,S,E)
Bradbury and Evans, London: No.1 1855 - No.5 c1864 (12-1/2x18", 100 pgs, illustrated hard-c, B&W)
nn (No.1) (1855) 35.00 70.00 150.00
2 (1858), 3 (1860) 35.00 70.00 150.00
4 (nd; c1862) 5 (nd; c1864) 35.00 70.00 150.00
nn (nd (late 1860's) 32.50 65.00 140.00
NOTE: 2-1/2x18-1/4", 494 pgs, green gilted-c) reprints 1-5 in one book
1-3 John Leech's... (nd; 12-3/8x10", ? pgs, red gilted-c). 25.00 50.00 100.00
NOTE: *Reprints John Leech cartoons from **Punch**. note that the Volume Number is mentioned only on the last page of these versions.*

PICTURES OF LIFE AND CHARACTER (E,M,S)
G.P. Putnam's Sons: 1880's (8-5/8x6-1/4", 218 pgs, hardcover, color-cr, B&W)
nn - John Leech (single panel **Punch** cartoon-r) 20.00 40.00 160.00
NOTE: *Leech reprints which extend back to the 1850s.*

PICTURES OF LIFE AND CHARACTER (Parchment-Paper Series) (E,M,S)
(see also Humerous Masterpieces)
D. Appleton & Co., NY: 1884 (30¢, 5-3/4 x 4-1/2", 104 pgs, paper-c, B&W)
nn - John Leech (single panel **Punch** cartoon-r) 20.00 40.00 160.00
NOTE: *An advertisment in the back refers to a cloth-bound edition for 50 cents.*

PIPPIN AMONG THE WIDE-AWAKES (O,S)
Werill & Chapin, 113 Nassau St, NYC, NY): 1860 (6x4-1/2", 36 pgs, 6 cents)
nn - Artist unknown (Very Rare) 100.00 200.00 400.00

PLISH AND PLUM (E.G)
Roberts Brothers, Boston: 1883 (8-1/8x5-3/4", 80 pgs, hardcover, B&W)
nn - By Wilhelm Busch 50.00 100.00 225.00

FR1.0 GD2.0 FN6.0

nn - Reprint (Roberts Brothers, 1895) 40.00 80.00 200.00
nn - Reprint (Little, Brown & Co., 1899) 40.00 80.00 200.00
NOTE: *The adventures of two dogs.*

POUNDS OF FUN
Frank Tousey, 34 North Moore St, NY: 1881 (6-1/2x9-1/2", 68pgs, B&W)
nn - Bellew, Worth, Woolf, Chips 40.00 80.00 200.00

PRESIDENTS MESSAGE, THE
G.P. Putnam's Sons, NY: 1887 (5-3/4x7-5/8, 44 pgs)
nn - (19) Thomas Nast single panel full page cartoons 40.00 80.00 200.00

PROTECT THE U.S. FROM JOHN BULL - PROTECTION PICTURES FROM JUDGE
Judge Publishing, New York: 1888 ((10 cents, 6-7/8x10-3/8", 36 pgs, paper-c, B&W)
nn - (Scarce) 30.00 60.00 130.00
NOTE: *Reprints both cartoons and commentary from **Puck**, concerning the issue of tariffs which were then being debated in Congress. Art by Gillam, Hamilton, Victor.*

PUCK (German language edition, St. Louis) (M,O) (see also Die Vehme)
Publisher unknown, St. Louis: No.1, March 18, 1871 - No. ??, Aug. 24, 1872 (B&W, paper-c)
1-?? (Very Rare) by Joseph Keppler (no known sales)
NOTE: *Joseph Keppler's second attempt at a weekly humor periodical, following **Die Vehme** one year earlier. This was his first attempt to launch using the title **Puck**. This German language version ran for a full year before being joined by an English language version.*

PUCK (English language edition, St. Louis) (M,O)
Publisher unknown, St. Louis: No.1, March ?? 1872 - No. ??, Aug. 24, 1872 (B&W, paper c)
1-?? (Very Rare) by Joseph Keppler (no known sales)
NOTE: *Same material as in the German language edition, but in English.*

PUCK, ILLUSTRIRTES HUMORISTISCHES WOCHENBLATT (German language edition, NYC) (M,O)
Keppler & Schwarzmann, New York: No.1 Sept (27) 1876 - 1164 Dec ?? 1899 (10 cents, color front/back-c and centerspread, remainder B&W, paper-c)
1-26 (Volume 1; Rare) by Joseph Keppler - these issues precede the English language version, and contain cartoons not found in them. Includes cartoons on the controversial Tilden-Hayes 1876 Presidential Election debacle. (no known sales)
27-52 (Volume 2; Rare) by Joseph Keppler - contains some cartoon material not found in the English language editions. Particularly in the earlier issues. (no known sales)
53-1164 15.00 30.00 60.00
Bound Volumes (six month, 26 issue run each):
Vol. 1 (Rare) (no known sales)
Vol. 2-4 (Rare) (no known sales)
Vol. 5-47 75.00 150.00 300.00
NOTE: *Joseph Keppler's second, and successful, attempt to launch **Puck**. In German. The first six months precede the launch of the English language edition. Soon after (but not immediately after) the launch of the English edition, both editions began sharing the same cartoons, but, their prose material always remained different. The German language edition ceased publication at the end of 1899, while the English language edition continued into the early 20th Century. First American periodical to feature printed color every issue.*

PUCK (English language edition, NYC) (M,O)
Keppler & Schwarzmann, New York: No.1 March (14) 1877 - 1190 Dec ?? 1899 (10 cents, color front/back-c and centerspread, remainder B&W, paper-c)
1 (Rare) by Joseph Keppler (no known sales)
2-26 (Rare) by Joseph Keppler (no known sales)
27-1190 12.50 25.00 50.00
(see Platinum Age section for year 1900+ issues)
Bound volumes (six month, 26 issue run each):
Vol. 1 (Rare) (one set sold on eBay for $2300.00)
Vol. 2 (Scarce) (one set sold on eBay for $1500.00)
Vol. 3-6 (pre-1880 issues) 175.00 375.00 750.00
Vol. 7-46 140.00 300.00 600.00
NOTE: *The English language editions began six months after the German editions, and so the English edition numbering is always one volume number, and 26 issue numbers, behind its parallel German language edition. Pre-1880 & post-1900 issues are more scarce than 1880's & 1890's.*

PUCK (miniature) (M,P,I)
Keppler & Schwarzmann, New York: nd (c1895) (7x5-1/8", 12 pgs, color front & back paper-c, B&W interior)
nn - Scarce 25.00 50.00 110.00
NOTE: *C.J.Taylor-c; F.M.Howarth-a; F.Opper-a; giveaway item promoting **Puck's** various publications. Mostly text, with art reprinted from **Puck**.*

PUCK, CARTOONS FROM (M,S)
Keppler & Schwarzmann, New York: 1893 (14-1/4x11-1/2", 244 pgs, hard-c, mostly B&W)
nn - by Joseph Keppler (Signed and Numbered) 105.00 225.00 450.00
NOTE: *Reprints Keppler cartoons from 1877 to 1893, mostly in B&W, though a few in color, with a text opposite each cartoon explaining the situation then being satirized. Issued only in an edition of 300 numbered issues, signed by Keppler. Only 1/4 of the pages are cartoons.*

PUCK'S LIBRARY (M)
Keppler & Schwarzmann, New York: No.1, July, 1887 - No. 174, Dec, 1899 (10 cents, 11-1/2x8-1/4", 36 pgs, color paper-c, B&W)
1- "The National Game" (Baseball) 50.00 100.00 210.00
2-149 10.00 20.00 50.00
NOTE: ***Puck's Library** was a monthly magazine reprinting cartoons & prose from **Puck**, with each issue's*

Rays of Light
1886 © Morse Bros., Canton, Mass.

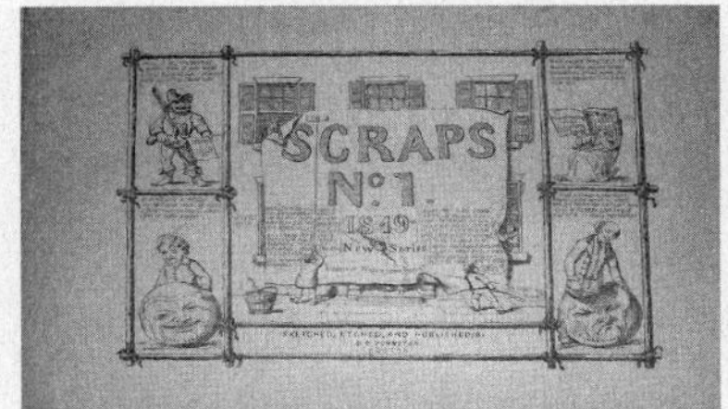

Scraps, New Series #1 by D.C. Johnston
1849 © D.C. Johnston, Boston

Shakespeare Would Ride The Bicycle If Alive Today
1896 © Cleveland Bicycles, Toledo, OH.

FR1.0 GD2.0 FN6.0

material organized around the same subject. The cover art was often original. All issues were kept in print for the duration of the series, so later issues are more scarce than earlier ones.

PUCK, PICKINGS FROM (M)
Keppler & Schwarzmann, New York: No.1, Sept, 1891 - No. 34, Dec, 1899 (25 cents, 13-1/4x10-1/4", 68 pgs, color paper-c, B&W)

1-34 Scarce 25.00 50.00 110.00
NOTE: *Similar to **Puck's Library**, except larger in size, and issued quarterly. All reprint material, except for the cover art. There also exist variations with "RAILROAD EDITION 30 CENTS" printed on the cover in place of the standard 25 cent price.*

PUCK'S OPPER BOOK (M)
Keppler & Schwarzmann, New York: 1888 (11-3/4x13-7/8", color paper-c, 68 pgs,interior B&W, 30¢)

nn - (Very Rare) by F. Opper 225.00 450.00 800.00
NOTE: *Puck's first book collecting work by a single artist.; mostly sequential comic strips.*

PUCK'S PRINTING BOOK FOR CHILDREN (S,O.I)
Keppler & Schwarzman, Pubs, NY: 1891 (10-3/8x7-7/8", 52 pgs, color-c, B&W and color)

nn - Frederick B Opper (Very Rare) (no known sales)

NOTE: *Left side printed in color; Right side B&W to be colored in.*

PUCK PROOFS (M,P,S)
Keppler & Schwarzmann, New York: nd (1906-1909) (74 pgs, paper cover; B&W) (all are Scarce)

nn - (c.1906, no price, 4-1/8x5-1/4") B&W painted -c of couple kissing over a chess board; 1905 & 1906-r 25.00 50.00 100.00
nn- (c.1909, 10 cents, 4-3/8x5-3/8") plain green paper-c; 76 pgs 1905-1909-r 25.00 50.00 100.00
NOTE: *Catalog of prints available from **Puck**, reprinting mostly cover & centerspread art from **Puck**. There likely exist more as yet unreported **Puck Proofs** catalogs. Art by Rose O'Neill.*

PUCK, THE TARIFF ?, CARTOONS AND COMMENTS FROM (M,S)
Keppler & Schwarzmann, New York: 1888 (10 cents, 6-7/8x10-3/8", 36 pgs, paper-c, B&W)

nn - (Scarce) 37.50 75.00 200.00
NOTE: *Reprints both cartoons and commentary from **Puck**, concerning the issue of tariffs which were then being debated in Congress. Art by Gillam, Keppler, Opper, Taylor.*

PUCK, WORLD'S FAIR
Keppler & Schwarzmann, PUCK BUILDING, World's Fair Grounds, Chicago: No.1 May 1, 1893 - No.26 Oct 30, 1893 (10 cents, 11-1/4x8-3/4, 14 pgs, paper-c, color front/back/center pages, rest B&W)(All issues Scarce to Rare)

1-26 35.00 70.00 140.00
1-26 bound volume: 500.00 1100.00 2300.00
NOTE: *Art by Joseph Keppler, F. Opper, F.M. Howarth, C.J. Taylor, W.A. Rogers. This was a separate, parallel run of **Puck**, published during the 1893 Chicago World's Fair from within the fairgrounds, and containing all new and different material than the regular weekly **Puck**. Smaller sized and priced the same, this originally sold poorly, and had not as wide distribution as **Puck**, and so consequently issues are much more rare than regular **Puck** issues from the same period. Not to be confused with the larger sized regular **Puck** issues from 1893 which sometimes also contained World's Fair related material, and sometimes had the words "World's Fair" appear on the cover. Can also be distinguished by the fact that **Puck's** issue numbering was in the 800's in 1893, while these issue number 1 through 26.*

PUNCHINELLO
Punchinello Publishing Co, NYC: April 2-Dec 24 1870 (weekly)

1-39 Henry L. Stephens, Frank Bellew, Bowlend 25.00 50.00 100.00
NOTE: *Funded by the Tweed Ring, mild politics attacking Grant Admin & other NYC newspapers. Bound copies exist.*

QUIDDITIES OF AN ALASKAN TRIP (O,G)
G.A. Steel & Co., Portland, OR: 1873 (6-3/4x10-1/2", 80 pgs, gilted hard-c, Red-c and Blue-c exist, B&W)

nn - By William H. Bell (Scarce) 350.00 750.00 1700.00
NOTE: *Highly sought Western Americana collectors. Parody of a trip from Washington DC to Alaska, by a member of the team which went to survey Alaska, purchase commonly known then as "Seward's Folly".*

"RAG TAGS" AND THEIR ADVENTURES, THE (N,S)
A. M. Robertson, San Francisco: 1899 (10-1/4x13-7/8, 84 pgs, color hard-c, B&W inside)

nn - By Arthur M. Lewis (SF Chronicle newspaper-r) (Scarce) 65.00 125.00 275.00

RAYS OF LIGHT (O,P)
Morse Bros., Canton, Mass.: No.1 1886 (7-1/8x5-1/8", 8 pgs, color paper-c, B&W)

1- (Rare) 50.00 100.00 200.00
NOTE: *Giveaway pamphlet in guise of an educational publication, consisting entirely of a sequential story in which a teacher instructs her classroom of young girls in the use of Rising Sun Stove Polish. Color front & back covers.*

RELIC OF THE ITALIAN REVOLUTION OF 1849, A
Gabici's Music Stores, New Orleans: 1849 (10-1/8x12-3/4", 144 pgs, hardcover)

nn - By G. Daelli (Scarce) 100.00 210.00 420.00
NOTE: *From the title page: "Album of fifty line engravings, executed on copper, by the most eminent artists at Rome in 1849; secreted from the papal police after the 'Restoration of Order,' And just imported into America."*

REMARKS ON THE JACOBINIAD (I,S)
E.W. Weld & W. Greenough, Boston: 1795-98 (8-1/4x5-1/8", 72 pgs, a number of B&W plates with text)

nn - Written by Rev. James Sylvester Gardner,artist unknown (Rare) (no known sales)
NOTE: *Early comics-type characters. Not sequential comics, but uses word balloons. Satire directed against "The Jacobin Club," supporters of the French Revolution and Radical Republicans. Gardner came to America from England in 1783, was minister of Trinity Church, Boston. There appears to be some reprints of this done as late as 1798.*

FR1.0 GD2.0 FN6.0

REV. MR. SOURBALL'S EUROPEAN TOUR, THE RECREATION OF A CITY, THE
Duffield Ashmead, Philadelphia: 1867 (7-5/8x6-1/4", 72 pgs, turquoise blue soft wrappers)

By Horace Cope (Rare) 50.00 100.00 225.00
NOTE: see **PARSON SOURBALL'S EUROPEAN TOUR** for the hard cover version.

RHYMES OF NONSENSE TRUTH & FICTION (S)
G.W. Carleton & Co, Publishers, NY: 1874 (10x7-3/4", 44 pgs, hard-c, B&W) (Very Rare)

nn - By Chaucer Jones and Michael Angelo Raphael Smith 100.00 200.00 450.00
NOTE: *Creator names obviously pseudonyms; looks like weak A.B. Frost.*

ROMANCE OF A HAMMOCK, THE - AS RECITED BY MR. GUS WILLIAMS IN "ONE OF THE FINEST" (O,P)
Unknown: 1880s (5-1/2x3-5/8" folded, 7 attached cardboard cards which fold out into a strip, color)

nn - By presently unknown Scarce 75.00 150.00 350.00
NOTE: *12-panel story, which one begins reading on one side of the folded-out strip, then flip to the other side to continue -- unlike the vast majority of folded strips, which are printed on only one side. This was a promotional handout, for a play titled "One of the Finest". The story pictured comes from a poem read in the play by then famous New York stage actor Gus Williams, who is pictured on the "cover"/title card."*

SAD TALE OF THE COURTSHIP OF CHEVALIER SLYFOX-WIKOF, SHOWING HIS HEART-RENDING ASTOUNDING & MOST WONDERFUL LOVE ADVENTURES WITH FANNY ELSSLER AND MISS GAMBOL, THE (O,G)
Garrett & Co., NY: Jan 1856 (25 ¢, 5-3/4x9-1/4", 100 pages, paper-c, B&W)

nn - By T.C. Bond ?? (Very Rare) 550.00 1100.00 2100.00
NOTE: *No surviving copies yet reported -- known via ads in Home Circle published by Garrett. Cover art by John McLenan and Samuel Avery. Graphic novel parodying the real-life romance between European actress/dancer Fanny Elssler and American aristocrat Henry Wikoff. The entire graphic novel is reprinted in the 1976 book "Fanny Elssler in America."*

SAD TALE OF THE COURTSHIP OF CHEVALIER SLYFOX-WIKOF, SHOWING HIS HEART-RENDING ASTOUNDING & MOST WONDERFUL LOVE ADVENTURES WITH FANNY ELSSLER AND MISS GUMBEL, THE (G) (25 cents printed on cover)
Dick And Fitzgerald, NY: 1870s-1888 (5-3/4x9-1/4", ??? pages, soft paper-c, B&W)

nn - By T.C. Bond ?? (Very Rare) 250.00 500.00 1050.00
NOTE: *Reprint of Garrett original printing before G,D&F partnership begins.*

SALT RIVER GUIDE FOR DISAPPOINTED POLITICIANS
Winchell, Small & Co., 113 Fulton St, NY: 1870s (16 pgs, 10¢)

nn - single panel cartoons from Wild Oats (Rare) 75.00 150.00 300.00

SAM SLICK'S COMIC ALMANAC
Philip J. Cozans, NYC: 1857 (7.5x4.5, 48 pgs, B&W) 100.00 200.00 400.00
NOTE: *Contains reprint of "Moses Keyser the Bowery Bully's Trip to the California Gold Mines" from Elton's Comic Almanac #17 1850.*

SCRAPS (O,S) (see also **F****** A*** K*****)**
D.C. Johnston, Boston: 1828 - No.8 1840; New Series No.1 1849 (12 pgs, printed one side only, paper-c, B&W)

1 - 1828 (9-1/4 x 11-3/4") (Very Rare) (no known sales)
2 - 1830 (9-3/4 x 12-3/4") (Very Rare) (no known sales)
3 - 1832 (10-7/8 x 13-1/8") (Very Rare) (no known sales)
4 - 1833 (11 x 13-5/8") (Very Rare) (no known sales)
5- 1834 (10-3/8 x 13-3/8") (Very Rare) (no known sales)
6 - 1835 (10-3/8 x 13-1/4") red lettering in title SCRAPS (Very Rare) 300.00 600.00 1200.00
6 - 1835 (10-3/8 x 13-1/4") no red lettering in title (Rare) 220.00 440.00 1000.00
7 - 1837 (10-3/4 x 13-7/8") 1st Edition (Very Rare) 200.00 400.00 880.00
7 - 1837 (10-3/4 x 13-3/4") 2nd Edition (so stated) 100.00 175.00 375.00
NOTE: *20 pgs. of text (double-sided), 4 pgs. of art (single-sided), plus the covers. There are no protective sheets between the art pages.*
8 - 1840 (10-1/2 x 13-7/8") (Rare) 200.00 400.00 880.00
New Series 1- 1849 (10-7/8 x 13-3/4") 125.00 250.00 475.00
NOTE: *By David Claypoole Johnston. All issues consist of four one-sided sheets with 9 to 12 single panel cartoons per sheet. The other pages are blank or text. With #1-5 the size of the pages can vary up to an inch. Contains 4 protective sheets (not part of page count) Only 1 3 4 and the 1849 New Series Number 1 has cover art along with 4 art pgs. (single sided) with 4 protective sheets and no text pages.New Series Number 1, as well as #6 with bo red lettering and the second printing of issue 7, have survived in higher numbers due to a 1940s warehouse discovery.*

THE SETTLEMENT OF RHODE ISLAND (O)
The Graphic Co. Photo-Lith 39 & 41, Park Place, New York: 1874 (11-3/8x10, 40 pgs, gilted blue hard-c

nn - Charles T. Miller & Walter F. Brown 75.00 150.00 300.00
NOTE: *This is also the Same Walter F. Brown that did "Hail Columbia".*

SHAKESPEARE WOULD RIDE THE BICYCLE IF ALIVE TODAY. "THE REASON WHY" (O,P,S)
Cleveland Bicycles H.A. Lozier & Co., Toledo, OH: 1896 (5-1/2x4",16 pgs, paper-c, color)

nn - By F. Opper (Rare) 75.00 150.00 325.00
NOTE: *Original cartoons of Shakespearian characters riding bicycles; also popular amongst collectors of bicycle ephemera.*

Stumping It
1876 © Collin & Lee, NY

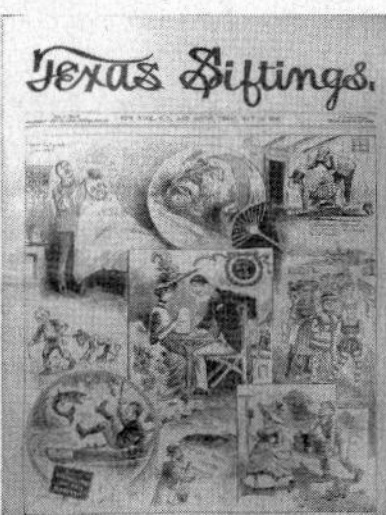

Texas Siftings v6 #2 May 15
1886 ©Texas Siftings Publishing Co.

The Adventures Of Mr. Tom Plump
1851 © Huestis & Cozans, NY

SHAKINGS - ETCHINGS FROM THE NAVAL ACADEMY BY A MEMBER OF THE CLASS OF '67 (O,S)
Lee & Shepard, Boston: 1867 (7-7/8x10", 132 pages, blue hard-c)
By: Park Benjamin 38.00 75.00 150.00
NOTE: *Park Benjamin later became editor of Harper's Bazaar magazine.*

SHOO FLY PICTORIAL (S)
John Stetson, Chestnut sT Theatre, Phila, PA: June 1870 (15-1/2x11-1/2", 8 pgs, B&W)
1 75.00 150.00 275.00

SHYS AT SHAKSPEARE
J.P. and T.C.P., Philadelphia: 1869 (9-1/4x6", 52 pgs)
nn - Artist unknown 75.00 150.00 310.00

SKETCHES OF LOWLY LIFE IN A GREAT CITY (M,S) (See 99 "Woolfs" From Truth)
G. P. Puntam's Sons: 1899 (8-5/8x11-1/4", 200 pgs, hard-c, B&W)
(reprints from Life and Judge of Woolf's cartoons of NYC slum children)
nn - By Michael Angelo Woolf 75.00 150.00 350.00
NOTE: *Woolf's cartoons are regarded as a primary influence on R.F. Outcault in the later development of The Yellow Kid newspaper strip.*

SNAP (O,S)
Valentine & Townsend, Tribune Bldg, NYC: March 13,1885 (17x11, 8 pgs, B&W)
1-Contains a sequential comic strip 50.00 100.00 200.00

SOCIETY PICTURES (M,S,E)
Charles H. Sergel Company, Chicago: 1895 (5-1/4x7-3/4", 168 pgs, printed 1 side, paper-c, B&W)
nn - By George du Maurier; reprints from **Punch**. 25.00 50.00 120.00

SOLDIERS AND SAILORS HALF DIME TALES OF THE LATE REBELLION
Soldiers & Sailors Publishing Co: 1868 (5-1/4x7-7/8", 32 pgs)
v1#1-#16 v2#1-#10 15.00 30.00 60.00
v2 #11 contains (5) page comic strip 25.00 50.00 100.00
NOTE: *Changes to Soldiers & Sailors Half Dime Magazine with v2 #1.*

SOUVENIR CONTAINING CARTOONS ISSUED BY THE PRESS BUREAU OF THE OHIO STATE REPUBLICAN EXECUTIVE COMMITTEE, A (S)
Ohio State Republican Executive Committee, Columbus, OH: 1899 (10-3/8x13-1/2, 248 pgs, Hard-c, B&W
nn - By William L. Bloomer (Scarce) 105.00 225.00 450.00

SOUVENIR OF SOHMER CARTOONS FROM PUCK, JUDGE, AND FRANK LESLIE'S (M,S,P)
Sohmer Piano Co.: nd(c.1893) (6x4-3/4", 16 pgs, paper-c, B&W)
nn 25.00 50.00 100.00
NOTE: *Reprints painted "cartoon" Sohmer Piano advertisements which appeared in the above publications. Artists include Keppler, Gillam, others.*

SPORTING NEW YORKER, THE
Ornum & Co, Beekman ST, NYC: 1870s
issues with sequential comic strips (Rare) 50.00 100.00 200.00

STORY OF THE MAN OF HUMANITY AND THE BULL CALF, THE
(see Bull Calf, The Story of The Man Of Humanity And The)
NOTE: *Reprints of two of A. B. Frost's mostfamous sequential comic strips.*

STREET & SMITH'S LITERARY ALBUM
Street & Smith, NY: #1 Dec 23 1865-#225 Apr 9 1870 (11-3/4x16-3/4", 16 pgs, B&W)
1 (23 Dec 1865) 15.00 50.00 100.00
2-129 131-225 (issues with short sequential strips) 15.00 50.00 100.00
130 (Steam Man satire parody) 100.00 200.00 300.00

STUFF AND NONSENSE (Harper's Monthly strip-r) (M)
Charles Scribner's Sons: 1884 (10-1/4x7-3/4", 100 pgs, hardcover, B&W)
nn - By Arthur Burdett Frost 125.00 200.00 400.00
nn - By A.B. Frost (1888 reprint, 104 pgs) 50.00 100.00 200.00
NOTE: *Earliest known anthology devoted to collecting the comic strips of a single American artist. 1888 2nd printing has a different cover and is layed out somewhat differently inside with a new title page, 3 added pages of cartoons, and a couple more illustrations. For more Frost, the 2nd is worth checki ng out also.*

STUMPING IT (LAUGHING SERIES BRICKTOP STORIES #8) (O,S)
Collin & Small, NY: 1876 (6-5/8x9-1/4, 68 pgs, perfect bound, B&W)
nn - Thomas Worth art abounds (some sequentials) 100.00 175.00 375.00
NOTE: *Mainly single panel cartoons w/text; however, some sequential comic strips inside worth picking up*

SUMMER SCHOOL OF PHILOSOPHY AT MT. DESERT, THE
Henry Holt & Co.: 1881 (10-3/8x8-5/8", 60 pgs, illus. gilt hard-c, B&W)
nn - By J. A. Mitchell 60.00 120.00 250.00
NOTE: *J.A.Mitchell went on to found **LIFE** two years later in 1883. Also, the long-running mascot for **LIFE** was Cupid - which you see multitudes of Cupids flying around in this story.*

SURE WATER CURE, THE
Carey Grey & Hart, Phila, PA: c1841-43 (8-/2x5, 32 pgs, B&W
nn - proto-comic-strip Very Rare 175.00 350.00 700.00

TAILOR-MADE GIRL, HER FRIENDS, HER FASHIONS, AND HER FOLLIES, THE
(see also IN THE "400" AND OUT) (M)
Charles Scribner's Sons, New York: 1888 (8-3/8x10-1/2", 68 pgs, hard-c, B&W)
nn - Art by C.J. Taylor 25.00 50.00 110.00
NOTE: *Format is a full page cartoon on every other page, with a script style vignette, written by Philip H. Welch, on every page opposite the art.*

TALL STUDENT, THE
Roberts Brothers, Boston: 1873 (7x5", 48 pgs, printed one side only, gilted hard-c, B&W)
nn - By Wilhelm Busch (Scarce) 37.50 75.00 150.00

TARIFF ?, CARTOONS AND COMMENTS FROM PUCK, THE (see Puck, The Tariff...)

TEASING TOM AND NAUGHTY NED WITH A SPOOL OF CLARK'S COTTON, THE ADVENTURES OF (O,P)
Clark's O.N.T. Spool Cotton: 1879 (4-1/4x3", 12 pgs, B&W, paper-c)
nn 17.50 35.00 80.00
NOTE: *Knock-off of the "First Trick" in Wilhelm Busch's **Max and Maurice**, modified to involve Clark's Spool Cotton in the story, with similar but new art by an artist identified as "HB". The back cover advertises the specific merchant who gave this booklet away -- multiple variations of back cover suspected.*

TEMPERANCE TALES; OR, SIX NIGHTS WITH THE WASHINGTONIANS, VOL I & II
W.A. Leary & Co., Philadelphia: 1848 (50¢, 6-1/8x4", 328 pgs, B&W, hard-c)
nn 125.00 250.00 525.00
NOTE: *Mostly text. This edition gathers Volume I & II together. The first 8 pages reprints George Cruikshank's **THE BOTTLE**, re-drawn & re-engraved by Phil A. Pilliner. Later editions of this book do not include **THE BOTTLE** reprint and are therefore of little interest to comics collectors.*

TEXAS SIFTINGS
Texas Siftings Publishing Co, Austin, Texas (1881-1887), **NYC** (1887-1897): 1881-1885 newspaper-size weekly; 1886-1897 folio weekly (15x10-3/4", 16 pgs, B&W 10¢

1881-1885 issues 25.00 50.00 110.00
v6#1 (5/8/86) (8) panel strip Afterwhich He Emigrated;
(16) panel The Tenor's Triumph Veni Vidi Vici 12.50 25.00 80.00
v6#2 (5/16/86 (5) panel sewuential 12.50 25.00 80.00
v6#3 no sequentials 12.50 25.00 80.00
v6#4 (5/29/86) Worth-c (4) panel Worth strip; (2) panel 12.50 25.00 80.00
v6#5 no sequentials 12.50 25.00 80.00
v6#6 (6/12/86) Comic Strip Cover (11) panels The Rise of a Great Artist
(5) panel sequential 50.00 100.00 205.00
v6#7 (6/19/86) Worth-c (2) panel Wiorth;
(10) panel Ha! Ha! The Honest Youth & the Lordly Villain 25.00 50.00 110.00
v6#8 (6/26/86) Worth-c; (15) panel The Kangaroo Hunter 25.00 50.00 110.00
v6#9 (7/3/86) Worth-c; Bellew (2) panel How Wives Get What They Want
12.50 25.00 80.00
v6#10 ((7/10/86) Baseball-c; (3) panel;
(5) panel A Story Without Words from Fliegende Blätter 12.50 25.00 80.00
v6 #11 12 13 Worth-c no sequentials 12.50 25.00 80.00
v6#14 (8/7/86) Wiorth-c; (7) panel Mrs Cleveland Presents
The President With A New Rocking Chair 12.50 25.00 80.00
v6#15 (8/14/86) Worth-c; (6) panel Worth strip 12.50 25.00 80.00
v6#16 (8/21/86) Worth-c Asleep At Post USA/Mexico Border
(6) panel sequential 12.50 25.00 80.00
v6#17 no sequrntials 12.50 25.00 80.00
v6#18 (9/4/86) Worth-c; (3) panel from Fliegende 12.50 25.00 80.00
v6#19 (9/11/86) Worth Anarchist & Uncle Sam-c;
(5) panel Duel of the Dudes 12.50 25.00 80.00
v6#20 (9/18/86) Worth-c (6) panel sequential 12.50 25.00 80.00
v6#21 (9/25/86) Worth-c; Verbeck single panel; (9) panel 12.50 25.00 80.00
v6#22 (10/2/86) Verbeck-c plus interiors 12.50 25.00 80.00
v6#23 (10/9/86) Worth-c Geronimo & Devil cover;
Verbeck and Chips singles 25.00 50.00 110.00
v6#24 (10/16/86) Worth-c Verbeck strip "Evolution" 12.50 25.00 80.00
v6#25 no sequential strips 12.50 25.00 80.00
v6#26 (10/30/86) Worth-c; (6) panel Verbeck "A Warning To Smokers"
12.50 25.00 80.00
NOTE: *Many Thomas Worth sequential comic strips. Frank Bellew and Dan McCarthy appear. Wilhelm Busch-r from German Fligende Blaetter. Later issues in 1890s comics become sporadic*

THAT COMIC PRIMER (S)
G.W. Carleton & Co., Publishers: 1877 (6-5/8x5", 52 pgs, paper soft-c, B&W)
nn - By Frank Bellew 75.00 150.00 300.00
NOTE: *Premium for the United States Life Insurance Company, New York.*

TIGER, THE LEFTENANT AND THE BOSUN, THE
Prudential Insurance Home Office, 878 & 880 Broad St, Newark, NJ: 1889 (4.5x3.25", 12 pgs) (Scarce)
nn - 8 panel sequential story in color 50.00 100.00 225.00

TOM PLUMP, THE ADVENTURES OF MR. (see also The Juvenile Gem) (O)
Huestis & Cozans, New York: nd (c1850-1851) (6x3-7/8", 12 pgs, hand colored paper-c, B&W)
nn- First printing(s) publisher's address is 104 Nassau Street (1850-1851)
(Very Rare) 750.00 1500.00 3100.00
NOTE: *California Gold Rush story. The hand colored outer cover is highly rare, with only 1 recorded copy possessing it. The front cover image and text is repeated precisely on page 3 (albeit b&w), and only interior pages are numbered, together leading owners of coverless copies to believe they have the cover. The true back*

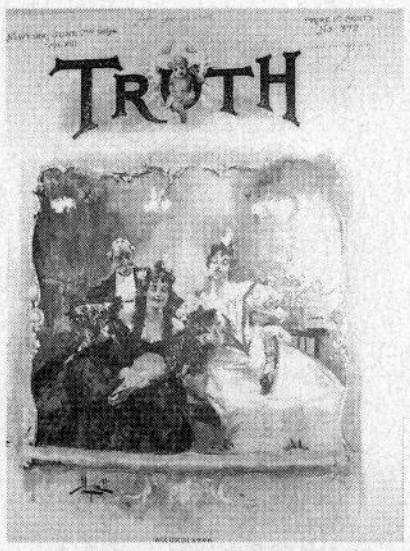

Truth #372 (first app. The Yellow Kid)
June 2 1894 © Truth Company, NY

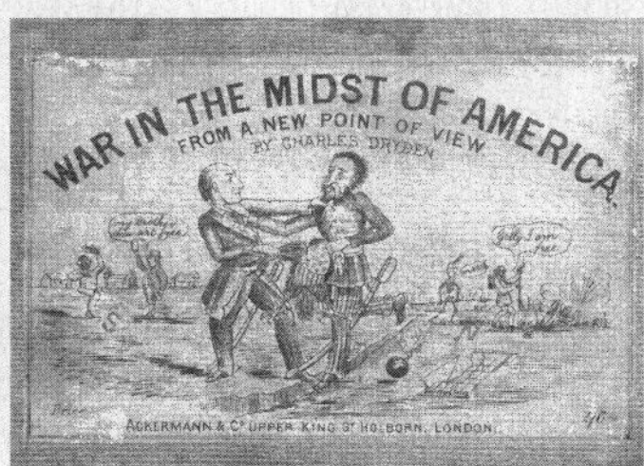

War in the Midst of America
1864 © Ackermann & Co.

Wild Oats #115 March 10
1875 © Winchell & Small, NYC

FR1.0 GD2.0 FN6.0

cover contains ads for the publisher. The cover was issued only with copies which were sold separately - booklets which were bound together as part of ***THE JUVENILE GEM*** *never had such covers.*

TOM PLUMP, THE ADVENTURES OF MR. (see also The Juvenile Gem) (O)
Philip J. Cozans: nd (1851-1852) (6x3-7/8", 12 pgs,hand colored paper-c, B&W)

nn- Second printing(s) publisher's address is 116 Nassau Street (1851-1852)
(Very Rare) 400.00 800.00 1600.00
nn- Third printing(s) publisher's address is 107 Nassau Street (1852+)
(Very Rare) 400.00 800.00 1600.00

TOM PLUMP, THE ADVENTURES OF MR.
Americana Review, Scotia, NY: nd(1960's) (6-1/4x4-1/8", 8 pgs, side-stapled, cardboard-c, B&W)

nn - Modern reprint - 25.00 50.00
NOTE: *Issued within a folder titled SIX CHILDREN'S BOOKS OF THE 1850'S. States "Reprinted by American Review" at bottom of front cover. Reprints the 104 Nassau Street address.)*
nn - Modern rep. (Scarce 1980s) (5-1/2x4-1/4", 8 pgs,side-stapled) - 10.00 20.00
NOTE: *Photocopy reprint by a comix zine publisher, from an Americana Review cop; vailable by mail order*

TOOTH-ACHE, THE (E,O)
D. Bogue, London: 1849 (5-1/4x3-3/4)

nn - By Cruikshank, B&W (Very Rare) 300.00 600.00 1300.00
nn - By Cruikshank, hand colored (Rare) (no known sales)
NOTE: *Scripted by Horace Mayhew, art by George Cruikshank. This is the British edition. Price 1/6 b&w, 3 hand colored. In British editions, the panels are not numbered. Publisher's name appears on cover. Booklet's "pages" unfold into a single, long, strip.*

J.L. Smith, Philadelphia, PA: nd (1849) (5-1/8"x 3-3/4" folded, 86-7/8" wide unfolded, 26 pgs, cardboard-c, color, 15¢)

nn - By Cruikshank, hand colored (Very Rare) 400.00 800.00 1700.00
NOTE: *Reprints the D. Bogue edition. In American editions, the panels are numbered (43 panels, not counting front & back cover). Publisher's name stamped on inside front cover, plus printed along left-hand side of first interior page. Page 1 is pasted to inside back cover, and unfolds from there. Front cover not attached to back cover by design. Booklet's "pages" unfold into a single, long, strip (made from four individual strips pasted together on the blank back side). There is a fairly common1974 British Arts Council reprint.*

TRAMP, THE: His Tricks, Tallies, and Tell-Tales, with His Signs, Countersigns, Grips, Passwords and Villainies Exposed (O,S)
Dick & Fitzgerald, New York: 1878 (11-3/8x8, 36 pgs, paper-c, B&W, 25¢) (Rare)

1 Frank Bellew 160.00 350.00 700.00
NOTE: *Edited by Frank Bellew, A Bee And A Chip (Bellew's daughter and son Frank).*

TRUTH (See Platinum Age section for 1900-1906 issues)
Truth Company, NY: 1886-1906? (13-11/16x10-5/16", 16 pgs, process color-c & center-folds, rest B&W)

	FR1.0	GD2.0	FN6.0
1886-1887 issues	20.00	40.00	100.00
1888-1895 issues non Outcault issues	15.00	30.00	80.00
Mar 10 1894 - precursor Yellow Kid RFO	60.00	180.00	425.00
#372 June 2 1894 - first app Yellow Kid RFO	200.00	600.00	1200.00
June 23 1894 - precursor Yellow Kid R. F. Outcault	60.00	180.00	425.00
July 14 1894 -2nd app Yellow Kid RFO	110.00	330.00	675.00
Sept 15 1894 - (2) 3rd app YK RFO plus YK precursor	110.00	330.00	675.00
Feb 9 1895 - 4th app Yellow Kid RFO	110.00	330.00	675.00
1896-1899 issues	10.00	20.00	55.00

NOTE: *This magazine contains the earliest known appearances of* ***The Yellow Kid*** *by Richard Felton Outcault. Feb 9 1895 issue's YK cartoon was reprinted one week later in the* ***New York World*** *Feb 17 1895 edition. We are still sorting out further Outcault appearances. Truth also contained full color sequential strips by Hy Mayer on the back plus Woolf, Verbeek, etc.*

TRUTH, SELECTIONS FROM
Truth Company, NY: 1894-Spr 1897 (13-11/16x10-1/4, color-c, quarterly)

	FR1.0	GD2.0	FN6.0
1-4	25.00	50.00	100.00
5-Outcault's early Yellow Kid	100.00	225.00	475.00
6-13	20.00	40.00	80.00

NOTE: *#5 reprints all early Outcault Yellow Kid appearances*

TURNER'S COMIC ALMANAC
Charles Strong, 298 Pearl St, NYC: ???-1843 (7.25x4.5", 36 pgs, B&W)

nn 65.00 125.00 250.00

TURNER'S COMICK ALMA-NACK
Turner & Fisher, NYC: 1844-?? (7.25x4.5", 36 pgs, B&W)

nn 65.00 125.00 250.00

TWO HUNDRED SKETCHES, HUMOROUS AND GROTESQUE, BY GUSTAVE DORE (E)
Frederick Warne & Co, London: 1867 (13-3/4x11-3/8, 94 pgs, hard-c, B&W)

	FR1.0	GD2.0	FN6.0
nn - (1867) by Gustave Dore	100.00	200.00	500.00
nn - (Second Edition; 1871)- by Gustave Dore	60.00	125.00	250.00
nn - (Third Edition; 1870's)- by Gustave Dore	60.00	125.00	250.00
nn - (Fourth Edition; 1870's- by Gustave Dore	60.00	125.00	250.00

NOTE: *Contains sequential comics stories, single panel cartoons, and sketches. Reprints and translates material which originally appeared in the French publications "Le Journal pour Rire", circa 1848-49. Although dated 1867, it was likely published & available for the 1866 Christmas Season, as has been confirmed for the American edition. Printed by Dalziel. The American & first British editions were printed simultaneously, the American edition is not a reprint of the British.*

TWO HUNDRED SKETCHES, HUMOROUS AND GROTESQUE, BY GUSTAVE DORE (E)
Roberts Brothers, Boston: 1867 (13-3/4x11-3/8", 96 pgs, hard-c, B&W)

nn - By Gustave Dore 100.00 200.00 600.00
NOTE: *Although dated 1867, it was published & available for the 1866 Christmas Season. Printed by Dalziel, in England, and imported to the USA expressly for a USA publisher.*

UNCLE JOSH'S TRUNK-FUL OF FUN
Dick & Fitzgerald, 18 Ann St, NY: 1870s (5-3/4x9", 68 pgs, B&W & Red-c, B&W inside)

nn - Rare 75.00 125.00 200.00
NOTE: *Many single panel cartoons; (2) pages of early boxing sequential strip*

UNCLE SAM'S COMIC ALMANAC
M.J. Meyers, NY: 1879 (11x8", 32 pgs)

nn - 50.00 100.00 200.00

UNDER THE GASLIGHT
Gaslight Publishing Co (Frank Tousey): Oct 13 1878-Apr 12 1879 (Folio, 16pgs)

1-27 75.00 125.00 200.00

UNITED STATES COMIC ALMANAC
King & Baird, Philadelphia: 1851-?? (7.5x4.5", 36 pgs, B&W)

nn 60.00 120.00 250.00

UPS AND DOWNS ON LAND AND WATER (O.G)
James R. Osgood & Co., Boston: 1871 ; **Houghton, Osgood & Co., Boston:** 1880 (108 pgs, gilted hard-c, B&W)

1st printing (1871; 10-3/4x16") - By Augustus Hoppin 50.00 100.00 200.00
2nd printing (1880; smaller sized) 32.50 65.00 130.00
NOTE: *Exists as blue or orange hard covers.*

VANITY FAIR
William A. Stephens (for Thompson & Camac): Dec 29 1859-July 4 1863 Quarto Weekly

average issues with comic strips 20.00 30.00 100.00

VERDICT, THE
Verdict Publishing Co: Dec 19 1898-Nov 12 1900 (Chromolithographic Weekly)

Average Issues 50.00 100.00 225.00
NOTE: *Artists included George B. Luks, Horace Taylor, MIRS. Striking anti-Republican weekly full o fsome of the most savage political cartoons of the era. The last brilliant burst of energy for the political cartoon weekly*

VERY VERY FUNNY (M,S)
Dick & Fitzgerald, New York: nd(c1880's) (10¢, 7-1/2x5", 68 pgs, paper-c, B&W)

nn - (Rare) 75.00 150.00 325.00
NOTE: *Unauthorized reprints of prose and cartoons extracted from Puck, Texas Siftings, and other publications. Includes art by Chips Bellew, Bisbee, Graetz, Opper, Wales, Zim.*

VIM
H. Wimmel, NYC: June 22-Aug 24 1898 (Chromolithographic Weekly)

average issue 50.00 100.00 200.00
Yellow Kid by Leon Barritt issues 75.00 150.00 350.00

WAR IN THE MIDST OF AMERICA. FROM A NEW POINT OF VIEW. (E,O,G)
Ackermann & Co., London: 1864 (4-3/8" x 5-7/8", folded, 36 feet wide unfolded, 80 pgs, hard-c, B&W)

nn- by Charles Dryden (rare) 425.00 850.00 1900.00
NOTE: *British graphic novel about the American Civil War, with a pro-Confederate bent. Adventures of a British artist who decides to visually summarize the American Civil War for his countrymen, from newspaper accounts. Reaching current events, he finds he can not finish the story until the War ends, and so he travels to America, to end it. Book unfolds into a single long strip (binding was issued split, to enable the unfolding).*

WASP, THE ILLUSTRATED SAN FRANCISCO
F. Korbel & Bros and Numerous Others: August 5 1876-April 25 1941 (Chromolithographic Weekly)

average 1800s issues with comic strips 50.00 100.00 200.00

WHAT I KNOW OF FARMING: Founded On The Experience of Horace Greeley (S)
The American News Company, New York: 1871 (7-1/4x4-1/2", paper-c, B&W)

nn - By Joseph Hull (Scarce) 35.00 70.00 175.00
NOTE: *Pay & Cox, Printers & Engravers, NY; political tract regarding Presidential elections.*

WILD FIRE
Wild Fire Co, NYC: Nov 30 1877-at least#16 Mar 1878 (Folio, 16 pgs)

1-16 30.00 60.00 125.00

WILD OATS, An Illustrated Weekly Journal of Fun, Satire, Burlesque, and Nits at Persons and Events of the Day (O)
Winchell & Small, 113 Fulton St /48 Ann St, NYC: Feb 1870-1881 (16-1/4x11", generally 16 pages, B&W, began as monthly, then bi-weekly, then weekly) All loose issues Very Rare (See *The Overstreet Price Guide* #35 2005 for a detailed index of single issue contents)

	FR1.0	GD2.0	FN6.0
1-25 Very Rare - contents to be indexed next year	50.00	100.00	225.00
26-28 30 32 35 36 39 40 41 43-46 1872 (sequential strips)	50.00	100.00	225.00
29 33 37 42 no sequential strips	40.00	80.00	160.00
31 34 38 47 Hopkins sequential comic strips	50.00	100.00	225.00
48 (1/16/73) Worth 13 panel sequential; first Woolf-c	50.00	100.00	225.00
49 51 53 54 60 62 61 64 65 66 67 69 1873 sequential strips	50.00	100.00	225.00
50 52 56 59 63 71 no sequential strips	40.00	80.00	160.00
51 (Worth 18 panel double page spread, Woolf 9 panel	50.00	100.00	225.00
55 Hopkins 22 panel double page spread; Bellew-c	50.00	150.00	320.00

57 intense unknown 6 panel "Two Relics of Barbarism, or A Few Contrasted Pictures,

Wild Oats #139 August 25
1875 © Winchell & Small, NY

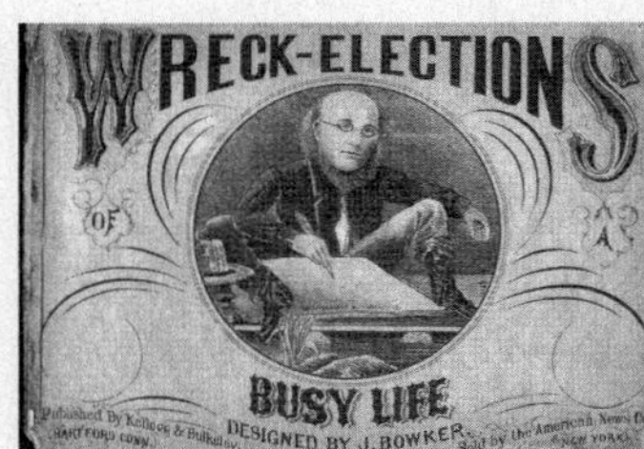

Wreck-Elections Of Busy Life
Kellogg & Buckeley © 1864?

Yankee Notions #7 (v2#1)
July 1852 © T.W. Strong, NY

FR1.0 GD2.0 FN6.0

Showing the origin of the North American Indian 50.00 100.00 225.00
58 (6/5/73) unknown 19 panel double pager "The Terrible Adventures of Messrs Buster & Stumps, About Exterminating the Indians" reads across both pages like Popeye #2095 (1933); Woolf-c 100.00 200.00 460.00
68 (10/16/73) unknown 9 panel "Adv of New jersey Mosquito" looks like Winsor McCay type style: early inspiration for McCay's animated cartoon? 50.00 100.00 250.00
70 unknown 6 panel; Hopkins 6 panel "Hopkins novel: A Tale of True Love, with all the variations"; Bellew-c 50.00 100.00 225.00
72 (12/11/73) Worth 11 panel; Wales President Grant war-c 50.00 100.00 225.00
73 74 75 Hopkins sequential comic strip 75.00 150.00 310.00
76 77 sequential strips 50.00 100.00 225.00
78 Bellew 5 panel double pager 50.00 100.00 225.00
79-105 (March 1874-Dec 1874) contents presently unknown 50.00 100.00 225.00
106 107 111 no sequentials;Bellew-c #106 110;Wales-c #107 50.00 100.00 225.00
108 (1/20/75) Wales 12 panel double pg spread; Bellew-c 50.00 100.00 225.00
109 (1/27/75) unknown 6 panel; Wales-c 50.00 100.00 225.00
111 Busch 13 panel "The Conundrum of the Day - Is Lager Beer Intoxicating?"; Bellew-c 50.00 100.00 225.00
112 116 sequential comic strips 50.00 100.00 225.00
113 114 115 no sequentials Worth-c #114 40.00 80.00 160.00
117 intense Wales 6 panel "One of the Oppresions of the Civil Rights Laws" Bellew-c 75.00 150.00 330.00
118-137 (3/31/75-8/4/75) no sequential comic strips 40.00 80.00 160.00
138 (8/18/75) Bellew Sr & Bellew "Chips" Jr singles appear 50.00 100.00 225.00
139-143 145-147 154-157 159 no sequentials 40.00 80.00 160.00
144 (9/29/75) Hopkins 8 panel sequential; Wales-c 50.00 100.00 225.00
148 (10/27/75) Opper's first cover; many Opper singles 75.00 150.00 320.00
149 150 151 152 153 all Opper-c and much interior work 50.00 100.00 225.00
158 (1/5/76) Palmer Cox 1rst comic strip 24 panel double page spread "The Adv of Mr & Mrs Sprowl And Their Christmas Turkey - A Crashing Chasing Tearful Tragedy But Happily Ending Well"; Opper-c 100.00 200.00 450.00
159 160 162 165 167 169-173 no sequentials 40.00 80.00 160.00
161 163 164 166 168 179 182 Palmer Cox sequential strips 100.00 200.00 450.00
174 (4/26/76) Cox 24 panel double pager "The Tramp's Progress; A Story of the West And the Union Pacific Railroad" 100.00 200.00 450.00
175-178 183-189 no sequentials 40.00 80.00 160.00
180 (6/7/76) Beard & Opper jam; Woolf, Bellew singles 50.00 100.00 225.00
181 more Mann two panel jobs; Opper-c 50.00 100.00 225.00
190 Bellew 9 panel "Rodger's Patent Mosquito Armour" 75.00 150.00 320.00
191-end contents to be indexed in the near future 40.00 80.00 160.00

NOTE: *There are very few lknown oose issues. All loose issues are Very Rare. Prices vary widely on this magazine. Issues with sequential comic strips would be in higher demand than issues with no comic strips. We present this index from the Library of Congress and New York Historical Society bound sets. We would love to hear from any one who turns up loose copies. This scarce humor bi-weekly contains easily a couple hundred original first-time published sequential comic strips found in most issues plus innumerable single panel cartoons in every issue*

WOMAN IN SEARCH OF HER RIGHTS, THE ADVENTURES OF (G)
Lee & Shepard, Boston And New York: early 1870s (8-3/8x13", 40 pgs, hard-c)

By Florence Claxton (Very Rare) 450.00 900.00 1900.00

NOTE: *Earliest known original comic book sequential story by a woman; contains "nearly 100 original drawings by the author, which have been reproduced in fac-simile by the graphotype process of engraving." Tinted two color lithography; orange tint printed first, then printed 2nd time with black ink; early women's sufferage.*

WORLD OVER, THE (I)
G. W. Dillingham Company, New York: 1897 (192 pgs, hard-c)

nn - By Joe Kerr; 80 illustrations by R.F. Outcault (Rare) 330.00 660.00 1250.00

NOTE: soft cover editions also exist

WRECK-ELECTIONS OF BUSY LIFE (S)
Kellogg & Bulkeley: 1867 (9-1/4x11-3/4", ??? pages, soft-c)

nn - By J. Bowker (Rare) 110.00 225.00 450.00

NOTE: *Says "Sold by American News Company, New York" on cover.*

WYMAN'S COMIC ALMANAC FOR THE TIMES
T.W. Strong, NY: 1854 (8x5", 24 pgs)

nn - 50.00 100.00 200.00

YANKEE DOODLE
W.H. Graham, Tribune Building, NYC: Oct 10 1846-Oct 2 1847 (Quarto weekly)

average issue 110.00 125.00 250.00

YANKEE NOTIONS, OR WHITTLINGS OF JONATHAN'S JACK-KNIFE
T.W. Strong, 98 Nassau St, NYC: Jan. 1852-1875 (11x8, 32 pgs, paper-c, 12.5¢, monthly)

1 Brother Jonathan character single panel cartoons 60.00 125.00 250.00

NOTE: *Begins continuing character sequential comic strip, "The Adventures of Jeremiah Oldpot" in "A Bird in the Hand Is Worth Two in The Bush"*

2-4 25.00 50.00 115.00
5 British X-Over 25.00 50.00 115.00

NOTE: *Single panel of John Bull & Brother Jonathan exchanging civilities (issues of Punch & Yankee Notions)*

6 end of Jeremiah Oldpot continued strip 25.00 50.00 115.00
v2#1 begin "Hoosier Bragg" sequential strip - six issue serial 25.00 50.00 115.00
v2#2 Feb 1853 two pg 12 panel sequential "Mr Vanity's Exploits, Arising Out Of A Valentine" 37.50 75.00 195.00
v2#3-v2#5 continues Hoosier Bragg 25.00 50.00 115.00
v2#6 Juen 1853 Lion Eats Hoosier Bragg, end of story 25.00 50.00 115.00

FR1.0 GD2.0 FN6.0

v3#1 begins referring to its cartoons as "Comic Art" 37.50 75.00 195.00
v4#1-V4#6 v5#1-v5#2 no sequential comic strips 20.00 40.00 100.00
v5#3 two sequential comic strips 37.50 75.00 195.00

NOTE: *Mr Take-A-Drop And The Maine Law (5) panels and The First Segar (7) panels (about smoking tobacco)*

v5#4 April 1856 begin Billy Vidkins 37.50 75.00 195.00

NOTE: *Begins reprinting "From Passages in the Life of Little Billy Vidkins, first issued as a stand alone proto-comic book in 1849 Illustrations of the Poets*

v5#5 The McBargem Guards (9) panel sequential; Vidkins 25.00 50.00 115.00
v5#6 v5 #9 no comics 20.00 40.00 100.00
v5#7 Billy Vidkins continues 25.00 50.00 115.00
v5#8 end of Vidkins By HL Stephens, Esq. 25.00 50.00 115.00
v5#10 (6) panel "How We Learn To Ride"; Timber is hero 25.00 50.00 115.00
v5#11 (7) panel "How Mr. Green Sparrowgrass Voted-A Warning For the Benefit of Quiet Citizens About To Excercize the Elective Franchise" plus Pt Two "How We Learn to Ride" 37.50 75.00 195.00
v5#12 (6) panel "How Mr Pipp Got Struck"; "The Eclipse" featuring Mr Phips; Pt 3 "How We Learn to Ride" 25.00 50.00 115.00
v6#1 (Jan 1857) (12) panel "A Tale of An Umbrella; (4) panel begins a serial "The Man Who Bought The Elephant; (8) panel How Our Young New Yorkers Celebrate New Years Day 25.00 50.00 115.00
v6#2 (Feb 1857) Pt 2 (4) panels The Man Who Bought the Elephant; (7) panel A Game of All Fours 25.00 50.00 115.00
v6#3 (Mar 1857) Pt 3 (4) panels The Man Who Bought the Elephant ending; (4) panel Ye Great Crinoline Monopoly 25.00 50.00 115.00
v6#4 no comic strips 25.00 50.00 115.00
v6#5 (May 1850) (3) panel A Short Trip to Mr Bumps, And How It Ended; (2) panel How mr Trembles Was Garrotted 25.00 50.00 115.00
v6#6 no comic strips 25.00 50.00 115.00
v6#7 (July 1857) (5) panel Alma Mater; (3) panel Three Tableaux In the Life of A Broadway Swell 25.00 50.00 115.00
v6 #8 9 no comic strips 25.00 50.00 115.00
v6#10 (Oct 1857) (3) panel Adv of Mr Near-Sight 25.00 50.00 115.00
v6#11 (Nov 1857) (11) panel Mrs Champignon's Dinner Party And the Way She Arranged Her Guests; (4) panel A Stroll in August 25.00 50.00 115.00
v6#12 (Dec 1857) (8) panel strip; (12) panel Young Fitz At A Blow Out in the Fifth Ave 25.00 50.00 115.00
v10#1 (Jan 1860) comic strip Bibbs at Central Park Skating Pond using word balloons 25.00 50.00 115.00

YE TRUE ACCOUNTE OF YE VISIT TO SPRINGFIELDE BY YE CONSTABEL HIS SPECIAL REPORTER
Frank Leslie: 1861 (5-1/8 x 5-1/4 or 93 inches when folded out, paper-c, B&W)

nn - Very Rare fold-out of 18 comic strip panels plus covers - - -

NOTE: *8 panels contain word balloons (Very Rare - only one copy known to exist.) First printed in Frank Leslie's Budget of Fun Jan 1 1861 issue. Abraham Lincoln Biography.*

YE VERACIOUS CHRONICLE OF GRUFF & POMPEY IN 7 TABLEAUX. (O,P)
Jackson's Best Chewing Tobacco & Donaldson Brothers: nd (c1870's) (5-1/8 tall x 3-3/8" wide folded, 27" wide unfolded, color cardboard)

nn - With all 8 panels attached (Scarce) 45.00 90.00 200.00
nn - Individual panels/cards 6.00 12.00 24.00

NOTE: *Black Americana interest. Consists of 8 attached cards, printed on one side, which unfold into a strip story of title card & 7 panels. Scrapbook hobbyists in the 19th Century tended to pull the panels apart and paste into their scrapbooks, making copies with all panels attached scarce.*

YOUNG AMERICA (continues as Yankee Doodle)
T.W. Strong, NYC: 1856

1-30 John McLennon 60.00 110.00 250.00

YOUNG AMERICA'S COMIC ALMANAC
T.W. Strong, NY: 1857 (7-1/2x5", 24 pgs)

nn 60.00 110.00 250.00

THE YOUNG MEN OF AMERICA (becomes Golden Weekly) (S)
Frank Tousey, NYC: 1887-88 (14x10-1/4", 16 pgs, B&W)

527 (10/13/87) Bellew strip "Story of A Black Eye" 25.00 50.00 110.00
530 (11/3/87) Thomas Worth (6) panel strip 32.00 64.00 125.00
531 (11/10/87) Thomas Worth(3) panel strip
537 (12/22/87) H.E. Patterson (3) panel strip
544 (2/9/88) Caran s'Ache (6) panel strip-r 37.50 75.00 110.00
555 (4/26/88) Thomas Worth (3) panel strip
556 (5/3/88) Thomas Worth (6) panel strip; Kit Carson-c 75.00 150.00 350.00
569 (8/21/88) Frank Bellew (2) panel strip
570 (8/9/88) Kemble (2) panel strip
571 (8/16/88) Kemble (2) panel strip; first Davy Crockett 75.00 150.00 350.00
Issues with just single panel cartoons 10.00 20.00 50.00

ZIM'S QUARTERLY (M)
(13-13/16x10-1/4", 60 pgs, color-c; most;y B&W, some interior color)

1 - Eugene Zimmerman 112.50 225.00 500.00

NOTE: *Approx. half sequential comic strips, other half single panel cartoons.*

Any addititions or corrections to this section are always welcome, very much encouraged and can be sent to **feedback@gemstonepub.com** to be processed for next year's Guide.

THE PLATINUM AGE

The American Comic Book: 1883-1938

A Concise History & Price Index Of The Field As Of 2017

NEWSPAPERS HARNESS COMICS POWER MYRIAD FORMATS COMPETE

by Robert Lee Beerbohm and Richard D. Olson, PhD ©2017

(This article was originally created by Robert L. Beerbohm and Richard D. Olson beginning in CBPG #27 1997 and is revised annually as new information comes to light.)

The story of the success of the modern comic strip as we know it today is tied closely to the companies who sponsored and bought licenses from the copyright holder for the purpose of advertising products. Platinum Age comic books have come back into their own after languishing mostly forgotten for a few decades. With this series of comics history research updates now marking its first decade, these historically important books are seem by many now as very collectible. Online sources such as eBay and bookfinder.com have demonstrate that many of these Platinum books are actually not scarce at all as previously thought, though they are in any type of higher-grade condition. Even so, most Platinum Age books are much rarer than so-called Golden Age comic books, yet despite this scarcity, *Mutt & Jeff, Bringing Up Father, The Katzenjammer Kids*, and many more were more popular than say Superman and Batman when they were introduced. Recent research has come up with some more amazing rediscoveries. There is much that can be learned and applied to today's comics market by a simple historical examination of the medium's evolution over more than 160 years.

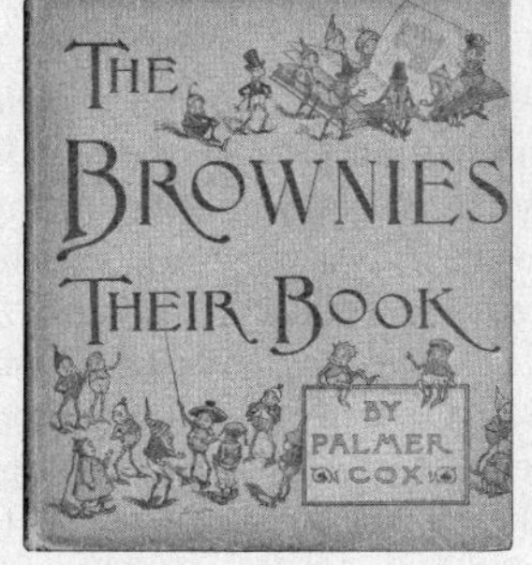

The Brownies' first book, 1887 by Palmer Cox, set a precedent for the Platinum Age, collecting and reprinting previously published material.

It should be noted that "ages" are applied to historical periods in the history of comics for convenience. In fact, ages typically overlap and there is no discrete beginning or ending for any given "age." This is the case with the Platinum Age, which clearly began with Palmer Cox's creation of *The Brownies* in 1883 even though it overlaps with the Victorian Age which ran through the end of the 19th Century. Cox introduced a qualitative change to the field, not an incremental quantitative change. Specifically, he produced art and verse for children in children's magazines and then merchandised those characters. He published work for children not only in books but in magazines and newspapers, and he merchandised his creations to an extent that had never been done previously.

Palmer Cox was born in 1840 near Granby, Quebec. He journeyed to Oakland, California in 1863, and began publishing cartoon, prose and poems in the local press and media outlets such as *The San Francisco Examiner* wherein by 1867 it has been reported he also began creating sequential comic strips, though none have yet surfaced.

His first book, *Squibs of California*, was published in 1874. He subsequently moved to New York in 1875 and almost immediately began working for the magazine *Wild Oats*, of which more is written about in the preceding Victorian Age history introduction as well as a sample of his sequential work. He drew dozens of sequential comic strips for *Wild Oats*, a humor magazine so scarce only one issue has been offered on eBay in the past six years.

Soon thereafter he became a major contributor to the Scribner publications, including *The St. Nicholas*, an illustrated magazine for young folk. His first cartoon for them was "The Wasp And The Bee," published in the March 1879 cover-

The Brownies in the Philippines by Palmer Cox, Oct 1904 - scarce original art from the book. President Roosevelt is pictured within these multitudes of Brownie madness, a Cox "signature trademark." Cox's stories are comic strip-oriented in nature of time sequence as he boldly took his Brownies around the world.

date issue. While it is now clear that Cox used elves and brownie-like characters in his art for several different magazines as early as 1877 in *Harper's Young People* magazine as well as using Brownies-type characters beginning in the Feb 1881 issue of *Wide Awake*, the first true appearance of the Brownies in their own story using that title, a combination of art and verse was February, 1883, in *St. Nicholas*. Palmer Cox's *The Brownies* were the first North American comics-type characters to be internationally merchandised. Even though Cox was continuously doing sequential comic strips in magazines like *Wild Oats*, he left the popular medium of comics when he hit paydirt with *The Brownies*. For over a quarter of a century, Cox deftly combined the popular advertising motifs of animals and fairies into a wonderful, whimsical world of society at its best and worst.

The Brownies' first book was issued in 1887, titled *The Brownies: Their Book*; many more followed. Cox also added a run of his hugely popular characters in *Ladies Home Journal* from October 1891 through February 1895, as well as a special for December 1910. With the 1892-93 World's Fair, the merchandising exploded with a host of products, including pianos, paper dolls and other figurines, chairs, stoves, puzzles, cough drops, coffee, soap, boots, candy, and many more. *Brownies* material was being produced in Europe as well as the United States of America.

Cox tried out *The Brownies* as a newspaper strip in the *San Francisco Examiner* during 1898, where he had begun his newspaper career over 30 years before, and then in the *New York World* in 1900. It was then syndicated from 1903 through 1907. He seems to have retired from regularly drawing *The Brownies* with the January 1914 issue of *St. Nicholas* when he was 74. A wealthy man, he lived to the ripe old age of 84, spending his last decade in his home he affectionately called Brownie Castle, back in Granby, Quebec.

By the mid-1890s, while keeping careful track of steadily rising circulations of magazines with graphic humor such as *Harper's, Puck, St. Nicholas, Judge, Life* and *Truth*, New York based newspaper publishers began to recognize that illustrated humor would sell extra papers. This is what *The Yellow Kid* taught these publishers. Thus was born the Sunday "comic supplement." Most of the super star favorites were under contract with these magazines. However, there was an artist working for *Truth* who wasn't. Roy L McCardell, then a staffer at *Puck*, informed Morrill Goddard, Sunday Editor of *The New York World*, that he knew someone who could fit what was needed at the then-largest newspaper in America.

Richard F. Outcault (1863-1928) first introduced his street children strip in *Truth* #372, June 2, 1894, somewhat inspired by Michael Angelo Woolf's slum kids single panel cartoons in **Life** which had begun in the mid 1880s. The interested collector should seek out a copy of Woolf's *Sketches of Lowly Life In A Great City* (1899) listed in the *Guide* for comparison study. Edward Harrigan's play "O'Reilly and the Four Hundred," which had a song beginning with the words "Down in Hogan's Alley..." also likely provided direct inspiration.

It's also probable that Outcault's *Hogan's Alley* cast, including the *Yellow Kid*, was inspired by Charles W. Saalburg's *The Ting Lings*, which began in the *Chicago Inter Ocean Jr* supplement post-dated May 1, 1894 in the April 29, 1894 edition of Chicago Inter Ocean. That first episode is titled: "The Brownies Welcome The Ting-Lings."

There is also a definite similarity in Mickey Dugan's appearance and clothing style to Saalburg's creation which we will now examine in more detail thanks to welcome, on-going research by long time comics historian Allan Holtz supplemented by living comics history legend Bill Blackbeard .

Charles Saalzburg was an artist who was also the genius behind color printing in newspapers. He seems to have pioneered the concept from whom all others learned their craft.

On June 23, 1892 the *Chicago Inter Ocean* introduced a section with mostly editorial cartoons titled the *Illustrated Supplement*, commemorating the Democratic National Convention held in that city. Early regulars included Thomas Nast and Art Young. Starting June 26, the *Inter Ocean* began steadily issuing this weekly four page supplement, typically featuring full page editorial cartoons on its front and back covers. In May 1893 the supplement began coming out twice a week, and even greater frequency to daily during the *World Columbian Exposition* held in Chicago later that same year as it was used as a wrapper to attract sales from fair goers. Art Young did some of the color cover art and comic strips for the early Fair supplements, printing them right at the Fair to goggle-eyed fair tourists. Thomas Nast did some art as well during a visit he made to the Fair.

By September 10, 1893 the *Inter Ocean* introduced color, a multi-panel editorial comic strip by Charles Saalburg. The supplement used yellow ink, a further nail in the coffin of various Yellow Kid myths which had clouded serious comics scholarship in earlier decades before being proven wrong.

On October 1, Tom E. Powers introduced their first sequential non-political comic strip in color, a humorous pantomime.

As the Exposition ended in November, the contents were soon aimed more at children, enhanced with color added to the center as well by December 24, 1893, then changing its title to *Inter Ocean Jr* in January 1894. This was accomplished easily by folding the single four page sheet into eight pages.

In the January 1894 Saalburg began using Brownies-inspired characters in his color comic strips. The present theory is the *Ting-Ling* characters took over solo five months later in response to a presumed cease and desist letter which inevitably must have been issued from Palmer Cox to the *Inter Ocean.*

However, on July 8 1894, the *Inter Ocean Jr* stopped color and full page comics-type work in this supplement, devolving back to simple small spot art works. By mid-1894, color comics printing genius Saalburg had been lured to Pulitzer's New York World, becoming Art Director in charge of coloring for the new color printing press at the *New York World.* The color supplement was soon to be unleashed in the largest city in America.

By the November 18, 1894 issue of the *World*, Outcault was working for Goddard and Saalburg. Outcault produced a successful Sunday newspaper sequential comic strip in color with "The Origin of a New Species" on the back page in the World's first colored Sunday supplement. Long time pro Walt McDougall, a famous cartoonist reputed to have turned the 1884 Presidential race with a single cartoon that ran in the *World*, handled the cartoon art on the front page. Earlier, *The World* began running full page color single panels on May 21, 1893. McDougall did various other page panels during 1893, but it was Jan. 28, 1894 when the first sequence of comic pictures in a New York World newspaper appeared in panels in the same format as our comic strips today. It was a full page cut up into nine panels. This historic sequence was drawn entirely in pantomime, with no words, by Mark Fenderson.

The second page to appear in panels was an eight panel strip from February 4, 1894, also lacking words except for the title. This page was a collaboration between Walt McDougall and Mark Fenderson titled "The Unfortunate Fate of a Well-Intentioned Dog." From then on, many full page color strips by McDougall and Fenderson appeared; they were the first cartoonists to draw for the Sunday newspaper comic section. It was Outcault, however, who soon became the most famous cartoonist featured. After first appearing in black and white in Pulitzer's *The New York World* on February 17, 1895 and again on March 10, 1895, *The Yellow Kid* was introduced to the public in color on May 5, 1895.

Some have erroneously reported in scholarly journals that perhaps it was Frank Ladendorf's "Uncle Reuben," first introduced May 26, 1895, which became the first regularly recurring comics character in newspapers. This is wrong, as even Outcault's "Yellow Kid" began in Pulitzer's paper a good three months before *Uncle Reuben*. Until firm evidence to the contrary comes to light, that honor will forever be enshrined with Jimmy Swinnerton's *Little Bears* cartoon characters, found all over inside Hearst's *San Francisco Examiner* beginning October 14, 1893 with the first one called "Baby Monarch. Though never actually a comic strip, they nonetheless were the earliest presently-known recurring comics-type characters in American newspapers. In June 1895, a semi-regular "Little Bears" feature began. On January 26, 1896, children were introduced, the title eventually changed to "Little Bears and Tykes," forever confusing some scholars decades later. There never was a strip titled *Little Bears and Tigers,* as the *Tigers* were strictly for New York consumption when Hearst ordered Swinnerton to move to the Big Apple to compete better in the brewing comic strip wars.

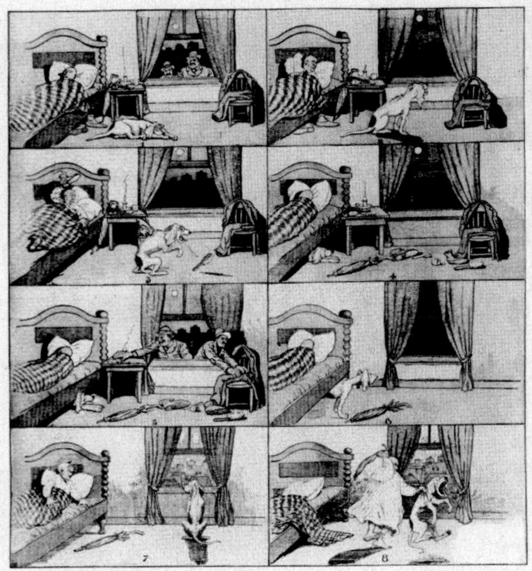

Walt McDougall & Mark Fenderson, the 2nd sequential comic strip in New York World, February 4, 1894, predates Yellow Kid in The World by over a year. Mark Fenderson drew the first NY World newspaper comic strip.

The Yellow Kid's importance is widely recognized today as the first newspaper comic strip to demonstrate without a doubt that the general public was ready for full color comics. *The Yellow Kid* was the first in the USA to show that comics could increase newspaper sales, and that comic characters could be merchandised. *The Yellow Kid* was the headlining spark of what was soon dubbed by Hearst as "eight pages of polychromatic effulgence that makes the rainbow look like a lead pipe."

Ongoing research suggests that Palmer Cox's fabulous success with *The Brownies* was a direct inspiration for Richard Outcault's future merchandising work. The ultimate proof lies in the fourth Yellow Kid cartoon, which appeared in the February 9, 1895 issue of *Truth*. It was reprinted in the *New York World* eight days later on February 17, 1895, becoming the first Yellow Kid cartoon in the newspapers. The caption read "FOURTH WARD BROWNIES. MICKEY, THE ARTIST (adding a finishing touch) Dere, Chimmy! If Palmer Cox wuz t' see yer, he'd git yer copyrighted in a minute." The Yellow Kid was widely licensed in the greater New York area for all kinds of products, including gum and cigarette cards, toys, pinbacks, cookies, postcards, tobacco products, and appliances. There was also a short-lived humor magazine from Street & Smith named *The Yellow Kid*, featuring exquisite Outcault covers, plus a 196-page comic book from Dillingham & Co. known as *The Yellow Kid in McFadden's Flats,* dated to early 1897. Check out the covers in "The Platinum Age" three-page comic strip elsewhere in this Guide. In addition, there were several Yellow Kid plays produced, spawning other collectibles like show posters, programs and illustrated sheet music. (For those interested in more information regarding the Yellow Kid, it is available on the Internet at www.neponset.com/yellowkid.)

Mickey Dugan burned brightly for a few years as Outcault secured a copyright on the character with the United States Government by September 1896. By the time he completed the necessary paperwork, however, hundreds of business people nationwide had pirated the image of The Yellow Kid and plastered it all over every product imaginable; mothers were even dressing their newborns to look like Dugan. Outcault, however, kept regularly utilizing images of *The Yellow Kid* in his comics style advertising work confirmed as late as 1915. Outcault soon found himself in a maelstrom not of his choosing, which probably pushed him to eventually drop the character. Outcault's creation went back and forth between newspaper giants Pulitzer and Hearst until Bennett's New York Herald mercifully snatched the cartoonist away in 1900 to do what amounted to a few relatively short-run strips. Later, he did one particular strip for a year–a satire of rural Black America titled *Pore Li'l Mose His Letters to his Mammy*, and then his newer creation, *Buster Brown*, debuted May 4, 1902. *Mose* had a very rare comic book collection published in 1902 by Cupples & Leon, now highly sought after by today's savvy collectors. Outcault continued drawing him in the background of occasional *Buster Brown* strips for many years to come.

William Randolph Hearst loved the comic strip medium ever since he was a little boy growing up on *Max & Moritz* by Wilhelm Busch in American collected book editions translated from the original German (these collections were first published in book form in 1871, serving as the influence for *The Katzenjammer Kids*). One of the ways Hearst responded to losing Outcault in 1900 was by purchasing the highly successful 23-year-old humor magazine *Puck* from the heirs of founder Joseph Keppler. With *Puck* and its exclusive cartoonist contracts, he commanded, among others, the very popular F. M. Howarth and Frederick Burr Opper's undivided attention. Opper first burst upon the comics scene in America back in 1880. Within a year Hearst had expanded this *National Lampoon* of its day into the colored Sunday comics section, *Puck-The Comic Weekly*. At first featuring Rudolph Dirk's *The Katzenjammer Kids* (1897), *Happy Hooligan* and other fine strips by the wildly popular Opper and a few others including Rudolph's brother Gus Dirks, the Hearst comic section steadily added more strips. For decades to come, there wasn't anything else that could compete with *Puck*. Hearst hired the best of the best and transformed *Puck* into the most popular comics section anywhere.

Outcault, meanwhile, followed in Palmer Cox's footprints a decade later by using

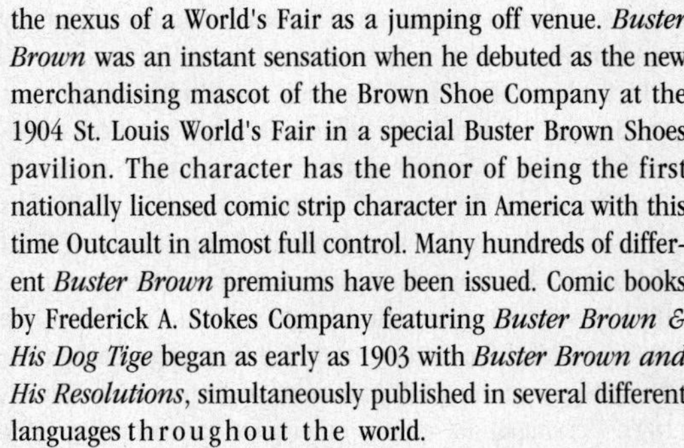

the nexus of a World's Fair as a jumping off venue. *Buster Brown* was an instant sensation when he debuted as the new merchandising mascot of the Brown Shoe Company at the 1904 St. Louis World's Fair in a special Buster Brown Shoes pavilion. The character has the honor of being the first nationally licensed comic strip character in America with this time Outcault in almost full control. Many hundreds of different *Buster Brown* premiums have been issued. Comic books by Frederick A. Stokes Company featuring *Buster Brown & His Dog Tige* began as early as 1903 with *Buster Brown and His Resolutions*, simultaneously published in several different languages throughout the world.

After a few years, Buster and Outcault returned to Hearst in late 1905, joining what soon became the flagship of the comics world. Buster's popularity quickly spread all over the United States and then the world as he single-handedly spawned the first great comic strip licensing dynasty. For years, there were little people traveling from town to town performing as *Buster Brown* and selling shoes while accompanied by small dogs named Tige. Many other highly competitive licensed strips would soon follow. We suggest getting *Hake's Price Guide to Character Toys* for info on several hundred *Buster Brown* competitors, as well as several pages of the more fascinating *Buster Brown* material.

Soon there were many comic strip syndicates not only offering hundreds of various comic strips but also offering to license the characters for any company interested in paying the fee. The history of the comic strip with wide popularity since *The Yellow Kid* has been intertwined with giveaway premiums and character-based, store-bought merchandise of all kinds. Since its infancy as a profitable art form unto itself with *The Yellow Kid*, the comic strip world has profited from selling all sorts of "stuff" to the public featuring their favorite character or strip as its motif. American business gladly responded to the desire for comic character memorabilia with

Left: The Yellow Kid #1, March 20, 1897, Street & Smith as Howard Ainslee, NY.
Right: A rare full color "The Yellow Kid in McFadden's Flats" advertising sign promoting the first comic book featuring the Yellow Kid. The sign is from 1896 and measures 12x18".

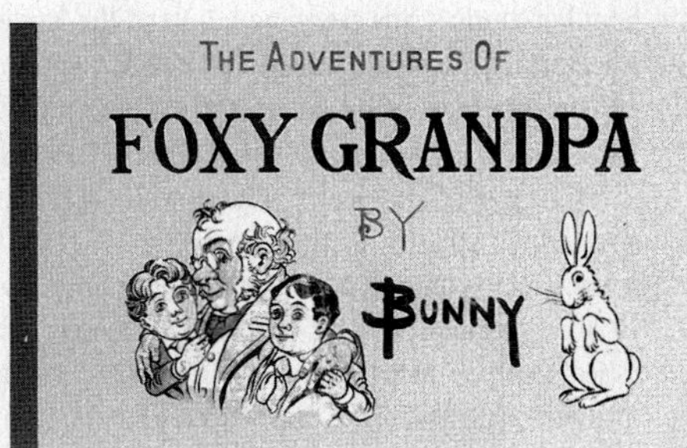

The Adventures of Foxy Grandpa, late 1900, cover for the rare earliest known first edition of Carl "Bunny" Schultze's famous creation. He was one of the newspaper comics' first superstars.

Pore Li'l Mose by Richard Outcault, 1901. Bridges in between Yellow Kid and Buster Brown. Becoming scarce because many copies have been cut up.

thousands of fun items to enjoy and collect. Most of the early comics were not aimed specifically at kids, though children understandably enjoyed them as well.

Comic books have generally been associated with almost all of the licensed merchandise in this century. In the Platinum Age section beginning right after this essay, you will find a great many comic books in varied formats and sizes published before the advent of the first successful monthly newsstand comic magazine, *Famous Funnies*. What drove each of these evolutionary format changes was the need by their producers to make money so more books could be issued.

A very significant format was F. M. Howarth's *Funny Folks*, published in 1899 by E. P. Dutton and drawn from color as well as black and white pages of *Puck*. This rather large hardcover volume measured 16 1/2" wide by 12" tall. It contains numerous sequential comic strip pages as well as single gag illustrations. Howarth's art was a joy to behold and deserves wider recognition.

By Oct. 1900, Hearst had already caused Opper's *Folks In Funnyville* to be collected by publisher R. H. Russell, NY in a 12x9 hard cover format from his *New York Journal American Humorist* section. At the end of 1900, Carl Shultze had a first edition of *Vaudevilles and Other Things* published by Isaac H. Blanchard Co., NY. It measures 10 1/2" wide by 13" tall with 22 pages including covers. Each interior page is a 2 to 7 panel comic strip with lots of color.

There were also recently unearthed format variation second and third printings of *Vaudevilles* with the inscription "From the Originator of the 'Foxy Grandpa' Series" at the bottom of its front cover of the third printing. This note is lacking on the earlier first two editions, and it also switches format size to 11" tall by 13" wide. Discovered last year was a heretofore undocumented *The Adventures of Foxy Grandpa* - also issued in 1900 - new to the Platinum listings. The second number dated 1901 drops the words "The Adventures of..." from the title.

E. W. Kemble's *The Blackberries* had a color collection by 1901, also published by R. H. Russell, NY, as well as a few other comic-related volumes by Kemble still to be unearthed and properly identified. An earlier one was titled *Coontown's 400* (1899) newly listed this year. While the title is definitely not "PC" by today's standards, Kemble's drawings are excellent slices of African-American life in the USA with some humor injected. Kemble did a good job documenting aspects of life.

Confirmed is the exact format of Hearst's 1902 *The Katzenjammer Kids and Happy Hooligan And His Brother Gloomy Gus*. They both measure 15 5/16" wide by 10" tall and contain 88 pages including covers. Confirmed also is the fact that there are two separate editions with different covers for the pictured 1902 first edition and a 1903 Frederick Stokes edition of *Katzenjammer Kids* and *Happy Hooligan* with differing contents. They both are two different books entirely, and what confuses many collectors is that they have identical indicia title pages, but so does an entirely different *KK* from 1905.

Settling on a popular size of 17" wide by 11" tall, comic books were soon available that featured Charles "Bunny" Schultze's *Foxy Grandpa*, Rudolph Dirk's *The Katzenjammer Kids*, Winsor McCay's *Little Sammy Sneeze, Rarebit Fiend* and *Little Nemo*, and Fred Opper's *Happy Hooligan* and *Maud*, in addition to dozens of *Buster Brown* comic books. For well over a decade, these large-size, full-color volumes were the norm, retailing for 60¢. These collections offered full-size Sunday comics with the back side blank per page.

Though not the first daily newspaper strip, the very rare *Brainy Bowers and Drowsy Dugan* by R. W. Taylor is now crowned the first collection of strip reprints from a daily newspaper published in America. There are now four different collections of Brainy Bower known to exist.

The Outbursts of Everett True by A. D. Condo and J. W. Raper was first published by Saalfield in 1907 in an 88-page hardcover collection. It qualifies as the second daily comic strip collection as it predates the first *Mutt & Jeff* collection from Ball by three years. Condo & Raper's creation began its regular run several times a week in 1905 daily newspapers and lasted until 1927, when Condo became too sick to continue. This same *Everett True* collection was later truncated a bit by Saalfield in 1921 to 56 strips in just 32 pages measuring the standard 10"x10" Cupples & Leon size.

By 1908 Stokes had a large backlist of full color comic books for sale at 60¢ each. Some of these titles date back to 1903 and were reprinted over and over as demand warranted. Note the number of titles in the advertisement pulled from the back of *The Three Fun Makers* shown below.

With the ever-increasing popularity of Bud Fisher's new daily strip sensation, *Mutt & Jeff,* a new format was created for reprinting daily strips in black and white, a hardcover book about 15" wide by 5" tall, published by Ball starting in 1910 for five volumes. In 1912, Ball also branched out with at least the now-obscure *Doings of the Van Loons* by Fred I. Leipziger, a rare comic book in the same format as the *Mutt & Jeffs.*

Cartoons Magazine also began in 1912 and ran through 1921 before undergoing a radical format change. It is notable as a wonderful source for information on early comics and their creators. See also the Platinum index.

The next significant evolutionary change occurred in 1919, when Cupples & Leon began issuing their black and white daily strip reprint books in a new aforementioned format, about 10" wide by 10" tall, with four panels reprinted per page in a two by two matrix. These books were 52 pages for 25¢. The first ones featured *Bringing Up Father* and *Mutt & Jeff;* there were about 100 others.

By 1921, the last of the oblong (11"x15") color comic books were issued, with Cupples & Leon's *Jimmie Dugan* and *The Reg'lar Fellers* by Gene Byrne, and EmBee's *The Trouble Of Bringing Up Father* by self publisher George McManus. Of special historical interest, Embee issued the first 10¢ monthly comic book, *Comic Monthly,* with the first issue dated January 1922. A dozen 8-1/2"x9" issues were published, each featuring solo adventures of popular King Features strips. The monthly 10¢ comic book concept had finally arrived, though it would be more than a decade before it became truly successful.

Skippy by Percy Crosby debuted in the long-running humor magazine *Life* in the March 22, 1923 issue. By 1924 the first hard cover collection, *Life Presents Skippy*, was published. The newspaper comic strip debuted June 23, 1925 with the McClure syndicate. Hearst soon picked up a Sunday page a year later in mid-1926, then added a daily strip in 1929. By the 1930s it was red hot - think *Calvin & Hobbes or Peanuts* in popularity. In its day, it was one of the most popular comic strips ever created. Read the Modern era essay for more on *Skippy's* immense popularity.

In 1926, Cupples & Leon added a new 7" wide by 9" tall format with *Little Orphan Annie, Smitty,* and others. These were issued in both softcover and hardcover editions with dust jackets, and became extremely popular at 60¢ per copy.

Dell began publishing all original material in *The Funnies* in late 1929 in a larger tabloid format. At least three dozen issues were published before Delacorte threw in the towel. Even the extremely popular *Big Little Book*, introduced in 1932, can be viewed as a smaller version of the existing formats. The competition amongst publishers now included Dell, McKay, Sonnet, Saalfield and Whitman. The 1930s saw a definite shift in merchandising comic strip material from adults to children. This was the decade when Kellogg's placed *Buck Rogers* on the map, when Ovaltine issued tons of *Little Orphan Annie* material. Merchandising from such pioneers as Sam Gold and Kay Kamen spearheaded this next transformation of the comics biz beginning in the early 1930s.

Upwards of a thousand of these *Funnies On Parade* precursors, in all formats, were published through 1935 and were very popular. Towards the end of this era of once-popular comic book formats, beautiful collections of *Popeye, Mickey Mouse, Dick Tracy*, and many others were published which today command ever higher prices on the open market as they are rediscovered by the advanced collector who appreciates and enjoys truly great classic comics.

END NOTE: Each year we strive to add to the many 1930s variant formats. This Platinum Age section has grown as a result of advanced collectors who continue to report in with new finds. We encourage interested collectors and scholars to help with this section of the book, as each new data entry is very important for recovering our history. For corrections and additions to next year's next edition of *The Overstreet Guide* of some treasures you may have uncovered, please feel free to contact Gemstone Publishing at feedback@gemstonepub.com.

For further information on this era of American comic books, check out the previous evolving comics history essays in Guides #27,29-#40. Happy Hunting!

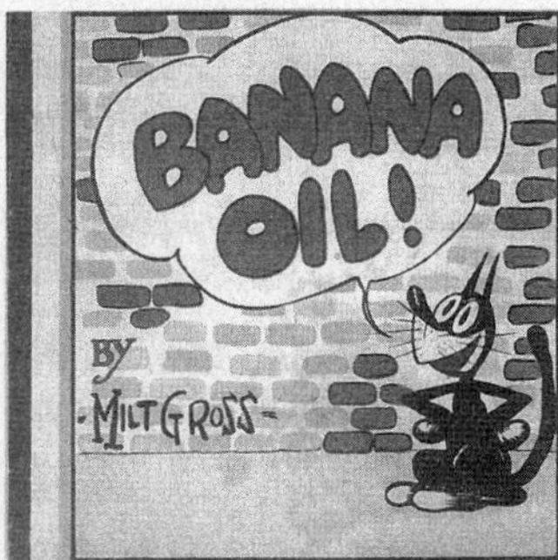

Banana Oil, a 1924 example of Cupples & Leon's then-revolutionary format from M.S. Publishers

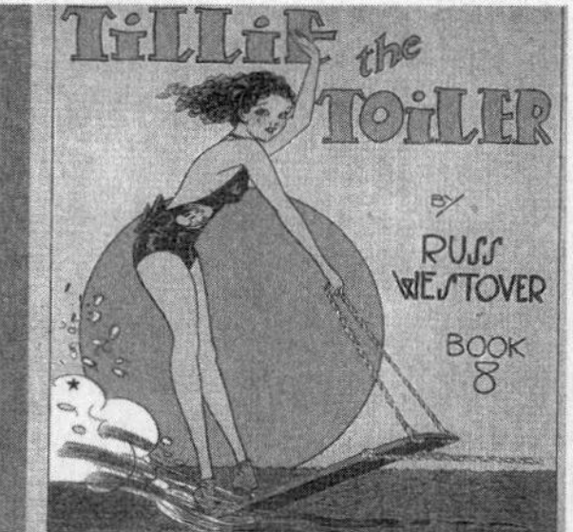

Tillie the Toiler #8 1933 from Cupples & Leon, another scarce number at the end of this once popular format.

David McKay published the last of the 10x10 comic books in 1935 as Famous Funnies grew in popularity.

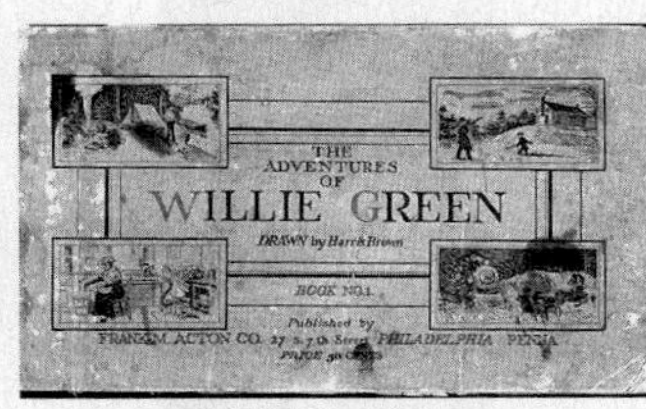

The Adventures of Willie Green
© Frank M. Acton

Alphonse and Gaston by Opper
1902 © Hearst's NY American & Journal

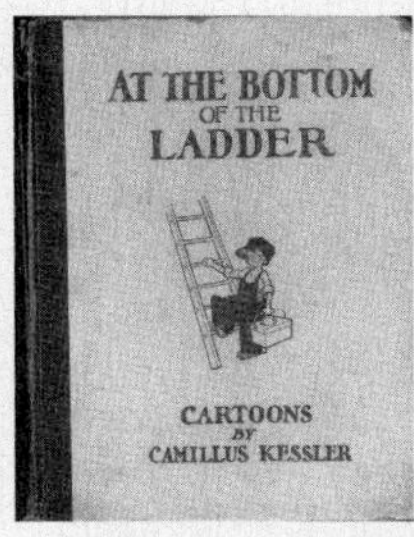

At The Bottom Of The Ladder
1926 © J.P. Lippincott Company

GD2.0 FN6.0 VF8.0 GD2.0 FN6.0 VF8.0

COLLECTOR'S NOTE: The books listed in this section were published many decades before organized comics fandom began archiving and helping to preserve these fragile popular culture artifacts. Consequently, copies of most all of these comics do not often surface in Fine+ or better shape. eBay has proven after more than a decade that many items once considered rare actually are not, though they almost always are in higher grades. For items marked scarce, we are trying to ascertain how many copies might still be in existence. Your input is always welcome.

Most Platinum Age comic books are in the Fair to VG range. If you want to collect these only in high grade, your collection will be extremely small. The prices given for Good, Fine and Very Fine categories are for strictly graded editions. If you need help grading your item, we refer you to the grading section in the front of this price guide or contact the authors of the Platinum essay. Most measurements are in inches. A few measurements are in centimeters. The first dimension given is Height and the second is Width.

For ease of ascertaining the contents of each item of this listing, there is a code letter or two following most titles we have been adding in over the years to aid you. A helpful list of categories pertaining to these codes can be found at the beginning of the Victorian Age pricing sections. This section created, revised, and expanded by Robert Beerbohm and Richard Olson with able assistance from Ray Agricola, Jon Berk, Bill Blackbeard, Roy Bonario, Ray Bottorff Jr., Chris Brown, Alfredo Castelli, Darrell Coons, Sol Davidson, Leonardo De Sá, Scott Deschaine, Mitchell Duval, Joe Evans, Tom Gordon III, Bruce Hamilton, Andy Konkykru, Don Kurtz, Gabriel Laderman, Bruce Mason, Donald Puff, Robert Quesinberry, Steve Rowe, Randy Scott, John Snyder, Art Spiegelman, Steve Thompson, Joan Crosby Tibbets, Richard Samuel West, Doug Wheeler, Richard Wright and Craig Yoe.

ADVENTURES OF EVA, PORA AND TED (M)
Evaporated Milk Association: 1932 (5x15", 16 pgs, B&W)

nn - By Steve 20.00 40.00 105.00
NOTE: *Appears to have had green, blue or white paper cover versions.*

ADVENTURES OF HAWKSHAW (N) (See Hawkshaw The Detective)
The Saalfield Publishing Co.: 1917 (9-3/4x13-1/2", 48 pgs., color & two-tone)

nn - By Gus Mager (only 24 pgs. of strips, reverse of each pg. is blank)
50.00 175.00 400.00
nn - 1927 Reprints 1917 issue 30.00 150.00 260.00
NOTE: *Started Feb 23, 1913-Sept 4, 1922, then begins again Dec 13, 1931-Feb 11, 1952.*

ADVENTURES OF SLIM AND SPUD, THE (M)
Prairie Farmer Publ. Co.: 1924 (3-3/4x 9-3/4", 104 pgs., B&W strip reprints)

nn 25.00 90.00 180.00
NOTE: *Illustrated mailing envelope exists postmarked out of Chicago, add 50%.*

ADVENTURES OF WILLIE WINTERS, THE (O,P)
Kelloggs Toasted Corn Flake Co.: 1912 (6-7/8x9-1/2", 20 pgs, full color)

nn - By Byron Williams & Dearborn Melvill 54.00 189.00 350.00

ADVENTURES OF WILLIE GREEN, THE (N) (see The Willie Green Comics)
Frank M. Acton Co.: 1915 (50¢, 52 pgs, 8-1/2X16", B&W, soft-c)

Book 1 - By Harris Brown; strip-r 54.00 189.00 350.00

A. E. F. IN CARTOONS BY WALLY, THE (N)
Don Sowers & Co.: 1933 (12x10-1/8", 88 pgs, hardcover B&W)

nn - By Wally Wallgren (WW One Stars & Stripes-r) 60.00 125.00 250.00

AFTER THE TOWN GOES DRY (I)
The Howell Publishing Co, Chicago: 1919 (48 pgs, 6-1/2x4", hardbound two color-c)

nn - By Henry C. Taylor; illus by Frank King 25.00 75.00 150.00

AIN'T IT A GRAND & GLORIOUS FEELING? (N) (Also see Mr. & Mrs.)
Whitman Publishing Co.: 1922 (9x9-3/4", 52 pgs., stiff cardboard-c)

nn - 1921 daily strip-r; B&W, color-c; Briggs-a 36.00 143.00 250.00
nn -(9x9-1/2", 28pgs., stiff cardboard-c)-Sunday strip-r in color (inside front-c says "More of the Married Life of Mr. & Mrs".) 36.00 143.00 250.00
NOTE: *Strip started in 1917; This is the 2nd Whitman comic book, after Brigg's MR. & MRS.*

ALL THE FUNNY FOLKS (I)
World Press Today, Inc.: 1926 (11-1/2x8-1/2", 112 pgs., color, hard-c)

nn-Barney Google, Spark Plug, Jiggs & Maggie, Tillie The Toiler, Happy Hooligan, Hans & Fritz, Toots & Casper, etc. 100.00 400.00 700.00
With Dust Jacket By Louis Biedermann 225.00 850.00 1500.00
NOTE: *Booklength race horse story masterfully enveloping all major King Features characters.*

ALPHONSE AND GASTON AND THEIR FRIEND LEON (N)
Hearst's New York American & Journal: 1902,1903 (10x15-1/4", Sunday strip reprints in color)

nn - (1902) - By Frederick Opper (scarce) 600.00 2000.00 -
nn - (1903) - By Frederick Opper (scarce) (72 pages) 600.00 2000.00 -
NOTE: *Strip ran Sept 22, 1901 to at least July 17, 1904.*

ALWAYS BELITTLIN' (see Skippy; That Rookie From the 13th Squad; Between Shots)
Henry Holt & Co.: 1927 (6x8", hard-c with DJ,

nn -By Percy Crosby (text with cartoons) 43.00 172.00 320.00

ALWAYS BELITTLIN' (I) (see Skippy; That Rookie From the 13th Squad, Between Shots)
Percy Crosby, Publisher: 1933 (14 1/4 x 11", 72 pgs, hard-c, B&W)

nn - By Percy Crosby 43.00 172.00 320.00
NOTE: *Self-published; primarily political cartoons with text pages denouncing prohibition's gang warfare effects and cuts in the national defense budget as Crosby saw war looming in Europe and with Japan.*

AMERICAN-JOURNAL-EXAMINER JOKE BOOK SPECIAL SUPPLEMENT (O)
New York American: 1911-12 (12 x 9 3/4", 16 pgs) (known issues) (Very Rare)

1 Tom Powers Joke Book(12/10/11) 80.00 320.00 -
2 Mutt & Jeff Joke Book (Bud Fisher 12/17/11) 100.00 365.00 -
3 TAD's Joke Book (Thomas Dorgan 12/24/11) 80.00 320.00 -
4 F. Opper's Joke Book (Frederick Burr Opper 12/31/11) (contains Happy Hooligan) 100.00 365.00 -
5 not known to exist
6 Swinnerton's Joke Book (Jimmy Swinnerton 01/14/12) (contains Mr. Jack) 100.00 375.00 -
7 The Monkey's Joke Book (Gus Mager 01/21/12) (contains Sherlocko the Monk) 100.00 365.00 -
8 Joys And Glooms Joke Book (T. E. Powers 01/28/12) 80.00 320.00 -
9 The Dingbat Family's Joke Book (George Herriman 02/04/12) (contains early Krazy Kat & Ignatz) 200.00 750.00 -
10 Valentine Joke Book, A (Opper, Howarth, Mager, T. E. Powers 02/11/12) 80.00 320.00 -
11 Little Hatchet Joke Book (T. E. Powers 02/18/12) 80.00 320.00 -
12 Jungle Joke Book (Dirks, McCay 02/25/12) 100.00 410.00 -
13 The Hayseeds Joke Book (03/03/12) 80.00 320.00 -
14 Married Life Joke Book (T.E. Powers 03/10/12) 80.00 320.00 -
NOTE: *These were insert newspaper supplements similar to Eisner's later Spirit sections. A Valentine Joke Book recently surfaced from Hearst's Boston Sunday American proving that other cities besides New York City had these special supplements. Each issue also contains work by other cartoonists besides the cover featured creator and those already listed above such as Sidney Smith, Winsor McCay, Hy Mayer, Grace Weiderseim (later Drayton), others.*

AMERICA'S BLACK & WHITE BOOK 100 Pictured Reasons Why We Are At War (N,S)
Cupples & Leon: 1917 (10 3/4 x 8", 216 pgs)

nn - W. A. Rogers (New York Herald-r) 35.00 118.00 210.00

AMONG THE FOLKS IN HISTORY
Rand McNally Print Guild: 1935 (192 pgs, 8-1/2x9-1/2", hard-c, B&W)

nn - By Gaar Williams 21.00 84.00 160.00

AMONG THE FOLKS IN HISTORY
The Book and Print Guild: 1935 (200 pgs, 8-1/2x9-1/2:,

nn - By Gaar Williams 21.00 84.00 160.00
NOTE: *Both the above are evidently different editions and contain largely full-page, single panel cartoons similar to Briggs' work of that sort. 8 or 10 pages are broken into panels, usually with a "this is how it was in the old days, this is how it is today theme."*

ANGELIC ANGELINA (N)
Cupples & Leon Company: 1909 (11-1/2x17", 56 pgs., 2 colors)

nn - By Munson Paddock 67.00 233.00 410.00
NOTE: *Strip ran March 22, 1908-Feb 7, 1909.*

ANDY GUMP, HIS LIFE STORY (I)
The Reilly & Lee Co, Chicago: 1924 (192 pgs, hardbound)

nn - By Sidney Smith (over 100 illustrations) 30.00 100.00 225.00

ANIMAL CIRCUS, THE (from Puggery Wee)
Rand McNally + Company: 1908 (48 pgs, 11x8-1/2", color-c, 3-color insides)

nn - By unknown 25.00 80.00 150.00
NOTE: *Illustrated verse, many pages with multiple illustrations.*

ANIMAL SERIALS
T. Y. Crowell: 1906 (9x6-7/8", 214 pgs, hard-c, B&W)

nn - By E Warde Blaisdell 20.00 80.00 160.00
NOTE: *Multi-page comic strip stories. Reprints of Sunday strip "Bunny Bright He's All-Right".*

A NOBODY'S SCRAP BOOK
Frederik A. Stokes Co., New York: 1900 (11" x 8-5/8", hard-c, color)

nn- (Scarce) 67.00 233.00 450.00
NOTE: *Designed in England, printed in Holland, on English paper -- which likely explains the mispelling of Frederick Stokes' name. Highly fragile paper. Strips and cartoons, all by the same unidentified artist, "A Nobody", almost certainly reprinted from somewhere, as they are very professional.*

AT THE BOTTOM OF THE LADDER (M)
J.P. Lippincott Company: 1926 (11x8-1/4", 296 pgs, hardcover, B&W)

nn - By Camillus Kessler 45.00 157.50 300.00
NOTE: *Hilarious single panel cartoons showing first jobs of then important "captains of industry."*

AUTO FUN, PICTURES AND COMMENTS FROM "LIFE"
Thomas Y. Crowell & Co.: 1905 (152 pgs, 9x7", hard-c, B&W)

nn -By various 45.00 157.00 375.00
NOTE: *The cover just has "Auto Fun" but the title page also has the subheading listed here. This is similar to other reprint books of Life cartoons printed in the guide. Largely single panel cartoons but also several sequential. One or more cartoons by Kemble, Levering, Dirks, Flagg, Sullivant. Sequential cartoons by Kemble, Levering, Sullivant, and the highpoint, a 2 pg 6 panel piece by Winsor McCay.*

BANANA OIL (N) (see also HE DONE HER WRONG)

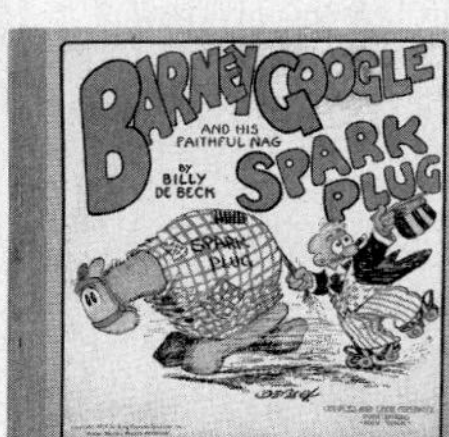

Barney Google and Spark Plug #1
© C&L

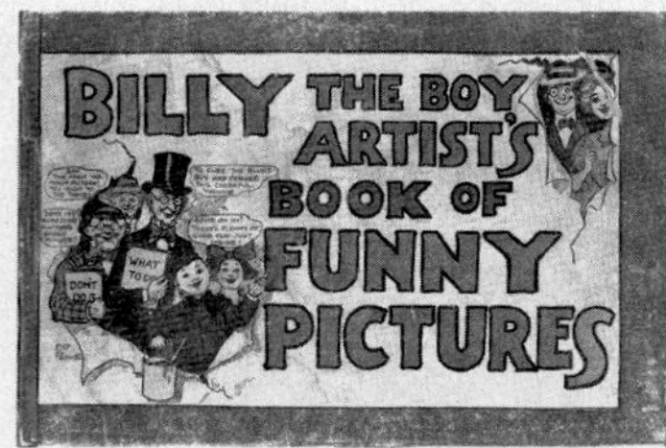

Bill the Boy Artist's Book by Ed Payne
1910 © C.M. Clark Publishing Co

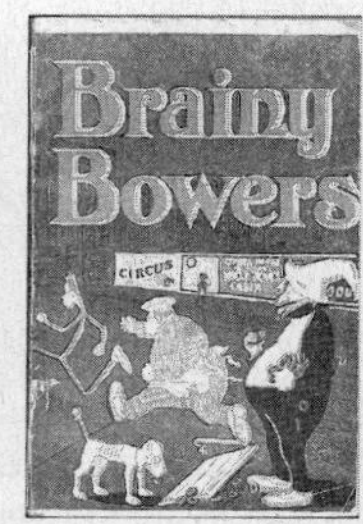

Brainy Bowers and Drowsy Duggan by R.W. Taylor
1905 © Star Publishing Co. - the first daily reprints

 GD2.0 FN6.0 VF8.0

MS Publ. Co.: 1924 (9-7/8x10", 52 pgs., B&W)

nn - Milt Gross comic strips; not reprints 150.00 450.00 880.00

BARKER'S ILLUSTRATED ALMANAC (O,P,S) (See Barkers in Victorian Era section)
Barker, Moore & Mein Medicine Co: 1900-1932+ (36 pgs, B&W, color paper-c)

1900-1932+ (7x5-7/8") 50.00 100.00 200.00

BARKER'S "KOMIC" PICTURE SOUVENIR (P,S) (see Barker's in Victorian)
Barker, Moore & Mein Medicine Co: nd (Parts 1-3, 1901-1903; Parts 1-4, 1906+) (color cardboard-c, B&W interior, 50 pages)

Parts 1-3 (Rare, earliest printing, nd (1901)) 125.00 375.00 750.00
NOTE: *Same cover as 4th edition in Victorian Age Section, except has "Part 1", "Part 2", or "Part 3" printed in the blank space beneath the crate on which central figure is sitting. States "Edition in 3 Parts" on the first interior page, beneath the picture of the Barker's Building.*
Parts 1-3 (nd, c1901-1903) 100.00 250.00 600.00
NOTE: *New cover art on all Parts. States "Edition in 3 Parts" on the first interior page.*
Parts 1-4 (nd, c1906+) 100.00 200.00 400.00
NOTE: *States "Edition in 4 Parts" on the first interior page. Various printings known.These have been confirmed as premium comic books, predating the Buster Brown premiums. They reprint advertising cartoons from Barker's Illustrated Almanac. For the 50 page booklets by this same name, numbered as "Part"s, without exception, were published after 1900. Some editions are found to have 54 pages.*

BARNEY GOOGLE AND SPARK PLUG (N) (See **Comic Monthly**)
Cupples & Leon Co.: 1923 - No.6, 1928 (9-7/8x9-3/4"; 52 pgs., B&W, daily-r)

1 (nn)-By Billy DeBeck 60.00 240.00 500.00
2-4 (#5 & #6 do not exist) 46.00 186.00 350.00
NOTE: *Started June 17, 1919 as newspaper strip; Spark Plug introduced July 17, 1922; strip still running making it one of the oldest still in existence.*

BART'S CARTOONS FOR 1902 FROM THE MINNEAPOLIS JOURNAL (N,S)
Minneapolis Journal: 1903 (11x9", 102 pgs, paperback, B&W)

nn - By Charles L. Bartholomew 30.00 100.00 175.00

BELIEVE IT OR NOT! by Ripley (N,S)
Simon & Schuster: 1929 (8x 5-1/4", 68 pgs, red, B&W cover, B&W interior)

nn - By Robert Ripley (strip-r text & art) 60.00 125.00 275.00
NOTE: *1929 was the first printing of many reprintings . Strip began Dec 19, 1918 and is still running.*

BEN WEBSTER (N)
Standard Printing Company: 1928-1931 (13-3/4x4-7/16", 768 pgs, soft-c)

1 - "Bound to Win" 50.00 125.00 300.00
2 - "...in old Mexico 50.00 125.00 300.00
3 - "...At Wilderness Lake 50.00 125.00 300.00
4 - "...in the Oil Fields 50.00 125.00 300.00
NOTE: *Self Published by Edwin Alger, also contains fan's letter pages.*

BIG SMOKER
W.T. Blackwell & Co.: 1908 (16 pgs, 5-1/2x3-1/2", color-c & interior)

nn - By unknown 20.00 55.00 100.00
NOTE: *Stated reprint of 1878 version. no known copies yet of original printing.*

BILLY BOUNCE (I)
Donohue & Co.: 1906 (288 pgs, hardbound)

nn - By W.W. Denslow & Dudley Bragdon 150.00 525.00 1000.00
NOTE: *Billy Bounce was created in 1901 as a comic strip by W. W. Denslow (strip ran from 1901 NOV 11 to 1905 DEC 3), but the series is best remembered in the C. W. Kahles version (from 1902 SEP 28). Denslow resumed his character in the above illustrated book.*

BILLY HON'S FAMOUS CARTOON BOOK (H)
Wasley Publishing Co.: 1927 (7-1/2x10", 68 pgs, softbound wraparound)

nn - By Billy Hon 15.00 50.00 100.00

BILLY THE BOY ARTIST'S BOOK OF FUNNY PICTURES (N)
C.M.Clark Publishing Co.: 1910 (9x12", hardcover-c, Boston Globe strip-r)

nn - By Ed Payne 125.00 400.00 750.00
NOTE: *This long lived strip ran in **The Boston Globe** from Nov 5 1899-Jan 7 1955; one of the longer run strips.*

BILLY THE BOY ARTIST'S PAINTING BOOK OF FUNNY PICTURES
(known to exist; more data required) - - -

BIRD CENTER CARTOONS: A Chronicle of Social Happenings (N,S)
A. C. McClurg & Co.: 1904 (12-3/8x9-1/2", 216 pgs, hardcover, B&W, single panels)

nn - By John McCutcheon 40.00 140.00 260.00
NOTE: *Strip began in **The Chicago Tribune** in 1903. Satirical cartoons and text concerning a mythical town.*

BLASTS FROM THE RAM'S HORN
The Rams Horn Company: 1902 (330 pgs, 7x9", B&W)

nn - By various 25.00 80.00 125.00
NOTE: *Cartoons reprinted from what was, apparently, a religious newspaper. Many cartoons by Frank Beard. Mostly single panel but occasionally sequential. Allegorical cartoons similar to the Christian Cartoons book. This book mixes cartoons and text sort of like the Caricature books. One or more cartoons on every page.*

BOBBY THATCHER & TREASURE CAVE (N)
Altemus Co.: 1932 (9x7", 86 pgs., B&W, hard-c)

nn - Reprints; Storm-a 54.00 189.00 400.00

BOBBY THATCHER'S ROMANCE (N)
The Bell Syndicate/Henry Altemus Co.: 1931 (8-3/4x7", color cover, B&W)

nn - By Storm 54.00 189.00 400.00

BOOK OF CARTOONS, A (M,S)
Edward T. Miller: 1903 (12-1/4x9-1/4", 120 pgs, hardcover, B&W)

nn - By Harry J. Westerman (Ohio State Journal-r) 20.00 70.00 125.00

BOOK OF DRAWINGS BY A.B. FROST, A (M,S)
P.F. Collier & Son: 1904 (15-3/8 x 11", 96 pgs, B&W)

nn - A.B. Frost 55.00 105.00 310.00
NOTE: *Pages alternate verses by Wallace Irwin and full-page plated by A.B.Frost. 39 plates.*

BOTTLE, THE (E) (see Victorian Age section for earlier printings)
Gowans & Gray, London & Glasgow: June 1905 (3-3/4x6", 72 pgs, printed one side only, paper cover, B&W)

nn - 1st printing (June 1905) 20.00 50.00 125.00
nn - 2nd printing (March 1906) 20.00 50.00 100.00
nn - 3rd printing (January 1911) 20.00 50.00 100.00
NOTE: *By George Cruikshank. Reprints both THE BOTTLE and THE DRUNKARD'S CHILDREN. Cover is text only - no cover art.*

BOTTLE, THE (E)
Frederick A. Stokes: nd (c1906) (3-3/4x6", 72 pgs, printed one side only, paper-c, B&W)

nn- by George Cruikshank 20.00 40.00 100.00
NOTE: *Reprint of the Gowans & Gray edition. Reprints both THE BOTTLE and THE DRUNKARD'S CHILDREN. Cover is text only - no cover art.*

BOYS AND FOLKS (N).
George H. Dornan Company: 1917 (10-1/4 x 8-1/4", 232 pgs. (single-sided), B&W strip-r.

nn - By Webster 21.00 64.00 150.00
NOTE: *Four sections: Life's Darkest Moments, Mostly About Folks, The Thrill That Comes Once in a Lifetime, and Our Boyhood Ambitions. Most are single-panel cartoons, but there are some sequential comic strips.*

BOY'S & GIRLS' BIG PAINTING BOOK OF INTERESTING COMIC PICTURES (N)
M. A. Donohue & Co.: 1914-16 (9x15, 70 pgs)

nn - By Carl "Bunny" Schultze (Foxy Grandpa-r) 81.00 284.00 –
#2 (1914) 81.00 284.00 –
#337 (1914) (sez "Big Painting & Drawing Book") 81.00 284.00 –
nn - (1916) (sez "Big Painting Book")(9-1/4x15") 81.00 284.00 –
NOTE: *These are all **Foxy Grandpa** items.*

BRAIN LEAKS: Dialogues of Mutt & Flea (N)
O. K. Printing Co. (Rochester Evening Times): 1911 (76 pgs, 6-5/8x4-5/8, hard-c, B&W)

nn - By Leo Edward O'Melia; newspaper strip-r 29.00 100.00 200.00

BRAINY BOWERS AND DROWSY DUGGAN (N)
Star Publishing: 1905 (7-1/4 x 4-9/16", 98 pgs., blue, brown & white color cover, B&W interior, 25¢) (daily strip-r 1902-04 Chicago Daily News)

#74 - By R. W. Taylor (Scarce) 600.00 1800.00 –
NOTE: *Part of a series of Atlantic Library Heart Series. Strip begins in 1901 and runs thru 1915. Taylor also created Yen the Janitor for the **New York World.***

BRAIN BOWERS AND DROWSY DUGAN (N)
Max Stein Pub. House, Chicago: 1905 (6-3/16x4-3/8", 64 pgs, B&W)

nn - By R.W. Taylor (Scarce) 600.00 1800.00 –
NOTE: *A coverless copy of this surfaced on eBay in 2002 selling for $700.00.;*

BRAINY BOWERS AND DROWSY DUGGAN GETTING ON IN THE WORLD WITH NO VISIBLE MEANS OF SUPPORT (STORIES TOLD IN PICTURES TO MAKE THEIR TELLING SHORT) (N)
Max Stein/Star Publishing: 1905 (7-3/8x5 1/8", 164 pgs, slick black, red & tan color cover, interior newsprint) (daily strip-r 1902-04 Chicago Daily News)

nn - By R. W. Taylor (Scarce) 500.00 1700.00 –
nn - Possible hard cover edition also? – – –
NOTE: *These Brainy Bowers editions are the earliest known daily newspaper strip reprint books.*

BRINGING UP FATHER (N)
Star Co. (King Features): 1917 (5-1/2x16-1/2", 100 pgs., B&W, cardboard-c)

nn - (Scarcer)-Daily strip- by George McManus 158.00 553.00 1050.00

BRINGING UP FATHER (N)
Cupples & Leon Co.: 1919 - No. 26, 1934 (10x10", 52 pgs., B&W, stiff cardboard-c)
(No. 22 is 9-1/4x9-1/2")

1-Daily strip-r by George McManus in all 30.00 110.00 375.00
2-10 28.00 105.00 285.00
11-20 40.00 200.00 400.00
21-26 (Scarcer) 65.00 310.00 600.00
The Big Book 1 (1926)-Thick book (hardcover, 142 pgs.) 127.00 508.00 1000.00
w/dust jacket (rare) 183.00 732.00 1400.00
The Big Book 2 (1929) 96.00 384.00 750.00
w/dust jacket (rare) 183.00 732.00 1375.00
NOTE: *The Big Books contain 3 regular issues rebound. Strip began Jan 2 1913-May 28 2000.*

BRINGING UP FATHER, THE TROUBLE OF (N)
Embee Publ. Co.: 1921 (9-3/4x15-3/4", 46 pgs, Sunday-r in color)

nn - (Rare) 100.00 350.00 700.00
NOTE: *Ties with Mutt & Jeff (EmBee) and Jimmie Dugan And The Reg'lar Fellers (C&L) as the last of the*

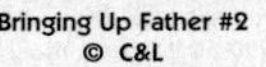
Bringing Up Father #2
© C&L

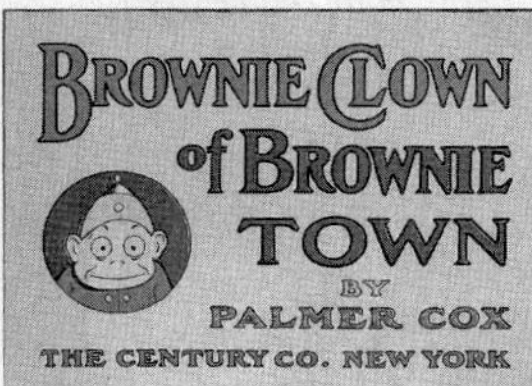

Brownie Clown of Brownie Town
© The Century Co.

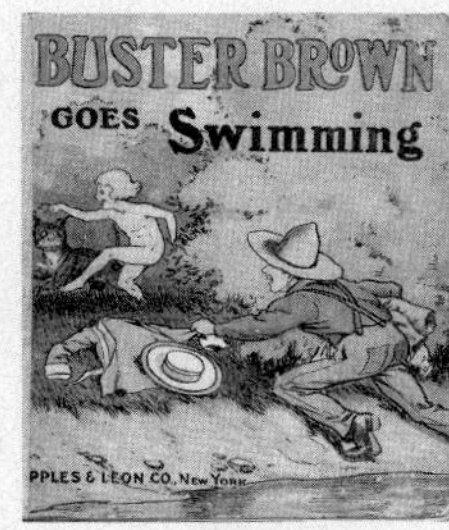

Buster Brown Nuggets - Goes Swimming
1907 © Cupples & Leon

GD2.0 FN6.0 VF8.0

oblong size era. This was self published by George McManus.

BRINGING UP FATHER (N) (see SAGARA'S ENGLISH CARTOONS)
Publisher unknown (actually, unreadable), Tokyo: October 1924 (9-7/8" x 7-1/2", 90 pgs, color hard-c, B&W)

nn- (Scarce) by George McManus C&A (no known sales)
NOTE: *Published in Tokyo, Japan, with all strips in both English and Japanese, to facilitate learning English. Introduction by George McManus. Scarce in USA.*

BRONX BALLADS (I)
Simon & Schuster, NY: 1927 (9-1/2x7-1/4", hard-c, B&W)

nn - By Robert Simon and Harry Hershfield 75.00 150.00 300.00

BROWNIES, THE (not sequential comic strips)
The Century Co.: 1887 - 1914 (all came with dust jackets; add $100-150 to value if original dust jacket is included and intact)

Book 1 - The Brownies: Their Book (1887) 200.00 800.00 1100.00
Book 2 - Another Brownies Book (1890) 150.00 635.00 1000.00
Book 3 - The Brownies at Home (1893) 125.00 530.00 825.00
Book 4 - The Brownies Around the World (1894) 100.00 425.00 675.00
Book 5 - The Brownies Through the Union (1895) 100.00 425.00 675.00
Book 6 - The Brownies Abroad (1899) 100.00 425.00 675.00
Book 7 - The Brownies in the Philippines (1904) 100.00 425.00 675.00
Book 8 - The Brownies' Latest Adventures (1910) 100.00 425.00 675.00
Book 9 - The Brownies Many More Nights (1914) 100.00 425.00 675.00
...Raid on Kleinmaier Bros. (c. 1910, 16 pages) Kleinmaier Bros. Clothing, Marion, Ohio (no known sales)

BROWNIE CLOWN OF BROWNIE TOWN (N)
The Century Co.: 1908 (6-7/8 x 9-3/8", 112 pgs, color hardcover & interior)

nn - By Palmer Cox (rare; 1907 newspaper comic strip-r) 250.00 800.00 1000.00
NOTE: *The Brownies created 1883 in* ***St Nicholas Magazine.***

BUDDY TUCKER & HIS FRIENDS (N) (Also see **Buster Brown Nuggets**)
Cupples & Leon Co.: 1906 (11-5/8 x17", 58 pgs, color) (Scarce)

nn - 1905 Sunday strip-r by R. F. Outcault 525.00 1550.00 2650.00
NOTE: *Strip began Apr 30, 1905 thru at least Oct 1905.*

BUFFALO BILL'S PICTURE STORIES
Street & Smith Publications: 1909 (Soft cardboard cover)

nn - Very rare 100.00 275.00 450.00

BUGHOUSE FABLES (N) (see also **Comic Monthly**)
Embee Distributing Co. (King Features): 1921 (10¢, 4x4-1/2", 48 pgs.)

1-By Barney Google (Billy DeBeck) 46.00 186.00 350.00

BUG MOVIES (O) (Also see Clancy The Cop & Deadwood Gulch)
Dell Publishing Co.: 1931 (9-13/16x9-7/8", 52 pgs., B&W)

nn - Original material; Stookie Allen-a 150.00 300.00 550.00

BULL
Bull Publishing Company, New York: No.1, March, 1916 - No.12, Feb, 1917 (10 cents, 10-3/4x8-3/4", 24 pgs, color paper-c, B&W)

1-12 (Very Rare) – – –
NOTE: *Pro-German, Anti-British cartoon/humor monthly, whose goal was to keep the U.S. neutral and out of World War I. We know of no copies which have sold in the past few years.*

BUNNY'S BLUE BOOK (see also Foxy Grandpa) (N)
Frederick A. Stokes Co.: 1911 (10x15, 60¢)

nn - By Carl "Bunny" Schultze strip-r 125.00 360.00 –

BUNNY'S RED BOOK (see also Foxy Grandpa) (N)
Frederick A. Stokes Co.: 1912 (10-1/4x15-3/4", 64 pgs.)

nn - By Carl "Bunny" Schultze strip-r 125.00 360.00 –

BUNNY'S GREEN BOOK (see also Foxy Grandpa) (N)
Frederick A. Stokes Co.: 1913 (10x15")

nn - By Carl "Bunny" Schultze 125.00 360.00 –

BUSTER BROWN (C) (Also see Brown's Blue Ribbon Book of Jokes and Jingles & Buddy Tucker & His Friends)
Frederick A. Stokes Co.: 1903 - 1916 (Daily strip-r in color)

1903...& His Resolutions (11-1/4x16", 66 pgs.) by R. F. Outcault (Rare)-1st nationally distributed comic. Distr. through Sears & Roebuck 1600.00 3400.00 –
1904...His Dog Tige & Their Troubles (11-1/4x16-1/4", 66 pgs.)(Rare) 600.00 1800.00 –
1905...Pranks (11-1/4x16-3/8", 66 pgs.) 400.00 1450.00 –
1906...Antics (11x16-3/8", 66 pgs.) 400.00 1450.00 –
1906...And Company (11x16-1/2", 66 pgs.) 300.00 1050.00 –
1906...Mary Jane & Tige (11-1/4x16, 66 pgs.) 300.00 1050.00 –
NOTE: ***Yellow Kid*** *pictured on two pages.*
1908 Collection of Buster Brown Comics 250.00 835.00 –
1909 Outcault's Real Buster and The Only Mary Jane (11x16, 66 pgs, Stokes) 250.00 835.00 –
1910...Up to Date (10-1/8x15-3/4", 66 pgs.) 208.00 729.00 1000.00

GD2.0 FN6.0 VF8.0

1911...Fun And Nonsense (10-1/8x15-3/4", 66 pgs.) 183.00 642.00 1100.00
1912...The Fun Maker (10-1/8x15-3/4", 66 pgs.) -Yellow Kid (4 pgs.) 183.00 642.00 1100.00
1913...At Home (10-1/8x15-3/4", 56 pgs.) 167.00 583.00 1000.00
1914...And Tige Here Again (10x16, 62 pgs, Stokes) 153.00 535.00 900.00
1915...And His Chum Tige (10x16, Stokes) 153.00 535.00 900.00
1916...The Little Rogue (10-1/8x15-3/4", 62 pgs.) 162.00 567.00 1025.00
1917...And the Cat (5-1/2x 6-1/2, 26 pgs, Stokes) 115.00 402.00 700.00
1917...Disturbs the Family (5-1/2x 6 1/2, 26 pgs, Stokes
NOTE: *Story featuring statue of "the Chinese Yellow Kid"* 115.00 402.00 700.00
1917...The Real Buster Brown (5-1/2x 6 -/2, 26 pgs, Stokes 115.00 402.00 700.00

Frederick A. Stokes Co. Hard Cover Series (I)

...Abroad (1904, 10-1/4x8", 86 pgs., B&W, hard-c)-R. F. Outcault-a (Rare) 200.00 700.00 1000.00
...Abroad (1904, B&W, 67 pgs.)-R. F. Outcault-a 200.00 700.00 1000.00
NOTE: *Buster Brown Abroad is not an actual comic book, but prose with illustrations.*
..."Tige" His Story 1905 (10x8", 63 pgs., B&W) (63 illos.)
nn-By RF Outcault 143.00 500.00 –
...My Resolutions 1906 (10x8", B&W, 68 pgs.)-R.F. Outcault-a (Rare) 233.00 817.00 1350.00
...Autobiography 1907 (10x8", B&W, 71 pgs.) (16 color plates & 36 B&W illos) 67.00 233.00 400.00
...And Mary Jane's Painting Book 1907 (10x13-1/4", 60 pgs, both card & hardcover versions exist
nn-RFO (first printing blank on top of cover) 67.00 233.00 440.00
First Series- this is a reprint if it says First Series 67.00 233.00 440.00
Volume Two - By RFO 67.00 233.00 440.00
... My Resolutions by Buster Brown (1907, 68 pgs, small size, cardboard covers) scarce 43.00 150.00 285.00
NOTE: *Not actual comic book per se, but a compilation of the Resolutions panels found at the end of Outcault's Buster Brown newspaper strips.*

BUSTER BROWN (N)
Cupples & Leon Co./N. Y. Herald Co.: 1906 - 1917 (11x17", color, strip-r)
NOTE: *Early issues by R. F. Outcault; most C&L editions are not by Outcault.*

1906...His Dog Tige And Their Jolly Times (11-3/8x16-5/8", 68 pgs.) 300.00 1100.00 1700.00
1906...His Dog Tige & Their Jolly Times (11x16, 46 pgs.) 163.00 600.00 1000.00
1907...Latest Frolics (11-3/8x16-5/8", 66 pgs., r/'05-06 strips) 163.00 600.00 1000.00
1908...Amusing Capers (58 pgs.) 129.00 475.00 800.00
1909...The Busy Body (11-3/8x16-5/8", 62 pgs.) 129.00 475.00 800.00
1910...On His Travels (11x16", 58 pgs.) 115.00 402.00 800.00
1911...Happy Days (11-3/8x16-5/8", 58 pgs.) 115.00 402.00 800.00
1912...In Foreign Lands (10x16", 58 pgs) 115.00 402.00 800.00
1913...And His Pets (11x16", 58 pgs.) STOKES???? 115.00 402.00 800.00
1913...And His Pets (26 pg partial reprint) – – –
1914...Funny Tricks (11-3/8x16-5/8", 58 pgs.) 115.00 402.00 800.00
1916...At Play (10x16, 58 pgs) 115.00 402.00 800.00

BUSTER BROWN NUGGETS (N)
Cupples & Leon Co./N.Y.Herald Co.: 1907 (1905, 7-1/2x6-1/2", 36 pgs., color, strip-r, hard-c)(By R. F. Outcault) (NOTE: books are all unnumbered)

Buster Brown Goes Fishing, Goes Swimming, Plays Indian, Goes Shooting, Plays Cowboy, On Uncle Jack's Farm, Tige And the Bull, And Uncle Buster 40.00 150.00 350.00
Buddy Tucker Meets Alice in Wonderland 56.00 200.00 400.00
Buddy Tucker Visits The House That Jack Built 40.00 150.00 350.00

BUSTER BROWN MUSLIN SERIES (N)
Saalfield: 1907 (also contain copyright Cupples & Leon)

...Goes Fishing, Plays Indian, And the Donkey (1907, 6-7/8x6-1/8", 24 pgs., color)-r/1905 Sunday comics page by Outcault (Rare) 50.00 175.00 325.00
...Plays Cowboy (1907, 6-3/4x6", 10 pgs., color)-r/1905 Sunday comics page by Outcault (Rare) 50.00 175.00 325.00
NOTE: *These are muslin versions of the C&L BB Nugget series. Muslin books are all cloth books, made to be washable so as not easily stained/destroyed by very young children. The Muslin books contain one strip each (the title strip), to the more common NUGGET's three strips.*

BUSTER BROWN PREMIUMS (Advertising premium booklets)
Various Publishers: 1904 - 1912 (3x5" to 5x7"; sizes vary)

American Fruit Product Company, Rochester, NY

Buster Brown Duffy's 1842 Cider (1904, 7x5". 12 pgs, C.E. Sherin Co, NYC)
nn - By R. F. Outcault (scarce) 100.00 350.00 600.00

The Brown Shoe Company, St. Louis, USA
Set of five books (5x7", 16 pgs., color)

Brown's Blue Ribbon Book of Jokes and Jingles Book 1 (nn, 1904)-By R. F. Outcault; Buster Brown & Tige, Little Tommy Tucker, Jack & Jill, Little Boy Blue, Dainty Jane; The Yellow Kid app. on back-c (1st BB comic book premium) 300.00 1050.00 2000.00
Buster Brown's Blue Ribbon Book of Jokes and Jingles Book 2 (1905)-

Buster Brown Nuggets -Buster Brown Plays Cowboy © C&L

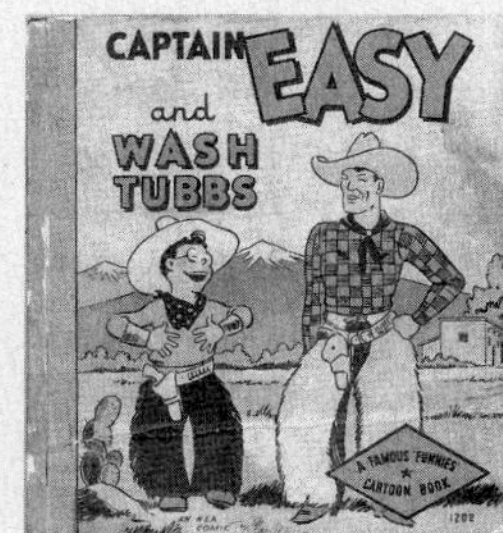

Captain Easy and Wash Tubbs by Roy Crane 1934 © Whitman Famous Comics Cartoon Book

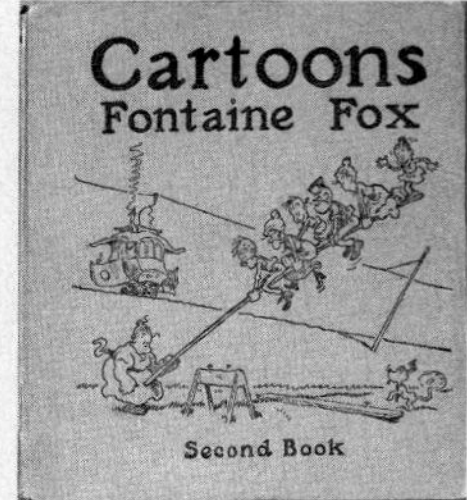

Cartoons Fontaine Fox Second Book early 1920s © Harper & Bros, NY

GD2.0 FN6.0 VF8.0

Original color art by Outcault 200.00 600.00 1200.00
Buster's Book of Jokes & Jingles Book 3 (1909)
not by R.F. Outcault 150.00 400.00 800.00
NOTE: *Reprinted from the Blue Ribbon post cards with advert jingles added.*
Buster's Book of Instructive Jokes and Jingles Book 4 (1910)-Original color art
not by R.F. Outcault 150.00 585.00 1000.00
...Book of Travels nn (1912, 3x5")-Original color art not signed by Outcault
117.00 408.00 735.00
NOTE: *Estimated 5 or 6 known copies exist of books #1-4.*

The Buster Brown Bread Company

"Buster Brown" Bread Book of Rhymes, The (1904, 4x6", 12 pgs., half color, half B&W)- Original color art not signed by RFO 158.00 553.00 1000.00

Buster Brown's Hosiery Mills

"How Buster Brown Got The Pie" nn (nd, 7x5-1/4". 16 pgs, color paper cover and color interior By R.F. Outcault 85.00 300.00 600.00
"The Autobiography of Buster Brown" nn (nd,9x6-1/8", 36 pgs, text story & art by R.F. Outcault 85.00 300.00 600.00
NOTE: *Similar to, but a distinctly different item than "Buster Brown's Autobiography."*

The Buster Brown Stocking Company

Buster Brown Drawing Book, The nn (nd, 5x6", 20 pgs.)-B&W reproductions of 1903 R.F. Outcault art to trace 50.00 150.00 350.00
NOTE: *Reprints a comic strip from Burr McIntosh Magazine, which includes Buster, Yellow Kid, and Pore Li'l Mose (only known story involving all three.)*
Buster Brown Stocking Magazine nn (Jan. 1906, 7-3/4x5-3/8", 36 pgs.) R.F. Outcault
50.00 100.00 225.00
NOTE: *This was actually a store bought item selling for 5 cents per copy.*

Collins Baking Company

Buster Brown Drawing Book nn (1904, 5x3", 12 pgs.)-Original B&W art to trace, not signed by R.F. Outcault 50.00 200.00 400.00

C. H. Morton, St. Albans, VT

Merry Antics of Buster Brown, Buddy Tucker & Tige nn (nd, 3-1/2x5-1/2", 16 pgs.) -Original B&W art by R.F. Outcault 83.00 292.00 525.00

Ivan Frank & Company

Buster Brown nn (1904, 3x5", 12 pgs.)-B&W repros of R. F. Outcault Sunday pages (First premium to actually reproduce Sunday comic pages – may be first premium comic strip-r book?) 125.00 438.00 800.00
Buster Brown's Pranks (1904, 3-1/2x5-1/8", 12 pgs.)-reprints intro of Buddy Tucker into the BB newspaper strip before he was spun off into his own short lived newspaper strip
125.00 438.00 800.00

Kaufmann & Strauss

Buster Brown Drawing Book (1906, 28 pages, 5x3-1/2") Color Cover, B+W original story signed by Outcault, tracing paper inserted as alternate pages. Back cover imprinted for Nox' Em All Shoes 50.00 150.00 325.00

Pond's Extract

Buster Brown's Experiences With Pond's Extract nn (1904, 6-3/4x4-1/2", 28 pgs.) Original color art by R.F. Outcault (may be the first BB premium comic book with original art) 100.00 250.00 575.00

C. A. Cross & Co.

Red Cross Drawing Book nn (1906, 4-7/8x3-1/2", color paper -c, B&W interior, 12 pgs.)
50.00 150.00 325.00
NOTE: *This is for Red Cross coffee; not the health organization.*

Ringen Stove Company

Quick Meal Steel Ranges nn (nd, 5x3", 16 pgs.)-Original B&W art not signed by R.F. Outcault 50.00 150.00 325.00

Steinwender Stoffregen Coffee Co.

"Buster Brown Coffee" (1905, 4-7/8x3", color paper cover, B&W interior, 12 printed pages, plus 1 tracing paper page above each interior image (total of 8 sheets) (Very Rare)
83.00 292.00 525.00
NOTE: *Part of a BB drawing contest. If instructions had been followed, most copies would have ended up destroyed.*

U. S. Playing Card Company

Buster Brown - My Own Playing Cards (1906, 2-1/2x1-3/4", full color)
nn - By R. F. Outcault 42.00 147.00 250.00
NOTE: *Series of full color panels tell stories, average about 5 cards per story.*

Publisher Unknown

The Drawing Book nn (1906, 3-9/16x5", 8 pgs.)-Original B&W art to trace not by R.F. Outcault 50.00 150.00 300.00

BUTLER BOOK A Series of Clever Cartoons of Yale Undergraduate Life
Yale Record: June 16, 1913 (10-3/4 x 17", 34 pgs, paper cover B&W)
nn - By Alban Bernard Butler 25.00 75.00 150.00
NOTE: *Cartoons and strips reprinted from The Yale Record student newspaper.*

BUTTONS & FATTY IN THE FUNNIES
Whitman Publishing Co.: nd 1927 (10-1/4x15-1/2", 28pg., color)
W936 - Signed "M.E.B.", probably M.E. Brady; strips in color copyright The Brooklyn Daily Eagle; (very rare) 61.00 244.00 425.00

BY BRIGGS (M,N,P) (see also OLD GOLD THE SMOOTHER AND BETTER CIGARETTE)
Old Gold Cigarettes: nd (c1920's) (11" x 9-11/16", 44 pgs, cardboard-c, B&W)
nn- (Scarce) 20.00 70.00 140.00
NOTE: *Collection reprinting strip cartoons by Clare Briggs, advertising Old Gold Cigarettes. These strips originally appeared in various magazines, play program booklets, newspapers, etc. Some of the strips involve regular Briggs strip series. Contains all of the strips in the smaller, color "OLD GOLD" giveaways, plus more.*

CAMION CARTOONS
Marshall Jones Company: 1919 (7-1/2x5", 136 pgs, B&W)
nn - By Kirkland H. Day (W.W.One occupation) 20.00 70.00 125.00

CANYON COUNTRY KIDDIES (M)
Doubleday, Page & Co: 1923 (8x10-1/4", 88 pgs, hard-c, B&W)
nn - By James Swinnerton 39.00 137.00 260.00

CARLO (H)
Doubleday, Page & Co.: 1913 (8 x 9-5/8, 120 pgs, hardcover, B&W)
nn - By A.B. Frost 40.00 140.00 300.00
NOTE: *Original sequential strips about a dog. Became short lived newspaper comic strip in 1914. Originally published with a dust jacket which increases value 50%.*

CARTOON BOOK, THE
Bureau of Publicity, War Loan Organization, Treasury Department, Washington, D.C.: 1918 (6-1/2x4-7/8", 48 pgs, paper cover, B&W)
nn - By various artists 31.00 108.00 200.00
NOTE: *U.S. government issued booklet of WW I propaganda cartoons by 46 artists promoting the third sale of Liberty Loan bonds. The artists include: Berryman, Clare Briggs, Cesare, J. N. "Ding" Darling, Rube Goldberg, Kemble, McCutcheon, George McManus, F. Opper, T. E. Powers, Ripley, Satterfield, H. T. Webster, Gaar Williams.*

CARTOON CATALOGUE (S)
The Lockwood Art School, Kalamazoo, Mich.: 1919 (11-5/8x9, 52 pgs, B&W)
nn - Edited by Mr. Lockwood 20.00 60.00 150.00
NOTE: *Jammed with 100s of single panel cartoons and some sequential comics; Mr Lockwood began the very first cartoonist school back in 1892. Clare Briggs was one of his students.*

CARTOON COMICS
Lasco Publications, Detroit, Mich: #1, April 1930 - #2, May 1930 (8-3/6x5-1/5")
1, 2 - By Lu Harris 20.00 60.00 120.00
NOTE: *Contains recurring characters Hollywood Horace, Campus Charlie, Pair-A-Dice Alley and Jocko Monkey. Not much is presently known about the creator(s) or publisher.*

CARTOON HISTORY OF ROOSEVELT'S CAREER, A
The Review of Reviews Company: 1910 (276 pgs, 8-1/4x11",
nn - By various 50.00 175.00 350.00
NOTE: *Reprints editorial cartoons about Teddy Roosevelt from U.S. and international newspapers and cartoons from the humor magaines (Puck, Judge, etc.). A few cartoonists whose work is included are Dalrymple, Opper, McDougall, McCutcheon, Remington, Rogers, Kemble. Mostly single panel but 10 or so are sequential strips.*

CARTOON HUMOR
Collegian Press: 1938 (102 pgs, squarebound, B&W)
nn 20.00 70.00 125.00
NOTE: *Contains cartoons & strips by Otto Soglow, Syd Hoff, Peter Arno, Abner Dean, others.*

CARTOONIST'S PHILOSOPHY, A
Percy Crosby: 1931, HC, 252 pgs, 5-1/2x7-1/2", hard-c, celluloid dust wrapper
nn - By Percy Crosby (10 plates, 6 are of Skippy) 30.00 70.00 140.00
NOTE: *Crosby's partial autobiography regarding his return to France in 1929, and portrayals of Normandy, the "cliff dwellers" on Normandy cliffs (destroyed in WWII), his visit to London, comments on art, philosophy, several poems, and political dialogue. His description of his Cockney driver, " Harold" is amusing. Also describes his experience visiting Chicago to speak out against Capone, his concerns over the evils of Prohibition, and the economy prior to the 1929 crash. This book reveals he was aware of the dangers of his outspoken views, and is prophetic, re: his later years as political prisoner. Also reveals his religious beliefs.*

CARTOONS BY BRADLEY: CARTOONIST OF THE CHICAGO DAILY NEWS
Rand McNally & Company: 1917 (11-1/4x8-3/4", 112 pgs, hardcover, B&W)
nn - By Luther D. Bradley (editorial) 20.00 70.00 120.00

CARTOONS BY FONTAINE FOX (Toonerville Trolley) (S)
Harper & Brothers Publishers: nd early '20s (9x7-7/8",102 pgs., hard-c, B&W)
Second Book- By Fontaine Fox (Toonerville-r) 150.00 300.00 550.00

CARTOONS BY HALLADAY (N,S)
Providence Journal Co., Rhode Island: Dec 1914 (116 pgs, 10-1/2x 7-3/4", hard-c, B&W)
nn- (Scarce) 50.00 125.00 250.00
NOTE: *Cartoons on Rhode Island politics, plus some Teddy Roosevelt & WW I cartoons.*

CARTOONS BY McCUTCHEON (S)
A. C. McClurg & Co.: 1903 (12-3/8x9-3/4", 212 pgs., hardcover, B&W)
nn - By John McCutcheon 20.00 70.00 125.00

CARTOONS BY W. A. IRELAND (S)
The Columbus-Evening Dispatch: 1907 (13-3/4 x 10-1/2", 66 pgs, hardcover)
nn - By W. A. Ireland (strip-r) 20.00 70.00 125.00

CARTOONS MAGAZINE (I,N,S)
H. H. Windsor, Publisher: Jan 1912-June 1921; July 1921-1923; 1923-1924; 1924-1927 (1912-July 1913 issues 12x9-1/4", 68-76 pgs; 1913-1921 issues 10x7", average 112 to 188 pgs, color covers)
1912-Jan-Dec 30.00 75.00 130.00
1913-1917 30.00 75.00 130.00

Cartoons Magazine Sept, 1917
by various creators © H. H. Windsor, Chicago

Charlie Chaplin in the Army by Segar
1917 © Essaney

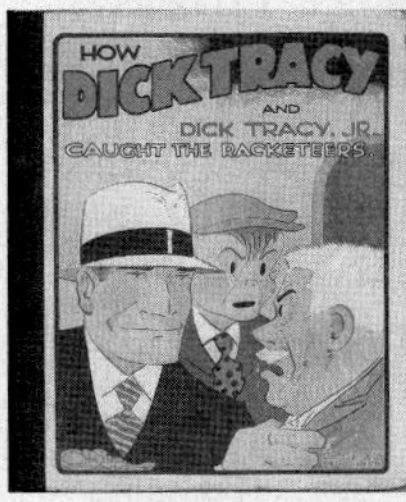

How Dick Tracy and Dick Tracy, Jr.
Caught the Racketeers by Chester Gould
1933 © Cupples & Leon

GD2.0 FN6.0 VF8.0

1917-(Apr) "How Comickers Regard Their Characters" 30.00 105.00 160.00
1917-(June) "A Genius of the Comic Page" - long article on George Herriman, Krazy Kat, etc with lots of Herriman art; "Cartoonists and Their Cars" 150.00 300.00 650.00
1918-1919 30.00 75.00 130.00
1920-June 1921 30.00 75.00 130.00
July 1921-1923 titled Wayside Tales & Cartoons Magazine 30.00 75.00 130.00
1923-1924 becomes Cartoons Magazine again 30.00 75.00 130.00
1924-1927 becomes Cartoons & Movie Magazine 30.00 75.00 130.00
NOTE: *Many issues contain a wealth of historical background on then current cartoonists of the day with an international slant; each issue profusely illustrated with many cartoons. We are unsure if this magazine continued after 1927.*

CARTOONS BY J. N. DARLING (S,N - some sequential strips)
The Register & Tribune Co., Des Moines, Iowa: 1909?-1920 (12x8-7/8",B&W)
Book 1 20.00 55.00 130.00
Book 2 Education of Alonzo Applegate (1910) 18.00 52.00 110.00
2nd printing 18.00 52.00 110.00
Book 3 Cartoons From The Files (1911) 18.00 52.00 110.00
Book 4 18.00 52.00 110.00
Book 5 In Peace And War (1916) 18.00 52.00 110.00
Book 6 Aces & Kings War Cartoons (Dec 1, 1918) 18.00 52.00 110.00
Book 7 The Jazz Era (Dec 1920) 18.00 52.00 110.00
Book 8 Our Own Outlines of History (1922) 18.00 52.00 110.00
NOTE: *Some of the most inspired hard hitting cartoons ever printed. Are there more?*

CARTOONS THAT MADE PRINCE HENRY FAMOUS, THE (N,S)
The Chicago Record-Herald: Feb/March 1902 (12-1/8" x 9", 32 pgs, paper-c, B&W)
nn- (Scarce) by McCutcheon 15.00 51.00 100.00
NOTE: *Cartoons about the visit of the British Prince Henry to the U.S.*

CAVALRY CARTOONS (O)
R. Montalboddi: nd (c1918) (14-1/4" x 11", 30 pgs, printed on one side, olive & black construction paper-c, B&W interior)
nn - By R.Montalboddi 20.00 55.00 100.00
NOTE: *Comics about life in the U.S.Cavalry during World War I, by a soldier who was in the 1st Cavalry.*

CHARLIE CHAPLIN (N)
Essanay/M. A. Donohue & Co.: 1917 (9x16", B&W, large size soft-c)
Series 1, #315-Comic Capers (9-3/4x15-3/4")-20 pgs. by Segar;
Series 1, #316-In the Movies 165.00 525.00 1150.00
#317-Up in the Air (20 pgs), #318-In the Army 165.00 525.00 1375.00
Funny Stunts-(12-1/2x16-3/8",16 color pgs) 165.00 525.00 1375.00
NOTE: *All contain pre-Thimble Theatre Segar art. The thin paper used makes high grade copies very scarce.*

CHASING THE BLUES
Doubleday Page: 1912 (7-1/2x10", 108 pgs., B&W, hard-c)
nn - By Rube Goldberg 150.00 525.00 1000.00
NOTE: *Contains a dozen Foolish Questions, baseball, a few Goldberg poems and lots of sequential strips.*

CHRISTIAN CARTOONS (N,S)
The Sunday School Times Company: 1922 (7-1/4 x 6-1/8,104 pgs, brown hard-c, B&W)
nn - E.J. Pace 15.00 51.00 100.00
NOTE: *Religious cartoons reprinted from The Sunday School Times.*

CLANCY THE COP (O))
Dell Publishing Co.: 1930 - No. 2, 1931 (10x10", 52 pgs., B&W, cardboard-c)
(Also see Bug Movies & Deadwood Gulch)
1, 2-By VEP Victor Pazimino (original material; not reprints) 10000 250.00 500.00

CLIFFORD MCBRIDE'S IMMORTAL NAPOLEON & UNCLE ELBY (N)
The Castle Press: 1932 (12x17"; soft-c cartoon book)
nn - Intro. by Don Herod 36.00 144.00 250.00

COLLECTED DRAWINGS OF BRUCE BAIRNSFATHER, THE
W. Colston Leigh: 1931 (11-1/4x8-1/4 ", 168 pages, hardcover, B&W)
nn - By Bruce Bairnsfather 24.00 96.00 175.00

COMICAL PEEP SHOW
McLoughlin Bros: 1902 (36 pgs, B&W)
nn 24.00 96.00 165.00
NOTE: *Comic stories of Wilhelm Busch redrawn; two versions with green or gold front cover logos; back covers different.*

COMIC ANIMALS (I)
Charles E. Graham & Co.: 1903 (9-3/4x7-1/4", 90 pgs, color cover)
nn - By Walt McDougall (not comic strips) 80.00 160.00 275.00

COMIC CUTS (O)
H. L. Baker Co., Inc.: 5/19/34-7/28/34 (Tabloid size 10-1/2x15-1/2", 24 pgs., 5¢)
(full color, not reprints; published weekly; created for news stand sales)
V1#1 - V1#7(6/30/34), V1#8(7/14/34), V1#9(7/28/34)-Idle Jack strips
250.00 500.00 1000.00
NOTE: *According to a 1958 Lloyd Jacquet interview, this short-lived comics mag was the direct inspiration for Major Malcolm Wheeler-Nicholson's* ***New Fun Comics****, not* ***Famous Funnies****.*

COMIC MONTHLY (N)
Embee Dist. Co.: Jan, 1922 - No. 12, Dec, 1922 (10¢, 8-1/2"x9", 28 pgs., 2-color covers)
(1st monthly newsstand comic publication) (Reprints 1921 B&W dailies)
1-Polly & Her Pals by Cliff Sterrett 400.00 1200.00 2500.00
2-Mike & Ike by Rube Goldberg 150.00 500.00 1125.00
3-S'Matter, Pop? 150.00 500.00 1125.00
4-Barney Google by Billy DeBeck 150.00 500.00 1125.00
5-Tillie the Toiler by Russ Westover 150.00 500.00 1125.00
6-Indoor Sports by Tad Dorgan 150.00 500.00 1125.00
NOTE: *#6 contains more Judge Rummy than Indoor Sports.*
7-Little Jimmy by James Swinnerton 150.00 500.00 1125.00
8-Toots and Casper b y Jimmy Murphy 150.00 500.00 1125.00
9-New Bughouse Fables by Barney Google 150.00 500.00 1125.00
10-Foolish Questions by Rube Goldberg 150.00 500.00 1125.00
11-Barney Google & Spark Plug by Billy DeBeck 150.00 500.00 1125.00
12-Polly & Her Pals by Cliff Sterrett 150.00 500.00 1125.00
NOTE: *This series was published by George McManus (Bringing Up Father) as Em & Rudolph Block, Jr., son of Hearst's cartoon editor for many years, as "Bee." One would have thought this series would have done very well considering the tremendous amount of talent assembled. All issues are extremely hard to find these days and rarely show up in any type of higher grade.*

COMIC PAINTING AND CRAYONING BOOK (H)
Saalfield Publ. Co.: 1917 (13-1/2x10", 32 pgs.) (No price on-c)
nn - Tidy Teddy by F. M. Follett, Clarence the Cop, Mr. & Mrs. Butt-In; regular comic stories to read or color 50.00 175.00 325.00

COMPLETE TRIBUNE PRIMER, THE (I)
Mutual Book Company: 1901 (7 1/4 x 5", 152 pgs, red hard-c)
nn - By Frederick Opper; has 75 Opper cartoons 25.00 75.00 150.00

COURTSHIP OF TAGS, THE (N)
McCormick Press: pre-1910 (9x4", 88 pgs, red & B&W-c, B&W interior)
nn - By O. E. Wertz (strip-r Wichita Daily Beacon) 25.00 75.00 150.00

DAFFYDILS (N)
Cupples & Leon Co.: 1911 (5-3/4x7-7/8", 52 pgs., B&W, hard-c)
nn - By "Tad" Dorgan 58.00 204.00 375.00
NOTE: *Also exists in self-published TAD edition: The T.A. Dorgan Company; unknown which is first printing.*

DAN DUNN SECRET OPERATIVE 48 (Also See Detective Dan) (N)
Whitman Publishing: 1937 ((5 1/2 x 7 1/4", 68pgs., color cardboard-c, B&W)
1010 And The Gangsters' Frame-Up 50.00 150.00 350.00
NOTE: *There are two versions of the book the later printing has a 5 cent cover price. Dick Tracy look-alike character by Norman Marsh.*

DANGERS OF DOLLY DIMPLE, THE (N)
Penn Tobacco Co.: nd (1930's) (9-3/8x7-7/8", 28 pgs, red cardboard-c, B&W)
nn - (Rare) by Walter Enright 25.00 88.00 150.00
NOTE: *Reprints newspaper comic strip advertisements, in which in every episode, Dolly Dimple's life is saved by Penn's Smoking Tobacco. - how very un-P.C. by today's standards.*

DEADWOOD GULCH (O) (See The Funnies 1929)(also see Bug Movies & Clancy The Cop)
Dell Publishing Co.: 1931 (10x10", 52 pgs., B&W, color covers, B&W interior)
nn - By Charles "Boody" Rogers (original material) 150.00 300.00 600.00

DESTINY A Novel In Pictures (O)
Farrar & Rinehart: 1930 (8x7", 424 pgs, B&W, hard-c, dust jacket?)
nn - By Otto Nuckel (original graphic novel) 25.00 100.00 200.00

DICK TRACY & DICK TRACY JR. CAUGHT THE RACKETEERS, HOW
Cupples & Leon Co.: 1933 (8-1/2x7", 88 pgs., hard-c) (See Treasure Box of Famous Comics) (N)
2-(Numbered on pg. 84)-Continuation of Stooge Viller book (daily strip reprints from 8/3/33 thru 11/8/33)(Rarer than #1) 100.00 400.00 800.00
With dust jacket... 175.00 500.00 1100.00

DICK TRACY & DICK TRACY JR. AND HOW THEY CAPTURED "STOOGE" VILLER (N)
Cupples & Leon Co.: 1933 (8-1/2x7", 100 pgs., hard-c, one-shot)
Reprints 1932 & 1933 Dick Tracy daily strips
nn(No.1)-1st app. of "Stooge" Viller 94.00 376.00 750.00
With dust jacket... 175.00 500.00 1000.00

DIMPLES By Grace Drayton (N) (See Dolly Dimples)
Hearst's International Library Co.: 1915 (6 1/4 x 5 1/4, 12 pgs) (5 known)
nn-Puppy and Pussy; nn-She Goes For a Walk; nn-She Had A Sneeze; nn-She Has a Naughty Play Husband; nn-Wait Till Fido Comes Home 21.00 74.00 175.00

DOINGS OF THE DOO DADS, THE (N)
Detroit News (Universal Feat. & Specialty Co.): 1922 (50¢, 7-3/4x7-3/4", 34 pgs, B&W, red & white-c, square binding)
nn-Reprints 1921 newspaper strip "Text & Pictures" given away as prize in the Detroit News Doo Dads contest; by Arch Dale 43.00 173.00 360.00

DOING THE GRAND CANYON
Fred Harvey: 1922 (7 x 4-3/4", 24 pgs, B&W, paper cover)
nn - John McCutcheon 25.00 55.00 110.00

'Erbie And 'Is Playmates By F. Opper
1932 © Democratic National Committee

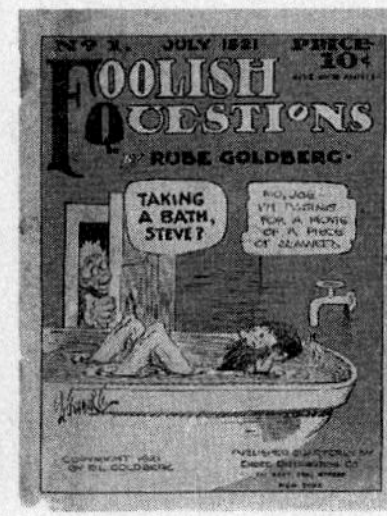

Foolish Questions by Rube Goldberg
1921 © EmBee Distributing Co., NY.

The Latest Adventures of Foxy Grandpa 1905
© Bunny Publ.

GD2.0 FN6.0 VF8.0

GD2.0 FN6.0 VF8.0

NOTE: *Text & 8 cartoons about visiting the Grand Canyon.*

DOINGS OF THE VAN-LOONS (N) (from same company as Mutt & Jeff #1-#5)
Ball Publications: 1912 (5-3/4X15-1/2", 68pg., B&W, hard-c)
nn - By Fred I. Leipziger (scarce) 72.00 252.00 600.00

DOLLY DIMPLES & BOBBY BOUNCE (See Dimples)
Cupples & Leon Co.: 1933 (8-3/4x7", color hardcover, B&W)
nn - Grace Drayton-a 24.00 96.00 165.00

DOO DADS, THE (Sleepy Sam and Tiny the Elephant)
Universal Feature * Specialty Co: 1922 (5-1/4x14", 36 pgs.,B&W, R&W-c,square binding)
nn - By Arch Dale 35.00 125.00 250.00

DRAWINGS BY HOWARD CHANDLER CHRISTIE (S, M)
Moffat, Yard & Company, NY: 1905 (11-7/8x16-1/2", 68 pgs, hard-c, B&W)
nn - Howard C. Christie 30.00 60.00 125.00
NOTE: *Reprints1898-1905 from Haprer & Bros, Ch. Scribners Sons, Leslie's, MacMillians, McLurg, Russell.*

DREAMS OF THE RAREBIT FIEND (N)
Frederick A. Stokes Co.:1905 (10-1/4x7-1/2", 68 pgs, thin paper cover all B&W) newspaper reprints from the New York Evening Telegram printed on yellow paper
nn-By Winsor "Silas" McCay (Very Rare) (Five copies known to exist)
Estimated value.... 1000.00 2500.00 –
NOTE: *A G/VG copy sold for $2,045 in May 2004. This item usually turns up with fragile paper.*

DRISCOLL'S BOOK OF PIRATES (O)
David McKay Publ.: 1934 (9x7", 124 pgs, B&W, hardcover)
nn - By Montford Amory ("Pieces of Eight strip-r) 21.00 64.00 150.00

DUCKY DADDLES
Frederick A. Stokes Co: July 1911 (15x10")
nn - By Grace Weiderseim (later Drayton) strip-r 50.00 175.00 300.00

DUMBUNNIES AND THEIR FRIENDS IN RABBITBORO, THE (O)
Albertine Randall Wheelan: 1931 (8-3/4x7-1/8", 82 pgs, color hardcover, B&W)
nn - By Albertine Randall Wheelan (self-pub) 75.00 125.00 250.00

EDISON - INSPIRATION TO YOUTH (N)(Also see Life of Thomas---)
Thomas A. Edison, Incorporated: 1939 (9-1/2 x 6-1/2, paper cover, B&W)
nn - Photo-c 50.00 150.00 250.00
NOTE: *Reprints strip material found in the 1928 Life of Thomas A. Edison in Word and Picture.*

'ERBIE AND 'IS PLAYMATES
Democratic National Committee: 1932 (8x9-1/2, 16 pgs, B&W)
nn - By Frederick Opper (Rare) 100.00 200.00 425.00
NOTE: *Anti-Hoover/Pro-Roosevelt political comics.*

EXPANSION BEING BART'S BEST CARTOONS FOR 1899
Minneapolis Journal: 1900 (10-1/4x8-1/4", 124 pgs, paperback, B&W)
v2#1 - By Charles L. Bartholomew 24.00 84.00 150.00

FAMOUS COMICS (N)
King Features Synd. (Whitman Pub. Co.): 1934 (100 pgs., daily newspaper-r) (3-1/2x8-1/2"; paper cover)(came in an illustrated box)
684 (#1) - Little Jimmy, Katz Kids & Barney Google 40.00 103.00 275.00
684 (#2) - Polly, Little Jimmy, Katzenjammer Kids 40.00 103.00 275.00
684 (#3) - Little Annie Rooney, Polly and Her Pals, Katzenjammer Kids
40.00 103.00 275.00
Box price... 75.00 150.00 425.00

FAMOUS COMICS CARTOON BOOKS (N)
Whitman Publishing Co.: 1934 (8x7-1/4", 72 pgs, B&W hard-c, daily strip-r)
1200-The Captain & the Kids; Dirks reprints credited to Bernard Dibble 29.00 86.00 210.00
1202-Captain Easy & Wash Tubbs by Roy Crane; 2 slightly different versions of cover exist 34.00 103.00 250.00
1203-Ella Cinders By Conselman & Plumb 28.00 84.00 210.00
1204-Freckles & His Friends 25.00 75.00 200.00
NOTE: *Called Famous Funnies Cartoon Books inside back area sales advertisement.*

FANTASIES IN HA-HA (M)
Meyer Bros & Co.: 1900 (14 x 11-7/8", 64 pgs, color cover hardcover, B&W)
nn - By Hy Mayer 50.00 150.00 300.00

FELIX (N)
Henry Altemus Company: 1931 (6-1/2"x8-1/4", 52 pgs., color, hard-c w/dust jacket)
1-3-Sunday strip reprints of Felix the Cat by Otto Messmer. Book No. 2 r/1931 Sunday panels mostly two to a page in a continuity format oddly arranged so each tier of panels reads across two pages, then drops to the next tier. (Books 1 & 3 have not been documented.)(Rare)
Each 250.00 500.00 1000.00
With dust jacket 250.00 750.00 1400.00

FELIX THE CAT BOOK (N)
McLoughlin Bros.: 1927 (8"x15-3/4", 52 pgs, half in color-half in B&W)
nn - Reprints 23 Sunday strips by Otto Messmer from 1926 & 1927, every other one in color, two pages per strip. (Rare) 200.00 800.00 1700.00
260-Reissued (1931), reformatted to 9-1/2"x10-1/4" (same color plates, but one strip per every three pages), retitled ("Book" dropped from title) and abridged (only eight strips repeated from first issue, 28 pgs.).(Rare) 90.00 350.00 650.00

F. FOX'S FUNNY FOLK (see Toonerville Trolley; Cartoons by Fontaine Fox) (C)
George H. Doran Company: 1917 (10-1/4x8-1/4", 228 pgs, red, B&W cover, B&W interior, hardcover; dust jacket?)
nn - By Fontaine Fox (Toonerville Trolley strip-r) 150.00 450.00 775.00

52 CAREY CARTOONS (O,S)
Carey Cartoon Service, NY: 1915 (25 cents, 6-3/4" x 10-1/2", 118 pgs, printed on one side, color cardboard-c, B&W)
nn - (1915) War – – –
NOTE: *The Carey Cartoon Service supplied a weekly, hand-colored single panel cartoon broadsheet, on current news events, starting in 1906 or 1907, for window display in Carey Fountain Pen chain stores. These broadsheets were 22-1/2" x 33" in size. Starting circa 1915, Carey Fountain Pens began offering subscriptions for the broadsheets to other merchants, for window display in their stores as well. This collects, in B&W, the cartoons for 1915. An "Edition Deluxe" was also advertised, with all cartoons hand colored. It is currently unknown whether a reprint collection was only issued in 1915, or if other editions exist.*

52 LETTERS TO SALESMEN
Steven-Davis Company: 1927 (???)
nn - (Rare) 25.00 100.00 150.00
NOTE: *52 motivational letters to salesmen, with page of comics for each week, bound into embossed leather binder.*

FOLKS IN FUNNYVILLE (S)
R.H. Russell: 1900 (12"x9-1/4", 48 pgs.)(cardboard-c)
nn - By Frederick Opper 300.00 1000.00 –
NOTE: *Reprinted from Hearst's NY Journal American Humorist supplements.*

FOOLISH QUESTIONS (S)
Small, Maynard & Co.: 1909 (6-7/8 x 5-1/2", 174 pgs, hardcover, B&W)
nn - By Rube Goldberg (first Goldberg item) 100.00 300.00 500.00
NOTE: *Comic strip began Oct 23, 1908 running thru 1941. Also drawn by George Frink in 1909.*

FOOLISH QUESTIONS THAT ARE ASKED BY ALL
Levi Strauss & Co./Small, Maynard & Co.: 1909 (5-1/2x5-3/4", 24 pgs, paper-c, B&W)
nn- (Rare) by Rube Goldberg 65.00 175.00 350.00

FOOLISH QUESTIONS (Boxed card set) (S)
Wallie Dorr Co., N.Y.: 1919 (5-1/4x3-3/4")(box & card backs are red)
nn - Boxed set w/52 B&W comics on cards; each a single panel gag complete set w/box
75.00 263.00 475.00
NOTE: *There are two diff sets put out simultaneously with the first set, by the same company. One set continues/picks up the numbering of the cards from the other set.*

FOOLISH QUESTIONS (S)
EmBee Distributing Co.: 1921 (10¢, 4x5 1/2; 52 pgs, 3 color covers; B&W)
1-By Rube Goldberg 46.00 160.00 300.00

FOXY GRANDPA
Foxy Grandpa Company, 33 Wall St, NY : 1900 (9x15", 84 pgs, full color, cardboard-c)
nn - By Carl Schultze (By Permission of New York Herald) 271.00 1200.00 –
NOTE: *This seminal comic strip began Jan 7, 1900 and was collected later that same year.*

FOXY GRANDPA (Also see The Funnies, 1st series) (N)
N. Y. Herald/Frederick A. Stokes Co./M. A. Donahue & Co./Bunny Publ. (L. R. Hammersly Co.): 1901 - 1916 (Strip-r in color, hard-c)
1901- 9x15" in color-N. Y. Herald 313.00 1000.00 –
1902- "Latest Larks of...", 32 pgs., 9-1/2x15-1/2" 164.00 575.00 –
1902- "The Many Advs. of...", 9x12", 148 pgs., Hammersly Co.
179.00 625.00 –
1903- "Latest Advs.", 9x15", 24 pgs., Hammersly Co. 164.00 575.00 –
1903- "...'s New Advs.", 11x15", 66 pgs., Stokes 164.00 575.00 –
1904- "Up to Date", 10x15", 66 pgs., Stokes 146.00 510.00 920.00
1904- "The Many Adventures of...", 9x15, 144pgs, Donohue 146.00 510.00 920.00
1905- "& Flip-Flaps", 9-1/2x15-1/2", 52 pgs. 146.00 510.00 920.00
1905- "The Latest Advs. of...", 9x15", 28, 52, & 68 pgs, M.A. Donohue Co.; re-issue of 1902 issue 104.00 365.00 725.00
1905- "Latest Larks of...", 9-1/2x15-1/2", 52 pgs., Donahue; re-issue of 1902 issue with more pages added 104.00 365.00 725.00
1905- "Latest Larks of...", 9-1/2x15-1/2", 24 pgs. edition, Donahue; re-issue of 1902 issue 104.00 365.00 725.00
1905- "Merry Pranks of...", 9-1/2x15-1/2", 28, 52 & 62 pgs., Donahue
104.00 365.00 725.00
1905-"...Surprises",10x15", color, 64 pg,Stokes, 60¢ 104.00 365.00 725.00
1906- "Frolics", 10x15", 30 pgs., Stokes 104.00 365.00 725.00
1907?-"...& His Boys",10x15", 64 color pgs, Stokes 104.00 365.00 725.00
1907- "Triumphs", 10x15", 62 pgs, Stokes 104.00 365.00 725.00
1908-"...Mother Goose", Stokes 104.00 365.00 725.00
1909- "...& Little Brother", 10x15, 58 pgs, Stokes 104.00 365.00 725.00

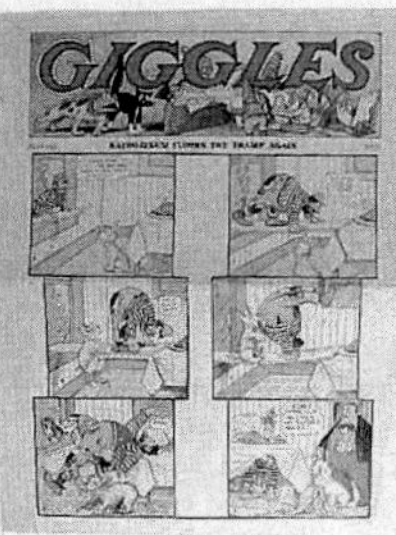
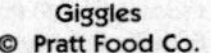
Giggles
© Pratt Food Co.

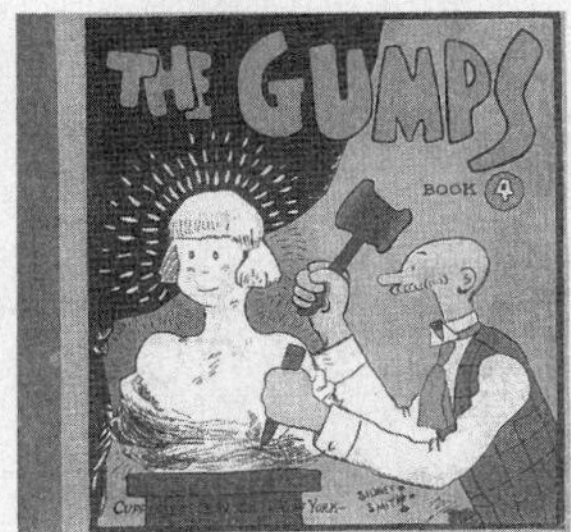

The Gumps by Sidney Smith
1927? © Cupples & Leon

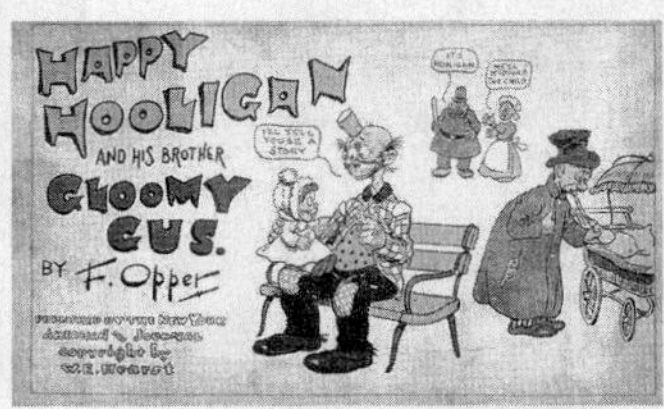

Happy Hooligan Book 1 1902
© Frederick A. Stokes

GD2.0 FN6.0 VF8.0

1911- "Latest Tricks", r-1910,1911 Sundays-Stokes Co. 104.00 365.00 725.00
1914-(9-1/2x15-1/2", 24 pgs.)-6 color cartoons/page, Bunny Publ. Co.
88.00 306.00 610.00
1915 - ...Always Jolly (10x16, Stokes) 88.00 306.00 610.00
1916- "Merry Book", (10x15", 64 pgs, Stokes) 88.00 306.00 610.00
1917-"...Adventures (5 1/2 x 6 1/2, 26 pgs, Stokes) 57.00 200.00 450.00
1917-"...Frolics (5 1/2 x 6 1/2, 26 pgs, Stokes) 57.00 200.00 450.00
1917-"...Triumphs (5 1/2 x 6 1/2, 26 pgs, Stokes) 57.00 200.00 450.00

FOXY GRANDPA, FUNNY TRICKS OF (The Stump Books)
M.A. Donahue Co, Chicago: approx 1903 (1-7/8x6-3/8", 44 pgs, blue hardcover)
nn - By Carl Schultze 54.00 189.00 330.00
NOTE: *One of a series of ten "stump" books; the only comics one.*

FOXY GRANDPA'S MOTHER GOOSE (I)
Stokes: October 1903 (10-11/16x8-1/2", 86 pgs, hard-c)
nn - By Carl Schultze (not comics - illustrated book) 54.00 189.00 330.00

FOXY GRANDPA SPARKLETS SERIES (N)
M. A. Donahue & Co.: 1908 (7-3/4x6-1/2"; 24 pgs., color)
"... Rides the Goat", "...& His Boys", "...Playing Ball", "...Fun on the Farm", "...Fancy Shooting", "...Show His Boys Up-To-Date Sports", "...Plays Santa Claus"
each.... 88.00 306.00 525.00
900- "Playing Ball"; Bunny illos; 8 pgs., linen like pgs., no date
73.00 254.00 435.00

FOXY GRANDPA VISITS RICHMOND (O,P)
Dietz Printing Co., Richmond, VA / Hotel Rueger: nd (c1920's) (5-7/8" x 4-1/2", 16 pgs, paper-c, B&W)
nn - (Scarce) By Bunny 50.00 100.00 250.00
NOTE: *Promotional comic given away to its guests by the Hotel Rueger, about Foxy Grandpa visiting and enjoying the Hotel. Originally came in an envelope, with the words "Foxy Grandpa Visits Richmond -- and Rueger's" printed on it.*

FOXY GRANDPA VISITS WASHINGTON, D.C. (P)
Dietz Printing Co., Richmond, VA / Hamilton Hotel: nd (c1920's) (5-7/8" x 4-1/2", 16 pgs, paper-c, B&W)
nn - (Scarce) By Bunny 50.00 100.00 185.00
NOTE: *Mostly reprints "... Visits Richmond", changing all references to Hotel Rueger, to Hamilton Hotel instead. Also, changes depictions of a waiter and a cook from black to white, plus incompletely erases the cover art on a book Foxy Grandpa falls asleep with (the latter is how we know that the Richmond version was first).*

FRAGMENTS FROM FRANCE (S)
G. P. Putnam & Sons: 1917 (9x6-1/4", 168 pgs, hardcover, $1.75)
nn - By Bruce Bairnsfather 25.00 88.00 150.00
NOTE: *WW1 trench warfare cartoons; color dust jacket.*

FUNNIES, THE (H) (See Clancy the Cop, Deadwood Gulch, Bug Movies)
Dell Publishing Co.: 1929 - No. 36, 10/18/30 (10¢; 5¢ No. 22 on) (16 pgs.)
Full tabloid size in color; not reprints; published every Saturday
1-My Big Brudder, Jonathan, Jazzbo & Jim, Foxy Grandpa, Sniffy, Jimmy Jams & other strips begin; first four-color comic newsstand publication; also contains magic, puzzles & stories 200.00 700.00 1425.00
2-21 (1930, 10¢) 150.00 300.00 600.00
22(nn-7/12/30-5¢) 150.00 300.00 600.00
23(nn-7/19/30-5¢), 24(nn-7/26/30-5¢), 25(nn-8/2/30), 26(nn-8/9/30), 27(nn-8/16/30), 28(nn-8/23/30), 29(nn-8/30/30), 30(nn-9/6/30), 31(nn-9/13/30), 32(nn-9/20/30), 33(nn-9/27/30), 34(nn-10/4/30), 35(nn-10/11/30), 36(nn, no date-10/18/30)
each.... 150.00 300.00 600.00

GASOLINE ALLEY (Also see Popular Comics & Super Comics) (N)
Reilly & Lee Publishers: 1929 (8-3/4x7", B&W daily strip-r, hard-c)
nn - By King (96 pgs.) 125.00 300.00 600.00
with scarce Dust Wrapper 250.00 500.00 1000.00
NOTE: *Of all the Frank King reprint books, this is the only one to reprint actual complete newspaper strips - all others are illustrated prose text stories.*

GIBSON'S PUBLISHED DRAWINGS, MR. (M,S) (see Victorian index for earlier issues)
R.H. Russell, New York: No.1 1894 - No. 9 1904 (11x17-3/4", hard-c, B&W)
nn (No.6; 1901) A Widow and her Friends (90 pgs.) 30.00 60.00 130.00
nn (No.7; 1902) The Social Ladder (88 pgs.) 30.00 60.00 130.00
8 - 1903 The Weaker Sex (88 pgs.) 30.00 60.00 130.00
9 - 1904 Everyday People (88 pgs.) 30.00 60.00 130.00
NOTE: *By Charles Dana Gibson cartoons, reprinted from magazines, primarily LIFE. The Education of Mr. Pipp tells a story. Series continues how long after 1904?*

GIGGLES
Pratt Food Co., Philadelphia, PA: 1908-09? (12x9", 8 pgs, color, 5 cents-c)
1-8: By Walt McDougall (#8 dated March 1909) 40.00 175.00 -
NOTE: *Appears to be monthly; almost tabloid size; yearly subscriptions was 25 cents.*

GOD'S MAN (H)
Jonathan Cape and Harrison Smith Inc.: 1929 (8-1/4x6", 298 pgs, B&W hardcover w/dust jacket) (original graphic novel in wood cuts)
nn - By Lynd Ward 43.00 171.00 300.00

GOLD DUST TWINS
N. K. Fairbank Co.: 1904 (4-5/8x6-3/4", 18 pgs, color and B&W)
nn - By E. W. Kemble (Rare) 50.00 100.00 200.00
NOTE: *Promo comic for Gold DustWashing Powder; includes page of watercolor paints.*

GOLF
Volland Co.: 1916 (9x12-3/4", 132 pgs, hard-c, B&W)
nn - By Clair Briggs 100.00 200.00 400.00

GUMPS, THE (N)
Landfield-Kupfer: No. 1, 1918 - No. 6, 1921; (B&W Daily strip-r)
Book No. 1(1918)(scarce)-cardboard-c, 5-1/4x13-1/3", 64 pgs., daily strip-r by Sidney Smith 75.00 250.00 500.00
Book No.2(1918)-(scarce); 5-1/4x13-1/3"; paper cover; 36 pgs. daily strip reprints by Sidney Smith 75.00 250.00 500.00
Book No. 3 100.00 350.00 700.00
Book No. 4 (1918) 5-3/8x13-7/8", 20 pgs. Color card-c 100.00 350.00 700.00
Book No. 5 10-1/4x13-1/2", 20 pgs. Color paper-c 100.00 350.00 700.00
Book No. 6 (Rare, 20 pgs, 8x13-3/8, strip-r 1920-21) 121.00 423.00 750.00

GUMPS, ANDY AND MIN, THE (N)
Landfield-Kupfer Printing Co., Chicago/Morrison Hotel: nd (1920s) (Giveaway, 5-1/2"x14", 20 pgs., B&W, soft-c)
nn - Strip-r by Sidney Smith; art & logo embossed on cover w/hotel restaurant menu on back-c or a hotel promo ad; 4 different contents of issues known
50.00 175.00 300.00

GUMPS, THE (N)
Cupples & Leon: 1924-1930 (10x10, 52 pgs, B&W)
1 - By Sidney Smith 75.00 250.00 400.00
2-7 39.00 154.00 275.00

THE GUMPS (P)
Cupples & Leon Company: 1924 (9 x 7-1/2", 28 pgs, paper cover)
nn (1924) 50.00 175.00 275.00
NOTE: *Promotional comic for Sunshine Andy Gump Biscuits. Daily strip-r from 1922-24.*

GUMP'S CARTOON BOOK, THE (N)
The National Arts Company: 1931 (13-7/8x10", 36 pgs, color covers, B&W)
nn - By Sidney Smith 57.00 228.00 400.00

GUMPS PAINTING BOOK, THE (N)
The National Arts Company: 1931 (11 x 15 1/4", 20 pgs, half in full color)
nn - By Sidney Smith 57.00 228.00 400.00

HALT FRIENDS! (see also **HELLO BUDDY**)
???: 1918? (4-3/8x5-3/4", 36 pgs, color-c, B&W, no cover price listed)
nn - Unknown 20.00 40.00 100.00
NOTE: *Says on front cover: "Comics of War Facts of Service Sold on its merits by Unemployed or Disabled Ex-Service Men. Credentials Shown On Request. Price - Pay What You Please." These are very common; contents vary widely.*

HAMBONE'S MEDITATIONS
Jahl & Co.: no date 1920 (6-1/8 x 7-1/2, 108 pgs, paper cover, B&W)
nn - By J. P. Alley 50.00 150.00 300.00
NOTE: *Reprint of racist single panel newspaper series, 2 cartoons per page.*

HAN OLA OG PER (N)
Anundsen Publishing Co, Decorah, Iowa: 1927 (10-3/8 x 15-3/4", 54 pgs, paper-c, B&W)
nn - American origin Norwegian language strips-r 33.00 131.00 230.00
NOTE: *1940s and modern reprints exist.*

HANS UND FRITZ (N)
The Saalfield Publishing Co.: 1917, 1927-29 (10x13-1/2", 28 pgs., B&W)
nn - By R. Dirks (1917, r-1916 strips) 96.00 335.00 600.00
nn - By R. Dirks (1923 edition- reprint of 1917 edition) 58.00 204.00 350.00
nn - By R. Dirks (1926 edition- reprint of 1917 edition) 58.00 204.00 350.00
The Funny Larks Of... By R. Dirks (©1917 outside cover; ©1916 inside indicia)
96.00 335.00 600.00
The Funny Larks Of... (1927) reprints 1917 edition of 1916 strips Halloween-c 58.00 204.00 350.00
The Funny Larks Of... 2 (1929) 58.00 204.00 350.00
193 - By R. Dirks; contains 1916 Sunday strip reprints of Katzenjammer Kids & Hawkshaw the Detective - reprint of 1917 nn edition (1929) this edition is not rare
58.00 204.00 350.00

HAPPY DAYS (S)
Coward-McCann Inc.: 1929 (12-1/2x9-5/8", 110 pgs, hardcover B&W)
nn - By Alban Butler (WW 1 cartoons) 20.00 60.00 125.00

HAPPY HOOLIGAN (See Alphonse...) (N)
Hearst's New York American & Journal: 1902,1903
Book 1-(1902)-"And His Brother Gloomy Gus", By Fred Opper; has 1901-02-r; (yellow & black)(86 pgs.)(10x15-1/4") 600.00 1800.00 3300.00
New Edition, 1903 -10x15" 82 pgs. in color 350.00 1400.00 -

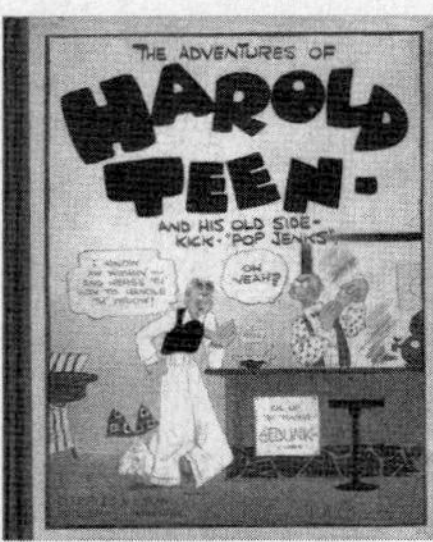

Harold Teen #2 by Carl Ed
1931 © Cupples & Leon

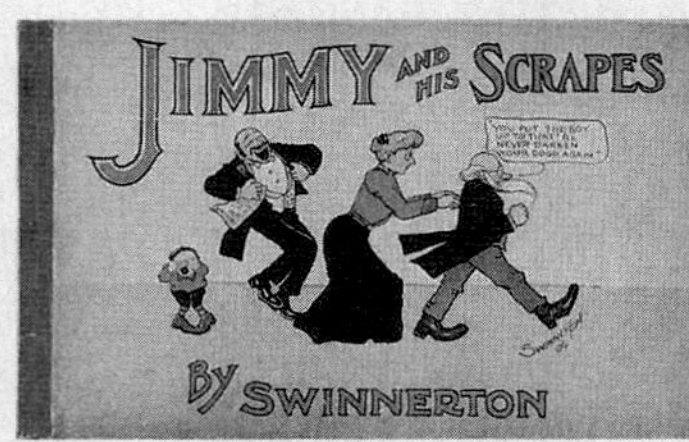

Jimmy and His Scrapes
© Frederick A. Stokes

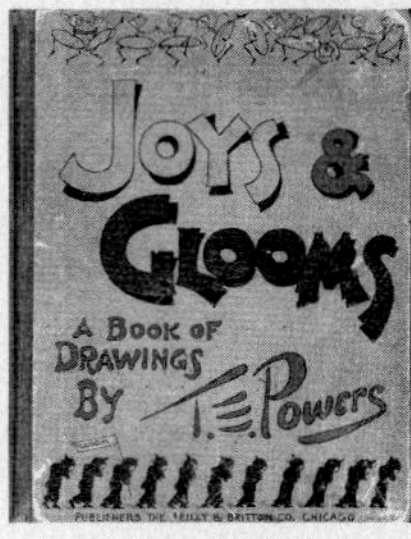

Joys & Glooms By T.E. Powers
1912 © Reilly & Britton Co.

GD2.0 FN6.0 VF8.0

NOTE: *Strip ran March 26, 1900-Aug 14, 1932 and is widely recognized as setting the format standard for all newspaper comic strips which came after it. Opper (1857-1937) was going blind towards the end.*

HAPPY HOOLIGAN (N) (By Fredrick Opper)
Frederick A. Stokes Co.: 1906-08 (10-1/4x15-3/4", cardboard color-c)
1906 - :Travels of...), 68 pgs,10-1/4x15-3/4", 1905-r 450.00 1000.00 –
1907 - "--Home Again", 68 pgs., 10x15-3/4", 60¢; full color-c 450.00 1000.00 –
1908 - "Handy--", 68 pgs, color 450.00 1000.00 –

HAPPY HOOLIGAN, THE STORY OF (G)
McLoughlin Bros.: No. 281, 1932 (12x9-1/2", 20 pgs., soft-c)
281-Three-color text, pictures on heavy paper 57.00 228.00 400.00
NOTE: *An homage to Opper's creation on its 30th Anniversary in 1932.*

HAROLD HARDHIKE'S REJUVENATION
O'Sullivan Rubber: 1917 (6-1/4x3-1/2, 16 pgs, B&W)
nn 25.00 100.00 200.00
NOTE: *Comic book to promote rubber shoe heels.*

HAROLD TEEN (N)
Cupples & Leon Co.: 1929 (9-7/8x9-7/8", 52 pgs, cardboard covers)
1 - By Carl Ed 50.00 200.00 500.00
nn - (1931, 8-11/16x6-7/8", 96 pgs, hardcover w/dj) 41.00 164.00 290.00
NOTE: *Title 2nd book:* ***HAROLD TEEN AND HIS OLD SIDE-KICK– POP JENKINS,*** *(Adv. of...). Precursor for Archie Andrews & crew; strip began May 4, 1919 running into 1959.*

HAROLD TEEN PAINT AND COLOR BOOK (N)
McLoughlin Bros Inc.: 1932 (13x9-3/4, 28 pgs, B&W and color)
#2054 25.00 100.00 200.00

HAWKSHAW THE DETECTIVE (See Advs. of..., Hans Und Fritz & Okay) (N)
The Saalfield Publishing Co.: 1917 (10-1/2x13-1/2", 24 pgs., B&W)
nn - By Gus Mager (Sunday strip-r) 54.00 190.00 325.00
nn - By Gus Mayer (1923 reprint of 1917 edition) 25.00 100.00 175.00
nn - By Gus Mager (1926 reprint of 1917 edition) 25.00 100.00 175.00
NOTE: *Runs Feb 23, 1913-Sept 4, 1922, starts again from Dec 13, 1931-Feb 11, 1952; Sherlock Holmes spoof.*

HEALTH IN PICTURES
American Public Health Association, NYC: 1930 (6-1/2" x 5-3/16", 76 pgs, green & black paper-c, B&W interior)
nn - By various 20.00 55.00 125.00
NOTE: *Collection of strips and cartoons put out by the Public Health Association, on topics ranging from boating and food safety, to small pox and typhoid prevention.*

HE DONE HER WRONG (O) (see also BANANA OIL)
Doubleday, Doran & Company: 1930 (8-1/4x 7-1/4", 276pgs, hard-c with dust jacket, B&W interiors)
nn - By Milt Gross 75.00 225.00 400.00
NOTE: *A seminal original-material wordless graphic novel, not reprints. Several modern reprints.*

HELLO BUDDY (see also **HALT FRIENDS**)
???: 1919? (4-3/8x5-3/4", 36 pgs, color-c, B&W, 15¢)
nn - Unknown 10.00 30.00 100.00
NOTE: *Says on front cover: "Comics of War Facts of Service Sold on its merits by Unemployed or Disabled Ex-Service Men." These are very common; contents vary widely.*

HENRY (N)
David McKay Co.: 1935 (25¢, soft-c)
Book 1 - By Carl Anderson 57.00 200.00 400.00
NOTE: *Strip began March 19 1932; this book ties with Popeye (David McKay) and Little Annie Rooney (David McKay) as the last of the 10x10" Platinum Age comic books.*

HENRY (M)
Greenberg Publishers Inc.: 1935 (11-1/4x 8-5/8", 72 pgs, red & blue color hard-c, dust jacket, B&W interiors) (strip-r from Saturday Evening Post)
nn - By Carl Anderson 57.00 200.00 400.00

HIGH KICKING KELLYS, THE (M)
Vaudeville News Corporation, NY: 1926 (5x11", B&W, two color soft-c)
nn - By Jack A. Ward (scarce) 40.00 160.00 280.00

HIGHLIGHTS OF HISTORY (N)
World Syndicate Publishing Co.: 1933-34 (4-1/2x4", 288 pgs)
nn - 5 different unnumbered issues; daily strip-r 25.00 50.00 100.00
NOTE: *Titles include Buffalo Bill, Daniel Boone, Kit Carson, Pioneers of the Old West, Winning of the Old Northwest. There are line drawing color covers and embossed hardcover versions. It is unknown which came out first.*

HOMER HOLCOMB AND MAY (N)
no publisher listed: 1920s (4 x 9-1/2", 40 pgs, paper cover, B&W)
nn - By Doc Bird Finch (strip-r) 10.00 40.00 70.00

HOME, SWEET HOME (N)
M.S. Publishing Co.: 1925 (10-1/4x10")
nn - By Tuthill 33.00 134.00 235.00

GD2.0 FN6.0 VF8.0

HOW THEY DRAW PROHIBITION (S)
Association Against Prohibition: 1930 (10x9", 100 pgs.)
nn - Single panel and multi-panel comics (rare) 71.00 285.00 500.00
NOTE: *Contains art by J.N. "Ding" Darling, James Flagg, Rollin Kirby, Winsor McCay, T.E. Powers, H.T. Webster, others. Also comes with a loose sheet listing all the newspapers where the cartoons originally appeared.*

HOW TO BE A CARTOONIST (H)
Saalfield Pub. Co: 1936 (10-3/8x12-1/2", 16 pgs, color-c, B&W)
nn - By Chas. H. Kuhn 15.00 50.00 100.00

HOW TO DRAW: A PRACTICAL BOOK OF INSTRUCTION (H)
Harper & Brothers: 1904 (9-1/4x12-3/8", 128 pgs, hardcover, B&W)
nn - Edited By Leon Barritt 57.00 228.00 400.00
NOTE: *Strips reprinted include: "Buster Brown" by Outcault, "Foxy Grandpa" by Bunny, "Happy Hooligan" by Opper, "Katzenjammer Kids" by Dirks, "Lady Bountiful" by Gene Carr, "Mr. Jack" by Swinnerton, "Panhandle Pete" by George McManus, "Mr E.Z. Mark" by F.M. Howarth others; non-character strips by Hy Mayer, Winsor McCay, T.E. Powers, others; single panel cartoons by Davenport, Frost, McDougall, Nast, W.A. Rogers, Sullivant, others.*

HOW TO DRAW CARTOONS (H)
Garden City Publishing Co.: 1926, 1937 (10 1/4 x 7 1/2, 150 pgs)
1926 first edition By Clare Briggs 25.00 75.00 150.00
1937 2nd edition By Clare Briggs 20.00 60.00 120.00
NOTE: *Seminal "how to" break into the comics syndicates with art by Briggs, Fisher, Goldberg, King, Webster, Opper, Tad, Hershfield, McCay, Ding, others. Came with Dust Jacket -add 50%.*

HOW TO DRAW FUNNY PICTURES: A Complete Course in Cartooning (H)
Frederick J. Drake & Co., Chicago: 1936 (10-3/8x6-7/8", 168 pgs, hardcover, B&W)
nn - By E.C. Matthews (200 illus by Eugene Zimmerman) 20.00 60.00 120.00

HY MAYER (M)
Puck Publishing: 1915 (13-1/2 x 20-3/4", 52 pgs, hardcover cover, color & B&W interiors)
nn - By Hy Mayer(strip reprints from Puck) 40.00 140.00 300.00

HYSTERICAL HISTORY OF THE CIVILIAN CONSERVATION CORPS
Peerless Engraving: 1934 (10-3/4x7-1/2", 104 pgs, soft-c, B&W)
nn - By various 20.00 60.00 125.00
NOTE: *Comics about CCC life, includes two color insert postcards in back.*

INDOOR SPORTS (N,S)
National Specials Co., New York: nd circa 1912 (25 cents, 6 x 9", 68 pgs, B&W)
nn - Tad 35.00 125.00 250.00
NOTE: *Cartoons reprinted from Hearst papers.*

IT HAPPENS IN THE BEST FAMILIES (N)
Powers Photo Engraving Co.: 1920 (52 pgs.)(9-1/2x10-3/4")
nn - By Briggs; B&W Sunday strips-r 29.00 114.00 220.00
Special Railroad Edition (30¢)-r/strips from 1914-1920 26.00 103.00 200.00

JIMMIE DUGAN AND THE REG'LAR FELLERS (N)
Cupples & Leon: 1921, 46 pgs. (11"x16")
nn - By Gene Byrne 71.00 284.00 500.00
NOTE: *Ties with EmBee's Mutt & Jeff and Trouble of Bringing Up Father as the last of this size.*

JIMMY (N) (see Little Jimmy Picture & Story Book)
N. Y. American & Journal: 1905 (10x15", 84 pgs., color)
nn - By Jimmy Swinnerton (scarce) 300.00 800.00 1700.00
NOTE: *James Swinnerton was one of the original first pioneers of the American newspaper comic strip.*

JIMMY AND HIS SCRAPES (N)
Frederick A. Stokes: 1906, (10-1/4x15-1/4", 66 pgs, cardboard-c, color)
nn - By Jimmy Swinnerton (scarce) 300.00 800.00 1600.00

JOE PALOOKA (N)
Cupples & Leon Co.: 1933 (9-13/16x10", 52 pgs., B&W daily strip-r)
nn - By Ham Fisher (scarce) 150.00 500.00 900.00

JOHN, JONATHAN AND MR. OPPER BY F. OPPER (S,I,N)
Grant, Richards, 48 Leicester Square, W.C.: 1903 (9-5/8x8-3/8", 108 pgs, hard-c B&W)
nn - Opper (Scarce) 50.00 200.00 400.00
NOTE: *British precursor-type companion to* Willie And His Poppa *reprints from Hearst's* NY American & Journal *Opper cartoons interfacing* Uncle Sam *precursor* Brother Jonathan, John Bull. *Uses name* Happy Hooligan *in one cartoon, has* John Bull *smoking opium in another.*

JOLLY POLLY'S BOOK OF ENGLISH AND ETIQUETTE (S)
Jos. J. Frisch: 1931 (60 cents, 8 x 5-1/8, 88 pgs, paper-c, B&W)
nn - By Jos. J. Frisch 20.00 60.00 125.00
NOTE: *Reprint of single panel newspaper series, 4 per page, of English and etiquette lessons taught by a flapper.*

JOYS AND GLOOMS (N)
Reilly & Britton Co.: 1912 (11x8", 72 pgs, hard-c, B&W interior)
nn - By T. E. Powers (newspaper strip-r) 39.00 156.00 325.00

JUDGE - yet to be indexed

JUDGE'S LIBRARY - yet to be indexed

The Cruise of the Katzenjammer Kids
© NY American & Journal

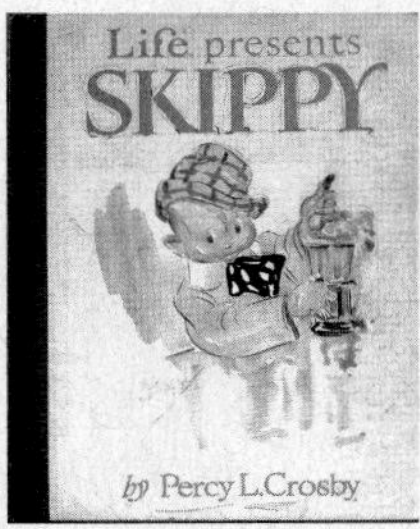

Life Presents Skippy by Percy L. Crosby
1924 © Life Publishing Company

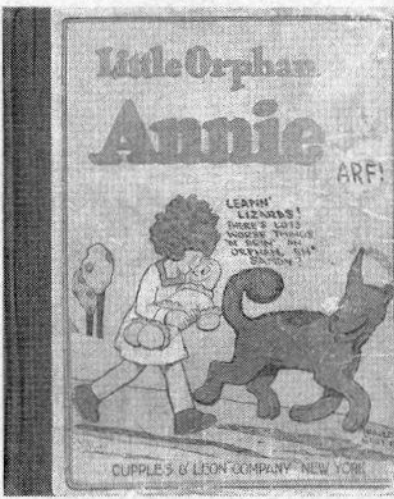

Little Orphan Annie 1926
© C&L

GD2.0 FN6.0 VF8.0 | **GD2.0 FN6.0 VF8.0**

JUST KIDS COMICS FOR CRAYON COLORING
King Features. NYC: 1928 (11x8-1/2, 16 pgs, soft-c)
nn - By Ad Carter 33.00 100.00 210.00
NOTE: *Porous better grade paper; top pics printed in color; lower in b&w to color.*

JUST KIDS, THE STORY OF (I)
McLoughlin Bros.: 1932 (12x9-1/2", 20 pgs., paper-c)
283-Three-color text, pictures on heavy paper 30.00 125.00 260.00

KAPTIN KIDDO AND PUPPO (N)
Frederick A. Stokes Co.: 1910-1913 (11x16-1/2", 62 pgs)
1910-By Grace Wiederseim (later Drayton) 50.00 150.00 260.00
1910-Turr-ble Tales of... By Grace Wiederseim (Edward Stern & Co., 11x16-1/2", 64 pgs.) 50.00 150.00 260.00
1913- ...'Speriences By Grace Drayton 50.00 150.00 260.00
NOTE: *Strip ran approx. 1909-1912.*

KATZENJAMMER KIDS, THE (Also see Hans Und Fritz) (N)
New York American & Journal: 1902,1903 (10x15-1/4", 86 pgs., color)
(By Rudolph Dirks; strip first appeared in 1897) © W.R. Hearst
NOTE: *All KK books 1902-1905 all have the same exact title page with a 1902 copyright by W.R. Hearst; almost always look instead on the front cover.*
1902 (Rare) (red & black); has 1901-02 strips 1000.00 2600.00 -
1903- **A New Edition** (Rare), 86 pgs 800.00 2100.00 -
1904- 10x15", 84 pgs 250.00 900.00 -
1905?-The Cruise of the, 10x15", 60¢, in color 250.00 900.00 -
1905-A Series of Comic Pictures, 10x15", 84 pgs. in color, possible reprint of 1904 edition 250.00 800.00 -
1905-Tricks of... (10x15", 66 pgs, Stokes) 250.00 800.00 -
1906-Stokes (10x16", 32 pgs. in color) 186.00 800.00 -
1907- The Cruise of the, 10x15", 62 pgs 1905-r? 186.00 800.00 -
1910-The Komical...(10x15) 150.00 450.00 800.00
1921-Embee Dist. Co., 10x16", 20 pgs. in color 150.00 450.00 800.00

KATZENJAMMER KIDS MAGIC DRAWING AND COLORING BOOK (N)
Sam L Gabriel Sons And Company: 1931 (8 1/2 x 12", 36 pages, stiff-c
838-By Knerr 50.00 200.00 350.00

KEEPING UP WITH THE JONESES (N)
Cupples & Leon Co.: 1920 - No. 2, 1921 (9-1/4x9-1/4",52 pgs.,B&W daily strip-r)
1,2-By Pop Momand 39.00 154.00 290.00

KID KARTOONS (N,S)
The Century Co.: 1922 (232 pgs, printed 1 side, 9-3/4 x 7-3/4", hard-c, B&W)
nn - By Gene Carr (Metropolitan Movies strip-r) 60.00 240.00 -

KING OF THE ROYAL MOUNTED (Also See Dan Dunn) (N)
Whitman Publishing: 1937 (5 1/2 x 7 1/4", 68 pgs., color cardboard-c, B&W)
1010 36.00 144.00 250.00

LADY BOUNTIFUL (N)
Saalfield Publ. Co./Press Publ. Co.: 1917 (13-3/8x10", 36 pgs, color cardboard-c, B&W interiors)
nn - By Gene Carr; 2 panels per page 50.00 150.00 280.00
193S - 2nd printing (13-1/8x10",28 pgs color-c, B&W) 33.00 117.00 200.00

LAUGHS YOU MIGHT HAVE HAD From The Comic Pages of Six Week Day Issues of the Post-Dispatch (N)
St. Louis Post-Dispatch: 1921 (9 x 10 1/2", 28 pgs, B&W, red ink cover)
nn - Various comic strips 39.00 154.00 270.00

LIFE, DOGS FROM (M)
Doubleday, Page & Company: nn 1920 - No.2 1926 (130 pgs, 11-1/4 x 9", color painted-c, hard-c, B&W)
nn (No.1) 120.00 360.00 -
Second Litter 80.00 320.00 -
NOTE: *Reprints strips & cartoons featuring dogs, from Life Magazine. Edited by Thomas L. Masson. Highly sought by collectors of dog ephemera. Art in both books is mostly by Robert L. Dickey. Other art: Carl Anderson-1,2; Barbes-1; Chip Bellew-1; Lang Campbell-1,2; Percy Crosby-1,2; Edwina-2; Frueh-2; R.B. Fuller-1; Gibson-1,2; Don Herold-2; Gus Mager-2; Orr-1; J.R. Shaver-1,2; T.S. Sullivant-2; Russ Westover-1,2; Crawford Young-1.*

LIFE OF DAVY CROCKETT IN PICTURE AND STORY, THE
Cupples & Leon: 1935 (8-3/4x7", 64 pgs, B&W hard-c, dust jacket)
nn - By C. Richard Schaare 29.00 116.00 235.00

LIFE OF THOMAS A. EDISON IN WORD AND PICTURE, THE (N)(Also see Edison...)
Thomas A. Edison Industries: 1928 (10x8", 56 pgs, paper cover, B&W)
nn - Photo-c 100.00 250.00 400.00
NOTE: *Reprints newspaper strip which ran August to November 1927.*

LIFE'S LITTLE JOKES (S)
M.S. Publ. Co.: No date (1924)(10-1/16x10", 52 pgs., B&W)
nn - By Rube Goldberg 64.00 257.00 550.00

LIFE, MINIATURE (see also LIFE (miniature reprint of of issue No. 1)) (M,P,S)
Life Publishing Co.: No. 1 - No. 4 1913, 1916, 1919 (5-3/4x4-5/8", 20 pgs, color paper-c
1- 3 (1913) 4 (1916) 5 (1919) (no known sales)
NOTE: *Giveaway item from Life, to promote subscriptions. All reprint material. No.2: James Montgomery Flagg-c; a-Chip Bellew, Gus Dirks, Gibson, F.M.Howarth, Art Young.*

LIFE'S PRINTS (was **LIFE'S PICTURE GALLERY** - See Victorian Age section) (M,S,P)
Life Publishing Company, New York: nd (c1907) (7x4-1/2", 132 pgs, paper cover, B&W)
nn - (nd; c1907) unillustrated black construction paper cover; reprints art from 1895-1907; art by J.M.Flagg, A.B.Frost, Gibson (Scarce) - - -
nn - (nd; c1908) b&w cardboard painted cover by Gibson, showing angel raising a champagne glass; reprints art from 1901-1908; art by J.M.Flagg, A.B.Frost, Gibson, Walt Kuhn, Art Young (Scarce) - - -
NOTE: *Catalog of prints reprinted from LIFE covers & centerspreads. There are likely more as yet unreported catalogs.*

LIFE, THE COMEDY OF LIFE
Life Publishing Company: 1907 (130 pgs, 11-3/4x9-1/4",embossed printed cloth covered board-c, B+W
nn - By various 30.00 100.00 150.00
NOTE: *Single cartoons and some sequential cartoons). Artists include Charles Dana Gibson, Harrison Cady, E.W. Kemble, James Montgomery Flagg.*

LILY OF THE ALLEY IN THE FUNNIES
Whitman Publishing Co.: No date (1927) (10-1/4x15-1/2"; 28 pgs., color)
W936 - By T. Burke (Rare) 57.00 228.00 400.00

LITTLE ANNIE ROONEY (N)
David McKay Co.: 1935 (25¢, soft-c)
Book 1 43.00 172.00 350.00
NOTE: *Ties with Henry & Popeye (David McKay) as the last of the 10x10" size Plat comic books.*

LITTLE ANNIE ROONEY WISHING BOOK (G) (See Happy Hooligan, Story of #281)
McLoughlin Bros.: 1932 (12x9-1/2", 16 pgs., soft-c, 3-color text, heavier paper)
282 - By Darrell McClure 41.00 144.00 280.00

LITTLE BIRD TOLD ME, A (E)
Life Publishing Co.: 1905? (96 pgs, hardbound)
nn - By Walt Kuhn (Life-r) 41.00 144.00 280.00

LITTLE FOLKS PAINTING BOOK (N)
The National Arts Company: 1931 (10-7/8 x 15-1/4", 20 pgs, half in full color)
nn - By "Tack" Knight (strip-r) 41.00 144.00 280.00

LITTLE JIMMY PICTURE AND STORY BOOK (I) (see Jimmy)
McLaughlin Bros., Inc.: 1932 (13-1/4 x 9-3/4", 20 pgs, cardstock color cover)
284 Text by Marion Kincaid; illus by Swinnerton 57.00 228.00 400.00

LITTLE JOHNNY & THE TEDDY BEARS (Judge-r) (M) (see Teddy Bear Books)
Reilly & Britton Co.: 1907 (10x14".; 68 pgs, green, red, black interior color)
nn - By J. R. Bray-a/Robert D. Towne-s 67.00 233.00 400.00

LITTLE JOURNEY TO THE HOME OF BRIGGS THE SKY-ROCKET, THE
Lockhart Art School: 1917 (10-3/4x7-7/8", 20 pgs, B&W) (I)
nn - About Clare Briggs (bio & lots of early art) 41.00 144.00 280.00

LITTLE KING, THE (see New Yorker Cartoon Albums for 1st appearance) (M)
Farrar & Reinhart, Inc: 1933 (10-1/4 x 8-3/4, 80 pgs, hardcover w/dust jacket
nn - By Otto Soglow (strip-r The New Yorker) 125.00 250.00 500.00
NOTE: *Copies with dust jacket are worth 50% more. Also exists in a 12x8-3/4 edition.*

LITTLE LULU BY MARGE (M)
Rand McNally & Company, Chicago: 1936 (6-9/16x6", 68 pgs, yellow hard-c, B&W)
nn - By Marjorie Henderson Buell 50.00 130.00 300.00
NOTE: *Begins reprinting single panel Little Lulu cartoons which began with Saturday Evening Post Feb. 23, 1935. This book was reprinted several times as late as 1940.*

LITTLE NAPOLEON
No publisher listed: 1924 , 50 pages, 10" by 10"; Color cardstock-c, B&W
nn - By Bud Counihan (Cupples &Leon format) 25.00 100.00 250.00

LITTLE NEMO (...in Slumberland) (N) (see also Little Sammy Sneeze, Dreams...Rarebit F)
Doffield & Co.(1906)/Cupples & Leon Co.(1909): 1906, 1909 (Sunday strip-r in color, cardboard covers)
1906-11x16-1/2" by Winsor McCay; 30 pgs. (scarce) 1500.00 5500.00 -
1909-10x14" by Winsor McCay (scarce) 1300.00 4000.00 -

LITTLE ORPHAN ANNIE (See Treasure Box of Famous Comics) (N)
Cupples & Leon Co.: 1926 - 1934 (8-3/4x7", 100 pgs., B&W daily strip-r, hard-c)
1 (1926)-Little Orphan Annie (softback see Treasure Box) 50.00 200.00 375.00
2 (1927)-In the Circus (softback see Wonder Box...) 36.00 144.00 275.00
3 (1928)-The Haunted House (softback see Wonder Box...) 36.00 144.00 275.00
4 (1929)-Bucking the World 36.00 144.00 275.00
5 (1930)-Never Say Die 30.00 120.00 225.00
6 (1931)-Shipwrecked 30.00 120.00 225.00
7 (1932)-A Willing Helper 25.00 100.00 175.00

The Trials of Lulu and Leander by Howarth
1906 © NY American & Journal

Maud the Mirthful Mule by Opper
1908 © Frederick A. Stokes

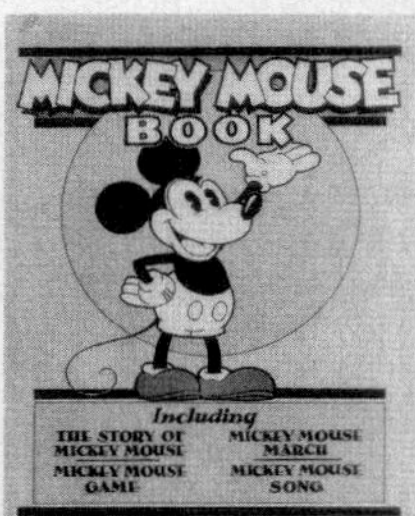

Mickey Mouse Book
1930 © Bibo & Lang

GD2.0 FN6.0 VF8.0

8 (1933)-In Cosmic City 25.00 100.00 175.00
9 (1934)-Uncle Dan (not rare) 25.00 100.00 175.00
NOTE: *Each book reprints dailies from the previous year. Each hardcover came with a dust jacket. Books without dust jackets are worth 50% less. Many of copies of #9 Uncle Dan have been turning up on eBay recently.*

LITTLE ORPHAN ANNIE RUMMY CARDS (N)
Whitman Publishing Co., Racine: 1935 (box: 5 x 6 1/2" Cards: 3 1/2 x 2 1/4")
nn-Harold Gray 20.00 60.00 125.00
NOTE: *36 cards, including 1 instruction card, 5 character cards and 30 cards forming 5 sequential stories (6 cards each).*

LITTLE SAMMY SNEEZE (N) (see also Little Nemo, Dreams of A Rarebit Fiend)
New York Herald Co.: Dec 1905 (11x16-1/2", 72 pgs., color)
nn - By Winsor McCay (Very Rare) 3500.00 7000.00 –
NOTE: *Rarely found in fine to mint condition.*

LIVE AND LET LIVE
Travelers Insurance Co.: 1936 (5-3/4x7/3/4", 16 pgs. color and B&W)
nn - Bill Holman, Carl Anderson, etc 20.00 60.00 120.00

LULU AND LEANDER (N) (see also Funny Folk, 1899, in Victorian section)
New York American & Journal: 1904 (76 pgs); **William A Stokes & Co:** 1906
nn - By F.M. Howarth 300.00 750.00 1500.00
nn - The Trials of...(1906, 10x16", 68 pgs. in color) 300.00 750.00 1500.00
NOTE: *F. M. Howarth helped pioneer the American comic strip in the pages of PUCK magazine in the early 1890s before the Yellow Kid.*

MADMAN'S DRUM (O)
Jonathan Cape and Harrison Smith Inc.: 1930 (8-1/4x6", 274 pgs, B&W hardcover w/dust jacket) (original graphic novel in wood cuts)
nn - By Lynd Ward 50.00 175.00 310.00

MAMA'S ANGEL CHILD IN TOYLAND (I)
Rand McNally, Chicago: 1915 (128 pgs, hardbound)
nn - By M.T. "Penny" Ross & Marie C, Sadler 40.00 140.00 240.00
NOTE: *Mamma's Angel Child published as a comic strip by the "Chicago Tribune" 1908 Mar 1 to 1920 Oct 17.This novel dedicated to Esther Starring Richartz, "the original Mamma's Angel Kid."*

MAUD (N) (see also **Happy Hooligan**)
Frederick A. Stokes Co.: 1906 - 1908? (10x15-1/2", cardboard-c)
1906-By Fred Opper (Scarce), 66 pgs. color 400.00 1300.00 –
1907-The Matchless, 10x15" 70 pgs in color 300.00 1100.00 –
1908-The Mirthful Mule, 10x15", 64 pgs in color 300.00 1100.00 –
NOTE: *First run of strip began July 24, 1904 to at least Oct 6, 1907, spun out of* ***Happy Hooligan.***

MEMORIAL EDITION The Drawings of Clare Briggs (S)
Wm H. Wise & Company: 1930 (7-1/2x8-3/4", 284 pgs, pebbled false black leather, B&W) (posthumous boxed set of 7 books by Clare Briggs)
nn - The Days of Real Sport; nn-Golf; nn-Real Folks at Home; nn-Ain't it a Grand and Glorious Feeling?; nn-That Guiltiest Feeling; nn-Somebody's Always Taking the Joy Out of Life; nn-When a Feller Needs a Friend
Each book... 30.00 110.00 160.00
NOTE: *Also exists in a whitish cream colored paper back edition; first edition unknown presently.*

MENACE CARTOONS (M, S)
Menace Publishing Company, Aurora, Missouri: 1914 (10-3/8x8", 80 pgs, cardboard-c, B&W)
nn - (Rare) 50.00 150.00 450.00
NOTE: *Reprints anti-Catholic cartoons from K.K.K. related publication* ***The Menace.***

MEN OF DARING (N)
Cupples & Leon Co.: 1933 (8-3/4x7", 100 pgs)
nn - By Stookie Allen, intro by Lowell Thomas 30.00 90.00 200.00

MICKEY MOUSE BOOK
Bibo & Lang: 1930-1931 (12x9", stapled-c, 20 pgs., 4 printings)
nn - First Disney licensed publication (a magazine, not a book–see first book, Adventures of Mickey Mouse). Contains story of how Mickey met Walt and got his name; games, cartoons & song "Mickey Mouse (You Cute Little Feller)," written by Irving Bibo; Minnie, Clarabelle Cow, Horace Horsecollar & caricature of Walt shaking hands with Mickey. The changes made with the 2nd printing have been verified by billing affidavits in the Walt Disney Archives and include:Two Win Smith Mickey strips from 4/15/30 and 4/17/30 added to page 8 & back-c; "Printed in U.S.A." added to front cover; Bobette Bibo's age of 11 years added to title page; faulty type on the word "tail" corrected top of page 3; the word "start" added to bottom of page 7, removing the words "start 1 2 3 4" from the top of page 7; music and lyrics were rewritten on pages 12-14. A green ink border was added beginning with 2nd printing and some covers have inking variations. Art by Albert Barbelle, drawn in an Ub Iwerks style. Total circulation : 97,938 copies varying from 21,000 to 26,000 per printing.
1st printing. Contains the song lyrics **censored** in later printings, "When little Minnie's pursued by a big bad villain we feel so bad then we're glad when you up and kill him." Attached to the Nov. 15, 1930 issue of the Official Bulletin of the Mickey Mouse Club notes: "Attached to this Bulletin is a new Mickey Mouse Book that has just been published." This is thought to be the reason why a slightly disproportionate larger number of copies of the first printing still exist 600.00 1300.00 5300.00

GD2.0 FN6.0 VF8.0

2nd printing with a theater/advertising. Christmas greeting added to inside front cover (1 copy known with Dec. 27, 1930 date) – 8000.00 –
2nd-4th printings 500.00 1100.00 3300.00
NOTE: *Theater/advertising copies do not qualify as separate printings. Most copies are missing pages 9 & 10 which had a puzzle to be cut out. Puzzle (pages 9 and 10) cut out or missing, subtract 60% to 75%.*

MICKEY MOUSE COLORING BOOK (S)
Saalfield Publishing Company:1931 (15-1/4x10-3/4", 32 pgs, color soft cover, half printed in full color interior, rest B&W
871 - By Ub Iwerks & Floyd Gottfredson (rare) 450.00 1300.00 2500.00
NOTE: *Contains reprints of first MM daily strip ever, including the "missing" speck the chicken is after found only on the original daily strip art by Iwerks plus other very early MM art. There were several other Saalfield Mickey Mouse coloring books manufactured around the same time.*

MICKEY MOUSE, THE ADVENTURES OF (I)
David McKay Co., Inc.: Book I, 1931 - Book II, 1932 (5-1/2"x8-1/2", 32 pgs.)
Book I-First Disney book, by strict definition (1st printing-50,000 copies)(see Mickey Mouse Book by Bibo & Lang). Illustrated text refers to Clarabelle Cow as "Carolyn" and Horace Horsecollar as "Henry". The name "Donald Duck" appears with a non-costumed generic duck on back cover & inside, not in the context of the character that later debuted in the Wise Little Hen.
Hardback w/characters on back-c 75.00 300.00 840.00
Softcover w/characters on back-c 40.00 165.00 420.00
Version without characters on back-c 50.00 200.00 460.00
Book II-Less common than Book I. Character development brought into conformity with the Mickey Mouse cartoon shorts and syndicated strips. Captain Church Mouse, Tanglefoot, Peg-Leg Pete and Pluto appear with Mickey & Minnie 50.00 200.00 460.00

MICKEY MOUSE COMIC (N)
David McKay Co.: 1931 - No. 4, 1934 (10"x9-3/4", 52 pgs., card board-c) (Later reprints exist)
1 (1931)-Reprints Floyd Gottfredson daily strips in black & white from 1930 & 1931, including the famous two week sequence in which Mickey tries to commit suicide 300.00 1000.00 2200.00
2 (1932)-1st app. of Pluto reprinted from 7/8/31 daily. All pgs. from 1931 164.00 656.00 1250.00
3 (1933)-Reprints 1932 & 1933 Sunday pages in color, one strip per page, including the "Lair of Wolf Barker" continuity pencilled by Gottfredson and inked by Al Taliaferro & Ted Thwaites. First app. Mickey's nephews, Morty & Ferdie, one identified by name of Mortimer Fieldmouse, not to be confused with Uncle Mortimer Mouse who is introduced in the Wolf Barker story 214.00 856.00 1700.00
4 (1934)-1931 dailies, include the only known reprint of the infamous strip of 2/4/31 where the villainous Kat Nipp snips off the end of Mickey's tail with a pair of scissors 140.00 560.00 1100.00

MICKEY MOUSE (N)
Whitman Publishing Co.: 1933-34 (10x8-3/4", 34 pgs, cardboard-c)
948-1932 & 1933 Sunday strips in color, printed from the same plates as Mickey Mouse Book #3 by David McKay, but only pages 5-17 & 32-48 (including all of the "Wolf Barker" continuity) 157.00 629.00 1300.00
NOTE: *Some copies bound with back cover upside down. Variance doesn't affect value. Same art appears on front and back covers of all copies. Height of Whitman reissue trimmed 1/2 inch.*

MILITARY WILLIE
J. I. Austen Co.: 1907 (7x9-1/2", 12 pgs., every other page in color, stapled)
nn - By F. R. Morgan 70.00 245.00 400.00

MINNEAPOLIS TRIBUNE CARTOON BOOK (S)
Minneapolis Tribune: 1899-1903 (11-3/8x9-3/8", B&W, paper cover)
nn (#1) (1899) 45.00 100.00 200.00
nn (#2) (1900) 45.00 100.00 200.00
nn (#3) (1901) (published Jan 01, 1901) 45.00 100.00 200.00
nn (#4) (1902) (114 pgs) 45.00 100.00 200.00
nn (#5) (1903) (9x10-3/4",110 pgs, B&W; color-c) 45.00 100.00 200.00
NOTE: *All by Roland C. Bowman (editorial-r).*

MINUTE BIOGRAPHIES: INTIMATE GLIMPSES INTO THE LIVES OF 150 FAMOUS MEN AND WOMEN
Grossett & Dunlap: 1931, 1933 (10-1/4x7-3/4", 168 pgs, hardcover, B&W)
nn - By Nisenson (art) & Parker(text) 25.00 75.00 160.00
More.... (1933) 25.00 75.00 160.00

MISCHIEVOUS MONKS OF CROCODILE ISLE, THE (N)
J. I. Austen Co., Chicago: 1908 (8-1/2x11-1/2", 12 pgs., 4 pgs. in color)
nn - By F. R. Morgan; reads longwise 125.00 375.00 600.00

MR. & MRS. (Also see Ain't It A Grand and Glorious Feeling?) (N)
Whitman Publishing Co.: 1922 (9x9-1/2", 52 & 28 pgs., cardboard-c)
nn - By Briggs (B&W, 52 pgs.) 37.00 149.00 260.00
nn - 28 pgs.-(9x9-1/2")-Sunday strips-r in color 41.00 163.00 285.00
NOTE: *The earliest presently-known Whitman comic books*

MR. BLOCK (N)
Industrial Workers of the World (IWW): 1913, 1919

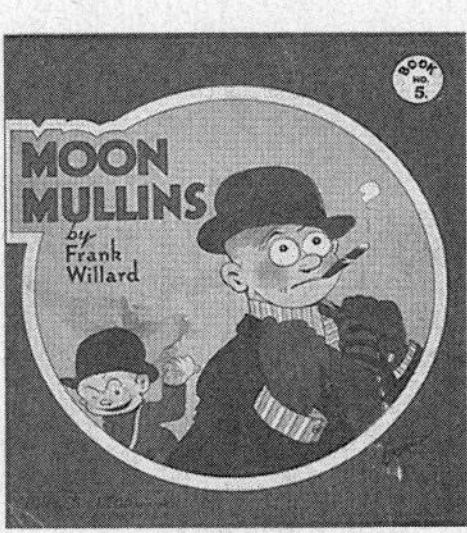

Moon Mullins #5 by Frank Willard
1931 @ Cupples & Leon

The Nebbs
© C&L

The Newlyweds by George McManus
1907 © Saalfield Publishing Co.

GD2.0 FN6.0 VF8.0

nn - By Ernest Riebe (C) 55.00 160.00 –
...And The Profiteers (original material) (H) 55.00 160.00 –
NOTE: *Mr Block was a daily strip published from 1912 NOV 7 to 1913 SEP ? by the socialist newspaper "Industrial Worker"; Mr Block was a "square" guy (his head was in fact a block) who enthusiastically supported the same system that exploited him. The noted Joe Hill wrote a song about him (Mr Block,1913, on the air of "It loooks me like a big time tonight") for the "Industrial Worker Songbook".*

MR. TWEE-DEEDLE (N)
Cupples & Leon: 1913, 1917 (11-3/8 x 16-3/4" color strips-r from NY Herald)
nn - By John B. Gruelle (later of Raggedy Ann fame) 350.00 900.00 2000.00
nn - "Further Adventures of..." By Gruelle 350.00 900.00 2000.00
NOTE: *Strip ran Feb 5, 1911-March 10, 1918.*

MONKEY SHINES OF MARSELEEN AND SOME OF HIS ADVENTURES (C)
McLaughlin Bros. New York: 1906 (10 x 12-3/8", 36 pgs, full color hardcover)
nn - By Norman E. Jennett strip-r NY Evening Telegram 100.00 250.00 475.00
NOTE: *Strip began in 1906 until at least March 13, 1910.*

MONKEY SHINES OF MARSELEEN (N)
Cupples & Leon Co.: 1909 (11-1/2 x 17", 58 pgs. in two colors)
nn - By Norman E. Jennett (strip-r New York Herald) 100.00 250.00 475.00

MOON MULLINS (N)
Cupples & Leon Co.: 1927 - 1933 (52 pgs., B&W daily strip-r)
Series 1 ('27)-By Willard 63.00 250.00 550.00
Series 2 ('28), Series 3 ('29), Series 4 ('30) 39.00 156.00 300.00
Series 5 ('31), 6 ('32), 7 ('33) 39.00 156.00 300.00
Big Book 1 ('30)-B&W (scarce) 100.00 400.00 750.00
w/dust jacket (rare) 183.00 732.00 1150.00

MOVING PICTURE FUNNIES
Saml Gabriel Sons & Company: 1918 (5-1/4 x 10-1/4", 52 pgs, B&W, illustrated hard-c)
nn 25.00 50.00 100.00
NOTE: *823 Comical illustrations that show a different scene when folded.*

MUTT & JEFF (...Cartoon, The) (N)
Ball Publications: 1911 - No. 5, 1916 (5-3/4 x 15-1/2", 72 pgs, B&W, hard-c)
1 (1910)(50¢) very common 71.00 286.00 550.00
2,3: 2 (1911)-Opium den panels; Jeff smokes opium (pipe dreams).
3 (1912) both very common 71.00 286.00 500.00
2-(1913) Reprint of 1911 edition with black ink cover 50.00 175.00 300.00
4 (1915) (50¢) (Scarce) 150.00 350.00 650.00
5 (1916) (Rare) -Photos of Fisher, 1st pg. (68 pages) 200.00 480.00 1000.00
5-Scarce 84 page reprint edition 150.00 450.00 850.00
NOTE: *Mutt & Jeff first appeared in newspapers in 1907. Cover variations exist showing Mutt & Jeff reading various newspapers; i.e., The Oregon Journal, The American, and The Detroit News. Reprinting of each issue began soon after publication. No. 4 and 5 may not have been reprinted. Values listed include the reprints. Mutt & Jeff was the first successful American daily newspaper comic strip and as such remains one of the seminal strips of all time.*

MUTT & JEFF (N)
Cupples & Leon Co.: No. 6, 1919 - No. 22, 1934? (9-1/2x9-1/2", 52 pgs., B&W dailies, stiff-c)
6, 7 - By Bud Fisher (very common) 32.00 128.00 225.00
8-10 46.00 186.00 325.00
11-18 (Somewhat Scarcer) (#19-#22 do not exist) 60.00 â240.00 420.00
nn (1920) (Advs. of...) 11x16"; 44 pgs.; full color reprints of 1919 Sunday strips
93.00 372.00 675.00
Big Book nn (1926, 144 pgs., hardcovers) 114.00 456.00 800.00
w/dust jacket 193.00 772.00 1350.00
Big Book 1 (1928) - Thick book (hardcovers) 114.00 456.00 800.00
w/dust jacket (rare) 182.00 729.00 1275.00
Big Book 2 (1929) - Thick book (hardcovers) 114.00 456.00 800.00
w/dust jacket (rare) 182.00 729.00 1275.00
NOTE: *The Big Books contain three previous issues rebound.*

MUTT & JEFF (N)
Embee Publ. Co.: 1921 (9x15", color cardboard-c & interior)
nn - Sunday strips in color (Rare)- BY Bud Fisher 150.00 600.00 1200.00
NOTE: *Ties with The Trouble of Bringing Up Father (EmBee) and Jimmie Dugan & The Reg'lar Fellers (C&L) as the last of this size.*

MYSTERIOUS STRANGER AND OTHER CARTOONS, THE
McClure, Phillips & Co.: 1905 (12-3/8x9-3/4", 338 pgs, hardcover, B&W)
nn - By John McCutcheon 32.00 128.00 250.00

MY WAR - Szeged (Szuts)
Wm. Morrow Co.: 1932 (7x10-1/2", 210 pgs, hard-c, B&W)
nn - (All story panels, no words - powerful) 32.00 128.00 250.00

NAUGHTY ADVENTURES OF VIVACIOUS MR. JACK, THE
New York American & Journal: 1904 (15x10", color strips)
nn - By James Swinnerton; (Very Rare - 3 known copies) 1000.00 1700.00 2500.00

NEBBS, THE (N)
Cupples & Leon Co.: 1928 (52 pgs., B&W daily strip-r)
nn - By Sol Hess; Carlson-a 40.00 160.00 300.00

GD2.0 FN6.0 VF8.0

NERVY NAT'S ADVENTURES (E)
Leslie-Judge Co.: 1911 (90 pgs, 85¢, 1903 strip reprints from **Judge**)
nn - By James Montgomery Flagg 75.00 263.00 450.00

THE NEWLYWEDS AND THEIR BABY (N)
Saalfield Publ. Co.: 1907 (13x10", 52 pgs., hardcover)
...& Their Baby' by McManus; daily strips 50% color 350.00 1100.00 –
NOTE: *Strip ran Apr 10, 1904 thru Jan 14, 1906 and then May 19, 1907-Dec 5, 1916; was a huge success with Baby Snookums long before McManus invented Bringing Up Father; Snookums brought back as a topper strip over BUF Nov 19, 1944-Dec 30, 1956.*

THE NEWLYWEDS AND THEIR BABY'S COMIC PICTURES FOR PAINTING AND CRAYONING (N)
Saalfield Publishign Company: 1916 (10-1/4x14-3/4", 52 pgs. Cardboard-c)
nn - 44 B&W pages, covers, and one color wrap glued to B&W title page.
Color wrap: color title pg. & 3 pgs of color strips 83.00 290.00 550.00
nn - (1917, 10x14", 20 pgs, oblong, cardboard-c) partial reprint of 1916 edition
31.00 124.00 300.00

THE NEWLYWEDS AND THEIR BABY (N)
Saalfield Publishing Company: 1917 (10-1/8x13-9/16 ", 52 pgs, full color cardstock-c, some pages full color, others two color (orange, blue))
nn 83.00 290.00 475.00

NEW YORKER CARTOON ALBUM, THE (M)
Doubleday, Doran & Company Inc.: (1928-1931); **Harper & Brothers.:** (1931-1933); **Random House** (1935-1937), 12x9", various pg counts, hardcovers w/dust jackets)
1928: nn-114 pgs Arno, Held, Soglow, Williams, etc 20.00 60.00 130.00
1928: SECOND-114 pgs Arno, Bairnsfather, Gross, Held, Soglow, Williams
10.00 30.00 75.00
1930: THIRD-172 pgs Arno, Bairnsfather, Held, Soglow, Art Young
10.00 30.00 75.00
1931: FOURTH-154 pgs Arno, Held, Soglow, Steig, Thurber, Williams, Art Young, "Little King" by Soglow begins 10.00 30.00 75.00
1932: FIFTH-156 pgs Arno, Bairnsfather, Held, Hoff, Soglow, Steig, Thurber, Williams 10.00 30.00 75.00
1933: SIXTH-156 pgs same as above 10.00 30.00 75.00
1935: SEVENTH-164 pgs 10.00 30.00 75.00
1937: 168 pgs; Charles Addams plus same as above but no Little King, two page "Gone With The Wind" parody strip 10.00 30.00 75.00
NOTE: *Some sequential strips but mostly single panel cartoons.*

NIPPY'S POP (N)
The Saalfield Publishing Co.: 1917 (10-1/2x13-1/2", 36 pgs., B&W, Sunday strip-r)
nn - Charles M Payne (better known as S'Matter Pop) 50.00 160.00 270.00

OH, MAN (A Bully Collection of Those Inimitable Humor Cartoons) (S)
P.F. Volland & Co.: 1919 (8-1/2x13"; 136 pgs.)
nn - By Briggs 50.00 160.00 270.00
NOTE: *Originally came in illustrated box with Briggs art (box is Rare - worth 50% more with box).*

OH SKIN-NAY! (S)
P.F. Volland & Co.: 1913 (8-1/2x13", 136 pgs.)
nn - The Days Of Real Sport by Briggs 43.00 152.00 250.00
NOTE: *Originally came in illustrated box with Briggs art (box is Rare - worth 50% more with box).*

OLD GOLD THE SMOOTHER AND BETTER CIGARETTE...NOT A COUGH IN A CARLOAD (M,N,P) (see also BY BRIGGS)
Old Gold Cigarettes: nd (c1920's) (16 pgs, paper-c, color) (both Scarce)
nn- (4-1/4" x 3-7/8") cover strip is "Oh, Man!"; also contains: "Real Folks at Home", "Ain't It a Grand and Glorious Feelin?", "It Happens in the Best Regulated Families", and "Mr. and Mrs." (no known sales)
1440- (5-9/16" x 5-1/4") cover strip is "Frank and Ernest"; also contains: "That Guiltiest Feeling", "Real Folks at Home", "Oh, Man!", "When a Feller Needs a Friend". (no known sales)
NOTE: *Collection reprinting strip cartoons by Clare Briggs, advertising Old Gold Cigarettes. These strips originally appeared in various magazines, play program booklets, newspapers, etc. Some of the strips involve regular Briggs strip series. The two booklets contain a completely different set of comics.*

ON AND OFF MOUNT ARARAT (also see **Tigers**) (N)
Hearst's New York American & Journal: 1902, 86pgs. 10x15-1/4"
nn - Rare Noah's Ark satire by Jimmy Swinnerton (rare) 450.00 1600.00 –

ON THE LINKS (N)
Associated Feature Service: Dec, 1926 (9x10", 48 pgs.)
nn - Daily strip-r 50.00 125.00 200.00

ONE HUNDRED WAR CARTOONS (S)
Idaho Daily Statesman: 1918 (7-3/4x10", 102 pgs, paperback, B&W)
nn - By Villeneuve (WW I cartoons) 20.00 60.00 130.00

OUR ANTEDILUVIAN ANCESTORS (N,S)
New York Evening Journal, NY: 1903 (11-3/8x8-7/8", hardcover)
nn - By F Opper 75.00 200.00 425.00
NOTE: *There is a simultaneously published British edition, identical size and contents, from C. Arthur Pearson*

The Adventures of Peck's Bad Boy With the Teddy Bear Show by McDougall
1907 © Charles C. Thompson, Co.

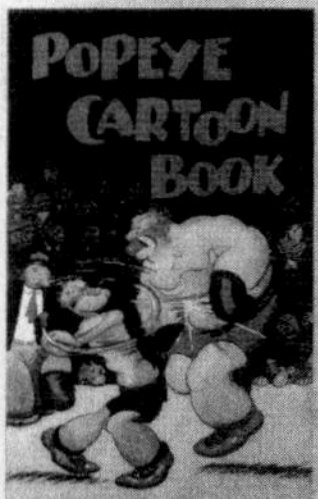

Popeye Cartoon Book
1934 © The Saalfield Co.

Roger Bean, R.G. #4
1917 © Indiana News Co., Distributors

Ltd, London. A collection of single panel cartoons about cavemen. Similar to an earlier British cartoon book "Prehistoric Peeps from Punch", by E.T. Reed.

OUTBURSTS OF EVERETT TRUE, THE (N)
Saalfield Publ. Co.(Werner Co.): 1907 (92 pgs, 9-7/16x5-1/4")

1907 (2-4 panel strips-r)-By Condo & Raper 125.00 350.00 700.00
1921-Full color-c; reprints 56 of 88 cartoons from 1907 ed. (10x10", 32 pgs B&W) 125.00 225.00 350.00

OVER THERE COMEDY FROM FRANCE
Observer House Printing: nd (WW 1 era) (6x14", 60 pgs, paper cover)

nn - Artist(s) unknown 15.00 53.00 100.00

OWN YOUR OWN HOME (I)
Bobbs-Merrill Company, Indianapolis: 1919 (7-7/16x5-1/4")

nn - By Fontaine Fox – – –

PECKS BAD BOY (N)
Charles C. Thompson Co, Chicago (by Walt McDougal): 1906-1908 (strip-r)

The Adventures of... (1906) 11-1/2x16-1/4", 68 pgs 100.00 400.00 820.00
...& His Country Cousin Cynthia (1907) 12x16-1/2," 34 pgs In color 100.00 400.00 820.00
Advs. of...And His Country Cousins (1907) 5-1/2x10 1/2", 18 pgs In color 50.00 175.00 375.00
Advs. of...And His Country Cousins (1907) 11-1/2x16-1/4", 36 pgs 50.00 175.00 375.00
...& Their Advs With The Teddy Bear (1907) 5-1/2x10-1/2", 18 pgs in color 50.00 175.00 375.00
...& Their Balloon Trip To the Country (1907) 5-1/2x 10-1/2, 18 pgs in color 50.00 175.00 375.00
...With the Teddy Bear Show (1907) 5-1/2x 10-1/2 50.00 175.00 375.00
...With The Billy Whiskers Goats (1907) 5-1/2 x 10-1/2, 18 pgs in color 50.00 175.00 375.00
...& His Chums (1908) - 11x16-3/8", 36 pgs. Stanton & Van Vliet Co 100.00 400.00 820.00
...& His Chums (1908)-Hardcover; full color;16 pgs. 100.00 350.00 660.00
Advs. of...in Pictures (1908) (11x17, 36 pgs)-In color; Stanton & Van V. Liet Co. 100.00 400.00 820.00

PERCY & FERDIE (N)
Cupples & Leon Co.: 1921 (10x10", 52 pgs., B&W dailies, cardboard-c)

nn - By H. A. MacGill (Rare) 61.00 244.00 500.00

PETER RABBIT (N)
John H. Eggers Co. The House of Little Books Publishers: 1922 - 1923

B1-B4-(Rare)-(Set of 4 books which came in a cardboard box)-Each book reprints half of a Sunday page per page and contains 8 B&W and 2 color pages; by Harrison Cady (9-1/4x6-1/4", paper-c) each.... 43.00 172.00 300.00
Box only 57.00 228.00 400.00

PHILATELIC CARTOONS (M)
Essex Publishing Company, Lynn, Mass.: 1916 (8-11/16" x 5-7/8", 40 pgs, light blue construction paper-c, B&W interior)

nn - By Leroy S. Bartlett 50.00 100.00 200.00
NOTE: *Comics reprinted from The New England Philatelist.*

PICTORIAL HISTORY OF THE DEPARTMENT OF COMMERCE UNDER HERBERT HOOVER (see Picture Life of a Great American) (O)
Hoover-Curtis Campaign Committee of New York State: no date, 1928 (3-1/4 x 5-1/4, 32 pgs, paper cover, B&W)

nn - By Satterfield (scarce) 50.00 150.00 300.00
NOTE: *1928 Presidential Campaign giveaway. Original material, contents completely different from Picture Life of a Great American.*

PICTURE LIFE OF A GREAT AMERICAN (see Pictorial History of the Department of Commerce under Herbert Hoover) (O)
Hoover-Curtis Campaign Committee of New York State: no date, 1928 (paper cover, B&W)

nn - (8-3/4 x 7, 20 pgs) Text cover, 2 page text introduction, 18 pgs of comics (scarcer first print) 43.00 129.00 260.00
nn - (9 x 6-3/4,24 pgs) Illustrated cover,5 page text introduction, 18 pgs of comics (scarce) 43.00 129.00 260.00
NOTE: *1928 Presidential Campaign giveaway. Unknown which above version was published first. Both contain the same original comics material by Satterfield.*

PINK LAFFIN (I)
Whitman Publishing Co.: 1922 (9x12")(Strip-r; some of these actually text joke books)

...the Lighter Side of Life, ...He Tells 'Em, ...and His Family, ...Knockouts; Ray Gleason-a (All rare) each... 26.00 104.00 200.00

POLLY (AND HER PALS) - (N)
Newspaper Feature Service: 1916 (3x2-1/2", color)

Altogether: Three Rahs and a Tiger! by Cliff Sterrett 35.00 75.00 150.00
There Is A Limit To Pa's Patience by Cliff Sterrett 35.00 75.00 150.00
Pa's Lil Book Has Some Uncut Pages by Sterrett 35.00 75.00 150.00

NOTE: *Single newsprint sheet printed in full color on both sides, unfolds to show 12 panel story.*

POPEYE PAINT BOOK (N)
McLaughlin Bros, Inc., Springfield, Mass.: 1932 (9-7/8x13", 28 pgs, color-c)

2052 - By E. C. Segar 90.00 300.00 650.00
NOTE: *Contains a full color panel above and the exact same art in below panel n B&W which one was to color in; strip-r panels.*

POPEYE CARTOON BOOK (N)
The Saalfield Co.: 1934 (8-1/2x13", 40 pgs, cardboard-c)

2095-(scarce)-1933 strip reprints in color by Segar. Each page contains a vertical half of a Sunday strip, so the continuity reads row by row completely across each double page spread. If each page is read by itself, the continuity makes no sense. Each double page spread reprints one complete Sunday page from 1933 350.00 1000.00 2800.00
12 Page Version 125.00 350.00 1100.00

POPEYE (See **Thimble Theatre** for earlier Popeye-r from Sonnett) (N)
David McKay Publications: 1935 (25¢; 52 pgs, B&W) (By Segar)

1-Daily strip reprints- "The Gold Mine Thieves" 200.00 400.00 900.00
2-Daily strip-r (scarce) 200.00 400.00 1000.00
NOTE: *Ties with Henry & Little Annie Rooney (David McKay) as the last of the 10x10" size books.*

PORE LI'L MOSE (N)
New York Herald Publ. by Grand Union Tea
Cupples & Leon Co.: 1902 (10-1/2x15", 78 pgs., color)

nn - By R. F. Outcault; Earliest known C&L comic book (scarce in high grade - very high demand) 1200.00 4000.00 –
NOTE: *Black Americana one page newspaper strips; falls in between Yellow Kid & Buster Brown. Complete copies have become scarce. Some have cut this book apart thinking that reselling individual pages will bring them more money.*

PRETTY PICTURES (M)
Farrar & Rinehart: 1931 (12 x 8-7/8", 104 pgs, color hardcover w/dust jacket, B&W; reprints from New Yorker, Judge, Life, Collier's Weekly)

nn - By Otto Soglow (contains "The Little King") 33.00 134.00 245.00

QUAINT OLD NEW ENGLAND (S)
Triton Syndicate: 1936 (5-1/4x6-1/4", 100 pgs, soft-c squarebound, B&W)

nn - By Jack Withycomb 36.00 144.00 250.00
NOTE: *Comics about weird doings in Old New England.*

RED CARTOONS (S)
Daily Worker Publishing Company: 1926 (12 x 9", 68 pgs,cardboard cover, B&W)

nn - By Various (scarce) 40.00 160.00 280.00
NOTE: *Reprint of American Communist Party editorial cartoons, from The Daily Worker, The Workers Monthly, and the Liberator. Art by Fred Ellis, William Gropper, Clive Weed, Art Young.*

REG'LAR FELLERS (See All-American Comics, Jimmie Dugan & The..., Popular Comics & Treasure Box of Famous Comics) (N)
Cupples & Leon Co./MS Publishing Co.: 1921-1929

1 (1921)-52 pgs. B&W dailies (Cupples & Leon, 10x10") 43.00 171.00 325.00
1925, 48 pgs. B&W dailies (MS Publ.) 39.00 157.00 300.00
Hardcover (1929, 8-3/4x7-1/2"; 96 pgs.)-B&W-r 54.00 214.00 400.00

REG'LAR FELLERS STORY PAINT BOOK
Whitman, Racine, Wisc.: 1932 (8-3/4x12-1/8", 132 pgs, red soft-c)

By Gene Byrnes 25.00 75.00 150.00

ROGER BEAN, R. G. (Regular Guy) (N)
The Indiana News Co, Distributers.: 1915 - No. 2, 1915 (5-3/8x17", 68 pgs., B&W, hardcovers); #3-#5 published by **Chas. B. Jackson:** 1916-1919
(No. 1 2 4 & 5 bound on side, No. 3 bound at top)

1-By Chas B. Jackson (68pgs.)(Scarce) 60.00 210.00 375.00
2- 5-5/8x17-1/8", 66 pgs (says 1913 inside - an obvious printing error) (red or green binding) 60.00 210.00 375.00
3-Along the Firing Line... (1916; 68 pgs, 6x17") 60.00 210.00 375.00
3-Along the Firing Line side-bound version 60.00 210.00 375.00
4-Into the Trenches and Out Again with... (1917, 68 pgs) 60.00 210.00 375.00
5 ...And The Reconstruction Period (1919, 5-3/8x15-1/2", 84 pgs) (Scarce) (has $1 printed on cover) 60.00 210.00 375.00
Baby Grand Editions 1-5 (10x10", cardboard-c) 60.00 210.00 375.00
NOTE: *No. 1 & 2 of the Twin Baby Grands (nd) 8-1/4x10-7/8", 52 pgs. #3 & #4 9x10-7/8" Cardboard cover. B&W strip reprints. Cover also says "Politics Pickles People Police."*
nn - 9x11, 68 pgs 60.00 210.00 375.00
NOTE: Has picture of Chic Jackson and a posthumous dedication from his three children. strip-r 1931-32

ROGER BEAN PHILOSOPHER
Schnull & Co: 1917 (5-1/2x17", 36 pgs., B&W, brown & black paper-c, square binding)

nn - By Chic Jackson (no known sales)

ROOKIE FROM THE 13TH SQUAD, THAT (N) (also Between Shots; Always Belittlin';Skippy)
Harper & Brothers Publishers: Feb. 1918 (8x9-1/4", 72 pgs, hardcover, B&W)

nn - By Lieut. P(ercy) L. Crosby 75.00 225.00 400.00
NOTE: *Strip began in 1917 at an Army base during basic training.*

ROUND THE WORLD WITH THE DOO-DADS (see Doings of the Doo-Dads, Doo Dads)
Universal Feature And Specialty Co, Chicago: 1922 (12x10-1/2", 52 pgs, B&W, red &

Seaman Si
© Pierce Publ. Co.

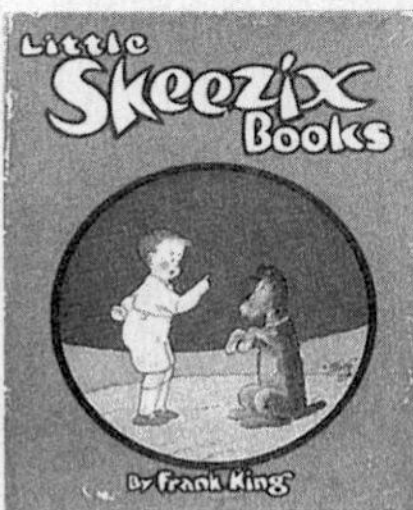

Little Skeezix Books by Frank King
1929 © Reilly & Lee

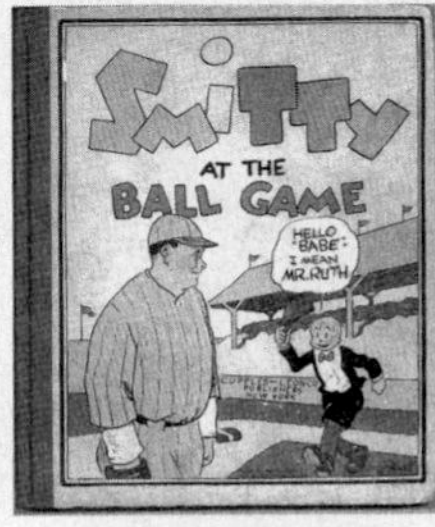

Smitty #2 By Walter Berndt
1929 © Cupples & Leon

GD2.0 FN6.0 VF8.0

light blue-c, square binding)
nn - By Arch Dale newspaper strip-r 43.00 173.00 300.00
NOTE: *Intermixed single panel and sequential comic strips with scenes from Scotland, Ireland, England, Holland, Italy, Spain, Egypt, Africa, and Lions & Elephants along the Nile River, China, Australia & back home.*

RUBAIYKT OF THE EGG
The John C Winston Co, Philadelphia: 1905 (7x5/12", 64 pgs, purple-c, B&W)
nn - By Clare Victor Dwiggins 35.00 75.00 160.00
NOTE: *Book is printed & cut into the shape of an egg.*

RULING CLAWSS, THE (N,S)
The Daily Worker: 1935 (192 pgs, 10-1/4 x 7-3/8", hard-c, B&W)
nn - By Redfield 60.00 240.00 -
NOTE: *Reprints cartoons from the American Communist Party newspaper The Daily Worker.*

SAGARA'S ENGLISH CARTOONS AND CARTOON STORIES (N)
Bunkosha, Tokyo: nd (c1925) (6-5/8" x 4-1/4", 272 pgs, hard-c, B&W)
nn- (Scarce) - - -
NOTE: *Published in Tokyo, Japan, with all strips in both English and Japanese, to facilitate learning English. Majority of book is Bringing Up Father by George McManus. Also contains Japanese strip Father Takes it Easy, by T. Sagara, reprinted from the Kokusai News Agency.*

SAM AND HIS LAUGH (N)
Frederick A. Stokes: 1906 (10x15", cardboard-c, Sunday strip-r in color)
nn - By Jimmy Swinnerton (Extremely Rare) 800.00 1400.00 3100.00
NOTE: *Strip ran July 24, 1904-Dec 26 1906; its ethnic humor might be considered racist by today's standards.*

SCHOOL DAYS (N)
Harper & Bros.: 1919 (9x8", 104 pgs.)
nn - By Clare Victor Dwiggins 75.00 150.00 300.00

SEAMAN SI - A Book of Cartoons About the Funniest "Gob" in the Navy (N)
Pierce Publishing Co.: 1916 (4x8-1/2, 200 pgs, hardcover, B&W); 1918 (4-1/8x8-1/4, 104 pgs, hardcover, B&W)
nn - By Perce Pearce (1916) 50.00 150.00 300.00
nn - 1918 - (Reilly & Britton Co.) 30.00 125.00 200.00
NOTE: *There exists two different covers for the 1918 reprints. The earlier edition was self published by the artist. The newspaper strip is sometimes also known as "The American Sailor."*

SECRET AGENT X-9 (N)
David McKay Pbll.: 1934 (Book 1: 84 pgs; Book 2: 124 pgs.) (8x7-1/2")
Book 1-Contains reprints of the first 13 weeks of the strip by Dashiell Hammett & Alex Raymond, complete except for 2 dailies 100.00 300.00 700.00
Book 2-Contains reprints immediately following contents of Book 1, for 20 weeks by Dashiell Hammett & Alex Raymond; complete except for two dailies. Last 5 strips misdated from 6/34, continuity correct 100.00 300.00 700.00

SILK HAT HARRY'S DIVORCE SUIT (N)
M. A. Donoghue & Co.: 1912 (5-3/4x15-1/2", oblong, B&W)
nn - Newspaper-r by Tad (Thomas A. Dorgan) 33.00 117.00 450.00

SINBAD A DOG'S LIFE (M)
Coward - McCann, Inc.: 1930 (11x 8-3/4", 104 pgs., single-sided, illustrated hard-c, B&W
nn - By Edwina 11.00 33.00 110.00
Sinbad...Again (1932, 10-15/16x 8-9/16", 104 pgs.) 11.00 33.00 110.00
NOTE: *Wordless comic strips from LIFE.*

SIS HOPKINS OWN BOOK AND MAGAZINE OF FUN
Leslie-Judge Co.: 1899-July 1911 (36 pgs, color-c, B&W) (merged into Judge's Library, later titled Film Fun)
any issue - By various 11.00 33.00 100.00
NOTE: *Zim, Flagg, Young, Newell, Adams, etc.*

SKEEZIX (Also see Gasoline Alley & Little Skeezix Books listed below) (I)
Reilly & Lee Co.: 1925 - 1928 (Strip-r, soft covers) (pictures & text)
...and Uncle Walt (1924)-Origin 26.00 104.00 225.00
...and Pal (1925), ...at the Circus (1926) 21.00 84.00 180.00
...& Uncle Walt (1927) (does this actually exist? reprint? never seen one yet)
...Out West (1928) 30.00 100.00 225.00
Hardback Editions... 34.00 136.00 245.00

SKEEZIX BOOKS, LITTLE (Also see Skeezix, Gasoline Alley) (G)
Reilly & Lee Co.: No date (1928, 1929) (Boxed set of three Skeezix books)
nn - Box with 3 issues of Skeezix. Skeezix & Pal, Skeezix at the Circus, Skeezix & Uncle Walt known. 1928 Set... 60.00 180.00 360.00
nn - Box with 4 issues of (3) above Skeezix plus "Out West" 80.00 330.00 550.00

SKEEZIX COLOR BOOK (N)
McLaughlin Bros. Inc, Springfield, Mass: 1929 (9-1/2x10-1/4", 28 pgs, one third in full color, rest in B&W)
2023 - By Frank King; strip-r to color 20.00 75.00 150.00

SKIPPY (see also Life Presents Skippy, Always Belittlin', That Rookie From 13th Squad)
No publisher listed: Circa 1920s (10x8", 16 pgs., color/B&W cartoons)
nn - By Percy Crosby 20.00 84.00 160.00

SKIPPY, LIFE PRESENTS (M)
Life Publishing Company & Henry Holt, NY: nd 1924 (134 pgs, 10-13/16x8-3/4", color hard-c, B&W
nn - By Percy L Crosby 100.00 300.00 550.00
NOTE: *Many sequential & single panel reprints from Skippy's earliest appearances in Life Magazine.*

SKIPPY
Greenberg, Publisher, Inc, NY: 1925. (11-14x8-5/8, 72 pgs, hard-c, B&W and color)
nn - By Percy L. Crosby 50.00 150.00 300.00
NOTE: *Some but not all of these comics were also in Life Presents Skippy; issued with dust wrapper.*

SKIPPY AND OTHER HUMOR
Greenberg: Publisher, NY: 1929 (11-1/4x8-1/2",72 pgs,tan hard-c, B&W and color)
nn - By Percy L. Crosby 25.00 75.00 160.00
NOTE: *Came with a dust jacket.*

SKIPPY (I)
Grossett & Dunlap: 1929 (7-3/8x6, 370 pgs, hardcover text with some art)
nn - By Percy Crosby (issued with a dust jacket) 23.00 92.00 190.00
NOTE: *This is worth very little without the dust wrapper; very common without athe dust jacket.*

SKIPPY
Greenberg Press: 1930 (soft cover, ca. 16 pp.,
nn - By Percy Crosby (scarce) 50.00 175.00 300.00
NOTE: *Reprints from LIFE cartoons, color, b/w. Crosby told Greenberg to withdraw from the market as it cheapened the hard cover prior editions. Greenberg then stopped publishing per agreement, and sent Crosby all the copper & zinc bookplates, which were in Crosby estate until 1996.*

SKIPPY CRAYON AND COLORING BOOK (N)
McLoughlin Bros, Inc., Springfield, MA: 1931 (13x9-3/4", 28 pgs, color-c, color & B&W)
2050 - By Percy Crosby 30.00 90.00 200.00
NOTE: *This item says on the front cover: "Licensed by Percy Crosby" because he owned his creation. About half the pages have one panel pre-printed in full color with same one b&w below for person to copy the colors.*

SKIPPY RAMBLES (I)
G.P. Putnam's Sons: 1932 (7 1/8 x 5 1/8, 202 pgs)
nn - By Percy Crosby 25.00 84.00 160.00
NOTE: *Issued with a dustjacket. Has Skippy plates by Crosby every 4 or 5 pages.*

SKUDDABUD STARRY STORY SERIES - FOLK FROM THE FUTURE (O,G)
no publisher listed: 1936 (9" x 11-7/8", 48 pgs, cardboard-c, B&W)
Book One (Rare) "Parachuting" 21.00 84.00 160.00
NOTE: *By Columba Krebs. Top half of each page is a continuing strip story, while bottom half are different stories, in prose, about the same characters -- a race of aliens who have migrated to Earth, from their dying world.*

S'MATTER POP? (N)
Saalfield Publ. Co.: 1917 (10x14", 44 pgs., B&W, cardboard-c,)
nn - By Charlie Payne; in full color; pages printed on one side 48.00 169.00 300.00

S'MATTER POP? (N) (25 ¢ cover price)
E.I. Company, New York: 1927 (8-15/16x7-1/8", 52 pgs, yellow soft-c perfect bound
nn - By C.M. Payne (scarce) 24.00 84.00 150.00
NOTE: *First comic book published by Hugo Gernsback, noted for inventing Amazing Stories among other memorable science fiction pulps. The World Science Fiction Convention Award, The Hugo, is named for him.*

SMITTY (See Treasure Box of Famous Comics) (N)
Cupples & Leon Co.: 1928 - 1933 (9x7", 96 pgs., B&W strip-r, hardcover)
1928-(96 pgs. 7x8-3/4") By Walter Berndt 50.00 185.00 350.00
1929-At the Ball Game (Babe Ruth on cover) 60.00 235.00 500.00
1930-The Flying Office Boy, 1931-The Jockey, 1932-In the North Woods each... 45.00 150.00 300.00
1933-At Military School 45.00 150.00 300.00
NOTE: *Each hardbound was published with a dust jacket; worth 50% more with dust jacket. The 1929 edition is very popular with baseball collectors. Strip debuted Nov 27, 1922.*

SMOKEY STOVER (See Dan Dunn & King of the Royal Mounted) (N)
Whitman Publishing: 1937 (5 1/2 x 7 1/4", 68pgs., color cardboard-c, B&W)
1010 36.00 150.00 300.00

SOCIAL COMEDY (M)
Life Publishing Company: 1902 (11-3/4 x 9-1/2", 128 pgs, B&W, illustrated hardcover)
nn - Artists include C.D. Gibson & Kemble. 25.00 75.00 150.00
NOTE: *Reprints cartoons and a few sequential comics from LIFE. Came in unmarked slipcase.*

SOCIAL HELL, THE (O)
Rich Hill: 1902
nn - By Ryan Walker 25.00 75.00 150.00
NOTE: *"The conditions of workers and the corruption of a political system beholden to corporate interests have been a major focus of human rights concerns since the 19th century. This early graphic novel depicts the social evils of unreformed capitalism. Ryan Walker was a syndicate cartoonist for many mainstream newspapers as well as for the communist Daily Worker." This description comes from http://www.lib.uconn.edu/DoddCenter/ascexh3.html, where you can find also a reproduction of the cover. I add that Ryan Walker was the editor of "The Saint Louis Republic" comic section since its inception in 1897; the supplement published "Alma and Oliver", George McManus's first series.*

SPORT AND THE KID (see The Umbrella Man) (N)
Lowman & Hanford Co.: 1913 (6-1/4x6-5/8",114 pgs, hardcover, B&W&orange)

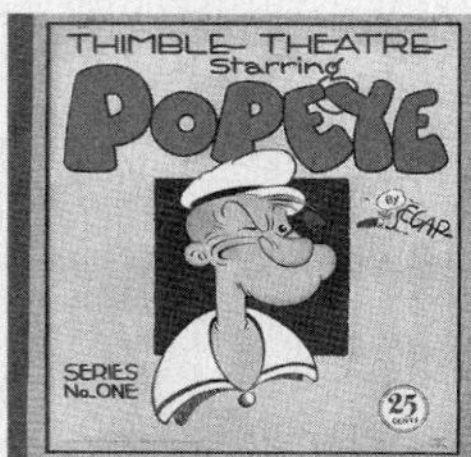

Thimble Theater #1 by E.C. Segar
1931 © Sonnet Publishing Co.

Tillie the Toiler #7 by Russ Westover
1932 © Cupples & Leon

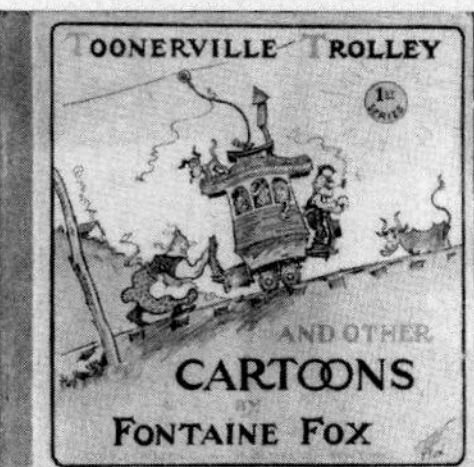

Toonerville Trolley And Other Cartoons
1921 © Cupples & Leon

GD2.0 FN6.0 VF8.0

nn - By J.R. "Dok" Hager 20.00 70.00 150.00

STORY OF CONNECTICUT (N)
The Hartford Times: Vol.1 1935 - Vol.3 1936 (10-1/2" x 7-3/8",304 pgs,color hard-c, B&W)

Vol.1 - 3 20.00 70.00 150.00
NOTE: *Collects a newspaper strip on Connecticut State history, which ran in the Hartford Times. Strip is in a similar format to "Texas History Movies". Also published in a plain, blue hardcover.*

STORY OF JAPAN IN CHINA, THE (N,S)
Trans-Pacific News Service, NYC: Vol. 3, No.1 March 10, 1938 (9" x 6", 36 pgs, construction paper-c, B&W)

Vol.3 No.1 21.00 64.00 150.00
NOTE: *Part of the "China Reference Series" of booklets, detailing the Japanese occupation and brutalization of China. Consists entirely of cartoons. The other booklets in the series have no cartoons. Art by: Ding, Fitzpatrick, Herblock, Herman, Rollin Kirby, Knox, Low, Manning, Orr, Shoemaker, Talburt.*

STRANGE AS IT SEEMS (S)
Blue-Star Publishing Co.: 1932 (64 pgs., B&W, square binding)

1-Newspaper-r (*Published with & without No. 1 and price on cover.*) 32.00 128.00 200.00
Ex-Lax giveaway (1936, B&W, 24 pgs., 5x7") - McNaught Synd.
20.00 55.00 110.00

SULLIVANT'S ABC ZOO (I)
The Old Wine Press: 1946 (11-3/4x9-3/8", hardcover)

nn - By T.S. Sullivant (Rare) – – –
NOTE: *Reprints Mitchell & Miller material 1895-1898 and Life Publishing 1898-1926.*

TAILSPIN TOMMY STORY & PICTURE BOOK (N)
McLoughlin Bros.: No. 266, 1931? (nd) (10x10-1/2", color strip-r)

266 - By Forrest 43.00 172.00 300.00

TAILSPIN TOMMY (Also see Famous Feature Stories & The Funnies)(N)
Cupples & Leon Co.: 1932 (100 pgs., hard-c) (B&W 1930 strip reprints)

nn - (Scarce)- by Hal Forrest & Glenn Chaffin 50.00 150.00 400.00

TALES OF DEMON DICK AND BUNKER BILL (O)
Whitman Publishing Co.: 1934 (5-1/4x10-1/2", 80 pgs, color hardcover, B&W)

793 - By Spencer 33.00 100.00 300.00

TARZAN BOOK (The Illustrated...) (N)
Grosset & Dunlap: 1929 (9x7", 80 pgs.)

1(Rare)-Contains 1st B&W Tarzan newspaper comics from 1929. By Hal Foster
Cloth reinforced spine & dust jacket (50¢); Foster-c
With dust jacket... 100.00 350.00 630.00
Without dust jacket... 55.00 200.00 325.00
2nd Printing(1934, 25¢, 76 pgs.)-4 Foster pgs. dropped; paper spine, circle in lower right cover with 25¢ price. The 25¢ is barely visible on some copies
40.00 145.00 250.00
1967-House of Greystoke reprint-7x10", using the complete 300 illustrations/text from the 1929 edition minus the original indicia, foreword, etc. Initial version bound in gold paper & sold for $5.00. Officially titled **Burroughs Bibliophile #2**. A very few additional copies were bound in heavier blue paper. Gold binding... 2.25 6.75 20.00
Blue binding... 2.50 7.50 27.00

TARZAN OF THE APES TO COLOR (N)
Saalfield Publishing Co.: No. 988, 1933 (15-1/4x10-3/4", 24 pgs)
(Coloring book)

988-(Very Rare)-Contains 1929 daily reprints with some new art by Hal Foster. Two panels blown up large on each page with one at the top of opposing pages on every other double-page spread. Believed to be the only time these panels appeared in color. Most color panels are reproduced a second time in B&W to be colored
275.00 1100.00 2200.00

TARZAN OF THE APES The Big Little Cartoon Book (N)
Whitman Publishing Company: 1933 (4-1/2x3 5/8", 320 pgs, color-c, B&W)

744 - By Hal Foster (comic strips on every page) 60.00 175.00 350.00

TECK HASKINS AT OHIO STATE (S)
Lea-Mar Press: 1908 (7-1/4x5-3/8", 84 pgs, B&W hardcover)

nn - By W.A. Ireland; football cartoons-r from Columbus Ohio Evening Dispatch
30.00 100.00 180.00
NOTE: *Small blue & white patch of cover art pasted atop a color cloth quilt patter; pasted patch can easily peel off some copies.*

TECK 1909 (S)
Lea-Mar Press: 1909 (8-5/8 x 8-1/8", 124 pgs., B&W hardcover, 25¢)

nn - By W.A. Ireland; Ohio State University baseball cartoons-r
from Columbus Evening Dispatch 30.00 100.00 180.00

TEDDY BEAR BOOKS, THE (M) (see also LITTLE JOHNNY AND THE TEDDY BEARS)
Reilly & Britton Co., Chicago: 1907 (7-1/16" x 5-3/8", 24 pgs, hard-c, color

The Teddy Bears Come to Life, The Teddy Bears at the Circus, The Teddy Bears in a Smashup, The Teddy Bears on a Lark, The Teddy Bears on a Toboggan, The Teddy Bears at School, The Teddy Bears Go Fishing, The Teddy Bears in Hot Water
25.00 75.00 150.00
NOTE: *Books are all unnumbered. C & A by J.R. Bray; s-Robert D. Towne. Reprints "Little Johnny & the Teddy Bears" strips, from Judge Magazine. Similar in format to the Buster Brown Nuggets series. All eight books debuted simultaneously.*

TEDDY BEARS IN FUN AND FROLIC (M) (see LITTLE JOHNNY & THE TEDDY BEARS)
Reilly & Britton Co., Chicago: 1908 (8-3/4" x 8-3/4", 50 pgs, cardboard-c, color)

nn - (Rare) by J.R. Bray-a; Robert D. Towne-s 100.00 400.00 725.00
NOTE: *Reprints "Little Johnny & the Teddy Bears" strips, from Judge Magazine. Unknown if there were any other "Teddy Bear" titles published in this format.*

THE TEENIE WEENIES
Reilly & Britton, Chicago: 1916 (16-3/8x10-1/2", 52 pgs, cardboard-c, full color)

nn - By Wm. Donahey (Chicago Tribune-r) 200.00 550.00 1000.00

TERROR OF THE TINY TADS (see also UPSIDE DOWNS OF LITTLE LADY LOVEKINS AND OLD MAN MUFFAROO)
Cupples & Leon: 1909 (11x17, 26 Sunday strips in Black & Red, Stiff cardboard-c)

nn - By Gustave Verbeek (Very Rare) (no known sales)

TEXAS HISTORY MOVIES (N)
Various editions, 1928 to 1986 (B&W)

Book I -1928 Southwest Press (7-1/4 x 5-3/8, 56 pgs, cardboard cover)
for the Magnolia Petroleum Company 50.00 125.00 275.00
nn - 1928 Southwest Press (12-3/8 x 9-1/4, 232 pgs, HC) 75.00 200.00 400.00
nn - 1935 Magnolia Petroleum Company (6 x 9, 132 pgs, paper cover)
21.00 63.00 140.00
NOTE: *Exists with either Wagon Train or Texas Flag & Lafitte/pirate covers.*
nn - 1943 Magnolia Petroleum Company (132 pgs, paper cover)
25.00 55.00 120.00
nn - 1963 Graphic Ideas Inc (11 x 8-1/2, softcover) 12.00 37.00 75.00
NOTE: *Reprints daily newspaper strips from the Dallas News, on Texas history. 1935 editions onward distributed within the Texas Public School System. Prior to that they appear to be giveaway comic books for the Magnolia Petroleum Company. There are many more editions than the ones pointed out above.*

THAT SON-IN-LAW OF PA'S! (N)
Newspaper Feature Service: 1914 (2-1/2 by 3", color)

nn - *Imprinted on back for THE LESTER SHOE STORE.* 15.00 30.00 60.00
NOTE: *Single sheet printed in full color on both sides, unfolds to show 12 panel story.*

THIMBLE THEATRE STARRING POPEYE (See also Popeye) (N)
Sonnet Publishing Co.: 1931 - No. 2, 1932 (25¢, B&W, 52 pgs.)(Rare)

1-Daily strip serial-r in both by Segar 165.00 700.00 1400.00
2 140.00 600.00 1200.00
NOTE: *The very first Popeye reprint book. The first Thimble Theatre Sunday page appeared Dec 19, 1919. Popeye first entered Thimble Theatre on Jan 17, 1929.*

THREE FUN MAKERS, THE (N)
Stokes and Company: 1908 (10x15", 64 pgs., color) (1904-06 Sunday strip-r)

nn - Maud, Katzenjammer Kids, Happy Hooligan 800.00 2100.00 –
NOTE: *This is the first comic book to compile more than one newspaper strip together.*

TIGERS (Also see On and Off Mount Ararat) (N)
Hearst's New York American & Journal: 1902, 86 pgs. 10x15-1/4"

nn - Funny animal strip-r by Jimmy Swinnerton 600.00 1700.00 –
NOTE: *The strip began as The Journal Tigers in The New York Journal Dec 12, 1897-Sept 28 1903*

TILLIE THE TOILER (N)
Cupples & Leon Co.: 1925 - No. 8, 1933 (52 pgs., B&W, daily strip-r)

nn (#1) By Russ Westover 54.00 216.00 425.00
2-8 50.00 175.00 360.00
NOTE: *First newspaper strip appearance was in January, 1921.*

TILLIE THE TOILER MAGIC DRAWING AND COLORING BOOK
Sam L Gabriel Sons And Company: 1931 (8-1/2 x 12", 36 pages, stiff-c)

838-By Russ Westover 39.00 156.00 275.00

TIMID SOUL, THE (N)
Simon & Schuster: 1931 (12-1/4x9", 136 pgs, B&W hardcover, dust jacket?)

nn - By H. T. Webster (newspaper strip-r) 40.00 120.00 260.00

TIM McCOY, POLICE CAR 17 (O)
Whitman Publishing Co.: 1934 (14-3/4x11", 32 pgs, stiff color covers)

674-1933 original material 75.00 300.00 475.00
NOTE: *Historically important as first movie adaptation in comic books.*

TOAST BOOK
John C. Winston Co: 1905 (7-1/4 x 6,104 pgs, skull-shaped book, feltcover, B&W)

nn - By Clare Dwiggins 50.00 175.00 300.00
NOTE: *Cartoon illustrations accompanying toasts/poems, most involving alcohol.*

TOM SAWYER & HUCK FINN (N)
Stoll & Edwards Co.:1925 (10x10-3/4", 52 pgs, stiff covers)

nn - By "Dwig" Dwiggins; 1923, 1924-r color Sunday strips 50.00 200.00 350.00
NOTE: *By Permission of the Estate of Samuel L. Clemons and the Mark Twain Company.*

TOONERVILLE TROLLEY AND OTHER CARTOONS (N) (See Cartoons by Fontaine Fox)
Cupples & Leon Co.: 1921 (10 x10", 52 pgs., B&W, daily strip-r)

1 - By Fontaine Fox 75.00 300.00 550.00

TRAINING FOR THE TRENCHES (M)

When a Feller Needs a Friend
© P.F. Volland & Co.

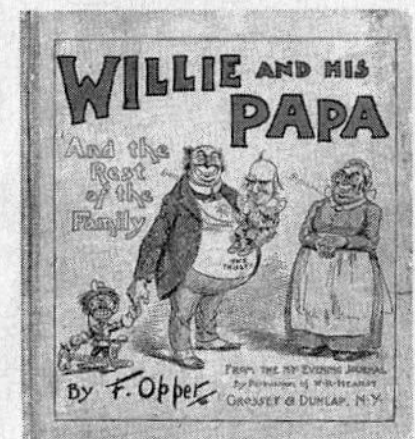

Willie and His Papa & the Rest of the Family by Opper
1901 © Grossett & Dunlap

The Yellow Kid #4 cover by Outcault
1897 © Howard, Ainslee & Co.

GD2.0 FN6.0 VF8.0

Palmer Publishing Company: 1917 (5-3/8 x 7", 20 pgs., paper-c, 10¢)
nn - By Lieut. Alban B. Butler, Jr. 21.00 84.00 150.00
NOTE: *Subtitle: "A book of humorous cartoons on a serious subject." Single-panels about military training.*

TREASURE BOX OF FAMOUS COMICS (N) (see Wonder Chest of Famous Comics)
Cupples & Leon Co.: 1934 8-1/2x(6-7/8", 36 pgs, soft covers) (Boxed set of 5 books)
Little Orphan Annie (1926) 21.00 84.00 180.00
Reg'lar Fellers (1928) 19.00 76.00 160.00
Smitty (1928) 19.00 76.00 160.00
Harold Teen (1931) 19.00 76.00 160.00
How Dick Tracy & Dick Tracy Jr. Caught The Racketeers (1933) 26.00 104.00 225.00
Softcover set of five books in box 160.00 640.00 1400.00
Box only 57.00 228.00 500.00
NOTE: *Dates shown are copyright dates; all books actually came out in 1934 or later. The softcovers are abbreviated versions of the hardcover editions listed under each character.*

T.R. IN CARTOONS (N)
A.C. McClurg & Co., Chicago: June 13, 1910 (10-5/8" x 8", 104? pgs, paper-c, B&W)
nn - By McCutcheon about Teddy Roosevelt - - -

TRUTH (See Victorian section for earlier issues including the first Yellow Kid appearances)
Truth Company, NY: 1886-1906? (13-11/16x10-5/16", 16 pgs, process color-c & center-folds, rest B&W)
1900-1906 issues 25.00 50.00 100.00

TRUTH SAVE IT FROM ABUSE & OVERWORK BEING THE EPISODE OF THE HIRED HAND & MRS. STIX PLASTER, CONCERTIST (N)
Radio Truth Society of WBAP: no date, 1924 (6-3/8 x 4-7/8, 40 pgs, paper cover, B&W)
nn - By V.T. Hamlin (Very Rare) 100.00 400.00 725.00
NOTE: *Radio station WBAP giveaway reprints strips from the Ft. Worth Texas Star-Telegram set at local radio station. 1st collected work by V.T. Hamlin, pre-Alley Oop.*

TWENTY FIVE YEARS AGO (see At The Bottom Of The Ladder) (M,S)
Coward-McCann: 1931 (5-3/4x8-1/4, 328 pgs, hardcover, B&W)
nn - By Camillus Kessler 32.00 128.00 250.00
NOTE: *Multi-image panel cartoons showing historical events for dates during the year.*

UMBRELLA MAN, THE (N) (See Sport And The Kid)
Lowman & Hanford Co.: 1911 (8-7/8x5-7/8",112 pgs, hard-c, B&W & orange)
nn - By J.R. "Dok" Hager (Seattle Times-r) 20.00 70.00 125.00

UNCLE REMUS AND BRER RABBIT (N)
Frederick A. Stokes Co.: 1907 (64 pgs, hardbound, color)
nn - By Joel C Harris & J.M. Conde 75.00 200.00 325.00

UPSIDE DOWNS OF LITTLE LADY LOVEKINS AND OLD MAN MUFFAROO
(see also TERROR OF THE TINY TADS)
New York Herald: 1905 (?) (N)
nn - By Gustav Verbeck 150.00 450.00 800.00

VAUDEVILLES AND OTHER THINGS (N)
Isaac H. Blandiard Co.: 1900 (13x10-1/2", 22 pgs., color) plus two reprints
nn - By Bunny (Scarce) 400.00 1000.00 -
nn - 2nd print "By the Creator of Foxy Grandpa" on-c but only has copyright info of 1900 (10-1/2x15 1/2, 28 pgs, color) 450.00 850.00 -
nn - 3rd print. "By the creator of Foxy Grandpa" on-c; has both 1900 and 1901 copyright info (11x13") 350.00 650.00 -

WALLY - HIS CARTOONS OF THE A.E.F. (N)
Stars & Stripes: 1917 (96 and 108 pgs, B&W)
nn - By Abian A "Wally" Wallgren (7x18; 96 pgs) 25.00 75.00 150.00
nn - another edition (108 pgs, 7x17-1/2) 25.00 75.00 150.00
NOTE: *World War One cartoons reprints from Stars & Stripes; sold to U.S. servicemen with profits to go to French War Orphans Fund. various editions from 1917-1920; there might be more than what we list here.*

WAR CARTOONS (S)
Dallas News: 1918 (11x9", 112 pgs, hardcover, B&W)
nn - By John Knott (WWOne cartoons) 20.00 70.00 130.00

WAR CARTOONS FROM THE CHICAGO DAILY NEWS (N,S)
Chicago Daily News: 1914 (10 cents, 7-3/4x10-3/4", 68 pgs, paper-c, B&W)
nn - By L.D. Bradley 20.00 70.00 130.00

WEBER & FIELD'S FUNNYISMS (S,M,O)
Arkell Comoany, NY: 1904 (10-7/8x8", 112 pgs, color-c, B&W)
1 - By various (only issue?) 20.00 70.00 150.00
NOTE: *Contains some sequential & many single panel strips by Outcault, George Luks, CA David, Houston, L Smith, Hy Mayer, Verbeck, Woolf, Sydney Adams, Frank "Chip" Bellew, Eugene "ZIM" Zimmerman, Phil May, FT Richards, Billy Marriner, Grosvenor and many others.*

WE'RE NOT HEROES (O,S)
E.C. Wells and J.W. Moss: 1933 (8-11/16" x 5-7/8", 52 pgs, B&W interior)
nn - By Eddie Wells; red & black paper-c 15.00 35.00 75.00
NOTE: *Amateurish cartoons about World War I vets in the Walter Reed Veteran's Hospital.*

WHEN A FELLER NEEDS A FRIEND (S)
P. F. Volland & Co.: 1914 (11-11/16x8-7/8)
nn - By Clare Briggs 37.00 131.00 220.00
NOTE: *Originally came in box with Briggs art (box is Rare); also numerous more modern reprints)*

WILD PILGRIMAGE (O)
Harrison Smith & Robert Haas: 1932 (9-7/8x7", 210 pgs, B&W hardcover w/dust jacket) (original wordless graphic novel in woodcuts)
nn - By Lynd Ward 50.00 175.00 300.00

WILLIE AND HIS PAPA AND THE REST OF THE FAMILY (I)
Grossett & Dunlap: 1901 (9-1/2x8", 200 pgs, hardcover from N.Y. Evening Journal by Permission of W. R. Hearst) (pictures & text)
nn - By Frederick Opper 100.00 260.00 400.00
NOTE: *Political satire series of single panel cartoons, involving whiny child Willie (President William McKinley), his rambunctious and uncontrollable cousin Teddy (Vice President Roosevelt), and Willie's Papa (trusts/monopolies) and their Maid (Senator) Hanna.*

WILLIE GREEN COMICS, THE (N) (see Adventures of Willie Green)
Frank M. Acton Co./Harris Brown: 1915 (8x15, 36 pgs); 1921 (6x10-1/8", 52 pgs, color paper cover, B&W interior, 25¢)
Book No. 1 By Harris Brown 45.00 158.00 300.00
Book 2 (#2 sold via mail order directly from the artist)(very rare) 45.00 172.00 325.00
NOTE: *Book No. 1 possible reprint of Adv. of Willie Green; definitely two different editions.*

WILLIE WESTINGHOUSE EDISON SMITH THE BOY INVENTOR (N)
William A. Stokes Co.: 1906 (10x16", 36 pgs. in color)
nn - By Frank Crane (Scarce) 375.00 900.00 1400.00
NOTE: *Comic strip began May 27, 1900 and ran thru 1914. Parody of inventors Westinghouse and Edison.*

WINNIE WINKLE (N)*Strip began as a daily Sept 20, 1920.*
Cupples & Leon Co.: 1930 - No. 4, 1933 (52 pgs., B&W daily strip-r)
1 40.00 160.00 360.00
2-4 25.00 110.00 300.00

WISDOM OF CHING CHOW, THE (see also The Gumps)
R. J. Jefferson Printing Co.: 1928 (4x3", 100 pgs, red & B&W cardboard cover) (newspaper strip-r The Chicago Tribune)
nn - By Sidney Smith (scarce) 30.00 90.00 150.00

WONDER CHEST OF FAMOUS COMICS (N) see Treasure Chest of Famous Comics)
Cupples & Leon Co.: 1935? 8-1/2x(6-7/8", 36 pgs, soft covers) (Boxed set of 5 books)
Little Orphan Annie #2 (1927) (Haunted House) 21.00 84.00 140.00
Little Orphan Annie #3 (1928) (in the Circus) 19.00 76.00 140.00
Smitty #2 (1929) (Babe Ruth app.) 19.00 76.00 140.00
Dolly Dimples and Bobby Bounce (1933) by Grace Drayton 19.00 76.00 140.00
How Dick Tracy & Dick Tracy Jr. Caught The Racketeers (1933) 26.00 104.00 200.00
Softcover set of five books in box 160.00 640.00 1250.00
Box only 57.00 228.00 425.00
NOTE: *Dates shown are original copyright dates of the first printings; all actually came out in 1934 or later. Extremely abbreviated versions of the hardcover editions listed under each character. It is suspected this came out the Christmas season following Teasure Chest of Famous Comics. which contains earlier editions.*

WORLD OF TROUBLE, A (S)
Minneapolis Journal: 1901 (10x8-3/4", 100 pgs, 40 pgs full color)
v3#1 - By Charles L. Bartholomew (editorial-r) 28.00 99.00 170.00

WRIGLEY'S "MOTHER GOOSE"
Wm. Wrigley Jr. Company, Chicago: 1915 (6" x 4", 28 pgs, full color)
nn - *Promotional comics for Wrigley's gum. Intro Wrigley's "Spearmen* 20.00 70.00 150.00
Book No. 2 20.00 70.00 150.00

YELLOW KID, THE (Magazine)(I) (becomes **The Yellow Book** #10 on)
Howard, Ainslee & Co., N.Y.: Mar. 20, 1897 - #9, July 17, 1897 (5¢, B&W w/color covers, 52p., stapled) (not a comic book)
1-R.F. Outcault Yellow kid on-c only #1-6. The same Yellow Kid color ad app. on back-c #1-6 (advertising the New York Sunday Journal) 875.00 3800.00 -
2-6 (#2 4/3/97, #5 5/22/97, #6, 6/5/97) 775.00 2950.00 -
7-9 (Yellow Kid not on-c) 145.00 500.00 -
NOTE: *Richard Outcault's Yellow Kid from the Hearst New York American represents the very first successful newspaper comic strip in America. Listed here due to historical importance.*

YELLOW KID IN MCFADDEN'S FLATS, THE (N)
G. W. Dillingham Co., New York: 1897 (50¢, 7-1/2x5-1/2", 196 pgs., B&W, squarebound)
nn - The first "comic" book featuring The Yellow Kid; E. W. Townsend narrative w/R. F. Outcault Sunday comic page art-r & some original drawings (Prices vary widely. Rare.) 7000.00 14,500.00 -
NOTE: *A Fair condition copy sold for $2,901 in August 2004.; restored app VF sold for $10,500 in 2005. A copy in Fine+ (spine intact) and loose back cover sold for $17,000 in 2006.*

YESTERDAYS (S)
The Reilly & Lee Co.: 1930 (8-3/4 x 7-1/2", 128 pgs, illustrated hard-c with dust jacket
nn - Text and cartoons about Victorian times by Frank Wing 25.00 50.00 100.00

Any addititions or corrections to this section are always welcome, very much encouraged and can be sent to **feedback@gemstonepub.com** to be processed for next year's Guide.

LEGENDS OF THE DARK KNIGHT
TOP 10 STORY ARCS
BY ED CATTO

Batman fans always want to know more. In the early days of the character, well-loved stories revealed past dark secrets, such as in *When Batman Was Robin* and *The First Batman*. By the '80s, Frank Miller's *Batman: Year One* would become the defect standard to reveal past stories about a present day character. In fact, *Year One* would set the premise of this series: *Batman: Legends of the Dark Knight*. Many fans would soon refer to it as simply *LOTDK* and thrill to the exciting premise: presenting the earliest tales of Batman's career by the industry's top creators.

The Legends of the Dark Knight stories would focus on Batman as an independent hero. James Gordon was never far away, usually serving as more of a colleague than a sidekick. Originally the series was clearly defined to avoid presenting tales featuring Robin, the Boy Wonder. These adventures take place before Batman recruited him into their ongoing war on crime. But even that rule would prove to be more of a general guideline as the series wore on. Borrowing the conceit from sister title *The Brave and the Bold*, sometimes Batman would enjoy a playdate with other heroes, such as the Viking Prince in *Destiny* (issues #35 and #36) and Ragman in *Snitch* (issue #51).

And while the tales were ostensibly to provide in-continuity stories from the early part of Batman's career, the series would often playfully sidestep those self-imposed rules. As the series continued, it would spark spin-offs and specials. Recently, a reboot would again provide opportunities for top creators to take their turn "at bat."

So please join me as we celebrate one of the most remarkable and enduring brand extensions in comics' history, and enjoy a look back at some of the very best and most memorable story arcs of *Batman: Legends of the Dark Knight*.

***Batman: Legends of the Dark Knight* #46 -49**
Heat
Writer: Doug Moench
Artist: Russ Heath

Be sure to have a cold lemonade at hand before you read this story. On the surface, *Heat* is the story of a killer on the loose in Gotham City during an oppressive heat wave. But just below the surface, you realize that it's also about the simmering passions and emotions that drive the main characters throughout this fast-paced four-parter.

In the earliest days of Batman's career, he works with an unexpectedly ally, the Catwoman, as they track down a serial killer.

Moench writes Catwoman as a strong-willed and focused woman. Although she is sexy, she is not anybody's plaything and makes that very clear. Batman and the Catwoman begin a dance that will last for years, and in many ways, this story serves as the springboard for their 75-year-old courtship.

Russ Heath is a classic comic artist, whose long career has provided an impressive body of work. In *Heat*, the great artist dazzles the reader with

LOTDK #47

strong figure work and detailed background. It's as if every action figure is placed "just so" in Heath's complex panorama of scenery. And he makes it look easy.

Heath is also known for having an appreciation of the female form. With Catwoman's sleek bodysuit and the many women in various stages of undress (due to the heat wave, of course) Heath is afforded several opportunities to illustrate one of his favorite subjects.

Interestingly, during the 2016 Baltimore Comic-Con panel honoring Russ Heath, the artist spoke about his distaste for excessive violence in comics. The panel moderator questioned Heath to explain further, and he re-told a violent scene from this story as an example of how far it had gone.

The story wraps up with a film noir-ish twist that's clever, wistful and memorable. The tales big finish almost seems more like a Will Eisner *Spirit* story than a mundane superhero story. But then hat's the magic of the LOTDK series.

TRIVIA: Although the villain is ostensibly Cat-Man, he looks more like the obscure Bat-Villain, the King of Cats.

BEST LINE: Catwoman to Batman, who is holding a scantily clad woman in his arms: "if you ask me, you need help…and I don't mean with her."

***Legends of the Dark Knight* #31**
Family
Writer: James D. Hudnall
Artist: Brent Anderson

So many of the *LOTDK* stories strip away the rich narrative tapestry that makes Batman unique. In this series, there's often very little of the rich supporting cast or familiar props and settings.

Family, a stylish done-in-one story by James D. Hudnall and Brent Anderson, follows that tradition to a degree. The tale showcases Batman's deep affection for his butler, Alfred. All the many roles that Alfred plays are touched on: mentor, invaluable detail man, Mother Hen, parental substitute and the close friend who keeps an accomplished man humble with gentle teasing.

In this tale, Bruce Wayne decides Alfred needs a vacation. He arranges to send him off to the mythical Corto Maltese, which seems to be the most dangerous place on earth outside of Gotham City. Clearly, the World's Greatest Detective is not the World's Greatest Travel Agent. When local bandits capture Alfred, it's up to Batman to don his cape and cowl to mount an international rescue.

Brent Anderson's art just sings in this tale. Anderson has always been a strong draftsman,

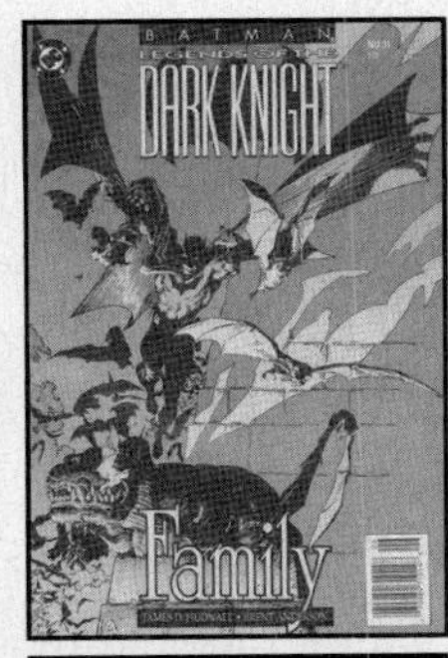

LOTDK #31

but here he provides the reader with innovative and fresh page layouts. Of note, Anderson clearly is having fun as he uses Batman's signature cape to create unique panel shapes.

Unlike heroes such as Hawkman, Batman does not use his avatar as a tool in his ongoing war on criminals. But Hudnall employs a clever trick with actual bats. It fits the story in a fun way and should have been used more by other writers.

TRIVIA: Batman recognizes the smell of marijuana on the villain's henchmen.

BEST LINE: Alfred teases Batman by saying, "Ah, finally! A new girlfriend and you want the mansion to yourself."

***Batman: Legends of the Dark Knight* #42 & 43**
Hot House
Writer: John Francis Moore
Artist P. Craig Russell

This sultry two-part adventure thrusts Batman into a tangled mystery full of deceit and misdirection. Russell's gorgeous art enthralls the reader, just as the villainess Poison Ivy enthralls men. Moore provides just enough plot twists to create a memorable drama that's refreshingly clever and yet firmly grounded in the established Batman mythology.

Unlike so many of the *LOTDK* story arcs, this one seems to be a product of the times. The fashion and hairstyles scream 1980s. Several story elements, including designer drugs and a *Fatal Attraction* reference, also date the story. And even by comic book standards, it was of the moment, too. This story weaves the then-recently-retrofitted Jason Woodrue character, freshly plucked from Alan Moore's *Swamp Thing*, into Poison Ivy's backstory.

Hot House uses the two issue format effectively. Part one reads like a complete mystery, where Poison Ivy is the victim, not villain. It makes you wonder if all men just want beautiful women to be inherently good. Part two turns the tables as Batman, Gordon and the readers slowly realize there's more to the story.

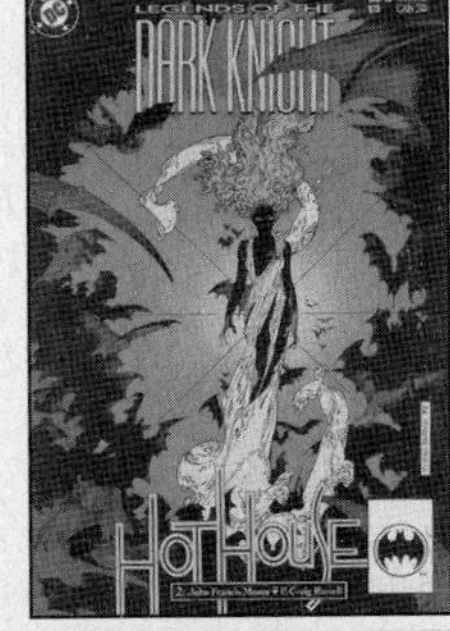

LOTDK #43

The interior art is lyrical and fluid, with wonderful motion imbued in every fabric and plant. Russell delights the reader with lovely portraits, intricate backgrounds, clever dramatic staging and flowing, poetical line work.

The gorgeous covers are exceptional. The first cover spotlights a gothic-style Batman in Ivy's environment: a verdant greenhouse stuffed with Ivy. By contrast, the second cover displays an alluring Poison Ivy against a background of angry crimson, surrounded by bats.

Moore and Russell portray the early friendship between James Gordon and Batman as comfortable and mature. They clearly respect and admire each others' skills, but do not encroach on the other's expertise. This is in stark contrast to Batman's opinions on the rest of the police force. At one point, Batman dismisses a local patrolman, abruptly telling the cop to "Call Gordon, I'll talk to him."

There's a sense of whimsy in the relationship too. A scene opens with Batman and Gordon going through the murder victim's files. It's a collaborative effort, as each detective rifles through the many papers. From their shoulder-to-shoulder search, they finally stumble upon a clue. As the scene is about to end, Batman nags his friend to stop smoking. Gordon gives it right back the Caped Crusader, saying he'll stop "when you quit your midnight ramblings."

Unlike so many encounters, Moore and Russell eschew the overused scene where Gordon inevitably turns around to find Batman is no longer there. Instead, we, see a crouching Batman responding with a "Hrmmph!" to his friend's gentle teasing.

TRIVIA: Pamela Isley doesn't appear as Poison Ivy in the story proper - only in a hallucinogenic dream/ fight sequence.

BEST LINE: "Maybe we all walk a narrow precipice, a thin rope, a shaky bridge, and try our best not to look down."

***Batman: Legends of the Dark Knight* #52 & 53**
TAO
Writer: Alan Grant
Artist: Arthur Ranson

I always enjoyed The Shadow's adventures in Chinatown. They seem to have a slightly different tone from the rest of the pulp crime fighter's adventures. And The Shadow even has a different appellation in Chinatown: Ying Ko. Readers naturally wondered if there was more to it all.

TAO, by longtime Batman scribe Alan Grant and new Batman artist Arthur Ranson, starts out as Batman's Chinatown adventure, following in the footsteps of his pulp predecessor. But it quickly becomes so much more, and reveals an untold chapter in the Batman mythology.

TAO begins in the past with young Bruce Wayne's journey around the world to expand and develop his crime fighting skill set is an odyssey that is all too infrequently touched upon in the Batman mythology. *TAO* adds backstory of a young man who is trying to learn and finds some struggles along the way.

In the flashback sequences, Bruce travels to the Tanggula Shan Mountains, on the border of China and Tibet, to study with an aged master. Repercussions of the sojourn impact Batman's present day adventures in the Gotham's Chinatown.

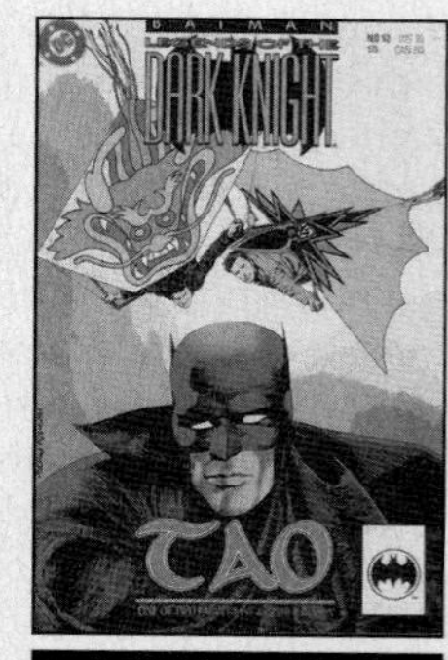

LOTDK #52

British artist Arthur Ranson was a new name to many American comic fans. His detailed artwork has the feel of classic illustration: solid figures, realistic castles and detailed backgrounds. But shifting it into high gear, he pushes the creative envelope with innovative panel layouts, inky shadow scenes and an impactful double page spread.

This all too-brief two-parter is memorable for the new characters it introduces, the engaging Kite-battle fight scenes, the modern day Chinatown sequences and the clever resolution of the secondary conflict.

TRIVIA: Ranson renders Bruce Wayne in such a way that he looks like actor Ron Ely.

BEST LINE: The aged master first speaks to Batman, and emasculates him with a teasing greeting: "Yes, Miss?"

***Batman: Legends of the Dark Knight* #69 & 70**
Criminals
Writer: Steven Grant
Artist: Mike Zeck

In *Criminals*, Steven Grant and Mike Zeck, fresh from their success on Marvel's *The Punisher*, deliver an intriguing two-part prison story, where Batman goes undercover to get to the bottom of things. The drama starts in a fresh way: from the point-of-view of a group of thieves, and showcases their fear of Batman, both warranted and irrational.

"Batman never really worked as a character for me - I realize I'm in the minority there - and I was trying to figure out a way to wrap my head around him," said Steven Grant.

"Back when Frank Miller was starting work on *The Dark Knight Returns*, he mentioned to me one day that he viewed Batman as a force of nature. That always struck me as a reasonably interesting idea, so this ended up being my take on it," Grant said. "That's what I was playing with in this story: the idea that Batman is a legendary, if not mythic, figure to Gotham's underworld, a sort of monster haunting them. He comes out of nowhere, places he couldn't possibly be. He's not human: that's why Bruce Wayne never appears in the story. So criminals don't say his name, it's like jinxing yourself."

"Criminals are a cowardly, suspicious lot, after all," he added.

But the action quickly shifts to the prison. "Coming up with a prison story idea was easy: Mike liked drawing prison stories." Grant said. "We'd already done *The Punisher* in a prison a couple of times, so when we were asked to do a Batman story, Mike suggested it. It was fine with me, I thought between those and Damned, I don't know how many more prison stories I have in me. I found it interesting because it's a very claustrophobic, restricted setting, so how does a character like Batman operate in that controlled environment? It was an interesting challenge."

LOTDK #69

Zeck's moody cover on the first issue starts it all off, but after that, it's a seamless collaboration. "By that point, Mike and I were finishing each other's sentences, so it was always a dream working with him. The only regret I've ever had about working with Mike is that we didn't do it a lot more times. I'd work with him again anytime he asked," Grant said.

TRIVIA: The cover to *Batman* #46, by Win Mortimer and George Roussous, was the first time a Batman comic showcased a prison.

BEST LINE: "There a rule in Gotham City, avoid his name. Do not invoke the devil. Call the devil and the devil will answer."

***Batman: Legends of the Dark Knight* #76-78**
Sleeping
Writer and Artist: Scott Hampton

So many of us find "the road not traveled" to be irresistible to explore, but in *Sleeping*, Scott Hampton reminds us how that trip can be tortuous and heartbreaking.

Sleeping, written and illustrated by Scott Hampton, is a wispy, dreamlike tale of love lost and purpose redefined. Hampton's gorgeous art, more illustrative and painterly than traditional comic art, is perfectly suited to this haunting tale.

On the way home from an event, the Wayne limousine crashes in a terrible accident, leaving millionaire playboy Bruce Wayne in a coma. While faithful Alfred waits and prays by his side, Batman embarks on a spiritual journey in a mythical, albeit hallucinogenic land.

LOTDK #77

While on this journey, he encounters two follow travelers. It is foretold that Batman is destined to meet his evil doppelganger. The story progresses in that tip-toe-y, meandering way that dreams do, and soon Hampton reveals that this evil doppelgänger is actually Batman's wife!

She explains that in her reality, Batman didn't embark on is crusade, and instead Bruce donated his fortune to charity, became a writer, and met the love of his life.

Like Alan Moore and Dave Gibbons' classic Superman story *For The Man Who Has Everything*, (from *Superman Annual* #11) a simpler, sweeter and more fulfilling life tor the hero is presented. The reader can't help but think that, although they enjoy the hero's adventures, perhaps the simpler family life would have been better.

At the story's conclusion, Batman and Mary, his wife from the road-not-traveled, both reaffirm who they are and the choices they have made. Hampton delivers a hauntingly poignant ending that stays with everyone who's ever wondered about their own life and asked, "what if..?"

BEST LINE: "Yes, Bruce, Mary...your wife. That is - I'm the wife you would have known if you hadn't chosen to become..."

TRIVIA: Hampton also offers a unique glimpse of Batman's parents in *Sleeping*, as the hero desperately seeks parental approval.

***Legends of the Dark Knight* #16 - 20**
Venom
Writer: Denny O'Neil
Layouts Trevor Von Eeden
Finished Pencils, Inks & Covers: José Luís Garcia-López

A fatal failure, a steep climb from the abyss, and a hero's ultimate resolve are memorably explored in the five-part *Venom* story arc. This story graphically shows the results of Batman wanting to accomplish too much, and subsequently giving into temptation to meet unrealistic goals. There are plenty of disturbing sequences in this story, and it's especially difficult for fans to watch Batman develop a nasty drug addiction.

Venom showcases several creators. Denny O'Neil, the long-time Batman scribe, should be applauded for trying something so new and different with the character. José Luís Garcia-López's covers are impactful and compelling. Colorist Steve Oliff creates especially striking colors on these covers. And the boundary-pushing artist, Trevor Von Eeden, is listed as layout artist in the credits.

LOTDK #17

"Although I'm credited as only layout artist, *Venom* was actually pretty comprehensively--albeit lightly--penciled by me, which the artist assigned the book, Russell Braun, pretty much just traced over in darker pencil," Von Eeden said.

"I really enjoyed drawing this Denny O'Neil script--and I was later told that the brilliant artist/inker José Luís Garcia-López kept xeroxes of my light pencils next to his board, while inking. Whether or not that's true, I'm very happy with the final results. Both Russell and José remained very true not only to my storytelling, but to my actual drawing style at the time," Von Eeden said.

"I was very fortunate to have José as inker again on the very last job I drew for DC Comics--the five-part Batman and Robin story arc in *LOTDK* #149-153. But as far as *Venom* goes, most importantly, I want to have everyone who reads that series to know that on the page where our Dark Knight druggie takes the pill for the first time--the blood running down from Batman's eye when he looks at the Venom pill were absolutely not my doing!" Von Eeden said. "To this day, I have no idea why those seemingly deliberately and clumsily done alterations were made to my work, and I'd really appreciate my fans out there knowing that those odd changes were certainly not my doing! I remain somewhat honored, nonetheless, to have drawn the story in which the great Batman finally personally faces and overcomes drug addiction. Now if only I could draw the story where the great nation of America finally faces and overcomes its hypocrisy addiction... but that's probably a tough call in a country born the land of the free and the home of the 'slave.'"

TRIVIA: The theme of Batman rescuing Alfred in a South American country would be revisited in *LOTDK* #31.

BEST LINE: Alfred has a heart to heart with Batman and says, "Your whole life testifies to a great capacity for obsession."

***Batman: Legends of the Dark Knight* #89- 90**
Clay
Writer: Alan Grant
Artist: Quique Alcatena

In a strange, yet beautiful tale, Alan Grant again returns to the Batman to provide a stage for the gorgeous artwork of Argentinian artist Quique Alcatena.

Alcatena's the type of illustrator that makes you want to linger over each page, and muse what the artwork would look like if it was hanging on your living room wall.

The two part adventure *Clay* tells an offbeat adventure from the earliest days of Batman's career. Interestingly, this story focuses on the second villain called Clayface to appear in the continuity, not the first. This version of the character is a slippery, sloppy bad guy, having been grotesquely transformed into living mud. And while many of the earlier *LOTDK* stories deal with Batman's focus on more realistic criminals and less on fantastic antagonists, this story is clearly a Batman vs. a monster story.

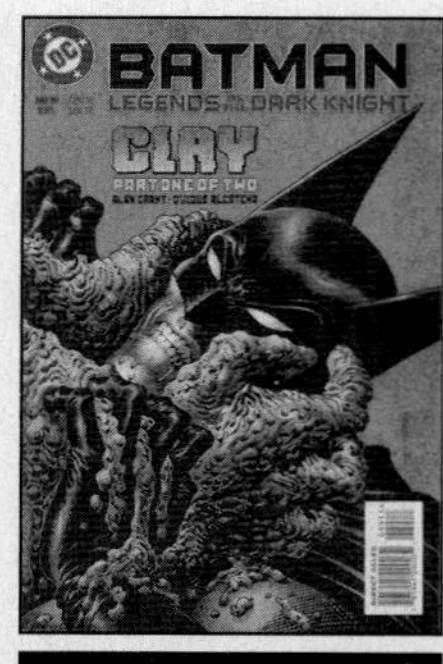

LOTDK #89

The strong page layouts, sympathetic retelling of the villain's origin and fantastic covers ensures this classic tale a spot on our best of *LOTDK* list.

TRIVIA: A retelling of the story "The Challenge of Clay-Face" in *Detective Comics* #298.

BEST LINE: "NOOOOOO!"

***Batman: Legends of the Dark Knight* #65-68**
Going Sane
Writer: J. M. DeMatteis
Artist: Joe Staton

Going Sane is one of the few *Batman: Legends of the Dark Knight* stories to feature the Dark Knight Detective's main antagonist, the Joker. Like an elaborate joke, this story has a clear plan and plenty of misdirection to surprise the reader. At first glance, it would seem to be the long-awaited origin of the Joker. But there's so much more to it.

DeMatteis is especially clever as he toys with

LOTDK #65

the readers, seemingly developing one of the most silly and simplistic alter egos for the Joker: Joe Kerr.

"I don't think we've ever really settled what happened to the guy who became the Joker. There were chemicals and the script says he takes pills to counter the skin color, but what about his grimace? How damaged are the muscles that make that grin?" Joe Staton said. "My main challenge was to have Joe Kerr's resting face look like it could go back to the Joker's image without losing the general look of the original."

DeMatteis explores the idea of the selfless hero here too. The female lead realizes that she must sacrifice her own potential happiness with Bruce, knowing that he will always pursue a selfless path of self-sacrifice. Fans may wonder if they are in fact, selfish, never permitting their hero to enjoy happiness as they always need to enjoy "more adventures."

TRIVIA: This story was originally submitted by J. M. DeMatteis years earlier, but shelved at the time because it was too close to another Joker story planned for publication: Moore & Bolland's *The Killing Joke*.

BEST LINE: "People struggle…break their backs…to make decent lives for themselves, for their children."

***Legends of the Dark Knight* #11- 15**
Prey
Writer: Dough Moench
Pencils: Paul Gulacy
Inks: Terry Austin

Prey, a quintessential *LOTDK* story showcasing an early adventure of Caped Crusader, is a breakneck adventure with gorgeous art by Paul Gulacy and an intricate story by Doug Moench.

Though populated by many characgters, Prey's scene stealer is the oddly-familiar Hugo Strange. He's one of Batman's earliest foes, but whenever fans read a story featuring him, they think, "Oh, yeah, that guy." And then that notion is immediately followed by "they should use him more." Here, Strange lives up to his name. He's wicked and twisted and hypocritical in every way. Although this adventure chronologically takes place before the classic *Detective Comics* storyline by Englehart and Rogers that featured Hugo Strange, this story feels like a sequel.

Paul Gulacy is a masterful creator who has illustrated many of the best loved Batman stories. To his credit, each time Gulacy draws a Batman story, he offers up a slightly different version of Batman. In *Prey*, his Batman is lean and rugged, focused on the matters at hand but, as you would expect from a millionaire playboy, doing it all with a sense of effortless style. And that's a great way to describe Gulacy's art on this art - he does it all with a sense of effortless style.

LOTDK #13

An important and easy-to-overlook element of this story arc are the brilliant inks by Terry Austin. A top-notch inker with a hard-edged artist voice, Terry Austin complements Gulacy's incredible pencils and binds them with a tight style. It's almost as if all the primal urges, fears and passions of all the main characters are trying to burst off the page, and are reined in by the no-nonsense Austin inking.

Gulacy's covers deserve credit for making this memorable series all the more memorable. Each one is like a secret code to hard-core and casual fans alike, with a prophecy that you are going to just love the story that unfolds within.

TRIVIA: Moench and Gulacy would reunite in *Terror*, in *Batman: Legends of the Dark Knight* #137-141.

BEST LINE: Batman reflecting on a difficult night of crime-fighting: "…And I had to walk all the way home."

(Re) Visting Gotham City

Picking up an issue of *Legends of the Dark Knight* is like being an invited to a great party attended by all the coolest people. It's both a celebration to a wonderful and versatile character and a great way for the industry's top professionals to contribute to an ongoing pop culture quilt of adventure stories.

The 10 stories selected may not be your top 10 favorites, but that's to be expected. I anticipate that these 10 might not even be my top 10 next year. We all change and grow, but it's nice to know that at one time, there was a place where passionate readers and top professionals could meet to share stories about a favorite character.

Ed Catto is the co-owner of Captain Action Enterprises and is co-founder of Bonfire Agency. He is a lifelong pop culture enthusiast.

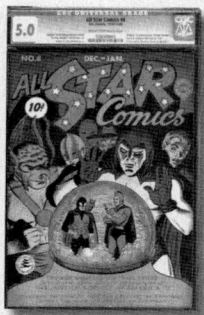

A&A: The Adventures of Archer & Armstrong #6 © VAL

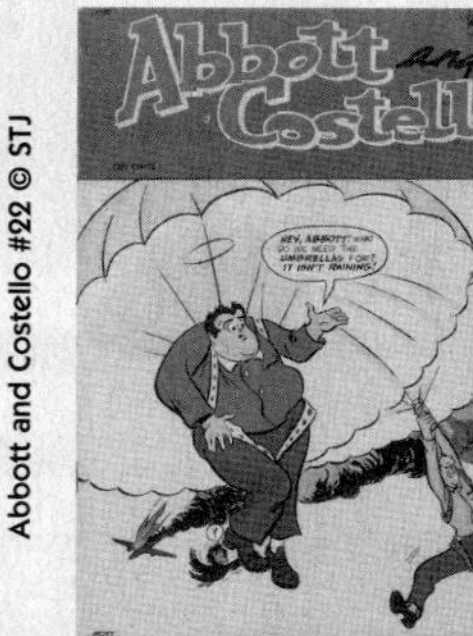

Abbott and Costello #22 © STJ

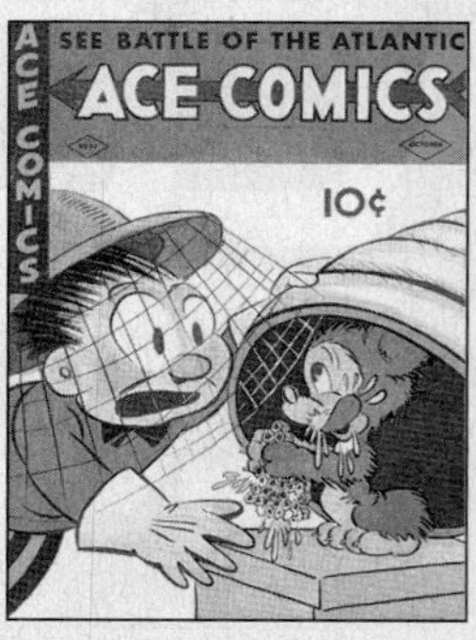

Ace Comics #55 © DMP

GD VG FN VF VF/NM NM-
2.0 4.0 6.0 8.0 9.0 9.2

The correct title listing for each comic book can be determined by consulting the indicia (publication data) on the beginning interior pages of the comic. The official title is determined by those words of the title in capital letters only, and not by what is on the cover. Titles are listed in this book as if they were one word, ignoring spaces, hyphens, and apostrophes, to make finding titles easier. Exceptions are made in rare cases. Comic books listed should be assumed to be in color unless noted "B&W".

Comic publishers are invited to send us sample copies for possible inclusion in future guides.

PRICING IN THIS GUIDE: Prices for **GD 2.0** (Good), **VG 4.0** (Very Good), **FN 6.0** (Fine), **VF 8.0** (Very Fine), **VF/NM 9.0** (Very Fine/Near Mint),and **NM– 9.2** (Near Mint–) are listed in whole U.S. dollars except for prices below $7 which show dollars and cents. **The minimum price listed is $3.00**, the cover price for current new comics. Many books listed at this price can be found in $1.00 boxes at conventions and dealers stores.

A-1 (See A-One)

A&A: THE ADVENTURES OF ARCHER & ARMSTRONG
Valiant Entertainment: Mar, 2016 - No. 12, Feb, 2017 ($3.99)

1-12: 1-Rafer Roberts-s/David Lafuente-a. 5-Faith app. 5-12-Norton-a 4.00
10-Cat cosplay photo variant-c 4.00

ABADAZAD
CrossGen (Code 6): Mar, 2004 - No. 3, May, 2004 ($2.95)

1-3-Ploog-a/c; DeMatteis-s 3.00
1-2nd printing with new cover 3.00

ABATTOIR
Radical Comics: Oct, 2010 - No. 6, Aug, 2011 ($3.99/$3.50, limited series)

1-($3.99) Cansino-a/Levin & Peteri-s 4.00
2-6-($3.50) 3.50

ABBIE AN' SLATS (...With Becky No. 1-4) (See Comics On Parade, Fight for Love, Giant Comics Edition 2, Giant Comics Editions #1, Sparkler Comics, Tip Topper, Treasury of Comics, & United Comics)
United Features Syndicate: 1940; March, 1948 - No. 4, Aug, 1948 (Reprints)

	GD	VG	FN	VF	VF/NM	NM-
Single Series 25 ('40)	40	80	120	246	411	575
Single Series 28	34	68	102	199	325	450
1 (1948)	17	34	51	98	154	210
2-4: 3-r/Sparkler #68-72	10	20	30	58	79	100

ABBOTT AND COSTELLO (...Comics)(See Giant Comics Editions #1 & Treasury of Comics)
St. John Publishing Co.: Feb, 1948 - No. 40, Sept, 1956 (Mort Drucker-a in most issues)

	GD	VG	FN	VF	VF/NM	NM-
1	81	162	243	518	884	1250
2	40	80	120	246	411	575
3-9 (#8, 8/49; #9, 2/50)	30	60	90	177	289	400
10-Son of Sinbad story by Kubert (new)	34	68	102	204	335	465
11,13-20 (#11, 10/50; #13, 8/51; #15, 12/52)	20	40	60	117	189	260
12-Movie issue	21	42	63	124	202	280
21-30: 28-r/#8. 29,30-Painted-c	15	30	45	86	133	180
31-40: 33,36,38-Reprints	13	26	39	74	105	135
3-D #1 (11/53, 25¢)-Infinity-c	32	64	96	188	307	425

ABBOTT AND COSTELLO (TV)
Charlton Comics: Feb, 1968 - No. 22, Aug, 1971 (Hanna-Barbera)

	GD	VG	FN	VF	VF/NM	NM-
1	7	14	21	46	86	125
2	4	8	12	27	44	60
3-10	3	6	9	21	33	45
11-22	3	6	9	17	26	35

ABC (See America's Best TV Comics)

ABC: A-Z (one-shots)
America's Best Comics: Nov, 2005 - July, 2006 ($3.99, one-shots)

... Greyshirt and Cobweb (1/06) character bios; Veitch-s/a; Gebbie-a; Dodson-c 4.00
... Terra Obscura and Splash Brannigan (3/06) character bios; Barta-a; Dodson-c 4.00
... Tom Strong and Jack B. Quick (11/05) character bios; Sprouse-a; Nowlan-a; Dodson-c 4.00
... Top Ten and Teams (7/06) character bios; Ha & Cannon-a; Veitch-a; Dodson-c 4.00

ABE SAPIEN... (Hellboy character)
Dark Horse Comics: Apr, 2013 - Present ($3.50/$3.99)

1-33: 1,2-Subtitled "Dark and Terrible"; Mignola & Allie-s/Fiumara-a/c. 8-Oeming-a. 23-Helboy app.; Nowlan-a 3.50
34-36-($3.99) 4.00
...: Drums of the Dead (3/98, $2.95) 1-Thompson-a. Hellboy back-up; Mignola-s/a/c 4.00
...: The Abyssal Plain (6/10 - No. 2, 7/10, $3.50) 1,2-Mignola & Arcudi-s/Snejbjerg-a 3.50
...: The Devil Does Not Jest (9/11 - No. 2, 10/11, $3.50) Mignola & Arcudi-s. 1-Two covers by Johnson & Francavilla 3.50
...: The Drowning (2/08 - No. 5, 6/08, $2.99) 1-5-Mignola-s/c; Alexander-a 3.50
...: The Haunted Boy (10/09, $3.50) 1-Mignola & Arcudi-s/Reynolds-a/Johnson-c 3.50

ABIGAIL AND THE SNOWMAN
Boom Entertainment (KaBOOM!): Dec, 2014 - No. 4, Mar, 2015 ($3.99, limited series)

1-4-Roger Langridge-s/a. 1-Covers by Langridge & Liew 4.00

A. BIZARRO
DC Comics: Jul, 1999 - No. 4, Oct, 1999 ($2.50, limited series)

1-4-Gerber-s/Bright-a 3.00

ABOMINATIONS (See Hulk)
Marvel Comics: Dec, 1996 - No. 3, Feb, 1997 ($1.50, limited series)

1-3-Future Hulk storyline 3.00

ABRAHAM LINCOLN LIFE STORY (See Dell Giants)

ABRAHAM STONE
Marvel Comics (Epic): July, 1995 - No. 2, Aug, 1995 ($6.95, limited series)

1,2-Joe Kubert-s/a 7.00

ABSENT-MINDED PROFESSOR, THE (see Shaggy Dog & The... under Movie Comics)

ABSOLUTE VERTIGO
DC Comics (Vertigo): Winter, 1995 (99¢, mature)

	GD	VG	FN	VF	VF/NM	NM-
nn-1st app. Preacher. Previews upcoming titles including Jonah Hex: Riders of the Worm, The Invisibles (King Mob), The Eaters, Ghostdancing & Preacher	2	4	6	10	14	18

ABYSS, THE (Movie)
Dark Horse Comics: June, 1989 - No. 2, July, 1989 ($2.25, limited series)

1,2-Adaptation of film; Kaluta & Moebius-a 3.00

ACCELERATE
DC Comics (Vertigo): Aug, 2000 - No. 4, Nov, 2000 ($2.95, limited series)

1-4-Pander Bros.-a/Kadrey-s 3.00

ACCLAIM ADVENTURE ZONE
Acclaim Books: 1997 ($4.50, digest size)

1-Short stories of Turok, Troublemakers, Ninjak and others 4.50

ACCUSED, THE (Civil War II tie-in)
Marvel Comics: Oct, 2016 ($4.99, one-shot)

1-The trial of Hawkeye; Matt Murdock app.; Guggenheim-s/Bachs & Brown-a/Mack-c 5.00

ACE COMICS
David McKay Publications: Apr, 1937 - No. 151, Oct-Nov, 1949 (All contain some newspaper strip reprints)

	GD	VG	FN	VF	VF/NM	NM-
1-Jungle Jim by Alex Raymond, Blondie, Ripley's Believe It Or Not, Krazy Kat begin (1st app. of each)	343	686	1029	2400	4200	6000
2	100	200	300	635	1093	1550
3-5	68	136	204	435	743	1050
6-10	52	104	156	328	552	775
11-The Phantom begins (1st app., 2/38) (in brown costume)	300	600	900	2010	3505	5000
12-20	41	82	123	256	428	600
21-25,27-30	37	74	111	222	361	500
26-Origin & 1st app. Prince Valiant (5/39); begins series?	139	278	417	883	1517	2150
31-40: 37-Krazy Kat ends	22	44	66	132	216	300
41-60	15	30	45	88	137	185
61-64,66-76-(7/43; last 68 pgs.)	14	28	42	80	115	150
65-(8/42)-Flag-c	15	30	45	88	137	185
77-84 (3/44; all 60 pgs.)	12	24	36	67	94	120
85-99 (52 pgs.)	11	22	33	60	83	105
100 (7/45; last 52 pgs.)	12	24	36	67	94	120
101-134: 128-(11/47)-Brick Bradford begins. 134-Last Prince Valiant (all 36 pgs.)	10	20	30	56	76	95
135-151: 135-(6/48)-Lone Ranger begins	9	18	27	52	69	85

ACE KELLY (See Tops Comics & Tops In Humor)

ACE KING (See Adventures of Detective...)

ACES
Acme Press (Eclipse): Apr, 1988 - No. 5, Dec, 1988 ($2.95, B&W, magazine)

1-5 3.00

ACES HIGH
E.C. Comics: Mar-Apr, 1955 - No. 5, Nov-Dec, 1955

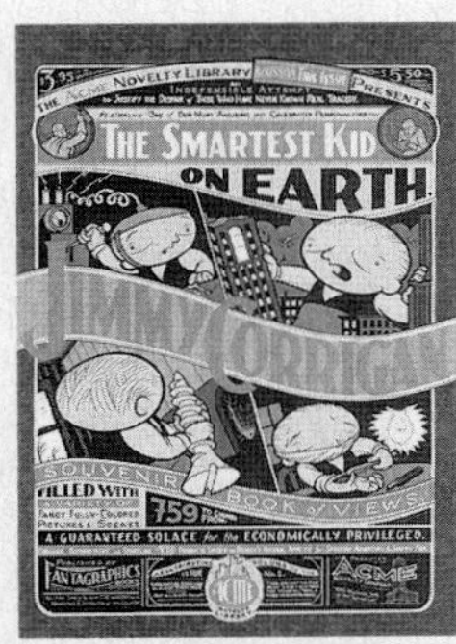

Acme Novelty Library #1 © Chris Ware

Action Comics #80 © DC

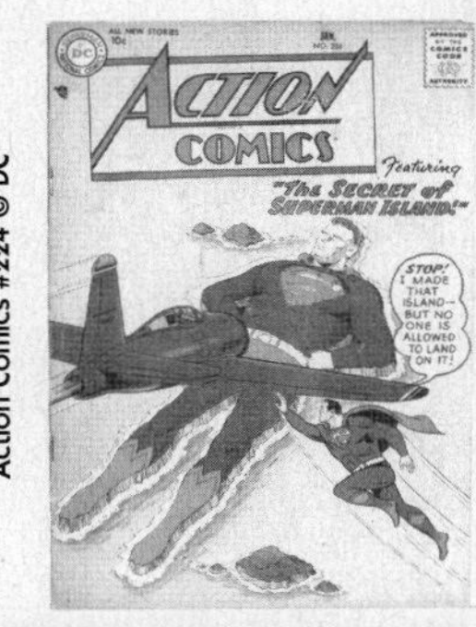

Action Comics #224 © DC

	GD 2.0	VG 4.0	FN 6.0	VF 8.0	VF/NM 9.0	NM- 9.2
1-Not approved by code	26	52	78	208	329	450
2	14	28	42	112	181	250
3-5	13	26	39	104	165	225

NOTE: *All have stories by* ***Davis***, ***Evans***, ***Krigstein***, *and* ***Wood***. ***Evans*** *c-1-5.*

ACES HIGH
Gemstone Publishing: Apr, 1999 - No. 5, Aug, 1999 ($2.50)

	GD 2.0	VG 4.0	FN 6.0	VF 8.0	VF/NM 9.0	NM- 9.2
1-5-Reprints E.C. issues						4.00
Annual 1 ($13.50) r/#1-5						14.00

ACME NOVELTY LIBRARY, THE
Fantagraphics Books: Winter 1993-94 - Present (quarterly, various sizes)

	GD 2.0	VG 4.0	FN 6.0	VF 8.0	VF/NM 9.0	NM- 9.2
1-Introduces Jimmy Corrigan; Chris Ware-s/a in all	3	6	9	16	23	30
1-2nd and later printings	1	2	3	5	6	8
2,3: 2-Quimby	2	4	6	9	13	16
4-Sparky's Best Comics & Stories	2	4	6	11	16	20
5-12: Jimmy Corrigan in all	2	4	6	8	10	12
13,15-($10.95-c)	2	4	6	10	14	18
14-($12.95-c) Concludes Jimmy Corrigan saga						20.00
16,19-($15.95, hardcover) Rusty Brown						20.00
17-($16.95, hardcover) Rusty Brown						20.00
18-($17.95, hardcover)						20.00
Jimmy Corrigan, The Smartest Kid on Earth (2000, Pantheon Books, Hardcover, $27.50, 380 pgs.) Collects Jimmy Corrigan stories; folded dust jacket						27.50
Jimmy Corrigan, The Smartest Kid on Earth (2003, Softcover, $17.95)						18.00

NOTE: *Multiple printings exist for most issues.*

ACROSS THE UNIVERSE: THE DC UNIVERSE STORIES OF ALAN MOORE (Also see DC Universe: The Stories of Alan Moore)
DC Comics: 2003 ($19.95, TPB)

	GD 2.0	VG 4.0	FN 6.0	VF 8.0	VF/NM 9.0	NM- 9.2
nn-Reprints selected Moore stories from '85-'87; Superman, Batman, Swamp Thing app.						20.00

ACTION ADVENTURE (War) (Formerly Real Adventure)
Gillmor Magazines: V1#2, June, 1955 - No. 4, Oct, 1955

	GD 2.0	VG 4.0	FN 6.0	VF 8.0	VF/NM 9.0	NM- 9.2
V1#2-4	7	14	21	35	43	50

ACTION COMICS (...Weekly #601-642) (Also see The Comics Magazine #1, More Fun #14-17 & Special Edition) (Also see Promotional Comics section)
National Periodical Publ./Detective Comics/DC Comics: 6/38 - No. 583, 9/86; No. 584, 1/87 - No. 904, Oct, 2011

	GD 2.0	VG 4.0	FN 6.0	VF 8.0	VF/NM 9.0	NM- 9.2
1-Origin & 1st app. Superman by Siegel & Shuster, Marco Polo, Tex Thompson, Pep Morgan, Chuck Dawson & Scoop Scanlon; 1st app. Zatara & Lois Lane; Superman story missing 4 pgs. which were included when reprinted in Superman #1; Clark Kent works for Daily Star; story continued in #2	185,000	370,000	650,000	1,300,000	2,250,000	3,200,000
1-Reprint, Oversize 13-1/2x10". **WARNING:** This comic is an exact reprint of the original except for its size. DC published it in 1974 with a second cover titling it as a Famous First Edition. There have been many reported cases of the outer cover being removed and the interior sold as the original edition. The reprint with the new outer cover removed is practically worthless. See Famous First Edition for value.						
2-O'Mealia non-Superman covers thru #6	10,270	20,540	30,810	77,025	133,513	190,000
3 (Scarce)-Superman apps. in costume in only one panel	7714	15,428	23,142	57,855	96,428	135,000
4-6: 6-1st Jimmy Olsen (called office boy)	3543	7086	10,629	26,573	44,287	62,000
7-1st time the name Superman is printed on a comic cover; 2nd Superman cover	35,000	70,000	105,000	210,000	315,000	420,000
8,9	2541	5082	7623	19,058	33,029	47,000
10-3rd Superman cover by Shuster; splash panel used as cover art for Superman #1	22,000	44,000	66,000	132,000	206,000	280,000
11,14: 1st X-Ray Vision? 14-Clip Carson begins, ends #41; Zatara-c	1135	2270	3405	8513	14,757	21,000
12-Has 1 panel Batman ad for Det. #27 (5/39); Zatara sci-fi cover	2378	4756	7134	17,835	30,918	44,000
13-Shuster Superman-c; last Scoop Scanlon; centerspread has a 2-page ad for Superman #1	14,000	28,000	42,000	80,000	120,000	160,000
15-Guardineer Superman-c; has ad mentioning Detective Comics and Batman; full page ad for New York World's Fair 1939 with 25¢-c	2432	4864	7296	18,240	31,620	45,000
16-Has full page ad and 1 panel ad for New York World's Fair 1939 25¢ cover edition	676	1352	2028	5070	8785	12,500
17-Superman cover; last Marco Polo; full page ad for New York World's Fair 1939 with 15¢-c	1622	3244	4866	12,165	21,083	30,000
18-Origin 3 Aces; has a 1 panel ad for New York World's Fair 1939 at the end of the Superman story (ad also in #16,17,19)	676	1352	2028	5070	8785	12,500
19-Superman covers begin	1568	3136	4704	11,760	20,380	29,000
20-The 'S' left off Superman's chest; Clark Kent works at 'Daily Star'	1514	3028	4542	11,355	19,678	28,000
21-Has 2 ads for More Fun #52 (1st Spectre)	622	1244	1866	4541	8021	11,500
22	595	1190	1785	4350	7675	11,000
23-1st app. Luthor (w/red hair) & Black Pirate; Black Pirate by Moldoff; 1st mention of The Daily Planet (4/40)-Has 1 panel ad for Spectre in More Fun	3500	7000	10,500	25,000	40,500	56,000
24,25: 24-Kent at Daily Planet. 25-Last app. Gargantua T. Potts, Tex Thompson's sidekick	497	994	1491	3628	6414	9200
26-28,30	443	886	1329	3234	5717	8200
29-1st Lois Lane-c (10/40)	486	972	1458	3550	6275	9000
31,32: 32-Intro/1st app. Krypto Ray Gun in Superman story by Burnley	309	618	927	2163	3782	5400
33-Origin Mr. America; Superman by Burnley; has half page ad for All Star Comics #3	326	652	978	2282	3991	5700
34,35,38,39	300	600	900	2070	3635	5200
36,40: 36-Classic robot-c. 40-(9/41)-Intro/1st app. Star Spangled Kid & Stripesy; Jerry Siegel photo	343	686	1029	2400	4200	6000
37-Origin Congo Bill	309	618	927	2163	3782	5400
41	297	594	891	1901	3251	4600
42-1st app./origin Vigilante; Bob Daley becomes Fat Man; origin Mr. America's magic flying carpet; The Queen Bee & Luthor app; Black Pirate ends; not in #41	300	600	900	1980	3440	4900
43-46,48-50: 44-Fat Man's i.d. revealed to Mr. America. 45-1st app. Stuff (Vigilante's oriental sidekick)	290	580	870	1856	3178	4500
47-1st Luthor cover in comics (4/42)	423	846	1269	3000	5250	7500
51-1st app. The Prankster	271	542	813	1734	2967	4200
52-Fat Man & Mr. America become the Ameri-commandos; origin Vigilante retold; classic Superman and back-ups-c	326	652	978	2282	3991	5700
53-56,59,60: 56-Last Fat Man. 60-First app. Lois Lane as Super-woman	245	490	735	1568	2684	3800
57-2nd Lois Lane-c in Action (3rd anywhere, 2/43)	252	504	756	1613	2757	3900
58-"Slap a Jap-c"	343	686	1029	2400	4200	6000
61-Historic Atomic Radiation-c (6/43)	284	568	852	1818	3109	4400
62-Japan war-c	232	464	696	1485	2543	3600
63-Japan war-c; last 3 Aces	271	542	813	1734	2967	4200
64-Intro Toyman	194	388	582	1242	2121	3000
65-70: 66-69-Kubert-i on Vigilante	161	322	483	1030	1765	2500
71-79: 74-Last Mr. America	129	258	387	826	1413	2000
80-2nd app. & 1st Mr. Mxyztplk-c (1/45)	158	316	474	1003	1727	2450
81-88,90: 83-Intro Hocus & Pocus	119	238	357	762	1306	1850
89-Classic rainbow cover	135	270	405	864	1482	2100
91-99: 93-X-Mas-c. 99-1st small logo (8/46)	100	200	300	635	1093	1550
100	135	270	405	864	1482	2100
101-Nuclear explosion-c (10/46)	226	452	678	1446	2473	3500
102-Mxyztplk-c	100	200	300	635	1093	1550
103-107,109-120: 105,117-X-Mas-c	90	180	270	576	988	1400
108-Classic molten metal-c	110	220	330	704	1202	1700
121,122,124-126,128-140: 135,136,138-Zatara by Kubert	87	174	261	553	952	1350
123-(8/48) 1st time Superman flies, not leaps	97	194	270	576	988	1500
127-Vigilante by Kubert; Tommy Tomorrow begins (12/48, see Real Fact #6)	89	178	267	565	970	1375
141-150,152-157,159-161: 156-Lois as Super Woman. 161- Last 52 pgs.	86	172	258	546	936	1325
151-Luthor/Mr. Mxyztplk/Prankster team-up	123	246	369	787	1344	1900
158-Origin Superman retold	142	284	426	909	1555	2200
162-180: 168,176-Used in **POP**, pg. 90. 173-Robot-c	82	164	246	528	902	1275
181-201: 191-Intro. Janu in Congo Bill. 198-Last Vigilante. 201-Last pre-code issue	77	154	231	493	847	1200
202-220,232: 212-(1/56)-Includes 1956 Superman calendar that is part of story. 232-1st Curt Swan-c in Action	60	120	180	381	653	925
221-231,233-240: 221-1st S.A. issue. 224-1st Golden Gorilla story. 228-(5/57)-Kongorilla in Congo Bill story (Congorilla try-out)	50	100	150	315	533	750
241,243-251: 241-Batman x-over. 248-Origin/1st app. Congorilla; Congo Bill renamed Congorilla. 251-Last Tommy Tomorrow	42	84	126	265	445	625
242-Origin & 1st app. Brainiac (7/58); 1st mention of Shrunken City of Kandor	500	1000	2000	6000	13,000	20,000
252-Origin & 1st app. Supergirl (5/59); 1st app. Metallo	550	1100	2200	6600	14,300	22,000
253-2nd app. Supergirl	81	162	243	518	884	1250
254-1st meeting of Bizarro & Superman-c/story; 3rd app. Supergirl	54	108	162	343	574	825
255-1st Bizarro Lois Lane-c/story & both Bizarros leave Earth to make Bizarro World; 4th app. Supergirl	47	94	141	296	498	700
256-260: 259-Red Kryptonite used	34	68	102	199	325	450
261-1st X-Kryptonite which gave Streaky his powers; last Congorilla in Action; origin & 1st app. Streaky The Super Cat	39	78	117	231	378	525

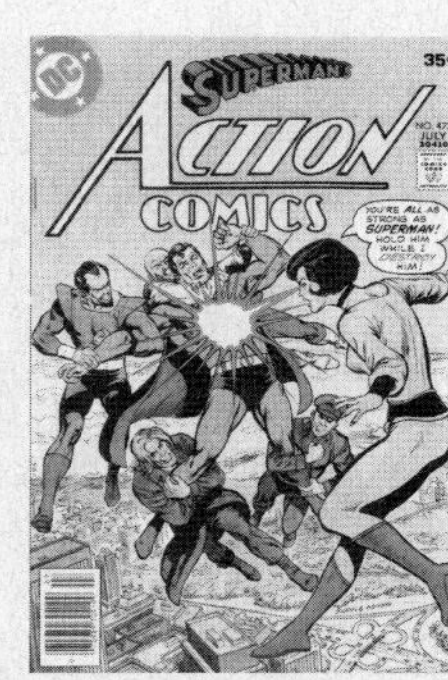

Action Comics #473 © DC

Action Comics #591 © DC

Action Comics #827 © DC

	GD 2.0	VG 4.0	FN 6.0	VF 8.0	VF/NM 9.0	NM- 9.2
262,264-266,268-270	30	60	90	177	289	400
263-Origin Bizarro World (continues in #264)	37	74	111	222	361	500
267(8/60)-3rd Legion app; 1st app. Chameleon Boy, Colossal Boy, & Invisible Kid, 1st app. of Supergirl as Superwoman.	68	136	204	435	743	1050
271-275,277-282: 274-Lois Lane as Superwoman. 280-Brief origin of Superman & Supergirl retold; Brainiac-c. 282-Last 10¢ issue	24	48	72	142	234	325
276(5/61)-6th Legion app; 1st app. Brainiac 5, Phantom Girl, Triplicate Girl, Bouncing Boy, Sun Boy, & Shrinking Violet; Supergirl joins Legion	54	108	162	343	574	825
283(12/61)-Legion of Super-Villains app. 1st 12¢	13	26	39	89	195	300
284(1/62)-Mon-El app.	13	26	39	89	195	300
285(2/62)-12th Legion app; Brainiac 5 cameo; Supergirl's existence revealed to world; JFK & Jackie cameos	25	50	75	175	388	600
286-287,289-292,294-299: 286(3/62)-Legion of Super Villains app. 287(4/62)-15th Legion app. (cameo). 289(6/62)-16th Legion app. (Adult); Lightning Man & Saturn Woman's marriage 1st revealed. 290(7/62)-Legion app. (cameo); Phantom Girl app. 1st Supergirl emergency squad. 291-1st meeting Supergirl & Mr. Mxyzptlk. 292-2nd app. Superhorse (see Adv.#293). 297-General Zod, Phantom Zone villains & Mon-El app. 298-General Zod app.; Legion cameo	11	22	33	76	163	250
288-Mon-El app.; r-origin Supergirl	12	24	36	79	170	260
293-Origin Comet (Superhorse)	13	26	39	89	195	300
300-(5/63)	13	26	39	86	188	290
301-303,305,307,308,310-312,315-320: 307-Saturn Girl app. 317-Death of Nor-Kan of Kandor. 319-Shrinking Violet app.	9	18	27	58	114	170
304,306,313: 304-Origin/1st app. Black Flame (9/63). 306-Brainiac 5, Mon-El app. 313-Batman app.	9	18	27	59	117	175
309-(2/64)-Legion app.; Batman & Robin-c & cameo; JFK app. (he died 11/22/63; on stands last week of Dec, 1963)	9	18	27	61	123	185
314-Retells origin Supergirl; J.L.A. x-over	9	18	27	59	117	175
321-333,335-339: 336-Origin Akvar (Flamebird)	7	14	21	48	89	130
334-Giant G-20; origin Supergirl, Streaky, Superhorse & Legion (all-r)	10	20	30	66	138	210
340-Origin, 1st app. of the Parasite; 2 pg. pin-up	15	30	45	100	220	340
341,344,350,358: 341-Batman app. in Supergirl back-up story. 344-Batman x-over. 350-Batman, Green Arrow & Green Lantern app. in Supergirl back-up story. 358-Superboy meets Supergirl	6	12	18	41	76	110
342,343,345,346,348,349,351-357,359: 342-UFO story. 345-Allen Funt/Candid Camera story.	6	12	18	40	73	105
347,360-Giant Supergirl G-33,G-45; 347-Origin Comet-r plus Bizarro story. 360-Legion app.-r; r/origin Supergirl	8	16	24	55	105	155
361-2nd app. Parasite	7	14	21	46	86	125
362-364,367-372,374-378: 362-366-Leper/Death story. 370-New facts about Superman's origin. 376-Last Supergirl in Action; last 12¢-c. 377-Legion begins (thru #392)	5	10	15	33	57	80
365,366: 365-JLA & Legion app. 366-JLA app.	5	10	15	34	60	85
373-Giant Supergirl G-57; Legion-r	8	16	24	51	96	140
379-399,401: 388-Sgt. Rock app. 392-Batman-c/app.; last Legion in Action; Saturn Girl gets new costume. 393-401-All Superman issues	3	6	9	19	30	40
400	4	8	12	23	37	50
402-Last 15¢ issue; Superman vs. Supergirl duel	3	6	9	20	31	42
403-413: All 52 pg. issues. 411-Origin Eclipso-(r). 413-Metamorpho begins, ends #418	3	6	9	19	30	40
414-424: 419-Intro. Human Target. 421-Intro Capt. Strong; Green Arrow begins. 422,423-Origin Human Target	2	4	6	9	13	16
425-Neal Adams-a(p); The Atom begins	3	6	9	15	22	28
426-431,433-436,438,439	2	4	6	8	10	12
432-1st Bronze Age Toyman app. (2/74)	2	4	6	13	18	22
437,443-(100 pg. Giants)	4	8	12	27	44	60
440-1st Grell-a on Green Arrow	2	4	6	10	14	18
441,442,444-448: 441-Grell-a on Green Arrow continues	2	4	6	8	10	12
449-(68 pgs.)	2	4	6	10	14	18
450-465,467-470,474-483,486,489-499: 454-Last Atom. 456-Grell Jaws-c. 458-Last Green Arrow	1	2	3	4	5	7
466,485,487,488: 466-Batman, Flash app. 485-Adams-c. 487,488-(44 pgs.). 487-Origin & 1st app. Microwave Man; origin Atom retold	1	2	3	5	7	9
471-(5/77) 1st app. Faora Hu-Ul	2	4	6	12	16	20
472,473-Faora app. 473-Faora, General Zod app.	2	4	6	9	13	16
481-483,485-492,495-499,501-505,507,508-Whitman variants (low print run; none show issue # on cover)	2	4	6	8	10	12
484-Earth II Superman & Lois Lane wed; 40th anniversary issue(6/78)	2	4	6	8	10	12
484-Variant includes 3-D Superman punchout doll in cello. pack; 4 different inserts; (Canadian promo?)	6	12	18	38	69	100

	GD 2.0	VG 4.0	FN 6.0	VF 8.0	VF/NM 9.0	NM- 9.2
500-($1.00, 68 pgs.)-Infinity-c; Superman life story retold; shows Legion statues in museum	2	4	6	8	10	12
501-520,522-543,545,547-551: 511-514-Airwave II solo stories. 513-The Atom begins. 517-Aquaman begins; ends #541. 532,536-New Teen Titans cameo. 535,536-Omega Men app. 551-Starfire becomes Red-Star						5.00
521-1st app. The Vixen	3	6	9	21	33	45
544-(6/83, Mando paper, 68 pgs.)-45th Anniversary issue; origins new Luthor & Brainiac; Omega Men cameo; Shuster-a (pin-up); article by Siegel	1	2	3	4	5	7
546-J.L.A., New Teen Titans app.	1	2	3	5	6	8
552,553-Animal Man-c & app. (2/84 & 3/84)						6.00
554-582						3.00
583-(9/86) Alan Moore scripts; last Earth 1 Superman story (cont'd from Superman #423)	2	4	6	11	16	20
584-(1/87) Byrne-a begins; New Teen Titans app.						6.00
585-599: 586-Legends x-over. 595-1st app. Silver Banshee. 596-Millennium x-over; Spectre app. 598-1st Checkmate						3.00
600-($2.50, 84 pgs., 5/88)						6.00
601-610,619-642: (#601-642 are weekly issues) ($1.50, 52 pgs.) 601-Re-intro The Secret Six; death of Katma Tui						4.00
611-618: 611-614-Catwoman stories (new costume in #611). 613-618-Nightwing stories						4.00
643-Superman & monthly issues begin again; Perez-c/a/scripts begin; swipes cover to Superman #1						6.00
644-649,651-661,663-666,668-673,675-683: 645-1st app. Maxima. 654-Part 3 of Batman storyline. 655-Free extra 8 pgs. 660-Death of Lex Luthor. 661-Begin $1.00-c. 675-Deathstroke cameo. 679-Last $1.00 issue. 683-Doomsday cameo						3.00
650,667: 650-($1.50, 52 pgs.)-Lobo cameo (last panel). 667-($1.75, 52 pgs.)						4.00
662-Clark Kent reveals i.d. to Lois Lane; story cont'd in Superman #53						4.00
674-Supergirl logo & c/story (reintro)						6.00
683-685-2nd & 3rd printings						3.00
684-Doomsday battle issue						4.00
685,686-Funeral for a Friend issues; Supergirl app.						4.00
687-($1.95)-Collector's Ed.w/die-cut-c						4.00
687-($1.50)-Newsstand Edition with mini-poster						3.00
688-699,701-703-($1.50): 688-Guy Gardner-c/story. 697-Bizarro-c/story. 703-(9/94)-Zero Hour						3.00
695-($2.50)-Collector's Edition w/embossed foil-c						4.00
700-($2.95, 68 pgs.)-Fall of Metropolis Pt 1, Guice-a; Pete Ross marries Lana Lang and Smallville flashbacks with Curt Swan art & Murphy Anderson inks						4.00
700-Platinum						15.00
700-Gold						18.00
0(10/94), 704(11/94)-719,721-731: 710-Begin $1.95-c. 714-Joker app. 719-Batman-c/app. 721-Mr. Mxyzptlk app. 723-Dave Johnson-c. 727-Final Night x-over.						3.00
720-Lois breaks off engagement w/Clark						4.00
720-2nd print.						3.00
732-749,751-764,767,767: 732-New powers. 733-New costume, Ray app. 738-Immonen-s/a(p) begins. 741-Legion app. 744-Millennium Giants x-over. 745-747-70's-style Superman vs. Prankster. 753-JLA-c/app. 757-Hawkman-c. 760-1st Encantadora. 761-Wonder Woman app. 766-Batman-c/app.						3.00
750-($2.95)						4.00
765-Joker & Harley-c/app.	1	2	3	5	6	8
768,769,771-774: 768-Begin $2.25-c; Marvel Family-c/app. 771-Nightwing-c/app. 772,773-Ra's al Ghul app. 774-Martian Manhunter-c/app.						3.00
770-($3.50) Conclusion of Emperor Joker x-over						4.00
775-($3.75) Bradstreet-c; intro. The Elite	2	4	6	8	10	12
775-(2nd printing)	1	2	3	5	6	8
776-799: 776-Farewell to Krypton; Rivoche-c. 780-782-Our Worlds at War x-over. 781-Hippolyta and Major Lane killed. 782-War ends. 784-Joker: Last Laugh; Batman & Green Lantern app. 793-Return to Krypton. 795-The Elite app. 798-Van Fleet-c						3.00
800-(4/03, $3.95) Struzan painted-c; guest artists include Ross, Jim Lee, Jurgens, Sale						4.00
801-811: 801-Raney-a. 809-The Creeper app. 811-Mr. Majestic app.						3.00
812-Godfall part 1; Turner-c; Caldwell-a(p)						4.00
812-2nd printing; B&W sketch-c by Turner						3.00
813-Godfall pt. 4; Turner-c; Caldwell-a(p)						4.00
814-824,826-828,830-834,836: 814-Reis-a/Art Adams-c; Darkseid app.; begin $2.50-c. 815,816-Teen Titans-c/app. 820-Doomsday app. 826-Capt. Marvel app. 827-Byrne-c/a begin. 831-Villains United tie-in. 836-Infinite Crisis; revised origin						3.00
825-($2.99, 40 pgs.) Doomsday app.						4.00
829-Omac Project x-over Sacrifice pt. 2						5.00
829-(2nd printing) red tone cover						4.00
835-1st Livewire app. in regular DCU	2	4	6	8	10	12
837-843-One Year Later; powers return after Infinite Crisis; Johns & Busiek-s						3.00
844-Donner & Johns-s/Adam Kubert-a/c begin; brown-toned cover						4.00
844-Andy Kubert variant-c						5.00

Action Comics #874 © DC

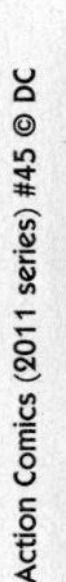
Action Comics (2011 series) #45 © DC

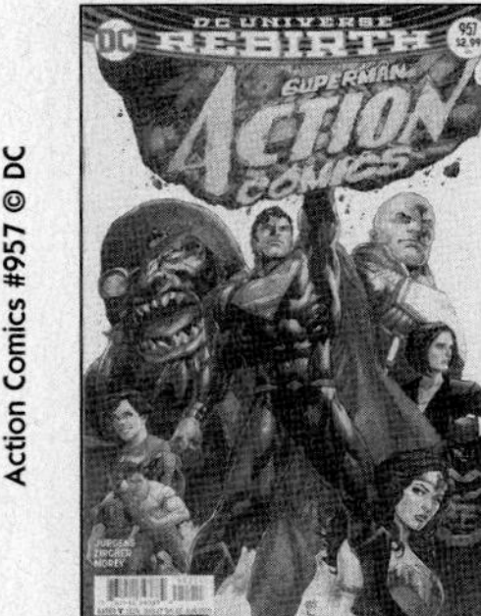

Action Comics #957 © DC

	GD	VG	FN	VF	VF/NM	NM-
	2.0	4.0	6.0	8.0	9.0	9.2

844-2nd printing with red-toned Adam Kubert cover 3.00
845-849,851-857: 845-Bizarro-c/app.; re-intro. General Zod, Ursa & Non. 846-Jax-Ur app. 847-849-No Kubert-a. 851-Kubert-a/c. 855-857-Bizarro app.; Powell-a/c 3.00
850-($3.99) Supergirl and LSH app., origin re-told; Guedes-a/c 4.00
858-($3.50) Legion of Super-Heroes app.; 1st meeting re-told; Johns-s/Frank-a/c 4.00
858-Variant-c (Superman & giant Brainiac robot) by Frank 5.00
858-Second printing with regular cover with red background instead of yellow 3.00
858-Special Edition (7/10, $1.00) r/#858 with "What's Next?" cover logo 3.00
859-878: 859-863-Legion of Super-Heroes app.; var-c on each (859-Andy Kubert. 860-Lightle. 861-Grell. 862-Giffen. 863-Frank) 864-Batman and Lightning Lad app. 866-Brainiac returns 869-"Soda Pop" cover edition, 870-Pa Kent dies. 871-New Krypton; Ross-c 3.00
869-Initial printing recalled because of beer bottles on cover
5 10 15 31 53 75
879-896: 879-($3.99) Back-up Capt. Atom feature begins. 890-Luthor stories begin. 893-Comics debut of Chloe Sullivan (Smallville TV show) in regular DCU. 894-Death (Sandman) app. 896-Secret Six app. 4.00
897-899, 901-903-($2.99) 897-Joker app. 898-Larfleeze app. 899-Brainiac app. 3.00
900 (6/11, $5.99, 96 pgs.) Conclusion of Luthor Black Ring saga; Doomsday app.; bonus short stories by various; Superman renounces U.S. citizenship 6.00
904-(10/11) Last issue of first volume; Doomsday app.; Rocafort-c 3.00
904-Variant-c by Ordway 5.00
#1,000,000 (11/98) Gene Ha-c; 853rd Century x-over 3.00
Annual 1 ('87, $2.95) Art Adams-c/a(p); Batman app. 5.00
Annual 2-6 ('89-'94, $2.95)-2-Pérez-c/a(i). 3-Armageddon 2001. 4-Eclipso vs. Shazam. 5-Bloodlines; 1st app. Loose Cannon. 6-Elseworlds story 4.00
Annual 7,9 ('95, '97, $3.95) 7-Year One story. 9-Pulp Heroes story 4.00
Annual 8 (1996, $2.95) Legends of the Dead Earth story 4.00
Annual 10 ('07, $3.99) Short stories by Johns & Donner and various incl. A. Adams, J. Kubert, Wight, Morales; origin of Phantom Zone, Mon-El; Metallo app.; Adam & Joe Kubert-c 4.00
Annual 11 (7/08, $4.99) Conclusion to General Zod story continued from #851; Kubert-a 5.00
Annual 12 (8/09, $4.99) Origin of Nightwing and Flamebird 5.00
Annual 13 (2/11, $4.99) 1st meeting of Luthor and Darkseid; Ra's al Ghul app. 5.00

NOTE:***Supergirl's*** *origin in 262, 280, 285, 291, 305, 309.* ***N. Adams*** *c-356, 358, 359, 361-364, 366, 367, 370-374, 377-379i, 398-400, 402, 404,405, 419p, 466, 468, 469, 473i, 485.* ***Aparo*** *a-642.* ***Austin*** *c/a-682i.* ***Baily*** *a-24, 25.* ***Boring*** *a-164, 194, 211, 223, 233, 241, 250, 261, 266-268, 346, 348, 352, 356, 357.* ***Burnley*** *a-28-33; c-48?, 53-55, 58, 59?, 60-63, 65, 66p, 67p, 70p, 71p, 79p, 82p, 84-86p, 90-92p, 93p?, 94p, 107p, 108p.* ***Byrne*** *a-584-598p, 599i, 600p; c-584-591, 596-600.* ***Ditko*** *a-642.* ***Giffen*** *a-560, 563, 565, 577, 579; c-539, 560, 563, 565, 577, 579.* ***Grell*** *a-440-442, 444-446, 450-452, 456-458; c-456.* ***Guardineer*** *a-24, 25; c-8, 11, 12, 14-16, 18. 25.* ***Guice*** *a(p)-676-681, 683-698, 700; c-683, 685, 686, 687(direct), 688-693i, 694-696, 697i, 698-700.* ***Infantino*** *a-642.* ***Kaluta*** *c-613.* ***Bob Kane's*** *Clip Carson-14-41.* ***Gil Kane*** *a-443r, 493r, 539-541, 544-546, 551-554, 601-605, 642; c-535p, 540, 541, 544p, 545-549, 551-554, 580, 627.* ***Kirby*** *c-638.* ***Meskin*** *a-42-121(most).* ***Mignola*** *a-600, Annual 2; c-c-614.* ***Moldoff*** *a-23-25, 443r.* ***Mooney*** *a-667p.* ***Mortimer*** *c-153, 154, 159-172, 174, 178-181, 184, 186-189, 191-193, 196, 200, 206.* ***Orlando*** *a-617p; c-621.* ***Perez*** *a-600i, 643-652p, Annual 2p; c-529p, 602, 643-651, Annual 2p.* ***Quesada*** *c-Annual 4p.* ***Fred Ray*** *c-34, 36-46, 50-52.* ***Siegel & Shuster*** *a-1-27.* ***Paul Smith*** *c-608.* ***Starlin*** *a-509; c-631.* ***Leonard Starr*** *a-597i(part),* ***Staton*** *a-525p, 526p, 531p, 535p, 536p.* ***Swan/Moldoff*** *c-281, 286, 287, 293, 298, 334.* ***Thibert*** *c-676, 677p, 678-681, 684.* ***Toth*** *a-406, 407, 413, 431; c-616.* ***Tuska*** *a-486p, 550.* ***Williamson*** *a-568i.* ***Zeck*** *c-Annual 5*

ACTION COMICS (2nd series)(DC New 52)(Numbering reverts to original V1 #957 after #52)
DC Comics: Nov, 2011 - No. 52, Jul, 2016; No. 957, Aug, 2016 - Present ($3.99)

1-Grant Morrison-s/Rags Morales-a/c; re-introduces Superman
1 3 4 6 8 10
1-Variant-c by Jim Lee of Superman in new armor costume
2 4 6 10 14 18
1-(2nd - 5th printings) 4.00
2-12: 2-Morales & Brent Anderson-a; behind the scenes sketch art and commentary. 3-Gene Ha & Morales-a. 4-Re-intro. Steel. 5-Flashback to Krypton; Andy Kubert-a. 6-Legion of Super-Heroes app.; Andy Kubert-a. 7-Gets the new costume; intro. Steel 4.00
2-12-Variant covers. 2-Van Sciver. 3-Ha. 4-Choi. 5,6-Morales. 8-Frank 5.00
13-17,19-23: 13-Re-intro of Krypto. 14-Neil deGrasse Tyson app. 15-Legion app. 4.00
18-($4.99) Last Morrison-s; Mxyzptlk, The Legion and the Wanderers app. 5.00
23.1, 23.2, 23.3, 23.4 (11/13, $2.99, regular covers) 3.00
23.1 (11/13, $3.99, 3-D cover) "Cyborg Superman #1" on cover; Zor-El & Brainiac app. 5.00
23.2 (11/13, $3.99, 3-D cover) "Zod #1" on cover; origin of Zod on Krypton; Faora app. 5.00
23.3 (11/13, $3.99, 3-D cover) "Lex Luthor #1" on cover; Kuder-c 5.00
23.4 (11/13, $3.99, 3-D cover) "Metallo #1" on cover; Fisch-s/Pugh-a 5.00
24-49,51,52: 25-Zero Year. 30-Doomsday app. 31-35-Doomed x-over. 40-Bizarro app. 51-Supergirl app. 52-Wonder Woman, Batman and pre-Flashpoint Superman app. 4.00
50-($4.99) Vandal Savage and the Justice League app. 5.00
#0 (11/12, $3.99) Flashback to Lois' 1st Superman sighting; Oliver-a; 4.00
Annual 1 (12/12, $4.99) Superman vs. K-Man; Fisch-s/Hamner-a; Atomic Skull app. 5.00
Annual 2 (12/13, $4.99) Rocafort & Jurgens-a; H'El & Faora app.; back-up Mad sampler 5.00
Annual 3 (9/14, $4.99) Superman Doomed x-over; Brainiac app. 5.00
...: Futures End 1 (11/14, $2.99, regular-c) Five years later; Alixe-a 3.00
...: Futures End 1 (11/14, $3.99, 3-D cover) 4.00

ACTION COMICS (Numbering reverts to original V1 #957 after #52 from 2011-2016 series)
DC Comics: No. 957, Aug, 2016 - Present ($2.99)

957-974: 957-Jurgens-s/Zircher-a; the pre-52 Superman vs. Lex Luthor & Doomsday. 960-962-Wonder Woman app. 973-Superwoman & Steel app. 3.00

ACTION COMICS
DC Comics: (no date)

1-Ashcan comic, not distributed to newsstands, only for in-house use. Cover art is the rejected art to Detective Comics #2 and interior from Detective Comics #1. A CGC certified 9.0 copy sold for $17,825 in 2002, $29,000 in 2008, and $50,000 in 2010.

ACTION FORCE (Also see G.I. Joe European Missions)
Marvel Comics Ltd. (British): Mar, 1987 - No. 50, 1988 ($1.00, weekly, magazine)

1,3: British G.I. Joe series. 3-w/poster insert 2 4 6 8 11 14
2,4 1 2 3 5 6 8
5-10 5.00
11-50 3.00
...Special 1 (7/87) Summer holiday special; Snake Eyes-c/app.
1 3 4 6 8 10
...Special 2 (10/87) Winter special 5.00

ACTION FUNNIES
DC Comics: 1937/1938

nn - Ashcan comic, not distributed to newsstands, only for in house use. Cover art is Action Comics #3 and interior from Detective Comics #10. The Mallette/Brown copy in VG+ condition sold for $15,000 in 2005. A VF+ copy sold for $10,157.50 in 2012.

ACTION GIRL
Slave Labor Graphics: Oct, 1994 - No. 19 ($2.50/$2.75/$2.95, B&W)

1-19: 4-Begin $2.75-c. 19-Begin $2.95-c 3.00
1-6 ($2.75, 2nd printings): All read 2nd Print in indicia. 1-(2/96). 2-(10/95). 3-(2/96). 4-(7/96). 5-(2/97). 6-(9/97) 3.00
1-4 ($2.75, 3rd printings): All read 3rd Print in indicia. 3.00

ACTION MAN (Based on the Hasbro G.I. Joe-type action figure)
IDW Publishing: Jun, 2016 - Present ($3.99)

1-4-John Barber-s/Paolo Villanelli-a 4.00
...: Revolution (110/16, $3.99) Tie-in to Hasbro toy titles x-over; Barber-s/Villanelli-a 4.00

ACTION PHILOSOPHERS!
Dark Horse Comics: Oct, 2014 ($1.00, one-shot)

1-Van Lente-s/Dunlavey-a 3.00

ACTION PLANET COMICS
Action Planet: 1996 - No. 3, Sept, 1997 ($3.95, B&W, 44 pgs.)

1-3: 1-Intro Monster Man by Mike Manley & other stories 4.00
Giant Size Action Planet Halloween Special (1998, $5.95, oversized) 6.00

ACTUAL CONFESSIONS (Formerly Love Adventures)
Atlas Comics (MPI): No. 13, Oct, 1952 - No. 14, Dec, 1952

13,14 12 24 36 67 94 120

ACTUAL ROMANCES (Becomes True Secrets #3 on?)
Marvel Comics (IPS): Oct, 1949 - No. 2, Jan, 1950 (52 pgs.)

1-Photo-c 18 36 54 107 169 230
2-Photo-c 13 26 39 74 105 135

A.D.: AFTER DEATH
Image Comics: Book 1, Nov, 2016 - Book 3 ($5.99, limited series, square-bound 8"x11")

1,2-Scott Snyder-s/Jeff Lemire-a 6.00

ADAM AND EVE
Spire Christian Comics (Fleming H. Revell Co.): 1975,1978 (35¢/39¢/49¢)

nn-By Al Hartley (1975 edition) 2 4 6 11 16 20
nn (1978 edition) 2 4 6 9 13 16

ADAM: LEGEND OF THE BLUE MARVEL
Marvel Comics: Jan, 2009 - No. 5, May, 2009 ($3.99, limited series)

1-5-Grevioux-s/Broome-a; Avengers app. 4.00

ADAM STRANGE (Also see Green Lantern #132, Mystery In Space #53 & Showcase #17)
DC Comics: 1990 - No. 3, 1990 ($3.95, 52 pgs, limited series, squarebound)

Book One - Three: Andy & Adam Kubert-c/a 4.00
...: The Man of Two Worlds (2003, $19.95, TPB) r/#1-3; sketch pages by Andy Kubert 20.00

ADAM STRANGE (Leads into the Rann/Thanagar War mini-series)
DC Comics: Nov, 2004 - No. 8, June, 2005 ($2.95, limited series)

1-8-Andy Diggle-s/Pascal Ferry-a/c. 1-Superman app. 3.00
...: Planet Heist TPB (2005, $19.99) r/series; sketch pages 20.00
... Special (11/08, $3.50) Takes place during Rann/Thanagar Holy War series; Starlin-s 4.00

ADAM-12 (TV)

Adam-12 #6 © GK

Adventure Comics #48 © DC

Adventure Comics #256 © DC

	GD 2.0	VG 4.0	FN 6.0	VF 8.0	VF/NM 9.0	NM- 9.2

Gold Key: Dec, 1973 - No. 10, Feb, 1976 (Photo-c)
1 6 12 18 37 66 95
2-10 3 6 9 21 33 45

ADDAMS FAMILY (TV cartoon)
Gold Key: Oct, 1974 - No. 3, Apr, 1975 (Hanna-Barbera)
1 7 14 21 46 86 125
2,3 5 10 15 33 57 80

ADLAI STEVENSON
Dell Publishing Co.: Dec, 1966
12-007-612-Life story; photo-c 3 6 9 21 33 45

ADOLESCENT RADIOACTIVE BLACK BELT HAMSTERS (See Clint)
Comic Castle/Eclipse Comics: 1986 - No. 9, Jan, 1988 ($1.50, B&W)
1-9: 1st & 2nd printings exist 3.00
1-Limited Edition 6.00
1-In 3-D (7/86), 2-4 ($2.50) 3.00
Massacre The Japanese Invasion #1 (8/89, $2.00) 3.00

ADOLESCENT RADIOACTIVE BLACK BELT HAMSTERS
Dynamite Entertainment: 2008 - No. 4, 2008 ($3.50, limited series)
1-4-Tom Nguyen-a/Keith Champagne-s; 2 covers by Nguyen and Oeming 3.50

ADRENALYNN (See The Tenth)
Image Comics: Aug, 1999 - No. 4, Feb, 2000 ($2.50)
1-4-Tony Daniel-s/Marty Egeland-a; origin of Adrenalynn 3.00

ADULT TALES OF TERROR ILLUSTRATED (See Terror Illustrated)

ADVANCED DUNGEONS & DRAGONS (Also see TSR Worlds)
DC Comics: Dec, 1988 - No. 36, Dec, 1991 (Newsstand #1 is Holiday, 1988-89) ($1.25-$1.75)
1-Based on TSR role playing game 4.00
2-36: 25-$1.75-c begins 3.00
Annual 1 (1990, $3.95, 68 pgs.) 4.00

ADVENTURE BOUND
Dell Publishing Co.: Aug, 1949
Four Color #239 6 12 18 37 66 95

ADVENTURE COMICS (Formerly New Adventure)(...Presents Dial H For Hero #479-490)
National Periodical Publications/DC Comics: No. 32, 11/38 - No. 490, 2/82; No. 491, 9/82 - No. 503, 9/83
32-Anchors Aweigh (ends #52), Barry O'Neil (ends #60, not in #33), Captain Desmo (ends #47), Dale Daring (ends #47), Federal Men (ends #70), The Golden Dragon (ends #36), Rusty & His Pals (ends #52) by Bob Kane, Todd Hunter (ends #38) and Tom Brent (ends #39) begin 500 1000 1500 2700 4000 5400
33-35,38 325 650 975 1750 2625 3500
36 (scarce) 550 1100 1650 3000 4500 6000
37-Cover used on Double Action #2 375 750 1125 2000 3000 4000
39(6/39)- Jack Wood begins, ends #42; early mention of Marijuana in comics 375 750 1125 2000 2625 3500
40-(Rare, 7/39, on stands 6/10/39)-The Sandman begins by Bert Christman (who died in WWII); believed to be 1st conceived story (see N.Y. World's Fair for 1st published app.); Socko Strong begins, ends #54 7000 14,000 21,000 52,000 106,000 160,000
41-O'Mealia shark-c 649 1298 1947 4738 8369 12,000
42,44-Sandman-c by Flessel. 44-Opium story 865 1730 2595 6315 11,158 16,000
43,45: 45-Full page ad for Flash Comics #1 459 918 1377 3350 5925 8500
46,47-Sandman covers by Flessel. 47-Steve Conrad Adventurer begins, ends #76 649 1298 1947 4738 8369 12,000
48-1st app. The Hourman by Bernard Baily; Baily-c (Hourman c-48,50,52-59) 2750 5500 8250 20,500 41,250 62,000
49 300 600 900 2010 3505 5000
50-2nd Hourman-c; -Cotton Carver by Jack Lehti begins, ends #64 314 628 942 2198 3849 5500
51,60-Sandman-c: 51-Sandman-c by Flessel. 389 778 1167 2723 4762 6800
52-59: 53-1st app. Jimmy "Minuteman" Martin & the Minutemen of America in Hourman; ends #78. 58-Paul Kirk Manhunter begins (1st app.), ends #72 271 542 813 1734 2967 4200
61-1st app. Starman by Jack Burnley (4/41); Starman c-61-72; Starman by Burnley in #61-80 1200 2400 3600 9000 17,000 25,000
62-65,67,68,70: 67-Origin & 1st app. The Mist; classic Burnley-c. 70-Last Federal Men 258 516 774 1651 2826 4000
66-Origin/1st app. Shining Knight (9/41) 300 600 900 1950 3375 4800
69-1st app. Sandy the Golden Boy (Sandman's sidekick) by Paul Norris (in a Bob Kane style); Sandman dons new costume 297 594 891 1901 3251 4600
71-Jimmy Martin becomes costumed aide to the Hourman; 1st app. Hourman's Miracle Ray machine 258 516 774 1651 2826 4000

	GD 2.0	VG 4.0	FN 6.0	VF 8.0	VF/NM 9.0	NM- 9.2

72-1st Simon & Kirby Sandman (3/42, 1st DC work) 975 1950 2919 7100 12,800 18,500
73-Origin Manhunter by Simon & Kirby; begin new series; Manhunter-c (scarce) 1275 2550 3825 9550 17,775 26,000
74-78,80: 74-Thorndyke replaces Jimmy, Hourman's assistant; new Sandman-c begin by S&K. 75-Thor app. by Kirby; 1st Kirby Thor (see Tales of the Unexpected #16). 77-Origin Genius Jones; Mist story. 80-Last S&K Manhunter & Burnley Starman 194 388 582 1242 2121 3000
79-Classic Manhunter-c 300 600 900 2010 3505 5000
81-90: 83-Last Hourman. 84-Mike Gibbs begins, ends #102 123 246 369 787 1344 1900
91-Last Simon & Kirby Sandman 119 238 357 762 1306 1850
92-99,101,102: 92-Last Manhunter. 101-Shining Knight origin retold. 102-Last Starman, Sandman, & Genius Jones; most-S&K-c (Genius Jones cont'd in More Fun #108) 97 194 291 621 1061 1500
100-S&K-c 135 270 405 864 1482 2100
103-Aquaman, Green Arrow, Johnny Quick & Superboy all move over from More Fun Comics #107; 8th app. Superboy; Superboy-c begin; 1st small logo (4/46) 309 618 927 2163 3782 5400
104 123 246 369 787 1344 1900
105-110 84 168 252 538 919 1300
111-120: 113-X-Mas-c 74 148 222 470 810 1150
121,122-126,128-130: 128-1st meeting Superboy & Lois Lane 69 138 207 442 759 1075
127-Brief origin Shining Knight retold 71 142 213 454 777 1100
131-141,143-149: 132-Shining Knight 1st return to King Arthur time; origin aide Sir Butch 61 122 183 390 670 950
142-Origin Shining Knight & Johnny Quick retold 65 130 195 416 708 1000
150,151,153,155,157,159,161,163-All have 6 pg. Shining Knight stories by Frank Frazetta. 159-Origin Johnny Quick. 161-1st Lana Lang app. in this title 74 148 222 470 810 1150
152,154,156,158,160,162,164-169: 166-Last Shining Knight. 168-Last 52 pg. issue 54 108 162 343 574 825
170-180 52 104 156 328 552 775
181-199: 189-B&W and color illo in **POP** 50 100 150 315 533 750
200 (5/54) 58 116 174 371 636 900
201-208: 207-Last Johnny Quick (not in 205) 47 94 141 296 498 700
209-Last pre-code issue; origin Speedy 48 96 144 302 514 725
210-1st app. Krypto (Superdog)-c/story (3/55) 550 1100 2200 5000 8750 12,500
211-213,215-219 43 86 129 271 461 650
214-2nd app. Krypto 84 168 252 538 919 1300
220-Krypto-c/sty 52 104 156 328 552 775
221-246: 229-1st S.A. issue; Green Arrow & Aquaman app. 237-1st Intergalactic Vigilante Squadron (6/57). 239-Krypto-c 37 74 111 222 361 500
247(4/58)-1st Legion of Super Heroes app.; 1st app. Cosmic Boy, Saturn Girl & Lightning Boy (later Lightning Lad in #267) (origin) 750 1500 3000 7500 15,750 24,000
248-252,254,255-Green Arrow in all: 255-Intro. Red Kryptonite in Superboy (used in #252 but with no effect) 34 68 102 199 325 450
253-1st meeting of Superboy & Robin; Green Arrow by Kirby in #250-255 (also see World's Finest #96-99) 39 78 117 231 378 525
256-Origin Green Arrow by Kirby 69 138 207 442 946 1450
257-259: 258-Green Arrow x-over in Superboy 27 54 81 158 259 360
260-1st Silver Age origin Aquaman (5/59) 90 180 270 720 1310 1900
261-265,268,270: 262-Origin Speedy in Green Arrow. 270-Congorilla begins, ends #281,283 22 44 66 128 209 290
266-(11/59)-Origin & 1st app. Aquagirl (tryout, not same as later character) 25 50 75 150 245 340
267(12/59)-2nd Legion of Super Heroes; Lightning Boy now called Lightning Lad; new costumes for Legion 97 194 291 611 1506 2400
269-Intro. Aqualad (2/60); last Green Arrow (not in #206) 47 94 141 296 498 700
271-Origin Luthor retold 42 84 126 265 445 625
272-274,277-280: 279-Intro White Kryptonite in Superboy. 280-1st meeting Superboy & Lori Lemaris 20 40 60 118 192 265
275-Origin Superman-Batman team retold (see World's Finest #94) 32 64 96 188 307 425
276-(9/60) Robinson Crusoe-like story 21 42 63 122 199 275
281,284,287-289: 281-Last Congorilla. 284-Last Aquaman in Adv.; Mooney-a. 287,288-Intro Dev-Em, the Knave from Krypton. 287-1st Bizarro Perry White & Jimmy Olsen. 288-Bizarro-c. 289-Legion cameo (statues) 19 38 57 111 176 240
282(3/61)-5th Legion app; intro/origin Star Boy 40 80 120 244 402 560
283-Intro. The Phantom Zone; 1st app. of General Zod (cameo in 2 panels) 71 142 213 454 777 1100
285-1st Tales of the Bizarro World-c/story (ends #299) in Adv. (see Action #255)

Adventure Comics #368 © DC

Adventure Comics (2009 series) #12 © DC

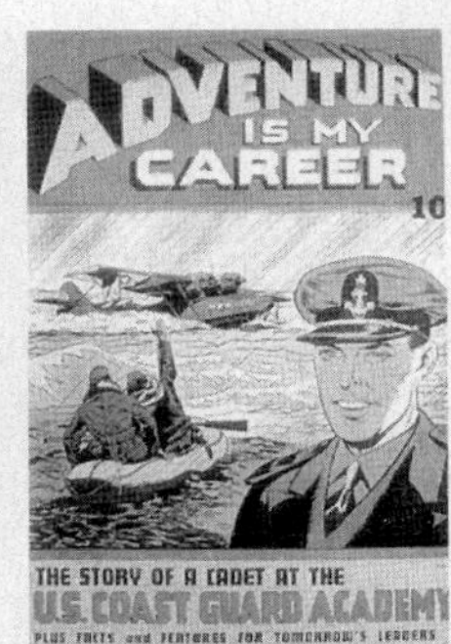

Adventure is My Career nn © CN

	GD 2.0	VG 4.0	FN 6.0	VF 8.0	VF/NM 9.0	NM- 9.2

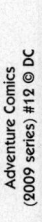

24 48 72 140 234 325
286-1st Bizarro Mxyzptlk; Bizarro-c 23 46 69 136 223 310
290(11/61)-9th Legion app; origin Sunboy in Legion (last 10¢ issue)
37 74 111 222 361 500
291,292,295-298: 291-1st 12¢ ish, (12/61). 292-1st Bizarro Lana Lang & Lucy Lane.
295-Bizarro-c; 1st Bizarro Titano 10 20 30 64 132 200
293(2/62)-13th Legion app; Mon-El app.; Legion of Super Pets 1st app./origin; 1st Superhorse; 2nd app. General Zod; 1st Bizarro Luthor & Kandor
37 74 111 222 361 500
294-1st Bizarro Marilyn Monroe, Pres. Kennedy. 12 24 36 83 182 280
299-1st Gold Kryptonite (8/62) 10 20 30 66 138 210
300-Tales of the Legion of Super-Heroes series begins (9/62); Mon-El leaves Phantom Zone (temporarily), joins Legion 54 108 162 432 1028 1600
301-Origin Bouncing Boy 15 30 45 105 233 360
302-305: 303-1st app. Matter-Eater Lad. 304-Death of Lightning Lad in Legion
12 24 36 83 182 280
306-310: 306-Intro. Legion of Substitute Heroes. 307-1st app. Element Lad in Legion.
308-1st app. Lightning Lass in Legion. 309-1st app. Legion of Super-Monsters
12 24 36 79 170 260
311-320: 312-Lightning Lad back in Legion. 315-Last new Superboy story; Colossal Boy app. 316-Origins & powers of Legion given. 317-Intro. Dream Girl in Legion; Lightning Lass becomes Light Lass; Hall of Fame series begins. 320-Dev-Em 2nd app.
10 20 30 64 132 200
321-Intro. Time Trapper 9 18 27 58 114 170
322-330: 327-Intro/1st app. Lone Wolf in Legion. 329-Intro The Bizarro Legionnaires; intro. Legion flight rings 8 16 24 55 105 155
331-340: 337-Chlorophyll Kid & Night Girl app. 340-Intro Computo in Legion
8 16 24 51 96 140
341-Triplicate Girl becomes Duo Damsel 7 14 21 44 82 120
342-345,347-351: 345-Last Hall of Fame; returns in 356,371. 348-Origin Sunboy; intro Dr. Regulus in Legion. 349-Intro Universo & Rond Vidar. 351-1st app. White Witch
6 12 18 42 79 115
346-1st app. Karate Kid, Princess Projectra, Ferro Lad, & Nemesis Kid.
13 26 39 89 195 300
352,354-360: 354,355-Superman meets the Adult Legion. 355-Insect Queen joins Legion (4/67)
6 12 18 38 69 100
353-Death of Ferro Lad in Legion 8 16 24 54 102 150
361-364,366,368-370: 369-Intro Mordru in Legion 5 10 15 35 63 90
365,367: 365-Intro Shadow Lass (memorial to Shadow Woman app. in #354's Adult Legion-s); lists origins & powers of L.S.H. 367-New Legion headquarters
6 12 18 37 66 95
371,372: 371-Intro. Chemical King (mentioned in #354's Adult Legion-s). 372-Timber Wolf & Chemical King join 6 12 18 37 66 95
373,374,376-380: 373-Intro. Tornado Twins (Barry Allen Flash descendants). 374-Article on comics fandom. 380-Last Legion in Adventure; last 12¢-c
5 10 15 34 60 85
375-Intro Quantum Queen & The Wanderers 5 10 15 35 63 90
381-Supergirl begins; 1st full length Supergirl story & her 1st solo book (6/69)
14 28 42 96 211 325
382-389 5 10 15 31 53 75
390-Giant Supergirl G-69 6 12 18 41 76 110
391-396,398 4 8 12 23 37 50
397-1st app. new Supergirl 5 10 15 31 53 75
399-Unpubbed G.A. Black Canary story 4 8 12 25 40 55
400-New costume for Supergirl (12/70) 5 10 15 31 53 75
401,402,404-408-(15¢-c) 3 6 9 17 26 35
403-68 pg. Giant G-81; Legion-r/#304,305,308,312 6 12 18 38 69 100
409-411,413-415,417-420-(52 pgs.): 413-Hawkman by Kubert r/B&B #44; G.A. Robotman-r/Det. #178; Zatanna by Morrow. 414-r-2nd Animal Man/Str. Advs. #184. 415-Animal Man-r/Str. Adv.#190 (origin recap). 417-Morrow Vigilante; Frazetta Shining Knight-r/Adv. #161; origin The Enchantress; no Zatanna. 418-Prev. unpub. Dr. Mid-Nite story from 1948; no Zatanna. 420-Animal Man-r/Str. Adv. #195 3 6 9 18 28 38
412-(52 pgs.) Reprints origin & 1st app. of Animal Man from Strange Adventures #180
3 6 9 18 28 38
416-Also listed as DC 100 Pg. Super Spectacular #10; Golden Age-r; r/1st app. Black Canary from Flash #86; no Zatanna 10 20 30 68 144 220
421-424: 424-Last Supergirl in Adventure 3 6 9 14 20 25
425-New look, content change to adventure; Kaluta-c; Toth-a, origin Capt. Fear
3 6 9 16 23 30
426,427: 426-1st Adventurers Club. 427-Last Vigilante 2 4 6 9 12 15
428-Origin/1st app. Black Orchid (c/story, 6-7/73) 5 10 15 35 63 90
429,430-Black Orchid-c/stories 3 6 9 20 31 42
431-Spectre by Aparo begins, ends #440. 5 10 15 35 63 90
432-439-Spectre app. 433-437-Cover title is Weird Adventure Comics. 436-Last 20¢ issue
3 6 9 21 33 45
440-New Spectre origin 4 8 12 23 37 50
441-458: 441-452-Aquaman app. 443-Fisherman app. 445-447-The Creeper app. 446-Flag-c. 449-451-Martian Manhunter app. 450-Weather Wizard app. in Aquaman story. 453-458-Superboy app. 453-Intro. Mighty Girl. 457,458-Eclipso app.
1 3 4 6 8 10
459,460 (68 pgs.): 459-New Gods/Darkseid storyline concludes from New Gods #19 (#459 is dated 9-10/78) without missing a month. 459-Flash (ends #466), Deadman (ends #466), Wonder Woman (ends #464), Green Lantern (ends #460). 460-Aquaman (ends #478)
3 6 9 14 20 26
461-($1.00, 68 pgs.) Justice Society begins; ends 466 4 8 12 25 40 55
462-($1.00, 68 pgs.) Death Earth II Batman 5 10 15 33 57 80
463-466 ($1.00 size, 68 pgs.) 2 4 6 10 14 18
467-Starman by Ditko & Plastic Man begins; 1st app. Prince Gavyn (Starman).
2 4 6 8 11 14
468-490: 470-Origin Starman. 479-Dial 'H' For Hero begins, ends #490. 478-Last Starman & Plastic Man. 480-490: Dial 'H' For Hero 5.00
491-503: 491-100pg. Digest size begins; r/Legion of Super Heroes/Adv. #247, 267; Spectre, Aquaman, Superboy, S&K Sandman, Black Canary-r & new Shazam by Newton begin. 492,495,496,499-S&K Sandman-r/Adventure in all. 493-Challengers of the Unknown begins by Tuska w/brief origin. 493-495,497-499-G.A. Captain Marvel-r. 494-499-Spectre-r/Spectre 1-3, 5-7. 496-Capt. Marvel Jr. new-s, Cockrum-a. 498-Mary Marvel new-s; Plastic Man-r begin; origin Bouncing Boy-r/ #301. 500-Legion-r (Digest size, 148 pgs.).
501-503: G.A.-r 2 4 6 9 13 16
... 80 Page Giant (10/98, $4.95) Wonder Woman, Shazam, Superboy, Supergirl, Green Arrow, Legion, Bizarro World stories 5.00

NOTE: *Bizarro covers-285, 286, 288, 294, 295, 329. Vigilante app.-420, 426, 427.* **N. Adams** *a(r)-495i-498i; c-365-369, 371-373, 375-379, 381-383.* **Aparo** *a-431-433, 434i, 435, 436, 437i, 438i, 439-452, 503r; c-431-452.* **Austin** *a-449i 451i.* **Bernard Baily** *c-48, 50, 52-59.* **Bolland** *c-475.* **Burnley** *c-61-72, 116-120p.* **Chaykin** *a-438.* **Ditko** *a-467-478p; c-467p.* **Creig Flessel** *c-32, 33, 40, 42, 44, 46, 47, 51, 60.* **Giffen** *c-491p-494p, 500p.* **Grell** *a-435-437, 440.* **Guardineer** *c-34, 35, 45.* **Infantino** *a-416r.* **Kaluta** *c-425.* **Bob Kane** *a-38.* **G. Kane** *a-414r, 425; c-496-499, 537.* **Kirby** *a-250-256.* **Kubert** *a-413.* **Meskin** *a-81,125,127.* **Moldoff** *a-494i; c-49.* **Morrow** *a-413-415, 417, 422, 502r, 503r.* **Netzer/Nasser** *a-449-451.* **Newton** *a-459-461, 464-466, 491p, 492p.* **Paul Norris** *a-69.* **Orlando** *a-457p, 458p.* **Perez** *c-484-486, 490p.* **Simon/Kirby** *a-503r; c-73-97, 100-102.* **Starlin** *c-471.* **Staton** *a-445-447i, 456-458p, 459, 460, 461p-465p, 466,467p-478p, 502p(r); c-458, 461(back).* **Toth** *a-418, 419, 425, 431, 495p-497p.* **Tuska** *a-494p.*

ADVENTURE COMICS (Also see All Star Comics 1999 crossover titles)
DC Comics: May, 1999 ($1.99, one-shot)
1-Golden Age Starman and the Atom; Snejbjerg-a 3.00

ADVENTURE COMICS (See Final Crisis: Legion of Three Worlds)
DC Comics: No. 0, Apr, 2009 - No. 12, Aug, 2010; No. 516, Sept, 2010 - No. 529, Oct, 2011 ($1.00/$3.99)
0-($1.00) R/Adventure Comics #247; new Luthor & Brainiac back-up-s; Lopresti-c 3.00
1-7-($3.99) Superboy stories; Johns-s/Manapul-a; Legion back-up-s. 5-7-Blackest Night 4.00
1-12-Variant 7-panel covers by various numbered with original #504-#515 5.00
8-12: 8-11-New Krypton x-over. 11-Mon-El leaves 21st century. 12-Legion; Levitz-s 4.00
516-521: 516-(9/10, resumes original numbering) flashback to Legion formation; Atom back-ups. 521-Adult Legion resumes; Mon-El joins Green Lanterns 4.00
522-529-($2.99) Legion Academy. 523-527-Jimenez-a/c 3.00

ADVENTURE COMICS SPECIAL (See New Krypton issues in 2009 Superman titles)
DC Comics: Jan, 2009 ($2.99, one-shot)
... Featuring the Guardian - James Robinson-s/Pere Pérez-a; origin re-told; intro. Gwen 3.00

ADVENTURE INTO MYSTERY
Atlas Comics (BFP No. 1/OPI No. 2-8): May, 1956 - No. 8, July, 1957
1-Powell s/f-a; Forte-a; Everett-c 61 122 183 390 670 950
2-Flying Saucer story 34 68 102 199 325 450
3,6-Everett-c 30 60 90 177 289 400
4,5,7: 4-Williamson-a, 4 pgs; Powell-a. 5-Everett-c/a, Orlando-a. 7-Torres-a; Everett-c 32 64 96 188 307 425
8-Moreira, Sale, Torres, Woodbridge-a, Severin-c 30 60 90 177 289 400

ADVENTURE IS MY CAREER
U.S. Coast Guard Academy/Street & Smith: 1945 (44 pgs.)
nn-Simon, Milt Gross-a 22 44 66 128 209 290

ADVENTURERS, THE
Aircel Comics/Adventure Publ.: Aug, 1986 - No. 10, 1987? ($1.50, B&W)
V2#1, 1987 - V2#9, 1988; V3#1, Oct, 1989 - V3#6, 1990
1-Peter Hsu-a 1 2 3 5 6 8
1-Cover variant, limited ed. 2 4 6 9 12 15
1-2nd print (1986); 1st app. Elf Warrior 3.00
2,3, 0 (#4, 12/86)-Origin, 5-10, Book II, reg. & Limited Ed. #1 3.50
Book II, #2,3,0,4-9 3.00
Book III, #1 (10/89, $2.25)-Reg. & limited-c, Book III, #2-6 3.00

Adventures in the DC Universe #12 © DC

Adventures Into Terror #31 © MAR

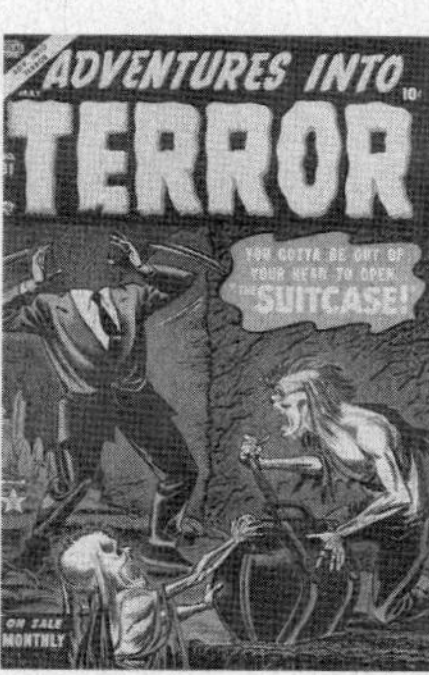

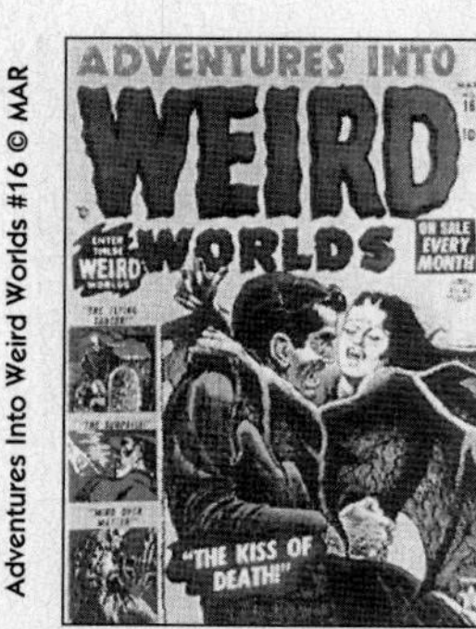

Adventures Into Weird Worlds #16 © MAR

ADVENTURES (No. 2 Spectacular… on cover)
St. John Publishing Co.: Nov, 1949 - No. 2, Feb, 1950 (No. 1 …in Romance on cover)
(Slightly larger size)

	GD 2.0	VG 4.0	FN 6.0	VF 8.0	VF/NM 9.0	NM- 9.2
1(Scarce); Bolle, Starr-a(2)	36	72	108	211	343	475
2(Scarce)-Slave Girl; China Bombshell app.; Bolle, L. Starr-a	45	90	135	284	480	675

ADVENTURES FOR BOYS
Bailey Enterprises: Dec, 1954

	GD 2.0	VG 4.0	FN 6.0	VF 8.0	VF/NM 9.0	NM- 9.2
nn-Comics, text, & photos	8	16	24	40	50	60

ADVENTURES IN PARADISE (TV)
Dell Publishing Co.: Feb-Apr, 1962

	GD 2.0	VG 4.0	FN 6.0	VF 8.0	VF/NM 9.0	NM- 9.2
Four Color #1301	6	12	18	37	66	95

ADVENTURES IN ROMANCE (See Adventures)

ADVENTURES IN SCIENCE (See Classics Illustrated Special Issue)

ADVENTURES IN THE DC UNIVERSE
DC Comics: Apr, 1997 - No. 19, Oct, 1998 ($1.75/$1.95/$1.99)

	GD 2.0	VG 4.0	FN 6.0	VF 8.0	VF/NM 9.0	NM- 9.2
1-Animated style in all: JLA-c/app						5.00
2-11,13-17,19: 2-Flash app. 3-Wonder Woman. 4-Green Lantern. 6-Aquaman. 7-Shazam Family. 8-Blue Beetle & Booster Gold. 9-Flash. 10-Legion. 11-Green Lantern & Wonder Woman. 13-Impulse & Martian Manhunter. 14-Superboy/Flash race						3.50
12,18-JLA-c/app						3.50
Annual 1(1997, $3.95)-Dr. Fate, Impulse, Rose & Thorn, Superboy, Mister Miracle app.						4.50

ADVENTURES IN THE RIFLE BRIGADE
DC Comics (Vertigo): Oct, 2000 - No. 3, Dec, 2000 ($2.50, limited series)

	GD 2.0	VG 4.0	FN 6.0	VF 8.0	VF/NM 9.0	NM- 9.2
1-3-Ennis-s/Ezquerra-a/Bolland-c						3.00
TPB (2004, $14.95) r/series and Operation Bollock series						15.00

ADVENTURES IN THE RIFLE BRIGADE: OPERATION BOLLOCK
DC Comics (Vertigo): Oct, 2001 - No. 3, Jan, 2002 ($2.50, limited series)

	GD 2.0	VG 4.0	FN 6.0	VF 8.0	VF/NM 9.0	NM- 9.2
1-3-Ennis-s/Ezquerra-a/Fabry-c						3.00

ADVENTURES IN 3-D (With glasses)
Harvey Publications: Nov, 1953 - No. 2, Jan, 1954 (25¢)

	GD 2.0	VG 4.0	FN 6.0	VF 8.0	VF/NM 9.0	NM- 9.2
1-Nostrand, Powell-a, 2-Powell-a	14	28	42	80	115	150

ADVENTURES INTO DARKNESS (See Seduction of the Innocent 3-D)
Better-Standard Publications/Visual Editions: No. 5, Aug, 1952- No. 14, 1954

	GD 2.0	VG 4.0	FN 6.0	VF 8.0	VF/NM 9.0	NM- 9.2
5-Katz-c/a; Toth-a(p)	52	104	156	328	552	775
6-Tuska, Katz-a	41	82	123	256	428	600
7-9: 7-Katz-c/a. 8,9-Toth-a(p)	39	78	117	240	395	550
10-12: 10,11-Jack Katz-a. 12-Toth-a; lingerie panel	37	74	111	222	361	500
13-Toth-a(p); Cannibalism story cited by T. E. Murphy articles	47	94	141	296	498	700
14	32	64	96	188	307	425

NOTE: ***Fawcette*** *a-13.* ***Moreira*** *a-5.* ***Sekowsky*** *a-10, 11, 13(2).*

ADVENTURES INTO TERROR (Formerly Joker Comics)
Marvel/Atlas Comics (CDS): No. 43, Nov, 1950 - No. 31, May, 1954

	GD 2.0	VG 4.0	FN 6.0	VF 8.0	VF/NM 9.0	NM- 9.2
43(#1)	84	168	252	538	919	1300
44(#2, 2/51)-Sol Brodsky-c	48	96	144	302	514	725
3(4/51), 4	40	80	120	246	411	575
5-Wolverton-c panel/Mystic #6; Rico-c panel also; Atom Bomb story	41	82	123	256	428	600
6,8: 8-Wolverton text illo r-/Marvel Tales #104; prototype of Spider-Man villain The Lizard	39	78	117	240	395	550
7-Wolverton-a "Where Monsters Dwell", 6 pgs.; Tuska-c; Maneely-c panels	68	136	204	435	743	1050
9,10,12-Krigstein-a. 9-Decapitation panels	39	78	117	231	378	525
11,13-20	36	72	108	211	343	475
21-24,26-31	34	68	102	199	325	450
25-Matt Fox-a	39	78	117	231	378	525

NOTE: ***Ayers*** *a-21.* ***Colan*** *a-3, 5, 14, 21, 24, 25, 28, 29; c-27.* ***Colletta*** *a-30.* ***Everett*** *c-13, 21, 25.* ***Fass*** *a-28, 29.* ***Forte*** *a-28.* ***Heath*** *a-43, 44, 4-6, 22, 24, 26; c-43, 9, 11.* ***Lazarus*** *a-7.* ***Maneely*** *a-7(3 pg.), 10, 11, 21., 22 c-15, 29.* ***Don Rico*** *a-4, 5(3 pg.).* ***Sekowsky*** *a-43, 3, 4.* ***Sinnott*** *a-8, 9, 11, 24, 28.* ***Tuska*** *a-14; c-7.*

ADVENTURES INTO THE UNKNOWN
American Comics Group: Fall, 1948 - No. 174, Aug, 1967 (No. 1-33: 52 pgs.)
(1st continuous series Supernatural comic; see Eerie #1)

	GD 2.0	VG 4.0	FN 6.0	VF 8.0	VF/NM 9.0	NM- 9.2
1-Guardineer-a; adapt. of 'Castle of Otranto' by Horace Walpole	265	530	795	1694	2897	4100
2,3: 3-Feldstein-a (9 pgs)	87	174	261	553	952	1350
4,5: 5- 'Spirit Of Frankenstein' series begins, ends #12 (except #11)	45	90	135	284	480	675
6-10	37	74	111	222	361	500
11-16,18-20: 13-Starr-a. 15-Hitler app.	32	64	96	188	307	425
17-Story similar to movie 'The Thing'	36	72	108	211	343	475
21-26,28-30	26	52	78	154	252	350
27-Williamson/Krenkel-a (8 pgs.)	32	64	96	188	307	425
31-50: 38-Atom bomb panels; Devil-c	20	40	60	118	192	265
51-(1/54)-(3-D effect-c/story)-Only white cover	50	100	150	315	533	750
52-58: (3-D effect-c/stories with black covers). 52-E.C. swipe/Haunt Of Fear #14	47	94	141	296	498	700
59-3-D effect story only; new logo	32	64	96	188	307	425
60-Wood*esque*-a by Landau	15	30	45	88	137	185
61-Last pre-code issue (1-2/55)	15	30	45	88	137	185
62-70	7	14	21	46	86	125
71-90: 80-Hydrogen bomb panel	6	12	18	37	66	95
91,96(#95 on inside),107,116-All have Williamson-a	6	12	18	40	73	105
92-95,97-99,101-106,108-115,117-128: 109-113,118-Whitney painted-c. 128-Williamson/Krenkel/Torres-a(r)/Forbidden Worlds #63; last 10¢ issue	5	10	15	31	53	75
100	5	10	15	34	60	85
129-153,157: 153,157-Magic Agent app.	4	8	12	23	37	50
154-Nemesis series begins (origin), ends #170	4	8	12	28	47	65
155,156,158-167,170-174: 174-Flying saucer-c	4	8	12	22	35	48
168-Ditko-a(p)	4	8	12	27	44	60
169-Nemesis battles Hitler	4	8	12	27	44	60
Nemesis Archives: Vol. One (Dark Horse Books, 9/08, $59.95) r/#154-170; creator bios						60.00

NOTE: *"Spirit of Frankenstein" series in 5, 6, 8-10, 12, 16.* ***Buscema*** *a-100, 106, 108-110, 158r, 165r.* ***Cameron*** *a-34.* ***Craig*** *a-152, 160.* ***Goode*** *a-45, 47, 60.* ***Landau*** *a-51, 59-63.* ***Lazarus*** *a-34, 48, 51, 52, 56, 58, 79, 87; c-31-56, 58.* ***Reinman*** *a-102, 111, 112, 115-118, 124, 130, 137, 141, 145, 164.* ***Whitney*** *c-12-30, 57, 59-on (most.)* ***Torres/Williamson*** *a-116.*

ADVENTURES INTO WEIRD WORLDS
Marvel/Atlas Comics (ACI): Jan, 1952 - No. 30, June, 1954

	GD 2.0	VG 4.0	FN 6.0	VF 8.0	VF/NM 9.0	NM- 9.2
1-Atom bomb panels	129	258	387	826	1413	2000
2-Sci/fic stories (2); one by Maneely	48	96	144	302	514	725
3-10: 7-Tongue ripped out. 10-Krigstein, Everett-a	41	82	123	256	428	600
11-20	37	74	111	222	361	500
21-Hitler in Hell story	42	84	126	265	445	625
22-26: 24-Man holds hypo & splits in two-c	36	72	108	211	343	475
27-Matt Fox end of world story-a; severed head-c	54	108	162	343	574	825
28-Atom bomb story; decapitation panels	39	78	117	231	378	525
29,30	32	64	96	188	307	425

NOTE: ***Ayers*** *a-8, 26.* ***Everett*** *a-4, 5; c-6, 8, 10-13, 18, 19, 22, 24, 25; a-4, 25.* ***Fass*** *a-7.* ***Forte*** *a-21, 24.* ***Al Hartley*** *a-2.* ***Heath*** *a-1, 4, 17, 22; c-7, 9, 20.* ***Maneely*** *a-2, 3, 11, 20, 22, 23, 25; c-1, 3, 22, 25-27, 29.* ***Reinman*** *a-24, 28.* ***Rico*** *a-13.* ***Robinson*** *a-13.* ***Sinnott*** *a-25, 30.* ***Tuska*** *a-1, 2, 12, 15.* ***Whitney*** *a-7.* ***Wildey*** *a-28. Bondage c-22.*

ADVENTURES IN WONDERLAND (Also see Uncle Charlies Fables)
Lev Gleason Publications: April, 1955 - No. 5, Feb, 1956 (Jr. Readers Guild)

	GD 2.0	VG 4.0	FN 6.0	VF 8.0	VF/NM 9.0	NM- 9.2
1-Maurer-a	12	24	36	67	94	120
2-4	8	16	24	40	50	60
5-Christmas issue	8	16	24	42	54	65

ADVENTURES OF ALAN LADD, THE
National Periodical Publ.: Oct-Nov, 1949 - No. 9, Feb-Mar, 1951 (All 52 pgs.)

	GD 2.0	VG 4.0	FN 6.0	VF 8.0	VF/NM 9.0	NM- 9.2
1-Photo-c	77	154	231	493	847	1200
2-Photo-c	40	80	120	246	411	575
3-6: Last photo-c	36	72	108	211	343	475
7-9	30	60	90	177	289	400

NOTE: ***Dan Barry*** *a-1.* ***Moreira*** *a-3-7.*

ADVENTURES OF ALICE (Also see Alice in Wonderland) (Becomes Alice at Monkey Island #3)
Civil Service Publ./Pentagon Publishing Co.: 1945

	GD 2.0	VG 4.0	FN 6.0	VF 8.0	VF/NM 9.0	NM- 9.2
1	15	30	45	85	130	175
2-Through the Magic Looking Glass	11	22	33	64	90	115

ADVENTURES OF BARON MUNCHAUSEN, THE
Now Comics: July, 1989 - No. 4, Oct, 1989 ($1.75, limited series)

	GD 2.0	VG 4.0	FN 6.0	VF 8.0	VF/NM 9.0	NM- 9.2
1-4: Movie adaptation						3.00

ADVENTURES OF BARRY WEEN, BOY GENIUS, THE
Image Comics: Mar, 1999 - No. 3, May, 1999 ($2.95, B&W, limited series)

	GD 2.0	VG 4.0	FN 6.0	VF 8.0	VF/NM 9.0	NM- 9.2
1-3-Judd Winick-s/a						3.00
…: Secret Crisis Origin Files (Oni, 7/04, Free Comic Book Day giveaway) - Winick-s/a						3.00
TPB (Oni Press, 11/99, $8.95) r/#1-3						9.00

ADVENTURES OF BARRY WEEN, BOY GENIUS 2.0, THE
Oni Press: Feb, 2000 - No. 3, Apr, 2000 ($2.95, B&W, limited series)

	GD 2.0	VG 4.0	FN 6.0	VF 8.0	VF/NM 9.0	NM- 9.2
1-3-Judd Winick-s/a						3.00
TPB (2000, $8.95)						9.00

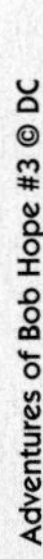
Adventures of Bob Hope #3 © DC

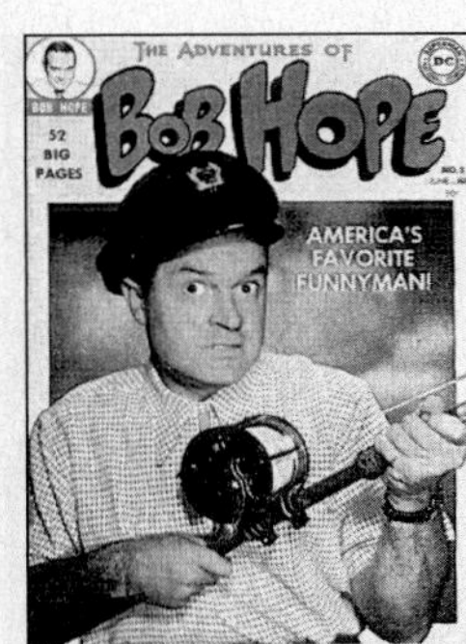

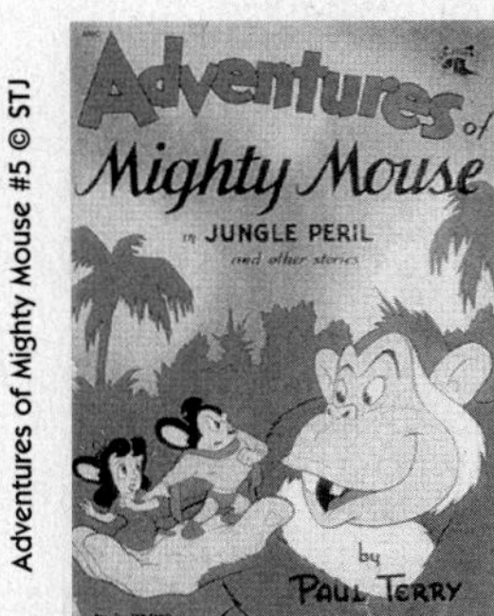

Adventures of Mighty Mouse #5 © STJ

Adventures of Rex The Wonder Dog #5 © DC

	GD 2.0	VG 4.0	FN 6.0	VF 8.0	VF/NM 9.0	NM- 9.2

ADVENTURES OF BARRY WEEN, BOY GENIUS 3, THE : MONKEY TALES
Oni Press: Feb, 2001 - No. 6, Feb, 2002 ($2.95, B&W, limited series)

	GD	VG	FN	VF	VF/NM	NM-
1-6-Judd Winick-s/a						3.00
TPB (2001, $8.95) r/#1-3; intro. by Peter David						9.00
...4 TPB (5/02, $8.95) r/#4-6						9.00

ADVENTURES OF BAYOU BILLY, THE (Based on video game)
Archie Comics: Sept, 1989 - No. 5, June, 1990 ($1.00)

	GD	VG	FN	VF	VF/NM	NM-
1-5: Esposito-c/a(i). 5-Kelley Jones-c						3.00

ADVENTURES OF BOB HOPE, THE (Also see True Comics #59)
National Per. Publ.: Feb-Mar, 1950 - No. 109, Feb-Mar, 1968 (#1-10: 52pgs.)

	GD	VG	FN	VF	VF/NM	NM-
1-Photo-c	258	516	774	1651	2826	4000
2-Photo-c	92	184	276	584	1005	1425
3,4-Photo-c	57	114	171	362	619	875
5-10: 9-Horror-c	41	82	123	256	428	600
11-20	29	58	87	170	278	385
21-31 (2-3/55; last precode)	20	40	60	117	189	260
32-40	9	18	27	61	123	185
41-50	8	16	24	54	102	150
51-70	7	14	21	46	86	125
71-93	5	10	15	35	63	90
94-Aquaman cameo	6	12	18	37	66	95
95-1st app. Super-Hip & 1st monster issue (11/65)	7	14	21	48	89	130
96-105: Super-Hip and monster stories in all. 103-Batman, Robin, Ringo Starr cameos	5	10	15	34	60	85
106-109-All monster-c/stories by N. Adams-c/a	7	14	21	49	92	135

NOTE: *Buzzy in #34. Kitty Karr of Hollywood in #15, 17-20, 23, 28. Liz in #26, 109. Miss Beverly Hills of Hollywood in #7, 8, 10, 13, 14. Miss Melody Lane of Broadway in #15. Rusty in #23, 25. Tommy in #24. No 2nd feature in #2-4, 6, 8, 11, 12, 28-108.*

ADVENTURES OF CAPTAIN AMERICA
Marvel Comics: Sept, 1991 - No. 4, Jan, 1992 ($4.95, 52 pgs., squarebound, limited series)

	GD	VG	FN	VF	VF/NM	NM-
1-4: 1-Origin in WW2; embossed-c; Nicieza scripts; Maguire-c/a(p) begins, ends #3. 2-4-Austin-c/a(i). 3,4-Red Skull app.						5.00

ADVENTURES OF CYCLOPS AND PHOENIX (Also See Askani'son & The Further Adventures of Cyclops And Phoenix)
Marvel Comics: May, 1994 - No. 4, Aug, 1994 ($2.95, limited series)

	GD	VG	FN	VF	VF/NM	NM-
1-4-Characters from X-Men; origin of Cable						4.00
Trade paperback ($14.95)-reprints #1-4						15.00

ADVENTURES OF DEAN MARTIN AND JERRY LEWIS, THE
(The Adventures of Jerry Lewis #41 on) (See Movie Love #12)
National Periodical Publications: July-Aug, 1952 - No. 40, Oct, 1957

	GD	VG	FN	VF	VF/NM	NM-
1	142	284	426	909	1555	2200
2-3 pg origin on how they became a team	60	120	180	381	653	925
3-10: 3- I Love Lucy text featurette	36	72	108	211	343	475
11-19: Last precode (2/55)	22	44	66	132	216	300
20-30	17	34	51	98	154	210
31-40	15	30	45	83	124	165

ADVENTURES OF DETECTIVE ACE KING, THE (Also see Bob Scully-- & Detective Dan)
Humor Publ. Corp.: No date (1933) (36 pgs., 9-1/2x12") (10¢, B&W, one-shot) (paper-c)

	GD	VG	FN	VF	VF/NM	NM-
Book 1-Along with Bob Scully & Detective Dan, the first comic w/original art & the first of a single theme.; Not reprints; Ace King by Martin Nadle (The American Sherlock Holmes). A Dick Tracy look-alike	625	1250	1875	5000	-	-

ADVENTURES OF EVIL AND MALICE, THE
Image Comics: June, 1999 - No. 3, Nov, 1999 ($3.50/$3.95, limited series)

	GD	VG	FN	VF	VF/NM	NM-
1-3-Jimmie Robinson-s/a. 3-($3.95-c)						4.00

ADVENTURES OF FELIX THE CAT, THE
Harvey Comics: May, 1992 ($1.25)

	GD	VG	FN	VF	VF/NM	NM-
1-Messmer-r						5.00

ADVENTURES OF FORD FAIRLANE, THE
DC Comics: May, 1990 - No. 4, Aug, 1990 ($1.50, limited series, mature)

	GD	VG	FN	VF	VF/NM	NM-
1-4: Andrew Dice Clay movie tie-in; Don Heck inks						4.00

ADVENTURES OF HOMER COBB, THE
Say/Bart Prod. : Sept, 1947 (Oversized) (Published in the U.S., but printed in Canada)

	GD	VG	FN	VF	VF/NM	NM-
1-(Scarce)-Feldstein-c/a	45	90	135	284	480	675

ADVENTURES OF HOMER GHOST (See Homer The Happy Ghost)
Atlas Comics: June, 1957 - No. 2, Aug, 1957

	GD	VG	FN	VF	VF/NM	NM-
V1#1,2: 2-Robot-c	16	32	48	94	147	200

ADVENTURES OF JERRY LEWIS, THE (Adventures of Dean Martin & Jerry Lewis No. 1-40)
(See Super DC Giant)
National Periodical Publ.: No. 41, Nov, 1957 - No. 124, May-June, 1971

	GD	VG	FN	VF	VF/NM	NM-
41	9	18	27	61	123	185
42-60	7	14	21	49	92	135
61-67,69-73,75-80	6	12	18	41	76	110
68,74-Photo-c (movie)	9	18	27	60	120	180
81,82,85-87,90,91,94,96,98,99	5	10	15	34	60	85
83,84,88: 83-1st Monsters-c/s. 84-Jerry as a Super-hero-c/s. 88-1st Witch, Miss Kraft	6	12	18	38	69	100
89-Bob Hope app.; Wizard of Oz & Alfred E. Neuman in MAD parody	6	12	18	41	76	110
92-Superman cameo	6	12	18	41	76	110
93-Beatles parody as babies	6	12	18	38	69	100
95-1st Uncle Hal Wack-A-Boy Camp-c/s	6	12	18	38	69	100
97-Batman/Robin/Joker-c/story; Riddler & Penguin app; Dick Sprang-c.	8	16	24	56	108	160
100	6	12	18	40	73	105
101,103,104-Neal Adams-c/a	7	14	21	46	86	125
102-Beatles app.; Neal Adams c/a	9	18	27	57	111	165
105-Superman x-over	6	12	18	41	76	110
106-111,113-116	4	8	12	28	47	65
112,117: 112-Flash x-over. 117-W. Woman x-over	6	12	18	40	73	105
118-124	4	8	12	27	44	60

NOTE: *Monster-c/s-90,93,96,98,101. Wack-A-Buy Camp-c/s-96,99,102,107,108.*

ADVENTURES OF JO-JOY, THE (See Jo-Joy)

ADVENTURES OF LASSIE, THE (See Lassie)

ADVENTURES OF LUTHER ARKWRIGHT, THE
Valkyrie Press/Dark Horse Comics: Oct, 1987 - No. 9, Jan, 1989 ($2.00, B&W) V2, #1, Mar, 1990 - V2#9, 1990 ($1.95, B&W)

	GD	VG	FN	VF	VF/NM	NM-
1-9: 1-Alan Moore intro., V2#1-9 (Dark Horse): r-1st series; new-c						4.00
TPB (1997, $14.95) r/#1-9 w/Michael Moorcock intro.						15.00

ADVENTURES OF MIGHTY MOUSE (Mighty Mouse Adventures No. 1)
St. John Publishing Co.: No. 2, Jan, 1952 - No. 18, May, 1955

	GD	VG	FN	VF	VF/NM	NM-
2	29	58	87	172	281	390
3-5	15	30	45	90	140	190
6-18	13	26	39	72	101	130

ADVENTURES OF MIGHTY MOUSE (2nd Series) (Becomes Mighty Mouse #161 on)
(Two No. 144's; formerly Paul Terry's Comics; No. 129-137 have nn's)
St. John/Pines/Dell/Gold Key: No. 126, Aug, 1955 - No. 160, Oct, 1963

	GD	VG	FN	VF	VF/NM	NM-
126(8/55), 127(10/55), 128(11/55)-St. John	10	20	30	56	76	95
nn(129, 4/56)-144(8/59)-Pines	5	10	15	30	50	70
144(10-12/59)-155(7-9/62) Dell	4	8	12	27	44	60
156(10/62)-160(10/63) Gold Key	4	8	12	27	44	60

NOTE: *Early issues titled "Paul Terry's Adventures of ...."*

ADVENTURES OF MIGHTY MOUSE (Formerly Mighty Mouse)
Gold Key: No. 166, Mar, 1979 - No. 172, Jan, 1980

	GD	VG	FN	VF	VF/NM	NM-
166-172	1	2	3	5	6	8

ADVS. OF MR. FROG & MISS MOUSE (See Dell Junior Treasury No. 4)

ADVENTURES OF OZZIE & HARRIET, THE (See Ozzie & Harriet)

ADVENTURES OF PATORUZU
Green Publishing Co.: Aug, 1946 - Winter, 1946

	GD	VG	FN	VF	VF/NM	NM-
nn's-Contains Animal Crackers reprints	6	12	18	28	34	40

ADVENTURES OF PINKY LEE, THE (TV)
Atlas Comics: July, 1955 - No. 5, Dec, 1955

	GD	VG	FN	VF	VF/NM	NM-
1	28	56	84	165	270	375
2-5	17	34	51	98	154	210

ADVENTURES OF PIPSQUEAK, THE (Formerly Pat the Brat)
Archie Publications (Radio Comics): No. 34, Sept, 1959 - No. 39, July, 1960

	GD	VG	FN	VF	VF/NM	NM-
34	3	6	9	21	33	45
35-39	3	6	9	17	26	35

ADVENTURES OF QUAKE & QUISP, THE (See Quaker Oats "Plenty of Glutton")

ADVENTURES OF REX THE WONDER DOG, THE (Rex...No. 1)
National Periodical Publ.: Jan-Feb, 1952 - No. 45, May-June, 1959; No. 46, Nov-Dec, 1959

	GD	VG	FN	VF	VF/NM	NM-
1-(Scarce)-Toth-c/a	206	412	618	1318	2259	3200
2-(Scarce)-Toth-c/a	81	162	243	518	884	1250
3-(Scarce)-Toth-a	60	120	180	380	653	925
4,5	47	94	141	296	498	700

Adventures of Supergirl #6 © DC

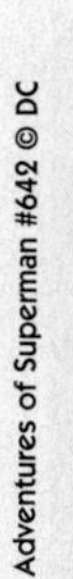
Adventures of Superman #642 © DC

Adventures of the Thing #3 © MAR

	GD 2.0	VG 4.0	FN 6.0	VF 8.0	VF/NM 9.0	NM- 9.2
6-10	39	78	117	240	395	550
11-Atom bomb-c/story; dinosaur-c/sty	43	86	129	271	461	650
12-19: 19-Last precode (1-2/55)	28	56	84	165	270	375
20-46	20	40	60	118	192	265

NOTE: ***Infantino, Gil Kane** art in 5-19 (most)*

ADVENTURES OF ROBIN HOOD, THE (Formerly Robin Hood)
Magazine Enterprises (Sussex Publ. Co.): No. 6, Jun, 1957 - No. 8, Nov, 1957 (Based on Richard Greene TV Show)

	GD	VG	FN	VF	VF/NM	NM-
6-8-Richard Greene photo-c. 6,7-Powell-a	15	30	45	83	124	165

ADVENTURES OF ROBIN HOOD, THE
Gold Key: Mar, 1974 - No. 7, Jan, 1975 (Disney cartoon) (36 pgs.)

	GD	VG	FN	VF	VF/NM	NM-
1(90291-403)-Part-r of $1.50 editions	2	4	6	13	18	22
2-7: 1-7 are part-r	2	4	6	8	11	14

ADVENTURES OF SNAKE PLISSKEN
Marvel Comics: Jan, 1997 ($2.50, one-shot)

1-Based on Escape From L.A. movie; Brereton-c 4.00

ADVENTURES OF SPAWN, THE
Image Comics (Todd McFarlane Prods.): Jan, 2007; Nov, 2008 ($5.99)

1,2-Printed adaptation of the Spawn.com web comic; Khary Randolph-a 6.00

ADVENTURES OF SPIDER-MAN, THE (Based on animated TV series)
Marvel Comics: Apr, 1996 - No. 12, Mar, 1997 (99¢)

1-12: 1-Punisher app. 2-Venom cameo. 3-X-Men. 6-Fantastic Four 3.00

ADVENTURES OF SUPERBOY, THE (See Superboy, 2nd Series)

ADVENTURES OF SUPERGIRL (Based on the TV series)
DC Comics: Early Jul, 2016 - No. 6, Sept, 2016 ($2.99)(Printing of stories first appearing online)

1-6: 1-Rampage app.; Bengal-a/Staggs-c 3.00

ADVENTURES OF SUPERMAN (Formerly Superman)
DC Comics: No. 424, Jan, 1987 - No. 499, Feb, 1993; No. 500, Early June, 1993 - No. 649, Apr, 2006 (This title's numbering continues with Superman #650, May, 2006)

424-Ordway-c/a; Wolfman-s begin following Byrne's Superman revamp; 1st Cat Grant 4.00
425-435,437-462: 426-Legends x-over. 432-1st app. Jose Delgado who becomes Gangbuster in #434. 437-Millennium x-over. 438-New Brainiac app. 440-Batman app. 449-Invasion 3.00
436-Byrne scripts begin; Millennium x-over 3.50
463-Superman/Flash race; cover swipe/Superman #199 5.00
464-Lobo-c & app. (pre-dates Lobo #1) 5.00

	GD	VG	FN	VF	VF/NM	NM-
465-1st app. Hank Henshaw (later becomes Cyborg Superman)	1	2	3	5	6	8

466-479,481-495: 467-Part 2 of Batman story. 473-Hal Jordan, Guy Gardner x-over. 477-Legion app. 491-Last $1.00-c. 495-Forever People-c/story; Darkseid app. 3.00
480,496,497: 480-($1.75, 52 pgs.). 496-Doomsday cameo. 497-Doomsday battle issue 4.00
496,497-2nd printings 3.00
498,499-Funeral for a Friend; Supergirl app. 4.00
498-2nd & 3rd printings 3.00
500-($2.95, 68 pgs.)-Collector's edition w/card 5.00
500-($2.50, 68 pgs.)-Regular edition w/different-c 4.00
500-Platinum edition 40.00
501-($1.95)-Collector's edition with die-cut-c 3.50
501-($1.50)-Regular edition w/mini-poster & diff.-c 3.00
502-516: 502-Supergirl-c/story. 508-Challengers of the Unknown app. 510-Bizarro-c/story. 516-(9/94)-Zero Hour 3.00
505-($2.50)-Holo-grafx foil-c edition 3.50
0,517-523: 0-(10/94). 517-(11/94) 3.00
524-549,551-580: 524-Begin $1.95-c. 527-Return of Alpha Centurion (Zero Hour). 533-Impulse-c/app. 535-Luthor-c/app. 536-Brainiac app. 537-Parasite app. 540-Final Night x-over. 541-Superboy-c/app.; Lois & Clark honeymoon. 545-New powers. 546-New costume. 555-Red & Blue Supermen battle. 557-Millennium Giants x-over. 558-560: Superman Silver Age-style story; Krypto app. 561-Begin $1.99-c. 565-JLA app. 3.00
550-($3.50)-Double sized 4.00
581-588: 581-Begin $2.25-c. 583-Emperor Joker. 588-Casey-s 3.00
589-595: 589-Return to Krypton; Rivoche-c. 591-Wolfman-s. 593-595-Our Worlds at War x-over. 593-New Suicide Squad formed. 594-Doomsday-c/app. 3.00
596-Aftermath of "War" x-over has panel showing damaged World Trade Center buildings; issue went on sale the day after the Sept. 11 attack 6.00
597-599,601-624: 597-Joker: Last Laugh. 604,605-Ultraman, Owlman, Superwoman app. 606-Return to Krypton. 612-616,619-623-Nowlan-c. 624-Mr. Majestic app. 3.00
600-($3.95) Wieringo-a; painted-c by Adel; pin-ups by various 4.00
625,626-Godfall parts 2,5; Turner-c; Caldwell-a(p) 4.00
627-641,643-648: 627-Begin $2.50-c, Rucka-s/Clark-a/Ha-c begin. 628-Wagner-c. 631-Bagged with Sky Captain CD; Lois shot. 634-Mxyzptlk visits DC offices. 639-Capt. Marvel & Eclipso app. 641-OMAC app. 643-Sacrifice aftermath; Batman & Wonder Woman app. 3.00
642-OMAC Project x-over Sacrifice pt. 3; JLA app. 5.00
642-(2nd printing) red tone cover 3.00
649-Last issue; Infinite Crisis x-over, Superman vs. Earth-2 Superman 4.00
#1,000,000 (11/98) Gene Ha-c; 853rd Century x-over 3.00
Annual 1 (1987, $1.25, 52 pgs.)-Starlin-c & scripts 4.00
Annual 2,3 (1990, 1991, $2.00, 68 pgs.): 2-Byrne-c/a(i); Legion '90 (Lobo) app. 3-Armageddon 2001 x-over 4.00
Annual 4-6 ('92-'94, $2.50, 68 pgs.): 4-Guy Gardner/Lobo-c/story; Eclipso storyline; Quesada-c(p). 5-Bloodlines storyline. 6-Elseworlds sty. 4.00
Annual 7,9('95, '97, $3.95)-7-Year One story. 9-Pulp Heroes sty 4.00
Annual 8 (1996, $2.95)-Legends of the Dead Earth story 4.00
NOTE: ***Erik Larsen** a-431.*

ADVENTURES OF SUPERMAN
DC Comics: Jul, 2013 - No. 17, Nov, 2014 ($3.99)

1-17-Short story anthology by various. 1-Lemire-s/a. 4-Timm-c. 6-Mongul app. 14-Joker app.; Sugar & Spike app.; Hester-a 4.00

ADVENTURES OF THE DOVER BOYS
Archie Comics (Close-up): September, 1950 - No. 2, 1950 (No month given)

	GD	VG	FN	VF	VF/NM	NM-
1,2	10	20	30	56	76	95

ADVENTURES OF THE FLY (The Fly #1-6; Fly Man No. 32-39; See The Double Life of Private Strong, The Fly, Laugh Comics & Mighty Crusaders)
Archie Publications/Radio Comics: Aug, 1959 - No. 30, Oct, 1964; No. 31, May, 1965

	GD	VG	FN	VF	VF/NM	NM-
1-Shield app.; origin The Fly; S&K-c/a	50	100	150	400	900	1400
2-Williamson, S&K-a	27	54	81	189	420	650
3-Origin retold; Davis, Powell-a	22	44	66	154	340	525
4-Neal Adams-a(p)(1 panel); S&K-c; Powell-a; 2 pg. Shield story	15	30	45	100	220	340
5,6,9,10: 9-Shield app. 9-1st app. Cat Girl. 10-Black Hood app.	10	20	30	68	144	220
7,8: 7-1st S.A. app. Black Hood (7/60). 8-1st S.A. app. Shield (9/60)	11	22	33	76	163	250
11-13,15-20: 13-1st app. Fly Girl w/o costume. 16-Last 10¢ issue. 20-Origin Fly Girl retold	7	14	21	49	92	135
14-Origin & 1st app. Fly Girl in costume	8	16	24	55	105	155
21-30: 23-Jaguar cameo. 27-29-Black Hood 1 pg. strips. 30-Comet x-over (1st S.A. app.) in Fly Girl	6	12	18	38	69	100
31-Black Hood, Shield, Comet app.	6	12	18	40	73	105

Vol. 1 TPB ('04, $12.95) r/#1-4 & Double Life of Private Strong #1,2; foreward by Joe Simon 13.00
NOTE: ***Simon** c-2-4. **Tuska** a-1. Cover title to #31 is Flyman; Advs. of the Fly inside.*

ADVENTURES OF THE JAGUAR, THE (See Blue Ribbon Comics, Laugh Comics & Mighty Crusaders)
Archie Publications (Radio Comics): Sept, 1961 - No. 15, Nov, 1963

	GD	VG	FN	VF	VF/NM	NM-
1-Origin Jaguar (1st app?) by J. Rosenberger	20	40	60	138	307	475
2,3: 3-Last 10¢ issue	10	20	30	69	147	225
4-6-Catgirl app. (#4's-c is same as splash pg.)	8	16	24	56	108	160
7-10: 10-Dinosaur-c	7	14	21	46	86	125
11-15:13,14-Catgirl, Black Hood app. in both	6	12	18	40	73	105

ADVENTURES OF THE MASK (TV cartoon)
Dark Horse Comics: Jan, 1996 - No. 12, Dec, 1996 ($2.50)

1-12: Based on animated series 3.00

ADVENTURES OF THE NEW MEN (Formerly Newmen #1-21)
Maximum Press: No. 22, Nov, 1996; No. 23, March, 1997 ($2.50)

22,23-Sprouse-c/a 3.00

ADVENTURES OF THE OUTSIDERS, THE (Formerly Batman & The Outsiders; also see The Outsiders)
DC Comics: No. 33, May, 1986 - No. 46, June, 1987

33-46: 39-45-r/Outsiders #1-7 by Aparo 3.00

ADVENTURES OF THE SUPER MARIO BROTHERS (See Super Mario Bros.)
Valiant: 1990 - No. 9, Oct, 1991 ($1.50)

	GD	VG	FN	VF	VF/NM	NM-
V2#1	2	4	6	10	14	18
2-9	1	2	3	5	6	8

ADVENTURES OF THE THING, THE (Also see The Thing)
Marvel Comics: Apr, 1992 - No. 4, July, 1992, ($1.25, limited series)

1-4: 1-r/Marvel Two-In-One #50 by Byrne; Kieth-c. 2-4-r/Marvel Two-In-One #80,51 & 77; 2-Ghost Rider-c/story; Quesada-c. 3-Miller-r/Quesada-c; new Perez-a (4 pgs.) 3.00

ADVENTURES OF THE X-MEN, THE (Based on animated TV series)

Adventures on the Planet of the Apes #7 © MAR

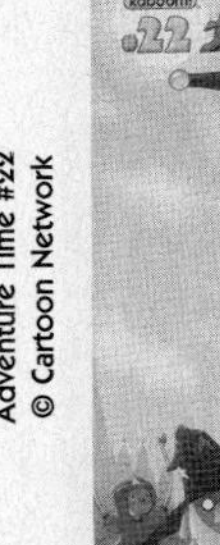

Adventure Time #22 © Cartoon Network

Afterlife With Archie #5 © ACP

GD VG FN VF VF/NM NM-
2.0 4.0 6.0 8.0 9.0 9.2

Marvel Comics: Apr, 1996 - No. 12, Mar, 1997 (99¢)
1-12: 1-Wolverine/Hulk battle. 3-Spider-Man-c. 5,6-Magneto-c/app. 3.00

ADVENTURES OF TINKER BELL (See Tinker Bell, 4-Color No. 896 & 982)

ADVENTURES OF TOM SAWYER (See Dell Junior Treasury No. 10)

ADVENTURES OF YOUNG DR. MASTERS, THE
Archie Comics (Radio Comics): Aug, 1964 - No. 2, Nov, 1964
1 3 6 9 21 33 45
2 3 6 9 15 22 28

ADVENTURES ON OTHER WORLDS (See Showcase #17 & 18)

ADVENTURES ON THE PLANET OF THE APES (Also see Planet of the Apes)
Marvel Comics Group: Oct, 1975 - No. 11, Dec, 1976
1-Planet of the Apes magazine-r in color; Starlin-c; adapts movie thru #6
4 8 12 23 37 50
2-5: 5-(25¢-c edition) 2 4 6 11 16 20
5-7-(30¢-c variants, limited distribution) 5 10 15 30 50 70
6-10: 6,7-(25¢-c edition). 7-Adapts 2nd movie (thru #11)
2 4 6 11 16 20
11-Last issue; concludes 2nd movie adaptation 3 6 9 15 22 28
NOTE: *Alcala* a-6-11r. *Buckler* c-2p. *Nasser* c-7. *Ploog* a-1-9. *Starlin* c-6. *Tuska* a-1-5r.

ADVENTURES WITH THE DC SUPER HEROES (Interior also inserted into some DC issues)
DC Comics/Geppi's Entertainment Museum: 2007 Free Comic Book Day giveaway
"The Batman and Cal Ripken, Jr. Hall of Fame Edition "A Rare Catch"" in indicia 3.00

ADVENTURE TIME (With Finn & Jake) (Based on the Cartoon Network animated series)
Boom Entertainment (KaBOOM!): Feb, 2012 - Present ($3.99)
1-Cover A 25.00
1-Covers B & C; interlocking image 25.00
1-Cover D variant by Jeffrey Brown 30.00
1-Cover E wraparound 35.00
1-Second & third printings 5.00
2-Four covers 10.00
3-24,26-49,51-62-Multiple covers on all 4.00
25-($4.99) Art by Dustin Nguyen, Jess Fink, Jeffrey Brown & others; multiple covers 5.00
50-($4.99) Hastings-s/McGinty-a; multiple covers 5.00
2013 Annual #1 (5/13, $4.99) Three covers; s/a by Langridge, Nguyen & others 5.00
2013 Spoooktacular (10/13, $4.99) Halloween-themed; s/a by Fraser Irving & others 5.00
2013 Summer Special (7/13, $4.99) Multiple covers 5.00
2014 Annual #1 (4/14, $4.99) Three covers; stories printed sideways 5.00
2014 Winter Special (1/14, $4.99) Multiple covers 5.00
2015 Spoooktacular (10/15, $4.99) a Marceline story; s/a by Hanna K 5.00
2016 Spoooktacular (9/16, $4.99) Short stories by various; 2 covers by Bartel & McClaren 5.00
... Cover Showcase (12/12, $3.99) Gallery of variant covers for #1-9; Paul Pope-c 4.00
... Free Comic Book Day Edition (5/12) Giveaway flip book with Peanuts 3.00

ADVENTURE TIME: BANANA GUARD ACADEMY (Cartoon Network)
Boom Entertainment (KaBOOM!): Jul, 2014 - No. 6, Dec, 2014 ($3.99, limited series)
1-6-Multiple covers on all; Mad Rupert-a 4.00

ADVENTURE TIME: CANDY CAPERS (Cartoon Network)
Boom Entertainment (KaBOOM!): Jul, 2013 - No. 6, Dec, 2013 ($3.99, limited series)
1-6-Multiple covers on all; McGinty-a 4.00

ADVENTURE TIME COMICS (Cartoon Network)
Boom Entertainment (KaBOOM!): Jul, 2016 - Present ($3.99)
1-8-Short stories by various. 1-Baltazar, Cook, Millionaire, Leyh-s/a 4.00

ADVENTURE TIME: ICE KING (Cartoon Network)
Boom Entertainment (KaBOOM!): Jan, 2016 - No. 6, Jun, 2016 ($3.99, limited series)
1-6-Multiple covers on all; Naujokaitis-s/Andrewson-a 4.00

ADVENTURE TIME: MARCELINE AND THE SCREAM QUEENS (Cartoon Network)
Boom Entertainment (KaBOOM!): Jul, 2012 - No. 6, Dec, 2012 ($3.99, limited series)
1-6-Multiple covers on all 4.00

ADVENTURE TIME: MARCELINE GONE ADRIFT (Cartoon Network)
Boom Entertainment (KaBOOM!): Jan, 2015 - No. 6, Jun, 2015 ($3.99, limited series)
1-6-Multiple covers on all; Meredith Gran-s/Carey Pietsch-a 4.00

ADVENTURE TIME: THE FLIP SIDE (Cartoon Network)
Boom Entertainment (KaBOOM!): Jan, 2014 - No. 6, Jun, 2014 ($3.99, limited series)
1-6-Multiple covers on all; Tobin & Coover-s; Wook Jin Clark-a 4.00

ADVENTURE TIME WITH FIONNA & CAKE (Cartoon Network)
Boom Entertainment (KaBOOM!): Jan, 2013 - No. 6, Jun, 2013 ($3.99, limited series)
1-6-Multiple covers on all 4.00

GD VG FN VF VF/NM NM-
2.0 4.0 6.0 8.0 9.0 9.2

ADVENTURE TIME WITH FIONNA & CAKE CARD WARS (Cartoon Network)
Boom Entertainment (KaBOOM!): Jul, 2015 - No. 6, Dec, 2015 ($3.99, limited series)
1-6-Multiple covers on all; Jen Wang-s/Britt Wilson-a. 1-Polybagged with a game card 4.00

AEON FLUX (Based on the 2005 movie which was based on the MTV animated series)
Dark Horse Comics: Oct, 2005 - No. 4, Jan, 2006 ($2.99, limited series)
1-4-Timothy Green II-a/Mike Kennedy-s 3.00
TPB (5/06, $12.95) r/series; cover gallery 13.00

A-FORCE (Secret Wars tie-in)
Marvel Comics: Jul, 2015 - No. 5, Dec, 2015 ($3.99, limited series)
1-5-All-Female Avengers team; Bennett & Willow Wilson-s/Molina-a. 1-Intro. Singularity 4.00

A-FORCE (Follows Secret Wars)
Marvel Comics: Mar, 2016 - No. 10, Dec, 2016 ($3.99)
1-10: 1-Medusa, She-Hulk, Dazzler, Nico, Capt. Marvel, Singularity team; Wilson-s/Molina-a. 5-7-Thompson-s/Caldwell-a. 8-10-Civil War II tie-in 4.00

AFRICA
Magazine Enterprises: 1955
1(A-1 #137)-Cave Girl, Thun'da; Powell-c/a(4) 29 58 87 170 278 385

AFRICAN LION (Disney movie)
Dell Publishing Co.: Nov, 1955
Four Color #665 5 10 15 34 60 85

AFTER DARK
Sterling Comics: No. 6, May, 1955 - No. 8, Sept, 1955
6-8-Sekowsky-a in all 9 18 27 52 69 85

AFTER DARK (Co-created by Wesley Snipes)
Radical Comics: No. 0, Jun, 2010 - No. 3 ($1.00/$4.99, limited series)
0-($1.00) Milligan-s/Nentrup & Mattina-a 3.00
1-3-($4.99) Milligan-s/Manco-a 5.00

AFTERLIFE WITH ARCHIE
Archie Comic Publications: Sept, 2013 - Present ($2.99/$3.99)
1-Aguirre-Sacasa-s/Francavilla-a; zombies in Riverdale; Sabrina app.; 4 covers 20.00
1-Second printing; new cover by Francavilla 6.00
2-Covers by Francavilla & Seeley; back-up short story r/Chilling Advs. in Sorcery 10.00
3-6: 3,4-Covers by Francavilla & Seeley on each; back-up r/Chilling Advs. in Sorcery. 5,6-Pepoy variant-c. 6-Back-up preview of Chilling Advs. of Sabrina #1 5.00
7-10-($3.99) 7-Covers by Francavilla & Pepoy; back-up r/Chilling Advs. in Sorcery 4.00
... Halloween ComicFest Edition 1 (2014, giveaway) Grey-toned reprint of #1 3.00
... Halloween ComicFest Edition 1 (2016, giveaway) Grey-toned reprint of #7 3.00

AFTERSHOCK GENESIS
AfterShock Comics: May, 2016 ($1.00, one-shot)
1-Short stories by various and previews of upcoming AfterShock titles 3.00

AFTER THE CAPE
Image Comics (Shadowline): Mar, 2007 - No. 3, May, 2007 ($2.99, B&W, limited series)
1-3-Jim Valentino-s/Marco Rudy-a 3.00
... Volume One TPB (9/07, $12.99) r/series; scripts, sketch pages, character profiles 13.00
...II (11/07 - No. 3, 1/08, $2.99) 1-3-Jim Valentino-s/Sergio Carrera-a 3.00

AGAINST BLACKSHARD 3-D (Also see SoulQuest)
Sirius Comics: August, 1986 ($2.25)
1 3.00

AGENCY, THE
Image Comics (Top Cow): August, 2001 - No. 6, Mar, 2002 ($2.50/$2.95/$4.95)
1-5: 1-Jenkins-s/Hotz-a; three covers by Hotz, Turner, Silvestri. 3-5-($2.95) 3.00
6-($4.95) Flip-c preview of Jeremiah TV series 5.00
Preview (2001, 16 pgs.) B&W pages, cover previews, sketch pages 3.00

AGENT CARTER: S.H.I.E.L.D. 50TH ANNIVERSARY
Marvel Comics: Nov, 2015 ($3.99, one-shot)
1-Kathryn Immonen-s/Rich Ellis-a; set in 1966; Sif, Dum Dum and Nick Fury app. 4.00

AGENT LIBERTY SPECIAL (See Superman, 2nd Series)
DC Comics: 1992 ($2.00, 52 pgs, one-shot)
1-1st solo adventure; Guice-c/a(i) 4.00

AGENTS, THE
Image Comics: Apr, 2003 - No. 6, Sept, 2003 ($2.95, B&W)
1-5-Ben Dunn-c/a in all 3.00
6-Five pg. preview of The Walking Dead #1 3 6 9 14 20 25

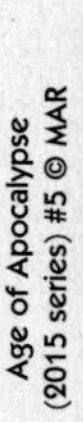
Agents of Law #2 © DH

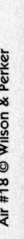

Age of Apocalypse (2015 series) #5 © MAR

Air #18 © Wilson & Perker

	GD 2.0	VG 4.0	FN 6.0	VF 8.0	VF/NM 9.0	NM- 9.2

AGENTS OF ATLAS
Marvel Comics: Oct, 2006 - No. 6, Mar, 2007 ($2.99, limited series)

1-6: 1-Golden Age heroes Marvel Boy & Venus app.; Kirk-a 3.00
... MGC 1 (7/10, $1.00) r/#1 with "Marvel's Greatest Comics" logo on cover 3.00
HC (2007, $24.99, dustjacket) r/#1-6, What If? #9, agents' debuts in '40s-'50s Atlas comics, creator interviews, character design art 25.00

AGENTS OF ATLAS (Dark Reign)
Marvel Comics: Apr, 2009 - No. 11, Nov, 2009 ($3.99)

1-11: 1-Pagulayan-a; 2 covers by Art Adams and McGuinness; back-up with Wolverine app. 5-New Avengers app. 8-Hulk app. 4.00

AGENTS OF LAW (Also see Comic's Greatest World)
Dark Horse Comics: Mar, 1995 - No. 6, Sept, 1995 ($2.50)

1-6: 5-Predator app. 6-Predator app.; death of Law 3.00

AGENTS OF P.A.C.T. (Also see Captain Canuck)
Chapterhouse Publishing: Jan, 2017 - Present ($3.99)

1-Andrasofszky & Northcott-s/Manfredi-a; Agent Fleur De Lys app. 4.00

AGENTS OF S.H.I.E.L.D. (Characters from the TV series)
Marvel Comics: Mar, 2016 - No. 10, Dec, 2016 ($3.99)

1-10: 1-Guggenheim-s/Peralta-a; Tony Stark app. 3,4-Standoff tie-in. 5-Spider-Man app. 7-10-Civil War II tie-in. 9,10-Elektra app. 4.00

AGENT X (Continued from Deadpool)
Marvel Comics: Sept. 2002 - No. 15, Dec, 2003 ($2.99/$2.25)

1-($2.99) Simone-s/Udon Studios-a; Taskmaster app. 4.00
2-9-($2.25) 2-Punisher app. 3.00
10-15-($2.99) 10,11-Evan Dorkin-s. 12-Hotz-a 3.00

AGE OF APOCALYPSE (See Uncanny X-Force)
Marvel Comics: May, 2012 - No. 14, Jun, 2013 ($2.99)

1-14: 1-Lapham-s/De La Torre-a/Ramos-c. 13-Leads into X-Termination x-over 3.00

AGE OF APOCALYPSE (Secret Wars tie-in)
Marvel Comics: Sept, 2015 - No. 5, Dec, 2015 ($4.99/$3.99, limited series)

1-($4.99) Nicieza-s/Sandoval-a; alternate X-Men vs. Apocalypse 5.00
2-5-($3.99) Covers #1-5 form one image; Blink, Sabretooth & Magneto app. 4.00

AGE OF APOCALYPSE: THE CHOSEN
Marvel Comics: Apr, 1995 ($2.50, one-shot)

1-Wraparound-c 5.00

AGE OF BRONZE
Image Comics: Nov, 1998 - Present ($2.95/$3.50, B&W)

1-6-Eric Shanower-c/s/a 3.50
7-33-($3.50) 3.50
...Behind the Scenes (5/02, $3.50) background info and creative process 3.50
Image Firsts: Age of Bronze #1 (4/10, $1.00) r/#1 with "Image Firsts" cover logo 3.00
...Special (6/99, $2.95) Story of Agamemnon and Menelaus 3.50
A Thousand Ships (7/01, $19.95, TPB) r/#1-9 20.00
Sacrifice (9/04, $19.95, TPB) r/#10-19 20.00

AGE OF HEROES, THE
Halloween Comics/Image Comics #3 on: 1996 - No. 5, 1999 ($2.95, B&W)

1-5: James Hudnall scripts; John Ridgway-c/a 3.00
...Special ($4.95) r/#1,2 5.00
...Special 2 ($6.95) r/#3,4 7.00
...Wex 1 ('98, $2.95) Hudnall-s/Angel Fernandez-a 3.00

AGE OF HEROES (The Heroic Age)
Marvel Comics: Jul, 2010 - No. 4, Oct, 2010 ($3.99, limited series)

1-4-Short stories of Avengers members by various. 4-Jae Lee-c 4.00

AGE OF INNOCENCE: THE REBIRTH OF IRON MAN
Marvel Comics: Feb, 1996 ($2.50, one-shot)

1-New origin of Tony Stark 3.00

AGE OF REPTILES
Dark Horse Comics: Nov, 1993 - No. 4, Feb, 1994 ($2.50, limited series)

1-4: Delgado-c/a/scripts in all 3.00
... Ancient Egyptians 1-4 (6/15 - No. 4, 9/15, $3.99) Delgado-c/a/scripts; wraparound-c 4.00
... The Hunt 1-5 (5/96 - No. 5, 9/96, $2.95) Delgado-c/a/scripts in all; wraparound-c 3.00
... The Journey 1-4 (11/09 - No. 4, 7/10, $3.50) Delgado-c/a/scripts in all; wraparound-c 3.50

AGE OF THE SENTRY, THE
Marvel Comics: Nov, 2008 - No. 6, Mar, 2010 ($2.99, limited series)

1-6-Silver Age style stories. 1-Origin retold; Bullock-c. 3-Coover-a 3.00

AGE OF ULTRON
Marvel Comics: May, 2013 - No. 10, Aug, 2013 ($3.99, limited series)

1-Wraparound cardstock foil-c; Hitch-a/c 6.00
2-9: 2-5-Hitch-a/c. 6-Peterson & Pacheco-a, Hank Pym killed 4.00
10-Polybagged; Angela joins the Marvel Universe 6.00

	GD	VG	FN	VF	VF/NM	NM-
10AU (8/13, $3.99) Waid-s/Aralijo-a/Pichelli-c; Hank Pym's origin re-told	1	3	4	6	8	10

AGE OF ULTRON VS. MARVEL ZOMBIES (Secret Wars tie-in)
Marvel Comics: Aug, 2015 - No. 4, Nov, 2015 ($3.99, limited series)

1-4-James Robinson-s/Steve Pugh-a; Vision, Wonder Man & Jim Hammond app. 4.00

AGE OF X (X-Men titles crossover)
Marvel Comics: ($3.99, limited series)

... Alpha 1 (3/11, $3.99) Short stories by various; covers by Bachalo & Coipel 4.00
...: Universe 1,2 (5/11 - No. 2, 6/11, $3.99) Pham-a; Bianchi-c; Avengers & Spider-Man app. 4.00

AGGIE MACK
Four Star Comics Corp./Superior Comics Ltd.: Jan, 1948 - No. 8, Aug, 1949

	GD	VG	FN	VF	VF/NM	NM-
1-Feldstein-a, "Johnny Prep"	45	90	135	284	480	675
2,3-Kamen-c	26	52	78	154	252	350
4-Feldstein "Johnny Prep"; Kamen-c	34	68	102	199	325	450
5-8-Kamen-c/a	28	56	84	165	270	375

AGGIE MACK
Dell Publishing Co.: Apr - Jun, 1962

	GD	VG	FN	VF	VF/NM	NM-
Four Color #1335	5	10	15	31	53	75

AIR
DC Comics (Vertigo): Oct, 2008 - No. 24, Oct, 2010 ($2.99)

1-6,8-24-G. Willow Wilson-s/M.K. Perker-a 3.00
7-($1.00) Includes story re-cap 3.00
... A History of the Future TPB (2011, $14.99) r/#18-24 15.00
... Flying Machine TPB (2009, $12.99) r/#6-10; Wilson intro. 13.00
... Letters From Lost Countries TPB (2009, $9.99) r/#1-5; character sketch pages 10.00
... Pure Land TPB (2010, $14.99) r/#11-17 15.00

AIR ACE (Formerly Bill Barnes No. 1-12)
Street & Smith Publications: V2#1, Jan, 1944 - V3#8(No. 20), Feb-Mar, 1947

	GD	VG	FN	VF	VF/NM	NM-
V2#1-Nazi concentration camp-c	52	104	156	328	552	775
V2#2-Classic Japanese WWII-c	206	412	618	1318	2259	3200
V2#3-12: 7-Powell-a	18	36	54	103	162	220
V3#1-6: 2-Atomic explosion on-c	14	28	42	82	121	160
V3#7-Powell bondage-c/a; all atomic issue	27	54	81	158	259	360
V3#8 (V5#8 on-c)-Powell-c/a	15	30	45	90	140	190

AIRBOY (Also see Airmaidens, Skywolf, Target: Airboy & Valkyrie)
Eclipse Comics: July, 1986 - No. 50, Oct, 1989 (#1-8, 50¢, 20 pgs., bi-weekly; #9-on, 36 pgs.; #34-on monthly)

1-4: 2-1st Marisa; Skywolf gets new costume. 3-The Heap begins 4.00

	GD	VG	FN	VF	VF/NM	NM-
5-Valkyrie returns; Dave Stevens-c	1	3	4	6	8	10

6-49: 9-Begin $1.25-c; Skywolf begins. 11-Origin of G.A. Airboy & his plane Birdie. 28-Mr. Monster vs. The Heap. 33-Begin $1.75-c. 38-40-The Heap by Infantino. 41-r/1st app. Valkyrie from Air Fighters. 42-Begin $1.95-c. 46,47-part-r/Air Fighters. 48-Black Angel-r/A.F 3.00
50 ($4.95, 52 pgs.)-Kubert-c 5.00

NOTE: ***Evans*** c-21. ***Gulacy*** c-7, 20. ***Spiegle*** a-34, 35, 37. ***Ken Steacy*** painted c-17, 33.

AIRBOY
Image Comics: Jun, 2015 - No. 4, Nov, 2015 ($2.99, limited series, mature)

1-4: 1-Airboy meets writer James Robinson and artist Greg Hinkle. 3,4-Valkyrie app. 3.00

AIRBOY COMICS (Air Fighters Comics No. 1-22)
Hillman Periodicals: V2#11, Dec, 1945 - V10#4, May, 1953 (No V3#3)

	GD	VG	FN	VF	VF/NM	NM-
V2#11	61	122	183	390	670	950
12-Valkyrie-c/app.	53	106	159	334	567	800
V3#1,2(no #3)	40	80	120	246	411	575
4-The Heap app. in Skywolf	37	74	111	222	361	500
5,7,8,10,11	33	66	99	194	317	440
6-Valkyrie-c/app.	36	72	108	216	351	485
9-Origin The Heap	37	74	111	222	361	500
12-Skywolf & Airboy x-over; Valkyrie-c/app.	39	78	117	240	395	550
V4#1-Iron Lady app.	33	66	99	194	317	440
2,3,12: 2-Rackman begins	26	52	78	154	252	350
4-Simon & Kirby-c	31	62	93	186	303	420
5-9,11-All S&K-a	30	60	90	177	289	400
10-Valkyrie-c/app.	32	64	96	192	314	435

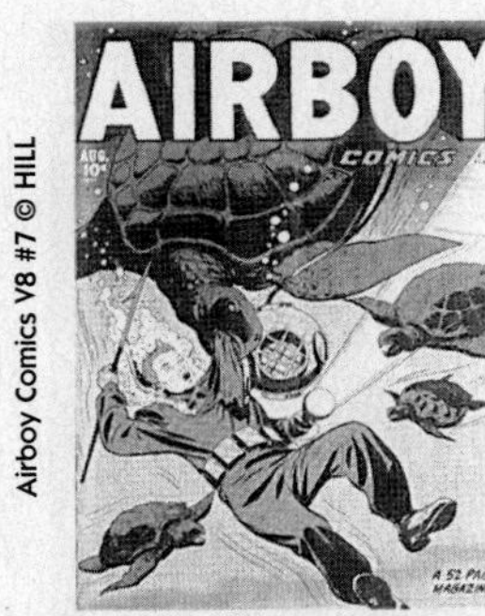

Airboy Comics V8 #7 © HILL

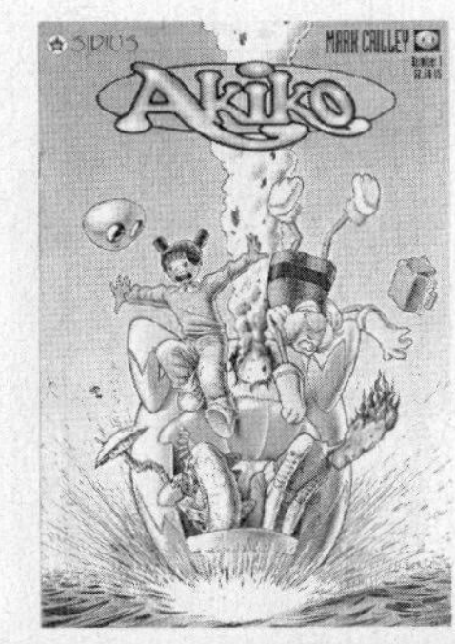

Akiko #1 © Mark Crilley

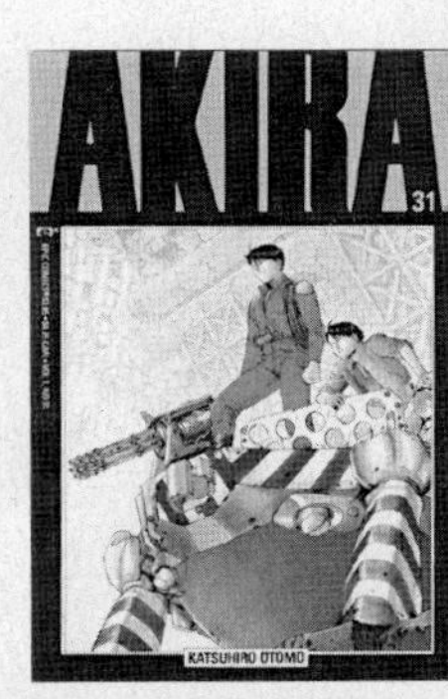

Akira #31 © Katsuhiro Otomo

	GD 2.0	VG 4.0	FN 6.0	VF 8.0	VF/NM 9.0	NM- 9.2
V5#1-4,6-11: 4-Infantino Heap. 10-Origin The Heap	20	40	60	120	195	270
5-Skull-c.	24	48	72	140	230	320
12-Krigstein-a(p)	21	42	63	124	202	280
V6#1-3,5-12: 6,8-Origin The Heap	20	40	60	114	182	250
4-Origin retold	22	44	66	132	216	300
V7#1-12: 7,8,10-Origin The Heap. 12-(1/51)	19	38	57	112	179	245
V8#1-3,5-12: 5-UFO-c (6/51)	18	36	54	105	165	225
4-Krigstein-a	19	38	57	109	172	235
V9#1,3,4,6-12: 7-One pg. Frazetta ad	15	30	45	90	140	190
2-Valkyrie app.	16	32	48	94	147	200
5(#100)	16	32	48	94	147	200
V10#1-4	15	30	45	85	130	175

NOTE: ***Barry** a-V2#3, 7. **Bolle** a-V4#12. **McWilliams** a-V3#7, 9. **Powell** a-V7#2, 3, V8#1, 6. **Starr** a-V5#1, 12. **Dick Wood** a-V4#12. Bondage-c V5#8.*

AIRBOY MEETS THE PROWLER
Eclipse Comics: Aug, 1987 ($1.95, one-shot)

	GD	VG	FN	VF	VF/NM	NM-
1-John Snyder, III-c/a						3.00

AIRBOY-MR. MONSTER SPECIAL
Eclipse Comics: Aug, 1987 ($1.75, one-shot)

	GD	VG	FN	VF	VF/NM	NM-
1						3.00

AIRBOY VERSUS THE AIR MAIDENS
Eclipse Comics: July, 1988 ($1.95)

	GD	VG	FN	VF	VF/NM	NM-
1						3.00

AIR FIGHTERS CLASSICS
Eclipse Comics: Nov, 1987 - No. 6, May, 1989 ($3.95, 68 pgs., B&W)

	GD	VG	FN	VF	VF/NM	NM-
1-6: Reprints G.A. Air Fighters #2-7. 1-Origin Airboy						4.00

AIR FIGHTERS COMICS (Airboy Comics #23 (V2#11) on)
Hillman Periodicals: Nov, 1941; No. 2, Nov, 1942 - V2#10, Fall, 1945

	GD	VG	FN	VF	VF/NM	NM-
V1#1-(Produced by Funnies, Inc.); No Airboy; Black Commander only app.	226	452	678	1446	2473	3500
2(11/42)-(Produced by Quality artists & Biro for Hillman); Origin & 1st app. Airboy & Iron Ace; Black Angel (1st app.), Flying Dutchman & Skywolf (1st app.) begin; Fuje-a; Biro-c/a	503	1006	1509	3672	6486	9300
3-Origin/1st app. The Heap; origin Skywolf; 2nd Airboy app./c	206	412	618	1318	2259	3200
4-Japan war-c	181	362	543	1158	1979	2800
5-Japanese octopus War-c	194	388	582	1242	2121	3000
6-Japanese soldiers as rats-c	219	438	657	1402	2401	3400
7-Classic Nazi swastika-c	200	400	600	1280	2190	3100
8-12: 8,10,11-War covers	90	180	270	576	988	1400
V2#1-Classic Nazi War-c	97	194	291	621	1061	1500
2-Skywolf by Giunta; Flying Dutchman by Fuje; 1st meeting Valkyrie & Airboy (she worked for the Nazis in beginning); 1st app. Valkyrie (11/43); Valkyrie-c	181	362	543	1158	1979	2800
3,4,6,8,9	61	122	183	390	670	950
5-Flag-c; Fuje-a	66	132	198	419	722	1025
7-Valkyrie app.	74	148	222	470	810	1150
10-Origin The Heap & Skywolf	69	138	207	442	759	1075

NOTE: ***Fuje** a-V1#2, 5, 7, V2#2, 3, 5, 7-9. **Giunta** a-V2#2, 3, 7, 9.*

AIRFIGHTERS MEET SGT. STRIKE SPECIAL, THE
Eclipse Comics: Jan, 1988 ($1.95, one-shot, stiff-c)

	GD	VG	FN	VF	VF/NM	NM-
1-Airboy, Valkyrie, Skywolf app.						3.00

AIR FORCES (See American Air Forces)

AIRMAIDENS SPECIAL
Eclipse Comics: August, 1987 ($1.75, one-shot, Baxter paper)

	GD	VG	FN	VF	VF/NM	NM-
1-Marisa becomes La Lupina (origin)						3.00

AIR RAIDERS
Marvel Comics (Star Comics)/Marvel #3 on: Nov, 1987- No. 5, Mar, 1988 ($1.00)

	GD	VG	FN	VF	VF/NM	NM-
1,5: Kelley Jones-a in all						4.00
2-4: 2-Thunderhammer app.						3.00

AIRTIGHT GARAGE, THE (Also see Elsewhere Prince)
Marvel Comics (Epic Comics): July, 1993 - No. 4, Oct, 1993 ($2.50, lim. series, Baxter paper)

	GD	VG	FN	VF	VF/NM	NM-
1-4: Moebius-c/a/scripts						5.00

AIR WAR STORIES
Dell Publishing Co.: Sept-Nov, 1964 - No. 8, Aug, 1966

	GD	VG	FN	VF	VF/NM	NM-
1-Painted-c; Glanzman-c/a begins	4	8	12	27	44	60
2-8: 2,3-Painted-c	3	6	9	17	26	35

A.K.A. GOLDFISH
Caliber Comics: 1994 - 1995 (B&W, $3.50/$3.95)

	GD	VG	FN	VF	VF/NM	NM-
...:Ace; ...:Jack; ...:Queen; ...:Joker; ...:King -Brian Michael Bendis-s/a						4.00
TPB (1996, $17.95)						20.00
Goldfish: The Definitive Collection (Image, 2001, $19.95) r/series plus promo art and new prose story; intro. by Matt Wagner						20.00
10th Anniversary HC (Image, 2002, $49.95)						50.00

AKIKO
Sirius: Mar, 1996 - No. 52, Feb, 2004 ($2.50/$2.95, B&W)

	GD	VG	FN	VF	VF/NM	NM-
1-Crilley-c/a/scripts in all						5.00
2						4.00
3-39: 25-($2.95, 32 pgs.)-w/Asala back-up pages						3.00
40-49,51,52: 40-Begin $2.95-c						3.00
50-($3.50)						3.50
Flights of Fancy TPB (5/02, $12.95) r/various features, pin-ups and gags						13.00
TPB Volume 1,4 ('97, 2/00, $14.95) 1-r/#1-7. 4-r/#19-25						15.00
TPB Volume 2,3 ('98, '99, $11.95) 2-r/#8-13. 3- r/#14-18						12.00
TPB Volume 5 (12/01, $12.95) r/#26-31						13.00
TPB Volume 6,7 (6/03, 4/04, $14.95) 6-r/#32-38. 7-r/#40-47						15.00

AKIKO ON THE PLANET SMOO
Sirius: Dec, 1995 ($3.95, B&W)

	GD	VG	FN	VF	VF/NM	NM-
V1#1-($3.95)-Crilley-c/a/scripts; gatefold-c						5.00
Ashcan ('95, mail offer)						3.00
Hardcover V1#1 (12/95, $19.95, B&W, 40 pgs.)						20.00
The Color Edition(2/00,$4.95)						5.00

AKIRA
Marvel Comics (Epic): Sept, 1988 - No. 38, Dec, 1995 ($3.50/$3.95/$6.95, deluxe, 68 pgs.)

	GD	VG	FN	VF	VF/NM	NM-
1-Manga by Katsuhiro Otomo	3	6	9	16	23	30
1,2-2nd printings (1989, $3.95)						5.00
2	2	4	6	9	12	15
3-5	2	4	6	8	10	12
6-16	1	2	3	5	7	9
17-33: 17-$3.95-c begins						6.00
34-36: 34-(1994)-$6.95-c begins. 35-(1995)	2	4	6	10	14	18
37-Texeira back-up, Gibbons, Williams pin-ups	3	6	9	14	20	25
38-Moebius, Allred, Pratt, Toth, Romita, Van Fleet, O'Neill, Madureira pin-ups	4	8	12	27	44	60

ALABASTER: THE GOOD, THE BAD AND THE BIRD
Dark Horse Comics: Dec, 2015 - No. 5, Apr, 2016 ($3.99, limited series)

	GD	VG	FN	VF	VF/NM	NM-
1-5-Caitlin Kiernan-s/Daniel Johnson-a						4.00

ALADDIN & HIS WONDERFUL LAMP (See Dell Jr Treasury #2)

ALAN LADD (See The Adventures of...)

ALAN MOORE'S AWESOME UNIVERSE HANDBOOK (Also see Across the Universe:...)
Awesome Entertainment: Apr, 1999 ($2.95, B&W)

	GD	VG	FN	VF	VF/NM	NM-
1-Alan Moore-text/ Alex Ross-sketch pages and 2 covers						5.00

ALAN MOORE...
DC Comics (WildStorm): TPB

	GD	VG	FN	VF	VF/NM	NM-
...'s Complete WildC.A.T.S. (2007, $29.99) r/#21-34,50; ...Homecoming & ...Gang War						30.00
...: Wild Worlds (2007, $24.99) r/various WildStorm one-shots and limited series						25.00

ALARMING ADVENTURES
Harvey Publications: Oct, 1962 - No. 3, Feb, 1963

	GD	VG	FN	VF	VF/NM	NM-
1-Crandall/Williamson-a	8	16	24	51	96	140
2-Williamson/Crandall-a	5	10	15	31	53	75
3-Torres-a	4	8	12	28	47	65

NOTE: ***Bailey** a-1, 3. **Crandall** a-1p, 2i. **Powell** a-2(2). **Severin** c-1-3. **Torres** a-2? **Tuska** a-1. **Williamson** a-1i, 2p.*

ALARMING TALES
Harvey Publications (Western Tales): Sept, 1957 - No. 6, Nov, 1958

	GD	VG	FN	VF	VF/NM	NM-
1-Kirby-c/a(4); Kamandi prototype story by Kirby	33	66	99	194	317	420
2-Kirby-a(4)	21	42	63	124	202	280
3,4-Kirby-a. 4-Powell, Wildey-a	17	34	51	98	154	210
5-Kirby/Williamson-a; Wildey-a; Severin-c	18	36	54	105	165	225
6-Williamson-a?; Severin-c	14	28	42	82	121	160

ALBEDO
Thoughts And Images: Summer, 1983 - No. 14, Spring, 1989 (B&W)
Antarctic Press: (Vol. 2) Jun, 1991 - No. 10 ($2.50)

	GD	VG	FN	VF	VF/NM	NM-
0-Yellow cover; 50 copies	15	30	45	103	227	350
0-White cover, 450 copies	8	16	24	56	108	160
0-Blue, 1st printing, 500 copies	7	14	21	49	92	135
0-Blue, 2nd printing, 1000 copies	4	8	12	27	44	60

Al Capp's Wolf Gal #1 © TOBY

Alex + Ada #13 © Luna & Vaughn

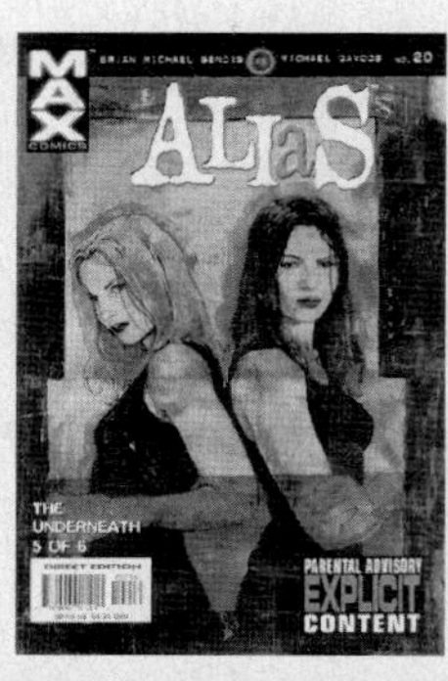

Alias #20 © MAR

	GD 2.0	VG 4.0	FN 6.0	VF 8.0	VF/NM 9.0	NM- 9.2
0-3rd & 4th printing	3	6	9	14	19	24
1-Dark red, 1st printing - low print run	10	20	30	64	132	200
1-Bright red, later printings - low print run	6	12	18	38	69	100
2-(11/84) 1st app. Usagi Yojimbo by Stan Sakai; 2000 copies - no 2nd printing	50	100	150	400	900	1400
3	3	6	9	21	33	45
4-Usagi Yojimbo-c	4	8	12	28	47	65
5-14						6.00
(Vol. 2) 1-10, Color Special						6.00

ALBEDO ANTHROPOMORPHICS
Antarctic Press: (Vol. 3) Spring, 1994 - No. 4, Jan, 1996 ($2.95, color); (Vol. 4) Dec, 1999 - No. 2, Jan, 1999 ($2.95/$2.99, B&W)

	GD 2.0	VG 4.0	FN 6.0	VF 8.0	VF/NM 9.0	NM- 9.2
V3#1-4-Steve Gallacci-c/a. V4#1,2						3.00

ALBERTO (See The Crusaders)

ALBERT THE ALLIGATOR & POGO POSSUM (See Pogo Possum)

ALBION (Inspired by 1960s IPC British comics characters)
DC Comics (WildStorm): Aug, 2005 - No. 6, Nov, 2006 ($2.99, limited series)

	GD 2.0	VG 4.0	FN 6.0	VF 8.0	VF/NM 9.0	NM- 9.2
1-6-Alan Moore, Leah Moore & John Reppion-s/Shane Oakley-a; Dave Gibbons-c						3.00
TPB (2007, $19.99) r/series; intro by Neil Gaiman; reprints from 1960s British comics						20.00

ALBUM OF CRIME (See Fox Giants)

ALBUM OF LOVE (See Fox Giants)

AL CAPP'S DOGPATCH (Also see Mammy Yokum)
Toby Press: No. 71, June, 1949 - No. 4, Dec, 1949

	GD 2.0	VG 4.0	FN 6.0	VF 8.0	VF/NM 9.0	NM- 9.2
71(#1)-Reprints from Tip Top #112-114	15	30	45	90	140	190
2-4: 4-Reprints from Li'l Abner #73	12	24	36	69	97	125

AL CAPP'S SHMOO (Also see Oxydol-Dreft & Washable Jones & Shmoo)
Toby Press: July, 1949 - No. 5, Apr, 1950 (None by Al Capp)

	GD 2.0	VG 4.0	FN 6.0	VF 8.0	VF/NM 9.0	NM- 9.2
1-1st app. Super-Shmoo	31	62	93	182	296	410
2-5: 3-Sci-fi trip to moon. 4-X-Mas-c	20	40	60	120	195	270

AL CAPP'S WOLF GAL
Toby Press: 1951 - No. 2, 1952

	GD 2.0	VG 4.0	FN 6.0	VF 8.0	VF/NM 9.0	NM- 9.2
1-Edited-r from Li'l Abner #63	23	46	69	136	223	310
2-Edited-r from Li'l Abner #64	18	36	54	103	162	220

ALEISTER ARCANE
IDW Publishing: Apr, 2004 - No. 3, June, 2004 ($3.99, limited series)

	GD 2.0	VG 4.0	FN 6.0	VF 8.0	VF/NM 9.0	NM- 9.2
1-3-Steve Niles-s/Breehn Burns-a						4.00
TPB (10/04, $17.99) r/series; sketch pages						18.00

ALEXANDER THE GREAT (Movie)
Dell Publishing Co.: No. 688, May, 1956

	GD 2.0	VG 4.0	FN 6.0	VF 8.0	VF/NM 9.0	NM- 9.2
Four Color 688-Buscema-a; photo-c	6	12	18	42	79	115

ALEX + ADA
Image Comics: Nov, 2013 - No. 15, Jun, 2015 ($2.99/$3.99)

	GD 2.0	VG 4.0	FN 6.0	VF 8.0	VF/NM 9.0	NM- 9.2
1-14-Jonathan Luna-a/c; Sarah Vaughn & Luna-s						3.00
15-($3.99) Conclusion						4.00

ALF (TV) (See Star Comics Digest)
Marvel Comics: Mar, 1988 - No. 50, Feb, 1992 ($1.00)

	GD 2.0	VG 4.0	FN 6.0	VF 8.0	VF/NM 9.0	NM- 9.2
1-Photo-c	1	3	4	6	8	10
1-2nd printing						3.00
2-19: 6-Photo-c						3.00
20-22: 20-Conan parody. 21-Marx Brothers. 22-X-Men parody						3.50
23-30: 24-Rhonda-c/app. 29-3-D cover						3.00
31-43,46,47,49						3.00
44,45: 44-X-Men parody. 45-Wolverine, Punisher, Capt. America-c						4.00
48-(12/91) Risqué Alf with seal cover	3	6	9	17	26	35
50-($1.75, 52 pgs.)-Final issue; photo-c						4.00
Annual 1-3: 1-Rocky & Bullwinkle app. 2-Sienkiewicz-c. 3-TMNT parody						4.00
...Comics Digest 1,2: 1-(1988)-Reprints Alf #1,2	1	3	4	6	8	10
Holiday Special 1,2 ('88, Wint. '89, 68 pgs.): 2-X-Men parody-c						4.00
Spring Special 1 (Spr/89, $1.75, 68 pgs.) Invisible Man parody						4.00
TPB (68 pgs.) r/#1-3; photo-c						5.00

ALFRED HARVEY'S BLACK CAT
Lorne-Harvey Productions: 1995 ($3.50, B&W/color)

	GD 2.0	VG 4.0	FN 6.0	VF 8.0	VF/NM 9.0	NM- 9.2
1-Origin by Mark Evanier & Murphy Anderson; contains history of Alfred Harvey & Harvey Publications; 5 pg. B&W Sad Sack story; Hildebrandts-c						6.00

ALGIE (LITTLE...)
Timor Publ. Co.: Dec, 1953 - No. 3, 1954

	GD 2.0	VG 4.0	FN 6.0	VF 8.0	VF/NM 9.0	NM- 9.2
1-Teenage	8	16	24	44	57	70
1-Algie #1 cover w/Secret Mysteries #19 inside	10	20	30	54	72	90
2,3	6	12	18	28	34	40
Accepted Reprint #2(nd)	3	6	8	12	14	16
Super Reprint #15	2	4	6	8	11	14

ALIAS:
Now Comics: July, 1990 - No. 5, Nov, 1990 ($1.75)

	GD 2.0	VG 4.0	FN 6.0	VF 8.0	VF/NM 9.0	NM- 9.2
1-5: 1-Sienkiewicz-c						3.00

ALIAS (Also see Jessica Jones apps. in New Avengers and The Pulse)
Marvel Comics (MAX Comics): Nov, 2001 - No. 28, Jan, 2004 ($2.99)

	GD 2.0	VG 4.0	FN 6.0	VF 8.0	VF/NM 9.0	NM- 9.2
1-Bendis-s/Gaydos-a/Mack-c; intro Jessica Jones; Luke Cage app.	4	8	12	23	37	50
2-4	1	2	3	4	5	7
5-23: 7,8-Sienkiewicz-a (2 pgs.) 16-21-Spider-Woman app. 22,23-Jessica's origin						3.00
24-28-Purple Man app.; Avengers app.; flashback-a by Bagley						5.00
... MGC 1 (6/10, $1.00) r/#1 with "Marvel's Greatest Comics" logo on cover						3.00
HC (2002, $29.99) r/#1-9; intro. by Jeph Loeb						30.00
Omnibus (2006, $69.99, hardcover with dustjacket) r/#1-28 and What If Jessica Jones Had Joined the Avengers?; original pitch, script and sketch pages						70.00
Vol. 1: TPB (2003, $19.99) r/#1-9						20.00
Vol. 2: Come Home TPB (2003, $13.99) r/#11-15						14.00
Vol. 3: The Underneath TPB (2003, $16.99) r/#10,16-21						17.00

ALICE (New Adventures in Wonderland)
Ziff-Davis Publ. Co.: No. 10, 7-8/51 - No. 11(#2), 11-12/51

	GD 2.0	VG 4.0	FN 6.0	VF 8.0	VF/NM 9.0	NM- 9.2
10-Painted-c; Berg-a	29	58	87	170	278	385
11-(#2 on inside) Dave Berg-a	19	38	57	109	172	235

ALICE AT MONKEY ISLAND (Formerly The Adventures of Alice)
Pentagon Publ. Co. (Civil Service): No. 3, 1946

	GD 2.0	VG 4.0	FN 6.0	VF 8.0	VF/NM 9.0	NM- 9.2
3	10	20	30	58	79	100

ALICE COOPER (Also see Last Temptation)
Dynamite Entertainment: 2014 - No. 6, 2015 ($3.99)

	GD 2.0	VG 4.0	FN 6.0	VF 8.0	VF/NM 9.0	NM- 9.2
1-6: 1-5-Joe Harris-s/Eman Casallos-a/David Mack-c. 6-Jerwa-s/Tenorio-a						4.00

ALICE COOPER VS. CHAOS!
Dynamite Entertainment: 2015 - No. 6, 2016 ($3.99, limited series)

	GD 2.0	VG 4.0	FN 6.0	VF 8.0	VF/NM 9.0	NM- 9.2
1-6-Chastity, Purgatori, Evil Ernie, Lady Demon & The Queen of Sorrows app.						4.00

ALICE IN WONDERLAND (Disney; see Advs. of Alice, Dell Jr. Treasury #1, The Dreamery, Movie Comics, Walt Disney Showcase #22, and World's Greatest Stories)
Dell Publishing Co.: No. 24, 1940; No. 331, 1951; No. 341, July, 1951

	GD 2.0	VG 4.0	FN 6.0	VF 8.0	VF/NM 9.0	NM- 9.2
Single Series 24 (#1)(1940)	54	108	162	343	574	825
Four Color 331, 341-"Unbirthday Party w/..."	14	28	42	96	211	325
1-(Whitman, 3/84, pre-pack only)-r/4-Color #331	3	6	9	14	20	25

ALIEN ENCOUNTERS (Replaces Alien Worlds)
Eclipse Comics: June, 1985 - No. 14, Aug, 1987 ($1.75, Baxter paper, mature)

	GD 2.0	VG 4.0	FN 6.0	VF 8.0	VF/NM 9.0	NM- 9.2
1-10: Nudity, strong language in all. 9-Snyder-a						4.00
11-14-Low print run						5.00

ALIEN LEGION (See Epic & Marvel Graphic Novel #25)
Marvel Comics (Epic Comics): Apr, 1984 - No. 20, Sept, 1987

	GD 2.0	VG 4.0	FN 6.0	VF 8.0	VF/NM 9.0	NM- 9.2
nn-With bound-in trading card; Austin-i						4.00
2-20: 2-$1.50-c. 7,8-Portacio-i						3.00

ALIEN LEGION (2nd Series)
Marvel Comics (Epic): Aug, 1987(indicia)(10/87 on-c) - No. 18, Aug, 1990

	GD 2.0	VG 4.0	FN 6.0	VF 8.0	VF/NM 9.0	NM- 9.2
V2#1-18-Stroman-a in all. 7-18-Farmer-i						3.00
...: Force Nomad TPB (Checker Book Pub. Group, 2001, $24.95) r/#1-11						25.00
...: Piecemaker TPB (Checker Book Pub. Group, 2002, $19.95) r/#12-18						20.00

ALIEN LEGION: (Series of titles; all Marvel/Epic Comics)

	GD 2.0	VG 4.0	FN 6.0	VF 8.0	VF/NM 9.0	NM- 9.2
--BINARY DEEP, 1993 ($3.50, one-shot, 52 pgs.), nn-With bound-in trading card						4.00
--JUGGER GRIMROD, 8/92 ($5.95, one-shot, 52 pgs.) Book 1						6.00
--ONE PLANET AT A TIME, 5/93 - Book 3, 7/93 ($4.95, squarebound, 52 pgs.) Book 1-3: Hoang Nguyen-a						5.00
--ON THE EDGE (The... #2 & 3), 11/90 - No. 3, 1/91 ($4.50, 52 pgs.) 1-3-Stroman & Farmer-a						4.50
--TENANTS OF HELL, '91 - No. 2, '91 ($4.50, squarebound, 52 pgs.) Book 1,2-Stroman-c/a(p)						4.50

ALIEN LEGION: UNCIVIL WAR
Titan Comics: Jul, 2014 - No. 4, Oct, 2014 ($3.99)

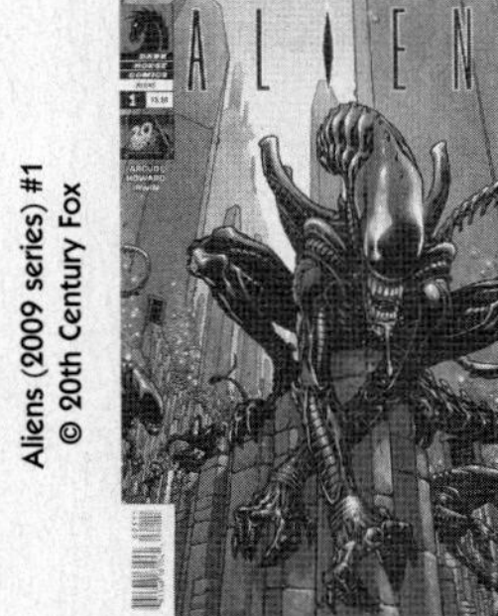
Aliens (2009 series) #1 © 20th Century Fox

Aliens: Rogue #3 © 20th Century Fox

Aliens: Survival #1 © 20th Century Fox

GD 2.0 | VG 4.0 | FN 6.0 | VF 8.0 | VF/NM 9.0 | NM- 9.2

1-4-Dixon-s/Stroman-a 4.00

ALIEN NATION (Movie)
DC Comics: Dec, 1988 ($2.50; 68 pgs.)
1-Adaptation of film; painted-c 4.00

ALIEN PIG FARM 3000
Image Comics (RAW Studios): Apr, 2007 - No. 4, July, 2007 ($2.99, limited series)
1-4-Steve Niles, Thomas Jane & Todd Farmer-s/Don Marquez-a 3.00

ALIEN RESURRECTION (Movie)
Dark Horse Comics: Oct, 1997 - No. 2, Nov, 1997 ($2.50; limited series)
1,2-Adaptation of film; Dave McKean-c 3.00

ALIENS, THE (Captain Johner and...)(Also see Magnus Robot Fighter...)
Gold Key: Sept-Dec, 1967; No. 2, May, 1982
1-Reprints from Magnus #1,3,4,6-10; Russ Manning-a in all
3 6 9 19 30 40
2-(Whitman) Same contents as #1 1 2 3 5 6 8

ALIENS (Movie) (See Alien: The Illustrated..., Dark Horse Comics & Dark Horse Presents #24)
Dark Horse Comics: May, 1988 - No. 6, July, 1989 ($1.95, B&W, limited series)
1-Based on movie sequel; 1st app. Aliens in comics 3 6 9 15 22 28
1-2nd - 6th printings; 4th w/new inside front-c 3.00
2 2 4 6 8 10 12
2-2nd & 3rd printing, 3-6-2nd printings 3.00
3 1 2 3 5 7 9
4-6 5.00
Mini Comic #1 (2/89, 4x6")-Was included with Aliens Portfolio 4.00
Collection 1 ($10.95,)-r/#1-6 plus Dark Horse Presents #24 plus new-a 12.00
Collection 1-2nd printing (1991, $11.95)-On higher quality paper than 1st print; Dorman painted-c 12.00
Hardcover ('90, $24.95, B&W)-r/1-6, DHP #24 30.00
... Omnibus Vol. 1 (7/07, $24.95, 9x6") r/1st & 2nd series and Aliens: Earth War 25.00
... Omnibus Vol. 2 (12/07, $24.95, 9x6") r/Genocide, Harvest and Colonial Marines series 25.00
... Omnibus Vol. 3 (3/08, $24.95, 9x6") r/Rogue, Salvation and Sacrifice, Labyrinth series 25.00
... Omnibus Vol. 4 (8/08, $24.95, 9x6") r/Music of the Spears, Stronghold, Berserker, Mondo Pest and Mondo Heat series and one-shots 25.00
... Omnibus Vol. 5 (11/08, $24.95, 9x6") r/Alchemy, Survival, Havoc series and various 25.00
... Omnibus Vol. 6 (2/09, $24.95, 9x6") r/Apocalypse GN, Xenogenesis & one-shots 25.00
... Outbreak (3rd printing, 8/96, $17.95)-Bolton-c 18.00
Platinum Edition - (See Dark Horse Presents: Aliens Platinum Edition) -

ALIENS
Dark Horse Comics: V2#1, Aug, 1989 - No. 4, 1990 ($2.25, limited series)
V2#1-Painted art by Denis Beauvais 5.00
1-2nd printing (1990), 2-4 3.00
...: Nightmare Asylum TPB (12/96, $16.95) r/series; Bolton-c 17.00

ALIENS
Dark Horse Comics: May, 2009 - No. 4, Nov, 2009 ($3.50, limited series)
1-4-John Arcudi-s/Zach Howard-a. 1,2-Howard-c. 3,4-Swanland-c 3.50

ALIENS: (Series of titles, all Dark Horse)
--ALCHEMY, 10/97 - No. 3, 11/97 ($2.95),1-3-Corben-c/a, Arcudi-s 3.00
--APOCALYPSE - THE DESTROYING ANGELS, 1/99 - No. 4, 4/99 ($2.95)
1-4-Doug Wheatly-a/Schultz-s 3.00
--BERSERKERS, 1/95 - No. 4, 4/95 ($2.50) 1-4 3.00
--COLONIAL MARINES, 1/93 - No. 10, 7/94 ($2.50) 1-10 3.00
--DEFIANCE, 4/16 - No. 4, 8/16 ($3.99) 1-9: 1,2-Brian Wood-s/Tristan Jones-a 4.00
--EARTH ANGEL, 8/94 ($2.95) 1-Byrne-a/story; wraparound-c 3.00
--EARTH WAR, 6/90 - No. 4, 10/90 ($2.50) 1-All have Sam Kieth-a & Bolton painted-c 5.00
1-2nd printing, 3,4 3.00
2 4.00
--GENOCIDE, 11/91 - No. 4, 2/92 ($2.50) 1-4-Suydam painted-c. 4-Wraparound-c, poster 3.00
--GLASS CORRIDOR, 6/98 ($2.95) 1-David Lloyd-s/a 3.00
--HARVEST (See Aliens: Hive)
--HAVOC, 6/97 - No. 2, 7/97 ($2.95) 1,2: Schultz-s, Kent Williams-c, 40 artists including Art Adams, Kelley Jones, Duncan Fegredo, Kevin Nowlan 3.00
--HIVE, 2/92 - No. 4,5/92 ($2.50) 1-4: Kelley Jones-c/a in all 3.00
...Harvest TPB ('98, $16.95) r/series; Bolton-c 17.00
--KIDNAPPED, 12/97 - No. 3, 2/98 ($2.50) 1-3 3.00
--LABYRINTH, 9/93 - No. 4, 1/94 ($2.50) 1-4: 1-Painted-c 3.00

GD 2.0 | VG 4.0 | FN 6.0 | VF 8.0 | VF/NM 9.0 | NM- 9.2

--LIFE AND DEATH, 9/16 - No. 4, 12/16 ($3.99) 1-4-Abnett-s/Moritat-a 4.00
--LOVESICK, 12/96 ($2.95) 1 3.00
--MONDO HEAT, 2/96 ($2.50) nn-Sequel to Mondo Pest 3.00
--MONDO PEST, 4/95 ($2.95, 44 pgs.) nn-r/Dark Horse Comics #22-24 4.00
--MUSIC OF THE SPEARS, 1/94 - No. 4, 4/94 ($2.50) 1-4 3.00
--NEWT'S TALE, 6/92 - No. 2, 7/92 ($4.95) 1,2-Bolton-c 5.00
--PIG, 3/97 ($2.95)1 3.00
--PREDATOR: THE DEADLIEST OF THE SPECIES, 7/93 - No. 12,8/95 ($2.50)
1-Bolton painted-c; Guice-a(p) 5.00
1-Embossed foil platinum edition 10.00
2-12: Bolton painted-c. 2,3-Guice-a(p) 3.00
--PURGE, 8/97 ($2.95) nn-Hester-a 3.00
--ROGUE, 4/93 - No. 4, 7/93 ($2.50)1-4: Painted-c 3.00
--SACRIFICE, 5/93 ($4.95, 52 pgs.) nn-P. Milligan scripts; painted-c/a 5.00
--SALVATION, 11/93 ($4.95, 52 pgs.) nn-Mignola-c/a(p); Gibbons script 5.00
--SPECIAL, 6/97 ($2.50) 1 3.00
--STALKER, 6/98 ($2.50)1-David Wenzel-s/a 3.00
--STRONGHOLD, 5/94 - No. 4, 9/94 ($2.50) 1-4 3.00
--SURVIVAL, 2/98 - No. 3, 4/98 ($2.95) 1-3-Tony Harris-c 3.00
--TRIBES, 1992 ($24.95, hardcover graphic novel) Bissette text-s with Dorman painted-a 25.00
...softcover ($9.95) 10.00

ALIENS: FIRE AND STONE (Crossover with AvP, Predator, and Prometheus)
Dark Horse Comics: Sept, 2014 - No. 4, Dec, 2014 ($3.50, limited series)
1-4-Roberson-s/Reynolds-a 3.50

ALIENS/ VAMPIRELLA (See Vampirella/Aliens)

ALIENS VS. PARKER (Not based on the Alien movie series)
BOOM! Studios: Mar, 2013 - No. 4, May, 2013 ($3.99, limited series)
1-4: 1-Paul Scheer & Nick Giovannetti-s; Bracchi-a/Noto-c 4.00

ALIENS VS. PREDATOR (See Dark Horse Presents #36)
Dark Horse Comics: June, 1990 - No. 4, Dec, 1990 ($2.50, limited series)
1-Painted-c 2 4 6 8 10 12
1-2nd printing 3.00
0-(7/90, $1.95, B&W)-r/Dark Horse Pres. #34-36 2 4 6 8 10 12
2,3 5.00
4-Dave Dorman painted-c 4.00
Annual (7/99, $4.95) Jae Lee-c 5.00
... : Booty (1/96, $2.50) painted-c 3.00
... Omnibus Vol. 1 (5/07, $24.95, 9x6") r/#1-4 & Annual; ...: War; ...: Eternal 25.00
... Omnibus Vol. 2 (10/07, $24.95, 9x6") r/...: Xenogenesis #1-4; ...: Deadliest of the Species; ...: Booty and stories from ... Annual 25.00
...: One For One (8/10, $1.00) r/#1 with red cover frame 3.00
... : Thrill of the Hunt (9/04, $6.95, digest-size TPB) Based on 2004 movie 7.00
... Wraith 1 (7/98, $2.95) Jay Stephens-s 3.00
--VS. PREDATOR: DUEL, 3/95 - No. 2, 4/95 ($2.50) 1,2 3.00
--VS. PREDATOR: ETERNAL, 6/98 - No. 4, 9/98 ($2.50)1-4: Edginton-s/Maleev-a; Fabry-c 3.00
--VS. PREDATOR: THREE WORLD WAR, 1/10 - No. 6, 9/10 ($3.50) 1-6-Leonardi-a 3.50
--VS. PREDATOR VS. THE TERMINATOR, 4/00 - No. 4, 7/00 ($2.95) 1-4: Ripley app. 3.00
--VS. PREDATOR: WAR, No. 0, 5/95 - No. 4, 8/95 ($2.50) 0-4: Corben painted-c 3.00
--VS. PREDATOR: XENOGENESIS, 12/99 - No. 4, 3/00 ($2.95) 1-4: Watson-s/Mel Rubi-a 3.00
--XENOGENESIS, 8/99 - No. 4, 11/99 ($2.95) 1-4: T&M Bierbaum-s 3.00

ALIENS VS. ZOMBIES (Not based on the Alien movie series)
Zenescope Entertainment: Jul, 2015 - No. 5, Dec, 2015 ($3.99, limited series)
1-5: 1-Brusha-s/Riccardi-a; multiple covers on each 4.00

ALIEN TERROR (See 3-D Alien Terror)

ALIEN: THE ILLUSTRATED STORY (Also see Aliens)
Heavy Metal Books: 1980 ($3.95, soft-c, 8x11")
nn-Movie adaptation; Simonson-a 3 6 9 16 23 30

ALIEN^3 (Movie)
Dark Horse Comics: June, 1992 - No. 3, July, 1992 ($2.50, limited series)
1-3: Adapts 3rd movie; Suydam painted-c 3.00

ALIEN VS. PREDATOR: FIRE AND STONE (Crossover with Aliens, Predator, and Prometheus)
Dark Horse Comics: Oct, 2014 - No. 4, Jan, 2015 ($3.50, limited series)

All-American Comics #16 © DC

All-American Comics #102 © DC

All-American Men of War #13 © DC

GD VG FN VF VF/NM NM-
2.0 4.0 6.0 8.0 9.0 9.2

1-4-Sebela-s/Olivetti-a 3.50

ALIEN VS. PREDATOR: LIFE AND DEATH (Crossover with Aliens, Predator, and Prometheus)
Dark Horse Comics: Dec, 2016 - No. 4, ($3.99, limited series)

1-3-Abnett-s/Theis-a 4.00

ALIEN WORLDS (Also see Eclipse Graphic Album #22)
Pacific Comics/Eclipse: Dec, 1982 - No. 9, Jan, 1985

1,2,4: 2,4-Dave Stevens-c/a 6.00
3,5-7 4.00
8,9 1 2 3 4 5 7
3-D No. 1-Art Adams 1st published art 1 2 3 4 5 7

ALISON DARE, LITTLE MISS ADVENTURES (Also see Return of ...)
Oni Press: Sept, 2000 ($4.50, B&W, one-shot)

1-J. Torres-s/J.Bone-c/a 4.50

ALISON DARE & THE HEART OF THE MAIDEN
Oni Press: Jan, 2002 - No. 2, Feb, 2002 ($2.95, B&W, limited series)

1,2-J. Torres-s/J.Bone-c/a 3.00

ALISTER THE SLAYER
Midnight Press: Oct, 1995 ($2.50)

1-Boris-c 3.00

ALL-AMERICAN COMICS (...Western #103-126, ...Men of War #127 on; also see The Big All-American Comic Book)
All-American/National Periodical Publ.: April, 1939 - No. 102, Oct, 1948

1-Hop Harrigan (1st app.), Scribbly by Mayer (1st DC app.), Toonerville Folks, Ben Webster, Spot Savage, Mutt & Jeff, Red White & Blue (1st app.), Adventures in the Unknown, Tippie, Reg'lar Fellers, Skippy, Bobby Thatcher, Mystery Men of Mars, Daiseybelle, Wiley of West Point begin 650 1300 1950 4600 7800 11,000
2-Ripley's Believe It or Not begins, ends #24 226 452 678 1446 2473 3500
3-5: 5-The American Way begins, ends #10 194 388 582 1242 2121 3000
6,7: 6-Last Spot Savage; Popsicle Pete begins, ends #26, 28. 7-Last Bobby Thatcher 132 264 396 838 1444 2050
8-The Ultra Man begins & 1st-c app. 432 864 1296 3154 5577 8000
9,10: 10-X-Mas-c 129 258 387 826 1413 2000
11,15: 11-Ultra Man-c. 15-Last Tippie & Reg'lar Fellars; Ultra Man-c 187 374 561 1197 2049 2900
12-14: 12-Last Toonerville Folks 126 252 378 806 1378 1950
16-(Rare)-Origin/1st app. Green Lantern by Sheldon Moldoff (c/a)(7/40) & begin series; appears in costume on-c & only one panel inside; created by Martin Nodell. Inspired in 1940 by a switchman's green lantern that would give trains the go ahead to proceed. G.L. cover pose swiped from last panel of a Jan, 1939 Flash Gordon Sunday page. 23,000 46,000 69,000 170,000 435,000 750,000
17-2nd Green Lantern 1250 2500 3750 9400 19,700 30,000
18-N.Y. World's Fair-c/story (scarce); The Atom app. in one panel announcing debut in next issue 1225 2450 3675 9200 19,100 29,000
19-Origin/1st app. The Atom (10/40); last Ultra Man 2400 4800 7200 18,000 37,000 56,000
20-Atom dons costume; Ma Hunkle becomes Red Tornado (1st app.)(1st DC costumed heroine, before Wonder Woman, 11/40); Rescue on Mars begins, ends #25; 1 pg. origin Green Lantern 622 1244 1866 4541 8021 11,500
21-Last Wiley of West Point & Skippy; classic Moldoff-c 524 1048 1572 3825 6763 9700
22,23: 23-Last Daiseybelle; 3 Idiots begin, end #82 366 732 1098 2562 4481 6400
24-Sisty & Dinky become the Cyclone Kids; Ben Webster ends; origin Dr. Mid-Nite & Sargon, The Sorcerer in text with app. 383 766 1149 2681 4691 6700
25-Origin & 1st story app. Dr. Mid-Nite by Stan Asch; Hop Harrigan becomes Guardian Angel; last Adventure in the Unknown (scarce) 1200 2400 3600 9000 18,500 28,000
26-Origin/1st story app. Sargon, the Sorcerer 389 778 1167 2723 4762 6800
27: #27-32 are misnumbered in indicia with correct No. appearing on-c. Intro. Doiby Dickles, Green Lantern's sidekick 400 800 1200 2800 4900 7000
28-Hop Harrigan gives up costumed i.d. 213 426 639 1363 2332 3300
29,30 213 426 639 1363 2332 3300
31-40: 35-Doiby learns Green Lantern's i.d. 177 354 531 1124 1937 2750
41-50: 50-Sargon ends 142 284 426 909 1555 2200
51-60: 59-Scribbly & the Red Tornado ends 119 238 357 762 1306 1850
61-Origin/1st app. Solomon Grundy (11/44) 1200 2400 3600 9000 18,000 27,000
62-70: 70-Kubert Sargon; intro Sargon's helper, Maximillian O'Leary 100 200 300 635 1093 1550
71-88: 71-Last Red White & Blue. 72-Black Pirate begins (not in #74-82); last Atom. 73-Winky, Blinky & Noddy begins, ends #82. 79,83-Mutt & Jeff-c. 85-1st Crusher Crock (becomes Sportsmaster); Hasen "Derby" cover 81 162 243 518 884 1250
89-Origin & 1st app. Harlequin 206 412 618 1318 2259 3200
90,92,96-99: 90-Origin/1st app. Icicle. 98-Sportsmaster-c. 99-Last Hop Harrigan 155 310 465 992 1696 2400
91,93,94,95-Harlequin-c 174 348 522 1114 1907 2700
100-1st app. Johnny Thunder by Alex Toth (8/48); western theme begins (Scarce) 206 412 618 1318 2259 3200
101-Last Mutt & Jeff (Scarce) 142 284 426 909 1555 2200
102-Last Green Lantern, Black Pirate & Dr. Mid-Nite (Scarce) 271 542 813 1734 2967 4200

NOTE: *No Atom in 47, 62-69.* ***Kinstler*** *Black Pirate-89.* ***Stan Aschmeier*** *a (Dr. Mid-Nite) 25-84; c-7.* ***Mayer*** *c-1, 2(part), 6, 10.* ***Moldoff*** *c-16-23.* ***Nodell*** *c-31.* ***Paul Reinman*** *a (Green Lantern)-53-55p, 56-84, 87; (Black Pirate)-83-88, 90; c-52, 55-76, 78, 80, 81, 87.* ***Toth*** *a-88, 92, 96, 98-102; c(p)-92, 96-102. Scribbly by* ***Mayer*** *in #1-59. Ultra Man by* ***Mayer*** *in #8-19.*

ALL AMERICAN COMICS
DC Comics: April 1939

nn - Ashcan comic, not distributed to newsstands, only for in house use. Cover art is Adventure Comics #33 and interior from Detective Comics #23. A CGC 7.5 copy sold for $7466 in December 2014.

ALL-AMERICAN COMICS (Also see All Star Comics 1999 crossover titles)
DC Comics: May, 1999 ($1.99, one-shot)

1-Golden Age Green Lantern and Johnny Thunder; Barreto-a 3.00

ALL-AMERICAN MEN OF WAR (Previously All-American Western)
National Periodical Publ.: No. 127, Aug-Sept, 1952 - No. 117, Sept-Oct, 1966

127 (#1, 1952) 132 264 396 1056 2378 3700
128 (1952) 56 112 168 448 999 1550
2(12-1/'52-53)-5 50 100 150 400 900 1400
6-Devil Dog story; Ghost Squadron story 38 76 114 285 641 1000
7-10: 8-Sgt. Storm Cloud-s 38 76 114 285 641 1000
11-16,18: 18-Last precode; 1st Kubert-c (2/55) 35 70 105 252 564 875
17-1st Frogman-s in this title 36 72 108 259 580 900
19,20,22-27 27 54 81 194 435 675
21-Easy Co. prototype 34 68 102 245 548 850
28 (12/55)-1st Sgt. Rock prototype; Kubert-a 54 108 162 432 966 1500
29,30,32-Wood-a 27 54 81 194 435 675
31,33,34,36-38,40: 34-Gunner prototype-s. 36-Little Sure Shot prototype-s. 38-1st S.A. issue 25 50 75 175 388 600
35-Greytone-c 29 58 87 207 464 720
39 (11/56)-2nd Sgt. Rock prototype; 1st Easy Co.? 38 76 114 281 628 975
41,43-47,49,50: 46-Tankbusters-c/s 21 42 63 150 330 510
42-Pre-Sgt. Rock Easy Co.-c/s 27 54 81 187 414 640
48-Easy Co.-c/s; Nick app.; Kubert-a 27 54 81 187 414 640
51-56,58-62,65,66: 61-Gunner-c/s 17 34 51 117 259 400
57(5/58),63,64-Pre-Sgt. Rock Easy Co.-c/s 23 46 69 161 356 550
67-1st Gunner & Sarge by Andru & Esposito 50 100 150 390 870 1350
68,69: 68-2nd app. Gunner & Sarge. 69-1st Tank Killer-c/s 22 42 63 147 324 500
70 14 28 42 96 211 325
71-80: 71,72,76-Tank Killer-c/s. 74-Minute Commandos-c/s 12 24 36 82 179 275
81-Greytone-c 12 24 36 81 176 270
82-Johnny Cloud begins(1st app.), ends #117 27 54 81 194 435 675
83-2nd Johnny Cloud 14 28 42 94 207 320
84-88: 88-Last 10¢ issue 10 20 30 69 147 225
89-100: 89-Battle Aces of 3 Wars begins, ends #98. 89,90-Panels from these issues used by artist Roy Lichtenstein for famous paintings 8 16 24 56 108 160
101-111,113-116: 110,11-Greytone-c. 111,114,115-Johnny Cloud 6 12 18 40 73 105
112-Balloon Buster series begins, ends #114,116 6 12 18 41 76 110
117-Johnny Cloud-c & 3-part story 6 12 18 41 76 110

NOTE: *Frogman stories in 17, 38, 44, 45, 50, 51, 53, 55-58, 63, 65, 66, 72, 76, 77.* ***Colan*** *a-112.* ***Drucker*** *a-47, 58, 61, 63, 65, 69, 71, 74, 77.* ***Grandenetti*** *c(p)-127, 128, 2-17(most).* ***Heath*** *a-14, 27, 32, 38, 41, 45, 47, 50, 51, 55-58, 62, 64, 71, 75, 76, 78, 95, 111-117; c-85, 91, 94-96, 100, 101, 110-112, others?* ***Infantino*** *a-8.* ***Kirby*** *a-29.* ***Krigstein*** *a-128('52), 2, 3, 5.* ***Kubert*** *a-22, 24, 28, 29, 33, 34, 36, 38, 39, 41-43, 47-50, 52, 53, 55, 56, 59, 60, 63-65, 69, 71-73, 76, 102, 103, 105, 106, 108, 114; c-41, 44, 52, 54, 55, 58, 64, 69, 76, 77, 79, 102-106, 108, 113-117, others? Tank Killer in 69, 71, 76 by* ***Kubert. P. Reinman*** *c-55, 57, 61, 62, 71, 72, 74-76, 80.* ***J. Severin*** *a-58.*

ALL AMERICAN MEN OF WAR
DC Comics: Aug/Sept. 1952

nn - Ashcan comic, not distributed to newsstands, only for in-house use. Cover art is All Star Western #58 and interior from Mr. District Attorney #21. A GD+ copy sold for $1195 in 2012.

ALL-AMERICAN SPORTS
Charlton Comics: Oct, 1967

1 3 6 9 19 30 45

All-American Western #103 © DC

All-Flash #13 © DC

All Good nn © STJ

ALL-AMERICAN WESTERN (Formerly All-American Comics; Becomes All-American Men of War)
National Periodical Publ.: No. 103, Nov, 1948 - No. 126, June-July, 1952 (103-121: 52 pgs.)

	GD 2.0	VG 4.0	FN 6.0	VF 8.0	VF/NM 9.0	NM- 9.2
103-Johnny Thunder & his horse Black Lightning continues by Toth, ends #126; Foley of The Fighting 5th, Minstrel Maverick, & Overland Coach begin; Captain Tootsie by Beck; mentioned in Love and Death	54	108	162	343	574	825
104-Kubert-a	39	78	117	234	385	535
105,107-Kubert-a	34	68	102	199	325	450
106,108-110,112: 112-Kurtzman's "Pot-Shot Pete" (1 pg.)	28	56	84	165	270	375
111,114-116-Kubert-a	29	58	87	172	281	390
113-Intro. Swift Deer, J. Thunder's new sidekick (4-5/50); classic Toth-c; Kubert-a	32	64	96	188	307	425
117-126: 121-Kubert-a; bondage-c	21	42	63	122	199	275

NOTE: *G. Kane c(p)-112, 119, 120, 123. Kubert a-103-105, 107, 111, 112(1 pg.), 113-116, 121. Toth a-103-125; c(p)-103-111,113-116, 121, 122, 124-126. Some copies of #125 have #12 on-c.*

ALL COMICS
Chicago Nite Life News: 1945

	GD	VG	FN	VF	VF/NM	NM-
1	15	30	45	85	130	175

ALLEGRA
Image Comics (WildStorm): Aug, 1996 - No. 4, Dec, 1996 ($2.50)

	GD	VG	FN	VF	VF/NM	NM-
1-4						3.00

ALLEY CAT (Alley Baggett)
Image Comics: July, 1999 - No. 6, Mar, 2000 ($2.50/$2.95)

	GD	VG	FN	VF	VF/NM	NM-
Preview Edition						6.00
Prelude						5.00
Prelude w/variant-c						6.00
1-Photo-c						3.00
1-Painted-c by Dorian						4.00
1-Another Universe Edition, 1-Wizard World Edition						7.00
2-4: 4-Twin towers on-c						3.00
5,6-($2.95)						3.00
Lingerie Edition (10/99, $4.95) Photos, pin-ups, cover gallery						5.00
...Vs. Lady Pendragon ('99, $3.00) Stinsman-c						3.00

ALLEY OOP (See The Comics, The Funnies, Red Ryder and Super Book #9)
Dell Publishing Co.: No. 3, 1942

	GD	VG	FN	VF	VF/NM	NM-
Four Color 3 (#1)	46	92	138	359	805	1250

ALLEY OOP
Argo Publ.: Nov, 1955 - No. 3, Mar, 1956 (Newspaper reprints)

	GD	VG	FN	VF	VF/NM	NM-
1	16	32	48	94	147	200
2,3	12	24	36	67	94	120

ALLEY OOP
Dell Publishing Co.: 12-2/62-63 - No. 2, 9-11/63

	GD	VG	FN	VF	VF/NM	NM-
1	5	10	15	35	63	90
2	5	10	15	31	53	75

ALLEY OOP
Standard Comics: No. 10, Sept, 1947 - No. 18, Oct, 1949

	GD	VG	FN	VF	VF/NM	NM-
10	32	64	96	188	307	425
11-18: 17,18-Schomburg-c	24	48	72	142	234	325

ALLEY OOP ADVENTURES
Antarctic Press: Aug, 1998 - No. 3, Dec, 1998 ($2.95)

	GD	VG	FN	VF	VF/NM	NM-
1-3-Jack Bender-s/a						3.00

ALLEY OOP ADVENTURES (Alley Oop Quarterly in indicia)
Antarctic Press: Sept, 1999 - No. 3, Mar, 2000 ($2.50/$2.99, B&W)

	GD	VG	FN	VF	VF/NM	NM-
1-3-Jack Bender-s/a						3.00

ALL-FAMOUS CRIME (2nd series - Formerly Law Against Crime #1-3; becomes All-Famous Police Cases #6 on)
Star Publications: No. 8, 5/51 - No. 10, 11/51; No. 4, 2/52 - No. 5, 5/52;

	GD	VG	FN	VF	VF/NM	NM-
8 (#1-1st series)	30	60	90	177	289	400
9 (#2)-Used in **SOTI**, illo- "The wish to hurt or kill couples in lovers' lanes is a not uncommon perversion;" L.B. Cole-c/a(r)/Law-Crime #3	42	84	126	265	445	625
10 (#3)	24	48	72	140	230	320
4 (#4-2nd series)-Formerly Law-Crime	22	44	66	132	216	300
5 (#5) Becomes All-Famous Police Cases #6	22	44	66	132	216	300

NOTE: *All have* **L.B. Cole** *covers.*

ALL FAMOUS CRIME STORIES (See Fox Giants)

ALL-FAMOUS POLICE CASES (Formerly All Famous Crime #5)
Star Publications: No. 6, Feb, 1952 - No. 16, Sept, 1954

	GD	VG	FN	VF	VF/NM	NM-
6	26	52	78	154	252	350
7,8: 7-Baker story. 8-Marijuana story	21	42	63	126	206	285
9-16	20	40	60	117	189	260

NOTE: ***L. B. Cole** c-all; a-15, 1pg.* ***Hollingsworth** a-15.*

ALL-FLASH (...Quarterly No. 1-5)
National Per. Publ./All-American: Summer, 1941 - No. 32, Dec-Jan, 1947-48

	GD	VG	FN	VF	VF/NM	NM-
1-Origin The Flash retold by E. E. Hibbard; Hibbard c-1-10,12-14,16,31p.	1250	2500	3750	8750	14,875	21,000
2-Origin recap	271	542	813	1734	2967	4200
3,4	161	322	483	1030	1765	2500
5-Winky, Blinky & Noddy begins (1st app.), ends #32	116	232	348	742	1271	1800
6-10: 6-Has full page ad for Wonder Woman #1	106	212	318	673	1162	1650
11,13: 13-The King app.	94	188	282	597	1024	1450
12-Origin/1st The Thinker	103	206	309	659	1130	1600
14-Green Lantern cameo	110	220	330	704	1202	1700
15-20: 18-Mutt & Jeff begins, ends #22	86	172	258	546	936	1325
21-31	71	142	213	454	777	1100
32-Origin/1st app. The Fiddler; 1st Star Sapphire	145	290	435	921	1586	2250

All-Flash Quarterly ashcan (a recently discovered CGC 7.0 copy sold for $8150 in 2012)

NOTE: *Book length stories in 2-13, 16. Bondage c-31, 32.* ***Martin Nodell** c-15, 17-28.*

ALL FLASH (Leads into Flash [2nd series] #231)
DC Comics: Sept, 2007 ($2.99, one-shot)

	GD	VG	FN	VF	VF/NM	NM-
1-Wally West hunts down Bart's killers; Waid-s; two covers by Middleton & Sienkiewicz						3.00

ALL FOR LOVE (Young Love V3#5-on)
Prize Publications: Apr-May, 1957 - V3#4, Dec-Jan, 1959-60

	GD	VG	FN	VF	VF/NM	NM-
V1#1	9	18	27	57	111	165
2-6: 5-Orlando-c	5	10	15	33	57	80
V2#1-5(1/59), 5(3/59)	5	10	15	30	50	70
V3#1(5/59), 1(7/59)-4: 2-Powell-a	4	8	12	27	44	60

ALL FUNNY COMICS
Tilsam Publ./National Periodical Publications (Detective): Winter, 1943-44 - No. 23, May-June, 1948

	GD	VG	FN	VF	VF/NM	NM-
1-Genius Jones (see Adventure #77 for debut), Buzzy (1st app., ends #4), Dover & Clover (see More Fun #93) begin; Bailey-a	48	96	144	302	514	725
2	22	44	66	132	216	300
3-10	15	30	45	85	130	175
11-13,15,18,19-Genius Jones app.	14	28	42	80	115	150
14,17,20-23	10	20	30	56	76	95
16-DC Super Heroes app.	31	62	93	182	296	410

ALL GOOD
St. John Publishing Co.: Oct, 1949 (50¢, 260 pgs.)

	GD	VG	FN	VF	VF/NM	NM-
nn-(8 St. John comics bound together)	110	220	330	704	1202	1700

NOTE: *Also see Li'l Audrey Yearbook & Treasury of Comics.*

ALL GOOD COMICS (See Fox Giants)
Fox Features Syndicate: No.1, Spring, 1946 (36 pgs.)

	GD	VG	FN	VF	VF/NM	NM-
1-Joy Family, Dick Transom, Rick Evans, One Round Hogan	27	54	81	158	259	360

ALL GREAT
William H. Wise & Co.: nd (1945?) (132 pgs.)

	GD	VG	FN	VF	VF/NM	NM-
nn-Capt. Jack Terry, Joan Mason, Girl Reporter, Baron Doomsday; Torture scenes	48	96	144	302	514	725

ALL GREAT COMICS (See Fox Giants)
Fox Feature Syndicate: 1946 (36 pgs.)

	GD	VG	FN	VF	VF/NM	NM-
1-Crazy House, Bertie Benson Boy Detective, Gussie the Gob	27	54	81	158	259	360

ALL GREAT COMICS (Formerly Phantom Lady #13? Dagar, Desert Hawk No. 14 on)
Fox Features Syndicate: No. 14, Oct, 1947 - No. 13, Dec, 1947 (Newspaper strip reprints)

	GD	VG	FN	VF	VF/NM	NM-
14(#12)-Brenda Starr & Texas Slim-r (Scarce)	57	114	171	362	621	880
13-Origin Dagar, Desert Hawk; Brenda Starr (all-r); Kamen-c; Dagar covers begin	65	130	195	416	708	1000

ALL-GREAT CONFESSION MAGAZINE (See Fox Giants)

ALL-GREAT CONFESSIONS (See Fox Giants)

ALL GREAT CRIME STORIES (See Fox Giants)

ALL GREAT JUNGLE ADVENTURES (See Fox Giants)

ALL HALLOW'S EVE
Innovation Publishing: 1991 ($4.95, 52 pgs.)

	GD	VG	FN	VF	VF/NM	NM-
1-Painted-c/a	1	2	3	4	5	7

All Humor Comics #11 © QUA

All-New Comics #8 © HARV

All-New Ghost Rider #1 © MAR

GD 2.0 | VG 4.0 | FN 6.0 | VF 8.0 | VF/NM 9.0 | NM- 9.2

GD 2.0 | VG 4.0 | FN 6.0 | VF 8.0 | VF/NM 9.0 | NM- 9.2

ALL HERO COMICS
Fawcett Publications: Mar, 1943 (100 pgs., cardboard-c)

1-Capt. Marvel Jr., Capt. Midnight, Golden Arrow, Ibis the Invincible, Spy Smasher, Lance O'Casey; 1st Banshee O'Brien; Raboy-c 190 380 570 1207 2079 2950

ALL HUMOR COMICS
Quality Comics Group: Spring, 1946 - No. 17, December, 1949

1 21 42 63 126 206 285
2-Atomic Tot story; Gustavson-a 14 28 42 76 108 140
3-9: 3-Intro Kelly Poole who is cover feature #3 on. 5-1st app. Hickory?
8-Gustavson-a 9 18 27 52 69 85
10-17 9 18 27 47 61 75

ALLIANCE, THE
Image Comics (Shadowline Ink): Aug, 1995 - No. 3, Nov, 1995 ($2.50)

1-3: 2-(9/95) 3.00

ALL LOVE (...Romances No. 26)(Formerly Ernie Comics)
Ace Periodicals (Current Books): No. 26, May, 1949 - No. 32, May, 1950

26 (No. 1)-Ernie, Lily Belle app. 13 26 39 74 105 135
27-L. B. Cole-a 15 30 45 83 124 165
28-32 10 20 30 56 76 95

ALL-NEGRO COMICS
All-Negro Comics: June, 1947 (15¢)

1 (Rare) 2000 4000 6000 11,000 15,000 19,000
NOTE: *Seldom found in fine or mint condition; many copies have brown pages.*

ALL-NEW ALL-DIFFERENT AVENGERS (Follows Secret Wars event)
Marvel Comics: Jan, 2016 - No. 15, Dec, 2015 ($4.99/$3.99)

1-($4.99) Spider-Man (Miles), Ms. Marvel, Nova join; Waid-s/Adam Kubert & Asrar-a 5.00
2-15-($3.99) Main cover by Alex Ross. 2,3-Warbringer app.; Kubert-a. 4-6,9,10-Asrar-a. 7,8-Standoff tie-ins; Adam Kubert-a. 9-Intro. new Wasp (Nadia). 13-15-Civil War II tie-in 4.00
Annual 1(10/16, $4.99) Fan-fic short stories by various incl. Waid/Zdarsky & Allegri 5.00

ALL-NEW ALL-DIFFERENT MARVEL UNIVERSE
Marvel Comics: May, 2016 ($4.99, one-shot)

1-Handbook-style entries; profiles of major characters; Marquez-c 5.00

ALL-NEW ALL-DIFFERENT POINT ONE (Follows Secret Wars event)
Marvel Comics: Dec, 2015 ($5.99, one-shot)

1-Preludes to new titles: Carnage, Daredevil, All-New Inhumans, Agents of S.H.I.E.L.D., Rocket Raccoon & Groot, and Contest of Champions; Del Mundo-c 6.00

ALL-NEW ATOM, THE (See The Atom and DCU Brave New World)
DC Comics: Sept, 2006 - No. 25, Sept, 2008 ($2.99)

1-25: 1-18-Simone-s. 1-Intro Ryan Choi; Byrne-a thru #3. 4-11-Barrows-a. 12,13-Chronos app. 14,15-Countdown x-over. 17,18-Wonder Woman app. 3.00
...: Future/Past TPB (2007, $14.99) r/#7-11 15.00
...: My Life in Miniature TPB (2007, $14.99) r/#1-6 and app. in DCU Brave New World #1 15.00
...: Small Wonder TPB (2008, $17.99) r/#17,18,21-25 18.00
...: The Hunt For Ray Palmer TPB (2008, $14.99) r/#12-16 15.00

ALL-NEW BATMAN: BRAVE & THE BOLD (See Batman: The Brave and the Bold)

ALL-NEW CAPTAIN AMERICA (See Captain America #25 - 2014 series)
Marvel Comics: Jan, 2015 - No. 6, Jun, 2015 ($3.99)

1-6: 1-Sam Wilson as Captain America, Ian as Nomad; Immonen-a 4.00
... Special 1 (7/15, $4.99) Loveness-s/Morgan-a; Inhumans & Spider-Man app. 5.00

ALL-NEW CAPTAIN AMERICA: FEAR HIM (Sam Wilson as Cap)
Marvel Comics: Jan, 2015 - No. 4, Apr, 2015 ($3.99, limited series)

1-4-Hopeless & Remender-s/Kudranski-a/Bianchi-c; The Scarecrow app. 4.00

ALL-NEW CLASSIC CAPTAIN CANUCK
Chapterhouse Comics: No. 0, Feb, 2016 - No. 3, Oct, 2016 ($4.99/$3.99)

0-($4.99) Short stories; Ed Brisson-s; art by various 5.00
1-3-($3.99) Brisson-s/Freeman-a; 2 covers on each 4.00

ALL-NEW COLLECTORS' EDITION (Formerly Limited Collectors' Edition: see for C-57, C-59)
DC Comics, Inc.: Jan, 1978 - Vol. 8, No. C-62, 1979 (No. 54-58: 76 pgs.)

C-53-Rudolph the Red-Nosed Reindeer 4 8 12 28 47 65
C-54-Superman Vs. Wonder Woman 4 8 12 27 44 60
C-55-Superboy & the Legion of Super-Heroes; Wedding of Lightning Lad & Saturn Girl; Grell-c/a 4 8 12 25 40 55
C-56-Superman Vs. Muhammad Ali: Wraparound Neal Adams-c/a; Adams & O'Neil-s (see "Superman Vs. Muhammad Ali" for reprint) 10 20 30 64 132 200
C-56-Superman Vs. Muhammad Ali (Whitman variant)-low print 11 22 33 76 163 250
C-57,C-59-(See Limited Collectors' Edition)
C-58-Superman Vs. Shazam; Buckler-c/a; Black Adam's 2nd Bronze Age app. 4 8 12 27 44 60
C-60-Rudolph's Summer Fun(8/78) 4 8 12 25 40 55
C-61-(See Famous First Edition-Superman #1)
C-62-Superman the Movie (68 pgs.; 1979)-Photo-c from movie plus photos inside (also see DC Special Series #25 for Superman II) 3 6 9 15 22 28

ALL-NEW COMICS (...Short Story Comics No. 1-3)
Family Comics (Harvey Publications): Jan, 1943 - No. 14, Nov, 1946; No. 15, Mar-Apr, 1947 (10 x 13-1/2")

1-Steve Case, Crime Rover, Johnny Rebel, Kayo Kane, The Echo, Night Hawk, Ray O'Light, Detective Shane begin (all 1st app.?); Red Blazer on cover only; Sultan-a; Nazi WWII-c 300 600 900 1980 3440 4900
2-Origin Scarlet Phantom by Kubert; Nazi WWII-c 135 270 405 864 1482 2100
3-Nazi WWII-c 119 238 357 762 1305 1850
4-Nazi WWII-c 107 214 321 680 1165 1650
5-Classic Schomburg Japanese WWII-c showing Japanese using Human Suicide bombs falling on the Capitol building 161 322 483 1030 1765 2500
6-11: Schomburg-c on all. 9-11-Japanese WWII-c. 6-8 Nazi WWII-c. 6-The Boy Heroes & Red Blazer (text story) begin, end #12; Black Cat app.; intro. Sparky in Red Blazer. 7-Kubert, Powell-a; Black Cat & Zebra app. 8,9: 8-Shock Gibson app.; Kubert, Powell-a; Schomburg-c. 9-Black Cat app.; Kubert-a. 10-The Zebra app. (from Green Hornet Comics); Kubert-a(3). 11-Girl Commandos, Man In Black app. 148 296 444 947 1624 2300
12-Kubert-a; Japanese WWII-c 61 122 183 390 670 950
13-Stuntman by Simon & Kirby; Green Hornet, Joe Palooka, Flying Fool app.; Green Hornet-c 50 100 150 315 533 750
14-The Green Hornet & The Man in Black Called Fate by Powell, Joe Flying Fool app.; Flying Fool app.; J. Palooka-c by Ham Fisher 41 82 123 256 428 600
15-(Rare)-Small size (5-1/2x8-1/2"; B&W; 32 pgs.). Distributed to mail subscribers only. Black Cat and Joe Palooka app. 174 348 522 1114 1907 2700
NOTE: *Also see Boy Explorers No. 2, Flash Gordon No. 5, and Stuntman No. 3.* ***Powell*** *a-11.* ***Schomburg*** *c-5-11. Captain Red Blazer & Spark on c-5-11 (w/Boy Heroes #12).*

ALL-NEW DOOP (X-Men)
Marvel Comics: Jun, 2014 - No. 5, Nov, 2014 ($3.99, limited series)

1-5-Milligan-s/Lafuente-a; Kitty Pryde and X-Men app. 3-5-The Anarchist app. 4.00

ALL-NEW EXECUTIVE ASSISTANT: IRIS (Volume 4) (Also see Executive Assistant: Iris)
Aspen MLT: Sept, 2013 - No. 5, Jun, 2014 ($1.00/$3.99)

1-($1.00) Buccellato-s/Qualano-a; multiple covers 3.00
2-5-($3.99) Multiple covers 4.00

ALL-NEW EXECUTIVE ASSISTANT: IRIS: ENEMIES AMONG US
Aspen MLT: Dec, 2016 - Present ($4.99)

1-Wohl-s/Cafaro-a; Hernandez-s/Green-a; multiple covers 5.00

ALL NEW FATHOM (See Fathom)

ALL-NEW GHOST RIDER (Also see the 2017 Ghost Rider series)
Marvel Comics: May, 2014 - No. 12, May, 2015 ($3.99)

1-12: 1-Felipe Smith-s/Tradd Moore-a; origin of Robbie Reyes. 6-10-Damion Scott-a 4.00

ALL-NEW HAWKEYE
Marvel Comics: May, 2015 - No. 5, Nov, 2015 ($3.99)

1-5-Jeff Lemire-s/Ramón Pérez-a/c; Kate Bishop app.; flashback to circus childhood 4.00

ALL-NEW HAWKEYE
Marvel Comics: Jan, 2016 - No. 6, Jun, 2016 ($3.99)

1-6-Lemire-s/Pérez-a/c; Kate Bishop app. 1-3-Flashforward 30 years; Mandarin app. 4.00

ALL-NEW INHUMANS
Marvel Comics: Feb, 2016 - No. 11, Nov, 2016 ($3.99)

1-($4.99)-Asmus & Soule-s/Caselli-a; Crystal & Gorgon app. 5.00
2-11-($3.99) 2-4-The Commissar app. 5,6-Spider-Man app. 4.00

ALL-NEW INVADERS
Marvel Comics: Mar, 2014 - No. 15, Apr, 2015 ($3.99)

1-15: 1-Capt. America, Bucky, Namor & Jim Hammond team; Robinson-s/Pugh-a. 6,7-Original Sin tie-in 4.00

ALL-NEW MARVEL NOW! POINT ONE
Marvel Comics: Mar, 2014 ($5.99, one-shot preview of upcoming series)

1-Previews of Loki, Silver Surfer, Black Widow, Ms. Marvel, Avengers, All-New Invaders 6.00

ALL-NEW OFFICIAL HANDBOOK OF THE MARVEL UNIVERSE A TO Z
Marvel Comics: 2006 - No. 12, 2006 ($3.99, limited series)

1-12-Profile pages of Marvel characters not covered in 2004-2005 Official Handbooks 4.00

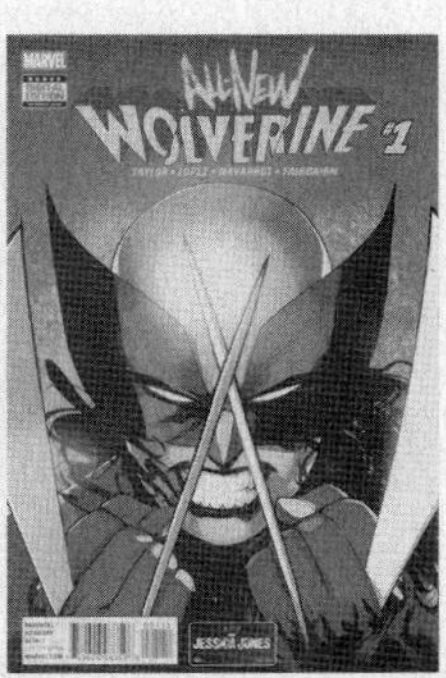

All-New Wolverine #1 © MAR

All-Select Comics #10 © MAR

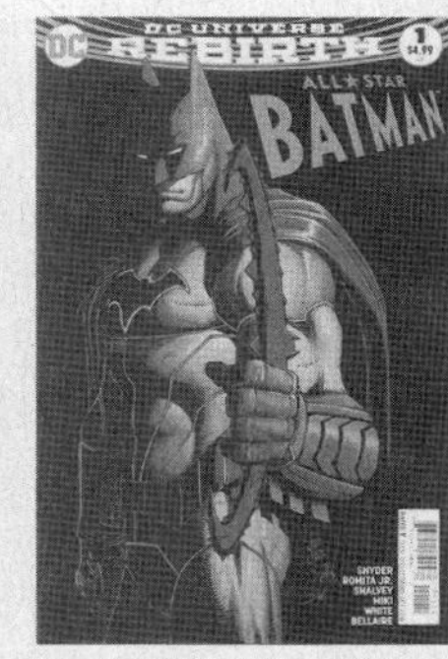

All Star Batman #1 © DC

GD VG FN VF VF/NM NM-
2.0 4.0 6.0 8.0 9.0 9.2

...: Update 1-4 (2007, $3.99) Profile pages 4.00

ALL-NEW ULTIMATES
Marvel Comics: Jun, 2014 - No. 12, Mar, 2015 ($3.99)
1-12: 1-Miles Morales Spider-Man, Spider-Woman, Cloak and Dagger, Kitty Pryde and Bombshell team. 5,6-Crossbones app. 4.00

ALL-NEW WOLVERINE (Laura Kinney X-23 as Wolverine)
Marvel Comics: Jan, 2016 - Present ($4.99/$3.99)
1-($4.99) Tom Taylor-s/David Lopez-a; Angel app. 5.00
2-17-($3.99) 2,3-Taskmaster app. 4-Doctor Strange app. 5-Janet Van Dyne app. 7-Squirrel Girl app. 8,9-Fin Fang Foom app. 10-12-Civil War II tie-in. 16,17-Gambit app. 4.00
Annual 1 (10/16, $4.99) Gwen Stacy app.; Tom Taylor-s/Marcio Takara-a 5.00

ALL-NEW X-FACTOR
Marvel Comics: Mar, 2014 - No. 20, Mar, 2015 ($3.99)
1-20: 1-12-David-s/DiGiandomenico-a; Gambit, Polaris, Quicksilver, Danger app. 13,14-Mhan-a. 14-Scarlet Witch app. 15-17-Axis tie-in 4.00

ALL-NEW X-MEN
Marvel Comics: Jan, 2013 - No. 41, Aug, 2015 ($3.99)
1-Bendis-s; Immonen-a and wraparound-c; original X-Men time travel to present 4.00
2-24: 6-8-Marquez-a; Mystique app. 8-Avengers app. 16,17-Battle of the Atom tie-ins. 18-New uniforms. 22-24-Trial of Jean Grey; Guardians of the Galaxy app. 4.00
25-($4.99) Art by Marquez with pages by Timm, Mack, Young, Campbell & many others 5.00
26-41: 30-Pichelli-a. 31-36-X-Men in Ultimate universe; Miles Morales app. 38,39-Black Vortex x-over; Ronan & Guardians of the Galaxy app.; Sorrentino-a. 40-Iceman revealed as gay 4.00
Annual 1 (2/15, $4.99) Sorrentino-a; Eva Bell and Morgana Le Fey in the past 5.00
Special #1 (12/13, $4.99) Superior Spider-Man and the Hulk app. 5.00

ALL-NEW X-MEN
Marvel Comics: Feb, 2016 - Present ($3.99)
1-8-Hopeless-s/Bagley-a; original X-Men, Wolverine (X-23), Kid Apocalypse app. 4.00
9-($4.99) Apocalypse Wars x-over; Beast & Kid Apocalypse in ancient Egypt 5.00
10-18: 10,11-Apocalypse Wars; young Apocalypse app. 17,18-Inhumans app. 4.00
Annual 1 (1/17, $4.99) Spotlight on Idie; Sina Grace-s/Cory Smith-a 5.00
#1.MU (4/17, $4.99) Monsters Unleashed tie-in; Barberi & Lim-a; Gambit app. 5.00

ALL NIGHTER
Image Comics: Jun, 2011 - No. 5, Oct, 2011 ($2.99, B&W, limited series)
1-5-David Haun-s/a/c 3.00

ALL-OUT WAR
DC Comics: Sept-Oct, 1979 - No. 6, Aug, 1980 ($1.00, 68 pgs.)
1-The Viking Commando (origin), Force Three(origin), & Black Eagle Squadron begin
2 4 6 13 18 22
2-6 2 4 6 8 10 12
NOTE: *Ayers a(p)-1-6. Elias r-2. Evans a-1-6. Kubert c-16.*

ALL PICTURE ADVENTURE MAGAZINE
St. John Publishing Co.: Oct, 1952 - No. 2, Nov, 1952 (100 pg. Giants, 25¢, squarebound)
1-War comics 47 94 141 296 498 700
2-Horror-crime comics 58 116 174 371 636 900
NOTE: *Above books contain three St. John comics rebound; variations possible. **Baker** art known in both.*

ALL PICTURE ALL TRUE LOVE STORY
St. John Publishing Co.: Oct., 1952 - No. 2, Nov., 1952 (100 pgs., 25¢)
1-Canteen Kate by Matt Baker 68 136 204 435 743 1050
2-Baker-c/a 65 130 195 416 708 1000

ALL-PICTURE COMEDY CARNIVAL
St. John Publishing Co.: October, 1952 (100 pgs., 25¢)(Contains 4 rebound comics)
1-Contents can vary; Baker-a 45 90 135 284 480 675

ALL REAL CONFESSION MAGAZINE (See Fox Giants)

ALL ROMANCES (Mr. Risk No. 7 on)
A. A. Wyn (Ace Periodicals): Aug, 1949 - No. 6, June, 1950
1 17 34 51 98 154 210
2 11 22 33 60 83 105
3-6 10 20 30 54 72 90

ALL-SELECT COMICS (Blonde Phantom No. 12 on)
Timely Comics (Daring Comics): Fall, 1943 - No. 11, Fall, 1946
1-Capt. America (by Rico #1), Human Torch, Sub-Mariner begin; Black Widow story (4 pgs.); Classic Schomburg-c 1800 3600 5400 12,000 25,000 38,000
2-Red Skull app. 676 1352 2028 4935 8718 12,500
3-The Whizzer begins 432 864 1296 3154 5577 8000

GD VG FN VF VF/NM NM-
2.0 4.0 6.0 8.0 9.0 9.2

4,5-Last Sub-Mariner 360 720 1080 2520 4410 6300
6-9: 6-The Destroyer app. 8-No Whizzer 297 594 891 1888 3244 4600
10-The Destroyer & Sub-Mariner app.; last Capt. America & Human Torch issue
297 594 891 1888 3244 4600
11-1st app. Blonde Phantom; Miss America app.; all Blonde Phantom-c by Shores
300 600 900 1980 3440 4900
NOTE: ***Schomburg** c-1-10. **Sekowsky** a-7. #7 & 8 show 1944 in indicia, but should be 1945.*

ALL SELECT COMICS 70th ANNIVERARY SPECIAL
Marvel Comics: Sept, 2009 ($3.99, one-shot)
1-New stories of Blonde Phantom and Marvex the Super Robot; r/Marvex G.A. app. 5.00

ALL SPORTS COMICS (Formerly Real Sports Comics; becomes All Time Sports Comics No. 4 on)
Hillman Periodicals: No. 2, Dec-Jan, 1948-49; No. 3, Feb-Mar, 1949
2-Krigstein-a(p), Powell, Starr-a 36 72 108 211 343 475
3-Mort Lawrence-a 22 44 66 132 216 300

ALL STAR BATMAN
DC Comics: Oct, 2016 - Present ($4.99)
1-5-Snyder-s/Romita Jr.-a; Two-Face app.; back-up with Shalvey-a 5.00
1-Director's Cut ($5.99) r/#1 with B&W art and original script; variant cover gallery 6.00
6,7-Back-up w/Francavilla-a. 6-Jock-a; Mr. Freeze app. 7-Lotay-a; Poison Ivy app 5.00

ALL STAR BATMAN & ROBIN, THE BOY WONDER
DC Comics: Sept, 2005 - No. 10, Aug, 2008 ($2.99)
1-Two covers; retelling of Robin's origin; Frank Miller-s/Jim Lee-a/c 4.00
1-Diamond Retailer Summit Edition (9/05) sketch-c 60.00
2-10: 2-7-Two covers by Lee and Miller. 3-Black Canary app. 4-Six pg. Batcave gatefold.
10-Edition without profanity 3.00
8-10: 8,9-Variant cover by Neal Adams. 10-Variant-c by Quitely 5.00
10-Recalled edition with insufficiently covered profanity inside; Jim Lee-c 20.00
10-Recalled edition with variant Quitely-c 40.00
... Special Edition (2/06, $3.99) r/#1 with Lee pencil pages and Miller script; new Miller-c 4.00
Vol. 1 HC (2008, $24.99, dustjacket) r/#1-9; cover gallery, sketch pages; Schreck intro. 25.00
Vol. 1 SC (2009, $19.99) r/#1-9; cover gallery, sketch pages; Schreck intro. 20.00

ALL STAR COMICS
DC Comics: Spring 1940
1-Ashcan comic, not distributed to newsstands, only for in-house use. Cover art is Flash Comics #1 and interior from Detective Comics #37. A CGC certified 7.0 copy sold for $15,600 in 2002 and for $21,000 in May 2014.

ALL STAR COMICS (All Star Western No. 58 on)
National Periodical Publ./All-American/DC Comics: Sum, 1940 - No. 57, Feb-Mar, 1951; No. 58, Jan-Feb, 1976 - No. 74, Sept-Oct, 1978
1-The Flash (#1 by E.E. Hibbard), Hawkman (by Shelly), Hourman (by Bernard Baily), The Sandman (by Creig Flessel), The Spectre (by Baily), Biff Bronson, Red White & Blue (ends #2) begin; Ultra Man's only app. (#1-3 are quarterly; #4 begins bi-monthly issues)
1200 2400 3600 9000 17,000 25,000
2-Green Lantern (by Martin Nodell), Johnny Thunder begin; Green Lantern figure swipe from the cover of All-American Comics #16; Flash figure swipe from cover of Flash Comics #8; Moldoff/Bailey-c (cut & paste-c.) 530 1060 1590 3869 6835 9800
3-Origin & 1st app. The Justice Society of America (Win/40); Dr. Fate & The Atom begin, Red Tornado cameo 5600 11,200 16,800 45,000 90,000 135,000
3-Reprint, Oversize 13-1/2x10". **WARNING:** This comic is an exact reprint of the original except for its size. DC published it in 1974 with a second cover titling it as a Famous First Edition. There have been many reported cases of the outer cover being removed and the interior sold as the original edition. The reprint with the new outer cover removed is practically worthless. See Famous First Edition for value.
4-1st adventure for J.S.A. 541 1082 1623 3950 6975 10,000
5-1st app. Shiera Sanders as Hawkgirl (1st costumed super-heroine, 6-7/41)
497 994 1491 3628 6414 9200
6-Johnny Thunder joins JSA 300 600 900 1980 3440 4900
7-First time ever Superman and Batman appear in a story together; Superman, Batman and Flash become honorary members; last Hourman; Doiby Dickles app.
423 846 1269 3000 5250 7500
8-Origin & 1st app. Wonder Woman (12-1/41-42)(added as 9 pgs. making book 76 pgs.; origin cont'd in Sensation #1; see W.W. #1 for more detailed origin); Dr. Fate dons new helmet; Hop Harrigan text stories & Starman begin; Shiera app.; Hop Harrigan JSA guest; Starman & Dr. Mid-Nite become members
15,000 30,000 45,000 120,000 190,000 260,000
9-11: 9-JSA's girlfriends cameo; Shiera app.; J. Edgar Hoover of FBI made associate member of JSA. 10-Flash, Green Lantern cameo; Sandman new costume. 11-Wonder Woman begins; Spectre cameo; Shiera app.; Moldoff Hawkman-c
300 600 900 2010 3505 5000
12-Wonder Woman becomes JSA Secretary 300 600 900 1950 3375 4800
13,15: Sandman w/Sandy in #14 & 15. 13-Hitler app. in book-length sci-fi story. 15-Origin &

All Star Comics #38 © DC

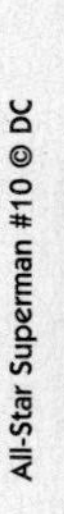
All-Star Superman #10 © DC

All Star Western (2011 series) #13 © DC

1st app. Brain Wave; Shiera app. 252 504 756 1613 2757 3900
14-(12/42) Junior JSA Club begins; w/membership offer & premiums
258 516 774 1651 2826 4000
16-20: 19-Sandman w/Sandy. 20-Dr. Fate & Sandman cameo
239 478 717 1530 2615 3700
21-23: 21-Spectre & Atom cameo; Dr. Fate by Kubert; Dr. Fate, Sandman end. 22-Last Hop Harrigan; Flag-c. 23-Origin/1st app. Psycho Pirate; last Spectre & Starman 181 362 543 1158 1979 2800
24-Flash & Green Lantern cameo; Mr. Terrific only app.; Wildcat, JSA guest; Kubert Hawkman begins; Hitler-c 187 374 561 1197 2049 2900
25-27: 25-Flash & Green Lantern start again. 26-Robot-c. 27-Wildcat, JSA guest (#24-26: only All-American imprint) 161 322 483 1030 1765 2500
28-32 148 296 444 947 1624 2300
33-Solomon Grundy & Doiby Dickles app; classic Solomon Grundy cover & last G.A. app.
400 800 1200 2800 4900 7000
34,35-Johnny Thunder cameo in both 135 270 405 864 1482 2100
36-Batman & Superman JSA guests 300 600 900 2010 3505 5000
37-Johnny Thunder cameo; origin & 1st app. Injustice Society; last Kubert Hawkman
187 374 561 1197 2049 2900
38-Black Canary begins; JSA Death issue 252 504 756 1613 2757 3900
39,40: 39-Last Johnny Thunder 129 258 387 826 1413 2000
41-Black Canary joins JSA; Injustice Society app. (2nd app.?)
129 258 387 826 1413 2000
42-Atom & the Hawkman don new costumes 129 258 387 826 1413 2000
43-49,51-56: 43-New logo; Robot-c. 55-Sci/Fi story. 56-Robot-c
129 258 387 826 1413 2000
50-Frazetta art, 3 pgs. 134 268 402 851 1463 2075
57-Kubert-a, 6 pgs. (Scarce); last app. G.A. Green Lantern, Flash & Dr. Mid-Nite
194 388 582 1242 2121 3000
V12 #58-(1976) JSA (Flash, Hawkman, Dr. Mid-Nite, Wildcat, Dr. Fate, Green Lantern, Robin & Star Spangled Kid) app.; intro. Power Girl 9 18 27 59 117 175
V12 #59,60: 59-Estrada & Wood-a 3 6 9 20 31 42
V12 #61-68: 62-65-Superman app. 64,65-Wood-c/a; Vandal Savage app. 66-Injustice Society app. 68-Psycho Pirate app. 3 6 9 20 31 42
V12 #69-1st Earth-2 Huntress (Helena Wayne) 6 12 18 40 73 105
V12 #70-73: 70-Full intro. of Huntress. 72-Thorn on-c 3 6 9 20 31 42
V12 #74-(44 pgs.) Last issue, story continues in Adventure Comics #461 & 462 (death of Earth-2 Batman; Staton-c/a 4 8 12 28 47 65
(See Justice Society Vol. 1 TPB for reprints of V12 revival)
NOTE: *No Atom-27, 36; no Dr. Fate-13; no Flash-8, 9, 11-23; no Green Lantern-8, 9,11-23; Hawkman in 1-57 (only one to app. in all 57 issues); no Johnny Thunder-5, 36; no Wonder Woman-9, 10, 23. Book length stories in 4-9, 11-14, 18-22, 25, 26, 29, 30, 32-36, 40, 42, 43. Johnny Peril in #42-46, 48, 49, 51, 52,54-57.* ***Baily*** *a-1-10, 12, 13, 14i, 15-20.* ***Burnley*** *Starman-8-13; c-12, 13.* ***Grell*** *c-58.* ***E.E. Hibbard*** *c-3, 4, 6-10.* ***Infantino*** *c-40.* ***Kubert*** *Hawkman-24-30, 33-37.* ***Lampert/Baily/Flessel*** *c-1, 2.* ***Moldoff*** *Hawkman-3-23; c-11.* ***Mart Nodell*** *c-25i, 26i, 27-32.* ***Purcell*** *c-5.* ***Simon & Kirby*** *Sandman 14-17, 19.* ***Staton*** *a-66-74p. c-74p.* ***Toth*** *a-37(2), 38(2), 40, 41; c-38, 41.* ***Wood*** *a-58i-63i, 64, 65; c-63i, 64, 65. Issues 1-7, 9-16 are 68 pgs.; #8 is 76 pgs.; #17-19 are 60 pgs.; #20-57 are 52 pgs.*

ALL STAR COMICS (Also see crossover 1999 editions of Adventure, All-American, National, Sensation, Smash, Star Spangled and Thrilling Comics)
DC Comics: May, 1999 - No. 2, May, 1999 ($2.95, bookends for JSA x-over)

1,2-Justice Society in World War 2; Robinson-s/Johnson-c 3.00
1-RRP Edition 45.00
...80-Page Giant (9/99, $4.95) Phantom Lady app. 5.00

ALL STAR INDEX, THE
Independent Comics Group (Eclipse): Feb, 1987 ($2.00, Baxter paper)

1 1 2 3 5 6 8

ALL-STAR SECTION EIGHT (Also see Sixpack and Dogwelder: Hard Travelin' Heroz)
DC Comics: Aug, 2015 - No. 6, Feb, 2016 ($2.99, limited series)

1-6-Ennis-s/McCrea-a/Conner-c. 1-Batman app. 4-Wonder Woman app. 6-Superman 3.00

ALL-STAR SQUADRON (See Justice League of America #193)
DC Comics: Sept, 1981 - No. 67, Mar, 1987

1-Original Atom, Hawkman, Dr. Mid-Nite, Robotman (origin), Plastic Man, Johnny Quick, Liberty Belle, Shining Knight begin 1 3 4 6 8 10
2-10: 3-Solomon Grundy app. 4,7-Spectre app. 8-Re-intro Steel, the Indestructable Man 5.00
11-24,26-46,48,49: 12-Origin G.A. Hawkman retold. 15-JLA, JSA & Crime Syndicate app. 23-Origin/1st app. The Amazing Man. 24-Batman app. 26-Origin Infinity, Inc.(2nd app.); Robin app. 27-Dr. Fate vs. The Spectre. 30-35-Spectre app. 33-Origin Freedom Fighters of Earth-X. 36,37-Superman vs. Capt. Marvel; Ordway-c. 41-Origin Starman 4.00
25-1st app. Nuklon (Atom Smasher) & Infinity, Inc. (9/83)
1 3 4 6 8 10
47-Origin Dr. Fate; McFarlane-a (1st full story)/part-c (7/85)
2 4 6 9 12 15
50-Double size; Crisis x-over 1 2 3 5 6 8
51-66: 51-56-Crisis x-over. 61-Origin Liberty Belle. 62-Origin The Shining Knight. 63-Origin Robotman. 65-Origin Johnny Quick. 66-Origin Tarantula 6.00
67-Last issue; retells first case of the Justice Society 1 2 3 5 6 8
Annual 1-3: 1(11/82)-Retells origin of G.A. Atom, Guardian & Wildcat; Jerry Ordway's 1st pencils for DC. (1st work was inking Carmine Infantino in Mystery in Space #117). 2(11/83)-Infinity, Inc. app. 3(9/84) 6.00
NOTE: ***Buckler*** *a-1-5; c-1, 3-5, 51.* ***Kubert*** *c-2, 7-18. JLA app. in 14, 15. JSA app. in 4, 14, 15, 19, 27, 28.*

ALL-STAR STORY OF THE DODGERS, THE
Stadium Communications: Apr, 1979 ($1.00)

1 2 4 6 9 13 16

ALL-STAR SUPERMAN (Also see FCBD edition in the Promotional Comics section)
DC Comics: Jan, 2006 - No. 12, Oct, 2008 ($2.99)

1-Grant Morrison-s/Frank Quitely-a/c 5.00
1-Variant-c by Neal Adams 20.00
1-Special Edition (2009, $1.00) r/#1 with "After Watchmen" cover logo frame 3.00
2-12: 3-Lois gets super powers. 7,8-Bizarro app. 3.00
Free Comic Book Day giveaway (6/08) reprints #1 3.00
Vol. 1 HC (2007, $19.99, dustjacket) r/#1-6; Bob Schreck intro. 20.00
Vol. 1 SC (2008, $12.99) r/#1-6; Schreck intro. 13.00
Vol. 2 HC (2009, $19.99, dustjacket) r/#7-12; Mark Waid intro. 20.00
Vol. 2 SC (2009, $12.99) r/#7-12; Mark Waid intro. 13.00

ALL STAR WESTERN (Formerly All Star Comics No. 1-57)
National Periodical Publ.: No. 58, Apr-May, 1951 - No. 119, June-July, 1961

58-Trigger Twins (ends #116), Strong Bow, The Roving Ranger & Don Caballero begin 52 104 156 328 552 775
59,60: Last 52 pgs. 31 62 93 186 303 420
61-66: 61-64-Toth-a 25 50 75 150 245 340
67-Johnny Thunder begins; Gil Kane-a 36 72 108 211 343 475
68-81: Last precode (2-3/55) 17 34 51 98 154 210
82-98: 97-1st S.A. issue 15 30 45 84 127 170
99-Frazetta-r/Jimmy Wakely #4 15 30 45 85 130 175
100 15 30 45 85 130 175
101-107,109-116,118,119: 103-Grey tone-c 14 28 42 80 115 150
108-Origin J. Thunder; J. Thunder logo begins 26 52 78 154 252 350
117-Origin Super Chief 16 32 48 94 147 200
NOTE: ***Gil Kane*** *c(p)-58, 59, 61, 63, 64, 68, 69, 70-95(most), 97-199(most).* ***Infantino*** *art in most issues. Madame .44 app.- #117-119.*

ALL-STAR WESTERN (Weird Western Tales No. 12 on)
National Periodical Publications: Aug-Sept, 1970 - No. 11, Apr-May, 1972

1-Pow-Wow Smith-r; Infantino-a 5 10 15 35 63 90
2-Outlaw begins; El Diablo by Morrow begins; has cameos by Williamson, Torres, Kane, Giordano & Phil Seuling 5 10 15 34 60 85
3-Origin El Diablo 5 10 15 31 53 75
4-6: 5-Last Outlaw issue. 6-Billy the Kid begins, ends #8
4 8 12 23 37 50
7-9-(52 pgs.) 9-Frazetta-a, 3pgs.(r) 4 8 12 25 40 55
10-(52 pgs.) Jonah Hex begins (1st app., 2-3/72) 34 68 102 245 548 850
11-(52 pgs.) 2nd app. Jonah Hex; 1st cover 13 26 39 89 195 300
NOTE: ***Neal Adams*** *c-2-5;* ***Aparo*** *a-5.* ***G. Kane*** *a-3, 4, 6, 8.* ***Kubert*** *a-4r, 7-9r.* ***Morrow*** *a-2-4, 10, 11. No. 7-11 have 52 pgs.*

ALL STAR WESTERN (DC New 52)
DC Comics: Nov, 2011 - No. 34, Oct, 2014 ($3.99)

1-34: 1-Jonah Hex in 1880s Gotham City; Gray & Palmiotti-s/Moritat-a. 2,3-El Diablo back-up. 9-11-Court of Owls. 10-Bat Lash back-up; Garcia-López-a. 13-16-Tomahawk back-up. 19-21-Booster Gold app. 21-28-Hex in present day. 22-Batman app. 27-Superman app. 30,31-Madame .44 back-up; Garcia-López-a. 34-Darwyn Cooke-c/a 4.00
#0 (11/12, $3.99) Jonah Hex's full origin; Gray & Palmiotti-s/Moritat-a 4.00

ALL SURPRISE (Becomes Jeanie #13 on) (Funny animal)
Timely/Marvel (CPC): Fall, 1943 - No. 12, Winter, 1946-47

1-Super Rabbit, Gandy & Sourpuss begin 55 110 165 352 601 850
2 23 46 69 136 223 310
3-10,12 19 38 57 111 176 240
11-Kurtzman "Pigtales" art 20 40 60 114 182 250

ALL TEEN (Formerly All Winners; All Winners & Teen Comics No. 21 on)
Marvel Comics (WFP): No. 20, January, 1947

20-Georgie, Mitzi, Patsy Walker, Willie app.; Syd Shores-c
34 68 102 199 325 450

ALL-TIME SPORTS COMICS (Formerly All Sports Comics)
Hillman Per.: V2, No. 4, Apr-May, 1949 - V2, No. 7, Oct-Nov, 1949 (All 52 pgs.)

V2#4 23 46 69 136 223 310
5-7: 5-(V1#5 inside)-Powell-a; Ty Cobb sty. 7-Krigstein-p; Walter Johnson &

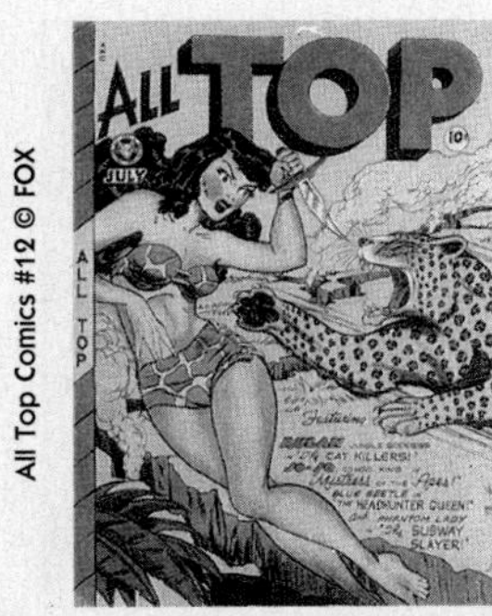

All Top Comics #12 © FOX

All Winners Comics #10 © MAR

Alpha: Big Time #1 © MAR

GD VG FN VF VF/NM NM-
2.0 4.0 6.0 8.0 9.0 9.2

Knute Rockne sty 18 36 54 105 165 225

ALL TOP
William H. Wise Co.: 1944 (132 pgs.)

nn-Capt. V, Merciless the Sorceress, Red Robbins, One Round Hogan, Mike the M.P., Snooky, Pussy Katnip app. 40 80 120 246 411 575

ALL TOP COMICS (My Experience No. 19 on)
Fox Features Synd./Green Publ./Norlen Mag.: 1945; No. 2, Sum, 1946 - No. 18, Jul, 1949; 1957 - 1959

1-Cosmo Cat & Flash Rabbit begin (1st app.) 33 66 99 194 317 440
2 (#1-7 are funny animal) 16 32 48 94 147 200
3-7: 7-Two diff. issues (7/47 & 9/47) 14 28 42 80 115 150
8-Blue Beetle, Phantom Lady, & Rulah, Jungle Goddess begin (11/47); Kamen-c 300 600 900 1950 3375 4800
9-Kamen-c 155 310 465 992 1696 2400
10-Classic Kamen bondage/torture/dwarf-c 187 374 561 1197 2049 2900
11-13,15,17: 11,12-Rulah-c. 15-No Blue Beetle 129 258 387 826 1413 2000
14-No Blue Beetle; used in **SOTI**, illo- "Corpses of colored people strung up by their wrists" 200 400 600 1280 2190 3100
16-Classic Good Girl octopus-c 168 336 504 1075 1838 2600
18-Dagar, Jo-Jo app; no Phantom Lady or Blue Beetle 87 174 261 553 952 1350
6(1957-Green Publ.)-Patoruzu the Indian; Cosmo Cat on cover only. 6(1958-Literary Ent.)-Muggy Doo; Cosmo Cat on cover only. 6(1959-Norlen)-Atomic Mouse; Cosmo Cat on-c only. 6(1959)-Little Eva. 6(Cornell)-Supermouse on-c 5 10 15 24 30 35
NOTE: *Jo-Jo by* ***Kamen****-12,18.*

ALL TRUE ALL PICTURE POLICE CASES
St. John Publishing Co.: Oct, 1952 - No. 2, Nov, 1952 (100 pgs.)

1-Three rebound St. John crime comics 53 106 159 334 567 800
2-Three comics rebound 41 82 123 256 428 600
NOTE: *Contents may vary.*

ALL-TRUE CRIME (...Cases No. 26-35; formerly Official True Crime Cases)
Marvel/Atlas Comics: No. 26, Feb, 1948 - No. 52, Sept, 1952
(OFI #26,27/CFI #28,29/LCC #30-46/LMC #47-52)

26(#1)-Syd Shores-c 39 78 117 231 378 525
27(4/48)-Electric chair-c 32 64 96 192 314 435
28-41,43-48,50-52: 35-37-Photo-c 15 30 45 86 133 180
42,49-Krigstein-a. 49-Used in **POP**, Pg 79 15 30 45 90 140 190
NOTE: ***Colan*** *a-46.* ***Keller*** *a-46.* ***Robinson*** *a-47, 50.* ***Sale*** *a-46.* ***Shores*** *c-26.* ***Tuska*** *a-48(3).*

ALL-TRUE DETECTIVE CASES (Kit Carson No. 5 on)
Avon Periodicals: #2, Apr-May, 1954 - No. 4, Aug-Sept, 1954

2(#1)-Wood-a 27 54 81 158 259 360
3-Kinstler-c 15 30 45 88 137 185
4-r/Gangsters And Gun Molls #2; Kamen-a 20 40 60 117 189 260
nn(100 pgs.)-7 pg. Kubert-a, Kinstler back-c 50 100 150 315 533 750

ALL TRUE ROMANCE (...Illustrated No. 3)
Artful Publ. #1-3/Harwell(Comic Media) #4-20?/Ajax-Farrell(Excellent Publ.) No. 22 on/Four Star Comic Corp.: 3/51 - No. 20, 12/54; No. 22, 3/55 - No. 30?, 7/57; No. 3(#31), 9/57;No. 4(#32), 11/57; No. 33, 2/58 - No. 34, 6/58

1 (3/51) 24 48 72 140 230 320
2 (10/51; 11/51 on-c) 14 28 42 82 121 160
3(12/51) - #5(5/52) 13 26 39 74 105 135
6-Wood-a, 9 pgs. (exceptional) 22 44 66 128 209 290
7-10 [two #7s: #7(11/52, 9/52 inside), #7(11/52, 11/52 inside)]. 10-Hollingsworth-c 12 24 36 69 97 125
11-13,16-19(9/54),20(12/54) (no #21): 11,13-Heck-a 11 22 33 60 83 105
14-Marijuana story 11 22 33 62 86 110
22: Last precode issue (1st Ajax, 3/55) 11 22 33 60 83 105
23-27,29,30(7/57): 29-Disbrow-a 9 18 27 52 68 90
28 (9/56)-L. B. Cole, Disbrow-a 14 28 42 76 108 140
3(#31, 9/57),4(#32, 11/57),33,34 (Farrell, '57- '58) 9 18 27 50 65 80

ALL WESTERN WINNERS (Formerly All Winners; becomes Western Winners with No. 5; see Two-Gun Kid No. 5)
Marvel Comics(CDS): No. 2, Winter, 1948-49 - No. 4, April, 1949

2-Black Rider (origin/1st app.) & his horse Satan, Kid Colt & his horse Steel, & Two-Gun Kid & his horse Cyclone begin; Shores c-2-4 76 152 228 486 831 1175
3-Anti-Wertham editorial 39 78 117 236 388 540
4-Black Rider i.d. revealed; Heath, Shores-a 39 78 117 236 388 540

ALL WINNERS COMICS (All Teen #20) (Also see Timely Presents: ...)
USA No. 1-7/WFP No. 10-19/YAI No. 21: Summer, 1941 - No. 19, Fall, 1946; No. 21, Winter, 1946-47; (No #20) (No. 21 continued from Young Allies No. 20)

GD VG FN VF VF/NM NM-
2.0 4.0 6.0 8.0 9.0 9.2

1-The Angel & Black Marvel only app.; Capt. America by Simon & Kirby, Human Torch & Sub-Mariner begin (#1 was advertised as All Aces); 1st app. All-Winners Squad in text story by Stan Lee 1900 3800 5700 13,500 24,750 36,000
2-The Destroyer & The Whizzer begin; Simon & Kirby Captain America 541 1082 1623 3950 6975 10,000
3 459 918 1377 3350 5925 8500
4-Classic War-c by Al Avison 519 1038 1557 3789 6695 9600
5 377 754 1131 2639 4620 6600
6-The Black Avenger only app.; no Whizzer story; Hitler, Hirohito & Mussolini-c 595 1190 1785 4350 7675 11,000
7-10 377 754 1131 2639 4620 6600
11,13-15: 11-1st Atlas globe on-c (Winter, 1943-44; also see Human Torch #14). 14,15-No Human Torch 297 594 891 1901 3251 4600
12-Red Skull story; last Destroyer; no Whizzer story 354 708 1062 2478 4339 6200
16-18: 16-No Human Torch 232 464 696 1485 2543 3600
19-(Scarce)-1st story app. & origin All Winners Squad (Capt. America & Bucky, Human Torch & Toro, Sub-Mariner, Whizzer, & Miss America; r-in Fantasy Masterpieces #10 892 1784 2676 6512 13,006 19,500
21-(Scarce)-All Winners Squad; bondage-c 687 1374 2061 5015 10,258 15,500
NOTE: ***Everett*** *Sub-Mariner-1, 3, 4;* ***Burgos*** *Torch-1, 3, 4.* ***Schomburg*** *c-1, 7-18.* ***Shores*** *c-19p, 21.*

(2nd Series - August, 1948, Marvel Comics (CDS))
(Becomes All Western Winners with No. 2)

1-The Blonde Phantom, Capt. America, Human Torch, & Sub-Mariner app. 303 606 909 2121 3711 5300

ALL WINNERS COMICS 70th ANNIVERARY SPECIAL
Marvel Comics: Oct, 2009 ($3.99, one-shot)

1-New story of All Winners Squad; r/G.A. Capt Anerica app. from All Winners #12 5.00

ALL-WINNERS SQUAD: BAND OF HEROES
Marvel Comics: Aug, 2011 - No. 5, Dec, 2011 ($2.99, unfinished limited series of 8 issues)

1-5-WWII story of the Young Avenger and Captain Flame; Jenkins-s/DiGiandomenico-a 3.00

ALL YOUR COMICS (See Fox Giants)
Fox Feature Syndicate (R. W. Voight): Spring, 1946 (36 pgs.)

1-Red Robbins, Merciless the Sorceress app. 22 44 66 128 209 290

ALMANAC OF CRIME (See Fox Giants)

AL OF FBI (See Little Al of the FBI)

ALOHA, HAWAIIAN DICK (Also see Hawaiian Dick)
Image Comics: Apr, 2016 - No. 5, Aug, 2016 ($3.99, limited series)

1-5-B. Clay Moore-s. 1-4-Jacob Wyatt-a. 5-Paul Reinwand-a 4.00

ALONE IN THE DARK (Based on video game)
Image Comics: Feb, 2003 ($4.95)

1-Matt Haley-c/a; Jean-Marc & Randy Lofficier-s 5.00

ALPHA AND OMEGA
Spire Christian Comics (Fleming H. Revell): 1978 (49¢)

nn 2 4 6 9 13 16

ALPHA: BIG TIME (See Amazing Spider-Man #692-694)
Marvel Comics: Apr, 2013 - No. 5, Aug, 2015 ($2.99)

1-5-Fialkov-s/Plati-a/Ramos-c. 1,3,5-Superior Peter Parker app. 4-Thor app. 3.00

ALPHA CENTURION (See Superman, 2nd Series & Zero Hour)
DC Comics: 1996 ($2.95, one-shot)

1 3.00

ALPHA FLIGHT (See X-Men #120,121 & X-Men/Alpha Flight)
Marvel Comics: Aug, 1983 - No. 130, Mar, 1994 (#52-on are direct sales only)

1-(52 pgs.) Byrne-a begins (thru #28) -Wolverine & Nightcrawler cameo 2 4 6 8 10 12
2-11,13-28: 2-Vindicator becomes Guardian; origin Marrina & Alpha Flight. 3-Concludes origin Alpha Flight. 6-Origin Shaman. 7-Origin Snowbird. 10,11-Origin Sasquatch. 13-Wolverine app. 16,17-Wolverine cameo. 17-X-Men x-over (mostly r-/X-Men #109). 20-New headquarters. 25-Return of Guardian. 28-Last Byrne issue 3.50
12-(52 pgs.)-Death of Guardian 4.00
29-32,35-49: 39-47,49-Portacio-a(i) 3.00
33-1st app. Lady Deathstrike; Wolverine app. 2 4 6 9 12 15
34-2nd app. Lady Deathstrike; origin Wolverine 6.00
50-Double size; Portacio-a(i) 4.00
51-Jim Lee's 1st work at Marvel (10/87); Wolverine cameo; 1st Lee Wolverine; Portacio-a(i) 1 2 3 5 6 8
52,53-Wolverine app.; Lee-a on Wolverine; Portacio-a(i); 53-Lee/Portacio-a 4.00
54-73,76-86,91-99,101-105: 54,63,64-No Jim Lee-a. 54-Portacio-a(i). 55-62-Jim Lee-a(p).

Alpha Flight V2 #11 © MAR

Altered Image #1 © Jim Valentino

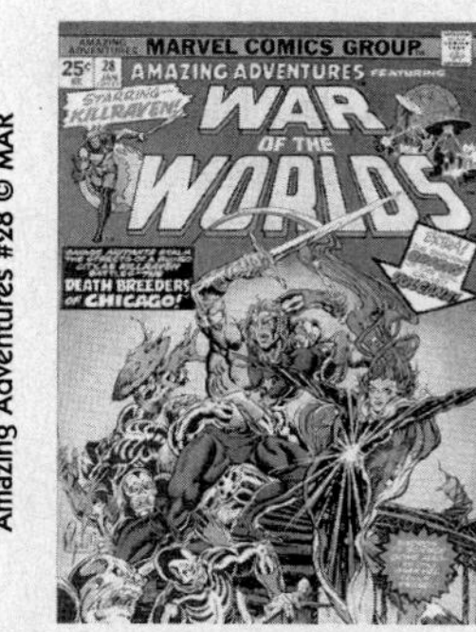

Amazing Adventures #28 © MAR

	GD 2.0	VG 4.0	FN 6.0	VF 8.0	VF/NM 9.0	NM- 9.2

71-Intro The Sorcerer (villain). 91-Dr. Doom app. 94-F.F. x-over. 99-Galactus, Avengers app. 102-Intro Weapon Omega 3.00
74,75,87-90,100: 74-Wolverine, Spider-Man & The Avengers app. 75-Double size ($1.95, 52 pgs.). 87-90-Wolverine. 4 part story w/Jim Lee-c. 89-Original Guardian returns. 100-($2.00, 52 pgs.)-Avengers & Galactus app. 4.00
106-Northstar revealed to be gay 3.50
106-2nd printing (direct sale only) 3.00
107-109,112-119,121-129: 107-X-Factor x-over. 112-Infinity War x-overs. 115-1st Wyre 3.00
110,111: Infinity War x-overs, Wolverine app. (brief). 111-Thanos cameo 3.00
120-($2.25)-Polybagged w/Paranormal Registration Act poster 4.00
130-($2.25, 52 pgs.) 4.00
Annual 1,2 (9/86, 12/87) 4.00
...Classics Vol. 1 TPB (2007, $24.99) r/#1-8; character profile pages; Byrne interview 25.00
Special V2#1(6/92, $2.50, 52 pgs.)-Wolverine-c/story 4.00
NOTE: ***Austin*** *c-1i, 2i, 53i.* ***Byrne*** *c-81, 82.* ***Guice*** *c-85, 91-99.* ***Jim Lee*** *a(p)-51, 53, 55-62, 64; c-53, 87-90.* ***Mignola*** *a-29-31p.* ***Whilce Portacio*** *a(i)-39-47, 49-54.*

ALPHA FLIGHT (2nd Series)
Marvel Comics: Aug, 1997 - No. 20, Mar, 1999 ($2.99/$1.99)

1-($2.99)-Wraparound cover 6.00
2,3: 2-Variant-c 4.00
4-11: 8,9-Wolverine-c/app. 3.00
12-($2.99) Death of Sasquatch; wraparound-c 4.00
13-15,18-20 3.00

	GD	VG	FN	VF	VF/NM	NM-
16-1st app. cameo Honey Lemon (Big Hero 6)	1	2	3	5	6	8
17-1st app. Big Hero 6	2	4	6	10	14	18

.../Inhumans '98 Annual ($3.50) Raney-a 4.00

ALPHA FLIGHT (3rd Series)
Marvel Comics: May, 2004 - No. 12, April, 2005 ($2.99)

1-12: 1-6-Lobdell-s/Henry-c/a 3.00
... Vol. 1: You Gotta Be Kiddin' Me (2004, $14.99) r/#1-6 15.00

ALPHA FLIGHT (4th Series)
Marvel Comics: No. 0.1, Jul, 2011 - No. 8, Mar, 2012 ($2.99)

0.1-Pak & Van Lente-s/Oliver & Green-a; Kara Killgrave app. 3.00
1-(8/11, $3.99) Fear Itself tie-in; Eaglesham-a/Jimenez-c; bonus design sketch pages 4.00
2-8-($2.99) Fear Itself tie-ins. 2-Puck returns. 5-Taskmaster app. 7,8-Wolverine app. 3.00

ALPHA FLIGHT: IN THE BEGINNING
Marvel Comics: July, 1997 ($1.95, one-shot)

(-1)-Flashback w/Wolverine 3.00

ALPHA FLIGHT SPECIAL
Marvel Comics: July, 1991 - No. 4, Oct, 1991 ($1.50, limited series)

1-4: 1-3-r-A. Flight #97-99 w/covers. 4-r-A.Flight #100 3.00

ALPHA KING (3 FLOYDS:...)
Image Comics: May, 2016 - Present ($3.99)

1-3-Azzarello & Floyd-s/Bisley-a/c 4.00

ALTERED IMAGE
Image Comics: Apr, 1998 - No. 3, Sept, 1998 ($2.50, limited series)

1-3-Spawn, Witchblade, Savage Dragon; Valentino-s/a 3.00

ALTERED STATES
Dynamite Entertainment: 2015 ($3.99, series of one-shots)

...: Doc Savage - Alternate reality Doc Savage in caveman past; Philip Tan-c 4.00
...: Red Sonja - Alternate reality Sonja in modern day New York City; Philip Tan-c 4.00
...: The Shadow - Alternate reality Shadow in sci-fi future; Philip Tan-c 4.00
...: Vampirella - Alternate reality Vampirella as a mortal on Drakulon; Collins-s 4.00

ALTER EGO
First Comics: May, 1986 - No. 4, Nov, 1986 (Mini-series)

1-4 3.00

ALTER NATION
Image Comics: Feb, 2004 - No. 4, Jun, 2004 ($2.95, limited series)

1-4: 1-Two covers by Art Adams and Barberi; Barberi-a 3.00

ALTERS
AfterShock Comics: Sept, 2016 - Present ($3.99)

1-4: 1-Paul Jenkins-s/Leila Leiz-a 4.00

ALVIN (TV) (See Four Color Comics No. 1042 or Three Chipmunks #1)
Dell Publishing Co.: Oct-Dec, 1962 - No. 28, Oct, 1973

	GD	VG	FN	VF	VF/NM	NM-
12-021-212 (#1)	8	16	24	51	96	140
2	5	10	15	31	53	75
3-10	4	8	12	28	47	65
11-"Chipmunks sing the Beatles' Hits"	5	10	15	31	53	75
12-28	4	8	12	23	37	50
Alvin For President (10/64)	4	8	12	28	47	65
...& His Pals in Merry Christmas with Clyde Crashcup & Leonardo 1 (25¢ Giant) (02-120-402)-(12-2/64)	6	12	18	42	79	115
Reprinted in 1966 (12-023-604)	4	8	12	23	37	50

ALVIN & THE CHIPMUNKS
Harvey Comics: July, 1992 - No. 5, May, 1994

1-5: 1-Richie Rich app. 5.00

AMALGAM AGE OF COMICS, THE: THE DC COMICS COLLECTION
DC Comics: 1996 ($12.95, trade paperback)

nn-r/Amazon, Assassins, Doctor Strangefate, JLX, Legends of the Dark Claw, & Super Soldier 13.00

AMANDA AND GUNN
Image Comics: Apr, 1997 - No. 4, Oct, 1997 ($2.95, B&W, limited series)

1-4 3.00

AMAZING ADULT FANTASY (Formerly Amazing Adventures #1-6; becomes Amazing Fantasy #15) (See Amazing Fantasy for Omnibus HC reprint of #1-15)
Marvel Comics Group (AMI): No. 7, Dec, 1961 - No. 14, July, 1962

	GD	VG	FN	VF	VF/NM	NM-
7-Ditko-c/a begins, ends #14	50	100	150	400	900	1400
8-Last 10¢ issue	45	90	135	333	754	1175
9-13: 12-1st app. Mailbag. 13-Anti-communist story	44	88	132	326	738	1150
13-2nd printing (1994)	2	4	6	8	10	12
14-Prototype issue (Professor X)	46	92	138	368	834	1300

AMAZING ADVENTURE FUNNIES (Fantoman No. 2 on)
Centaur Publications: June, 1940 - No. 2, Sept. 1940

	GD	VG	FN	VF	VF/NM	NM-
1-The Fantom of the Fair by Gustavson (r/Amaz. Mystery Funnies V2#7,V2#8), The Arrow, Skyrocket Steele From the Year X by Everett (r/AMF #2); Burgos-a	200	400	600	1280	2190	3100
2-Reprints; Published after Fantoman #2	129	258	387	826	1413	2000

NOTE: ***Burgos*** *a-1(2).* ***Everett*** *a-1(3).* ***Gustavson*** *a-1(5), 2(3).* ***Pinajian*** *a-2.*

AMAZING ADVENTURES (Also see Boy Cowboy & Science Comics)
Ziff-Davis Publ. Co.: 1950; No. 1, Nov, 1950 - No. 6, Fall, 1952 (Painted covers)

	GD	VG	FN	VF	VF/NM	NM-
1950 (no month given) (8-1/2x11) (8 pgs.) Has the front & back cover plus Schomburg story used in Amazing Advs. #1 (Sent to subscribers of Z-D s/f magazines & ordered through mail for 10¢. Used to test market)	77	154	231	493	847	1200
1-Wood, Schomburg, Anderson, Whitney-a	97	194	291	621	1061	1500
2,3,5: 2-Schomburg-a. 2,5-Anderson-a. 3,5-Starr-a	47	94	141	296	498	700
4-Classic-c; Anderson-a	61	122	183	390	670	950
6-Krigstein-a	48	96	144	302	514	725

AMAZING ADVENTURES (Becomes Amazing Adult Fantasy #7 on) (See Amazing Fantasy for Omnibus HC reprint of #1-15)
Atlas Comics (AMI)/Marvel Comics No. 3 on: June, 1961 - No. 6, Nov, 1961

	GD	VG	FN	VF	VF/NM	NM-
1-Origin Dr. Droom (1st Marvel-Age Superhero) by Kirby; Kirby/Ditko-a (5 pgs.) Ditko & Kirby-a in all; Kirby monster c-1-6	129	258	387	1032	2316	3600
2	50	100	150	384	867	1350
3-6: 6-Last Dr. Droom	46	92	138	350	788	1225

AMAZING ADVENTURES
Marvel Comics Group: Aug, 1970 - No. 39, Nov, 1976

	GD	VG	FN	VF	VF/NM	NM-
1-Inhumans by Kirby(p) & Black Widow (1st app. in Tales of Suspense #52) double feature begins	7	14	21	49	92	135
2-4: 2-F.F. brief app. 4-Last Inhumans by Kirby	3	6	9	21	33	45
5-8: Adams-a(p); 8-Last Black Widow; last 15¢-c	5	10	15	30	50	70
9,10: Magneto app. 10-Last Inhumans (origin-r by Kirby)	4	8	12	25	40	55
11-New Beast begins(1st app. in mutated form; origin in flashback); X-Men cameo in flashback (#11-17 are X-Men tie-ins)	18	36	54	124	275	425
12-17: 12-Beast battles Iron Man. 13-Brotherhood of Evil Mutants x-over from X-Men. 15-X-Men app. 16-Rutland Vermont - Bald Mountain Halloween x-over; Juggernaut app. 17-Last Beast (origin); X-Men app.	7	14	21	48	89	130
18-War of the Worlds begins (5/73); 1st app. Killraven; Neal Adams-a(p)	4	8	12	27	44	60
19-35,38,39: 19-Chaykin-a. 25-Buckler-a. 35-Giffen's first published story (art), along with Deadly Hands of Kung-Fu #22 (3/76)	1	3	4	6	8	10
36,37-(Regular 25¢ edition)(7-8/76)	1	3	4	6	8	10
36,37-(30¢-c variants, limited distribution)	4	8	12	27	44	60

NOTE: ***N. Adams*** *c-6-8.* ***Buscema*** *a-1p, 2p.* ***Colan*** *a-3-5p, 26p.* ***Ditko*** *a-24r.* ***Everett*** *a(i)3-5, 7-9.* ***Giffen*** *a-35i, 38p.* ***G. Kane*** *c-11, 25p, 29p.* ***Ploog*** *a-12i.* ***Russell*** *a-27-32, 34-37, 39; c-28, 30-32, 33i, 34, 35, 37, 39i.* ***Starlin*** *a-17.* ***Starlin*** *c-15p, 16, 17, 27.* ***Sutton*** *a-11-15p.*

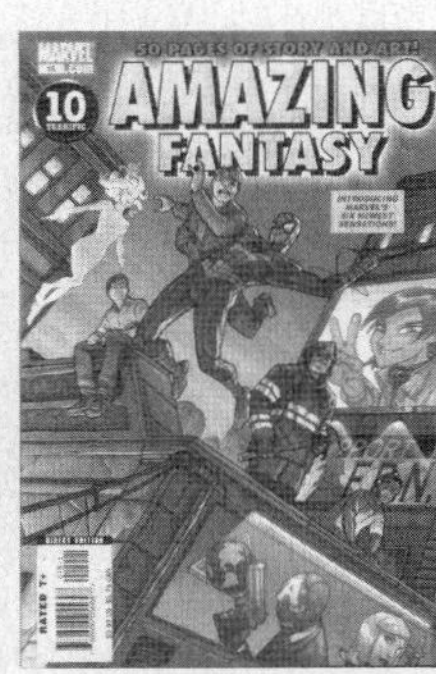

Amazing Fantasy (2004 series) #15 © MAR

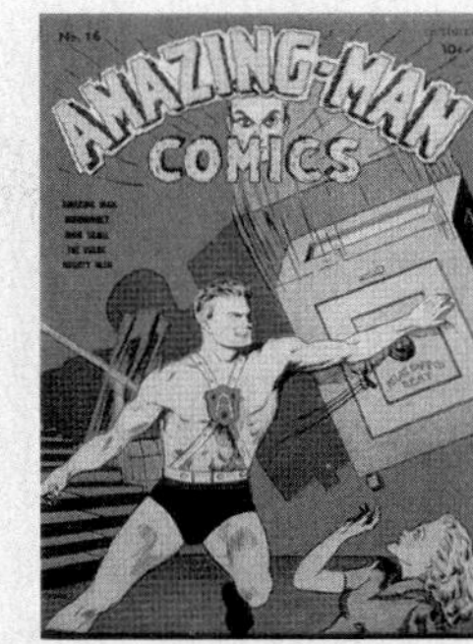

Amazing-Man Comics #16 © CEN

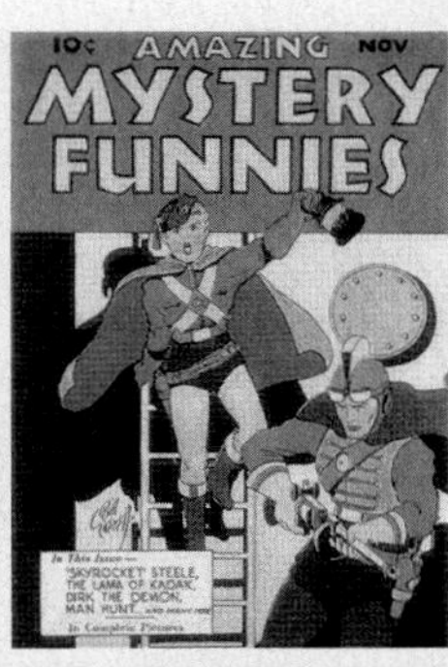

Amazing Mystery Funnies #3 © CEN

GD 2.0 VG 4.0 FN 6.0 VF 8.0 VF/NM 9.0 NM- 9.2

AMAZING ADVENTURES
Marvel Comics Group: Dec, 1979 - No. 14, Jan, 1981

V2#1-Reprints story/X-Men #1 & 38 (origins) 3 6 9 14 20 25
2-14: 2-6-Early X-Men-r. 7,8-Origin Iceman 2 4 6 8 10 12
NOTE: ***Byrne*** *c-6p, 9p.* ***Kirby*** *a-1-14r; c-7, 9.* ***Steranko*** *a-12r.* ***Tuska*** *a-7-9.*

AMAZING ADVENTURES
Marvel Comics: July, 1988 ($4.95, squarebound, one-shot, 80 pgs.)

1-Anthology; Austin, Golden-a 5.00

AMAZING ADVENTURES OF CAPTAIN CARVEL AND HIS CARVEL CRUSADERS, THE
(See Carvel Comics in the Promotional Comics section)

AMAZING CHAN & THE CHAN CLAN, THE (TV)
Gold Key: May, 1973 - No. 4, Feb, 1974 (Hanna-Barbera)

1-Warren Tufts-a in all 3 6 9 21 33 45
2-4 3 6 9 16 23 30

AMAZING COMICS (Complete Comics No. 2)
Timely Comics (EPC): Fall, 1944

1-The Destroyer, The Whizzer, The Young Allies (by Sekowsky), Sergeant Dix;
Schomburg-c 290 580 870 1856 3178 4500

AMAZING DETECTIVE CASES (Formerly Suspense No. 2?)
Marvel/Atlas Comics (CCC): No. 3, Nov, 1950 - No. 14, Sept, 1952

3 34 68 102 199 325 450
4-6: 6-Jerry Robinson-a 20 40 60 114 182 250
7-10 18 36 54 105 165 225
11,12: 11-(3/52)-Horror format begins. 12-Krigstein-a 53 106 159 334 567 800
13-(Scarce)-Everett-a; electrocution-c/story 58 116 174 371 636 900
14 50 100 150 315 533 750
NOTE: ***Colan*** *a-9.* ***Maneely*** *c-13.* ***Sekowsky*** *a-12.* ***Sinnott*** *a-13.* ***Tuska*** *a-10.*

AMAZING FANTASY (Formerly Amazing Adult Fantasy #7-14)
Atlas Magazines/Marvel: #15, Aug, 1962 (Sept, 1962 shown in indicia); #16, Dec, 1995 - #18, Feb, 1996

15-Origin/1st app. of Spider-Man by Steve Ditko (11 pgs.); 1st app. Aunt May & Uncle Ben;
Kirby/Ditko-c 7000 14,000 28,000 80,000 215,000 350,000
16-18 ('95-'96, $3.95): Kurt Busiek scripts; painted-c/a by Paul Lee 4.00
Amazing Fantasy #15: Spider-Man! (8/12, $3.99) recolored rep. of #15 and ASM #1 4.00
Amazing Fantasy Omnibus HC ("Amazing Adult Fantasy" on-c) (2007, $75.00, dustjacket)
r/Amazing Adventures #1-6, Amazing Adult Fantasy #7-14 and Amazing Fantasy #15 with
letter pages; foreword by Bissette; cover gallery from '70s reprint titles 75.00

AMAZING FANTASY (Continues from #6 in Araña: The Heart of the Spider)
Marvel Comics: Aug, 2004 - No. 20, June, 2006 ($2.99)

1-Intro. Anya Corazon; Fiona Avery-s/Mark Brooks-c/a 4.00
2-14,16-20: 3,4-Roger Cruz-a. 7-Intro. new Scorpion; Kirk-a. 10-Intro. Vampire By Night
13,14-Back-up Captain Universe stories. 16-20-Death's Head 3.00
15-($3.99, 1/06) Spider-Man app.; intro 6 new characters incl. Amadeus Cho/Mastermind
Excello seen in World War Hulk series; s/a by various
3 6 9 16 23 30
Death's Head 3.0: Unnatural Selection TPB (2006, $13.99) r/#16-20 14.00
Scorpion: Poison Tomorrow (2005, $7.99, digest) r/#7-13 8.00

AMAZING GHOST STORIES (Formerly Nightmare)
St. John Publishing Co.: No. 14, Oct, 1954 - No. 16, Feb, 1955

14-Pit & the Pendulum story by Kinstler; Baker-c 41 82 123 256 428 600
15-r/Weird Thrillers #5; Baker-c, Powell-a 36 72 108 211 343 475
16-Kubert reprints of Weird Thrillers #4; Baker-c; Roussos, Tuska-a;
Kinstler-a (1 pg.) 36 72 108 211 343 475

AMAZING HIGH ADVENTURE
Marvel Comics: 8/84; No. 2, 10/85; No. 3, 10/86 - No. 5, 1986 ($2.00)

1-5: Painted-c on all. 3,4-Baxter paper. 4-Bolton-c/a. 5-Bolton-a 4.00
NOTE: ***Bissette*** *a-4.* ***Severin*** *a-1, 3.* ***Sienkiewicz*** *a-1,2.* ***Paul Smith*** *a-2.* ***Williamson*** *a-2i.*

AMAZING JOY BUZZARDS
Image Comics: 2005 - No. 4, 2005 ($2.95, B&W with pink spot color in #1)

1-4-Mark Andrew Smith-s/Dan Hipp-a. 1-Mahfood back-c. 2-Morse back-c 3.00
Vol. 1 TPB (2005, $11.95) r/#1-4; bonus art and character design sketches 12.00
TPB (2008, $19.99) r/#1-4 and Vol. 2 #1-5 20.00

AMAZING JOY BUZZARDS (Volume 2)
Image Comics: Oct, 2005 - No. 5, Aug, 2006 ($2.99, B&W)

1-5: 1-Mark Andrew Smith-s/Dan Hipp-a. 4-Mahfood-a; Crosland-a. 5-Holgate-a 3.00
Vol. 2 TPB (2006, $12.99) r/#1-4; bonus art, pin-ups and character sketches 13.00

AMAZING-MAN COMICS (Formerly Motion Picture Funnies Weekly?)
(Also see Stars And Stripes Comics)
Centaur Publications: No. 5, Sept, 1939 - No. 26, Jan, 1942

5(#1)(Rare)-Origin/1st app. A-Man the Amazing Man by Bill Everett; The Cat-Man by Tarpe
Mills (also #8), Mighty Man by Filchock, Minimidget & sidekick Ritty, & The Iron Skull by
Burgos begins 2100 4200 6300 17,000 28,500 40,000
6-Origin The Amazing Man retold; The Shark begins; Ivy Menace by Tarpe Mills app.
423 846 1269 3000 5250 7500
7-Magician From Mars begins; ends #11 300 600 900 2010 3505 5000
8-Cat-Man dresses as woman 239 478 717 1530 2615 3700
9-Magician From Mars battles the 'Elemental Monster,' swiped into The Spectre in More Fun
#54 & 55. Ties w/Marvel Mystery #4 for 1st Nazi War-c on a comic (2/40)
252 504 756 1613 2757 3900
10,11: 11-Zardi, the Eternal Man begins; ends #16; Amazing Man dons costume;
last Everett issue 181 362 543 1158 1979 2800
12,13 168 336 504 1075 1838 2600
14-Reef Kinkaid, Rocke Wayburn (ends #20), & Dr. Hypno (ends #21) begin;
no Zardi or Chuck Hardy 142 284 426 909 1555 2200
15,17-20: 15-Zardi returns; no Rocke Wayburn. 17-Dr. Hypno returns; no Zardi
126 252 378 806 1378 1950
16-Mighty Man's powers of super strength & ability to shrink & grow explained; Rocke Wayburn
returns; no Dr. Hypno; Al Avison (a character) begins, ends #18 (a tribute to the famed
artist) 132 264 396 838 1444 2050
21-Origin Dash Dartwell (drug-use story); origin & only app. T.N.T.
142 284 426 909 1555 2200
22-Dash Dartwell, the Human Meteor & The Voice app; last Iron Skull & The Shark;
Silver Streak app. (classic-c) 432 864 1296 3154 5577 8000
23-Two Amazing Man stories; intro/origin Tommy the Amazing Kid; The Marksman only app.
123 246 369 787 1344 1900
24-King of Darkness, Nightshade, & Blue Lady begin; end #26; 1st app. Super-Ann
123 246 369 787 1344 1900
25 (Scarce) Meteor Martin by Wolverton 423 846 1269 3000 5250 7500
26 (Scarce) Meteor Martin by Wolverton; Electric Ray app.
459 918 1377 3350 5925 8500
NOTE: ***Everett*** *a-5-11; c-5-11.* ***Gilman*** *a-14-20.* ***Giunta/Mirando*** *a-7-10.* ***Sam Glanzman*** *a-14-16, 18-21, 23.* ***Louis Glanzman*** *a-6, 9-11, 14-21; c-13-19, 21.* ***Robert Golden*** *a-9.* ***Gustavson*** *a-6; c-22, 23.* ***Lubbers*** *a-14-21.* ***Simon*** *a-10.* ***Frank Thomas*** *a-6, 9-11, 14, 15, 17-21.*

AMAZING MYSTERIES (Formerly Sub-Mariner Comics No. 31)
Marvel Comics (CCC): No. 32, May, 1949 - No. 35, Jan, 1950 (1st Marvel Horror Comic)

32-The Witness app. 116 232 348 742 1271 1800
33-Horror format 53 106 159 334 567 800
34,35: Changes to Crime. 34,35-Photo-c 23 46 69 136 223 310

AMAZING MYSTERY FUNNIES
Centaur Publications: Aug, 1938 - No. 24, Sept, 1940 (All 52 pgs.)

V1#1-Everett-c(1st); Dick Kent Adv. story; Skyrocket Steele in the Year X on cover only
514 1028 1542 3750 6625 9500
2-Everett 1st-a (Skyrocket Steele) 314 628 942 2198 3849 5500
3 194 388 582 1242 2121 3000
3(#4, 12/38)-nn on cover, #3 on inside; bondage-c
226 452 678 1446 2473 3500
V2#1,3,4,6: 3-Air-Sub DX begins by Burgos. 4-Dan Hastings, Sand Hog begins (ends #5).
6-Last Skyrocket Steele 181 362 543 1158 1979 2800
2-Classic-c; drug use story 245 490 735 1568 2684 3800
5-Classic Everett-c 400 800 1200 2800 4900 7000
7 (Scarce)-Intro. The Fantom of the Fair & begins; Everett, Gustavson, Burgos-a
432 864 1296 3154 5577 8000
8-Origin & 1st app. Speed Centaur 181 362 543 1158 1979 2800
9-11: 11-Self portrait and biog. of Everett; Jon Linton begins; early Robot cover (11/39)
142 284 426 909 1555 2200
12 (Scarce)-1st Space Patrol; Wolverton-a (12/39); new costume Phantom of the Fair
232 464 696 1485 2543 3600
V3#1(#17, 1/40)-Intro. Bullet; Tippy Taylor serial begins, ends #24
(continued in The Arrow #2) 123 246 369 787 1344 1900
18,20: 18-Fantom of the Fair by Gustavson 119 238 357 762 1306 1850
19,21-24: Space Patrol by Wolverton in all 135 270 405 864 1482 2100
NOTE: ***Burgos a****-V2#3-9.* ***Eisner*** *a-V1#2, 3(2).* ***Everett*** *a-V1#2-4, V2#1, 3-6; c-V1#1-4,V2#3, 5, 18.* ***Filchock*** *a-V2#9.* ***Flessel*** *a-V2#6.* ***Guardineer*** *a-V1#4, V2#4-6;* ***Gustavson*** *a-V2#4, 5, 9-12, V3#1, 18, 19; c-V2#7, 9, 12, V3#1, 21, 22;* ***McWilliams*** *a-V2#9, 10.* ***TarpeMills*** *a-V2#2, 4-6, 9-12, V3#1.* ***Leo Morey****(Pulp artist) c-V2#10; text illo-V2#11.* ***FrankThomas*** *a-6-V2#11.* ***Webster*** *a-V2#4.*

AMAZING SAINTS
Logos International: 1974 (39¢)

nn-True story of Phil Saint 2 4 6 9 13 16

AMAZING SCARLET SPIDER
Marvel Comics: Nov, 1995 - No. 2, Dec, 1995 ($1.95, limited series)

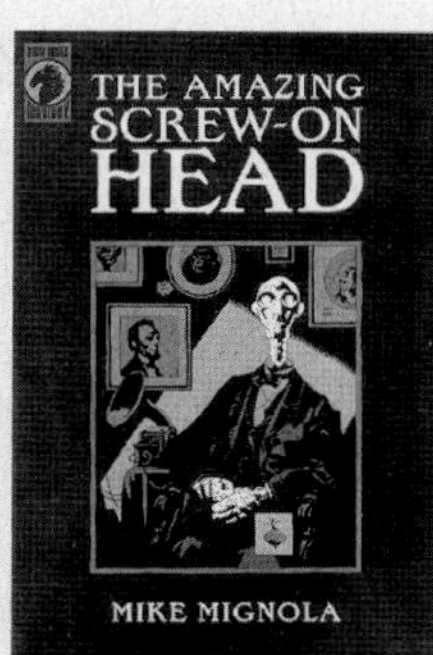

The Amazing Screw-On Head #1 © Mike Mignola

Amazing Spider-Man #2 © MAR

Amazing Spider-Man #43 © MAR

GD VG FN VF VF/NM NM-
2.0 4.0 6.0 8.0 9.0 9.2

1,2: Replaces "Amazing Spider-Man" for two issues. 1-Venom/Carnage cameos.
2-Green Goblin & Joystick-c/app. 3.00

AMAZING SCREW-ON HEAD, THE
Dark Horse Comics (Maverick): May, 2002 ($2.99, one-shot)

1-Mike Mignola-s/a/c 3.00

AMAZING SPIDER-GIRL (Also see Spider-Girl and What If...? (2nd series) #105)
Marvel Comics: No. 0, 2006; No. 1, Dec, 2006 - No. 30, May, 2009 ($2.99)

0-($1.99) Recap of the Spider-Girl series and character profiles; A.F. #15 cover swipe 3.00
1-14,16-24,26-($2.99) Frenz & Buscema-a. 9-Carnage returns. 19-Has #17 on cover 3.00
15,25,30-($3.99) 15-10th Anniversary issue. 25-Three covers 4.00
... Vol. 1: What Ever Happened to the Daughter of Spider-Man? TPB (2007, $14.99) r/#0-6 15.00
... Vol. 2: Comes the Carnage! TPB (2007, $13.99) r/#7-12 14.00
... Vol. 3: Mind Games TPB (2008, $13.99) r/#13-18 14.00

AMAZING SPIDER-MAN, THE (See All Detergent Comics, Amazing Fantasy, America's Best TV Comics, Aurora, Deadly Foes of..., Fireside Book Series, Friendly Neighborhood..., Giant-Size..., Giant Size Super-Heroes Featuring..., Marvel Age..., Marvel Collectors Item Classics, Marvel Fanfare, Marvel Graphic Novel, Marvel Knoghts..., Marvel Spec. Ed., Marvel Tales, Marvel Team-Up, Marvel Treasury Ed., New Avengers, Nothing Can Stop the Juggernaut, Official Marvel Index To..., Peter Parker..., Power Record Comics, Spectacular..., Spider-Man, Spider-Man Digest, Spider-Man Saga, Spider-Man 2099, Spider-Man Vs. Wolverine, Spidey Super Stories, Strange Tales Annual #2, Superior Spider-Man, Superman Vs. ..., Try-Out Winner Book, Ultimate Marvel Team-Up, Ultimate Spider-Man, Web of Spider- Man & Within Our Reach)

AMAZING SPIDER-MAN, THE
Marvel Comics Group: March, 1963 - No. 441, Nov, 1998

1-Retells origin by Steve Ditko; 1st Fantastic Four x-over (ties with F.F. #12 as first Marvel x-over); intro. John Jameson & The Chameleon; Spider-Man's 2nd app.; Kirby/Ditko-c; Ditko-c/a #1-38 2200 4400 6600 17,000 42,500 68,000
1-Reprint from the Golden Record Comic set 28 56 84 202 451 700
With record (1966) 40 80 120 296 673 1050
2-1st app. the Vulture & the Terrible Tinkerer 433 866 1299 3681 8341 13,000
3-1st app. Doc Octopus; 1st full-length story; Human Torch cameo;
Spider-Man pin-up by Ditko 350 700 1050 2975 6738 10,500
4-Origin & 1st app. The Sandman (see Strange Tales #115 for 2nd app.); 1st monthly issue; intro. Betty Brant & Liz Allen 283 566 849 2335 5268 8200
5-Dr. Doom app. 224 448 672 1848 4174 6500
6-1st app. Lizard 190 380 570 1568 3534 5500
7-Vs. The Vulture 132 264 396 1056 2378 3700
8-Fantastic Four app. in back-up story by Kirby & Ditko
96 192 288 768 1734 2700
9-Origin & 1st app. Electro (2/64) 132 264 396 1056 2378 3700
10-1st app. Big Man & The Enforcers 98 196 294 784 1767 2750
11-1st app. Bennett Brant 118 236 354 944 2122 3300
12-Doc Octopus unmasks Spider-Man-c/story 89 178 267 712 1606 2500
13-1st app. Mysterio 141 282 423 1142 2571 4000
14-(7/64)-1st app. The Green Goblin (c/story)(Norman Osborn); Hulk x-over
207 414 621 1708 3854 6000
15-1st app. Kraven the Hunter; 1st mention of Mary Jane Watson (not shown)
93 186 279 744 1672 2600
16-Spider-Man battles Daredevil (1st x-over 9/64); still in old yellow costume
75 150 225 600 1350 2100
17-2nd app. Green Goblin (c/story); Human Torch x-over (also in #18 & #21)
79 158 237 632 1416 2200
18-1st app. Ned Leeds who later becomes Hobgoblin; Fantastic Four cameo;
3rd app. Sandman 49 98 147 376 851 1325
19-Sandman app. 38 76 114 281 628 975
20-Origin & 1st app. The Scorpion 68 136 204 544 1222 1900
21-2nd app. The Beetle (see Strange Tales #123) 40 80 120 296 673 1050
22-1st app. Princess Python 39 78 117 289 657 1025
23-3rd app. The Green Goblin-c/story; Norman Osborn app.; Marvel Masterwork pin-up by Ditko; fan letter by Jim Shooter 46 92 138 368 834 1300
24 36 72 108 266 596 925
25-(6/65)-1st brief app. Mary Jane Watson (face not shown); 1st app. Spencer Smythe;
Norman Osborn app. 40 80 120 296 673 1050
26-4th app. The Green Goblin-c/story; 1st app. Crime Master; dies in #27
41 82 123 303 689 1075
27-5th app. The Green Goblin-c/story; Norman Osborn app.
40 80 120 296 673 1050
28-Origin & 1st app. Molten Man (9/65, scarcer in high grade)
89 178 267 712 1606 2500
29,30 28 56 84 202 451 700
31-(12/65)-1st app. Gwen Stacy, Harry Osborn who later becomes 2nd Green Goblin & Prof. Warren. 46 92 138 340 770 1200
32-38: 34-4th app. Kraven the Hunter. 36-1st app. Looter. 37-Intro. Norman Osborn.
38-(7/66)-2nd brief app. Mary Jane Watson (face not shown); last Ditko issue
23 46 69 161 356 550
39-The Green Goblin-c/story; Green Goblin's i.d. revealed as Norman Osborn; Romita-a begins (8/66; see Daredevil #16 for 1st Romita-a on Spider-Man)
42 84 126 311 706 1100
40-1st told origin The Green Goblin-c/story 38 76 114 285 641 1000
41-1st app. Rhino 42 84 126 311 706 1100
42-(11/66)-3rd app. Mary Jane Watson (cameo in last 2 panels); 1st time face is shown 23 46 69 161 356 550
43-45,47-49: 43-Origin of the Rhino. 44,45-2nd & 3rd app. The Lizard. 47-M.J. Watson & Peter Parker 1st date. 47-Green Goblin cameo; Harry & Norman Osborn app.
47,49-5th & 6th app. Kraven the Hunter. 48-1st new Vulture (Blackie Drago)
18 36 54 124 275 425
46-Intro/origin The Shocker 23 46 69 161 356 550
50-1st app. Kingpin (7/67) 79 168 237 632 1416 2200
51-2nd app. Kingpin; Joe Robertson 1-panel cameo 22 44 66 154 340 525
52-58,60: 52-1st app. Joe Robertson & 3rd app. Kingpin. 56-1st app. Capt. George Stacy.
57,58-Ka-Zar app. 12 24 36 84 185 285
59-1st app. Brainwasher (alias Kingpin); 1st-c app. M. J. Watson
13 26 39 89 195 300
61-74: 61-1st Gwen Stacy cover app. 67-1st app. Randy Robertson. 69-Kingpin-c.
69,70-Kingpin app. 70-1st app. Vanessa Fisk (Kingpin's wife)(only seen in shadow).
73-1st app. Silvermane. 74-Last 12¢ issue 10 20 30 66 138 210
75-77,79-83,87-89,91,92,95,99: 79-The Prowler app. 83-1st app. Schemer; Vanessa Fisk app. (only previously seen in shadow in #70) 9 18 27 58 114 170
78-1st app. The Prowler 10 20 30 64 132 200
84,85,93: 84,85-Kingpin-c/story. 93-1st app. Arthur Stacy
9 18 27 59 117 175
86-Re-intro & origin Black Widow in new costume 11 22 33 73 157 240
90-Death of Capt. Stacy 11 22 33 73 157 240
94-Origin retold 10 20 30 64 132 200
96-98-Green Goblin app. (97,98-Green Goblin-c); drug books not approved by CCA
10 20 30 69 147 225
100-Anniversary issue (9/71); Green Goblin cameo (2 pgs.)
13 26 39 91 201 310
101-1st app. Morbius the Living Vampire; Lizard cameo; Stan Lee co-plots with Roy Thomas; last 15¢ issue (10/71) 24 48 72 168 372 575
101-Silver ink 2nd printing (9/92, $1.75) 2 4 6 8 10 12
102-Origin & 2nd app. Morbius (25¢, 52 pgs.) 12 24 36 79 170 260
103-118: 103,104-Roy Thomas-s. 104,111-Kraven the Hunter-c/stories. 105-109-Stan Lee-s.
108-1st app. Sha-Shan. 109-Dr. Strange-c/story. 110-1st app. Gibbon; Conway-s begin.
113-1st app. Hammerhead. 116-118-Reprints story from Spectacular Spider-Man Mag. in color with some changes 6 12 18 41 76 110
119,120-Spider-Man vs. Hulk (4 & 5/73) 9 18 27 58 114 170
121-Death of Gwen Stacy (6/73) (killed by Green Goblin) (reprinted in Marvel Tales #98 & 192)
29 58 87 209 467 725
122-Death of The Green Goblin-c/story (7/73) (reprinted in Marvel Tales #99 & 192)
24 48 72 168 372 575
123-Cage app. 7 14 21 44 82 120
124-1st app. Man-Wolf (9/73) 7 14 21 49 92 135
125-Man-Wolf origin 6 12 18 40 73 105
126-128: 126-1st mention of Harry Osborn becoming Green Goblin
6 12 18 38 69 100
129-1st app. The Punisher (2/74); 1st app. Jackal 150 300 450 750 1125 1500
130-133: 131-Last 20¢ issue 5 10 15 34 60 85
134-(7/74); 1st app. Tarantula; Harry Osborn discovers Spider-Man's ID; Punisher cameo
6 12 18 41 76 110
135-2nd full Punisher app. (8/74) 10 20 30 64 132 200
136-1st app. Harry Osborn Green Goblin in costume 8 16 24 51 96 140
137-Green Goblin-c/story (2nd Harry Osborn Goblin) 6 12 18 37 66 95
138-141: 139-1st Grizzly. 140-1st app. Glory Grant 4 8 12 25 40 55
142,143-Gwen Stacy clone cameos: 143-1st app. Cyclone
4 8 12 25 40 55
144-147: 144-Full app. of Gwen Stacy clone. 145,146-Gwen Stacy clone storyline continues.
147-Spider-Man learns Gwen Stacy is clone 4 8 12 25 40 55
148-Jackal revealed 4 8 12 28 47 65
149-Spider-Man clone story begins, clone dies (?); origin of Jackal
8 16 24 51 96 140
150-Spider-Man decides he is not the clone 4 8 12 28 47 65
151-Spider-Man disposes of clone body; Len Wein-s begins; thru #180
5 10 15 31 53 75
152-160-(Regular 25¢ editions). 152-vs. the Shocker. 154-vs. Sandman. 156-1st Mirage.
157-159-Doc Octopus & Hammerhead app. 159-Last 25¢ issue(8/76). 160-Spider-Mobile destroyed 3 6 9 19 30 40
155-159-(30¢-c variants, limited distribution) 7 14 21 48 89 130

Amazing Spider-Man #194 © MAR

Amazing Spider-Man #243 © MAR

Amazing Spider-Man #368 © MAR

GD VG FN VF VF/NM NM-
2.0 4.0 6.0 8.0 9.0 9.2

161-Nightcrawler app. from X-Men; Punisher cameo; Wolverine & Colossus app. 4 8 12 25 40 55
162-Punisher, Nightcrawler app.; 1st Jigsaw 4 8 12 25 40 55
163-168: 163-164-vs. the Kingpin. 165-vs. Stegron. 166-Stegron & the Lizard app. 167-1st app. Will O' The Wisp. 168-Will O' The Wisp app. 3 6 9 16 23 30
169-170,172-173: 169-Clone story recapped; Stan Lee Cameo. 170-Dr. Faustus app. 172-1st Rocket Racer. 173-vs Molten Man 3 6 9 16 23 30
171-Nova app. x-over w/Nova #12 3 6 9 17 26 35
169-173-(35¢-c variants, limited dist.)(6-10/77) 17 34 51 117 259 400
174,175-Punisher app. 3 6 9 19 30 40
176-180-Green Goblin app. 3 6 9 18 28 38
181-186: 181-Origin retold; gives life history of Spidey; Punisher cameo in flashback (1 panel). 182-(7/78)-Peter's first proposal to Mary Jane, but she declines (in #183). 183-Rocket Racer & the Big Wheel app. 184-vs. the second White Dragon. 185-Peter graduates college 3 6 9 14 20 25
187,188: 187-Captain America app. 188-vs. Jigsaw 3 6 9 16 23 30
189,190-Byrne-a; Man-Wolf app. 3 6 9 16 23 30
191-193,196-199: 191-vs. the Spider-Slayer. 192-Death of Spencer Smythe. 193-Peter & Mary Jane break up; the Fly app. 196-Faked death of Aunt May. 197-vs. the Kingpin. 198,199-Mysterio app. 2 4 6 11 16 20
NOTE: *Whitman 3-packs containing #192-194,196 exist.*
194-1st app. Black Cat 9 18 27 60 120 180
195-2nd app. Black Cat & origin Black Cat 3 6 9 19 30 40
200-Giant origin issue (1/80); death of the burglar (from Amazing Fantasy #15) 3 6 9 21 33 45
201,202-Punisher app. 3 6 9 14 19 24
203-208,210-219: 203-3rd Dazzler (4/80). 204,205-Black Cat app. 204-last Wolfman-s. 206-Byrne-a. 207-vs Mesmero. 210-1st app. Madame Web. 211-Sub-Mariner app. 212-1st app. & origin Hydro-Man. 214,215-New Frightful Four app: Wizard, Trapster, Sandman & Llyra (Namor foe). 216-Madame Web app. 217-Sandman vs Hydro-Man. 219-Grey Gargoyle app. Frank Miller-c 2 4 6 9 12 15
209-Kraven the Hunter app; 1st app. origin Calypso 2 4 6 11 16 20
220-225,228: 220-Moon Knight app. 222-1st app. of the Whizzer as Speed Demon. 223-vs. The Red Ghost & the Super-Apes; Roger Stern-s begins. 224-Vulture app. 225-Foolkiller II-c/story. 1 3 4 6 8 10
226,227-Black Cat returns 2 4 6 9 12 15
229,230: Classic 'Nothing can stop the Juggernaut' story 2 4 6 13 18 22
231-237: 231,232-Cobra & Mr Hyde app. 233-Tarantula app. 234-Free 16 pg. insert "Marvel Guide to Collecting Comics", Tarantula & Will O' The Wisp app. 235-Origin Will 'O The Wisp. 236-Tarantula dies. 237-Stilt-Man app. 1 3 4 6 8 10
238-(3/83)-1st app. Hobgoblin (Ned Leeds); came with skin "Tattooz" decal.
NOTE: The same decal appears in the more common Fantastic Four #252 which is being removed & placed in this issue as incentive to increase value. (No "Tattooz" were included in the Canadian edition)
(Value with tattooz) 8 16 24 54 102 150
(Value without tattooz) 5 10 15 23 57 80
239-2nd app. Hobgoblin & 1st battle w/Spidey 4 8 12 27 44 60
240-243,246-248: 240,241-Vulture app. (origin in #241). 242-Mary Jane Watson cameo (last panel). 243-Reintro Mary Jane after 4 year absence. 248-'The Kid Who Collects Spider-Man' story 1 3 4 6 8 10
244-3rd app. Hobgoblin (cameo) 2 4 6 9 12 15
245-(10/83)-4th app. Hobgoblin (cameo); Lefty Donovan gains powers of Hobgoblin & battles Spider-Man 2 4 6 9 12 15
249-251: 3 part Hobgoblin/Spider-Man battle. 249-Retells origin & death of 1st Green Goblin. 251-Last old costume 2 4 6 9 13 16
252-Spider-Man dons new black costume (5/84); ties with Marvel Team-Up #141 & Spectacular Spider-Man #90 for 1st new costume in regular title (See Marvel Super-Heroes Secret Wars #8 (12/84) for acquisition of costume); last Roger Stern-s 5 10 15 35 63 90
253-1st app. The Rose; Tom DeFalco-s begin 2 4 6 9 12 15
254,255,257,258: 254-Jack O' Lantern app. 255-1st app Black Fox. 257-Hobgoblin cameo; 2nd app. Puma; M.J. Watson reveals she knows Spidey's i.d. 258-Hobgoblin app. 1 3 4 6 8 10
256-1st app. Puma 2 4 6 9 12 15
259-Full Hobgoblin app.; Spidey back to old costume; origin Mary Jane Watson 2 4 6 9 12 15
260-Hobgoblin app. 2 4 6 8 10 12
261-Hobgoblin-c/story; painted-c by Vess 2 4 6 9 11 14
262-Spider-Man unmasked; photo-c 1 3 4 6 8 10
263,264,266-268: 266-Toad & Frogman app.; Peter David-s. 268-Secret Wars II x-over 1 2 3 5 6 8
265-1st app. Silver Sable (6/85) 3 6 9 16 23 30
265-Silver ink 2nd printing ($1.25) 1 2 3 4 5 7
269-270: 269-Spider-Man vs Firelord. 270 Avengers app. 1 3 4 6 8 10
271-274,277-280,282-283: 272-1st app. Slyde. 273-Secret Wars II x-over; Beyonder app. 274-Secret Wars II x-over; Zarathos app. (The Spirit of Vengeance). 277-Vess-c & back-up art. 278-Scourge app; death of the Wraith. 279-Jack O' Lantern-c/s. 280-1st Sinister Syndicate: Beetle, Boomerang, Hydro-Man, Rhino, Speed Demon. 282-X-Factor app. 1 2 3 5 6 8
275-($1.25, 52 pgs.)-Hobgoblin-c/story; origin-r by Ditko 3 6 9 14 20 25
276-Hobgoblin app. 1 3 4 6 8 10
281-Hobgoblin battles Jack O'Lantern 1 3 4 6 8 10
284,285: 284-Punisher cameo; Gang War Pt. 1; Hobgoblin-c/story. 285-Punisher app.; minor Hobgoblin app.; last Tom DeFalco-s; Gang War Pt. 2 1 3 4 6 8 10
286-288: Gang War Parts 3-5. 286-Hobgoblin-c & app. (minor). 287-Hobgoblin app. (minor). 288-Full Hobgoblin app.; Gang War ends 1 3 4 6 8 10
289-(6/87, $1.25, 52 pgs.)-Hobgoblin's i.d. revealed as Ned Leeds; death of Ned Leeds; Macendale (Jack O'Lantern) becomes new Hobgoblin (1st app.) 3 6 9 14 20 25
290-292,295-297: 290-Peter proposes to Mary Jane; 1st David Michelinie-s. 291,292-Spider-Slayer app. 292-She accepts; leads into wedding in Amazing Spider-Man Annual #21. 295-'Mad Dog Ward' Pt.2; x-over w/Web of Spider-Man #33 & Spectacular Spider-Man #133. 296-297-Doc Octopus app. 1 2 3 5 6 8
293,294-Part 2 & 5 of Kraven story from Web of Spider-Man. 293-Continued from Web of Spider-Man #31; continues into Spectacular Spider-Man #131. 294-Death of Kraven; continued from Web of Spider-Man #32; continues in Spectacular Spider-Man #132 2 4 6 9 12 15
298-Todd McFarlane-c/a begins (3/88); 1st brief app. Eddie Brock who becomes Venom; (last pg.) 5 10 15 33 57 80
299-1st brief app. Venom with costume 4 8 12 27 44 60
300 ($1.50, 52 pgs.; 25th Anniversary)-1st full Venom app.; last black costume (5/88) 30 60 90 150 200 250
301-$1.00 issues begin. Classic McFarlane-c 3 6 9 16 23 30
302-305: 302-303-Silver Sable app. 304,305-Black Fox app. 304-1st bi-weekly issue 2 4 6 10 14 18
306-311,313,314: 306-Swipes-c from Action #1. 307-Chameleon app. 308-Taskmaster app. 309-1st app. Styx & Stone. 310-Killer Shrike app. 311-Inferno x-over; Mysterio app. 2 4 6 9 13 16
312-Hobgoblin battles Green Goblin; Inferno x-over 2 4 6 13 18 22
315,317-Venom app. 3 6 9 16 23 30
316-Classic Venom-c 3 6 9 21 33 45
318-323,325: 318-Scorpion app. 319-Bi-weekly begins again; Scorpion, Rhino, Backlash app. 320-'Assassination Nation Plot' Pt.1 (ends in issue #325); Paladin & Silver Sable app. 321-Paladin & Silver Sable app. 322-Silver Sable app. 323-Captain America app. 325-Captain America & Red Skull app. 1 3 4 6 8 10
324-Sabretooth app.; McFarlane cover only 2 4 6 8 10 12
326,327,329: 326-Acts of Vengeance x-over; vs Graviton. 327-Acts of Vengeance x-over; vs. Magneto; Cosmic storyline continues from Spectacular Spider-Man; Erik Larsen-a. 329-Acts of Vengeance x-over; vs. the Tri-Sentinel; Sebastian Shaw app.; Erik Larsen-a (continuous through issue #344) 6.00
328-Acts of Vengeance x-over; vs. the Hulk; last McFarlane issue 2 4 6 9 12 15
330,331-Punisher app. 331-Minor Venom app. 6.00
332,333-Venom-c/story 2 4 6 8 10 12
334-336,338-343: 334-339-Return of the Sinister Six. 341-Tarantula app; Spider-Man loses his cosmic powers. 342,343-Black Cat app. 4.00
337-Hobgoblin app. 5.00
344-(2/91) 1st app. Cletus Kasady (Carnage) 3 6 9 15 22 28
345-1st full app. Cletus Kasady; Venom cameo on last pg.; 1st Mark Bagley-a on Spider-Man 2 4 6 9 12 15
346,347-Venom app. 2 4 6 9 12 15
348,349,351-359: 348-Avengers x-over. 351-Bagley-a begins. 351,352-Nova of New Warriors app. 353-Darkhawk app.; brief Punisher app. 354-Punisher cameo & Nova, Night Thrasher (New Warriors), Darkhawk & Moon Knight app. 357,358-Punisher, Darkhawk, Moon Knight, Night Thrasher, Nova x-over. 358-3 part gatefold-c; last $1.00-c 4.00
350-($1.50, 52pgs.)-Origin retold; Spidey vs. Dr. Doom; last Erik Larsen-a pin-ups; Uncle Ben app. 5.00
360-Carnage cameo 1 3 4 6 8 10
361-(4/92) Intro. Carnage (the Spawn of Venom); begin 3 part story; recap of how Spidey's alien costume became Venom 4 8 12 27 44 60
361-($1.25)-2nd printing; silver-c 3 6 9 17 26 35
362,363-Carnage & Venom-c/story 2 4 6 9 12 15
362-2nd printing 2 4 6 9 12 15
364,366-373,376,377,381-387: 364-The Shocker app. (old villain). 366-Peter's parents-c/story; Red Skull, Viper & Taskmaster app. 367-Red Skull, Viper & Taskmaster app. 368-Invasion of the Spider-Slayers Pt.1 (through Pt.6 in #373). 369-Harry Osborn back-up (Gr. Goblin II).

Amazing Spider-Man #435 © MAR

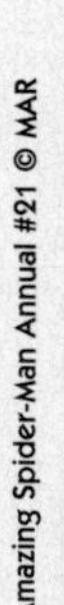

Amazing Spider-Man Annual #21 © MAR

Amazing Spider-Man: Skating on Thin Ice © MAR

	GD 2.0	VG 4.0	FN 6.0	VF 8.0	VF/NM 9.0	NM- 9.2

Electro app. 370-Black Cat & Scorpion app. 373-Venom back-up. 376,377-Cardiac app. 381,382-Hulk app. 383-The Jury app. 383-385-vs The Jury. 384-Venom/Carnage app. 386-Vulture app. 387-Vulture is de-aged & gets new costume 3.00

365-($3.95, 84 pgs.)-30th anniversary issue w/silver hologram on-c; Spidey/Venom/Carnage pull-out poster; contains 5 pg. preview of Spider-Man 2099 (1st app.); Spidey's origin retold; Lizard app.; reintro Peter's parents in Stan Lee 3 pg. text w/illo (story continues thru #370) 2 4 6 10 14 18

374-Venom-c/story 6.00

375-($3.95, 68 pgs.)-Holo-grafx foil-c; vs. Venom story; ties into Venom: Lethal Protector #1; Pat Olliffe-a. 1 3 4 6 8 10

378-380: Parts 3,7 and 11 of Maximum Carnage. 378-Continued from Web of Spider-Man #101; Venom vs Carnage; continues in Spider-Man #35. 379-Continued from Web of Spider-Man #102; Deathlok, Firestar, Black Cat & Morbius app.; continued in Spider-Man #36. 380-Continued from Web of Spider-Man #103; Captain America & Cloak and Dagger app.; continued in Spider-Man #37 5.00

388-($2.25, 68 pgs.)-Newsstand edition; Venom back-up & Cardiac & chance back-up; last David Michelinie-s (6-year run) 4.00

388-($2.95, 68 pgs.)-Collector's edition w/foil-c 5.00

389-1st JM DeMatteis-s; Trading Card insert (3 cards) attached to the staples; harder to find in true high grade due to indents caused by the cards; Green Goblin app. 4.00

390-393,395,396: 390-393-vs. Shriek. 395-Puma app. 396-Daredevil & the Owl app. 3.00

390-($2.95)-Collector's edition polybagged w/16 pg. insert of new animated Spidey TV show plus animation cel 5.00

394-($2.95, 48 pgs.)-Deluxe edition; flip book w/Birth of a Spider-Man Pt. 2; silver foil both-c; Power & Responsibility Pt. 2; Judas Traveller, the Jackal and the Gwen Stacy Clone app. 1st app. Scrier 5.00

394-Newstand edition ($1.50-c) 7.00

397-($2.25)-Flip book w/Ultimate Spider-Man 4.00

398,399: 398-Web of Death Pt.3; continued from Spectacular Spider-Man #220; Doc Octopus & Kaine app.; continued in Spectacular Spider-Man #221. 399-Smoke and Mirrors Pt.2; continued from Web of Spider-Man #122; Jackal, Scarlet Spider, Gwen Stacy Clone app; continued in Spider-Man #56 5.00

400-($2.95)-Death of Aunt May; newsstand edition 3 6 9 16 24 32

400-($3.95)-Death of Aunt May; embossed grey overlay cover 2 4 6 11 16 20

400-Collector's Edition; white embossed-c; (10,000 print run) 5 10 15 30 50 70

401,402,405,406-409: 401-The Mark of Kaine Pt.2; continued from Web of Spider-Man #124; Scarlet Spider app; continues in Spider-Man #58. 402-Judas Traveller & Scrier app. 405-Exiled Pt.2; continued from Web of Spider-Man #128; Scarlet Spider app.; continues in Spider-Man #62. 406-1st full app. of the female Doc Octopus (Carolyn Trainer); continues in Spider-Man #63; Marvel Overpower card insert; harder to find in higher grades due to card indenting; last JM DeMatteis-s. 407-Human Torch, Sandman & Silver Sable app. Tom DeFalco-s (returns to Spider-Man; last-s in 1987). 408-Regular ed; Media Blizzard pt.2; Mysterio app; continued from Sensational Spider-Man #1; continues in Spider-Man #65. 409-The Return of Kaine Pt.3; continued from Spectacular Spider-Man #231; Kaine & Rhino app.; continues in Spider-Man #66 4.00

403-The Trial of Peter Parker Pt. 2; continued from Web of Spider-Man #126; Carnage app; continues in Spider-Man #60. 1 2 3 5 6 8

404-Maximum Clonage Pt.3; continued from Web of Spider-Man #127; Scarlet Spider, Jackal, Scrier & Kaine app; continued in Spider-Man #61 5.00

408-($2.95)-Polybagged version with TV theme song cassette; scarce in high grade due to damage caused by the cassette indenting the actual comic 9 18 27 58 114 170

408-Direct edition (without cassette & out of polybag) 5 10 15 34 60 85

408-Newsstand edition; variant cover 5 10 15 35 63 90

410-Web of Carnage Pt.2; continued from Sensational Spider-Man #3; Carnage app; continues in Spider-Man #67 3 6 9 15 22 28

411,412,414,417-419,421-424: 411-Blood Brothers Pt.2; continued from Sensational Spider-Man #4; Gaunt app; continued in Spider-Man #68. 412-Blood Brothers Pt.6; continued from Sensational Spider-Man #5; vs Gaunt. 414-The Rose app. 417-Death of Scrier. 418-Revelations Pt.3; continued from Spectacular Spider-Man #240; Norman Osborn returns; 'death' of Peter and Mary Jane's baby (May Parker); continued in Spider-Man #75. 419-1st minor app. of The Black Tarantula. 422,423-Electro app. 424-Elektra app. 4.00

413-Contains a free packet of Island Twists Kool-Aid and Spider-Man For Kids magazine subscriber card; harder to find in true high grade 6.00

415-Onslaught Impact 2; Green Goblin (Phil Urich) app. vs. Mark IV Sentinels; last Mark Bagley-a (5 year run) 6.00

416-Epilogue to Onslaught; harder to find in high grade due to Marvel Overpower card insert 1 3 4 6 8 10

420-X-Man app. 1 2 3 4 5 7

425-($2.99)-48 pgs., wraparound-c; X-Man app 1 2 3 4 5 7

426,428,429,432,435-437,440: 426-Female Dr. Octopus app. 428-Dr. Octopus app. 429-Absorbing Man app. 432-Spider-Hunt Pt.2; continued from Sensational Spider-Man #25; Black Tarantula & Norman Osborn app. 433-Mr. Hyde app. 435-Identity Crisis; Black Tarantula & Kaine app. 436-Black Tarantula app. 437-Plantman app. 440-Gathering of Five Pt.2; continued from Sensational Spider-Man #32; John Byrne-s; Molten Man & Norman Osborn app; continued in Spider-Man #96 6.00

427-Return of Dr. Octopus; double-gatefold-c. 1 2 3 4 5 7

430-Carnage & Silver Surfer app. 3 6 9 14 20 25

431-Cosmic-Carnage vs Silver Surfer; Galactus cameo 3 6 9 21 33 45

432-Variant yellow-c 'Wanted Dead or Alive' 2 4 6 9 12 15

434-Identity Crisis; Black Tarantula app. 1 3 4 6 8 10

434-Variant 'Amazing Ricochet #1'-c 2 4 6 9 12 15

438-Daredevil app. 7.00

439-Alternate future story; Avengers app; last Tom DeFalco-s 1 2 3 5 6 8

441-The Final Chapter Pt.1; John Byrne-s; Norman Osborn app; last issue (Dec. 1998); story continues in Spider-Man #97 1 2 3 5 7 9

#500-up (See Amazing Spider-Man Vol. 2; series resumed original numbering after Vol. 2 #58)

#(-1) Flashback issue (7/97, $1.95-c) 3.00

Annual 1 (1964, 72 pgs.) Origin Spider-Man; 1st app. Sinister Six (Dr. Octopus, Electro, Kraven the Hunter, Mysterio, Sandman, Vulture) (new 41 pg. story); plus gallery of Spidey foes; early X-Men app. 136 272 408 1088 2444 3800

Annual 2 (1965, 25¢, 72 pgs.) Reprints from #1,2,5 plus new Doctor Strange story 34 68 102 245 548 850

Special 3 (11/66, 25¢, 72 pgs.) New Avengers story & Hulk x-over; Doctor Octopus-r from #11,12; Romita-a 17 34 51 117 259 400

Special 4 (11/67, 25¢, 68 pgs.) Spidey battles Human Torch (new 41 pg. story) 13 26 39 89 195 300

Special 5 (11/68, 25¢, 68 pgs.) New 40 pg. Red Skull story; 1st app. Peter Parker's parents; last annual with new-a 11 22 33 73 157 240

Special 5-2nd printing (1994) 2 4 6 8 10 12

Special 6 (11/69, 25¢, 68 pgs.) Reprints 41 pg. Sinister Six story from annual #1 plus 2 Kirby/Ditko stories (r) 6 12 18 41 76 110

Special 7 (12/70, 25¢, 68 pgs.) All-r(#1,2) new Vulture-c 5 10 15 35 63 90

Special 8 (12/71) All-r 5 10 15 35 63 90

King Size 9 ('73) Reprints Spectacular Spider-Man (mag.) #2; 40 pg. Green Goblin-c/story (re-edited from 58 pgs.) 5 10 15 35 63 90

Annual 10 (1976) Origin Human Fly (vs. Spidey); new-a begins 3 6 9 16 23 30

Annual 11-13 ('77-'79): 12-Spidey vs. Hulk-r/#119,120. 13-New Byrne/Austin-a; Dr. Octopus x-over w/Spectacular S-M Ann. #1 2 4 6 11 16 20

Annual 14 (1980) Miller-c/a(p); Dr. Strange app. 3 6 9 14 20 25

Annual 15 (1981) Miller-c/a(p); Punisher app. 3 6 9 17 26 35

Annual 16 (1982)-Origin/1st app. new Capt. Marvel (female heroine) 2 4 6 8 10 12

Annual 17-20: 17 ('83)-Kingpin app. 18 ('84)-Scorpion app.; JJJ weds. 19 ('85). 20 ('86)-Origin Iron Man of 2020 1 2 3 4 5 7

Annual 21 (1987) Special wedding issue; newsstand & direct sale versions exist & are worth same 2 4 6 13 18 22

Annual 22 (1988, $1.75, 68 pgs.) 1st app. Speedball; Evolutionary War x-over; Daredevil app. 2 4 6 8 11 14

Annual 23 (1989, $2.00, 68 pgs.) Atlantis Attacks; origin Spider-Man retold; She-Hulk app.; Byrne-c; Liefeld-a(p), 23 pgs. 5.00

Annual 24 (1990, $2.00, 68 pgs.) -Ant-Man app. 4.00

Annual 25 (1991, $2.00, 68 pgs.) 3 pg. origin recap; Iron Man app.; 1st Venom solo story; Ditko-a (6 pgs.) 5.00

Annual 26 (1992, $2.25, 68 pgs.) New Warriors-c/story; Venom solo story cont'd in Spectacular Spider-Man Annual #12 5.00

Annual 27 ('93, $2.95, 68 pgs.) Bagged w/card; 1st app. Annex 4.00

Annual 28 ('94, $2.95, 68 pgs.) Carnage-c/story 1 3 4 6 8 10

'96 Special-($2.95, 64 pgs.)-"Blast From The Past" 4.00

'97 Special-($2.99)-Wraparound-c,Sundown app. 4.00

... : Carnage (6/93, $6.95)-r/ASM #344,345,359-363 1 3 4 6 8 10

Marvel Graphic Novel - Parallel Lives (3/89, $8.95) 2 4 6 8 10 12

...: Parallel Lives 1 (2012, $4.99) r/1989 GN 5.00

Marvel Graphic Novel - Spirits of the Earth (1990, $18.95, HC) 3 6 9 15 22 28

Super Special 1 (4/95, $3.95)-Flip Book 4.00

...: Skating on Thin Ice 1(1990, $1.25, Canadian)-McFarlane-c; anti-drug issue; Electro app. 1 2 3 5 7 9

...: Skating on Thin Ice 1 (2/93, $1.50, American) 4.00

...: Double Trouble 2 (1990, $1.25, Canadian) 6.00

...: Double Trouble 2 (2/93, $1.50, American) 3.00

Amazing Spider-Man V2 #41 © MAR

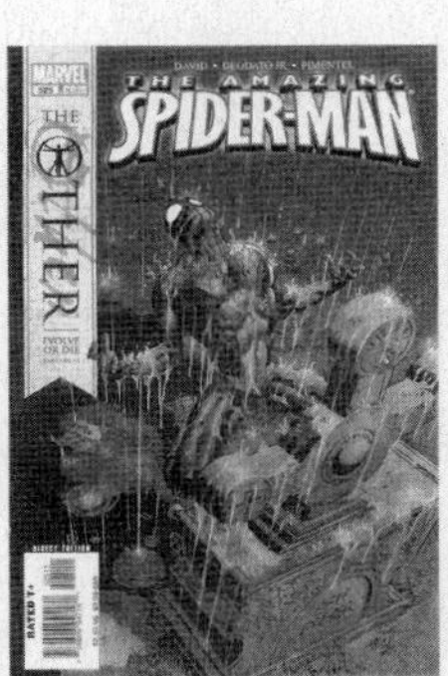

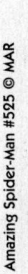

Amazing Spider-Man #525 © MAR

Amazing Spider-Man #667 © MAR

GD 2.0 | VG 4.0 | FN 6.0 | VF 8.0 | VF/NM 9.0 | NM- 9.2

....: Hit and Run 3 (1990, $1.25, Canadian)-Ghost Rider-c/story 1 2 3 5 7 9
....: Hit and Run 3 (2/93. $1.50, American) 3.00
....: Chaos in Calgary 4 (Canadian; part of 5 part series)-Turbine,Night Rider, Frightful app. 2 4 6 8 11 14
....: Chaos in Calgary 4 (2/93, $1.50, American) 3.00
....: Deadball 5 (1993, $1.60, Canadian)-Green Goblin-c/story; features Montreal Expos 2 4 6 10 14 18
Note: Prices listed above are for English Canadian editions. French editions are worth double.
....: Soul of the Hunter nn (8/92, $5.95, 52 pgs.)-Zeck-c/a(p) 6.00
Wizard #1 Ace Edition ($13.99) r/#1 w/ new Ramos acetate-c 14.00
Wizard #129 Ace Edition ($13.99) r/#129 w/ new Ramos acetate-c 14.00

NOTE: ***Austin*** *a(i)-248, 335, 337, Annual 13; c(i)-188, 241, 242, 248, 331, 334, 343, Annual 25.* ***J. Buscema*** *a(p)-72, 73, 76-81, 84, 85.* ***Byrne*** *a-189p, 190p, 206p, Annual 3r, 6r, 7r, 13p; c-189p, 268, 296, Annual 12.* ***Ditko*** *a-1-38, Annual 1, Special 3(r), 2, 24(2); c-1i, 2-38.* ***Guice*** *c/a-Annual 18i.* ***Gil Kane*** *a(p)-89-105, 120-124, 150, Annual 10, 12i, 24p; c-90p, 96, 98, 99, 101-105p, 129p, 131p, 132p, 137-140p, 143p, 148p, 149p, 151p, 153p, 160p, 161p, Annual 10p, 24.* ***Kirby*** *a-8.* ***Erik Larsen*** *a-324, 327, 329-350; c-327, 329-350, 354i, Annual 25.* ***McFarlane*** *a-298p, 299p, 300-303, 304-323p, 325p, 328; c-298-325, 328.* ***Miller*** *c-218, 219.* ***Mooney*** *a-65i, 67-82i, 84-88i, 173i, 178i, 189i, 190i, 192i, 193i, 196-202i, 207i, 211-219i, 221i, 222i, 226i, 227i, 229-233i, Annual 11i, 17i.* ***Nasser*** *c-228p.* ***Nebres*** *a-Annual 24i.* ***Russell*** *c-357i.* ***Simonson*** *c-222, 337i.* ***Starlin*** *a-113i, 114i, 187p.* ***Williamson*** *a-365i.*

AMAZING SPIDER-MAN (Volume 2) (Some issues reprinted in "Spider-Man, Best Of" hardcovers)
Marvel Comics: Jan, 1999 - No. 700, Feb, 2013 ($2.99/$1.99/$2.25)

1-($2.99)-Byrne-a; Avengers, Fantastic Four & Green Goblin app. 6.00
1-Sunburst variant-c 1 3 4 6 8 10
1-($6.95) Dynamic Forces variant-c by the Romitas 2 4 6 9 12 15
1-Marvel Matrix sketch variant-c 1 3 4 6 8 10
2-($1.99) Two covers -by John Byrne and Andy Kubert 4.00
3-11: 4-Fantastic Four app. 5-Spider-Woman-c 3.00
12-($2.99) Sinister Six return (cont. in Peter Parker #12) 4.00
13-17: 13-Mary Jane's plane explodes 3.00
18,19,21-24,26-28: 18-Begin $2.25-c. 19-Venom-c. 24-Maximum Security 3.00
20-($2.99, 100 pgs.) Spider-Slayer issue; new story and reprints 4.00
25-($2.99) Regular cover; Peter Parker becomes the Green Goblin 4.00
25-($3.99) Holo-foil enhanced cover 5.00
29-Peter is reunited with Mary Jane 4.00
30-Straczynski-s/Campbell-c begin; intro. Ezekiel 6.00
31-35: Battles Morlun 4.00
36-Black cover; aftermath of the Sept. 11 tragedy in New York 3 6 9 17 26 35
37-49: 39-'Nuff Said issue 42-Dr. Strange app. 43-45-Doctor Octopus app. 46-48-Cho-c 3.00
50-Peter and MJ reunite; Captain America & Dr. Doom app.; Campbell-c 4.00
51-58: 51,52-Campbell-c. 55,56-Avery scripts. 57,58-Avengers, FF, Cyclops app. 3.00
(After #58 [Nov, 2003] numbering reverts back to original Vol. 1 with #500, Dec, 2003)
500-($3.50) J. Scott Campbell-c; Romita Jr. & Sr.-a; Uncle Ben app. 1 3 4 6 8 10
501-524: 501-Harris-c. 503-504-Loki app. 506-508-Ezekiel app. 509-514-Sins Past; intro. Gabriel and Sarah Osborn; Deodato-a. 519-Moves into Avengers HQ. 521-Begin $2.50-c 524-Harris-c 3.00
525,526-Evolve or Die x-over. 525-David-s. 526-Hudlin-s; Spider-Man loses eye 4.00
525-528-2nd printings with variant-c. 525-Ben Reilly costume. 526-Six-Armed Spidey. 527-Spider-Man 2099. 528-Spider-Ham 5.00
527,528: Evolve or Die pt. 9,12 3.00
529-Debut of red and gold costume (Iron Spider); Garney-a 18.00
529-2nd printing 5.00
529-3rd printing with Wieringo-c 3.00
530,531-Titanium Man app.; Kirkham-a. 531-Begin $2.99-c 6.00
532-538-Civil War tie-in. 538-Aunt May shot 5.00
539-543-Back in Black. 539-Peter wears the black costume 3.00
544-($3.99) "One More Day" pt. 1; Quesada-a/Straczynski-s 4.00
545-(12/08, $3.99) "One More Day" pt. 4; Quesada-a/Straczynski-s, Peter & MJ's marriage un-done; r/wedding from ASM Annual #21; 2 covers by Quesada and Djurdjevic 4.00
546-($3.99) Brand New Day begins; McNiven-a; Deodato, Winslade, Land, Romita Jr.-a; 1st app. Mr. Negative 5.00
546-Variant-c by Bryan Hitch 8.00
546-Second printing with new McNiven-c of Peter Parker 4.00
546-MGC (7/10, $1.00) r/#546 with "Marvel's Greatest Comics" logo on cover 3.00
547-567: 547,548-McNiven-a. 549-551-Larroca-a. 550-Intro. Menace. 555-557-Bachalo-a. 559-Intro. Screwball. 560,561-MJ app. 565-New Kraven intro. 566,567-Spidey in Daredevil costume 3.00
568-($3.99) Romita Jr.-a begins; two covers by Romita Jr. and Alex Ross 6.00
568-Variant-c by John Romita Sr. 20.00
568-2nd printing with Romita Jr. Anti-Venom costume cover 4.00
569-Debut of Anti-Venom; Norman Osborn and Thunderbolts app.;Romita Jr.-c 4.00
569-Variant Venom-c by Granov 6.00
570-572-Two covers on each 3.00
573-($3.99) New Ways to Die conclusion; Spidey meets Stephen Colbert back-up; Ollife-a; two covers by Romita Jr. and Maguire 5.00
573-Variant cover with Stephen Colbert; cover swipe of AF #15 by Quesada 10.00
574-582: 577-Punisher app. 3.00
583-($3.99) Spidey meets Obama back-up story; regular Romita Sr. "Cougars" cover 10.00
583-($3.99) Obama variant-c with Spidey on left; Spidey meets Obama back-up story 40.00
583-($3.99) Second printing Obama variant-c with Spidey on right and yellow bkgrd 8.00
583-($3.99) 3rd-5th printings Obama variant-c: 3rd-Blue bkgrd w/flag. 4th-White bkgrd w/flag. 5th-Lincoln Memorial bkgrd 5.00
584-587, 589-599: 585-Menace ID revealed. 590,591-Fantastic Four app. 594-Aunt May engaged. 595-599-American Son; Osborn Avengers app. app. 3.00
588-($3.99) Conclusion to "Character Assassination"; Romita Jr.-a 4.00
600-(9/09, $4.99) Aunt May's wedding; Romita Jr.-a; Doc Octopus, FF app.; Mary Jane cameo; back-up story by Stan Lee; back-up with Doran-a; 2 covers by Romita Jr. & Ross 8.00
600-Variant covers by Romita Sr. and Quesada 12.00
601-604,606-611,613-616,618-621,623-627: 601-Back-up w/Quesada-a. 606,607-Black Cat app.; Campbell-c. 611-Deadpool-c/app. 612-The Gauntlet begins; Waid-s. 615,616-Sandman app. 621-Black Cat app. 624-Peter Parker fired. 626-Gaydos-a 3.00
605,612,617,622,628-($3.99): 605-Mayhew-c. 613-Rhino back-up story. 617-New Rhino. 622-Bianchi-c; Morbius app. 628-Captain Universe app. 4.00
629-633-($2.99)-Bachalo-a; Lizard app. 3.00
634-641-($3.99) 634-637-Grim Hunt; Kaine app. 635-Kraven returns. 638-641-"One Moment in Time" wedding flashback/ret-con; Quesada-s 4.00
638-641-Variant covers by Quesada 15.00
642-646-($2.99) Waid-s/Azaceta-a; interlocking covers by Djurdjevic 3.00
647-($4.99) Short stories by various; Djurdjevic-c; cover gallery of Brand New Day issues 5.00
648-691-($3.99) 648-Big Time begins; Ramos-a; Hobgoblin app. 654-Flash Thompson becomes Venom; Marla Jameson killed. 655-Martin-a. 657-660-Fantastic Four app. 666-673-Spider Island. 667-672-Ramos-a; Avengers app. 677-X-over w/Daredevil #8. 682-687-Avengers app. 4.00
654.1-(4/11, $2.99) Flash Thompson as Venom; Ramos-a 3.00
679.1-(4/12, $2.99) Morbius the Living Vampire app. 3.00
692-($5.99) Debut of Alpha; Ramos-a; back-up short stories 6.00
693-697: 694-Cover swipe of Superman vs. Spider-Man 4.00
698, 699, 699.1: 698-Doctor Octopus brain switch revealed. 699.1-Morbius origin 4.00
700-($7.99) Collage cover; Leads into Superior Spider-Man #1; back-up short stories 20.00
700-Variant skyline-c by Marcos 40.00
700-Second printing cover with Doctor Octopus on an ASM #300 swipe 8.00
700.1 - 700.5 (2/14, weekly limited series, $3.99) 700.1-Janson-a/Ferry-c 4.00
1999, 2000 Annual (6/99, '00, $3.50) 1999-Buscema-a 4.00
2001 Annual ($2.99) Follows Peter Parker: S-M #29; last Mackie-s 4.00
Annual 1 (2008, $3.99) McKone-a; secret of Jackpot revealed; death of Jackpot 4.00
Annual 36 (9/09, $3.99) Debut of Raptor; Olliffe-a 4.00
Annual 37 (7/10, $3.99) Untold 1st meeting with Captain America; back-up w/Olliffe-a 4.00
Annual 38 (6/11, $3.99) Deadpool & Hulk app.; Garbett-a/McNiven-c 4.00
Annual 39 (7/12, $3.99) Avengers app.; Garbett-a/c 4.00
...: Big Time 1 (8/11, $5.99) r/#648-650 6.00
Collected Edition #30-32 ($3.95) reprints #30-32 w/cover #30 4.00
... 500 Covers HC (2004, $49.99) reprints covers for #1-500 & Annuals; yearly re-caps 50.00
...: Ends of the Earth (7/12, $3.99) Silas-a/Fiumara-c; Big Hero Six app. 4.00
...: Family Business HC (2014, $24.99) Kingpin app.; Waid & Robinson-s/Dell'Otto-a 25.00
Free Comic Book Day 2011 (Spider-Man) 1-Ramos-c/a; Spider-Woman & Shang-Chi app. 3.00
.../Ghost Rider: Motorstorm 1 ('11, $2.99) r/#558-560 3.00
...: Hooky 1 (2012, $4.99) r/Marvel Graphic Novel #22 (1986) with Wrightson-a 5.00
...: Infested 1 (11/11, $3.99) Spider Island tie-in; short stories by various; Ramos-c 4.00
... Omnibus HC (2007, $99.99, dustjacket) r/Amazing Fantasy #15, Amazing Spider-Man #1-38, Annual #1,2, Strange Tales Annual #2 & Fantastic Four Annual #1; letter pages, bonus art, intro. by Stan Lee; bios, essays, Marvel Tales cover gallery 100.00
Spider-Man: Brand New Day - Extra!! #1 (9/08, $3.99) short stories; Bachalo,Olliffe-a 4.00
Spider-Man: Brand New Day Yearbook #1 (2008, $4.99) plot synopses; profile pages 5.00
... Spidey Sunday Spectacuar (7/11, $3.99) collects back-ups from ASM #634-645 4.00
...: Swing Shift (2007 FCBD Edition) Jimenez-c/a; Slott-s 4.00
...: Swing Shift Director's Cut (2008, $3.99) story from 2007 FCBD; Brand New Day info 4.00
The Many Loves of the Amazing Spider-Man (7/10, $3.99) short stories of Black Cat, Gwen & Carlie, and Mary Jane; s/a by various 4.00
...: The Short Halloween (7/09, $3.99) Bill Hader & Seth Meyers-s/Maguire-a 4.00
...: You're Hired 1 (5/11, $3.99) r/story from New York Daily News insert 4.00
...Vol. 1: Coming Home (2001, $15.95) r/#30-35; J. Scott Campbell-c 16.00
...Vol. 2: Revelations (2002, $8.99) r/#36-39; Kaare Andrews-c 9.00
...Vol. 3: Until the Stars Turn Cold (2002, $12.99) r/#40-45; Romita Jr.-c 13.00
...Vol. 4: The Life and Death of Spiders (2003, $11.99) r/#46-50; Campbell-c 12.00
...Vol. 5: Unintended Consequences (2003, $12.99) r/#51-56; Dodson-c 13.00
...Vol. 6: Happy Birthday (2003, $12.99) r/#57,58,500-502 13.00
...Vol. 7: The Book of Ezekiel (2004, $12.99) r/#503-508; Romita Jr.-c 13.00

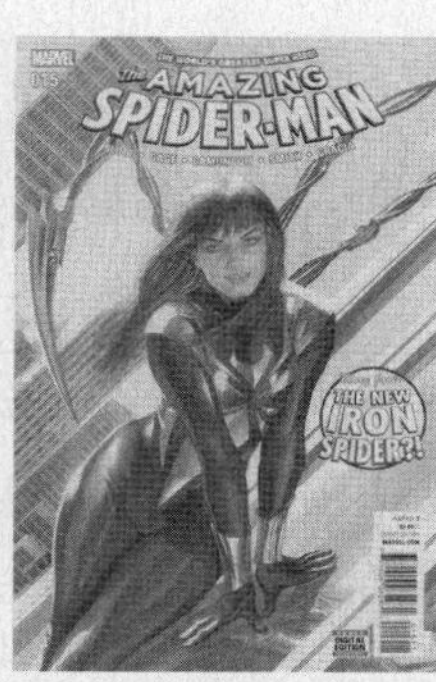

Amazing Spider-Man (2015 series) #15 © MAR

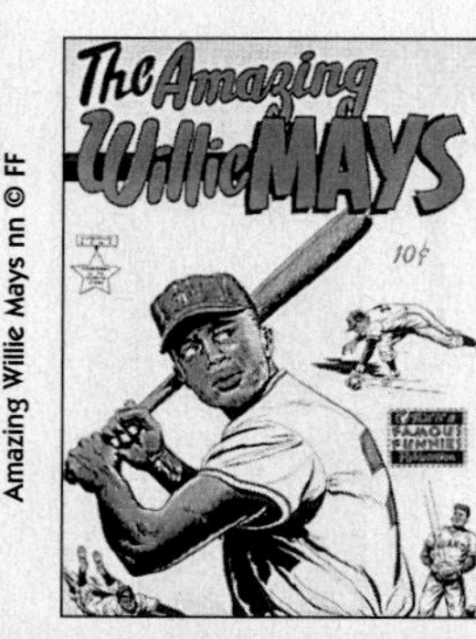

Amazing Willie Mays nn © FF

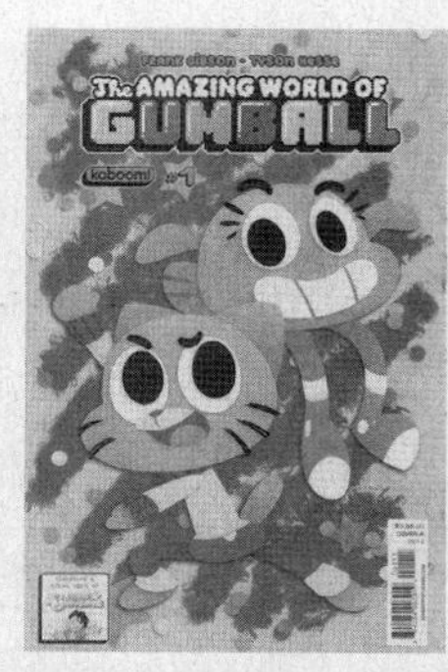

Amazing World of Gumball #1 © TBS

GD 2.0 | VG 4.0 | FN 6.0 | VF 8.0 | VF/NM 9.0 | NM- 9.2

...Vol. 8: Sins Past (2005, $12.99) r/#509-514; cover sketch gallery 13.00
...Vol. 9: Skin Deep (2005, $9.99) r/#515-518 10.00
...Vol. 10: New Avengers (2005, $14.99) r/#519-524 15.00
Brand New Day #1-3 (11/08-1/09, $3.99) reprints #546-551 4.00
Civil War: Amazing Spider-Man TPB (2007, $17.99) r/#532-538; variant covers 18.00

AMAZING SPIDER-MAN (Follows Superior Spider-Man)(Also see Spider-Verse Team-Up)
Marvel Comics: Jun, 2014 - No. 20.1 , Oct, 2015 ($3.99)(there was no #19 or 20)

1-($5.99) 1st app. Cindy Moon (cameo, becomes Silk in #3); Slott-s/Ramos-a; bonus shorts with Electro, Black Cat, Spider-Man 2099, Kaine; bonus r/Inhuman #1; Ramos-c 6.00
1-Variant-c by J. Scott Campbell 8.00
2,3-Cindy Moon app.; Electro app. 2-Avengers app. 3-Black Cat app. 4.00
4-1st app. Silk (Cindy Moon); Original Sin tie-in 20.00
5-8: 5,6-Silk, Black Cat app. 7,8-Ms. Marvel app.; back-up Spider-Verse; Morlun app. 4.00
9-($4.99) Spider-Verse part 1; Variant Spider-Men & Spider-Gwen app.; Coipel-a 6.00
10-15-Spider-Verse; Superior Spider-Man returns. 13,14-Uncle Ben app.; Camuncoli-a 4.00
16-18-Ghost app.; Ramos-a; back-up with Black Cat 4.00
16.1, 17.1, 18.1, 19.1, 20.1-($3.99) Spiral parts 1-5; Conway-s/Barberi-a 4.00
Annual 1 (2/15, $4.99) Sean Ryan-s/Peterson-a/c; Nitz-s/Salas-a 5.00
Special 1(5/15, $4.99) Crossover with Inhumans and All-New Captain America specials 5.00
#1.1-1.5 (Learning to Crawl) (7/14-11/14, $3.99) Re-tells early career; Alex Ross-c 4.00

AMAZING SPIDER-MAN (Follows Secret Wars)
Marvel Comics: Dec, 2015 - Present ($5.99/$3.99)

1-($5.99) Slott-s/Camuncoli-a; main-c by Alex Ross; back-up previews of Spider-titles 6.00
2-18-($3.99) 3,5-Human Torch app. 6-8-Cloak & Dagger app. 13-15-Iron Man app. 15-Mary Jane in the Iron Spider suit. 17-New female Electro 4.00
19-($4.99) Clone Conspiracy tie-in; Kingpin & Rhino app. 5.00
20-24: Clone Conspiracy tie-ins. 20-Doctor Octopus gets his body back. 21-Kaine returns 4.00
#1.1-1.6 (Amazing Grace) (2/16-9/16, $3.99) The Santerians app.; Bianchi-a 4.00
Annual 1 (1/17, $4.99) Short stories by various incl. Wayne Brady, Ramos, Gage, Asmus 5.00

AMAZING SPIDER-MAN & SILK: THE SPIDER(FLY) EFFECT
Marvel Comics: May, 2016 - No. 4, Aug, 2016 ($4.99, limited series)

1-4: 1-Robbie Thompson-s/Todd Nauck-a; time-travelling Peter & Silk meet Ben Parker 5.00

AMAZING SPIDER-MAN EXTRA! (Continued from Spider-Man: Brand New Day - Extra!! #1)
Marvel Comics: No. 2, Mar, 2009 - No. 3, May, 2009 ($3.99)

2,3: 2-Anti-Venom app.; Bachalo-a. 3-Ana Kraven app.; Jimenez-a 4.00

AMAZING SPIDER-MAN FAMILY (Also see Spider-Man Family)
Marvel Comics: Oct, 2008 - No. 8, Sept, 2009 ($4.99, anthology)

1-8-New tales and reprints. 1-Includes r/ASM #300; Granov-c. 2-Deodato-c. 5-Spider-Girl new story. 6-Origin of Jackpot 5.00

AMAZING SPIDER-MAN PRESENTS: AMERICAN SON
Marvel Comics: Jul, 2010 - No. 4, Oct, 2010 ($3.99, limited series)

1-4-Reed-s/Briones-a/Djurdjevic-c; Gabriel Stacy app. 4.00

AMAZING SPIDER-MAN PRESENTS: ANTI-VENOM - NEW WAYS TO LIVE
Marvel Comics: Nov, 2009 - No. 3, Feb, 2010 ($3.99, limited series)

1-3-Wells-s/Siqueira-a; Punisher app. 4.00

AMAZING SPIDER-MAN PRESENTS: JACKPOT
Marvel Comics: Mar, 2010 - No. 3, Jun, 2010 ($3.99, limited series)

1-3-Guggenheim-s/Melo-a; Boomerang and White Rabbit app. 4.00

AMAZING SPIDER-MAN: RENEW YOUR VOWS (Secret Wars tie-in)
Marvel Comics: Aug, 2015 - No. 5, Nov, 2015 ($3.99, limited series)

1-5-Adam Kubert-a; wife Mary Jane and daughter Annie app. 1-Venom app. 4.00

AMAZING SPIDER-MAN: RENEW YOUR VOWS (Series)
Marvel Comics: Jan, 2017 - Present ($4.99/$3.99)

1-($4.99) Conway-s/Stegman-a; Mole Man app.; back-up Holden-s/a; Leth-s/Sauvage-a 5.00
2-4-($3.99) Conway-s/Stegman-a 4.00

AMAZING SPIDER-MAN: THE MOVIE
Marvel Comics: Aug, 2012 - No. 2, Aug, 2012 ($3.99, limited series)

1,2-Partial adaptation of the 2012 movie; Neil Edwards-a; photo covers 4.00

AMAZING SPIDER-MAN: THE MOVIE ADAPTATION
Marvel Comics: Mar, 2014 - No. 2, Apr, 2014 ($2.99, limited series)

1,2-Adaptation of the 2012 movie; Wellington Alves-a; photo covers 3.00

AMAZING WILLIE MAYS, THE
Famous Funnies Publ.: No date (Sept, 1954)

nn 84 168 252 538 919 1300

AMAZING WORLD OF DC COMICS
DC Comics: Jul, 1974 - No. 17, 1978 ($1.50, B&W, mail-order DC Pro-zine)

1-Kubert interview; unpublished Kirby-a; Infantino-c 6 12 18 42 79 115
2-4: 3-Julie Schwartz profile. 4-Batman; Robinson-c 5 10 15 31 53 75
5-Sheldon Mayer 4 8 12 28 47 65
6,8,13: 6-Joe Orlando; EC-r; Wrightson pin-up. 8-Infantino; Batman-r from Pop Tart giveaway. 13-Humor; Aragonés-c; Wood/Ditko-a; photos from serials of Superman, Batman, Captain Marvel 4 8 12 22 35 48
7,10-12: 7-Superman; r/1955 Pep comic giveaway. 10-Behind the scenes at DC; Showcase article. 11-Super-Villains; unpubl. Secret Society of S.V. story. 12-Legion; Grell-c/interview; 4 8 12 23 37 50
9-Legion of Super-Heroes; lengthy bios and history; Cockrum-c 6 12 18 42 79 115
14-Justice League 4 8 12 25 40 55
15-Wonder Woman; Nasser-c 5 10 15 30 50 70
16-Golden Age heroes 4 8 12 28 47 65
17-Shazam; G.A., 70s, TV and Fawcett heroes 4 8 12 25 40 55
Special 1 (Digest size) 3 6 9 20 31 42

AMAZING WORLD OF GUMBALL, THE (Based on the Cartoon Network series)
Boom Entertainment (kaBOOM!): Jun, 2014 - No. 8, Mar, 2015 ($3.99)

1-8-Multiple covers on each 4.00
... 2015 Grab Bag Special (9/15, $4.99) Short stories and pin-ups by various; 3 covers 5.00
... 2015 Special (1/15, $4.99) Short stories by various; 3 covers 5.00
... 2016 Grab Bag Special (8/16, $4.99) Short stories and pin-ups by various 5.00

AMAZING WORLD OF SUPERMAN (See Superman)

AMAZING X-MEN
Marvel Comics: Mar, 1995 - No. 4, July, 1995 ($1.95, limited series)

1-Age of Apocalypse; Andy Kubert-c/a 4.00
2-4 3.00

AMAZING X-MEN
Marvel Comics: Jan, 2014 - No. 19, Jun, 2015 ($3.99)

1-19: 1-Nightcrawler returns; Aaron-s/McGuinness-a; wraparound-c. 7-Firestar, Iceman and Spider-Man app. 8-12-World War Wendigo. 19-Colossus vs. The Juggernaut 4.00
Annual 1 (8/14, $4.99) Larroca-a/c; back-up w/Juan Doe-a 5.00

AMAZON
Comico: Mar, 1989 - No. 3, May, 1989 ($1.95, limited series)

1-3: Ecological theme; Steven Seagle-s/Tim Sale-a 3.00
1-3-(Dark Horse, 3/09 - No. 3, 5/09, $3.50) recolored reprint with creator interviews 3.50

AMAZON (Also see Marvel Versus DC #3 & DC Versus Marvel #4)
DC Comics (Amalgam): Apr, 1996 ($1.95, one-shot)

1-John Byrne-c/a/scripts 3.00

AMAZON ATTACK 3-D
The 3-D Zone: Sept, 1990 ($3.95, 28 pgs.)

1-Chaykin-a 6.00

AMAZONS ATTACK (See Wonder Woman #8 - 2006 series)
DC Comics: Jun, 2007 - No. 6, Late Oct, 2007 ($2.99, limited series)

1-6-Queen Hippolyta and Amazons attacks Wash., DC; Pfeifer-s/Woods-a 3.00

AMAZON WOMAN (1st Series)
FantaCo: Summer, 1994 - No. 2, Fall, 1994 ($2.95, B&W, limited series, mature)

1,2: Tom Simonton-c/a/scripts 3.00

AMAZON WOMAN (2nd Series)
FantaCo: Feb, 1996 - No. 4, May, 1996 ($2.95, B&W, limited series, mature)

1-4: Tom Simonton-a/scripts 3.00
...: Invaders of Terror ('96, $5.95) Simonton-a/s 6.00

AMBUSH BUG (Also see Son of...)
DC Comics: June, 1985 - No. 4, Sept, 1985 (75¢, limited series)

1-4: Giffen-c/a in all 4.00
Nothing Special 1 (9/92, $2.50, 68 pg.)-Giffen-c/a 4.00
Stocking Stuffer (2/86, $1.25)-Giffen-c/a 4.00

AMBUSH BUG: YEAR NONE
DC Comics: Sept, 2008 - No. 5, Jan, 2009; No. 7, Dec, 2009 ($2.99, limited series, no #6)

1-5,7-Giffen-s/a; Jonni DC app. 4-Conner-c. 7-Baltazar & Franco-a; Giffen-a 3.00

AME-COMI GIRLS (Based on the Anime-styled statue series)
DC Comics: Dec, 2012 - No. 5, Apr, 2013 ($3.99, printed version of digital-first series)

1-5: 1-Wonder Woman; Conner-c/a. 2-Batgirl. 3-Duela Dent; Naifeh-a 4.00

AME-COMI GIRLS (Based on the Anime-styled statue series)

America #1 © MAR

American Century #1 © Chaykin & DC

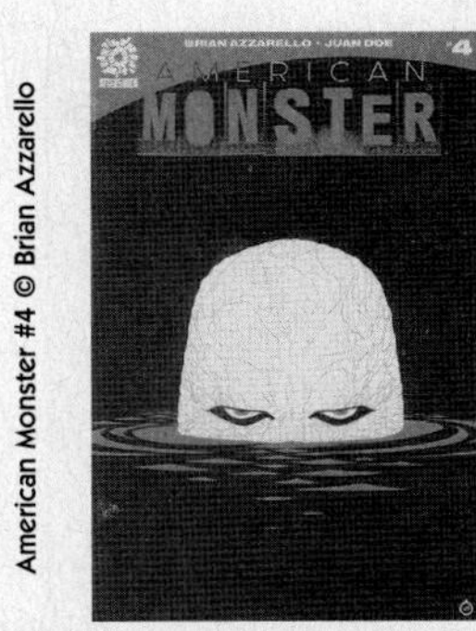

American Monster #4 © Brian Azzarello

	GD 2.0	VG 4.0	FN 6.0	VF 8.0	VF/NM 9.0	NM- 9.2

DC Comics: May, 2013 - No. 8, Dec, 2013 ($3.99)
1-8: 1-Palmiotti & Gray-s/Francisco-a; story continues from earlier series 4.00

AMERICA (From Young Avengers and The Ultimates)
Marvel Comics: May, 2017 - Present ($3.99)
1-Gabby Rivera-s/Joe Quinones-a; Captain Marvel & Spectrum app. 4.00

AMERICA AT WAR - THE BEST OF DC WAR COMICS (See Fireside Book Series)

AMERICA IN ACTION
Dell (Imp. Publ. Co.)/ Mayflower House Publ.: 1942; Winter, 1945 (36 pgs.)
1942-Dell-(68 pgs.) 19 38 57 111 176 240
1-(1945)-Has 3 adaptations from American history; Kiefer, Schrotter & Webb-a 14 28 42 82 121 160

AMERICAN, THE
Dark Horse Comics: July, 1987 - No. 8, 1989 ($1.50/$1.75, B&W)
1-8: ($1.50) 3.00
Collection ($5.95, B&W)-Reprints 6.00
Special 1 (1990, $2.25, B&W) 3.00

AMERICAN AIR FORCES, THE (See A-1 Comics)
William H. Wise(Flying Cadet Publ. Co./Hasan(No.1)/Life's Romances/ Magazine Ent. No. 5 on): Sept-Oct, 1944-No. 4, 1945; No. 5, 1951-No. 12, 1954
1-Article by Zack Mosley, creator of Smilin' Jack; German war-c 42 84 126 265 445 625
2-Classic-Japan war-c 84 168 252 538 919 1300
3,4-Japan war-c 20 40 60 114 182 250
NOTE: *All part comic, part magazine. Art by* **Whitney, Chas. Quinlan, H. C. Kiefer,** *and* **Tony Dipreta.**
5(A-1 45)(Formerly Jet Powers), 6(A-1 54), 7(A-1 58), 8(A-1 65), 9(A-1 67), 10(A-1 74), 11(A-1 79), 12(A-1 91) 10 20 30 54 72 90
NOTE: **Powell** *c/a-5-12.*

AMERICAN CENTURY
DC Comics (Vertigo): May, 2001 - No. 27, Oct, 2003 ($2.50/$2.75)
1-Chaykin-s/painted-c; Tischman-a 4.00
2-27: 5-New story arc begins. 10-16,22-27-Orbik-c. 17-21-Silke-c. 18-$2.75-c begins 3.00
Hollywood Babylon (2002, $12.95, TPB) r/#5-9; w/sketch-to-art pages 13.00
Scars & Stripes (2001, $8.95, TPB) r/#1-4; Tischman intro. 9.00

AMERICAN DREAM (From the M2 Avengers)
Marvel Comics: Jul, 2008 - No. 5, Sept, 2008 ($2.99, limited series)
1-5-DeFalco-s/Nauck-a 3.00

AMERICAN FLAGG! (See First Comics Graphic Novel 3,9,12,21 & Howard Chaykin's..)
First Comics: Oct, 1983 - No. 50, Mar, 1988
1,21-27: 1-Chaykin-c/a begins. 21-27-Alan Moore scripts 4.00
2-20,28-49: 31-Origin Bob Violence 3.00
50-Last issue 4.00
Special 1 (11/86)-Introduces Chaykin's Time² 4.00
...: Hard Times TPB (6/85, $11.95) r/#1-7; intro. by Michael Moorcock; bonus materials 12.00
...: Definitive Collection Volume 1 HC (2008, $49.99) r/#1-14 and material from the...: Hard Times TPB; intro by Michael Chabon; afterword by Jim Lee 50.00

AMERICAN FREAK: A TALE OF THE UN-MEN
DC Comics (Vertigo): Feb, 1994 - No. 5, Jun, 1994 ($1.95, mini-series, mature)
1-5 3.00

AMERICAN GRAPHICS
Henry Stewart: No. 1, 1954; No. 2, 1957 (25¢)
1-The Maid of the Mist, The Last of the Eries (Indian Legends of Niagara) (sold at Niagara Falls) 11 22 33 64 90 115
2-Victory at Niagara & Laura Secord (Heroine of the War of 1812) 8 16 24 40 50 60

AMERICAN INDIAN, THE (See Picture Progress)

AMERICAN LEGENDS
Image Comics (Top Cow): Nov, 2014 - Present ($3.99)
1-Studio Hive-a; multiple covers 4.00

AMERICAN LIBRARY
David McKay Publ.: 1943 - No. 6, 1944 (15¢, 68 pgs., B&W, text & pictures)
nn (#1)-Thirty Seconds Over Tokyo (movie) 47 94 141 296 498 700
nn (#2)-Guadalcanal Diary; painted-c (only 10¢) 34 68 102 206 336 465
3-6: 3-Look to the Mountain. 4-Case of the Crooked Candle (Perry Mason). 5-Duel in the Sun. 6-Wingate's Raiders 18 36 54 105 165 225

AMERICAN: LOST IN AMERICA, THE
Dark Horse Comics: July, 1992 - No. 4, Oct, 1992 ($2.50, limited series)
1-4: 1-Dorman painted-c. 2-Phillips painted-c. 3-Mignola-c. 4-Jim Lee-c 3.00

AMERICAN MONSTER
AfterShock Comics: Jan, 2016 - Present ($3.99)
1-5-Brian Azzarello-s/Juan Doe-a 4.00

AMERICAN MYTHOLOGY DARK: WEREWOLVES VS DINOSAURS
American Mythology Prods.: 2016 - Present ($3.99)
1-Chris Scalf & Eric Dobson-s/a; 3 covers 4.00

AMERICAN SPLENDOR: (Series of titles)
Dark Horse Comics: Aug, 1996 - Apr, 2001 (B&W, all one-shots)
--**COMIC-CON COMICS** (8/96) 1-H. Pekar script. --**MUSIC COMICS** (11/97) nn-H. Pekar-s/ Sacco-a; r/Village Voice jazz strips. --**ODDS AND ENDS** (12/97) 1-Pekar-s. --**ON THE JOB** (5/97) 1-Pekar-s. --**A STEP OUT OF THE NEST** (8/94) 1-Pekar-s. --**TERMINAL** (9/99) 1-Pekar-s. --**TRANSATLANTIC** (7/98) 1-"American Splendour" on cover; Pekar-s 3.00
--**A PORTRAIT OF THE AUTHOR IN HIS DECLINING YEARS** (4/01, $3.99) 1-Photo-c. --**BEDTIME STORIES** (6/00, $3.95) 4.00

AMERICAN SPLENDOR
DC Comics: Nov, 2006 - No. 4, Feb, 2007 ($2.99, B&W)
1-4-Pekar-s/art by Haspiel and various. 1-Fabry-c 3.00
...: Another Day TPB (2007, $14.99) r/#1-4 15.00

AMERICAN SPLENDOR (Volume 2)
DC Comics (Vertigo): Jun, 2008 - No. 4, Sept, 2008 ($2.99, B&W)
1-4-Pekar-s/art by Haspiel and various. 1-Bond-c. 3-Cooke-c 3.00
...: Another Dollar TPB (2009, $14.99) r/#1-4 15.00

AMERICAN SPLENDOR: UNSUNG HERO
Dark Horse Comics: Aug, 2002 - No. 3, Oct, 2002 ($3.99, B&W, limited series)
1-3-Pekar script/Collier-a; biography of Robert McNeill 4.00
TPB (8/03, $11.95) r/#1-3 12.00

AMERICAN SPLENDOR: WINDFALL
Dark Horse Comics: Sept, 1995 - No. 2, Oct,1995 ($3.95, B&W, limited series)
1,2-Pekar script 4.00

AMERICAN TAIL: FIEVEL GOES WEST, AN
Marvel Comics: Early Jan, 1992 - No. 3, Early Feb, 1992 ($1.00, limited series)
1-3-Adapts Universal animated movie; Wildman-a 3.00
1-($2.95-c, 69 pgs.) Deluxe squarebound edition 5.00

AMERICAN VAMPIRE
DC Comics (Vertigo): May, 2010 - Present ($3.99/$2.99)
1-10: 1-9-Snyder-s/Albuquerque-a. 1-5-Back-up story by Stephen King 4.00
1-5-Variant-c: 1-Jim Lee. 2-Berni Wrightson. 3-Andy Kubert. 5-Paul Pope 6.00
11-34-($2.99) 11-Santolouco-a. 12-Zezelj-a. 19-21-Bernet-a 3.00
... Anthology 1 (10/13, $7.99) Short stories by various; Albuquerque-c 8.00
...: The Long Road to Hell 1 (8/13, $6.99) Snyder-s/Albuquerque-a 7.00
HC (2010, $24.99, d.j.) r/#1-5; intro. by Stephen King; script pages and sketch art 25.00
...Volume Two HC (2011, $24.99, d.j.) r/#6-11; cover design art 25.00

AMERICAN VAMPIRE: LORD OF NIGHTMARES
DC Comics (Vertigo): Aug, 2012 - No. 5, Dec, 2012 ($2.99, limited series)
1-5-Set in 1954 England; Snyder-s/Nguyen-a/c. 2-Origin of Dracula 3.00

AMERICAN VAMPIRE: SECOND CYCLE
DC Comics (Vertigo): May, 2014 - No. 11, Jan, 2016 ($3.99/$2.99, limited series)
1,8-10-($3.99) Snyder-s/Albuquerque-a/c 4.00
2-7-($2.99) 5-Bergara-a 3.00
11-($4.99) Snyder-s/Albuquerque-a/c 5.00

AMERICAN VAMPIRE: SURVIVAL OF THE FITTEST
DC Comics (Vertigo): Aug, 2011 - No. 5, Dec, 2011 ($2.99, limited series)
1-5-Set during WWII; Snyder-s/Murphy-a/c 3.00

AMERICAN VIRGIN
DC Comics (Vertigo): May, 2006 - No. 23, Mar, 2008 ($2.99)
1-23-Steven Seagle-s/Becky Cloonan-a in most. 1-3-Quitely-c. 4-14-Middleton-c 3.00
...: Head (2006, $9.99, TPB) r/#1-4; interviews with the creators and page development 10.00
...: Going Down (2007, $14.99, TPB) r/#5-9 15.00
...: Wet (2007, $12.99, TPB) r/#10-14 13.00
...: Around the World (Vol. 4) (2008, $17.99, TPB) r/#15-23 18.00

AMERICAN WAY, THE
DC Comics (WildStorm): Apr, 2006 - No. 8, Nov, 2006 ($2.99, limited series)
1-8-John Ridley-s/Georges Jeanty-a/c 3.00
TPB (2007, $19.99) r/series; covers; Jeanty sketch pages 20.00

America's Best Comics #12 © Nedor

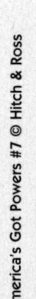

America's Got Powers #7 © Hitch & Ross

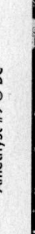

Amethyst #9 © DC

GD 2.0 VG 4.0 FN 6.0 VF 8.0 VF/NM 9.0 NM- 9.2

AMERICA'S BEST COMICS
Nedor/Better/Standard Publications: Feb, 1942; No. 2, Sept, 1942 - No. 31, July, 1949 (New logo with #9)

1-The Woman in Red, Black Terror, Captain Future, Doc Strange, The Liberator, & Don Davis, Secret Ace begin 371 742 1113 2600 4550 6500
2-Origin The American Eagle; The Woman in Red ends 161 322 483 1030 1765 2500
3-Pyroman begins (11/42, 1st app.; also see Startling Comics #18, 12/42) 155 310 465 992 1696 2400
4-6: 5-Last Capt. Future (not in #4); Lone Eagle app. 6-American Crusader app. 116 232 348 742 1271 1800
7-Hitler, Mussolini & Hirohito-c 314 628 942 2198 3849 5500
8-Last Liberator 113 226 339 718 1234 1750
9-The Fighting Yank begins; The Ghost app. 115 230 345 738 1253 1775
10-Flag-c 110 220 330 704 1202 1700
11-Hirohito & Tojo-c. (10/44) 129 258 387 826 1413 2000
12 86 172 258 546 936 1325
13-Japanese WWII-c 103 206 309 659 1130 1600
14-17: 14-American Eagle ends; Doc Strange vs. Hitler story 71 142 213 454 777 1100
18-Classic-c 97 194 291 621 1061 1500
19-21: 21-Infinity-c 63 126 189 403 689 975
22-Capt. Future app. 55 110 165 352 601 850
23-Miss Masque begins; last Doc Strange 77 154 231 493 847 1200
24-Miss Masque bondage-c 74 148 222 470 810 1150
25-Last Fighting Yank; Sea Eagle app. 58 116 174 371 636 900
26-Miss Masque motorcycle-c; The Phantom Detective & The Silver Knight app.; Frazetta text illo & some panels in Miss Masque 65 130 195 416 708 1000
27-31: 27,28-Commando Cubs. 27-Doc Strange. 28-Tuska Black Terror. 29-Last Pyroman 53 106 159 334 567 800

NOTE: *American Eagle not in 3, 8, 9, 13. Fighting Yank not in 10, 12. Liberator not in 2, 6, 7. Pyroman not in 9, 11, 14-16, 23, 25-27.* ***Schomburg (Xela)*** *c-5, 7-31. Bondage c-18, 24.*

AMERICA'S BEST COMICS
America's Best Comics: 1999 - 2008

... Preview (1999, Wizard magazine supplement) - Previews Tom Strong, Top Ten, Promethea, Tomorrow Stories 3.00
... Primer (2008, $4.99, TPB) r/Tom Strong #1, Tom Strong's Terrific Tales, Top Ten #1, Promethea #1, Tomorrow Stories #1,6 5.00
... Sketchbook (2002, $5.95, square-bound)-Design sketches by Sprouse, Ross, Adams, Nowlan, Ha and others 6.00
Special 1 (2/01, $6.95)-Short stories of Alan Moore's characters; art by various; Ross-c 7.00
TPB (2004, $17.95) Reprints short stories and sketch pages from ABC titles 18.00

AMERICA'S BEST TV COMICS (TV)
American Broadcasting Co. (Prod. by Marvel Comics): 1967 (25¢, 68 pgs.)

1-Spider-Man, Fantastic Four (by Kirby/Ayers), Casper, King Kong, George of the Jungle, Journey to the Center of the Earth stories (promotes new TV cartoon show) 10 20 30 69 147 225

AMERICA'S BIGGEST COMICS BOOK
William H. Wise: 1944 (196 pgs., one-shot)

1-The Grim Reaper, The Silver Knight, Zudo, the Jungle Boy, Commando Cubs, Thunderhoof app. 48 96 144 302 514 725

AMERICA'S FUNNIEST COMICS
William H. Wise: 1944 - No. 2, 1944 (15¢, 80 pgs.)

nn(#1), 2-Funny Animal 24 48 72 142 234 325

AMERICA'S GOT POWERS
Image Comics: Apr, 2012 - No. 7, Oct, 2013 ($2.99, limited series)

1-7-Jonathan Ross-s/Bryan Hitch-a/c. 1-Wraparound-c 3.00

AMERICA'S GREATEST COMICS
Fawcett Publications: May?, 1941 - No. 8, Summer, 1943 (15¢, 100 pgs., soft cardboard-c)

1-Bulletman, Spy Smasher, Capt. Marvel, Minute Man & Mr. Scarlet begin; Classic Mac Raboy-c. 1st time that Fawcett's major super-heroes appear together as a group on a cover. Fawcett's 1st squarebound comic 343 686 1029 2400 4200 6000
2 145 290 435 921 1586 2250
3 113 226 339 718 1234 1750
4,5: 4-Commando Yank begins; Golden Arrow, Ibis the Invincible & Spy Smasher cameo in Captain Marvel 77 154 231 489 837 1185
6,7: 7-Balbo the Boy Magician app.; Captain Marvel, Bulletman cameo in Mr. Scarlet 68 136 204 435 743 1050
8-Capt. Marvel Jr. & Golden Arrow app.; Spy Smasher x-over in Capt. Midnight; no Minute Man or Commando Yank 68 136 204 435 743 1050

GD 2.0 VG 4.0 FN 6.0 VF 8.0 VF/NM 9.0 NM- 9.2

AMERICA'S SWEETHEART SUNNY (See Sunny, ...)

AMERICA VS. THE JUSTICE SOCIETY
DC Comics: Jan, 1985 - No. 4, Apr, 1985 ($1.00, limited series)

1-Double size; Alcala-a(i) in all 2 4 6 8 10 12
2-4: 3,4-Spectre cameo 1 2 3 5 7 9

AMERICOMICS
Americomics: April, 1983 - No. 6, Mar, 1984 ($2.00, Baxter paper/slick paper)

1-Intro/origin The Shade; Intro. The Slayer, Captain Freedom and The Liberty Corps; Perez-c 5.00
1,2-2nd printings ($2.00) 3.00
2-6: 2-Messenger app. & 1st app. Tara on Jungle Island. 3-New & old Blue Beetle battle. 4-Origin Dragonfly & Shade. 5-Origin Commando D. 6-Origin the Scarlet Scorpion 3.00
Special 1 (8/83, $2.00)-Sentinels of Justice (Blue Beetle, Captain Atom, Nightshade & The Question) 5.00

AMETHYST
DC Comics: Jan, 1985 - No. 16, Aug, 1986 (75¢)

1-16: 8-Fire Jade's i.d. revealed 3.00
Special 1 (10/86, $1.25) 4.00
1-4 (11/87 - 2/88)(Limited series) 3.00

AMETHYST, PRINCESS OF GEMWORLD (See Legion of Super-Heroes #298)
DC Comics: May, 1983 - No. 12, Apr, 1984 (Maxi-series)

1-(60¢) 5.00
1,2-(35¢): tested in Austin & Kansas City 5 10 15 31 53 75
2-12, Annual 1(9/84): 5-11-Pérez-c(p) 4.00

NOTE: *Issues #1 & 2 also have Canadian variants with a 75¢ cover price.*

AMORY WARS (Based on the Coheed and Cambria album The Second Stage Turbine Blade)
Image Comics: Jun, 2007 - No. 5, Jan, 2008 ($2.99, limited series)

1-5: 1-Claudio Sanchez-s/Gus Vasquez-a 3.00

AMORY WARS II
Image Comics: Jun, 2008 - No. 5, Oct, 2008 ($2.99, limited series)

1-5-Claudio Sanchez-s/Gabriel Guzman-a 3.00

AMORY WARS IN KEEPING SECRETS OF SILENT EARTH: 3
BOOM! Studios: May, 2010 - No. 12, Jun, 2011 ($3.99)

1-12: 1-Claudio Sanchez & Peter David-s/Chris Burnham-a. 1-Four covers 4.00

AMY RACECAR COLOR SPECIAL (See Stray Bullets)
El Capitán Books: July, 1997; Oct, 1999 ($2.95/$3.50)

1,2-David Lapham-a/scripts. 2-($3.50) 3.50

ANARCHO DICTATOR OF DEATH (See Comics Novel)

ANARKY (See Batman titles)
DC Comics: May, 1997 - No. 4, Aug, 1997 ($2.50, limited series)

1 3.50
2-4 3.00

ANARKY (See Batman titles)
DC Comics: May, 1999 - No. 8, Dec, 1999 ($2.50)

1-8: 1-JLA app.; Grant-s/Breyfogle-a. 3-Green Lantern app. 7-Day of Judgment; Haunted Tank app. 8-Joker-c/app. 3.00

ANCHORS ANDREWS (The Saltwater Daffy)
St. John Publishing Co.: Jan, 1953 - No. 4, July, 1953 (Anchors the Saltwater... No. 4)

1-Canteen Kate by Matt Baker (9 pgs.) 24 48 72 142 234 325
2-4 10 20 30 56 76 95

ANDY & WOODY (See March of Comics No. 40, 55, 76)

ANDY BURNETT (TV, Disney)
Dell Publishing Co.: Dec, 1957

Four Color 865-Photo-c 8 16 24 52 99 145

ANDY COMICS (Formerly Scream Comics; becomes Ernie Comics)
Current Publications (Ace Magazines): No. 20, June, 1948-No. 21, Aug, 1948

20,21: Archie-type comic 10 20 30 56 76 95

ANDY DEVINE WESTERN
Fawcett Publications: Dec, 1950 - No. 2, 1951

1-Photo-c 47 94 141 296 498 700
2-Photo-c 32 64 96 192 314 435

ANDY GRIFFITH SHOW, THE (TV)(1st show aired 10/3/60)
Dell Publishing Co.: #1252, Jan-Mar, 1962; #1341, Apr-Jun, 1962

Four Color 1252(#1) 36 72 108 259 580 900

Andy Panda FC #409 © Walter Lantz

A-Next #11 © MAR

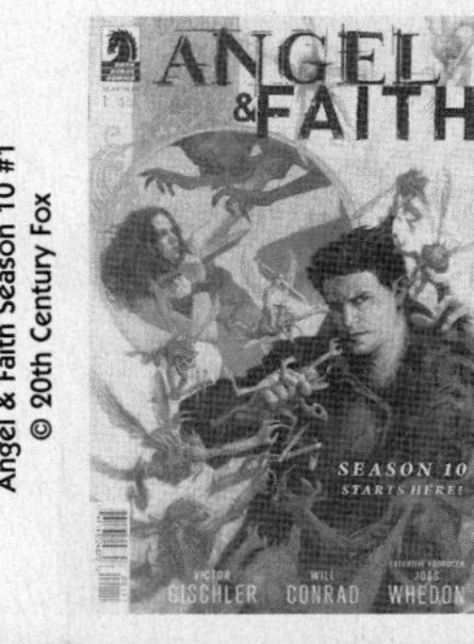

Angel & Faith Season 10 #1 © 20th Century Fox

	GD 2.0	VG 4.0	FN 6.0	VF 8.0	VF/NM 9.0	NM- 9.2
Four Color 1341-Photo-c	33	66	99	238	532	825

ANDY HARDY COMICS (See Movie Comics #3 by Fiction House)
Dell Publishing Co.: April, 1952 - No. 6, Sept-Nov, 1954

	GD 2.0	VG 4.0	FN 6.0	VF 8.0	VF/NM 9.0	NM- 9.2
Four Color 389(#1)	5	10	15	35	63	90
Four Color 447,480,515, #5,#6	4	8	12	27	44	60

ANDY PANDA (Also see Crackajack Funnies #39, The Funnies, New Funnies & Walter Lantz...)
Dell Publishing Co.: 1943 - No. 56, Nov-Jan, 1961-62 (Walter Lantz)

	GD 2.0	VG 4.0	FN 6.0	VF 8.0	VF/NM 9.0	NM- 9.2
Four Color 25(#1, 1943)	46	92	138	368	834	1300
Four Color 54(1944)	25	50	75	175	388	600
Four Color 85(1945)	15	30	45	103	227	350
Four Color 130(1946),154,198	10	20	30	70	150	230
Four Color 216,240,258,280,297	8	16	24	55	105	155
Four Color 326,345,358	6	12	18	41	76	110
Four Color 383,409	5	10	15	35	63	90
16(11-1/52-53) - 30	4	8	12	28	47	65
31-56	4	8	12	23	37	50

(See March of Comics #5, 22, 79, & Super Book #4, 15, 27.)

A-NEXT (See Avengers)
Marvel Comics: Oct, 1998 - No. 12, Sept, 1999 ($1.99)

	GD 2.0	VG 4.0	FN 6.0	VF 8.0	VF/NM 9.0	NM- 9.2
1-6,8-12: 1-Next generation of Avengers; Frenz-a. 2-Two covers. 3-Defenders app.						3.00
7-1st app. of Hope Pym						5.00
Spider-Girl Presents Avengers Next Vol. 1: Second Coming (2006, $7.99, digest) r/#1-6						8.00

ANGEL
Dell Publishing Co.: Aug, 1954 - No. 16, Nov-Jan, 1958-59

	GD 2.0	VG 4.0	FN 6.0	VF 8.0	VF/NM 9.0	NM- 9.2
Four Color 576(#1, 8/54)	5	10	15	30	50	70
2(5-7/55) - 16	3	6	9	17	26	35

ANGEL (TV) (Also see Buffy the Vampire Slayer)
Dark Horse Comics: Nov, 1999 - No. 17, Apr, 2001 ($2.95/$2.99)

	GD 2.0	VG 4.0	FN 6.0	VF 8.0	VF/NM 9.0	NM- 9.2
1-17: 1-3,5-7,10-14-Zanier-a. 1-4,7,10-Matsuda & photo-c. 16-Buffy-c/app.						3.00
...: Earthly Possessions TPB (4/01, $9.95) r/#5-7, photo-c						10.00
...: Surrogates TPB (12/00, $9.95) r/#1-3; photo-c						10.00

ANGEL (Buffy the Vampire Slayer)
Dark Horse Comics: Sept, 2001 - No. 4, May, 2002 ($2.99, limited series)

	GD 2.0	VG 4.0	FN 6.0	VF 8.0	VF/NM 9.0	NM- 9.2
1-4-Joss Whedon & Matthews-s/Rubi-a; photo-c and Rubi-c on each						3.00

ANGEL (Buffy the Vampire Slayer) (Previously titled Angel: After the Fall)
IDW Publishing: No. 18, Feb, 2009 - No. 44, Apr, 2011 ($3.99)

	GD 2.0	VG 4.0	FN 6.0	VF 8.0	VF/NM 9.0	NM- 9.2
18-44: Multiple covers on all. 25-Juliet Landau-s						4.00

ANGEL (one-shots) (Buffy the Vampire Slayer)
IDW Publishing: ($3.99/$7.49)

	GD 2.0	VG 4.0	FN 6.0	VF 8.0	VF/NM 9.0	NM- 9.2
...: Connor (8/06, $3.99) Jay Faerber-s/Bob Gill-a; 4 covers + 1 retailer cover						4.00
...: Doyle (7/06, $3.99) Jeff Mariotte-s/David Messina-a; 4 covers + 1 retailer cover						4.00
...: Gunn (5/06, $3.99) Dan Jolley-s/Mark Pennington-a; 4 covers + 2 retailer covers						4.00
...: Illyria (4/06, $3.99) Peter David-s/Nicola Scott-a; 4 covers + 2 retailer covers						4.00
...: Masks (10/06, $7.49) short stories of Angel, Illyria, Cordilia & Lindsay; puppet Angel app.						8.00
... 100-Page Spectacular (4/11, $7.99) reprints of 4 issues; Runge-c						8.00
... Special • Lorne (3/10, $7.99) John Byrne-s/a; The Groosalugg app.						8.00
Team Angel 100-Page Spectacular (4/11, $7.99) reprints; Runge-c						8.00
...: Vs. Frankenstein (10/09, $3.99) John Byrne-s/a/c						4.00
...: Vs. Frankenstein II (10/10, $3.99) John Byrne-s/a/c						4.00
...: Wesley (6/06, $3.99) Scott Tipton-s/Mike Norton-a; 4 covers + 1 retailer cover						4.00
Spotlight TPB (12/06, $19.99) r/Connor, Doyle, Gunn, Illyria & Wesley one-shots						20.00
... Yearbook (5/11, $7.99) short stories by various; 3 covers						8.00

ANGELA
Image Comics (Todd McFarlane Prod.): Dec, 1994 - No. 3, Feb, 1995 ($2.95, lim. series)

	GD 2.0	VG 4.0	FN 6.0	VF 8.0	VF/NM 9.0	NM- 9.2
1-Gaiman scripts & Capullo-c/a in all; Spawn app.	1	2	3	5	6	8
2						6.00
3						5.00
Special Edition (1995)-Pirate Spawn-c	3	6	9	14	20	25
Special Edition (1995)-Angela-c	3	6	9	14	20	25
TPB ($9.95, 1995) reprints #1-3 & Special Ed. w/additional pin-ups						10.00

ANGELA: ASGARD'S ASSASSIN (The Image Comics character in the Marvel Universe)
Marvel Comics: Feb, 2015 - No. 6, Jul, 2015 ($3.99)

	GD 2.0	VG 4.0	FN 6.0	VF 8.0	VF/NM 9.0	NM- 9.2
1-6: 1-Gillen-s/Jimenez-a; multiple covers. 4-6-Guardians of the Galaxy app.						4.00

ANGEL: AFTER THE FALL (Buffy the Vampire Slayer) (Follows the last TV episode)
IDW Publishing: Nov, 2007 - No. 17, Feb, 2009 ($3.99)(Continues as Angel with #18)

	GD 2.0	VG 4.0	FN 6.0	VF 8.0	VF/NM 9.0	NM- 9.2
1-Whedon & Lynch-s; multiple covers						5.00
2-17: Multiple covers on all						4.00

ANGELA/GLORY: RAGE OF ANGELS (See Glory/Angela: Rage of Angels)
Image Comics (Todd McFarlane Productions): Mar, 1996 ($2.50, one-shot)

	GD 2.0	VG 4.0	FN 6.0	VF 8.0	VF/NM 9.0	NM- 9.2
1-Liefeld-c/Cruz-a(p); Darkchylde preview flip book						4.00
1-Variant-c						4.00

ANGEL: A HOLE IN THE WORLD (Adaptation of the 2-part TV episode)
IDW Publishing: Dec, 2009 - No. 5, Apr, 2010 ($3.99, limited series)

	GD 2.0	VG 4.0	FN 6.0	VF 8.0	VF/NM 9.0	NM- 9.2
1-5-Fred becomes Illyria; Casagrande-a/c						4.00

ANGEL & FAITH (Follows Buffy the Vampire Slayer Season Eight)
Dark Horse Comics: Aug, 2011 - No. 25, Aug, 2013 ($2.99)

	GD 2.0	VG 4.0	FN 6.0	VF 8.0	VF/NM 9.0	NM- 9.2
1-Gage-s/Isaacs-a; two covers by Morris & Chen						3.00
2-25-Two covers by Morris & Isaacs. 5-Harmony & Clem app.; Noto-a. 7-Drusilla app. 11-14-Willow & Connor app. 20-Spike app.; Archie style-c						3.00

ANGEL & FAITH SEASON 10 (Buffy the Vampire Slayer)
Dark Horse Comics: Apr, 2014 - No. 25, Apr, 2016 ($3.50/$3.99)

	GD 2.0	VG 4.0	FN 6.0	VF 8.0	VF/NM 9.0	NM- 9.2
1-15-Two covers on each. 1-Gischler-s/Conrad-a. 5-Santacruz-a. 6-10-Amy app. 10-Fred returns						3.50
16-25-($3.99) 17-Drusilla returns						4.00

ANGEL AND THE APE (Meet Angel No. 7) (See Limited Collector's Edition C-34 & Showcase No. 77)
National Periodical Publications: Nov-Dec, 1968 - No. 6, Sept-Oct, 1969

	GD 2.0	VG 4.0	FN 6.0	VF 8.0	VF/NM 9.0	NM- 9.2
1-(11-12/68)-Not Wood-a	4	8	12	28	47	65
2-5-Wood inks in all. 4-Last 12¢ issue	3	6	9	19	30	40
6-Wood inks	3	6	9	21	33	45

ANGEL AND THE APE (2nd Series)
DC Comics: Mar, 1991 - No. 4, June, 1991 ($1.00, limited series)

	GD 2.0	VG 4.0	FN 6.0	VF 8.0	VF/NM 9.0	NM- 9.2
1-4						3.00

ANGEL AND THE APE (3rd Series)
DC Comics (Vertigo): Oct, 2001 - No. 4, Jan 2002 ($2.95, limited series)

	GD 2.0	VG 4.0	FN 6.0	VF 8.0	VF/NM 9.0	NM- 9.2
1-4-Chaykin & Tischman-s/Bond-a/Art Adams-c						3.00

ANGELA: QUEEN OF HEL (The Image Comics character in the Marvel Universe)
Marvel Comics: Dec, 2015 - No. 7, Jun, 2016 ($3.99)

	GD 2.0	VG 4.0	FN 6.0	VF 8.0	VF/NM 9.0	NM- 9.2
1-5: 1-Bennett-s/Jacinto & Hans-a. 4,5-Hela app. 6,7-Thor (Jane) app.						4.00

ANGEL: AULD LANG SYNE (Buffy the Vampire Slayer)
IDW Publishing: Nov, 2006 - No. 5, Mar, 2007 ($3.99, limited series)

	GD 2.0	VG 4.0	FN 6.0	VF 8.0	VF/NM 9.0	NM- 9.2
1-5: 1-Three covers plus photo-c; Tipton-s/Messina-a						4.00

ANGEL: BARBARY COAST (Buffy the Vampire Slayer)
IDW Publishing: Apr, 2010 - No. 3, Jun, 2010 ($3.99, limited series)

	GD 2.0	VG 4.0	FN 6.0	VF 8.0	VF/NM 9.0	NM- 9.2
1-3-Angel in 1906 San Francisco; Tischman-s/Urru-a; 2 covers on each						4.00

ANGEL: BLOOD & TRENCHES (Buffy the Vampire Slayer)
IDW Publishing: Mar, 2009 - No. 4, June, 2009 ($3.99, B&W&Red, limited series)

	GD 2.0	VG 4.0	FN 6.0	VF 8.0	VF/NM 9.0	NM- 9.2
1-4-Angel in World War II Europe; John Byrne-s/a/c						4.00

ANGEL: ILLYRIA: HAUNTED (Buffy the Vampire Slayer)
IDW Publishing: Nov, 2010 - No. 4, Feb, 2011 ($3.99, limited series)

	GD 2.0	VG 4.0	FN 6.0	VF 8.0	VF/NM 9.0	NM- 9.2
1-4-Tipton & Huehner-s/Casagrande-a; 2 covers						4.00

ANGEL LOVE
DC Comics: Aug, 1986 - No. 8, Mar, 1987 (75¢, limited series)

	GD 2.0	VG 4.0	FN 6.0	VF 8.0	VF/NM 9.0	NM- 9.2
1-8, Special 1 (1987, $1.25, 52 pgs.)						4.00

ANGEL: NOT FADE AWAY (Buffy the Vampire Slayer)
IDW Publishing: May, 2009 - No. 3, July, 2009 ($3.99, limited series)

	GD 2.0	VG 4.0	FN 6.0	VF 8.0	VF/NM 9.0	NM- 9.2
1-3-Adaptation of TV show's final episodes; Mooney-a						4.00

ANGEL OF LIGHT, THE (See The Crusaders)

ANGEL: OLD FRIENDS (Buffy the Vampire Slayer)
IDW Publishing: Nov, 2005 - No. 5, Mar, 2006 ($3.99, limited series)

	GD 2.0	VG 4.0	FN 6.0	VF 8.0	VF/NM 9.0	NM- 9.2
1-5: Four covers plus photo-c on each; Mariotte-s/Messina-a; Gunn, Spike and Illyria app.						4.00
... Cover Gallery (6/06, $3.99) gallery of variant covers for the series						4.00
... Cover Gallery (12/06, $3.99) gallery of variant covers; preview of Angel: Auld Lang Syne						4.00
TPB (2006, $19.99) r/series; gallery of Messina covers						20.00

ANGEL: ONLY HUMAN (Buffy the Vampire Slayer)
IDW Publishing: Aug, 2009 - No. 5, Dec, 2009 ($3.99, limited series)

	GD 2.0	VG 4.0	FN 6.0	VF 8.0	VF/NM 9.0	NM- 9.2
1-5-Lobdell-s/Messina-a; covers by Messina and Dave Dorman						4.00

ANGEL: REVELATIONS (X-Men character)
Marvel Comics: July, 2008 - No. 5, Nov, 2008 ($3.99, limited series)

	GD 2.0	VG 4.0	FN 6.0	VF 8.0	VF/NM 9.0	NM- 9.2
1-5-Origin from childhood re-told; Adam Pollina-a/Aquirre-Sacasa-s						4.00

Angry Birds Comics V2 #7 © Rovio

Animal Adventures #2 © Timor

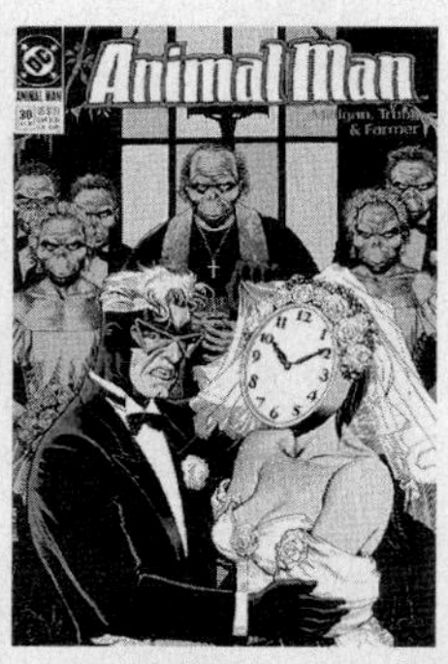

Animal Man #30 © DC

GD VG FN VF VF/NM NM-
2.0 4.0 6.0 8.0 9.0 9.2

ANGEL SEASON 11 (Buffy the Vampire Slayer)
Dark Horse Comics: Jan, 2017 - Present ($3.99)
1,2-Bechko-s/Borges-a; Fred & Illyria app. 4.00

ANGEL: SMILE TIME (Buffy the Vampire Slayer)
IDW Publishing: Dec, 2008 - No. 3, Apr, 2009 ($3.99, limited series)
1-3-Adaptation of TV episode; Messina-a; Messina and photo covers for each 4.00

ANGEL: THE CURSE (Buffy the Vampire Slayer)
IDW Publishing: June, 2005 - No. 5, Oct, 2005 ($3.99, limited series)
1-5-Four covers on each; Mariotte-s/Messina-a 4.00
TPB (1/06, $19.99) r/#1-5; cover gallery of Messina covers 20.00

ANGELTOWN
DC Comics (Vertigo): Jan, 2005 - No. 5, May, 2005 ($2.95, limited series)
1-5-Gary Phillips-s/Shawn Martinbrough-a 3.00

ANGELUS
Image Comics (Top Cow): Dec, 2007; Dec, 2009 - Nov, 2010 ($2.99)
... Pilot Season 1-(12/07) Sejic-a/c; Edington-s; origin re-told 3.00
1-6-Marz-s/Sejic-a; multiple covers on each 3.00

ANGRY BIRDS COMICS (Based on the Rovio videogame)(Also see Super Angry Birds)
IDW Publishing: Jun, 2014 - No. 12, Jun, 2015 ($3.99)
1-12-Short stories by Jeff Parker, Paul Tobin and various; wraparound-c on most 4.00
Volume 2 (1/16 - 12/16, $3.99) 1-12-Wraparound-c on all 4.00
...: Holiday Special (12/14, $5.99) Terence in charge of the North Pole 6.00

ANGRY BIRDS: FLIGHT SCHOOL (Based on the Rovio videogame)
IDW Publishing: Feb, 2017 - Present ($3.99)
1-Short stories by various 4.00

ANGRY BIRDS GAME PLAY (Based on the Rovio videogame)
IDW Publishing: Jan, 2017 - Present ($3.99)
1-Short stories by various; wraparound-c 4.00

ANGRY BIRDS TRANSFORMERS (Based on the Rovio videogame)
IDW Publishing: Nov, 2014 - No. 4, Feb, 2015 ($3.99, limited series)
1-4-Barber-s; the Eggspark lands on Piggy Island 4.00

ANGRY CHRIST COMIX (See Cry For Dawn)

ANIMA
DC Comics: Mar, 1994 - No. 15, July, 1995 ($1.75/$1.95/$2.25)
1-7,0,8-15: 7-(9/94)-Begin $1.95-c; Zero Hour x-over 3.00

ANIMAL ADVENTURES
Timor Publications/Accepted Publ. (reprints): Dec, 1953 - No. 3, May?, 1954
1-Funny animal 8 16 24 42 54 65
2,3: 2-Featuring Soopermutt (2/54) 6 12 18 31 38 45
1-3 (reprints, nd) 3 6 8 11 13 15

ANIMAL ANTICS
DC Comics: Feb, 1946
nn - Ashcan comic, not distributed to newsstands, only for in-house use. Cover art is Star Spangled Comics #49 and interior is Boy Commandos #12; a NM cover sold for $1000 in 2012, and FN/VF copy sold for $1553.50 in 2012.

ANIMAL ANTICS (Movietown... No. 24 on)
National Periodical Publ: Mar-Apr, 1946 - No. 23, Nov-Dec, 1949 (All 52 pgs.?)
1-Raccoon Kids begins by Otto Feuer; many-c by Grossman; Seaman Sy Wheeler by Kelly in some issues; Grossman-a in most issues 45 90 135 284 480 675
2 25 50 75 147 241 335
3-10: 10-Post-c/a 16 32 48 94 147 200
11-23: 14,15,18,19-Post-a 12 24 36 69 97 125

ANIMAL COMICS
Dell Publishing Co.: Dec-Jan, 1941-42 - No. 30, Dec-Jan, 1947-48
1-1st Pogo app. by Walt Kelly (Dan Noonan art in most issues)
123 246 369 787 1344 1900
2-Uncle Wiggily begins 55 110 165 352 601 850
3,5 26 52 78 182 404 625
4,6,7-No Pogo 15 30 45 103 227 350
8-10 18 36 54 124 275 425
11-15 11 22 33 76 163 250
16-20 8 16 24 56 108 160
21-30: 24-30- "Jigger" by John Stanley 7 14 21 48 89 130
NOTE: *Dan Noonan a-18-30. Gollub art in most later issues; c-29, 30. Kelly c-7-26, part #27-30.*

ANIMAL CRACKERS (Also see Adventures of Patoruzu)
Green Publ. Co./Norlen/Fox Feat.(Hero Books): 1946; No. 31, July, 1950; No. 9, 1959
1-Super Cat begins (1st app.) 20 40 60 120 195 270
2 11 22 33 64 90 115
31(Fox)-Formerly My Love Secret 9 18 27 50 65 80
9(1959-Norlen)-Infinity-c 5 10 15 22 26 30
nn, nd ('50s), no publ.; infinity-c 5 10 15 22 26 30

ANIMAL FABLES
E. C. Comics (Fables Publ. Co.): July-Aug, 1946 - No. 7, Nov-Dec, 1947
1-Freddy Firefly (clone of Human Torch), Korky Kangaroo, Petey Pig, Danny Demon begin 65 130 195 416 708 1000
2-Aesop Fables begin 39 78 117 231 378 525
3-6 34 68 102 199 325 450
7-Origin Moon Girl 81 162 243 518 884 1250

ANIMAL FAIR (Fawcett's...)
Fawcett Publications: Mar, 1946 - No. 11, Feb, 1947
1-Hoppy the Marvel Bunny-c 29 58 87 170 278 385
2 14 28 42 82 121 160
3-6 12 24 36 67 94 120
7-11 10 20 30 54 72 90

ANIMAL FUN
Premier Magazines: 1953 (25¢, came w/glasses)
1-(3-D)-Ziggy Pig, Silly Seal, Billy & Buggy Bear 39 78 117 236 388 540

ANIMAL MAN (See Action Comics #552, 553, DC Comics Presents #77, 78, Last Days of Animal Man, Secret Origins #39, Strange Adventures #180 & Wonder Woman #267, 268)
DC Comics (Vertigo imprint #57 on): Sept, 1988 - No. 89, Nov, 1995 ($1.25/$1.50/$1.75/$1.95/$2.25, mature)
1-Grant Morrison scripts begin, ends #26 2 4 6 8 10 12
2-10: 2-Superman cameo. 6-Invasion tie-in. 9-Manhunter-c/story. 10-Psycho Pirate app. 1 2 3 4 5 7
11-49,51-55,57-89: 23,24-Psycho Pirate app. 24-Arkham Asylum story; Bizarro Superman app. 25-Inferior Five app. 26-Morrison apps. in story; part photo-c (of Morrison?) 3.00
50-($2.95, 52 pgs.)-Last issue w/Veitch scripts 5.00
56-($3.50, 68 pgs.) 5.00
Annual 1 (1993, $3.95, 68 pgs.)-Bolland-c; Children's Crusade Pt. 3 6.00
...: Deus Ex Machina TPB (2003, $19.95) r/#18-26; Morrison-s; new Bolland-c 20.00
...: Origin of the Species TPB (2002, $19.95) r/#10-17 & Secret Origins #39 20.00
NOTE: *Bolland c-1-63. 71-Sutton-a(i)*

ANIMAL MAN (DC New 52)
DC Comics: Nov, 2011 - No. 29, May, 2014 ($2.99)
1-Jeff Lemire-s/Travel Foreman-a/c; 1st printing with yellow cover background 8.00
1-Second printing (red cover background), Third printing (grey cover background) 3.00
2-29: 2-4 Foreman-a. 5-Huat-a. 10 Justice League Dark app. 13-17-Rotworld 3.00
#0 (11/12, $2.99) Lemire-s/Pugh-a/c; Buddy Baker's origin re-told 3.00
Annual 1 (7/12, $4.99) Swamp Thing app.; Lemire-s/Green-a 5.00
Annual 2 (9/13, $4.99) Lemire-s/Foreman-a 5.00

ANIMAL MYSTIC (See Dark One...)
Cry For Dawn/Sirius: 1993 - No. 4, 1995 ($2.95?/$3.50, B&W)
1 3 6 9 14 19 24
1-Alternate 4 8 12 22 34 45
1-2nd printing 5.00
2 2 4 6 10 14 18
2,3-2nd prints (Sirius) 3.50
3 ,4: 4-Color poster insert, Linsner-s 1 2 3 5 7 9
TPB ($14.95) r/series 18.00

ANIMAL MYSTIC WATER WARS
Sirius: 1996 - No. 6 ($2.95, limited series)
1-6-Dark One-c/a/scripts 5.00

ANIMAL WORLD, THE (Movie)
Dell Publishing Co.: No. 713, Aug, 1956
Four Color 713 4 8 12 28 47 65

ANIMANIACS (TV)
DC Comics: May, 1995 - No. 59, Apr, 2000 ($1.50/$1.75/$1.95/$1.99)
1 1 2 3 4 5 7
2-20: 13-Manga issue. 19-X-Files parody; Miran Kim-c; Adlard-a (4 pgs.) 4.00
21-59: 26-E.C. parody-c. 34-Xena parody. 43-Pinky & the Brain take over 3.00
A Christmas Special (12/94, $1.50, "1" on-c) 5.00

ANIMATED COMICS

Animosity #1 © Marguerite Bennett

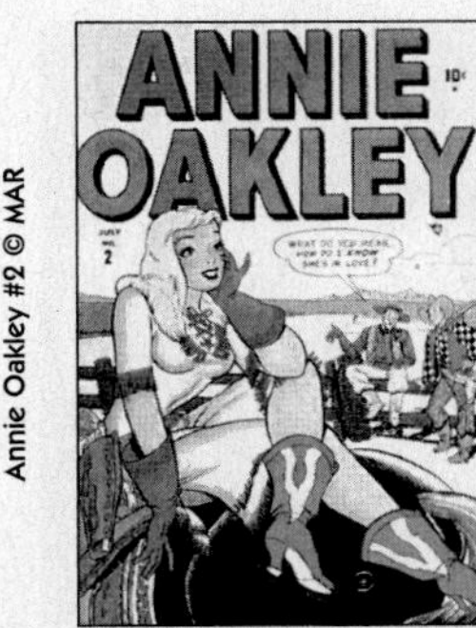

Annie Oakley #2 © MAR

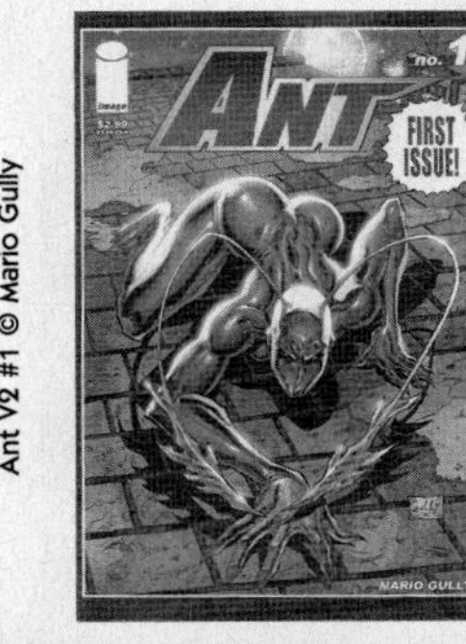

Ant V2 #1 © Mario Gully

	GD 2.0	VG 4.0	FN 6.0	VF 8.0	VF/NM 9.0	NM- 9.2

E. C. Comics: No date given (Summer, 1947?)
1 (Rare) Funny Animal 97 194 291 621 1061 1500

ANIMATED FUNNY COMIC TUNES (See Funny Tunes)

ANIMATED MOVIE-TUNES (Movie Tunes No. 3)
Margood Publishing Corp. (Timely): Fall, 1945 - No. 2, Sum, 1946
1,2-Super Rabbit, Ziggy Pig & Silly Seal 40 80 120 246 411 575

ANIMAX
Marvel Comics (Star Comics): Dec, 1986 - No. 4, June, 1987
1-4: Based on toys; Simonson-a 3.00

ANIMOSITY
AfterShock Comics: Aug, 2016 - Present ($3.99)
1-Marguerite Bennett-s/Rafael de Latorre-a; 2 covers 15.00
2 8.00
3-5 4.00
...: The Rise (1/17, $3.99) Bennett-s/Juan Doe-a; the day the animals awoke 4.00

ANITA BLAKE (Circus of the Damned - The Charmer on cover)
Marvel Comics: July, 2010 - No. 5, Dec, 2010 ($3.99, limited series)
1-5-Laurell K. Hamilton & Jess Ruffner-s/Ron Lim-a/ Brett Booth-c 4.00
... - The Ingenue 1-5 (3/11 - No. 5, 10/11, $3.99) Hamilton & Ruffner-s/Lim-a/Booth-c 4.00
... - The Scoundrel 1-4 (11/11 - No. 5, 5/12, $3.99) Hamilton & Ruffner-s/Lim-a/Booth-c 4.00

ANITA BLAKE: VAMPIRE HUNTER GUILTY PLEASURES
Marvel Comics (Dabel Brothers): Dec, 2006 - No. 12, Aug, 2008 ($2.99)
1-Laurell K. Hamilton-s/Brett Booth-a; blue cover 6.00
1-Variant-c by Greg Horn 20.00
1-Sketch cover 25.00
1-2nd printing with red cover 3.00
2-Two covers 5.00
3-12 3.00
...: Handbook (2007, $3.99) profile pages of characters; glossary 4.00
....Volume One HC (6/07, $19.99, dust jacket) r/#1-6; cover gallery 20.00

ANITA BLAKE: VAMPIRE HUNTER THE FIRST DEATH, (LAURELL K. HAMILTON'S...)
Marvel Comics (Dabel Brothers): July, 2007 - No. 2, Dec, 2007 ($3.99)
1,2-Laurell K. Hamilton & Jonathon Green-s/Wellington Alves-a. 2-Marvel Zombie var-c 4.00
... HC (2008, $19.99, dust jacket) r/#1,2 & Guilty Pleasures Handbook 20.00

ANITA BLAKE, VAMPIRE HUNTER: THE LAUGHING CORPSE
Marvel Comics: Dec, 2008 - No. 5, Apr, 2009 ($3.99)
... - Book One (12/08 - No. 5, 4/09) 1-5-Laurell K. Hamilton-s/Ron Lim-a/c 4.00
... - Necromancer 1-5 (6/09 - No. 5, 11/09, $3.99) Lim-a/c 4.00
Anita Blake (Executioner on-c) #11-15 (12/09 - No. 15, 5/10) numbering continued; Lim-a 4.00

ANNE RICE'S INTERVIEW WITH THE VAMPIRE
Innovation Books: 1991 - No. 12, Jan, 1994 ($2.50, limited series)
1-12: Adapts novel; Moeller-a 3.00

ANNE RICE'S THE MASTER OF RAMPLING GATE
Innovation Books: 1991 ($6.95, one-shot)
1-Bolton painted-c; Colleen Doran painted-a 7.00

ANNE RICE'S THE MUMMY OR RAMSES THE DAMNED
Millennium Publications: Oct, 1990 - No. 12, Feb, 1992 ($2.50, limited series)
1-12: Adapts novel; Mooney-p in all 3.00

ANNE RICE'S THE WITCHING HOUR
Millennium Publ./Comico: 1992 - No. 13, Jan, 1993 ($2.50, limited series)
1-13 3.00

ANNETTE (Disney, TV)
Dell Publishing Co.: No. 905, May, 1958; No. 1100, May, 1960
(Mickey Mouse Club)
Four Color 905-Annette Funicello photo-c 21 42 63 147 324 500
Four Color 1100-...'s Life Story (Movie); A. Funicello photo-c
17 34 51 117 259 400

ANNEX (See Amazing Spider-Man Annual #27 for 1st app.)
Marvel Comics: Aug, 1994 - No. 4, Nov, 1994 ($1.75)
1-4: 1,4-Spider-Man app. 3.00

ANNIE
Marvel Comics Group: Oct, 1982 - No. 2, Nov, 1982 (60¢)
1,2-Movie adaptation 4.00
Treasury Edition ($2.00, tabloid size) 3 6 9 17 26 35

ANNIE OAKLEY (See Tessie The Typist #19, Two-Gun Kid & Wild Western)
Marvel/Atlas Comics(MPI No. 1-4/CDS No. 5 on): Spring, 1948 - No. 4, 11/48; No. 5, 6/55 - No. 11, 6/56
1 (1st Series, 1948)-Hedy Devine app. 57 114 171 362 619 875
2 (7/48, 52 pgs.)-Kurtzman-a, "Hey Look", 1 pg; Intro. Lana; Hedy Devine
app; Captain Tootsie by Beck 34 68 102 199 325 450
3,4 27 54 81 158 259 360
5 (2nd Series, 1955)-Reinman-a; Maneely-c 20 40 60 114 182 250
6-9: 6,8-Woodbridge-a. 9-Williamson-a (4 pgs.) 15 30 45 85 130 175
10,11: 11-Severin-c 14 28 42 82 121 160

ANNIE OAKLEY AND TAGG (TV)
Dell Publishing Co./Gold Key: 1953 - No. 18, Jan-Mar, 1959; July, 1965 (Gail Davis photo-c #3 on)
Four Color 438 (#1) 13 26 39 89 195 300
Four Color 481,575 (#2,3) 9 18 27 59 117 175
4(7-9/55)-10 7 14 21 46 86 125
11-18(1-3/59) 6 12 18 38 69 100
1(7/65-Gold Key)-Photo-c (c-r/#6) 4 8 12 27 44 60
NOTE: *Manning a-13. Photo back c-4, 9, 11.*

ANNIHILATION
Marvel Comics: May, 2006 - No. 6, Mar, 2007 ($3.99/$2.99, limited x-over series)
Prologue (5/06, $3.99, one-shot) Nova, Thanos and Silver Surfer app. 4.00
1-6: 1-(10/06) Giffen-s/DiVito-a; Annihilus app. 3.00
...: Heralds of Galactus 1,2 (4/07-5/07, $3.99) 2-Silver Surfer app. 4.00
...: Nova 1-4 (6/06-9/06, $2.99) Abnett & Lanning-s/Walker-a/Dell'Otto-c. 2,3-Quasar app. 3.00
...: Ronan 1-4 (6/06-9/06, $2.99) Furman-s/Lucas-a/Dell'Otto-c 3.00
... Saga (2007, $1.99) re-cap of the series; DiVito-c 3.00
...: Silver Surfer 1-4 (6/06-9/06, $2.99) Giffen-s/Arlem-a/Dell'Otto-c 3.00
...: Super-Skrull 1-4 (6/06-9/06, $2.99) Grillo-Marxuach-s/Titus-a/Dell'Otto-c 3.00
...: The Nova Corps Files (2006, $3.99) profile pages of characters and alien races 4.00
Annihilation Book 1 HC (2007, $29.99, dustjacket) r/Drax the Destroyer #1-4, Annihilation Prologue and Annihilation: Nova #1-4; sketch and layout pages 30.00
Annihilation Book 1 SC (2007, $24.99) same content as HC 25.00
Annihilation Book 2 HC (2007, $29.99, dustjacket) r/Annihilation: Silver Surfer #1-4, ...: Super Skrull #1-4 and ...: Ronan #1-4; sketch and layout pages 30.00
Annihilation Book 2 SC (2007, $24.99) same content as HC 25.00
Annihilation Book 3 HC (2007, $29.99, dustjacket) r/Annihilation #1-6, Annihilation: Heralds of Galactus #1,2 and Annihilation: Nova Corps Files; sketch pages 30.00
Annihilation Book 3 SC (2007, $24.99) same content as HC 25.00

ANNIHILATION: CONQUEST (Also see Nova 2007 series)
Marvel Comics: Jan, 2008 - No. 6, Jun, 2008 ($3.99/$2.99, limited x-over series)
Prologue (8/07, $3.99, one-shot) the new Quasar, Moondragon app.; Perkins-a 4.00
1-5-Raney-a; Ultron app. 3-Moondragon dies 5.00
6-($3.99) Guardians of the Galaxy team forms 3 6 9 15 22 28
... - Quasar 1-4 (9/07-No. 4, 12/07, $2.99) Gage-s/Lilly-a. 1-Super-Adaptoid app. 3.00
... - Starlord 1-4 (9/07-No. 4, 12/07, $2.99) Giffen-s/Green-a 6.00
... - Wraith 1-4 (9/07-No. 4, 12/07, $2.99) Hotz-a/Grillo-Marxuach-s 3.00
Annihilation: Conquest Book 1 HC (2008, $29.99, dustjacket) r/Prologue; ...Quasar #1-4, ...Star-Lord #1-4; Annihilation Saga; design pages 30.00

ANNIHILATOR
Legendary Comics: Sept, 2014 - No. 6, Jun, 2015 ($3.99)
1-6-Grant Morrison-s/Frazer Irving-a/c 4.00

ANNIHILATORS
Marvel Comics: May, 2011 - No. 4, Aug, 2011 ($4.99, limited series)
1-4: Quasar, Silver Surfer, Beta-Ray Bill, Ronan, Gladiator app.; Huat-a 5.00

ANNIHILATORS: EARTHFALL
Marvel Comics: Nov, 2011 - No. 4, Feb, 2012 ($3.99, limited series)
1-4-Avengers app.; Abnett & Lanning-s/Huat-a/Christopher-c 4.00

ANOTHER WORLD (See Strange Stories From...)

ANSWER!, THE
Dark Horse Comics: Jan, 2013 - No. 4 ($3.99, limited series)
1-3-Dennis Hopeless-s/Mike Norton-a 4.00

ANT
Image Comics: Aug, 2005 - No. 11 ($2.99)
1-11: 1-Mario Gulley-s/a. 2-Savage Dragon & Spawn app. 3-Spawn-c/app. 3.00
Vol. 1: Reality Bites TPB (2006, $12.99) r/#1-4; sketch and concept art 13.00

ANTHRO (See Showcase #74)
National Periodical Publications: July-Aug, 1968 - No. 6, July-Aug, 1969

Ant-Man & Wasp #1 © MAR

A-1 Comics #7 © ME

A-1 Comics #133 © ME

	GD 2.0	VG 4.0	FN 6.0	VF 8.0	VF/NM 9.0	NM- 9.2
1-(7-8/68)-Howie Post-a in all	5	10	15	33	57	80
2-5: 5-Last 12¢ issue	3	6	9	21	33	45
6-Wood-c/a (inks)	4	8	12	23	37	50

ANTI-HITLER COMICS
New England Comics Press: Summer, 1992 ($2.75, B&W, one-shot)

1-Reprints Hitler as Devil stories from wartime comics 6.00

ANT-MAN (See Irredeemable Ant-Man, The)

ANT-MAN (Also see Astonishing Ant-Man)
Marvel Comics: Mar, 2015 - No. 5, Jul, 2015 ($3.99)

1-($4.99) Scott Lang as Ant-Man; Spencer-s/Rosanas-a; main-c by Brooks 5.00
2-5-($3.99) 2,3-Taskmaster app. 4-Darren Cross returns 4.00
Annual 1 (9/15, $4.99) Giant-Man & Egghead app.; intro. Raz Malhotra 5.00
...: Larger Than Life 1 (8/15, $3.99) movie Hank Pym story; r/Tales to Astonish #27 & #35 4.00
...: Last Days 1 (10/15, $3.99) Secret Wars tie-in; Spencer-s; Miss Patroit app. 4.00

ANT-MAN & WASP
Marvel Comics: Jan, 2011 - No. 3, Mar, 2011 ($3.99, limited series)

1-3-Tim Seeley-s/a; Espin-c; Tigra app. 4.00

ANT-MAN'S BIG CHRISTMAS
Marvel Comics: Feb, 2000 ($5.95, square-bound, one-shot)

1-Bob Gale-s/Phil Winslade-a; Avengers app. 6.00

ANT-MAN: SEASON ONE
Marvel Comics: 2012 ($24.99, hardcover graphic novel)

HC - Origin story; DeFalco-s/Domingues-a/Tedesco painted-c 25.00

ANTONY AND CLEOPATRA (See Ideal, a Classical Comic)

ANYTHING GOES
Fantagraphics Books: Oct, 1986 - No. 6, 1987 ($2.00, #1-5 color & B&W/#6 B&W, lim. series)

1-6: 1-Flaming Carrot app. (1st in color?); G. Kane-c. 2-6: 2-Miller-c(p); Alan Moore scripts; Kirby-a; early Sam Kieth-a (2 pgs.). 3-Capt. Jack, Cerebus app.; Cerebus-c by N. Adams. 4-Perez-c. 5-3rd color Teenage Mutant Ninja Turtles app. 3.50

A-1
Marvel Comics (Epic Comics): 1992 - No. 4, 1993 ($5.95, limited series, mature)

	GD	VG	FN	VF	VF/NM	NM-
1-4: 1-Fabry-c/a, Russell-a, S. Hampton-a. 3-Bisley-c; Kent Williams-a. 4-McKean-a; Dorman-s/a	1	2	3	4	5	7

A-1 COMICS (A-1 appears on covers No. 1-17 only)(See individual title listings for #11-139) (1st two issues not numbered.)
Life's Romances Publ.-No. 1/Compix/Magazine Ent.: 1944 - No. 139, Sept-Oct, 1955 (No #2)

nn-(1944) (See Kerry Drake Detective Cases)

	GD	VG	FN	VF	VF/NM	NM-
1-Dotty Dripple (1 pg.), Mr. Ex, Bush Berry, Rocky, Lew Loyal (20 pgs.)	20	40	60	114	182	250
3-8,10: Texas Slim & Dirty Dalton, The Corsair, Teddy Rich, Dotty Dripple, Inca Dinca, Tommy Tinker, Little Mexico & Tugboat Tim, The Masquerader & others. 7-Corsair-c/s. 8-Intro Rodeo Ryan	12	24	36	69	97	125
9-All Texas Slim	13	26	39	72	101	130

(See Individual Alphabetical listings for prices)

11-Teena; Ogden Whitney-c
13-Guns of Fact & Fiction (1948). Used in **SOTI**, pg. 19; Ingels & Johnny Craig-a
17-Tim Holt #2; photo-c; last issue to carry A-1 on cover (9-10/48)
19-Tim Holt #3; photo-c
22-Dick Powell (1949)-Photo-c
23-Cowboys and Indians #6; Doc Holiday-c/story
25-Fibber McGee & Molly (1949) (Radio)
26-Trail Colt #2-Ingels-c
28-Christmas-(Koko & Kola #6) ("50)
30-Jet Powers #1-Powell-a
32-Jet Powers #2
33-Muggsy Mouse #1(`51)
35-Jet Powers #3-Williamson/Evans-a
37-Ghost Rider #5-Frazetta-c (1951)
39-Muggsy Mouse #3
41-Cowboys 'N' Indians #7 (1951)
43-Dogface Dooley #2
45-American Air Forces #5-Powell-c/a
47-Thun'da, King of the Congo #1-Frazetta-c/a('52)

12,15-Teena
14-Tim Holt Western Adventures #1
16-Vacation Comics; The Pixies, Tom Tom, Flying Fredd, & Koko & Kola
18,20-Jimmy Durante; photo covers on both
21-Joan of Arc (1949)-Movie adaptation; Ingrid Bergman photo-covers & interior photos; Whitney-a
24-Trail Colt #1-Frazetta-r in-Manhunt #13; Ingels-c; L. B. Cole-a
27-Ghost Rider #1(1950)-Origin
29-Ghost Rider #2-Frazetta-c (1950)
31-Ghost Rider #3-Frazetta-c & origin ('51)
34-Ghost Rider #4-Frazetta-c (1951)
36-Muggsy Mouse #2; Racist-c
38-Jet Powers #4-Williamson/Wood-a
40-Dogface Dooley #1('51)
42-Best of the West #1-Powell-a
44-Ghost Rider #6
46-Best of the West #2
48-Cowboys 'N' Indians #8
49-Dogface Dooley #3

50-Danger Is Their Business #11 ('52)-Powell-a
53-Dogface Dooley #4
55-U.S. Marines #5-Powell-a
56-Thun'da #2-Powell-c/a
58-American Air Forces #7-Powell-a
60-The U.S. Marines #6-Powell-a
62-Starr Flagg, Undercover Girl #5 (#1) reprinted from A-1 #24
65-American Air Forces #8-Powell-a
67-American Air Forces #9-Powell-a
69-Ghost Rider #9(10/52)
71-Ghost Rider #10(12/52)-Vs. Frankenstein
74-American Air Forces #10-Powell-a
76-Best of the West #7
78-Thun'da #4-Powell-c/a
80-Ghost Rider #12(6/52)-One-eyed Devil-c
83-Thun'da #5-Powell-c/a
84-Ghost Rider #13(7-8/53)
86-Thun'da #6-Powell-c/a
88-Bobby Benson's B-Bar-B Riders #20
90-Red Hawk #11(1953)-Powell-c/a
91-American Air Forces #12-Powell-a
93-Great Western #8('54)-Origin The Ghost Rider; Powell-a
95-Muggsy Mouse #4
96-Cave Girl #12, with Thun'da; Powell-c/a
99-Muggsy Mouse #5
101-White Indian #12-Frazetta-a(r)
101-Dream Book of Romance #6 (4-6/54); Marlon Brando photo-c; Powell, Bolle, Guardineer-a
105-Great Western #9-Ghost Rider app.; Powell-a, 6 pgs.; Bolle-c
107-Hot Dog #1
108-Red Fox #15 (1954)-L.B. Cole-c/a; Powell-a
110-Dream Book of Romance #8 (10/54)-Movie photo-c
112-Ghost Rider #14 ('54)
114-Dream Book of Love #2- Guardineer, Bolle-a; Piper Laurie, Victor Mature photo-c
118-Undercover Girl #7-Powell-c
120-Badmen of the West #2
121-Mysteries of Scotland Yard #1; reprinted from Manhunt (5 stories)
124-Dream Book of Romance #8 (10-11/54)
126-I'm a Cop #2-Powell-a
128-I'm a Cop #3-Powell-a
130-Strongman #1-Powell-a (2-3/55)
132-Strongman #2
134-Strongman #3
136-Hot Dog #4
138-The Avenger #4-Powell-c/a

51-Ghost Rider #7 ('52)
52-Best of the West #3
54-American Air Forces #6(8/52)-Powell-a
57-Ghost Rider #8
59-Best of the West #4
61-Space Ace #5('53)-Guardineer-a
63-Manhunt #13-Frazetta
64-Dogface Dooley #5
66-Best of the West #5
68-U.S. Marines #7-Powell-a
70-Best of the West #6
72-U.S. Marines #8-Powell-a(3)
73-Thun'da #3-Powell-c/a
75-Ghost Rider #11(3/52)
77-Manhunt #14
79-American Air Forces #11-Powell-a
81-Best of the West #8
82-Cave Girl #11(1953)-Powell-c/a; origin (#1)
85-Best of the West #9
87-Best of the West #10(9-10/53)
89-Home Run #3-Powell-a; Stan Musial photo-c
92-Dream Book of Romance #5-Photo-c; Guardineer-a
94-White Indian #11-Frazetta-a(r); Powell-c
97-Best of the West #11
98-Undercover Girl #6-Powell-c
100-Badmen of the West #1-Meskin-a(?)
103-Best of the West #12-Powell-a
104-White Indian #13-Frazetta-a(r) ('54)
106-Dream Book of Love #1 (6-7/54) -Powell, Bolle-a; Montgomery Clift, Donna Reed photo-c
109-Dream Book of Romance #7 (7-8/54). Powell-a; movie photo-c
111-I'm a Cop #1 ('54); drug mention story; Powell-a
113-Great Western #10; Powell-a
115-Hot Dog #3
116-Cave Girl #13-Powell-c/a
117-White Indian #14
119-Straight Arrow's Fury #1 (origin); Fred Meagher-c/a
122-Black Phantom #1 (11/54)
123-Dream Book of Love #3 (10-11/54)-Movie photo-c
125-Cave Girl #14-Powell-c/a
127-Great Western #11('54)-Powell-a
129-The Avenger #1('55)-Powell-c
131-The Avenger #2('55)-Powell-c/a
133-The Avenger #3-Powell-c/a
135-White Indian #15
137-Africa #1-Powell-c/a(4)
139-Strongman #4-Powell-a

NOTE: *Bolle a-110. Photo-c-17-22, 89, 92, 101, 106, 109, 110, 114, 123, 124.*

APACHE
Fiction House Magazines: 1951

	GD	VG	FN	VF	VF/NM	NM-
1	23	46	69	136	223	310
I.W. Reprint No. 1-r/#1 above	3	6	9	17	26	35

APACHE KID (Formerly Reno Browne; Western Gunfighters #20 on) (Also see Two-Gun Western & Wild Western)
Marvel/Atlas Comics(MPC No. 53-10/CPS No. 11 on): No. 53, 12/50 - No. 10, 1/52; No. 11, 12/54 - No. 19, 4/56

	GD	VG	FN	VF	VF/NM	NM-
53(#1)-Apache Kid & his horse Nightwind (origin), Red Hawkins by Syd Shores begins	39	78	117	231	378	525
2(2/51)	19	38	57	111	176	240
3-5	14	28	42	82	121	160
6-10 (1951-52): 7-Russ Heath-a	13	26	39	72	101	130

Aphrodite IX V2 #7 © TCOW

A+X #16 © MAR

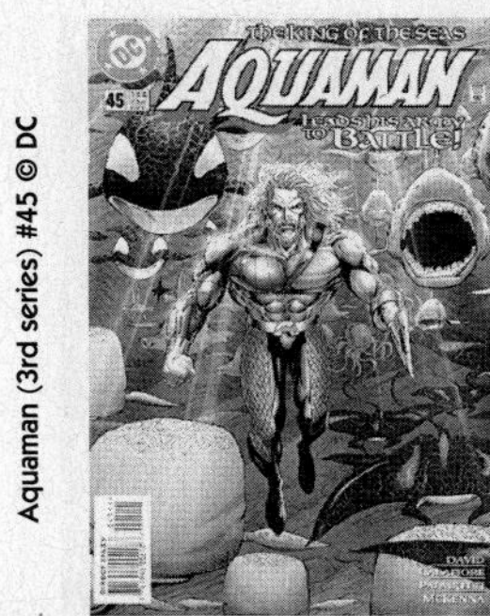

Aquaman (3rd series) #45 © DC

	GD 2.0	VG 4.0	FN 6.0	VF 8.0	VF/NM 9.0	NM- 9.2
11-19 (1954-56)	11	22	33	60	83	105

NOTE: ***Heath** a-7. c-11, 13. **Maneely** a-53; c-53(#1), 12, 14-16. **Powell** a-14. **Severin** c-17.*

APACHE MASSACRE (See Chief Victorio's...)

APACHE SKIES
Marvel Comics: Sept, 2002 - No. 4, Dec, 2002 ($2.99, limited series)

	GD 2.0	VG 4.0	FN 6.0	VF 8.0	VF/NM 9.0	NM- 9.2
1-4-Apache Kid app.; Ostrander-s/Manco-c/a						3.00
TPB (2003, $12.99) r/#1-4						13.00

APACHE TRAIL
Steinway/America's Best: Sept, 1957 - No. 4, June, 1958

	GD 2.0	VG 4.0	FN 6.0	VF 8.0	VF/NM 9.0	NM- 9.2
1	11	22	33	64	90	115
2-4: 2-Tuska-a	8	16	24	40	50	60

APE (Magazine)
Dell Publishing Co.: 1961 (52 pgs., B&W)

	GD 2.0	VG 4.0	FN 6.0	VF 8.0	VF/NM 9.0	NM- 9.2
1-Comics and humor	5	10	15	30	50	70

APHRODITE IX
Image Comics (Top Cow): Sept, 2000 - No. 4, Mar, 2002 ($2.50)

	GD 2.0	VG 4.0	FN 6.0	VF 8.0	VF/NM 9.0	NM- 9.2
1-3: 1-Four covers by Finch, Turner, Silvestri, Benitez						4.00
1-Tower Record Ed.; Finch-c						3.00
1-DF Chrome ($14.99)						15.00
4-($4.95) Double-sized issue; Finch-c						5.00
Convention Preview						10.00
...: Time Out of Mind TPB (6/04, $14.99) r/#1-4, & #0; cover gallery						15.00
Wizard #0 (4/00, bagged w/Tomb Raider magazine) Preview & sketchbook						5.00
#0-(6/01, $2.95) r/Wizard #0 with cover gallery						3.00

APHRODITE IX (Volume 2)
Image Comics (Top Cow): May, 2013 - No. 11, Jun, 2014 ($2.99/$3.99)

	GD 2.0	VG 4.0	FN 6.0	VF 8.0	VF/NM 9.0	NM- 9.2
1-Free Comic Book Day giveaway; Hawkins-s/Sejic-a						3.00
2-10-($2.99) Hawkins-s/Sejic-a						3.00
11-($3.99) Leads into Aphrodite IX Cyber Force #1						4.00
... Cyber Force #1 (7/14, $5.99) Hawkins-s/Sejic-a; leads into IXth Generation #1						6.00
... Hidden Files 1 (1/14, $2.99) Character profiles; Sejic-a						3.00

A+X (Avengers Plus X-Men)
Marvel Comics: Dec, 2012 - No. 18, May, 2014 ($3.99)

	GD 2.0	VG 4.0	FN 6.0	VF 8.0	VF/NM 9.0	NM- 9.2
1-18: 1-Hulk & Wolverine team-up; Keown-c. 2-Black Widow/Rogue; Bachalo-c/a. 14-Superior Spider-Man app.						4.00
1-Variant baby-c by Skottie Young						5.00

APOCALYPSE AL
Image Comics: Feb, 2014 - No. 4 ($2.99, B&W)

	GD 2.0	VG 4.0	FN 6.0	VF 8.0	VF/NM 9.0	NM- 9.2
1-3-Straczynski-s/Kotian-a; 2 covers on each						3.00

APOCALYPSE NERD
Dark Horse Comics: January, 2005 - No. 6, Oct, 2007 ($2.99, B&W)

	GD 2.0	VG 4.0	FN 6.0	VF 8.0	VF/NM 9.0	NM- 9.2
1-6-Peter Bagge-s/a						3.00

APOLLO IX (See Aphrodite IX)
Image Comics (Top Cow): Aug, 2015 ($3.99, one-shot)

	GD 2.0	VG 4.0	FN 6.0	VF 8.0	VF/NM 9.0	NM- 9.2
1-Ashley Robinson-s/Fernando Argosino-a; 2 covers						4.00

APPARITION
Caliber Comics: 1995 ($3.95, 52 pgs., B&W)

	GD 2.0	VG 4.0	FN 6.0	VF 8.0	VF/NM 9.0	NM- 9.2
1 ($3.95)						4.00
V2#1-6 ($2.95)						3.00
Visitations						4.00

APPLESEED
Eclipse Comics: Sept, 1988 - Book 4, Vol. 4, Aug, 1991 ($2.50/$2.75/$3.50, 52/68 pgs, B&W)

	GD 2.0	VG 4.0	FN 6.0	VF 8.0	VF/NM 9.0	NM- 9.2
Book One, Vol. 1-5: 5-(1/89), Book Two, Vol. 1(2/89) -5(7/89): Art Adams-c, Book Three, Vol. 1(8/89) -4 ($2.75), Book Three, Vol. 5 ($3.50), Book Four, Vol. 1 (1/91) - 4 (8/91) ($3.50, 68 pgs.)						6.00

APPLESEED DATABOOK
Dark Horse Comics: Apr, 1994 - No. 2, May, 1994 ($3.50, B&W, limited series)

	GD 2.0	VG 4.0	FN 6.0	VF 8.0	VF/NM 9.0	NM- 9.2
1,2: 1-Flip book format						4.00

APPROVED COMICS (Also see Blue Ribbon Comics)
St. John Publishing Co. (Most have no c-price): March, 1954 - No. 12, Aug, 1954 (Painted-c on #1-5,7,8,10)

	GD 2.0	VG 4.0	FN 6.0	VF 8.0	VF/NM 9.0	NM- 9.2
1-The Hawk #5-r	10	20	30	56	76	95
2-Invisible Boy (3/54)-Origin; Saunders-c	16	32	48	92	144	195
3-Wild Boy of the Congo #11-r (4/54)	10	20	30	56	76	95
4,5: 4-Kid Cowboy-r. 5-Fly Boy-r	10	20	30	56	76	95
6-Daring Adv.-r (5/54); Krigstein-a(2); Baker-c	14	28	42	82	121	160
7-The Hawk #6-r	10	20	30	56	76	95
8-Crime on the Run (6/54); Powell-a; Saunders-c	10	20	30	56	76	95
9-Western Bandit Trails #3-r, with new-c; Baker-c/a	15	30	45	85	130	175
10-Dinky Duck (Terrytoons)	7	14	21	35	43	50
11-Fightin' Marines #3-r (8/54); Canteen Kate app; Baker-c/a	20	40	60	114	182	250
12-Northwest Mounties #4-r(8/54); new Baker-c	15	30	45	85	130	175

AQUAMAN (See Adventure Comics #260, Brave & the Bold, DC Comics Presents #5, DC Special #28, DC Special Series #1, DC Super Stars #7, Detective Comics, JLA, Justice League of America, More Fun #73, Showcase #30-33, Super DC Giant, Super Friends, and World's Finest Comics)

AQUAMAN (1st Series)
National Periodical Publications/DC Comics: Jan-Feb, 1962 - No. 56, Mar-Apr, 1971; No. 57, Aug-Sept, 1977 - No. 63, Aug-Sept, 1978

	GD 2.0	VG 4.0	FN 6.0	VF 8.0	VF/NM 9.0	NM- 9.2
1-(1-2/62)-Intro. Quisp	155	310	465	1279	2890	4500
2	33	66	99	238	532	825
3-5	19	38	57	131	291	450
6-10	13	26	39	89	195	300
11-1st app. Mera	38	76	114	285	641	1000
12-17,19,20	10	20	30	69	147	225
18-Aquaman weds Mera; JLA cameo	13	26	39	89	195	300
21-28,30-32: 23-Birth of Aquababy. 26-Huntress app.(3-4/66). 30-Batman & Superman-c & cameo	7	14	21	49	92	135
29-1st app. Ocean Master, Aquaman's step-brother	36	72	108	259	580	900
33-1st app. Aqua-Girl (see Adventure #266)	12	24	36	82	179	275
34,36-40: 40-Jim Aparo's 1st DC work (8/68)	6	12	18	41	76	110
35-1st app. Black Manta	46	92	138	340	770	1200
41,43-46,47,49: 45-Last 12¢-c	5	10	15	35	63	90
42-Black Manta-c	11	22	33	76	163	250
48-Origin reprinted	6	12	18	37	66	95
50-52-Deadman by Neal Adams	8	16	24	51	96	140
53-56('71): 56-1st app. Crusader; last 15¢-c	3	6	9	21	33	45
57-('77) Black Manta-c	3	6	9	14	20	25
58-63: 58-Origin retold	2	4	6	9	12	15
...: Death of a Prince TPB (2011, $29.99) r/#58-63 and Adventure #435-437,441-455						30.00

NOTE: ***Aparo** a-40-45, 46p, 47-59; c-58-63. **Nick Cardy** c-1-40. **Newton** a-60-63.*

AQUAMAN (1st limited series)
DC Comics: Feb, 1986 - No. 4, May, 1986 (75¢, limited series)

	GD 2.0	VG 4.0	FN 6.0	VF 8.0	VF/NM 9.0	NM- 9.2
1-New costume; 1st app. Nuada of Thierna Na Oge	1	2	3	4	5	7
2-4: 3-Retelling of Aquaman & Ocean Master's origins.						5.00
Special 1 (1988, $1.50, 52 pgs.)						4.00

NOTE: ***Craig Hamilton** c/a-1-4p. **Russell** c-2-4i.*

AQUAMAN (2nd limited series)
DC Comics: June, 1989 - No. 5, Oct, 1989 ($1.00, limited series)

	GD 2.0	VG 4.0	FN 6.0	VF 8.0	VF/NM 9.0	NM- 9.2
1-5: Giffen plots/breakdowns; Swan-a(p).						4.00
Special 1 (Legend of..., $2.00, 1989, 52 pgs.)-Giffen plots/breakdowns; Swan-a(p)						4.00

AQUAMAN (2nd Series)
DC Comics: Dec, 1991 - No. 13, Dec, 1992 ($1.00/$1.25)

	GD 2.0	VG 4.0	FN 6.0	VF 8.0	VF/NM 9.0	NM- 9.2
1-5						3.00
6-13: 6-Begin $1.25-c. 9-Sea Devils app.						3.00

AQUAMAN (3rd Series)(Also see Atlantis Chronicles)
DC Comics: Aug, 1994 - No. 75, Jan, 2001 ($1.50/$1.75/$1.95/$1.99/$2.50)

	GD 2.0	VG 4.0	FN 6.0	VF 8.0	VF/NM 9.0	NM- 9.2
1-(8/94)-Peter David scripts begin; reintro Dolphin						6.00
2-(9/94)-Aquaman loses hand						6.50
0-(10/94)-Aquaman replaces lost hand with hook.						6.50
3-8: 3-(11/94)-Superboy-c/app. 4-Lobo app. 6-Deep Six app.						3.50
9-69: 9-Begin $1.75-c. 10-Green Lantern app. 11-Reintro Mera. 15-Re-intro Kordax. 16-vs. JLA. 18-Reintro Ocean Master & Atlan (Aquaman's father). 19-Reintro Garth (Aqualad). 23-1st app. Deep Blue (Neptune Perkins & Tsunami's daughter). 23,24-Neptune Perkins, Nuada, Tsunami, Arion, Power Girl, & The Sea Devils app. 26-Final Night. 28-Martian Manhunter-c/app. 29-Black Manta-c/app. 32-Swamp Thing-c/app. 37-Genesis x-over. 41-Maxima-c/app. 43-Millennium Giants x-over; Superman-c/app. 44-G.A. Flash & Sentinel app. 50-Larsen-s begins. 53-Superman app. 60-Tempest marries Dolphin; Teen Titans app. 63-Kaluta covers begin. 66-JLA app.						3.00
70-75: 70-Begin $2.50-c. 71-73-Warlord-c/app. 75-Final issue						3.00
#1,000,000 (11/98) 853rd Century x-over						3.00
Annual 1 (1995, $3.50)-Year One story						4.00
Annual 2 (1996, $2.95)-Legends of the Dead Earth story						4.00
Annual 3 (1997, $3.95)-Pulp Heroes story						4.00
Annual 4,5 ('98, '99, $2.95)-4-Ghosts; Wrightson-c. 5-JLApe						4.00
...Secret Files 1 (12/98, $4.95) Origin-s and pin-ups						5.00

NOTE: ***Art Adams**-c, Annual 5. **Mignola** c-6. **Simonson** c-15.*

Aquaman (2016 series) #1 © DC

Arcanum #2 © Brandon Peterson

Archie #4 © ACP

	GD 2.0	VG 4.0	FN 6.0	VF 8.0	VF/NM 9.0	NM- 9.2

AQUAMAN (4th Series)(Titled Aquaman: Sword of Atlantis #40-on) (Also see JLA #69-75)
DC Comics: Feb, 2003 - No. 57, Dec, 2007 ($2.50/$2.99)

1-Veitch-s/Guichet-a/Maleev-c 4.00
2-14: 2-Martian Manhunter app. 8-11-Black Manta app. 3.00
15-39: 15-San Diego flooded; Pfeifer-s/Davis-c begin. 23,24-Sea Devils app. 33-Mera returns. 39-Black Manta app. 3.00
40-Sword of Atlantis; One Year Later begins ($2.99-c) Guice-a ; two covers 4.00
41-49,51-57: 41-Two covers. 42-Sea Devils app. 44-Ocean Master app. 3.00
50-($3.99) Tempest app.; McManus-a 4.00
...Secret Files 2003 (5/03, $4.95) background on Aquaman's new powers; pin-ups 5.00
...: Once and Future TPB (2006, $12.99) r/#40-45 13.00
...: The Waterbearer TPB (2003, $12.95) r/#1-4, stories from Aquaman Secret Files and JLA/JSA Secret Files #1; JG Jones-c 13.00

AQUAMAN (DC New 52)
DC Comics: Nov, 2011 - No. 52, Jul, 2016 ($2.99/$3.99)

1-23,24: 1-Geoff Johns-s/Ivan Reis-a/c. 7-13-Black Manta app. 14-17-Throne of Atlantis. 15,16-Justice League app. 24-Story of Atlan 3.00
23.1, 23.2 (11/13, $2.99, regular covers) 3.00
23.1 (11/13, $3.99, 3-D cover) "Black Manta #1" on cover; Crime Syndicate app. 5.00
23.2 (11/13, $3.99, 3-D cover) "Ocean Master #1" on cover; Crime Syndicate app. 5.00
25-($3.99) "Death of a King" finale; last Johns-s 4.00
26-49,51,52: 26-Pelletier-a. 31-Swamp Thing app. 37-Grodd app. 41-($3.99-c begin) 4.00
50-($4.99) Booth-a 5.00
#0 (11/12, $2.99) Aquaman & Vulko's return to Atlantis; Johns-s/Reis-a/c 3.00
Annual 1 (12/13, $4.99) The Others app.; Pelletier-c/Ostrander-s 5.00
Annual 2 (9/14, $4.99) Wonder Woman app.; Parker-s/Guichet-a 5.00
...: Futures End 1 (11/14, $2.99, regular-c) Five years later; Jurgens-s 3.00
...: Futures End 1 (11/14, $3.99, 3-D cover) 4.00

AQUAMAN (DC Rebirth)
DC Comics: Aug, 2016 - Present ($2.99)

1-18: 1-Abnett-s/Walker-a; Black Manta app. 5,6-Superman app. 14,15-Black Manta app. 3.00
...: Rebirth (8/16, $2.99) Abnett-s/Eaton & Jiménez-a; Black Manta app. 3.00

AQUAMAN AND THE OTHERS (DC New 52)
DC Comics: Jun, 2014 - No. 11, May, 2015 ($2.99)

1-11: 1-Jurgens-s/Medina-a 3.00
...: Futures End 1 (11/14, $2.99, regular-c) Five years later; Cont'd from Aquaman: FE #1 3.00
...: Futures End 1 (11/14, $3.99, 3-D cover) 4.00

AQUAMAN: TIME & TIDE (3rd limited series) (Also see Atlantis Chronicles)
DC Comics: Dec, 1993 - No. 4, Mar, 1994 ($1.50, limited series)

1-4: Peter David scripts; origin retold. 3.00
Trade paperback ($9.95) 10.00

AQUANAUTS (TV)
Dell Publishing Co.: May - July, 1961

Four Color 1197-Photo-c 6 12 18 41 76 110

ARABIAN NIGHTS (See Cinema Comics Herald)

ARACHNOPHOBIA (Movie)
Hollywood Comics (Disney Comics): 1990 ($5.95, 68 pg. graphic novel)

nn-Adaptation of film; Spiegle-a 6.00
Comic edition ($2.95, 68 pgs.) 4.00

ARAK/SON OF THUNDER (See Warlord #48)
DC Comics: Sept, 1981 - No. 50, Nov, 1985

1,24,50: 1-1st app. Angelica, Princess of White Cathay. 24,50-(52 pgs.) 4.00
2-23,25-49: 3-Intro Valda. 12-Origin Valda. 20-Origin Angelica 3.00
Annual 1(10/84) 4.00

ARAÑA THE HEART OF THE SPIDER (See Amazing Fantasy (2004) #1-6)
Marvel Comics: March, 2005 - No. 12, Feb, 2006 ($2.99)

1-12: 1-Avery-s/Cruz-a. 4-Spider-Man-c/app. 3.00
Vol. 1: Heart of the Spider (2005, $7.99, digest) r/Amazing Fantasy (2004) #1-6 8.00
Vol. 2: In the Beginning (2005, $7.99, digest) r/#1-6 8.00
Vol. 3: Night of the Hunter (2006, $7.99, digest) r/#7-12 8.00

ARCADIA
BOOM! Studios: May, 2015 - No. 8, Feb, 2016 ($3.99)

1-8-Paknadel-s/Pfeiffer-a 4.00

ARCANA (Also see Books of Magic limited & ongoing series and Mister E)
DC Comics (Vertigo): 1994 ($3.95, 68 pgs., annual)

1-Bolton painted-c; Children's Crusade/Tim Hunter story 4.00

ARCANUM
Image Comics (Top Cow Productions): Apr, 1997 - No. 8, Feb, 1998 ($2.50)

1/2 Gold Edition 12.00
1-Brandon Peterson-s/a(p), 1-Variant-c, 4-American Ent. Ed. 3.50
2-8 3.00
3-Variant-c 4.00
...: Millennium's End TPB (2005, $16.99) r/#1-8 & #1/2; cover gallery and sketch pages 17.00

ARCHANGEL (See Uncanny X-Men, X-Factor & X-Men)
Marvel Comics: Feb, 1996 ($2.50, B&W, one-shot)

1-Milligan story 3.00

ARCHARD'S AGENTS (See Ruse)
CrossGeneration Comics: Jan, 2003; Nov, 2003; Apr, 2004 ($2.95)

1-Dixon-s/Perkins-a 3.00
...: The Case of the Puzzled Pugilist (11/03) Dixon-s/Perkins-a 3.00
Vol. 3 - Deadly Dare (4/04) Dixon-s/McNiven-a; preview of Lady Death: The Wild Hunt 3.00

ARCHENEMIES
Dark Horse Comics: Apr, 2006 - No. 4, July, 2006 ($2.99, limited series)

1-4-Melbourne-s/Guichet-a 3.00

ARCHER & ARMSTRONG
Valiant: July (June inside), 1992 - No. 26, Oct, 1994 ($2.50)

0-(7/92)-B. Smith-c/a; Reese-i assists 6.00
0-(with Gold Valiant Logo) 5 10 15 33 57 80
1,2: 1-(8/92)-Origin & 1st app. Archer; Miller-c; B. Smith/Layton-a. 2-2nd app. Turok (c/story); Smith/Layton-a; Simonson-c 5.00
3-7: 3,4-Smith-c&a(p) & scripts 4.00
8-($4.50, 52 pgs.)-Combined with Eternal Warrior #8; B. Smith-c/a & scripts; 1st app. Ivar the Time Walker 5.00
9-26: 10-2nd app. Ivar. 10,11-B. Smith-c. 21,22-Shadowman app. 22-w/bound-in trading card. 25-Eternal Warrior app. 26-Flip book w/Eternal Warrior #26 3.00
...: First Impressions HC (2008, $24.95) recolored reprints #0-6; new "Formation of the Sect" story by Jim Shooter and Sal Velutto; Shooter commentary; new cover by Golden 25.00

ARCHER & ARMSTRONG
Valiant Entertainment: Aug, 2012 - Present ($3.99)

1-24: 1-Van Lente-s/Henry-a; two covers; origin. 5-8-Eternal Warrior app. 4.00
1,4-8-Pullbox variants: 1-Clayton Henry. 4-Juan Doe. 7,8-Emanuela Lupacchino 4.00
1-Variant-c by David Aja 10.00
1-Variant-c by Neal Adams 25.00
25-($4.99) Van Lente-s/Henry-a; back-up short stories by various; cover gallery 5.00
#0-(5/13, $3.99) Van Lente-s/Henry-a 4.00
...Archer #0-(2/14, $3.99) Van Lente-s/Pere Pérez-a; childhood origin 4.00
...: The One Percent #1 (11/14, $3.99) Fawkes-s/Eisma-a/Juan Doe-c 4.00

ARCHIE (See Archie Comics) (Also see Afterlife With..., Christmas & Archie, Everything's..., Explorers of the Unknown, Jackpot, Life With..., Little..., Oxydol-Dreft, Pep, Riverdale High, Teenage Mutant Ninja Turtles Adventures & To Riverdale and Back Again)

ARCHIE
Archie Comic Publications: Sept, 2015 - Present ($3.99)

1-17-Mark Waid-s; multiple covers on all; back-up classic reprints. 1-3-Fiona Staples-a. 4-Annie Wu-a. 5-10-Veronica Fish-a. 13-Re-intro. Cheryl Blossom; back-up r/1st app. from B&V #320. 13-17-Eisma-a 4.00
... Collector's Edition (2/16, $9.99) r/#1-3 with creator intros and variant cover gallery 10.00
FCBD Edition (2016, giveaway) r/#1; Staples-c; back-up Jughead story 3.00

ARCHIE ALL CANADIAN DIGEST
Archie Publications: Aug, 1996 ($1.75, 96 pgs.)

1 1 2 3 5 6 8

ARCHIE AMERICANA SERIES, BEST OF THE FORTIES
Archie Publications: 1991, 2002 ($10.95, trade paperback)

Vol. 1,2-r/early strips from 1940s 1-Intro. by Steven King. 2-Intro. by Paul Castiglia 12.00

ARCHIE AMERICANA SERIES, BEST OF THE FIFTIES
Archie Publications: 1991 ($8.95, trade paperback)

Vol. 2-r/strips from 1950's 12.00
2nd printing (1998, $9.95) 12.00
Book 2 (2003, $10.95) 12.00

ARCHIE AMERICANA SERIES, BEST OF THE SIXTIES
Archie Publications: 1995 ($9.95, trade paperback)

Vol. 3-r/strips from 1960s; intro. by Frankie Avalon 12.00

ARCHIE AMERICANA SERIES, BEST OF THE SEVENTIES
Archie Publications: 1997, 2008 ($9.95/$10.95, trade paperback)

Vol. 4 (1997, $9.95)-r/strips from 1970s 12.00

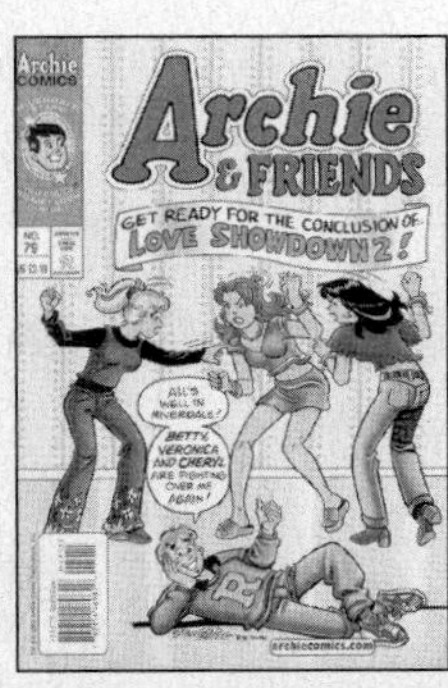

Archie & Friends #79 © ACP

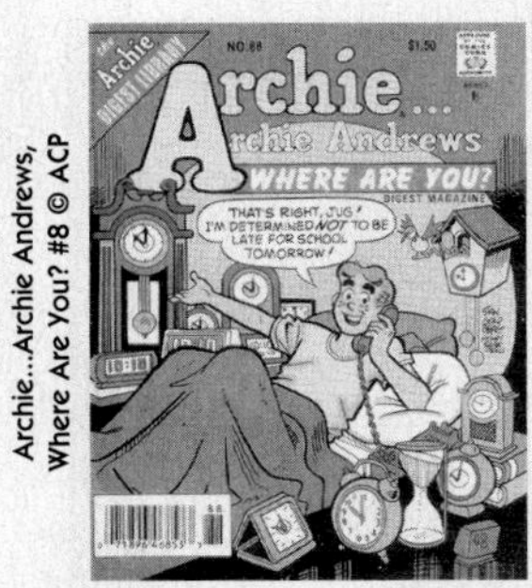

Archie...Archie Andrews, Where Are You? #8 © ACP

Archie Comics #9 © ACP

	GD 2.0	VG 4.0	FN 6.0	VF 8.0	VF/NM 9.0	NM- 9.2
Vol. 8 Book 2 (2008, $10.95)-r/other strips from 1970s						12.00

ARCHIE AMERICANA SERIES, BEST OF THE EIGHTIES
Archie Publications: 2001 ($10.95, trade paperback)

	GD 2.0	VG 4.0	FN 6.0	VF 8.0	VF/NM 9.0	NM- 9.2
Vol. 5-r/strips from 1980s; foreward by Steve Geppi						12.00

ARCHIE AMERICANA SERIES, BEST OF THE '90S
Archie Publications: 2008 ($11.95, trade paperback)

	GD 2.0	VG 4.0	FN 6.0	VF 8.0	VF/NM 9.0	NM- 9.2
Vol. 9-r/strips from 1990s; new Lindsey cover						12.00

ARCHIE AND BIG ETHEL
Spire Christian Comics (Fleming H. Revell Co.): 1982 (69¢)

	GD 2.0	VG 4.0	FN 6.0	VF 8.0	VF/NM 9.0	NM- 9.2
nn-(Low print run)	2	4	6	13	18	22

ARCHIE & FRIENDS
Archie Comics: Dec, 1992 - No. 159, Feb, 2012 ($1.25-$2.99)

	GD 2.0	VG 4.0	FN 6.0	VF 8.0	VF/NM 9.0	NM- 9.2
1						5.00
2,4,10-14,17,18,20-Sabrina app. 20-Archie's Band-c						4.00
3,5-9,16						3.00
15-Babewatch-s with Sabrina app.						6.00
19-Josie and the Pussycats app.; E.T. parody-c/s						5.00
21-46						3.00
47-All Josie and the Pussycats issue; movie and actress profiles/photos						4.00
48-142: 48-56,58,60,96-Josie and the Pussycats-c/s. 79-Cheryl Blossom returns. 100-The Veronicas-c/app. 101-Katy Keene begins. 129-Begin $2.50. 130,131-Josie and the Pussycats. 137-Cosmo, Super Duck, Pat the Brat and other old characters app.						3.00
143-159: 143-Begin $2.99-c. 145-Jersey Shore spoof. 146,147-Twilite. 154-Little Archie						3.00

ARCHIE & FRIENDS DOUBLE DIGEST MAGAZINE
Archie Comics: Feb, 2011 - No. 33, Jan, 2014 ($3.99, digest-size)

	GD 2.0	VG 4.0	FN 6.0	VF 8.0	VF/NM 9.0	NM- 9.2
1-32: 1-Staton-a. 7-13-SuperTeens app.						4.00
33-($5.99, 320 pages) Double Double Digest						6.00

ARCHIE AND ME (See Archie Giant Series Mag. #578, 591, 603, 616, 626)
Archie Publications: Oct, 1964; No. 2, Aug, 1965 - No. 161, Feb, 1987

	GD 2.0	VG 4.0	FN 6.0	VF 8.0	VF/NM 9.0	NM- 9.2
1	15	30	45	103	227	350
2-(8/65)	8	16	24	56	108	160
3-5: 3-(12/65)	6	12	18	40	73	105
6-10: 6-(8/66)	5	10	15	30	50	70
11-20: 11-(4/68)	3	6	9	21	33	45
21(6/68)-26,28-30: 21-UFO story. 26-X-Mas-c	3	6	9	16	24	32
27-Groovyman & Knowman superhero-s; UFO-sty	3	6	9	19	30	40
31-42: 37-Japan Expo '70-c/s	3	6	9	14	19	24
43-48,50-63-(All Giants): 43-(8/71) Mummy-s. 44-Mermaid-s. 62-Elvis cameo-c. 63-(2/74)	3	6	9	15	22	28
49-(Giant) Josie & the Pussycats-c/app.	3	6	9	20	31	42
64-66,68-99-(Regular size): 85-Bicentennial-s. 98-Collectors Comics	2	4	6	8	10	12
67-Sabrina app.(8/74)	2	4	6	10	14	18
100-(4/78)	2	4	6	8	11	14
101-120: 107-UFO-s	1	2	3	5	6	8
121(8/80)-159: 134-Riverdale 2001						6.00
160,161: 160-Origin Mr. Weatherbee; Caveman Archie gang story. 161-Last issue	1	2	3	5	6	8

ARCHIE AND MR. WEATHERBEE
Spire Christian Comics (Fleming H. Revell Co.): 1980 (59¢)

	GD 2.0	VG 4.0	FN 6.0	VF 8.0	VF/NM 9.0	NM- 9.2
nn - (Low print run)	2	4	6	13	18	22

ARCHIE...ARCHIE ANDREWS, WHERE ARE YOU? (...Comics Digest #9, 10; ...Comics Digest Mag. No. 11 on)
Archie Publications: Feb, 1977 - No. 114, May, 1998 (Digest size, 160-128 pgs., quarterly)

	GD 2.0	VG 4.0	FN 6.0	VF 8.0	VF/NM 9.0	NM- 9.2
1	3	6	9	17	26	35
2,3,5,7-9-N. Adams-a; 8-r-/origin The Fly by S&K. 9-Steel Sterling-r	2	4	6	10	14	18
4,6,10 ($1.00/$1.50)	2	4	6	8	11	14
11-20: 17-Katy Keene story	2	3	4	6	8	10
21-50,100	1	2	3	5	6	8
51-70						4.00
71-99,101-114: 113-Begin $1.95-c						3.00

ARCHIE AS PUREHEART THE POWERFUL (Also see Archie Giant Series #142, Jughead as Captain Hero, Life With Archie & Little Archie)
Archie Publications (Radio Comics): Sept, 1966 - No. 6, Nov, 1967

	GD 2.0	VG 4.0	FN 6.0	VF 8.0	VF/NM 9.0	NM- 9.2
1-Super hero parody	11	22	33	76	163	250
2	6	12	18	41	76	110
3-6	6	12	18	37	66	95

NOTE: *Evilheart cameos in all. Title: Archie As Pureheart the Powerful #1-3; ...As Capt. Pureheart-#4-6.*

ARCHIE AT RIVERDALE HIGH (See Archie Giant Series Magazine #573, 586, 604 & Riverdale High)
Archie Publications: Aug, 1972 - No. 113, Feb, 1987

	GD 2.0	VG 4.0	FN 6.0	VF 8.0	VF/NM 9.0	NM- 9.2
1	6	12	18	41	76	110
2	4	8	12	23	37	50
3-5	3	6	9	16	23	30
6-10	2	4	6	11	16	20
11-30	2	4	6	8	10	12
31(12/75)-46,48-50(12/77)	1	3	4	6	8	10
47-Archie in drag-s; Betty mud wrestling-s	2	4	6	10	14	18
51-80,100 (12/84)	1	2	3	5	6	8
81(8/81)-88, 91,93-95,98						6.00
89,90-Early Cheryl Blossom app. 90-Archies Band app.	3	6	9	14	20	26
92,96,97,99-Cheryl Blossom app. 96-Anti-smoking issue	2	4	6	11	16	20
101,102,104-109,111,112: 102-Ghost-c						6.00
103-Archie dates Cheryl Blossom-s	2	4	6	11	16	20
110,113: 110-Godzilla-s. 113-Last issue	1	2	3	5	6	8

ARCHIE COMICS (See Pep Comics #22 [12/41] for Archie's debut) (1st Teen-age comic; Radio show first aired 6/2/45 by NBC)
MLJ Magazines No. 1-19/Archie Publ. No. 20 on: Winter, 1942-43 - No. 19, 3-4/46; No. 20, 5-6/46 - No. 666, Jul, 2015

	GD 2.0	VG 4.0	FN 6.0	VF 8.0	VF/NM 9.0	NM- 9.2
1 (Scarce)-Jughead, Veronica app.; 1st app. Mrs. Andrews	12,000	24,000	42,000	85,000	135,000	185,000
2 (Scarce)	1700	3400	5100	12,500	20,750	29,000
3 (60 pgs.)(scarce)	838	1676	2514	6117	10,809	15,500
4-Article about Archie radio series	514	1028	1542	3750	6625	9500
5-Halloween-c	459	918	1377	3350	5925	8500
6,8-10: 6-X-Mas-c. 9-1st Miss Grundy cover	300	600	900	2010	3505	5000
7-1st definitive love triangle story	371	742	1113	2600	4550	6500
11-15: 15-Dotty & Ditto by Woggon	158	316	474	1003	1727	2450
16-20: 15,17,18-Dotty & Ditto by Woggon. 16,19-Woggon-a. 18-Halloween pumpkin-c.	145	290	435	921	1586	2250
21-30: 23-Betty & Veronica by Woggon. 25-Woggon-a. 30-Coach Piffle app., a Coach Kleats prototype. 34-Pre-Dilton try-out (named Dilbert)	87	174	261	553	952	1350
31-40	53	106	159	334	567	800
41-49	41	82	123	256	428	600
50-Classic Montana Betty-c (5-6/51)	97	194	291	621	1061	1500
51-60	18	36	54	124	275	425
61-70 (1954): 65-70, Katy Keene app.	13	26	39	89	195	300
71-80: 72-74-Katy Keene app.	11	22	33	73	157	240
81-93,95-99	9	18	27	60	120	180
94-1st Coach Kleats in this title (see Pep #24)	10	20	30	64	132	200
100	10	20	30	66	138	210
101-122,126,128-130 (1962)	6	12	18	40	73	105
123-125,127-Horror/SF covers. 123-UFO-c/s	9	18	27	59	117	175
131,132,134-157,159,160: 137-1st Caveman Archie gang story	4	8	12	27	44	60
133 (12/62)-1st app. Cricket O'Dell	5	10	15	30	50	70
158-Archie in drag story	4	8	12	28	47	65
161(2/66)-184,186-188,190-195,197-199: 168-Superhero gag-c. 176,178-Twiggy-c 183-Caveman Archie gang story	3	6	9	17	26	35
185-1st "The Archies" Band story	4	8	12	25	40	55
189 (3/69)-Archie's band meets Don Kirshner who developed the Monkees	3	6	9	19	30	40
196 (12/69)-Early Cricket O'Dell app.	3	6	9	19	30	40
200 (6/70)	3	6	9	18	28	38
201-230(11/73): 213-Sabrina/Josie-c cameos. 229-Lost Child issue	2	4	6	11	16	20
231-260(3/77): 253-Tarzan parody	2	4	6	8	11	14
261-282, 284-299	1	3	4	6	8	10
283(8/79)-Cover/story plugs "International Children's Appeal" which was a fraudulent charity, according to TV's 20/20 news program broadcast July 20, 1979	2	4	6	8	10	12
300(1/81)-Anniversary issue	2	4	6	8	11	14
301-321,323-325,327-335,337-350: 323-Cheryl Blossom pin-up. 325-Cheryl Blossom app.						6.00
322-E.T. story	1	2	3	5	6	8
326-Early Cheryl Blossom story	2	4	6	11	16	20
336-Michael Jackson/Boy George parody	2	4	6	8	10	12
351-399: 356-Calgary Olympics Special. 393-Infinity-c; 1st comic book printed on recycled paper						5.00
400 (6/92)-Shows 1st meeting of Little Archie and Veronica						6.00

Archie Comics #630 © ACP

Archie Comics Digest #272 © ACP

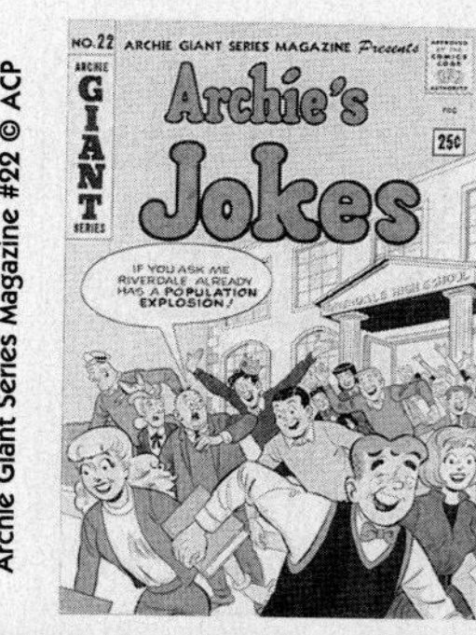

Archie Giant Series Magazine #22 © ACP

401-428 4.00
429-Love Showdown part 1 5.00
430-599: 467- "A Storm Over Uniforms" x-over parts 3,4. 538-Comic-Con issue 3.00
600-602: 600-(10/09) Archie proposes to Veronica. 601-Marries Veronica. 602-Twins born 4.00
603-605: 603-(1/10) Archie proposes to Betty. 604-Marries Betty. 605-Twins born 4.00
606-615,618-626: 609-Begin $2.99-c. 610-613-Man From RIVERDALE. 625-70th Anniversary. 626-Michael Strahan app. 3.00
616,617-Obama & Palin app.; two covers on each 4.00
627-630-Archie Meets KISS; 2 covers on each by Parent & Francavilla 4.00
631-658: 632-634-Archie marries Valerie from the Pussycats. 635-Jill Thompson var-c. 636-Gender swap. 641-644-Crossover with Glee; 2 covers. 648-Simonson var-c. 655-Cosmo the Merry Martian app. 656-Intro. Harper Lodge 3.00
650-Variant "Battle of the Bands" cover by Fiona Staples 5.00
659-665-($3.99) Two covers on each. 664-Game of Thrones parody. 665-Harper app. 4.00
666-Last issue; 6 interlocking covers with vintage title logos (Archie Comics, Blue Ribbon Comics, Top-Notch Comics, Pep Comics, Zip Comics, and Jackpot Comics) 4.00
Annual 1 ('50)-116 pgs. (Scarce) 300 600 900 1950 3975 6000
Annual 2 ('51) 116 232 348 742 1421 2100
Annual 3 ('52) 66 132 198 419 785 1150
Annual 4,5 (1953-54) 46 92 138 290 520 750
Annual 6-10 (1955-59): 8,9-(100 pgs.). 10-(84 pgs.) Elvis record on-c 16 32 48 110 243 375
Annual 11-15 (1960-65): 12,13-(84 pgs.) 14,15-(68 pgs.) 9 18 27 62 126 190
Annual 16-20 (1966-70)(all 68 pgs.): 20-Archie's band-c 6 12 18 38 69 100
Annual 21,22,24-26 (1971-75): 21,22-(68 pgs.). 22-Archie's band-s. 24-26-(52 pgs.). 25-Cavemen-s 4 8 12 23 37 50
Annual 23-Archie's band-c/s; Josie/Sabrina-c 5 10 15 30 50 70
Annual Digest 27 ('75) 4 8 12 23 37 50
...28-30 3 6 9 14 20 25
...31-34 2 4 6 9 13 16
...35-40 (...Magazine #35 on) 1 3 4 6 8 10
...41-65 ('94) 5.00
...66-69 3.00
...All-Star Specials (Winter '75, $1.25)-6 remaindered Archie comics rebound in each; titles: "The World of Giant Comics", "Giant Grab Bag of Comics", "Triple Giant Comics" & "Giant Spec. Comics 5 10 15 30 50 70

NOTE: *Archies Band-s-185, 188-192, 197, 198, 201, 204, 205, 208, 209, 215, 329, 330; Band-c-191, 330. Cavemen Archie Gang-s-183, 192, 197, 208, 210, 220, 223, 282, 333, 335, 338, 340.* ***Al Fagly*** *c-17-35.* ***Bob Montana*** *c-38, 41-50, 58, Annual 1-4.* ***Bill Woggon*** *c-53, 54.*

ARCHIE COMICS DIGEST (...Magazine No. 37-95)
Archie Publications: Aug, 1973 - No. 267, Nov, 2010 (Digest-size, 160-128 pgs.)

1-1st Archie digest 9 18 27 58 114 170
2 5 10 15 30 50 70
3-5 4 8 12 23 37 50
6-10 3 6 9 16 23 30
11-33: 32,33-The Fly-r by S&K 2 4 6 10 14 18
34-60 1 3 4 6 8 10
61-80,100 1 2 3 5 6 8
81-99 5.00
101-140: 36-Katy Keene story 4.00
141-165 3.00
166-235,237-267: 194-Begin $2.39-c. 225-Begin $2.49-c 3.00
236-65th Anniversary issue, r/1st app. in Pep #22 and entire Archie Comics #1 (1942) 5.00

NOTE: ***Neal Adams*** *a-1, 2, 4, 5, 19-21, 24, 25, 27, 29, 31, 33. X-mas c-88, 94, 100, 106.*

ARCHIE COMICS DIGEST (Continues from Archie's Double Digest #252)
Archie Publications: No. 253, Sept, 2014 - Present ($4.99-$6.99, digest-size)

253,254,257-259,261,262,264,267,269,270,272,273,275-($4.99) 5.00
255,260,266,274,276-($6.99) Titled Archie Jumbo Comics Digest 7.00
256,263,265,268,271-($5.99): 256,263,268-Titled Archie Comics Annual 6.00

ARCHIE COMICS (Free Comic Book Day editions) (Also see Pep Comics)
Archie Publications: 2003 - Present

... Free Comic Book Day Edition 1,2: 1-(7/03). 2-(9/04) 3.00
Little Archie "The Legend of the Lost Lagoon" FCBD Edition (5/07) Bolling-s/a 3.00
... Presents the Mighty Archie Art Players ('09) Free Comic Book Day giveaway 3.00
...'s 65th Anniversary Bash ('06) Free Comic Book Day giveaway 3.00
...'s Summer Splash FCBD Edition (5/10) Parent-a; Cheryl Blossom app. 3.00

ARCHIE COMICS PRESENTS: THE LOVE SHOWDOWN COLLECTION
Archie Publications: 1994 ($4.95, squarebound)

nn-r/Archie #429, Betty #19, Betty & Veronica #82, & Veronica #39 1 2 3 5 6 8

GD VG FN VF VF/NM NM-
2.0 4.0 6.0 8.0 9.0 9.2

ARCHIE COMICS SUPER SPECIAL
Archie Publications: Dec, 2012 - Present ($9.99, squarebound magazine-sized, quarterly)

1-7: 1-Christmas themed. 2-Valentine's themed 10.00

ARCHIE DIGEST (Free Comic Book Day edition)
Archie Comic Publications: June/July 2014 (digest-size giveaway)

1-Reprints; Parent-c 3.00

ARCHIE DOUBLE DIGEST (See Archie's Double Digest Quarterly Magazine)

ARCHIE GETS A JOB
Spire Christian Comics (Fleming H. Revell Co.): 1977

nn 2 4 6 13 18 22

ARCHIE GIANT SERIES MAGAZINE
Archie Publications: 1954 - No. 632, July, 1992 (No #36-135, no #252-451) (#1 not code approved) (#1-233 are Giants; #12-184 are 68 pgs.,#185-194,197-233 are 52 pgs.; #195,196 are 84 pgs.; #234-up are 36 pgs.)

1-Archie's Christmas Stocking 158 316 474 1003 1727 2450
2-Archie's Christmas Stocking('55) 77 154 231 493 847 1200
3-6-Archie's Christmas Stocking('56- '59) 53 106 159 334 567 800
7-10: 7-Katy Keene Holiday Fun(9/60); Bill Woggon-c. 8-Betty & Veronica Summer Fun (10/60); baseball story w/Babe Ruth & Lou Gehrig. 9-The World of Jughead (12/60); Neal Adams-a. 10-Archie's Christmas Stocking(1/61) 39 78 117 240 395 550
11,13,16,18: 11-Betty & Veronica Spectacular (6/61). 13-Betty & Veronica Summer Fun (10/61). 16-Betty & Veronica Spectacular (6/62). 18-Betty & Veronica Summer Fun (10/62) 25 50 75 150 245 340
12,14,15,17,19,20: 12-Katy Keene Holiday Fun (9/61). 14-The World of Jughead (12/61); Vampire-s. 15-Archie's Christmas Stocking (1/62). 17-Archie's Jokes (9/62); Katy Keene app. 19-The World of Jughead (12/62). 20-Archie's Christmas Stocking (1/63) 19 38 57 112 179 245
21,23,28: 21-Betty & Veronica Spectacular (6/63). 23-Betty & Veronica Summer Fun (10/63). 28-Betty & Veronica Summer Fun (9/64) 9 18 27 59 117 175
22,24,25,27,29,30: 22-Archie's Jokes (9/63). 24-The World of Jughead (12/63). 25-Archie's Christmas Stocking (1/64). 27-Archie's Jokes (8/64). 29-Around the World with Archie (10/64); Doris Day-s. 30-The World of Jughead (12/64) 8 16 24 54 102 150
26-Betty & Veronica Spectacular (6/64); all pin-ups; DeCarlo-c/a 9 18 27 60 120 180
31,33-35: 31-Archie's Christmas Stocking (1/65). 33-Archie's Jokes (8/65). 34-Betty & Veronica Summer Fun (9/65). 35-Around the World with Archie (10/65). 6 12 18 38 69 100
32-Betty & Veronica Spectacular (6/65); all pin-ups; DeCarlo-c/a 7 14 21 46 86 125
36-135-**Do not exist**
136-141: 136-The World of Jughead (12/65). 137-Archie's Christmas Stocking (1/66). 138-Betty & Veronica Spect. (6/66). 139-Archie's Jokes (6/66). 140-Betty & Veronica Summer Fun (8/66). 141-Around the World with Archie (9/66) 6 12 18 38 69 100
142-Archie's Super-Hero Special (10/66)-Origin Capt. Pureheart, Capt. Hero, and Evilheart 7 14 21 49 92 135
143-The World of Jughead (12/66); Capt. Hero-c/s; Man From R.I.V.E.R.D.A.L.E., Pureheart, Superteen app. 6 12 18 38 69 100
144-160: 144-Archie's Christmas Stocking (1/67). 145-Betty & Veronica Spectacular (6/67). 146-Archie's Jokes (6/67). 147-Betty & Veronica Summer Fun (8/67) 148-World of Archie (9/67). 149-World of Jughead (10/67). 150-Archie's Christmas Stocking (1/68). 151-World of Archie (2/68). 152-World of Jughead (2/68). 153-Betty & Veronica Spectacular (6/68). 154-Archie Jokes (6/68). 155-Betty & Veronica Summer Fun (8/68). 156-World of Archie (10/68). 157-World of Jughead (12/68). 158-Archie's Christmas Stocking (1/69). 159-Betty & Veronica Christmas Spectacular (1/69). 160-World of Archie (2/69); Frankenstein-s each... 4 8 12 23 37 50
161-World of Jughead (2/69); Super-Jughead-s; 11 pg. early Cricket O'Dell-s 4 8 12 25 40 55
162-183: 162-Betty & Veronica Spectacular (6/69). 163-Archie's Jokes(8/69). 164-Betty & Veronica Summer Fun (9/69). 165-World of Archie (9/69). 166-World of Jughead (9/69). 167-Archie's Christmas Stocking (1/70). 168-Betty & Veronica Christmas Spect. (1/70). 169-Archie's Christmas Love-In (1/70). 170-Jughead's Eat-Out Comic Book Mag. (12/69). 171-World of Archie (2/70). 172-World of Jughead (2/70). 173-Betty & Veronica Spectacular (6/70). 174-Archie's Jokes (8/70). 175-Betty & Veronica Summer Fun (9/70). 176-Li'l Jinx Giant Laugh-Out (8/70). 177-World of Archie (9/70). 178-World of Jughead (9/70). 179-Archie's Christmas Stocking(1/71). 180-Betty & Veronica Christmas Spect. (1/71). 181-Archie's Christmas Love-In (1/71). 182-World of Archie (2/71). 183-World of Jughead (2/71)-Last squarebound each... 3 6 9 17 26 35
184-189,193,194,197-199 (52 pgs.): 184-Betty & Veronica Spectacular (6/71). 185-Li'l Jinx Giant Laugh-Out (6/71). 186-Archie's Jokes (8/71). 187-Betty & Veronica Summer Fun (9/71). 188-World of Archie (9/71). 189-World of Jughead (9/71). 193-World of Archie (3/72).194-World of Jughead (4/72). 197-Betty & Veronica Spectacular (6/72). 198-Archie's Jokes (8/72). 199-Betty & Veronica Summer Fun (9/72)

Archie Giant Series Magazine #472 © ACP

Archie Giant Series Magazine #611 © ACP

Archie Meets Ramones #1 © ACP

	GD 2.0	VG 4.0	FN 6.0	VF 8.0	VF/NM 9.0	NM- 9.2

each... 3 6 9 15 22 28
190-Archie's Christmas Stocking (12/71); Sabrina-c 4 8 12 27 44 60
191-Betty & Veronica Christmas Spect.(2/72); Sabrina app.
4 8 12 23 37 50
192-Archie's Christmas Love-In (1/72); Archie Band-c/s
3 6 9 20 31 42
195-(84 pgs.)-Li'l Jinx Christmas Bag (1/72). 3 6 9 21 33 45
196-(84 pgs.)-Sabrina's Christmas Magic (1/72) 5 10 15 33 57 80
200-(52 pgs.)-World of Archie (10/72) 3 6 9 20 31 42
201-206,208-219,221-230,232,233 (All 52 pgs.): 201-Betty & Veronica Spectacular (10/72). 202-World of Jughead (11/72). 203-Archie's Christmas Stocking (12/72). 204-Betty & Veronica Christmas Spectacular (2/73). 205-Archie's Christmas Love-In (1/73). 206-Li'l Jinx Christmas Bag (12/72). 208-World of Archie (3/73). 209-World of Jughead (4/73). 210-Betty & Veronica Spectacular (6/73). 211-Archie's Jokes (8/73). 212-Betty & Veronica Summer Fun (9/73). 213-World of Archie (10/73). 214-Betty & Veronica Spectacular (10/73). 215-World of Jughead (11/73). 216-Archie's Christmas Stocking (12/73). 217-Betty & Veronica Christmas Spectacular (2/74). 218-Archie's Christmas Love-In (1/74). 219-Li'l Jinx Christmas Bag (12/73). 221-Betty & Veronica Spectacular (Advertised as World of Archie) (6/74). 222-Archie's Jokes (advertised as World of Jughead) (8/74). 223-Li'l Jinx (8/74). 224-Betty & Veronica Summer Fun (9/74). 225-World of Archie (9/74). 226-Betty & Veronica Spectacular (10/74). 227-World of Jughead (10/74). 228-Archie's Christmas Stocking (12/74). 229-Betty & Veronica Christmas Spectacular (12/74). 230-Archie's Christmas Love-In (1/75). 232-World of Archie (3/75). 233-World of Jughead (4/75)
each... 2 4 6 11 16 20
207,220,231,243: Sabrina's Christmas Magic. 207-(12/72). 220-(12/73). 231-(1/75). 243-(1/76)
each... 3 6 9 16 24 32
234-242,244-251 (36 pgs.): 234-Betty & Veronica Spectacular (6/75). 235-Archie's Jokes (8/75). 236-Betty & Veronica Summer Fun (9/75). 237-World of Archie (9/75) 238-Betty & Veronica Spectacular (10/75). 239-World of Jughead (10/75). 240-Archie's Christmas Stocking (12/75). 241-Betty & Veronica Christmas Spectacular (12/75). 242-Archie's Christmas Love-In (1/76). 244-World of Archie (3/76). 245-World of Jughead (4/76). 246-Betty & Veronica Spectacular (6/76). 247-Archie's Jokes (8/76). 248-Betty & Veronica Summer Fun (9/76). 249-World of Archie (9/76). 250-Betty & Veronica Spectacular (10/76). 251-World of Jughead each.... 2 4 6 9 12 15
252-451-**Do not exist**
452-454,456-466,468-478, 480-490,492-499: 452-Archie's Christmas Stocking (12/76). 453-Betty & Veronica Christmas Spectacular (12/76). 454-Archie's Christmas Love-In (1/77). 456-World of Archie (3/77). 457-World of Jughead (4/77). 458-Betty & Veronica Spectacular (6/77). 459-Archie's Jokes (8/77)-Shows 8/76 in error. 460-Betty & Veronica Summer Fun (9/77). 461-World of Archie (9/77). 462-Betty & Veronica Spectacular (10/77). 463-World of Jughead (10/77). 464-Archie's Christmas Stocking (12/77). 465-Betty & Veronica Christmas Spectacular (12/77). 466-Archie's Christmas Love-In (1/78). 468-World of Archie (2/78). 469-World of Jughead (2/78). 470-Betty & Veronica Spectacular(6/78). 471-Archie's Jokes (8/78). 472-Betty & Veronica Summer Fun (9/78). 473-World of Archie (9/78). 474-Betty & Veronica Spectacular (10/78). 475-World of Jughead (10/78). 476-Archie's Christmas Stocking (12/78). 477-Betty & Veronica Christmas Spectacular (12/78). 478-Archie's Christmas Love-In (1/79). 480-The World of Archie (3/79). 481-World of Jughead (4/79). 482-Betty & Veronica Spectacular (6/79). 483-Archie's Jokes (8/79). 484-Betty & Veronica Summer Fun(9/79). 485-The World of Archie (9/79). 486-Betty & Veronica Spectacular (10/79). 487-The World of Jughead (10/79). 488-Archie's Christmas Stocking (12/79). 489-Betty & Veronica Christmas Spectacular (1/80). 490-Archie's Christmas Love-in (1/80). 492-The World of Archie (2/80). 493-The World of Jughead (4/80). 494-Betty & Veronica Spectacular (6/80). 495-Archie's Jokes (8/80). 496-Betty & Veronica Summer Fun (9/80). 497-The World of Archie (9/80). 498-Betty & Veronica Spectacular (10/80). 499-The World of Jughead (10/80) each... 2 4 6 8 10 12
455,467,479,491,503-Sabrina's Christmas Magic: 455-(1/77). 467-(1/78). 479-(1/79) Dracula/Werewolf-s. 491-(1/80), 503(1/81) 2 4 6 11 16 20
500-Archie's Christmas Stocking (12/80) 2 4 6 8 11 14
501-514,516-527,529-532,534-539,541-543,545-550: 501-Betty & Veronica Christmas Spectacular (12/80). 502-Archie's Christmas Love-in (1/81). 504-The World of Archie (3/81). 505-The World of Jughead (4/81). 506-Betty & Veronica Spectacular (6/81). 507-Archie's Jokes (8/81). 508-Betty & Veronica Summer Fun (9/81). 509-The World of Archie (9/81). 510-Betty & Vernonica Spectacular (9/81). 511-The World of Jughead (10/81). 512-Archie's Christmas Stocking (12/81). 513-Betty & Veronica Christmas Spectacular (12/81). 514-Archie's Christmas Love-in (1/82). 516-The World of Archie(3/82). 517-The World of Jughead (4/82). 518-Betty & Veronica Spectacular (6/82). 519-Archie's Jokes (8/82). 520-Betty & Veronica Summer Fun (9/82). 521-The World of Archie (9/82). 522-Betty & Veronica Spectacular (10/82). 523-The World of Jughead (10/82).524-Archie's Christmas Stocking (1/83). 525-Betty and Veronica Christmas Spectacular (1/83). 526-Betty and Veronica Spectacular (5/83). 527-Little Archie (8/83). 529-Betty and Veronica Summer Fun (8/83). 530-Betty and Veronica Spectacular (9/83). 531-The World of Jughead (9/83). 532-The World of Archie (10/83). 534-Little Archie (1/84). 535-Archie's Christmas Stocking (1/84). 536-Betty and Veronica Christmas Spectacular (1/84). 537-Betty and Veronica Spectacular (6/84). 538-Little Archie (8/84). 539-Betty and Veronica Summer Fun (8/84). 541-Betty and Veronica Spectacular (9/84). 542-The World of Jughead (9/84). 543-The World of Archie (10/84). 545-Little Archie (12/84). 546-Archie's Christmas Stocking (12/84). 547-Betty and Veronica Christmas Spectacular (12/84). 548-Betty and Veronica Spectacular (6/85). 549-Little Archie. 550-Betty and Veronica Summer Fun
each... 1 2 3 5 7 9
515,528,533,540,544: 515-Sabrina's Christmas Magic (1/82). 528-Josie and the Pussycats (8/83). 533-Sabrina; Space Pirates by Frank Bolling (10/83). 540-Josie and the Pussycats (8/84). 544-Sabrina the Teen-Age Witch (10/84).
each... 2 4 6 10 14 18
551,562,571,584,597-Josie and the Pussycats 2 4 6 8 10 12
552-561,563-570,572-583,585-596,598-600: 552-Betty & Veronica Spectacular. 553-The World of Jughead. 554-The World of Archie. 555-Betty's Diary. 556-Little Archie (1/86). 557-Archie's Christmas Stocking (1/86). 558-Betty & Veronica Christmas Spectacular (1/86). 559-Betty & Veronica Spectacular. 560-Little Archie. 561-Betty & Veronica Summer Fun. 563-Betty & Veronica Spectacular. 564-World of Jughead. 565-World of Archie. 566-Little Archie. 567-Archie's Christmas Stocking. 568-Betty & Veronica Christmas Spectacular. 569-Betty & Veronica Spring Spectacular. 570-Little Archie. 571-Dracula-c/s. 572-Betty & Veronica Summer Fun. 573-Archie At Riverdale High. 574-World of Archie. 575-Betty & Veronica Spectacular. 576-Pep. 577-World of Jughead. 578-Archie And Me. 579-Archie's Christmas Stocking. 580-Betty and Veronica Christmas Spectacular. 581-Little Archie Christmas Special. 582-Betty & Veronica Spring Spectacular. 583-Little Archie. 585-Betty & Veronica Summer Fun. 586-Archie At Riverdale High. 587-The World of Archie (10/88); 1st app. Explorers of the Unknown. 588-Betty & Veronica Spectacular. 589-Pep (10/88). 590-The World of Jughead. 591-Archie & Me. 592-Archie's Christmas Stocking. 593-Betty & Veronica Christmas Spectacular. 594-Little Archie. 595-Betty & Veronica Spring Spectacular. 596-Little Archie. 598-Betty & Veronica Summer Fun. 599-The World of Archie (10/89); 2nd app. Explorers of the Unknown. 600-Betty and Veronica Spectacular
each.... 6.00
601,602,604-609,611-629: 601-Pep. 602-The World of Jughead. 604-Archie at Riverdale High. 605-Archie's Christmas Stocking. 606-Betty and Veronica Christmas Spectacular. 607-Little Archie. 608-Betty and Veronica Spectacular. 609-Little Archie. 611-Betty and Veronica Summer Fun. 612-The World of Archie. 613-Betty and Veronica Spectacular. 614-Pep (10/90). 615-Veronica's Summer Special. 616-Archie and Me. 617-Archie's Christmas Stocking. 618-Betty & Veronica Christmas Spectacular. 619-Little Archie. 620-Betty and Veronica Spectacular. 621-Betty and Veronica Summer Fun. 622-Josie & the Pussycats; not published. 623-Betty and Veronica Spectacular. 624-Pep Comics. 625-Veronica's Summer Special. 626-Archie and Me. 627-World of Archie. 628-Archie's Pals 'n' Gals Holiday Special. 629-Betty & Veronica Christmas Spectacular.
each.... 4.00
603-Archie and Me; Titanic app. 5.00
610-Josie and the Pussycats 1 2 3 4 5 7
630-631: 630-Archie's Christmas Stocking. 631-Archie's Pals 'n' Gals 4.00
632-Last issue; Betty & Veronica Spectacular 1 2 3 4 5 7
NOTE: *Archies Band-c-173,180,192; s-189,192. Archie Cavemen-165,225,232,244,249. Little Sabrina-527,534, 538,545,556,566. UFO-s-178,487,594.*

ARCHIE MEETS RAMONES
Archie Comic Publications: 2016 ($4.99, one-shot)
1-Segura & Rosenberg-s/Lagacé-a; multiple covers; The Archies go to 1976; Sabrina app. 5.00

ARCHIE MEETS THE PUNISHER (Same contents as The Punisher Meets Archie)
Marvel Comics & Archie Comics Publ.: Aug, 1994 ($2.95, 52 pgs., one-shot)
1-Batton Lash story, John Buscema-a on Punisher, Stan Goldberg-a on Archie
1 2 3 5 6 8

ARCHIE'S ACTIVITY COMICS DIGEST MAGAZINE
Archie Enterprises: 1985 - No. 4 (Annual, 128 pgs., digest size)
1 (Most copies are marked) 2 4 6 9 13 16
2-4 1 2 3 5 7 9

ARCHIE'S CAR
Spire Christian Comics (Fleming H. Revell co.): 1979 (49¢)
nn 2 4 6 13 18 22

ARCHIE'S CHRISTMAS LOVE-IN (See Archie Giant Series Mag. No. 169, 181,192, 205, 218, 230, 242, 454, 466, 478, 490, 502, 514)

ARCHIE'S CHRISTMAS STOCKING (See Archie Giant Series Mag. No. 1-6,10, 15, 20, 25, 31, 137, 144, 150, 158, 167, 179, 190, 203, 216, 228, 240, 452, 464, 476, 488, 500, 512, 524, 535, 546, 557, 567, 579, 592, 605, 617, 630)

ARCHIE'S CHRISTMAS STOCKING
Archie Comics: 1993 - No. 7, 1999 ($2.00-$2.29, 52 pgs.)(Bound-in calendar poster in all)
1-Dan DeCarlo-c/a 5.00
2-5 4.00
6,7: 6-(1998, $2.25). 7-(1999, $2.29) 4.00

ARCHIE'S CIRCUS
Barbour Christian Comics: 1990 (69¢)

Archie's Dougle Digest #97 © ACP

Archie's Girls, Betty and Veronica #1 © ACP

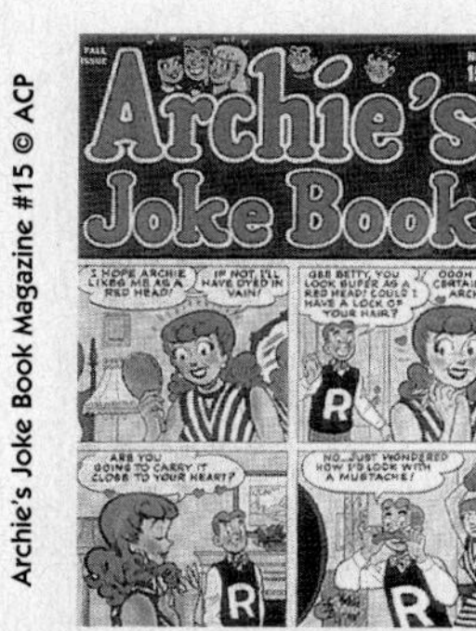

Archie's Joke Book Magazine #15 © ACP

	GD 2.0	VG 4.0	FN 6.0	VF 8.0	VF/NM 9.0	NM- 9.2
nn	2	4	6	10	14	18

ARCHIE'S CLASSIC CHRISTMAS STORIES
Archie Comics: 2002 ($10.95, TPB)

Volume 1 - Reprints stories from 1955-1964 Archie's Christmas Stocking issues						12.00

ARCHIE'S CLEAN SLATE
Spire Christian Comics (Fleming H. Revell Co.): 1973 (35/49¢)

1-(35¢-c edition)(Some issues have nn)	3	6	9	14	19	24
1-(49¢-c edition)	2	4	6	10	14	18

ARCHIE'S DATE BOOK
Spire Christian comics (Fleming H. Revell Co.): 1981

nn-(Low print)	2	4	6	13	18	22

ARCHIE'S DOUBLE DIGEST QUARTERLY MAGAZINE
Archie Comics: 1981 - No. 252, Aug, 2014 ($1.95-$3.99, 256 pgs.) (Archie's Double Digest Magazine No. 10 on)(Title becomes Archie's Comics Digest #253 on)

1	3	6	9	16	23	30
2-10; 6-Katy Keene story.	2	4	6	10	14	18
11-30: 29-Pureheart story	2	4	6	8	10	12
31-50	1	2	3	4	5	7
51-70,100						5.00
71-99						4.00
101-237,239-251: 123-Begin $3.29-c. 170-Begin $3.69. 197-Begin $3.99-c.						4.00
238-Titled Archie Double Double Digest (4/13, $5.99, 320 pages)						6.00
252-($4.99) Title changes to Archie's Comics Digest with #253						5.00

ARCHIE'S FAMILY ALBUM
Spire Christian Comics (Fleming H. Revell Co.): 1978 (39¢/49¢, 36 pgs.)

nn	2	4	6	13	18	22
nn (49¢-c edition)	2	4	6	9	13	16

ARCHIE'S FESTIVAL
Spire Christian Comics (Fleming H. Revell Co.): 1980 (49¢)

nn	2	4	6	13	18	22

ARCHIE'S FUNHOUSE DOUBLE DIGEST
Archie Comics: Feb, 2014 - Present ($3.99-$7.99, digest-size)

1-5						4.00
6,19,21: 6,19-Titled Archie's Funhouse Double Double Digest ($5.99, 320 pgs.)						6.00
7-10,12-14,16,18-($4.99) Title becomes Archie's Funhouse Comics Digest						5.00
11-($7.99) Titled Archie's Funhouse Jumbo Comics Digest						8.00
15,17,20,22-($6.99) Archie's Funhouse Jumbo Comics Digest						7.00
23,24-($5.99) 23-Titled Archie's Funhouse Christmas Annual Double Digest						6.00

ARCHIE'S GIRLS, BETTY AND VERONICA (Becomes Betty & Veronica)(Also see Veronica)
Archie Publications (Close-Up): 1950 - No. 347, Apr, 1987

1	326	652	978	2282	3991	5700
2	135	270	405	864	1482	2100
3-5: 3-Betty's 1st ponytail. 4-Dan DeCarlo's 1st Archie work	81	162	243	518	884	1250
6-10: 10-Katy Keene app. (2 pgs.)	58	116	174	371	636	900
11-20: 11,13,14,17-19-Katy Keene app. 17-Last pre-code issue (3/55). 20-Debbie's Diary (2 pgs.)	42	84	126	265	445	625
21-30: 27,30-Katy Keene app. 29-Tarzan	34	68	102	199	325	450
31-43,45-50: 41-Marilyn Monroe and Brigitte Bardot mentioned. 45-Fabian 1 pg. photo & bio. 46-Bobby Darin 1 pg. photo & bio	21	42	63	126	206	285
44-Elvis Presley 1 pg. photo & bio	24	48	72	144	237	330
51-55,57-74: 67-Jackie Kennedy homage. 73-Sci-fi-c	9	18	27	57	111	165
56-Elvis and Bobby Darin records parody	10	20	30	66	138	210
75-Betty & Veronica sell souls to Devil	21	42	63	147	324	500
76-99: 82-Bobby Rydell 1 pg. illustrated bio; Elvis mentioned on-c. 83-Rick Nelson illo/text page. 84-Connie Francis 1 pg. illustrated bio	6	12	18	38	69	100
100	6	12	18	42	79	115
101-104, 106-117,120 (12/65): 113-Monsters-s	4	8	12	28	47	65
105-Beatles wig parody (5 pg. story)(9/64)	5	10	15	31	53	75
118-(10/65) 1st app./origin Superteen (also see Betty & Me #3)	6	12	18	41	76	110
119-2nd app./last Superteen story	5	10	15	31	53	75
121,122,124-126,128-140 (8/67): 135,140-Mod-c. 136-Slave Girl-s	3	6	9	19	30	40
123-"Jingo"-Ringo parody-c	4	8	12	23	37	50
127-Beatles Fan Club-s	5	10	15	31	53	75
141-156,158-163,165-180 (12/70)	3	6	9	15	22	28
157,164-Archies Band	3	6	9	18	28	38
181-193,195-199	2	4	6	11	16	20
194-Sabrina-c/s	3	6	9	18	28	38
200-(8/72)	3	6	9	14	19	24
201-205,207,209,211-215,217-240	2	4	6	8	10	12
206,208,210, 216: 206,208,216-Sabrina c/app. 206-Josie-c. 210-Sabrina app.	3	6	9	15	22	28
241 (1/76)-270 (6/78)	1	3	4	6	8	10
271-299: 281-UFO-s	1	2	3	5	7	9
300 (12/80)-Anniversary issue	2	4	6	8	10	12
301-309	1	2	3	4	5	7
310-John Travolta parody story	1	3	4	6	8	10
311-319						6.00
320 (10/82)-Intro. of Cheryl Blossom on cover and inside story (she also appears, but not on the cover, in Jughead #325 with same 10/82 publication date)	17	34	51	117	259	400
321-Cheryl Blossom app.	6	12	18	38	69	100
322-Cheryl Blossom app.; Cheryl meets Archie for the 1st time	7	14	21	46	86	125
323,326,329,330,331,333-338: 333-Monsters-s						6.00
324,325-Crickett O'Dell app.	2	4	6	9	12	15
327,328-Cheryl Blossom app.	3	6	9	19	30	40
332,339: 332-Superhero costume party. 339-(12/85) Betty dressed as Madonna.	2	4	6	9	12	15
340-346 Low print	1	3	4	6	8	10
347 (4/87) Last issue; low print	2	4	6	8	10	12
Annual 1 (1953)	129	258	387	826	1413	2000
Annual 2 (1954)	50	100	150	315	533	750
Annual 3-5 (1955-1957)	39	78	117	240	395	550
Annual 6-8 (1958-1960)	28	56	84	165	270	375

ARCHIE'S HOLIDAY FUN DIGEST
Archie Comics: 1997 - Present ($1.75/$1.95/$1.99/$2.19/$2.39/$2.49, annual)

1-12-Christmas stories						3.00

ARCHIE'S JOKEBOOK COMICS DIGEST ANNUAL (See Jokebook...)

ARCHIE'S JOKE BOOK MAGAZINE (See Joke Book ...)
Archie Publ: 1953 - No. 3, Sum, 1954; No. 15, Fall, 1954 - No. 288, 11/82 (subtitled...Laugh-In #127-140; ...Laugh-Out #141-194)

1953-One Shot (#1)	142	284	426	909	1555	2200
2	53	106	159	334	567	800
3 (no #4-14)	41	82	123	256	428	600
15-20: 15-Formerly Archie's Rival Reggie #14; last pre-code issue (Fall/54). 15-17-Katy Keene app.	27	54	81	158	259	360
21-30	16	32	48	94	147	200
31-43: 42-Bio of Ed "Kookie" Byrnes. 43-story about guitarist Duane Eddy	14	28	42	76	108	140
44-1st professional comic work by Neal Adams, 4 pgs.	32	64	96	192	314	435
45-47-N. Adams-a in all, 2-6 pgs.	19	38	57	111	176	240
48-Four pgs. N. Adams-a	19	38	57	111	176	240
49,50	6	12	18	41	66	90
51-56,60 (1962)	4	8	12	27	44	60
57-Elvis mentioned; Marilyn Monroe cameo	6	12	18	37	66	95
58,59-Horror/Sci-Fi-c	7	14	21	48	89	130
61-80 (8/64): 66-(12¢ cover). 76-Robot-c	3	6	9	17	26	35
66-(15¢ cover variant)	4	8	12	23	37	50
81-89,91,92,94-99	3	6	9	14	20	25
90,93: 90-Beatles gag. 93-Beatles cameo	3	6	9	16	24	32
100 (5/66)	3	6	9	16	23	30
101,103-117,119-123,127,129,131-140 (9/69): 105-Superhero gag-c. 108-110-Archies Archers Band-s. 116-Beatles/Monkees/Bob Dylan cameos (posters)	2	4	6	11	16	20
102 (7/66) Archie Band prototype-c; Elvis parody panel, Rolling Stones mention	3	6	9	17	26	35
118,124,125,126,128,130: 118-Archie Band-c; Veronica & Groovers band-s. 124-Archies Band-c/app. 125-Beatles cameo (poster). 126,130-Monkees cameo. 128-Veronica/Archies Band app.	3	6	9	16	23	30
141-173,175-181,183-199	2	4	6	8	11	14
174-Sabrina-c. 182-Sabrina cameo	2	4	6	9	13	16
200 (9/74)	2	4	6	9	13	16
201-230 (3/77)	1	2	3	5	6	8
231-239,241-287						6.00
240-Elvis record-c	2	3	4	6	8	10
288-Last issue	1	2	3	4	5	7

NOTE: *Archies Band-c-118,124,147,172; 1 pg.-s-127,128,138,140,143,147,167; 2 pg.-s-124,131, 155. Sabrina app.-247,248,252-259,261,262,264,266-270,274,277,284-286.*

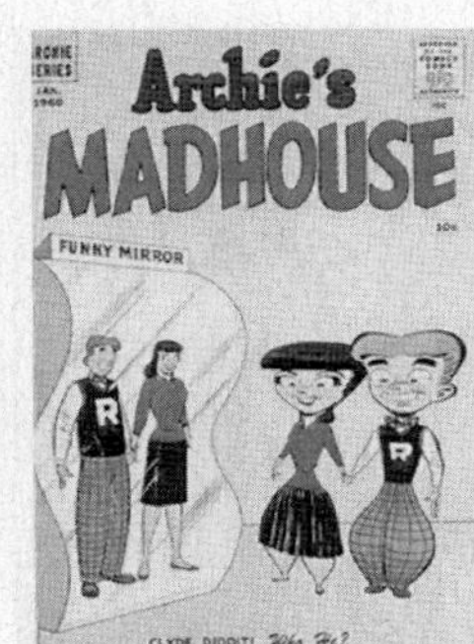

Archie's Madhouse #3 © ACP

Archie's Pal Jughead Comics #46 © ACP

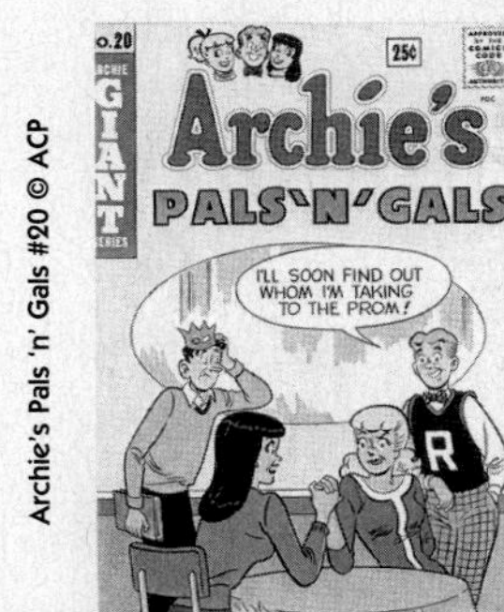

Archie's Pals 'n' Gals #20 © ACP

ARCHIE'S JOKES (See Archie Giant Series Mag. No. 17, 22, 27, 33, 139, 146, 154, 163, 174, 186, 198, 211, 222, 235, 247, 459, 471, 483, 495, 519)

ARCHIE'S LOVE SCENE
Spire Christian Comics (Fleming H. Revell Co.): 1973 (35¢/39¢/49¢/no price)

	GD 2.0	VG 4.0	FN 6.0	VF 8.0	VF/NM 9.0	NM- 9.2
1-(35¢ Edition)	3	6	9	14	19	24
1-(39¢/49¢ Edition/no price) (Some copies have nn)	2	4	6	10	14	18

ARCHIE'S LOVE SHOWDOWN SPECIAL
Archie Publications: 1994 ($2.00, one-shot)

	GD 2.0	VG 4.0	FN 6.0	VF 8.0	VF/NM 9.0	NM- 9.2
1-Concludes x-over from Archie #429, Betty #19, B&V #82, Veronica #39						4.00

ARCHIE'S MADHOUSE (Madhouse Ma-ad No. 67 on)
Archie Publications: Sept, 1959 - No. 66, Feb, 1969

	GD 2.0	VG 4.0	FN 6.0	VF 8.0	VF/NM 9.0	NM- 9.2
1-Archie begins	24	48	72	172	379	585
2	12	24	36	82	179	275
3-5	9	18	27	58	114	170
6-10	6	12	18	41	76	110
11-17 (Last w/regular characters)	5	10	15	35	63	90
18-21,23,29: 18-New format begins. 23-No Sabrina. 29-Flying saucer-c	5	10	15	31	53	75
22-1st app. Sabrina, the Teen-age Witch (10/62)	107	214	321	856	1928	3000
24-2nd app.Sabrina a	14	28	42	96	211	325
25,26,28-Sabrina app. 25-1st app. Captain Sprocket (4/63); 3rd app. Sabrina; sci-fi/horror-c	10	20	30	69	147	225
27-Sabrina-c; no story	8	16	24	54	102	150
30,34,38-40: No Sabrina. 34-Bordered-c begin.	4	8	12	25	40	55
31-33,37-Sabrina app.	8	16	24	51	96	140
35-Beatles cameo. No Sabrina	4	8	12	28	47	65
36-1st Salem the Cat w/Sabrina story	11	22	33	76	163	250
41-48,51,52,54,56,57,60-62,64-66; No Sabrina 43-Mighty Crusaders cameo. 44-Swipes Mad #4 (Super-Duperman) in "Bird Monsters From Outer Space"	3	6	9	20	31	42
49,50,53,55,58,59,63-Sabrina stories	6	12	18	37	66	95
Annual 1 (1962-63) no Sabrina	8	16	24	51	96	140
Annual 2 (1964) no Sabrina	5	10	15	31	53	75
Annual 3 (1965)-r/1st app. Sabrina from #22	11	22	33	76	163	250
Annual 4,5('66-68)(Becomes Madhouse Ma-ad Annual #7 on); no Sabrina	4	8	12	27	44	60
Annual 6 (1969)-Sabrina the Teen-Age Witch-sty	6	12	18	38	69	100

NOTE: *Cover title to #61-65 is "Madhouse" and to #66 is "Madhouse Ma-ad Jokes". Sci-Fi/Horror covers 6, 8, 11, 13, 15-26, 29, 35, 36, 38, 42, 43, 48, 51, 58, 60.*

ARCHIE'S MECHANICS
Archie Publications: Sept, 1954 - No. 3, 1955

	GD 2.0	VG 4.0	FN 6.0	VF 8.0	VF/NM 9.0	NM- 9.2
1-(15¢; 52 pgs.)	107	214	321	680	1165	1650
2-(10¢)-Last pre-code issue	57	114	171	362	619	875
3-(10¢)	48	96	144	302	514	725

ARCHIE'S MYSTERIES (Continued from Archie's Weird Mysteries)
Archie Comics: No. 25, Feb, 2003 - No. 34, June, 2004 ($2.19)

	GD 2.0	VG 4.0	FN 6.0	VF 8.0	VF/NM 9.0	NM- 9.2
25-34- Archie and gang as "Teen Scene Investigators"						3.00

ARCHIE'S ONE WAY
Spire Christian Comics (Fleming H. Revell Co.): 1972 (35¢/39¢/49¢, 36 pgs.)

	GD 2.0	VG 4.0	FN 6.0	VF 8.0	VF/NM 9.0	NM- 9.2
nn-(35¢ Edition)	3	6	9	14	19	24
nn-(39¢, 49¢, no price editions)	2	4	6	10	14	18

ARCHIE'S PAL, JUGHEAD (Jughead No. 127 on)
Archie Publications: 1949 - No. 126, Nov, 1965

	GD 2.0	VG 4.0	FN 6.0	VF 8.0	VF/NM 9.0	NM- 9.2
1 (1949)-1st app. Moose (see Pep #33)	300	600	900	1920	3310	4700
2 (1950)	103	206	309	659	1130	1600
3-5	58	116	174	371	636	900
6-10: 7-Suzie app.	39	78	117	240	395	550
11-20: 20-Jughead as Sherlock Holmes parody	26	52	78	154	252	350
21-30: 23-25,28-30-Katy Keene app. 23-Early Dilton-s. 28-Debbie's Diary app.	18	36	54	103	162	220
31-50: 49-Archies Rock 'N' Rollers band-c	7	14	21	48	89	130
51-57,59-70: 59- Bio of Will Hutchins of TV's Sugarfoot. 68-Early Archie Gang Cavemen-s	5	10	15	34	60	85
58-Neal Adams-a	6	12	18	40	73	105
71-76,83,89-99: 72-Jughead dates Betty & Veronica. 83 (4/62) 1st mention of Secret Society of Jughead Hating Girls. 95-2nd app. Cricket O'Dell	4	8	12	27	44	60
77,78,80-82,85,86,88-Horror/Sci-Fi-c. 86(7/62) 1st app. The Brain	8	16	24	51	96	140
79-Creature From the Black Lagoon-c	9	18	27	57	111	165
84-1st app. Big Ethyl (5/62)	5	10	15	33	57	80
87-2nd app. of Big Ethyl; UGAJ (United Girls Against Jughead)-s	5	10	15	30	50	70
100	4	8	12	28	47	65
101-Return of Big Ethyl	4	8	12	27	44	60
102-126	3	6	9	19	30	40
Annual 1 (1953, 25¢)	94	188	282	597	1024	1450
Annual 2 (1954, 25¢)-Last pre-code issue	45	90	135	284	480	675
Annual 3-5 (1955-57, 25¢)	34	68	102	199	325	450
Annual 6-8 (1958-60, 25¢)	21	42	63	126	206	285

ARCHIE'S PAL JUGHEAD COMICS (Formerly Jughead #1-45)
Archie Comic Publ.: No. 46, June, 1993 - No. 214, Sept, 2012 ($1.25-$2.99)

	GD 2.0	VG 4.0	FN 6.0	VF 8.0	VF/NM 9.0	NM- 9.2
46-214: 100-"A Storm Over Uniforms" x-over part 1,2. 166-Three Geeks cameo. 200-Tom Root-s; Sabrina cameo. 201-Begin $2.99-c						3.00

ARCHIE'S PALS 'N' GALS (Also see Archie Giant Series Magazine #628)
Archie Publ: 1952-53 - No. 6, 1957-58; No. 7, 1958 - No. 224, Sept, 1991
(...All News Stories on-c #49-59)

	GD 2.0	VG 4.0	FN 6.0	VF 8.0	VF/NM 9.0	NM- 9.2
1-(116 pgs., 25¢)	119	238	357	762	1306	1850
2(Annual)('54, 25¢)	50	100	150	315	533	750
3-5(Annual, '55-57, 25¢): 3-Last pre-code issue	37	74	111	222	361	500
6-10('58-'60)	22	44	66	132	216	300
11,13,14,16,17,20-(84 pgs.): 17-B&V paper dolls	14	28	42	80	115	150
12,15-(84 pgs.) Neal Adams-a. 12-Harry Belafonte 2 pg. photos & bio.	15	30	45	90	140	190
18-(84 pgs.) Horror/Sci-Fi-c	16	32	48	94	147	200
19-Marilyn Monroe app.	20	40	60	114	182	250
21,22,24-28,30 (68 pgs.)	6	12	18	41	76	110
23-(Wint./62) 6 pg. Josie-s with Pepper and Melody (1st app.) by DeCarlo; Betty in towel pin-up	46	92	138	340	770	1200
29-Beatles satire (68 pgs.)	9	18	27	60	120	180
31(Wint. 64/65)-39 -(68 pgs.)	5	10	15	33	57	80
40-Early Superteen-s; with Pureheart	6	12	18	41	76	110
41(8/67)-43,45-50(2/69) (68 pgs.)	4	8	12	25	40	55
44-Archies Band-s; WEB cameo	4	8	12	28	47	65
51(4/69),52,55-64(6/71): 62-Last squarebound	3	6	9	18	28	38
53-Archies Band-c/s	3	6	9	21	33	45
54-Satan meets Veronica-s	5	10	15	34	60	85
65(8/70),67-70,73,74,76-81,83(6/74) (52 pgs.)	3	6	9	21	33	45
66,82-Sabrina-c	4	8	12	22	34	45
71,72-Two part drug story (8/72,9/72)	3	6	9	21	33	45
75-Archies Band-s	3	6	9	16	24	32
84-99	2	4	6	8	10	12
100 (12/75)	2	4	6	9	13	16
101-130(3/79): 125,126-Riverdale 2001-s	1	2	3	5	6	8
131-160,162-170 (7/84)						6.00
161 (11/82) 3rd app./1st solo Cheryl Blossom-s and pin-up; 2nd Jason Blossom	5	10	15	30	50	70
171-173,175,177-197,199: 197-G. Colan-a						5.00
174,176,198: 174-New Archies Band-s. 176-Cyndi Lauper-c. 198-Archie gang on strike at Archie Ent. offices						6.00
200(9/88)-Illiteracy-s						6.00
201,203-223: Later issues $1.00 cover						4.00
202-Explains end of Archie's jalopy; Dezerland-c/s; James Dean cameo						6.00
224-Last issue						6.00

NOTE: *Archies Band-c-45,47,49,53,56; s-44,53,75,174. UFO-s-50,63,209,220.*

ARCHIE'S PALS 'N' GALS DOUBLE DIGEST MAGAZINE
Archie Comic Publications: Nov, 1992 - No. 146, Dec, 2010 ($2.50-$3.99)

	GD 2.0	VG 4.0	FN 6.0	VF 8.0	VF/NM 9.0	NM- 9.2
1-Capt. Hero story; Pureheart app.	2	4	6	8	10	12
2-10: 2-Superduck story; Little Jinx in all. 4-Begin $2.75-c	1	2	3	4	5	7
11-29						4.00
30-146: 40-Begin $2.99-c. 48-Begin $3.19-c. 56-Begin $3.29-c. 72-Begin $3.59-c. 100-Story uses screen captures from classic animated series. 102-Begin $3.69-c 125-128-"New Look" art; Moose and Midge break up. 130-Begin $3.99-c. 133-Reggie spotlight, also reprints early apps.						4.00

ARCHIE'S PARABLES
Spire Christian Comics (Fleming H. Revell Co.): 1973,1975 (39/49¢, 36 pgs.)

	GD 2.0	VG 4.0	FN 6.0	VF 8.0	VF/NM 9.0	NM- 9.2
nn-By Al Hartley; 39¢ Edition	3	6	9	14	19	24
49¢, no price editions	2	4	6	9	13	16

ARCHIE'S R/C RACERS (Radio controlled cars)
Archie Comics: Sept, 1989 - No. 10, Mar, 1991 (95¢/$1)

Archie's Super Teens #4 © ACP

Archie vs. Predator #3 © ACP & 20th Century Fox

Aria Angela #1 © Avalon & Todd McFarlane

	GD 2.0	VG 4.0	FN 6.0	VF 8.0	VF/NM 9.0	NM- 9.2

1 6.00
2,5-7,10: 5-Elvis parody. 7-Supervillain-c/s. 10-UFO-c/s 4.00
3,4,8,9 3.00

ARCHIE'S RIVAL REGGIE (Reggie & Archie's Joke Book #15 on)
Archie Publications: 1949 - No. 14, Aug, 1954

1-Reggie 1st app. in Jackpot Comics #5 103 206 309 659 1130 1600
2 47 94 141 296 498 700
3-5 36 72 108 211 343 475
6-10 24 48 72 142 234 325
11-14: Katy Keene in No. 10-14, 1-2 pgs. 19 38 57 111 176 240

ARCHIE'S RIVERDALE HIGH (See Riverdale High)

ARCHIE'S ROLLER COASTER
Spire Christian Comics (Fleming H. Revell Co.): 1981 (69¢)

nn-(Low print) 2 4 6 13 18 22

ARCHIE'S SOMETHING ELSE
Spire Christian Comics (Fleming H. Revell Co.): 1975 (39/49¢, 36 pgs.)

nn-(39¢-c) Hell's Angels Biker on motorcycle-c 3 6 9 14 19 24
nn-(49¢-c) 2 4 6 10 14 18
Barbour Christian Comics Edition ('86, no price listed) 2 3 4 6 8 10

ARCHIE'S SONSHINE
Spire Christian Comics (Fleming H. Revell Co.): 1973, 1974 (39/49¢, 36 pgs.)

39¢ Edition 3 6 9 14 19 24
49¢, no price editions 2 4 6 9 13 16

ARCHIE'S SPORTS SCENE
Spire Christian Comics (Fleming H. Revell Co.): 1983 (no cover price)

nn-(Low print) 2 4 6 13 18 22

ARCHIE'S SPRING BREAK
Archie Comics: 1996 - No. 5, 2000 ($2.00/$2.49, 48 pgs., annual)

1-5: 1,2-Dan DeCarlo-c 4.00

ARCHIE'S STORY & GAME COMICS DIGEST MAGAZINE
Archie Enterprises: Nov, 1986 - No. 39, Jan, 1998 ($1.25-$1.95, 128 pgs., digest-size)

1: Marked-up copies are common 2 4 6 11 16 20
2-10 2 4 6 8 10 12
11-20 1 2 3 4 5 7
21-39: 39-($1.95) 4.00

ARCHIE'S SUPER HERO SPECIAL (See Archie Giant Series Mag. No. 142)

ARCHIE'S SUPER HERO SPECIAL (...Comics Digest Mag. 2)
Archie Publications (Red Circle): Jan, 1979 - No. 2, Aug, 1979 (95¢, 148 pgs.)

1-Simon & Kirby r-/Double Life of Pvt. Strong #1,2; Black Hood, The Fly, Jaguar, The Web app. 2 4 6 11 16 20
2-Contains contents to the never published Black Hood #1; origin Black Hood; N. Adams, Wood, Channing, McWilliams, Morrow, S&K-a(r); N. Adams-c. The Shield, The Fly, Jaguar, Hangman, Steel Sterling, The Web, The Fox-r 2 4 6 11 16 20

ARCHIE'S SUPER TEENS
Archie Comic Publications, Inc.: 1994 - No. 4, 1996 ($2.00, 52 pgs.)

1-Staton/Esposito-c/a; pull-out poster 5.00
2-4: 2-Fred Hembeck script; Bret Blevins/Terry Austin-a 4.00

ARCHIE'S TV LAUGH-OUT ("...Starring Sabrina" on-c #1-50)
Archie Publications: Dec, 1969 - No. 105, Feb, 1986 (#1-7: 68 pgs.)

1-Sabrina begins, thru #105 10 20 30 66 138 210
2 (68 pgs.) 5 10 15 35 63 90
3-6 (68 pgs.) 5 10 15 30 50 70
7-Josie begins, thru #105; Archie's & Josie's Bands cover logos begin 7 14 21 46 86 125
8-23 (52 pgs.): 10-1st Josie on-c. 12-1st Josie and Pussycats on-c. 14-Beatles cameo on poster 4 8 12 25 40 55
24-40: 37,39,40-Bicentennial-c 3 6 9 14 20 25
41,47,56: 41-Alexandra rejoins J&P band. 47-Fonz cameo; voodoo-s. 56-Fonz parody; B&V with Farrah hair-c 3 6 9 15 22 28
42-46,48-55,57-60 2 4 6 9 12 15
61-68,70-80: 63-UFO-s. 79-Mummy-s 1 3 4 6 8 10
69-Sherlock Holmes parody 1 3 4 6 8 10
81-90,94,95,97-99: 84 Voodoo-s 1 2 3 5 6 8
91-Early Cheryl Blossom-s; Sabrina/Archies Band-c 3 6 9 19 30 40
92-A-Team parody 1 3 4 6 8 10
93-(2/84) Archie in drag-s; Hill Street Blues-s; Groucho Marx parody; cameo parody app. of Batman, Spider-Man, Wonder Woman and others 2 4 6 9 12 15
96-MASH parody-s; Jughead in drag; Archies Band-c 1 3 4 6 8 10
100-(4/85) Michael Jackson parody-c/s; J&P band and Archie band on-c 2 4 6 10 14 18
101-104-Lower print run. 104-Miami Vice parody-c 1 2 3 5 7 9
105-Wrestling/Hulk Hogan parody-c; J&P band-s 2 4 6 9 12 15

NOTE: ***Dan DeCarlo-a*** *78-up(most),* ***c****-89-up(most).* ***Archies Band-s*** *2,7,9-11,15,20,25,37,64,65,67,68,70,73,76,78,79,83,84,86,90,96,100,101;* ***Archies Band-c*** *2,17,20,91,94,96,99-103.* ***Josie-s*** *12,21,26,35,52,78,80,90.* ***Josie-c*** *10,91,94.* ***Josie and the Pussycats (as a band in costume)-s*** *7,9,10,37,38,41,42,66,84,99-101,105.* ***Josie w/Pussycats member Valerie &/or Melody-s*** *17,20,22,25,27-29,31,33,36,39,40,43-51,53-65,67-77,79,81-83,85-89,92-94,102-104.* ***Josie w/Pussycats band-c*** *12,14,17,18,22,24.* ***Sabrina-s*** *1-9,11-86,88-106.* ***Sabrina-c*** *1-18,21,23,27,49,91,94.*

ARCHIE'S VACATION SPECIAL
Archie Publications: Winter, 1994 - Present ($2.00/$2.25/$2.29/$2.49, annual)

1 5.00
2-8: 8-(2000, $2.49) 4.00

ARCHIE'S WEIRD MYSTERIES (Continues as Archie's Mysteries)
Archie Comics: Feb, 2000 - No. 24, Dec, 2002 ($1.79/$1.99)

1 3.50
2-24: 3-Mighty Crusaders app. 14-Super Teens-c/app.; Mighty Crusaders app. 3.00

ARCHIE'S WORLD
Spire Christian Comics (Fleming H. Revell Co.): 1973, 1976 (39/49¢)

39¢ Edition 3 6 9 14 19 24
49¢ Edition, no price editions 2 4 6 9 13 16

ARCHIE 3000
Archie Comics: May, 1989 - No. 16, July, 1991 (75¢/95¢/$1.00)

1,16: 16-Aliens-c/s 4.00
2-15: 6-Begin $1.00-c; X-Mas-c 3.00

ARCHIE VS. PREDATOR
Dark Horse Comics: Apr, 2015 - No. 4, Jul, 2015 ($3.99, limited series)

1-4-The Archie gang hunted by the Predator; de Campi-s/Ruiz-a; 3 covers on each 4.00

ARCHIE VS. SHARKNADO
Archie Comics: 2015 ($4.99, one-shot)

1-Based on the Sharknado movie series; Ferrante-s/Parent-a; 3 covers 5.00

ARCOMICS PREMIERE
Arcomics: July, 1993 ($2.95)

1-1st lenticular-c on a comic (flicker-c) 4.00

AREA 52
Image Comics: Jan, 2001 - No. 4, June, 2001 ($2.95)

1-4-Haberlin-s/Henry-a 3.00

ARES
Marvel Comics: Mar, 2006 - No. 5, July, 2006 ($2.99, limited series)

1-5-Oeming-s/Foreman-a 3.00
...: God of War TPB (2006, $13.99) r/series 14.00

ARGUS (See Flash, 2nd Series) (Also see Showcase '95 #1,2)
DC Comics: Apr, 1995 - No. 6, Oct, 1995 ($1.50, limited series)

1-6: 4-Begin $1.75-c 3.00

ARIA
Image Comics (Avalon Studios): Jan, 1999 - No. 4, Nov, 1999 ($2.50)

Preview (11/98, $2.95) 5.00
1-Anacleto-c/a 1 2 3 5 6 8
1-Variant-c by Michael Turner 1 2 3 5 6 8
1-($10.00) Alternate-c by Turner 1 3 4 6 8 10
1,2-(Blanc & Noir) Black and white printing of pencil art 3.00
1-(Blanc & Noir) DF Edition 5.00
2-4: 2,4-Anacleto-c/a. 3-Martinez-a 3.00
4-($6.95) Glow in the Dark-c 1 3 4 6 8 10
Aria Angela 1 (2/00, $2.95) Anacleto-a; 4 covers by Anacleto, JG Jones, Portacio and Quesada 3.00
Aria Angela Blanc & Noir 1 (4/00, $2.95) Anacleto-c 3.00
Aria Angela European Ashcan 10.00
Aria Angela 2 (10/00, $2.95) Anacleto-a/c 3.00
...: A Midwinter's Dream 1 (1/02, $4.95, 7"x7") text-s w/Anacleto panels 5.00
...: The Enchanted Collection (5/04, $16.95) r/Summer's Spell & The Uses of Enchantment 17.00

ARIA: SUMMER'S SPELL
Image Comics (Avalon Studios): Mar, 2002 - No. 2, Jun, 2002 ($2.95)

1,2-Anacleto-c/Holguin-s/Pajarillo & Medina-a 3.00

ARIA: THE SOUL MARKET

Arkham Asylum: Madness HC © DC

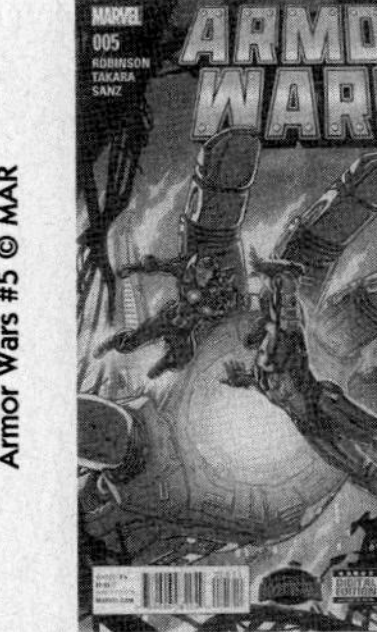

Armor Wars #5 © MAR

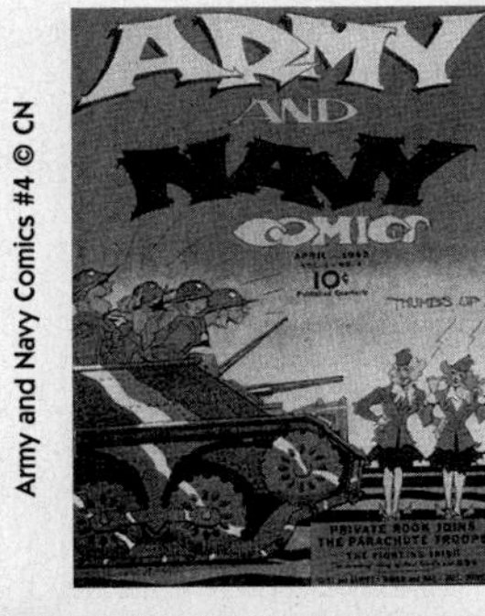

Army and Navy Comics #4 © CN

	GD 2.0	VG 4.0	FN 6.0	VF 8.0	VF/NM 9.0	NM- 9.2

Image Comics (Avalon Studios): Mar, 2001 - No. 6, Dec, 2001 ($2.95)

1-6-Anacleto-c/Holguin-s 3.00
HC (2002, $26.95, 8.25" x 12.25") oversized r/#1-6 27.00
SC (2004, $16.95, 8.25" x 12.25") oversized r/#1-6 17.00

ARIA: THE USES OF ENCHANTMENT
Image Comics (Avalon Studios): Feb, 2003 - No. 4, Sept, 2003 ($2.95)

1-4-Anacleto-c/Holguin-s/Medina-a 3.00

ARIANE AND BLUEBEARD (See Night Music #8)

ARIEL & SEBASTIAN (See Cartoon Tales & The Little Mermaid)

ARION, LORD OF ATLANTIS (Also see Warlord #55)
DC Comics: Nov, 1982 - No. 35, Sept, 1985

1-Story cont'd from Warlord #62 4.00
2-35 3.00
... Special #1 (11/85) 4.00

ARION THE IMMORTAL (Also see Showcase '95 #7)
DC Comics: July, 1992 - No. 6, Dec, 1992 ($1.50, limited series)

1-6: 4-Gustovich-a(i) 3.00

ARISTOCATS (See Movie Comics & Walt Disney Showcase No. 16)

ARISTOKITTENS, THE (...Meet Jiminy Cricket No. 1)(Disney)
Gold Key: Oct, 1971 - No. 9, Oct, 1975

	GD	VG	FN	VF	VF/NM	NM-
1	3	6	9	19	30	40
2-5,7-9	3	6	9	14	19	24
6-(52 pgs.)	3	6	9	15	22	28

ARIZONA KID, THE (Also see The Comics & Wild Western)
Marvel/Atlas Comics(CSI): Mar, 1951 - No. 6, Jan, 1952

	GD	VG	FN	VF	VF/NM	NM-
1	24	48	72	144	237	330
2-4: 2-Heath-a(3)	14	28	42	76	108	140
5,6	11	22	33	62	86	110

NOTE: *Heath a-1-3; c-1-3. Maneely c-4-6. Morisi a-4-6. Sinnott a-6.*

ARK, THE (See The Crusaders)

ARKAGA
Image Comics: Sept, 1997 ($2.95, one-shot)

1-Jorgensen-s/a 3.00

ARKANIUM
Dreamwave Productions: Sept, 2002 - No. 5 ($2.95)

1-5: 1-Gatefold wraparound-c 3.00

ARKHAM ASYLUM: LIVING HELL
DC Comics: July, 2003 - No. 6, Dec, 2003 ($2.50, limited series)

1-6-Ryan Sook-a; Batman app. 3-Batgirl-c/app. 3.00

ARKHAM ASYLUM: MADNESS
DC Comics: 2010 ($19.99, HC graphic novel, dustjacket)

HC-Sam Kieth-s/a/c; Joker, Two-Face, Harley and Ivy app. 20.00
SC-(2011, $14.99) Sam Kieth-s/a/c; Joker, Two-Face, Harley and Ivy app. 15.00

ARKHAM MANOR (Follows events in Batman Eternal #30)
DC Comics: Dec, 2014 - No. 6, May, 2015 ($2.99)

1-6-Arkham Asylum re-opens in Wayne Manor; Duggan-s/Crystal-a 3.00
...: Endgame 1 (6/15, $2.99) Tieri-s/Albuquerque-c; tie-in with other Batman titles 3.00

ARKHAM REBORN
DC Comics: Dec, 2009 - No. 3, Feb, 2010 ($2.99, limited series)

1-3-David Hine-s/Jeremy Haun-a 3.00
Batman: Arkham Reborn TPB (2010, $12.99) r/#1-3, Detective Comics #864,865 and Batman: Battle For the Cowl: Arkham Asylum #1 13.00

ARMAGEDDON
Chaos! Comics: Oct, 1999 - No. 4, Jan, 2000 ($2.95, limited series)

Preview 5.00
1-4-Lady Death, Evil Ernie, Purgatori app. 3.00

ARMAGEDDON: ALIEN AGENDA
DC Comics: Nov, 1991 - No. 4, Feb, 1992 ($1.00, limited series)

1-4 3.00

ARMAGEDDON FACTOR, THE
AC Comics: 1987 - No. 2, 1987; No. 3, 1990 ($1.95)

1,2: Sentinels of Justice, Dragonfly, Femforce 3.00
3-($3.95, color)-Almost all AC characters app. 4.00

ARMAGEDDON: INFERNO
DC Comics: Apr, 1992 - No. 4, July, 1992 ($1.00, limited series)

1-4: Many DC heroes app. 3-A. Adams/Austin-a 3.00

ARMAGEDDON 2001
DC Comics: May, 1991 - No. 2, Oct, 1991 ($2.00, squarebound, 68 pgs.)

1-Features many DC heroes; intro Waverider 5.00
1-2nd & 3rd printings; 3rd has silver ink-c 4.00
2 4.00

ARMED & DANGEROUS
Acclaim Comics (Armada): Apr, 1996 - No.4, July, 1996 ($2.95, B&W)

1-4-Bob Hall-c/a & scripts 3.00
Special 1 (8/96, $2.95, B&W)-Hall-c/a & scripts. 3.00

ARMED & DANGEROUS HELL'S SLAUGHTERHOUSE
Acclaim Comics (Armada): Oct, 1996 - No. 4, Jan, 1997 ($2.95, B&W)

1-4: Hall-c/a/scripts. 3.00

ARMOR (AND THE SILVER STREAK) (Revengers Featuring... in indicia for #1-3)
Continuity Comics: Sept, 1985 - No.13, Apr, 1992 ($2.00)

1-13: 1-Intro/origin Armor & the Silver Streak; Neal Adams-c/a. 7-Origin Armor; Nebres-i 3.50

ARMOR (DEATHWATCH 2000)
Continuity Comics: Apr, 1993 - No. 6, Nov, 1993 ($2.50)

1-6: 1-3-Deathwatch 2000 x-over 3.00

ARMOR HUNTERS
Valiant Entertainment: Jun, 2014 - No. 4, Sept, 2014 ($3.99)

1-4-Venditti-s/Braithwaite-a; X-O vs. the Hunters. 2-4-Bloodshot app. 4-Ninjak app. 4.00
...: Aftermath 1 (10/14, $3.99) Venditti-s/Cafu-a; leads into Unity #0 4.00

ARMOR HUNTERS: BLOODSHOT
Valiant Entertainment: Jul, 2014 - No. 3, Sept, 2014 ($3.99, limited series)

1-3-Joe Harris-s/Hairsine-a; Malgam app. 4.00

ARMOR HUNTERS: HARBINGER
Valiant Entertainment: Jul, 2014 - No. 3, Sept, 2014 ($3.99, limited series)

1-3-Dysart-s/Gill-a 4.00

ARMORINES (See X-O Manowar #25 for 16 pg. bound-in Armorines #0)
Valiant: June, 1994 - No. 12, June, 1995 ($2.25)

0-Stand-alone edition with cardstock-c 30.00
0-Gold 25.00
1 4.00
2-12: 7-Wraparound-c. 12-Byrne-c/swipe (X-Men, 1st Series #138) 3.00

ARMORINES (Volume 2)
Acclaim Comics: Oct, 1999 - No. 4 ($3.95/$2.50, limited series)

1-($3.95) Calafiore & P. Palmiotti-a 4.00
2,3-($2.50) 3.00

ARMOR WARS (Secret Wars tie-in)
Marvel Comics: Aug, 2015 - No. 5, Nov, 2015 ($3.99, limited series)

1-5-Tony Stark and other armor-clad citizens of Technopolis; Robinson-s/Takara-a 4.00

ARMOR X
Image Comics: March, 2005 - No. 4, June, 2005 ($2.95, limited series)

1-Keith Champagne-s/Andy Smith-a; flip covers on #2-4 3.00

ARMY AND NAVY COMICS (Supersnipe No. 6 on)
Street & Smith Publications: May, 1941 - No. 5, July, 1942

	GD	VG	FN	VF	VF/NM	NM-
1-Cap Fury & Nick Carter	54	108	162	343	574	825
2-Cap Fury & Nick Carter	32	64	96	188	307	425
3,4: 4-Jack Farr-c/a	24	48	72	142	234	325
5-Supersnipe app.; see Shadow V2#3 for 1st app.; Story of Douglas MacArthur; George Marcoux-c/a	53	106	159	334	567	800

ARMY @ LOVE
DC Comics (Vertigo): May, 2007 - No. 12, Apr, 2008; V2 #1, Oct, 2008 - No. 6, Mar, 2009 ($2.99)

1-12-Rick Veitch-s/a(p); Gary Erskine-a(i) 3.00
(Vol. 2) 1-6-Veitch-s/a(p); Erskine-a(i) 3.00
...: Generation Pwned TPB (2008, $12.99) r/#6-12 13.00
...: The Hot Zone Club TPB (2007, $9.99) r/#1-5; intro. by Peter Kuper 10.00

ARMY ATTACK
Charlton Comics: July, 1964 - No. 4, Feb, 1965; V2#38, July, 1965 - No. 47, Feb, 1967

	GD	VG	FN	VF	VF/NM	NM-
V1#1	5	10	15	30	50	70

Army of Darkness #3 © Raimi/Renegade

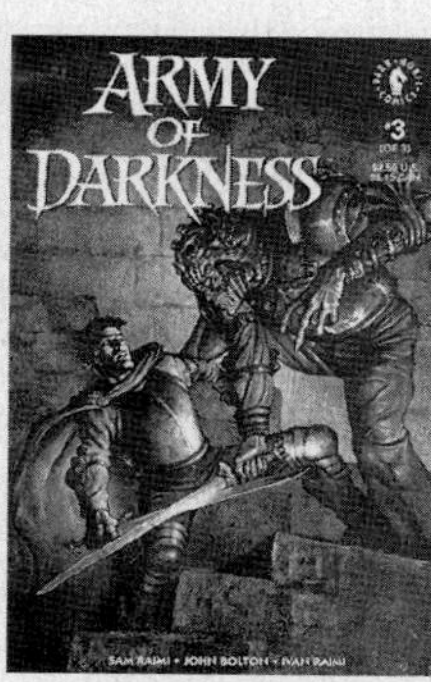

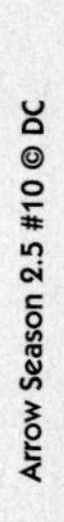
Arrow Season 2.5 #10 © DC

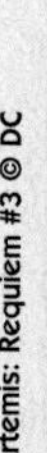
Artemis: Requiem #3 © DC

	GD 2.0	VG 4.0	FN 6.0	VF 8.0	VF/NM 9.0	NM- 9.2
2-4(2/65)	3	6	9	19	30	40
V2#38(7/65)-47 (formerly U.S. Air Force #1-37)	3	6	9	16	23	30

NOTE: ***Glanzman** a-1-3. **Montes/Bache** a-44.*

ARMY AT WAR (Also see Our Army at War & Cancelled Comic Cavalcade)
DC Comics: Oct-Nov, 1978

	GD 2.0	VG 4.0	FN 6.0	VF 8.0	VF/NM 9.0	NM- 9.2
1-Kubert-c; all new story and art	2	4	6	11	16	20

ARMY OF DARKNESS (Movie)
Dark Horse Comics: Nov, 1992 - No. 2, Dec, 1992; No. 3, Oct, 1993 ($2.50, limited series)

	GD 2.0	VG 4.0	FN 6.0	VF 8.0	VF/NM 9.0	NM- 9.2
1-3-Bolton painted-c/a	2	4	6	9	12	15
... Movie Adaptation TPB (2006, $14.99) r/#1-3; intro. by Busiek; Bruce Campbell interview						15.00

ARMY OF DARKNESS (Also see Marvel Zombies vs. Army of Darkness)
Dynamite Entertainment: 2005 - No. 13, 2007 ($2.99)

1-4 (Vs. Re-Animator):1,2-Four covers; Greene-a/Kuhoric-s. 3,4-Three covers 4.00
5-13: 5-7-Kuhoric-s/Sharpe-a; four covers. 8-11-Ash Vs. Dracula. 12,13-Death of Ash 4.00

ARMY OF DARKNESS: ...
Dynamite Entertainment: 2007 - No. 27, 2010 ($3.50/$3.99)

... From the Ashes 1-4-Kuhoric-s/Blanco-a; covers by Blanco & Suydam 4.00
5-8-(The Long Road Home); two covers on each 4.00
9-25: 9-12-(Home Sweet Hell), 13-King For a Day. 14-17-Hellbillies and Deadnecks 4.00
26,27-($3.99) Raicht-s/Cohn-a/c 4.00
#1992.1 (2014, $7.99, squarebound) Short stories by Kuhoric, Niles and others 8.00
...: Ash's Christmas Horror Special (2008, $4.99) Kuhoric-s/Simons-a; 2 covers 5.00
...: Convention Invasion (2014, $7.99, squarebound) Moreci-s/Peeples-a 8.00
... Election Special 1 (2016, $5.99) Serrano-s/Galindo-a 6.00
.../ Reanimator One Shot (2013, $4.99) Rahner-s/Valiente-a 5.00

ARMY OF DARKNESS VOLUME 3
Dynamite Entertainment: 2012 - No. 13, 2013 ($3.99)

1-13: 1-Female Ash; Michaels-a 4.00

ARMY OF DARKNESS VOLUME 4
Dynamite Entertainment: 2014 - No. 5, 2015 ($3.99)

1-5-Ash in space; Bunn-s/Watts-a; multiple covers 4.00

ARMY OF DARKNESS: ASHES 2 ASHES (Movie)
Devil's Due Publ.: July, 2004 - No. 4, 2004 ($2.99, limited series)

1-4-Four covers for each; Nick Bradshaw-a 4.00
1-Director's Cut (12/04, $4.99) r/#1, cover gallery, script and sketch pages 5.00
TPB (2005, $14.99) r/series; cover gallery; Bradshaw interview and sketch pages 15.00

ARMY OF DARKNESS: ASH GETS HITCHED
Dynamite Entertainment: 2014 - No. 4, 2014 ($3.99, limited series)

1-4-Ash in medieval times; Niles-s/Tenorio-a; multiple covers 4.00

ARMY OF DARKNESS: ASH SAVES OBAMA
Dynamite Entertainment: 2009 - No. 4, 2009 ($3.50, limited series)

1-4-Serrano-s/Padilla-a; covers by Parrillo and Nauck. 4-Obama app. 4.00

ARMY OF DARKNESS FURIOUS ROAD
Dynamite Entertainment: 2016 - No. 6, 2016 ($3.99, limited series)

1-6-Nancy Collins-s/Kewber Baal-a. 1-Multiple covers 4.00

ARMY OF DARKNESS: SHOP TILL YOU DROP DEAD (Movie)
Devil's Due Publ.: Jan, 2005 - No. 4, July, 2005 ($2.99, limited series)

1-4:1-Five covers; Bradshaw-a/Kuhoric-s. 2-4: Two covers. 3-Greene-a 4.00

ARMY OF DARKNESS VS. HACK/SLASH
Dynamite Entertainment: 2013 - No. 6, 2014 ($3.99, limited series)

1-6-Tim Seeley-s/Daniel Leister-a; multiple covers on each 4.00

ARMY OF DARKNESS / XENA
Dynamite Entertainment: 2008 - No. 4, 2008 ($3.50, limited series)

1-4-Layman-s/Montenegro-a; two covers on each 4.00

ARMY OF DARKNESS XENA: WARRIOR PRINCESS FOREVER... AND A DAY
Dynamite Entertainment: 2016 -Present ($3.99, limited series)

1-5-Lobdell-s. 1-Multiple covers. 1,2-Fernandez-a. 3-5-Galindo-a 4.00

ARMY SURPLUS KOMIKZ FEATURING CUTEY BUNNY
Army Surplus Komikz/Eclipse Comics: 1982 - No. 5, 1985 ($1.50, B&W)

	GD 2.0	VG 4.0	FN 6.0	VF 8.0	VF/NM 9.0	NM- 9.2
1-Cutey Bunny begins	2	4	6	8	10	12
2-5: 5-(Eclipse)-JLA/X-Men/Batman parody						4.50

ARMY WAR HEROES (Also see Iron Corporal)
Charlton Comics: Dec, 1963 - No. 38, June, 1970

	GD 2.0	VG 4.0	FN 6.0	VF 8.0	VF/NM 9.0	NM- 9.2
1	5	10	15	35	63	90
2-10	3	6	9	21	33	45
11-21,23-30: 24-Intro. Archer & Corp. Jack series	3	6	9	16	23	30
22-Origin/1st app. Iron Corporal series by Glanzman	5	10	15	30	50	70
31-38	2	4	6	10	14	18
Modern Comics Reprint 36 ('78)						5.00

NOTE: ***Montes/Bache** a-1, 16, 17, 21, 23-25, 27-30.*

AROUND THE BLOCK WITH DUNC & LOO (See Dunc and Loo)

AROUND THE WORLD IN 80 DAYS (Movie) (See A Golden Picture Classic)
Dell Publishing Co.: Feb, 1957

	GD 2.0	VG 4.0	FN 6.0	VF 8.0	VF/NM 9.0	NM- 9.2
Four Color 784-Photo-c	7	14	21	46	86	125

AROUND THE WORLD UNDER THE SEA (See Movie Classics)

AROUND THE WORLD WITH ARCHIE (See Archie Giant Series Mag. #29, 35, 141)

AROUND THE WORLD WITH HUCKLEBERRY & HIS FRIENDS (See Dell Giant No. 44)

ARRGH! (Satire)
Marvel Comics Group: Dec, 1974 - No. 5, Sept, 1975 (25¢)

	GD 2.0	VG 4.0	FN 6.0	VF 8.0	VF/NM 9.0	NM- 9.2
1-Dracula story; Sekowsky-a(p)	3	6	9	19	30	40
2-5: 2-Frankenstein. 3-Mummy. 4-Nightstalker(TV); Dracula-c/app., Hunchback. 5-Invisible Man, Dracula	3	6	9	14	20	25

NOTE ***Alcala** a-2; c-3. **Everett** a-1r, 2r. **Grandenetti** a-4. **Maneely** a-4r. **Sutton** a-1-3.*

ARROW (See Protectors)
Malibu Comics: Oct, 1992 ($1.95, one-shot)

1-Moder-a(p) 3.00

ARROW (Based on the 2012 television series)
DC Comics: Jan, 2013 - No. 12, Dec, 2013 ($3.99, printings of digital-first stories)

	GD 2.0	VG 4.0	FN 6.0	VF 8.0	VF/NM 9.0	NM- 9.2
1-Photo-c; origin retold; Grell-a	1	2	3	5	6	8
1-Special Edition (2012, giveaway) Grell-c; back-up preview of Green Arrow #0						3.00
2-12: 8-12-Photo-c						4.00

ARROW SEASON 2.5 (Follows the second season of the 2012 television series)
DC Comics: Dec, 2014 - No. 12, Nov, 2015 ($2.99, printings of digital-first stories)

1-12-Photo-c on most. 1-5-Brother Blood app. 5,6-Suicide Squad app. 3.00

ARROW, THE (See Funny Pages)
Centaur Publications: Oct, 1940 - No. 2, Nov, 1940; No. 3, Oct, 1941

	GD 2.0	VG 4.0	FN 6.0	VF 8.0	VF/NM 9.0	NM- 9.2
1-The Arrow begins(r/Funny Pages)	383	766	1149	2681	4691	6700
2,3: 2-Tippy Taylor serial continues from Amazing Mystery Funnies #24. 3-Origin Dash Dartwell, the Human Meteor; origin The Rainbow-r; bondage-c	194	388	582	1242	2121	3000

NOTE: ***Gustavson** a-1, 2; c-3.*

ARROWHEAD (See Black Rider and Wild Western)
Atlas Comics (CPS): April, 1954 - No. 4, Nov, 1954

	GD 2.0	VG 4.0	FN 6.0	VF 8.0	VF/NM 9.0	NM- 9.2
1-Arrowhead & his horse Eagle begin	18	36	54	107	169	230
2-4: 4-Forte-a	11	22	33	64	90	115

NOTE: ***Heath** c-3. **Jack Katz** a-3. **Maneely** c-2. **Pakula** a-2. **Sinnott** a-1-4; c-1.*

ARROWSMITH (Also see Astro City/Arrowsmith flip book)
DC Comics (Cliffhanger): Sept, 2003 - No. 6, May, 2004 ($2.95)

1-6-Pacheco-a/Busiek-s 3.00
...: So Smart in Their Fine Uniforms TPB (2004, $14.95) r/#1-6 15.00

ARSENAL (Teen Titans' Speedy)
DC Comics: Oct, 1998 - No. 4, Jan, 1999 ($2.50, limited series)

1-4: Grayson-s. 1-Black Canary app. 2-Green Arrow app. 3.00

ARSENAL SPECIAL (See New Titans, Showcase '94 #7 & Showcase '95 #8)
DC Comics: 1996 ($2.95, one-shot)

1 3.00

ARTBABE
Fantagraphics Books: May, 1996 - Apr, 1999 ($2.50/$2.95/$3.50, B&W)

V1 #5, V2 #1-3 3.00
#4-($3.50) 3.50

ARTEMIS IX (See Aphrodite IX)
Image Comics (Top Cow): Aug, 2015 ($3.99, one-shot)

1-Dan Wickline-s/Johnny Desjardins-a; 2 covers 4.00

ARTEMIS: REQUIEM (Also see Wonder Woman, 2nd Series #90)
DC Comics: June, 1996 - No. 6, Nov, 1996 ($1.75, limited series)

1-6: Messner-Loebs scripts & Benes-c/a in all. 1,2-Wonder Woman app. 3.00

ARTIFACTS
Image Comics (Top Cow): Jul, 2010 - No. 40, Nov, 2014 ($3.99, intended as a limited series)

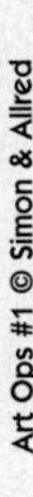

Art Ops #1 © Simon & Allred

Ash #4 © Q&P

The Assignment #1 © Rue de Sevres

GD VG FN VF VF/NM NM-
2.0 4.0 6.0 8.0 9.0 9.2

0-(5/10, free) Free Comic Book Day edition; Sejic-a 3.00
1-39: 1-6-Marz-s/Broussard-a. 1-Multiple covers; back-up origin of Witchblade. 7,8-Portacio-a. 9-12-Haun-a. 10-Wraparound-c by Sejic. 13-Keown-a. 14-25-Sejic-a 4.00
40-($5.99) Steve Foxe-s/Adalor Alvarez-a/Sejic-c; back-up stories 6.00
... Lost Tales 1 (5/15, $3.99) Short stories by Talent Hunt runners-up 4.00
...Origins (1/12, $3.99) Two-page spread origins of the 13 artifacts; wraparound-c 4.00

ART OF HOMAGE STUDIOS, THE
Image Comics: Dec, 1993 ($4.95, one-shot)
1-Short stories and pin-ups by Jim Lee, Silvestri, Williams, Portacio & Chiodo 5.00

ART OF ZEN INTERGALACTIC NINJA, THE
Entity Comics: 1994 - No. 2, 1994 ($2.95)
1,2 3.00

ART OPS
DC Comics (Vertigo): Dec, 2015 - No. 12, Dec, 2016 ($3.99)
1-12: Shaun Simon-s/Mike Allred-c. 1-5,8,9,12-Mike Allred-a. 6,7-Eduardo Risso-a 4.00

ARZACH (See Moebius…)
Dark Horse Comics: 1996 ($6.95, one-shot)
nn-Moebius-c/a/scripts 1 2 3 4 5 7

ASCENSION
Image Comics (Top Cow Productions): Oct, 1997 - No. 22, Mar, 2000 ($2.50)
Preview 5.00
Preview Gold Edition 8.00
Preview San Diego Edition 2 4 6 8 10 12
0 4.00
1/2 6.00
1-David Finch-s/a(p)/Batt-s/a(i) 4.00
1-Variant-c w/Image logo at lower right 6.00
2-22 3.00
... Collected Edition 1,2 (1998 - No. 2, $4.95, squarebound) 1-r/#1,2. 2-r/#3,4 5.00
Fan Club Edition 5.00

ASH
Event Comics: Nov, 1994 - No. 6, Dec, 1995; No. 0, May, 1996 ($2.50/$3.00)
0-Present & Future (Both 5/96, $3.00, foil logo-c)-w/pin-ups 3.00
0-Blue Foil logo-c (Present and Future) (1000 each) 4.00
0-Silver Prism logo-c (Present and Future) (500 each) 10.00
0-Red Prism logo-c (Present and Future) (250 each) 20.00
0-Gold Hologram logo-c (Present and Future) (1000 each) 8.00
1-Quesada-p/story; Palmiotti-i/story: Barry Windsor-Smith pin-up 2 4 6 8 10 12
2-Mignola Hellboy pin-up 1 2 3 4 5 7
3,4: 3-Big Guy pin-up by Geoff Darrow. 4-Jim Lee pin-up 4.00
4-Fahrenheit Gold 7.00
4-6-Fahrenheit Red (5,6-1000) 8.00
4-6-Fahrenheit White 12.00
5, 6-Double-c w/Hildebrandt Bros.-a, Quesada & Palmiotti. 6-Texeira-c 3.00
5,6-Fahrenheit Gold (2000) 4.00
6-Fahrenheit White (500)-Texeira-c 12.00
Volume 1 (1996, $14.95, TPB)-r/#1-5, intro by James Robinson 15.00
Wizard Mini-Comic (1996, magazine supplement) 3.00
Wizard #1/2 (1997, mail order) 4.00

ASH AND THE ARMY OF DARKNESS (Leads into Army of Darkness: Ash Gets Hitched)
Dynamite Entertainment: 2013 - No. 8, 2014 ($3.99)
1-8: 1-5-Niles-s/Calero-a. 1-Three covers. 2-8-Two covers. 6-8-Tenorio-a 4.00

ASH: CINDER & SMOKE
Event Comics: May, 1997 - No. 6, Oct, 1997 ($2.95, limited series)
1-6: Ramos-a/Waid, Augustyn-s in all. 2-6-variant covers by Ramos and Quesada 3.00

ASH: FILES
Event Comics: Mar, 1997 ($2.95, one-shot)
1-Comics w/text 3.00

ASH: FIRE AND CROSSFIRE
Event Comics: Jan, 1999 - No. 5 ($2.95, limited series)
1,2-Robinson-s/Quesada & Palmiotti-c/a 3.00

ASH: FIRE WITHIN, THE
Event Comics: Sept, 1996 - No. 2, Jan, 1997 ($2.95, unfinished limited series)
1,2: Quesada & Palmiotti-c/s/a 3.00

ASH/ 22 BRIDES
Event Comics: Dec, 1996 - No. 2, Apr, 1997 ($2.95, limited series)
1,2: Nicieza-s/Ramos-c/a 3.00

ASKANI'SON (See Adventures of Cyclops & Phoenix limited series)
Marvel Comics: Jan, 1996 - No. 4, May, 1996 ($2.95, limited series)
1-4: Story cont'd from Advs. of Cyclops & Phoenix; Lobdell/Loeb story; Gene Ha-c/a(p) 3.00
TPB (1997, $12.99) r/#1-4; Gene Ha painted-c 13.00

ASPEN (MICHAEL TURNER PRESENTS:...) (Also see Fathom)
Aspen MLT, Inc.: July, 2003 - No. 3, Aug, 2003 ($2.99)
1-Fathom story; Turner-a/Johns-s; interviews w/Turner & Johns; two covers by Turner 3.00
2,3:2-Fathom story; Turner-a/Johns-s; two covers by Turner; pin-ups and interviews 3.00
... Presents: The Adventures of the Aspen Universe (10/16, free) coloring book; Oum-a 3.00
... Seasons: Fall 2005 (12/05, $2.99) short stories by various; Turner-c 3.00
... Seasons: Spring 2005 (4/05, $2.99) short stories by various; Turner-c 3.00
... Seasons: Summer 2006 (10/06, $2.99) short stories by various; Turner-c 3.00
... Seasons: Winter 2009 (3/09, $2.99) short stories by various; Benitez-c 3.00
... Showcase: Aspen Matthews 1 (7/08, $2.99) Caldwell-a 3.00
... Showcase: Kiani 1 (10/09, $2.99) Scott Clark-a; covers by Clark and Caldwell 3.00
... Sketchbook 1 (2003, $2.99) sketch pages by Michael Turner and Talent Caldwell 3.00
... Splash: 2006 Swimsuit Spectacular 1 (3/06, $2.99) pin-up pages by various; Turner-c 3.00
... Splash: 2007 Swimsuit Spectacular 1 (8/07, $2.99) pin-up pages by various; Turner-c 3.00
... Splash: 2008 Swimsuit Spectacular 1 (7/08, $2.99) pin-up pages by various; Turner-c 3.00
... Splash: 2010 Swimsuit Spectacular 1 (8/10, $2.99) pin-up pages by various; 2 covers 3.00
... Universe Sourcebook 1 (7/16, $5.99) Character profiles for Fathom, Soulfire, Iris 6.00

ASPEN SHOWCASE
Aspen MLT: Oct, 2008 ($2.99)
...: Benoist 1 (10/08) - Krul-s/Gunnell-a; two covers by Gunnell & Manapul 3.00
...: Ember 1 (2/09) - Randy Green-a; two covers by Gunnell & Green 3.00

ASPEN UNIVERSE: REVELATIONS
Aspen MLT: Jul, 2016 - No. 5, Dec, 2016 ($3.99)
1-5-Fathom & Soulfire crossover; Fialkov & Krul-s/Gunderson-a; multiple covers 4.00

ASSASSINS
DC Comics (Amalgam): Apr, 1996 ($1.95)
1 3.00

ASSASSIN'S CREED (Based on the Ubisoft Entertainment videogame)
Titan Comics: Nov, 2015 - No. 14, Feb, 2017 ($3.99/$4.99)
1-12: 1-Del Col & McCreery-s/Edwards-a; multiple-c. 1-5-Trial By Fire. 6-11-Setting Sun 4.00
13,14-($4.99) Homecoming 5.00
... Free Comic Book Day (5/16, giveaway) Alves-a; Great Wall back-up w/Calero-a 3.00

ASSASSIN'S CREED: AWAKENING (Based on the Ubisoft Entertainment videogame)
Titan Comics: Dec, 2016 - No. 6 ($4.99, B&W manga style, reads right to left)
1-4-Takashi Yano-s/Kenji Oiwa-a 5.00

ASSASSIN'S CREED: LOCUS (Based on the Ubisoft Entertainment videogame)
Titan Comics: Oct, 2016 - Present ($3.99)
1-4-Edginton-s/Wijngaard-a 4.00

ASSASSIN'S CREED: THE FALL (Based on the Ubisoft Entertainment videogame)
DC Comics: Jan, 2011 - No. 3, Mar, 2011 ($3.99, limited series)
1-3-Cam Stewart & Karl Kerschl-s/a 4.00

ASSASSIN'S CREED: UPRISING (Based on the Ubisoft Entertainment videogame)
Titan Comics: Feb, 2017 - Present ($3.99)
1-Paknadel & Watters-s/Holder-a; multiple covers 4.00

ASSIGNMENT, THE (Adapts screenplay of 2017 movie The Assignment)
Titan Comics (Hard Case Crime): Feb, 2017 - Present ($5.99)
1-3-Walter Hill & Denis Hamill-s/Jef-a; English version of French comic 6.00

ASSAULT ON NEW OLYMPUS PROLOGUE
Marvel Comics: Jan, 2010 ($3.99, one-shot)
1-Spider-Man, Hercules, Amadeus Cho app.; Granov-c; leads into Inc. Hercules #138 4.00

ASTONISHING (Formerly Marvel Boy No. 1, 2)
Marvel/Atlas Comics(20CC): No. 3, Apr, 1951 - No. 63, Aug, 1957
3-Marvel Boy continues; 3-5-Marvel Boy-c 135 270 405 864 1482 2100
4-6-Last Marvel Boy; 4-Stan Lee app. 90 180 270 576 988 1400
7-10: 7-Maneely s/f story. 10-Sinnott s/f story 50 100 150 315 533 750
11,12,15,17,20 43 86 129 271 461 650
13,14,16,18,19-Krigstein-a. 18-Jack The Ripper sty 44 88 132 277 469 660
21,22,24 37 74 111 222 361 500
23-E.C. swipe "The Hole In The Wall" from Vault Of Horror #16 39 78 117 231 378 525
25,29: 25-Crandall-a. 29-Decapitation-c 37 74 111 218 354 490

Astonishing Ant-Man #6 © MAR

Astonishing X-Men #1 © MAR

Astro City #27 © Jukebox

GD 2.0 | VG 4.0 | FN 6.0 | VF 8.0 | VF/NM 9.0 | NM- 9.2

26-28 34 68 102 206 336 465
30-Tentacled eyeball-c/story; classic-c 65 130 195 416 708 1000
31-Classic story: man develops atomic powers after exposure to A-bomb; four A-bomb panels 32 64 96 188 307 425
32-37-Last pre-code issues 30 60 90 177 289 400
38-43,46,48-52,56,58,59,61 24 48 72 142 234 325
44,45,47,53-55,57,60: 44-Crandall swipe/Weird Fantasy #22. 45,47-Krigstein-a. 53-Ditko-a. 54-Torres-a, 55-Crandall, Torres-a. 57-Williamson/Krenkel-a (4 pgs.). 60-Williamson/Mayo-a (4 pgs.) 25 50 75 150 245 340
62,63: 62-Torres, Powell-a. 63-Woodbridge-a 25 50 75 147 241 335

NOTE: ***Ayers** a-16, 49. **Berg** a-36, 53, 56. **Cameron** a-50. **Gene Colan** a-12, 20, 29, 56. **Ditko** a-53. **Drucker** a-41, 62. **Everett** a-3-6(3), 6, 10, 12, 37, 47, 48, 58; c-3-5, 13,15, 16, 18, 29, 47, 49, 51, 53-55, 57, 59-63. **Fass** a-11, 34. **Forte** a-26, 48, 53, 58, 60. **Fuje** a-11. **Heath** a-8, 29; c-8, 9, 19, 22, 25, 26. **Kirby** a-56. **Lawrence** a-28, 37, 38, 42. **Maneely** a-7(2), 19; c-7, 31, 33, 34, 56. **Moldoff** a-33. **Morisi** a-10, 60. **Morrow** a-52, 61. **Orlando** a-47, 58, 61. **Pakula** a-10. **Powell** a-43, 44, 48. **Ravielli** a-26, 28. **Reinman** a-32, 34, 38. **Robinson** a-20. **J. Romita** a-7, 18, 24, 43, 57,61. **Roussos** a-55. **Sale** a-28, 38, 59; c-32. **Sekowsky** a-13. **Severin** c-46. **Shores** a-16, 60. **Sinnott** a-11, 30, 31. **Whitney** a-13. **Ed Win** a-20. Canadian reprints exist.*

ASTONISHING ANT-MAN (Scott Lang)
Marvel Comics: Dec, 2015 - No. 13, Dec, 2016($3.99)

1-12: 1-Spencer-s/Rosanas-a; Cassie Lang app. 2,3-Capt. America (Sam Wilson) app. 4.00
13-($4.99) Spencer-s/Schoonover & Rosanas-a; Yellowjacket app. 5.00

ASTONISHING SPIDER-MAN AND WOLVERINE
Marvel Comics: Jul, 2010 - No. 6, Jul. 2011 ($3.99, limited series)

1-6-Adam Kubert-a/Jason Aaron-s. 1-Bonus pin-up gallery; wraparound-c 4.00
1-Director's Cut (10/10, $4.99) r/#1 with full script & B&W art 5.00
...: Another Fine Mess (6/11, $4.99) r/#1-3; wraparound-c 5.00

ASTONISHING TALES (See Ka-Zar)
Marvel Comics Group: Aug, 1970 - No. 36, July, 1976 (#1-7: 15¢; #8: 25¢)

1-Ka-Zar (by Kirby(p) #1,2; by B. Smith #3-6) & Dr. Doom (by Wood #1-4; by Tuska #5,6; by Colan #7,8; 1st Marvel villain solo series) double feature begins; Kraven the Hunter-c/story; Nixon cameo 6 12 18 38 69 100
2-Kraven the Hunter-c/story; Kirby, Wood-a 3 6 9 21 33 45
3-5: B. Smith-p; Wood-a-#3,4. 5-Red Skull app. 4 8 12 23 37 50
6-1st app. Bobbi Morse (later becomes Mockingbird); Doctor Doom vs. Black Panther-c/sty; 5 10 15 33 57 80
7-Last 15¢ issue; Black Panther app. 3 6 9 17 26 35
8-(25¢, 52 pgs.)-Last Dr. Doom of series 4 8 12 23 37 50
9-All Ka-Zar issues begin; Lorna-r/Lorna #14 2 4 6 11 16 20
10-B. Smith/Sal Buscema-a. 3 6 9 14 20 25
11-Origin Ka-Zar & Zabu; death of Ka-Zar's father 2 4 6 13 18 22
12-2nd app.Man-Thing; by Neal Adams (see Savage Tales #1 for 1st app.) 5 10 15 33 57 80
13-3rd app.Man-Thing 4 8 12 25 40 55
14-20: 14-Jann of the Jungle-r (1950s); reprints censored Ka-Zar-s from Savage Tales #1. 17-S.H.I.E.L.D. begins. 19-Starlin-a(p). 20-Last Ka-Zar (continues into 1974 Ka-Zar series) 1 3 4 6 8 10
21-(12/73)-It! the Living Colossus begins, ends #24 (see Supernatural Thrillers #1) 4 8 12 23 37 50
22 3 6 9 17 26 35
23,24-It! the Living Colossus vs. Fin Fang Foom 4 8 12 23 37 50
25-1st app. Deathlok the Demolisher; full length stories begin, end #36; Perez's 1st work, 2 pgs. (8/74) 8 16 24 51 96 140
26-28,30 3 6 9 14 20 25
29-Reprints origin/1st app. Guardians of the Galaxy from Marvel Super-Heroes #18 plus-c w/4 pgs. omitted; no Deathlok story 3 6 9 19 30 40
31-34: 31-Watcher-r/Silver Surfer #3 2 4 6 10 14 18
35,36-(Regular 25¢ edition)(5,7/76) 2 4 6 10 14 18
35,36-(30¢-c, low distribution) 5 10 15 33 57 80

NOTE: ***Buckler** a-13i, 16p, 25, 26p, 27p, 28, 29p-36p; c-13, 25p, 26-30, 32-35p, 36. **John Buscema** a-9, 12p-14p, 16p; c-4-6p, 12p. **Colan** a-7p, 8p. **Ditko** a-21r. **Everett** a-6i. **G. Kane** a-11p, 15p; c-9, 10p, 11p, 14, 15p, 21p. **McWilliams** a-30i. **Starlin** a-19p; c-16p. **Sutton & Trimpe** a-8. **Tuska** a-5p, 6p, 8p. **Wood** a-1-4. **Wrightson** c-31i.*

ASTONISHING TALES (Anthology)
Marvel Comics: Apr, 2009 - No. 6, Sept, 2009 ($3.99, limited series)

1-6-Wolverine, Punisher, Iron Man and Iron Man 2020 app. 1-Wraparound-c 4.00

ASTONISHING THOR
Marvel Comics: Jan, 2011 - No. 5, Sept, 2011 ($3.99, limited series)

1-5: 1-Robert Rodi-s/Mike Choi-a/Esad Ribic-c 4.00

ASTONISHING X-MEN
Marvel Comics: Mar, 1995 - No. 4, July, 1995 ($1.95, limited series)

1-Age of Apocalypse; Magneto-c 4.00
2-4 3.00

ASTONISHING X-MEN
Marvel Comics: Sept, 1999 - No.3, Nov, 1999 ($2.50, limited series)

1-3-New team, Cable & X-Man app.; Peterson-a 3.00
TPB (11/00, $15.95) r/#1-3, X-Men #92 & #95, Uncanny X-Men #375 16.00

ASTONISHING X-MEN (See Giant-Size Astonishing X-Men for story folllowing #24)
Marvel Comics: July, 2004 - No. 68, Dec, 2013 ($2.99/$3.99)

1-Whedon-s/Cassaday-c/a; team of Cyclops, Beast, Wolverine, Emma Frost & Kitty Pryde 4.00
1-Director's Cut (2004, $3.99) different Cassaday partial sketch-c; cover gallery, sketch pages and script excerpt 5.00
1-Variant-c by Cassaday 10.00
1-Variant-c by Dell'Otto 5.00
2,3,5,6-X-Men battle Ord 3.00
4-Colossus returns 4.00
4-Variant Colossus cover by Cassaday 5.00
7-24: 7-Fantastic Four app. 9,10-X-Men vs. the Danger Room 3.00
7,9,10-12,19-24-Second printing variant covers 3.00
25-35: 25-Ellis-s/Bianchi-a begins; Bianchi wraparound-c. 31-Jimenez-a begins 3.00
36-68-($3.99): 36-Pearson wraparound-c; Way-s/Pearson-a. 44-47-McKone-a. 51-Northstar wedding; wraparound-c. 60-X-Termination tie-in 4.00
Annual 1 (1/13, $4.99) Gage-s/Baldeon-a; bonus r/Alpha Flight #106 5.00
.../Amazing Spider-Man: The Gauntlet Sketchbook ('09, giveaway) flip book preview 3.00
...: Ghost Boxes 1,2 (12/08-1/09, $3.99) Ellis-s/Davis & Granov-a; full Ellis script 4.00
... Saga (2006, $3.99) reprints highlights from #1-12; sketch pages and cover gallery 4.00
... Sketchbook Special ('08, $2.99) Costume sketches & blueprints by Bianchi & Larroca 3.00
...Vol. 1 HC (2006, $29.99, dust jacket) r/#1-12; interviews, sketch pages and covers 30.00
...Vol. 1: Gifted (2004, $14.99) r/#1-6; variant cover gallery 15.00
...Vol. 2: Dangerous (2005, $14.99) r/#7-12; variant cover gallery 15.00
...Vol. 3: Torn (2007, $14.99) r/#13-18; variant & sketch cover gallery 15.00

ASTONISHING X-MEN: XENOGENESIS
Marvel Comics: July, 2010 - No. 5, Apr, 2011 ($3.99, limited series)

1-5-Warren Ellis-s/Kaare Andrews-a/c. 1-Wraparound-c; script 4.00
1-Director's Cut (10/10, $4.99) r/#1 with full script & B&W art; cover sketches 5.00

ASTOUNDING SPACE THRILLS: THE COMIC BOOK
Image Comics: Apr, 2000 - No. 4, Dec, 2000 ($2.95, limited series)

1-4-Steve Conley-s/a. 2,3-Flip book w/Crater Kid 3.00
Galaxy-Sized Astounding Space Thrills 1 (10/01, $4.95) 5.00

ASTOUNDING WOLF-MAN
Image Comics: Jun, 2007 - No. 25, Nov, 2010 ($2.99)

1-Free Comic Boy Day issue; Kirkman-s/Howard-a; origin story 3.00
2-24: 11-Invincible x-over from Invincble #57 3.00
25-($4.99) Wraparound-c; Wolfcorps app. 5.00
Vol. 1 TPB (2008, $14.99) r/#1-7; sketch pages; Kirkman intro. 15.00

ASTRA
CPM Manga: 2001 - No. 8 ($2.95, B&W, limited series)

1-8: Created by Jerry Robinson; Tanaka-a. 1-Balent variant-c 3.00
TPB (2002, $15.95) r/#1-8; JH Williams III-c from #3 16.00

ASTRO BOY (TV) (See March of Comics #285 & The Original...)
Gold Key: August, 1965 (12¢)

1(10151-508) 1st app. Astro Boy in comics 26 52 78 182 404 625

ASTRO BOY THE MOVIE (Based on the 2009 CGI movie)
IDW Publishing: 2009 ($3.99, limited series)

...Official Movie Adaptation 1-4 (8/09 - No. 4, 9/09, $3.99) EJ Su-a 4.00
...Official Movie Prequel 1-4 (5/09 - No. 4, 8/09) Jourdan-a/c; Ashley Wood var-c on each 4.00

ASTRO CITY (Also see Kurt Busiek's Astro City)
DC Comics (WildStorm Productions): Dec, 2004 - Dec, 2009 (one-shots)

...#1 Special Edition (8/10, $1.00) reprints first issue with "What's Next? cover logo 3.00
...: Astra Special 1,2 (11/09, 12/09, $3.99) Busiek-s/Anderson-a/Ross-c 4.00
... A Visitor's Guide (12/04, $5.95) short story, city guide and pin-ups by various; Ross-c 6.00
...: Beautie (4/08, $3.99) Busiek-s/Anderson-a/Ross-c; origin 4.00
...: Samaritan (9/06, $3.99) Busiek-s/Anderson-a/Ross-c; origin of Infidel 4.00
...: Shining Stars HC (2011, $24.99, d.j) r/...: Astra Special 1,2, ...: Beautie, ...: Samaritan, and ...: Silver Agent 1,2; bonus design art and Ross cover sketch art 25.00
...: Silver Agent 1,2 (8,9/10, $3.99) Busiek-s/Anderson-a/Ross-c 4.00

ASTRO CITY (Also see Kurt Busiek's Astro City)
DC Comics (Vertigo): Aug, 2013 - Present ($3.99)

1-41-Busiek-s/Ross-c; Anderson-a in most. 12-Nolan-a. 17-Grummett-a. 22,25-Merino-a. 35,36-Ron Randall-a; Jack-In-The Box app. 39,40-Carnero-a 4.00

ASTRO CITY / ARROWSMITH (Flip book)
DC Comics (WildStorm Productions): Jun, 2004 ($2.95, one-shot flip book)

Astronauts in Trouble #1 © Young & Adlard

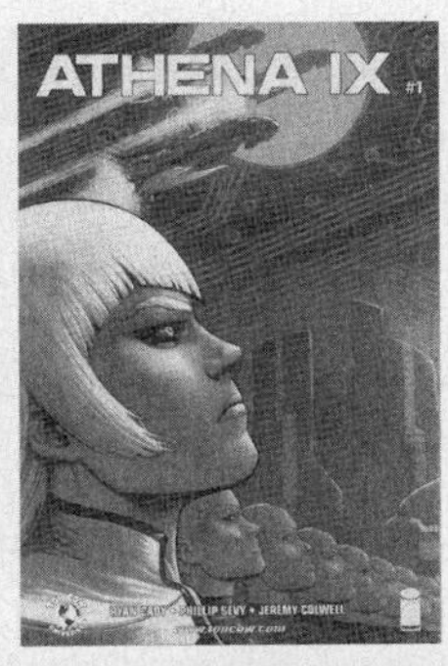

Athena IX #1 © TCOW

The Atom #36 © DC

	GD 2.0	VG 4.0	FN 6.0	VF 8.0	VF/NM 9.0	NM- 9.2

1-Intro. Black Badge; Ross-c; Arrowsmith a/c by Pacheco 3.00

ASTRO CITY: DARK AGE
DC Comics (WildStorm Productions): Aug, 2005 - No. 4, Dec, 2005 ($2.95, limited series)

Book One 1-4-Busiek-s/Anderson-a/Ross-c; Silver Agent and The Blue Knight app. 3.00
Book Two #1-4 (1/07-11/07, $2.99) Busiek-s/Anderson-a/Ross-c 3.00
Book Three #1-4 (7/09-10/09, $3.99) Busiek-s/Anderson-a/Ross-c 4.00
Book Four #1-4 (3/10-6/10, $3.99) Busiek-s/Anderson-a/Ross-c 4.00
... 1: Brothers and Other Strangers HC (2008, $29.99, d.j.) r/Book One #1-4, Book Two #1-4, and story from Astro City/Arrowsmith #1; Marc Guggenheim intro.; new Ross-c 30.00
... 1: Brothers and Other Strangers SC (2009, $19.99) same contents as HC 20.00
... 2: Brothers in Arms HC ('10, $29.99, d.j.) r/Book Three #1-4, Book Four #1-4, Ross-c 30.00

ASTRO CITY: LOCAL HEROES
DC Comics (WildStorm Productions): Apr, 2003 - No. 5, Feb, 2004 ($2.95, limited series)

1-5-Busiek-s/Anderson-a/Ross-c 3.00
HC (2005, $24.95) r/series; Kurt Busiek's Astro City V2 #21,22; stories from Astro City/ Arrowsmith #1; and 9-11, The World's Finest... Vol. 2; Alex Ross sketch pages 25.00
SC (2005, $17.99) same contents as HC 18.00

ASTRONAUTS IN TROUBLE
Image Comics: Jun, 2015 - No. 11 ($2.99, B&W, reprints of earlier Astronauts in Trouble)

1-11-Larry Young-s. 1-3-Reprints the Space: 1959 series; Charlie Adlard-a. 4-9-Reprints the Live From the Moon series. 4-6-Matt Smith-a. 7-11-Adlard-a 3.00

ASYLUM
Millennium Publications: 1993 ($2.50)

1-3: 1-Bolton-c/a; Russell 2-pg. illos 3.00

ASYLUM
Maximum Press: Dec, 1995 - No. 11, Jan, 1997 ($2.95/$2.99, anthology)
(#1-6 are flip books)

1-11: 1-Warchild by Art Adams, Beanworld, Avengelyne, Battlestar Galactica. 2-Intro Mike Deodato's Deathkiss. 4-1st app.Christian; painted Battlestar Galactica story begins. 6-Intro Bionix (Six Million Dollar Man & the Bionic Woman). 7-Begin $2.99-c. 8-B&W-a. 9- Foot Soldiers & Kid Supreme. 10-Lady Supreme by Terry Moore-c/app. 4.00

ATARI FORCE (Also see Promotional comics section)
DC Comics: Jan, 1984 - No. 20, Aug, 1985 (Mando paper)

1-(1/84)-Intro Tempest, Packrat, Babe, Morphea, & Dart 4.00
2-20 3.00
Special 1 (4/86) 4.00
NOTE: *Byrne c-Special 1i. Giffen a-12p, 13i. Rogers a-18p, Special 1p.*

A-TEAM, THE (TV) (Also see Marvel Graphic Novel)
Marvel Comics Group: Mar, 1984 - No. 3, May, 1984 (limited series)

	GD	VG	FN	VF	VF/NM	NM-
1-3						6.00
1,2-(Whitman bagged set) w/75¢-c	2	4	6	8	10	12
3-(Whitman, no bag) w/75¢-c	1	2	3	5	6	8

A-TEAM: SHOTGUN WEDDING (Based on the 2010 movie)
IDW Publishing: Mar, 2010 - No. 4, Apr, 2010 ($3.99, limited series)

1-4-Co-plotted by Joe Carnahan; Stephen Mooney-a; Snyder III-c 4.00

A-TEAM: WAR STORIES (Based on the 2010 movie)
IDW Publishing: Mar, 2010 - Apr, 2010 ($3.99, series of one-shots)

...: B.A. (3/10) Dixon & Burnham-s/Maloney-a/Gaydos & photo-c 4.00
...: Face (4/10) Dixon & Burnham-s/Muriel-a/Gaydos & photo-c 4.00
...: Hannibal (3/10) Dixon & Burnham-s/Petrus-a/Gaydos & photo-c 4.00
...: Murdock (4/10) Dixon & Burnham-s/Vilanova-a/Gaydos & photo-c 4.00

ATHENA INC. THE MANHUNTER PROJECT
Image Comics: Dec, 2001; Apr, 2002 - No. 6 ($2.95/$4.95/$5.95)

...The Beginning (12/01, $5.95) Anacleto-c/a; Haberlin-s 6.00
1-5: 1-(4/02, $2.95) two covers by Anacleto 3.00
6-($4.95) 5.00
...: Agents Roster #1 (11/02, $5.95, 8 1/2 x 11") bios and sketch pages by Anacleto 6.00
Vol. 1 TPB (4/03, $19.95) r/#1-6 & Agents Roster; cover gallery 20.00

ATHENA
Dynamite Entertainment: 2009 - No. 4, 2010 ($3.50)

1-4-Murray-s/Neves-a; multiple covers on each. 1-Obama flip cover 3.50

ATHENA IX (See Aphrodite IX)
Image Comics (Top Cow): Jul, 2015 ($3.99, one-shot)

1-Ryan Cady-s/Phillip Sevy; 3 covers 4.00

ATLANTIS CHRONICLES, THE (Also see Aquaman, 3rd Series & Aquaman: Time & Tide)
DC Comics: Mar, 1990 - No. 7, Sept, 1990 ($2.95, limited series, 52 pgs.)

1-7: 1-Peter David scripts. 7-True origin of Aquaman; nudity panels 4.00

ATLANTIS, THE LOST CONTINENT
Dell Publishing Co.: May, 1961

	GD	VG	FN	VF	VF/NM	NM-
Four Color #1188-Movie, photo-c	9	18	27	59	117	175

ATLAS (See 1st Issue Special)

ATLAS
Dark Horse Comics: Feb, 1994 - No. 4, 1994 ($2.50, limited series)

1-4 3.00

ATLAS (Agents of Atlas)(The Heroic Age)
Marvel Comics: Jul, 2010 - No. 5, Nov, 2010 ($3.99/$2.99)

1-($3.99) Parker-s/Hardman-a/Dodson-c; 3-D Man app.; profile page 4.00
2-5-($2.99) 2,3,5-Pagulayan-c. 4-Jae Lee-c 3.00

ATLAS UNIFIED
Atlas Comics: No. 0, Oct, 2011 - No. 2, Feb, 2012 ($2.99, unfinished limited series)

0 Prelude: Midnight (10/11) Phoenix, Kromag, Sgt. Hawk app.; bonus sketch pages 3.00
1,2: 1-Three covers; Peyer-s/Salgado-a; x-over of Grim Ghost, Wulf, Phoenix & others 3.00

ATMOSPHERICS
Avatar Press: June, 2002 ($5.95, B&W, one-shot graphic novel)

1-Warren Ellis-s/Ken Meyer Jr.-painted-a/c 6.00

ATOM, THE (See Action #425, All-American #19, Brave & the Bold, D.C. Special Series #1, Detective Comics, Flash Comics #80, Hawkman, Identity Crisis, JLA, Power Of The Atom, Showcase #34 -36, Super Friends, Sword of The Atom, Teen Titans & World's Finest)

ATOM, THE (...& the Hawkman No. 39 on)
National Periodical Publ.: June-July, 1962 - No. 38, Aug-Sept, 1968

	GD	VG	FN	VF	VF/NM	NM-
1-(6-7/62)-Intro Plant-Master; 1st app. Maya	100	200	300	800	1800	2800
2	31	62	93	223	499	775
3-1st Time Pool story; 1st app. Chronos (origin)	21	42	63	147	324	500
4,5: 4-Snapper Carr x-over	15	30	45	103	227	350
6,9,10	11	22	33	76	163	250
7-Hawkman x-over (6-7/63; 1st Atom & Hawkman team-up); 1st app. Hawkman since Brave & the Bold tryouts	23	46	69	161	356	550
8-Justice League, Dr. Light app.	12	24	36	79	170	260
11-15: 13-Chronos-c/story	9	18	27	60	120	180
16-18,20	7	14	21	46	86	125
19-Zatanna x-over; 2nd app.	9	18	27	59	117	175
21-28,30: 26-Two-page pin-up. 28-Chronos-c/story	6	12	18	41	76	110
29-1st solo Golden Age Atom x-over in S.A.	13	26	39	89	195	300
31-35,37,38: 31-Hawkman x-over. 37-Intro. Major Mynah; Hawkman cameo	5	10	15	35	63	90
36-G.A. Atom x-over	6	12	18	41	76	110

NOTE: *Anderson a-1-11i, 13i; c-inks-1-25, 31-35, 37. Sid Greene a-8i-37i. Gil Kane a-1p-37p; c-1p-28p, 29, 33p, 34; c-26i. George Roussos a-38i. Mike Sekowsky a-38p. Time Pool stories also in 6, 9,12, 17, 21, 27, 35.*

ATOM, THE (See All New Atom and Tangent Comics/ The Atom)

ATOM AGE (See Classics Illustrated Special Issue)

ATOM-AGE COMBAT
St. John Publishing Co.: June, 1952 - No. 5, Apr, 1953; Feb, 1958

	GD	VG	FN	VF	VF/NM	NM-
1-Buck Vinson in all	55	110	165	352	601	850
2-Flying saucer story	34	68	102	199	325	450
3,5: 3-Mayo-a (6 pgs.). 5-Flying saucer-c/story	30	60	90	177	289	400
4 (Scarce)	34	68	102	199	325	450
1(2/58-St. John)	26	52	78	154	252	350

ATOM-AGE COMBAT
Fago Magazines: No. 2, Jan, 1959 - No. 3, Mar, 1959

	GD	VG	FN	VF	VF/NM	NM-
2-A-Bomb explosion-c;	31	62	93	182	296	410
3	22	44	66	132	216	300

ATOMAN
Spark Publications: Feb, 1946 - No. 2, April, 1946

	GD	VG	FN	VF	VF/NM	NM-
1-Origin & 1st app. Atoman; Robinson/Meskin-a; Kidcrusaders, Wild Bill Hickok, Marvin the Great app.	71	142	213	454	777	1100
2-Robinson/Meskin-a; Robinson c-1,2	43	86	129	271	461	650

ATOM & HAWKMAN, THE (Formerly The Atom)
National Periodical Publ: No. 39, Oct-Nov, 1968 - No. 45, Oct-Nov, 1969; No. 46, Mar, 2010

	GD	VG	FN	VF	VF/NM	NM-
39-43: 40-41-Kubert/Anderson-a. 43-(7/69)-Last 12¢ issue; 1st S.A. app. Gentleman Ghost	5	10	15	34	60	85
44,45: 44-(9/69)-1st 15¢-c; origin Gentleman Ghost	5	10	15	34	60	85
46-(3/10, $2.99) Blackest Night crossover one-shot; Geoff Johns-s/Ryan Sook-a/c						3.00

NOTE: *M. Anderson a-39, 40i, 41i, 43, 44. Sid Greene a-40i-45i. Kubert a-40p, 41p; c-39-45.*

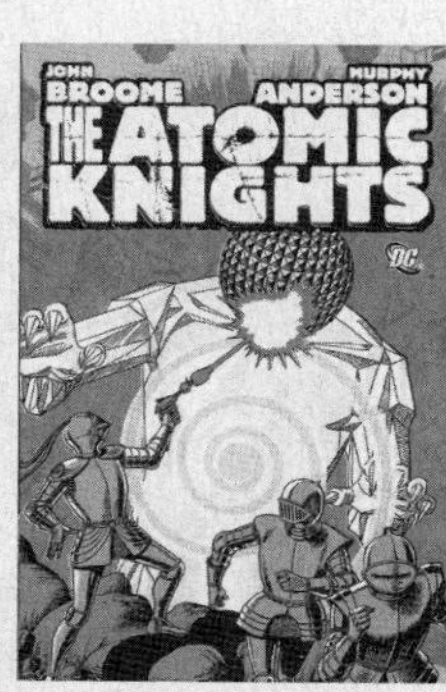

The Atomic Knights HC © DC

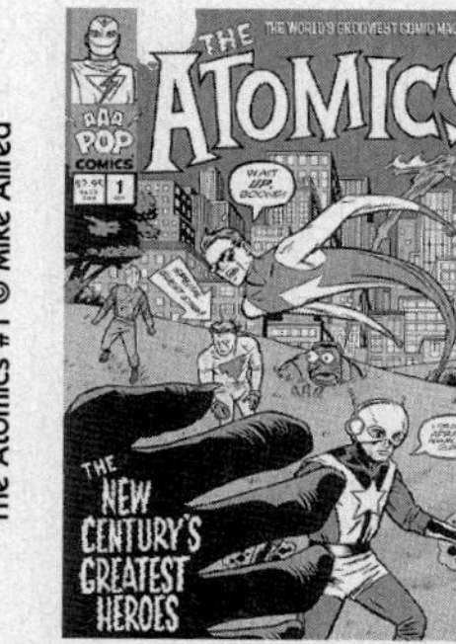

The Atomics #1 © Mike Allred

Attack #3 © YM

GD 2.0 VG 4.0 FN 6.0 VF 8.0 VF/NM 9.0 NM- 9.2

ATOM ANT (TV) (See Golden Comics Digest #2) (Hanna-Barbera)
Gold Key: January, 1966 (12¢)
1(10170-601)-1st app. Atom Ant, Precious Pup, and Hillbilly Bears 15 30 45 103 227 350

ATOM ANT & SECRET SQUIRREL (See Hanna-Barbera Presents)

ATOMIC AGE
Marvel Comics (Epic Comics): Nov, 1990 - No. 4, Feb, 1991 ($4.50, limited series, square-bound, 52 pgs.)
1-4: Williamson-a(i); sci-fi story set in 1957 4.50

ATOMIC ATTACK (True War Stories; formerly Attack, first series)
Youthful Magazines: No. 5, Jan, 1953 - No. 8, Oct, 1953 (1st story is sci/fi in all issues)
5-Atomic bomb-c; science fiction stories in all 45 90 135 284 480 675
6-8 31 62 93 182 296 410

ATOMIC BOMB
Jay Burtis Publications: 1945 (36 pgs.)
1-Superheroes Airmale & Stampy (scarce) 71 142 213 454 777 1100

ATOMIC BUNNY (Formerly Atomic Rabbit)
Charlton Comics: No. 12, Aug, 1958 - No. 19, Dec, 1959
12 12 24 36 69 97 125
13-19 8 16 24 42 54 65

ATOMIC COMICS
Daniels Publications (Canadian): Jan, 1946 (Reprints, one-shot)
1-Rocketman, Yankee Boy, Master Key app. 42 84 126 265 445 625

ATOMIC COMICS
Green Publishing Co.: Jan, 1946 - No. 4, July-Aug, 1946 (#1-4 were printed w/o cover gloss)
1-Radio Squad by Siegel & Shuster; Barry O'Neal app.; Fang Gow cover-r/ Detective Comics (Classic-c) 81 162 243 518 884 1250
2-Inspector Dayton; Kid Kane by Matt Baker; Lucky Wings, Congo King, Prop Powers (only app.) begin; atomic monster-c 55 110 165 352 601 850
3,4: 3-Zero Ghost Detective app.; Baker-a(2) each; 4-Baker-c 40 80 120 244 402 560

ATOMIC KNIGHTS (See Strange Adventures #117)
DC Comics: 2010 ($39.99, HC with dustjacket)
HC-Reprints the original 1960-64 run from debut in Strange Adventures #117 to S.A. #160; new intro. by Murphy Anderson 40.00

ATOMIC MOUSE (TV, Movies) (See Blue Bird, Funny Animals, Giant Comics Edition & Wotalife Comics)
Capitol Stories/Charlton Comics: 3/53 - No. 52, 2/63; No. 1, 12/84; V2#10, 9/85 - No. 12, 1/86
1-Origin & 1st app.; Al Fago-c/a in most 37 74 111 222 361 500
2 15 30 45 86 133 180
3-10: 5-Timmy The Timid Ghost app.; see Zoo Funnies 10 20 30 58 79 100
11-13,16-25 8 16 24 40 50 60
14,15-Hoppy The Marvel Bunny app. 9 18 27 50 65 80
26-(68 pgs.) 12 24 36 67 94 120
27-40: 36,37-Atom The Cat app. 6 12 18 29 36 42
41-52 5 10 15 22 26 30
1 (1984)-Low print run; rep/#7-c w/diff. stories 2 4 6 8 10 12
V2#10 (9/85) -12(1/86)-Low print run 1 3 4 6 8 10

ATOMIC RABBIT (Atomic Bunny #12 on; see Giant Comics #3 & Wotalife)
Charlton Comics: Aug, 1955 - No. 11, Mar, 1958
1-Origin & 1st app.; Al Fago-c/a in all? 32 64 96 188 307 425
2 14 28 42 80 115 150
3-10 10 20 30 56 76 95
11-(68 pgs.) 14 28 42 80 115 150

ATOMICS, THE
AAA Pop Comics: Jan, 2000 - No. 15, Nov, 2001 ($2.95)
1-11-Mike Allred-s/a; 1-Madman-c/app. 3.00
12-15-($3.50): 13-15-Savage Dragon-c/app. 15-Afterword by Alex Ross; colored reprint of 1st Frank Einstein story 3.50
...King-Size Giant Spectacular: Jigsaw (2000, $10.00) r/#1-4 10.00
...King-Size Giant Spectacular: Lessons in Light, Lava, & Lasers (2000, $8.95) r/#5-8 9.00
...King-Size Giant Spectacular: Running With the Dragon ('02, $8.95) r/#13-15 and r/1st Frank Einstein app. in color 9.00
...King-Size Giant Spectacular: Worlds Within Worlds ('01, $8.95) r/#9-12 9.00
Madman and the Atomics, Vol. 1 TPB (2007, $24.99) r/#1-15, cover gallery, pin-ups, afterword by Alex Ross 25.00
...: Spaced Out & Grounded in Snap City TPB (10/03, $12.95) r/one-shots - It Girl, Mr. Gum, Spaceman and Crash Metro & the Star Squad; sketch pages 13.00

ATOMIC SPY CASES
Avon Periodicals: Mar-Apr, 1950 (Painted-c)
1-No Wood-a; A-bomb blast panels; Fass-a 41 82 123 256 428 600

ATOMIC THUNDERBOLT, THE
Regor Company: Feb, 1946 (one-shot) (scarce)
1-Intro. Atomic Thunderbolt & Mr. Murdo 77 154 231 493 847 1200

ATOMIC TOYBOX
Image Comics: Dec, 1999 ($2.95)
1- Aaron Lopresti-c/s/a 3.00

ATOMIC WAR!
Ace Periodicals (Junior Books): Nov, 1952 - No. 4, Apr, 1953
1-Atomic bomb-c 174 348 522 1114 1907 2700
2,3: 3-Atomic bomb-c 70 140 210 445 765 1085
4-Used in **POP**, pg. 96 & illo. 70 140 210 445 765 1085

ATOMIKA
Speakeasy Comics/Mercury Comics: Mar, 2005 - No. 6 ($2.99)
1-6: 1-Alex Ross-c/Sal Abbinanti-a/Dabb-s. 3-Fabry-c. 4-Four covers; Romita back-c 3.00
... God is Red TPB (5/06, $19.99) r/#1-6; cover gallery; Dabb foreword 20.00

ATOMIK ANGELS
Crusade Comics: May, 1996 - No. 4, Nov. 1996 ($2.50)
1-4: 1-Freefall from Gen 13 app. 3.00
1-Variant-c 4.00
Intrep-Edition (2/96, B&W, giveaway at launch party)-Previews Atomik Angels #1; includes Billy Tucci interview. 4.00

ATOM SPECIAL (See Atom & Justice League of America)
DC Comics: 1993/1995 ($2.50/$2.95)(68pgs.)
1,2: 1-Dillon-c/a. 2-McDonnell-a/Bolland-c/Peyer-s 4.00

ATOM THE CAT (Formerly Tom Cat; see Giant Comics #3)
Charlton Comics: No. 9, Oct, 1957 - No. 17, Aug, 1959
9 10 20 30 54 72 90
10,13-17 7 14 21 35 43 50
11,12: 11(64 pgs)-Atomic Mouse app. 12(100 pgs.) 11 22 33 62 86 110

ATTACK
Youthful Mag./Trojan No. 5 on: May, 1952 - No. 4, Nov, 1952; No. 5, Jan, 1953 - No. 5, Sept, 1953
1-(1st series)-Extreme violence 47 94 141 296 498 700
2,3-Both Harrison-c/a; bondage, whipping 28 56 84 165 270 375
4-Krenkel-a (7 pgs.); Harrison-a (becomes Atomic Attack #5 on) 28 56 84 165 270 375
5-(#1, Trojan, 2nd series) 18 36 54 105 165 225
6-8 (#2-4), 5 14 28 42 80 115 150

ATTACK
Charlton Comics: No. 54, 1958 - No. 60, Nov, 1959
54 (25¢, 100 pgs.) 12 24 36 69 97 125
55-60 7 14 21 35 43 50

ATTACK!
Charlton Comics: 1962 - No. 15, 3/75; No. 16, 8/79 - No. 48, 10/84
nn(#1)-('62) Special Edition 6 12 18 38 69 100
2('63), 3(Fall, '64) 4 8 12 23 37 50
V4#3(10/66), 4(10/67)-(Formerly Special War Series #2; becomes Attack At Sea V4#5): 3-Tokyo Rose story 3 6 9 19 30 40
1(9/71)-D-Day story 3 6 9 16 23 30
2-5: 2-Hitler app. 4-American Eagle app. 2 4 6 9 12 15
6-15(3/75): 8-Nixon app. 1 3 4 6 8 10
16(8/79) - 40 5.00
41-47 Low print run 7.00
48(10/84)-Wood-r; S&K-c (low print) 1 3 4 6 8 10
Modern Comics 13('78)-r 5.00
NOTE: *Sutton a-9,10,13.*

ATTACK!
Spire Christian Comics (Fleming H. Revell Co.): 1975 (39¢/49¢, 36 pgs.)
nn 2 4 6 10 14 18

ATTACK AT SEA (Formerly Attack!, 1967)
Charlton Comics: V4#5, Oct, 1968 (one-shot)

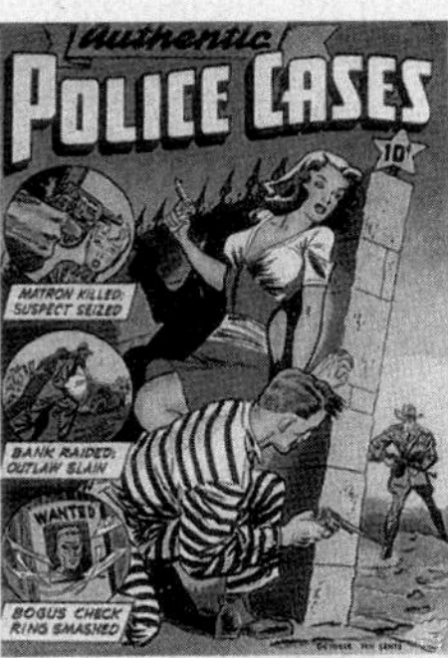

Authentic Police Cases #5 © STJ

The Authority (2008 series) #22 © DC

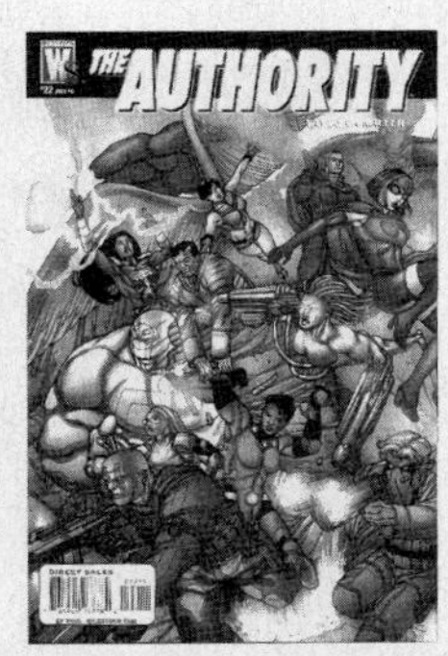

Automatic Kafka #7 © WSP

	GD 2.0	VG 4.0	FN 6.0	VF 8.0	VF/NM 9.0	NM- 9.2
V4#5	3	6	9	19	30	40

ATTACK ON PLANET MARS (See Strange Worlds #18)
Avon Periodicals: 1951

	GD	VG	FN	VF	VF/NM	NM-
nn-Infantino, Fawcette, Kubert & Wood-a; adaptation of Tarrano the Conqueror by Ray Cummings	100	200	300	635	1093	1550

ATTITUDE LAD
Slave Labor Graphics: Apr, 1994 - No. 3, Nov, 1994 ($2.95, B&W)

1-3 3.00

AUDREY & MELVIN (Formerly Little...)(See Little Audrey & Melvin)
Harvey Publications: No. 62, Sept, 1974

	GD	VG	FN	VF	VF/NM	NM-
62	2	4	6	9	13	16

AUGIE DOGGIE (TV) (See Hanna-Barbera Band Wagon, Quick-Draw McGraw, Spotlight #2, Top Cat & Whitman Comic Books)
Gold Key: October, 1963 (12¢)

	GD	VG	FN	VF	VF/NM	NM-
1-Hanna-Barbera character	15	30	45	100	220	340

AUTHENTIC POLICE CASES
St. John Publishing Co.: 2/48 - No. 6, 11/48; No. 7, 5/50 - No. 38, 3/55

	GD	VG	FN	VF	VF/NM	NM-
1-Hale the Magician by Tuska begins	58	116	174	371	636	900
2-Lady Satan, Johnny Rebel app.	39	78	117	240	395	550
3-Veiled Avenger app.; blood drainage story plus 2 Lucky Coyne stories; used in **SOTI**, illo. from Red Seal #16	61	122	183	390	670	950
4,5: 4-Masked Black Jack app. 5-Late 1930s Jack Cole-a(r); transvestism story	39	78	117	240	395	550
6-Matt Baker-c; used in **SOTI**, illo- "An invitation to learning", r-in Fugitives From Justice #3; Jack Cole-a; also used by the N.Y. Legis. Comm.	116	232	348	742	1271	1800
7,8,10-14: 7-Jack Cole-a; Matt Baker-a begins #8, ends #?; Vic Flint in #10-14. 10-12-Baker-a(2 each)	50	100	150	315	533	750
9-No Vic Flint	48	96	144	302	514	725
15-Drug-c/story; Vic Flint app.; Baker-c	50	100	150	315	533	750
16,17,19,22-Baker-c	41	82	123	256	428	600
18,20,21,23: Baker-a(i)	34	68	102	199	325	450
24-28 (All 100 pgs.): 26-Transvestism	53	106	159	334	567	800
29,31,32-Baker-c	37	74	111	222	361	500
30	26	52	78	154	252	350
33-38: 33-Baker-c. 34-Baker-c; r/#9. 35-Baker-c/a(2); r/#10. 36-r/#11; Vic Flint strip-r; Baker-c/a(2) unsigned. 37-Baker-c; r/#17. 38- Baker-c/a; r/#18	37	74	111	222	361	500

NOTE: ***Matt Baker** c-6-16, 17, 19, 22, 27, 29, 31-38; a-13, 16. Bondage c-1, 3.*

AUTHORITY, THE (See Stormwatch and Jenny Sparks: The Secret History of...)
DC Comics (WildStorm): May, 1999 - No. 29, Jul, 2002 ($2.50)

	GD	VG	FN	VF	VF/NM	NM-
1-Wraparound-c; Warren Ellis-s/Bryan Hitch and Paul Neary-a	1	2	3	4	5	7
1-Special Edition (7/10, $1.00) r/#1 with "What's Next?" logo on cover						3.00
2-4						5.00
5-12: 12-Death of Jenny Sparks; last Ellis-s						4.00
13-Mark Millar-s/Frank Quitely-c/a begins						6.00
14-16-Authority vs. Marvel-esque villains						4.00
17-29: 17,18-Weston-a. 19,20,22-Quitely-a. 21-McCrea-a. 23-26-Peyer-s/Nguyen-a; new Authority. 25,26-Jenny Sparks app. 27,28-Millar-s/Art Adams-a/c						3.00
Annual 2000 ($3.50) Devil's Night x-over; Hamner-a/Bermejo-c						4.00
Absolute Authority Slipcased Hardcover (2002, $49.95) oversized r/#1-12 plus script pages by Ellis and sketch pages by Hitch						50.00
...: Earth Inferno and Other Stories TPB (2002, $14.95) r/#17-20, Annual 2000, and Wildstorm Summer Special; new Quitely-c						15.00
...: Human on the Inside HC (2004, $24.95, dust jacket) Ridley-s/Oliver-a/c						25.00
...: Human on the Inside SC (2004, $17.99) Ridley-s/Oliver-a/c						18.00
...: Kev (10/02, $4.95) Ennis-s/Fabry-c/a						5.00
...: Relentless TPB (2000, $17.95) r/#1-8						18.00
...: Scorched Earth (2/03, $4.95) Robbie Morrison-s/Frazer Irving-a/Ashley Wood-c						5.00
...: Transfer of Power TPB (2002, $17.95) r/#22-29						18.00
...: Under New Management TPB (2000, $17.95) r/#9-16; new Quitely-c						18.00

AUTHORITY, THE (See previews in Sleeper, Stormwatch: Team Achilles and Wildcats Version 3.0)
DC Comics (WildStorm): Jul, 2003 - No. 14, Oct, 2004 ($2.50)

1-14: 1-Robbie Morrison-s/Dwayne Turner-a. 5-Huat-a. 14-Portacio-a 3.00
#0 (10/03, $2.95) r/preview back-up-s listed above; Turner sketch pages 3.00
...: Fractured Worlds TPB (2005, $17.95) r/#6-14; cover gallery 18.00
...: Harsh Realities TPB (2004, $14.95) r/#0-5; cover gallery 15.00
.../Lobo: Jingle Hell (2/04, $4.95) Bisley-c/a; Giffen & Grant-s 5.00
.../Lobo: Spring Break Massacre (8/05, $4.99) Bisley-c/a; Giffen & Grant-s 5.00

AUTHORITY, THE (Volume 4) (The Lost Year)
DC Comics (WildStorm): Dec, 2006 - No. 2, May 2007; No. 3, Jan, 2010 - No. 12, Oct, 2010 ($2.99)

1,2-Grant Morrison-s/Gene Ha-a/c 3.00
1-Variant cover by Art Adams 5.00
3-12: 3-(1/10) Morrison & Giffen-s/Robertson-a. 3-12-Ha-c. 12-Ordway-a 3.00
...Reader: The Lost Year (1/10, $2.99) r/#1,2 3.00
... Book One (2010, $17.99) r/#1-7; cover sketch art 18.00

AUTHORITY, THE (Volume 5) (World's End)
DC Comics (WildStorm): Oct, 2008 - No. 29, Jan, 2011 ($2.99)

1-29: 1-5-Simon Coleby-a/c; Lynch back-up story w/Hairsine-a/Gage-s. 21-Simonson-c 3.00
...: Rule Britannia TPB (2010, $19.99) r/#8-17 20.00
...: World's End TPB (2009, $17.99) r/#1-7 18.00

AUTHORITY, THE: MORE KEV
DC Comics (WildStorm): Jul, 2004 - No. 4, Dec, 2004 ($2.95, limited series)

1-4-Garth Ennis-s/Glenn Fabry-c/a 3.00
...: Kev TPB (2005, $14.99) r/Authority: Kev one-shot and Authority: More Kev series 15.00

AUTHORITY, THE: PRIME
DC Comics (WildStorm): Dec, 2007 - No. 6, May, 2008 ($2.99, limited series)

1-6-Gage-s/Robertson-c/a; Bendix app. 3.00
TPB (2008, $17.99) r/#1-6 18.00

AUTHORITY, THE: REVOLUTION
DC Comics (WildStorm): Dec, 2004 - No. 12, Dec, 2005 ($2.95/$2.99)

1-12-Brubaker-s/Nguyen-a. 5-Henry Bendix returns. 7-Jenny Sparks app. 3.00
...: Book One TPB (2005, $14.99) r/#1-6; cover gallery and Nguyen sketch pages 15.00
...: Book Two TPB (2006, $14.99) r/#7-12; cover gallery and Nguyen sketch pages 15.00

AUTHORITY, THE: THE MAGNIFICENT KEV
DC Comics (WildStorm): Nov, 2005 - No. 5, Feb, 2006 ($2.99, limited series)

1-5-Garth Ennis-s/Carlos Ezquerra-a/Glenn Fabry-c 3.00
TPB (2006, $14.99) r/#1-5 15.00

AUTOMATIC KAFKA
DC Comics (WildStorm): Sept, 2002 - No. 9, Jul, 2003 ($2.95)

1-9-Ashley Wood-c/a; Joe Casey-s 3.00

AUTUMN ADVENTURES (Walt Disney's...)
Disney Comics: Autumn, 1990; No. 2, Autumn, 1991 ($2.95, 68 pgs.)

1-Donald Duck-r(2) by Barks, Pluto-r, & new-a 4.00
2-D. Duck-r by Barks; new Super Goof story 4.00

AUTUMNLANDS: TOOTH & CLAW (Titled Tooth & Claw for issue #1)
Image Comics: Nov, 2014 - Present ($2.99)

1-14: 1-Busiek-s/Dewey-a. 2-Variant-c by Alex Ross 3.00

AVATAARS: COVENANT OF THE SHIELD
Marvel Comics: Sept, 2000 - No. 3, Nov, 2000 ($2.99, limited series)

1-3-Kaminski-s/Oscar Jimenez-a 3.00

AVATAR
DC Comics: Feb, 1991 - No. 3, Apr, 1991 ($5.95, limited series, 100 pgs.)

1-3: Based on TSR's Forgotten Realms 6.00

AVENGELYNE
Maximum Press: May, 1995 - No. 3, July, 1995 ($2.50/$3.50, limited series)

	GD	VG	FN	VF	VF/NM	NM-
1/2	2	4	6	8	10	12
1/2 Platinum						15.00
1-Newstand ($2.50)-Photo-c; poster insert						6.00
1-Direct Market ($3.50)-Chromium-c; poster	1	2	3	4	5	7
1-Glossy edition	2	4	6	12	16	20
1-Gold						12.00
2-3: 2-Polybagged w/card						3.00
3-Variant-c; Deodato pin-up						5.00
...Bible (10/96, $3.50)						4.00
.../Glory (9/95, $3.95) 2 covers						4.00
.../Glory Swimsuit Special (6/96, $2.95) photo and illos. covers						3.00
.../Glory: The Godyssey (9/96, $2.99) 2 covers (1 photo)						3.00
...Revelation One (Avatar, 1/01, $3.50) 3 covers by Haley, Rio, Shaw; Shaw-a						3.50
.../Shi (Avatar, 11/01, $3.50) Eight covers; Waller-a						3.50
...Swimsuit (8/95, $2.95)-Pin-ups/photos. 3-Variant-c exist (2 photo, 1 Liefeld-a)						4.00
...Swimsuit (1/96, $3.50, 2nd printing)-photo-c						4.00
Trade paperback (12/95, $9.95)						10.00
.../Warrior Nun Areala 1 (11/96, $2.99) also see Warrior Nun/Avengelyne						3.00

AVENGELYNE

Avengelyne: Deadly Sins #1 © Rob Liefeld

Avengers #2 © MAR

Avengers #42 © MAR

GD VG FN VF VF/NM NM-
2.0 4.0 6.0 8.0 9.0 9.2

Maximum Press: V2#1, Apr, 1996 - No. 14, Apr, 1997 ($2.95/$2.50)

V2#1-Four covers exist (2 photo-c). 4.00
V2#2-Three covers exist (1 photo-c); flip book w/Darkchylde 5.00
V2#0, 3-14: 0-(10/96).3-Flip book w/Priest preview. 5-Flip book w/Blindside 3.00

AVENGELYNE (Volume 3)
Awesome Comics: Mar, 1999 ($2.50)

1-Fraga & Liefeld-a 3.00

AVENGELYNE (4th series)
Image Comics: Jul, 2011 - No. 8, May, 2012 ($2.99)

1-8-Liefeld & Poulson-s/Gieni-a. 1-Three covers by Liefeld, Gieni, and Benitez 3.00

AVENGELYNE: ARMAGEDDON
Maximum Press: Dec, 1996 - No. 3, Feb, 1997 ($2.99, limited series)

1-3-Scott Clark-a(p) 3.00

AVENGELYNE: DEADLY SINS
Maximum Press: Feb, 1996 - No. 2, Mar, 1996 ($2.95, limited series)

1,2: 1-Two-c exist (1 photo, 1 Liefeld-a). 2-Liefeld-c; Pop Mhan-a(p) 3.00

AVENGELYNE/POWER
Maximum Press: Nov, 1995 - No.3, Jan, 1996 ($2.95, limited series)

1-3: 1,2-Liefeld-c. 3-Three variant-c. exist (1 photo-c) 3.00

AVENGELYNE · PROPHET
Maximum Press: May, 1996; No. 2, Feb. 1997 ($2.95, unfinished lim. series)

1,2-Liefeld-c/a(p) 3.00

AVENGER, THE (See A-1 Comics)
Magazine Enterprises: Feb-Mar, 1955 - No. 4, Aug-Sept, 1955

1(A-1 #129)-Origin 40 80 120 244 402 560
2(A-1 #131), 3(A-1 #133) Robot-c, 4(A-1 #138) 27 54 81 160 263 365
IW Reprint #9('64)-Reprints #1 (new cover) 3 6 9 19 30 40
NOTE: ***Powell** a-2-4; c-1-4.*

AVENGER, THE (Pulp Hero from Justice Inc.)
Dynamite Entertainment: 2014 ($7.99)

... Special 2014: The Television Killers - Rahner-s/Menna-a/Hack-c 8.00

AVENGERS, THE (TV)(Also see Steed and Mrs. Peel)
Gold Key: Nov, 1968 ("John Steed & Emma Peel" cover title) (15¢)

1-Photo-c 13 26 39 89 195 300
1-(Variant with photo back-c) 17 34 51 117 259 400

AVENGERS, THE (See Essential..., Giant-Size..., JLA/..., Kree/Skrull War Starring..., Marvel Graphic Novel #27, Marvel Super Action, Marvel Super Heroes('66), Marvel Treasury Ed., Marvel Triple Action, New Avengers, Solo Avengers, Tales Of Suspense #49, West Coast Avengers & X-Men Vs....)

AVENGERS, THE (The Mighty Avengers on cover only #63-69)
Marvel Comics Group: Sept, 1963 - No. 402, Sept, 1996

1-Origin & 1st app. The Avengers (Thor, Iron Man, Hulk, Ant-Man, Wasp); Loki app. 800 1600 3200 9000 22,000 40,000
2-Hulk leaves Avengers 114 228 342 912 2056 3200
3-2nd Sub-Mariner x-over outside the F.F. (see Strange Tales #107 for 1st); Sub-Mariner & Hulk team-up & battle Avengers; Spider-Man cameo (1/64) 89 178 267 712 1606 2500
4-Revival of Captain America who joins the Avengers; 1st Silver Age app. of Captain America & Bucky (3/64) 259 518 777 2137 4819 7500
4-Reprint from the Golden Record Comic set 15 30 45 100 220 340
With Record (1966) 21 42 63 150 330 510
5-Hulk app. 50 100 150 400 900 1400
6-1st app. original Zemo & his Masters of Evil 44 88 132 326 738 1150
7-Rick Jones app. in Bucky costume 40 80 120 296 673 1050
8-Intro Kang 38 76 114 285 641 1000
9-Intro Wonder Man who dies in same story 56 112 168 448 999 1550
10-Intro/1st app. Immortus; early Hercules app. (11/64) 29 58 87 209 467 725
11-Spider-Man-c & x-over (12/64) 37 74 111 274 612 950
12-15: 15-Death of original Zemo 19 38 57 131 291 450
16-New Avengers line-up (Hawkeye, Quicksilver, Scarlet Witch join; Thor, Iron Man, Giant-Man, Wasp leave) 35 70 105 252 564 875
17,18: 17-Minor Hulk app. 13 26 39 89 195 300
19-1st app. Swordsman; origin Hawkeye (8/65) 15 30 45 103 227 350
20-22: Wood inks. 20-Intro. Power Man (Erik Josten) 10 20 30 69 147 225
23,24,26,27,29,30: 23-Romita Sr. inks (1st Silver Age Marvel work). 23,24-Avengers vs. Kang. 9 18 27 61 123 185
25-Dr. Doom-c/story 18 36 54 124 275 425
28-(5/66) First app. of The Collector; Giant-Man becomes Goliath

GD VG FN VF VF/NM NM-
2.0 4.0 6.0 8.0 9.0 9.2

27 54 81 194 435 675
31-40: 32-1st Sons of the Serpent. 34-Last full Stan Lee plot/script. 35-1st Roy Thomas script w/Stan Lee plot. 38-40-Hercules app. 40-Sub-Mariner app. 8 16 24 51 96 140
41-46,50: 43-1st app. Red Guardian (dies in #44). 45-Hercules joins. 46-Ant-Man returns (re-intro, 11/67) 7 14 21 46 86 125
47,49-Magneto-c/story 7 14 21 48 89 130
48-Origin/1st app. new Black Knight (1/68) 7 14 21 48 89 130
51-The Collector app. 8 16 24 51 96 140
52-Black Panther joins; 1st app. The Grim Reaper 8 16 24 56 108 160
53-X-Men app. 9 18 27 61 123 185
54-1st Ultron app. (1 panel); new Masters of Evil 11 22 33 76 163 250
55-1st full app. Ultron (8/68) (1 panel reveal in #54) 19 38 57 131 291 450
56-Zemo app; story explains how Capt. America became imprisoned in ice during WWII, only to be rescued in Avengers #4 8 16 24 56 108 160
57-1st app. S.A. Vision (10/68); death of Ultron-5 46 92 138 359 805 1250
58-Origin The Vision 10 20 30 69 147 225
59-Intro. Yellowjacket 11 22 33 76 163 250
60-65: 60-Wasp & Yellowjacket wed. 61-Dr. Strange app. 62-1st Man-Ape. 63-Goliath becomes Yellowjacket; Hawkeye becomes the new Goliath. 65-Last 12¢ issue 6 12 18 41 76 110
66-B. Smith-a; vs. Ultron-6; 1st mention of adamantium metal 8 16 24 51 96 140
67-Ultron-6 cvr/sty; B. Smith-a 9 18 27 61 123 185
68-Buscema-a 6 12 18 38 69 100
69-1st brief app. Squadron Sinister (Dr. Spectrum, Hyperion, Nighthawk) 8 16 24 54 102 150
70-1st full app. Nighthawk 7 14 21 46 86 125
71-1st app. The Invaders (12/69); Black Knight joins 9 18 27 61 123 185
72-79,81,82,84,86,90-91: 72-1st Zodiak; Captain Marvel & Nick Fury app. 73,74-Sons of the Serpent. 75-1st app. Arkon. 78-1st app. Lethal Legion (Man-Ape, Living Laser, Power Man, Grimm Reaper, Swordsman). 82-Daredevil app. 86-2nd Squadron Supreme app. 5 10 15 35 63 90
80-1st app. Red Wolf 7 14 21 44 82 120
83-Intro. The Liberators (Wasp, Valkyrie, Scarlet Witch, Medusa & the Black Widow) 11 22 33 76 163 250
85-1st app. Squadron Supreme (American Eagle, Dr. Spectrum, Hawkeye (Wyatt McDonald), Hyperion, Lady Lark, Nighthawk (Kyle Richmond), Tom Thumb, Whizzer) 6 12 18 41 76 110
87-Origin The Black Panther 9 18 27 59 117 175
88-Written by Harlan Ellison; Hulk app. 6 12 18 37 66 95
88-2nd printing (1994) 2 4 6 8 10 12
89-Classic Captain Marvel execution-c; beginning of Kree/Skrull War (runs through issue #97) 7 14 21 44 82 120
92-Last 15¢ issue; Neal Adams-c 6 12 18 41 76 110
93-(52 pgs.)-Neal Adams-c/a 15 30 45 100 220 340
94-96-Neal Adams-c/a 8 16 24 54 102 150
97-G.A. Capt. America, Sub-Mariner, Human Torch, Patriot, Vision, Blazing Skull, Fin, Angel, & new Capt. Marvel x-over 7 14 21 46 86 125
98,99: 98-Goliath becomes Hawkeye; Smith c/a(i). 99-Smith-c, Smith/Sutton-a 5 10 15 31 53 75
100-(6/72)-Smith-c/a; featuring everyone who was an Avenger 9 18 27 61 123 185
101-Harlan Ellison scripts 4 8 12 27 44 60
102-106,108,109 4 8 12 23 37 50
107-Starlin-a(p) 4 8 12 25 40 55
110,111-X-Men and Magneto app. 5 10 15 35 63 90
112-1st app. Mantis 13 26 39 89 195 300
113-115,119-124,126,128-130: 114-Swordsman returns; joins Avengers, first Mantis-c. 115-Prologue to Avengers/Defenders War. 119-Rutland, Vermont Halloween issue. 120-123-vs. Zodiac. 123,124-Mantis origin. 124-1st Star-Stalker. 126-Klaw & Solarr app. 129-Kang app; story continues in Giant-Size Avengers #2 3 6 9 19 30 40
116-118-Avengers/Defenders War; x-over w/Defenders #8-11. 116-Silver Surfer vs Vision. 117-Captain America vs. Sub-Mariner. 118-Avengers & Defenders vs. Loki & Dormammu 5 10 15 33 57 80
125-Thanos-c & brief app.; story continues in Captain Marvel #33 5 10 15 33 57 80
127-Ultron-7 app; story continues in Fantastic Four #150 4 8 12 23 37 50
131-133,136-140: 131,132-Vs. Kang. 131-1st Legion of the Unliving. 132-Continues in Giant-Size Avengers #3. 133-Origin of the Kree. 136-Ploog-r/Amazing Advs. #12. 137-Moondragon joins; Beast app; becomes provisional member; officially joins in #151; Wasp & Yellowjacket return 3 6 9 16 23 30

Avengers #183 © MAR

Avengers #241 © MAR

Avengers #378 © MAR

GD VG FN VF VF/NM NM-
2.0 4.0 6.0 8.0 9.0 9.2

GD VG FN VF VF/NM NM-
2.0 4.0 6.0 8.0 9.0 9.2

134,135-Origin of the Vision revised (also see Avengers Forever mini-series). 135-Continues in Giant-Size Avengers #4 4 8 12 23 37 50
141-143: 141-Squadron Supreme app; Pérez-a(p) begins. 142,143-Marvel Western heroes app. (Kid Colt, Rawhide Kid, Two-Gun Kid, Ringo Kid, Night Rider). 143-Vs. Kang (last 1970s app.) 2 4 6 12 15 20
144-Origin & 1st app. Hellcat (Patsy Walker) 5 10 15 35 63 90
145,146: Published out of sequence; Tony Isabella-s; originally intended to be in Giant-Size Avengers #5 2 4 6 9 12 15
146-149-(30¢-c variants, limited distribution) 5 10 15 31 53 75
147-149-(Reg. 25¢ editions)(5-7/76) Squadron Supreme app. 2 4 6 11 16 20
150-Kirby-a(r) pgs. 7-18 (from issue #16); pgs. 1-6 feature new-a by Pérez; new line-up: Capt. America, Iron Man, Scarlet Witch, Wasp, Yellowjacket, Vision & The Beast 2 4 6 13 18 22
150-(30¢-c variant, limited distribution) 5 10 15 35 53 75
151-Wonder Man returns w/new costume; Champions app.; The Collector app. 3 6 9 14 19 24
152-154,157,159,160,163: 152-1st app Black Talon. 154-vs. Attuma; continues in Super-Villain Team-up #9. 160-Grimm Reaper app. 163-Vs. The Champions 2 4 6 9 12 15
155,156-Dr. Doom app. 2 4 6 10 14 18
158-1st app. Graviton; Wonder Man vs. Vision; Jim Shooter plots begin 2 4 6 11 16 20
160-164-(35¢-c variants, limited dist.)(6-10/77) 8 16 24 51 96 140
161,162-Ultron-8 app; Henry Pym appears as Ant-Man. 162-1st app. Jocasta 3 6 9 14 20 25
164,165-Byrne-a; vs. Lethal Legion 2 4 6 10 14 18
166-Byrne-a; vs. Count Nefaria 2 4 6 13 18 22
167,168-Guardians of the Galaxy app. 2 4 6 11 16 20
169,172,178-180: 172-Hawkeye rejoins 1 3 4 6 8 10
170,171-Ultron & Jocasta app. 170-Minor Guardians of the Galaxy app. 2 4 6 11 16 20
173-177-Korvac Saga issues; 173-175-The Collector app. 173,177-Guardians of the Galaxy app. 174-Thanos cameo. 176-Starhawk app. 2 4 6 8 10 12
181-(3/79) Byrne-a/Pérez-c; new line-up: Capt. America, Scarlet Witch, Iron Man, Wasp, Vision, Beast & The Falcon; debut of Scott Lang who becomes Ant-Man in Marvel Premiere #47 (4/79) 6 12 18 40 73 105
182-191-Byrne-a: 183-Ms. Marvel joins. 184-vs. Absorbing Man. 185-Origin Quicksilver & Scarlet Witch. 186-187-vs. Morded the Mystic. 188-Intro. The Elements of Doom. 189-Deathbird app. 190,191-vs. Grey Gargoyle 2 4 6 8 10 12
192-194,197-199: 197-199-vs Red Ronin 1 2 3 5 6 8
195-1st Taskmaster cameo 2 4 6 9 12 15
196-1st full Taskmaster app. 5 10 15 35 63 90
200-(10/80, 52 pgs.)-Ms. Marvel leaves; 1st actual app. of Marcus Immortus 2 4 6 10 14 18
201,203-210,212: 204,205-vs. Yellow Claw 5.00
202-Ultron app. 2 4 6 10 14 18
211-New line-up: Capt. America, Iron Man, Tigra, Thor, Wasp & Yellowjacket; Angel, Beast, Dazzler app. 1 2 3 4 5 7
213,215,216,239,240,250: 213-Controversial Yellowjacket slapping Wasp issue; Yellowjacket leaves. 215,216-Silver Surfer app. 216-Tigra leaves. 239-(1/84) Avengers app. on David Letterman show. 240-Spider-Woman revived. 250-($1.00, 52 pgs; West Coast Avengers app. vs. Maelstrom 6.00
214-Ghost Rider app. 1 2 3 4 5 7
217-218,222,224-235,238: 217-Yellowjacket & Wasp return. 222-1st app. Egghead's Masters of Evil. 225,226-Black Knight app. 227-Roger Stern plots begin; Captain Marvel (Monica Rambeau) joins. 229-Death of Egghead. 230-Yellowjacket quits. 231-Iron Man leaves. 232-Starfox (Eros) joins. 233-Byrne-a. 234-Origin Quicksilver & Scarlet Witch. 238-Origin Blackout 5.00
219,220-Drax the Destroyer app. 220-Moondragon vs. Drax 1 2 3 5 6 8
221-Hawkeye & She-Hulk join; Spider-Man, Spider-Woman, Dazzler app. 6.00
223-Taskmaster app. 2 4 6 11 16 20
236,237-Spider-Man tries to join the Avengers 6.00
241-249,251-256,258-262: 242-Dr. Strange app. 243-Vision becomes chairman. 244,245-vs. Dire Wraiths. 246-248-Eternals app. 249-x-over with Thor #350. 252-vs. the Blood Brothers. 253-Vision vs. Quasimodo. 254-West Coast Avengers app. 255-John Buscema & Tom Palmer return as artists; 1st app Nebula's pirate crew. 256-Terminus app. 258-x-over with Amazing Spider-Man #269-270; Spider-Man & Firelord app. 258-260-Nebula app. 260-261-Secret Wars II X-over; Beyonder app. 262-Hercules vs. Sub-Mariner 4.00
257-1st app. Nebula (from the Guardians of the Galaxy movie) 3 6 9 17 26 35
263-(1/86) Return of Jean Grey, leading into X-Factor #1(story continues in FF #286) 6.00
264-265,267-269: 264-1st new Yellowjacket (Rita Demara) 266-Secret Wars II x-over; vs. The Beyonder. 267-269-Kang app. 3.00
266-Secret Wars II epilogue; Silver Surfer & Molecule Man app. 4.00
270-273-Baron Zemo and the new Masters of Evil app. 272-Alpha Flight app. 4.00
274-277-Baron Zemo and the new Masters of Evil app. in 'Siege of Avengers mansion'. 274-Hercules injured. 275-Jarvis severely beaten. 276-Thor returns. 277-Capt. America vs. Baron Zemo 5.00
278-283: 279-Capt. Marvel (Monica Rambeau) becomes Avengers leader; Dr. Druid joins. 280-Jarvis flashback issue. 281-283-Olympian Gods app. 282-Sub-Mariner rejoins 3.00
284,285-vs. the Olympian Gods. 285 Avengers vs. Zeus; Hercules recovers 4.00
286-299: 286-Fixer app. Awesome Android & Super Adaptoid app. 287-Mentallo app. 288-1st app. 'Heavy Metal' (TESS-One, Intergalactic Sentry #459, Machine Man, Super-Adaptoid). 290-West Coast Avengers app. 291-$1.00 issues begin. 292-1st app. the Leviathan (Marrina). 293-Death of Marrina. 294-Capt. Marvel (Monica Rambeau) leaves. 295-vs. the Cross-Time Kangs. 297-Dr. Druid leaves; Thor, Black Knight & She-Hulk resign. 298-Inferno x-over. 299-Inferno x-over; New Mutants app. 3.00
300-(2/89, $1.75, 68 pgs., squarebound) New line-up; the Captain (Steve Rogers), Thor, Invisible Woman, Mr. Fantastic & Gilgamesh (formerly the Forgotten one) Inferno x-over; Simonson-a 4.00
301-304,306-313,319-325,327,330-343: 301-Firelord app; 1st app. Super-Nova. 302-Re-intro Quasar; Firelord app. 303-vs. Super-Nova. Quasar, Firelord & West Coast Avengers app.; Mr. Fantastic & Invisible Woman leave. 308-310-Eternals app. 311-313-Acts of Vengeance x-over. 312-Freedom Force app. 320-324-Alpha Flight app. 327-2nd app. Rage. 332,333-Dr. Doom app. 334-Intro. Thane Ector & the Brethren; Inhumans & Quicksilver app. 335-339-vs. the Brethren. 335-1st Steve Epting art. 341,342-New Warriors & Sons of the Serpent app. 343-Intro. the Gatherers; Bob Harras scripts begin (end #395); last $1.00-c 3.00
305,314-318: 305-Byrne scripts begin; most current & non-active Avengers app. 314-318-Spider-Man x-over. 4.00
326-1st app. Rage (11/90) 5.00
328,329: 328-Origin Rage. 329-New line-up (Capt. America, Quasar, Sersi, She-Hulk, Thor, Vision, Black Widow) Spider-Man becomes a reserve member; Rage & Sandman become probationary members 4.00
344,348-349,351-359: 344-1st app. Proctor, leader of the Gatherers. 349-Thor vs. Hercules. 351-Starjammers app. 352-354-Grimm Reaper app. 3.00
345,346-Operation Galactic Storm x-overs. 345-Pt.5-Deathbird app. 346-Pt.12-Intro. Starforce (super-powered Kree warriors) 4.00
347-Double-sized issue ($1.75, 39, pgs.) Operation Galactic Storm conclusion (Pt.19) end of the Kree/Shi'ar War; 'death' of the Supreme Intelligence 5.00
350-($2.50, 68 pgs.) Double gatefold-c showing-c to #1; r/#53 w/cover in flip book format; vs. The Starjammers 5.00
360-($2.95, 52 pgs.) Embossed all-foil-c; 30th ann. 5.00
361,362,364,365,367: 361-362-vs. the Gatherers. 364-365-vs. Galen-Kor of the Kree 4.00
363-($2.95, 52 pgs.)-All silver foil-c; vs. Proctor & the Gatherers; 1st cameo app. Deathcry (unnamed) 5.00
366-($3.95, 68 pgs.)-Embossed all gold foil-c; Deadpool app. in back-up story 5.00
368,376-378: 368-Bloodties pt.1; Avengers/X-Men x-over 3.00
369-($2.95)-Foil embossed-c; Bloodties pt.5; X-Men/Avengers vs. Exodus 5.00
370-373: 370-371-Ghaur the Deviant app. 372-373-vs. Proctor & the Gatherers 4.00
374-Bound-in trading card sheet; origin of Proctor as an alternate-Earth Black Knight revealed (scarcer in NM due to the card insert) 5.00
375-($2.00, 52 pgs.)-Regular ed.; Thunderstrike returns; leads into Malibu Comic's Black September; end of the Gatherers saga (since #343); death of Proctor; Black Knight & Sersi leave; last Epting-a 4.00
375-($2.50, 52 pgs.)-Collectors ed. 5.00
379-382-Regular editions: 379-Galen Kor & Kree Lunatic Legion app. 380-382-High Evolutionary app. 380-1st Mike Deodato-a. 381-Exodus app. 3.00
379-382-Marvel Double Feature editions ($2.50, 45 pgs.)-all have Giant-Man stories in a flip-book format 4.00
383-385: 383-Fantastic Force app. 384-Hercules stripped of immortality & banished from Olympus. 385-Red Skull app. 4.00
386-389, 398-399: 386-Red Skull app.; 'Taking of AIM' prelude; continues in Capt. America #440. 387-Taking of AIM Pt.2; Red Skull app.; re-intro Modok; continues in Capt. America #441. 388-Taking of AIM Pt.4; Red Skull & Modok app. 6.00
390-393: 390-'The Crossing' prelude; leads into Avengers: the Crossing #1. 391,392-The Crossing. 391-Overpower game card insert; scarcer in NM. 392-393-The Crossing 5.00
394,397: 394-The Crossing; 1st new Wasp; story cont. in Avengers Timeslide #1; 397-x-over w/Hulk #440-441 1 2 3 4 5 7
395-The Crossing/Timeslide; 'death' of Tony Stark; Bob Harras co-plot only, last work on Avengers 1 2 3 5 6 8
396-First Sign Pt.4; vs. the Zodiac 8.00
400-(Double-size, 32 pgs.)-Mark Waid scripts; Loki app. 7.00
401,402: 401-Onslaught Impact #1; Magneto app. 402-Onslaught Impact #2; vs. Onslaught & Holocaust; last issue; continues in X-Men #56 6.00

Avengers Annual #8 © MAR

Avengers V3 #5 © MAR

Avengers V3 #66 © MAR

GD VG FN VF VF/NM NM-
2.0 4.0 6.0 8.0 9.0 9.2

#500-503 (See Avengers Vol. 3; series resumed original numbering after Vol. 3 #84)
Special 1 (9/67, 25¢, 68 pgs.)-New-a; original & new Avengers team-up 12 24 36 83 182 280
Special 2 (9/68, 25¢, 68 pgs.)-New-a; original vs. new Avengers 9 18 27 57 111 165
Special 3 (9/69, 25¢, 68 pgs.)-r/Avengers #4 plus 3 Capt. America stories by Kirby (art); origin Red Skull 5 10 15 34 60 85
Special 4 (1/71, 25¢, 68 pgs.)-Kirby-r/Avengers #5,6 3 6 9 21 33 45
Special 5 (1/72, 52 pgs.)-All-reprint issue; Kirby-r Avengers #8/Heck-r w/Spider-Man from issue #11 3 6 9 21 33 45
Annual 6 (11/76) Pérez-a; Kirby-c; vs. Nuklo 2 4 6 11 16 20
Annual 7 (11/77)-Starlin-c/a; Warlock dies; Thanos app.; x-over w/Marvel Two-in-one Ann #2 5 10 15 35 63 90
Annual 8 (1978)-Dr. Strange, Ms. Marvel app. vs. Hyperion, Dr. Spectrum & Whizzer 2 4 6 8 11 14
Annual 9 (1979)-Newton-a(p); Intro. Arsenal 2 3 4 6 8 10
Annual 10 (1981)-Golden-a; X-Men cameo; 1st app. Rogue & Madelyne Pryor 5 10 15 33 57 80
Annual 11-13: 11 (1982)-Vs. The Defenders. 12 ('83)-Inhumans app. 13 ('84)-Ditko/Byrne-a 5.00
Annual 14-15,17-18: 14 ('85)-x-over w/Fantastic Four Ann. #19; vs. the Skrulls. 15 ('86)-vs. Freedom Force; x-over w/Avengers West Coast Ann. #1. 17('88)-Evolutionary War x-over. 18('89)-Atlantis Attacks 4.00
Annual 16 (1987)-x-over w/Avengers West Coast Ann. #2; Silver Surfer app. vs. the Grandmaster and Legion of the Unliving (including Drax, Captain Marvel & Green Goblin) 5.00
Annual 19-22: 19 ('90)-Terminus Factor Pt.5 (conclusion) continued from Avengers West Coast Ann. #5. 20 ('91)-Subterranean Saga Pt.1; cont. in Hulk Ann. #17. 21 ('92)-Citizen Kang pt.4; vs. Terminatrix. 22 ('93)-Bagged w/card; 1st app. Bloodwraith 4.00
Annual 23 (1994)-Buscema-a; Roy Thomas-s; vs. Loki & Pluto; x-over w/Thor Ann. #19 5.00
Avengers 1: The Coming of the Avengers! (2012, $3.99) recolored reprint/#1 5.00
...: Galactic Storm Vol. 1 ('06, $29.99, TPB) r/Kree-Shi'ar war from Avengers #345-346, Capt. America #398-399, Avengers West Coast #80-81, Quasar #32-33, Wonder Man #7-8, Iron Man #278 and Thor #445; new Epting-c 30.00
...: Galactic Storm Vol. 2 ('06, $29.99, TPB) r/Kree-Shi'ar war from Avengers #347, Capt. America #400-401, Avengers West Coast #82, Quasar #34-36, Wonder Man #9, Iron Man #279, Thor #446 and What If #55-56 30.00
...: Kang - Time and Time Again ('05, $19.99, TPB) r/Avengers #69-71 & 267-269, Thor #140 and Incredible Hulk #135 20.00
...Kree-Skrull War ('00, $24.95, TPB) new Neal Adams-c 25.00
...: Legends Vol. 3: George Perez ('03, $16.99)-r/#161,162,194-196,201, Ann. #6 & 8 17.00
Marvel Double Feature...Avengers/Giant-Man #379 ($2.50, 52 pgs.)-Same as Avengers #379 w/Giant-Man flip book 4.00
Marvel Graphic Novel - Deathtrap: The Vault (1991, $9.95) Venom-c/app. 2 4 6 8 11 14
The Korvac Saga TPB (2003, $19.95)-r/#167,168,170-177; Perez-c 20.00
The Serpent Crown TPB (2005, $15.99)-r/#141-144,147-149; Hellcat app. 16.00
The Yesterday Quest ($6.95)-r/#181,182,185-187 1 2 3 4 5 7
Under Siege ('98, $16.95, TPB) r/#270,271,273-277 17.00
...: Vision and the Scarlet Witch TPB (2005, $15.99) r/wedding from Giant-Size Avengers #4 and "Vision and the Scarlet Witch" mini-series #1-4 16.00
...: Visionaries ('99, $16.95)-r/early George Perez art 17.00

NOTE: ***Austin** c(i)-157, 167, 168, 170-177, 181, 183-188, 198-201, Annual 8. **John Buscema** a-41-44p, 46p, 47p, 49, 50, 51-62p, 74-77, 79-85, 87-91, 97, 105p, 121p, 124p,125p, 152, 153p, 255-279p, 281-302p; c-41-66, 68-71, 73-91, 97-99, 178, 256-259p, 261-279p, 281-302p. **Byrne** a-164-166p, 181-191p, 233p, Annual 13i, 14p; c-186-190p, 233p, 260, 305p; scripts-305-312. **Colan** a(p)-63-65, 111, 206-208, 210, 211; c(p)-65, 206-208, 210, 211. **Ditko** a-Annual 13. **Guice** a-Annual 12p. **Don Heck** a-9-15, 17-40, 157. **Kane** c-37p, 159p. **Kane/Everett** c-97. **Kirby** a-1-8p, Special 3r, 4r(p); c-1-30, 148, 151-158; layouts-14-16. **Ron Lim** c(p)-335-341. **Miller** c-193p. **Mooney** a-86i, 179p, 180p. **Nebres** a-178i; c-179i. **Newton** a-204p, Annual 9p. **Perez** a(p)-141, 143, 144, 148, 150, 154, 155, 160, 161, 162, 167,168, 170, 171, 194-196, 198-202, Annual 6, 8; c(p)-160-162, 164-166, 170-174, 181,183-185, 191, 192, 194-201, 379-382, Annual 8. **Starlin** c-121, 135. **Staton** a-127-134i. **Tuska** a-47i,48i, 51i, 53i, 54i, 106p, 107p, 135p, 137-140p, 163p. Guardians of the Galaxy app. in #167, 168, 170, 173, 175, 181.*

AVENGERS, THE (Volume Two)
Marvel Comics: V2#1, Nov, 1996 - No. 13, Nov, 1997 ($2.95/$1.95/$1.99) (Produced by Extreme Studios)

1-($2.95)-Heroes Reborn begins; intro new team (Captain America, Swordsman, Scarlet Witch, Vision, Thor, Hellcat & Hawkeye); 1st app. Avengers Island; Loki & Enchantress app.; Rob Liefeld-p & plot; Chap Yaep-p; Jim Valentino scripts; variant-c exists 5.00
1-($1.95)-Variant-c 6.00
2-13: 2,3-Jeph Loeb scripts begin, Kang app. 4-Hulk-c/app. 5-Thor/Hulk battle; 2 covers. 10,11,13-"World War 3"-pt. 2, x-over w/Image characters. 12-($2.99) "Heroes Reunited"-pt. 2 4.00
Heroes Reborn: Avengers (2006, $29.99, TPB) r/#1-12; pin-up and cover gallery 30.00

AVENGERS, THE (Volume Three)(See New Avengers for next series)
Marvel Comics: Feb, 1998 - No. 84, Aug, 2004; No. 500, Sept, 2004 - No. 503, Dec, 2004

GD VG FN VF VF/NM NM-
2.0 4.0 6.0 8.0 9.0 9.2

($2.99/$1.99/$2.25)
1-($2.99, 48 pgs.) Busiek-s/Pérez-a/wraparound-c; Avengers reassemble after Heroes Return; many Avengers app. vs. Morgan Le Fey 5.00
1-Variant Heroes Return sunburst cover 1 2 3 4 5 7
1-Dynamic Forces Ltd Edition (1500 copies); sunburst-c signed by Perez 4 8 12 23 37 50
1-Rough Cut-Features original script and pencil pages 4.00
2-($1.99) Pérez-c; vs. Morgan Le Fey, alternate painted-c by Lago 4.00
3,4: 3-Wonder Man-c/app. & "dies". 4-Final roster chosen; Captain America, Thor, Hawkeye, Iron Man, Scarlet Witch, Vision, Warbird (formally Ms. Marvel: Carol Danvers) 3.00
5-6,8-11; 5-6: Squadron Supreme-c/app.: Hyperion, Dr. Spectrum, Power Princess, Whizzer, Haywire, Lady Lark, Shape & Moonglow. 8-1st app; Triathlon & Silverclaw; vs. Moses Magnum. 9-1st mention of the Triune Understanding. 10-Grimm Reaper & Ultron app; return of the Legion of the Unliving: Captain Mar-Vell, Dr. Druid, Mockingbird, Swordsman, Wonder Man & Thunderstrike. 11-Legion of the Unliving app; Hellcat, Spider-Man, Daredevil & Fantastic Four guest app; Wonder Man returns to life 3.00
7-Live Kree or Die pt. 4; continued from Quicksilver #10; Warbird leaves; vs. Kree Lunatic Legion 4.00
12-($2.99, 38 pgs.) Thunderbolts app; Firebird and Justice (of the New Warriors) join the Avengers. 4.00
12-Alternate-c of Avengers w/white background; no logo 3 6 9 16 23 30
12-Dynamic Forces alternate-c; ltd. to 5000 copies 1 3 4 6 8 10
12-Dynamic Forces alternate-c; ltd. to 1500 copies; signed by Pérez, Vey and Smith 3 6 9 14 20 25
13-18,23,26: 13-New Warriors app.; 1st app. Lord Templar; 1st (shadowed) app. Jonathan Tremont – leader of the Triune Understanding. 14-Beast app vs. Lord Templar; 1st app. Pagan. 15-1st full app. of Jonathan Tremont; Pagan and Lord Templar, the Wrecking Crew and Ultron app. 16-18-Ordway-s/a; vs. the Doomsday Man in #17; vs. the Wrecking Crew in #18. 23-Vision & Scarlet Witch history retold. 26-Immonen-a; Lord Templar & Taskmaster app. 3.00
16-Variant-c w/purple background 5.00
19,20: Ultron Unlimited pt. 1-2; Black Panther app.; Giant-Man (Henry Pym app. in #20-22) 1 3 4 6 8 10
21,22-Ultron Unlimited pt. 3-4; vs. Ultron; Black Panther app. 6.00
24-Continued from Juggernaut: the Eighth Day #1; vs. the Exemplars 4.00
25-Vs. the Exemplars; Spider-Man, New Warriors, Juggernaut and Quicksilver app. 5.00
27-($2.99, 100 pgs. 'Monster') New line up - Justice, Firestar & Thor leave, Triathlon & She-Hulk join, Wonder Man becomes a reserve member; Ant-Man app.; reprints issues (all Vol.1) #101,150,151, Annual #19; Note: Due to the 100 pages, this issue often suffers from tears around the staples. 6.00
28-32: 28-30-vs. Kulan Gath. 31-Vision rejoins; vs. Grimm Reaper. 32-Life story & secret origin of Madame Masque revealed 3.00
33-Thunderbolts x-over w/Thunderbolts #44; Madame Masque & Count Nefaria app. 1 3 4 6 9 12
34-($2.99, 38 pgs.) Last Perez-a; continued from Thunderbolts #44; vs. Count Nefaria; Black Widow app 6.00
35-37: 35-Maximum Security x-over; Romita Jr.-a; 36-37; vs. Bloodwraith; Epting-a 4.00
38-Davis-a begins ($1.99-c); new line-up: Captain America, Goliath (Henry Pym), Thor, Quicksilver, Wasp, Iron Man, Vision, Scarlet Witch, Triathlon, Wonder Man & Warbird (Carol Danvers) 4.00
39,40: Hulk app. 5.00
41-47,49: 41-Vs. Scarlet Centurion; Kang app. 42-44-Kang, Scarlet Centurion & the Presence app. 43-Jack of Hearts joins; last Davis-a. 45-Origin of the Scarlet Centurion; Kang & the Master of the World (from Alpha Flight issues) app. 46-Vs. Kang and his army; Scarlet Centurion & the Master of the World app. 47-Origin of Scarlet Centurion continued with flashback to issue #200 w/Ms. Marvel (Carol Danvers); 1st full app of the Triple Evil (ancient cosmic menace). 49-'Nuff Said story; Kang attacks Washington DC 3.00
48-($3.50, 100 pgs); vs. Kang and his legions; Scarlet Centurion app; death of Master of the World; Triple Evil app.; r/#98-100 4.00
50-($3.50); vs. the Triple Evil (destroyed); Lord Pagan & Templar app. (both die); Jonathan Tremont & the Triune Understanding revealed as villains; 3-D Man app. 5.00
51,52: 51-Kang app. as ruler of the Earth; Wonder Man and Scarlet Witch app.; features 2 pg. tribute to the late John Buscema who passed away on January 10th 2002. 52-Avengers vs. Kang; Scarlet Centurion & the Presence app. 4.00
53-Avengers vs. Kang; death of Jonathan Tremont. 6.00
54-56: 54-Conclusion of the Kang war w/Kang defeated; death of Scarlet Centurion. 55-Kang war aftermath; Thor leaves. 56-Beast app; last Busiek issue 4.00
57-62,65-84: 57-Geoff Johns-s begins; 'World Trust' pt. 1; ends with pt. 4 in issue #60. 64-Solo Falcon story; vs. Scarecrow. 65-70-Red Zone pt. 1-6; vs. the Red Skull. Wasp and Yellowjacket (Henry Pym) story; vs. Plantman and Whirlwind. 71-74; Search for She-Hulk pt. 1-4; Hulk app. in #73-74. 77-Last Johns issue. 78-81; Chuck Austen-s begin; Lionheart of Avalon pt. 1-5; special 50-¢t issue. 79-81; Captain Britain (Brian Braddock) app. 82-84-Once an Invader pt. 1-4; intro. New invaders team: Blazing Skull, Spitfire,

Avengers (2010 series) #1 © MAR

Avengers (2017 series) #4 © MAR

Avengers Arena #6 © MAR

GD 2.0 | VG 4.0 | FN 6.0 | VF 8.0 | VF/NM 9.0 | NM- 9.2

US Agent & Union Jack; Namor app. in #83-84 4.00
63-Standoff pt. 3; continued from Thor (Vol. 2) #58; Thor vs. Iron Man; Dr. Doom app. 2 4 6 9 12 15
(After #84 [Aug, 2004], numbering reverted back to original Vol. 1 with #500, Sept, 2004)
500-($3.50) "Avengers Disassembled" begins; Bendis-s/Finch-a; Ant-Man (Scott Lang) and Jack of Hearts killed, Vision destroyed by the Scarlet Witch 5.00
500-Director's Cut ($4.99) Cassaday foil variant-c plus interviews and galleries 1 3 4 6 8 10
501, 502-($2.25): 501-Numerous Avengers and ex-team members app. 502-Hawkeye killed 5.00
503-($3.50) "Avengers Disassembled" ends; reprint pages from Avengers V1#16; Dr. Strange and Magneto app; story continues in Avengers Finale #1 4.00
#11/2 (12/99, $2.50) Timm-c/a; Stern-s; 1963-style issue 3.00
.../ Squadron Supreme '98 Annual ($2.99) 4.00
1999, 2000 Annual (7/99, '00, $3.50) 1999-Manco-a. 2000-Breyfogle-a 4.00
2001 Annual ($2.99) Reis-a; back-up-s art by Churchill 4.00
...: Above and Beyond TPB ('05, $24.99) r/#36-40,56, Annual 2001, & Avengers: The Ultron Imperative; Alan Davis-c 25.00
... Assemble HC ('04, $29.95, oversized) r/#1-11 & '98 Annual; Busiek intro.; Pérez pencil art and Busiek script from Avengers #1 30.00
... Assemble Vol. 2 HC ('05, $29.95, oversized) r/#12-22, #0 & Ann. 1999; Ordway intro. 30.00
... Assemble Vol. 3 HC ('06, $34.99, oversized) r/#23-34, #1 1/2 & Thunderbolts #42-44 35.00
... Assemble Vol. 4 HC ('07, $34.99, oversized) r/#35-40, Avengers 2000, Avengers 2001, Avengers: The Ultron Imperative, Maximum Security #1-3 & ...Dangerous Planet 35.00
... Assemble Vol. 5 HC ('07, $39.99, oversized) r/#41-56 and Avengers 2001 40.00
...: Clear and Present Dangers TPB ('01, $19.95) r/#8-15 20.00
...: Defenders War HC ('07, $19.99) r/#115-118 & Defenders #8-11; Englehart intro. 20.00
...: Disassembled HC ('06, $24.99) r/#500-503 & Avengers Finale; Director's Cut extras 25.00
...: Disassembled TPB ('05, $15.99) r/#500-503 & Avengers Finale; Director's Cut extras 16.00
...Finale 1 (1/05, $3.50) Epilogue to Avengers Disassembled; Neal Adams-c; art by various incl. Peréz, Maleev, Oeming, Powell, Mayhew, Mack, McNiven, Cheung, Frank 4.00
Free Comic Book Day (5/09, giveaway) New Avengers 1st battle vs. Dark Avengers 3.00
...: Living Legends TPB ('04, $19.99) r/#23-30; last Busiek/Pérez arc 20.00
...Supreme Justice TPB (4/01, $17.95) r/Squadron Supreme appearances in Avengers #5-7, '98 Annual, Iron Man #7, Capt. America #8, Quicksilver #10; Pérez-c 18.00
The Kang Dynasty TPB ('02, $29.99) r/#41-55 & 2001 Annual 30.00
The Morgan Conquest TPB ('00, $14.95) r/#1-4 15.00
.../Thunderbolts Vol. 1: The Nefaria Protocols (2004, $19.99) r/#31-34, 42-44 20.00
Ultron Unleashed TPB (8/99, $3.50) reprints early app. 4.00
Ultron Unlimited TPB (4/01, $14.95) r/#19-22 & #0 prelude 15.00
Wizard #0-Ultron Unlimited prelude 3.00
Vol. 1: World Trust TPB ('03, $14.99) r/#57-62 & Marvel Double-Shot #2 15.00
Vol. 2: Red Zone TPB ('04, $14.99) r/#64-70 15.00
Vol. 3: The Search For She-Hulk TPB ('04, $12.99) r/#71-76 13.00
Vol. 4: The Lionheart of Avalon TPB ('04, $11.99) r/#77-81 12.00
Vol. 5: Once an Invader TPB ('04, $14.99) r/#82-84, V1 #71; Invaders #0 & Ann #1 ('77) 15.00

AVENGERS (The Heroic Age)
Marvel Comics: July, 2010 - No. 34, Jan, 2013 ($3.99)

1-New team assembled; Bendis-s/Romita Jr.-a; Kang app.; back-up text Avengers history 6.00
1-Variant-c by Land 8.00
1-Variant covers by Djurdjevic and John Romita Sr. 12.00
1-3-Second printings 4.00
2,3: 2-Wonder Man app. 5.00
4-12: 4-6-Ultron app. 7-Red Hulk app. 12-Red Hulk joins 4.00
12.1 -(6/11, $2.99) Hitch & Neary-c/a; The Wizard & The Intelligencia app.; Ultron returns 3.00
13-24: 13-17-Fear Itself tie-ins. 13,15-Bachalo-a. 17-New Avengers app. 18-20-Acuña-a. 19-Vision returns, Storm joins 4.00
24.1 -(5/12, $2.99) Peterson-a; Magneto, She-Hulk app. 3.00
25-33: 25-30-Avengers vs. X-Men tie-in; Simonson-a. 31-34-Janet Van Dyne app. 4.00
34-($4.99) Art by Peterson, Mayhew & Dodson; Deodato, Simonson, Yu, Cheung, Coipel art pages; Bendis afterword 5.00
... Annual 1 (3/12, $4.99) Bendis-s/Dell'Otto-c/a; Wonder Man app. 5.00
... Assemble 1 (7/10, $3.99) Handbook-style profiles of Avengers, enemies, allies 4.00
...: Infinity Quest 1 (8/11, $4.99) r/#7-9 with variant covers 5.00
... Roll Call 1 (2012, $4.99) Updated handbook-style profiles of Avengers & enemies 5.00
... Spotlight (7/10, $3.99) Creator interviews, previews, history of the team; trivia 4.00

AVENGERS (Marvel NOW!)
Marvel Comics: Feb, 2013 - No. 44, Jun, 2015 ($3.99)

1-13: 1-Hickman-s/Opeña-a/Weaver-c. 4-6-Adam Kubert-a 4.00
14-23: 14-17-Prelude to Infinity. 18-23-Infinity tie-ins 4.00
24-($4.99) Rogue Planet; Ribic-a; Iron Man 3030 app. 5.00
25-28-Hickman-s/Larroca-a. 27-Includes reprint of All-New Invaders #1 4.00
29-($4.99) Original Sin tie-in; Yu-a/Cho-c 5.00
30-34-Original Sin tie-in; Hickman-s/Yu-a 4.00
34.1 (11/14), 34.2 (3/15), 35-($4.99) 34.1-Spotlight on Hyperion; Keown-a. 34.2-Spotlight on Starbrand; Bengal-a. 35-Cheung, Medina-a 5.00
36-39,41-43: 37,39,41-Deodato-a. 39-Leads into New Avengers #28 4.00
40-($4.99) Thanos-c/app.; Caselli-a 5.00
44-($4.99) Follows New Avengers #33; Thanos app.; leads into Secret Wars #1 5.00
Annual (2/14, $4.99) Christmas-themed; Lafuente-a 5.00
...: Endless Wartime HC (2013, $24.99, OGN) Ellis-s/McKone-a; intro by Clark Gregg 25.00
...: No More Bullying (3/15, $1.99) Short stories; Avengers, Spider-Man, GOTG app. 3.00
... Now! Handbook 1 (2/15, $4.99) Updated version with new characters from 2014 5.00
...: The Enemy Within (7/13, $2.99) DeConnick-s/Hepburn-a; Captain Marvel tie-in 3.00
...: Vs 1 (7/15, $5.99) Printing of 4 digital-first stories; Raney-c 6.00
100th Anniversary Special: Avengers 1 (9/14, $3.99) James Stokoe-s/a 4.00

AVENGERS (After Secret Wars)
Marvel Comics: No. 0, Dec, 2015 ($5.99)

0-Short story preludes for the various Avengers 2016 titles; Deadpool app. 6.00

AVENGERS (Follows events of Civil War II)
Marvel Comics: Jan, 2017 - Present ($4.99/$3.99)

1-($4.99) Spider-Man, Capt. America (Sam), Thor (Jane), Wasp, Vision, Hercules team 5.00
2-5-($3.99) Kang app.; Waid-s/del Mundo-a 4.00
#1.MU (3/17, $4.99) Monsters Unleashed tie-in; Zub-s/Izaakse-a 5.00

AVENGERS (Flashback to new team roster from Avengers #16 [1965])
Marvel Comics: No. 1.1, Jan, 2017 - Present ($3.99)

1.1, 1.2, 1.3, 1.4- Hawkeye, Quicksilver and Scarlet Witch join team; Waid-s/Kitson-a 4.00

AVENGERS ACADEMY (The Heroic Age)(Also see Avengers Arena)
Marvel Comics: Aug, 2010 - No. 39, Jan, 2013 ($3.99/$2.99)

1-($3.99) Gage-s/McKone-a/c; Intro. team of Veil, Hazmat, Striker, Mettle, Finesse, Reptil 4.00
1-Variant-c by Djurdjevic 8.00
2-14,14.1 -($2.99) 3,4-Juggernaut app. 5-Molina-a. 7-Absorbing Man app.; Raney-a. 3.00
15-39: 15-20-Fear Itself tie-in. 22-Magneto app. 27,28-Runaways app. 29-33-Tie in to Avengers vs. X-Men event 3.00
... Giant Size 1 (7/11, $7.99) Young Allies and Arcade app.; Tobin-s/Baldeon-a 8.00

AVENGERS: AGE OF ULTRON POINT ONE (Free Comic Book Day)
Marvel Comics: 2012 (Free giveaway)

#0.1 - Reprints Avengers 12.1 (6/11); Bendis-s/Hitch & Neary-c/a 4.00

AVENGERS: A.I. (Follows Age of Ultron series)
Marvel Comics: Sept, 2013 - No. 12, Jun, 2014 ($2.99)

1-12: 1-Humphries-s/Araújo-a; Hank Pym, Vision app. 7-Daredevil app. 3.00

AVENGERS AND POWER PACK ASSEMBLE!
Marvel Comics: June, 2006 - No. 4, Sept, 2006 ($2.99, limited series)

1-4-GuriHiru-a/Sumerak-s. 1-Capt. America app. 2-Iron Man. 3-Spider-Man, Kang app. 3.00
TPB (2006, $6.99, digest-size) r/#1-4 7.00

AVENGERS AND THE INFINITY GAUNTLET
Marvel Comics: Oct, 2010 - No. 4, Jan, 2011 ($2.99, limited series)

1-4: 1-Clevinger-s/Churilla-a; Dr. Doom and Thanos app. 1-Ramos-c. 2-Lim-c 3.00

AVENGERS & X-MEN: AXIS
Marvel Comics: Dec, 2014 - No. 9, Feb, 2015 ($4.99/$3.99, limited series)

1-($4.99) Remender-s/Adam Kubert-a; Red Skull as Red Onslaught 5.00
2-8-($3.99): 2,7-Kubert-a. 3,4,8-Yu-a. 3-Adult Apocalypse app. 5,6-Dodson-a 4.00
9-($4.99) Cheung, Dodson, Yu & Kubert-a 5.00

AVENGERS ARENA
Marvel Comics: Feb, 2013 - No. 18, Jan, 2014 ($2.99)

1-18: 1-Avengers Academy members & Runaways in Arcade's Murder World; Walker-a 3.00

AVENGERS ASSEMBLE (Also see Marvel Universe Avengers Assemble)
Marvel Comics: May, 2012 - No. 25, May, 2014 ($3.99)

1-25: 1-Bendis-s/Bagley-a/c; movie roster in regular Marvel universe. 3-Thanos returns. 4-8-Guardians of the Galaxy app. 9-DeConnick-s begin. 13,14-Age of Ultron tie-in. 18-20-Infinity tie-in. 21-23-Inhumanity 4.00
Annual 1 (3/13, $4.99) Gage-s/Coker-a; spotlight on The Vision 5.00

AVENGERS: CELESTIAL QUEST
Marvel Comics: Nov, 2001 - No. 8, June, 2002 ($2.50/$3.50, limited series)

1-7-Englehart-s/Santamaría-a; Thanos app. 3.00
8-($3.50) 4.00

AVENGERS: CLASSIC
Marvel Comics: Aug, 2007 - No. 12, Juy, 2008 ($3.99/$2.99)

1,12-($3.99) 1-Reprints Avengers #1 ('63) with new stories about that era; Art Adams-c 4.00

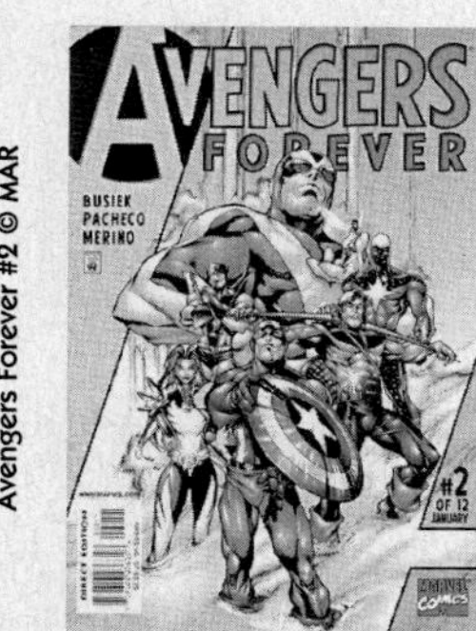

Avengers Forever #2 © MAR

Avengers 1959 #1 © MAR

Avengers Prime #1 © MAR

GD VG FN VF VF/NM NM-
2.0 4.0 6.0 8.0 9.0 9.2

2-11-($2.99) R/#2-11 with back-up w/art by Oeming and others 3.00

AVENGERS COLLECTOR'S EDITION, THE
Marvel Comics: 1993 (Ordered through mail w/candy wrapper, 20 pgs.)

1-Contains 4 bound-in trading cards 5.00

AVENGERS: EARTH'S MIGHTIEST HEROES
Marvel Comics: Jan, 2005 - No. 8, Apr, 2005 ($3.50, limited series)

1-8-Retells origin; Casey-s/Kolins-a 4.00
HC (2005, $24.99, 7 1/2" x 11" with dustjacket) r/#1-8 25.00

AVENGERS: EARTH'S MIGHTIEST HEROES (Based on the Disney animated series)
Marvel Comics: Jan, 2011 - No. 4, Apr, 2011 ($3.99)

1-4-Yost-s/Wegener-a. 1-Hero profile pages. 2-Villain profile pages 4.00

AVENGERS EARTH'S MIGHTIEST HEROES (Titled Marvel Universe... for #1)
Marvel Comics: Jun, 2012 - No. 17, Oct, 2013 ($2.99)

1-17-All ages title. 13-FF & Dr. Doom app. 17-Ant-Man, Luke Cage & Iron Fist app. 4.00

AVENGERS: EARTH'S MIGHTIEST HEROES II
Marvel Comics: Jan, 2007 - No. 8, May, 2007 ($3.99, limited series)

1-8-Retells time when the Vision joined; Casey-s/Rosado-a. 6-Hank & Janet's wedding 4.00
HC (2007, $24.99, 7 1/2" x 11" with dustjacket) r/#1-8; cover sketches 25.00

AVENGERS FAIRY TALES
Marvel Comics: May, 2008 - No. 4, Dec, 2008 ($2.99, limited series)

1-4: 1-Peter Pan-style tale; Cebulski-a/Lemos-a. 2-The Vision. 3-Miyazawa-a 3.00

AVENGERS FOREVER
Marvel Comics: Dec, 1998 - No. 12, Feb, 2000 ($2.99)

1-Busiek-s/Pacheco-a in all 4.00
2-12: 4-Four covers. 6-Two covers. 8-Vision origin revised. 12-Rick Jones becomes Capt. Marvel 3.00
TPB (1/01, $24.95) r/#1-12; Busiek intro.; new Pacheco-c 25.00

AVENGERS INFINITY
Marvel Comics: Sept, 2000 - No. 4, Dec, 2000 ($2.99, limited series)

1-4-Stern-s/Chen-a 3.00

AVENGERS/ INVADERS
Marvel Comics: Jul, 2008 - No. 12, Aug, 2009 ($2.99, limited series)

1-Invaders journey to the present; Alex Ross-c/Sadowski-a; Thunderbolts app. 3.00
2-12: 2-New Avengers app.; Perkins variant-c. 3-12-Variant-c on each 3.00
... Sketchbook (2008, giveaway) Ross and Sadowski sketch art; Krueger commentary 3.00

AVENGERS/ JLA (See JLA/Avengers for #1 & #3)
DC Comics: No, 2, 2003; No. 4, 2003 ($5.95, limited series)

2-Busiek-s/Pérez-a; wraparound-c; Krona, Galactus app. 6.00
4-Busiek-s/Pérez-a; wraparound-c 6.00

AVENGERS LOG, THE
Marvel Comics: Feb, 1994 ($1.95)

1-Gives history of all members; Pérez-c 3.00

AVENGERS: MILLENNIUM
Marvel Comics: Jun, 2015 - No. 4, Jun, 2015 ($3.99, weekly limited series)

1-4-Di Giandomenico-a; Scarlet Witch & Quicksilver app. 1-Yu-c. 2-4-Deodato-c. 4.00

AVENGERS NEXT (See A-Next and Spider-Girl)
Marvel Comics: Jan, 2007 - No. 5, Mar, 2007 ($2.99, limited series)

1-5-Lim-a/Wieringo-c; Spider-Girl app. 1-Avengers vs. zombies. 2-Thena app. 3.00
...: Rebirth TPB (2007, $13.99) r/#1-5 14.00

AVENGERS 1959
Marvel Comics: Dec, 2011 - No. 5, Mar, 2012 ($2.99, limited series)

1-5-Chaykin-s/a/c; Nick Fury, Kraven, Namora, Sabretooth, Dominic Fortune app. 3.00

AVENGERS: OPERATION HYDRA
Marvel Comics: Jun, 2015 ($3.99, one-shot)

1-Movie team; Pilgrim-s/Di Vito-a; bonus reprint of Avengers #16 (1965) 4.00

AVENGERS ORIGINS (Series of one-shots)
Marvel Comics: Jan, 2012 ($3.99)

...: Ant-Man & The Wasp 1 (1/12) Aguirre-Sacasa-s/Hans-a/Djurdjevic-c; origin of both 4.00
...: Luke Cage 1 (1/12) Glass & Benson-s/Talajic-a/Djurdjevic-c; 4.00
...: Scarlet Witch & Quicksilver 1 (1/12) McKeever-s/Pierfederici-a/Djurdjevic-c 4.00
...: Thor 1 (1/12) K. Immonen-s/Barrionuevo-a/Djurdjevic-c 4.00
...: Vision 1 (1/12) Higgins & Siegel-s/Perger-a/Djurdjevic-c; Ultron-5 app. 4.00

AVENGERS PRIME (The Heroic Age)
Marvel Comics: Aug, 2010 - No. 5, Mar, 2011 ($3.99, limited series)

1-5-Thor, Iron Man & Steve Rogers; Bendis-s/Davis-a; Enchantress app. 4.00
1-Variant-c by Djurdjevic 8.00

AVENGERS: RAGE OF ULTRON
Marvel Comics: 2015 ($24.99, hardcover graphic novel)

HC - Remender-s/Opeña-a; intro by Busiek 25.00

AVENGERS: SEASON ONE
Marvel Comics: 2013 ($24.99, hardcover graphic novel)

HC - Origin story; Peter David-a/Tedesco painted-c; bonus script outline 25.00

AVENGERS: SOLO
Marvel Comics: Dec, 2011 - No. 5, Apr, 2012 ($3.99, limited series)

1-5-Hawkeye; back-up Avengers Academy 4.00

AVENGERS SPOTLIGHT (Formerly Solo Avengers #1-20)
Marvel Comics: No. 21, Aug, 1989 - No. 40, Jan, 1991 (75¢/$1.00)

21-Byrne-c/a 3.50
22-40: 26-Acts of Vengeance story. 31-34-U.S. Agent series. 36-Heck-i. 37-Mortimer-i. 40-The Black Knight app. 3.00

AVENGERS STANDOFF (Crossover with Avengers titles and other Marvel titles)
Marvel Comics: Apr, 2016 - Jun, 2016 ($4.99)

...: Assault on Pleasant Hill Alpha 1 (5/16) Part 2 of crossover; Spencer-s/Saiz-a 5.00
...: Assault on Pleasant Hill Omega 1 (6/16) Part 3 of crossover; Spencer-s/Acuña-a; new Quasar debut; Red Skull app. 5.00
...: Welcome to Pleasant Hill 1 (4/16) Part 1 of crossover; Spencer-s/Bagley-a/Acuña-c 5.00

AVENGERS STRIKEFILE
Marvel Comics: Jan, 1994 ($1.75, one-shot)

1 3.00

AVENGERS: THE CHILDREN'S CRUSADE
Marvel Comics: Sept, 2010 - No. 9, May, 2012 ($3.99, limited series)

1-9-Young Avengers search for Scarlet Witch; Heinberg-s/Cheung-a. 6-9-X-Men app. 4.00
1-4-Variant-c. 1-Jelena Djurdjevic. 2-Travis Charest. 3,4-Art Adams 6.00
... - Young Avengers (5/11, $3.99) Takes place between #4&5; Alan Davis-a/c 4.00

AVENGERS: THE CROSSING
Marvel Comics: July, 1995 ($4.95, one-shot)

1-Deodato-c/a; 1st app. Thor's new costume 5.00

AVENGERS: THE INITIATIVE (See Civil War and related titles)
Marvel Comics: Jun, 2007 - No. 35, Jun, 2010 ($2.99)

1-Caselli-a/Slott-s/Cheung-c; War Machine app. 4.00
2-35: 4,5-World War Hulk. 6-Uy-a. 14-19-Secret Invasion; 3-D Man app. 16-Skrull Kill Krew returns. 20-Tigra pregnancy revealed, 21-25-Ramos-a. 32-35-Siege 3.00
Annual 1 (1/08, $3.99) Secret Invasion tie-in; Cheung-c 4.00
... Featuring Reptil (5/09, $3.99) Gage-s/Uy-a 4.00
... Special 1 (1/09, $3.99) Slott & Gage-s/Uy-a 4.00
...: Vol. 1 - Basic Training HC (2007, $19.99, d.j.) r/#1-6 20.00
...: Vol. 1 - Basic Training SC (2008, $14.99) r/#1-6 15.00

AVENGERS: THE ORIGIN
Marvel Comics: Jun, 2010 - No. 5, Oct, 2010 ($3.99, limited series)

1-5-Casey-s/Noto-a/c; team origin (pre-Capt. America) re-told; Loki app. 4.00

AVENGERS: THE TERMINATRIX OBJECTIVE
Marvel Comics: Sept, 1993 - No. 4, Dec, 1993 ($1.25, limited series)

1 ($2.50)-Holo-grafx foil-c 4.00
2-4-Old vs. current Avengers 3.00

AVENGERS: THE ULTRON IMPERATIVE
Marvel Comics: Nov, 2001 ($5.99, one-shot)

1-Follow-up to the Ultron Unlimited ending in Avengers #42; BWS-c 6.00

AVENGERS, THOR & CAPTAIN AMERICA: OFFICIAL INDEX TO THE MARVEL UNIVERSE
Marvel Comics: Jun, 2010 - No. 15, 2001 ($3.99)

1-15-Each issue has chronological synopsies, creator credits, character lists for 30-40 issues of Avengers, Captain America and Journey Into Mystery starting with debuts 4.00

AVENGERS/THUNDERBOLTS
Marvel Comics: May, 2004 - No. 6, Sept, 2004 ($2.99, limited series)

1-6: Busiek & Nicieza-s/Kitson-c. 1,2-Kitson-a. 3-6-Grummett-a 3.00
Vol. 2: Best Intentions (2004, $14.99) r/#1-6 15.00

AVENGERS: TIMESLIDE
Marvel Comics: Feb, 1996 ($4.95, one-shot)

Avengers: X-Sanction #1 © MAR

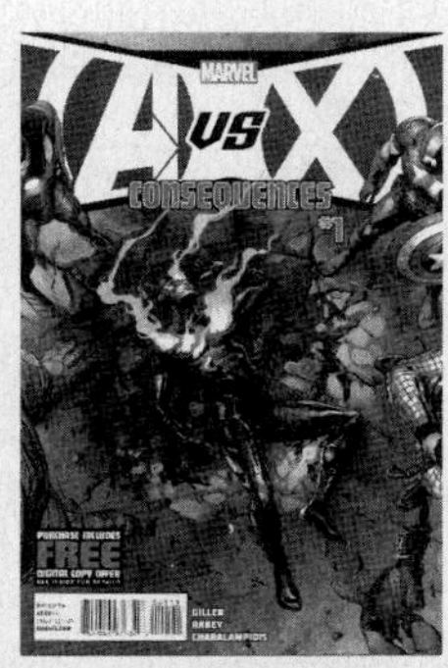

AVX: Consequences #1 © MAR

Axcend #2 © Shane Davis

	GD 2.0	VG 4.0	FN 6.0	VF 8.0	VF/NM 9.0	NM- 9.2

1-Foil-c 5.00

AVENGERS TWO: WONDER MAN & BEAST
Marvel Comics: May, 2000 - No. 3, July, 2000 ($2.99, limited series)
1-3: Stern-s/Bagley-c/a 3.00

AVENGERS/ULTRAFORCE (See Ultraforce/Avengers)
Marvel Comics: Oct, 1995 ($3.95, one-shot)
1-Wraparound foil-c by Pérez 4.00

AVENGERS: ULTRON FOREVER
Marvel Comics: Jun, 2015 ($4.99)(Continues in New Avengers: Ultron Forever)
1-Part 1 of 3-part crossover with New Avengers and Uncanny Avengers; Ewing-s/ Alan Davis-a; team-up of past, present and future Avengers vs. Ultron 5.00

AVENGERS UNDERCOVER (Follows Avengers Arena series)
Marvel Comics: May, 2014 - No. 10, Nov, 2014 ($2.99)
1-10: Hopeless-s in all; Masters of Evil app. 1,2,4,5,7,Kev Walker-a. 3,6,9-Green-a 3.00

AVENGERS UNITED THEY STAND
Marvel Comics: Nov, 1999 - No. 7, June, 2000 ($2.99/$1.99)
1-Based on the animated series 4.00
2-6-($1.99) 2-Avengers battle Hydra. 6-The Collector app. 3.00
7-($2.99) Devil Dinosaur-c/app.; The Collector app.; r/Avengers Action Figure Comic 4.00

AVENGERS UNIVERSE
Marvel Comics: Jun, 2000 - No. 3, Oct, 2000 ($3.99)
1-3-Reprints recent stories 4.00

AVENGERS UNPLUGGED
Marvel Comics: Oct, 1995 - No. 6, Aug, 1996 (99¢, bi-monthly)
1-6 3.00

AVENGERS VS. ATLAS (Leads into Atlas #1)
Marvel Comics: Mar, 2010 - No. 4, Jun, 2010 ($3.99, limited series)
1-4-Hardman-a; Ramos-c. 1-Back-up w/Miyazawa-a. 2-4-Original Avengers app. 4.00

AVENGERS VS INFINITY
Marvel Comics: Jan, 2016 ($5.99, one-shot)
1-Short stories with The Wrecker, Doctor Doom, Bossman & Dracula; Alves & Lim-a 6.00

AVENGERS VS. PET AVENGERS
Marvel Comics: Dec, 2010 - No. 4, Mar, 2011 ($2.99, limited series)
1-4-Eliopoulos-s/Guara-a; Fin Fang Foom app. 3.00

AVENGERS VS. X-MEN (Also see AVX: VS and AVX: Consequences)
Marvel Comics: No. 0, May, 2012 - No. 12, Dec, 2012 ($3.99/$4.99, bi-weekly limited series)
0-Bendis & Aaron-s; Frank Cho-a/c; Scarlet Witch and Hope featured 4.00
1-11: 1-5-Romita Jr. -a. 6,7,11-Coipel-a. 8-10-Adam Kubert-a. 11-Hulk app. 4.00
12-($4.99) Adam Kubert-a; Cyclops as Dark Phoenix 5.00

AVENGERS WEST COAST (Formerly West Coast Avengers)
Marvel Comics: No. 48, Sept, 1989 - No. 102, Jan, 1994 ($1.00/$1.25)
48,49: 48-Byrne-c/a & scripts continue thru #57 3.50
50-Re-intro original Human Torch 4.00
51-69,71-74,76-83,85,86,89-99: 54-Cover swipe/F.F. #1. 78-Last $1.00-c. 79-Dr. Strange x-over. 93-95-Darkhawk app. 3.00
70,75,84,87,88: 70-Spider-Woman app. 75 (52 pgs.)-Fantastic Four x-over. 84-Origin Spider-Woman retold; Spider-Man app. (also in #85,86). 87,88-Wolverine-c/story 4.00
100-($3.95, 68 pgs.)-Embossed all red foil-c 4.00
101,102: 101-X-Men x-over 5.00
Annual 5-8 ('90- '93, 68 pgs.)-5,6-West Coast Avengers in indicia. 7-Darkhawk app. 8-Polybagged w/card 4.00
...: Darker Than Scarlet TPB (2008, $24.99) r/#51-57,60-62; Byrne-s/a 25.00
...: Vision Quest TPB (2005, $24.99) r/#42-50; Byrne-s/a 25.00

AVENGERS WORLD
Marvel Comics: Mar, 2014 - No. 21, Jul, 2015 ($3.99)
1-21: 1-Hickman & Spencer-s/Caselli-a. 6-Neal Adams-c. 15,16-Doctor Doom app. 16-Cassie Lang brought back to life. 21-Leads into Secret Wars #1 4.00

AVENGERS: X-SANCTION
Marvel Comics: Feb, 2012 - No. 4, May, 2012 ($3.99, limited series)
1-4-Loeb-s/McGuinness-a/c; Cable battles the Avengers. 3,4-Wolverine & Spidey app. 4.00

AVENGING SPIDER-MAN (Spider-Man and Avengers member team-ups)
Marvel Comics: Jan, 2012 - No. 22, Aug, 2013 ($3.99)
1-8,10-15: 1-3-Madureira-a/Wells-s; Madureira-c. 1-3-Red Hulk & Avengers app. 4-Hawkeye. 5-Captain America app.; Yu-a. 11-Dillon-a. 12,13-Deadpool app. 14,15-Devil Dinosaur 4.00
1-Variant-c by Ramos 1 2 3 5 6 8
1-Variant-c by J. Scott Campbell 1 2 3 5 6 8
9-(9/12) Carol Danvers (Ms. Marvel) takes the name Captain Marvel 3 6 9 21 33 45
15.1 (2/13, $2.99) Follows Amazing Spider-Man #700; 1st Superior Spider-Man 5.00
16-22-Superior Spider-Man. 16-Wolverine & X-Men app. 18-Thor app. 22-Punisher app. 4.00
Annual 1 (12/12, $4.99) Spider-Man (Peter Parker) and The Thing; Zircher-c 5.00

AVIATION ADVENTURES AND MODEL BUILDING (True Aviation Advs. ...No. 15)
Parents' Magazine Institute: No. 16, Dec, 1946 - No. 17, Feb, 1947
16,17-Half comics and half pictures 8 16 24 42 54 65

AVIATION CADETS
Street & Smith Publications: 1943
nn 19 37 57 111 176 240

A-V IN 3-D
Aardvark-Vanaheim: Dec, 1984 ($2.00, 28 pgs. w/glasses)
1-Cerebus, Flaming Carrot, Normalman & Ms. Tree 4.00

AVX: CONSEQUENCES (Aftermath of Avengers Vs. X-Men series)
Marvel Comics: Dec, 2012 - No. 5, Jan, 2013 ($3.99, weekly limited series)
1-5-Cyclops in prison; Gillen-s/art by various 4.00

AVX: VS (Tie-in to Avengers Vs. X-Men series)
Marvel Comics: Jun, 2012 - No. 6, Nov, 2012 ($3.99, limited series)
1-6-Spotlight on the individual fights from Avengers Vs. X-Men #2; art by various 4.00

AWESOME ADVENTURES
Awesome Entertainment: Aug, 1999 ($2.50)
1-Alan Moore-s/ Steve Skroce-a; Youngblood story 3.00

AWESOME HOLIDAY SPECIAL
Awesome Entertainment: Dec, 1997 ($2.50, one-shot)
1-Flip book w/covers of Fighting American & Coven. Holiday stories also featuring Kaboom and Shaft by regular creators. 3.00
1-Gold Edition 5.00

AWFUL OSCAR (Formerly & becomes Oscar Comics with No. 13)
Marvel Comics: No. 11, June, 1949 - No. 12, Aug, 1949
11,12 16 32 48 94 147 200

AW YEAH COMICS: ACTION CAT & ADVENTURE BUG
Dark Horse Graphics: Mar, 2016 - No. 4, Jun, 2016 ($2.99, limited series)
1-4-Art Baltazar & Franco-s/a 3.00

AXA
Eclipse Comics: Apr, 1987 - No. 2, Aug, 1987 ($1.75)
1,2 3.00

AXCEND
Image Comics: Oct, 2015 - Present ($3.50/$3.99)
1-3-Shane Davis-s/a 3.50
4,5-($3.99) 4.00

AXE COP: BAD GUY EARTH
Dark Horse Comics: Mar, 2011 - No. 3, May, 2011 ($3.50, limited series)
1-3-Malachai Nicolle-s/Ethan Nicolle-a 3.50

AXE COP: PRESIDENT OF THE WORLD
Dark Horse Comics: Jul, 2012 - No. 3, Sept, 2012 ($3.50, limited series)
1-3-Malachai Nicolle-s/Ethan Nicolle-a 3.50

AXE COP: THE AMERICAN CHOPPERS
Dark Horse Comics: May, 2014 - No. 3, Jul, 2014 ($3.99, limited series)
1-3-Malachai Nicolle-s/Ethan Nicolle-a. 3-Origin of Axe Cop 4.00

AXEL PRESSBUTTON (Pressbutton No. 5; see Laser Eraser &...)
Eclipse Comics: Nov, 1984 - No. 6, July, 1985 ($1.50/$1.75, Baxter paper)
1-6: Reprints Warrior (British mag.). 1-Bolland-c; origin Laser Eraser & Pressbutton 3.00

AXIS ALPHA
Axis Comics: Feb, 1994 ($2.50, one-shot)
V1-Previews Axis titles including, Tribe, Dethgrip, B.E.A.S.T.I.E.S. & more; Pitt app. in Tribe story. 3.00

AXIS: CARNAGE (Tie-in to Avengers & X-Men Axis series)
Marvel Comics: Dec, 2014 - No. 3, Feb, 2015 ($3.99, limited series)
1-3-Spears-s/Peralta-a; Carnage as a hero; Sin-Eater app. 4.00

AXIS: HOBGOBLIN (Tie-in to Avengers & X-Men Axis series)

Azrael: Agent of the Bat #91 © DC

Aztek: The Ultimate Man #10 © DC

Baby Huey, The Baby Giant #4 © HARV

	GD 2.0	VG 4.0	FN 6.0	VF 8.0	VF/NM 9.0	NM- 9.2
Marvel Comics: Dec, 2014 - No. 3, Feb, 2015 ($3.99, limited series)						
1-3-Shinick-s/Rodriguez-a; Hobgoblin as a hero; Goblin King app.						4.00
AXIS: RESOLUTIONS (Tie-in to Avengers & X-Men Axis series)						
Marvel Comics: Dec, 2014 - No. 4, Feb, 2015 ($3.99, limited series)						
1-4-Two stories per issue; s/a by various. 1-Lashley-a. 4-Chaykin-s/a						4.00
AZRAEL (...Agent of the Bat #47 on)(Also see Batman: Sword of Azrael)						
DC Comics: Feb, 1995 - No. 100, May, 2003 ($1.95/$2.25/$2.50/$2.95)						
1-Dennis O'Neil scripts begin						5.00
2,3						3.50
4-46,48-62: 5,6-Ras Al Ghul app. 13-Nightwing-c/app. 15-Contagion Pt. 5 (Pt. 4 on-c). 16-Contagion Pt. 10. 22-Batman-c/app. 23,27-Batman app. 27,28-Joker app. 35-Hitman app. 36-39-Batman, Bane app. 50-New costume. 53-Joker-c/app. 56,57,60-New Batgirl app.						3.00
47-($3.95) Flip book with Batman: Shadow of the Bat #80						4.00
63-74,76-92: 63-Huntress-c/app.; Azrael returns to old costume. 67-Begin $2.50-c. 70-79-Harris-c. 83-Joker x-over. 91-Bruce Wayne: Fugitive pt. 15						3.00
75-($3.95) New costume; Harris-c						4.00
93-100: 93-Begin $2.95-c. 95,96-Two-Face app. 100-Last issue; Zeck-c						3.00
#1,000,000 (11/98) Giarrano-a						3.00
Annual 1 (1995, $3.95)-Year One story						4.00
Annual 2 (1996, $2.95)-Legends of the Dead Earth story						4.00
Annual 3 (1997, $3.95)-Pulp Heroes story; Orbik-c						4.00
.../Ash (1997, $4.95) O'Neil-s/Quesada, Palmiotti-a						5.00
Plus (12/96, $2.95)-Question-c/app.						4.00
AZRAEL						
DC Comics: Dec, 2009 - No. 18, May, 2011 ($2.99)						
1-18: 1-9-Nicieza-s/Bachs-a. 1-Covers by Jock & Irving. 2,3-Jock-c. 5-Ragman app.						3.00
...: Angel in the Dark TPB (2010, $17.99) r/#1-6; cover gallery						18.00
AZRAEL: DEATH'S DARK KNIGHT						
DC Comics: May, 2009 - No. 3, Jul, 2009 ($2.99, limited series)						
1-Battle For the Cowl tie-in; Nicieza-s/Irving-a/March-c						3.00
TPB (2010, $14.99) r/#1-3, Batman Annual #27 and Detective Annual #11						15.00
AZTEC ACE						
Eclipse Comics: Mar, 1984 - No. 15, Sept, 1985 ($2.25/$1.50/$1.75, Baxter paper)						
1-$2.25-c (52 pgs.)						4.00
2-15: 2-Begin 36 pgs.						3.00
NOTE: ***N. Redondo** a-1i-8i, 10i. c-6-8i.*						
AZTEK: THE ULTIMATE MAN						
DC Comics: Aug, 1996 - No. 10, May 1997 ($1.75)						
1-1st app. Aztek & Synth; Grant Morrison & Mark Millar scripts in all						6.00
2-9: 2-Green Lantern app. 3-1st app. Death-Doll. 4-Intro The Lizard King. 5-Origin. 6-Joker app.; Batman cameo. 7-Batman app. 8-Luthor app. 9-vs. Parasite-c/app.						4.00
10-Joins the JLA; JLA-c/app.	1	2	4	6	8	10
JLA Presents: Aztek the Ultimate Man TPB (2008, $19.99) r/#1-10						20.00
NOTE: ***Breyfogle** c-5p. **N. Steven Harris** a-1-5p. **Porter** c-1p. **Wieringo** c-2p.*						
BABE (...Darling of the Hills, later issues)(See Big Shot and Sparky Watts)						
Prize/Headline/Feature: June-July, 1948 - No. 11, Apr-May, 1950						
1-Boody Rogers-a	47	94	141	296	498	700
2-Boody Rogers-a	26	52	78	154	252	350
3-11-All by Boody Rogers	22	44	66	132	216	300
BABE						
Dark Horse Comics (Legend): July, 1994 - No. 4, Jan, 1994 ($2.50, lim. series)						
1-4: John Byrne-c/a/scripts; ProtoTykes back-up story						3.00
BABE RUTH SPORTS COMICS (Becomes Rags Rabbit #11 on?)						
Harvey Publications: April, 1949 - No. 11, Feb, 1951						
1-Powell-a	40	80	120	246	411	575
2-Powell-a	27	54	81	158	259	360
3-11: Powell-a in most	22	44	66	130	213	295
NOTE: *Baseball c-2-4, 9. Basketball c-1, 6. Football c-5. Yogi Berra c/story-8. Joe DiMaggio c/story-3. Bob Feller c/story-4. Stan Musial c-9.*						
BABES IN TOYLAND (Disney, Movie) (See Golden Pix Story Book ST-3)						
Dell Publishing Co.: No. 1282, Feb-Apr, 1962						
Four Color 1282-Annette Funicello photo-c	12	24	36	83	182	280
BABES OF BROADWAY						
Broadway Comics: May, 1996 ($2.95, one-shot)						
1-Pin-ups of Broadway Comics' female characters; Alan Davis, Michael Kaluta, J. G. Jones, Alan Weiss, Guy Davis & others-a; Giordano-c.						3.00

	GD 2.0	VG 4.0	FN 6.0	VF 8.0	VF/NM 9.0	NM- 9.2
BABE 2						
Dark Horse Comics (Legend): Mar, 1995 - No. 2, May, 1995 ($2.50, lim. series)						
1,2: John Byrne-c/a/scripts						3.00
BABY HUEY						
Harvey Comics: No. 1, Oct, 1991 - No. 9, June, 1994 ($1.00/$1.25/$1.50, quarterly)						
1 ($1.00): 1-Cover says "Big Baby Huey"						5.00
2-9 ($1.25-$1.50)						3.00
BABY HUEY AND PAPA (See Paramount Animated...)						
Harvey Publications: May, 1962 - No. 33, Jan, 1968 (Also see Casper The Friendly Ghost)						
1	13	26	39	86	188	290
2	7	14	21	49	92	135
3-5	5	10	15	33	57	80
6-10	3	6	9	20	31	42
11-20	3	6	9	15	22	28
21-33	2	4	6	13	18	22
BABY HUEY DIGEST						
Harvey Publications: June, 1992 (Digest-size, one-shot)						
1-Reprints	1	3	4	6	8	10
BABY HUEY DUCKLAND						
Harvey Publications: Nov, 1962 - No. 15, Nov, 1966 (25¢ Giants, 68 pgs.)						
1	10	20	30	66	138	210
2-5	5	10	15	34	60	85
6-15	3	6	9	21	33	45
BABY HUEY, THE BABY GIANT (Also see Big Baby Huey, Casper, Harvey Hits #22, Harvey Comics Hits #60, & Paramount Animated Comics)						
Harvey Publ: 9/56 - #97, 10/71; #98, 10/72; #99, 10/80; #100, 10/90; #101, 11/90						
1-Infinity-c	50	100	150	400	900	1400
2	21	42	63	147	324	500
3-Baby Huey takes anti-pep pills	13	26	39	89	195	300
4,5	9	18	27	61	123	185
6-10	6	12	18	40	73	105
11-20	5	10	15	31	53	75
21-40	4	8	12	23	37	50
41-60	3	6	9	16	23	30
61-79 (12/67)	2	4	6	13	18	22
80(12/68) - 95-All 68 pg. Giants	3	6	9	16	24	32
96,97-Both 52 pg. Giants	3	6	9	14	19	24
98-Regular size	2	4	6	9	12	15
99-Regular size	1	2	3	5	6	8
100,101 ($1.00)						4.00
BABYLON 5 (TV)						
DC Comics: Jan, 1995 - No. 11, Dec, 1995 ($1.95/$2.50)						
1	2	4	6	8	11	14
2-5	1	2	3	5	7	9
6-11: 7-Begin $2.50-c	1	2	3	4	5	7
... The Price of Peace (1998, $9.95, TPB) r/#1-4,11						10.00
BABYLON 5: IN VALEN'S NAME						
DC Comics: Mar, 1998 - No. 3, May, 1998 ($2.50, limited series)						
1-3						4.00
BABY SNOOTS (Also see March of Comics #359,371,396,401,419,431,443,450,462,474,485)						
Gold Key: Aug, 1970 - No. 22, Nov, 1975						
1	3	6	9	19	30	40
2-11	2	4	6	11	16	20
12-22: 22-Titled Snoots, the Forgetful Elefink	2	4	6	8	10	12
BACCHUS (Also see Eddie Campbell's ...)						
Harrier Comics (New Wave): 1988 - No. 2, Aug, 1988 ($1.95, B&W)						
1,2: Eddie Campbell-c/a/scripts.						3.00
BACHELOR FATHER (TV)						
Dell Publishing Co.: No. 1332, 4-6/62 - No. 2, Sept.-Nov., 1962						
Four Color 1332 (#1), 2-Written by Stanley	6	12	18	42	79	115
BACHELOR'S DIARY						
Avon Periodicals: 1949 (15¢)						
1(Scarce)-King Features panel cartoons & text-r; pin-up, girl wrestling photos; similar to Sideshow	129	258	387	826	1413	2000
BACKLASH (Also see The Kindred)						
Image Comics (WildStorm Prod.): Nov,1994 - No. 32, May, 1997 ($1.95/$2.50)						

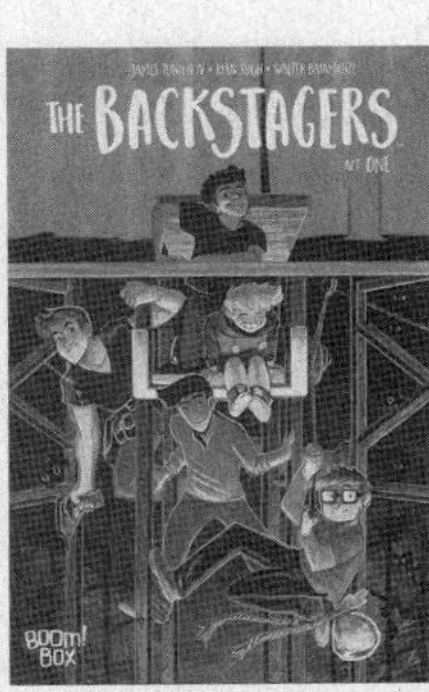

The Backstagers #1 © Sygh & Tynion IV

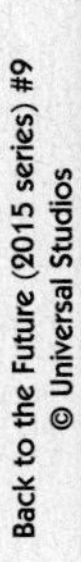
Back to the Future (2015 series) #9 © Universal Studios

Baffling Mysteries #9 © ACE

	GD 2.0	VG 4.0	FN 6.0	VF 8.0	VF/NM 9.0	NM- 9.2

1-Double-c; variant-double-c 4.00
2-24,26-32: 5-Intro Mindscape; 2 pinups. 8-Wildstorm Rising Pt 8 (newsstand & Direct Market versions. 19-Fire From Heaven Pt 2. 20-Fire From Heaven Pt 10. 31-WildC.A.T.S app. 3.00
25-($3.95)-Double-size 4.00
...& Taboo's African Holiday (9/99, $5.95) Booth-s/a(p) 6.00

BACKLASH/SPIDER-MAN
Image Comics (WildStorm Productions): Aug, 1996 - No. 2, Sept, 1996 ($2.50, lim. series)
1,2: Pike (villain from WildC.A.T.S) & Venom app. 3.00

BACKPACK MARVELS (B&W backpack-sized reprint collections)
Marvel Comics: Nov, 2000 ($6.95, B&W, digest-size)
Avengers 1 -r/Avengers #181-189; profile pages 7.00
Spider-Man 1-r/ASM #234-240 7.00
X-Men 1-r/Uncanny X-Men #167-173 7.00
X-Men 2-r/Uncanny X-Men #174-179; new painted-c by Greg Horn 7.00

BACKSTAGERS, THE
Boom Entertainment (BOOM! Box): Aug, 2016 - No. 8 ($3.99)
1-7: 1-James Tynion IV-s/Rian Sygh-a/Veronica Fish-c 4.00

BACK TO THE FUTURE (Movie, TV cartoon)
Harvey Comics: Nov, 1991 - No. 4, June, 1992 ($1.25)
1-4: 1,2-Gil Kane-c; based on animated cartoon 3.00

BACK TO THE FUTURE (Movie, TV cartoon)
IDW Publishing: Oct, 2015 - Present ($3.99)
1-Story by Bob Gale; multiple covers; Doc & Marty's first meeting 6.00
2-17-Multiple covers. 3-Archie variant-c 4.00

BACK TO THE FUTURE: BIFF TO THE FUTURE
IDW Publishing: Jan, 2017 - Present ($3.99, limited series)
1-Biff's rise to power with the sports almanac; Gale & Fridolfs-s/Alan Robinson-a 4.00

BACK TO THE FUTURE: CITIZEN BROWN (Based on the Telltale Games video game)
IDW Publishing: May, 2016 - No. 5, Sept, 2016 ($4.99, limited series)
1-5-Erik Burnham-s/Alan Robinson-a; multiple covers on all 5.00

BACK TO THE FUTURE: FORWARD TO THE FUTURE
Harvey Comics: Oct, 1992 - No. 3, Feb, 1993 ($1.50, limited series)
1-3 3.00

BAD ASS
Dynamite Entertainment: 2014 - No. 4. 2014 ($3.99)
1-4-Hanna-s/Bessadi-a 4.00

BAD BLOOD
Dark Horse Comics: Jan, 2014 - No. 5, May, 2014 ($3.99, limited series)
1-5-Vampire story; Jonathan Maberry-s/Tyler Crook-a 4.00

BAD BOY
Oni Press: Dec, 1997 ($4.95, one-shot)
1-Frank Miller-s/Simon Bisley-a/painted-c 5.00

BAD COMPANY
Quality Comics/Fleetway Quality #15 on: Aug, 1988 - No. 19?, 1990 ($1.50/$1.75, high quality paper)
1-19: 5,6-Guice-c 3.00

BADGE OF JUSTICE (Formerly Crime And Justice #21)
Charlton Comics: No. 22, Jan, 1955; No. 2, Apr, 1955 - No. 4, Oct, 1955

	GD	VG	FN	VF	VF/NM	NM-
22(#1)-Giordano-c	10	20	30	58	79	100
2-4	7	14	21	35	43	50

BADGER, THE
Capital Comics(#1-4)/First Comics: Dec, 1983 - No. 70, Apr, 1991; V2#1, Spring, 1991
1 5.00
2-49,51-70: 52-54-Tim Vigil-c/a 3.00
50-($3.95, 52 pgs.) 4.00
V2#1 (Spring, 1991, $4.95) 5.00

BADGER, THE
Image Comics: V3#78, May, 1997 - V3#88 ($2.95, B&W)
78-Cover lists #1, Baron-s 3.00
79/#2, 80/#3, 81(indicia lists #80)/#4,82-88/#5-11 3.00

BADGER, THE
Devil's Due/1First Comics: 2016 - Present ($3.99)
1-5: 1-Mike Baron-s/Jim Fern-a/Val Mayerik-c; origin story. 2-5-Putin app. 4.00

BADGER GOES BERSERK
First Comics: Sept, 1989 - No. 4, Dec, 1989 ($1.95, lim. series, Baxter paper)
1-4: 2-Paul Chadwick-c/a(2pgs.) 3.00

BADGER: SHATTERED MIRROR
Dark Horse Comics: July, 1994 - No. Oct, 1994 ($2.50, limited series)
1-4 3.00

BADGER: ZEN POP FUNNY-ANIMAL VERSION
Dark Horse Comics: July, 1994 - No. 2, Aug, 1994 ($2.50, limited series)
1,2 3.00

BAD GIRLS
DC Comics: Oct, 2003 - No. 5, Feb, 2004 ($2.50, limited series)
1-5-Steve Vance-s/Jennifer Graves-a/Darwyn Cooke-c 3.00
TPB (2009, $14.99) r/#1-5; Graves sketch pages 15.00

BAD IDEAS
Image Comics: Apr, 2004 - No. 2, July, 2004 ($5.95, B&W, limited series)
1,2-Chinsang-s/Mahfood & Crosland-a 6.00
..., Vol. 1: Collected! (2005, $12.99) r/#1,2 13.00

BAD KITTY ONE SHOT (CHAOS!...)
Dynamite Entertainment: 2014 ($5.99)
1-Spence-s/Rafael-a/c; origin 6.00

BADLANDS
Vortex Comics: May, 1990 ($3.00, glossy stock, mature)
1-Chaykin-c 3.00

BADLANDS
Dark Horse Comics: July, 1991 - No. 6, Dec, 1991 ($2.25, B&W, limited series)
1-6: 1-John F. Kennedy-c; reprints Vortex Comics issue 3.00

BADMEN OF THE WEST
Avon Periodicals: 1951 (Giant) (132 pgs., painted-c)

	GD	VG	FN	VF	VF/NM	NM-
1-Contains rebound copies of Jesse James, King of the Bad Men of Deadwood, Badmen of Tombstone; other combinations possible. Issues with Kubert-a...	43	86	129	271	461	650

BADMEN OF THE WEST! (See A-1 Comics)
Magazine Enterprises: 1953 - No. 3, 1954

	GD	VG	FN	VF	VF/NM	NM-
1 (A-1 100)-Meskin-a?	22	44	66	132	216	300
2 (A-1 120), 3: 2-Larsen-a	15	30	45	85	130	175

BADMEN OF TOMBSTONE
Avon Periodicals: 1950

	GD	VG	FN	VF	VF/NM	NM-
nn	19	38	57	111	176	240

BAD PLANET
Image Comics (Raw Studios): Dec, 2005 - No. 6, Nov, 2008 ($2.99)
1-6: 1-Thomas Jane & Steve Niles-s/Larosa & Bradstreet-a/c. 2-Wrightson-c. 3-3-D pages 3.00

BADROCK (Also see Youngblood)
Image Comics (Extreme Studios): Mar, 1995 - No. 2, Jan, 1996 ($1.75/$2.50)
1-Variant-c (3) 3.50
2-Liefeld-c/a & story; Savage Dragon app, flipbook w/Grifter/Badrock #2; variant-c exist 3.00
Annual 1(1995,$2.95)-Arthur Adams-c 4.00
Annual 1 Commemorative ($9.95)-3,000 printed 10.00
.../Wolverine (6/96, $4.95, squarebound)-Sauron app; pin-ups; variant-c exists 5.00
.../Wolverine (6/96)-Special Comicon Edition 5.00

BADROCK AND COMPANY (Also see Youngblood)
Image Comics (Extreme Studios): Sept, 1994 - No.6, Feb, 1995 ($2.50)
1-6 : 6-Indicia reads "October 1994"; story cont'd in Shadowhawk #17 3.00

BAFFLING MYSTERIES (Formerly Indian Braves No. 1-4; Heroes of the Wild Frontier No. 26-on)
Periodical House (Ace Magazines): No. 5, Nov, 1951 - No. 26, Oct, 1955

	GD	VG	FN	VF	VF/NM	NM-
5	47	94	141	296	498	700
6-19,21-24: 8-Woodish-a by Cameron. 10-E.C. Crypt Keeper swipe on-c. 24-Last pre-code issue	34	68	102	199	325	450
20-Classic bondage-c	41	82	123	256	428	600
25-Reprints; surrealistic-c	24	48	72	142	234	325
26-Reprints	22	44	66	132	216	300

*NOTE: **Cameron** a-8, 10, 16-18, 20-22. **Colan** a-5, 11, 25r/5. **Sekowsky** a-5, 6, 22. Bondage c-20, 23. Reprints in 18(1), 19(1), 24(3).*

BAKER STREET PECULIARS, THE
Boom Entertainment (kaboom!): Mar, 2016 - No. 4, Jun, 2016 ($3.99, limited series)

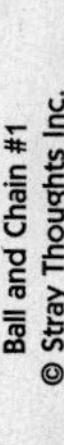
Ball and Chain #1 © Stray Thoughts Inc.

Baltimore: Empty Graves #3 © Mignola & Golden

Barbie #9 © Mattel

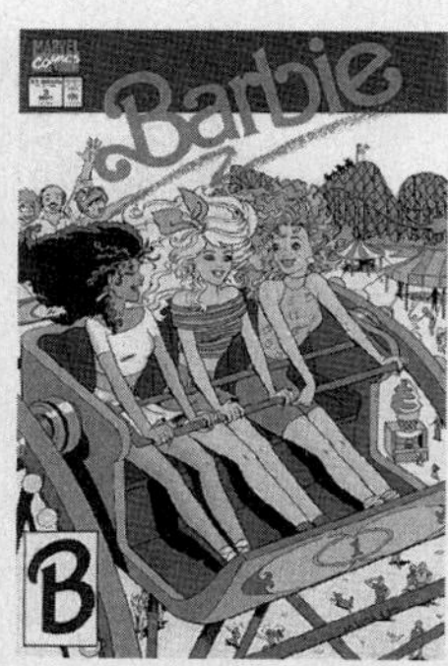

GD 2.0 | VG 4.0 | FN 6.0 | VF 8.0 | VF/NM 9.0 | NM- 9.2

1-4-Roger Langridge-s/Andy Hirsch-a 4.00

BALBO (See Master Comics #33 & Mighty Midget Comics)

BALDER THE BRAVE
Marvel Comics Group: Nov, 1985 - No. 4, 1986 (Limited series)
1-4: Simonson-c/a; character from Thor 4.00

BALLAD OF HALO JONES, THE
Quality Comics: Sept, 1987 - No. 12, Aug, 1988 ($1.25/$1.50)
1-12: Alan Moore scripts in all 3.00

BALL AND CHAIN
DC Comics (Homage): Nov, 1999 - No. 4, Feb, 2000 ($2.50, limited series)
1-4-Lobdell-s/Garza-a 3.00

BALLISTIC (Also See Cyberforce)
Image Comics (Top Cow Productions): Sept, 1995 - No. 3, Dec, 1995 ($2.50, limited series)
1-3: Wetworks app, Turner-c/a 3.00
... Action (5/96, $2.95) Pin-ups of Top Cow characters participating in outdoor sports 3.00
... Imagery (1/96, $2.50, anthology) Cyberforce app. 3.00
.../ Wolverine (2/97, $2.95) Devil's Reign pt. 4; Witchblade cameo (1 page) 4.00

BALOO & LITTLE BRITCHES (Disney)
Gold Key: Apr, 1968
1-From the Jungle Book 4 8 12 23 37 50

BALTIMORE: ... (One-shots)
Dark Horse Comics: ($3.50)
... The Inquisitor (6/13) Mignola & Golden-s; Stenbeck-a/c 3.50
... The Play (11/12) Mignola & Golden-s; Stenbeck-a/c 3.50
... The Widow and the Tank (2/13) Mignola & Golden-s; Stenbeck-a/c 3.50

BALTIMORE: CHAPEL OF BONES
Dark Horse Comics: Jan, 2014 - No. 2, Feb, 2014 ($3.50, limited series)
1,2-Mignola & Golden-s; Stenbeck-a/c 3.50

BALTIMORE: EMPTY GRAVES
Dark Horse Comics: Apr, 2016 - No. 5, Aug, 2016 ($3.99, limited series)
1-5-Mignola & Golden-s; Bergting-a; Stenbeck-c 4.00

BALTIMORE: DR. LESKOVAR'S REMEDY
Dark Horse Comics: Jun, 2012 - No. 2, Jul, 2012 ($3.50, limited series)
1,2-Mignola & Golden-s; Stenbeck-a/c 3.50

BALTIMORE: THE CULT OF THE RED KING
Dark Horse Comics: May, 2015 - No. 5, Sept, 2015 ($3.99, limited series)
1-5-Mignola & Golden-s; Bergting-a; Stenbeck-c 4.00

BALTIMORE: THE CURSE BELLS
Dark Horse Comics: Aug, 2011 - No. 5, Dec, 2011 ($3.50, limited series)
1-5-Mignola-s/c; Stenbeck-a. 1-Variant-c by Francavilla 3.50

BALTIMORE: THE INFERNAL TRAIN
Dark Horse Comics: Sept, 2013 - No. 3, Nov, 2013 ($3.50, limited series)
1-3-Mignola & Golden-s; Stenbeck-a/c 3.50

BALTIMORE: THE PLAGUE SHIPS
Dark Horse Comics: Aug, 2010 - No. 5, Dec, 2010 ($3.50, limited series)
1-5-Mignola-s/c; Stenbeck-a; Lord Baltimore hunting vampires in 1916 Europe 3.50

BALTIMORE: THE RED KINGDOM
Dark Horse Comics: Feb, 2017 - No. 5 ($3.99, limited series)
1,2-Mignola & Golden-s; Bergting-a; Stenbeck-c 4.00

BALTIMORE: THE WITCH OF HARJU
Dark Horse Comics: Jul, 2014 - No. 3, Sept, 2014 ($3.50, limited series)
1-3-Mignola & Golden-s; Bergting-a; Stenbeck-c 3.50

BALTIMORE: THE WOLF AND THE APOSTLE
Dark Horse Comics: Oct, 2014 - No. 2, Nov, 2014 ($3.50, limited series)
1,2-Mignola & Golden-s; Stenbeck-a/c 3.50

BAMBI (Disney) (See Movie Classics, Movie Comics, and Walt Disney Showcase No. 31)
Dell Publishing Co.: No. 12, 1942; No. 30, 1943; No. 186, Apr, 1948; 1984
Four Color 12-Walt Disney's... 46 92 138 340 770 1200
Four Color 30-Bambi's Children (1943) 40 80 120 296 673 1050
Four Color 186-Walt Disney's...; reprinted as Movie Classic Bambi #3 (1956)
14 28 42 96 211 325
1-(Whitman, 1984; 60¢)-r/Four Color #186 (3-pack) 2 4 6 10 14 18

GD 2.0 | VG 4.0 | FN 6.0 | VF 8.0 | VF/NM 9.0 | NM- 9.2

BAMBI (Disney)
Grosset & Dunlap: 1942 (50¢, 7"x8-1/2", 32pg, hard-c w/dust jacket)
nn-Given away w/a copy of Thumper for a $2.00, 2-yr. subscription to WDC&S in 1942 (Xmas offer). Book only 22 44 66 132 216 300
w/dust jacket 39 78 117 240 395 550

BAMM BAMM & PEBBLES FLINTSTONE (TV)
Gold Key: Oct, 1964 (Hanna-Barbera)
1 8 16 24 51 96 140

BANANA SPLITS, THE (TV) (See Golden Comics Digest & March of Comics No. 364)
Gold Key: June, 1969 - No. 8, Oct, 1971 (Hanna-Barbera)
1-Photo-c on all 8 16 24 56 108 160
2-8 5 10 15 34 60 85

BANANA SUNDAY
Oni Press: July, 2005 - No. 4, Oct, 2005 ($2.99, B&W, limited series)
1-4-Root Nibot-s/Colleen Coover-a 3.00
TPB (3/06, $11.95) r/#1-4; sketch gallery 12.00

BAND WAGON (See Hanna-Barbera Band Wagon)

BANG! TANGO
DC Comics (Vertigo): Apr, 2009 - No. 6, Sept, 2009 ($2.99, limited series)
1-6-Kelly-s/Sibar-a/Chaykin-c 3.00

BANG-UP COMICS
Progressive Publishers: Dec, 1941 - No. 3, June, 1942
1-Nazi WWII-c; Cosmo Mann & Lady Fairplay begin; Buzz Balmer by Rick Yager in all (origin #1) 116 232 348 742 1271 1800
2-Nazi zeppelin WWII-c 68 136 204 435 743 1050
3-Japanese WWII-c 61 122 183 390 670 950

BANISHED KNIGHTS (See Warlands)
Image Comics: Dec, 2001 - No. 4, June, 2002 ($2.95)
1-4-Two covers (Alvin Lee, Pat Lee) 3.00

BANNER COMICS (Becomes Captain Courageous No. 6)
Ace Magazines: No. 3, Sept, 1941 - No. 5, Jan, 1942
3-Captain Courageous (1st app.) & Lone Warrior & Sidekick Dicky begin; Nazi WWII-c by Jim Mooney 206 412 618 1318 2259 3200
4,5: 4-Flag-c 142 284 426 909 1555 2200

BARACK OBAMA (See Presidential Material: Barack Obama, Amazing Spider-Man #583, Savage Dragon #137)

BARACK THE BARBARIAN
Devil's Due Publishing: Jun, 2009 - No. 4, Oct, 2009 ($3.50/$3.99, limited series)
...Quest For The Treasure of Stimuli 1-3-($3.50) Conan spoof with Barack Obama; Hama-s 3.50
...Quest For The Treasure of Stimuli 4-($3.99) 4.00
...: The Red of Red Sarah 1 ($5.99, B&W) Sarah Palin satire; Hama-s 6.00

BARBARIANS, THE
Atlas Comics/Seaboard Periodicals: June, 1975
1-Origin, only app. Andrax; Iron Jaw app.; Marcos-a 2 4 6 13 18 22

BARBIE
Marvel Comics: Jan, 1991 - No. 63, Mar, 1996 ($1.00/$1.25/$1.50)
1-Polybagged w/doorknob hanger; Romita-c 2 4 6 9 12 15
2-49,51-62 1 2 3 5 7 9
50,63: 50-(Giant). 63-Last issue 2 4 6 8 10 12
... And Baby Sister Kelly (1995, 99¢-c, part of a Marvel 4-pack) scarce
3 6 9 14 20 25

BARBIE & KEN
Dell Publishing Co.: May-July, 1962 - No. 5, Nov-Jan, 1963-64
01-053-207(#1)-Based on Mattel toy dolls 36 72 108 259 580 900
2-4 26 52 78 182 404 625
5 (Last issue) 27 54 81 189 420 650

BARBIE FASHION
Marvel Comics: Jan, 1991 - No. 53, May, 1995 ($1.00/$1.25/$1.50)
1-Polybagged w/Barbie Pink Card 2 4 6 9 12 15
2-49,51,52: 4-Contains preview to Sweet XVI 1 2 3 5 7 9
50,53: 50-(Giant). 53-Last issue 2 4 6 8 10 12

BARB WIRE (See Comics' Greatest World)
Dark Horse Comics: Apr, 1994 - No. 9, Feb, 1995 ($2.00/$2.50)
1-9: 1-Foil logo 3.00
Trade paperback (1996, $8.95)-r/#2,3,5,6 w/Pamela Anderson bio 9.00

BARB WIRE (Volume 2)

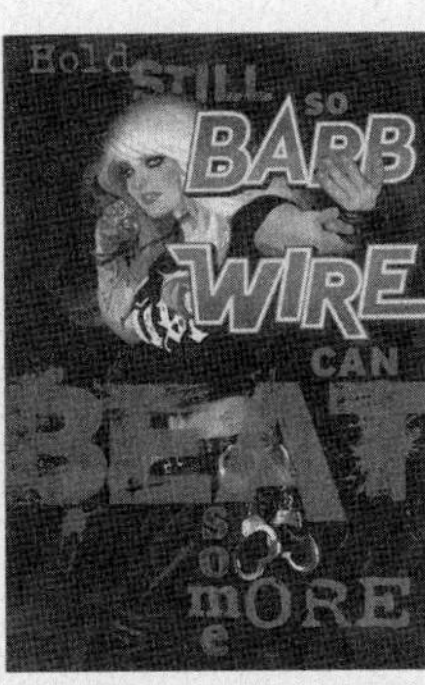

Barb Wire (2015 series) #6 © DH

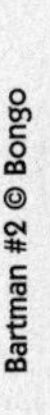

Bartman #2 © Bongo

Baseball's Greatest Heroes #2 © MC

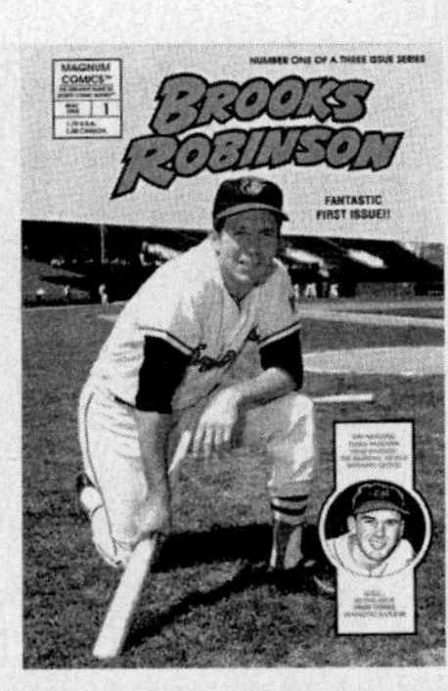

	GD 2.0	VG 4.0	FN 6.0	VF 8.0	VF/NM 9.0	NM- 9.2

Dark Horse Comics: Jul, 2015 - No. 8, Feb, 2016 ($3.99)

Issue	GD 2.0	VG 4.0	FN 6.0	VF 8.0	VF/NM 9.0	NM- 9.2
1-8-Adam Hughes-c on all. 1-Warner-s/Olliffe-a; two covers by Hughes						4.00

BARB WIRE: ACE OF SPADES
Dark Horse Comics: May, 1996 - No. 4, Sept, 1996 ($2.95, limited series)

Issue	GD 2.0	VG 4.0	FN 6.0	VF 8.0	VF/NM 9.0	NM- 9.2
1-4: Chris Warner-c/a(p)/scripts; Tim Bradstreet-c/a(i) in all						3.00

BARB WIRE COMICS MAGAZINE SPECIAL
Dark Horse Comics: May, 1996 ($3.50, B&W, magazine, one-shot)

Issue	GD 2.0	VG 4.0	FN 6.0	VF 8.0	VF/NM 9.0	NM- 9.2
nn-Adaptation of film; photo-c; poster insert.						3.50

BARB WIRE MOVIE SPECIAL
Dark Horse Comics: May, 1996 ($3.95, one-shot)

Issue	GD 2.0	VG 4.0	FN 6.0	VF 8.0	VF/NM 9.0	NM- 9.2
nn-Adaptation of film; photo-c; 1st app. new look						4.00

BARKER, THE (Also see National Comics #42)
Quality Comics Group/Comic Magazine: Autumn, 1946 - No. 15, Dec, 1949

Issue	GD 2.0	VG 4.0	FN 6.0	VF 8.0	VF/NM 9.0	NM- 9.2
1	27	54	81	158	259	360
2	15	30	45	86	133	180
3-10	13	26	39	72	101	130
11-14	10	20	30	54	72	90
15-Jack Cole-a(p)	10	20	30	56	76	95

NOTE: *Jack Cole* art in some issues.

BARNABY
Civil Service Publications Inc.: 1945 (25¢,102 pgs., digest size)

Issue	GD 2.0	VG 4.0	FN 6.0	VF 8.0	VF/NM 9.0	NM- 9.2
V1#1-r/Crocket Johnson strips from 1942	5	10	14	20	24	28

BARNEY AND BETTY RUBBLE (TV) (Flintstones' Neighbors)
Charlton Comics: Jan, 1973 - No. 23, Dec, 1976 (Hanna-Barbera)

Issue	GD 2.0	VG 4.0	FN 6.0	VF 8.0	VF/NM 9.0	NM- 9.2
1	4	8	12	23	37	50
2-11: 11(2/75)-1st Mike Zeck-a (illos)	3	6	9	14	20	25
12-23: 17-Columbo parody	2	4	6	10	14	18
Digest Annual (1972, B&W, 100 pgs.) (scarce)	4	8	12	25	40	55

BARNEY BAXTER (Also see Magic Comics)
David McKay/Dell Publishing Co./Argo: 1938 - No. 2, 1956

Issue	GD 2.0	VG 4.0	FN 6.0	VF 8.0	VF/NM 9.0	NM- 9.2
Feature Books 15(McKay-1938)	42	84	126	268	452	635
Four Color 20(1942)	24	48	72	170	378	585
1,2 (1956-Argo)	9	18	27	50	65	80

BARNEY BEAR ...
Spire Christian Comics (Fleming H. Revell Co.): 1977-1982

Issue	GD 2.0	VG 4.0	FN 6.0	VF 8.0	VF/NM 9.0	NM- 9.2
...Home Plate nn-(1979, 49¢), ...In Toyland nn-(1982, 49¢),...Lost and Found nn-(1979, 49¢), Out of The Woods nn-(1980, 49¢), Sunday School Picnic nn-(1981, 69¢), The Swamp Gang!-(1977, 39¢)	2	4	6	9	13	16

BARNEY GOOGLE & SNUFFY SMITH
Dell Publishing Co./Gold Key: 1942 - 1943; April, 1964

Issue	GD 2.0	VG 4.0	FN 6.0	VF 8.0	VF/NM 9.0	NM- 9.2
Four Color 19(1942)	52	104	156	323	549	775
Four Color 40(1944)	20	40	60	135	300	465
Large Feature Comic 11(1943)	39	78	117	240	395	550
1(10113-404)-Gold Key (4/64)	4	8	12	25	40	55

BARNEY GOOGLE & SNUFFY SMITH
Toby Press: June, 1951 - No. 4, Feb, 1952 (Reprints)

Issue	GD 2.0	VG 4.0	FN 6.0	VF 8.0	VF/NM 9.0	NM- 9.2
1	14	28	42	80	115	150
2,3	9	18	27	47	61	75
4-Kurtzman-a "Pot Shot Pete", 5 pgs.; reprints John Wayne #5	12	24	36	69	97	125

BARNEY GOOGLE AND SNUFFY SMITH
Charlton Comics: Mar, 1970 - No. 6, Jan, 1971

Issue	GD 2.0	VG 4.0	FN 6.0	VF 8.0	VF/NM 9.0	NM- 9.2
1	3	6	9	16	24	32
2-6	2	4	6	11	16	20

BARNUM!
DC Comics (Vertigo): 2003; 2005 ($29.95, $19.95)

Issue	GD 2.0	VG 4.0	FN 6.0	VF 8.0	VF/NM 9.0	NM- 9.2
Hardcover (2003, $29.95, with dust jacket)-Chaykin & Tischman-s/Henrichon-a						30.00
Softcover (2005, $19.95)-Chaykin & Tischman-s/Henrichon-a						20.00

BARNYARD COMICS (Dizzy Duck No. 32 on)
Nedor/Polo Mag./Standard(Animated Cartoons): June, 1944 - No. 31, Sept, 1950; No. 10, 1957

Issue	GD 2.0	VG 4.0	FN 6.0	VF 8.0	VF/NM 9.0	NM- 9.2
1 (nn, 52 pgs.)-Funny animal	25	50	75	150	245	340
2 (52 pgs.)	15	30	45	84	127	170
3-5	11	22	33	64	90	115
6-12,16	10	20	30	58	79	100
13-15,17,21,23,26,27,29-All contain Frazetta text illos	11	22	33	64	90	115
18-20,22,24,25-All contain Frazetta-a & text illos	14	28	42	80	115	150
28,30,31	9	18	27	52	69	85
10 (1957)(Exist?)	4	7	10	14	17	20

BARRY M. GOLDWATER
Dell Publishing Co.: Mar, 1965 (Complete life story)

Issue	GD 2.0	VG 4.0	FN 6.0	VF 8.0	VF/NM 9.0	NM- 9.2
12-055-503-Photo-c	4	8	12	23	37	50

BARRY WINDSOR-SMITH: STORYTELLER
Dark Horse Comics: Oct, 1996 - No. 9, July, 1997 ($4.95, oversize)

Issue	GD 2.0	VG 4.0	FN 6.0	VF 8.0	VF/NM 9.0	NM- 9.2
1-9: 1-Intro Young Gods, Paradox Man & the Freebooters; Barry Smith-c/a/scripts						5.00
Preview						4.00

BAR SINISTER (Also see Shaman's Tears)
Acclaim Comics (Windjammer): Jun, 1995 - No. 4, Sept, 1995 ($2.50, lim. series)

Issue	GD 2.0	VG 4.0	FN 6.0	VF 8.0	VF/NM 9.0	NM- 9.2
1-4: Mike Grell-c/a/scripts						3.00

BARTMAN (Also see Simpsons Comics & Radioactive Man)
Bongo Comics: 1993 - No. 6, 1994 ($1.95/$2.25)

Issue	GD 2.0	VG 4.0	FN 6.0	VF 8.0	VF/NM 9.0	NM- 9.2
1-($2.95)-Foil-c; bound-in jumbo Bartman poster						6.00
2-6: 3-w/trading card						4.00

BART SIMPSON (See Simpsons Comics Presents Bart Simpson)

BASEBALL COMICS
Will Eisner Productions: Spring, 1949 (Reprinted later as a Spirit section)

Issue	GD 2.0	VG 4.0	FN 6.0	VF 8.0	VF/NM 9.0	NM- 9.2
1-Will Eisner-c/a	70	140	210	445	765	1085

BASEBALL COMICS
Kitchen Sink Press: 1991 ($3.95, coated stock)

Issue	GD 2.0	VG 4.0	FN 6.0	VF 8.0	VF/NM 9.0	NM- 9.2
1-r/1949 ish. by Eisner; contains trading cards						6.00

BASEBALL HEROES
Fawcett Publications: 1952 (one-shot)

Issue	GD 2.0	VG 4.0	FN 6.0	VF 8.0	VF/NM 9.0	NM- 9.2
nn (Scarce)-Babe Ruth photo-c; baseball's Hall of Fame biographies	86	172	258	546	936	1325

BASEBALL'S GREATEST HEROES
Magnum Comics: Dec, 1991 - No. 2, May, 1992 ($1.75)

Issue	GD 2.0	VG 4.0	FN 6.0	VF 8.0	VF/NM 9.0	NM- 9.2
1-Mickey Mantle #1; photo-c; Sinnott-a(p)						5.00
2-Brooks Robinson #1; photo-c; Sinnott-a(i)						4.00

BASEBALL THRILLS
Ziff-Davis Publ. Co.: No. 10, Sum, 1951 - No. 3, Sum, 1952 (Saunders painted-c No.1,2)

Issue	GD 2.0	VG 4.0	FN 6.0	VF 8.0	VF/NM 9.0	NM- 9.2
10(#1)-Bob Feller, Musial, Newcombe & Boudreau stories	44	88	132	277	469	660
2-Powell-a(2)(Late Sum, '51); Feller, Berra & Mathewson stories	32	64	96	188	307	425
3-Kinstler-c/a; Joe DiMaggio story	32	64	96	188	307	425

BASEBALL THRILLS 3-D
The 3-D Zone: May, 1990 ($2.95, w/glasses)

Issue	GD 2.0	VG 4.0	FN 6.0	VF 8.0	VF/NM 9.0	NM- 9.2
1-New L.B. Cole-c; life stories of Ty Cobb & Ted Williams						6.00

BASICALLY STRANGE (Magazine)
John C. Comics (Archie Comics Group): Dec, 1982 ($1.95, B&W)

Issue	GD 2.0	VG 4.0	FN 6.0	VF 8.0	VF/NM 9.0	NM- 9.2
1-(21,000 printed; all but 1,000 destroyed; pgs. out of sequence)	3	6	9	16	23	30
1-Wood, Toth-a; Corben-c; reprints & new art	2	4	6	13	18	22

BASIC HISTORY OF AMERICA ILLUSTRATED
Pendulum Press: 1976 (B&W) (Soft-c $1.50; Hard-c $4.50)

07-1999-America Becomes a World Power 1890-1920. 07-2251-The Industrial Era 1865-1915. 07-226x-Before the Civil War 1830-1860. 07-2278-Americans Move Westward 1800-1850. 07-2286-The Civil War 1850-1876; Redondo-a. 07-2294-The Fight for Freedom 1750-1783. 07-2308-The New World 1500-1750. 07-2316-Problems of the New Nation 1800-1830. 07-2324-Roaring Twenties and the Great Depression 1920-1940. 07-2332-The United States Emerges 1783-1800. 07-2340-America Today 1945-1976. 07-2359-World War II 1940-1945

Issue	GD 2.0	VG 4.0	FN 6.0	VF 8.0	VF/NM 9.0	NM- 9.2
Softcover editions each	1	2	3	4	5	7
Hardcover editions each						14.00

BASIL (...the Royal Cat)
St. John Publishing Co.: Jan, 1953 - No. 4, Sept, 1953

Issue	GD 2.0	VG 4.0	FN 6.0	VF 8.0	VF/NM 9.0	NM- 9.2
1-Funny animal	9	18	27	47	61	75
2-4	6	12	18	28	34	40
I.W. Reprint 1	2	4	6	9	12	15

BASIL WOLVERTON'S FANTASTIC FABLES
Dark Horse Comics: Oct, 1993 - No. 2, Dec, 1993 ($2.50, B&W, limited series)

Issue	GD 2.0	VG 4.0	FN 6.0	VF 8.0	VF/NM 9.0	NM- 9.2
1,2-Wolverton-c/a(r)						6.00

Batgirl #41 © DC

Batgirl (2016 series) #1 © DC

Batman #6 © DC

GD VG FN VF VF/NM NM-
2.0 4.0 6.0 8.0 9.0 9.2

BASIL WOLVERTON'S GATEWAY TO HORROR
Dark Horse Comics: June, 1988 ($1.75, B&W, one-shot)
1-Wolverton-r 6.00

BASIL WOLVERTON'S PLANET OF TERROR
Dark Horse Comics: Oct, 1987 ($1.75, B&W, one-shot)
1-Wolverton-r; Alan Moore-c 6.00

BASTARD SAMURAI
Image Comics: Apr, 2002 - No. 3, Aug, 2002 ($2.95)
1-3-Oeming & Gunter-s; Shannon-a/Oeming-i 3.00
TPB (2003, $12.95) r/#1-3; plus sketch pages and pin-ups 13.00

BATGIRL (See Batman: No Man's Land stories)
DC Comics: Apr, 2000 - No. 73, Apr, 2006 ($2.50)
1-Scott & Campanella-a 6.00
1-(2nd printing) 3.00
2-10: 8-Lady Shiva app. 4.50
11-24: 12-"Officer Down" x-over. 15-Joker-c/app. 24-Bruce Wayne: Murderer pt. 2. 4.00
25-($3.25) Batgirl vs Lady Shiva 4.50
26-29: 27- Bruce Wayne: Fugitive pt. 5; Noto-a. 29-B.W.:F. pt. 13 3.50
30-49,51-73: 30-32-Connor Hawke app. 39-Intro. Black Wind. 41-Superboy-c/app. 53-Robin (Spoiler) app. 54-Bagged with Sky Captain CD. 55-57-War Games. 63,64-Deathstroke app. 67-Birds of Prey app. 70-1st app. Lazara (Nora Fries). 73-Lady Shiva origin; Sale-c 3.00
50-($3.25) Batgirl vs Batman 4.00
Annual 1 ('00, $3.50) Planet DC; intro. Aruna 5.00
...: A Knight Alone (2001, $12.95, TPB) r/#7-11,13,14 13.00
...: Death Wish (2003, $14.95, TPB) r/#17-20,22,23,25 & Secret Files and Origins #1 15.00
...: Destruction's Daughter (2006, $19.99, TPB) r/#65-73 20.00
...: Fists of Fury (2004, $14.95, TPB) r/#15,16,21,26-28 15.00
...: Kicking Assassins (2005, $14.99, TPB) r/#60-64 15.00
... Secret Files and Origins (8/02, $4.95) origin-s Noto-a; profile pages and pin-ups 5.00
...: Silent Running (2001, $12.95, TPB) r/#1-6 13.00

BATGIRL (Cassandra Cain)
DC Comics: Sept, 2008 - No. 6, Feb, 2009 ($2.99)
1-6-Beechen-s/Calafiore-a 3.00

BATGIRL (Spoiler/Stephanie Brown)(Batman: Reborn)
DC Comics: Oct, 2009 - No. 24, Oct, 2011 ($2.99)
1-24: 1-7-Garbett-a/Noto-c. 3-New costume. 8-Caldwell-a. 9-14-Lau-c. 14-Supergirl app. 3.00
1-Variant-c by Hamner 5.00
...: Batgirl Rising TPB (2010, $17.99) r/#1-7 20.00
...: The Flood TPB (2011, $14.99) r/#9-14 15.00

BATGIRL (Barbara Gordon)(DC New 52)(See Secret Origins #10)
DC Comics: Nov, 2011 - No. 52, Jul, 2016 ($2.99)
1-Barbara Gordon back in costume; Simone-s/Syaf-a/Hughes-c 6.00
1-Second & Third printings 3.00
2-12: 2-6-Hughes-c. 3-Nightwing app. 7-12-Syaf-c. 9-Night of the Owls. 12-Batwoman app. 3.00
13-Die-cut cover; Death of the Family tie-in; Batwoman app. 10.00
13-24: 14-16-Death of the Family tie-in; Joker app. 20,21-Intro. The Ventriloquist 3.00
25-($3.99) Zero Year tie-in; Bennett-s/Pasarin-a 4.00
26-34: 27-Gothtopia tie-in. 28,29-Strix app. 31-34-Simone-s. 31-Ragdoll app. 3.00
35-49,51,52: 35-New costume; Tarr-a/Stewart-c. 37-Dagger Type app. 41,42-Batman (Gordon) & Livewire app. 45-Dick Grayson app. 48,49-Black Canary app. 3.00
50-($4.99) Black Canary, Spoiler & Bluebird app.; Tarr-a 5.00
#0 (11/12, $2.99) Batgirl origin updated; Simone-s/Benes-a 3.00
Annual 1 (12/12, $4.99) Catwoman and the Talons app.; Simone-s/Wijaya-a/Benes-c 5.00
Annual 2 (6/14, $4.99) Poison Ivy app.; Simone-s/Gill-a/Benes-c 5.00
Annual 3 (9/15, $4.99) Dick Grayson, Spoiler & Batwoman app. 5.00
...: Endgame 1 (5/15, $2.99) Tie-in with other Endgame stories in Batman titles 3.00
...: Futures End 1 (11/14, $2.99, regular-c) Five years later; Bane app.; Simone-s 3.00
...: Futures End 1 (11/14, $3.99, 3-D cover) 4.00

BATGIRL (DC Rebirth)
DC Comics: Sept, 2016 - Present ($2.99)
1-8: 1-Hope Larson-s/Rafael Albuquerque-a. 6-Poison Ivy app. 3.00

BATGIRL ADVENTURES (See Batman Adventures, The)
DC Comics: Feb, 1998 ($2.95, one-shot) (Based on animated series)
1-Harley Quinn and Poison Ivy app.; Timm-c 3 6 9 21 33 45

BATGIRL AND THE BIRDS OF PREY (DC Rebirth)
DC Comics: Aug, 2016 - Present ($2.99)
1-7: 1-Julie & Shawna Benson-s/Claire Roe-a. 3-6-Antonio-a 3.00
...: Rebirth 1 (9/16, $2.99) Batgirl, Black Canary & Huntress team up; Claire Roe-a 3.00

BATGIRL SPECIAL
DC Comics: 1988 ($1.50, one-shot, 52 pgs)
1-Kitson-a/Mignola-c 1 2 3 5 7 9

BATGIRL: YEAR ONE
DC Comics: Feb, 2003 - No. 9, Oct, 2003 ($2.95, limited series)
1-9-Barbara Gordon becomes Batgirl; Killer Moth app.; Beatty & Dixon-s 3.00
TPB (2003, $17.95) r/#1-9 18.00

BAT LASH (See DC Special Series #16, Showcase #76, Weird Western Tales)
National Periodical Publications: Oct-Nov, 1968 - No. 7, Oct-Nov, 1969 (12¢/15¢)
1-(10-11/68, 12¢-c)-2nd app. Bat Lash; classic Nick Cardy-c/a in all
6 12 18 42 79 115
2-7: 6,7-(15¢-c) 4 8 12 27 44 60

BAT LASH
DC Comics: Feb, 2008 - No. 6, Jul, 2008 ($2.99, limited series)
1-6-Aragonés & Brandvold-s/John Severin-a. 1-Two covers by Severin and Simonson 3.00
...: Guns and Roses TPB (2008, $17.99) r/#1-6 18.00

BATMAN (See All Star Batman & Robin, Anarky, Aurora [in Promo. Comics section], Azrael, The Best of DC #2, Blind Justice, The Brave & the Bold, Cosmic Odyssey, DC 100-Page Super Spec. #14,20, DC Special, DC Special Series, Detective, Dynamic Classics, 80-Page Giants, Gotham By Gaslight, Gotham Nights, Greatest Batman Stories Ever Told, Greatest Joker Stories Ever Told, Heroes Against Hunger, JLA,The Joker, Justice League of America, Justice League Int., Legends of the Dark Knight, Limited Coll. Ed., Man-Bat, Nightwing, Power Record Comics, Real Fact #5, Robin, Saga of Ra's al Ghul, Shadow of the..., Star Spangled, Super Friends, 3-D Batman, Untold Legend of..., Wanted... & World's Finest Comics)

BATMAN
National Per. Publ./Detective Comics/DC Comics: Spring, 1940 - No. 713, Oct, 2011 (#1-5 were quarterly)
1-Origin The Batman reprinted (2 pgs.) from Det. #33 w/splash from #34 by Bob Kane; see Detective #33 for 1st origin; 1st app. Joker (2 stories intended for 2 separate issues of Det. Comics which would have been 1st & 2nd app.); splash pg. to 2nd Joker story is similar to cover of Det. #40 (story intended for #40); 1st app. The Cat (Catwoman) (1st villainess in comics); has Batman story (w/Hugo Strange) without Robin originally planned for Det. #38; mentions location (Manhattan) where Batman lives (see Det. #31). This book was created entirely from the inventory of Det. Comics; 1st Batman/Robin pin-up on back-c; has text piece & photo of Bob Kane
40,000 80,000 120,000 270,000 460,000 650,000
1-Reprint, oversize 13-1/2x10". **WARNING**: This comic is an exact duplicate reprint of the original except for its size. DC published it in 1974 with a second cover titling it as a Famous First Edition. There have been many reported cases of the outer cover being removed and the interior sold as the original edition. The reprint with the new outer cover removed is practically worthless. See Famous First Edition for value.
2-2nd app. The Joker; 2nd app. Catwoman (out of costume) in Joker story; 1st time called Catwoman (NOTE: A 15¢-c for Canadian distr. exists.)
2400 4800 7200 18,000 34,000 50,000
3-3rd app Catwoman (1st in costume & 1st costumed villainess); 1st Puppet Master app.; classic Kane & Robinson-c 1200 2400 3600 9000 17,500 26,000
4-4th app. The Joker (see Det. #45 for 3rd); 1st mention of Gotham City in a Batman comic (on newspaper)(Win/40) 1000 2000 3000 7500 13,500 19,500
5-1st app. the Batmobile with its bat-head front 784 1568 2352 5723 10,112 14,500
6,7: 7-Bullseye-c; Joker app. 622 1244 1866 4541 8021 11,500
8-Infinity-c by Fred Ray; Joker app. 514 1028 1542 3750 6625 9500
9-10:9-1st Batman x-mas story; Burnley-c. 10-Catwoman story (gets new costume)
486 972 1458 3550 6275 9000
11-Classic Joker-c by Ray/Robinson (3rd Joker-c, 6-7/42); Joker & Penguin app.
1150 2300 3450 8740 15,870 23,000
12,15: 12-Joker app. 15-New costume Catwoman 377 754 1131 2639 4620 6600
13-Jerry Siegel (Superman's co-creator) appears in a Batman story; Batman parachuting on black-c 417 834 1251 2919 5110 7300
14-2nd Penguin-c; Penguin app. (12-1/42-43) 389 778 1167 2723 4762 6800
16-Intro/origin Alfred (4-5/43); cover is a reverse of #9 cover by Burnley; 1st small logo
703 1406 2109 5132 9066 13,000
17,20: 17-Classic war-c; Penguin app. 20-1st Batmobile-c (12-1/43-44); Joker app.
331 662 993 2317 4059 5800
18-Hitler, Hirohito, Mussolini-c. 432 864 1296 3154 5577 8000
19-Joker app. 245 490 735 1568 2684 3800
21,22,24,26,28-30: 21-1st skinny Alfred in Batman (2-3/44). 21,30-Penguin app. 22-1st Alfred solo-c/story (Alfred solo stories in 22-32,36); Catwoman & The Cavalier app. 28-Joker story
194 388 582 1242 2121 3000
23-Joker-c/story; classic black-c 400 800 1200 2800 4900 7000
25-Only Joker/Penguin team-up; 1st team-up between two major villains
300 600 900 2010 3505 5000
27-Classic Burnley Christmas-c; Penguin app. 248 496 744 1575 2713 3850

Batman #55 © DC

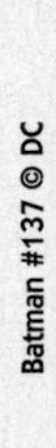

Batman #137 © DC

Batman #227 © DC

	GD 2.0	VG 4.0	FN 6.0	VF 8.0	VF/NM 9.0	NM- 9.2
31,32,34-36,39: 32-Origin Robin retold; Joker app. 35-Catwoman story (in new costume w/o cat head mask). 36-Penguin app.	142	284	426	909	1555	2200
33-Christmas-c	171	342	513	1086	1868	2650
37-Joker spotlight on black-c	271	542	813	1734	2967	4200
38-Penguin-c/story	181	362	543	1158	1979	2800
40-Joker-c/story	252	504	756	1613	2757	3900
41-1st Sci-fi cover/story in Batman; Penguin app.(6-7/47)	135	270	405	864	1482	2100
42-2nd Catwoman-c (1st in Batman)(8-9/47); Catwoman story also.	271	542	813	1734	2967	4200
43-Penguin-c/story	152	304	456	965	1658	2350
44-Classic Joker-c	290	580	870	1856	3178	4500
45,46: 45-Christmas-c/story; Catwoman story. 46-Joker app.	119	238	357	762	1306	1850
47-1st detailed origin The Batman (6-7/48); 1st Bat-signal-c this title (see Detective #108); Batman tracks down his parent's killer and reveals i.d. to him	568	1136	1704	4146	7323	10,500
48-1000 Secrets of the Batcave; r-in #203; Penguin story	155	310	465	992	1696	2400
49-Joker-c/story; 1st app. Mad Hatter; 1st app. Vicki Vale	300	600	900	2010	3505	5000
50-Two-Face impostor app.	168	336	504	1075	1838	2600
51,54,56,57,60: 57-Centerfold is a 1950 calendar; Joker app.	113	226	339	718	1234	1750
52-Joker-c/story	232	464	696	1485	2543	3600
53-Joker story	116	232	348	742	1271	1800
55-Joker-c/stories	219	438	657	1402	2401	3400
58,61: 58-Penguin-c. 61-Origin Batman Plane II	129	258	387	826	1413	2000
59-1st app. Deadshot; Batman in the future-c/sty	300	600	900	2010	3505	5000
62-Origin Catwoman; Catwoman-c	239	478	717	1530	2615	3700
63-1st app. Killer Moth; Joker story; flying saucer story(2-3/51)	123	246	369	787	1344	1900
64,70-72,74-77,79: 70-Robot-c. 72-Last 52 pg. issue. 74-Used in **POP**, Pg. 90. 75-Gorilla-c. 76-Penguin story. 79-Vicki Vale in "The Bride of Batman"	97	194	291	621	1061	1500
65,69-Catwoman-c/stories	174	348	522	1114	1907	2700
66,73-Joker-c/stories. 66-Pre-2nd Batman & Robin team try-out. 73-Vicki Vale story	187	374	561	1197	2049	2900
67-Joker story	110	220	330	704	1202	1700
68,81-Two-Face-c/stories	123	246	369	787	1344	1900
78-(8-9/53)-Roh Kar, The Man Hunter from Mars story-the 1st lawman of Mars to come to Earth (green skinned)	116	232	348	742	1271	1800
80-Joker stories	110	220	330	704	1202	1700
82,83,87-89: 89-Last pre-code issue	90	180	270	576	988	1400
84-Catwoman-c/story; Two-Face app.	155	310	465	992	1696	2400
85,86-Joker story. 86-Intro Batmarine (Batman's submarine)	94	188	282	597	1024	1450
90,91,93-96,98,99: 99-(4/56)-Last G.A. Penguin app.	77	154	231	493	847	1200
92-1st app. Bat-Hound-c/story	181	362	543	1158	1979	2800
97-2nd app. Bat-Hound-c/story; Joker story	90	180	270	576	988	1400
100-(6/56)	309	618	927	2163	3782	5400
101-(8/56)-Clark Kent x-over who protects Batman's i.d. (3rd story)	77	154	231	493	847	1200
102-104,106-109: 103-1st S.A. issue; 3rd Bat-Hound-c/story	73	146	219	467	796	1125
105-1st Batwoman in Batman (2nd anywhere)	148	296	444	947	1624	2300
110-Joker story	74	148	222	470	810	1150
111-120: 112-1st app. Signalman (super villain). 113-1st app. Fatman; Batman meets his counterpart on Planet X w/a chest plate similar to S.A. Batman's design (yellow oval w/black design inside).	63	126	189	403	689	975
121- Origin/1st app. of Mr. Zero (Mr. Freeze).	343	686	1029	2400	4200	6000
122,124-126,128,130: 122,126-Batwoman-c/story. 124-2nd app. Signal Man. 128-Batwoman cameo. 130-Lex Luthor app.	53	106	159	334	567	800
123,127: 123-Joker story; Bat-Hound app. 127-(10/59)-Batman vs. Thor the Thunder God c/story; Joker story; Superman cameo	54	108	162	343	574	825
129-Origin Robin retold; bondage-c; Batwoman-c/story (reprinted in Batman Family #8)	63	126	189	403	689	975
131-135,137,138,141-143: 131-Intro 2nd Batman & Robin series (see #66; also in #135,145, 154,159,163). 133-1st Bat-Mite in Batman (3rd app. anywhere). 134-Origin The Dummy (not Vigilante's villain). 141-2nd app. original Bat-Girl. 143-(10/61)-Last 10¢ issue	43	86	129	271	461	650
136-Joker-c/story	52	104	156	328	552	775
139-Intro 1st original Bat-Girl; only app. Signalman as the Blue Bowman	90	180	270	576	988	1400
140-Joker story, Batwoman-c/s; Superman cameo	47	94	141	296	498	700
144-(12/61)-1st 12¢ issue; Joker story	27	54	81	194	435	675
145,148-Joker-c/stories	29	58	87	209	467	725
146,147,149,150	21	42	63	147	324	500
151-154,156-158,160-162,164-168,170: 152-Joker story. 156-Ant-Man/Robin team-up(6/63). 164-New Batmobile(6/64) new look & Mystery Analysts series begins	17	34	51	117	259	400
155-1st S.A. app. The Penguin (5/63)	42	84	126	311	706	1100
159,163-Joker-c/stories. 159-Bat-Girl app. 163-Last Bat-Girl app. until Teen Titans #50	23	46	69	161	356	550
169-2nd SA Penguin app.	20	40	60	138	307	475
171-1st Riddler app.(5/65) since Dec. 1948	61	122	183	488	1094	1700
172-175,177,178,180,184	10	20	30	70	150	230
176-(80-Pg. Giant G-17); Joker-c/story; Penguin app. in strip-r; Catwoman reprint	12	24	36	83	182	280
179-2nd app. Silver Age Riddler	18	36	54	124	275	425
181-Intro. Poison Ivy; Batman & Robin poster insert	57	114	171	456	1028	1600
182,187-(80 Pg. Giants G-24, G-30); Joker-c/stories	11	22	33	75	160	245
183-2nd app. Poison Ivy	15	30	45	103	227	350
185-(80 Pg. Giant G-27)	11	22	33	73	157	240
186-Joker-c/story	11	22	33	75	160	245
188,191,192,194-196,199	9	18	27	58	114	170
189-1st S.A. app. Scarecrow; retells origin of G.A. Scarecrow from World's Finest #3(1st app.)	27	54	81	189	420	650
190-Penguin-c/app.	11	22	33	76	163	250
193-(80-Pg. Giant G-37)	10	20	30	68	144	220
197-4th S.A. Catwoman app. cont'd from Det. #369; 1st new Batgirl app. in Batman (5th anywhere)	15	30	45	103	227	350
198-(80-Pg. Giant G-43); Joker-c/story-r/World's Finest #61; Catwoman-r/Det. #211; Penguin-r; origin-r/#47	10	20	30	70	150	230
200-(3/68)-Joker cameo; retells origin of Batman & Robin; 1st Neal Adams work this title (cover only)	12	24	36	84	185	285
201-Joker story	7	14	21	46	86	125
202,204-207,209-212: 210-Catwoman-c/app. 212-Last 12¢ issue	6	12	18	42	79	115
203-(80 Pg. Giant G-49); r/#48, 61, & Det. 185; Batcave Blueprints	8	16	24	56	108	160
208-(80 Pg. Giant G-55); New origin Batman by Gil Kane plus 3 G.A. Batman reprints w/Catwoman, Vicki Vale & Batwoman	8	16	24	56	108	160
213-(80-Pg. Giant G-61); 30th anniversary issue (7-8/69); origin Alfred (r/Batman #16), Joker(r/Det. #168), Clayface; new origin Robin with new facts	9	18	27	61	123	185
214-217: 214-Alfred given a new last name- "Pennyworth" (see Detective #96)	6	12	18	37	66	95
218-(68 pg. Giant G-67)	7	14	21	48	89	130
219-Neal Adams-a	9	18	27	60	120	180
220,221,224-226,229-231	5	10	15	34	60	85
222-Beatles take-off; art lesson by Joe Kubert	16	32	48	110	243	375
223,228,233: 223,228-(68 pg. Giants G-73,G-79). 233-G-85-(68 pgs., "64 pgs." on-c)	7	14	21	46	86	125
227-Neal Adams cover swipe of Detective #31	36	72	108	259	580	900
232-(6/71) Adams-a. Intro/1st app. Ra's al Ghul; origin Batman & Robin retold; last 15¢ issue (see Detective #411 (5/71) for Talia's debut)	32	64	96	230	515	800
234-(9/71)-1st modern app. of Harvey Dent/Two-Face with origin re-told in brief; (see World's Finest #173 for Batman as Two-Face; only S.A. mention of character); N. Adams-a; 52 pg. issues begin, end #242	21	42	63	147	324	500
235,236,239-242: 239-XMas-c. 241-Reprint/#5	6	12	18	41	76	110
237-N. Adams-a. 1st Rutland Vermont - Bald Mountain Halloween x-over. G.A. Batman-r/ Det. #37; 1st app. The Reaper; Wrightson/Ellison plots	15	30	45	100	220	340
238-Also listed as DC 100 Page Super Spectacular #8; Batman, Legion, Aquaman-r; G.A. Atom, Sargon (r/Sensation #57), Plastic Man (r/Police #14) stories; Doom Patrol origin-r; N. Adams wraparound-c	12	24	36	84	185	285
243-245-Neal Adams-a	9	18	27	61	123	185
246-250,252,253: 246-Scarecrow app. 253-Shadow-c & app.	5	10	15	34	60	85
251-(9/73)-N. Adams-c/a; Joker-c/story	36	72	108	259	580	900
254,256,257,259,261-All 100 pg. editions; part-r: 254-(2/74)-Man-Bat-c/app. 256-Catwoman app. 257-Joker & Penguin app. 259-Shadow-c/app.	7	14	21	44	82	120
255-(100 pgs.)-N. Adams-c/a; tells of Bruce Wayne's father who wore bat costume & fought crime (r/Det. #235); r/story Batman #22	8	16	24	51	96	140
258-First mention of Arkham (Hospital, renamed Arkham Asylum in #260)	8	16	24	54	102	150

Batman #311 © DC

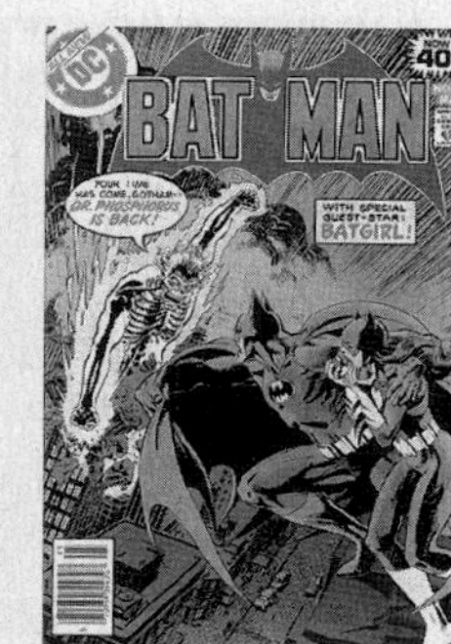

Batman #540 © DC

Batman #620 © DC

	GD 2.0	VG 4.0	FN 6.0	VF 8.0	VF/NM 9.0	NM- 9.2
260-(100 pgs.) Joker-c/story; 2nd Arkham Asylum (see #258 for 1st mention)	8	16	24	51	96	140
262 (68 pgs.)	5	10	15	33	57	80
263,264,266-285,287-290,292,293,295-299: 266-Catwoman back to old costume	3	6	9	14	20	25
265-Wrightson-a(i)	3	6	9	15	22	28
286,291,294: 294-Joker-c/stories	3	6	9	17	26	35
300-Double-size	4	8	12	23	37	50
301-(7/78)-306,308-310,312-315,317-320,325-331,333-352: 304-(44 pgs.). 306-3rd app. Black Spider. 308-Mr. Freeze app. 310-1st modern app. The Gentleman Ghost in Batman; Kubert-c. 312,314,346-Two-Face-c/stories. 313-2nd app. Calendar Man. 318-Intro Firebug. 319-2nd modern age app. The Gentleman Ghost; Kubert-c. 331-1st app./death original Electrocutioner. 344-Poison Ivy app. 345-1st app. new Dr. Death. 345,346,351-Catwoman back-ups	2	4	6	9	12	15
306-308,311-320,323,324,326-(Whitman variants; low print run; none show issue # on cover)	2	4	6	13	18	22
307-1st app. Lucius Fox (1/79)	2	4	6	11	16	20
311,316,322-324: 311-Batgirl-c/story; Batgirl reteams w/Batman. 316-Robin returns. 322-324-Catwoman (Selina Kyle) app. 322,323-Cat-Man cameos (1st in Batman, 1 panel each). 323-1st meeting Catwoman & Cat-Man. 324-1st full app. Cat-Man this title	2	4	6	10	14	18
321,353,359-Joker-c/stories	3	6	9	14	20	25
332-Catwoman's 1st solo	2	4	6	11	16	20
354-356,358,360,362-365,369,370: 362-Riddler-c/story with origin retold in brief	1	3	4	6	8	10
357-1st app. Jason Todd (3/83); see Det. #524; brief app. Croc (see Detective #523 (2/83) for earlier cameo	7	14	21	49	92	135
361-Debut of Harvey Bullock (7/83)(see Detective #441,('74) for a similar Lt. Bullock, no first name given, appeared in 3 panels)	3	6	9	14	20	25
366-Jason Todd 1st in Robin costume; Joker-c/story	3	6	9	19	30	40
367-Jason in red & green costume (not as Robin)	2	4	6	8	11	14
368-1st new Robin in costume (Jason Todd)	3	6	9	17	26	35
371-385,388-399,401-403: 371-Cat-Man-c/story; brief origin Cat-Man (cont'd in Det. #538). 390-391-Catwoman app. 398-Catwoman & Two-Face app. 401-2nd app. Magpie (see Man of Steel #3 for 1st). 403-Joker cameo	1	2	3	5	6	8

NOTE: *Issues 397-399, 401-403, 408-416, 421-425, 430-432 all have 2nd printings in 1989; some with up to 8 printings. Some are not identified as reprints but have newer ads copyrighted after cover dates. All reprints have different back-c ads. All reprints are scarcer than 1st prints and have same value to variant collectors.*

	GD 2.0	VG 4.0	FN 6.0	VF 8.0	VF/NM 9.0	NM- 9.2
386-Intro Black Mask (villain)	4	8	12	28	47	65
387-Intro Black Mask continues	2	4	6	11	16	20
400 ($1.50, 68pgs.)-Dark Knight special; intro by Stephen King; Art Adams/Austin-a	3	6	9	17	26	35
404-Miller scripts begin (end 407); Year 1; 1st modern app. Catwoman (2/87)	3	6	9	19	30	40
405-407: 407-Year 1 ends (See Detective Comics #575-578 for Year 2)	3	6	9	14	20	25
408-410: New Origin Jason Todd (Robin)	2	4	6	13	18	22
411-416,421,422,424,425: 411-Two-face app. 412-Origin/1st app. Mime. 414-Starlin scripts begin, end #429. 416-Nightwing-c/story						6.00
417-420: "Ten Nights of the Beast" storyline	2	4	6	8	10	12
423-McFarlane-c	3	6	9	16	23	30
426-($1.50, 52 pgs.)- "A Death In The Family" storyline begins, ends #429	3	6	9	16	23	30
427- "A Death In The Family" part 2. (Direct Sales version has inside back-c page for phone poll; newsstand version has an ad on inside back-c and UPC code on front-c)	2	4	6	11	16	20
428-Death of Robin (Jason Todd)	3	6	9	21	33	45
429-Joker-c/story; Superman app.	2	4	6	11	16	20
430-432						5.00
433-435-Many Deaths of the Batman story by John Byrne-c/scripts						5.00
436-Year 3 begins (ends #439); origin original Robin retold by Nightwing (Dick Grayson); 1st app. Timothy Drake (8/89)	2	4	6	9	12	15
436-441: 436-2nd printing. 437-Origin Robin cont. 440,441: "A Lonely Place of Dying" Parts 1 & 3						5.00
442-1st app. Timothy Drake in Robin costume	1	2	3	5	6	8
443-456,458,459,462-464: 445-447-Batman goes to Russia. 448,449-The Penguin Affair Pts 1 & 3. 450-Origin Joker. 450,451-Joker-c/stories. 452-454-Dark Knight Dark City storyline; Riddler app. 455-Alan Grant scripts begin, ends #466, 470. 464-Last solo Batman story; free 16 pg. preview of Impact Comics line						4.00
457-Timothy Drake officially becomes Robin & dons new costume	2	4	6	8	10	12
457-Direct sale edition (has #000 in indicia)	2	4	6	8	10	12
460,461,465-487: 460,461-Two part Catwoman story. 465-Robin returns to action with Batman. 470-War of the Gods x-over. 475-1st app. Renee Montoya. 475,476-Return of Scarface. 476-Last $1.00-c. 477,478-Photo-c						4.00
488-Cont'd from Batman: Sword of Azrael #4; Azrael-c & app.	1	2	3	5	6	8
489-Bane-c/story; 1st app. Azrael in Bat-costume	1	3	4	6	8	10
490-Riddler-c/story; Azrael & Bane app.						6.00
491,492: 491-Knightfall lead-in; Joker-c/story; Azrael & Bane app.; Kelley Jones-c begin. 492-Knightfall part 1; Bane app.						6.00
492-Platinum edition (promo copy)	2	4	6	9	12	15
493-496: 493-Knightfall Pt. 3. 494-Knightfall Pt. 5; Joker-c & app. 495-Knightfall Pt. 7; brief Bane & Joker apps. 496-Knightfall Pt. 9, Joker-c/story; Bane cameo						6.00
497-(Late 7/93)-Knightfall Pt. 11; Bane breaks Batman's back; B&W outer-c; Aparo-a(p); Giordano-a(i)	2	4	6	8	10	12
497-499: 497-2nd printing. 497-Newsstand edition w/o outer cover. 498-Knightfall part 15; Bane & Catwoman-c & app. (see Showcase 93 #7 & 8) 499-Knightfall Pt. 17; Bane app.						5.00
500-($2.50, 68 pgs.)-Knightfall Pt. 19; Azrael in new Bat-costume; Bane-c/story						5.00
500-($3.95, 68 pgs.)-Collector's Edition w/die-cut double-c w/foil by Joe Quesada & 2 bound-in post cards	1	2	3	5	6	8
501-508,510,511: 501-Begin $1.50-c. 501-508-Knightquest. 503,504-Catwoman app. 507-Ballistic app.; Jim Balent-a(p). 510-KnightsEnd Pt. 7. 511-(9/94)-Zero Hour; Batgirl-c/story						3.00
509-($2.50, 52 pgs.)-KnightsEnd Pt. 1						4.00
512-514,516-518: 512-(11/94)-Dick Grayson assumes Batman role						3.00
515-Special Ed.($2.50)-Kelley Jones-a begins; all black embossed-c; Troika Pt. 1						5.00
515-Regular Edition						3.00
519-534,536-549: 519-Begin $1.95-c. 521-Return of Alfred, 522-Swamp Thing app. 525-Mr. Freeze app. 527,528-Two Face app. 529-Contagion Pt. 6. 530-532-Deadman app. 533-Legacy prelude. 534-Legacy Pt. 5. 536-Final Night x-over; Man-Bat-c/app. 540,541-Spectre-c-app. 544-546-Joker & The Demon. 548,549-Penguin-c/app.						3.00
530-532 ($2.50)-Enhanced edition; glow-in-the-dark-c.						4.00
535-(10/96, $2.95)-1st app. The Ogre						4.00
535-(10/96, $3.95)-1st app. The Ogre; variant, cardboard, foldout-c						5.00
550-($3.50)-Collector's Ed., includes 4 collector cards; intro. Chase, return of Clayface; Kelley Jones-c						5.00
550-($2.95)-Standard Ed.; Williams & Gray-c						4.00
551,552,554-562: 551,552-Ragman c/app. 554-Cataclysm pt. 12.						3.00
553-Cataclysm pt.3						4.00
563-No Man's Land; Joker-c by Campbell; Bob Gale-s						5.00
564-569,571-574: 567-1st Cassandra Cain. 569-New Batgirl-c/app.						3.00
570-Joker and Harley Quinn story	3	6	9	14	20	25
575-579: 575-New look Batman begins; McDaniel-a						3.00
580-598: 580-Begin $2.25-c. 587-Gordon shot. 591,592-Deadshot-c/app.						3.00
599-Bruce Wayne: Murderer pt. 7						3.50
600-($3.95) Bruce Wayne: Fugitive pt. 1; back-up homage stories in '50s, 60's, & 70s styles; by Aragonés, Gaudiano, Shanower and others						5.00
600-(2nd printing)						4.00
601-604, 606,607: 601,603-Bruce Wayne: Fugitive pt.3,13. 606,607-Deadshot-c/app.						3.00
605-($2.95) Conclusion to Bruce Wayne: Fugitive x-over; Noto-c						4.00
608-(12/02) Hush begins; Jim Lee-a/c & Jeph Loeb-s begin; Poison Ivy & Catwoman app.						15.00
608-2nd printing; has different cover with Batman standing on gargoyle						70.00
608-Special Edition; has different cover; 200 printed; used for promotional purposes (a CGC certified 9.2 copy sold for $700, and a CGC certified 9.8 copy sold for $2,100)						
608-Special Edition (9/09, $1.00) printing has new "After Watchmen" logo cover frame						5.00
609-Huntress app.						9.00
610,611: 610-Killer Croc-c/app.; Batman & Catwoman kiss						8.00
612-Batman vs. Superman; 1st printing with full color cover						20.00
612-2nd printing with B&W sketch cover						30.00
613,614: 614-Joker-c/app.						8.00
615-617: 615-Reveals ID to Catwoman. 616-Ra's al Ghul app. 617-Scarecrow app.						5.00
618-Batman vs. "Jason Todd"						4.00
619-Newsstand cover; Hush story concludes; Riddler app.						5.00
619-Two variant tri-fold covers; one Heroes group, one Villains group						5.00
619-2nd printing with Riddler chess cover						5.00
620-Broken City pt. 1; Azzarello-s/Risso-a/c begin; Killer Croc app.						4.00
621-633: 621-625-Azzarello-s/Risso-a/c. 626-630-Winick-s/Nguyen-a/Wagner-c; Penguin & Scarecrow app. 631-633-War Games. 633-Conclusion to War Games x-over						3.00
634,636-638-Winick-s/Nguyen-a/Wagner-c; Red Hood app. 637-Amazo app. 638-Red Hood unmasked as Jason Todd						4.00
635-1st app. Red Hood (later revealed as Jason Todd in #638)						30.00
639-650: 640-Superman app. 641-Begin $2.50-c. 643,644-War Crimes; Joker app. 650-Infinite Crisis; Joker and Jason Todd app.						3.00
651-654-One Year Later; Bianchi-c						3.50
655-Begin Grant Morrison-s/Andy Kubert-a; Kubert-c w/red background						20.00
655-Variant cover by Adam Kubert, brown-toned image						50.00
656-Intro. Damian, son of Talia and Batman (see Batman: Son of the Demon)						15.00

Batman #666 © DC

Batman (2011 series) #15 © DC

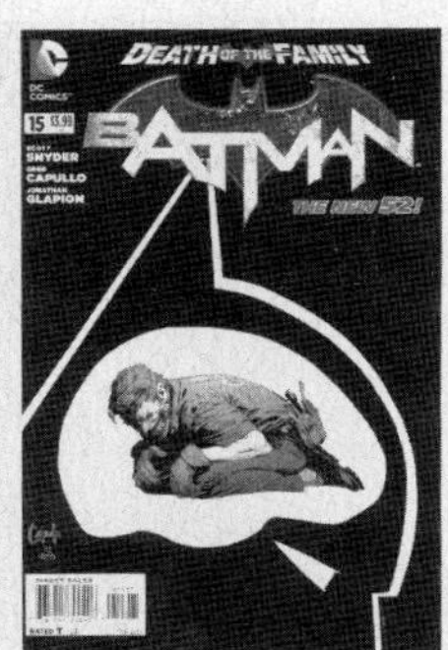

Batman (2016 series) #7 © DC

GD VG FN VF VF/NM NM-
2.0 4.0 6.0 8.0 9.0 9.2

657-Damian in Robin costume 5.00
658-665: 659-662-Mandrake-a. 663-Van Fleet-a. 664-Bane app. 3.00
666-675: 666-Future story of adult Damian; Andy Kubert-a. 667-669-Williams III-a. 670,671-Resurrection of Ra's al Ghul; Daniel-a. 671-2nd printing 3.00
676-Batman R.I.P. begins; Morrison-s/Daniel-a/Alex Ross-c 4.00
676-Variant-c by Tony Daniel 12.00
676-Second (red-tinted Daniel-c) & third (B&W Daniel-c) printings 3.00
677-680,682-685: Batman R.I.P.; Alex Ross-c. 678-Bat-Mite app. 682-685-Last Rites 3.00
677-Variant-c with Red Hood by Tony Daniel 10.00
677-Second printing with B&W&red-tinted Daniel-c 3.00
681-($3.99) Batman R.I.P. conclusion 4.00
686-($3.99) Gaiman-s/Andy Kubert-a; continues in Detective #853; Kubert sketch pgs.; covers by Kubert and Ross; 2nd & 3rd printings exist 4.00
687-($3.99) Batman: Reborn begins; Dick Grayson becomes Batman; Winick-s/Benes-a 4.00
688-699: 688-691-Bagley-a. 692-697,699-Tony Daniel-s/a. 692-Catwoman app. 3.00
700-(8/10, $4.99) Morrison-s; art by Daniel, Quitely, Finch & Andy Kubert; Finch-c 6.00
700-Variant-c by Mignola 10.00
701-712: 701,702-Morrison-s; R.I.P story. 704-Batman Inc. begins; Daniel-s/a 3.00
713-(10/11) Last issue of first volume; Nicieza-s; Robin flashbacks 3.00
#0 (10/94)-Zero Hour issue released between #511 & #512; Origin retold 3.00
#1,000,000 (11/98) 853rd Century x-over 3.00
Annual 1 (8-10/61)-Swan-c 53 106 159 413 932 1450
Annual 2 24 48 72 168 372 575
Annual 3 (Summer, '62)-Joker-c/story 25 50 75 175 388 600
Annual 4,5 12 24 36 84 185 285
Annual 6,7 (7/64, 25¢, 80 pgs.) 10 20 30 69 147 225
Annual V5#8 (1982)-Painted-c 1 3 4 6 8 10
Annual 9,10,12: 9(7/85). 10(1986). 12(1988, $1.50) 1 2 3 4 5 7
Annual 11 (1987, $1.25)-Penguin-c/story; Moore-s 1 2 3 5 7 9
Annual 13 (1989, $1.75, 68 pgs.)-Gives history of Bruce Wayne, Dick Grayson, Jason Todd, Alfred, Comm. Gordon, Barbara Gordon (Batgirl) & Vicki Vale; Morrow-i 6.00
Annual 14-17 ('90-'93, 68 pgs.)-14-Origin Two-Face. 15-Armageddon 2001 x-over; Joker app. 15 (2nd printing). 16-Joker-c/s; Kieth-c. 17 (1993, $2.50, 68 pgs.)-Azrael in Bat-costume; intro Ballistic 4.00
Annual 18 (1994, $2.95) 4.00
Annual 19 (1995, $3.95)-Year One story; retells Scarecrow's origin 4.00
Annual 20 (1996, $2.95)-Legends of the Dead Earth story; Giarrano-a 4.00
Annual 21 (1997, $3.95)-Pulp Heroes story 4.00
Annual 22,23 ('98, '99, $2.95)-22-Ghosts; Wrightson-c. 23-JLApe; Art Adams-c 4.00
Annual 24 ('00, $3.50) Planet DC; intro. The Boggart; Aparo-a 4.00
Annual 25 ('06, $4.99) Infinite Crisis-revised story of Jason Todd; unused Aparo page 6.00
Annual 26 ('07, $3.99) Origin of Ra's al Ghul; Damian app. 4.00
Annual 27 ('09, $4.99) Azrael app.; Calafiore-a; back-up story w/Kelley Jones-a 5.00
Annual 28 (2/11, $4.99) The Question, Nightrunner and Veil app.; Lau-c 5.00

NOTE: ***Art Adams*** *a-400p.* ***Neal Adams*** *c-200, 203, 210, 217, 219-222, 224-227, 229, 230, 232, 234, 236-241, 243-246, 251, 255, Annual 14.* ***Aparo*** *a-414-420, 426-435, 440-448, 450, 451, 480-483, 486-491, 494-500; c-414-416, 481, 482, 463i, 486, 487i.* ***Bolland*** *a-400; c-445-447.* ***Burnley*** *a-10, 12-18, 20, 22, 25, 27; c-9, 15, 16, 27, 28p, 40p, 42p.* ***Byrne*** *c-401, 433-435, 533-535, Annual 11.* ***Travis Charest*** *c-488-490p.* ***Colan*** *a-340p, 343-345p, 348-351p, 373p, 383p; c-343p, 345p, 350p.* ***J. Cole*** *a-238r.* ***Cowan*** *a-Annual 10p.* ***Golden*** *a-295p, 303p, 484, 485.* ***Alan Grant*** *scripts-455-466, 470, 474-476, 479, 480, Annual 16(part).* ***Grell*** *a-287, 288p, 289p, 290; c-287-290.* ***Infantino/Anderson*** *c-167, 173, 175, 181, 186, 191, 192, 194, 195, 198, 199.* ***Infantino/Giella*** *c-190.* ***Kelley Jones*** *a-513-519, 521-525, 527; c-491-499, 500(newsstand), 501-510, 513.* ***Kaluta*** *c-242, 248, 253, Annual 12.* ***G. Kane/Anderson*** *c-178-180.* ***Bob Kane*** *a-1, 2, 5; c-1-5, 7, 17.* ***G. Kane*** *a-(r)-254, 255, 259, 261, 353i.* ***Kubert*** *a-238r, 400; c-310, 319p, 327, 328, 344.* ***McFarlane*** *c-423.* ***Mignola*** *c-426-429, 452-454, Annual 18.* ***Moldoff*** *c-101-140.* ***Moldoff/Giella*** *a-164-175, 177-181, 183, 184, 186.* ***Moldoff/Greene*** *a-169, 172-174, 177-179, 181, 184.* ***Mooney*** *a-255r.* ***Morrow*** *a-Annual 13i.* ***Newton*** *a-305, 306, 328p, 331p, 332p, 337p, 338p, 346p, 352-357p, 360-372p, 374-378p; c-374p, 378p.* ***Nino*** *a-Annual 9.* ***Irv Novick*** *c-201, 202.* ***Perez*** *a-400; c-436-442.* ***Fred Ray*** *c-8, 10; w/Robinson-11.* ***Robinson/Roussos*** *a-12-17, 20, 22, 24, 25, 27, 28, 31, 33, 37.* ***Robinson*** *a-12, 14, 18, 22-32,34, 36, 37, 255r, 260r, 261r; c-6, 10, 12-14, 18, 21, 24, 26, 30, 37, 39.* ***Simonson*** *a-300p, 312p, 321p; c-300p, 312p, 366, 413i.* ***P. Smith*** *a-Annual 9.* ***Dick Sprang*** *c-19, 20, 22, 23, 25, 29, 31-36, 38, 51, 55, 66, 73, 76.* ***Starlin*** *c/a-402.* ***Staton*** *a-334.* ***Sutton*** *a-400.* ***Wrightson*** *a-265i, 400; c-320r. Bat-Hound app. in 92, 97, 103, 123, 125, 133, 156, 158. Bat-Mite app. in 133, 136, 144, 146, 158, 161. Batwoman app. in 105, 116, 122, 125, 128, 129, 131, 133, 139, 140, 141, 144, 145, 150, 151, 153, 154, 157, 159, 162, 163.* ***Zeck*** *c-417-420. Catwoman back-ups in 332, 345, 346, 348-351. Joker app. in 1, 2, 4, 5, 7-9, 11-13, 19, 20, 23, 25, 28, 32 & many more. Robin solo back-up stories in 337-339, 341-343.*

BATMAN (DC New 52)
DC Comics: Nov, 2011 - No. 52, Jul, 2016 ($2.99/$3.99)

1-Snyder-s/Capullo-a/c 5 10 15 31 53 75
1-Variant-c by Van Sciver 4 8 12 28 47 65
1-2nd-5th printings 3 6 9 17 26 35
2-4 2 4 6 9 12 15
2-5-Variant covers. 2-Jim Lee. 3-Ivan Reis. 4-Mike Choi, 5-Burnham. 6-Gary Frank 2 4 6 9 12 15
5-7-Court of Owls. 7-Debut Harper Row 1 3 4 6 8 10
5-7 Combo Pack ($3.99) polybagged with digital download code 1 3 4 6 8 10
8-11: 8-Begin $3.99-c. 8,9-Night of the Owls. 11-Court of the Owls finale 6.00

GD VG FN VF VF/NM NM-
2.0 4.0 6.0 8.0 9.0 9.2

12-Story of Harper Row; Cloonan-a 5.00
13-Death of the Family; Joker and Harley Quinn app.; die-cut-c 2 4 6 8 10 12
14-20: 14-17-Death of the Family. 17-Death of the Family conclusion. 18-Andy Kubert-a 5.00
21-23: 21-Zero Year begins; 1st app. Duke Thomas (unnamed) 5.00
23.1, 23.2, 23.3, 23.4 (11/13, $2.99, regular covers) 4.00
23.1 (11/13, $3.99, 3-D cover) "Joker #1" on cover; Andy Kubert-s/Andy Clarke-a 10.00
23.2 (11/13, $3.99, 3-D cover) "Riddler #1" on cover; Jeremy Haun-a 6.00
23.3 (11/13, $3.99, 3-D cover) "Penguin #1" on cover; Tieri-s/Duce-a/Fabok-c 6.00
23.4 (11/13, $3.99, 3-D cover) "Bane #1" on cover; Nolan-a/March-c 6.00
24-(12/13, $6.99) Batman vs. Red Hood at Ace Chemicals re-told; Dark City begins 7.00
24-New York Comic Con variant with Detective #27 cover swipe 2 4 6 9 12 15
25,29,33-($4.99) 25-All black cover; Doctor Death app. 33-Zero Year finale 6.00
26-28,30-32,34: 28-Nguyen-a; Harper Row as Bluebird; Stephanie Brown returns 4.00
35-($4.99) Endgame pt. 1; Justice League app.; back-up with Kelley Jones-a 5.00
36-39-Endgame; Joker app.; (back-up stories in each; 37-McCrea-a, 38-Kieth-a, 39-Nguyen) 39-Alfred attacked 4.00
40-($4.99) Endgame conclusion 5.00
41-43,45-49,51,52: 41-Gordon dons the robot suit. 49-Paquette-a. 52-Tynion-s 4.00
44-($4.99) Snyder & Azzarello-s/Jock-a 5.00
50-($5.99) Bruce Wayne back as Batman; new costume 6.00
#0 (11/12, $3.99) Flashbacks; Red Hood gang app. 5.00
Annual 1 (7/12, $4.99) Origin of Mr. Freeze; Snyder-s/Fabok-a 2 4 6 11 16 20
Annual 2 (9/13, $4.99) Origin of the Anchoress; Jock-c 6.00
Annual 3 (2/15, $4.99) Joker app.; Tynion-s/Antonio-a/Albuquerque-c 5.00
Annual 4 (11/15, $4.99) Joker app.; Tynion-s/Antonio-a/Murphy-c 5.00
... Endgame 40 Director's Cut 1 (1/16, $5.99) Pencil art and original script for #40 6.00
...: Futures End 1 (11/14, $2.99, regular-c) Five years later; Fawkes-s; Bizarro app. 3.00
...: Futures End 1 (11/14, $3.99, 3-D cover) 4.00
... Zero Year Director's Cut (9/13, $5.99) Reprints Batman #21 original pencil art pages with word balloons; Scott Snyder's script 6.00

BATMAN (DC Rebirth)
DC Comics: Aug, 2016 - Present ($2.99)

1-King-s/Finch-a/c; intro. Gotham and Gotham Girl 5.00
1-Director's Cut (1/17, $5.99) r/#1 in pencil-a; original script; variant cover gallery 6.00
2-18: 2-Hugo Strange app. 3-Psycho Pirate returns. 5-Justice League app. 7,8-Night of the Monster Men x-overs; Batwoman & Nightwing app. 9-13-I Am Suicide; Bane app. 3.00
Annual 1 (1/17, $4.99) Short stories by various incl. Adams, Dini, Snyder Finch; Finch-c 5.00
...: Rebirth 1 (8/16, $2.99) King & Snyder-s/Janín-a; Duke Thomas & Calendar Man app. 3.00

BATMAN (Hardcover books and trade paperbacks)
...: ABSOLUTION (2002, $24.95)-Hard-c.; DeMatteis-s/Ashmore painted-a 25.00
...: ABSOLUTION (2003, $17.95)-Soft-c.; DeMatteis-s/Ashmore painted-a 18.00
...: A LONELY PLACE OF DYING (1990, $3.95, 132 pgs.)-r/Batman #440-442 & New Titans #60,61; Perez-c 6.00
...: ANARKY TPB (1999, $12.95) r/early appearances 13.00
...AND DRACULA: RED RAIN nn (1991, $24.95)-Hard-c.; Elseworlds storyline 32.00
...AND DRACULA: RED RAIN nn (1992, $9.95)-SC 12.00
...AND SON HC (2007, $24.99, dustjacket) r/Batman #655-658,663-666 25.00
...AND SON SC (2008, $14.99) r/Batman #655-658,663-666 15.00
...ANNUALS (See DC Comics Classics Library for reprints of early Annuals)
ARKHAM ASYLUM Hard-c; Morrison-s/McKean-a (1989, $24.95) 35.00
ARKHAM ASYLUM Soft-c ($14.95) 20.00
ARKHAM ASYLUM 15TH ANNIVERSARY EDITION Hard-c (2004, $29.95) reprint with Morrison's script and annotations, original page layouts; Karen Berger afterword 30.00
ARKHAM ASYLUM 15TH ANNIVERSARY EDITION Soft-c (2005, $17.99) 18.00
...: AS THE CROW FLIES-(2004, $12.95) r/#626-630; Nguyen sketch pages 13.00
BIRTH OF THE DEMON Hard-c (1992, $24.95)-Origin of Ra's al Ghul 35.00
BIRTH OF THE DEMON Soft-c (1993, $12.95) 15.00
BLIND JUSTICE nn (1992, $7.50)-r/Det. #598-600 8.00
BLOODSTORM (1994, $24.95,HC) Kelley Jones-c/a 28.00
BRIDE OF THE DEMON Hard-c (1990, $19.95) 25.00
BRIDE OF THE DEMON Soft-c ($12.95) 15.00
...: BROKEN CITY HC-(2004, $24.95) r/#620-625; new Johnson-c; intro by Schreck 25.00
...: BROKEN CITY SC-(2004, $14.99) r/#620-625; new Johnson-c; intro by Schreck 15.00
...: BRUCE WAYNE: FUGITIVE Vol. 1 ('02, $12.95)-r/ story arc 13.00
...: BRUCE WAYNE: FUGITIVE Vol. 2 ('03, $12.95)-r/ story arc 13.00
...: BRUCE WAYNE: FUGITIVE Vol. 3 ('03, $12.95)-r/ story arc 13.00
...: BRUCE WAYNE-MURDERER? ('02, $19.95)-r/ story arc 20.00
...: BRUCE WAYNE - THE ROAD HOME HC ('11, $24.99) r/Bruce Wayne: The Road Home one-shots 25.00
...: CASTLE OF THE BAT ($5.95)-Elseworlds story 6.00

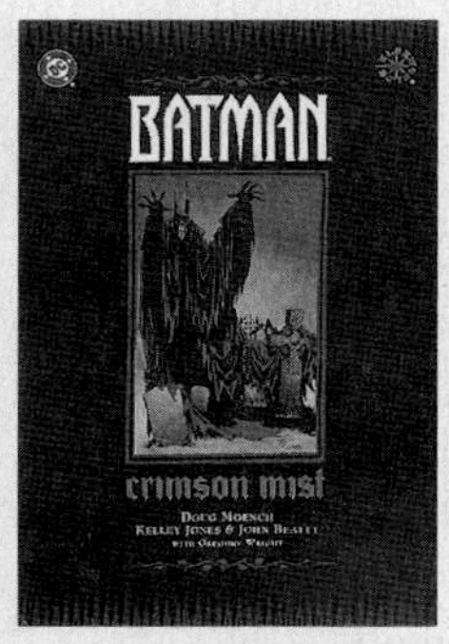

Batman: Crimson Mist HC © DC

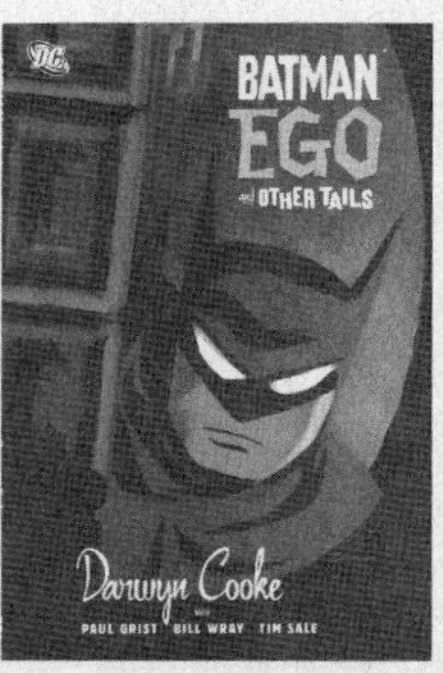

Batman: Ego and Other Tales HC © DC

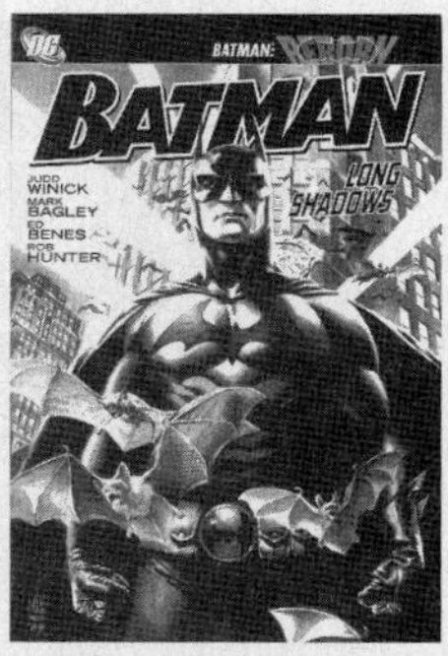

Batman: Long Shadows HC © DC

	GD 2.0	VG 4.0	FN 6.0	VF 8.0	VF/NM 9.0	NM- 9.2

...: CATACLYSM ('99, $17.95)-r/ story arc 18.00
...: CHILD OF DREAMS (2003, $24.95, B&W, HC) Reprint of Japanese manga with Kia Asamiya-s/a/c; English adaptation by Max Allan Collins; Asamiya interview 25.00
...: CHILD OF DREAMS (2003, $19.95, B&W, SC) 20.00
...CHRONICLES VOL. 1 (2005, $14.99)-r/apps. in Detective Comics #27-38; Batman #1 15.00
...CHRONICLES VOL. 2 (2006, $14.99)-r/apps. in Detective Comics #39-45 and NY World's Fair 1940; Batman #2,3 15.00
...CHRONICLES VOL. 3 (2007, $14.99)-r/apps. in Detective Comics #46-50 and World's Best Comics #1; Batman #4,5 15.00
...CHRONICLES VOL. 4 (2007, $14.99)-r/apps. in Detective Comics #51-56 and World's Finest Comics #2,3; Batman #6,7 15.00
...CHRONICLES VOL. 5 (2008, $14.99)-r/apps. in Detective Comics #57-61 and World's Finest Comics #4; Batman #8,9 15.00
...CHRONICLES VOL. 6 (2008, $14.99)-r/apps. in Detective Comics #62-65 and World's Finest Comics #5,6; Batman #10,11 15.00
...CHRONICLES VOL. 7 (2009, $14.99)-r/apps. in Detective Comics #66-70 and World's Finest Comics #7; Batman #12,13 15.00
...CHRONICLES VOL. 8 (2009, $14.99)-r/apps. in Detective Comics #71-74 and World's Finest Comics #8,9; Batman #14,15 15.00
...CHRONICLES VOL. 9 (2010, $14.99)-r/apps. in Detective Comics #75-77 and World's Finest Comics #10; Batman #16,17 15.00
...CHRONICLES VOL. 10 (2010, $14.99)-r/apps. in Detective Comics #78-81 and World's Finest Comics #11; Batman #18,19 15.00
...: CITY OF CRIME (2006, $19.99) r/Detective Comics #800-808,811-814; Lapham-s 20.00
...: COLLECTED LEGENDS OF THE DARK KNIGHT nn (1994, $12.95)-r/Legends of the Dark Knight #32-34,38,42,43 13.00
...: CRIMSON MIST (1999, $24.95,HC)-Vampire Batman Elseworlds story Doug Moench-s/Kelley Jones-c/a 25.00
...: CRIMSON MIST (2001, $14.95,SC) 15.00
...: DARK JOKER-THE WILD (1993, $24.95,HC)-Elseworlds story; Moench-s/Jones-c/a 30.00
...: DARK JOKER-THE WILD (1993, $9.95,SC) 12.00
...DARK KNIGHT DYNASTY nn (1997, $24.95)-Hard-c.; 3 Elseworlds stories; Barr-s/ S. Hampton painted-a, Gary Frank, McDaniel-a(p) 28.00
...DARK KNIGHT DYNASTY Softcover (2000, $14.95) Hampton-c 15.00
...DEADMAN: DEATH AND GLORY nn (1996, $24.95)-Hard-c.; Robinson-s/ Estes-c/a 28.00
...DEADMAN: DEATH AND GLORY ($12.95)-SC 15.00
DEATH AND THE CITY (2007, $14.99, TPB)-r/Detective #827-834 15.00
DEATH BY DESIGN (2012, $24.99, HC)-Chip Kidd-s/Dave Taylor-s 25.00
DEATH IN THE FAMILY (1988, $3.95, trade paperback)-r/Batman #426-429 by Aparo 10.00
DEATH IN THE FAMILY: (2nd - 5th printings) 6.00
...: DETECTIVE (2007, $14.99, SC)-r/Detective Comics #821-826 15.00
...: DETECTIVE #27 HC (2003, $19.95)-Elseworlds; Uslan-s/Snejbjerg-a 20.00
...: DETECTIVE #27 SC (2004, $12.95)-Elseworlds; Uslan-s/Snejbjerg-a 13.00
DIGITAL JUSTICE nn (1990, $24.95, Hard-c.)-Computer generated art 30.00
... EARTH ONE HC (2012, $22.99)-Updated re-imagining of Batman's origin & debut; Geoff Johns-s/Gary Frank-a 23.00
... : EGO AND OTHER TALES HC (2007, $24.99)-r/Batman: Ego, Catwoman: Selina's Big Score, and stories from Batman Black and White and Solo; Darwyn Cooke-s/a 25.00
... : EGO AND OTHER TALES SC (2008, $17.99) same contents as HC 18.00
... :EVOLUTION (2001, $12.95, SC)-r/Detective Comics #743-750 13.00
... FACES (1995, $9.95, TPB) r/Legends of the Dark Knight #28-30 15.00
... FACES (2008, $12.99, TPB) Second printing 13.00
...: FACE THE FACE (2006, $14.99, TPB)-r/Batman #651-654, Detective #817-820 15.00
...: FALSE FACES HC (2008, $19.99)-r/Batman #588-590, Wonder Woman #160,161; Batman: Gotham City Secret Files #1 and Detective #787; Brian K. Vaughn intro. 20.00
...: FALSE FACES SC (2008, $14.99)-r/Batman #588-590, Wonder Woman #160,161; Batman: Gotham City Secret Files #1 and Detective #787; Brian K. Vaughn intro. 15.00
...: FORTUNATE SON HC (1999, $24.95) Gene Ha-a 25.00
...: FORTUNATE SON SC (2000, $14.95) Gene Ha-a 15.00
FOUR OF A KIND TPB (1998, $14.95)-r/1995 Year One Annuals featuring Poison Ivy, Riddler, Scarecrow, & Man-Bat 15.00
... GOING SANE (2008, $14.95, TPB) r/Legends of the Dark Knight #65-68,200 15.00
...: GOTHAM BY GASLIGHT (2006, $12.99, TPB) r/Gotham By Gaslight & Master of the Future one-shots; Elseworlds Batman vs. Jack the Ripper 13.00
...GOTHIC (1992, $12.95, TPB)-r/Legends of the Dark Knight #6-10 15.00
...GOTHIC (2007, $14.99, TPB)-r/Legends of the Dark Knight #6-10 15.00
...: HARVEST BREED-(2000, $24.95) George Pratt-s/painted-a 25.00
...: HARVEST BREED-(2003, $17.95) George Pratt-s/painted-a 18.00
...: HAUNTED KNIGHT-(1997, $12.95) r/ Halloween specials 15.00
...: HEART OF HUSH HC-(2009, $19.99) r/#Detective #846-850; pin-ups 20.00
...: HEART OF HUSH SC-(2010, $14.99) r/#Detective #846-850; pin-ups 15.00
...: HONG KONG HC (2003, $24.95, with dustjacket) Doug Moench-s/Tony Wong-a 25.00
...: HONG KONG SC (2004, $17.95) Doug Moench-s/Tony Wong-a 18.00
...: HUSH DOUBLE FEATURE-(2003, $3.95) r/#608,609(1st 2 Jim Lee-a issues) 6.00
...: HUSH SC-(2009, $24.99) r/#608-619; Wizard 0; variant cover gallery; Loeb intro 25.00
...: HUSH UNWRAPPED-(2011, $39.99, HC) r/#608-619's original Jin Lee pencil art 40.00
...: HUSH VOLUME 1 HC-(2003, $19.95) r/#608-612; & new 2 pg. origin w/Lee-a 20.00
...: HUSH VOLUME 1 SC-(2004, $12.95) r/#608-612; includes CD of DC GN art 13.00
...: HUSH VOLUME 2 HC-(2003, $19.95) r/#613-619; Lee intro & sketchpages 20.00
...: HUSH VOLUME 2 SC-(2004, $12.95) r/#613-619; Lee intro & sketchpages 13.00
...: ILLUSTRATED BY NEAL ADAMS VOLUME 1 HC-(2003, $49.95) r/Batman, Brave and the Bold, and Detective Comics stories and covers 50.00
...: ILLUSTRATED BY NEAL ADAMS VOLUME 2 HC-(2004, $49.95) r/Adams' Batman art from 1969-71; intro. by Dick Giordano 50.00
...: ILLUSTRATED BY NEAL ADAMS VOLUME 3 HC-(2006, $49.99) r/Adams' Batman art from 1971-74; covers, pin-ups and design art; intro. by Denny O'Neil 50.00
... IMPOSTERS TPB (2011, $14.99) r/Detective Comics #867-870 15.00
... INTERNATIONAL TPB (2010, $17.99) R/Batman: Scottish Connection, Batman in Barcelona: Dragon's Knight and Batman: Legends of the DK #52,53; Jim Lee-c 18.00
... IN THE FORTIES TPB ($19.95) Intro. by Bill Schelly 20.00
... IN THE FIFTIES TPB ($19.95) Intro. by Michael Uslan 20.00
... IN THE SIXTIES TPB ($19.95) Intro. by Adam West 20.00
... IN THE SEVENTIES TPB ($19.95) Intro. by Dennis O'Neil 20.00
... IN THE EIGHTIES TPB ($19.95) Intro. by John Wells 20.00
.../ JUDGE DREDD FILES (2004, $14.95) reprints cross-overs 15.00
... :KING TUT'S TOMB TPB (2010, $14.99) r/Batman Confidential #26-28, Batman #353 and Brave and the Bold #164,171 15.00
... LEGACY-(1996, $17.95) reprints Legacy 18.00
...: LIFE AFTER DEATH HC-(2010, $19.99, dustjacket) r/#Batman #692-699 20.00
...: LONG SHADOWS HC-(2010, $19.99, dustjacket) r/#Batman #687-691 20.00
...: LONG SHADOWS SC-(2011, $14.99) r/#Batman #687-691 15.00
...: LOVERS & MADMEN-(See Batman Confidential)
...: MAD LOVE AND OTHER STORIES HC (2009, $19.99) r/Batman Adventures: Mad Love, Batman Advs. Holiday Special and other Dini/Timm collaborations; commentary 20.00
...: THE MANY DEATHS OF THE BATMAN (1992, $3.95, 84 pgs.)-r/Batman #433-435 w/new Byrne-c 6.00
...: MONSTERS (2009, $19.99, TPB)-r/Legends of the Dark Knight #71-73,83,84,89,90 20.00
...: THE MOVIES (1997, $19.95)-r/movie adaptations of Batman, Batman Returns, Batman Forever, Batman and Robin 20.00
...: NINE LIVES HC (2002, $24.95, sideways format) Motter-s/Lark-a 25.00
...: NINE LIVES SC (2003, $17.95, sideways format) Motter-s/Lark-a 18.00
...: OFFICER DOWN (2001, $12.95)-r/Commissioner shot x-over; Talon-c 13.00
.../ PLANETARY DELUXE HC (2011, $22.99)-r/Planetary/Batman: Night on Earth; script 23.00
...: PREY (1992, $12.95)-Gulacy/Austin-a 15.00
...: PRIVATE CASEBOOK HC (2008, $19.99)-r/Detective Comics #840-845 and story from DC Infinite Halloween Special #1 20.00
...: PRODIGAL (1997, $14.95)-Gulacy/Austin-a 15.00
...: R.I.P.: THE DELUXE EDITION HC (2009, $24.99)-r/Batman #676-683 and story from DC Universe #0 25.00
...: R.I.P.: SC (2010, $14.99)-r/Batman #676-683 and story from DC Universe #0 15.00
... SCARECROW TALES (2005, $19.99, TPB) r/Scarecrow stories & pin-ups from World's Finest #3 to present 20.00
...: SECRETS OF THE BATCAVE (2007, $17.99, TPB) r/Batcave stories 18.00
SHAMAN (1993, $12.95)-r/Legends/D.K. #1-5 15.00
...: SNOW (2007, $14.99, TPB)-r/Legends of the Dark Knight #192-196; Fisher-a 15.00
...: SON OF THE DEMON Hard-c (9/87, $14.95) (see Batman #655-658) 35.00
...: SON OF THE DEMON limited signed & numbered Hard-c (1,700) 60.00
...: SON OF THE DEMON Soft-c w/new-c ($8.95) 15.00
...: SON OF THE DEMON Soft-c (1989, $9.95, 2nd printing - 5th printing) 10.00
... : STRANGE APPARITIONS ($12.95) r/'77-'78 Englehart/Rogers stories from Detective #469-479; also Simonson-a 13.00
...: TALES OF THE DEMON (1991, $17.95, 212 pgs.)-Intro by Sam Hamm; reprints by Neal Adams(3) & Golden; contains Saga of Ra's al Ghul #1 20.00
TALES OF THE MULTIVERSE: BATMAN - VAMPIRE (2007, $19.99) r/Batman & Dracula: Red Rain, Batman: Bloodstorm and Batman: Crimson Mist; Van Lustbader foreword 20.00
...: TEN NIGHTS OF THE BEAST (1994, $5.95)-r/Batman #417-420 8.00
...: TERROR (2003, $12.95, TPB)-r/Legends of the Dark Knight #137-141; Gulacy-c 13.00
...: THE BLACK GLOVE (2009, $17.99, TPB) r/Batman #667-669,672-675 18.00
...: THE CHALICE (HC, '99, $24.95) Van Fleet painted-a 25.00
...: THE CHALICE (SC, '00, $14.95) Van Fleet painted-a 15.00
...: THE GREATEST STORIES EVER TOLD (2005, $19.99, TPB) Les Daniels intro. 20.00
...: THE GREATEST STORIES EVER TOLD VOLUME TWO (2007, $19.99, TPB) 20.00
...: THE JOKER'S LAST LAUGH ('08, $17.99) r/Joker's Last Laugh series #1-6 18.00
...: THE LAST ANGEL (1994, $12.95, TPB) Lustbader-s 15.00
...: THE RESURRECTION OF RA'S AL GHUL (2008, $29.99, HC w/DJ) r/x-over 30.00
...: THE RESURRECTION OF RA'S AL GHUL (2009, $19.99, SC) r/x-over 20.00
...: THE RING, THE ARROW AND THE BAT (2003, $19.95, TPB) r/Legends of the DCU #7-9 & Batman: Legends of the Dark Knight #127-131; Green Lantern & Green Arrow app. 20.00

Batman: Year One TPB © DC

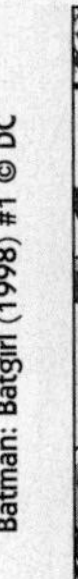

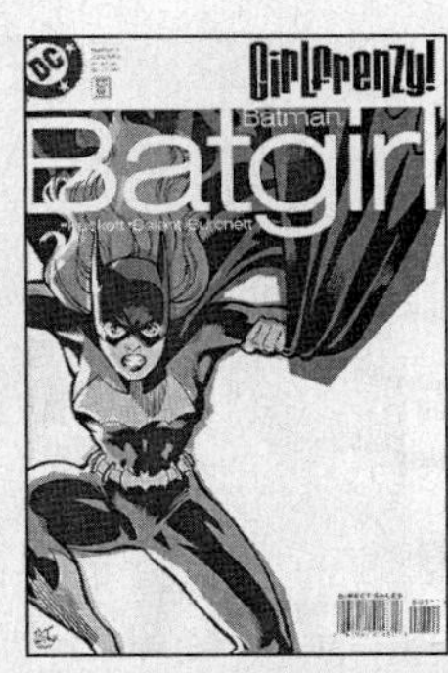

Batman: Batgirl (1998) #1 © DC

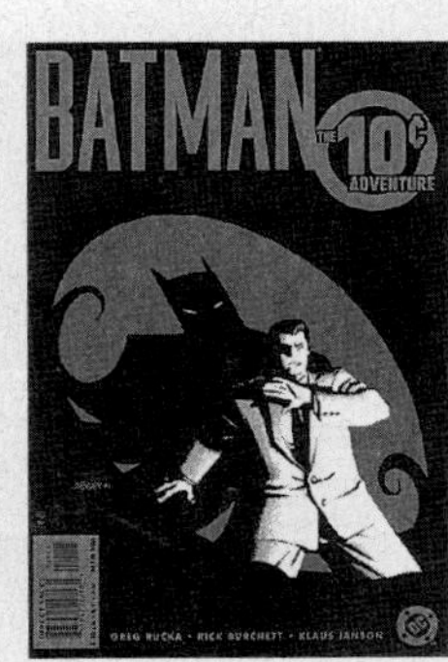

Batman: The 10-Cent Adventure © DC

GD 2.0 | VG 4.0 | FN 6.0 | VF 8.0 | VF/NM 9.0 | NM- 9.2

...: THE STRANGE DEATHS OF BATMAN ('09, $19.99) r/Batman #291-294, Det. #347, World's Finest #184,269, Brave & the Bold #115, Nightwing #52; Aparo-c 20.00
...: THE WRATH ('09, $17.99) r/Batman Special #1 and Batman Confidential #13-16 18.00
...: THRILLKILLER (1998, $12.95, TPB)-r/series & Thrillkiller '62 15.00
...: TIME AND THE BATMAN HC ('11, $19.99) r/Batman #700-703; cover gallery 20.00
...: TWO-FACE AND SCARECROW YEAR ONE (2009, $19.99, TPB)-r/Year One: Batman Scarecrow #1,2 and Two Face: Year One #1,2 20.00
...: UNDER THE COWL (2010, $17.99, TPB)-r/app. Dick Grayson, Tim Drake, Damian Wayne, Jean Paul Valley and Terry McGinnis as Batman 18.00
...: UNDER THE HOOD (2005, $9.99, TPB)-r/Batman #635-641 10.00
...: UNDER THE HOOD Vol. 2 (2006, $9.99, TPB)-r/Batman #645-650 & Annual #25 10.00
...: UNDER THE RED HOOD (2011, $29.99, TPB)-r/Batman #635-641,645-650, Ann. #25 30.00
...: VENOM (1993, $9.95, TPB)-r/Legends of the Dark Knight #16-20; embossed-c 15.00
... VS. TWO-FACE (2008, $19.99, TPB) r/initial (Det. #80) & classic battles; Bianchi-c 20.00
...: WAR CRIMES (2006, $12.99, TPB) r/x-over; James Jean-c 13.00
... WAR DRUMS (2004, $17.95) r/Detective #790-796 & Robin #126-128 18.00
...: WAR GAMES ACT 1,2,3 (2005, $14.95/$14.99, TPB) r/x-over; James Jean-c; each.. 15.00
...: WHATEVER HAPPENED TO THE CAPED CRUSADER? HC-(2009, $24.99, d.j.) r/Batman #686, Detective #853 and other Gaiman Batman stories; Gaiman intro.; Andy Kubert sketch pages; new Kubert cover 25.00
...: WHATEVER HAPPENED TO THE CAPED CRUSADER? SC-(2010, $14.99) 15.00
YEAR ONE Hard-c (1988, $12.95) r/Batman #404-407 25.00
YEAR ONE (1988, $9.95, TPB)-r/Batman #404-407 by Miller; intro by Miller 15.00
YEAR ONE (TPB, 2nd & 3rd printings) 10.00
YEAR ONE Deluxe HC (2005, $19.99, die-cut d.j.) new intro. by Miller and developmental material from Mazzucchelli; script pages and sketches 20.00
YEAR ONE (Deluxe) SC (2007, $14.99) r/story plus bonus material from 2005 HC 15.00
YEAR TWO (1990, $9.95, TPB)-r/Det. 575-578 by McFarlane; wraparound-c 15.00

BATMAN (one-shots)
... ABDUCTION, THE (1998, $5.95) 6.00
... ALLIES SECRET FILES AND ORIGINS 2005 (8/05, $4.99) stories/pin-ups by various 5.00
... & ROBIN (1997, $5.95)-Movie adaptation 6.00
...: ARKHAM ASYLUM - TALES OF MADNESS (5/98, $2.95) Cataclysm x-over pt. 16 4.00
... : BANE (1997, $4.95)-Dixon-s/Burchett-a; Stelfreeze-c; cover art interlocks w/Batman:(Batgirl, Mr. Freeze, Poison Ivy) 6.00
... : BATGIRL (1997, $4.95)-Puckett-s/Haley,Kesel-a; Stelfreeze-c; cover art interlocks w/Batman:(Bane, Mr. Freeze, Poison Ivy) 6.00
... : BATGIRL (6/98, $1.95)-Girlfrenzy; Balent-a 4.00
... : BLACKGATE (1/97, $3.95) Dixon-s 5.00
... : BLACKGATE - ISLE OF MEN (4/98, $2.95) Cataclysm x-over pt. 8; Moench-s/Aparo-a 4.00
... BOOK OF SHADOWS, THE (1999, $5.95) 6.00
BROTHERHOOD OF THE BAT (1995, $5.95)-Elseworlds-s 6.00
... BULLOCK'S LAW (8/99, $4.95) Dixon-s 5.00
.../CAPTAIN AMERICA (1996, $5.95, DC/Marvel) Elseworlds story; Byrne-c/s/a 8.00
... : CATWOMAN DEFIANT nn (1992, $4.95, prestige format)-Milligan scripts; cover art interlocks w/Batman: Penguin Triumphant; special foil logo 6.00
.../CATWOMAN: FOLLOW THE MONEY (1/11, $4.99) Chaykin-c/s/a 5.00
... /DANGER GIRL (2/05, $4.95)-Leinil Yu-a/c; Joker, Harley Quinn & Catwoman app. 8.00
... /DAREDEVIL (2000, $5.95)-Barreto-a 6.00
...: DARK ALLEGIANCES (1996, $5.95)-Elseworlds story, Chaykin-c/a 7.00
...: DARK KNIGHT GALLERY (1/96, $3.50)-Pin-ups by Pratt, Balent, & others 4.00
...:DAY OF JUDGMENT (11/99, $3.95) 5.00
...:DEATH OF INNOCENTS (12/96, $3.95)-O'Neil-s/ Staton-a(p) 5.00
.../DEMON (1996, $4.95)-Alan Grant scripts 6.00
.../DEMON: A TRAGEDY (2000, $5.95)-Grant-s/Murray painted-a 6.00
...:D.O.A. (1999, $6.95)-Bob Hall-s/a 7.00
...:/DOC SAVAGE SPECIAL (2010, $4.99)-Azzarello-s/Noto-a/covers by JG Jones & Morales; preview of First Wave line (Batman, Doc Savage, The Spirit, Blackhawks) 5.00
...:DREAMLAND (2000, $5.95)-Grant-s/Breyfogle-a 6.00
... : EGO (2000, $6.95)-Darwyn Cooke-s/a 7.00
... 80-PAGE GIANT (8/98, $4.95) Stelfreeze-c 6.00
... 80-PAGE GIANT 1 (2/10, $5.99) Andy Kubert-c; Catwoman, Poison Ivy app. 6.00
... 80-PAGE GIANT 2 (10/99, $4.95) Luck of the Draw 6.00
... 80-PAGE GIANT 3 (7/00, $5.95) Calendar Man 6.00
... 80-PAGE GIANT 2011 (2/11, $5.95) Nguyen-c; short stories of villains by various 6.00
... 80-PAGE GIANT 2011 (10/11, $5.99) Nguyen-c; art by Naifeh & others 6.00
... FOREVER (1995, $5.95, direct market) 6.00
... FOREVER (1995, $3.95, newsstand) 4.00
FULL CIRCLE nn (1991, $5.95, 68 pgs.)-Sequel to Batman: Year Two 8.00
...GALLERY, The 1 (1992, $2.95)-Pin-ups by Miller, N. Adams & others 4.00
...GOLDEN STREETS OF GOTHAM (2003, $6.95) Elseworlds in early 1900s 7.00
...GOTHAM BY GASLIGHT (1989, $3.95) Elseworlds; Mignola-a/Augustyn-s 8.00
...GOTHAM CITY SECRET FILES 1 (4/00, $4.95) Batgirl app. 6.00
...: GOTHAM NOIR (2001, $6.95)-Elseworlds; Brubaker-s/Phillips-c/a 7.00

.../GREEN ARROW: THE POISON TOMORROW nn (1992, $5.95, square-bound, 68 pgs.) Netzer-c/a 8.00
...: HIDDEN TREASURES 1 (12/10, $4.99) unpubl. story Wrightson-a; r/Swamp Thing #7 5.00
HOLY TERROR nn (1991, $4.95, 52 pgs.)-Elseworlds story 6.00
.../HOUDINI: THE DEVIL'S WORKSHOP (1993, $5.95) 7.00
... :HUNTRESS/SPOILER - BLUNT TRAUMA (5/98, $2.95) Cataclysm pt. 13; Dixon-s/Barreto & Sienkiewicz-a 4.00
...: I, JOKER nn (1998, $4.95)-Elseworlds story; Bob Hall-s/a 6.00
...: IN BARCELONA: DRAGON'S KNIGHT 1 (7/09, $3.99) Waid-s/Olmos-a/Jim Lee-c 4.00
...: IN DARKEST KNIGHT nn (1994, $4.95, 52 pgs.)-Elseworlds story; Batman w/Green Lantern's ring. 6.00
...:JOKER'S APPRENTICE (5/99, $3.95) Von Eeden-a 5.00
...:JOKER'S DAUGHTER (4/14, $4.99) Bennett-s/Hetrick-a/Jeanty-c 5.00
.../ JOKER: SWITCH (2003, $6.95)-Bolton-a/Grayson-s 7.00
...:JUDGE DREDD: JUDGEMENT ON GOTHAM nn (1991, $5.95, 68 pgs.) Simon Bisley-c/a; Grant/Wagner scripts 8.00
...:JUDGE DREDD: JUDGEMENT ON GOTHAM nn (2nd printing) 6.00
...:JUDGE DREDD: THE ULTIMATE RIDDLE (1995, $4.95) 6.00
...:JUDGE DREDD: VENDETTA IN GOTHAM (1993, $5.95) 7.00
...: KNIGHTGALLERY (1995, $3.50)-Elseworlds sketchbook. 4.00
.../ LOBO (2000, $5.95)-Elseworlds; Joker app.; Bisley-a 6.00
...: MASK OF THE PHANTASM (1994, $2.95)-Movie adapt. 4.00
...: MASK OF THE PHANTASM (1994, $4.95)-Movie adapt. 6.00
...: MASQUE (1997, $6.95)-Elseworlds; Grell-c/s/a 7.00
...: MASTER OF THE FUTURE nn (1991, $5.95, 68 pgs.)-Elseworlds; sequel to Gotham By Gaslight; Barreto-a; embossed-c 6.00
...: MITEFALL (1995, $4.95)-Alan Grant script, Kevin O'Neill-a 6.00
... : MR. FREEZE (1997, $4.95)-Dini-s/Buckingham-a; Stelfreeze-c; cover art interlocks w/Batman:(Bane, Batgirl, Poison Ivy) 6.00
... /NIGHTWING: BLOODBORNE (2002, $5.95) Cypress-a; McKeever-c 6.00
...: NOEL (2011, $22.99, HC graphic novel with dustjacket) Lee Bermejo-s/a; Jim Lee intro.; Catwoman, Superman & The Joker app.; bonus sketch & layout art pages 23.00
...: NOSFERATU (1999, $5.95) McKeever-a 6.00
...: OF ARKHAM (2000, $5.95)-Elseworlds; Grant-s/Alcatena-a 6.00
...: OUR WORLDS AT WAR (8/01, $2.95)-Jae Lee-c 3.00
...: PENGUIN TRIUMPHANT nn (1992, $4.95)-Staton-a(p); foil logo 6.00
...•PHANTOM STRANGER nn (1997, $4.95) nn-Grant-s/Ransom-a 6.00
... : PLUS (2/97, $2.95) Arsenal-c/app. 4.00
... : POISON IVY (1997, $4.95)-J.F. Moore-s/Apthorp-a; Stelfreeze-c; cover art interlocks w/Batman:(Bane, Batgirl, Mr. Freeze) 6.00
.../POISON IVY: CAST SHADOWS (2004, $6.95) Van Fleet-c/a; Nocenti-s 7.00
.../PUNISHER: LAKE OF FIRE (1994, $4.95, DC/Marvel) 6.00
... :REIGN OF TERROR ('99, $4.95) Elseworlds 6.00
...RETURNS MOVIE SPECIAL (1992, $3.95) 4.00
...RETURNS MOVIE PRESTIGE (1992, $5.95, squarebound)-Dorman painted-c 6.00
...:RIDDLER-THE RIDDLE FACTORY (1995, $4.95)-Wagner script 6.00
...: ROOM FULL OF STRANGERS (2004, $5.95) Scott Morse-s/c/a 6.00
...: SCARECROW 3-D (12/98, $3.95) w/glasses 5.00
.../ SCARFACE: A PSYCHODRAMA (2001, $5.95)-Adlard-a/Sienkiewicz-c 6.00
...: SCAR OF THE BAT nn (1996, $4.95)-Elseworlds; Max Allan Collins script; Barreto-a 6.00
... :SCOTTISH CONNECTION (1998, $5.95) Quitely-a 6.00
... :SEDUCTION OF THE GUN nn (1992, $2.50, 68 pgs.) 5.00
.../SPAWN: WAR DEVIL nn (1994, $4.95, 52 pgs.) 6.00
... SPECIAL 1 (4/84)-Mike W. Barr story; Golden-c/a 1 2 3 5 6 8
.../SPIDER-MAN (1997, $4.95) Dematteis-s/Nolan & Kesel-a 6.00
... : THE ABDUCTION ('98, $5.95) 6.00
... : THE BLUE, THE GREY, & THE BAT (1992, $5.95)-Weiss/Lopez-a 7.00
... :THE HILL (5/00, $2.95)-Priest-s/Martinbrough-a 3.00
... :THE KILLING JOKE (1988, deluxe 52 pgs., mature readers)-Bolland-c/a; Alan Moore scripts; Joker cripples Barbara Gordon 4 8 12 28 47 65
...: THE KILLING JOKE (2nd thru 14th printings) 2 4 6 13 18 22
...: THE KILLING JOKE : THE DELUXE EDITION (2008, $17.99, HC) re-colored version along with Bolland-s/a from Batman Black and White #4; sketch pages; Tim Sale intro. 18.00
...: THE MAN WHO LAUGHS (2005, $6.95)-Retells 1st meeting with the Joker; Mahnke-a 7.00
...: THE OFFICIAL COMIC ADAPTATION OF THE WARNER BROS. MOTION PICTURE (1989, $2.50, regular format, 68 pgs.)-Ordway-c 4.00
...: THE OFFICIAL COMIC ADAPTATION OF THE WARNER BROS. MOTION PICTURE (1989, $4.95, prestige format, 68 pgs.)-same interiors but different-c 6.00
...: THE ORDER OF BEASTS (2004, $5.95)-Elseworlds; Eddie Campbell-a 6.00
...: THE SPIRIT (1/07, $4.99)-Loeb-s/Cooke-a; P'Gell & Commissioner Dolan app. 5.00
...: THE 10-CENT ADVENTURE (3/02, 10¢) intro. to the "Bruce Wayne: Murderer" x-over; Rucka-s/Burchett & Janson-a/Dave Johnson-c 3.00

NOTE: (Also see Promotional Comics section for alternate copies with special outer half-covers promoting local comic shops)

...: THE 12-CENT ADVENTURE (10/04, 12¢) intro. to the "War Games" x-over;

Batman Adventures (2003 series) #2 © DC

Batman and Robin #12 © DC

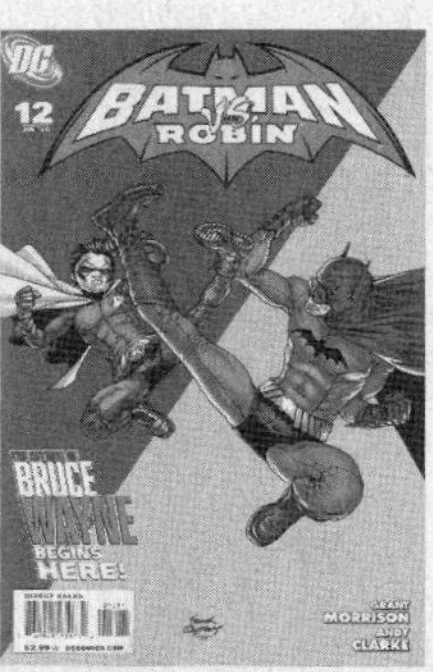

Batman and the Outsiders (2007 series) #1 © DC

	GD 2.0	VG 4.0	FN 6.0	VF 8.0	VF/NM 9.0	NM- 9.2

Grayson-s/Bachs-a; Catwoman & Spoiler app. 3.00
...: TWO-FACE-CRIME AND PUNISHMENT-(1995, $4.95)-McDaniel-a 6.00
... : TWO FACES (11/98, $4.95) Elseworlds 6.00
...Vs. THE INCREDIBLE HULK (1995, $3.95)-r/DC Special Series #27 6.00
...: VILLAINS SECRET FILES (10/98, $4.95) Origin-s 6.00
... VILLAINS SECRET FILES AND ORIGINS 2005 (7/05, $4.99) Clayface origin w/ Mignola-a; Black Mask story, pin-up of villains by various; Barrionuevo-c 6.00

BATMAN ADVENTURES, THE (Based on animated series)
DC Comics: Oct, 1992 - No. 36, Oct, 1995 ($1.25/$1.50)

1-Penguin-c/story 1 3 4 6 8 10
1 ($1.95, Silver Edition)-2nd printing 3.00
2,4-6,8-11,13-15,17-19: 2-Catwoman-c/story. 5-Scarecrow-c/story. 10-Riddler-c/story. 11-Man-Bat-c/story. 18-Batgirl-c/story. 19-Scarecrow-c/story 4.00
3-Joker-c/story 2 4 6 8 10 12
7-Special edition polybagged with Man-Bat trading card 6.00
12-(9/93) 1st Harley Quinn app. in comics; 1st animated-version Batgirl app. in title 40 80 120 200 325 450
16-Joker-c/story; begin $1.50-c 3 6 9 16 23 30
20-24,26,27,29-32: 26-Batgirl app. 3.00
25-($2.50, 52 pgs.)-Superman app. 4.00
28-Joker & Harley Quinn-c; 2nd app. Harley Quinn 3 6 9 16 23 30
33-36: 33-Begin $1.75-c 3.00
Annual 1 ('94) 3rd app. Harley Quinn 3 6 9 19 30 40
Annual 2 ('95) Demon-c/story; Ra's al Ghul app. 4.00
...: Dangerous Dames & Demons (2003, $14.95, TPB) r/Annual 1,2, Mad Love & Adventures in the DC Universe #3; Bruce Timm painted-c 30.00
Holiday Special 1 (1995, $2.95) Harley Quinn app. 2 4 6 11 16 20
The Collected Adventures Vol. 1,2 ('93, '95, $5.95) 10.00
TPB ('98, $7.95) r/#1-6; painted wraparound-c 10.00

BATMAN ADVENTURES (Based on animated series)
DC Comics: Jun, 2003 - No. 17, Oct, 2004 ($2.25)

1-Timm-c 1 2 3 5 6 8
1-Free Comic Book Day edition (6/03) Timm-c 4.00
1-Halloween Fest Special Edition (12/15) Timm-c 3.00
2,4-9,11-15,17: 4-Ra's al Ghul app. 6-8-Phantasm app. 14-Grey Ghost app. 3.00
3-Joker & Harley Quinn-c/app. 3 6 9 16 23 30
10-Catwoman-c/app. 2 4 6 11 16 20
16-Joker & Harley Quinn-c/app. 4 8 12 23 37 50
Batman/Scooby-Doo Halloween Fest 1 (12/12, giveaway flipbook with Scooby-Doo) r/#1 5.00
Vol. 1: Rogues Gallery (2004, $6.95, digest size) r/#1-4 & Batman: Gotham Advs. #50 7.00
Vol. 2: Shadows & Masks (2004, $6.95, digest size) r/#5-9 7.00

BATMAN ADVENTURES, THE: MAD LOVE
DC Comics: Feb, 1994 ($3.95/$4.95)

1-Origin of Harley Quinn; Dini-s/Timm-c/a 7 14 21 44 82 120
1-($4.95, Prestige format) new Timm painted-c 4 8 12 23 37 50

BATMAN ADVENTURES, THE: THE LOST YEARS (TV)
DC Comics: Jan, 1998 - No. 5, May, 1998 ($1.95) (Based on animated series)

1-5-Leads into Fall '97's new animated episodes. 4-Tim Drake becomes Robin. 5-Dick becomes Nightwing 3.00
TPB-(1999, $9.95) r/series 12.00

BATMAN/ALIENS
DC Comics/Dark Horse: Mar, 1997 - No. 2, Apr, 1997 ($4.95, limited series)

1,2: Wrightson-c/a. 6.00
TPB-(1997, $14.95) w/prequel from DHP #101,102 15.00

BATMAN/ALIENS II
DC Comics/Dark Horse: 2003 - No. 3, 2003 ($5.95, limited series)

1-3-Edginton-s/Staz Johnson-a 6.00
TPB-(2003, $14.95) r/#1-3 15.00

BATMAN AND... (See Batman and Robin [2011 series] #19-on)

BATMAN AND ROBIN (See Batman R.I.P. and Batman: Battle For The Cowl series)
DC Comics: Aug, 2009 - No. 26, Oct, 2011 ($2.99)

1-Grant Morrison-s/Frank Quitely-a/c; Dick Grayson & Damian Wayne team 8.00
1-Variant cover by J.G. Jones 20.00
1-Second thru Fourth printings - recolored Quitely covers 3.00
2-16-Quitely-c. 2-Three printings. 4-6-Tan-a. 7-9-Stewart-a; Batwoman & Squire app. 13-15-Joker app.; Irving-a. 16-Bruce Wayne returns; Batman Inc. announced 3.00
2-Variant-c by Adam Kubert 10.00
17-26: 17-McDaniel-a/March-c. 21,22-Gleason-a. 23-25-Red Hood app. 3.00
... #1 Special Edition (6/10, $1.00) r/#1 with "What's Next?" cover logo 3.00
...: Batman and Robin Must Die - The Deluxe Edition HC (2011, $24.99) r/#13-16; cover and costume design sketch art 25.00
...: Batman Reborn - The Deluxe Edition HC (2010, $24.99) r/#1-6; design sketch art 25.00
...: Batman Reborn SC (2011, $14.99) r/#1-6; cover and character design sketch art 15.00
...: Batman vs. Robin - The Deluxe Edition HC (2010, $24.99) r/#7-12; cover sketch art 25.00

BATMAN AND ROBIN (DC New 52)(Cover title changes each issue from #19-32)
DC Comics: Nov, 2011 - No. 40, May, 2015 ($2.99)

1-Bruce and Damian Wayne in costume; Tomasi-s/Gleason-a 4.00
2-14: 5,6-Ducard flashback. 9-Night of the Owls 3.00
15-Death of the Family tie-in; die-cut Joker cover 5.00
16-18: 16-Death of the Family tie-in. 18-Requiem 3.00
19-23: 19-Red Robin. 20-Red Hood. 21-Batgirl. 22-Catwoman. 23-Nightwing 3.00
23.1, 23.2, 23.3, 23.4 (11/13, $2.99, regular covers) 3.00
23.1 (11/13, $3.99, 3-D cover) "Two Face #1" on cover; March-a; Scarecrow app. 6.00
23.2 (11/13, $3.99, 3-D cover) "Court of Owls #1" on cover; history of the Owls 5.00
23.3 (11/13, $3.99, 3-D cover) "Ra's al Ghul #1" on cover; history of Ra's retold 5.00
23.4 (11/13, $3.99, 3-D cover) "Killer Croc #1" on cover; Croc's origin 5.00
24-40: 24-28-Two-Face. 25-Matches Malone app. 29-Aquaman. 30-Wonder Woman. 31-Frankenstein. 32-Ra's al Ghul. 33-38-Title back to Batman and Robin. 37-Darkseid app.; Damien returns; cont'd in Robin Rises: Alpha. 39,40-Justice League app. 3.00
#0 (11/12, $2.99) Damian's childhood training with Talia; Tomasi-s/Gleason-a 3.00
Annual 1 (3/13, $4.99) Damian in the Batman #666 costume; Andy Kubert-c 5.00
Annual 2 (3/14, $4.99) Mahnke-a; flashback to Dick Grayson's first week as Robin 5.00
Annual 3 (6/15, $4.99) Ryp-a/Syaf-c 5.00
...: Futures End 1 (11/14, $2.99, regular-c) Five years later; Nguyen-a; 1st app. Duke Thomas as future Robin 3.00
...: Futures End 1 (11/14, $3.99, 3-D cover) 4.00

BATMAN AND ROBIN ADVENTURES (TV)
DC Comics: Nov, 1995 - No. 25, Dec, 1997 ($1.75) (Based on animated series)

1-Dini-s. 4.00
2-4,6,7,9-15,17,19,20,22,23: 2-4-Dini script. 4-Penguin-c/app. 9-Batgirl & Talia-c/app. 10-Ra's al Ghul-c/app. 11-Man-Bat app. 12-Bane-c/app. 13-Scarecrow-c/app. 15 Deadman-c/app. 3.00
5-Joker-c/story 6.00
8-Poison Ivy & Harley Quinn-c/app. 2 4 6 13 18 22
16,18,24: 16-Catwoman-c/app. 18-Joker-c/app. 24-Poison Ivy app. 1 2 3 5 6 8
21-Batgirl-c 3 6 9 16 23 30
25-($2.95, 48 pgs.) 4.00
Annual 1,2 (11/96, 11/97): 1-Phantasm-c/app. 2-Zatara & Zatanna-c/app. 4.00
...: Sub-Zero(1998, $3.95) Adaptation of animated video 4.00

BATMAN & ROBIN ETERNAL (Sequel to Batman Eternal)
DC Comics: Dec, 2015 - No. 26, May, 2016 ($3.99/$2.99, weekly series)

1-($3.99) Tynion IV & Snyder-s/Daniel-a; Cassandra Cain app. 4.00
2-25-($2.99) Dick Grayson, Red Hood, Red Robin, Bluebird, Spoiler app. 6-1st app. Mother. 9,10,15,16,24,25-Azrael app. 23-25-Midnighter app. 3.00
26-($3.99) Conclusion; Tony Daniel-c 4.00

BATMAN AND SUPERMAN ADVENTURES: WORLD'S FINEST
DC Comics: 1997 ($6.95, square-bound, one-shot) (Based on animated series)

1-Adaptation of animated crossover episode; Dini-s/Timm-c 2 4 6 8 11 14

BATMAN AND SUPERMAN: WORLD'S FINEST
DC Comics: Apr, 1999 - No. 10, Jan, 2000 ($4.95/$1.99, limited series)

1,10-($4.95, squarebound) Taylor-a 5.00
2-9-($1.99) 5-Batgirl app. 8-Catwoman-c/app. 3.00
TPB (2003, $19.95) r/#1-10 20.00

BATMAN AND THE OUTSIDERS (The Adventures of the Outsiders #33 on)
(Also see Brave & The Bold #200 & The Outsiders) (Replaces The Brave and the Bold)
DC Comics: Aug, 1983 - No. 32, Apr, 1986 (Mando paper #5 on)

1-Batman, Halo, Geo-Force, Katana, Metamorpho & Black Lightning begin 5.00
2-32: 5-New Teen Titans x-over. 9-Halo begins. 11,12-Origin Katana. 18-More info on Metamorpho's origin. 28-31-Lookers origin. 32-Team disbands 3.00
Annual 1,2 (9/84, 9/85): 2-Metamorpho & Sapphire Stagg wed 4.00
NOTE: ***Aparo** a-1-9, 11-13p, 16-20; c-1-4, 5i, 6-21, Annual 1, 2.* ***B. Kane** a-3r.* ***Layton** a-19i, 20i.* ***Lopez** a-3p.* ***Miller** c-Annual 1.* ***Perez** c-5p.* ***B. Willingham** a-14p.*

BATMAN AND THE OUTSIDERS (Continues as The Outsiders for #15-39)
DC Comics: Dec, 2007 - No. 14, Feb, 2009; No. 40, Jul, 2011 ($2.99)

1-14: 1-Batman, Catwoman, Martian Manhunter, Katana, Metamorpho, Thunder & Grace begin. 4-Batgirl joins. 11-13-Batman R.I.P. 3.00
40 (7/11) Final issue; Didio-s/Tan-a; history of the team 3.00

Batman: Arkham Knight #2 © DC

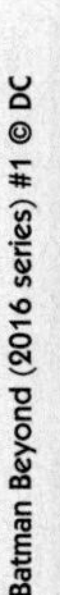
Batman Beyond (2016 series) #1 © DC

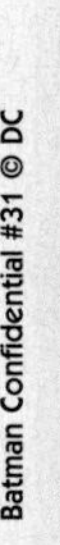
Batman Confidential #31 © DC

GD VG FN VF VF/NM NM-
2.0 4.0 6.0 8.0 9.0 9.2

GD VG FN VF VF/NM NM-
2.0 4.0 6.0 8.0 9.0 9.2

... Special (3/09, $3.99) Alfred assembles a new team; Andy Kubert-a; two covers 4.00
...: The Chrysalis TPB (2008, $14.99) r/#1-5 15.00
...: The Snare TPB (2008, $14.99) r/#6-10 15.00

BATMAN: ARKHAM CITY (Prequel to the video game)
DC Comics: Early Jul, 2011 - No. 5, Oct, 2011 ($2.99, limited series)

1-5-Dini-s/D'Anda-a; Joker app. 3.00
...: End Game (1/13, $6.99) Story bridges Arkham City and Arkham Unhinged series 7.00

BATMAN: ARKHAM KNIGHT (Prequel to the Arkham video game trilogy finale)
DC Comics: May, 2015 - No. 12, Feb, 2016 ($3.99)

1-Tomasi-s/Bogdanovic-a/Panosian-c; 1st comic app. of Arkham Knight 6.00
2-12: 2-Harley Quinn cover 4.00
Annual 1 (11/15, $4.99) Tomasi-s/Segovia-a; Firefly app. 5.00
...: Robin 1 (1/16, $2.99) Tomasi-s/Rocha-a 3.00

BATMAN: ARKHAM KNIGHT: GENESIS
DC Comics: Oct, 2015 - No. 6 ($2.99, limited series)

1-4: 1-Tomasi-s/Borges-a/Sejic-c; Jason Todd's origin. 4-Harley Quinn cover 3.00

BATMAN: ARKHAM UNHINGED (Based on the Batman: Arkham City video game)
DC Comics: Jun, 2012 - No. 20, Jan, 2014 ($2.99)

1-20: 1-Wilkins-c; Catwoman, Two-Face & Hugo Strange app. 3.00

BATMAN: BANE OF THE DEMON
DC Comics: Mar, 1998 - No. 4, June, 1998 ($1.95, limited series)

1-4-Dixon-s/Nolan-a; prelude to Legacy x-over 3.00

BATMAN: BATTLE FOR THE COWL (Follows Batman R.I.P. storyline)
DC Comics: May, 2009 - No. 3, Jul, 2009 ($3.99, limited series)

1-3-Tony Daniel-s/a/c; 2 covers on each 4.00
...: Arkham Asylum (6/09, $2.99) Hine-s/Haun-a/Ladronn-c 3.00
...: Commissioner Gordon (5/09, $2.99) Mandrake-a/Ladronn-c; Mr. Freeze app. 3.00
...: Man-Bat (6/09, $2.99) Harris-s/Calafiore-a/Ladronn-c; Dr. Phosphorus app. 3.00
...: The Network (7/09, $2.99) Nicieza-s/Calafiore & Kramer-a/Ladronn-c 3.00
...: The Underground (6/09, $2.99) Yost-s/Raimondi-a/Ladronn-c; Harley Quinn app. 3.00
Companion SC (2009, $14.99) r/ five one-shots 15.00
HC (2009, $19.99) r/#1-3 & Gotham Gazette: Batman Dead & Gotham Gazette: Batman Alive; gallery of variant covers and sketch art 20.00
SC (2010, $14.99) same contents as HC 15.00

BATMAN BEYOND (Based on animated series)
DC Comics: Mar, 1999 - No. 6, Aug, 1999 ($1.99, limited series)

1-Adaptation of pilot episode, Timm-c 3 6 9 15 22 28
2-6: 2-Adaptation of pilot episode continues, Timm-c 5.00
TPB (1999, $9.95) r/#1-6 15.00

BATMAN BEYOND (Based on animated series)(Continuing series)
DC Comics: Nov, 1999 - No. 24, Oct, 2001 ($1.99)

1-Rousseau-a; Batman vs. Batman 6.00
2-24: 14-Demon-c/app. 21,22-Justice League Unlimited-c/app. 4.00
...: Return of the Joker (2/01, $2.95) adaptation of video release 3 6 9 19 30 40

BATMAN BEYOND (Animated series)(See Superman/Batman Annual #4)
DC Comics: Aug, 2010 - No. 6, Jan, 2011 ($2.99, limited series)

1-6: 1-Benjamin-a; Nguyen-c; return of Hush 3.00
1-Variant-c by J.H. Williams III 6.00
...: Hush Beyond TPB (2011, $14.99) r/#1-6 15.00

BATMAN BEYOND
DC Comics: Mar, 2011 - No. 8, Oct, 2011 ($2.99)

1-8: 1-3-Justice League app.; Beechen-s/Benjamin-a/Nguyen-c. 8-Inque app. 3.00
1-Variant-c by Darwyn Cooke 4.00

BATMAN BEYOND (Tim Drake as Batman)
DC Comics: Aug, 2015 - No. 16, Nov. 2016 ($2.99)

1-16: 1-Jurgens-s/Chang-a. 2-Inque app. 5-New suit. 7,16-Stephen Thompson-a. 10-Tuftan app. 11-Superman's son app. 12-Tan-a. 16-Terry McGinnis back as Batman 3.00

BATMAN BEYOND (DC Rebirth)
DC Comics: Dec, 2016 - Present ($2.99)

1-5: 1-3-Dan Jurgens-s/Bernard Chang-a. 4,5-Pete Woods-a 3.00
...: Rebirth 1 (11/16, $2.99) Terry McGinnis in the suit; Jurgens-s/Sook-a 3.00

BATMAN BEYOND UNIVERSE
DC Comics: Oct, 2013 - No. 16, Jan, 2015 ($3.99)

1-12: 1-Superman & the JLB app.; Sean Murphy-c. 8-12-Wonder Woman app. 9-12-Justice Lords app. 13,14-Phantasm returns. 15-Royal Flush Gang app. 4.00

BATMAN BEYOND UNLIMITED
DC Comics: Apr, 2012 - No. 18, Sept, 2013 ($3.99)

1-18: 1-Beechen-s/Breyfogle-a; Superman & Justice League back-ups; Nguyen-c. 17-Metal Men return; Marvel Family app. 18-New Batgirl 4.00

BATMAN: BLACK & WHITE
DC Comics: June, 1996 - No. 4, Sept, 1996 ($2.95, B&W, limited series)

1-Stories by McKeever, Timm, Kubert, Chaykin, Goodwin; Jim Lee-c; Allred inside front-c; Moebius inside back-c 4.00
2-4: 2-Stories by Simonson, Corben, Bisley & Gaiman; Miller-c. 3-Stories by M. Wagner, Janson, Sienkiewicz, O'Neil & Kristiansen; B. Smith-c; Russell inside front-c; Silvestri inside back-c. 4-Stories by Bolland, Goodwin & Gianni, Strnad & Nowlan, O'Neil & Stelfreeze; Toth-c; pin-ups by Neal Adams & Alex Ross 3.00
Hardcover ('97, $39.95) r/series w/new art & cover plate 40.00
Softcover ('00, $19.95) r/series 20.00
Volume 2 HC ('02, $39.95, 7 3/4"x12") r/B&W back-up-s from Batman: Gotham Knights #1-16; stories and art by various incl. Ross, Buscema, Byrne, Ellison, Sale; Mignola-c 40.00
Volume 2 SC ('03, $19.95, 7 3/4"x12") same contents as HC 20.00
Volume 2 SC ('08, $19.99, reg. size) same contents as HC 20.00
Volume 3 HC ('07, $24.99, reg. size) r/B&W back-up-s from Batman: Gotham Knights #17-49; stories and art by various incl. Davis, DeCarlo, Morse, Schwartz, Thompson; Miller-c 25.00

BATMAN: BLACK & WHITE
DC Comics: Nov, 2013 - No. 6, Apr, 2014 ($4.99, B&W, limited series)

1-6-Short story anthology by various. 1-Silvestri-c; Neal Adams-a. 2-Steranko-c; Nino-a. 3-Bermejo-s/a. 4-Conner-c; Allred-s/a. 6-Mahnke-c; Hughes, Cloonan, Chiang-a 5.00

BATMAN: BOOK OF THE DEAD
DC Comics: Jun, 1999 - No. 2, July, 1999 ($4.95, limited series, prestige format)

1,2-Elseworlds; Kitson-a 6.00

BATMAN CACOPHONY
DC Comics: Jan, 2009 - No. 3, Mar, 2009 ($3.99, limited series)

1-3-Kevin Smith-s/Walt Flanagan-a; Joker and Onomatoapoeia app.; Adam Kubert-c 4.00
1-3-Variant-c by Sienkiewicz 15.00
HC (2009, $19.99, d.j.) r/#1-3; Kevin Smith intro.; script for #3, cover gallery 20.00
SC (2010, $14.99) r/#1-3; Kevin Smith intro.; script for #3, cover gallery 15.00

BATMAN: CATWOMAN DEFIANT (See Batman one-shots)

BATMAN/ CATWOMAN: TRAIL OF THE GUN
DC Comics: 2004 - No. 2, 2004 ($5.95, limited series, prestige format)

1,2-Elseworlds; Van Sciver-a/Nocenti-s 6.00

BATMAN CHRONICLES, THE (See the Batman TPB listings for the Golden Age reprint series that shares this title)
DC Comics: Summer, 1995 - No. 23, Winter, 2001 ($2.95, quarterly)

1-3,5-19: 1-Dixon/Grant/Moench script. 3-Bolland-c. 5-Oracle Year One story, Richard Dragon app., Chaykin-c. 6-Kaluta-c; Ra's al Ghul story. 7-Superman-c/app.11-Paul Pope-s/a. 12-Cataclysm pt. 10. 18-No Man's Land 5.00
4-Hitman story by Ennis, Contagion tie-in; Balent-c 2 4 6 9 12 15
20-23: 20-Catwoman and Relative Heroes-c/app. 21-Pander Bros.-a 4.00
...Gallery (3/97, $3.50) Pin-ups 4.00
...Gauntlet, The (1997, $4.95, one-shot) 6.00

BATMAN: CITY OF LIGHT
DC Comics: Dec, 2003 - No. 8, July, 2004 ($2.95, limited series)

1-8-Pander Brothers-a/s; Paniccia-s 3.00

BATMAN CONFIDENTIAL
DC Comics: Feb, 2007 - No. 54, May, 2011 ($2.99)

1-49,51-54: 1-6-Diggle-s/Portacio-a/c. 7-12-Cowan-a; Joker's origin. 13-16-Morales-a. 17-21-Batgirl vs. Catwoman; Maguire-a. 22-25-McDaniel-a; Joker app. 26-28-King Tut app.; Garcia-Lopez-a. 40-43-Kieth-s/a. 44-48-Mandrake-a/c 3.00
50-($4.99) Bingham-a; back-up Silver Age-style JLA story 5.00
...: Dead to Rights SC (2010, $14.99) r/#22-25,29,30 15.00
...: Lovers and Madmen HC (2008, $24.99, dustjacket) r/#7-12; Brad Meltzer intro. 25.00
...: Lovers and Madmen SC (2009, $14.99) r/#7-12; Brad Meltzer intro. 15.00
...: Rules of Engagement HC (2007, $24.99, dustjacket) r/#1-6 25.00
...: The Bat and the Beast SC (2010, $12.99) r/#31-35 13.00
...: The Cat and the Bat SC (2009, $12.99) r/#17-21 13.00
...: Vs. The Undead SC (2010, $14.99) r/#44-48 15.00

BATMAN: DARK DETECTIVE
DC Comics: Early July, 2005 - No. 6, Late September, 2005 ($2.99, limited series)

1-6-Englehart-s/Rogers & Austin-a; Silver St. Cloud and The Joker app. 3.00

BATMAN: DARK KNIGHT OF THE ROUND TABLE

Batman: Death Mask #1 © DC

Batman Eternal #1 © DC

Batman: Harley and Ivy #2 © DC

GD VG FN VF VF/NM NM-
2.0 4.0 6.0 8.0 9.0 9.2

DC Comics: 1999 - No. 2, 1999 ($4.95, limited series, prestige format)
1,2-Elseworlds; Giordano-a 7.00

BATMAN: DARK VICTORY
DC Comics: 1999 - No. 13, 2000 ($4.95/$2.95, limited series)
Wizard #0 Preview 3.00
1-($4.95) Loeb-s/Sale-c/a 5.00
2-12-($2.95) 3.00
13-($4.95) 5.00
Hardcover (2001, $29.95) with dust jacket; r/#0,1-13 30.00
Softcover (2002, $19.95) r/#0,1-13 20.00

BATMAN: DEATH AND THE MAIDENS
DC Comics: Oct, 2003 - No. 9, Aug, 2004 ($2.95, limited series)
1-Ra's al Ghul app.; Rucka-s/Janson-a 4.00
2-9: 9-Ra's al Ghul dies 3.00
TPB (2004, $19.95) r/#1-9 & Detective #783 20.00

BATMAN/ DEATHBLOW: AFTER THE FIRE
DC Comics/WildStorm: 2002 - No. 3, 2002 ($5.95, limited series)
1-3-Azzarello-s/Bermejo & Bradstreet-a 6.00
TPB (2003, $12.95) r/#1-3; plus concept art 13.00

BATMAN: DEATH MASK
DC Comics/CMX: Jun, 2008 - No. 4, Sept, 2008 ($2.99, B&W, limited series, right-to-left manga style)
1-4-Yoshinori Natsume-s/a 3.00
TPB (2008, $9.99, digest size) r/#1-4; interview with Yoshinori Natsume 10.00

BATMAN ETERNAL (Also see Arkham Manor series)
DC Comics: Jun, 2014 - No. 52, Jun, 2015 ($2.99, weekly series)
1-Snyder-s/Fabok-a; Professor Pyg & Jason Bard app. 5.00
2-51: 2-Carmine Falcone returns. 3-Stephanie Brown app. 6,14-17,26,29,30,37-Joker's Daughter app. 20-Spoiler dons costume. 30-Arkham Asylum destroyed. 41-Bluebird in costume 3.00
52-($3.99) Jae Lee-c; art by various 4.00

BATMAN: EUROPA
DC Comics: Jan, 2016 - No. 4, Apr, 2016 ($4.99, limited series)
1-4: 1-Joker app.; Casali & Azzarello-a/Camuncoli & Jim Lee-a. 2-Camuncoli-a 5.00
... Director's Cut 1 (8/16, $5.99) r/#1 with Jim Lee's pencil art; bonus original script 6.00

BATMAN FAMILY, THE
National Periodical Pub./DC Comics: Sept-Oct, 1975 - No. 20, Oct-Nov, 1978 (#1-4, 17-on: 68 pgs.) (Combined with Detective Comics with No. 481)
1-Origin/2nd app. Batgirl-Robin team-up (The Dynamite Duo); reprints plus one new story begins; N. Adams-a(r); r/1st app. Man-Bat from Det. #400
5 10 15 30 50 70
2-5: 2-r/Det. #369. 3-Batgirl & Robin learn each's i.d.; r/Batwoman app. from Batman #105. 4-r/1st Fatman app. from Batman #113. 5-r/1st Bat-Hound app. from Batman #92
3 6 9 16 23 30
6-(7-8/76) Joker's daughter on cover (1st app.) 7 14 21 46 86 125
7,8,14-16: 8-r/Batwoman app.14-Batwoman app. 15-3rd app. Killer Moth. 16-Bat-Girl cameo (last app. in costume until New Teen Titans #47) 2 4 6 13 18 22
9-Joker's daughter-c/app. 4 8 12 28 47 65
10-1st revival Batwoman; Cavalier app.; Killer Moth app.
3 6 9 18 28 38
11-13,17-20: 11-13-Rogers-a(p): 11-New stories begin; Man-Bat begins. 13-Batwoman cameo. 17-($1.00 size)-Batman, Huntress begin; Batwoman & Catwoman 1st meet. 18-20: Huntress by Staton in all. 20-Origin Ragman retold
3 6 9 17 26 35

NOTE: *Aparo* a-17; c-11-16. *Austin* a-12i. *Chaykin* a-14p. *Michael Golden* a-15-17,18-20p. *Grell* a-1; c-1. *Gil Kane* a-2r. *Kaluta* c-17, 19. *Newton* a-13. *Robinson* a-1r, 3i(r), 9r. *Russell* a-18i, 19i. *Starlin* a-17; c-18, 20.

BATMAN: FAMILY
DC Comics: Dec, 2002 - No. 8, Feb, 2003 ($2.95/$2.25, weekly limited series)
1,8-($2.95): 1-John Francis Moore-s/Hoberg & Gaudiano-a 4.00
2-7-($2.25): 3-Orpheus & Black Canary app. 3.00

BATMAN: GATES OF GOTHAM
DC Comics: Jul, 2011 - No. 5, Late Oct, 2011 ($2.99, limited series)
1-5-Flashbacks to 1880s Gotham City; Snyder-s/Higgins-a 3.00

BATMAN: GCPD
DC Comics: Aug, 1996 - No. 4, Nov, 1996 ($2.25, limited series)
1-4: Features Jim Gordon; Aparo/Sienkiewicz-a 3.00

BATMAN: GORDON OF GOTHAM

GD VG FN VF VF/NM NM-
2.0 4.0 6.0 8.0 9.0 9.2

DC Comics: June, 1998 - No. 4, Sept, 1998 ($1.95, limited series)
1-4: Gordon's early days in Chicago 3.00

BATMAN: GORDON'S LAW
DC Comics: Dec, 1996 - No. 4, Mar, 1997 ($1.95, limited series)
1-4: Dixon-s/Janson-c/a 3.00

BATMAN: GOTHAM ADVENTURES (TV)
DC Comics: June, 1998 - No. 60, May, 2003 ($2.95/$1.95/$1.99/$2.25)
1-($2.95) Based on Kids WB Batman animated series 6.00
2-3-($1.95): 2-Two-Face-c/app. 3.00
4-9,11-13,15-28: 4-Begin $1.99-c. 5-Deadman-c. 13-MAD #1 cover swipe 3.00
10,14-Harley Quinn c/app. 2 4 6 10 14 18
29,43-Harley Quinn c/app. 2 4 6 11 16 20
30,32-42,44,46-52,54-59: 50-Catwoman-c/app. 58-Creeper-c/app. 3.00
31-Joker-c/app. 6.00
45-Harley Quinn c/app. 3 6 9 16 23 30
53-Poison Ivy-c/app.; Harley Quinn cameo 1 3 4 6 8 10
60-Joker-c/app. 1 3 4 6 8 10
TPB (2000, $9.95) r/#1-6 15.00

BATMAN: GOTHAM AFTER MIDNIGHT
DC Comics: July, 2008 - No. 12, Jun, 2009 ($2.99, limited series)
1-12-Steve Niles-s/Kelley Jones-a/c. 1-Scarecrow app. 2-Man-Bat app. 5,6-Joker app. 3.00
TPB (2009, $19.99) r/#1-12; John Carpenter intro.; Jones sketch pages 20.00

BATMAN: GOTHAM COUNTY LINE
DC Comics: 2005 - No. 3, 2005 ($5.99, square-bound, limited series)
1-3-Steve Niles-s/Scott Hampton-a. 2,3-Deadman app. 6.00
TPB (2006, $17.99) r/#1-3 18.00

BATMAN: GOTHAM KNIGHTS
DC Comics: Mar, 2000 - No. 74, Apr, 2006 ($2.50/$2.75)
1-Grayson-s; B&W back-up by Warren Ellis & Jim Lee 4.00
2-10-Grayson-s; B&W back-ups by various. 6-Killing Joke flashback 3.00
11-($3.25) Bolland-c; Kyle Baker back-up story 4.00
12-24: 13-Officer Down x-over; Ellison back-up-s. 15-Colan back-up. 20-Superman-c/app.3.00
25,26-Bruce Wayne: Murderer pt. 4,10 3.50
27-31: 28,30,31-Bruce Wayne: Fugitive pt. 7,14,17 3.00
32-49: 32-Begin $2.75-c; Kaluta-a back-up. 33,34-Bane-c/app. 35-Mahfood-a back-up. 38-Bolton-a back-up. 43-Jason Todd & Batgirl app. 44-Jason Todd flashback 3.00
50-54-Hush returns-Barrionuevo-a/Bermejo-c. 53,54-Green Arrow app. 4.00
55-($3.75) Batman vs. Hush; Joker & Riddler app. 5.00
56-74: 56-58-War Games; Jae Lee-c. 60-65-Hush app. 66-Villains United tie-in; Talia app.3.00
Batman: Hush Returns TPB (2006, $12.99) r/#50-55,66; cover gallery 13.00

BATMAN: GOTHAM NIGHTS II (First series listed under Gotham Nights)
DC Comics: Mar, 1995 - No. 4, June, 1995 ($1.95, limited series)
1-4 3.00

BATMAN/GRENDEL (1st limited series)
DC Comics: 1993 - No. 2, 1993 ($4.95, limited series, squarebound; 52 pgs.)
1,2: Batman vs. Hunter Rose. 1-Devil's Riddle; Matt Wagner-c/a/scripts. 2-Devil's Masque; Matt Wagner-c/a/scripts 7.00

BATMAN/GRENDEL (2nd limited series)
DC Comics: June, 1996 - No. 2, July, 1996 ($4.95, limited series, squarebound)
1,2: Batman vs. Grendel Prime. 1-Devil's Bones. 2-Devil's Dance; Wagner-c/a/s 6.00

BATMAN: HARLEY & IVY
DC Comics: Jun, 2004 - No. 3, Aug, 2004 ($2.50, limited series)
1-Paul Dini-s/Bruce Timm-c/a in all 3 6 9 17 26 35
2,3 3 6 9 14 20 25
TPB (2007, $14.99) r/series; newly colored story from Batman: Gotham Knights #14 and Harley and Ivy: Love on the Lam series 15.00

BATMAN: HARLEY QUINN
DC Comics: 1999 ($5.95, prestige format)
1-Intro. of Harley Quinn into regular DC continuity; Dini-s/Alex Ross-c
7 14 21 48 89 130
1-(2nd printing) 3 6 9 21 33 45

BATMAN: HAUNTED GOTHAM
DC Comics: 2000 - No. 4, 2000 ($4.95, limited series, squarebound)
1-4-Doug Moench-s/Kelley Jones-c/a 6.00
TPB (2009, $19.99) r/#1-4 20.00

BATMAN/ HELLBOY/STARMAN

Batman Incorporated #1 © DC

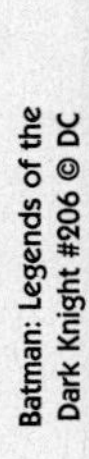

Batman: Legends of the Dark Knight #206 © DC

Batman: Li'l Gotham #12 © DC

GD	VG	FN	VF	VF/NM	NM-
2.0	4.0	6.0	8.0	9.0	9.2

DC Comics/Dark Horse: Jan, 1999 - No. 2, Feb, 1999 ($2.50, limited series)
1,2: Robinson-s/Mignola-a. 2-Harris-c 5.00

BATMAN: HOLLYWOOD KNIGHT
DC Comics: Apr, 2001 - No. 3, Jun, 2001 ($2.50, limited series)
1-3-Elseworlds Batman as a 1940's movie star; Giordano-a/Layton-s 3.00

BATMAN/ HUNTRESS: CRY FOR BLOOD
DC Comics: Jun, 2000 - No. 6, Nov, 2000 ($2.50, limited series)
1-6: Rucka-s/Burchett-a; The Question app. 3.00
TPB (2002, $12.95) r/#1-6 13.00

BATMAN, INC.
DC Comics: Jan, 2011 - No. 8, Aug, 2011 ($3.99/$2.99)
1-3-Morrison-s/Paquette-a; covers by Paquette & Williams 4.00
4-8-($2.99) 4-Burnham-a, original Batwoman (Kathy Kane) app. 3.00
...: Leviathan Strikes (2/12, $6.99) Morrison-s/Burnham & Stewart-a; cover gallery 7.00

BATMAN INCORPORATED
DC Comics: Jul, 2012 - No. 13, Sept, 2013 ($2.99)
1-7-Morrison-s/Burnham-a/c. 2-Origin of Talia. 3-Matches Malone returns 3.00
1-Variant-c by Quitely 5.00
8-Death of Damian 5.00
9-13: 9,10,12,13-Morrison-s/Burnham-a/c 3.00
#0 (11/12, $2.99) Frazer Irving-a; the start of Batman Incorporated 3.00
... Special 1 (10/13, $4.99) Short stories about international Batmen; s/a by various 5.00

BATMAN: JEKYLL & HYDE
DC Comics: June, 2005 - No. 6, Nov, 2005 ($2.99, limited series)
1-6-Paul Jenkins-s; Two-Face app. 1-3-Jae Lee-a. 4-6-Sean Phillips-a 3.00
TPB (2008, $14.99) r/#1-6 15.00

BATMAN: JOKER TIME (...: It's Joker Time! on cover)
DC Comics: 2000 - No. 3 ($4.95, limited series, squarebound)
1-3-Bob Hall-s/a 6.00

BATMAN: JOURNEY INTO KNGHT
DC Comics: Oct, 2005 - No. 12, Nov, 2006 ($2.50/$2.99, limited series)
1-9-Andrew Helfer-s/Tan Eng Huat-a/Pat Lee-c 3.00
10-12-($2.99) Joker app. 3.00

BATMAN/ JUDGE DREDD "DIE LAUGHING"
DC Comics: 1998 - No. 2, 1999 ($4.95, limited series, squarebound)
1,2: 1-Fabry-c/a. 2-Jim Murray-c/a 6.00

BATMAN: KNIGHTGALLERY (See Batman one-shots)

BATMAN: LEAGUE OF BATMEN
DC Comics: 2001 - No. 2, 2001 ($5.95, limited series, squarebound)
1,2-Elseworlds; Moench-s/Bright & Tanghal-a/Van Fleet-c 6.00

BATMAN: LEGENDS OF THE DARK KNIGHT (Legends of the Dark...#1-36)
DC Comics: Nov, 1989 - No. 214, Mar, 2007 ($1.50/$1.75/$1.95/$1.99/$2.25/$2.50/$2.99)
1- "Shaman" begins, ends #5; outer cover has four different color variations, all worth same 5.00
2-10: 6-10- "Gothic" by Grant Morrison (scripts) 4.00
11-15: 11-15-Gulacy/Austin-a. 13-Catwoman app. 4.00
16-Intro drug Bane uses; begin Venom story 6.00
17-20 5.00
21-49,51-63: 38-Bat-Mite-c/story. 46-49-Catwoman app. w/Heath-c/a. 51-Ragman app.; Joe Kubert-c. 59,60,61-Knightquest x-over. 62,63-KnightsEnd Pt. 4 & 10 3.00
50-($3.95, 68 pgs.)-Bolland embossed gold foil-c; Joker-c/story; pin-ups by Chaykin, Simonson, Williamson, Kaluta, Russell, others 5.00
64-99: 64-(9/94)-Begin $1.95-c. 71-73-James Robinson-s,Watkiss-c/a. 74,75-McKeever-c/a/s. 76-78-Scott Hampton-c/a/s. 81-Card insert. 83,84-Ellis-s. 85-Robinson-s. 91-93-Ennis-s. 94-Michael T. Gilbert-s/a. 3.00
100-($3.95) Alex Ross painted-c; gallery by various 5.00
101-115: 101-Ezquerra-a. 102-104-Robinson-s 3.00
116-No Man's Land stories begin; Huntress-c 4.00
117-119,121-126: 122-Harris-c 3.00
120-ID of new Batgirl revealed 4.00
127-131: Return to Legends stories; Green Arrow app. 3.00
132-199, 201-204: 132-136 ($2.25-c) Archie Goodwin-s/Rogers-a. 137-141-Gulacy-a. 142-145-Joker and Ra's al Ghul app. 146-148-Kitson-a. 158-Begin $2.50-c 169-171-Tony Harris-c/a. 182-184-War Games. 182-Bagged with Sky Captain CD 3.00
200-($4.99) Joker-c/app. 5.00
205-214: 205-Begin $2.99-c. 207,208-Olivetti-a. 214-Deadshot app. 3.00
#0-(10/94)-Zero Hour; Quesada/Palmiotti-c; released between #64&65 3.00

GD	VG	FN	VF	VF/NM	NM-
2.0	4.0	6.0	8.0	9.0	9.2

Annual 1-7 ('91-'97, $3.50-$3.95, 68 pgs.): 1-Joker app. 2-Netzer-c/a. 3-New Batman (Azrael) app. 4-Elseworlds story. 5-Year One; Man-Bat app. 6-Legend of the Dead Earth story. 7-Pulp Heroes story 4.00
... Halloween Special 1 (12/93, $6.95, 84 pgs.)-Embossed & foil stamped-c
1 2 3 5 6 8
... Halloween Special Edition 1 (12/14, giveaway) Sale-a/c 3.00
Batman Madness-...Halloween Special (1994, $4.95) 6.00
Batman Ghosts-...Halloween Special (1995, $4.95) 6.00
NOTE: ***Aparo** a-Annual 1. **Chaykin** scripts-24-26. **Giffen** a-Annual 1. **Golden** a-Annual 1. **Alan Grant** scripts-38, 52, 53. **Gil Kane** c/a-24-26. **Mignola** a-54; c-54, 62. **Morrow** a-Annual 3i. **Quesada** a-Annual 1. **James Robinson** scripts- 71-73. **Russell** c/a-42, 43. **Sears** a-21, 23; c-21, 23. **Zeck** a-69, 70; c-69, 70.*

BATMAN-LEGENDS OF THE DARK KNIGHT: JAZZ
DC Comics: Apr, 1995 - No. 3, June, 1995 ($2.50, limited series)
1-3 3.00

BATMAN: LI'L GOTHAM
DC Comics: Jun, 2013 - No. 12, May, 2014 ($2.99, printings of stories that 1st appeared online)
1-12-Dustin Nguyen-a/c; Nguyen & Fridolfs-s; holiday themed short stories 3.00
Halloween Comic Fest 2013 (12/13, no cover price) Halloween giveaway; r/#1 3.00

BATMAN/LOBO
DC Comics: Oct, 2007 - No. 2, Nov, 2007 ($5.99, squarebound, limited series)
1,2-Sam Kieth-s/a 6.00

BATMAN: MANBAT
DC Comics: Oct, 1995 - No. 3, Dec, 1995 ($4.95, limited series)
1-3-Elseworlds-Delano-script; Bolton-a 6.00
TPB-(1997, $14.95) r/#1-3 15.00

BATMAN: MITEFALL (See Batman one-shots)

BATMAN MINIATURE (See Batman Kellogg's)

BATMAN: NEVERMORE
DC Comics: June, 2003 - No. 5, Oct, 2003 ($2.50, limited series)
1-5-Elseworlds Batman & Edgar Allan Poe; Wrightson-c/Guy Davis-a/Len Wein-s 3.00

BATMAN: NO MAN'S LAND (Also see 1999 Batman titles)
DC Comics: (one shots)
nn (3/99, $2.95) Alex Ross-c; Bob Gale-s; begins year-long story arc 4.00
Collector's Ed. (3/99, $3.95) Ross lenticular-c 6.00
#0 (: Ground Zero on cover) (12/99, $4.95) Orbik-c 6.00
...: Gallery (7/99, $3.95) Jim Lee-c 4.00
...: Secret Files (12/99, $4.95) Maleev-c 6.00
TPB ('99, $12.95) r/early No Man's Land stories; new Batgirl early app. 13.00
No Law and a New Order TPB(1999, $5.95) Ross-c 8.00
Volume 2 ('00, $12.95) r/later No Man's Land stories; Batgirl(Huntress) app.; Deodato-c 13.00
Volume 3-5 ('00,'01 $12.95) 3-Intro. new Batgirl. 4-('00). 5-('01) Land-c 13.00

BATMAN: ODYSSEY
DC Comics: Sept, 2010 - No. 6, Feb, 2011 ($3.99, limited series)
1-6-Neal Adams-s/a/c. 1-Man-Bat app.; bonus sketch pages. 5,6-Joker app. 4.00
1-6-Variant B&W-version cover 5.00
Vol. 2 (12/11 - No. 7, 6/12) 1-7-Neal Adams-s/a/c 4.00

BATMAN: ORPHANS
DC Comics: Early Feb, 2011 - No. 2, Late Feb, 2011 ($3.99, limited series)
1,2-Berganza-s/Barberi-a/c 4.00

BATMAN: ORPHEUS RISING
DC Comics: Oct, 2001 - No. 5, Feb, 2002 ($2.50, limited series)
1-5-Intro. Orpheus; Simmons-s/Turner & Miki-a 3.00

BATMAN: OUTLAWS
DC Comics: 2000 - No. 3, 2000 ($4.95, limited series)
1-3-Moench-s/Gulacy-a 6.00

BATMAN: PENGUIN TRIUMPHANT (See Batman one-shots)

BATMAN/PREDATOR III: BLOOD TIES
DC Comics/Dark Horse Comics: Nov, 1997 - No. 4, Feb, 1998 ($1.95, lim. series)
1-4: Dixon-s/Damaggio-c/a 4.00
TPB-(1998, $7.95) r/#1-4 10.00

BATMAN/RA'S AL GHUL (See Year One:...)

BATMAN RETURNS MOVIE SPECIAL (See Batman one-shots)

BATMAN: RIDDLER-THE RIDDLE FACTORY (See Batman one-shots)

BATMAN: RUN, RIDDLER, RUN
DC Comics: 1992 - Book 3, 1992 ($4.95, limited series)

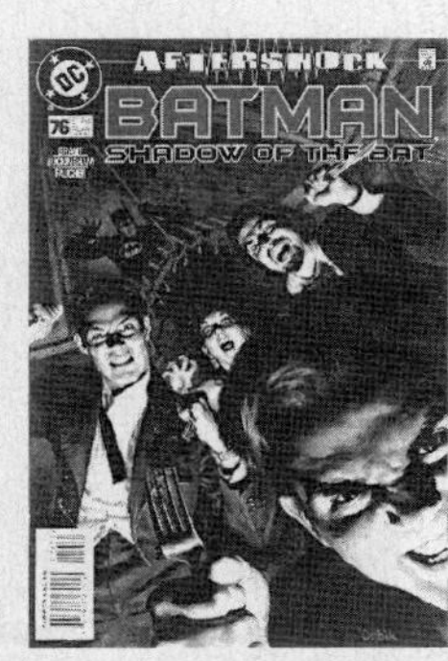

Batman: Shadow of the Bat #76 © DC

Batman '66 #20 © DC

Batman/Superman #14 © DC

Book 1-3: Mark Badger-a & plot 6.00

BATMAN SCARECROW (See Year One:...)

BATMAN: SECRET FILES
DC Comics: Oct, 1997 ($4.95)
1-New origin-s and profiles 6.00

BATMAN: SECRETS
DC Comics: May, 2006 - No. 5, Sept, 2006 ($2.99, limited series)
1-5-Sam Kieth-s/a/c; Joker app. 3.00
TPB (2007, $12.99) r/series 13.00

BATMAN: SHADOW OF THE BAT
DC Comics: June, 1992 - No. 94, Feb, 2000 ($1.50/$1.75/$1.95/$1.99)
1-The Last Arkham-c/story begins; Alan Grant scripts in all 5.00
1-($2.50)-Deluxe edition polybagged w/poster, pop-up & book mark 6.00
2-7: 4-The Last Arkham ends. 7-Last $1.50-c 3.00
8-28: 14,15-Staton-a(p). 16-18-Knightfall tie-ins. 19-28-Knightquest tie-ins w/Azrael as Batman. 25-Silver ink-c; anniversary issue 3.00
29-($2.95, 52 pgs.)-KnightsEnd Pt. 2 4.00
30-72: 30-KnightsEnd Pt. 8. 31-(9/94)-Begin $1.95-c; Zero Hour. 32-(11/94). 33-Robin-c. 35-Troika-Pt.2. 43,44-Cat-Man & Catwoman-c. 48-Contagion Pt. 1; card insert. 49-Contagion Pt.7. 56,57,58-Poison Ivy-c/app. 62-Two-Face app. 69,70-Fate app. 3.00
35-($2.95)-Variant embossed-c 4.00
73,74,76-78: Cataclysm x-over pts. 1,9. 76-78-Orbik-c 3.00
75-($2.95) Mr. Freeze & Clayface app.; Orbik-c 4.00
79,81,82: 79-Begin $1.99-c; Orbik-c 3.00
80-($3.95) Flip book with Azrael #47 4.00
83-No Man's Land; intro. new Batgirl (Huntress) 5.00
84,85-No Man's Land 4.00
86-92,94: 87-Deodato-a. 90-Harris-c. 92-Superman app. 94-No Man's Land ends 3.00
93-Joker and Harley app. 5.00
#0 (10/94) Zero Hour; released between #31&32 3.00
#1,000,000 (11/98) 853rd Century x-over; Orbik-c 3.00
Annual 1-5 ('93-'97 $2.95-$3.95, 68 pgs.): 3-Year One story; Poison Ivy app. 4-Legends of the Dead Earth story; Starman cameo. 5-Pulp Heroes story; Poison Ivy app. 4.00

BATMAN '66 (Characters and likenesses based on the 1966 television series)
DC Comics: Sept, 2013 - No. 30, Feb, 2016 ($3.99/$2.99, printings of stories that first appeared online)
1-Jeff Parker-s/Jonathan Case-a/Mike Allred-c; Riddler & Catwoman app. 4.00
1-Variant-c by Jonathan Case 6.00
1-San Diego Comic-Con variant action figure photo-c 3 6 9 14 20 25
2-12: 2-Penguin & Mr. Freeze app.; Templeton-a. 3,11,20-Joker app. 5,10,11-Batgirl app. 8-King Tut app. 4.00
13-24,26-30: 14-Selfie variant-c. 16,20-Egghead app. 18,21,27,29-Batgirl app. 21-Lord Death Man app. 22-Oeming-a. 26-Poison Ivy app. 27-Bane app. 30-Allred-a 3.00
25-1st app. The Harlequin; back-up Mad Men spoof with Batgirl 5.00
... The Lost Episode 1 (1/15, $9.99) Harlan Ellison 1960s script adapted by Len Wein; García-López-a; Two-Face app.; covers by García-López & Ross; original pencil art 10.00

BATMAN '66 MEETS STEED AND MRS. PEEL (TV's The Avengers)
DC Comics: Sept, 2016 - No. 6, Feb, 2017 ($2.99, printings of stories that first appeared online)
1-6-Edginton-s/Dow Smith-a/Allred-c. 1,2-Catwoman app. 3-6-Mr. Freeze app. 3.00

BATMAN '66 MEETS THE GREEN HORNET
DC Comics: Aug, 2014 - No. 6, Jan, 2015 ($2.99, printings of stories that first appeared online)
1-6-Kevin Smith & Ralph Garman-s/Ty Templeton-a/Alex Ross-c 3.00

BATMAN '66 MEETS THE MAN FROM U.N.C.L.E.
DC Comics: Feb, 2016 - No. 6, Jul, 2016 ($2.99, limited series)
1-6-Jeff Parker-s/David Haun-a/Allred-c. 1-Olga and Penguin app. 3.00

BATMAN '66 MEETS WONDER WOMAN '77
DC Comics: Mar, 2017 - No. 6 ($3.99, limited series)
1,2-Parker & Andreyko-s/Haun-a; Ra's al Ghul & Talia app. 4.00

BATMAN: SON OF THE DEMON (Also see Batman #655-658 and Batman Hardcovers)
DC Comics: 2006 ($5.99, reprints the 1987 HC in comic book format)
nn-Talia has Batman's son; Mike W. Barr-s/Jerry Bingham-a; new Andy Kubert-c 6.00

BATMAN-SPAWN: WAR DEVIL (See Batman one-shots)

BATMAN SPECTACULAR (See DC Special Series No. 15)

BATMAN: STREETS OF GOTHAM (Follows Batman: Battle For The Cowl series)
DC Comics: Aug, 2009 - No. 21, May, 2011 ($3.99$2.99)
1-18: 1-Dini-s/Nguyen-a; back-up Manhunter feature; Jeanty-a. 10,11-Zsasz app. 4.00
19-21-($2.99) 19-Joker app. 3.00
...- Hush Money HC (2010, $19.99) r/#1-4, Detective #852 and Batman #685 20.00
...- Hush Money SC (2011, $14.99) r/#1-4, Detective #852 and Batman #685 15.00
...- Leviathan HC (2010, $19.99) r/#5-11 20.00
...- The House of Hush HC (2011, $22.99) r/#12-14,16-21 23.00

BATMAN STRIKES!, THE (Based on the 2004 animated series)
DC Comics: Nov, 2004 - No. 50, Dec, 2008 ($2.25)
1,2,4-27,29-31,33,34,36-38,40,42,44,46,48-50: 1,11-Penguin app. 2-Man-Bat app. 4-Bane app. 9-Joker app. 18-Batgirl debut. 29-Robin debuts. 33-Cal Ripken 8-pg. insert. 44-Superman app. 3.00
1-Free Comic Book Day edition (6/05) Penguin app. 3.00
3-($2.95) Joker-c/app.; Catwoman & Wonder Woman-r from Advs. in the DCU 4.00
28,32-Joker-c/app. 32-Cal Ripken 8-pg. insert. 5.00
35-Joker & Harley Quinn-c/app. 2 4 6 9 12 15
39,47-Black Mask-c/app. 6.00
41-Harley Quinn & Poison Ivy-c/app. 2 4 6 9 12 15
43-Harley Quinn-c/app. 2 4 6 9 12 15
45-Harley Quinn, Poison Ivy, Catwoman-c/app. 2 4 6 10 14 18
Jam Packed Action (2005, $7.99, digest) adaptations of two TV episodes 8.00
... Vol. 1: Crime Time (2005, $6.99, digest) r/#1-5 7.00
... Vol. 2: In Darkest Knight (2005, $6.99, digest) r/#6-10 7.00

BATMAN/ SUPERMAN
DC Comics: Aug, 2013 - No. 32, Jul, 2016 ($3.99)
1-4-Greg Pak-s/Jae Lee-a/c; Catwoman & Wonder Woman app. 4.00
3.1 (11/13, $2.99, regular cover) 3.00
3.1 (11/13, $3.99, 3-D cover) "Doomsday #1" on cover; Booth-a; Zod app. 6.00
5-7-Booth-a; reads sideways; Mongul app. 4.00
8,9-First Contact x-over with Worlds' Finest #20,21; Power Girl & Huntress app.; Lee-a 4.00
10-31: 11-Doomed tie-in. 13-Jae Lee-a. 13-15-Catwoman app. 17-Lobo app. 21-Batman (Gordon in robot suit). 23,24-Aquaman app. 25-27-Vandal Savage app. 4.00
32-The Great Ten app.; 1st app. Chinese Super-Man (Kong Kenan) 5.00
Annual 1 (5/14, $5.99) Supergirl, Krypto, Cyborg, Batgirl, Red Hood app.; Jae Lee-c 6.00
Annual 2 (5/15, $4.99) Killer Croc, Cheshire & Bane app.; Syaf-c 5.00
...: Futures End 1 (11/14, $2.99, regular-c) Five years later; Pak-s 3.00
...: Futures End 1 (11/14, $3.99, 3-D cover) 4.00

BATMAN/ SUPERMAN/WONDER WOMAN: TRINITY
DC Comics: 2003 - No. 3, 2003 ($6.95, limited series, squarebound)
1-3-Matt Wagner-s/a/c. 1-Ra's al Ghul & Bizarro app. 7.00
HC (2004, $24.95, with dust-jacket) r/series; intro. by Brad Meltzer 30.00
SC (2004, $17.99) r/series; intro. by Brad Meltzer 18.00

BATMAN: SWORD OF AZRAEL (Also see Azrael & Batman #488,489)
DC Comics: Oct, 1992 - No. 4, Jan, 1993 ($1.75, limited series)
1-Wraparound gatefold-c; Quesada-c/a(p) in all; 1st app. Azrael
2 4 6 10 14 18
2-4: 4-Cont'd in Batman #488 1 2 3 5 6 8
Silver Edition 1-4 (1993, $1.95)-Reprints #1-4 3.00
Trade Paperback (1993, $9.95)-Reprints #1-4 12.00
Trade Paperback Gold Edition 18.00

BATMAN/ TARZAN: CLAWS OF THE CAT-WOMAN
Dark Horse Comics/DC Comics: Sept, 1999 - No. 4, Dec, 1999 ($2.95, limited series)
1-4: Marz-s/Kordey-a 3.00

BATMAN/ TEENAGE MUTANT NINJA TURTLES
DC Comics: Feb, 2016 - No. 6, Jul, 2016 ($3.99, limited series)
1-6-Tynion IV-s/Williams II-a; Penguin, Croc & Shredder app. 4.00
... Director's Cut 1 (11/16, $5.99) r/#1 in B&W and pencil-a; original script 6.00

BATMAN/ TEENAGE MUTANT NINJA TURTLES ADVENTURES
IDW Publishing: Nov, 2016 - Present ($3.99, limited series)
1-4-Manning-s/Sommariva-a; Clayface, Joker and Harley Quinn app.; multiple covers 4.00
... Director's Cut 1 (2/17, $4.99) r/#1 in B&W and pencil-a; original script 5.00

BATMAN: TENSES
DC Comics: 2003 - No. 2, 2003 ($6.95, limited series)
1,2-Joe Casey-s/Cully Hamner-a; Bruce Wayne's first year back in Gotham 7.00

BATMAN: THE ANKH
DC Comics: 2002 - No. 2, 2002 ($5.95, limited series)
1,2-Dixon-s/Van Fleet-a 6.00

BATMAN: THE BRAVE AND THE BOLD (Based on the 2008 animated series)
DC Comics: Mar, 2009 - No. 22, Dec, 2010 ($2.50/$2.99)
1-18: 1-Power Girl app. 4-Sugar & Spike cameo. 7-Doom Patrol app. 9-Catman app. 3.00
19-22-($2.99) Cyborg Superman and the Green Lantern Corps app. 22-Aquaman app. 3.00

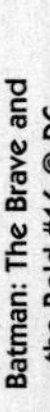
Batman: The Brave and the Bold #16 © DC

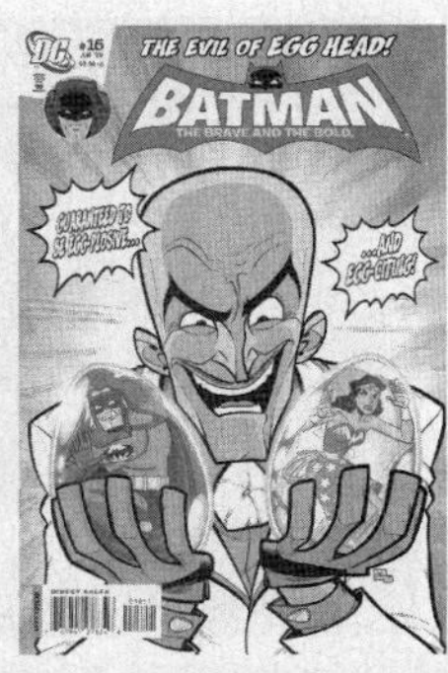

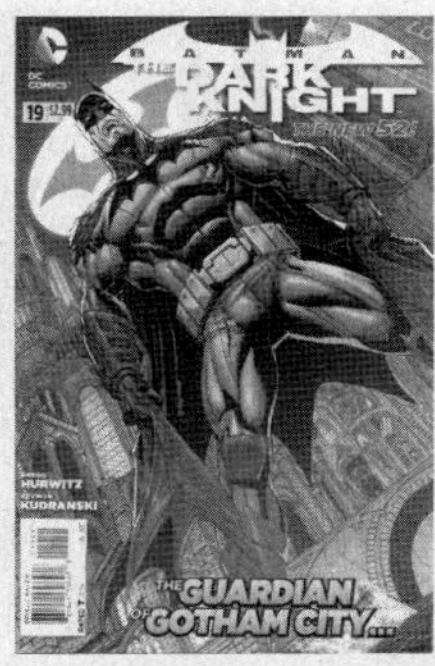

Batman: The Dark Knight (2011 series) #19 © DC

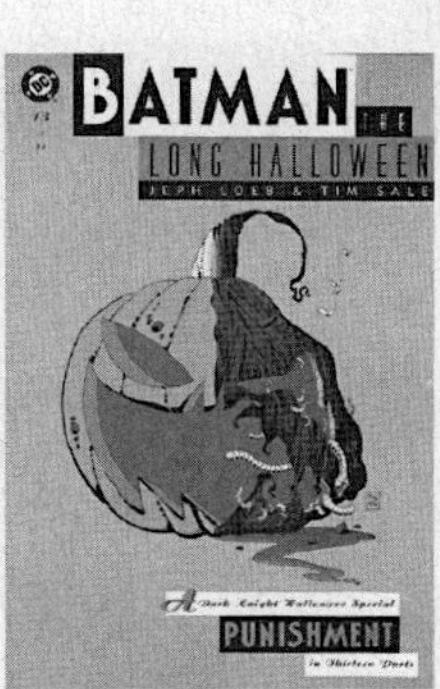

Batman: The Long Halloween #13 © DC

GD 2.0 | VG 4.0 | FN 6.0 | VF 8.0 | VF/NM 9.0 | NM- 9.2

TPB (2009, $12.99) r/#1-6 13.00
...: Emerald Knight TPB (2011, $12.99) r/#13,14,16,18,19,21 13.00
...: The Fearsome Fangs Strike Again TPB (2010, $12.99) r/#7-12 13.00

BATMAN: THE BRAVE AND THE BOLD (Titled "All New Batman: Brave & the Bold" for #1-13)
DC Comics: Jan, 2011 - No. 16, Apr, 2012 ($2.99)
1-16: 1-Superman. 4-Wonder Woman app. 8-Aquaman app. 9-Hawkman app. 3.00

BATMAN: THE CULT
DC Comics: 1988 - No. 4, Nov, 1988 ($3.50, deluxe limited series)
1-Wrightson-a/painted-c in all 1 2 3 5 6 8
2-4 6.00
Trade Paperback (1991, $14.95)-New Wrightson-c; Starlin intro. 25.00
Trade Paperback (2009, $19.99) 20.00

BATMAN: THE DARK KNIGHT
DC Comics: Jan, 2011 - No. 5, Oct, 2011 ($3.99/$2.99)
1-David Finch-s/a; Penguin & Killer Croc app.; covers by Finch and Clarke 4.00
2-5-($2.99) Demon app. 3.00

BATMAN: THE DARK KNIGHT (DC New 52)
DC Comics: Nov, 2011 - No. 29, May, 2014 ($2.99)
1-29: 1-Jenkins & Finch-s/Finch-a/c; White Rabbit debut. 3-Flash app. 5,6-Superman app. 6,7-Bane app. 9-Night of the Owls. 22-25-Maleev-a. 28-Van Sciver-a/c 3.00
23.1, 23.2, 23.3, 23.4 (11/13, $2.99, regular covers) 3.00
23.1 (11/13, $3.99, 3-D cover) "Ventriloquist #1" on cover; Simone-s/Santacruz-a 6.00
23.2 (11/13, $3.99, 3-D cover) "Mr. Freeze #1" on cover; Gray & Palmiotti-s 5.00
23.3 (11/13, $3.99, 3-D cover) "Clayface#1" on cover; Richards-a 5.00
23.4 (11/13, $3.99, 3-D cover) "Joker's Daughter #1" on cover; origin story; Jeanty-a 12.00
#0 (11/12, $2.99) Hurwitz-s/Suayan & Ryp-a; flashback to aftermath of parents' murder 3.00
Annual 1 (7/13, $4.99) Hurwitz-s/Kudranski-a/Maleev-c; Scarecrow, Penguin Mad Hatter 5.00

BATMAN: THE DARK KNIGHT RETURNS (Also see Dark Knight Strikes Again)
DC Comics: Mar, 1986 - No. 4, 1986 ($2.95, squarebound, limited series)
1-Miller story & c/a(p); set in the future 6 12 18 42 79 115
1,2-2nd & 3rd printings, 3-2nd printing 2 4 6 10 14 18
2-Carrie Kelley becomes 1st female Robin 4 8 12 23 37 50
3-Death of Joker; Superman app. 3 6 9 16 24 32
4-Death of Alfred; Superman app. 3 6 9 16 24 32
Hardcover, signed & numbered edition ($40.00)(4000 copies) 275.00
Hardcover, trade edition 60.00
Softcover, trade edition (1st printing only) 2 4 6 11 16 20
Softcover, trade edition (2nd thru 8th printings) 2 4 6 8 10 12
10th Anniv. Slipcase set ('96, $100.00): Signed & numbered hard-c edition (10,000 copies), sketchbook, copy of script for #1, 2 color prints 135.00
10th Anniv. Hardcover ('96, $45.00) 50.00
10th Anniv. Softcover ('97, $14.95) 18.00
Hardcover 2nd printing ('02, $24.95) with 3 1/4" tall partial dustjacket 25.00
NOTE: *The #2 second printings can be identified by matching the grey background colors on the inside front cover and facing page. The inside front cover of the second printing has a dark grey background which does not match the lighter grey of the facing page. On the true 1st printings, the backgrounds are both light grey. All other issues are clearly marked.*

BATMAN: THE DOOM THAT CAME TO GOTHAM
DC Comics: 2000 - No. 3, 2001 ($4.95, limited series)
1-3-Elseworlds; Mignola-c/s; Nixey-a; Etrigan app. 6.00

BATMAN: THE KILLING JOKE (See Batman one-shots)

BATMAN: THE LONG HALLOWEEN
DC Comics: Oct, 1996 - No. 13, Oct, 1997 ($2.95/$4.95, limited series)
1-($4.95)-Loeb-s/Sale-c/a in all 1 3 4 6 8 10
2-5($2.95): 2-Solomon Grundy-c/app. 3-Joker-c/app., Catwoman, Poison Ivy app. 6.00
6-10: 6-Poison Ivy-c. 7-Riddler-c/app. 5.00
11,12 4.00
13-($4.95, 48 pgs.)-Killer revelations 6.00
Special Edition (Halloween Comic Fest 2013) (12/13, free giveaway) r/#1 3.00
Absolute Batman: The Long Halloween (2007, $75.00, oversized HC) r/series; interviews with the creators; Sale sketch pages; action figure line; unpubbed 4-page sequence 75.00
HC-($29.95) r/series 50.00
SC-($19.95) 20.00

BATMAN: THE MAD MONK ("Batman & the Mad Monk" on cover)
DC Comics: Oct, 2006 - No. 6, Mar, 2007 ($3.50, limited series)
1-6-Matt Wagner-s/a/c. 1-Catwoman app. 3.50
TPB (2007, $14.99) r/#1-6 15.00

BATMAN: THE MONSTER MEN ("Batman & the Monster Men" on cover)
DC Comics: Jan, 2006 - No. 6, June, 2006 ($2.99, limited series)
1-6-Matt Wagner-s/a/c 3.00
TPB (2006, $14.99) r/#1-6 15.00

BATMAN: THE OFFICIAL COMIC ADAPTATION OF THE WARNER BROS. MOTION PICTURE (See Batman one-shots)

BATMAN: THE RETURN
DC Comics: Jan, 2011 ($4.99, one-shot)
1-Morrison-s/Finch-a; covers by Finch & Ha; costume design sketch art; script pages 5.00

BATMAN: THE RETURN OF BRUCE WAYNE (Follows Batman's "death" in Final Crisis #6)
DC Comics: Early Jul, 2010 - No. 6, Dec, 2010 ($3.99, limited series)
1-6-Bruce Wayne's time travels; Morrison-s/Andy Kubert-c. 1-Sprouse-a. 4-Jeanty-a 4.00
1-Second & third printings; 4.00
1-6-Variant covers: 1-Sprouse. 2-Irving. 3-Paquette. 4-Jeanty. 5-Sook. 6-Garbett 8.00
... - The Deluxe Edition HC (2011, $29.99) r/#1-6; sketch pages 30.00

BATMAN: THE ULTIMATE EVIL
DC Comics: 1995 ($5.95, limited series, prestige format)
1,2-Barrett, Jr. adaptation of Vachss novel. 6.00

BATMAN: THE WIDENING GYRE
DC Comics: Oct, 2009 - No. 6, Sept, 2010 ($3.99/$2.99/$4.99, limited series)
1-($3.99) Kevin Smith-s/Walt Flanagan-a; debut Baphomet; Demon app.; Sienkiewicz-c 4.00
1-5-Variant covers by Gene Ha 8.00
2-5-($2.99) 2-Silver St. Cloud returns. 5-Catwoman app. 3.00
6-($4.99) Joker, Deadshot & Catwoman app. 5.00
6-Variant cover by Gene Ha 10.00
HC (2010, $19.99, dj) r/#1-6; variant covers; afterword by Kevin Smith 20.00

BATMAN 3-D (Also see 3-D Batman)
DC Comics: 1990 ($9.95, w/glasses, 8-1/8x10-3/4")
nn-Byrne-a/scripts; Riddler, Joker, Penguin & Two-Face app. plus r/1953 3-D Batman; pin-ups by many artists 2 4 6 8 10 12

BATMAN: TOYMAN
DC Comics: Nov, 1998 - No. 4, Feb, 1999 ($2.25, limited series)
1-4-Hama-s 3.00

BATMAN: TURNING POINTS
DC Comics: Jan, 2001 - No. 5, Jan, 2001 ($2.50, weekly limited series)
1-5: 2-Giella-a. 3-Kubert-c/Giordano-a. 4-Chaykin-c/Brent Anderson-a. 5-Pope-c/a 3.00
TPB (2007, $14.99) r/#1-5 15.00

BATMAN: TWO-FACE-CRIME AND PUNISHMENT (See Batman one-shots)

BATMAN: TWO-FACE STRIKES TWICE
DC Comics: 1993 - No. 2, 1993 ($4.95, 52 pgs.)
1,2-Flip book format w/Staton-a (G.A. side) 6.00

BATMAN UNSEEN
DC Comics: Early Dec, 2009 - No. 5, Feb, 2010 ($2.99, limited series)
1-5-Doug Moench-s/Kelley Jones-a/c. Black Mask app. 3.00
SC (2010, $14.99) r/#1-5 15.00

BATMAN: VENGEANCE OF BANE (Also see Batman #491)
DC Comics: Jan, 1993; 1995 ($2.50, 68 pgs.)
... Special 1 - Origin & 1st app. Bane; Dixon-s/Nolan & Barreto-a/Fabry-c 4 8 12 28 47 65
... Special 1 (2nd printing) 2 4 6 9 12 15
.... II nn (1995, $3.95)-sequel; Dixon-s/Nolan & Barreto-a/Fabry-c 2 4 6 9 12 15

BATMAN VERSUS PREDATOR
DC Comics/Dark Horse Comics: 1991 - No. 3, 1992 ($4.95/$1.95, limited series)
(1st DC/Dark Horse x-over)
1 (Prestige format, $4.95)-1 & 3 contain 8 Batman/Predator trading cards; Andy & Adam Kubert-a; Suydam painted-c 1 2 3 5 6 8
1-3 (Regular format, $1.95)-No trading cards 4.00
2,3-(Prestige)-2-Extra pin-ups inside; Suydam-c 6.00
TPB (1993, $5.95, 132 pgs.)-r/#1-3 w/new introductions & forward plus new wraparound-c by Dave Gibbons 1 3 4 6 8 10

BATMAN VERSUS PREDATOR II: BLOODMATCH
DC Comics: Late 1994 - No. 4, 1995 ($2.50, limited series)
1-4-Huntress app.; Moench scripts; Gulacy-a 4.00
TPB (1995, $6.95)-r/#1-4 1 3 4 6 8 10

BATMAN VS. THE INCREDIBLE HULK (See DC Special Series No. 27)

Bat-Mite #1 © DC

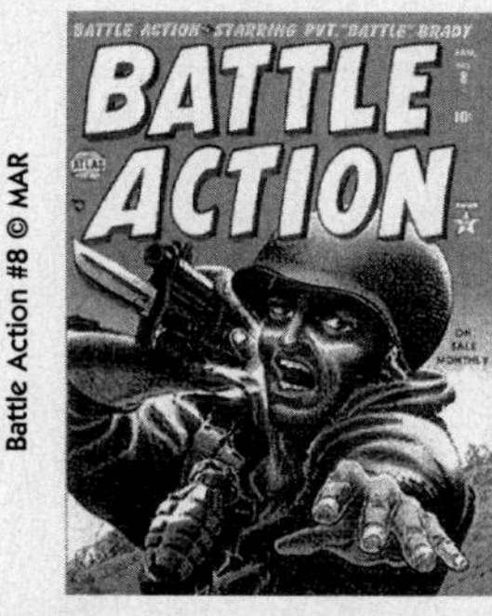

Battle Action #8 © MAR

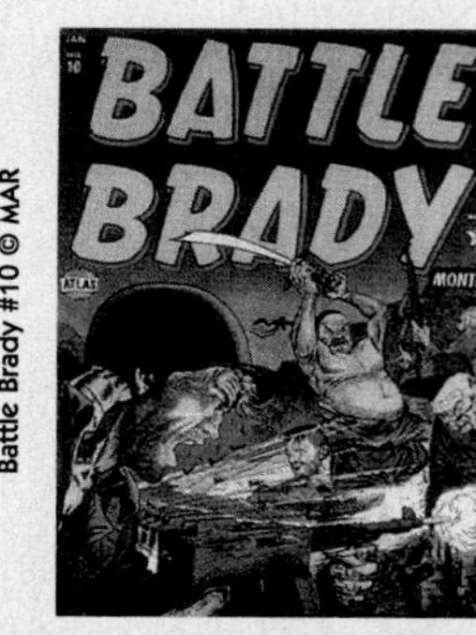

Battle Brady #10 © MAR

BATMAN: WAR ON CRIME
DC Comics: Nov, 1999 ($9.95, treasury size, one-shot)

	GD 2.0	VG 4.0	FN 6.0	VF 8.0	VF/NM 9.0	NM- 9.2
nn-Painted art by Alex Ross; story by Alex Ross and Paul Dini						10.00

BATMAN/ WILDCAT
DC Comics: Apr, 1997 - No. 3, June, 1997 ($2.25, mini-series)

	GD 2.0	VG 4.0	FN 6.0	VF 8.0	VF/NM 9.0	NM- 9.2
1-3: Dixon/Smith-s: 1-Killer Croc app.						3.00

BATMAN: YEAR 100
DC Comics: 2006 - No. 4, 2006 ($5.99, squarebound, limited series)

	GD 2.0	VG 4.0	FN 6.0	VF 8.0	VF/NM 9.0	NM- 9.2
1-4-Paul Pope-s/a/c						6.00
TPB (2007, $19.99) r/series						20.00

BAT MASTERSON (TV) (Also see Tim Holt #28)
Dell Publishing Co.: Aug-Oct, 1959; Feb-Apr, 1960 - No. 9, Nov-Jan, 1961-62

	GD 2.0	VG 4.0	FN 6.0	VF 8.0	VF/NM 9.0	NM- 9.2
Four Color 1013 (#1) (8-10/59)	10	20	30	66	138	210
2-9: Gene Barry photo-c on all. 2,3,6-Two different back-c exist; variants have a comic strip on the back-c	6	12	18	38	69	100

BAT-MITE
DC Comics: Aug, 2015 - No. 6, Jan, 2016 ($2.99, limited series)

	GD 2.0	VG 4.0	FN 6.0	VF 8.0	VF/NM 9.0	NM- 9.2
1-6: 1-Jurgens-s/Howell-a; Batman app. 4-Booster Gold app. 5-Inferior Five app.						3.00

BATS (See Tales Calculated to Drive You Bats)

BATS, CATS & CADILLACS
Now Comics: Oct, 1990 - No. 2, Nov, 1990 ($1.75)

	GD 2.0	VG 4.0	FN 6.0	VF 8.0	VF/NM 9.0	NM- 9.2
1,2: 1-Gustovich-a(i); Snyder-c						3.00

BAT-THING
DC Comics (Amalgam): June, 1997 ($1.95, one-shot)

	GD 2.0	VG 4.0	FN 6.0	VF 8.0	VF/NM 9.0	NM- 9.2
1-Hama-s/Damaggio & Sienkiewicz-a						3.00

BATTLE
Marvel/Atlas Comics(FPI #1-62/ Male #63 on): Mar, 1951 - No. 70, Jun, 1960

	GD 2.0	VG 4.0	FN 6.0	VF 8.0	VF/NM 9.0	NM- 9.2
1	58	116	174	371	636	900
2	32	64	96	188	307	425
3-10: 4-1st Buck Pvt. O'Toole. 10-Pakula-a	26	52	78	154	252	350
11-20: 11-Check-a. 17-Classic Hitler story	21	42	63	122	199	275
21,23-Krigstein-a	21	42	63	124	202	280
22,24-36: 32-Tuska-a. 36-Everett-a	20	40	60	114	182	250
37-Kubert-a (Last precode, 2/55)	20	40	60	117	189	260
38-40,42-48	18	36	54	103	162	220
41,49: 41-Kubert/Moskowitz-a. 49-Davis-a	18	36	54	107	169	230
50-54,56-58: 56-Colan-a; Ayers-a	17	34	51	100	158	215
55-Williamson-a (5 pgs.)	18	36	54	107	169	230
59-Torres-a	18	36	54	103	162	220
60-62: 60,62-Combat Kelly app. 61-Combat Casey app.	17	34	51	100	158	215
63-Ditko-a	24	48	72	140	230	320
64-66-Kirby-a. 66-Davis-a; has story of Fidel Castro in pre-Communism days (an admiring profile)	27	54	81	160	263	365
67,68: 67-Williamson/Crandall-a (4 pgs.); Kirby, Davis-a. 68-Kirby/Williamson-a (4 pgs.); Kirby/Ditko-a	28	56	84	165	270	375
69,70: 69-Kirby-a. 70-Kirby/Ditko-a	27	54	81	160	263	365

NOTE: ***Andru*** *a-37.* ***Berg*** *a-8, 38, 14, 60-62.* ***Colan*** *a-19, 33, 43, 55.* ***Everett*** *a-36, 50, 70; c-56, 57.* ***Heath*** *a-6, 9, 13, 31, 69; c-6, 9, 12, 26, 35, 37.* ***Kirby*** *c-64-69.* ***Maneely*** *a-4, 6, 7, 31, 61; c-4, 22, 27, 33, 43, 48, 59, 61.* ***Orlando*** *a-47.* ***Powell*** *a-53, 55.* ***Reinman*** *a-4, 8-10, 14, 26, 32, 48.* ***Robinson*** *a-9, 39.* ***Romita*** *a-14, 26.* ***Severin*** *a-28, 32-34, 66-69; c-36, 50, 55.* ***Sinnott*** *a-33, 37, 63, 66.* ***Whitney*** *s-10.* ***Woodbridge*** *a-52, 55.*

BATTLE ACTION
Atlas Comics (NPI): Feb, 1952 - No. 12, 5/53; No. 13, 10/54 - No. 30, 8/57

	GD 2.0	VG 4.0	FN 6.0	VF 8.0	VF/NM 9.0	NM- 9.2
1-Pakula-a	42	84	126	265	445	625
2	22	44	66	132	216	300
3,4,6,7,9,10: 6-Robinson-c/a. 7-Partial nudity	17	34	51	98	154	210
5-Used in **POP**, pg. 93,94	17	34	51	100	158	215
8-Krigstein-a	18	36	54	103	162	220
11-15 (Last precode, 2/55)	16	32	48	94	147	200
16-30: 20-Romita-a. 22-Pakula-a. 27,30-Torres-a	15	30	45	85	130	175

NOTE: *Battle Brady app. 5-7, 10-12.* ***Berg*** *a-3.* ***Check*** *a-11.* ***Everett*** *a-7; c-13, 25.* ***Heath*** *a-3, 8, 18; c-3,15, 18, 21.* ***Maneely*** *a-1; c-5.* ***Reinman*** *a-1, 2, 20.* ***Robinson*** *a-6, 7; c-6.* ***Shores*** *a-7(2), 12, 20; c-11.* ***Sinnott*** *a-3, 27.* ***Woodbridge*** *a-28, 30.*

BATTLE ATTACK
Stanmor Publications: Oct, 1952 - No. 8, Dec, 1955

	GD 2.0	VG 4.0	FN 6.0	VF 8.0	VF/NM 9.0	NM- 9.2
1	15	30	45	90	140	190
2	10	20	30	54	72	90
3-8: 3-Hollingsworth-a	9	18	27	50	65	80

BATTLEAXES
DC Comics (Vertigo): May, 2000 - No. 4, Aug, 2000 ($2.50, limited series)

	GD 2.0	VG 4.0	FN 6.0	VF 8.0	VF/NM 9.0	NM- 9.2
1-4: Terry LaBan-s/Alex Horley-a						3.00

BATTLE BEASTS
Blackthorne Publishing: Feb, 1988 - No. 4, 1988 ($1.50/$1.75, B&W/color)

	GD 2.0	VG 4.0	FN 6.0	VF 8.0	VF/NM 9.0	NM- 9.2
1-4: 1-3- (B&W)-Based on Hasbro toys. 4-Color						3.00

BATTLE BEASTS
IDW Publishing: Jul, 2012 - No. 4, Oct, 2012 ($3.99, limited series)

	GD 2.0	VG 4.0	FN 6.0	VF 8.0	VF/NM 9.0	NM- 9.2
1-4-Curnow-s/Schiti-a; 2 covers on each						4.00

BATTLE BRADY (Formerly Men in Action No. 1-9; see 3-D Action)
Atlas Comics (IPC): No. 10, Jan, 1953 - No. 14, June, 1953

	GD 2.0	VG 4.0	FN 6.0	VF 8.0	VF/NM 9.0	NM- 9.2
10: 10-12-Syd Shores-c	24	48	72	142	234	325
11-Used in **POP**, pg. 95 plus B&W & color illos	17	34	51	98	154	210
12-14	15	30	45	86	133	180

BATTLE CHASERS
Image Comics (Cliffhanger): Apr, 1998 - No. 4, Dec, 1998;
DC Comics (Cliffhanger): No. 5, May, 1999 - No. 8, May, 2001 ($2.50)
Image Comics: No. 9, Sept, 2001 ($3.50)

	GD 2.0	VG 4.0	FN 6.0	VF 8.0	VF/NM 9.0	NM- 9.2
Prelude (2/98)	1	3	4	6	8	10
Prelude Gold Ed.	1	3	4	6	8	10
1-Madureira & Sharrieff-s/Madureira-a(p)/Charest-c	1	2	3	5	7	9
1-American Ent. Ed. w/"racy" cover	1	3	4	6	8	10
1-Gold Edition						9.00
1-Chromium cover						20.00
1-2nd printing						3.00
2						5.00
2-Dynamic Forces BattleChrome cover	2	4	6	8	10	12
3-Red Monika cover by Madureira						4.00
4-8: 4-Four covers. 6-Back-up by Adam Warren-s/a. 7-Three covers (Madureira, Ramos, Campbell)						3.00
9-($3.50, Image) Flip cover/story by Adam Warren						4.00
...: A Gathering of Heroes HC ('99, $24.95) r/#1-5, Prelude, Frank Frazetta Fantasy III.; cover gallery						25.00
...: A Gathering of Heroes SC ('99, $14.95)						15.00
...Collected Edition 1,2 (11/98, 5/99, $5.95) 1-r/#1,2. 2-r/#3,4						6.00

BATTLE CLASSICS (See Cancelled Comic Cavalcade)
DC Comics: Sept-Oct, 1978 (44 pgs.)

	GD 2.0	VG 4.0	FN 6.0	VF 8.0	VF/NM 9.0	NM- 9.2
1-Kubert-r; new Kubert-c	2	4	6	8	10	12

BATTLE CRY
Stanmor Publications: 1952 (May) - No. 20, Sept, 1955

	GD 2.0	VG 4.0	FN 6.0	VF 8.0	VF/NM 9.0	NM- 9.2
1	20	40	60	117	189	260
2-(7/52)	12	24	36	69	97	125
3,5-10: 8-Pvt. Ike begins, ends #13,17	10	20	30	58	76	95
4-Classic E.C. swipe	11	22	33	62	86	110
11-20	9	18	27	52	69	85

NOTE: ***Hollingsworth*** *a-9; c-20.*

BATTLEFIELD (War Adventures on the...)
Atlas Comics (ACI): April, 1952 - No. 11, May, 1953

	GD 2.0	VG 4.0	FN 6.0	VF 8.0	VF/NM 9.0	NM- 9.2
1-Pakula, Reinman-a	39	78	117	240	395	550
2-5: 2-Heath, Maneely, Pakula, Reinman-a	20	40	60	114	182	250
6-11	16	32	48	94	147	200

NOTE: ***Colan*** *a-11.* ***Everett*** *a-8.* ***Heath*** *a-1, 2, 5p,7; c-2, 8, 9, 11.* ***Ravielli*** *a-11.*

BATTLEFIELD ACTION (Formerly Foreign Intrigues)
Charlton Comics: No. 16, Nov, 1957 - No. 62, 2-3/66; No. 63, 7/80 - No. 89, 11/84

	GD 2.0	VG 4.0	FN 6.0	VF 8.0	VF/NM 9.0	NM- 9.2
V2#16	9	18	27	47	61	75
17,20-30: 29-D-Day story	6	12	18	28	34	40
18,19-Check-a (2 stories in #18)	3	6	9	21	33	45
31-34,36-62(1966): 40-Panel from this issue used by artist Roy Lichtenstein for famous painting. 55,61-Hitler app.	3	6	9	16	23	30
35-Hitler-c	4	8	12	23	37	50
63-80(1983-84)						5.00
81-83,85-89 (Low print run)	1	2	3	4	5	7
84-Kirby reprints; 3 stories	1	3	4	6	8	10

NOTE: ***Montes/Bache*** *a-43, 55, 62.* ***Glanzman*** *a-87r.*

BATTLEFIELDS
Dynamite Entertainment: 2008 - No. 9, 2010 ($3.50, limited series then numbered issues)

	GD 2.0	VG 4.0	FN 6.0	VF 8.0	VF/NM 9.0	NM- 9.2
...: Dear Billy 1-3 ('09 - No. 3, '09, $3.50) Ennis-s/Snejbjerg-a/Cassaday-c.1-Leach var-c						3.50
...: Happy Valley 1-3 ('09 - No. 3, '09, $3.50) Ennis-s/Holden-a/Leach-c						3.50
...: The Night Witches 1-3 ('08 - No. 3, '09, $3.50) Ennis-s/Braun-a/Cassaday-c; Russian female pilots in WW2. 1-Leach var-c						3.50

Battlefields V2 #4 © Spitfire & D. Robertson

Battlefront #29 © MAR

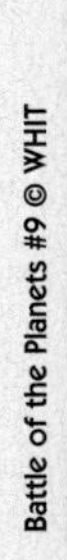
Battle of the Planets #9 © WHIT

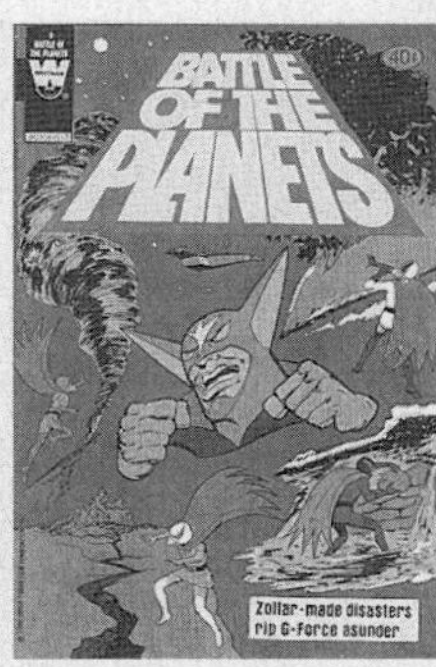

GD VG FN VF VF/NM NM-
2.0 4.0 6.0 8.0 9.0 9.2

...: The Tankies 1-3 ('09 - No. 3, '09, $3.50) Ennis-s/Ezquerra-a/Cassaday-c.1-Leach var-c 3.50
4-9: 4-6-Ezquerra-a/Leach-c. 7-9-Sequel to "The Night Witches"; Braun-a 3.50

BATTLEFIELDS (Volume 2)
Dynamite Entertainment: 2012 - No. 6, 2013 ($3.99, limited series)

1-6: 1-3-Ennis-s/Ezquerra-a/Leach-c. 4-6-Braun-a 4.00

BATTLE FIRE
Aragon Magazine/Stanmor Publications: Apr, 1955 - No. 7, 1955

1 15 30 45 85 130 175
2-(6/55) 9 18 27 52 69 85
3-7 9 18 27 47 61 75

BATTLE FOR A THREE DIMENSIONAL WORLD
3D Cosmic Publications: May, 1983 (20 pgs., slick paper w/stiff-c, $3.00)

nn-Kirby c/a in 3-D; shows history of 3-D 2 4 6 8 11 14

BATTLEFORCE
Blackthorne Publishing: Nov, 1987 - No. 2, 1988 ($1.75, color/B&W)

1,2: Based on game. 1-In color. 2-B&W 3.00

BATTLE FOR INDEPENDENTS, THE (Also See Cyblade/Shi & Shi/Cyblade: The Battle For Independents)
Image Comics (Top Cow Productions)/Crusade Comics: 1995 ($29.95)

nn-Boxed set of all editions of Shi/Cyblade & Cyblade/Shi plus new variant
3 6 9 19 30 40

BATTLE FOR THE PLANET OF THE APES (See Power Record Comics)

BATTLEFRONT
Atlas Comics (PPI): June, 1952 - No. 48, Aug, 1957

1-Heath-c 47 94 141 296 498 700
2-Robinson-a(4) 25 50 75 150 245 340
3-5-Robinson-a 21 42 63 122 199 275
6-10: Combat Kelly in No. 6-10. 6-Romita-a 19 38 57 109 172 235
11-22,24-28: 14,16-Battle Brady app. 22-Teddy Roosevelt & His Rough Riders
story. 28-Last pre-code (2/55) 17 34 51 98 154 210
23,43-Check-a 17 34 51 100 158 215
29-39,41,44-47 15 30 45 90 140 190
40,42-Williamson-a 17 34 51 98 154 210
48-Crandall-a 16 32 48 94 147 200

NOTE: ***Ayers** a-18, 19, 32, 35. **Berg** a-44. **Colan** a-21, 22, 32, 33, 35, 38, 40, 42, 43, 45. **Drucker** a-28, 29. **Everett** a-44. **Heath** c-23, 26, 27, 29, 32. **Maneely** a-21-23, 26; c-2, 7, 13, 22, 34, 35, 41. **Morisi** a-42. **Morrow** a-41.**Orlando** a-47. **Powell** a-19, 21, 25, 29, 32, 40, 47. **Robinson** a-1-3, 4&5(4); c-4, 5. **Robert Sale** a-19. **Severin** a-32; c-40, 42, 45. **Sinnott** a-26, 45, 48. **Woodbridge** a-45, 46.*

BATTLEFRONT
Standard Comics: No. 5, June, 1952

5-Toth-a 15 30 45 90 140 190

BATTLE GODS: WARRIORS OF THE CHAAK
Dark Horse Comics: Apr, 2000 - No. 4, July, 2000 ($2.95)

1-4-Francisco Ruiz Velasco-s/a 3.00

BATTLE GROUND
Atlas Comics (OMC): Sept, 1954 - No. 20, Sept, 1957

1 37 74 111 222 361 500
2-Jack Katz-a (11/54) 20 40 60 114 182 250
3,4: 3-Jack Katz-a. 4-Last precode (3/55) 17 34 51 98 154 210
5-8,10 (3/56) 15 30 45 90 140 190
9,11,13,18: 9-Krigstein-a. 11,13,18-Williamson-a in each
17 34 51 98 154 210
12,15-17,19,20 15 30 45 86 133 180
14-Kirby-a 19 38 57 112 179 245

NOTE: ***Ayers** a-4, 13, 16. **Colan** a-3, 11, 13. **Drucker** a-7, 12, 13, 20. **Heath** c-2, 3, 5, 7, 13. **Maneely** a-3, 14, 19; c-1, 18, 19. **Orlando** a-17. **Pakula** a-11. **Reinman** a-2. **Severin** a-4, 5, 12, 19. c-20. **Sinnott** a-7, 16. **Tuska** a-11.*

BATTLE HEROES
Stanley Publications: Sept, 1966 - No. 2, Nov, 1966 (25¢, squarebound giants)

1 4 8 12 23 37 50
2 3 6 9 17 26 35

BATTLE HYMN
Image Comics: Jan, 2005 - No. 5, Oct, 2005 ($2.95/$2.99, limited series)

1-5-WW2 super team; B. Clay Moore-s/Jeremy Haun-a; flip cover on #1-4 3.00

BATTLE OF THE BULGE (See Movie Classics)

BATTLE OF THE PLANETS (Based on syndicated cartoon by Sandy Frank)
Gold Key/Whitman No. 6 on: 6/79 - No. 10, 12/80

1: Mortimer a-1-4,7-10 5 10 15 34 60 85

GD VG FN VF VF/NM NM-
2.0 4.0 6.0 8.0 9.0 9.2

2-6,10 3 6 9 21 33 45
7-Low print run 5 10 15 35 63 90
8,9-Low print run: 8(11/80). 9-(3-pack only?) 5 10 15 33 57 80

BATTLE OF THE PLANETS (Also see Thundercats/...)
Image Comics (Top Cow): Aug, 2002 - No. 12, Sept, 2003 ($2.95/$2.99)

1-($2.95) Alex Ross-c & art director; Tortosa-a(p); re-intro. G-Force 3.00
1-($5.95) Holofoil-c by Ross 6.00
2-11-($2.99) Ross-c on all 3.00
12-($4.99) 5.00
#1/2 (7/03, $2.99) Benitez-c; Alex Ross sketch pages 3.00
... Battle Book 1 (5/03, $4.99) background info on characters, equipment, stories 5.00
... : Jason 1 (7/03, $4.99) Ross-c; Erwin David-a; preview of Tomb Raider: Epiphany 5.00
... : Mark 1 (5/03, $4.99) Ross-c; Erwin David-a; preview of BotP: Jason 5.00
.../Thundercats 1 (Image/WildStorm, 5/03, $4.99) 2 covers by Ross & Campbell 5.00
.../Witchblade 1 (2/03, $5.95) Ross-c; Christina and Jo Chen-a 6.00
Vol. 1: Trial By Fire (2003, $7.99) r/#1-3 8.00
Vol. 2: Blood Red Sky (9/03, $16.95) r/#4-9 17.00
Vol. 3: Destroy All Monsters (11/03, $19.95) r/#10-12, ...: Jason, ...: Mark, .../Witchblade 20.00
Vol. 1: Digest (1/04, $9.99, 7-3/8x5", B&W) r/#1-9 & ...: Mark 10.00
Vol. 2: Digest (8/04, $9.99, B&W) r/#10-12, ...: Jason, ...: Manga #1-3, .../Witchblade 10.00

BATTLE OF THE PLANETS: MANGA
Image Comics (Top Cow): Nov, 2003 - No. 3, Jan, 2004 ($2.99, B&W)

1-3-Edwin David-a/David Wohl-s; previews for Wanted & Tomb Raider #35 3.00

BATTLE OF THE PLANETS: PRINCESS
Image Comics (Top Cow): Nov, 2004 - No. 6, May, 2005 ($2.99, B&W, limited series)

1-6-Tortosa-a/Wohl-s. 1-Ross-c. 2-Tortosa-c 3.00

BATTLE POPE
Image Comics: June, 2005 - No. 14, Apr, 2007 ($2.99/$3.50, reprints 2000 B&W series in color)

1-5-Kirkman-s/Moore-a 3.50
6-10,12-14-($3.50) 14-Wedding 3.50
11-($4.99) Christmas issue 5.00
... Vol. 1: Genesis TPB (2006, $12.95) r/#1-4; sketch pages 13.00
... Vol. 2: Mayhem TPB (2006, $12.99) r/#5-8; sketch pages 13.00
... Vol. 3: Pillow Talk TPB (2007, $12.99) r/#9-11; sketch pages 13.00

BATTLER BRITTON (British comics character who debuted in 1956)
DC Comics (WildStorm): Sept, 2006 - No. 5, Jan, 2007 ($2.99, limited series)

1-5-WWII fighter pilots; Garth Ennis-s/Colin Wilson-a 3.00
TPB (2007, $19.99) r/#1-5; background of the character's British origins in the 1950s 20.00

BATTLE REPORT
Ajax/Farrell Publications: Aug, 1952 - No. 6, June, 1953

1 15 30 45 84 127 170
2-6 9 18 27 52 69 85

BATTLE SCARS
Marvel Comics: Jan, 2012 - No. 6, Jun, 2012 ($2.99, limited series)

1-Intro. Marcus Johnson and Cheese (later ID'd as Phil Coulson in #6); Eaton-a/Pagulayan-c
2 4 6 8 10 12
2-5: 4-Deadpool app. 5-Nick Fury app. 4.00
6-Marcus Johnson becomes Nick Fury Jr.; resembles movie version; Cheese joins SHIELD and is ID'd as Agent Coulson 2 4 6 8 10 12

BATTLE SQUADRON
Stanmor Publications: April, 1955 - No. 5, Dec, 1955

1 14 28 42 80 115 150
2-5: 3-Iwo Jima & flag-c 9 18 27 47 61 75

BATTLESTAR GALACTICA (TV) (Also see Marvel Comics Super Special #8)
Marvel Comics Group: Mar, 1979 - No. 23, Jan, 1981

1: 1-5 adapt TV episodes 2 4 6 11 16 20
2-23: 1-3-Partial-r 1 3 4 6 8 10

NOTE: ***Austin** c-9i, 10i. **Golden** c-18. **Simonson** a(p)-4, 5, 11-13, 15-20, 22, 23; c(p)-4, 5,11-17, 19, 20, 22, 23.*

BATTLESTAR GALACTICA (TV) (Also see Asylum)
Maximum Press: July, 1995 - No. 4, Nov, 1995 ($2.50, limited series)

1-4: Continuation of 1978 TV series 4.00
Trade paperback (12/95, $12.95)-reprints series 13.00

BATTLESTAR GALACTICA (1978 TV series)
Realm Press: Dec, 1997 - No. 5, July, 1998 ($2.99)

1-5-Chris Scalf-s/painted-a/c 3.00
...Search For Sanctuary (9/98, $2.99) Scalf & Kuhoric-s 3.00
...Search For Sanctuary Special (4/00, $3.99) Kuhoric-s/Scalf & Scott-a 4.00

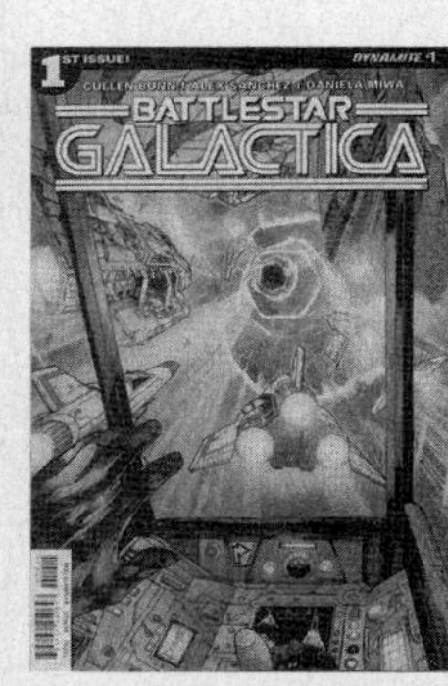

Battlestar Galactica V3 #1 © Universal

Battletide II #2 © MAR

Batwing #1 © DC

GD 2.0 | VG 4.0 | FN 6.0 | VF 8.0 | VF/NM 9.0 | NM- 9.2

GD 2.0 | VG 4.0 | FN 6.0 | VF 8.0 | VF/NM 9.0 | NM- 9.2

BATTLESTAR GALACTICA (2003-2009 TV series)
Dynamite Entertainment: No. 0, 2006 - No. 12, 2007 (25¢/$2.99)

0-(25¢-c) Two covers; Pak-s/Raynor-a 3.00
1-($2.99) Covers by Turner, Tan, Raynor & photo-c; Pak-s/Raynor-a 3.00
2-12-Four covers on each 3.00
... Pegasus (2007, $4.99) story of Battlestar Pegasus & Admiral Cain; 2 covers 5.00
... Volume 1 HC (2007, $19.99) r/#0-4; cover gallery; Raynor sketch pages; commentary 20.00
... Volume 1 TPB (2007, $14.99) r/#0-4; cover gallery; Raynor sketch pages; commentary 15.00
... Volume 2 HC (2007, $19.99) r/#5-8; cover gallery; Raynor sketch pages 20.00
... Volume 2 TPB (2007, $14.99) r/#5-8; cover gallery; Raynor sketch pages 15.00

BATTLESTAR GALACTICA, (Classic...) (1978 TV series characters)
Dynamite Entertainment: 2006 - No. 5,2006 ($2.99)

1-5: 1-Two covers by Dorman & Caldwell; Rafael-a. 2-Two covers 3.00

BATTLESTAR GALACTICA, (Classic...) (Volume 2) (1978 TV series characters)
Dynamite Entertainment: 2013 - No. 12, 2014 ($3.99)

1-12: 1-5-Two covers by Alex Ross & Chris Eliopoulos on each; Abnett & Lanning-s 4.00

BATTLESTAR GALACTICA, (Classic...) (Volume 3) (1978 TV series characters)
Dynamite Entertainment: 2016 - Present ($3.99)

1-5: 1-Cullen Bunn-s/Alex Sanchez-a; multiple covers 4.00

BATTLESTAR GALACTICA: APOLLO'S JOURNEY (1978 TV series)
Maximum Press: Apr, 1996 - No. 3, June, 1996 ($2.95, limited series)

1-3: Richard Hatch scripts 4.00

BATTLESTAR GALACTICA: CYLON APOCALYPSE (1978 TV series characters)
Dynamite Entertainment: 2007 - No. 4, 2007 ($2.99, limited series)

1-4-Carlos Rafael-a; 4 covers on each 3.00
TPB (2007, $14.99) r/series with cover gallery 15.00

BATTLESTAR GALACTICA: CYLON WAR (2003-2009 TV series)
Dynamite Entertainment: 2009 - No. 4, 2010 ($3.99, limited series)

1-3-First cylon war 40 years before the Caprica attack; Raynor-a; 2 covers 4.00

BATTLESTAR GALACTICA 1880, STEAMPUNK... (1978 TV series characters)
(Title changes from "(Classic) Battlestar Galactica Vol. 2" after #1)
Dynamite Entertainment: 2014 - No. 4, 2014 ($3.99, limited series)

1-4-Tony Lee-s/Aneke-a; multiple covers 4.00

BATTLESTAR GALACTICA: GHOSTS (2003-2009 TV series)
Dynamite Entertainment: 2008 - No. 4, 2009 ($4.99, 40 pgs., limited series)

1-4-Intro. of the Ghost Squadron; Jerwa-s/Lau-a/Calero-c 5.00

BATTLESTAR GALACTICA: GODS AND MONSTERS (2003-2009 TV series)
Dynamite Entertainment: 2016 - Present ($3.99, limited series)

1-4-Karl Kesel-s/Alec Morgan & Dan Schkade-a 4.00

BATTLESTAR GALACTICA: JOURNEY'S END (1978 TV series)
Maximum Press: Aug, 1996 - No. 4, Nov, 1996 ($2.99, limited series)

1-4-Continuation of the T.V. series 4.00

BATTLESTAR GALACTICA: ORIGINS (2003-2009 TV series)
Dynamite Entertainment: 2007 - No. 11, 2008 ($3.50)

1-11: 1-4-Baltar's origin; multiple covers. 5-8-Adama's origin. 9-11-Starbuck & Helo 3.50

BATTLESTAR GALACTICA: SEASON III
Realm Press: June/July, 1999 - No. 3, Sept, 1999 ($2.99)

1-3: 1-Kuhoric-s/Scalf & Scott-a; two covers by Scalf & Jae Lee. 2,3-Two covers 3.00
Gallery (4/00, $3.99) short story and pin-ups 4.00
1999 Tour Book (5/99, $2.99) 3.00
1999 Tour Book Convention Edition (6.99) 7.00
...Special: Centurion Prime (12/99, $3.99) Kuhoric-s 4.00

BATTLESTAR GALACTICA: SEASON ZERO (2003-2009 TV series)
Dynamite Entertainment: 2007 - No. 12, 2008 ($2.99)

1-12-Set 2 years before the Cylon attack; multiple covers 3.00
.../The Lone Ranger 2007 Free Comic Book Day Edition; flip book with Cassaday Lone Ranger-c 3.00

BATTLESTAR GALACTICA: SIX (2003-2009 TV series)
Dynamite Entertainment: No. 1, 2014 - No. 5, 2015 ($3.99, limited series)

1-5: 1-J.T. Krul-s/Igor Lima-a; multiple covers. 3-5-Rodolfo-a. 5-Baltar app. 4.00

BATTLESTAR GALACTICA: SPECIAL EDITION (TV)
Maximum Press: Jan, 1997 ($2.99, one-shot)

1-Fully painted; Scalf-c/s/a; r/Asylum 3.00

BATTLESTAR GALACTICA: STARBUCK (TV)
Maximum Press: Dec, 1995 - No. 3, Mar, 1996 ($2.50, limited series)

1-3 4.00

BATTLESTAR GALACTICA: STARBUCK, (Classic...) (1978 TV series characters)
Dynamite Entertainment: 2013 - No. 4, 2014 ($3.99, limited series)

1-4-Tony Lee-s/Eman Casallos-a. 1-Childhood flashback 4.00

BATTLESTAR GALACTICA: THE COMPENDIUM (TV)
Maximum Press: Feb, 1997 ($2.99, one-shot)

1 3.00

BATTLESTAR GALACTICA: THE DEATH OF APOLLO, (Classic...) (1978 TV series)
Dynamite Entertainment: 2014 - No. 6, 2015 ($3.99, limited series)

1-6-Dan Abnett-s/Dietrich Smith-a; multiple covers on each 4.00

BATTLESTAR GALACTICA: THE ENEMY WITHIN (TV)
Maximum Press: Nov, 1995 - No. 3, Feb, 1996 ($2.50, limited series)

1-3: 3-Indicia reads Feb, 1995 in error. 4.00

BATTLESTAR GALACTICA: THE FINAL FIVE (2003 series)
Dynamite Entertainment: 2009 - No. 4, 2009 ($3.99, limited series)

1-4-Raynor-a; 2 covers on each 4.00

BATTLESTAR GALACTICA ZAREK (2003 series)
Dynamite Entertainment: 2007 - No. 4, 2007 ($3.50, limited series)

1-4-Origin story of political activist Tom Zarek; 2 covers on each 3.50

BATTLE STORIES (See XMas Comics)
Fawcett Publications: Jan, 1952 - No. 11, Sept, 1953

	GD 2.0	VG 4.0	FN 6.0	VF 8.0	VF/NM 9.0	NM- 9.2
1-Evans-a (Korean War)	17	34	51	98	154	210
2	10	20	30	58	79	100
3-11	9	18	27	50	65	80

BATTLE STORIES
Super Comics: 1963 - 1964

	GD 2.0	VG 4.0	FN 6.0	VF 8.0	VF/NM 9.0	NM- 9.2
Reprints #10-13,15-18: 10-r/U.S Tank Commandos #? 11-r/? 11, 12,17-r/Monty Hall #?; 13-Kintsler-a (1pg).15-r/American Air Forces #7 by Powell; Bolle-r. 18-U.S. Fighting Air Force #?	2	4	6	9	13	16

BATTLETECH (See Blackthorne 3-D Series #41 for 3-D issue)
Blackthorne Publishing: Oct, 1987 - No. 6, 1988 ($1.75/$2.00)

1-6: Based on game. 1-Color. 2-Begin B&W 3.00
Annual 1 ($4.50, B&W) 5.00

BATTLETECH
Malibu Comics: Feb, 1995 ($2.95)

0 3.00

BATTLETECH FALLOUT
Malibu Comics: Dec, 1994 - No. 4, Mar, 1995 ($2.95)

1-4-Two edi. exist #1; normal logo 3.00
1-Gold version w/foil logo stamped "Gold Limited Edition 8.00
1-Full-c holographic limited edition 6.00

BATTLETIDE (Death's Head II & Killpower...)
Marvel Comics UK, Ltd.: Dec, 1992 - No. 4, Mar, 1993 ($1.75, mini-series)

1-4: Wolverine, Psylocke, Dark Angel app. 3.00

BATTLETIDE II (Death's Head II & Killpower...)
Marvel Comics UK, Ltd.: Aug, 1993 - No. 4, Nov, 1993 ($1.75, mini-series)

1-($2.95)-Foil embossed logo 4.00
2-4: 2-Hulk-c/story 3.00

BATWING (DC New 52)
DC Comics: Nov, 2011 - No. 34, Oct, 2014 ($2.99)

1-24: 1-3,5-Judd Winick-s/Ben Oliver-a. 4-Origin; Chriscross-a. 9-Night of the Owls 3.00
25-($3.99) Zero Year tie-in; Luke Fox's first meeting with Batman; Conner-c 4.00
26-34: 26,27-Darwyn Cooke-c 3.00
#0 (11/12, $2.99) origin of David Zavimbe; Winick-s/To-a 3.00
...: Futures End 1 (11/14, $2.99, regular-c) Five years later; Panosian-c 3.00
...: Futures End 1 (11/14, $3.99, 3-D cover) 4.00

BATWOMAN (See 52 #9 & 11 for debut and Detective Comics #854-860)
DC Comics: No. 0, Jan, 2011; No. 1, Nov, 2011 - No. 40, May, 2015 ($2.99)

0-(1/11) Williams III-s; art by Williams III and Reeder; Williams III-c 3.00
0-(1/11)-Variant-c by Reeder 5.00
1-New DC 52; Williams III-a; Williams III & Blackman-s; Bette Kane app. 5.00
2-24: 2-Cameron Chase returns. 6-8-Reeder-a/c. 9-11,15,18-20,22,23-McCarthy-a. 12-17-Wonder Woman app. 21-Francavilla-a; Killer Croc app. 3.00

Batwoman: Rebirth #1 © DC

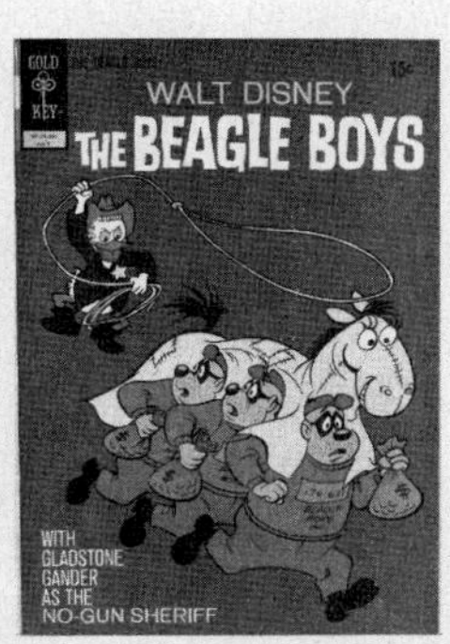

The Beagle Boys #13 © DIS

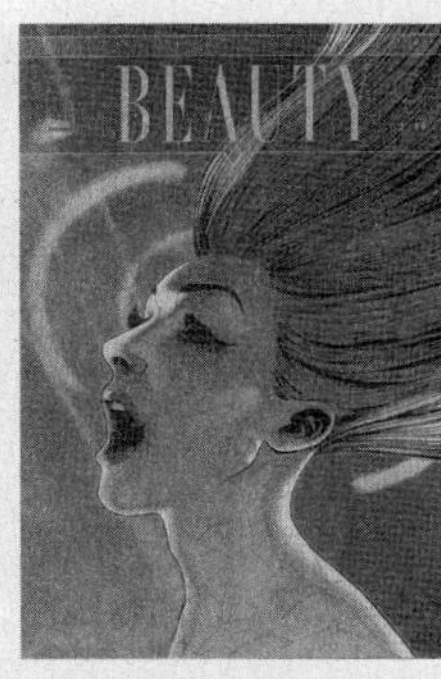

The Beauty #9 © Haun & Hurley

GD 2.0 | VG 4.0 | FN 6.0 | VF 8.0 | VF/NM 9.0 | NM- 9.2

25-($3.99) Zero Year tie-in; Maggie Sawyer & Bruce Wayne app. 4.00
26-40: 26-31-Wolf Spider. 35-Etrigan, Clayface, Ragman & Alice app. 3.00
#0 (11/12, $2.99) Flashback to Kate's training; Williams III-a 3.00
Annual 1 (6/14, $4.99) Continued from #24; Batman app.; McCarthy & Moritat-a 5.00
Annual 2 (6/15, $4.99) Continued from #40; Jeanty-c/a 5.00
... Elegy The Deluxe Edition HC (2010, $24.99, d.j.) r/Detective #854-860; gallery of variant covers, sketch art and script pages; intro. by Rachel Maddow 25.00
... Elegy SC (2011, $17.99) same contents as Deluxe HC 18.00
...: Futures End 1 (11/14, $2.99, regular-c) Five years later; Red Alice app. 3.00
...: Futures End 1 (11/14, $3.99, 3-D cover) 4.00

BATWOMAN (DC Rebirth)
DC Comics: Apr, 2017 - Present ($2.99)

...: Rebirth 1 (4/17, $2.99) Bennett & Tynion-s/Epting-a; origin re-capped 3.00

BAY CITY JIVE
DC Comics (WildStorm): Jul, 2001 - No. 3, Sept, 2001 ($2.95, limited series)

1-3: Intro Sugah Rollins in 1970s San Francisco; Layman-s/Johnson-a 3.00

BAYWATCH COMIC STORIES (TV) (Magazine)
Acclaim Comics (Armada): May, 1996 - No. 4, 1997 ($4.95) (Photo-c on all)

1-4: Photo comics based on TV show 5.00

BEACH BLANKET BINGO (See Movie Classics)

BEAGLE BOYS, THE (Walt Disney)(See The Phantom Blot)
Gold Key: 11/64; No. 2, 11/65; No. 3, 8/66 - No. 47, 2/79 (See WDC&S #134)

	GD	VG	FN	VF	VF/NM	NM-
1	5	10	15	30	50	70
2-5	3	6	9	17	26	35
6-10	3	6	9	15	22	28
11-20: 11,14,19-r	2	4	6	11	16	20
21-30: 27-r	2	4	6	8	11	14
31-47	1	3	4	6	8	10

BEAGLE BOYS VERSUS UNCLE SCROOGE
Gold Key: Mar, 1979 - No. 12, Feb, 1980

	GD	VG	FN	VF	VF/NM	NM-
1	2	4	6	9	13	16
2-12: 9-r	1	2	3	5	6	8

BEANBAGS
Ziff-Davis Publ. Co. (Approved Comics): Winter, 1951 - No. 2, Spring, 1952

	GD	VG	FN	VF	VF/NM	NM-
1,2	14	28	42	82	121	160

BEANIE THE MEANIE
Fago Publications: No. 3, May, 1959

	GD	VG	FN	VF	VF/NM	NM-
3	5	10	15	24	30	35

BEANY AND CECIL (TV) (Bob Clampett's...)
Dell Publishing Co.: Jan, 1952 - 1955; July-Sept, 1962 - No. 5, July-Sept, 1963

	GD	VG	FN	VF	VF/NM	NM-
Four Color 368	21	42	63	147	324	500
Four Color 414,448,477,530,570,635(1/55)	12	24	36	84	185	285
01-057-209 (#1)	11	22	33	77	166	255
2-5	9	18	27	58	114	170

BEAR COUNTRY (Disney)
Dell Publishing Co.: No. 758, Dec, 1956

	GD	VG	FN	VF	VF/NM	NM-
Four Color 758-Movie	5	10	15	33	57	80

BEAST (See X-Men)
Marvel Comics: May, 1997 - No. 3, 1997 ($2.50, mini-series)

1-3-Giffen-s/Nocon-a 3.00

BEAST BOY (See Titans)
DC Comics: Jan, 2000 - No. 4, Apr, 2000 ($2.95, mini-series)

1-4-Justiano-c/a; Raab & Johns-s 3.00

B.E.A.S.T.I.E.S. (Also see Axis Alpha)
Axis Comics: Apr, 1994 ($1.95)

1-Javier Saltares-c/a/scripts 3.00

BEASTS OF BURDEN (See Dark Horse Book of Hauntings, ...Monsters, ...The Dead, ...Witchcraft)
Dark Horse Comics: Sept, 2009 - No. 4, Dec, 2009 ($2.99, limited series)

1-4-Evan Dorkin-s/Jill Thompson-a/c 3.00
...: Hunters & Gatherers (3/14, $3.50) Evan Dorkin-s/Jill Thompson-a/c 3.50
...: Neighborhood Watch (8/12, $3.50) Evan Dorkin-s/Jill Thompson-a/c 3.50
...: What the Cat Dragged In (5/16, $3.99) Evan Dorkin & Sarah Dyer-s/Jill Thompson-a/c 4.00
Volume 1: Animal Rites HC (6/10, $19.99) r/#1-4 & short stories from Dark Horse Books 20.00

BEATLES, THE (See Girls' Romances #109, Go-Go, Heart Throbs #101, Herbie #5, Howard the Duck Mag. #4, Laugh #166, Marvel Comics Super Special #4, My Little Margie #54, Not Brand Echh, Strange Tales #130, Summer Love, Superman's Pal Jimmy Olsen #79, Teen Confessions #37, Tippy's Friends & Tippy Teen)

GD 2.0 | VG 4.0 | FN 6.0 | VF 8.0 | VF/NM 9.0 | NM- 9.2

BEATLES, THE (Life Story)
Dell Publishing Co.: Sept-Nov, 1964 (35¢)

	GD	VG	FN	VF	VF/NM	NM-
1-(Scarce)-Stories with color photo pin-ups; Paul S. Newman-s (photo-c)	46	92	138	368	834	1300

BEATLES EXPERIENCE, THE
Revolutionary Comics: Mar, 1991 - No. 8, 1991 ($2.50, B&W, limited series)

1-8: 1-Gold logo 5.00

BEATLES YELLOW SUBMARINE (See Movie Comics under Yellow...)

BEAUTIFUL KILLER
Black Bull Comics: Sept., 2002 - No. 3, Jan, 2003 ($2.99, limited series)

...Limited Preview Edition (5/02, $5.00) preview pgs. & creator interviews 5.00
1-Noto-a/Palmiotti-s; Hughes-c; intro Brigit Cole 3.00
2,3: 2-Jusko-c. 3-Noto-c 3.00
TPB (5/03, $9.99) r/#1-3; cover gallery and Adam Hughes sketch pages 10.00

BEAUTIFUL PEOPLE
Slave Labor Graphics: Apr, 1994 ($4.95, 8-1/2x11", one-shot)

nn 5.00

BEAUTIFUL STORIES FOR UGLY CHILDREN
DC Comics (Piranha Press): 1989 - No. 30, 1991 ($2.00/$2.50, B&W, mature)

Vol. 1-20: 12-$2.50-c begins 4.00
21-25 5.00

	GD	VG	FN	VF	VF/NM	NM-
26-30-(Lower print run)	1	2	3	4	5	7

A Cotton Candy Autopsy ($12.95, B&W)-Reprints 1st two volumes 13.00

BEAUTY, THE (Also see Pilot Season: The Beauty)
Image Comics: Aug, 2015 - Present ($3.50/$3.99)

1-6-Jeremy Haun & Jason Hurley-s/Haun-a. 1-Three covers; reprints Pilot Season issue 3.50
7-12-($3.99) 7-Huddleston-a. 8-10-Weldele-a. 12-Haun-a 4.00

BEAUTY AND THE BEAST, THE
Marvel Comics Group: Jan, 1985 - No. 4, Apr, 1985 (limited series)

1-4: Dazzler & the Beast from X-Men; Sienkiewicz-c on all 4.00

BEAUTY AND THE BEAST (Graphic novel)(Also see Cartoon Tales & Disney's New Adventures of...)
Disney Comics: 1992

nn-($4.95, prestige edition)-Adapts animated film 7.00
nn-($2.50, newsstand edition) 4.00

BEAUTY AND THE BEAST
Disney Comics: Sept., 1992 - No. 2, 1992 ($1.50, limited series)

1,2 3.00

BEAUTY AND THE BEAST: PORTRAIT OF LOVE (TV)
First Comics: May, 1989 - No. 2, Mar, 1990 ($5.95, 60 pgs., squarebound)

1,2: 1-Based on TV show, Wendy Pini-a/scripts. 2-...: Night of Beauty; by Wendy Pini 6.00

BEAVER VALLEY (Movie)(Disney)
Dell Publishing Co.: No. 625, Apr, 1955

	GD	VG	FN	VF	VF/NM	NM-
Four Color 625	6	12	18	37	66	95

BEAVIS AND BUTTHEAD (MTV's...)(TV cartoon)
Marvel Comics: Mar, 1994 - No. 28, June, 1996 ($1.95)

	GD	VG	FN	VF	VF/NM	NM-
1-Silver ink-c. 1, 2-Punisher & Devil Dinosaur app.	1	3	4	6	8	10

1-2nd printing 4.00
2,3: 2-Wolverine app. 3-Man-Thing, Spider-Man, Venom, Carnage, Mary Jane & Stan Lee cameos; John Romita, Sr. art (2 pgs.) 5.00
4-28: 5-War Machine, Thor, Loki, Hulk, Captain America & Rhino cameos. 6-Psylocke, Polaris, Daredevil & Bullseye app. 7-Ghost Rider & Sub-Mariner app. 8-Quasar & Eon app. 9-Prowler & Nightwatch app. 11-Black Widow app. 12-Thunderstrike & Bloodaxe app. 13-Night Thrasher app. 14-Spider-Man 2099 app. 15-Warlock app. 16-X-Factor app. 25-Juggernaut app. 4.00

BECK & CAUL INVESTIGATIONS
Gauntlet Comics (Caliber): Jan, 1994 - No. 5, 1995? ($2.95, B&W)

1-5 3.00
Special 1 ($4.95) 5.00

BEDKNOBS AND BROOMSTICKS (See Walt Disney Showcase No. 6 & 50)

BEDLAM!
Eclipse Comics: Sept, 1985 - No. 2, Sept, 1985 (B&W-r in color)

1,2: Bissette-a 4.00

BEDTIME STORIES FOR IMPRESSIONABLE CHILDREN
Moonstone Books/American Mythology: Nov, 2010; Feb, 2017 ($3.99, B&W)

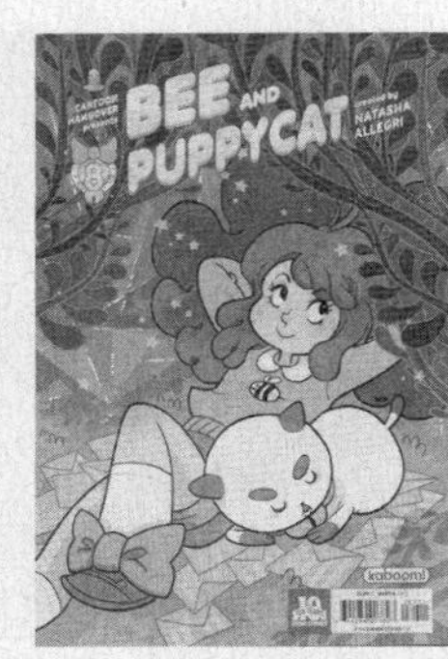

Bee and Puppycat #8 © Frederator

Beetle Bailey #70 © CC

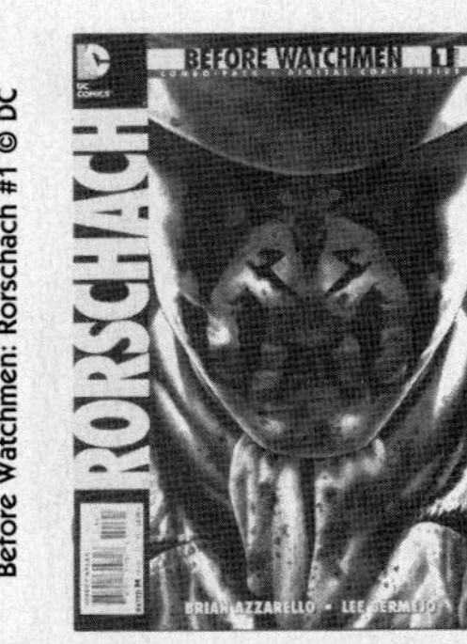

Before Watchmen: Rorschach #1 © DC

	GD 2.0	VG 4.0	FN 6.0	VF 8.0	VF/NM 9.0	NM- 9.2
1-(11/10) Short story anthology; Vaughn, Kuhoric & Tinnell-s; 3 covers						4.00
1-(2/17) Short story anthology; Vaughn, Shooter & Nelms-s; 4 covers						4.00

BEDTIME STORY (See Cinema Comics Herald)

BEE AND PUPPYCAT
Boom Entertainment (KaBOOM!): May, 2014 - No. 11, Apr, 2016 ($3.99)

	GD	VG	FN	VF	VF/NM	NM-
1-11: Multiple covers on each. 1,2-Natasha Allegri-s/a						4.00

BEELZELVIS
Slave Labor Graphics: Feb, 1994 ($2.95, B&W, one-shot)

	GD	VG	FN	VF	VF/NM	NM-
1						3.00

BEEP BEEP, THE ROAD RUNNER (TV) (See Dell Giant Comics Bugs Bunny Vacation Funnies #8 for 1st app.) (Also see Daffy & Kite Fun Book)
Dell Publishing Co./Gold Key No. 1-88/Whitman No. 89 on: July, 1958 - No. 14, Aug-Oct, 1962; Oct, 1966 - No. 105, 1984

	GD	VG	FN	VF	VF/NM	NM-
Four Color 918 (#1, 7/58)	12	24	36	81	176	270
Four Color 1008,1046 (11-1/59-60)	7	14	21	49	92	135
4(2-4/60)-14(Dell)	6	12	18	37	66	95
1(10/66, Gold Key)	6	12	18	41	76	110
2-5	4	8	12	27	44	60
6-14	3	6	9	19	30	40
15-18,20-40	3	6	9	16	23	30
19-With pull-out poster	4	8	12	25	40	55
41-50	3	6	9	14	19	24
51-70	2	4	6	9	13	16
71-88	2	3	4	6	8	10
89,90,94-101: 100(3/82), 101(4/82)	2	4	6	8	10	12
91(8/80), 92(9/80), 93 (3-pack?) (low printing)	7	14	21	49	92	135
102-105 (All #90189 on-c; nd or date code; pre-pack) 102(6/83), 103(7/83), 104(5/84), 105(6/84)	3	6	9	19	30	40
#63-2970 (Now Age Books/Pendulum Pub. Comic Digest, 1971, 75¢, 100 pages, B&W) collection of one-page gags	4	8	12	27	44	60

NOTE: *See March of Comics #351, 353, 375, 387, 397, 416, 430, 442, 455. #5, 8-10, 35, 53, 59-62, 68-r; 96-102, 104 are 1/3-r.*

BEETLE BAILEY (See Giant Comic Album, Sarge Snorkel; also Comics Reading Libraries in the Promotional Comics section)
Dell Publishing Co./Gold Key #39-53/King #54-66/Charlton #67-119/Gold Key #120-131/ Whitman #132: #459, 5/53 - #38, 5-7/62; #39, 11/62 - #53, 5/66; #54, 8/66 - #65, 12/67;#67, 2/69 - #119, 11/76; #120, 4/78 - #132, 4/80

	GD	VG	FN	VF	VF/NM	NM-
Four Color 469 (#1)-By Mort Walker	12	24	36	83	182	280
Four Color 521,552,622	7	14	21	49	92	135
5(2-4/56)-10(5-7/57)	5	10	15	35	63	90
11-20(4-5/59)	4	8	12	28	47	65
21-38(5-7/62)	3	6	9	20	31	42
39-53(5/66)	3	6	9	17	26	35
54-65 (No. 66 publ. overseas only?)	3	6	9	16	23	30
67-69: 69-Last 12¢ issue	3	6	9	14	20	25
70-99	2	4	6	9	13	16
100	2	4	6	11	16	20
101-111,114-119	1	3	4	6	8	10
112,113-Byrne illos. (4 each)	2	4	6	9	12	18
120-132	1	2	3	4	5	7

BEETLE BAILEY
Harvey Comics: V2#1, Sept, 1992 - V2#9, Aug, 1994 ($1.25/$1.50)

	GD	VG	FN	VF	VF/NM	NM-
V2#1						5.00
2-9-($1.50)						3.50
Big Book 1(11/92),2(5/93)(Both $1.95, 52 pgs.)						4.00
Giant Size V2#1(10/92),2(3/93)(Both $2.25,68 pgs.)						4.00

BEETLEJUICE (TV)
Harvey Comics: Oct, 1991 ($1.25)

	GD	VG	FN	VF	VF/NM	NM-
1						5.00

BEETLEJUICE CRIMEBUSTERS ON THE HAUNT
Harvey Comics: Sept, 1992 - No. 3, Jan, 1993 ($1.50, limited series)

	GD	VG	FN	VF	VF/NM	NM-
1-3						4.00

BEE 29, THE BOMBARDIER
Neal Publications: Feb, 1945

	GD	VG	FN	VF	VF/NM	NM-
1-(Funny animal)	37	74	111	222	361	500

BEFORE THE FANTASTIC FOUR: BEN GRIMM AND LOGAN
Marvel Comics: July, 2000 - No. 3, Sept, 2000 ($2.99, limited series)

	GD	VG	FN	VF	VF/NM	NM-
1-3-The Thing and Wolverine app.; Hama-s						3.00

BEFORE THE FANTASTIC FOUR: REED RICHARDS
Marvel Comics: Sept, 2000 - No. 3, Dec, 2000 ($2.99, limited series)

	GD	VG	FN	VF	VF/NM	NM-
1-3-Peter David-s/Duncan Fegredo-c/a						3.00

BEFORE THE FANTASTIC FOUR: THE STORMS
Marvel Comics: Dec, 2000 - No. 3, Feb, 2001 ($2.99, limited series)

	GD	VG	FN	VF	VF/NM	NM-
1-3-Adlard-a						3.00

BEFORE WATCHMEN: COMEDIAN (Prequel to 1986 Watchmen series)
DC Comics: Aug, 2012 - No. 6, Jun, 2013 ($3.99, limited series)

	GD	VG	FN	VF	VF/NM	NM-
1-6-Brian Azzarello-s/J.G. Jones-a/c; The Comedian during the Vietnam War; back-up Crimson Corsair serial in #1-4; Higgins-a						4.00
1-Variant-c by Jim Lee						30.00
1-6-Variant covers. 1-Risso. 2-Bradstreet. 3-Leon. 4-Stelfreeze. 5-Frank. 6-Albuquerque						8.00

BEFORE WATCHMEN: DOLLAR BILL (Prequel to 1986 Watchmen series)
DC Comics: Mar, 2013 ($3.99, one-shot)

	GD	VG	FN	VF	VF/NM	NM-
1-Len Wein-s/Steve Rude-a/c; origin and demise of Dollar Bill						4.00
1-Variant-c by Jim Lee						60.00
1-Variant-c by Darwyn Cooke						8.00

BEFORE WATCHMEN: DR. MANHATTAN (Prequel to 1986 Watchmen series)
DC Comics: Oct, 2012 - No. 4, Apr, 2013 ($3.99, limited series)

	GD	VG	FN	VF	VF/NM	NM-
1-4-Straczynski-s/Hughes-a/c; back-up Crimson Corsair serial in #1-3; Higgins-a						4.00
1-Variant-c by Jim Lee						30.00
1-4-Variant covers. 1-Pope. 2-Russell. 3-Neal Adams. 4-Sienkiewicz						8.00

BEFORE WATCHMEN: MINUTEMEN (Prequel to 1986 Watchmen series)
DC Comics: Aug, 2012 - No. 6, Mar, 2013 ($3.99, limited series)

	GD	VG	FN	VF	VF/NM	NM-
1-6-Darwyn Cooke-a/c; The team flashback to 1939; back-up Crimson Corsair serial in #1-5; Higgins-a						4.00
1-Variant-c by Jim Lee						20.00
1-6-Variant covers. 1-Golden. 2-Garcia-Lopez-c. 3-Chiang. 4-Rude. 6-Cloonan						8.00

BEFORE WATCHMEN: MOLOCH (Prequel to 1986 Watchmen series)
DC Comics: Jan, 2013 - No. 2, Feb, 2013 ($3.99, limited series)

	GD	VG	FN	VF	VF/NM	NM-
1,2-Straczynski-s/Risso-a/c; origin; back-up Crimson Corsair serial in both; Higgins-a						4.00
1-Variant-c by Jim Lee						30.00
1,2-Variant covers. 1-Matt Wagner. 2-Olly Moss						6.00

BEFORE WATCHMEN: NITE OWL (Prequel to 1986 Watchmen series)
DC Comics: Aug, 2012 - No. 4, Feb, 2013 ($3.99, limited series)

	GD	VG	FN	VF	VF/NM	NM-
1-4-Straczynski-s/Andy Kubert-a/c; Joe Kubert-a(i) in #1-3; back-up Crimson Corsair serial in #1-3; Higgins-a						4.00
1-Variant-c by Jim Lee						20.00
1-4-Variant covers. 1-Nowlan. 2-Finch. 3-Samnee. 4-Van Sciver						8.00

BEFORE WATCHMEN: OZYMANDIAS (Prequel to 1986 Watchmen series)
DC Comics: Sept, 2012 - No. 6, Apr, 2013 ($3.99, limited series)

	GD	VG	FN	VF	VF/NM	NM-
1-6-Len Wein-s/Jae Lee-a/c; origin of master plan; back-up Crimson Corsair serial in #1-4; Higgins-a						4.00
1-Variant-c by Jim Lee						20.00
1-6-Variant covers. 1-Jimenez. 2-Noto. 3-Carnevale. 4-Kaluta. 5-Thompson. 6-Sook						8.00

BEFORE WATCHMEN: RORSCHACH (Prequel to 1986 Watchmen series)
DC Comics: Oct, 2012 - No. 4, Apr, 2013 ($3.99, limited series)

	GD	VG	FN	VF	VF/NM	NM-
1-4-Azzarello-s/Bermejo-a/c; back-up Crimson Corsair serial in #1-3; Higgins-a						4.00
1-Variant-c by Jim Lee						40.00
1-4-Variant covers. 1-Steranko. 2-Jock. 3-Kidd. 4-Reis						8.00

BEFORE WATCHMEN: SILK SPECTRE (Prequel to 1986 Watchmen series)
DC Comics: Aug, 2012 - No. 4, Dec, 2013 ($3.99, limited series)

	GD	VG	FN	VF	VF/NM	NM-
1-4-Cooke & Conner-s/Conner-a/c; back-up Crimson Corsair serial in all; Higgins-a						4.00
1-Variant-c by Jim Lee						40.00
1-4-Variant covers. 1-Dave Johnson. 2-Middleton. 3-Allred. 4-Timm						8.00

BEHIND PRISON BARS
Realistic Comics (Avon): 1952

	GD	VG	FN	VF	VF/NM	NM-
1-Kinstler-c	39	78	117	231	378	525

BEHOLD THE HANDMAID
George Pflaum: 1954 (Religious) (25¢ with a 20¢ sticker price)

	GD	VG	FN	VF	VF/NM	NM-
nn	6	12	18	31	38	45

BELIEVE IT OR NOT (See Ripley's...)

BEN AND ME (Disney)
Dell Publishing Co.: No. 539, Mar, 1954

	GD	VG	FN	VF	VF/NM	NM-
Four Color 539	5	10	15	30	50	70

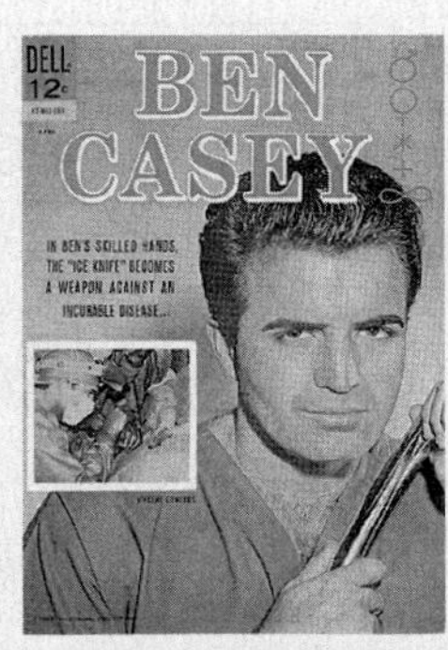

Ben Casey #5 © Bing Crosby Prods.

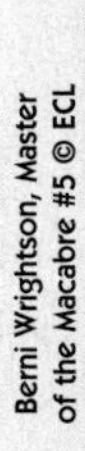
Berni Wrightson, Master of the Macabre #5 © ECL

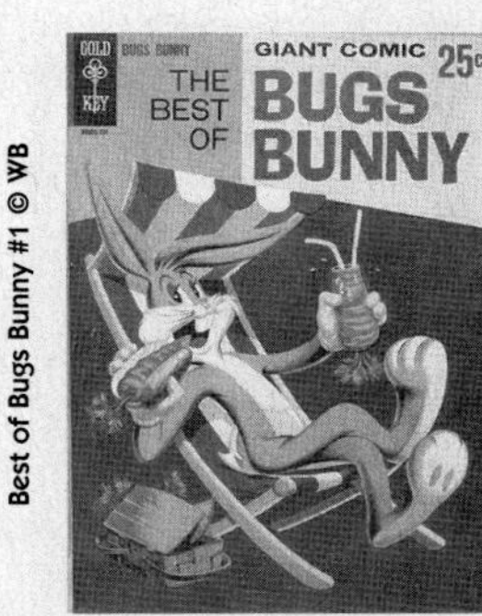

Best of Bugs Bunny #1 © WB

	GD 2.0	VG 4.0	FN 6.0	VF 8.0	VF/NM 9.0	NM- 9.2
BEN BOWIE AND HIS MOUNTAIN MEN						
Dell Publishing Co.: 1952 - No. 17, Nov-Jan, 1958-59						
Four Color 443 (#1)	9	18	27	58	114	170
Four Color 513,557,599,626,657	5	10	15	34	60	85
7(5-7/56)-11: 11-Intro/origin Yellow Hair	4	8	12	25	40	55
12-17	4	8	12	23	37	50
BEN CASEY (TV)						
Dell Publishing Co.: June-July, 1962 - No. 10, June-Aug, 1965 (Photo-c)						
12-063-207 (#1)	5	10	15	35	63	90
2(10/62),3,5-10	4	8	12	23	37	50
4-Marijuana & heroin use story	4	8	12	27	44	60
BEN CASEY FILM STORIES (TV)						
Gold Key: Nov, 1962 (25¢) (Photo-c)						
30009-211-All photos	6	12	18	38	69	100
BENEATH THE PLANET OF THE APES (See Movie Comics & Power Record Comics)						
BEN FRANKLIN (See Kite Fun Book)						
BEN HUR						
Dell Publishing Co.: No. 1052, Nov, 1959						
Four Color 1052-Movie, Manning-a	9	18	27	61	123	185
BEN ISRAEL						
Logos International: 1974 (39¢)						
nn-Christian religious	2	4	6	10	14	18
BEN 10 (Cartoon Network)						
IDW Publishing: Nov, 2013 - No. 4, Feb, 2014 ($3.99, limited series)						
1-4: Henderson-s/Purcell-a; multiple covers on each						4.00
BEOWULF (Also see First Comics Graphic Novel #1)						
National Periodical Publications: Apr-May, 1975 - No. 6, Feb-Mar, 1976						
1	2	4	6	9	12	15
2,3,5,6: 5-Flying saucer-c/story	1	2	3	5	6	8
4-Dracula-c/s	1	3	4	6	8	10
BERNI WRIGHTSON, MASTER OF THE MACABRE						
Pacific Comics/Eclipse Comics No. 5: July, 1983 - No. 5, Nov, 1984 ($1.50, Baxter paper)						
1-5: Wrightson-c/a(r). 4-Jeff Jones-r (11 pgs.)						6.00
BERRYS, THE (Also see Funny World)						
Argo Publ.: May, 1956						
1-Reprints daily & Sunday strips & daily Animal Antics by Ed Nofziger	6	12	18	29	36	42
BERZERKER (Milo Ventimiglia Presents...)						
Image Comics (Top Cow): No. 0, Feb, 2009 - No. 6, Jun, 2010 ($2.99/$3.99)						
0-3-Jeremy Haun-a/Rick Loverd-s/Dale Keown-c. 0-Creator interviews						3.00
4-6-($3.99) Covers by Haun & Keown						4.00
BERZERKERS (See Youngblood V1#2)						
Image Comics (Extreme Studios): Aug, 1995 - No. 3, Oct, 1995 ($2.50, limited series)						
1-3: Beau Smith scripts, Fraga-a						3.00
BEST COMICS						
Better Publications: Nov, 1939 - No. 4, Feb, 1940(10-11/16" wide x 8" tall, reads sideways)						
1-(Scarce)-Red Mask begins(1st app.) & c/s-all	258	516	774	1651	2826	4000
2-4: 4-Cannibalism story	142	284	426	909	1555	2200
BEST FROM BOY'S LIFE, THE						
Gilberton Company: Oct, 1957 - No. 5, Oct, 1958 (35¢)						
1-Space Conquerors & Kam of the Ancient Ones begin, end #5; Bob Cousy photo/story	13	26	39	72	101	130
2,3,5	8	16	24	42	54	65
4-L.B. Cole-a	8	16	24	44	57	70
BEST LOVE (Formerly Sub-Mariner Comics No. 32)						
Marvel Comics (MPI): No. 33, Aug, 1949 - No. 36, April, 1950 (Photo-c 33-36)						
33-Kubert-a	16	32	48	94	147	200
34 (10/49)	12	24	36	67	94	120
35,36-Everett-a	13	26	39	74	105	135
BEST OF ARCHIE, THE						
Perigee Books: 1980 ($7.95, softcover TPB)						
nn-Intro by Michael Uslan & Jeffrey Mendel	5	10	15	34	60	85
BEST OF BUGS BUNNY, THE						
Gold Key: Oct, 1966 - No. 2, Oct, 1968						

	GD 2.0	VG 4.0	FN 6.0	VF 8.0	VF/NM 9.0	NM- 9.2
1,2-Giants	4	8	12	27	44	60
BEST OF DC, THE (Blue Ribbon Digest) (See Limited Coll. Ed. C-52)						
DC Comics: Sept-Oct, 1979 - No. 71, Apr, 1986 (100-148 pgs; mostly reprints)						
1-Superman, w/"Death of Superman"-r	2	4	6	11	16	20
2,5-9: 2-Batman 40th Ann. Special. 5-Best of 1979. 6,8-Superman. 7-Superboy. 9-Batman, Creeper app.	2	4	6	8	10	12
3-Superfriends	2	4	6	9	12	15
4-Rudolph the Red Nosed Reindeer	2	4	6	9	13	16
10-Secret Origins of Super Villains; 1st ever Penguin origin-s	3	6	9	15	22	28
11-16,18-20: 11-The Year's Best Stories. 12-Superman Time and Space Stories.13-Best of DC Comics Presents. 14-New origin stories of Batman villains. 15-Superboy. 16-Superman Anniv. 18-Teen Titans new-s., Adams, Kane-a; Perez-c. 19-Superman. 20-World's Finest	1	2	3	5	7	9
17-Supergirl	2	4	6	8	10	12
21,22: 21-Justice Society. 22-Christmas; unpublished Sandman story w/Kirby-a	2	4	6	10	14	18
23-27: 23-(148 pgs.)-Best of 1981. 24 Legion, new story and 16 pgs. new costumes. 25-Superman. 26-Brave & Bold. 27-Superman vs. Luthor	2	4	6	9	12	15
28,29: 28-Binky, Sugar & Spike app. 29-Sugar & Spike, 3 new stories; new Stanley & his Monster story	2	4	6	9	13	16
30,32-36,38,40: 30-Detective Comics. 32-Superman. 33-Secret origins of Legion Heroes and Villains. 34-Metal Men; has #497 on-c from Adv. Comics. 35-The Year's Best Comics Stories (148 pgs.). 36-Superman vs. Kryptonite. 38-Superman. 40-World of Krypton	2	4	6	9	12	15
31-JLA	2	4	6	10	14	18
34-Corrected version with "#34" on cover	2	4	6	10	14	18
37,39: 37-"Funny Stuff", Mayer-a. 39-Binky	2	4	6	10	14	18
41,43,45,47,49,53,55,58,60,63,65,68,70: 41-Sugar & Spike new stories with Mayer-a. 43,49,55-Funny Stuff. 45,53,70-Binky. 47,65,68-Sugar & Spike. 58-Super Jrs. Holiday Special; Sugar & Spike. 60-Plop!; Wood-c(r) & Aragonés-r (5/85). 63-Plop!; Wrightson-a(r)	3	6	9	14	19	24
42,44,46,48,50-52,54,56,57,59,61,62,64,66,67,69,71: 42,56-Superman vs. Aliens. 44,57,67-Superboy & LSH. 46-Jimmy Olsen. 48-Superman Team-ups. 50-Year's best Superman. 51-Batman Family. 52 Best of 1984. 54,56,59-Superman. 61-(148 pgs.)Year's best. 62-Best of Batman 1985. 69-Year's best Team stories. 71-Year's best	2	4	6	10	14	18
NOTE: ***N. Adams*** *a-2r, 14r, 18r, 26, 51.* ***Aparo*** *a-9, 14, 26, 30; c-9, 14, 26.* ***Austin*** *a-51i.* ***Buckler*** *a-40p; c-16, 22.* ***Giffen*** *a-50, 52; c-33p.* ***Grell*** *a-33p.* ***Grossman*** *a-37.* ***Heath*** *a-26.* ***Infantino*** *a-10r, 18.* ***Kaluta*** *a-40.* ***G. Kane*** *a-10r, 18r; c-40, 44.* ***Kubert*** *a-10r, 21, 26.* ***Layton*** *a-21.* ***S. Mayer*** *c-29, 37, 41, 43, 47; a-28, 29, 37, 41, 43, 47, 58, 65, 68.* ***Moldoff*** *c-64p.* ***Morrow*** *a-40; c-40.* ***W. Mortimer*** *a-39p.* ***Newton*** *a-5, 51.* ***Perez*** *a-24, 50p; c-18, 21, 23.* ***Rogers*** *a-14, 51p.* ***Simonson*** *a-11r.* ***Spiegle*** *a-52.* ***Starlin*** *a-51.* ***Staton*** *a-5, 21.* ***Tuska*** *a-24.* ***Wolverton*** *a-60.* ***Wood*** *a-60, 63; c-60, 63.* ***Wrightson*** *a-60. New art in #14, 18, 24.*						
BEST OF DENNIS THE MENACE, THE						
Hallden/Fawcett Publications: Summer, 1959 - No. 5, Spring, 1961 (100 pgs.)						
1-All reprints; Wiseman-a	7	14	21	44	72	100
2-5: 2-Christmas-c	4	8	12	28	44	60
BEST OF DONALD DUCK, THE						
Gold Key: Nov, 1965 (12¢, 36 pgs.)(Lists 2nd printing in indicia)						
1-Reprints Four Color #223 by Barks	7	14	21	46	86	125
BEST OF DONALD DUCK & UNCLE SCROOGE, THE						
Gold Key: Nov, 1964 - No. 2, Sept, 1967 (25¢ Giants)						
1(30022-411)('64)-Reprints 4-Color #189 & 408 by Carl Barks; cover of F.C. #189 redrawn by Barks	8	16	24	54	102	150
2(30022-709)('67)-Reprints 4-Color #256 & "Seven Cities of Cibola" & U.S. #8 by Barks	7	14	21	44	82	120
BEST OF HORROR AND SCIENCE FICTION COMICS						
Bruce Webster: 1987 ($2.00)						
1-Wolverton, Frazetta, Powell, Ditko-r	1	3	4	6	8	10
BEST OF JOSIE AND THE PUSSYCATS						
Archie Comics: 2001 ($10.95, TPB)						
1-Reprints 1st app. and noteworthy stories						12.00
BEST OF MARMADUKE, THE						
Charlton Comics: 1960						
1-Brad Anderson's strip reprints	3	6	9	19	30	40
BEST OF MS. TREE, THE						
Pyramid Comics: 1987 - No. 4, 1988 ($2.00, B&W, limited series)						
1-4						3.00
BEST OF THE BRAVE AND THE BOLD, THE (See Super DC Giant)						

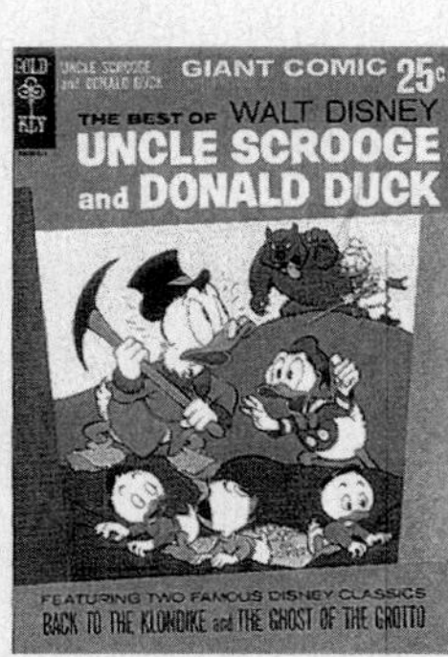

Best of Uncle Scrooge & Donald Duck nn © DIS

Betty and Me #37 © ACP

Betty and Veronica V3 #1 © ACP

	GD 2.0	VG 4.0	FN 6.0	VF 8.0	VF/NM 9.0	NM- 9.2

DC Comics: Oct, 1988 - No. 6, Jan, 1989 ($2.50, limited series)

1-6: Neal Adams-r, Kubert-r & Heath-r in all 4.00

BEST OF THE SPIRIT, THE
DC Comics: 2005 ($14.99, TPB)

nn-Reprints 1st app. and noteworthy stories; intro by Neil Gaiman; Eisner bio. 15.00

BEST OF THE WEST (See A-1 Comics)
Magazine Enterprises: 1951 - No. 12, April-June, 1954

1(A-1 42)-Ghost Rider, Durango Kid, Straight Arrow, Bobby Benson begin
41 82 123 256 428 600
2(A-1 46) 22 44 66 128 209 290
3(A-1 52), 4(A-1 59), 5(A-1 66) 18 36 54 105 165 225
6(A-1 70), 7(A-1 76), 8(A-1 81), 9(A-1 85), 10(A-1 87), 11(A-1 97),
12(A-1 103) 15 30 45 84 127 170

NOTE: *Bolle a-9. Borth a-12. Guardineer a-5, 12. Powell a-1, 12.*

BEST OF UNCLE SCROOGE & DONALD DUCK, THE
Gold Key: Nov, 1966 (25¢)

1(30030-611)-Reprints part 4-Color #159 & 456 & Uncle Scrooge #6,7 by Carl Barks
7 14 21 44 82 120

BEST OF WALT DISNEY COMICS, THE
Western Publishing Co.: 1974 ($1.50, 52 pgs.) (Walt Disney)
(8-1/2x11" cardboard covers; 32,000 printed of each)

96170-Reprints 1st two stories less 1 pg. each from 4-Color #62
6 12 18 37 66 95
96171-Reprints Mickey Mouse and the Bat Bandit of Inferno Gulch from 1934
(strips) by Gottfredson 6 12 18 37 66 95
96172-r/Uncle Scrooge #386 & two other stories 6 12 18 37 66 95
96173-Reprints "Ghost of the Grotto" (from 4-Color #159) & "Christmas on
Bear Mountain" (from 4-Color #178) 6 12 18 37 66 95

BEST ROMANCE
Standard Comics (Visual Editions): No. 5, Feb-Mar, 1952 - No. 7, Aug, 1952

5-Toth-a; photo-c 16 32 48 94 147 200
6,7-Photo-c 11 22 33 62 86 110

BEST SELLER COMICS (See Tailspin Tommy)

BEST WESTERN (Formerly Terry Toons? or Miss America Magazine
Marvel Comics (IPC): V7#24(#57)?; Western Outlaws & Sheriffs No. 60 on)
No. 58, June, 1949 - No. 59, Aug, 1949

58,59-Black Rider, Kid Colt, Two-Gun Kid app.; both have Syd Shores-c
21 42 63 122 199 275

BETA RAY BILL: GODHUNTER
Marvel Comics: Aug, 2009 - No. 3, Oct, 2009 ($3.99, limited series)

1-3-Kano-a; Thor and Galactus app.; reprints form Thor #337-339. 2,3-Silver Surfer app. 4.00

BETRAYAL OF THE PLANET OF THE APES (Set 20 years before the first movie)
BOOM! Studios: Nov, 2011 - No. 4, Feb, 2012 ($3.99, limited series)

1-4-Dr. Zaius app.; Bechko-s/Hardman-a. 1-Three covers. 2-Two covers 4.00

BETTIE PAGE COMICS
Dark Horse Comics: Mar, 1996 ($3.95)

1-Dave Stevens-c; Blevins & Heath-a; Jaime Hernandez pin-up
2 4 6 11 16 20

BETTIE PAGE COMICS: QUEEN OF THE NILE
Dark Horse Comics: Dec, 1999 - No. 3, Apr, 2000 ($2.95, limited series)

1-3-Silke-s/a; Stevens-c 2 4 6 8 10 12

BETTIE PAGE COMICS: SPICY ADVENTURE
Dark Horse Comics: Jan, 1997 ($2.95, one-shot, mature)

nn-Silke-c/s/a 2 4 6 8 10 12

BETTY (See Pep Comics #22 for 1st app.)
Archie Comics: Sept, 1992 - No. 195, Jan, 2012 ($1.25-$2.99)

1 6.00
2-18,20-24: 20-1st Super Sleuther-s 4.00
19-Love Showdown part 2 5.00
25-Pin-up page of Betty as Marilyn Monroe, Madonna, Lady Di 5.00
26-50 3.00
51-195: 57- "A Storm Over Uniforms" x-over part 5,6. 186-Begin $2.99-c 3.00

BETTY AND HER STEADY (Going Steady with Betty No. 1)
Avon Periodicals: No. 2, Mar-Apr, 1950

2 13 26 39 72 101 130

BETTY AND ME
Archie Publications: Aug, 1965 - No. 200, Aug, 1992

1 11 22 33 73 157 240
2,3: 3-Origin Superteen 6 12 18 38 69 100
4-8: Superteen in new costume #4-7; dons new helmet in #5,
ends #8. 5 10 15 31 53 75
9,10: Girl from R.I.V.E.R.D.A.L.E. 9-UFO-s 4 8 12 27 44 60
11-15,17-20(4/69) 3 6 9 21 33 45
16-Classic cover; w/risqué cover dialogue 7 14 21 46 86 125
21,24-35: 33-Paper doll page 3 6 9 16 23 30
22-Archies Band-s 3 6 9 16 24 32
23-I Dream of Jeannie parody 3 6 9 19 30 40
36(8/71),37,41-55 (52 pgs.): 42-Betty as vamp-s 3 6 9 16 23 30
38-Sabrina app. 4 8 12 23 37 50
39-Josie and Sabrina cover cameos 3 6 9 19 30 40
40-Archie & Betty share a cabin 3 6 9 17 26 35
56(4/71)-80(12/76): 79 Betty Cooper mysteries thru #86. 79-81-Drago the Vampire-s
2 4 6 9 13 16
81-99: 83-Harem-c. 84-Jekyll & Hyde-c/s 2 4 6 8 10 12
100(3/79) 2 4 6 9 12 15
101,118: 101-Elvis mentioned. 118-Tarzan mentioned 1 2 3 5 7 9
102-117,119-130(9/82): 103,104-Space-s. 124-DeCarlo-c begins 7.00
131-138,140,142-147,149-154,156-158: 135,136-Jason Blossom app. 136-Cheryl Blossom
cameo. 137-Space-s. 138-Tarzan parody 5.00
139,141,148: 139-Katy Keene collecting-s; Archie in drag-s. 141-Tarzan parody-s.
148-Cyndi Lauper parody-s 6.00
155,159,160(8/87): 155-Archie in drag-s. 159-Superhero gag-c. 160-Wheel of Fortune parody
6.00
161-169,171-199 4.00
170,200: 170-New Archie Superhero-s 6.00

BETTY AND VERONICA (Also see Archie's Girls...)
Archie Enterprises: June, 1987 - No. 278, Dec, 2015 (75¢-$3.99)

1 2 3 4 6 8 10
2-10 6.00
11-30 4.00
31-81 3.00
82-Love Showdown part 3 5.00
83-271: 242-Begin $2.50-c. 247-Begin $2.99-c. 264-271-Two covers 3.00
267-Mermaid variant-c by Fiona Staples 10.00
272-274,276-278-($3.99): 272-274,276,277-Two covers. 278-Last issue; 6 covers 4.00
275-($4.99) Five covers by Adam Hughes, Ramona Fradon & others 5.00
... Free Comic Book Day Edition #1 (6/05) Katy Keene-c/app.; Cheryl Blossom app. 3.00

BETTY AND VERONICA (Volume 3)
Archie Comic Publications: Sept, 2016 - Present ($3.99)

1,2-Adam Hughes-s/a; multiple covers on each; back-up classic pin-ups 4.00

BETTY & VERONICA ANNUAL DIGEST (...Digest Magazine #1-4, 44 on; ...Comics Digest
Mag. #5-43)(Continues as Betty & Veronica Friends Double Digest #209-on)
Archie Publications: Nov, 1980 - No. 208, Nov, 2010 ($1.00/-$2.69, digest size)

1 3 6 9 15 22 28
2-10: 2(11/81-Katy Keene story), 3(8/82) 2 4 6 9 13 16
11-30 1 3 4 6 8 10
31-50 1 2 3 4 5 7
51-70 4.00
71-191: 110-Begin $2.19-c. 135-Begin $2.39-c. 165-Begin $2.49. 185-Includes reprint of
Archie's Girls B&V #1 (1950) and new story where 1950 & 2008 B&V meet 3.00
192-208: 192-Begin $2.69-c 3.00

BETTY & VERONICA ANNUAL DIGEST MAGAZINE
Archie Comics: Sept, 1989 - No. 16, Aug, 1997 ($1.50/$1.75/$1.79, 128 pgs.)

1 1 2 3 5 7 9
2-10: 9-Neon ink logo 5.00
11-16: 16-Begin $1.79-c 3.00

BETTY & VERONICA CHRISTMAS SPECTACULAR (See Archie Giant Series Magazine #159, 168, 180, 191, 204, 217, 229, 241, 453, 465, 477, 489, 501, 513, 525, 536, 547, 558, 568, 580, 593, 606, 618)

BETTY & VERONICA DOUBLE DIGEST MAGAZINE
Archie Enterprises: 1987 - Present ($2.25-$6.99, digest size, 256 pgs.)(...Digest #12 on)

1 2 4 6 8 10 12
2-10 1 2 3 4 5 7
11-25: 5,17-Xmas-c. 16-Capt. Hero story 5.00
26-50 4.00
51-150: 87-Begin $3.19-c. 95-Begin $3.29-c. 114-Begin $3.59-c. 142-Begin $3.69-c 4.00
151-211,213-222: 151-(7/07)-Realistic style Betty & Veronica debuts (thru #154). 160-Cheryl

Beverly Hillbillies #7 © Filmway

Beware the Creeper #1 © DC

The Beyond #7 © ACE

GD VG FN VF VF/NM NM-
2.0 4.0 6.0 8.0 9.0 9.2

GD VG FN VF VF/NM NM-
2.0 4.0 6.0 8.0 9.0 9.2

Blossom spotlight. 170-173-Realistic style 4.00
212,223,237,240-($5.99) Titled Betty & Veronica Double Double Digest (320 pages) 6.00
224-($5.99) Titled Betty & Veronica Comics Annual (192 pgs.) 6.00
225,228,238,242,247,250-($6.99) Titled Betty & Veronica Jumbo Comics Digest (320 pgs.) 7.00
226,227,229-232,234-236,239,241,243,245,246,249,251-($4.99) Titled Betty & Veronica Comics Digest or Comics Double Digest 5.00
244,248-($5.99) 244-Titled Betty & Veronica Summer Annual. 248-Holiday Annual 6.00
Betty & Veronica: in Bad Boy Trouble Vol.1 TPB (2007, $7.49) r/new style from #151-154 8.00

BETTY & VERONICA FRIENDS DOUBLE DIGEST (Continues from B&V Digest Mag. #208)
Archie Publications: No. 209, Jan, 2011 - Present ($3.99-$6.99, digest size)

209-236,238: 209-Cheryl Blossom app. 4.00
237,246-Titled Betty & Veronica Friends Double Double Digest ($5.99, 320 pages) 6.00
239-($4.99) Double Digest 5.00
240,245,250,252-($6.99) Titled Betty & Veronica Friends Jumbo Comics Digest (320 pgs.) 7.00
241-244,248-($4.99) Titled Betty & Veronica Friends Comics Digest. 244-Pussycats app. 5.00
247,249,251,253-($5.99) 247-Easter Annual. 251-Halloween Annual 6.00

BETTY & VERONICA SPECTACULAR (See Archie Giant Series Mag. #11, 16, 21, 26, 32, 138, 145, 153, 162, 173, 184, 197, 201, 210, 214, 221, 226, 234, 238, 246, 250, 458, 462, 470, 482, 486, 494, 498, 506, 510, 518, 522, 526, 530, 537, 552, 559, 563, 569, 575, 582, 588, 600, 608, 613, 620, 623, and Betty & Veronica)

BETTY AND VERONICA SPECTACULAR
Archie Comics: Oct, 1992 - No. 90, Sept, 2009 ($1.25/$1.50/$1.75/$1.99/$2.19/$2.25/$2.50)

1-Dan DeCarlo-c/a 5.00
2-90: 48-Cheryl Blossom leaves Riverdale. 64-Cheryl Blossom returns 3.00

BETTY & VERONICA SPRING SPECTACULAR (See Archie Giant Series Magazine #569, 582, 595)

BETTY & VERONICA SUMMER FUN (See Archie Giant Series Mag. #8, 13, 18, 23, 28, 34, 140, 147, 155, 164, 175, 187, 199, 212, 224, 236, 248, 460, 484, 496, 508, 520, 529, 539, 550, 561, 572, 585, 598, 611, 621)
Archie Comics: 1994 - Present ($2.00/$2.25/$2.29)

1-($2.00, 52 pgs. plus poster) 4.00
2-6: 5-($2.25-c). 6-($2.29-c) 3.00
Vol. 1 (2003, $10.95) reprints stories from Archie Giant Series editions 12.00

BETTY BOOP (Volume 1)
Dynamite Entertainment: 2016 - No. 4, 2017 ($3.99)

1-4-Langridge-s/Lagacé-a; Koko app.; multiple covers on each 4.00

BETTY BOOP'S BIG BREAK
First Publishing: 1990 ($5.95, 52 pgs.)

nn-By Joshua Quagmire; 60th anniversary ish. 6.00

BETTY PAGE 3-D COMICS
The 3-D Zone: 1991 ($3.95, "7-1/2x10-1/4," 28 pgs., no glasses)

1-Photo inside covers; back-c nudity 2 4 6 8 11 14

BETTY'S DIARY (See Archie Giant Series Magazine No. 555)
Archie Enterprises: April, 1986 - No. 40, Apr, 1991 (#1:65¢; 75¢/95¢)

1 1 2 3 4 5 7
2-10 4.00
11-40 3.00

BETTY'S DIGEST
Archie Enterprises: Nov, 1996 - No. 2 ($1.75/$1.79)

1,2 3.00

BEVERLY HILLBILLIES (TV)
Dell Publishing Co.: 4-6/63 - No. 18, 8/67; No. 19, 10/69; No. 20, 10/70; No. 21, Oct, 1971

1-Photo-c 12 24 36 83 182 280
2-Photo-c 8 16 24 51 96 140
3-9: All have photo covers 6 12 18 40 73 105
10: No photo cover 5 10 15 30 50 70
11-21: All have photo covers. 18-Last 12¢ issue. 19-21-Reprint #1-3 (covers and insides) 5 10 15 33 57 80

NOTE: *#1-9, 11-21 are photo covers.*

BEWARE (Formerly Fantastic; Chilling Tales No. 13 on)
Youthful Magazines: No. 10, June, 1952 - No. 12, Oct, 1952

10-E.A. Poe's Pit & the Pendulum adaptation by Wildey; Harrison/Bache-a; atom bomb and shrunken head-c 68 136 204 435 743 1050
11-Harrison-a; Ambrose Bierce adapt. 47 94 141 296 498 700
12-Used in **SOTI**, pg. 388; Harrison-a 47 94 141 296 498 700

BEWARE
Trojan Magazines/Merit Publ. No. ?: No. 13, 1/53 - No. 16, 7/53; No. 5, 9/53 - No. 15, 5/55

13(#1)-Harrison-a 68 136 204 435 743 1050
14(#2, 3/53)-Krenkel/Harrison-c; dismemberment, severed head panels 47 94 141 296 498 700
15,16(#3, 5/53; #4, 7/53)-Harrison-a 42 84 126 265 445 625
5,9,12,13(1/55) 41 82 123 256 428 600
6-Ill. in **SOTI**- "Children are first shocked and then desensitized by all this brutality." Corpse on cover swipe/V.O.H. #26; girl on cover swipe/Advs. Into Darkness #10 81 162 243 518 884 1250
7,8-Check-a 42 84 126 265 445 675
10-Frazetta/Check-c; Disbrow, Check-a 161 322 483 1030 1765 2500
11-Disbrow-a; heart torn out, blood drainage 47 94 141 296 498 700
14,15: 14-Myron Fass-c. 15-Harrison-a 39 78 117 240 395 550

NOTE: ***Fass** a-5, 6, 8; c-6, 11, 14. **Forte** a-8. **Hollingsworth** a-15(#3), 16(#4), 9; c-16(#4), 8, 9. **Kiefer** a-16(#4), 5, 6, 10.*

BEWARE (Becomes Tomb of Darkness No. 9 on)
Marvel Comics Group: Mar, 1973 - No. 8, May, 1974 (All reprints)

1-Everett-c; Kirby & Sinnott-r ('54) 4 8 12 25 40 55
2-8: 2-Forte, Colan-r. 6-Tuska-a. 7-Torres-r/Mystical Tales #7 3 6 9 16 24 32

NOTE: ***Infantino** a-4r. **Gil Kane** c-4. **Wildey** a-7r.*

BEWARE TERROR TALES
Fawcett Publications: May, 1952 - No. 8, July, 1953

1-E.C. art swipe/Haunt of Fear #5 & Vault of Horror #26 55 110 165 352 601 850
2 39 78 117 231 378 525
3-5,7 34 68 102 199 325 450
6-Classic skeleton-c 40 80 120 246 411 575
8-Tothish-a; people being cooked-c 43 86 129 271 461 650

NOTE: ***Andru** a-2. **Bernard Bailey** a-1; c-1-5. **Powell** a-1, 2, 8. **Sekowsky** a-2.*

BEWARE THE BATMAN (Based on the Cartoon Network series)
DC Comics: Dec, 2013 - No. 6, May, 2014 ($2.99)

1-6: 1-Anarky app. 4-Man-Bat app. 6-Killer Croc app. 3.00

BEWARE THE CREEPER (See Adventure, Best of the Brave & the Bold, Brave & the Bold, 1st Issue Special, Flash #318-323, Showcase #73, World's Finest Comics #249)
National Periodical Publications: May-June, 1968 - No. 6, Mar-Apr, 1969 (All 12¢ issues)

1-(5-6/68)-Classic Ditko-c; Ditko-a in all 8 16 24 54 102 150
2-6: 2-5-Ditko-c. 2-Intro. Proteus. 6-Gil Kane-c 5 10 15 31 53 75

BEWARE THE CREEPER
DC Comics (Vertigo): June, 2003 - No. 5, Oct, 2003 ($2.95, limited series)

1-5-Female vigilante in 1920s Paris; Jason Hall-s/Cliff Chiang-a 3.00

BEWITCHED (TV)
Dell Publishing Co.: 4-6/65 - No. 11, 10/67; No. 12, 10/68 - No. 13, 1/69; No. 14, 10/69

1-Photo-c 12 24 36 84 185 285
2-No photo-c 7 14 21 46 86 125
3-13-All have photo-c. 12-Rep. #1. 13-Last 12¢-c 6 12 18 40 73 105
14-No photo-c; reprints #2 5 10 15 31 53 75

BEYOND!
Marvel Comics: Sept, 2006 - No. 6, Feb, 2007 ($2.99, limited series)

1-6-McDuffie-s/Kolins-a; Spider-Man, Venom, Gravity, Wasp app. 6-Gravity dies 3.00

BEYOND, THE
Ace Magazines: Nov, 1950 - No. 30, Jan, 1955

1-Bakerish-a(p) 54 108 162 343 574 825
2-Bakerish-a(p) 37 74 111 222 361 500
3-10: 10-Woodish-a by Cameron 30 60 90 177 289 400
11-20: 18-Used in **POP**, pgs. 81,82 24 48 72 142 234 325
21-26,28-30 22 44 66 132 216 300
27-Used in **SOTI**, pg. 111 24 48 72 142 234 325

NOTE: ***Cameron** a-10, 11p, 12p, 15, 16, 21-27, 30; c-20. **Colan** a-6, 13, 17. **Sekowsky** a-2, 3, 5, 7, 11, 14, 27r. No. 1 was to appear as Challenge of the Unknown No. 7.*

BEYOND THE FRINGE (Based on the TV series Fringe)
DC Comics: May, 2012 ($3.99, one-shot)

1-Joshua Jackson-s/Jorge Jimenez-a/Drew Johnson-c 4.00

BEYOND THE GRAVE
Charlton Comics: July, 1975 - No. 6, June, 1976; No. 7, Jan, 1983 - No. 17, Oct, 1984

1-Ditko-a (6 pgs.); Sutton painted-c 4 8 12 25 40 55
2-6: 2-5-Ditko-a; Ditko c-2,3,6 3 6 9 16 23 30
7-17: ('83-'84) Reprints. 8,11,16-Ditko-a. 11-Staton-a. 13-Aparo-c(r). 15-Sutton-c (low print run). 16-Palais-a 1 2 3 5 6 8
Modern Comics Reprint 2('78) 6.00

NOTE: ***Howard** a-4. **Kim** a-1. **Larson** a-4, 6.*

BIBLE, THE: EDEN
IDW Publishing: 2003 ($21.99, hardcover graphic novel)

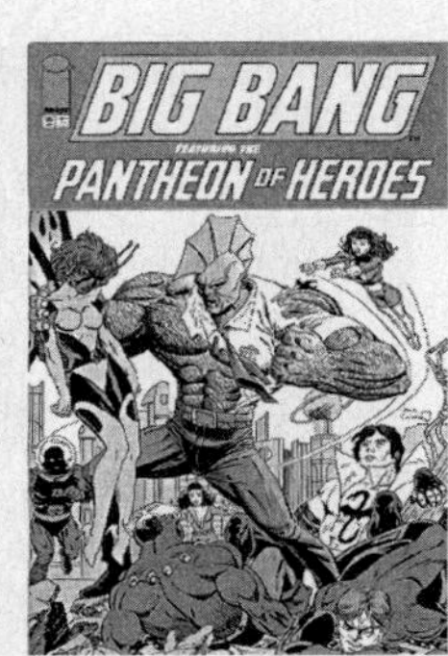

Big Bang Comics V2 #18 © Carlson

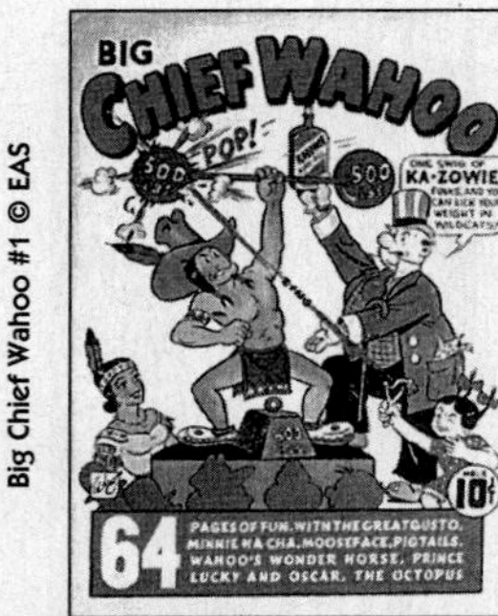

Big Chief Wahoo #1 © EAS

Big Hero 6 #2 © MAR

	GD 2.0	VG 4.0	FN 6.0	VF 8.0	VF/NM 9.0	NM- 9.2

HC-Scott Hampton painted-a; adaptation of Genesis by Dave Elliot and Keith Giffen 22.00

BIBLE TALES FOR YOUNG FOLK (...Young People No. 3-5)
Atlas Comics (OMC): Aug, 1953 - No. 5, Mar, 1954

	GD	VG	FN	VF	VF/NM	NM-
1	29	58	87	170	278	385
2-Everett, Krigstein-a; Robinson-c	18	36	54	105	165	225
3-5: 4,5-Robinson-c	15	30	45	88	137	185

BIG (Movie)
Hit Comics (Dark Horse Comics): Mar, 1989 ($2.00)

1-Adaptation of film; Paul Chadwick-c 3.00

BIG ALL-AMERICAN COMIC BOOK, THE (See All-American Comics)
All-American/National Per. Publ.: 1944 (132 pgs., one-shot) (Early DC Annual)

	GD	VG	FN	VF	VF/NM	NM-
1-Wonder Woman, Green Lantern, Flash, The Atom, Wildcat, Scribbly, The Whip, Ghost Patrol, Hawkman by Kubert (1st on Hawkman), Hop Harrigan, Johnny Thunder, Little Boy Blue, Mr. Terrific, Mutt & Jeff app.; Sargon on cover only; cover by Kubert/Hibbard/Mayer and others	650	1300	1950	4750	8625	12,500

BIG BABY HUEY (See Baby Huey)

BIG BANG COMICS (Becomes Big Bang #4)
Caliber Press: Spring, 1994 - No. 4, Feb, 1995; No. 0, May, 1995 ($1.95, lim. series)

1-4-($1.95-c) 3.00
0-(5/95, $2.95) Alex Ross-c; color and B&W pages 3.00
Your Big Book of Big Bang Comics TPB ('98, $11.00) r/#0-2 11.00

BIG BANG COMICS (Volume 2)
Image Comics (Highbrow Ent.): V2#1, May, 1996 - No. 35, Jan, 2001 ($1.95-$3.95)

1-23,26: 1-Mighty Man app. 2-4-S.A. Shadowhawk app. 5-Begin $2.95-c. 6-Curt Swan/Murphy Anderson-c. 7-Begin B&W. 12-Savage Dragon-c/app. 16,17,21-Shadow Lady 3.00
24,25,27-35-($3.95): 35-Big Bang vs. Alan Moore's "1963" characters 4.00
...Presents the Ultiman Family (2/05, $3.50) 3.50
...Round Table of America (2/04, $3.95) Don Thomas-a 4.00
...Summer Special (8/03, $4.95) World's Nastiest Nazis app. 5.00

BIG BANG PRESENTS (Volume 3)
Big Bang Comics: July, 2006 - No. 5 ($2.95/$3.95, B&W)

1,2: 1-Protoplasman (Plastic Man homage) 3.00
3-5-($3.95) 3-Origin of Protoplasman. 4-Flip book 4.00

BIG BANG UNIVERSE
AC Comics: 2015 ($9.95, B&W)

1-Four new stories; Ultiman, Knight Watchman, Galahad & Whiz Kids app. 10.00

BIG BLACK KISS
Vortex Comics: Sep, 1989 - No, 3, Nov, 1989 ($3.75, B&W, lim. series, mature)

1-3-Chaykin-s/a 4.00

BIG BLOWN BABY (Also see Dark Horse Presents)
Dark Horse Comics: Aug, 1996 - No. 4, Nov, 1996 ($2.95, lim. series, mature)

1-4: Bill Wray-c/a/scripts 3.00

BIG BOOK OF ..., THE
DC Comics (Paradox Press): 1994 - 1999 (B&W)($12.95 - $14.95)

nn-...**BAD**,1998 ($14.95),...**CONSPIRACIES**, 1995 ($12.95), ...**DEATH**,1994 ($12.95), ...**FREAKS**, 1996 ($14.95), ...**GRIMM**, 1999 ($14.95), ...**HOAXES**, 1996 ($14.95), ...**LITTLE CRIMINALS**, 1996 ($14.95), ...**LOSERS**,1997 ($14.95), **MARTYRS**, 1997 ($14.95), ...**SCANDAL**,1997 ($14.95), ...**THE WEIRD WILD WEST**,1998 ($14.95), ...**THUGS**, 1997 ($14.95), ...**UNEXPLAINED**, 1997 ($14.95), ...**URBAN LEGENDS**, 1994 ($12.95), ...**VICE**, 1999 ($14.95), ...**WEIRDOS**, 1995 ($12.95) cover price

BIG BOOK OF FUN COMICS (See New Book of Comics)
National Periodical Publications: Spring, 1936 (Large size, 52 pgs.)
(1st comic book annual & DC annual)

	GD	VG	FN	VF	VF/NM	NM-
1 (Very rare)-r/New Fun #1-5	2300	4600	6900	15,000	-	-

BIG BOOK ROMANCES
Fawcett Publications: Feb, 1950 (no date given) (148 pgs.)

	GD	VG	FN	VF	VF/NM	NM-
1-Contains remaindered Fawcett romance comics - several combinations possible	77	154	231	493	847	1200

BIG CHIEF WAHOO
Eastern Color Printing/George Dougherty (distr. by Fawcett): July, 1942 - No. 7, Wint., 1943/44?(no year given)(Quarterly)

	GD	VG	FN	VF	VF/NM	NM-
1-Newspaper-r (on sale 6/15/42)	42	84	126	265	445	625
2-Steve Roper app.	23	46	69	136	223	310
3-5: 4-Chief is holding a Katy Keene comic in one panel	18	36	54	105	165	225
6-7	14	28	42	82	121	160

NOTE: *Kerry Drake in some issues.*

BIG CIRCUS, THE (Movie)
Dell Publishing Co.: No. 1036, Sept-Nov, 1959

	GD	VG	FN	VF	VF/NM	NM-
Four Color 1036-Photo-c	6	12	18	40	73	105

BIG CON JOB, THE (PALMIOTTI & BRADY'S...)
BOOM! Studios: Mar, 2015 - No. 4, Jun, 2015 ($3.99, limited series)

1-4-Palmiotti & Brady-s/Stanton-a/Conner-c 4.00

BIG COUNTRY, THE (Movie)
Dell Publishing Co.: No. 946, Oct, 1958

	GD	VG	FN	VF	VF/NM	NM-
Four Color 946-Photo-c	6	12	18	42	79	115

BIG DADDY DANGER
DC Comics: Oct, 2002 - No. 9, June, 2003 ($2.95, limited series)

1-9-Adam Pollina-s/a/c 3.00

BIG DADDY ROTH (Magazine)
Millar Publications: Oct-Nov, 1964 - No. 4, Apr-May, 1965 (35¢)

	GD	VG	FN	VF	VF/NM	NM-
1-Toth-a; Batman & Robin parody	17	34	51	117	259	400
2-4-Toth-a	11	22	33	76	163	250

BIGFOOT
IDW Publishing: Feb, 2005 - No. 4, May, 2005 ($3.99, limited series)

1-4-Steve Niles & Rob Zombie-s/Richard Corben-a/c 4.00

BIGG TIME
DC Comics (Vertigo): 2002 ($14.95, B&W, graphic novel)

nn-Ty Templeton-s/c/a 15.00

BIG GUY AND RUSTY THE BOY ROBOT, THE (Also See Madman Comics #6,7 & Martha Washington Stranded In Space)
Dark Horse (Legend): July, 1995 - No. 2, Aug, 1995 ($4.95, oversize, limited series)

	GD	VG	FN	VF	VF/NM	NM-
1,2-Frank Miller scripts & Geoff Darrow-c/a	1	2	3	4	5	7

BIG HAIR PRODUCTIONS
Image Comics: Feb, 2000 - No. 2, Mar, 2000 ($3.50, B&W)

1,2 3.50

BIG HERO ADVENTURES (See Jigsaw)

BIG HERO 6 (Also see Sunfire & Big Hero Six)
Marvel Comics: Nov, 2008 - No. 5, Mar, 2009 ($3.99, limited series)

	GD	VG	FN	VF	VF/NM	NM-
1-Claremont-s/Nakayama-a; 1-Character design pages & Handbook entries	3	6	9	15	22	28
2-5	1	2	3	5	6	8

...: Brave New Heroes 1 (11/12, $8.99) r/#1-5 9.00

BIG JON & SPARKIE (Radio)(Formerly Sparkie, Radio Pixie)
Ziff-Davis Publ. Co.: No. 4, Sept-Oct, 1952 (Painted-c)

	GD	VG	FN	VF	VF/NM	NM-
4-Based on children's radio program	19	38	57	111	176	240

BIG LAND, THE (Movie)
Dell Publishing Co.: No. 812, July, 1957

	GD	VG	FN	VF	VF/NM	NM-
Four Color 812-Alan Ladd photo-c	8	16	24	52	99	145

BIG LIE, THE
Image Comics: Sept, 2011 ($3.99, one-shot)

1-Revisits the 9-11 attacks; Rick Veitch-s/a(p); Thomas Yeates-c 4.00

BIG MAN PLANS
Image Comics: Mar, 2015 - No. 4 ($3.50, limited series)

1-4-Eric Powell & Tim Wiesch-s/Powell-a/c 3.50

BIG RED (See Movie Comics)

BIG SHOT COMICS
Columbia Comics Group: May, 1940 - No. 104, Aug, 1949

	GD	VG	FN	VF	VF/NM	NM-
1-Intro. Skyman; The Face (1st app.; Tony Trent), The Cloak (Spy Master), Marvelo, Monarch of Magicians, Joe Palooka, Charlie Chan, Tom Kerry, Dixie Dugan, Rocky Ryan begin; Charlie Chan moves over from Feature Comics #31 (4/40)	297	594	891	1901	3251	4600
2	100	200	300	635	1093	1550
3-The Cloak called Spy Chief; Skyman-c	90	180	270	576	988	1400
4,5	61	122	183	390	670	950
6-10: 8-Christmas-c	50	100	150	315	533	750
11-13	47	94	141	296	498	700
14-Origin & 1st app. Sparky Watts (6/41)	50	100	150	315	533	750
15-Origin The Cloak	55	110	165	352	601	850
16-20	39	78	117	240	395	550

Big Thunder Mountain Railroad #4 © DIS

Big Trouble in Little China #1 © 20th Century Fox

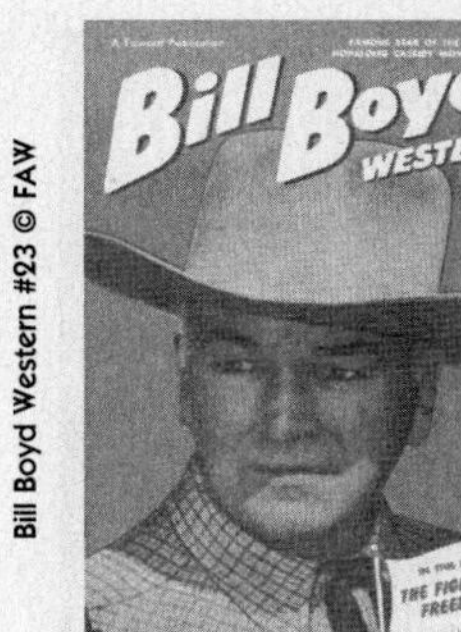
Bill Boyd Western #23 © FAW

	GD 2.0	VG 4.0	FN 6.0	VF 8.0	VF/NM 9.0	NM- 9.2
21-23,27,30: 30-X-Mas-c, WWII-c	34	68	102	204	332	460
24-Classic Tojo-c.	119	238	357	762	1306	1850
25-Hitler-c	81	162	243	518	884	1250
26,29-Japanese WWII-c. 29-Intro. Capt. Yank; Bo (a dog) newspaper strip-r by Frank Beck begin, ends #104.	41	82	123	250	418	585
28-Hitler, Tojo & Mussolini-c	123	246	369	787	1344	1900
31,33-40	24	48	72	142	234	325
32-Vic Jordan newspaper strip reprints begin, ends #52; Hitler, Tojo & Mussolini-c	110	220	330	704	1202	1700
41,42,44,45,47-50: 42-No Skyman. 50-Origin The Face retold	21	42	63	122	199	275
43-Hitler-c	97	194	291	621	1061	1500
46-Hitler, Tojo-c (6/44)	95	190	285	603	1039	1475
51-Tojo Japanese war-c	39	78	117	231	378	525
52-56,58-60:	18	36	54	105	165	225
57-Hitler, Tojo Halloween mask-c	41	82	123	256	428	600
61-70: 63 on-Tony Trent, the Face	14	28	42	82	121	160
71-80: 73-The Face cameo. 74-(2/47)-Mickey Finn begins. 74,80-The Face app. in Tony Trent. 78-Last Charlie Chan strip-r	14	28	42	76	108	140
81-90: 85-Tony Trent marries Babs Walsh. 86-Valentines-c	11	22	33	62	86	110
91-99,101-104: 69-94-Skyman in Outer Space. 96-Xmas-c	10	20	30	56	76	95
100	11	22	33	64	90	115

NOTE: ***Mart Bailey*** *art on "The Face" No. 1-104.* ***Guardineer*** *a-5. Sparky Watts by* ***Boody Rogers****-No. 14-42, 77-104, (by others No. 43-76). Others than Tony Trent wear "The Face" mask in No. 46-63, 93. Skyman by* ***Ogden Whitney****-No. 1, 2, 4, 12-37, 49, 70-101. Skyman covers-No. 1, 3, 7-12, 14, 16, 20, 27, 89, 95, 100.*

BIG SMASH BARGAIN COMICS
No publisher listed: Early 1950s (25¢, 160pgs., Canadian reprints)

	GD	VG	FN	VF	VF/NM	NM-
1-4: Contains 4 comics from various companies bundled with new cover (scarce)	41	82	123	256	428	600

BIG TEX
Toby Press: June, 1953

	GD	VG	FN	VF	VF/NM	NM-
1-Contains (3) John Wayne stories-r with name changed to Big Tex	13	26	39	74	105	135

BIG-3
Fox Features Syndicate: Fall, 1940 - No. 7, Jan, 1942

	GD	VG	FN	VF	VF/NM	NM-
1-Blue Beetle, The Flame, & Samson begin	245	490	735	1568	2684	3800
2	97	194	291	621	1061	1500
3-5	71	142	213	454	777	1100
6,7: 6-Last Samson. 7-V-Man app.	55	100	165	352	601	850

BIG THUNDER MOUNTAIN RAILROAD (Disney Kingdoms)
Marvel Comics: May, 2015 - No. 5, Oct, 2015 ($3.99, limited series)

1-5: 1-Dennis Hopeless-s/Tigh Walker-a/Pasqual Ferry-c. 3-Ruiz-a 4.00

BIG TOP COMICS, THE (TV's Great Circus Show)
Toby Press: 1951 - No. 2, 1951 (No month)

	GD	VG	FN	VF	VF/NM	NM-
1	12	24	36	67	94	120
2	9	18	27	50	65	80

BIG TOWN (Radio/TV) (Also see Movie Comics, 1946)
National Periodical Publ: Jan, 1951 - No. 50, Mar-Apr, 1958 (No. 1-9: 52pgs.)

	GD	VG	FN	VF	VF/NM	NM-
1-Dan Barry-a begins	69	138	207	442	759	1075
2	37	74	111	222	361	500
3-10	22	44	66	132	216	300
11-20	18	36	54	105	165	225
21-31: Last pre-code (1-2/55)	14	28	42	76	108	140
32-50: 46-Grey tone cover	10	20	30	56	76	95

BIG TROUBLE IN LITTLE CHINA (Based on the 1986 Kurt Russell movie)
BOOM! Studios: Jun, 2014 - No. 25, Jun, 2016 ($3.99)

1-12-Continuing advs. of Jack Burton; John Carpenter & Eric Powell-s; Brian Churilla-a; multiple covers by Powell and others on each 4.00
13-24: 13-16-Van Lente-s/Eisma-a. 17-20-McDaid-a. 21-24-Santos-a 4.00
25-($4.99) Van Lente-s/Santos-a 5.00

BIG TROUBLE IN LITTLE CHINA / ESCAPE FROM NEW YORK (Based on the movies)
BOOM! Studios: Oct, 2016 - No. 6, Mar, 2017 ($3.99)

1-6-Jack Burton meets Snake Plisskin; Greg Pak-s/Daniel Bayliss-a 4.00

BIG VALLEY, THE (TV)
Dell Publishing Co.: June, 1966 - No. 5, Oct, 1967; No. 6, Oct, 1969

	GD	VG	FN	VF	VF/NM	NM-
1: Photo-c #1-5	5	10	15	31	53	75
2-6: 6-Reprints #1	3	6	9	21	33	45

BIKER MICE FROM MARS (TV)
Marvel Comics: Nov, 1993 - No. 3, Jan, 1994 ($1.50, limited series)

1-3: 1-Intro Vinnie, Modo & Throttle. 2-Origin 4.00

BILL & TED GO TO HELL (Movie)
BOOM! Studios: Feb, 2016 - No. 4, May, 2016 ($3.99, limited series)

1-4-Joines-s/Bachan-a 4.00

BILL & TED'S BOGUS JOURNEY
Marvel Comics: Sept, 1991 ($2.95, squarebound, 84 pgs.)

1-Adapts movie sequel 4.00

BILL & TED'S EXCELLENT COMIC BOOK (Movie)
Marvel Comics: Dec, 1991 - No. 12, 1992 ($1.00/$1.25)

1-12: 3-Begin $1.25-c 3.00

BILL & TED'S MOST TRIUMPHANT RETURN (Movie)
BOOM! Studios: Mar, 2015 - No. 6, Aug, 2015 ($3.99, limited series)

1-6: 1-Follows the end of the second movie; Lynch-s/Gaylord-a/Guillory-c 4.00

BILL BARNES COMICS (...America's Air Ace Comics No. 2 on) (Becomes Air Ace V2#1 on; also see Shadow Comics)
Street & Smith Publications: Oct, 1940(No. month given) - No. 12, Oct, 1943

	GD	VG	FN	VF	VF/NM	NM-
1-23 pgs.-comics; Rocket Rooney begins	103	206	309	659	1130	1600
2-Barnes as The Phantom Flyer app.; Tuska-a	53	106	159	334	567	800
3-5	42	84	126	269	452	635
6,8,10,12	39	78	117	233	384	535
7-(1942) Story about dropping atomic bomb on Japan	50	100	150	315	533	750
9-Classic WWII cover	55	110	165	352	601	850
11-Japanese WWII Gremlin cover	40	80	120	244	402	560

BILL BATTLE, THE ONE MAN ARMY (Also see Master Comics No. 133)
Fawcett Publications: Oct, 1952 - No. 4, Apr, 1953 (All photo-c)

	GD	VG	FN	VF	VF/NM	NM-
1	14	28	42	82	121	160
2	9	18	27	47	61	75
3,4	8	16	24	42	54	65

BILL BLACK'S FUN COMICS
Paragon #1-3/Americomics #4: Dec, 1982 - No. 4, Mar, 1983 ($1.75/$2.00, Baxter paper) (1st AC comic)

	GD	VG	FN	VF	VF/NM	NM-
1-(B&W fanzine; 7x8-1/2"; low print) Intro. Capt. Paragon, Phantom Lady & Commando D	2	4	6	13	18	22
2-4: 2,3-(B&W fanzines; 8-1/2x11"). 3-Kirby-c. 4-($2.00, color)-Origin Nightfall (formerly Phantom Lady); Nightveil app.; Kirby-a	1	3	4	6	8	10

BILL BOYD WESTERN (Movie star; see Hopalong Cassidy & Western Hero)
Fawcett Publ: Feb, 1950 - No. 23, June, 1952 (1-3,7,11,14-on: 36 pgs.)

	GD	VG	FN	VF	VF/NM	NM-
1-Bill Boyd & his horse Midnite begin; photo front/back-c	30	60	90	177	289	400
2-Painted-c	16	32	48	94	147	200
3-Photo-c begin, end #23; last photo back-c	14	28	42	80	115	150
4-6(52 pgs.)	12	24	36	69	97	125
7,11(36 pgs.)	10	20	30	56	76	95
8-10,12,13(52 pgs.)	10	20	30	58	79	100
14-22	9	18	27	52	69	85
23-Last issue	10	20	30	56	76	95

BILL BUMLIN (See Treasury of Comics No. 3)

BILL ELLIOTT (See Wild Bill Elliott)

BILLI 99
Dark Horse Comics: Sept, 1991 - No. 4, 1991 ($3.50, B&W, lim. series, 52 pgs.)

1-4: Tim Sale-c/a 4.00

BILL STERN'S SPORTS BOOK
Ziff-Davis Publ. Co.(Approved Comics): Spring-Sum, 1951 - V2#2, Win, 1952

	GD	VG	FN	VF	VF/NM	NM-
V1#10-(1951) Whitney painted-c	21	42	63	122	199	275
2-(Sum/52; reg. size)	16	32	48	94	147	200
V2#2-(1952, 96 pgs.)-Krigstein, Kinstler-a	21	42	63	126	206	285

BILL THE BULL: ONE SHOT, ONE BOURBON, ONE BEER
Boneyard Press: Dec, 1994 ($2.95, B&W, mature)

1 3.00

BILLY AND BUGGY BEAR (See Animal Fun)
I.W. Enterprises/Super: 1958; 1964

I.W. Reprint #1, #7('58)-All Surprise Comics #?(Same issue-r for both)

Billy Batson and the Magic of Shazam! #14 © DC

Billy the Kid and Oscar #1 © FAW

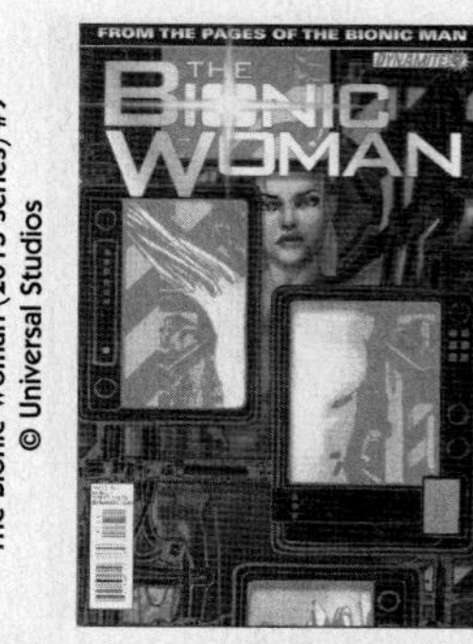

The Bionic Woman (2013 series) #9 © Universal Studios

	GD 2.0	VG 4.0	FN 6.0	VF 8.0	VF/NM 9.0	NM- 9.2
	2	4	6	10	14	18
Super Reprint #10(1964)	2	4	6	8	11	14

BILLY BATSON AND THE MAGIC OF SHAZAM! (Follows Shazam: The Monster Society of Evil mini-series)
DC Comics: Sept, 2008 - No. 21, Dec, 2010 ($2.25/$2.50, all ages title)

	GD	VG	FN	VF	VF/NM	NM-
1-17: 1-4-Mike Kunkel-s/a/c; Theo (Black) Adam app. 5-DeStefano-a. 13-16-Black Adam						4.00
1-Variant B&W sketch cover						4.00
18-21 ($2.99) 21-Justice League cameo						4.00
TPB (2010, $12.99) r/#1-6; cover and haracter sketches						13.00
...: Mr. Mind Over Matter TPB (2011, $12.99) r/#7-12						13.00

BILLY BUCKSKIN WESTERN (2-Gun Western No. 4)
Atlas Comics (IMC No. 1/MgPC No. 2,3): Nov, 1955 - No. 3, Mar, 1956

	GD	VG	FN	VF	VF/NM	NM-
1-Mort Drucker-a; Maneely-c/a	18	36	54	107	169	230
2-Mort Drucker-a	11	22	33	64	90	115
3-Williamson, Drucker-a	14	28	42	76	108	140

BILLY BUNNY (Black Cobra No. 6 on)
Excellent Publications: Feb-Mar, 1954 - No. 5, Oct-Nov, 1954

	GD	VG	FN	VF	VF/NM	NM-
1	10	20	30	56	76	95
2	7	14	21	35	43	50
3-5	6	12	18	28	34	40

BILLY BUNNY'S CHRISTMAS FROLICS
Farrell Publications: 1952 (25¢ Giant, 100 pgs.)

	GD	VG	FN	VF	VF/NM	NM-
1	22	44	66	132	216	300

BILLY MAKE BELIEVE
United Features Syndicate: No. 14, 1939

	GD	VG	FN	VF	VF/NM	NM-
Single Series 14	32	64	96	192	314	435

BILLY NGUYEN, PRIVATE EYE
Caliber Press: V2#1, 1990 ($2.50)

	GD	VG	FN	VF	VF/NM	NM-
V2#1						3.00

BILLY THE KID (Formerly The Masked Raider; also see Doc Savage Comics & Return of the Outlaw)
Charlton Publ. Co.: No. 9, Nov, 1957 - No. 121, Dec, 1976; No. 122, Sept, 1977 - No. 123, Oct, 1977; No. 124, Feb, 1978 - No. 153, Mar, 1983

	GD	VG	FN	VF	VF/NM	NM-
9	10	20	30	58	79	100
10,12,14,17-19: 12-2 pg Check-sty	8	16	24	40	50	60
11-(68 pgs.)-Origin & 1st app. The Ghost Train	9	18	27	50	65	80
13-Williamson/Torres-a	8	16	24	44	57	70
15-Origin; 2 pgs. Williamson-a	8	16	24	44	57	70
16-Williamson-a, 2 pgs.	8	16	24	42	54	65
20-26-Severin-a(3-4 each)	8	16	24	44	57	70
27-30: 30-Masked Rider app.	3	6	9	18	28	38
31-40	3	6	9	15	22	28
41-60	2	4	6	13	18	22
61-65	2	4	6	10	14	18
66-Bounty Hunter series begins.	3	6	9	14	20	25
67-80: Bounty Hunter series; not in #79,82,84-86	2	4	6	10	14	18
81-84,86-90: 87-Last Bounty Hunter. 88-1st app. Mr. Young of the Boothill Gazette	2	4	6	8	10	12
85-Early Kaluta-a (4 pgs.)	2	4	6	9	13	16
91-123: 110-Mr. Young of Boothill app. 111-Origin The Ghost Train. 117-Gunsmith & Co., The Cheyenne Kid app.	1	2	3	5	6	8
124(2/78)-153						6.00
Modern Comics 109 (1977 reprint)						5.00

NOTE: *Boyette a-88-110.* ***Kim*** *a-73.* ***Morsi*** *a-12,14.* ***Sattler*** *a-118-123.* ***Severin*** *a(r)-121-129, 134; c-23, 25.* ***Sutton*** *a-111.*

BILLY THE KID ADVENTURE MAGAZINE
Toby Press: Oct, 1950 - No. 29, 1955

	GD	VG	FN	VF	VF/NM	NM-
1-Williamson/Frazetta-a (2 pgs) r/from John Wayne Adventure Comics #2; photo-c	31	62	93	182	296	410
2-Photo-c	12	24	36	69	97	125
3-Williamson/Frazetta "The Claws of Death", 4 pgs. plus Williamson art	34	68	102	199	325	450
4,5,7,8,10: 4,7-Photo-c	9	18	27	52	69	85
6-Frazetta assist on "Nightmare"; photo-c	15	30	45	83	124	165
9-Kurtzman Pot-Shot Pete; photo-c	11	22	33	64	90	115
11,12,15-20: 11-Photo-c	8	16	24	42	54	65
13-Kurtzman-r/John Wayne #12 (Genius)	9	18	27	47	61	75
14-Williamson/Frazetta; r-of #1 (2 pgs.)	10	20	30	56	76	95
21,23-29	7	14	21	37	46	55
22-Williamson/Frazetta-r(1pg.)/#1; photo-c	8	16	24	42	54	65

BILLY THE KID AND OSCAR (Also see Fawcett's Funny Animals)
Fawcett Publications: Winter, 1945 - No. 3, Fall, 1946 (Funny animal)

	GD	VG	FN	VF	VF/NM	NM-
1	15	30	45	86	133	180
2,3	10	20	30	58	79	100

BILLY THE KID'S OLD TIMEY ODDITIES
Dark Horse Comics: Apr, 2005 - No. 4, July, 2005 ($2.99, limited series)

	GD	VG	FN	VF	VF/NM	NM-
1-4-Eric Powell-s/c; Kyle Hotz-a						4.00
TPB (2005, $13.95) r/series						14.00
... and the Ghostly Fiend of London (9/10 - No. 4, 12/10, $3.99) 1-4-Powell-s/c; Kyle Hotz-a; Goon back-up; Powell-s/a						4.00
... and the Orm of Loch Ness (10/12 - No. 4, 1/13, $3.50) 1-4-Powell-s/Hotz-a/c						4.00

BILLY WEST (Bill West No. 9,10)
Standard Comics (Visual Editions): 1949-No. 9, Feb, 1951; No. 10, Feb, 1952

	GD	VG	FN	VF	VF/NM	NM-
1	17	34	51	98	154	210
2	11	22	33	60	83	105
3-6,9,10	10	20	30	54	72	90
7,8-Schomburg-c	11	22	33	60	83	105

NOTE: ***Celardo*** *a-1-6, 9; c-1-3.* ***Moreira*** *a-3.* ***Roussos*** *a-2.*

BING CROSBY (See Feature Films)

BINGO (...Comics) (H. C. Blackerby)
Howard Publ.: 1945 (Reprints National material)

	GD	VG	FN	VF	VF/NM	NM-
1-L. B. Cole opium-c; blank back-c	39	78	117	231	378	525

BINGO, THE MONKEY DOODLE BOY
St. John Publishing Co.: Aug, 1951; Oct, 1953

	GD	VG	FN	VF	VF/NM	NM-
1(8/51)-By Eric Peters	9	18	27	52	69	85
1(10/53)	7	14	21	37	46	55

BINKY (Formerly Leave It to...)
National Periodical Publ./DC Comics: No. 72, 4-5/70 - No. 81, 10-11/71; No. 82, Summer/77

	GD	VG	FN	VF	VF/NM	NM-
72-76	4	8	12	27	44	60
77-79: (68 pgs.). 77-Bobby Sherman 1pg. story w/photo. 78-1 pg. sty on Barry Williams of Brady Bunch. 79-Osmonds 1pg. story	5	10	15	35	63	90
80,81 (52 pgs.)-Sweat Pain story	5	10	15	31	53	75
82 (1977, one-shot)	4	8	12	27	44	60

BINKY'S BUDDIES
National Periodical Publications: Jan-Feb, 1969 - No. 12, Nov-Dec, 1970

	GD	VG	FN	VF	VF/NM	NM-
1	7	14	21	46	86	125
2-12: 3-Last 12¢ issue	4	8	12	27	44	60

BIONIC MAN (TV)
Dynamite Entertainment: 2011 - No. 26, 2013 ($3.99)

	GD	VG	FN	VF	VF/NM	NM-
1-26: 1-Kevin Smith & Phil Hester-s; Lau-a; multiple covers. 12-15-Bigfoot app.						4.00
Annual 1 (2013, $4.99) The Venus Probe; Beatty-s/Mayhew-c						5.00

BIONIC MAN VS. THE BIONIC WOMAN (TV)
Dynamite Entertainment: 2013 - No. 5, 2013 ($3.99, limited series)

	GD	VG	FN	VF	VF/NM	NM-
1-5-Champagne-s/Luis-a; 3 covers on each						4.00

BIONIC WOMAN, THE (TV)
Charlton Publications: Oct, 1977 - No. 5, June, 1978

	GD	VG	FN	VF	VF/NM	NM-
1	4	8	12	28	47	65
2-5	3	6	9	17	26	35

BIONIC WOMAN, THE (TV)
Dynamite Entertainment: 2013 - No. 10, 2013 ($3.99)

	GD	VG	FN	VF	VF/NM	NM-
1-10: 1-Tobin-s/Renaud-c/Carvalho-a; origin re-told						4.00

BIONIC WOMAN, THE: SEASON FOUR (TV)
Dynamite Entertainment: 2014 - No. 4, 2014 ($3.99, limited series)

	GD	VG	FN	VF	VF/NM	NM-
1-4-Jerwa-s/Cabrera-a. 1-Reg & photo-c						4.00

BIRDS OF PREY (Also see Black Canary/Oracle: Birds of Prey)
DC Comics: Jan, 1999 - No. 127, Apr, 2009 ($1.99/$2.50/$2.99)

	GD	VG	FN	VF	VF/NM	NM-
1-Dixon-s/Land-c/a	1	3	4	6	8	10
2-4						6.00
5-7,9-15: 15-Guice-a begins.						4.00
8-Nightwing-c/app.; Barbara & Dick's circus date	3	6	9	21	33	45
16-38: 23-Grodd-c/app. 26-Bane app. 32-Noto-c begin						3.00
39,40-Bruce Wayne: Murderer pt. 5,12						3.50
41-Bruce Wayne: Fugitive pt. 2						4.00
42-46: 42-Fabry-a. 45-Deathstroke-c/app.						3.00

Birds of Prey (2010 series) #8 © DC

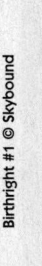

Birthright #1 © Skybound

The Black Bat #8 © DYN

	GD	VG	FN	VF	VF/NM	NM-
	2.0	4.0	6.0	8.0	9.0	9.2

47-74,76-91: 47-49-Terry Moore-s/Conner & Palmiotti-a; Noto-c. 50-Gilbert Hernandez-s begin. 52,54-Metamorpho app. 56-Simone-s/Benes-a begin. 65,67,68,70-Land-c. 76-Debut of Black Alice (from Day of Vengeance). 86-Timm-a (7 pgs.) 3.00
75-($2.95) Pearson-c; back-up story of Lady Blackhawk 4.00
92-99,101-127: 92-One Year Later. 94-Begin $2.99-c; Prometheus app. 96,97-Black Alice app. 98,99-New Batgirl app. 99-Black Canary leaves the team. 104-107-Secret Six app. 3.00
100-($3.99) new team recruited; Black Canary origin re-told 4.00
TPB (1999, $17.95) r/ previous series and one-shots 18.00
...: Batgirl 1 (2/98, $2.95) Dixon-s/Frank-c 5.00
...: Batgirl/Catwoman 1 ('03, $5.95) Robertson-a; cont'd in BOP: Catwoman/Oracle 1 6.00
...: Between Dark & Dawn TPB (2006, $14.99) r/#69-75 15.00
...: Blood and Circuits TPB (2007, $17.99) r/#96-103 18.00
...: Catwoman/Oracle 1 ('03, $5.95) Cont'd from BOP: Batgirl/Catwoman 1; David Ross-a 6.00
...: Club Kids TPB (2008, $17.99) r/#109-112,118 18.00
...: Dead of Winter TPB (2008, $17.99) r/#104-108 18.00
...: Metropolis or Dust TPB (2008, $17.99) r/#113-117 18.00
...: Of Like Minds TPB (2004, $14.95) r/#55-61 15.00
...: Old Friends, New Enemies TPB (2003, $17.95) r/#1-6, ...: Batgirl, ...: Wolves 18.00
...: Perfect Pitch TPB (2007, $17.99) r/#86-90,92-95 18.00
...: Platinum Flats TPB (2009, $17.99) r/#119-124 18.00
...: Revolution 1 (1997, $2.95) Frank-c/Dixon-s 5.00
... Secret Files 2003 (8/03, $4.95) Short stories, pin-ups and profile pages; Noto-c 5.00
...: Sensei and Student TPB (2005, $17.95) r/#62-68 18.00
...: The Battle Within TPB (2006, $17.99) r/#76-85 18.00
...: The Ravens 1 (6/98, $1.95)-Dixon-s; Girlfrenzy issue 4.00
...: Wolves 1 (10/97, $2.95) Dixon-s/Giordano & Faucher-a 5.00

BIRDS OF PREY (Brightest Day)
DC Comics: Jul, 2010 - No. 15, Oct, 2011 ($2.99)

1-Simone-s/Benes-a/c; Hawk and Dove join team, Penguin app. 3.00
1-Variant cover by Chiang 5.00
2-15: 2-4-Penguin app. 7-10-"Death of Oracle". 11-Catman app. 14,15-Tucci-a 3.00
... End Run HC (2011, $22.99, d.j.) r/#1-6 23.00

BIRDS OF PREY (DC New 52)
DC Comics: Nov, 2011 - No. 34, Oct, 2014 ($2.99)

1-24: 1-Swierczynski-s/Saiz-a; intro. Starling. 2-Katana & Poison Ivy join. 4-Batgirl joins. 9-Night of the Owls. 16-Strix joins. 18-20-Mr. Freeze app. 3.00
25-($3.99) Zero Year tie-in; flashback to Dinah's childhood; John Lynch app. 4.00
26-34: 26-Birds vs. Basilisk. 28-Gothtopia tie-in; Ra's al Ghul app. 32-34-Suicide Squad 3.00
#0 (11/12, $2.99) Black Canary and Batgirl first meeting; Molenaar-a/Lau-c 3.00
...: Futures End 1 (11/14, $2.99, regular-c) Five years later; The Red League 3.00
...: Futures End 1 (11/14, $3.99, 3-D cover) 4.00

BIRDS OF PREY: MANHUNT
DC Comics: Sept, 1996 - No. 4, Dec, 1996 ($1.95, limited series)

1-Features Black Canary, Oracle, Huntress, & Catwoman; Chuck Dixon scripts; Gary Frank-c on all. 1-Catwoman cameo only 1 2 3 5 6 8
2-4 6.00
NOTE: *Gary Frank c-1-4. Matt Haley a-1-4p. Wade Von Grawbadger a-1i.*

BIRTH CAUL, THE
Eddie Campbell Comics: 1999 ($5.95, B&W, one-shot)

1-Alan Moore-s/Eddie Campbell-a 6.00

BIRTH OF THE DEFIANT UNIVERSE, THE
Defiant Comics: May, 1993

nn-Contains promotional artwork & text; limited print run of 1000 copies.
2 4 6 10 14 18

BIRTHRIGHT
Image Comics (Skybound): Oct, 2014 - Present ($2.99)

1-22-Joshua Williamson-s/Andrei Bressan-a 3.00

BISHOP (See Uncanny X-Men & X-Men)
Marvel Comics: Dec, 1994 - No.4, Mar, 1995 ($2.95, limited series)

1-4: Foil-c; Shard & Mountjoy in all. 1-Storm app. 4.00

BISHOP THE LAST X-MAN
Marvel Comics: Oct, 1999 - No. 16, Jan, 2001 ($2.99/$1.99/$2.25)

1-($2.99)-Jeanty-a 4.00
2-8-($1.99): 2-Two covers 3.00
9-11,13-16: 9-Begin $2.25-c. 15-Maximum Security x-over; Xavier app. 3.00
12-($2.99) 4.00

BISHOP: XAVIER SECURITY ENFORCER
Marvel Comics: Jan, 1998 - No.3, Mar, 1998 ($2.50, limited series)

1-3: Ostrander-s 3.00

BITCH PLANET
Image Comics: Dec, 2014 - Present ($3.50/$3.99)

1-DeConnick-s/De Landro-a/c 5.00
2-9: 3-Origin of Penny Rolle. 5-Begin $3.99-c. 6-Meiko flashback 4.00

BITE CLUB
DC Comics (Vertigo): Jun, 2004 - No. 6, Nov, 2004 ($2.95, limited series)

1-6-Chaykin-s/Tischman-a/Quitely-c 3.00
TPB Digest (2005, $9.99) r/#1-6; cover gallery 10.00
The Complete Bite Club TPB (2007, $19.99) r/#1-6 and ...: Vampire Crime Unit #1-5 20.00

BITE CLUB: VAMPIRE CRIME UNIT
DC Comics (Vertigo): Jun, 2006 - No. 5 ($2.99, limited series)

1-5:1-Chaykin & Tischman-s/Hahn-a/Quitely-c. 4-Chaykin-c 3.00

BIZARRE ADVENTURES (Formerly Marvel Preview)
Marvel Comics Group: No. 25, 3/81 - No. 34, 2/83 (#25-33: Magazine-$1.50)

25,26: 25-Lethal Ladies. 26-King Kull; Bolton-c/a 2 4 6 8 10 12
27,28: 27-Phoenix, Iceman & Nightcrawler app. 28-The Unlikely Heroes; Elektra by Miller; Neal Adams-a 2 4 6 10 14 18
29,30,32,33: 29-Stephen King's Lawnmower Man. 30-Tomorrow; 1st app. Silhouette. 32-Gods; Thor-c/s. 33-Horror; Dracula app.; photo-c 2 3 4 6 8 10
31-After The Violence Stops; new Hangman story; Miller-a
2 4 6 8 10 12
34 ($2.00, Baxter paper, comic size)-Son of Santa; Christmas special; Howard the Duck by Paul Smith 1 2 3 5 7 9
NOTE: *Alcala a-27i. Austin a-25i, 28i. Bolton a-26, 32. J. Buscema a-27p, 29, 30p; c-26. Byrne a-31 (2 pg.). Golden a-25p, 28p. Perez a-27p. Rogers a-25p. Simonson a-29; c-29. Paul Smith a-34.*

BIZARRO
DC Comics: Aug, 2015 - No. 6, Jan, 2016 ($2.99, limited series)

1-6-Corson-s/Duarte-a; Jimmy Olsen app. 4-Zatanna app. 6-Superman app. 3.00

BIZARRO COMICS!
DC Comics: 2001 ($29.95, hardcover, one-shot)

HC-Short stories of DC heroes by various alternative cartoonists including Dorkin, Pope, Haspiel, Kidd, Kochalka, Millionaire, Stephens, Wray; includes "Superman's Babysitter" by Kyle Baker from Elseworlds 80-Page Giant recalled by DC; Groening-c 30.00
Softcover (2003, $19.95) 20.00

BIZARRO WORLD
DC Comics: 2005 ($29.95, hardcover, one-shot)

HC-Short stories by various alternative cartoonists including Bagge, Baker, Dorkin, Dunn, Kupperman, Morse, Oswalt, Pekar, Simpson, Stewart; Jaime Hernandez-c 30.00
Softcover (2006, $19.99) 20.00

BLACK ADAM (See 52 and Countdown)
DC Comics: Oct, 2007 - No. 6, Mar, 2008 ($2.99, limited series)

1-6: 1-Mahnke-a/c; Isis returns; Felix Faust app. 5.00
...: The Dark Age TPB (2008, $17.99) r/#1-6; Alex Ross-c 18.00

BLACK AND WHITE (See Large Feature Comic, Series I)

BLACK & WHITE (Also see Codename: Black & White)
Image Comics (Extreme): Oct, 1994 - No. 3, Jan, 1995 ($1.95, limited series)

1-3: Thibert-c/story 3.00

BLACK & WHITE MAGIC
Innovation Publishing: 1991 ($2.95, 98 pgs., B&W w/30 pgs. color, squarebound)

1-Contains rebound comics w/covers removed; contents may vary 4.00

BLACK AXE
Marvel Comics (UK): Apr, 1993 - No. 7, Oct, 1993 ($1.75)

1-4: 1-Romita Jr.-c. 2-Sunfire-c/s 3.00
5-7: 5-Janson-c; Black Panther app. 6,7-Black Panther-c/s 3.00

BLACK BAG
Legendary Comics: Nov, 2015 - Present ($3.99)

1-3-Roberson-s/Bastos-a 4.00

BLACKBALL COMICS
Blackball Comics: Mar, 1994 ($3.00)

1-Trencher-c/story by Giffen; John Pain by O'Neill 3.00

BLACK BAT, THE
Dynamite Entertainment: 2013 - No. 12, 2014 ($3.99)

1-12-Buccellato-s/Cliquet-a; multiple covers on each 4.00

BLACKBEARD'S GHOST (See Movie Comics)

BLACK BEAUTY (See Son of Black Beauty)

Black Canary (2015 series) #3 © DC

Black Cat Comics #5 © HARV

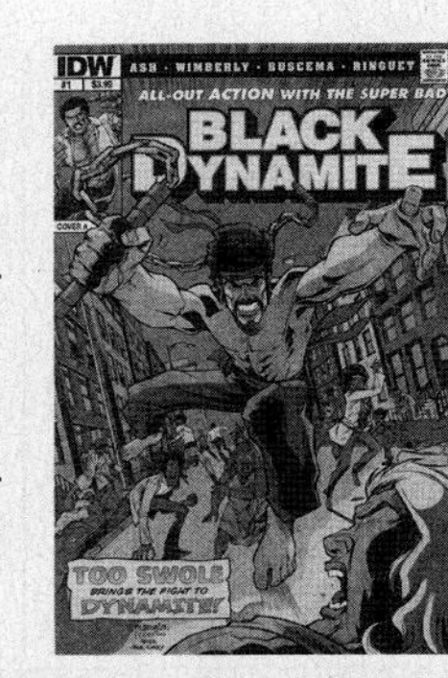

Black Dynamite #1 © Dynamite Ent.

	GD 2.0	VG 4.0	FN 6.0	VF 8.0	VF/NM 9.0	NM- 9.2

Dell Publishing Co.: No. 440, Dec, 1952

Four Color 440 5 10 15 33 57 80

BLACK BEETLE, THE
Dark Horse Comics: Jan, 2013 - No. 4, Jun, 2013 ($3.99, limited series)

1-4-Francavilla-s/a/c 4.00

BLACK BOLT: SOMETHING INHUMAN THIS WAY COMES
Marvel Comics: Sept, 2013 ($7.99, one-shot)

1-Reprints Black Bolt app. in Amazing Adventures #5-10 & Avengers #95 8.00

BLACKBURNE COVENANT, THE
Dark Horse Comics: Apr, 2003 - No. 4, July, 2003 ($2.99, limited series)

1-4-Nicieza-s/Raffaele-a 3.00
TPB (2003, $12.95) r/#1-4 13.00

BLACK CANARY (See All Star Comics #38, Flash Comics #86, Justice League of America #75 & World's Finest #244)
DC Comics: Nov, 1991 - No. 4, Feb, 1992 ($1.75, limited series)

1-4 3.00

BLACK CANARY
DC Comics: Jan, 1993 - No. 12, Dec, 1993 ($1.75)

1-7 3.00
8-12: 8-The Ray-c/story. 9,10-Huntress-c/story 3.00

BLACK CANARY (Follows Oliver Queen's marriage proposal in Green Arrow #75)
DC Comics: Early Sept, 2007 - No. 4, Late Oct, 2007 ($2.99, bi-weekly limited series)

1-4-Bedard-s/Siqueira-a 3.00
... Wedding Planner 1 (11/07, $2.99) Roux-c/Ferguson & Norrie-a 3.00

BLACK CANARY
DC Comics: Aug, 2015 - No. 12, Aug, 2016 ($2.99)

1-12: 1-Fletcher-s/Annie Wu-a/c. 4,5-Guerra-a. 8-Vixen app. 9-Moritat-a. 10-Batgirl app. 3.00

BLACK CANARY AND ZATANNA; BLOODSPELL
DC Comics: 2014 ($22.99, hardcover graphic novel, dustjacket)

HC-Paul Dini-s/Joe Quinones-a; includes script and sketch art 23.00

BLACK CANARY/ORACLE: BIRDS OF PREY (Also see Showcase '96 #3)
DC Comics: 1996 ($3.95, one-shot)

1-Chuck Dixon scripts & Gary Frank-c/a. 2 4 6 11 16 20

BLACK CAT (AMAZING SPIDER-MAN PRESENTS...)
Marvel Comics: Aug, 2010 - No. 4, Dec, 2010 ($3.99, limited series)

1-4-Van Meter-s/Pulido-a/Conner-c; Spider-Man & Ana Kraven app. 4.00

BLACK CAT COMICS (...Western #16-19; ...Mystery #30 on)
(See All-New #7,9, The Original Black Cat, Pocket & Speed Comics)
Harvey Publications (Home Comics): June-July, 1946 - No. 29, June, 1951

1-Kubert-a; Joe Simon c-1,2 84 168 252 538 919 1300
2-Kubert-a 41 82 123 256 428 600
3,4: 4-The Red Demons begin (The Demon #4 & 5)
34 68 102 206 336 465
5,6,7: 5,6-The Scarlet Arrow app. in ea. by Powell; S&K-a in both. 6-Origin Red Demon. 7-Vagabond Prince by S&K plus 1 more story 39 78 117 240 395 550
8-S&K-a; Kerry Drake begins, ends #13 36 72 108 216 351 485
9-Origin Stuntman (r/Stuntman #1) 39 78 117 231 378 525
10-20: 14,15,17-Mary Worth app. plus Invisible Scarlet O'Neil-#15,20,24
27 54 81 160 263 365
21-26 22 44 66 128 209 290
27,28: 27-Used in **SOTI**, pg. 193; X-Mas-c; 2 pg. John Wayne story. 28-Intro. Kit, Black Cat's new sidekick 24 48 72 140 230 320
29-Black Cat bondage-c; Black Cat stories 22 44 66 132 216 300

BLACK CAT MYSTERY (Formerly Black Cat; ...Western Mystery #54; ...Western #55,56; ...Mystery #57; ...Mystic #58-62; Black Cat #63-65)
Harvey Publications: No. 30, Aug, 1951 - No. 65, Apr, 1963

30-Black Cat on cover and first page only 39 78 117 231 378 525
31,32,34,37,38,40 31 62 93 182 296 410
33-Used in **POP**, pg. 89; electrocution-c 39 78 117 240 395 550
35-Atomic disaster cover/story 40 80 120 244 402 560
36,39-Used in **SOTI**: #36-Pgs. 270,271; #39-Pgs. 386-388
39 78 117 231 378 525
41-43 30 60 90 177 289 400
44-Eyes, ears, tongue cut out; Nostrand-a 36 72 108 211 343 475
45-Classic "Colorama" by Powell; Nostrand-a 77 154 231 493 847 1200
46-49,51-Nostrand-a in all. 51-Story has blank panel covering censored art (post-Code)
34 68 102 199 325 450
50-Check-a; classic Warren Kremer-c showing a man's face & hands burning away
371 742 1113 2600 4550 6500
52,53 (r/#34 & 35) 20 40 60 114 182 250
54-Two Black Cat stories (2/55, last pre-code) 21 42 63 122 199 275
55,56-Black Cat app. 20 40 60 114 182 250
57(7/56)-Kirby-c 21 42 63 124 202 280
58-60-Kirby-a(4). 58,59-Kirby-c. 60,61-Simon-c 24 48 72 144 237 330
61-Nostrand-a; "Colorama" r/#45 22 44 66 132 216 300
62 (3/58)-E.C. story swipe 20 40 60 114 182 250
63-65: Giants(10/62,1/63, 4/63); Reprints; Black Cat app. 63-origin Black Kitten. 65-1 pg. Powell-a 21 42 63 126 206 285

NOTE: ***Kremer** a-37, 39, 43; c-36, 37, 47. **Meskin** a-51. **Palais** a-30, 31(2), 32(2), 33-35, 37-40. **Powell** a-32-35, 36(2), 40, 41, 43-53, 57. **Simon** c-63-65. **Sparling** a-44. Bondage c-32, 34, 43.*

BLACK COBRA (Bride's Diary No. 4 on) (See Captain Flight #8)
Ajax/Farrell Publications(Excellent Publ.): No. 1, 10-11/54; No. 6(No. 2), 12-1/54-55; No. 3, 2-3/55

1-Re-intro Black Cobra & The Cobra Kid (costumed heroes)
39 78 117 233 384 535
6(#2)-Formerly Billy Bunny 20 40 60 118 192 265
3-(Pre-code)-Torpedoman app. 20 40 60 114 182 250

BLACK CONDOR (Also see Crack Comics, Freedom Fighters & Showcase '94 #10,11)
DC Comics: June, 1992 - No. 12, May, 1993 ($1.25)

1-8-Heath-c 3.00
9-12: 9,10,12-Heath-c. 9,10-The Ray app. 12-Batman-c/app. 3.00

BLACK CROSS SPECIAL (See Dark Horse Presents)
Dark Horse Comics: Jan, 1988 ($1.75, B&W, one-shot)(Reprints & new-a)

1-1st printing 4.00
1-(2nd printing) has 2 pgs. new-a 3.00

BLACK CROSS: DIRTY WORK (See Dark Horse Presents)
Dark Horse Comics: Apr, 1997 ($2.95, one-shot)

1-Chris Warner-c/s/a 3.00

BLACK DIAMOND
Americomics: May, 1983 - No. 5, 1984 (no month)($2.00-$1.75, Baxter paper)

1-3-Movie adapt.; 1-Colt back-up begins 4.00
4,5 3.00

NOTE: ***Bill Black** a-1i; c-1. **Gulacy** c-2-5. Sybil Danning photo back-c-1.*

BLACK DIAMOND WESTERN (Formerly Desperado No. 1-8)
Lev Gleason Publ: No. 9, Mar, 1949 - No. 60, Feb, 1956 (No. 9-28: 52 pgs.)

9-Black Diamond & his horse Reliapon begin; origin & 1st app. Black Diamond
21 42 63 122 199 275
10 12 24 36 69 97 125
11-15 10 20 30 54 72 90
16-28(11/49-11/51)-Wolverton's Bingbang Buster 14 28 42 76 108 140
29-40: 31-One pg. Frazetta anti-drug ad 9 18 27 47 61 75
41-50,53-59 8 16 24 40 50 60
51-3-D effect-c/story 15 30 45 85 130 175
52-3-D effect story 14 28 42 81 118 155
60-Last issue 8 16 24 44 57 70

NOTE: ***Biro** c-9-35?. **Cooper** a-12. **Myron Foss** a-54-58, c-54-56, 58. **Guardineer** a-9, 12, 15, 18. **Jack Keller** a-12. **Kida** a-9. **Maurer** a-10. **Ed Moore** a-16. **Morisi** a-55. **William Overgard** a-9-23. **Tuska** a-10, 48. **Bill Walton** a-57.*

BLACK DRAGON, THE
Marvel Comics (Epic Comics): May, 1985 - No. 6, Oct, 1985 (Baxter paper, mature)

1-6: 1-Chris Claremont story & John Bolton painted-c/a in all 4.00
TPB (Dark Horse, 4/96, $17.95, B&W, trade paperback) r/#1-6; intro by Anne McCaffrey 18.00

BLACK DYNAMITE (Based on the Michael Jai White film)
IDW Publishing: Dec, 2013 - No. 4, Aug, 2014 ($3.99)

1-4: 1-Ash-s/Wimberly-a; multiple covers. 2,3-Ferreira-a 4.00

BLACKEST NIGHT (2009 Green Lantern & DC crossover) (Leads into Brightest Day series)
DC Comics: No. 0, Jun, 2009 - No. 8, May, 2010 ($3.99, limited series)

0-Free Comic Book Day edition; Johns-s/Reis-a; profile pages of different corps 3.00
1-8: 1-($3.99) Black Lantern Corps arises; Johns-s/Reis-c/a; Hawkman & Hawkgirl killed. 4-Nekron rises. 8-Dead heroes return 5.00
1-Variant cover by Van Sciver 10.00
1-3,5: 2nd-4th printings 4.00
2-8: 2-Cascioli variant-c. 3-Van Sciver variant-c. 4-7-Migliari variant-c. 8-Mahnke var-c 8.00
... Director's Cut (6/10, $5.99) Commentary with story panels; cover gallery, script pgs. 6.00
HC (2010, $29.99, d.j.) r/#0-8 & Blackest Night Director's Cut; variant cover gallery 30.00
SC (2011, $19.99) r/#0-8 & Blackest Night Director's Cut; variant cover gallery 20.00

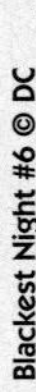
Blackest Night #6 © DC

Black-Eyed Kids #1 © Joe Pruett

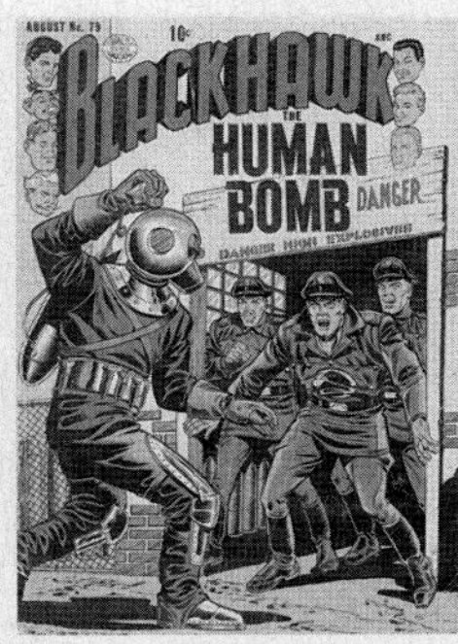

Blackhawk #79 © QUA

	GD	VG	FN	VF	VF/NM	NM-
	2.0	4.0	6.0	8.0	9.0	9.2

...: Black Lantern Corps Vol. 1 HC (2010, $24.99, d.j.) r/BN: Batman, BN: Superman, and BN: Titans series; cover gallery and character sketch designs 25.00
...: Black Lantern Corps Vol. 1 SC (2011, $19.99) same contents as HC edition 20.00
...: Black Lantern Corps Vol. 2 HC (2010, $24.99, d.j.) r/BN: The Flash, BN: JSA, and BN: Wonder Woman series; cover gallery and character sketch designs 25.00
...: Rise of the Black Lanterns HC (2010, $24.99) r/one-shots Atom and Hawkman #46, Catwoman #83, Phantom Stranger #42, Power of Shazam #48, The Question #37, Starman #81, Weird Western Tales #71, Green Arrow #30 & Adventure Comics #7; sketch art 25.00
...: Rise of the Black Lanterns SC (2011, $19.99) same contents as HC edition 20.00

BLACKEST NIGHT: BATMAN (2009 Green Lantern & DC crossover)
DC Comics: Oct, 2009 - No. 3, Dec, 2009 ($2.99, limited series)

1-3: 1-Bat-parents rise as Black Lanterns; Deadman app.; Syaf-a/Andy Kubert-c; 2 printings. 3-Flying Graysons return 3.00
1-3-Variant-c by Sienkiewicz 5.00

BLACKEST NIGHT: JSA (2009 Green Lantern & DC crossover)
DC Comics: Feb, 2010 - No. 3, Apr, 2010 ($2.99, limited series)

1-3-Original Sandman, Dr. Midnite and Mr. Terrific rise; Barrows-a/c 3.00
1-3-Variant-c by Gene Ha 5.00

BLACKEST NIGHT: SUPERMAN (2009 Green Lantern & DC crossover)
DC Comics: Oct, 2009 - No. 3, Dec, 2009 ($2.99, limited series)

1-3-Earth-2 Superman and Lois become Black Lanterns; Barrows-a/c; 2 printings 3.00
1-3-Variant-c by Shane Davis 5.00

BLACKEST NIGHT: TALES OF THE CORPS (2009 Green Lantern & DC crossover)
DC Comics: Sept, 2009 - No. 3, Sept, 2009 ($3.99, weekly limited series)

1-3-Short stories by various; interlocking cover images. 3-Commentary on B.N. #0 4.00
HC (2010, $24.99) r/#1-3 & Adventure Comics #4,5 & Green Lantern #49; sketch art 25.00
SC (2011, $19.99) r/#1-3 & Adventure Comics #4,5 & Green Lantern #49; sketch art 20.00

BLACKEST NIGHT: THE FLASH (2009 Green Lantern & DC crossover)
DC Comics: Feb, 2010 - No. 3, Apr, 2010 ($2.99, limited series)

1-3-Rogues vs. Dead Rogues; Johns-s/Kolins-a 3.00
1-3-Variant-c by Manapul 5.00

BLACKEST NIGHT: TITANS (2009 Green Lantern & DC crossover)
DC Comics: Oct, 2009 - No. 3, Dec, 2009 ($2.99, limited series)

1-3-Terra and the original Hawk return; Benes-a/c 3.00
1-3-Variant-c by Brian Haberlin 5.00

BLACKEST NIGHT: WONDER WOMAN (2009 Green Lantern & DC crossover)
DC Comics: Feb, 2010 - No. 3, Apr, 2010 ($2.99, limited series)

1-3-Maxwell Lord returns; Rucka-s/Scott-a/Horn-c. 2,3-Mera app.; Star Sapphire 3.00
1-3-Variant-c by Ryan Sook 5.00

BLACK-EYED KIDS
AfterShock Comics: Apr, 2016 - Present ($3.99)

1-11: 1-($1.99) Joe Pruett-s/Szymon Kudranski-a/Francesco Francavilla-c. 2-11-($3.99) 4.00

BLACK FLAG (See Asylum #5)
Maximum Press: Jan, 1995 - No.4, 1995; No. 0, July, 1995 ($2.50, B&W) (No. 0 in color)

Preview Edition (6/94, $1.95, B&W)-Fraga/McFarlane-c. 3.00
0-4: 0-(7/95)-Liefeld/Fraga-c. 1-(1/95). 3.00
1-Variant cover 5.00
2,4-Variant covers 3.00

NOTE: ***Fraga** a-0-4, Preview Edition; c-1-4. **Liefeld/Fraga** c-0. **McFarlane/Fraga** c-Preview Edition.*

BLACK FURY (Becomes Wild West No. 58) (See Blue Bird)
Charlton Comics Group: May, 1955 - No. 57, Mar-Apr, 1966 (Horse stories)

	GD	VG	FN	VF	VF/NM	NM-
1	12	24	36	67	94	120
2	7	14	21	37	46	55
3-10	6	12	18	28	34	40
11-15,19,20	4	8	10	18	22	25
16-18-Ditko-a	12	24	36	67	94	120
21-30	4	7	10	14	17	20
31-57	3	6	8	12	14	16

BLACK GOLIATH (See Avengers #32-35,41,54 and Civil War #4)
Marvel Comics Group: Feb, 1976 - No. 5, Nov, 1976

	GD	VG	FN	VF	VF/NM	NM-
1-Tuska-a(p) thru #3	3	6	9	17	26	35
2-5: 2-4-(Regular 25¢ editions). 4-Kirby-c/Buckler-a	2	4	6	9	13	16
2-4-(30¢-c variants, limited distribution)(4,6,8/76)	4	8	12	23	37	50

BLACK HAMMER
Dark Horse Comics: Jul, 2016 - Present ($3.99)

1-6-Lemire-s/Ormston-a; covers by Ormston & Lemire 4.00
... Giant-Sized Annual (1/17, $5.99) Short stories by various incl. Nguyen, Allred, Kindt 6.00

	GD	VG	FN	VF	VF/NM	NM-
	2.0	4.0	6.0	8.0	9.0	9.2

BLACKHAWK (Formerly Uncle Sam #1-8; see Military Comics & Modern Comics)
Comic Magazines(Quality)No. 9-107(12/56); National Periodical Publications No. 108 (1/57) -250; DC Comics No. 251 on: No. 9, Winter, 1944 - No. 243, 10-11/68; No. 244, 1-2/76 - No. 250, 1-2/77; No. 251, 10/82 - No. 273, 11/84

	GD	VG	FN	VF	VF/NM	NM-
9 (1944)	258	516	774	1651	2826	4000
10 (1946)	113	226	339	718	1234	1750
11-15: 14-Ward-a; 13,14-Fear app.	81	162	243	518	884	1250
16-19	68	136	204	435	743	1050
20-Classic Crandall bondage-c; Ward Blackhawk	103	206	309	659	1130	1600
21-30 (1950)	52	104	156	328	552	775
31-40: 31-Chop Chop by Jack Cole	41	82	123	250	418	585
41-49,51-60: 42-Robot-c	36	72	108	216	351	485
50-1st Killer Shark; origin in text	39	78	117	236	388	540
61,62: 61-Used in **POP**, pg. 91. 62-Used in **POP**, pg. 92 & color illo	32	64	96	192	314	435
63-70,72-80: 65-H-Bomb explosion panel. 66-B&W & color illos **POP**. 67-Hitler-s. 70-Return of Killer Shark; atomic explosion panel. 75-Intro. Blackie the Hawk	31	62	93	182	296	410
71-Origin retold; flying saucer-c; A-Bomb panels	35	70	105	208	339	470
81-86: Last precode (3/55)	27	54	81	162	266	370
87-92,94-99,101-107: 91-Robot-c. 105-1st S.A.	22	44	66	132	216	300
93-Origin in text	23	46	69	136	223	310
100	27	54	81	162	266	370
108-1st DC issue (1/57); re-intro. Blackie, the Hawk, their mascot; not in #115	38	76	114	281	628	975
109-117: 117-(10/57)-Mr. Freeze app.	15	30	45	100	220	340
118-(11/57)-Frazetta-r/Jimmy Wakely #4 (3 pgs.)	15	30	45	103	227	350
119-130 (11/58): 120-Robot-c	12	24	36	79	170	260
131,132,134-140 (9/59)	10	20	30	66	138	210
133-Intro. Lady Blackhawk	37	74	111	222	361	500
141-150,152-163,165,166: 141-Cat-Man returns-c/s. 143-Kurtzman-r/Jimmy Wakely #4. 150-(7/60)-King Condor returns. 166-Last 10¢ issue	8	16	24	54	102	150
151-Lady Blackhawk receives & loses super powers	8	16	24	56	108	160
164-Origin retold	8	16	24	56	108	160
167-180	6	12	18	37	66	95
181-190	5	10	15	31	53	75
191-196,199: 196-Combat Diary series begins	4	8	12	27	44	60
197,198,200: 197-New look for Blackhawks. 198-Origin retold	4	8	12	28	47	65
201,202,204-210	3	6	9	21	33	45
203-Origin Chop Chop (12/64)	4	8	12	25	40	55
211-227,229-243(1968): 230-Blackhawks become superheroes; JLA cameo 242-Return to old costumes	3	6	9	17	26	35
228-Batman, Green Lantern, Superman, The Flash cameos.	3	6	9	21	33	45
244 ('76) -250: 250-Chuck dies	1	2	3	5	6	8

251-273: 251-Origin retold; Black Knights return. 252-Intro Domino. 253-Part origin Hendrickson. 258-Blackhawk's Island destroyed. 259-Part origin Chop-Chop. 265-273 (75¢ cover price) 4.00

NOTE: ***Chaykin** a-260; c-257-260, 262. **Crandall** a-10, 11, 13, 16?, 18-20, 22-26, 30-33, 35p, 36(2), 37, 38?, 39-44, 46-50, 52-58, 60, 63, 64, 66, 67; c-14-20, 22-63(most except #28-33, 36, 37, 39). **Evans** a-244, 245,246i, 248-250i. **G. Kane** c-263, 264. **Kubert c**-244, 245. **Newton** a-266p. **Severin** a-257.**Spiegle** a-261-267, 269-273; c-265-272. **Toth** a-260p. **Ward** a-16-27(Chop Chop, 8pgs. ea.); pencilled stories-No. 17-63(approx.). **Wildey** a-268. Chop Chop solo stories in #10-95?*

BLACKHAWK
DC Comics: Mar, 1988 - No. 3, May, 1988 ($2.95, limited series, mature)

1-3: Chaykin painted-c/a/scripts 4.00

BLACKHAWK (Also see Action Comics #601)
DC Comics: Mar, 1989 - No. 16, Aug, 1990 ($1.50, mature)

1 4.00
2-6,8-16: 16-Crandall-c swipe 3.00
7-($2.50, 52 pgs.)-Story-r/Military #1 4.00
Annual 1 (1989, $2.95, 68 pgs.)-Recaps origin of Blackhawk, Lady Blackhawk, and others 4.00
Special 1 (1992, $3.50, 68 pgs.)-Mature readers 4.00

BLACKHAWK INDIAN TOMAHAWK WAR, THE
Avon Periodicals: 1951 (Also see Fighting Indians of the Wild West)

	GD	VG	FN	VF	VF/NM	NM-
nn-Kinstler-c; Kit West story	21	42	63	124	202	280

BLACKHAWKS (DC New 52)
DC Comics: Nov, 2011 - No. 8, Jun, 2012 ($2.99)

1-8: 1-Costa-s/Nolan & Lashley-a 3.00

BLACK HOLE (See Walt Disney Showcase #54) (Disney, movie)

The Black Hood V2 #1 © ACP

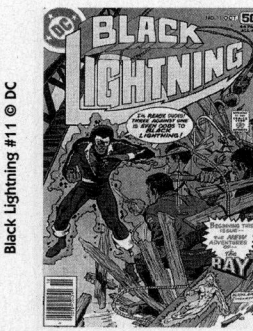

Black Lightning #11 © DC

Black Magick #3 © Rucka & Scott

GD 2.0 | VG 4.0 | FN 6.0 | VF 8.0 | VF/NM 9.0 | NM- 9.2

Whitman Publishing Co.: Mar, 1980 - No. 4, Sept, 1980
11295(#1) (1979, Golden, $1.50-c, 52 pgs., graphic novel; 8 1/2x11") Photo-c;
Spiegle-a. 3 6 9 14 20 25
1-3: 1,2-Movie adaptation. 2,3-Spiegle-a. 3-McWilliams-a; photo-c.
3-New stories 2 4 6 10 14 18
4-Sold only in pre-packs; new story; Spiegle-a 23 46 69 161 356 550

BLACK HOOD, THE (See Blue Ribbon, Flyman & Mighty Comics)
Red Circle Comics (Archie): June, 1983 - No. 3, Oct, 1983 (Mandell paper)
1-Morrow, McWilliams, Wildey-a; Toth-c 6.00
2,3: The Fox by Toth-c/a; Boyette-a. 3-Morrow-a; Toth wraparound-c 4.00
NOTE: *Also see Archie's Super-Hero Special Digest #2*

BLACK HOOD
DC Comics (Impact Comics): Dec, 1991 - No. 12, Dec, 1992 ($1.00)
1 4.00
2-12: 11-Intro The Fox. 12-Origin Black Hood 3.00
Annual 1 (1992, $2.50, 68 pgs.)-w/Trading card 4.00

BLACK HOOD, THE
Archie Comic Publications (Dark Circle Comics): Apr, 2015 - No. 11, Aug, 2016 ($3.99)
1-11: 1-Origin retold; Swierczynski-s/Gaydos-a; five covers. 6-Chaykin-a. 8-Hack-a 4.00

BLACK HOOD, THE (Volume 2)
Archie Comic Publications (Dark Circle Comics): Dec, 2016 - Present ($3.99)
1-3-Swierczynski-s/Greg Scott-a 4.00

BLACK HOOD COMICS (Formerly Hangman #2-8; Laugh Comics #20 on; also see Black Swan, Jackpot, Roly Poly & Top-Notch #9)
MLJ Magazines: No. 9, Wint., 1943-44 - No. 19, Sum., 1946 (on radio in 1943)
9-The Hangman & The Boy Buddies cont'd 129 258 387 826 1413 2000
10-Hangman & Dusty, the Boy Detective app. 77 154 231 493 847 1200
11-Dusty app.; no Hangman 65 130 195 416 708 1000
12,13,15-18: 17-Hal Foster swipe from Prince Valiant; 1st issue with "An Archie
Magazine" on-c 58 116 174 371 636 900
14-Kinstler blood-c 103 206 309 659 1130 1600
19-I.D. exposed; last issue 65 130 195 416 708 1000
NOTE: *Hangman by* ***Fuje*** *in 9, 10.* ***Kinstler*** *a-15, c-14-16.*

BLACK JACK (Rocky Lane's…; formerly Jim Bowie)
Charlton Comics: No. 20, Nov, 1957 - No. 30, Nov, 1959
20 9 18 27 52 69 85
21,27,29,30 6 12 18 31 38 45
22,23: 22-(68 pgs.). 23-Williamson/Torres-a 8 16 24 42 54 65
24-26,28-Ditko-a 10 20 30 56 76 95

BLACK JACK KETCHUM
Image Comics: Dec, 2015 - No. 4, Mar, 2016 ($3.99)
1-4: 1-Brian Schirmer-s/Claudia Balboni-a 4.00

BLACK KNIGHT, THE
Toby Press: May, 1953; 1963
1-Bondage-c 36 72 108 211 343 475
Super Reprint No. 11 (1963)-Reprints 1953 issue 3 6 9 19 25 32

BLACK KNIGHT, THE
Atlas Comics (MgPC): May, 1955 - No. 5, April, 1956
1-Origin Crusader; Maneely-c/a 135 270 405 864 1482 2100
2-Maneely-c/a(4) 81 162 243 518 884 1250
3-5: 4-Maneely-c/a. 5-Maneely-c, Shores-a 65 130 195 416 708 1000

BLACK KNIGHT (See The Avengers #48, Marvel Super Heroes & Tales To Astonish #52)
Marvel Comics: June, 1990 - No. 4, Sept, 1990 ($1.50, limited series)
1-4: 1-Original Black Knight returns. 3,4-Dr. Strange app. 3.00
... (MDCU) 1 (01/10, $3.99) Origin re-told; Frenz-a; originally from Marvel Digital Comics 4.00
NOTE: *Buckler c-1-4p*

BLACK KNIGHT (See Weirdworld and Secret Wars 2015 series)
Marvel Comics: Jan, 2016 - No. 5, May, 2016 ($3.99)
1-5: 1-Tieri-s/Pizzari-a. 2-5-Uncanny Avengers app. 4.00

BLACK KNIGHT: EXODUS
Marvel Comics: Dec, 1996 ($2.50, one-shot)
1-Raab-s; Apocalypse-c/app. 3.00

BLACK LAMB, THE
DC Comics (Helix): Nov, 1996 - No, 6, Apr, 1997 ($2.50, limited series)
1-6: Tim Truman-c/a/scripts 3.00

BLACKLIGHT (From ShadowHawk)
Image Comics: June, 2005 - No. 2, Jul, 2005 ($2.99)
1,2-Toledo & Deering-a/Wherle-s 3.00

BLACK LIGHTNING (See The Brave & The Bold, Cancelled Comic Cavalcade, DC Comics Presents #16, Detective #490 and World's Finest #257)
National Periodical Publ./DC Comics: Apr, 1977 - No. 11, Sept-Oct, 1978
1-Origin Black Lightning 3 6 9 19 30 40
2,3,6-10 1 3 4 6 8 10
4,5-Superman-c/s. 4-Intro Cyclotronic Man 2 4 6 8 10 12
11-The Ray new solo story 2 4 6 9 12 15
NOTE: ***Buckler*** *c-1-3p, 6-11p. #11 is 44 pgs.*

BLACK LIGHTNING (2nd Series)
DC Comics: Feb, 1995 - No. 13, Feb, 1996 ($1.95/$2.25)
1-5-Tony Isabella scripts begin, ends #8 3.00
6-13: 6-Begin $2.25-c. 13-Batman-c/app. 3.00

BLACK LIGHTNING: YEAR ONE
DC Comics: Mar, 2009 - No. 6, May, 2009 ($2.99, bi-weekly limited series)
1-6-Van Meter-s/Hamner-a. 1-Two printings (white and yellow cover title logos) 3.00
TPB (2009, $17.99) r/#1-6 18.00

BLACK LIST, THE (Based on the TV show)
Titan Comics: Aug, 2015 - No. 10, Jul, 2016 ($3.99)
1-10-Art & photo-c for each: 1-Nicole Phillips-s/Beni Lobel-a. 4.00

BLACK MAGIC (…Magazine) (Becomes Cool Cat V8#6 on)
Crestwood Publ. V1#1-4,V6#1-V7#5/Headline V1#5-V5#3,V7#6-V8#5: 10-11/50 - V4#1, 6-7/53: V4#2, 9-10/53 - V5#3, 11-12/54; V6#1, 9-10/57 - V7#2, 11-12/58: V7#3, 7-8/60 - V8#5, 11-12/61 (V1#1-5, 52pgs.; V1#6-V3#3, 44pgs.)
V1#1-S&K-a, 10 pgs.; Meskin-a(2) 174 348 522 1114 1907 2700
2-S&K-a, 17 pgs.; Meskin-a 74 148 222 470 810 1150
3-6(8-9/51)-S&K, Roussos, Meskin-a 61 122 183 390 670 950
V2#1(10-11/51),4,5,7(#13),9(#15),12(#18)-S&K-a 41 82 123 250 418 585
2,3,6,8,10,11(#17) 34 68 102 204 332 460
V3#1(#19, 12/52) - 6(#24, 5/53)-S&K-a 35 70 105 208 339 470
V4#1(#25, 6-7/53), 2(#26, 9-10/53)-S&K-a(3-4) 37 74 111 218 354 490
3(#27, 11-12/53)-S&K-a; Ditko-a (2nd published-a); also see Captain 3-D, Daring Love #1, Strange Fantasy #9, & Fantastic Fears #5 (Fant. Fears was 1st drawn, but not 1st publ.)
68 136 204 435 743 1050
4(#28)-Eyes ripped out/story-S&K, Ditko-a 50 100 150 315 533 750
5(#29, 3-4/54)-S&K, Ditko-a 39 78 117 229 375 520
6(#30, 5-6/54)-S&K, Powell?-a 31 62 93 186 303 420
V5#1(#31, 7-8/54 - 3(#33, 11-12/54)-S&K-a 21 42 63 122 199 275
V6#1(#34, 9-10/57), 2(#35, 11-12/57) 12 24 36 69 97 125
3(1-2/58) - 6(7-8/58) 12 24 36 69 97 125
V7#1(9-10/58) - 3(7-8/60), 4(9-10/60) 10 20 30 56 76 95
5(11-12/60)-Hitler-c; Torres-a 20 40 60 114 182 250
6(1-2/61)-Powell-a(2) 10 20 30 56 76 95
V8#1(3-4/61)-Powell-c/a 10 20 30 56 76 95
2(5-6/61)-E.C. story swipe/W.F. #22; Ditko, Powell-a
11 22 33 60 83 105
3(7-8/61)-E.C. story swipe/W.F. #22; Powell-a(2) 11 22 33 60 83 105
4(9-10/61)-Powell-a(5) 10 20 30 56 76 95
5-E.C. story swipe/W.S.F. #28; Powell-a(3) 11 22 33 60 83 105
NOTE: ***Bernard Baily*** *a-V4#6?, V5#3(2).* ***Grandenetti*** *a-V2#3, 11.* ***Kirby*** *c-V1#1-6, V2#1-12, V3#1-6, V4#1, 2, 4-6, V5#1-3.* ***McWilliams*** *a-V3#2i.* ***Meskin*** *a-V1#1(2), 2, 3, 4(2), 5(2), 6, V2/1, 2, 3(2), 4(3), 5, 6(2), 7-9, 11, 12i, V3#1(2), 5, 6, V5#1(2), 2.* ***Orlando*** *a-V6#1, 4, V7#2; c-V6/1-6.* ***Powell*** *a-V5#1?.* ***Roussos*** *a-V1#3-5, 6(2), V2#3(2), 4, 5(2), 6, 8, 9, 10(2), 11, 12p, V3#1(2), 2i, 5, V5#2.* ***Simon*** *a-V2#12, V3#2, V7#5? c-V4#3?, V7#3?, 4, 5?, 6?, V8#1-5.* ***Simon & Kirby*** *a-V1#1, 2(2), 3-6, V2#1, 4, 5, 7, 9, 12, V3#1-6, V4#1(3), 2(4), 3(2), 4(2), 5, 6, V5#1-3; c-V2#1.* ***Leonard Starr*** *a-V1#1.* ***Tuska*** *a-V6#3, 4.* ***Woodbridge*** *a-V7#4.*

BLACK MAGIC
National Periodical Publications: Oct-Nov, 1973 - No. 9, Apr-May, 1975
1-S&K reprints 3 6 9 16 24 32
2-8-S&K reprints 2 4 6 10 14 18
9-S&K reprints 2 4 6 11 16 20

BLACK MAGICK
Image Comics: Oct, 2015 - Present ($3.99)
1-5-Greg Rucka-s/Nicola Scott-a 4.00

BLACKMAIL TERROR (See Harvey Comics Library)

BLACK MARKET
BOOM! Studios: Jul, 2014 - No. 4, Oct, 2014 ($3.99, limited series)
1-4-Barbiere-s/Santos-a 4.00

BLACK MASK

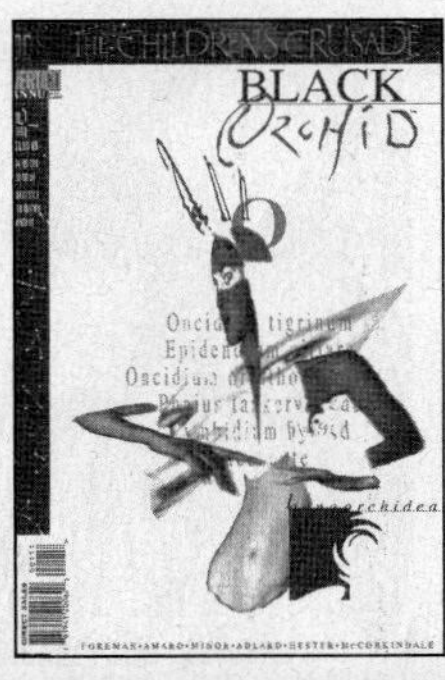

Black Orchid Annual #1 © DC

Black Panther (2016 series) #1 © MAR

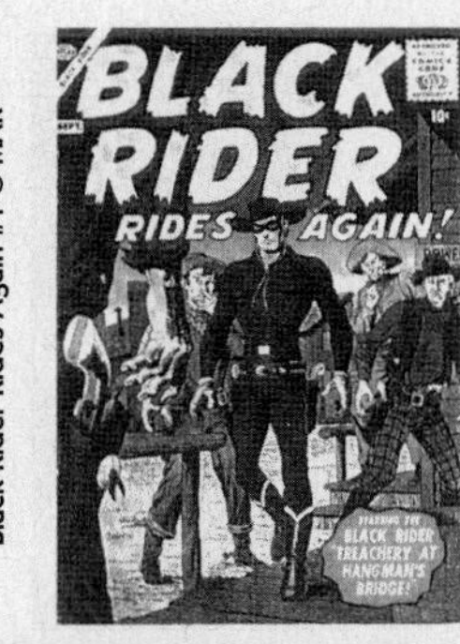

Black Rider Rides Again #1 © MAR

GD 2.0 | VG 4.0 | FN 6.0 | VF 8.0 | VF/NM 9.0 | NM- 9.2

DC Comics: 1993 - No. 3, 1994 ($4.95, limited series, 52 pgs.)
1-3 5.00

BLACK MONDAY MURDERS, THE
Image Comics: Aug, 2016 - No. 4, Nov, 2016 ($4.99, limited series)
1-4-Jonathan Hickman-s/Tomm Coker-a 5.00

BLACK OPS
Image Comics (WildStorm): Jan, 1996 - No. 5, May, 1996 ($2.50, lim. series)
1-5 3.00

BLACK ORCHID (See Adventure Comics #428 & Phantom Stranger)
DC Comics: Holiday, 1988-89 - No. 3, 1989 ($3.50, lim. series, prestige format)
Book 1,3: Gaiman scripts & McKean painted-a in all 6.00
Book 2-Arkham Asylum story; Batman app. 1 2 3 5 6 8
TPB (1991, $19.95) r/#1-3; new McKean-c 20.00

BLACK ORCHID
DC Comics: Sept, 1993 - No. 22, June, 1995 ($1.95/$2.25)
1-22: Dave McKean-c all issues 3.00
1-Platinum Edition 12.00
Annual 1 (1993, $3.95, 68 pgs.)-Children's Crusade 4.00

BLACKOUT
Dark Horse Comics: Mar, 2014 - No. 4, Jul, 2014 ($2.99, limited series)
1-4-Barbiere-s/Lorimer-a; King Tiger back-up by Stradley-s/Doug Wheatley-a 3.00

BLACKOUTS (See Broadway Hollywood...)

BLACK PANTHER, THE (Also see Avengers #52, Fantastic Four #52, Jungle Action & Marvel Premiere #51-53)
Marvel Comics Group: Jan, 1977 - No. 15, May, 1979
1-Jack Kirby-s/a thru #12 6 12 18 38 69 100
2-13: 4,5-(Regular 30¢ editions). 8-Origin 3 6 9 16 23 30
4,5-(35¢-c variants, limited dist.)(7,9/77) 8 16 24 54 102 150
14,15-Avengers x-over. 14-Origin 3 6 9 17 26 35
...By Jack Kirby Vol. 1 TPB (2005, $19.99) r/#1-7; unused covers and sketch pages 20.00
...By Jack Kirby Vol. 2 TPB (2006, $19.99) r/#8-12 by Kirby and #13 non-Kirby 20.00
NOTE: *J. Buscema c-15p. Layton c-13i.*

BLACK PANTHER
Marvel Comics Group: July, 1988 - No. 4, Oct, 1988 ($1.25)
1-4-Gillis-s/Cowan & Delarosa-a 4.00

BLACK PANTHER (Marvel Knights)
Marvel Comics: Nov, 1998 - No. 62, Sept, 2003 ($2.50)
1-Texeira-a/c; Priest-s 6.00
1-($6.95) DF edition w/Quesada & Palmiotti-c 1 2 3 5 6 8
2-4: 2-Two covers by Texeira and Timm. 3-Fantastic Four app. 4.00
5-35,37-40: 5-Evans-a. 6-8-Jusko-a. 8-Avengers-c/app. 15-Hulk app. 22-Moon Knight app. 23-Deadpool & the Avengers app. 25-Maximum Security x-over. 26-Storm-c/app. 28-Magneto & Sub-Mariner-c/app. 29-WWII flashback meeting w/Captain America. 35-Defenders-c/app. 37-Luke Cage and Falcon-c/app. 3.00
36-($3.50, 100 pgs.) 35th Anniversary issue incl. r/1st app. in FF #52 4.00
41-56: 41-44-Wolverine app. 47-Thor app. 48,49-Magneto app. 3.00
57-62: 57-Begin $2.99-c. 59-Falcon app. 3.00
...: The Client (6/01, $14.95, TPB) r/#1-5 15.00
... 2099 #1 (11/04, $2.99) Kirkman-s/Hotz-a/Pat Lee-c 3.00

BLACK PANTHER (Marvel Knights)
Marvel Comics: Apr, 2005 - No. 41, Nov, 2008 ($2.99)
1-Reginald Hudlin-s/John Romita Jr. & Klaus Janson-a; covers by Romita & Ribic 5.00
1-2nd printing; variant-c by Ribic 3.00
2-7,9-15,17-20: 7-House of M; Hairsine-a. 10-14-Luke Cage app. 12,13-Blade app. 17-Linsner-c. 19-Doctor Doom app. 3.00
8-Cho-c; X-Men app. 4.00
8-2nd printing variant-c 3.00
16-($3.99) Wedding of T'Challa and Storm; wraparound Cho-c; Hudlin-s/Eaton-a 4.00
21-Civil War x-over; Namor app. 8.00
21-2nd printing with new cover and Civil War logo 3.00
22-25-Civil War: 23-25-Turner-c 4.00
26-41: 26-30-T'Challa and Storm join the Fantastic Four. 27-30-Marvel Zombies app. 28-30-Suydam-c. 39-41-Secret Invasion 3.00
Annual 1 (4/08, $3.99) Hudlin-s/Stroman & Lashley-a; alternate future; Uatu app. 4.00
...: Bad Mutha TPB (2006, $10.99) r/#10-13 11.00
...: Civil War TPB (2007, $17.99) r/#19-25 18.00
...: Four the Hard Way TPB (2007, $13.99) r/#26-30; page layouts and character designs 14.00
...: Little Green Men TPB (2008, $10.99) r/#31-34 11.00
...: The Bride TPB (2006, $14.99) r/#14-18; interview with the dress designer 15.00
...: Who Is The Black Panther HC (2005, $21.99) r/#1-6; Hudlin afterword; cover gallery 22.00
...: Who Is The Black Panther SC (2006, $14.99) r/#1-6; Hudlin afterword; cover gallery 15.00

BLACK PANTHER
Marvel Comics: Apr, 2009 - No. 12, Mar, 2010 ($3.99/$2.99)
1-($3.99) Hudlin-s/Lashley-a; covers by Campbell & Lashley; Dr. Doom app. 4.00
2-12-($2.99) 2-6-Campbell-c. 6-Shuri becomes female Black Panther 3.00

BLACK PANTHER
Marvel Comics: Jun, 2016 - Present ($4.99/$3.99)
1-($4.99) Ta-Nehisi Coates-s/Brian Stelfreeze-a; bonus Stelfreeze interview & art 5.00
2-11-($3.99) 2-4,9-Stelfreeze-a. 5-8,10,11-Sprouse-a 4.00

BLACK PANTHER/CAPTAIN AMERICA: FLAGS OF OUR FATHERS
Marvel Comics: Jun, 2010 - No. 4, Sept, 2010 ($3.99, limited series)
1-4-Hudlin-s/Cowan-a; WW2 story; Howling Commandos & Red Skull app. 4.00

BLACK PANTHER: PANTHER'S PREY
Marvel Comics: May, 1991 - No. 4, Oct, 1991 ($4.95, squarebound, lim. series, 52 pgs.)
1-4: McGregor-s/Turner-a 5.00

BLACK PANTHER: THE MAN WITHOUT FEAR (Continues from Daredevil #512)
Marvel Comics: No. 513, Feb, 2011 - No. 523, Nov, 2011 ($2.99)
513-523: 513-Shadowland aftermath; Liss-s/Francavilla-a/Bianchi-c. 521-523-Fear Itself 3.00
513-Variant-c by Francavilla 5.00

BLACK PANTHER: THE MOST DANGEROUS MAN ALIVE
Marvel Comics: No. 523.1, Nov, 2011 - No. 529, Apr, 2012 ($2.99)
523.1, 524-529: 523.1-Palo-a/Zircher-c. 524-Spider Island tie-in; Lady Bullseye app. 3.00

BLACK PANTHER: WORLD OF WAKANDA
Marvel Comics: Jan, 2017 - Present ($4.99/$3.99)
1-($4.99) Roxanne Gay-s/Alitha E. Martinez-a; spotlight on The Dora Milaje 5.00
2-4-($3.99) 4.00

BLACK PEARL, THE
Dark Horse Comics: Sept, 1996 - No. 5, Jan, 1997 ($2.95, limited series)
1-5: Mark Hamill scripts 3.00

BLACK PHANTOM (See Tim Holt #25, 38)
Magazine Enterprises: Nov, 1954 (one-shot) (Female outlaw)
1 (A-1 #122)-The Ghost Rider story plus 3 Black Phantom stories; Headlight-c/a 39 78 117 231 378 525

BLACK PHANTOM
AC Comics: 1989 - No. 3, 1990 ($2.50, B&W; #2 color)(Reprints & new-a)
1-3: 1-Ayers-r, Bolle-r/B.P. #1-3-Redmask-r 3.00

BLACK PHANTOM, RETURN OF THE (See Wisco)

BLACK RIDER (Western Winners #1-7; Western Tales of Black Rider #28-31; Gunsmoke Western #32 on)(See All Western Winners, Best Western, Kid Colt, Outlaw Kid, Rex Hart, Two-Gun Kid, Two-Gun Western, Western Gunfighters, Western Winners, & Wild Western)
Marvel/Atlas Comics(CDS No. 8-17/CPS No. 19 on): No. 8, 3/50 - No. 18, 1/52; No. 19, 11/53 - No. 27, 3/55
8 (#1)-Black Rider & his horse Satan begin; 36 pgs; Stan Lee photo-c as Black Rider) 48 96 144 302 514 725
9-52 pgs. begin, end #14 26 52 78 154 252 350
10-Origin Black Rider 32 64 96 192 314 435
11-14: 14-Last 52pgs. 19 38 57 111 176 240
15-19: 19-Two-Gun Kid app. 16 32 48 94 147 200
20-Classic-c; Two-Gun Kid app. 18 36 54 107 169 230
21-27: 21-23-Two-Gun Kid app. 24,25-Arrowhead app. 26-Kid Colt app. 27-Last issue; last precode. Kid Colt app. The Spider (a villain) burns to death 15 30 45 86 133 180
NOTE: *Ayers c-22. Jack Keller a-15, 26, 27. Maneely a-14; c-16, 17, 25, 27. Syd Shores a-19, 21, 22, 23(3), 24(3), 25-27; c-19, 21, 23. Sinnott a-24, 25. Tuska a-12, 19-21.*

BLACK RIDER RIDES AGAIN!, THE
Atlas Comics (CPS): Sept, 1957
1-Kirby-a(3); Powell-a; Severin-c 30 60 90 177 289 400

BLACK ROAD
Image Comics: Apr, 2016 - Present ($3.99)
1-7-Brian Wood-s/Garry Brown-a 4.00

BLACK SEPTEMBER (Also see Avengers/Ultraforce, Ultraforce (1st series) #10 & Ultraforce/Avengers)
Malibu Comics (Ultraverse): 1995 ($1.50, one-shot)

Black Science #22 © Remender & Scalera

The Black Terror #21 © Pub. Ent. Ltd.

Black Widow (2016 series) #1 © MAR

GD 2.0 | VG 4.0 | FN 6.0 | VF 8.0 | VF/NM 9.0 | NM- 9.2

Infinity-Intro to the new Ultraverse; variant-c exists. 3.00

BLACK SCIENCE
Image Comics: Nov, 2013 - Present ($3.50/$3.99)
1-Remender-s/Scalera-a; multiple covers 10.00
2 6.00
3-28: 11,16,21-28-$3.99-c 4.00

BLACKSTONE (See Super Magician Comics & Wisco Giveaways)

BLACKSTONE, MASTER MAGICIAN COMICS
Vital Publ./Street & Smith Publ.: Mar-Apr, 1946 - No. 3, July-Aug, 1946
1 39 78 117 231 378 525
2,3 21 42 63 126 206 285

BLACKSTONE, THE MAGICIAN (...Detective on cover only #3 & 4)
Marvel Comics (CnPC): No. 2, May, 1948 - No. 4, Sept, 1948 (No #1) (Cont'd from E.C. #1?)
2-The Blonde Phantom begins, ends #4 90 180 270 576 988 1400
3,4: 3-Blonde Phantom by Sekowsky 53 106 159 334 567 800

BLACKSTONE, THE MAGICIAN DETECTIVE FIGHTS CRIME
E. C. Comics: Fall, 1947
1-1st app. Happy Houlihans 57 114 171 362 619 875

BLACK SUN (X-Men Black Sun on cover)
Marvel Comics: Nov, 2000 - No. 5, Nov, 2000 ($2.99, weekly limited series)
1-(...: X-Men), 2-(...: Storm), 3-(...: Banshee and Sunfire), 4-(...: Colossus and Nightcrawler), 5-(...: Wolverine and Thunderbird); Claremont-s in all; Evans interlocking painted covers; Magik returns 3.00

BLACK SUN
DC Comics (WildStorm): Nov, 2002 - No. 6, Jun, 2003 ($2.95, limited series)
1-6-Andreyko-s/Scott-a 3.00

BLACK SWAN COMICS
MLJ Magazines (Pershing Square Publ. Co.): 1945
1-The Black Hood reprints from Black Hood No. 14; Bill Woggon-a; Suzie app. Caribbean Pirates-c 22 44 66 132 216 300

BLACK TARANTULA (See Feature Presentations No. 5)

BLACK TERROR (See America's Best Comics & Exciting Comics)
Better Publications/Standard: Winter, 1942-43 - No. 27, June, 1949
1-Black Terror, Crime Crusader begin; Japanese WWII-c 400 800 1200 2800 4900 7000
2 174 348 522 1114 1907 2700
3-Nazi WWII-c 161 322 483 1030 1765 2500
4,5-Nazi & Japanese WWII-c 142 284 426 909 1555 2200
6-8: 6,8-Classic Nazi WWII-c. 7-Classic Japanese WWII-c; The Ghost app. 161 322 483 1030 1765 2500
9,10-Nazi & Japanese WWII-c 123 246 369 787 1344 1900
11,13-19 61 122 183 390 670 950
12-Japanese WWII-c 77 154 231 493 847 1200
20-Classic-c; The Scarab app. 90 180 270 576 988 1400
21-Miss Masque app. 65 130 195 416 708 1000
22-Part Frazetta-a on one Black Terror story 61 122 183 390 670 950
23,25-27 54 108 162 343 574 825
24-Frazetta-a (1/4 pg.) 65 130 195 416 708 1000
NOTE: *Schomburg (Xela) c-2-27; bondage c-2, 17, 24.* ***Meskin** a-27.* ***Moreira** a-27.* ***Robinson/Meskin** a-23, 24(3), 25, 26.* ***Roussos/Mayo** a-24.* ***Tuska** a-26, 27.*

BLACK TERROR, THE (Also see Total Eclipse)
Eclipse Comics: Oct, 1989 - No. 3, June, 1990 ($4.95, 52 pgs., squarebound, limited series)
1-3: Beau Smith & Chuck Dixon scripts; Dan Brereton painted-c/a 5.00

BLACK TERROR (Also see Project Superpowers)
Dynamite Entertainment: 2008 - No. 14, 2011 ($3.50/$3.99)
1-14-Golden Age hero. 1-Alex Ross-c/Mike Lilly-a; various variant-c exist 4.00

BLACKTHORNE 3-D SERIES
Blackthorne Publishing Co.: May, 1985 - No. 80, 1989 ($2.25/$2.50)
1-Sheena in 3-D #1. D. Stevens-c/retouched-a 1 2 3 5 6 8
2-10: 2-MerlinRealm in 3-D #1. 3-3-D Heroes #1. Goldyn in 3-D #1. 5-Bizarre 3-D Zone #1. 6-Salimba in 3-D #2. 7-Twisted Tales in 3-D #1. 8-Dick Tracy in 3-D #1. 9-Salimba in 3-D #2. 10-Gumby in 3-D #1 6.00
11-19: 11-Betty Boop in 3-D #1. 12-Hamster Vice in 3-D #1. 13-Little Nemo in 3-D #1. 14-Gumby in 3-D #2. 15-Hamster Vice #6 in 3-D. 16-Laffin' Gas #6 in 3-D. 17-Gumby in 3-D #3. 18-Bullwinkle and Rocky in 3-D #1. 19-The Flintstones in 3-D #1 6.00
20(#1),26(#2),35(#3),39(#4),52(#5),62,71(#6)-G.I. Joe in 3-D. 62-G.I. Joe Annual 2 4 6 8 11 14
21-24,27-28: 21-Gumby in 3-D #4. 22-The Flintstones in 3-D #2. 23-Laurel & Hardy in 3-D #1. 24-Bozo the Clown in 3-D #1. 27-Bravestarr in 3-D #1. 28- Gumby in 3-D #5 6.00
25,29,37-The Transformers in 3-D 2 4 6 10 14 18
30-Star Wars in 3-D #1 3 6 9 16 23 30
31-34,36,38,40: 31-The California Raisins in 3-D #1. 32-Richie Rich & Casper in 3-D #1. 33-Gumby in 3-D #6. 34-Laurel & Hardy in 3-D #2. 36-The Flintstones in 3-D #3. 38-Gumby in 3-D #7. 40-Bravestarr in 3-D #2 6.00
41-46,49,50: 41-Battletech in 3-D #1. 42-The Flintstones in 3-D #4. 43-Underdog in 3-D #1 44-The California Raisins in 3-D #2. 45-Red Heat in 3-D #1 (movie adapt.). 46-The California Raisins in 3-D #3. 49-Rambo in 3-D #1. 49-Sad Sack in 3-D #1. 50-Bullwinkle For President in 3-D #1 6.00
47,48-Star Wars in 3-D #2,3 2 4 6 11 16 20
51,53-60: 51-Kull in 3-D #1. 53-Red Sonja in 3-D #1. 54-Bozo in 3-D #2. 55-Waxwork in 3-D #1 (movie adapt.). 57-Casper in 3-D #1. 58-Baby Huey in 3-D #1. 59-Little Dot in 3-D #1. 60-Solomon Kane in 3-D #1 6.00
61,63-70,72-74,76-80: 61-Werewolf in 3-D #1. 63-The California Raisins in 3-D #4. 64-To Die For in 3-D #1. 65-Capt. Holo in 3-D #1. 66-Playful Little Audrey in 3-D #1. 67-Kull in 3-D #2. 69-The California Raisins in 3-D #5. 70-Wendy in 3-D #1. 72-Sports Hall of Shame #1. 74-The Noid in 3-D #1. 80-The Noid in 3-D #2 1 2 3 4 5 7
75-Moonwalker in 3-D #1 (Michael Jackson movie adapt.) 4 8 12 27 44 60

BLACK VORTEX (See Guardians of the Galaxy & X-Men: The Black Vortex)

BLACK WIDOW (Marvel Knights) (Also see Marvel Graphic Novel)
Marvel Comics: May, 1999 - No. 3, Aug, 1999 ($2.99, limited series)
1-(June on-c) Devin Grayson-s/J.G. Jones-c/a; Daredevil app. 5.00
1-Variant-c by J.G. Jones 6.00
2,3 4.00
...Web of Intrigue (6/99, $3.50) r/origin & early appearances 4.00
TPB (7/01, $15.95) r/Vol. 1 & 2; Jones-c 16.00

BLACK WIDOW (Marvel Knights) (Volume 2)
Marvel Comics: Jan, 2001 - No. 3, May, 2001 ($2.99, limited series)
1-3-Grayson & Rucka-s/Scott Hampton-c/a; Daredevil app. 3.00

BLACK WIDOW (Marvel Knights)
Marvel Comics: Nov, 2004 - No. 6, Apr, 2005 ($2.99, limited series)
1-6-Sienkiewicz-a/Land-c 3.00

BLACK WIDOW (Continues in Widowmaker #1)
Marvel Comics: Jun, 2010 - No. 8, Jan, 2011 ($3.99/$2.99)
1-($3.99) Liu-s/Acuña-a; Wolverine app.; back-up history text 4.00
1-Variant photo-c of Scarlett Johansson from Iron Man 2 movie 3 6 9 14 20 25
2-8-($2.99) 2-5-Acuña-a. 2,3-Elektra app. 3.00

BLACK WIDOW (All-New Marvel Now!)
Marvel Comics: Mar, 2014 - No. 20, Sept, 2015 ($3.99)
1-20: 1-Edmonson-s/Noto-a/c. 7-Daredevil app. 8-Winter Soldier app. 11-X-23 app. 4.00

BLACK WIDOW
Marvel Comics: May, 2016 - Present ($3.99)
1-11: 1-Waid-s/Samnee-s&a. 6-Iron Man app. 9,10-Winter Soldier app. 4.00

BLACK WIDOW & THE MARVEL GIRLS
Marvel Comics: Feb, 2010 - No. 4, Apr, 2010 ($2.99, limited series)
1-4-Tobin-s. 1-Enchantress app. 2-Avengers app. 4-Storm app.; Miyazawa-a 3.00

BLACK WIDOW: DEADLY ORIGIN
Marvel Comics: Jan, 2010 - No. 4, Apr, 2010 ($3.99, limited series)
1-4-Granov-c; origin retold. 1-Wolverine and Bucky app. 3-Daredevil app. 4.00

BLACK WIDOW: PALE LITTLE SPIDER (Marvel Knights) (Volume 3)
Marvel Comics: Jun, 2002 - No. 3, Aug, 2002 ($2.99, limited series)
1-3-Rucka-s/Kordey-a/Horn-c 3.00

BLACK WIDOW 2 (THE THINGS THEY SAY ABOUT HER) (Marvel Knights)
Marvel Comics: Nov, 2005 - No. 6, Apr, 2006 ($2.99, limited series)
1-6-Phillips & Sienkiewicz-a/Morgan-s; Daredevil app. 3.00
TPB (2006, $15.99) r/#1-6 16.00

BLACKWULF
Marvel Comics: June, 1994 - No. 10, Mar, 1995 ($1.50)
1-($2.50)-Embossed-c; Angel Medina-a 4.00
2-10 3.00

BLADE (The Vampire Hunter)
Marvel Comics

Blade of the Immortal #64 © H. Samura

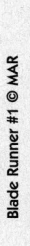

Blade Runner #1 © MAR

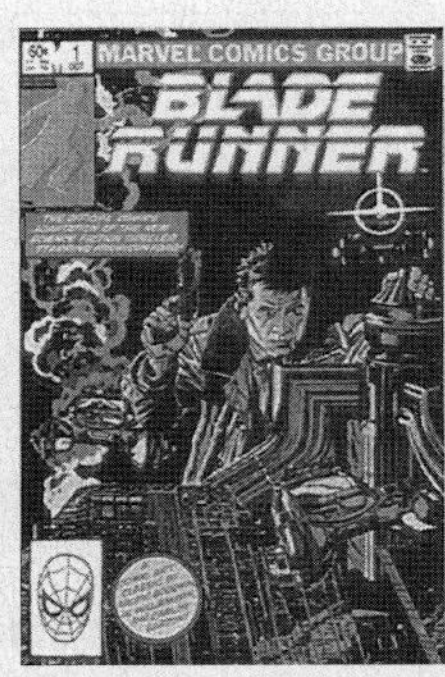

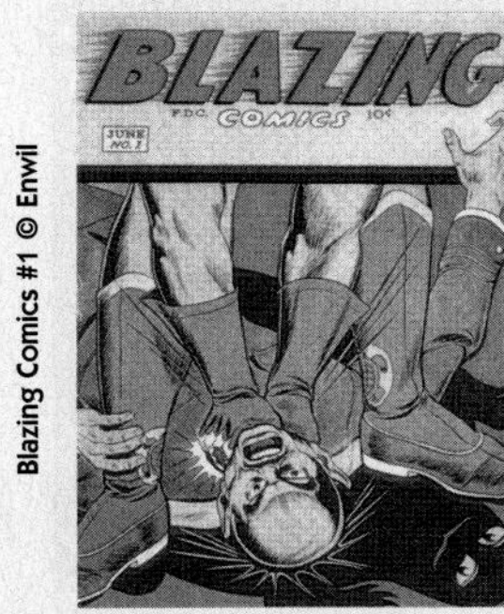

Blazing Comics #1 © Enwil

GD 2.0 | VG 4.0 | FN 6.0 | VF 8.0 | VF/NM 9.0 | NM- 9.2

1-(3/98, $3.50) Colan-a(p)/Christopher Golden-s 4.00
... Black & White TPB (2004, $15.99, B&W) reprints from magazines Vampire Tales #8,9; Marvel Preview #3,6; Crescent City Blues #1 and Marvel Shadow and Light #1 16.00
San Diego Con Promo (6/97) Wesley Snipes photo-c 3.00
...Sins of the Father (10/98, $5.99) Sears-a; movie adaption 6.00
Blade 2: Movie Adaptation (5/02, $5.95) Ponticelli-a/Bradstreet-c 6.00

BLADE (The Vampire Hunter)
Marvel Comics: Nov, 1998 - No. 3, Jan, 1999 ($3.50/$2.99)

1-($3.50) Contains Movie insider pages; McKean-a 4.00
2,3-($2.99): 2-Two covers 3.00

BLADE (Volume 2)
Marvel Comics (MAX): May, 2002 -No. 6, Oct, 2002 ($2.99)

1-6-Bradstreet-c/Hinz-s. 1-5-Pugh-a. 6-Homs-a 3.00

BLADE
Marvel Comics: Nov, 2006 - No. 12, Oct, 2007 ($2.99)

1-12: 1-Chaykin-a/Guggenheim-s; origin retold; Spider-Man app. 2-Dr. Doom-c/app. 5-Civil War tie-in; Wolverine app. 6-Blade loses a hand. 10-Spider-Man app. 3.00
...: Sins of the Father TPB (2007, $14.99) r/#7-12; afterword by Guggenheim 15.00
...: Undead Again TPB (2007, $14.99) r/#1-6; letters pages from #1&2 15.00

BLADE OF THE IMMORTAL (Manga)
Dark Horse Comics: June, 1996 - No. 131, Nov, 2007 ($2.95/$2.99/$3.95, B&W)

1-Hiroaki Samura-s/a in all 1 3 4 6 8 10
2-5: 2-#1 on cover in error 6.00
6-10 5.00
11,19,20,34-($3.95, 48 pgs.): 34-Food one-shot 4.00
12-18,21-33,35-41,43-105,107-131: 12-20-Dreamsong. 21-28-On Silent Wings. 29-33-Dark Shadow. 35-42-Heart of Darkness. 43-57-The Gathering 3.00
42-($3.50) Ends Heart of Darkness 3.50
106-($3.99) 4.00

BLADE RUNNER (Movie)
Marvel Comics Group: Oct, 1982 - No. 2, Nov, 1982

1,2-r/Marvel Super Special #22; 1-Williamson-c/a. 2-Williamson-a
1 3 4 6 8 10

BLADE: THE VAMPIRE-HUNTER
Marvel Comics: July, 1994 - No. 10, Apr, 1995 ($1.95)

1-($2.95)-Foil-c; Dracula returns; Wheatley-c/a 4.00
2-10: 2,3,10-Dracula-c/app. 8-Morbius app. 3.00

BLADE: VAMPIRE-HUNTER
Marvel Comics: Dec, 1999 - No. 6, May, 2000 ($3.50/$2.50)

1-($3.50)-Bart Sears-s; Sears and Smith-a 4.00
2-6-($2.50): 2-Regular & Wesley Snipes photo-c 3.00

BLAIR WITCH CHRONICLES, THE
Oni Press: Mar, 2000 - No. 4, July, 2000 ($2.95, B&W, limited series)

1-4-Van Meter-s.1-Guy Davis-a. 2-Mireault-a 3.00
1-DF Alternate-c by John Estes 4.00
TPB (9/00, $15.95) r/#1-4 & Blair Witch Project one-shot 16.00

BLAIR WITCH: DARK TESTAMENTS
Image Comics: Oct, 2000 ($2.95, one-shot)

1-Edington-s/Adlard-a; story of murderer Rustin Parr 3.00

BLAIR WITCH PROJECT, THE (Movie companion, not adaptation)
Oni Press: July, 1999 ($2.95, B&W, one-shot)

1-(1st printing) History of the Blair Witch, art by Edwards, Mireault, and Davis; Van Meter-s; only the stick figure is red on the cover 5.00
1-(2nd printing) Stick figure and title lettering are red on cover 4.00
1-(3rd printing) Stick figure, title, and creator credits are red on cover 3.00
DF Glow in the Dark variant-c ($10.00) 10.00

BLAST (Satire Magazine)
G & D Publications: Feb, 1971 - No. 2, May, 1971

1-Wrightson & Kaluta-a/Everette-c 7 14 21 48 89 130
2-Kaluta-c/a 5 10 15 35 63 90

BLAST CORPS
Dark Horse Comics: Oct, 1998 ($2.50, one-shot, based on Nintendo game)

1-Reprints from Nintendo Power magazine; Mahn-a 3.00

BLASTERS SPECIAL
DC Comics: 1989 ($2.00, one-shot)

1-Peter David scripts; Invasion spin-off 4.00

BLAST-OFF (Three Rocketeers)
Harvey Publications (Fun Day Funnies): Oct, 1965 (12¢)

1-Kirby/Williamson-a(2); Williamson/Crandall-a; Williamson/Torres/Krenkel-a; Kirby/Simon-c
6 12 18 41 76 110

BLAZE
Marvel Comics: Aug, 1994 - No. 12, July, 1995 ($1.95)

1-($2.95)-Foil embossed-c 4.00
2-12: 2-Man-Thing-c/story. 11,12-Punisher app. 3.00

BLAZE CARSON (Rex Hart #6 on)(See Kid Colt, Tex Taylor, Wild Western, Wisco)
Marvel Comics (USA): Sept, 1948 - No. 5, June, 1949

1-Tex Taylor app.; Shores-c 31 62 93 182 296 410
2,4,5: 2-Tex Morgan app.; Shores-c. 4-Two-Gun Kid app. 5-Tex Taylor app.
20 40 60 114 182 250
3-Used by N.Y. State Legis. Comm. (injury to eye splash); Tex Morgan app.
20 40 60 118 192 265

BLAZE: LEGACY OF BLOOD (See Ghost Rider & Ghost Rider/Blaze)
Marvel Comics (Midnight Sons imprint): Dec, 1993 - No. 4, Mar, 1994 ($1.75, limited series)

1-4 3.00

BLAZE OF GLORY
Marvel Comics: Feb, 2000 - No. 4, Mar, 2000 ($2.99, limited series)

1-4-Ostrander-s/Manco-a; Two-Gun Kid, Rawhide Kid, Red Wolf and Ghost Rider app. 3.00
TPB (7/02, $9.99) r/#1-4 10.00

BLAZE THE WONDER COLLIE (Formerly Molly Manton's Romances #1?)
Marvel Comics(SePI): No. 2, Oct, 1949 - No. 3, Feb, 1950 (Both have photo-c)

2(#1), 3-(Scarce) 28 56 84 165 270 375

BLAZING BATTLE TALES
Seaboard Periodicals (Atlas): July, 1975

1-Intro. Sgt. Hawk & the Sky Demon; Severin, McWilliams, Sparling-a; Nazi-c by Thorne
3 6 9 14 19 24

BLAZING COMBAT (Magazine)
Warren Publishing Co.: Oct, 1965 - No. 4, July, 1966 (35¢, B&W)

1-Frazetta painted-c on all 25 50 75 175 388 600
2 8 16 24 51 96 140
3,4: 4-Frazetta half pg. ad 7 14 21 44 82 120
nn-Anthology (reprints from No. 1-4) (low print) 8 16 24 51 96 140

NOTE: ***Adkins** a-4. **Colan** a-3,4,nn. **Crandall** a-all. **Evans** a-1,4. **Heath** a-4,nn. **Morrow** a-1-3,nn. **Orlando** a-1-3,nn. **J. Severin** a-all. **Torres** a-1-4. **Toth** a-all. **Williamson** a-2. and **Wood** a-3,4,nn.*

BLAZING COMBAT: WORLD WAR I AND WORLD WAR II
Apple Press: Mar, 1994 ($3.75, B&W)

1,2: 1-r/Colan, Toth, Goodwin, Severin, Wood-a. 2-r/Crandall, Evans, Severin, Torres, Williamson-a 4.00

BLAZING COMICS (Also see Blue Circle Comics and Red Circle Comics)
Enwil Associates/Rural Home: 6/44 - #3, 9/44; #4, 2/45; #5, 3/45; #5(V2#2), 3/55 - #6(V2#3), 1955?

1-The Green Turtle, Red Hawk, Black Buccaneer begin; origin Jun-Gal; classic Japanese WWII splash 57 114 171 362 619 875
2-5: 3-Briefer-a. 5-(V2#2 inside) 39 78 117 231 378 525
5(3/55, V2#2-inside)-Black Buccaneer-c, 6(V2#3-inside, 1955)-Indian/Japanese-c; cover is from Apr. 1945 21 42 63 126 206 285

NOTE: *No. 5 & 6 contain remaindered comics rebound and the contents can vary. Cloak & Dagger, Will Rogers, Superman 64, Star Spangled 130, Kaanga known. Value would be half of contents.*

BLAZING SIXGUNS
Avon Periodicals: Dec, 1952

1-Kinstler-c/a; Larsen/Alascia-a(2), Tuska?-a; Jesse James, Kit Carson, Wild Bill Hickok app. 20 40 60 114 182 250

BLAZING SIXGUNS
I.W./Super Comics: 1964

I.W. Reprint #1,8,9: 1-r/Wild Bill Hickok #26, Western True Crime #? & Blazing Sixguns #1 by Avon; Kinstler-c. 8-r/Blazing Western #?; Kinstler-c. 9-r/Blazing Western #1; Ditko-r; Kintsler-c reprinted from Dalton Boys #1 2 4 6 10 14 18
Super Reprint #10,11,15-17: 10,11-r/The Rider #2,1. 15-r/Silver Kid Western #?. 16-r/Buffalo Bill #?; Wildey-r; Severin-c. 17(1964)-r/Western True Crime #?
2 4 6 10 14 18
12-Reprints Bullseye #3; S&K-a 3 6 9 18 28 38
18-r/Straight Arrow #? by Powell; Severin-c 2 4 6 10 14 18

BLAZING SIX-GUNS (Also see Sundance Kid)
Skywald Comics: Feb, 1971 - No. 2, Apr, 1971 (52 pgs.)

Blazing West #7 © ACG

Blitzkrieg #4 © DC

Blood Blister #1 © Hester & Harris

	GD 2.0	VG 4.0	FN 6.0	VF 8.0	VF/NM 9.0	NM- 9.2
1-The Red Mask (3-D effect, not true 3-D), Sundance Kid begin (new-s), Avon's Geronimo reprint by Kinstler; Wyatt Earp app.	3	6	9	14	20	25
2-Wild Bill Hickok, Jesse James, Kit Carson-r plus M.E. Red Mask-r (3-D effect)	2	4	6	10	14	18

BLAZING WEST (The Hooded Horseman #21 on)(52 pgs.)
American Comics Group (B&I Publ./Michel Publ.): Fall, 1948 - No. 20, Nov-Dec, 1951

	GD 2.0	VG 4.0	FN 6.0	VF 8.0	VF/NM 9.0	NM- 9.2
1-Origin & 1st app. Injun Jones, Tenderfoot & Buffalo Belle; Texas Tim & Ranger begins, ends #13	20	40	60	120	195	270
2,3 (1-2/49)	12	24	36	67	94	120
4-Origin & 1st app. Little Lobo; Starr-a (3-4/49)	11	22	33	60	83	105
5-10: 5-Starr-a	9	18	27	52	69	85
11-13	8	16	24	44	57	70
14(11-12/50)-Origin/1st app. The Hooded Horseman	14	28	42	80	115	150
15-20: 15,16,18,19-Starr-a	9	18	27	52	69	85

BLAZING WESTERN
Timor Publications: Jan, 1954 - No. 5, Sept, 1954

	GD 2.0	VG 4.0	FN 6.0	VF 8.0	VF/NM 9.0	NM- 9.2
1-Ditko-a (1st Western-a?); text story by Bruce Hamilton	20	40	60	118	192	265
2-4	10	20	30	54	72	90
5-Disbrow-a; L.B. Cole-c	10	20	30	56	76	95

BLINDSIDE
Image Comics (Extreme Studios): Aug, 1996 ($2.50)

1-Variant-c exists 3.00

BLINK (See X-Men Age of Apocalypse storyline)
Marvel Comics: March, 2001 - No. 4, June, 2001 ($2.99, limited series)

1-4-Adam Kubert-c/Lobdell-s/Winick-script; leads into Exiles #1 3.00

BLIP
Marvel Comics Group: 2/1983 - 1983 (Video game mag. in comic format)

	GD 2.0	VG 4.0	FN 6.0	VF 8.0	VF/NM 9.0	NM- 9.2
1-1st app. Donkey Kong & Mario Bros. in comics, 6pgs. comics; photo-c	2	3	4	6	8	10
2-Spider-Man photo-c; 6pgs. Spider-Man comics w/Green Goblin	2	4	6	8	10	12
3,4,6						6.00
5-E.T., Indiana Jones; Rocky-c	1	2	3	4	5	7
7-6pgs. Hulk comics; Pac-Man & Donkey Kong Jr. Hints	1	2	3	5	6	8

BLISS ALLEY
Image Comics: July, 1997 - No. 2, Sept, 1997 ($2.95, B&W)

1,2-Messner-Loebs-s/a 3.00

BLITZKRIEG
National Periodical Publications: Jan-Feb, 1976 - No. 5, Sept-Oct, 1976

	GD 2.0	VG 4.0	FN 6.0	VF 8.0	VF/NM 9.0	NM- 9.2
1-Kubert-c on all	4	8	12	25	40	55
2-5	3	6	9	16	24	32

BLOCKBUSTERS OF THE MARVEL UNIVERSE
Marvel Comics: March, 2011 ($4.99, one-shot)

1-Handbook-style summaries of Marvel crossover events like Civil War & Heroes Reborn 5.00

BLONDE PHANTOM (Formerly All-Select #1-11; Lovers #23 on)(Also see Blackstone, Marvel Mystery, Millie The Model #2, Sub-Mariner Comics #25 & Sun Girl)
Marvel Comics (MPC): No. 12, Winter, 1946-47 - No. 22, Mar, 1949

	GD 2.0	VG 4.0	FN 6.0	VF 8.0	VF/NM 9.0	NM- 9.2
12-Miss America begins, ends #14	206	412	618	1318	2259	3200
13-Sub-Mariner begins (not in #16)	119	238	357	762	1306	1850
14,15: 15-Kurtzman's "Hey Look"	113	226	339	718	1234	1750
16-Captain America with Bucky story by Rico(p), 6 pgs.; Kurtzman's "Hey Look" (1 pg.)	142	284	426	909	1555	2200
17-22: 22-Anti Wertham editorial	100	200	300	635	1093	1550

NOTE: *Shores c-12-18.*

BLONDIE (See Ace Comics, Comics Reading Libraries (Promotional Comics section), Dagwood, Daisy & Her Pups, Eat Right to Work..., King & Magic Comics)
David McKay Publications: 1942 - 1946

	GD 2.0	VG 4.0	FN 6.0	VF 8.0	VF/NM 9.0	NM- 9.2
Feature Books 12 (Rare)	89	178	267	565	970	1375
Feature Books 27-29,31,34(1940)	22	44	66	128	209	290
Feature Books 36,38,40,42,43,45,47	20	40	60	114	182	250
...1944 (Hard-c, 1938, B&W, 128 pgs.)-1944 daily strip-r	16	32	48	94	147	200

BLONDIE & DAGWOOD FAMILY
Harvey Publ. (King Features Synd.): Oct, 1963 - No. 4, Dec, 1965 (68 pgs.)

	GD 2.0	VG 4.0	FN 6.0	VF 8.0	VF/NM 9.0	NM- 9.2
1	5	10	15	30	50	70
2-4	3	6	9	19	30	40

BLONDIE COMICS (...Monthly No. 16-141)
David McKay #1-15/Harvey #16-163/King #164-175/Charlton #177 on:
Spring, 1947 - No. 163, Nov, 1965; No. 164, Aug, 1966 - No. 175, Dec, 1967; No. 177, Feb, 1969 - No. 222, Nov, 1976

	GD 2.0	VG 4.0	FN 6.0	VF 8.0	VF/NM 9.0	NM- 9.2
1	40	80	120	246	411	575
2	20	40	60	114	182	250
3-5	15	30	45	90	140	190
6-10	14	28	42	80	115	150
11-15	10	20	30	56	76	95
16-(3/50; 1st Harvey issue)	11	22	33	62	86	110
17-20: 20-(3/51)-Becomes Daisy & Her Pups #21 & Chamber of Chills #21	5	10	15	34	60	85
21-30	5	10	15	31	53	75
31-50	4	8	12	27	44	60
51-80	4	8	12	23	37	50
81-99	3	6	9	21	33	45
100	4	8	12	25	40	55
101-124,126-130	3	6	9	17	26	35
125 (80 pgs.)	4	8	12	27	44	60
131-136,138,139	3	6	9	16	24	32
137,140-(80 pgs.)	4	8	12	25	40	55
141-147,149-154,156,160,164-167	3	6	9	16	23	30
148,155,157-159,161-163 are 68 pgs.	3	6	9	21	33	45
168-175	2	4	6	11	16	20
177-199 (no #176)-Moon landing-c/s	2	4	6	9	13	16
200-Anniversary issue; highlights of the Bumsteads	2	4	6	10	14	18
201-210,213-222	2	4	6	8	10	12
211,212-1st & 2nd app. Super Dagwood	2	4	6	9	13	16
Blondie, Dagwood & Daisy by Chic Young #1(Harvey, 1953, 100 pg. squarebound giant) new stories; Popeye (1 pg.) and Felix (1pg.) app.	36	72	108	211	343	475

BLOOD
Marvel Comics (Epic Comics): Feb, 1988 - No. 4, Apr, 1988 ($3.25, mature)

1-4: DeMatteis scripts & Kent Williams-c/a 5.00

BLOOD AND GLORY (Punisher & Captain America)
Marvel Comics: Oct, 1992 - No. 3, Dec, 1992 ($5.95, limited series)

1-3: 1-Embossed wraparound-c by Janson; Chichester & Clarke-s 6.00

BLOOD & ROSES: FUTURE PAST TENSE (Bob Hickey's...)
Sky Comics: Dec, 1993 ($2.25)

1-Silver ink logo 3.00

BLOOD & ROSES: SEARCH FOR THE TIME-STONE (Bob Hickey's...)
Sky Comics: Apr, 1994 ($2.50)

1 3.00

BLOOD AND SHADOWS
DC Comics (Vertigo): 1996 - Book 4, 1996 ($5.95, squarebound, mature)

Books 1-4: Joe R. Lansdale scripts; Mark A. Nelson-c/a. 6.00

BLOOD AND WATER
DC Comics (Vertigo): May, 2003 - No. 5, Sept, 2003 ($2.95, limited series)

1-5-Judd Winick-s/Tomm Coker-a/Brian Bolland-c 3.00
TPB (2009, $14.99) r/#1-5 15.00

BLOOD: A TALE
DC Comics (Vertigo): Nov, 1996 - No. 4, Feb, 1997 ($2.95, limited series)

1-4: Reprints Epic series w/new-c; DeMatteis scripts; Kent Williams-c/a 3.00
TPB (2004, $19.95) r/#1-4 20.00

BLOODBATH
DC Comics: Early Dec, 1993 - No. 2, Late Dec, 1993 ($3.50, 68 pgs.)

	GD 2.0	VG 4.0	FN 6.0	VF 8.0	VF/NM 9.0	NM- 9.2
1-Neon ink-c; Superman app.; new Batman-c /app.						4.00
2-Hitman 2nd app.	1	2	3	4	5	7

BLOOD BLISTER
AfterShock Comics: Jan, 2017 - Present ($3.99)

1-Phil Hester-s/Tony Harris-a 4.00

BLOODHOUND
DC Comics: Sept, 2004 - No. 10, June, 2005 ($2.95)

1-10: 1-Jolley-s/Kirk-a/Johnson-c. 5-Firestorm app. (cont. from Firestorm #7) 3.00

BLOODHOUND: CROWBAR MEDICINE
Dark Horse Comics: Oct, 2013 - No. 5, Mar, 2014 ($3.99)

1-5-Jolley-s/Kirk-a/c 4.00

Bloodlines #6 © DC

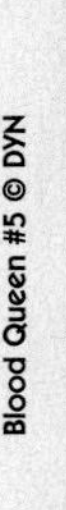
Blood Queen #5 © DYN

Bloodshot Reborn #2 © VAL

GD VG FN VF VF/NM NM-
2.0 4.0 6.0 8.0 9.0 9.2

GD VG FN VF VF/NM NM-
2.0 4.0 6.0 8.0 9.0 9.2

BLOOD LEGACY
Image Comics (Top Cow): May, 2000 - No. 4, Nov, 2000; Apr, 2003 ($2.50/$4.99)
...: The Story of Ryan 1-4-Kerri Hawkins-s. 1-Andy Park-a(p); 3 covers 3.00
...: The Young Ones 1 (4/03, $4.99, one-shot) Basaldua-c/a 5.00
Preview Special ('00, $4.95) B&W flip-book w/The Magdalena Preview 5.00

BLOODLINES
DC Comics: Jun, 2016 - No. 6, Nov, 2016 ($2.99, limited series)
1-6: 1-Krul-s/Marion-a 3.00

BLOODLINES: A TALE FROM THE HEART OF AFRICA (See Tales From the Heart of Africa)
Marvel Comics (Epic Comics): 1992 ($5.95, 52 pgs.)
1-Story cont'd from Tales From… 6.00

BLOOD OF DRACULA
Apple Comics: Nov, 1987 - No. 20?, 1990 ($1.75/$1.95, B&W)($2.25 #14,16 on)
1-3,5-14,20: 1-10-Chadwick-c 4.00
4,16-19-Lost Frankenstein pgs. by Wrightson 1 2 3 4 5 7
15-Contains stereo flexidisc ($3.75) 5.00

BLOOD OF THE DEMON (Etrigan the Demon)
DC Comics: May, 2005 - No. 17, Sept, 2006 ($2.50/$2.99)
1-14-Byrne-a(p) & plot/Pfeifer-script. 3,4-Batman app. 13-One Year Later 3.00
15-17-($2.99) 3.00

BLOOD OF THE INNOCENT (See Warp Graphics Annual)
WaRP Graphics: 1/7/86 - No. 4, 1/28/86 (Weekly mini-series, mature)
1-4 3.00

BLOODPACK
DC Comics: Mar, 1995 - No. 4, June,1995 ($1.50, limited series)
1-4 3.00

BLOODPOOL
Image Comics (Extreme): Aug, 1995 - No. 4, Nov, 1995 ($2.50, limited series)
1-4: Jo Duffy scripts in all 3.00
Special (3/96, $2.50)-Jo Duffy scripts 3.00
Trade Paperback (1996, $12.95)-r/#1-4 13.00

BLOOD QUEEN, THE
Dynamite Entertainment: 2014 - No. 6, 2014 ($3.99, limited series)
1-6-Brownfield-s/Casas-a/Anacleto-c; variant covers on each 4.00
Annual 2014 ($7.99) Prequel stories to the series 8.00

BLOOD QUEEN VS. DRACULA
Dynamite Entertainment: 2015 - No. 4, 2015 ($3.99, limited series)
1-4-Brownfield-s/Baal-a/Anacleto-c; variant covers on each 4.00

BLOOD RED DRAGON (Stan Lee and Yoshiki's...)
Image Comics: No. 0, Aug, 2011 - No. 3, Nov, 2011 ($3.99)
0-3-Goff-s/Soriano-a 4.00

BLOODSCENT
Comico: Oct, 1988 ($2.00, one-shot, Baxter paper)
1-Colan-p 3.00

BLOODSEED
Marvel Comics (Frontier Comics): Oct, 1993 - No. 2, Nov, 1993 ($1.95)
1,2: Sharp/Cam Smith-a 3.00

BLOODSHOT (See Eternal Warrior #4 & Rai #0)
Valiant/Acclaim Comics (Valiant): Feb, 1993 - No. 51, Aug, 1996 ($2.25/$2.50)
0-(3/94, $3.50)-Wraparound chromium-c by Quesada(p); origin 5.00
0-Gold variant; no cover price 30.00
Note: There is a "Platinum variant" ; press run error of Gold ed. (25 copies exist)
(A CGC certified 9.8 copy sold for $2,067 in 2004)
1-($3.50)-Chromium embossed-c by B. Smith w/poster
1 2 3 5 6 8
2-5,8-14: 3-$2.25-c begins; cont'd in Hard Corps #5. 4-Eternal Warrior-c/story. 5-Rai & Eternal Warrior app. 14-(3/94)-Reese-c(i) 4.00
6,7: 6-1st app. Ninjak (out of costume). 7-Ninjak in costume
1 3 4 6 8 10
15(4/94)-50: 16-w/bound-in trading card 3.00
51-Bloodshot dies? 3 6 9 19 30 40
Yearbook 1 (1994, $3.95) 4.00
Special 1 (3/94, $5.95)-Zeck-c/a(p); Last Stand 6.00
...: Blood of the Machine HC (2012, $24.99) r/#1-8; new 8 pg. story; intro. by VanHook 25.00

BLOODSHOT (Volume Two)
Acclaim Comics (Valiant): July, 1997 - No. 16, Oct, 1998 ($2.50)
1-16: 1-Two covers. 5-Copycat-c. X-O Manowar-c/app 3.00

BLOODSHOT (Re-titled Bloodshot and H.A.R.D.Corps for #14-23)
Valiant Entertainment: July, 2012 - No. 25, Nov, 2014 ($3.99)
1-13: 1-Sweirczynski-s/Garcia & Lozzi-a. 10-13-Harbinger Wars tie-ins 4.00
1-9-Pullbox variants 4.00
1-Variant-c by David Aja 15.00
1-Variant-c by Esad Ribic 20.00
14-24: 14-23-Bloodshot and H.A.R.D.Corps 4.00
25-($4.99) Milligan-s/Larosa-a; back-up Chaykin-s/a; short features by various 5.00
#0 (8/13) Kindt-s/ChrisCross-a; covers by Lupacchino & Bullock 4.00
Bloodshot and H.A.R.D.Corps #0 (2/14, $3.99) History of Project Rising Spirit 4.00

BLOODSHOT REBORN
Valiant Entertainment: Apr, 2015 - No. 18, Oct, 2016 ($3.99)
1-18: 1-4-Lemire-s/Suayan-a. 1-1st app. Bloodsquirt. 6-9-Guice-a. 10-13-Set 30 years later. 14-1st app. Deathmate 4.00
Annual 2016 #1 (3/16, $5.99) Short stories by various incl. Kano, Lemire, Bennett 6.00
...: Bloodshot Island - Director's Cut 1 (6/16, $4.99) r/#1 in B&W; original script 5.00

BLOODSHOT U.S.A.
Valiant Entertainment: Oct, 2016 - No. 4, Jan, 2017 ($3.99, limited series)
1-4-Lemire-s/Braithwaite-a; Ninjak and Deathmate app. 4.00

BLOODSTONE
Marvel Comics: Dec, 2001 - No. 4, Mar, 2002 ($2.99)
1-4-Intro. Elsa Bloodstone; Abnett & Lanning-s/Lopez-a 3.00

BLOODSTREAM
Image Comics: Jan, 2004 - No. 4, Dec, 2004 ($2.95)
1-4-Adam Shaw painted-a 3.00

BLOODSTRIKE (See Supreme V2#3)
Image Comics (Extreme Studios): 1993 - No. 22, May, 1995; No. 25, May, 1994 ($1.95/$2.50)
1-22, 25: Liefeld layouts in early issues. 1-Blood Brothers prelude. 2-1st app. Lethal. 5-1st app. Noble. 9-Black and White part 6 by Art Thibert; Liefeld pin-up. 9,10-Have coupon #3 & 7 for Extreme Prejudice #0. 10-(4/94). 11-(7/94). 16:Platt-c; Prophet app. 17-19-polybagged w/card . 25-(5/94)-Liefeld/Fraga-c 3.00
NOTE: *Giffen story/layouts-4-6.* ***Jae Lee*** *c-7, 8.* ***Rob Liefeld*** *layouts-1-3.* ***Art Thibert*** *c-6i.*

BLOODSTRIKE
Image Comics: No. 26, Mar, 2012 - No. 33, Dec, 2012 ($2.99/$3.99)
26-29: 26-Two covers by Seeley & Liefeld; Seeley-s/Gaston-a 3.00
30-33-($3.99) 32,33-Suprema app. 4.00

BLOODSTRIKE (Volume 2)
Image Comics: Jul, 2015 - Present ($2.99/$3.99)
1-($3.99) Liefeld-s/a 4.00
2-(9/15, $2.99) Liefeld-s/a 3.00

BLOODSTRIKE ASSASSIN
Image Comics (Extreme Studios): June, 1995 - No. 3, Aug, 1995; No. 0, Oct, 1995 ($2.50, limited series)
0-3: 3-(8/95)-Quesada-c. 0-(10/95)-Battlestone app. 3.00

BLOOD SWORD, THE
Jademan Comics: Aug, 1988 - No. 53, Dec, 1992 ($1.50/$1.95, 68 pgs.)
1-53-Kung Fu stories in all 4.00

BLOOD SWORD DYNASTY
Jademan Comics: 1989 -No. 41, Jan, 1993 ($1.25, 36 pgs.)
1-Ties into Blood Sword 4.00
2-41: Ties into Blood Sword 3.00

BLOOD SYNDICATE
DC Comics (Milestone): Apr, 1993 - No. 35, Feb, 1996 ($1.50/-$3.50)
1-($2.95)-Collector's Edition; polybagged with poster, trading card, & acid-free backing board (direct sale only) 4.00
1-9,11-24,26,27,29,33-34: 8-Intro Kwai. 15-Byrne-c. 16-Worlds Collide Pt. 6; Superman-c/app. 17-Worlds Collide Pt. 13. 29-(99¢); Long Hot Summer x-over 3.00
10,28,30-32: 10-Simonson-c. 30-Long Hot Summer x-over 3.00
25-($2.95, 52 pgs.) 4.00
35-Kwai disappears; last issue 4.00

BLOODWULF
Image Comics (Extreme): Feb, 1995 - No. 4, May, 1995 ($2.50, limited series)
1-4: 1-Liefeld-c w/4 diferent captions & alternate-c. 3.00
Summer Special (8/95, $2.50)-Jeff Johnson-c/a; Supreme app; story takes place

Bloody Mary #2 © Ennis & Ezquerra

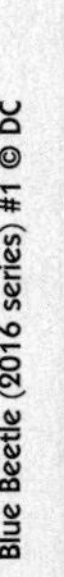

Blue Beetle (2016 series) #1 © DC

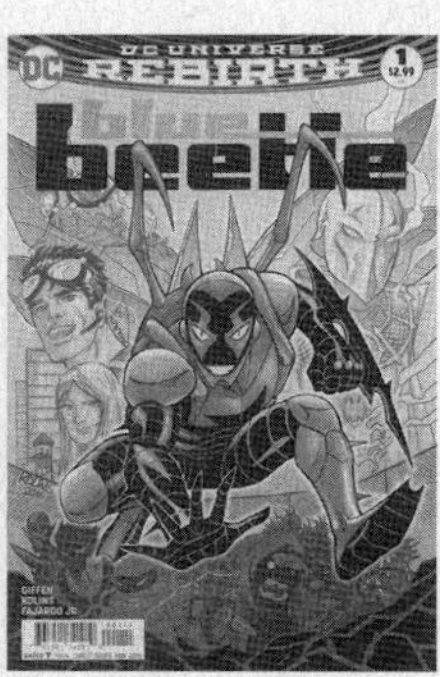

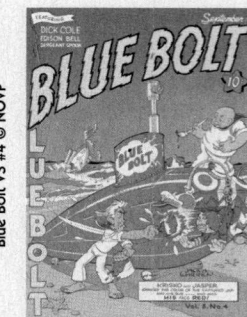

Blue Bolt V3 #4 © NOVP

	GD 2.0	VG 4.0	FN 6.0	VF 8.0	VF/NM 9.0	NM- 9.2
between Legend of Supreme #3 & Supreme #23.						3.00

BLOODY MARY
DC Comics (Helix): Oct, 1996 - No. 4, Jan, 1997 ($2.25, limited series)

	GD 2.0	VG 4.0	FN 6.0	VF 8.0	VF/NM 9.0	NM- 9.2
1-4: Garth Ennis scripts; Ezquerra-c/a in all						3.50
TPB (2005, $19.99) r/#1-4 and Bloody Mary: Lady Liberty #1-4						20.00

BLOODY MARY: LADY LIBERTY
DC Comics (Helix): Sept, 1997 - No. 4, Dec, 1997 ($2.50, limited series)

	GD 2.0	VG 4.0	FN 6.0	VF 8.0	VF/NM 9.0	NM- 9.2
1-4: Garth Ennis scripts; Ezquerra-c/a in all						3.00

BLUE
Image Comics (Action Toys): Aug, 1999 - No. 2, Apr, 2000 ($2.50)

	GD 2.0	VG 4.0	FN 6.0	VF 8.0	VF/NM 9.0	NM- 9.2
1,2-Aronowitz-s/Struzan-c						3.00

BLUEBEARD
Slave Labor Graphics: Nov, 1993 - No. 3, Mar, 1994 ($2.95, B&W, lim. series)

	GD 2.0	VG 4.0	FN 6.0	VF 8.0	VF/NM 9.0	NM- 9.2
1-3: James Robinson scripts. 2-(12/93)						3.00
Trade paperback (6/94, $9.95)						13.00
Trade paperback (2nd printing, 7/96, $12.95)-New-c						13.00

BLUE BEETLE, THE (Also see All Top, Big-3, Mystery Men & Weekly Comic Magazine)
Fox Publ. No. 1-11, 31-60; Holyoke No. 12-30: Winter, 1939-40 - No. 57, 7/48; No. 58, 4/50 - No. 60, 8/50

	GD 2.0	VG 4.0	FN 6.0	VF 8.0	VF/NM 9.0	NM- 9.2
1-Reprints from Mystery Men #1-5; Blue Beetle origin; Yarko the Great-r/from Wonder Comics /Wonderworld #2-5 all by Eisner; Master Magician app.; (Blue Beetle in 4 different costumes)	514	1028	1542	3750	6625	9500
2-K-51-r by Powell/Wonderworld #8,9	239	478	717	1530	2615	3700
3-Simon-c	161	322	483	1030	1765	2500
4-Marijuana drug mention story	119	238	357	762	1306	1850
5-Zanzibar The Magician by Tuska	97	194	291	621	1061	1500
6-Dynamite Thor begins (1st); origin Blue Beetle	94	188	282	597	1024	1450
7,8-Dynamo app. in both. 8-Last Thor	90	180	270	576	988	1400
9-12: 9,10-The Blackbird & The Gorilla app. 10-Bondage/hypo-c. 11(2/42)-Bondage-c; The Gladiator app. 12(6/42)-The Black Fury app.	81	162	243	518	884	1250
13-V-Man begins (1st app.), ends #19; Kubert-a; centerfold spread	84	168	252	538	919	1300
14,15-Kubert-a in both. 14-Intro. side-kick (c/text only), Sparky (called Spunky #17-19); BB vs. The Red Robe (Red Skull swipe)	74	148	222	470	810	1150
16-18: 17-Brodsky-c	57	114	171	362	619	875
19-Kubert-a	58	116	174	371	636	900
20-Origin/1st app. Tiger Squadron; Arabian Nights begin	60	120	180	381	653	925
21-26: 24-Intro. & only app. The Halo. 26-General Patton story & photo	50	100	150	315	533	750
27-Tamaa, Jungle Prince app.	43	86	129	271	461	650
28-30(2/44): 29-WWII Nazi bondage-c(1/44)	41	82	123	256	428	600
31(6/44), 33,34,36-40: 34-38-"The Threat from Saturn" serial. 40-Shows #20 in indicia	36	72	108	211	343	475
32-Hitler-c	116	232	348	742	1271	1800
35-Extreme violence	40	80	120	246	411	575
41-45 (#43 exist?)	34	68	102	206	336	465
46-The Puppeteer app.	39	78	117	231	378	525
47-Kamen & Baker-a begin	174	348	522	1114	1907	2700
48-50	126	252	378	806	1378	1950
51,53	110	220	330	704	1202	1700
52-Kamen bondage-c; true crime stories begin	181	362	543	1158	1979	2800
54-Used in **SOTI**. Illo, "Children call these 'headlights' comics"; classic-c	400	800	1200	2800	4900	7000
55-57: 56-Used in **SOTI**, pg. 145. 57(7/48)-Last Kamen issue; becomes Western Killers?	107	214	321	680	1165	1650
58(4/50)-60-No Kamen-a	23	46	69	136	223	310

NOTE: ***Kamen** a-47-51, 53, 55-57; c-47, 49-52. **Powell** a-4(2). Bondage-c 9-12, 46, 52. Headlight-c 46, 48, 57.*

BLUE BEETLE (Formerly The Thing; becomes Mr. Muscles No. 22 on) (See Charlton Bullseye & Space Adventures)
Charlton Comics: No. 18, Feb, 1955 - No. 21, Aug, 1955

	GD 2.0	VG 4.0	FN 6.0	VF 8.0	VF/NM 9.0	NM- 9.2
18,19-(Pre-1944-r). 18-Last pre-code issue. 19-Bouncer, Rocket Kelly-r	23	46	69	136	223	310
20-Joan Mason by Kamen	29	58	87	170	278	385
21-New material	22	44	66	132	216	300

BLUE BEETLE (Unusual Tales #1-49; Ghostly Tales #55 on)(See Captain Atom #83 & Charlton Bullseye)
Charlton Comics: V2#1, June, 1964 - V2#5, Mar-Apr, 1965; V3#50, July, 1965 - V3#54, Feb-Mar, 1966; #1, June, 1967 - #5, Nov, 1968

	GD 2.0	VG 4.0	FN 6.0	VF 8.0	VF/NM 9.0	NM- 9.2
V2#1-Origin/1st S.A. app. Dan Garrett-Blue Beetle	21	42	63	147	324	500
2-5: 5-Weiss illo; 1st published-a?	6	12	18	37	66	95
V3#50-54-Formerly Unusual Tales	5	10	15	34	60	85
1(1967)-Question series begins by Ditko	19	38	57	131	291	450
2-Origin Ted Kord-Blue Beetle (see Capt. Atom #83 for 1st Ted Kord Blue Beetle); Dan Garrett x-over	7	14	21	44	82	120
3-5 (All Ditko-c/a in #1-5)	6	12	18	37	66	95
1,3(Modern Comics-1977)-Reprints	2	4	6	9	12	15

NOTE: *#6 only appeared in the fanzine 'The Charlton Portfolio.'*

BLUE BEETLE (Also see Americomics, Crisis On Infinite Earths, Justice League & Showcase '94 #2-4)
DC Comics: June, 1986 - No. 24, May, 1988

	GD 2.0	VG 4.0	FN 6.0	VF 8.0	VF/NM 9.0	NM- 9.2
1-Origin retold; intro. Firefist						5.00
2-10,15-19,21-24: 2-Origin Firefist. 5-7-The Question app. 21-Millennium tie-in						3.00
11-14-New Teen Titans x-over						3.50
20-Justice League app.; Millennium tie-in						3.50

BLUE BEETLE (See Infinite Crisis, Teen Titans, and Booster Gold #21)
DC Comics: May, 2006 - No. 36, Apr, 2009 ($2.99)

	GD 2.0	VG 4.0	FN 6.0	VF 8.0	VF/NM 9.0	NM- 9.2
1-Hamner-a/Giffen & Rogers-s; Guy Gardner app.						4.00
1-2nd & 3rd printings						3.00
2-36: 2-2nd printing exists. 2-4-Oracle app. 5-Phantom Stranger app. 16-Eclipso app. 18,33-Teen Titans app. 20-Sinestro Corps. 21-Spectre app. 26-Spanish issue						3.00
...: Black and Blue TPB (2010, $17.99) r/#27,28,35,36 & Booster Gold #21-25,28,29						18.00
...: Boundaries TPB (2009, $14.99) r/#29-34						15.00
...: End Game TPB (2008, $14.99) r/#20-26; English script for #26						15.00
...: Reach For the Stars TPB (2008, $14.99) r/#13-19						15.00
...: Road Trip TPB (2007, $12.99) r/#7-12						13.00
...: Shellshocked TPB (2006, $12.99) r/#1-6						13.00

BLUE BEETLE (DC New 52) (Also see Threshold)
DC Comics: Nov, 2011 - No. 16, Mar, 2013 ($2.99)

	GD 2.0	VG 4.0	FN 6.0	VF 8.0	VF/NM 9.0	NM- 9.2
1-16: 1-Bedard-s/Ig Guara-a; new origin. 9-Green Lantern (Kyle) app. 11-Booster Gold						3.00
#0 (11/12, $2.99) Origin of the scarab						3.00

BLUE BEETLE (DC Rebirth)
DC Comics: Nov, 2016 - Present ($2.99)

	GD 2.0	VG 4.0	FN 6.0	VF 8.0	VF/NM 9.0	NM- 9.2
1-6-Giffen-s/Kolins-a. 4-6-Doctor Fate app.						3.00
...: Rebirth 1 (10/16, $2.99) Giffen-s/Kolins-a; Ted Kord & Doctor Fate app.						3.00

BLUEBERRY (See Lt. Blueberry & Marshal Blueberry)
Marvel Comics (Epic Comics): 1989 - No. 5, 1990 ($12.95/$14.95, graphic novel)

	GD 2.0	VG 4.0	FN 6.0	VF 8.0	VF/NM 9.0	NM- 9.2
1,3,4,5-($12.95)-Moebius-a in all	3	6	9	14	19	24
2-($14.95)	3	6	9	14	20	26

BLUE BOLT
Funnies, Inc. No. 1/Novelty Press/Premium Group of Comics: June, 1940 - No. 101 (V10#2), Sept-Oct, 1949

	GD 2.0	VG 4.0	FN 6.0	VF 8.0	VF/NM 9.0	NM- 9.2
V1#1-Origin Blue Bolt by Joe Simon, Sub-Zero Man, White Rider & Super Horse, Dick Cole, Wonder Boy & Sgt. Spook (1st app. of each)	389	778	1167	2723	4762	6800
2-Simon & Kirby's 1st art & 1st super-hero (Blue Bolt)	258	516	774	1651	2826	4000
3-1 pg. Space Hawk by Wolverton; 2nd S&K-a on Blue Bolt (same cover date as Red Raven #1); Simon-c	239	478	717	1530	2615	3700
4-S&K-a; classic Everett shark-c	213	426	639	1363	2332	3300
5-S&K-a; Everett-a begins on Sub-Zero; 1st time S&K names app. in a comic	181	362	543	1158	1979	2800
6,8-10-S&K-a	155	310	465	992	1696	2400
7-Classic S&K-c/a (scarce)	226	452	678	1446	2473	3500
11-Classic Everett Giant Robot-c (scarce)	194	388	582	1242	2121	3000
12-Nazi submarine-c	155	310	465	992	1696	2400
V2#1-Origin Dick Cole & The Twister; Twister x-over in Dick Cole, Sub-Zero, & Blue Bolt; origin Simba Karno who battles Dick Cole thru V2#5 & becomes main supporting character V2#6 on; battle-c	47	94	141	296	498	700
2-Origin The Twister retold in text	39	78	117	240	395	550
3-5: 5-Intro. Freezum	34	68	102	199	325	450
6-Origin Sgt. Spook retold	30	60	90	177	289	400
7-12: 7-Lois Blake becomes Blue Bolt's costume aide; last Twister. 12-Text-sty by Mickey Spillaine	24	48	72	144	237	330
V3#1-3	20	40	60	117	189	260
4-12: 4-Blue Bolt abandons costume	17	34	51	98	154	210
V4#1-Hitler, Tojo, Mussolini-c	90	180	270	576	988	1400
V4#2-Liberty Bell-c	16	32	48	94	147	200
V4#3-12: 3-Shows V4#3 on-c, V4#4 inside (9-10/43). 5-Infinity-c. 8-Last Sub-Zero	14	28	42	82	121	160
V5#1-8, V6#1-3,5-7,9,10, V7#1-12	14	28	42	76	108	140
V6#4-Racist cover	34	68	102	199	325	450

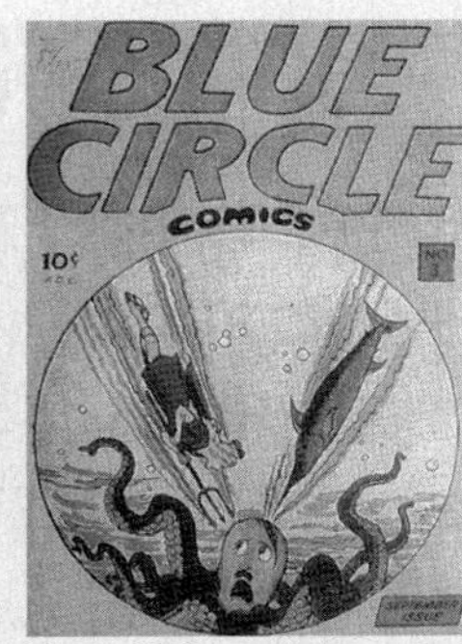

Blue Circle Comics #3 © Enwil

Blue Monday: Lovecats © Chynna Clugston

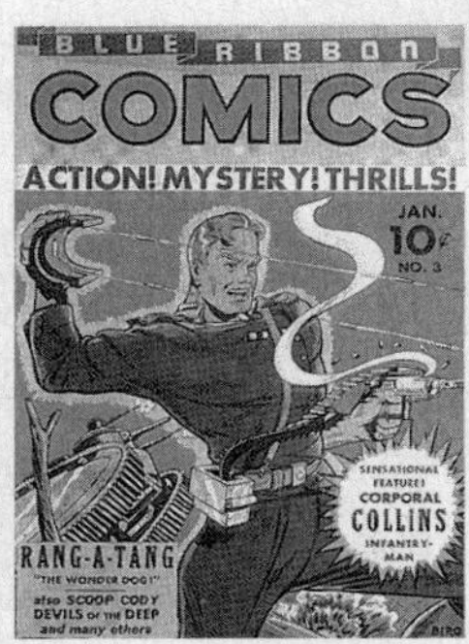

Blue Ribbon Comics #3 © MLJ

	GD 2.0	VG 4.0	FN 6.0	VF 8.0	VF/NM 9.0	NM- 9.2
V6#8-Girl fight-c	15	30	45	85	130	175
V8#1-6,8-12, V9#1-4,7,8, V10#1(#100),V10#2(#101)-Last Dick Cole, Blue Bolt	11	22	33	60	83	105
V8#7,V9#6,9-L. B. Cole-c	22	44	66	128	209	290
V9#5-Classic fish in the face-c	26	52	78	154	252	350

NOTE: ***Everett*** *c-V1#4, 11, V2#1, 2.* ***Gustavson*** *a-V1#1-12, V2#1-7.* ***Kiefer*** *c-V3#1.* ***Rico*** *a-V6#10, V7#4. Blue Bolt not in V9#8.*

BLUE BOLT (Becomes Ghostly Weird Stories #120 on; continuation of Novelty Blue Bolt) (...Weird Tales of Terror #111,112,...Weird Tales #113-119)
Star Publications: No. 102, Nov-Dec, 1949 - No. 119, May-June, 1953

	GD	VG	FN	VF	VF/NM	NM-
102-The Chameleon, & Target app.	39	78	117	240	395	550
103,104-The Chameleon app. 104-Last Target	39	78	117	231	378	525
105-Origin Blue Bolt (from #1) retold by Simon; Chameleon & Target app.; opium den story	103	206	309	659	1130	1600
106-Blue Bolt by S&K begins; Spacehawk reprints from Target by Wolverton begin, ends #110; Sub-Zero begins; ends #109	77	154	231	493	847	1200
107-110: 108-Last S&K Blue Bolt reprint. 109-Wolverton-c(r)/inside Spacehawk splash. 110-Target app.	74	148	222	470	810	1150
111,112: 111-Red Rocket & The Mask-r; last Blue Bolt; 1pg. L. B. Cole-a. 112-Last Torpedo Man app.	71	142	213	454	777	1100
113-Wolverton's Spacehawk-r/Target V3#7	73	146	219	467	796	1125
114,116: 116-Jungle Jo-r	71	142	213	454	777	1100
115-Sgt. Spook app.	81	162	243	518	884	1250
117-Jo-Jo & Blue Bolt-r; Hollingsworth-a	74	148	222	470	810	1150
118-"White Spirit" by Wood	73	146	219	467	796	1125
119-Disbrow/Cole-c; Jungle Jo-r	71	142	213	454	777	1100
Accepted Reprint #103(1957?, nd)	14	28	42	80	115	150

NOTE: ***L. B. Cole*** *c-102-108, 110 on.* ***Disbrow*** *a-112(2), 113(3), 114(2), 115(2), 116-118.* ***Hollingsworth*** *a-117.* ***Palais*** *a-112r. Sci/Fi c-105-110. Horror c-111.*

BLUE BULLETEER, THE (Also see Femforce Special)
AC Comics: 1989 ($2.25, B&W, one-shot)

1-Origin by Bill Black; Bill Ward-a — 4.00

BLUE BULLETEER (Also see Femforce Special)
AC Comics: 1996 ($5.95, B&W, one-shot)

1-Photo-c — 6.00

BLUE CIRCLE COMICS (Also see Red Circle Comics, Blazing Comics & Roly Poly Comic Book)
Enwil Associates/Rural Home: June, 1944 - No. 6, Apr, 1945

	GD	VG	FN	VF	VF/NM	NM-
1-The Blue Circle begins (1st app.); origin & 1st app. Steel Fist	37	74	111	222	361	500
2	21	42	63	126	206	285
3-Hitler parody-c	48	96	144	302	514	725
4-6: 5-Last Steel Fist.	20	40	60	117	189	260
6-(Dated 4/45, Vol. 2#3 inside)-Leftover covers to #6 were later restapled over early 1950's coverless comics; variations of the coverless comics exist. Colossal Features known.	20	40	60	117	189	260

BLUE DEVIL (See Fury of Firestorm #24, Underworld Unleashed, Starman (2nd) #38, Infinite Crisis and Shadowpact)
DC Comics: June, 1984 - No. 31, Dec, 1986 (75¢/$1.25)

1 — 4.00
2-16,19-31: 4-Origin Nebiros. 7-Gil Kane-a. 8-Giffen-a — 3.00
17,18-Crisis x-over — 3.50
Annual 1 (11/85)-Team-ups w/Black Orchid, Creeper, Demon, Madame Xanadu, Man-Bat & Phantom Stranger — 4.00

BLUE MONDAY: ... (one-shots)
Oni Press: Feb, 2002 - Present (B&W, Chynna Clugston-Major-s/a/c in all)

Dead Man's Party (10/02, $2.95) Dan Brereton painted back-c — 3.00
Inbetween Days (9/03, $9.95, 8" x 5-1/2") r/Dead Man's Party, Lovecats, & Nobody's Fool — 10.00
Lovecats (2/02, $2.95) Valentine's Day themed — 3.00
Nobody's Fool (2/03, $2.95) April Fool's Day themed — 3.00
Thieves Like Us (12/08, $3.50) Part 1 of an unfinished 5-part series — 3.50

BLUE MONDAY: ABSOLUTE BEGINNERS
Oni Press: Feb, 2001 - No. 4, Sept, 2001 ($2.95, B&W, limited series)

1-4-Chynna Clugston-Major-s/a/c — 3.00
TPB (12/01, $11.95, 8" x 6") r/series — 12.00

BLUE MONDAY: PAINTED MOON
Oni Press: Feb, 2004 - No. 4, Mar, 2005 ($2.99, B&W, limited series)

1-4-Chynna Clugston-Major-s/a/c — 3.00
TPB (4/05, $11.95, digest-sized) r/series; sketch pages — 12.00

BLUE MONDAY: THE KIDS ARE ALRIGHT
Oni Press: Feb, 2000 - No. 3, May, 2000 ($2.95, B&W, limited series)

1-3-Chynna Clugston-Major-s/a/c. 1-Variant-c by Warren. 2-Dorkin-c — 3.00
3-Variant cover by J. Scott Campbell — 4.00
TPB (12/00, $10.95, digest-sized) r/#1-3 & earlier short stories — 11.00

BLUE PHANTOM, THE
Dell Publishing Co.: June-Aug, 1962

	GD	VG	FN	VF	VF/NM	NM-
1(01-066-208)-by Fred Fredericks	3	6	9	20	31	42

BLUE RIBBON COMICS (...Mystery Comics No. 9-18)
MLJ Magazines: Nov, 1939 - No. 22, Mar, 1942 (1st MLJ series)

	GD	VG	FN	VF	VF/NM	NM-
1-Dan Hastings, Richy the Amazing Boy, Rang-A-Tang the Wonder Dog begin (1st app. of each); Little Nemo app. (not by W. McCay); Jack Cole-a(3) (1st MLJ comic)	252	504	756	1613	2757	3900
2-Bob Phantom, Silver Fox (both in #3), Rang-A-Tang Club & Cpl. Collins begin (1st app. of each); Jack Cole-a	123	246	369	787	1344	1900
3-J. Cole-a	84	168	252	538	919	1300
4-Doc Strong, The Green Falcon, & Hercules begin (1st app. each); origin & 1st app. The Fox & Ty-Gor, Son of the Tiger	92	184	276	584	1005	1425
5-8: 8-Last Hercules; 6,7-Biro, Meskin-a. 7-Fox app. on-c	74	148	222	470	810	1150
9-(Scarce)-Origin & 1st app. Mr. Justice (2/41)	331	662	993	2317	4059	5800
10-13: 12-Last Doc Strong. 13-Inferno, the Flame Breather begins, ends #19; Devil-c	135	270	405	864	1482	2100
14,15,17,18: 15-Last Green Falcon	119	238	357	762	1306	1850
16-Origin & 1st app. Captain Flag (9/41)	171	342	513	1086	1868	2650
19-22: 20-Last Ty-Gor. 22-Origin Mr. Justice retold	107	214	321	680	1165	1650

NOTE: ***Biro*** *c-3-5; a-2 (Cpl. Collins & Scoop Cody).* ***S. Cooper*** *c-9-17. 20-22 contain "Tales From the Witch's Cauldron" (same strip as "Stories of the Black Witch" in Zip Comics). Mr. Justice c-9-18. Captain Flag c-16-18 (w/Mr. Justice), 19-22.*

BLUE RIBBON COMICS (Becomes Teen-Age Diary Secrets #4)
(Also see Approved Comics, Blue Ribbon Comics and Heckle & Jeckle)
Blue Ribbon (St. John): Feb, 1949 - No. 6, Aug, 1949

	GD	VG	FN	VF	VF/NM	NM-
1-Heckle & Jeckle (Terrytoons)	15	30	45	90	140	190
2(4/49)-Diary Secrets; Baker-c	55	110	165	352	601	850
3-Heckle & Jeckle (Terrytoons)	11	22	33	62	86	110
4(6/49)-Diary Secrets; Baker c/a(2)	58	116	174	371	636	900
5(8/49)-Teen-Age Diary Secrets; Oversize; photo-c; Baker-a(2)- Continues as Teen-Age Diary Secrets	74	148	222	470	810	1150
6-Dinky Duck(8/49)(Terrytoons)	8	16	24	44	57	70

BLUE RIBBON COMICS
Red Circle Prod./Archie Ent. No. 5 on: Nov, 1983 - No. 14, Dec, 1984

	GD	VG	FN	VF	VF/NM	NM-
1-S&K-r/Advs. of the Fly #1,2; Williamson/Torres-r/Fly #2; Ditko-c	1	2	3	5	6	8
2-7,9,10: 3-Origin Steel Sterling. 5-S&K Shield-r; new Kirby-c. 6,7-The Fox app.						6.00
8-Toth centerspread; Black Hood app.; Neal Adams-a(r)	1	2	3	4	5	7
11,13,14: 11-Black Hood. 13-Thunder Bunny. 14-Web & Jaguar						6.00
12-Thunder Agents; Noman new Ditko-a	1	2	3	5	6	8

NOTE: ***N. Adams*** *a(r)-8.* ***Buckler*** *a-4i.* ***Nino*** *a-2i.* ***McWilliams*** *a-8.* ***Morrow*** *a-8.*

BLUE STREAK (See Holyoke One-Shot No. 8)

BLUNTMAN AND CHRONIC TPB(Also see Jay and Silent Bob, Clerks, and Oni Double Feature)
Image Comics: Dec, 2001 ($14.95, TPB)

nn-Tie-in for "Jay & Silent Bob Strike Back" movie; new Kevin Smith-s/Michael Oeming-a; r/app. from Oni Double Feature #12 in color; Ben Affleck & Jason Lee afterwords — 15.00

BLYTHE (Marge's)
Dell Publishing Co.: No. 1072, Jan-Mar, 1960

	GD	VG	FN	VF	VF/NM	NM-
Four Color 1072	5	10	15	34	60	85

B-MAN (See Double-Dare Adventures)

BO (Tom Cat #4 on) (Also see Big Shot #29 & Dixie Dugan)
Charlton Comics Group: June, 1955 - No. 3, Oct, 1955 (A dog)

	GD	VG	FN	VF	VF/NM	NM-
1-3: Newspaper reprints by Frank Beck; Noodnik the Eskimo app.	8	16	24	40	50	60

BOATNIKS, THE (See Walt Disney Showcase No. 1)

BOB BURDEN'S ORIGINAL MYSTERYMEN PRESENTS
Dark Horse Comics: 1999 - No. 4 ($2.95/$3.50)

1-3-Bob Burden-s/Sadowski-a(p) — 3.50
4-($3.50) All Villain issue — 3.50

BOBBY BENSON'S B-BAR-B RIDERS (Radio) (See Best of The West, The Lemonade Kid &

Bob Colt #9 © FAW

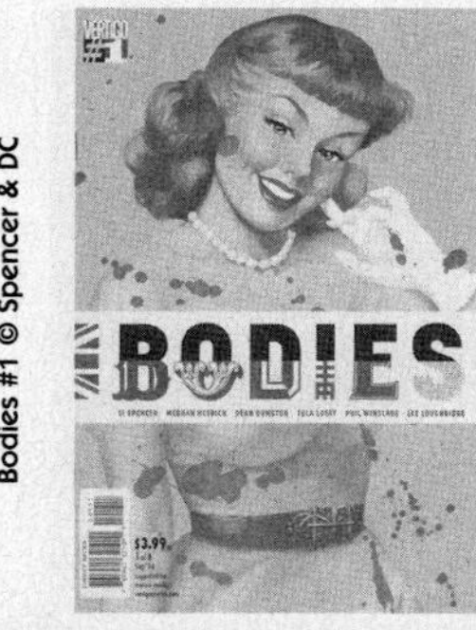

Bodies #1 © Spencer & DC

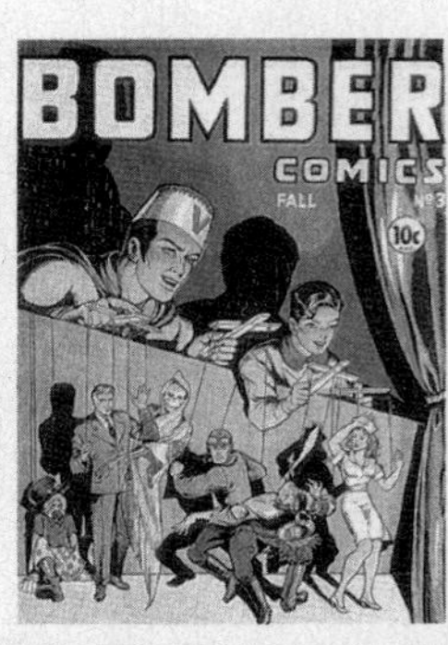

Bomber Comics #3 © EP

GD 2.0 | VG 4.0 | FN 6.0 | VF 8.0 | VF/NM 9.0 | NM- 9.2

GD 2.0 | VG 4.0 | FN 6.0 | VF 8.0 | VF/NM 9.0 | NM- 9.2

Model Fun)
Magazine Enterprises/AC Comics: May-June, 1950 - No. 20, May-June, 1953
1-The Lemonade Kid begins; Powell-a (Scarce) 42 84 126 267 451 635
2 18 36 54 103 162 220
3-5: 4,5-Lemonade Kid-c (#4-Spider-c) 14 28 42 78 112 145
6-8,10 13 26 39 74 105 135
9,11,13-Frazetta-c; Ghost Rider in #13-15 by Ayers-a. 13-Ghost Rider-c
39 78 117 236 388 540
12,17-20: 20-(A-1 #88) 12 24 36 67 94 120
14-Decapitation/Bondage-c & story; classic horror-c 30 60 90 177 289 400
15-Ghost Rider-c 23 46 69 136 223 310
16-Photo-c 14 28 42 81 118 155
1 (1990, $2.75, B&W)-Reprints; photo-c & inside covers 3.00
NOTE: ***Ayers** a-13-15, 20. **Powell** a-1-12(4 ea.), 13(3), 14-16(Red Hawk only); c-1-8,1 0, 12. Lemonade Kid in most 1-13.*

BOBBY COMICS
Universal Phoenix Features: May, 1946
1-By S. M. Iger 13 26 39 74 105 135

BOBBY SHERMAN (TV)
Charlton Comics: Feb, 1972 - No. 7, Oct, 1972
1-Based on TV show "Getting Together" 5 10 15 33 57 80
2-7: Photo-c on all. 7-Bobby Sherman for President 4 8 12 23 37 50

BOB COLT (See XMas Comics)
Fawcett Publications: Nov, 1950 - No. 10, May, 1952
1-Bob Colt, his horse Buckskin & sidekick Pablo begin; photo front/back-c
begin 24 48 72 142 234 325
2 14 28 42 80 115 150
3-5 12 24 36 67 94 120
6-Flying Saucer story 10 20 30 58 79 100
7-10: 9-Last photo back-c 9 18 27 52 69 85

BOB HOPE (See Adventures of... & Calling All Boys #12)

BOB MARLEY, TALE OF THE TUFF GONG (Music star)
Marvel Comics: Aug, 1994 - No, 3, Nov, 1994 ($5.95, limited series)
1-3 6.00

BOB POWELL'S TIMELESS TALES
Eclipse Comics: March, 1989 ($2.00, B&W)
1-Powell-r/Black Cat #5 (Scarlet Arrow), 9 & Race for the Moon #1 3.00

BOB'S BURGERS (TV)
Dynamite Entertainment: 2014 - No. 5, 2014 ($3.99)
1-5-Short stories by various. 1-Multiple covers 4.00

BOB'S BURGERS (Volume 2)(TV)
Dynamite Entertainment: 2015 - No. 16, 2016 ($3.99)
1-16-Short stories by various; multiple covers on all 4.00
... Free Comic Book Day 2015 (giveaway) Reprints various short stories from Vol. 1 3.00
... Free Comic Book Day 2016 (giveaway) Reprints various short stories 3.00

BOB SCULLY, THE TWO-FISTED HICK DETECTIVE (Also see Advs. of Detective Ace King and Detective Dan)
Humor Publ. Co.: No date (1933) (36 pgs., 9-1/2x11", B&W, paper-c; 10¢-c)
nn-By Howard Dell; not reprints; along with Advs. of Det. Ace King and Detective Dan, the first comic w/original art & the first of a single theme; has a blue 2-tone cover
600 1200 1800 4800 - -

BOB SON OF BATTLE
Dell Publishing Co.: No. 729, Nov, 1956
Four Color 729 4 8 12 27 44 60

BOB STEELE WESTERN (Movie star)
Fawcett Publications/AC Comics: Dec, 1950 - No. 10, June, 1952; 1990
1-Bob Steele & his horse Bullet begin; photo front/back-c begin
37 74 111 222 361 500
2 19 38 57 109 172 235
3-5: 4-Last photo back-c 14 28 42 82 121 160
6-10: 10-Last photo-c 13 26 39 72 101 130
1 (1990, $2.75, B&W)-Bob Steele & Rocky Lane reprints; photo-c & inside covers 3.00

BOB SWIFT (Boy Sportsman)
Fawcett Publications: May, 1951 - No. 5, Jan, 1952
1 10 20 30 58 79 100
2-5: Saunders painted-c #1-5 7 14 21 35 43 50

BOB, THE GALACTIC BUM
DC Comics: Feb, 1995 - No. 4, June, 1995 ($1.95, limited series)
1-4: 1-Lobo app. 3.00

BODIES
DC Comics (Vertigo): Sept, 2014 - No. 8, Apr, 2015 ($3.99, limited series)
1-8-Spencer-s; art by Hetrick, Ormston, Lotay & Winslade 4.00

BODY BAGS
Dark Horse Comics (Blanc Noir): Sept, 1996 - No. 4, Jan, 1997 ($2.95, mini-series, mature) (1st Blanc Noir series)
1,2-Jason Pearson-c/a/scripts in all. 1-Intro Clownface & Panda 5.00
3,4 4.00
Body Bags 1 (Image Comics, 7/05, $5.99) r/#1&2 6.00
Body Bags 2 (Image Comics, 8/05, $5.99) r/#3&4 6.00
...: 3 The Hard Way (Image, 2/06, $5.99) new story & r/Dark Horse Presents Annual 1997 and Dark Horse Maverick 2000; Pearson-c 6.00
...: One Shot (Image, 11/08, $5.99) wraparound-c; Pearson-c/a/s 6.00

BODYCOUNT (Also see Casey Jones & Raphael)
Image Comics (Highbrow Entertainment): Mar, 1996 - No. 4, July, 1996 ($2.50, lim. series)
1-4: Kevin Eastman-a(p)/scripts; Simon Bisley-c/a(i); Turtles app. 3.00

BODY DOUBLES (See Resurrection Man)
DC Comics: Oct, 1999 - No. 4, Jan, 2000 ($2.50, limited series)
1-4-Lanning & Abnett-s. 2-Black Canary app. 4-Wonder Woman app. 3.00
... (Villains) (2/98, $1.95, one-shot) 1-Pearson-c; Deadshot app. 3.00

BOFFO LAFFS
Paragraphics: 1986 - No. 5 ($2.50/$1.95)
1-($2.50) First comic cover with hologram 4.00
2-5 3.00

BOLD ADVENTURE
Pacific Comics: Nov, 1983 - No. 3, June, 1984 ($1.50)
1-Time Force, Anaconda, & The Weirdling begin 3.00
2,3: 2-Soldiers of Fortune begins. 3-Spitfire 3.00
NOTE: ***Kaluta** c-3. **Nebres** a-1-3. **Nino** a-2, 3. **Severin** a-3.*

BOLD STORIES (Also see Candid Tales & It Rhymes With Lust)
Kirby Publishing Co.: Mar, 1950 - July, 1950 (Digest size, 144 pgs.)
March issue (Very Rare) - Contains "The Ogre of Paris" by Wood
258 516 774 1651 2826 4000
May issue (Very Rare) - Contains "The Cobra's Kiss" by Graham Ingels (21 pgs.) 213 426 639 1363 2332 3300
July issue (Very Rare) - Contains "The Ogre of Paris" by Wood
194 388 582 1242 2121 3000

BOLT AND STAR FORCE SIX
Americomics: 1984 ($1.75)
1-Origin Bolt & Star Force Six 3.00
Special 1 (1984, $2.00, 52pgs., B&W) 4.00

BOMBARDIER (See Bee 29, the Bombardier & Cinema Comics Herald)

BOMBAST
Topps Comics: 1993 ($2.95, one-shot) (Created by Jack Kirby)
1-Polybagged w/Kirbychrome trading card; Savage Dragon app.; Kirby-c; has coupon for Amberchrome Secret City Saga #0 4.00

BOMBA THE JUNGLE BOY (TV)
National Periodical Publ.: Sept-Oct, 1967 - No. 7, Sept-Oct, 1968 (12¢)
1-Intro. Bomba; Infantino/Anderson-c 4 8 12 23 37 50
2-7 3 6 9 16 23 30

BOMBER COMICS
Elliot Publ. Co./Melverne Herald/Farrell/Sunrise Times: Mar, 1944 - No. 4, Winter, 1944-45
1-Wonder Boy, & Kismet, Man of Fate begin 97 194 291 621 1061 1500
2-Hitler-c and 8 pg. story 129 258 387 826 1413 2000
3: 2-4-Have Classics Comics ad to HRN 20 53 106 159 334 567 800
4-Hitler, Tojo & Mussolini-c; Sensation Comics #13-c/swipe; has Classics Comics ad to HRN 20. 123 246 369 787 1344 1900

BOMB QUEEN
Image Comics (Shadowline): Feb, 2006 - No. 4, May, 2006 ($3.50, mature)
1-4-Jimmie Robinson-s/a 3.50
... Vs. Blacklight One Shot #1 (8/06, $3.50) Robinson-a; Shadowhawk app. 3.50
..., Vol. 1: WMD: Woman of Mass Destruction TPB (7/06, $12.99) r/#1-4; bonus art 13.00

BOMB QUEEN II
Image Comics (Shadowline): Oct, 2006 - No. 3, Dec, 2006 ($3.50, mature)

Bonanza #16 © GK

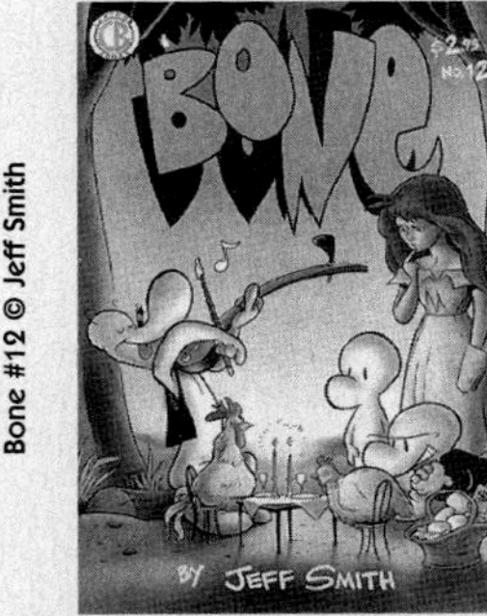

Bone #12 © Jeff Smith

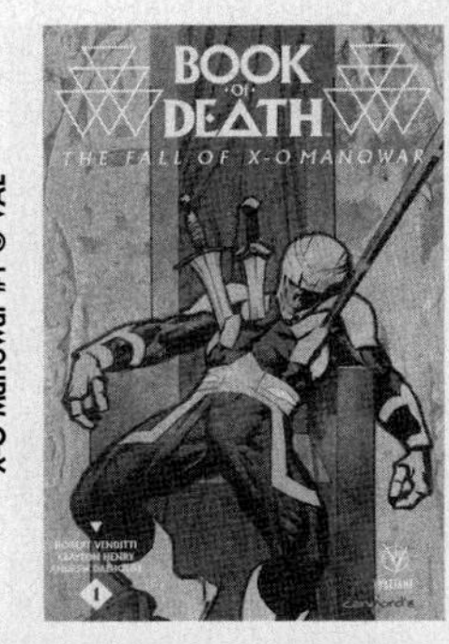

Book of Death: Fall of X-O Manowar #1 © VAL

GD 2.0 | VG 4.0 | FN 6.0 | VF 8.0 | VF/NM 9.0 | NM- 9.2

1-3-Jimmie Robinson-s/a; intro. The Four Queens 3.50
..., Vol. 2: Dirty Bomb - Queen of Hearts TPB (7/07, $14.99) r/#1-3 & Blacklight One Shot; bonus art; Robinson interview 15.00

BOMB QUEEN III THE GOOD, THE BAD & THE LOVELY
Image Comics (Shadowline): Mar, 2007 - No. 4, Jun, 2007 ($3.50, mature)
1-4-Jimmie Robinson-a/Jim Valentino-s; Blacklight & Rebound app. 1-Linsner-c 3.50

BOMB QUEEN IV SUICIDE BOMBER
Image Comics (Shadowline): Aug, 2007 - No. 4, Dec, 2007 ($3.50, mature)
1-4-Jim Robinson-s/a. 3-She-Spawn app. 3.50

BOMB QUEEN (Volume 5)
Image Comics (Shadowline): May, 2008 - No. 6, Mar, 2009 ($3.50, mature)
Vol. 5 #1-6-Jim Robinson-s/a 3.50
Vol. 6 #1-4: 1-(9/09 - No. 4, 1/11, $3.50) Obama satire 3.50
Vol. 7 #1-4 (12/11 - No. 4, 5/12) Bomb Queen returns in 2112 3.50
... Presents: All Girl Comics (5/09, $3.50) Dee Rail, Blacklight, Rebound, Tempest app. 3.50
... Presents: All Girl Special (7/11, $3.50) President Palin app. 3.50
... vs. Hack/Slash (2/11, $3.50) Cassie and Vlad app.; Robinson-s/a 3.50

BONANZA (TV)
Dell/Gold Key: June-Aug, 1960 - No. 37, Aug, 1970 (All Photo-c)

	GD 2.0	VG 4.0	FN 6.0	VF 8.0	VF/NM 9.0	NM- 9.2
Four Color 1110 (6-8/60)	28	56	84	202	451	700
Four Color 1221,1283, & #01070-207, 01070-210	15	30	45	100	220	340
1(12/62-Gold Key)	16	32	48	110	243	375
2	9	18	27	58	114	170
3-10	7	14	21	44	82	120
11-20	5	10	15	34	60	85
21-37: 29-Reprints	5	10	15	30	50	70

BONE
Cartoon Books #1-20, 28 on/Image Comics #21-27: Jul, 1991 - No. 55, Jun, 2004 ($2.95, B&W)

	GD 2.0	VG 4.0	FN 6.0	VF 8.0	VF/NM 9.0	NM- 9.2
1-Jeff Smith-c/a in all	32	64	96	230	515	800
1-2nd printing	2	4	6	9	12	15
1-3rd thru 5th printings						4.00
2-1st printing	8	16	24	54	102	150
2-2nd & 3rd printings						4.00
3-1st printing	6	12	18	37	66	95
3-2nd thru 4th printings						4.00
4,5	4	8	12	28	47	65
6-10	2	4	6	13	18	22
11-20						6.00
13 1/2 (1/95, Wizard)	2	4	6	8	10	12
13 1/2 (Gold)	2	4	6	9	12	15
21-37: 21-1st Image issue						5.00
38-($4.95) Three covers by Miller, Ross, Smith	1	2	3	4	5	7
39-55-($2.95)						4.00
1-27-($2.95): 1-Image reprints begin w/new-c. 2-Allred pin-up.						3.00
... Holiday Special (1993, giveaway)	2	3	4	6	8	10
... Reader -($9.95) Behind the scenes info						10.00
... Sourcebook-San Diego Edition						3.00
...10th Anniversary Edition (8/01, $5.95) r/#1 in color; came with figure						6.00
Complete Bone Adventures Vol 1,2 ('93, '94, $12.95, r/#1-6 & #7-12)						15.00
...: One Volume Edition (2004, $39.95, 1300 pgs.) r/#1-54; extra material						40.00
Volume 1-($19.95, hard-c)-"Out From Boneville"						20.00
Volume 1-($12.95, soft-c)						13.00
Volume 2,5-($22.95, hard-c)-"The Great Cow Race" & "Rock Jaw"						23.00
Volume 2,5-($14.95, soft-c)						15.00
Volume 3,4-($24.95, hard-c)-"Eyes of the Storm" & "The Dragonslayer"						25.00
Volume 3,4,7-($16.95, soft-c)						17.00
Volume 6-($15.95, soft-c)-"Old Man's Cave"						16.00
Volume 7-($24.95, hard-c)-"Ghost Circles"						25.00
Volume 8-($23.95, hard-c)-"Treasure Hunters"						24.00

NOTE: *Printings not listed sell for cover price.*

BONGO (See Story Hour Series)

BONGO & LUMPJAW (Disney, see Walt Disney Showcase #3)
Dell Publishing Co.: No. 706, June, 1956; No. 886, Mar, 1958

	GD 2.0	VG 4.0	FN 6.0	VF 8.0	VF/NM 9.0	NM- 9.2
Four Color 706 (#1)	6	12	18	37	66	95
Four Color 886	4	8	12	28	47	65

BONGO COMICS ...
Bongo Comics: 2005 - Present (Free Comic Book Day giveaways)
Gimme Gimme Giveaway! (2005) - Short stories from Simpsons Comics, Futurama Comics and Radioactive Man 3.00
Free-For-All! (2006, 2007, 2008, 2009, 2010, 2011, 2013-2016) - Short stories 3.00
Free-For-All! 2012 - Flip book with SpongeBob Comics 3.00

BONGO COMICS PRESENTS RADIOACTIVE MAN (See Radioactive Man)

BON VOYAGE (See Movie Classics)

BOOF
Image Comics (Todd McFarlane Prod.): July, 1994 - No. 6, Dec, 1994 ($1.95)
1-6 3.00

BOOF AND THE BRUISE CREW
Image Comics (Todd McFarlane Prod.): July, 1994 - No. 6, Dec, 1994 ($1.95)
1-6 3.00

BOOK AND RECORD SET (See Power Record Comics)

BOOK OF ALL COMICS
William H. Wise: 1945 (196 pgs.)(Inside f/c has Green Publ. blacked out)

	GD 2.0	VG 4.0	FN 6.0	VF 8.0	VF/NM 9.0	NM- 9.2
nn-Green Mask, Puppeteer & The Bouncer	63	126	189	403	689	975

BOOK OF ANTS, THE
Artisan Entertainment: 1998 ($2.95, B&W)
1-Based on the movie Pi; Aronofsky-s 3.00

BOOK OF BALLADS AND SAGAS, THE
Green Man Press: Oct, 1995 - No. 4 ($2.95/$3.50/$3.25, B&W)
1-4: 1-Vess-c/a; Gaiman story. 3.50

BOOK OF COMICS, THE
William H. Wise: No date (1944) (25¢, 132 pgs.)

	GD 2.0	VG 4.0	FN 6.0	VF 8.0	VF/NM 9.0	NM- 9.2
nn-Captain V app.	48	96	144	302	514	725

BOOK OF DEATH
Valiant Entertainment: Jul, 2015 - No. 4, Oct, 2015 ($3.99, limited series)
1-4-Venditti-s/Gill & Braithwaite-a; multiple covers on each. 4-Flip book with preview for Wrath of the Eternal Warrior series 4.00
...: Fall of Bloodshot (7/15, $3.99) Lemire-s/Braithwaite-a; Armstrong app. 4.00
...: Fall of Harbinger (9/15, $3.99) Dysart-s/Kano-a; future deaths of the team 4.00
...: Fall of Ninjak (8/15, $3.99) Kindt-s/Hairsine-a 4.00
...: Fall of X-O Manowar (10/15, $3.99) Venditti-s/Henry-a; future death of Aric 4.00

BOOK OF FATE, THE (See Fate)
DC Comics: Feb, 1997 - No. 12, Jan, 1998 ($2.25/$2.50)
1-12: 4-Two-Face-c/app. 6-Convergence. 11-Sentinel app. 3.00

BOOK OF LOST SOULS, THE
Marvel Comics (Icon): Dec, 2005 - No. 6, June, 2006 ($2.99)
1-6-Colleen Doran-a/c; J. Michael Straczynski-s 3.00
... Vol. 1: Introductions All Around (2006, $16.99, TPB) r/series 17.00

BOOK OF LOVE (See Fox Giants)

BOOK OF NIGHT, THE
Dark Horse Comics: July, 1987 - No. 3, 1987 ($1.75, B&W)
1-3: Reprints from Epic Illustrated; Vess-a 3.00
TPB-r/#1-3 15.00
Hardcover-Black-c with red crest 100.00
Hardcover w/slipcase (1991) signed and numbered 50.00

BOOK OF THE DEAD
Marvel Comics: Dec, 1993 - No. 4, Mar, 1994 ($1.75, limited series, 52 pgs.)

	GD 2.0	VG 4.0	FN 6.0	VF 8.0	VF/NM 9.0	NM- 9.2
1-4: 1-Ploog Frankenstein & Morrow Man-Thing-r begin; Wrightson-r/Chamber of Darkness #7. 2-Morrow new painted-c; Chaykin/Morrow Man-Thing; Krigstein-r/Uncanny Tales #54; r/Fear #10. 3-r/Astonishing Tales #10 & Starlin Man-Thing. 3,4-Painted-c	1	2	3	5	6	8

BOOKS OF DOOM (Dr. Doom from Fantastic Four)
Marvel Comics: Jan, 2006 - No. 6, June, 2006 ($2.99, limited series)
1-6-Life story/origin of Dr. Doom; Brubaker-s/Raimondi-a/Rivera-c 3.00
Fantastic Four: Books of Doom HC (2006, $19.99) r/#1-6 20.00
Fantastic Four: Books of Doom SC (2007, $14.99) r/#1-6 15.00

BOOKS OF FAERIE, THE
DC Comics (Vertigo): Mar, 1997 - No. 3, May, 1997 ($2.50, limited series)
1-3-Gross-a 3.00
TPB (1998, $14.95) r/#1-3 & Arcana Annual #1 15.00

BOOKS OF FAERIE, THE : AUBERON'S TALE
DC Comics (Vertigo): Aug, 1998 - No. 3, Oct, 1998 ($2.50, limited series)
1-3-Gross-a 3.00

BOOKS OF FAERIE, THE : MOLLY'S STORY

Books of Magic #52 © DC

Booster Gold #7 © DC

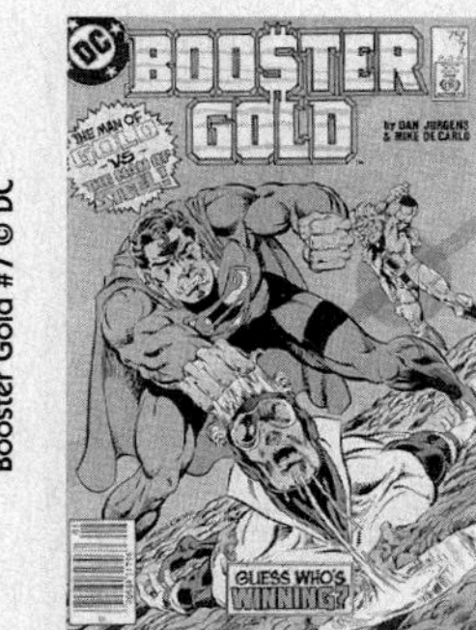

Borderlands #7 © Gearbox

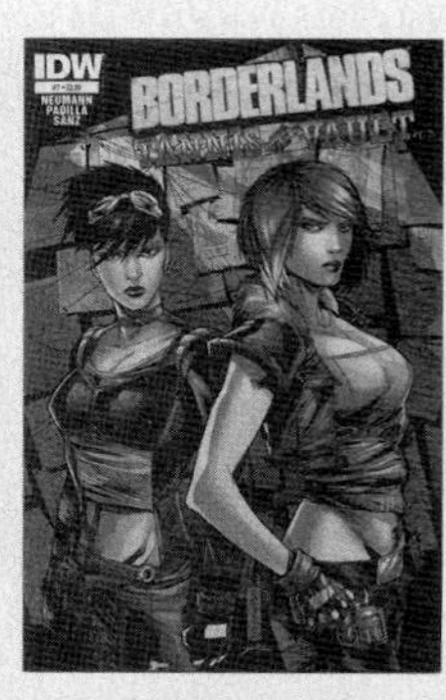

GD VG FN VF VF/NM NM-
2.0 4.0 6.0 8.0 9.0 9.2

DC Comics (Vertigo): Sept, 1999 - No. 4, Dec, 1999 ($2.50, limited series)
1-4-Ney Rieber-s/Mejia-a 3.00

BOOKS OF MAGIC
DC Comics: 1990 - No. 4, 1991 ($3.95, 52 pgs., limited series, mature)
1-Bolton painted-c/a; Phantom Stranger app.; Gaiman scripts in all
1 3 4 6 8 10
2,3: 2-John Constantine, Dr. Fate, Spectre, Deadman app. 3-Dr. Occult app.; minor Sandman app. 1 2 3 4 5 7
4-Early Death-c/app. (early 1991) 1 2 3 5 6 8
Trade paperback-($19.95)-Reprints limited series 20.00

BOOKS OF MAGIC (Also see Hunter: The Age of Magic and Names of Magic)
DC Comics (Vertigo): May, 1994 - No. 75, Aug, 2000 ($1.95/$2.50, mature)
1-Charles Vess-c 2 4 6 8 10 12
1-Platinum 2 4 6 13 18 22
2-4: 4-Death app. 1 2 3 4 5 7
5-14; Charles Vess-c 4.00
15-75: 15-$2.50-c begins. 22-Kaluta-c. 25-Death-c/app; Bachalo-c. 51-Peter Gross-s/a begins. 55-Medley-a 3.00
Annual 1-3 (2/97, 2/98, '99, $3.95) 4.00
Bindings (1995, $12.95, TPB)-r/#1-4 13.00
Death After Death (2001, $19.95, TPB)-r/#42-50 20.00
Girl in the Box (1999, $14.95, TPB)-r/#26-32 15.00
Reckonings (1997, $12.95, TPB)-r/#14-20 13.00
Summonings (1996, $17.50, TPB)-r/#5-13, Vertigo Rave #1 17.50
The Burning Girl (2000, $17.95, TPB)-r/#33-41 18.00
Transformations (1998, $12.95, TPB)-r/#21-25 13.00

BOOKS OF MAGICK, THE : LIFE DURING WARTIME (See Books of Magic)
DC Comics (Vertigo): Sept, 2004 - No. 15, Dec, 2005 ($2.50/$2.75)
1-15: 1-Spencer-s/Ormston-a/Quitely-c; Constantine app. 2-Bagged with Sky Captain CD 6-Fegredo-a. 7-Constantine & Zatanna-c 3.00
... Book One TPB (2005, $9.95) r/#1-5 10.00

BOOM! STUDIOS...
BOOM! Studios
... Ten Year Celebration 2015 Free Comic Book Day Special (5/15, giveaway) short stories of Adventure Time, Peanuts, Garfield, Lumberjanes, Regular Show & others 3.00
... Summer Blast (5/16, FCBD giveaway) Mouse Guard, Labyrinth, Adventure Time 3.00

BOONDOCK SAINTS (Based on the movie)
12-Gauge Comics: May, 2010 - No. 2, Jun, 2010 ($3.99, limited series)
...: In Nomine Patris 1,2-Troy Duffy-s/Guus Floor-a 4.00
...: In Nomine Patris Vol. 2 (10/10 - No. 2, 11/10): 1,2-Duffy-s/Floor-a 4.00
...: In Nomine Patris Vol. 3 (3/11 - No. 2, 4/11): 1,2-Duffy-s/Floor-a 4.00

BOOSTER GOLD (See Justice League #4)
DC Comics: Feb, 1986 - No. 25, Feb, 1988 (75¢)
1-Dan Jurgens-s/a(p); 1st app. of Booster Gold 3 6 9 16 23 30
2-25: 4-Rose & Thorn app. 6-Origin. 6,7,23-Superman app. 8,9-LSH app. 22-JLI app. 24,25-Millennium tie-ins 5.00
NOTE: *Austin c-22i. Byrne c-23i.*

BOOSTER GOLD (See DC's weekly series 52)
DC Comics: Oct, 2007 - No. 47, Oct, 2011 ($3.50/$2.99/$3.99)
1-Geoff Johns-s/Dan Jurgens-a(p); covers by Jurgens and Art Adams; Rip Hunter app. 5.00
2-4,6-20: 3-Jonah Hex app. 4-Barry Allen app. 8-Superman app. 3.00
5-Joker and Batgirl app.; Killing Joke-style-c 5.00
21-29-($3.99) 21-Blue Beetle back-ups begin. 22-New Teen Titans app. 23-Photo-c. 26,27-Blackest Night; Ted Kord rises. 29-Cyborg Superman app. 4.00
30-47-($2.99): 32-34-Giffen & DeMatteis-s. 32-Emerald Empress app. 40-Origin retold. 43-Legion of S.H. app. 44-47-Flashpoint tie-in; Doomsday app. 3.00
#0-(4/08) Blue Beetle (Ted Cord) returns; takes place between #6&7 3.00
#1,000,000-(9/08) Michelle Carter returns; takes place between #10&11 3.00
...: Futures End 1 (11/14, $2.99, regular-c) Jurgens-s; Kamandi, LSH, Captain Atom app. 3.00
...: Futures End 1 (11/14, $3.99, 3-D cover) 4.00

BOOTS AND HER BUDDIES
Standard Comics/Visual Editions/Argo (NEA Service):
No. 5, 9/48 - No. 9, 9/49; 12/55 - No. 3, 1956
5-Strip-r 18 36 54 107 169 230
6,8 13 26 39 72 101 130
7-(Scarce) 15 30 45 85 130 175
9-(Scarce)-Frazetta-a (2 pgs.) 28 56 84 168 274 380
1-3(Argo-1955-56)-Reprints 6 12 18 31 38 45

BOOTS & SADDLES (TV)

GD VG FN VF VF/NM NM-
2.0 4.0 6.0 8.0 9.0 9.2

Dell Publ. Co.: No. 919, July, 1958; No. 1029, Sept, 1959; No. 1116, Aug, 1960
Four Color 919 (#1)-Photo-c 7 14 21 46 86 125
Four Color 1029, 1116-Photo-c 5 10 15 33 57 80

BORDERLANDS: ... (Based on the video game)
IDW Publishing: Jul, 2014 - No. 8, Feb, 2015 ($3.99)
1-8: 1-4-The Fall of Fyerstone. 5-8-Tannis and the Vault 4.00

BORDERLANDS: ORIGINS (Based on the video game)
IDW Publishing: Nov, 2012 - No. 4, Feb, 2013 ($3.99, limited series)
1-4: 1-Spotlight on Roland. 2-Lilith. 3-Mordecai. 4-Brick 4.00

BORDER PATROL
P. L. Publishing Co.: May-June, 1951 - No. 3, Sept-Oct, 1951
1 15 30 45 85 130 175
2,3 10 20 30 56 76 95

BORDER WORLDS (Also see Megaton Man)
Kitchen Sink Press: 7/86 - No. 7, 1987; V2#1, 1990 - No. 4, 1990 ($1.95-$2.00, B&W, mature)
1-7, V2#1-4: Donald Simpson-c/a/scripts 3.00

BORIS KARLOFF TALES OF MYSTERY (TV) (...Thriller No. 1,2)
Gold Key: No. 3, April, 1963 - No. 97, Feb, 1980
3-5-(Two #5's, 10/63,11/63): 5-(10/63)-11 pgs. Toth-a.
5 10 15 31 53 75
6-8,10: 10-Orlando-a 4 8 12 25 40 55
9-Wood-a 4 8 12 27 44 60
11-Williamson-a, 8 pgs.; Orlando-a, 5 pgs. 4 8 12 27 44 60
12-Torres, McWilliams-a; Orlando-a(2) 4 8 12 21 33 45
13,14,16-20 3 6 9 18 28 38
15-Crandall 3 6 9 19 30 40
21-Jeff Jones-a(3 pgs.) "The Screaming Skull" 3 6 9 19 30 40
22-Last 12¢ issue 3 6 9 16 23 30
23-30: 23-Reprint; photo-c 3 6 9 15 22 28
31-50: 36-Weiss-a 3 6 9 14 19 24
51-74: 74-Origin & 1st app. Taurus 2 4 6 10 14 18
75-79,87-97: 90-r/Torres, McWilliams-a/#12; Morrow-c 2 4 6 9 12 15
80-86-(52 pgs.) 2 4 6 10 14 18
Story Digest 1(7/70-Gold Key)-All text/illos.; 148 pp. 5 10 15 31 53 75
(See Mystery Comics Digest No. 2, 5, 8, 11, 14, 17, 20, 23, 26)
NOTE: *Bolle a-51-54, 56, 58, 59. McWilliams a-12, 14, 18, 19, 72, 80, 81, 93. Orlando a-11-15, 21. Reprints: 78, 81-86, 88, 90, 92, 95, 97.*

BORIS KARLOFF THRILLER (TV) (Becomes Boris Karloff Tales...)
Gold Key: Oct, 1962 - No. 2, Jan, 1963 (84 pgs.)
1-Photo-c 10 20 30 64 132 200
2 6 12 18 40 73 105

BORIS THE BEAR
Dark Horse Comics/Nicotat Comics #13 on: Aug, 1986 - No. 34, 1990 ($1.50/$1.75/$1.95, B&W)
1, 8, Annual 1 (1988, $2.50): 8-(44 pgs.) 4.00
1 (2nd printing),2,3,4A,4B,5-12, 14-34 3.00
13-1st Nicotat Comics issue 3.00

BORIS THE BEAR INSTANT COLOR CLASSICS
Dark Horse Comics: July, 1987 - No. 3, 1987 ($1.75/$1.95)
1-3 3.00

BORN
Marvel Comics: 2003 - No. 4, 2003 ($3.50, limited series)
1-4-Frank Castle (the Punisher) in 1971 Vietnam; Ennis-s/Robertson-a 3.50
HC (2004, $17.99) oversized reprint of series; proposal, layout pages 18.00
Punisher: Born SC (2004, $13.99) r/series; proposal, layout pages 14.00

BORN AGAIN
Spire Christian Comics (Fleming H. Revell Co.): 1978 (39¢)
nn-Watergate, Nixon, etc. 3 6 9 19 30 40

BOUNCE, THE
Image Comics: May, 2013 - No. 12, May, 2014 ($2.99)
1-12-Casey-s/Messina-a 3.00

BOUNCER, THE (Formerly Green Mask #9)
Fox Features Syndicate: 1944 - No. 14, Jan, 1945
nn(1944, #10?) 34 68 102 199 325 450
11 (9/44)-Origin; Rocket Kelly, One Round Hogan app.
24 48 72 142 234 325

Box Office Poison Color Comics #1 © Alex Robinson

Boy Comics #41 © LEV

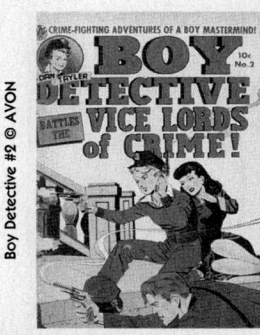

Boy Detective #2 © AVON

	GD 2.0	VG 4.0	FN 6.0	VF 8.0	VF/NM 9.0	NM- 9.2

12-14: 14-Reprints no # issue 20 40 60 114 182 250

BOUNTY
Dark Horse Comics: Jul, 2016 - No. 5, Dec, 2016 ($3.99, limited series)
1-5-Kurtis Wiebe-s/Mindy Lee-a 4.00

BOUNTY GUNS (See Luke Short's..., Four Color 739)

BOX OFFICE POISON
Antarctic Press: 1996 - No. 21, Sept, 2000 ($2.95, B&W)
1-Alex Robinson-s/a in all 1 2 3 4 5 7
2-5 4.00
6-21, ...Kolor Karnival 1 (5/99, $2.99) 3.00
...Super Special 0 (5/97, $4.95) 5.00
Sherman's March: Collected BOP Vol. 1 (9/98, $14.95) r/#0-4 15.00
TPB (2002, $29.95, 608 pgs.) r/entire series 30.00

BOX OFFICE POISON COLOR COMICS
IDW Publishing: Jan, 2017 - Present ($3.99)
1,2-Colored reprints of 1996 series; Alex Robinson-s/a in all; bonus commentary 4.00

BOY AND THE PIRATES, THE (Movie)
Dell Publishing Co.: No. 1117, Aug, 1960
Four Color 1117-Photo-c 6 12 18 37 66 95

BOY COMICS (Captain Battle No. 1 & 2; Boy Illustories No. 43-108) (Stories by Charles Biro) (Also see Squeeks)
Lev Gleason Publ. (Comic House): No. 3, Apr, 1942 - No. 119, Mar, 1956
3 (No.1)-1st app. & origin Crimebuster (ends #110), Bombshell (ends #8) Young Robin Hood (ends # 32), Yankee Longago (ends #28), Hero of the Month (ends #31), Case 1001-1005, 1006-1009 (ends #10); Swoop Storm begins (ends #32); Pepper Casey only app.; 1st app. Iron Jaw; Crimebuster's pet monkey Squeeks begins 326 652 978 2282 3991 5700
4-Hitler, Tojo Mussolini-c; Iron Jaw app. Little Wise Guys (prototype of later version) begins, ends #5 194 388 582 1242 2121 3000
5-Japanese war-c 129 258 387 826 1413 2000
6-Origin Iron Jaw; origin & death of Iron Jaw's son killed by his father; Hitler app.; Little Dynamite begins, ends #39; 1st Iron Jaw-c 326 652 978 2282 3991 5700
7-Flag & Hitler, Tojo, Mussolini-c; Dickey Dean app. 194 388 582 1242 2121 3000
8-Death of Iron Jaw; Iron Jaw-c & spash pg. 103 206 309 659 1130 1600
9-Iron Jaw classic-c (does not appear in story) 168 336 504 1075 1838 2600
10-Return of Iron Jaw; classic Biro Iron Jaw/Nazi-c 194 388 582 1242 2121 3000
11-Iron Jaw sty/classic-c 129 258 387 826 1413 2000
12-Classic Japanese WWII bondage torture interrogation-c 116 232 348 742 1271 1800
13-Nazi firing squad-c 84 168 252 538 919 1300
14-Iron Jaw-c 84 168 252 538 919 1300
15-Death of Iron Jaw, killed by The Rodent 97 194 291 621 1061 1500
16,18,20 (2/45) 47 94 141 296 498 700
17-(8/44)-Flag-c; The Moth app. 50 100 150 315 533 750
19-One of the greatest all-time stories 53 106 159 334 567 800
21-24: 24-Concentration camp story 34 68 102 199 325 450
25-Devil-c; hanging story (52 pgs.) 40 80 120 246 411 575
26-Bondage, torture-c/story (68 pgs.) 47 94 141 296 498 700
27-29,31,32-(All 68 pgs.). 28-Yankee Longago ends. 32-Swoop Storm & Young Robin Hood end 36 72 108 211 343 475
30-(10/46, 68 pgs.)-Origin Crimebuster retold from #3 w/Iron Jaw; Nazi work camp story 40 80 120 246 411 575
33-40: 34-Crimebuster story (2); suicide-c/story 22 44 66 132 216 300
41-50-41-Daredevil illus. text story 19 38 57 111 176 240
51-59: 57(9/50)-Dilly Duncan begins, ends #71 16 32 48 94 147 200
60-(12/50)-Iron Jaw returns c/sty 18 36 54 105 165 225
61-Origin Crimebuster & Iron Jaw retold c/sty 20 40 60 114 182 250
62-(2/51)-Death of Iron Jaw explained w/Iron Jaw-c 19 38 57 111 176 240
63-67,69-72: 63-McWilliams-a 14 28 42 76 108 140
68,73-Iron Jaw c/sty; 73-Frazetta 1 pg. ad 14 28 42 80 115 150
74,78,81-Iron Jaw c/sty (2-3) 12 24 36 67 94 120
75-77,84 11 22 33 62 86 110
79,80-Iron Jaw sty: 80(8/52)-1st app. Rocky X of the Rocketeers; becomes "Rocky X" #101; Iron Jaw, Sniffer & the Deadly Dozen in #80-118 11 22 33 64 90 115
82-Iron Jaw-c (apps. in one panel) 11 22 33 62 86 110
83,85-88-Iron Jaw c/sty. 87-The Deadly Dozen begins; becomes Iron Jaw #88 (4/53) 11 22 33 64 90 115
89(5/53)-92-The Claw serial app. in Rocky X (also see Silver Streak & Daredevil); on-c. 89-"Iron Jaw" becomes "Sniffrer & Iron Jaw" (ends #118); Iron Jaw c/story in all 12 24 36 67 94 120
93-Claw cameo & last app.; Woodesque-a on Rocky X by Sid Check; Iron Jaw-c/sty 11 22 33 64 90 115
94-97-Iron Jaw-c/sty in all 11 22 33 60 83 105
98,100:(4/54): 98-Rocky X by Sid Check 11 22 33 62 86 110
99,101-107,109,111,119: 101-Rocky X becomes spy strip. 106-Robin Hood app. 111-Crimebuster becomes Chuck Chandler, ends #119 10 20 30 54 72 90
108-(2/55)-Kubert & Ditko-a (Crimebuster, 8 pgs.) 11 22 33 62 86 110
110,112-118-Kubert-a 10 20 30 58 79 100
(See Giant Boy Book of Comics)
NOTE: *Boy Movies in 3-5,40,41. Iron Jaw app. 3,4,6,8,10,11,13-15; returns-60,62, 68, 69, 72-79, 81-118; c-60-62, 73, 74, 78, 81-83, 85-97.* ***Biro** c-all.* ***Jack Alderman** a-26.* ***Dan Barry** a-31,32, 35-38.* ***Al Borth** a- 51.* ***Dick Briefer** a-3-28, 124.* ***Sid Check** a-93, 98.* ***Ditko** a-108.* ***Bob Fujitani (Fuje)** a-55, 18pgs.* ***Jerry Gandenetti** a-52.* ***R. W. Hall** a-19-22.* ***Hubbell** a-30, 106, 108, 110, 111.* ***Joe Kubert** a-108, 110, 112-118.* ***Kenneth Landau** a-92.* ***George Mandel** a-3-30.* ***Norman Maurer** a-4-9, 11-13, 31, 32, 35, 41, 43, 46, 51, 57, 61, 73, 74, 78-83.* ***Bob Montana** a-4, 16, 19.* ***Pete Morisi** a-111.* ***William Overgard** a-68, 71, 74, 86, 88.* ***Palais** a-14, 16, 17, 19, 20, 25, 26. among others.* ***Tuska** a-30.* ***Bob Wood** a-8-13.*

BOY COMMANDOS (See Detective #64 & World's Finest Comics #8)
National Periodical Publications: Winter, 1942-43 - No. 36, Nov-Dec, 1949
1-Origin Liberty Belle; The Sandman & The Newsboy Legion x-over in Boy Commandos; S&K-a, 48 pgs.; S&K cameo? (classic WWII-c) 400 800 1200 2800 4900 7000
2-Last Liberty Belle; Hitler-c; S&K-a, 46 pgs.; WWII-c 239 478 717 1530 2615 3700
3-S&K-a, 45 pgs.; WWII-c 135 270 405 864 1482 2100
4-6: All WWII-c. 6-S&K-a 84 168 252 538 919 1300
7-10: All WWII-c 53 106 159 334 567 800
11-13: All WWII-c. 11-Infinity-c 39 78 117 240 395 550
14,16,18-19-All have S&K-a. 18-2nd Crazy Quilt-c 34 68 102 199 325 450
15-1st app. Crazy Quilt, their arch nemesis 41 82 123 256 428 600
17,20-Sci/fi-c/stories 39 78 117 240 395 550
21,22,25: 22-3rd Crazy Quilt-c; Judy Canova x-over 27 54 81 158 259 360
23-S&K-c/a(all) 36 72 108 214 347 480
24-1st costumed superhero satire-c (11-12/47). 31 62 93 186 303 420
26-Flying Saucer story (3-4/48)-4th of this theme; see The Spirit 9/28/47(1st), Shadow Comics V7#10 (2nd, 1/48) & Captain Midnight #60 (3rd, 2/48) 32 64 96 190 310 430
27,28,30: 30-Cleveland Indians story 26 52 78 154 252 350
29-S&K story (1) 27 54 81 162 266 370
31-35: 32-Dale Evans app. on-c & in story. 33-Last Crazy Quilt-c. 34-Intro. Wolf, their mascot 23 46 69 136 223 310
36-Intro The Atomobile c/sci-fi story (Scarce) 41 82 123 256 428 600
The Boy Commandos by Joe Simon & Jack Kirby Volume One HC (2010, $49.99) reprints apps. in Detective #64-72, World's Finest #8,9 & Boy Commandos #1,2; Buhle intro. 50.00
NOTE: *Most issues signed by **Simon & Kirby** are not by them.* ***S&K** c-1-9, 13, 14, 17, 21, 23, 24, 30-32.* ***Feller** c-30.*

BOY COMMANDOS
National Per. Publ.: Sept-Oct, 1973 - No. 2, Nov-Dec, 1973 (G.A. S&K reprints)
1,2: 1-Reprints story from Boy Commandos #1 plus-c & Detective #66 by S&K. 2-Infantino/Orlando-c 2 4 6 10 14 18

BOY COMMANDOS COMICS
DC Comics: Sept/Oct. 1942
1-Ashcan comic, not distributed to newsstands, only for in-house use. Cover art is the splash page from the Boy Commandos story in Detective Comics #68 interior is from an unidentified issue of Detective Comics (A FN- copy sold for $1912 in 2012)
nn - (9-10/42) Ashcan comic, not distributed to newsstands, only for in-house use. Cover art is the splash page from the Boy Commandos story in Detective Comics #68 interior is from Detective Comics #68 (no known sales)

BOY COWBOY (Also see Amazing Adventures & Science Comics)
Ziff-Davis Publ. Co.: 1950 (8 pgs. in color)
nn-Sent to subscribers of Ziff-Davis mags. & ordered through mail for 10¢; used to test market for Kid Cowboy 36 72 108 211 343 475

BOY DETECTIVE
Avon Periodicals: May-June, 1951 - No. 4, May, 1952
1 22 44 66 132 216 300
2-4: 3,4-Kinstler-c 15 30 45 85 130 175

BOY EXPLORERS COMICS (Terry and The Pirates No. 3 on)
Family Comics (Harvey Publ.): May-June, 1946 - No. 2, Sept-Oct, 1946
1-Intro The Explorers, Duke of Broadway, Calamity Jane & Danny Dixon...Cadet; S&K-c/a, 24 pgs. 77 154 231 493 847 1200
2-(Rare)-Small size (5-1/2x8-1/2"; B&W; 32 pgs.) Distributed to mail subscribers only; S&K-a 155 310 465 992 1696 2400
(Also see All New No. 15, Flash Gordon No. 5, and Stuntman No. 3)

BOY ILLUSTORIES (See Boy Comics)

Boy Meets Girl #17 © LEV

The Boys #31 © Spitfire

B.P.R.D.: Hell on Earth #134 © Mike Mignola

	GD 2.0	VG 4.0	FN 6.0	VF 8.0	VF/NM 9.0	NM- 9.2

BOY LOVES GIRL (Boy Meets Girl No. 1-24)
Lev Gleason Publications: No. 25, July, 1952 - No. 57, June, 1956

	GD	VG	FN	VF	VF/NM	NM-
25(#1)	14	28	42	82	121	160
26,27,29-33: 30-33-Serial, 'Loves of My Life	10	20	30	56	76	95
34-42: 39-Lingerie panels	10	20	30	54	72	90
28-Drug propaganda story	10	20	30	56	76	95
43-Toth-a	10	20	30	58	79	100
44-50: 47-Toth-a? 49-Roller Derby-c. 50-Last pre-code (2/55)	9	18	27	52	69	85
51-57: 57-Ann Brewster-a	9	18	27	47	61	75

BOY MEETS GIRL (Boy Loves Girl No. 25 on)
Lev Gleason Publications: Feb, 1950 - No. 24, June, 1952 (No. 1-17: 52 pgs.)

	GD	VG	FN	VF	VF/NM	NM-
1-Guardineer-a	21	42	63	122	199	275
2	13	26	39	74	105	135
3-10	12	24	36	67	94	120
11-24	11	22	33	60	83	105

NOTE: *Briefer a-24. Fuje c-3,7. Painted-c 1-17. Photo-c 19-21, 23.*

BOYS, THE
DC Comics (WildStorm)/Dynamite Ent. #7 on: Oct, 2006 - No. 72, 2012 ($2.99/$3.99)

	GD	VG	FN	VF	VF/NM	NM-
1-Garth Ennis-s/Darick Robertson-a	1	3	4	6	8	10
2-6						5.00
7-42-(Dynamite Ent.,). 19-Origin of the Homelander. 23-Variant-c by Cassaday						3.00
43-64,66-71-($3.99) Russ Braun-a in most. 54,55-McCrea-a						4.00
65,72-($4.99): 65-End of the Homelander. 72-Last issue; bonus pin-ups; cover gallery						5.00
#1: Dynamite Edition (2009, $1.00) r/#1; flip book with Battlefields Night Witches						3.00
...: Herogasm 1-6 (2009 - No. 6, 2009, $2.99) Ennis-s/McCrea-a						3.00
... Volume 1: The Name of the Game TPB (2007, $14.99) r/#1-6; intro. by Simon Pegg						15.00
... Volume 2: Get Some TPB (2008, $19.99) r/#7-14						20.00
... Volume 3: Good For The Soul TPB (2008, $19.99) r/#15-22						20.00
... Volume 4: We Gotta Go Now TPB (2009, $19.99) r/#23-30; cover gallery						20.00
... Volume 5: Herogasm TPB (2009, $19.99) r/#Herogasm #1-6						20.00

BOYS, THE: BUTCHER, BAKER, CANDLESTICKMAKER
Dynamite Entertainment: 2011 - No. 6, 2011 ($3.99, mature)

1-6-Garth Ennis-s/Darick Robertson-a; Billy Butcher's early years — 4.00

BOYS, THE: HIGHLAND LADDIE
Dynamite Entertainment: 2010 - No. 6, 2011 ($3.99, mature)

1-6-Garth Ennis-s/John McCrea-a — 4.00

BOYS' AND GIRLS' MARCH OF COMICS (See March of Comics)

BOYS' RANCH (Also see Western Tales & Witches' Western Tales)
Harvey Publ.: Oct, 1950 - No. 6, Aug, 1951 (No.1-3, 52 pgs.; No. 4-6, 36 pgs.)

	GD	VG	FN	VF	VF/NM	NM-
1-S&K-c/a(3)	58	116	174	371	636	900
2-S&K-c/a(3)	40	80	120	246	411	575
3-S&K-c/a(2); Meskin-a	39	78	117	231	378	525
4-S&K-c/a, 5 pgs.	34	68	102	199	325	450
5,6-S&K-c, splashes & centerspread only; Meskin-a	20	40	60	114	182	250

BOZO (Larry Harmon's Bozo, the World's Most Famous Clown)
Innovation Publishing: 1992 ($6.95, 68 pgs.)

	GD	VG	FN	VF	VF/NM	NM-
1-Reprints Four Color #285(#1)	1	2	3	4	5	7

BOZO THE CLOWN (TV) (Bozo No. 7 on)
Dell Publishing Co.: July, 1950 - No. 4, Oct-Dec, 1963

	GD	VG	FN	VF	VF/NM	NM-
Four Color 285(#1)	17	34	51	117	259	400
2(7-9/51)-7(10-12/52)	9	18	27	63	129	195
Four Color 464,508,551,594(10/54)	9	18	27	58	114	170
1(nn, 5-7/62)	7	14	21	44	82	120
2 - 4(1963)	5	10	15	35	63	90

BOZZ CHRONICLES, THE
Marvel Comics (Epic Comics): Dec, 1985 - No. 6, 1986 (Lim. series, mature)

1-6-Logan/Wolverine look alike in 19th century. 1,3,5-Blevins-a — 3.00

B.P.R.D. (Bureau of Paranormal Research and Defense) (Also see Hellboy titles)
Dark Horse Comics: (one-shots)

... Dark Waters (7/03, $2.99) Guy Davis-c/a; Augustyn-s — 3.00
... Night Train (9/03, $2.99) Johns & Kolins-s; Kolins & Stewart-a — 3.00
... The Ectoplasmic Man (6/08, $2.99) Stenbeck-a/Mignola-c; origin of Johann Kraus — 3.00
... There's Something Under My Bed (11/03, $2.99) Pollina-a/c — 3.00
... The Soul of Venice (5/03, $2.99) Oeming-a/c; Gunter & Oeming-s — 3.00
... The Soul of Venice and Other Stories TPB (8/04, $17.95) r/one-shots & new story by Mignola and Cam Stewart; sketch pages by various — 18.00
... War on Frogs (6/08,12/08, 6/09, 12/09, $2.99) 1-Trimpe-a/Mignola-c; Abe Sapien app. 2-Severin-a. 3-Moline-a. 4-Snejbjerg — 3.00

B.P.R.D.: GARDEN OF SOULS
Dark Horse Comics: Mar, 2007 - No. 5, July, 2007 ($2.99, limited series)

1-5-Mignola & Arcudi-s/Guy Davis-a/Mignola-c — 3.00

B.P.R.D.: HELL ON EARTH
Dark Horse Comics: ($3.50, limited series)

... Exorcism (6/12 - No. 2, 7/12) 1,2-Mignola-s/Stewart-a/Kalvachev -c — 3.50
... Gods (1/11 - No. 3, 3/11) 1-Mignola & Arcudi-s/Guy Davis-a; Ryan Sook-c — 3.50
... Monsters (7/11 - No. 2, 8/11) 1,2-Mignola & Arcudi-s. 1-Sook & Francavilla covers — 3.50
... New World (8/10 - No. 5, 12/10) 1-5-Mignola & Arcudi-s/Guy Davis-a/c — 3.50
... Russia (9/11 - No. 5, 1/12) 1-5-Mignola & Arcudi-s/Crook-a — 3.50
... The Devil's Engine (5/12 - No. 3, 7/12) 1-3-Mignola & Arcudi-s/Crook-a/Fegredo-c — 3.50
... The Long Death (2/12 - No. 3, 4/12) 1-3-Mignola & Arcudi-s/Harren-a/Fegredo-c — 3.50
... The Pickens County Horror (3/12 - No. 2, 4/12) 1,2-Mignola & Allie-s/Latour-a — 3.50
... The Transformation of J.H. O'Donnell (5/12) 1-Mignola & Allie-s/Fiumara-a — 3.50
... The Return of the Master (8/12 - No. 5, 12/12) 1-5-Mignola & Arcudi-s/Crook-a; 3-5-Also numbered as #100-102 on cover and indicia — 3.50
103-141: 103-(1/13). 103,104-The Abyss of Time. 105,106-A Cold Day in Hell — 3.50
142-147-($3.99) — 4.00

B.P.R.D.: HOLLOW EARTH (Mike Mignola's...)
Dark Horse Comics: Jan, 2002 - No. 3, June, 2002 ($2.99, limited series)

1-3-Mignola, Golden & Sniegoski-s/Sook-a/Mignola-c; Hellboy and Abe Sapien app. — 3.00
... and Other Stories TPB (1/03; 7/04, $17.95) r/#1-3, Hellboy: Box Full of Evil, Abe Sapien: Drums of the Dead, and Dark Horse Extra; plus sketch pages — 18.00

B.P.R.D.: KILLING GROUND
Dark Horse Comics: Aug, 2007 - No. 5, Dec, 2007 ($2.99, limited series)

1-5-Mignola & Arcudi-s/Guy Davis-a/c — 3.00

B.P.R.D.: KING OF FEAR
Dark Horse Comics: Jan, 2010 - No. 5, May, 2010 ($2.99, limited series)

1,2-Mignola & Arcudi-s/Guy Davis-a; Mignola-c — 3.00

B.P.R.D.: 1946
Dark Horse Comics: Jan, 2008 - No. 5, May, 2008 ($2.99, limited series)

1-5-Mignola & Dysart-s/Azaceta-a; Mignola-c — 3.00

B.P.R.D.: 1947
Dark Horse Comics: Jul, 2009 - No. 5, Nov, 2009 ($2.99, limited series)

1-5-Mignola & Dysart-s/Bá & Moon-a; Mignola-c — 3.00

B.P.R.D.: 1948
Dark Horse Comics: Oct, 2012 - No. 5, Feb, 2013 ($3.50, limited series)

1-5-Mignola & Arcudi-s/Fiumara-a; Johnson-c — 3.50

B.P.R.D.: PLAGUE OF FROGS
Dark Horse Comics: Mar, 2004 - No. 5, July, 2004 ($2.99, limited series)

1-5-Mignola-s/Guy Davis-c/a — 3.00
TPB (1/05, $17.95) r/series; sketchbook pages & afterword by Davis & Mignola — 18.00

B.P.R.D.: THE BLACK FLAME
Dark Horse Comics: Sept, 2005 - No. 6, Jan, 2006 ($2.99, limited series)

1-6-Mignola & Arcudi-s/Guy Davis-a/ Mignola-c — 3.00
TPB (7/06, $17.95) r/series; sketchbook pages & afterword by Davis & Mignola — 18.00

B.P.R.D.: THE BLACK GODDESS
Dark Horse Comics: Jan, 2009 - No. 5, May, 2009 ($2.99, limited series)

1-5-Mignola & Arcudi-s/Guy Davis-a/Nowlan-c — 3.00

B.P.R.D.: THE DEAD
Dark Horse Comics: Nov, 2004 - No. 5, Mar, 2005 ($2.99, limited series)

1-5-Mignola-s/Guy Davis-c/a — 3.00

B.P.R.D.: THE DEAD REMEMBERED
Dark Horse Comics: Apr, 2011 - No. 3, Jun, 2011 ($3.50, limited series)

1-3-Mignola-s; Moline-a; Jo Chen-c. 1-Variant-c by Moline — 3.50

B.P.R.D.: THE UNIVERSAL MACHINE
Dark Horse Comics: Apr, 2006 - No. 5, Aug, 2006 ($2.99, limited series)

1-5-Mignola & Arcudi-s/Guy Davis-a/Mignola-c. 5-Mignola-a (5 pgs.) — 3.00
TPB (1/07, $17.95) r/series; sketchbook pages by Davis; Mignola afterword — 18.00

B.P.R.D.: THE WARNING
Dark Horse Comics: July, 2008 - No. 5, Nov, 2008 ($2.99, limited series)

1-5-Mignola & Arcudi-s/Guy Davis-c/a — 3.00

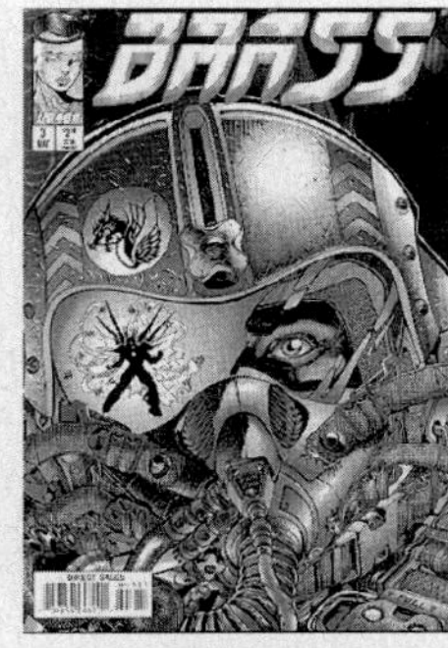

Brass #3 © WSP

The Brave and the Bold #21 © DC

The Brave and the Bold #56 © DC

B.P.R.D.: VAMPIRE
Dark Horse Comics: Mar, 2013 - No. 5, Jul, 2013 ($3.50, limited series)

	GD 2.0	VG 4.0	FN 6.0	VF 8.0	VF/NM 9.0	NM- 9.2
1-5-Mignola-s/Bá & Moon-a; Moon-c						3.50

BRADLEYS, THE (Also see Hate)
Fantagraphics Books: Apr, 1999 - No. 6, Jan, 2000 ($2.95, B&W, limited series)

	GD 2.0	VG 4.0	FN 6.0	VF 8.0	VF/NM 9.0	NM- 9.2
1-6-Reprints Peter Bagge's-s/a						3.00

BRADY BUNCH, THE (TV)(See Kite Fun Book and Binky #78)
Dell Publishing Co.: Feb, 1970 - No. 2, May, 1970 (photo-c)

	GD 2.0	VG 4.0	FN 6.0	VF 8.0	VF/NM 9.0	NM- 9.2
1	10	20	30	69	147	225
2	8	16	24	54	102	150

BRAIN, THE
Sussex Publ. Co./Magazine Enterprises: Sept, 1956 - No. 7, 1958

	GD 2.0	VG 4.0	FN 6.0	VF 8.0	VF/NM 9.0	NM- 9.2
1-Dan DeCarlo-a in all including reprints	13	26	39	74	105	135
2,3	9	18	27	47	61	75
4-7	4	8	12	27	44	60
I.W. Reprints #1-4,8-10('63),14: 2-Reprints Sussex #2 with new cover added	2	4	6	9	13	16
Super Reprint #17,18(nd)	2	4	6	9	13	16

BRAINBANX
DC Comics (Helix): Mar, 1997 - No. 6, Aug, 1997 ($2.50, limited series)

	GD 2.0	VG 4.0	FN 6.0	VF 8.0	VF/NM 9.0	NM- 9.2
1-6: Elaine Lee-s/Temujin-a						3.00

BRAIN BOY
Dell Publishing Co.: Apr-June, 1962 - No. 6, Sept-Nov, 1963 (Painted c-#1-6)

	GD 2.0	VG 4.0	FN 6.0	VF 8.0	VF/NM 9.0	NM- 9.2
Four Color 1330(#1)-Gil Kane-a; origin	10	20	30	64	132	200
2(7-9/62),3-6: 4-Origin retold	6	12	18	41	76	110

BRAIN BOY
Dark Horse Comics: Sept, 2013 - No. 3, Nov, 2013 ($2.99, limited series)

	GD 2.0	VG 4.0	FN 6.0	VF 8.0	VF/NM 9.0	NM- 9.2
1-3-Van Lente-s/Silva-a/Olivetti-c						3.00
#0-(12/13, $2.99) Reprints stories from Dark Horse Presents #23-25; Olivetti-c						3.00

BRAIN BOY: THE MEN FROM G.E.S.T.A.L.T.
Dark Horse Comics: May, 2014 - No. 4, Aug, 2014 ($2.99, limited series)

	GD 2.0	VG 4.0	FN 6.0	VF 8.0	VF/NM 9.0	NM- 9.2
1-4-Van Lente-s/Freddie Williams II-a/c						3.00

BRAM STOKER'S DRACULA (Movie)(Also see Dracula: Vlad the Impaler)
Topps Comics: Oct, 1992 - No. 4, Jan, 1993 ($2.95, limited series, polybagged)

	GD 2.0	VG 4.0	FN 6.0	VF 8.0	VF/NM 9.0	NM- 9.2
1-(1st & 2nd printing)-Adaptation of film begins; Mignola-c/a in all; 4 trading cards & poster; photo scenes of movie						5.00
1-Crimson foil edition (limited to 500)						15.00
2-4: 2-Bound-in poster & cards. 4 trading cards in both. 3-Contains coupon to win 1 of 500 crimson foil-c edition of #1. 4-Contains coupon to win 1 of 500 uncut sheets of all 16 trading cards						4.00

BRAND ECHH (See Not Brand Echh)

BRAND OF EMPIRE (See Luke Short's...Four Color 771)

BRASS
Image Comics (WildStorm Productions): Aug, 1996 - No. 3, May, 1997 ($2.50, lim. series)

	GD 2.0	VG 4.0	FN 6.0	VF 8.0	VF/NM 9.0	NM- 9.2
1-($4.50) Folio Ed.; oversized						4.50
1-3: Wiesenfeld-s/Bennett-a. 3-Grunge & Roxy(Gen 13) cameo						3.00

BRASS
DC Comics (WildStorm): Aug, 2000 - No. 6, Jan, 2001 ($2.50, limited series)

	GD 2.0	VG 4.0	FN 6.0	VF 8.0	VF/NM 9.0	NM- 9.2
1-6-Arcudi-s						3.00

BRATH
CrossGeneration Comics: Feb, 2003 - No. 14, June, 2004 ($2.95)

	GD 2.0	VG 4.0	FN 6.0	VF 8.0	VF/NM 9.0	NM- 9.2
Prequel-Dixon-s/Di Vito-a						3.00
1-14: 1-(3/03)-Dixon-s/Di Vito-a						3.00
Vol. 1: Hammer of Vengeance (2003, $9.95) Digest-sized reprint of Prequel & #1-6						10.00

BRATS BIZARRE
Marvel Comics (Epic/Heavy Hitters): 1994 - No. 4, 1994 ($2.50, limited series)

	GD 2.0	VG 4.0	FN 6.0	VF 8.0	VF/NM 9.0	NM- 9.2
1-4: All w/bound-in trading cards						3.00

BRAVADOS, THE (See Wild Western Action)
Skywald Publ. Corp.: Aug, 1971 (52 pgs., one-shot)

	GD 2.0	VG 4.0	FN 6.0	VF 8.0	VF/NM 9.0	NM- 9.2
1-Red Mask, The Durango Kid, Billy Nevada-r; Bolle-a; 3-D effect story	3	6	9	14	19	24

BRAVE AND THE BOLD, THE (See Best Of... & Super DC Giant) (Replaced by Batman & The Outsiders)
National Periodical Publ./DC Comics: Aug-Sept, 1955 - No. 200, July, 1983

	GD 2.0	VG 4.0	FN 6.0	VF 8.0	VF/NM 9.0	NM- 9.2
1-Viking Prince by Kubert, Silent Knight, Golden Gladiator begin; part Kubert-c	317	634	951	2695	6098	9500
2	132	264	396	1056	2378	3700
3,4	70	140	210	560	1255	1950
5-Robin Hood begins (4-5/56, 1st DC app.), ends #15; see Robin Hood Tales #7	71	142	213	568	1284	2000
6-10: 6-Robin Hood by Kubert; last Golden Gladiator app.; Silent Knight; no Viking Prince. 8-1st S.A. issue	46	92	138	368	834	1300
11-22,24: 12,14-Robin Hood-c. 18,21-23-Grey tone-c. 22-Last Silent Knight. 24-Last Viking Prince by Kubert (2nd solo book)	38	76	114	281	628	975
23-Viking Prince origin by Kubert; 1st B&B single theme issue & 1st Viking Prince solo book	46	92	138	359	805	1250
25-1st app. Suicide Squad (8-9/59)	276	552	828	2277	5139	8000
26,27-Suicide Squad	40	80	120	296	673	1050
28-(2-3/60)-Justice League intro./1st app.; origin/1st app. Snapper Carr	1400	2800	5600	17,000	48,500	80,000
29-Justice League (4-5/60)-2nd app. battle the Weapons Master; robot-c	276	552	828	2277	5139	6800
30-Justice League (6-7/60)-3rd app.; vs. Amazo	190	380	570	1568	3534	5500
31-1st app. Cave Carson (8-9/60); scarce in high grade; 1st try-out series	44	88	132	326	738	1150
32,33-Cave Carson	23	46	69	164	362	560
34-Origin/1st app. Silver-Age Hawkman, Hawkgirl & Byth (2-3/61); Gardner Fox story, Kubert-c/a ; 1st S.A. Hawkman tryout series; 2nd in #42-44; both series predate Hawkman #1 (4-5/64)	159	318	477	1312	2956	4600
35-Hawkman by Kubert (4-5/61)-2nd app.	37	74	111	274	612	950
36-Hawkman by Kubert; origin & 1st app. Shadow Thief (6-7/61)-3rd app.	34	68	102	245	548	850
37-Suicide Squad (2nd tryout series)	22	44	66	154	340	525
38,39-Suicide Squad. 38-Last 10¢ issue	18	36	54	124	275	425
40,41-Cave Carson Inside Earth (2nd try-out series). 40-Kubert-a. 41-Meskin-a	12	24	36	84	185	285
42-Hawkman by Kubert (2nd tryout series); Hawkman earns helmet wings; Byth app.	19	38	57	133	297	460
43-Hawkman by Kubert; more detailed origin	23	46	69	161	356	550
44-Hawkman by Kubert; grey-tone-c	19	38	57	133	297	460
45-49-Strange Sports Stories by Infantino	8	16	24	56	108	160
50-The Green Arrow & Manhunter From Mars (10-11/63); 1st Manhunter x-over outside of Detective Comics (pre-dates House of Mystery #143); team-ups begin	17	34	51	117	259	400
51-Aquaman & Hawkman (12-1/63-64); pre-dates Hawkman #1	18	36	54	124	275	425
52-(2-3/64)-3 Battle Stars; Sgt. Rock, Haunted Tank, Johnny Cloud, & Mlle. Marie team-up for 1st time by Kubert (c/a)	21	42	63	147	324	500
53-Atom & The Flash by Toth	9	18	27	59	117	175
54-Kid Flash, Robin & Aqualad; 1st app./origin Teen Titans (6-7/64)	64	128	192	512	1156	1800
55-Metal Men & The Atom	8	16	24	54	102	150
56-The Flash & Manhunter From Mars	8	16	24	54	102	150
57-Origin & 1st app. Metamorpho (12-1/64-65)	19	38	57	131	291	450
58-2nd app. Metamorpho by Fradon	9	18	27	61	123	185
59-Batman & Green Lantern; 1st Batman team-up in Brave and the Bold	11	22	33	73	157	240
60-Teen Titans (2nd app.)-1st app. new Wonder Girl (Donna Troy), who joins Titans (6-7/65)	40	80	120	296	673	1050
61-Origin Starman & Black Canary by Anderson	12	24	36	82	179	275
62-Origin Starman & Black Canary cont'd. 62-1st S.A. app. Wildcat (10-11/65); 1st S.A. app. of G.A. Huntress (W.W. villain)	10	20	30	69	147	225
63-Supergirl & Wonder Woman	8	16	24	56	108	160
64-Batman Versus Eclipso (see H.O.S. #61)	8	16	24	51	96	140
65-Flash & Doom Patrol (4-5/66)	6	12	18	37	66	95
66-Metamorpho & Metal Men (6-7/66)	6	12	18	37	66	95
67-Batman & The Flash by Infantino; Batman team-ups begin, end #200 (8-9/66)	6	12	18	42	79	115
68-Batman/Metamorpho/Joker/Riddler/Penguin-c/story; Batman as Bat-Hulk (Hulk parody)	8	16	24	51	96	140
69-Batman & Green Lantern	6	12	18	38	69	100
70-Batman & Hawkman; Craig-a(p)	6	12	18	38	69	100
71-Batman & Green Arrow	6	12	18	38	69	100
72-Spectre & Flash (6-7/67); 4th app. The Spectre; predates Spectre #1	6	12	18	40	73	105
73-Aquaman & The Atom	6	12	18	37	66	95
74-Batman & Metal Men	6	12	18	37	66	95

75-Batman & The Spectre (12-1/67-68); 6th app. Spectre; came out between

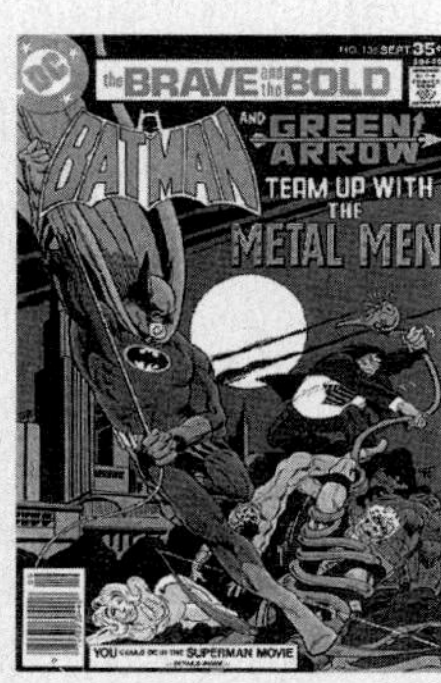

The Brave and the Bold #136 © DC

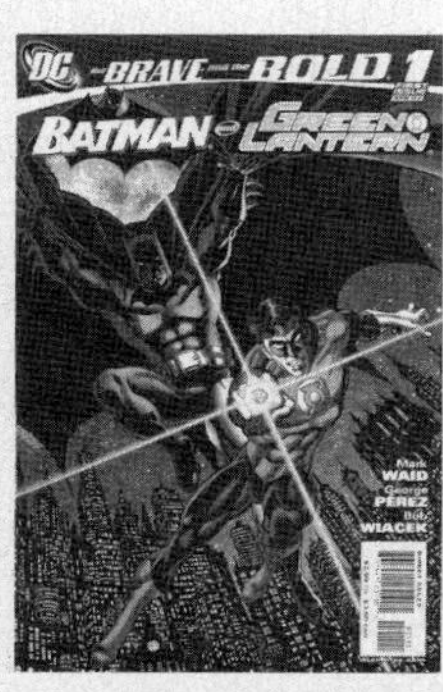

The Brave and the Bold (2007 series) #1 © DC

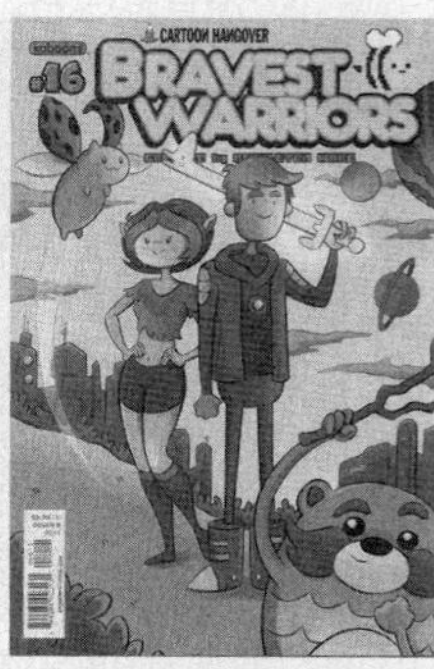

Bravest Warriors #16 © Frederator

GD VG FN VF VF/NM NM-
2.0 4.0 6.0 8.0 9.0 9.2

Spectre #1 & #2 6 12 18 41 76 110
76-Batman & Plastic Man (2-3/68); came out between Plastic Man #8 & #9
6 12 18 37 66 95
77-Batman & The Atom 6 12 18 37 66 95
78-Batman, Wonder Woman & Batgirl 6 12 18 41 76 110
79-Batman & Deadman by Neal Adams (8-9/68); early Deadman app.
9 18 27 61 123 185
80-Batman & Creeper (10-11/68); N. Adams-a; early app. The Creeper; came out between Creeper #3 & #4 8 16 24 52 99 145
81-Batman & Flash; N. Adams-a 8 16 24 52 99 145
82-Batman & Aquaman; N. Adams-a; origin Ocean Master retold (2-3/69)
8 16 24 55 105 155
83-Batman & Teen Titans; N. Adams-a (4-5/69) 8 16 24 52 99 145
84-Batman (G.A., 1st S.A. app.) & Sgt. Rock; N. Adams-a; last 12¢ issue (6-7/69)
8 16 24 52 99 145
85-Batman & Green Arrow; 1st new costume for Green Arrow by Neal Adams (8-9/69)
12 24 36 82 179 275
86-Batman & Deadman (10-11/69); N. Adams-a; story concludes from Strange Adventures #216 (1-2/69) 8 16 24 52 99 145
87-Batman & Wonder Woman 4 8 12 27 44 60
88-Batman & Wildcat 4 8 12 27 44 60
89-Batman & Phantom Stranger (4-5/70); early Phantom Stranger app. (came out between Phantom Stranger #6 & 7 4 8 12 25 40 55
90-Batman & Adam Strange 4 8 12 25 40 55
91-Batman & Black Canary (8-9/70) 4 8 12 25 40 55
92-Batman; intro the Bat Squad 4 8 12 25 40 55
93-Batman-House of Mystery; N. Adams-a 7 14 21 49 92 135
94-Batman-Teen Titans 4 8 12 27 44 60
95-Batman & Plastic Man 3 6 9 20 31 42
96-Batman & Sgt. Rock; last 15¢ issue 3 6 9 21 33 45
97-Batman & Wildcat; 52 pg. issues begin, end #102; reprints origin & 1st app. Deadman from Strange Advs. #205 3 6 9 21 33 45
98-Batman & Phantom Stranger; 1st Jim Aparo Batman-a?
3 6 9 21 33 45
99-Batman & Flash 3 6 9 21 33 45
100-(2-3/72, 25¢, 52 pgs.)-Batman-Green Lantern-Green Arrow-Black Canary-Robin; Deadman-r by Adams/Str. Advs. #210 5 10 15 35 63 90
101-Batman & Metamorpho; Kubert Viking Prince 3 6 9 20 31 42
102-Batman-Teen Titans; N. Adams-a(p) 5 10 15 30 50 70
103-107,109,110: Batman team-ups: 103-Metal Men. 104-Deadman. 105-Wonder Woman. 106-Green Arrow. 107-Black Canary. 109-Demon. 110-Wildcat
3 6 9 14 20 26
108-Sgt. Rock 3 6 9 15 22 28
111-Batman/Joker-c/story 3 6 9 20 31 42
112-117: All 100 pgs.; Batman team-ups: 112-Mr. Miracle. 113-Metal Men; reprints origin/1st Hawkman from Brave and the Bold #34; r/origin Multi-Man/Challengers #14. 114-Aquaman. 115-Atom; r/origin Viking Prince from #23; r/Dr. Fate/Hourman/Solomon Grundy/Green Lantern from Showcase #55. 116-Spectre. 117-Sgt. Rock; last 100 pg. issue
5 10 15 30 50 70
118-Batman/Wildcat/Joker-c/story 3 6 9 16 24 32
119,121-123,125-128,132-140: Batman team-ups: 119-Man-Bat. 121-Metal Men. 122-Swamp Thing. 123-Plastic Man/Metamorpho. 125-Flash. 126-Aquaman. 127-Wildcat. 128-Mr. Miracle. 132-Kung-Fu Fighter. 133-Deadman. 134-Green Lantern. 135-Metal Men. 136-Metal Men/Green Arrow. 137-Demon. 138-Mr. Miracle. 139-Hawkman. 140-Wonder Woman 2 4 6 8 10 12
120-Kamandi (68 pgs.) 3 6 9 14 19 24
124-Sgt. Rock; Jim Aparo app. on cover & in story` 2 4 6 9 12 15
129,130-Batman/Green Arrow/Atom parts 1 & 2; Joker & Two Face-c/stories
3 6 9 15 22 28
131-Batman & Wonder Woman vs. Catwoman-c/sty 2 4 6 10 14 18
141-Batman/Black Canary vs. Joker-c/story 2 4 6 13 18 22
142-160: Batman team-ups: 142-Aquaman. 143-Creeper; origin Human Target (44 pgs.). 144-Green Arrow; origin Human Target part 2 (44 pgs.). 145-Phantom Stranger. 146-G.A. Batman/Unknown Soldier. 147-Supergirl. 148-Plastic Man; X-Mas-c. 149-Teen Titans. 150-Anniversary issue; Superman. 151-Flash. 152-Atom. 153-Red Tornado. 154-Metamorpho. 155-Green Lantern. 156-Dr. Fate. 157-Batman vs. Kamandi (ties into Kamandi #59). 158-Wonder Woman. 159-Ra's Al Ghul. 160-Supergirl.
1 3 4 6 8 10
145(11/79)-147,150-159,165(8/80)-(Whitman variants; low print run; none show issue # on cover) 2 4 6 10 14 18
161-181,183-190,192-195,198,199: Batman team-ups: 161-Adam Strange. 162-G.A. Batman/Sgt. Rock. 163-Black Lightning. 164-Hawkman. 165-Man-Bat. 166-Black Canary; Nemesis (intro) back-up story begins, ends #192; Penguin-c/story. 167-G.A. Batman/Blackhawk; origin Nemesis. 168-Green Arrow. 169-Zatanna. 170-Nemesis. 171-Scalphunter. 172-Firestorm. 173-Guardians of the Universe. 174-Green Lantern. 175-Lois Lane. 176-Swamp Thing. 177-Elongated Man. 178-Creeper. 179-Legion. 180-Spectre. 181-Hawk & Dove. 183-Riddler. 184-Huntress & Earth II Batman. 185-Green Arrow. 186-Hawkman. 187-Metal Men. 188,189-Rose & the Thorn. 190-Adam Strange. 192-Superboy vs. Mr. I.Q. 194-Flash. 195-I...Vampire. 198-Karate Kid. 199-Batman vs. The Spectre 6.00
182-G.A. Robin; G.A. Starman app.; 1st modern app. G.A. Batwoman
2 4 6 8 11 14
191-Batman/Joker-c/story; Nemesis app. 2 4 6 9 13 16
196-Ragman; origin Ragman retold. 1 2 3 5 6 8
197-Catwoman; Earth II Batman & Catwoman marry; 2nd modern app. of G.A. Batwoman; Scarecrow story in Golden Age style 2 4 6 13 18 22
200-Double-sized (64 pgs.); printed on Mando paper; Earth One & Earth Two Batman app. in separate stories; intro/1st app. Batman & The Outsiders; 1st app. Katana
3 6 9 14 20 25

NOTE: ***Neal Adams** a-79-86, 93, 100r, 102; c-75, 76, 79-86, 88-90, 93, 95, 99, 100r. **M. Anderson** a-115r; c-72i, 96i. **Andru/Esposito** c-25-27. **Aparo** a-98, 100-102, 104-125, 126i, 127-136, 138-145, 147, 148i, 149-152, 154, 155, 157-162, 168-170, 173-178, 180-182, 184, 186i-189i, 191i-193i, 195, 196, 200; c-105-109, 111-136, 137i, 138-175, 177, 180-184, 186-200. **Austin** a-166i. **Bernard Baily** c-32, 33, 58. **Buckler** a-185, 186p; c-137, 178p, 185p, 186p. **Giordano** a-143, 144. **Infantino** a-67p, 72p, 97r, 98r, 115r, 172p, 183p, 190p, 194p; c-45-49, 67p, 69p, 70p, 72p, 96p, 98r. **Kaluta** c-176. **Kane** a-115r; c-59, 64. **Kubert** &/or **Heath** a-1-24; reprints-101, 113, 115, 117. **Kubert** a-99r; c-22-24, 34-36, 40, 42-44, 52. **Mooney** a-114r. **Mortimer** a-64, 69. **Newton** a-153p, 156p, 165p. **Irv Novick** c-1(part), 2-21. **Fred Ray** a-78r. **Roussos** a-50, 76i, 114r. **Staton** 148p. 52 pgs.-97, 100; 68 pgs.-120; 100 pgs.-112-117.*

BRAVE AND THE BOLD, THE
DC Comics: Dec, 1991 - No. 6, June, 1992 ($1.75, limited series)

1-6: Green Arrow, The Butcher, The Question in all; Grell scripts in all 4.00
NOTE: *Grell c-3, 4-6.*

BRAVE AND THE BOLD, THE
DC Comics: Apr, 2007 - No. 35, Aug, 2010 ($2.99)

1-Batman & Green Lantern team-up; Roulette app.; Waid-s/Peréz-c/a; 2 covers 4.00
2-32,34,35: 2-GL & Supergirl. 3-Batman & Blue Beetle vs. Fatal Five; Lobo app. 4-6-LSH app. 12-Megistus conclusion; Ordway-a. 14-Kolins-a. 16-Superman & Catwoman. 28-Blackhawks app. 29-Batman/Brother Power the Geek. 31-Atom/Joker 3.00
33-Batgirl, Zatanna & W.W.; prelude to Killing Joke 3 6 9 14 20 25
...: Demons and Dragons HC (2009, $24.99, dustjacket) r/#13-16; Brave & the Bold V1 #181, Flash V3 #107 and Impulse #17; Mark Waid commentary 25.00
...: Demons and Dragons SC (2010, $17.99) same contents as HC 18.00
...: Milestone SC (2010, $17.99) r/#24-26 and Static #12, Hardware #16, Xombi #6 18.00
Team-ups of the Brave and the Bold HC (2010, $24.99) r/#27-33 25.00
...: The Book of Destiny HC (2008, $24.99, dustjacket) r/#7-12; Ordway sketch pages 25.00
...: The Book of Destiny SC (2009, $17.99) r/#7-12; Ordway sketch pages 18.00
...: The Lords of Luck HC (2007, $24.99, dustjacket) r/#1-6 with Waid intro & annotations 25.00
...: The Lords of Luck SC (2008, $17.99) r/#1-6 with Waid intro & annotations 18.00
...: Without Sin SC (2009, $17.99) r/#17-22 18.00

BRAVE AND THE BOLD ANNUAL NO. 1 1969 ISSUE, THE
DC Comics: 2001 ($5.95, one-shot)

1-Reprints Silver Age team-ups in 1960s-style 80 pg. Giant format 6.00

BRAVE AND THE BOLD SPECIAL, THE (See DC Special Series No. 8)

BRAVE EAGLE (TV)
Dell Publishing Co.: No. 705, June, 1956 - No. 929, July, 1958

Four Color 705 (#1)-Photo-c 6 12 18 42 79 115
Four Color 770, 816, 879 (2/58), 929-All photo-c 5 10 15 31 53 75

BRAVE NEW WORLD (See DCU Brave New World)

BRAVE OLD WORLD (V2K)
DC Comics (Vertigo): Feb, 2000 - No. 4, May, 2000 ($2.50, mini-series)

1-4-Messner-Loeb-s/Guy Davis & Phil Hester-a 3.00

BRAVE ONE, THE (Movie)
Dell Publishing Co.: No. 773, Mar, 1957

Four Color 773-Photo-c 5 10 15 34 60 85

BRAVEST WARRIORS (Based on the animated web series)
BOOM! Entertainment (KaBOOM): Oct, 2012 - No. 36, Sept, 2015 ($3.99)

1-36-Multiple covers on each 4.00
2014 Annual (1/14, $4.99) Short stories featuring Catbug; multiple covers 5.00
2014 Impossibear Special 1 (6/14, $4.99) Short stories; multiple covers 5.00
... Paralyzed Horse Giant 1 (11/14, $4.99) Short stories; multiple covers 5.00
...: Tales From the Holo John 1 (5/15, $4.99) Short stories; multiple covers 5.00

BRAVURA
Malibu Comics (Bravura): 1995 (mail-in offer)

0-wraparound holographic-c; short stories and promo pin-ups of Chaykin's Power & Glory, Gil Kane's & Steven Grant's Edge, Starlin's Breed, & Simonson's Star Slammers 5.00

Breakfast After Noon #6 © Andi Watson

Brickleberry #1 © 20th Century Fox

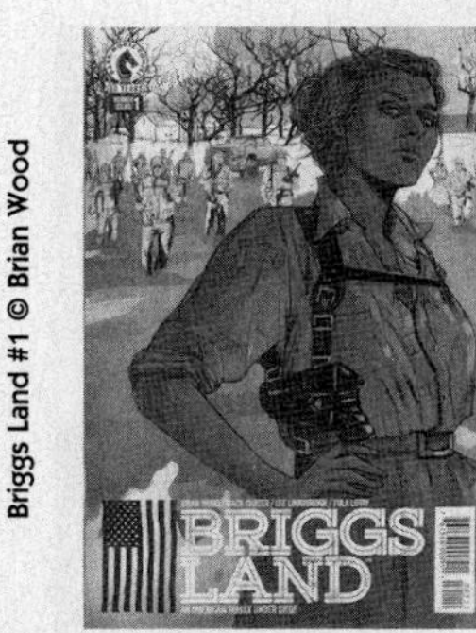

Briggs Land #1 © Brian Wood

	GD 2.0	VG 4.0	FN 6.0	VF 8.0	VF/NM 9.0	NM- 9.2

1 1/2 7.00

BREACH
DC Comics: Mar, 2005 - No. 11, Jan, 2006 ($2.95/$2.50)
1-11: 1-Marcos Martin-a/Bob Harras-s; origin. 4-JLA-c/app. 3.00

BREAKDOWN
Devil's Due Publ.: Oct, 2004 - No. 6, Apr, 2005 ($2.95)
1-6: 1-Two covers by Dave Ross and Leinil Yu; Dixon-s/Ross-a 3.00

BREAKFAST AFTER NOON
Oni Press: May, 2000 - No. 6, Jan, 2001 ($2.95, B&W, limited series)
1-6-Andi Watson-s/a 3.00
TPB (2001, $19.95) r/series 20.00

BREAKING INTO COMICS THE MARVEL WAY
Marvel Comics: May, 2010 - No. 2, May, 2010 ($3.99, limited series)
1,2-Short stories by various newcomer artists; artist profiles 4.00

BREAKNECK BLVD.
MotioN Comics/Slave Labor Graphics Vol. 2: No. 0, Feb, 1994 - No. 2, Nov, 1994; Vol. 2#1, Jul, 1995 - #6, Dec., 1996 ($2.50/$2.95, B&W)
0-2, V2#1-6: 0-Pérez/Giordano-c 3.00

BREAK-THRU (Also see Exiles V1#4)
Malibu Comics (Ultraverse): Dec, 1993 - No. 2, Jan, 1994 ($2.50, 44 pgs.)
1,2-Pérez-c/a(p); has x-overs in Ultraverse titles 4.00

BREATH OF BONES: A TALE OF THE GOLEM
Dark Horse Comics: Jun, 2013 - No. 3, Aug, 2013 ($3.99, B&W, limited series)
1-3-Niles-s/Wachter-a 4.00

BREATHTAKER
DC Comics: 1990 - No. 4, 1990 ($4.95, 52 pgs., prestige format, mature)
Book 1-4: Mark Wheatley-painted-c/a & scripts; Marc Hempel-a 5.00
TPB (1994, $14.95) r/#1-4; intro by Neil Gaiman 15.00

'BREED
Malibu Comics (Bravura): Jan, 1994 - No. 6, 1994 ($2.50, limited series)
1-(48 pgs.)-Origin/1st app. of 'Breed by Starlin; contains Bravura stamps; spot varnish-c 4.00
2-6: 2-5-contains Bravura stamps. 6-Death of Rachel 3.00
...:Book of Genesis (1994, $12.95)-reprints #1-6 13.00

'BREED II
Malibu Comics (Bravura): Nov, 1994 - No. 6, Apr, 1995 ($2.95, limited series)
1-6: Starlin-c/a/scripts in all. 1-Gold edition 3.00

'BREED III
Image Comics: May, 2011 - No. 7, Dec, 2011 ($2.99)
1-7: Starlin-c/a/scripts in all 3.00

BREEZE LAWSON, SKY SHERIFF (See Sky Sheriff)

BRENDA LEE'S LIFE STORY
Dell Publishing Co.: July-Sept., 1962
01-078-209 8 16 24 51 86 120

BRENDA STARR (Also see All Great)
Four Star Comics Corp./Superior Comics Ltd.: No. 13, 9/47; No. 14, 3/48; V2#3, 6/48 - V2#12, 12/49
V1#13-By Dale Messick 100 200 300 635 1093 1550
14-Classic Kamen bondage-c 400 800 1200 2800 4900 7000
V2#3-Baker-a? 77 154 231 493 847 1200
4-Used in **SOTI**, pg. 21; Kamen-c 94 188 282 597 1024 1450
5-10 71 142 213 454 777 1100
11,12 (Scarce) 74 148 222 470 810 1150
NOTE: *Newspaper reprints plus original material through #6. All original #7 on.*

BRENDA STARR (...Reporter)(Young Lovers No. 16 on?)
Charlton Comics: No. 13, June, 1955 - No. 15, Oct, 1955
13-15-Newspaper-r 32 64 96 188 307 425

BRENDA STARR REPORTER
Dell Publishing Co.: Oct, 1963
1 10 20 30 68 144 220

BRER RABBIT (See Kite Fun Book, Walt Disney Showcase #28 and Wheaties)
Dell Publishing Co.: No. 129, 1946; No. 208, Jan, 1949; No. 693, 1956 (Disney)
Four Color 129 (#1)-Adapted from Disney movie "Song of the South"
23 46 69 164 362 560
Four Color 208 (1/49) 10 20 30 66 138 210
Four Color 693-Part-r #129 7 14 21 49 92 135

BRIAN PULIDO'S LADY DEATH... (See Lady Death)

BRICK BRADFORD (Also see Ace Comics & King Comics)
King Features Syndicate/Standard: No. 5, July, 1948 - No. 8, July, 1949 (Ritt & Grey reprints)
5 20 40 60 114 182 250
6-Robot-c (by Schomburg?). 47 94 141 296 498 700
7-Schomburg-c. 8-Says #7 inside, #8 on-c 17 34 51 98 154 210

BRICKLEBERRY (Based on the animated series)
Dynamite Entertainment: 2016 - No. 4, 2016 ($3.99, limited series)
1-4-Waco O'Guin & Roger Black-s 4.00

BRIDE'S DIARY (Formerly Black Cobra No. 3)
Ajax/Farrell Publ.: No. 4, May, 1955 - No. 10, Aug, 1956
4 (#1) 11 22 33 64 90 115
5-8 9 18 27 47 61 75
9,10-Disbrow-a 10 20 30 56 76 95

BRIDES IN LOVE (Hollywood Romances & Summer Love No. 46 on)
Charlton Comics: Aug, 1956 - No. 45, Feb, 1965
1 13 26 39 74 105 135
2 8 16 24 40 50 60
3-6,8-10 3 6 9 21 33 45
7-(68 pgs.) 4 8 12 27 44 60
11-20 3 6 9 16 23 30
21-45 2 4 6 11 16 20

BRIDES OF HELHEIM
Oni Press: Oct, 2014 - No. 6, May, 2015 ($3.99)
1-6-Cullen Bunn-s/Joëlle Jones-a 4.00

BRIDES ROMANCES
Quality Comics Group: Nov, 1953 - No. 23, Dec, 1956
1 20 40 60 114 182 250
2 12 24 36 67 94 120
3-10: Last precode (3/55) 11 22 33 62 86 110
11-17,19-22: 15-Baker-a(p)?; Colan-a 10 20 30 56 76 95
18-Baker-a 13 26 39 74 105 135
23-Baker-c/a 20 40 60 114 182 250

BRIDE'S SECRETS
Ajax/Farrell(Excellent Publ.)/Four-Star: Apr-May, 1954 - No. 19, May, 1958
1 16 32 48 94 147 200
2 10 20 30 58 79 100
3-6: Last precode (3/55) 9 18 27 52 69 85
7-11,13-19: 18-Hollingsworth-a 9 18 27 47 61 75
12-Disbrow-a 10 20 30 54 72 90

BRIDE-TO-BE ROMANCES (See True...)

BRIGADE
Image Comics (Extreme Studios): Aug, 1992 - No. 4, 1993 ($1.95, lim. series)
1-Liefeld part plots/scripts in all, Liefeld-c(p); contains 2 Brigade trading cards 4.00
1-Gold foil stamped logo edition 8.00
2-Contains coupon for Image Comics #0 & 2 trading cards 3.00
2-With coupon missing 2.00
3,4: 3-Contains 2 trading cards; 1st Birds of Prey. 4-Flip book featuring Youngblood #5 3.00

BRIGADE
Image Comics (Extreme): V2#1, May, 1993 - V2#22, July, 1995, V2#25, May, 1996 ($1.95/$2.50)
V2#1-22,25: 1-Gatefold-c; Liefeld co-plots; Blood Brothers part 1; Bloodstrike app. 2-(6/93, V2#1 on inside)-Foil merricote-c (newsstand ed. w/out foil-c exists). 3-Perez-c(i); Liefeld scripts. 8,9-Coupons #2 & 6 for Extreme Prejudice #0 bound-in. 11-(8/94, $2.50) WildC.A.T.S app. 16-Polybagged w/ trading card. 22-"Supreme Apocalypse" Pt. 4; w/ trading card 3.00
0-(9/93)-Liefeld scripts; 1st app. Warcry; Youngblood & Wildcats app.; 3.00
20-Variant-c. by Quesada & Palmiotti 3.00
Sourcebook 1 (8/94, $2.95) 3.00
1-(Awesome Ent., 7/00, $2.99) Flip book w/Century preview 4.00
1-(6/10, $3.99) Liefeld-s/Mychaels-a; covers by Liefeld & Mychaels 4.00

BRIGAND, THE (See Fawcett Movie Comics No. 18)

BRIGGS LAND
Dark Horse Comics: Aug, 2016 - Present ($3.99)
1-6-Brian Wood-s/Mack Chater-a/Tula Lotay-c 4.00

BRIGHTEST DAY (Also see Blackest Night and Green Lantern)

Brilliant #1 © Jinxworld

Britannia #4 © VAL

The Brotherhood #5 © MAR

GD VG FN VF VF/NM NM-
2.0 4.0 6.0 8.0 9.0 9.2

DC Comics: No. 0, Jun, 2010 - No. 24, Late Jun, 2011 ($3.99/$2.99)
0-($3.99) Johns & Tomasi-s/Pasarin-a/Finch-c 4.00
0-Variant-c by Reis 8.00
1-23-($2.99) 1-Black Manta returns. 4-Intro. Jackson (new Aqualad) 16-Aqualad origin. 18-Hawkman & Hawkgirl killed. 20-Aquaman killed 3.00
1-23: Variant covers. 1-6,9-18,20-23-by Reis, 7,8 White Lantern by Sook. 19-by Frank 6.00
24-($4.99) Swamp Thing and John Constantine return to DC universe 5.00
24-($4.99) Variant cover by Reis 8.00
...: The Atom Special (9/10, $2.99) Lemire-s/Asrar-a/Frank-c 3.00
... Volume 1 HC (2010, $29.99) r/#0-7; cover gallery 30.00
... Volume 2 HC (2011, $29.99) r/#8-16; cover gallery 30.00

BRIGHTEST DAY AFTERMATH: THE SEARCH FOR SWAMP THING
DC Comics: Aug, 2011 - No. 3, Oct, 2011 ($2.99, limited series)
1-3-Vankin-s/Castiello-a; covers by Syaf & Jones; John Constantine & Zatanna app. 3.00

BRILLIANT
Marvel Comics (Icon): Jul, 2011 - No. 5, Mar, 2014 ($3.95, limited series)
1-5-Bendis-s/Bagley-a/c 4.00

BRING BACK THE BAD GUYS (Also see Fireside Book Series)
Marvel Comics: 1998 ($24.95, TPB)
1-Reprints stories of Marvel villains' secrets 25.00

BRINGING UP FATHER
Dell Publishing Co.: No. 9, 1942 - No. 37, 1944
Large Feature Comic 9 34 68 102 199 325 450
Four Color 37 18 36 54 124 275 425

BRING ON THE BAD GUYS (See Fireside Book Series)

BRING THE THUNDER
Dynamite Entertainment: 2010 - No. 4, 2011 ($3.99)
1-4-Alex Ross-c/Ross & Nitz-s/Tortosa-a 4.00

BRITANNIA
Valiant Entertainment: Sept, 2016 - No. 4, Dec, 2016 ($3.99, limited series)
1-MIlligan-a/Ryp-a; set in 60-66 A.D.; Emperor Nero app. 4.00

BROADWAY HOLLYWOOD BLACKOUTS
Stanhall: Mar-Apr, 1954 - No. 3, July-Aug, 1954
1 22 44 66 132 216 300
2,3 15 30 45 85 130 175

BROADWAY ROMANCES
Quality Comics Group: January, 1950 - No. 5, Sept, 1950
1-Ward-c/a (9 pgs.); Gustavson-a 41 82 123 256 428 600
2-Ward-a (9 pgs.); photo-c 29 58 87 170 278 385
3-5: All-Photo-c 16 32 48 94 147 200

BROKEN ARROW (TV)
Dell Publishing Co.: No. 855, Oct, 1957 - No. 947, Nov, 1958
Four Color 855 (#1)-Photo-c 6 12 18 37 66 95
Four Color 947-Photo-c 5 10 15 31 53 75

BROKEN CROSS, THE (See The Crusaders)

BROKEN MOON
American Gothic Press: Sept, 2015 - No. 4, Jan, 2016 ($3.99, limited series)
1-4-Steve Niles-s/Nat Jones-a; covers by Jones & Sanjulian 4.00

BROKEN PIECES
Aspen MLT: No. 0, Sept, 2011; Oct, 2011 - No. 5, Dec, 2012 ($2.50/$3.50, limited series)
0-($2.50)-Roslan-s/Kaneshiro-a; three covers 3.00
1-5: 1-($3.50)-Roslan-s/Kaneshiro-a; three covers 3.50

BROKEN TRINITY
Image Comics (Top Cow): July, 2008 - No. 3, Nov, 2008 ($2.99, limited series)
1-3-Witchblade, Darkness & Angelus app.; Marz-s/Sejic & Hester-a; two covers 3.00
...: Aftermath 1 (4/09, $2.99) Marz & Hill-s/Lucas & Kirkham-a 3.00
...: Angelus 1 (12/08, $2.99) Marz-s/Stelfreeze-a; two covers 3.00
...: Pandora's Box 1-6 (2/10 - No. 6, 4/11 $3.99) Tommy Lee Edwards-c 4.00
...: The Darkness 1 (8/08, $2.99) Hester-s/Lucas-a; two covers 3.00
...: Witchblade 1 (12/08, $2.99) Marz-s/Blake-a; two covers 3.00

BRONCHO BILL (See Comics On Parade, Sparkler & Tip Top Comics)
United Features Syndicate/Standard(Visual Editions) No. 5-on: 1939 - 1940; No. 5, 1?/48 - No. 16, 8?/50
Single Series 2 ('39) 54 108 162 343 574 825
Single Series 19 ('40)(#2 on cvr) 42 84 126 267 451 635

5 15 30 45 85 130 175
6(4/48)-10(4/49) 10 20 30 56 76 95
11(6/49)-16 9 18 27 50 65 80
NOTE: *Schomburg c-6, 7, 9-13, 15, 16.*

BROOKLYN ANIMAL CONTROL
IDW Publishing: Dec, 2015 ($7.99, square-bound, one-shot)
1-J.T. Petty-s/Stephen Thompson-a; werewolves in Brooklyn 8.00

BROOKS ROBINSON (See Baseball's Greatest Heroes #2)

BROTHER BILLY THE PAIN FROM PLAINS
Marvel Comics Group: 1979 (68pgs.)
1-B&W comics, satire, Jimmy Carter-c & x-over w/Brother Billy peanut jokes. Joey Adams-a (scarce) 5 10 15 31 53 75

BROTHERHOOD, THE (Also see X-Men titles)
Marvel Comics: July, 2001 - No. 9, Mar, 2002 ($2.25)
1-Intro. Orwell & the Brotherhood; Ribic-a/X-s/Sienkiewicz-c 3.00
2-9: 2-Two covers (JG Jones & Sienkiewicz). 4-6-Fabry-c. 7-9-Phillips-c/a 3.00

BROTHER POWER, THE GEEK (See Saga of Swamp Thing Annual & Vertigo Visions)
National Periodical Publications: Sept-Oct, 1968 - No. 2, Nov-Dec, 1968
1-Origin; Simon-c(i?) 5 10 15 31 53 75
2 3 6 9 19 30 40

BROTHERS, HANG IN THERE, THE
Spire Christian Comics (Fleming H. Revell Co.): 1979 (49¢)
nn 2 4 6 13 18 22

BROTHERS IN ARMS (Based on the World War II military video game)
Dynamite Entertainment: 2008 - No. 4, 2008 ($3.99/$3.50)
1-($3.99) Fabbri-a; two covers by Fabbri & Sejic 4.00
2-4-($3.50) Two covers by Fabbri & Sejic on each 3.50

BROTHERS OF THE SPEAR (Also see Tarzan)
Gold Key/Whitman No. 18: June, 1972 - No. 17, Feb, 1976; No. 18, May, 1982
1 5 10 15 31 53 75
2-Painted-c begin, end #17 3 6 9 18 28 38
3-10 3 6 9 15 22 28
11-18: 12-Line drawn-c. 13-17-Spiegle-a. 18(5/82)-r/#2; Leopard Girl-r 2 4 6 11 16 20

BROTHERS, THE CULT ESCAPE, THE
Spire Christian Comics (Fleming H. Revell Co.): 1980 (49¢)
nn 3 6 9 14 19 24

BROWNIES (See New Funnies)
Dell Publishing Co.: No. 192, July, 1948 - No. 605, Dec, 1954
Four Color 192(#1)-Kelly-a 13 26 39 89 195 300
Four Color 244(9/49), 293 (9/50)-Last Kelly c/a 10 20 30 64 132 200
Four Color 337(7-8/51), 365(12-1/51-52), 398(5/52) 6 12 18 38 69 100
Four Color 436(11/52), 482(7/53), 522(12/53), 605 5 10 15 35 63 90

BRUCE GENTRY
Better/Standard/Four Star Publ./Superior No. 3: Jan, 1948 - No. 8, Jul, 1949
1-Ray Bailey strip reprints begin, end #3; E.C. emblem appears as a monogram on stationery in story; negligee panels 65 130 195 416 708 1000
2,3 39 78 117 240 395 550
4-8 28 56 84 165 270 375
NOTE: *Kamenish a-2-7; c-1-8.*

BRUCE JONES' OUTER EDGE
Innovation: 1993 ($2.50, B&W, one-shot)
1-Bruce Jones-c/a/script 3.00

BRUCE LEE (Also see Deadly Hands of Kung Fu)
Malibu Comics: July, 1994 - No. 6, Dec, 1994 ($2.95, 36 pgs.)
1-6: 1-(44 pgs.)-Mortal Kombat prev., 1st app. in comics. 2,6-(36 pgs.) 5.00

BRUCE WAYNE: AGENT OF S.H.I.E.L.D. (Also see Marvel Vs. DC #3 & DC Vs. Marvel #4)
Marvel Comics (Amalgam): Apr, 1996 ($1.95, one-shot)
1-Chuck Dixon scripts & Cary Nord-c/a. 3.00

BRUCE WAYNE: THE ROAD HOME (See Batman: The Return of Bruce Wayne)
(See Batman: Bruce Wayne - The Road Home HC for reprints)
DC Comics: Dec, 2010 ($2.99, series of one-shots with interlocking covers)
...: Batgirl 1 - Bryan Miller-s/Pere Pérez-a 3.00
...: Batman and Robin 1 - Nicieza-s/Richards-a; Vicki Vale app. 3.00
...: Catwoman 1 - Fridolfs-s/Nguyen-a; Harley & Ivy app. 3.00

Brutal Nature #2 © Saracino & Olivetti

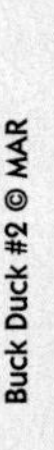
Buck Duck #2 © MAR

Buck Rogers (2013 series) #4 © Dille Family

GD VG FN VF VF/NM NM-
2.0 4.0 6.0 8.0 9.0 9.2

...: Commissioner Gordon 1 - Beechen-s/Kudranski-a; Penguin app. 3.00
...: Oracle 1 - Andreyko-s/Padilla-a; Man-Bat & Manhunter app. 3.00
...: Outsiders 1 - Barr-s/Saltares-a 3.00
...: Ra's al Ghul 1 - Nicieza-s/McDaniel-a 3.00
...: Red Robin 1 - Nicieza-s/Bachs-a; Ra's al Ghul app. 3.00

BRUISER
Anthem Publications: Feb, 1994 ($2.45)
1 3.00

BRUTAL NATURE
IDW Publishing: May, 2016 - No. 4, Aug, 2016 ($3.99, limited series)
1-4-Ariel Olivetti-a/Luciano Saracino-s 4.00

BRUTE, THE
Seaboard Publ. (Atlas): Feb, 1975 - No. 3, July, 1975
1-Origin & 1st app; Sekowsky-a(p) 3 6 9 15 22 28
2-Sekowsky-a(p); Fleisher-s 2 4 6 10 14 18
3-Brunner/Starlin/Weiss-a(p) 2 4 6 13 18 22

BRUTE & BABE
Ominous Press: July, 1994 - No. 2, Aug, 1994
1-($3.95, 8 tablets plus-c)-"...It Begins..."; tablet format 4.00
2-($2.50, 36 pgs.)-"Mael's Rage", 2-(40 pgs.)-Stiff additional variant-c 3.00

BRUTE FORCE
Marvel Comics: Aug, 1990 - No. 4, Nov, 1990 ($1.00, limited series)
1-4: Animal super-heroes; Delbo & DeCarlo-a 3.00

B-SIDES (The Craptacular...)
Marvel Comics: Nov, 2002 - No. 3, Jan, 2003 ($2.99, limited series)
1-3-Kieth-c/Weldele-a. 2-Dorkin-a (1 pg.) 2-FF cameo. 3-FF app. 3.00

BUBBLEGUM CRISIS: GRAND MAL
Dark Horse Comics: Mar, 1994 - No. 4, June, 1994 ($2.50, limited series)
1-4-Japanese manga 3.00

BUBBLEGUN
Aspen MLT: Jun, 2013 - No. 5, Mar, 2014 ($1.00/$3.99)
1-($1.00) Roslan-s/Bowden-a; multiple covers 3.00
2-5-($3.99) Multiple covers on each 4.00

BUCCANEER
I. W. Enterprises: No date (1963)
I.W. Reprint #1(r-/Quality #20), #8(r-/#23): Crandall-a in each
3 6 9 16 23 30

BUCCANEERS (Formerly Kid Eternity)
Quality Comics: No. 19, Jan, 1950 - No. 27, May, 1951 (No. 24-27: 52 pgs.)
19-Captain Daring, Black Roger, Eric Falcon & Spanish Main begin;
Crandall-a 48 96 144 302 514 725
20,23-Crandall-a 36 72 108 215 350 485
21-Crandall-c/a 39 78 117 236 388 540
22-Bondage-c 28 56 84 165 270 375
24-26: 24-Adam Peril, U.S.N. begins. 25-Origin & 1st app. Corsair Queen.
26-Last Spanish Main 24 48 72 142 234 325
27-Crandall-c/a 34 68 102 205 335 465
Super Reprint #12 (1964)-Crandall-r/#21 3 6 9 16 23 30

BUCCANEERS, THE (TV)
Dell Publishing Co.: No. 800, 1957
Four Color 800-Photo-c 6 12 18 42 79 115

BUCKAROO BANZAI (Movie)
Marvel Comics Group: Dec, 1984 - No. 2, Feb, 1985
1,2-Movie adaptation; r/Marvel Super Special #33; Texiera-c/a 4.00

BUCKAROO BANZAI: RETURN OF THE SCREW
Moonstone: 2006 - No. 3, 2006 ($3.50, limited series)
1-3: 1-Three covers by Haley, Stribling, Beck; Thompson-a 3.50
Preview (2006, 50¢) B&W preview; history of movie and spin-off projects 3.00

BUCK DUCK
Atlas Comics (ANC): June, 1953 - No. 4, Dec, 1953
1-Funny animal stories in all 20 40 60 117 189 260
2-4: 2-Ed Win-a(5) 13 26 39 72 101 130

BUCK JONES (Also see Crackajack Funnies, Famous Feature Stories, Master Comics #7 & Wow Comics #1, 1936)
Dell Publishing Co.: No. 299, Oct, 1950 - No. 850, Oct, 1957 (All Painted-c)
Four Color 299(#1)-Buck Jones & his horse Silver-B begin; painted back-c begins, ends #5
12 24 36 82 179 275
2(4-6/51) 7 14 21 44 82 120
3-8(10-12/52) 6 12 18 37 66 95
Four Color 460,500,546,589 6 12 18 41 76 110
Four Color 652,733,850 5 10 15 35 63 90

BUCK ROGERS (Also see Famous Funnies, Pure Oil Comics, Salerno Carnival of Comics, 24 Pages of Comics, & Vicks Comics)
Famous Funnies: Winter, 1940-41 - No. 6, Sept, 1943
NOTE: Buck Rogers first appeared in the pulp magazine Amazing Stories Vol. 3 #5 in Aug, 1928.
1-Sunday strip reprints by Rick Yager; begins with strip #190; Calkins-c
343 686 1029 2400 4200 6000
2 (7/41)-Calkins-c 142 284 426 909 1555 2200
3 (12/41), 4 (7/42) 119 238 357 762 1306 1850
5,6: 5-Story continues with Famous Funnies No. 80; Buck Rogers, Sky Roads. 6-Reprints of 1939 dailies; contains B.R. story "Crater of Doom" (2 pgs.) by Calkins not-r from Famous Funnies 100 200 300 635 1093 1550

BUCK ROGERS
Toby Press: No. 100, Jan, 1951 - No. 9, May-June, 1951
100(#7)-All strip-r begin; Anderson, Chatton-a 32 64 96 188 307 425
101(#8), 9-All Anderson-a(1947-49-r/dailies) 24 48 72 142 234 325

BUCK ROGERS (...in the 25th Century No. 5 on) (TV)
Gold Key/Whitman No. 7 on: Oct, 1964; No. 2, July, 1979 - No. 16, May, 1982 (No #10; story was written but never released. #17 exists only as a press proof without covers and was never published)
1(10128-410, 12¢)-1st S.A. app. Buck Rogers & 1st new B. R. in comics
since 1933 giveaway; painted-c; back-c pin-up 10 20 30 70 150 230
2(7/79)-6: 3,4,6-Movie adaptation; painted-c 2 4 6 9 12 15
7,11 (Whitman) 2 4 6 11 16 20
8,9 (prepack)(scarce) 4 8 12 27 44 60
12-16: 14(2/82), 15(3/82), 16(5/82) 2 4 6 8 10 12
Giant Movie Edition 11296(64pp, Whitman, $1.50), reprints GK #2-4 minus cover;
tabloid size; photo-c (See Marvel Treasury) 3 6 9 17 26 35
Giant Movie Edition 02489(Western/Marvel, $1.50), reprints GK #2-4 minus cover
3 6 9 16 24 32
NOTE: *Bolle a-2p,3p, Movie Ed.(p). McWilliams a-2i,3i, 5-11, Movie Ed.(i). Painted c-1-9,11-13.*

BUCK ROGERS (Comics Module)
TSR, Inc.: 1990 - No. 10, 1991 ($2.95, 44 pgs.)
1-10 (1990): 1-Begin origin in 3 parts. 2-Indicia says #1. 2,3-Black Barney back-up story. 4-All Black Barney issue; B. B.-c. 5-Indicia says #6; Black Barney-c & lead story; Buck Rogers back-up story. 10-Flip book (72pgs.) 4.00

BUCK ROGERS
Dynamite Entertainment: No. 0, 2009 - No. 12, 2010 (25¢/$3.50)
0-(25¢) Beatty-s/Rafael-a/Cassaday-c 3.00
1-12: 1-($3.50) Three covers by Cassaday, Ross and Wagner; origin re-told 3.50
Annual 1 (2011, $4.99) Rafael-a; covers by Rafael & Sadowski 5.00

BUCK ROGERS
Hermes Press: 2013 - No. 4, 2013 ($3.99)
1-4-Howard Chaykin-s/a/c 4.00

BUCKSKIN (TV)
Dell Publishing Co.: No. 1011, July, 1959 - No. 1107, June-Aug, 1960
Four Color 1011 (#1)-Photo-c 7 14 21 44 82 120
Four Color 1107-Photo-c 6 12 18 40 73 105

BUCKY BARNES: THE WINTER SOLDIER (See Captain America titles)
Marvel Comics: Dec, 2014 - No. 11, Nov, 2015 ($3.99)
1-11: 1-Ales Kot-s/Marco Rudy-a; Daisy Johnson app. 2,8,9,10-Loki app. 4-7,9-Crossbones app. 7-Foss-a 4.00

BUCKY O'HARE (Funny Animal)
Continuity Comics: 1988 ($5.95, graphic novel)
1-Golden-c/a(r); r/serial-Echo of Futurepast #1-6 1 2 3 4 5 7
Deluxe Hardcover ($40.00, 52 pg., 8 x 11") 40.00

BUCKY O'HARE
Continuity Comics: Jan, 1991 - No. 5, 1991 ($2.00)
1-6: 1-Michael Golden-c/a 3.00

BUDDIES IN THE U.S. ARMY
Avon Periodicals: Nov, 1952 - No. 2, 1953
1-Lawrence-c 15 30 45 85 130 175

Buffalo Bill #3 © YM

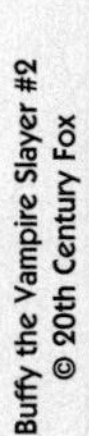

Buffy the Vampire Slayer #2 © 20th Century Fox

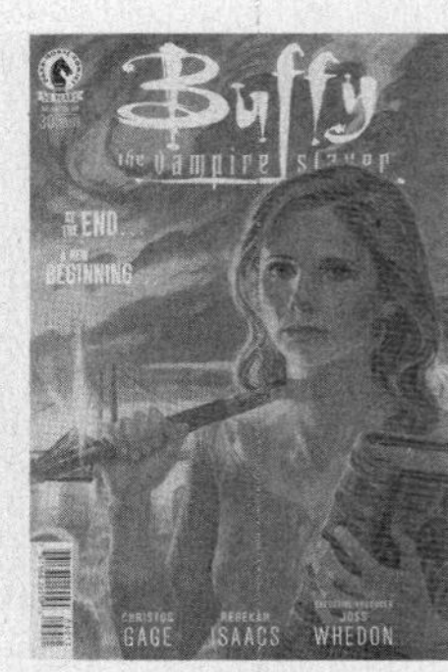

Buffy the Vampire Slayer (Season 10) #30 © 20th Century Fox

	GD 2.0	VG 4.0	FN 6.0	VF 8.0	VF/NM 9.0	NM- 9.2
2-Mort Lawrence-c/a	11	22	33	60	83	105

BUFFALO BEE (TV)
Dell Publishing Co.: No. 957, Nov, 1958 - No. 1061, Dec-Feb, 1959-60

	GD 2.0	VG 4.0	FN 6.0	VF 8.0	VF/NM 9.0	NM- 9.2
Four Color 957 (#1)	8	16	24	52	99	145
Four Color 1002 (8-10/59), 1061	6	12	18	40	73	105

BUFFALO BILL (See Frontier Fighters, Super Western Comics & Western Action Thrillers)
Youthful Magazines: No. 2, Oct, 1950 - No. 9, Dec, 1951

	GD 2.0	VG 4.0	FN 6.0	VF 8.0	VF/NM 9.0	NM- 9.2
2-Annie Oakley story	15	30	45	84	127	170
3-9: 2-4-Walter Johnson-c/a. 9-Wildey-a	11	22	33	60	83	105

BUFFALO BILL CODY (See Cody of the Pony Express)

BUFFALO BILL, JR. (TV) (See Western Roundup)
Dell/Gold Key: Jan, 1956 - No. 13, Aug-Oct, 1959; 1965 (All photo-c)

	GD 2.0	VG 4.0	FN 6.0	VF 8.0	VF/NM 9.0	NM- 9.2
Four Color 673 (#1)	8	16	24	56	108	160
Four Color 742,766,798,828,856(11/57)	5	10	15	35	63	90
7(2-4/58)-13	5	10	15	31	53	75
1(6/65, Gold Key)-Photo-c(r/F.C. #798); photo-b/c	4	8	12	23	37	50

BUFFALO BILL PICTURE STORIES
Street & Smith Publications: June-July, 1949 - No. 2, Aug-Sept, 1949

	GD 2.0	VG 4.0	FN 6.0	VF 8.0	VF/NM 9.0	NM- 9.2
1,2-Wildey, Powell-a in each	14	28	42	80	115	150

BUFFY: THE HIGH SCHOOL YEARS (Based on the TV series)
Dark Horse Comics

	GD 2.0	VG 4.0	FN 6.0	VF 8.0	VF/NM 9.0	NM- 9.2
... – Glutton For Punishment (10/16, $10.99, 6" x 9") McDonald-s/Li-a						11.00

BUFFY THE VAMPIRE SLAYER (Based on the TV series)(Also see Angel and Faith, Spike, Tales of the Vampires and Willow)
Dark Horse Comics: 1998 - No. 63, Nov, 2003 ($2.95/$2.99)

	GD 2.0	VG 4.0	FN 6.0	VF 8.0	VF/NM 9.0	NM- 9.2
1-Bennett-a/Watson-s; Art Adams-c	1	2	3	6	8	10
1-Variant photo-c	1	2	3	6	8	10
1-Gold foil logo Art Adams-c						15.00
1-Gold foil logo photo-c						20.00
2-4-Photo-c	1	3	4	6	8	10
5-15-Regular and photo-c. 4-7-Gomez-a. 5,8-Green-c						5.00
16-48: 29,30-Angel x-over. 43-45-Death of Buffy. 47-Lobdell-s begin. 48-Pike returns						3.00
50-($3.50) Scooby gang battles Adam; back-up story by Watson						4.00
51-63: 51-54-Viva Las Buffy; pre-Sunnydale Buffy & Pike in Vegas						3.00
Annual '99 ($4.95)-Two stories and pin-ups	1	2	3	4	5	7
...: A Stake to the Heart TPB (3/04, $12.95) r/#60-63						13.00
...: Chaos Bleeds (6/03, $2.99) Based on the video game; photo & Campbell-c						3.00
...: Creatures of Habit (3/02, $17.95) text with Horton & Paul Lee-a						18.00
...: Jonathan 1 (1/01, $2.99) two covers; Richards-a						3.00
...: Lost and Found 1 (3/02, $2.99) aftermath of Buffy's death; Richards-a						3.00
... Lovers Walk (2/01, $2.99) short stories by various; Richards & photo-c						3.00
...: Note From the Underground (3/03, $12.95) r/#47-50						13.00
...: Omnibus Vol. 1 (7/07, $24.95, 9x6") r/Spike & Dru #3, Origin #1-3 and Buffy #51-59						25.00
...: Omnibus Vol. 2 (9/07, $24.95, 9x6") r/Buffy #60-63 and various one-shots & specials						25.00
...: Omnibus Vol. 3 (1/08, $24.95, 9x6") r/Buffy #1-8,12,16, Annual '99						25.00
...: Omnibus Vol. 4 (5/08, $24.95, 9x6") r/Buffy #9-11,13-15,17-20,50 and various						25.00
...: Omnibus Vol. 5 (9/08, $24.95, 9x6") r/Buffy #21-28 and various one-shots & specials						25.00
...: Omnibus Vol. 6 (2/09, $24.95, 9x6") r/Buffy #29-38 and various one-shots & specials						25.00
...: One For One (9/10, $1.00) r/#1 with red cover frame						3.00
...: Reunion (6/02, $3.50) Buffy & Angel's; Espenson-s; art by various						3.50
...: Slayer Interrupted TPB (2003, $14.95) r/#56-59						15.00
...: Tales of the Slayers (10/02, $3.50) art by Matsuda and Colan; art & photo-c						3.50
...: The Death of Buffy TPB (8/02, $15.95) r/#43-46						16.00
...: Viva Las Buffy TPB (7/03, $12.95) r/#51-54						13.00
Wizard #1/2	1	2	3	6	8	9

BUFFY THE VAMPIRE SLAYER ("Season Eight" of the TV series)
Dark Horse Comics: Mar, 2007 - No. 40, Jan, 2011 ($2.99)

	GD 2.0	VG 4.0	FN 6.0	VF 8.0	VF/NM 9.0	NM- 9.2
1-Joss Whedon-s/Georges Jeanty-a/Jo Chen-c						6.00
1-Variant cover by Jeanty						6.00
1-RRP with B&W Jeanty cover (edition of 1000)						85.00
1-4: 1-2nd thru 5th printings. 2-2nd-4th printings. 3,4-2nd & 3rd printings						3.00
2-5-Jeanty-a; covers by Chen & Jeanty						4.00
6-13,16-19-Two covers by Chen & Jeanty. 6-9-Faith app.; Vaughan-s. 10,11-Whedon-s. 12-15-Goddard-s; Dracula app. 16-19-Fray app.; Whedon-s/Moline-a						3.00
20-40: 20-28,31-40-Two covers by Chen and Jeanty. 20-Animation style flashback. 21,26-30-Espenson-s. 30-Hughes-c. 31-Whedon-s. 32-35-Meltzer-s. 36-40-Whedon-s						3.00
...: Riley (8/10, $3.50) Espensen-s/Moline-a; Riley Finn and Sam; Angel app.						3.50
... Tales of the Vampires (6/09, $2.99) Cloonan-s/Lolos-a; covers by Chen & Bá/Moon						3.00
...: Willow (12/09, $3.50) Whedon-s/Moline-a; Willow meets the Snake Guide						3.50

BUFFY THE VAMPIRE SLAYER ("Season Nine" of the TV series)
Dark Horse Comics: Sept, 2011 - No. 25, Sept, 2013 ($2.99)

	GD 2.0	VG 4.0	FN 6.0	VF 8.0	VF/NM 9.0	NM- 9.2
1-25: 1-Whedon-s/Jeanty-a; covers by Morris & Chen. 2-5-Chambliss-s; two covers by Morris & Jeanty. 5-Moline-a; Nikki flashback. 6,7-Two covers by Jeanty & Noto. 8-10-Richards-a. 14-Espenson-s; intro. Billy. 16-19-Illyria app.						3.00
....: Buffyverse Sampler (1/13, $4.99) r/#1, Angel & Faith #1, Spike #1, Willow #1						5.00
FCBD (5/12, giveaway) Buffy vs. Alien; Jeanty-a; flip book with The Guild						3.00

BUFFY THE VAMPIRE SLAYER (SEASON TEN)
Dark Horse Comics: Mar, 2014 - No. 30, Aug, 2016 ($3.50/$3.99)

	GD 2.0	VG 4.0	FN 6.0	VF 8.0	VF/NM 9.0	NM- 9.2
1-16: 1-Gage-s/Isaacs-a; covers by Morris & Isaacs. 2-5-Dracula app. 3-5,7,12,13-Nicholas Brendon & Gage-s. 8-Corben-a (3 pgs)						3.50
17-30-($3.99) 19-Nicholas Brendon & Gage-s. 25-Levens-a						4.00

BUFFY THE VAMPIRE SLAYER SEASON ELEVEN
Dark Horse Comics: Nov, 2016 - Present ($3.99)

	GD 2.0	VG 4.0	FN 6.0	VF 8.0	VF/NM 9.0	NM- 9.2
1-4: 1-Gage-s/Isaacs-a; covers by Morris & Isaacs						4.00

BUFFY THE VAMPIRE SLAYER: ANGEL
Dark Horse Comics: May, 1999 - No. 3, July, 1999 ($2.95, limited series)

	GD 2.0	VG 4.0	FN 6.0	VF 8.0	VF/NM 9.0	NM- 9.2
1-3-Gomez-a; Matsuda-c & photo-c for each						3.00

BUFFY THE VAMPIRE SLAYER: GILES
Dark Horse Comics: Oct, 2000 ($2.95, one-shot)

	GD 2.0	VG 4.0	FN 6.0	VF 8.0	VF/NM 9.0	NM- 9.2
1-Eric Powell-a; Powell & photo-c						3.00

BUFFY THE VAMPIRE SLAYER: HAUNTED
Dark Horse Comics: Dec, 2001 - No. 4, Mar, 2002 ($2.99, limited series)

	GD 2.0	VG 4.0	FN 6.0	VF 8.0	VF/NM 9.0	NM- 9.2
1-4-Faith and the Mayor app.; Espenson-s/Richards-a						3.00
TPB (9/02, $12.95) r/series; photo-c						13.00

BUFFY THE VAMPIRE SLAYER: OZ
Dark Horse Comics: July, 2001 - No. 3, Sept, 2001 ($2.99, limited series)

	GD 2.0	VG 4.0	FN 6.0	VF 8.0	VF/NM 9.0	NM- 9.2
1-3-Totleben & photo-c; Golden-s						3.00

BUFFY THE VAMPIRE SLAYER: SPIKE AND DRU
Dark Horse Comics: Apr, 1999; No. 2, Oct, 1999; No. 3, Dec, 2000 ($2.95)

	GD 2.0	VG 4.0	FN 6.0	VF 8.0	VF/NM 9.0	NM- 9.2
1-3: 1,2-Photo-c. 3-Two covers (photo & Sook)						3.00

BUFFY THE VAMPIRE SLAYER: THE ORIGIN (Adapts movie screenplay)
Dark Horse Comics: Jan, 1999 - No. 3, Mar, 1999 ($2.95, limited series)

	GD 2.0	VG 4.0	FN 6.0	VF 8.0	VF/NM 9.0	NM- 9.2
1-3-Brereton-s/Bennett-a; reg & photo-c for each						3.00

BUFFY THE VAMPIRE SLAYER: WILLOW & TARA
Dark Horse Comics: Apr, 2001 ($2.99, one-shot)

	GD 2.0	VG 4.0	FN 6.0	VF 8.0	VF/NM 9.0	NM- 9.2
1-Terry Moore-a/Chris Golden & Amber Benson-s; Moore-c & photo-c						3.00
TPB (4/03, $9.95) r/#1 & W&T - Wilderness; photo-c						10.00

BUFFY THE VAMPIRE SLAYER: WILLOW & TARA - WILDERNESS
Dark Horse Comics: Jul, 2002 - No. 2, Sept, 2002 ($2.99, limited series)

	GD 2.0	VG 4.0	FN 6.0	VF 8.0	VF/NM 9.0	NM- 9.2
1,2-Chris Golden & Amber Benson-s; Jothikaumar-c & photo-c						3.00

BUG
Marvel Comics: Mar, 1997 ($2.99, one-shot)

	GD 2.0	VG 4.0	FN 6.0	VF 8.0	VF/NM 9.0	NM- 9.2
1-Micronauts character						3.00

BUGALOOS (Sid & Marty Krofft TV show)
Charlton Comics: Sept, 1971 - No. 4, Feb, 1972

	GD 2.0	VG 4.0	FN 6.0	VF 8.0	VF/NM 9.0	NM- 9.2
1	5	10	15	30	50	70
2-4	3	6	9	19	30	40

NOTE: *No. 3(1/72) went on sale late in 1972 (after No. 4) with the 1/73 issues.*

BUGHOUSE (Satire)
Ajax/Farrell (Excellent Publ.): Mar-Apr, 1954 - No. 4, Sept-Oct, 1954

	GD 2.0	VG 4.0	FN 6.0	VF 8.0	VF/NM 9.0	NM- 9.2
V1#1	25	50	75	150	245	340
2-4	15	30	45	84	127	170

BUGS BUNNY (See The Best of..., Camp Comics, Comic Album #2, 6, 10, 14, Dell Giant #28, 32, 46, Dynabrite, Golden Comics Digest #1, 3, 5, 6, 8, 10, 14, 15, 17, 21, 26, 30, 34, 39, 42, 47, Kite Fun Book, Large Feature Comic #8, Looney Tunes and Merry Melodies, March of Comics #44, 59, 75, 83, 97, 115, 132, 149, 160, 179, 188, 201, 220, 231, 245, 259, 273, 287, 301, 315, 329, 343, 363, 367, 380, 392, 403, 415, 428, 440, 452, 464, 476, 487, Porky Pig, Puffed Wheat, Story Hour Series #802, Super Book #14, 26 and Whitman Comic Books)

BUGS BUNNY (See Dell Giants for annuals)
Dell Publishing Co./Gold Key No. 86-218/Whitman No. 219 on: 1942 - No. 245, April, 1984

	GD 2.0	VG 4.0	FN 6.0	VF 8.0	VF/NM 9.0	NM- 9.2
Large Feature Comic 8(1942)-(Rarely found in fine-mint condition)	297	594	891	1888	3244	4600
Four Color 33 ('43)	107	214	321	856	1928	3000
Four Color 51	35	70	105	252	564	875

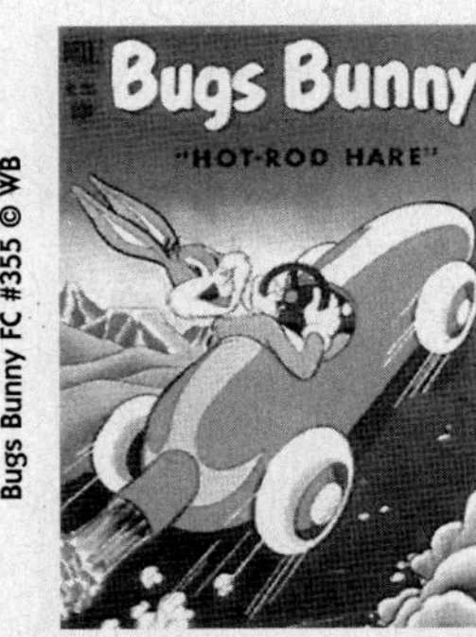

Bugs Bunny FC #355 © WB

Bulletman #1 © FAW

Bullseye (2017 series) #2 © MAR

	GD 2.0	VG 4.0	FN 6.0	VF 8.0	VF/NM 9.0	NM- 9.2
Four Color 88	23	46	69	156	348	540
Four Color 123('46),142,164	15	30	45	105	233	360
Four Color 187,200,217,233	11	22	33	76	163	250
Four Color 250-Used in **SOTI**, pg. 309	12	24	36	79	170	260
Four Color 266,274,281,289,298('50)	9	18	27	61	123	185
Four Color 307,317(#1),327(#2),338,347,355,366,376,393	8	16	24	55	105	155
Four Color 407,420,432(10/52)	7	14	21	48	89	130
Four Color 498(9/53),585(9/54), 647(9/55)	6	12	18	38	69	100
Four Color 724(9/56),838(9/57),1064(12/59)	5	10	15	34	60	85
28(12-1/52-53)-30	5	10	15	34	60	85
31-50	4	8	12	28	47	65
51-85(7-9/62)	4	8	12	23	37	50
86(10/62)-88-Bugs Bunny's Showtime-(25¢, 80pgs.)	5	10	15	35	63	90
89-99	3	6	9	16	24	32
100	3	6	9	17	26	35
101-118: 108-1st Honey Bunny. 118-Last 12¢ issue	3	6	9	14	19	24
119-140	2	4	6	11	16	20
141-170	2	4	6	9	12	15
171-218: 218-Publ. by Whitman only?	2	4	6	8	10	12
219,220,225-237(5/82): 229-Swipe of Barks story/WDC&S #223. 233(2/82)	2	4	6	8	10	12
221(9/80),222(11/80)-Pre-pack? (Scarce)	4	8	12	28	47	65
223 (1/81, 50¢-c), 224 (3/81)-Low distr.	3	6	9	14	20	25
223 (1/81, 40¢-c) Cover price error variant	3	6	9	17	26	35
238-245 (#90070 on-c, nd, nd code; pre-pack): 238(5/83), 239(6/83), 240(7/83), 241(7/83), 242(8/83), 243(8/83), 244(3/84), 245(4/84)	3	6	9	15	22	28

NOTE: *Reprints-100,102-104,110,115,123,143,144,147,167,173,175-177,179-185,187,190.*

	GD	VG	FN	VF	VF/NM	NM-
nn (Xerox Pub. Comic Digest, 1971, 100 pages, B&W) collection of one-page gags	4	8	12	23	37	50
...Comic-Go-Round 11196-(224 pgs.)($1.95)(Golden Press, 1979)	4	8	12	25	40	55
...Winter Fun 1(12/67-Gold Key)-Giant	5	10	15	30	50	70

BUGS BUNNY
DC Comics: June, 1990 - No. 3, Aug, 1990 ($1.00, limited series)

1-3: Daffy Duck, Elmer Fudd, others app. — 4.00

BUGS BUNNY (...Monthly on-c)
DC Comics: 1993 - No. 3, 1994? ($1.95)

1-3-Bugs, Porky Pig, Daffy, Road Runner — 3.50

BUGS BUNNY (Digest-size reprints from Looney Tunes)
DC Comics: 2005 - Present ($6.99, digest)

Vol. 1: What's Up Doc? - Reprints from Looney Tunes #37,41,43-45,48,52,55,57-59,63 — 7.00

BUGS BUNNY & PORKY PIG
Gold Key: Sept, 1965 (Paper-c, giant, 100 pgs.)

	GD	VG	FN	VF	VF/NM	NM-
1(30025-509)	6	12	18	38	69	100

BUGS BUNNY'S ALBUM (See Bugs Bunny, Four Color No. 498,585,647,724)

BUGS BUNNY LIFE STORY ALBUM (See Bugs Bunny, Four Color No. 838)

BUGS BUNNY MERRY CHRISTMAS (See Bugs Bunny, Four Color No. 1064)

BUILDING, THE
Kitchen Sink Press: 1987; 2000 (8 1/2" x 11" sepia toned graphic novel)

nn-Will Eisner-s/c/a — 15.00
nn-(DC Comics, 9/00, $9.95) reprints 1987 edition — 10.00

BULLET CROW, FOWL OF FORTUNE
Eclipse Comics: Mar, 1987 - No. 2, Apr, 1987 ($2.00, B&W, limited series)

1,2-The Comic Reader-r & new-a — 3.00

BULLETMAN (See Fawcett Miniatures, Master Comics, Mighty Midget Comics, Nickel Comics & XMas Comics)
Fawcett Publications: Sum, 1941 - #12, 2/12/43; #14, Spr, 1946 - #16, Fall, 1946 (No #13)

	GD	VG	FN	VF	VF/NM	NM-
1-Silver metallic-c	400	800	1200	2800	4900	7000
2-Raboy-c	177	354	531	1124	1937	2750
3,5-Raboy-c each	142	284	426	909	1555	2200
4	98	196	294	622	1074	1525
6,8-10: 10-Intro. Bulletdog	84	168	252	538	919	1300
7-Ghost Stories told by night watchman of cemetery begins; Eisnerish-a; hidden message "Chic Stone is a jerk".	94	188	282	597	1024	1450
11,12,14-16 (nn 13): 12-Robot-c	61	122	183	390	670	950

NOTE: ***Mac Raboy** c-1-3, 5, 6, 10. "Bulletman the Flying Detective" on cover #8 on.*

BULLET POINTS
Marvel Comics: Jan, 2007 - No. 5, May, 2007 ($2.99, limited series)

1-5: 1-Steve Rogers becomes Iron Man; Straczynski-s/Edwards-a. 4,5-Galactus app. — 3.00
TPB (2007, $13.99) r/#1-5; layout pages by Edwards — 14.00

BULLETPROOF MONK (Inspired the 2003 film)
Image Comics (Flypaper Press): 1998 - No. 3, 1999 ($2.95, limited series)

1-3-Oeming-a — 3.00
...: Tales of the BPM (3/03, $2.95) Flip book; 2 covers by Sale; art by Sale, Oeming, Dave Johnson; Seann William Scott afterword — 3.00
TPB (2002, $9.95) r/#1-3; foreword by John Woo — 10.00

BULLETS AND BRACELETS (Also see Marvel Versus DC #3 & DC Versus Marvel #4)
Marvel Comics (Amalgam): Apr, 1996 ($1.95)

1-John Ostrander script & Gary Frank-c/a — 3.00

BULLSEYE (Daredevil villain)
Marvel Comics: Apr, 2017 - Present ($4.99/$3.99)

1-($4.99) Brisson-s/Sanna-a; back-up with Wolfman-s/Morgan-a — 5.00
2-($3.99) Brisson-s/Sanna-a — 4.00

BULLS-EYE (Cody of The Pony Express No. 8 on)
Mainline No. 1-5/Charlton No. 6,7: 7-8/54-No. 5, 3-4/55; No. 6, 6/55; No. 7, 8/55

	GD	VG	FN	VF	VF/NM	NM-
1-S&K-c, 2 pgs.-a	74	148	222	470	810	1150
2-S&K-c/a	54	108	162	343	574	825
3-5-S&K-c/a(2 each). 4-Last pre-code issue (1-2/55). 5-Censored issue with tomahawks removed in battle scene	45	90	135	284	480	675
6-S&K-c/a	40	80	120	246	411	575
7-S&K-c/a(3)	45	90	135	284	480	675

BULLS-EYE COMICS (Formerly Komik Pages #10; becomes Kayo #12)
Harry 'A' Chesler: No. 11, 1944

	GD	VG	FN	VF	VF/NM	NM-
11-Origin K-9, Green Knight's sidekick, Lance; The Green Knight, Lady Satan, Yankee Doodle Jones app.	77	154	231	493	847	1200

BULLSEYE: GREATEST HITS (Daredevil villain)
Marvel Comics: Nov, 2004 - No. 5, Mar, 2005 ($2.99, limted series)

1-5-Origin of Bullseye; Steve Dillon-a/Deodato-c. 3-Punisher app. — 3.00
TPB (2005, $13.99) r/#1-5 — 14.00

BULLSEYE: PERFECT GAME (Daredevil villain)
Marvel Comics: Jan, 2011 - No. 2, Feb, 2011 ($3.99, limited series)

1,2-Huston-s/Martinbrough-a; Bullseye as baseball pitcher — 4.00

BULLWHIP GRIFFIN (See Movie Comics)

BULLWINKLE (...and Rocky No. 22 on; See March of Comics #233 and Rocky & Bullwinkle) (TV) (Jay Ward)
Dell/Gold Key: 3-5/62 - #11, 4/74; #12, 6/76 - #19, 3/78; #20, 4/79 - #25, 2/80

	GD	VG	FN	VF	VF/NM	NM-
Four Color 1270 (3-5/62)	16	32	48	110	243	375
01-090-209 (Dell, 7-9/62)	13	26	39	86	188	290
1(11/62, Gold Key)	12	24	36	80	173	265
2(2/63)	8	16	24	54	102	150
3(4/72)-11(4/74-Gold Key)	5	10	15	31	53	75
12-14: 12(6/76)-Reprints. 13(9/76), 14-New stories	3	6	9	17	26	35
15-25	2	4	6	11	16	20
Mother Moose Nursery Pomes 01-530-207 (5-7/62, Dell)	15	30	45	100	220	340

NOTE: *Reprints: 6, 7, 20-24.*

BULLWINKLE AND ROCKY (TV)
Charlton Comics: July, 1970 - No. 7, July, 1971

	GD	VG	FN	VF	VF/NM	NM-
1-Has 1 pg. pin-up	6	12	18	40	73	105
2-7: 3-Snidely Whiplash app.	5	10	15	30	50	70

BULLWINKLE AND ROCKY
Star Comics/Marvel Comics No. 3 on: Nov, 1987 - No. 9, Mar, 1989

	GD	VG	FN	VF	VF/NM	NM-
1-9: Boris & Natasha in all. 3,5,8-Dudley Do-Right app. 4-Reagan-c						5.00
Marvel Moosterworks (1/92, $4.95)	2	4	6	8	10	12

BUMMER
Fantagraphics Books: June, 1995 ($3.50, B&W, mature)

1 — 3.50

BUNNY (Also see Harvey Pop Comics and Fruitman Special)
Harvey Publications: Dec, 1966 - No. 20, Dec, 1971; No. 21, Nov, 1976

	GD	VG	FN	VF	VF/NM	NM-
1-68 pg. Giants begin	7	14	21	49	92	135
2-10: 3-1st app. Fruitman. 6,8-10-Fruitman	4	8	12	28	47	65
11-18: 18-Last 68 pg. Giant	4	8	12	27	44	60
19-21-52 pg. Giants: 21-Fruitman app.	4	8	12	25	40	55

BURKE'S LAW (TV)

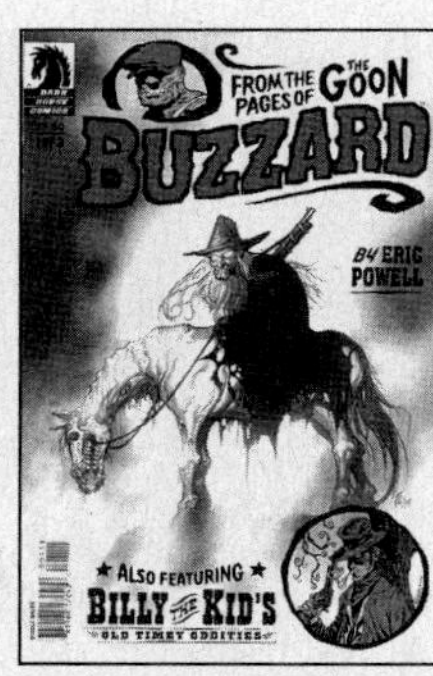

The Buzzard #1 © Eric Powell

Buzzy #6 © DC

Cable #75 © MAR

Dell Publ.: 1-3/64; No. 2, 5-7/64; No. 3, 3-5/65 (All have Gene Barry photo-c)

	GD 2.0	VG 4.0	FN 6.0	VF 8.0	VF/NM 9.0	NM- 9.2
1-Photo-c	5	10	15	31	53	75
2,3-Photo-c	4	8	12	23	37	50

BURNING FIELDS
BOOM! Studios: Jan, 2015 - No. 8, Sept, 2015 ($3.99, limited series)

	GD 2.0	VG 4.0	FN 6.0	VF 8.0	VF/NM 9.0	NM- 9.2
1-6-Moreci & Daniel-s/Lorimer-a						4.00

BURNING ROMANCES (See Fox Giants)

BUSTER BEAR
Quality Comics Group (Arnold Publ.): Dec, 1953 - No. 10, June, 1955

	GD 2.0	VG 4.0	FN 6.0	VF 8.0	VF/NM 9.0	NM- 9.2
1-Funny animal	13	26	39	72	101	130
2	7	14	21	37	46	55
3-10	6	12	18	31	38	45
I.W. Reprint #9,10 (Super on inside)	2	4	6	9	13	16

BUSTER BROWN COMICS (See Promotional Comics section)

BUSTER BUNNY
Standard Comics(Animated Cartoons)/Pines: Nov, 1949 - No. 16, Oct, 1953

	GD 2.0	VG 4.0	FN 6.0	VF 8.0	VF/NM 9.0	NM- 9.2
1-Frazetta 1 pg. text illo.	13	26	39	74	105	135
2	7	14	21	37	46	55
3-14,16	6	12	18	31	38	45
15-Racist-c	12	24	36	67	94	120

BUSTER CRABBE (TV)
Famous Funnies Publ.: Nov, 1951 - No. 12, 1953

	GD 2.0	VG 4.0	FN 6.0	VF 8.0	VF/NM 9.0	NM- 9.2
1-1st app.(?) Frazetta anti-drug ad; text story about Buster Crabbe & Billy the Kid	40	80	120	246	411	575
2-Williamson/Evans-c; text story about Wild Bill Hickok & Pecos Bill	38	76	114	225	368	510
3-Williamson/Evans-c/a	39	78	117	240	395	550
4-Frazetta-c/a, 1pg.; bondage-c	53	106	159	334	567	800
5-Frazetta-c; Williamson/Krenkel/Orlando-a, 11pgs. (per Mr. Williamson)	155	310	465	992	1696	2400
6,8	20	40	60	117	189	260
7-Frazetta one pg. ad	20	40	60	118	192	265
9-One pg. Frazetta Boy Scouts ad (1st?)	17	34	51	98	154	210
10-12	13	26	39	72	101	130

NOTE: Eastern Color sold 3 dozen each NM file copies of #s 9-12 a few years ago.

BUSTER CRABBE (The Amazing Adventures of...)(Movie star)
Lev Gleason Publications: Dec, 1953 - No. 4, June, 1954

	GD 2.0	VG 4.0	FN 6.0	VF 8.0	VF/NM 9.0	NM- 9.2
1,4: 1-Photo-c. 4-Flash Gordon-c	21	42	63	126	206	285
2,3-Toth-a	19	38	57	111	176	240

BUTCH CASSIDY
Skywald Comics: June, 1971 - No. 3, Oct, 1971 (52 pgs.)

	GD 2.0	VG 4.0	FN 6.0	VF 8.0	VF/NM 9.0	NM- 9.2
1-Pre-code reprints and new material; Red Mask reprint, retitled Maverick; Bolle-a; Sutton-a	3	6	9	15	22	28
2,3: 2-Whip Wilson-r. 3-Dead Canyon Days reprint/Crack Western No. 63; Sundance Kid app.; Crandall-a	2	4	6	10	14	18

BUTCH CASSIDY (...& the Wild Bunch)
Avon Periodicals: 1951

	GD 2.0	VG 4.0	FN 6.0	VF 8.0	VF/NM 9.0	NM- 9.2
1-Kinstler-c/a	21	42	63	124	202	280

NOTE: *Reinman* story; Issue number on inside spine.

BUTCH CASSIDY (See Fun-In No. 11 & Western Adventure Comics)

BUTCHER, THE (Also see Brave and the Bold, 2nd Series)
DC Comics: May, 1990 - No. 5, Sept, 1990 ($1.50, mature)

	GD 2.0	VG 4.0	FN 6.0	VF 8.0	VF/NM 9.0	NM- 9.2
1-5: 1-No indicia inside						3.00

BUTCHER KNIGHT
Image Comics (Top Cow): Jan, 2001 - No. 4, June, 2001 ($2.95, limited series)

	GD 2.0	VG 4.0	FN 6.0	VF 8.0	VF/NM 9.0	NM- 9.2
Preview (B&W, 16 pgs.) Dwayne Turner-c/a						3.00
1-4-Dwayne Turner-c/a						3.00

BUTTERFLY
Archaia: Sept, 2014 - No. 4, Dec, 2014 ($3.99, limited series)

	GD 2.0	VG 4.0	FN 6.0	VF 8.0	VF/NM 9.0	NM- 9.2
1-4: Phil Noto-c on all. 1-Marguerite Bennett-s/Antonio Fuso-a. 3,4-Simeone-a						4.00

BUZ SAWYER (Sweeney No. 4 on)
Standard Comics: June, 1948 - No. 3, 1949

	GD 2.0	VG 4.0	FN 6.0	VF 8.0	VF/NM 9.0	NM- 9.2
1-Roy Crane-a	30	60	90	177	289	400
2-Intro his pal Sweeney	17	34	51	98	154	210
3	13	26	39	72	101	130

BUZ SAWYER'S PAL, ROSCOE SWEENEY (See Sweeney)

BUZZ, THE (Also see Spider-Girl)
Marvel Comics: July, 2000 - No. 3, Sept, 2000 ($2.99, limited series)

	GD 2.0	VG 4.0	FN 6.0	VF 8.0	VF/NM 9.0	NM- 9.2
1-3-Buscema-a/DeFalco & Frenz-s						3.00

BUZZARD (See The Goon)
Dark Horse Comics: Jun, 2010 - No. 3, Aug, 2010 ($3.50, limited series)

	GD 2.0	VG 4.0	FN 6.0	VF 8.0	VF/NM 9.0	NM- 9.2
1-3-Eric Powell-c; Buzzard story w/Powell-s/a; Billy The Kid back-up; Powell-s/Hotz-a						3.50

BUZZ BUZZ COMICS MAGAZINE
Horse Press: May, 1996 ($4.95, B&W, over-sized magazine)

	GD 2.0	VG 4.0	FN 6.0	VF 8.0	VF/NM 9.0	NM- 9.2
1-Paul Pope-c/a/scripts; Moebius-a						5.00

BUZZY (See All Funny Comics)
National Periodical Publications/Detective Comics: Winter, 1944-45 - No. 75, 1-2/57; No. 76, 10/57; No. 77, 10/58

	GD 2.0	VG 4.0	FN 6.0	VF 8.0	VF/NM 9.0	NM- 9.2
1 (52 pgs. begin); "America's favorite teenster"	39	78	117	231	378	525
2 (Spr, 1945)	20	40	60	117	189	260
3-5	15	30	45	90	140	190
6-10	14	28	42	80	115	150
11-20	13	26	39	74	105	135
21-30	12	24	36	67	94	120
31,35-38	11	22	33	60	83	105
32-34,39-Last 52 pgs. Scribbly story by Mayer in each (these four stories were done for Scribbly #14 which was delayed for a year)	11	22	33	64	90	115
40-77: 62-Last precode (2/55)	10	20	30	57	79	100

BUZZY THE CROW (See Harvey Comics Hits #60 & 62, Harvey Hits #18 & Paramount Animated Comics #1)

BY BIZARRE HANDS
Dark Horse Comics: Apr, 1994 - No. 3, June, 1994 ($2.50, B&W, mature)

	GD 2.0	VG 4.0	FN 6.0	VF 8.0	VF/NM 9.0	NM- 9.2
1-3: Lansdale stories						3.00

CABBOT: BLOODHUNTER (Also see Bloodstrike & Bloodstrike: Assassin)
Maximum Press: Jan, 1997 ($2.50, one-shot)

	GD 2.0	VG 4.0	FN 6.0	VF 8.0	VF/NM 9.0	NM- 9.2
1-Rick Veitch-a/script; Platt-c; Thor, Chapel & Prophet cameos						3.00

CABLE (See Ghost Rider &..., & New Mutants #87) (Title becomes Soldier X)
Marvel Comics: May, 1993 - No. 107, Sept, 2002 ($3.50/$1.95/$1.50-$2.25)

	GD 2.0	VG 4.0	FN 6.0	VF 8.0	VF/NM 9.0	NM- 9.2
1-($3.50, 52 pgs.)-Gold foil & embossed-c; Thibert a-1-4p; c-1-3						5.00
2,4-15: 4-Liefeld-a assist; last Thibert-a(p). 6-8-Reveals that Baby Nathan is Cable; gives background on Stryfe. 9-Omega Red-c/story. 11-Bound-in trading card sheet						4.00
3-1st Weasel; extra 16 pg. X-Men/Avengers ann. preview	1	2	3	5	6	8
16-Newsstand edition						3.00
16-Enhanced edition						5.00
17-20-($1.95)-Deluxe edition, 20-w/bound in '95 Fleer Ultra cards						4.00
17-20-($1.50)-Standard edition						3.00
21-24, 26-44, -1(7/97): 21-Begin $1.95-c; return from Age of Apocalyse. 24-Grizzly dies. 28-vs. Sugarman; Mr. Sinister app. 30-X-Man-c/app.; Exodus app. 31-vs. X-Man. 32-Post app. 33-Post-c/app; Mandarin app (flashback); includes "Onslaught Update". 34-Onslaught x-over; Hulk-c/app; Apocalypse app. (cont'd in Hulk #444). 35-Onslaught x-over; Apocalypse vs. Cable. 36-w/card insert. 38-Weapon X-c/app; Psycho Man & Micronauts app. 40-Scott Clark-a(p). 41-Bishop-c/app.						3.00
25 ($3.95)-Foil gatefold-c						5.00
45-49,51-74: 45-Operation Zero Tolerance. 51-1st Casey-s. 54-Black Panther. 55-Domino-c/app. 62-Nick Fury-c/app.63-Stryfe-c/app. 67,68-Avengers-c/app. 71,73-Liefeld-a						3.00
50-($2.99) Double sized w/wraparound-c						4.00
75 -($2.99) Liefeld-c/a; Apocalypse: The Twelve x-over						4.00
76-79: 76-Apocalypse: The Twelve x-over						3.00
80-96: 80-Begin $2.25-c. 87-Mystique-c/app.						3.00
97-99,101-107: 97-Tischman-s/Kordey-a/c begin						3.00
100-($3.99) Dialogue-free 'Nuff Said back-up story						4.00
... Classic Vol. 1 TPB (2008, $29.99) r/#1-4, New Mutants #87, Cable: Blood & Metal #1,2						30.00
.../Machine Man '98 Annual ($2.99) Wraparound-c						4.00
.../X-Force '96 Annual ($2.95) Wraparound-c						4.00
...'99 Annual ($3.50) vs. Sinister; computer photo-c						4.00
...Second Genesis 1 (9/99, $3.99) r/New Mutants #99, 100 and X-Force #1; Liefeld-c						4.00
...: The End (2002, $14.99, TPB) r/#101-107						15.00

CABLE
Marvel Comics: May, 2008 - No. 25, Jun, 2010 ($2.99/$3.99)

	GD 2.0	VG 4.0	FN 6.0	VF 8.0	VF/NM 9.0	NM- 9.2
1-23: 1-10-Olivetti-c/a. 1-Liefeld var-c. 2-Finch var-c. 3-Romita Jr. var-c. 4-Bishop app.; Djurdjevic var-c. 5-Silvestri var-c. 6-Liefeld var-c. 13-15-Messiah War x-over; Deadpool app. 16,17-Gulacy-a						3.00
24,25-($3.99) 24-Bishop app. 25-Deadpool app.; Medina-a						4.00

CABLE AND X-FORCE (Marvel NOW!)
Marvel Comics: Feb, 2013 - Present ($3.99)

Cable / Deadpool #39 © MAR

Cage! #1 © MAR

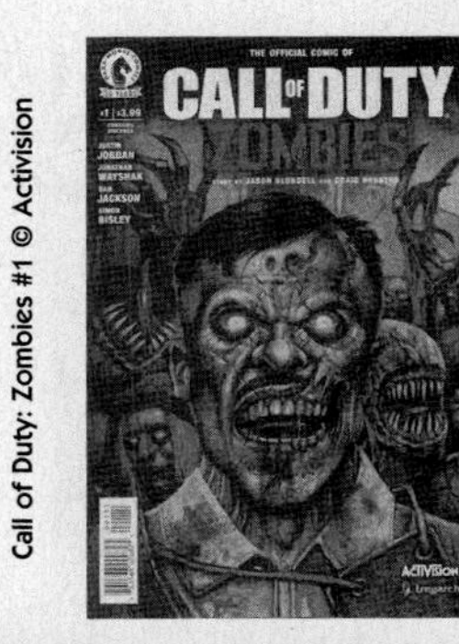

Call of Duty: Zombies #1 © Activision

GD VG FN VF VF/NM NM-
2.0 4.0 6.0 8.0 9.0 9.2

1-19: 1-Hopeless-s/Larroca-a; Cable, Colossus, Domino, Forge & Dr. Nemesis team 4.00

CABLE - BLOOD AND METAL (Also see New Mutants #87 & X-Force #8)
Marvel Comics: Oct, 1992 - No. 2, Nov, 1992 ($2.50, limited series, 52 pgs.)
1-Fabian Nicieza scripts; John Romita, Jr.-c/a in both; Cable vs. Stryfe; 2nd app. of The Wild Pack (becomes The Six Pack); wraparound-c 5.00
2-Prelude to X-Cutioner's Song 5.00

CABLE/DEADPOOL ("Cable & Deadpool" on cover)
Marvel Comics: May, 2004 - No. 50, Apr, 2008 ($2.99)
1-Nicieza-s/Liefeld-c 4 8 12 25 40 55
2,3 1 3 4 6 8 10
4-37: 7-9-X-Men app. 17-House of M. 21-Heroes For Hire app. 30,31-Civil War. 30-Great Lakes Avengers app. 33-Liefeld-c 5.00
38-1st Bob, Agent fo HYDRA 2 4 6 13 18 22
39-49: 43,44-Wolverine app. 4.00
50-($3.99) Final issue; Spider-Man and the Avengers app. 2 4 6 8 10 12
Cable & Deadpool MCG 1 (7/11, $1.00) r/#1 with "Marvel's Greatest Comics" cover logo 3.00
... Vol. 1: If Looks Could Kill TPB (2004, $14.99) r/#1-6 15.00
... Vol. 2: The Burnt Offering TPB (2005, $14.99) r/#7-12 15.00
... Vol. 3: The Human Race TPB (2005, $14.99) r/#13-18 15.00
... Vol. 4: Bosom Buddies TPB (2006, $14.99) r/#19-24 15.00
... Vol. 5: Living Legends TPB (2006, $13.99) r/#25-29 14.00
... Vol. 6: Paved With Good Intentions TPB (2007, $14.99) r/#30-35 15.00
... Vol. 7: Separation Anxiety TPB (2007, $17.99) r/#36-42; sketch pages 18.00
Deadpool Vs. The Marvel Universe TPB (2008, $24.99) r/#43-50 25.00

CADET GRAY OF WEST POINT (See Dell Giants)

CADILLACS & DINOSAURS (TV)
Marvel Comics (Epic Comics): Nov, 1990 - No. 6, Apr, 1991 ($2.50, limited series)
1-6: r/Xenozoic Tales in color w/new-c 3.00
...In 3-D #1 (7/92, $3.95, Kitchen Sink)-With glasses 6.00

CADILLACS AND DINOSAURS (TV)
Topps Comics: V2#1, Feb, 1994 - V2#9, 1995 ($2.50, limited series)
V2#1-($2.95)-Collector's edition w/Stout-c & bound-in poster; Buckler-a; foil stamped logo; Giordano-a in all 6.00
V2#1-9: 1-Newsstand edition w/Giordano-c. 2,3-Collector's editions w/Stout-c & posters. 2,3-Newsstand ed. w/Giordano-c; w/o posters. 4-6-Collectors & Newsstand editions; Kieth-c. 7-9-Linsner-c 3.00

CAGE (Also see Hero for Hire, Power Man & Punisher)
Marvel Comics: Apr, 1992 - No. 20, Nov, 1993 ($1.25)
1,3,10,12: 3-Punisher-c & minor app. 10-Rhino & Hulk-c/app. 12-(52 pgs.)-Iron Fist app. 4.00
2,4-9,11,13-20: 9-Rhino-c/story; Hulk cameo 3.00

CAGE (Volume 3)
Marvel Comics (MAX): Mar, 2002 - No. 5, Sept, 2002 ($2.99, mature)
1-5-Corben-c/a; Azzarello-s 3.00
HC (2002, $19.99, with dustjacket) r/#1-5; intro. by Darius James; sketch pages 20.00
SC (2003, $13.99) r/#1-5; intro. by Darius James 14.00

CAGE! (Luke Cage)
Marvel Comics: Dec, 2016 - No. 4, Mar, 2017 ($3.99, limited series)
1-4-Genndy Tartakovsky-s/a; set in 1977 4.00

CAGED HEAT 3000 (Movie)
Roger Corman's Cosmic Comics: Nov, 1995 - No. 3, Jan, 1996 ($2.50)
1-3: Adaptation of film 3.00

CAGE HERO
Dynamite Entertainment: 2015 - No. 4, 2016 ($3.99, limited series)
1-4-Kevin Eastman & Ian Parker-s/Renalto Rei-a 4.00

CAGES
Tundra Publ.: 1991 - No. 10, May, 1996 ($3.50/$3.95/$4.95, limited series)
1-Dave McKean-c/a in all 2 4 6 8 10 12
2-Misprint exists 1 2 3 5 6 8
3-9: 5-$3.95-c begins 4.00
10-($4.95) 5.00

CAIN'S HUNDRED (TV)
Dell Publishing Co.: May-July, 1962 - No. 2, Sept-Nov, 1962
nn(01-094-207) 3 6 9 19 30 40
2 3 6 9 15 22 28

CAIN/VAMPIRELLA FLIP BOOK
Harris Comics: Oct, 1994 ($6.95, one-shot, squarebound)
nn-contains Cain #3 & #4; flip book is r/Vampirella story from 1993 Creepy Fearbook 1 2 3 5 7 9

CALIBER PRESENTS
Caliber Press: Jan, 1989 - No. 24, 1991 ($1.95/$2.50, B&W, 52 pgs.)
1-Anthology; 1st app. The Crow; Tim Vigil-c/a 8 16 24 54 102 150
2-Deadworld story; Tim Vigil-a 2 4 6 10 14 18
3-24: 15-24 ($3.50, 68 pgs.) 4.00

CALIBER PRESENTS: CINDERELLA ON FIRE
Caliber Press: 1994 ($2.95, B&W, mature)
1 3.00

CALIBER SPOTLIGHT
Caliber Press: May, 1995 ($2.95, B&W)
1-Kabuki app 3.50

CALIFORNIA GIRLS
Eclipse Comics: June, 1987 - No. 8, May, 1988 ($2.00, 40 pgs, B&W)
1-8: All contain color paper dolls 4.00

CALL, THE
Marvel Comics: June, 2003 - No. 4, Sept, 2003 ($2.25)
1-4-Austen-s/Olliffe-a 3.00

CALLING ALL BOYS (Tex Granger No. 18 on)
Parents' Magazine Institute: Jan, 1946 - No. 17, May, 1948 (Photo c-1-5,7,8)
1 18 36 54 103 162 220
2-Contains Roy Rogers article 11 22 33 60 83 105
3-7,9,11,14-17: 6-Painted-c. 11-Rin Tin Tin photo on-c; Tex Granger begins. 14-J. Edgar Hoover photo on-c. 15-Tex Granger-c begin 9 18 27 50 65 80
8-Milton Caniff story 11 22 33 60 83 105
10-Gary Cooper photo on-c 11 22 33 60 83 105
12-Bob Hope photo on-c 15 30 45 85 130 175
13-Bing Crosby photo on-c 14 28 42 80 115 150

CALLING ALL GIRLS
Parents' Magazine Institute: Sept, 1941 - No. 89, Sept, 1949 (Part magazine, part comic)
1 25 50 75 150 245 340
2-Photo-c 14 28 42 80 115 150
3-Shirley Temple photo-c 19 38 57 109 172 235
4-10: 4,5,7,9-Photo-c. 9-Flag-c 12 24 36 69 97 125
11-Tina Thayer photo-c; Mickey Rooney photo-b/c; B&W photo inside of Gary Cooper as Lou Gehrig in "Pride of Yankees" 14 28 42 80 115 150
12-20 10 20 30 56 76 95
21-39,41-43(10-11/45)-Last issue with comics 9 18 27 52 69 85
40-Liz Taylor photo-c 27 54 81 160 263 365
44-51(7/46)-Last comic book size issue 8 16 24 44 57 70
52-89 8 16 24 40 50 60
NOTE: ***Jack Sparling** art in many issues; becomes a girls' magazine "Senior Prom" with #90.*

CALLING ALL KIDS (Also see True Comics)
Parents' Magazine Institute: Dec-Jan, 1945-46 - No. 26, Aug, 1949
1-Funny animal 18 36 54 103 162 220
2 11 22 33 60 83 105
3-10 9 18 27 52 69 85
11-26 9 18 27 47 61 75

CALL OF DUTY: BLACK OPS III (Based on the Activision video game)
Dark Horse Comics: Nov, 2015 - No. 6, Oct, 2016 ($3.99, limited series)
1-6-Prequel to the game; Hama-s/Ferreira-a 4.00

CALL OF DUTY: ZOMBIES (Based on the Activision video game)
Dark Horse Comics: Oct, 2016 - No. 3, Mar, 2017 ($3.99, limited series)
1-3-Justin Jordan-s/Jonathan Wayshak-a/Simon Bisley-c 4.00

CALL OF DUTY, THE : THE BROTHERHOOD
Marvel Comics: Aug, 2002 - No. 6, Jan, 2003 ($2.25)
1-Exploits of NYC Fire Dept.; Finch-c/a; Austen & Bruce Jones-s 4.00
2-6-Austen-s 3.00
...Vol 1: The Brotherhood & The Wagon TPB (2002, $14.99) r/#1-6 & ...The Wagon #1-4 15.00

CALL OF DUTY, THE : THE PRECINCT
Marvel Comics: Sept, 2002 - No. 5, Jan, 2003 ($2.25, limited series)
1-Exploits of NYC Police Dept.; Finch-c; Bruce Jones-s/Mandrake-a 3.00
2-4 3.00
...Vol 2: The Precinct TPB (2003, $9.99) r/#1-4 10.00

Camp Candy #2 © DIC

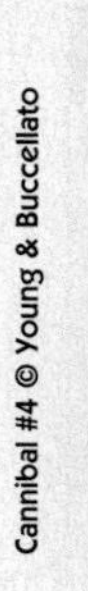
Cannibal #4 © Young & Buccellato

Captain Action Season 2 #1 © Captain Action Ents.

GD 2.0 | VG 4.0 | FN 6.0 | VF 8.0 | VF/NM 9.0 | NM- 9.2

CALL OF DUTY, THE : THE WAGON
Marvel Comics: Oct, 2002 - No. 4, Jan, 2003 ($2.25, limited series)
1-4-Exploits of NYC EMS Dept.; Finch-c; Austen-s/Zelzej-a 3.00

CALVIN (See Li'l Kids)

CALVIN & THE COLONEL (TV)
Dell Publishing Co.: No. 1354, Apr-June, 1962 - No. 2, July-Sept, 1962
Four Color 1354(#1) (The last Four Color issue) 8 16 24 54 102 150
2 5 10 15 35 63 90

CAMELOT 3000
DC Comics: Dec, 1982 - No. 11, July, 1984; No. 12, Apr, 1985 (Direct sales, maxi series, Mando paper)
1-12: 1-Mike Barr scripts & Brian Bolland-c/a begin. 5-Intro Knights of New Camelot 5.00
TPB (1988, $12.95) r/#1-12 15.00
...: The Deluxe Edition (2008, $34.99, HC) r/#1-12; oversized & recolored; Barr intro.; design and promotional art; original proposal page 40.00
NOTE: *Austin* a-7i-12i. *Bolland* a-1-12p; c-1-12.

CAMERA COMICS
U.S. Camera Publishing Corp./ME: July, 1944 - No. 9, Summer, 1946
nn (7/44) 37 74 111 222 361 500
nn (9/44) 26 52 78 154 252 350
1(10/44)-The Grey Comet (slightly smaller page size than subsequent issues) 30 60 90 177 289 400
2-16 pgs. of photos with 32 pgs. of comics 20 40 60 114 182 250
3-Nazi WW II-c; photos 24 48 72 142 234 325
4-9: All 1/3 photos 16 32 48 94 147 200

CAMP CANDY (TV)
Marvel Comics: May, 1990 - No. 6, Oct, 1990 ($1.00, limited series)
1-6: Post-c/a(p); featuring John Candy 5.00

CAMP COMICS
Dell Publishing Co.: Feb, 1942 - No. 3, April, 1942 (All have photo-c)(All issues are scarce)
1- "Seaman Sy Wheeler" by Kelly, 7 pgs.; Bugs Bunny app.; Mark Twain adaptation 84 168 252 538 919 1300
2-Kelly-a, 12 pgs.; Bugs Bunny app.; classic-c 84 168 252 538 919 1300
3-(Scarce)-Dave Berg & Walt Kelly-a 63 126 189 403 689 975

CAMP RUNAMUCK (TV)
Dell Publishing Co.: Apr, 1966
1-Photo-c 3 6 9 21 33 45

CAMPUS LOVES
Quality Comics Group (Comic Magazines): Dec, 1949 - No. 5, Aug, 1950
1-Ward-c/a (9 pgs.) 39 78 117 240 395 550
2-Ward-c/a 30 60 90 177 289 400
3-5 16 32 48 94 147 200
NOTE: *Gustavson* a-1-5. Photo c-3-5.

CAMPUS ROMANCE (...Romances on cover)
Avon Periodicals/Realistic: Sept-Oct, 1949 - No. 3, Feb-Mar, 1950
1-Walter Johnson-a; c-/Avon paperback #348 39 78 117 240 395 550
2-Grandenetti-a; c-/Avon paperback #151 28 56 84 165 270 375
3-c-/Avon paperback #201 28 56 84 165 270 375
Realistic reprint 16 32 48 94 147 200

CANADA DRY PREMIUMS (See Swamp Fox, The & Terry & The Pirates in the Promotional Comics section)

CANCELLED COMIC CAVALCADE (See the Promotional Comics section)

CANDID TALES (Also see Bold Stories & It Rhymes With Lust)
Kirby Publ. Co.: April, 1950; June, 1950 (Digest size) (144 pgs.) (Full color)
nn-(Scarce) Contains Wood female pirate story, 15 pgs., and 14 pgs. in June issue; Powell-a 174 348 522 1114 1907 2700
NOTE: *Another version exists with Dr. Kilmore by Wood; no female pirate story.*

CANDY (Teen-age)(Also see Police Comics #37)
Quality Comics Group (Comic Magazines): Autumn, 1947 - No. 64, Jul, 1956
1-Gustavson-a 30 60 90 177 289 400
2-Gustavson-a 15 30 45 88 137 185
3-10 11 22 33 62 86 110
11-30 9 18 27 50 65 80
31-64: 64-Ward-c(p)? 8 16 24 42 54 65
Super Reprint No. 2,10,12,16,17,18('63- '64):17-Candy #12 2 4 6 10 14 18
NOTE: *Jack Cole* 1-2 pg. art in many issues.

CANDY COMICS
William H. Wise & Co.: Fall, 1944 - No. 3, Spring, 1945
1-Two Scoop Scuttle stories by Wolverton 39 78 117 240 395 550
2,3-Scoop Scuttle by Wolverton, 2-4 pgs. 26 52 78 154 252 350

CANNON (See Heroes, Inc. Presents Cannon)

CANNIBAL
Image Comics: Oct, 2016 - Present ($3.99)
1-4-Young & Buccellato-s/Bergara-a 4.00

CANNON: DAWN OF WAR (Michael Turner's...)
Aspen MLT, Inc.: Nov, 2004 ($2.99)
1-Turnbull-a; two covers by Turnbull and Turner 3.00

CANNONBALL COMICS
Rural Home Publishing Co.: Feb, 1945 - No. 2, Mar, 1945
1-The Crash Kid, Thunderbrand, The Captive Prince & Crime Crusader begin; skull-c 142 284 426 909 1555 2200
2-Devil-c 110 220 330 704 1202 1700

CANTEEN KATE (See All Picture All True Love Story & Fightin' Marines)
St. John Publishing Co.: June, 1952 - No. 3, Nov, 1952
1-Matt Baker-c/a 84 168 252 538 919 1300
2-Matt Baker-c/a 52 104 156 328 552 775
3-(Rare)-Used in **POP**, pg. 75; Baker-c/a 60 120 180 381 653 925

CAPE, THE
IDW Publishing: Dec, 2010; Jul, 2011 - No. 4, Jan, 2012 ($3.99)
1-(12/10) Zach Howard-c/a; Jason Ciaramella-s 4.00
1-4: 1-(7/11) Story continues from 12/10 issue 4.00
...: Legacy Edition (6/11, $5.99) r/#1 (12/10) with Joe Hill's original short story 6.00
...: 1969 (7/12 - No. 4, 10/12, $3.99) 1-4-Ciaramella-s; origin in Vietnam 4.00

CAPER
DC Comics: Dec, 2003 - No. 12, Nov, 2004 ($2.95, limited series)
1-12: 1-4-Judd Winick-s/Farel Dalrymple-a. 5-8-John Severin-a. 9-12-Fowler-a 3.00

CAPES
Image Comics: Sept, 2003 - No. 3, Nov, 2003 ($3.50)
1-Robert Kirkman-s; 5 pg. preview of The Walking Dead #1 3 6 9 19 30 40
2,3-Robert Kirkman-s/Mark Englert-a/c 3.50

CAP'N QUICK & A FOOZLE (Also see Eclipse Mag. & Monthly)
Eclipse Comics: July, 1984 - No. 3, Nov, 1985 ($1.50, color, Baxter paper)
1-3-Rogers-c/a 3.00

CAPTAIN ACTION (Toy)
National Periodical Publications: Oct-Nov, 1968 - No. 5, June-July, 1969 (Based on Ideal toy)
1-Origin; Wally Wood-a; Superman-c app. 6 12 18 38 69 100
2,3,5-Gil Kane/Wally Wood-a 5 10 15 31 53 75
4- Gil Kane-c 4 8 12 27 44 60

CAPTAIN ACTION CAT: THE TIMESTREAM CATASTROPHE
Dynamite Entertainment: 2014 - No. 4, 2014 ($3.99, limited series)
1-4-Art Baltazar-s/a; Franco & Smits-s; all ages cat version of Capt. Action characters; Ghost, X, Captain Midnight, Skyman & The Occultist app. 4.00

CAPTAIN ACTION COMICS (Toy)
Moonstone: No. 0, 2008 - Present (Based on the Ideal toy)
0-($1.99) Origin re-told; Sparacio-a; three covers; character history by Michael Eury 3.00
1-5: 1-($3.99) Sparacio-a; intro. by Jim Shooter 4.00
... Comics Special 1 (2010, $5.99) 3 covers by Barreto, Ordway & Spiegle 6.00
... Exclusive Special 1 (2011, no price) Gulacy-c; Barreto-a 4.00
...: First Mission, Last Day (2008, $3.99) origin story re-told; Nicieza-s/Procopio-a 4.00
... King Size Special 1 (2011, $6.99) 1-Covers by Byrne, Wheatley & M. Benes 7.00
... Season 2 (2010, $3.99) 1-3: 1-Covers by Allred & Texiera; Obama app. 4.00
... Winter Special (2011, $4.99) Green Hornet & Kato on-c & text story 5.00

CAPTAIN AERO COMICS (Samson No. 1-6; also see Veri Best Sure Fire & Veri Best Sure Shot Comics)
Holyoke Publishing Co.: V1#7(#1), Dec, 1941 - V2#4(#10), Jan, 1943; V3#9(#11), Sept, 1943 -V4#3(#17), Oct, 1944; #21, Dec, 1944 - #26, Aug, 1946 (No #18-20)
V1#7(#1)-Flag-Man & Solar, Master of Magic, Captain Aero, Cap Stone, Adventurer begin; Nazi WWII-c 200 400 600 1280 2190 3100
8,10: 8(#2)-Pals of Freedom app. 10(#4)-Origin The Gargoyle; Kubert-a 97 194 291 621 1061 1500
9(#3)-Hitler-sty; Catman back-c; Alias X begins; Pals of Freedom app.; Nazi WWII-c 111 222 333 705 1215 1725

Captain Aero Comics #25 © CON

Captain America #100 © MAR

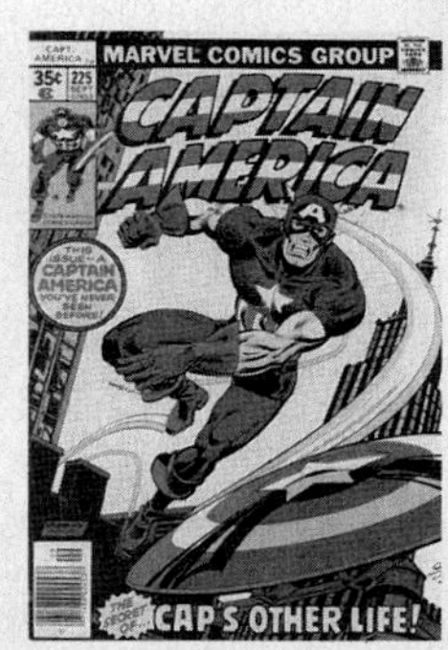

Captain America #225 © MAR

	GD 2.0	VG 4.0	FN 6.0	VF 8.0	VF/NM 9.0	NM- 9.2
11,12(#5,6)-Kubert-a; Miss Victory in #6	79	158	237	502	864	1225
V2#1,2(#7,8): 8-Origin The Red Cross; Miss Victory app.; Brodsky-c(i)	61	122	183	390	670	950
3(#9)-Miss Victory app.	103	206	309	659	1130	1600
4(#10)-Miss Victory app.; Japanese WWII-c	90	180	270	576	988	1400
V3#9 - V3#12(#11-14): All Quinlan Japanese WWII-c. 9-Miss Victory app.	77	154	231	493	847	1200
V3#13(#15),V4#2(#16): Schomburg Japanese WWII-c. 13-Miss Victory app.	90	180	270	576	988	1400
V4#3(#17)-Miss Victory app.; L.B. Cole Japanese WWII-c	68	136	204	435	743	1050
21-24-L.B. Cole Japanese WWII covers. 22-Intro/origin Mighty Mite	58	116	174	371	636	900
25-L.B. Cole Sci-fi-c	71	142	213	454	777	1100
26-L.B. Cole Sci-fi-c; Palais-a(2) (scarce)	232	464	696	1485	2543	3600

NOTE: ***L.B. Cole** c-17, 21-26. **Hollingsworth** a-23. **Infantino** a-23, 26. **Schomburg** c-15, 16.*

CAPTAIN AMERICA (See Adventures of..., All-Select, All Winners, Aurora, Avengers #4, Blood and Glory, Captain Britain 16-20, Giant-Size..., The Invaders, Marvel Double Feature, Marvel Fanfare, Marvel Mystery, Marvel Super-Action, Marvel Super Heroes V2#3, Marvel Team-Up, Marvel Treasury Special, Power Record Comics, Ultimates, USA Comics, Young Allies & Young Men)

CAPTAIN AMERICA (Formerly Tales of Suspense #1-99) (Captain America and the Falcon #134-223 & Steve Rogers: Captain America #444-454 appears on cover only)
Marvel Comics Group: No. 100, Apr, 1968 - No. 454, Aug, 1996

	GD 2.0	VG 4.0	FN 6.0	VF 8.0	VF/NM 9.0	NM- 9.2
100-Flashback on Cap's revival with Avengers & Sub-Mariner; story continued from Tales of Suspense #99; Kirby-c/a begins	50	100	150	350	625	900
101-The Sleeper-c/story; Red Skull app.	9	18	27	59	117	175
102-104: 102-Sleeper-c/s. 103,104-Red Skull-c/sty	7	14	21	48	89	130
105-108: 107-Red Skull & Hitler-c	6	12	18	37	66	95
109-Origin Capt. America retold in detail	9	18	27	59	117	175
109-2nd printing (1994)	2	4	6	8	10	12
110-Rick Jones dons Bucky's costume & becomes Cap's partner; Hulk x-over; Steranko-a Classic Steranko-c	10	20	30	66	138	210
111,113-Classic Steranko-c/a: 111-Death of Steve Rogers. 113-Cap's funeral; Avengers app.	9	18	27	59	117	175
112-S.A. recovery retold; last Kirby-c/a	6	12	18	41	76	110
114-116,119,120: 114-Red Skull Cosmic Cube story. 115,116-Red Skull app; last 12c issue. 119-Cap vs. Red Skull; Cosmic Cube "destroyed"; Falcon app.	4	8	12	28	47	65
117-1st app. The Falcon (9/69)	27	54	81	189	420	650
118-2nd app. The Falcon	8	16	24	54	102	150
121-136,139,140: 121-Retells origin; Avengers app. 122-Cap vs. Scorpion. 124-Modok app. 125-Mandarin app. 129-Red Skull app. 133-The Falcon becomes Cap's partner; origin Modok. 139,140-Grey Gargoyle app; origin in #140	3	6	9	21	33	45
137,138-Spider-Man x-over	4	8	12	27	44	60
141,142-Grey Gargoyle app. 141-Last Stan Lee issue. 142-Last 15¢ issue	3	6	9	17	26	35
143-(52 pgs) Cap vs. Red Skull	3	6	9	21	33	45
144-New costume Falcon	3	6	9	19	30	40
145-152: 145-147-Cap vs. the Supreme Hydra. 148-Red Skull app. 151,152- Cap vs. Mr. Hyde	3	6	9	14	20	25
153-155: 153-1st brief app. Jack Monroe; return of 1950s Captain America. 154-1st full app. Jack Monroe (Nomad); 1950s Captain America and Avengers app. 155-Origin retold; origin Jack Monroe and the 1950s Captain America	3	6	9	19	30	40
156-Cap vs. the 1950s Captain America; Jack Monroe app; classic Cap vs Cap cover	3	6	9	16	23	30
157-170,177-179: 160-1st app. Solarr. 161,162-Peggy Carter app. 163-1st Serpent Squad: Viper, Eel and Cobra. 164-1st Nightshade. 165-167-Cap vs. Yellow Claw. 168-1st Helmut Zemo (as the Phoenix). 169,170-Vs. original Moonstone	2	4	6	9	12	15
171-Black Panther app.	3	6	9	16	23	30
172,173: X-Men x-over	3	6	9	16	23	30
174,175: X-Men x-over	2	4	6	18	22	25
176-End of Cap. Avengers app.	2	4	6	13	18	22
180-Intro/origin of Nomad (Steve Rogers)	3	6	9	17	26	35
181-Intro/origin new Cap.	2	4	6	11	16	20
182,184,185,187-192: 182,184,185-Red Skull app. 189,190-Cap vs. Nightshade. 191-Iron Man app. 192-Intro Dr. Karla Sofen (later becomes Moonstone)	2	4	6	8	10	12
183-Death of new Cap; Steve Rogers drops Nomad I.D; returns to being Capt. America	2	4	6	9	12	15
186-True origin The Falcon; Red Skull app.	2	4	6	11	16	20
193-Kirby-c/a begins	3	6	9	16	23	30

	GD 2.0	VG 4.0	FN 6.0	VF 8.0	VF/NM 9.0	NM- 9.2
194-199-(Regular 25¢ edition)(4-7/76)	2	4	6	10	14	18
196-199-(30¢-c variants, limited distribution)	5	10	15	31	53	75
200-(Regular 25¢ edition)(8/76)	2	4	6	11	16	20
200-(30¢-c variant, limited distribution)	5	10	15	34	60	85
201-214-Kirby-c/a. 208-1st Arnim Zola. 209,210- Arnim Zola app. 210-212 –vs Red Skull	2	4	6	8	11	14
210-214-(35¢-c variants, limited dist.)(6-10/77)	9	18	27	59	117	175
215,216,218-229: 215-Origin retold. 216-r/Strange Tales #114. 226,227-Red Skull app. 228-Cap vs. Constrictor. 229-Marvel Man app.	1	2	4	5	6	9
217-Intro. Marvel Boy (Wendell Vaughan); becomes Marvel Man in #218; later becomes Quasar (2/78)	4	8	12	28	47	65
230,235: 230-Battles Hulk-c/story cont'd in Inc. Hulk #232. 235-(7/79) Daredevil x-over; Miller-a(p)	1	2	4	5	7	10
231-233,236-240,242-246: 233-"Death" of Sharon Carter. 244,245-Miller-c	1	2	3	4	5	7
234-Daredevil app.	1	2	3	4	6	8
241-Punisher app.; Miller-c	4	8	12	27	44	60
241-2nd print	1	2	3	5	6	8
247-252-Byrne-a	1	3	4	6	8	10
253,255: 253-Byrne-a; Baron Blood app. 255-Origin retold; Miller-c	2	4	6	9	12	15
254-Byrne-a; death of Baron Blood; intro new Union Jack	2	4	6	13	18	22
256-262: 257-Hulk app. 258-Zeck-a begins. 259-Cap vs. Dr. Octopus. 261,262-Red Skull app.						5.00
263-266: 263-Red Skull-c/story. 264-Original X-Men app. 265,266-Spider-Man app.						6.00
267-280: 267-1st app. Everyman. 268-Defenders app. 269-1st Team America. 272-1st Vermin. 273,274-Baron Strucker. 275-1st Baron Zemo (formally the Phoenix). 276-278-Cap vs. Baron Zemo. 279-(3/83)-Contains Tattooz skin decals. 280-Scarecrow app.						5.00
281-1950's Bucky returns. Spider-Woman and Viper app.	1	2	3	4	6	8
282-Bucky becomes new Nomad (Jack Monroe)	1	3	4	6	8	10
282-Silver ink 2nd print ($1.75) w/original date (6/83)						3.00
283-Cap vs. Viper						5.00
284,285,289,291-300: 284-Patriot (Jack Mace) app. 285-Death of Patriot. 293,294-Nomad app. 293-299-Red Skull and Baron Zemo app. 298-Origin Red Skull. 300- "Death" of Red Skull.						4.00
286-288-Deathlok app.						5.00
290-1st Mother Superior (Red Skull's daughter, later becomes Sin)	1	2	3	4	6	8
301-304,307-318,322,324-326,328-331: 301-Avengers app. 307-1st Madcap; 1st Mark Gruenwald-s (begins 8-year run). 308-Secret Wars II x-over. 310-1st Serpent Society. 312-1st Flag Smasher. 313-Death of Modok. 314-Squadron Supreme x-over. 317-Hawkeye & Mockingbird app. 318-Scourge app; death of Blue Streak and Adder. 322-Cap vs. Flag Smasher. 325-Nomad app. 328,330-Demolition Man (D-Man) app.						3.00
305,306-Captain Britain app.						4.00
319-321,327: 319-Scourge kills numerous villians 320-"Death"of Scourge. 321-Cap vs. Flag Smasher; classic Zeck cover Cap with machine gun. 327-Cap vs Super-Patriot						4.00
323-1st app. new Super-Patriot (see Nick Fury)						5.00
332-Old Captain America resigns	2	4	6	8	10	12
333-340; 333- Super Patriot becomes new Cap. 334-Intro new Bucky; Freedom Force app. 337-Serpent Society app; Avengers #4 homage-c; Steve Rogers becomes 'the Captain'; becomes Captain America again in issue #350. 339-Fall of the Mutants tie-in						4.00
341-343,345-349: 341-Cap vs Iron Man; x-over with Iron Man #228. 342-Cap vs. Viper and the Serpent Squad						3.00
344-($1.50, 52 pgs.)-Ronald Reagan cameo as a snake man						4.00
350-($1.75, 68 pgs.)-Return of Steve Rogers (original Cap) to original costume						6.00
351-358,360-382,384-396: 351-Nick Fury app. 357-Bloodstone hunt Pt. 1 (of 6). 358-Baron Zemo app. 365,366-Acts of Vengeance x-overs. 367-Magneto vs Red Skull. 372-378-Streets of Poison. 374-Bullseye app. 375-Daredevil app. 376-Black Widow app. 377-Bullseye vs. Crossbones; Red Skull app. 379-Quasar app. 380-382-Serpent Society app. 386-U.S. Agent app. 387-392-Superia Stratagem. 387-389-Red Skull back-up stories. 394-Red Skull app. 395-Thor app. (Eric Masterson; also in 396-397); Red Skull app. 396-Red Skull and new (1st) Jack O Lantern app; last $1.00-c						3.00
359-Crossbones debut (cameo); Baron Zemo app.	1	3	4	6	8	10
360-1st app. Crossbones; Baron Zemo app.	3	6	9	16	23	30
383-($2.00, 68 pgs., squarebound)-50th anniversary issue; Red Skull story; Jim Lee-c(i)						5.00
397-399,401-424: 397-New Jack O Lantern app. 398,399-Operation Galactic Storm x-overs. 401-Operation Galactic storm epilogue. 402-Begin 6 part Man-Wolf story w/Wolverine in #403-407. 405-410-New Jack O Lantern app. in back-up story. 406-Cable & Shatterstar cameo. 407-Capwolf vs. Cable-c/story. 408-Infinity War x-over; Falcon back-up story. 409-Red Skull & Crossbones app. 410-Crossbones app. 414-Black Panther app. 419-Red Skull app; x-over with Silver Sable #15. 423- Cap vs. Namor-c/story						3.00

400-($2.25, 84 pgs.) Flip book format w/double gatefold-c; Operation Galactic Storm x-over;

Captain America V3 #1 © MAR

Captain America V4 #4 © MAR

Captain America #600 © MAR

GD 2.0 | VG 4.0 | FN 6.0 | VF 8.0 | VF/NM 9.0 | NM- 9.2

r/Avengers #4 plus-c contains cover pin-ups 1 2 3 5 6 8
425-($2.95, 52 pgs.)-Embossed Foil-c edition; Fighting Chance Pt. 1 4.00
425-($1.75, 52 pgs.)-non-embossed-c edition; Fighting Chance Pt. 1 5.00
426-439,442,443: 426-437-Fighting Chance Pt. 2-12. 427-Begins $1.50-c; bound-in trading card sheet. 428-1st Americop. 431-1st Free Spirit. 434-1st Jack Flag. 438-Fighting Chance epilogue. 443-Last Gruenwald issue 4.00
440,441-Avengers x-overs; 'Taking A.I.M" story 5.00
444-Mark Waid scripts & Ron Garney-c/a(p) begins, ends #454; Avengers app. 5.00
445-Operation rebirth Pt.1; vs Red Skull; Sharon Carter returns 5.00
446,447 – Operation Rebirth; Red Skull app. 446-Hitler app. 6.00
448-($2.95, double-sized issue) Waid script & Garney-c/a; Red Skull "dies" 5.00
449-Thor app; story x-overs with Thor, Iron Man and Avengers titles 5.00
450- "Man Without a Country" begins; Steve Rogers-c 4.00
450-Captain America-c with white background 6.00
451-453: 451-1st app. Cap's new costume. 453-Cap gets old costume back; Bill Clinton app. 4.00
454-Last issue of the regular series (8/96) 5.00
#600-up (See Captain America 2005 series, resumed original numbering after #50)
Special 1(1/71)-All reprint issue from Tales Of Suspense #63,69,70,71,75 5 10 15 35 63 90
Special 2(1/72, 52 pgs.)-All reprint issue from Tales Of Suspense #72-74 and Not Brand Echh #5 4 8 12 23 37 50
Annual 3('76, 52 pgs.)-Kirby-c/a(new) 3 6 9 16 23 30
Annual 4('77, 34 pgs.)-Magneto-c/story 3 6 9 16 23 30
Annual 5-7: (52 pgs.)('81-'83) 5.00
Annual 8(9/86)-Wolverine-c/story 3 6 9 19 30 40
Annual 9-13('90-'94, 68 pgs.)-9-Nomad back-up. 10-Origin retold (2 pgs.). 11-Falcon solo story. 12-Bagged w/card. 13-Red Skull-c/story 4.00
...Ashcan Edition ('95, 75¢) 3.00
... and the Falcon: Madbomb TPB (2004, $16.99) r/#193-200; Kirby-s/a 17.00
... and the Falcon: Nomad TPB (2006, $24.99) r/#177-186; Cap becomes Nomad 25.00
... and the Falcon: Secret Empire TPB (2005, $19.99) r/#169-176 20.00
... and the Falcon: The Swine TPB (2006, $29.99) r/#206-214 & Annual #3,4 30.00
... By Jack Kirby: Bicentennial Battles TPB (2005, $19.99) r/#201-205 & Marvel Treasury Special Featuring Captain America's Bicentennial Battles; Kirby-s/a 20.00
...: Deathlok Lives! nn(10/93, $4.95)-r/#286-288 6.00
...Drug War 1-(1994, $2.00, 52 pgs.)-New Warriors app. 4.00
...Man Without a Country(1998, $12.99, TPB)-r/#450-453 13.00
...Medusa Effect 1 (1994, $2.95, 68 pgs.)-Origin Baron Zemo 4.00
...Operation Rebirth (1996, $9.95)-r/#445-448 10.00
... 65th Anniversary Special (5/06, $3.99) WWII flashback with Bucky; Brubaker-s 5.00
...Streets of Poison ($15.95)-r/#372-378 16.00
...: The Movie Special nn (5/92, $3.50, 52 pgs.)-Adapts movie; printed on coated stock; The Red Skull app. 4.00

NOTE: ***Austin*** *c-225i, 239i, 246i.* ***Buscema*** *a-115p, 217p; c-136p, 217, 297.* ***Byrne*** *c-223(part), 238, 239, 247p-254p, 290, 291, 313p; a-247-254p, 255, 313p, 350.* ***Colan*** *a(p)-116-137, 256, Annual 5; c(p)-116-123, 126, 129.* ***Everett*** *a-136i, 137i; c-126i.* ***Garney*** *a(p)-444-454.* ***Gil Kane*** *a-145p; c-147p, 149p, 150p, 170p, 172-174, 180, 181p, 183-190p, 215, 216, 220, 221.* ***Kirby*** *a(p)-100-109, 112, 193-214, 216, Special 1, 2(layouts), Annual 3, 4; c-100-109, 112, 126p, 193-214.* ***Ron Lim*** *a(p)-366, 368-378, 380-386; c-366p, 368-378p, 379, 380-393p.* ***Miller*** *c-241p, 244p, 245p, 255p, Annual 5.* ***Mooney*** *a-149i.* ***Morrow*** *a-144.* ***Perez*** *c-243p, 246p.* ***Robbins*** *c(p)-183-187, 189-192, 225.* ***Roussos*** *a-140i, 168i.* ***Shores*** *a-102i, 107i, 109i.* ***Starlin/Sinnott*** *c-162.* ***Sutton*** *a-244i.* ***Tuska*** *a-112i, 215p, Special 2.* ***Waid*** *scripts-444-454.* ***Williamson*** *a-313i.* ***Wood*** *a-127i.* ***Zeck*** *a-263-289; c-300.*

CAPTAIN AMERICA (Volume Two)
Marvel Comics: V2#1, Nov, 1996 - No. 13, Nov, 1997($2.95/$1.95/$1.99)
(Produced by Extreme Studios)

1-($2.95)-Heroes Reborn begins; Liefeld-c/a; Loeb scripts; reintro Nick Fury 1 2 3 5 6 8
1-($2.95)-(Variant-c)-Liefeld-c/a 1 2 3 5 6 8
1-(7/96, $2.95)-(Exclusive Comicon Ed.)-Liefeld-c/a 2 4 6 8 10 12
2-11,13: 5-Two-c. 6-Cable-c/app. 13-"World War 3"-pt. 4, x-over w/Image 3.00
12-($2.99) "Heroes Reunited"-pt. 4 4.00
Heroes Reborn: Captain America (2006, $29.99, TPB) r/#1-12 & Heroes Reborn #1/2 30.00

CAPTAIN AMERICA (Vol. Three) (Also see Capt. America: Sentinel of Liberty)
Marvel Comics: Jan, 1998 - No. 50, Feb, 2002 ($2.99/$1.99/$2.25)

1-($2.99) Mark Waid-s/Ron Garney-a 4.00
1-Variant cover 6.00
2-($1.99): 2-Two covers 3.00
3-11: 3-Returns to old shield. 4-Hawkeye app. 5-Thor-c/app. 7-Andy Kubert-c/a begin. 9-New shield 3.00
12-($2.99) Battles Nightmare; Red Skull back-up story 4.00
13-17,19-Red Skull returns 3.00
18-($2.99) Cap vs. Korvac in the Future 4.00
20-24,26-29: 20,21-Sgt. Fury back-up story painted by Evans 3.00
25-($2.99) Cap & Falcon vs. Hatemonger 4.00

GD 2.0 | VG 4.0 | FN 6.0 | VF 8.0 | VF/NM 9.0 | NM- 9.2

30-49: 30-Begin $2.25-c. 32-Ordway-a. 33-Jurgens-s/a begins; U.S. Agent app. 36-Maximum Security x-over. 41,46-Red Skull app. 3.00
50-($5.95) Stories by various incl. Jurgens, Quitely, Immonen; Ha-c 6.00
.../Citizen V '98 Annual ($3.50) Busiek & Kesel-s 4.00
1999 Annual ($3.50) Flag Smasher app. 4.00
2000 Annual ($3.50) Continued from #35 vs. Protocide; Jurgens-s 4.00
2001 Annual ($2.99) Golden Age flashback; Invaders app. 4.00
...: To Serve and Protect TPB (2/02, $17.95) r/Vol. 3 #1-7 18.00

CAPTAIN AMERICA (Volume 4)
Marvel Comics: Jun, 2002 - No. 32, Dec, 2004 ($3.99/$2.99)

1-Ney Rieber-s/Cassaday-c/a 4.00
2-9-($2.99) 3-Cap reveals Steve Rogers ID. 7-9-Hairsine-a 3.00
10-32: 10-16-Jae Lee-a. 17-20-Gibbons-s/Weeks-a. 21-26-Bachalo-a. 26-Bucky flashback. 27,28-Eddie Campbell-a. 29-32-Red Skull app. 3.00
...Vol. 1: The New Deal HC (2003, $22.99) r/#1-6; foreward by Max Allan Collins 23.00
...Vol. 2: The Extremists TPB (2003, $13.99) r/#7-11; Cassaday-c 14.00
...Vol. 3: Ice TPB (2003, $12.99) r/#12-16; Jae Lee-a; Cassaday-c 13.00
...Vol. 4: Cap Lives TPB (2004, $12.99) r/#17-22 & Tales of Suspense #66 13.00
Avengers Disassembled: Captain America TPB (2004, $17.99) r/#29-32 and Captain America and the Falcon #5-7 18.00

CAPTAIN AMERICA
Marvel Comics: Jan, 2005 - No. 619, Aug, 2011 ($2.99/$3.99)

1-Brubaker-s/Epting-c/a; Red Skull app. 2 4 6 9 12 15
2-5 5.00
6-1st full app. of the Winter Soldier; Swastika-c 3 6 9 17 26 35
6-Retailer variant cover 3 6 9 19 30 40
7-24: 10-House of M. 11-Origin of the Winter Soldier. 13-Iron Man app. 24-Civil War 4.00
8-Variant Red Skull cover 2 4 6 8 10 12
25-($3.99) Captain America shot dead; handcuffed red glove cover by Epting 12.00
25-($3.99) Variant edition with running Cap cover by McGuinness 8.00
25-($3.99) 2nd printing with "The Death of The Dream" cover by Epting 5.00
25-Director's Cut-($4.99) w/script with Brubaker commentary; pencil pages, variant and un-used covers gallery; article on media hype 6.00
26-33-Falcon & Winter Soldier app. 3.00
34-(3/08) Bucky becomes the new Captain America; Alex Ross-c 10.00
34-Variant-c by Steve Epting 8.00
34-($3.99) Director's Cut; includes script; pencil art, costume designs, cover gallery 5.00
34-DF Edition with Alex Ross portrait cover; signed by Ross 30.00
35-49-Bucky as Captain America. 43-45-Batroc app. 46,47-Sub-Mariner app. 3.00
50-(7/09, $3.99) Bucky's birthday flashbacks; Captain America's life synopsis; Martin-a 4.00
(After #50, numbering reverts to original with #600, Aug, 2009)
600-(8/09, $4.99) Covers by Ross and Epting; leads into Captain America: Reborn series; art by Guice, Chaykin, Ross, Eaglesham; commentary by Joe Simon; cover gallery 5.00
601-615,617-619-($3.99) 601-Gene Colan-a; 3 covers. 602-Nomad back-up feature begins. 606-Baron Zemo returns. 611-615-Trial of Captain America 4.00
615.1 (5/11, $2.99) Brubaker-s/Breitweiser-a/Acuña-c 3.00
616-(5/11, $4.99) 70th Anniversary Issue; short stories by Brubaker, Chaykin, Deodato, McGuinness, Grist and others, Charest-c 5.00
616-Variant-c by Epting 8.00
...: America's Avenger (8/11, $4.99) Handbook format profiles of friends and foes 5.00
... and Batroc (5/11, $3.99) Gillen-s/Arlem-a; Bucky vs. Batroc in Paris 4.00
... and Crossbones (5/11, $3.99) Harms-s/Shalvey-a/Tocchini-c 4.00
... and Falcon (5/11, $3.99) Williams-s/Isaacs-a/Tocchini-c 4.00
... and the First Thirteen (5/11, $3.99) Peggy Carter in WWII France 1943 4.00
... and the Secret Avengers (5/11, $3.99) DeConnick-s/Tocchini-a/c; Black Widow app. 4.00
... and Thor: Avengers 1 (9/11, $4.99) Movie version Cap; prequel to Thor movie; Lim-c 5.00
... By Ed Brubaker Omnibus Vol. 1 HC (2007, $74.99, dustjacket) r/#1-25; Capt. America 65th Anniv. Spec. and Winter Soldier: Winter Kills; Brubaker intro.; bonus material 75.00
Civil War: Captain America TPB (2007, $11.99) r/#22-24 & Winter Soldier: Winter Kills 12.00
...: Fighting Avenger (6/11, $4.99) 1st WWII mission; Gurihiru-a/c; Kitson var-c 5.00
...MGC #1 (5/10, $1.00) r/#1 with "Marvel's Greatest Comics" cover logo 3.00
...: Rebirth 1 (8/11, $4.99) r/origin & Red Skull apps. from Tales of Suspense #63,65-68 5.00
...: Red Menace Vol. 1 SC (2006, $11.99) r/#15-17 and 65th Anniversary Special 12.00
...: Red Menace Vol. 2 SC (2006, $10.99) r/#18-21; Brubaker interview 11.00
... Spotlight (7/11, $3.99) creator interviews; features on the movie and The Invaders 4.00
... Theater of War: America First! (2/09, $4.99) 1950s era tale; Chaykin-s/a; reprints 5.00
... Theater of War: America the Beautiful (3/09, $4.99) WW2 tale; Jenkins-s/Erskine-a 5.00
... Theater of War: Operation Zero-Point (12/08, $3.99) WW2 tale; Breitweiser-a 4.00
...: The Death of Captan America Vol. 1 HC (2007, $19.99) r/#25-30; variant covers 20.00
...: The Death of Captan America Vol. 2 HC (2008, $19.99) r/#31-36; variant covers 20.00
...Vol. 1: Winter Soldier HC (2005, $21.99) r/#1-7; concept sketches 22.00
...Vol. 1: Winter Soldier SC (2006, $16.99) r/#1-7; concept sketches 17.00
...: Who Won't Wield the Shield (6/10, $3.99) Deadpool & Forbush Man app. 4.00

Captain America (2013 series) #6 © MAR

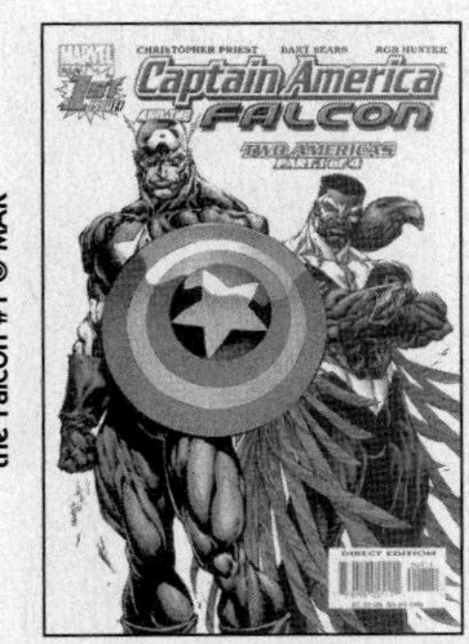

Captain America and the Falcon #1 © MAR

Captain America Comics #73 © MAR

GD 2.0 VG 4.0 FN 6.0 VF 8.0 VF/NM 9.0 NM- 9.2

...: Winter Soldier Vol. 2 HC (2006, $19.99) r/#8,9,11-14 20.00
...: Winter Soldier Vol. 2 SC (2006, $14.99) r/#8,9,11-14 15.00

CAPTAIN AMERICA
Marvel Comics: Sept, 2011 - No. 19, Dec, 2012 ($3.99)

1-19: 1-5-Brubaker-s/McNiven-c/a. 1-Nick Fury & Baron Zemo app. 6-10-Davis-a/c 4.00
1-Variant-c by John Romita Sr. 8.00
1-Movie photo variant-c of Chris Evans in costume 5.00

CAPTAIN AMERICA (Marvel NOW!)
Marvel Comics: Jan, 2013 - No. 25, Dec, 2014 ($3.99)

1-10-Remender-s/Romita Jr.-a/c; Cap in Dimension Z; Arnim Zola app.; 1st app. Jet Black. 10-Sharon Carter supposedly killed 4.00
11-24: 11,12,14,15-Pacheco-a; Nuke returns. 16-Red Skull app.; Alixe-a. 21-Steve Rogers rapidly aged. 22-24-Pacheco-a; Avengers app. 23-Sharon Carter returns 4.00
25-($4.99) Sam Wilson becomes the new Captain America; Pacheco-a 5.00
...: Homecoming 1 (5/14, $3.99) Van Lente-s/Grummett-a; bonus rep of Capt. Am. #117 4.00
...: Peggy Carter, Agent of S.H.I.E.L.D. (2014, $7.99) r/notable appearances 8.00

CAPTAIN AMERICA AND ... (Numbering continues from Captain America #619)
Marvel Comics: No. 620, Sept, 2011 - No. 640, Feb, 2013 ($2.99)

... Bucky 620-628: 620-624-Brubaker & Andreyko-s/Samnee-a/McGuinness-c. 620-Bucky's early WWII days. 625-628-Francavilla-c/a 3.00
... Hawkeye 629-632: 629-(6/12) Bunn-s/Vitti-aDell'Otto-c 3.00
... Iron Man 633-635: 635-(8/12) Bunn-s/Kitson-a/Andrasofszky-c; Batroc app. 3.00
... Namor 635.1 (10/12) World War II flashback; Will Conrad-a/Immonen-c 3.00
... Black Widow 636-640: 636-(11/12) Bunn-s/Francavilla-a/c 3.00

CAPTAIN AMERICA AND THE FALCON
Marvel Comics: May, 2004 - No. 14, June, 2005 ($2.99, limited series)

1-4-Priest-s/Sears-a 3.00
5-14: 5-8-Avengers Disassembled x-over. 6,7-Scarlet Witch app. 8-12-Modok app. 3.00
... Vol. 1: Two Americas (2005, $9.99) r/#1-4 10.00
... Vol. 2: Brothers and Keepers (2005, $17.99) r/#8-14 18.00

CAPTAIN AMERICA & THE KORVAC SAGA
Marvel Comics: Feb, 2011 - No. 4, May, 2011 ($2.99, limited series)

1-4-McCool-s/Rousseau-a/c. 4-Galactus app. 3.00

CAPTAIN AMERICA & THE MIGHTY AVENGERS (Sam Wilson as Captain America)
Marvel Comics: Jan, 2015 - No. 9, Aug, 2015 ($3.99)

1-9: 1-3-AXIS tie-ins; Luke Ross-a. 8,9-Secret Wars tie-in 4.00

CAPTAIN AMERICA/BLACK PANTHER (See Black Panther/Captain America: Flags of Our Fathers)

CAPTAIN AMERICA COMICS
Timely/Marvel Comics (TCI 1-20/CmPS 21-68/MjMC 69-75/Atlas Comics (PrPI 76-78):
Mar, 1941 - No. 75, Feb, 1950; No. 76, 5/54 - No. 78, 9/54
(No. 74 & 75 titled Capt. America's Weird Tales)

1-Origin & 1st app. Captain America & Bucky by Simon & Kirby; Hurricane, Tuk the Caveboy begin by S&K; 1st app. Red Skull; Hitler-c (by Simon?); intro of the "Capt. America Sentinels of Liberty Club" (advertised on inside front-c.); indicia reads Vol. 2, Number 1 21,000 42,000 63,000 140,000 230,000 400,000
2-S&K Hurricane; Tuk by Avison (Kirby splash); classic Hitler-c; 1st app. Cap's round shield 2400 4800 7200 18,000 38,000 58,000
3-Classic Red Skull-c & app; Stan Lee's 1st text (1st work for Marvel) 2400 4800 7200 18,000 35,000 52,000
4-Early use of full pg. panel in comic; back-c pin-up of Captain America and Bucky 1150 2300 3450 8600 16,300 24,000
5-Classic Kirby Nazi/torture Wheel of Death/Red Skull-c 1050 2100 3150 7800 14,400 21,000
6-Origin Father Time; Tuk the Caveboy ends 1000 2000 3000 7300 12,900 18,500
7-Red Skull app.; classic-c 1050 2100 3150 7800 14,400 21,000
8-10-Last S&K issue, (S&K centerfold #6-10) 811 1622 2433 5920 10,460 15,000
11-Last Hurricane, Headline Hunter; Al Avison Captain America begins, ends #20; Avison-c(p) 541 1082 1623 3950 6975 10,000
12-The Imp begins, ends #16; last Father Time 541 1082 1623 3950 6975 10,000
13-Origin The Secret Stamp; classic "Remember Pearl Harbor"-c 865 1730 2595 6315 11,158 16,000
14,15: 14-"Remember Pearl Harbor" Japanese bondage/torture-c 541 1082 1623 3950 6975 10,000
16-Red Skull unmasks Cap; Red Skull-c 811 1622 2433 5920 10,460 15,000
17-The Fighting Fool only app. 486 972 1458 3550 6275 9000
18-Classic-c 514 1028 1542 3750 6625 9500
19-Human Torch begins #19 459 918 1377 3350 5925 8500
20-Sub-Mariner app.; no Human Torch 454 908 1362 3314 5857 8400
21-25: 25-Cap drinks liquid opium 449 898 1347 3278 5789 8300

GD 2.0 VG 4.0 FN 6.0 VF 8.0 VF/NM 9.0 NM- 9.2

26-30: 27-Last Secret Stamp; last 68 pg. issue. 28-60 pg. issues begin. 443 886 1329 3234 5717 8200
31-35,38-40: 34-Centerfold poster of Cap 415 830 1245 2905 5103 7300
36-Classic Hitler-c 676 1352 2028 4935 8718 12,500
37-Red Skull app. 649 1298 1947 4738 8369 12,000
41-Last Japan War-c 343 686 1029 2400 4200 6000
42-45 290 580 870 1856 3178 4500
46-German Holocaust-c; classic 1200 2400 3600 8000 14,000 20,000
47-Last German War-c 314 628 942 2198 3849 5500
48-58,60 213 426 639 1363 2332 3300
59-Origin retold 354 708 1062 2478 4339 6200
61-Red Skull-c/story 411 822 1233 2877 5039 7200
62,64,65: 65-Kurtzman's "Hey Look" 258 516 774 1651 2826 4000
63-Intro/origin Asbestos Lady 271 542 813 1734 2967 4200
66-Bucky is shot; Golden Girl teams up with Captain America & learns his i.d; origin Golden Girl 343 686 1029 2400 4200 6000
67-69: 67-Captain America/Golden Girl team-up; Mxyztplk swipe; last Toro in Human Torch. 68-Sub-Mariner/Namora, and Captain America/Golden Girl team-up. 69-Human Torch/ Sun Girl team-up. 326 652 978 2282 3991 5700
70-73: 70-Sub-Mariner/Namora, and Captain America/Golden Girl team-up. 70-SciFi-c/story. 71-Anti Wertham editorial; The Witness, Bucky app. 371 742 1113 2600 4550 6500
74-(Scarce)(10/49)-Titled "Captain America's Weird Tales"; Red Skull-c & app.; classic-c 1600 3200 4800 12,000 22,500 33,000
75(2/50)-Titled "C.A.'s Weird Tales"; no C.A. app.; horror cover/stories 354 708 1062 2478 4339 6200
76-78(1954): Human Torch/Toro stories; all have communist-c/stories 245 490 735 1568 2684 3800
132-Pg. Issue (B&W-1942)(Canadian)-Very rare. Has blank inside-c and back-c; contains Marvel Mystery #33 & Captain America #18 w/cover from Captain America #22; same contents as one version of the Marvel Mystery annuals 5000 10,000 15,000 37,000 - -

NOTE: ***Crandall*** *a-2i, 3i, 9i, 10i.* ***Kirby*** *c-1, 2, 5-8p.* ***Rico*** *c-69-71.* ***Romita*** *c-77, 78.* ***Schomburg*** *c-3, 4, 26-29, 31, 33, 37-39, 41, 42, 45-54, 58.* ***Sekowsky*** *c-55, 56.* ***Shores*** *c-1i, 2i, 5-7i, 11i, 20-25, 30, 32, 34, 35, 40, 57, 59-67.* ***S&K*** *c-9, 10. Bondage c-3, 7, 15, 16, 34, 38.*

CAPTAIN AMERICA COMICS #1 70TH ANNIVERSARY EDITION
Marvel Comics: May, 2011 ($4.99, one-shot)

1-Recolored reprint of entire 1941 issue including Hurricane & Tuk stories; Ching-c 6.00

CAPTAIN AMERICA COMICS 70TH ANNIVERSARY SPECIAL
Marvel Comics: June, 2009 ($3.99, one-shot)

1-WWII flashback; Marcos Martin-a; Marcos-2 covers; r/Capt. America Comics #7 5.00

CAPTAIN AMERICA CORPS
Marvel Comics: Aug, 2011 - No. 5, Dec, 2011 ($2.99, limited series)

1-5-Stern-s/Briones-a/Jimenez-a; various versions of Captain America team-up 3.00

CAPTAIN AMERICA: DEAD MEN RUNNING
Marvel Comics: Mar, 2002 - No. 3, May, 2002 ($2.99, limited series)

1-3-Macan-s/Zezelj-a 3.00

CAPTAIN AMERICA: FIRST VENGEANCE (Based on the 2011 movie version)
Marvel Comics: Jul, 2011 - No. 4, Aug, 2011 ($2.99, limited series)

1-4-Van Lente-s; art by Luke Ross & others. 2-Movie photo-c 3.00

CAPTAIN AMERICA: FOREVER ALLIES
Marvel Comics: Oct, 2010 - No. 4, Jan, 2011 ($3.99, limited series)

1-4-Stern-s/Dragotta-a; Bucky in present & WW2 flashbacks; Young Allies app. 4.00

CAPTAIN AMERICA: HAIL HYDRA
Marvel Comics: Mar, 2011 - No. 5, Jul, 2011 ($2.99, limited series)

1-5-Cap vs. Hydra; Granov-c. 1-WWII flashback. 2-Kirby-style art by Scioli. 4-Hotz-a 3.00

CAPTAIN AMERICA: LIVING LEGEND
Marvel Comics: Dec, 2013 - No. 4, Feb, 2014 ($3.99, limited series)

1-4: 1-Diggle-s/Granov-a/c. 2-4-Alessio-a 4.00

CAPTAIN AMERICA: MAN OUT OF TIME
Marvel Comics: Jan, 2011 - No. 5, May, 2011 ($3.99, limited series)

1-5-Waid-s/Molina-a/Hitch-c; Cap's unfreezing in modern times re-told 4.00

CAPTAIN AMERICA/NICK FURY: BLOOD TRUCE
Marvel Comics: Feb, 1995 ($5.95, one-shot, squarebound)

nn-Chaykin story 6.00

CAPTAIN AMERICA/NICK FURY: THE OTHERWORLD WAR
Marvel Comics: Oct, 2001 ($6.95, one-shot, squarebound)

nn-Manco-a; Bucky and Red Skull app. 7.00

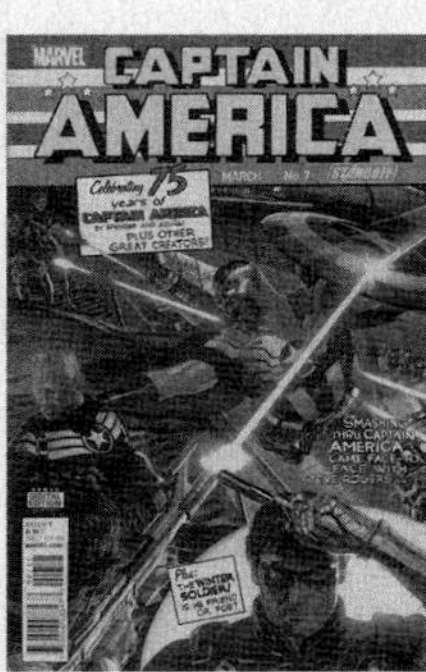

Captain America: Sam Wilson #7 © MAR

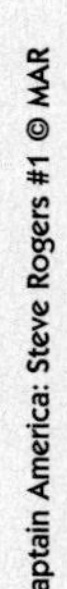
Captain America: Steve Rogers #1 © MAR

Captain Atom: Armageddon #7 © DC

	GD 2.0	VG 4.0	FN 6.0	VF 8.0	VF/NM 9.0	NM- 9.2

CAPTAIN AMERICA: PATRIOT
Marvel Comics: Nov, 2010 - No. 4, Feb, 2011 ($3.99, limited series)

1-4-Kesel-s/Breitweiser-a; 1-WW2 story; Patriot & the Liberty Legion app. 4.00

CAPTAIN AMERICA: REBORN (Titled Reborn in #1-3)
Marvel Comics: Sept, 2009 - No. 6, Mar, 2010 ($3.99, limited series)

1-6-Steve Rogers returns from the dead; Brubaker-s/Hitch & Guice-a. 1-Covers by Hitch, Ross & Quesada. 2-Origin re-told. 4-Joe Kubert var-c. 5-Cassaday var-c 4.00
1-4-Variant-c by Cassaday. 2-Variant-c by Sale. 5-Finch var-c 10.00
... MGC #1 (5/11, $1.00) r/#1 with "Marvel's Greatest Comics" logo on cover 3.00
...: Who Will Wield the Shield? (2/10, $3.99) Aftermath of series; Guice & Luke Ross-a 4.00

CAPTAIN AMERICA: RED, WHITE & BLUE
Marvel Comics: Sept, 2002 ($29.99, one-shot, hardcover with dustjacket)

nn-Reprints from Lee & Kirby, Steranko, Miller and others; and new short stories and pin-ups by various incl. Ross, Dini, Timm, Waid, Dorkin, Sienkiewicz, Miller, Bruce Jones, Collins, Piers-Rayner, Pope, Deodato, Quitely, Nino; Stelfreeze-c 30.00
TPB (2007, $19.99) 20.00

CAPTAIN AMERICA: ROAD TO WAR
Marvel Comics: Jun, 2016 ($4.99, one-shot)

1-Prelude to Captain America: Civil War movie; bonus r/Tales of Suspense #58 5.00

CAPTAIN AMERICA: SAM WILSON
Marvel Comics: Dec, 2015 - Present ($3.99)

1-6: 1-Spencer-s/Acuña-a; Misty Knight & D-Man app. 3-6-Sam as CapWolf 4.00
7-($5.99) 75th Anniversary issue; Steve Rogers regains his youth; Standoff tie-in; bonus short stories by Whedon & Cassaday, Tim Sale, and Rucka & Perkins 6.00
8-19: 8-Standoff tie-in; Baron Zemo app. 10-13-Civil War II tie-in. 11-13-U.S. Agent app. 4.00

CAPTAIN AMERICA, SENTINEL OF LIBERTY (See Fireside Book Series)

CAPTAIN AMERICA: SENTINEL OF LIBERTY
Marvel Comics: Sept, 1998 - No. 12, Aug, 1999 ($1.99)

1-Waid-s/Garney-a 3.00
1-Rough Cut ($2.99) Features original script and pencil pages 3.00
2-5: 2-Two-c; Invaders WW2 story 3.00
6-($2.99) Iron Man-c/app. 4.00
7-11: 8-Falcon-c/app. 9-Falcon poses as Cap 3.00
12-($2.99) Final issue; Bucky-c/app. 4.00

CAPTAIN AMERICA SPECIAL EDITION
Marvel Comics Group: Feb, 1984 - No. 2, Mar, 1984 ($2.00, Baxter paper)

1-Steranko-c/a(r) in both; r/ Captain America #110,111 6.00
2-Reprints the scarce Our Love Story #5, and C.A. #113 1 2 3 5 6 8

CAPTAIN AMERICA: STEVE ROGERS (Also see Captain America: Sam Wilson)
Marvel Comics: Jul, 2016 - Present ($4.99/$3.99)

1-Spencer-s/Saiz-a; childhood flashbacks to Hydra recruitment; Red Skull app. 5.00
2-12-($3.99) 2-Kobik app. 4-6-Civil War II tie-in 4.00

CAPTAIN AMERICA THEATER OF WAR
Marvel Comics: 2009 - 2010 ($3.99, series of one-shots)

...: A Brother in Arms (6/09) Jenkins-s/McCrea-a; WWII story 4.00
...: Ghosts of My Country (12/09) Jenkins-s/Bonetti-a/Guice-c 4.00
...: Prisoners of Duty (2/10) Higgins & Siegel-s/Padilla-a; WWII story 4.00
...: To Soldier On (10/09) Jenkins-s/Blanco-a/Noto-c; Captain America in Iraq 4.00

CAPTAIN AMERICA: THE CHOSEN
Marvel Comics: Nov, 2007 - No. 6, Mar, 2008 ($3.99, limited series)

1-6-Breitweiser-a/Morrell-s 4.00

CAPTAIN AMERICA: THE CLASSIC YEARS
Marvel Comics: Jun, 1998 - No. 2 (trade paperbacks)

1-($19.95) Reprints Captain America Comics #1-5 25.00
2-($24.95) Reprints Captain America Comics #6-10 25.00

CAPTAIN AMERICA: THE FIRST AVENGER ADAPTATION (MARVEL'S...)
Marvel Comics: Jan, 2014 - No. 2, Feb, 2014 ($2.99, limited series)

1,2-Adaptation of the 2011 movie; Peter David-s/Wellinton Alves-a/photo-c 3.00

CAPTAIN AMERICA: THE LEGEND
Marvel Comics: Sept, 1996 ($3.95, one-shot)

1-Tribute issue; wraparound-c 5.00

CAPTAIN AMERICA: THE 1940S NEWSPAPER STRIP
Marvel Comics: Aug, 2010 - No. 3, Oct, 2010 ($3.99, limited series)

1-3-Karl Kesel-s/a; new stories set in WW2, formatted like 1940s newspaper comics 4.00

CAPTAIN AMERICA: WHAT PRICE GLORY
Marvel Comics: May, 2003 - No. 4, May, 2003 ($2.99, weekly limited series)

1-4-Bruce Jones-s/Steve Rude & Mike Royer-a 3.00

CAPTAIN AMERICA: WHITE
Marvel Comics: No. 0, Sept, 2008; No. 1, Nov, 2015 - No. 5, Feb, 2016 (limited series)

0-Bucky's origin retold; Loeb-s/Sale-a in all; interviews with creators; Sale sketch art 3.00
1-($4.99) Flashback to 1941; Sgt. Fury and the Howling Commandos app. 5.00
2-5-($3.99) 3-5-Red Skull app. 4.00

CAPTAIN AMERICA: WINTER SOLDIER DIRECTOR'S CUT
Marvel Comics: Jun, 2014 ($4.99, one-shot)

1-Reprints Captain America (2005) #1; bonus Brubaker script & series proposal 5.00

CAPTAIN AND THE KIDS, THE (See Famous Comics Cartoon Books)

CAPTAIN AND THE KIDS, THE (See Comics on Parade, Katzenjammer Kids, Okay Comics & Sparkler Comics)
United Features Syndicate/Dell Publ. Co.: 1938 -12/39; Sum, 1947 - No. 32, 1955; Four Color No. 881, Feb, 1958

	GD 2.0	VG 4.0	FN 6.0	VF 8.0	VF/NM 9.0	NM- 9.2
Single Series 1(1938)	116	232	348	742	1271	1800
Single Series 1(Reprint)(12/39- "Reprint" on-c)	48	96	144	302	514	725
1(Summer, 1947-UFS)-Katzenjammer Kids	19	38	57	111	176	240
2	11	22	33	62	86	110
3-10	10	20	30	54	72	90
11-20	8	16	24	44	57	70
21-32 (1955)	8	16	24	40	50	60
50th Anniversary issue-(1948)-Contains a 2 pg. history of the strip, including an account of the famous Supreme Court decision allowing both Pulitzer & Hearst to run the same strip under different names	19	38	57	111	176	240
Special Summer issue, Fall issue (1948)	12	24	36	69	97	125
Four Color 881 (Dell)	5	10	15	30	50	70

CAPTAIN ATOM
Nationwide Publishers: 1950 - No. 7, 1951 (5¢, 5x7-1/4", 52 pgs.)

	GD 2.0	VG 4.0	FN 6.0	VF 8.0	VF/NM 9.0	NM- 9.2
1-Science fiction	42	84	126	265	445	625
2-7	26	52	78	154	252	350

CAPTAIN ATOM (Formerly Strange Suspense Stories #77)(Also see Space Adventures and Thunderbolt)
Charlton Comics: V2#78, Dec, 1965 - V2#89, Dec, 1967

	GD 2.0	VG 4.0	FN 6.0	VF 8.0	VF/NM 9.0	NM- 9.2
V2#78-Origin retold; Bache-a (3 pgs.)	8	16	24	51	96	140
79-81: 79-1st app. Dr. Spectro; 3 pg. Ditko cut & paste /Space Adventures #24.	5	10	15	35	63	90
82-Intro. Nightshade (9/66)	10	20	30	69	147	225
83-(11/66)-1st app. Ted Kord/Blue Beetle	34	68	102	245	548	850
84-86: Ted Kord Blue Beetle in all. 84-1st app. new Captain Atom. 85-1st app. Punch and Jewelee	5	10	15	33	57	80
87-89: Nightshade by Aparo in all	5	10	15	33	57	80
83-(Modern Comics-1977)-reprints	3	6	9	19	30	40
84,85-(Modern Comics-1977)-reprints	1	2	3	5	6	8

NOTE: *Aparo a-87-89. Ditko c/a(p) 78-89. #90 only published in fanzine 'The Charlton Bullseye' #1, 2.*

CAPTAIN ATOM (Also see Americomics & Crisis On Infinite Earths)
DC Comics: Mar, 1987 - No. 57, Sept, 1991 (Direct sales only #35 on)

1-(44 pgs.)-Origin/1st app. with new costume 5.00
2-49: 5-Firestorm x-over. 6-Intro. new Dr. Spectro. 11-Millennium tie-in. 14-Nightshade app. 16-Justice League app. 17-$1.00-c begins; Swamp Thing app. 20-Blue Beetle x-over. 24,25-Invasion tie-in 3.00
50-($2.00, 52 pgs.) 4.00
51-57: 57-War of the Gods x-over 3.00
Annual 1,2 ('88, '89)-1-Intro Major Force 4.00

CAPTAIN ATOM (DC New 52)
DC Comics: Nov, 2011 - No. 12, Oct, 2012; No. 0, Nov, 2012 ($2.99)

1-12-J.T. Krul-s/Freddie Williams II-a. 3-Flash app. 3.00
#0 (11/12, $2.99) origin of Captain Atom re-told 3.00

CAPTAIN ATOM: ARMAGEDDON (Restarts the WildStorm Universe)
DC Comics (WildStorm): Dec, 2005 - No. 9, Aug, 2006 ($2.99, limited series)

1-9-Captain Atom appears in WildStorm Universe; Pfeifer-s/Camuncoli-a. 1-Lee-c 3.00
TPB (2007, $19.99) r/series 20.00

CAPTAIN BATTLE (Boy Comics #3 on) (See Silver Streak Comics)
New Friday Publ./Comic House: Summer, 1941 - No. 2, Fall, 1941

	GD 2.0	VG 4.0	FN 6.0	VF 8.0	VF/NM 9.0	NM- 9.2
1-Origin Blackout by Rico; Captain Battle begins (1st appeared in Silver Streak #10, 5/41) classic hooded villain bondage/torture-c	194	388	582	1242	2121	3000
2-Doctor Horror only app.	90	180	270	576	988	1400

Captain Britain and MI:13 #1 © MAR

Captain Canuck (2015 series) #2 © Richard Comely

Captain Eo 3-D #1 © DIS

GD	VG	FN	VF	VF/NM	NM-
2.0	4.0	6.0	8.0	9.0	9.2

CAPTAIN BATTLE (2nd Series)
Magazine Press/Picture Scoop No. 5: No. 3, Wint, 1942-43; No. 5, Sum, 1943 (No #4)

3-Origin Silver Streak-r/SS#3; origin Lance Hale-r/Silver Streak; Simon-a(r) (52 pgs., nd) 84 168 252 538 919 1300
5-Origin Blackout retold (68 pgs.); Japanese WWII-c 84 168 252 538 919 1300

CAPTAIN BATTLE, JR.
Comic House (Lev Gleason): Fall, 1943 - No. 2, Winter, 1943-44

1-Nazi WWII-c by Rico. Hitler/Claw sty; The Claw vs. The Ghost 142 284 426 909 1555 2200
2-Wolverton's Scoop Scuttle; Don Rico-c/a; The Green Claw story is reprinted from Silver Streak #6; Japanese WWII bondage/torture-c by Rico 84 168 252 538 919 1300

CAPTAIN BEN DIX (See Promotional Comics section)

CAPTAIN BRITAIN (Also see Marvel Team-Up No. 65, 66)
Marvel Comics International: Oct. 13, 1976 - No. 39, July 6, 1977 (Weekly)

1-1st app & origin of Captain Britain (Brian Broddock); with Capt. Britain's face mask inside Claremont-s/Trimpe-a 8 16 24 56 108 160
2-Origin, part II; Capt. Britain's Boomerang inside 3 6 9 17 26 35
3-7: 3-Vs. Bank Robbers. 4-7-Vs. Hurricane 2 4 6 8 10 12
8-(12/76) 1st app. Betsy Braddock, the sister of Capt. Britain (Brian Braddock) who later becomes Psylocke (X-Men); 1st app. Dr. Synne 12 24 36 79 170 260
9-11-Battles Dr. Synne. 9,10-Betsy Braddock app. 2 4 6 8 10 12
12-23,25-27: (low print run)-12,13-Vs. Dr. Synne. 14,15-Vs. Mastermind. 16-23,25,26-With Captain America. 17-Misprinted & color section reprinted in #18. 27-Origin retold 3 6 9 14 20 25
24-With Capt. Britain's Jet Plane inside 3 6 9 19 30 40
28-32,36-39: 28-32-Vs. Lord Hawk. 30-32-Inhumans app. 35-Dr. Doom app. 37-39-Vs. Highwayman & Munipulator 1 2 3 5 6 8
33-35-More on origin 1 2 3 5 7 9
Annual (1978, Hardback, 64 pgs.)-Reprints #1-7 with pin-ups of Marvel characters 3 6 9 15 22 28
Summer Special (1980, 52 pgs.)-Reprints 1 2 3 5 6 8

NOTE: *No. 1, 2, & 24 are rarer in mint due to inserts. Distributed in Great Britain only. Nick Fury-r by* ***Steranko*** *in 1-20, 24-31, 35-37. Fantastic Four-r by* ***J. Buscema*** *in all. New* ***Buscema****-a in 24-30. Story from No. 39 continues in Super Spider-Man (British weekly) No. 231-247. Following cancellation of his series, new Captain Britain stories appeared in "Super Spider-Man" (British weekly) No. 231-247. Captain Britain stories which appear in Super-Spider-Man No 248-253 are reprints of Marvel Team-Up No. 65&66. Capt. Britain strips also appeared in Hulk Comic (weekly) 1, 3-30, 42-55, 57-60, in Marvel Superheroes (monthly) 377-388, in Daredevils (monthly) 1-11, Mighty World of Marvel (monthly) 7-16 & Captain Britain (monthly) 1-14. Issues 1-23 have B&W & color, paper-c, & are 32 pgs. Issues 24 on are all B&W w/glossy-c & are 36 pgs.*

CAPTAIN BRITAIN AND MI: 13 (Also see Secret Invasion x-over titles)
Marvel Comics: Jul, 2008 - No. 15, Sept, 2009 ($2.99)

1-Skrull invasion; Black Knight app.; Kirk-a 4.00
1-2nd printing with Kirk variant-c; 3rd printing with B&W cover 3.00
2-15: 5-Blade app. 9,10-Dracula app. 3.00
... Annual 1 (8/09, $3.99) Land-c; Meggan in Hell; Dr. Doom cameo; Collins-a 4.00

CAPTAIN BRITAIN AND THE MIGHTY DEFENDERS (Secret Wars tie-in)
Marvel Comics: Sept, 2015 - No. 2, Oct, 2015 ($3.99, limited series)

1,2-Ho Yinsen, Faiza Hussain, White Tiger, She-Hulk app.; Al Ewing-s/Alan Davis-a 4.00

CAPTAIN CANUCK
Comely Comix (Canada)(All distr. in U. S.): Jul,1975 - No. 4, Jul, 1977; No. 4, Jul-Aug, 1979 - No. 14, Mar-Apr, 1981

1-1st app. Captain Canuck, C.I.S.O. & Bluefox; Richard Comely-c/a 2 4 6 9 12 15
2,3(5-7/76): 2-1st app. Dr. Walker, Redcoat & Kebec. 3-1st app. Heather 6.00
4 (1st printing-2/77)-10x14-1/2"; (5.00); B&W; 300 copies serially numbered and signed with one certificate of authenticity 9 18 27 61 123 185
4 (2nd printing-7/77)-11x17", B&W; only 15 copies printed; signed by creator Richard Comely, serially #'d and two certificates of authenticity inserted; orange cardboard covers (Very Rare) 12 24 36 84 185 285
4-14: 4(7-8/79)-1st app. Tom Evans & Mr. Gold; origin The Catman. 5-Origin Capt. Canuck's powers; 1st app. Earth Patrol & Chaos Corps. 5-7-Three-part neo-Nazi story set in 1994. 8-Jonn 'The Final Chapter'; 1st app. Mike & Saskia. 9-1st World Beyond. 11-1st 'Chariots of Fire' story. 12-A-bomb explosion panel 6.00
15-(8/04, $15.00) Limited edition of unpublished issue from 1981; serially #'d edition of 150; signed by creator Richard Comely 7 14 21 44 82 120
... Legacy 1 (9-10/06) Comely-s/a 4.00
... Legacy Special Edition ($7.95, 52 pgs., limited ed. of 1000) Comely-s/a 1 3 4 6 8 10
Special Collectors Pack (#1 & #2 polybagged) 2 4 6 8 10 12
Summer Special 1(7-9/80, 95¢, 64 pgs.) George Freeman-c/a; pin-ups by Gene Day, Tom Grummett, Dave Sim and others 6.00
Summer Special / Canada Day Edition #1 (2014, no cover price) 2 new stories, background on animated web series; regular-c shows a parade; variants exist 5.00

NOTE: *30,000 copies of No. 2 were destroyed in Winnipeg.*

CAPTAIN CANUCK
Chapterhouse Comics: May, 2015 - Present ($3.99)

1-11: 1-Kalman Andrasofszky-s/a; 3 covers. 3-11-Leonard Kirk-a 4.00
#0/FCBD Edition (5/15, giveaway) previews #1; origin re-told; character profiles 3.00

CAPTAIN CANUCK: UNHOLY WAR
Comely Comix: Oct, 2004 - No. 3, Jan, 2005; No. 4, Sept, 2007 ($2.50, limited series)

1-3-Riel Langlois-s/Drue Langlois-a: 1-1st app. David Semple (West Coast Capt. Canuck); Clair Sinclair as Bluefox 3.00
4-(Low print run) Black Mack the Lumberjack, Torchie, Splatter app. 6.00

CAPTAIN CARROT AND HIS AMAZING ZOO CREW (Also see New Teen Titans & Oz-Wonderland War)
DC Comics: Mar, 1982 - No. 20, Nov, 1983

1-Superman app. 6.00
2-20: 3-Re-intro Dodo & The Frog. 9-Re-intro Three Mouseketeers, the Terrific Whatzit. 10,11-Pig Iron reverts back to Peter Porkchops. 20-Changeling app. 4.00

CAPTAIN CARROT AND THE FINAL ARK (DC Countdown tie-in)
DC Comics: Dec, 2007 - No. 3, Feb, 2008 ($2.99, limited series)

1-3-Bill Morrison-s/Scott Shaw!-a. 3-Batman, Red Arrow, Hawkgirl & Zatanna app. 3.00
TPB (2008, $19.99) r/#1-3; Captain Carrot and His Amazing Zoo Crew #1,14,15; New Teen Titans #16 and stories from Teen Titans (2003 series) #30,31; cover gallery 20.00

CAPTAIN CARVEL AND HIS CARVEL CRUSADERS (See Carvel Comics)

CAPTAIN CONFEDERACY
Marvel Comics (Epic Comics): Nov, 1991 - No. 4, Feb, 1992 ($1.95)

1-4: All new stories 3.00

CAPTAIN COURAGEOUS COMICS (Banner #3-5; see Four Favorites #5)
Periodical House (Ace Magazines): No. 6, March, 1942

6-Origin & 1st app. The Sword; Lone Warrior, Capt. Courageous app.; Capt. moves to Four Favorites #5 in May 110 220 330 704 1202 1700

CAPT'N CRUNCH COMICS (See Cap'n...)

CAPTAIN DAVY JONES
Dell Publishing Co.: No. 598, Nov, 1954

Four Color 598 5 10 15 35 63 90

CAPTAIN EASY (See The Funnies & Red Ryder #3-32)
Hawley/Dell Publ./Standard(Visual Editions)/Argo: 1939 - No. 17, Sept, 1949; April, 1956

nn-Hawley(1939)-Contains reprints from The Funnies & 1938 Sunday strips by Roy Crane 90 180 270 576 988 1400
Four Color 24 (1943) 54 108 162 343 574 825
Four Color 111(6/46) 12 24 36 82 179 275
10(Standard-10/47) 14 28 42 76 108 140
11,12,14,15,17: 11-17 all contain 1930s & '40s strip-r 10 20 30 56 76 95
13,16: Schomburg-c 12 24 36 69 97 125
Argo 1(4/56)-Reprints 7 14 21 37 46 55

CAPTAIN EASY & WASH TUBBS (See Famous Comics Cartoon Books)

CAPTAIN ELECTRON
Brick Computer Science Institute: Aug, 1986 ($2.25)

1-Disbrow-a 3.00

CAPTAIN EO 3-D (Michael Jackson Disney theme parks movie)
Eclipse Comics: July, 1987 (Eclipse 3-D Special #18, $3.50, Baxter)

1-Adapts 3-D movie; Michael Jackson-c/app. 3 6 9 14 20 25
1-2-D limited edition 5 10 15 31 53 75
1-Large size (11x17", 8/87)-Sold only at Disney Theme parks ($6.95) 4 8 12 23 37 50

CAPTAIN FEARLESS COMICS (Also see Holyoke One-Shot #6, Old Glory Comics & Silver Streak #1)
Helnit Publishing Co. (Holyoke Publ. Co.): Aug, 1941 - No. 2, Sept, 1941

1-Origin Mr. Miracle, Alias X, Captain Fearless, Citizen Smith Son of the Unknown Soldier; Miss Victory (1st app.) begins (1st patriotic heroine? before Wonder Woman) 103 206 309 659 1130 1600
2-Grit Grady, Captain Stone app. 54 108 162 343 574 825

CAPTAIN FLAG (See Blue Ribbon Comics #16)

CAPTAIN FLASH
Sterling Comics: Nov, 1954 - No. 4, July, 1955

Captain Flight Comics #8 © Four Star

Captain Marvel #17 © MAR

Captain Marvel (1994) #1 © MAR

	GD 2.0	VG 4.0	FN 6.0	VF 8.0	VF/NM 9.0	NM- 9.2
1-Origin; Sekowsky-a; Tomboy (female super hero) begins; only pre-code issue; atomic rocket-c	43	86	129	271	461	650
2-4: 4-Flying saucer invasion-c	26	52	78	154	252	350

CAPTAIN FLEET (Action Packed Tales of the Sea)
Ziff-Davis Publishing Co.: Fall, 1952

	GD 2.0	VG 4.0	FN 6.0	VF 8.0	VF/NM 9.0	NM- 9.2
1-Painted-c	18	36	54	103	162	220

CAPTAIN FLIGHT COMICS
Four Star Publications: May, 1944 - No. 10, Dec, 1945; No. 11, Feb-Mar, 1947

	GD 2.0	VG 4.0	FN 6.0	VF 8.0	VF/NM 9.0	NM- 9.2
nn-Captain Flight begins	68	136	204	435	743	1050
2-4: 4-Rock Raymond begins, ends #7	47	94	141	296	498	700
5-Bondage, classic torture-c; Red Rocket begins; the Grenade app. (scarce)	206	412	618	1318	2259	3200
6-L. B. Cole-a, 8 pgs.	41	82	123	256	428	600
7-10: 7-L. B. Cole covers begin, end #11. 7-9-Japanese WWII-c. 8-Yankee Girl begins; intro. Black Cobra & Cobra Kid & begins. 9-Torpedoman app.; last Yankee Girl; Kinstler-a. 10-Deep Sea Dawson, Zoom of the Jungle, Rock Raymond, Red Rocket, & Black Cobra app; bondage-c	60	120	180	381	653	925
11-Torpedoman, Blue Flame (Human Torch clone) app.; last Black Cobra, Red Rocket; classic L. B. Cole sci-fi robot-c (scarce)	245	490	735	1568	2684	3800

CAPTAIN GALLANT (...of the Foreign Legion) (TV) (Texas Rangers in Action No. 5 on?)
Charlton Comics: 1955; No. 2, Jan, 1956 - No. 4, Sept, 1956

	GD 2.0	VG 4.0	FN 6.0	VF 8.0	VF/NM 9.0	NM- 9.2
Non-Heinz version (#1)-Buster Crabbe photo on-c; full page Buster Crabbe photo inside front-c	8	16	24	44	57	70
(Heinz version is listed in the Promotional Comics section)						
2-4: Buster Crabbe in all. 2-Crabbe photo back-c	6	12	18	31	38	45

CAPTAIN GLORY
Topps Comics: Apr, 1993 ($2.95) (Created by Jack Kirby)

	GD 2.0	VG 4.0	FN 6.0	VF 8.0	VF/NM 9.0	NM- 9.2
1-Polybagged w/Kirbychrome trading card; Ditko-a & Kirby-c; has coupon for Amberchrome Secret City Saga #0						4.00

CAPTAIN HERO (See Jughead as...)

CAPTAIN HERO COMICS DIGEST MAGAZINE
Archie Publications: Sept, 1981

	GD 2.0	VG 4.0	FN 6.0	VF 8.0	VF/NM 9.0	NM- 9.2
1-Reprints of Jughead as Super-Guy	2	4	6	10	14	18

CAPTAIN HOBBY COMICS
Export Publication Ent. Ltd. (Dist. in U.S. by Kable News Co.): Feb, 1948 (Canadian)

	GD 2.0	VG 4.0	FN 6.0	VF 8.0	VF/NM 9.0	NM- 9.2
1	12	24	36	67	94	120

CAPT. HOLO IN 3-D (See Blackthorne 3-D Series #65)

CAPTAIN HOOK & PETER PAN (Movie)(Disney)
Dell Publishing Co.: No. 446, Jan, 1953

	GD 2.0	VG 4.0	FN 6.0	VF 8.0	VF/NM 9.0	NM- 9.2
Four Color 446	9	18	27	58	114	170

CAPTAIN JET (Fantastic Fears No. 7 on)
Four Star Publ./Farrell/Comic Media: May, 1952 - No. 5, Jan, 1953

	GD 2.0	VG 4.0	FN 6.0	VF 8.0	VF/NM 9.0	NM- 9.2
1-Bakerish-a	25	50	75	150	245	340
2	15	30	45	86	133	180
3-5,6(?)	12	24	36	69	97	125

CAPTAIN JOHNER & THE ALIENS
Valiant: May, 1995 - No. 2, May, 1995 ($2.95, shipped in same month)

	GD 2.0	VG 4.0	FN 6.0	VF 8.0	VF/NM 9.0	NM- 9.2
1,2: Reprints Magnus Robot Fighter 4000 A.D. back-up stories; new Paul Smith-c						3.00

CAPTAIN JUSTICE (TV)
Marvel Comics: Mar, 1988 - No. 2, Apr, 1988 (limited series)

	GD 2.0	VG 4.0	FN 6.0	VF 8.0	VF/NM 9.0	NM- 9.2
1,2-Based on the 1987 "Once a Hero" television series						3.00

CAPTAIN KANGAROO (TV)
Dell Publishing Co.: No. 721, Aug, 1956 - No. 872, Jan, 1958

	GD 2.0	VG 4.0	FN 6.0	VF 8.0	VF/NM 9.0	NM- 9.2
Four Color 721 (#1)-Photo-c	13	26	39	86	188	290
Four Color 780, 872-Photo-c	11	22	33	73	157	240

CAPTAIN KID
AfterShock Comics: Jul, 2016 - No. 5 ($3.99)

	GD 2.0	VG 4.0	FN 6.0	VF 8.0	VF/NM 9.0	NM- 9.2
1-4-Mark Waid & Tom Peyer-s/Wilfredo Torres-a						4.00

CAPTAIN KIDD (Formerly Dagar; My Secret Story #26 on)(Also see Comic Comics & Fantastic Comics)
Fox Feature Syndicate: No. 24, June, 1949 - No. 25, Aug, 1949

	GD 2.0	VG 4.0	FN 6.0	VF 8.0	VF/NM 9.0	NM- 9.2
24,25: 24-Features Blackbeard the Pirate	15	30	45	85	130	175

CAPTAIN MARVEL (See All Hero, All-New Collectors' Ed., America's Greatest, Fawcett Miniature, Gift, JSA, Kingdom Come, Legends, Limited Collectors' Ed., Marvel Family, Master No. 21, Mighty Midget Comics, Power of Shazam!, Shazam, Special Edition Comics, Whiz, Wisco (in Promotional Comics section), World's Finest #253 and XMas Comics)

CAPTAIN MARVEL (Becomes ...Presents the Terrible 5 No. 5)
M. F. Enterprises: April, 1966 - No. 4, Nov, 1966 (25¢ Giants)

	GD 2.0	VG 4.0	FN 6.0	VF 8.0	VF/NM 9.0	NM- 9.2
nn-(#1 on pg. 5)-Origin; created by Carl Burgos	5	10	15	31	53	75
2-4: 3-(#3 on pg. 4)-Fights the Bat	3	6	9	21	33	45

CAPTAIN MARVEL (Marvel's Space-Born Super-Hero! Captain Marvel #1-6; see Giant-Size..., Life Of..., Marvel Graphic Novel #1, Marvel Spotlight V2#1 & Marvel Super-Heroes #12)
Marvel Comics Group: May, 1968 - No. 19, Dec, 1969; No. 20, June, 1970 - No. 21, Aug, 1970; No. 22, Sept, 1972 - No. 62, May, 1979

	GD 2.0	VG 4.0	FN 6.0	VF 8.0	VF/NM 9.0	NM- 9.2
1	16	32	48	110	243	375
2-Super Skrull-c/story	8	16	24	51	96	140
3-5: 4-Captain Marvel battles Sub-Mariner	6	12	18	38	69	100
6-11: 11-Capt. Marvel given great power by Zo the Ruler; Smith/Trimpe-c; Death of Una	4	8	12	25	40	55
12,13,15,19,20	3	6	9	17	26	35
14-Capt. Marvel vs. Iron Man; last 12¢ issue.	4	8	12	28	47	65
16-1st new Captain Marvel (cameo)	4	8	12	28	47	65
17-1st new Captain Marvel app.	8	16	24	51	96	140
18-Carol Danvers gets powers	7	14	21	44	82	120
21-Capt. Marvel battles Hulk; last 15¢ issue	4	8	12	28	47	65
22-24	3	6	9	17	26	35
25-Starlin-c/a begins; Starlin's 1st Thanos saga begins (3/73), ends #34; Thanos cameo (5 panels)	7	14	21	48	89	130
26-2nd app. Thanos (see Iron Man #55); 1st Thanos-c	8	16	24	54	102	150
27-3rd app. Thanos	7	14	21	44	82	120
28-Thanos-c/s (4th app.); Avengers app.	8	16	24	54	102	150
29,30-Thanos cameos. 29-C.M. gains more powers	4	8	12	28	47	65
31-Thanos app.; last 20¢ issue; Avengers app.	5	10	15	30	50	70
32-Thanos-c & app.; Avengers app.	5	10	15	31	53	75
33-Thanos-c & app.; Capt. Marvel battles Thanos; Thanos origin re-told	8	16	24	54	102	150
34-1st app. Nitro; C.M. contracts cancer which eventually kills him; last Starlin-c/a	4	8	12	25	40	55
35,37-40,42,46-48,50,53-56,59-62: 39-Origin Watcher. 42-Drax app.	2	4	6	8	10	12
36,41,43,49: 36-R-origin/1st app. Capt. Marvel from Marvel Super-Heroes #12. 41,43-Drax app.; Wrightson part inks; #43-c(i). 49-Starlin & Weiss-p assists	2	4	6	8	11	14
44,45-(Regular 25¢ editions)(5,7/76)	2	4	6	8	10	12
44,45-(30¢-c variants, limited distribution)	4	8	12	27	44	60
51,52-(Regular 30¢ editions)(7,9/77)	2	4	6	8	10	12
51,52-(35¢-c variants, limited distribution)	7	14	21	44	82	120
57-Thanos appears in flashback	2	4	6	13	18	22
58-Thanos cameo	2	4	6	10	14	18

NOTE: ***Alcala** a-35. **Austin** a-46i, 49-53i; c-52i. **Buscema** a-18p-21p. **Colan** a(p)-1-4; c(p)-1-4, 8, 9. **Heck** a-5-10p, 16p. **Gil Kane** a-17-21p; c-17-24p, 37p, 53. **Starlin** a-36. **McWilliams** a-40i. #25-34 were reprinted in The Life of Captain Marvel.*

CAPTAIN MARVEL
Marvel Comics: Nov, 1989 ($1.50, one-shot, 52 pgs.)

	GD 2.0	VG 4.0	FN 6.0	VF 8.0	VF/NM 9.0	NM- 9.2
1-Super-hero from Avengers; new powers						4.00

CAPTAIN MARVEL
Marvel Comics: Feb, 1994 ($1.75, 52 pgs.)

	GD 2.0	VG 4.0	FN 6.0	VF 8.0	VF/NM 9.0	NM- 9.2
1-(Indicia reads Vol 2 #2)-Minor Captain America app.						4.00

CAPTAIN MARVEL
Marvel Comics: Dec, 1995 - No. 6, May, 1996 ($2.95/$1.95)

	GD 2.0	VG 4.0	FN 6.0	VF 8.0	VF/NM 9.0	NM- 9.2
1 ($2.95)-Advs. of Mar-Vell's son begins; Fabian Nicieza scripts; foil-c						4.00
2-6: 2-Begin $1.95-c						3.00

CAPTAIN MARVEL (Vol. 3) (See Avengers Forever)
Marvel Comics: Jan, 2000 - No. 35, Oct, 2002 ($2.50)

	GD 2.0	VG 4.0	FN 6.0	VF 8.0	VF/NM 9.0	NM- 9.2
1-Peter David-s in all; two covers						4.00
2-10: 2-Two covers; Hulk app. 9-Silver Surfer app.						3.00
11-35: 12-Maximum Security x-over. 17,18-Starlin-a. 27-30-Spider-Man 2099 app.						3.00
Wizard #0-Preview and history of Rick Jones						4.00
...: First Contact (8/01, $16.95, TPB) r/#0,1-6						17.00

CAPTAIN MARVEL (Vol. 4) (See Avengers Forever)
Marvel Comics: Nov, 2002 - No. 25, Sept, 2004 ($2.25/$2.99)

	GD 2.0	VG 4.0	FN 6.0	VF 8.0	VF/NM 9.0	NM- 9.2
1-Peter David-s/Chriscross-a ; 3 covers by Ross, Jusko & Chriscross						4.00
2-7: 2,3-Punisher app. 3-Alex Ross-c; new costume debuts. 4-Noto-c. 7-Thor app.						3.00
3-Sketchbook Edition-($3.50) includes Ross' concept design pages for new costume						4.00

Captain Marvel (2014 series) #15 © MAR

Captain Marvel Adventures #27 © FAW

Captain Marvel, Jr. #8 © FAW

	GD 2.0	VG 4.0	FN 6.0	VF 8.0	VF/NM 9.0	NM- 9.2
8-25: 8-Begin $2.99-c; Thor app.; Manco-c. 10-Spider-Man-c/app. 15-Neal Adams-c						3.00
Vol. 1: Nothing To Lose (2003, $14.99, TPB) r/#1-6						15.00
Vol. 2: Coven (2003, $14.99, TPB) r/#7-12						15.00
Vol. 3: Crazy Like a Fox (2004, $14.99, TPB) r/#13-18						15.00
Vol. 4: Odyssey (2004, $16.99, TPB) r/#19-25						17.00

CAPTAIN MARVEL (Vol. 5) (See Secret Invasion x-over titles)
Marvel Comics: Jan, 2008 - No. 5, Jun, 2008 ($2.99)

	GD	VG	FN	VF	VF/NM	NM-
1-5-Mar-Vell "from the past in the present"; McGuinness-c/Weeks-a						3.00
3,4-Skrull variant-c						4.00

CAPTAIN MARVEL
Marvel Comics: Sept, 2012 - No. 17, Jan, 2014 ($2.99)

	GD	VG	FN	VF	VF/NM	NM-
1-Carol Danvers as Captain Marvel; DeConnick-s/Soy-a	2	4	6	9	12	15
2-5						6.00
6-13,15,16: 13-The Enemy Within. 15,16-Infinity tie-in						5.00
14-1st cameo of Kamala Khan (new Ms. Marvel); Andrade-a; The Enemy Within cont'd	3	6	9	19	30	40
17-($3.99) Cameo of Kamala Khan (new Ms. Marvel); Andrade-a	2	4	6	10	14	18
17-($3.99, 2nd printing) Kamala Khan (new Ms. Marvel) in costume on cover	8	16	24	54	102	150

CAPTAIN MARVEL
Marvel Comics: May, 2014 - No. 15, Jul, 2015 ($3.99)

	GD	VG	FN	VF	VF/NM	NM-
1-Carol Danvers; DeConnick-s/Lopez-a	2	4	6	10	14	18
2,3-Guardians of the Galaxy app.						6.00
4-9,11-15: 7,8-Rocket Raccoon app. 14-Black Vortex x-over						4.00
10-($4.99) 100th issue; War Machine & Spider-Woman app.; Lopez & Takara-a						5.00

CAPTAIN MARVEL (Follows Secret Wars event)(Also see Mighty Captain Marvel)
Marvel Comics: Mar, 2016 - No. 10, ($3.99)

	GD	VG	FN	VF	VF/NM	NM-
1-5-Carol Danvers; Fazekas & Butters-s/Anka-a; Aurora, Sasquatch & Puck app.						4.00
6-9-Civil War II tie-ins						4.00
10-($4.99) Civil War II tie-in; Gage & Gage-s/Silas-a; Alpha Flight app.						5.00

CAPTAIN MARVEL ADVENTURES (See Special Edition Comics for pre #1)
Fawcett Publications: 1941 (March) - No. 150, Nov, 1953 (#1 on stands 1/16/41)

	GD	VG	FN	VF	VF/NM	NM-
nn(#1)-Captain Marvel & Sivana by Jack Kirby. The cover was printed on unstable paper stock and is rarely found in Fine or Mint condition; blank back inside-c	4000	8000	16,000	32,000	56,000	80,000
2-(Advertised as #3, which was counting Special Edition Comics as the real #1); Tuska-a	459	918	1377	3350	5925	8500
3-Metallic silver-c	331	662	993	2317	4059	5800
4-Three Lt. Marvels app.	226	452	678	1446	2473	3500
5	174	348	522	1114	1907	2700
6-10: 9-1st Otto Binder scripts on Capt. Marvel	129	258	387	826	1413	2000
11-15: 12-Capt. Marvel joins the Army. 13-Two pg. Capt. Marvel pin-up. 15-Comix Cards on back-c begin, end #26	103	206	309	659	1130	1600
16,17: 17-Painted-c	94	188	282	597	1024	1450
18-Origin & 1st app. Mary Marvel & Marvel Family (12/11/42); classic painted-c; Mary Marvel by Marcus Swayze	432	864	1296	3154	5577	8000
19-Mary Marvel x-over; Christmas-c	84	168	252	538	919	1300
20,21,23-Attached to the cover, each has a miniature comic just like the Mighty Midget Comics #11, except that each has a full color promo ad on the back cover. Most copies were circulated without the miniature comic. These issues with miniatures attached are very rare, and should not be mistaken for copies with the similar Mighty Midget glued in its place. The Mighty Midgets had blank back covers except for a small victory stamp seal. Only the Capt. Marvel, Captain Marvel Jr. and Golden Arrow No. 11 miniatures have been positively documented as having been affixed to these covers. Each miniature was only partially glued by its back cover to the Captain Marvel comic making it easy to see if it's the genuine miniature rather than a Mighty Midget. with comic attached....	432	864	1296	3154	5577	8000
20,23-Without miniature	71	142	213	454	777	1100
21-Without miniature; Hitler-c	132	264	396	838	1444	2050
22-Mr. Mind serial begins; Mr. Mind first heard	97	194	291	621	1061	1500
24,25	68	136	204	432	746	1060
26-28,30: 26-Flag-c; subtle Mr. Mind 2-panel cameo. 27-1st full Mr. Mind app. (his voice was only heard over the radio before now) (9/43)	57	114	171	362	619	875
29-1st Mr. Mind-c (11/43)	63	126	189	403	689	975
31-35: 35-Origin Radar (5/44, see Master #50)	51	102	153	318	539	760
36-40: 37-Mary Marvel x-over	47	94	141	296	498	700
41-46: 42-Christmas-c. 43-Capt. Marvel 1st meets Uncle Marvel; Mary Batson cameo. 46-Mr. Mind serial ends	39	78	117	240	395	550
47-50	37	74	111	222	361	500
51-53,55-60: 51-63-Bi-weekly issues. 52-Origin & 1st app. Sivana Jr.; Capt. Marvel Jr. x-over	34	68	102	199	325	450
54-Special oversize 68 pg. issue	34	68	102	204	332	460
61-The Cult of the Curse serial begins	36	72	108	216	351	485
62-65-Serial cont.; Mary Marvel x-over in #65	34	68	102	199	325	450
66-Serial ends; Atomic War-c	39	78	117	233	384	535
67-77,79: 69-Billy Batson's Christmas; Uncle Marvel, Mary Marvel, Capt. Marvel Jr. x-over. 71-Three Lt. Marvels app. 79-Origin Mr. Tawny	31	62	93	182	296	410
78-Origin Mr. Atom	34	68	102	204	322	460
80-Origin Capt. Marvel retold; origin scene-c	97	194	291	621	1061	1500
81-84,86-90: 81,90-Mr. Atom app. 82-Infinity-c. 82,86,88,90-Mr. Tawny app.	31	62	93	182	296	410
85-Freedom Train issue	34	68	102	199	325	450
91-99: 92-Mr. Tawny app. 96-Gets 1st name "Tawky"	30	60	90	177	289	400
100-Origin retold; silver metallic-c	50	100	150	315	533	750
101-115,117-120	30	60	90	177	289	400
116-Flying Saucer issue (1/51)	34	68	102	199	325	450
121-Origin retold	37	74	111	222	361	500
122-137,139,140	30	60	90	177	289	400
138-Flying Saucer issue (11/52)	34	68	102	204	332	460
141-Pre-code horror story "The Hideous Head-Hunter"	34	68	102	199	325	450
142-149: 142-used in **POP**, pgs. 92,96	33	66	99	194	317	440
150-(Low distribution)	58	116	174	371	636	900

NOTE: *Swayze a-12, 14, 15, 18, 19, 40; c-12, 15, 19.*

CAPTAIN MARVEL AND THE CAROL CORPS (Secret Wars tie-in)
Marvel Comics: Aug, 2015 - No. 4, Nov, 2015 ($3.99, limited series)

	GD	VG	FN	VF	VF/NM	NM-
1-4: 1-Carol Danvers' squad; DeConnick & Thompson-s/Lopez-a. 4-Braga-a						4.00

CAPTAIN MARVEL AND THE GOOD HUMOR MAN (Movie)
Fawcett Publications: 1950

	GD	VG	FN	VF	VF/NM	NM-
nn-Partial photo-c w/Jack Carson & the Captain Marvel Club Boys	47	94	141	296	498	700

CAPTAIN MARVEL COMIC STORY PAINT BOOK (See Comic Story...)

CAPTAIN MARVEL, JR. (See Fawcett Miniatures, Marvel Family, Master Comics, Mighty Midget Comics, Shazam & Whiz Comics)

CAPTAIN MARVEL, JR.
Fawcett Publications: Nov, 1942 - No. 119, June, 1953 (No #34)

	GD	VG	FN	VF	VF/NM	NM-
1-Origin Capt. Marvel Jr. retold (Whiz #25); Capt. Nazi app. Classic Raboy-c	595	1190	1785	4350	7675	11,000
2-Vs. Capt. Nazi; origin Capt. Nippon	210	420	630	1334	2292	3250
3	116	232	348	742	1271	1800
4-Classic Raboy-c	123	246	369	787	1344	1900
5-Vs. Capt. Nazi	97	194	291	621	1061	1500
6-8: 8-Vs. Capt. Nazi	81	162	243	518	884	1250
9-Classic flag-c	97	194	291	621	1061	1500
10-Hitler-c	174	348	522	1114	1907	2700
11,12,15-Capt. Nazi app.	68	136	204	435	743	1050
13-Classic Hitler, Tojo and Mussolini football-c	174	348	522	1114	1907	2700
14,16-20: 14-Christmas-c. 16-Capt. Marvel & Sivana x-over. 17-Futuristic city-c. 19-Capt. Nazi & Capt. Nippon app.	57	114	171	362	619	875
21-30: 25-Flag-c	45	90	135	284	480	675
31-33,36-40: 37-Infinity-c	33	66	99	194	317	440
35-#34 on inside; cover shows origin of Sivana Jr. which is not on inside. Evidently the cover to #35 was printed out of sequence and bound with contents to #34	33	66	99	194	317	440
41-70: 42-Robot-c. 53-Atomic Bomb-c/story	27	54	81	160	263	365
71-99,101-104: 87,93-Robot-c. 104-Used in **POP**, pg. 89	24	48	72	142	234	325
100	29	58	87	170	278	385
105-114,116-118: 116-Vampira, Queen of Terror app.	28	56	84	165	270	375
115-Classic injury to eye-c; Eyeball story w/injury-to-eye panels	142	284	426	909	1555	2200
119-Electric chair-c (scarce)	81	162	243	518	884	1250

NOTE: *Mac Raboy c-1-28, 30-32, 57, 59 among others.*

CAPTAIN MARVEL PRESENTS THE TERRIBLE FIVE
M. F. Enterprises: Aug, 1966; V2#5, Sept, 1967 (No #2-4) (25¢)

	GD	VG	FN	VF	VF/NM	NM-
1	5	10	15	30	50	70
V2#5-(Formerly Captain Marvel)	3	6	9	21	33	45

CAPTAIN MARVEL'S FUN BOOK
Samuel Lowe Co.: 1944 (1/2" thick) (cardboard covers)(25¢)

	GD	VG	FN	VF	VF/NM	NM-
nn-Puzzles, games, magic, etc.; infinity-c	43	86	129	271	461	650

CAPTAIN MARVEL SPECIAL EDITION (See Special Edition)

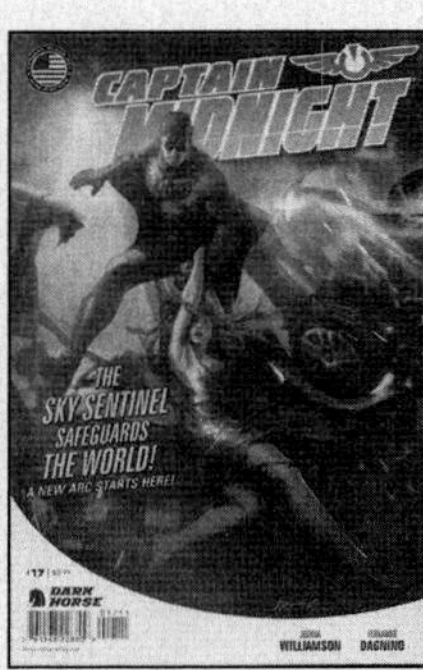

Captain Midnight (2013 series) #17 © DH

Captain Science #3 © YM

Captain 3-D #1 © HARV

GD 2.0 | VG 4.0 | FN 6.0 | VF 8.0 | VF/NM 9.0 | NM- 9.2

CAPTAIN MARVEL STORY BOOK
Fawcett Publications: Summer, 1946 - No. 4, Summer?, 1948

1-Half text 58 116 174 371 636 900
2-4 41 82 123 256 428 600

CAPTAIN MARVEL THRILL BOOK (Large-Size)
Fawcett Publications: 1941 (B&W w/color-c)

1-Reprints from Whiz #8,10, & Special Edition #1 (Rare)
350 700 1050 3500 - -
NOTE: *Rarely found in Fine or Mint condition.*

CAPTAIN MIDNIGHT (TV, radio, films) (See The Funnies, Popular Comics & Super Book of Comics)(Becomes Sweethearts No. 68 on)
Fawcett Publications: Sept, 1942 - No. 67, Fall, 1948 (#1-14: 68 pgs.)

1-Origin Captain Midnight, star of radio and movies; Captain Marvel cameo on cover
320 640 960 2240 3920 5600
2-Smashes the Jap Juggarnaut 158 316 474 1003 1727 2450
3-Classic Nazi war-c 145 290 435 921 1586 2250
4,5: 4-Grapples the Gremlins 116 232 348 742 1271 1800
6-8 69 138 207 442 759 1075
9-Raboy-c 73 146 219 467 796 1125
10-Raboy Flag-c 74 148 222 470 810 1150
11-20: 11,17,18-Raboy-c. 16 (1/44) 50 100 150 315 533 750
21-Classic WWII-c 58 116 174 371 636 900
22,25-30: 22-War savings stamp-c 40 80 120 246 411 575
23-WWII Concentration Camp-c 55 110 165 352 601 850
24-Japan flag sunburst-c 61 122 183 390 670 950
31-40 32 64 96 188 307 425
41-59,61-67: 50-Sci/fi theme begins? 25 50 75 150 245 340
60-Flying Saucer issue (2/48)-3rd of this theme; see The Spirit 9/28/47 (1st), Shadow Comics V7#10 (2nd, 1/48) & Boy Commandos #26 (4th, 3-4/48)
39 78 117 233 384 535

CAPTAIN MIDNIGHT
Dark Horse Comics: No. 0, Jun, 2013 - No. 24, Jun, 2015 ($2.99)

0-24: 0-Williamson-s/Ibáñez-a; WWII hero appears in modern times. 4,5-Skyman app. 3.00
One For One: Captain Midnight #1 (1/14, $1.00) r/#1 3.00

CAPTAIN NICE (TV)
Gold Key: Nov, 1967 (one-shot)

1(10211-711)-Photo-c 6 12 18 37 66 95

CAPTAIN N: THE GAME MASTER (TV)
Valiant Comics: 1990 - No. 6? ($1.95, thick stock, coated-c)

1-6: 4-6-Layton-c 5.00

CAPTAIN PARAGON (See Bill Black's Fun Comics)
Americomics: Dec, 1983 - No. 4, 1985

1-Intro/1st app. Ms. Victory 4.00
2-4 3.00

CAPTAIN PARAGON AND THE SENTINELS OF JUSTICE
AC Comics: April, 1985 - No. 6, 1986 ($1.75)

1-6: 1-Capt. Paragon, Commando D., Nightveil, Scarlet Scorpion, Stardust & Atoman 3.00

CAPTAIN PLANET AND THE PLANETEERS (TV cartoon)
Marvel Comics: Oct, 1991 - No. 12, Oct, 1992 ($1.00/$1.25)

1-N. Adams painted-c 4.00
2-12: 3-Romita-c 3.00

CAPTAIN POWER AND THE SOLDIERS OF THE FUTURE (TV)
Continuity Comics: Aug, 1988 - No. 2, 1988 ($2.00)

1,2: 1-Neal Adams-c/layouts/inks; variant-c exists. 3.00

CAPTAIN PUREHEART (See Archie as...)

CAPTAIN ROCKET
P. L. Publ. (Canada): Nov, 1951

1 53 106 159 334 567 800

CAPT. SAVAGE AND HIS LEATHERNECK RAIDERS (...And His Battlefield Raiders #9 on)
Marvel Comics Group (Animated Timely Features): Jan, 1968 - No. 19, Mar, 1970 (See Sgt. Fury No. 10)

1-Sgt. Fury & Howlers cameo 6 12 18 38 69 100
2,7,11: 2-Origin Hydra. 7-Pre-"Thing" Ben Grimm story. 11-Sgt. Fury app.
3 6 9 17 26 35
3-6,8-10,12-14: 4-Origin Hydra. 14-Last 12¢ issue 3 6 9 16 23 30
15-19 3 6 9 14 19 24
NOTE: ***Ayres/Shores** a-1-8,11. **Ayres/Severin** a-9,10,17-19. **Heck/Shores** a-12-15.*

CAPTAIN SCIENCE (Fantastic No. 8 on)
Youthful Magazines: Nov, 1950; No. 2, Feb, 1951 - No. 7, Dec, 1951

1-Wood-a; origin; 2 pg. text w/ photos of George Pal's "Destination Moon."
97 194 291 621 1061 1500
2-Flying saucer-c swiped Weird Science #13(#2)-c 54 108 162 343 574 825
3,6,7; 3,6-Bondage c-swipes/Wings #94,91 50 100 150 315 533 750
4,5-Wood/Orlando-c/a(2) each 87 174 261 553 952 1350
NOTE: ***Fass** a-4. Bondage c-3, 6, 7.*

CAPTAIN SILVER'S LOG OF SEA HOUND (See Sea Hound)

CAPTAIN SINBAD (Movie Adaptation) (See Fantastic Voyages of... & Movie Comics)

CAPTAIN STERNN: RUNNING OUT OF TIME
Kitchen Sink Press: Sept, 1993 - No. 5, 1994 ($4.95, limited series, coated stock, 52 pgs.)

1-5: Berni Wrightson-c/a/scripts 6.00
1-Gold ink variant 10.00

CAPTAIN STEVE SAVAGE (...& His Jet Fighters, No. 2-13)
Avon Periodicals: 1950 - No. 8, 1/53; No. 5, 9-10/54 - No. 13, 5-6/56

nn(1st series)-Harrison/Wood art, 22 pgs. (titled "...Over Korea")
45 90 135 284 480 675
1(4/51)-Reprints nn issue (Canadian) 21 42 63 124 202 280
2-Kamen-a 18 36 54 103 162 220
3-11 (#6, 11-12/54, last precode) 15 30 45 83 124 165
12-Wood-a (6 pgs.) 18 36 54 103 162 220
13-Check, Lawrence-a 15 30 45 84 127 170
NOTE: ***Kinstler** c-2-5, 7-9, 11. **Lawrence** a-8. **Ravielli** a-5, 9.*
5(9-10/54-2nd series)(Formerly Sensational Police Cases)
12 24 36 67 94 120
6-Reprints nn issue; Harrison/Wood-a 12 24 36 69 97 125
7-13: 9,10-Kinstler-c. 10-r/cover #2 (1st series). 13-r/cover #8 (1st series)
10 20 30 56 76 95

CAPTAIN STONE (See Holyoke One-Shot No. 10)

CAPT. STORM (Also see G. I. Combat #138)
National Periodical Publications: May-June, 1964 - No. 18, Mar-Apr, 1967

1-Origin 10 20 30 69 147 225
2-7,9-18: 3,6,13-Kubert-a. 4-Colan-a. 12-Kubert-c 7 14 21 44 82 120
8-Grey-tone-c 8 16 24 54 102 150

CAPTAIN 3-D (Super hero)
Harvey Publications: December, 1953 (25¢, came with 2 pairs of glasses)

1-Kirby/Ditko-a (Ditko's 3rd published work tied with Strange Fantasy #9, see also Daring Love #1 & Black Magic V4 #3); shows cover in 3-D on inside;
Kirby/Meskin-c 12 24 36 69 97 125
NOTE: *Half price without glasses*

CAPTAIN THUNDER AND BLUE BOLT
Hero Comics: Sept, 1987 - No. 10, 1988 ($1.95)

1-10: 1-Origin Blue Bolt. 3-Origin Capt. Thunder. 6-1st app. Wicket. 8-Champions x-over 3.00

CAPTAIN TOOTSIE & THE SECRET LEGION (Advs. of...)(Also see Monte Hale #30,39 & Real Western Hero)
Toby Press: Oct, 1950 - No. 2, Dec, 1950

1-Not Beck-a; both have sci/fi covers 32 64 96 188 307 425
2-The Rocketeer Patrol app.; not Beck-a 20 40 60 114 182 250

CAPTAIN TRIUMPH (See Crack Comics #27)

CAPTAIN UNIVERSE... (5-part x-over)
Marvel Comics: 2005; Jan, 2006

.../ Daredevil 1 (1/06, $2.99) Part 2; Faerber-s/Santacruz-a 3.00
.../ Hulk 1 (1/06, $2.99) Part 1; Faerber-s/Magno-a 3.00
.../ Invisible Woman 1 (1/06, $2.99) Part 4; Faerber-s/Raiz-a; Gladiator app. 3.00
.../ Silver Surfer 1 (1/06, $2.99) Part 5; Faerber-s/Magno-a 3.00
.../ X-23 1 (1/06, $2.99) Part 3; Faerber-s/Portella-a; Scorpion app. 3.00
...: Power Unimaginable TPB (2005, $19.99)-Reprints from Marvel Spotlight #9-11, Incredible Hulk Ann. #10, Marvel Fanfare #25, Web of Spider-Man Ann. #5&6, Marvel Comics Presents #148, Cosmic Power Unlimited #5 20.00
...: The Hero Who Could Be You 1 (7/13, $7.99) r/Marvel Spotlight #9-11 & early apps. 8.00
...: Universal Heroes TPB (2005, $13.99) reprints .../Hulk, .../Daredevil, ...X-23 and back-up stories from Amazing Fantasy (2005) #13,14 14.00

CAPTAIN VENTURE & THE LAND BENEATH THE SEA (See Space Family Robinson)
Gold Key: Oct, 1968 - No. 2, Oct, 1969

1-r/Space Family Robinson serial; Spiegle-a 4 8 12 27 44 60
2-Spiegle-a 4 8 12 23 37 50

CAPTAIN VICTORY AND THE GALACTIC RANGERS (Also see Kirby: Genesis)

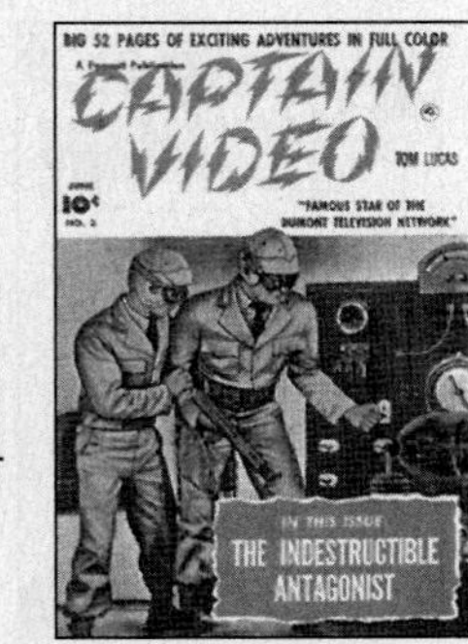

Captain Video #3 © FAW

Carnage (2016 series) #7 © MAR

Cars #0 © DIS/Pixar

	GD 2.0	VG 4.0	FN 6.0	VF 8.0	VF/NM 9.0	NM- 9.2

Pacific Comics: Nov, 1981 - No. 13, Jan, 1984 ($1.00, direct sales, 36-48 pgs.) (Created by Jack Kirby)

1-1st app. Mr. Mind						4.00
2-13: 3-N. Adams-a						3.00
Special 1-(10/83)-Kirby c/a(p)						4.00

NOTE: ***Conrad** a-10, 11. **Ditko** a-6. **Kirby** a-1-3p; c-1-13.*

CAPTAIN VICTORY AND THE GALACTIC RANGERS
Jack Kirby Comics: July, 2000 - No. 2, Sept, 2000 ($2.95, B&W)

1,2-New Jeremy Kirby-s with reprinted Jack Kirby-a; Liefeld pin-up art 3.00

CAPTAIN VICTORY AND THE GALACTIC RANGERS
Dynamite Entertainment: 2014 - No. 6, 2015 ($3.99)

1-6-Joe Casey-s; art by various. 3-Dalrymple & Mahfood-a 4.00

CAPTAIN VIDEO (TV) (See XMas Comics)
Fawcett Publications: Feb, 1951 - No. 6, Dec, 1951 (No. 1,5,6-36 pgs.; 2-4, 52 pgs.)

1-George Evans-a(2); 1st TV hero comic	103	206	309	659	1130	1600
2-Used in **SOTI**, pg. 382	66	132	198	419	722	1025
3-6-All Evans-a except #5 mostly Evans	55	110	165	352	601	850

NOTE: *Minor **Williamson** assists on most issues. Photo c-1, 5, 6; painted c-2-4.*

CAPTAIN WILLIE SCHULTZ (Also see Fightin' Army)
Charlton Comics: No. 76, Oct, 1985 - No. 77, Jan, 1986

76,77-Low print run	1	2	3	5	6	8

CAPTAIN WIZARD COMICS (See Meteor, Red Band & Three Ring Comics)
Rural Home: 1946

1-Capt. Wizard dons new costume; Impossible Man, Race Wilkins app.	39	78	117	240	395	550

CAPTAIN WONDER
Image Comics: Feb, 2011 ($4.99, 3-D comic with glasses)

1-Haberlin-s/Tan-a; sketch pages, crossword puzzle, paper dolls 5.00

CAPTURE CREATURES
BOOM! Entertainment (kaboom!): Nov, 2014 - No. 4, May, 2015 ($3.99)

1-4-Frank Gibson-s/Becky Dreistadt-a; multiple covers on each 4.00

CARBON GREY
Image Comics: Mar, 2011 - No. 3, May, 2011 ($2.99, limited series)

1-3-Khari Evans, Kinsun Loh & Hoang Nguyen-a; Nguyen-c	3.00
... Origins 1,2 (11/11 - No. 2, 3/12, $3.99) 1-Pop Mhan-a	4.00
Vol. 2 (7/12 - No. 3, 2/13, $3.99) 1-3-Gardner-s/Evans & Nguyen-a	4.00
Vol. 3 (12/13 - Present) 1,2-Gardner-s/Evans & Nguyen-a	4.00

CARE BEARS (TV, Movie)(See Star Comics Magazine)
Star Comics/Marvel Comics No. 15 on: Nov, 1985 - No. 20, Jan, 1989

1-Post-a begins	2	4	6	9	12	15
2-20: 11-$1.00-c begins. 13-Madballs app.	1	3	4	6	8	10

CAREER GIRL ROMANCES (Formerly Three Nurses)
Charlton Comics: June, 1964 - No. 78, Dec, 1973

V4#24-31	3	6	9	14	20	25
32-Elvis Presley, Herman's Hermits, Johnny Rivers line drawn-c	9	18	27	62	126	190
33-37,39-50: 39-Tiffany Sinn app.	2	4	6	13	18	22
38-(2/67) 1st app. Tiffany Sinn, C.I.A. Sweetheart, Undercover Agent (also see Secret Agent #10; Dominguel-a	3	6	9	16	24	32
51-78: 54-Jonnie Love anti-drup PSA. 67-Susan Dey pin-up. 70-David Cassidy pin-up	2	4	6	10	14	18

CAR 54, WHERE ARE YOU? (TV)
Dell Publishing Co.: Mar-May, 1962 - No. 7, Sept-Nov, 1963; 1964 - 1965 (All photo-c)

Four Color 1257(#1, 3-5/62)	8	16	24	54	102	150
2(6-8/62)-7	5	10	15	30	50	70
2,3(10-12/64), 4(1-3/65)-Reprints #2,3,&4 of 1st series	3	6	9	19	30	40

CARL BARKS LIBRARY OF WALT DISNEY'S GYRO GEARLOOSE COMICS AND FILLERS IN COLOR, THE
Gladstone: 1993 ($7.95, 8-1/2x11", limited series, 52 pgs.)

1-6: Carl Barks reprints	1	3	4	6	8	10

CARL BARKS LIBRARY OF WALT DISNEY'S COMICS AND STORIES IN COLOR, THE
Gladstone: Jan, 1992 - No. 51, Mar, 1996 ($8.95, 8-1/2x11", 60 pgs.)

1,2,6,8-51: 1-Barks Donald Duck-r/WDC&S #31-35; 2-r/#36,38-41; 6-r/#57-61; 8-r/#67-71; 9-r/#72-76; 10-r/#77-81; 11-r/#82-86; 12-r/#87-91; 13-r/#92-96; 14-r/#97-101; 15-r/#102-106; 16-r/#107-111; 17-r/#112,114,117,124,125; 18-r/#126-130; 19-r/#131,132(2),133,134; 20-r/#135-139; 21-r/#140-144; 22-r/#145-149; 23-r/#150-154; 24-r/#155-159; 25-r/#160-164; 26-r/#165-169; 27-r/#170-174;28-r/#175-179; 29-r/#180-184; 30-r/#185-189; 31-r/#190-194; 32-r/#195-199;33-r/#200-204; 34-r/#205-209; 35-r/#210-214; 36-r/#215-219; 37-r/#220-224; 38-r/#225-229; 39-r/#230-234; 40-r/#235-239; 41-r/#240-244; 42r/#245-249; 43-r/#250-254; 44-50; All contain one Heroes & Villains trading card each	2	4	6	9	12	15
3,4,7: 3-r/#42-46. 4-r/#47-51. 7-r/#62-66.	2	4	6	11	16	20
5-r/#52-56	3	6	9	16	23	30

CARL BARKS LIBRARY OF WALT DISNEY'S DONALD DUCK ADVENTURES IN COLOR, THE
Gladstone: Jan, 1994 - No. 25, Jan, 1996 ($7.95-$9.95, 44-68 pgs., 8-1/2"x11") (all contain one Donald Duck trading card each)

1-5,7-25-Carl Barks-r: 1-r/FC #9; 2-r/FC #29; 3-r/FC #62; 4-r/FC #108; 5-r/FC #147 & #79(Mickey Mouse); 7-r/FC #159. 8-r/FC #178 & 189. 9-r/FC #199 & 203; 10-r/FC 223 & 238; 11-r/Christmas Parade #1 & 2; 12-r/FC #296; 13-r/FC #263; 14-r/MOC #20 & 41; 15-r/FC 275 & 282; 16-r/FC #291&300; 17-r/FC #308 & 318; 18-r/Vac. Parade #1 & Summer Fun #2; 19-r/FC #328 & 367	2	4	6	9	12	15
6-r/MOC #4, Cheerios "Atom Bomb," D.D. Tells About Kites	3	6	9	14	20	25

CARL BARKS LIBRARY OF WALT DISNEY'S DONALD DUCK CHRISTMAS STORIES IN COLOR, THE
Gladstone: 1992 ($7.95, 44pgs., one-shot)

nn-Reprints Firestone giveaways 1945-1949	2	4	6	10	14	18

CARL BARKS LIBRARY OF WALT DISNEY'S UNCLE SCROOGE COMICS ONE PAGERS IN COLOR, THE
Gladstone: 1992 - No. 2, 1993 ($8.95, limited series, 60 pgs., 8-1/2x11")

1-Carl Barks one pg. reprints	3	6	9	16	23	30
2-Carl Barks one pg. reprints	2	4	6	10	14	18

CARNAGE
Marvel Comics: Dec, 2010 - No. 5, Aug, 2011 ($3.99, limited series)

1-5-Spider-Man & Iron Man app.; Clayton Crain-a/c; Wells-s	4.00
...: It's a Wonderful Life (10/96, $1.95) David Quinn scripts	3.00
...: Mind Bomb (2/96, $2.95) Warren Ellis script; Kyle Hotz-a	4.00

CARNAGE
Marvel Comics: Jan, 2016 - No. 16, Mar, 2017 ($3.99)

1-16: 1-Conway-s/Perkins-a; Eddie Brock app. 3-Man-Wolf app. 4,5-Toxin app. 4.00

CARNAGE, U.S.A.
Marvel Comics: Feb, 2012 - No. 5, Jun, 2012 ($3.99, limited series)

1-4-Clayton Crain-a/c; Wells-s; Spider-Man & Avengers app. 3,4-Venom app. 4.00

CARNATION MALTED MILK GIVEAWAYS (See Wisco)

CARNEYS, THE
Archie Comics: Summer, 1994 ($2.00, 52 pgs)

1-Bound-in pull-out poster 4.00

CARNIVAL COMICS (Formerly Kayo #12; becomes Red Seal Comics #14)
Harry 'A' Chesler/Pershing Square Publ. Co.: 1945

nn (#13)-Guardineer-a	20	40	60	114	182	250

CAROLINE KENNEDY
Charlton Comics: 1961 (one-shot)

nn-Interior photo covers of Kennedy family	8	16	24	54	102	150

CAROUSEL COMICS
F. E. Howard, Toronto: V1#8, April, 1948

V1#8	12	24	36	67	94	120

CARS (Based on the 2006 Pixar movie)
Boom Entertainment: No. 0, Nov, 2009 - No. 7, Jun, 2010 ($2.99)

0-7: 0,1-Three covers on each. 2-7-Two covers on each	3.00
...: Adventures of Tow Mater 1-4 (7/10 - No. 4, 10/10, $2.99) 1-Two covers	3.00
...: Radiator Springs 1-4 (7/09 - No. 4, 10/09, $2.99) Two covers on each	3.00
...: The Rookie 1-4 (3/09 - No. 4, 6/09, $2.99) Origin of Lightning McQueen	3.00

CARS 2 (Based on the 2011 Pixar movie)
Marvel Worldwide (Disney Comics): Aug, 2011 - No. 2, Aug, 2011 ($3.99)

1,2-Movie adaptation; car profile pages 4.00

CARS, WORLD OF (Free Comic Book Day giveaway)
BOOM Kids!: May, 2009

1-Based on the Disney/Pixar movie 3.00

CARTOON CARTOONS (Anthology)
DC Comics: Mar, 2001 - No. 33, Oct, 2004 ($1.99/$2.25)

Cartoon Network Action Pack #18 © CN

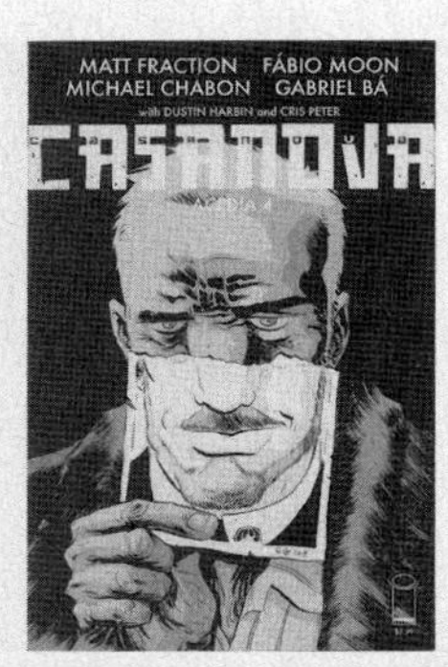
Casanova: Acedia #4 © Milkfed Criminals

Casper and Nightmare #14 © Paramount

	GD 2.0	VG 4.0	FN 6.0	VF 8.0	VF/NM 9.0	NM- 9.2

1-33-Short stories of Cartoon Network characters. 3,6,10,13,15-Space Ghost. 13-Begin $2.25-c. 17-Dexter's Laboratory begins 3.00

CARTOON KIDS
Atlas Comics (CPS): 1957 (no month)

1-Maneely-c/a; Dexter The Demon, Willie The Wise-Guy, Little Zelda app. 14 28 42 80 115 150

CARTOON NETWORK ACTION PACK (Anthology)
DC Comics: July, 2006 - No. 67, May, 2012 ($2.25/$2.50/$2.99)

1-31-Short stories of Cartoon Network characters. 1,4,6-Rowdyruff Boys app. 3.00
32-67: 32-Begin $2.50-c. 50-Ben 10/Generator Rex team-up 3.00

CARTOON NETWORK BLOCK PARTY (Anthology)
DC Comics: Nov, 2004 - No. 59, Sept, 2009 ($2.25/$2.50)

1,2,4-51-Short stories of Cartoon Network characters 3.00
3-($2.95) Bonus pages 4.00
52-59: 52-Begin $2.50-c. 59-Last issue; Powerpuff Girls app. 3.00
Cartoon Network 2-in-1: Ben 10 Alien Force/The Secret Saturdays TPB (2010, $12.99) reprints stories from #26-42 13.00
Cartoon Network 2-in-1: Foster's Home For Imaginary Friends/Powerpuff Girls TPB (2010, $12.99) reprints stories from #19-21,23,25,26,28,30-32,34-38,41 13.00
... Vol. 1: Get Down! (2005, $6.99, digest) reprints from Dexter's Lab and Cartoon Cartoons 7.00
... Vol. 2: Read All About It! (2005, $6.99, digest) reprints 7.00
... Vol. 3: Can You Dig It?; ... Vol. 4: Blast Off! (2006, $6.99, digest) reprints 7.00

CARTOON NETWORK PRESENTS
DC Comics: Aug, 1997 - No. 24, Aug, 1999 ($1.75-$1.99, anthology)

1-Dexter's Lab 5.00
1-Platinum Edition 1 2 3 5 7 9
2-10: 2-Space Ghost 3.50
11-24: 12-Bizarro World 3.00

CARTOON NETWORK PRESENTS SPACE GHOST
Archie Comics: Mar, 1997 ($1.50)

1-Scott Rosema-p 6.00

CARTOON NETWORK STARRING... (Anthology)
DC Comics: Sept, 1999 - No. 18, Feb, 2001 ($1.99)

1-Powerpuff Girls 5.00
2-18: 2,8,11,14,17-Johnny Bravo. 12,15,18-Space Ghost 3.00

CARTOON TALES (Disney's...)
W.D. Publications (Disney): nd, nn (1992) ($2.95, 6-5/8x9-1/2", 52 pgs.)

nn-Ariel & Sebastian-Serpent Teen; Beauty and the Beast; A Tale of Enchantment; Darkwing Duck - Just Us Justice Ducks; 101 Dalmatians - Canine Classics; Tale Spin - Surprise in the Skies; Uncle Scrooge - Blast to the Past 4.00

CARVERS
Image Comics (Flypaper Press): 1998 - No. 3, 1999 ($2.95)

1-3-Pander Bros.-a/Fleming-s 3.00

CAR WARRIORS
Marvel Comics (Epic): June, 1991 - No. 4, Sept, 1991 ($2.25, lim. series)

1-4: 1-Says April in indicia 3.00

CASANOVA
Image Comics: June, 2006 - No. 14, May, 2008 ($1.99, B&W & olive green or blue)

1-14: 1-7-Matt Fraction-s/Gabriel Bá-a/c. 8-14-Fabio Moon-a 3.00
...: Luxuria TPB (2008, $12.99) r/#1-7; sketch pages and cover gallery 13.00
1-4 (Marvel Comics, 10/10 - No. 4, 12/10, $3.99) Recolored reprints Image series #1-7 4.00
...: Acedia 1-7 (Image, 1/15 - Present) Fraction-s/Moon-a; back-up by Chabon-s/Bá-a 4.00
...: Avaritia (III) 1-4 (Marvel, 11/11 - No. 4, 8/12, $4.99) new story; Fraction-s/Bá-a 5.00
...: Gula (Marvel, 1/11 - No. 4, 4/11) r/Image series #8-14. 4-New story pages 4.00

CASE FILES: SAM & TWITCH (Also see the Spawn titles)
Image Comics: May, 2003 - No. 25, July, 2006 ($2.50/$2.95, color #1-6/B&W #7-on)

1-25: 1-5-Scott Morse-a/Marc Andreyko-s. 7-13-Paul Lee-a. 13-Niles-s 3.00

CASE OF THE SHOPLIFTER'S SHOE (See Perry Mason, Feature Book No.50)

CASE OF THE WINKING BUDDHA, THE
St. John Publ. Co.: 1950 (132 pgs.; 25¢; B&W; 5-1/2x7-5-1/2x8")

nn-Charles Raab-a; reprinted in Authentic Police Cases No. 25 43 86 129 271 461 650

CASEY BLUE
DC Comics (WildStorm): Jul, 2008 - No. 6, Dec, 2008 ($2.99, limited series)

1-6-B. Clay Moore-s/Carlos Barberi-a 3.00
...: Beyond Tomorrow TPB (2009, $19.99) r/#1-6; Barberi sketch pages 20.00

CASEY-CRIME PHOTOGRAPHER (Two-Gun Western No. 5 on)(Radio)
Marvel Comics (BFP): Aug, 1949 - No. 4, Feb, 1950

1-Photo-c; 52 pgs. 30 60 90 177 289 400
2-4: Photo-c 20 40 60 118 192 265

CASEY JONES (TV)
Dell Publishing Co.: No. 915, July, 1958

Four Color 915-Alan Hale photo-c 5 10 15 34 60 85

CASEY JONES & RAPHAEL (See Bodycount)
Mirage Studios: Oct, 1994 ($2.75, unfinished limited series)

1-Bisley-c; Eastman story & pencils 3.00

CASEY JONES: NORTH BY DOWNEAST
Mirage Studios: May, 1994 - No. 2, July, 1994 ($2.75, limited series)

1,2-Rick Veitch script & pencils; Kevin Eastman story & inks 3.00

CASPER ADVENTURE DIGEST
Harvey Comics: V2#1, Oct, 1992 - V2#8, Apr, 1994 ($1.75/$1.95, digest-size)

V2#1: Casper, Richie Rich, Spooky, Wendy 5.00
2-8 3.50

CASPER AND...
Harvey Comics: Nov, 1987 - No. 12, June, 1990 (.75/$1.00, all reprints)

1-Ghostly Trio 5.00
2-12: 2-Spooky; begin $1.00-c. 3-Wendy. 4-Nightmare. 5-Ghostly Trio. 6-Spooky. 7-Wendy. 8-Hot Stuff. 9-Baby Huey. 10-Wendy.11-Ghostly Trio. 12-Spooky 3.00

CASPER AND FRIENDS
Harvey Comics: Oct, 1991 - No. 5, July, 1992 ($1.00/$1.25)

1-Nightmare, Ghostly Trio, Wendy, Spooky 4.00
2-5 3.00

CASPER AND FRIENDS MAGAZINE: Mar, 1997 - No. 3, July, 1997 ($3.99)

1-3 4.00

CASPER AND NIGHTMARE (See Harvey Hits# 37, 45, 52, 56, 59, 62, 65, 68,71, 75)

CASPER AND NIGHTMARE (Nightmare & Casper No. 1-5)
Harvey Publications: No. 6, 11/64 - No. 44, 10/73; No. 45, 6/74 - No. 46, 8/74 (25¢)

6: 68 pg. Giants begin, ends #32 5 10 15 31 53 75
7-10 3 6 9 21 33 45
11-20 3 6 9 17 26 35
21-37: 33-37-(52 pg. Giants) 3 6 9 14 20 26
38-46 2 4 6 10 14 18
NOTE: *Many issues contain reprints.*

CASPER AND SPOOKY (See Harvey Hits No. 20)
Harvey Publications: Oct, 1972 - No. 7, Oct, 1973

1 3 6 9 17 26 35
2-7 2 4 6 10 14 18

CASPER AND THE GHOSTLY TRIO
Harvey Pub.: Nov, 1972 - No. 7, Nov, 1973; No. 8, Aug, 1990 - No. 10, Dec, 1990

1 3 6 9 17 26 35
2-7 2 4 6 10 14 18
8-10 6.00

CASPER AND WENDY
Harvey Publications: Sept, 1972 - No. 8, Nov, 1973

1: 52 pg. Giant 3 6 9 17 26 35
2-8 2 4 6 10 14 18

CASPER BIG BOOK
Harvey Comics: V2#1, Aug, 1992 - No. 3, May, 1993 ($1.95, 52 pgs.)

V2#1-Spooky app. 4.00
2,3 4.00

CASPER CAT (See Dopey Duck)
I. W. Enterprises/Super: 1958; 1963

1,7: 1-Wacky Duck #?.7-Reprint, Super No. 14('63) 2 4 6 9 13 16

CASPER DIGEST (...Magazine #?; ...Halloween Digest #8, 10)
Harvey Publications: Oct, 1986 - No. 18, Jan, 1991 ($1.25/$1.75, digest-size)

1 1 3 4 6 8 10
2-18: 11-Valentine-c. 18-Halloween-c 6.00

CASPER DIGEST (...Magazine #? on)
Harvey Comics: V2#1, Sept, 1991 - V2#14, Nov, 1994 ($1.75/$1.95, digest-size)

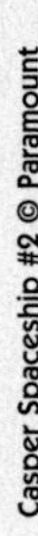
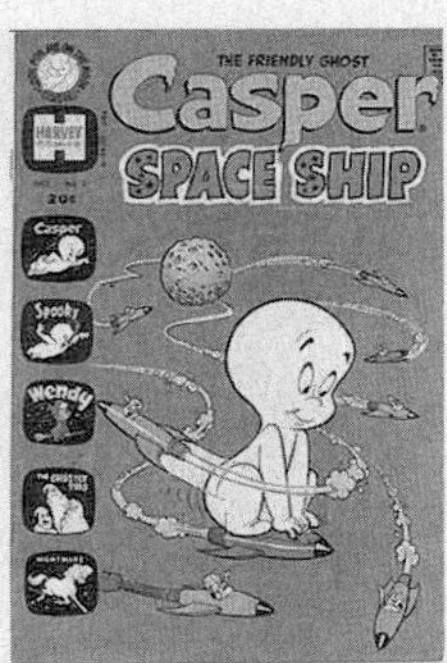

Casper Spaceship #2 © Paramount

Casper, The Friendly Ghost #15 © Paramount

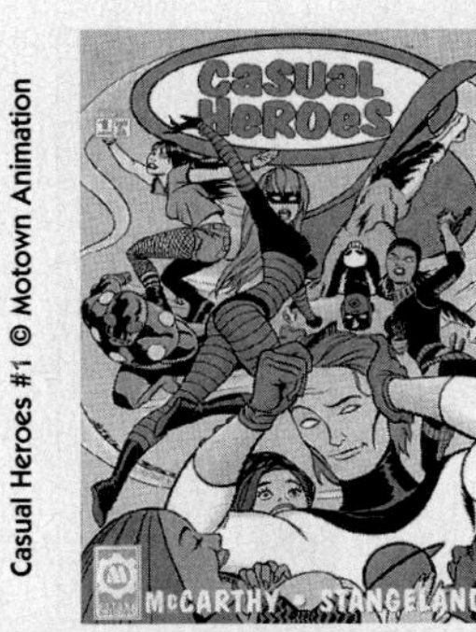

Casual Heroes #1 © Motown Animation

	GD 2.0	VG 4.0	FN 6.0	VF 8.0	VF/NM 9.0	NM- 9.2

V2#1 5.00
2-14 3.50

CASPER DIGEST STORIES
Harvey Publications: Feb, 1980 - No. 4, Nov, 1980 (95¢, 132 pgs., digest size)
1 2 4 6 9 13 16
2-4 1 2 3 5 7 9

CASPER DIGEST WINNERS
Harvey Publications: Apr, 1980 - No. 3, Sept, 1980 (95¢, 132 pgs., digest size)
1 2 4 6 9 13 16
2,3 1 2 3 5 7 9

CASPER ENCHANTED TALES DIGEST
Harvey Comics: May, 1992 - No. 10, Oct, 1994 ($1.75, digest-size, 98 pgs.)
1-Casper, Spooky, Wendy stories 5.00
2-10 4.00

CASPER GHOSTLAND
Harvey Comics: May, 1992 ($1.25)
1 3.00

CASPER GIANT SIZE
Harvey Comics: Oct, 1992 - No. 4, Nov, 1993 ($2.25, 68 pgs.)
V2#1-Casper, Wendy, Spooky stories 5.00
2-4 4.00

CASPER HALLOWEEN TRICK OR TREAT
Harvey Publications: Jan, 1976 (52 pgs.)
1 3 6 9 17 26 35

CASPER IN SPACE (Formerly Casper Spaceship)
Harvey Publications: No. 6, June, 1973 - No. 8, Oct, 1973
6-8 2 4 6 10 14 18

CASPER'S GHOSTLAND
Harvey Publications: Winter, 1958-59 - No. 97, 12/77; No. 98, 12/79 (25¢)
1-84 pgs. begin, ends #10 17 34 51 117 259 400
2 9 18 27 59 117 175
3-10 7 14 21 44 82 120
11-20: 11-68 pgs. begin, ends #61. 13-X-Mas-c 5 10 15 35 63 90
21-40 4 8 12 28 47 65
41-61 3 6 9 16 24 32
62-77: 62-52 pgs. begin 2 4 6 9 13 16
78-98: 94-X-Mas-c 2 4 6 8 10 12
NOTE: *Most issues contain reprints w/new stories.*

CASPER SPACESHIP (Casper in Space No. 6 on)
Harvey Publications: Aug, 1972 - No. 5, April, 1973
1: 52 pg. Giant 3 6 9 18 28 38
2-5 2 4 6 11 16 20

CASPER'S SCARE SCHOOL
Ape Entertainment: 2011 - No. 4 ($3.99, limited series)
1,2-New short stories and classic reprints 4.00

CASPER STRANGE GHOST STORIES
Harvey Publications: October, 1974 - No. 14, Jan, 1977 (All 52 pgs.)
1 3 6 9 18 28 38
2-14 2 4 6 11 16 20

CASPER, THE FRIENDLY GHOST (See America's Best TV Comics, Famous TV Funday Funnies, The Friendly Ghost..., Nightmare &..., Richie Rich and..., Tastee-Freez, Treasury of Comics, Wendy the Good Little Witch & Wendy Witch World)

CASPER, THE FRIENDLY GHOST (Becomes Harvey Comics Hits No. 61 (No. 6), and then continued with Harvey issue No. 7)(1st Series)
St. John Publishing Co.: Sept, 1949 - No. 5, Aug, 1951
1(1949)-Origin & 1st app. Baby Huey & Herman the Mouse (1st comic app. of Casper and the 1st time the name Casper app. in any media, even films)
486 972 1458 3550 6275 9000
2,3 (2/50 & 8/50) 135 270 405 864 1482 2100
4,5 (3/51 & 8/51) 90 180 270 576 988 1400

CASPER, THE FRIENDLY GHOST (Paramount Picture Star...)(2nd Series)
Harvey Publications (Family Comics): No. 7, Dec, 1952 - No. 70, July, 1958
Note: No. 6 is Harvey Comics Hits No. 61 (10/52)
7-Baby Huey begins, ends #9 37 74 111 274 612 950
8,9 21 42 63 147 324 500
10-Spooky begins (1st app., 6/53), ends #70? 36 72 108 259 580 900
11,12: 2nd & 3rd app. Spooky 15 30 45 100 220 340
13-18: Alfred Harvey app. in story 12 24 36 79 170 260
19-1st app. Nightmare (4/54) 24 48 72 168 372 575
20-Wendy the Witch begins (1st app., 5/54) 42 84 126 311 706 1100
21-30: 24-Infinity-c 9 18 27 59 117 175
31-40: 38-Early Wendy app. 39-1st app. Samson Honeybun. 40-1st app. Dr. Brainstorm
7 14 21 46 86 125
41-1st Wendy app. on-c 11 22 33 76 163 250
42-50: 43-2nd Wendy-c. 46-1st app. Spooky's girl Pearl.
6 12 18 37 66 95
51-70 (Continues as Friendly Ghost... 8/58) 58-Early app. Bat Balfrey. 63-2nd app. Something the Baby Ghost. 66-1st app. Wildcat Witch 5 10 15 31 53 75
Harvey Comics Classics Vol. 1 TPB (Dark Horse Books, 6/07, $19.95) Reprints Casper's earliest appearances in this title, Little Audrey, and The Friendly Ghost Casper, mostly B&W with some color stories; history, early concept drawings and animation art 20.00
NOTE: *Baby Huey app. 7-9, 11, 121, 14, 16, 20. Buzzy app. 14, 16, 20. Nightmare app. 19, 27, 36, 37, 42, 46, 51, 53, 56, 70. Spooky app. 10-70. Wendy app. 20, 29-31, 35, 37, 38, 41-49, 51, 52, 54-58, 61, 64, 68.*

CASPER THE FRIENDLY GHOST (Formerly The Friendly Ghost...)(3rd Series)
Harvey Comics: No. 254, July, 1990 - No. 260, Jan, 1991 ($1.00)
254-260 3.00

CASPER THE FRIENDLY GHOST (4th Series)
Harvey Comics: Mar, 1991 - No. 28, Nov, 1994 ($1.00/$1.25/$1.50)
1-Casper becomes Mighty Ghost; Spooky & Wendy app. 5.00
2-28: 7,8-Post-a. 11-28-($1.50) 3.00

CASPER T.V. SHOWTIME
Harvey Comics: Jan, 1980 - No. 5, Oct, 1980
1 2 4 6 9 13 16
2-5 1 2 3 5 7 9

CASSETTE BOOKS (Classics Illustrated)
Cassette Book Co./I.P.S. Publ.: 1984 (48 pgs, b&w comic with cassette tape)
NOTE: *This series was illegal. The artwork was illegally obtained, and the Classics Illustrated copyright owner, Twin Circle Publ. sued to get an injunction to prevent the continued sale of this series. Many C.I. collectors obtained copies before the 1987 injunction, but now they are already scarce. Here again the market is just developing, but sealed mint copies of com ic and tape should be worth at least $25.*
1001 (CI#1-A2)New-PC 1002(CI#3-A2)CI-PC 1003(CI#13-A2)CI-PC
1004(CI#25)CI-LDC 1005(CI#10-A2)New-PC 1006(CI#64)CI-LDC

CASTILIAN (See Movie Classics)

CASTLE: A CALM BEFORE STORM (Based on the ABC TV series Castle)
Marvel Comics: Feb, 2013 - No. 5, Jul, 2013 ($3.99, limited series)
1-5-Peter David-s/Robert Atkins-a/Mico Suayan-c 4.00

CASTLE: RICHARD CASTLE'S ... (Based on the ABC TV series Castle)
Marvel Comics: 2011, 2012 ($19.99, hardcover graphic novels with dustjacket)
Deadly Storm HC (2011) - An "adaptation" of the show's fictional Derrick Storm novel; Bendis & DeConnick-s 20.00
Storm Season HC (2012) - Bendis & DeConnick-s/Lupacchino-a 20.00

CASTLEVANIA: THE BELMONT LEGACY
IDW Publishing: March 2005 - No. 5, July, 2005 ($3.99, limited series)
1-5-Marc Andreyko-s/E.J. Su-a 4.00

CASTLE WAITING
Olio: 1997 - No. 7, 1999 ($2.95, B&W)
Cartoon Books: Vol. 2, Aug, 2000 - No. 16 ($2.95/$3.95, B&W)
Fantagraphics Books: Vol. 3, 2006 - Present ($5.95/$3.95, B&W)
1-Linda Medley-s/a in all 1 2 3 5 6 8
2 4.00
3-7 3.00
The Lucky Road TPB r/#1-7 17.00
Hiatus Issue (1999) Crilley-c; short stories and previews 3.00
Vol. 2 #1-6,14-16 (#5&6 also have #12&13 on cover, for series numbering) 3.00
Vol. 3 #1 ($5.95) r/#15,16 and new story 6.00
Vol. 3 #2-15 ($3.95) 4.00

CASUAL HEROES
Image Comics (Motown Machineworks): Apr, 1996 ($2.25, unfinished lim. series)
1-Steve Rude-c 3.00

CAT, T.H.E. (TV) (See T.H.E. Cat)

CAT, THE (See Movie Classics)

CAT, THE (Female hero)
Marvel Comics Group: Nov, 1972 - No. 4, June, 1973
1-Origin & 1st app. The Cat (who later becomes Tigra); Mooney-a(i); Wood-c(i)/a(i)

Catalyst Comix #4 © DH

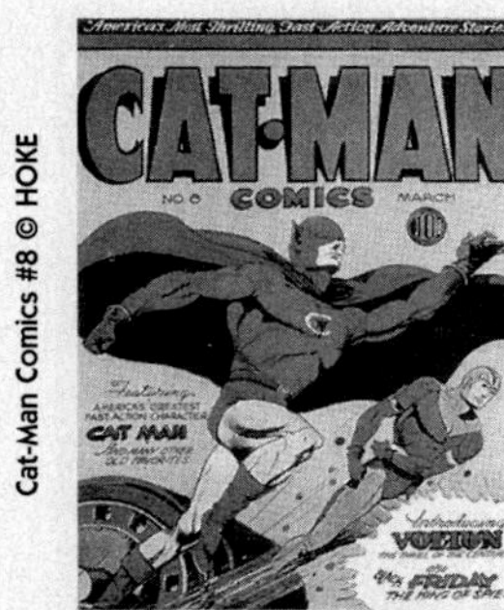

Cat-Man Comics #8 © HOKE

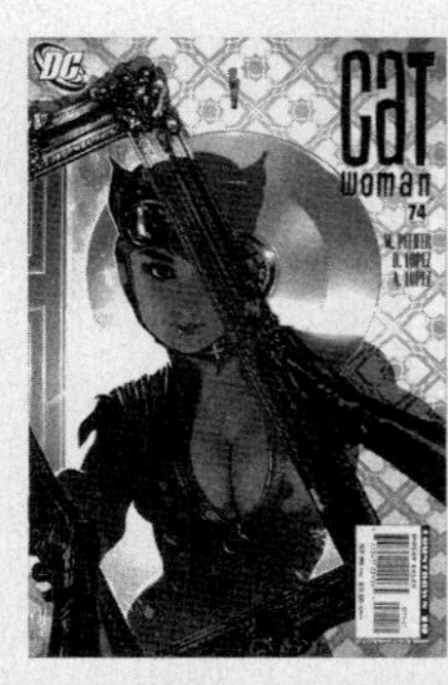

Catwoman (2nd series) #74 © DC

	GD 2.0	VG 4.0	FN 6.0	VF 8.0	VF/NM 9.0	NM- 9.2
	8	16	24	54	102	150
2,3: 2-Marie Severin/Mooney-a. 3-Everett inks	3	6	9	16	24	32
4-Starlin/Weiss-a(p)	3	6	9	17	26	35

CATACLYSM
Marvel Comics: No. 0.1, Dec, 2013 ($3.99)

0.1-Fialkov-s; Galactus threatens the Ultimate Universe 4.00

CATACLYSM: THE ULTIMATES LAST STAND (Leads into Survive #1)
Marvel Comics: Jan, 2014 - No. 5, Apr, 2014 ($3.99, limited series)

1-5-Galactus in the Ultimate Universe; Ultimates & Spider-Man app.; Bendis-s/Bagley-a 4.00

CATACLYSM: ULTIMATES
Marvel Comics: Jan, 2014 - No. 3, Mar, 2014 ($3.99, limited series)

1-3-Ultimates vs. Galactus; Fialkov-s/Giandomenico-a 4.00

CATACLYSM: ULTIMATE SPIDER-MAN
Marvel Comics: Jan, 2014 - No. 3, Mar, 2014 ($3.99, limited series)

1-3-Spider-Man vs. Galactus; Bendis-s/Marquez-a 4.00

CATACLYSM: ULTIMATE X-MEN
Marvel Comics: Jan, 2014 - No. 3, Mar, 2014 ($3.99, limited series)

1-3-Fialkov-s/Martinez-a; Captain Marvel app. 4.00

CATALYST: AGENTS OF CHANGE (Also see Comics' Greatest World)
Dark Horse Comics: Feb, 1994 - No.7, Nov, 1994 ($2.00, limited series)

1-7: 1-Foil stamped logo 3.00

CATALYST COMIX (From Comics' Greatest World)
Dark Horse Comics: Jul, 2013 - Present ($2.99)

1-9: Amazing Grace, Frank Wells, and Agents of Change app.; Casey-s/Grampá-c 3.00

CATECHISM IN PICTURES
Catechetical Guild: Jan, 1958

	GD	VG	FN	VF	VF/NM	NM-
311-Addison Burbank-a	8	16	24	40	50	60

CAT FROM OUTER SPACE (See Walt Disney Showcase #46)

CATHOLIC COMICS (See Heroes All Catholic...)
Catholic Publications: June, 1946 - V3#10, July, 1949

	GD	VG	FN	VF	VF/NM	NM-
1	30	60	90	177	289	400
2	16	32	48	94	147	200
3-13(7/47): 11-Hollingsworth-a	14	28	42	82	121	160
V2#1-10	11	22	33	62	86	110
V3#1-10: Reprints 10-part Treasure Island serial from Target V2#2-11 (see Key Comics #5)	11	22	33	64	90	115

NOTE: *Orlando c-V2#10, V3#5, 6, 8.*

CATHOLIC PICTORIAL
Catholic Guild: 1947

	GD	VG	FN	VF	VF/NM	NM-
1-Toth-a(2) (Rare)	39	78	117	240	395	550

CAT-MAN COMICS (Formerly Crash Comics No. 1-5)
Holyoke Publishing Co./Continental Magazines V2#12, 7/44 on:
5/41 - No. 17, 1/43; No. 18, 7/43 - No. 22, 12/43; No. 23, 3/44 - No. 26, 11/44; No. 27, 4/45 - No. 30, 12/45; No. 31, 6/46 - No. 32, 8/46

	GD	VG	FN	VF	VF/NM	NM-
1(V1#6)-The Cat-Man new costume (see Crash Comics for 1st app.) by Charles Quinlan; Origin The Deacon & Sidekick Mickey, Dr. Diamond & Rag-Man; The Black Widow app. Blaze Baylor begins	514	1028	1542	3750	6625	9500
2(V1#7)	245	490	735	1568	2684	3800
3(V1#8)-The Pied Piper begins; classic Hitler, Stalin & Mussolini-c	300	600	900	2010	3505	5000
4(V1#9)	206	412	618	1318	2259	3200
5(V2#10, 12/41)-Origin/1st app. The Kitten, Cat-Man's sidekick; The Hood begins. (cover re-dated w/cat image printed over Nov. date). Most of The Kitten's cover image blocked with sidebar	258	516	774	1651	2826	4000
6(V2#11), 7(V2#12)	206	412	618	1318	2259	3200
8(V2#13,3/42)-Origin Little Leaders; Volton by Kubert begins (his 1st comic book work)	290	580	870	1856	3178	4500
9 (V2#14, 4/42)-Classic-c showing a laughing Kitten slaughtering Japanese soldiers with a machine gun	300	600	900	2010	3505	5000
10 (V2#15, 5/42)-Origin Blackout; Phantom Falcon begins	194	388	582	1242	2121	3000
11 (V3#1, 6/42)-Kubert-a	194	388	582	1242	2121	3000
12 (V3#2),15,17(1/43): 12-Volton by Brodsky, not Kubert	187	374	561	1197	2049	2900
13-(9/42)(scarce) Weed of Doom (marijuana)	769	1538	2307	4037	7019	10,000
14-(10/42) World War II-c; Brodsky-a	200	400	600	1280	2190	3100
16 (V3#5, 12/42)-Hitler, Tojo, Mussolini, Goehring-c	615	1230	1845	3229	5615	8000
18 (V3#8, 7/43)-(scarce)	246	492	738	1292	2246	3200
19 (V2#6, 9/43)-Hitler, Tojo, Mussolini-c	577	1154	1731	3029	5265	7500
20 (V2#7, 10/43)-Classic Hitler-c	923	1846	2769	4846	8423	12,000
21,22 (V2#8, V2#9)	161	322	483	1030	1765	2500
23 (V2#10, 3/44) World War II-c	181	362	543	1158	1979	2800
nn(V3#13, 5/44) Rico-a; Schomburg Japanese WWII bondage-c (Rare)	314	628	942	2198	3849	5500
nn(V2#12, 7/44) L.B. Cole-a (4 pgs)	129	258	387	826	1413	2000
nn(V3#1, 9/44)-Origin The Golden Archer; Leatherface app.	129	258	387	826	1413	2000
nn(V3#2, 11/44)-L. B. Cole-c	148	296	444	947	1624	2300
27-Origins Catman & Kitten retold; L. B. Cole Flag-c; Infantino-a	194	388	582	1242	2121	3000
28-Dr. Macabre app.; L. B. Cole-c/a	290	580	870	1856	3178	4500
29-32-L. B. Cole-c; bondage-#30	194	388	582	1242	2121	3000

NOTE: *Fuje a-11, 27, 28(2), 29(3), 30.* ***Palais*** *a-11, 16, 27, 28, 29(2), 30(2), 32; c-25(7/44).* ***Rico*** *a-11(2), 23, 27, 28.*

CAT TALES (3-D)
Eternity Comics: Apr, 1989 ($2.95)

1-Felix the Cat-r in 3-D 5.00

CATWOMAN (Also see Action Comics Weekly #611, Batman #404-407, Detective Comics, & Superman's Girlfriend Lois Lane #70, 71)
DC Comics: Feb, 1989 - No. 4, May, 1989 ($1.50, limited series, mature)

	GD	VG	FN	VF	VF/NM	NM-
1	1	3	4	6	8	10
2-4: 3-Batman cameo. 4-Batman app.	1	2	3	5	7	9
Her Sister's Keeper (1991, $9.95, trade paperback)-r/#1-4						12.00

CATWOMAN (Also see Showcase '93, Showcase '95 #4, & Batman #404-407)
DC Comics: Aug, 1993 - No. 94, Jul, 2001 ($1.50-$2.25)

	GD	VG	FN	VF	VF/NM	NM-
0-(10/94)-Zero Hour; origin retold. Released between #14&15						4.00
1-($1.95)-Embossed-c; Bane app.; Balent c-1-10; a-1-10p						6.00
2-20: 3-Bane flashback cameo. 4-Brief Bane app. 6,7-Knightquest tie-ins; Batman (Azrael) app. 8-1st app. Zephyr. 12-KnightsEnd pt. 6. 13-new Knights End Aftermath. 14-(9/94)-Zero Hour						4.00
21-24, 26-30, 33-49: 21-$1.95-c begins. 28,29-Penguin cameo app. 36-Legacy pt. 2. 38-40-Year Two; Batman, Joker, Penguin & Two-Face app. 46-Two-Face app.						3.00
25,31,32: 25-($2.95)-Robin app. 31,32-Contagion pt. 4 (Reads pt. 5 on-c) & pt. 9.						4.00
50-($2.95, 48 pgs.)-New armored costume						4.00
50-($2.95, 48 pgs.)-Collector's Ed.w/metallic ink-c						5.00
51-77: 51-Huntress-c/app. 54-Grayson-s begins. 56-Cataclysm pt.6. 57-Poison Ivy-c/app. 63-65-Joker-c/app. 72-No Man's Land; Ostrander-s begins						3.00
78-82: 80-Catwoman goes to jail						3.00
83,84,89-Harley Quinn-c/app. 83-Begin $2.25-c	1	3	4	6	8	10
85-88,90-94						3.00
#1,000,000 (11/98) 853rd Century x-over						3.00
Annual 1 (1994, $2.95, 68 pgs.)-Elseworlds story; Batman app.; no Balent-a						4.00
Annual 2,4 ('95, '97, $3.95) 2-Year One story. 4-Pulp Heroes						4.00
Annual 3 (1996, $2.95)-Legends of the Dead Earth story						4.00
...Plus 1 (11/97, $2.95) Screamqueen (Scare Tactics) app.						4.00
TPB ($9.95) r/#15-19, Balent-c						12.00

CATWOMAN (Also see Detective Comics #759-762)
DC Comics: Jan, 2002 - No. 82, Oct, 2008; No. 83, Mar, 2010 ($2.50/$2.99)

	GD	VG	FN	VF	VF/NM	NM-
1-Darwyn Cooke & Mike Allred-a; Ed Brubaker-s						6.00
2-4						4.00
5-43: 5-9-Rader-a/Paul Pope-c. 10-Morse-c. 16-JG Jones-c. 22-Batman-c/app. 34-36-War Games. 43-Killer Croc app.						3.00
44-Adam Hughes-c begin						5.00
45,46	2	4	6	10	14	18
47,49,52-57,59-68,71,73,75-79: 52-Catwoman kills Black Mask. 53-One Year Later; Helena born. 55-Begin $2.99-c. 56-58-Wildcat app. 75-78-Salvation Run						5.00
48,69	1	2	3	5	6	8
50,58,72-Zatanna-c/app.	1	3	4	6	8	10
51-Classic Selina Kyle mugshot-c	5	10	15	31	53	75
70-Classic-c; "Amazons Attack" tie-in	3	6	9	14	20	25
74-Zatanna app.	3	6	9	17	26	35
80-82	1	3	4	6	8	10
83-(3/10, $2.99) Blackest Night one-shot; Harley Quinn & Black Mask app.; Hughes-c						3.00
...: Catwoman Dies TPB (2008, $14.99) r/#66-72; Hughes cover gallery						15.00
...: Crime Pays TPB (2008, $14.99) r/#73-77						15.00
...: Crooked Little Town TPB (2003, $14.95) r/#5-10 & Secret Files; Oeming-c						15.00
...: It's Only a Movie TPB (2007, $19.99) r/#59-65						20.00
...: Relentless TPB (2005, $19.95) r/#12-19 & Secret Files						20.00

Catwoman (2011 series) #18 © DC

Caught #4 © MAR

Cave Carson Has a Cybernetic Eye #1 © DC

GD 2.0 VG 4.0 FN 6.0 VF 8.0 VF/NM 9.0 NM- 9.2

... Secret Files and Origins (10/02, $4.95) origin-s Oeming-a; profiles and pin-ups 5.00
...Selina's Big Score HC (2002, $24.95) Cooke-s/a; pin-ups by various 25.00
...Selina's Big Score SC (2003, $17.95) Cooke-s/a; pin-ups by various 18.00
...: The Dark End of the Street TPB (2002, $12.95) r/#1-4 & Slam Bradley back-up stories from Detective Comics #759-762 13.00
...: The Long Road Home TPB (2009, $17.99) r/#78-82 18.00
...: The Replacements TPB (2007, $14.99) r/#53-58 15.00
...: Wild Ride TPB (2005, $14.99) r/#20-24 & Secret Files #1 15.00

CATWOMAN (DC New 52)
DC Comics: Nov, 2011 - No. 52, Jul, 2016 ($2.99)

1-Winick-s/March-a; Batman app. 5.00
2-12: 2-6-March-a. 7,8-Melo-a. 9-Night of the Owls 3.00
13-(12/12) Death of the Family tie-in; die-cut Joker mask-c 12.00
13-Second printing with chessboard-c 5.00
14-22: 14-Death of the Family tie-in; Joker app 3.00
23,24: 23-(10/13) Debut of Joker's Daughter in final panel. 24-Joker's Daughter app. 5.00
25,26,28-49: 25-Zero Year. 26-Joker's Daughter app. 28-Gothtopia. 35-40-Jae Lee-c 3.00
27-($3.99) Gothtopia x-over with Detective Comics #27; Olliffe & Richards-a 4.00
50-($4.99) Harley Quinn, Poison Ivy app.; back-up origin of Black Mask's mask 5.00
51,52: Black Mask & the False Face Society app.; Middleton-c 3.00
#0 (11/12, $2.99) Origin re-told; Nocenti-s/Melo-a/March-c 3.00
Annual 1 (7/13, $4.99) Nocenti-s/Duce-a; Penguin app. 5.00
Annual 2 (2/15, $4.99) Olliffe & McCrea-a 5.00
...: Election Night 1 (1/17, $4.99) Meredith Finch-s/Shane Davis-a; Prez app. 5.00
...: Futures End 1 (11/14, $2.99, regular-c) Five years later; Olliffe-a/Dodson-c 3.00
...: Futures End 1 (11/14, $3.99, 3-D cover) 4.00

CATWOMAN/ GUARDIAN OF GOTHAM
DC Comics: 1999 - No. 2, 1999 ($5.95, limited series)

1,2-Elseworlds; Moench-s/Balent-a 6.00

CATWOMAN: NINE LIVES OF A FELINE FATALE
DC Comics: 2004 ($14.95, TPB)

nn-Reprints notable stories from Batman #1 to the present; pin-ups by various; Bolland-c 15.00

CATWOMAN: THE MOVIE (2004 Halle Berry movie)
DC Comics: 2004 ($4.95/$9.95)

1-($4.95) Movie adaptation; Jim Lee-c and sketch pages; Derenick-a 5.00
... & Other Cat Tales TPB (2004, $9.95)-r/Movie adaptation; Jim Lee sketch pages, r/Catwoman #0, Catwoman (2nd series) #11 & 25; photo-c 10.00

CATWOMAN/VAMPIRELLA: THE FURIES
DC Comics/Harris Publ.: Feb, 1997 ($4.95, squarebound, 46 pgs.) (1st DC/Harris x-over)

nn-Reintro Pantha; Chuck Dixon scripts; Jim Balent-c/a 6.00

CATWOMAN: WHEN IN ROME
DC Comics: Nov, 2004 - No. 6, Aug, 2005 ($3.50, limited series)

1-6-Jeph Loeb-s/Tim Sale-a/c; Riddler app. 3.50
HC (2005, $19.99, dustjacket) r/series; intro by Mark Chiarello; sketch pages 20.00
SC (2007, $12.99) r/series; intro by Mark Chiarello; sketch pages 13.00

CATWOMAN/WILDCAT
DC Comics: Aug, 1998 - No. 4, Nov, 1998 ($2.50, limited series)

1-4-Chuck Dixon & Beau Smith-s; Stelfreeze-c 3.00

CAUGHT
Atlas Comics (VPI): Aug, 1956 - No. 5, Apr, 1957

1 25 50 75 150 245 340
2-4: 3-Maneely, Pakula, Torres-a. 4-Maneely-a 14 28 42 82 121 160
5-Crandall, Krigstein-a 15 30 45 84 127 170
NOTE: ***Drucker** a-2. **Heck** a-4. **Severin** c-1, 2, 4, 5. **Shores** a-4.*

CAVALIER COMICS
A. W. Nugent Publ. Co.: 1945; 1952 (Early DC reprints)

2(1945)-Speed Saunders, Fang Gow 20 40 60 117 189 260
2(1952) 12 24 36 67 94 120

CAVALRY, THE : S.H.I.E.L.D. 50TH ANNIVERSARY
Marvel Comics: Nov, 2015 ($3.99, one-shot)

1-Agent Melinda May on a training mission; Luke Ross-a; Keown-c 4.00

CAVE CARSON HAS A CYBERNETIC EYE
DC Comics (Young Animal): Dec, 2016 - Present ($3.99)

1-5-Jonathan Rivera & Gerald Way-s/Michael Avon Oeming-a; back-up Tom Scioli-s/a 4.00

CAVE GIRL (Also see Africa)
Magazine Enterprises: No. 11, 1953 - No. 14, 1954

11(A-1 82)-Origin; all Cave Girl stories 50 100 150 315 533 750
12(A-1 96), 13(A-1 116), 14(A-1 125)-Thunda by Powell in each 39 78 117 231 378 525
NOTE: ***Powell** c/a in all.*

CAVE GIRL
AC Comics: 1988 ($2.95, 44 pgs.) (16 pgs. of color, rest B&W)

1-Powell-r/Cave Girl #11; Nyoka photo back-c from movie; Powell/Bill Black-c; Special Limited Edition on-c 4.00

CAVE KIDS (TV) (See Comic Album #16)
Gold Key: Feb, 1963 - No. 16, Mar, 1967 (Hanna-Barbera)

1 6 12 18 38 69 100
2-5 4 8 12 23 37 50
6-16: 7,12-Pebbles & Bamm Bamm app. 16-1st Space Kidettes 3 6 9 19 30 40

CAVEWOMAN
Basement Comics: Jan, 1994 - No. 6, 1995 ($2.95)

1 5 10 15 35 63 90
2 3 6 9 19 30 40
3-6 2 4 6 9 13 16
...: Meets Explorers ('97, $2.95) 5.00
...: One-Shot Special (7/00, $2.95) Massey-s/a 5.00

CBLDF (Comic Book Legal Defense Fund) (See Liberty Comics)

CELESTINE (See Violator Vs. Badrock #1)
Image Comics (Extreme): May, 1996 - No. 2, June, 1996 ($2.50, limited series)

1,2: Warren Ellis scripts 3.00

CENTURION OF ANCIENT ROME, THE
Zondervan Publishing House: 1958 (no month listed) (B&W, 36 pgs.)

(Rare) All by Jay Disbrow 110 220 330 704 1202 1700

CENTURIONS (TV)
DC Comics: June, 1987 - No. 4, Sept, 1987 (75¢, limited series)

1-4 4.00

CENTURY: DISTANT SONS
Marvel Comics: Feb, 1996 ($2.95, one-shot)

1-Wraparound-c 4.00

CENTURY OF COMICS (See Promotional Comics section)

CENTURY WEST
Image Comics: Sept, 2013 ($7.99, squarebound, graphic novel)

nn-Haward Chaykin-s/a/c 8.00

CEREBUS BI-WEEKLY
Aardvark-Vanaheim: Dec. 2, 1988 - No. 27, Nov. 24, 1989 ($1.25, B&W)

Reprints Cerebus The Aardvark #1-27
1-16, 18, 19, 21-27: 3.00
17-Hepcats app. 2 4 6 8 10 12
20-Milk & Cheese app. 2 4 6 10 12 15

CEREBUS: CHURCH & STATE
Aardvark-Vanaheim: Feb, 1991 - No. 30, Apr, 1992 ($2.00, B&W, bi-weekly)

1-30: r/Cerebus #51-80 3.00

CEREBUS: HIGH SOCIETY
Aardvark-Vanaheim: Feb, 1990 - No. 25, 1991 ($1.70, B&W)

1-25: r/Cerebus #26-50 3.00

CEREBUS IN HELL?
Aardvark-Vanaheim: No. 0, 2016; No. 1, Jan, 2017 - No. 4 ($4.00, B&W)

0-2-Sim & Atwal-s; Cerebus figures placed over original Gustave Doré artwork of Hell 4.00

CEREBUS JAM
Aardvark-Vanaheim: Apr, 1985

1-Eisner, Austin, Dave Sim-a (Cerebus vs. Spirit) 6.00

CEREBUS THE AARDVARK (See A-V in 3-D, Nucleus, Power Comics)
Aardvark-Vanaheim: Dec, 1977 - No. 300, March, 2004 ($1.70/$2.00/$2.25, B&W)

0 3.00
0-Gold 20.00
1-1st app. Cerebus; 2000 print run; most copies poorly printed 100 200 300 800 1800 2800
Note: *There is a counterfeit version known to exist. It can be distinguished from the original in the following ways: inside cover is glossy instead of flat, black background on the front cover is blotted or spotty. Reports show that a counterfeit #2 also exists.*
2-Dave Sim art in all 13 26 39 91 201 310

Cerebus #171 © Dave Sim

Challengers of the Unknown #27 © DC

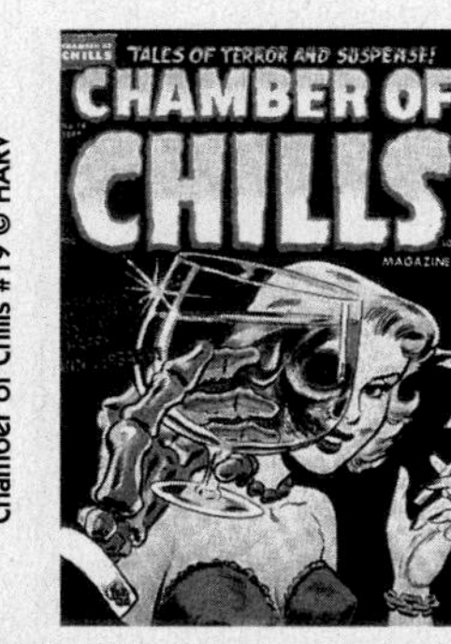

Chamber of Chills #19 © HARV

	GD 2.0	VG 4.0	FN 6.0	VF 8.0	VF/NM 9.0	NM- 9.2
3-Origin Red Sophia	11	22	33	73	157	240
4-Origin Elrod the Albino	9	18	27	60	120	180
5,6	7	14	21	49	92	135
7-10	6	12	18	37	66	95
11,12: 11-Origin The Cockroach	5	10	15	31	53	75
13-15: 14-Origin Lord Julius	4	8	12	28	47	65
16-20	3	6	9	21	33	45
21-B. Smith letter in letter column	5	10	15	35	63	90
22-Low distribution; no cover price	4	8	12	25	40	55
23-30: 23-Preview of Wandering Star by Teri S. Wood. 26-High Society begins, ends #50	3	6	9	16	23	30
31-Origin Moonroach	3	6	9	16	24	32
32-40, 53-Intro. Wolveroach (brief app.)	2	4	6	8	10	12
41-50,52: 52-Church & State begins, ends #111; Cutey Bunny app.	1	2	3	5	7	9
51,54: 51-Cutey Bunny app. 54-1st full Wolveroach story	2	4	6	8	11	14
55,56-Wolveroach app.; Normalman back-ups by Valentino	1	3	4	6	8	10
57-100: 61,62: Flaming Carrot app. 65-Gerhard begins						4.00
101-160: 104-Flaming Carrot app. 112/113-Double issue. 114-Jaka's Story begins, ends #136. 139-Melmoth begins, ends #150. 151-Mothers & Daughters begins, ends #200						3.00
161-Bone app.	1	3	4	6	8	10
162-231: 175-($2.25, 44 pgs). 186-Strangers in Paradise cameo. 201-Guys storyline begins; Eddie Campbell's Bacchus app. 220-231-Rick's Story						3.00
232-265-Going Home						3.00
266-288,291-299-Latter Days: 267-Five-Bar Gate. 276-Spore (Spawn spoof)						3.00
289&290 ($4.50) Two issues combined						5.00
300-Final issue						3.00
Free Cerebus (Giveaway, 1991-92?, 36 pgs.)-All-r						4.00

CHAIN GANG WAR
DC Comics: July, 1993 - No. 12, June, 1994 ($1.75)

	GD 2.0	VG 4.0	FN 6.0	VF 8.0	VF/NM 9.0	NM- 9.2
1-($2.50)-Embossed silver foil-c, Dave Johnson-c/a						4.00
2-4,6-12: 3-Deathstroke app. 4-Brief Deathstroke app. 6-New Batman (Azrael) cameo. 11-New Batman-c/story. 12-New Batman app.						3.00
5-($2.50)-Foil-c; Deathstroke app; new Batman cameo (1 panel)						4.00

CHAINS OF CHAOS
Harris Comics: Nov, 1994 - No. 3, Jan, 1995 ($2.95, limited series)

	GD 2.0	VG 4.0	FN 6.0	VF 8.0	VF/NM 9.0	NM- 9.2
1-3-Re-Intro of The Rook w/ Vampirella						5.00

CHALLENGE OF THE UNKNOWN (Formerly Love Experiences)
Ace Magazines: No. 6, Sept, 1950 (See Web Of Mystery No. 19)

	GD 2.0	VG 4.0	FN 6.0	VF 8.0	VF/NM 9.0	NM- 9.2
6- "Villa of the Vampire" used in N.Y. Joint Legislative Comm. Publ; Sekowsky-a	47	94	141	296	498	700

CHALLENGER, THE
Interfaith Publications/T.C. Comics: 1945 - No. 4, Oct-Dec, 1946

	GD 2.0	VG 4.0	FN 6.0	VF 8.0	VF/NM 9.0	NM- 9.2
nn; nd; 32 pgs.; Origin the Challenger Club; Anti-Fascist with funny animal filler	90	180	270	576	988	1400
2-Classic Pandora's Box demons-c; Kubert-a	77	154	231	493	847	1200
3,4: Kubert-a; 4-Fuje-a	48	96	144	302	514	725

CHALLENGERS OF THE FANTASTIC
Marvel Comics (Amalgam): June 1997 ($1.95, one-shot)

	GD 2.0	VG 4.0	FN 6.0	VF 8.0	VF/NM 9.0	NM- 9.2
1-Karl Kesel-s/Tom Grummett-a						3.00

CHALLENGERS OF THE UNKNOWN (See Showcase #6, 7, 11, 12, Super DC Giant, and Super Team Family) (See Showcase Presents for B&W reprints)
National Per. Publ./DC Comics: 4-5/58 - No. 77, 12-1/70-71; No. 78, 2/73 - No. 80, 6-7/73; No. 81, 6-7/77 - No. 87, 6-7/78

	GD 2.0	VG 4.0	FN 6.0	VF 8.0	VF/NM 9.0	NM- 9.2
1-(4-5/58)-Kirby/Stein-a(2); Kirby-c	231	462	693	1906	4303	6700
2-Kirby/Stein-a(2)	64	128	192	512	1156	1800
3-Kirby/Stein-a(2); Rocky returns from space with powers similar to the Fantastic Four (9/58)	59	118	177	472	1061	1650
4-8-Kirby/Wood-a plus cover to #8	42	84	126	311	706	1100
9,10	25	50	75	175	388	600
11-Grey tone-c	30	60	90	216	483	750
12-15: 14-Origin/1st app. Multi-Man (villain)	17	34	51	119	265	410
16-22: 18-Intro. Cosmo, the Challengers Spacepet. 22-Last 10¢ issue	12	24	36	81	176	270
23-30	8	16	24	56	108	160
31-Retells origin of the Challengers	9	18	27	57	111	165
32-40	6	12	18	41	76	110
41-47,49,50,52-60: 43-New look begins. 47-1st Sponge-Man. 49-Intro. Challenger Corps. 55-Death of Red Ryan. 60-Red Ryan returns	5	10	15	31	53	75
48,51: 48-Doom Patrol app. 51-Sea Devils app.	5	10	15	33	57	80
61-68: 64,65-Kirby origin-r, parts 1 & 2. 66-New logo. 68-Last 12¢ issue.	4	8	12	23	37	50
69-73,75-80: 69-1st app. Corinna. 77-Last 15¢ issue	3	6	9	16	23	30
74-Deadman by Tuska/Adams; 1 pg. Wrightson-a	6	12	18	38	69	100
81,83-87: 81-(6-7/77). 83-87-Swamp Thing app. 84-87-Deadman app.	2	4	6	8	10	12
82-Swamp Thing begins (thru #87, c/s	2	4	6	9	12	15

NOTE: ***N. Adams** c-67, 68, 70, 72, 74i, 81i. **Buckler** c-83-86p. **Giffen** a-83-87p. **Kirby** a-75-80r; c-75, 77, 78. **Kubert** c-64, 66, 69, 76, 79. **Nasser** c/a-81p, 82p. **Tuska** a-73. **Wood** r-76.*

CHALLENGERS OF THE UNKNOWN
DC Comics: Mar, 1991 - No. 8, Oct, 1991 ($1.75, limited series)

	GD 2.0	VG 4.0	FN 6.0	VF 8.0	VF/NM 9.0	NM- 9.2
1-Jeph Loeb scripts & Tim Sale-a in all (1st work together); Bolland-c						4.00
2-8: 2-Superman app. 3-Dr. Fate app. 6-G. Kane-c(p). 7-Steranko-c/swipe by Art Adams						3.00
... Must Die! (2004, $19.95, TPB) r/series; intro by Bendis; Sale sketch pages						20.00

NOTE: *Art **Adams** c-7. **Hempel** c-5. **Gil Kane** c-6p. **Sale** a-1-8; c-3, 8. **Wagner** c-4.*

CHALLENGERS OF THE UNKNOWN
DC Comics: Feb, 1997 - No. 18, July, 1998 ($2.25)

	GD 2.0	VG 4.0	FN 6.0	VF 8.0	VF/NM 9.0	NM- 9.2
1-18: 1-Intro new team; Leon-c/a(p) begins. 4-Origin of new team. 11,12-Batman app. 15-Millennium Giants x-over; Superman-c/app.						3.00

CHALLENGERS OF THE UNKNOWN
DC Comics: Aug, 2004 - No. 6, Jan, 2005 ($2.95, limited series)

	GD 2.0	VG 4.0	FN 6.0	VF 8.0	VF/NM 9.0	NM- 9.2
1-6-Intro. new team; Howard Chaykin-s/a						3.00

CHALLENGE TO THE WORLD
Catechetical Guild: 1951 (10¢, 36 pgs.)

	GD 2.0	VG 4.0	FN 6.0	VF 8.0	VF/NM 9.0	NM- 9.2
nn	6	12	18	31	38	45

CHAMBER (See Generation X and Uncanny X-Men)
Marvel Comics: Oct, 2002 - No. 4, Jan, 2003 ($2.99, limited series)

	GD 2.0	VG 4.0	FN 6.0	VF 8.0	VF/NM 9.0	NM- 9.2
1-4-Bachalo-c/Vaughan-s/Ferguson-a. 1-Cyclops app.						3.00

CHAMBER OF CHILLS (Formerly Blondie Comics #20; ...of Clues No. 27 on)
Harvey Publications/Witches Tales: No. 21, June, 1951 - No. 26, Dec, 1954

	GD 2.0	VG 4.0	FN 6.0	VF 8.0	VF/NM 9.0	NM- 9.2
21 (#1)	58	116	174	371	636	900
22,24 (#2,4)	41	82	123	256	428	600
23 (#3)-Excessive violence; eyes torn out	42	84	126	265	445	625
5(2/52)-Decapitation, acid in face scene	42	84	126	265	445	625
6-Woman melted alive	41	82	123	256	428	600
7-Used in **SOTI**, pg. 389; decapitation/severed head panels	40	80	120	246	411	575
8-10: 8-Decapitation panels	37	74	111	222	361	500
11,12,14: 14-Spider-Man precursor (11/52)	32	64	96	188	307	425
13,15-18,20-24-Nostrand-a in all. 13,21-Decapitation panels. 18-Atom bomb panels. 20-Nostrand-c	37	74	111	222	361	500
19-Classic-c; Nostrand-a	161	322	483	1030	1765	2500
25,26	24	48	72	142	234	325

NOTE: *About half the issues contain bondage, torture, sadism, perversion, gore, cannibalism, eyes ripped out, acid in face, etc. **Elias** c-4-11, 14-19, 21-26. **Kremer** a-12, 17. **Palais** a-21(1), 23. **Nostrand/Powell** a-13, 15, 16. **Powell** a-21, 23, 24('51), 5-8, 11, 13, 18-21, 23-25. Bondage-c-21, 24('51), 7. 25-r/#5; 26-r/#9.*

CHAMBER OF CHILLS
Marvel Comics Group: Nov, 1972 - No. 25, Nov, 1976

	GD 2.0	VG 4.0	FN 6.0	VF 8.0	VF/NM 9.0	NM- 9.2
1-Harlan Ellison adaptation	5	10	15	31	53	75
2-5: 2-1st app. John Jakes' Brak the Barbarian	3	6	9	17	26	35
6-25: 22,23-(Regular 25¢ editions)	3	6	9	16	23	30
22,23-(30¢-c variants, limited distribution)(5,7/76)	5	10	15	33	57	80

NOTE: ***Adkins** a-1i, 2i. **Brunner** a-2-4; c-4. **Chaykin** a-4. **Ditko** r-14, 16, 19, 23, 24. **Everett** a-3i, 11r,21r. **Heath** a-1r. **Gil Kane** c-2p. **Kirby** r-11, 18, 19, 22. **Powell** a-13r. **Russell** a-1p, 2p. **Shores** a-5 . **Williamson/Mayo** a-13r. **Robert E. Howard** horror story adaptation-2, 3.*

CHAMBER OF CLUES (Formerly Chamber of Chills)
Harvey Publications: No. 27, Feb, 1955 - No. 28, April, 1955

	GD 2.0	VG 4.0	FN 6.0	VF 8.0	VF/NM 9.0	NM- 9.2
27-Kerry Drake-r/#19; Powell-a; last pre-code	7	14	21	35	43	50
28-Kerry Drake	6	12	18	28	34	40

CHAMBER OF DARKNESS (Monsters on the Prowl #9 on)
Marvel Comics Group: Oct, 1969 - No. 8, Dec, 1970

	GD 2.0	VG 4.0	FN 6.0	VF 8.0	VF/NM 9.0	NM- 9.2
1-Buscema-a(p)	7	14	21	48	89	130
2,3: 2-Neal Adams scripts. 3-Smith, Buscema-a	4	8	12	28	47	65
4-A Conan-esque tryout by Smith (4/70); reprinted in Conan #16; Marie Severin/Everett-c	8	16	24	56	108	160
5,8: 5-H.P. Lovecraft adaptation. 8-Wrightson-c	4	8	12	25	40	55
6	3	6	9	21	33	45

7-Wrightson-c/a, 7pgs. (his 1st work at Marvel); Wrightson draws himself in

Champions (2016 series) #1 © MAR

The Chaos Effect Omega © VAL

Charismagic #0 © Aspen MLT

	GD 2.0	VG 4.0	FN 6.0	VF 8.0	VF/NM 9.0	NM- 9.2
1st & last panels; Kirby/Ditko-r; last 15¢-c	5	10	15	35	63	90
1-(1/72; 25¢ Special, 52 pgs.)	4	8	12	25	40	55

*NOTE: **Adkins/Everett** a-8. **Buscema** a-Special 1r. **Craig** a-5. **Ditko** a-6-8r. **Heck** a-1, 2, 8, Special 1r. **Kirby** a(p)-4, 5, 7r. **Kirby/Everett** c-5. **Severin/Everett** c-6. **Shores** a-2, 3i, Special 1r. **Sutton** a-1, 2i, 4, 7, Special 1r. **Wrightson** c-7, 8.*

CHAMP COMICS (Formerly Champion No. 1-10)
Worth Publ. Co./Champ Publ./Family Comics(Harvey Publ.): No. 11, Oct, 1940 - No. 24, Dec, 1942; No. 25, April, 1943

	GD 2.0	VG 4.0	FN 6.0	VF 8.0	VF/NM 9.0	NM- 9.2
11-Human Meteor cont'd. from Champion	135	270	405	864	1482	2100
12-17,20: 14,15-Crandall-c. 20-The Green Ghost app.	110	220	330	704	1202	1700
18,19-Simon-c. 19-The Wasp app.	135	270	405	864	1482	2100
21-23,25: 22-The White Mask app. 23-Flag-c	84	168	252	538	919	1300
24-Hitler, Tojo & Mussolini-c	155	310	465	992	1696	2400

CHAMPION (See Gene Autry's...)

CHAMPION COMICS
Worth Publ. Co.: Oct, 1939 (ashcan)

nn-Ashcan comic, not distributed to newsstands, only for in house use. A FN/VF copy sold for $2,261.76 in 2010.

CHAMPION COMICS (Formerly Speed Comics #1?; Champ Comics No. 11 on)
Worth Publ. Co.(Harvey Publications): No. 2, Dec, 1939 - No. 10, Aug, 1940 (no No.1)

	GD 2.0	VG 4.0	FN 6.0	VF 8.0	VF/NM 9.0	NM- 9.2
2-The Champ, The Blazing Scarab, Neptina, Liberty Lads, Jungleman, Bill Handy, Swingtime Sweetie begin	129	258	387	826	1413	2000
3-7: 7-The Human Meteor begins?	84	168	252	538	919	1300
8,10: 8-Simon-c. 10-Bondage-c by Kirby	271	542	813	1734	2967	4200
9-1st S&K-c (1st collaboration together)	300	600	900	1950	3375	4800

CHAMPIONS, THE
Marvel Comics Group: Oct, 1975 - No. 17, Jan, 1978

	GD 2.0	VG 4.0	FN 6.0	VF 8.0	VF/NM 9.0	NM- 9.2
1-Origin & 1st app. The Champions (The Angel, Black Widow, Ghost Rider, Hercules, Iceman); Venus x-over	4	8	12	23	37	50
2-10,16: 2,3-Venus x-over. 5-7-(Regular 25¢ edition)(4-8/76). 6-Kirby-c	2	4	6	11	16	20
5-7-(30¢-c variants, limited distribution)	4	8	12	28	47	65
11-15,17-Byrne-a. 14,15-(Regular 30¢ edition	2	4	6	13	18	22
14,15-(35¢-c variant, limited distribution)	5	10	15	35	63	90
... Classic Vol. 1 TPB (2006, $19.99) r/#1-11; unused cover to #7						20.00
... Classic Vol. 2 TPB (2007, $19.99) r/#12-17, Iron Man Ann. #4, Avengers #163, Super-Villain Team-Up #14 and Peter Parker, The Spectacular Spider-Man #17-18						20.00
...: No Time For Losers (2016, $7.99) r/#1-3,14,15; art by Heck, Tuska & Byrne						8.00

*NOTE: **Buckler/Adkins** c-3. **Byrne** a-11-15, 17. **Kane/Adkins** c-1. **Kane/Layton** c-11. **Tuska** a-3p, 4p, 6p, 7p. Ghost Rider c-1-4, 7, 8, 10, 14, 16, 17 (4, 10, 14 are more prominent).*

CHAMPIONS (Game)
Eclipse Comics: June, 1986 - No. 6, Feb, 1987 (limited series)

	NM- 9.2
1-6: 1-Intro Flare; based on game. 5-Origin Flare	3.00

CHAMPIONS (Also see The League of Champions)
Hero Comics: Sept, 1987 - No. 12, 1989 ($1.95)

	NM- 9.2
1-12: 1-Intro The Marksman & The Rose. 14-Origin Malice	3.00
Annual 1(1988, $2.75, 52 pgs.)-Origin of Giant	4.00

CHAMPIONS
Marvel Comics: Dec, 2016 - Present ($4.99/$3.99)

	NM- 9.2
1-($4.99) Ms. Marvel, Spider-Man (Miles), Hulk (Amadeus), Nova, Viv Vision team	5.00
2-6-($3.99) 3-Young Cyclops joins. 5-Gwenpool app.	4.00
#1.MU (4/17, $4.99) Monsters Unleashed tie-in; Whitely-s/Stein & Brandt-a	5.00

CHAMPION SPORTS
National Periodical Publications: Oct-Nov, 1973 - No. 3, Feb-Mar, 1974

	GD 2.0	VG 4.0	FN 6.0	VF 8.0	VF/NM 9.0	NM- 9.2
1	3	6	9	16	23	30
2,3	2	4	6	9	12	15

CHANNEL ZERO
Image Comics: Feb, 1998 - No. 5 ($2.95, B&W, limited series)

	NM- 9.2
1-5, ...Dupe (1/99) -Brian Wood-s/a	3.00

CHAOS (See The Crusaders)

CHAOS!
Dynamite Entertainment: 2014 - No. 6, 2014 ($3.99, limited series)

	NM- 9.2
1-6-Seeley-s/Andolfo-a; multiple covers on each. Purgatori, Evil Ernie, Chastity app.	4.00
... Holiday Special 2014 ($5.99) Short stories by various; Lupacchino-c	6.00
...: Smiley The Psychotic Button 1 (2015, $4.99) origin re-told; Andolfo-c	5.00

CHAOS! BIBLE
Chaos! Comics: Nov, 1995 ($3.30, one-shot)

	NM- 9.2
1-Profiles of characters & creators	3.50

CHAOS! CHRONICLES
Chaos! Comics: Feb, 2000 ($3.50, one-shot)

	NM- 9.2
1-Profiles of characters, checklist of Chaos! comics and products	3.50

CHAOS EFFECT, THE
Valiant: 1994

	NM- 9.2
Alpha (Giveaway w/trading card checklist)	3.00
Alpha-Gold variant, Alpha-Red variant, Omega-Gold variant	5.00
Omega (11/94, $2.25); Epilogue Pt. 1, 2 (12/94, 1/95; $2.95)	3.00

CHAOS! GALLERY
Chaos! Comics: Aug, 1997 ($2.95, one-shot)

	NM- 9.2
1-Pin-ups of characters	3.00

CHAOS! QUARTERLY
Chaos! Comics: Oct, 1995 -No. 3, May, 1996 ($4.95, quarterly)

	NM- 9.2
1-3: 1-Anthology; Lady Death-c by Julie Bell. 2-Boris "Lady Demon"-c	5.00
1-Premium Edition (7,500)	25.00

CHAOS WAR
Marvel Comics: Dec, 2010 - No. 4, Mr, 2011 ($3.99, limited series)

	NM- 9.2
1-5-Hercules, Thor and others vs. Chaos King; Pham-a. 3-5-Galactus app.	4.00
...: Alpha Flight 1 (1/11, $3.99) McCann-s/Brown-a	4.00
...: Ares 1 (2/11, $3.99) Oeming-s/Segovia-a	4.00
...: Chaos King 1 (1/11, $3.99) Kaluta-a/c; Monclair-s	4.00
...: Dead Avengers 1-3 (1/11 - No. 3, 3/11, $3.99) Grummett-a; Capt. Marvel app.	4.00
...: God Squad 1 (2/11, $3.99) Sumerak-s/Panosian-a	4.00
...: Thor 1,2 (1/11 - No. 2, 2/11, $3.99) DeMatteis-s/Ching-a	4.00
...: X-Men 1,2 (2/11 - No. 2, 3/11, $3.99) Braithwaite-a; Thunderbird, Banshee app.	4.00

CHAPEL (Also see Youngblood & Youngblood Strikefile #1-3)
Image Comics (Extreme Studios): No. 1 Feb, 1995 - No. 2, Mar, 1995 ($2.50, limited series)

	NM- 9.2
1,2	3.00

CHAPEL (Also see Youngblood & Youngblood Strikefile #1-3)
Image Comics (Extreme Studios): V2 #1, Aug, 1995 - No. 7, Apr, 1996 ($2.50)

	NM- 9.2
V2#1-7: 4-Babewatch x-over. 5-vs. Spawn. 7-Shadowhawk-c/app; Shadowhunt x-over	3.00
#1-Quesada & Palmiotti variant-c	3.00

CHAPEL (Also see Youngblood & Youngblood Strikefile #1-3)
Awesome Entertainment: Sept, 1997 ($2.99, one-shot)

	NM- 9.2
1 (Reg. & alternate covers)	3.00

CHARISMAGIC
Aspen MLT: No. 0, Mar, 2011 - No. 6, Jul, 2012 ($1.99/$2.99/$3.50)

	NM- 9.2
0-($1.99) Khary Randolph-a/ Vince Hernandez-s; 3 covers	3.00
1-4-($2.99) 1-4-Four covers on each	3.00
5,6-($3.50) Multiple covers on each	3.50
...: The Death Princess 1-3 (11/12 - No. 3, 7/13, $3.99) Hernandez-s/Emilio Lopez-a	4.00

CHARISMAGIC (Volume 2)
Aspen MLT: May, 2013 - No. 6, Nov, 2013 ($1.00/$3.99)

	NM- 9.2
1-($1.00) Vincenzo Cucca-a/ Vince Hernandez-s; multiple covers	3.00
2-6-($3.99) Multiple covers on each	4.00

CHARLEMAGNE (Also see War Dancer)
Defiant: Mar, 1994 - No. 5, July, 1994 ($2.50)

	NM- 9.2
1-(3/94, $3.50, 52 pgs.)-Adam Pollina-c/a.	4.00
2,3,5: Adam Pollina-c/a. 2-War Dancer app. 5-Pre-Schism issue.	3.00
4-($3.25, 52 pgs.)	4.00
#0 (Hero Illustrated giveaway)-Adam Pollina-c/a; 1st app. of Ngu	3.00

CHARLIE CHAN (See Big Shot Comics, Columbia Comics, Feature Comics & The New Advs. of...)

CHARLIE CHAN (The Adventures of...) (Zaza The Mystic No. 10 on) (TV)
Crestwood(Prize) No. 1-5; Charlton No. 6(6/55) on: 6-7/48 - No. 5, 2-3/49; No.6, 6/55 - No. 9, 3/56

	GD 2.0	VG 4.0	FN 6.0	VF 8.0	VF/NM 9.0	NM- 9.2
1-S&K-c, 2 pgs.; Infantino-a	87	174	261	553	952	1350
2-5-S&K-c: 3-S&K-c/a	50	100	150	315	533	750
6 (6/55-Charlton)-S&K-c	37	74	111	222	361	500
7-9	20	40	60	118	192	265

CHARLIE CHAN
Dell Publishing Co.: Oct-Dec, 1965 - No. 2, Mar, 1966

	GD 2.0	VG 4.0	FN 6.0	VF 8.0	VF/NM 9.0	NM- 9.2
1-Springer-a/c	5	10	15	31	53	75
2-Springer-a/c	3	6	9	21	33	45

CHARLIE McCARTHY (See Edgar Bergen Presents...)

Charlton Bullseye #3 © CC

Chassis #3 © Hurricane Ent.

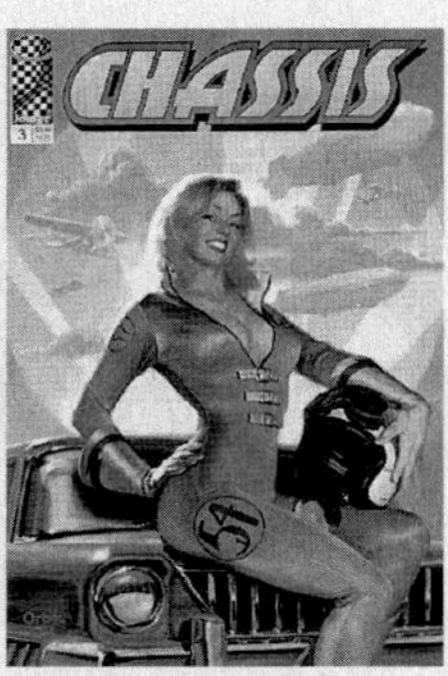

Cheryl Blossom #21 © ACP

	GD 2.0	VG 4.0	FN 6.0	VF 8.0	VF/NM 9.0	NM- 9.2
Dell Publishing Co.: No. 171, Nov, 1947 - No. 571, July, 1954 (See True Comics #14)						
Four Color 171	24	48	72	170	378	585
Four Color 196-Part photo-c; photo back-c	15	30	45	105	233	360
1(3-5/49)-Part photo-c; photo back-c	12	24	36	82	179	275
2-9(7/52; #5,6-52 pgs.)	7	14	21	48	89	130
Four Color 445,478,527,571	6	12	18	40	73	105
CHARLTON ACTION: FEATURING "STATIC" (Also see Eclipse Monthly)						
Charlton Comics: No, 11, Oct, 1985 - No. 12, Dec, 1985						
11,12-Ditko-c/a; low print run	1	2	3	5	6	8
CHARLTON BULLSEYE						
CPL/Gang Publications: 1975 - No. 5, 1976 ($1.50, B&W, bi-monthly, magazine format)						
1: 1 & 2 are last Capt. Atom by Ditko/Byrne intended for the never published Capt. Atom #90; Nightshade app.; Jeff Jones-a	5	10	15	30	50	70
2-Part 2 Capt. Atom story by Ditko/Byrne	3	6	9	21	33	45
3-Wrong Country by Sanho Kim	2	4	6	13	18	22
4-Doomsday + 1 by John Byrne	3	6	9	16	24	32
5-Doomsday + 1 by Byrne, The Question by Toth; Neal Adams back-c; Toth-c	5	10	15	31	53	75
CHARLTON BULLSEYE						
Charlton Publications: June, 1981 - No. 10, Dec, 1982; Nov, 1986						
1-1st Blue Beetle app. since '74, 1st app. The Question since '75; 1st app. Rocket Rabbit; Neil The Horse shown on preview page	3	6	9	17	26	35
2-5: 2-Charlton debut of Neil The Horse; Rocket Rabbit app. 4-Vanguards						6.00
6-10: Low print run. 6-Origin & 1st app. Thunderbunny. 7-1st apps. of Captain Atom & Nightshade since '75. 9-1st app. Bludd.	2	4	6	8	10	12
NOTE: *Material intended for issue #11-up was published in* ***Scary Tales*** *#37-up.*						
CHARLTON CLASSICS						
Charlton Comics: Apr, 1980 - No. 9, Aug, 1981						
1-Hercules-r by Glanzman in all						6.00
2-9						5.00
CHARLTON CLASSICS LIBRARY (1776)						
Charlton Comics: V10 No.1, Mar, 1973 (one-shot)						
1776 (title) - Adaptation of the film musical "1776"; given away at movie theatres; also a newsstand version	3	6	9	14	19	24
CHARLTON PREMIERE (Formerly Marine War Heroes)						
Charlton Comics: V1#19, July, 1967; V2#1, Sept, 1967 - No. 4, May, 1968						
V1#19, V2#1,2,4: V1#19-Marine War Heroes. V2#1-Trio; intro. Shape, Tyro Team & Spookman. 2-Children of Doom; Boyette classic-a. 4-Unlikely Tales; Aparo, Ditko-a	3	6	9	15	22	28
V2#3-Sinistro Boy Fiend; Blue Beetle & Peacemaker x-over	3	6	9	17	26	35
CHARLTON SPORT LIBRARY - PROFESSIONAL FOOTBALL						
Charlton Comics: Winter, 1969-70 (Jan. on cover) (68 pgs.)						
1	3	6	9	19	30	40
CHARMED (TV)						
Zenescope Entertainment: No. 0, Jun, 2010 - No. 24, Oct, 2012 ($3.50)						
0-24-Multiple covers on most						3.50
CHARMED SEASON 10 (TV)						
Zenescope Entertainment: Oct, 2014 - Present ($3.99)						
1-15: 1-Shand-s/Feliz-a/Seidman-c						4.00
CHASE (See Batman #550 for 1st app.)(Also see Batwoman)						
DC Comics: Feb, 1998 - No. 9, Oct, 1998; #1,000,000 Nov, 1998 ($2.50)						
1-9: Williams III & Gray-a. 1-Includes 4 Chase cards. 4-Teen Titans app. 7,8-Batman app. 9-GL Hal Jordan-c/app.						3.00
#1,000,000 (11/98) Final issue; 853rd Century x-over						3.00
CHASING DOGMA (See Jay and Silent Bob)						
CHASSIS						
Millenium Publications: 1996 - No. 3 ($2.95)						
1-3: 1-Adam Hughes-c. 2-Conner var-c.						3.00
CHASSIS						
Hurricane Entertainment: 1998 - No. 3 ($2.95)						
0,1-3: 1-Adam Hughes-c. 0-Green var-c.						3.00
CHASSIS (Vol. 3)						
Image Comics: Nov, 1999 - No. 4 ($2.95, limited series)						
1-4: 1-Two covers by O'Neil and Green. 2-Busch var-c.						3.00

	GD 2.0	VG 4.0	FN 6.0	VF 8.0	VF/NM 9.0	NM- 9.2
1-($6.95) DF Edition alternate-c by Wieringo						7.00
CHASTITY						
Chaos! Comics: (one-shots)						
#1/2 (1/01, $2.95) Batista-a						3.00
Heartbreaker (3/02, $2.99) Adrian-a/Molenaar-c						3.00
Love Bites (3/01, $2.99) Vale-a/Romano-c						3.00
Reign of Terror 1 (10/00, $2.95) Grant-s/Ross-a/Rio-c						3.00
Re-Imagined 1 (7/02, $2.99) Conner-c; Toledo-a						3.00
CHASTITY						
Dynamite Entertainment: 2014 - No. 6, 2014 ($3.99, limited series)						
1-6: 1-Andreyko-s/Acosta-a; origin retold. Multiple covers on each						4.00
CHASTITY: CRAZYTOWN						
Chaos! Comics: Apr, 2002 - No. 3, June, 2002 ($2.99, limited series)						
1-3-Nicieza-s/Batista-c/a						3.00
CHASTITY: LUST FOR LIFE						
Chaos! Comics: May, 1999 - No. 3, July, 1999 ($2.95, limited series)						
1-3-Nutman-s/Benes-c/a						3.00
CHASTITY: ROCKED						
Chaos! Comics: Nov, 1998 - No. 4, Feb, 1999 ($2.95, limited series)						
1-4-Nutman-s/Justiniano-c/a						3.00
CHASTITY: SHATTERED						
Chaos! Comics: Jun, 2001 - No. 3, Sept, 2001 ($2.99, limited series)						
1-3-Kaminski & Pulido-s/Batista-c/a						3.00
CHASTITY: THEATER OF PAIN						
Chaos! Comics: Feb, 1997 - No. 3, June, 1997 ($2.95, limited series)						
1-3-Pulido-s/Justiniano-c/a						3.00
TPB (1997, $9.95) r/#1-3						10.00
CHECKMATE (TV)						
Gold Key: Oct, 1962 - No. 2, Dec, 1962						
1-Photo-c on both	5	10	15	33	57	80
2	5	10	15	30	50	70
CHECKMATE! (See Action Comics #598 and The OMAC Project)						
DC Comics: Apr, 1988 - No. 33, Jan, 1991 ($1.25)						
1-33: 13: New format begins						3.00
NOTE: ***Gil Kane*** *c-2, 4, 7, 8, 10, 11, 15-19.*						
CHECKMATE (See Infinite Crisis and The OMAC Project)						
DC Comics: Jun, 2006 - No. 31, Dec, 2008 ($2.99)						
1-Rucka-s/Saiz-a/Bermejo-c; Alan Scott, Mr. Terrific, Sasha Bordeaux app.						4.00
1-2nd printing with B&W cover						3.00
2-31: 2,3-Kobra, King Faraday, Amanda Waller, Fire app. 4-The Great Ten app. 13-15-Outsiders app. 26-Chimera origin						3.00
...: A King's GameTPB (2007, $14.99) r/#1-7						15.00
...: Chimera TPB (2009, $17.99) r/#26-31						18.00
...: Fall of the Wall TPB (2008, $14.99) r/#16-22						15.00
...: Pawn Breaks TPB (2007, $14.99) r/#8-12						15.00
CHERYL BLOSSOM (See Archie's Girls, Betty and Veronica #320 for 1st app.)						
Archie Publications: Sept, 1995 - No. 3, Nov, 1995 ($1.50, limited series)						
1	2	4	6	9	12	15
2,3	1	2	3	5	7	9
Special 1-4 ('95, '96, $2.00)	1	2	3	5	7	9
CHERYL BLOSSOM (Cheryl's Summer Job)						
Archie Publications: July, 1996 - No. 3, Sept, 1996 ($1.50, limited series)						
1-3	1	2	3	4	5	7
CHERYL BLOSSOM (...Goes Hollywood)						
Archie Publications: Dec, 1996 - No. 3, Feb, 1997 ($1.50, limited series)						
1-3	1	2	3	4	5	7
CHERYL BLOSSOM						
Archie Publications: Apr, 1997 - No. 37, Mar, 2001 ($1.50/$1.75/$1.79/$1.99)						
1-Dan DeCarlo-c/a	2	4	6	8	10	12
2-10: 2-7-Dan DeCarlo-c/a						6.00
11-37: 32-Begin $1.99-c. 34-Sabrina app.						4.00
CHESTY SANCHEZ						
Antarctic Press: Nov, 1995 - No. 2, Mar, 1996 ($2.95, B&W)						
1,2						3.00
...Super Special (2/99, $5.99)						6.00

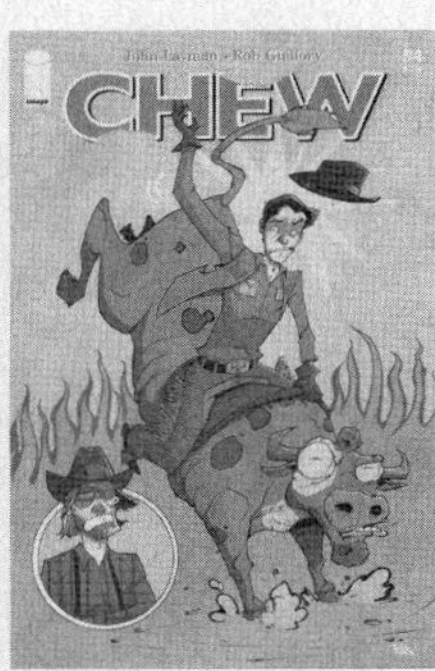

Chew #54 © John Layman

Chewbacca #1 © Lucasfilm

Chilling Adventures of Sabrina #6 © ACP

CHEVAL NOIR
Dark Horse Comics: 1989 - No. 48, Nov, 1993 ($3.50, B&W, 68 pgs.)

	GD 2.0	VG 4.0	FN 6.0	VF 8.0	VF/NM 9.0	NM- 9.2
1 ($3.50) Dave Stevens-c	2	4	6	10	14	18
2-6,8,10 ($3.50): 6-Moebius poster insert						5.00
7-Dave Stevens-c	2	4	6	8	10	12
9,11,13,15,17,20,22 ($4.50, 84 pgs.)						6.00
12,18,19,21,23 ($3.95): 12-Geary-a; Mignola-c						5.00
14 ($4.95, 76 pgs.)(7 pgs. color)						6.00
16,24 ($3.75): 16-19-Contain trading cards						5.00
25,26 ($3.95): 26-Moebius-a begins						5.00
27-48 ($2.95): 33-Snyder III-c						4.00

NOTE: ***Bolland** a-2, 6, 7, 13, 14. **Bolton** a-2, 4, 45; c-4, 20. **Chadwick** c-13. **Dorman** painted c-16. **Geary** a-13, 14. **Kelley Jones** c-27. **Kaluta** a-6; c-6, 18. **Moebius** c-5, 9, 26. **Dave Stevens** c-1, 7. **Sutton** painted c-36.*

CHEW (See Walking Dead #61 for preview)
Image Comics: Jun, 2009 - No. 60, Nov, 2016 ($2.99/$3.50/$3.99)

	GD 2.0	VG 4.0	FN 6.0	VF 8.0	VF/NM 9.0	NM- 9.2
1-Layman-s/Guillory-a	10	20	30	69	147	225
1-(2nd-4th printings)	2	4	6	9	12	15
2-1st printing	3	6	9	19	30	40
2-5-(2nd & 3rd printings)						6.00
3-1st printing	2	4	6	11	16	20
4,5-1st printings	2	4	6	9	12	15
6-10	1	3	4	6	8	10
11-15: 15-Gatefold wraparound-c	1	2	3	5	6	8
16-24: 19-Neon green cover ink						5.00
25-44,46-49: 27-(6/12) Second Helping Edition						3.00
27-(5/11) Future issue released between #18 & #19						5.00
45,50-55-($3.50) 49-Poyo cover. 53-Flintstones cover						3.50
56-59-($3.99)						4.00
60-($5.99) Final issue; double cover with gatefold; set in the future						6.00
...: Demon Chicken Poyo One-Shot (4/16, $3.99) Layman-s/Guillory-a; pin-up gallery						4.00
.../ Revival One Shot (5/14, $4.99) Flip book: Layman-s/Guillory-a & Selley-s/Norton-a						5.00
...: Warrior Chicken Poyo (7/14, $3.50) Layman-s/Guillory-a; bonus pin-up gallery						3.50
Image Firsts: Chew #1 (4/10, $1.00) r/#1 with "Image Firsts" cover logo						5.00

CHEWBACCA (Star Wars)
Marvel Comics: Dec, 2015 - No. 5, Feb, 2016 ($3.99, limited series)

	GD 2.0	VG 4.0	FN 6.0	VF 8.0	VF/NM 9.0	NM- 9.2
1-5-Duggan-s/Noto-a; takes place after Episode 4 Battle of Yavin						4.00

CHEYENNE (TV)
Dell Publishing Co.: No. 734, Oct, 1956 - No. 25, Dec-Jan, 1961-62

	GD 2.0	VG 4.0	FN 6.0	VF 8.0	VF/NM 9.0	NM- 9.2
Four Color 734(#1)-Clint Walker photo-c	13	26	39	86	188	290
Four Color 772,803: Clint Walker photo-c	8	16	24	51	96	140
4(8-10/57) - 20: 4-9,13-20-Clint Walker photo-c. 10-12-Ty Hardin photo-c	6	12	18	37	66	95
21-25-Clint Walker photo-c on all	6	12	18	38	69	100

CHEYENNE AUTUMN (See Movie Classics)

CHEYENNE KID (Formerly Wild Frontier No. 1-7)
Charlton Comics: No. 8, July, 1957 - No. 99, Nov, 1973

	GD 2.0	VG 4.0	FN 6.0	VF 8.0	VF/NM 9.0	NM- 9.2
8 (#1)	8	16	24	42	54	65
9,15-19	6	12	18	29	36	42
10-Williamson/Torres-a(3); Ditko-c	11	22	33	60	83	105
11-(68 pgs.)-Cheyenne Kid meets Geronimo	10	20	30	58	79	100
12-Williamson/Torres-a(2)	10	20	30	58	79	100
13-Williamson/Torres-a (5 pgs.)	8	16	24	44	57	70
14-Williamson-a (5 pgs.?)	8	16	24	42	54	65
20-22,24,25-Severin c/a(3) each	4	8	12	21	33	45
23,27-29	3	6	9	15	22	28
26,30-Severin-a	3	6	9	17	26	35
31-59	2	4	6	10	14	18
60-65	2	4	6	8	11	14
66-Wander by Aparo begins, ends #87	2	4	6	10	14	18
67-80	2	4	6	8	11	14
81-99: Apache Red begins #88, origin in #89	2	4	6	8	11	14
Modern Comics Reprint 87,89(1978)						5.00

CHIAROSCURO (THE PRIVATE LIVES OF LEONARDO DA VINCI)
DC Comics (Vertigo): July, 1995 - No. 10, Apr, 1996 ($2.50/$2.95, limited series, mature)

	GD 2.0	VG 4.0	FN 6.0	VF 8.0	VF/NM 9.0	NM- 9.2
1-9: McGreal and Rawson-s/Truog & Kayanan-a						3.00
10-($2.95)						3.00
TPB (2005, $24.99) r/series; intro. by Alisa Kwitney, afterword by Pat McGreal						25.00

CHICAGO MAIL ORDER (See C-M-O Comics in the Promotional Comics section)

CHIEF, THE (Indian Chief No. 3 on)
Dell Publishing Co.: No. 290, Aug, 1950 - No. 2, Apr-June, 1951

	GD 2.0	VG 4.0	FN 6.0	VF 8.0	VF/NM 9.0	NM- 9.2
Four Color 290(#1)	7	14	21	49	92	135
2	5	10	15	35	63	90

CHIEF CRAZY HORSE (See Wild Bill Hickok #21)
Avon Periodicals: 1950 (Also see Fighting Indians of the Wild West!)

	GD 2.0	VG 4.0	FN 6.0	VF 8.0	VF/NM 9.0	NM- 9.2
nn-Fawcette-c	24	48	72	142	234	325

CHIEF VICTORIO'S APACHE MASSACRE (See Fight Indians of/Wild West!)
Avon Periodicals: 1951

	GD 2.0	VG 4.0	FN 6.0	VF 8.0	VF/NM 9.0	NM- 9.2
nn-Williamson/Frazetta-a (7 pgs.); Larsen-a; Kinstler-c	58	116	174	371	636	900

CHILD IS BORN, A
Apostle Arts: Nov, 2011 ($5.99, one-shot)

	GD 2.0	VG 4.0	FN 6.0	VF 8.0	VF/NM 9.0	NM- 9.2
nn-Story of the birth of Jesus; Billy Tucci-s/a; cover by Tucci & Sparacio						6.00
HC (7/12, $15.99) Includes bonus interview with Billy Tucci and sketch art						16.00

CHILDREN OF FIRE
Fantagor Press: Nov, 1987 - No. 3, 1988 ($2.00, limited series)

	GD 2.0	VG 4.0	FN 6.0	VF 8.0	VF/NM 9.0	NM- 9.2
1-3: by Richard Corben						4.00

CHILDREN OF THE VOYAGER (See Marvel Frontier Comics Unlimited)
Marvel Frontier Comics: Sept, 1993 - No. 4, Dec, 1993 ($1.95, limited series)

	GD 2.0	VG 4.0	FN 6.0	VF 8.0	VF/NM 9.0	NM- 9.2
1-($2.95)-Embossed glow-in-the-dark-c; Paul Johnson-c/a						4.00
2-4						3.00

CHILDREN'S BIG BOOK
Dorene Publ. Co.: 1945 (25¢, stiff-c, 68 pgs.)

	GD 2.0	VG 4.0	FN 6.0	VF 8.0	VF/NM 9.0	NM- 9.2
nn-Comics & fairy tales; David Icove-a	15	30	45	90	140	90

CHILDREN'S CRUSADE, THE
DC Comics (Vertigo): Dec, 1993 - No. 2, Jan, 1994 ($3.95, limited series)

	GD 2.0	VG 4.0	FN 6.0	VF 8.0	VF/NM 9.0	NM- 9.2
1,2-Gaiman scripts & Bachalo-a; framing issues for Children's Crusade x-over						4.00

CHILD'S PLAY: THE SERIES (Movie)
Innovation Publishing: May, 1991 - #3, 1991 ($2.50, 28pgs.)

	GD 2.0	VG 4.0	FN 6.0	VF 8.0	VF/NM 9.0	NM- 9.2
1-3						3.00

CHILD'S PLAY 2 THE OFFICIAL MOVIE ADAPTATION (Movie)
Innovation Publishing: 1990 - No. 3, 1990 ($2.50, bi-weekly limited series)

	GD 2.0	VG 4.0	FN 6.0	VF 8.0	VF/NM 9.0	NM- 9.2
1-3: Adapts movie sequel						3.00

CHILI (Millie's Rival)
Marvel Comics Group: 5/69 - No. 17, 9/70; No. 18, 8/72 - No. 26, 12/73

	GD 2.0	VG 4.0	FN 6.0	VF 8.0	VF/NM 9.0	NM- 9.2
1	9	18	27	58	114	170
2,4,5	5	10	15	34	60	85
3-Millie & Chili visit Marvel and meet Stan Lee & Stan Goldberg (6 pgs.)	6	12	18	37	66	95
6-17	5	10	15	30	50	70
18-26	4	8	12	27	44	60
Special 1(12/71, 52 pgs.)	5	10	15	35	63	90

CHILLER
Marvel Comics (Epic): Nov, 1993 - No. 2, Dec, 1993 ($7.95, lim. series)

	GD 2.0	VG 4.0	FN 6.0	VF 8.0	VF/NM 9.0	NM- 9.2
1,2-(68 pgs.)	1	2	3	5	6	8

CHILLING ADVENTURES IN SORCERY (...as Told by Sabrina #1, 2)
(Red Circle Sorcery No. 6 on)
Archie Publications (Red Circle Prods.): 9/72 - No. 2, 10/72; No. 3, 10/73 - No. 5, 2/74

	GD 2.0	VG 4.0	FN 6.0	VF 8.0	VF/NM 9.0	NM- 9.2
1-Sabrina cameo as narrator	5	10	15	30	50	70
2-Sabrina cameo as narrator	3	6	9	17	26	35
3-5: Morrow-c/a, all. 4,5-Alcazar-a	2	4	6	11	16	20

CHILLING ADVENTURES OF SABRINA
Archie Comic Publications: Dec, 2014 - Present ($3.99)

	GD 2.0	VG 4.0	FN 6.0	VF 8.0	VF/NM 9.0	NM- 9.2
1-6: 1-Aguirre-Sacasa-s/Hack-a; two covers; origin re-told, set in the 1960s						4.00
... - Halloween ComicFest Edition 1 (2015, free) r/#1 in B&W						3.00

CHILLING TALES (Formerly Beware)
Youthful Magazines: No. 13, Dec, 1952 - No. 17, Oct, 1953

	GD 2.0	VG 4.0	FN 6.0	VF 8.0	VF/NM 9.0	NM- 9.2
13(No.1)-Harrison-a; Matt Fox-c/a	97	194	291	621	1061	1500
14-Harrison-a	65	130	195	416	708	1000
15-Matt Fox-c; Harrison-a	77	154	231	493	847	1200
16-Poe adapt.-'Metzengerstein'; Rudyard Kipling adapt.- 'Mark of the Beast,' by Kiefer; bondage-c	77	154	231	493	847	1200
17-Matt Fox-c; Sir Walter Scott & Poe adapt.	71	142	213	454	777	1100

CHILLING TALES OF HORROR (Magazine)
Stanley Publications: V1#1, 6/69 - V1#7, 12/70; V2#2, 2/71 - V2#6, 10/71(50¢, B&W, 52 pgs.)

Chin Music #1 © Niles & Harris

Chip 'n' Dale #17 © DIS

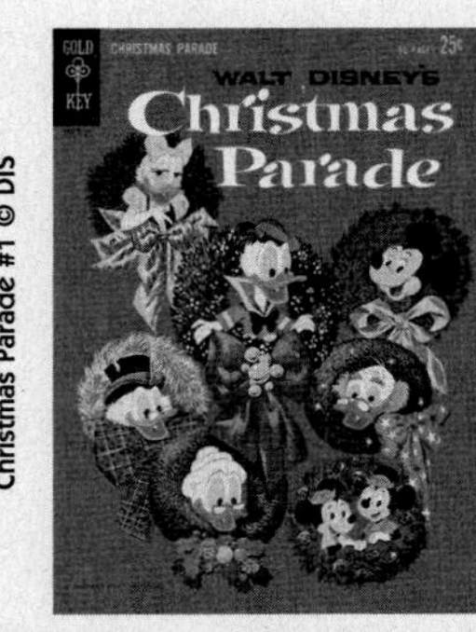

Christmas Parade #1 © DIS

	GD 2.0	VG 4.0	FN 6.0	VF 8.0	VF/NM 9.0	NM- 9.2
V1#1	9	18	27	57	111	165
2-4,(no #5),6,7: 7-Cameron-a	6	12	18	38	69	100
V2#2-6: 2-Two different #2 issues exist (2/71 & 4/71). 2-(2/71) Spirit of Frankenstein -r/Adventures into the Unknown #16. 4-(8/71) different from other V2#4(6/71)	5	10	15	35	63	90
V2#4-(6/71) r/9 pg. Feldstein-a from Adventures into the Unknown #3	6	12	18	37	66	95

NOTE: *Two issues of V2#2 exist, Feb, 1971 and April, 1971. Two issues of V2#4 exist, Jun, 1971 and Aug, 1971.*

CHILLY WILLY (Also see New Funnies #211)
Dell Publ. Co.: No. 740, Oct, 1956 - No. 1281, Apr-June, 1962 (Walter Lantz)

	GD	VG	FN	VF	VF/NM	NM-
Four Color 740 (#1)	8	16	24	51	96	140
Four Color 852 (2/58),967 (2/59),1017 (9/59),1074 (2-4/60),1122 (8/60), 1177 (4-6/61),1212 (7-9/61),1281	5	10	15	34	60	85

CHIMERA
CrossGeneration Comics: Mar, 2003 - No. 4, July, 2003 ($2.95, limited series)

1-4-Marz-s/Peterson-c/a 3.00
Vol. 1 TPB (2003, $15.95) r/#1-4 plus sketch pages, 3-D models, how-to guides 16.00

CHIMICHANGA
Albatross Exploding Funny Books: 2010 ($3.00, B&W)

1-3-Eric Powell-s/a/c 3.00

CHIMICHANGA: THE SORROW OF THE WORLD'S WORST FACE
Dark Horse Comics: Oct, 2016 - No. 4 ($3.99, limited series)

1-3-Eric Powell-s/Stephanie Buscema-a 4.00

CHINA BOY (See Wisco in the Promotional Comics section)

CHIN MUSIC
Image Comics: May, 2013 - Present ($2.99)

1,2-Steve Niles-s/Tony Harris-a/c 3.00

CHIP 'N' DALE (Walt Disney)(See Walt Disney's C&S #204)
Dell Publishing Co./Gold Key/Whitman No. 65 on: Nov, 1953 - No. 30, June-Aug, 1962; Sept, 1967 - No. 83, July, 1984

	GD	VG	FN	VF	VF/NM	NM-
Four Color 517(#1)	11	22	33	73	157	240
Four Color 581,636	6	12	18	42	79	115
4(12/55-2/56)-10	5	10	15	33	57	80
11-30	4	8	12	28	47	65
1(Gold Key, 1967)-Reprints	3	6	9	19	30	40
2-10	2	4	6	13	18	22
11-20	2	4	6	9	12	15
21-40	2	4	6	8	10	12
41-64,70-77: 75(2/82), 76(2-3/82), 77(3/82)	1	2	3	5	7	9
65,66 (Whitman)	2	4	6	8	11	14
67-69 (3-pack? 1980): 67(8/80), 68(10/80) (scarce)	4	8	12	28	47	65
78-83 (All #90214; 3-pack, nd, nd code): 78(4/83), 79(5/83), 80(7/83), 81(8/83), 82(5/84), 83(7/84)	3	6	9	15	22	28

NOTE: *All Gold Key/Whitman issues have reprints except No. 32-35, 38-41, 45-47. No. 23-28, 30-42, 45-47, 49 have new covers.*

CHIP 'N DALE RESCUE RANGERS
Disney Comics: June, 1990 - No. 19, Dec, 1991 ($1.50)

1-New stories; origin begins 4.00
2-19: 2-Origin continued 3.00

CHIP 'N DALE RESCUE RANGERS
BOOM! Studios: Dec, 2010 - No. 8, Jul, 2011 ($3.99)

1-8: 1-Brill-s/Castellani-a; 3 covers 4.00
... Free Comic Book Day Edition (5/11) Flip book with Darkwing Duck 3.00

CHITTY CHITTY BANG BANG (See Movie Comics)

C.H.I.X.
Image Comics (Studiosaurus): Jan, 1998 ($2.50)

1-Dodson, Haley, Lopresti, Randall, and Warren-s/c/a 3.00
1-($5.00) "X-Ray Variant" cover 5.00
C.H.I.X. That Time Forgot 1 (8/98, $2.95) 3.00

CHOICE COMICS
Great Publications: Dec, 1941 - No. 3, Feb, 1942

	GD	VG	FN	VF	VF/NM	NM-
1-Origin Secret Circle; Atlas the Mighty app.; Zomba, Jungle Fight, Kangaroo Man, & Fire Eater begin	155	310	465	992	1696	2400
2	77	154	231	493	847	1200
3-Double feature; Features movie "The Lost City" (classic cover); continued from Great Comics #3	194	388	582	1242	2121	3000

CHOLLY AND FLYTRAP (Arthur Suydam's...)(Also see New Adventures of...)

GD VG FN VF VF/NM NM-
2.0 4.0 6.0 8.0 9.0 9.2

Image Comics: Nov, 2004 - No. 4, June, 2005 ($4.95/$5.95, limited series)

1-($4.95) Arthur Suydam-s/a/c 6.00
2-4-($5.95) 6.00

CHOO CHOO CHARLIE
Gold Key: Dec, 1969

	GD	VG	FN	VF	VF/NM	NM-
1-John Stanley-a	5	10	15	35	63	90

CHOSEN
Dark Horse Comics: Jan, 2004 - No. 3, Aug, 2004 ($2.99, limited series)

1-Story of the second coming; Mark Millar-s/Peter Gross-a 4.00
2,3 3.00

CHRISTIAN (See Asylum)
Maximum Press: Jan, 1996 ($2.99, one-shot)

1-Pop Mhan-a 3.00

CHRISTIAN HEROES OF TODAY
David C. Cook: 1964 (36 pgs.)

	GD	VG	FN	VF	VF/NM	NM-
nn	3	6	9	17	26	35

CHRISTMAS (Also see A-1 Comics)
Magazine Enterprises: No. 28, 1950

	GD	VG	FN	VF	VF/NM	NM-
A-1 28	10	20	30	56	76	95

CHRISTMAS ADVENTURE, A (See Classics Comics Giveaways, 12/69)

CHRISTMAS ALBUM (See March of Comics No. 312)

CHRISTMAS ANNUAL
Golden Special: 1975 ($1.95, 100 pgs., stiff-c)

	GD	VG	FN	VF	VF/NM	NM-
nn-Reprints Mother Goose stories with Walt Kelly-a	3	6	9	21	33	45

CHRISTMAS & ARCHIE
Archie Comics: Jan, 1975 ($1.00, 68 pgs., 10-1/4x13-1/4" treasury-sized)

	GD	VG	FN	VF	VF/NM	NM-
1-(scarce)	5	10	15	34	60	85

CHRISTMAS BELLS (See March of Comics No. 297)

CHRISTMAS CARNIVAL
Ziff-Davis Publ. Co./St. John Publ. Co. No. 2: 1952 (25¢, one-shot, 100 pgs.)

	GD	VG	FN	VF	VF/NM	NM-
nn	37	74	111	222	361	500
2-Reprints Ziff-Davis issue plus-c	18	36	54	103	162	220

CHRISTMAS CAROL, A (See March of Comics No. 33)

CHRISTMAS EVE, A (See March of Comics No. 212)

CHRISTMAS IN DISNEYLAND (See Dell Giants)

CHRISTMAS PARADE (See Dell Giant No. 26, Dell Giants, March of Comics No. 284, Walt Disney Christmas Parade & Walt Disney's...)

CHRISTMAS PARADE (Walt Disney's)
Gold Key: 1962 (no month listed) - No. 9, Jan, 1972 (#1,5: 80 pgs.; #2-4,7-9: 36 pgs.)

	GD	VG	FN	VF	VF/NM	NM-
1 (30018-301)-Giant	8	16	24	51	96	140
2-6: 2-r/F.C. #367 by Barks. 3-r/F.C. #178 by Barks. 4-r/F.C. #203 by Barks. 5-r/Christmas Parade #1 (Dell) by Barks; giant. 6-r/Christmas Parade #2 (Dell) by Barks (64 pgs.); giant	5	10	15	35	63	90
7-Pull-out poster (half price w/o poster)	5	10	15	30	50	70
8-r/F.C. #367 by Barks; pull-out poster	5	10	15	35	63	90
9	4	8	12	25	40	55

CHRISTMAS PARTY (See March of Comics No. 256)

CHRISTMAS STORIES (See Little People No. 959, 1062)

CHRISTMAS STORY (See March of Comics No. 326 in the Promotional Comics section)

CHRISTMAS STORY, THE
Catechetical Guild: 1955 (15¢)

	GD	VG	FN	VF	VF/NM	NM-
393-Addison Burbank-a	8	16	24	40	50	60

CHRISTMAS STORY BOOK (See Woolworth's Christmas Story Book)

CHRISTMAS TREASURY, A (See Dell Giants & March of Comics No. 227)

CHRISTMAS WITH ARCHIE
Spire Christian Comics (Fleming H. Revell Co.): 1973, 1974 (49¢, 52 pgs.)

	GD	VG	FN	VF	VF/NM	NM-
nn-Low print run	3	6	9	15	22	28

CHRISTMAS WITH MOTHER GOOSE
Dell Publishing Co.: No. 90, Nov, 1945 - No. 253, Nov, 1949

	GD	VG	FN	VF	VF/NM	NM-
Four Color 90 (#1)-Kelly-a	15	30	45	103	227	350
Four Color 126 ('46), 172 (11/47)-By Walt Kelly	11	22	33	76	163	250
Four Color 201 (10/48), 253-By Walt Kelly	10	20	30	64	132	200

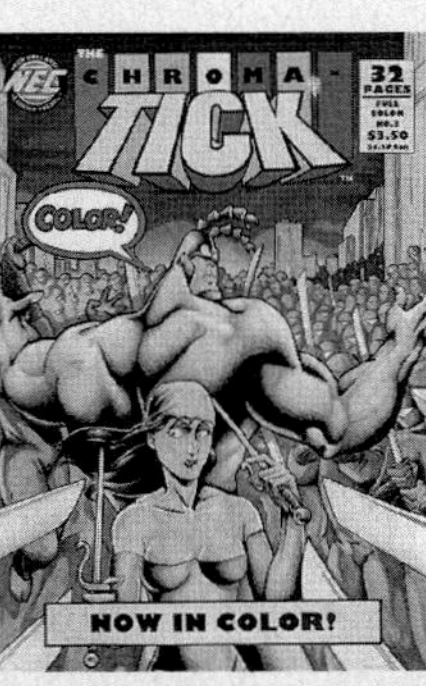

The Chroma-Tick #3 © Ben Edlund

Chrononauts #4 © MillarWorld & Murphy

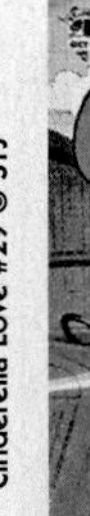
Cinderella Love #29 © STJ

	GD	VG	FN	VF	VF/NM	NM-
	2.0	4.0	6.0	8.0	9.0	9.2

CHRISTMAS WITH SANTA (See March of Comics No. 92)

CHRISTMAS WITH THE SUPER-HEROES (See Limited Collectors' Edition)
DC Comics: 1988; No. 2, 1989 ($2.95)

1,2: 1-(100 pgs.)-All reprints; N. Adams-r, Byrne-c; Batman, Superman, JLA, LSH Christmas stories; r-Miller's 1st Batman/DC Special Series #21. 2-(68 pgs.)-Superman by Chadwick; Batman, Wonder Woman, Deadman, Green Lantern, Flash app.; Morrow-a; Enemy Ace by Byrne; all new-a 6.00

CHROMA-TICK, THE (...Special Edition, #1,2) (Also see The Tick)
New England Comics Press: Feb, 1992 - No. 8, Nov, 1993 ($3.95/$3.50, 44 pgs.)

1,2-Includes serially numbered trading card set 5.00
3-8 ($3.50, 36 pgs.): 6-Bound-in card 4.00

CHROME
Hot Comics: 1986 - No. 3, 1986 ($1.50, limited series)

1-3 3.00

CHROMIUM MAN, THE
Triumphant Comics: Aug, 1993 - No.10, May, 1994 ($2.50)

1-1st app. Mr. Death; all serially numbered 3.00
2-10: 2-1st app. Prince Vandal. 3-1st app. Candi, Breaker & Coil. 4,5-Triumphant Unleashed x-over. 8,9-(3/94). 10-(5/94) 3.00
0-(4/94)-Four color-c, 0-All pink-c & all blue-c; no cover price 3.00

CHROMIUM MAN: VIOLENT PAST, THE
Triumphant Comics: Jan, 1994 - No. 2, Jan, 1994 ($2.50, limited series)

1,2-Serially numbered to 22,000 each 3.00

CHRONICLES OF CONAN, THE (See Conan the Barbarian)

CHRONICLES OF CORUM, THE (Also see Corum...)
First Comics: Jan, 1987 - No. 12, Nov, 1988 ($1.75/$1.95, deluxe series)

1-12: Adapts Michael Moorcock's novel 3.00

CHRONONAUTS
Image Comics: Mar, 2015 - No. 4, Jun, 2015 ($3.50/$5.99)

1-3-Mark Millar-s/Sean Murphy-a 3.50
4-($5.99) 6.00

CHRONOS
DC Comics: Mar, 1998 - No. 11, Feb. 1999 ($2.50)

1-11-J.F. Moore-s/Guinan-a 3.00
#1,000,000 (11/98) 853rd Century x-over 3.00

CHUCK (Based on the NBC TV series)
DC Comics (WildStorm): Aug, 2008 - No. 6, Jan, 2009 ($2.99, limited series)

1-6-Jeremy Haun-a/Kristian Donaldson-c; Noto back-up-a 3.00
TPB (2009, $19.99) r/#1-6; photo-c 20.00

CHUCKLE, THE GIGGLY BOOK OF COMIC ANIMALS
R. B. Leffingwell Co.: 1945 (132 pgs., one-shot)

1-Funny animal 24 48 72 144 237 330

CHUCK NORRIS (TV)
Marvel Comics (Star Comics): Jan, 1987 - No. 4, July, 1987

1-Ditko-a 2 4 6 10 14 18
2,3: Ditko-a 6.00
4-No Ditko-a (low print run) 1 2 3 4 5 8

CHUCK WAGON (See Sheriff Bob Dixon's...)

CHUCKY (Based on the 1988 killer doll movie Child's Play)
Devil's Due Publishing: Apr, 2007 - No. 4, Nov, 2007 ($3.50/$5.50)

1-3-Pulido-s/Medors-a; art & photo covers 5.00
4-($5.50) 1 2 3 4 5 7
TPB (2007, $18.99) r/series; gallery of variant covers; 4 pages of script and sketch art 19.00

CHYNA (WWF Wrestling)
Chaos! Comics: Sept, 2000; July, 2001 ($2.95/$2.99, one-shots)

1-Grant-s/Barrows-a; photo-c 3.00
1-($9.95) Premium Edition; Cleavenger-c 10.00
II -(7/01, $2.99) Deodato-a; photo-c 3.00

CICERO'S CAT
Dell Publishing Co.: July-Aug, 1959 - No. 2, Sept-Oct, 1959

1-Cat from Mutt & Jeff 4 8 12 28 47 65
2 4 8 12 25 40 55

CIMARRON STRIP (TV)
Dell Publishing Co.: Jan, 1968

1-Stuart Whitman photo-c 4 8 12 23 37 50

CINDER AND ASHE
DC Comics: May, 1988 - No. 4, Aug, 1988 ($1.75, limited series)

1-4: Mature readers 3.00

CINDERELLA (Disney) (See Movie Comics)
Dell Publishing Co.: No. 272, Apr, 1950 - No. 786, Apr, 1957

Four Color 272 12 24 36 82 179 275
Four Color 786-Partial-r #272 6 12 18 41 76 110

CINDERELLA
Whitman Publishing Co.: Apr, 1982

nn-Reprints 4-Color #272 1 2 3 4 5 7

CINDERELLA: FABLES ARE FOREVER (See Fables)
DC Comics (Vertigo): Apr, 2011 - No. 6, Sept, 2011 ($2.99, limited series)

1-6-Roberson-s/McManus-a/Zullo-c; Dorothy Gale app. 3.00

CINDERELLA: FROM FABLETOWN WITH LOVE (See Fables)
DC Comics (Vertigo): Jan, 2010 - No. 6, Jun, 2010 ($2.99, limited series)

1-6: Roberson-s/McManus-a/Zullo-c 3.00
TPB (2010, $14.99) r/#1-6 15.00

CINDERELLA LOVE
Ziff-Davis/St. John Publ. Co. No. 12 on: No. 10, 1950; No. 11, 4-5/51; No. 12, 9/51; No. 4, 10-11/51 - No. 11, Fall, 1952; No. 12, 10/53 - No. 15, 8/54; No. 25, 12/54 - No. 29, 10/55 (No #16-24)

10(#1)(1st Series, 1950)-Painted-c 24 48 72 142 234 325
11(#2, 4-5/51)-Crandall-a; Saunders painted-c 16 32 48 94 147 200
12(#3, 9/51)-Photo-c 15 30 45 86 133 180
4-8: 4,6,7-Photo-c 15 30 45 84 127 170
9-Kinstler-a; photo-c 15 30 45 88 137 185
10,11(Fall/'52): 10,11-Photo-c 15 30 45 84 127 170
12(St. John-10/53)-#13:13-Painted-c. 15 30 45 83 124 165
14-Matt Baker-a 26 52 78 154 252 350
15(8/54)-Matt Baker-c 77 154 231 493 847 1200
25(2nd Series)(Formerly Romantic Marriage) Classic Matt Baker-c 129 258 387 826 1413 2000
26-Matt Baker-c; last precode (2/55) 97 194 291 621 1061 1500
27-29: Matt Baker-c 77 154 231 493 847 1200

CINDY COMICS (...Smith No. 39, 40; Crime Can't Win No. 41 on)(Formerly Krazy Komics) (See Junior Miss & Teen Comics)
Timely Comics: No. 27, Fall, 1947 - No. 40, July, 1950

27-Kurtzman-a, 3 pgs: Margie, Oscar begin 37 74 111 222 361 500
28-31-Kurtzman-a 20 40 60 114 182 250
32-36,38-40: 33-Georgie story; anti-Wertham editorial 16 32 48 94 147 200
37-Classic greytone-c 200 400 600 1000 1500 2000

NOTE: *Kurtzman's "Hey Look"-#27(3), 29(2), 30(2), 31; "Giggles 'n' Grins"-28.*

CINNAMON: EL CICLO
DC Comics: Oct, 2003 - No. 5, Feb, 2004 ($2.50, limited series)

1-5-Van Meter-s/Chaykin-c/Paronzini-a 3.00

CIRCUS (...the Comic Riot)
Globe Syndicate: June, 1938 - No. 3, Aug, 1938

1-(Scarce)-Spacehawks (2 pgs.), & Disk Eyes by Wolverton (2 pgs.), Pewee Throttle by Cole (2nd comic book work; see Star Comics V1#11), Beau Gus, Ken Craig & The Lords of Crillon, Jack Hinton by Eisner, Van Bragger by Kane 503 1006 1509 3672 6486 9300
2,3-(Scarce)-Eisner, Cole, Wolverton, Bob Kane-a in each 284 568 852 1818 3109 4400

CIRCUS BOY (TV) (See Movie Classics)
Dell Publishing Co.: No. 759, Dec, 1956 - No. 813, July, 1957

Four Color 759 (#1)-The Monkees' Mickey Dolenz photo-c 12 24 36 79 170 260
Four Color 785 (4/57), 813-Mickey Dolenz photo-c 9 18 27 62 126 190

CIRCUS COMICS
Farm Women's Pub. Co./D. S. Publ.: Apr, 1945 - No. 2, Jun, 1945; Wint., 1948-49

1-Funny animal 15 30 45 84 127 170
2 10 20 30 54 72 90
1(1948)-D.S. Publ.; 2 pgs. Frazetta 25 50 75 150 245 340

CIRCUS OF FUN COMICS
A. W. Nugent Publ. Co.: 1945 - No. 3, Dec, 1947 (A book of games & puzzles)

1 15 30 45 88 137 185

The Cisco Kid #4 © DELL

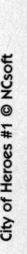

City of Heroes #1 © NCsoft

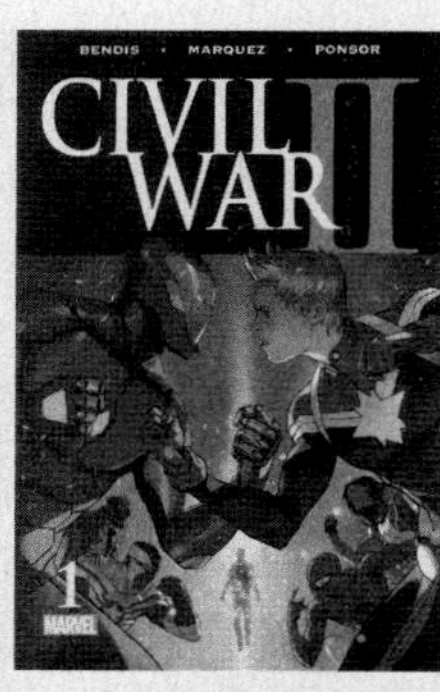

Civil War II #1 © MAR

GD 2.0 | VG 4.0 | FN 6.0 | VF 8.0 | VF/NM 9.0 | NM- 9.2

2,3 10 20 30 54 72 90

CISCO KID, THE (TV)
Dell Publishing Co.: July, 1950 - No. 41, Oct-Dec, 1958

Four Color 292(#1)-Cisco Kid, his horse Diablo, & sidekick Pancho & his horse Loco begin; line drawn cover 20 40 60 138 307 475
2(1/51) Painted-c begin 10 20 30 64 132 200
3-5 9 18 27 59 117 175
6-10 8 16 24 51 96 140
11-20 7 14 21 44 82 120
21-36-Last painted-c 6 12 18 37 66 95
37-41: All photo-c 7 14 21 46 86 125
NOTE: *Buscema a-40. Ernest Nordli painted c-5-16, 20, 35.*

CISCO KID COMICS
Bernard Bailey/Swappers Quarterly: Winter, 1944 (one-shot)

1-Illustrated Stories of the Operas: Faust; Funnyman by Giunta; Cisco Kid (1st app.) & Superbaby begin; Giunta-c 47 94 141 296 498 700

CITIZEN JACK
Image Comics: Nov, 2015 - No. 6, May, 2016 ($3.99, limited series)

1-6-Sam Humphries-s/Tommy Patterson-a 4.00

CITIZEN SMITH (See Holyoke One-Shot No. 9)

CITIZEN V AND THE V-BATTALION (See Thunderbolts)
Marvel Comics: June, 2001 - No. 3, Aug, 2001 ($2.99, limited series)

1-3-Nicieza-a; Michael Ryan-c/a 3.00
...: The Everlasting 1-4 (3/02 - No. 4, 7/02) Nicieza-s/LaRosa-a(p) 3.00

CITY OF HEROES (Online game)
Dark Horse Comics/Blue King Studios: Sept, 2002; May, 2004 - No. 7 ($2.95)

1-(no cover price) Dakan-s/Zombo-a 3.00
1-7-($2.95) 3.00

CITY OF HEROES (Online game)
Image Comics: June, 2005 - No. 20, Aug, 2007 ($2.99)

1-20: 1-Waid-s; Pérez-c. 6-Flip-c with City of Villains. 7-9-Jurgens-s 3.00

CITY OF OTHERS
Dark Horse Comics: Apr, 2007 - No. 4, Aug, 2007 ($2.99, limited series)

1-4-Bernie Wrightson-a/c; Steve Niles & Wrightson-s 3.00
TPB (2/08, $14.95) r/#1-4; Wrightson sketch pages 15.00

CITY OF SILENCE
Image Comics: May, 2000 - No. 3, July, 2000 ($2.50)

1-3-Ellis-s/Erskine-a 3.00
TPB (6/04, $9.95) r/#1-3; pin-up gallery 10.00

CITY OF THE LIVING DEAD (See Fantastic Tales No. 1)
Avon Periodicals: 1952

nn-Hollingsworth-c/a 65 130 195 416 708 1000

CITY OF TOMORROW
DC Comics (WildStorm): June, 2005 - No. 6, Nov, 2005 ($2.99, limited series)

1-6-Howard Chaykin-s/a 3.00
TPB (2006, $19.99) r/#1-6 20.00

CITY PEOPLE NOTEBOOK
Kitchen Sink Press: 1989 ($9.95, B&W, magazine sized)

nn-Will Eisner-s/a 15.00
nn-(DC Comics, 2000) Reprint 10.00

CITY SURGEON (Blake Harper...)
Gold Key: August, 1963

1(10075-308)-Painted-c 4 8 12 23 37 50

CITY: THE MIND IN THE MACHINE
IDW (Darby Pop Publishing): Feb, 2014 - No. 4, May, 2014 ($3.99)

1-4-Eric Garcia-s; 2 covers on each. 1-Fernandez-a. 3-Drew Moss-a. 4-Montenat-a 4.00

CIVIL WAR (Also see Amazing Spider-Man for TPB)
Marvel Comics: July, 2006 - No. 7, Jan, 2007 ($3.99/$2.99, limited series)

1-($3.99) Millar-s/McNiven-a & wraparound-c 2 4 6 11 16 20
1-Variant cover by Michael Turner 3 6 9 17 26 35
1-Aspen Comics Variant cover by Turner 3 6 9 19 30 40
1-Sketch Variant cover 4 8 12 23 37 50
1-Director's Cut (2006, $4.99) r/#1 plus promo art, variant covers, sketches and script 1 2 3 5 6 8
2-($2.99) Spider-Man unmasks 2 4 6 8 10 12
2-Turner variant cover 2 4 6 11 16 20
2-B&W sketch variant cover 3 6 9 17 26 35
2-2nd printing 5.00
3-7: 3-Thor returns. 4-Goliath killed 1 2 3 5 6 8
3-7-Turner variant covers 1 2 3 6 8 10
3-7-B&W sketch variant covers 3 6 9 14 20 25
TPB (2007, $24.99) r/#1-7; gallery of variant covers 25.00
...: Battle Damage Report (2007, $3.99) Post-Civil War character profiles; McGuinness-c 4.00
...: Choosing Sides (2/07, $3.99) Colan-c; Howard the Duck app.; 2 covers by Yu & Colan 5.00
... Companion TPB (2007, $13.99) r/Civil War Files, ...:Battle Damage Report, Marvel Spotlight: Millar/McNiven, Marvel Spotlight: Civil War Aftermath and Daily Bugle CW 14.00
Daily Bugle Civil War Newspaper Special #1 (9/06, 50¢, newsprint) Daily Bugle "newspaper" overview of the crossover; Mayhew-a 3.00
...Files (2006, $3.99) profile pages of major Civil War characters; McNiven-c 4.00
...: Marvel Universe TPB (2007, $11.99) r/Civil War: Choosing Sides, CW: The Return, She-Hulk #8, CW: The Initiative; She-Hulk sketch page; variant cover gallery 12.00
...: MGC #1 (6/10, $1.00) r/#1 with "Marvel's Greatest Comics" cover logo 3.00
...: The Confession (5/07, $2.99) Maleev-c/a; Bendis-s 3.00
...: The Initiative (4/07, $4.99) Silvestri-c/a; previews of post-Civil War series 5.00
...: The Return (3/07, $2.99) Captain Marvel returns; The Sentry app.; Raney-a 3.00
...: The Road to Civil War TPB (2007, $14.99) r/New Avengers: Illuminati, Fantastic Four #536 & 537, Amazing Spider-Man #529-531; Spider-Man costume sketches by Bachalo 15.00
... War Crimes (2/07, $3.99) Kingpin in prison; Tieri-s/Staz Johnson-a 4.00
... War Crimes TPB (2007, $17.99) r/Civil War: War Crimes one-shot and Underworld #1-5 18.00
... X-Men Universe TPB (2007, $13.99) r/Cable & Deadpool #30-32; X-Factor #8,9 14.00

CIVIL WAR (Secret Wars tie-in)
Marvel Comics: Sept, 2015 - No. 5, Dec, 2015 ($4.99/$3.99, limited series)

1-($4.99) Soule-s/Yu-a; Stark vs. Rogers on Battleworld 5.00
2-5-($3.99) 4.00

CIVIL WAR CHRONICLES (Reprints of Civil War and related Marvel issues)
Marvel Comics: Oct, 2007 - No. 12, Sept, 2008 ($4.99, limited series)

1-12: Reprints Civil War, Civil War: Frontline and x-over issues 5.00

CIVIL WAR: FRONTLINE (Tie-in to Civil War and related Marvel issues)
Marvel Comics: Aug, 2006 - No. 11, Apr, 2007 ($2.99, limited series)

1-Jenkins-s/Bachs-a/Watson-c; back-up stories by various 4.00
2-11: 3-Green Goblin app. 11-Aftermath of Civil War #7 3.00
... Book 1 TPB (2007, $14.99) r/#1-6 15.00
... Book 2 TPB (2007, $14.99) r/#7-11 15.00

CIVIL WAR: HOUSE OF M
Marvel Comics: Nov, 2008 - No. 5, Mar, 2009 ($2.99, limited series)

1-5-Gage-s/DiVito-a 3.00

CIVIL WAR MUSKET, THE (Kadets of America Handbook)
Custom Comics, Inc.: 1960 (25¢, half-size, 36 pgs.)

nn 3 6 9 15 22 28

CIVIL WAR II
Marvel Comics: No. 0, Jul, 2016 - No. 8, Feb, 2017 ($4.99/$5.99, limited series)

0-($4.99) Bendis-s/Coipel-a; intro. Ulysses 5.00
1-($5.99) Bendis-s/Marquez-a; Thanos kills War Machine 6.00
2-8-($4.99) 3-Banner killed. 4,5-Guardians of the Galaxy app. 7-Sorrentino-a (2 pgs.) 5.00
...: The Oath 1 (3/17, $4.99) Spencer-s; Capt. America named Director of SHIELD 5.00

CIVIL WAR II: AMAZING SPIDER-MAN
Marvel Comics: Aug, 2016 - No. 4, Nov, 2016 ($3.99, limited series)

1-4-Gage-s/Foreman-a; Ulysses app.; Clash returns 4.00

CIVIL WAR II: CHOOSING SIDES
Marvel Comics: Aug, 2016 - No. 6, Nov, 2016 ($4.99/$3.99, limited series)

1-($4.99) Short stories; Nick Fury, Night Thrasher & Damage Control app. 5.00
2-6-($3.99) Nick Fury story in all. 2-War Machine. 4-Punisher. 6-Jessica Jones 4.00

CIVIL WAR II: GODS OF WAR
Marvel Comics: Aug, 2016 - No. 4, Nov, 2016 ($3.99, limited series)

1-4-Abnett-s/Laiso-a/Anacleto-c. 1-Amadeus Cho app. 3-Avengers app. 4.00

CIVIL WAR II: KINGPIN
Marvel Comics: Sept, 2016 - No. 4, Dec, 2016 ($4.99/$3.99, limited series)

1-($4.99) Two stories; Rosenberg-s/Ortiz-a; Talajic-a; intro./origin Janus Jardeesh 5.00
2-4-($3.99) Rosenberg-s/Ortiz-a. 3-Punisher app. 4.00

CIVIL WAR II: ULYSSES
Marvel Comics: Oct, 2016 - No. 3, Dec, 2016 ($4.99, limited series)

1-3-Ewing-s/Kesel & Palo-a/Francavilla-c; Karnak and the Inhumans app. 4.00

Civil War II: X-Men #1 © MAR

Clandestine (2008 series) #1 © MAR

Clarence #4 © Cartoon Network

	GD 2.0	VG 4.0	FN 6.0	VF 8.0	VF/NM 9.0	NM- 9.2

CIVIL WAR II: X-MEN
Marvel Comics: Aug, 2016 - No. 4, Nov, 2016 ($3.99, limited series)

1-4-Bunn-s/Broccardo-a; Magneto app. 2-The Brood & Fantomex app. 4-Ulysses app. 4.00

CIVIL WAR: X-MEN (Tie-in to Civil War)
Marvel Comics: Sept, 2006 - No. 4, Dec, 2006 ($2.99, limited series)

1-4-Paquette-a/Hine-s; Bishop app. 3.00
1-Variant cover by Michael Turner 10.00
TPB (2007, $11.99) r/#1-4, profile pages of minor characters 12.00

CIVIL WAR: YOUNG AVENGERS & RUNAWAYS (Tie-in to Civil War)
Marvel Comics: Sept, 2006 - No. 4, Dec, 2006 ($2.99, limited series)

1-4-Caselli-a/Wells-s/Cheung-c 3.00
TPB (2007, $11.99) r/#1-4, profile pages of characters 12.00

CLAIRE VOYANT (Also see Keen Teens)
Leader Publ./Standard/Pentagon Publ.: 1946 - No. 4, 1947 (Sparling strip reprints)

	GD	VG	FN	VF	VF/NM	NM-
nn	81	162	243	518	884	1250
2-Kamen-c	58	116	174	371	636	900
3-Kamen bridal-c; contents mentioned in Love and Death, a book by Gershom Legman(1949) referenced by Dr. Wertham in **SOTI**	90	180	270	576	988	1400
4-Kamen bondage-c	77	154	231	493	847	1200

CLANDESTINE (Also see Marvel Comics Presents & X-Men: ClanDestine)
Marvel Comics: Oct, 1994 - No.12, Sept, 1995 ($2.95/$2.50)

1-($2.95)-Alan Davis-c/a(p)/scripts & Mark Farmer-c/a(i) begin, ends #8; Modok app.; Silver Surfer cameo; gold foil-c 4.00
2-12: 2-Wraparound-c. 2,3-Silver Surfer app. 5-Origin of ClanDestine. 6-Capt. America, Hulk, Spider-Man, Thing & Thor-c; Spider-Man cameo. 7-Spider-Man-c/app; Punisher cameo. 8-Invaders & Dr. Strange app. 10-Captain Britain-c/app. 11-Sub-Mariner app. 3.00
Preview (10/94, $1.50) 3.00
... Classic HC (2008, $29.99, DJ) r/#1-8, Marvel Comics Presents #158, X-Men and Clandestine #1&2, sketch pages and cover gallery; Alan Davis afterword 30.00

CLANDESTINE
Marvel Comics: Apr, 2008 - No. 5, Aug, 2008 ($2.99, limited series)

1-5: 1-Alan Davis-c/a(p)/scripts & Mark Farmer-c/a(i). 2-5-Excalibur app. 3.00

CLARENCE (Based on the Cartoon Network series)
BOOM! Studios (kaboom): Jun, 2015 - No. 4, Sept, 2015 ($3.99)

1-4-Short stories by various; multiple covers on each 4.00
...: Quest 1 (6/16, $4.99) Cron-DeVico-s; art by Smigiel & Omac 5.00
...: Rest Stops 1 (12/15, $4.99) Short stories by various; two covers 5.00

CLASH
DC Comics: 1991 - No. 3, 1991 ($4.95, limited series, 52 pgs.)

Book One - Three: Adam Kubert-c/a 5.00

CLASSIC BATTLESTAR GALACTICA (See Battlestar Galactica, Classic...)

CLASSIC COMICS/ILLUSTRATED - INTRODUCTION
by Dan Malan

Since the first publication of this special introduction to the **Classics** section, a number of revisions have been made to further clarify the listings. **Classics** reprint editions prior to 1963 had either incorrect dates or no dates listed. Those reprint editions should be identified only by the highest number on the reorder list (HRN). Past *Guides* listed what were calculated to be approximately correct dates, but many people found it confusing for the *Guide* to list a date not listed in the comic itself.

We have also attempted to clear up confusion about edition variations, such as color, printer, etc. Such variations are identified by letters. Editions are determined by three categories. Original edition variations are designated as Edition 1A, 1B, etc. All reprint editions prior to 1963 are identified by HRN only. All reprint editions from 9/63 on are identified by the correct date listed in the comic.

Information is also included on four reprintings of **Classics**. From 1968-1976, Twin Circle, the Catholic newspaper, serialized over 100 **Classics** titles. That list can be found under non-series items at the end of this section. In 1972, twelve **Classics** were reissued as **Now Age Books Illustrated**. They are listed under **Pendulum Illustrated Classics**. In 1982, 20 **Classics** were reissued, adapted for teaching English as a second language. They are listed under **Regents Illustrated Classics**. Then in 1984, six **Classics** were reissued with cassette tapes. See the listing under **Cassette Books**.

UNDERSTANDING CLASSICS ILLUSTRATED
by Dan Malan

Since **Classics Illustrated** is the most complicated comic book series, with all its reprint editions and variations, changes in covers and artwork, a variety of means of identifying editions, and the most extensive worldwide distribution of any comic-book series, this introductory section is provided to assist you in gaining expertise about this series.

THE HISTORY OF CLASSICS

The **Classics** series was the brain child of Albert L. Kanter, who saw in the new comic-book medium a means of introducing children to the great classics of literature. In October of 1941 his Gilberton Co. began the **Classic Comics** series with **The Three Musketeers**, with 64 pages of storyline. In those early years, the struggling series saw irregular schedules and numerous printers, not to mention variable art quality and liberal story adaptations. With No.13 the page total was reduced to 56 (except for No. 33, originally scheduled to be No. 9), and with No. 15 the coming-next ad on the outside back cover moved inside. In 1945 the Jerry Iger Shop began producing all new CC titles, beginning with No. 23. In 1947 the search for a classier logo resulted in **Classics Illustrated**, beginning with No. 35, **Last Days of Pompeii**. With No. 45 the page total dropped again to 48, which was to become the standard.

Two new developments in 1951 had a profound effect upon the success of the series. One was the introduction of painted covers, instead of the old line drawn covers, beginning with No. 81, **The Odyssey**. The second was the switch to the major national distributor Curtis. They raised the cover price from 10 to 15 cents, making it the highest priced comic-book, but it did not slow the growth of the series, because they were marketed as books, not comics. Because of this higher quality image, **Classics** flourished during the fifties while other comic series were reeling from outside attacks. They diversified with their new **Juniors**, **Specials**, and **World Around Us** series.

Classics artwork can be divided into three distinct periods. The pre-Iger era (1941-44) was mentioned above for its variable art quality. The Iger era (1945-53) was a major improvement in art quality and adaptations. It came to be dominated by artists Henry Kiefer and Alex Blum, together accounting for some 50 titles. Their styles gave the first real personality to the series. The EC era (1954-62) resulted from the demise of the EC horror series, when many of their artists made the major switch to classical art.

But several factors brought the production of new CI titles to a complete halt in 1962. Gilberton lost its 2nd class mailing permit. External factors like television, cheap paperback books, and Cliff Notes were all eating away at their market. Production halted with No.167, **Faust**, even though many more titles were already in the works. Many of those found their way into foreign series, and are very desirable to collectors. In 1967, **Classics Illustrated** was sold to Patrick Frawley and his Catholic publication, Twin Circle. They issued two new titles in 1969 as part of an attempted revival, but succumbed to major distribution problems in 1971. In 1988, First Publishing acquired the rights to use the old CI series art, logo, and name from the Frawley Group, and released a short-lived series featuring contributions of modern creators. Acclaim Books and Twin Circles issued a series of **Classics** reprints from 1997-1998.

One of the unique aspects of the **Classics Illustrated** (CI) series was the proliferation of reprint variations. Some titles had as many as 25 editions. Reprinting began in 1943. Some **Classic Comics** (CC) reprints (r) had the logo format revised to a banner logo, and added a motto under the banner. In 1947 CC titles changed to the CI logo, but kept their line drawn covers (LDC). In 1948, Nos. 13, 18, 29 and 41 received second covers (LDC2), replacing covers considered too violent, and reprints of Nos. 13-44 had pages reduced to 48, except for No. 26, which had 48 pages to begin with.

Starting in the mid-1950s, 70 of the 80 LDC titles were reissued with new painted covers (PC). Thirty of them also received new interior artwork (A2). The new artwork was generally higher quality with larger art panels and more faithful but abbreviated storylines. Later on, there were 29 second painted covers (PC2), mostly by Twin Circle. Altogether there were 199 interior art variations (169 (O)s and 30 A2 editions) and 272 different covers (169 (O)s, four LDC2s, 70 new PCs of LDC (O)s, and 29 PC2s). It is mildly astounding to realize that there are nearly 1400 different editions in the U.S. CI series.

FOREIGN CLASSICS ILLUSTRATED

If U.S. Classics variations are mildly astounding, the veritable plethora of foreign CI variations will boggle your imagination. While we still anticipate additional discoveries, we presently know about series in 25 languages and 27 countries. There were 250 new CI titles in foreign series, and nearly 400 new foreign covers of U.S. titles. The 1400 U.S. CI editions pale in comparison to the 4000 plus foreign editions. The very nature of CI lent itself to flourishing as an international series. Worldwide, they published over one billion copies! The first foreign CI series consisted of six Canadian Classic Comic reprints in 1946.

The following chart shows when CI series first began in each country:
1946: Canada. 1947: Australia. 1948: Brazil/The Netherlands. 1950: Italy. 1951: Greece/Japan/Hong Kong(?)/England/Argentina/Mexico. 1952: West Germany. 1954: Norway. 1955: New Zealand/South Africa. 1956: Denmark/Sweden/Iceland. 1957: Finland/France. 1962: Singapore(?). 1964: India (8 languages). 1971: Ireland (Gaelic). 1973: Belgium(?)/Philippines(?) & Malaysia(?).

Significant among the early series were Brazil and Greece. In 1950, Brazil was the first country to begin doing its own new titles. They issued nearly 80 new CI titles by Brazilian authors. In Greece in 1951 they actually had debates in parliament about the effects of Classics Illustrated on Greek culture, leading to the inclusion of 88 new Greek History & Mythology titles in the CI series.

But by far the most important foreign CI development was the joint European series which began in 1956 in 10 countries simultaneously. By 1960, CI had the largest European distribu-

Classic Comics #1 © GIL

Classic Comics #2 © GIL

Classic Comics #3 © GIL

tion of any American publication, not just comics! So when all the problems came up with U.S. distribution, they literally moved the CI operation to Europe in 1962, and continued producing new titles in all four CI series. Many of them were adapted and drawn in the U.S., the most famous of which was the British CI #158A. Dr. No, drawn by Norman Nodel. Unfortunately, the British CI series ended in late 1963, which limited the European CI titles available in English to 15. Altogether there were 82 new CI art titles in the joint European series, which ran until 1976.

IDENTIFYING CLASSICS EDITIONS

HRN: This is the highest number on the reorder list. It should be listed in ( ) after the title number. It is crucial to understanding various CI editions.

ORIGINALS (O): This is the all-important First Edition. To determine (O)s,there is one primary rule and two secondary rules (with exceptions):

Rule No. 1: All (O)s and only (O)s have coming-next ads for the next number. **Exceptions**: No. 14(15) (reprint) has an ad on the last inside text page only. No. 14(0) also has a full-page outside back cover ad (also rule 2). Nos.55(75) and 57(75) have coming-next ads. (Rules 2 and 3 apply here). Nos. 168(0) and 169(0) do not have coming-next ads. No.168 was never reprinted; No. 169(0) has HRN (166). No. 169(169) is the only reprint.

Rule No. 2: On nos.1-80, all (O)s and only (O)s list 10c on the front cover. **Exceptions**: Reprint variations of Nos. 37(62), 39(71), and 46(62) list 10c on the front cover. (Rules 1 and 3 apply here.)

Rule No. 3: All (O)s have HRN close to that title No. **Exceptions**: Some reprints also have HRNs close to that title number: a few CC(r)s, 58(62), 60(62), 149(149), 152(149) 153(149), and title nos. in the 160's. (Rules 1 and 2 apply here.)

DATES: Many reprint editions list either an incorrect date or no date. Since Gilberton apparently kept track of CI editions by HRN, they often left the (O) date on reprints. Often, someone with a CI collection for sale will swear that all their copies are originals. That is why we are so detailed in pointing out how to identify original editions. Except for original editions, which should have a coming-next ad, etc., all CI dates prior to 1963 are incorrect! So you want to go by HRN only if it is (165) or below, and go by listed date if it is 1963 or later. There are a few (167) editions with incorrect dates. They could be listed either as (167) or (62/3), which is meant to indicate that they were issued sometime between late 1962 and early 1963.

COVERS: A change from CC to LDC indicates a logo change, not a cover change; while a change from LDC to LDC2, LDC to PC, or from PC to PC2 does indicate a new cover. New PCs can be identified by HRN, and PC2s can be identified by HRN and date. Several covers had color changes, particularly from purple to blue.

Notes: If you see 15 cents in Canada on a front cover, it does not necessarily indicate a Canadian edition. Editions with an HRN between 44 and 75, with 15 cents on the cover are Canadian. Check the publisher's address. An HRN listing two numbers with a / between them indicates that there are two different reorder lists in the front and back covers. Official Twin Circle editions have a full-page back cover ad for their TC magazine, with no CI reorder list. Any CI with just a Twin Circle sticker on the front is not an official TC edition.

TIPS ON LISTING CLASSICS FOR SALE

It may be easy to just list Edition 17, but Classics collectors keep track of CI editions in terms of HRN and/or date, (O) or (r), CC or LDC, PC or PC2, A1 or A2, soft or stiff cover, etc. Try to help them out. For originals, just list (0), unless there are variations such as color (Nos. 10 and 61), printer (Nos. 18-22), HRN (Nos. 95, 108, 160), etc. For reprints, just list HRN if it's (165) or below. Above that, list HRN and date. Also, please list type of logo/cover/art for the convenience of buyers. They will appreciate it.

CLASSIC COMICS (Also see Best from Boys Life, Cassette Books, Famous Stories, Fast Fiction, Golden Picture Classics, King Classics, Marvel Classics Comics, Pendulum Illustrated Classics, Picture Parade, Picture Progress, Regents Ill. Classics, Spitfire, Stories by Famous Authors, Superior Stories, and World Around Us.)

CLASSIC COMICS (Classics Illustrated No. 35 on)
Elliot Publishing #1-3 (1941-1942)/Gilberton Publications #4-167 (1942-1967) /Twin Circle Pub. (Frawley) #168-169 (1968-1971):
10/41 - No. 34, 2/47; No. 35, 3/47 - No. 169, Spring 1969
(Reprint Editions of almost all titles 5/43 - Spring 1971)
(Painted Covers (0)s No. 81 on, and (r)s of most Nos. 1-80)

Abbreviations:
A–Art; C or c–Cover; CC–Classic Comics; CI–Classics Ill.; Ed–Edition; LDC–Line Drawn Cover; PC–Painted Cover; r–Reprint

1. The Three Musketeers

Ed	HRN	Date	Details	A	C	GD 2.0	VG 4.0	FN 6.0	VF 8.0	VF/NM 9.0	NM- 9.2
1	–	10/41	Date listed-1941; Elliot Pub; 68 pgs.	1	1	486	972	1458	3550	6275	9000
2	10	–	10¢ price removed on all (r)s; Elliot Pub; CC-r	1	1	36	72	108	211	343	475
3	15	–	Long Isl. Ind. Ed.; CC-r	1	1	26	52	78	154	252	350
4	18/20	–	Sunrise Times Ed.; CC-r	1	1	19	38	57	109	172	235
5	21	–	Richmond Courier Ed.; CC-r	1	1	17	34	51	98	154	210
6	28	1946	CC-r	1	1	14	28	42	80	115	150
7	36	–	LDC-r	1	1	8	16	24	42	54	65
8	60	–	LDC-r	1	1	6	12	18	27	33	38
9	64	–	LDC-r	1	1	5	10	15	22	26	30
10	78	–	C-price 15¢;LDC-r	1	1	4	9	13	18	22	26
11	93	–	LDC-r	1	1	4	9	13	18	22	26
12	114	–	Last LDC-r	1	1	4	8	11	16	19	22
13	134	–	New-c; old-a; 64 pg. PC-r	1	2	3	6	9	18	28	38
14	143	–	Old-a; PC-r; 64 pg.	1	2	2	4	6	11	16	20
15	150	–	New-a; PC-r; Evans/Crandall-a	2	2	3	6	9	16	24	32
16	149	–	PC-r	2	2	2	4	6	8	11	14
17	167	–	PC-r	2	2	2	4	6	8	11	14
18	167	4/64	PC-r	2	2	2	4	6	8	11	14
19	167	1/65	PC-r	2	2	2	4	6	8	11	14
20	167	3/66	PC-r	2	2	2	4	6	8	11	14
21	166	11/67	PC-r	2	2	2	4	6	8	11	14
22	166	Spr/69	C-price 25¢ ; stiff-c; PC-r	2	2	2	4	6	8	11	14
23	169	Spr/71	PC-r; stiff-c	2	2	2	4	6	8	11	14

2. Ivanhoe

Ed	HRN	Date	Details	A	C	GD 2.0	VG 4.0	FN 6.0	VF 8.0	VF/NM 9.0	NM- 9.2
1	(O)	12/41?	Date listed-1941; Elliot Pub; 68 pgs.	1	1	239	478	717	1530	2615	3700
2	10	–	Price & 'Presents' removed; Elliot Pub; CC-r	1	1	32	64	96	188	307	425
3	15	–	Long Isl. Ind. ed.; CC-r	1	1	21	42	63	124	202	280
4	18/20	–	Sunrise Times ed.; CC-r	1	1	18	36	54	103	162	225
5	21	–	Richmond Courier ed.; CC-r	1	1	16	32	48	94	147	200
6	28	1946	Last 'Comics'-r	1	1	14	28	42	80	115	150
7	36	–	1st LDC-r	1	1	9	18	27	47	61	75
8	60	–	LDC-r	1	1	6	12	18	27	33	38
9	64	–	LDC-r	1	1	5	10	15	22	26	30
10	78	–	C-price 15¢; LDC-r	1	1	4	9	13	18	22	26
11	89	–	LDC-r	1	1	4	8	12	17	21	24
12	106	–	LDC-r	1	1	4	7	10	14	17	20
13	121	–	Last LDC-r	1	1	4	7	10	14	17	20
14	136	–	New-c&a; PC-r	2	2	5	10	15	25	31	36
15	142	–	PC-r	2	2	2	4	6	9	13	16
16	153	–	PC-r	2	2	2	4	6	9	13	16
17	149	–	PC-r	2	2	2	4	6	9	13	16
18	167	–	PC-r	2	2	2	4	6	8	11	14
19	167	5/64	PC-r	2	2	2	4	6	8	11	14
20	167	1/65	PC-r	2	2	2	4	6	8	11	14
21	167	3/66	PC-r	2	2	2	4	6	8	11	14
22A	166	9/67	PC-r	2	2	2	4	6	8	11	14
22B	166	–	Center ad for Children's Digest & Young Miss; rare; PC-r	2	2	6	12	18	40	73	105
23	166	R/68	C-Price 25¢; PC-r	2	2	2	4	6	8	11	14
24	169	Win/69	Stiff-c	2	2	2	4	6	8	11	14
25	169	Win/71	PC-r; stiff-c	2	2	2	4	6	8	11	14

3. The Count of Monte Cristo

Ed	HRN	Date	Details	A	C	GD 2.0	VG 4.0	FN 6.0	VF 8.0	VF/NM 9.0	NM- 9.2
1	(O)	3/42	Elliot Pub; 68 pgs.	1	1	155	310	465	992	1696	2400
2	10	–	Conray Prods; CC-r	1	1	27	54	81	158	259	360
3	15	–	Long Isl. Ind. ed.; CC-r	1	1	20	40	60	120	195	270
4	18/20	–	Sunrise Times ed.; CC-r	1	1	18	36	54	107	169	230
5	20	–	Sunrise Times ed.; CC-r	1	1	17	34	51	98	154	210
6	21	–	Richmond Courier ed.; CC-r	1	1	16	32	48	94	147	200
7	28	1946	CC-r; new Banner logo	1	1	14	28	42	80	115	150

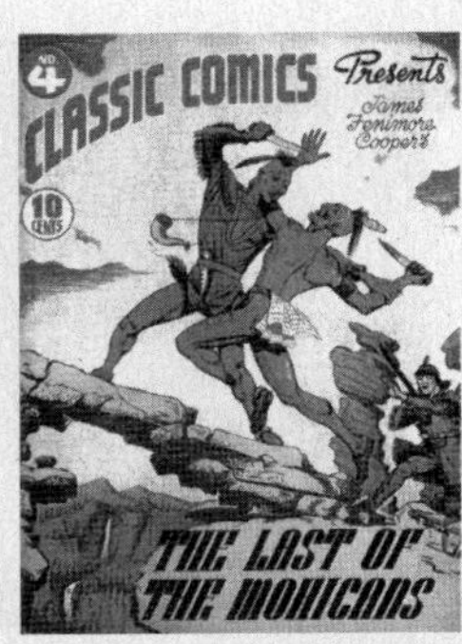

Classic Comics #4 © GIL

Classic Comics #5 © GIL

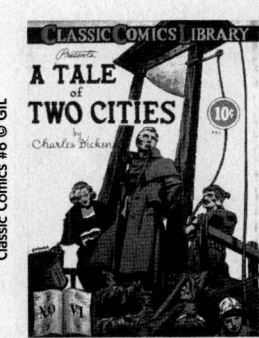

Classic Comics #6 © GIL

Ed	HRN	Date	Details	A	C	GD 2.0	VG 4.0	FN 6.0	VF 8.0	VF/NM 9.0	NM- 9.2
8	36	–	1st LDC-r	1	1	9	18	27	47	61	75
9	60	–	LDC-r	1	1	6	12	18	27	33	38
10	62	–	LDC-r	1	1	6	12	18	29	36	42
11	71	–	LDC-r	1	1	5	10	14	20	24	28
12	87	–	C-price 15¢; LDC-r	1	1	4	9	13	18	22	26
13	113	–	LDC-r	1	1	4	7	10	14	17	20
14	135	–	New-c&a; PC-r; Cameron-a	2	2	3	6	9	17	26	35
15	143	–	PC-r	2	2	2	4	6	8	13	16
16	153	–	PC-r	2	2	2	4	6	8	13	16
17	161	–	PC-r	2	2	2	4	6	8	13	16
18	167	–	PC-r	2	2	2	4	6	8	11	14
19	167	7/64	PC-r	2	2	2	4	6	8	11	14
20	167	7/65	PC-r	2	2	2	4	6	8	11	14
21	167	7/66	PC-r	2	2	2	4	6	8	11	14
22	166	R/68	C-price 25¢; PC-r	2	2	2	4	6	8	11	14
23	169	–	Win/69 Stiff-c; PC-r	2	2	2	4	6	8	11	14

4. The Last of the Mohicans

Ed	HRN	Date	Details	A	C	GD 2.0	VG 4.0	FN 6.0	VF 8.0	VF/NM 9.0	NM- 9.2
1	(O)	8/42	Date listed-1942; Gilberton #4(0) on; 68 pgs.	1	1	132	264	396	838	1444	2050
2	12	–	Elliot Pub; CC-r	1	1	27	54	81	158	259	360
3	15	–	Long Isl. Ind. ed.; CC-r	1	1	20	40	60	120	195	270
4	20	–	Long Isl. Ind. ed.; CC-r; banner logo	1	1	18	36	54	105	165	225
5	21	–	Queens Home News ed.; CC-r	1	1	16	32	48	94	147	200
6	28	1946	Last CC-r; new	1	1	14	28	42	80	115	150
7	36	–	1st LDC-r	1	1	9	18	27	47	61	75
8	60	–	LDC-r	1	1	6	12	18	27	33	38
9	64	–	LDC-r	1	1	5	10	14	20	24	28
10	78	–	C-price 15¢; LDC-r	1	1	4	9	13	18	22	26
11	89	–	LDC-r	1	1	4	8	12	17	21	24
12	117	–	Last LDC-r	1	1	4	7	10	14	17	20
13	135	–	New-c; PC-r	1	2	5	10	15	24	30	35
14	141	–	PC-r	1	2	4	7	9	14	16	18
15	150	–	New-a; PC-r; Severin, L.B. Cole-a	2	2	6	12	18	27	33	38
16	161	–	PC-r	2	2	2	4	6	8	11	14
17	167	–	PC-r	2	2	2	4	6	8	11	14
18	167	6/64	PC-r	2	2	2	4	6	8	11	14
19	167	8/65	PC-r	2	2	2	4	6	8	11	14
20	167	8/66	PC-r	2	2	2	4	6	8	11	14
21	166	R/67	C-price 25¢; PC-r	2	2	2	4	6	8	11	14
22	169	Spr/69	Stiff-c; PC-r	2	2	2	4	6	8	11	14

5. Moby Dick

Ed	HRN	Date	Details	A	C	GD 2.0	VG 4.0	FN 6.0	VF 8.0	VF/NM 9.0	NM- 9.2
1A	(O)	9/42	Date listed-1942; Gilberton; 68 pgs.	1	1	161	322	483	1030	1765	2500
1B			inside-c, rare free promo			245	490	735	1568	2684	3800
2	10	–	Conray Prods; Pg. 64 changed from 105 title list to letter from Editor; CC-r	1	1	28	56	84	165	270	375
3	15	–	Long Isl. Ind. ed.; Pg. 64 changed from Letter to the Editor to Ill. poem-Concord Hymn; CC-r	1	1	23	46	69	136	223	310
4	18/20	–	Sunrise Times ed.; CC-r	1	1	19	38	57	109	172	235
5	20	–	Sunrise Times ed.; CC-r	1	1	18	36	54	105	165	225
6	21	–	Sunrise Times ed.; CC-r	1	1	16	32	48	94	147	200
7	28	1946	CC-r; new banner logo	1	1	14	28	42	81	118	155
8	36	–	1st LDC-r	1	1	9	18	27	47	61	75
9	60	–	LDC-r	1	1	6	12	18	27	33	38
10	62	–	LDC-r	1	1	6	12	18	29	36	42
11	71	–	LDC-r	1	1	5	10	15	22	26	30
12	87	–	C-price 15¢; LDC-r	1	1	5	10	14	20	24	28
13	118	–	LDC-r	1	1	4	8	12	17	21	24
14	131	–	New c&a; PC-r	2	2	5	10	15	25	31	36
15	138	–	PC-r	2	2	2	4	6	9	12	16
16	148	–	PC-r	2	2	2	4	6	9	12	16
17	158	–	PC-r	2	2	2	4	6	9	12	16
18	167	–	PC-r	2	2	2	4	6	8	11	14
19	167	6/64	PC-r	2	2	2	4	6	8	11	14
20	167	7/65	PC-r	2	2	2	4	6	8	11	14
21	167	3/66	PC-r	2	2	2	4	6	8	11	14
22	166	9/67	PC-r	2	2	2	4	6	8	11	14
23	166	Win/69	New-c & c-price 25¢; Stiff-c; PC-r	2	3	3	6	9	16	23	30
24	169	Win/71	PC-r	2	3	3	6	9	14	19	24

6. A Tale of Two Cities

Ed	HRN	Date	Details	A	C	GD 2.0	VG 4.0	FN 6.0	VF 8.0	VF/NM 9.0	NM- 9.2
1	(O)	10/42	Date listed-1942; 68 pgs. Zeckerberg c/a	1	1	129	258	387	826	1413	2000
2	14	–	Elliot Pub; CC-r	1	1	24	48	72	142	234	325
3	18	–	Long Isl. Ind. ed.; CC-r	1	1	20	40	60	114	182	250
4	20	–	Sunrise Times ed.; CC-r	1	1	18	36	54	105	165	225
5	28	1946	Last CC-r; new banner logo	1	1	14	28	42	80	115	150
6	51	–	1st LDC-r	1	1	8	16	24	42	54	65
7	64	–	LDC-r	1	1	5	10	15	23	28	32
8	78	–	C-price 15¢; LDC-r	1	1	5	10	14	20	24	28
9	89	–	LDC-r	1	1	4	7	10	14	17	20
10	117	–	LDC-r	1	1	4	7	10	14	17	20
11	132	–	New-c&a; PC-r; Joe Orlando-a	2	2	5	10	15	25	31	36
12	140	–	PC-r	2	2	2	4	6	8	11	14
13	147	–	PC-r	2	2	2	4	6	8	11	14
14	152	–	PC-r; very rare	2	2	17	34	51	98	154	210
15	153	–	PC-r	2	2	2	4	6	9	13	16
16	149	–	PC-r	2	2	2	4	6	9	13	16
17	167	–	PC-r	2	2	2	4	6	8	11	14
18	167	6/64	PC-r	2	2	2	4	6	8	11	14
19	167	8/65	PC-r	2	2	2	4	6	8	11	14
20	166	5/67	PC-r	2	2	2	4	6	8	11	14
21	166	Fall/68	New-c & 25¢; PC-r	2	3	3	6	9	16	24	32
22	169	Sum/70	Stiff-c; PC-r	2	3	2	4	6	13	18	22

7. Robin Hood

Ed	HRN	Date	Details	A	C	GD 2.0	VG 4.0	FN 6.0	VF 8.0	VF/NM 9.0	NM- 9.2
1	(O)	12/42	Date listed-1942; first Gift Box ad-bc; 68 pgs.	1	1	100	200	300	635	1093	1550
2	12	–	Elliot Pub; CC-r	1	1	24	48	72	140	230	320
3	18	–	Long Isl. Ind. ed.; CC-r	1	1	19	38	57	111	176	240
4	20	–	Nassau Bulletin ed.; CC-r	1	1	18	36	54	103	162	220
5	22	–	Queens Cty. Times ed.; CC-r	1	1	16	32	48	94	147	200
6	28	–	CC-r	1	1	14	28	42	81	118	155
7	51	–	LDC-r	1	1	8	16	24	42	54	65
8	64	–	LDC-r	1	1	5	10	15	24	30	35
9	78	–	LDC-r	1	1	4	9	13	18	22	26
10	97	–	LDC-r	1	1	4	8	12	17	21	24
11	106	–	LDC-r	1	1	4	7	10	14	17	20
12	121	–	LDC-r	1	1	4	7	10	14	17	20
13	129	–	New-c; PC-r	1	2	5	10	15	25	31	36
14	136	–	New-a; PC-r	2	2	5	10	15	24	29	34
15	143	–	PC-r	2	2	2	4	6	9	13	16
16	153	–	PC-r	2	2	2	4	6	9	13	16
17	164	–	PC-r	2	2	2	4	6	8	11	14
18	167	–	PC-r	2	2	2	4	6	8	11	14
19	167	6/64	PC-r	2	2	2	4	6	8	11	14
20	167	5/65	PC-r	2	2	2	4	6	8	11	14
21	167	7/66	PC-r	2	2	2	4	6	8	11	14
22	166	12/67	PC-r	2	2	2	4	6	8	11	14

Classic Comics #9 © GIL

Classic Comics #11 © GIL

Classic Comics #12 © GIL

Ed	HRN	Date	Details	A	C	GD 2.0	VG 4.0	FN 6.0	VF 8.0	VF/NM 9.0	NM- 9.2
23	169	Sum/69	Stiff-c; c-price 25¢; PC-r	2	2	2	4	6	8	11	14

8. Arabian Nights

Ed	HRN	Date	Details	A	C	GD 2.0	VG 4.0	FN 6.0	VF 8.0	VF/NM 9.0	NM- 9.2
1	(O)	2/43	Original; 68 pgs. Lilian Chestney-c/a	1	1	152	304	456	965	1658	2350
2	17	–	Long Isl. ed.; pg. 64 changed from Gift Box ad to Letter from British Medical Worker; CC-r	1	1	52	104	156	323	549	775
3	20	–	Nassau Bulletin; Pg. 64 changed from letter to article-Three Men Named Smith; CC-r	1	1	42	84	126	265	445	625
4A	28	1946	CC-r; new banner logo, slick-c	1	1	31	62	93	182	296	410
4B	28	1946	Same, but w/stiff-c	1	1	31	62	93	182	296	410
5	51	–	LDC-r	1	1	22	44	66	128	209	290
6	64	–	LDC-r	1	1	19	38	57	111	176	240
7	78	–	LDC-r	1	1	18	36	54	105	165	225
8	164	–	New-c&a; PC-r	2	2	15	30	45	90	140	190

9. Les Miserables

Ed	HRN	Date	Details	A	C	GD 2.0	VG 4.0	FN 6.0	VF 8.0	VF/NM 9.0	NM- 9.2
1A	(O)	3/43	Original; slick paper cover; 68 pgs.	1	1	97	194	291	621	1061	1500
1B	(O)	3/43	Original; rough, pulp type-c; 68 pgs.	1	1	116	232	348	742	1271	1800
2	14	–	Elliot Pub; CC-r	1	1	26	52	78	154	252	350
3	18	3/44	Nassau Bul. Pg. 64 changed from Gift Box ad to Bill of Rights article; CC-r	1	1	22	44	66	128	209	290
4	20	–	Richmond Courier ed.; CC-r	1	1	19	38	57	111	176	240
5	28	1946	Gilberton; pgs. 60-64 rearranged/ illos added; CC-r	1	1	14	28	42	81	118	155
6	51	–	LDC-r	1	1	9	18	27	47	61	75
7	71	–	LDC-r	1	1	6	12	18	29	36	42
8	87	–	C-price 15¢; LDC-r	1	1	6	12	18	27	33	38
9	161	–	New-c&a; PC-r	2	2	7	14	21	37	46	55
10	167	9/63	PC-r	2	2	2	4	6	11	16	20
11	167	12/65	PC-r	2	2	2	4	6	11	16	20
12	166	R/1968	New-c & price 25¢; PC-r	2	3	3	6	9	17	26	35

10. Robinson Crusoe (Used in **SOTI**, pg. 142)

Ed	HRN	Date	Details	A	C	GD 2.0	VG 4.0	FN 6.0	VF 8.0	VF/NM 9.0	NM- 9.2
1A	(O)	4/43	Original; Violet-c; 68 pgs; Zuckerberg c/a	1	1	86	172	258	546	936	1325
1B	(O)	4/43	Original; blue-grey-c, 68 pgs.	1	1	94	188	282	597	1024	1450
2A	14	–	Elliot Pub; violet-c; 68 pgs; CC-r	1	1	29	58	87	170	278	385
2B	14	–	Elliot Pub; blue-grey-c; CC-r	1	1	25	50	75	147	241	335
3	18	–	Nassau Bul. Pg. 64 changed from Gift Box ad to Bill of Rights article; CC-r	1	1	19	38	57	111	176	240
4	20	–	Queens Home News ed.; CC-r	1	1	16	32	48	94	147	200
5	28	1946	Gilberton; pg. 64 changes from Bill of Rights to WWII article-One Leg Shot Away; last CC-r	1	1	14	28	42	80	115	150
6	51	–	LDC-r	1	1	8	16	24	42	54	65
7	64	–	LDC-r	1	1	6	12	18	27	33	38
8	78	–	C-price 15¢; LDC-r	1	1	5	10	14	20	24	28
9	97	–	LDC-r	1	1	4	9	13	18	22	26
10	114	–	LDC-r	1	1	4	7	10	14	17	20
11	130	–	New-c; PC-r	1	2	5	10	15	25	31	36
12	140	–	New-a; PC-r	2	2	5	10	15	24	29	34
13	153	–	PC-r	2	2	2	4	6	8	11	14
14	164	–	PC-r	2	2	2	4	6	8	11	14
15	167	–	PC-r	2	2	2	4	6	8	11	14
16	167	7/64	PC-r	2	2	2	4	6	10	14	18
17	167	5/65	PC-r	2	2	2	4	6	10	14	18
18	167	6/66	PC-r	2	2	2	4	6	8	11	14
19	166	Fall/68	C-price 25¢; PC-r	2	2	2	4	6	8	11	14
20	166	R/68	(No Twin Circle ad)	2	2	2	4	6	9	13	16
21	169	Sm/70	Stiff-c; PC-r	2	2	2	4	6	9	13	16

11. Don Quixote

Ed	HRN	Date	Details	A	C	GD 2.0	VG 4.0	FN 6.0	VF 8.0	VF/NM 9.0	NM- 9.2
1	10	5/43	First (O) with HRN list; 68 pgs.	1	1	89	178	267	565	970	1375
2	18	–	Nassau Bulletin ed.; CC-r	1	1	23	46	69	136	223	310
3	21	–	Queens Home News ed.; CC-r	1	1	19	38	57	111	176	240
4	28	–	CC-r	1	1	14	28	42	81	118	155
5	110	–	New-PC; PC-r	1	2	7	14	21	35	43	50
6	156	–	Pgs. reduced 68 to 52; PC-r	1	2	4	7	10	14	17	20
7	165	–	PC-r	1	2	2	4	6	9	13	16
8	167	1/64	PC-r	1	2	2	4	6	9	13	16
9	167	11/65	PC-r	1	2	2	4	6	9	13	16
10	166	R/1968	New-c & price 25¢; PC-r	1	3	3	6	9	18	27	36

12. Rip Van Winkle and the Headless Horseman

Ed	HRN	Date	Details	A	C	GD 2.0	VG 4.0	FN 6.0	VF 8.0	VF/NM 9.0	NM- 9.2
1	11	6/43	Original; 68 pgs.	1	1	92	184	276	584	1005	1425
2	15	–	Long Isl. Ind. ed.; CC-r	1	1	24	48	72	142	234	325
3	20	–	Long Isl. Ind. ed.;	1	1	20	40	60	114	182	250
4	22	–	Queens Cty. Times ed.; CC-r	1	1	16	32	48	94	147	200
5	28	–	CC-r	1	1	14	28	42	80	115	150
6	60	–	1st LDC-r	1	1	8	16	24	40	50	60
7	62	–	LDC-r	1	1	5	10	15	23	28	32
8	71	–	LDC-r	1	1	4	9	13	18	22	26
9	89	–	C-price 15¢; LDC-r	1	1	4	8	12	17	21	24
10	118	–	LDC-r	1	1	4	7	10	14	17	20
11	132	–	New-c; PC-r	1	2	5	10	15	25	31	36
12	150	–	New-a; PC-r	2	2	5	10	15	24	29	34
13	158	–	PC-r	2	2	2	4	6	9	13	16
14	167	–	PC-r	2	2	2	4	6	9	13	16
15	167	12/63	PC-r	2	2	2	4	6	8	11	14
16	167	4/65	PC-r	2	2	2	4	6	8	11	14
17	167	4/66	PC-r	2	2	2	4	6	8	11	14
18	166	R/1968	New-c&price 25¢; PC-r; stiff-c	2	3	3	6	9	14	20	26
19	169	Sm/70	PC-r; stiff-c	2	3	2	4	6	10	14	18

13. Dr. Jekyll and Mr. Hyde (Used in **SOTI**, pg. 143)(1st horror comic?)

Ed	HRN	Date	Details	A	C	GD 2.0	VG 4.0	FN 6.0	VF 8.0	VF/NM 9.0	NM- 9.2
1	12	8/43	Original 60 pgs.	1	1	139	278	417	883	1517	2150
2	15	–	Long Isl. Ind. ed.; CC-r	1	1	36	72	108	211	343	475
3	20	–	Long Isl. Ind. ed.; CC-r	1	1	24	48	72	142	234	325
4	28	–	No c-price; CC-r	1	1	18	36	54	105	165	225
5	60	–	New-c; Pgs. reduced from 60 to 52; H.C. Kiefer-c; LDC-r	1	2	9	18	27	47	61	75
6	62	–	LDC-r	1	2	6	12	18	28	34	40
7	71	–	LDC-r	1	2	5	10	15	23	28	32
8	87	–	Date returns (erroneous); LDC-r	1	2	5	10	15	22	26	30
9	112	–	New-c&a; PC-r; Cameron-a	2	3	7	14	21	35	43	50
10	153	–	PC-r	2	3	2	4	6	9	13	16
11	161	–	PC-r	2	3	2	4	6	9	13	16
12	167	–	PC-r	2	3	2	4	6	8	11	14

Classic Comics #14 © GIL

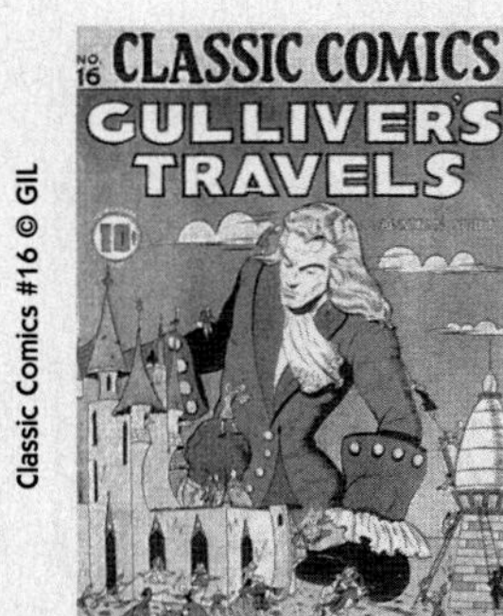

Classic Comics #16 © GIL

Classic Comics #18 © GIL

Ed	HRN	Date	Details	A	C	GD 2.0	VG 4.0	FN 6.0	VF 8.0	VF/NM 9.0	NM- 9.2
13	167	8/64	PC-r	2	3	2	4	6	8	11	14
14	167	11/65	PC-r	2	3	2	4	6	8	11	14
15	166	R/68	C-price 25¢; PC-r	2	3	2	4	6	8	11	14
16	169	Wn/69	PC-r; stiff-c	2	3	2	4	6	8	11	14

14. Westward Ho!

Ed	HRN	Date	Details	A	C	GD 2.0	VG 4.0	FN 6.0	VF 8.0	VF/NM 9.0	NM- 9.2
1	13	9/43	Original; last outside bc coming-next ad; 60 pgs.	1	1	194	388	582	1242	2121	3000
2	15	–	Long Isl. Ind. ed.; CC-r	1	1	58	116	174	371	636	900
3	21	–	Queens Home News; Pg. 56 changed from coming-next ad to Three Men Named Smith; CC-r	1	1	46	92	138	290	488	685
4	28	1946	Gilberton; Pg. 56 changed again to WWII article-Speaking for America; last CC-r	1	1	39	78	117	242	401	560
5	53	–	Pgs. reduced from 60 to 52; LDC-r	1	1	36	72	108	216	351	485

15. Uncle Tom's Cabin (Used in **SOTI**, pgs. 102, 103)

Ed	HRN	Date	Details	A	C	GD 2.0	VG 4.0	FN 6.0	VF 8.0	VF/NM 9.0	NM- 9.2
1	14	11/43	Original; Outside-bc ad: 2 Gift Boxes; 60 pgs.; color var. on-c; green trunk,root on left & brown trunk, root on left	1	1	82	164	246	528	902	1275
2	15	–	Long Isl. Ind. listed- bottom inside-fc; also Gilberton listed bottom-pg. 1; CC-r; portion of root to the left of the price circle can be green or brown	1	1	26	52	78	154	252	350
3	21	–	Nassau Bulletin ed.; CC-r	1	1	20	40	60	117	189	260
4	28	–	No c-price; CC-r	1	1	14	28	42	82	121	160
5	53	–	Pgs. reduced 60 to 52; LDC-r	1	1	8	16	24	42	54	65
6	71	–	LDC-r	1	1	6	12	18	27	33	38
7	89	–	C-price 15¢; LDC-r	1	1	5	10	15	24	30	35
8	117	–	New-c/lettering changes; PC-r	1	2	5	10	15	25	31	36
9	128	–	'Picture Progress' promo; PC-r	1	2	2	4	6	10	14	18
10	137	–	PC-r	1	2	2	4	6	9	13	16
11	146	–	PC-r	1	2	2	4	6	9	13	16
12	154	–	PC-r	1	2	2	4	6	9	13	16
13	161	–	PC-r	1	2	2	4	6	8	11	14
14	167	–	PC-r	1	2	2	4	6	8	11	14
15	167	6/64	PC-r	1	2	2	4	6	8	11	14
16	167	5/65	PC-r	1	2	2	4	6	8	11	14
17	166	5/67	PC-r	1	2	2	4	6	8	11	14
18	166	Wn/69	New-stiff-c; PC-r	1	3	3	6	9	15	22	28
19	169	Sm/70	PC-r; stiff-c	1	3	2	4	6	10	14	18

16. Gulliver's Travels

Ed	HRN	Date	Details	A	C	GD 2.0	VG 4.0	FN 6.0	VF 8.0	VF/NM 9.0	NM- 9.2
1	15	12/43	Original-Lilian Chestney c/a; 60 pgs.	1	1	77	154	231	493	847	1200
2	18/20	–	Price deleted; Queens Home News ed; CC-r	1	1	22	44	66	128	209	290
3	22	–	Queens Cty. Times ed.; CC-r	1	1	18	36	54	105	165	225
4	28	–	CC-r	1	1	14	28	42	80	115	150
5	60	–	Pgs. reduced to 48; LDC-r	1	1	6	12	18	31	38	45
6	62	–	LDC-r	1	1	5	10	15	23	28	32
7	78	–	C-price 15¢; LDC-r	1	1	5	10	14	20	24	28
8	89	–	LDC-r	1	1	4	8	12	17	21	24
9	155	–	New-c; PC-r	1	2	5	10	15	25	31	36
10	165	–	PC-r	1	2	2	4	6	8	11	14
11	167	5/64	PC-r	1	2	2	4	6	8	11	14
12	167	11/65	PC-r	1	2	2	4	6	8	11	14
13	166	R/1968	C-price 25¢; PC-r	1	2	2	4	6	8	11	14
14	169	Wn/69	PC-r; stiff-c	1	2	2	4	6	8	11	14

17. The Deerslayer

Ed	HRN	Date	Details	A	C	GD 2.0	VG 4.0	FN 6.0	VF 8.0	VF/NM 9.0	NM- 9.2
1	16	1/44	Original; Outside-bc ad: 3 Gift Boxes; 60 pgs.	1	1	66	132	198	419	872	1025
2A	18	–	Queens Cty Times (inside-fc); CC-r	1	1	23	46	69	136	223	310
2B	18	–	Gilberton (bottom-pg. 1); CC-r; Scarce	1	1	33	66	99	194	317	440
3	22	–	Queens Cty. Times ed.; CC-r	1	1	19	38	57	109	172	235
4	28	–	CC-r	1	1	14	28	42	81	118	155
5	60	–	Pgs.reduced to 52; LDC-r	1	1	7	14	21	37	46	55
6	64	–	LDC-r	1	1	5	10	15	22	26	30
7	85	–	C-price 15¢; LDC-r	1	1	4	8	12	17	21	24
8	118	–	LDC-r	1	1	4	7	10	14	17	20
9	132	–	LDC-r	1	1	4	7	10	14	17	20
10	167	11/66	Last LDC-r	1	1	2	4	6	11	16	20
11	166	R/1968	New-c & price 25¢; PC-r	1	2	3	6	9	17	26	35
12	169	Spr/71	Stiff-c; letters from parents & educators; PC-r	1	2	2	4	6	10	14	18

18. The Hunchback of Notre Dame

Ed	HRN	Date	Details	A	C	GD 2.0	VG 4.0	FN 6.0	VF 8.0	VF/NM 9.0	NM- 9.2
1A	17	3/44	Orig.; Gilberton ed; 60 pgs.	1	1	94	188	282	597	1024	1450
1B	17	3/44	Orig.; Island Pub. Ed.; 60 pgs.	1	1	84	168	252	538	919	1300
2	18/20	–	Queens Home News ed.; CC-r	1	1	28	56	84	165	270	375
3	22	--	Queens Cty. Times ed.; CC-r	1	1	22	44	66	132	216	300
4	28	–	CC-r	1	1	21	42	63	122	199	275
5	60	–	New-c; 8pgs. deleted; Kiefer-c; LDC-r	1	2	9	18	27	50	65	80
6	62	–	LDC-r	1	2	5	10	15	22	26	30
7	78	–	C-price 15¢; LDC-r	1	2	5	10	14	20	24	28
8A	89	–	H.C.Kiefer on bottom right-fc; LDC-r	1	2	4	9	13	18	22	26
8B	89	–	Name omitted; LDC-r	1	2	5	10	15	24	30	35
9	118	–	LDC-r	1	2	4	8	12	17	21	24
10	140	–	New-c; PC-r	1	3	7	14	21	35	43	50
11	146	–	PC-r	1	3	4	9	13	18	22	26
12	158	–	New-c&a; PC-r; Evans/Crandall-a	2	4	5	10	15	25	31	36
13	165	–	PC-r	2	4	2	4	6	9	13	16
14	167	9/63	PC-r	2	4	2	4	6	9	13	16
15	167	10/64	PC-r	2	4	2	4	6	9	13	16
16	167	4/66	PC-r	2	4	2	4	6	8	11	14
17	166	R/1968	New price 25¢; PC-r	2	4	2	4	6	8	11	14
18	169	Sp/70	Stiff-c; PC-r	2	4	2	4	6	8	11	14

19. Huckleberry Finn

Ed	HRN	Date	Details	A	C	GD 2.0	VG 4.0	FN 6.0	VF 8.0	VF/NM 9.0	NM- 9.2
1A	18	4/44	Orig.; Gilberton ed.; 60 pgs.	1	1	54	108	162	343	574	825
1B	18	4/44	Orig.; Island Pub.; 60 pgs.	1	1	57	114	171	362	619	875
2	18	–	Nassau Bulletin ed.; fc-price 15¢-Canada; no coming-next ad; CC-r	1	1	23	46	69	136	223	310
3	22	–	Queens City Times ed.; CC-r	1	1	19	38	57	111	176	240

Classic Comics #20 © GIL

Classic Comics #23 © GIL

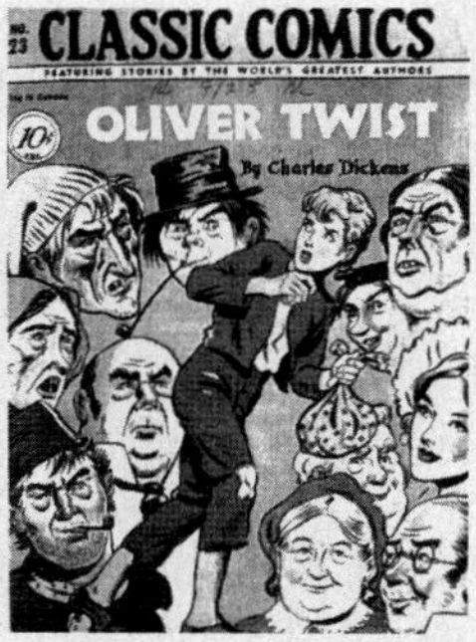

Classic Comics #25 © GIL

Ed	HRN	Date	Details	A	C	GD 2.0	VG 4.0	FN 6.0	VF 8.0	VF/NM 9.0	NM- 9.2
4	28	–	CC-r	1	1	14	28	42	80	115	150
5	60	–	Pgs. reduced to 48; LDC-r	1	1	6	12	18	31	38	45
6	62	–	LDC-r	1	1	5	10	15	23	28	32
7	78	–	LDC-r	1	1	4	9	13	18	22	26
8	89	–	LDC-r	1	1	4	8	12	17	21	24
9	117	–	LDC-r	1	1	4	7	10	14	17	20
10	131	–	New-c&a; PC-r	2	2	5	10	15	24	30	35
11	140	–	PC-r	2	2	2	4	6	9	13	16
12	150	–	PC-r	2	2	2	4	6	9	13	16
13	158	–	PC-r	2	2	2	4	6	9	13	16
14	165	–	PC-r (scarce)	2	2	3	6	9	14	19	24
15	167	–	PC-r	2	2	2	4	6	8	11	14
16	167	6/64	PC-r	2	2	2	4	6	8	11	14
17	167	6/65	PC-r	2	2	2	4	6	8	11	14
18	167	10/65	PC-r	2	2	2	4	6	8	11	14
19	166	9/67	PC-r	2	2	2	4	6	8	11	14
20	166	Win/69	C-price 25¢; PC-r; stiff-c	2	2	2	4	6	8	11	14
21	169	Sm/70	PC-r; stiff-c	2	2	2	4	6	8	11	14

20. The Corsican Brothers

Ed	HRN	Date	Details	A	C	GD 2.0	VG 4.0	FN 6.0	VF 8.0	VF/NM 9.0	NM- 9.2
1A	20	6/44	Orig.; Gilberton ed.; bc-ad: 4 Gift Boxes; 60 pgs.	1	1	48	96	114	302	514	725
1B	20	6/44	Orig.; Courier ed.; 60 pgs.	1	1	41	82	123	256	428	600
1C	20	6/44	Orig.; Long Island Ind. ed.; 60 pgs.	1	1	41	82	123	256	428	600
2	22	–	Queens Cty. Times ed.; white logo banner; CC-r	1	1	20	40	60	114	182	250
3	28	–	CC-r	1	1	19	38	57	109	172	235
4	60	–	CI logo; no price; 48 pgs.; LDC-r	1	1	15	30	45	90	140	190
5A	62	–	LDC-r; Classics Ill. logo at top of pgs.	1	1	15	30	45	83	124	165
5B	62	–	w/o logo at top of pg. (scarcer)	1	1	15	30	45	86	133	180
6	78	–	C-price 15¢; LDC-r	1	1	14	28	42	81	118	155
7	97	–	LDC-r	1	1	14	28	42	78	112	145

21. 3 Famous Mysteries ("The Sign of the 4", "The Murders in the Rue Morgue", "The Flayed Hand")

Ed	HRN	Date	Details	A	C	GD 2.0	VG 4.0	FN 6.0	VF 8.0	VF/NM 9.0	NM- 9.2
1A	21	7/44	Orig.; Gilberton ed.; 60 pgs.	1	1	98	196	294	630	1078	1525
1B	21	7/44	Orig. Island Pub. Co.; 60 pgs.	1	1	102	204	306	650	1113	1575
1C	21	7/44	Original; Courier Ed.; 60 pgs.	1	1	89	178	267	565	970	1375
2	22	–	Nassau Bulletin ed.; CC-r	1	1	40	80	120	244	402	560
3	30	–	CC-r	1	1	28	56	84	165	270	375
4	62	–	LDC-r; 8 pgs. deleted; LDC-r	1	1	22	44	66	128	209	290
5	70	–	LDC-r	1	1	20	40	60	117	189	260
6	85	–	C-price 15¢; LDC-r	1	1	18	36	54	107	169	230
7	114	–	New-c; PC-r	1	2	18	36	54	107	169	230

22. The Pathfinder

Ed	HRN	Date	Details	A	C	GD 2.0	VG 4.0	FN 6.0	VF 8.0	VF/NM 9.0	NM- 9.2
1A	22	10/44	Orig.; No printer listed; ownership statement inside fc lists Gilberton & date; 60 pgs.	1	1	47	94	141	296	498	700
1B	22	10/44	Orig.; Island Pub. ed.; 60 pgs.	1	1	41	82	123	256	428	600
1C	22	10/44	Orig.; Queens Cty Times ed. 60 pgs.	1	1	41	82	123	256	428	600
2	30	–	C-price removed; CC-r	1	1	15	30	45	85	130	175
3	60	–	Pgs. reduced to 52; LDC-r	1	1	6	12	18	27	33	38
4	70	–	LDC-r	1	1	5	10	15	22	26	30
5	85	–	C-price 15¢; LDC-r	1	1	4	9	13	18	22	26
6	118	–	LDC-r	1	1	4	8	12	17	21	24
7	132	–	LDC-r	1	1	4	7	10	14	17	20
8	146	–	LDC-r	1	1	4	7	10	14	17	20
9	167	11/63	New-c; PC-r	1	2	4	8	12	23	37	50
10	167	12/65	PC-r	1	2	2	4	6	11	16	20
11	166	8/67	PC-r	1	2	2	4	6	11	16	20

23. Oliver Twist (1st Classic produced by the Iger Shop)

Ed	HRN	Date	Details	A	C	GD 2.0	VG 4.0	FN 6.0	VF 8.0	VF/NM 9.0	NM- 9.2
1	23	7/45	Original; 60 pgs.	1	1	47	94	141	296	498	700
2A	30	–	Printers Union logo on bottom left-fc same as 23(Orig.) (very rare); CC-r	1	1	30	60	90	177	289	400
2B	30	–	Union logo omitted; CC-r	1	1	15	30	45	84	127	170
3	60	–	Pgs. reduced to 48; LDC-r	1	1	6	12	18	29	36	42
4	62	–	LDC-r	1	1	5	10	15	23	28	32
5	71	–	LDC-r	1	1	5	10	14	20	24	28
6	85	–	C-price 15¢; LDC-r	1	1	4	9	13	18	22	26
7	94	–	LDC-r	1	1	4	7	10	14	17	20
8	118	–	LDC-r	1	1	4	7	10	14	17	20
9	136	–	New-PC, old-a; PC-r	1	2	5	10	15	24	30	35
10	150	–	Old-a; PC-r	1	2	4	7	10	14	17	20
11	164	–	Old-a; PC-r	1	2	4	8	11	16	19	22
12	164	–	New-a; PC-r; Evans/Crandall-a	2	2	4	8	12	23	37	50
13	167	–	PC-r	2	2	2	4	6	11	16	20
14	167	8/64	PC-r	2	2	2	4	6	8	11	14
15	167	12/65	PC-r	2	2	2	4	6	8	11	14
16	166	R/1968	New 25¢; PC-r	2	2	2	4	6	8	11	14
17	169	Win/69	Stiff-c; PC-r	2	2	2	4	6	8	11	14

24. A Connecticut Yankee in King Arthur's Court

Ed	HRN	Date	Details	A	C	GD 2.0	VG 4.0	FN 6.0	VF 8.0	VF/NM 9.0	NM- 9.2
1	–	9/45	Original	1	1	41	82	123	256	428	600
2	30	–	No price circle; CC-r	1	1	15	30	45	84	127	170
3	60	–	8 pgs. deleted; LDC-r	1	1	6	12	18	27	33	38
4	62	–	LDC-r	1	1	5	10	15	23	28	32
5	71	–	LDC-r	1	1	5	10	15	22	26	30
6	87	–	C-price 15¢; LDC-r	1	1	4	9	13	18	22	26
7	121	–	LDC-r	1	1	4	8	12	17	21	24
8	140	–	New-c&a; PC-r	2	2	5	10	15	25	31	36
9	153	–	PC-r	2	2	2	4	6	9	13	16
10	164	–	PC-r	2	2	2	4	6	8	11	14
11	167	–	PC-r	2	2	2	4	6	8	11	14
12	167	7/64	PC-r	2	2	2	4	6	8	11	14
13	167	6/66	PC-r	2	2	2	4	6	8	11	14
14	166	R/1968	C-price 25¢; PC-r	2	2	2	4	6	8	11	14
15	169	Spr/71	PC-r; stiff-c	2	2	2	4	6	8	11	14

25. Two Years Before the Mast

Ed	HRN	Date	Details	A	C	GD 2.0	VG 4.0	FN 6.0	VF 8.0	VF/NM 9.0	NM- 9.2
1	–	10/45	Original; Webb/Heames-a&c	1	1	41	82	123	256	428	600
2	30	–	Price circle blank; CC-r	1	1	15	30	45	84	127	170
3	60	–	8 pgs. deleted; LDC-r	1	1	6	12	18	27	33	38
4	62	–	LDC-r	1	1	5	10	15	23	28	32
5	71	–	LDC-r	1	1	4	9	13	18	22	26
6	85	–	C-price 15¢; LDC-r	1	1	4	8	12	17	21	24
7	114	–	LDC-r	1	1	4	7	10	14	17	20
8	156	–	3 pgs. replaced by fillers; new-c; PC-r	1	2	5	10	15	25	31	36
9	167	12/63	PC-r	1	2	2	4	6	8	11	14
10	167	12/65	PC-r	1	2	2	4	6	8	11	14
11	166	9/67	PC-r	1	2	2	4	6	8	11	14
12	169	Win/69	C-price 25¢; stiff-c PC-r	1	2	2	4	6	8	11	14

Classic Comics #27 © GIL

Classic Comics #29 © GIL

Classic Comics #33 © GIL

26. Frankenstein (2nd horror comic?)

Ed	HRN	Date	Details	A	C	GD 2.0	VG 4.0	FN 6.0	VF 8.0	VF/NM 9.0	NM- 9.2
1	26	12/45	Orig.; Webb/Brewster a&c; 52 pgs.	1	1	115	230	345	730	1253	1775
2A	30	–	Price circle blank; no indicia; CC-r	1	1	32	64	96	192	314	435
2B	30	–	With indicia; scarce; CC-r	1	1	37	74	111	222	361	500
3	60	–	LDC-r	1	1	17	34	51	98	154	210
4	62	–	LDC-r	1	1	15	30	45	88	137	185
5	71	–	LDC-r	1	1	8	16	24	42	54	65
6A	82	–	C-price 15¢; soft-c LDC-r	1	1	7	14	21	37	46	55
6B	82	–	Stiff-c; LDC-r	1	1	8	16	24	42	54	65
7	117	–	LDC-r	1	1	5	10	15	22	26	30
8	146	–	New Saunders-c; PC-r	1	2	6	12	18	31	38	45
9	152	–	Scarce; PC-r	1	2	8	16	24	42	54	65
10	153	–	PC-r	1	2	2	4	6	10	14	18
11	160	–	PC-r	1	2	2	4	6	10	14	18
12	165	–	PC-r	1	2	2	4	6	9	13	16
13	167	–	PC-r	1	2	2	4	6	9	13	16
14	167	6/64	PC-r	1	2	2	4	6	9	13	16
15	167	6/65	PC-r	1	2	2	4	6	9	13	16
16	167	10/65	PC-r	1	2	2	4	6	9	13	16
17	166	9/67	PC-r	1	2	2	4	6	9	13	16
18	169	Fall/69	C-price 25¢; stiff-c PC-r	1	2	2	4	6	9	13	16
19	169	Spr/71	PC-r; stiff-c	1	2	2	4	6	9	13	16

27. The Adventures of Marco Polo

Ed	HRN	Date	Details	A	C	GD 2.0	VG 4.0	FN 6.0	VF 8.0	VF/NM 9.0	NM- 9.2
1	–	4/46	Original	1	1	41	82	123	256	428	600
2	30	–	Last 'Comics' reprint; CC-r	1	1	15	30	45	84	127	170
3	70	–	8 pgs. deleted; no c-price; LDC-r	1	1	5	10	15	24	30	35
4	87	–	C-price 15¢; LDC-r	1	1	4	9	13	18	22	26
5	117	–	LDC-r	1	1	4	7	10	14	17	20
6	154	–	New-c; PC-r	1	2	5	10	15	24	30	35
7	165	–	PC-r	1	2	2	4	6	8	11	14
8	167	4/64	PC-r	1	2	2	4	6	8	11	14
9	167	6/66	PC-r	1	2	2	4	6	8	11	14
10	169	Spr/69	New price 25¢; stiff-c; PC-r	1	2	2	4	6	8	11	14

28. Michael Strogoff

Ed	HRN	Date	Details	A	C	GD 2.0	VG 4.0	FN 6.0	VF 8.0	VF/NM 9.0	NM- 9.2
1	–	6/46	Original	1	1	41	82	123	256	428	600
2	51	–	8 pgs. cut; LDC-r	1	1	15	30	45	84	127	170
3	115	–	New-c; PC-r	1	2	6	12	18	31	38	45
4	155	–	PC-r	1	2	4	7	10	14	17	20
5	167	11/63	PC-r	1	2	2	4	6	9	13	16
6	167	7/66	PC-r	1	2	2	4	6	9	13	16
7	169	Sm/69	C-price 25¢; stiff-c PC-r	1	3	3	6	9	15	21	26

29. The Prince and the Pauper

Ed	HRN	Date	Details	A	C	GD 2.0	VG 4.0	FN 6.0	VF 8.0	VF/NM 9.0	NM- 9.2
1	–	7/46	Orig.; "Horror"-c	1	1	60	120	180	381	653	925
2	60	–	8 pgs. cut; new-c by Kiefer; LDC-r	1	2	9	18	27	52	69	85
3	62	–	LDC-r	1	2	5	10	15	24	30	35
4	71	–	LDC-r	1	2	4	9	13	18	22	26
5	93	–	LDC-r	1	2	4	8	12	17	21	24
6	114	–	LDC-r	1	2	4	7	10	14	17	20
7	128	–	New-c; PC-r	1	3	5	10	15	24	30	35
8	138	–	PC-r	1	3	2	4	6	9	13	16
9	150	–	PC-r	1	3	2	4	6	9	13	16
10	164	–	PC-r	1	3	2	4	6	8	11	14
11	167	–	PC-r	1	3	2	4	6	8	11	14
12	167	7/64	PC-r	1	3	2	4	6	8	11	14
13	167	11/65	PC-r	1	3	2	4	6	8	11	14
14	166	R/68	C-price 25¢; PC-r	1	3	2	4	6	8	11	14
15	169	Sm/70	PC-r; stiff-c	1	3	2	4	6	8	11	14

30. The Moonstone

Ed	HRN	Date	Details	A	C	GD 2.0	VG 4.0	FN 6.0	VF 8.0	VF/NM 9.0	NM- 9.2
1	–	9/46	Original; Rico-c/a	1	1	41	82	123	256	428	600
2	60	–	LDC-r; 8pgs. cut	1	1	9	18	27	50	65	80
3	70	–	LDC-r	1	1	8	16	24	42	54	65
4	155	–	New L.B. Cole-c; PC-r	1	2	4	8	12	28	44	60
5	165	–	PC-r; L.B. Cole-c	1	2	3	6	9	16	23	30
6	167	1/64	PC-r; L.B. Cole-c	1	2	2	4	6	11	16	20
7	167	9/65	PC-r; L.B. Cole-c	1	2	2	4	6	10	14	18
8	166	R/1968	C-price 25¢; PC-r	1	2	2	4	6	9	13	16

31. The Black Arrow

Ed	HRN	Date	Details	A	C	GD 2.0	VG 4.0	FN 6.0	VF 8.0	VF/NM 9.0	NM- 9.2
1	30	10/46	Original	1	1	39	78	117	235	385	535
2	51	–	CI logo; LDC-r 8pgs. deleted	1	1	6	12	18	33	41	48
3	64	–	LDC-r	1	1	4	9	13	18	22	26
4	87	–	C-price 15¢; LDC-r	1	1	4	8	12	17	21	24
5	108	–	LDC-r	1	1	4	7	10	14	17	20
6	125	–	LDC-r	1	1	4	7	10	14	17	20
7	131	–	New-c; PC-r	1	2	5	10	15	24	30	35
8	140	–	PC-r	1	2	2	4	6	9	13	16
9	148	–	PC-r	1	2	2	4	6	9	13	16
10	161	–	PC-r	1	2	2	4	6	8	11	14
11	167	–	PC-r	1	2	2	4	6	8	11	14
12	167	7/64	PC-r	1	2	2	4	6	8	11	14
13	167	11/65	PC-r	1	2	2	4	6	8	11	14
14	166	R/1968	C-price 25¢; PC-r	1	2	2	4	6	8	11	14

32. Lorna Doone

Ed	HRN	Date	Details	A	C	GD 2.0	VG 4.0	FN 6.0	VF 8.0	VF/NM 9.0	NM- 9.2
1	–	12/46	Original; Matt Baker c&a	1	1	41	82	123	250	418	585
2	53/64	–	8 pgs. deleted; LDC-r	1	1	9	18	27	47	61	75
3	85	1951	C-price 15¢; LDC-r; Baker c&a	1	1	7	14	21	37	46	55
4	118	–	LDC-r	1	1	4	9	13	18	22	26
5	138	–	New-c; old-c becomes new title pg.; PC-r	1	2	6	12	18	28	34	40
6	150	–	PC-r	1	2	2	4	6	8	11	14
7	165	–	PC-r	1	2	2	4	6	8	11	14
8	167	1/64	PC-r	1	2	2	4	6	9	13	16
9	167	11/65	PC-r	1	2	2	4	6	9	13	16
10	166	R/1968	New-c; PC-r	1	3	3	6	9	16	24	32

33. The Adventures of Sherlock Holmes

Ed	HRN	Date	Details	A	C	GD 2.0	VG 4.0	FN 6.0	VF 8.0	VF/NM 9.0	NM- 9.2
1	33	1/47	Original; Kiefer-c; contains Study in Scarlet & Hound of the Baskervilles; 68 pgs.	1	1	132	264	396	838	1444	2050
2	53	–	"A Study in Scarlet" (17 pgs.) deleted; LDC-r	1	1	48	96	144	302	514	725
3	71	–	LDC-r	1	1	39	78	117	231	378	525
4A	89	–	C-price 15¢; LDC-r	1	1	30	60	90	117	289	400
4B	89	–	Kiefer's name omitted from-c	1	1	31	62	93	186	303	420

34. Mysterious Island (Last "Classic Comic")

Ed	HRN	Date	Details	A	C	GD 2.0	VG 4.0	FN 6.0	VF 8.0	VF/NM 9.0	NM- 9.2
1	35	2/47	Original; Webb/ Heames-c/a	1	1	41	82	123	250	418	585
2	60	–	8 pgs. deleted; LDC-r	1	1	7	14	21	37	46	55
3	62	–	LDC-r	1	1	5	10	15	23	28	32
4	71	–	LDC-r	1	1	6	12	18	31	38	45
5	78	–	C-price 15¢ in circle; LDC-r	1	1	5	10	14	20	24	28
6	92	–	LDC-r	1	1	4	9	13	18	22	26
7	117	–	LDC-r	1	1	4	7	10	14	17	20
8	140	–	New-c; PC-r	1	2	5	10	15	24	30	35
9	156	–	PC-r	1	2	2	4	6	9	13	16
10	167	10/63	PC-r	1	2	2	4	6	8	11	14

Classics Illustrated #37 © GIL

Classics Illustrated #39 © GIL

Classics Illustrated #44 © GIL

Ed	HRN	Date	Details	A	C	GD 2.0	VG 4.0	FN 6.0	VF 8.0	VF/NM 9.0	NM- 9.2
11	167	5/64	PC-r	1	2	2	4	6	8	11	14
12	167	6/66	PC-r	1	2	2	4	6	8	11	14
13	166	R/1968	C-price 25¢; PC-r	1	2	2	4	6	8	11	14

35. Last Days of Pompeii (First "Classics Illustrated")

Ed	HRN	Date	Details	A	C	GD 2.0	VG 4.0	FN 6.0	VF 8.0	VF/NM 9.0	NM- 9.2
1	35	3/47	Original; LDC; Kiefer-c/a	1	1	41	82	123	250	418	585
2	161	–	New c&a; 15¢; PC-r; Kirby/Ayers-a	2	2	5	10	15	32	51	70
3	167	1/64	PC-r	2	2	3	6	9	16	22	28
4	167	7/66	PC-r	2	2	3	6	9	16	22	28
5	169	Spr/70	New price 25¢; stiff-c; PC-r	2	2	3	6	9	16	22	28

36. Typee

Ed	HRN	Date	Details	A	C	GD 2.0	VG 4.0	FN 6.0	VF 8.0	VF/NM 9.0	NM- 9.2
1	36	4/47	Original	1	1	29	58	87	170	278	385
2	64	–	No c-price; 8 pg. ed.; LDC-r	1	1	7	14	21	37	46	55
3	155	–	New-c; PC-r	1	2	5	10	15	24	30	35
4	167	9/63	PC-r	1	2	2	4	6	9	13	16
5	167	7/65	PC-r	1	2	2	4	6	9	13	16
6	169	Sm/69	C-price 25¢; stiff-c PC-r	1	2	2	4	6	9	13	16

37. The Pioneers

Ed	HRN	Date	Details	A	C	GD 2.0	VG 4.0	FN 6.0	VF 8.0	VF/NM 9.0	NM- 9.2
1	37	5/47	Original; Palais-c/a	1	1	27	54	81	158	259	360
2A	62	–	8 pgs. cut; LDC-r; price circle blank	1	1	6	12	18	28	34	40
2B	62	–	10¢; LDC-r;	1	1	29	58	87	170	278	385
3	70	–	LDC-r	1	1	4	8	12	17	21	24
4	92	–	15¢; LDC-r	1	1	4	8	11	16	19	22
5	118	–	LDC-r	1	1	4	7	10	14	17	20
6	131	–	LDC-r	1	1	4	7	10	14	17	20
7	132	–	LDC-r	1	1	4	7	10	14	17	20
8	153	–	LDC-r	1	1	4	7	10	14	17	20
9	167	5/64	LDC-r	1	1	2	4	6	9	13	16
10	167	6/66	LDC-r	1	1	2	4	6	9	13	16
11	166	R/1968	New-c; 25¢; PC-r	1	2	3	6	9	18	27	36

38. Adventures of Cellini

Ed	HRN	Date	Details	A	C	GD 2.0	VG 4.0	FN 6.0	VF 8.0	VF/NM 9.0	NM- 9.2
1	–	6/47	Original; Froehlich c/a	1	1	32	64	96	192	314	435
2	164	–	New-c&a; PC-r	2	2	3	6	9	18	27	36
3	167	12/63	PC-r	2	2	2	4	6	10	14	18
4	167	7/66	PC-r	2	2	2	4	6	10	14	18
5	169	Spr/70	Stiff-c; new price 25¢; PC-r	2	2	2	4	6	11	16	20

39. Jane Eyre

Ed	HRN	Date	Details	A	C	GD 2.0	VG 4.0	FN 6.0	VF 8.0	VF/NM 9.0	NM- 9.2
1	–	7/47	Original	1	1	31	62	93	186	303	420
2	60	–	No c-price; 8 pgs. cut; LDC-r	1	1	6	12	18	31	38	45
3	62	–	LDC-r	1	1	5	10	15	24	30	35
4	71	–	LDC-r; c-price 10¢	1	1	5	10	15	22	26	30
5	92	–	C-price 15¢; LDC-r	1	1	4	9	13	18	22	26
6	118	–	LDC-r	1	1	4	8	12	17	21	24
7	142	–	New-c; old-a; PC-r	1	2	6	12	18	28	34	40
8	154	–	Old-a; PC-r	1	2	4	8	12	17	21	24
9	165	–	New-a; PC-r	2	2	3	6	9	17	26	35
10	167	12/63	PC-r	2	2	3	6	9	14	19	24
11	167	4/65	PC-r	2	2	2	4	6	13	18	22
12	167	8/66	PC-r	2	2	2	4	6	13	18	22
13	166	R/1968	New-c; PC-r	2	3	5	10	15	31	53	75

40. Mysteries ("The Pit and the Pendulum", "The Advs. of Hans Pfall" & "The Fall of the House of Usher")

Ed	HRN	Date	Details	A	C	GD 2.0	VG 4.0	FN 6.0	VF 8.0	VF/NM 9.0	NM- 9.2
1	40	8/47	Original; Kiefer-c/a, Froehlich, Griffiths-a	1	1	58	116	174	371	636	900
2	62	–	LDC-r; 8pgs. cut	1	1	24	48	72	142	234	325
3	75	–	LDC-r	1	1	19	38	57	111	176	240
4	92	–	C-price 15¢; LDC-r	1	1	15	30	45	94	147	200

41. Twenty Years After

Ed	HRN	Date	Details	A	C	GD 2.0	VG 4.0	FN 6.0	VF 8.0	VF/NM 9.0	NM- 9.2
1	–	9/47	Original; 'horror'-c	1	1	39	78	117	235	385	535
2	62	–	New-c; no c-price 8 pgs. cut; LDC-r; Kiefer-c	1	2	7	14	21	37	46	55
3	78	–	C-price 15¢; LDC-r	1	2	5	10	15	23	28	32
4	156	–	New-c; PC-r	1	3	5	10	15	24	30	35
5	167	12/63	PC-r	1	3	2	4	6	8	11	14
6	167	11/66	PC-r	1	3	2	4	6	8	11	14
7	169	Spr/70	New price 25¢; stiff-c; PC-r	1	3	2	4	6	8	11	14

42. Swiss Family Robinson

Ed	HRN	Date	Details	A	C	GD 2.0	VG 4.0	FN 6.0	VF 8.0	VF/NM 9.0	NM- 9.2
1	42	10/47	Orig.; Kiefer-c&a;	1	1	24	48	72	140	230	320
2A	62	–	8 pgs. cut; outside bc: Gift Box ad; LDC-r	1	1	6	12	18	31	38	45
2B	62	–	8 pgs. cut; outside-bc: Reorder list; scarce; LDC-r	1	1	10	20	30	58	79	100
3	75	–	LDC-r	1	1	5	10	14	20	24	28
4	93	–	LDC-r	1	1	5	10	14	20	24	28
5	117	–	LDC-r	1	1	3	6	9	14	19	24
6	131	–	New-c; old-a; PC-r	1	2	3	6	9	15	21	26
7	137	–	Old-a; PC-r	1	2	2	4	6	10	14	18
8	141	–	Old-a; PC-r	1	2	2	4	6	10	14	18
9	152	–	New-a; PC-r	2	2	3	6	9	16	23	30
10	158	–	PC-r	2	2	2	4	6	8	11	14
11	165	–	PC-r	2	2	3	6	9	16	24	32
12	167	12/63	PC-r	2	2	2	4	6	8	11	14
13	167	4/65	PC-r	2	2	2	4	6	8	11	14
14	167	5/66	PC-r	2	2	2	4	6	8	11	14
15	166	11/67	PC-r	2	2	2	4	6	8	11	14
16	169	Spr/69	PC-r; stiff-c	2	2	2	4	6	8	11	14

43. Great Expectations (Used in **SOTI**, pg. 311)

Ed	HRN	Date	Details	A	C	GD 2.0	VG 4.0	FN 6.0	VF 8.0	VF/NM 9.0	NM- 9.2
1	43	11/47	Original; Kiefer-a/c	1	1	90	180	270	576	988	1400
2	62	–	No c-price; 8 pgs. cut; LDC-r	1	1	57	114	171	362	624	885

44. Mysteries of Paris (Used in **SOTI**, pg. 323)

Ed	HRN	Date	Details	A	C	GD 2.0	VG 4.0	FN 6.0	VF 8.0	VF/NM 9.0	NM- 9.2
1A	44	12/47	Original; 56 pgs.; Kiefer-c/a	1	1	65	130	195	416	708	1000
1B	44	12/47	Orig.; printed on white/heavier paper; (rare)	1	1	76	152	228	486	831	1175
2A	62	–	8 pgs. cut; outside-bc: Gift Box ad; LDC-r	1	1	30	60	90	177	289	400
2B	62	–	8 pgs. cut; outside-bc: reorder list; LDC-r	1	1	30	60	90	177	289	400
3	78	–	C-price 15¢; LDC-r	1	1	25	50	75	147	241	335

45. Tom Brown's School Days

Ed	HRN	Date	Details	A	C	GD 2.0	VG 4.0	FN 6.0	VF 8.0	VF/NM 9.0	NM- 9.2
1	44	1/48	Original; 1st 48pg. issue	1	1	20	40	60	114	182	250
2	64	–	No c-price; LDC-r	1	1	7	14	21	35	43	50
3	161	–	New-c&a; PC-r	2	2	3	6	9	16	24	32
4	167	2/64	PC-r	2	2	2	4	6	9	13	16
5	167	8/66	PC-r	2	2	2	4	6	9	13	16
6	166	R/1968	C-price 25¢; PC-r	2	2	2	4	6	9	13	16

46. Kidnapped

Ed	HRN	Date	Details	A	C	GD 2.0	VG 4.0	FN 6.0	VF 8.0	VF/NM 9.0	NM- 9.2
1	47	4/48	Original; Webb-c/a	1	1	20	40	60	114	182	250
2A	62	–	Price circle blank; LDC-r	1	1	7	14	21	35	43	50
2B	62	–	C-price 10¢; rare; LDC-r	1	1	31	62	93	182	296	410
3	78	–	C-price 15¢; LDC-r	1	1	5	10	14	20	24	28
4	87	–	LDC-r	1	1	4	9	13	18	22	26
5	118	–	LDC-r	1	1	4	7	10	14	17	20

Classics Illustrated #48 © GIL

Classics Illustrated #51 © GIL

Classics Illustrated #53 © GIL

Ed	HRN	Date	Details	A	C	GD 2.0	VG 4.0	FN 6.0	VF 8.0	VF/NM 9.0	NM- 9.2
6	131	–	New-c; PC-r	1	2	5	10	15	23	28	32
7	140	–	PC-r	1	2	2	4	6	9	13	16
8	150	–	PC-r	1	2	2	4	6	9	13	16
9	164	–	Reduced pg.width; PC-r	1	2	2	4	6	8	11	14
10	167	–	PC-r	1	2	2	4	6	8	11	14
11	167	3/64	PC-r	1	2	2	4	6	8	11	14
12	167	6/65	PC-r	1	2	2	4	6	8	11	14
13	167	12/65	PC-r	1	2	2	4	6	8	11	14
14	166	9/67	PC-r	1	2	2	4	6	8	11	14
15	166	Win/69	New price 25¢; PC-r; stiff-c	1	2	2	4	6	8	11	14
16	169	Sm/70	PC-r; stiff-c	1	2	2	4	6	8	11	14

47. Twenty Thousand Leagues Under the Sea

Ed	HRN	Date	Details	A	C	GD 2.0	VG 4.0	FN 6.0	VF 8.0	VF/NM 9.0	NM- 9.2
1	47	5/48	Orig.; Kiefer-a&c;	1	1	20	40	60	120	195	270
2	64	–	No c-price; LDC-r	1	1	6	12	18	28	34	40
3	78	–	C-price 15¢; LDC-r	1	1	4	9	13	18	22	26
4	94	–	LDC-r	1	1	4	8	12	17	21	24
5	118	–	LDC-r	1	1	4	7	10	14	17	20
6	128	–	New-c; PC-r	1	2	5	10	15	24	30	35
7	133	–	PC-r	1	2	2	4	6	10	14	18
8	140	–	PC-r	1	2	2	4	6	9	13	16
9	148	–	PC-r	1	2	2	4	6	9	13	16
10	156	–	PC-r	1	2	2	4	6	9	13	16
11	165	–	PC-r	1	2	2	4	6	9	13	16
12	167	–	PC-r	1	2	2	4	6	9	13	16
13	167	3/64	PC-r	1	2	2	4	6	9	13	16
14	167	8/65	PC-r	1	2	2	4	6	9	13	16
15	167	10/66	PC-r	1	2	2	4	6	9	13	16
16	166	R/1968	C-price 25¢; new-c PC-r	1	3	3	6	9	15	22	28
17	169	Spr/70	Stiff-c; PC-r	1	3	2	4	6	13	18	22

48. David Copperfield

Ed	HRN	Date	Details	A	C	GD 2.0	VG 4.0	FN 6.0	VF 8.0	VF/NM 9.0	NM- 9.2
1	47	6/48	Original; Kiefer-c/a	1	1	20	40	60	114	182	250
2	64	–	Price circle replaced by motif of boy reading; LDC-r	1	1	6	12	18	28	34	40
3	87	–	C-price 15¢; LDC-r	1	1	4	8	12	17	21	24
4	121	–	New-c; PC-r	1	2	5	10	15	22	26	30
5	130	–	PC-r	1	2	2	4	6	9	13	16
6	140	–	PC-r	1	2	2	4	6	9	13	16
7	148	–	PC-r	1	2	2	4	6	9	13	16
8	156	–	PC-r	1	2	2	4	6	9	13	16
9	167	–	PC-r	1	2	2	4	6	8	11	14
10	167	4/64	PC-r	1	2	2	4	6	8	11	14
11	167	6/65	PC-r	1	2	2	4	6	8	11	14
12	166	5/67	PC-r	1	2	2	4	6	8	11	14
13	166	R/67	PC-r; C-price 25¢	1	2	2	4	6	10	14	18
14	166	Spr/69	C-price 25¢; stiff-c PC-r	1	2	2	4	6	8	11	14
15	169	Win/69	Stiff-c; PC-r	1	2	2	4	6	8	11	14

49. Alice in Wonderland

Ed	HRN	Date	Details	A	C	GD 2.0	VG 4.0	FN 6.0	VF 8.0	VF/NM 9.0	NM- 9.2
1	47	7/48	Original; 1st Blum a & c	1	1	24	48	72	140	230	320
2	64	–	No c-price; LDC-r	1	1	8	16	24	44	57	70
3A	85	–	C-price 15¢; soft-c LDC-r	1	1	8	16	24	40	50	60
3B	85	–	Stiff-c; LDC-r	1	1	8	16	24	42	54	65
4	155	–	New PC, similar to orig.; PC-r	1	2	4	8	12	27	44	60
5	165	–	PC-r	1	2	3	6	9	18	28	38
6	167	3/64	PC-r	1	2	3	6	9	16	24	32
7	167	6/66	PC-r	1	2	4	8	12	28	47	65
8A	166	Fall/68	New-c; soft-c; 25¢ c-price; PC-r	1	3	4	8	12	27	44	60
8B	166	Fall/68	New-c; stiff-c; 25¢ c-price; PC-r	1	3	6	12	18	40	73	105

50. Adventures of Tom Sawyer (Used in **SOTI**, pg. 37)

Ed	HRN	Date	Details	A	C	GD 2.0	VG 4.0	FN 6.0	VF 8.0	VF/NM 9.0	NM- 9.2
1A	51	8/48	Orig.; Aldo Rubano a&c	1	1	20	40	60	114	182	250
1B	51	9/48	Orig.; Rubano c&a	1	1	20	40	60	114	182	250
1C	51	9/48	Orig.; outside-bc: blue & yellow only; rare	1	1	25	50	75	147	241	335
2	64	–	No c-price; LDC-r	1	1	5	10	15	23	28	32
3	78	–	C-price 15¢; LDC-r	1	1	4	8	12	17	21	24
4	94	–	LDC-r	1	1	4	7	10	14	17	20
5	117	–	LDC-r	1	1	2	4	6	10	14	18
6	132	–	LDC-r	1	1	2	4	6	10	14	18
7	140	–	New-c; PC-r	1	2	3	6	9	17	26	35
8	150	–	PC-r	1	2	2	4	6	9	13	16
9	164	–	New-a; PC-r	2	2	3	6	9	17	26	35
10	167	–	PC-r	2	2	2	4	6	9	13	16
11	167	1/65	PC-r	2	2	2	4	6	8	11	14
12	167	5/66	PC-r	2	2	2	4	6	8	11	14
13	166	12/67	PC-r	2	2	2	4	6	8	11	14
14	169	Fall/69	C-price 25¢; stiff-c; PC-r	2	2	2	4	6	8	11	14
15	169	Win/71	PC-r	2	2	2	4	6	8	11	14

51. The Spy

Ed	HRN	Date	Details	A	C	GD 2.0	VG 4.0	FN 6.0	VF 8.0	VF/NM 9.0	NM- 9.2
1A	51	9/48	Original; inside-bc illo: Christmas Carol	1	1	19	38	57	109	172	235
1B	51	9/48	Original; inside-bc illo: Man in Iron Mask	1	1	19	38	57	109	172	235
1C	51	8/48	Original; outside-bc: full color	1	1	19	38	57	109	172	235
1D	51	8/48	Original; outside-bc: blue & yellow only; scarce	1	1	20	40	60	115	185	255
2	89	–	C-price 15¢; LDC-r	1	1	5	10	14	20	24	28
3	121	–	LDC-r	1	1	4	8	12	17	21	24
4	139	–	New-c; PC-r	1	2	3	6	9	18	27	35
5	156	–	PC-r	1	2	2	4	6	9	13	16
6	167	11/63	PC-r	1	2	2	4	6	8	11	14
7	167	7/66	PC-r	1	2	2	4	6	8	11	14
8A	166	Win/69	C-price 25¢; soft-c; scarce; PC-r	1	2	3	6	9	15	21	26
8B	166	Win/69	C-price 25¢; stiff-c; PC-r	1	2	2	4	6	8	11	14

52. The House of the Seven Gables

Ed	HRN	Date	Details	A	C	GD 2.0	VG 4.0	FN 6.0	VF 8.0	VF/NM 9.0	NM- 9.2
1	53	10/48	Orig.; Griffiths a&c	1	1	19	38	57	109	172	235
2	89	–	C-price 15¢; LDC-r	1	1	5	10	14	20	24	28
3	121	–	LDC-r	1	1	4	8	12	17	21	24
4	142	–	New-c&a; PC-r; Woodbridge-a	2	2	5	10	15	25	31	36
5	156	–	PC-r	2	2	2	4	6	9	13	16
6	165	–	PC-r	2	2	2	4	6	8	11	14
7	167	5/64	PC-r	2	2	2	4	6	9	13	16
8	167	3/66	PC-r	2	2	2	4	6	8	11	14
9	166	R/1968	C-price 25¢; PC-r	2	2	2	4	6	8	11	14
10	169	Spr/70	Stiff-c; PC-r	2	2	2	4	6	8	11	14

53. A Christmas Carol

Ed	HRN	Date	Details	A	C	GD 2.0	VG 4.0	FN 6.0	VF 8.0	VF/NM 9.0	NM- 9.2
1	53	11/48	Original & only ed; Kiefer-c/a	1	1	24	48	72	142	234	325

54. Man in the Iron Mask

Ed	HRN	Date	Details	A	C	GD 2.0	VG 4.0	FN 6.0	VF 8.0	VF/NM 9.0	NM- 9.2
1	55	12/48	Original; Froehlich-a, Kiefer-c	1	1	19	38	57	109	172	235
2	93	–	C-price 15¢; LDC-r	1	1	5	10	15	23	28	32
3A	111	–	(O) logo lettering; scarce; LDC-r	1	1	6	12	18	31	38	45
3B	111	–	New logo as PC; LDC-r	1	1	5	10	15	23	28	32
4	142	–	New-c&a; PC-r	2	2	5	10	15	24	30	35
5	154	–	PC-r	2	2	2	4	6	9	13	16
6	165	–	PC-r	2	2	2	4	6	8	11	14
7	167	5/64	PC-r	2	2	2	4	6	8	11	14
8	167	4/66	PC-r	2	2	2	4	6	8	11	14

Classics Illustrated #57 © GIL

Classics Illustrated #59 © GIL

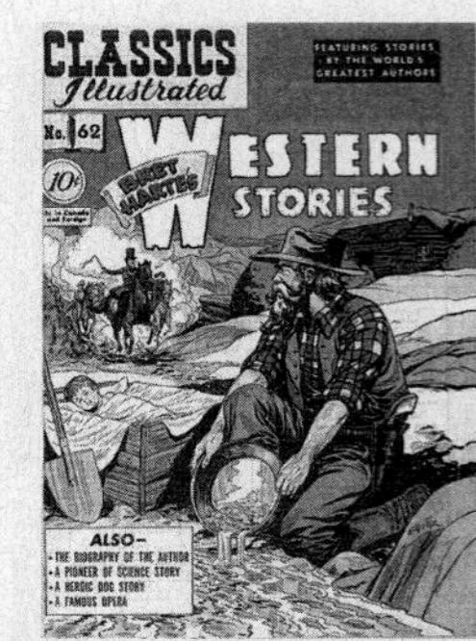

Classics Illustrated #62 © GIL

Ed	HRN	Date	Details	A	C	GD 2.0	VG 4.0	FN 6.0	VF 8.0	VF/NM 9.0	NM- 9.2
9A	166	Win/69	C-price 25¢; soft-c PC-r	2	2	3	6	9	15	21	26
9B	166	Win/69	Stiff-c	2	2	2	4	6	8	11	14

55. Silas Marner (Used in **SOTI**, pgs. 311, 312)

Ed	HRN	Date	Details	A	C	GD 2.0	VG 4.0	FN 6.0	VF 8.0	VF/NM 9.0	NM- 9.2
1	55	1/49	Original-Kiefer-c	1	1	19	38	57	109	172	235
2	75	–	Price circle blank; 'Coming Next' ad; LDC-r	1	1	5	10	15	24	30	35
3	97	–	LDC-r	1	1	3	6	9	14	19	24
4	121	–	New-c; PC-r	1	2	3	6	9	18	27	35
5	130	–	PC-r	1	2	2	4	6	9	13	16
6	140	–	PC-r	1	2	2	4	6	9	13	16
7	154	–	PC-r	1	2	2	4	6	9	13	16
8	165	–	PC-r	1	2	2	4	6	8	11	14
9	167	2/64	PC-r	1	2	2	4	6	8	11	14
10	167	6/65	PC-r	1	2	2	4	6	8	11	14
11	166	5/67	PC-r	1	2	2	4	6	8	11	14
12A	166	Win/69	C-price 25¢; soft-c PC-r	1	2	3	6	9	15	21	26
12B	166	Win/69	C-price 25¢; stiff-c PC-r	1	2	2	4	6	8	11	14

56. The Toilers of the Sea

Ed	HRN	Date	Details	A	C	GD 2.0	VG 4.0	FN 6.0	VF 8.0	VF/NM 9.0	NM- 9.2
1	55	2/49	Original; A.M. Froehlich-c/a	1	1	24	48	72	142	234	325
2	165	–	New-c&a; PC-r; Angelo Torres-a	2	2	8	16	24	40	50	60
3	167	3/64	PC-r	2	2	3	6	9	16	23	30
4	167	10/66	PC-r	2	2	3	6	9	16	23	30

57. The Song of Hiawatha

Ed	HRN	Date	Details	A	C	GD 2.0	VG 4.0	FN 6.0	VF 8.0	VF/NM 9.0	NM- 9.2
1	55	3/49	Original; Alex Blum-c/a	1	1	18	36	54	103	162	220
2	75	–	No c-price w/15¢ sticker; 'Coming Next' ad; LDC-r	1	1	5	10	15	24	30	35
3	94	–	C-price 15¢; LDC-r	1	1	5	10	14	20	24	28
4	118	–	LDC-r	1	1	3	6	9	14	19	24
5	134	–	New-c; PC-r	1	2	3	6	9	17	26	35
6	139	–	PC-r	1	2	2	4	6	9	13	16
7	154	–	PC-r	1	2	2	4	6	9	13	16
8	167	–	Has orig.date; PC-r	1	2	2	4	6	8	11	14
9	167	9/64	PC-r	1	2	2	4	6	8	11	14
10	167	10/65	PC-r	1	2	2	4	6	8	11	14
11	166	F/1968	C-price 25¢; PC-r	1	2	2	4	6	8	11	14

58. The Prairie

Ed	HRN	Date	Details	A	C	GD 2.0	VG 4.0	FN 6.0	VF 8.0	VF/NM 9.0	NM- 9.2
1	60	4/49	Original; Palais c/a	1	1	18	36	54	103	162	220
2A	62	–	No c-price; no coming-next ad; LDC-r	1	1	9	18	27	47	61	75
2B	62		10¢ (rare)	1	1	19	38	57	112	179	245
3	78	–	C-price 15¢ in dbl. circle; LDC-r	1	1	5	10	15	22	26	30
4	114	–	LDC-r	1	1	4	8	12	17	21	24
5	131	–	LDC-r	1	1	4	7	10	14	17	20
6	132	–	LDC-r	1	1	4	7	10	14	17	20
7	146	–	New-c; PC-r	1	2	5	10	15	23	28	32
8	155	–	PC-r	1	2	2	4	6	9	13	16
9	167	5/64	PC-r	1	2	2	4	6	8	11	14
10	167	4/66	PC-r	1	2	2	4	6	8	11	14
11	169	Sm/69	New price 25¢; stiff-c; PC-r	1	2	2	4	6	8	11	14

59. Wuthering Heights

Ed	HRN	Date	Details	A	C	GD 2.0	VG 4.0	FN 6.0	VF 8.0	VF/NM 9.0	NM- 9.2
1	60	5/49	Original; Kiefer-c/a	1	1	19	38	57	109	172	235
2	85	–	C-price 15¢; LDC-r	1	1	6	12	18	28	34	40
3	156	–	New-c; PC-r	1	2	5	10	15	25	31	36
4	167	1/64	PC-r	1	2	2	4	6	9	13	16
5	167	10/66	PC-r	1	2	2	4	6	9	13	16
6	169	Sm/69	C-price 25¢; stiff-c; PC-r	1	2	2	4	6	9	13	16

60. Black Beauty

Ed	HRN	Date	Details	A	C	GD 2.0	VG 4.0	FN 6.0	VF 8.0	VF/NM 9.0	NM- 9.2
1	62	6/49	Original; Froehlich-c/a	1	1	18	36	54	103	162	220
2	62	–	No c-price; no coming-next ad; LDC-r (rare)	1	1	20	40	60	114	182	250
3	85	–	C-price 15¢; LDC-r	1	1	5	10	15	23	28	32
4	158	–	New L.B. Cole-c/a; PC-r	2	2	7	14	21	35	43	50
5	167	2/64	PC-r	2	2	2	4	6	11	16	20
6	167	3/66	PC-r	2	2	2	4	6	11	16	20
7	166	R/1968	New-c&price, 25¢; PC-r	2	3	5	10	15	30	50	70

61. The Woman in White

Ed	HRN	Date	Details	A	C	GD 2.0	VG 4.0	FN 6.0	VF 8.0	VF/NM 9.0	NM- 9.2
1A	62	7/49	Original; Blum-c/a fc-purple; bc: top illos light blue	1	1	19	38	57	109	172	235
1B	62	7/49	Original; Blum-c/a fc-pink; bc: top illos light violet	1	1	19	38	57	109	172	235
2	156	–	New-c; PC-r	1	2	6	12	18	28	34	40
3	167	1/64	PC-r	1	2	2	4	6	11	16	20
4	166	R/1968	C-price 25¢; PC-r	1	2	2	4	6	11	16	20

62. Western Stories ("The Luck of Roaring Camp" and "The Outcasts of Poker Flat")

Ed	HRN	Date	Details	A	C	GD 2.0	VG 4.0	FN 6.0	VF 8.0	VF/NM 9.0	NM- 9.2
1	62	8/49	Original; Kiefer-c/a	1	1	17	34	51	98	154	210
2	89	–	C-price 15¢; LDC-r	1	1	5	10	15	23	28	32
3	121	–	LDC-r	1	1	3	6	9	15	21	26
4	137	–	New-c; PC-r	1	2	3	6	9	17	26	35
5	152	–	PC-r	1	2	2	4	6	8	11	14
6	167	10/63	PC-r	1	2	2	4	6	8	11	14
7	167	6/64	PC-r	1	2	2	4	6	8	11	14
8	167	11/66	PC-r	1	2	2	4	6	8	11	14
9	166	R/1968	New-c&price 25¢; PC-r	1	3	3	6	9	16	24	32

63. The Man Without a Country

Ed	HRN	Date	Details	A	C	GD 2.0	VG 4.0	FN 6.0	VF 8.0	VF/NM 9.0	NM- 9.2
1	62	9/49	Original; Kiefer-c/a	1	1	18	36	54	103	162	220
2	78	–	C-price 15¢ in double circle; LDC-r	1	1	5	10	15	23	28	32
3	156	–	New-c, old-a; PC-r	1	2	6	12	18	28	34	40
4	165	–	New-a & text pgs.; PC-r; A. Torres-a	2	2	5	10	15	23	28	32
5	167	3/64	PC-r	2	2	2	4	6	8	11	14
6	167	8/66	PC-r	2	2	2	4	6	8	11	14
7	169	Sm/69	New price 25¢; stiff-c; PC-r	2	2	2	4	6	8	11	14

64. Treasure Island

Ed	HRN	Date	Details	A	C	GD 2.0	VG 4.0	FN 6.0	VF 8.0	VF/NM 9.0	NM- 9.2
1	62	10/49	Original; Blum-c/a	1	1	19	38	57	109	172	235
2A	82	–	C-price 15¢; soft-c LDC-r	1	1	5	10	15	22	26	30
2B	82	–	Stiff-c; LDC-r	1	1	5	10	15	23	28	32
3	117	–	LDC-r	1	1	3	6	9	15	21	26
4	131	–	New-c; PC-r	1	2	3	6	9	17	26	35
5	138	–	PC-r	1	2	2	4	6	9	13	16
6	146	–	PC-r	1	2	2	4	6	9	13	16
7	158	–	PC-r	1	2	2	4	6	9	13	16
8	165	–	PC-r	1	2	2	4	6	8	11	14
9	167	–	PC-r	1	2	2	4	6	8	11	14
10	167	6/64	PC-r	1	2	2	4	6	8	11	14
11	167	12/65	PC-r	1	2	2	4	6	8	11	14
12A	166	10/67	PC-r	1	2	2	4	6	8	11	14
12B	166	10/67	w/Grit ad stapled in book	1	2	10	20	30	66	138	210
13	169	Spr/69	New price 25¢; stiff-c; PC-r	1	2	2	4	6	9	13	16
14	–	1989	Long John Silver's Seafood Shoppes; $1.95, First/Berkley	1	2						5.00

Classics Illustrated #66 © GIL

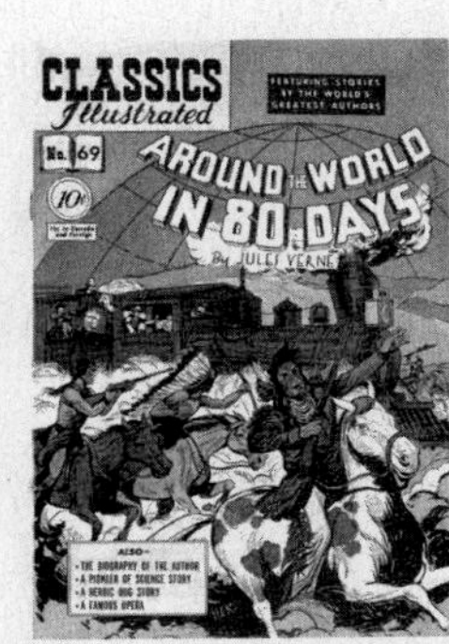

Classics Illustrated #69 © GIL

Classics Illustrated #73 © GIL

Publ.; Blum-r

65. Benjamin Franklin

Ed	HRN	Date	Details	A	C	GD 2.0	VG 4.0	FN 6.0	VF 8.0	VF/NM 9.0	NM- 9.2
1	64	11/49	Original; Kiefer-c; Iger Shop-a	1	1	10	20	30	68	144	220
2	131	–	New-c; PC-r	1	2	5	10	15	24	30	35
3	154	–	PC-r	1	2	2	4	6	9	13	16
4	167	2/64	PC-r	1	2	2	4	6	9	13	16
5	167	4/66	PC-r	1	2	2	4	6	9	13	16
6	169	Fall/69	New price 25¢; stiff-c; PC-r	1	2	2	4	6	9	13	16

66. The Cloister and the Hearth

Ed	HRN	Date	Details	A	C	GD 2.0	VG 4.0	FN 6.0	VF 8.0	VF/NM 9.0	NM- 9.2
1	67	12/49	Original & only ed; Kiefer-a & c	1	1	32	64	96	192	314	435

67. The Scottish Chiefs

Ed	HRN	Date	Details	A	C	GD 2.0	VG 4.0	FN 6.0	VF 8.0	VF/NM 9.0	NM- 9.2
1	67	1/50	Original; Blum-a&c	1	1	15	30	45	90	140	190
2	85	–	C-price 15¢; LDC-r	1	1	5	10	15	23	28	32
3	118	–	LDC-r	1	1	3	6	9	15	21	26
4	136	–	New-c; PC-r	1	2	3	6	9	18	27	36
5	154	–	PC-r	1	2	2	4	6	9	13	16
6	167	11/63	PC-r	1	2	2	4	6	10	14	18
7	167	8/65	PC-r	1	2	2	4	6	9	13	16

68. Julius Caesar (Used in **SOTI**, pgs. 36, 37)

Ed	HRN	Date	Details	A	C	GD 2.0	VG 4.0	FN 6.0	VF 8.0	VF/NM 9.0	NM- 9.2
1	70	2/50	Original; Kiefer-c/a	1	1	15	30	45	90	140	190
2	85	–	C-price 15¢; LDC-r	1	1	5	10	15	22	26	30
3	108	–	LDC-r	1	1	4	9	13	18	22	26
4	156	–	New L.B. Cole-c; PC-r	1	2	6	12	18	28	34	40
5	165	–	New-a by Evans, Crandall; PC-r	2	2	5	10	15	24	30	35
6	167	2/64	PC-r	2	2	2	4	6	8	11	14
7	167	10/65	Tarzan books inside cover; PC-r	2	2	2	4	6	8	11	14
8	166	R/1967	PC-r	2	2	2	4	6	8	11	14
9	169	Win/69	PC-r; stiff-c	2	2	2	4	6	8	11	14

69. Around the World in 80 Days

Ed	HRN	Date	Details	A	C	GD 2.0	VG 4.0	FN 6.0	VF 8.0	VF/NM 9.0	NM- 9.2
1	70	3/50	Original; Kiefer-c/a	1	1	15	30	45	90	140	190
2	87	–	C-price 15¢; LDC-r	1	1	5	10	15	22	26	30
3	125	–	LDC-r	1	1	4	9	13	18	22	26
4	136	–	New-c; PC-r	1	2	5	10	15	25	31	36
5	146	–	PC-r	1	2	2	4	6	9	13	16
6	152	–	PC-r	1	2	2	4	6	9	13	16
7	164	–	PC-r	1	2	2	4	6	8	11	14
8	167	–	PC-r	1	2	2	4	6	8	11	14
9	167	7/64	PC-r	1	2	2	4	6	8	11	14
10	167	11/65	PC-r	1	2	2	4	6	8	11	14
11	166	7/67	PC-r	1	2	2	4	6	8	11	14
12	169	Spr/69	C-price 25¢; stiff-c; PC-r	1	2	2	4	6	8	11	14

70. The Pilot

Ed	HRN	Date	Details	A	C	GD 2.0	VG 4.0	FN 6.0	VF 8.0	VF/NM 9.0	NM- 9.2
1	71	4/50	Original; Blum-c/a	1	1	14	28	42	81	118	155
2	92	–	C-price 15¢; LDC-r	1	1	5	10	15	23	28	32
3	125	–	LDC-r	1	1	4	9	13	18	22	26
4	156	–	New-c; PC-r	1	2	6	12	18	28	34	40
5	167	2/64	PC-r	1	2	2	4	6	11	16	20
6	167	5/66	PC-r	1	2	2	4	6	9	13	16

71. The Man Who Laughs

Ed	HRN	Date	Details	A	C	GD 2.0	VG 4.0	FN 6.0	VF 8.0	VF/NM 9.0	NM- 9.2
1	71	5/50	Original; Blum-c/a	1	1	20	40	60	114	182	250
2	165	–	New-c&a; PC-r	2	2	14	28	42	80	115	155
3	167	4/64	PC-r	2	2	11	22	33	62	86	115

72. The Oregon Trail

Ed	HRN	Date	Details	A	C	GD 2.0	VG 4.0	FN 6.0	VF 8.0	VF/NM 9.0	NM- 9.2
1	73	6/50	Original; Kiefer-c/a	1	1	14	28	42	81	118	155
2	89	–	C-price 15¢; LDC-r	1	1	5	10	15	23	28	32
3	121	–	LDC-r	1	1	4	9	13	18	22	26
4	131	–	New-c; PC-r	1	2	5	10	15	25	31	36
5	140	–	PC-r	1	2	2	4	6	9	13	16
6	150	–	PC-r	1	2	2	4	6	9	13	16
7	164	–	PC-r	1	2	2	4	6	8	11	14
8	167	–	PC-r	1	2	2	4	6	8	11	14
9	167	8/64	PC-r	1	2	2	4	6	8	11	14
10	167	10/65	PC-r	1	2	2	4	6	8	11	14
11	166	R/1968	C-price 25¢; PC-r	1	2	2	4	6	8	11	14

73. The Black Tulip

Ed	HRN	Date	Details	A	C	GD 2.0	VG 4.0	FN 6.0	VF 8.0	VF/NM 9.0	NM- 9.2
1	75	7/50	1st & only ed.; Alex Blum-c/a	1	1	38	76	114	228	369	510

74. Mr. Midshipman Easy

Ed	HRN	Date	Details	A	C	GD 2.0	VG 4.0	FN 6.0	VF 8.0	VF/NM 9.0	NM- 9.2
1	75	8/50	1st & only edition	1	1	38	76	114	228	369	510

75. The Lady of the Lake

Ed	HRN	Date	Details	A	C	GD 2.0	VG 4.0	FN 6.0	VF 8.0	VF/NM 9.0	NM- 9.2
1	75	9/50	Original; Kiefer-c/a	1	1	14	28	42	81	118	155
2	85	–	C-price 15¢; LDC-r	1	1	5	10	15	24	30	35
3	118	–	LDC-r	1	1	5	10	14	20	24	28
4	139	–	New-c; PC-r	1	2	5	10	15	25	31	36
5	154	–	PC-r	1	2	2	4	6	9	13	16
6	165	–	PC-r	1	2	2	4	6	8	11	14
7	167	4/64	PC-r	1	2	2	4	6	8	11	14
8	167	5/66	PC-r	1	2	2	4	6	8	11	14
9	169	Spr/69	New price 25¢; stiff-c; PC-r	1	2	2	4	6	8	11	14

76. The Prisoner of Zenda

Ed	HRN	Date	Details	A	C	GD 2.0	VG 4.0	FN 6.0	VF 8.0	VF/NM 9.0	NM- 9.2
1	75	10/50	Original; Kiefer-c/a	1	1	14	28	42	81	118	155
2	85	–	C-price 15¢; LDC-r	1	1	5	10	15	23	28	32
3	111	–	LDC-r	1	1	3	6	9	16	21	26
4	128	–	New-c; PC-r	1	2	3	6	9	17	26	35
5	152	–	PC-r	1	2	2	4	6	9	13	16
6	165	–	PC-r	1	2	2	4	6	8	11	14
7	167	4/64	PC-r	1	2	2	4	6	8	11	14
8	167	9/66	PC-r	1	2	2	4	6	8	11	14
9	169	Fall/69	New price 25¢; stiff-c; PC-r	1	2	2	4	6	8	11	14

77. The Iliad

Ed	HRN	Date	Details	A	C	GD 2.0	VG 4.0	FN 6.0	VF 8.0	VF/NM 9.0	NM- 9.2
1	78	11/50	Original; Blum-c/a	1	1	14	28	42	81	118	155
2	87	–	C-price 15¢; LDC-r	1	1	5	10	15	24	30	35
3	121	–	LDC-r	1	1	3	6	9	15	21	26
4	139	–	New-c; PC-r	1	2	3	6	9	16	24	32
5	150	–	PC-r	1	2	2	4	6	9	13	16
6	165	–	PC-r	1	2	2	4	6	8	11	14
7	167	10/63	PC-r	1	2	2	4	6	8	11	14
8	167	7/64	PC-r	1	2	2	4	6	8	11	14
9	167	5/66	PC-r	1	2	2	4	6	8	11	14
10	166	R/1968	C-price 25¢; PC-r	1	2	2	4	6	8	11	14

78. Joan of Arc

Ed	HRN	Date	Details	A	C	GD 2.0	VG 4.0	FN 6.0	VF 8.0	VF/NM 9.0	NM- 9.2
1	78	12/50	Original; Kiefer-c/a	1	1	14	28	42	81	118	155
2	87	–	C-price 15¢; LDC-r	1	1	5	10	15	23	28	32
3	113	–	LDC-r	1	1	3	6	9	15	21	26
4	128	–	New-c; PC-r	1	2	3	6	9	17	26	35
5	140	–	PC-r	1	2	2	4	6	9	13	16
6	150	–	PC-r	1	2	2	4	6	9	13	16
7	159	–	PC-r	1	2	2	4	6	9	13	16
8	167	–	PC-r	1	2	2	4	6	8	11	14
9	167	12/63	PC-r	1	2	2	4	6	8	11	14
10	167	6/65	PC-r	1	2	2	4	6	8	11	14
11	166	6/67	PC-r	1	2	2	4	6	8	11	14
12	166	Win/69	New-c&price, 25¢; PC-r; stiff-c	1	3	3	6	9	16	24	32

79. Cyrano de Bergerac

Ed	HRN	Date	Details	A	C	GD 2.0	VG 4.0	FN 6.0	VF 8.0	VF/NM 9.0	NM- 9.2
1	78	1/51	Orig.; movie promo inside front-c; Blum-c/a	1	1	14	28	42	81	118	155
2	85	–	C-price 15¢; LDC-r	1	1	5	10	15	23	28	32
3	118	–	LDC-r	1	1	3	6	9	17	23	28

Classics Illustrated #81 © GIL

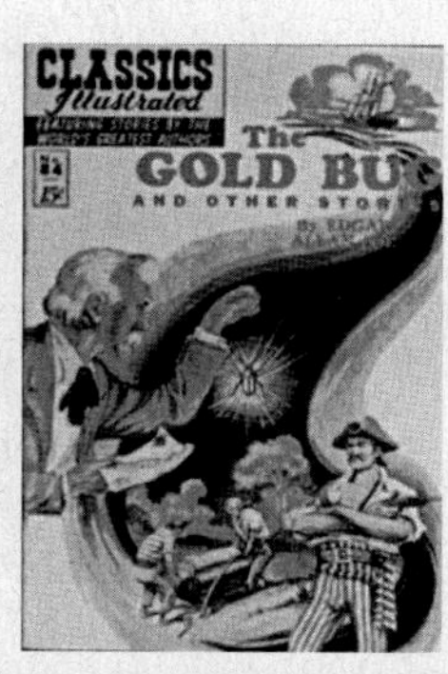

Classics Illustrated #84 © GIL

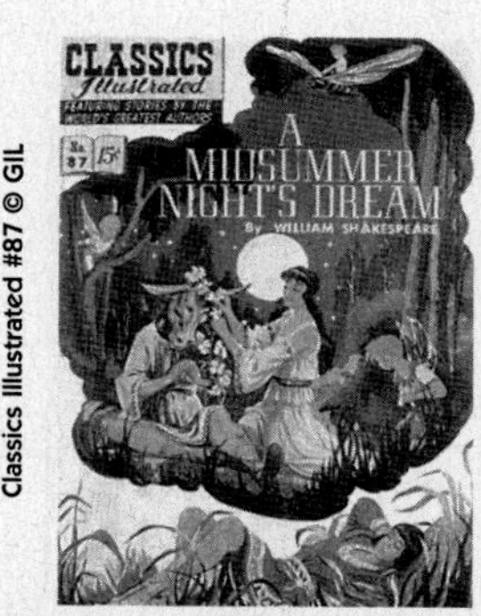

Classics Illustrated #87 © GIL

Ed	HRN	Date	Details	A	C	GD 2.0	VG 4.0	FN 6.0	VF 8.0	VF/NM 9.0	NM- 9.2
4	133	–	New-c; PC-r	1	2	3	6	9	16	24	32
5	156	–	PC-r	1	2	2	4	6	11	16	20
6	167	8/64	PC-r	1	2	2	4	6	11	16	20

80. White Fang (Last line drawn cover)

Ed	HRN	Date	Details	A	C	GD 2.0	VG 4.0	FN 6.0	VF 8.0	VF/NM 9.0	NM- 9.2
1	79	2/51	Orig.; Blum-c/a	1	1	14	28	42	81	118	155
2	87	–	C-price 15¢; LDC-r	1	1	5	10	15	24	30	35
3	125	–	LDC-r	1	1	3	6	9	15	21	26
4	132	–	New-c; PC-r	1	2	3	6	9	16	24	32
5	140	–	PC-r	1	2	2	4	6	9	13	16
6	153	–	PC-r	1	2	2	4	6	9	13	16
7	167	–	PC-r	1	2	2	4	6	8	11	14
8	167	9/64	PC-r	1	2	2	4	6	8	11	14
9	167	7/65	PC-r	1	2	2	4	6	8	11	14
10	166	6/67	PC-r	1	2	2	4	6	8	11	14
11	169	Fall/69	New price 25¢; PC-r; stiff-c	1	2	2	4	6	8	11	14

81. The Odyssey (1st painted cover)

Ed	HRN	Date	Details	A	C	GD 2.0	VG 4.0	FN 6.0	VF 8.0	VF/NM 9.0	NM- 9.2
1	82	3/51	First 15¢ Original; Blum-c	1	1	14	28	42	81	118	155
2	167	8/64	PC-r	1	1	2	4	6	11	16	20
3	167	10/66	PC-r	1	1	2	4	6	11	16	20
4	169	Spr/69	New, stiff-c; PC-r	1	2	3	6	9	18	27	36

82. The Master of Ballantrae

Ed	HRN	Date	Details	A	C	GD 2.0	VG 4.0	FN 6.0	VF 8.0	VF/NM 9.0	NM- 9.2
1	82	4/51	Original; Blum-c	1	1	13	26	39	72	101	130
2	167	8/64	PC-r	1	1	3	6	9	14	19	24
3	166	Fall/68	New, stiff-c; PC-r	1	2	3	6	9	18	27	36

83. The Jungle Book

Ed	HRN	Date	Details	A	C	GD 2.0	VG 4.0	FN 6.0	VF 8.0	VF/NM 9.0	NM- 9.2
1	85	5/51	Original; Blum-c Bossert/Blum-a	1	1	13	26	39	72	101	130
2	110	–	PC-r	1	1	2	4	6	10	14	18
3	125	–	PC-r	1	1	2	4	6	9	13	16
4	134	–	PC-r	1	1	2	4	6	9	13	16
5	142	–	PC-r	1	1	2	4	6	9	13	16
6	150	–	PC-r	1	1	2	4	6	9	13	16
7	159	–	PC-r	1	1	2	4	6	9	13	16
8	167	–	PC-r	1	1	2	4	6	8	11	14
9	167	3/65	PC-r	1	1	2	4	6	8	11	14
10	167	11/65	PC-r	1	1	2	4	6	8	11	14
11	167	5/66	PC-r	1	1	2	4	6	8	11	14
12	166	R/1968	New c&a; stiff-c; PC-r	2	2	3	6	9	18	28	38

84. The Gold Bug and Other Stories ("The Gold Bug", "The Tell-Tale Heart", "The Cask of Amontillado")

Ed	HRN	Date	Details	A	C	GD 2.0	VG 4.0	FN 6.0	VF 8.0	VF/NM 9.0	NM- 9.2
1	85	6/51	Original; Blum-c/a; Palais, Laverly-a	1	1	15	30	45	84	127	170
2	167	7/64	PC-r	1	1	11	22	33	62	86	110

85. The Sea Wolf

Ed	HRN	Date	Details	A	C	GD 2.0	VG 4.0	FN 6.0	VF 8.0	VF/NM 9.0	NM- 9.2
1	85	7/51	Original; Blum-c/a	1	1	11	22	33	64	90	115
2	121	–	PC-r	1	1	2	4	6	9	13	16
3	132	–	PC-r	1	1	2	4	6	9	13	16
4	141	–	PC-r	1	1	2	4	6	9	13	16
5	161	–	PC-r	1	1	2	4	6	8	11	14
6	167	2/64	PC-r	1	1	2	4	6	8	11	14
7	167	11/65	PC-r	1	1	2	4	6	8	11	14
8	169	Fall/69	New price 25¢; stiff-c; PC-r	1	1	2	4	6	8	11	14

86. Under Two Flags

Ed	HRN	Date	Details	A	C	GD 2.0	VG 4.0	FN 6.0	VF 8.0	VF/NM 9.0	NM- 9.2
1	87	8/51	Original; first delBourgo-a	1	1	11	22	33	64	90	115
2	117	–	PC-r	1	1	2	4	6	10	14	18
3	139	–	PC-r	1	1	2	4	6	9	13	16
4	158	–	PC-r	1	1	2	4	6	9	13	16
5	167	2/64	PC-r	1	1	2	4	6	8	11	14
6	167	8/66	PC-r	1	1	2	4	6	8	11	14
7	169	Sm/69	New price 25¢; stiff-c; PC-r	1	1	2	4	6	8	11	14

87. A Midsummer Nights Dream

Ed	HRN	Date	Details	A	C	GD 2.0	VG 4.0	FN 6.0	VF 8.0	VF/NM 9.0	NM- 9.2
1	87	9/51	Original; Blum c/a	1	1	11	22	33	64	90	115
2	161	–	PC-r	1	1	2	4	6	9	13	16
3	167	4/64	PC-r	1	1	2	4	6	8	11	14
4	167	5/66	PC-r	1	1	2	4	6	8	11	14
5	169	Sm/69	New price 25¢; stiff-c; PC-r	1	1	2	4	6	8	11	14

88. Men of Iron

Ed	HRN	Date	Details	A	C	GD 2.0	VG 4.0	FN 6.0	VF 8.0	VF/NM 9.0	NM- 9.2
1	89	10/51	Original	1	1	11	22	33	64	90	115
2	154	–	PC-r	1	1	2	4	6	9	13	16
3	167	1/64	PC-r	1	1	2	4	6	8	11	14
4	166	R/1968	C-price 25¢; PC-r	1	1	2	4	6	8	11	14

89. Crime and Punishment (Cover illo. in **POP**)

Ed	HRN	Date	Details	A	C	GD 2.0	VG 4.0	FN 6.0	VF 8.0	VF/NM 9.0	NM- 9.2
1	89	11/51	Original; Palais-a	1	1	13	26	39	72	101	130
2	152	–	PC-r	1	1	2	4	6	9	13	16
3	167	4/64	PC-r	1	1	2	4	6	8	11	14
4	167	5/66	PC-r	1	1	2	4	6	8	11	14
5	169	Fall/69	New price 25¢ stiff-c; PC-r	1	1	2	4	6	8	11	14

90. Green Mansions

Ed	HRN	Date	Details	A	C	GD 2.0	VG 4.0	FN 6.0	VF 8.0	VF/NM 9.0	NM- 9.2
1	89	12/51	Original; Blum-c/a	1	1	11	22	33	64	90	115
2	148	–	New L.B. Cole-c; PC-r	1	2	5	10	15	22	26	30
3	165	–	PC-r	1	2	2	4	6	8	11	14
4	167	4/64	PC-r	1	2	2	4	6	8	11	14
5	167	9/66	PC-r	1	2	2	4	6	8	11	14
6	169	Sm/69	New price 25¢; stiff-c; PC-r	1	2	2	4	6	8	11	14

91. The Call of the Wild

Ed	HRN	Date	Details	A	C	GD 2.0	VG 4.0	FN 6.0	VF 8.0	VF/NM 9.0	NM- 9.2
1	92	1/52	Orig.; delBourgo-a	1	1	11	22	33	64	90	115
2	112	–	PC-r	1	1	2	4	6	9	13	16
3	125	–	'Picture Progress' on back-c; PC-r	1	1	2	4	6	9	13	16
4	134	–	PC-r	1	1	2	4	6	9	13	16
5	143	–	PC-r	1	1	2	4	6	9	13	16
6	165	–	PC-r	1	1	2	4	6	9	13	16
7	167	–	PC-r	1	1	2	4	6	8	11	14
8	167	4/65	PC-r	1	1	2	4	6	8	11	14
9	167	3/66	PC-r	1	1	2	4	6	8	11	14
10	166	11/67	PC-r	1	1	2	4	6	8	11	14
11	169	Spr/70	New price 25¢; stiff-c; PC-r	1	1	2	4	6	8	11	14

92. The Courtship of Miles Standish

Ed	HRN	Date	Details	A	C	GD 2.0	VG 4.0	FN 6.0	VF 8.0	VF/NM 9.0	NM- 9.2
1	92	2/52	Original; Blum-c/a	1	1	11	22	33	64	90	115
2	165	–	PC-r	1	1	2	4	6	9	13	16
3	167	3/64	PC-r	1	1	2	4	6	9	13	16
4	166	5/67	PC-r	1	1	2	4	6	9	13	16
5	169	Win/69	New price 25¢ stiff-c; PC-r	1	1	2	4	6	9	13	16

93. Pudd'nhead Wilson

Ed	HRN	Date	Details	A	C	GD 2.0	VG 4.0	FN 6.0	VF 8.0	VF/NM 9.0	NM- 9.2
1	94	3/52	Orig.; Kiefer-c/a;	1	1	11	22	33	64	90	115
2	165	–	New-c; PC-r	1	2	2	4	6	11	16	25
3	167	3/64	PC-r	1	2	2	4	6	9	13	16
4	166	R/1968	New price 25¢; soft-c; PC-r	1	2	2	4	6	9	13	16

94. David Balfour

Ed	HRN	Date	Details	A	C	GD 2.0	VG 4.0	FN 6.0	VF 8.0	VF/NM 9.0	NM- 9.2
1	94	4/52	Original; Palais-a	1	1	11	22	33	64	90	115
2	167	5/64	PC-r	1	1	2	4	6	11	16	20
3	166	R/1968	C-price 25¢; PC-r	1	1	2	4	6	13	18	22

95. All Quiet on the Western Front

Ed	HRN	Date	Details	A	C	GD 2.0	VG 4.0	FN 6.0	VF 8.0	VF/NM 9.0	NM- 9.2
1A	96	5/52	Orig.; del Bourgo-a	1	1	14	28	42	81	118	155

Classics Illustrated #97 © GIL

Classics Illustrated #101 © GIL

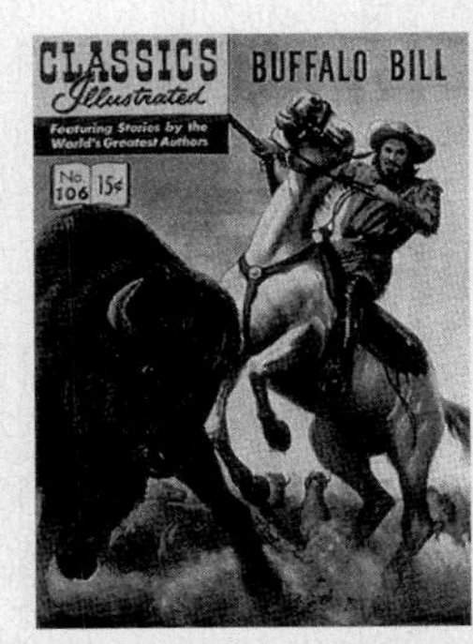

Classics Illustrated #106 © GIL

Ed	HRN	Date	Details	A	C	GD 2.0	VG 4.0	FN 6.0	VF 8.0	VF/NM 9.0	NM- 9.2
1B	99	5/52	Orig.; del Bourgo-a	1	1	13	26	39	72	101	130
2	167	10/64	PC-r	1	1	3	6	9	15	22	28
3	167	11/66	PC-r	1	1	3	6	9	15	22	28

96. Daniel Boone

Ed	HRN	Date	Details	A	C	GD 2.0	VG 4.0	FN 6.0	VF 8.0	VF/NM 9.0	NM- 9.2
1	97	6/52	Original; Blum-a	1	1	11	22	33	62	86	110
2	117	–	PC-r	1	1	2	4	6	9	13	16
3	128	–	PC-r	1	1	2	4	6	9	13	16
4	132	–	PC-r	1	1	2	4	6	9	13	16
5	134	–	"Story of Jesus" on back-c; PC-r	1	1	2	4	6	9	13	16
6	158	–	PC-r	1	1	2	4	6	9	13	16
7	167	1/64	PC-r	1	1	2	4	6	8	11	14
8	167	5/65	PC-r	1	1	2	4	6	8	11	14
9	167	11/66	PC-r	1	1	2	4	6	8	11	14
10	166	Win/69	New-c; price 25¢; PC-r; stiff-c	1	2	3	6	9	15	22	28

97. King Solomon's Mines

Ed	HRN	Date	Details	A	C	GD 2.0	VG 4.0	FN 6.0	VF 8.0	VF/NM 9.0	NM- 9.2
1	96	7/52	Orig.; Kiefer-a	1	1	11	22	33	62	86	110
2	118	–	PC-r	1	1	2	4	6	9	13	16
3	131	–	PC-r	1	1	2	4	6	9	13	16
4	141	–	PC-r	1	1	2	4	6	9	13	16
5	158	–	PC-r	1	1	2	4	6	9	13	16
6	167	2/64	PC-r	1	1	2	4	6	8	11	14
7	167	9/65	PC-r	1	1	2	4	6	8	11	14
8	169	Sm/69	New price 25¢; stiff-c; PC-r	1	1	2	4	6	8	11	14

98. The Red Badge of Courage

Ed	HRN	Date	Details	A	C	GD 2.0	VG 4.0	FN 6.0	VF 8.0	VF/NM 9.0	NM- 9.2
1	98	8/52	Original	1	1	11	22	33	62	86	110
2	118	–	PC-r	1	1	2	4	6	9	13	16
3	132	–	PC-r	1	1	2	4	6	9	13	16
4	142	–	PC-r	1	1	2	4	6	9	13	16
5	152	–	PC-r	1	1	2	4	6	9	13	16
6	161	–	PC-r	1	1	2	4	6	9	13	16
7	167	–	Has orig.date; PC-r	1	1	2	4	6	9	13	16
8	167	9/64	PC-r	1	1	2	4	6	9	13	16
9	167	10/65	PC-r	1	1	2	4	6	9	13	16
10	166	R/1968	New-c&price 25¢; PC-r; stiff-c	1	2	3	6	9	16	23	30

99. Hamlet (Used in **POP**, pg. 102)

Ed	HRN	Date	Details	A	C	GD 2.0	VG 4.0	FN 6.0	VF 8.0	VF/NM 9.0	NM- 9.2
1	98	9/52	Original; Blum-a	1	1	11	22	33	64	90	115
2	121	–	PC-r	1	1	2	4	6	9	13	16
3	141	–	PC-r	1	1	2	4	6	9	13	16
4	158	–	PC-r	1	1	2	4	6	9	13	16
5	167	–	Has orig.date; PC-r	1	1	2	4	6	8	11	14
6	167	7/65	PC-r	1	1	2	4	6	8	11	14
7	166	4/67	PC-r	1	1	2	4	6	8	11	14
8	169	Spr/69	New-c&price 25¢; PC-r; stiff-c	1	2	3	6	9	16	23	30

100. Mutiny on the Bounty

Ed	HRN	Date	Details	A	C	GD 2.0	VG 4.0	FN 6.0	VF 8.0	VF/NM 9.0	NM- 9.2
1	100	10/52	Original	1	1	11	22	33	62	86	110
2	117	–	PC-r	1	1	2	4	6	9	13	16
3	132	–	PC-r	1	1	2	4	6	9	13	16
4	142	–	PC-r	1	1	2	4	6	9	13	16
5	155	–	PC-r	1	1	2	4	6	9	13	16
6	167	–	Has orig. date;PC-r	1	1	2	4	6	8	11	14
7	167	5/64	PC-r	1	1	2	4	6	8	11	14
8	167	3/66	PC-r	1	1	2	4	6	8	11	14
9	169	Spr/70	PC-r; stiff-c	1	1	2	4	6	8	11	14

101. William Tell

Ed	HRN	Date	Details	A	C	GD 2.0	VG 4.0	FN 6.0	VF 8.0	VF/NM 9.0	NM- 9.2
1	101	11/52	Original; Kiefer-c delBourgo-a	1	1	11	22	33	62	86	110
2	118	–	PC-r	1	1	2	4	6	9	13	16
3	141	–	PC-r	1	1	2	4	6	9	13	16
4	158	–	PC-r	1	1	2	4	6	9	13	16
5	167	–	Has orig.date; PC-r	1	1	2	4	6	8	11	14
6	167	11/64	PC-r	1	1	2	4	6	8	11	14
7	166	4/67	PC-r	1	1	2	4	6	8	11	14
8	169	Win/69	New price 25¢; stiff-c; PC-r	1	1	2	4	6	8	11	14

102. The White Company

Ed	HRN	Date	Details	A	C	GD 2.0	VG 4.0	FN 6.0	VF 8.0	VF/NM 9.0	NM- 9.2
1	101	12/52	Original; Blum-a	1	1	14	28	42	76	108	140
2	165	–	PC-r	1	1	3	6	9	16	23	30
3	167	4/64	PC-r	1	1	3	6	9	16	23	30

103. Men Against the Sea

Ed	HRN	Date	Details	A	C	GD 2.0	VG 4.0	FN 6.0	VF 8.0	VF/NM 9.0	NM- 9.2
1	104	1/53	Original; Kiefer-c; Palais-a	1	1	11	22	33	64	90	115
2	114	–	PC-r	1	1	4	8	11	16	19	22
3	131	–	New-c; PC-r	1	2	5	10	15	24	30	35
4	158	–	PC-r	1	2	4	7	10	14	17	20
5	149	–	White reorder list; came after HRN-158; PC-r	1	2	5	10	15	22	26	30
6	167	3/64	PC-r	1	2	2	4	6	9	13	16

104. Bring 'Em Back Alive

Ed	HRN	Date	Details	A	C	GD 2.0	VG 4.0	FN 6.0	VF 8.0	VF/NM 9.0	NM- 9.2
1	105	2/53	Original; Kiefer-c/a	1	1	11	22	33	62	86	110
2	118	–	PC-r	1	1	2	4	6	9	13	16
3	133	–	PC-r	1	1	2	4	6	9	13	16
4	150	–	PC-r	1	1	2	4	6	9	13	16
5	158	–	PC-r	1	1	2	4	6	9	13	16
6	167	10/63	PC-r	1	1	2	4	6	8	11	14
7	167	9/65	PC-r	1	1	2	4	6	8	11	14
8	169	Win/69	New price 25¢; stiff-c; PC-r	1	1	2	4	6	8	11	14

105. From the Earth to the Moon

Ed	HRN	Date	Details	A	C	GD 2.0	VG 4.0	FN 6.0	VF 8.0	VF/NM 9.0	NM- 9.2
1	106	3/53	Original; Blum-a	1	1	11	22	33	62	86	110
2	118	–	PC-r	1	1	2	4	6	9	13	16
3	132	–	PC-r	1	1	2	4	6	9	13	16
4	141	–	PC-r	1	1	2	4	6	9	13	16
5	146	–	PC-r	1	1	2	4	6	9	13	16
6	156	–	PC-r	1	1	2	4	6	9	13	16
7	167	–	Has orig. date; PC-r	1	1	2	4	6	8	11	14
8	167	5/64	PC-r	1	1	2	4	6	8	11	14
9	167	5/65	PC-r	1	1	2	4	6	8	11	14
10A	166	10/67	PC-r	1	1	2	4	6	8	11	14
10B	166	10/67	w/Grit ad stapled in book	1	1	9	18	27	59	117	175
11	169	Sm/69	New price 25¢; stiff-c; PC-r	1	1	2	4	6	8	11	14
12	169	Spr/71	PC-r	1	1	2	4	6	8	11	14

106. Buffalo Bill

Ed	HRN	Date	Details	A	C	GD 2.0	VG 4.0	FN 6.0	VF 8.0	VF/NM 9.0	NM- 9.2
1	107	4/53	Orig.; delBourgo-a	1	1	11	22	33	60	83	105
2	118	–	PC-r	1	1	2	4	6	9	13	16
3	132	–	PC-r	1	1	2	4	6	9	13	16
4	142	–	PC-r	1	1	2	4	6	9	13	16
5	161	–	PC-r	1	1	2	4	6	8	11	14
6	167	3/64	PC-r	1	1	2	4	6	8	11	14
7	166	7/67	PC-r	1	1	2	4	6	8	11	14
8	169	Fall/69	PC-r; stiff-c	1	1	2	4	6	8	11	14

107. King of the Khyber Rifles

Ed	HRN	Date	Details	A	C	GD 2.0	VG 4.0	FN 6.0	VF 8.0	VF/NM 9.0	NM- 9.2
1	108	5/53	Original	1	1	11	22	33	60	83	105
2	118	–	PC-r	1	1	2	4	6	9	13	16
3	146	–	PC-r	1	1	2	4	6	9	13	16
4	158	–	PC-r	1	1	2	4	6	9	13	16
5	167	–	Has orig.date; PC-r	1	1	2	4	6	8	11	14
6	167	10/66	PC-r	1	1	2	4	6	8	11	14

108. Knights of the Round Table

Ed	HRN	Date	Details	A	C	GD 2.0	VG 4.0	FN 6.0	VF 8.0	VF/NM 9.0	NM- 9.2
1A	108	6/53	Original; Blum-a	1	1	11	22	33	64	90	115
1B	109	6/53	Original; scarce	1	1	12	24	36	67	94	120
2	117	–	PC-r	1	1	2	4	6	9	13	16

Classics Illustrated #111 © GIL

Classics Illustrated #118 © GIL

Classics Illustrated #124 © GIL

Ed	HRN	Date	Details	A	C	GD 2.0	VG 4.0	FN 6.0	VF 8.0	VF/NM 9.0	NM- 9.2
3	165	–	PC-r	1	1	2	4	6	8	11	14
4	167	4/64	PC-r	1	1	2	4	6	8	11	14
5	166	4/67	PC-r	1	1	2	4	6	8	11	14
6	169	Sm/69	New price 25¢; stiff-c; PC-r	1	1	2	4	6	8	11	14

109. Pitcairn's Island

Ed	HRN	Date	Details	A	C	GD 2.0	VG 4.0	FN 6.0	VF 8.0	VF/NM 9.0	NM- 9.2
1	110	7/53	Original; Palais-a	1	1	11	22	33	64	90	115
2	165	–	PC-r	1	1	2	4	6	9	13	16
3	167	3/64	PC-r	1	1	2	4	6	9	13	16
4	166	6/67	PC-r	1	1	2	4	6	9	13	16

110. A Study in Scarlet

Ed	HRN	Date	Details	A	C	GD 2.0	VG 4.0	FN 6.0	VF 8.0	VF/NM 9.0	NM- 9.2
1	111	8/53	Original	1	1	15	30	45	84	127	170
2	165	–	PC-r	1	1	11	22	33	62	86	110

111. The Talisman

Ed	HRN	Date	Details	A	C	GD 2.0	VG 4.0	FN 6.0	VF 8.0	VF/NM 9.0	NM- 9.2
1	112	9/53	Original; last H.C. Kiefer-a	1	1	11	22	33	64	90	115
2	165	–	PC-r	1	1	2	4	6	9	13	16
3	167	5/64	PC-r	1	1	2	4	6	9	13	16
4	166	Fall/68	C-price 25¢; PC-r	1	1	2	4	6	9	13	16

112. Adventures of Kit Carson

Ed	HRN	Date	Details	A	C	GD 2.0	VG 4.0	FN 6.0	VF 8.0	VF/NM 9.0	NM- 9.2
1	113	10/53	Original; Palais-a	1	1	11	22	33	62	86	110
2	129	–	PC-r	1	1	2	4	6	9	13	16
3	141	–	PC-r	1	1	2	4	6	9	13	16
4	152	–	PC-r	1	1	2	4	6	9	13	16
5	161	–	PC-r	1	1	2	4	6	8	11	14
6	167	–	PC-r	1	1	2	4	6	8	11	14
7	167	2/65	PC-r	1	1	2	4	6	8	11	14
8	167	5/66	PC-r	1	1	2	4	6	8	11	14
9	166	Win/69	New-c&price 25¢; PC-r; stiff-c	1	2	3	6	9	14	20	25

113. The Forty-Five Guardsmen

Ed	HRN	Date	Details	A	C	GD 2.0	VG 4.0	FN 6.0	VF 8.0	VF/NM 9.0	NM- 9.2
1	114	11/53	Orig.; delBourgo-a	1	1	14	28	42	76	108	140
2	166	7/67	PC-r	1	1	4	8	12	23	37	50

114. The Red Rover

Ed	HRN	Date	Details	A	C	GD 2.0	VG 4.0	FN 6.0	VF 8.0	VF/NM 9.0	NM- 9.2
1	115	12/53	Original	1	1	14	28	42	76	108	140
2	166	7/67	PC-r	1	1	4	8	12	23	37	50

115. How I Found Livingstone

Ed	HRN	Date	Details	A	C	GD 2.0	VG 4.0	FN 6.0	VF 8.0	VF/NM 9.0	NM- 9.2
1	116	1/54	Original	1	1	14	28	42	80	115	150
2	167	1/67	PC-r	1	1	4	8	12	27	44	60

116. The Bottle Imp

Ed	HRN	Date	Details	A	C	GD 2.0	VG 4.0	FN 6.0	VF 8.0	VF/NM 9.0	NM- 9.2
1	117	2/54	Orig.; Cameron-a	1	1	14	28	42	80	115	150
2	167	1/67	PC-r	1	1	4	8	12	27	44	60

117. Captains Courageous

Ed	HRN	Date	Details	A	C	GD 2.0	VG 4.0	FN 6.0	VF 8.0	VF/NM 9.0	NM- 9.2
1	118	3/54	Orig.; Costanza-a	1	1	13	26	39	74	105	135
2	167	2/67	PC-r	1	1	3	6	9	14	20	26
3	169	Fall/69	New price 25¢; stiff-c; PC-r	1	1	3	6	9	14	20	26

118. Rob Roy

Ed	HRN	Date	Details	A	C	GD 2.0	VG 4.0	FN 6.0	VF 8.0	VF/NM 9.0	NM- 9.2
1	119	4/54	Original; Rudy & Walter Palais-a	1	1	14	28	42	80	115	150
2	167	2/67	PC-r	1	1	4	8	12	27	44	60

119. Soldiers of Fortune

Ed	HRN	Date	Details	A	C	GD 2.0	VG 4.0	FN 6.0	VF 8.0	VF/NM 9.0	NM- 9.2
1	120	5/54	Schaffenberger-a	1	1	13	26	39	72	101	130
2	166	3/67	PC-r	1	1	3	6	9	14	20	26
3	169	Spr/70	New price 25¢; stiff-c; PC-r	1	1	3	6	9	14	20	26

120. The Hurricane

Ed	HRN	Date	Details	A	C	GD 2.0	VG 4.0	FN 6.0	VF 8.0	VF/NM 9.0	NM- 9.2
1	121	6/54	Orig.; Cameron-a	1	1	13	26	39	72	101	130
2	166	3/67	PC-r	1	1	4	8	12	22	34	50

121. Wild Bill Hickok

Ed	HRN	Date	Details	A	C	GD 2.0	VG 4.0	FN 6.0	VF 8.0	VF/NM 9.0	NM- 9.2
1	122	7/54	Original	1	1	11	22	33	60	83	105
2	132	–	PC-r	1	1	2	4	6	9	13	16
3	141	–	PC-r	1	1	2	4	6	9	13	16
4	154	–	PC-r	1	1	2	4	6	9	13	16
5	167	–	PC-r	1	1	2	4	6	8	11	14
6	167	8/64	PC-r	1	1	2	4	6	8	11	14
7	166	4/67	PC-r	1	1	2	4	6	8	11	14
8	169	Win/69	PC-r; stiff-c	1	1	2	4	6	8	11	14

122. The Mutineers

Ed	HRN	Date	Details	A	C	GD 2.0	VG 4.0	FN 6.0	VF 8.0	VF/NM 9.0	NM- 9.2
1	123	9/54	Original	1	1	11	22	33	64	90	115
2	136	–	PC-r	1	1	2	4	6	9	13	16
3	146	–	PC-r	1	1	2	4	6	9	13	16
4	158	–	PC-r	1	1	2	4	6	9	13	16
5	167	11/63	PC-r	1	1	2	4	6	8	11	14
6	167	3/65	PC-r	1	1	2	4	6	8	11	14
7	166	8/67	PC-r	1	1	2	4	6	8	11	14

123. Fang and Claw

Ed	HRN	Date	Details	A	C	GD 2.0	VG 4.0	FN 6.0	VF 8.0	VF/NM 9.0	NM- 9.2
1	124	11/54	Original	1	1	11	22	33	64	90	115
2	133	–	PC-r	1	1	2	4	6	9	13	16
3	143	–	PC-r	1	1	2	4	6	9	13	16
4	154	–	PC-r	1	1	2	4	6	9	13	16
5	167	–	Has orig.date; PC-r	1	1	2	4	6	8	11	14
6	167	9/65	PC-r	1	1	2	4	6	8	11	14

124. The War of the Worlds

Ed	HRN	Date	Details	A	C	GD 2.0	VG 4.0	FN 6.0	VF 8.0	VF/NM 9.0	NM- 9.2
1	125	1/55	Original; Cameron-c/a	1	1	14	28	42	80	115	150
2	131	–	PC-r	1	1	2	4	6	10	14	18
3	141	–	PC-r	1	1	2	4	6	10	14	18
4	148	–	PC-r	1	1	2	4	6	10	14	18
5	156	–	PC-r	1	1	2	4	6	10	14	18
6	165	–	PC-r	1	1	2	4	6	13	18	22
7	167	–	PC-r	1	1	2	4	6	9	13	16
8	167	11/64	PC-r	1	1	2	4	6	10	14	18
9	167	11/65	PC-r	1	1	2	4	6	9	13	16
10	166	R/1968	C-price 25¢; PC-r	1	1	2	4	6	9	13	16
11	169	Sm/70	PC-r; stiff-c	1	1	2	4	6	9	13	16

125. The Ox Bow Incident

Ed	HRN	Date	Details	A	C	GD 2.0	VG 4.0	FN 6.0	VF 8.0	VF/NM 9.0	NM- 9.2
1	–	3/55	Original; Picture Progress replaces reorder list	1	1	11	22	33	60	83	105
2	143	–	PC-r	1	1	2	4	6	9	13	16
3	152	–	PC-r	1	1	2	4	6	9	13	16
4	149	–	PC-r	1	1	2	4	6	9	13	16
5	167	–	PC-r	1	1	2	4	6	8	11	14
6	167	11/64	PC-r	1	1	2	4	6	8	11	14
7	166	4/67	PC-r	1	1	2	4	6	8	11	14
8	169	Win/69	New price 25¢; stiff-c; PC-r	1	1	2	4	6	8	11	14

126. The Downfall

Ed	HRN	Date	Details	A	C	GD 2.0	VG 4.0	FN 6.0	VF 8.0	VF/NM 9.0	NM- 9.2
1	–	5/55	Orig.; 'Picture Progress' replaces reorder list; Cameron-c/a	1	1	11	22	33	64	90	115
2	167	8/64	PC-r	1	1	2	4	6	13	18	22
3	166	R/1968	C-price 25¢; PC-r	1	1	2	4	6	13	18	22

127. The King of the Mountains

Ed	HRN	Date	Details	A	C	GD 2.0	VG 4.0	FN 6.0	VF 8.0	VF/NM 9.0	NM- 9.2
1	128	7/55	Original	1	1	11	22	33	64	90	115
2	167	6/64	PC-r	1	1	2	4	6	11	16	20
3	166	F/1968	C-price 25¢; PC-r	1	1	2	4	6	11	16	20

128. Macbeth (Used in **POP**, pg. 102)

Ed	HRN	Date	Details	A	C	GD 2.0	VG 4.0	FN 6.0	VF 8.0	VF/NM 9.0	NM- 9.2
1	128	9/55	Orig.; last Blum-a	1	1	11	22	33	64	90	115
2	143	–	PC-r	1	1	2	4	6	9	13	16

Classics Illustrated #130 © GIL

Classics Illustrated #138 © GIL

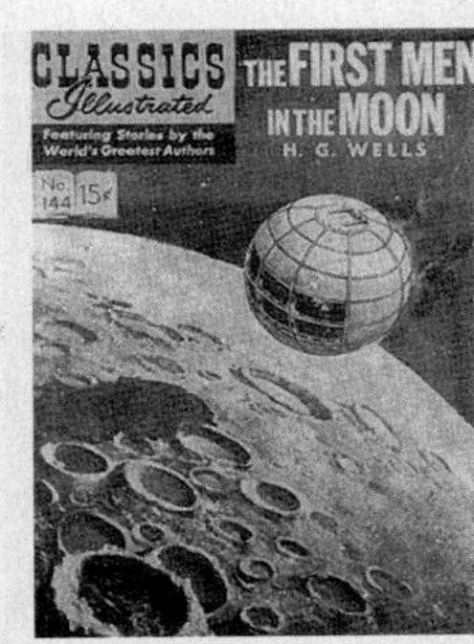

Classics Illustrated #144 © GIL

Ed	HRN	Date	Details	A	C	GD 2.0	VG 4.0	FN 6.0	VF 8.0	VF/NM 9.0	NM- 9.2
3	158	–	PC-r	1	1	2	4	6	9	13	16
4	167	–	PC-r	1	1	2	4	6	8	11	14
5	167	6/64	PC-r	1	1	2	4	6	8	11	14
6	166	4/67	PC-r	1	1	2	4	6	8	11	14
7	166	R/1968	C-Price 25¢; PC-r	1	1	2	4	6	8	11	14
8	169	Spr/70	Stiff-c; PC-r	1	1	2	4	6	8	11	14

129. Davy Crockett

Ed	HRN	Date	Details	A	C	GD 2.0	VG 4.0	FN 6.0	VF 8.0	VF/NM 9.0	NM- 9.2
1	129	11/55	Orig.; Cameron-a	1	1	14	28	42	82	121	160
2	167	9/66	PC-r	1	1	11	22	33	62	86	110

130. Caesar's Conquests

Ed	HRN	Date	Details	A	C	GD 2.0	VG 4.0	FN 6.0	VF 8.0	VF/NM 9.0	NM- 9.2
1	130	1/56	Original; Orlando-a	1	1	11	22	33	64	90	115
2	142	–	PC-r	1	1	2	4	6	9	13	16
3	152	–	PC-r	1	1	2	4	6	9	13	16
4	149	–	PC-r	1	1	2	4	6	9	13	16
5	167	–	PC-r	1	1	2	4	6	8	11	14
6	167	10/64	PC-r	1	1	2	4	6	8	11	14
7	167	4/66	PC-r	1	1	2	4	6	8	11	14

131. The Covered Wagon

Ed	HRN	Date	Details	A	C	GD 2.0	VG 4.0	FN 6.0	VF 8.0	VF/NM 9.0	NM- 9.2
1	131	3/56	Original	1	1	6	12	18	40	73	105
2	143	–	PC-r	1	1	2	4	6	9	13	16
3	152	–	PC-r	1	1	2	4	6	9	13	16
4	158	–	PC-r	1	1	2	4	6	9	13	16
5	167	–	PC-r	1	1	2	4	6	8	11	14
6	167	11/64	PC-r	1	1	2	4	6	8	11	14
7	167	4/66	PC-r	1	1	2	4	6	8	11	14
8	169	Win/69	New price 25¢; stiff-c; PC-r	1	1	2	4	6	8	11	14

132. The Dark Frigate

Ed	HRN	Date	Details	A	C	GD 2.0	VG 4.0	FN 6.0	VF 8.0	VF/NM 9.0	NM- 9.2
1	132	5/56	Original	1	1	11	22	33	64	90	115
2	150	–	PC-r	1	1	2	4	6	9	13	16
3	167	1/64	PC-r	1	1	2	4	6	9	13	16
4	166	5/67	PC-r	1	1	2	4	6	9	13	16

133. The Time Machine

Ed	HRN	Date	Details	A	C	GD 2.0	VG 4.0	FN 6.0	VF 8.0	VF/NM 9.0	NM- 9.2
1	132	7/56	Orig.; Cameron-a	1	1	7	14	21	46	86	125
2	142	–	PC-r	1	1	2	4	6	10	14	18
3	152	–	PC-r	1	1	2	4	6	10	14	18
4	158	–	PC-r	1	1	2	4	6	9	13	16
5	167	–	PC-r	1	1	2	4	6	9	13	16
6	167	6/64	PC-r	1	1	2	4	6	10	14	18
7	167	3/66	PC-r	1	1	2	4	6	9	13	16
8	166	12/67	PC-r	1	1	2	4	6	9	13	16
9	169	Win/71	New price 25¢; stiff-c; PC-r	1	1	2	4	6	9	13	16

134. Romeo and Juliet

Ed	HRN	Date	Details	A	C	GD 2.0	VG 4.0	FN 6.0	VF 8.0	VF/NM 9.0	NM- 9.2
1	134	9/56	Original; Evans-a	1	1	6	12	18	42	79	115
2	161	–	PC-r	1	1	2	4	6	9	13	16
3	167	9/63	PC-r	1	1	2	4	6	8	11	14
4	167	5/65	PC-r	1	1	2	4	6	8	11	14
5	166	6/67	PC-r	1	1	2	4	6	8	11	14
6	166	Win/69	New c&price 25¢; stiff-c; PC-r	1	2	3	6	9	17	25	32

135. Waterloo

Ed	HRN	Date	Details	A	C	GD 2.0	VG 4.0	FN 6.0	VF 8.0	VF/NM 9.0	NM- 9.2
1	135	11/56	Orig.; G. Ingels-a	1	1	6	12	18	42	79	115
2	153	–	PC-r	1	1	2	4	6	9	13	16
3	167	–	PC-r	1	1	2	4	6	8	11	14
4	167	9/64	PC-r	1	1	2	4	6	8	11	14
5	166	R/1968	C-price 25¢; PC-r	1	1	2	4	6	8	11	14

136. Lord Jim

Ed	HRN	Date	Details	A	C	GD 2.0	VG 4.0	FN 6.0	VF 8.0	VF/NM 9.0	NM- 9.2
1	136	1/57	Original; Evans-a	1	1	6	12	18	42	79	115
2	165	–	PC-r	1	1	2	4	6	8	11	14
3	167	3/64	PC-r	1	1	2	4	6	8	11	14
4	167	9/66	PC-r	1	1	2	4	6	8	11	14
5	169	Sm/69	New price 25 ¢; stiff-c; PC-r	1	1	2	4	6	8	11	14

137. The Little Savage

Ed	HRN	Date	Details	A	C	GD 2.0	VG 4.0	FN 6.0	VF 8.0	VF/NM 9.0	NM- 9.2
1	136	3/57	Original; Evans-a	1	1	6	12	18	42	79	115
2	148	–	PC-r	1	1	2	4	6	9	13	16
3	156	–	PC-r	1	1	2	4	6	9	13	16
4	167	–	PC-r	1	1	2	4	6	8	11	14
5	167	10/64	PC-r	1	1	2	4	6	8	11	14
6	166	8/67	PC-r	1	1	2	4	6	8	11	14
7	169	Spr/70	New price 25¢; stiff-c; PC-r	1	1	2	4	6	8	11	14

138. A Journey to the Center of the Earth

Ed	HRN	Date	Details	A	C	GD 2.0	VG 4.0	FN 6.0	VF 8.0	VF/NM 9.0	NM- 9.2
1	136	5/57	Original	1	1	8	16	24	51	96	140
2	146	–	PC-r	1	1	2	4	6	11	16	20
3	156	–	PC-r	1	1	2	4	6	11	16	20
4	158	–	PC-r	1	1	2	4	6	9	13	16
5	167	–	PC-r	1	1	2	4	6	8	11	14
6	167	6/64	PC-r	1	1	2	4	6	13	18	22
7	167	4/66	PC-r	1	1	2	4	6	13	18	22
8	166	R/68	C-price 25¢; PC-r	1	1	2	4	6	10	14	18

139. In the Reign of Terror

Ed	HRN	Date	Details	A	C	GD 2.0	VG 4.0	FN 6.0	VF 8.0	VF/NM 9.0	NM- 9.2
1	139	7/57	Original; Evans-a	1	1	6	12	18	40	73	105
2	154	–	PC-r	1	1	2	4	6	9	13	16
3	167	–	Has orig.date; PC-r	1	1	2	4	6	8	11	14
4	167	7/64	PC-r	1	1	2	4	6	8	11	14
5	166	R/1968	C-price 25¢; PC-r	1	1	2	4	6	8	11	14

140. On Jungle Trails

Ed	HRN	Date	Details	A	C	GD 2.0	VG 4.0	FN 6.0	VF 8.0	VF/NM 9.0	NM- 9.2
1	140	9/57	Original	1	1	6	12	18	40	73	105
2	150	–	PC-r	1	1	2	4	6	9	13	16
3	160	–	PC-r	1	1	2	4	6	9	13	16
4	167	9/63	PC-r	1	1	2	4	6	8	11	14
5	167	9/65	PC-r	1	1	2	4	6	8	11	14

141. Castle Dangerous

Ed	HRN	Date	Details	A	C	GD 2.0	VG 4.0	FN 6.0	VF 8.0	VF/NM 9.0	NM- 9.2
1	141	11/57	Original	1	1	7	14	21	44	82	120
2	152	–	PC-r	1	1	2	4	6	9	13	16
3	167	–	PC-r	1	1	2	4	6	9	13	16
4	166	7/67	PC-r	1	1	2	4	6	9	13	16

142. Abraham Lincoln

Ed	HRN	Date	Details	A	C	GD 2.0	VG 4.0	FN 6.0	VF 8.0	VF/NM 9.0	NM- 9.2
1	142	1/58	Original	1	1	6	12	18	42	79	115
2	154	–	PC-r	1	1	2	4	6	9	13	16
3	158	–	PC-r	1	1	2	4	6	9	13	16
4	167	10/63	PC-r	1	1	2	4	6	8	11	14
5	167	7/65	PC-r	1	1	2	4	6	8	11	14
6	166	11/67	PC-r	1	1	2	4	6	8	11	14
7	169	Fall/69	New price 25¢; stiff-c; PC-r	1	1	2	4	6	8	11	14

143. Kim

Ed	HRN	Date	Details	A	C	GD 2.0	VG 4.0	FN 6.0	VF 8.0	VF/NM 9.0	NM- 9.2
1	143	3/58	Original; Orlando-a	1	1	6	12	18	40	73	105
2	165	–	PC-r	1	1	2	4	6	8	11	14
3	167	11/63	PC-r	1	1	2	4	6	8	11	14
4	167	8/65	PC-r	1	1	2	4	6	8	11	14
5	169	Win/69	New price 25¢; stiff-c; PC-r	1	1	2	4	6	8	11	14

144. The First Men in the Moon

Ed	HRN	Date	Details	A	C	GD 2.0	VG 4.0	FN 6.0	VF 8.0	VF/NM 9.0	NM- 9.2
1	143	5/58	Original; Woodbridge/Williamson/Torres-a	1	1	7	14	21	46	86	125
2	152	–	(Rare)-PC-r	1	1	8	16	24	51	96	140
3	153	–	PC-r	1	1	2	4	6	9	13	16
4	161	–	PC-r	1	1	2	4	6	8	11	14
5	167	–	PC-r	1	1	2	4	6	8	11	14
6	167	12/65	PC-r	1	1	2	4	6	8	11	14
7	166	Fall/68	New-c&price 25¢; PC-r; stiff-c	1	2	3	6	9	16	23	30
8	169	Win/69	Stiff-c; PC-r	1	2	2	4	6	10	16	20

145. The Crisis

Classics Illustrated #149 © GIL

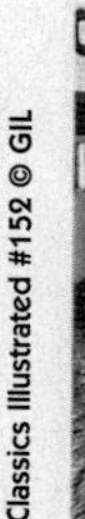
Classics Illustrated #152 © GIL

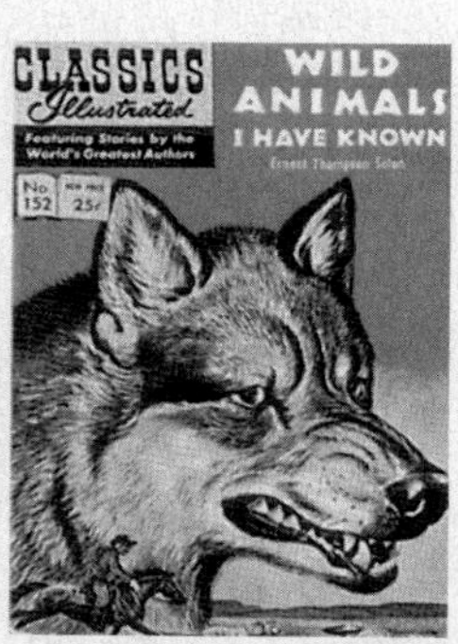

Classics Illustrated #161 © GIL

Ed	HRN	Date	Details	A	C	GD 2.0	VG 4.0	FN 6.0	VF 8.0	VF/NM 9.0	NM- 9.2
1	143	7/58	Original; Evans-a	1	1	6	12	18	42	79	115
2	156	–	PC-r	1	1	2	4	6	9	13	16
3	167	10/63	PC-r	1	1	2	4	6	8	11	14
4	167	3/65	PC-r	1	1	2	4	6	8	11	14
5	166	R/68	C-price 25¢; PC-r	1	1	2	4	6	8	11	14

146. With Fire and Sword

Ed	HRN	Date	Details	A	C	GD 2.0	VG 4.0	FN 6.0	VF 8.0	VF/NM 9.0	NM- 9.2
1	143	9/58	Original; Woodbridge-a	1	1	6	12	18	42	79	115
2	156	–	PC-r	1	1	2	4	6	10	14	18
3	167	11/63	PC-r	1	1	2	4	6	9	13	16
4	167	3/65	PC-r	1	1	2	4	6	9	13	16

147. Ben-Hur

Ed	HRN	Date	Details	A	C	GD 2.0	VG 4.0	FN 6.0	VF 8.0	VF/NM 9.0	NM- 9.2
1	147	11/58	Original; Orlando-a	1	1	6	12	18	41	76	110
2	152	–	Scarce; PC-r	1	1	6	12	18	42	79	115
3	153	–	PC-r	1	1	2	4	6	9	13	16
4	158	–	PC-r	1	1	2	4	6	9	13	16
5	167	–	Orig.date; but PC-r	1	1	2	4	6	8	11	14
6	167	2/65	PC-r	1	1	2	4	6	8	11	14
7	167	9/66	PC-r	1	1	2	4	6	8	11	14
8A	166	Fall/68	New-c&price 25¢; PC-r; soft-c	1	2	3	6	9	16	24	32
8B	166	Fall/68	New-c&price 25¢; PC-r; stiff-c; scarce	1	2	3	6	9	21	33	45

148. The Buccaneer

Ed	HRN	Date	Details	A	C	GD 2.0	VG 4.0	FN 6.0	VF 8.0	VF/NM 9.0	NM- 9.2
1	148	1/59	Orig.; Evans/Jenny-a; Saunders-c	1	1	6	12	18	40	73	105
2	568	–	Juniors list only PC-r	1	1	2	4	6	9	13	16
3	167	–	PC-r	1	1	2	4	6	8	11	14
4	167	9/65	PC-r	1	1	2	4	6	8	11	14
5	169	Sm/69	New price 25¢; PC-r; stiff-c	1	1	2	4	6	8	11	14

149. Off on a Comet

Ed	HRN	Date	Details	A	C	GD 2.0	VG 4.0	FN 6.0	VF 8.0	VF/NM 9.0	NM- 9.2
1	149	3/59	Orig.;G.McCann-a; blue reorder list	1	1	6	12	18	42	79	115
2	155	–	PC-r	1	1	2	4	6	9	13	16
3	149	–	PC-r; white reorder list; no coming-next ad	1	1	2	4	6	9	13	16
4	167	12/63	PC-r	1	1	2	4	6	8	11	14
5	167	2/65	PC-r	1	1	2	4	6	8	11	14
6	167	10/66	PC-r	1	1	2	4	6	8	11	14
7	166	Fall/68	New-c & price 25¢; PC-r	1	2	3	6	9	16	23	30

150. The Virginian

Ed	HRN	Date	Details	A	C	GD 2.0	VG 4.0	FN 6.0	VF 8.0	VF/NM 9.0	NM- 9.2
1	150	5/59	Original	1	1	7	14	21	44	82	120
2	164	–	PC-r	1	1	2	4	6	11	16	20
3	167	10/63	PC-r	1	1	3	6	9	15	21	26
4	167	12/65	PC-r	1	1	2	4	6	11	16	20

151. Won By the Sword

Ed	HRN	Date	Details	A	C	GD 2.0	VG 4.0	FN 6.0	VF 8.0	VF/NM 9.0	NM- 9.2
1	150	7/59	Original	1	1	6	12	18	42	79	115
2	164	–	PC-r	1	1	2	4	6	10	14	18
3	167	10/63	PC-r	1	1	2	4	6	10	14	18
4	166	7/67	PC-r	1	1	2	4	6	10	14	18

152. Wild Animals I Have Known

Ed	HRN	Date	Details	A	C	GD 2.0	VG 4.0	FN 6.0	VF 8.0	VF/NM 9.0	NM- 9.2
1	152	9/59	Orig.; L.B. Cole c/a	1	1	7	14	21	46	86	125
2A	149	–	PC-r; white reorder list; no coming-next ad; IBC: Jr. list #572	1	1	2	4	6	9	13	16
2B	149	–	PC-r; inside-bc: Jr. list to #555	1	1	2	4	6	9	13	16
2C	149	–	PC-r; inside-bc: has World Around Us ad; scarce	1	1	3	6	9	15	21	26
3	167	9/63	PC-r	1	1	2	4	6	8	11	14
4	167	8/65	PC-r	1	1	2	4	6	8	11	14
5	169	Fall/69	New price 25¢; stiff-c; PC-r	1	1	2	4	6	8	11	14

153. The Invisible Man

Ed	HRN	Date	Details	A	C	GD 2.0	VG 4.0	FN 6.0	VF 8.0	VF/NM 9.0	NM- 9.2
1	153	11/59	Original	1	1	7	14	21	49	92	135
2A	149	–	PC-r; white reorder list; no coming-next ad; inside-bc: Jr. list to #572	1	1	2	4	6	11	16	20
2B	149	–	PC-r; inside-bc: Jr. list to #555	1	1	2	4	6	13	18	22
3	167	–	PC-r	1	1	2	4	6	9	13	16
4	167	2/65	PC-r	1	1	2	4	6	9	13	16
5	167	9/66	PC-r	1	1	2	4	6	9	13	16
6	166	Win/69	New price 25¢; PC-r; stiff-c	1	1	2	4	6	9	13	16
7	169	Spr/71	Stiff-c; letters spelling 'Invisible Man' are 'solid' not 'invisible;' PC-r	1	1	2	4	6	9	13	16

154. The Conspiracy of Pontiac

Ed	HRN	Date	Details	A	C	GD 2.0	VG 4.0	FN 6.0	VF 8.0	VF/NM 9.0	NM- 9.2
1	154	1/60	Original	1	1	7	14	21	41	82	120
2	167	11/63	PC-r	1	1	2	4	6	13	18	22
3	167	7/64	PC-r	1	1	2	4	6	13	18	22
4	166	12/67	PC-r	1	1	2	4	6	13	18	22

155. The Lion of the North

Ed	HRN	Date	Details	A	C	GD 2.0	VG 4.0	FN 6.0	VF 8.0	VF/NM 9.0	NM- 9.2
1	154	3/60	Original	1	1	6	12	18	42	79	115
2	167	1/64	PC-r	1	1	2	4	6	11	16	20
3	166	R/1967	C-price 25¢; PC-r	1	1	2	4	6	10	14	18

156. The Conquest of Mexico

Ed	HRN	Date	Details	A	C	GD 2.0	VG 4.0	FN 6.0	VF 8.0	VF/NM 9.0	NM- 9.2
1	156	5/60	Orig.; Bruno Premiani-c/a	1	1	6	12	18	42	79	115
2	167	1/64	PC-r	1	1	2	4	6	10	14	18
3	166	8/67	PC-r	1	1	2	4	6	10	14	18
4	169	Spr/70	New price 25¢; stiff-c; PC-r	1	1	2	4	6	9	13	16

157. Lives of the Hunted

Ed	HRN	Date	Details	A	C	GD 2.0	VG 4.0	FN 6.0	VF 8.0	VF/NM 9.0	NM- 9.2
1	156	7/60	Orig.; L.B. Cole-c	1	1	7	14	21	44	82	120
2	167	2/64	PC-r	1	1	2	4	6	13	18	22
3	166	10/67	PC-r	1	1	2	4	6	13	18	22

158. The Conspirators

Ed	HRN	Date	Details	A	C	GD 2.0	VG 4.0	FN 6.0	VF 8.0	VF/NM 9.0	NM- 9.2
1	156	9/60	Original	1	1	7	14	21	44	82	120
2	167	7/64	PC-r	1	1	2	4	6	13	18	22
3	166	10/67	PC-r	1	1	2	4	6	13	18	22

159. The Octopus

Ed	HRN	Date	Details	A	C	GD 2.0	VG 4.0	FN 6.0	VF 8.0	VF/NM 9.0	NM- 9.2
1	159	11/60	Orig.; Gray Morrow-a; L.B. Cole-c	1	1	7	14	21	44	82	120
2	167	2/64	PC-r	1	1	2	4	6	13	18	22
3	166	R/1967	C-price 25¢; PC-r	1	1	2	4	6	13	18	22

160. The Food of the Gods

Ed	HRN	Date	Details	A	C	GD 2.0	VG 4.0	FN 6.0	VF 8.0	VF/NM 9.0	NM- 9.2
1A	159	1/61	Original	1	1	7	14	21	46	86	125
1B	160	1/61	Original; same, except for HRN	1	1	7	14	21	44	82	120
2	167	1/64	PC-r	1	1	2	4	6	13	18	22
3	166	6/67	PC-r	1	1	2	4	6	13	18	22

161. Cleopatra

Ed	HRN	Date	Details	A	C	GD 2.0	VG 4.0	FN 6.0	VF 8.0	VF/NM 9.0	NM- 9.2
1	161	3/61	Original	1	1	7	14	21	44	82	120
2	167	1/64	PC-r	1	1	3	6	9	14	19	24
3	166	8/67	PC-r	1	1	3	6	9	14	19	24

162. Robur the Conqueror

Classics Illustrated #167 © GIL

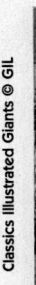

Classics Illustrated Giants © GIL

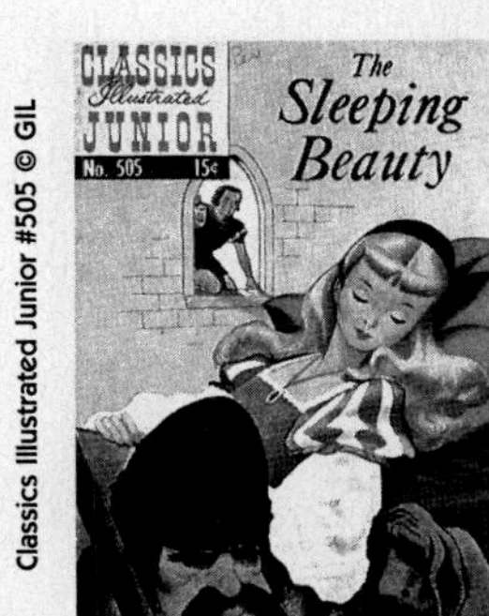

Classics Illustrated Junior #505 © GIL

Ed	HRN	Date	Details	A	C	GD 2.0	VG 4.0	FN 6.0	VF 8.0	VF/NM 9.0	NM- 9.2
1	162	5/61	Original	1	1	7	14	21	44	82	120
2	167	7/64	PC-r	1	1	3	6	9	14	19	24
3	166	8/67	PC-r	1	1	3	6	9	14	19	24

163. Master of the World

Ed	HRN	Date	Details	A	C	GD 2.0	VG 4.0	FN 6.0	VF 8.0	VF/NM 9.0	NM- 9.2
1	163	7/61	Original; Gray Morrow-a	1	1	7	14	21	44	82	120
2	167	1/65	PC-r	1	1	2	4	6	13	18	22
3	166	R/1968	C-price 25¢; PC-r	1	1	2	4	6	13	18	22

164. The Cossack Chief

Ed	HRN	Date	Details	A	C	GD 2.0	VG 4.0	FN 6.0	VF 8.0	VF/NM 9.0	NM- 9.2
1	164	(1961)	Orig.; nd(10/61?)	1	1	6	12	18	41	76	110
2	167	4/65	PC-r	1	1	2	4	6	13	18	22
3	166	Fall/68	C-price 25¢; PC-r	1	1	2	4	6	13	18	22

165. The Queen's Necklace

Ed	HRN	Date	Details	A	C	GD 2.0	VG 4.0	FN 6.0	VF 8.0	VF/NM 9.0	NM- 9.2
1	164	1/62	Original; Morrow-a	1	1	7	14	21	44	82	120
2	167	4/65	PC-r	1	1	2	4	6	13	18	22
3	166	Fall/68	C-price 25¢; PC-r	1	1	2	4	6	13	18	22

166. Tigers and Traitors

Ed	HRN	Date	Details	A	C	GD 2.0	VG 4.0	FN 6.0	VF 8.0	VF/NM 9.0	NM- 9.2
1	165	5/62	Original	1	1	8	16	24	55	105	155
2	167	2/64	PC-r	1	1	3	6	9	21	33	45
3	167	11/66	PC-r	1	1	3	6	9	21	33	45

167. Faust

Ed	HRN	Date	Details	A	C	GD 2.0	VG 4.0	FN 6.0	VF 8.0	VF/NM 9.0	NM- 9.2
1	165	8/62	Original	1	1	11	22	33	75	160	245
2	167	2/64	PC-r	1	1	5	10	15	34	60	85
3	166	6/67	PC-r	1	1	5	10	15	34	60	85

168. In Freedom's Cause

Ed	HRN	Date	Details	A	C	GD 2.0	VG 4.0	FN 6.0	VF 8.0	VF/NM 9.0	NM- 9.2
1	169	Win/69	Original; Evans/ Crandall-a; stiff-c; 25¢; no coming-next ad;	1	1	13	26	39	86	188	290

169. Negro Americans The Early Years

Ed	HRN	Date	Details	A	C	GD 2.0	VG 4.0	FN 6.0	VF 8.0	VF/NM 9.0	NM- 9.2
1	166	Spr/69	Orig. & last issue; 25¢; Stiff-c; no coming-next ad; other sources indicate publication date of 5/69	1	1	12	24	36	80	173	265
2	169	Spr/69	Stiff-c	1	1	7	14	21	44	82	120

NOTE: *Many other titles were prepared or planned but were only issued in British/European series.*

CLASSIC POPEYE (See Popeye, Classic)

CLASSIC PUNISHER (Also see Punisher)
Marvel Comics: Dec, 1989 ($4.95, B&W, deluxe format, 68 pgs.)

1-Reprints Marvel Super Action #1 & Marvel Preview #2 plus new story 5.00

CLASSIC RED SONJA
Dynamite Entertainment: 2010 - No. 4, 2010 ($3.99)

1-4-Newly colored reprints of stories from Savage Sword of Conan magazine 4.00

CLASSICS ILLUSTRATED
First Publishing/Berkley Publishing: Feb, 1990 - No. 27, July, 1991 ($3.75/$3.95, 52 pgs.)

1-27: 1-Gahan Wilson-c/a. 4-Sienkiewicz painted-c/a. 6-Russell scripts/layouts. 7-Spiegle-a. 9-Ploog-c/a. 16-Staton-a. 18-Gahan Wilson-c/a; 20-Geary-a. 26-Aesop's Fables (6/91). 26,27-Direct sale only 5.00

CLASSICS ILLUSTRATED
Acclaim Books/Twin Circle PublishingCo.: Feb, 1997 - Jan, 1998 ($4.99, digest-size) (Each book contains study notes)

A Christmas Carol-(12/97), A Connecticut Yankee in King Arthur's Court-(5/97), All Quiet on the Western Front-(1/98), A Midsummer's Night Dream-(4/97) Around the World in 80 Days-(1/98), A Tale of Two Cities-(2/97)Joe Orlando-r, Captains Courageous-(11/97), Crime and Punishment-(3/97), Dr. Jekyll and Mr. Hyde-(10/97), Don Quixote-(12/97), Frankenstein-(10/97), Great Expectations-(4/97), Hamlet-(3/97), Huckleberry Finn-(3/97), Jane Eyre-(2/97), Kidnapped-(1/98), Les Miserables-(5/97), Lord Jim-(9/97), Macbeth-(5/97), Moby Dick-(4/97), Oliver Twist-(5/97), Robinson Crusoe-(9/97), Romeo & Juliet-(2/97), Silas Marner-(11/97), The Call of the Wild-(9/97), The Count of Monte Cristo-(1/98), The House of the Seven Gables-(9/97), The Iliad-(12/97), The Invisible Man-(10/97), The Last of the Mohicans-(12/97), The Master of Ballantrae-(11/97), The Odyssey-(3/97), The Prince and the Pauper-(4/97), The Red Badge Of Courage-(9/97), Tom Sawyer-(2/97) Wuthering Heights-(11/97) 5.00

NOTE: *Stories reprinted from the original Gilberton Classic Comics and Classics Illustrated.*

CLASSICS ILLUSTRATED GIANTS
Gilberton Publications: Oct, 1949 (One-Shots - "OS")

These Giant Editions, all with new front and back covers, were advertised from 10/49 to 2/52. They were 50¢ on the newsstand and 60¢ by mail. They are actually four Classics in one volume. All the stories are reprints of the Classics Illustrated Series.
NOTE: There were also British hardback Adventure & Indian Giants in 1952, with the same covers but different contents: Adventure - 2, 7, 10; Indian - 17, 22, 37, 58. They are also rare.

	GD 2.0	VG 4.0	FN 6.0	VF 8.0	VF/NM 9.0	NM- 9.2
"An Illustrated Library of Great Adventure Stories" - reprints of No. 6,7,8,10 (Rare); Kiefer-c	158	316	474	1003	1727	2450
"An Illustrated Library of Exciting Mystery Stories" - reprints of No. 30,21,40, 13 (Rare); Blum-c	168	336	504	1075	1838	2600
"An Illustrated Library of Great Indian Stories" - reprints of No. 4,17,22,37 (Rare); Blum-c	158	316	474	1003	1727	2450

INTRODUCTION TO CLASSICS ILLUSTRATED JUNIOR

Collectors of Juniors can be put into one of two categories: those who want any copy of each title, and those who want all the originals. Those seeking every original and reprint edition are a limited group, primarily because Juniors have no changes in art or covers to spark interest, and because reprints are so low in value it is difficult to get dealers to look for specific reprint editions.

In recent years it has become apparent that most serious Classics collectors seek Junior originals. Those seeking reprints seek them for low cost. This has made the previous note about the comparative market value of reprints inadequate. Three particular reprint editions are worth even more. For the 535-Twin Circle edition, see Giveaways. There are also reprint editions of 501 and 503 which have a full-page bc ad for the very rare Junior record. Those may sell as high as $10-$15 in mint. Original editions of 557 and 558 also have that ad.

There are no reprint editions of 577. The only edition, from 1969, is a 25 cent stiff-cover edition with no ad for the next issue. All other original editions have coming-next ad. But 577, like C.I. #168, was prepared in 1962 but not issued. Copies of 577 can be found in 1963 British/European series, which then continued with dozens of additional new Junior titles.

PRICES LISTED BELOW ARE FOR ORIGINAL EDITIONS, WHICH HAVE AN AD FOR THE NEXT ISSUE.

NOTE: *Non HRN 576 copies- many are written on or colored . Reprints with 576 HRN are worth about 1/3 original prices. All other HRN #'s are 1/2 original price*

CLASSICS ILLUSTRATED JUNIOR
Famous Authors Ltd. (Gilberton Publications): Oct, 1953 - Spring, 1971

	GD 2.0	VG 4.0	FN 6.0	VF 8.0	VF/NM 9.0	NM- 9.2
501-Snow White & the Seven Dwarfs; Alex Blum-a	12	24	36	69	97	125
502-The Ugly Duckling	9	18	27	47	61	75
503-Cinderella	8	16	24	40	50	60
504-512: 504-The Pied Piper. 505-The Sleeping Beauty. 506-The Three Little Pigs. 507-Jack & the Beanstalk. 508-Goldilocks & the Three Bears. 509-Beauty and the Beast. 510-Little Red Riding Hood. 511-Puss-N Boots. 512-Rumpelstiltskin	6	12	18	27	33	38
513-Pinocchio	7	14	21	37	46	55
514-The Steadfast Tin Soldier	8	16	24	44	57	70
515-Johnny Appleseed	6	12	18	27	33	38
516-Aladdin and His Lamp	6	12	18	29	36	42
517-519: 517-The Emperor's New Clothes. 518-The Golden Goose. 519-Paul Bunyan	6	12	18	27	33	38
520-Thumbelina	6	12	18	29	36	42
521-King of the Golden River	6	12	18	27	33	38
522,523,530: 522-The Nightingale. 523-The Gallant Tailor. 530-The Golden Bird	5	10	15	24	30	35
524-The Wild Swans	6	12	18	29	36	42
525,526: 525-The Little Mermaid. 526-The Frog Prince	6	12	18	29	36	42
527-The Golden-Haired Giant	6	12	18	27	33	38
528-The Penny Prince	6	12	18	27	33	38
529-The Magic Servants	6	12	18	27	33	38
531-Rapunzel	6	12	18	27	33	38
532-534: 532-The Dancing Princesses. 533-The Magic Fountain. 534-The Golden Touch	5	10	15	23	28	32
535-The Wizard of Oz	8	16	24	44	57	70
536-The Chimney Sweep	6	12	18	27	33	38
537-The Three Fairies	6	12	18	28	34	40
538-Silly Hans	5	10	15	23	28	32
539-The Enchanted Fish	6	12	18	31	38	45
540-The Tinder-Box	6	12	18	31	38	45
541-Snow White & Rose Red	5	10	15	24	30	35
542-The Donkey's Tale	5	10	15	24	30	35
543-The House in the Woods	6	12	18	27	33	38

Classics Illustrated Junior #569 © GIL

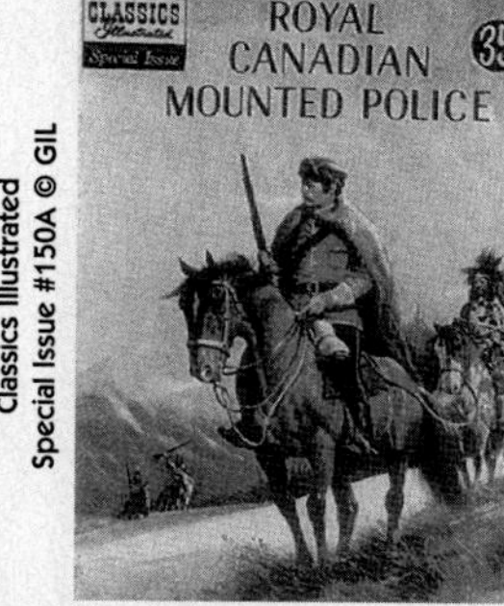

Classics Illustrated Special Issue #150A © GIL

Clean Room #4 © Gail Simone

	GD 2.0	VG 4.0	FN 6.0	VF 8.0	VF/NM 9.0	NM- 9.2
544-The Golden Fleece	6	12	18	31	38	45
545-The Glass Mountain	5	10	15	24	30	35
546-The Elves & the Shoemaker	5	10	15	24	30	35
547-The Wishing Table	6	12	18	27	33	38
548-551: 548-The Magic Pitcher. 549-Simple Kate. 550-The Singing Donkey. 551-The Queen Bee	5	10	15	23	28	32
552-The Three Little Dwarfs	6	12	18	27	33	38
553,556: 553-King Thrushbeard. 556-The Elf Mound	5	10	15	23	28	32
554-The Enchanted Deer	6	12	18	29	36	42
555-The Three Golden Apples	5	10	15	24	30	35
557-Silly Willy	6	12	18	28	34	40
558-The Magic Dish; L.B. Cole-c; soft and stiff-c exist on original	7	14	21	35	43	50
559-The Japanese Lantern; 1 pg. Ingels-a; L.B. Cole-c	7	14	21	35	43	50
560-The Doll Princess; L.B. Cole-c	7	14	21	35	43	50
561-Hans Humdrum; L.B. Cole-c	6	12	18	29	36	42
562-The Enchanted Pony; L.B. Cole-c	7	14	21	35	43	50
563,565-568,570: 563-The Wishing Well; L.B. Cole-c. 565-The Silly Princess; L.B. Cole-c. 566-Clumsy Hans; L.B. Cole-c. 567-The Bearskin Soldier; L.B. Cole-c. 570-The Pearl Princess	6	12	18	27	33	38
564-The Salt Mountain; L.B.Cole-c. 568-The Happy Hedgehog; L.B. Cole-c.	6	12	18	28	34	40
569,573: 569-The Three Giants.573-The Crystal Ball	5	10	15	23	28	32
571,572: 571-How Fire Came to the Indians. 572-The Drummer Boy	6	12	18	29	36	42
574-Brightboots	5	10	15	24	30	35
575-The Fearless Prince	6	12	18	28	34	40
576-The Princess Who Saw Everything	7	14	21	35	43	50
577-The Runaway Dumpling	8	16	24	44	57	70

NOTE: *Prices are for original editions. Last reprint - Spring, 1971.* ***Costanza*** *&* ***Schaffenberger*** *art in many issues.*

CLASSICS ILLUSTRATED SPECIAL ISSUE
Gilberton Co.: (Came out semi-annually) Dec, 1955 - Jul, 1962 (35¢, 100 pgs.)

	GD 2.0	VG 4.0	FN 6.0	VF 8.0	VF/NM 9.0	NM- 9.2
129-The Story of Jesus (titled ...Special Edition) "Jesus on Mountain" cover	18	36	54	105	165	225
"Three Camels" cover (12/58)	19	38	57	109	172	235
"Mountain" cover (no date)-Has checklist on inside b/c to HRN #161 & different testimonial on back-c	14	28	42	76	108	140
"Mountain" cover (1968 re-issue; has white 50¢ circle)	10	20	30	56	76	95
132A-The Story of America (6/56); Cameron-a	12	24	36	67	94	120
135A-The Ten Commandments(12/56)	11	22	33	64	90	115
138A-Adventures in Science(6/57); HRN to 137	11	22	33	60	83	105
138A-(6/57)-2nd version w/HRN to 149	7	14	21	35	43	50
138A-(12/61)-3rd version w/HRN to 149	7	14	21	35	43	50
141A-The Rough Rider (Teddy Roosevelt)(12/57); Evans-a	11	22	33	62	86	110
144A-Blazing the Trails West(6/58)- 73 pgs. of Crandall/Evans plus Severin-a	11	22	33	64	90	115
147A-Crossing the Rockies(12/58)-Crandall/Evans-a	11	22	33	62	86	110
150A-Royal Canadian Police(6/59)-Ingels, Sid Check-a	11	22	33	62	86	110
153A-Men, Guns & Cattle(12/59)-Evans-a (26 pgs.); Kinstler-a	11	22	33	62	86	110
156A-The Atomic Age(6/60)-Crandall/Evans, Torres-a	11	22	33	62	86	110
159A-Rockets, Jets and Missiles(12/60)-Evans, Morrow-a	11	22	33	62	86	110
162A-War Between the States(6/61)-Kirby & Crandall/Evans-a; Ingels-a	17	34	51	100	158	215
165A-To the Stars(12/61)-Torres, Crandall/Evans, Kirby-a	14	28	42	76	108	140
166A-World War II('62)-Torres, Crandall/Evans, Kirby-a	15	30	45	83	124	165
167A-Prehistoric World(7/62)-Torres & Crandall/Evans-a; two versions exist (HRN to 165 & HRN to 167)	14	28	42	81	118	155
nn Special Issue-The United Nations (1964; 50¢; scarce); this is actually part of the European Special Series, which cont'd on after the U.S. series stopped issuing new titles in 1962. This English edition was prepared specifically for sale at the U.N. It was printed in Norway	50	100	150	315	533	750

NOTE: *There was another U.S. Special Issue prepared in 1962 with artwork by* ***Torres*** *entitled World War I. Unfortunately, it was never issued in any English-language edition. It was issued in 1964 in West Germany, The Netherlands, and some Scandanavian countries, with another edition in 1974 with a new cover.*

CLASSICS LIBRARY (See King Classics)

CLASSIC STAR WARS (Also see Star Wars)

Dark Horse Comics: Aug, 1992 - No. 20, June, 1994 ($2.50)

	GD 2.0	VG 4.0	FN 6.0	VF 8.0	VF/NM 9.0	NM- 9.2
1-Begin Star Wars strip-r by Williamson; Williamson redrew portions of the panels to fit comic book format						6.00
2-10: 8-Polybagged w/Star Wars Galaxy trading card. 8-M. Schultz-c						4.00
11-19: 13-Yeates-c. 17-M. Schultz-c. 19-Evans-c						3.00
20-($3.50, 52 pgs.)-Polybagged w/trading card						4.00
Escape To Hoth TPB ($16.95) r/#15-20						17.00
The Rebel Storm TPB - r/#8-14						17.00
Trade paperback ($29.95, slip-cased)-Reprints all movie adaptations						30.00

NOTE: *Williamson c-1-5,7,9,10,14,15,20.*

CLASSIC STAR WARS: (Title series). **Dark Horse Comics**

	GD 2.0	VG 4.0	FN 6.0	VF 8.0	VF/NM 9.0	NM- 9.2
--A NEW HOPE, 6/94 - No. 2, 7/94 ($3.95) 1,2: 1-r/Star Wars #1-3, 7-9 publ; 2-r/Star Wars #4-6, 10-12 publ. by Marvel Comics						4.00
--DEVILWORLDS, 8/96 - No.2, 9/96 ($2.50s)1,2: r/Alan Moore-s						3.00
--HAN SOLO AT STARS' END, 3/97 - No. 3, 5/97 ($2.95) 1-3: r/strips by Alfredo Alcala						3.00
--RETURN OF THE JEDI, 10/94 - No.2, 11/94 ($3.50) 1,2: 1-r/1983-84 Marvel series; polybagged with w/trading card						3.50
--THE EARLY ADVENTURES, 8/94 - No. 9, 4/95 ($2.50)1-9						3.00
--THE EMPIRE STRIKES BACK, 8/94 - No. 2, 9/94 ($3.95) 1-r/Star Wars #39-44 published by Marvel Comics						4.00

CLASSIC X-MEN (Becomes X-Men Classic #46 on)
Marvel Comics Group: Sept, 1986 - No. 45, Mar, 1990

	GD 2.0	VG 4.0	FN 6.0	VF 8.0	VF/NM 9.0	NM- 9.2
1-Begins-r of New X-Men	2	4	6	8	10	12
2-10: 10-Sabretooth app.						4.00
11-42,44,45: 11-1st origin of Magneto in back-up story. 17-Wolverine-c. 27-r/X-Men #121. 26-r/X-Men #120; Wolverine-c/app. 35-r/X-Men #129. 39-New Jim Lee back-up story (2nd-a on X-Men)						3.00
43-Byrne-c/a(r); ($1.75, double-size)						4.00

NOTE: ***Art Adams*** *c(p)-1-10, 12-16, 18-23.* ***Austin*** *c-10,15-21,24-28i.* ***Bolton*** *back up stories in 1-28,30-35.* ***Williamson*** *c-12-14i.*

CLAW (See Capt. Battle, Jr., Daredevil Comics & Silver Streak Comics)

CLAWS (See Wolverine & Black Cat: Claws 2 for sequel)
Marvel Comics: Oct, 2006 - No. 3, Dec, 2006 ($3.99, limited series)

	GD 2.0	VG 4.0	FN 6.0	VF 8.0	VF/NM 9.0	NM- 9.2
1-3-Wolverine and Black Cat team-up; Linsner-a/c.						4.00
Wolverine & Black Cat: Claws HC (2007, $17.99, dustjacket) r/#1-3 & bonus Linsner art						18.00

CLAW THE UNCONQUERED (See Cancelled Comic Cavalcade)
National Periodical Publications/DC Comics: 5-6/75 - No. 9, 9-10/76; No. 10, 4-5/78 - No. 12, 8-9/78

	GD 2.0	VG 4.0	FN 6.0	VF 8.0	VF/NM 9.0	NM- 9.2
1-1st app. Claw	2	4	6	8	10	12
2-12: 3-Nudity panel. 9-Origin	1	2	3	4	5	7

NOTE: ***Giffen*** *a-8-12p.* ***Kubert*** *c-10-12.* ***Layton*** *a-9i, 12i.*

CLAW THE UNCONQUERED (See Red Sonja/Claw: The Devil's Hands)
DC Comics: Aug, 2006 - No. 6, Jan, 2007 ($2.99)

	GD 2.0	VG 4.0	FN 6.0	VF 8.0	VF/NM 9.0	NM- 9.2
1-6: 1,2-Chuck Dixon-s/Andy Smith; two covers by Smith & Van Sciver						3.00
TPB (2007, $17.99) r/#1-6; cover gallery						18.00

CLAY CODY, GUNSLINGER
Pines Comics: Fall, 1957

	GD 2.0	VG 4.0	FN 6.0	VF 8.0	VF/NM 9.0	NM- 9.2
1-Painted-c	6	12	18	31	38	45

CLEAN FUN, STARRING "SHOOGAFOOTS JONES"
Specialty Book Co.: 1944 (10¢, B&W, oversized covers, 24 pgs.)

	GD 2.0	VG 4.0	FN 6.0	VF 8.0	VF/NM 9.0	NM- 9.2
nn-Humorous situations involving Negroes in the Deep South						
White cover issue...	25	50	75	150	245	340
Dark grey cover issue...	26	52	78	154	252	350

CLEAN ROOM
DC Comics (Vertigo): Dec, 2015 - Present ($3.99)

	GD 2.0	VG 4.0	FN 6.0	VF 8.0	VF/NM 9.0	NM- 9.2
1-16: 1-Gail Simone-s/Jon Davis-Hunt-a/Jenny Frison-c						4.00

CLEMENTINA THE FLYING PIG (See Dell Jr. Treasury)

CLEOPATRA (See Ideal, a Classical Comic No. 1)

CLERKS: THE COMIC BOOK (Also see Tales From the Clerks and Oni Double Feature #1)
Oni Press: Feb, 1998 ($2.95, B&W, one-shot)

	GD 2.0	VG 4.0	FN 6.0	VF 8.0	VF/NM 9.0	NM- 9.2
1-Kevin Smith-s	2	4	6	11	16	20
1-Second printing						4.00
...Holiday Special (12/98, $2.95) Smith-s						5.00
...The Lost Scene (12/99, $2.95) Smith-s/Hester-a						5.00

CLIFFHANGER (See Battle Chasers, Crimson, and Danger Girl)

Climax! #1 © Gilmore

Cloak and Dagger (2010 series) #1 © MAR

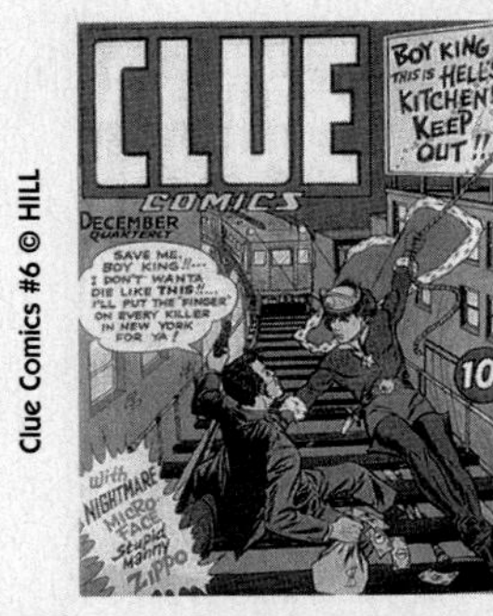
Clue Comics #6 © HILL

GD VG FN VF VF/NM NM-
2.0 4.0 6.0 8.0 9.0 9.2

GD VG FN VF VF/NM NM-
2.0 4.0 6.0 8.0 9.0 9.2

WildStorm Prod./Wizard Press: 1997 (Wizard supplement)
0-Sketchbook preview of Cliffhanger titles 6.00

CLIMAX! (Mystery)
Gillmor Magazines: July, 1955 - No. 2, Sept, 1955
1 17 34 51 98 154 210
2 14 28 42 76 108 140

CLINT (Also see Adolescent Radioactive Black Belt Hamsters)
Eclipse Comics: Sept, 1986 - No. 2, Jan, 1987 ($1.50, B&W)
1,2 3.00

CLINT & MAC (TV, Disney)
Dell Publishing Co.: No. 889, Mar, 1958
Four Color 889-Alex Toth-a, photo-c 10 20 30 64 132 200

CLIVE BARKER'S BOOK OF THE DAMNED: A HELLRAISER COMPANION
Marvel Comics (Epic): Oct, 1991 - No. 3, Nov, 1992 ($4.95, semi-annual)
Volume 1-3-(52 pgs.): 1-Simon Bisley-c. 2-(4/92). 3-(11/92)-McKean-a (1 pg.) 5.00

CLIVE BARKER'S HELLRAISER (Also see Epic, Hellraiser Nightbreed –Jihad, Revelations, Son of Celluloid, Tapping the Vein & Weaveworld)
Marvel Comics (Epic Comics): 1989 - No. 20, 1993 ($4.50-6.95, mature, quarterly, 68 pgs.)
Book 1-4,10-16,18,19: Based on Hellraiser & Hellbound movies; Bolton-c/a; Spiegle & Wrightson-a (graphic album). 10-Foil-c. 12-Sam Kieth-a 6.00
Book 5-9 ($5.95): 7-Bolton-a. 8-Morrow-a 6.00
Book 17-Alex Ross-a, 34 pgs. 2 4 6 8 10 12
Book 20-By Gaiman/McKean 1 2 3 5 6 8
...Collected Best (Checker Books, '02, $21.95)-r/by various incl. Ross, Gaiman, Mignola 22.00
...Collected Best II ('03, $19.95)-r/by various incl. Bolton, L. Wachowski, Dorman 20.00
...Collected Best III ('04, $26.95)-r/by various incl. Bolton, L. Wachowski, Wrightson 27.00
...Dark Holiday Special ('92, $4.95)-Conrad-a 6.00
...Spring Slaughter 1 ('94, $6.95, 52 pgs.)-Painted-c 7.00
...Summer Special 1 ('92, $5.95, 68 pgs.) 6.00

CLIVE BARKER'S HELLRAISER
BOOM! Studios: Mar, 2011 - No. 20, Nov, 2012 ($3.99)
1-20: 1-Barker & Monfette-s/Manco-a; preview of Hellraiser Masterpieces; 3 covers 4.00
Annual 1 (3/12, $4.99) Hervás-a; three covers 5.00
2013 Annual (10/13, $4.99) Seifert-s/Hervás-a; Barker & Meares-s/Ordon-a 5.00
...: Bestiary 1-6 (8/14 - No. 6, 1/15, $3.99) short stories by various; multiple covers 4.00
... Masterpieces 1-12 (11/11 - No. 12, 4/12, $3.99) reps from Marvel series. 1-Wrightson-a 4.00
...: The Dark Watch 1-12 (2/13 - No. 12, 1/14, $3.99) Tom Garcia-a; multiple covers 4.00
...: The Road Below 1-4 (10/12 - No. 4, 1/13, $3.99) Haemi Jang-a; multiple covers 4.00

CLIVE BARKER'S NEXT TESTAMENT
BOOM! Studios: May, 2013 - No. 12, Aug, 2014 ($3.99)
1-12: 1-Clive Barker & Mark Miller-s/Haemi Jang-a. 1-Four covers 4.00

CLIVE BARKER'S NIGHTBREED (Also see Epic)
Marvel Comics (Epic Comics): Apr, 1990 - No. 25, Mar, 1993 ($1.95/$2.25/$2.50, mature)
1-25: 1-4-Adapt horror movie. 5-New stories; Guice-a(p) 3.00

CLIVE BARKER'S NIGHTBREED
BOOM! Studios: May, 2014 - No. 12, Apr, 2015 ($3.99)
1-12: 1-8-Andreyko-s/Kowalski-a. 9-11-Javier & Pramanik-a 4.00

CLIVE BARKER'S THE HARROWERS
Marvel Comics (Epic Comics): Dec, 1993 - No. 6, May, 1994 ($2.50)
1-($2.95)-Glow-in-the-dark-c; Colan-c/a in all 4.00
2-6 3.00
NOTE: *Colan a(p)-1-6; c-1-3, 4p, 5p.* ***Williamson*** *a(i)-2, 4, 5(part).*

CLOAK AND DAGGER
Ziff-Davis Publishing Co.: Fall, 1952
1-Saunders painted-c 36 72 108 211 343 475

CLOAK AND DAGGER (Also see Marvel Fanfare and Spectacular Spider-Man #64)
Marvel Comics Group: Oct, 1983 - No. 4, Jan, 1984 (Mini-series)
1-4-Austin-c/a(i) in all. 4-Origin 4.00

CLOAK AND DAGGER (2nd Series)(Also see Marvel Graphic Novel #34 & Strange Tales)
Marvel Comics Group: July, 1985 - No. 11, Jan, 1987
1-11: 7,8-Mignola-c. 9-Art Adams-p 3.00
...And Power Pack (1990, $7.95, 68 pgs.) 8.00

CLOAK AND DAGGER (3rd Series listed as Mutant Misadventures Of...)

CLOAK AND DAGGER
Marvel Comics: May, 2010 ($3.99, one-shot)
1-Stuart Moore-s/Mark Brooks-a; X-Men app. 4.00

CLOAKS
BOOM! Studios: Sept, 2014 - No. 4, Dec, 2014 ($3.99, limited series)
1-4-Monroe-s/Navarro-a 4.00

CLOBBERIN' TIME
Marvel Comics: Sept, 1995 ($1.95) (Based on card game)
nn-Overpower game guide; Ben Grimm story 3.00

CLOCK MAKER, THE
Image Comics: Jan, 2003 - No. 4, May, 2003 ($2.50, comic unfolds to 10"x13" pages)
1-4-Krueger-s 3.00
... Act Two (4/04, $4.95, standard format) Krueger-s/Matt Smith-c 5.00

CLOCKWORK ANGELS (Based on Neil Peart's story and lyrics from Rush's album)
BOOM! Studios: Mar, 2014 - No. 6, Nov, 2014 ($3.99, limited series)
1-6-Kevin J. Anderson-s/Nick Robles-a; two covers on each 4.00

CLONE CONSPIRACY, THE (Also see Amazing Spider-Man [2017] #18)
Marvel Comics: Dec, 2016 - Present ($4.99/$3.99)
1-($4.99) Slott-s/Cheung-a; Miles Warren, Gwen Stacy, Doc Ock & Rhino app. 5.00
2-5-($3.99) Kaine app. 3-Ben Reilly returns 4.00
...: Omega 1 (5/17, $4.99) Three short stories by various; aftermath of series 5.00

CLONEZONE SPECIAL
Dark Horse Comics/First Comics: 1989 ($2.00, B&W)
1-Back-up series from Badger & Nexus 3.00

CLOSE ENCOUNTERS (See Marvel Comics Super Special & Marvel Special Edition)

CLOSE SHAVES OF PAULINE PERIL, THE (TV cartoon)
Gold Key: June, 1970 - No. 4, March, 1971
1 4 8 12 23 37 50
2-4 3 6 9 16 23 30

CLOUDBURST
Image Comics: June, 2004 ($7.95, squarebound)
1-Gray & Palmiotti-s/Shy & Gouveia-a 8.00

CLOUDFALL
Image Comics: Nov, 2003 ($4.95, B&W, squarebound)
1-Kirkman-s/Su-a/c 5.00

CLOWN COMICS (No. 1 titled Clown Comic Book)
Clown Comics/Home Comics/Harvey Publ.: 1945 - No. 3, Win, 1946
nn (#1) 14 28 42 82 121 160
2,3 9 18 27 50 65 80

CLOWNS, THE (I Pagliacci)
Dark Horse Comics: 1998 ($2.95, B&W, one-shot)
1-Adaption of the opera; P. Craig Russell-script 3.00

CLUBHOUSE RASCALS (#1 titled ...Presents?) (Also see Three Rascals)
Sussex Publ. Co. (Magazine Enterprises): June, 1956 - No. 2, Oct, 1956
1-The Brain app. in both; DeCarlo-a 8 16 24 44 57 70
2 7 14 21 35 43 50

CLUB "16"
Famous Funnies: June, 1948 - No. 4, Dec, 1948
1-Teen-age humor 14 28 42 76 108 140
2-4 8 16 24 44 57 70

CLUE COMICS (Real Clue Crime V2#4 on)
Hillman Periodicals: Jan, 1943 - No. 15(V2#3), May, 1947
1-Origin The Boy King, Nightmare, Micro-Face, Twilight, & Zippo
184 368 552 1168 2009 2850
2 (scarce) 87 174 261 553 952 1350
3-5 (9/43) 47 94 141 296 498 700
6,8,9: 8-Palais-c/a(2) 36 72 108 211 343 475
7-Classic concentration camp torture-c (3/44) 84 168 252 538 919 1300
10-Origin/1st app. The Gun Master & begin series; content changes to crime (10/46) 37 74 111 222 361 500
11 (12/46) 26 52 78 154 252 350
12-Origin Rackman; McWilliams-a, Guardineer-a(2) 36 72 108 211 343 475
V2#1-Nightmare new origin; Iron Lady app.; Simon & Kirby-a (3/47)
55 110 165 352 601 850
V2#2-S&K-a(2)-Bondage/torture-c; man attacks & kills people with electric iron. Infantino-a 81 162 243 518 884 1250
V2#3-S&K-a(3) 57 114 171 362 619 875

Cluster #5 © Brisson & Couceiro

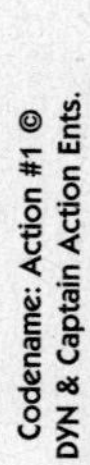
Codename: Action #1 © DYN & Captain Action Ents.

Colder: Toss the Bones #3 © Tobin & Ferreyra

	GD 2.0	VG 4.0	FN 6.0	VF 8.0	VF/NM 9.0	NM- 9.2

CLUELESS SPRING SPECIAL (TV)
Marvel Comics: May, 1997 ($3.99, magazine sized, one-shot)
1-Photo-c from TV show 4.00

CLUSTER
BOOM! Studios: Feb, 2015 - No. 8, Oct, 2015 ($3.99, limited series)
1-8-Ed Brisson-s/Damian Couceiro-a 4.00

CLUTCHING HAND, THE
American Comics Group: July-Aug, 1954
1-Gustavson, Moldoff-a 47 94 141 296 498 700

CLYDE BEATTY COMICS (Also see Crackajack Funnies)
Commodore Productions & Artists, Inc.: October, 1953 (84 pgs.)
1-Photo front/back-c; movie scenes and comics 22 44 66 132 216 300

CLYDE CRASHCUP (TV)
Dell Publishing Co.: Aug-Oct, 1963 - No. 5, Sept-Nov, 1964
1-All written by John Stanley 6 12 18 41 76 110
2-5 4 8 12 27 44 60

COBB
IDW Publishing: May, 2006 - No. 3, July, 2007 ($3.99, B&W)
1-3-Beau Smith-s/Eduardo Barreto-a/c; regular and retailer incentive covers 4.00

COBRA (G.I. Joe)
IDW Publishing: No. 10, Feb, 2012 - No. 21, Jan, 2013 ($3.99)
10-21 4.00
... Annual 2012: The Origin of Cobra Commander (1/12, $7.99) Dixon-s 8.00

CODENAME: ACTION
Dynamite Entertainment: 2013 - No. 5, 2014 ($3.99, limited series)
1-5-Captain Action; Chris Roberson-s/Jonathan Lau-a; multiple covers on each 4.00

CODE NAME: ASSASSIN (See 1st Issue Special)

CODENAME: BABOUSHKA
Image Comics: Oct, 2015 - Present ($3.99)
1-5: 1-Antony Johnston-s/Shari Chankhamma-a 4.00

CODENAME: DANGER
Lodestone Publishing: Aug, 1985 - No. 4, May, 1986 ($1.50)
1-4 3.00

CODENAME: FIREARM (Also see Firearm)
Malibu Comics (Ultraverse): June, 1995 - No. 5, Sept, 1995 ($2.95, bimonthly limited series)
0-5: 0-2-Alec Swan back-up story by James Robinson. 0-Pérez-c 3.00

CODENAME: GENETIX
Marvel Comics UK: Jan, 1993 - No. 4, May, 1993 ($1.75, limited series)
1-4: Wolverine in all 3.00

CODENAME: KNOCKOUT
DC Comics (Vertigo): No. 0, Jun, 2001 - No. 23, June, 2003 ($2.50/$2.75)
0-15: Rodi-s in all. 0-5-Small Jr. -a. 1-Two covers by Chiodo & Cho. 7,8,10,11,12-Paquette-a. 6,9,13,14-Conner-a 3.00
16-23: 16-Begin $2.75-c. 23-Last issue; JG Jones-c 3.00

CODENAME SPITFIRE (Formerly Spitfire And The Troubleshooters)
Marvel Comics Group: No. 10, July, 1987 - No. 13, Oct, 1987
10-13: 10-Rogers-c/a (low printing) 3.50

CODENAME: STRYKE FORCE (Also See Cyberforce V1#4 & Cyberforce/Stryke Force: Opposing Forces
Image Comics (Top Cow Productions): Jan, 1994 - No. 14, Sept, 1995 ($1.95-$2.25)
0,1-14: 1-12-Silvestri stories, Peterson-a. 4-Stormwatch app. 14-Story continues in Cyberforce/Stryke Force: Opposing Forces; Turner-a 3.00
1-Gold, 1-Blue 4.00

CODE OF HONOR
Marvel Comics: Feb, 1997 - No. 4, May, 1997 ($5.95, limited series)
1-4-Fully painted by various; Dixon-s 6.00

CODY OF THE PONY EXPRESS (See Colossal Features Magazine)
Fox Features Syndicate: Sept, 1950 (See Women Outlaws)(One shot)
1-Painted-c 15 30 45 85 130 175

CODY OF THE PONY EXPRESS (Buffalo Bill...) (Outlaws of the West #11 on; Formerly Bullseye)
Charlton Comics: No. 8, Oct, 1955; No. 9, Jan, 1956; No. 10, June, 1956
8-Bullseye on splash pg; not S&K-a 8 16 24 44 57 70
9,10: Buffalo Bill app. in all 6 12 18 29 36 42

CODY STARBUCK (1st app. in Star Reach #1)
Star Reach Productions: July, 1978
nn-Howard Chaykin-c/a 3 6 9 14 20 25
2nd printing 2 4 6 8 10 12
NOTE: *Both printings say First Printing. True first printing is on lower-grade paper, somewhat off-register, and snow in snow sequence has green tint.*

CO-ED ROMANCES
P. L. Publishing Co.: November, 1951
1 12 24 36 67 94 120

COFFEE WORLD
World Comics: Oct, 1995 ($1.50, B&W, anthology)
1-Shannon Wheeler's Too Much Coffee Man story 3.00

COFFIN, THE
Oni Press: Sept, 2000 - No. 4, May, 2001 ($2.95, B&W, limited series)
1-4-Hester-s/Huddleston-a 3.00

COFFIN HILL
DC Comics (Vertigo): Dec, 2013 - No. 20, Sept, 2015 ($2.99/$3.99)
1-18: 1-Caitlin Kittredge-s/Inaki Miranda-a; covers by Dave Johnson & Gene Ha 3.00
19,20-($3.99) Johnson-c 4.00

COLDER
Dark Horse Comics: Nov, 2012 - No. 5, Mar, 2013 ($3.99, limited series)
1-5-Tobin-s/Ferreyra-a/c 4.00

COLDER: THE BAD SEED
Dark Horse Comics: Oct, 2014 - No. 5, Feb, 2015 ($3.99, limited series)
1-5-Tobin-s/Ferreyra-a/c 4.00

COLDER: TOSS THE BONES
Dark Horse Comics: Sept, 2015 - No. 5, Jan, 2016 ($3.99, limited series)
1-5-Tobin-s/Ferreyra-a/c 4.00

COLD WAR
IDW Publishing: Oct, 2011 - No. 4, Jan, 2012 ($3.99, limited series)
1-4-John Byrne-s/a/c; two covers on each 4.00

COLLIDER (See FBP: Federal Bureau Of Physics; title changed after issue #1)

COLLECTORS DRACULA, THE
Millennium Publications: 1994 - No. 2, 1994 ($3.95, color/B&W, 52 pgs., limited series)
1,2-Bolton-a (7 pgs.) 4.00

COLLECTORS ITEM CLASSICS (See Marvel Collectors Item Classics)

COLONIZED, THE
IDW Publishing: Apr, 2013 - No. 4, Jul, 2013 ($3.99, limited series)
1-4-Aliens vs. Zombies; Dave Sim-c/Chris Ryall-s/Drew Moss-a 4.00

COLORS IN BLACK
Dark Horse Comics: Mar, 1995 - No. 4, June, 1995 ($2.95, limited series)
1-4 3.00

COLOSSAL FEATURES MAGAZINE (Formerly I Loved) (See Cody of the Pony Express)
Fox Features Syndicate: No. 33, 5/50 - No. 34, 7/50; No. 3, 9/50 (Based on Columbia serial)
33,34: Cody of the Pony Express begins. 33-Painted-c. 34-Photo-c 15 30 45 84 127 170
3-Authentic criminal cases 15 30 45 84 127 170

COLOSSAL SHOW, THE (TV cartoon)
Gold Key: Oct, 1969
1 5 10 15 30 50 70

COLOSSUS (See X-Men)
Marvel Comics: Oct, 1997 ($2.99, 48 pgs., one-shot)
1-Raab-s/Hitch & Neary-a, wraparound-c 4.00

COLOSSUS COMICS (See Green Giant & Motion Picture Funnies Weekly)
Sun Publications (Funnies, Inc.?): March, 1940
1-(Scarce)-Tulpa of Tsang(hero); Colossus app. 1000 2000 3000 7600 13,800 20,000
NOTE: *Cover by artist that drew Colossus in Green Giant Comics.*

COLOUR OF MAGIC, THE (Terry Pratchett's...)
Innovation Publishing: 1991 - No. 4, 1991 ($2.50, limited series)
1-4: Adapts 1st novel of the Discworld series 3.00

Combat #7 © DELL

Combat Kelly and the Deadly Dozen #2 © MAR

Comedy Comics #17 © MAR

COLT .45 (TV)
Dell Publishing Co.: No. 924, 8/58 - No. 1058, 11-1/59-60; No. 4, 2-4/60 - No. 9, 5-7/61

	GD 2.0	VG 4.0	FN 6.0	VF 8.0	VF/NM 9.0	NM- 9.2
Four Color 924(#1)-Wayde Preston photo-c on all	9	18	27	62	126	190
Four Color 1004,1058: 1004-Photo-b/c	7	14	21	48	89	130
4,5,7-9	7	14	21	48	89	130
6-Toth-a	8	16	24	51	96	140

COLUMBIA COMICS
William H. Wise Co.: 1943

	GD 2.0	VG 4.0	FN 6.0	VF 8.0	VF/NM 9.0	NM- 9.2
1-Joe Palooka, Charlie Chan, Capt. Yank, Sparky Watts, Dixie Dugan app.	31	62	93	182	296	410

COMANCHE
Dell Publishing Co.: No. 1350, Apr-Jun, 1962

	GD 2.0	VG 4.0	FN 6.0	VF 8.0	VF/NM 9.0	NM- 9.2
Four Color 1350-Disney movie; reprints FC #966 with title change from "Tonka" to "Comanche"; Sal Mineo photo-c	5	10	15	33	57	80

COMANCHEROS, THE
Dell Publishing Co.: No. 1300, Mar-May, 1962

	GD 2.0	VG 4.0	FN 6.0	VF 8.0	VF/NM 9.0	NM- 9.2
Four Color 1300-Movie, John Wayne photo-c	14	28	42	94	207	320

COMBAT
Atlas Comics (ANC): June, 1952 - No. 11, April, 1953

	GD 2.0	VG 4.0	FN 6.0	VF 8.0	VF/NM 9.0	NM- 9.2
1	41	82	123	256	428	600
2-Heath-c/a	22	44	66	132	216	300
3,5-9,11: 3-Romita-a. 6-Robinson-c; Romita-a	17	34	51	98	154	210
4-Krigstein-a	17	34	51	100	158	215
10-B&W and color illos. in **POP**; Sale-a, Forte-a	18	36	54	103	162	220

NOTE: *Combat Casey in 7-11.* ***Heath*** *a-2, 3; c-1, 2, 5, 9.* ***Maneely*** *a-1; c-3, 10.* ***Pakula*** *a-1.* ***Reinman*** *a-1.*

COMBAT
Dell Publishing Co.: Oct-Nov, 1961 - No. 40, Oct, 1973 (No #9)

	GD 2.0	VG 4.0	FN 6.0	VF 8.0	VF/NM 9.0	NM- 9.2
1	6	12	18	38	69	100
2,3,5	4	8	12	25	40	55
4-John F. Kennedy c/story (P.T. 109)	5	10	15	31	53	75
6,7,8(4-6/63), 8(7-9/63)	4	8	12	23	37	50
10-26: 26-Last 12¢ issue	3	6	9	19	30	40
27-40(reprints #1-14). 30-r/#4	3	6	9	14	19	24

COMBAT CASEY (Formerly War Combat)
Atlas Comics (SAI): No. 6, Jan, 1953 - No. 34, July, 1957

	GD 2.0	VG 4.0	FN 6.0	VF 8.0	VF/NM 9.0	NM- 9.2
6 (Indicia shows 1/52 in error)	30	60	90	177	289	400
7-R.Q. Sale-a	18	36	54	103	162	220
8-Used in **POP**, pg. 94	17	34	51	98	154	210
9,10,13-19-Violent art by R.Q. Sale; Battle Brady x-over #10	20	40	60	114	182	250
11,12,20-Last Precode (2/55)	15	30	45	85	130	175
21-34: 22,25-R.Q. Sale-a	14	28	42	82	121	160

NOTE: ***Everett*** *a-6.* ***Heath*** *c-10, 17, 19, 23, 30.* ***Maneely*** *c-6, 8, 15.* ***Powell*** *a-29(5), 30(5), 34.* ***Severin*** *c-26, 33, 34.*

COMBAT KELLY
Atlas Comics (SPI): Nov, 1951 - No. 44, Aug, 1957

	GD 2.0	VG 4.0	FN 6.0	VF 8.0	VF/NM 9.0	NM- 9.2
1-1st app. Combat Kelly; Heath-a	42	84	126	265	445	625
2	22	44	66	132	216	300
3-10	18	36	54	105	165	225
11-Used in **POP**, pgs. 94,95 plus color illo.	18	36	54	105	165	225
12-Color illo. in **POP**	17	34	51	98	154	210
13-16	15	30	45	88	137	185
17-Violent art by R. Q. Sale; Combat Casey app.	19	38	57	111	176	240
18-20,22-28: 18-Battle Brady app. 28-Last precode (1/55)	15	30	45	85	130	175
21-Transvestism-c	16	32	48	94	147	200
29-44: 38-Green Berets story (8/56)	14	28	42	82	121	160

NOTE: ***Berg*** *a-8, 12-14, 15-17, 19-23, 25, 26, 28, 31-37, 39, 41-44; c-2.* ***Colan*** *a-42.* ***Heath*** *a-4, 18; c-31.* ***Lawrence*** *a-23.* ***Maneely*** *a-4(2), 6, 7(3), 8; c-4, 5, 7, 8, 10, 25, 29, 39.* ***R.Q. Sale*** *a-17, 25.* ***Severin*** *c-41, 42.* ***Whitney*** *a-5.*

COMBAT KELLY (...and the Deadly Dozen)
Marvel Comics Group: June, 1972 - No. 9, Oct, 1973

	GD 2.0	VG 4.0	FN 6.0	VF 8.0	VF/NM 9.0	NM- 9.2
1-Intro & origin new Combat Kelly; Ayers/Mooney-a; Severin-c (20¢)	3	6	9	19	30	40
2,5-8	2	4	6	11	16	20
3,4: 3-Origin. 4-Sgt. Fury-c/s	3	6	9	14	19	24
9-Death of the Deadly Dozen	3	6	9	16	23	30

COMBAT ZONE: TRUE TALES OF GIS IN IRAQ
Marvel Comics: 2005 ($19.99, squarebound)

	GD 2.0	VG 4.0	FN 6.0	VF 8.0	VF/NM 9.0	NM- 9.2
Vol. 1-Karl Zinsmeister scripts adapted from his non-fiction books; Dan Jurgens-a						20.00

COMBINED OPERATIONS (See The Story of the Commandos)

COMEBACK (See Zane Grey 4-Color 357)

COMEDY CARNIVAL
St. John Publishing Co.: no date (1950's) (100 pgs.)

	GD 2.0	VG 4.0	FN 6.0	VF 8.0	VF/NM 9.0	NM- 9.2
nn-Contains rebound St. John comics	37	74	111	222	361	500

COMEDY COMICS (1st Series) (Daring Mystery #1-8) (Becomes Margie Comics #35 on)
Timely Comics (TCI 9,10): No. 9, April, 1942 - No. 34, Fall, 1946

	GD 2.0	VG 4.0	FN 6.0	VF 8.0	VF/NM 9.0	NM- 9.2
9-(Scarce)-The Fin by Everett, Capt. Dash, Citizen V, & The Silver Scorpion app.; Wolverton-a; 1st app. Comedy Kid; satire on Hitler & Stalin; The Fin, Citizen V & Silver Scorpion cont. from Daring Mystery	300	600	900	2040	3570	5100
10-(Scarce)-Origin The Fourth Musketeer, Victory Boys; Monstro, the Mighty app.	232	464	696	1485	2543	3600
11-Vagabond, Stuporman app.	65	130	195	416	708	1000
12,13	30	60	90	177	289	400
14-Origin/1st app. Super Rabbit (3/43) plus-c	84	168	252	538	919	1300
15-19	28	56	84	165	270	375
20-Hitler parody-c	65	130	195	416	708	1000
21-Tojo-c	53	106	159	334	567	800
22-Hitler parody-c	90	180	270	576	988	1400
23-32	20	40	60	117	189	260
33-Kurtzman-a (5 pgs.)	21	42	63	122	199	275
34-Intro Margie; Wolverton-a (5 pgs.)	39	78	117	231	378	525

COMEDY COMICS (2nd Series)
Marvel Comics (ACI): May, 1948 - No. 10, Jan, 1950

	GD 2.0	VG 4.0	FN 6.0	VF 8.0	VF/NM 9.0	NM- 9.2
1-Hedy, Tessie, Millie begin; Kurtzman's "Hey Look" (he draws himself)	53	106	159	334	567	800
2	24	48	72	142	234	325
3,4-Kurtzman's "Hey Look" (?&3)	25	50	75	150	245	340
5-10	17	34	51	98	154	210

COMET, THE (See The Mighty Crusaders & Pep Comics #1)
Red Circle Comics (Archie): Oct, 1983 - No. 2, Dec, 1983

	GD 2.0	VG 4.0	FN 6.0	VF 8.0	VF/NM 9.0	NM- 9.2
1-Re-intro & origin The Comet; The American Shield begins. Nino & Infantino art in both. Hangman in both						6.00
2-Origin continues.						5.00

COMET, THE
DC Comics (Impact Comics): July, 1991 - No. 18, Dec, 1992 ($1.00/$1.25)

	GD 2.0	VG 4.0	FN 6.0	VF 8.0	VF/NM 9.0	NM- 9.2
1						4.00
2-18: 4-Black Hood app. 6-Re-intro Hangman. 8-Web x-over. 10-Contains Crusaders trading card. 4-Origin. Netzer (Nasser) c(p)-11,14-17						3.00
Annual 1 (1992, $2.50, 68 pgs.)-Contains Impact trading card; Shield back-up story						4.00

COMET MAN, THE (Movie)
Marvel Comics Group: Feb, 1987 - No. 6, July, 1987 (limited series)

	GD 2.0	VG 4.0	FN 6.0	VF 8.0	VF/NM 9.0	NM- 9.2
1-6: 3-Hulk app. 4-She-Hulk shower scene-c/s. Fantastic 4 app. 5-Fantastic 4 app.						3.00

NOTE: ***Kelley Jones*** *a-1-6p.*

COMIC ALBUM (Also see Disney Comic Album)
Dell Publishing Co.: Mar-May, 1958 - No. 18, June-Aug, 1962

	GD 2.0	VG 4.0	FN 6.0	VF 8.0	VF/NM 9.0	NM- 9.2
1-Donald Duck	8	16	24	51	96	140
2-Bugs Bunny	5	10	15	30	50	70
3-Donald Duck	6	12	18	40	73	105
4-6,8-10: 4-Tom & Jerry. 5-Woody Woodpecker. 6,10-Bugs Bunny. 8-Tom & Jerry. 9-Woody Woodpecker	4	8	12	27	44	60
7,11,15: Popeye. 11-(9-11/60)	4	8	12	28	47	65
12-14: 12-Tom & Jerry. 13-Woody Woodpecker. 14-Bugs Bunny	4	8	12	27	44	60
16-Flintstones (12-2/61-62)-3rd app. Early Cave Kids app.	7	14	21	46	86	125
17-Space Mouse (3rd app.)	5	10	15	30	50	70
18-Three Stooges; photo-c	7	14	21	46	86	125

COMIC BOOK
Marvel Comics-#1/Dark Horse Comics-#2: 1995 ($5.95, oversize)

	GD 2.0	VG 4.0	FN 6.0	VF 8.0	VF/NM 9.0	NM- 9.2
1-Spumco characters by John K.	1	2	3	4	5	7
2-(Dark Horse)						6.00

COMIC BOOK GUY: THE COMIC BOOK (BONGO COMICS PRESENTS...) (Simpsons)
Bongo Comics: 2010 - No. 5, 2010 ($3.99/$2.99, limited series)

	GD 2.0	VG 4.0	FN 6.0	VF 8.0	VF/NM 9.0	NM- 9.2
1-($3.99) Four-layer cover w/classic swipes incl. FF#1; intro Graphic Novel Kid	2	4	6	11	16	20
2-5-($2.99) 2-Stan Lee cameo. 3-Includes Little Lulu spoof. 4-Comic Book Guy origin						6.00

COMIC CAPERS

Comic Cavalcade #2 © DC

Comics and Stories #1 © DH

Comics on Parade #13 © UFS

	GD	VG	FN	VF	VF/NM	NM-
	2.0	4.0	6.0	8.0	9.0	9.2

Red Circle Mag./Marvel Comics: Fall, 1944 - No. 6, Fall, 1946

1-Super Rabbit, The Creeper, Silly Seal, Ziggy Pig, Sharpy Fox begin	40	80	120	246	411	575
2	21	42	63	126	206	285
3-6: 4-(Summer 1945)	20	40	60	117	189	260

COMIC CAVALCADE
All-American/National Periodical Publications: Winter, 1942-43 - No. 63, June-July, 1954 (Contents change with No. 30, Dec-Jan, 1948-49 on)

1-The Flash, Green Lantern, Wonder Woman, Wildcat, The Black Pirate by Moldoff (also #2), Ghost Patrol, and Red White & Blue begin; Scribbly app.; Minute Movie	946	1892	2838	6906	12,203	17,500
2-Mutt & Jeff begin; last Ghost Patrol & Black Pirate; Minute Movies	271	542	813	1734	2967	4200
3-Hop Harrigan & Sargon, the Sorcerer begin; The King app.	181	362	543	1158	1979	2800
4,5: 4-The Gay Ghost, The King, Scribbly, & Red Tornado app. 5-Christmas-c. 5-Prints ad for Jr. JSA membership kit that includes "The Minute Man Answers The Call"	174	348	522	1114	1907	2700
6-10: 7-Red Tornado & Black Pirate app.; last Scribbly. 9-Fat & Slat app.; X-Mas-c	148	296	444	947	1624	2300
11-Wonder Woman vs. The Cheetah	119	238	357	762	1306	1850
12,14: 12-Last Red White & Blue	110	220	330	704	1202	1700
13-Solomon Grundy app.; X-Mas-c	213	426	639	1363	2332	3300
15-Just a Story begins	111	222	333	705	1215	1725
16-20: 19-Christmas-c	103	206	309	659	1130	1600
21-23: 22-Johnny Peril begins. 23-Harry Lampert-c (Toth swipes)	94	188	282	597	1024	1450
24-Solomon Grundy x-over in Green Lantern	123	246	369	787	1344	1900
25-28: 25-Black Canary app.; X-Mas-c. 26-28-Johnny Peril app. 28-Last Mutt & Jeff	87	174	261	553	952	1350
29-(10-11/48)-Last Flash, Wonder Woman, Green Lantern & Johnny Peril; Wonder Woman invents "Thinking Machine"; 2nd computer in comics (after Flash Comics #52); Leave It to Binky story (early app.)	110	220	330	704	1202	1700
30-(12-1/48-49)-The Fox & the Crow, Dodo & the Frog & Nutsy Squirrel begin	42	84	126	265	445	625
31-35	23	46	69	136	223	310
36-49: 41-Last squarebound issue	17	34	51	100	158	215
50-62(Scarce)	21	42	63	122	199	275
63(Rare)	34	68	102	204	332	460

NOTE: ***Grossman** a-30-63. **E.E. Hibbard** c-(Flash only)-1-4, 7-14, 16-19, 21. **Sheldon Mayer** a(2-3)-40-63. **Moulson** c(G.L.)-7, 15. **Nodell** c(G.L.)-9. **H.G. Peter** c(W. Woman only)-1, 3-21, 24. **Post** a-31, 36. **Purcell** c(G.L.)-2-5, 10. **Reinman** a(Green Lantern)-4-6, 8, 9, 13, 15-21; c(Gr. Lantern)-6, 8, 19. **Toth** a(Green Lantern)-26-28; c-27. Atom app.-22, 23.*

COMIC COMICS
Fawcett Publications: Apr, 1946 - No. 10, Feb, 1947

1-Captain Kid; Nutty Comics #1 in indicia	15	30	45	85	130	175
2-10-Wolverton-a, 4 pgs. each. 5-Captain Kidd app. Mystic Moot by Wolverton in #2-10?	15	30	45	84	127	170

COMIC LAND
Fact and Fiction Publ.: March, 1946

1-Sandusky & the Senator, Sam Stupor, Sleuth, Marvin the Great, Sir Passer, Phineas Gruff app.; Irv Tirman & Perry Williams art	15	30	45	85	130	175

COMICO CHRISTMAS SPECIAL
Comico: Dec, 1988 ($2.50, 44 pgs.)

1-Rude/Williamson-a; Dave Stevens-c 5.00

COMICO COLLECTION (Also see Grendel)
Comico: 1987 ($9.95, slipcased collection)

nn-Contains exclusive Grendel: Devil's Vagary, 9 random Comico comics, a poster and newsletter in black slipcase w/silver ink 25.00

COMICO PRIMER (See Primer)

COMIC PAGES (Formerly Funny Picture Stories)
Centaur Publications: V3#4, July, 1939 - V3#6, Dec, 1939

V3#4-Bob Wood-a	90	180	270	576	988	1400
5,6: 6-Schwab-c	77	154	231	493	847	1200

COMICS (See All Good)

COMICS, THE
Dell Publ. Co.: Mar, 1937 - No. 11, Nov, 1938 (Newspaper strip-r; bi-monthly)

1-1st app. Tom Mix in comics; Wash Tubbs, Tom Beatty, Myra North, Arizona Kid, Erik Noble & International Spy w/Doctor Doom begin	187	374	561	1197	2049	2900
2	84	168	252	538	919	1300
3-11: 3-Alley Oop begins	68	136	204	435	743	1050

COMICS AND STORIES (See Walt Disney's Comics and Stories)

COMICS & STORIES (Also see Wolf & Red)
Dark Horse Comics: Apr, 1996 - No. 4, July, 1996 ($2.95, lim. series) (Created by Tex Avery)

1-4: Wolf & Red app; reads Comics and Stories on-c. 1-Terry Moore-a. 2-Reed Waller-a 3.00

COMICS CALENDAR, THE (The 1946...)
True Comics Press (ordered through the mail): 1946 (25¢, 116 pgs.) (Stapled at top)

nn-(Rare) Has a "strip" story for every day of the year in color	40	80	120	242	401	560

COMICS DIGEST (Pocket size)
Parents' Magazine Institute: Winter, 1942-43 (B&W, 100 pgs)

1-Reprints from True Comics (non-fiction World War II stories)	10	20	30	54	72	90

COMICS EXPRESS
Eclipse Comics: Nov, 1989 - No. 2, Jan, 1990 ($2.95, B&W, 68pgs.)

1,2: Collection of strip-r; 2(12/89-c, 1/90 inside) 4.00

COMICS FOR KIDS
London Publ. Co./Timely: 1945 (no month); No. 2, Sum, 1945 (Funny animal)

1-Puffy Pig, Sharpy Fox	34	68	102	199	325	450
2-Puffy Pig, Sharpy Fox	23	46	69	136	223	310

COMICS' GREATEST WORLD
Dark Horse Comics: Jun, 1993 - V4#4, Sept, 1993 ($1.00, weekly, lim. series)

Arcadia (Wk 1): V1#1,2,4: 1-X: Frank Miller-c. 2-Pit Bulls. 4-Monster.						3.00
1-B&W Press Proof Edition (1500 copies)	1	3	4	6	8	10
1-Silver-c; distr. retailer bonus w/print & cards	1	2	3	5	6	8
3-Ghost, Dorman-c; Hughes-a						4.00
Retailer's Prem. Emb. Silver Foil Logo-r/V1#1-4	1	3	4	6	8	10
Golden City (Wk 2: V2#1-4: 1-Rebel; Ordway-c. 2-Mecha; Dave Johnson-c.						
3-Titan; Walt Simonson-c. 4-Catalyst; Perez-c.						3.00
1-Gold-c; distr. retailer bonus w/print & cards.						6.00
Retailer's Prem. Embos. Gold Foil Logo-r/V2#1-4	1	2	3	5	6	8
Steel Harbor (Week 3): V3#1-Barb Wire; Dorman-c; Gulacy-a(p)						4.00
2-4: 2-The Machine. 3-Wolfgang. 4-Motorhead						3.00
1-Silver-c; distr. retailer bonus w/print & cards	1	2	3	5	6	8
Retailer's Prem. Emb. Red Foil Logo-r/V3#1-4.	1	3	4	6	8	10
Vortex (Week 4): V4#1-4: 1-Division 13; Dorman-c. 2-Hero Zero; Art Adams-c.						
3-King Tiger; Chadwick-a(p); Darrow-c. 4-Vortex; Miller-c.						3.00
1-Gold-c; distr. retailer bonus w/print & cards.						6.00
Retailer's Prem. Emb. Blue Foil Logo-r/V4#1-4.	1	2	3	5	6	8

COMICS' GREATEST WORLD: OUT OF THE VORTEX (See Out of The Vortex)

COMICS HITS (See Harvey Comics Hits)

COMICS MAGAZINE, THE (...Funny Pages #3)(Funny Pages #6 on)
Comics Magazine Co. (1st Comics Mag./Centaur Publ.): May, 1936 - No. 5, Sept, 1936 (Paper covers)

1-1st app. Dr. Mystic (a.k.a. Dr. Occult) by Siegel & Shuster (the 1st app. of a Superman prototype in comics). Dr. Mystic is not in costume but later appears in costume as a more pronounced prototype in More Fun #14-17. (1st episode of "The Koth and the Seven"; continues in More Fun #14; originally scheduled for publication at DC). 1 pg. Kelly-a; Sheldon Mayer-a	3700	7400	11,100	22,000	-	-
2-Federal Agent (a.k.a. Federal Men) by Siegel & Shuster; 1 pg. Kelly-a	400	800	1200	2400	3200	4000
3-5	350	700	1050	2100	2800	3500

COMICS NOVEL (Anarcho, Dictator of Death)
Fawcett Publications: 1947

1-All Radar; 51 pg anti-fascism story	37	74	111	222	361	500

COMICS ON PARADE (No. 30 on are a continuation of Single Series)
United Features Syndicate: Apr, 1938 - No. 104, Feb, 1955

1-Tarzan by Foster; Captain & the Kids, Little Mary Mixup, Abbie & Slats, Ella Cinders, Broncho Bill, Li'l Abner begin	389	778	1167	2723	4762	6800
2 (Tarzan & others app. on-c of #1-3,17)	139	278	417	883	1517	2150
3	110	220	330	704	1202	1700
4,5	81	162	243	518	884	1250
6-10	55	110	165	352	601	850
11-16,18-20	42	84	126	267	451	635
17-Tarzan-c	54	108	162	343	574	825

Commando Adventures #2 © MAR

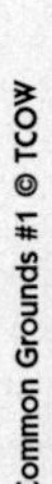

Common Grounds #1 © TCOW

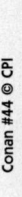

Conan #44 © CPI

	GD 2.0	VG 4.0	FN 6.0	VF 8.0	VF/NM 9.0	NM- 9.2
21-29: 22-Son of Tarzan begins. 22,24,28-Tailspin Tommy-c. 29-Last Tarzan issue	36	72	108	216	351	485
30-Li'l Abner	20	40	60	114	182	250
31-The Captain & the Kids	15	30	45	85	130	175
32-Nancy & Fritzi Ritz	14	28	42	78	112	145
33,36,39,42-Li'l Abner	16	32	48	94	147	200
34,37,40-The Captain & the Kids (10/41,6/42,3/43)	15	30	45	83	124	165
35,38-Nancy & Fritzi Ritz. 38-Infinity-c	14	28	42	76	108	140
41-Nancy & Fritzi Ritz	12	24	36	67	94	120
43-The Captain & the Kids	15	30	45	83	124	165
44 (3/44),47,50: Nancy & Fritzi Ritz	12	24	36	67	94	120
45-Li'l Abner	15	30	45	84	127	170
46,49-The Captain & the Kids	13	26	39	74	105	135
48-Li'l Abner (3/45)	15	30	45	84	127	170
51,54-Li'l Abner	14	28	42	76	108	140
52-The Captain & the Kids (3/46)	12	24	36	69	97	125
53,55,57-Nancy & Fritzi Ritz	11	22	33	62	86	110
56-The Captain & the Kids (r/Sparkler)	11	22	33	62	86	110
58-Li'l Abner; continues as Li'l Abner #61?	14	28	42	76	108	140
59-The Captain & the Kids	10	20	30	54	72	90
60-70-Nancy & Fritzi Ritz	9	18	27	47	61	75
71-99,101-104-Nancy & Sluggo: 71-76-Nancy only	8	16	24	42	54	65
100-Nancy & Sluggo	14	28	42	76	108	140
Special Issue, 7/46; Summer, 1948 - The Captain & the Kids app.	14	28	42	76	108	140
NOTE: Bound Volume (Very Rare) includes No. 1-12; bound by publisher in pictorial comic boards & distributed at the 1939 World's Fair and through mail order from ads in comic books (also see Tip Top)	300	600	900	2010	3505	5000

NOTE: *Li'l Abner reprinted from Tip Top.*

COMICS READING LIBRARIES (See the Promotional Comics section)

COMICS REVUE
St. John Publ. Co. (United Features Synd.): June, 1947 - No. 5, Jan, 1948

	GD	VG	FN	VF	VF/NM	NM-
1-Ella Cinders & Blackie	14	28	42	80	115	150
2,4: 2-Hap Hopper (7/47). 4-Ella Cinders (9/47)	9	18	27	50	65	80
3,5: 3-Iron Vic (8/47). 5-Gordo No. 1 (1/48)	9	18	27	47	61	75

COMIC STORY PAINT BOOK
Samuel Lowe Co.: 1943 (Large size, 68 pgs.)

	GD	VG	FN	VF	VF/NM	NM-
1055-Captain Marvel & a Captain Marvel Jr. story to read & color; 3 panels in color per pg. (reprints)	82	164	246	528	902	1275

COMING OF RAGE
Liquid Comics: 2015 - No. 5, 2016 ($3.99, limited series)

1-5-Wes Craven & Steve Niles-s/Francesco Biagini-a. 1-Afterword by Wes Craven 4.00

COMIX BOOK
Marvel Comics Group/Krupp Comics Works No. 4,5: 1974 - No. 5, 1976 ($1.00, B&W, magazine) (#1-3 newsstand; #4,5 were direct distribution only)

	GD	VG	FN	VF	VF/NM	NM-
1-Underground comic artists; 2 pgs. Wolverton-a	3	6	9	15	22	28
2,3: 2-Wolverton-a (1 pg.)	3	6	9	14	19	24
4(2/76), 4(5/76), 5 (Low distribution)	3	6	9	16	23	30

NOTE: *Print run No. 1-3: 200,000-250,000; No. 4&5: 10,000 each.*

COMIX INTERNATIONAL
Warren Magazines: Jul, 1974 - No. 5, Spring, 1977 (Full color, stiff-c, mail only)

	GD	VG	FN	VF	VF/NM	NM-
1-Low distribution; all Corben story remainders from Warren; Corben-c on all	9	18	27	62	126	190
2,4: 2-Two Dracula stories; Wood, Wrightson-r; Crandall-a; Maroto-a. 4-Printing w/ 3 Corben sty	6	12	18	37	66	95
3-5: 3-Dax story. 4-(printing without Corben story). 4-Crandall-a. 4,5-Vampirella stories. 5-Spirit story; Eisner-a	5	10	15	33	57	80

NOTE: *No. 4 had two printings with extra* ***Corben*** *story in one. No. 3 may also have a variation. No. 3 has two Jeff Jones reprints from Vampirella.*

COMMANDER BATTLE AND THE ATOMIC SUB
Amer. Comics Group (Titan Publ. Co.): Jul-Aug, 1954 - No. 7, Aug-Sep, 1955

	GD	VG	FN	VF	VF/NM	NM-
1 (3-D effect)-Moldoff flying saucer-c	58	116	174	371	636	900
2,4-7: 2-Moldoff-c. 4-(1-2/55)-Last pre-code; Landau-a. 5-3-D effect story (2 pgs.). 6,7-Landau-a. 7-Flying saucer-c	38	76	114	226	368	510
3-H-Bomb-c; Atomic Sub becomes Atomic Spaceship	39	78	117	231	378	525

COMMANDO ADVENTURES
Atlas Comics (MMC): June, 1957 - No. 2, Aug, 1957

	GD	VG	FN	VF	VF/NM	NM-
1-Severin-c	16	32	48	94	147	200
2-Severin-c; Reinman & Romita-a; Drucker-a?	12	24	36	67	94	120

COMMANDOS
DC Comics: Oct. 1942

1-Ashcan comic, not distributed to newsstands, only for in-house use. Cover art is Boy Commandos #1 with interior being a Boy Commandos story from an unidentified issue of Detective Comics (a VF copy sold for $1254.75 in 2012)

COMMANDO YANK (See The Mighty Midget Comics & Wow Comics)

COMMON GROUNDS
Image Comics (Top Cow): Feb, 2004 - No. 6, July, 2004 ($2.99)

1-6: 1-Two covers; art by Jurgens and Oeming. 3-Bachalo, Jurgens-a. 4-Peréz-a 3.00
...: Baker's Dozen TPB (12/04, $14.99) r/#1-6; cover gallery; Holey Crullers pages 15.00

COMPLETE ALICE IN WONDERLAND (Adaptation of Carroll's original story)
Dynamite Entertainment: 2009 - Present ($4.99, limited series)

1-4-Leah Moore & John Reppion-s/Erica Awano-a/John Cassaday-c 5.00

COMPLETE BOOK OF COMICS AND FUNNIES
William H. Wise & Co.: 1944 (25¢, one-shot, 196 pgs.)

	GD	VG	FN	VF	VF/NM	NM-
1-Origin Brad Spencer, Wonderman; The Magnet, The Silver Knight by Kinstler, & Zudo the Jungle Boy app.	55	110	165	352	601	850

COMPLETE BOOK OF TRUE CRIME COMICS
William H. Wise & Co.: No date (Mid 1940's) (25¢, 132 pgs.)

	GD	VG	FN	VF	VF/NM	NM-
nn-Contains Crime Does Not Pay rebound (includes #22)	174	348	522	1114	1907	2700

COMPLETE COMICS (Formerly Amazing Comics No. 1)
Timely Comics (EPC): No. 2, Winter, 1944-45

	GD	VG	FN	VF	VF/NM	NM-
2-The Destroyer, The Whizzer, The Young Allies & Sergeant Dix; Schomburg-c	181	362	543	1158	1979	2800

COMPLETE DRACULA (Adaptation of Stoker's original story)
Dynamite Entertainment: 2009 - No. 5, 2009 ($4.99, limited series)

1-5-Leah Moore & John Reppion-s/Colton Worley-a/John Cassaday-c 5.00

COMPLETE FRANK MILLER BATMAN, THE
Longmeadow Press: 1989 ($29.95, hardcover, silver gilded pages)

HC-Reprints Batman: Year One, Wanted: Santa Claus--Dead or Alive, and The Dark Knight Returns 45.00

COMPLETE GUIDE TO THE DEADLY ARTS OF KUNG FU AND KARATE
Marvel Comics: 1974 (68 pgs., B&W magazine)

	GD	VG	FN	VF	VF/NM	NM-
V1#1-Bruce Lee-c and 5 pg. story (scarce)	7	14	21	44	82	120

COMPLETE LOVE MAGAZINE (Formerly a pulp with same title)
Ace Periodicals (Periodical House): V26#2, May-June, 1951 - V32#4(#191), Sept, 1956

	GD	VG	FN	VF	VF/NM	NM-
V26#2-Painted-c (52 pgs.)	15	30	45	84	127	170
V26#3-6(2/52), V27#1(4/52)-6(1/53)	11	22	33	62	86	110
V28#1(3/53), V28#2(5/53), V29#3(7/53)-6(12/53)	10	20	30	58	79	100
V30#1(2/54), V30#1(#176, 4/54),2,4-6(#181, 1/55)	10	20	30	58	79	100
V30#3(#178)-Rock Hudson photo-c	11	22	33	60	83	105
V31#1(#182, 3/55)-Last precode	10	20	30	56	76	95
V31#2(5/55)-6(#187, 1/56)	10	20	30	54	72	90
V32#1(#188, 3/56)-4(#191, 9/56)	10	20	30	54	72	90

NOTE: *(34 total issues). Photo-c V27#5-on. Painted-c V26#3.*

COMPLETE MYSTERY (True Complete Mystery No. 5 on)
Marvel Comics (PrPI): Aug, 1948 - No. 4, Feb, 1949 (Full length stories)

	GD	VG	FN	VF	VF/NM	NM-
1-Seven Dead Men	54	108	162	343	574	825
2-4: 2-Jigsaw of Doom!; Shores-a. 3-Fear in the Night; Burgos-c/a (28 pgs.). 4-A Squealer Dies Fast	41	82	123	256	428	600

COMPLETE ROMANCE
Avon Periodicals: 1949

	GD	VG	FN	VF	VF/NM	NM-
1-(Scarce)-Reprinted as Women to Love	55	110	165	352	601	850

CONAN (See Chamber of Darkness #4, Giant-Size..., Handbook of..., King Conan, Marvel Graphic Novel #19, 28, Marvel Treasury Ed., Power Record Comics, Robert E. Howard's..., Savage Sword of Conan, and Savage Tales)

CONAN
Dark Horse Comics: Feb, 2004 - No. 50, May, 2008 ($2.99)

0-(11/03, 25¢-c) Busiek-s/Nord-a 3.00
1-($2.99) Linsner-c/Busiek-s/Nord-a 5.00
1-(2nd printing) J. Scott Campell-c 3.00
1-(3rd printing) Nord-c 3.00
2-49: 18-Severin & Timm-a. 22-Kaluta-a (6 pgs.) 24-Harris-c. 29-31-Mignola-s 3.00
24-Variant-c with nude woman (also see Conan and the Demons of Khitai #3 for ad) 35.00
50-($4.99) Harris-c; new story and reprint from Conan the Barbarian #30 5.00

Conan Classic #5 © CPI

Conan the Avenger #2 © CPI

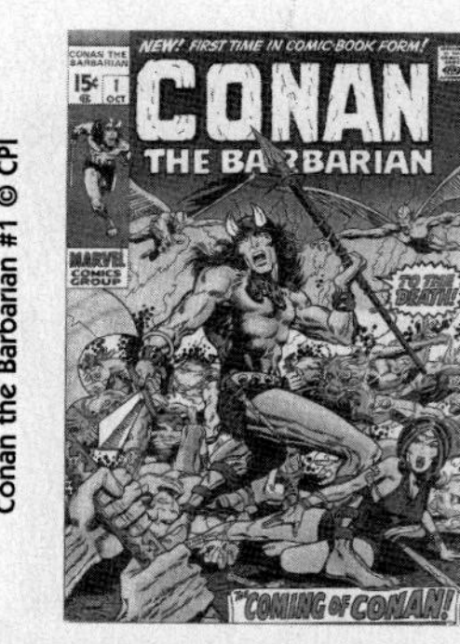

NEW! FIRST TIME IN COMIC-BOOK FORM!
CONAN
THE BARBARIAN
TO THE DEATH!
COMING of CONAN!

Conan the Barbarian #1 © CPI

GD 2.0 VG 4.0 FN 6.0 VF 8.0 VF/NM 9.0 NM- 9.2

...: and the Daughters of Midora (10/04, $4.99) Texiera-a/c 5.00
...: Born on the Battlefield TPB (6/08, $17.95) r/#0,8,15,23,32,45,46; Ruth sketch pages 18.00
...: FCBD 2006 Special (5/06) Paul Lee-a; flip book with Star Wars FCBD 2006 Special 3.00
...: One For One (8/10, $1.00) r/#1 with red cover frame 3.00
...: The Blood-Stained Crown and Other Stories TPB (1/08, $14.95) r/#18,26-28,39 15.00
...: The Weight of the Crown (1/10, $3.50) Darick Robertson-s/a; 2 covers by Robertson 3.50
HC Vol. 1: The Frost Giant's Daughter and Other Stories (2005, $24.95) r/#1-6, partial #7; signed by Busiek; Nord sketch pages 25.00
Vol. 1: The Frost Giant's Daughter and Other Stories (2005, $15.95) r/#1-6, partial #7 16.00
Vol. 2: The God in the Bowl and Other Stories HC (2005, $24.95) r/#9-14 25.00
Vol. 2: The God in the Bowl and Other Stories SC (2006, $15.95) r/#9-14 16.00
Vol. 3: The Tower of the Elephant and Other Stories HC (5/06, $24.95) r/#0,16,17,19-22 25.00
Vol. 3: The Tower of the Elephant and Other Stories SC (6/06, $15.95) r/#0,16,17,19-22 16.00
Vol. 4: The Hall of the Dead and Other Stories HC (5/07, $24.95) r/#0,24,25,29-31,33,34 25.00
Vol. 4: The Hall of the Dead and Other Stories SC (6/07, $17.95) r/#0,24,25,29-31,33,34 18.00
Vol. 5: Rogues in the House and Other Stories SC (3/08, $17.95) r/#0,37,38,41-44 18.00
Vol. 6: The Hand of Nergal HC (10/08, $24.95) r/#0,47-50; sketch pages 25.00

CONAN AND THE DEMONS OF KHITAI
Dark Horse Comics: Oct, 2005 - No. 4, Jan, 2006 ($2.99, limited series)

1,2,4-Paul Lee-a/Akira Yoshida-s/Pat Lee-c 3.00
3-1st printing with red cover logo; letters page has image of Conan #24 nude variant-c 5.00
3-2nd printing with black cover logo; letters page has image of Conan #24 regular-c 3.00
TPB (7/06, $12.95) r/series 13.00

CONAN AND THE JEWELS OF GWAHLUR
Dark Horse Comics: Apr, 2005 - No. 3, June, 2005 ($2.99, limited series)

1-3-P. Craig Russell-s/a/c 3.00
HC (12/05, $13.95) r/series; P. Craig Russell interview and sketch pages 14.00

CONAN AND THE MIDNIGHT GOD
Dark Horse Comics: Dec, 2006 - No. 5, May, 2007 ($2.99, limited series)

1-5-Dysart-s/Conrad-a/Alexander-c 3.00
TPB (10/07, $14.95) r/#1-5 and Age of Conan: Hyborian Adventures one-shot 15.00

CONAN AND THE PEOPLE OF THE BLACK CIRCLE
Dark Horse Comics: Oct, 2013 - No. 4, Jan, 2014 ($3.50, limited series)

1-4-Van Lente-s/Olivetti-a/c 3.50

CONAN AND THE SONGS OF THE DEAD
Dark Horse Comics: July, 2006 - No. 5, Nov, 2006 ($2.99, limited series)

1-5-Timothy Truman-a/c; Joe Lansdale-s 3.00
TPB (4/07, $14.95) r/series; Truman sketch pages 15.00

CONAN: (Title Series): Marvel Comics

CONAN, 8/95 - No. 11, 6/96 ($2.95), 1-11: 4-Malibu Comic's Rune app. 3.00
...CLASSIC, 6/94 - No. 11, 4/95 ($1.50), 1-11: 1-r/Conan #1 by B. Smith, r/covers w/changes. 2-11-r/Conan #2-11 by Smith. 2-Bound w/cover to Conan The Adventurer #2 by mistake 3.00
...DEATH COVERED IN GOLD, 9/99 - No. 3, 11/99 ($2.99), 1-3-Roy Thomas-s/ John Buscema-a 3.00
...FLAME AND THE FIEND, 8/00 - No. 3, 10/00 ($2.99), 1-3-Thomas-s 3.00
...RETURN OF STYRM, 9/98 - No. 3, 11/98 ($2.99), 1-3-Parente & Soresina-a; painted-c 3.00
...RIVER OF BLOOD, 6/98 - No. 3, 8/98 ($2.50), 1-3 3.00
...SCARLET SWORD, 12/98 - No. 3, 2/99 ($2.99), 1-3-Thomas-s/Raffaele-a 3.00

CONAN: ISLAND OF NO RETURN
Dark Horse Comics: Jun, 2011 - No. 2, Jul, 2011 ($3.50, limited series)

1,2-Marz-s/Sears-a 3.50

CONAN RED SONJA
Dark Horse Comics: Jan, 2015 - No. 4, Apr, 2015 ($3.99, limited series)

1-4-Gail Simone & Jim Zub-s/Dan Panosian-a/c 4.00

CONAN: ROAD OF KINGS
Dark Horse Comics: Dec, 2010 - No. 12, Jan, 2012 ($3.50)

1-12: 1-Roy Thomas-s/Mike Hawthorne-a; covers by Wheatley & Keown 3.50

CONAN SAGA, THE
Marvel Comics: June, 1987 - No. 97, Apr, 1995 ($2.00/$2.25, B&W, magazine)

1-Barry Smith-r; new Smith-c 2 4 6 8 11 14
2-27: 2-9,11-new Barry Smith-c. 13,15-Boris-c. 17-Adams-r.18,25-Chaykin-r. 22-r/Giant-Size Conan 1,2 4.00
28-90: 28-Begin $2.25-c. 31-Red Sonja-r by N. Adams/SSOC #1; 1 pg. Jeff Jones-r. 32-Newspaper strip-r begin by Buscema. 33-Smith/Conrad-a. 39-r/Kull #1('71) by Andru & Wood. 44-Swipes-c/Savage Tales #1. 57-Brunner-r/SSOC #30. 66-r/Conan Annual #2 by Buscema. 79-r/Conan #43-45 w/Red Sonja. 85-Based on Conan #57-63 3.00
91-96 5.00
97-Last issue 1 2 3 5 6 8

NOTE: ***J. Buscema*** *r-32-on; c-86.* ***Chaykin*** *r-34.* ***Chiodo*** *painted c-63, 65, 66, 82.* ***G. Colan*** *a-47p.* ***Jusko*** *painted c-64, 83.* ***Kaluta*** *c-84.* ***Nino*** *a-37.* ***Ploog*** *a-50.* ***N. Redondo*** *painted c-48, 50, 51, 53, 57, 62.* ***Simonson*** *r-50-54, 56.* ***B. Smith*** *r-51.* ***Starlin*** *c-34.* ***Williamson*** *r-50i.*

CONAN THE ADVENTURER
Marvel Comics: June, 1994 - No. 14, July, 1995 ($1.50)

1-($2.50)-Embossed foil-c; Kayaran-a 4.00
2-14 3.00
2-Contents are Conan Classics #2 by mistake 3.00

CONAN THE AVENGER
Dark Horse Comics: Apr, 2014 - No. 25, Apr, 2016 ($3.99/$3.50)

1-25: 1-Van Lente-s/Ching-a. 4-Staples-c. 13-15-Powell-c. 25-Bisley-c 4.00

CONAN THE BARBARIAN
Marvel Comics: Oct, 1970 - No. 275, Dec, 1993

1-Origin/1st app. Conan (in comics) by Barry Smith; 1st brief app. Kull; #1-9 are 15¢ issues 24 48 72 168 372 575
2 9 18 27 59 117 175
3-(Low distribution in some areas) 12 24 36 84 185 285
4,5 7 14 21 49 92 135
6-9: 8-Hidden panel message, pg. 14. 9-Last 15¢-c 6 12 18 37 66 95
10,11 (25¢ 52 pg. giants): 10-Black Knight-r; Kull story by Severin 6 12 18 42 79 115
12,13: 12-Wrightson-c(i) 5 10 15 34 60 85
14,15-Elric app. 6 12 18 38 69 100
16,19,20: 16-Conan-r/Savage Tales #1 5 10 15 33 57 80
17,18-No Barry Smith-a 4 8 12 27 44 60
21,22: 22-Has reprint from #1 4 8 12 28 47 65
23-1st app. Red Sonja (2/73) 7 14 21 46 86 125
24-1st full Red Sonja story; last Smith-a 6 12 18 40 73 105
25-John Buscema-c/a begins 3 6 9 16 23 30
26-30: 28-Centerfold ad by Mark Jewelers 2 4 6 13 18 22
31-36,38-40 2 4 6 9 12 15
37-Neal Adams-c/a; last 20¢ issue; contains pull-out subscription form 3 6 9 16 24 32
41-43,46-50: 48-Origin retold 2 4 6 8 10 12
44,45-N. Adams-i(Crusty Bunkers). 45-Adams-c 2 4 6 9 12 15
51-57,59,60: 59-Origin Belit 1 2 3 5 6 8
58-2nd Belit app. (see Giant-Size Conan #1) 2 4 6 8 11 14
61-65-(Regular 25¢ editions)(4-8/76) 1 2 3 4 5 7
61-65-(30¢-c variants, limited distribution) 5 10 15 30 50 70
66-99: 68-Red Sonja story cont'd from Marvel Feature #7. 75-79-(Reg. 30¢-c). 84-Intro. Zula. 85-Origin Zula. 87-r/Savage Sword of Conan #3 in color 6.00
75-79-(35¢-c variants, limited distribution) 6 12 18 41 76 110
100-(52 pg. Giant)-Death of Belit 1 3 4 6 8 10
101-114 4.00
115-Double size 5.00
116-199,201-231,233-249: 116-r/Power Record Comic PR31. 244-Zula returns 4.00
200,232: 200-(52 pgs.). 232-Young Conan storyline begins; Conan is born 5.00
250-(60 pgs.) 6.00
251-270: 262-Adapted from R.E. Howard story 5.00
271-274 1 2 3 5 6 8
275-($2.50, 68 pgs.)-Final issue; painted-c (low print) 3 6 9 19 30 40
King Size 1(1973, 35¢)-Smith-r/#2,4; Smith-c 3 6 9 19 30 40
Annual 2(1976, 50¢)-New full length story 2 4 6 10 14 18
Annual 3,4: 3('78)-Chaykin/N. Adams-r/SSOC #2. 4('78)-New full length story 2 4 6 8 10 12
Annual 5,6: 5(1979)-New full length Buscema story & part-c, 6(1981)-Kane-c/a 6.00
Annual 7-12: 7('82)-Based on novel "Conan of the Isles" (new-a). 8(1984). 9(1984). 10(1986). 11(1986). 12(1987) 4.00
Special Edition 1 (Red Nails) 4.00
The Chronicles of Conan Vol. 1: Tower of the Elephant and Other Stories (Dark Horse, 2003, $15.95) r/#1-8; afterword by Roy Thomas 16.00
The Chronicles of Conan Vol. 2: Rogues in the House and Other Stories (Dark Horse, 2003, $15.95) r/#9-13,16; afterword by Roy Thomas 16.00
The Chronicles of Conan Vol. 3: The Monster of the Monoliths and Other Stories (Dark Horse, 2003, $15.95) r/#14,15,17-21; afterword by Roy Thomas 16.00
The Chronicles of Conan Vol. 4: The Song of Red Sonja and Other Stories (Dark Horse, 2004, $15.95) r/#23-26 & "Red Nails" from Savage Tales; afterword by Roy Thomas 16.00
The Chronicles of Conan Vol. 5: The Shadow in the Tomb and Other Stories (Dark Horse, 2004, $15.95) r/#27-34; afterword by Roy Thomas 16.00
The Chronicles of Conan Vol. 6: The Curse of the Skull and Other Stories (Dark Horse,

Conan the Barbarian (2012 series) #11 © CPI

Conan the Slayer #1 © CPI

Confessions of Love #12 © STAR

GD VG FN VF VF/NM NM-
2.0 4.0 6.0 8.0 9.0 9.2

GD VG FN VF VF/NM NM-
2.0 4.0 6.0 8.0 9.0 9.2

2004, $15.95) r/#35-42; afterword by Roy Thomas 16.00
The Chronicles of Conan Vol. 7: The Dweller in the Pool and Other Stories (Dark Horse, 2005, $15.95) r/#43-51; afterword by Roy Thomas 16.00
The Chronicles of Conan Vol. 8: Brothers of the Blade and Other Stories (Dark Horse, 2005, $16.95) r/#52-59; afterword by Roy Thomas 17.00
The Chronicles of Conan Vol. 9: Riders of the River-Dragons and Other Stories (Dark Horse, 11/05, $16.95) r/#60-63,65,69-71; afterword by Roy Thomas 17.00
The Chronicles of Conan Vol. 10: When Giants Walk the Earth and Other Stories (Dark Horse, 3/06, $16.95) r/#72-77,79-82; afterword by Roy Thomas 17.00
The Chronicles of Conan Vol. 11: The Dance of the Skull and Other Stories (Dark Horse, 2/07, $16.95) r/#82-86,88-90; afterword by Roy Thomas 17.00
The Chronicles of Conan Vol. 12: The King Beast of Abombi and Other Stories (Dark Horse, 7/07, $16.95) r/#91,93-100; afterword by Roy Thomas 17.00
The Chronicles of Conan Vol. 13: Whispering Shadows and Other Stories (Dark Horse, 12/07, $16.95) r/#92,100-107; afterword by Roy Thomas 17.00
The Chronicles of Conan Vol. 14: Shadow of the Beast and Other Stories (Dark Horse, 3/08, $16.95) r/#92,108-115; afterword by Roy Thomas 17.00
The Chronicles of Conan Vol. 15: The Corridor of Mullah-Kajar and Other Stories (Dark Horse, 7/08, $16.95) r/#116-121 & Annual #2; afterword by Roy Thomas 17.00

NOTE: ***Arthur Adams*** *c-248, 249.* ***Neal Adams*** *a-116r(i); c-49i.* ***Austin*** *a-125, 126; c-125i, 126i.* ***Brunner*** *c-17i. c-40.* ***Buscema*** *a-25-36p, 38, 39, 41-56p, 58-63p, 65-67p, 68, 70-78p, 84-86p, 88-91p, 93-126p, 136p, 140, 141-144p, 146-158p, 159, 161, 162, 163p, 165-185p, 187-190p, Annual 2(3pgs.). 3-5p, 7p; c(p)-26, 36, 44, 46, 52, 56, 58, 59, 64, 65, 72, 78-80, 83-91, 93-103, 105-126, 136-151, 155-159, 161, 162, 168, 169, 171, 172, 174, 175, 178-185, 188, 189, Annual 4, 5, 7.* ***Chaykin*** *a-79-83.* ***Golden*** *c-152.* ***Kaluta*** *c-167.* ***Gil Kane*** *a-12p, 17p, 18p, 127-130, 131-134p; c-12p, 17p, 18p, 23, 25, 27-32, 34, 35, 38, 39, 41-43, 45-51, 53-55, 57, 60-63, 65-71, 73p, 76p, 127-134.* ***Jim Lee*** *c-242.* ***McFarlane*** *c-241p.* ***Ploog*** *a-57.* ***Russell*** *a-21; c-251i.* ***Simonson*** *c-135.* ***B. Smith*** *a-1-11p, 12, 13-15p, 16, 19-21, 23, 24; c-1-11, 13-16, 19-24p.* ***Starlin*** *a-64.* ***Wood*** *a-47r. Issue Nos. 3-5, 7-9, 11, 16-18, 21, 23, 25, 27-30, 35, 37, 38, 42, 45, 52, 57, 58, 65, 69-71, 73, 79-83, 99, 100, 104, 114, Annual 2 have original Robert E. Howard stories adapted. Issues #32-34 adapted from Norvell Page's novel* ***Flame Winds****.*

CONAN THE BARBARIAN (Volume 2)
Marvel Comics: July, 1997 - No. 3, Oct, 1997 ($2.50, limited series)
1-3-Castellini-a 3.00

CONAN THE BARBARIAN
Dark Horse Comics: Feb, 2012 - No. 25, Feb, 2014 ($3.50)
1-25: 1-3-Brian Wood-s/Becky Cloonan-a. 1-Two covers by Carnevale & Cloonan 3.50
One for One: Conan the Barbarian #1 (1/14, $1.00) r/#1 3.00

CONAN THE BARBARIAN MOVIE SPECIAL (Movie)
Marvel Comics Group: Oct, 1982 - No. 2, Nov, 1982
1,2-Movie adaptation; Buscema-a 4.00

CONAN THE BARBARIAN: THE MASK OF ACHERON (Based on the 2011 movie)
Dark Horse Comics: Jul, 2011 ($6.99, one-shot)
1-Stuart Moore-s/Gabriel Guzman-a/c 7.00

CONAN THE BARBARIAN: THE USURPER
Marvel Comics: Dec, 1997 - No. 3, Feb, 1998 ($2.50, limited series)
1-3-Dixon-s 3.00

CONAN: THE BOOK OF THOTH
Dark Horse Comics: Mar, 2006 - No. 4, June, 2006 ($4.99, limited series)
1-4-Origin of Thoth-amon; Len Wein & Kurt Busiek-s/Kelley Jones-a/c 5.00
TPB (12/06, $17.95) r/#1-4 18.00

CONAN THE CIMMERIAN
Dark Horse Comics: No. 0, Jun, 2008 - No. 25, Nov, 2010 (99¢/$2.99)
0-Follows Conan #50; Truman-s/Giorello-a/c 3.00
1-(7/08, $2.99) Two covers by Joe Kubert and Cho; Giorello & Corben-a 3.00
2-25: 2-7-Cho-c; Giorello & Corben-a. 8-18-Linsner-c. 14-Joe Kubert-a (7 pgs.) 3.00

CONAN THE DESTROYER (Movie)
Marvel Comics Group: Jan, 1985 - No. 2, Mar, 1985
1,2-r/Marvel Super Special 4.00

CONAN THE FRAZETTA COVER SERIES
Dark Horse Comics: Dec, 2007 - No. 8 ($3.50/$5.99/$6.99)
1-($3.50) Reprints from Dark Horse series with Frazetta covers 6.00
2,3-($5.99) 6.00
4-8-($6.99) 7.00

CONAN THE KING (Formerly King Conan)
Marvel Comics Group: No. 20, Jan, 1984 - No. 55, Nov, 1989
20-49 4.00
50-54 5.00
55-Last issue 1 3 4 6 8 10
NOTE: ***Kaluta*** *c-20-23, 24i, 26, 27, 30, 50, 52.* ***Williamson*** *a-37i; c-37i, 38i.*

CONAN: THE LEGEND (See Conan 2004 series)

CONAN: THE LORD OF THE SPIDERS
Marvel Comics: Mar, 1998 - No. 3, May, 1998 ($2.50, limited series)
1-3-Roy Thomas-s/Raffaele-a 3.00

CONAN THE SAVAGE
Marvel Comics: Aug, 1995 - No. 10, May, 1996 ($2.95, B&W, Magazine)
1-10: 1-Bisley-c. 4-vs. Malibu Comics' Rune. 5,10-Brereton-c 4.00

CONAN THE SLAYER
Dark Horse Comics: Jul, 2016 - Present ($3.99)
1-6: 1-Bunn-s/Dávila-a/Bermejo-c 4.00

CONAN VS. RUNE (Also See Conan #4)
Marvel Comics: Nov, 1995 ($2.95, one-shot)
1-Barry Smith-c/a/scripts 4.00

CONCRETE (Also see Dark Horse Presents & Within Our Reach)
Dark Horse Comics: March, 1987 - No. 10, Nov, 1988 ($1.50, B&W)
1-Paul Chadwick-c/a in all 2 4 6 8 10 12
1-2nd print 3.00
2 6.00
3-Origin 5.00
4-10 4.00
A New Life 1 (1989, $2.95, B&W)-r/#3,4 plus new-a (11 pgs.) 4.00
Celebrates Earth Day 1990 ($3.50, 52 pgs.) 6.00
Color Special 1 (2/89, $2.95, 44 pgs.)-r/1st two Concrete apps. from Dark Horse Presents #1,2 plus new-a 6.00
Depths TPB (7/05, $12.95)-r/#1-5, stories from DHP #1,8,10,150; other short stories 13.00
Land And Sea 1 (2/89, $2.95, B&W)-r/#1,2 6.00
Odd Jobs 1 (7/90, $3.50)-r/5,6 plus new-a 4.00
...Vol. 1: Depths ('05, $12.95, 9"x6") r/#1-5 & short stories 13.00
...Vol. 2: Heights ('05, $12.95, 9"x6") r/#6-10 & short stories 13.00
...Vol. 3: Fragile Creatures (1/06, $12.95, 9"x6") r/mini-series & short stories from DHP 13.00
...Vol. 4: Killer Smile (3/06, $12.95, 9"x6") r/mini-series & short stories from various 13.00
...Vol. 5: Think Like a Mountain (5/06, $12.95, 9"x6") r/mini-series & short stories 13.00
...Vol. 6: Strange Armor (7/06, $12.95, 9"x6") r/mini-series & short stories 13.00
...Vol. 7: The Human Dilemma (4/06, $12.95, 9"x6") r/mini-series 13.00

CONCRETE: (Title series), **Dark Horse Comics**
--ECLECTICA, 4/93 - No. 2, 5/93 ($2.95) 1,2 4.00
--FRAGILE CREATURE, 6/91 - No. 4, 2/92 ($2.50) 1-4 4.00
--KILLER SMILE, (Legend), 7/94 - No. 4, 10/94 ($2.95) 1-4 4.00
--STRANGE ARMOR, 12/97 - No. 5, 5/98 ($2.95, color) 1-5-Chadwick-s/c/a; retells origin 4.00
--THE HUMAN DILEMMA, 12/04 - No. 6, 5/05 ($3.50)
1-6: Chadwick-a/c & scripts; Concrete has a child 3.50
--THINK LIKE A MOUNTAIN, (Legend), 3/96 - No. 6, 8/96 ($2.95)
1-6: Chadwick-a/scripts & Darrow-c in all 4.00

CONDORMAN (Walt Disney)
Whitman Publishing: Oct, 1981 - No. 3, Jan, 1982
1-3: 1,2-Movie adaptation; photo-c 1 3 4 6 8 10

CONEHEADS
Marvel Comics: June, 1994 - No. 4, 1994 ($1.75, limited series)
1-4 3.00

CONFESSIONS ILLUSTRATED (Magazine)
E. C. Comics: Jan-Feb, 1956 - No. 2, Spring, 1956
1-Craig, Kamen, Wood, Orlando-a 30 60 90 177 289 400
2-Craig, Crandall, Kamen, Orlando-a 22 44 66 132 216 300

CONFESSIONS OF LOVE
Artful Publ.: Apr, 1950 - No. 2, July, 1950 (25¢, 7-1/4x5-1/4", 132 pgs.)
1-Bakerish-a 71 142 213 454 777 1100
2-Art & text; Bakerish-a 47 94 141 296 498 700

CONFESSIONS OF LOVE (Formerly Startling Terror Tales #10; becomes Confessions of Romance No. 7 on)
Star Publications: No. 11, 7/52 - No. 14, 1/53; No. 4, 3/53- No. 6, 8/53
11-13: 12,13-Disbrow-a 20 40 60 118 192 265
14,5,6 17 34 51 98 154 210
4-Disbrow-a 18 36 54 103 162 220
NOTE: *All have* ***L. B. Cole*** *covers.*

CONFESSIONS OF ROMANCE (Formerly Confessions of Love)
Star Publications: No. 7, Nov, 1953 - No. 11, Nov, 1954

Congo Bill (1999 series) #1 © DC

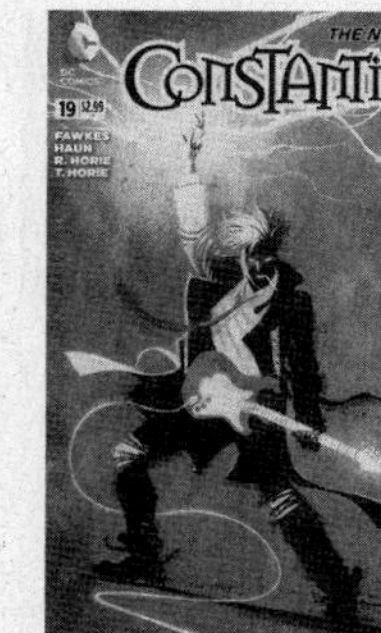

Constantine #19 © DC

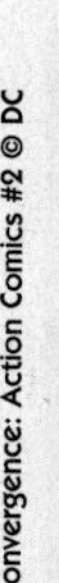
Convergence: Action Comics #2 © DC

	GD 2.0	VG 4.0	FN 6.0	VF 8.0	VF/NM 9.0	NM- 9.2
7	20	40	60	120	195	270
8	17	34	51	98	154	210
9-Wood-a	19	38	57	109	172	235
10,11-Disbrow-a	18	36	54	103	162	220

NOTE: *All have* ***L. B. Cole*** *covers.*

CONFESSIONS OF THE LOVELORN (Formerly Lovelorn)
American Comics Group (Regis Publ./Best Synd. Features): No. 52, Aug, 1954 - No. 114, June-July, 1960

	GD	VG	FN	VF	VF/NM	NM-
52 (3-D effect)	37	74	111	222	361	500
53,55	14	28	42	80	115	150
54 (3-D effect)	34	68	102	199	325	450
56-Anti-communist propaganda story, 10 pgs; last pre-code (2/55)	16	32	48	94	147	200
57-90,100	10	20	30	56	76	95
91-Williamson-a	11	22	33	62	86	110
92-99,101-114	9	18	27	47	61	75

NOTE: ***Whitney*** *a-most issues; c-52, 53. Painted c-106, 107.*

CONFIDENTIAL DIARY (Formerly High School Confidential Diary; Three Nurses #18 on)
Charlton Comics: No. 12, May, 1962 - No. 17, Mar, 1963

12-17 3 6 9 15 21 26

CONGO BILL (See Action Comics & More Fun Comics #56)
National Periodical Publication: Aug-Sept, 1954 - No. 7, Aug-Sept, 1955

	GD	VG	FN	VF	VF/NM	NM-
1	200	400	600	1600	-	-
2,7	125	250	375	1000	-	-
3-6: 4-Last pre-Code issue	100	200	300	800	-	-

NOTE: *(Rarely found in fine to mint condition.)* ***Nick Cardy*** *c-1-7.*

CONGO BILL
DC Comics (Vertigo): Oct, 1999 - No. 4, Jan, 2000 ($2.95, limited series)

1-4-Corben-c 3.00

CONGORILLA (Also see Actions Comics #224)
DC Comics: Nov, 1992 - No. 4, Feb, 1993 ($1.75, limited series)

1-4: 1,2-Brian Bolland-c 3.00

CONJURORS
DC Comics: Apr, 1999 - No. 3, Jun, 1999 ($2.95, limited series)

1-3-Elseworlds; Phantom Stranger app.; Barreto-c/a 3.00

CONNECTICUT YANKEE, A (See King Classics)

CONNOR HAWKE: DRAGON'S BLOOD (Also see Green Arrow titles)
DC Comics: Jan, 2007 - No. 6, Jun, 2007 ($2.99, limited series)

1-6-Chuck Dixon-s/Derec Donovan-a/c 3.00
SC (2008, $19.99) r/#1-6 20.00

CONQUEROR, THE
Dell Publishing Co.: No., 690, Mar, 1956

Four Color 690-Movie, John Wayne photo-c 15 30 45 103 227 350

CONQUEROR COMICS
Albrecht Publishing Co.: Winter, 1945

nn 24 48 72 142 234 325

CONQUEROR OF THE BARREN EARTH (See The Warlord #63)
DC Comics: Feb, 1985 - No. 4, May, 1985 (Limited series)

1-4: Back-up series from Warlord 3.00

CONQUEST
Store Comics: 1953 (6¢)

1-Richard the Lion Hearted, Beowulf, Swamp Fox 7 14 21 37 46 55

CONQUEST
Famous Funnies: Spring, 1955

1-Crandall-a, 1 pg.; contains contents of 1953 ish. 5 10 15 22 26 30

CONSPIRACY
Marvel Comics: Feb, 1998 - No. 2, Mar, 1998 ($2.99, limited series)

1,2-Painted art by Korday/Abnett-s 3.00

CONSTANTINE (Also see Hellblazer)
DC Comics (Vertigo): 2005 (Based on the 2005 Keanu Reeves movie)

...: The Hellblazer Collection (2005, $14.95) Movie adaptation and r/#1, 27, 41; photo-c 15.00
...: The Official Movie Adaptation (2005, $6.95) Seagle-s/Randall-a/photo-c 7.00

CONSTANTINE (Also see Justice League Dark)
DC Comics: May, 2013 - No. 23, May, 2015 ($2.99)

1-Lemire & Fawkes-s/Guedes-a; two covers by Reis & Guedes 1 2 3 5 6 8
2-20: 2-The Spectre app. 5-Trinity War tie-in; Shazam app. 9-Forever Evil tie-in. 20-23-Constantine on Earth 2. 23-Darkseid app. 3.00
...: Futures End 1 (11/14, $2.99, regular-c) Five years later; Ferreyra-a/c 3.00
...: Futures End 1 (11/14, $3.99, 3-D cover) 4.00
.../Hellblazer Special Edition 1 (12/14, $1.00) Flipbook r/#1 and Hellblazer #1 3.00

CONSTANTINE: THE HELLBLAZER
DC Comics: Aug, 2015 - No. 13, Aug, 2016 ($2.99)

1-13: 1-Doyle & Tynion IV-s/Rossmo-a, covers by Rossmo & Doyle. 3,4-Doyle-a. 7-Swamp Thing app. 8-12-Neron app. 10,11-Foreman-a 3.00

CONSTRUCT
Caliber (New Worlds): 1996 - No. 6, 1997 ($2.95, B&W, limited series)

1-6: Paul Jenkins scripts 3.00

CONSUMED
Platinum Studios: July, 2007 - No. 4, Oct, 2007 ($2.99, limited series)

1-4-Linsner-c/Budd-a/Shumskas-Tait-s 3.00

CONTACT COMICS
Aviation Press: July, 1944 - No. 12, May, 1946

	GD	VG	FN	VF	VF/NM	NM-
nn-Black Venus, Flamingo, Golden Eagle, Tommy Tomahawk begin	68	136	204	435	743	1050
2-Classic-c	65	130	195	416	708	1000
3-5: 3-Last Flamingo. 3,4-Black Venus by L. B. Cole. 5-The Phantom Flyer app.	48	96	144	302	514	725
6,11-Kurtzman's Black Venus; 11-Last Golden Eagle, last Tommy Tomahawk; Feldstein-a	52	104	156	328	552	775
7-10	41	82	123	256	428	600
12-Sky Rangers, Air Kids, Ace Diamond app.; L.B. Cole sci-fi cover	174	348	522	1114	1907	2700

NOTE: ***L. B. Cole*** *a-3, 9; c-1-12.* ***Giunta*** *a-3.* ***Hollingsworth*** *a-5, 7, 10.* ***Palais*** *a-11, 12.*

CONTEMPORARY MOTIVATORS
Pendelum Press: 1977 - 1978 ($1.45, 5-3/8x8", 31 pgs., B&W)

14-3002 The Caine Mutiny; 14-3010 Banner in the Sky; 14-3029 God Is My Co-Pilot; 14-3037 Guadalcanal Diary; 14-3045 Hiroshima; 14-3053 Hot Rod; 14-3061 Just Dial a Number; 14-3088 The Diary of Anne Frank; 14-3096 Lost Horizon 2 4 6 8 10 12

NOTE: *Also see Pendulum Illustrated Classics. Above may have been distributed the same.*

CONTEST OF CHAMPIONS (See Marvel Super-Hero...)

CONTEST OF CHAMPIONS
Marvel Comics: Dec, 2015 - No. 10, Sept, 2016 ($4.99/$3.99, limited series)

1-($4.99) The Collector, Venom, Mr. Fixit, Iron Man, Gamora & Maestro app.; Medina-a 5.00
2-9-($3.99) 2-Ares and Punisher 2099 app. 3-5-The Sentry app. 7,8-Ultimates app. 9-Revisits Civil War 4.00
10-($4.99) Finale; Ewing-s/Marcellius-a 5.00

CONTEST OF CHAMPIONS II
Marvel Comics: Sept, 1999 - No. 5, Nov, 1999 ($2.50, limited series)

1-5-Claremont-s/Jimenez-a 3.00

CONTRACT WITH GOD, A
Baronet Publishing Co./Kitchen Sink Press: 1978 ($4.95/$7.95, B&W, graphic novel)

nn-Will Eisner-s/a 3 6 9 14 20 25
Reprint (DC Comics, 2000, $12.95) 13.00

CONVERGENCE
DC Comics: No. 0, Jun, 2015 - No. 8, July, 2015 ($4.99/$3.99, weekly limited series)

0-Superman & multiple Brainiacs app.; intro Telos; Van Sciver-a/Jurgens & King-s 5.00
1-($4.99) Earth-2 heroes vs. Telos; Pagulayan-a; wraparound-c by Reis 5.00
2-7-($3.99) 2-Intro. Deimos; Pagulayan-a. 4,5-Warlord app. 5-Andy Kubert-a 4.00
8-($4.99) Conclusion; art by Segovia, Pagulayan, Pansica & Van Sciver 5.00

CONVERGENCE
DC Comics: June, 2015 - July, 2015 ($3.99, 2-part tie-in miniseries, each issue has a variant cover designed by Chip Kidd)

... Action Comics 1,2 - Pre-Crisis Earth Two Superman & Power Girl; Red Son Superman, Wonder Woman & Lex Luthor app.; Conner-c. 2-Bonus preview of Sinestro #12 4.00
... Adventures of Superman 1,2 - Pre-Crisis Earth One Superman & Supergirl app.; Wolfman-s. 2-Kamandi app.; bonus preview of Martian Manhunter #1 4.00
... Aquaman 1,2 - Harpoon-hand Aquaman & Deathblow app.; Cloonan-c; Richards-a. 2-Bonus preview of Doctor Fate #1 4.00
... Atom 1,2 - Pre-Flashpoint Ray Palmer & Deathstroke app.; Dillon-c/Yeowell-a. 2-Ryan Choi app.; bonus preview of Green Lantern #41 4.00

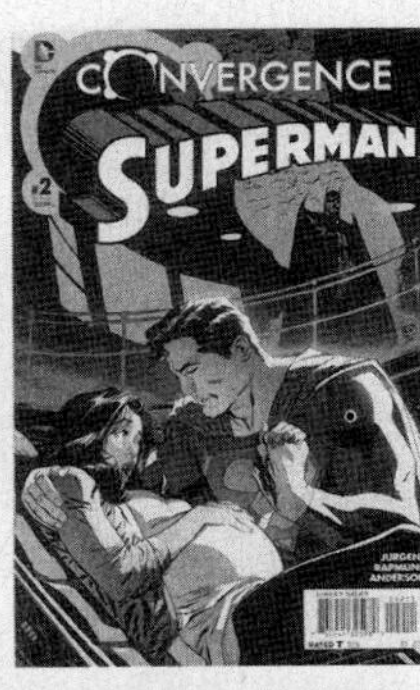

Convergence: Superman #2 © DC

Coo Coo Comics #42 © STD

Copperhead #7 © Faerber & Godlewski

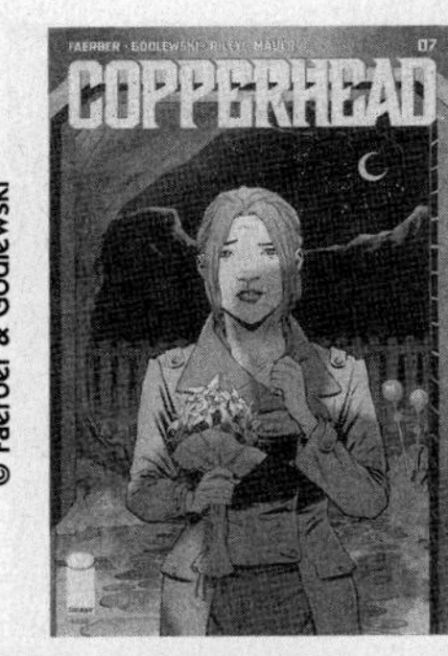

GD VG FN VF VF/NM NM-
2.0 4.0 6.0 8.0 9.0 9.2

... Batgirl 1,2 - Stephanie Brown, Cassadra Cain, Tim Drake & Catman app; Leonardi-a. 2-Grodd app.; bonus preview of Prez #1 4.00
... Batman and Robin 1,2 - Pre-Flashpoint Batman, Damian & Red Hood app.; Cowan & Janson-a. 2-Superman app.; bonus preview of Omega Men #1 4.00
... Batman and The Outsiders 1,2 - Pre-Crisis Outsiders and Omac app.; Andy Kubert-c. 2-Bonus preview of Batman Beyond #1 4.00
... Batman: Shadow of the Bat 1,2 - Pre-Zero Hour Batman & Azrael app. 1-Philip Tan-a/c. 2-Leonardi-a; bonus preview of Deathstroke #7 4.00
... Blue Beetle 1,2 - Charlton Blue Beetle, Captain Atom & The Question app.; Blevins-c. 2-Legion of Super-Heroes app.; bonus preview of Black Canary #1 4.00
... Booster Gold 1,2 - Rip Hunter & the Legion of Super-Heroes app.; Jurgens-c. 2-Blue Beetle app.; bonus preview of Earth-2: Society #1 4.00
... Catwoman 1,2 - Pre-Zero Hour purple suit Catwoman & Kingdom Come Batman app.; Ron Randall-a. Bonus preview of Gotham By Midnight #6 4.00
... Crime Syndicate 1,2 - Earth-Three villains & 853rd Century JLA app.; Winslade-a. 2-Bonus preview of Cyborg #1 4.00
... Detective Comics 1,2 - Earth-Two pre-Crisis Robin & Huntress vs. Red Son Superman; Cowan & Sienkiewicz-a. 2-Red Son Batman app.; bonus preview of Flash #41 4.00
... Flash 1,2 - Earth-One pre-Crisis Barry Allen vs. Tangent Superman; Abnett-s/Dallocchio-a; 2-Bonus preview of New Suicide Squad #9 4.00
... Green Arrow 1,2 - Pre-Zero Hour Oliver Queen & Connor Hawke vs. Kingdom Come Black Canary & Dinah Lance; Morales-a; 2-Bonus preview of G.L.C. Lost Army #1 4.00
... Green Lantern Corps 1,2 - Earth-One pre-Crisis Guy Gardner, John Stewart & Hal Jordan; Hercules from Durvale app. 2-Bonus preview of Gotham Academy #7 4.00
... Green Lantern/Parallax 1,2 - Pre-Zero Hour Hal Jordan & Kyle Rayner; Ron Wagner-a. Princess Fern of Electropolis app. 2-Bonus preview of Lobo #7 4.00
... Harley Quinn 1,2 - Pre-Flashpoint Harley, Poison Ivy & Catwoman; Winslade-a. 2-Harley battles Captain Carrot. 2-Bonus preview of Section Eight #1 4.00
... Hawkman 1,2 - Earth-One pre-Crisis Katar Hol & Shayera; Parker-s/Truman-a. 2-Bonus preview of Grayson #9 4.00
... Infinity Inc. 1,2 - Earth-Two pre-Crisis Infinity Inc. vs. Future Jonah Hex & The Dogs of War; Ordway-s, 1-Ben Caldwell-a. 2-Bonus preview of Batgirl #41 4.00
... Justice League 1,2 - Pre-Flashpoint female Justice League vs. Flashpoint Aquaman; Buckingham-c. 2-Bonus preview of Detective Comics #41 4.00
... Justice League International 1,2 - Pre-Zero Hour JLI vs. Kingdom Come; Manley-a. 2-Bonus preview of Justice League 3001 #1 4.00
... Justice League of America 1,2 - Earth-One pre-Crisis Detroit JLA vs. Tangent Secret Six; ChrisCross-a. 2-Bonus preview of Batman/Superman #21 4.00
... Justice Society of America 1,2 - Earth-Two pre-Crisis JSA vs. Weaponers of Qward; Derenick-a. 2-Bonus preview of Superman/Wonder Woman #18 4.00
... New Teen Titans 1,2 - Earth-One pre-Crisis Teen Titans vs. Tangent Doom Patrol; Nicola Scott-a. 2-Bonus preview of Robin: Son of Batman #1 4.00
... Nightwing and Oracle 1,2 - Pre-Flashpoint version vs. Flashpoint Hawkman; Duursema-a/Thompson-c. 2-Bonus preview of Midnighter #1 4.00
... Plastic Man and the Freedom Fighters 1,2 - Earth-X team vs. Futures End cyborgs; Silver Ghost app.; McCrea-a/Barta-c. 2-Bonus preview of Harley Quinn #17 4.00
... The Question 1,2 - Pre-Flashpoint Question (Renee Montoya); Huntress, Batwoman & Two-Face app.; Rucka-s/Hamner-a. 2-Bonus preview of Starfire #1 4.00
... Shazam! 1,2 - Earth-S Marvel Family vs. Gotham By Gaslight Batman; Shaner-a Sivana, Ibac, Mr. Atom app. 2-Bonus preview of Constantine The Hellblazer #1 4.00
... Speed Force 1,2 - Pre-Flashpoint Flash (Wally West) vs. Flashpoint Wonder Woman Grummett-a; Fastback (Zoo Crew) app. 2-Bonus preview of Green Arrow #41 4.00
... Suicide Squad 1,2 - Pre-Zero Hour vs. Kingdom Come Green Lantern Mandrake-a; Lex Luthor app. 2-Bonus preview of Aquaman #41 4.00
... Superboy 1,2 - Pre-Zero Hour Kon-El vs. Kingdom Come Superman, Flash & Red Robin; Moline-a/Tarr-c. 2-Bonus preview of Action Comics #41 4.00
... Superboy and the Legion of Super-Heroes 1,2 - Pre-Crisis Legion vs. The Atomic Knights; Storms-a/Guerra-c. 2-Bonus preview of Teen Titans #9 4.00
... Supergirl: Matrix 1,2 - Pre-Zero Hour Supergirl vs. Lady Quark (Electropolis); Ambush Bug app.; Giffen-s/Green II-a/Porter-c. 2-Bonus preview of Bat-Mite #1 4.00
... Superman 1,2 - Pre-Flashpoint Superman & Lois vs. Flashpoint heroes; Jurgens-s/Weeks-a; 2-Baby born (Jonathan Kent); bonus preview of Doomed #1 (See Superman: Lois & Clark series) 4.00
... Superman: Man of Steel 1,2 - Pre-Zero Hour Steel vs. Gen-13; Parasite app.; Louise Simonson-s/June Brigman-a/Walt Simonson-c. 2-Bonus preview of Bizarro #1 4.00
... Swamp Thing 1,2 - Earth-One pre-Crisis Swamp Thing vs. Red Rain vampire Batman; Len Wein-s/Kelley Jones-a. 2-Bonus preview of Catwoman #41 4.00
... Titans 1,2 - Pre-Flashpoint Titans vs. The Extremists; Nicieza-s/Wagner-a; 2-Bonus preview of Red Hood & Arsenal #1 4.00
... Wonder Woman 1,2 - Earth-One pre-Crisis Wonder Woman vs. Red Rain vampire Joker, Catwoman & Poison Ivy. 1-Middleton-a/c. 2-Lopresti-a; bonus preview of Secret Six 4.00
... World's Finest 1,2 - Earth-Two pre-Crisis Seven Soldiers of Victory vs. Weaponers of Qward; Scribbly Jibbet app.; Levitz-s. 2-Bonus preview of We Are Robin #1 4.00

CONVOCATIONS: A MAGIC THE GATHERING GALLERY
Acclaim Comics (Armada): Jan, 1996 ($2.50, one-shot)
1-pin-ups by various artists including Kaluta, Vess, and Dringenberg 3.00

COO COO COMICS (...the Bird Brain No. 57 on)
Nedor Publ. Co./Standard (Animated Cartoons): Oct, 1942 - No. 62, Apr, 1952
1-Origin/1st app. Super Mouse & begin series (cloned from Superman); the first funny animal super hero series (see Looney Tunes #5 for 1st funny animal super hero)
43 86 129 271 461 650
2 20 40 60 114 182 250
3-10: 10-(3/44) 15 30 45 83 124 165
11-33: 33-1 pg. Ingels-a 12 24 36 67 94 120
34-40,43-46,48-50Text illos by Frazetta in all. 36-Super Mouse covers begin
15 30 45 85 130 175
41-Frazetta-a (6-pg. story & 3 text illos) 24 48 72 144 237 330
42,47-Frazetta-a & text illos. 18 36 54 107 169 230
51-62: 56-58,61-Super Mouse app. 11 22 33 60 83 105

"COOKIE" (Also see Topsy-Turvy)
Michel Publ./American Comics Group(Regis Publ.): Apr, 1946 - No. 55, Aug-Sept, 1955
1-Teen-age humor 28 56 84 165 270 375
2-1st app. Tee-Pee Tim who takes over Ha Ha Comics later
15 30 45 88 137 185
3-10: 8-Bing Crosby app. 13 26 39 74 105 135
11-20: 12-Hedy Lamarr app. 13-Jackie Robinson mentioned. 15-Gregory Peck app. 16-Ub Iwerks (a creator of Mickey Mouse) name used. 18-Jane Russell-type Jane Bustle. 19-Cookie takes a dog to see Lassie movie 11 22 33 64 90 115
21-23,26,28-30: 26-Milt Gross & Starlett O'Hara stories. 28,30-Starlett O'Hara stories
10 20 30 54 72 90
24,25,27-Starlett O'Hara stories 10 20 30 56 76 95
31-34,37-48,52-55 9 18 27 47 61 75
35,36-Starlett O'Hara stories 9 18 27 52 69 85
49-51: 49-(6-7/54)-3-D effect-c/s. 50-3-D effect. 51-(10-11/54) 8pg. TrueVision 3-D effect story
14 28 42 82 121 160

COOL CAT (What's Cookin' With...) (Formerly Black Magic)
Prize Publications: V8#6, Mar-Apr, 1962 - V9#2, July-Aug, 1962
V8#6, nn(V9#1, 5-6/62), V9#2 3 6 9 19 30 40

COOL WORLD (Movie by Ralph Bakshi)
DC Comics: Apr, 1992 - No. 4, Sept, 1992 ($1.75, limited series)
1-4: Prequel to animated/live action movie. 1-Bakshi-c. Bill Wray inks in all 3.00
Movie Adaptation nn ('92, $3.50, 68pg.)-Bakshi-c 4.00

COPPER CANYON (See Fawcett Movie Comics)

COPPERHEAD
Image Comics: Sept, 2014 - Present ($3.50)
1-10: 1-Faerber-s/Godlewski-a; multiple covers 3.50

COPS (TV)
DC Comics: Aug, 1988 - No. 15, Aug, 1989 ($1.00)
1 ($1.50, 52 pgs.)-Based on Hasbro Toys 4.00
2-15: 14-Orlando-c(p) 3.00

COPS: THE JOB
Marvel Comics: June, 1992 - No. 4, Sept, 1992 ($1.25, limited series)
1-4: All have Jusko scripts & Golden-c 3.00

CORBEN SPECIAL, A
Pacific Comics: May, 1984 (one-shot)
1-Corben-c/a; E.A. Poe adaptation 6.00

CORE, THE
Image Comics: July, 2008 ($3.99)
Pilot Season - Hickman-s/Rocafort-a 4.00

CORKY & WHITE SHADOW (Disney, TV)
Dell Publishing Co.: No. 707, May, 1956 (Mickey Mouse Club)
Four Color 707-Photo-c 6 12 18 41 76 110

CORLISS ARCHER (See Meet Corliss Archer)

CORMAC MAC ART (Robert E. Howard's...)
Dark Horse Comics: 1990 - No. 4, 1990 ($1.95, B&W, mini-series)
1-4: All have Bolton painted-c; Howard adapts. 3.00

CORPORAL RUSTY DUGAN (See Holyoke One-Shot #2)

CORPSES OF DR. SACOTTI, THE (See Ideal a Classical Comic)

CORSAIR, THE (See A-1 Comics No. 5, 7, 10 under Texas Slim)

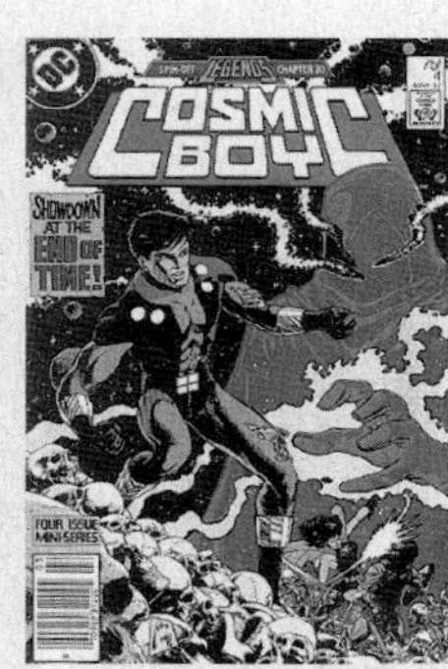

Cosmic Boy #4 © DC

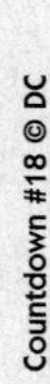
Countdown #18 © DC

Coup D'Etat: Stormwatch #2 © WSP

	GD 2.0	VG 4.0	FN 6.0	VF 8.0	VF/NM 9.0	NM- 9.2

CORUM: THE BULL AND THE SPEAR (See Chronicles Of Corum)
First Comics: Jan, 1989 - No. 4, July, 1989 ($1.95)

1-4: Adapts Michael Moorcock's novel 3.00

COSMIC BOOK, THE
Ace Comics: Dec, 1986 - No. 1, 1987 ($1.95)

1,2: 1-(44pgs.)-Wood, Toth-a. 2-(B&W) 4.00

COSMIC BOY (Also see The Legion of Super-Heroes)
DC Comics: Dec, 1986 - No. 4, Mar, 1987 (limited series)

1-4: Legends tie-ins all issues 4.00

COSMIC GUARD
Devil's Due Publ.: Aug, 2004 - No. 6, Dec, 2005 ($2.99)

1-6-Jim Starlin-s/a 3.00

COSMIC HEROES
Eternity/Malibu Graphics: Oct, 1988 - No. 11, Dec, 1989 ($1.95, B&W)

1-11: Reprints 1934-1936's Buck Rogers newspaper strips #1-728 3.00

COSMIC ODYSSEY
DC Comics: 1988 - No. 4, 1988 ($3.50, limited series, squarebound)

1-4: Reintro. New Gods into DC continuity; Superman, Batman, Green Lantern (John Stewart) app; Starlin scripts, Mignola-c/a in all. 2-Darkseid merges Demon & Jason Blood (separated in Demon limited series #4) 5.00
TPB (1992,2009, $19.99) r/#1-4; Robert Greenberger intro. 20.00

COSMIC POWERS
Marvel Comics: Mar, 1994 - No. 6, Aug, 1994 ($2.50, limited series)

1,2-Thanos app. 1-Ron Lim-c/a(p). 2-Terrax 5.00
3-6: 3-Ganymede & Jack of Hearts app. 4.00

COSMIC POWERS UNLIMITED
Marvel Comics: May, 1995 - No. 5, May, 1996 ($3.95, quarterly)

1-5 4.00

COSMIC SLAM
Ultimate Sports Entertainment: 1999 ($3.95, one-shot)

1-McGwire, Sosa, Bagwell, Justice battle aliens; Sienkiewicz-c 4.00

COSMO CAT (Becomes Sunny #11 on; also see All Top & Wotalife Comics)
Fox Publications/Green Publ. Co./Norlen Mag.: July-Aug, 1946 - No. 10, Oct, 1947; 1957; 1959

	GD	VG	FN	VF	VF/NM	NM-
1	29	58	87	170	278	385
2	15	30	45	86	133	180
3-Origin (11-12/46)	19	38	57	111	176	240
4-Robot-c	15	30	45	83	124	165
5-10	11	22	33	60	83	105
2-4(1957-Green Publ. Co.)	6	12	18	27	33	38
2-4(1959-Norlen Mag.)	5	10	15	23	28	32
I.W. Reprint #1	2	4	6	11	16	20

COSMO THE MERRY MARTIAN
Archie Publications (Radio Comics): Sept, 1958 - No. 6, Oct, 1959

	GD	VG	FN	VF	VF/NM	NM-
1-Bob White-a in all	18	36	54	103	162	220
2-6	12	24	36	67	94	120

COTTON WOODS (All-American athlete)
Dell Publishing Co.: No. 837, Sept, 1957

	GD	VG	FN	VF	VF/NM	NM-
Four Color 837	5	10	15	30	50	70

COUGAR, THE (Cougar No. 2)
Seaboard Periodicals (Atlas): April, 1975 - No. 2, July, 1975

	GD	VG	FN	VF	VF/NM	NM-
1,2: 1-Vampire; Adkins-a(p). 2-Cougar origin; werewolf-s; Buckler-c(p)	2	4	6	11	16	20

COUNTDOWN (See Movie Classics)

COUNTDOWN
DC Comics (WildStorm): June, 2000 - No. 8, Jan, 2001 ($2.95)

1-8-Mariotte-s/Lopresti-a 3.00

COUNTDOWN (Continued from 52 weekly series)
DC Comics: No. 51, July, 2007 - No. 1, June, 2008 ($2.99, weekly, limited series) (issue #s go in reverse)

51-Gatefold wraparound-c by Andy Kubert; Duela Dent killed; the Monitors app. 3.00
50-1: 50-Joker-c. 48-Lightray dies. 47-Mary Marvel gains Black Adam's powers. 46-Intro. Forerunner. 43-Funeral for Bart Allen. 39-Karate Kid-c 3.00
Countdown to Final Crisis Vol. 1 TPB (2008, $19.99) r/#51-39 20.00
Countdown to Final Crisis Vol. 2 TPB (2008, $19.99) r/#38-26 20.00
Countdown to Final Crisis Vol. 3 TPB (2008, $19.99) r/#25-13 20.00
Countdown to Final Crisis Vol. 4 TPB (2008, $19.99) r/#12-1 20.00

COUNTDOWN: ARENA (Takes place during Countdown #21-18)
DC Comics: Feb, 2008 - No. 4, Feb, 2008 ($3.99, weekly, limited series)

1-4-Battles between alternate Earth heroes; McDaniel-a; Andy Kubert variant-c on each 4.00
TPB (2008, $17.99) r/#1-4; variant covers 18.00

COUNTDOWN PRESENTS: LORD HAVOK & THE EXTREMISTS
DC Comics: Dec, 2007 - No. 8 ($2.99, limited series)

1-6: 1-Tieri-s/Sharp-a/c; Challengers From Beyond app. 3.00
TPB (2008, $17.99) r/#1-6 18.00

COUNTDOWN PRESENTS THE SEARCH FOR RAY PALMER (Leads into Countdown #18)
DC Comics: Nov, 2007 - Feb, 2008 ($2.99, series of one-shots)

...: Wildstorm (11/07) Part 1; The Authority app.; Art Adams-c/Unzueta-a 3.00
...: Crime Society (12/07) Earth-3 Owlman & Jokester app.; Igle-a 3.00
...: Red Rain (1/08) Vampire Batman app.; Kelley Jones-c; Jones, Battle & Unzueta-a 3.00
...: Gotham By Gaslight (1/08) Victorian Batman app.; Tocchini-a/Nguyen-c 3.00
...: Red Son (2/08) Soviet Superman app.; Foreman-a 3.00
...: Superwoman/Batwoman (2/08) Conclusion; gender-reversed heroes; Sook-c 3.00
TPB (2008, $17.99) r/one-shots 18.00

COUNTDOWN SPECIAL
DC Comics: Dec, 2007 - Jun, 2008 ($4.99, collection of reprints related to Countdown)

...: Eclipso (5/08) r/Eclipso #10 & Spectre #17,18 (1994); Sook-c 5.00
...: Jimmy Olsen (1/08) r/Superman's Pal, Jimmy Olsen #136,147,148; Kirby-s/a; Sook-c 5.00
...: Kamandi (6/08) r/Kamandi: The Last Boy on Earth #1,10,29; Kirby-s/a; Sook-c 5.00
...: New Gods (3/08) r/Forever People #1, Mr. Miracle #1, New Gods #7; Kirby-s/a; Sook-c 5.00
...: Omac (4/08) r/Omac (1974) #1, Warlord #37-39, DC Comics Presents #61; Sook-c 5.00
...: The Atom 1,2 (2/08) r/stories from Super-Team Family #11-14; Sook-c on both 5.00
...: The Flash (12/07) r/Rogues Gallery in Flash (1st series) #106,113,155,174; Sook-c 5.00

COUNTDOWN TO ADVENTURE
DC Comics: Oct, 2007 - No. 8, May, 2008 ($3.99, limited series)

1-8: 1-Adam Strange, Animal Man and Starfire app.; origin of Forerunner 4.00
TPB (2008, $17.99) r/#1-8 18.00

COUNTDOWN TO INFINITE CRISIS (See DC Countdown)

COUNTDOWN TO MYSTERY (See Eclipso: The Music of the Spheres TPB for reprint)
DC Comics: Nov, 2007 - No. 8, Jun, 2008 ($3.99, limited series)

1-8: 1-Doctor Fate, Eclipso, The Spectre and Plastic Man app. 4.00
TPB (2008, $17.99) r/#1-8 18.00

COUNT DUCKULA (TV)
Marvel Comics: Nov, 1988 - No. 15, Jan, 1991 ($1.00)

1,8: 1-Dangermouse back-up. 8-Geraldo Rivera photo-c/& app.; Sienkiewicz-a(i) 5.00
2-7,9-15: Dangermouse back-ups in all 4.00

COUNT OF MONTE CRISTO, THE
Dell Publishing Co.: No. 794, May, 1957

	GD	VG	FN	VF	VF/NM	NM-
Four Color 794-Movie, Buscema-a	8	16	24	51	96	140

COUP D'ETAT (Oneshots)
DC Comics (WildStorm): April, 2004 ($2.95, weekly limited series)

...: Sleeper 1 (part 1 of 4) Jim Lee-a; 2 covers by Lee and Bermejo 3.00
...: Stormwatch 1 (part 2 of 4) D'Anda-a; 2 covers by D'Anda and Bermejo 3.00
...: Wildcats Version 3.0 1 (part 3 of 4) Garza-a; 2 covers by Garza and Bermejo 3.00
...: The Authority 1 (part 4 of 4) Portacio-a; 2 covers by Portacio and Bermejo 3.00
...: Afterword 1 (5/04) Profile pages and prelude stories for Sleeper & Wetworks 3.00
TPB (2004, $12.95) r/series and profile pages from Afterword 13.00

COURAGE COMICS
J. Edward Slavin: 1945

	GD	VG	FN	VF	VF/NM	NM-
1,2,77	16	32	48	94	147	200

COURTNEY CRUMRIN
Oni Press: Apr, 2012 - No. 10, Feb, 2013 ($3.99)

1-10-Ted Naifeh-s/a 4.00
#1 (5/14, Free Comic Book Day giveaway) r/#1 3.00

COURTNEY CRUMRIN...
Oni Press: July, 2005; July 2007; Dec, 2008 ($5.95, B&W, series of one-shots)

... And The Fire Thief's Tale (7/07) Naifeh-s/a 6.00
... And The Prince of Nowhere (12/08) Naifeh-s/a 6.00
... Tales (5/11) sequel to Tales Portrait of the Warlock...; Naifeh-s/a 6.00
... Tales Portrait of the Warlock as a Young Man (7/05) origin Uncle Aloysius; Naifeh-s/a 6.00

Courtney Crumrin & The Night Things FCBD © Ted Naifeh

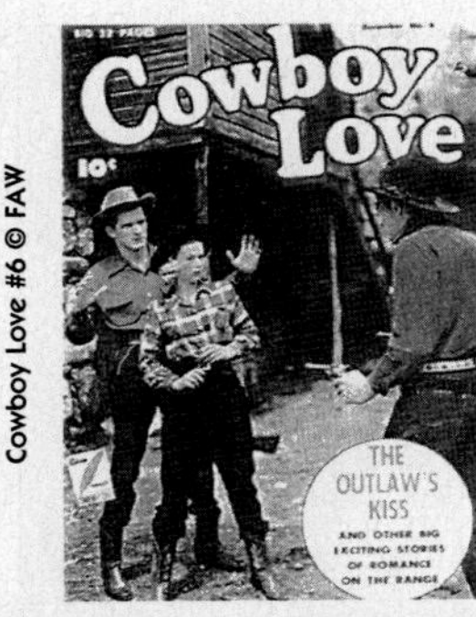

Cowboy Love #6 © FAW

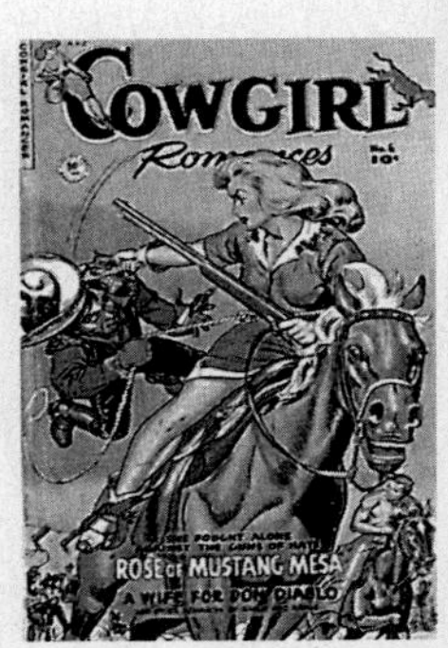

Cowgirl Romances #6 © FH

GD 2.0 | VG 4.0 | FN 6.0 | VF 8.0 | VF/NM 9.0 | NM- 9.2

COURTNEY CRUMRIN & THE COVEN OF MYSTICS
Oni Press: Dec, 2002 - No. 4, March, 2003 ($2.95, B&W, limited series)
1-4-Ted Naifeh-s/a 3.00
TPB (9/03, $11.95, 8" x 5-1/2") r/#1-4 12.00

COURTNEY CRUMRIN & THE NIGHT THINGS
Oni Press: Mar, 2002 - No. 4, June, 2002 ($2.95, B&W, limited series)
1-4-Ted Naifeh-s/a 3.00
Free Comic Book Day Edition (5/03) Naifeh-s/a 3.00
TPB (12/02, $11.95) r/#1-4 12.00

COURTNEY CRUMRIN IN THE TWILIGHT KINGDOM
Oni Press: Dec, 2003 - No. 4, May, 2004 ($2.99, B&W, limited series)
1-4-Ted Naifeh-s/a 3.00
TPB (9/04, $11.95, digest-size) r/#1-4 12.00

COURTSHIP OF EDDIE'S FATHER (TV)
Dell Publishing Co.: Jan, 1970 - No. 2, May, 1970
1-Bill Bixby photo-c on both 5 10 15 33 57 80
2 4 8 12 23 37 50

COVEN
Awesome Entertainment: Aug, 1997 - No. 5, Mar, 1998 ($2.50)
Preview 1 2 3 5 6 8
1-Loeb-s/Churchill-a; three covers by Churchill, Liefeld, Pollina
1 2 3 5 6 8
1-Fan Appreciation Ed.(3/98); new Churchill-c 3.00
1+ :Includes B&W art from Kaboom 1 3 4 6 8 10
2-Regular-c w/leaping Fantom 6.00
2-Variant-c w/circle of candles 1 2 3 5 6 8
3-6-Contains flip book preview of ReGex 3.00
3-White variant-c 1 2 3 4 5 7
3,4: 3-Halloween wraparound-c. 4-Purple variant-c 3.00
...Black & White (9/98) Short stories 3.00
...Fantom Special (2/98) w/sketch pages 5.00

COVEN
Awesome Entertainment: Jan, 1999 - No. 3, June, 1999 ($2.50)
1-3: 1-Loeb-s/Churchill-a; 6 covers by various. 2-Supreme-c/app. 3-Flip book w/Kaboom preview 3.00
... Dark Origins (7/99, 2.50) w/Lionheart gallery 3.00

COVENANT, THE
Image Comics (Top Cow): 2005 ($9.99, squarebound, one-shot)
nn-Tone Rodriguez-a/Aron Coleite-s 10.00

COVENANT, THE
Image Comics: Jun, 2015 - No. 5, Dec, 2015 ($3.99)
1-5-Rob Liefeld-s/c; Matt Horak-a; story of the Ark of the Covenant 4.00

COVERED WAGONS, HO (Disney, TV)
Dell Publishing Co.: No. 814, June, 1957 (Donald Duck)
Four Color 814-Mickey Mouse app. 5 10 15 34 60 85

COWBOY ACTION (Formerly Western Thrillers No. 1-4; Becomes Quick-Trigger Western No. 12 on)
Atlas Comics (ACI): No. 5, March, 1955 - No. 11, March, 1956
5 15 30 45 88 137 185
6-10: 6-8-Heath-c 11 22 33 64 90 115
11-Williamson-a (4 pgs.); Baker-a 13 26 39 74 105 135
NOTE: *Ayers a-8. Drucker a-6. Maneely c/a-5, 6. Severin c-10. Shores a-7.*

COWBOY COMICS (Star Ranger #12, Stories #14)(Star Ranger Funnies #15)
Centaur Publishing Co.: No. 13, July, 1938 - No. 14, Aug, 1938
13-(Rare)-Ace and Deuce, Lyin Lou, Air Patrol, Aces High, Lee Trent, Trouble Hunters begin
206 412 618 1318 2259 3200
14-(Rare)-Filchock-c 142 284 426 909 1555 2200
NOTE: *Guardineer a-13, 14. Gustavson a-13, 14.*

COWBOY IN AFRICA (TV)
Gold Key: Mar, 1968
1(10219-803)-Chuck Connors photo-c 4 8 12 25 40 55

COWBOY LOVE (Becomes Range Busters?)
Fawcett Publications/Charlton Comics No. 28 on: 7/49 - V2#10, 6/50; No. 11, 1951; No. 28, 2/55 - No. 31, 8/55
V1#1-Rocky Lane photo back-c 15 30 45 88 137 185
2 8 16 24 44 57 70
V1#3,4,6 (12/49) 8 16 24 40 50 60
5-Bill Boyd photo back-c (11/49) 9 18 27 47 61 75
V2#7-Williamson/Evans-a 10 20 30 54 72 90
V2#8-11 7 14 21 35 43 50
V1#28 (Charlton)-Last precode (2/55) (Formerly Romantic Story?)
6 12 18 31 38 45
V1#29-31 (Charlton; becomes Sweetheart Diary #32 on)
6 12 18 28 34 40
NOTE: *Powell a-10. Marcus Swayze a-2, 3. Photo c-1-11. No. 1-3, 5-7, 9, 10 are 52 pgs.*

COWBOY ROMANCES (Young Men No. 4 on)
Marvel Comics (IPC): Oct, 1949 - No. 3, Mar, 1950 (All photo-c & 52 pgs.)
1-Photo-c 26 52 78 154 252 350
2-William Holden, Mona Freeman "Streets of Laredo" photo-c
18 36 54 107 169 230
3-Photo-c 15 30 45 90 140 190

COWBOYS 'N' INJUNS (...and Indians No. 6 on)
Compix No. 1-5/Magazine Enterprises No. 6 on: 1946 - No. 5, 1947; No. 6, 1949 - No. 8, 1952
1-Funny animal western 15 30 45 90 140 190
2-5-All funny animal western 10 20 30 56 76 95
6(A-1 23)-Half violent, half funny; Ayers-a 15 30 45 84 127 170
7(A-1 41, 1950), 8(A-1 48)-All funny 9 18 27 50 65 80
I.W. Reprint No. 1,7,10 (Reprinted in Canada by Superior, No. 7), 10('63)
2 4 6 11 16 20

COWBOY WESTERN COMICS (TV)(Formerly Jack In The Box; Becomes Space Western No. 40-45 & Wild Bill Hickok & Jingles No. 68 on; title: Cowboy Western Heroes No. 47 & 48; Cowboy Western No. 49 on)
Charlton (Capitol Stories): No. 17, 7/48 - No. 39, 8/52; No. 46, 10/53; No. 47, 12/53; No. 48, Spr, '54; No. 49, 5-6/54 - No. 67, 3/58 (nn 40-45)
17-Jesse James, Annie Oakley, Wild Bill Hickok begin; Texas Rangers app.
16 32 48 94 147 200
18,19-Orlando-c/a. 18-Paul Bunyan begins. 19-Wyatt Earp story
10 20 30 58 79 100
20-25: 21-Buffalo Bill story. 22-Texas Rangers-c/story. 24-Joel McCrea photo-c & adaptation from movie "Three Faces West". 25-James Craig photo-c & adaptation from movie "Northwest Stampede" 9 18 27 52 69 85
26-George Montgomery photo-c and adaptation from movie "Indian Scout"; 1 pg. bio on Will Rogers 10 20 30 58 79 100
27-Sunset Carson photo-c & adapts movie "Sunset Carson Rides Again" plus 1 other Sunset Carson story 39 78 117 240 395 550
28-Sunset Carson line drawn-c; adapts movies "Battling Marshal" & "Fighting Mustangs" starring Sunset Carson 20 40 60 114 182 250
29-Sunset Carson line drawn-c; adapts movies "Rio Grande" with Sunset Carson & "Winchester '73" w/James Stewart plus 5 pg. life history of Sunset Carson featuring Tom Mix 20 40 60 114 182 250
30-Sunset Carson photo-c; adapts movie "Deadline" starring Sunset Carson plus 1 other Sunset Carson story 39 78 117 240 395 550
31-34,38,39,47-50 (no #40-45): 50-Golden Arrow, Rocky Lane & Blackjack (r?) stories
9 18 27 47 61 75
35,36-Sunset Carson-c/stories (2 in each). 35-Inside front-c photo of Sunset Carson plus photo on-c 20 40 60 120 195 270
37-Sunset Carson stories (2) 15 30 45 94 147 200
46-(Formerly Space Western)-Space western story 15 30 45 94 147 200
51-57,59-66: 51-Golden Arrow(r?) & Monte Hale-r renamed Rusty Hall. 53,54-Tom Mix-r. 55-Monte Hale story(r?). 66-Young Eagle story. 67-Wild Bill Hickok and Jingles-c/story
7 14 21 35 43 50
58-(1/56)-Wild Bill Hickok, Annie Oakley & Jesse James stories; Forgione-a
8 16 24 44 57 70
67-(15¢, 68 pgs.)-Williamson/Torres-a, 5 pgs. 9 18 27 50 65 80
NOTE: *Many issues trimmed 1" shorter. Maneely a-67(5). Inside front/back photo c-29.*

COWGIRL ROMANCES
Marvel Comics (CCC): No. 28, Jan, 1950 (52 pgs.)
28(#1)-Photo-c 23 46 69 136 223 310

COWGIRL ROMANCES
Fiction House Magazines: 1950 - No. 12, Winter, 1952-53 (No. 1-3: 52 pgs.)
1-Kamen-a 48 96 144 302 514 725
2 26 52 78 154 252 350
3-5: 5-12-Whitman-c (most) 22 44 66 132 216 300
6-9,11,12 21 42 63 126 206 285
10-Frazetta?/Williamson?-a; Kamen?/Baker-a; r/Mitzi story from Movie Comics #4 w/all new dialogue 37 74 111 222 361 500

C.O.W.L. #1 © Higgins & Siegel

Crackajack Funnies #40 © DELL

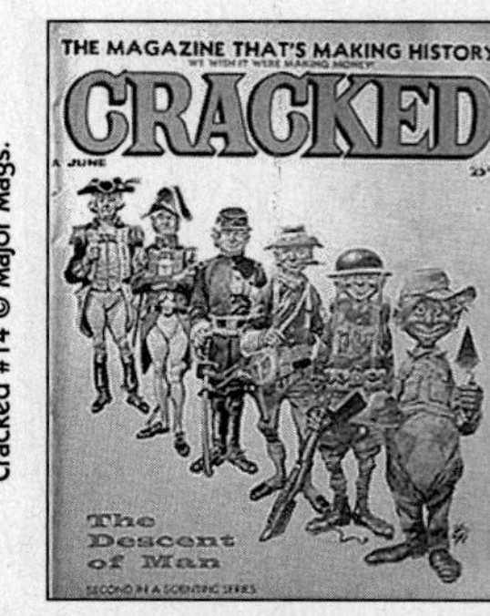

Cracked #14 © Major Mags.

GD VG FN VF VF/NM NM-
2.0 4.0 6.0 8.0 9.0 9.2

C.O.W.L.
Image Comics: May, 2014 - No. 11, Jul, 2015 ($3.50)
1-11: 1-Higgins & Siegel-s/Reis-a. 6-Origin of Grey Raven; Charretier-a 3.50

COW PUNCHER (...Comics)
Avon Periodicals: Jan, 1947; No. 2, Sept, 1947 - No. 7, 1949
1-Clint Cortland, Texas Ranger, Kit West, Pioneer Queen begin; Kubert-a; Alabam stories begin 55 110 165 352 601 850
2-Kubert, Kamen/Feldstein-a; Kamen-c 47 94 141 296 498 700
3-5,7: 3-Kiefer story 36 72 108 211 343 475
6-Opium drug mention story; bondage, headlight-c; Reinman-a 43 86 129 271 461 650

COWPUNCHER
Realistic Publications: 1953 (nn) (Reprints Avon's No. 2)
nn-Kubert-a 15 30 45 84 127 170

COWSILLS, THE (See Harvey Pop Comics)

COW SPECIAL, THE
Image Comics (Top Cow): Spring-Summer 2000; 2001 ($2.95)
1-Previews upcoming Top Cow projects; Yancy Butler photo-c 3.00
Vol. 2 #1-Witchblade-c; previews and interviews 3.00

COYOTE
Marvel Comics (Epic Comics): June, 1983 - No. 16, Mar, 1986
1-10,15: 7-10-Ditko-a 4.00
11-1st McFarlane-a. 2 4 6 10 14 18
12-14,16: 12-14-McFarlane-a. 14-Badger x-over. 16-Reagan c/app. 6.00
Coyote Collection Vol. 1 (2005, $14.99) reprints from Coyote #1-7 & Scorpio Rose #1,2 plus Rogers layout pages for unpublished #3; Englehart intro. 15.00
Coyote Collection Vol. 2 (2005, $12.99) reprints from Coyote #1-4 13.00
Coyote Collection Vol. 3 (2006, $12.99) reprints from Coyote #5-8 13.00
Coyote Collection Vol. 4 (2007, $14.99) reprints from Coyote #9-12 15.00
Coyote Collection Vol. 5 (2007, $12.99) reprints from Coyote #13-16 13.00

CRACKAJACK FUNNIES (Also see The Owl)
Dell Publishing Co.: June, 1938 - No. 43, Jan, 1942
1-Dan Dunn, Freckles, Myra North, Wash Tubbs, Apple Mary, The Nebbs, Don Winslow, Tom Mix, Buck Jones, Major Hoople, Clyde Beatty, Boots begin 190 380 570 1207 2079 2950
2 76 152 228 486 831 1175
3 57 114 171 362 619 875
4 47 94 141 296 498 700
5-Nude woman on cover (10/38) 53 106 159 334 567 800
6-8,10: 8-Speed Bolton begins (1st app.) 41 82 123 256 428 600
9-(3/39)-Red Ryder strip-r begin by Harman; 1st app. in comics & 1st cover app. 174 348 522 1114 1907 2700
11-14 36 72 108 216 351 485
15-Tarzan text feature begins by Burroughs (9/39); not in #26,35 39 78 117 234 385 535
16-24: 18-Stratosphere Jim begins (1st app., 12/39). 23-Ellery Queen begins plus-c (1st comic book app., 5/40) 32 64 96 188 307 425
25-The Owl begins (1st app., 7/40); in new costume #26 by Frank Thomas (also see Popular Comics #72) 84 168 252 538 919 1300
26,27,29,30 50 100 150 315 533 750
28-Part Owl-c 58 116 174 371 636 900
31-Owl covers begin, end #42 61 122 183 390 670 950
32-Origin Owl Girl 63 126 189 403 689 975
33-37: 36-Last Tarzan issue. 37-Cyclone & Midge begin (1st app.) 55 110 165 352 601 850
38-(scarce) Classic giant gorilla vs. Owl-c 77 154 231 493 847 1200
39-Andy Panda begins (intro/1st app., 9/41) 68 136 204 435 743 1050
40-42: 42-Last Owl-c. 53 106 159 334 567 800
43-Terry & the Pirates-r 26 52 78 154 252 350
NOTE: *McWilliams art in most issues.*

CRACK COMICS (Crack Western No. 63 on)
Quality Comics Group: May, 1940 - No. 62, Sept, 1949
1-Origin & 1st app. The Black Condor by Lou Fine, Madame Fatal, Red Torpedo, Rock Bradden & The Space Legion; The Clock, Alias the Spider (by Gustavson), Wizard Wells, & Ned Brant begin; Powell-a; Note: Madame Fatal is a man dressed as a woman 465 930 1395 3395 5998 8600
2 219 438 657 1402 2401 3400
3 155 310 465 992 1696 2400
4 126 252 378 806 1378 1950
5-10: 5-Molly The Model begins. 10-Tor, the Magic Master begins 103 206 309 659 1130 1600
11-20: 13-1 pg. J. Cole-a. 15-1st app. Spitfire 87 174 261 553 952 1350
21-24: 23-Pen Miller begins; continued from National Comics #22. 24-Last Fine Black Condor 68 136 204 435 743 1050
25 54 108 162 343 574 825
26-Flag-c 68 136 204 435 743 1050
27-(1/43)-Intro & origin Captain Triumph by Alfred Andriola (Kerry Drake artist) & begin series 116 232 348 742 1271 1800
28-30 42 84 126 265 445 625
31-39: 31-Last Black Condor 24 48 72 142 234 325
40-46 17 34 51 100 158 215
47-57,59,60-Capt. Triumph by Crandall 18 36 54 107 169 230
58,61,62-Last Captain Triumph 15 30 45 85 130 175
NOTE: *Black Condor by* ***Fine****: No. 1, 2, 5, 6, 8, 10-24; by* ***Sultan****: No. 3, 7; by* ***Fugitani****: No. 9.* ***Cole*** *a-34.* ***Crandall*** *a-61(unsigned); c-48, 49, 51-61.* ***Guardineer*** *a-17.* ***Gustavson*** *a-1, 2, 4, 7, 13, 17, 23.* ***McWilliams*** *a-15-27. Black Condor c-2, 4, 6, 8, 10, 12, 14, 16, 18, 20-26. Capt. Triumph c-27-62. The Clock c-1, 3, 5, 7, 9, 11, 13, 15, 17, 19.*

CRACK COMICS (Next Issue Project)
Image Comics: No. 63, Oct, 2011 ($4.99, one-shot)
63-Mimics style & format of a 1949 issue; Weiss-c; s/a by various; Capt Triumph app. 5.00

CRACK COMICS
Quality Comics: May 1940
1-Ashcan comic, not distributed to newsstands, only for in-house use. Cover art is the same as published version of Crack Comics #1with exception of text panel on bottom left of cover. A CGC certified 4.0 copy sold for $1,495 in 2005.

CRACKED (Magazine) (Satire) (Also see The 3-D Zone #19)
Major Magazines(#1-212)/Globe Communications(#213-346/American Media #347 on):
Feb-Mar, 1958 - No. 365, Nov, 2004
1-One pg. Williamson-a; Everett-c; Gunsmoke-s 32 64 96 230 515 800
2-1st Shut-Ups & Bonus Cut-Outs; Superman parody-c by Severin (his 1st cover on the title) Frankenstein-s 15 30 45 103 227 350
3-5 11 22 33 76 163 250
6-10: 7-Reprints 1st 6 covers on-c. 8-Frankenstein-c. 10-Wolverton-a 9 18 27 61 123 185
11-12, 13(nn,3/60), 7 14 21 48 89 130
14-Kirby-a 8 16 24 54 102 150
15-17, 18(nn,2/61), 19,20 6 12 18 40 73 105
21-27(11/62), 27(No.28, 2/63; mis-#d), 29(5/63) 5 10 15 35 63 90
30-40(11/64): 37-Beatles and Superman cameos 4 8 12 27 44 60
41-45,47-56,59,60: 47,49,52-Munsters. 51-Beatles inside-c. 59-Laurel and Hardy photos 4 8 12 23 37 50
46,57,58: 46,58-Man From U.N.C.L.E. 46-Beatles. 57-Rolling Stones 4 8 12 25 40 55
61-80: 62-Beatles cameo. 69-Batman, Superman app. 70-(8/68) Elvis cameo. 71-Garrison's Gorillas; W.C. Fields photos 3 6 9 16 23 30
81-99: 99-Alfred E. Neuman on-c 3 6 9 14 20 25
100 3 6 9 17 26 35
101-119: 104-Godfather-c/s. 108-Archie Bunker-s. 112,119-Kung Fu (TV). 113-Tarzan-s. 115-MASH. 117-Cannon. 118-The Sting-c/s 2 4 6 10 14 18
120(12/74) Six Million Dollar Man-c/s; Ward-a 2 4 6 13 18 22
121,122,124-126,128-133,136-140: 121-American Graffiti. 122-Korak-c/s. 124,131-Godfather-c/s. 128-Capone-c. 129,131-Jaws. 132-Baretta-c/s. 133-Space 1999. 136-Laverne and Shirley/Fonz-c. 137-Travolta/Kotter-c/s. 138-Travolta/Laverne and Shirley/Fonz-c. 139-Barney Miller-c/s. 140-King Kong-c/s; Fonz-s 2 4 6 10 14 18
123-Planet of the Apes-c/s; Six Million Dollar Man 2 4 6 13 18 22
127,134,135: 127-Star Trek-c/s; Ward-a. 134-Fonz-c/s; Starsky and Hutch. 135-Bionic Woman-c/s; Ward-a 2 4 6 11 16 20
141,151-Charlie's Angels-c/s. 151-Frankenstein 2 4 6 11 16 20
142,143,150,152-155,157: 142-MASH-c/s. 143-Rocky-c/s; King Kong-s. 150-(5/78) Close Encounters-c/s. 152-Close Enc./Star Wars-c/s. 153-Close Enc./Fonz-c/s. 154-Jaws II-c/s; Star Wars-s. 155-Star Wars/Fonz-c 2 4 6 9 13 16
144,149,156,158-160: 144-Fonz/Happy Days-c. 149-Star Wars/Six Mil.$ Man-c/s. 156-Grease/Travolta-c. 158-Mork & Mindy. 159-Battlestar Galactica-c/s; MASH-s. 160-Superman-c/s 2 4 6 11 16 20
145,147-Both have insert postcards: 145-Fonz/Rocky/L&S-c/s. 147-Star Wars-s; Farrah photo page (missing postcards-1/2 price) 3 6 9 14 20 26
146,148: 46-Star Wars-c/s with stickers insert (missing stickers-1/2 price). 148-Star Wars-c/s with inside-c color poster 3 6 9 16 23 30
161,170-Ward-a: 161-Mork & Mindy-c/s. 170-Dukes of Hazzard-c/s 2 4 6 8 11 14
162,165-168,171,172,175-178,180-Ward-a: 162-Sherlock Holmes-s. 165-Dracula-c/s. 167-Mork-c/s. 168,175-MASH-c/s. 168-Mork-s. 172-Dukes of Hazzard/CHiPs-c/s. 176-Barney Miller-c/s 2 4 6 8 10 12

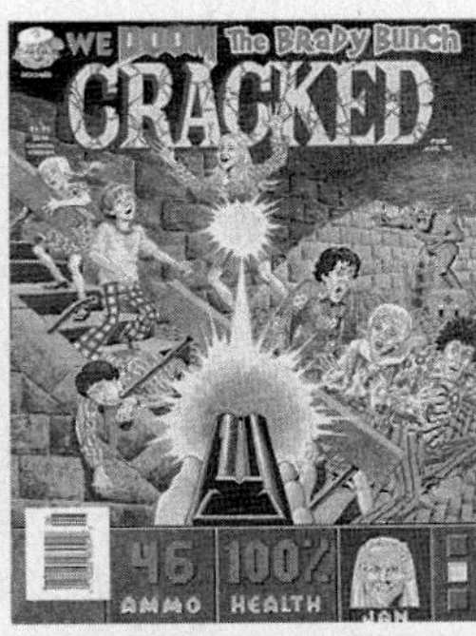

Cracked #300 © Globe CC

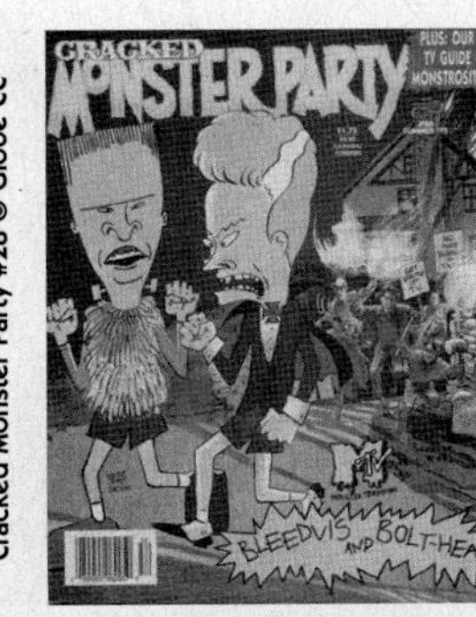

Cracked Monster Party #28 © Globe CC

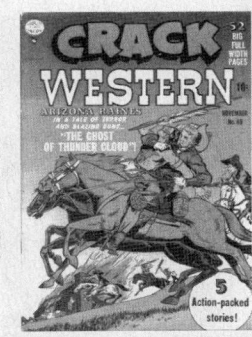

Crack Western #69 © QUA

	GD 2.0	VG 4.0	FN 6.0	VF 8.0	VF/NM 9.0	NM- 9.2
163,179:163-Postcard insert; Mork & Mindy-c/s. 179-Insult cards insert; Popeye, Dukes of Hazzard-c/s	3	6	9	14	19	24
164,169,173,174: 164-Alien movie-c/s; Mork & Mindy-s. 169-Star Trek. 173,174-Star Wars-Empire Strikes Back. 173-SW poster	2	4	6	9	13	16
181,182,185-191,193,194,196-198-most Ward-a: 182-MASH-c/s. 185-Dukes of Hazzard-c/s; Jefferson-s. 187-Love Boat. 188-Fall Guy-s. 189-Fonz/Happy Days-c. 190,194-MASH-c/s. 191-Magnum P.I./Rocky-c; Magnum-s. 193-Knight Rider-s. 196-Dukes of Hazzard/Knight Rider-c/s. 198-Jaws III-c/s; Fall Guy-s	1	2	3	5	7	9
183,184,192,195,199,200-Ward-a in all: 183-Superman-c/s. 184-Star Trek-c/s. 192-E.T.-c/s; Rocky-s. 195-E.T.-c/s. 199-Jabba-c; Star Wars-s. 200-(12/83)	1	3	4	6	8	10
201,203,210-A-Team-c/s						6.00
202,204-206,211-224,226,227,230-233: 202-Knight Rider-s. 204-Magnum P.I.; A-Team-s. 206-Michael Jackson/Mr. T-c/s. 212-Prince-s; Cosby-s. 213-Monsters issue-c/s. 215-Hulk Hogan/Mr. T-c/s. 216-Miami Vice-s; James Bond-s. 217-Rambo-s; Cosby-s; A-Team-s. 218-Rocky-c/s. 219-Arnold/Commando-c/s; Rocky-s; Godzilla. 220-Rocky-c/s. 221-Stephen King app. 223-Miami Vice-s. 224-Cosby-s. 226-29th Anniv.; Tarzan-s; Aliens-s; Family Ties-s. 227-Cosby, Family Ties, Miami Vice-s. 230-Monkees-c/s; Elvis on-c; 232-Alf, Cheers, StarTrek-s. 233-Superman/James Bond-c/s; Robocop, Predator-s						5.00
207-209,225,234: 207-Michael Jackson-c/s. 208-Indiana Jones-c/s. 209-MichaelJackson/ Gremlins-c/s; Star Trek III-s. 225-Schwarzenegger/Stallone/G.I. Joe-c/s. 234-Don Martin-a begins; Batman/Robocop/Clint Eastwood-c/s						6.00
228,229: 228-Star Trek-c/s; Alf, Pee Wee Herman-s. 229-Monsters issue-c/s; centerfold with many superheroes						6.00
235,239,243,249: 235-1st Martin-c; Star Trek:TNG-s; Alf-s. 239-Beetlejuice-c/s; Mike Tyson-s. 243-X-Men and other heroes app. 249-Batman/Indiana Jones/Ghostbusters-c/s						6.00
236,244,245,248: 236-Madonna/Stallone-c/s; Twilight Zone-s. 244-Elvis-c/s; Martin-c. 245-Roger Rabbit-c/s. 248-Batman issue						6.00
237,238,240-242,246,247,250: 237-Robocop-s. 238-Rambo-c/s; Star Trek-s. 242-Dirty Harry-s, Ward-a. 246-Alf-s; Star Trek-s., Ward-a. 247-Star Trek-s. 250-Batman/Ghostbusters-s						4.00
251-253,255,256,259,261-265,275-278,281,284,286-297,299: 252-Star Trek-s. 253-Back to the Future-c/s. 255-TMNT-c/s. 256-TMNT-c/s; Batman, Bart Simpson on-c. 259-Die Hard II, Robocop-s. 261-TMNT, Twin Peaks-s. 262-Rocky-c/s; Rocky Horror-s. 265-TMNT-s. 276-Aliens III, Batman-s. 277-Clinton-c. 284-Bart Simpson-c; 90210-s. 297-Van Damme-s/photo-c. 299-Dumb & Dumber-c/s						4.00
254,257,266,267,272,280,282,285,298,300: 254-Back to the Future, Punisher-s; Wolverton-a, Batman-s, Ward-a. 257-Batman, Simpsons-s; Spider-Man and other heroes app. 266-Terminator-c/s. 267-Toons-c/s. 272-Star Trek VI-s. 280-Swimsuit issue. 282-Cheers-c/s. 285-Jurassic Park-c/s. 298-Swimsuit issue; Martin-c. 300-(8/95) Brady Bunch-c/s						5.00
258,260,274,279,283: 258-Simpsons-c/s; Back to the Future-s. 260-Spider-Man-c/s; Simpsons-s. 274-Batman-c/s. 279-Madonna-c/s. 283-Jurassic Park-c/s; Wolverine app. inside back-c						5.00
301-305,307-365: 365-Freas-c						3.00
306-Toy Story-c/s						4.00
Biggest... (Winter, 1977)	2	4	6	13	18	22
Biggest, Greatest... nn('65)	4	8	12	28	47	65
Biggest, Greatest... 2('66/67) - #5('69/70)	3	6	9	19	30	40
Biggest, Greatest... 6('70) - #12(Wint. '77)	3	6	9	14	19	24
Biggest, Greatest...13(Fall '78) - #21(Fall/Wint. '86)	2	4	6	8	11	14
...Blockbuster 1(Sum '87), 2('88), 3(Sum. '89)	1	3	4	6	8	10
...Blockbuster 4 - 6(Sum. '92)						6.00
...Collectors' Edition 4 ('73; formerly ...Special)	2	4	6	13	18	22
5-9,10(10/75)	2	4	6	11	16	20
11-19,20(11/17)	2	4	6	8	11	14
21,22,23(5/78): 23-Ward-a	2	4	6	8	11	14
(#24-62,64 not numbered)						
1978 (nn; July, Sept, Nov, Dec) (#24-27)	2	4	6	8	11	14
1979 (nn; May, July, Sept, Nov, Dec) (#28-33)	2	4	6	8	11	14
1980 (nn; Feb, May, July, Sept, Nov, Dec) (#34-39)	1	3	4	6	8	10
1981 (nn; Feb, May, July, Sept, Nov, Dec) (#40-45)	1	3	4	6	8	10
1982 (nn; Feb, May, July, Sept, Nov, Dec) (#46-51)	1	3	4	6	8	10
1983 (nn; Feb, May, Sept, Nov, Dec) (#52-56)	1	3	4	6	8	10
1984 (nn; Feb, May, July, Nov) (#57-60)	1	2	3	4	5	7
1985 (nn; Feb) (#61)	1	2	3	4	5	7
62(9/85), nn(#63,11/85), 64(12/85), 65-69, 70(4/87)	1	2	3	4	5	7
71,72,73(100 pgs., 1/88), 74-79, 80(9/89)						5.00
81-96, 97(two diff. issues), 98-115: 83-Elvis, Batman parodies						5.00
116('98)-Last issue?						6.00
...Digest 1(Fall, '86, 148 pgs.), 2(1/87)	1	2	3	6	8	10
...Digest 3-5	1	2	3	4	5	7
...Party Pack 1,2('88) - 4('90)						4.00
...Shut-Ups 1(2/72)	3	6	9	17	26	35
...Shut-Ups 2('72) becomes Cracked Spec. #3	3	6	9	14	19	24
...Special 3('73; formerly Cracked Shut-Ups; ...Collectors' Edition#4 on)	2	4	6	13	18	22
... Summer Special 1(Sum. '91), 2(Sum. '92)-Don Martin-a						4.00
... Summer Special 3(Sum. '93) - 8(Sum. '98)						3.00
... Super (Vol. 2, formerly Super Cracked) 5(Wint. '91/92) - 14(Wint.'97/98)						3.00
Extra Special... 1(Spr. '76)	2	4	6	11	16	20
Extra Special... 2(Spr./Sum. '77)	2	4	6	10	14	18
Extra Special... 3(Wint. '79) - 9(Wint. '86)	1	2	3	4	5	7
Giant... nn('65)	5	10	15	33	57	80
Giant... 2('66) - 5('69)	3	6	9	21	33	45
Giant...6('70) - 12('76)	3	6	9	16	24	32
Giant...nn(9/77, #13), nn(1/78, #14), nn(3/78, #15), nn(5/78, #16), nn(7/78, #17), nn(11/78, #18), nn(3/79, #19), nn(7/79, #20), nn(10/79, #21), nn(12/79, #22), nn(3/80, #23), nn(7/80, #24)	2	4	6	11	16	20
Giant...nn(10/80, #25), nn(12/80, #26), nn(3/81, #27), nn(7/81, #28), nn(10/81, #29), nn(12/81, #30), nn(7/82, #31), nn(10/82, #32), nn(12/82, #33), nn(7/83, #34),	2	4	6	8	11	14
Giant...nn(10/83, #35), nn(12/83, #36), nn(3/84, #37), nn(7/84, #38), nn(10/84, #39), nn(3/85, #40), nn(7/85, #41), nn(10/85, #42)	1	2	3	5	7	9
Giant...43(3/86) - 46(1/87), 47(Wint. '88), 48(Wint. '89)	1	2	3	4	5	7
King Sized... 1('67)	4	8	12	25	40	55
King Sized... 2('68) - 5('71)	3	6	9	17	26	35
King Sized... 6('72) - 11('77)	3	6	9	14	20	26
King Sized... 12(Fall '78) - 17(Sum. '83)	2	4	6	8	11	14
King Sized... 18-20 (Sum/'86) (#21,22 exist?)	1	3	4	6	8	10
Spaced Out... 1-4 ('93 - '94)						5.00
Super... 1('68)	4	8	12	25	40	55
Super... 2('69) - 6('73)	3	6	9	19	30	40
Super... 7('74), 8(Spr. '75) - 10(Spr. '77)	3	6	9	15	22	28
Super... 11(Sum. '78) - 16(Fall '81)	2	4	6	11	16	20
Super... 17(Spr. '82) - 22(Fall '83)	2	4	6	8	11	14
Super... 23(Sum. '84, mis-numbered as #24)	2	4	6	8	11	14
Super... 24(Fall '84, correctly numbered)	2	4	6	8	11	14
Super... 25(Wint. '85) - 32(Fall '86)	2	4	6	8	10	12
Super... (Vol. 2) 1('87, 100 pgs.)-Severin & Elder-a	1	3	4	6	8	10
Super... (Vol. 2) 2(Sum. '88), 3(Wint. '89), 4(exist?)(Becomes Cracked Super)						6.00

NOTE: ***Burgos*** *a-1-10.* ***Colan*** *a-257.* ***Davis*** *a-5, 11-17, 24, 40, 80; c-12-14, 16.* ***Elder*** *a-5, 6, 10-13; c-10.* ***Everett*** *a-1-10, 23-25, 61; c-1.* ***Heath*** *a-1-3, 6, 13, 14, 17, 110; c-6.* ***Jaffee*** *a-5, 6.* ***Don Martin*** *c-235, 244, 247, 259, 261, 264.* ***Morrow*** *a-8-10.* ***Reinman*** *a-1-4.* ***Severin*** *c/a-in most all issues.* ***Shores*** *a-3-7.* ***Torres*** *a-7-10.* ***Ward*** *a-22-24, 27, 35, 40, 120-193, 195, 197-205, 242, 244, 246, 247, 250, 252-257.* ***Williamson*** *a-1 (1 pg.).* ***Wolverton*** *a-10 (2 pgs.), Giant nn('65).* ***Wood*** *a-27, 35, 40. Alfred E. Neuman c-177, 200, 202. Batman c-234, 248, 249, 256, 274. Captain America c-256. Christmas c-234, 243. Spider-Man c-260. Star Trek c-127, 169, 207, 228. Star Wars c-145, 146, 148, 149, 152, 155, 173, 174, 199. Superman c-183, 233. #144, 146 have free full-color pre-glued stickers. #145, 147, 155, 163 have free full-color postcards. #123, 137, 154, 157 have free iron-ons.*

CRACKED MONSTER PARTY
Globe Communications: July, 1988 - No. 27, Wint. 1999/2000

	GD 2.0	VG 4.0	FN 6.0	VF 8.0	VF/NM 9.0	NM- 9.2
1	2	4	6	10	14	18
2-10	2	4	6	8	10	12
11-26	1	2	3	4	5	7
27-Interview with a Vampire-c/s	2	4	6	8	10	12

CRACKED'S FOR MONSTERS ONLY
Major Magazines: Sept, 1969 - No. 9, Sept, 1969; June, 1972

	GD 2.0	VG 4.0	FN 6.0	VF 8.0	VF/NM 9.0	NM- 9.2
1	4	8	12	28	47	65
2-9, nn(6/72)	3	6	9	19	30	40

CRACK WESTERN (Formerly Crack Comics; Jonesy No. 85 on)
Quality Comics Group: No. 63, Nov, 1949 - No. 84, May, 1953 (36 pgs., 63-68,74-on)

	GD 2.0	VG 4.0	FN 6.0	VF 8.0	VF/NM 9.0	NM- 9.2
63(#1)-Ward-c; Two-Gun Lil (origin & 1st app.)(ends #84), Arizona Ames, his horse Thunder (with sidekick Spurs & his horse Calico), Frontier Marshal (ends #70), & Dead Canyon Days (ends #69) begin; Crandall-a	18	36	54	107	169	230
64,65: 64-Ward-c. Crandall-a in both.	15	30	45	83	124	165
66,68-Photo-c. 66-Arizona Ames becomes A. Raines (ends #84)	13	26	39	72	101	130
67-Randolph Scott photo-c; Crandall-a	14	28	42	80	115	150
69(52pgs.)-Crandall-a	13	26	39	72	101	130
70(52pgs.)-The Whip (origin & 1st app.) & his horse Diablo begin (ends #84); Crandall-a	13	26	39	72	101	130
71(52pgs.)-Frontier Marshal becomes Bob Allen F. Marshal (ends #84); Crandall-c/a	14	28	42	80	115	150
72(52pgs.)-Tim Holt photo-c	12	24	36	67	94	120
73(52pgs.)-Photo-c	10	20	30	58	79	100
74-76,78,79,81,83-Crandall-c. 83-Crandall-a(p)	11	22	33	62	86	110
77,80,82	8	16	24	44	57	70
84-Crandall-c/a	12	24	36	67	94	120

NOTE: ***Crandall*** *c-71p, 74-81, 83p(w/****Cuidera****-i).*

CRASH COMICS (Cat-Man Comics No. 6 on)

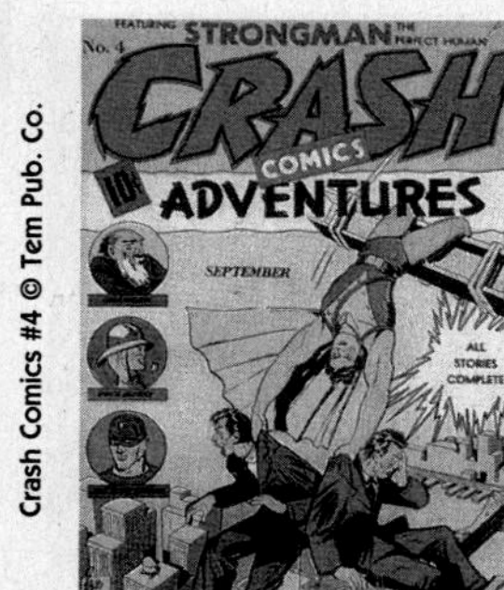

Crash Comics #4 © Tem Pub. Co.

Crazy #54 © MAR

Crazyman #2 © Continuity

	GD 2.0	VG 4.0	FN 6.0	VF 8.0	VF/NM 9.0	NM- 9.2

Tem Publishing Co.: May, 1940 - No. 5, Nov, 1940

	GD	VG	FN	VF	VF/NM	NM-
1-The Blue Streak, Strongman (origin), The Perfect Human, Shangra begin (1st app. of each); Kirby-a	354	708	1062	2478	4339	6200
2-Simon & Kirby-a	194	388	582	1242	2121	3000
3-Simon & Kirby-a	174	348	522	1114	1907	2700
4-Origin & 1st app. The Cat-Man; S&K-a	432	864	1296	3154	5577	8000
5-1st Cat-Man-c & 2nd app.; Simon & Kirby-a	245	490	735	1568	2684	3800

NOTE: *Solar Legion by* ***Kirby*** *No. 1-5 (5 pgs. each). Strongman c-1-4. Catman c-5.*

CRASH DIVE (See Cinema Comics Herald)

CRASH METRO AND THE STAR SQUAD
Oni Press: May, 1999 ($2.95, B&W, one-shot)

1-Allred-s/Ontiveros-a 3.00

CRASH RYAN (Also see Dark Horse Presents #44)
Marvel Comics (Epic): Oct, 1984 - No. 4, Jan, 1985 (Baxter paper, lim. series)

1-4 3.00

CRAZY (Also see This Magazine is Crazy)
Atlas Comics (CSI): Dec, 1953 - No. 7, July, 1954

	GD	VG	FN	VF	VF/NM	NM-
1-Everett-c/a	43	86	129	271	461	650
2	28	56	84	165	270	375
3-7: 4-I Love Lucy satire. 5-Satire on censorship	24	48	72	142	234	325

NOTE: ***Ayers*** *a-5.* ***Berg*** *a-1, 2.* ***Burgos*** *c-5, 6.* ***Drucker*** *a-6.* ***Everett*** *a-1-4.* ***Al Hartley*** *a-4.* ***Heath*** *a-3, 7; c-7.* ***Maneely*** *a-1-7, c-3, 4.* ***Post*** *a-3-6. Funny monster c-1-4.*

CRAZY (Satire)
Marvel Comics Group: Feb, 1973 - No. 3, June, 1973

	GD	VG	FN	VF	VF/NM	NM-
1-Not Brand Echh-r; Beatles cameo (r)	3	6	9	16	23	30
2,3-Not Brand Echh-r; Kirby-a	2	4	6	10	16	20

CRAZY MAGAZINE (Satire)
Oct, 1973 - No. 94, Apr, 1983 (40-90¢, B&W magazine)
Marvel Comics: (#1, 44 pgs; #2-90, reg. issues, 52 pgs; #92-95, 68 pgs)'

	GD	VG	FN	VF	VF/NM	NM-
1-Wolverton(1 pg.), Bode-a; 3 pg. photo story of Neal Adams & Dick Giordano; Harlan Ellison story; TV Kung Fu sty.	4	8	12	28	47	65
2-"Live & Let Die" c/s; 8pgs; Adams/Buscema-a; McCloud w5 pgs. Adams-a; Kurtzman's "Hey Look" 2 pg.-r	3	6	9	19	30	40
3-5: 3-"High Plains Drifter" w/Clint Eastwood c/s; Waltons app; Drucker, Reese-a. 4-Shaft-c/s; Ploog-a; Nixon 3 pg. app; Freas-a. 5-Michael Crichton's "Westworld" c/s; Nixon app.	3	6	9	16	24	32
6,7,18: 6-Exorcist c/s; Nixon app. 7-TV's Kung Fu c/s; Nixon app.; Ploog & Freas-a. 18-Six Million Dollar Man/Bionic Woman c/s; Welcome Back Kotter story	3	6	9	15	22	28
8-10: 8-Serpico c/s; Casper parody; TV's Police Story. 9-Joker cameo; Chinatown story; Eisner s/a begins; Has 1st 8 covers on-c. 10-Playboy Bunny-c; M. Severin-a; Lee Marrs-a begins; "Deathwish" story	3	6	9	14	20	26
11-17,19: 11-Towering Inferno. 12-Rhoda. 13-"Tommy" the Who Rock Opera. 14-Mandingo. 15-Jaws story. 16-Santa/Xmas-c; "Good Times" TV story; Jaws. 17-Bicentennial issue; Baretta; Woody Allen. 19-King Kong c/s; Reagan, J. Carter, Howard the Duck cameos, "Laverne & Shirley"	2	4	6	11	16	20
20,24,27: 20-Bicentennial-c; Space 1999 sty; Superheroes song sheet, 4pgs. 24-Charlie's Angels. 27-Charlie's Angels/Travolta/Fonz-c; Bionic Woman sty	3	6	9	14	19	24
21-23,25,26,28-30: 21-Starsky & Hutch. 22-Mount Rushmore/J. Carter-c; TV's Barney Miller; Superheroes spoof. 23-Santa/Xmas-c; "Happy Days" sty; "Omen" sty. 25-J. Carter-c/s; Grandenetti-a begins; TV's Alice; Logan's Run. 26-TV Stars-c; Mary Hartman, King Kong. 28-Donny & Marie Osmond-c/s; Marathon Man. 29-Travolta/Kotter-c; "One Day at a Time", Gong Show. 30-1977, 84 pgs. w/bonus; Jaws, Baretta, King Kong, Happy Days	2	4	6	9	12	15
31,33-35,38,40: 31-"Rocky"-c/s; TV game shows. 33-Peter Benchley's "Deep". 34-J. Carter-c; TV's "Fish". 35-Xmas-c with Fonz/Six Million Dollar Man/Wonder Woman/Darth Vader/ Travolta, TV's "Mash" & "Family Matters". 38-Close Encounters of the Third Kind-c/s. 40-"Three's Company-c/s	1	3	4	6	8	11
32-Star Wars/Darth Vader-c/s; "Black Sunday"	3	6	9	14	19	24
36,42,47,49: 36-Farrah Fawcett/Six Million Dollar Man-c; TV's Nancy Drew & Hardy Boys; 1st app. Howard The Duck in Crazy, 2 pgs. 42-84 pgs. w/bonus; TV Hulk/Spider-Man-c; Mash, Gong Show, One Day at a Time, Disco, Alice. 47-Battlestar Galactica xmas-c; movie "Foul Play". 49-1979, 84 pgs. w/bonus; Mork & Mindy-c; Jaws, Saturday Night Fever, Three's Company	2	4	6	9	12	15
37-1978, 84 pgs. w/bonus. Darth Vader-c; Barney Miller, Laverne & Shirley, Good Times, Rocky, Donny & Marie Osmond, Bionic Woman	2	4	6	13	18	22
39,44: 39-Saturday Night Fever-c/s. 44-"Grease"-c w/Travolta/O. Newton-John	2	4	6	11	16	20
41-Kiss-c & 1pg. photos; Disaster movies, TV's "Family", Annie Hall	4	8	12	27	44	60
43,45,46,48,51: 43-Jaws-c; Saturday Night Fever. 43-E.C. swipe from Mad #131. 45-Travolta/O. Newton-John/J. Carter-c; Eight is Enough. 46-TV Hulk-c/s; Punk Rock. 48-"Wiz"-c, Battlestar Galactica-s. 51-Grease/Mork & Mindy/D&M Osmond-c, Mork & Mindy-sty. "Boys from Brazil"	1	3	4	6	8	11
50,58: 50-Superman movie-c/sty, Playboy Mag., TV Hulk, Fonz; Howard the Duck, 1 pg. 58-1980, 84 pgs. w/32 pg. color comic bonus insert-Full reprint of Crazy Comic #1, Battlestar Galactica, Charlie's Angels, Starsky & Hutch	2	4	6	11	16	20
52,59,60,64: 52-1979, 84 pgs. w/bonus. Marlon Brando-c; TV Hulk, Grease. Kiss, 1 pg. photos. 59-Santa Ptd-c by Larkin; "Alien", "Moonraker", Rocky-2, Howard the Duck, 1 pg. 60-Star Trek w/Muppets-c; Star Trek sty; 1st app/origin Teen Hulk; Severin-a. 64-84 pgs. w/bonus Monopoly game satire. "Empire Strikes Back", 8 pgs., One Day at a Time	2	4	6	11	16	20
53,54,65,67-70: 53-"Animal House"-c/sty; TV's "Vegas", Howard the Duck, 1 pg. 54-Love at First Bite-c/sty, Fantasy Island sty, Howard the Duck 1 pg. 65-(Has #66 on-c, Aug/'80). "Black Hole" w/Janson-a; Kirby,Wood/Severin-a(r), 5 pgs. Howard the Duck, 3 pgs.; Broderick-a; Buck Rogers, Mr. Rogers. 67-84 pgs. w/bonus; TV's Kung Fu, Exorcist; Ploog-a(r). 68-American Gigolo, Dukes of Hazzard, Teen Hulk; Howard the Duck, 3 pgs. Broderick-a; Monster sty/5 pg. Ditko-a(r). 69-Obnoxio the Clown-c/sty; Stephen King's "Shining", Teen Hulk, Richie Rich, Howard the Duck, 3pgs; Broderick-a. 70-84 pgs. Towering Inferno, Daytime TV; Trina Robbins-a	1	3	4	6	8	10
55-57,61,63: 55-84 pgs. w/bonus; Love Boat, Mork & Mindy, Fonz, TV Hulk. 56-Mork/Rocky/ J. Carter-c; China Syndrome. 57-TV Hulk with Miss Piggy-c, Dracula, Taxi, Muppets. 61-1980, 84 pgs. Adams-a(r), McCloud, Pro wrestling, Casper, TV's Police Story. 63-Apocalypse Now-Coppola's cult movie; 3rd app. Teen Hulk, Howard the Duck, 3 pgs.	2	4	6	8	11	14
62-Kiss-c & 2 pg. app; Quincy, 2nd app. Teen Hulk	4	8	12	23	37	50
66-Sept/'80, Empire Strikes Back-c/sty; Teen Hulk by Severin, Howard the Duck, 3pgs. by Broderick	2	4	6	10	14	18
71,72,75-77,79: 71-Blues Brothers parody, Teen Hulk, Superheroes parody, WKRP in Cincinnati, Howard the Duck, 3pgs. by Broderick. 72-Jackie Gleason/Smokey & the Bandit II-c/sty, Shogun, Teen Hulk. Howard the Duck, 3pgs. by Broderick. 75-Flash Gordon movie c/sty; Teen Hulk, Cat in the Hat, Howard the Duck 3pgs. by Broderick. 76-84 pgs. w/bonus; Monster-sty w/ Crandall-a(r), Monster-stys(2) w/Kirby-a(r), 5pgs. ea; Mash, TV Hulk, Chinatown. 77-Popeye movie/R. Williams-c/sty; Teen Hulk, Love Boat, Howard the Duck 3 pgs. 79-84 pgs. w/bonus color stickers; has new material; "9 to 5" w/Dolly Parton, Teen Hulk, Magnum P.I., Monster-sty w/5pgs, Ditko-a(r), "Rat" w/Sutton-a(r), Everett-a, 4 pgs.(r)	1	3	4	6	8	10
73,74,78,80: 73-84 pgs. w/bonus Hulk/Spiderman Finger Puppets-c & bonus; "Live & Let Die, Jaws, Fantasy Island. 74-Dallas/"Who Shot J.R."-c/sty; Elephant Man, Howard the Duck 3pgs. by Broderick. 78-Clint Eastwood-c/sty; Teen Hulk, Superheroes parody, Lou Grant. 80-Star Wars, 2 pg. app; "Howling", TV's "Greatest American Hero"	2	4	6	8	11	14
81,84,86,87,89: 81-.Superman Movie II-c/sty; Wolverine cameo, Mash, Teen Hulk. 84-American Werewolf in London, Johnny Carson app; Teen Hulk. 86-Time Bandits-c/sty; Private Benjamin. 87-Rubix Cube-c; Hill Street Blues, "Ragtime", Origin Obnoxio the Clown; Teen Hulk. 89-Burt Reynolds "Sharkey's Machine", Teen Hulk	1	3	4	6	8	10
82-X-Men-c w/new Byrne-a, 84 pgs. w/new material; Fantasy Island, Teen Hulk, "For Your Eyes Only", Spiderman/Human Torch-r by Kirby/Ditko; Sutton-a(r); Rogers-a; Hunchback of Notre Dame, 5 pgs.	2	4	6	11	16	20
83-Raiders of the Lost Ark-c/sty; Hart to Hart; Reese-a; Teen Hulk	2	4	6	9	13	20
85,88: 85-84 pgs; Escape from New York, Teen Hulk; Kirby-a(r), 5 pgs, Poseidon Adventure, Flintstones, Sesame Street. 88-84 pgs. w/bonus Dr. Strange Game; some new material; Jeffersons, X-Men/Wolverine, 10 pgs.; Byrne-a; Apocalypse Now, Teen Hulk	1	3	4	6	8	11
90-94: 90-Conan-c/sty; M. Severin-a; Teen Hulk. 91-84 pgs, some new material; Bladerunner-c/sty, "Deathwish-II, Teen Hulk, Black Knight, 10 pgs.-'50s-r w/Maneely-a. 92-Wrath of Khan Star Trek-c/sty; Joanie & Chachi, Teen Hulk. 93-"E.T."-c/sty, Teen Hulk, Archie Bunkers Place, Dr. Doom Game. 94-Poltergeist, Smurfs, Teen Hulk, Casper, Avengers parody-8pgs. Adams-a	2	4	6	10	14	18
Crazy Summer Special #1 (Sum, '75, 100 pgs.)-Nixon, TV Kung Fu, Babe Ruth, Joe Namath, Waltons, McCloud, Chariots of the Gods	3	6	9	14	19	24

NOTE: ***N. Adams*** *a-2, 61r, 94p.* ***Austin*** *a-82i.* ***Buscema*** *a-2, 82.* ***Byrne*** *c-82p.* ***Nick Cardy*** *c-7, 8, 10, 12-16, Super Special 1.* ***Crandall*** *a-76r.* ***Ditko*** *a-68r, 79r, 82r.* ***Drucker*** *a-3.* ***Eisner*** *a-9-16.* ***Kelly Freas*** *c-1-6, 9, 11; a-7.* ***Kirby/Wood*** *a-65r.* ***Ploog*** *a-1, 4, 7, 67r, 73r.* ***Rogers*** *a-82.* ***Sparling*** *a-92.* ***Wood*** *a-65r. Howard the Duck in 36, 50, 51, 53, 54, 59, 63, 65, 66, 68, 69, 71, 72, 74, 75, 77. Hulk in 46, c-42, 46, 57, 73. Star Wars in 32, 66; c-37.*

CRAZYMAN
Continuity Comics: Apr, 1992 - No. 3, 1992 ($2.50, high quality paper)

1-($3.95, 52 pgs.)-Embossed-c; N. Adams part-i 4.00
2,3 ($2.50): 2-N. Adams/Bolland-c 3.00

CRAZYMAN
Continuity Comics: V2#1, 5/93 - No. 4, 1/94 ($2.50, high quality paper)

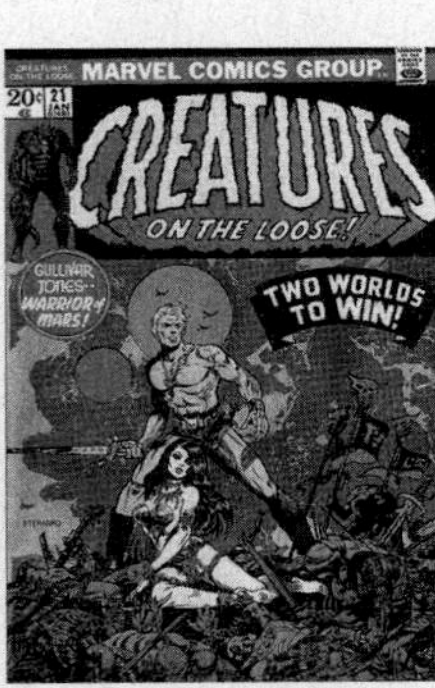

Creatures on the Loose #21 © MAR

Creeps #3 © Mishkin & Mandrake

Creepy #73 © WP

V2#1-4: 1-Entire book is die-cut. 2-(12/93)-Adams-c(p) & part scripts. 3-(12/93). 4-Indicia says #3, Jan. 1993 — 3.00

CRAZY, MAN, CRAZY (Magazine) (Becomes This Magazine is...?) (Formerly From Here to Insanity)
Humor Magazines (Charlton): V2#1, Dec, 1955 - V2#2, June, 1956
V2#1,V2#2-Satire; Wolverton-a, 3 pgs. — 19 38 57 109 172 235

CREATOR-OWNED HEROES
Image Comics: Jun, 2012 - No. 8, Jan, 2013 ($3.99)
1-8-Anthology of short stories by various and creator interviews — 4.00

CREATURE, THE (See Movie Classics)

CREATURE COMMANDOS (See Weird War Tales #93 for 1st app.)
DC Comics: May, 2000 - No. 8, Dec, 2000 ($2.50, limited series)
1-8: Truman-s/Eaton-a — 3.00

CREATURES OF THE ID
Caliber Press: 1990 ($2.95, B&W)
1-Frank Einstein (Madman) app.; Allred-a — 4 8 12 27 44 60

CREATURES OF THE NIGHT
Dark Horse Books: Nov, 2004 ($12.95, hardcover graphic novel)
HC-Neil Gaiman-s/Michael Zulli-a/c — 13.00

CREATURES ON THE LOOSE (Formerly Tower of Shadows No. 1-9)(See Kull)
Marvel Comics: No. 10, March, 1971 - No. 37, Sept, 1975 (New-a & reprints)
10-(15¢)-1st full app. King Kull; see Kull the Conqueror; Wrightson-a — 8 16 24 51 96 140
11-Classic story about an underground comic artist going to Hell — 4 8 12 27 44 60
12-15: 13-Last 15¢ issue — 4 8 12 23 37 50
16-Origin Warrior of Mars (begins, ends #21) — 3 6 9 15 22 28
17-20 — 2 4 6 9 13 16
21-Steranko-c — 3 6 9 16 24 32
22-Steranko-c; Thongor stories begin — 3 6 9 17 26 35
23-29-Thongor-c/stories — 1 3 4 6 8 10
30-Manwolf begins — 3 6 9 19 30 40
31-33 — 2 4 6 9 13 16
34-37 — 2 4 6 8 10 12

NOTE: *Crandall a-13.* ***Ditko*** *r-15, 17, 18, 20, 22, 24, 27, 28.* ***Everett*** *a-16i(new).* ***Matt Fox*** *r-21i.* ***Howard*** *a-26i.* ***Gil Kane*** *a-16p, 17p, 19i; c-16, 17, 19, 20, 25, 29, 33p, 35p, 36p.* ***Kirby*** *a-10-15r, 16(2)r, 17r, 19r.* ***Morrow*** *a-20, 21.* ***Perez*** *a-33-37; c-34p.* ***Shores*** *a-11.* ***Innott*** *r-21.* ***Sutton*** *c-10.* ***Tuska*** *a-30-32p.*

CREECH, THE
Image Comics: Oct, 1997 - No. 3, Dec, 1997 ($1.95/$2.50, limited series)
1-3: 1-Capullo-s/c/a(p) — 3.00
TPB (1999, $9.95) r/#1-3, McFarlane intro. — 10.00
Out for Blood 1-3 (7/01 - No. 3, 11/01; $4.95) Capullo-s/c/a — 5.00

CREED
Hall of Heroes Comics: Dec, 1994 - No. 2, Jan, 1995 ($2.50, B&W)
1 — 2 4 6 10 14 18
2 — 2 4 6 8 10 12

CREED
Lightning Comics: June, 1995 - No. 3 ($2.75/$3.00, B&W/color)
1-($2.75) — 4.00
1-($3.00, color) — 5.00
1-($9.95)-Commemorative Edition — 10.00
1-TwinVariant Edition (1250? print run) — 10.00
1-Special Edition; polybagged w/certificate — 4.00
1 Gold Collectors Edition; polybagged w/certificate — 3.00
2,3-($3.00, color)-Butt Naked Edition & regular-c — 3.00
3-($9.95)-Commemorative Edition; polybagged w/certificate & card — 10.00

CREED: CRANIAL DISORDER
Lightning Comics: Oct, 1996 ($3.00, limited series)
1-3-Two covers — 3.00
1-($5.95)-Platinum Edition — 6.00
2,3-($9.95)Ltd. Edition — 10.00

CREED/TEENAGE MUTANT NINJA TURTLES
Lightning Comics: May, 1996 ($3.00, one-shot)
1-Kaniuga-a(p)/scripts; Laird-c; variant-c exists — 3.00
1-($9.95)-Platinum Edition — 10.00
1-Special Edition; polybagged w/certificate — 5.00

CREEP, THE
Dark Horse Books: No. 0, Aug, 2012 - No. 4, Dec, 2012 ($2.99/$3.50)
0-Frank Miller-c; Arcudi-s/Case-a — 3.50
1-4-($3.50): 1-Mignola-c. 2-Sook-c — 3.50

CREEPER BY STEVE DITKO, THE
DC Comics: 2010 ($39.99, hardcover with dustjacket)
HC-Reprints Showcase #73, Beware the Creeper #1-6, First Issue Special #7 and apps. in World's Finest #249-255 and Cancelled Comic Cavalcade #2; intro. by Steve Niles — 40.00

CREEPER, THE (See Beware... , Showcase #73 & 1st Issue Special #7)
DC Comics: Dec, 1997 - No. 11; #1,000,000 Nov, 1998 ($2.50)
1-11-Kaminski-s/Martinbrough-a(p). 7,8-Joker-c/app. — 3.00
#1,000,000 (11/98) 853rd Century x-over — 3.00

CREEPER, THE (See DCU Brave New World)
DC Comics: Oct, 2006 - No. 6, Mar, 2007 ($2.99, limited series)
1-6-Niles-s/Justiniano-a/c; Jack Ryder becomes the Creeper. 2-6-Batman app. — 3.00
... - Welcome to Creepsville TPB ('07, $19.99) r/#1-6 & story from DCU Brave New World — 20.00

CREEPS
Image Comics: Oct, 2001 - No. 4, May, 2002 ($2.95)
1-4-Mandrake-a/Mishkin-s — 3.00

CREEPSHOW
Plume/New American Library Pub.: July, 1982 (softcover graphic novel)
1st edition-nn-(68 pgs.) Kamen-c/Wrightson-a; screenplay by Stephen King for the George Romero movie — 5 10 15 31 53 75
2nd-7th printings — 3 6 9 17 26 35

CREEPY (See Warren Presents)
Warren Publishing Co./Harris Publ. #146: 1964 - No. 145, Feb, 1983; No. 146, 1985 (B&W, magazine)
1-Frazetta-a (his last story in comics?); Jack Davis-c; 1st Warren all comics magazine; 1st app. Uncle Creepy — 12 24 36 84 185 285
2-Frazetta-c & 1 pg. strip — 8 16 24 56 108 160
3-8,11-13,15-17: 3-7,9-11,15-17-Frazetta-c. 7-Frazetta 1 pg. strip. 15,16-Adams-a. 16-Jeff Jones-a — 6 12 18 37 66 95
9-Creepy fan club sketch by Wrightson (1st published-a); has 1/2 pg. anti-smoking strip by Frazetta; Frazetta-c; 1st Wood and Ditko art on this title; Toth-a (low print) — 7 14 21 49 92 135
10-Brunner fan club sketch (1st published work) — 6 12 18 38 69 100
14-Neal Adams 1st Warren work — 6 12 18 38 69 100
18-28,30,31: 27-Frazetta-c — 4 8 12 28 47 65
29,34: 29-Jones-a — 5 10 15 30 50 70
32-(scarce) Frazetta-c; Harlan Ellison sty — 8 16 24 51 96 140
33,35,37,39,40,42-47,49: 35-Hitler/Nazi-s. 39-1st Uncle Creepy solo-s, Cousin Eerie app.; early Brunner-a. 42-1st San Julian-c. 44-1st Ploog-a. 46-Corben-a — 4 8 12 23 37 50
36-(11/70)1st Corben art at Warren — 5 10 15 30 50 70
38,41-(scarce): 38-1st Kelly-c. 41-Corben-a — 5 10 15 33 57 80
48,55,65-(1972, 1973, 1974 Annuals) #55 & 65 contain an 8 pg. slick comic insert. 48-(84 pgs.). 55-Color poster bonus (1/2 price if missing). 65-(100 pgs.) Summer Giant — 5 10 15 30 50 70
50-Vampirella/Eerie/Creepy-c — 5 10 15 33 57 80
51,54,56-61,64: All contain an 8 pg. slick comic insert in middle. 59-Xmas horror. 54,64-Chaykin-a — 4 8 12 27 44 60
52,53,66,71,72,75,76,78-80: 71-All Bermejo-a; Space & Time issue. 72-Gual-a. 78-Fantasy issue. 79,80-Monsters issue — 3 6 9 19 30 40
62,63-1st & 2nd full Wrightson story art; Corben-a; 8 pg. color comic insert — 4 8 12 27 44 60
67,68,73 — 3 6 9 21 33 45
69,70-Edgar Allan Poe issues; Corben-a — 4 8 12 23 37 50
74,77: 74-All Crandell-a. 77-Xmas Horror issue; Corben-a,Wrightson-a — 4 8 12 23 37 50
81,84,85,88-90,92-94,96-99,102,104-112,114-118,120,122-130: 84,93-Sports issue. 85,97,102-Monster issue. 89-All war issue; Nino-a. 94-Weird Children issue. 96,109-Aliens issue. 99-Disasters. 103-Corben-a. 104-Robots issue. 106-Sword & Sorcery.107-Sci-fi. 116-End of Man. 125-Xmas Horror — 2 4 6 10 14 18
82,100,101: 82-All Maroto issue. 100-(8/78) Anniversary. 101-Corben-a — 3 6 9 14 20 26
83,95-Wrightson-a. 83-Corben-a. 95-Gorilla/Apes. — 2 4 6 13 18 22
86,87,91,103-Wrightson-a. 86-Xmas Horror — 2 4 6 13 18 22
113-All Wrightson-r issue — 3 6 9 19 29 38
119,121: 119-All Nino issue.121-All Severin-r issue — 2 4 6 13 18 22
131,133-136,138,140: 135-Xmas issue — 2 4 6 13 18 22
132,137,139: 132-Corben. 137-All Williamson-r issue. 139-All Toth-r issue

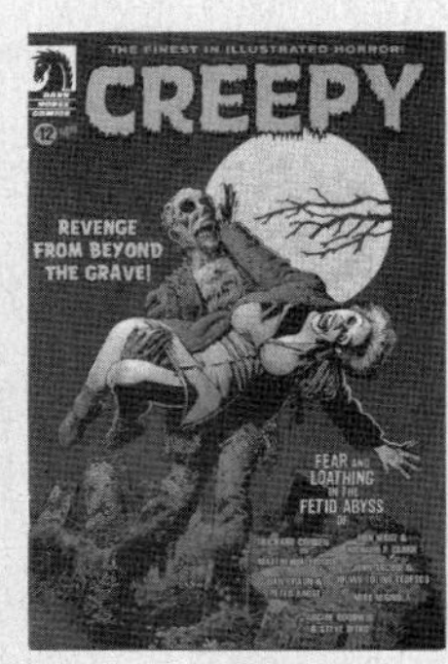

Creepy (2009 series) #12 © New Comic Co.

Crime and Justice #9 © CC

Crime Detector #5 © Timor

	GD 2.0	VG 4.0	FN 6.0	VF 8.0	VF/NM 9.0	NM- 9.2
	3	6	9	14	20	26
141,143,144 (low dist.): 144-Giant, $2.25; Frazetta-c	3	6	9	17	26	35
142,145 (low dist.): 142-(10/82, 100 pgs.) All Torres issue. 145-(2/83) last Warren issue	3	6	9	19	30	40
146 ($2.95)-1st from Harris; resurrection issue	6	12	18	41	76	110
Year Book '68-'70: '70-Neal Adams, Ditko-a(r)	5	10	15	33	57	80
Annual 1971,1972	5	10	15	31	53	75
1993 Fearbook ($3.95)-Harris Publ.; Brereton-c; Vampirella by Busiek-s/Art Adams-a; David-s; Paquette-a	3	6	9	17	26	35
...:The Classic Years TPB (Harris/Dark Horse, '91, $12.95) Kaluta-c; art by Frazetta,Torres, Crandall, Ditko, Morrow, Williamson, Wrightson						25.00

NOTE: *All issues contain many good artists works:* ***Neal Adams, Brunner, Corben, Craig (Taycee), Crandall, Ditko, Evans, Frazetta, Heath, Jeff Jones, Krenkel, McWilliams, Morrow, Nino, Orlando, Ploog, Severin, Torres, Toth, Williamson, Wood, & Wrightson****; covers by* ***Crandall, Davis, Frazetta, Morrow, San Julian, Todd/Bode****; Otto Binder's "Adam Link" stories in No. 2, 4, 6, 8, 9, 12, 13, 15 with* ***Orlando*** *art.* ***Frazetta*** *c-2-7, 9-11, 15-17, 27, 32, 83r, 89r, 91r.* ***E.A. Poe*** *adaptations in 66, 69, 70.*

CREEPY (Mini-series)
Harris Comics/Dark Horse: 1992 - Book 4, 1992 (48 pgs, B&W, squarebound)

	GD 2.0	VG 4.0	FN 6.0	VF 8.0	VF/NM 9.0	NM- 9.2
Book 1-4: Brereton painted-c on all. Stories and art by various incl. David (all), Busiek(2), Infantino(2), Guice(3), Colan(1)	2	4	6	8	10	12

CREEPY
Dark Horse Comics: July, 2009 - Present ($4.99/$3.99, 48 pgs, B&W, quarterly)

	GD 2.0	VG 4.0	FN 6.0	VF 8.0	VF/NM 9.0	NM- 9.2
1-13: 1-Powell-c; art by Wrightson, Toth, Alexander. 8,12-Corben-c.						5.00
14-24-($3.99) 18-Nguyen-c. 20,23,24-Corben-a						4.00

CREEPY THINGS
Charlton Comics: July, 1975 - No. 6, June, 1976

	GD 2.0	VG 4.0	FN 6.0	VF 8.0	VF/NM 9.0	NM- 9.2
1-Sutton-c/a	3	6	9	14	19	24
2-6: Ditko-a in 3,5. Sutton c-3,4. 6-Zeck-c	2	4	6	8	10	12
Modern Comics Reprint 2-6(1977)						5.00

NOTE: ***Larson*** *a-2,6.* ***Sutton*** *a-1,2,4,6.* ***Zeck*** *a-2.*

CREW, THE
Marvel Comics: July, 2003 - No. 7, Jan, 2004 ($2.50)

	GD 2.0	VG 4.0	FN 6.0	VF 8.0	VF/NM 9.0	NM- 9.2
1-7-Priest-s/Bennett-a; James Rhodes (War Machine) app.						3.00

CRIME AND JUSTICE (Badge Of Justice #22 on; Rookie Cop? No. 27 on)
Capitol Stories/Charlton Comics: March, 1951 - No. 21, Nov, 1954; No. 23, Mar, 1955 - No. 26, Sept, 1955 (No #22)

	GD 2.0	VG 4.0	FN 6.0	VF 8.0	VF/NM 9.0	NM- 9.2
1	41	82	123	256	428	600
2	20	40	60	117	189	260
3-8,10-13: 6-Negligee panels	18	36	54	103	162	220
9-Classic story "Comics Vs. Crime"	36	72	108	211	343	475
14-Color illos in **POP**; story of murderer who beheads women	32	64	96	188	307	425
15-17,19-21,23,24: 15-Negligee panels. 23-Rookie Cop (1st app.)	14	28	42	76	108	140
18-Ditko-a	31	62	93	186	303	420
25,26: (scarce)	20	40	60	114	182	250

NOTE: ***Alascia*** *c-20.* ***Ayers*** *a-17.* ***Shuster*** *a-19-21; c-19. Bondage c-11, 12.*

CRIME AND PUNISHMENT (Title inspired by 1935 film)
Lev Gleason Publications: April, 1948 - No. 74, Aug, 1955

	GD 2.0	VG 4.0	FN 6.0	VF 8.0	VF/NM 9.0	NM- 9.2
1-Mr. Crime app. on-c	41	82	123	256	428	600
2-Narrator, Officer Common Sense (a ghost) begins, ends #27? (see Crime Does Not Pay #41)	21	42	63	122	199	275
3-(6/48)-Used in **SOTI**, pg. 112; contains Biro & Gleason self censorship code of 12 listed restrictions	22	44	66	132	216	300
4,5	15	30	45	90	140	190
6-10	14	28	42	80	115	150
11-20	12	24	36	69	97	125
21-30	11	22	33	60	83	105
31-38,40-44,46: 46-One pg. Frazetta-a	10	20	30	54	72	90
39-Drug mention story "The Five Dopes"	16	32	48	94	147	200
45- "Hophead Killer" drug story	16	32	48	94	147	200
47-53,55,57,60-65,70-74:	9	18	27	52	69	85
54-Electric Chair-c	10	20	30	56	76	95
56-Classic dagger/torture-c	11	22	33	64	90	115
58-Used in **POP**, pg. 79	11	22	33	62	86	110
59-Used in **SOTI**, illo "What comic-book America stands for"	36	72	108	216	351	485
66-Toth-c/a(4); 3-D effect issue (3/54); 1st "Deep Dimension" process	41	82	123	250	418	585
67- "Monkey on His Back" heroin story; 3-D effect issue	39	78	117	231	378	525
68-3-D effect issue; Toth-c (7/54)	32	64	96	188	307	425
69- "The Hot Rod Gang" dope crazy kids	15	30	45	85	130	175

NOTE: ***Belfi*** *a- 2, 3, 5.* ***Biro*** *c-most.* ***Al Borth*** *a-9, 35.* ***Cooper*** *a-9.* ***Joe Certa*** *a-8.* ***Tony Dipreta*** *a-3, 5, 15, 34.* ***Everett*** *a-31.* ***Bob Fujitani (Fuje)*** *a-2-20, 26, 27.* ***Joseph Gaguardi*** *a-15, 18, 20.* ***Fred Guardineer*** *a-2-5, 10-12, 14, 15, 17, 18, 20, 26-28, 32, 34, 35, 38-44, 51, 54.* ***Jack Keller*** *a-18.* ***Kinstler*** *c-69.* ***Martinott*** *a-13.* ***Al McWilliams*** *a-36, 41, 48, 49.* ***William Overgard*** *a-36.* ***Dick Rockwell*** *a-35, 51.* ***Robert Q. Sale*** *a-43.* ***George Tuska*** *a-28, 30, 51, 64, 70. Painted-c-31.*

CRIME AND PUNISHMENT: MARSHALL LAW TAKES MANHATTAN
Marvel Comics (Epic Comics): 1989 ($4.95, 52 pgs., direct sales only, mature)

	GD 2.0	VG 4.0	FN 6.0	VF 8.0	VF/NM 9.0	NM- 9.2
nn-Graphic album featuring Marshall Law						5.00

CRIME BIBLE: THE FIVE LESSONS (Aftermath of DC's 52 series)
DC Comics: Dec, 2007 - No. 5, Apr, 2008 ($2.99, limited series)

	GD 2.0	VG 4.0	FN 6.0	VF 8.0	VF/NM 9.0	NM- 9.2
1-5-Rucka-s; The Question (Renee Montoya) app. 3-Batwoman app.						3.00
The Question: The Five Books of Blood HC (2008, $19.99) r/#1-5						20.00
The Question: The Five Books of Blood SC (2009, $14.99) r/#1-5						15.00

CRIME CAN'T WIN (Formerly Cindy Smith)
Marvel/Atlas Comics (TCI 41/CCC 42,43,4-12): No. 41, 9/50 - No. 43, 2/51; No. 4, 4/51 - No. 12, 9/53

	GD 2.0	VG 4.0	FN 6.0	VF 8.0	VF/NM 9.0	NM- 9.2
41(#1)-"The Girl Who Planned Her Own Murder"	31	62	93	186	303	420
42(#2)	18	36	54	103	162	220
43(#3)-Horror story	21	42	63	124	202	280
4(4/51),5-12: 10-Possible use in **SOTI**, pg. 161	15	30	45	85	130	175

NOTE: ***Robinson*** *a-9-11.* ***Tuska*** *a-43.*

CRIME CASES COMICS (Formerly Willie Comics)
Marvel/Atlas Comics(CnPC No.24-8/MJMC No.9-12): No. 24, 8/50 - No. 27, 3/51; No. 5, 5/51 - No. 12, 7/52

	GD 2.0	VG 4.0	FN 6.0	VF 8.0	VF/NM 9.0	NM- 9.2
24 (#1, 52 pgs.)-True police cases	23	46	69	136	223	310
25-27(#2-4): 27-Morisi-a	17	34	51	98	154	210
5-12: 11-Robinson-a. 12-Tuska-a	15	30	45	85	130	175

CRIME CLINIC
Ziff-Davis Publishing Co.: No. 10, July-Aug, 1951 - No. 5, Summer, 1952

	GD 2.0	VG 4.0	FN 6.0	VF 8.0	VF/NM 9.0	NM- 9.2
10(#1)-Painted-c; origin Dr. Tom Rogers	31	62	93	186	303	420
11(#2),4,5: 4,5-Painted-c	20	40	60	120	195	270
3-Used in **SOTI**, pg. 18	21	42	63	124	202	280

NOTE: *All have painted covers by* ***Saunders. Starr*** *a-10.*

CRIME CLINIC
Slave Labor Graphics: May, 1995 - No. 2, Oct, 1995 ($2.95, B&W, limited series)

	GD 2.0	VG 4.0	FN 6.0	VF 8.0	VF/NM 9.0	NM- 9.2
1,2						3.00

CRIME DETECTIVE COMICS
Hillman Periodicals: Mar-Apr, 1948 - V3#8, May-June, 1953

	GD 2.0	VG 4.0	FN 6.0	VF 8.0	VF/NM 9.0	NM- 9.2
V1#1-The Invisible 6, costumed villains app; Fuje-c/a, 15 pgs.	37	74	111	222	361	500
2,5: 5-Krigstein-a	18	36	54	103	162	220
3,4,6,7,10-12: 6-McWilliams-a	15	30	45	88	137	185
8-Kirbyish-a by McCann	15	30	45	88	137	185
9-Used in **SOTI**, pg. 16 & "Caricature of the author in a position comic book publishers wish he were in permanently" illo.	42	84	126	265	445	625
V2#1,4,7-Krigstein-a: 1-Tuska-a	14	28	42	81	118	155
2,3,5,6,8-12 (1-2/52)	13	26	39	74	105	135
V3#1-Drug use-c	14	28	42	78	112	145
2-8	11	22	33	62	86	110

NOTE: ***Briefer*** *a-11, V3#1.* ***Kinstlerish****-a by* ***McCann****-V2#7, V3#2.* ***Powell*** *a-10, 11.* ***Starr*** *a-10.*

CRIME DETECTOR
Timor Publications: Jan, 1954 - No. 5, Sept, 1954

	GD 2.0	VG 4.0	FN 6.0	VF 8.0	VF/NM 9.0	NM- 9.2
1	26	52	78	154	252	350
2	15	30	45	85	130	175
3,4	14	28	42	80	115	150
5-Disbrow-a (classic)	26	52	78	154	252	350

CRIME DOES NOT PAY (Formerly Silver Streak Comics No. 1-21)
Comic House/Lev Gleason/Golfing: No. 22, June, 1942 - No. 147, July, 1955 (1st crime comic)(Title inspired by film)

	GD 2.0	VG 4.0	FN 6.0	VF 8.0	VF/NM 9.0	NM- 9.2
22 (23 on cover, 22 on indicia)-Origin The War Eagle & only app.; Chip Gardner begins; #22 was rebound in Complete Book of True Crime (Scarce)	649	1298	1947	4738	8369	12,000
23-(7/42) (Scarce)	314	628	942	2198	3849	5500
24-(11/42) Intro. & 1st app. Mr. Crime; classic Biro-c showing woman's head on fire being pushed onto hot stovetop burner	900	1800	2700	4500	8000	11,500
25-(1/43) 2nd app. Mr. Crime; classic '40s crime-c	135	270	405	864	1482	2100
26-(3/43) 3rd app. Mr. Crime	113	226	339	718	1234	1750
27-Classic Biro-c pushing man into hot oven	135	270	405	864	1482	2100
28-30: 30-Wood and Biro app.	82	164	246	528	902	1275

Crime Fighters #6 © MAR

Crime Mysteries #2 © TM

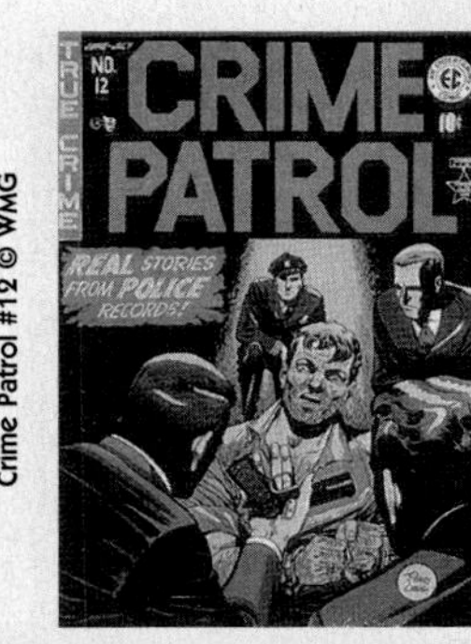

Crime Patrol #12 © WMG

	GD 2.0	VG 4.0	FN 6.0	VF 8.0	VF/NM 9.0	NM- 9.2
31,32,34-40	45	90	135	284	480	675
33-(5/44) Classic Biro hanging & hatchet-c	206	412	618	1318	2259	3200
41-(9/45) Origin & 1st app. Officer Common Sense	41	82	123	256	428	600
42-(11/45) Classic electrocution-c	71	142	213	454	777	1100
43-46,48-50: 44-50 are 68 pg. issues. 44-"Legs" Diamond story. 50-(3/47)-1st issue to advertise 5 million readers on front-c. 58-(12/47)-shows 6 million readers (these ads believed to have influenced the crime comic wave of 1948)	29	58	87	170	278	385
47-(9/46)-Electric chair-c	45	90	135	284	480	675
51-70: 58(12/47)-Thomas Dun, killer of thousands (1565) story. 63,64-Possible use in **SOTI**, pg. 306. 63-Contains Biro & Gleason self censorship code of 12 listed restrictions (5/48)	21	42	63	122	199	275
71-99: 87-Chip Gardner begins, ends #100. 87-99-Painted-c	17	34	51	98	154	210
100-Painted-c	19	38	57	109	172	235
101-104,107-110: 101,102-Painted-c. 102-Chip Gardner app.	14	28	42	81	118	155
105-Used in **POP**, pg. 84	15	30	45	85	130	175
106,114-Frazetta-a, 1 pg.	14	28	42	82	121	160
111-Used in **POP**, pgs. 80 & 81; injury-to-eye sty illo	16	32	48	94	147	200
112,113,115-130	12	24	36	67	94	120
131-140	11	22	33	60	83	105
141,142-Last pre-code issue; Kubert-a(1)	12	24	36	69	97	125
143-Kubert-a in one story	12	24	36	69	97	125
144-146	11	22	33	60	83	105
147-Last issue (scarce); Kubert-a	17	34	51	98	154	210
1(Golfing-1945)	10	20	30	54	72	90
The Best of...(1944, 128 pgs.)-Series contains 4 rebound issues	113	226	339	718	1234	1750
...1945 issue	74	148	222	470	810	1150
...1946-48 issues	55	110	165	352	601	850
...1949-50 issues	47	94	147	296	498	700
...1951-53 issues (25¢)	40	80	120	246	411	575

NOTE: *Many issues contain violent covers and stories. Who Dunit by* ***Guardineer****-39-42, 44-105, 108-110; Chip Gardner by* ***Bob Jujitani (Fuge)****-88-103.* ***Alderman*** *a-29, 41-44, 49.* ***Dan Barry*** *a-67, 75.* ***Charles Biro*** *c-1-76, 122, 142.* ***Dick Briefer*** *a-29(2), 30, 31, 33, 37, 39.* ***G. Colan*** *a-105.* ***Tony Dipreta*** *a-79, 90, 92.* ***Fuje*** *c-88, 89, 91-94, 96, 98, 99, 102, 103.* ***Fred Guardineer*** *a-51, 57, 58(2), 66-68, 71, 74, 79, 81, 90, 92.* ***Joe Kubert*** *c-143.* ***Landau*** *a-118.* ***Al Mandell*** *a-37.* ***Norman Maurer*** *a-29, 39, 41, 42.* ***McWilliams*** *a-91, 93, 95, 100-103.* ***Rudy Palais*** *a-30, 33,* ***Bob Powell*** *a-146, 147.* ***George Tuska*** *a-48-50(2ea.), 51, 52 56, 57(2), 58, 60-64, 66-68, 71, 74, 81. Painted c-87-103. Bondage c-43, 62, 98.*

CRIME EXPOSED
Marvel Comics (PPI)/Marvel Atlas Comics (PrPI): June, 1948; Dec, 1950 - No. 14, June, 1952

	GD	VG	FN	VF	VF/NM	NM-
1(6/48)	39	78	117	231	378	525
1(12/50)	25	50	75	150	245	340
2	16	32	48	94	147	200
3-9,11,14	15	30	45	84	127	170
10-Used in **POP**, pg. 81	15	30	45	86	133	180
12-Krigstein & Robinson-a	15	30	45	86	133	180
13-Used in **POP**, pg. 81; Krigstein-a	15	30	45	88	137	185

NOTE: ***Keller*** *a-8, 10.* ***Maneely*** *c-8.* ***Robinson*** *a-11, 12.* ***Sale*** *a-4.* ***Tuska*** *a-3, 4.*

CRIMEFIGHTERS
Marvel Comics (CmPS 1-3/CCC 4-10): Apr, 1948 - No. 10, Nov, 1949

	GD	VG	FN	VF	VF/NM	NM-
1-Some copies are undated & could be reprints	30	60	90	177	189	400
2,3: 3-Morphine addict story	16	32	48	94	147	200
4-10: 4-Early John Buscema-a. 6-Anti-Wertham editorial. 9,10-Photo-c	15	30	45	84	127	170

CRIME FIGHTERS (...Always Win)
Atlas Comics (CnPC): No. 11, Sept, 1954 - No. 13, Jan, 1955

	GD	VG	FN	VF	VF/NM	NM-
11-13: 11-Maneely-a,13-Pakula, Reinman, Severin-a	14	28	42	80	115	150

CRIME-FIGHTING DETECTIVE (Shock Detective Cases No. 20 on; formerly Criminals on the Run)
Star Publications: No. 11, Apr-May, 1950 - No. 19, June, 1952 (Based on true crime cases)

	GD	VG	FN	VF	VF/NM	NM-
11-L. B. Cole-c/a (2 pgs.); L. B. Cole-c on all	21	42	63	126	206	285
12,13,15-19: 17-Young King Cole & Dr. Doom app.	17	34	51	98	154	210
14-L. B. Cole-c/a, r/Law-Crime #2	19	38	57	109	172	235

CRIME FILES
Standard Comics: No. 5, Sept, 1952 - No. 6, Nov, 1952

	GD	VG	FN	VF	VF/NM	NM-
5-1pg. Alex Toth-a; used in **SOTI**, pg. 4 (text)	26	52	78	154	252	350
6-Sekowsky-a	15	30	45	85	130	175

CRIME ILLUSTRATED (Magazine)
E. C. Comics: Nov-Dec, 1955 - No. 2, Spring, 1956 (25¢, Adult Suspense Stories on-c)

	GD	VG	FN	VF	VF/NM	NM-
1-Ingels & Crandall-a	20	40	60	117	189	260
2-Ingels & Crandall-a	15	30	45	88	137	185

NOTE: ***Craig*** *a-2.* ***Crandall*** *a-1, 2; c-2.* ***Evans*** *a-1.* ***Davis*** *a-2.* ***Ingels*** *a-1, 2.* ***Krigstein/Crandall*** *a-1.* ***Orlando*** *a-1, 2; c-1.*

CRIME INCORPORATED (Formerly Crimes Incorporated)
Fox Features Syndicate: No. 2, Aug, 1950; No. 3, Aug, 1951

	GD	VG	FN	VF	VF/NM	NM-
2	30	60	90	177	289	400
3(1951)-Hollingsworth-a	20	40	60	117	189	260

CRIME MACHINE (Magazine reprints pre-code crime and gangster comics)
Skywald Publications: Feb, 1971 - No. 2, May, 1971 (B&W, 68 pgs., roundbound)

	GD	VG	FN	VF	VF/NM	NM-
1-Kubert-a(2)(r)(Avon); bikini girl in cake-c	5	10	15	35	63	90
2-Torres, Wildey-a; violent-c/a	4	8	12	27	44	60

CRIME MUST LOSE! (Formerly Sports Action?)
Sports Action (Atlas Comics): No. 4, Oct, 1950 - No. 12, April, 1952

	GD	VG	FN	VF	VF/NM	NM-
4-Ann Brewster-a in all; c-used in N.Y. Legis. Comm. documents	22	44	66	132	216	300
5-10,12: 9-Robinson-a	15	30	45	90	140	190
11-Used in **POP**, pg. 89	16	32	48	94	147	200

CRIME MUST PAY THE PENALTY (Formerly Four Favorites; Penalty #47, 48)
Ace Magazines (Current Books): No. 33, Feb, 1948; No. 2, Jun, 1948 - No. 48, Jan, 1956

	GD	VG	FN	VF	VF/NM	NM-
33(#1, 2/48)-Becomes Four Teeners #34?	43	86	129	271	461	650
2(6/48)-Extreme violence; Palais-a?	28	56	84	165	270	375
3,4,8: 3- "Frisco Mary" story used in Senate Investigation report, pg. 7. 4,8-Transvestism stories	21	42	63	126	206	285
5-7,9,10	17	34	51	98	154	210
11-19	15	30	45	90	140	190
20-Drug story "Dealers in White Death"	24	48	72	142	234	325
21-32,34-40,42-48: 44-Last pre-code	14	28	42	76	108	140
33(7/53)- "Dell Fabry-Junk King" drug story; mentioned in Love and Death	20	40	60	114	182	250
41-reprints "Dealers in White Death"	14	28	42	80	115	150

NOTE: ***Cameron*** *a-29-31, 34, 35, 39-41.* ***Colan*** *a-20, 31.* ***Kremer*** *a-3, 37r.* ***Larsen*** *a-32.* ***Palais*** *a-5?,37.*

CRIME MUST STOP
Hillman Periodicals: October, 1952 (52 pgs.)

	GD	VG	FN	VF	VF/NM	NM-
V1#1(Scarce)-Similar to Monster Crime; Mort Lawrence, Krigstein-a	123	246	369	787	1344	1900

CRIME MYSTERIES (Secret Mysteries #16 on; combined with Crime Smashers #7 on)
Ribage Publ. Corp. (Trojan Magazines): May, 1952 - No. 15, Sept, 1954

	GD	VG	FN	VF	VF/NM	NM-
1-Transvestism story; crime & terror stories begin	86	172	258	546	936	1325
2-Marijuana story (7/52)	55	110	165	352	601	850
3-One pg. Frazetta-a	47	94	141	296	498	700
4-Cover shows girl in bondage having her blood drained; 1 pg. Frazetta-a	123	246	369	787	1344	1900
5-10	41	82	123	256	428	600
11,12,14	39	78	117	231	378	525
13-(5/54)-Angelo Torres 1st comic work (inks over Check's pencils); Check-a	41	82	123	259	435	610
15-Acid in face-c	54	108	162	343	574	825

NOTE: ***Fass*** *a-13; c-4, 6, 10.* ***Hollingsworth*** *a-10-13, 15; c-2, 12, 13, 15.* ***Kiefer*** *a-4.* ***Woodbridge*** *a-13? Bondage-c-1, 8, 12.*

CRIME ON THE RUN (See Approved Comics #8)

CRIME ON THE WATERFRONT (Formerly Famous Gangsters)
Realistic Publications: No. 4, May, 1952 (Painted cover)

	GD	VG	FN	VF	VF/NM	NM-
4	32	64	96	188	307	425

CRIME PATROL (Formerly International #1-5; International Crime Patrol #6; becomes Crypt of Terror #17 on)
E. C. Comics: No. 7, Summer, 1948 - No. 16, Feb-Mar, 1950

	GD	VG	FN	VF	VF/NM	NM-
7-Intro. Captain Crime	84	168	252	538	919	1300
8-14: 12-Ingels-a	77	154	231	493	847	1200
15-Intro. of Crypt Keeper (inspired by Witches Tales radio show) & Crypt of Terror (see Tales From the Crypt #33 for origin); used by N.Y. Legis. Comm.; last pg. Feldstein-a	274	548	822	2192	3496	4800
16-2nd Crypt Keeper app.; Roussos-a	177	354	531	1416	2258	3100

NOTE: ***Craig*** *c/a in most issues.* ***Feldstein*** *a-9-16.* ***Kiefer*** *a-8, 10, 11.* ***Moldoff*** *a-7.*

CRIME PATROL
Gemstone Publishing: Apr, 2000 - No. 10, Jan, 2001 ($2.50)

	NM-
1-10: E.C. reprints	4.00
Volume 1,2 (2000, $13.50) 1-r/#1-5. 2-r/#6-10	14.00

Crimes By Women #11 © FOX

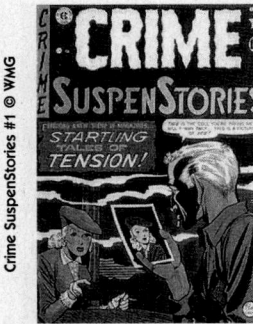

Crime SuspenStories #1 © WMG

Crimson #1 © Aegis

	GD 2.0	VG 4.0	FN 6.0	VF 8.0	VF/NM 9.0	NM- 9.2

CRIME PHOTOGRAPHER (See Casey...)

CRIME REPORTER
St. John Publ. Co.: Aug, 1948 - No. 3, Dec, 1948 (Indicia shows Oct.)

1-Drug club story	77	154	231	493	847	1200
2-Used in **SOTI**: illo- "Children told me what the man was going to do with the red-hot poker;" r/Dynamic #17 with editing; Baker-c; Tuska-a	123	246	369	787	1344	1900
3-Baker-c; Tuska-a	71	142	213	454	777	1100

CRIMES BY WOMEN
Fox Features Syndicate: June, 1948 - No. 15, Aug, 1951; 1954 (True crime cases)

1-True story of Bonnie Parker	129	258	387	826	1413	2000
2	77	154	231	493	847	1200
3-Used in **SOTI**, pg. 234	103	206	309	659	1130	1600
4,5,7-9,11-15: 8-Used in **POP**. 14-Bondage-c	69	138	207	442	759	1075
6-Classic girl fight-c; acid-in-face panel	103	206	309	659	1130	1600
10-Used in **SOTI**, pg. 72; girl fight-c	77	154	231	493	847	1200
54(M.S. Publ.-'54)-Reprint; (formerly My Love Secret)	28	56	84	165	270	375

CRIMES INCORPORATED (Formerly My Past)
Fox Features Syndicate: No. 12, June, 1950 (Crime Incorporated No. 2 on)

12	32	64	96	188	307	425

CRIMES INCORPORATED (See Fox Giants)

CRIME SMASHER (See Whiz #76)
Fawcett Publications: Summer, 1948 (one-shot)

1-Formerly Spy Smasher	41	82	123	256	428	600

CRIME SMASHERS (Becomes Secret Mysteries No. 16 on)
Ribage Publishing Corp.(Trojan Magazines): Oct, 1950 - No. 15, Mar, 1953

1-Used in **SOTI**, pg. 19,20, & illo "A girl raped and murdered;" Sally the Sleuth begins	90	180	270	576	988	1400
2-Kubert-c	48	96	144	302	514	725
3,4	39	78	117	240	395	550
5-Wood-a	47	94	141	296	498	700
6,8-11: 8-Lingerie panel	32	64	96	188	307	425
7-Female heroin junkie story	36	72	108	211	343	475
12-Injury to eye panel; 1 pg. Frazetta-a	34	68	102	204	332	460
13-Used in **POP**, pgs. 79,80; 1 pg. Frazetta-a	34	68	102	204	332	460
14,15	26	52	78	154	252	350

NOTE: ***Hollingsworth** a-14. **Kiefer** a-15. Bondage c-7, 9.*

CRIME SUSPENSTORIES (Formerly Vault of Horror No. 12-14)
E. C. Comics: No. 15, Oct-Nov, 1950 - No. 27, Feb-Mar, 1955

15-Identical to #1 in content; #1 printed on outside front cover. #15 (formerly "The Vault of Horror") printed and blackened out on inside front cover with Vol. 1, No. 1 printed over it. Evidently, several of No. 15 were printed before a decision was made not to drop the Vault of Horror and Haunt of Fear series. The print run was stopped on No. 15 and continued on No. 1. All of the No. 15 issues were changed as described above.

15	200	400	600	1600	2550	3500
1	154	308	462	1232	1966	2700
2	74	148	222	592	946	1300
3-5: 3-Poe adaptation. 3-Old Witch stories begin	54	108	162	432	691	950
6-10: 9-Craig bio.	49	98	147	392	621	850
11,12,14,15: 15-The Old Witch guest stars	37	74	111	296	473	650
13,16-Williamson-a	39	78	117	312	494	675
17-Classic "bullet in the head" cover; Williamson/Frazetta-a (6 pgs.); Williamson bio.	71	142	213	568	909	1250
18,19: 19-Used in **SOTI**, pg. 235	33	66	99	264	420	575
20-Classic hanging cover used in **SOTI**, illo "Cover of a children's comic book"	80	160	240	640	1020	1400
21,24-26: 24- "Food For Thought" similar to "Cave In" in Amazing Detective Cases #13 (1952)	26	52	78	208	329	450
22-Classic ax decapitation-c; exhibited in the 1954 Senate Investigation on juvenile delinquency trial; decapitation story	514	1028	1542	4112	6556	9000

NOTE: *Senator Kefauver questioning Bill Gaines: "Here is your May issue. This seems to be a man with a bloody ax holding a woman's head up which has been severed from her body. Do you think that's in good taste?" Gaines: "Yes I do - for the cover of a horror comic. A cover in bad taste, for example, might be defined as holding her head a little higher so that blood could be seen dripping from it and moving the body over a little further so that the neck of the body could be seen to be bloody." It was actually drawn this way first and Gaines had Craig change it to the published version.*

23-Used in Senate investigation on juvenile delinquency	34	68	102	272	436	600
27-Last issue (Low distribution)	31	62	93	248	399	550

NOTE: ***Craig** a-1-21; c-1-18, 20-22. **Crandall** a-18-26. **Davis** a-4, 5, 7, 9-12, 20. **Elder** a-17,18. **Evans** a-15, 19, 21, 23, 25, 27; c-23, 24. **Feldstein** c-19. **Ingels** a-1-12, 14, 15, 27. **Kamen** a-2, 4-18, 20-27; c-25-27. **Krigstein** a-22, 24, 25, 27. **Kurtzman** a-1, 3. **Orlando** a-16, 22, 24, 26. **Wood** a-1, 3. Issues No. 1-3 were printed in Canada as "Weird Suspenstories." Issues No. 11-15 have E. C. "quickie" stories. No. 25 contains the famous "Are You a Red Dupe?" editorial. Ray Bradbury adaptations-15, 17.*

	GD 2.0	VG 4.0	FN 6.0	VF 8.0	VF/NM 9.0	NM- 9.2

CRIME SUSPENSTORIES
Russ Cochran/Gemstone Publ.: Nov, 1992 - No. 27, May, 1999 ($1.50/$2.00/$2.50)

1-27: Reprints Crime SuspenStories series 4.00

CRIMINAL (Also see Criminal: The Sinners)
Marvel Comics (Icon): Oct, 2006 - No. 10, Oct, 2007 ($2.99)
Volume 2: Feb, 2008 - No. 7, Nov, 2008 ($3.50)

1-10-Ed Brubaker-s/Sean Phillips-a/c 3.00
Volume 2: 1-7-Brubaker-s/Phillips-a 3.50
...: The Special Edition (Image Comics, 2/15, $4.99) Brubaker-s/Phillips-a; 1970s Conan B&W magazine pastishe within story 5.00
... Vol. 1: Coward TPB (2007, $14.99) r/#1-5; intro. by Tom Fontana 15.00
... Vol. 2: Lawless TPB (2007, $14.99) r/#6-10; intro. by Frank Miller 15.00
... Vol. 3: The Dead and the Dying TPB (2008, $11.99) r/V2#1-4; intro. by John Singleton 12.00

CRIMINAL MACABRE: (limited series and one-shots)
Dark Horse Comics: ($2.99)

...: Cellblock 666 (9/08 - No. 4, 5/09)(#25-28 in series) 1-4-Niles-s/Stakal-a/Bradstreet-c 3.00
...: Die, Die, My Darling (4/12, $3.50) reprints serial from DHP #4-6; Staples-c 3.50
...: Feat of Clay (6/06, $2.99) Niles-s/Hotz-a/c 3.00
Free Comic Book Day: Criminal Macabre - Call Me Monster (5/11) flip book w/Baltimore 3.00
...: My Demon Baby (9/07 - No. 4, 4/08)(#21-24 in the series) 1-4-Niles-s/Stakal-a 3.00
...: No Peace For Dead Men (9/11, $3.99) Niles-s/Mitten-a/Staples-c 4.00
...: The Eyes of Frankenstein (9/13 - No. 4, 12/13 $3.99) 1-4-Niles-s/Mitten-a 4.00
...: The Goon (7/11, $3.99) Niles-s/Mitten-a; covers by Powell & Staples 4.00
...: They Fight By Night (11/12, $3.99) reprints serial from DHP #10-13; Staples-c 4.00
...: Two Red Eyes (12/06 - No. 4, 3/07) 1-4-Niles-s/Hotz-a/Bradstreet-c 3.00

CRIMINAL MACABRE: A CAL MCDONALD MYSTERY (Also see Last Train to Deadsville)
Dark Horse Comics: May, 2003 - No. 5, Sept, 2003 ($2.99)

1-5-Niles-s/Templesmith-a 3.00

CRIMINAL MACABRE: FINAL NIGHT - THE 30 DAYS OF NIGHT CROSSOVER
Dark Horse Comics: Dec, 2012 - No. 4, Mar, 2013 ($3.99, limited series)

1-4-Niles-s/Mitten-a/Erickson-c 4.00

CRIMINAL MACABRE:THE THIRD CHILD
Dark Horse Comics: Sept, 2014 - No. 4, Dec, 2014 ($3.99, limited series)

1-4-Niles-s/Mitten-a/Erickson-c 4.00

CRIMINALS ON THE RUN (Formerly Young King Cole) (Crime Fighting Detective No. 11 on)
Premium Group (Novelty Press): V4#1, Aug-Sep, 1948-#10, Dec-Jan, 1949-50

V4#1-Young King Cole continues	29	58	87	170	278	385
2-6: 6-Dr. Doom app.	24	48	72	142	234	325
7-Classic "Fish in the Face" c by L. B. Cole	61	122	183	390	670	950
V5#1,2 (#8,9),10: 9,10-L. B. Cole-c	22	44	66	128	209	290

NOTE: *Most issues have **L. B. Cole** covers. **McWilliams** a-V4#6, 7, V5#2, 10; c-V4#5.*

CRIMINAL: THE LAST OF THE INNOCENT
Marvel Comics (Icon): Jun, 2011 - No. 4, Sept, 2011 ($3.50)

1-4-Ed Brubaker-s/Sean Phillips-a/c 3.50

CRIMINAL: THE SINNERS
Marvel Comics (Icon): Sept, 2009 - No. 5, Mar, 2010 ($3.50)

1-5-Ed Brubaker-s/Sean Phillips-a/c 3.50

CRIMSON (Also see Cliffhanger #0)
Image Comics (Cliffhanger Productions): May, 1998 - No. 7, Dec, 1998;
DC Comics (Cliffhanger Prod.): No. 8, Mar, 1999 - No. 24, Apr, 2001 ($2.50)

1-Humberto Ramos-a/Augustyn-s 5.00
1-Variant-c by Warren 8.00
1-Chromium-c 15.00
2-Ramos-c with street crowd, 2-Variant-c by Art Adams 4.00
2-Dynamic Forces CrimsonChrome cover 15.00
3-7: 3-Ramos Moon background-c. 7-Three covers by Ramos, Madureira, & Campbell 3.50
8-23: 8-First DC issue 3.00
24-($3.50) Final issue; wraparound-c 4.00
DF Premiere Ed. 1998 ($6.95) covers by Ramos and Jae Lee 7.00
Crimson: Scarlet X Blood on the Moon (10/99, $3.95) 4.00
Crimson Sourcebook (11/99, $2.95) Pin-ups and info 3.00
Earth Angel TPB (2001, $14.95) r/#13-18 15.00
Heaven and Earth TPB (1/00, $14.95) r/#7-12 15.00
Loyalty and Loss TPB ('99, $12.95) r/#1-6 15.00
Redemption TPB ('01, $14.95) r/#19-24 15.00

CRIMSON AVENGER, THE (See Detective Comics #20 for 1st app.)(Also see Leading Comics #1 & World's Best/Finest Comics)
DC Comics: June, 1988 - No. 4, Sept, 1988 ($1.00, limited series)

Crisis on Infinite Earths #7 © DC

Cross #4 © Andrew Vachss

Crossing Midnight #17 © Carey & Fern

GD 2.0 | VG 4.0 | FN 6.0 | VF 8.0 | VF/NM 9.0 | NM- 9.2

1-4 4.00

CRIMSON DYNAMO
Marvel Comics (Epic): Oct, 2003 - No. 6, Apr, 2004 ($2.50/$2.99)
1-4,6: 1-John Jackson Miller-s/Steve Ellis-a/c 3.00
5-($2.99) Iron Man-c/app. 4.00

CRIMSON PLAGUE
Event Comics: June, 1997 ($2.95, unfinished mini-series)
1-George Perez-a 3.00

CRIMSON PLAGUE (George Pérez's...)
Image Comics (Gorilla): June, 2000 - No. 2, Aug, 2000 ($2.95, mini-series)
1-George Pérez-a; reprints 6/97 issue with 16 new pages 3.00
2-($2.50) 3.00

CRISIS AFTERMATH: THE BATTLE FOR BLUDHAVEN (Also see Infinite Crisis)
DC Comics: Jun, 2006 - No. 6, Sept, 2006 ($2.99, limited series)
1-Atomic Knights return; Teen Titans app.; Jurgens-a/Acuna-c 4.00
1-2nd printing with pencil cover 3.00
2-6: 2-Intro S.H.A.D.E. (new Freedom Fighters) 3.00
TPB (2007, $12.99) r/#1-6 13.00

CRISIS AFTERMATH: THE SPECTRE (Also see Infinite Crisis, Gotham Central and Tales of the Unexpected)
DC Comics: Jul, 2006 - No. 3, Sept, 2006 ($2.99, limited series)
1-3-Crispus Allen becomes the Spectre; Pfeifer-s/Chiang-a/c 3.00
TPB (2007, $12.99) r/#1-3 and Tales of the Unexpected #1-3 13.00

CRISIS ON INFINITE EARTHS (Also see Official... Index and Legends of the DC Universe)
DC Comics: Apr, 1985 - No. 12, Mar, 1986 (maxi-series)
1-1st DC app. Blue Beetle & Detective Karp from Charlton; Pérez-c on all 2 4 6 10 14 18
2-6: 6-Intro Charlton's Capt. Atom, Nightshade, Question, Judomaster, Peacemaker & Thunderbolt into DC Universe 2 4 6 8 10 12
7-Double size; death of Supergirl 3 6 9 15 22 28
8-Death of the Flash (Barry Allen) 3 6 9 15 22 28
9-11: 9-Intro. Charlton's Ghost into DC Universe. 10-Intro. Charlton's Banshee, Dr. Spectro, Image, Punch & Jewelee into DC Universe; Starman (Prince Gavyn) dies 2 4 6 8 10 12
12-(52 pgs.)-Deaths of Dove, Kole, Lori Lemaris, Sunburst, G.A. Robin & Huntress; Kid Flash becomes new Flash; 3rd & final DC app. of the 3 Lt. Marvels; Green Fury gets new look (becomes Green Flame in Infinity, Inc. #32) 2 4 6 9 13 16
Slipcased Hardcover (1998, $99.95) Wraparound dust-jacket cover pencilled by Pérez and painted by Alex Ross; sketch pages by Pérez; Wolfman intro.; afterword by Giordano 125.00
TPB (2000, $29.95) Wraparound-c by Pérez and Ross 30.00
NOTE: *Crossover issues: All Star Squadron 50-56,60; Amethyst 13; Blue Devil 17,18; DC Comics Presents 78,86-88,95; Detective Comics 558; Fury of Firestorm 41,42; G.I. Combat 274; Green Lantern 194-196,198; Infinity, Inc. 18-25 & Annual 1, Justice League of America 244,245 & Annual 3; Legion of Super-Heroes 16,18; Losers Special 1; New Teen Titans 13,14; Omega Men 31,33; Superman 413-415; Swamp Thing 44,46; Wonder Woman 327-329.*

CRISIS ON MULTIPLE EARTHS
DC Comics: 2002 - 2010 ($14.95, trade paperbacks)
TPB-(2003) Reprints 1st 4 Silver Age JLA/JSA crossovers from J.L.ofA. #21,22; 29,30; 37,38; 46,47; new painted-c by Alex Ross; intro. by Mark Waid 15.00
Volume 2 (2003, $14.95) r/J.L.ofA. #55,56; 64,65; 73,74; 82,83; new Ordway-c 15.00
Volume 3 (2004, $14.95) r/J.L.ofA. #91,92; 100-102; 107,108; 113; Wein intro., Ross-c 15.00
Volume 4 (2006, $14.99) r/J.L.ofA. #123-124 (Earth-Prime),135-137 (Fawcett's Shazam characters), 147-148 (Legion of Super-Heroes); Ross-c 15.00
Volume 5 (2010, $19.99) r/J.L.ofA. #159-160 (Jonah Hex, Enemy Ace), #171-172 (Murder of Mr. Terrific), 1#83-185 (New Gods & Darkseid); Pérez-c 20.00
... The Team-Ups Volume 1 (2005, $14.99) r/Flash #123,129,137,151; Showcase #55,56; Green Lantern #40, Brave and the Bold #61 and Spectre #7; new Ordway-c 15.00

CRITICAL MASS (See A Shadowline Saga: Critical Mass)

CRITTER
Big Dog Press: Jul, 2011 - No. 4, 2011; Jun, 2012 - No. 20, Apr, 2014 ($3.50)
1-4-Multiple covers on all 3.50
Vol. 2 1-20-Multiple covers on all 3.50

CRITTER
Aspen MLT: Jul, 2015 - No. 4, Oct, 2015 ($3.99)
1-4-Reprints the 2011 series; multiple covers on all 4.00

CRITTERS (Also see Usagi Yojimbo Summer Special)
Fantagraphics Books: 1986 - No. 50, 1990 ($1.70/$2.00, B&W)
1-Cutey Bunny, Usagi Yojimbo app. 2 4 6 10 14 18
2,4,5,8,9 6.00
3,6,7,10-Usagi Yojimbo app. 1 2 3 5 6 8
11,14-Usagi Yojimbo app. 11-Christmas Special (68 pgs.) 5.00
12,13,15-22,24-37,39,40: 22-Watchmen parody; two diff. covers exist 3.00
23-With Alan Moore Flexi-disc ($3.95) 5.00
38-($2.75-c) Usagi Yojimbo app. 5.00
41-49 4.00
50 ($4.95, 84 pgs.)-Neil the Horse, Capt. Jack, Sam & Max & Usagi Yojimbo app.; Quagmire, Shaw-a 1 2 3 4 5 7
Special 1 (1/88, $2.00) 4.00

CROSS
Dark Horse Comics: No. 0, Oct, 1995 - No. 6, Apr, 1995 ($2.95, limited series, mature)
0-6: Darrow-c & Vachss scripts in all 3.00

CROSS AND THE SWITCHBLADE, THE
Spire Christian Comics (Fleming H. Revell Co.): 1972 (35-49¢)
1-Some issues have nn 3 6 9 17 26 35

CROSS BRONX, THE
Image Comics: Sept, 2006 - No. 4, Dec, 2006 ($2.99, limited series)
1-4: 1-Oeming-a/c; Oeming & Brandon-s; Ribic var-c. 2-Johnson var-c. 4-Mack var-c 3.00

CROSSFIRE
Spire Christian Comics (Fleming H. Revell Co.): 1973 (39/49¢)
nn 2 4 6 13 18 22

CROSSFIRE (Also see DNAgents)
Eclipse Comics: 5/84 - No. 17, 3/86; No. 18, 1/87 - No. 26, 2/88 ($1.50, Baxter paper) (#18-26 are B&W)
1-11,14-26: 1-DNAgents x-over; Spiegle-c/a begins 3.00
12-Death of Marilyn Monroe; Dave Stevens-c 2 4 6 11 16 20
13-Death of Marilyn Monroe 1 2 3 5 6 8

CROSSFIRE AND RAINBOW (Also see DNAgents)
Eclipse Comics: June, 1986 - No. 4, Sept, 1986 ($1.25, deluxe format)
1-3: Spiegle-a 3.00
4-Dave Stevens-c 6.00

CROSSGEN...
CrossGeneration Comics
CrossGenesis (1/00) Previews CrossGen universe; cover gallery 3.00
...Primer (1/00) Wizard supplement; intro. to the CrossGen universe 3.00
...Sampler (2/00) Retailer preview book 3.00

CROSSGEN CHRONICLES
CrossGeneration Comics: June, 2000 - No. 8 ($3.95)
1-Intro. to CrossGen characters & company 4.00
1-(no cover price) same contents, customer preview 4.00
2-8: 2-(3/01) George Pérez-c/a. 3-5-Pérez-a/Waid-s. 6,7-Nebres-c/a 4.00

CROSSING MIDNIGHT
DC Comics (Vertigo): Jan, 2007 - No. 19, Jul, 2008 ($2.99)
1-19: 1-Carey-s/Fern-a/Williams III-c. 10-12-Nguyen-a 3.00
...: Cut Here TPB (2007, $9.99) r/#1-5 10.00
...: A Map of Midnight TPB (2008, $14.99) r/#6-12; afterword by Carey 15.00
...: The Sword in the Soul TPB (2008, $14.99) r/#13-19 15.00

CROSSING THE ROCKIES (See Classics Illustrated Special Issue)

CROSSOVERS, THE
CrossGeneration Comics: Feb, 2003 - No. 12 ($2.95)
1-12-Robert Rodi-s. 1-6-Mauricet & Ernie Colon-a. 7-Staton-a begins 3.00
Vol. 1: Cross Currents (2003, $9.95) digest-sized reprints #1-6 10.00

CROW, THE (Also see Caliber Presents)
Caliber Press: Feb, 1989 - No. 4, 1989 ($1.95, B&W, limited series)
1-James O'Barr-c/a/scripts 8 16 24 56 108 160
1-3-2nd printing 2 4 6 10 14 18
2-4 4 8 12 28 47 65
2-3rd printing 5.00

CROW, THE
Tundra Publishing, Ltd.: Jan, 1992 - No. 3, 1992 ($4.95, B&W, 68 pgs.)
1-r/#1,2 of Caliber series 2 4 6 11 16 20
2,3: 2-r/#3 of Caliber series w/new material. 3-All new material 2 4 6 8 10 12

CROW, THE
Kitchen Sink Press: 1/96 - No. 3, 3/96 ($2.95, B&W)

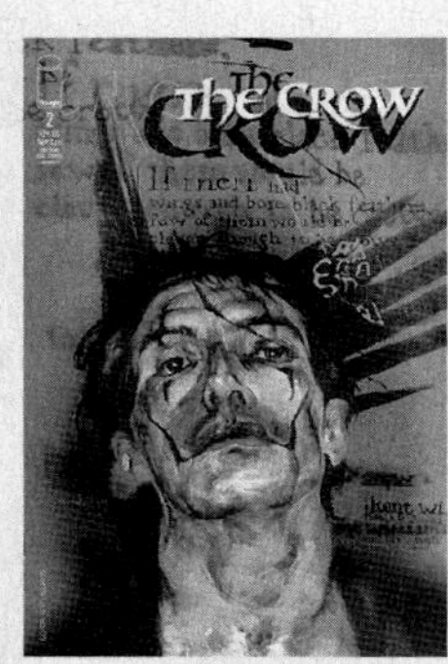

The Crow (1999 series) #2 © TMP

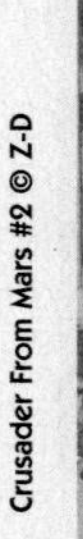
Crusader From Mars #2 © Z-D

Cry Havoc #2 © Spurrier & Kelly

	GD 2.0	VG 4.0	FN 6.0	VF 8.0	VF/NM 9.0	NM- 9.2
1-3: James O'Barr-c/scripts						5.00
#0-A Cycle of Shattered Lives (12/98, $3.50) new story by O'Barr						4.00

CROW, THE
Image Comics (Todd McFarlane Prod.): Feb, 1999 - No. 10, Nov, 1999 ($2.50)

	GD 2.0	VG 4.0	FN 6.0	VF 8.0	VF/NM 9.0	NM- 9.2
1-10: 1-Two covers by McFarlane and Kent Williams; Muth-s in all. 2-6,10-Paul Lee-a						3.00
Book 1 - Vengeance (2000, $10.95, TPB) r/#1-3,5,6						11.00
Book 2 - Evil Beyond Reach (2000, $10.95, TPB) r/#4,7-10						11.00
Todd McFarlane Presents The Crow Magazine 1 (3/00, $4.95)						5.00

CROW, THE: CITY OF ANGELS (Movie)
Kitchen Sink Press: July, 1996 - No. 3, Sept, 1996 ($2.95, limited series)

	GD 2.0	VG 4.0	FN 6.0	VF 8.0	VF/NM 9.0	NM- 9.2
1-3: Adaptation of film; two-c (photo & illos.). 1-Vincent Perez interview						3.00

CROW, THE: CURARE
IDW Publishing: Jun, 2013 - No. 3, Aug, 2013 ($3.99, limited series)

	GD 2.0	VG 4.0	FN 6.0	VF 8.0	VF/NM 9.0	NM- 9.2
1-3-James O'Barr-s/Antoine Dodé-a; multiple covers on each						4.00

CROW, THE: DEATH AND REBIRTH
IDW Publishing: Jul, 2012 - No. 5, Nov, 2012 ($3.99, limited series)

	GD 2.0	VG 4.0	FN 6.0	VF 8.0	VF/NM 9.0	NM- 9.2
1-5-Shirley-s/Colden-a; multiple covers on each						4.00

CROW, THE: FLESH AND BLOOD
Kitchen Sink Press: May, 1996 - No. 3, July, 1996 ($2.95, limited series)

	GD 2.0	VG 4.0	FN 6.0	VF 8.0	VF/NM 9.0	NM- 9.2
1-3: O'Barr-c						3.00

CROW, THE: RAZOR - KILL THE PAIN
London Night Studios: Apr, 1998 - No. 3, July, 1998 ($2.95, B&W, lim. series)

	GD 2.0	VG 4.0	FN 6.0	VF 8.0	VF/NM 9.0	NM- 9.2
1-3-Hartsoe-s/O'Barr-painted-c						3.00
0(10/98) Dorien painted-c, Finale (2/99)						3.00
The Lost Chapter (2/99, $4.95), Tour Book-(12/97) pin-ups; 4 diff.-c						5.00

CROW, THE: PESTILENCE
IDW Publishing: Mar, 2014 - No. 4, Jun, 2014 ($3.99, limited series)

	GD 2.0	VG 4.0	FN 6.0	VF 8.0	VF/NM 9.0	NM- 9.2
1-4-Frank Bill-s/Drew Moss-a; two covers						4.00

CROW, THE: SKINNING THE WOLVES
IDW Publishing: Dec, 2012 - No. 3, Feb, 2013 ($3.99, limited series)

	GD 2.0	VG 4.0	FN 6.0	VF 8.0	VF/NM 9.0	NM- 9.2
1-3-James O'Barr-s/Jim Terry-s/a; multiple covers on each						4.00

CROW, THE: WAKING NIGHTMARES
Kitchen Sink Press: Jan, 1997 - No. 4, 1998 ($2.95, B&W, limited series)

	GD 2.0	VG 4.0	FN 6.0	VF 8.0	VF/NM 9.0	NM- 9.2
1-4-Miran Kim-c						5.00

CROW, THE: WILD JUSTICE
Kitchen Sink Press: Oct, 1996 - No. 3, Dec, 1996 ($2.95, B&W, limited series)

	GD 2.0	VG 4.0	FN 6.0	VF 8.0	VF/NM 9.0	NM- 9.2
1-3-Prosser-s/Adlard-a						3.00

CROWN COMICS (Also see Vooda)
Golfing/McCombs Publ.: Wint, 1944-45; No. 2, Sum, 1945 - No. 19, July, 1949

	GD 2.0	VG 4.0	FN 6.0	VF 8.0	VF/NM 9.0	NM- 9.2
1- "The Oblong Box" E.A. Poe adaptation	47	94	141	296	498	700
2-Baker-a	34	68	102	204	332	460
3-Baker-a; Voodah by Baker	41	82	123	256	428	600
4-6-Baker-c/a; Voodah app. #4,5	39	78	117	231	378	525
7-Feldstein, Baker, Kamen-a; Baker-c	39	78	117	240	395	550
8-Baker-a; Voodah app.	29	58	87	170	278	385
9-11,13-19: Voodah in #10-19. 13-New logo	20	40	60	114	182	250
12-Master Marvin by Feldstein, Starr-a; Voodah-c	20	40	60	117	189	260

NOTE: *Bolle a-11, 13-16, 18, 19; c-11p, 15. Powell a-19. Starr a-11-13; c-11i.*

CRUCIBLE
DC Comics (Impact): Feb, 1993 - No. 6, July, 1993 ($1.25, limited series)

	GD 2.0	VG 4.0	FN 6.0	VF 8.0	VF/NM 9.0	NM- 9.2
1-6: 1-(99¢)-Neon ink-c. 1,2-Quesada-c(p). 1-4-Quesada layouts						3.00

CRUEL AND UNUSUAL
DC Comics (Vertigo): June, 1999 - No. 4, Sept, 1999 ($2.95, limited series)

	GD 2.0	VG 4.0	FN 6.0	VF 8.0	VF/NM 9.0	NM- 9.2
1-4-Delano & Peyer-s/McCrea-c/a						3.00

CRUSADER FROM MARS (See Tops in Adventure)
Ziff-Davis Publ. Co.: Jan-Mar, 1952 - No. 2, Fall, 1952 (Painted-c)

	GD 2.0	VG 4.0	FN 6.0	VF 8.0	VF/NM 9.0	NM- 9.2
1-Cover is dated Spring	84	168	252	538	919	1300
2-Bondage-c	58	116	174	371	636	900

CRUSADER RABBIT (TV)
Dell Publishing Co.: No. 735, Oct, 1956 - No. 805, May, 1957

	GD 2.0	VG 4.0	FN 6.0	VF 8.0	VF/NM 9.0	NM- 9.2
Four Color 735 (#1)	21	42	63	147	324	500
Four Color 805	16	32	48	111	246	380

CRUSADERS, THE (Religious)
Chick Publications: 1974 - Vol. 17, 1988 (39/69¢, 36 pgs.)

	GD 2.0	VG 4.0	FN 6.0	VF 8.0	VF/NM 9.0	NM- 9.2
Vol.1-Operation Bucharest ('74). Vol.2-The Broken Cross ('74). Vol.3-Scarface ('74). Vol.4-Exorcists ('75). Vol.5-Chaos ('75)	3	6	9	16	23	30
Vol.6-Primal Man? ('76)-(Disputes evolution theory). Vol.7-The Ark-(claims proof of existence, destroyed by Bolsheviks). Vol.8-The Gift-(Life story of Christ). Vol.9-Angel of Light-(Story of the Devil). Vol.10-Spellbound?-(Tells how rock music is Satanic & produced by witches). 11-Sabotage?. 12-Alberto. 13-Double Cross. 14-The Godfathers. (No. 6-14 low in distribution; loaded with religious propaganda.). 15-The Force. 16-The Four Horsemen	3	6	9	16	23	30
Vol. 17-The Prophet (low print run)	3	6	9	17	26	35

CRUSADERS (Southern Knights No. 2 on)
Guild Publications: 1982 (B&W, magazine size)

	GD 2.0	VG 4.0	FN 6.0	VF 8.0	VF/NM 9.0	NM- 9.2
1-1st app. Southern Knights	2	4	6	10	14	18

CRUSADERS, THE (Also see Black Hood, The Jaguar, The Comet, The Fly, Legend of the Shield, The Mighty... & The Web)
DC Comics (Impact): May, 1992 - No. 8, Dec, 1992 ($1.00/$1.25)

	GD 2.0	VG 4.0	FN 6.0	VF 8.0	VF/NM 9.0	NM- 9.2
1-8-Contains 3 Impact trading cards						4.00

CRUSADES, THE
DC Comics (Vertigo): 2001 - No. 20, Dec, 2002 ($3.95/$2.50)

	GD 2.0	VG 4.0	FN 6.0	VF 8.0	VF/NM 9.0	NM- 9.2
...: Urban Decree ('01, $3.95) Intro. the Knight; Seagle-s/Kelley Jones-c/a						4.00
1-(5/01, $2.50) Sienkiewicz-c						3.00
2-20: 2-Moeller-c. 18-Begin $2.95-c						3.00

CRUSH
Dark Horse Comics: Oct, 2003 - No. 4, Jan, 2004 ($2.99, limited series)

	GD 2.0	VG 4.0	FN 6.0	VF 8.0	VF/NM 9.0	NM- 9.2
1-4-Jason Hall-s/Sean Murphy-a						3.00

CRUSH, THE
Image Comics (Motown Machineworks): Jan, 1996 - No. 5, July, 1996 ($2.25, limited series)

	GD 2.0	VG 4.0	FN 6.0	VF 8.0	VF/NM 9.0	NM- 9.2
1-5: Baron scripts						3.00

CRUX
CrossGeneration Comics: May, 2001 - No. 33, Feb, 2004 ($2.95)

	GD 2.0	VG 4.0	FN 6.0	VF 8.0	VF/NM 9.0	NM- 9.2
1-33: 1-Waid-s/Epting & Magyar-a/c. 6-Pelletier-a. 13-Dixon-s begin. 25-Cover has fake creases and other aging						3.00
Atlantis Rising Vol. 1 TPB (2002, $15.95) r/#1-6						16.00
Test of Time Vol. 2 TPB (12/02, $15.95) r/#7-12						16.00
Vol. 3: Strangers in Atlantis (2003, $15.95) r/#13-18						16.00
Vol. 4: Chaos Reborn (2003, $15.95) r/#19-24						16.00

CRY FOR DAWN
Cry For Dawn Pub.: 1989 - No. 9 ($2.25, B&W, mature)

	GD 2.0	VG 4.0	FN 6.0	VF 8.0	VF/NM 9.0	NM- 9.2
1	7	14	21	46	86	125
1-2nd printing	3	6	9	19	30	40
1-3rd printing	3	6	9	14	20	25
2	4	8	12	23	37	50
2-2nd printing	2	4	6	11	16	20
3	3	6	9	16	23	30
3a-HorrorCon Edition (1990, less than 400 printed, signed inside-c)						200.00
4-6	2	4	6	11	16	20
5-2nd printing	1	2	3	5	6	8
7-9	2	4	6	9	12	15
4-9-Signed & numbered editions	3	6	9	14	20	25
Angry Christ Comix HC (4/03, $29.99) reprints various stories; and 30 pgs. new material						30.00
...Calendar (1993)						35.00

CRY HAVOC
Image Comics: Jan, 2016 - No. 6, Jun, 2016 ($3.99)

	GD 2.0	VG 4.0	FN 6.0	VF 8.0	VF/NM 9.0	NM- 9.2
1-6-Simon Spurrier-s/Ryan Kelly-a; 2 covers on each						4.00

CRYIN' LION COMICS
William H. Wise Co.: Fall, 1944 - No. 3, Spring, 1945

	GD 2.0	VG 4.0	FN 6.0	VF 8.0	VF/NM 9.0	NM- 9.2
1-Funny animal	18	36	54	107	169	230
2-Hitler and Tojo app.	15	30	45	84	127	170
3	11	22	33	62	86	110

CRYPT
Image Comics (Extreme): Aug, 1995 - No.2, Oct. 1995 ($2.50, limited series)

	GD 2.0	VG 4.0	FN 6.0	VF 8.0	VF/NM 9.0	NM- 9.2
1,2-Prophet app.						3.00

CRYPTIC WRITINGS OF MEGADETH
Chaos! Comics: Sept, 1997 - No. 4, Jun, 1998 ($2.95, quarterly)

	GD 2.0	VG 4.0	FN 6.0	VF 8.0	VF/NM 9.0	NM- 9.2
1-4-Stories based on song lyrics by Dave Mustaine						3.00

CRYPTOCRACY
Dark Horse Comics: Jun, 2016 - No. 6, Nov, 2016 ($3.99)

Cryptocracy #1 © BCC & Woods

C•23 #2 © Wizards of the Coast

Curse Words #1 © Silent E Prods.

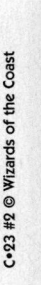

	GD 2.0	VG 4.0	FN 6.0	VF 8.0	VF/NM 9.0	NM- 9.2

1-6: 1-Van Jensen-s/Pete Woods-a 4.00

CRYPT OF DAWN (see Dawn)
Sirius: 1996 ($2.95, B&W, limited series)

1-Linsner-c/s; anthology.						5.00
2, 3 (2/98)						4.00
4,5: 4- (6/98), 5-(11/98)						3.00
Ltd. Edition						20.00

CRYPT OF SHADOWS
Marvel Comics Group: Jan, 1973 - No. 21, Nov, 1975 (#1-9 are 20¢)

1-Wolverton-r/Advs. Into Terror #7	4	8	12	27	44	60
2-10: 2-Starlin/Everett-c	3	6	9	16	24	32
11-21: 18,20-Kirby-a	3	6	9	15	22	28

NOTE: ***Briefer*** *a-2r.* ***Ditko*** *a-13r, 18-20r.* ***Everett*** *a-6, 14r; c-2i.* ***Heath*** *a-1r.* ***Gil Kane*** *c-1, 6.* ***Mort Lawrence*** *a-1r, 8r.* ***Maneely*** *a-2r.* ***Moldoff*** *a-8.* ***Powell*** *a-12r, 14r.* ***Tuska*** *a-2r.*

CRYPT OF TERROR (Formerly Crime Patrol; Tales From the Crypt No. 20 on)
(Also see EC Archives • Tales From the Crypt)
E. C. Comics: No. 17, Apr-May, 1950 - No. 19, Aug-Sept, 1950

17-1st New Trend to hit stands	343	686	1029	2744	4372	6000
18,19	183	366	549	1464	2332	3200

NOTE: ***Craig*** *c/a-17-19.* ***Feldstein*** *a-17-19.* ***Ingels*** *a-19.* ***Kurtzman*** *a-18.* ***Wood*** *a-18. Canadian reprints known; see Table of Contents.*

CRYPTOZOIC MAN (Comic Book Men)
Dynamite Entertainment: 2013 - No. 4, 2014 ($3.99, limited series)

1-Bryan Johnson-s/Walt Flanagan-a/c	2	4	6	10	14	18
2-4	1	3	4	6	8	10

CRYSIS (Based on the EA videogame)
IDW Publishing: Jun, 2011 - No. 6, Oct, 2011 ($3.99, limited series)

1-6: 1-Richard K. Moran-s/Peter Bergting-a; two covers 4.00

CSI: CRIME SCENE INVESTIGATION (Based on TV series)
IDW Publishing: Jan, 2003 - No. 5, May, 2003 ($3.99, limited series)

1-Two covers (photo & Ashley Wood); Max Allan Collins-s	4.00
2-5	4.00
Free Comic Book Day edition (7/04) Previews CSI: Bad Rap; The Shield: Spotlight; 24: One Shot; and 30 Days of Night	3.00
...: Case Files Vol. 1 TPB (8/06, $19.99) B&W rep/Serial TPB, CSI - Bad Rap and CSI - Demon House limited series	20.00
...: Serial TPB (2003, $19.99) r/#1-5; bonus short story by Collins/Wood	20.00
...: Thicker Than Blood (7/03, $6.99) Mariotte-s/Rodriguez-a	7.00

CSI: CRIME SCENE INVESTIGATION - BAD RAP
IDW Publishing: Aug, 2003 - No. 5, Dec, 2003 ($3.99, limited series)

1-5-Two photo covers; Max Allan Collins-s/Rodriguez-a	4.00
TPB (3/04, $19.99) r/#1-5	20.00

CSI: CRIME SCENE INVESTIGATION - DEMON HOUSE
IDW Publishing: Feb, 2004 - No. 5, Jun, 2004 ($3.99, limited series)

1-5-Photo covers on all; Max Allan Collins-s/Rodriguez-a	4.00
TPB (10/04, $19.99) r/#1-5	20.00

CSI: CRIME SCENE INVESTIGATION - DOMINOS
IDW Publishing: Aug, 2004 - No. 5, Dec, 2004 ($3.99, limited series)

1-5-Photo covers on all; Oprisko-s/Rodriguez-a 4.00

CSI: CRIME SCENE INVESTIGATION - DYING IN THE GUTTERS
IDW Publishing: Aug, 2006 - No. 5, Dec, 2006 ($3.99, limited series)

1-5-"Rich Johnston" murdered; comic creators (Quesada, Rucka, David, Brubaker, Silvestri and others) appear as suspects; Stephen Mooney-a; photo-c 4.00

CSI: CRIME SCENE INVESTIGATION - SECRET IDENTITY
IDW Publishing: Feb, 2005 - No. 5, Jun, 2005 ($3.99, limited series)

1-5-Photo covers on all; Steven Grant-s/Gabriel Rodriguez-a 4.00

CSI: MIAMI
IDW Publishing: Oct, 2003; Apr, 2004 ($6.99, one-shots)

... - Blood Money (9/04)-Oprisko-s/Guedes & Perkins-a	7.00
... - Smoking Gun (10/03)-Mariotte-s/Avilés & Wood-a	7.00
... - Thou Shalt Not... (4/04)-Oprisko-s/Guedes & Wood-a	7.00
TPB (2/05, $19.99) reprints one-shots	20.00

CSI: NY - BLOODY MURDER
IDW Publishing: July, 2005 - No. 5, Nov, 2005 ($3.99, limited series)

1-5-Photo covers on all; Collins-s/Woodward-a 4.00

C•23 (Jim Lee's...) (Based on Wizards of the Coast card game)
Image Comics: Apr, 1998 - No. 8, Nov, 1998 ($2.50)

1-8: 1,2-Choi & Mariotte-s/ Charest-c. 2-Variant-c by Jim Lee. 4-Ryan Benjamin-c. 5,8-Corben var-c. 6-Flip book with Planetary preview; Corben-c 3.00

CUD
Fantagraphics Books: 8/92 - No. 8, 12/94 ($2.25-$2.75, B&W, mature)

1-8: Terry LaBan scripts & art in all. 6-1st Eno & Plum 3.00

CUD COMICS
Dark Horse Comics: Jan, 1995 - No. 8, Sept, 1997 ($2.95, B&W)

1-8: Terry LaBan-c/a/scripts. 5-Nudity; marijuana story	3.00
Eno and Plum TPB (1997, $12.95) r/#1-4, DHP #93-95	13.00

CUPID
Marvel Comics (U.S.A.): Dec, 1949 - No. 2, Mar, 1950

1-Photo-c	22	44	66	132	216	300
2-Bettie Page ('50s pin-up queen) photo-c; Powell-a (see My Love #4)	71	142	213	454	777	1100

CURB STOMP
BOOM! Studios: Feb, 2015 - No. 4, May, 2015 ($3.99, limited series)

1-4-Ryan Ferrier-s/Devaki Neogi-a 4.00

CURIO
Harry 'A' Chesler: 1930's(?) (Tabloid size, 16-20 pgs.)

nn	20	40	60	120	195	270

CURLY KAYOE COMICS (Boxing)
United Features Syndicate/Dell Publ. Co.: 1946 - No. 8, 1950; Jan, 1958

1 (1946)-Strip-r (Fritzi Ritz); biography of Sam Leff, Kayoe's artist	22	44	66	132	216	300
2	16	32	48	94	147	200
3-8	14	28	42	80	115	150
United Presents...(Fall, 1948)	14	28	42	80	115	150
Four Color 871 (Dell, 1/58)	5	10	15	30	50	70

CURSED
Image Comics (Top Cow): Oct, 2003 - No. 4, Feb, 2004 ($2.99)

1-4-Avery & Blevins-s/Molenaar-a 3.00

CURSE OF DRACULA, THE
Dark Horse Comics: July, 1998 - No. 3, Sept, 1998 ($2.95, limited series)

1-3-Marv Wolfman-s/Gene Colan-a	3.00
TPB (2005, $9.95) r/series; intro. by Marv Wolfman	10.00

CURSE OF RUNE (Becomes Rune, 2nd Series)
Malibu Comics (Ultraverse): May, 1995 - No. 4, Aug, 1995 ($2.50, lim. series)

1-4: 1-Two covers form one image 3.00

CURSE OF THE SPAWN
Image Comics (Todd McFarlane Prod.): Sept, 1996 - No. 29, Mar, 1999 ($1.95)

1-Dwayne Turner-a(p)	1	3	4	6	8	10
1-B&W Edition	2	4	6	10	14	18
2-3						5.00
4-29: 12-Movie photo-c of Melinda Clarke (Priest)						4.00
Blood and Sutures ('99, $9.95, TPB) r/#5-8						10.00
Lost Values ('00, $10.95, TPB) r/#12-14,22; Ashley Wood-c						11.00
Sacrifice of the Soul ('99, $9.95, TPB) r/#1-4						10.00
Shades of Gray ('00, $9.95, TPB) r/#9-11,29						10.00
The Best of the Curse of the Spawn (6/06, $16.99, TPB) B&W r/#1-8,12-16,20-29						17.00

CURSE OF THE WEIRD
Marvel Comics: Dec, 1993 - No. 4, Mar, 1994 ($1.25, limited series)
(Pre-code horror-r)

1-4: 1,3,4-Wolverton-r(1-Eye of Doom; 3-Where Monsters Dwell; 4-The End of the World). 2-Orlando-r. 4-Zombie-r by Everett; painted-c	1	2	3	5	6	8

NOTE: ***Briefer*** *r-2.* ***Davis*** *a-4r.* ***Ditko*** *a-1r, 2r, 4r; c-1r.* ***Everett*** *r-1.* ***Heath*** *r-1-3.* ***Kubert*** *r-3.* ***Wolverton*** *a-1r, 3r, 4r.*

CURSE WORDS
Image Comics: Jan, 2017 - Present ($3.99)

1,2-Charles Soule-s/Ryan Browne-a 4.00

CUSTER'S LAST FIGHT
Avon Periodicals: 1950

nn-Partial reprint of Cowpuncher #1	17	34	51	98	154	210

CUTEY BUNNY (See Army Surplus Komikz Featuring...)

CUTIE PIE
Junior Reader's Guild (Lev Gleason): May, 1955 - No. 3, Dec, 1955; No. 4, Feb, 1956;

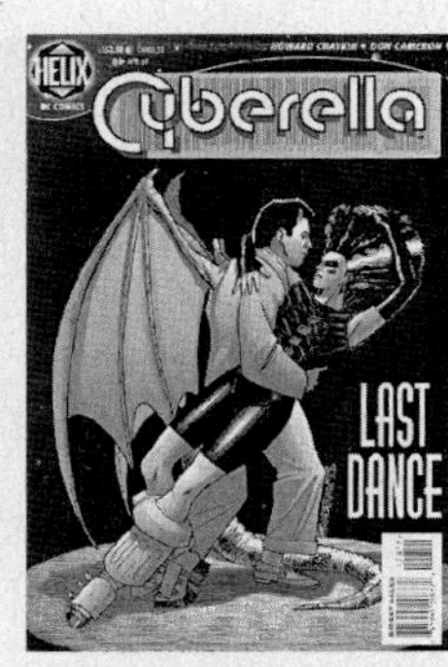

Cyberella #8 © Chaykin & Cameron

Cyberforce V2 #3 © TCOW

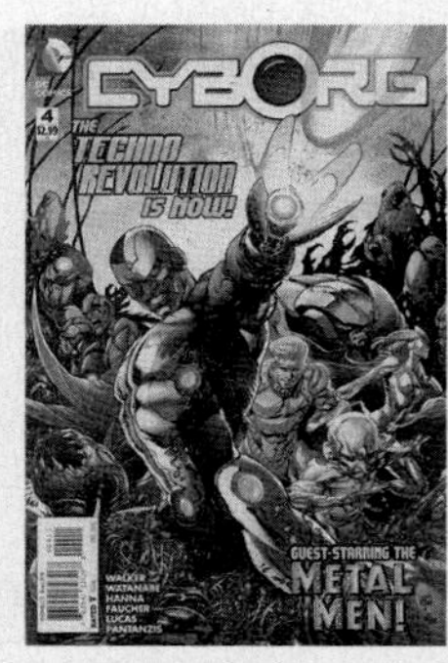

Cyborg #4 © DC

	GD 2.0	VG 4.0	FN 6.0	VF 8.0	VF/NM 9.0	NM- 9.2

No. 5, Aug, 1956

1	9	18	27	52	69	85
2-5: 4-Misdated 2/55	6	12	18	31	38	45

CUTTING EDGE
Marvel Comics: Dec, 1995 ($2.95)

1-Hulk-c/story; Messner-Loebs scripts 3.00

CVO: COVERT VAMPIRIC OPERATIONS
IDW Publishing: June, 2003 ($5.99, one-shot)

1-Alex Garner-s/Mindy Lee-a(p) 6.00
... - Human Touch 1 (8/04, $3.99, one-shot) Hernandez & Garner-a 4.00
... - 100-Page Spectacular (4/11, $7.99) r/#1, African Blood #2 Rogue State #5 8.00
TPB (9/04, $19.99) r/#1 and ... - Artifact #1-3; intro. by Garner 20.00

CVO: COVERT VAMPIRIC OPERATIONS - AFRICAN BLOOD
IDW Publishing: Sept, 2006 - No. 4, May, 2007 ($3.99, limited series)

1-4-El Torres-s/Luis Czerniawski-a 4.00

CVO: COVERT VAMPIRIC OPERATIONS - ARTIFACT
IDW Publishing: Oct, 2003 - No. 3, Dec, 2003 ($3.99, limited series)

1-3-Jeff Mariotte-s/Gabriel Hernandez-a/Alex Garner-c 4.00

CVO: COVERT VAMPIRIC OPERATIONS - ROGUE STATE
IDW Publishing: Nov, 2004 - No. 5, Mar, 2005 ($3.99, limited series)

1-5-Jeff Mariotte-s/Vazquez-a 4.00
TPB (7/05, $19.99) r/#1-5; cover gallery 20.00

CYBERELLA
DC Comics (Helix): Sept, 1996 - No. 12, Aug, 1997 ($2.25/$2.50)(1st Helix series)

1-12: 1-5-Chaykin & Cameron-a. 1,2-Chaykin-c. 3-5-Cameron-c 3.00

CYBERFORCE
Image Comics (Top Cow Productions): Oct, 1992 - No. 4, 1993; No. 0, Sept, 1993 ($1.95, limited series)

1-Silvestri-c/a in all; coupon for Image Comics #0; 1st Top Cow Productions title 6.00
1-With coupon missing 2.00
2-4,0: 2-(3/93). 3-Pitt-c/story. 4-Codename: Stryke Force back-up (1st app.); foil-c. 0-(9/93)-Walt Simonson-c/a/scripts 3.00

CYBERFORCE
Image Comics (Top Cow Productions)/Top Cow Comics No. 28 on:
V2#1, Nov, 1993 - No. 35, Sept. 1997 ($1.95)

V2#1-24: 1-7-Marc Silvestri/Keith Williams-c/a. 8-McFarlane-c/a. 10-Painted variant-c exists. 18-Variant-c exists. 23-Velocity-c. 3.00
1-3: 1-Gold Logo-c. 2-Silver embossed-c. 3-Gold embossed-c 10.00
1-(99¢, 3/96, 2nd printing) 3.00
25-($3.95)-Wraparound, foil-c 4.00
26-35: 28-(11/96)-1st Top Cow Comics iss. Quesada & Palmiotti's Gabriel app. 27-Quesada & Palmiotti's Ash app. 3.00
Annual 1,2 (3/95, 8/96, $2.50, $2.95) 4.00
NOTE: *Annuals read Volume One in the indica.*

CYBERFORCE (Volume 3)
Image Comics (Top Cow): Apr, 2006 - No. 6, Nov, 2006 ($2.99)

1-6: 1-Pat Lee-a/Ron Marz-s; three covers by Pat Lee, Marc Silvestri and Dave Finch 3.00
#0-(6/06, $2.99) reprints origin story from Image Comics Hardcover Vol. 1 3.00
.../X-Men 1 (1/07, $3.99) Pat Lee-a/Ron Marz-s; 2 covers by Lee and Silvestri 4.00
Vol. 1 TPB (12/06, $14.99) r/#1-6, #0 & story from The Cow Quarterly; cover gallery 15.00

CYBER FORCE (Volume 4)
Image Comics (Top Cow): Dec, 2012 - Present (no cover price/$2.99)

1-11: 1-Silvestri & Hawkins-s/Pham-a; multiple covers on each 3.00
...: Artifacts #0 (12/16, $3.99) Short stories by various; Khoi Pham-c 4.00

CYBERFORCE/HUNTER-KILLER
Image Comics (Top Cow Productions): July, 2009 - No. 5, Mar, 2010 ($2.99)

1-5-Waid-s/Rocafort-a; multiple covers on each 3.00

CYBERFORCE ORIGINS
Image Comics (Top Cow Productions): Jan, 1995 - No. 3, Nov, 1995 ($2.50)

1-Cyblade (1/95) 5.00
1-Cyblade (3/96, 99¢, 2nd printing) 3.00
1A-Exclusive Ed.; Tucci-c 4.00
2,3: 2-Stryker (2/95)-1st Mike Turner-a. 3-Impact 3.00
(#4) Misery (12/95, $2.95) 3.00

CYBERFORCE/STRYKEFORCE: OPPOSING FORCES (See Codename: Stryke Force #15)
Image Comics (Top Cow Productions): Sept, 1995 - No. 2, Oct, 1995 ($2.50, limited series)

1,2: 2-Stryker disbands Strykeforce. 3.00

CYBERFORCE UNIVERSE SOURCEBOOK
Image Comics (Top Cow Productions): Aug, 1994/Feb, 1995 ($2.50)

1,2-Silvestri-c 3.00

CYBERFROG
Hall of Heroes: June, 1994 - No. 2, Dec, 1994 ($2.50, B&W, limited series)

1-Ethan Van Sciver-c/a/scripts	3	6	9	15	22	28
2	2	4	6	8	10	12

CYBERFROG
Harris Comics: Feb, 1996 - No. 3, Apr, 1996 ($2.95)

0-3: Van Sciver-c/a/scripts. 2-Variant-c exists 6.00

CYBERFROG: (Title series), **Harris Comics**

--RESERVOIR FROG, 9/96 - No. 2, 10/96 ($2.95) 1,2: Van Sciver-c/a/scripts; wraparound-c 4.00
--3RD ANNIVERSARY SPECIAL, 1/97 - #2, ($2.50, B&W) 1,2 4.00
--VS. CREED, 7/97 ($2.95, B&W)1 4.00

CYBERNARY (See Deathblow #1)
Image Comics (WildStorm Productions): Nov, 1995 - No.5, Mar, 1996 ($2.50)

1-5 3.00

CYBERNARY 2.0
DC Comics (WildStorm): Sept, 2001 - No. 6, Apr, 2002 ($2.95, limited series)

1-6: Joe Harris-s/Eric Canete-a. 6-The Authority app. 3.00

CYBERPUNK
Innovation Publishing: Sept, 1989 - No. 2, Oct, 1989 ($1.95, 28 pgs.) Book 2, #1, May, 1990 - No. 2, 1990 ($2.25, 28 pgs.)

1,2, Book 2 #1,2:1,2-Ken Steacy painted-covers (Adults) 3.00

CYBERPUNK: THE SERAPHIM FILES
Innovation Publishing: Nov, 1990 - No. 2, Dec, 1990 ($2.50, 28 pgs., mature)

1,2: 1-Painted-c; story cont'd from Seraphim 3.00

CYBERPUNX
Image Comics (Extreme Studios): Mar, 1996 ($2.50)

1 3.00

CYBERRAD
Continuity Comics: 1991 - No. 7, 1992 ($2.00)(Direct sale & newsstand-c variations) V2#1, 1993 ($2.50)

1-7: 5-Glow-in-the-dark-c by N. Adams (direct sale only). 6-Contains 4 pg. fold-out poster; N. Adams layouts 3.00
V2#1-($2.95, direct sale ed.)-Die-cut-c w/B&W hologram on-c; Neal Adams sketches 4.00
V2#1-($2.50, newsstand ed.)-Without sketches 3.00

CYBERRAD DEATHWATCH 2000 (Becomes CyberRad w/#2, 7/93)
Continuity Comics: Apr, 1993 - No. 2, 1993 ($2.50)

1,2: 1-Bagged w/2 cards; Adams-c & layouts & plots. 2-Bagged w/card; Adams scripts 3.00

CYBER 7
Eclipse Comics: Mar, 1989 - #7, Sept, 1989; V2#1, Oct, 1989 - #10, 1990 ($2.00, B&W)

1-7, Book 2 #1-10: Stories translated from Japanese 3.00

CYBLADE
Image Comics (Top Cow Productions): Oct, 2008 - No. 4, Mar, 2009 ($2.99)

1-4: 1,2-Mays-a/Fialkov-s. 1-Two covers. 3,4-Ferguson-a 3.00
.../ Ghost Rider 1 (Marvel/Top Cow, 1/97, $2.95) Devil's Reign pt. 2 4.00
...: Pilot Season 1 (9/07, $2.99) Rick Mays-a 3.00

CYBLADE/SHI (Also see Battle For The Independents & Shi/Cyblade: The Battle For The Independents)
Image Comics (Top Cow Productions): 1995 ($2.95, one-shot)

San Diego Preview	2	4	6	10	14	18
1-($2.95)-1st app. Witchblade	2	4	6	8	10	12
1-($2.95)-variant-c; Tucci-a						5.00

CYBORG (From Justice League)
DC Comics: Sept, 2015 - No. 12, Aug, 2016 ($2.99)

1-12: 1-Walker-s/Reis-a. 3-6-Metal Men app. 9,10-Shazam app. 3.00

CYBORG (DC Rebirth)
DC Comics: Nov, 2016 - Present ($2.99)

1-10: 1-Semper Jr.-s/Pelletier-a; Kilg%re app. 6-Intro. Variant 3.00
...: Rebirth 1 (11/16, $2.99) Semper Jr.-s/Pelletier-a; origin retold 3.00

Cyclone Comics #2 © Bilbara

Dagar, Desert Hawk #16 © FOX

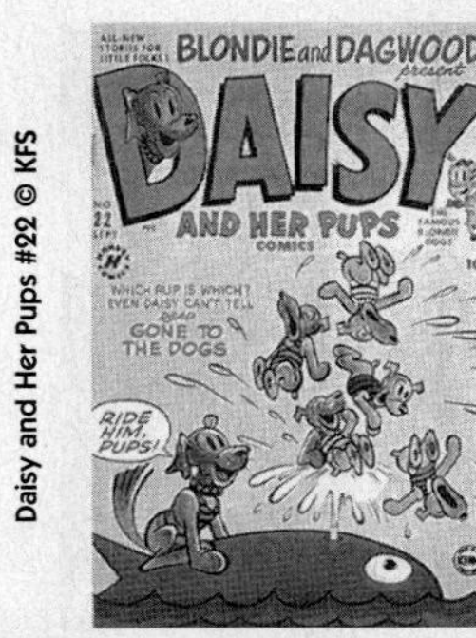

Daisy and Her Pups #22 © KFS

GD 2.0 | VG 4.0 | FN 6.0 | VF 8.0 | VF/NM 9.0 | NM- 9.2

CYBRID
Maximum Press: July, 1995; No. 0, Jan, 1997 ($2.95/$3.50)

1-(7/95) 3.50
0-(1/97)-Liefeld-a/script; story cont'd in Avengelyne #4 3.50

CYCLONE COMICS (Also see Whirlwind Comics)
Bilbara Publishing Co.: June, 1940 - No. 5, Nov, 1940

1-Origin Tornado Tom; Volton (the human generator), Tornado Tom, Kingdom of the Moon, Mister Q begin (1st app. of each) 77 154 231 493 847 1200
2 55 110 165 352 601 850
3-Classic-c (scarce) 123 246 369 787 1344 1900
4-(9/40) 61 122 183 390 670 950
5-(Scarce) 90 180 270 576 988 1400
Ashcan - (5/40) Not distributed to newsstands, only for in house use. Cover produced on green stock paper. A CGC certified FN (6.0) copy sold for $2,000 in 2006.

CYCLOPS (X-Men)
Marvel Comics: Oct, 2001 - No. 4, Jan, 2002 ($2.50, limited series)

1-4-Texeira-c/a. 1,2-Black Tom and Juggernaut app. 3.00
1-(5/11, $2.99, one-shot) Haspiel-a; Batroc and the Circus of Crime app. 3.00

CYCLOPS (All-New X-Men)
Marvel Comics: Jul, 2014 - No. 12, Jun, 2015 ($3.99)

1-10: 1-Rucka-s/Dauterman-a; Corsair app. 6-12-Layman-s. 12-Black Vortex x-over 4.00

CYCLOPS: RETRIBUTION
Marvel Comics: 1994 ($5.95, trade paperback)

nn-r/Marvel Comics Presents #17-24 1 2 3 5 6 8

CY-GOR (See Spawn #38 for 1st app.)
Image Comics (Todd McFarlane Prod.): July, 1999 - No. 6, Dec, 1999 ($2.50)

1-6-Veitch-s 3.00

CYNTHIA DOYLE, NURSE IN LOVE (Formerly Sweetheart Diary)
Charlton Publications: No. 66, Oct, 1962 - No. 74, Feb, 1964

66-74 3 6 9 14 19 24

DAFFODIL
Marvel Comics (Soleil): 2010 - No. 3, 2010 ($5.99, limited series)

1-3-English version of French comic; Brrémaud-s/Rigano-a 6.00

DAFFY (Daffy Duck No. 18 on)(See Looney Tunes)
Dell Publishing Co./Gold Key No. 31-127/Whitman No. 128 on: #457, 3/53 - #30, 7-9/62; #31, 10-12/62 - #145, 6/84 (No #132,133)

Four Color 457(#1)-Elmer Fudd x-overs begin 12 24 36 79 170 260
Four Color 536,615('55) 7 14 21 48 89 130
4(1-3/56)-11('57) 5 10 15 33 57 80
12-19(1958-59) 4 8 12 28 47 65
20-40(1960-64) 3 6 9 20 31 42
41-60(1964-68) 3 6 9 16 23 30
61-90(1969-74)-Road Runner in most. 76-82-"Daffy Duck and the Road Runner" on-c 2 4 6 11 16 20
90-Whitman variant 3 6 9 14 19 24
91-110 2 4 6 8 11 14
111-127 1 3 4 6 8 10
128,134-141: 139(2/82), 140(2-3/82), 141(4/82) 2 4 6 8 10 12
129(8/80),130,131 (pre-pack?) (scarce). 129-Sherlock Holmes parody-s 4 8 12 28 47 65
142-145(#90029 on-c; nd, nd code, pre-pack): 142(6/83), 143(8/83), 144(3/84), 145(6/84) 3 6 9 17 26 35
Mini-Comic 1 (1976; 3-1/4x6-1/2") 1 3 4 6 8 10

NOTE: *Reprint issues-No.41-46, 48, 50, 53-55, 58, 59, 65, 67, 69, 73, 81, 96, 103-108; 136-142, 144, 145(1/3-2/3-r). (See March of Comics No. 277, 288, 303, 313, 331, 347, 357,375, 387, 397, 402, 413, 425, 437, 460).*

DAFFY DUCK (Digest-size reprints from Looney Tunes)
DC Comics: 2005 ($6.99, digest)

Vol. 1: You're Despicable! - Reprints from Looney Tunes #38,43,45,47,51,53,54,58,61,62,66,70 7.00

DAFFY TUNES COMICS
Four-Star Publications: June, 1947; No. 12, Aug, 1947

nn 11 22 33 62 86 110
12-Al Fago-c/a; funny animal 10 20 30 56 76 95

DAGAR, DESERT HAWK (Captain Kidd No. 24 on; formerly All Great)
Fox Features Syndicate: No. 14, Feb, 1948 - No. 23, Apr, 1949 (No #17,18)

14-Tangi & Safari Cary begin; Good bondage-c/a 103 206 309 659 1130 1600
15,16-E. Good-a; 15-Headlight-c 57 114 171 362 619 875
19,20,22: 19-Used in **SOTI**, pg. 180 (Tangi) 53 106 159 334 567 800
21,23: 21-Bondage-c; "Bombs & Bums Away" panel in "Flood of Death" story used in **SOTI**. 23-Bondage-c 55 110 165 352 601 850

NOTE: *Tangi by **Kamen**-14-16, 19, 20; c-20, 21.*

DAGAR THE INVINCIBLE (Tales of Sword & Sorcery...) (Also see Dan Curtis Giveaways & Gold Key Spotlight)
Gold Key: Oct, 1972 - No. 18, Dec, 1976; No. 19, Apr, 1982

1-Origin; intro. Villains Olstellon & Scor 4 8 12 23 37 50
2-5: 3-Intro. Graylin, Dagar's woman; Jarn x-over 3 6 9 14 19 24
6-1st Dark Gods story 2 4 6 9 13 16
7-10: 9-Intro. Torgus. 10-1st Three Witches story 2 4 6 9 13 16
11-18: 13-Durak & Torgus x-over; story continues in Dr. Spektor #15. 14-Dagar's origin retold. 18-Origin retold 2 4 6 8 10 12
19(4/82)-Origin-r/#18 6.00

NOTE: *Durak app. in 7, 12, 13. Tragg app. in 5, 11.*

DAGWOOD (Chic Young's) (Also see Blondie Comics)
Harvey Publications: Sept, 1950 - No. 140, Nov, 1965

1 16 32 48 110 243 375
2 8 16 24 56 108 160
3-10 7 14 21 44 82 120
11-20 5 10 15 35 63 90
21-30 5 10 15 31 53 75
31-50: 33-Sci-Fi-c 4 8 12 28 47 65
51-70 3 6 9 21 33 45
71-100 3 6 9 17 26 35
101-121,123-128,130,135 3 6 9 16 23 30
122,129,131-134,136-140-All are 68-pg. issues 3 6 9 21 33 45

NOTE: *Popeye and other one page strips appeared in early issues.*

DAI KAMIKAZE!
Now Comics: June, 1987 - No. 12, Aug, 1988 ($1.75)

1-1st app. Speed Racer 5.00
1-Second printing 3.00
2-12 3.00

DAILY BUGLE (See Spider-Man)
Marvel Comics: Dec, 1996 - No. 3, Feb, 1997 ($2.50, B&W, limited series)

1-3-Paul Grist-s 3.00

DAISY AND DONALD (See Walt Disney Showcase No. 8)
Gold Key/Whitman No. 42 on: May, 1973 - No. 59, July, 1984 (no No. 48)

1-Barks-r/WDC&S #280,308 3 6 9 21 33 45
2-5: 4-Barks-r/WDC&S #224 2 4 6 11 16 20
6-10 2 4 6 9 12 15
11-20 1 3 4 6 8 10
21-41: 32-r/WDC&S #308 1 2 3 5 6 8
36,42-44 (Whitman) 2 4 6 8 11 14
45 (8/80),46-(pre-pack?)(scarce) 4 8 12 27 44 60
47-(12/80)-Only distr. in Whitman 3-pack (scarce) 5 10 15 35 63 90
48(3/81)-50(8/81): 50-r/#3 2 4 6 10 14 18
51-54: 51-Barks-r/4-Color #1150. 52-r/#2. 53(2/82), 54(4/82) 2 4 6 9 13 16
55-59-(all #90284 on-c, nd, nd code, pre-pack): 55(5/83), 56(7/83), 57(8/83), 58(8/83), 59(7/84) 3 6 9 19 30 40

DAISY & HER PUPS (Dagwood & Blondie's Dogs)(Formerly Blondie Comics #20)
Harvey Publications: No. 21, 7/51 - No. 27, 7/52; No. 8, 9/52 - No. 18, 5/54

21 (#1)-Blondie's dog Daisy and her 5 pups led by Elmer begin. Rags Rabbit app. 5 10 15 35 63 90
22-27 (#2-7): 26 has No. 6 on cover but No. 26 on inside. 23,25-The Little King app. 24-Bringing Up Father by McManus app. 25-27-Rags Rabbit app. 4 8 12 27 44 60
8-18: 8,9-Rags Rabbit app. 8,17-The Little King app. 11-The Flop Family Swan begins. 22-Cookie app. 11-Felix The Cat app. by 17,18-Popeye app. 4 8 12 25 40 55

DAISY DUCK & UNCLE SCROOGE PICNIC TIME (See Dell Giant #33)

DAISY DUCK & UNCLE SCROOGE SHOW BOAT (See Dell Giant #55)

DAISY DUCK'S DIARY (See Dynabrite Comics, & Walt Disney's C&S #298)
Dell Publishing Co.: No. 600, Nov, 1954 - No. 1247, Dec-Fef, 1961-62 (Disney)

Four Color 600 (#1) 8 16 24 51 96 140
Four Color 659, 743 (11/56) 6 12 18 40 73 105
Four Color 858 (11/57), 948 (11/58), 1247 (12-2/61-62) 5 10 15 35 63 90
Four Color 1055 (11-1/59-60), 1150 (12-1/60-61)-By Carl Barks 8 16 24 56 108 160

Daken: Dark Wolverine #1 © MAR

Damsels #8 © DYN

Danger #3 © Comic Media

	GD 2.0	VG 4.0	FN 6.0	VF 8.0	VF/NM 9.0	NM- 9.2

DAISY HANDBOOK
Daisy Manufacturing Co.: 1946; No. 2, 1948 (10¢, pocket-size, 132 pgs.)

1-Buck Rogers, Red Ryder; Wolverton-a (2 pgs.)	21	42	63	122	199	275
2-Captain Marvel & Ibis the Invincible, Red Ryder, Boy Commandos & Robotman; Wolverton-a (2 pgs.); contains 8 pg. color catalog	21	42	63	122	199	275

DAISY MAE (See Oxydol-Dreft)

DAISY'S RED RYDER GUN BOOK
Daisy Manufacturing Co.: 1955 (25¢, pocket-size, 132 pgs.)

nn-Boy Commandos, Red Ryder; 1pg. Wolverton-a	15	30	45	85	130	175

DAKEN: DARK WOLVERINE
Marvel Comics: Nov, 2010 - No. 23, May, 2012 ($3.99/$2.99)

1-Camuncoli-a/c; Way & Liu-s; back-up history of the character 4.00
2-9, 9.1, 10-23-($2.99) 3,4-Fantastic Four app. 7-9-Crossover with X-23 #8,9; Gambit app. 9.1-Avengers app. 13-16-Moon Knight app. 17-19-Runaways app. 3.00

DAKKON BLACKBLADE ON THE WORLD OF MAGIC: THE GATHERING
Acclaim Comics (Armada): June, 1996 ($5.95, one-shot)

1-Jerry Prosser scripts; Rags Morales-c/a. 6.00

DAKOTA LIL (See Fawcett Movie Comics)

DAKTARI (Ivan Tors) (TV)
Dell Publishing Co.: July, 1967 - No. 3, Oct, 1968; No. 4, Oct, 1969

1-Marshall Thompson photo-c on all	4	8	12	23	37	50
2-4	3	6	9	17	26	35

DALE EVANS COMICS (Also see Queen of the West...)(See Boy Commandos #32)
National Periodical Publications: Sept-Oct, 1948 - No. 24, Jul-Aug, 1952 (No. 1-19: 52 pgs.)

1-Dale Evans & her horse Buttermilk begin; Sierra Smith begins by Alex Toth	58	116	174	371	636	900
2-Alex Toth-a	30	60	90	177	289	400
3-11-Alex Toth-a	20	40	60	114	182	250
12-20: 12-Target-c	14	28	42	80	115	150
21-24	14	28	42	82	121	160

NOTE: *Photo-c-1, 2, 4-14.*

DALGODA
Fantagraphics Books: Aug, 1984 - No. 8, Feb, 1986 (High quality paper)

1,8: 1- Fujitake-c/a in all. 8-Alan Moore story 4.00
2-7: 2,3-Debut Grimwood's Daughter. 3.00

DALTON BOYS, THE
Avon Periodicals: 1951

1-(Number on spine)-Kinstler-c	20	40	60	114	182	250

DAMAGE
DC Comics: Apr, 1994 - No. 20, Jan, 1996 ($1.75/$1.95/$2.25)

1-20: 6-(9/94)-Zero Hour. 0-(10/94). 7-(11/94). 14-Ray app. 3.00

DAMAGE CONTROL (See Marvel Comics Presents #19)
Marvel Comics: 5/89 - No. 4, 8/89; V2#1, 12/89 - No. 4, 2/90 ($1.00)
V3#1, 6/91 - No. 4, 9/91 ($1.25, all are limited series)

V1#1-4,V2#1-4,V3#1-4: V1#4-Wolverine app. V2#2,4-Punisher app. 1-Spider-Man app. 2-New Warriors app. 3,4-Silver Surfer app. 4-Infinity Gauntlet parody 3.00

DAMAGED
Radical Comics: Jul, 2011 - No. 6 ($3.99/$3.50, limited series)

1-($3.99) Lapham-s/Manco-a; covers by Maleev & Manco 4.00
2-4-($3.50) Maleev-c 3.50

DAMIAN: SON OF BATMAN
DC Comics: Dec, 2013 - No. 4, Mar, 2014 ($3.99, limited series)

1-4-Andy Kubert-s/c/a; near-future Damian; Ra's al Ghul & Talia app. 4.00
1-Variant-c by Tony Daniel 8.00

DAMNED
Image Comics (Homage Comics): June, 1997 - No. 4, Sept, 1997 ($2.50, limited series)

1-4-Steven Grant-s/Mike Zeck-c/a in all 3.00

DAMN NATION
Dark Horse Comics: Feb, 2005 - No. 3, Apr, 2005 ($2.99, limited series)

1-3-J. Alexander-a/Andrew Cosby-s 3.00

DAMSELS
Dynamite Entertainment: 2012 - No. 13, 2014 ($3.99)

1-13: 1-Leah Moore & John Reppion-s/Aneke-a. 1-Campbell-c. 2-8-Linsner-c 4.00
... Giant Killer One Shot (2013, $4.99) Leah Moore & John Reppion-s/Dietrich Smith-a 5.00

	GD 2.0	VG 4.0	FN 6.0	VF 8.0	VF/NM 9.0	NM- 9.2

DAMSELS IN EXCESS
Aspen MLT: Jul, 2014 - No. 5, May, 2015 ($3.99, limited series)

1-5-Vince Hernandez-s/Mirka Andolfo-a; multiple covers on each 4.00

DAMSELS: MERMAIDS
Dynamite Entertainment: No. 0, 2013 - No. 5, 2013 ($3.99)

0-Free Comic Book Day giveaway; Sturges-s/Deshong-a/Hans-c 3.00
1-5-($3.99) Sturges-s/Deshong-a. 1-Two covers by Anacleto & Renaud. 2-5-Renaud-c 4.00

DANCES WITH DEMONS (See Marvel Frontier Comics Unlimited)
Marvel Frontier Comics: Sept, 1993 - No. 4, Dec, 1993 ($1.95, limited series)

1-($2.95)-Foil embossed-c; Charlie Adlard & Rod Ramos-a 4.00
2-4 3.00

DAN DARE
Virgin Comics: Nov, 2007 - No. 7, July, 2008 ($2.99/$5.99)

1-6-Ennis-s/Erskine-a. 1-Two covers by Talbot and Horn. 2-6-Two covers on each 3.00
7-($5.99) Double sized finale with wraparound Erskine-c; Gibbons variant-c 6.00

DANDEE: Four Star Publications: 1947 (Advertised, not published)

DAN DUNN (See Crackajack Funnies, Detective Dan, Famous Feature Stories & Red Ryder)

DANDY COMICS (Also see Happy Jack Howard)
E. C. Comics: Spring, 1947 - No. 7, Spring, 1948

1-Funny animal; Vince Fago-a in all; Dandy in all	45	90	135	284	480	675
2	32	64	96	192	314	435
3-7: 3-Intro Handy Andy who is c-feature #3 on	27	54	81	158	259	360

DANGER
Comic Media/Allen Hardy Assoc.: Jan, 1953 - No. 11, Aug, 1954

1-Heck-c/a	34	68	102	199	325	450
2,3,5,7,9-11:	18	36	54	107	169	230
4-Marijuana cover/story	21	42	63	124	202	280
6- "Narcotics" story; begin spy theme	20	40	60	114	182	250
8-Bondage/torture/headlights panels	22	44	66	128	209	290

NOTE: ***Morisi** a-2, 5, 6(3), 10; c-2. Contains some reprints from Danger & Dynamite.*

DANGER (Formerly Comic Media title)
Charlton Comics Group: No. 12, June, 1955 - No. 14, Oct, 1955

12(#1)	14	28	42	80	115	150
13,14: 14-r/#12	11	22	33	62	86	110

DANGER
Super Comics: 1964

Super Reprint #10-12 (Black Dwarf; #10-r/Great Comics #1 by Novack. #11-r/Johnny Danger #1. #12-r/Red Seal #14), #15-r/Spy Cases #26. #16-Unpublished Chesler material (Yankee Girl), #17-r/Scoop #8 (Capt. Courage & Enchanted Dagger), #18(nd)-r/Guns Against Gangsters #5 (Gun-Master, Annie Oakley, The Chameleon; L.B. Cole-r)	2	4	6	11	16	20

DANGER AND ADVENTURE (Formerly This Magazine Is Haunted; Robin Hood and His Merry Men No. 28 on)
Charlton Comics: No. 22, Feb, 1955 - No. 27, Feb, 1956

22-Ibis the Invincible-c/story (last G.A. app.); Nyoka app.; last pre-code issue	11	22	33	62	86	110
23-Lance O'Casey-c/sty; Nyoka app.; Ditko-a thru #27	13	26	39	72	101	130
24-27: 24-Mike Danger & Johnny Adventure begin	9	18	27	50	65	80

DANGER GIRL (Also see Cliffhanger #0)
Image Comics (Cliffhanger Productions): Mar, 1998 - No. 4, Dec, 1998;
DC Comics (Cliffhanger Prod.): No. 5, July, 1999 - No. 7, Feb, 2001

Preview-Bagged in DV8 #14 Voyager Pack						4.00
Preview Gold Edition						10.00
1-($2.95) Hartnell & Campbell-s/Campbell/Garner-a	1	2	3	5	6	8
1-($4.95) Chromium cover						50.00
1-American Entertainment Ed.						8.00
1-American Entertainment Gold Ed., 1-Tourbook edition						12.00
1-"Danger-sized" ed.; over-sized format	3	6	9	16	24	32
2-($2.50)						4.00
2-Smoking Gun variant cover	4	8	12	25	40	55
2-Platinum Ed.	5	10	15	33	57	80
2-Dynamic Forces Omnichrome variant-c	2	4	6	10	14	18
2-Gold foil cover						9.00
2-Ruby red foil cover	12	24	36	79	170	260
3,4: 3-c by Campbell, Charest and Adam Hughes. 4-Big knife variant-c						3.00
3,5: 3-Gold foil cover. 5-DF Bikini variant-c						5.00
4-6						3.00

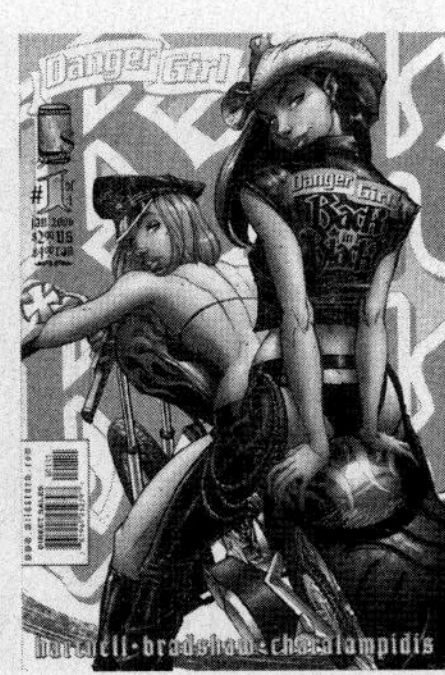

Danger Girl: Back in Black #1 © JSC

Danger Unlimited #1 © DH

Daomu #1 © Concept Art House

GD 2.0 | VG 4.0 | FN 6.0 | VF 8.0 | VF/NM 9.0 | NM- 9.2

GD 2.0 | VG 4.0 | FN 6.0 | VF 8.0 | VF/NM 9.0 | NM- 9.2

7-($5.95) Wraparound gatefold-c; Last issue 6.00
...: Danger-Sized Treasury Edition #1 (IDW, 1/12, $9.99, 13" x 8-1/2") r/#1,2 & Preview 10.00
...: Hawaiian Punch (5/03, $4.95) Campbell-c; Phil Noto-a 5.00
...: Odd Jobs TPB (2004, $14.95) r/one-shots Hawaiian Punch, Viva Las Danger & Special; Campbell-c 15.00
San Diego Preview (8/98, B&W) flip book w/Wildcats preview 5.00
Sketchbook (2001, $6.95) Campbell-a; sketches for comics, toys, games 7.00
...Special (2/00, $3.50) art by Campbell, Chiodo, and Art Adams 3.50
... 3-D #1 (4/03, $4.95, bagged with 3-D glasses) r/ Preview & #1 in 3-D 5.00
...: Viva Las Danger (1/04, $4.95) Noto-a/Campbell-c 5.00
... :The Dangerous Collection nn (8/98; r-#1) 6.00
... :The Dangerous Collection 2,3: 2-(11/98, $5.95) r/#2,3. 3-('99) r/#4,5 6.00
... :The Dangerous Collection nn, 2-($10.00) Gold foil logo 10.00
... :The Ultimate Collection HC ($29.95) r/#1-7; intro by Bruce Campbell 30.00
... :The Ultimate Collection SC ($19.95) r/#1-7; intro by Bruce Campbell 20.00

DANGER GIRL AND THE ARMY OF DARKNESS
Dynamite Entertainment/ IDW Publ.: 2011 - No. 6, 2012 ($3.99, limited series)

1-6-Hartnell-s/Bolson-a. 1,2 Covers by Campbell, Bradshaw & Renaud 4.00

DANGER GIRL: BACK IN BLACK
DC Comics (Cliffhanger): Jan, 2006 - No. 4, Apr, 2006 ($2.99, limited series)

1-4-Hartnell-s/Bradshaw-a. 1-Campbell-c 3.00
TPB (2007, $12.99) r/series & covers 13.00

DANGER GIRL: BODY SHOTS
DC Comics (WildStorm): Jun, 2007 - No. 4, Sept, 2007 ($2.99, limited series)

1-4-Hartnell-s/Bradshaw-a 3.00
TPB (2007, $12.99) r/series & covers 13.00

DANGER GIRL/ G.I. JOE
IDW Publishing: Jul, 2012 - No. 5, Nov, 2012 ($3.99, limited series)

1-5-Hartnell-s/Royle-a; 2 covers by Campbell on each 4.00

DANGER GIRL KAMIKAZE
DC Comics (Cliffhanger): Nov, 2001 - No. 2, Dec., 2001 ($2.95, lim. series)

1,2-Tommy Yune-s/a 3.00

DANGER GIRL: MAYDAY
IDW Publishing: Apr, 2014 - No. 4, Aug, 2014 ($3.99, limited series)

1-4-Hartnell-s/Royle-a; 2 covers by Royle on each 4.00

DANGER GIRL: RENEGADE
IDW Publishing: Sept, 2015 - No. 4, Jan, 2016 ($3.99, limited series)

1-4-Hartnell-s/Molnar-a/Campbell-c 4.00

DANGER GIRL: REVOLVER
IDW Publishing: Jan, 2012 - No. 4, Apr, 2012 ($3.99, limited series)

1-4-Hartnell-s/Madden-a; covers by Campbell & Madden 4.00

DANGER GIRL: THE CHASE
IDW Publishing: Sept, 2013 - No. 4, Dec, 2013 ($3.99, limited series)

1-4-Hartnell-s/Tolibao-a. 1-Three covers (Panosian, Wallace & photo) 4.00

DANGER GIRL: TRINITY
IDW Publishing: Apr, 2013 - No. 4, Jul, 2013 ($3.99, limited series)

1-4-Hartnell-s/Campbell-c; art by Royle, Tolibao, & Molnar. 1-Variant-c by Garner 4.00

DANGER IS OUR BUSINESS!
Toby Press: 1953(Dec.) - No. 10, June, 1955

1-Captain Comet by Williamson/Frazetta-a, 6 pgs. (science fiction) 50 100 150 315 533 750
2 15 30 45 85 130 175
3-10 14 28 42 76 108 140
I.W. Reprint #9('64)-Williamson/Frazetta-r/#1; Kinstler-c 8 16 24 51 96 140

DANGER IS THEIR BUSINESS (Also see A-1 Comic)
Magazine Enterprises: No. 50, 1952

A-1 50-Powell-a 15 30 45 83 124 165

DANGER MAN (TV)
Dell Publishing Co.: No. 1231, Sept-Nov, 1961

Four Color 1231-Patrick McGoohan photo-c 10 20 30 66 138 210

DANGER TRAIL (Also see Showcase #50, 51)
National Periodical Publ.: July-Aug, 1950 - No. 5, Mar-Apr, 1951 (52 pgs.)

1-King Faraday begins, ends #4; Toth-a in all 139 278 417 883 1517 2150
2 95 190 285 603 1039 1475
3-(Rare) one of the rarest early '50s DCs 155 310 465 992 1696 2400
4,5: 5-Johnny Peril-c/story (moves to Sensation Comics #107); new logo (also see Comic Cavalcade #15-29) 73 146 219 467 796 1125

DANGER TRAIL
DC Comics: Apr, 1993 - No. 4, July, 1993 ($1.50, limited series)

1-4: Gulacy-c on all 3.00

DANGER UNLIMITED (See San Diego Comic Con Comics #2 & Torch of Liberty Special)
Dark Horse (Legend): Feb, 1994 - No. 4, May, 1994 ($2.00, limited series)

1-4: Byrne-c/a/scripts in all; origin stories of both original team (Doc Danger, Thermal, Miss Mirage, & Hunk) & future team (Thermal, Belebet, & Caucus). 1-Intro Torch of Liberty & Golgotha (cameo) in back-up story. 4-Hellboy & Torch of Liberty cameo in lead story 3.00
TPB (1995, $14.95)-r/#1-4; includes last pg. originally cut from #4 15.00

DAN HASTINGS (See Syndicate Features)

DANIEL BOONE (See The Exploits of..., Fighting... Frontier Scout...,The Legends of... & March of Comics No. 306)
Dell Publishing Co.: No. 1163, Mar-May, 1961

Four Color 1163-Marsh-a 5 10 15 35 63 90

DANIEL BOONE (TV) (See March of Comics No. 306)
Gold Key: Jan, 1965 - No. 15, Apr, 1969 (All have Fess Parker photo-c)

1-Back-c and last eight pages fold in half to form "Official Handbook Fess Parker as Daniel Boone Trail Blazers Club" 7 14 21 48 89 130
2-Back-c pin-up 5 10 15 30 50 70
3-5-Back-c pin-ups 4 8 12 25 40 55
6-15: 7,8-Back-c pin-up 3 6 9 19 30 40

DAN'L BOONE
Sussex Publ. Co.: Sept, 1955 - No. 8, Sept, 1957

1 14 28 42 80 115 150
2 10 20 30 54 72 90
3-8 8 16 24 40 50 60

DANNY BLAZE (...Firefighter) (Nature Boy No. 3 on)
Charlton Comics: Aug, 1955 - No. 2, Oct, 1955

1-Authentic stories of fire fighting 13 26 39 74 105 135
2 9 18 27 50 65 80

DANNY DINGLE (See Sparkler Comics)
United Features Syndicate: No. 17, 1940

Single Series 17 28 56 84 165 270 375

DANNY THOMAS SHOW, THE (TV)
Dell Publishing Co.: No. 1180, Apr-June, 1961 - No. 1249, Dec-Feb, 1961-62

Four Color 1180-Toth-a, photo-c 13 26 39 89 195 300
Four Color 1249-Manning-a, photo-c 12 24 36 80 173 265

DANTE
Image Comics (Top Cow): Jan, 2017 - Present ($5.99)

1-Matt Hawkins-s/Darick Robertson-a/c 6.00

DANTE'S INFERNO (Based on the video game)
DC Comics (WildStorm): Feb, 2010 - No. 6, Jul, 2010 ($3.99, limited series)

1-6-Christos Gage-s/Diego Latorre-a 4.00
TPB (2010, $19.99) r/#1-6 20.00

DAOMU (Based on a novel series from China)
Image Comics: Feb, 2011 - No. 8, Dec, 2011 ($2.99)

1-8-Kennedy Xu-s/Ken Chou-a 3.00

DARBY O'GILL & THE LITTLE PEOPLE (Movie)(See Movie Comics)
Dell Publishing Co.: 1959 (Disney)

Four Color 1024-Toth-a; photo-c. 9 18 27 57 111 165

DAREDEVIL ("Daredevil Comics" on cover of #2) (See Silver Streak Comics)
Lev Gleason Publications (Funnies, Inc. No. 1): July, 1941 - No. 134, Sept, 1956 (52 pgs. #52-80; 64 pgs. #35-41)(Charles Biro stories)

1-No. 1 titled "Dardedevil Battles Hitler," Classic battle issue as Daredevil teams up in each strip - The Silver Streak, Lance Hale, Cloud Curtis, Dickey Dean & Pirate Prince to battle Hitler; The Claw unites with Hitler and Japanese and battles Daredevil; Origin of Hitler feature story "The Man of Hate." Classic Hitler photo app. on-c 1275 2550 3825 9500 16,750 24,000
2-London (by Jerry Robinson), Pat Patriot (by Reed Crandall), Nightro, Real American No. 1 (by Briefer #2-11), Dash Dillon, Whirlwind begin; Dickie Dean, Pirate Prince end; intro. & only app. Pioneer, Champion of America & Times Square. The Claw

Daredevil #17 © LEV

Daredevil #63 © LEV

Daredevil #10 © MAR

	GD 2.0	VG 4.0	FN 6.0	VF 8.0	VF/NM 9.0	NM- 9.2
continues #2-4	383	766	1149	2681	4691	6700
3-Intro./origin of 13. Newspaper editor has name "Roussos." Daredevil battles the Claw ill. text story	258	516	774	1651	2826	4000
4-The Claw captured and taken to New York Central Park Zoo. Whirlwind, the Blond Bomber begins, ends #6	219	438	657	1402	2401	3400
5-Ghost vs. Claw begins by Bob Wood, ends #20; 13 & Jinx begin; origin 13 retold in text; intro./origin Jinx, 13's sidekick; intro. Sniffer in Daredevil	181	362	543	1158	1979	2800
6-(12/41)-Daredevil battles wolf with human brain. Dash Dillon ends	161	322	483	1030	1765	2500
7,9: 7-(2/42), shows #6 on cover; delayed one month due to Pearl Harbor attack. 9-Daredevil vs. Daredevil-c; Sniffer strip begins, ends #69	119	238	357	762	1306	1850
8-Nazi WWII war-c. Nightro ends. Sniffer/Daredevil fight Nazi insurgents;	129	258	387	826	1413	2000
10-(5-42), "Remember Pearl Harbor" Japanese WWII-c; classic splash page w/American flag. Daredevil joins Air Corps. to fight Japanese. Ghost Battles Claw & Japanese. Last Whirlwind	161	322	483	1030	1765	2500
11-Classic Quasimodo (hunchback of Notre Dame) bondage/torture-c/sty. London, Pat Patriot, Real America #1 end	460	920	1380	2944	4622	6300
12-Origin of The Claw; Scoop Scuttle by Wolverton begins (2-4 pgs.), ends #22, not in #21. Charles Biro biography. Dickey Dean, Pirate Prince return (both end #32)	139	278	417	883	1517	2150
13-Intro of Little Wise Guys (10/42)(also see Boy #4); Daredevil fights Nazi hooded cult; Ghost battles Claw, Hitler & Nazis in Britain; Bob Wood biography	108	216	324	686	1181	1675
14-Classic Daredevil facial portrait-c; Hitler app.; "Slap the Jap" game included	87	174	261	553	952	1350
15-Death of Meatball	107	214	321	680	1165	1650
16-WWII-c w/freighter hit by German torpedo. Meatball is buried & Curly joins Little Wise Guys team	79	158	237	502	864	1225
17-Little Wise Guys hanging and beating Japanese soldiers on cover	129	258	387	826	1413	2000
18-New origin of Daredevil (not same as Silver Streak #6). Hitler, Mussolini Tojo and Mickey Mouse app. on-c at carnival	129	258	387	826	1413	2000
19,20: Last Ghost vs. Claw	65	130	195	416	708	1000
21-Reprints cover of Silver Streak #6 (on inside) plus intro. of The Claw from Silver Streak #1. The Claw strip begins by Bob Q. Siege, ends #31	84	168	252	538	919	1300
22,23: 22-Daredevil fights the Tramp. 23-Dickie Dean by Bob Montana	46	92	138	290	488	685
24-Bloody puppet show-c	53	106	159	334	567	800
25-1st Little Wise Guys-c without Daredevil	37	74	111	222	361	500
26,28-30	41	82	123	256	428	600
27-Bondage/torture-c	97	194	291	621	1061	1500
31-Death of The Claw	84	168	252	538	919	1300
32-34: 32,33-Egbert app. 33-Roger Wilco begins, ends #35	34	68	102	206	336	465
35-37,39-41: 35-Two Daredevil stories begin, end #68; Chauncey app. 37-39-Go Along Gallagher app. (#35-41 are 64 pgs.); 41-Dickie Dean ends	36	72	108	216	351	485
38-Origin Daredevil retold from #18	47	94	141	296	498	700
42-Intro. Kilroy in Daredevil who unveils Daredevil's I.D.-c/sty	31	62	93	182	296	410
43-45,47,48-All Daredevil-c. 43-Daredevil in costume on-c & 1 panel only inside; 44-DD back in costume; i.d. revealed on-c.	29	58	87	172	281	390
46,50: DD not on-c	24	48	72	142	234	325
49-Wise Guys fight secret hooded group c/sty. DD not on-c	29	58	87	172	281	390
51,52,56-60,63-66,68,69-Last Daredevil & Sniffer (12/50). 56-Wise Guys start their own circus. DD not on-c	20	40	60	115	185	255
53-Daredevil/Wise Guys find lost palace of Zanzarah, an underground Egyptian tomb w/mummy & treasure; classic c/story. DD-c	22	44	66	128	209	290
54,55-Daredevil-c	21	42	63	124	202	280
61-Daredevil & Wise Guys in haunted house classic c/story. Daredevil/Wise Guys fly rocket into stratosphere. DD not on-c	22	44	66	128	209	290
62-Wise Guys in medieval times, a dream by Peewee locked in a medieval museum; classic c/story. DD not on-c	22	44	66	128	209	290
67-Last Daredevil-c	21	42	63	124	202	280
70-Little Wise Guys take over book without Daredevil. Daredevil removed from-c & logo; Air Devils w/Hot Rock Flanagan begins, ends #80	14	28	42	80	115	150
71-78,81: 81-Dilly Duncan begins, ends #134	11	22	33	60	83	105
79,80: 79-(10/51)-Daredevil returns; Wise Guys go to Africa. 80-Daredevil & Wise Guys blast into space & land on Mars; last Daredevil app. in title	12	24	36	69	97	125
82,90: One pg. Frazetta ad in both	11	22	33	60	83	105
83-89,91-99,101-134	10	20	30	56	76	95
100-(7/53)	12	24	36	69	97	125

NOTE: ***Biro** a-1-22, 38; c-1-134; script-1-134. **Dan Barry** a(Daredevil) 40-48; **Roy Belft**-a (Daredevil) 49-55. **Bolle** a-125. **Al Borth**-a(Daredevil) #57-59. **Briefer** a-1-11 (Real American #1); Pirate Prince-#1, 2, 12-31. **Tony Dipreta**-a(Wise Guys) #108-110, 112-134. **R.W. Hall** a-22. **Carl Hubbell** a-9-21, 23-26, 27(Daredevil), 28-32. **Al Mandel** a-13. **Hy Mankin**-a(Wise Guys)-#80, 81. **Maurer**-a(Daredevil)-23, 31, 37, 38, 41, 43-51, 53-67, 69; (Little Wise Guys)-70-89. **McWilliams** a-70, 73-80. **Bob Montana** a-12, 23, 27, 28, 31-33. **Wm. Overgard**-a(Daredevil) #67, (Wise Guys) 74-79, 83-85, 87. **Jerry Robinson** a(London) #2-8. **Roussos** a(Nightro)-2-8. **Bob Q. Siege**-a(Claw) 27-31; (Daredevil)-#35. **Wolverton** a-12-22. **Bob Wood**-a(The Claw)-1-20; (The Ghost)-5-20. **Dick Wood** sty-2-10, 13-22, 27-32. **Daredevil** not on-c #46,49-52,56-66,68-134.*

DAREDEVIL (...& the Black Widow #92-107 on-c only; see Giant-Size...,Marvel Advs., Marvel Graphic Novel #24, Marvel Super Heroes, '66 & Spider-Man &...)
Marvel Comics Group: Apr, 1964 - No. 380, Oct, 1998

	GD 2.0	VG 4.0	FN 6.0	VF 8.0	VF/NM 9.0	NM- 9.2
1-Origin/1st app. Daredevil; intro Foggy Nelson & Karen Page; death of Battling Murdock; Bill Everett-c/a; reprinted in Marvel Super Heroes #1 (1966)	500	1000	1500	3500	7000	10,500
2-Fantastic Four cameo; 2nd app. Electro (Spidey villain); Thing guest star	71	142	213	568	1284	2000
3-Origin & 1st app. The Owl (villain)	41	82	123	303	689	1075
4-Origin & 1st app. The Purple Man	36	72	108	266	596	925
5-Minor costume change; Wood-a begins	28	56	84	196	441	685
6-Mr. Fear app.	20	40	60	138	307	475
7-Daredevil battles Sub-Mariner & dons red costume for 1st time (4/65); Marvel Masterwork pin-up by Wood	77	154	231	616	1383	2150
8-10: 8-Origin/1st app. Stilt Man. 10-1st app. Cat Man, Bird Man, Ape Man & Frog Man	15	30	45	103	227	350
11-15: 11-Last Wally Wood. 12-1st app. Plunderer; Ka-Zar app. Kirby/Romita-a begins. 13-Facts about Ka-Zar's origin; vs. the Plunderer; Kirby/Romita-a. 14-Romita-a begins; Ka-Zar & the Plunderer app. 15-1st app. the Ox	10	20	30	66	138	210
16,17- Spider-Man x-over. 16-1st Romita-a on Spider-Man (5/66)	19	38	57	131	291	450
18-Origin & 1st app. Gladiator	10	20	30	69	147	225
19,20: 19-DD vs. the Gladiator. 20-DD vs. the Owl; 1st Gene Colan-a	8	16	24	56	108	160
21-26,28-30: 21-DD vs. the Owl. 22-DD vs. the Owl, Gladiator & and Masked Marauder; 1st app the Tri-Man. 23-Owl, Gladiator, Masked Marauder & Tri-Man app. 24-Ka-Zar app. 25-1st app. Leap-Frog; 1st app. 'Mike Murdock' Daredevil's fake twin brother. 26-Stilt-Man app. 30-Thor app. vs. Cobra and Mr. Hyde	6	12	18	41	76	110
27-Spider-Man x-over; Stilt-Man & the Masked Marauder app.	7	14	21	48	89	150
31-36,39,40: 31,32-DD vs. Cobra & Mr. Hyde. 33,34-DD vs. the Beetle. 35-DD vs. the Trapster. 36-DD vs. the Trapster; Dr. Doom cameo. 39-1st app. Exterminator (later becomes Death-Stalker); Ape Man, Cat Man & Bird Man app. as the Unholy Three. 40-DD vs. the Unholy Three	6	12	18	37	66	95
37,38: 37-Daredevil vs. Dr. Doom. 38-Dr. Doom app; Fantastic Four x-over; continued in Fantastic Four #73	6	12	18	41	76	110
41,42-44-49: 41- 'Death' of Mike Murdock; Daredevil drops the fake twin persona; DD vs. the Exterminator and the Unholy Three. 42-1st app. Jester. 44-46-DD vs. the Jester. 48-DD vs. Stilt-Man. 49-1st app. Star Saxon & the Plastoid	5	10	15	34	60	85
43-Daredevil vs. Captain America; origin partially retold; Kirby-c	8	16	24	56	108	160
50-51,53: 50-Barry Smith-a; last Stan Lee-s; vs. Star Saxon & the Plastoid. 51-1st Roy Thomas-s; Barry Smith-a; vs. Star Saxon & the Plastoid. 53-Gene Colan-a returns; origin retold	5	10	15	35	63	90
52-Barry Smith-a; Black Panther app.; learns Daredevil's secret identity	6	12	18	41	76	110
54-56,58-60: 54-Spider-Man cameo; vs. Mr. Fear. 55-DD vs. Mr. Fear. 56-1st app. Death's Head (Star Saxon) (9/69); story continued in #57. 58-1st app. Stunt-Master. 59-1st app. Torpedo (dies this issue)	4	8	12	27	44	60
57-Reveals i.d. to Karen Page; Death's Head app.	6	12	18	37	66	95
61,63-68,70-72,74-76,78-80: 61-DD vs. the Jester, Cobra & Mr. Hyde. 63-vs. Gladiator. 64-Stunt-Master app. 67-Stilt-Man app. 71-Last Roy Thomas-s. 72-1st app Tagak 'Lord of Leopards'; 1st Gerry Conway-s. 75-1st app. El Condor. 76-Death El Condor. 78-1st app. Man-Bull. 79-DD vs. Man-Bull. 80-vs the Owl	4	8	12	23	37	50
62,69,73: 62-Origin of Nighthawk (Kyle Richmond). 69-Black Panther app. 73-Continued from Iron Man #35; Nick Fury app. vs. the Zodiac; concluded in Iron Man #36.	4	8	12	27	44	60
77-Spider-Man & Sub-Mariner app.; story continues in Sub-Mariner #40	5	10	15	30	50	70
81-(52 pgs.)-Black Widow becomes regular guest star (11/71); receives co-billing w/issue #92 through issue #107; vs. Mr. Kline and the Owl	8	12	18	38	69	125
82,84-87,89-98: 82-DD vs. Mr. Kline. 84-Conclusion of the Mr. Kline story; see Iron Man #41-45 & Sub-Mariner #42. 85-DD vs. Gladiator. 86-Death of the Ox.						

Daredevil #111 © MAR

Daredevil #200 © MAR

Daredevil #319 © MAR

GD VG FN VF VF/NM NM-
2.0 4.0 6.0 8.0 9.0 9.2

GD VG FN VF VF/NM NM-
2.0 4.0 6.0 8.0 9.0 9.2

87-Daredevil & the Black Widow relocate to San Francisco; Electro app. 89-Purple Man & Electro app. 90-Mr. Fear app. 91-Death of Mr. Fear. 92-Black Widow gets co-billing as of this issue. 93,94-DD vs. the Indestructible Man. 95,96-DD vs. the Man-Bull. 97-99-DD vs. the Dark Messiah; Steve Gerber co-script; 98-Last Conway-s 3 6 9 19 30 40

83,99: 83-Barry Smith layouts/Weiss-p. 99-Hawkeye app; Steve Gerber-s begin; plot continues in Avengers #111 3 6 9 21 33 45

88-Purple Man app; early life of Black Widow revealed 4 8 12 23 37 50

100-1st app. Angar the Screamer; origin retold; Jann Wenner, editor of Rolling Stone app. 4 8 12 28 47 65

101,102,104,106,108-110: 101-vs Angar the Screamer. 102-vs. Stilt Man. 104-Kraven the Hunter app. 106-Moondragon app; vs. Terrex. 108-Title returns to 'Daredevil'. Moondragon app.; 1st app. Black Spectre; Beetle app; Daredevil and Black Widow break-up. 109-Shanna the She-Devil app.; vs. Nekra & Black Spectre; story continues in Marvel Two-in-One #3. 110-Continued from Marvel Two-in-One #3; vs. the Mandrill, Nekra & Black Spectre; brief Thing app. 3 6 9 16 23 30

103-1st app. & origin of Ramrod; Spider-Man app. 3 6 9 19 30 40

105-Origin of Moondragon by Starlin (12/73) Thanos cameo in flashback (early app.) 5 10 15 35 63 90

107-Starlin-c; Thanos cameo; Moondragon & Captain Marvel app; death of Terrex 3 6 9 17 26 35

111-1st app. Silver Samurai; Shanna the She-Devil, Mandrill, Nekra & Black Spectre app. 6 12 18 38 69 100

112-114,116-120: 112-Conclusion of the Black Spectre story; Mandrill & Nekra app. 113-1st brief app. Death-Stalker; Gladiator app. 114-1st full Death-Stalker app; Man-Thing & Gladiator app. 116,117-DD vs. the Owl; 117-Last Gerber-s. 118-1st app. Blackwing; vs. the Circus of Crime. 119-Tony Isabella-s begin. 120-1st app. El Jaguar Agent of HYDRA 3 6 9 16 23 30

115-Death-Stalker app.; advertisement for Wolverine in Incredible Hulk #181 (on pg. 19) 3 6 9 17 26 35

121-123,125-130,137: 121-vs. HYDRA; El Jaguar and the Dreadnaught app; Nick Fury app. 122-Return of Silvermane as the new Supreme HYDRA. 123-Silvermane, El Jaguar, Dreadnaught, Mentallo & HYDRA app; Nick Fury and SHIELD app; last Isabella-s. 125-Death of Copperhead; Wolfman-s begin. 126-1st app. the second and third Torpedos; 1st app. Heather Glenn. 127-vs. the third Torpedo (Brock Jones). 128-Death-Stalker app. 129-vs the Man-Bull 3 6 9 14 20 25

124-1st app. Copperhead; Black Widow leaves; Len Wein & Marv Wolfman co-plot 3 6 9 17 26 35

131-Origin/1st app. Bullseye (see Nick Fury #15) 15 30 45 100 220 340

132-2nd Bullseye app. new Bullseye (regular 25c edition) 5 10 15 35 63 90

132-(30¢-c variant, limited distribution)(4/76) 10 20 30 64 132 200

133-136: 133-Uri Geller & the Jester app. 134-Torpedo app. vs. the Chameleon. 135,136-vs. the Jester 3 6 9 14 20 25

133-136-(30¢-c variants, limited distribution)(5-8/76) 4 8 12 28 47 65

138-Ghost Rider-c/story; Death's Head is reincarnated; Byrne-a 3 6 9 19 30 40

139,140,142-145,147-154: 140-vs the Beetle & Gladiator. 142-vs. Cobra & Hyde; Nova cameo. 143-Cobra & Hyde app; last Wolfman-s. 144-vs the Man-Bull & Owl. 145-vs the Owl. 147-Purple Man app. 148-Death-Stalker app. 149-1st app. the third Smasher. 150-1st app. Paladin. 151-Reveals i.d. to Heather Glenn. 152-vs Death-Stalker; Roger McKenzie-s begin. 153-vs Cobra & Hyde. 154-vs Purple Man, Cobra & Hyde & Jester 2 4 6 13 18 22

141,146-Bullseye app. 4 8 12 23 37 50

146-(35¢-c variant, limited distribution) 10 20 30 64 132 200

147,148-(35¢-c variants, limited distribution) 8 16 24 54 102 150

155-157-DD vs. Death-Stalker; Black Widow, Hercules, Captain America & the Beast app. 3 6 9 14 20 25

158-Frank Miller-a begins (5/79) origin/death of Death-Stalker (see Captain America #235 & Spectacular Spider-Man #27) 8 16 24 56 108 160

159-Brief Bullseye app. 5 10 15 30 50 70

160,161-Bullseye and Black Widow app. 4 8 12 25 40 55

162-Ditko-a; no Miller-a; origin retold 3 6 9 14 20 25

163,164: 163-vs. the Hulk. 164-Origin retold and expanded 3 6 9 18 28 38

165-167,170: 165-1st Miller co-plot w/McKenzie; Dr. Octopus app. 166-vs. Gladiator. 167-Last McKenzie co-plot; 1st app. Mauler. 170-Kingpin app. 3 6 9 16 24 32

168-(1/81) Origin/1st app. Elektra; 1st Miller scripts 11 22 33 73 157 240

169-2nd Elektra app; Bullseye app. 4 8 12 27 44 60

171-173: 171,172-vs. the Kingpin 3 6 9 17 16 35

174-1st app. the Hand (Ninjas who trained Elektra) 3 6 9 21 33 45

175-Elektra & Daredevil vs. the Hand 3 6 9 19 30 40

176-180-Elektra app: 176-1st app. Stick (Daredevil's mentor). 177-Kingpin & the Hand app. 178-Kingpin & Power Man & Iron Fist app. 179-Anti-smoking issue mentioned in the Congressional Record 3 6 9 16 24 32

181-(4/82, 52-pgs)-Death of Elektra; Punisher cameo out of costume 4 8 12 25 40 55

182-184: 182-Bullseye app. 183,184 -'Angel Dust' drug story; Punisher app. 3 6 9 16 23 30

185-191: 186-Stilt-Man app. 187-New Black Widow vs. the Hand. 188-Black Widow app. 189-Death of Stick; Black Widow app. 190-Elektra returns, part origin; 2 pin-ups. 191-Classic 'Russian Roulette' story with Bullseye; last Miller Daredevil 2 4 6 8 10 12

192-195,198,199: 192-Alan Brennert story; Klaus Janson (p)&(i) begin. 193-Larry Hama-s. 194-Denny O'Neil-s begin. 198-Bullseye receives Adamantium bones. 199-Bullseye app; death of Dark Wind 4.00

196-Wolverine-c/app; 1st app. Dark Wind. Bullseye app. 2 4 6 9 13 16

197-Bullseye-c/app; 1st app, Yuriko Oyama (becomes Lady Deathstrike in Alpha Flight #33) 1 2 3 5 6 8

200-Bulleye vs. Daredevil; Byrne-c 1 2 3 5 6 8

201-207,209-218: 201-Black Widow solo story. 202-1st app. Micah Synn. 203-1st app. the Trump; Byrne-c. 204-1st app. Crossbow (Green Arrow homage?) 205-1st app. Gael (Irish Republican Army hitman). 206-DD vs. Micah Synn; 1st Mazzucchelli-p on DD. Kingpin app. 207-HYDRA & Black Widow app. 209-Harlan Ellison plot. 210-Crossbow & Kingpin app. 211,212-DD & Kingpin team-up vs. Micah Synn. 215-Two-Gun Kid flashback. 216-Gael app. 217-Gael app; 1st app. the Cossack; Barry-Windsor-Smith-c. 218-DD appears as the Jester 4.00

208,219: 208-Harlan Ellison scripts borrowed from Avengers TV episode 'House that Jack Built'. 219-Miller-c/script 5.00

220-226,234-237: 220-Death of Heather Glenn. 222-Black Widow app. 223-Secret Wars II crossover; Beyonder gives DD his sight back; DD rejects the gift. 225-Vulture app. 226-Gladiator app.; last Denny O'Neil-s. 234-Madcap app. 235-DD vs. Mr. Hyde. 237-DD vs. Klaw; Black Widow app. 4.00

227-(2/86, 36 pgs.)-Miller scripts begin; classic 'Born Again' Pt.1 story begins; Kingpin learns DD's secret identity. 6.00

228-233: 'Born Again'; Kingpin ruins Matt Murdock's life. 232-1st app Nuke. 233-Last Miller script; Captain America app.; death of Nuke 5.00

238-Mutant massacre; Sabretooth app; 1st Ann Nocenti-s 6.00

239,240,242-247: 239-1st app. Rotgut. 243-1st app. Nameless One. 245-Black Panther app. 246-1st app. Chance. 247-Black Widow app. 3.00

241-Todd McFarlane-a(p) 5.00

248-Wolverine cameo; 1st app. Bushwacker. 249-DD vs. Wolverine; Bushwacker app. 6.00

250,251,253,258: 250-1st app. Bullet; Romita Jr-a begins. 251-vs. Bullet. 253-Kingpin app. 258-1st app. Bengal 3.00

252-(52 pgs)-Fall of the Mutants tie-in; 1st app. Ammo. 260-(52 pgs)-Bushwacker, Bullet, Ammo & Typhoid Mary vs. DD 5.00

254-Origin & 1st app. Typhoid Mary (5/88) 3 6 9 19 30 40

255,256:2nd.3rd app. Typhoid Mary app. 259-Typhoid Mary app. 5.00

257-Punisher app. (x-over w/Punisher #10) 2 4 6 8 10 12

261-269,271-281: 261-Typhoid Mary & Human Torch app. 262-Inferno tie-in. 263-Inferno tie-in; 1st new look 'monstrous' Mephisto. 264-vs the Owl. 265-Inferno tie-in; Mephisto app. 266-Mephisto app. 267-Bullet app. 269-Blob & Pyro (from Freedom Force) app. 272-1st app. Shotgun; Inhumans app. 273-DD vs. Shotgun; Inhumans app. 274-Black Bolt & the Inhumans app. 275,276-'Acts of Vengeance' x-over; Ultron app. 278-Mephisto & Blackheart app. 279-Mephisto app. 280-DD in Hell; Mephisto app. 281-Silver Surfer cameo; Mephisto & Blackheart app. 3.00

270-1st app. Blackheart (the son of Mephisto); Spider-Man app. 5.00

282-DD escapes Hell; Silver Surfer, Mephisto & Blackheart app. 4.00

283-287,289 294-299: 283-Captain America app. 284-287,289-Bullseye impersonates DD; 284-1st Lee Weeks-a. 291-vs. Bullet; last Nocenti-s. 292,293-Punisher app. 295-Ghost Rider app. 297-'Last Rights' Pt.1; Typhoid Mary app. 298-Pt.2; Nick Fury & SHIELD app. 299-Pt. 3; Baron Strucker & Hydra vs. the Kingpin 3.00

287-Bulleye-c/s; Kingpin app; Elektra dream sequence 5.00

290-Bullseye vs. Daredevil 1 3 4 6 8 10

300-(52 pgs.)-'Last Rights' Pt.4; Kingpin loses criminal empire; last Weeks-a 4.00

301-318: 301-303-vs. the Owl. 305-306-Spider-Man app. 307-'Dead Man's Hand' Pt. 1; Nomad & Tombstone app.; continued in Nomad #4. 308-'Dead Man's Hand' Pt. 5; continued from Punisher War Journal #45; Punisher app; continues in Punisher War Journal #46. 309-'Dead Man's Hand' Pt. 7; continued from Nomad #5; continued in Punisher War Journal #47. 310-Infinity War tie-in; Calypso vs. DD doppelganger. 311-Calypso & Brother Voodoo app. 314,315-Shock & Mr. Fear app. 317,318-Taskmaster, Stilt-Man & Tatterdemalion app. 3.00

319-Prologue to Fall From Grace Pt. 1; Elektra returns; Silver Sable app. 6.00

319-2nd printing w/black-c 3.00

320-(9/93) Fall From Grace Pt. 1; Silver Sable app. 5.00

Daredevil #375 © MAR

Daredevil V2 #5 © MAR

Daredevil (2011 series) #32 © MAR

GD VG FN VF VF/NM NM-
2.0 4.0 6.0 8.0 9.0 9.2

321-Fall From Grace regular ed; Pt. 2 new armored costume; Venom app. 3.00
321-($2.00)-Wraparound Glow-in-the-dark-c 5.00
322-Fall From Grace Pt. 3; Eddie Brock app. 4.00
323,324: Fall From Grace Pt. 4 & 5; 323-vs. Venom-c/story; 324-Morbius-c/story 4.00
325-($2.50, 52 pgs.) Fall From Grace ends; contains bound-in poster; Elektra app. 4.00
326-338: 326-New logo; Captain America app. 327-Captain America-c/story. 328-Captain America & Baron Strucker app. 329-Iron Fist app. 330-Gambit app. 331,332-vs. Baron Strucker. 334-336-Bushwacker app. 338-Kingpin app. 3.00
339-343: 339-342-Kingpin app. 4.00
344-(9/95)-Title becomes part of the 'Marvel Edge' imprint; story continued from Double Edge: Alpha; Punisher & Nick Fury app.; continued in Ghost Rider #65 5.00
345-Original red costume returns; Marvel Overpower card insert 6.00
346-349: 348-1st Cary Nord-a in DD (1/96) 'Dec' on-c 4.00
350-($2.95)-Double-Sized 4.00
350-($3.50)-Double-Sized; gold ink-c 5.00
351-353,355-360: 351-Last 'Marvel Edge' imprint issue. 353-Karl Kessel scripts; Nord-c/a begins. 354-Bullseye (illusion)-c. 355-Pyro app. 357-Enforcers app. 358-Mysterio app. 360-Absorbing Man app. 4.00
354-Spider-Man app.; $1.50-c begins 1 2 3 5 6 8
361,365-367: 361-Black Widow & DD vs. Grey Gargoyle. 365-367: 365-Molten Man & Mr. Fear app. 366-Mr. Fear app.; Colan-c/a. 367-Colan-c/a; Mr. Fear & Gladiator app. 5.00
362-364: 363-Colan-c/a. 364-Mr. Fear app. 4.00
368-Omega Red & Black Widow app. 1 3 4 6 8 10
369-Black Widow app. 6.00
370-374: 370-Darkstar, Vanguard & Ursa Major app; last Colan-a. 371-Black Widow app. 372-Ghost Rider (Daniel Ketch) app. 373,374-Mr. Fear app. 5.00
375-($2.99)-Wraparound-c; Mr. Fear-c/app. 5.00
376-379: "Flying Blind", DD goes undercover for SHIELD 3.00
380-($2.99) Final issue; flashback story; Kingpin, Bullseye & Bushwacker app. 1 3 4 6 8 10
#(-1) Flashback issue (7/97, $1.95); Gene Colan-c/a 3.00
Special 1 (9/67, 25¢, 68-pgs)-New art/story by Lee/Colan; DD vs. the 'Emissaries of Evil' (Electro, Leapfrog, Stilt-Man, Matador & Gladiator) 7 14 21 46 86 125
Special 2,3: 2 (2/71, 25¢, 52 pgs.) Reprints issues #10-11 by Wood. 3-(1/72, 25¢, 52 pgs.) Reprints issues #16-17 3 6 9 21 33 45
Annual 4 (10/76, squarebound) Sub-Mariner & Black Panther app. 3 6 9 17 26 35
Annual 4 (#5, 1989) Atlantis Attacks; continued from Spectacular Spider-Man Annual #9; Spider-Man app.; continued in Avengers Annual #18 5.00
Annual 6-9: 6-('90) Lifeform Pt. 2; continued from Punisher Annual #3; continues in Silver Surfer Annual #3. 7-('91) The Von Strucker Gambit Pt. 1; continued in Punisher Annual #4. Guice-a (7 pgs.). 8-('92) System Bites Pt. 2; Deathlok & Bushwacker app; continued in Wonder Man Annual #1. 9-('93) Polybagged w/card; 1st app. Devourer 4.00
Annual 10-('94) Elektra, Nick Fury, Shang-Chi (Master of Kung-Fu) vs. Ghostmaker 5.00
...: Born Again TPB ($17.95)-r/#227-233; Miller-s/Mazzucchelli-a & new-c 20.00
... By Frank Miller and Klaus Janson Omnibus HC (2007, $99.99, dustjacket) r/#158-161, 163-191 and What If...? #28; intros by Miller and Janson; interviews, bonus art 100.00
... By Frank Miller and Klaus Janson Omnibus Companion HC (2007, $59.99, die-cut d.j.) r/#219,226-233, Daredevil: The Man Without Fear #1-5, Daredevil: Love and War, and Peter Parker, the Spect. Spider-Man #27-28; bonus materials 60.00
.../Deadpool (Annual '97, $2.99)-Wraparound-c 6.00
...: Fall From Grace TPB ($19.95)-r/#319-325 20.00
...: Gang War TPB ($15.95)-r/#169-172,180; Miller-s/a(p) 16.00
...Legends: (Vol. 4) Typhoid Mary TPB (2003, $19.95) r/#254-257,259-263 20.00
... :Love's Labors Lost TPB ($19.99)-r/#215-217,219-222,225,226; Mazzucchelli-c 20.00
.../Punisher TPB (1988, $4.95)-r/D.D. #182-184 (all printings) 6.00
...Visionaries: Frank Miller Vol. 1 TPB ($17.95) r/#158-161,163-167 18.00
...Visionaries: Frank Miller Vol. 2 TPB ($24.95) r/#168-182; new Miller-c 25.00
...Visionaries: Frank Miller Vol. 3 TPB ($24.95) r/#183-191, What If? #28,35 & Bizarre Adventures #28; new Miller-c 25.00
... Vs. Bullseye Vol. 1 TPB (2004, $15.99) r/#131-132,146,169,181,191 16.00
Wizard Ace Edition: Daredevil (Vol. 1) #1 (4/03, $13.99) Acetate Campbell-c 14.00
NOTE: ***Art Adams*** *c-238p, 239.* ***Austin*** *a-191i; c-151i, 200i.* ***John Buscema*** *a-136, 137p, 234p, 235p; c-86p, 136i, 137p, 142, 219.* ***Byrne*** *c-200p, 201, 203, 223.* ***Capullo*** *a-286p.* ***Colan*** *a(p)-20-49, 53-82, 84-98, 100, 110, 112, 124, 153, 154, 156, 157, 363, 366-370, Spec. 1p; c(p)-20-42, 44-49, 53-60, 71, 92, 98, 138, 153, 154, 156, 157, Annual 1.* ***Craig*** *a-50i, 52i.* ***Ditko*** *a-162, 234p, 235p, 264p; c-162.* ***Everett*** *c/a-1; inks-21, 83.* ***Garney*** *c/a-304.* ***Gil Kane*** *a-141p, 146-148p, 151p; c(p)-85, 90, 91, 93, 94, 115, 116, 119, 120, 125-128, 133, 139, 147, 152.* ***Kirby*** *c-2-4, 5p, 12p, 13p, 43.* ***Layton*** *c-202.* ***Miller*** *scripts-168-182, 183(part), 184-191, 219, 227-233; a-158-161p, 163-184p, 191p; c-158-161p, 163-184p, 185-189, 190p, 191.* ***Orlando*** *a-2-4p.* ***Powell*** *a-9p, 11p, Special 1r, 2r.* ***Simonson*** *c-199, 236p.* ***B. Smith*** *a-236p; c-51p, 52p, 217.* ***Starlin*** *a-105p.* ***Steranko*** *c-44i.* ***Tuska*** *a-39i, 145p.* ***Williamson*** *a(i)-237, 239, 240, 243, 248-257, 259-282, 283(part), 284, 285, 287, 288(part), 289(part), 293-300; c(i)-237, 243, 244, 248-257, 259-263, 265-278, 280-289, Annual 8.* ***Wood*** *a-5-8, 9i, 10, 11i, Spec. 2i; c-5i, 6-11, 164i.*

DAREDEVIL (Volume 2)(Marvel Knights)(Becomes Black Panther: The Man Without Fear #513)
Marvel Comics: Nov, 1998 - No. 512, Feb, 2011 ($2.50/$2.99)

1-Kevin Smith-s/Quesada & Palmiotti-a 12.00

GD VG FN VF VF/NM NM-
2.0 4.0 6.0 8.0 9.0 9.2

1-($6.95) DF Edition w/Quesada & Palmiotti var.-c 15.00
1-($6.00) DF Sketch Ed. w/B&W-c 10.00
2-Two covers by Campbell and Quesada/Palmiotti 9.00
3-8: 4,5-Bullseye app. 5-Variant-c exists. 8-Spider-Man-c/app.; last Smith-s 6.00
9-15: 9-11-David Mack-s; intro Echo. 12-Begin $2.99-c; Haynes-a. 13,14-Quesada-a 4.00
16-19-Direct editions; Bendis-s/Mack-c/painted-a 4.00
18,19,21,22-Newsstand editions with variant cover logo "Marvel Unlimited Featuring... 4.00
20-($3.50) Gale-s/Winslade-a; back-up by Stan Lee-s/Colan-a; Mack-c 5.00
21-40: 21-25-Gale-s. 26-38-Bendis-s/Maleev-a. 32-Daredevil's ID revealed. 35-Spider-Man-c/app. 38-Iron Fist & Luke Cage app. 40-Dodson-a 3.50
41-(25¢-c) Begins "Lowlife" arc; Maleev-a; intro Milla Donovan 3.00
41-(Newsstand edition with 2.99¢-c) 3.00
42-45-"Lowlife" arc; Maleev-a 3.00
46-50-($2.99). 46-Typhoid Mary returns. 49-Bullseye app. 50-Art panels by various incl. Romita, Colan, Mack, Janson, Oeming, Quesada 3.00
51-64,66-74,76-81: 51-55-Mack-s/a; Echo app. 54-Wolverine-c/app. 61-64-Black Widow app. 71-Decalogue begins. 76-81-The Murdock Papers. 81-Last Bendis-s/Maleev-a 3.00
65-($3.99) 40th Anniversary issue; Land-c; art by Maleev, Horn, Bachalo and others 4.00
75-($3.99) Decalogue ends; Jester app. 4.00
82-99,101-119: 82-Brubaker-s/Lark-a begin; Foggy "killed". 84-86-Punisher app. 87-Other Daredevil ID revealed. 94-Romita-c. 111-Lady Bullseye debut 3.00
82-Variant-c by McNiven 4.00
100-($3.99) Three covers (Djurdjevic, Bermejo and Turner); art by Romita Sr., Colan, Lark, Sienkiewicz, Maleev, Bermejo & Djurdjevic; sketch art gallery; r/Daredevil #90 (1972) 4.00
(After Vol. 2 #119, Aug, 2009, numbering reverts to original Vol. 1 with #500)
500-(10/09, $4.99) Kingpin, Lady Bullseye app.; back-up stories, pin-up & cover galleries; r/#191; five covers by Djurdjevic, Darrow, Dell'Otto, Ross and Zircher 5.00
501-512: 501-Daredevil takes over The Hand; Diggle-s begins; Ribic-c. 508-Shadowland begins. 512-Black Panther app. 3.00
Annual #1 (12/07, $3.99) Brubaker-s/Fernandez-a/Djurdjevic-c; Black Tarantula app. 4.00
... & Captain America: Dead on Arrival (2008, $4.99) English version of Italian story 5.00
... Black & White 1 (10/10, $3.99) B&W short stories by various; Aja-c 4.00
... Blood of the Tarantula (6/08, $3.99) Parks & Brubaker-s/Samnee-a/Djurdjevic-c 4.00
... By Brian Michael Bendis Omnibus Vol. 1 HC (2008, $99.99) oversized r/#16-19,26-50, and 56-60 100.00
... By Ed Brubaker Saga (2008, giveaway) synopsis of issues #82-110, preview of #111 3.00
... Cage Match 1 (7/10, $2.99) flashback early Luke Cage team-up; Chen-a 3.00
... MGC #26 (8/10, $1.00) r/#26 with "Marvel's Greatest Comics" logo on cover 3.00
...2099 #1 (11/04, $2.99) Kirkman-s/Moline-a 3.00
TPB ($9.95) r/#1-3 10.00
...Vol. 1 HC (2001, $29.99, with dustjacket) r/#1-11,13-15 30.00
...Vol. 1 HC (2003, $29.99, with dustjacket) r/#1-11,13-15; larger page size 30.00
...Vol. 2 HC (2002, $29.99, with dustjacket) r/#26-37; afterword by Bendis 30.00
...Vol. 3 HC (2004, $29.99, with dustjacket) r/#38-50; Maleev sketch pages 30.00
...Vol. 4 HC (2005, $29.99, with dustjacket) r/#56-65; Vol. 1 #81 (1971) Black Widow 30.00
...Vol. 5 HC (2006, $29.99, with dustjacket) r/#66-75 30.00
...Vol. 6 HC (2006, $34.99, with dustjacket) r/#76-81 & What If Karen Page Had Lived? 35.00
(Vol. 1) Visionaries TPB ($19.95) r/#1-8; Ben Affleck intro. 20.00
(Vol. 2) Parts of a Hole TPB (1/02, $17.95) r/#9-15; David Mack intro. 18.00
(Vol. 3) Wake Up TPB (7/02, $9.99) r/#16-19 10.00
...Vol. 4: Underboss TPB (8/02, $14.99) r/#26-31 15.00
...Vol. 5: Out TPB (2003, $19.99) r/#32-40 20.00
...Vol. 6: Lowlife TPB (2003, $13.99) r/#41-45 14.00
...Vol. 7: Hardcore TPB (2003, $13.99) r/#46-50 14.00
...Vol. 8: Echo - Vision Quest TPB (2004, $13.99) r/#51-55; David Mack-s/a 14.00
...Vol. 9: King of Hell's Kitchen TPB (2004, $13.99) r/#56-60 14.00
...Vol. 10: The Widow TPB (2004, $16.99) r/#61-65 & Vol. 1 #81 17.00
...Vol. 11: Golden Age TPB (2005, $13.99) r/#66-70 14.00
...Vol. 12: Decalogue TPB (2005, $14.99) r/#71-75 15.00
...Vol. 13: The Murdock Papers TPB (2006, $14.99) r/#76-81 15.00
...: The Devil Inside and Out Vol. 1 (2006, $14.99) r/#82-87; Brubaker & Lark interview 15.00
...: The Devil Inside and Out Vol. 2 (2007, $14.99) r/#88-93; Bermejo cover sketches 15.00
...: Hell To Pay Vol. 1 TPB (2007, $14.99) r/#94-99; Djurdjevic cover sketches 15.00
...: Hell To Pay Vol. 2 TPB (2008, $15.99) r/#100-105 16.00

DAREDEVIL (Volume 3)
Marvel Comics: Sept, 2011 - No. 36, Apr, 2014 ($3.99/$2.99)

1-($3.99) Mark Waid-s/Paolo Rivera-a; back-up tale with Marcos Martin-a 4.00
1-Variant-c by Marcos Martin 8.00
1-Variant-c by Neal Adams 10.00
2-10,10.1,11-20,23,24,25,27-36-($2.99) 2-Capt. America app. 3-Klaw returns. 4-6-Marcos Martin-a. 8-X-over w/Amazing Spider-Man #677; Spider-Man and Black Cat app. 11-Spider-Man app. 17-Allred-a. 30-Silver Surfer app. 32,33-Satana & monsters app. 3.00
21,22: 21-1st Superior Spider-Man app. (cameo). 22-Superior Spider-Man app. 5.00
26-($3.99) Bullseye and Lady Bullseye app.; back-up "Fighting Cancer" story 4.00

Daredevil (2014 series) #7 © MAR

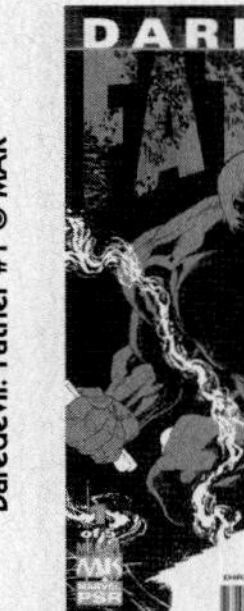
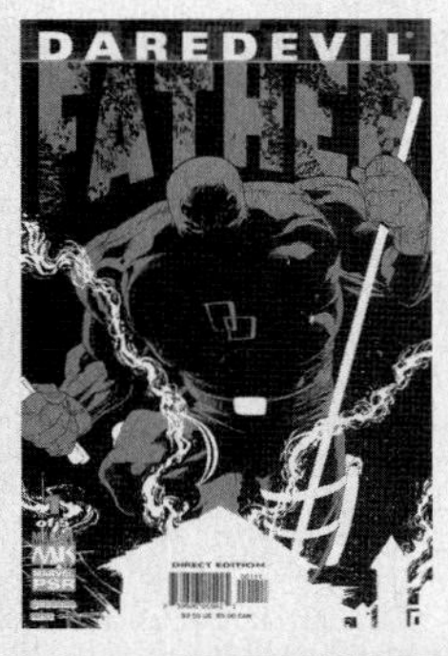

Daredevil: Father #1 © MAR

Daredevil: Redemption #1 © MAR

GD 2.0 | VG 4.0 | FN 6.0 | VF 8.0 | VF/NM 9.0 | NM- 9.2

Annual 1 (10/12, $4.99) Alan Davis-s/a/c; Dr. Strange & ClanDestine app. 5.00

DAREDEVIL (Volume 4)
Marvel Comics: May, 2014 - No. 18, Nov, 2015 ($3.99)

1-18-($3.99) Mark Waid-s/Chris Samnee-a; Murdock moves to San Francisco. 6,7-Original Sin tie-in. 8-10-Purple Man app. 14-Owl's daughter app. 15-18-Kingpin app. 4.00
#0.1-(9/14, $4.99) Waid-s/Krause-a/Samnee-c 5.00
#1.50-($4.99) 50th Anniversary issue; Murdock at 50; back-up Bendis-s/Maleev-a 5.00
#15.1-(7/15, $4.99) Waid-s/Samnee-a; Guggenheim-s/Krause-a 5.00

DAREDEVIL (Follows Secret Wars)
Marvel Comics: Feb, 2016 - Present ($3.99)

1-17: 1-Soule-s/Garney-a; Blindspot app. 2,3-The Hand app. 4-Steve Rogers app. 6,7-Elektra app.; Sienkiewicz-c. 9-Spider-Man app.16-Bullseye app. 4.00
Annual 1 (10/16, $4.99) Echo returns; Vanesa Del Ray-a 5.00

DAREDEVIL/ BATMAN (Also see Batman/Daredevil)
Marvel Comics/ DC Comics: 1997 ($5.99, one-shot)

nn-McDaniel-c/a 6.00

DAREDEVIL BATTLES HITLER (See Daredevil #1 [1941 series])

DAREDEVIL: BATTLIN' JACK MURDOCK
Marvel Comics: Aug, 2007 - No. 4, Nov, 2007 ($3.99, limited series)

1-4-Wells-s/DiGiandomenico-a; flashback to the fixed fight 4.00
TPB (2007, $12.99) r/#1-4; page layouts and cover inks 13.00

DAREDEVIL COMICS (Golden Age title) (See Daredevil)

DAREDEVIL: DARK NIGHTS
Marvel Comics: Aug, 2013 - No. 8, Mar, 2014 ($3.99, limited series)

1-8: 1-3-Lee Weeks-s/a. 4,5-David Lapham-s/a; The Shocker app. 6-8-Conner-c 4.00

DAREDEVIL/ ELEKTRA: LOVE AND WAR
Marvel Comics: 2003 ($29.99, hardcover with dust jacket)

HC-Larger-size reprints of Daredevil: Love and War (Marvel Graphic Novel #24) & Elektra: Assassin; Frank Miller-s; Bill Sienkiewicz-a 30.00

DAREDEVIL: END OF DAYS
Marvel Comics: Dec, 2012 - No. 8, Aug, 2013 ($3.99, limited series)

1-8-Bendis & Mack-s/Janson & Sienkiewicz-a; death of Daredevil in the future 4.00

DAREDEVIL: FATHER
Marvel Comics: June, 2004 - No. 6, Feb, 2007 ($3.50/$2.99, limited series)

1-Quesada-s/a; Isanove-painted color 3.50
1-Director's Cut ($2.99) cover and page development art; partial sketch-c 3.00
2-6: 2-($2.99,10/05). 3-Santerians app. 3.00
HC (2006, $24.99) r/series; Lindelof intro.; sketch pages, cover pencils and bonus art 25.00

DAREDEVIL: NINJA
Marvel Comics: Dec, 2000 - No. 3, Feb, 2001 ($2.99, limited series)

1-3: Bendis-s/Haynes-a 3.00
1-Dynamic Forces foil-c 10.00
TPB (7/01, $12.95) r/#1-3 with cover and sketch gallery 13.00

DAREDEVIL NOIR
Marvel Comics: June, 2009 - No. 4, Sept, 2009 ($3.99, limited series)

1-4-Irvine-s/Coker-a; covers by Coker and Calero 4.00

DAREDEVIL / PUNISHER: SEVENTH CIRCLE
Marvel Comics: Jul, 2016 - Present ($4.99, limited series)

1-4-Soule-s/Kudranski-a; Blindspot app. 3,4-Crimson Dynamo app. 5.00

DAREDEVIL: REBORN (Follows Shadowland x-over)
Marvel Comics: Mar, 2011 - No. 4, Jul, 2011 ($3.99, limited series)

1-4-Diggle-s/Gianfelice-a 4.00

DAREDEVIL: REDEMPTION
Marvel Comics: Apr, 2005 - No. 6, Aug, 2005 ($2.99, limited series)

1-6-Hine-s/Gaydos-a/Sienkiewicz-c 3.00
TPB (2005, $14.99) r/#1-6 15.00

DAREDEVIL: SEASON ONE
Marvel Comics: 2012 ($24.99, hardcover graphic novel)

HC - Story of early career, yellow costume; Johnston-s/Alves-a/Tedesco painted-c 25.00

DAREDEVIL/ SHI (See Shi/ Daredevil)
Marvel Comics/ Crusade Comics: Feb,1997 ($2.95, one-shot)

1 3.00

DAREDEVIL/ SPIDER-MAN
Marvel Comics: Jan, 2001 - No. 4, Apr, 2001 ($2.99, limited series)

1-4-Jenkins-s/Winslade-a/Alex Ross-c; Stilt Man app. 3.00
TPB (8/01, $12.95) r/#1-4; Ross-c 13.00

DAREDEVIL THE MAN WITHOUT FEAR
Marvel Comics: Oct, 1993 - No. 5, Feb, 1994 ($2.95, limited series) (foil embossed covers)

1-Miller scripts; Romita, Jr./Williamson-c/a 6.00
2-5 5.00
Hardcover 100.00
Trade paperback 20.00

DAREDEVIL: THE MOVIE (2003 movie adaptation)
Marvel Comics: March, 2003 ($3.50/$12.95, one-shot)

1-Photo-c of Ben Affleck; Bruce Jones-s/Manuel Garcia-a 3.50
TPB ($12.95) r/movie adaptation; Daredevil #32; Ultimate Daredevil & Elektra #1 and Spider-Man's Tangled Web #4; photo-c of Ben Affleck 13.00

DAREDEVIL: THE TARGET (Daredevil Bullseye on cover)
Marvel Comics: Jan, 2003 ($3.50, unfinished limited series)

1-Kevin Smith-s/Glenn Fabry-c/a 3.50

DAREDEVIL VS. PUNISHER
Marvel Comics: Sept, 2005 - No. 6, Jan, 2006 ($2.99, limited series)

1-5-David Lapham-s/a 3.00
TPB (2005, $15.99) r/#1-6 16.00

DAREDEVIL: YELLOW
Marvel Comics: Aug, 2001 - No. 6, Jan, 2002 ($3.50, limited series)

1-6-Jeph Loeb-s/Tim Sale-a/c; origin & yellow costume days retold 3.50
HC (5/02, $29.95) r/#1-6 with dustjacket; intro by Stan Lee; sketch pages 30.00
Daredevil Legends Vol. 1: Daredevil Yellow (2002, $14.99, TPB) r/#1-6 15.00

DARING ADVENTURES (Also see Approved Comics)
St. John Publishing Co.: Nov, 1953 (25¢, 3-D, came w/glasses)

1 (3-D)-Reprints lead story from Son of Sinbad #1 by Kubert 26 52 78 154 252 350

DARING ADVENTURES
I.W. Enterprises/Super Comics: 1963 - 1964

I. W. Reprint #8-r/Fight Comics #53; Matt Baker-a 4 8 12 28 47 65
I.W. Reprint #9-r/Blue Bolt #115; Disbrow-a(3) 5 10 15 30 50 70
Super Reprint #10,11('63)-r/Dynamic #24,16; 11-Marijuana story; Yankee Boy app.; Mac Raboy-a 4 8 12 21 33 45
Super Reprint #12('64)-Phantom Lady from Fox (r/#14 only? w/splash pg. omitted); Matt Baker-a 9 18 27 57 111 165
Super Reprint #15('64)-r/Hooded Menace #1 6 12 18 37 66 95
Super Reprint #16('64)-r/Dynamic #12 3 6 9 19 30 40
Super Reprint #17('64)-r/Green Lama #3 by Raboy 4 8 12 25 40 55
Super Reprint #18-Origin Atlas from unpublished Atlas Comics #1 4 8 12 23 37 50

DARING COMICS (Formerly Daring Mystery) (Jeanie Comics No. 13 on)
Timely Comics (HPC): No. 9, Fall, 1944 - No. 12, Fall, 1945

9-Human Torch, Toro & Sub-Mariner begin 194 388 582 1242 2121 3000
10-12: 10-The Angel only app. 11,12-The Destroyer app. 168 336 504 1075 1838 2600

NOTE: ***Schomburg*** *c-9-11.* ***Sekowsky*** *c-12? Human Torch, Toro & Sub-Mariner c-9-12.*

DARING CONFESSIONS (Formerly Youthful Hearts)
Youthful Magazines: No. 4, 11/52 - No. 7, 5/53; No. 8, 10/53

4-Doug Wildey-a; Tony Curtis story 20 40 60 120 195 270
5-8: 5-Ray Anthony photo on-c. 6,8-Wildey-a 15 30 45 86 133 180

DARING ESCAPES
Image Comics: Sept, 1998 - No. 4, Mar, 1999 ($2.95/$2.50, mini-series)

1-Houdini; following app. in Spawn #19,20 3.00
2-4-($2.50) 3.00

DARING LOVE (Radiant Love No. 2 on)
Gilmor Magazines: Sept-Oct, 1953

1–Steve Ditko's 1st published work (1st drawn was Fantastic Fears #5)(Also see Black Magic #27)(scarce) 258 516 774 1651 2826 4000

DARING LOVE (Formerly Youthful Romances)
Ribage/Pix: No. 15, 12/52; No. 16, 2/53-c, 4/53-Indicia; No. 17-4/53-c & indicia

15 15 30 45 86 133 180
16,17: 17-Photo-c 14 28 42 80 115 150

NOTE: ***Colletta*** *a-15.* ***Wildey*** *a-17.*

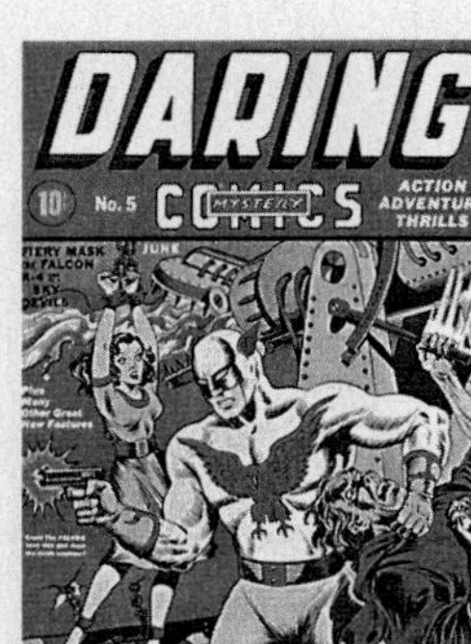

Daring Mystery Comics #5 © MAR

Darkchylde: The Legacy #1 © Randy Queen

Dark Days #1 © Niles & Templesmith

GD VG FN VF VF/NM NM-
2.0 4.0 6.0 8.0 9.0 9.2

GD VG FN VF VF/NM NM-
2.0 4.0 6.0 8.0 9.0 9.2

DARING LOVE STORIES (See Fox Giants)

DARING MYSTERY COMICS (Comedy Comics No. 9 on; title changed to Daring Comics with No. 9)
Timely Comics (TPI 1-6/TCI 7,8): 1/40 - No. 5, 6/40; No. 6, 9/40; No. 7, 4/41 - No. 8, 1/42

1-Origin The Fiery Mask (1st app.) by Joe Simon; Monako, Prince of Magic (1st app.), John Steele, Soldier of Fortune (1st app.), Doc Denton (1st app.) begin; Flash Foster & Barney Mullen, Sea Rover only app; bondage-c 2200 4400 6600 17,000 33,500 50,000
2-(Rare)-Origin The Phantom Bullet (1st & only app.); The Laughing Mask & Mr. E only app.; Trojak the Tiger Man begins, ends #6; Zephyr Jones & K-4 & His Sky Devils app., also #4 1150 2300 3450 8700 16,600 24,500
3-The Phantom Reporter, Dale of FBI, Captain Strong only app.; Breeze Barton, Marvex the Super-Robot, The Purple Mask begin 622 1244 1866 4541 8021 11,500
4,5: 4-Last Purple Mask; Whirlwind Carter begins; Dan Gorman, G-Man app. 5-The Falcon begins (1st app.); The Fiery Mask, Little Hercules app. by Sagendorf in the Segar style; bondage-c 459 918 1377 3350 5925 8500
6-Origin & only app. Marvel Boy by S&K; Flying Flame, Dynaman, & Stuporman only app.; The Fiery Mask by S&K; S&K-c 514 1028 1542 3750 6625 9500
7-Origin and 1st app. The Blue Diamond, Captain Daring by S&K, The Fin by Everett, The Challenger, The Silver Scorpion & The Thunderer by Burgos; Mr. Millions app 423 846 1269 3000 5250 7500
8-Origin Citizen V; Last Fin, Silver Scorpion, Capt. Daring by Borth, Blue Diamond & The Thunderer; Kirby & part solo Simon-c; Rudy the Robot only app.; Citizen V, Fin & Silver Scorpion continue in Comedy #9 371 742 1113 2600 4550 6500

NOTE: ***Schomburg** c-1-4, 7. **Simon** a-2, 3, 5. Cover features: 1-Fiery Mask; 2-Phantom Bullet; 3-Purple Mask; 4-G-Man; 5-The Falcon; 6-Marvel Boy; 7, 8-Multiple characters.*

DARING MYSTERY COMICS 70th ANNIVERARY SPECIAL
Marvel Comics: Nov, 2009 ($3.99, one-shot)

1-New story of The Phantom Reporter; r/app. in Daring Mystery #3 (1940); 2 covers 5.00

DARING NEW ADVENTURES OF SUPERGIRL, THE
DC Comics: Nov, 1982 - No. 13, Nov, 1983 (Supergirl No. 14 on)

1-Origin retold; Lois Lane back-ups in #2-12 2 4 6 10 14 18
2-13: 8,9-Doom Patrol app. 13-New costume; flag-c 5.00

NOTE: ***Buckler** c-1p, 2p. **Giffen** c-3p, 4p. **Gil Kane** c-6,8, 9, 11-13.*

DARK, THE
Continum Comics: Nov, 1990 - No. 4, Feb, 1993; V2#1, May, 1993 - V2#7, Apr?, 1994 ($1.95)

1-4: 1-Bright-p; Panosian, Hanna-i; Stroman-c. 2-(1/92)-Stroman-c/a(p). 4-Perez-c & part-i 3.00
V2#1,V2#2-6: V2#1-Red foil Bart Sears-c. V2#1-Red non-foil variant-c. V2#1-2nd printing w/blue foil Bart Sears-c. V2#2-Stroman/Bryant-a. 3-Perez-c(i). 3-6-Foil-c. 4-Perez-c & part-i; bound-in trading cards. 5,6-(2,3/94)-Perez-c(i). 7-(B&W)-Perez-c(i) 3.00
Convention Book 1 ,2(Fall/94, 10/94)-Perez-c 3.00

DARK AGES
Dark Horse Comics: Aug, 2014 - No. 4, Nov, 2014 ($3.99, limited series)

1-4-Abnett-s/Culbard-a/c 4.00

DARK AND BLOODY, THE
DC Comics (Vertigo): Apr, 2016 - No. 6, Sept, 2016 ($3.99, limited series)

1-6-Aldridge-s/Godlewski-a 4.00

DARK ANGEL (Formerly Hell's Angel)
Marvel Comics UK, Ltd.: No. 6, Dec, 1992 - No. 16, Dec, 1993 ($1.75)

6-8,13-16: 6-Excalibur-c/story. 8-Psylocke app. 3.00
9-12-Wolverine/X-Men app. 3.50

DARK ANGEL: PHOENIX RESURRECTION (Kia Asamiya's...)
Image Comics: May, 2000 - No. 4, Oct, 2001 ($2.95)

1-4-Kia Asamiya-s/a. 3-Van Fleet variant-c 3.00

DARK AVENGERS (See Secret Invasion and Dark Reign titles)
Marvel Comics: Mar, 2009 - No. 16, Jul, 2010 ($3.99)

1-Norman Osborn assembles his Avengers; Bendis-s/Deodato-a/c 4.00
1-Variant Iron Patriot armor cover by Djurdjevic 8.00
2-16: 2-6-Bendis-s/Deodato-a/c. 2-4 Dr. Doom app. 7,8-Utopia x-over; X-Men app. 9-Nick Fury app. 11,12-Deodato & Horn-a. 13-16-Siege. 13-Sentry origin 4.00
Annual 1 (2/10, $4.99) Bendis-s/Bachalo-a; Marvel Boy new costume; Siege preview 5.00
,,,/ Uncanny X-Men: Exodus (11/09, $3.99) Conclusion of x-over; Deodato & Dodson-a 4.00
,,,/ Uncanny X-Men: Utopia (8/09, $3.99) Part 1 of x-over w/Uncanny X-Men #513,514 4.00

DARK AVENGERS (Title continues from Thunderbolts #174)
Marvel Comics: No. 175, Aug, 2012 - No. 190, Jul, 2013 ($2.99)

175-190: 175-New team assembles; Parker-s/Shalvey-a/Deodato-c 3.00

DARK AVENGERS: ARES
Marvel Comics: Dec, 2009 - No. 3, Feb, 2010 ($3.99, limited series)

1-3-Garcia-a/Gillen-s. 1-Nord-c. 2-Tan-c. 3-McGuinness-c 4.00

DARKCHYLDE (Also see Dreams of the Darkchylde)
Maximum Press #1-3/ Image Comics #4 on: June, 1996 - No. 5, Sept, 1997 ($2.95/ $2.50)

1-Randy Queen-c/a/scripts; "Roses" cover 6.00
1-American Entertainment Edition-wraparound-c 6.00
1-"Fashion magazine-style" variant-c 1 2 3 4 5 7
1-Special Comicon Edition (contents of #1) Winged devil variant-c 5.00
1-($2.50)-Remastered Ed.-wraparound-c 4.00
2(Reg-c),2-Spiderweb and Moon variant-c 6.00
3(Reg-c),3-"Kalvin Clein" variant-c by Drew 4.00
4,5(Reg-c), 4-Variant-c 4.00
5-B&W Edition, 5-Dynamic Forces Gold Ed. 8.00
0-(3/98, $2.50) 3.00
0-Remastered (1/01, $2.95) includes Darkchylde: Redemption preview 3.00
1/2-WIzard offer 4.00
1/2 Variant-c 6.00
... The Descent TPB ('98, $19.95) r/#1-5; bagged with Darkchylde The Legacy Preview Special 1998; listed price is for TPB only 20.00

DARKCHYLDE LAST ISSUE SPECIAL
Darkchylde Entertainment: June, 2002 ($3.95)

1-Wraparound-c; cover gallery 4.00

DARKCHYLDE REDEMPTION
Darkchylde Entertainment: Feb, 2001 - No. 2, Dec, 2001 ($2.95)

1,2: 1-Wraparound-c 3.00
1-Dynamic Forces alternate-c 6.00
1-Dynamic Forces chrome-c 16.00

DARKCHYLDE SKETCH BOOK
Image Comics (Dynamic Forces): 1998

1-Regular-c 8.00
1-DarkChrome cover 16.00

DARKCHYLDE SUMMER SWIMSUIT SPECTACULAR
DC Comics (WildStorm): Aug, 1999 ($3.95, one-shot)

1-Pin-up art by various 4.00

DARKCHYLDE SWIMSUIT ILLUSTRATED
Image Comics: 1998 ($2.50, one-shot)

1-Pin-up art by various 3.00
1-(6.95) Variant cover 7.00
1-Chromium cover 15.00

DARKCHYLDE THE DIARY
Image Comics: June, 1997 ($2.50, one-shot)

1-Queen-c/s/ art by various 3.00
1-Variant-c 5.00
1-Holochrome variant-c 8.00

DARKCHYLDE THE LEGACY
Image Comics/DC (WildStorm) #3 on: Aug, 1998 - No. 3, June, 1999 ($2.50)

1-3: 1-Queen-c. 2-Two covers by Queen and Art Adams 3.00

DARK CLAW ADVENTURES
DC Comics (Amalgam): June, 1997 ($1.95, one-shot)

1-Templeton-c/s/a & Burchett-a 3.00

DARK CROSSINGS: DARK CLOUDS RISING
Image Comics (Top Cow): June, 2000; Oct, 2000 ($5.95, limited series)

1-Witchblade, Darkness, Tomb Raider crossover; Dwayne Turner-a 6.00
1-(Dark Clouds Overhead) 6.00

DARK CRYSTAL, THE (Movie)
Marvel Comics Group: April, 1983 - No. 2, May, 1983

1,2-Adaptation of film 4.00

DARK DAYS (See 30 Days of Night)
IDW Publishing: June, 2003 - No. 6, Dec, 2003 ($3.99, limited series)

1-6-Sequel to 30 Days of Night; Niles-s/Templesmith-a 4.00
1-Retailer variant (Diamond/Alliance Fort Wayne 5/03 summit) 15.00
TPB (2004, $19.99) r/#1-6; cover gallery; intro. by Eric Red 20.00

DARKDEVIL (See Spider-Girl)
Marvel Comics: Nov, 2000 - No. 3, Jan, 2001 ($2.99, limited series)

1-3: 1-Origin of Darkdevil; Kingpin-c/app. 3.00

Darker Image #1 © Image

Darkhawk #6 © MAR

Dark Horse Presents #50 © DH

GD 2.0 | VG 4.0 | FN 6.0 | VF 8.0 | VF/NM 9.0 | NM- 9.2

DARK DOMINION
Defiant: Oct, 1993 - No. 10, July, 1994 ($2.50)
1-10-Len Wein scripts begin. 1-Intro Chasm. 4-Free extra 16 pgs. 7-9-J.G. Jones-c/a (his 1st pro work). 10-Pre-Schism issue; Shooter/Wein script; John Ridgway-a 3.00

DARK ENGINE
Image Comics: Jul, 2014 - No. 5, Mar, 2015 ($3.50)
1-5-Burton-s/Bivens-a 3.50

DARKER IMAGE (Also see Deathblow, The Maxx, & Bloodwulf)
Image Comics: Mar, 1993 ($1.95, one-shot)
1-The Maxx by Sam Kieth begins; Bloodwulf by Rob Liefeld & Deathblow by Jim Lee begin (both 1st app.); polybagged w/1 of 3 cards by Kieth, Lee or Liefeld 3.00
1-B&W interior pgs. w/silver foil logo 6.00

DARK FANTASIES
Dark Fantasy: 1994 - No. 8, 1995 ($2.95)
1-Test print Run (3,000)-Linsner-c 1 2 3 5 6 8
1-Linsner-c 5.00
2-8: 2-4 (Deluxe), 2-4 (Regular), 5-8 (Deluxe; $3.95) 4.00
5-8 (Regular; $3.50) 3.50

DARK GUARD
Marvel Comics UK: Oct, 1993 - No. 4, Jan, 1994 ($1.75)
1-($2.95)-Foil stamped-c 4.00
2-4 3.00

DARKHAWK (Also see War of Kings)
Marvel Comics: Mar, 1991 - No. 50, Apr, 1995 ($1.00/$1.25/$1.50)
1-Origin/1st app. Darkhawk; Hobgoblin cameo 2 4 6 9 12 15
2,3,13,14: 2-Spider-Man & Hobgoblin app. 3-Spider-Man & Hobgoblin app. 13,14-Venom-c/story 4.00
4-12,15-24,26-49: 6-Capt. America & Daredevil x-over. 9-Punisher app. 11,12-Tombstone app. 19-Spider-Man & Brotherhood of Evil Mutants-c/story. 20-Spider-Man app. 22-Ghost Rider-c/story. 23-Origin begins, ends #25. 27-New Warriors-c/story. 35-Begin 3 part Venom story. 39-Bound-in trading card sheet 3.00
25,50: (52 pgs.)-Red holo-grafx foil-c w/double gatefold poster; origin of Darkhawk armor 4.00
Annual 1-3 ('92-'94,68 pgs.)-1-Vs. Iron Man. 2 -Polybagged w/card 4.00

DARKHOLD: PAGES FROM THE BOOK OF SINS (See Midnight Sons Unlimited)
Marvel Comics (Midnight Sons imprint #15 on): Oct, 1992 - No. 16, Jan, 1994
1-($2.75, 52 pgs.)-Polybagged w/poster by Andy & Adam Kubert; part 4 of Rise of the Midnight Sons storyline 4.00
2-10,12-16: 3-Reintro Modred the Mystic (see Marvel Chillers #1). 4-Sabertooth-c/sty. 5-Punisher & Ghost Rider app. 15-Spot varnish-c. 15,16-Siege of Darkness pt. 4&12 3.00
11-($2.25)-Outer-c is a Darkhold envelope made of black parchment w/gold ink 4.00

DARK HORSE BOOK OF..., THE
Dark Horse Comics: Aug, 2003 - Nov, 2006 ($14.95/$15.95, HC, 9 1/4" x 6 1/4")
... Hauntings (8/03, $14.95)-Short stories by various incl. Mignola (Hellboy), Thompson, Dorkin, Russell; Gianni-c 15.00
... Monsters (11/06, $15.95)-Short-s by Mignola, Thompson, Dorkin, Giffen, Busiek; Gianni-c 16.00
... The Dead (6/05, $14.95)-Short-s by Mignola, Thompson, Dorkin, Powell; Gianni-c 15.00
... Witchcraft (6/04, $14.95)-Short-s by Mignola, Thompson, Dorkin, Millionaire; Gianni-c 15.00

DARK HORSE CLASSICS (Title series), **Dark Horse Comics**
1992 ($3.95, B&W, 52 pgs. nn's): The Last of the Mohicans. 20,000 Leagues Under the Sea 4.00

DARK HORSE CLASSICS, 5/96 ($2.95) 1-r/Predator: Jungle Tales 3.00
--ALIENS VERSUS PREDATOR, 2/97 - No. 6, 7/97 ($2.95,) 1-6: r/Aliens Versus Predator 3.00
--GODZILLA: KING OF THE MONSTERS, 4/98 ($2.95) 1-6: 1-r/Godzilla: Color Special; Art Adams-a 3.00
--STAR WARS: DARK EMPIRE, 3/97 - No. 6, 8/97 ($2.95) 1-6: r/Star Wars: Dark Empire 3.00
--TERROR OF GODZILLA, 8/98 - No. 6, 1/99 ($2.95) 1-6-r/manga Godzilla in color; Art Adams-c 3.00

DARK HORSE COMICS
Dark Horse Comics: Aug, 1992 - No. 25, Sept, 1994 ($2.50)
1-Dorman double gategold painted-c; Predator, Robocop, Timecop (3-part) & Renegade stories begin 4.00
2-6,11-25: 2-Mignola-c. 3-Begin 3-part Aliens story; Aliens-c. 4-Predator-c. 6-Begin 4 part Robocop story. 12-Begin 2-part Aliens & 3-part Predator stories. 13-Thing From Another World begins w/Nino-a(i). 15-Begin 2-part Aliens: Cargo story. 16-Begin 3-part Predator story. 17-Begin 3-part Star Wars: Droids story & 3-part Aliens: Alien story; Droids-c. 19-Begin 2-part X story; X cover 3.00
7-Begin Star Wars: Tales of the Jedi 3-part story 1 2 3 4 5 7
8-1st app. X and begins; begin 4-part James Bond 6.00
9,10: 9-Star Wars ends. 10-X ends; Begin 3-part Predator & Godzilla stories 4.00
NOTE: *Art Adams c-11.*

DARK HORSE DAY SAMPLER 2016
Dark Horse Comics: Jun, 2016 (no price, promotional one-shot)
nn-New Buffy the Vampire Slayer story; reprint stories of Sin City, AvP, Umbrella Academy 3.00

DARK HORSE DOWN UNDER
Dark Horse Comics: Jun, 1994 - No. 3, Oct, 1994 ($2.50, B&W, limited series)
1-3 3.00

DARK HORSE MAVERICK
Dark Horse Comics: July, 2000; July, 2001; Sept, 2002 (B&W, annual)
2000-($3.95) Short stories by Miller, Chadwick, Sakai, Pearson 4.00
2001-($4.99) Short stories by Sakai, Wagner and others; Miller-c 5.00
...: Happy Endings (9/02, $9.95) Short stories by Bendis, Oeming, Mahfood, Mignola, Miller, Kieth and others; Miller-c 10.00

DARK HORSE MONSTERS
Dark Horse Comics: Feb, 1997 ($2.95, one-shot)
1-Reprints 3.00

DARK HORSE PRESENTS
Dark Horse Comics: July, 1986 - No. 157, Sept, 2000 ($1.50-$2.95, B&W)
1-1st app. Concrete by Paul Chadwick 2 4 6 10 14 18
1-2nd printing (1988, $1.50) 3.00
1-Silver ink 3rd printing (1992, $2.25)-Says 2nd printing inside 3.00
2-9: 2-6,9-Concrete app. 6.00
10-1st app. The Mask; Concrete app. 2 4 6 9 12 15
11-19,21-23: 11-19,21-Mask stories. 12,14,16,18,22-Concrete app. 15(2/88). 17-All Roachmill issue 6.00
20-(68 pgs.)-Concrete, Flaming Carrot, Mask 1 3 4 6 8 10
24-Origin Aliens-c/story (11/88); Mr. Monster app. 2 4 6 13 18 22
25-27,29-31,37-39,41,44,45,47-49: 38-Concrete. 44-Crash Ryan. 48,49-Contain 2 trading cards 3.00
28,33,40: 28-(52 pgs.)-Concrete app.; Mr. Monster story (homage to Graham Ingels). 33-(44 pgs.). 40-(52 pgs.)-1st Argosy story 4.00
32,34,35: 32-(68 pgs.)-Annual; Concrete, American. 34-Aliens-c/story. 35-Predator-c/app. 4.00
36-1st Aliens Vs. Predator story; painted-c 2 4 6 10 14 18
36-Variant line drawn-c 3 6 9 16 23 30
42,43,46: 42,43-Aliens-c/stories. 46-Prequel to new Predator II mini-series 3.00
50-S/F story by Perez; contains 2 trading cards 4.00
51-53-Sin City by Frank Miller, parts 2-4; 51,53-Miller-c (see D.H.P. Fifth Anniversary Special for pt. 1) 1 2 3 4 6 8
54-61: 54-(9/91) The Next Men begins (1st app.) by Byrne; Miller-a/Morrow-c. Homocide by Morrow (also in #55). 55-2nd app. The Next Men; parts 5 & 6 of Sin City by Miller; Miller-c. 56-(68 pg. annual)-part 7 of Sin City by Miller; part prologue to Aliens: Genocide; Next Men by Byrne. 57-(52 pgs.)-Part 8 of Sin City by Miller; Next Men by Byrne; Byrne & Miller-c; Alien Fire story; swipes cover to Daredevil #1. 58,59-Alien Fire stories. 58-61- Part 9-12 Sin City by Miller 5.00
62-Last Sin City (entire book by Miller, c/a; 52 pgs.) 2 4 6 8 10 12
63-66,68-79,81-84-($2.25): 64-Dr. Giggles begins (1st app.), ends #66; Boris the Bear story. 66-New Concrete-c/story by Chadwick. 71-Begin 3 part Dominque story by Jim Balent; Balent-c. 72-(3/93)-Begin 3-part Eudaemon (1st app.) story by Nelson 3.00
67-($3.95, 68 pgs.)-Begin 3-part prelude to Predator: Race War mini-series; Oscar Wilde adapt. by Russell 4.00
80-Art Adams-c/a (Monkeyman & O'Brien) 4.00
85-87,92-99: 85-Begin $2.50-c. 92, 93, 95-Too Much Coffee Man 3.00
88-Hellboy by Mignola. 2 4 6 8 10 12
89-91-Hellboy by Mignola. 1 2 3 5 6 8
NOTE: *There are 5 different Dark Horse Presents #100 issues*
100-1-Intro Lance Blastoff by Miller; Milk & Cheese by Evan Dorkin 4.00
100-2-Hellboy-c by Wrightson; Hellboy story by Mignola; includes Roberta Gregory & Paul Pope stories 6.00
100-3-100-5: 100-3-Darrow-c, Concrete by Chadwick; Pekar story. 100-4-Gibbons-c: Miller story, Geary story/a. 100-5-Allred-c, Adams, Dorkin, Pope 3.00
101-125: 101-Aliens c/a by Wrightson, story by Pope. 103-Kirby gatefold-c. 106-Big Blown Baby by Bill Wray. 107-Mignola-c/a. 109-Begin $2.95-c; Paul Pope-c. 110-Ed Brubaker-a/s. 114-Flip books begin; Lance Blastoff by Miller; Star Slammers by Simonson. 115-Miller-c. 117-Aliens-c/app. 118-Evan Dorkin-c/a. 119-Monkeyman & O'Brien. 124-Predator. 125-Nocturnals 3.00
126-($3.95, 48 pgs.)-Flip book: Nocturnals, Starship Troopers 4.00
127-134,136-140: 127-Nocturnals. 129-The Hammer. 132-134-Warren-a 3.00
135-($3.50) The Mark 3.50
141-All Buffy the Vampire Slayer issue 4.00

Dark Horse Presents V3 #3 © DH

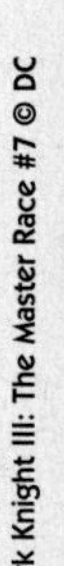
Dark Knight III: The Master Race #7 © DC

The Darkness #10 © TCOW

GD 2.0 | VG 4.0 | FN 6.0 | VF 8.0 | VF/NM 9.0 | NM- 9.2

142-149: 142-Mignola-c. 143-Tarzan. 146,147-Aliens vs. Predator. 148-Xena 3.00
150-($4.50) Buffy-c by Green; Buffy, Concrete, Fish Police app. 4.50
151-157: 151-Hellboy-c/app. 153-155-Angel flip-c. 156,157-Witch's Son 3.00
Annual 1997 ($4.95, 64 pgs.)-Flip book; Body Bags, Aliens. Pearson-c; stories by Allred & Stephens, Pope, Smith & Morrow 1 2 3 5 6 8
Annual 1998 ($4.95, 64 pgs.) 1st Buffy the Vampire Slayer comic app.; Hellboy story and cover by Mignola 1 2 3 5 6 8
Annual 1999 (7/99, $4.95) Stories of Xena, Hellboy, Ghost, Luke Skywalker, Groo, Concrete, the Mask and Usagi Yojimbo in their youth. 5.00
Annual 2000 ($4.95) Girl sidekicks; Chiodo-c and flip photo Buffy-c 5.00
...Aliens Platinum Edition (1992)-r/DHP #24,43,43,56 & Special 11.00
...Fifth Anniversary Special nn (4/91, $9.95)-Part 1 of Sin City by Frank Miller (c/a); Aliens, Aliens vs. Predator, Concrete, Roachmill, Give Me Liberty & The American stories 35.00
The One Trick Rip-off (1997, $12.95, TPB)-r/stories from #101-112 13.00
NOTE: *Geary a-59, 60. Miller a-Special, 51-53, 55-62; c-59-62, 100-1; c-51, 53, 55, 59-62, 100-1. Moebius a-63; c-63, 70. Vess a-78; c-75, 78.*

DARK HORSE PRESENTS
Dark Horse Comics: Apr, 2011 - No. 36, May, 2014 ($7.99, anthology)
1-36: 1-Frank Miller-c & Xerxes preview; Neal Adams-s/a. 1-3-Concrete by Chadwick. 1-8-Chaykin-s/a. 2,3,9-Corben-a. 3-Steranko interview. 7-Hellboy app. 10-Milk & Cheese. 12-17-Aliens; Kieth-a. 14-Flipbook. 18-Capt. Midnight. 23-26,29-34-Nexus. 25,26-Buffy. 28,29-Neal Adams-s/a. 31,32-Hellboy; McMahon-a 8.00

DARK HORSE PRESENTS (Volume 3)
Dark Horse Comics: Aug, 2014 - Present ($4.99, anthology)
1-6: 1-Two covers. 1,2-Rusty & Big Guy by Darrow-s/a. 2-Aliens. 5-Alex Ross-c 5.00
7-(2/15) 200th Issue; Hellboy by Mignola & Bá, Groo, Mind Mgmt; Gibbons, Darrow-a 5.00
8-15,17-31: 8-10-Tarzan by Grell. 14,15-The Rook; Gulacy-a. 17,18-Levitz-s 5.00
16-($5.99) Flip book with Hellboy by Mignola; art by Calero, Ordway, McCarthy 6.00

DARK HORSE TWENTY YEARS
Dark Horse Comics: 2006 (25¢, one-shot)
nn-Pin-ups by Dark Horse artists of other artists' Dark Horse characters; Mignola-c 3.00

DARK IVORY
Image Comics: Mar, 2008 - No. 4, Jan, 2009 ($2.99, limited series)
1-4-Eva Hopkins & Joseph Michael Linsner-s/Linsner-a/c 3.00

DARK KNIGHT (See Batman: The Dark Knight Returns & Legends of the...)

DARK KNIGHT RETURNS, THE: THE LAST CRUSADE
DC Comics: Aug, 2016 ($6.99, squarebound, one-shot)
1-Miller & Azzarello-s/Romita Jr.-a; Jason Todd Robin vs. The Joker; Poison Ivy app. 7.00

DARK KNIGHT STRIKES AGAIN, THE (Also see Batman: The Dark Knight Returns)
DC Comics: 2001 - No. 3, 2002 ($7.95, prestige format, limited series)
1-Frank Miller-s/a/c; sequel set 3 years after Dark Knight Returns; 2 covers 10.00
2,3 10.00
HC (2002, $29.95) intro. by Miller; sketch pages and exclusive artwork; cover has 3 1/4" tall partial dustjacket 30.00
SC (2002, $19.95) intro. by Miller; sketch pages 20.00

DARK KNIGHT III: THE MASTER RACE (Also see Batman: The Dark Knight Returns)
DC Comics: Jan, 2016 - No. 9 ($5.99, cardstock cover, limited series)
1-7: 1-Miller & Azzarello-s/Andy Kubert-a; Dark Knight Universe Presents: The Atom mini-comic attached at centerfold, Miller-a. 2-Wonder Woman mini-comic. 3-Superman returns; Green Lantern mini-comic. 4-Batgirl mini-comic. 5-Lara mini-comic. 6-World's Finest mini-comic. 7-Strange Adventures mini-comic 6.00
1-7-Deluxe Edition ($12.99, HC) reprints story plus mini-comic at full size; cover gallery 13.00
... Book One - Director's Cut (11/16, $7.99) r/ #1 in B&W art; script, variant cover gallery 8.00

DARKLON THE MYSTIC (Also see Eerie Magazine #79,80)
Pacific Comics: Oct, 1983 (one-shot)
1-Starlin-c/a(r) 4.00

DARKMAN (Movie)
Marvel Comics: Sept, 1990; Oct, 1990 - No. 3, Dec, 1990 ($1.50)
1 (9/90, $2.25, B&W mag., 68 pgs.)-Adaptation of film 4.00
1-3: Reprints B&W magazine 3.00

DARKMAN
Marvel Comics: V2#1, Apr, 1993 -No. 6, Sept, 1993 ($2.95, limited series)
V2#1 ($3.95, 52 pgs.) 4.00
2-6 3.00

DARK MANSION OF FORBIDDEN LOVE, THE (Becomes Forbidden Tales of Dark Mansion No. 5 on)
National Periodical Publ.: Sept-Oct, 1971 - No. 4, Mar-Apr, 1972 (52 pgs.)
1-Greytone-c on all 17 34 51 119 265 410
2-4: 2-Adams-c. 3-Jeff Jones-c 9 18 27 60 120 180

DARKMAN VS. THE ARMY OF DARKNESS (Movie crossover)
Dynamite Entertainment: 2006 - No. 4, 2007 ($3.50)
1-4: 1-Busiek & Stern-s/Fry-a; photo-c and Perez and Bradshaw covers 3.50

DARKMINDS
Image Comics (Dreamwave Prod.): July, 1998 - No. 8, Apr, 1999 ($2.50)
1-Manga; Pat Lee-s/a; 2 covers 1 3 4 6 8 10
1-2nd printing 3.00
2, 0-(1/99, $5.00) Story and sketch pages 5.00
3-8, 1/2-(5/99, $2.50) Story and sketch pages 3.00
... Collected 1,2 (1/99,3/99; $7.95) 1-r/#1-3. 2-r/#4-6 8.00
... Collected 3 (5/99; $5.95) r/#7,8 6.00

DARKMINDS (Volume 2)
Image Comics (Dreamwave Prod.): Feb, 2000 - No. 10, Apr, 2001 ($2.50)
1-10-Pat Lee-c 3.00
0-(7/00) Origin of Mai Murasaki; sketchbook 3.00

DARKMINDS: MACROPOLIS
Image Comics (Dreamwave Prod.): Jan, 2002 - No. 4, Dec, 2002 ($2.95)
Preview (8/01) Flip book w/Banished Knights preview 3.00
1-4-Jo Chen-a 3.00

DARKMINDS: MACROPOLIS (Volume 2)
Dreamwave Prod.: Sept, 2003 - No. 4, Jul, 2004 ($2.95)
1-4-Chris Sarracini-s/Kwang Mook Lim-a 3.00

DARKMINDS / WITCHBLADE (Also see Witchblade/Dark Minds)
Image Comics (Top Cow/Dreamwave Prod.): Aug, 2000 ($5.95, one-shot)
1-Wohl-s/Pat Lee-a; two covers by Silvestri and Lee 6.00

DARK MYSTERIES (Thrilling Tales of Horror & Suspense)
"Master" - "Merit" Publications: June-July, 1951 - No. 24, July, 1955
1-Wood-c/a (8 pgs.) 142 284 426 909 1555 2200
2-Classic skull-c; Wood/Harrison-c/a (8 pgs.) 142 284 426 909 1555 2200
3-9: 7-Dismemberment, hypo blood drainage stys 58 116 174 371 636 900
10-Cannibalism story; witch burning-c 103 206 309 659 1130 1600
11-13,15-17: 11-Severed head panels. 13-Dismemberment-c/story. 17-The Old Gravedigger host 53 106 159 334 567 800
14-Several E.C. Craig swipes 54 108 162 343 574 825
18-Bondage, skeletons-c 77 154 231 493 847 1200
19-Injury-to-eye panel; E.C. swipe; torture-c 226 452 678 1446 2473 3500
20-Female bondage, blood drainage story 61 122 183 390 670 950
21,22: 21-Devil-c. 22-Last pre-code issue, misdated 3/54 instead of 3/55 42 84 126 265 445 625
23,24 34 68 102 199 325 450
NOTE: *Cameron a-1, 2. Myron Fass c/a-21. Harrison a-3, 7; c-3. Hollingsworth a-7-17, 20, 21, 23. Wildey a-5. Woodish art by Fleishman-9; c-10, 14-17. Bondage c-10, 18, 19.*

DARK NEMESIS (VILLAINS) (See Teen Titans)
DC Comics: Feb, 1998 ($1.95, one-shot)
1-Jurgens-s/Pearson-c 3.00

DARKNESS, THE (See Witchblade #10)
Image Comics (Top Cow Productions): Dec, 1996 - No. 40, Aug, 2001 ($2.50)
Special Preview Edition-(7/96, B&W)-Ennis script; Silvestri-a(p) 2 4 6 9 13 16
0 2 4 6 8 10 12
0-Gold Edition 16.00
1/2 1 3 4 6 8 10
1/2-Christmas-c 3 6 9 14 19 24
1/2-(3/01, $2.95) r/#1/2 w/new 6 pg. story & Silvestri-c 3.00
1-Ennis-s/Silvestri-a, 1-Black variant-c 2 4 6 9 12 15
1-Platinum variant-c 20.00
1-DF Green variant-c 12.00
1,2: 1-Fan Club Ed. 1 3 4 6 8 10
3-5 6.00
6-10: 9,10-Witchblade "Family Ties" x-over pt. 2,3 4.00
7-Variant-c w/concubine 1 2 3 5 7 9
8-American Entertainment 6.00
8-10-American Entertainment Gold Ed. 7.00
11-Regular Ed.; Ennis-s/Silverstri & D-Tron-c 3.00
11-Nine (non-chromium) variant-c (Benitez, Cabrera, the Hildebrandts, Finch, Keown, Peterson, Portacio, Tan, Turner 4.50
11-Chromium-c by Silvestri & Batt 20.00

Darkness #84 © TCOW

Dark Reign: Young Avengers #5 © MAR

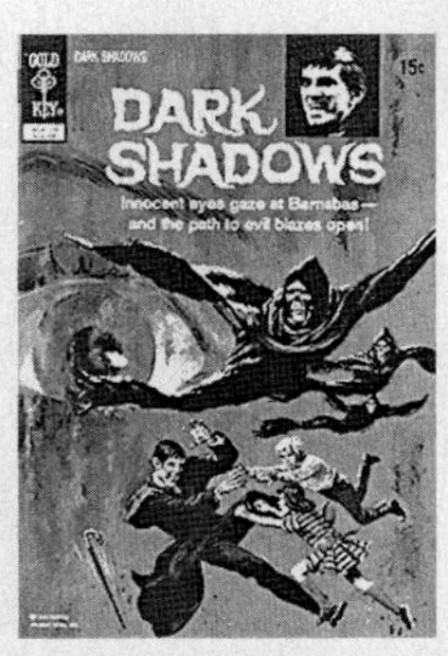

Dark Shadows #15 © Dan Curtis

GD 2.0 | VG 4.0 | FN 6.0 | VF 8.0 | VF/NM 9.0 | NM- 9.2

12-19: 13-Begin Benitez-a(p) 3.00
20-24,26-40: 34-Ripclaw app. 3.00
25-($3.99) Two covers (Benitez, Silvestri) 4.00
25-Chromium-c variant by Silvestri 8.00
.../ Batman (8/99, $5.95) Silvestri, Finch, Lansing-a(p) 6.00
...Collected Editions #1-4 ($4.95,TPB) 1-r/#1,2. 2-r/#3,4. 3- r/#5,6. 4- r/#7,8 6.00
...Collected Editions #5,6 ($5.95, TPB)5- r/#11,12. 6-r/#13,14 6.00
Deluxe Collected Editions #1 (12/98, $14.95, TPB) r/#1-6 & Preview 15.00
...: Heart of Darkness (2001, $14.95, TPB) r/ #7,8, 11-14 15.00
Holiday Pin-up-American Entertainment 5.00
Holiday Pin-up Gold Ed.-American Entertainment 7.00
Image Firsts: Darkness #1 (9/10, $1.00) r/#1 with "Image Firsts" logo on cover 3.00
Infinity #1 (8/99, $3.50) Lobdell-s 3.50
Prelude-American Entertainment 4.00
Prelude Gold Ed.-American Entertainment 9.00
Volume 1 Compendium (2006, $59.99) r/#1-40, V2 #1, Tales of the Darkness #1-4; #1/2, Darkness/Witchblade #1/2, Darkness: Wanted Dead; cover and sketch gallery 60.00
...: Wanted Dead 1 (8/03, $2.99) Texiera-a/Tieri-s 3.00
Wizard ACE Ed.- Reprints #1 2 4 6 8 10 12

DARKNESS (Volume 2)
Image Comics (Top Cow Productions): Dec, 2002 - No. 24, Oct, 2004 ($2.99)

1-24: 1-6-Jenkins-s/Keown-a. 17-20-Lapham-s. 23,24-Magdalena app. 3.00
... Black Sails (3/05, $2.99) Marz-s/Cha-a; Hunter-Killer preview 3.00
... and Tomb Raider (4/05, $2.99) r/Darkness Prelude & Tomb Raider/Darkness Special 3.00
...: Resurrection TPB (2/04, $16.99) r/#1-6 & Vol. 1 #40 17.00
.../ The Incredible Hulk (7/04, $2.99) Keown-a/Jenkins-s 3.00
.../ Vampirella (7/05, $2.99) Terry Moore-s; two covers by Basaldua and Moore 3.00
... Vol. 5 TPB (2006, $19.99) r/#7-16 & The Darkness: Wanted Dead #1; cover gallery 20.00
... vs. Mr Hyde Monster War 2005 (9/05, $2.99) x-over w/Witchblade, Tomb Raider and Magdalena; two covers 3.00
.../ Wolverine (2006, $2.99) Kirkham-a/Tieri-s 3.00

DARKNESS (Volume 3) (Numbering jumps from #10 to #75)
Image Comics (Top Cow Productions): Dec, 2007 - Present ($2.99)

1-10: 1-Hester-s/Broussard-a. 1-Three covers. 7-9-Lucas-a. 8-Aphrodite IV app. 3.00
75 (2/09, $4.99) Four covers; Hester-s/art by various 5.00
76-99,101-113,115-($2.99) 76-99,101-Multiple covers on each 3.00
100 (2/12, $4.99) Four covers; Hester-s/art by various; cover gallery; series timeline 5.00
114-($4.99) The Age of Reason Part 1; Hine-s/Haun-a; bonus Darkness timeline 5.00
116-($3.99) The Age of Reason Part 3; Hine-s/Haun-a 4.00
... : Butcher (4/08, $3.99) Story of Butcher Joyce; Levin-s/Broussard-a/c 4.00
... : Close Your Eyes (6/14, $3.99) Story of Adelmo Estacado in 1912; Kot-s/Oleksicki-a/c 4.00
...: Confession (5/11) Free Comic Boy Day giveaway; Broussard & Molnar-a 3.00
... / Darkchylde: Kingdom Pain 1 (5/10, $4.99) Randy Queen-s/a 5.00
... First Look (11/07, 99¢) Previews series; sketch pages 3.00
... : Hope (4/16, $3.99) Harmon-s/Dwyer-a/Linda Sejic-c 4.00
... : Lodbrok's Hand (12/08, $2.99) Hester-s/Oeming-a/c; variant-c by Carnevale 3.00
... : Shadows and Flame 1 (1/10, $2.99) Lucas-c/a 3.00
... : Vicious Traditions 1 (3/14, $3.99) Ales Kot-s/Dean Ormston-a/Dale Keown-c 4.00

DARKNESS: FOUR HORSEMEN
Image Comics (Top Cow): Aug, 2010 - No. 4, May, 2011 ($3.99, limited series)

1-4-Hine-s/Wamester-a 4.00

DARKNESS: LEVEL...
Image Comics (Top Cow): No. 0, Dec, 2006 - No. 5, Aug, 2007 ($2.99, limited series)

0-5: 0-Origin of The Darkness in WW1; Jenkins-s. 1-Jackie's origin retold; Sejic-a 3.00

DARKNESS/ PITT
Image Comics (Top Cow): Dec, 2006; Aug, 2009 - No. 3, Nov, 2009 ($2.99)

...: First Look (12/06) Jenkins script pages with Keown B&W and color art 3.00
1-3: 1-(8/09) Jenkins-s/Keown-a; covers by Keown and Sejic. 2,3-Two covers 3.00

DARKNESS/ SUPERMAN
Image Comics (Top Cow Productions): Jan, 2005 - No. 2, Feb, 2005 ($2.99, limited series)

1,2-Marz-s/Kirkham & Banning-a/Silvestri-c 3.00

DARKNESS VISIBLE
IDW Publishing: Feb, 2017 - Present ($3.99)

1-Mike Carey & Arvind David-s/Brendan Cahill-a 4.00

DARKNESS VS. EVA: DAUGHTER OF DRACULA
Dynamite Entertainment: 2008 - No. 4, 2008 ($3.50, limited series)

1-4-Leah Moore & John Reppion-s/Salazar-a; three covers on each 3.50

DARK NIGHT: A TRUE BATMAN STORY
DC Comics: 2016 ($22.99, HC Graphic Novel)

HC - Paul Dini-s/Eduardo Risso-a 23.00

DARK REIGN (Follows Secret Invasion crossover)
Marvel Comics: 2009 ($3.99/$4.99, one-shots)

...: Files 1 (2009, $4.99) profile pages of villains tied in to Dark Reign x-over 5.00
...: Made Men 1 (11/09, $3.99) short stories by various incl. Pham, Leon, Oliver 4.00
...: New Nation 1 (2/09, $3.99) previews of various series tied in to Dark Reign x-over 4.00
...: The Cabal 1 (6/09, $3.99) Cabal members stories by various incl. Granov, Acuña 4.00
...: The Goblin Legacy 1 (2009, $3.99) r/ASM #39,40; Osborn history; Mayhew-a 4.00

DARK REIGN: ELEKTRA
Marvel Comics: May, 2009 - No. 5, Oct, 2009 ($3.99, limited series)

1-5-Mann-a/Bermejo-c; Elektra after the Skrull replacement. 2,3-Bullseye app. 4.00

DARK REIGN: FANTASTIC FOUR
Marvel Comics: May, 2009 - No. 5, Sept, 2009 ($2.99, limited series)

1-5-Chen-a 3.00

DARK REIGN: HAWKEYE
Marvel Comics: June, 2009 - No. 5, Mar, 2010 ($3.99, limited series)

1-5-Bullseye in the Dark Avengers; Raney-a/Langley-c. 5-Guinaldo-a 4.00

DARK REIGN: LETHAL LEGION
Marvel Comics: Aug, 2009 - No. 3, Nov, 2009 ($3.99, limited series)

1-3-Santolouco-a/Edwards-c; Grim Reaper and Wonder Man app. 4.00

DARK REIGN: MR. NEGATIVE (Also see Amazing Spider-Man #546)
Marvel Comics: Aug, 2009 - No. 3, Oct, 2009 ($3.99, limited series)

1-3-Jae Lee-c/Gugliotta-a; Spider-Man app. 4.00

DARK REIGN: SINISTER SPIDER-MAN
Marvel Comics: Aug, 2009 - No. 4, Nov, 2009 ($3.99, limited series)

1-4-Bachalo-c/a; Venom/Scorpion as Dark Avenger Spider-Man 4.00

DARK REIGN: THE HOOD
Marvel Comics: Jul, 2009 - No. 5, Nov, 2009 ($3.99, limited series)

1-5-Hotz-a/Djurdjevic-c 4.00

DARK REIGN: THE LIST
Marvel Comics: 2009 - 2010 ($3.99, one-shots)

... - Amazing Spider-Man (1/10, $3.99) Adam Kubert-c/a; back-up r/Pulse #5 4.00
... - Avengers (11/09, $3.99) Bendis-s/Djurdjevic-c/a; Ronin (Hawkeye) app. 4.00
... - Daredevil (11/09, $3.99) Diggle-s/Tan-c/a; Bullseye app.; leads into Daredevil #501 4.00
... - Hulk (12/09, $3.99) Pak-s/Oliver-a; Skaar app.; back-up r/Amaz. Spider-Man #14 4.00
... - Punisher (12/09, $3.99) Romita Jr.-a/c; Castle killed by Daken; preview of Franken-Castle in Punisher #11 6.00
... - Secret Warriors (12/09, $3.99) McGuinness-a/c; Nick Fury; back-up r/Steranko-a 4.00
... - Wolverine (12/09, $3.99) Ribic-a/c; Marvel Boy and Fantomex app. 4.00
... - X-Men (11/09, $3.99) Alan Davis-a/c; Namor app.; back-up r/Kieth-a 4.00

DARK REIGN: YOUNG AVENGERS
Marvel Comics: Jul, 2009 - No. 5, Dec, 2009 ($3.99, limited series)

1-5-Brooks-a; Osborn's Young Avengers vs. original Young Avengers 4.00

DARK REIGN: ZODIAC
Marvel Comics: Aug, 2009 - No. 3, Nov, 2009 ($3.99, limited series)

1-3-Casey-s/Fox-a. 1-Human Torch app. 4.00

DARKSEID (VILLAINS) (See Jack Kirby's New Gods and New Gods)
DC Comics: Feb, 1998 ($1.95, one-shot)

1-Byrne-s/Pearson-c 3.00

DARKSEID VS. GALACTUS: THE HUNGER
DC Comics: 1995 ($4.95, one-shot) (1st DC/Marvel x-over by John Byrne)

nn-John Byrne-c/a/script 6.00

DARK SHADOWS
Steinway Comic Publ. (Ajax)(America's Best): Oct, 1957 - No. 3, May, 1958

	GD 2.0	VG 4.0	FN 6.0	VF 8.0	VF/NM 9.0	NM- 9.2
1	32	64	96	188	307	425
2,3	21	42	63	122	199	275

DARK SHADOWS (TV) (See Dan Curtis Giveaways)
Gold Key: Mar, 1969 - No. 35, Feb, 1976 (Photo-c: 1-7)

	GD 2.0	VG 4.0	FN 6.0	VF 8.0	VF/NM 9.0	NM- 9.2
1(30039-903)-With pull-out poster (25¢)	21	42	63	147	324	500
1-With poster missing	7	14	21	48	89	130
2	8	16	24	54	102	150
3-With pull-out poster	9	18	27	60	120	180
3-With poster missing	5	10	15	35	63	90
4-7: 7-Last photo-c	6	12	18	38	69	100

Dark Shadows Volume 1 #18 © Curtis Holdings

Dark Tower: The Gunslinger Born #3 © Stephen King

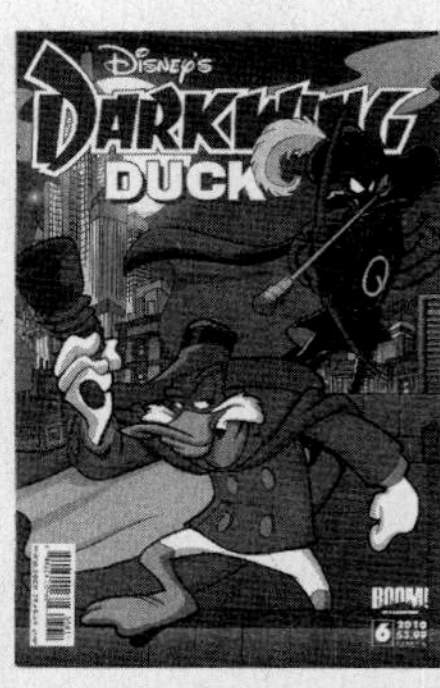

Darkwing Duck (2010 series) #6 © DIS

	GD 2.0	VG 4.0	FN 6.0	VF 8.0	VF/NM 9.0	NM- 9.2
8-10	5	10	15	30	50	70
11-20	4	8	12	27	44	60
21-35: 30-Last painted-c	4	8	12	23	37	50
Story Digest 1 (6/70, 148pp.)-Photo-c (low print)	7	14	21	46	86	125

DARK SHADOWS (TV) (See Nightmare on Elm Street)
Innovation Publishing: June, 1992 - No. 4, Spring, 1993 ($2.50, limited series, coated stock)
1-Based on 1991 NBC TV mini-series; painted-c 5.00
2-4 4.00

DARK SHADOWS: BOOK TWO
Innovation Publishing: 1993 - No. 4, July, 1993 ($2.50, limited series)
1-4-Painted-c. 4-Maggie Thompson scripts 4.00

DARK SHADOWS: BOOK THREE
Innovation Publishing: Nov, 1993 ($2.50)
1-(Whole #9) 4.00

DARK SHADOWS/VAMPIRELLA
Dynamite Entertainment: 2012 - No. 5, 2012 ($3.99, limited series)
1-5-Andreyko-s/Berkenkotter-a/Neves-c 4.00

DARK SHADOWS, VOLUME 1
Dynamite Entertainment: 2011 - No. 23, 2013 ($3.99)
1-23-Set in 1971. 1-Aaron Campbell-a; covers by Campbell & Francavilla 4.00

DARK SHADOWS: YEAR ONE
Dynamite Entertainment: 2013 - No. 6, 2013 ($3.99, limited series)
1-6-Origin of Barnabas Collins; Andreyko-s/Vilanova-a 4.00

DARK SOULS: LEGENDS OF THE FLAME (Based on the Bandai Namco video game)
Titan Comics: Sept, 2016 - No. 2, Nov, 2016 ($3.99, limited series)
1,2-Short stories by various; multiple covers on each 4.00

DARK SOULS: THE BREATH OF ANDOLUS (Based on the Bandai Namco video game)
Titan Comics: May, 2016 - No. 4, Sept, 2016 ($3.99, limited series)
1-4-George Mann-s/Alan Quah-a; multiple covers on each 4.00

DARK SOULS: WINTER'S SPITE (Based on the Bandai Namco video game)
Titan Comics: Dec, 2016 - Present ($3.99, limited series)
1-3-George Mann-s/Alan Quah-a; multiple covers on each 4.00

DARKSTAR AND THE WINTER GUARD
Marvel Comics: Aug, 2010 - No. 3, Oct, 2010 ($3.99, limited series)
1-3-Gallaher-s/Ellis-a/Henry-c; back-up reprint from X-Men Unlimited #28 4.00

DARKSTARS, THE
DC Comics: Oct, 1992 - No. 38, Jan, 1996 ($1.75/$1.95)
1-1st app. The Darkstars 4.00
2-24,0,25-38: 5-Hawkman & Hawkwoman app. 18-20-Flash app. 24-(9/94)-Zero Hour. 0-(10/94). 25-(11/94). 30-Green Lantern app. 31-...vs. Darkseid. 32-Green Lantern app. 3.00
NOTE: ***Travis Charest** a(p)-4-7; c(p)-2-5; c-6-11. **Stroman** a-1-3; c-1.*

DARK TALES FROM THE VOKESVERSE
American Mythology: 2016 ($4.99, B&W)
1-Short horror stories by Neil Vokes and various; 2 covers 5.00

DARK TOWER: THE BATTLE OF JERICHO HILL (Based on Stephen King's Dark Tower)
Marvel Comics: Feb, 2010 - No. 5, Jun, 2010 ($3.99, limited series)
1-5-Peter David & Robin Furth-s/Jae Lee & Richard Isanove-a/c; variant-c for each 4.00

DARK TOWER: THE DRAWING OF THE THREE - BITTER MEDICINE (Stephen King)
Marvel Comics: Jun, 2016 - No. 5, Oct, 2016 ($3.99, limited series)
1-5-Peter David & Robin Furth-s/Jonathan Marks-a/Nimit Malavia-c 4.00

DARK TOWER: THE DRAWING OF THE THREE - HOUSE OF CARDS (Stephen King)
Marvel Comics: May, 2015 - No. 5, Sept, 2015 ($3.99, limited series)
1-5-Peter David & Robin Furth-s/Piotr Kowalski-a/J.T. Tedesco-c 4.00

DARK TOWER: THE DRAWING OF THE THREE - LADY OF SHADOWS (Stephen King)
Marvel Comics: Nov, 2015 - No. 5, Mar, 2016 ($3.99, limited series)
1-5-Peter David & Robin Furth-s/Jonathan Marks-a/Nimit Malavia-c 4.00

DARK TOWER: THE DRAWING OF THE THREE - THE PRISONER (Stephen King)
Marvel Comics: Nov, 2014 - No. 5, Feb, 2015 ($3.99, limited series)
1-5-Peter David & Robin Furth-s/Piotr Kowalski-a/J.T. Tedesco-c 4.00

DARK TOWER: THE DRAWING OF THE THREE - THE SAILOR (Stephen King)
Marvel Comics: Dec, 2016 - No. 5, Apr, 2017 ($3.99, limited series)
1-5-Peter David & Robin Furth-s/Ramirez-a/Anacleto-c 4.00

DARK TOWER: THE FALL OF GILEAD (Based on Stephen King's Dark Tower)
Marvel Comics: July, 2009 - No. 6, Jan, 2010 ($3.99, limited series)
1-6-Peter David & Robin Furth-s/Richard Isanove-a/Jae Lee-c; variant-c for each 4.00
Dark Tower: Guide to Gilead (2009, $3.99) profile pages of people and places 4.00

DARK TOWER: THE GUNSLINGER BORN (Based on Stephen King's Dark Tower series)
Marvel Comics: Apr, 2007 - No. 7, Oct, 2007 ($3.99, limited series)
1-Peter David & Robin Furth-s/Jae Lee & Richard Isanove-a; boyhood of Roland Deschain; afterword by Ralph Macchio; map of New Canaan 6.00
1-Variant cover by Quesada 8.00
1-Second printing with variant-c by Quesada 5.00
1-Sketch cover variant by Jae Lee 40.00
2-6-Jae Lee-c 4.00
2-Second printing with variant-c by Immonen 4.00
2-7-Variant covers. 2-Finch-c. 3-Yu-c. 4-McNiven-c. 5-Land-c. 6-Campbell. 7-Coipel 6.00
2-7-B&W sketch-c by Jae Lee 20.00
... MGC #1 (5/11, $1.00) r/#1 with "Marvel's Greatest Comics" logo on cover 3.00
... Sketchbook (2006, no cover price) pencil art and designs by Lee; coloring process 5.00
Dark Tower: Gunslinger's Guidebook (2007, $3.99) profile pages with Jae Lee-a 4.00
HC (2007, $24.99) r/#1-7; variant covers and sketch pages; Macchio intro. 25.00

DARK TOWER: THE GUNSLINGER - EVIL GROUND (Stephen King's Dark Tower)
Marvel Comics: Jun, 2013 - No. 2, Aug, 2013 ($3.99, limited series)
1,2-Robin Furth & Peter David-s/Richard Isanove-a/c 4.00

DARK TOWER: THE GUNSLINGER - SHEEMIE'S TALE (Stephen King's Dark Tower)
Marvel Comics: Mar, 2013 - No. 2, Apr, 2013 ($3.99, limited series)
1,2-Robin Furth-s/Richard Isanove-a/c 4.00

DARK TOWER: THE GUNSLINGER - SO FELL LORD PERTH (Stephen King's Dark Tower)
Marvel Comics: Sept, 2013 ($3.99, one-shot)
1-Robin Furth & Peter David-s/Richard Isanove-a/c 4.00

DARK TOWER: THE GUNSLINGER - THE BATTLE OF TULL (Stephen King's Dark Tower)
Marvel Comics: Aug, 2011 - No. 5, Dec, 2011 ($3.99, limited series)
1-5-Peter David & Robin Furth-s/Michael Lark-a/c 4.00

DARK TOWER: THE GUNSLINGER - THE JOURNEY BEGINS (Stephen King's Dark Tower)
Marvel Comics: Jul, 2010 - No. 5, Nov, 2010 ($3.99, limited series)
1-5-Peter David & Robin Furth-s/Sean Phillips-a/c 4.00
1-Variant cover by Jae Lee 5.00

DARK TOWER: THE GUNSLINGER - THE LITTLE SISTERS OF ELURIA (Stephen King)
Marvel Comics: Feb, 2011 - No. 5, Jun, 2011 ($3.99, limited series)
1-5: 1-Peter David & Robin Furth-s/Luke Ross-a/c 4.00

DARK TOWER: THE GUNSLINGER - THE MAN IN BLACK (Stephen King)
Marvel Comics: Aug, 2012 - No. 5, Dec, 2012 ($3.99, limited series)
1-5-Peter David & Robin Furth-s/Maleev-a/c 4.00

DARK TOWER: THE GUNSLINGER - THE WAY STATION (Stephen King)
Marvel Comics: Feb, 2012 - No. 5, Jun, 2012 ($3.99, limited series)
1-5-Peter David & Robin Furth-s/Laurence Campbell-a/c 4.00

DARK TOWER: THE LONG ROAD HOME (Based on Stephen King's Dark Tower series)
Marvel Comics: May, 2008 - No. 5, Sept, 2008 ($3.99, limited series)
1-Peter David & Robin Furth-s/Jae Lee & Richard Isanove-a 4.00
1-Variant cover by Deodato 6.00
1-Sketch cover variant by Jae Lee 40.00
2-5-Jae Lee-c 4.00
2-5: 2-Variant-c by Quesada. 3-Djurdjevic var-c. 4-Garney var-c. 5-Bermejo var-c 6.00
2-5-B&W sketch-c by Jae Lee 20.00
2-Second printing with variant-c by Lee 4.00
Dark Tower: End-World Almanac (2008, $3.99) guide to locations and inhabitants 4.00

DARK TOWER: THE SORCEROR (Based on Stephen King's Dark Tower)
Marvel Comics: June, 2009 ($3.99, one-shot)
1-Robin Furth-s/Richard Isanove-a/c; the story of Marten Broadcloak 4.00

DARK TOWER: TREACHERY (Based on Stephen King's Dark Tower series)
Marvel Comics: Nov, 2008 - No. 6, Apr, 2009 ($3.99, limited series)
1-6-Peter David & Robin Furth-s/Jae Lee & Richard Isanove-a 4.00
1-Variant cover by Dell'otto 10.00

DARKWING DUCK (TV cartoon) (Also see Cartoon Tales)
Disney Comics: Nov, 1991 - No. 4, Feb, 1992 ($1.50, limited series)
1-4: Adapts hour-long premiere TV episode 3.00

DARKWING DUCK (TV cartoon)

Darling Love #3 © ACP

Darth Vader #13 © Lucasfilm

Dawn #2 © J.M. Linsner

	GD 2.0	VG 4.0	FN 6.0	VF 8.0	VF/NM 9.0	NM- 9.2

BOOM! Studios (KABOOM!): Jun, 2010 - No. 18, Nov, 2011 ($3.99)

1-Brill-s/Silvani-a; Launchpad McQuack app.; 3 covers						5.00
2-18-Multiple covers on all. 7-Batman #1 cover swipe. 8-Detective #31 cover swipe						4.00
Annual 1 (3/11, $4.99) Three covers; Quackerjack app.						5.00
... Free Comic Book Day Edition (5/11) Flip book with Chip 'N' Dale Rescue Rangers						3.00

DARK WOLVERINE (See Wolverine 2003 series)

DARK X-MEN (See Dark Avengers and the Dark Reign mini-series)
Marvel Comics: Jan, 2010 - No. 5, May, 2010 ($3.99, limited series)

1-5-Cornell-s/Kirk-a. 1-3-Bianchi-c. 1-Nate Grey returns						4.00
...: The Confession (11/09, $3.99) Cansino-a; Paquette-c						4.00

DARK X-MEN: THE BEGINNING (See Dark Avengers and the Dark Reign mini-series)
Marvel Comics: Sept, 2009 - No. 3, Oct, 2009 ($3.99, limited series)

1-3: 1-Cornell-s/Kirk-a; Jae Lee-c on all. 2-Daken app. 3-Mystique app.; Jock-a						4.00

DARLING LOVE
Close Up/Archie Publ. (A Darling Magazine): Oct-Nov, 1949 - No. 11, 1952 (no month) (52 pgs.)(Most photo-c)

1-Photo-c	25	50	75	150	245	340
2-Photo-c	15	30	45	83	124	165
3-8,10,11: 3-6-photo-c	13	26	39	74	105	135
9-Krigstein-a	14	28	42	78	112	145

DARLING ROMANCE
Close Up (MLJ Publications): Sept-Oct, 1949 - No. 7, 1951 (All photo-c)

1-(52 pgs.)-Photo-c	27	54	81	162	266	370
2	15	30	45	83	124	165
3-7	13	26	39	74	105	135

DARQUE PASSAGES (See Master Darque)
Acclaim (Valiant): April, 1998 ($2.50)

1-Christina Z.-s/Manco-c/a						3.00

DART (Also see Freak Force & Savage Dragon)
Image Comics (Highbrow Entertainment): Feb, 1996 - No. 3, May, 1996 ($2.50, lim. series)

1-3						3.00

DARTH MAUL
Marvel Comics: Apr, 2015 - Present ($4.99)

1-Cullen Bunn-s/Luke Ross-a; back-up by Eliopoulos-s/a						5.00

DARTH VADER (Follows after the end of Star Wars Episode IV)
Marvel Comics: Apr, 2015 - No. 25, Dec, 2016 ($4.99/$3.99)

1-($4.99) Gillen-s/Larroca-a/Granov-c; Jabba the Hut & Boba Fett app.						5.00
2,4-12-($3.99) 6-Boba Fett app.						4.00
3-Intro. Doctor Aphra and Triple Zero						5.00
13-19,21-24: 13-15-Vader Down x-over pts. 2,4,6. 24-Flashbacks to Episode III						4.00
20-($4.99) The Emperor app.; back-up Triple-Zero & Beetee story w/Norton-a						5.00
25-($5.99) Gillen-s/Larroca-a; back-up story with Fiumara-a; bonus cover gallery						6.00
Annual 1 (2/16, $4.99) Gillen-s/Yu-a/c						5.00
...: Doctor Aphra No. 1 Halloween Comic Fest 2016 (12/16, giveaway) r/#3						3.00

DASTARDLY & MUTTLEY (See Fun-In No. 1-4, 6 and Kite Fun Book)

DATE WITH DANGER
Standard Comics: No. 5, Dec, 1952 - No. 6, Feb, 1953

5,6-Secret agent stories: 6-Atom bomb story	10	20	30	54	72	90

DATE WITH DEBBI (Also see Debbi's Dates)
National Periodical Publ.: Jan-Feb, 1969 - No. 17, Sept-Oct, 1971; No. 18, Oct-Nov, 1972

1-Teenage	7	14	21	48	89	130
2-5,17-(52 pgs) James Taylor sty.	4	8	12	25	40	55
6-12,18-Last issue	4	8	12	23	37	50
13-16-(68 pgs.): 14-1 pg. story on Jack Wild. 15-Marlo Thomas/"That Girl" story	4	8	12	27	44	60

DATE WITH JUDY, A (Radio/TV, and 1948 movie)
National Periodical Publications: Oct-Nov, 1947 - No. 79, Oct-Nov, 1960 (No. 1-25: 52 pgs.)

1-Teenage	34	68	102	199	325	450
2	16	32	48	94	147	200
3-10	14	28	42	80	115	150
11-20	11	22	33	62	86	110
21-40	10	20	30	58	79	100
41-45: 45-Last pre-code (2-3/55)	10	20	30	54	72	90
46-79: 79-Drucker-c/a	9	18	27	50	65	80

DATE WITH MILLIE, A (Life With Millie No. 8 on)(Teenage)
Atlas/Marvel Comics (MPC): Oct, 1956 - No. 7, Aug, 1957; Oct, 1959 - No. 7, Oct, 1960

1(10/56)-(1st Series)-Dan DeCarlo-a in #1-7	41	82	123	256	428	600
2	22	44	66	132	216	300
3-7	19	38	57	111	176	240
1(10/59)-(2nd Series)	22	44	66	132	216	300
2-7	15	30	45	85	130	175

DATE WITH PATSY, A (Also see Patsy Walker)
Atlas Comics: Sept, 1957 (One-shot)

1-Starring Patsy Walker	20	40	60	114	182	250

DAUGHTERS OF THE DRAGON (See Heroes For Hire)
Marvel Comics: 2005; Mar, 2006 - No. 6, Aug, 2006 ($2.99, limited series)

1-6-Palmiotti & Gray-s/Evans-a. 1-Rhino app. 5,6-Iron Fist app.						3.00
... Deadly Hands Special (2005, $3.99) reprints app. from Deadly Hands of Kung Fu #32,33 & Bizarre Adventures #25; Claremont-s/Rogers-a; new Rogers-c & interview						4.00
...: Samurai Bullets TPB (2006, $15.99) r/#1-6						16.00

DAVID AND GOLIATH (Movie)
Dell Publishing Co.: No. 1205, July, 1961

Four Color 1205-Photo-c	6	12	18	42	79	115

DAVID BORING (See Eightball)
Pantheon Books: 2000 ($24.95, hardcover w/dust jacket)

Hardcover - reprints David Boring stories from Eightball; Clowes-s/a						25.00

DAVID CASSIDY (TV)(See Partridge Family, Swing With Scooter #33 & Time For Love #30)
Charlton Comics: Feb, 1972 - No. 14, Sept, 1973

1-Most have photo covers	6	12	18	38	69	100
2-5	4	8	12	25	40	55
6-14	4	8	12	23	37	50

DAVID LADD'S LIFE STORY (See Movie Classics)

DAVY CROCKETT (See Dell Giants, Fightin..., Frontier Fighters, It's Game Time, Power Record Comics, Western Tales & Wild Frontier)

DAVY CROCKETT (Frontier Fighter...)
Avon Periodicals: 1951

nn-Tuska?, Reinman-a; Fawcette-c	20	40	60	114	182	250

DAVY CROCKETT (...King of the Wild Frontier No. 1,2)(TV)
Dell Publishing Co./Gold Key: 5/55 - No. 671, 12/55; No. 1, 12/63; No. 2, 11/69 (Walt Disney)

Four Color 631(#1)-Fess Parker photo-c	14	28	42	96	211	325
Four Color 639-Photo-c	11	22	33	76	163	260
Four Color 664,671(Marsh-a)-Photo-c	11	22	33	75	160	245
1(12/63-Gold Key)-Fess Parker photo-c; reprints	7	14	21	46	86	125
2(11/69)-Fess Parker photo-c; reprints	4	8	12	28	44	60

DAVY CROCKETT (...Frontier Fighter #1,2; Kid Montana #9 on)
Charlton Comics: Aug, 1955 - No. 8, Jan, 1957

1	10	20	30	58	79	100
2	7	14	21	37	46	55
3-8	6	12	18	28	34	40

DAWN
Sirius Entertainment/Image Comics: June, 1995 - No. 6, 1996 ($2.95)

1/2-w/certificate	1	2	3	5	6	8
1/2-Variant-c	2	4	6	10	14	18
1-Linsner-c/a	1	2	3	5	6	8
1-Black Light Edition	2	4	6	9	13	16
1-White Trash Edition	3	6	9	16	23	30
1-Look Sharp Edition	3	6	9	18	28	38
2-4: Linsner-c/a						4.50
2-Variant-c, 3-Limited Edition	2	4	6	13	18	22
4-6-Vibrato-c						3.50
4, 5-Limited Edition	2	4	6	8	10	12
6-Limited Edition	2	4	6	8	10	12
...Convention Sketchbook (Image Comics, 2002, $2.95) pin-ups						3.00
...2003 Convention Sketchbook (Image Comics, 3/03, $2.95) pin-ups						3.00
...2004 Convention Sketchbook (Image Comics, 4/04, $2.95) pin-ups						3.00
...2005 Convention Sketchbook (Image Comics, 5/05, $2.95) pin-ups						3.00
Genesis Edition ('99, Wizard supplement) previews Return of the Goddess						3.00
Lucifer's Halo TPB (11/97, $19.95) r/Drama, Dawn #1-6 plus 12 pages of new artwork						20.00
...: Not to Touch The Earth (9/10, $5.99) Linsner-s/c/a; pin-ups by various incl. Turner						6.00
...: Tenth Anniversary Special (9/99, $2.95) Interviews						3.00
The Portable Dawn ($9.95, 5"x4", 64 pgs.) Pocket-sized cover gallery						10.00
...: The Swordmaster's Daughter & Other Stories (2013, $3.99) Linsner-s/c/a						4.00

DAWN OF THE DEAD (George A. Romaro's...)

Dawn of the Planet of the Apes #2 © 20th Century Fox

Dazzler #26 © MAR

DC Comics Bombshells #8 © DC

GD VG FN VF VF/NM NM-
2.0 4.0 6.0 8.0 9.0 9.2

GD VG FN VF VF/NM NM-
2.0 4.0 6.0 8.0 9.0 9.2

IDW Publishing: Apr, 2004 - No. 3, Jun, 2004 ($3.99, limited series)

1-3-Adaptation of the 2004 movie; Niles-s 4.00
TPB (9/04, $17.99) r/#1-3; intro. by George A. Romero 18.00

DAWN OF THE PLANET OF THE APES
BOOM! Studios: Nov, 2014 - No. 6, Apr, 2015 ($3.99, limited series)

1-6: 1-Takes place between the 2011 and 2014 movies; Moreci-s/McDaid-a 4.00

DAWN: THE RETURN OF THE GODDESS
Sirius Entertainment: Apr, 1999 - No. 4, July, 2000 ($2.95, limited series)

1-4-Linsner-s/a 3.00
TPB (4/02, $12.95) r/#1-4; intro. by Linsner 13.00

DAWN: THREE TIERS
Image Comics: Jun, 2003 - No. 6, Aug, 2005 ($2.95, limited series)

1-6-Linsner-s/a. 2-Preview of Vampire's Christmas 3.00

DAWN / VAMPIRELLA
Dynamite Entertainment: 2014 - No. 5, 2015 ($3.99, limited series)

1-5-Linsner-s/a/c. 3-Vampirella origin re-told 4.00

DAYDREAMERS (See Generation X)
Marvel Comics: Aug, 1997 - No. 3, Oct, 1997 ($2.50, limited series)

1-3-Franklin Richards, Howard the Duck, Man-Thing app. 3.00

DAY MEN
BOOM! Studios: Jul, 2013 - No. 8, Oct, 2015 ($3.99)

1-Stelfreeze-a/c; Gagnon & Nelson-s 5.00
2-8: 2-Covers by Stelfreeze & Pérez 4.00
...: Pen & Ink No. 1 (12/13, $9.99, 11"x17") Pen and ink art for #1&2 with commentary 10.00

DAY OF JUDGMENT
DC Comics: Nov, 1999 - No. 5, Nov, 1999 ($2.95/$2.50, limited series)

1-($2.95) Spectre possessed; Matt Smith-a 3.00
2-5: Parallax returns. 5-Hal Jordan becomes the Spectre 3.00
...Secret Files 1 (11/99, $4.95) Harris-c 5.00

DAY OF VENGEANCE (Prelude to Infinite Crisis)(Also see Birds of Prey #76 for 1st app. of Black Alice)
DC Comics: June, 2005 - No. 6, Nov, 2005 ($2.50, limited series)

1-6: 1-Jean Loring becomes Eclipso; Spectre, Ragman, Enchantress, Detective Chimp, Shazam app.; Justiniano-a. 2,3-Capt. Marvel app. 4-6-Black Alice app. 3.00
...: Infinite Crisis Special 1 (3/06, $4.99) Justiniano-a/Simonson-c 5.00
TPB (2005, $12.99) r/series & Action #826, Advs. of Superman #639, Superman #216 13.00

DAYS OF THE DEFENDERS (See Defenders, The)
Marvel Comics: Mar, 2001 ($3.50, one-shot)

1-Reprints early team-ups of members, incl. Marvel Feature #1; Larsen-c 3.50

DAYS OF THE MOB (See In the Days of the Mob)

DAYTRIPPER
DC Comics (Vertigo): Feb, 2010 - No. 10, Nov, 2010 ($2.99, limited series)

1-10-Gabriel Bá & Fábio Moon-s/a 3.00
TPB (2010, $19.99) r/#1-10; sketch art pages 20.00

DAZEY'S DIARY
Dell Publishing Co.: June-Aug, 1962

01-174-208: Bill Woggon-c/a 4 8 12 27 44 60

DAZZLER, THE (Also see Marvel Graphic Novel & X-Men #130)
Marvel Comics Group: Mar, 1981 - No. 42, Mar, 1986

1-X-Men app. 2 4 6 8 10 12
2-20,23,25,26,29-32,34-37,39-41: 2-X-Men app. 10,11-Galactus app. 23-Rogue/Mystique 1 pg. app. 26-Jusko-c. 40-Secret Wars II 4.00
21,22,24,27,28,38,42: 21-Double size; photo-c. 22 (12/82)-vs. Rogue Battle-c/sty. 24-Full app. Rogue w/Powerman (Iron Fist). 27-Rogue app. 28-Full app. Rogue; Mystique app. 38-Wolverine-c/app.; X-Men app. 42-Beast-c/app. 5.00
33-Michael Jackson "Thriller" swipe-c/sty 1 3 4 6 8 10
One-shot (7/10, $3.99) Andrasofszky-a/c; Arcade app. 4.00
NOTE: *No. 1 distributed only through comic shops.* ***Alcala*** *a-1i, 2i.* ***Chadwick*** *a-38-42p; c(p)-39, 41, 42.* ***Guice*** *a-38i, 42i; c-38, 40.*

DC CHALLENGE (Most DC superheroes appear)
DC Comics: Nov, 1985 - No. 12, Oct, 1986 ($1.25/$2.00, maxi-series)

1-11: 1-Colan-a. 2,8-Batman-c/app. 4-Gil Kane-c/a 3.00
12-($2.00-c) Giant; low print 4.00
NOTE: *Batman app. in 1-4, 6-12. Joker app. in 7.* ***Infantino*** *a-3.* ***Ordway*** *c-12.* ***Swan/Austin*** *c-10.*

DC COMICS: BOMBSHELLS
DC Comics: Oct, 2015 - Present ($3.99, printings of digital-first stories)

1-23: 1-Bennett-s/Sauvage-a/Lucia-a; set in 1940 WWII. 4,14-18-Harley Quinn-c/app. 4.00
Annual 1 (10/16, $4.99) Bennett-s/Charretier-a; origin of vampire Batgirl 5.00

DC COMICS CLASSICS LIBRARY (Hardcover collections of classic DC stories)
DC Comics: 2009 - Present ($39.99, hardcover with dustjacket)

Batman: A Death in the Family ('09)- r/Batman #426-429, 440-442, New Titans #60,61 40.00
Batman Annuals ('09)- r/Batman Annual #1-3; afterword by Richard Bruning 40.00
Batman Annuals Volume 2 ('10)- r/Batman Annual #4-7; intro. by Michael Uslan 40.00
Flash of Two Worlds ('09)- r/Flash #123,129,137,151,170&173 team-ups with G.A. Flash 40.00
Justice League of America by George Pérez ('09) r/J.L.of A. #184-186, 192-194 40.00
Justice League of America by George Pérez Vol. 2 ('10) r/J.L.of A. #195-197,200 40.00
Legion of Super-Heroes: The Life and Death of Ferro Lad ('09) - r/Adventure Comics # 346, 347,352-355,357; intro. by Paul Levitz; afterword by Jim Shooter 40.00
Roots of the Swamp Thing ('09)- r/House of Secrets #92 & Swamp Thing #1-13; Wein intro. 40.00
Superman: Kryptonite Nevermore ('09)- r/Superman #233-238,240-242; afterword by Denny O'Neil 40.00

DC COMICS ESSENTIALS
DC Comics: ($1.00, flipbooks with DC Graphic Novel catalog of recommended titles)

...: Action Comics #1 (2/14, $1.00) Reprints Action #1 (2011) with flipbook of DC GNs 3.00
...: Batman #1 (12/13, $1.00) Reprints Batman #1 (2011) with flipbook of DC GNs 3.00
...: Batman and Robin #1 (4/16, $1.00) Reprints Batman and Robin #1 (2011) with flipbook 3.00
...: Batman and Son Special Ed. ('14, $1.00) Reprints Batman #655 with flipbook 3.00
...: Batman: Death of the Family (6/16, $1.00) Reprints Batman #13 (2011) with flipbook 3.00
...: Batman: Hush Spec. Ed. ('14, $1.00) Reprints Batman #608 with flipbook of DC GNs 3.00
...: Batman: The Black Mirror Special Ed. ('14, $1.00) Reprints Detective #871 w/flipbook 3.00
...: Batman: The Dark Knight Returns #1 (5/16, $1.00) Reprints #1 with flipbook 3.00
...: Batman: The Dark Knight Returns Special Ed. ('14, $1.00) Reprints #1 with flipbook 3.00
...: Batman: Year One #1 ('14, $1.00) Reprints Batman #404 with flipbook of DC GNs 3.00
...: DC: The New Frontier #1 (3/16, $1.00) Reprints first issue with flipbook 3.00
...: Green Lantern #1 (1/14, $1.00) Reprints Green Lantern #1 (2011) with flipbook 3.00
...: JLA #1 (6/16, $1.00) Reprints JLA #1 with flipbook of DC GNs 3.00
...: Justice League #1 (1/14, $1.00) Reprints Justice League #1 (2011) with flipbook 3.00
...: Superman Unchained #1 (5/16, $1.00) Reprints Superman Unchained #1 with flipbook 3.00
...: Watchmen #1 (2/14, $1.00) Reprints Watchmen #1 (1986) with flipbook 3.00
...: Wonder Woman #1 (12/13, $1.00) Reprints Wonder Woman #1 (2011) with flipbook 3.00

DC COMICS MEGA SAMPLER
DC Comics: 2009; Jul, 2010 (6-1/4" x 9-1/2", FCBD giveaways)

1, 2010- Short stories of kid-friendly titles; Tiny Titans, Billy Batson, Super Friends app. 3.00

DC COMICS PRESENTS
DC Comics: July-Aug, 1978 - No. 97, Sept, 1986 (Superman team-ups in all)

1-4th Superman/Flash race 4 8 12 28 47 65
1-(Whitman variant) 5 10 15 33 57 80
2-Part 2 of Superman/Flash race 3 6 9 15 22 28
2-(Whitman variant) 3 6 9 17 26 35
3,4,9-12,14-16,19,21,22-(Whitman variants, low print run, none have issue # on cover) 3 6 9 14 20 25
3-10: 3-Adam Strange. 4-Metal Men. 5-Aquaman. 6-Green Lantern. 7-Red Tornado. 8-Swamp Thing. 9-Wonder Woman. 10-Sgt. Rock 2 4 6 8 10 12
11-25,28-40: 12-Mister Miracle. 13-Legion of Super-Heroes. 19-Batgirl. 21-Elongated Man. 23-Dr. Fate. 24-Deadman. 30-Black Canary. 31-Robin. 34-Marvel Family. 35-Man-Bat. 36-Starman. 37-Hawkgirl. 38-The Flash 6.00
26-(10/80)-Green Lantern; intro Cyborg, Starfire, Raven (1st app. New Teen Titans in 16 pg. preview); Starlin-c/a; Sargon the Sorcerer back-up 8 16 24 56 108 160
27-1st app. Mongul 3 6 9 21 33 45
41-Superman/Joker-c/story; 1st app. New Wonder Woman in 16 pg. preview; Colan-a 1 3 4 6 8 10
42-46,48,50,52-71,73-76,79-83: 42-Sandman. 43,80-Legion of Super-Heroes. 52-Doom Patrol; 1st app. Ambush Bug. 58-Robin. 82-Adam Strange. 83-Batman & Outsiders 4.00
47-(7/82) He-Man-c/s (1st app. in comics) 6 12 18 38 69 100
49-Black Adam & Captain Marvel app. 3 6 9 17 26 35
51-Preview insert (16 pgs.) of He-Man (2nd app.) 2 4 6 9 12 15
72,77,78,97: 72-Joker/Phantom Stranger-c/story. 77,78-Animal Man app. (77-c also). 97-Phantom Zone 6.00
84-Challengers of the Unknown; Kirby-c/s. 6.00
85-Swamp Thing; Alan Moore scripts 6.00
86,88-96: 86-88-Crisis x-over. 88-Creeper 4.00
87-Origin/1st app. Superboy of Earth Prime 2 4 6 8 10 12
Annual 1(9/82)-G.A. Superman; 1st app. Alexander Luthor 1 2 3 5 6 8
Annual 2,3: 2(7/83)-Intro/origin Superwoman. 3(9/84)-Shazam 4.00
Annual 4(10/85)-Superwoman 4.00
NOTE: ***Adkins*** *a-2, 54; c-2.* ***Buckler*** *a-33, 34; c-30, 33, 34.* ***Giffen*** *a-39; c-59.* ***Gil Kane*** *a-28, 35, Annual 3; c-48p,*

DC Comics Presents: Batman #1 © DC

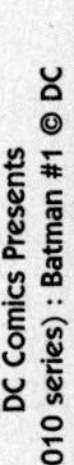

DC Comics Presents (2010 series) : Batman #1 © DC

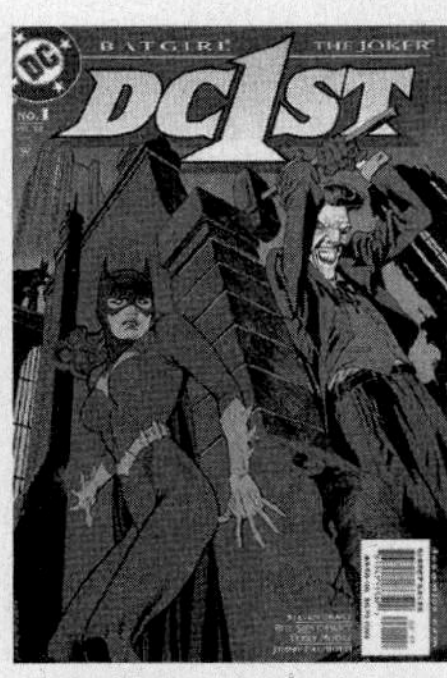

DC First: Batgirl / Joker © DC

GD 2.0 VG 4.0 FN 6.0 VF 8.0 VF/NM 9.0 NM- 9.2

GD 2.0 VG 4.0 FN 6.0 VF 8.0 VF/NM 9.0 NM- 9.2

56, 58, 60, 62, 64, 68, Annual 2, 3. ***Kirby*** *c/a-84.* ***Kubert*** *c/a-66.* ***Morrow*** *c/a-65.* ***Newton*** *c/a-54p.* ***Orlando*** *c-53i.* ***Perez*** *a-26p, 61p; c-38, 61, 94.* ***Starlin*** *a-26-29p, 36p, 37p; c-26-29, 36, 37, 93.* ***Toth*** *a-84.* ***Williamson*** *i-79, 85, 87.*

DC COMICS PRESENTS: ...(Julie Schwartz tribute series of one-shots based on classic covers)
DC Comics: Sept, 2004 - Oct, 2004 ($2.50)

The Atom -(Based on cover of Atom #10) Gibbons-s/Oliffe-a; Waid-s/Jurgens-a; Bolland-c 3.00
Batman -(Batman #183) Johns-s/Infantino-a; Wein-s/Kuhn-a; Hughes-c 3.00
The Flash -(Flash #163) Loeb-s/McGuinness-a; O'Neil-s/Mahnke-a; Ross-c 3.00
Green Lantern -(Green Lantern #31) Azzarello-s/Breyfogle-a; Pasko-s/McDaniel-a; Bolland-c 3.00
Hawkman -(Hawkman #6) Bates-s/Byrne-a; Busiek-s/Simonson-a; Garcia-Lopez-c 3.00
Justice League of America -(J.L. of A. #53) Ellison & David-s/Giella-a; Wolfman-s/Nguyen-a; Garcia-Lopez-c 3.00
Mystery in Space -(M.I.S. #82) Maggin-s/Williams-a; Morrison-s/Ordway-a; Ross-c 3.00
Superman -(Superman #264) Stan Lee-s/Cooke-a; Levitz-s/Giffen-a; Hughes-c 3.00

DC COMICS PRESENTS: ...
DC Comics: Dec, 2010 - Present ($7.99/$9.99, squarebound, one-shot reprints)

The Atom 1 (3/11) r/Legends of the DC Universe #28,29,40,41; Gil Kane-a 8.00
Batman 1 (12/10) r/Batman #582-585,600 8.00
Batman 2 (1/11) r/Batman #591-594 8.00
Batman 3 (2/11) r/Batman #595-598 8.00
Batman Adventures 1 (9/14) reprints; Burchett, Parobeck, Templeton, Timm-a 8.00
Batman: Arkham 1 (6/11) r/Batman Chronicles #6, Batman; Arkham Asylum - Tales of Madness #1, Batman Villains Secret Files #1 & Justice Leagues: J.L. of Arkham #1 8.00
Batman - Bad 1 (1/12) r/Batman: Legends of the D.K. #146-148 8.00
Batman Beyond 1 (2/11) r/Batman Beyond #13,14,21,22 8.00
Batman: Blaze of Glory 1 (2/12) r/Batman: Legends of the D.K. #197-199,212 8.00
Batman - Blink 1 (12/11) r/Batman: Legends of the D.K. #156-158 8.00
Batman/Catwoman 1 (12/10) r/Batman and Catwoman: Trail of the Gun 8.00
Batman - Conspiracy 1 (4/11) r/Batman: Legends of the D.K. #86-88; Detective #821 8.00
Batman - Dark Knight, Dark City 1 (7/11) r/Batman #452-454; Detective #633 8.00
Batman - Don't Blink 1 (1/12) r/Batman: Legends of the D.K. #164-167 8.00
Batman: Gotham Noir 1 (9/11) r/Batman: Gotham Noir #1 & Batman #604 8.00
Batman - Irresistible 1 (5/11) r/Batman: Legends of the D.K. #169-171; Hourman #22 8.00
Batman - The Demon Laughs 1 (12/11) r/Batman: Legends of the D.K. #142-145; Aparo-a 8.00
Batman: The Secret City 1 (2/12) r/Batman: Legends of the D.K. #180,181,190,191 8.00
Batman: Urban Legends 1 (2/12) r/Batman: Legends of the D.K. #168,177-179 8.00
Brightest Day 1 (12/10) r/Strange Advs. #205, Hawkman #27,34,36, Solo #8, DC Hol. '09 8.00
Brightest Day 2 (1/11) r/Firestorm #11-13 & Martian Manhunter #11,24 8.00
Brightest Day 3 (2/11) r/Legends of the DC Univ. #25-27 & Teen Titans #27,28 8.00
Captain Atom 1 (2/12) r/back-up stories from Action Comics #879-889 8.00
Catwoman - Guardian of Gotham 1 (12/11) r/Catwoman: Guardian of Gotham #1,2 8.00
Chase 1 (1/11) r/Chase #1,6-8 8.00
Darkseid War 1 (2/16, $7.99) r/New Gods #1,7, Mister Miracle #1 & Forever People #1 8.00
Demon Driven Out, The 1 (7/14, $9.99) r/The Demon: Driven Out #1-6 10.00
Elseworlds 80-Page Giant 1 (1/12) r/Elseworlds 80-Page Giant (pulled from distribution) 8.00
Flash 1 (7/11) r/Showcase #4,14 and Flash #125,130,139 8.00
Flash/Green Lantern: Faster Friends (1/11) r/G.L./Flash: Faster Friends & Flash/G.L. : FF 8.00
Green Lantern 1 (12/10) r/Green Lantern #137-140 (2001) 8.00
Green Lantern - Fear Itself 1 (4/11) r/Green Lantern: Fear Itself GN 8.00
Green Lantern - Willworld 1 (7/11) r/Green Lantern: Willworld GN 8.00
Harley Quinn 1 (4/14) r/Batman: Harley Quinn #1, Joker's Asylum II: HQ #1 and others 8.00
Impulse 1 (8/11) r/Impulse #50-53 8.00
Jack Kirby Omnibus Sampler 1 (12/11) r/Kirby art stories from 1957,1958 8.00
JLA 1 (2/11) r/JLA #90-93 8.00
JLA - Age of Wonder 1 (12/11) r/JLA: Age of Wonder 8.00
JLA: Black Baptism 1 (8/11) r/JLA: Black Baptism #1-4 8.00
JLA Heaven's Ladder 1 (10/11) comic-sized reprint; and r/Green Lantern #1,000,000 8.00
Legion of Super-Heroes 1 (6/11) r/Legion of Super-Heroes #122,123 & Legionnaires 79,80 8.00
Legion of Super-Heroes 2 (2/12) r/Adv. #247 and recent Legion short stories 8.00
Lobo 1 (3/11) r/Lobo #63,64 & DC First: Superman/Lobo #1 8.00
Metal Men 1 (4/11) r/Doom Patrol ('09) #1-7 and Silver Age: The Brave and the Bold #1 8.00
Night Force 1 (4/11) r/Night Force #1-4; Gene Colan-a 8.00
Ninja Boy 1 (6/11) r/Ninja Boy #1-4 8.00
Robin War 100-Page Super Spectacular 1 (2/16) Ryan Sook-c 8.00
Shazam! 1,2 (9/11,10/11) 1-r/Power of Shazam #38-41. 2-r/ #42-46 8.00
Son of Superman 1 (7/11) r/Son of Superman GN 8.00
Superboy's Legion 1 (12/11) r/Superboy's Legion #1,2 (Elseworlds) 8.00
Superman 1 (12/10) r/Superman: The Man of Steel #121 & Superman #179,180,185 8.00
Superman 2 (1/11) r/Action #798, Superman: The Man of Steel #133, Superman #189 & Advs. of Superman #611 8.00
Superman 3 (2/11) r/Superman #177,178,181,182 8.00
Superman 4 (9/11) r/Action #768,771-773 8.00
Superman Adventures 1 (8/12) r/Superman Adventures #16,19,22,23 8.00
Superman/Doomsday 1 (5/11) r/Doomsday Annual #1 & Superman #175 8.00
Superman - Infestation 1 (8/11) r/Action #778, Advs. of Superman #591, Superman #169 and Superman: The Man of Steel #113 8.00
Superman: Lois and Clark 100-Page S.S. 1 (1/16) r/Superman: The Wedding Album 8.00
Superman - Secret Identity 1 (12/11) r/Superman: Secret Identity #1,2 8.00
Superman - Secret Identity 2 (1/12) r/Superman: Secret Identity #3,4 8.00
Superman - Sole Survivor 1 (3/11) r/Legends of the DC Universe #1-3,39 8.00
Superman - The Kents 1,2 (1/12, 2/12) 1-r/The Kents #1-4. 2-The Kents #5-8 8.00
Teen Titans 1 (10/11) Teen Titans Lost Annual #1 and Solo #7; Allred-a 8.00
Titans Hunt 100-Page Super Spectacular 1 (1/16) r/Teen Titans early apps.; Sook-c 8.00
The Life Story of the Flash 1 (1/12) r/The Life Story of the Flash GN 8.00
T.H.U.N.D.E.R. Agents 1 (2/11) r/T.H.U.N.D.E.R. Agents #1,2,7 (1966) 8.00
Wonder Woman 1 (4/11) r/Wonder Woman #139-142 (1998) 8.00
Wonder Woman Adventures 1 (9/12) r/Advs. in the DC Universe #1,3,11,19 8.00
Young Justice 1 (12/10) r/JLA World Without Grownups #1,2 8.00
Young Justice 2 (1/11) r/Y.J: The Secret, Y.J. Secret Files #1, Y.J. In No Man's Land 8.00
Young Justice 3 (2/11) r/Young Justice #7 & Y.J Secret Origins 80-Page Giant #1 8.00

DC COMICS - THE NEW 52 FCBD SPECIAL EDITION
DC Comics: Jun, 2012 (giveaway one-shot)

1-Origin of The Trinity of Sin (Pandora, The Question, Phantom Stranger); Justice League app.; Jim Lee, Reis, Ha, Rocafort-a; previews Earth 2, G.I. Combat, Ravagers 3.00

DC COMICS THE NEW 52 PRESENTS: ...
DC Comics: Mar, 2012 - Present ($7.99, squarebound, one-shot reprints)

The Dark 1 (3/12) r/Animal Man #1, Swamp Thing #1, I, Vampire #1, and J.L. Dark #1 8.00

DC COUNTDOWN (To Infinite Crisis)
DC Comics: May, 2005 ($1.00, 80 pages, one-shot)

1-Death of Blue Beetle; prelude to OMAC Project, Day of Vengeance, Rann/Thanagar War and Villains United mini-series; s/a by various; Jim Lee/Alex Ross-c 4.00

DC FIRST: ...(series of one-shots)
DC Comics: July, 2002 ($3.50)

Batgirl/Joker 1-Sienkiewicz & Terry Moore-a; Nowlan-c 3.50
Green Lantern/Green Lantern 1-Alan Scott & Hal Jordan vs. Krona 3.50
Flash/Superman 1-Superman races Jay Garrick; Abra Kadabra app. 3.50
Superman/Lobo 1-Giffen-s; Nowlan-c 3.50

DC GOES APE
DC Comics: 2008 ($19.99, trade paperback)

Vol. 1 - Reprints app. of Grodd, Beppo, Titano and other monkey tales; Art Adams-c 20.00

DC GRAPHIC NOVEL (Also see DC Science Fiction...)
DC Comics: Nov, 1983 - No. 7, 1986 ($5.95, 68 pgs.)

1-3,5,7: 1-Star Raiders. 2-Warlords; not from regular Warlord series. 3-The Medusa Chain; Ernie Colon story/a. 5-Me and Joe Priest; Chaykin-c. 7-Space Clusters; Nino-c/a 2 4 6 9 12 15
4-The Hunger Dogs by Kirby; Darkseid kills Himon from Mister Miracle & destroys New Genesis 5 10 15 31 53 75
6-Metalzoic; Sienkiewicz-c ($6.95) 2 4 6 9 12 15

DC HOLIDAY SPECIAL '09
DC Comics: Feb, 2010 ($5.99, one-shot)

1-Christmas short stories by various incl. Dragotta, Tucci, Chaykin; Dustin Nguyen-c 6.00

DC INFINITE HALLOWEEN SPECIAL
DC Comics: Dec, 2007 ($5.99, one-shot)

1-Halloween short stories by various incl. Dini, Waid, Hairsine, Kelley Jones; Gene Ha-c 6.00

DC KIDS MEGA SAMPLER
DC Comics: June, 2009 (Free Comic Book Day giveaway, one-shot)

1-Tiny Titans, Batman: The Brave and the Bold, Billy Batson/Shazam short stories 3.00

DC/MARVEL: ALL ACCESS (Also see DC Versus Marvel & Marvel Versus DC)
DC Comics: 1996 - No. 4, 1997 ($2.95, limited series)

1-4: 1-Superman & Spider-Man app. 2-Robin & Jubilee app. 3-Dr. Strange & Batman-c/app., X-Men, JLA app. 4-X-Men vs. JLA-c/app. rebirth of Amalgam 3.00

DC/MARVEL: CROSSOVER CLASSICS
DC Comics: 1998; 2003 ($14.95, TPB)

Vol. II-Reprints Batman/Punisher: Lake of Fire, Punisher/Batman: Deadly Knights, Silver Surfer/Superman, Batman & Capt. America 15.00
Vol. 4 (2003, $14.95) Reprints Green Lantern/Silver Surfer: Unholy Alliances, Darkseid/Galactus: The Hunger, Batman & Spider-Man, and Superman/Fantastic Four 15.00

DC NATION FCBD SUPER SAMPLER
DC Comics: (Giveaway)

.../ Superman Adventures Flip Book (6/12) stories from Superman Family Adventures,

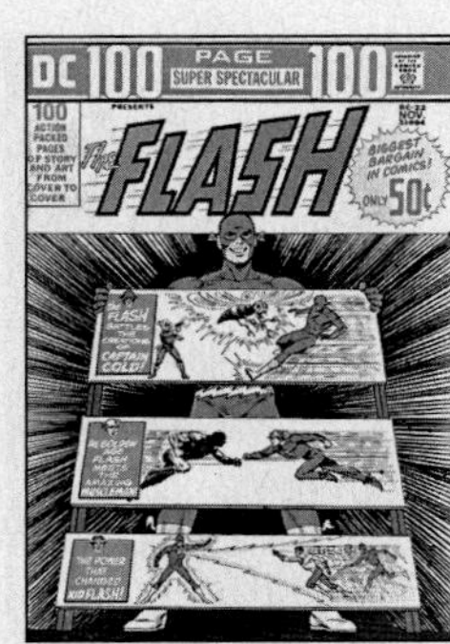

DC 100 Page Super Spectacular #22 © DC

DC Special #1 © DC

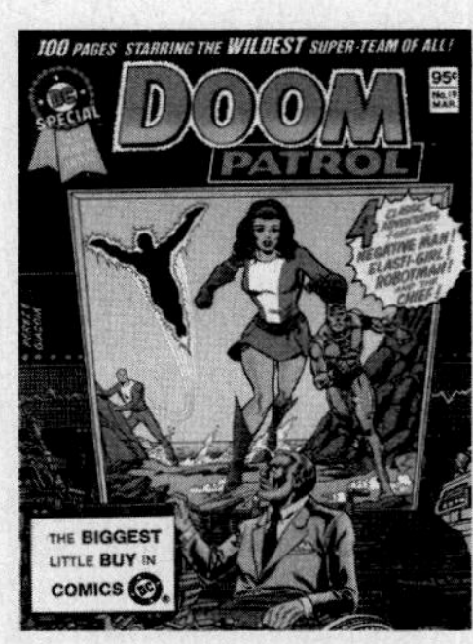

DC Special Blue Ribbon Digest #19 © DC

GD VG FN VF VF/NM NM-
2.0 4.0 6.0 8.0 9.0 9.2

GD VG FN VF VF/NM NM-
2.0 4.0 6.0 8.0 9.0 9.2

Young Justice, Green Lantern: The Animated Series 3.00
... (7/13) Stories from Beware the Batman and Teen Titans Go! 3.00

DC 100 PAGE SUPER SPECTACULAR
(Title is 100 Page... No. 14 on)(Square bound) (Reprints, 50¢)
National Periodical Publications: No. 4, Summer, 1971 - No. 13, 6/72; No. 14, 2/73 - No. 22, 11/73 (No #1-3)

4-Weird Mystery Tales; Johnny Peril & Phantom Stranger; cover & splashes by Wrightson; origin Jungle Boy of Jupiter 24 48 72 168 372 575
5-Love Stories; Wood inks (7 pgs.)(scarcer) 46 92 138 340 770 1200
6- "World's Greatest Super-Heroes"; JLA, JSA, Spectre, Johnny Quick, Vigilante & Hawkman; contains unpublished Wildcat story; N. Adams wrap-around-c; r/JLA #21,22 17 34 51 119 265 410
6-Replica Edition (2004, $6.95) complete reprint w/wraparound-c 7.00
7-(Also listed as Superman #245) Air Wave, Kid Eternity, Hawkman-r; Atom-r/Atom #3 9 18 27 60 120 180
8-(Also listed as Batman #238) Batman, Legion, Aquaman-r; G.A. Atom, Sargon (r/Sensation #57), Plastic Man (r/Police #14) stories; Doom Patrol origin-r; Neal Adams wraparound-c 12 24 36 84 185 285
9-(Also listed as Our Army at War #242) Kubert-c 9 18 27 58 114 170
10-(Also listed as Adventure Comics #416) Golden Age-reprints; r/1st app. Black Canary from Flash #86; no Zatanna 10 20 30 68 144 220
11-(Also listed as Flash #214) origin Metal Men-r/Showcase #37; never before published G.A. Flash story. 8 16 24 54 102 150
12,14: 12-(Also listed as Superboy #185) Legion-c/story; Teen Titans, Kid Eternity (r/Hit #46), Star Spangled Kid-r(S.S. #55). 14-Batman-r/Detective #31,32,156; Atom-r/Showcase #34 7 14 21 46 86 125
13-(Also listed as Superman #252) Ray(r/Smash #17), Black Condor, (r/Crack #18), Hawkman(r/Flash #24); Starman-r/Adv. #67; Dr. Fate & Spectre-r/More Fun #57; Neal Adams-c 10 20 30 66 138 210
15,16,18,19,21,22: 15-r/2nd Boy Commandos/Det. #64. 16-Sgt. Rock; r/Capt. Storm #1, 1st Johnny Cloud/All-American Men of War #82. 18-Superman. 21-Superboy; r/Brave & the Bold #54. 22-r/All-Flash #13 6 12 18 37 66 95
17,20: 17-JSA-r/All Star #37 (10-11/47, 38 pgs.), Sandman-r/Adv. #65 (8/41), JLA #23 (11/63) & JLA #43 (3/66). 20-Batman-r/Det. #66,68, Spectre; origin Two-Face 6 12 18 38 69 100
... : Love Stories Replica Edition (2000, $6.95) reprints #5 7.00

NOTE: ***Anderson*** *r-11, 14, 18i, 22.* ***B. Baily*** *r-18, 20.* ***Burnley*** *r-18, 20.* ***Crandall*** *r-14p, 20.* ***Drucker*** *r-4.* ***Grandenetti*** *a-22(2)r.* ***Heath*** *a-22r.* ***Infantino*** *r-17, 20, 22.* ***G. Kane*** *r-18.* ***Kirby*** *r-15.* ***Kubert*** *r-6, 7, 16, 17; c-16, 19.* ***Manning*** *a-19r.* ***Meskin*** *r-4, 22.* ***Mooney*** *r-15, 21.* ***Toth*** *r-17, 20.*

DC ONE MILLION (Also see crossover #1,000,000 issues and JLA One Million TPB)
DC Comics: Nov, 1998 - No. 4, Nov, 1998 ($2.95/$1.99, weekly lim. series)

1-($2.95) JLA travels to the 853rd century; Morrison-s 4.00
2-4-($1.99) 3.00
... Eighty-Page Giant (8/99, $4.95) 5.00
TPB ('99, $14.95) r/#1-4 and several x-over stories 15.00

DC REBIRTH HOLIDAY SPECIAL
DC Comics: Feb, 2017 ($9.99, one-shot)

1-Short stories by various; framing pages of Harley Quinn by Dini-s/Charretier-a 10.00

DC RETROACTIVE (New stories done in old style plus reprint from decade)
DC Comics: Sept, 2011 - Oct, 2011 ($4.99, series of one-shots)

...: Batman - The '70s (9/11, $4.99) Len Wein-s/Tom Mandrake-a; r/Batman #307 5.00
...: Batman - The '80s (10/11, $4.99) Mike Barr-s/Jerry Bingham-a; The Reaper app. 5.00
...: Batman - The '90s (10/11, $4.99) Grant-s/Breyfogle-a; Scarface & Ventriloquist app. 5.00
...: Flash - The '70s (9/11, $4.99) Bates-s/Gallego-a; r/DC Comics Presents #1,2 5.00
...: Flash - The '80s (10/11, $4.99) Messner-Loebs-s/LaRocque-a; r/Flash v2 #18 5.00
...: Flash - The '90s (10/11, $4.99) Augustyn-s/Bowden-a; r/Flash v2 #142 5.00
...: Green Lantern - The '70s (9/11, $4.99) O'Neil-s/Grell-a; r/Green Lantern #76 5.00
...: Green Lantern - The '80s (10/11, $4.99) Wein-s/Staton-a; r/Green Lantern #172 5.00
...: Green Lantern - The '90s (10/11, $4.99) Marz-s/Banks-a; r/Green Lantern v3 #78 5.00
...: JLA - The '70s (9/11, $4.99) Bates-s; Adam Strange app.; r/J.L. of A. #123 5.00
...: JLA - The '80s (10/11, $4.99) Conway-s/Randall-a; Felix Faust app.; r/J.L.of A. #239 5.00
...: JLA - The '90s (10/11, $4.99) Giffen & DeMatteis-s/Maguire-a; r/J.L.A. #6 5.00
...: Superman - The '70s (9/11, $4.99) Pasko-s/Barreto-a; r/Action Comics #484 5.00
...: Superman - The '80s (10/11, $4.99) Wolfman-s/Cariello-a; r/Superman #352 5.00
...: Superman - The '90s (10/11, $4.99) L. Simonson-s/Bogdanove-a; Guardian app. 5.00
...: Wonder Woman - The '70s (9/11, $4.99) O'Neil-s/J. Bone-a; r/Wonder Woman #201 5.00
...: Wonder Woman - The '80s (10/11, $4.99) Thomas-s/Buckler-a; r/W.W. #288 5.00
...: Wonder Woman - The '90s (10/11, $4.99) Messner-Loebs-s/Moder-a; r/W.W. v2 #66 5.00

DC SCIENCE FICTION GRAPHIC NOVEL
DC Comics: 1985 - No. 7, 1987 ($5.95)

SF1-SF7: SF1-Hell on Earth by Robert Bloch; Giffen-p. SF2-Nightwings by Robert Silverberg; G. Colan-p. SF3-Frost & Fire by Bradbury. SF4-Merchants of Venus. SF5-Demon With A Glass Hand by Ellison; M. Rogers-a. SF6-The Magic Goes Away by Niven. SF7-Sandkings by George R.R. Martin 2 4 6 8 11 14

DC SILVER AGE CLASSICS
DC Comics: 1992 ($1.00, all reprints)

...Action Comics #252-r/1st Supergirl. Adventure Comics #247-r/1st Legion of Super-Heroes. The Brave and the Bold #28-r/1st JLA. Detective Comics #225-r/1st Martian Manhunter. Detective Comics #327-r/1st new look Batman. Green Lantern #76-r/1st Green Lantern/ Green Arrow. House of Secrets #92-r/1st Swamp Thing. Showcase #4-r/1st S.A. Flash. Showcase #22-r/1st S.A. Green Lantern 4.00
...Sugar and Spike #99; includes 2 unpublished stories 5.00

DC SPECIAL (Also see Super DC Giant)
National Per. Publ.: 10-12/68 - No. 15, 11-12/71; No. 16, Spr/75 - No. 29, 8-9/77

1-All Infantino issue; Flash, Batman, Adam Strange-r; begin 68 pg. issues, end #21 8 16 24 54 102 150
2-Teen humor; Binky, Buzzy, Harvey app. 9 18 27 62 126 190
3-All-Girl issue; unpubl. GA Wonder Woman story 9 18 27 57 111 165
4,11: 4-Horror (1st Abel, brief). 11-Monsters 5 10 15 33 57 80
5-10,12-15: 5-All Kubert issue; Viking Prince, Sgt. Rock-r. 6-Western. 7,9,13-Strangest Sports. 12-Viking Prince; Kubert-c/a (r/B&B almost entirely). 15-G.A. Plastic Man origin-r/ Police #1; origin Woozy by Cole; 14,15-(52 pgs.) 4 8 12 27 44 60
16-27: 16-Super Heroes Battle Super Gorillas. 17-Early S.A. Green Lantern-r. 22-Origin Robin Hood. 26-Enemy Ace. 27-Captain Comet story 3 6 9 16 23 30
28-Earth Shattering Disaster Stories; Legion of Super-Heroes story 3 6 9 16 24 32
29-New "The Untold Origin of the Justice Society"; Staton-a/Neal Adams-c; Hitler app. in story and on cover 5 10 15 31 53 75

NOTE: ***N. Adams*** *c-3, 4, 6, 11, 29.* ***Grell*** *a-20; c-17, 20.* ***Heath*** *a-12r.* ***G. Kane*** *a-6p, 13r, 17r, 19-21r.* ***Kirby*** *a-4,11.* ***Kubert*** *a-6r, 12r, 22.* ***Meskin*** *a-10.* ***Moreira*** *a-10.* ***Staton*** *a-29p.* ***Toth*** *a-13, 20r. #1-15: 25¢; 16-27: 50¢; 28, 29: 60¢. #1-13, 16-21: 68 pgs.; 14, 15: 52 pgs.; 25-27: oversized.*

DC SPECIAL BLUE RIBBON DIGEST
DC Comics: Mar-Apr, 1980 - No. 24, Aug, 1982

1,2,4,5: 1-Legion reprints. 2-Flash. 4-Green Lantern. 5-Secret Origins; new Zatara and Zatanna 2 4 6 8 11 14
3-Justice Society reprints; new Dr. Fate story 2 4 6 10 14 18
6,8-10: 6-Ghosts. 8-Legion. 9-Secret Origins. 10-Warlord-"The Deimos Saga"-Grell-s/c/a 2 4 6 8 11 14
7-Sgt. Rock's Prize Battle Tales 2 4 6 13 18 22
11,16: 11-Justice League. 16-Green Lantern/Green Arrow-r; all Adams-a 2 4 6 11 16 20
12-Haunted Tank; reprints 1st app. 2 4 6 13 18 22
13-15,17-19: 13-Strange Sports Stories. 14-UFO Invaders; Adam Strange app. 15-Secret Origins of Super Villains; JLA app. 17-Ghosts. 18-Sgt. Rock; Kubert front & back-c. 19-Doom Patrol; new Perez-c 2 4 6 9 13 16
20-Dark Mansion of Forbidden Love (scarce) 4 8 12 28 47 65
21-Our Army at War 3 6 9 15 22 28
22-24: 22-Secret Origins. 23-Green Arrow, w/new 7 pg. story (Spiegle-a). 24-House of Mystery; new Kubert wraparound-c 2 4 6 13 18 22

NOTE: ***N. Adams*** *a-16(6)r, 17r, 23r; c-16.* ***Aparo*** *a-6r, 24r; c-23.* ***Grell*** *a-8, 10; c-10.* ***Heath*** *a-14.* ***Infantino*** *a-15r.* ***Kaluta*** *a-17r.* ***Gil Kane*** *a-15r, 22r.* ***Kirby*** *a-5, 9, 23r.* ***Kubert*** *a-3, 18r, 21r; c-7, 12, 14, 17, 18, 21, 24.* ***Morrow*** *a-24r.* ***Orlando*** *a-17r, 22r; c-1, 20.* ***Toth*** *a-21r, 24r.* ***Wood*** *a-3, 17r, 24r.* ***Wrightson*** *a-16r, 17r, 24r.*

DC SPECIAL: CYBORG (From Teen Titans) (See Teen Titans 2003 series for TPB collection)
DC Comics: Jul, 2008 - No. 6, Dec, 2008 ($2.99, limited series)

1-6: 1-Sable-s/Lashley-a; origin re-told. 3-6-Magno-a 3.00

DC SPECIAL: RAVEN (From Teen Titans) (See Teen Titans 2003 series for TPB collection)
DC Comics: May, 2008 - No. 5, Sept, 2008 ($2.99, limited series)

1-5-Marv Wolfman-s/Damion Scott-a 3.00

DC SPECIAL SERIES
National Periodical Publications/DC Comics: 9/77 - No. 16, Fall, 1978; No. 17, 8/79 - No. 27, Fall, 1981 (No. 18, 19, 23, 24 - digest size, 100 pgs.; No. 25-27 - Treasury sized)

1-"5-Star Super-Hero Spectacular 1977"; Batman, Atom, Flash, Green Lantern, Aquaman, in solo stories, Kobra app.; 1st app. Patty Spivot in Flash story; N. Adams-c 5 10 15 33 57 80
2(#1)-"The Original Swamp Thing Saga 1977"-r/Swamp Thing #1&2 by Wrightson; new Wrightson wraparound-c. 2 4 6 11 16 20
3,4,6-8: 3-Sgt Rock. 4-Unexpected. 6-Secret Society of Super Villains, Jones-a. 7-Ghosts Special. 8-Brave and Bold w/ new Batman, Deadman & Sgt Rock team-up 2 4 6 13 18 22
5-"Superman Spectacular 1977"-(84 pg, $1.00)-Superman vs. Brainiac & Lex Luthor, new 63 pg. story 3 6 9 15 22 28
9-Wonder Woman; Ditko-a (11 pgs.) 3 6 9 15 22 28

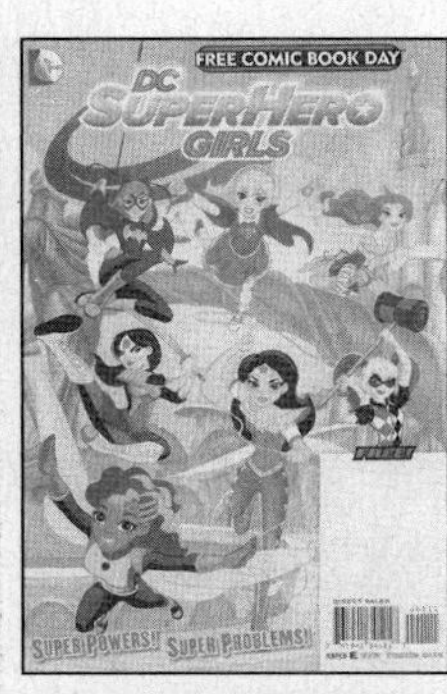

DC Superhero Girls #1 FCBD © DC

DC: The New Frontier #1 © DC

DC Universe Presents #7 © DC

	GD 2.0	VG 4.0	FN 6.0	VF 8.0	VF/NM 9.0	NM- 9.2

10-"Secret Origins of Superheroes Special 1978"-(52 pgs.)-Dr. Fate, Lightray & Black Canary on-c/new origin stories; Staton, Newton-a 3 6 9 14 20 26
11-"Flash Spectacular 1978"-(84 pgs.) Flash, Kid Flash, GA Flash & Johnny Quick vs. Grodd; Wood-i on Kid Flash chapter 2 4 6 13 18 22
12-"Secrets of Haunted House Special Spring 1978" 2 4 6 13 18 22
13-"Sgt. Rock Special Spring 1978", 50 pg new story 3 6 9 14 19 24
14,17,20-"Original Swamp Thing Saga", Wrightson-a: 14-Sum '78, r/#3,4. 17-Sum '79 r/#5-7. 20-Jan/Feb '80, r/#8-10 2 4 6 9 13 16
15-"Batman Spectacular Summer 1978", Ra's Al Ghul-app.; Golden-a. Rogers-a/front & back-c 4 8 12 25 40 55
16-"Jonah Hex Spectacular Fall 1978"; death of Jonah Hex, Heath-a; Bat Lash and Scalphunter stories 6 12 18 37 66 95
18,19-Digest size: 18-"Sgt. Rock's Prize Battle Tales Fall 1979". 19-"Secret Origins of Super-Heroes Fall 1979"; origins Wonder Woman (new-a),r/Robin, Batman-Superman team, Aquaman, Hawkman and others 2 4 6 13 18 22
21-"Super-Star Holiday Special Spring 1980", Frank Miller-a in "Batman--Wanted Dead or Alive" (1st Batman story); Jonah Hex, Sgt. Rock, Superboy & LSH and House of Mystery/ Witching Hour-c/stories 5 10 15 30 50 70
22-"G.I. Combat Sept. 1980", Kubert-c. Haunted Tank-s 3 6 9 14 19 24
23,24-Digest size: 23-World's Finest-r. 24-Flash 2 4 6 11 16 20
V5#25-($2.95)-"Superman II, the Adventure Continues Summer 1981"; photos from movie & photo-c (see All-New Coll. Ed. C-62 for first Superman movie) 3 6 9 14 19 24
26-($2.50)-"Superman and His Incredible Fortress of Solitude Summer 1981" 3 6 9 14 19 24
27-($2.50)-"Batman vs. The Incredible Hulk Fall 1981" 4 8 12 23 37 50

*NOTE: **Aparo** c-8. **Heath** a-12i, 16. **Infantino** a-19r. **Kirby** a-23, 19r. **Kubert** c-13, 19r. **Nasser/Netzer** a-1, 10i, 15. **Newton** a-10. **Nino** a-4, 7. **Starlin** c-12. **Staton** a-1. **Tuska** a-19r. #25 & 26. were advertised as All-New Collectors' Edition C-63, C-64. #26 was originally planned as All-New Collectors' Ed. C-30?; has C-630 & A.N.C.E. on cover.*

DC SPECIAL: THE RETURN OF DONNA TROY
DC Comics: Aug, 2005 - No. 4, Late Oct, 2005 ($2.99, limited series)

1-4-Jimenez-s/Garcia-Lopez-a(p)/Pérez-i 3.00

DC SUPERHERO GIRLS
DC Comics: May, 2016 (All-ages FCBD giveaway)

1 Special Edition (5/16); teenage girl heroes at Super Hero High; Fontana-s/Labat-a 3.00
... Halloween Fest Special Edition (12/16); teenage girl heroes at Super Hero High 3.00

DC SUPER-STARS
National Periodical Publ./DC Comics: March, 1976 - No. 18, Winter, 1978 (No. 3-18: 52 pgs.)

1-(68 pgs.)-Re-intro Teen Titans (predates T. T. #44 (11/76); tryout iss.) plus r/Teen Titans; W.W. as girl was original Wonder Girl 3 6 9 19 30 40
2-6,9,11,12,16: 2,4,6,8-Adam Strange; 2-(68 pgs.)-r/1st Adam Strange/Hawkman team-up from Mystery in Space #90 plus Atomic Knights origin-r. 3-Legion issue. 4-r/Tales/Unexpected #45. 11-Zatanna-c 2 4 6 8 11 14
7-Aquaman spotlight; Aqualad, Aquagirl, Ocean Master & Black Manta app.; Aparo-c 3 6 9 21 33 45
8-r/1st Space Ranger from Showcase #15, Adam Strange-r/Mystery in Space #89 & Star Rovers-r/M.I.S. #80 2 4 6 9 13 16
10-Strange Sports Stories; Batman/Joker-c/story 2 4 6 10 14 18
13-Sergio Aragonés Special 3 6 9 15 22 28
14,15,18: 15-Sgt. Rock 2 4 6 9 13 16
17-Secret Origins of Super-Heroes (origin of The Huntress); origin Green Arrow by Grell; Legion app.; Earth II Batman & Catwoman marry (1st revealed; also see B&B #197 & Superman Family #211) 8 16 24 54 102 150

*NOTE: **M. Anderson** r-2, 4, 6. **Aparo** c-7, 14, 18. **Austin** a-11i. **Buckler** a-14p; c-10. **Grell** a-17. **G. Kane** a-1r, 10r. **Kubert** c-15. **Layton** c/a-16i, 17i. **Mooney** a-4r, 6r. **Morrow** c/a-11r. **Nasser** a-11. **Newton** c/a-16p. **Staton** a-17; c-17. No. 10, 12-18 contain all new material; the rest are reprints. #1 contains new and reprint material.*

DC: THE NEW FRONTIER (Also see Justice League: The New Frontier Special)
DC Comics: Mar, 2004 - No. 6, Nov, 2004 ($6.95, limited series)

1-6-DCU in the 1940s-60s; Darwyn Cooke-c/s/a in all. 1-Hal Jordan and The Losers app. 2-Origin Martian Manhunter; Barry Allen app. 3-Challengers of the Unknown 7.00
...Volume One (2004, $19.95, TPB) r/#1-3; cover gallery & intro. by Paul Levitz 20.00
...Volume Two (2005, $19.99, TPB) r/#4-6; cover gallery & afterword by Cooke 20.00

DC TOP COW CROSSOVERS
DC Comics/Top Cow Productions: 2007 ($14.99, TPB)

SC-r/The Darkness/Batman; JLA/Witchblade; The Darkness/Superman; JLA/Cyberforce 15.00

DC 2000
DC Comics: 2000 - No. 2, 2000 ($6.95, limited series)

1,2-JLA visit 1941 JSA; Semeiks-a 7.00

DCU BRAVE NEW WORLD (See Infinite Crisis and tie-ins)
DC Comics: Aug, 2006 ($1.00, 80 pgs., one-shot)

1-Previews 2006 series Martian Manhunter, OMAC, The Creeper, The All-New Atom, The Trials of Shazam, and Uncle Sam and the Freedom Fighters; the Monitor app. 4.00

DCU (Halloween and Christmas one-shot anthologies)
DC Comics

... Halloween Special '09 (12/09, $5.99) Ha-c; art from Bagley, Tucci, K. Jones, Nguyen 6.00
... Halloween Special 2010 (12/10, $4.99) Ha-c; art from Tucci, Garbett; I...Vampire app. 5.00
... Holiday Special (2/09, $5.99) Christmas by various incl. Dini, Maguire, Reis; Quitely-c 6.00
... Holiday Special 2010 (2/11, $4.99) Jonah Hex, Spectre, Legion of S.H., Anthro app. 5.00
... Infinite Halloween Special (12/08, $5.99) Ralph & Sue Dibny app.; Gene Ha-c 6.00
... Infinite Holiday Special (2/07, $4.99) by various; Batwoman app.; Porter-c 5.00

DCU HEROES SECRET FILES
DC Comics: Feb, 1999 ($4.95, one-shot)

1-Origin-s and pin-ups; new Star Spangled Kid app. 5.00

DCU: LEGACIES
DC Comics: Jul, 2010 - No. 10, Apr, 2011 ($3.99, limited series)

1-10: 1,2-Andy Kubert-c; JSA app.; two covers on each. 3-JLA app.; Garcia-Lopez-a. 4-Sgt. Rock back-up; Joe Kubert-a. 5-Pérez-a. 8-Back-up Quitely-a 4.00

DC UNIVERSE CHRISTMAS, A
DC Comics: 2000 ($19.95)

TPB-Reprints DC Christmas stories by various 20.00

DC UNIVERSE: DECISIONS
DC Comics: Early Nov, 2008 - No. 4, Late Dec, 2008 ($2.99, limited series)

1-4-Assassination plot in the Presidential election; Winick & Willingham-s/Porter-a 3.00

DC UNIVERSE HOLIDAY BASH
DC Comics: 1997- 1999 ($3.95)

I,II-(X-mas '96,'97) Christmas stories by various 5.00
III (1999, for Christmas '98, $4.95) 5.00

DC UNIVERSE ILLUSTRATED BY NEAL ADAMS (Also see Batman Illustrated by Neal Adams HC Vol. 1-3)
DC Comics: 2008 ($39.99, hardcover with dustjacket)

Vol. 1 - Reprints Adams' non-Batman/non-Green Lantern work from 1967-1972; incl. Teen Titans, DC war, Enemy Ace, Superman and PSAs; promo art; Levitz foreword 40.00

DC UNIVERSE: LAST WILL AND TESTAMENT
DC Comics: Oct, 2008 ($3.99, one-shot)

1-Geo-Force vs. Deathstroke; DC heroes prepare for Final Crisis; Brad Meltzer-s; Adam Kubert & Joe Kubert-a; two covers 4.00

DC UNIVERSE ONLINE LEGENDS (Based on the online game)
DC Comics: Early Apr. 2011 - Late May, 2012 ($2.99)

1-26: 1-Wolfman & Bedard-s/Porter-a; DC heroes & Luthor vs. Brainiac. 1-Wraparound-c 3.00

DC UNIVERSE: ORIGINS
DC Comics: 2009 ($14.99, TPB)

nn-Reprints 2-page origins of DC characters from back-ups in 52, Countdown and Justice League: Cry For Justice #1-3; s/a by various; Alex Ross-c 15.00

DC UNIVERSE PRESENTS (DC New 52)
DC Comics: Nov, 2011 - No. 19, Jun, 2013 ($2.99)

1-5-Deadman. 1-Deadman origin re-told; Jenkins-s/Chang-a/Sook-c 3.00
6-8-Challengers of the Unknown; DiDio-s/Ordway-a/Sook-c 3.00
9-19: 9-11-Savage; Chang-a. 12-Kid Flash. 13-16-Black Lightning & Blue Devil 3.00
#0 (11/12, $5.99) O.M.A.C., Mr. Terrific, Hawk & Dove, Blackhawks, Deadman origins 6.00

DC UNIVERSE: REBIRTH
DC Comics: Jul, 2016 ($2.99, one-shot)

1-($2.99) Wally West returns; Johns-s; art by Frank, Van Sciver, Reis & Jimenez; wraparound-c by Gary Frank 3.00
1-2nd printing ($5.99, squarebound) same wraparound-c by Gary Frank 6.00
1-3rd printing ($5.99, squarebound) variant Kid Flash cover by Gary Frank 6.00

DC UNIVERSE SPECIAL
DC Comics: July, 2008 - Aug, 2008 ($4.99, collection of reprints related to Final Crisis)

...: Justice League of America (7/08) r/J.L. of A. #111,166-168 & Detective #274; Sook-c 5.00
...: Reign in Hell (8/08) r/Blaze/Satanus War x-over; Sook-c 5.00
...: Superman (7/08) r/Mongul app. in Superman #32, Showcase '95 #7,8, Flash #102 5.00

DC UNIVERSE: THE STORIES OF ALAN MOORE (Also see Across the Universe:...)
DC Comics: 2006 ($19.99)

TPB-Reprints Batman: The Killing Joke, "Whatever Happened to the Man of Tomorrow", "For The Man Who Has Everything, and other classic Moore DC stories; Bolland-c 20.00

DC UNIVERSE: TRINITY
DC Comics: Aug, 1993 - No. 2, Sept, 1993 ($2.95, 52 pgs, limited series)

Dead Boy Detectives #12 © DC

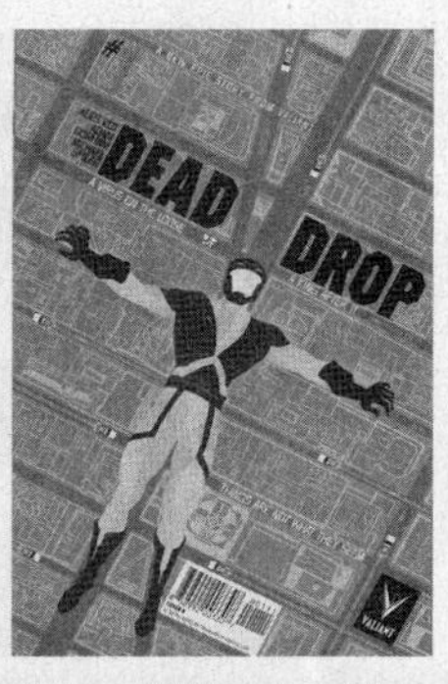

Dead Drop #1 © VAL

Deadly Hands of Kung Fu #17 © MAR

GD 2.0 | VG 4.0 | FN 6.0 | VF 8.0 | VF/NM 9.0 | NM- 9.2

1,2-Foil-c; Green Lantern, Darkstars, Legion app. 4.00

DC UNIVERSE VS. MASTERS OF THE UNIVERSE
DC Comics: Oct, 2013 - No. 6, May, 2014 ($2.99, limited series)

1-6: 1-3-Giffen-s/Soy-a/Benes-c; Constantine app. 4-6-Mhan-a 3.00

DCU VILLAINS SECRET FILES
DC Comics: Apr, 1999 ($4.95, one-shot)

1-Origin-s and profile pages 5.00

DC VERSUS MARVEL (See Marvel Versus DC) (Also see Amazon, Assassins, Bruce Wayne: Agent of S.H.I. E. L.D., Bullets & Bracelets, Doctor Strangefate, JLX, Legend of the Dark Claw, Magneto & The Magnetic Men, Speed Demon, Spider-Boy, Super Soldier, X-Patrol)
DC Comics: No. 1, 1996, No. 4, 1996 ($3.95, limited series)

1,4: 1-Marz script, Jurgens-a(p); 1st app. of Access. 5.00
.../Marvel Versus DC ($12.95, trade paperback) r/1-4 13.00

DC/WILDSTORM DREAMWAR
DC Comics: Jun, 2008 - No. 6, Nov, 2008 ($2.99, limited series)

1-6-Giffen-s; Silver Age JLA, Teen Titans, JSA, Legion app. on WildStorm Earth 3.00
1-Variant-c of Superman & Midnighter by Garbett 6.00
TPB (2009, $19.99) r/series 20.00

DC: WORLD WAR III (See 52/WWIII)

D-DAY (Also see Special War Series)
Charlton Comics (no No. 3): Sum/63; No. 2, Fall/64; No. 4, 9/66; No. 5, 10/67; No. 6, 11/68

1,2: 1(1963)-Montes/Bache-c. 2(Fall '64)-Wood-a(4) 3 6 9 21 33 45
4-6('66-'68)-Montes/Bache-a #5 3 6 9 14 20 25

DEAD AIR
Slave Labor Graphics: July, 1989 ($5.95, graphic novel)

nn-Mike Allred's 1st published work 1 2 3 5 6 8

DEAD BOY DETECTIVES
DC Comics (Vertigo): Feb, 2014 - No. 12, Feb, 2015 ($2.99, limited series)

1-12-Litt-s/Buckingham-a. 1-Covers by Buckingham & Chiang 3.00

DEAD CORPSE
DC Comics (Helix): Sept, 1998 - No. 4, Dec, 1998 ($2.50, limited series)

1-4-Pugh-a/Hinz-s 3.00

DEAD DROP
Valiant Entertainment: May, 2015 - No. 4, Aug, 2015 ($3.99, limited series)

1-4-Ales Kot-s/Adam Gorham-a; X-O Manowar app. 2-Archer app. 4.00

DEAD END CRIME STORIES
Kirby Publishing Co.: April, 1949 (52 pgs.)

nn-(Scarce)-Powell, Roussos-a; painted-c 60 120 180 381 653 925

DEAD ENDERS
DC Comics (Vertigo): Mar, 2000 - No. 16, June, 2001 ($2.50)

1-16-Brubaker-s/Pleece & Case-a 3.00
Stealing the Sun (2000, $9.95, TPB) r/#1-4, Vertigo Winter's Edge #3 10.00

DEAD-EYE WESTERN COMICS
Hillman Periodicals: Nov-Dec, 1948 - V3#1, Apr-May, 1953

V1#1-(52 pgs.)-Krigstein, Roussos-a 22 44 66 128 209 290
V1#2,3-(52 pgs.) 14 28 42 78 112 145
V1#4-12-(52 pgs.) 10 20 30 56 76 95
V2#1,2,5-8,10-12: 1-7-(52 pgs.) 8 16 24 44 57 70
3,4-Krigstein-a 9 18 27 50 65 80
9-One pg. Frazetta ad 8 16 24 44 57 70
V3#1 8 16 24 44 57 70

NOTE: ***Briefer** a-V1#8. Kinstleresque stories by **McCann**-12, V2#1, 2, V3#1. **McWilliams** a-V1#5. **Ed Moore** a-V1#4.*

DEADFACE: DOING THE ISLANDS WITH BACCHUS
Dark Horse Comics: July, 1991 - No. 3, Sept, 1991 ($2.95, B&W, lim. series)

1-3: By Eddie Campbell 3.00

DEADFACE: EARTH, WATER, AIR, AND FIRE
Dark Horse Comics: July, 1992 - No. 4, Oct, 1992 ($2.50, B&W, limited series; British-r)

1-4: By Eddie Campbell 3.00

DEAD INSIDE
Dark Horse Comics: Dec, 2016 - Present ($3.99)

1-3-Arcudi-s/Fejzula-a/Dave Johnson-c 4.00

DEAD IN THE WEST
Dark Horse Comics: Oct, 1993 - No. 2, Mar, 1994 ($3.95, B&W, 52 pgs.)

1,2-Timothy Truman-c 4.00

DEAD IRONS
Dynamite Entertainment: 2009 - No. 4, 2009 ($3.99)

1-4-Kuhoric-s/Alexander-a/Jae Lee-c 4.00

DEADLANDER (Becomes Dead Rider for #2)
Dark Horse Comics: Oct, 2007 - No. 4, ($2.99, limited series)

1-2-Kevin Ferrara-s/a 3.00

DEADLANDS (Old West role playing game)
Image Comics: Jul, 2011; Aug, 2011; Jan, 2012 ($2.99, one-shots)

...: Black Water (1/12) Mariotte-s/Brook Turner-a 3.00
...: Death Was Silent (8/11) Marz-s/Sears-a/c 3.00
...: Massacre at Red Wing (7/11) Palmiotti & Gray-s/Moder-a/c 3.00

DEADLIEST HEROES OF KUNG FU (Magazine)
Marvel Comics Group: Summer, 1975 (B&W)(76 pgs.)

1-Bruce Lee vs. Carradine painted-c; TV Kung Fu, 4pgs. photos/article; Enter the Dragon, 24 pgs. photos/article w/ Bruce Lee; Bruce Lee photo pinup 5 10 15 31 53 75

DEADLINE
Marvel Comics: June, 2002 - No. 4, Sept, 2002 ($2.99, limited series)

1-4: 1-Intro. Kat Farrell; Bill Rosemann-s/Guy Davis-a; Horn painted-c 3.00
TPB (2002. $9.99) r/#1-4 10.00

DEADLY DUO, THE
Image Comics (Highbrow Entertainment): Nov, 1994 - No. 3, Jan, 1995 ($2.50, lim. series)

1-3: 1-1st app. of Kill Cat 3.00

DEADLY DUO, THE
Image Comics (Highbrow Entertainment): June, 1995 - No. 4, Oct, 1995 ($2.50, lim. series)

1-4: 1-Spawn app. 2-Savage Dragon app. 3-Gen 13 app. 3.00

DEADLY FOES OF SPIDER-MAN (See Lethal Foes of...)
Marvel Comics: May, 1991 - No. 4, Aug, 1991 ($1.00, limited series)

1-4: 1-Punisher, Kingpin, Rhino app. 3.00

DEADLY HANDS OF KUNG FU, THE (See Master of Kung Fu)
Marvel Comics Group: April, 1974 - No. 33, Feb, 1977 (75¢) (B&W, magazine)

1(V1#4 listed in error)-Origin Sons of the Tiger; Shang-Chi, Master of Kung Fu begins (ties w/Master of Kung Fu #17 as 3rd app. Shang-Chi); Bruce Lee painted-c by Neal Adams; 2pg. memorial photo pinup w/8 pgs. photos/articles; TV Kung Fu, 9 pgs. photos/articles; 15 pgs. Starlin-a 5 10 15 35 63 90
2-Adams painted-c; 1st time origin of Shang-Chi, 34 pgs. by Starlin. TV Kung Fu, 6 pgs. photos & article w/2 pg. pinup. Bruce Lee, 11 pgs. ph/a 4 8 12 28 47 65
3,4,7,10: 3-Adams painted-c; Gulacy-a. Enter the Dragon, photos/articles, 8 pgs. 4-TV Kung Fu painted-c by Neal Adams; TV Kung Fu 7 pg. article/art; Fu Manchu; Enter the Dragon, 10 pg. photos/article w/Bruce Lee. 7-Bruce Lee painted-c & 9 pgs. photos/articles-Return of Dragon plus 1 pg. photo pinup. 10-(3/75)-Iron Fist painted-c & 34 pg. sty-Early app. 3 6 9 21 33 45
5,6: 5-1st app. Manchurian, 6 pgs. Gulacy-a. TV Kung Fu, 4 pg. article; reprints books w/Barry Smith-a. Capt. America-sty, 10 pgs. Kirby-a(r). 6-Bruce Lee photos/article, 6 pgs.; 15 pgs. early Perez-a 3 6 9 20 31 42
8,9,11: 9-Iron Fist, 2 pg. Preview pinup; Nebres-a. 11-Billy Jack painted-c by Adams; 17 pgs. photos/article 3 6 9 18 28 38
12,13: 12-James Bond painted-c by Adams; 14 pg. photos/article. 13-16 pgs. early Perez-a; Piers Anthony, 7 pgs. photos/article 3 6 9 17 26 35
14-Classic Bruce Lee painted-c by Adams. Lee pinup by Chaykin. Lee 16 pg. photos/article w/2 pgs. Green Hornet TV 6 12 18 37 66 95
15,19: 15-Sum, '75 Giant Annual #1. 20pgs. Starlin-a. Bruce Lee photo pinup & 3 pg. photos/ article re book; Man-Thing app. Iron Fist-c/sty; Gulacy-a 18pgs. 19-Iron Fist painted-c & series begins; 1st White Tiger 3 6 9 18 28 38
16,18,20: 16-1st app. Corpse Rider, a Samurai w/Sanho Kim-a. 20-Chuck Norris painted-c & 16 pgs. interview w/photos/article; Bruce Lee vs. C. Norris pinup by Ken Barr. Origin The White Tiger, Perez-a 3 6 9 16 24 32
17-Bruce Lee painted-c by Adams; interview w/R. Clouse, director Enter Dragon 7 pgs. w/B. Lee app. 1st Giffen-a (1pg. 11/75) 4 8 12 28 47 65
21-Bruce Lee 1pg. photos/article 3 6 9 16 24 32
22-1st brief app. Jack of Hearts. 1st Giffen sty-a (along w/Amazing Adv. #35, 3/76) 3 6 9 19 30 40
23-1st full app. Jack of Hearts 4 8 12 23 37 50
24-26,29: 24-Iron Fist-c & centerfold pinup. early Zeck-a; Shang Chi pinup; 6 pgs. Piers Anthony text sty w/Perez/Austin-a; Jack of Hearts app. early Giffen-a. 25-1st app. Shimuru, "Samurai", 20 pgs. Mantlo-sty/Broderick-a; "Swordquest"-c & begins 17 pg. sty by Sanho

Deadman: Dead Again #5 © DC

Deadpool #11 © MAR

Deadpool (2008 series) #1 © MAR

GD 2.0 | VG 4.0 | FN 6.0 | VF 8.0 | VF/NM 9.0 | NM- 9.2

Kim; 11 pg. photos/article; partly Bruce Lee. 26-Bruce Lee painted-c & pinup; 16 pgs. interviews w/Kwon & Clouse; talk about Bruce Lee re-filming of Lee legend. 29-Ironfist vs. Shang Chi battle-c/sty; Jack of Hearts app. 3 6 9 18 28 38
27 3 6 9 15 22 28
28-All Bruce Lee Special Issue; (1st time in comics). Bruce Lee painted-c by Ken Barr & pinup. 36 pgs. comics chronicaling Bruce Lee's life; 15 pgs. B. Lee photos/article (Rare in high grade) 7 14 21 46 86 125
30-32: 30-Swordquest-c/sty & conclusion; Jack of Hearts app. 31-Jack of Hearts app; Staton-a. 32-1st Daughters of the Dragon-c/sty, 21 pgs. M. Rogers-a/Claremont-sty; Iron Fist pinup 3 6 9 16 23 30
33-Shang Chi-c/sty; Classic Daughters of the Dragon, 21 pgs. M. Rogers-a/Claremont-story with nudity; Bob Wall interview, photos/article, 14 pgs. 3 6 9 20 31 42
...Special Album Edition 1(Summer, '74)-Iron Fist-c/story (early app., 3rd?); 10 pgs. Adams-i; Shang Chi/Fu Manchu, 10 pgs.; Sons of Tiger, 11 pgs.; TV Kung Fu, 6 pgs. photos/article 4 8 12 23 37 50

NOTE: ***Bruce Lee:*** *1-7, 14, 15, 17, 25, 26, 28.* ***Kung Fu (TV):*** *1, 2, 4.* ***Jack of Hearts****: 22, 23, 29-33.* ***Shang Chi Master of Kung Fu****: 1-9, 11-18, 29, 31, 33.* ***Sons of Tiger:*** *1, 3, 4, 6-14, 16-19.* ***Swordquest:*** *25-27, 29-33.* ***White Tiger:*** *19-24, 26, 27, 29-33.* ***N. Adams*** *a-1i(part), 27i; c-1, 2-4, 11, 12, 14, 17.* ***Giffen*** *a-22p, 24p.* ***G. Kane*** *a-23p.* ***Kirby*** *a-5r.* ***Nasser*** *a-27p, 28.* ***Perez*** *a(p)-6-14, 16, 17, 19, 21.* ***Rogers*** *a-26, 32, 33.* ***Starlin*** *a-1, 2r, 15r.* ***Staton*** *a-28p, 31, 32.*

DEADLY HANDS OF KUNG FU
Marvel Comics: Jul, 2014 - No. 4, Oct, 2014 ($3.99, limited series)
1-4-Benson-s/Huat-a/Johnson-c. 2-4-Misty Knight & Colleen Wing app. 4.00

DEADMAN (See The Brave and the Bold & Phantom Stranger #39)
DC Comics: May, 1985 - No. 7, Nov, 1985 ($1.75, Baxter paper)
1-7: 1-Deadman-r by Infantino, N. Adams in all. 5-Batman-c/story-r/Strange Adventures. 7-Batman-r 4.00
... Book One TPB (2011, $19.99) r/apps. in Strange Adventures #205-213 20.00

DEADMAN
DC Comics: Mar, 1986 - No. 4, June, 1986 (75¢, limited series)
1-4: Lopez-c/a. 4-Byrne-c(p) 4.00

DEADMAN
DC Comics: Feb, 2002 - No. 9, Oct, 2002 ($2.50)
1-9: 1-4-Vance-s/Beroy-a. 3,4-Mignola-c. 5,6-Garcia-Lopez-a 3.00

DEADMAN
DC Comics (Vertigo): Oct, 2006 - No. 13, Oct, 2007 ($2.99)
1-13: 1-Bruce Jones-s/John Watkiss-a/c; intro Brandon Cayce 3.00
...: Deadman Walking TPB (2007, $9.99) r/#1-5 10.00

DEADMAN: DARK MANSION OF FORBIDDEN LOVE
DC Comics: Dec, 2016 - No. 3, Apr, 2017 ($5.99, limited series, squarebound)
1-3-Sarah Vaughn-s/Lan Medina-a/Stephanie Hans-c 6.00

DEADMAN: DEAD AGAIN (Leads into 2002 series)
DC Comics: Oct, 2001 - No. 5, Oct, 2001 ($2.50, weekly limited series)
1-5: Deadman at the deaths of the Flash, Robin, Superman, Hal Jordan 3.00

DEADMAN: EXORCISM
DC Comics: 1992 - No. 2, 1992 ($4.95, limited series, 52 pgs.)
1,2: Kelley Jones-c/a in both 5.00

DEADMAN: LOVE AFTER DEATH
DC Comics: 1989 - No. 2, 1990 ($3.95, 52 pgs., limited series, mature)
Book One, Two: Kelley Jones-c/a in both. 1-Contains nudity 5.00

DEAD MAN'S RUN
Aspen MLT: No. 0, Dec, 2011 - No. 6, Jul, 2013 ($2.50/$3.50)
0-($2.50) Greg Pak-s/Tony Parker-a; 3 covers; bonus design sketch art 3.00
1-6: 1-(2/12, $3.50) Greg Pak-s/Tony Parker-a; 2 covers 3.50

DEAD OF NIGHT
Marvel Comics Group: Dec, 1973 - No. 11, Aug, 1975
1-Horror reprints 4 8 12 28 47 65
2-10: 10-Kirby-a. 6-Jack the Ripper-c/s 3 6 9 17 26 35
11-Intro Scarecrow; Kane/Wrightson-c 4 8 12 27 44 60
NOTE: ***Ditko*** *r-7, 10.* ***Everett*** *c-2.* ***Sinnott*** *r-1.*

DEAD OF NIGHT FEATURING DEVIL-SLAYER
Marvel Comics (MAX): Nov, 2008 - No. 4, Feb, 2009 ($3.99, limited series)
1-4-Keene-s/Samnee-a/Andrews-c 4.00

DEAD OF NIGHT FEATURING MAN-THING
Marvel Comics (MAX): Apr, 2008 - No. 4, July, 2008 ($3.99, limited series)
1-4: 1-Man-Thing origin re-told; Kano-a. 2-4-Jennifer Kale app. 4.00

DEAD OF NIGHT FEATURING WEREWOLF BY NIGHT
Marvel Comics (MAX): Mar, 2009 - No. 4, Jun, 2009 ($3.99, limited series)
1-4: 1-Werewolf By Night origin re-told; Swierczynski-s/Suayan-a 4.00

DEAD OR ALIVE - A CYBERPUNK WESTERN
Image Comics (Shok Studio): Apr, 1998 - No. 4, July, 1998 ($2.50, limited series)
1-4 3.00

DEADPOOL (See New Mutants #98 for 1st app.)
Marvel Comics: Aug, 1994 - No. 4, Nov, 1994 ($2.50, limited series)
1-Mark Waid's 1st Marvel work; Ian Churchill-c/a 2 4 6 11 16 20
2-4 1 2 3 5 6 8

DEADPOOL (... : Agent of Weapon X on cover #57-60) (title becomes Agent X)
Marvel Comics: Jan, 1997 - No. 69, Sept, 2002 ($2.95/$1.95/$1.99)
1-($2.95)-Wraparound-c; Kelly-s/McGuinness-a 6 12 18 37 66 95
2-Begin-$1.95-c. 2 4 6 9 12 15
3,5-10,12,13,15-22,24: 12-Variant-c. 22-Cable app. 6.00
4-Hulk-c/app. 2 4 6 11 16 20
11-($3.99)-Deadpool replaces Spider-Man from Amazing Spider-Man #47; Kraven, Gwen Stacy app. 3 6 9 17 26 35
14-1st Ajax; begin McDaniel-a 3 6 9 14 20 25
23,25-($2.99); 23-Dead Reckoning pt. 1; wraparound-c 1 2 3 4 5 7
26-40: 27-Wolverine-c/app. 37-Thor app. 5.00
41,43-49,51-53,56-60: 41-Begin $2.25-c. 44-Black Panther-c/app. 46-49-Chadwick-a 51-Cover swipe of Detective #38. 57-60-BWS-c 4.00
42-G.I. Joe #21 cover swipe; silent issue 2 4 6 11 16 20
50-1st Kid Deadpool 2 4 6 11 16 20
54,55-Punisher-c/app. 54-Dillon-c. 55-Bradstreet-c 3 6 9 14 20 25
61-64,66-68: 61-64-Funeral For a Freak on cover. 66-69-Udon Studios-a. 67-Dazzler-c/app. 1 3 4 6 8 10
65-Girl in bunny suit-c; Udon Studios-a 3 6 9 19 30 40
69-Udon Studios-a 2 4 6 9 12 15
#(-1) Flashback (7/97) Lopresti-a; Wade Wilson's early days 2 4 6 9 12 15
.../Death '98 Annual ($2.99) Kelly-s 3 6 9 16 23 30
... Team-Up (12/98, $2.99) Widdle Wade-c/app. 2 4 6 8 10 12
Baby's First Deadpool Book (12/98, $2.99) 3 6 9 16 23 30
Encyclopædia Deadpoolica (12/98, $2.99) Synopses 3 6 9 14 20 25
.../GLI - Summer Fun Spectacular #1 (9/07, $3.99) short stories; Pelletier-c 1 3 4 6 8 10
... Classic Vol. 1 TPB (2008, $29.99) r/#1, New Mutants #98, Deadpool: The Circle Chase #1-4 and Deadpool (1994 series) #1-4 30.00
Mission Improbable TPB (9/98, $14.95) r/#1-5 20.00
Wizard #0 ('98, bagged with Wizard #87) 6.00

DEADPOOL
Marvel Comics: Nov, 2008 - No. 63, Dec, 2012 ($3.99/$2.99)
1-($3.99) Medina-a; Secret Invasion x-over; Crain-c 3 6 9 16 23 30
1-Variant cover by Liefeld 4 8 12 27 44 60
2 1 3 4 6 8 10
3-10: 4-10-Pearson-c. 8,9-Thunderbolts x-over. 10-Dark Reign 6.00
11-24,26-33, 33.1, 34-44,46-49-($2.99): 11-20-Pearson-c. 16-18-X-Men app. 19-21-Spider-Man & Hit-Monkey app. 26-Ghost Rider app. 27-29-Secret Avengers app. 30,31-Curse of the Mutants. 37-39-Hulk app. 4.00
25-($3.99) 3-D cover, fake 3-D glasses on back-c; back-up story w/Bond-a 5.00
45-1st full app. of Evil Deadpool 2 4 6 9 12 15
49.1, 51-63 ($2.99) 49-McCrea-a. 51-Garza-a. 61-Hit-Monkey app. 4.00
50-($3.99) Uncanny X-Force & Kingpin app.; Barberi-a 1 2 3 5 6 8
900-(12/09, $4.99) Stories by various incl. Liefeld, Baker; wraparound-c by Johnson 6.00
1000-(10/10, $4.99) Stories by various; gallery of variant covers; Johnson-c 6.00
Annual 1 (7/11, $3.99) "Identity Wars" crossover; Spider-Man & Hulk app. 5.00
... & Cable #26 (4/11, $3.99) Swierczynski-s/Fernandez-a 4.00
... Family 1 (6/11, $3.99) short stories by various; Pearson-c 4.00
...: Games of Death 1 (5/09, $3.99) Benson-s/Crystal-a/Land-c 4.00
... MCG (7/10, $1.00) r/#1 with "Marvel's Greatest Comics" logo on cover 3.00

DEADPOOL
Marvel Comics: Jan, 2013 - No. 45, Jun, 2015 ($2.99)
1-Posehn & Duggan-s/Tony Moore-a/Darrow-c; Deadpool vs. Zombie ex-Presidents 2 4 6 8 10 12
2-5 6.00
6-26: 7-Iron Man app.; spoof in 1980s style; Koblish-a/Maguire-c. 10-Spider-Man app.

Deadpool (2016 series) #27 © MAR

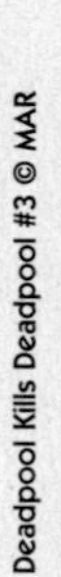

Deadpool Kills Deadpool #3 © MAR

Deadpool vs. X-Force #2 © MAR

GD	VG	FN	VF	VF/NM	NM-
2.0	4.0	6.0	8.0	9.0	9.2

13-Spoof in 1970s style; Heroes For Hire app. 15-19-Wolverine & Capt. America app. 4.00
27-($9.99) Wedding of Deadpool & Shiklah; wraparound-c with 236 characters 15.00
28-33,35-44-($3.99): 30-32-Dazzler app. 36-39-AXIS tie-in. 40-Gracking issue 4.00
34-($4.99) Original Sin tie-in; flashback in 1990s style; Sabretooth & Alpha Flight app. 1 2 3 5 6 8
45-(#250 on cover, 5/15, $9.99) Death of Deadpool; back-up short stories by various 10.00
Annual 1 (1/14, $4.99) Madcap and Avengers app.; Acker & Blacker-s/Shaner-a 5.00
Annual 2 (7/14, $4.99) Spider-Man and The Chameleon app.; Camagni-a/Nakayama-c 5.00
Bi-Annual 1 (11/14, $4.99) Scheer & Giovannetti-s/Espin-a; Brute Force app. 5.00
...: The Gauntlet (3/14, giveaway) printing of Marvel digital comics content; Cho-c 3.00

DEADPOOL
Marvel Comics: Jan, 2016 - Present ($4.99/$3.99)

1-($4.99) Duggan-s/Hawthorne-a; Deadpool starts a Heroes For Hire 5.00
2-6,8-12-($3.99) 3,4-Steve Rogers app. 6-Intro. Deadpool 2099; Koblish-a. 8-11-Sabretooth app. 12-Deadpool 2099 app. 4.00
7-($9.99) 25th Anniversary issue; back-up short stories about the Mercs For Money 10.00
13-($9.99) Crossover with Daredevil & Power Man and Iron Fist 10.00
14-20,22-24,26-28: 14-17-Civil War II tie-ins. 14-Ulysses app. 15-Black Panther app. 4.00
21-($9.99) Duggan-s/Lolli-a; Shakespeare-style story by Doescher-s/Oliveira-a 10.00
25-($5.99) Duggan-s/Koblish-a; Deadpool 2099 story 6.00
#3.1-(2/16, $3.99) All-Spanish issue about the Mexican Deadpool Masacre; Koblish-a 4.00
Annual 1 (11/16, $4.99) Spoof of Spider-Man and His Amazing Friends cartoon; Koblish-a 5.00
...: Last Days of Magic 1 (7/16, $4.99) Koblish-a/Ramos-c; Doctor Strange app. 5.00
...: Masacre 1 (7/16, $3.99) Reprints #3.1 in English 4.00

DEADPOOL & CABLE: SPLIT SECOND
Marvel Comics: Feb, 2016 - No. 3, Apr, 2016 ($3.99, limited series)

1-3-Nicieza-s/Reilly Brown-a 4.00

DEADPOOL & THE MERCS FOR MONEY
Marvel Comics: Apr, 2016 - No. 5, Aug, 2016 ($3.99)

1-5: 1-Bunn-s/Espin-a; bonus reprint of Spidey #1 4.00

DEADPOOL & THE MERCS FOR MONEY
Marvel Comics: Sept, 2016 - Present ($3.99)

1-8: 1-Bunn-s/Coello-a; Negasonic Teenage Warhead app. 4.00

DEADPOOL: BACK IN BLACK (Deadpool with the Venom symbiote right before ASM #300)
Marvel Comics: Dec, 2016 - No. 5, Feb, 2017 ($3.99, limited series)

1-5: 2-Power Pack app. 5-Spider-Man in black costume app.; Eddie Brock app. 4.00

DEADPOOL: DRACULA'S GAUNTLET (Printing of Marvel digital comic mini-series)
Marvel Comics: Sept, 2014 - No. 7, Oct, 2014 ($3.99, weekly limited series)

1-7-Duggan & Posehn-s; Deadpool meets Shiklah. 2,3,6-Blade app. 4-Frightful Four app. 4.00

DEADPOOL CORPS (Continues from Prelude to Deadpool Corps series)
Marvel Comics: Jun, 2010 - No. 12, May, 2011 ($3.99/$2.99)

1-($3.99) Liefeld-a/c; Gischler-s; 2 covers by Liefeld 1 2 3 5 6 8
2-12-($2.99) 2-5,7,9-Liefeld-a. 6-Mychaels-a 3.00
...: Rank and Foul 1 (5/10, $3.99) Handbook-style profile pages of allies and enemies 4.00

DEADPOOL KILLS DEADPOOL
Marvel Comics: Sept, 2013 - No. 4, Dec, 2013 ($2.99, limited series)

1-Bunn-s/Espin-a; Deadpool Corps app. 1 2 3 5 6 8
2-4 3.00

DEADPOOL KILLS THE MARVEL UNIVERSE
Marvel Comics: Oct, 2012 - No. 4, Oct, 2012 ($2.99, weekly limited series)

1-Bunn-s/Talajic-a/Andrews-c 3 6 9 16 23 30
2-4 2 4 6 8 10 12

DEADPOOL KILLUSTRATED
Marvel Comics: Mar, 2013 - No. 4, Jun, 2013 ($2.99, limited series)

1-Bunn-s/Lolli-a/Del Mundo-c; stories/covers styled like Classics Illustrated 1 2 3 5 6 8
2-4 4.00

DEADPOOL MAX
Marvel Comics (MAX): Dec, 2010 - No. 12, Nov, 2011 ($3.99)

1-12: 1-8,10-12-David Lapham-s/Kyle Baker-a/c. 6,7-Domino app. 9-Crystal-a 4.00
... X-Mas Special 1 (2/12, $4.99) Lapham-s; art by Lapham, Baker & Crystal; Baker-c 5.00

DEADPOOL MAX 2
Marvel Comics (MAX): Dec, 2011 - No. 6, May, 2012 ($3.99)

1-6: 1,2-David Lapham-s/Kyle Baker-a/c. 3-Crystal-a 4.00

DEADPOOL: MERC WITH A MOUTH
Marvel Comics: Sept, 2009 - No. 13, Sept, 2010 ($3.99/$2.99)

1-($3.99) Suydam-c/Dazo-a; Zombie-head Deadpool & Ka-Zar app.; r/Deadpool #4 ('97) 1 3 4 6 8 10
2-6,8-12-($2.99) Suydam-c on all. 8-Deadpool goes to Zombie dimension 4.00
7-($3.99) Covers by Suydam & Liefeld; art by Liefeld, Baker, Pastoras, Dazo; 1st app. Lady Deadpool 3 6 9 19 30 40
13-($3.99) Silence of the Lambs-c 2 4 6 10 14 18

DEADPOOL PULP
Marvel Comics: Nov, 2010 - No. 4, Feb, 2011 ($3.99, limited series)

1-4-Alternate Deadpool in 1955; Glass & Benson-s/Laurence Campbell-a/Jae Lee-c 4.00

DEADPOOL'S ART OF WAR
Marvel Comics: Dec, 2014 - No. 4, Mar, 2015 ($3.99, limited series)

1-4-David-s/Koblish-a; Loki and Thor app. 4.00

DEADPOOL'S SECRET SECRET WARS (Secret Wars tie-in)
Marvel Comics: Jul, 2015 - No. 4, Oct, 2015 ($4.99/$3.99, limited series)

1-($4.99) Deadpool inserts himself into the 1984 Secret Wars series; Bunn-s/Harris-c 5.00
2-4-($3.99) Spider-Man, Avengers & X-Men app. 3-Black costume created 4.00
2-Gwenpool variant-c by Bachalo; 1st app. of Gwenpool 20.00

DEADPOOL: SUICIDE KINGS
Marvel Comics: Jun, 2009 - No. 5, Oct, 2009 ($3.99, limited series)

1-Barberi-a; Punisher, Daredevil, & Spider-Man app. 1 3 4 6 8 10
2-5 5.00

DEADPOOL TEAM-UP
Marvel Comics: No. 899, Jan, 2010 - No. 883, May, 2011 ($2.99, numbering runs in reverse)

899-883: 899-Hercules app.; Ramos-c. 897-Ghost Rider app. 894-Franken-Castle app. 887-Thor app. 883-Galactus & Silver Surfer app. 3.00

DEADPOOL: THE CIRCLE CHASE (See New Mutants #98)
Marvel Comics: Aug, 1993 - No. 4, Nov, 1993 ($2.00, limited series)

1-($2.50)-Embossed-c 3 6 9 14 20 25
2-4 1 3 4 6 8 10

DEADPOOL: THE DUCK
Marvel Comics: Mar, 2017 - Present ($3.99, limited series)

1-4-Deadpool & Howard the Duck merge; Rocket Raccoon app.; Camagni-a 4.00

DEADPOOL: TOO SOON
Marvel Comics: Dec, 2016 - No. 4, Mar, 2017 ($4.99, limited series)

1-4-Corin-s/Nauck-a; Squirrel Girl, Howard the Duck, Punisher, Forbush Man app. 5.00

DEADPOOL V GAMBIT
Marvel Comics: Aug, 2016 - No. 5, Nov, 2016 ($3.99, limited series)

1-5-Acker & Blacker-s/Beyruth-s. 1-Spider-Man & Daredevil app. 4.00

DEADPOOL VS. CARNAGE
Marvel Comics: Jun, 2014 - No. 4, Aug, 2014 ($3.99, limited series)

1-Bunn-s/Espin-a/Fabry-c 2 4 6 8 10 12
2-4 6.00

DEADPOOL VS. THANOS
Marvel Comics: Nov, 2015 - No. 4, Dec, 2015 ($3.99, limited series)

1-4-Seeley-s/Bondoc-a; Death app. 2-Guardians of the Galaxy app. 4.00

DEADPOOL VS. THE PUNISHER
Marvel Comics: Jun, 2017 - No. 5 ($3.99, limited series)

1-Van Lente-s/Pere Pérez-a/Shalvey-c 4.00

DEADPOOL VS. X-FORCE
Marvel Comics: Sept, 2014 - No. 4, Nov, 2014 ($3.99, limited series)

1-4-Swierczynski-s/Larraz-a/Shane Davis-c 4.00

DEADPOOL: WADE WILSON'S WAR
Marvel Comics: Aug, 2010 - No. 4, Nov, 2010 ($3.99, limited series)

1-4-Swierczynski-s/Pearson-a/c; Bullseye, Domino & Silver Sable app. 4.00

DEAD RIDER (See Deadlander)

DEAD ROMEO
DC Comics: June, 2009 - No. 6, Nov, 2009 ($2.99, limited series)

1-6-Ryan Benjamin-a/Jesse Snider-s 3.00
TPB (2010, $19.99) r/#1-6; cover gallery 20.00

DEAD, SHE SAID
IDW Publishing: May, 2008 - No. 3, Sept, 2008 ($3.99, limited series)

1-3-Bernie Wrightson-a/Steve Niles-s 4.00

DEADSHOT (See Batman #59, Detective Comics #474, & Showcase '93 #8)

Dead Vengeance #2 © Bill Morrison

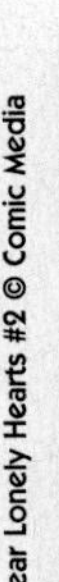
Dear Lonely Hearts #2 © Comic Media

Death Head #1 © Zack & Nick Keller

	GD 2.0	VG 4.0	FN 6.0	VF 8.0	VF/NM 9.0	NM- 9.2

DC Comics: Nov, 1988 - No. 4, Feb, 1989 ($1.00, limited series)

1-Ostrander & Yale-s/Luke McDonnell-a	1	2	3	5	6	8
2-4						5.00

DEADSHOT
DC Comics: Feb, 2005 - No. 5, June 2005 ($2.95, limited series)

1-5-Zeck-c/Gage-s/Cummings-a. 3-Green Arrow app. 4.00

DEAD SPACE (Based on the Electronics Arts videogame)
Image Comics: Mar, 2008 - No. 6, Sept, 2008 ($2.99, limited series)

1-6-Templesmith-a/Johnston-s 3.00
... Extraction (9/09, $3.50) Templesmith-a/Johnston-s 3.50

DEAD SQUAD
IDW Publishing (Darby Pop): Oct, 2014 - Present ($3.99)

1-4-Federman-s/Scaia-a. 1-Two covers 4.00

DEAD VENGEANCE
Dark Horse Comics: Oct, 2015 - No. 4, Jan, 2016 ($3.99, limited series)

1-4-Bill Morrison-s. 1-Morrison-a. 2-4-Tone Rodriguez-a 4.00

DEAD WHO WALK, THE (See Strange Mysteries-Super Reprint #15,16 {1963-64})
Realistic Comics: 1952 (one-shot)

nn	74	148	222	470	810	1150

DEADWORLD (Also see The Realm)
Arrow Comics/Caliber Comics: Dec, 1986 - No. 26 ($1.50/$1.95/#15-28: $2.50, B&W)

1-4 4.00
5-26-Graphic cover version 4.00
5-26-Tame cover version 3.00
...Archives 1-3 (1992, $2.50) 3.00

DEAN KOONTZ'S FRANKENSTEIN: STORM SURGE
Dynamite Entertainment: 2015 - No. 6, 2016 ($3.99)

1-6-Chuck Dixon-s/Andres Ponce-a 4.00

DEAN MARTIN & JERRY LEWIS (See Adventures of...)

DEAR BEATRICE FAIRFAX
Best/Standard Comics (King Features): No. 5, Nov, 1950 - No. 9, Sept, 1951 (Vern Greene art)

5-All have Schomburg air brush-c	17	34	51	98	154	210
6-9	14	28	42	76	108	140

DEAR HEART (Formerly Lonely Heart)
Ajax: No. 15, July, 1956 - No. 16, Sept, 1956

15,16	9	18	27	52	69	85

DEAR LONELY HEART (...Illustrated No. 1-6)
Artful Publications: Mar, 1951; No. 2, Oct, 1951 - No. 8, Oct, 1952

1	20	40	60	120	195	270
2	12	24	36	67	94	120
3-Matt Baker Jungle Girl story	22	44	66	128	209	290
4-8	11	22	33	60	83	105

DEAR LONELY HEARTS (Lonely Heart #9 on)
Harwell Publ./Mystery Publ. Co. (Comic Media): Aug, 1953 -No. 8, Oct, 1954

1	15	30	45	88	137	185
2-8	11	22	33	64	90	115

DEARLY BELOVED
Ziff-Davis Publishing Co.: Fall, 1952

1-Photo-c	19	38	57	111	176	240

DEAR NANCY PARKER
Gold Key: June, 1963 - No. 2, Sept, 1963

1-Painted-c on both	4	8	12	23	37	50
2	3	6	9	17	26	35

DEATH, THE ABSOLUTE... (From Neil Gaiman's Sandman titles)
DC Comics (Vertigo): 2009 ($99.99, oversized hardcover in slipcase)

nn-Reprints 1st app. in Sandman #8, Sandman #20, Death: The High Cost of Living #1-3, Death: the Time of Your Life #1-3, Death Talks About Life; short stories and pin-ups; merchandise pics; script and sketch art for Sandman #8; Gaiman afterword 100.00

DEATH: AT DEATH'S DOOR (See Sandman: The Season of Mists)
DC Comics (Vertigo): 2003 ($9.95, graphic novel one-shot, B&W, 7-1/2" x 5")

1-Jill Thompson-s/a/c; manga-style; Morpheus and the Endless app. 10.00

DEATH BE DAMNED
BOOM! Studios: Feb, 2017 - No. 4, ($3.99, limited series)

1-Ben Acker, Ben Blacker & Andrew Miller-s/Hannah Christenson-a 4.00

DEATHBLOW (Also see Batman/Deathblow and Darker Image)
Image Comics (WildStorm Productions): May (Apr. inside), 1993 - No. 29, Aug, 1996 ($1.75/$1.95/$2.50)

0-(8/96, $2.95, 32 pgs.)-r/Darker Image w/new story & art; Jim Lee & Trevor Scott-a; new Jim Lee-c 3.00
1-($2.50)-Red foil stamped logo on black varnish-c; Jim Lee-c/a; flip-book side has Cybernary -c/story (#2 also) 4.00
1-($1.95)-Newsstand version w/o foil-c & varnish 3.00
2-29: 2-(8/93)-Lee-a; with bound-in poster. 2-($1.75)-Newsstand version w/o poster. 4-Jim Lee-c/Tim Sale-a begin. 13-W/pinup poster by Tim Sale & Jim Lee. 16-($1.95 Newsstand & $2.50 Direct Market editions)-Wildstorm Rising Pt. 6. 17-Variant "Chicago Comicon" edition exists. 20,21-Gen 13 app. 23-Backlash-c/app. 24,25-Grifter-c/app; Gen 13 & Dane from Wetworks app. 28-Deathblow dies. 29-Memorial issue 3.00
5-Alternate Portacio-c (Forms larger picture when combined with alternate-c for Gen 13 #5, Kindred #3, Stormwatch #10, Team 7 #1, Union #0, Wetworks #2 & WildC.A.T.S #11) 6.00
...:Sinners and Saints TPB ('99, $19.95) r/#1-12; Sale-c 20.00

DEATHBLOW (Volume 2)
DC Comics (WildStorm): Dec, 2006 - No. 9, Apr, 2008 ($2.99)

1-9: 1-Azzarello-s/D'Anda-a; two covers by D'Anda & Platt 3.00
...: And Then You Live! TPB (2008, $19.99) r/#1-9 20.00

DEATHBLOW BY BLOWS
DC Comics (WildStorm): Nov, 1999 - No. 3, Jan, 2000 ($2.95, limited series)

1-3-Alan Moore-s/Jim Baikie-a 3.00

DEATHBLOW/WOLVERINE
Image Comics (WildStorm Productions)/ Marvel Comics: Sept, 1996 - No. 2, Feb, 1997 ($2.50, limited series)

1,2: Wiesenfeld-s/Bennett-a 3.00
TPB (1997, $8.95) r/#1,2 9.00

DEATH DEALER (Also see Frank Frazetta's...)
Verotik: July, 1995 - No. 4, July, 1997 ($5.95)

1-Frazetta-c; Bisley-a	2	4	6	8	10	12
1-2nd print, 2-4-($6.95)-Frazetta-c; embossed logo	1	2	3	4	5	7

DEATH-DEFYING 'DEVIL, THE (Also see Project Superpowers)
Dynamite Entertainment: 2008 - No. 4, 2009 ($3.50, limited series)

1-4-Casey & Ross-s/Salazar-a; multiple covers; the Dragon app. 3.50

DEATH-DEFYING DOCTOR MIRAGE, THE
Valiant Entertainment: Sept, 2014 - No. 5, Jan, 2015 ($3.99, limited series)

1-5-Van Meter-s/de la Torre-a. 1-3-Foreman-c. 4,5-Wada-c 4.00

DEATH-DEFYING DOCTOR MIRAGE, THE: SECOND LIVES
Valiant Entertainment: Dec, 2015 - No. 4, Mar, 2016 ($3.99, limited series)

1-4-Van Meter-s/de La Torre-a 4.00

DEATH HEAD
Dark Horse Comics: Jul, 2015 - No. 6, Feb, 2016 ($3.99, limited series)

1-6-Zach & Nick Keller-s/Joanna Estep-a 4.00

DEATH, JR.
Image Comics: Apr, 2005 - No. 3, Aug, 2005 ($4.99, squarebound, limited series)

1-3-Gary Whitta-s/Ted Naifeh-a 5.00
Vol. 1 TPB (2005, $14.99) r/series; concept and promotional art 15.00

DEATH, JR. (Volume 2)
Image Comics: Jul, 2006 - No. 3, May, 2007 ($4.99, squarebound, limited series)

1-3-Gary Whitta-s/Ted Naifeh-a. 1-Dan Brereton-c 5.00
Vol. 2 TPB (2007, $14.99) r/series; Halloween story w/Guy Davis-a; promotional art 15.00

DEATHLOK (Also see Astonishing Tales #25)
Marvel Comics: July, 1990 - No. 4, Oct, 1990 ($3.95, limited series, 52 pgs.)

1-4: 1,2-Guice-a(p). 3,4-Denys Cowan-a, c-4 5.00

DEATHLOK
Marvel Comics: July, 1991 - No. 34, Apr, 1994 ($1.75)

1-Silver ink cover; Denys Cowan-c/a(p) begins 4.00
2-18,20-24,26-34: 2-Forge (X-Men) app. 3-Vs. Dr. Doom. 5-X-Men & F.F. x-over. 6,7-Punisher x-over. 9,10-Ghost Rider-c/story. 16-Infinity War x-over. 17-Jae Lee-c. 22-Black Panther app. 27-Siege app. 3.00
19-($2.25)-Foil-c 4.00

Deathlok (2014 series) #7 © MAR

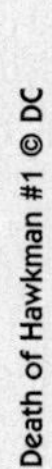
Death of Hawkman #1 © DC

Deathstroke (2014 series) #3 © DC

GD 2.0	VG 4.0	FN 6.0	VF 8.0	VF/NM 9.0	NM- 9.2

25-($2.95, 52 pgs.)-Holo-grafx foil-c 4.00
Annual 1 (1992, $2.25, 68 pgs.)-Guice-p; Quesada-c(p) 4.00
Annual 2 (1993, $2.95, 68 pgs.)-Bagged w/card; intro Tracer 4.00
NOTE: ***Denys Cowan*** *a(p)-9-13, 15, Annual 1; c-9-12, 13p, 14.* ***Guice/Cowan*** *c-8.*

DEATHLOK
Marvel Comics: Sept, 1999 - No. 11, June, 2000 ($1.99)
1-11: 1-Casey-s/Manco-a. 2-Two covers. 4-Canete-a 3.00

DEATHLOK (... The Demolisher on cover)
Marvel Comics: Jan, 2010 - No. 7, Jul, 2010 ($3.99, limited series)
1-7-Huston-s/Medina-a/Peterson-c 4.00

DEATHLOK
Marvel Comics: Dec, 2014 - No. 10, Sept, 2015 ($3.99)
1-10: 1-Edmonson-s/Perkins-a; intro. Henry Hayes. 2-5,8-10-Domino app. 4.00

DEATHLOK SPECIAL
Marvel Comics: May, 1991 - No. 4, June, 1991 ($2.00, bi-weekly lim. series)
1-4: r/1-4(1990) w/new Guice-c #1,2; Cowan c-3,4 3.00
1-2nd printing w/white-c 3.00

DEATHMASK
Future Comics: Mar, 2003 - No. 3, June, 2003 ($2.99)
1-3-Giordano-a(p)/Michelinie & Layton-s 3.00

DEATHMATCH
BOOM! Studios: Dec, 2012 - No. 12, Nov, 2013 ($2.99)
1-($1.00) Jenkins-s/Magno-a; multiple covers 3.00
2-12 ($3.99) Multiple covers on each 4.00

DEATHMATE
Valiant (Prologue/Yellow/Blue)/Image Comics (Black/Red/Epilogue):
Sept, 1993 - Epilogue (#6), Feb, 1994 ($2.95/$4.95, limited series)
Preview-(7/93, 8 pgs.) 3.00
Prologue (#1)–Silver foil; Jim Lee/Layton-c; B. Smith/Lee-a; Liefeld-a(p) 3.00
Prologue–Special gold foil ed. of silver ed. 4.00
Black (#2)-(9/93, $4.95, 52 pgs.)-Silvestri/Jim Lee-c; pencils by Peterson/Silvestri/Capullo/ Jim Lee/Portacio; 1st story app. Gen 13 telling their rebellion against the Troika (see WildC.A.T.S. Trilogy) 6.00
Black-Special gold foil edition 7.00
Yellow (#3)-(10/93, $4.95, 52 pgs)-Yellow foil-c; Indicia says Prologue Sept 1993 by mistake; 3rd app. Ninjak; Thibert-c(i) 5.00
Yellow-Special gold foil edition 6.00
Blue (#4)-(10/93, $4.95, 52 pgs.)-Thibert blue foil-c(i); Reese-a(i) 5.00
Blue-Special gold foil edition 6.00
Red (#5), Epilogue (#6)-(2/94, $2.95)-Silver foil Quesada/Silvestri-c; Silvestri-a(p) 3.00

DEATH METAL
Marvel Comics UK: Jan, 1994 - No. 4, Apr, 1994 ($1.95, limited series)
1-4: 1-Silver ink-c. Alpha Flight app. 3.00

DEATH METAL VS. GENETIX
Marvel Comics UK: Dec, 1993 - No. 2, Jan, 1994 (Limited series)
1-($2.95)-Polybagged w/2 trading cards 3.00
2-($2.50)-Polybagged w/2 trading cards 3.00

DEATH OF CAPTAIN MARVEL (See Marvel Graphic Novel #1)

DEATH OF DRACULA
Marvel Comics: Aug, 2010 ($3.99, one shot)
1-Gischler-s/Camuncoli-a/c 4.00

DEATH OF HAWKMAN, THE
DC Comics: Dec, 2016 - No. 6, May, 2017 ($3.99, limited series)
1-6-Andreyko-s/Lopresti-a; Adam Strange app. 2-6-Despero app. 4.00

DEATH OF MR. MONSTER, THE (See Mr. Monster #8)

DEATH OF SUPERMAN (See Superman, 2nd Series)

DEATH OF THE NEW GODS (Tie-in to the Countdown series)
DC Comics: Early Dec, 2007 - No. 8, Jun, 2008 ($3.50, limited series)
1-8-Jim Starlin-s/a/c. 1-Barda killed. 6-Orion dies. 7-Scott Free and Metron die 3.50
TPB (2009, $19.99) r/#1-8; Starlin intro.; cover gallery 20.00

DEATH OF WOLVERINE
Marvel Comics: Nov, 2014 - No. 4, Dec, 2014 ($4.99, limited series)
1-4-Soule-s/McNiven-a; multiple covers on each; bonus art & commentary in each 5.00
...: Deadpool & Captain America (12/14, $4.99) Duggan-s/Kolins-a 5.00
...: Life After Logan (1/15, $4.99) Short stories by various; Cyclops, Nightcrawler app. 5.00

DEATH OF WOLVERINE: THE LOGAN LEGACY (Continues in Wolverines #1)
Marvel Comics: Dec, 2014 - No. 7, Feb, 2015 ($3.99, bi-weekly limited series)
1-7: 1-Soule-s; X-23, Daken, Deathstrike, Mystique & Sabretooth app. 4.00

DEATH OF WOLVERINE: THE WEAPON X PROGRAM
Marvel Comics: Jan, 2015 - No. 5, Mar, 2015 ($3.99, bi-weekly limited series)
1-5-Soule-s. 1-3-Larroca-a. 3-Sabretooth app. 4.00

DEATH OF X (Leads into X-Men vs. Inhumans)
Marvel Comics: Dec, 2016 - No. 4, Jan, 2017 ($4.99/$3.99, limited series)
1-($4.99) Soule & Lemire-s; Kuder-a; X-Men, Inhumans & Hydra app. 5.00
2-4-($3.99) 2-Kuder-a. 3,4-Kuder & Garrón-a. 4-Death of Cyclops 4.00

DEATH RACE 2020
Roger Corman's Cosmic Comics: Apr, 1995 - No. 8, Nov, 1995 ($2.50)
1-8: Sequel to the Movie 3.00

DEATH RATTLE (Formerly an Underground)
Kitchen Sink Press: V2#1, 10/85 - No. 18, 1988, 1994 ($1.95, Baxter paper, mature); V3#1, 11/95 - No. 5, 6/96 ($2.95, B&W)
V2#1-7,9-18: 1-Corben-c. 2-Unpubbed Spirit story by Eisner. 5-Robot Woman-r by Wolverton. 6-B&W issues begin. 10-Savage World-r by by Williamson/Torres/Krenkel/Frazetta from Witzend #1. 16-Wolverton Spacehawk-r 5.00
8-(12/86)-1st app. Mark Schultz's Xenozoic Tales/Cadillacs & Dinosaurs 2 4 6 11 16 20
8-(1994)-r plus interview w/Mark Schultz 3.50
V3#1-5 ($2.95-c): 1-Mark Schultz-c 3.50

DEATH SENTENCE
Titan Comics: Nov, 2003 - No. 6, Apr, 2014 ($3.99)
1-6-Montynero-s/c; Dowling-a 4.00

DEATH SENTENCE LONDON
Titan Comics: Jun, 2015 - No. 6, Jan, 2016 ($3.99)
1-6-Montynero-s/c; Simmonds-a 4.00

DEATH'S HEAD (See Daredevil #56, Dragon's Claws #5 & Incomplete...)(See Amazing Fantasy (2004) for Death's Head 3.0)
Marvel Comics: Dec, 1988 - No. 10, Sept, 1989 ($1.75)
1-Dragon's Claws spin-off 3.00
2-Fantastic Four app.; Dragon's Claws x-over 3.00
3-10: 8-Dr. Who app. 9-F. F. x-over; Simonson-c(p) 3.00

DEATH'S HEAD II (Also see Battletide)
Marvel Comics UK, Ltd.: Mar, 1992 - No. 4, June (May inside), 1992 ($1.75, color, lim. series)
1-4: 2-Fantastic Four app. 4-Punisher, Spider-Man, Daredevil, Dr. Strange, Capt. America & Wolverine in the year 2020 3.00
1,2-Silver ink 2nd printiings 3.00

DEATH'S HEAD II (Also see Battletide)
Marvel Comics UK, Ltd.: Dec, 1992 - No. 16, Mar, 1994 ($1.75/$1.95)
V2#1-13,15,16: 1-Gatefold-c. 1-4-X-Men app.15-Capt. America & Wolverine app. 3.00
14-($2.95)-Foil flip-c w/Death's Head II Gold #0 4.00
...Gold 1 (1/94, $3.95, 68 pgs.)-Gold foil-c 4.00

DEATH'S HEAD II & THE ORIGIN OF DIE CUT
Marvel Comics UK, Ltd.: Aug, 1993 - No. 2, Sept, 1993 (limited series)
1-($2.95)-Embossed-c 4.00
2 ($1.75) 3.00

DEATHSTROKE (DC New 52)
DC Comics: Nov, 2011 - No. 20, Jul, 2013 ($2.99)
1-Higgins-s/Bennett-a/Bisley-c 6.00
2-20: 4-Blackhawks app. 9-12-Liefeld-s/a/c; Lobo app. 3.00
#0 (11/12, $2.99) Origin story, Team 7 app.; Liefeld-s/a/c 3.00

DEATHSTROKE (DC New 52)
DC Comics: Dec, 2014 - No. 20, Sept, 2016 ($2.99)
1-20: 1-Tony Daniel-s/a; I Ching app. 3-6-Harley Quinn app. 7-10-Wonder Woman app. 11-13-Harley Quinn & Suicide Squad app. 3.00
Annual 1 (9/15, $4.99) Takes place between #8 & 9; Wonder Woman app.; Kirkham-a 5.00
Annual 1 (8/16, $4.99) Hester-s/Colak & Viacava-a 5.00

DEATHSTROKE (DC Rebirth)
DC Comics: Oct, 2016 - Present ($2.99)
1-13: 1-Priest-s/Pagulayan-a; Clock King app. 4,5-Batman & Robin (Damian) app. 8-Superman app. 11-The Creeper app.; Cowan & Sienkiewicz-a 3.00
... Rebirth 1 (10/16, $2.99) Priest-s/Pagulayan-a; Clock King app. 3.00

Death: The Time of Your Life #3 © DC

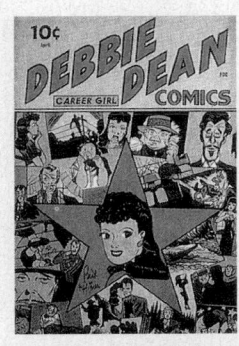

Debbie Dean, Career Girl #1 © Civil

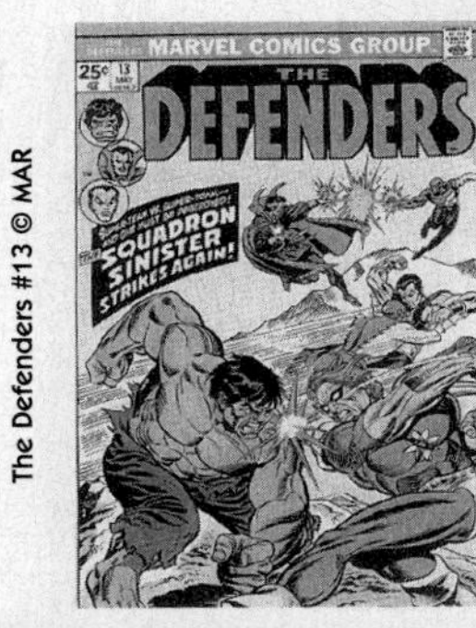

The Defenders #13 © MAR

GD 2.0 | VG 4.0 | FN 6.0 | VF 8.0 | VF/NM 9.0 | NM- 9.2

DEATHSTROKE: THE TERMINATOR (Deathstroke: The Hunted #0-47; Deathstroke #48-60) (Also see Marvel & DC Present, New Teen Titans #2, New Titans, Showcase '93 #7,9 & Tales of the Teen Titans #42-44)
DC Comics: Aug, 1991 - No. 60, June, 1996 ($1.75-$2.25)

1-New Titans spin-off; Mike Zeck c-1-28 2 4 6 9 12 15
1-Gold ink 2nd printing ($1.75) 1 2 3 5 6 8
2 5.00
3-40,0(10/94),41(11/94)-49,51-60: 6,8-Batman cameo. 7,9-Batman-c/story. 9-1st brief app. new Vigilante (female). 10-1st full app. new Vigilante; Perez-i. 13-Vs. Justice League; Team Titans cameo on last pg. 14-Total Chaos, part 1; Team Titans-c/story cont'd in New Titans #90. 15-1st app. Rose Wilson. 40-(9/94). 0-(10/94)-Begin Deathstroke, The Hunted, ends #47. 3.00
50 ($3.50) 4.00
Annual 1-4 ('92-'95, 68 pgs.): 1-Nightwing & Vigilante app.; minor Eclipso app. 2-Bloodlines Deathstorm; 1st app. Gunfire. 3-Elseworlds story. 4-Year One story 4.00
NOTE: ***Golden** a-12. **Perez** a-11i. **Zeck** c-Annual 1, 2.*

DEATH: THE HIGH COST OF LIVING (See Sandman #8) (Also see the Books of Magic limited & ongoing series)
DC Comics (Vertigo): Mar, 1993 - No. 3, May, 1993 ($1.95, limited series)

1-Bachalo/Buckingham-a; Dave McKean-c; Neil Gaiman scripts in all 6.00
1-Platinum edition 40.00
2 3.50
3-Pgs. 19 & 20 had wrong placement 3.00
3-Corrected version w/pgs. 19 & 20 facing each other 4.00
Death Talks About Life-giveaway about AIDS prevention 5.00
Hardcover (1994, $19.95)-r/#1-3 & Death Talks About Life; intro. by Tori Amos 20.00
Trade paperback (6/94, $12.95, Titan Books)-r/#1-3 & Death Talks About Life; prism-c 13.00

DEATH: THE TIME OF YOUR LIFE (See Sandman #8)
DC Comics (Vertigo): Apr, 1996 - No. 3, July, 1996 ($2.95, limited series)

1-3: Neil Gaiman story & Bachalo/Buckingham-a; Dave McKean-c. 2-(5/96) 3.00
Hardcover (1997, $19.95)-r/#1-3 w/3 new pages & gallery art by various 20.00
TPB (1997, $12.95)-r/#1-3 & Visions of Death gallery; Intro. by Claire Danes 13.00

DEATH 3
Marvel Comics UK: Sept, 1993 - No. 4, Dec, 1993 ($1.75, limited series)

1-($2.95)-Embossed-c 4.00
2-4 3.00

DEATH VALLEY (Cowboys and Indians)
Comic Media: Oct, 1953 - No. 6, Aug, 1954

1-Billy the Kid; Morisi-a; Andru/Esposito-c/a 24 48 72 140 230 320
2-Don Heck-c 15 30 45 85 130 175
3-6: 3,5-Morisi-a. 5-Discount-a 14 28 42 80 115 150

DEATH VALLEY (Becomes Frontier Scout, Daniel Boone No.10-13)
Charlton Comics: No. 7, 6/55 - No. 9, 10/55 (Cont'd from Comic Media series)

7-9: 8-Wolverton-a (half pg.) 11 22 33 62 86 110

DEATH VIGIL
Image Comics (Top Cow): Jul, 2014 - No. 8, Sept, 2015 ($3.99)

1-8-Stjepan Sejic-s/a/c 4.00

DEATHWISH
DC Comics (Milestone Media): Dec, 1994 - No. 4, Mar, 1995 ($2.50, lim. series)

1-4 3.00

DEATH WRECK
Marvel Comics UK: Jan, 1994 - No. 4, Apr, 1994 ($1.95, limited series)

1-4: 1-Metallic ink logo; Death's Head II app. 3.00

DEBBIE DEAN, CAREER GIRL
Civil Service Publ.: April, 1945 - No. 2, July, 1945

1,2-Newspaper reprints by Bert Whitman 14 28 42 82 121 160

DEBBI'S DATES (Also see Date With Debbi)
National Periodical Publications: Apr-May, 1969 - No. 11, Dec-Jan, 1970-71

1 7 14 21 46 86 125
2,3,5,7-11: 2-Last 12¢ issue 4 8 12 25 40 55
4-Neal Adams text illo 4 8 12 28 47 65
6-Superman cameo 6 12 18 37 66 95

DECADE OF DARK HORSE, A
Dark Horse Comics: Jul, 1996 - No. 4, Oct, 1996 ($2.95, B&W/color, lim. series)

1-4: 1-Sin City-c/story by Miller; Grendel by Wagner; Predator. 2-Star Wars wraparound-c. 3-Aliens-c/story; Nexus, Mask stories 3.00

DECAPITATOR (Randy Bowen's...)
Dark Horse Comics: Jun, 1998 - No. 4, ($2.95)

1-4-Bowen-s/art by various. 1-Mahnke-c. 3-Jones-c 4.00

DECEPTION, THE
Image Comics (Flypaper Press): 1999 - No. 3, 1999 ($2.95, B&W, mini-series)

1-3-Horley painted-c 3.00

DECIMATION: THE HOUSE OF M
Marvel Comics: Jan, 2006 ($3.99)

... - The Day After (one-shot) Claremont-s/Green-a 4.00

DECISION 2012 (Biographies of the main 2012 presidential candidates)
BOOM! Studios: Nov, 2011 ($3.99, series of one-shots)

...: Barack Obama 1 (11/11, $3.99) biography; Damian Couceiro-a; 2 covers 4.00
...: Michelle Bachman 1 (11/11) biography; Aaron McConnell-a; 2 covers 4.00
...: Ron Paul 1 (11/11) biography; Dean Kotz-a; 2 covers 4.00
...: Sarah Palin 1 (11/11) biography; Damian Couceiro-a; 2 covers 4.00

DEEP, THE (Movie)
Marvel Comics Group: Nov, 1977 (Giant)

1-Infantino-c/a 1 3 4 6 8 10

DEEP GRAVITY
Dark Horse Comics: Jul, 2014 - No. 4, Oct, 2014 ($3.99, limited series)

1-4-Hardman & Bechko-s/Baldó-a/Hardman-c 4.00

DEEP SLEEPER
Oni Press/Image Comics: Feb, 2004 - No. 4, Sept, 2004 ($3.50/$2.95, B&W, limited series)

1,2-(Oni Press, $3.50)-Hester-s/Huddleston-a 3.50
3,4-(Image Comics, $2.95) 3.00
... Omnibus (Image, 8/04, $5.95) r/#1,2 6.00
... Vol. 1 TPB (2005, $12.95) r/#1-4; cover gallery 13.00

DEEP STATE
BOOM! Studios: Nov, 2014 - No. 8, Jul, 2015 ($3.99)

1-8-Justin Jordan-s/Ariela Kristantina-a 4.00

DEFCON 4
Image Comics (WildStorm Productions): Feb, 1996 - No. 4, Sept, 1996 ($2.50, lim. series)

1/2 1 2 3 5 7 9
1/2 Gold-(1000 printed) 14.00
1-Main Cover by Mat Broome & Edwin Rosell 3.00
1-Hordes of Cymulants variant-c by Michael Golden 5.00
1-Backs to the Wall variant-c by Humberto Ramos & Alex Garner 5.00
1-Defcon 4-Way variant-c by Jim Lee 1 2 3 4 5 7
2-4 3.00

DEFEND COMICS (The CBLDF Presents...)
Comic Book Legal Defense Fund: May, 2015 (giveaway)

FCBD Edition - Short stories incl. Kevin Keller, Beanworld; art by Liew, Parent, Watson 3.00

DEFENDERS, THE (TV)
Dell Publishing Co.: Sept-Nov, 1962 - No. 2, Feb-Apr, 1963

12-176-211(#1) 4 8 12 25 40 55
12-176-304(#2) 3 6 9 20 31 42

DEFENDERS, THE (Also see Giant-Size..., Marvel Feature, Marvel Treasury Edition, Secret Defenders & Sub-Mariner #34, 35; The New...#140-on)
Marvel Comics Group: Aug, 1972 - No. 152, Feb, 1986

1-The Hulk, Doctor Strange, Sub-Mariner begin 13 26 39 86 188 290
2-Silver Surfer x-over 7 14 21 44 82 120
3-5: 3-Silver Surfer x-over. 4-Valkyrie joins 5 10 15 31 53 75
6,7: 6-Silver Surfer x-over 3 6 9 21 33 45
8,9,11: 8-11-Defenders vs. the Avengers (Crossover with Avengers #115-118)
8,11-Silver Surfer x-over 4 8 12 28 47 65
10-Hulk vs. Thor battle 8 16 24 54 102 150
12-14: 12-Last 20¢ issue 3 6 9 14 20 25
15,16-Magneto & Brotherhood of Evil Mutants app. from X-Men 3 6 9 16 23 30
17-20: 17-Power Man x-over (11/74); 1st app. of the Wrecking Crew 2 4 6 9 12 15
21-25: 24,25-Son of Satan app. 1 3 4 6 8 10
26,29-Guardians of the Galaxy app. (#26 is 8/75; pre-dates Marvel Presents #3).
29-Starhawk joins Guardians 2 4 6 9 12 15
27-1st brief app. Starhawk; Guardians of the Galaxy app. 3 6 9 14 20 25
28-1st full app. Starhawk; Guardians of the Galaxy app.

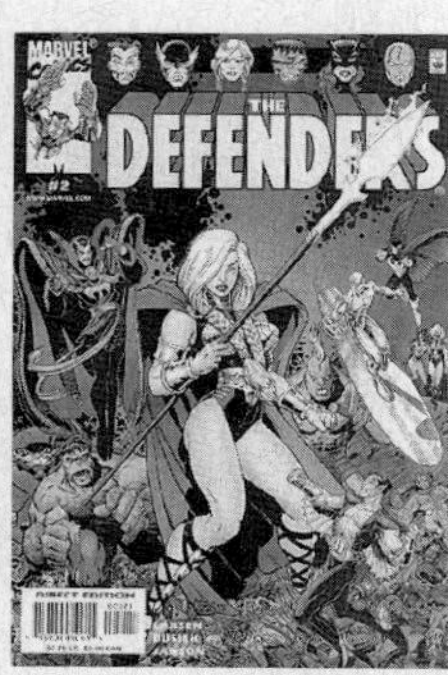

The Defenders V2 #2 © MAR

Dejah Thoris (2016 series) #1 © DYN

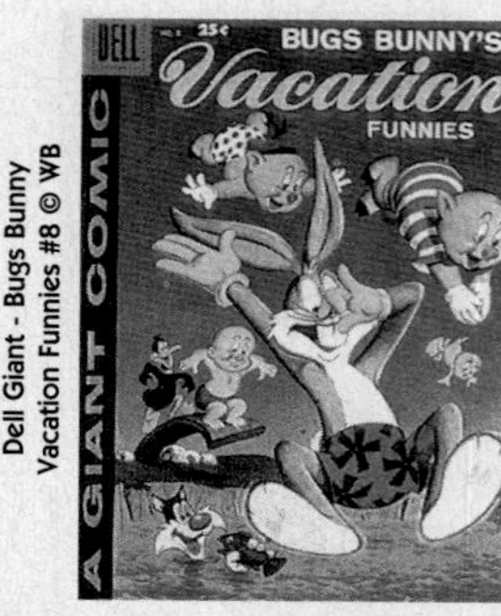

Dell Giant - Bugs Bunny Vacation Funnies #8 © WB

	GD 2.0	VG 4.0	FN 6.0	VF 8.0	VF/NM 9.0	NM- 9.2
	5	10	15	34	60	85
30-33,39-50: 31,32-Origin Nighthawk. 44-Hellcat joins. 45-Dr. Strange leaves. 47-49-Early Moon Knight app. (5/77). 48-50-(Reg. 30¢-c)						6.00
34-38-(Regular 25¢ editions): 35-Intro New Red Guardian						6.00
34-38-(30¢-c variants, limited distribution)(4-8/76)	4	8	12	25	40	55
48-52-(35¢-c variants, limited distribution)(6-10/77)	7	14	21	44	82	120
51-60: 51,52-(Reg. 30¢-c). 53-1st brief app. Lunatik (Lobo lookalike). 55-Origin Red Guardian; Lunatik cameo. 56-1st full Lunatik story						5.00
61-75: 61-Lunatik & Spider-Man app. 70-73-Lunatik (origin #71). 73-75-Foolkiller II app. (Greg Salinger). 74-Nighthawk resigns						4.00
76-93,95,97-99,102-119,123,124,126-149,151: 77-Origin Omega. 78-Original Defenders return thru #101. 104-The Beast joins. 105-Son of Satan joins. 106-Death of Nighthawk. 129-New Mutants cameo (3/84, early x-over)						3.00
94-1st Gargoyle	1	2	3	5	6	8
96-Ghost Rider app.						4.00
100-(52 pgs.)-Hellcat (Patsy Walker) revealed as Satan's daughter	1	3	4	6	8	10
101,120-122: 101-Silver Surfer-c & app. 120,121-Son of Satan-c/stories. 122-Final app. Son of Satan (2 pgs.)						4.00
125,150: 125-(52 pgs.)-Intro new Defenders. 150-(52 pgs.)-Origin Cloud						4.00
152-(52 pgs.)-Ties in with X-Factor & Secret Wars II						6.00
Annual 1 (1976, 52 pgs.)-New book-length story	3	6	9	19	30	40

NOTE: *Art Adams c-142p. Austin a-53i; c-65i, 119i, 145i. Frank Bolle a-7i, 10i, 11i. Buckler c(p)-34, 38, 76, 77, 79-86, 90, 91. J. Buscema c-66. Giffen a-42-49p, 50, 51-54p. Golden a-53p, 54p; c-94, 96. Guice c-129. G. Kane c(p)-13, 16, 18, 19, 21-26, 31-33, 35-37, 40, 41, 52, 55. Kirby c-42-45. Mooney a-3i, 31-34i, 62i, 63i, 85i. Nasser c-88p. Perez c(p)-51, 53, 54. Rogers c-98. Starlin c-110. Tuska a-57p. Silver Surfer in No. 2, 3, 6, 8-11, 92, 98-101, 107, 112-115, 122-125.*

DEFENDERS, THE (Volume 2) (Continues in The Order)
Marvel Comics: Mar, 2001 - No. 12, Feb, 2002 ($2.99/$2.25)

1-Busiek & Larsen-s/Larsen & Janson-a/c						3.00
2-11: 2-Two covers by Larsen & Art Adams; Valkyrie app. 4-Frenz-a						3.00
12-($3.50) 'Nuff Said issue; back-up-s Reis-a						4.00
...: From the Vault (9/11, $2.99) Previously unpublished story; Bagley-a						3.00

DEFENDERS, THE
Marvel Comics: Sept, 2005 - No. 5, Jan, 2006 ($2.99, limited series)

1-5-Giffen & DeMatteis-s/Maguire-a. 2-Dormammu app.						3.00
...: Indefensible HC (2006, $19.99, dust jacket) r/#1-5; Giffen & Maguire sketch page						20.00
...: Indefensible SC (2007, $13.99) r/#1-5; Giffen & Maguire sketch page						14.00

DEFENDERS, THE
Marvel Comics: Feb, 2012 - No. 12, Jan, 2013 ($3.99)

1-12: 1-Dr. Strange, Namor, Silver Surfer, Red She-Hulk, Iron Fist team; Dodson-a						4.00
...: Strange Heroes 1 (2/12, $4.99) Handbook-style profiles of team members and foes						5.00
...: The Coming of the Defenders 1 (2/12, $5.99) r/Marvel Feature #1-3; recolored-c of #1						6.00
...: Tournament of Heroes 1 (3/12, $5.99) r/Defenders #62-65 (1978); recolored-c of #62						6.00

DEFENDERS OF DYNATRON CITY
Marvel Comics: Feb, 1992 - No. 6, July, 1992 ($1.25, limited series)

1-6-Lucasarts characters. 2-Origin						3.00

DEFENDERS OF THE EARTH (TV)
Marvel Comics (Star Comics): Jan, 1987 - No. 4, July, 1987

1-4: The Phantom, Mandrake The Magician, Flash Gordon begin. 3-Origin Phantom. 4-Origin Mandrake						4.00

DEFEX
Devil's Due Publ.: Oct, 2004 - No. 6, Apr, 2005 ($2.95)

1-6: 1-Wolfman-s/Caselli-a. 6-Pérez-c						3.00

DEFIANCE
Image Comics: Feb, 2002 - No. 8, Jun, 2003 ($2.95)

Preview Edition (12/01)						3.00
1-8-Barré-s/Kang & Suh-a						3.00

DEFINITIVE DIRECTORY OF THE DC UNIVERSE, THE (See Who's Who...)

DEJAH OF MARS (Warlord of Mars)
Dynamite Entertainment: 2014 - No. 4, 2014 ($3.99)

1-4-Rahner-s/Morales-a; multiple covers on each						4.00

DEJAH THORIS (Warlord of Mars)
Dynamite Entertainment: 2016 - No. 6, 2016 ($3.99)

1-6-Barbarie-s/Manna-a; multiple covers						4.00

DEJAH THORIS AND THE GREEN MEN OF MARS (Warlord of Mars)
Dynamite Entertainment: 2013 - No. 12, 2014 ($3.99)

1-12: 1-8-Rahner-s/Antonio-a; multiple covers on each. 9-12-Morales-a						4.00

DEJAH THORIS AND THE WHITE APES OF MARS (Warlord of Mars)
Dynamite Entertainment: 2012 - No. 3, 2012 ($3.99)

1-3-Rahner-s/Antonio-a; 2 covers by Peterson & Garza						4.00

DELECTA OF THE PLANETS (See Don Fortune & Fawcett Miniatures)

DELETE
1First Comics: 2016 - No. 4, 2016 ($4.99, limited series)

1-4-Palmiotti & Gray-s/Timms-a/Conner-c						5.00

DELICATE CREATURES
Image Comics (Top Cow): 2001 ($16.95, hardcover with dust jacket)

nn-Fairy tale storybook; J. Michael Straczynski-s; Michael Zulli-a						17.00

DELINQUENTS
Valiant Entertainment: Aug, 2014 - No. 4, Nov, 2014 ($3.99, limited series)

1-4-Quantum & Woody meet Archer & Armstrong; Asmus & Van Lente-s/Kano-a						4.00

DELIRIUM'S PARTY: A LITTLE ENDLESS STORYBOOK (Characters from The Sandman titles and The Little Endless Storybook)
DC Comics: 2011 ($14.99, hardcover, one-shot)

HC-Jill Thompson-s/painted-a/c; Little Delirium throws a party; watercolor page process						15.00

DELLA VISION (...The Television Queen) (Patty Powers #4 on)
Atlas Comics: April, 1955 - No. 3, Aug, 1955

1-Al Hartley-c	24	48	72	142	234	325
2,3	15	30	45	85	130	175

DELLEC
Aspen MLT.: Aug, 2009 - No. 6, Oct, 2011 ($2.50)

1-6-Gunnell-a/c						3.00

DELL GIANT COMICS

Dell Publishing began to release square bound comics in 1949 with a 132-page issue called Christmas Parade #1. The covers were of a heavier stock to accommodate the increased number of pages. The books proved profitable at 25 cents, but the average number of pages was quickly reduced to 100. Ten years later they were converted to a numbering system similar to the Four Color Comics, for greater ease in distribution and the page counts cut back to mostly 84 pages. The label "Dell Giant" began to appear on the covers in 1954. Because of the size of the books and the heavier, less pliant cover stock, they are rarely found in high grade condition, and with the exception of a small quantity of copies released from Western Publishing's warehouse–are almost never found in near mint.

Abraham Lincoln Life Story 1(3/58)	8	16	24	64	107	150
Bugs Bunny Christmas Funnies 1(11/50, 116pp)	21	42	63	168	289	410
...Christmas Funnies 2(11/51, 116pp)	12	24	36	96	171	245
...Christmas Funnies 3-5(11/52-11/54,)-Becomes Christmas Party #6	10	20	30	80	140	200
...Christmas Funnies 7-9(12/56-12/58)	9	18	27	72	124	175
...Christmas Party 6(11/55)-Formerly Bugs Bunny Christmas Funnies	9	18	27	72	124	175
...County Fair 1(9/57)	11	22	33	88	149	210
...Halloween Parade 1(10/53)	12	24	36	96	166	235
...Halloween Parade 2(10/54)-Trick 'N' Treat Halloween Fun #3 on	10	20	30	80	135	190
...Trick 'N' Treat Halloween Fun 3,4(10/55-10/56)-Formerly Halloween Parade #2	9	18	27	72	129	185
...Vacation Funnies 1(7/51, 112pp)	20	40	60	160	280	400
...Vacation Funnies 2('52)	13	26	39	104	180	255
...Vacation Funnies 3-5('53-'55)	10	20	30	80	138	195
...Vacation Funnies 6,7,9('56-'59)	9	18	27	72	124	175
...Vacation Funnies 8('58) 1st app. Beep Beep the Road Runner, Wile E. Coyote (1st meeting), Mathilda (Mrs. Beep Beep) and their 3 children who hatch from eggs; one month before Four Color #918	11	22	33	88	157	225
Cadet Gray of West Point 1(4/58)-Williamson-a, 10pgs.; Buscema-a; photo-c	8	16	24	64	107	150
Christmas In Disneyland 1(12/57)-Barks-a, 18 pgs.	25	50	75	200	350	500
Christmas Parade 1(11/49)(132 pgs.)(1st Dell Giant)-Donald Duck (25 pgs. by Barks, r-in G.K. Christmas Parade #5); Mickey Mouse & other film oriented stories; Cinderella (prior to movie), 7 Dwarfs, Bambi & Thumper, So Dear To My Heart, Flying Mouse, Dumbo, Cookieland & others	63	126	189	504	877	1250
Christmas Parade 2('50)-Donald Duck (132 pgs.)(25 pgs. by Barks, r-in Gold Key's Christmas Parade #6). Mickey, Pluto, Chip & Dale, etc. Contents shift to a holiday expansion of W.D. C&S type format	42	84	126	336	588	840
Christmas Parade 3-7('51-'55, #3-116pgs; #4-7, 100 pgs.)	14	28	42	112	196	280
Christmas Parade 8(12/56)-Barks-a, 8 pgs.	22	44	66	176	306	435
Christmas Parade 9(12/58)-Barks-a, 20 pgs.	25	50	75	200	350	500

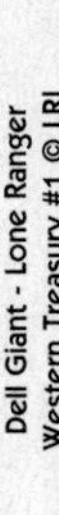
Dell Giant - Lone Ranger Western Treasury #1 © LRI

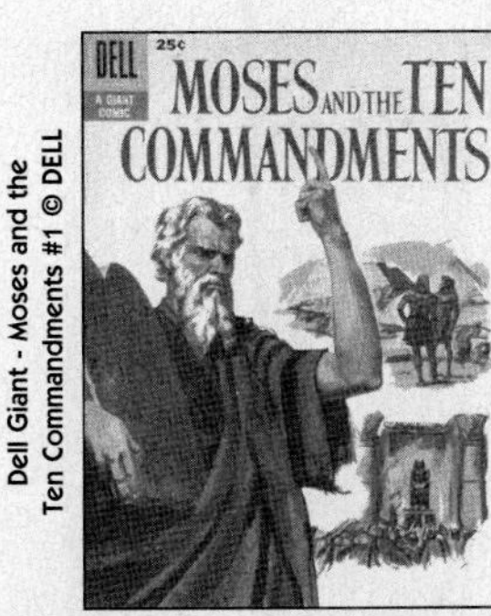

Dell Giant - Moses and the Ten Commandments #1 © DELL

Dell Giant - Summer Fun #2 © DIS

	GD 2.0	VG 4.0	FN 6.0	VF 8.0	VF/NM 9.0	NM- 9.2
Christmas Treasury, A 1(11/54)	10	20	30	80	135	190
Davy Crockett, King Of The Wild Frontier 1(9/55)-Fess Parker photo-c; Marsh-a	19	38	57	152	269	385
Disneyland Birthday Party 1(10/58)-Barks-a, 16 pgs. r-by Gladstone	25	50	75	200	350	500
Donald and Mickey In Disneyland 1(5/58)	11	22	33	88	157	225
Donald Duck Beach Party 1(7/54)-Has an Uncle Scrooge story (not by Barks) that prefigures the later rivalry with Flintheart Glomgold and tells of Scrooge's wild rivalry with another millionaire	16	32	48	128	224	320
...Beach Party 2(1955)-Lady & Tramp	11	22	33	88	157	225
...Beach Party 3-5(1956-58)	11	22	33	88	152	215
...Beach Party 6(8/59, 84pp)-Stapled	8	16	24	64	115	165
Donald Duck Fun Book 1,2 (1953 & 10/54)-Games, puzzles, comics & cut-outs (very rare in unused condition)(most copies commonly have defaced interior pgs.)	63	126	189	504	877	1250
Donald Duck In Disneyland 1(9/55)-1st Disneyland Dell Giant	15	30	45	120	210	300
Golden West Rodeo Treasury 1(10/57)	10	20	30	80	135	190
Huey, Dewey and Louie Back To School 1(9/58)	9	18	27	72	126	180
Lady and The Tramp 1(6/55)	17	34	51	136	233	330
Life Stories of American Presidents 1(11/57)-Buscema-a	8	16	24	64	107	150
Lone Ranger Golden West 3(8/55)-Formerly Lone Ranger Western Treasury	18	36	54	144	255	365
Lone Ranger Movie Story nn(3/56)-Origin Lone Ranger in text; Clayton Moore photo-c	36	72	108	288	507	725
...Western Treasury 1(9/53)-Origin Lone Ranger, Silver, & Tonto; painted cover	23	46	69	184	325	465
...Western Treasury 2(8/54)-Becomes Lone Ranger Golden West #3	18	36	54	144	255	365
Marge's Little Lulu & Alvin Story Telling Time 1(3/59)-r/#2,5,3,11,30,10,21,17,8, 14,16; Stanley-a	14	28	42	112	196	280
...& Her Friends 4(3/56)-Tripp-a	14	28	42	112	191	270
...& Her Special Friends 3(3/55)-Tripp-a	15	30	45	120	210	300
...& Tubby At Summer Camp 5,2: 5(10/57)-Tripp-a. 2(10/58)-Tripp-a	13	26	39	104	182	260
...& Tubby Halloween Fun 6,2: 6(10/57)-Tripp-a. 2(10/58)-Tripp-a	13	26	39	104	182	260
...& Tubby In Alaska 1(7/59)-Tripp-a	13	26	39	104	177	250
...On Vacation 1(7/54)-r/4C-110,14,4C-146,5,4C-97,4,4C-158,3,1;Stanley-a	25	50	75	200	350	500
...& Tubby Annual 1(3/53)-r/4C-165,4C-74,4C-146,4C-97,4C-158, 4C-139, 4C-131; Stanley-a (1st Lulu Dell Giant)	30	60	90	240	420	600
...& Tubby Annual 2('54)-r/4C-139,6,4C-115,4C-74,5,4C-97,3,4C-146,18; Stanley-a	25	50	75	200	350	500
Marge's Tubby & His Clubhouse Pals 1(10/56)-1st app. Gran'pa Feeb;1st app. Janie; written by Stanley; Tripp-a	15	30	45	120	210	300
Mickey Mouse Almanac 1(12/57)-Barks-a, 8pgs.	27	54	81	216	378	540
...Birthday Party 1(9/53)-r/entire 48pgs. of Gottfredson's "Mickey Mouse in Love Trouble" from WDC&S 36-39. Quality equal to original. Also reprints one story each from Four Color 27, 79, & 181 plus 6 panels of highlights in the career of Mickey Mouse	31	62	93	248	434	620
...Club Parade 1(12/55)-r/4-Color 16 with some death trap scenes redrawn by Paul Murry & recolored with night turned into day; quality less than original	22	44	66	176	308	440
...In Fantasy Land 1(5/57)	13	26	39	104	180	255
...In Frontier Land 1(5/56)-Mickey Mouse Club iss.	13	26	39	104	180	255
...Summer Fun 1(8/58)-Mobile cut-outs on back-c; becomes Summer Fun with #2; Canadian version exists with 30¢-c price	13	26	39	104	180	255
Moses & The Ten Commandments 1(8/57)-Not based on movie; Dell's adaptation; Sekowsky-a; variant version has "Gods of Egypt" comic back-c	8	16	24	64	107	150
Nancy & Sluggo Travel Time 1(9/58)	8	16	24	64	115	165
Peter Pan Treasure Chest 1(1/53, 212pp)-Disney; contains 54-page movie adaptation & other Peter Pan stories; plus Donald & Mickey stories w/P. Pan; a 32-page retelling of "D. Duck Finds Pirate Gold" with yellow beak, called "Capt. Hook & the Buried Treasure"	140	280	420	1120	1960	2800
Picnic Party 6,7(7/55-6/56)(Formerly Vacation Parade)-Uncle Scrooge, Mickey & Donald	12	24	36	96	166	235
Picnic Party 8(7/57)-Barks-a, 6pgs	21	42	63	168	289	410
Pogo Parade 1(9/53)-Kelly-a(r-/Pogo from Animal Comics in this order: #11,13,21,14,27,16,23,9,18,15,17)	25	50	75	200	350	500
Raggedy Ann & Andy 1(2/55)	16	32	48	128	224	320
Santa Claus Funnies 1(11/52)-Dan Noonan -A Christmas Carol adaptation	9	18	27	72	126	180

	GD 2.0	VG 4.0	FN 6.0	VF 8.0	VF/NM 9.0	NM- 9.2
Silly Symphonies 1(9/52)-Redrawing of Gotfredson's Mickey Mouse strip of "The Brave Little Tailor;" 2 Good Housekeeping pages (from 1943); Lady and the Two Siamese Cats, three years before "Lady & the Tramp;" a retelling of Donald Duck's first app. in "The Wise Little Hen" & other stories based on 1930's Silly Symphony cartoons	33	66	99	264	457	650
Silly Symphonies 2(9/53)-M. Mouse in "The Sorcerer's Apprentice", 2 Good Housekeeping pages (from 1944); The Pelican & the Snipe, Elmer Elephant, Peculiar Penguins, Little Hiawatha, & others	24	48	72	192	339	485
Silly Symphonies 3(2/54)-r/Mickey & The Beanstalk (4-Color #157, 39pgs.), Little Minnehaha, Pablo, The Flying Gauchito, Pluto, & Bongo, & 2 Good Housekeeping pages (1944)	20	40	60	160	275	390
Silly Symphonies 4(8/54)-r/Dumbo (4-Color 234), Morris The Midget Moose, The Country Cousin, Bongo, & Clara Cluck	20	40	60	160	275	390
Silly Symphonies 5-8: 5(2/55)-r/Cinderella (4-Color 272), Bucky Bug, Pluto, Little Hiawatha, The 7 Dwarfs & Dumbo, Pinocchio. 6(8/55)-r/Pinocchio (WDC&S 63), The 7 Dwarfs & Thumper (WDC&S 45), M. Mouse "Adventures With Robin Hood" (40 pgs.), Johnny Appleseed, Pluto & Peter Pan, & Bucky Bug; Cut-out on back-c. 7(2/57)-r/Reluctant Dragon, Ugly Duckling, M. Mouse & Peter Pan, Jiminy Cricket, Peter & The Wolf, Brer Rabbit, Bucky Bug; Cut-out on back-c. 8(2/58)-r/Thumper Meets The 7 Dwarfs (4-Color #19), Jiminy Cricket, Niok, Brer Rabbit; Cut-out on back-c	16	32	48	128	224	320
Silly Symphonies 9(2/59)-r/Paul Bunyan, Humphrey Bear, Jiminy Cricket, The Social Lion, Goliath II; cut-out on back-c	15	30	45	120	210	300
Sleeping Beauty 1(4/59)	25	50	75	200	350	500
Summer Fun 2(8/59, 84pp, stapled binding)(Formerly Mickey Mouse...)-Barks-a(2), 24 pgs.	24	48	72	192	336	480
Tarzan's Jungle Annual 1(8/52)-Lex Barker photo on-c of #1,2	15	30	45	120	210	300
...Annual 2(8/53)	11	22	33	88	152	215
...Annual 3-7('54-9/58)(two No. 5s)-Manning-a-No. 3,5-7; Marsh-a in No. 1-7 plus painted-c 1-7	9	18	27	72	124	175
Tom And Jerry Back To School 1(9/56) 2 different back-c, variant has "Apple for the Teacher" cut-out	12	24	36	96	168	240
...Picnic Time 1(7/58)	10	20	30	80	135	190
...Summer Fun 1(7/54)-Droopy written by Barks	15	30	45	120	205	290
...Summer Fun 2-4(7/55-7/57)	8	16	24	64	107	150
...Toy Fair 1(6/58)	9	18	27	72	126	180
...Winter Carnival 1(12/52)-Droopy written by Barks	20	40	60	160	280	400
...Winter Carnival 2(12/53)-Droopy written by Barks	16	32	48	128	224	320
...Winter Fun 3(12/54)	8	16	24	64	115	165
...Winter Fun 4-7(12/55-11/58)	7	14	21	56	101	145
Treasury of Dogs, A 1(10/56)	8	16	24	64	107	150
Treasury of Horses, A (9/55)	8	16	24	64	107	150
Uncle Scrooge Goes To Disneyland 1(8/57p)-Barks-a, 20 pgs. r-by Gladstone; 2 different back-c; variant shows 6 snapshots of Scrooge	26	52	78	208	359	510
Vacation In Disneyland 1(8/58)	11	22	33	88	157	225
Vacation Parade 1(7/50, 132pp)-Donald Duck & Mickey Mouse; Barks-a, 55 pgs.	95	190	285	760	1330	1900
Vacation Parade 2(7/51,116pp)	25	50	75	200	350	500
Vacation Parade 3-5(7/52-7/54)-Becomes Picnic Party No. 6 on. #4-Robin Hood Advs.	14	28	42	112	194	275
Western Roundup 1(6/52)-Photo-c; Gene Autry, Roy Rogers, Johnny Mack Brown, Rex Allen, & Bill Elliott begin; photo back-c begin, end No. 14,16,18	25	50	75	200	350	500
Western Roundup 2(2/53)-Photo-c	14	28	42	112	196	280
Western Roundup 3-5(7-9/53 - 1-3/54)-Photo-c	11	22	33	88	157	225
Western Roundup 6-10(4-6/54 - 4-6/55)-Photo-c	11	22	33	88	149	210
Western Roundup 11-17,25: 11-17-Photo-c; 11-13,16,17-Manning-a. 11-Flying A's Range Rider, Dale Evans begin	9	18	27	72	129	185
Western Roundup 18-Toth-a; last photo-c; Gene Autry ends	11	22	33	88	149	210
Western Roundup 19-24-Manning-a. 19-Buffalo Bill Jr. begins (7-9/57; early app.). 19,20,22-Toth-a. 21-Rex Allen, Johnny Mack Brown end. 22-Jace Pearson's Texas Rangers, Rin Tin Tin, Tales of Wells Fargo (2nd app., 4-6/58) & Wagon Train (2nd app.) begin	9	18	27	72	129	185
Woody Woodpecker Back To School 1(10/52)	10	20	30	80	140	200
...Back To School 2-4,6('53-10/57)-County Fair No. 5	8	16	24	64	112	160
...County Fair 5(9/56)-Formerly Back To School	8	16	24	64	112	160
...County Fair 2(11/58)	7	14	21	56	101	145

DELL GIANTS (Consecutive numbering)
Dell Publishing Co.: No. 21, Sept, 1959 - No. 55, Sept, 1961 (Most 84 pgs., 25¢)

	GD 2.0	VG 4.0	FN 6.0	VF 8.0	VF/NM 9.0	NM- 9.2
21-(#1)-M.G.M.'s Tom & Jerry Picnic Time (84pp, stapled binding)-Painted-c	11	22	33	88	157	225
22-Huey, Dewey & Louie Back to School (Disney; 10/59, 84pp, square binding begins)						

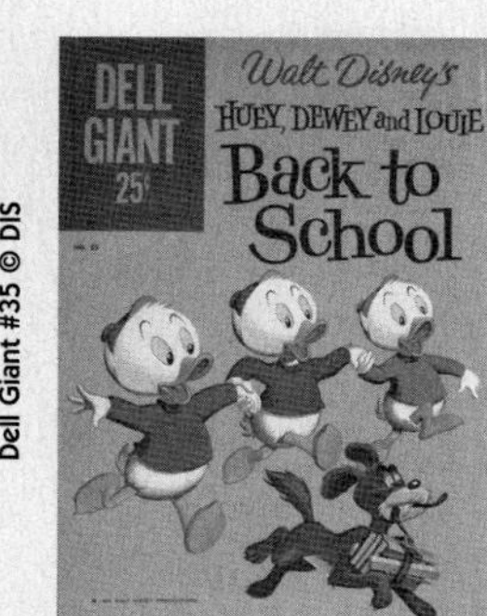

Dell Giant #35 © DIS

The Demon #5 © DC

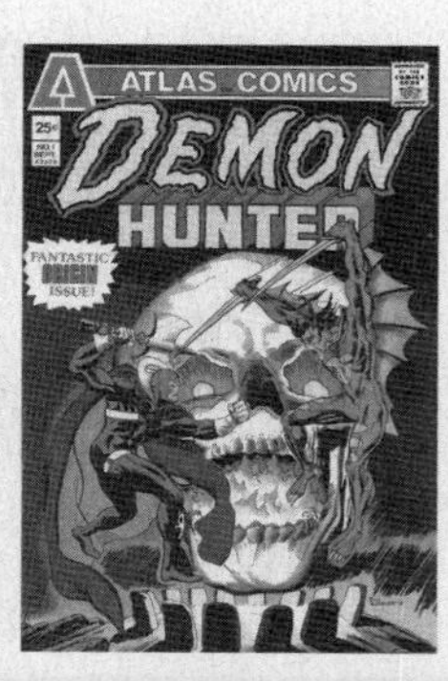

Demon-Hunter #1 © Seaboard

	GD 2.0	VG 4.0	FN 6.0	VF 8.0	VF/NM 9.0	NM- 9.2
	9	18	27	72	129	185
23-Marge's Little Lulu & Tubby Halloween Fun (10/59)-Tripp-a	12	24	36	96	168	240
24-Woody Woodpecker's Family Fun (11/59)(Walter Lantz)	8	16	24	64	112	160
25-Tarzan's Jungle World(11/59)-Marsh-a; painted-c	11	22	33	88	152	215
26-Christmas Parade(Disney; 12/59)-Barks-a, 16pgs.; Barks draws himself on wanted poster on pg. 13	21	42	63	168	289	410
27-Walt Disney's Man in Space (10/59) r-/4-Color 716,866, & 954 (100 pgs., 35¢)(TV)	9	18	27	72	129	185
28-Bugs Bunny's Winter Fun (2/60)	9	18	27	72	126	180
29-Marge's Little Lulu & Tubby in Hawaii (4/60)-Tripp-a	12	24	36	96	166	235
30-Disneyland USA(Disney; 6/60)	9	18	27	72	124	175
31-Huckleberry Hound Summer Fun (7/60)(TV)(HannaBarbera)-Yogi Bear & Pixie & Dixie app.	12	24	36	96	173	250
32-Bugs Bunny Beach Party	7	14	21	56	101	145
33-Daisy Duck & Uncle Scrooge Picnic Time (Disney; 9/60)	9	18	27	72	124	175
34-Nancy & Sluggo Summer Camp (8/60)	7	14	21	56	101	145
35-Huey, Dewey & Louie Back to School (Disney; 10/60)-1st app. Daisy Duck's Nieces, April, May & June	12	24	36	96	163	230
36-Marge's Little Lulu & Witch Hazel Halloween Fun (10/60)-Tripp-a	11	22	33	88	157	225
37-Tarzan, King of the Jungle (11/60)-Marsh-a; painted-c	9	18	27	72	129	185
38-Uncle Donald & His Nephews Family Fun (Disney; 11/60)-Cover painting based on a pencil sketch by Barks	12	24	36	96	173	250
39-Walt Disney's Merry Christmas (Disney; 12/60)-Cover painting based on a pencil sketch by Barks	12	24	36	96	173	250
40-Woody Woodpecker Christmas Parade (12/60)(Walter Lantz)	6	12	18	48	87	125
41-Yogi Bear's Winter Sports (12/60)(TV)(Hanna-Barbera)-Huckleberry Hound, Pixie & Dixie, Augie Doggie app.	12	24	36	96	173	250
42-Marge's Little Lulu & Tubby in Australia (4/61)	11	22	33	88	157	225
43-Mighty Mouse in Outer Space (5/61)	18	36	54	144	252	360
44-Around the World with Huckleberry and His Friends (7/61)(TV)(Hanna-Barbera)-Yogi Bear, Pixie & Dixie, Quick Draw McGraw, Augie Doggie app.; 1st app. Yakky Doodle	13	26	39	104	182	260
45-Nancy & Sluggo Summer Camp (8/61)	7	14	21	56	96	135
46-Bugs Bunny Beach Party (8/61)	7	14	21	56	96	135
47-Mickey & Donald in Vacationland (Disney; 8/61)	8	16	24	64	115	165
48-The Flintstones (No. 1)(Bedrock Bedlam)(7/61)(TV)(Hanna-Barbera) 1st app. in comics	21	42	63	168	294	420
49-Huey, Dewey & Louie Back to School (Disney; 9/61)	9	18	27	72	124	175
50-Marge's Little Lulu & Witch Hazel Trick 'N' Treat (10/61)	11	22	33	88	157	225
51-Tarzan, King of the Jungle by Jesse Marsh (11/61)-Painted-c	8	16	24	64	110	155
52-Uncle Donald & His Nephews Dude Ranch (Disney; 11/61)	8	16	24	64	115	165
53-Donald Duck Merry Christmas (Disney; 12/61)	8	16	24	64	112	160
54-Woody Woodpecker's Christmas Party (12/61)-Issued after No. 55	7	14	21	56	98	140
55-Daisy Duck & Uncle Scrooge Showboat (Disney; 9/61)	8	16	24	64	117	170

NOTE: All issues printed with & without ad on back cover.

DELL JUNIOR TREASURY
Dell Publishing Co.: June, 1955 - No. 10, Oct, 1957 (15¢) (All painted-c)

	GD 2.0	VG 4.0	FN 6.0	VF 8.0	VF/NM 9.0	NM- 9.2
1-Alice in Wonderland; r/4-Color #331 (52 pgs.)	8	16	24	54	102	150
2-Aladdin & the Wonderful Lamp	6	12	18	41	76	110
3-Gulliver's Travels (1/56)	6	12	18	37	66	95
4-Adventures of Mr. Frog & Miss Mouse	6	12	18	38	69	100
5-The Wizard of Oz (7/56)	6	12	18	41	76	110
6-10: 6-Heidi (10/56). 7-Santa and the Angel. 8-Raggedy Ann and the Camel with the Wrinkled Knees. 9-Clementina the Flying Pig. 10-Adventures of Tom Sawyer	6	12	18	37	66	95

DEMOLITION MAN
DC Comics: Nov, 1993 - No. 4, Feb, 1994 ($1.75, color, limited series)

	GD 2.0	VG 4.0	FN 6.0	VF 8.0	VF/NM 9.0	NM- 9.2
1-4-Movie adaptation						3.00

DEMON, THE (See Detective Comics No. 482-485)
National Periodical Publications: Aug-Sept, 1972 - V3#16, Jan, 1974

	GD 2.0	VG 4.0	FN 6.0	VF 8.0	VF/NM 9.0	NM- 9.2
1-Origin; Kirby-s/c/a in all; 1st Morgaine Le Fey	10	20	30	64	132	200
2-5	4	8	12	27	44	60
6-16: 7-1st app. Klarion the Witch Boy	3	6	9	19	30	40

DEMON, THE (1st limited series)(Also see Cosmic Odyssey #2)
DC Comics: Nov, 1986 - No. 4, Feb, 1987 (75¢, limited series)(#2 has #4 of 4 on-c)

	GD 2.0	VG 4.0	FN 6.0	VF 8.0	VF/NM 9.0	NM- 9.2
1-4: Matt Wagner-a(p) & scripts in all. 4-Demon & Jason Blood become separate entities.						4.00

DEMON, THE (2nd Series)
DC Comics: July, 1990 - No. 58, May, 1995 ($1.50/$1.75/$1.95)

	GD 2.0	VG 4.0	FN 6.0	VF 8.0	VF/NM 9.0	NM- 9.2
1-Grant scripts begin, ends #39: 1-4-Painted-c						5.00
2-18,20-27,29-39,41,42: 3,8-Batman app. (cameo #4). 12-Bisley painted-c. 12-15,21-Lobo app. (1 pg. cameo #11). 23-Robin app. 29-Superman app. 31,33-39-Lobo app.						3.00
19-($2.50, 44 pgs.)-Lobo poster stapled inside						5.00
28,40: 28-Superman-c/story; begin $1.75-c. 40-Garth Ennis scripts begin						4.00
43-45-Hitman app.	1	2	3	5	7	9
46-48 Return of The Haunted Tank-c/s. 48-Begin $1.95-c.						5.00
49,51,0-(10/94),55-58: 51-(9/94)						3.00
50 ($2.95, 52 pgs.)						4.00
52-54-Hitman-s						5.00
Annual 1 (1992, $3.00, 68 pgs.)-Eclipso-c/story						4.00
Annual 2 (1993, $3.50, 68 pgs.)-1st app. of Hitman	2	4	6	13	18	22

NOTE: *Alan Grant scripts in #1-16, 20, 21, 23-25, 30-39, Annual 1. **Wagner** a/scripts-22.*

DEMON DREAMS
Pacific Comics: Feb, 1984 - No. 2, May, 1984

	GD 2.0	VG 4.0	FN 6.0	VF 8.0	VF/NM 9.0	NM- 9.2
1,2-Mostly r-/Heavy Metal						3.00

DEMON: DRIVEN OUT
DC Comics: Nov, 2003 - No. 6, Apr, 2004 ($2.50, limited series)

	GD 2.0	VG 4.0	FN 6.0	VF 8.0	VF/NM 9.0	NM- 9.2
1-6-Dysart-s/Mhan-a						3.00

DEMON-HUNTER
Seaboard Periodicals (Atlas): Sept, 1975

	GD 2.0	VG 4.0	FN 6.0	VF 8.0	VF/NM 9.0	NM- 9.2
1-Origin/1st app. Demon-Hunter; Buckler-c/a	2	4	6	11	16	20

DEMON KNIGHT: A GRIMJACK GRAPHIC NOVEL
First Publishing: 1990 ($8.95, 52 pgs.)

	GD 2.0	VG 4.0	FN 6.0	VF 8.0	VF/NM 9.0	NM- 9.2
nn-Flint Henry-a						9.00

DEMON KNIGHTS (New DC 52) (Set in the Dark Ages)
DC Comics: Nov, 2011 - No. 23, Oct, 2013 ($2.99)

	GD 2.0	VG 4.0	FN 6.0	VF 8.0	VF/NM 9.0	NM- 9.2
1-23: 1-Cornell-s/Neves-a/Daniel-c; Etrigan, Madame Xanadu & The Shining Knight app.						3.00
#0 (11/12, $2.99) Origin of Etrigan The Demon; Merlin app.; Cornell-s/Chang-a						3.00

DENNIS THE MENACE (TV with 1959 issues) (Becomes ...Fun Fest Series; See The Best of... & The Very Best of...)(...Fun Fest on-c only to #156-166)
Standard Comics/Pines No.15-31/Hallden (Fawcett) No.32 on: 8/53 - #14, 1/56; #15, 3/56 - #31, 11/58; #32, 1/59 - #166, 11/79

	GD 2.0	VG 4.0	FN 6.0	VF 8.0	VF/NM 9.0	NM- 9.2
1-1st app. Dennis, Mr. & Mrs. Wilson, Ruff & Dennis' mom & dad; Wiseman-a, written by Fred Toole-most issues	194	388	582	1242	2121	3000
2	58	116	174	371	636	900
3-5	37	74	111	222	361	500
6-10: 8-Last pre-code issue	30	60	90	177	289	400
11-20	20	40	60	114	182	250
21,23-30	13	26	39	74	105	135
22-1st app. Margaret w/blonde hair	16	32	48	94	147	200
31-1st app. Joey	16	32	48	94	147	200
32-38,40(1/60): 37-A-Bomb blast panel	9	18	27	52	69	85
39-1st app. Gina (11/59)	12	24	36	67	94	120
41-60(7/62)	4	8	12	22	34	45
61-80(9/65),100(1/69)	3	6	9	14	20	25
81-99	2	4	6	11	16	20
101-117: 102-Last 12¢ issue	2	4	6	9	12	15
118(1/72)-131 (All 52 pages)	2	4	6	10	14	18
132(1/74)-142,144-160	1	2	3	5	7	9
143(3/76) Olympic-c/s; low print	2	4	6	10	14	18
161-166	1	3	4	6	8	10

NOTE: ***Wiseman** c/a-1-46, 53, 68, 69.*

DENNIS THE MENACE (Giants) (No. 1 titled Giant Vacation Special; becomes Dennis the Menace Bonus Magazine No. 76 on)
(#1-8,18,23,25,30,38: 100 pgs.; rest to #41: 84 pgs.; #42-75: 68 pgs.)
Standard/Pines/Hallden(Fawcett): Summer, 1955 - No. 75, Dec, 1969

	GD 2.0	VG 4.0	FN 6.0	VF 8.0	VF/NM 9.0	NM- 9.2
nn-Giant Vacation Special(Summ/55-Standard)	18	36	54	103	162	220
nn-Christmas issue (Winter '55)	15	30	45	88	137	185
2-Giant Vacation Special (Summer '56-Pines)	14	28	42	78	112	145

Dennis the Menace and the Bible Kids #3 © Word Books

Dept. H #7 © Matt Kindt

Descender #11 © 171 Studios & Dustin Nguyen

GD VG FN VF VF/NM NM-
2.0 4.0 6.0 8.0 9.0 9.2

3-Giant Christmas issue (Winter '56-Pines) 13 26 39 72 101 130
4-Giant Vacation Special (Summer '57-Pines) 12 24 36 67 94 120
5-Giant Christmas issue (Winter '57-Pines) 12 24 36 67 94 120
6-In Hawaii (Giant Vacation Special)(Summer '58-Pines)
11 22 33 62 86 110
6-In Hawaii (Summer '59-Hallden)-2nd printing; says 3rd large printing on-c
6-In Hawaii (Summer '60)-3rd printing; says 4th large printing on-c
6-In Hawaii (Summer '62)-4th printing; says 5th large printing on-c
each.... 8 16 24 42 54 65
6-Giant Christmas issue (Winter '58) 11 22 33 62 86 110
7-In Hollywood (Winter '59-Hallden) 5 10 15 30 50 70
7-In Hollywood (Summer '61)-2nd printing 3 6 9 20 31 42
8-In Mexico (Winter '60, 100 pgs.-Hallden/Fawcett) 5 10 15 30 50 70
8-In Mexico (Summer '62, 2nd printing) 3 6 9 20 31 42
9-Goes to Camp (Summer '61, 84 pgs.)-1st CCA approved issue
5 10 15 30 50 70
9-Goes to Camp (Summer '62)-2nd printing 3 6 9 20 31 42
10-12: 10-X-Mas issue (Winter '61), 11-Giant Christmas issue (Winter '62),
12-Triple Feature (Winter '62) 5 10 15 33 57 80
13-17: 13-Best of Dennis the Menace (Spring '63)-Reprints, 14-And His Dog Ruff (Summer '63), 15-In Washington, D.C. (Summer '63), 16-Goes to Camp (Summer '63)-Reprints No. 9, 17-& His Pal Joey (Winter '63) 4 8 12 23 37 50
18-In Hawaii (Reprints No. 6) 3 6 9 19 30 40
19-Giant Christmas issue (Winter '63) 4 8 12 23 37 50
20-Spring Special (Spring '64) 4 8 12 23 37 50
21-40 (Summer '66): 30-r/#6. #35-Xmas spec.Wint,'65
3 6 9 17 26 35
41-60 (Fall '68) 3 6 9 14 19 24
61-75 (12/69): 68-Partial-r/#6 2 4 6 11 16 20
NOTE: *Wiseman c/a-1-8, 12, 14, 15, 17, 20, 22, 27, 28, 31, 35, 36, 41, 49.*

DENNIS THE MENACE
Marvel Comics Group: Nov, 1981 - No. 13, Nov, 1982
1-New-a 2 4 6 9 12 15
2-13: 2-New art. 3-Part-r. 4,5-r. 5-X-Mas-c & issue, 7-Spider Kid-c/sty
1 2 3 4 5 7
NOTE: *Hank Ketcham c-most; a-3, 12. Wiseman a-4, 5.*

DENNIS THE MENACE AND HIS DOG RUFF
Hallden/Fawcett: Summer, 1961
1-Wiseman-c/a 5 10 15 34 60 85

DENNIS THE MENACE AND HIS FRIENDS
Fawcett Publ.: 1969; No. 5, Jan, 1970 - No. 46, April, 1980 (All reprints)
Dennis the Menace & Joey No. 2 (7/69) 2 4 6 13 18 22
Dennis the Menace & Ruff No. 2 (9/69) 2 4 6 13 18 22
Dennis the Menace & Mr. Wilson No. 1 (10/69) 3 6 9 15 22 28
Dennis & Margaret No. 1 (Winter '69) 3 6 9 15 22 28
5-12: 5-Dennis the Menace & Margaret. 6-...& Joey. 7-...& Ruff. 8-...& Mr. Wilson
2 4 6 8 11 14
13-21-(52 pg Giants): 13-(1/72). 21-(1/74) 2 4 6 10 14 18
22-37 1 3 4 6 8 10
38-46 (Digest size, 148 pgs., 4/78, 95¢) 2 4 6 8 11 14
NOTE: *Titles rotate every four issues, beginning with No. 5. Joey issues: #2(7/69),6,10,14,18,22,26,30,34. Ruff issues: #2(9/69), 7,11,15,19,23,27,31,35. Mr. Wilson issues: #1(10/69),8,12,16,20,24,28,32,36. Margaret issues: #1(Wint./69),5,9,13,17,21,25,29,33,37.*

DENNIS THE MENACE AND HIS PAL JOEY
Fawcett Publ.: Summer, 1961 (10¢) (See Dennis the Menace Giants No. 45)
1-Wiseman-c/a 5 10 15 34 60 85

DENNIS THE MENACE AND THE BIBLE KIDS
Word Books: 1977 (36 pgs.)
1-6: 1-Jesus. 2-Joseph. 3-David. 4-The Bible Girls. 5-Moses. 6-More About Jesus
2 4 6 9 12 15
7-9-Low print run: 7-The Lord's Prayer. 8-Stories Jesus told. 9-Paul, God's Traveller
3 6 9 19 30 40
10-Low print run; In the Beginning 5 10 15 33 57 80
NOTE: *Ketcham c/a in all.*

DENNIS THE MENACE BIG BONUS SERIES
Fawcett Publications: No. 10, Feb, 1980 - No. 11, Apr, 1980
10,11 1 2 3 5 6 8

DENNIS THE MENACE BONUS MAGAZINE (Formerly Dennis the Menace Giants Nos. 1-75)
(...Big Bonus Series on-c for #174-194)
Fawcett Publications: No. 76, 1/70 - No. 95, 7/71; No. 95, 7/71; No. 97, '71; No. 194, 10/79; (No. 76-124: 68 pgs.; No. 125-163: 52 pgs.; No. 164 on: 36 pgs.)

GD VG FN VF VF/NM NM-
2.0 4.0 6.0 8.0 9.0 9.2

76-90(3/71) 2 4 6 10 14 18
91-95, 97-110(10/72): Two #95's with same date(7/71) A-Summer Games, and
B-That's Our Boy. No #96 2 4 6 9 13 16
111-124 2 4 6 8 10 12
125-163-(52 pgs.) 2 4 6 8 10 12
164-194: 166-Indicia printed backwards 1 2 3 4 5 7

DENNIS THE MENACE COMICS DIGEST
Marvel Comics Group: April, 1982 - No. 3, Aug, 1982 ($1.25, digest-size)
1-3-Reprints 1 3 4 6 8 10
1-Mistakenly printed with DC emblem on cover 2 4 6 10 12 15
NOTE: *Ketcham c-all. Wiseman a-all. A few thousand #1's were published with a DC emblem on cover.*

DENNIS THE MENACE FUN BOOK
Fawcett Publications/Standard Comics: 1960 (100 pgs.)
1-Part Wiseman-a 5 10 15 35 63 90

DENNIS THE MENACE FUN FEST SERIES (Formerly Dennis the Menace #166)
Hallden (Fawcett): No. 16, Jan, 1980 - No. 17, Mar, 1980 (40¢)
16,17-By Hank Ketcham 1 2 3 4 5 7

DENNIS THE MENACE POCKET FULL OF FUN!
Fawcett Publications (Hallden): Spring, 1969 - No. 50, March, 1980 (196 pgs.) (Digest size)
1-Reprints in all issues 5 10 15 33 57 80
2-10 4 8 12 23 37 50
11-20 3 6 9 15 22 28
21-28 2 4 6 11 16 20
29-50: 35,40,46-Sunday strip-r 2 4 6 8 11 14
NOTE: *No. 1-28 are 196 pgs.; No. 29-36: 164 pgs.; No. 37: 148 pgs.; No. 38 on: 132 pgs. No. 8, 11, 15, 21, 25, 29 all contain strip reprints.*

DENNIS THE MENACE TELEVISION SPECIAL
Fawcett Publ. (Hallden Div.): Summer, 1961 - No. 2, Spring, 1962 (Giant)
1 5 10 15 34 60 85
2 3 6 9 21 33 45

DENNIS THE MENACE TRIPLE FEATURE
Fawcett Publications: Winter, 1961 (Giant)
1-Wiseman-c/a 5 10 15 34 60 85

DEPT. H
Dark Horse Comics: Apr, 2016 - Present ($3.99)
1-11-Matt Kindt-s/a. 1-Two covers 4.00

DEPUTY, THE (TV)
Dell Publishing Co.: No. 1077, Feb-Apr, 1960 - No. 1225, Oct-Dec, 1961
(all-Henry Fonda photo-c)
Four Color 1077 (#1)-Buscema-a 10 20 30 64 132 200
Four Color 1130 (9-11/60)-Buscema-a,1225 8 16 24 54 102 150

DEPUTY DAWG (TV) (Also see New Terrytoons)
Dell Publishing Co./Gold Key: Oct-Dec, 1961 - No. 1299, 1962; No. 1, Aug, 1965
Four Color 1238,1299 9 18 27 63 129 195
1(10164-508)(8/65)-Gold Key 9 18 27 63 129 195

DEPUTY DAWG PRESENTS DINKY DUCK AND HASHIMOTO-SAN (TV)
Gold Key: August, 1965
1(10159-508) 9 18 27 57 111 165

DESCENDER
Image Comics: Mar, 2015 - Present ($2.99/$3.99)
1-Lemire-s/Nguyen-a/c in all; bonus concept-a 5.00
1-Variant-c by Lemire 6.00
2-18-Lemire-s/Nguyen-a/c 3.00
19-($3.99) 4.00

DESERT GOLD (See Zane Grey 4-Color 467)

DESIGN FOR SURVIVAL (Gen. Thomas S. Power's...)
American Security Council Press: 1968 (36 pgs. in color) (25¢)
nn-Propaganda against the Threat of Communism-Aircraft cover; H-Bomb panel
3 6 9 17 26 35
Twin Circle Edition-Cover shows panels from inside 2 4 6 13 18 22

DESOLATION JONES
DC Comics (WildStorm): July, 2005 - No. 8, Feb, 2007 ($2.95/$2.99)
1-8: 1-6-Warren Ellis-s/J.H. Williams-a. 7,8-Zezelj-a 3.00

DESPERADO (Becomes Black Diamond Western No. 9 on)
Lev Gleason Publications: June, 1948 - No. 8, Feb, 1949 (All 52 pgs.)

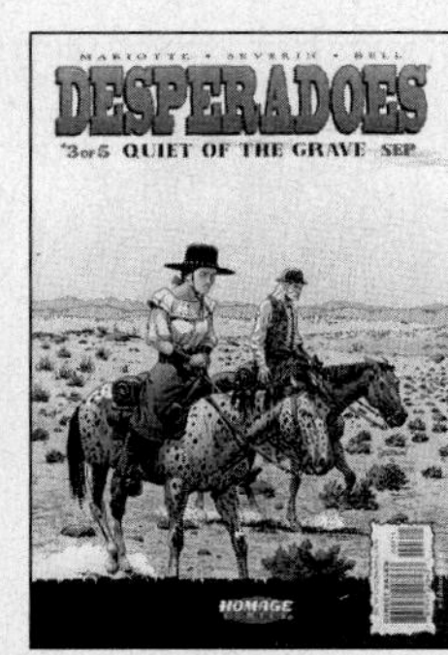

Desperadoes: Quiet of the Grave #3 © WSP

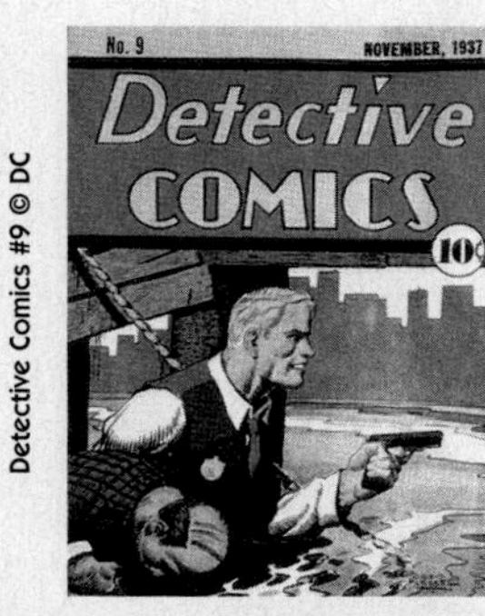

Detective Comics #9 © DC

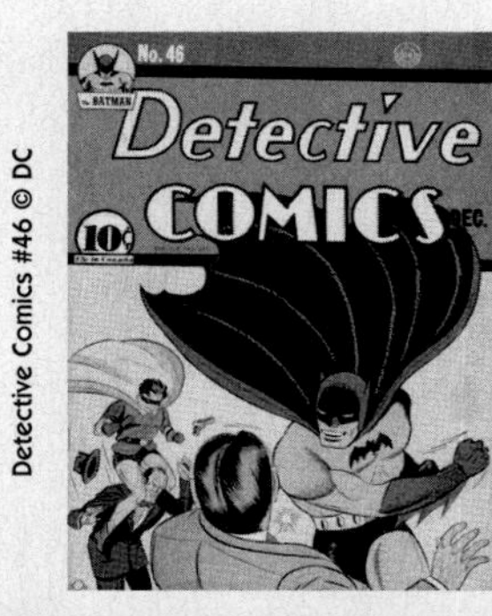

Detective Comics #46 © DC

	GD 2.0	VG 4.0	FN 6.0	VF 8.0	VF/NM 9.0	NM- 9.2
1-Biro-c on all; contains inside photo-c of Charles Biro, Lev Gleason & Bob Wood	16	32	48	94	147	200
2	10	20	30	56	76	95
3-Story with over 20 killings	10	20	30	58	79	100
4-8	8	16	24	44	57	70

NOTE: ***Barry** a-2. **Fuje** a-4, 8. **Guardineer** a-5-7. **Kida** a-3-7. **Ed Moore** a-4, 6.*

DESPERADO PRIMER
Image Comics (Desperado): Apr, 2005 ($1.99, one-shot)

1-Previews of Roundeye, World Traveler, A Mirror To The Soul; Bolland-c 3.00

DESPERADOES
Image Comics (Homage): Sept, 1997 - No. 5, June, 1998 ($2.50/$2.95)

1-5-Mariotte-s/Cassaday-c/a: 1-($2.50-c). 2-5-($2.95) 3.00
...: A Moment's Sunlight TPB ('98, $16.95) r/#1-5 17.00
...: Epidemic! (11/99, $5.95) Mariotte-s 6.00

DESPERADOES: BANNERS OF GOLD
IDW Publishing: Dec, 2004 - No. 5, Apr, 2005 ($3.99, limited series)

1-5: Mariotte-s/Haun-a. 1-Cassaday-c 4.00

DESPERADOES: BUFFALO DREAMS
IDW Publishing: Jan, 2007 - No. 4, Apr, 2007 ($3.99, limited series)

1-4: Mariotte-s/Dose-a/c 4.00

DESPERADOES: QUIET OF THE GRAVE
DC Comics (Homage): Jul, 2001 - No. 5, Nov, 2001 ($2.95)

1-5-Jeff Mariotte-s/John Severin-c/a 3.00
TPB (2002, $14.95) r/#1-5; intro. by Brian Keene 15.00

DESPERATE TIMES (See Savage Dragon)
Image Comics: Jun, 1998 - No. 4, Dec, 1998; Nov, 2000 - No. 4, July, 2001 ($2.95, B&W)

1-4-Chris Eliopoulos-s/a 3.00
(Vol. 2) 1-4 3.00
(Vol. 3) 0-(1/04, $3.50) Pages read sideways 3.50
(Vol. 3) 1-Pages read sideways 3.00

DESTINATION MOON (See Fawcett Movie Comics, Space Adventures #20, 23, & Strange Adventures #1)

DESTINY: A CHRONICLE OF DEATHS FORETOLD (See Sandman)
DC Comics (Vertigo): 1997 - No.3, 1998 ($5.95, limited series)

1-3-Alisa Kwitney-s in all: 1-Kent Williams & Michael Zulli-a, Williams painted-c. 2-Williams & Scott Hampton-painted-c/a. 3-Williams & Guay-a 6.00
TPB (2000, $14.95) r/series 15.00

DESTROY!!
Eclipse Comics: 1986 ($4.95, B&W, magazine-size, one-shot)

1 5.00
3-D Special 1-r-/#1 ($2.50) 5.00

DESTROYER
Marvel Comics: June, 2009 - No. 5, Oct, 2009 ($3.99, limited series)

1-5-Kirkman-s/Walker-a/Pearson-c 4.00

DESTROYER, THE
Marvel Comics (MAX): Nov, 1989 - No. 9, Jun, 1990 ($2.25, B&W, magazine, 52 pgs.)

1-Based on Remo Williams movie, paperbacks 6.00
2-9: 2-Williamson part inks. 4-Ditko-a 4.00

DESTROYER, THE
Marvel Comics: V2#1, March, 1991 ($1.95, 52 pgs.)
V3#1, Dec, 1991 - No. 4, Mar, 1992 ($1.95, mini-series)

V2#1,V3#1-4: Based on Remo Williams paperbacks. V3#1-4-Simonson-c. 3-Morrow-a 4.00

DESTROYER, THE (Also see Solar, Man of the Atom)
Valiant: Apr, 1995 ($2.95, color, one-shot)

0-Indicia indicates #1 3.00

DESTROYER DUCK
Eclipse Comics: Feb, 1982 - No. 7, May, 1984 (#2-7: Baxter paper) ($1.50)

	GD	VG	FN	VF	VF/NM	NM-
1-Origin Destroyer Duck; 1st app. Groo; Kirby-c/a(p)	2	4	6	9	12	15
2-5: 2-Starling back-up begins; Kirby-c/a(p) thru #5						5.00
6,7						4.00

NOTE: ***Neal Adams** c-1i. **Kirby** c/a-1-5p. **Miller** c-7.*

DESTRUCTOR, THE
Atlas/Seaboard: February, 1975 - No. 4, Aug, 1975

	GD	VG	FN	VF	VF/NM	NM-
1-Origin/1st app.; Ditko/Wood-a; Wood-c(i)	2	4	6	13	18	22
2-4: 2-Ditko/Wood-a. 3,4-Ditko-a(p)	2	4	6	9	13	16

DETECTIVE COMICS (Also see other Batman titles)
National Periodical Publications/DC Comics: Mar, 1937 - No. 881, Oct, 2011

	GD 2.0	VG 4.0	FN 6.0	VF 8.0	VF/NM 9.0	NM- 9.2
1-(Scarce)-Slam Bradley & Spy by Siegel & Shuster, Speed Saunders by Stoner and Flessel, Cosmo, the Phantom of Disguise, Buck Marshall, Bruce Nelson begin; Chin Lung in 'Claws of the Red Dragon' serial begins; Vincent Sullivan-c	13,500	27,000	40,500	100,000	-	-
2 (Rare)-Creig Flessel-c begin; new logo	6000	12,000	18,000	39,000	-	-
3 (Rare)	3700	7400	11,000	27,000	-	-
4,5: 5-Larry Steele begins	1900	3800	5700	10,450	14,725	19,000
6,7,9,10	1350	2700	4050	7425	10,463	13,500
8-Mister Chang-c; classic-c	1900	3800	5700	10,450	14,725	19,000
11-14,17,19: 17-1st app. Fu Manchu in Detective	1150	2300	3450	6325	8913	11,500
15,16-Have interior ad for Action Comics #1	1350	2700	4050	7425	10,463	13,500
18-Classic Fu Manchu-c; last Flessel-c	1800	3600	5400	9900	13,950	18,000
20-The Crimson Avenger begins (1st app.)	1350	2700	4050	7425	10,463	13,500
21,23-25	950	1900	2850	5225	7363	9500
22-1st Crimson Avenger-c by Chambers (12/38)	1150	2300	3450	6325	8913	11,500
26	1100	2200	3300	6050	8525	11,000
27-The Bat-Man & Commissioner Gordon begin (1st app.), created by Bill Finger & Bob Kane (5/39); Batman-c (1st)(by Kane). Bat-Man's secret identity revealed as Bruce Wayne in six pg. story. Signed Rob't Kane (also see Det. PIcture Stories #5 & Funny Pages V3#1)	150,000	300,000	450,000	1,000,000	1,600,000	2,200,000

27-Reprint, Oversize 13-1/2x10". WARNING: This comic is an exact duplicate reprint of the original except for its size. DC published it in 1974 with a second cover titling it as Famous First Edition. There have been many reported cases of the outer cover being removed and the interior sold as the original edition. The reprint with the new outer cover removed is practically worthless; see Famous First Edition for value.

	GD	VG	FN	VF	VF/NM	NM-
28-2nd app. The Batman (6 pg. story); non-Bat-Man-c; signed Rob't Kane	8000	16,000	24,000	44,000	72,000	100,000
29-1st app. Doctor Death-c/story, Batman's 1st name villain. 1st 2 part story (10 pgs.). 2nd Batman-c by Kane	16,000	32,000	48,000	90,000	155,000	220,000
30-Dr. Death app. Story concludes from issue #29. Classic Batman splash panel by Kane.	2000	4000	6000	14,000	23,000	32,000
31-Classic Batman over castle cover; 1st app. The Monk & 1st Julie Madison (Bruce Wayne's 1st love interest); 1st Batplane (Bat-Gyro) and Batarang; 2nd 2-part Batman adventure. Gardner Fox takes over script from Bill Finger. 1st mention of locale (New York City) where Batman lives	25,000	50,000	75,000	140,000	205,000	270,000
32-Batman story concludes from issue #31. 1st app. Dala (Monk's assistant). Batman uses gun for 1st time to slay The Monk and Dala. This was the 1st time a costumed hero used a gun in comic books. 1st Batman head logo on cover	1600	3200	4800	11,000	19,500	28,000
33-Origin The Batman (2 pgs.)(1st told origin); Batman gun holster-c; Batman w/smoking gun panel at end of story. Batman story now 12 pgs. Classic Batman-c	12,000	24,000	36,000	75,000	132,500	190,000
34-2nd Crimson Avenger-c by Creig Flessel and last non Batman-c. Story from issue #32 x-over as Bruce Wayne sees Julie Madison off to America from Paris. Classic Batman splash panel used later in Batman #1 for origin story. Steve Malone begins	1250	2500	3750	9000	15,000	21,000
35-Classic Batman hypodermic needle-c that reflects story in issue #34. Classic Batman with smoking .45 automatic splash panel. Batman-c begin	14,000	28,000	42,000	90,000	130,000	170,000
36-Batman-c that reflects adventure in issue #35. Origin/1st app. of Dr. Hugo Strange (1st major villain, 2/40). 1st finned-gloves worn by Batman	5500	11,000	16,500	40,000	60,000	80,000
37-Last solo Golden-Age Batman adventure in Detective Comics. Panel at end of story reflects solo Batman adventure in Batman #1 that was originally planned for Detective #38. Cliff Crosby begins	4200	8400	12,600	30,000	47,500	65,000
38-Origin/1st app. Robin the Boy Wonder (4/40); Batman and Robin-c begin; cover by Kane	10,000	20,000	30,000	70,000	102,000	135,000
39-Opium story; Clayface app. in 1 panel ad at the end of the Batman story	946	1892	2838	6906	12,203	17,500
40-Origin & 1st app. Clayface (Basil Karlo); 1st Joker cover app. (6/40); Joker story intended for this issue was used in Batman #1 instead; cover is similar to splash page in 2nd Joker story in Batman #1	1800	3600	5400	12,000	21,000	30,000
41-Robin's 1st solo	459	918	1377	3350	5925	8500
42-44: 44-Crimson Avenger-new costume	383	766	1149	2681	4691	6700
45-1st Joker story in Det. (3rd book app. & 4th story app. over all, 11/40)	486	972	1458	3350	6275	9000
46-50: 46-Death of Hugo Strange. 48-1st time car called Batmobile (2/41); Gotham City 1st mention in Detective (1st mentioned in Wow #1; also see Batman #4). 49-Last Clayface	343	686	1029	2400	4200	6000
51-53,55-57	271	542	813	1734	2967	4200
54-Cover mimics Detective #33 cover	284	568	852	1818	3109	4400
58-1st Penguin app. (12/41); last Speed Saunders; Fred Ray-c	1200	2400	3600	9000	13,500	18,000

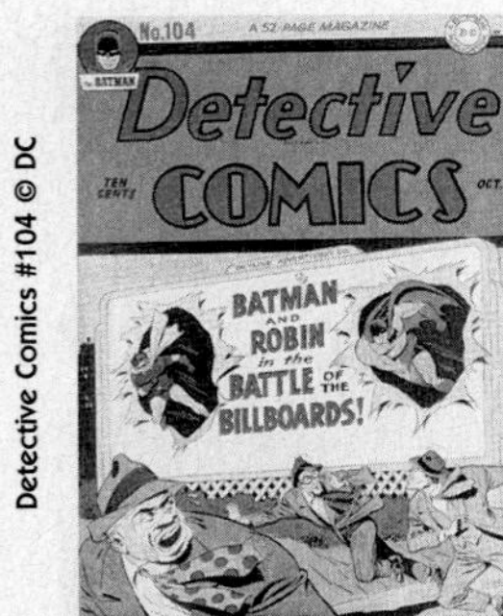

Detective Comics #104 © DC

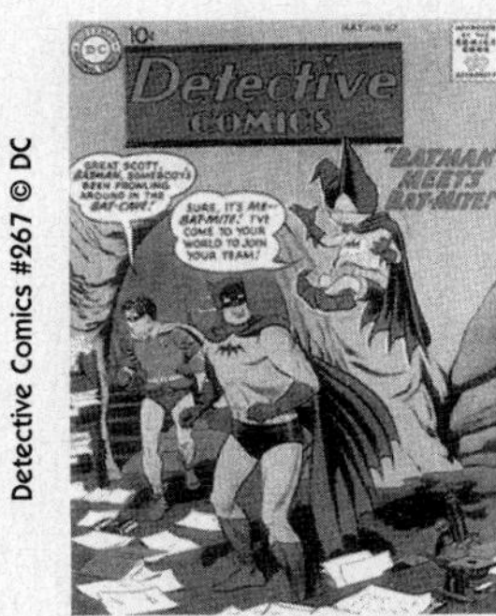

Detective Comics #267 © DC

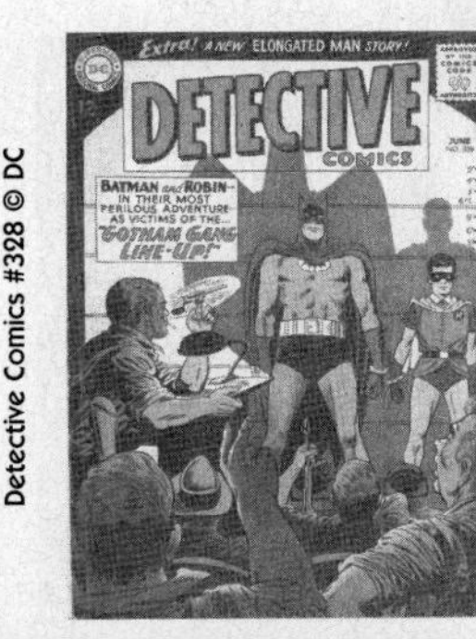

Detective Comics #328 © DC

	GD 2.0	VG 4.0	FN 6.0	VF 8.0	VF/NM 9.0	NM- 9.2
59,60: 59-Last Steve Malone; 2nd Penguin; Wing becomes Crimson Avenger's aide. 60-Intro. Air Wave; Joker app. (2nd in Det.)	271	542	813	1734	2967	4200
61,63: 63-Last Cliff Crosby; 1st app. Mr. Baffle	245	490	735	1568	2684	3800
62-Joker-c/story (2nd Joker-c, 4/42)	595	1190	1785	4350	7675	11,000
64-Origin & 1st app. Boy Commandos by Simon & Kirby (6/42); Joker app.	432	864	1296	3154	5577	8000
65-1st Boy Commandos-c (S&K-a on Boy Commandos & Ray/Robinson-a on Batman & Robin on-c; 4 artists on one-c)	314	628	942	2198	3849	5500
66-Origin & 1st app. Two-Face (originally named Harvey Kent)	1400	2800	4200	10,000	16,000	22,000
67-1st Penguin-c (9/42)	377	754	1131	2639	4620	6600
68-Two-Face-c/story; 1st Two-Face-c	423	846	1269	3000	5250	7500
69-Classic Joker with 2 guns in his hands-c	1100	2200	3300	7500	11,250	15,000
70	245	490	735	1568	2684	3800
71-Classic Joker black background calendar-c	750	1500	2250	5000	7500	10,000
72,74,75: 74-1st Tweedledum & Tweedledee plus-c; S&K-a	194	388	582	1242	2121	3000
73-Scarecrow-c/story (1st Scarecrow-c)	750	1500	2250	5000	7500	10,000
76-Newsboy Legion & The Sandman x-over in Boy Commandos; S&K-a; Joker-c/story	343	686	1029	2400	4200	6000
77-79: All S&K-a	168	336	504	1075	1838	2600
80-Two-Face-c/sty; S&K-a	245	490	735	1568	2684	3800
81,82,84,86-90: 81-1st Cavalier-c & app. 87-Penguin app. 89-Last Crimson Avenger; 2nd Cavalier-c & app.	135	270	405	864	1482	2100
83-1st "skinny" Alfred (1/44)(see Batman #21; last S&K Boy Commandos (also #92,128); most issues #84 on signed S&K are not by them	148	296	444	947	1624	2300
85-Joker-c/story; last Spy; Kirby/Klech Boy Commandos	284	568	852	1818	3109	4400
91,102,109-Joker-c/stories	271	542	813	1734	2967	4200
92-98: 96-Alfred's last name 'Beagle' revealed, later changed to 'Pennyworth' in #214	113	226	339	718	1234	1750
99-Penguin-c/story	174	348	522	1114	1907	2700
100 (6/45)	148	296	444	947	1624	2300
101,103-107,110-113,115-117,119	100	200	300	635	1093	1550
108-1st Bat-signal-c (2/46)	116	232	348	742	1271	1800
114,118-Joker-c/stories. 114-1st small logo (8/46)	232	464	696	1485	2543	3600
120-Penguin-c/story	181	362	543	1158	1979	2800
121,123,125,127,129,130	97	194	291	621	1061	1500
122-1st Catwoman-c (4/47)	300	600	900	2010	3505	5000
124,128-Joker-c/stories	194	388	582	1242	2121	3000
126-Penguin-c	155	310	465	992	1696	2400
131-134,136,139	90	180	270	576	988	1400
135-Frankenstein-c/story	113	226	339	718	1234	1750
137-Joker-c/story; last Air Wave	194	388	582	1242	2121	3000
138-Origin Robotman (see Star Spangled #7 for 1st app.); series ends #202	135	270	405	864	1482	2100
140-The Riddler-c/story (1st app., 10/48)	1800	3600	5400	12,000	21,000	30,000
141,143-148,150: 150-Last Boy Commandos	90	180	270	576	988	1400
142-2nd Riddler-c/story	300	600	900	2010	3505	5000
149-Joker-c/story	181	362	543	1158	1979	2800
151-Origin & 1st app. Pow Wow Smith, Indian lawman (9/49) & begins series	100	200	300	635	1093	1550
152,154,155,157-160: 152-Last Slam Bradley	90	180	270	576	988	1400
153-1st app. Roy Raymond TV Detective (11/49); origin The Human Fly	94	188	282	597	1024	1450
156(2/50)-The new classic Batmobile	155	310	465	992	1696	2400
161-167,169,170,172-176: Last 52 pg. issue	87	174	261	553	952	1350
168-Origin the Joker	2200	4400	6600	14,000	24,000	34,000
171-Penguin-c	119	238	357	762	1306	1850
177-179,181-186,188,189,191,192,194-199,201,202,204,206-210,212,214-216: 184-1st app. Fire Fly. 185-Secret of Batman's utility belt. 202-Last Robotman & Pow Wow Smith. 215-1st app. of Batmen of all Nations. 216-Last precode (2/55)	84	168	252	538	919	1300
180,193-Joker-c/story	155	310	465	992	1696	2400
187-Two-Face-c/story	226	452	678	1446	2473	3500
190-Origin Batman retold	107	214	321	680	1165	1650
200(10/53), 205: 205-Origin Batcave	100	200	300	635	1093	1550
203,211-Catwoman-c/stories	116	232	348	742	1271	1800
213-Origin & 1st app. Mirror Man	97	194	291	621	1061	1500
217-224: 218-Batman Jr. & Robin Sr. app.	71	142	213	454	777	1100
225-(11/55)-1st app. Martian Manhunter (J'onn J'onzz); origin begins; also see Batman #78	1000	2000	3000	7000	12,500	18,000
226-Origin Martian Manhunter cont'd (2nd app.)	194	388	582	1242	2121	3000
227-229: Martian Manhunter stories in all	84	168	252	538	919	1300
230-1st app. Mad Hatter (imposter, not the one from Batman #49, this one's appearance inspired the 1966 TV version); brief recap origin of Martian Manhunter	116	232	348	742	1271	1800
231-Brief origin recap Martian Manhunter	63	126	189	403	689	975
232,234,237,238,240	60	120	180	380	653	925
233-Origin & 1st app. Batwoman (7/56)	343	686	1029	2400	4200	6000
235-Origin Batman & his costume; tells how Bruce Wayne's father (Thomas Wayne) wore Bat costume & fought crime (reprinted in Batman #255)	100	200	300	635	1093	1550
236-1st S.A. issue; J'onn J'onzz talks to parents and Mars-1st since being stranded on Earth; 1st app. Bat-Tank?	63	126	189	403	689	975
239-Early DC grey tone-c	90	180	270	576	988	1400
241-260: 246-Intro. Diane Meade, John Jones' girl. 249-Batwoman-c/app. 253-1st app. The Terrible Trio. 254-Bat-Hound-c/story. 257-Intro. & 1st app. Whirly Bats. 259-1st app. The Calendar Man	47	94	141	296	498	700
261-264,266,268-271: 261-J. Jones tie-in to sci/fi movie "Incredible Shrinking Man"; 1st app. Dr. Double X. 262-Origin Jackal. 268,271-Manhunter origin recap	39	78	117	231	378	525
265-Batman's origin retold with new facts	53	106	159	334	567	800
267-Origin & 1st app. Bat-Mite (5/59)	97	194	291	621	1061	1500
272,274,275,277-280	34	68	102	199	325	450
273-J'onn J'onzz i.d. revealed for 1st time	34	68	102	206	336	465
276-2nd app. Bat-Mite	43	86	129	271	461	650
281-292, 294-297: 286,292-Batwoman-c/app. 287-Origin J'onn J'onzz retold. 289-Bat-Mite-c/story. 292-Last Roy Raymond. 297-Last 10¢ issue (11/61)	26	52	78	154	252	350
293-(7/61)-Aquaman begins (pre #1); ends #300	27	54	81	158	259	360
298-(12/61)-1st modern Clayface (Matt Hagen)	46	92	138	359	805	1250
299, 300-(2/62)-Aquaman ends	14	28	42	94	207	320
301-(3/62)-J'onn J'onzz returns to Mars (1st time since stranded on Earth six years before)	12	24	36	82	179	275
302-Batwoman-c/app.	12	24	36	82	179	275
303-306,308-310,312-317,319-321,323,324,326,329,330: 321-2nd Terrible Trio. 326-Last J'onn J'onzz, story cont'd in House of Mystery #143; intro. Idol-Head of Diabolu	10	20	30	64	132	200
307-Batwoman-c/app.	10	20	30	66	138	210
311-1st app. Cat-Man; intro. Zook in John Jones	20	40	60	138	307	475
318,322,325: 318,325-Cat-Man-c/story (2nd & 3rd app.); also 1st & 2nd app. Batwoman as the Cat-Woman. 322-Bat-Girl's 1st/only app. in Det. (6th in all); Batman cameo in J'onn J'onzz (only hero to app. in series)	12	24	36	82	179	275
327-(5/64)-Elongated Man begins, ends #383; 1st new look Batman with new costume; Infantino/Giella new look-a begins; Batman with gun	16	32	48	111	246	375
328-Death of Alfred; Bob Kane biog, 2 pgs.	12	24	36	81	176	270
331,333-340: 334-1st app. The Outsider	8	16	24	54	102	150
332,341,365-Joker-c/stories	11	22	33	73	157	240
342-358,360,361,366-368: 345-Intro Block Buster. 347-"What If" theme story (1/66). 350-Elongated Man new costume. 355-Zatanna x-over in Elongated Man. 356-Alfred brought back in Batman, early SA app.	7	14	21	49	92	135
359-Intro/origin Batgirl (Barbara Gordon)-c/story (1/67); 1st Silver Age app. Killer Moth; classic Batgirl-c	125	250	500	1200	2200	3600
362,364-S.A. Riddler app. (early)	9	18	27	58	114	170
363-2nd app. new Batgirl	12	24	36	82	179	275
369(11/67)-N. Adams-a (Elongated Man); 3rd app. S.A. Catwoman (cameo; leads into Batman #197); 4th app. new Batgirl	14	28	42	94	207	320
370-1st Neal Adams-a on Batman (cover only, 12/67)	9	18	27	61	123	185
371-(1/68) 1st new Batmobile from TV show; classic Batgirl-c	10	20	30	68	144	220
372-376,378-386,389,390: 375-New Batmobile-c	6	12	18	38	69	100
377-S.A. Riddler-c/sty	7	14	21	46	86	125
387-r/1st Batman story from #27 (30th anniversary, 5/69); Joker-c; last 12¢ issue	9	18	27	59	117	175
388-Joker-c/story	9	18	27	60	120	180
391-394,396,398,399,401,403,406,409: 392-1st app. Jason Bard. 401-2nd Batgirl/Robin team-up	6	12	18	37	66	95
395,397,402,404,407,408,410-Neal Adams-a. 402-Man-Bat-c/app. (2nd app.). 404-Tribute to Enemy Ace	11	22	33	72	154	235
400-(6/70)-Origin & 1st app. Man-Bat; 1st Batgirl/Robin team-up (cont'd in #401); Neal Adams-a	25	50	75	175	388	600
405-Debut League of Assassins	15	30	45	103	227	350
411-(5/71) Intro. Talia, daughter of Ra's al Ghul (Ra's mentioned, but doesn't appear until Batman #232 (6/71); Bob Brown-a	32	64	96	230	515	800
412-413: 413-Last 15¢ issue	6	12	18	37	66	95

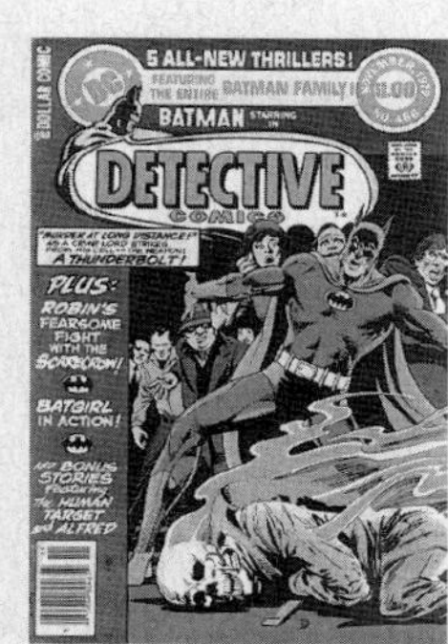

Detective Comics #486 © DC

Detective Comics #554 © DC

Detective Comics #831 © DC

GD 2.0 VG 4.0 FN 6.0 VF 8.0 VF/NM 9.0 NM- 9.2

414-424: All-25¢, 52 pgs. 418-Creeper x-over. 424-Last Batgirl. 6 12 18 38 69 100
425-436: 426,430,436-Elongated Man app. 428,434-Hawkman begins, ends #467 5 10 15 30 50 70
437-New Manhunter begins (10-11/73, 1st app.) by Simonson, ends #443 5 10 15 34 60 85
438-440,442-445 (All 100 Page Super Spectaculars): 438-Kubert Hawkman-r. 439-Origin Manhunter. 440-G.A. Manhunter(Adv. #79) by S&K, Hawkman, Dollman, Green Lantern; Toth-a. 442-G.A. Newsboy Legion, Black Canary, Elongated Man, Dr. Fate-r. 443-Origin The Creeper-r; death of Manhunter; G.A. Green Lantern, Spectre-r; Batman-r/Batman #18. 444-G.A. Kid Eternity-r. 445-G.A. Dr. Midnite-r. 6 12 18 38 69 100
441-(6,7/74)(100 Page S.S.) 1st app. Lt. (Harvey) Bullock, first name not given, appears in only 3 panels; G.A. Plastic Man, Batman, Ibis-r 7 14 21 44 82 120
446-460: 457-Origin retold & updated 3 6 9 17 26 35
461-465,470,480: 480-(44 pgs.). 463-1st app. Black Spider. 464-2nd app. Black Spider 470-Intro. Silver St. Cloud. 3 6 9 16 23 30
466-468,471-473,478,479-Rogers-a in all: 466-1st app. Signalman since Batman #139. 470,471-1st modern app. Hugo Strange. 478-1st app. 3rd Clayface (Preston Payne). 479-(44 pgs.) 4 8 12 25 40 55
469-Intro/origin Dr. Phosphorous; Simonson-a 4 8 12 23 37 50
474-1st app. new Deadshot 6 12 18 41 76 110
475,476-Joker-c/stories; Rogers-a 7 14 21 48 89 130
477-Neal Adams-a(r); Rogers-a (3 pgs.) 4 8 12 23 37 50
481-(Combined with Batman Family, 12-1/78-79, begin $1.00, 68 pg. issues, ends #495); 481-495-Batgirl, Robin solo stories 3 6 9 21 33 45
482-Starlin/Russell, Golden-a; The Demon begins (origin-r), ends #485 (by Ditko #483-485) 3 6 9 14 20 25
483-40th Anniversary issue; origin retold; Newton Batman begins 3 6 9 15 22 28
484-495 (68 pgs): 484-Origin Robin. 485-Death of Batwoman. 486-Killer Moth app. 487-The Odd Man by Ditko. 489-Robin/Batgirl team-up. 490-Black Lightning begins. 491-(#492 on inside). 493-Intro. The Swashbuckler 2 4 6 9 13 16
496-499: 496-Clayface app. 2 4 6 8 10 12
500-($1.50, 52 pgs.)-Batman/Deadman team-up with Infantino-a; new Hawkman story by Joe Kubert; incorrectly says 500th Anniv. of Det. 2 4 6 13 18 22
501-503,505-522: 509-Catman-c. 510-Mad Hatter-c. 512-2nd app. new Dr. Death. 513-Two-Face app. 519-Last Batgirl. 521-Green Arrow series begins 1 2 3 5 6 8
504-Joker-c/story 2 4 6 10 14 18
523-1st Killer Croc (cameo); Solomon Grundy app. 3 6 9 19 30 40
524-2nd app. Jason Todd (cameo)(3/83) 2 4 6 9 12 15
525-3rd app. Jason Todd (See Batman #357) 2 4 6 9 12 15
526-Batman's 500th app. in Detective Comics ($1.50, 68 pgs.); Death of Jason Todd's parents, Joker-c/story (55 pgs.); Bob Kane pin-up 3 6 9 15 22 28
527-531,533,534,536-553,555-568,571,573: 538-Cat-Man-c/story cont'd from Batman #371. 542-Jason Todd quits as Robin (becomes Robin again #547). 549,550-Alan Moore scripts (Green Arrow). 566-Batman villains profiled. 567-Harlan Ellison scripts 6.00
532,569,570-Joker-c/stories 2 4 6 9 13 16
535-Intro new Robin (Jason Todd)-1st appeared in Batman 1 3 4 6 8 10
554-1st new Black Canary (9/85) 1 2 3 5 6 8
572-(3/87, $1.25, 60 pgs.)-50th Anniv. of Det. Comics 1 3 4 6 8 10
574-Origin Batman & Jason Todd retold 2 4 6 8 10 12
575-Year 2 begins, ends #578 3 6 9 15 22 28
576-578: McFarlane-c/a; The Reaper app. 3 6 9 15 22 28
579-597,599,601-607,609,610: 579-New bat wing logo. 583-1st app. villains Scarface & Ventriloquist. 589-595-(52 pgs.)-Each contain free 16 pg. Batman stories. 604-607-Mudpack storyline; 604,607-Contain Batman mini-posters. 610-Faked death of Penguin; artists names app. on tombstone on-c 4.00
598-($2.95, 84 pgs.)- "Blind Justice" storyline begins by Batman movie writer Sam Hamm, ends #600 6.00
600-(5/89, $2.95, 84 pgs.)-50th Anniv. of Batman in Det.; 1 pg. Neal Adams pin-up, among other artists 6.00
608-1st app. Anarky 6.00
611-626,628-646,649-658: 612-1st new look Cat-Man; Catwoman app. 615- "The Penguin Affair" part 2 (See Batman #448,449). 617-Joker-c/story. 624-1st new Catwoman (w/death) & 1st new Batwoman. 626-Batman's 600th app. in Detective. 642-Return of Scarface, part 2. 644-Last $1.00-c. 644-646-The (2nd) Electrocutioner (Lester Buchinsky) app. 652,653-Huntress-c/story w/new costume plus Charest-c on both 4.00
627-($2.95, 84 pgs.)-Batman's 601st app. in Det.; reprints 1st story/#27 plus 3 versions (2 new) of same story 6.00
647-1st app. Stephanie Brown 2 4 6 9 12 15
648-1st full app. Spoiler (Stephanie Brown) 5.00
659-664: 659-Knightfall part 2; Kelley Jones-c. 660-Knightfall part 4; Bane-c by Sam Kieth. 661-Knightfall part 6; brief Joker & Riddler app. 662-Knightfall part 8; Riddler app.; Sam Kieth-c. 663-Knightfall part 10; Kelley Jones-c. 664-Knightfall part 12; Bane-c/story; Joker app.; continued in Showcase 93 #7 & 8; Jones-c 6.00

GD 2.0 VG 4.0 FN 6.0 VF 8.0 VF/NM 9.0 NM- 9.2

665-675: 665,666-Knightfall parts 16 & 18; 666-Bane-c/story. 667-Knightquest: The Crusade & new Batman begins (1st app. in Batman #500). 669-Begin $1.50-c; Knightquest, cont'd in Robin #1. 671,673-Joker app. 4.00
675-($2.95)-Collectors edition w/foil-c 5.00
676-($2.50, 52 pgs.)-KnightsEnd pt. 3 5.00
677,678: 677-KnightsEnd pt. 9. 678-(9/94)-Zero Hour tie-in. 4.00
679-685: 679-(11/94). 682-Troika pt. 3 3.00
682-($2.50) Embossed-c Troika pt. 3 4.00
686-699,701-719: 686-Begin $1.95-c. 693,694-Poison Ivy-c/app. 695-Contagion pt. 2; Catwoman, Penguin app. 696-Contagion pt. 8. 698-Two-Face-c/app. 701-Legacy pt. 6; Batman vs. Bane-c/app. 702-Legacy Epilogue. 703-Final Night x-over. 705-707-Riddler-app. 714,715-Martian Manhunter-app. 3.00
700-($4.95, Collectors Edition)-Legacy pt. 1; Ra's Al Ghul-c/app; Talia & Bane app; book displayed at shops in envelope 6.00
700-($2.95, Regular Edition)-Different-c 4.00
720-736,738,739: 720,721-Cataclysm pts. 5,14. 723-Green Arrow app. 730-740-No Man's Land stories. 735-1st app. Mercy Graves in regular DCU 3.00
737-Harley Quinn-c/app. (1st app. in Detective); No Man's Land 2 4 6 9 12 15
740-Joker, Bane-c/app.; Harley Quinn app.; No Man's Land 1 3 4 6 8 10
741-($2.50) Endgame; Joker-c/app.; Harley Quinn app. 5.00
742-749,751-765: 742-New look Batman begins; 1st app. Crispus Allen (who later becomes the Spectre). 751,752-Poison Ivy app. 756-Superman-c/app. 759-762-Catwoman back-up 3.00
750-($4.95, 64 pgs.) Ra's al Ghul-c 6.00
766-772: 766,767-Bruce Wayne: Murderer pt. 1,8. 769-772-Bruce Wayne: Fugitive pts. 4,8,12,16 3.00
773,774,776-782,784-799: 773-Begin $2.75-c; Sienkiewicz-c. 777-784-Sale-c. 784-786-Alan Scott app. 787-Mad Hatter app. 797-799-War Games 3.00
775-($3.50) Sienkiewicz-c 4.00
783-1st Nyssa 5.00
800-($3.50) Jock-c; aftermath of War Games; back-up by Lapham 4.00
801-816: 801-814-Lapham-s. 804-Mr. Freeze app. 809-War Crimes 3.00
817-830,832-836,838-849,851,852: 817-820: One Year Later 8-part x-over with Batman #651-654; Robinson-s/Bianchi-c. 819-Begin $2.99-c. 820-Dini-s/Williams III-a. 821-Harley Quinn app. 825-Doctor Phosphorus app. 827-Debut of new Scarface. 833,834-Zatanna & Joker app. 838,839-Resurrection of Ra's al Ghul x-over. 846-847-Batman R.I.P. x-over 3.00
817,818,838,839-2nd printings. 817-Combo-c of #817̳ cover images. 818-Combo-c of #818 and Batman #653 cover images. 838-Andy Kubert variant-c. 839-Red bkgd-c 3.00
831,837-Harley Quinn-c/app. 831-Dini-s 1 3 4 6 8 10
850-($3.99) Batman vs. Hush; Dini-s/Nguyen-a 6.00
853-($3.99) Gaiman-s/Andy Kubert-a; continued from Batman #686; Kubert sketch pgs. 4.00
853-Variant-c with red background by Andy Kubert 12.00
854-872-($3.99) 854-Batwoman features begin; Rucka-a/J.H. Williams-a/c; The Question back-ups begin. 858-860-Batwoman origin. 871-1st Scott Snyder Batman-s 4.00
854,858,859,860-Variant-c: 854-JG Jones. 858-Hughes. 859-Jock. 860-Alex Ross 6.00
854-Special Edition (8/10, $1.00) reprints issue with "What's Next?" logo on cover 3.00
873-880-($2.99) 874,875,879-Francavilla-a. 880-Jock-a 3.00
881-(10/11) Last issue of first volume; Snyder-s/Jock & Francavilla-a 3.00
#0-(10/94) Zero Hour tie-in, released between #678 & 679 3.00
#1,000,000 (11/98) 853rd Century x-over 3.00
Annual 1 (1988, $1.50) 5.00
Annual 2-7,9 ('89-'94, '96, 68 pgs.)-4-Painted-c. 5-Joker-c/story (54 pgs.) continued in Robin Annual #1; Sam Kieth-c; Eclipso app. 6-Azrael as Batman in new costume; intro Geist the Twilight Man; Bloodlines storyline. 7-Elseworlds story. 9-Legends of the Dead Earth story 5.00
Annual 8 (1995, $3.95, 68 pgs.)-Year One story 5.00
Annual 10 (1997, $3.95)-Pulp Heroes story 5.00
Annual 11 (12/09, $4.99)-Azrael & The Question app.; continued from Batman Ann. #27 5.00
Annual 12 (2/11, $4.99)-Nightrunner & The Question app.; continued in Batman Ann. #28 5.00

NOTE: **Neal Adams** *c-370, 372, 385, 389, 391, 392, 394-422, 439.* **Aparo** *a-437, 438, 444-446, 500, 625-632p, 638-643p; c-430, 437, 440-446, 448, 468-470, 480, 484(back), 492-502,508, 509, 515, 518-522, 641, 716, 719, 722, 724.* **Austin** *a(i)-450, 451, 463-468, 471-476; c(i)-474-476, 478.* **Baily** *a-443r.* **Buckler** *a-434, 446p, 479p; c(p)-467, 482, 505-507, 511, 513-516, 518.* **Burnley** *a(Batman)-65, 75, 78, 83, 100, 103, 125; c-62i, 63i, 64, 73i, 78, 83p, 96p, 103p, 105p, 106, 108, 121p, 123p, 125p.* **Chaykin** *a-441.* **Colan** *a(p)-510, 512, 517, 523, 528-538, 540-546, 555-567; c(p)-510, 512, 528, 530-535, 537, 538, 540, 541, 543-545, 556-558, 560-564.* **J. Craig** *a-488.* **Ditko** *a-443r, 483-485, 487.* **Golden** *a-482p; c-625, 626, 628-631, 633, 644-646.* **Alan Grant** *scripts-584-597, 601-621, 641, 642, Annual 5.* **Grell** *a-445, 455, 463p, 464p; c-455.* **Guardineer** *c-23, 24, 26, 28, 30, 32.* **Gustavson** *a-441r.* **Infantino** *a-354, 442(2)r, 500, 572.* **Infantino/Anderson** *c-333, 337-340, 343, 344, 347, 351, 352, 359, 361-368, 371.* **Kelley Jones** *c-651, 657i, 658i, 659, 661, 663-675.* **Kaluta** *c-423, 424, 426-428, 431, 434, 438, 484, 486, 572.* **Bob Kane** *a-Most early issues #27 on, 297r, 356r, 438-440r, 442r, 443r.* **Kane/Robinson** *c-33.* **Gil Kane** *a(p)-368, 370-374, 384, 385, 388-407, 438r, 439r, 520.* **Kane/Anderson** *c-369.* **Sam Kieth** *c-654-656 (657, 658 w/***Kelley Jones***), 660, 662, Annual #5.* **Kubert** *a-438r, 439r, 500; c-348-350.* **McFarlane** *c/a(p)-576-578.* **Meskin** *a-420r.* **Mignola** *c-583.*

Detective Comics (2011 series) #8 © DC

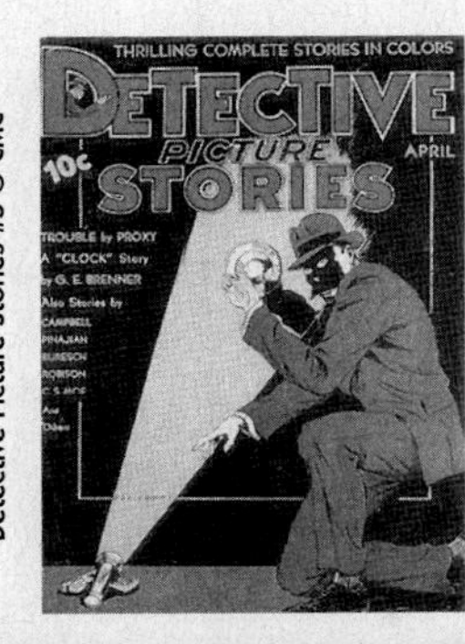

Detective Picture Stories #5 © CMC

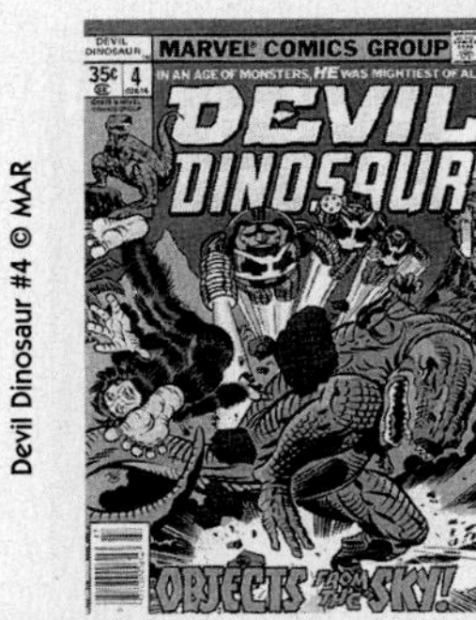

Devil Dinosaur #4 © MAR

GD 2.0 | VG 4.0 | FN 6.0 | VF 8.0 | VF/NM 9.0 | NM- 9.2

***Moldoff** c-233-354, 259, 266, 267, 275, 287, 289, 290, 297, 300. **Moldoff/Giella** a-328, 330, 332, 334, 336, 338, 340, 342, 344, 346, 348, 350, 352, 354, 356. **Mooney** a-444r. **Moreira** a-153-300, 419r, 444r, 445r. **Nasser/Netzer** a-654, 655, 657, 658. **Newton** a(p)-480, 481, 483-499, 501-509, 511, 513-516, 518-520, 524, 526, 539; c-526p. **Irv Novick** c-375-377, 383. **Robbins** a-426p, 429p. **Robinson** a-part: 66, 68, 71-73; all: 74-76, 79, 80; c-62, 64, 66, 68-74, 76, 79, 82, 86, 88, 442r, 443r. **Rogers** a-466-468, 471-479p, 481p; c-471p, 472p, 473, 474-479p. **Roussos** Airwave-76-105(most); c(i)-71, 72, 74-76, 79, 107. **Russell** a-481i, 482i. **Simon/Kirby** a-440r, 442r. **Simonson** a-437-443, 450, 469, 470, 500. **Dick Sprang** c-77, 82, 84, 85, 87, 89-93, 95-100, 102, 103i, 104i, 106, 108, 114, 117, 118, 122, 123, 128, 129, 131, 133, 135, 141, 148, 149, 168, 622-624. **Starlin** a-481p, 482p; c-503, 504, 567p. **Starr** a-444r. **Toth** a-442; r-414, 416, 418, 424, 440-441, 443, 444. **Tuska** a-486p, 490p. **Matt Wagner** c-647-649. **Wrightson** c-425.*

DETECTIVE COMICS (DC New 52)(Numbering reverts to original series #934 after #52)
DC Comics: Nov, 2011 - Present ($2.99/$3.99)

1-Joker app.; Tony Daniel-s/a/c 3 6 9 14 20 25
2-7: 2-Intro of The Dollmaker. 5-7-Penguin app. 5.00
8,10-14,16-18: 8-($3.99) Catwoman & Scarecrow app.; back-up Two-Face story begins 4.00
9-Night of the Owls 5.00
15-Die-cut Joker cover; Death of the Family tie-in 8.00
19-(6/13, $7.99) 900th issue of Detective; bonus back-up stories and pin-up art 8.00
20-24,26: 21-23-Man-Bat back-up story. 26-Man-Bat app. 4.00
23.1, 23.2, 23.3, 23.4 (11/13, $2.99, regular covers) 3.00
23.1 (11/13, $3.99, 3-D cover) "Poison Ivy #1" on cover; Fridolfs-s/Pina-a 1 3 4 6 8 10
23.2 (11/13, $3.99, 3-D cover) "Harley Quinn #1" on cover; Googe-a/Kindt-s; origin 2 4 6 11 16 20
23.3 (11/13, $3.99, 3-D cover) "Scarecrow #1" on cover; Kudranski-a 5.00
23.4 (11/13, $3.99, 3-D cover) "Man-Bat #1" on cover; Tieri-s/Eaton-a 5.00
25-($3.99) Zero Year focus on Lt. Gordon; Fabok-a/c; Man-Bat back-up 4.00
27-($7.99) Start of Gothtopia; short stories by Meltzer, Hitch, Neal Adams, Francavilla, Murphy 8.00
28-49,51,52: 28,29-Gothtopia. 30-34,37-40-Manupul-a. 37-40-Anarky app. 43,44-Joker's Daughter. 45,46-Justice League app. 47-"Robin War" tie-in 4.00
50-($4.99) Bonus pin-up swipes of classic Detective covers by various 5.00
#0 (11/12, $3.99) Flashback to training and return to Alfred 4.00
Annual 1 (10/12, $4.99) Black Mask app.; Daniel-s/c; Molenaar-a 5.00
Annual 2 (9/13, $4.99) The Wrath app.; Eaton-a/Clarke-c 5.00
Annual 3 (9/14, $4.99) March-c 5.00
...: Endgame 1 (5/15, $2.99) Tie-in to Endgame story in Batman #35-40; Anarky app. 3.00
...: Futures End 1 (11/14, $2.99, regular-c) Five years later; Riddler app. 3.00
...: Futures End 1 (11/14, $3.99, 3-D cover) 4.00

DETECTIVE COMICS (Numbering reverts to original V1 #934 after #52 from 2011-2016 series)
DC Comics: No. 934, Aug, 2016 - Present ($2.99)

934-Tynion IV-s/Barrows-a; Batwoman, Spoiler, Red Robin, Clayface app. 3.00
935-949,951: 936-938-Alvaro Martinez-a. 937-Intro. Ulysses Armstrong. 940-Apparent death of Tim Drake. 941,942-Night of the Monster Men x-over. 944-Batwing returns. 948,949-Batwoman begins. 951-"League of Shadows" 3.00
950-($3.99) Prologue to "League of Shadows"; Takara-a; Shiva & Azrael app. 4.00

DETECTIVE DAN, SECRET OP. 48 (Also see Adventures of Detective Ace King and Bob Scully, The Two-Fisted Hick Detective)
Humor Publ. Co. (Norman Marsh): 1933 (10¢, 10x13", 36 pgs., B&W, one-shot) (3 color, cardboard-c)

nn-By Norman Marsh, 1st comic w/ original-a; 1st newsstand-c; Dick Tracy look-alike; forerunner of Dan Dunn. (Title and Wu Fang character inspired Detective Comics #1 four years later.) (1st comic of a single theme) 2000 4000 6000 12,000 - -

DETECTIVE EYE (See Keen Detective Funnies)
Centaur Publications: Nov, 1940 - No. 2, Dec, 1940

1-Air Man (see Keen Detective) & The Eye Sees begins; The Masked Marvel & Dean Denton app. 271 542 813 1734 2967 4200
2-Origin Don Rance and the Mysticape; Binder-a; Frank Thomas-c 181 362 543 1158 1979 2800

DETECTIVE PICTURE STORIES (Keen Detective Funnies No. 8 on?)
Comics Magazine Company: Dec, 1936 - No. 5, Apr, 1937

1 (All issues are very scarce) 575 1150 1725 3300 5400 7500
2-The Clock app. (1/37, early app.) 270 540 810 1550 2525 3500
3,4: 4-Eisner-a 160 320 480 912 1556 2200
5-The Clock-c/story (4/37); "The Case of the Missing Heir" 1st detective/adventure art by Bob Kane; Bruce Wayne prototype app. (story reprinted in Funny Pages V3 #1) 385 770 1155 2200 3600 5000

DETECTIVES, THE (TV)
Dell Publishing Co.: No. 1168, Mar-May, 1961 - No. 1240, Oct-Dec, 1961

Four Color 1168 (#1)-Robert Taylor photo-c 9 18 27 61 123 185
Four Color 1219-Robert Taylor, Adam West photo-c 9 18 27 61 123 185
Four Color 1240-Tufts-a; Robert Taylor photo-c; 2 different back-c 8 16 24 51 96 140

DETECTIVES, INC. (See Eclipse Graphic Album Series)
Eclipse Comics: Apr, 1985 - No. 2, Apr, 1985 ($1.75, both w/April dates)

1,2: 2-Nudity 3.00

DETECTIVES, INC.: A TERROR OF DYING DREAMS
Eclipse Comics: Jun, 1987 - No. 3, Dec, 1987 ($1.75, B&W& sepia)

1-3: Colan-a 3.00
TPB ('99, $19.95) r/series 20.00

DETENTION COMICS
DC Comics: Oct, 1996 ($3.50, 56 pgs., one-shot)

1-Robin story by Dennis O'Neil & Norm Breyfogle; Superboy story by Ron Marz & Ron Lim; Warrior story by Ruben Diaz & Joe Phillips; Phillips-c 5.00

DETHKLOK (Based on the animated series Metalocalypse)
Dark Horse Comics: Oct, 2010 - No. 3, Feb, 2011 ($3.99, limited series)

1-3-Small & Schnepp-s; covers by Schnepp & Eric Powell 4.00
...: Versus the Goon 1-(7/09, $3.50) Powell-s/a/c; Dethklok visits the Goon universe 3.50
...: Versus the Goon 1-Variant cover by Jon Schnepp 5.00
HC (7/11, $19.99) r/#1-3 & Dethklok: Versus the Goon 20.00

DETONATOR (Mike Baron's...)
Image Comics: Nov, 2004 - No. 4 ($2.50/$2.95)

1-4-Mike Baron-s/Mel Rubi-a 3.00

DEUS EX (Based on the Square Enix videogame)
DC Comics: Apr, 2011 - No. 6, Sept, 2011 ($2.99, limited series)

1-6-Robbie Morrison-s/Trevor Hairsine-a 3.00

DEUS EX: CHILDREN'S CRUSADE (Based on the Square Enix videogame)
Titan Comics: Mar, 2016 - No. 5, Jul, 2016 ($3.99, limited series)

1-5-Alex Irvine-s/John Aggs-a; 3 covers on each 4.00

DEVASTATOR
Image Comics/Halloween: 1998 - No. 3 ($2.95, B&W, limited series)

1,2-Hudnall-s/Horn-c/a 3.00

DEVI (Shekhar Kapur's...)
Virgin Comics: July, 2006 - No. 20, Jun, 2008 ($2.99)

1-20: 1-Mukesh Singh-a/Siddharth Kotian-s. 2-Greg Horn-c 3.00
.../Witchblade (4/08, $2.99) Singh-a/Land-c; continued from Witchblade/Devi 3.00
... Vol. 1 TPB (5/07, $14.99) r/#1-5 and Story from Virgin Comics Preview #0 15.00
... Vol. 2 TPB (9/07, $14.99) r/#6-10; character and cover sketches 15.00

DEVIL CHEF
Dark Horse Comics: July, 1994 ($2.50, B&W, one-shot)

nn 3.00

DEVIL DINOSAUR
Marvel Comics Group: Apr, 1978 - No. 9, Dec, 1978

1-Kirby/Royer-a in all; all have Kirby-c 3 6 9 19 30 40
2-9: 4-7-UFO/sci. fic. 8-Dinoriders-c/sty 2 4 6 10 14 18
... By Jack Kirby Omnibus HC (2007, $29.99, dustjacket) r/#1-9; intro. by Brevoort 30.00

DEVIL DINOSAUR SPRING FLING
Marvel Comics: June, 1997 ($2.99. one-shot)

1-(48 pgs.) Moon-Boy-c/app. 4.00

DEVIL-DOG DUGAN (Tales of the Marines No. 4 on)
Atlas Comics (OPI): July, 1956 - No. 3, Nov, 1956

1-Severin-c 20 40 60 114 182 250
2-Iron Mike McGraw x-over; Severin-c 13 26 39 72 101 130
3 12 24 36 67 94 120

DEVIL DOGS
Street & Smith Publishers: 1942

1-Boy Rangers, U.S. Marines 39 78 117 231 378 525

DEVILERS
Dynamite Entertainment: 2014 - No. 7, 2015 ($2.99)

1-7-Fialkov-s/Triano-a/Jock-c 3.00

DEVILINA (Magazine)
Atlas/Seaboard: Feb, 1975 - No. 2, May, 1975 (B&W)

1-Art by Reese, Marcos; "The Tempest" adapt. 4 8 12 27 44 60
2 (Low printing) 4 8 12 28 47 65

DEVIL KIDS STARRING HOT STUFF

Devolution #1 © DYN

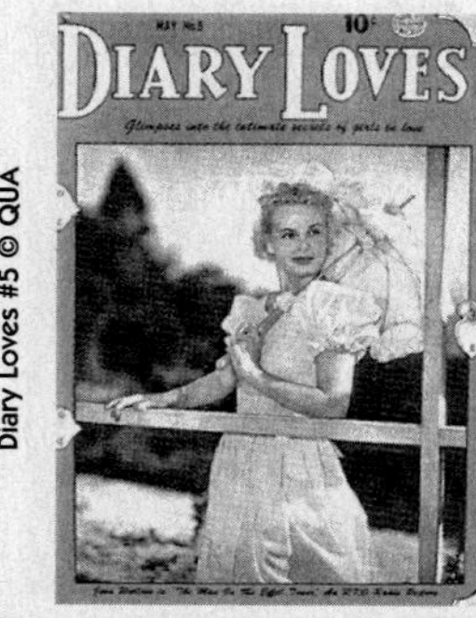

Diary Loves #5 © QUA

Dick Cole #2 © STAR

	GD 2.0	VG 4.0	FN 6.0	VF 8.0	VF/NM 9.0	NM- 9.2
Harvey Publications (Illustrated Humor): July, 1962 - No. 107, Oct, 1981 (Giant-Size #41-55)						
1 (12¢ cover price #1-#41-9/69)	28	56	84	202	451	700
2	10	20	30	69	147	225
3-10 (1/64)	8	16	24	51	96	140
11-20	5	10	15	33	57	80
21-30	4	8	12	25	40	55
31-40: 40-(6/69)	3	6	9	19	30	40
41-50: All 68 pg. Giants	3	6	9	21	33	45
51-55: All 52 pg. Giants	3	6	9	19	30	40
56-70	2	4	6	11	16	20
71-90	2	4	6	8	11	14
91-107	1	2	3	5	6	8

DEVIL'S DUE FREE COMIC BOOK DAY
Devil's Due Publ.: May, 2005 (Free Comic Book Day giveaway)
nn-Short stories of G.I. Joe, Defex and Darkstalkers; Darkstalkers flip cover 3.00

DEVIL'S FOOTPRINTS, THE
Dark Horse Comics: March, 2003 - No. 4, June, 2003 ($2.99, limited series)
1-4-Paul Lee-c/a; Scott Allie-s 3.00

DEVI / WITCHBLADE
Graphic India Pte, Ltd.: Jan, 2016 ($4.99, one-shot)
1-Ron Marz & Samit Basu-s/Eric & Rick Basuldua & Mukesh Singh-a; multiple covers 5.00

DEVOLUTION
Dynamite Entertainment: 2016 - No. 5, 2016 ($3.99)
1-5-Remender-s/Wayshak-a/Jae Lee-c 4.00

DEXTER (Character from the novels and Showtime series)
Marvel Comics: Sept, 2013 - No. 5, Jan, 2014 ($3.99, limited series)
1-5-Jeff Linsday-s/Dalibor Talajic-a/Mike Del Mundo-c 4.00

DEXTER COMICS
Dearfield Publ.: Summer, 1948 - No. 5, July, 1949

	GD	VG	FN	VF	VF/NM	NM-
1-Teen-age humor	16	32	48	94	147	200
2-Junie Prom app.	12	24	36	67	94	120
3-5	10	20	30	58	79	100

DEXTER DOWN UNDER (Character from the novels and Showtime series)
Marvel Comics: Apr, 2014 - No. 5, Aug, 2014 ($3.99, limited series)
1-5-Jeff Linsday-s/Dalibor Talajic-a/Mike Del Mundo-c 4.00

DEXTER'S LABORATORY (Cartoon Network)
DC Comics: Sept, 1999 - No. 34, Apr, 2003 ($1.99/$2.25)
1 4.00
2-10: 2-McCracken-s 3.00
11-24, 26-34: 31-Begin $2.25-c. 32-34-Wray-c 3.00
25-(50¢-c) Tartakovsky-s/a; Action Hank-c/app. 3.00

DEXTER'S LABORATORY (Cartoon Network)
IDW Publishing: Apr, 2014 - No. 4, Jul, 2014 ($3.99)
1-4-Fridolfs-s/Jampole-a; three covers on each 4.00

DEXTER THE DEMON (Formerly Melvin The Monster)(See Cartoon Kids & Peter the Little Pest)
Atlas Comics (HPC): No. 7, Sept, 1957

	GD	VG	FN	VF	VF/NM	NM-
7	10	20	30	56	76	105

DHAMPIRE: STILLBORN
DC Comics (Vertigo): 1996 ($5.95, one-shot, mature)
1-Nancy Collins script; Paul Lee-c/a 6.00

DIABLO
DC Comics: Jan, 2012 - No. 5, Oct, 2012 ($2.99, limited series)
1-5-Aaron Williams-s/Joseph Lacroix-a/c 3.00

DIAL H (Dial H for HERO)(Also see Justice League #23.3)
DC Comics: Jul, 2012 - No. 15, Oct, 2013 ($2.99/$4.99)
1-14: 1-6-China Miéville-s/Mateus Santolouco-a/Brian Bolland-c. 1-Variant-c by Finch 3.00
15-($4.99) Mieville-s/Ponticelli-a/Bolland-c 5.00
#0 (11/12, $2.99) Origin of the dial; Miéville-s/Burchielli-a/Bolland-c 3.00

DIARY CONFESSIONS (Formerly Ideal Romance)
Stanmor/Key Publ.(Medal Comics): No. 9, May, 1955 - No. 14, Apr, 1955

	GD	VG	FN	VF	VF/NM	NM-
9	12	24	36	67	94	120
10-14	10	20	30	54	72	90

DIARY LOVES (Formerly Love Diary #1; G. I. Sweethearts #32 on)
Quality Comics Group: No. 2, Nov, 1949 - No. 31, April, 1953

	GD 2.0	VG 4.0	FN 6.0	VF 8.0	VF/NM 9.0	NM- 9.2
2-Ward-c/a, 9 pgs.	21	42	63	124	202	280
3 (1/50)-Photo-c begin, end #27?	13	26	39	72	101	130
4-Crandall-a	14	28	42	78	112	145
5-7,10	11	22	33	64	90	115
8,9-Ward-a 6,8 pgs. 8-Gustavson-a; Esther Williams photo-c	15	30	45	86	133	180
11,13,14,17-20	11	22	33	62	86	110
12,15,16-Ward-a 9,7,8 pgs.	15	30	45	83	124	165
21-Ward-a, 7 pgs.	14	28	42	80	115	150
22-31: 31-Whitney-a	11	22	33	60	83	105

NOTE: *Photo c-3-10, 12-28.*

DIARY OF HORROR
Avon Periodicals: December, 1952

	GD	VG	FN	VF	VF/NM	NM-
1-Hollingsworth-c/a; bondage-c	71	142	213	454	777	1100

DIARY SECRETS (Formerly Teen-Age Diary Secrets)(See Giant Comics Ed.)
St. John Publishing Co.: No. 10, Feb, 1952 - No. 30, Sept, 1955

	GD	VG	FN	VF	VF/NM	NM-
10-Baker-c/a most issues	61	122	183	390	670	950
11-16,18,19	55	110	165	352	601	850
17,20: Kubert-r/Hollywood Confessions #1. 17-r/Teen Age Romances #9	58	116	174	371	636	900
21-30: 22,27-Signed stories by Estrada. 28-Last precode (3/55)	50	100	150	315	533	750
nn-(25¢ giant, nd (1950?)-Baker-c & rebound St. John comics	142	284	426	909	1555	2200

DICK COLE (Sport Thrills No. 11 on)(See Blue Bolt & Four Most #1)
Curtis Publ./Star Publications: Dec-Jan, 1948-49 - No. 10, June-July, 1950

	GD	VG	FN	VF	VF/NM	NM-
1-Sgt. Spook; L. B. Cole-c; McWilliams-a; Curt Swan's 1st work	34	68	102	199	325	450
2,5	15	30	45	92	144	195
3,4,6-10: All-L.B. Cole-c. 10-Joe Louis story	22	44	66	130	213	295
Accepted Reprint #7(V1#6 on-c)(1950's)-Reprints #7; L.B. Cole-c	9	18	27	47	61	75
Accepted Reprint #9(nd)-(Reprints #9 & #8-c)	9	18	27	47	61	75

NOTE: ***L. B. Cole** c-1, 3, 4, 6-10. **Al McWilliams** a-6. Dick Cole in 1-9. Baseball c-10. Basketball c-9. Football c-8.*

DICKIE DARE
Eastern Color Printing Co.: 1941 - No. 4, 1942 (#3 on sale 6/15/42)

	GD	VG	FN	VF	VF/NM	NM-
1-Caniff-a, bondage-c by Everett	63	126	189	403	689	975
2	30	60	90	177	289	400
3,4-Half Scorchy Smith by Noel Sickles who was very influential in Milton Caniff's development	32	64	96	188	307	425

DICK POWELL (Also see A-1 Comics)
Magazine Enterprises: No. 22, 1949 (one shot)

	GD	VG	FN	VF	VF/NM	NM-
A-1 22-Photo-c	22	44	66	132	216	300

DICK QUICK, ACE REPORTER (See Picture News #10)

DICKS
Caliber Comics: 1997 - No. 4, 1998 ($2.95, B&W)
1-4-Ennis-s/McCrea-c/a; r/Fleetway 3.00
TPB ('98, $12.95) r/series 13.00

DICK'S ADVENTURES
Dell Publishing Co.: No. 245, Sept, 1949

	GD	VG	FN	VF	VF/NM	NM-
Four Color 245	6	12	18	37	66	95

DICK TRACY (See Famous Feature Stories, Harvey Comics Library, Limited Collectors' Ed., Mammoth Comics, Merry Christmas, The Original..., Popular Comics, Super Book No. 1, 7, 13, 25, Super Comics & Tastee-Freez)

DICK TRACY
David McKay Publications: May, 1937 - Jan, 1938

	GD	VG	FN	VF	VF/NM	NM-
Feature Books nn - 100 pgs., partially reprinted as 4-Color No. 1 (appeared before Large Feature Comics, 1st Dick Tracy comic book) (Very Rare-five known copies; two incomplete)	1350	2700	4050	10,000	18,500	27,000
Feature Books 4 - Reprints nn issue w/new-c	152	304	456	965	1658	2350
Feature Books 6,9	107	214	321	680	1165	1650

DICK TRACY (...Monthly #1-24)
Dell Publishing Co.: 1939 - No. 24, Dec, 1949

	GD	VG	FN	VF	VF/NM	NM-
Large Feature Comic 1 (1939) -Dick Tracy Meets The Blank	226	452	678	1446	2473	3500
Large Feature Comic 4,8	113	226	339	718	1234	1750
Large Feature Comic 11,13,15	103	206	309	659	1130	1600
Four Color 1(1939)('35-r)	1100	2200	3300	8360	15,680	23,000
Four Color 6(1940)('37-r)-(Scarce)	258	516	774	1651	2826	4000

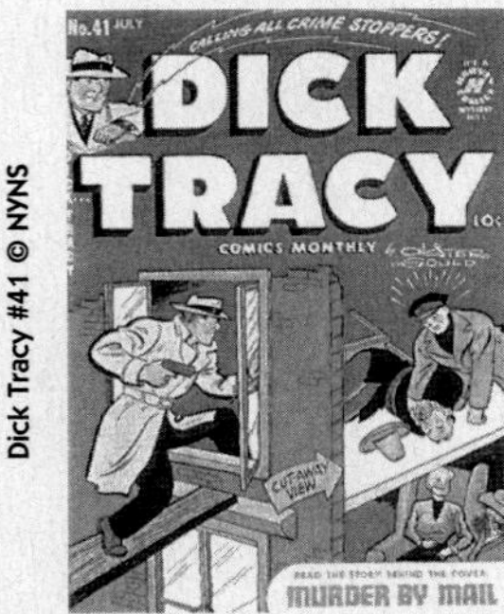

Dick Tracy #41 © NYNS

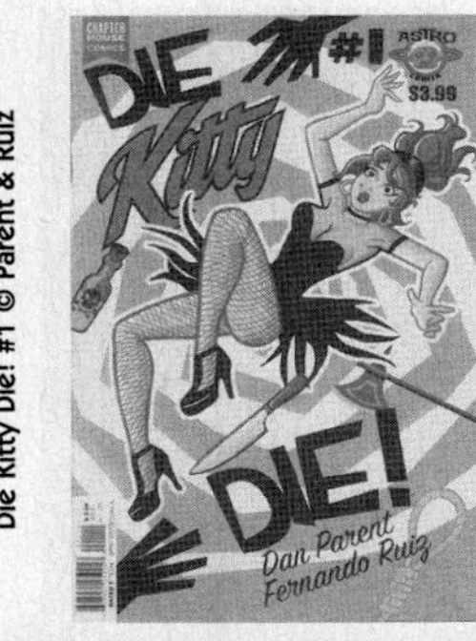

Die Kitty Die! #1 © Parent & Ruiz

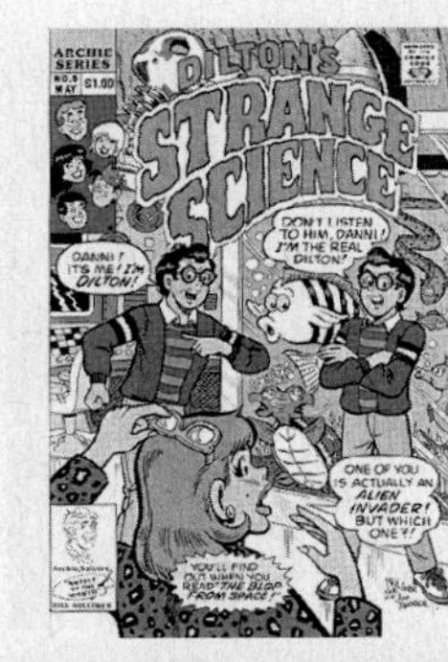

Dilton's Strange Science #5 © ACP

	GD 2.0	VG 4.0	FN 6.0	VF 8.0	VF/NM 9.0	NM- 9.2
Four Color 8(1940)('38-'39-r)	135	270	405	864	1482	2100
Large Feature Comic 3(1941, Series II)	100	200	300	635	1093	1550
Four Color 21('41)('38-r)	92	184	276	584	1005	1425
Four Color 34('43)('39-'40-r)	38	76	114	282	634	985
Four Color 56('44)('40-r)	34	68	102	247	554	860
Four Color 96('46)('40-r)	23	46	69	161	356	550
Four Color 133('47)('40-'41-r)	18	36	54	124	275	425
Four Color 163('47)('41-r)	16	32	48	110	243	375
1(1/48)('34-r)	42	84	126	311	706	1100
2,3	22	44	66	154	340	525
4-10	18	36	54	126	281	435
11-18: 13-Bondage-c	14	28	42	97	214	330
19-1st app. Sparkle Plenty, B.O. Plenty & Gravel Gertie in a 3-pg. strip not by Gould	15	30	45	103	227	350
20-1st app. Sam Catchem; c/a not by Gould	13	26	39	91	201	310
21-24-Only 2 pg. Gould-a in each	13	26	39	89	195	300

NOTE: *No. 19-24 have a 2 pg. biography of a famous villain illustrated by* ***Gould****: 19-Little Face; 20-Flattop; 21-Breathless Mahoney; 22-Measles; 23-Itchy; 24-The Brow.*

DICK TRACY (Continued from Dell series)(...Comics Monthly #25-140)
Harvey Publications: No. 25, Mar, 1950 - No. 145, April, 1961

	GD	VG	FN	VF	VF/NM	NM-
25-Flat Top-c/story (also #26,27)	11	22	33	76	163	250
26-28,30: 28-Bondage-c. 28,29-The Brow-c/stories	9	18	27	61	123	185
29-1st app. Gravel Gertie in a Gould-r	10	20	30	69	147	225
31,32,34,35,37-40: 40-Intro/origin 2-way wrist radio (6/51)	8	16	24	52	99	145
33- "Measles the Teen-Age Dope Pusher"	9	18	27	61	123	185
36-1st app. B.O. Plenty in a Gould-r	9	18	27	61	123	185
41-50	7	14	21	46	86	125
51-56,58-80: 51-2pgs Powell-a	6	12	18	40	73	105
57-1st app. Sam Catchem in a Gould-r	7	14	21	46	86	125
81-99,101-140: 99-109-Painted-c	6	12	18	37	66	95
100, 141-145 (25¢)(titled "Dick Tracy")	6	12	18	40	73	105

NOTE: ***Powell*** *a(1-2pgs.)-43, 44, 104, 108, 109, 145. No. 110-120, 141-145 are all reprints from earlier issues.*

DICK TRACY ("Reuben Award" series)
Blackthorne Publishing: 12/84 - No. 24, 6/89 (1-12: $5.95; 13-24: $6.95, B&W, 76 pgs.)

	GD	VG	FN	VF	VF/NM	NM-
1-8-1st printings; hard-c ed. ($14.95)						20.00
1-3-2nd printings, 1986; hard-c ed.						20.00
1-12-1st & 2nd printings; squarebound. thick-c						12.00
13-24 ($6.95): 21,22-Regular-c & stapled						14.00

NOTE: ***Gould*** *daily & Sunday strip-r in all. 1-12 r-12/31/45-4/5/49; 13-24 r-7/13/41-2/20/44.*

DICK TRACY (Disney)
WD Publications: 1990 - No. 3, 1990 (color) (Book 3 adapts 1990 movie)

	GD	VG	FN	VF	VF/NM	NM-
Book One ($3.95, 52pgs.)-Kyle Baker-c/a						6.00
Book Two, Three ($5.95, 68pgs.)-Direct sale						6.00
Book Two, Three ($2.95, 68pgs.)-Newsstand						4.00

DICK TRACY ADVENTURES
Gladstone Publishing: May, 1991 ($4.95, 76 pgs.)

	GD	VG	FN	VF	VF/NM	NM-
1-Reprints strips 2/1/42-4/18/42						5.00

DICK TRACY, EXPLOITS OF
Rosdon Books, Inc.: 1946 ($1.00, hard-c strip reprints)

	GD	VG	FN	VF	VF/NM	NM-
1-Reprints the near complete case of "The Brow" from 6/12/44 to 9/24/44 (story starts a few weeks late)	25	50	75	147	241	335
with dust jacket...	39	78	117	240	395	550

DICK TRACY MONTHLY/WEEKLY
Blackthorne Publishing: May, 1986 - No. 99, 1989 ($2.00, B&W)
(Becomes Weekly #26 on)

	GD	VG	FN	VF	VF/NM	NM-
1-60: Gould-r. 30,31-Mr. Crime app.						4.00
61-90						4.00
91-95						6.00
96-99-Low print	1	2	3	5	7	9

NOTE: *#1-10 reprint strips 3/10/40-7/13/41; #10(pg.8)-51 reprint strips 4/6/49-12/31/55; #52-99 reprint strips 12/26/56-4/26/64.*

DICK TRACY SPECIAL
Blackthorne Publ.: Jan, 1988 - No. 3, Aug. (no month), 1989 ($2.95, B&W)

	GD	VG	FN	VF	VF/NM	NM-
1-3: 1-Origin D. Tracy; 4/strips 10/12/31-3/30/32						4.00

DICK TRACY: THE EARLY YEARS
Blackthorne Publishing: Aug, 1987 - No. 4, Aug (no month) 1989 ($6.95, B&W, 76 pgs.)

	GD	VG	FN	VF	VF/NM	NM-
1-3: 1-4-r/strips 10/12/31(1st daily)-8/31/32 & Sunday strips 6/12/32-8/28/32; Big Boy apps. in #1-3	1	2	3	4	5	7
4 ($2.95, 52pgs.)						4.00

DICK TRACY UNPRINTED STORIES
Blackthorne Publishing: Sept, 1987 - No. 4, June, 1988 ($2.95, B&W)

	GD	VG	FN	VF	VF/NM	NM-
1-4: Reprints strips 1/1/56-12/25/56						4.00

DICK TURPIN (See Legend of Young...)

DIE-CUT
Marvel Comics UK, Ltd: Nov, 1993 - No. 4, Feb, 1994 ($1.75, limited series)

	GD	VG	FN	VF	VF/NM	NM-
1-4: 1-Die-cut-c; The Beast app.						3.00

DIE-CUT VS. G-FORCE
Marvel Comics UK, Ltd: Nov, 1993 - No. 2, Dec, 1993 ($2.75, limited series)

	GD	VG	FN	VF	VF/NM	NM-
1,2-($2.75)-Gold foil-c on both						4.00

DIE HARD: YEAR ONE (Based on the John McClane character)
BOOM! Studios: Aug, 2009 - No. 8, Mar, 2010 ($3.99, limited series)

	GD	VG	FN	VF	VF/NM	NM-
1-8-Chaykin-s; Officer McClane in 1976 NYC; multiple covers on each						4.00

DIE KITTY DIE
Chapterhouse Comics: Oct, 2016 - Present ($3.99/$4.99)

	GD	VG	FN	VF	VF/NM	NM-
1,3,4-($3.99) Fernando Ruiz-s/Dan Parent-a; Harvey-style spoof						4.00
2-($4.99) Bonus faux 1969 reprint; Li'l Satan app.						5.00

DIE, MONSTER, DIE (See Movie Classics)

DIESEL (TYSON HESSE'S...)
Boom Entertainment (BOOM! Box): Sept, 2015 - No. 4, Dec, 2015 ($3.99, limited series)

	GD	VG	FN	VF	VF/NM	NM-
1-4-Tyson Hesse-s/a in all. 1-Three covers						4.00

DIGIMON DIGITAL MONSTERS (TV)
Dark Horse Comics: May, 2000 - No. 12, Nov, 2000 ($2.95/$2.99)

	GD	VG	FN	VF	VF/NM	NM-
1-12						3.00

DIGITEK
Marvel UK, Ltd: Dec, 1992 - No. 4, Mar, 1993 ($1.95/$2.25, mini-series)

	GD	VG	FN	VF	VF/NM	NM-
1-4: 3-Deathlock-c/story						3.00

DILLY (Dilly Duncan from Daredevil Comics; see Boy Comics #57)
Lev Gleason Publications: May, 1953 - No. 3, Sept, 1953

	GD	VG	FN	VF	VF/NM	NM-
1-Teenage; Biro-c	8	16	24	42	54	65
2,3-Biro-c	6	12	18	31	38	45

DILTON'S STRANGE SCIENCE (See Pep Comics #78)
Archie Comics: May, 1989 - No. 5, May, 1990 (75¢/$1.00)

	GD	VG	FN	VF	VF/NM	NM-
1-5						3.00

DIME COMICS
Newsbook Publ. Corp.: 1945; 1951

	GD	VG	FN	VF	VF/NM	NM-
1-Silver Streak/Green Dragon-c/sty; Japanese WWII-c by L. B. Cole (Rare)	187	374	561	1197	2049	2900
1(1951)	20	40	60	117	189	260

DINGBATS (See 1st Issue Special)

DING DONG
Compix/Magazine Enterprises: Summer?, 1946 - No. 5, 1947 (52 pgs.)

	GD	VG	FN	VF	VF/NM	NM-
1-Funny animal	37	74	111	222	361	500
2 (9/46)	16	32	48	94	147	200
3 (Wint '46-'47) - 5	14	28	42	80	115	150

DINKY DUCK (Paul Terry's...) (See Approved Comics, Blue Ribbon, Giant Comics Edition #5A & New Terrytoons)
St. John Publishing Co./Pines No. 16 on: Nov, 1951 - No. 16, Sept, 1955; No. 16, Fall, 1956; No. 17, May, 1957 - No. 19, Summer, 1958

	GD	VG	FN	VF	VF/NM	NM-
1-Funny animal	14	28	42	81	118	155
2	8	16	24	44	57	70
3-10	6	12	18	31	38	45
11-16(9/55)	6	12	18	28	34	40
16 (Fall, '56) - 19	5	10	15	23	28	32

DINKY DUCK & HASHIMOTO-SAN (See Deputy Dawg Presents...)

DINO (TV)(The Flintstones)
Charlton Publications: Aug, 1973 - No. 20, Jan, 1977 (Hanna-Barbera)

	GD	VG	FN	VF	VF/NM	NM-
1	3	6	9	17	26	35
2-10	2	4	6	10	14	18
11-20	2	4	6	8	10	12
Digest nn (w/Xerox Pub., 1974) (low print run)	2	4	6	11	16	20

DINO ISLAND
Mirage Studios: Feb, 1994 - No. 2, Mar, 1994 ($2.75, limited series)

Dinosaurs For Hire #11 © Tom Mason

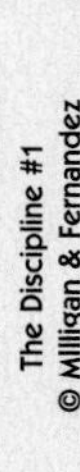

Disney Magic Kingdom Comics #1 © DIS

	GD	VG	FN	VF	VF/NM	NM-
	2.0	4.0	6.0	8.0	9.0	9.2

	GD	VG	FN	VF	VF/NM	NM-
	2.0	4.0	6.0	8.0	9.0	9.2

1,2-By Jim Lawson 3.00

DINO RIDERS
Marvel Comics: Feb, 1989 - No. 3, 1989 ($1.00)

1-3: Based on toys 3.00

DINOSAUR REX
Upshot Graphics (Fantagraphics): 1986 - No. 3, 1986 ($2.00, limited series)

1-3 3.00

DINOSAURS, A CELEBRATION
Marvel Comics (Epic): Oct, 1992 - No. 4, Oct, 1992 ($4.95, lim. series, 52 pgs.)

1-4: 2-Bolton painted-c 5.00

DINOSAURS ATTACK! (Based on Topps trading card set)
IDW Publishing: Jul, 2013 - No. 5, Nov, 2013 ($3.99, limited series)

1-5: 1,2-Remastered version of 1991 graphic novel. 3-5-New continuation of story 4.00

DINOSAURS ATTACK! THE GRAPHIC NOVEL
Eclipse Comics: 1991 ($3.95, coated stock, stiff-c)

Book One- Based on Topps trading cards 5.00

DINOSAURS FOR HIRE
Malibu Comics: Feb, 1993 - No. 12, Feb, 1994 ($1.95/$2.50)

1-12: 1,10-Flip bk. 8-Bagged w/Skycap; Staton-c. 10-Flip book 3.00

DINOSAURS GRAPHIC NOVEL (TV)
Disney Comics: 1992 - No. 2, 1993 ($2.95, 52 pgs.)

1,2-Staton-a; based on Dinosaurs TV show 4.00

DINOSAURUS
Dell Publishing Co.: No. 1120, Aug, 1960

Four Color 1120-Movie, painted-c 8 16 24 51 96 140

DIPPY DUCK
Atlas Comics (OPI): October, 1957

1-Maneely-a; code approved 14 28 42 80 115 150

DIRECTORY TO A NONEXISTENT UNIVERSE
Eclipse Comics: Dec, 1987 ($2.00, B&W)

1 3.00

DIRK GENTLY'S HOLISTIC DETECTIVE AGENCY
IDW Publishing: May, 2015 - No. 5, Oct, 2015 ($3.99, limited series)

1-5: 1-Ryall-s/Kyriazis-a; multiple covers on each 4.00
...: A Spoon Too Short 1-5 (2/16 - No. 5, 6/16, $3.99) A.E. David-s/Kyriazis-a 4.00
...: The Salmon of Doubt 1-5 (10/16 - No. 5, 2/17, $3.99) A.E. David-s/Kyriazis-a 4.00

DIRTY DOZEN (See Movie Classics)

DIRTY PAIR (Manga)
Eclipse Comics: Dec, 1988 - No. 4, Apr, 1989 ($2.00, B&W, limited series)

1-4: Japanese manga with original stories 3.00
...: Start the Violence (Dark Horse, 9/99, $2.95) r/B&W stories in color from Dark Horse Presents #132-134; covers by Warren & Pearson 3.00

DIRTY PAIR: FATAL BUT NOT SERIOUS (Manga)
Dark Horse Comics: July, 1995 - No. 5, Nov, 1995 ($2.95, limited series)

1-5 3.00

DIRTY PAIR: RUN FROM THE FUTURE (Manga)
Dark Horse Comics: Jan, 2000 - No. 4, Mar, 2000 ($2.95, limited series)

1-4-Warren-s/c/a. Var.-c by Hughes(1), Stelfreeze(2), Timm(3), Ramos(4) 3.00

DIRTY PAIR: SIM HELL (Manga)
Dark Horse Comics: May, 1993 - No. 4, Aug, 1993 ($2.50, B&W, limited series)

1-4 3.00
...Remastered #1-4 (5/01 - 8/01) reprints in color, with pin-up gallery 3.00

DIRTY PAIR II (Manga)
Eclipse Comics: June, 1989 - No. 5, Mar, 1990 ($2.00, B&W, limited series)

1-5: 3-Cover is misnumbered as #1 3.00

DIRTY PAIR III, THE (A Plague of Angels) (Manga)
Eclipse Comics: Aug, 1990 - No. 5, Aug, 1991 ($2.00/$2.25, B&W, lim. series)

1-5 3.00

DISCIPLINE
Image Comics: Mar, 2016 - No. 6, Aug, 2016 ($2.99)

1-6-Peter Milligan-s/Leandro Fernández-a 3.00

DISNEY AFTERNOON, THE (TV)
Marvel Comics: Nov, 1994 - No. 10?, Aug, 1995 ($1.50)

1-10: 3-w/bound-in Power Ranger Barcode Card 3.00

DISNEY COMIC ALBUM
Disney Comics: 1990(no month, year) - No. 8, 1991 ($6.95/$7.95)

1,2 ($6.95): 1-Donald Duck and Gyro Gearloose by Barks(r). 2-Uncle Scrooge by Barks(r); Jr. Woodchucks app. 9.00
3-8: 3-Donald Duck-r/F.C. 308 by Barks; begin $7.95-c. 4-Mickey Mouse Meets the Phantom Blot; r/M.M Club Parade (censored 1956 version of story). 5-Chip `n' Dale Rescue Rangers; new-a. 6-Uncle Scrooge. 7-Donald Duck in Too Many Pets; Barks-r(4) including F.C. #29. 8-Super Goof; r/S.G. #1, D.D. #102 9.00

DISNEY COMIC HITS
Marvel Comics: Oct, 1995 - No. 16, Jan, 1997 ($1.50/$2.50)

1-16: 4-Toy Story. 6-Aladdin. 7-Pocahontas. 10-The Hunchback of Notre Dame (Same story in Disney's The Hunchback of Notre Dame). 13-Aladdin and the Forty Thieves 4.00

DISNEY COMICS
Disney Comics: June, 1990

Boxed set of #1 issues includes Donald Duck Advs., Ducktales, Chip 'n Dale Rescue Rangers, Roger Rabbit, Mickey Mouse Advs. & Goofy Advs.; limited to 10,000 sets 2 4 6 11 16 20

DISNEY GIANT HALLOWEEN HEX
IDW Publishing: Oct, 2016 ($6.99)

1-Halloween-themed reprints of U.S., Dutch and Italian stories; three covers 7.00

DISNEY KINGDOMS: FIGMENT 2 (Sequel to Figment series)
Marvel Comics: Nov, 2015 - No. 5, Mar, 2016 ($3.99)

1-5: 1-Jim Zub-s/Ramon Bachs-a/J. T. Christopher-c 4.00

DISNEY KINGDOMS: SEEKERS OF THE WEIRD
Marvel Comics: Mar, 2014 - No. 5, Jul, 2014 ($3.99)

1-5: 1-Seifert-s/Moline-a/Del Mundo-c. 3-Andrade-a 4.00

DISNEYLAND BIRTHDAY PARTY (Also see Dell Giants)
Gladstone Publishing Co.: Aug, 1985 ($2.50)

1-Reprints Dell Giant with new-photo-c 2 4 6 8 10 12
...Comics Digest #1-(Digest) 2 4 6 8 11 14

DISNEYLAND MAGAZINE
Fawcett Publications: Feb. 15, 1972 - ? (10-1/4"x12-5/8", 20 pgs, weekly)

1-One or two page painted art features on Dumbo, Snow White, Lady & the Tramp, the Aristocats, Brer Rabbit, Peter Pan, Cinderella, Jungle Book, Alice & Pinocchio. Most standard characters app. 3 6 9 16 23 30

DISNEYLAND, USA (See Dell Giant No. 30)

DISNEY MAGIC KINGDOM COMICS
IDW Publishing: May, 2016 - Present ($6.99, squarebound, quarterly)

1,2-Reprints inspired by the theme parks; Barks-a 7.00

DISNEY MOVIE BOOK
Walt Disney Productions (Gladstone): 1990 ($7.95, 8-1/2"x11", 52 pgs.) (w/pull-out poster)

1-Roger Rabbit in Tummy Trouble; from the cartoon film strips adapted to the comic format. Ron Dias-c 2 4 6 8 10 12

DISNEY'S ACTION CLUB
Acclaim Books: 1997 - No. 4 ($4.50, digest size)

1-4: 1-Hercules. 4-Mighty Ducks 4.50

DISNEY'S ALADDIN (Movie)
Marvel Comics: no date (Oct, 1994) - No. 11, 1995 ($1.50)

1-11 3.00

DISNEY'S BEAUTY AND THE BEAST (Movie)
Marvel Comics: Sept, 1994 - No. 13, 1995 ($1.50)

1-13 3.00

DISNEY'S BEAUTY AND THE BEAST HOLIDAY SPECIAL
Acclaim Books: 1997 ($4.50, digest size, one-shot)

1-Based on The Enchanted Christmas video 4.50

DISNEY'S COLOSSAL COMICS COLLECTION
Disney Comics: 1991 - No. 10, 1993 ($1.95, digest-size, 96/132 pgs.)

1-10: Ducktales, Talespin, Chip 'n Dale's Rescue Rangers. 4-r/Darkwing Duck #1-4. 6-Goofy begins. 8-Little Mermaid 5.00

DISNEY'S COMICS IN 3-D
Disney Comics: 1992 ($2.95, w/glasses, polybagged)

Disney's The Lion King #1 © DIS

District X #1 © MAR

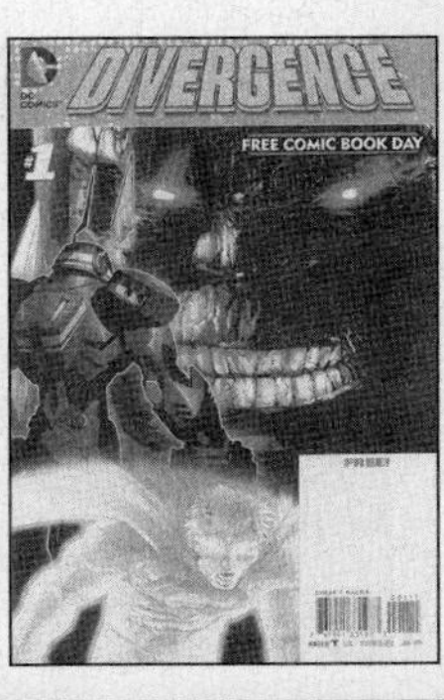

Divergence FCBD Special Ed. #1 © DC

1-Infinity-c; Barks, Rosa, Gottfredson-r 5.00

DISNEY'S ENCHANTING STORIES
Acclaim Books: 1997 - No. 5 ($4.50, digest size)
1-5: 1-Hercules. 2-Pocahontas 4.50

DISNEY'S HERO SQUAD
BOOM! Studios: Jan, 2010 - No. 8, Aug, 2010 ($2.99)
1-8: 1-3-Phantom Blot app. 1-Back-up reprint of Super Goof #1 3.00

DISNEY'S NEW ADVENTURES OF BEAUTY AND THE BEAST (Also see Beauty and the Beast & Disney's Beauty and the Beast)
Disney Comics: 1992 - No. 2, 1992 ($1.50, limited series)
1,2-New stories based on movie 3.00

DISNEY'S POCAHONTAS (Movie)
Marvel Comics: 1995 ($4.95, one-shot)
1-Movie adaptation 1 2 3 4 5 7

DISNEY'S TALESPIN LIMITED SERIES: "TAKE OFF" (TV) (See Talespin)
W. D. Publications (Disney Comics): Jan, 1991 - No. 4, Apr, 1991 ($1.50, lim. series, 52 pgs.)
1-4: Based on animated series; 4 part origin 4.00

DISNEY'S TARZAN (Movie)
Dark Horse Comics: June, 1999 - No. 2, July, 1999 ($2.95, limited series)
1,2: Movie adaptation 3.00

DISNEY'S THE LION KING (Movie)
Marvel Comics: July, 1994 - No. 2, July, 1994 ($1.50, limited series)
1,2: 2-part movie adaptation 3.00
1-($2.50, 52 pgs.)-Complete story 5.00

DISNEY'S THE LITTLE MERMAID (Movie)
Marvel Comics: Sept, 1994 - No. 12, 1995 ($1.50)
1-12 4.00

DISNEY'S THE LITTLE MERMAID LIMITED SERIES (Movie)
Disney Comics: Feb, 1992 - No. 4, May, 1992 ($1.50, limited series)
1-4: Peter David scripts 4.00

DISNEY'S THE LITTLE MERMAID: UNDERWATER ENGAGEMENTS
Acclaim Books: 1997 ($4.50, digest size)
1-Flip book 4.50

DISNEY'S THE HUNCHBACK OF NOTRE DAME (Movie)(See Disney's Comic Hits #10)
Marvel Comics: July, 1996 ($4.95, squarebound, one-shot)
1-Movie adaptation. 1 2 3 4 5 7
NOTE: *A different edition of this series was sold at Wal-Mart stores with new covers depicting scenes from the 1989 feature film. Inside contents and price were identical.*

DISNEY'S THE PRINCE AND THE PAUPER
W. D. Publications: no date ($5.95, 68 pgs., squarebound)
nn-Movie adaptation 6.00

DISNEY'S THE THREE MUSKETEERS (Movie)
Marvel Comics: Jan, 1994 - No. 2, Feb, 1994 ($1.50, limited series)
1,2-Morrow-c; Spiegle-a; Movie adaptation 3.00

DISNEY'S TOY STORY (Movie)
Marvel Comics: Dec, 1995 ($4.95, one-shot)
nn-Adaptation of film 1 2 3 4 5 7

DISTANT SOIL, A (1st Series)
WaRP Graphics: Dec, 1983 - No. 9, Mar 1986 ($1.50, B&W)
1-Magazine size 6.00
2-9: 2-4 are magazine size 4.00
NOTE: *Second printings exist of #1, 2, 3 & 6.*

DISTANT SOIL, A
Donning (Star Blaze): Mar, 1989 ($12.95, trade paperback)
nn-new material 13.00

DISTANT SOIL, A (2nd Series)
Aria Press/Image Comics (Highbrow Entertainment) #15 on:
June, 1991 - Present ($1.75/$2.50/$2.95/$3.50/$3.95, B&W)
1-27: 13-$2.95-c begins. 14-Sketchbook. 15-(8/96)-1st Image issue 4.00
29-33,35,37-($3.95) 4.00
34-($4.95, 64 pages) includes sketchbook pages 5.00
36,38-($4.50) 36-Back-up story by Darnall & Doran. 38-Includes sketch pages 4.50
39-42-($3.50) 3.50
The Aria ('01, $16.95,TPB) r/#26-31 17.00
The Ascendant ('98, $18.95,TPB) r/#13-25 19.00
The Gathering ('97, $18.95,TPB) r/#1-13; intro. Neil Gaiman 19.00
Vol. 4: Coda (2005, $17.99, TPB) r/#32-38 18.00
NOTE: *Four separate printings exist for #1 and are clearly marked. Second printings exist of #2-4 and are also clearly marked.*

DISTANT SOIL, A: IMMIGRANT SONG
Donning (Star Blaze): Aug, 1987 ($6.95, trade paperback)
nn-new material 7.00

DISTRICT X (Also see X-Men titles) (Also see Mutopia X)
Marvel Comics: July, 2004 - No. 14, Aug, 2005 ($2.99)
1-14: 1-3-Bishop app.; Yardin-a/Hine-s 3.00
...Vol. 1: Mr. M (2005, $14.99) r/#1-6; sketch page by Yardin 15.00
...Vol. 2: Underground (2005, $19.99) r/#7-14; prologue from X-Men Unlimited #2 20.00

DIVER DAN (TV)
Dell Publishing Co.: Feb-Apr, 1962 - No. 2, June-Aug, 1962
Four Color 1254(#1), 2 5 10 15 31 53 75

DIVERGENCE FCBD SPECIAL EDITION
DC Comics: Jun, 2015 (Free Comic Book Day giveaway)
1-Previews Batman #41, Superman #41, Justice League Darkseid War 3.00

DIVINE RIGHT
Image Comics (WildStorm Prod.): Sept, 1997 - No. 12, Nov, 1999 ($2.50)
Preview 5.00
1,2: 1-Jim Lee-s/a(p)/c, 1-Variant-c by Charest 4.00
1-($3.50)-Voyager Pack w/Stormwatch preview 4.00
1-American Entertainment Ed. 6.00
2-Variant-c of Exotica & Blaze 5.00
3-Chromium-c by Jim Lee 5.00
3-12: 3-5-Fairchild & Lynch app. 4-American Entertainment Ed. 8-Two covers. 9-1st DC issue. 11,12-Divine Intervention pt. 1,4 3.00
5-Pacific Comicon Ed. 6.00
6-Glow in the dark variant-c, European Tour Edition 20.00
...Book One TPB (2002, $17.95) r/#1-7 18.00
...Book Two TPB (2002, $17.95) r/#8-12 & Divine Intervention Gen13, ...Wildcats 18.00
...Collected Edition #1-3 ($5.95, TPB) 1-r/#1,2. 2-r/#3,4. 3-r/#5,6 6.00
Divine Intervention/Gen 13 (11/99, $2.50) Part 3; D'Anda-a 3.00
Divine Intervention/Wildcats (11/99, $2.50) Part 2; D'Anda-a 3.00

DIVINITY
Valiant Entertainment: Feb, 2015 - No. 4, May, 2015 ($3.99, limited series)
1-4-Kindt-s/Hairsine-a 4.00

DIVINITY II
Valiant Entertainment: Apr, 2016 - No. 4, Jul, 2016 ($3.99, limited series)
1-4-Kindt-s/Hairsine-a; 1-Origin of Myshka 4.00

DIVINITY III: STALINVERSE
Valiant Entertainment: Dec, 2016 - No. 4 ($3.99, limited series)
1-3-Kindt-s/Hairsine-a 4.00
Divinity III: Aric, Son of the Revolution 1 (1/17, $3.99) Joe Harris-s/Cafu-a 4.00
Divinity III: Komandar Bloodshot 1 (12/16, $3.99) Jeff Lemire-s/Clayton Crain-a 4.00
Divinity III: Shadowman and the Battle for New Stalingrad 1 (2/17, $3.99) Robert Gill-a 4.00

DIVISION 13 (See Comic's Greatest World)
Dark Horse Comics: Sept, 1994 - Jan, 1995 ($2.50, color)
1-4: Giffen story in all. 1-Art Adams-c 3.00

DIXIE DUGAN (See Big Shot, Columbia Comics & Feature Funnies)
McNaught Syndicate/Columbia/Publication Ent.: July, 1942 - No. 13, 1949
(Strip reprints in all)

	GD 2.0	VG 4.0	FN 6.0	VF 8.0	VF/NM 9.0	NM- 9.2
1-Joe Palooka x-over by Ham Fisher	28	56	84	165	270	375
2	15	30	45	88	137	185
3(1943)	13	26	39	72	101	130
4,5(1945-46)-Bo strip-r	10	20	30	56	76	95
6-13(1/47-49): 6-Paperdoll cut-outs	9	18	27	50	65	80

DIXIE DUGAN
Prize Publications (Headline): V3#1, Nov, 1951 - V4#4, Feb, 1954

	GD 2.0	VG 4.0	FN 6.0	VF 8.0	VF/NM 9.0	NM- 9.2
V3#1	10	20	30	58	79	100
2-4	7	14	21	37	46	55
V4#1-4(#5-8)	6	12	18	31	38	45

DIZZY DAMES
American Comics Group (B&M Distr. Co.): Sept-Oct, 1952 - No. 6, Jul-Aug, 1953

Django Unchained #7
© Visiona Romantica

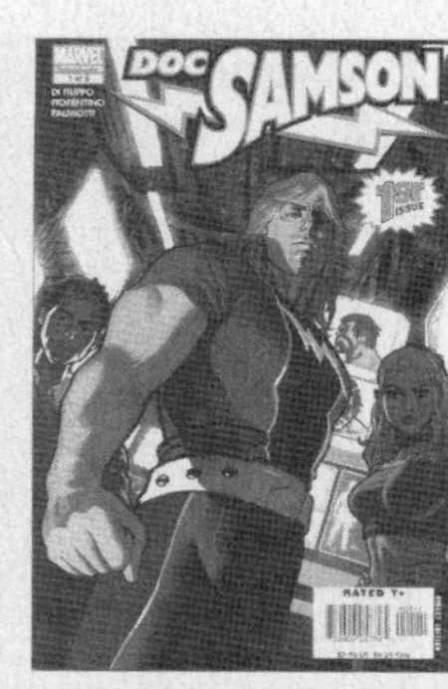

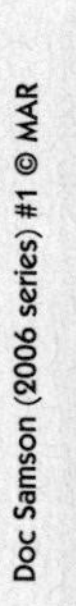
Doc Samson (2006 series) #1 © MAR

Doc Savage Comics V2 #5 © CN

	GD 2.0	VG 4.0	FN 6.0	VF 8.0	VF/NM 9.0	NM- 9.2
1-Whitney-c	58	116	174	371	636	900
2	22	44	66	132	216	300
3-6	20	40	60	114	182	250

DIZZY DON COMICS
F. E. Howard Publications/Dizzy Don Ent. Ltd (Canada): 1942 - No. 22, Oct, 1946; No. 3, Apr, 1947 - No. 4, Sept./Oct., 1947 (Most B&W)

	GD 2.0	VG 4.0	FN 6.0	VF 8.0	VF/NM 9.0	NM- 9.2
1 (B&W)	50	100	150	315	533	750
2 (B&W)	34	68	102	199	325	450
4-21 (B&W)	30	60	90	177	289	400
22-Full color, 52 pgs.	34	68	102	199	325	450
3 (4/47), 4 (9-10/47)-Full color, 52 pgs.	34	68	102	199	325	450

DIZZY DUCK (Formerly Barnyard Comics)
Standard Comics: No. 32, Nov, 1950 - No. 39, Mar, 1952

	GD 2.0	VG 4.0	FN 6.0	VF 8.0	VF/NM 9.0	NM- 9.2
32-Funny animal	11	22	33	64	90	115
33-39	8	16	24	40	50	60

DJANGO UNCHAINED (Adaptation of the 2012 movie)
DC Comics (Vertigo): Feb, 2013 - No. 7, Oct, 2013 ($3.99, limited series)

	GD 2.0	VG 4.0	FN 6.0	VF 8.0	VF/NM 9.0	NM- 9.2
1-Adaptation of Quentin Tarantino's script; Guéra-a; Tarantino foreword; sketch pages						20.00
1-Variant-c by Jim Lee						80.00
2-Cowan-c; bonus concept art and cover sketch art						8.00
2-Variant-c by Mark Chiarello						35.00
3-7: 5-Quitely-c. 7-Alex Ross-c						5.00

DJANGO / ZORRO (Django from the 2012 Taratino movie)
Dynamite Entertainment: 2014 - No. 7, 2015 ($3.99/$5.99, limited series)

	GD 2.0	VG 4.0	FN 6.0	VF 8.0	VF/NM 9.0	NM- 9.2
1-6-Tarantino & Matt Wagner-s/Esteve Polls-a; multiple covers on each						4.00
7-($5.99) Covers by Jae Lee & Francesco Francavilla						6.00

DMZ
DC Comics (Vertigo): Jan, 2006 - No. 72, Feb, 2012 ($2.99)

	GD 2.0	VG 4.0	FN 6.0	VF 8.0	VF/NM 9.0	NM- 9.2
1-Brian Wood-s/Riccardo Burchielli-a						4.00
1-(2008, no cover price) Convention Exclusive promotional edition						3.00
2-49,51-72: 2-10-Brian Wood-s/Riccardo Burchielli-a. 11-Donaldson-a. 12-Wood-s/a						3.00
50-($3.99) Short stories by various incl. Risso, Moon, Gibbons, Bermejo, Jim Lee						4.00
...: Blood in the Game TPB (2009, $12.99) r/#29-34; intro. by Greg Palast						13.00
...: Body of a Journalist TPB (2007, $12.99) r/#6-12; intro. by D. Randall Blythe						13.00
...: Collective Punishment TPB (2011, $14.99) r/#55-59						15.00
...: Friendly Fire TPB (2008, $12.99) r/#18-22; intro. by Sgt. John G. Ford						13.00
...: Hearts and Minds TPB (2010, $16.99) r/#42-49; intro. by Morgan Spurlock						17.00
...: M.I.A. TPB (2011, $14.99) r/#50-54						15.00
...: On the Ground TPB (2006, $9.99) r/#1-5; intro. by Brian Azzarello						10.00
...: Public Works TPB (2007, $12.99) r/#13-17; intro. by Cory Doctorow						13.00
...: The Hidden War TPB (2008, $12.99) r/#23-28						13.00
...: War Powers TPB (2009, $14.99) r/#35-41						15.00

DNAGENTS (The New DNAgents V2/1 on)(Also see Surge)
Eclipse Comics: March, 1983 - No. 24, July, 1985 ($1.50, Baxter paper)

	GD 2.0	VG 4.0	FN 6.0	VF 8.0	VF/NM 9.0	NM- 9.2
1-Origin.						4.00
2-23: 4-Amber app. 8-Infinity-c						3.00
24-Dave Stevens-c	1	2	3	5	6	8
... Industrial Strength Edition TPB (Image, 2008, $24.99) B&W r/#1-14; Evanier intro.						25.00

DOBERMAN (See Sgt. Bilko's Private...)

DOBERMAN
IDW Publishing (Darby Pop): Jul, 2014 - No. 5, Jan, 2015 ($3.99)

	GD 2.0	VG 4.0	FN 6.0	VF 8.0	VF/NM 9.0	NM- 9.2
1-5-Marder, Rosell, & Lambert-s/McKinney-a						4.00

DOBIE GILLIS (See The Many Loves of...)

DOC FRANKENSTEIN
Burlyman Entertainment: Nov, 2004 - No. 6 ($3.50)

	GD 2.0	VG 4.0	FN 6.0	VF 8.0	VF/NM 9.0	NM- 9.2
1-6-Wachowski brothers-s/Skroce-a						3.50

DOCK WALLOPER (Ed Burns' ...)
Virgin Comics: Nov, 2007 - No. 5, Jun, 2008 ($2.99)

	GD 2.0	VG 4.0	FN 6.0	VF 8.0	VF/NM 9.0	NM- 9.2
1-5-Burns & Palmiotti-s/Siju Thomas-a; Prohibition time						3.00

DOC MACABRE
IDW Publishing: Dec, 2010 - No. 3, Feb, 2011 ($3.99)

	GD 2.0	VG 4.0	FN 6.0	VF 8.0	VF/NM 9.0	NM- 9.2
1-3-Steve Niles-s/Bernie Wrightson-a/c						4.00

DOC SAMSON (Also see Incredible Hulk)
Marvel Comics: Jan, 1996 - No. 4, Apr, 1996 ($1.95, limited series)

	GD 2.0	VG 4.0	FN 6.0	VF 8.0	VF/NM 9.0	NM- 9.2
1-4: 1-Hulk c/app. 2-She-Hulk-c/app. 3-Punisher-c/app. 4-Polaris-c/app.						3.00

DOC SAMSON (Incredible Hulk)
Marvel Comics: Mar, 2006 - No. 5, July, 2006 ($2.99, limited series)

	GD 2.0	VG 4.0	FN 6.0	VF 8.0	VF/NM 9.0	NM- 9.2
1-5: 1-DiFilippo-s/Fiorentino-a. 3-Conner-c						3.00

DOC SAVAGE
Gold Key: Nov, 1966

	GD 2.0	VG 4.0	FN 6.0	VF 8.0	VF/NM 9.0	NM- 9.2
1-Adaptation of the Thousand-Headed Man; James Bama c-r/1964 Doc Savage paperback	11	22	33	76	163	250

DOC SAVAGE (Also see Giant-Size...)
Marvel Comics Group: Oct, 1972 - No. 8, Jan, 1974

	GD 2.0	VG 4.0	FN 6.0	VF 8.0	VF/NM 9.0	NM- 9.2
1	4	8	12	23	37	50
2,3-Steranko-c	3	6	9	15	22	28
4-8	2	4	6	9	13	16
...: The Man of Bronze TPB (DC Comics, 2010, $17.99) r/#1-8						18.00

NOTE: *Gil Kane c-5, 6. Mooney a-1i. No. 1, 2 adapts pulp story "The Man of Bronze"; No. 3, 4 adapts "Death in Silver"; No. 5, 6 adapts "The Monsters"; No. 7, 8 adapts "The Brand of The Werewolf".*

DOC SAVAGE (Magazine) (See Showcase Presents for reprint)
Marvel Comics Group: Aug, 1975 - No. 8, Spring, 1977 ($1.00, B&W)

	GD 2.0	VG 4.0	FN 6.0	VF 8.0	VF/NM 9.0	NM- 9.2
1-Cover from movie poster; Ron Ely photo-c	3	6	9	15	22	28
2-5: 3-Buscema-a. 5-Adams-a(1 pg.), Rogers-a(1 pg)	2	4	6	9	13	16
6-8	2	4	6	10	14	18

DOC SAVAGE
DC Comics: Nov, 1987 - No. 4, Feb, 1988 ($1.75, limited series)

	GD 2.0	VG 4.0	FN 6.0	VF 8.0	VF/NM 9.0	NM- 9.2
1-4: Dennis O'Neil-s/Adam & Andy Kubert-a/c in all						4.00
...: The Silver Pyramid TPB (2009, $19.99) r/#1-4						20.00

DOC SAVAGE
DC Comics: Nov, 1988 - No. 24, Oct, 1990 ($1.75/$2.00: #13-24)

	GD 2.0	VG 4.0	FN 6.0	VF 8.0	VF/NM 9.0	NM- 9.2
1-16,19-24						4.00
17,18-Shadow x-over						5.00
Annual 1 (1989, $3.50, 68 pgs.)						5.00

DOC SAVAGE (First Wave)
DC Comics: Jun, 2010 - No. 18, Nov, 2011 ($3.99/$2.99)

	GD 2.0	VG 4.0	FN 6.0	VF 8.0	VF/NM 9.0	NM- 9.2
1-9: 1-4-Malmont-s/Porter-a/J.G. Jones-c. Justice Inc. back-up; S. Hampton-a						4.00
1-6-Variant covers by Cassaday						5.00
10-17-($2.99) 10,16,17-Winslade-a						3.00

DOC SAVAGE
Dynamite Entertainment: 2013 - No. 8, 2014 ($3.99)

	GD 2.0	VG 4.0	FN 6.0	VF 8.0	VF/NM 9.0	NM- 9.2
1-8: 1-Roberson-s/Evely-a; covers by Ross & Cassaday						4.00
Annual 2014 ($5.99) Denton-s/Castro-a						6.00
Special 2014: Woman of Bronze ($7.99, squarebound) Walker-s/Baal-a; Patricia Savage						8.00

DOC SAVAGE COMICS (Also see Shadow Comics)
Street & Smith Publ.: May, 1940 - No. 20, Oct, 1943 (1st app. in Doc Savage pulp, 3/33)

	GD 2.0	VG 4.0	FN 6.0	VF 8.0	VF/NM 9.0	NM- 9.2
1-Doc Savage, Cap Fury, Danny Garrett, Mark Mallory, The Whisperer, Captain Death, Billy the Kid, Sheriff Pete & Treasure Island begin; Norgil, the Magician app.	568	1136	1704	4146	7323	10,500
2-Origin & 1st app. Ajax, the Sun Man; Danny Garrett, The Whisperer end; classic sci-fi cover	226	452	678	1446	2473	3500
3	148	296	444	947	1624	2300
4-Treasure Island ends; Tuska-a	116	232	348	742	1271	1800
5-Origin & 1st app. Astron, the Crocodile Queen, not in #9 & 11; Norgi the Magician app.; classic-c	103	206	309	659	1130	1600
6-10: 6-Cap Fury ends; origin & only app. Red Falcon in Astron story. 8-Mark Mallory ends; Charlie McCarthy app. on-c plus true life story. 9-Supersnipe app. 10-Origin & only app. The Thunderbolt	64	128	192	406	696	985
11,12	53	106	159	334	567	800
V2#1-6,8(#13-18,20): 15-Origin of Ajax the Sun Man; Jack Benny on-c; Hitler app. 16-The Pulp Hero, The Avenger app.; Fanny Brice story. 17-Sun Man ends; Nick Carter begins; Duffy's Tavern part photo-c & story. 18-Huckleberry Finn part-c/story. 19-Henny Youngman part photo-c & life story. 20-Only all funny-c w/Huckleberry Finn	48	96	144	301	511	720
V2#7-Classic Devil-c	53	106	159	334	567	800

DOC SAVAGE: CURSE OF THE FIRE GOD
Dark Horse Comics: Sept, 1995 - No, 4, Dec, 1995 ($2.95, limited series)

	GD 2.0	VG 4.0	FN 6.0	VF 8.0	VF/NM 9.0	NM- 9.2
1-4						3.00

DOC SAVAGE: THE MAN OF BRONZE
Skylark Pub: Mar, 1979, 68pgs. (B&W comic digest, 5-1/4x7-5/8")(low print)

	GD 2.0	VG 4.0	FN 6.0	VF 8.0	VF/NM 9.0	NM- 9.2
15406-0: Whitman-a, 60 pgs., new comics	4	8	12	23	37	50

DOC SAVAGE: THE MAN OF BRONZE
Millennium Publications: 1991 - No. 4, 1991 ($2.50, limited series)

Doctor Aphra #1 © Lucasfilm

Doctor Mid-Nite #2 © DC

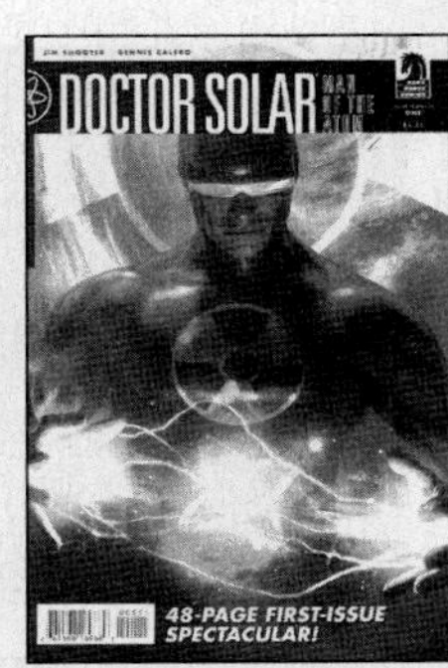

Doctor Solar (2010 series) #1 © RH

GD 2.0 | VG 4.0 | FN 6.0 | VF 8.0 | VF/NM 9.0 | NM- 9.2

1-4: 1-Bronze logo 3.00
...: The Manual of Bronze 1 ($2.50, B&W, color, one-shot)-Unpublished proposed Doc Savage strip in color, B&W strip-r 3.00

DOC SAVAGE: THE MAN OF BRONZE, DOOM DYNASTY
Millennium Publ.: 1992 (Says 1991) - No. 2, 1992 ($2.50, limited series)

1,2 3.00

DOC SAVAGE: THE MAN OF BRONZE - REPEL
Innovation Publishing: 1992 ($2.50)

1-Dave Dorman painted-c 3.00

DOC SAVAGE: THE MAN OF BRONZE THE DEVIL'S THOUGHTS
Millennium Publ.: 1992 (Says 1991) - No. 3, 1992 ($2.50, limited series)

1-3 3.00

DOC SAVAGE: THE SPIDER'S WEB
Dynamite Entertainment: 2015 - No. 5, 2016 ($3.99, limited series)

1-5-Roberson-s/Razek-a. 1-Multiple covers 4.00

DOC STEARN...MR. MONSTER (See Mr. Monster)

DR. ANTHONY KING, HOLLYWOOD LOVE DOCTOR
Minoan Publishing Corp./Harvey Publications No. 4: 1952(Jan) - No. 3, May, 1953; No. 4, May, 1954

1 17 34 51 98 154 210
2-4: 4-Powell-a 11 22 33 60 83 105

DR. ANTHONY'S LOVE CLINIC (See Mr. Anthony's...)

DOCTOR APHRA (Star Wars)(See Darth Vader #3 for debut)
Marvel Comics: Feb, 2017 - Present ($4.99/$3.99)

1-Gillen-s/Walker-a; back-up with Larroca-a; BT-1, Triple-Zero and Black Krrsantan app. 5.00
2-4-($3.99) Walker-a 4.00

DR. BOBBS
Dell Publishing Co.: No. 212, Jan, 1949

Four Color 212 6 12 18 38 69 100

DOCTOR DOOM AND THE MASTERS OF EVIL (All ages title)
Marvel Comics: Mar, 2009 - No. 4, Jun, 2009 ($2.99)

1-4: 1-Sinister Six app. 4-Magneto app. 3.00

DR. DOOM'S REVENGE
Marvel Comics: 1989 (Came w/computer game from Paragon Software)

V1#1-Spider-Man & Captain America fight Dr. Doom 3.00

DR. FATE (See 1st Issue Special, The Immortal..., Justice League, More Fun #55, & Showcase)

DOCTOR FATE
DC Comics: July, 1987 - No. 4, Oct, 1987 ($1.50, limited series, Baxter paper)

1-4: Giffen-c/a in all 4.00

DOCTOR FATE
DC Comics: Winter, 1988-'89 - No. 41, June, 1992 ($1.25/$1.50 #5 on)

1,15: 15-Justice League app. 4.00
2-14 3.00
16-41: 25-1st new Dr. Fate. 36-Original Dr. Fate returns 3.00
Annual 1(1989, $2.95, 68 pgs.)-Sutton-a 4.00

DOCTOR FATE
DC Comics: Oct, 2003 - No. 5, Feb, 2004 ($2.50, limited series)

1-5-Golden-s/Kramer-a 3.00

DOCTOR FATE
DC Comics: Aug, 2015 - No. 18, Jan, 2017 ($2.99)

1-18: 1-Levitz-s/Liew-a; Khalid Nassour chosen as new Doctor. 12-15-Kent Nelson app. 3.00

DR. FU MANCHU (See The Mask of...)
I.W. Enterprises: 1964

1-r/Avon's "Mask of Dr. Fu Manchu"; Wood-a 6 12 18 41 76 110

DR. GIGGLES (See Dark Horse Presents #64-66)
Dark Horse Comics: Oct, 1992 - No. 2, Oct, 1992 ($2.50, limited series)

1,2-Based on movie 3.00

DOCTOR GRAVES (Formerly The Many Ghosts of...)
Charlton Comics: No. 73, Sept, 1985 - No. 75, Jan, 1986

73-75-Low print run. 73,74-Ditko-a 1 2 3 5 6 8
... Magic Book nn (Charlton Press/Xerox Education, 1977, 68 pgs., digest) Ditko-c/a; Staton-a 4 8 12 23 37 50

DR. HORRIBLE (Based on Joss Whedon's internet feature)
Dark Horse Comics: Nov, 2009 ($3.50, one-shot)

1-Zack Whedon-s/Joëlle Jones-a; Captain Hammer pin-up by Gene Ha; 3 covers 3.50
... and other Horrible Stories TPB (9/10, $9.99) r/#1 and 3 stories from MySpace DHP 10.00

DR. JEKYLL AND MR. HYDE (See A Star Presentation & Supernatural Thrillers #4)

DR. KILDARE (TV)
Dell Publishing Co.: No. 1337, 4-6/62 - No. 9, 4-6/65 (All Richard Chamberlain photo-c)

Four Color 1337(#1, 1962) 8 16 24 52 99 145
2-9 6 12 18 37 66 95

DR. MASTERS (See The Adventures of Young...)

DOCTOR MID-NITE (Also see All-American #25)
DC Comics: 1999 - No. 3, 1999 ($5.95, square-bound, limited series)

1-3-Matt Wagner-s/John K. Snyder III-painted art 6.00
TPB (2000, $19.95) r/series 20.00

DOCTOR OCTOPUS: NEGATIVE EXPOSURE
Marvel Comics: Dec, 2003 - No. 5, Apr, 2004 ($2.99, limited series)

1-5-Vaughan-s/Staz Johnson-a; Spider-Man app. 3.00
Spider-Man/Doctor Octopus: Negative Exposure TPB (2004, $13.99) r/series 14.00

DR. ROBOT SPECIAL
Dark Horse Comics: Apr, 2000 ($2.95, one-shot)

1-Bernie Mireault-s/a; some reprints from Madman Comics #12-15 3.00

DOCTOR SOLAR, MAN OF THE ATOM (See The Occult Files of Dr. Spektor #14 & Solar)
Gold Key/Whitman No. 28 on: 10/62 - No. 27, 4/69; No. 28, 4/81 - No. 31, 3/82 (1-27 have painted-c)

1-(#10000-210)-Origin/1st app. Dr. Solar (1st original Gold Key character) 37 74 111 274 612 950
2-Prof. Harbinger begins 10 20 30 69 147 225
3,4 8 16 24 51 96 140
5-Intro. Man of the Atom in costume 8 16 24 56 108 160
6-10 5 10 15 35 63 90
11-14,16-20 4 8 12 28 47 65
15-Origin retold 5 10 15 30 50 70
21-23: 23-Last 12¢ issue 4 8 12 25 40 55
24-27 3 6 9 21 33 45
28-31: 29-Magnus Robot Fighter begins. 31-(3/82)The Sentinel app. 3 6 9 14 20 25
Hardcover Vol. One (Dark Horse Books, 2004, $49.95) r/#1-7; creator bios 50.00
Hardcover Vol. Two (Dark Horse Books, 6/05, $49.95) r/#8-14; Jim Shooter foreword 50.00
Hardcover Vol. Three (Dark Horse Books, 9/05, $49.95) r/#15-22; Mike Baron foreword 50.00
Hardcover Vol. Four (Dark Horse Books, 11/07, $49.95) r/#23-31 and The Occult Files of Dr. Spektor #14; Batton Lash foreword 50.00
NOTE: *Frank Bolle a-6-19, 29-31; c-29i, 30i. Bob Fugitani a-1-5. Spiegle a-29-31. Al McWilliams a-20-23.*

DOCTOR SOLAR, MAN OF THE ATOM
Valiant Comics: 1990 - No. 2, 1991 ($7.95, card stock-c, high quality, 96 pgs.)

1,2: Reprints Gold Key series 1 2 3 5 6 8

DOCTOR SOLAR, MAN OF THE ATOM
Dark Horse Comics: Jul, 2010 - No. 8, Sept, 2011 ($3.50)

1-(48 pgs.) Shooter-s/Calero-a; back-up reprint of origin/1st app. in D.S. #1 (1962) 4.00
2-8: 2-7-Roger Robinson-a 3.50
Free Comic Book Day Doctor Solar, Man of the Atom & Magnus, Robot Fighter (5/10, free) short story re-intros of Solar & Magnus; Shooter-s/Swanland-c; Calero & Reinhold-a 3.00

DOCTOR SPECTRUM (See Supreme Power)
Marvel Comics: Oct, 2004 - No. 6, Mar, 2005 ($2.99, limited series)

1-6-Origin; Sara Barnes-s/Travel Foreman-a 3.00
TPB (2005, $16.99) r/#1-6 17.00

DOCTOR SPEKTOR (See The Occult Files of..., & Spine-Tingling Tales)

DOCTOR SPEKTOR: MASTER OF THE OCCULT
Dynamite Entertainment: 2014 - No. 4, 2014 ($3.99)

1-4-Mark Waid-s; multiple covers on each 4.00

DOCTOR STRANGE (Formerly Strange Tales #1-168) (Also see The Defenders, Giant-Size..., Marvel Fanfare, Marvel Graphic Novel, Marvel Premiere, Marvel Treasury Edition, Strange & Strange Tales, 2nd Series)
Marvel Comics Group: No. 169, 6/68 - No. 183, 11/69; 6/74 - No. 81, 2/87

169(#1)-Origin retold; panel swipe/M.D. #1-c 27 54 81 189 420 650
170-176 5 10 15 35 63 90
177-New costume 7 14 21 46 86 125
178-183: 178-Black Knight app. 179-Spider-Man story-r. 180-Photo montage-c.

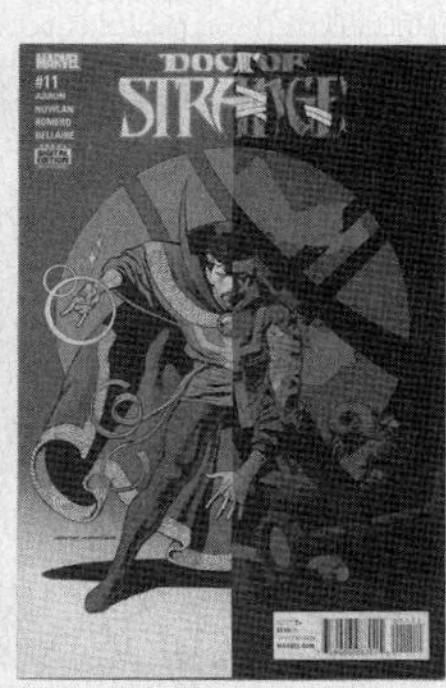

Doctor Strange (2015 series) #11 © MAR

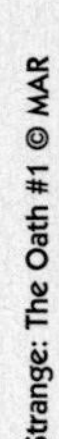

Doctor Strange: The Oath #1 © MAR

Doctor Who (2009 series) #16 © BBC

GD 2.0 | VG 4.0 | FN 6.0 | VF 8.0 | VF/NM 9.0 | NM- 9.2

181-Brunner-c(part-i), last 12¢ issue 5 10 15 33 57 80
1(6/74, 2nd series)-Brunner-c/a 10 20 30 64 132 200
2 5 10 15 34 60 85
3-5 3 6 9 17 26 35
6-10 2 4 6 10 14 18
11-13,15-20: 13,15-17-(Regular 25¢ editions) 1 3 4 6 8 10
13,15-17-(30¢-c variants, limited distribution) 4 8 12 25 40 55
14-(5/76) Dracula app.; (regular 25¢ edition) 2 4 6 10 14 18
14-(30¢-c variant, limited distribution) 5 10 15 33 57 80
21-40: 21-Origin-r/Doctor Strange #169. 23-25-(Regular 30¢ editions). 31-Sub-Mariner-c/story 6.00
23-25-(35¢-c variants, limited distribution)(6,8,10/77) 6 12 18 38 69 100
41-57,63-77,79-81: 56-Origin retold 4.00
58-62: 58-Re-intro Hannibal King (cameo). 59-Hannibal King full app. 59-62-Dracula app. (Darkhold storyline). 61,62-Doctor Strange, Blade, Hannibal King & Frank Drake team-up to battle. Dracula. 62-Death of Dracula & Lilith 6.00
78-New costume 1 2 3 5 6 8
Annual 1(1976, 52 pgs.)-New Russell-a (35 pgs.) 3 6 9 14 20 25
...: From the Marvel Vault (4/11, $2.99) Stern-s/Vokes-a 3.00
.../Silver Dagger Special Edition 1 (3/83, $2.50)-r/#1,2,4,5; Wrightson-c 4.00
... Vs. Dracula TPB (2006, $19.99) r/#14,58-62 and Tomb of Dracula #44 20.00
...What Is It That Disturbs You, Stephen? #1 (10/97, $5.99, 48 pgs.) Russell-a/Andreyko & Russell-s, retelling of Annual #1 story 6.00

NOTE: ***Adkins** a-169, 170, 171i; c-169-171, 172i, 173. **Adams** a-4i. **Austin** a(i)-48-60, 66, 68, 70, 73; c(i)-38, 47-53, 55, 58-60, 70. **Brunner** a-1-5p; c-1-6, 22, 28-30, 33. **Colan** a(p)-172-178, 180-183, 6-18, 36-45, 47; c(p)-172, 174-183, 11-21, 23, 27, 35, 36, 47. **Ditko** a-179r, 3r. **Everett** c-183i. **Golden** a-46p, 55p; c-42-44, 46, 55p. **G. Kane** c(p)-8-10. **Miller** c-46p. **Nebres** a-20, 22, 23, 24i, 26i, 32i; c-32i, 34. **Rogers** a-48-53p; c-47p-53p. **Russell** a-34i, 46i, Annual 1. **B. Smith** c-179. **Paul Smith** a-54p, 56p, 65, 66p, 68p, 69, 71-73; c-56, 65, 66, 68, 71. **Starlin** a-23p, 26; c-25, 26. **Sutton** a-27-29p, 31i, 33, 34p. Painted c-62, 63.*

DOCTOR STRANGE (Volume 2)
Marvel Comics: Feb, 1999 - No. 4, May, 1999 ($2.99, limited series)

1-4: 1,2-Tony Harris-a/painted cover. 3,4-Chadwick-a 3.00

DOCTOR STRANGE (Follows Secret Wars event)
Marvel Comics: Dec, 2015 - Present ($4.99/$3.99)

1-($4.99) Aaron-s/Bachalo-a; back-up with Nowlan-a 5.00
2-5,7-18-($3.99) Aaron-s/Bachalo-a. 7-10-The Last Days of Magic 4.00
6-($4.99) The Last Days of Magic 5.00
#1.MU (4/17, $4.99) Monsters Unleashed tie-in; Chip Zdarsky-s/Julian Lopez-a 5.00
Annual 1 (11/16, $4.99) K. Immonen-s/Romero-a; Clea app. 5.00
...: Last Days of Magic 1 (6/16, $5.99) Story between #6 & 7; Doctor Voodoo & The Wu 6.00
...: Mystic Apprentice 1 (12/16, $3.99) New story w/Di Vito-a; r/Strange Tales #115, 110 4.00

DOCTOR STRANGE AND THE SORCERERS SUPREME (Prelude in Doctor Strange Annual #1)
Marvel Comics: Dec, 2016 - Present ($3.99)

1-5-Thompson-s/Rodriguez-a; The Ancient One, Wiccan & Merlin app. 5.00

DOCTOR STRANGE CLASSICS
Marvel Comics Group: Mar, 1984 - No. 4, June, 1984 ($1.50, Baxter paper)

1-4: Ditko-r; Byrne-c. 4-New Golden pin-up 4.00
NOTE: ***Byrne** c-1i, 2-4.*

DOCTOR STRANGEFATE (See Marvel Versus DC #3 & DC Versus Marvel #4)
DC Comics (Amalgam): Apr, 1996 ($1.95)

1-Ron Marz script w/Jose Garcia-Lopez-(p) & Kevin Nowlan-(i). Access & Charles Xavier app. 3.00

DOCTOR STRANGE MASTER OF THE MYSTIC ARTS (See Fireside Book Series)

DOCTOR STRANGE/PUNISHER: MAGIC BULLETS
Marvel Comics: Feb, 2017 - No. 4 ($4.99, limited series)

1-3-Barber-s/Broccardo-a 5.00

DOCTOR STRANGE, SORCERER SUPREME
Marvel Comics (Midnight Sons imprint #60 on): Nov, 1988 - No. 90, June, 1996 ($1.25/$1.50/$1.75/$1.95, direct sales only, Mando paper)

1 ($1.25) 1 3 4 6 8 10
2-9,12-14,16-25,27,29-40,42-49,51-64: 3-New Defenders app. 5-Guice-c/a begins. 14-18-Morbius story line. 31-36-Infinity Gauntlet x-overs. 31-Silver Surfer app. 33-Thanos-c & cameo. 36-Warlock app. 37-Silver Surfer app. 40-Daredevil x-over. 42-47-Infinity War x-overs. 47-Gamora app. 52,53-Morbius-c/stories. 60,61-Siege of Darkness pt. 7 & 15. 60-Spot varnish-c. 61-New Doctor Strange begins (cameo, 1st app.). 62-Dr. Doom & Morbius app. 3.00
10,11,26,28,41: 10-Re-intro Morbius w/new costume (11/89). 11-Hobgoblin app. 26-Werewolf by Night app. 28-Ghost Rider-s cont'd from G.R. #12; published at same time as Doctor Strange/Ghost Rider Special #1(4/91). 41-Wolverine-c/story 4.00
15-Unauthorized Amy Grant photo-c 5.00
50-($2.95, 52 pgs.)-Holo-grafx foil-c; Hulk, Ghost Rider & Silver Surfer app.; leads into new Secret Defenders series 4.00
65-74, 76-90: 65-Begin $1.95-c; bound-in card sheet. 72-Silver ink-c. 80-82- Ellis-s. 84-DeMatteis story begins. 87-Death of Baron Mordo 3.00
75 ($2.50) 4.00
75 ($3.50)-Foil-c 5.00
Annual 2-4 ('92-'94, 68 pgs.)-2-Defenders app. 3-Polybagged w/card 4.00
Ashcan (1995, 75¢) 3.00
.../Ghost Rider Special 1 (4/91, $1.50)-Same book as D.S.S.S. #28 3.00
...Vs. Dracula 1 (3/94, $1.75, 52 pgs.)-r/Tomb of Dracula #44 & Dr. Strange #14 4.00
NOTE: ***Colan** c/a-19. **Golden** c-28. **Guice** a-5-16, 18, 20-24; c-5-12, 20-24. See 1st series for Annual #1.*

DOCTOR STRANGE: THE OATH
Marvel Comics: Dec, 2006 - No. 5, Apr, 2007 ($2.99, limited series)

1-5-Vaughan-s/Martin-a; Night Nurse app. 1-Origin re-told 3.00
1-Halloween Comic Fest 2015 (12/15, giveaway) r/#1 with logo on cover 3.00
TPB (2007, $13.99) r/#1-5; sketch pages and promotional art 14.00

DR. TOM BRENT, YOUNG INTERN
Charlton Publications: Feb, 1963 - No. 5, Oct, 1963

1 3 6 9 16 23 30
2-5 2 4 6 11 16 20

DR. TOMORROW
Acclaim Comics (Valiant): Sept, 1997 - No. 12 ($2.50)

1-12: 1-Mignola-c 3.00

DR. VOLTZ (See Mighty Midget Comics)

DOCTOR VOODOO: AVENGER OF THE SUPERNATURAL
Marvel Comics: Dec, 2009 - No. 5, Apr, 2010 ($2.99, limited series)

1-5-Dr. Doom, Son of Satan & Ghost Rider app.; Palo-a 3.00
Doctor Voodoo: The Origin of Jericho Drumm (1/10, $4.99) r/Strange Tales #169,170 5.00

DR. WEIRD
Big Bang Comics: Oct, 1994 - No. 2, May, 1995 ($2.95, B&W)

1,2: 1-Frank Brunner-c 4.00
... Special (2/94, $3.95, B&W, 68 pgs.) Origin-r by Starlin; Starlin-c 4.00

DOCTOR WHO (Also see Marvel Premiere #57-60)
Marvel Comics Group: Oct, 1984 - No. 23, Aug, 1986 ($1.50, direct sales, Baxter paper)

1-British-r 2 4 6 8 11 14
2-15-British-r 5.00
16-23 6.00
Graphic Novel Voyager (1985, $8.95) color reprints of B&W comic pages from Doctor Who Magazine #88-99; Colin Baker afterword 15.00

DOCTOR WHO (Based on the 2005 TV series with David Tennant)
IDW Publishing: Jan, 2008 - No. 6, Jun, 2008 ($3.99)

1-6: 1-Nick Roche-a/Gary Russell-s; two covers 4.00

DOCTOR WHO (Based on the 2005 TV series with David Tennant)
IDW Publishing: Jul, 2009 - No. 16, Oct, 2010 ($3.99)

1-16-Grist-c on all. 3-5,13-16-Art by Matt Smith (not the actor) 4.00
... Annual 2010 (7/10, $7.99) short stories by various; Yates-c; cameo by 11th Doctor 8.00
...: Autopia (6/09, $3.99) Ostrander-s; Yates-a/c; variant photo-c 4.00
...: Black Death White Life (9/09, $3.99) Mandrake-a; Guy Davis- c; variant photo-c 4.00
...: Cold-Blooded War (8/09, $3.99) Salmon-a/c; variant photo-c 4.00
...: Room With a Déjà View (6/09, $3.99) Eric J-a; Mandrake-c; variant photo-c 4.00
...: The Whispering Gallery (2/09, $3.99) Moore & Reppion-s; Templesmith-a/2 covers 4.00
...: Time Machination (5/09, $3.99) Paul Grist-a/c; variant photo-c 4.00

DOCTOR WHO (Based on the 2010 TV series with Matt Smith)
IDW Publishing: Jan, 2011 - No. 12, Apr, 2012 ($3.99)

1-16: 1-Edwards & photo-c; Currie-a. 5-Buckingham-a. 12-Grist-a 4.00
Annual 2011 (8/11, $7.99) short stories by Fialkov, Shedd, Smith, McDaid and others 8.00
... Convention Special (7/11, no cover price, BBC America Shop Exclusive) The Doctor, Amy, and Rory at the San Diego Comic-Con; Matthew Dow Smith-s/Domingues-a 15.00
... 100 Page Spectacular 1 (7/12, $7.99) Short story reprints from various eras 8.00

DOCTOR WHO (Volume 3)(Based on the 2010 TV series with Matt Smith)
IDW Publishing: Sept, 2012 - No. 16, Dec, 2013 ($3.99)

1-16-Regular & photo-c on each: 1,2-Diggle-s/Buckingham-a. 3,4-Bond-a 4.00
...: 2016 Convention Exclusive (7/16, $10.00) Short stories of the various doctors 10.00
... Special 2012 (8/12, $7.99) Short stories by various incl. Wein, Diggle; Buckingham-c 8.00
... Special 2013 (12/13, $7.99) Cornell-s/Broxton-a; The Doctor visits the real world 8.00

DOCTOR WHO: A FAIRYTALE LIFE (Based on the 2010 TV series with Matt Smith)
IDW Publishing: Apr, 2011 - No. 4, Jul, 2011 ($3.99, limited series)

1-4: 1-Sturges-s/Yeates-a; covers by Buckingham & Mebberson. 3-Shearer-a 4.00

Doctor Who: The Eighth Doctor #1 © BBC

Doctor Who: The Third Doctor #1 © BBC

Doll Man Quarterly #1 © QUA

	GD 2.0	VG 4.0	FN 6.0	VF 8.0	VF/NM 9.0	NM- 9.2

DR. WHO & THE DALEKS (See Movie Classics)

DOCTOR WHO CLASSICS
IDW Publishing: Nov, 2005 - Oct, 2013 ($3.99)

1-10: Reprints from Doctor Who Weekly (1979); art by Gibbons, Neary and others 4.00
Series 2 (12/08 - No. 12, 11/09, $3.99) 1-12 4.00
Series 3 (3/10 - No. 6, 8/10, $3.99) 1-6 4.00
Series 4 (2/12 - No. 6, 7/12, $3.99) 1-6: Colin Baker era 4.00
Series 5 (3/13 - No. 5, 10/13 $3.99) 1-5: Sylvester McCoy era 4.00
...: The Seventh Doctor (2/11, $3.99) 1-5: 1-Furman-s/Ridgway-a; Sylvester McCoy-era 4.00

DOCTOR WHO EVENT 2015: FOUR DOCTORS
Titan Comics: Sept, 2015 - No. 5, Oct, 2015 ($3.99, weekly limited series)

1-5-Paul Cornell-s/Neil Edwards-a; 10th, 11th, 12th and War Doctor app. 4.00

DOCTOR WHO EVENT 2016: SUPREMACY OF THE CYBERMEN
Titan Comics: Aug, 2016 - No. 5, Dec, 2016 ($3.99, limited series)

1-5-Mann & Scott-s; 9th, 10th, 11th, 12th Doctors app.; multiple covers on each 4.00

DOCTOR WHO: FREE COMIC BOOK DAY
Titan Comics: Jun, 2015; Jun, 2016; Jun, 2017 (giveaways)

1-Short stories with the 10th, 11th & 12th Doctors; Paul Cornell interview 3.00
2016 - (6/16) Short stories with the 9th, 10th, 11th & 12th Doctors 3.00

DOCTOR WHO: PRISONERS OF TIME
IDW Publishing: Feb, 2013 - No. 12, Nov, 2013 ($3.99, limited series)

1-50th Anniversary series with each issue spotlighting one Doctor; Francavilla-c 6.00
1-12-Photo covers 5.00
2-12: Francavilla-c on all. 5-12-Dave Sim variant-c. 8-Langridge-a 4.00

DOCTOR WHO: THE EIGHTH DOCTOR (Based on the Paul McGann version)
Titan Comics: Nov, 2015 - No. 5, Apr, 2016 ($3.99, limited series)

1-5: 1-Intro. Josephine; Vieceli-a; multiple covers on each 4.00

DOCTOR WHO: THE ELEVENTH DOCTOR (Based on the Matt Smith version)
Titan Comics: Aug, 2014 - No. 15, Sept, 2015 ($3.99)

1-15: 1-Intro. Alice; Fraser-a; multiple covers on each 4.00

DOCTOR WHO: THE ELEVENTH DOCTOR YEAR TWO (Matt Smith version)
Titan Comics: Oct, 2015 - No. 15, Dec, 2016 ($3.99)

1-15: 1-War Doctor & Abslom Daak app.; multiple covers on each 4.00

DOCTOR WHO: THE ELEVENTH DOCTOR YEAR THREE (Matt Smith version)
Titan Comics: Feb, 2017 - Present ($3.99)

1-3: 1-The Doctor and Alice; Rob Williams-s; multiple covers on each 4.00

DOCTOR WHO: THE FORGOTTEN (Based on the 2005 TV series with David Tennant)
IDW Publishing: Aug, 2008 - No. 6, Jan, 2009 ($3.99)

1-6: 1,2-Pia Guerra-a/Tony Lee-s; two covers 4.00

DOCTOR WHO: THE FOURTH DOCTOR (Based on the Tom Baker version)
Titan Comics: Apr, 2016 - No. 5, Oct, 2016 ($3.99)

1-5: Sarah Jane app.; Brian Williamson-a; multiple covers on each 4.00

DOCTOR WHO: THE NINTH DOCTOR (Based on the Christopher Eccleston version)
Titan Comics: Apr, 2015 - No. 5, Dec, 2015 ($3.99)

1-5: 1-Rose & Capt. Jack app.; Cavan Scott-s; multiple covers on each 4.00

DOCTOR WHO: THE NINTH DOCTOR ONGOING (Christopher Eccleston version)
Titan Comics: May, 2016 - Present ($3.99)

1-10: 1-Rose & Capt. Jack app.; Cavan Scott-s; multiple covers on each 4.00

DOCTOR WHO: THE TENTH DOCTOR (Based on the David Tennant version)
Titan Comics: Aug, 2014 - No. 15, Sept, 2015 ($3.99)

1-15: 1-5-Casagrande-a; multiple covers on each. 1-Intro. Gabby. 6,7-Weeping Angels 4.00

DOCTOR WHO: THE TENTH DOCTOR YEAR TWO (David Tennant version)
Titan Comics: Oct, 2015 - No. 17, Jan, 2017 ($3.99)

1-17: 1-Abadzis-s/Carlini-a; multiple covers on each. 3-Captain Jack app. 4.00

DOCTOR WHO: THE TENTH DOCTOR YEAR THREE (David Tennant version)
Titan Comics: Feb, 2017 - Present ($3.99)

1,2-The Doctor & Gabby; Abadzis-s; multiple covers on each 4.00

DOCTOR WHO: THE THIRD DOCTOR (Based on the Jon Pertwee version)
Titan Comics: Oct, 2016 - Present ($3.99)

1-5-Jo and The Brigadier app.; multiple covers on each 4.00

DOCTOR WHO: THE TWELFTH DOCTOR (Based on the Peter Capaldi version)
Titan Comics: Nov, 2014 - No. 15, Jan, 2016 ($3.99)

1-15: 1-The Doctor and Clara; Dave Taylor-a; multiple covers on each 4.00

DOCTOR WHO: THE TWELFTH DOCTOR YEAR TWO (Based on the Peter Capaldi version)
Titan Comics: Feb, 2016 - Present ($3.99)

1-14: 1-The Doctor and Clara. 6-Intro. Hattie 4.00

DR. WONDER
Old Town Publishing: June, 1996 - No. 5 ($2.95, B&W)

1-5: 1-Intro & origin of Dr. Wonder; Dick Ayers-c/a; Irwin Hasen-a 3.00

DOCTOR ZERO
Marvel Comics (Epic Comics): Apr, 1988 - No. 8, Aug, 1989 ($1.25/$1.50)

1-8: 1-Sienkiewicz-c. 6,7-Spiegle-a 3.00
NOTE: *Sienkiewicz a-3i, 4i; c-1. Spiegle a-6, 7.*

DO-DO (Funny Animal Circus Stories)
Nation-Wide Publishers: 1950 - No. 7, 1951 (5¢, 5x7-1/4" Miniature)

	GD 2.0	VG 4.0	FN 6.0	VF 8.0	VF/NM 9.0	NM- 9.2
1 (52 pgs.)	28	56	84	165	270	375
2-7	16	32	48	94	147	200

DODO & THE FROG, THE (Formerly Funny Stuff; also see It's Game Time #2)
National Periodical Publications: No. 80, 9-10/54 - No. 88, 1-2/56; No. 89, 8-9/56; No. 90, 10-11/56; No. 91, 9/57; No. 92, 11/57 (See Comic Cavalcade and Captain Carrot)

	GD 2.0	VG 4.0	FN 6.0	VF 8.0	VF/NM 9.0	NM- 9.2
80-1st app. Doodles Duck by Sheldon Mayer	20	40	60	114	182	250
81-91: Doodles Duck by Mayer in #81,83-90	14	28	42	76	108	140
92-(Scarce)-Doodles Duck by S. Mayer	18	36	54	105	165	225

DOGFACE DOOLEY
Magazine Enterprises: 1951 - No. 5, 1953

	GD 2.0	VG 4.0	FN 6.0	VF 8.0	VF/NM 9.0	NM- 9.2
1(A-1 40)	8	16	24	40	50	60
2(A-1 43), 3(A-1 49), 4(A-1 53), 5(A-1 64)	6	12	18	28	34	40
I.W. Reprint #1('64), Super Reprint #17	2	4	6	9	13	16

DOG MOON
DC Comics (Vertigo): 1996 ($6.95, one-shot)

1-Robert Hunter-scripts; Tim Truman-c/a. 7.00

DOG OF FLANDERS, A
Dell Publishing Co.: No. 1088, Mar, 1960

	GD 2.0	VG 4.0	FN 6.0	VF 8.0	VF/NM 9.0	NM- 9.2
Four Color 1088-Movie, photo-c	5	10	15	31	53	75

DOGPATCH (See Al Capp's... & Mammy Yokum)

DOGS OF WAR (Also see Warriors of Plasm #13)
Defiant: Apr, 1994 - No. 5, Aug, 1994 ($2.50)

1-5: 5-Schism x-over 3.00

DOGS-O-WAR
Crusade Comics: June, 1996 - No. 3, Jan, 1997 ($2.95, B&W, limited series)

1-3: 1,2-Photo-c 3.00

DOLLFACE & HER GANG (Betty Betz'...)
Dell Publishing Co.: No. 309, Jan, 1951

	GD 2.0	VG 4.0	FN 6.0	VF 8.0	VF/NM 9.0	NM- 9.2
Four Color 309	6	12	18	37	66	95

DOLLHOUSE
Dark Horse Comics: Mar, 2011; Jul, 2011 - No. 5, Nov, 2011 ($3.50, limited series)

1-5-Richards-a; two covers on each 4.00
...: Epitaphs (3/11, $3.50) reprints story from DVD collection; covers by Noto & Morris 4.00

DOLLMAN (Movie)
Eternity Comics: Sept, 1991 - No. 4, Dec, 1991 ($2.50, limited series)

1-4: Adaptation of film 3.00

DOLL MAN QUARTERLY, THE (Doll Man #17 on; also see Feature Comics #27 & Freedom Fighters)
Quality Comics: Fall, 1941 - No. 7, Fall, '43; No. 8, Spr, '46 - No. 47, Oct, 1953

	GD 2.0	VG 4.0	FN 6.0	VF 8.0	VF/NM 9.0	NM- 9.2
1-Dollman (by Cassone), Justin Wright begin	343	686	1029	2400	4200	6000
2-The Dragon begins; Crandall-a(5)	155	310	465	992	1696	2400
3,4	97	194	291	621	1061	1500
5-Crandall-a	94	188	282	597	1024	1450
6,7(1943)	55	110	165	352	601	850
8(1946)-1st app. Torchy by Bill Ward	174	348	522	1114	1907	2700
9(Summer 1946)	55	110	165	352	601	850
10-20	42	84	126	265	445	625
21-26,28-30: 28-Vs. The Flame	39	78	117	240	395	550
27-Sci-fi bondage-c	42	84	126	265	445	625
31-(12/50)-Intro Elmo, the wonder dog (Dollman's faithful dog)	43	86	129	271	461	650
32-35,38,40: 32-34-Jeb Rivers app. 34-Crandall-a(p)						

Dominion Factor #2.3 © MAR

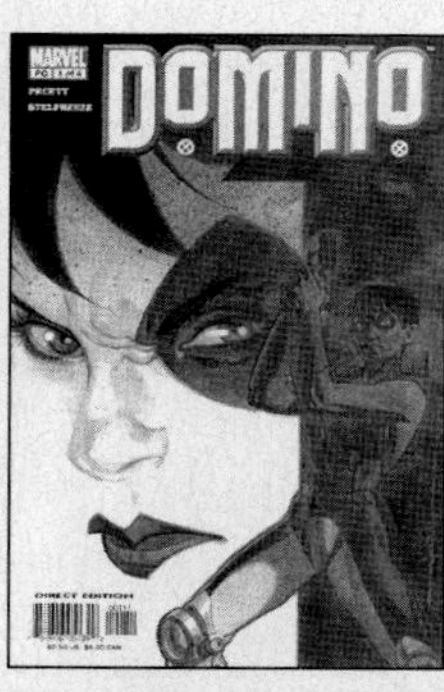

Domino (2003 series) #1 © MAR

Donald Duck #46 © DIS

	GD 2.0	VG 4.0	FN 6.0	VF 8.0	VF/NM 9.0	NM- 9.2
	40	80	120	246	411	575
36-Giant shark-c	43	86	129	271	461	650
37-Origin & 1st app. Dollgirl; Dollgirl bondage-c	65	130	195	416	708	1000
39- "Narcotics...the Death Drug" c-/story	47	94	141	296	498	700
41-47	34	68	102	199	325	450

Super Reprint #11('64, r/#20),15(r/#23),17(r/#28): 15,17-Torchy app.; Andru/Esposito-c
3 6 9 20 30 40

NOTE: ***Ward*** *Torchy in 8, 9, 11, 12, 14-24, 27; by Fox-#26, 30, 35-47.* ***Crandall*** *a-2, 5, 10, 13 & Super #11, 17, 18.* ***Crandall/Cuidera*** *c-40-42.* ***Guardineer*** *a-3. Bondage c-27, 37, 38, 39.*

DOLLY
Ziff-Davis Publ. Co.: No. 10, July-Aug, 1951 (Funny animal)
10-Painted-c 11 22 33 58 79 105

DOLLY DILL
Marvel Comics/Newsstand Publ.: 1945
1 21 42 63 122 199 275

DOLLZ, THE
Image Comics: Apr, 2001 - No. 2, June, 2001 ($2.95)
1,2: 1-Four covers; Sniegoski & Green-s/Green-a 3.00

DOMINATION FACTOR
Marvel Comics: Nov, 1999 - 4.8, Feb, 2000 ($2.50, interconnected mini-series)
1.1, 2.3, 3.5, 4.7-Fantastic Four; Jurgens-s/a 3.00
1.2, 2.4, 3.6, 4.8-Avengers; Ordway-s/a 3.00

DOMINIC FORTUNE
Marvel Comics (MAX): Oct, 2009 - No. 4, Jan, 2010 ($3.99, limited series)
1-4-Howard Chaykin-s/a/c 4.00

DOMINION
Image Comics: Jan, 2003 - No. 2 ($2.95)
1,2-Keith Giffen-s/a 3.00

DOMINION (Manga)
Eclipse Comics: Dec, 1990 - No. 6., July, 1990 ($2.00, B&W, limited series)
1-6 3.00

DOMINION: CONFLICT 1 (Manga)
Dark Horse Comics: Mar, 1996 - No. 6, Aug, 1996 ($2.95, B&W, limited series)
1-6: Shirow-c/a/scripts 3.00

DOMINIQUE LAVEAU: VOODOO CHILD
DC Comics (Vertigo): May, 2012 - No. 7, Nov, 2012 ($2.99, limited series)
1-7-Selwyn Seyfu Hinds-s/Denys Cowan-a 3.00

DOMINO (See X-Force)
Marvel Comics: Jan, 1997 - No. 3, Mar, 1997 ($1.95, limited series)
1-3: 2-Deathstrike-c/app. 3.00

DOMINO (See X-Force)
Marvel Comics: June, 2003 - No. 4, Aug, 2003 ($2.50, limited series)
1-4-Stelfreeze-c/a; Pruett-s. 3.00

DOMINO CHANCE
Chance Enterprises: May-June, 1982 - No. 9, May, 1985 (B&W)
1-9: 7-1st app. Gizmo, 2 pgs. 8-1st full Gizmo story. 1-Reprint, May, 1985 4.00

DONALD AND MICKEY IN DISNEYLAND (See Dell Giants)

DONALD AND SCROOGE
Disney Comics: 1992 ($8.95, squarebound, 100 pgs.)
nn-Don Rosa reprint special; r/U.S., D.D. Advs. 1 3 4 6 8 10
1-3 (1992, $1.50)-r/D.D. Advs. (Disney) #1,22,24 & U.S. #261-263,269 3.00

DONALD AND THE WHEEL (Disney)
Dell Publishing Co.: No. 1190, Nov, 1961
Four Color 1190-Movie, Barks-c 7 14 21 49 92 135

DONALD DUCK (See Adventures of Mickey Mouse, Cheerios, Donald & Mickey, Ducktales, Dynabrite Comics, Gladstone Comic Album, Mickey & Donald, Mickey Mouse Mag., Story Hour Series, Uncle Scrooge, Walt Disney's Comics & Stories, W. D.'s Donald Duck, Wheaties & Whitman Comic Books, Wise Little Hen, The)

DONALD DUCK
Whitman Publishing Co./Grosset & Dunlap/K.K.: 1935, 1936 (All pages on heavy linen-like finish cover stock in color;1st book ever devoted to Donald Duck; see Advs. of Mickey Mouse for 1st app.) (9-1/2x13")
978(1935)-16 pgs.; Illustrated text story book 206 412 618 1318 2259 3200
nn(1936)-36 pgs.plus hard cover & dust jacket. Story completely rewritten with B&W illos added. Mickey appears and his nephews are named Morty & Monty
Book only 194 388 582 1242 2121 3000
Dust jacket only.... 39 78 117 240 395 550

DONALD DUCK (Walt Disney's) (10¢)
Whitman/K.K. Publications: 1938 (8-1/2x11-1/2", B&W, cardboard-c)
(Has D. Duck with bubble pipe on-c)
nn-The first Donald Duck & Walt Disney comic book; 1936 & 1937 Sunday strip-r(in B&W); same format as the Feature Books; 1st strips with Huey, Dewey & Louie from 10/17/37
314 628 942 2198 3849 5500

DONALD DUCK (Walt Disney's...#262 on; see 4-Color listings for titles & Four Color No. 1109 for origin story)
Dell Publ. Co./Gold Key #85-216/Whitman #217-245/Gladstone #246 on: 1940 - No. 84, Sept-Nov, 1962; No. 85, Dec, 1962 - No. 245, July, 1984; No. 246, Oct, 1986 - No. 279, May, 1990; No. 280, Sept, 1993 - No. 307, Mar,1998
Four Color 4(1940)-Daily 1939 strip-r by Al Taliaferro
2000 4000 6000 15,000 27,500 40,000
Large Feature Comic 16(1/41?)-1940 Sunday strips-r in B&W
881 1762 2643 6431 11,366 16,300
Large Feature Comic 20('41)-Comic Paint Book, r-single panels from Large Feature #16 at top of each pg. to color; daily strip-r across bottom of each pg. (Rare)
1000 2000 3000 7400 13,200 19,000
Four Color 9('42)- "Finds Pirate Gold"; 64 pgs. by Carl Barks & Jack Hannah (pgs. 1,2,5,12-40 are by Barks, his 1st Donald Duck comic book art work; © 8/17/42)
1000 2000 3000 7600 13,800 20,000
Four Color 29(9/43)- "Mummy's Ring" by Barks; reprinted in Uncle Scrooge & Donald Duck #1('65), W. D. Comics Digest #44('73) & Donald Duck Advs. #14
795 1590 2385 5804 10,252 14,700
Four Color 62(1/45)- "Frozen Gold"; 52 pgs. by Barks, reprinted in The Best of W.D. Comics & Donald Duck Advs. #4 224 448 672 1848 4174 6500
Four Color 108(1946)- "Terror of the River"; 52 pgs. by Carl Barks; reprinted in Gladstone Comic Album #2 148 296 444 1221 2761 4300
Four Color 147(5/47)-in "Volcano Valley" by Barks 104 208 312 832 1866 2900
Four Color 159(8/47)-in "The Ghost of the Grotto";52 pgs. by Carl Barks; reprinted in Best of Uncle Scrooge & Donald Duck #1 ('66) & The Best of W.D. Comics & D.D. Advs. #9; two Barks stories 89 178 267 712 1606 2500
Four Color 178(12/47)-1st app. Uncle Scrooge by Carl Barks; reprinted in Gold Key Christmas Parade #3 & The Best of Walt Disney Comics 136 272 408 1088 2444 3800
Four Color 189(6/48)-by Carl Barks; reprinted in Best of Donald Duck & Uncle Scrooge #1('64) & D.D. Advs. #19 79 158 237 632 1416 2200
Four Color 199(10/48)-by Carl Barks; mentioned in Love and Death; r/in Gladstone Comic Album #5 84 168 252 672 1511 2350
Four Color 203(12/48)-by Barks; reprinted as Gold Key Christmas Parade #4
59 118 177 472 1061 1650
Four Color 223(4/49)-by Barks; reprinted as Best of Donald Duck #1 & Donald Duck Advs. #3
77 154 231 616 1383 2150
Four Color 238(8/49)-in "Voodoo Hoodoo" by Barks 57 114 171 456 1028 1600
Four Color 256(12/49)-by Barks; reprinted in Best of Donald Duck & Uncle Scrooge #2('67), Gladstone Comic Album #16 & W.D. Comics Digest 44('73)
46 92 138 368 834 1300
Four Color 263(2/50)-Two Barks stories; r-in D.D. #278
46 92 138 359 805 1250
Four Color 275(5/50), 282(7/50), 291(9/50), 300(11/50)-All by Carl Barks; 275, 282 reprinted in W.D. Comics Digest #44('73). #275 r/in Gladstone Comic Album #10. #291 r/in D. Duck Advs. #16 46 92 138 350 788 1225
Four Color 308(1/51), 318(3/51)-by Barks; #318-reprinted in W.D. Comics Digest #34 & D.D. Advs. #2,19 44 88 132 326 738 1150
Four Color 328(5/51)-by Carl Barks 43 86 129 318 722 1125
Four Color 339(7-8/51), 379-2nd Uncle Scrooge-c; art not by Barks.
14 28 42 96 211 325
Four Color 348(9-10/51), 356,394-Barks-c only 22 44 66 154 340 525
Four Color 367(1-2/52)-by Barks; reprinted as Gold Key Christmas Parade #2 & #8
34 68 102 245 548 850
Four Color 408(7-8/52), 422(9-10/52)-All by Carl Barks. #408-r-in Best of Donald Duck & Uncle Scrooge #1('64) & Gladstone Comic Album #13
34 68 102 245 548 850
26(11-12/52)-In "Trick or Treat" (Barks-a, 36pgs.) 1st story r-in Walt Disney Digest #16 & Gladstone C.A. #23 33 66 99 238 532 825
27-30-Barks-c only 12 24 36 80 173 265
31-44,47-50 7 14 21 46 86 125
45-Barks-a (6 pgs.) 13 26 39 89 195 300
46- "Secret of Hondorica" by Barks, 24 pgs.; reprinted in Donald Duck #98 & 154
17 34 51 119 265 410
51-Barks-a,1/2 pg. 7 14 21 46 86 125
52- "Lost Peg-Leg Mine" by Barks, 10 pgs. 13 26 39 89 195 300

Donald Duck #264 © DIS

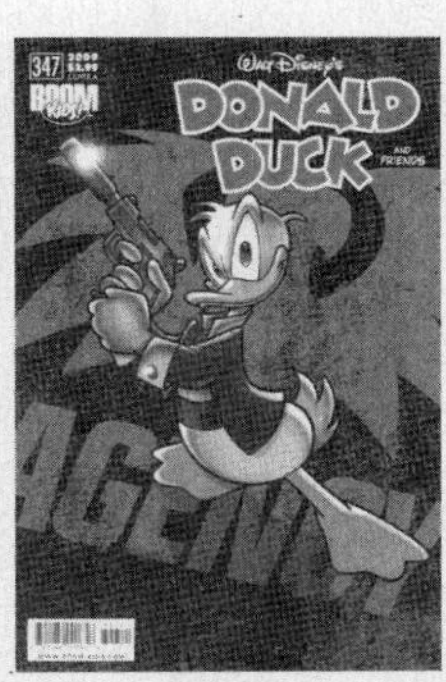

Donald Duck and Friends #347 © DIS

Don Fortune Magazine #5 © Don Fortune Pub.

	GD 2.0	VG 4.0	FN 6.0	VF 8.0	VF/NM 9.0	NM- 9.2
53,55-59	6	12	18	38	69	100
54- "Forbidden Valley" by Barks, 26 pgs. (10¢ & 15¢ versions exist)	14	28	42	98	217	335
60- "Donald Duck & the Titanic Ants" by Barks, 20 pgs. plus 6 more pgs.	14	28	42	98	217	335
61-67,69,70	5	10	15	34	60	85
68-Barks-a, 5 pgs.	9	18	27	62	126	190
71-Barks-r, 1/2 pg.	5	10	15	34	60	85
72-78,80,82-97,99,100: 96-Donald Duck Album	5	10	15	33	57	80
79,81-Barks-a, 1pg.	5	10	15	34	60	85
98-Reprints #46 (Barks)	5	10	15	34	60	85
101,103-111,113-135: 120-Last 12¢ issue. 134-Barks-r/#52 & WDC&S 194. 135-Barks-r/WDC&S 198, 19 pgs.	4	8	12	22	35	48
102-Super Goof. 112-1st Moby Duck	4	8	12	23	37	50
136-153,155,156,158: 149-20¢-c begin	3	6	9	14	20	26
154-Barks-r(#46)	3	6	9	16	24	32
157,159,160,164: 157-Barks-r(#45); 25¢-c begin. 159-Reprints/WDC&S #192 (10 pgs.). 160-Barks-r(#26). 164-Barks-r(#79)	3	6	9	14	20	26
161-163,165-173,175-187,189-191: 175-30¢-c begin. 187-Barks r/#68.	2	4	6	13	18	22
174,188: 174-r/4-Color #394.	3	6	9	14	19	24
175-177-Whitman variants	3	6	9	14	19	24
192-Barks-r(40 pgs.) from Donald Duck #60 & WDC&S #226,234 (52 pgs.)	3	6	9	15	22	28
193-200,202-207,209-211,213-216	2	4	6	9	13	16
201,208,212: 201-Barks-r/Christmas Parade #26, 16pgs. 208-Barks-r/#60 (6 pgs.). 212-Barks-r/WDC&S #130	2	4	6	9	13	16
217-219: 217 has 216 on-c. 219-Barks-r/WDC&S #106,107, 10 pgs. ea.	2	4	6	10	14	18
220,225-228: 228-Barks-r/F.C. #275	2	4	6	13	18	22
221,223,224: Scarce; only sold in pre-packs. 221(8/80), 223(11/80), 224(12/80)	5	10	15	35	63	90
222-(9-10/80)-(Very low distribution)	16	32	48	112	249	385
229-240: 229-Barks-r/F.C. #282. 230-Barks-r/ #52 & WDC&S #194. 236(2/82), 237(2-3/82), 238(3/82), 239(4/82), 240(5/82)	2	4	6	9	13	16
241-245: 241(4/83), 242(5/83), 243(3/84), 244(4/84), 245(7/84)(low print)	3	6	9	14	19	24
246-(1st Gladstone issue)-Barks-r/FC #422	3	6	9	15	21	26
247-249,251: 248,249-Barks-r/DD #54 & 26. 251-Barks-r/1945 Firestone	2	4	6	9	13	16
250-($1.50, 68 pgs.)-Barks-r/4-Color #9	2	4	6	10	14	18
252-277,280: 254-Barks-r/FC #328. 256-Barks-r/FC #147. 257-($1.50, 52 pgs.)-Barks-r/ Vacation Parade #1. 261-Barks-r/FC #300. 275-Kelly-r/FC #92. 280 (#1, 2nd Series)	1	2	3	5	6	8
278,279,286: 278,279 ($1.95, 68 pgs.): 278-Rosa-a; Barks-r/FC #263. 279-Rosa-c; Barks-r/MOC #4. 286-Rosa-a	1	2	3	5	7	9
281,282,284	1	2	3	4	5	7
283-Don Rosa-a, part-c & scripts	1	2	3	5	6	8
285,287-307						5.00
286 ($2.95, 68 pgs.)-Happy Birthday, Donald						6.00
Mini-Comic #1(1976)-(3-1/4x6-1/2"); r/D.D. #150	2	4	6	8	11	14

*NOTE: **Carl Barks** wrote all issues he illustrated, but #117, 126, 138 contain his script only. Issues 4-Color #189, 199, 203, 223, 238, 256, 263, 275, 282, 308, 348, 356, 367, 394, 408, 422, 26-30, 35, 44, 46, 52, 55, 57, 60, 65, 70-73, 77-80, 83, 101, 103, 105, 106, 111, 126, 246r, 266r, 268r, 271r, 275r, 278r(F.C. 263) all have **Barks** covers. **Barks** r-263-267, 269-278-282, 284, 285. #96 titled "Comic Album", #99-"Christmas Album". New art issues (not reprints)-106-46, 148-63, 167, 169, 170, 172, 173, 175, 178, 179, 196, 209, 223, 225, 236. **Taliaferro** daily newspaper strips #258-260, 264, 284, 285; Sunday strips #247, 280-283.*

DONALD DUCK (Numbering continues from Donald Duck and Friends #362)
BOOM! Studios (Kaboom!): No. 363, Feb, 2011 - No. 367, Jun, 2011 ($3.99)

363-367: 363-Barks reprints incl. "Mystery of the Loch". 364-Rosa-c — 4.00

DONALD DUCK
IDW Publishing: May, 2015 - No. 18, Oct, 2016 ($3.99)

1-Legacy numbered #368; art by Scarpa and others; multiple covers — 4.00
2-18-Reprints of Italian & Dutch stories; multiple covers on each. 8-Christmas issue — 4.00
...'s Halloween Scream (10/15, Halloween giveaway) r/Donald Duck Advs. #7,8 (1990) — 3.00

DONALD DUCK ADVENTURES (See Walt Disney's Donald Duck Adventures)

DONALD DUCK ALBUM (See Comic Album No. 1,3 & Duck Album)
Dell Publishing Co./Gold Key: 5-7/59 - F.C. No. 1239, 10-12/61; 1962; 8/63 - No. 2, Oct, 1963

	GD	VG	FN	VF	VF/NM	NM-
Four Color 995 (#1)	6	12	18	42	79	115
Four Color 1099,1140,1239-Barks-c	6	12	18	42	79	115
Four Color 1182, 01204-207 (1962-Dell)	5	10	15	34	60	85
1(8/63-Gold Key)-Barks-c	5	10	15	34	60	85
2(10/63)	4	8	12	28	47	65

DONALD DUCK AND FRIENDS (Numbering continues from Walt Disney's ...)
BOOM! Studios: No. 347, Oct, 2009 - No. 362, Jan, 2011 ($2.99)

347-362: Two covers on most. Retitled "Donald Duck" with #363 — 3.00

DONALD DUCK AND THE BOYS (Also see Story Hour Series)
Whitman Publishing Co.: 1948 (5-1/4x5-1/2", 100pgs., hard-c; art & text)

845-(49) new illos by Barks based on his Donald Duck 10-pager in WDC&S #74, Expanded text not written by Barks; Cover not by Barks — 50 100 150 350 600 850
(Prices vary widely on this book)

DONALD DUCK AND THE CHRISTMAS CAROL
Whitman Publishing Co.: 1960 (A Little Golden Book, 6-3/8"x7-5/8", 28 pgs.)

nn-Story book pencilled by Carl Barks with the intended title "Uncle Scrooge's Christmas Carol." Finished art adapted by Norman McGary. (Rare)-Reprinted in Uncle Scrooge in Color. — 20 40 60 100 185 270

DONALD DUCK BEACH PARTY (Also see Dell Giants)
Gold Key: Sept, 1965 (12¢)

1(#10158-509)-Barks-r/WDC&S #45; painted-c — 6 12 18 37 66 95

DONALD DUCK BOOK (See Story Hour Series)

DONALD DUCK COMICS DIGEST
Gladstone Publishing: Nov, 1986 - No. 5, July, 1987 ($1.25/$1.50, 96 pgs.)

1,3: 1-Barks-c/a-r — 1 3 4 6 8 10
2,4,5: 4,5-$1.50-c — 6.00

DONALD DUCK FUN BOOK (See Dell Giants)

DONALD DUCK IN DISNEYLAND (See Dell Giants)

DONALD DUCK MARCH OF COMICS (See March of Comics #4,20,41,56,69,263)

DONALD DUCK MERRY CHRISTMAS (See Dell Giant No. 53)

DONALD DUCK PICNIC PARTY (See Picnic Party listed under Dell Giants)

DONALD DUCK TELLS ABOUT KITES (See Kite Fun Book)

DONALD DUCK, THIS IS YOUR LIFE (Disney, TV)
Dell Publishing Co.: No. 1109, Aug-Oct, 1960

Four Color 1109-Gyro flashback to WDC&S #141; origin Donald Duck (1st told) — 12 24 36 81 176 270

DONALD DUCK XMAS ALBUM (See regular Donald Duck No. 99)

DONALD IN MATHMAGIC LAND (Disney)
Dell Publishing Co.: No. 1051, Oct-Dec, 1959 - No. 1198, May-July, 1961

	GD	VG	FN	VF	VF/NM	NM-
Four Color 1051 (#1)-Movie	8	16	24	56	108	160
Four Color 1198-Reprint of above	6	12	18	37	66	95

DONALD QUEST (Donald Duck in parallel universe of Feudarnia)
IDW Publishing: Nov, 2016 - No. 5 ($3.99, limited series)

1-4-English version of Italian story; multiple covers on each. 1-Ambrosio-s/Freccero-a — 4.00

DONATELLO, TEENAGE MUTANT NINJA TURTLE
Mirage Studios: Aug, 1986 ($1.50, B&W, one-shot, 44 pgs.)

1 — 2 4 6 10 14 18

DONDI
Dell Publishing Co.: No. 1176, Mar-May, 1961 - No. 1276, Dec, 1961

	GD	VG	FN	VF	VF/NM	NM-
Four Color 1176 (#1)-Movie; origin, photo-c	5	10	15	35	63	90
Four Color 1276	4	8	12	27	44	60

DON FORTUNE MAGAZINE
Don Fortune Publishing Co.: Aug, 1946 - No. 6, Feb, 1947

	GD	VG	FN	VF	VF/NM	NM-
1-Delecta of the Planets by C.C. Beck in all	29	58	87	170	278	385
2	15	30	45	85	130	175
3-6: 3-Bondage-c	14	28	42	76	108	140

DONG XOAI, VIETNAM 1965
DC Comics: 2010 ($19.95, B&W graphic novel)

SC-Joe Kubert-s/a/c; includes report of actual events that inspired the story — 20.00

DONKEY KONG (See Blip #1)

DONNA MATRIX
Reactor, Inc.: Aug, 1993 ($2.95, 52 pgs.)

1-Computer generated-c/a by Mike Saenz; 3-D effects — 4.00

DON NEWCOMBE
Fawcett Publications: 1950 (Baseball)

Don Winslow of the Navy #2 © Merwil

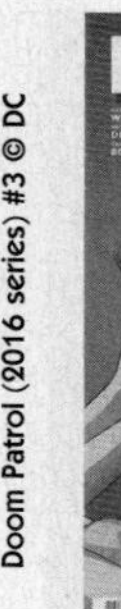

Doom Patrol (2016 series) #3 © DC

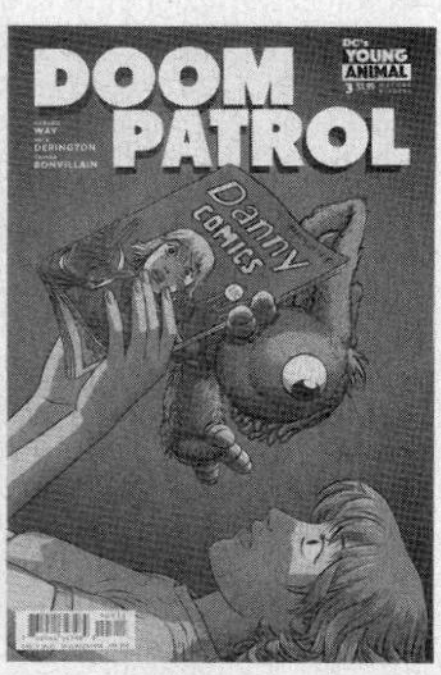

Doom 2099 #19 © MAR

	GD 2.0	VG 4.0	FN 6.0	VF 8.0	VF/NM 9.0	NM- 9.2
nn-Photo-c	53	106	159	334	567	800

DON ROSA'S COMICS AND STORIES
Fantagraphics Books (CX Comics): 1983 ($2.95)

	GD	VG	FN	VF	VF/NM	NM-
1,2: 1-(68 pgs.) Reprints Rosa's The Pertwillaby Papers episodes #128-133.						
2-(60 pgs.) Reprints episodes #134-138	2	4	6	11	16	20

DON SIMPSON'S BIZARRE HEROES (Also see Megaton Man)
Fiasco Comics: May, 1990 - No. 17, Sept, 1996 ($2.50/$2.95, B&W)

	GD	VG	FN	VF	VF/NM	NM-
1-10,0,11-17: 0-Begin $2.95-c; r/Bizarre Heroes #1. 17-(9/96)-Indicia also reads Megaton Man #0; intro Megaton Man and the Fiascoverse to new readers						3.00

DON'T GIVE UP THE SHIP
Dell Publishing Co.: No. 1049, Aug, 1959

	GD	VG	FN	VF	VF/NM	NM-
Four Color 1049-Movie, Jerry Lewis photo-c	9	18	27	58	114	170

DON WINSLOW OF THE NAVY
Merwil Publishing Co.: Apr, 1937 - No. 2, May, 1937 (96 pgs.)(A pulp/comic book cross; stapled spine)

	GD	VG	FN	VF	VF/NM	NM-
V1#1-Has 16 pgs. comics in color. Captain Colorful & Jupiter Jones by Sheldon Mayer; complete Don Winslow novel	653	1306	1959	4900	-	-
2-Sheldon Mayer-a	177	354	531	1325	-	-

DON WINSLOW OF THE NAVY (See Crackajack Funnies, Famous Feature Stories, Popular Comics & Super Book #5,6)
Dell Publishing Co.: No. 2, Nov, 1939 - No. 22, 1941

	GD	VG	FN	VF	VF/NM	NM-
Four Color 2 (#1)-Rare	223	446	669	1416	2433	3450
Four Color 22	52	104	156	328	552	775

DON WINSLOW OF THE NAVY (See TV Teens; Movie, Radio, TV) (Fightin' Navy No. 74 on)
Fawcett Publications/Charlton No. 70 on: 2/43 - #64, 12/48; #65, 1/51 - #69, 9/51; #70, 3/55 - #73, 9/55

	GD	VG	FN	VF	VF/NM	NM-
1-(68 pgs.)-Captain Marvel on cover	123	246	369	787	1344	1900
2	45	90	135	284	480	675
3	37	74	111	222	361	500
4-6: 6-Flag-c	30	60	90	177	289	400
7-10: 8-Last 68 pg. issue?	22	44	66	132	216	300
11-20	19	38	57	111	176	240
21-40	16	32	48	94	147	200
41-43,45-64: 51,60-Singapore Sal (villain) app. 64-(12/48)	15	30	45	85	130	175
44-Classic spider-c	39	78	117	231	378	525
65(1/51)-Flying Saucer attack; photo-c	23	46	69	136	223	310
66 - 69(9/51): All photo-c. 66-sci-fi story	15	30	45	85	130	175
70(3/55)-73: 70-73 r-/#26,58 & 59	10	20	30	56	76	95

DOODLE JUMP (Based on the game app)
Dynamite Entertainment: 2014 - No. 6, 2015 ($3.99, limited series)

	GD	VG	FN	VF	VF/NM	NM-
1-6-Steve Uy-a; multiple covers on each						4.00

DOOM
Marvel Comics: Oct, 2000 - No. 3, Dec, 2000 ($2.99, limited series)

	GD	VG	FN	VF	VF/NM	NM-
1-3-Dr. Doom; Dixon-s/Manco-a						3.00

DOOMED (Also see Teen Titans #14 (2016))
DC Comics: Aug, 2015 - No. 6, Jan, 2016 ($2.99, limited series)

	GD	VG	FN	VF	VF/NM	NM-
1-6: 1-Lobdell-s/Fernandez-a. 3-Alpha Centurion app. 4-6-Superman app.						3.00

DOOM FORCE SPECIAL
DC Comics: July, 1992 ($2.95, 68 pgs., one-shot, mature) (X-Force parody)

	GD	VG	FN	VF	VF/NM	NM-
1-Morrison scripts; Simonson, Steacy, & others-a; Giffen/Mignola-c						4.00

DOOM PATROL, THE (Formerly My Greatest Adventure No. 1-85; see Brave and the Bold, DC Special Blue Ribbon Digest 19, Official... Index & Showcase No. 94-96)
National Periodical Publ.: No. 86, 3/64 - No. 121, 9-10/68; No. 122, 2/73 - No. 124, 6-7/73

	GD	VG	FN	VF	VF/NM	NM-
86-1 pg. origin (#86-121 are 12¢ issues)	21	42	63	147	324	500
87-98: 88-Origin The Chief. 91-Intro. Mento	8	16	24	56	108	160
99-Intro. Beast Boy (later becomes the Changeling in New Teen Titans)	50	100	150	300	500	700
100-Origin Beast Boy; Robot-Maniac series begins (12/65)	10	20	30	69	147	225
101-110: 102-Challengers of the Unknown app. 104-Wedding issue. 105-Robot-Maniac series ends. 106-Negative Man begins (origin)	6	12	18	38	69	100
111-120	5	10	15	33	57	80
121-Death of Doom Patrol; Orlando-c.	11	22	33	73	157	240
122-124: All reprints	2	4	6	8	11	14

DOOM PATROL
DC Comics (Vertigo imprint #64 on): Oct, 1987 - No, 87, Feb, 1995 (75¢-$1.95, new format)

	GD	VG	FN	VF	VF/NM	NM-
1-Wraparound-c; Lightle-a						6.00
2-18: 3-1st app. Lodestone. 4-1st app. Karma. 8,15,16-Art Adams-c(i). 18-Invasion tie-in						4.00
19-(2/89)-Grant Morrison scripts begin, ends #63; 1st app Crazy Jane; $1.50-c & new format begins.	1	2	3	5	6	8
20-30: 29-Superman app. 30-Night Breed fold-out						5.00
31-34,37-41,45-49,51-56,58-60: 39-World Without End preview						3.00
35-1st brief app. of Flex Mentallo	1	2	3	5	6	8
36-1st full app. of Flex Mentallo	1	2	3	5	7	9
42-44-Origin of Flex Mentallo						4.00
50,57 ($2.50, 52 pgs.)						4.00
61-87: 61,70-Photo-c. 73-Death cameo (2 panels)						3.00
...And Suicide Squad 1 (3/88, $1.50, 52 pgs.)-Wraparound-c						4.00
Annual 1 (1988, $1.50, 52 pgs.)						4.00
Annual 2 (1994, $3.95, 68 pgs.)-Children's Crusade tie-in.						4.00
...: Crawling From the Wreckage TPB (2004, $19.95) r/#19-25; Morrison-s						20.00
...: Down Paradise Way TPB (2005, $19.99) r/#35-41; Morrison-s						20.00
...: Magic Bus TPB (2007, $19.99) r/#51-57; Morrison-s; new Bolland-c						20.00
...: Musclebound TPB (2006, $19.99) r/#42-50; Morrison-s; new Bolland-c						20.00
...: Planet Love TPB (2008, $19.99) r/#58-63 & Doom Force Special #1; Morrison-s						20.00
...: The Painting That Ate Paris TPB (2004, $19.95) r/#26-34; Morrison-s						20.00

NOTE: ***Bisley*** *painted c-26-48, 55-58.* ***Bolland*** *c-64, 75.* ***Dringenberg*** *a-42(p).* ***Steacy*** *a-53.*

DOOM PATROL
DC Comics: Dec, 2001 - No. 22, Sept, 2003 ($2.50)

	GD	VG	FN	VF	VF/NM	NM-
1-Intro. new team with Robotman; Tan Eng Huat-c/a; John Arcudi-s						4.00
2-22: 4,5-Metamorpho & Elongated Man app. 13,14-Fisher-a. 20-Geary-a						3.00

DOOM PATROL (see JLA #94-99)
DC Comics: Aug, 2004 - No. 18, Jan, 2006 ($2.50)

	GD	VG	FN	VF	VF/NM	NM-
1-18-John Byrne-s/a. 1-Green Lantern, Batman app.						3.00

DOOM PATROL
DC Comics: Oct, 2009 - No. 22, Jul, 2011 ($3.99/$2.99)

	GD	VG	FN	VF	VF/NM	NM-
1-7: 1-Giffen-s/Clark-a; back-up Metal Men feature w/Maguire-a. 1-Two covers. 4-5-Blackest Night. 6-Negative Man origin re-told						4.00
8-22-($2.99) 11,12-Ambush Bug app. 16-Giffen-a. 21-Robotman origin retold						3.00
...: Brotherhood TPB (2011, $17.99) r/#7-13						18.00
...: We Who Are About to Die TPB (2010, $14.99) r/#1-6; cover gallery; design art						15.00

DOOM PATROL
DC Comics (Young Animal): Nov, 2016 - Present ($3.99)

	GD	VG	FN	VF	VF/NM	NM-
1-4: 1-Gerald Way-s/Nick Derington-a; main cover has peel-off gyro sticker						4.00

DOOM PATROL (See Tangent Comics/ Doom Patrol)

DOOMSDAY
DC Comics: 1995 ($3.95, one-shot)

	GD	VG	FN	VF	VF/NM	NM-
1-Year One story by Jurgens, L. Simonson, Ordway, and Gil Kane; Superman app.						5.00

DOOMSDAY + 1 (Also see Charlton Bullseye)
Charlton Comics: July, 1975 - No. 6, June, 1976; No. 7, June, 1978 - No. 12, May, 1979

	GD	VG	FN	VF	VF/NM	NM-
1: #1-5 are 25¢ issues	3	6	9	15	22	28
2-6: 4-Intro Lor. 5-Ditko-a(1 pg.) 6-Begin 30¢-c	2	4	6	10	14	18
V3#7-12 (reprints #1-6)						6.00
5 (Modern Comics reprint, 1977)						6.00

NOTE: ***Byrne*** *c/a-1-12; Painted covers-2-7.*

DOOMSDAY.1
IDW Publishing: May, 2013 - No. 4, Aug, 2013 ($3.99)

	GD	VG	FN	VF	VF/NM	NM-
1-4-John Byrne-s/a/c						4.00

DOOMSDAY SQUAD, THE
Fantagraphics Books: Aug, 1986 - No. 7, 1987 ($2.00)

	GD	VG	FN	VF	VF/NM	NM-
1,2,4-7: Byrne-a in all. 1,2-New Byrne-c. 4-Neal Adams-c. 5-7-Gil Kane-c						4.00
3-Usagi Yojimbo app. (1st in color); new Byrne-c						6.00

DOOM'S IV
Image Comics (Extreme): July, 1994 - No.4, Oct, 1994 ($2.50, limited series)

	GD	VG	FN	VF	VF/NM	NM-
1-4-Liefeld story						3.00
1,2-Two alternate Liefeld-c each, 4 covers form 1 picture						5.00

DOOM: THE EMPEROR RETURNS
Marvel Comics: Jan, 2002 - No. 3, Mar, 2002 ($2.50, limited series)

	GD	VG	FN	VF	VF/NM	NM-
1-3-Dixon-s/Manco-a; Franklin Richards app.						3.00

DOOM 2099 (See Marvel Comics Presents #118 & 2099: World of Tomorrow)
Marvel Comics: Jan, 1993 - No. 44, Aug, 1996 ($1.25/$1.50/$1.95)

	GD	VG	FN	VF	VF/NM	NM-
1-Metallic foil stamped-c						4.00
1-2nd printing						3.00

Double Dragon #1 © MAR

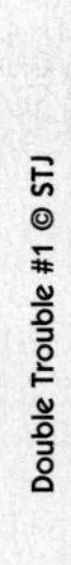

Double Trouble #1 © STJ

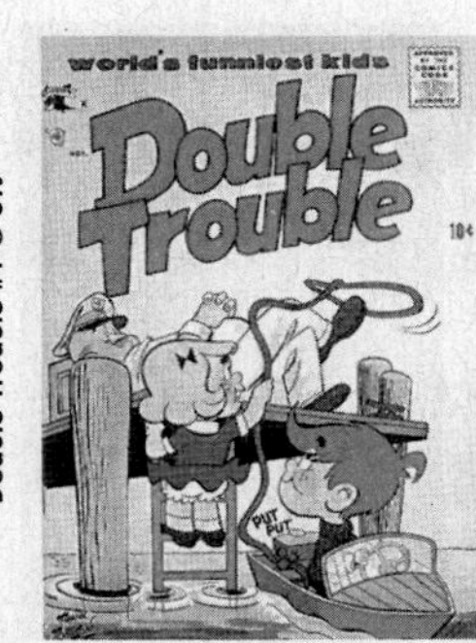

Down With Crime #5 © FAW

GD VG FN VF VF/NM NM-
2.0 4.0 6.0 8.0 9.0 9.2

GD VG FN VF VF/NM NM-
2.0 4.0 6.0 8.0 9.0 9.2

2-24,26-44: 4-Ron Lim-c(p). 17-bound-in trading card sheet. 40-Namor & Doctor Strange app. 41-Daredevil app., Namor-c/app. 44-Intro The Emissary; story contin'd in 2099: World of Tomorrow 3.00
18-Variant polybagged with Sega Sub-Terrania poster 4.00
25 ($2.25, 52 pgs.) 4.00
25 ($2.95, 52pgs.) Foil embossed cover 5.00
29 ($3.50)-acetate-c. 4.00

DOOMWAR
Marvel Comics: Apr, 2010 - No. 6, Sept, 2010 ($3.99, limited series)
1-6-Doctor Doom invades Wakanda; Black Panther & X-Men app.; Romita Jr.-c/Eaton-a 4.00

DOORWAY TO NIGHTMARE (See Cancelled Comic Cavalcade and Madame Xanadu)
DC Comics: Jan-Feb, 1978 - No. 5, Sept-Oct, 1978
1-Madame Xanadu in all 2 4 6 11 16 20
2-5: 4-Craig-a 2 4 6 8 11 14
NOTE: ***Kaluta*** *covers on all. Merged into The Unexpected with No. 190.*

DOPEY DUCK COMICS (Wacky Duck No. 3) (See Super Funnies)
Timely Comics (NPP): Fall, 1945 - No. 2, Apr, 1946
1-Casper Cat, Krazy Krow 40 80 120 246 411 575
2-Casper Cat, Krazy Krow 30 60 90 177 289 400

DORK
Slave Labor: June, 1993 - No. 11 ($2.50-$3.50, B&W, mature)
1-7,9-11: Evan Dorkin-c/a/scripts in all. 1(8/95),2(1/96)-(2nd printings). 1(3/97) (3rd printing). 1-Milk & Cheese app. 3-Eltingville Club starts. 6-Reprints 1st Eltingville Club app. from Instant Piano #1 3.00
8-($3.50) 4.00
Who's Laughing Now? TPB (2001, $11.95) reprints most of #1-5 12.00
The Collected Dork, Vol. 2: Circling the Drain (6/03, $13.95) r/most of #7-10 & other-s 14.00

DOROTHY & THE WIZARD IN OZ (Adaptation of the original 1908 L. Frank Baum book) (Also see Wonderful Wizard of Oz, Marvelous Land of Oz, and Ozma of Oz)
Marvel Comics: Nov, 2011 - No. 8, Aug, 2012 ($3.99, limited series)
1-8-Eric Shanower-a/Skottie Young-a/c 4.00

DOROTHY LAMOUR (Formerly Jungle Lil)(Stage, screen, radio)
Fox Features Syndicate: No. 2, June, 1950 - No. 3, Aug, 1950
2-Wood-a(3), photo-c 37 74 111 222 361 500
3-Wood-a(3), photo-c 30 60 90 177 289 400

DOROTHY OF OZ PREQUEL
IDW Publishing: Mar, 2012 - No. 4, Aug, 2012 ($3.99, limited series)
1-4-Tipton-s/Shedd-a 4.00

DOT DOTLAND (Formerly Little Dot Dotland)
Harvey Publications: No. 62, Sept, 1974 - No. 63, Nov, 1974
62,63 2 4 6 9 12 15

DOTTY (...& Her Boy Friends)(Formerly Four Teeners; Glamorous Romances No. 41 on)
Ace Magazines (A. A. Wyn): No. 35, June, 1948 - No. 40, May, 1949
35-Teen-age 11 22 33 60 83 105
36-40: 37-Transvestism story 8 16 24 44 57 70

DOTTY DRIPPLE (Horace & Dotty Dripple No. 25 on)
Magazine Ent.(Life's Romances)/Harvey No. 3 on: 1946 - No. 24, June, 1952 (Also see A-1 No. 1, 3-8, 10)
1 (nd) (10¢) 14 28 42 82 121 160
2 9 18 27 50 65 80
3-10: 3,4-Powell-a 7 14 21 35 43 50
11-24 6 12 18 28 34 40

DOTTY DRIPPLE AND TAFFY
Dell Publishing Co.: No. 646, Sept, 1955 - No. 903, May, 1958
Four Color 646 (#1) 6 12 18 37 66 95
Four Color 691,718,746,801,903 4 8 12 28 47 65

DOUBLE ACTION COMICS
National Periodical Publications: No. 2, Jan, 1940 (68 pgs., B&W)
2-Contains original stories(?); pre-hero DC contents; same cover as Adventure No. 37. (seven known copies, four in high grade) (not an ashcan) 3200 6400 9600 19,200 25,600 32,000
NOTE: *The cover to this book was probably reprinted from Adventure #37. #1 exists as an ash can copy with B&W cover; contains a coverless comic on inside with 1st & last page missing. There is proof of at least limited news-stand distribution. #2 cover proof only sold in 2005 for $4,000.*

DOUBLE COMICS
Elliot Publications: 1940 - 1944 (132 pgs.)
1940 issues; Masked Marvel-c & The Mad Mong vs. The White Flash covers known 300 600 900 2010 3505 5000
1941 issues; Tornado Tim-c, Nordac-c, & Green Light covers known 200 400 600 1280 2190 3100
1942 issues 145 290 435 921 1586 2250
1943,1944 issues 123 246 369 787 1344 1900
NOTE: *Double Comics consisted of an almost endless combination of pairs of remaindered, unsold issues of comics representing most publishers and usually mixed publishers in the same book; e.g., a Captain America with a Silver Streak, or a Feature with a Detective, etc., could appear inside the same cover. The actual contents would have to determine its price. Prices listed are for average contents. Any containing rare origin or first issues are worth much more. Covers also vary in same year. Value would be approximately 50 percent of contents.*

DOUBLE-CROSS (See The Crusaders)

DOUBLE-DARE ADVENTURES
Harvey Publications: Dec, 1966 - No. 2, Mar, 1967 (35¢/25¢, 68 pgs.)
1-Origin Bee-Man, Glowing Gladiator, & Magic-Master; Simon/Kirby-a 6 12 18 37 66 95
2-Torres-a; r/Alarming Adv. #3('63) 4 8 12 28 47 65
NOTE: ***Powell*** *a-1.* ***Simon/Sparling*** *c-1, 2.*

DOUBLE DRAGON
Marvel Comics: July, 1991 - No. 6, Dec, 1991 ($1.00, limited series)
1-6: Based on video game. 2-Art Adams-c 3.00

DOUBLE EDGE
Marvel Comics: Alpha, 1995; Omega, 1995 ($4.95, limited series)
Alpha ($4.95)- Punisher story, Nick Fury app. 5.00
Omega ($4.95)-Punisher, Daredevil, Ghost Rider app. Death of Nick Fury 5.00

DOUBLE IMAGE
Image Comics: Feb, 2001 - No. 5, July, 2001 ($2.95)
1-5: 1-Flip covers of Codeflesh (Casey-s/Adlard-a) and The Bod (Young-s). 2-Two covers. 5-"Trust in Me" begins; Chaudhary-a 3.00

DOUBLE LIFE OF PRIVATE STRONG, THE
Archie Publications/Radio Comics: June, 1959 - No. 2, Aug, 1959
1-Origin & re-intro The Shield; Simon & Kirby-c/a, their re-entry into the super-hero genre; intro./1st app. The Fly; 1st S.A. super-hero for Archie Publ. 30 60 90 216 483 750
2-S&K-c/a; Tuska-a; The Fly app. (2nd or 3rd?) 18 36 54 124 275 425

DOUBLE TROUBLE
St. John Publishing Co.: Nov, 1957 - No. 2, Jan-Feb, 1958
1,2: Tuffy & Snuffy by Frank Johnson; dubbed "World's Funniest Kids" 6 12 18 31 38 45

DOUBLE TROUBLE WITH GOOBER
Dell Publishing Co.: No. 417, Aug, 1952 - No. 556, May, 1954
Four Color 417 5 10 15 33 57 80
Four Color 471,516,556 4 8 12 27 44 60

DOUBLE UP COMICS
Elliott Publications: 1941 (Pocket size, 192 pgs., 10¢)
1-Contains rebound copies of digest sized issues of Pocket Comics, Speed Comics, & Spitfire Comics; Japanese WWII-c 155 310 465 992 1696 2400

DOVER & CLOVER (See All Funny & More Fun Comics #93)

DOVER BOYS (See Adventures of the...)

DOVER THE BIRD
Famous Funnies Publishing Co.: Spring, 1955
1-Funny animal; code approved 7 14 21 35 43 50

DOWN
Image Comics (Top Cow): Dec, 2005 - No. 4, Mar, 2006 ($2.99)
1-4-Warren Ellis-s. 1-Tony Harris-a/c. 2-4-Cully Hamner-a 3.00
Down & Top Cow's Best of Warren Ellis TPB (6/06, $15.99) r/#1-4 & Tales of the Witchblade #3,4; Ellis-s; script for Down #1 with Harris sketch pages 16.00

DOWN WITH CRIME
Fawcett Publications: Nov, 1952 - No. 7, Nov, 1953
1 37 74 111 222 361 500
2,4,5: 2,4-Powell-a in each. 5-Bondage-c 19 38 57 111 176 240
3-Used in **POP**, pg. 106; "H is for Heroin" drug story 21 42 63 126 206 285
6,7: 6-Used in **POP**, pg. 80 18 36 54 105 165 225

DO YOU BELIEVE IN NIGHTMARES?
St. John Publishing Co.: Nov, 1957 - No. 2, Jan, 1958

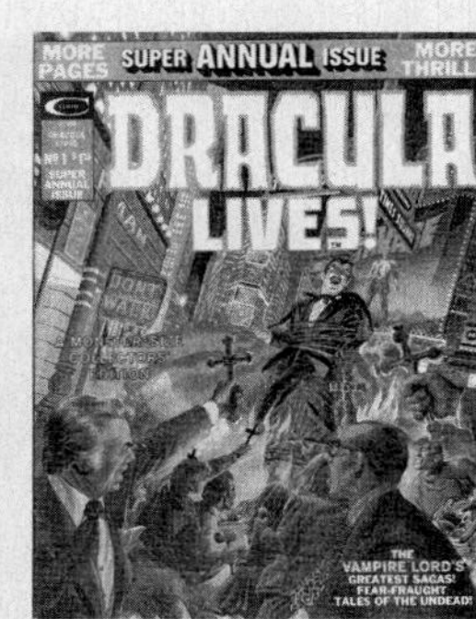

Dracula Lives! #1 © MAR

The Dragon #5 © Erik Larsen

Dragon Age #2 © EA

	GD 2.0	VG 4.0	FN 6.0	VF 8.0	VF/NM 9.0	NM- 9.2
1-Mostly Ditko-c/a	60	120	180	381	653	925
2-Ayers-a	36	72	108	211	343	475

D.P. 7
Marvel Comics Group (New Universe): Nov, 1986 - No. 32, June, 1989

1-20, 3.00
21-32-Low print 4.00
Annual #1 (11/87)-Intro. The Witness 4.00
... Classic Vol. 1 TPB (2007, $24.99) r/#1-9; Mark Gruenwald-s/Paul Ryan-a in all 25.00
NOTE: *Williamson a-9i, 11i; c-9i.*

DRACULA (See Bram Stoker's Dracula, Giant-Size..., Little Dracula, Marvel Graphic Novel, Requiem for Dracula, Spider-Man Vs...., Stoker's..., Tomb of... & Wedding of...; also see Movie Classics under Universal Presents as well as Dracula)

DRACULA (See Movie Classics for #1)(Also see Frankenstein & Werewolf)
Dell Publ. Co.: No. 2, 11/66 - No. 4, 3/67; No. 6, 7/72 - No. 8, 7/73 (No #5)

	GD	VG	FN	VF	VF/NM	NM-
2-Origin & 1st app. Dracula (11/66) (super hero)	4	8	12	28	47	65
3,4: 4-Intro. Fleeta ('67)	3	6	9	19	30	40
6-('72)-r/#2 w/origin	3	6	9	15	21	26
7,8-r/#3, #4	2	4	6	11	16	20

DRACULA (Magazine)
Warren Publishing Co.: 1979 (120 pgs., full color)

	GD	VG	FN	VF	VF/NM	NM-
Book 1-Maroto art; Spanish material translated into English (mail order only)	6	12	18	37	66	95

DRACULA
Marvel Comics: Jul, 2010 - No. 4, Sept, 2010 ($3.99, limited series)

1-4-Colored reprint of Bram Stoker's Classic Dracula adapt. from Dracula Lives!, Legion of Monsters and Stoker's Dracula; Thomas-s/Giordano-a; J. Djurdjevic-c 4.00

DRACULA CHRONICLES
Topps Comics: Apr, 1995 - No. 3, June, 1995 ($2.50, limited series)

1-3-Linsner-c 3.00

DRACULA LIVES! (Magazine)(Also see Tomb of Dracula) (Reprinted in Stoker's Dracula)
Marvel Comics Group: 1973(no month) - No. 13, July, 1975 (75¢, B&W) (76 pgs.)

	GD	VG	FN	VF	VF/NM	NM-
1-Boris painted-c	8	16	24	51	96	140
2 (7/73)-1st time origin Dracula; Adams, Starlin-a	5	10	15	31	53	75
3-1st app. Robert E. Howard's Soloman Kane; Adams-c/a	5	10	15	31	53	75
4,5: 4-Ploog-a. 5(V2#1)-Bram Stoker's Classic Dracula adapt. begins	4	8	12	23	37	50
6-9: 6-8-Bram Stoker adapt. 9-Bondage-c	4	8	12	23	37	50
10 (1/75)-16 pg. Lilith solo (1st?)	4	8	12	27	44	60
11-13: 11-21 pg. Lilith solo sty. 12-31 pg. Dracula sty	4	8	12	23	37	50
Annual 1(Summer, 1975, $1.25, 92 pgs.)-Morrow painted-c; 6 Dracula stys. 25 pgs. Adams-a(r)	4	8	12	25	40	55

NOTE: ***N. Adams** a-2, 3i, 10i, Annual 1r(2, 3i). **Alcala** a-9. **Buscema** a-3p, 6p, Annual 1p. **Colan** a(p)-1, 2, 5, 6, 8. **Evans** a-7. **Gulacy** a-9. **Heath** a-1r, 13. **Pakula** a-6r. Sutton a-13. **Weiss** r-Annual 1p. 4 **Dracula** stories each in 1, 609; 3 **Dracula** stories each in 2, 4, 5,, 13.*

DRACULA: LORD OF THE UNDEAD
Marvel Comics: Dec, 1998 - No. 3, Dec, 1998 ($2.99, limited series)

1-3-Olliffe & Palmer-a 3.00

DRACULA: RETURN OF THE IMPALER
Slave Labor Graphics: July, 1993 - No. 4, Oct, 1994 ($2.95, limited series)

1-4 3.00

DRACULA'S REVENGE
IDW Publishing: Apr, 2004 - No. 3 ($3.99, limited series)

1,2-Forbeck-s/Kudranski-a 4.00

DRACULA: THE COMPANY OF MONSTERS
BOOM! Studios: Aug, 2010 - No. 12, Jul, 2011 ($3.99)

1-12: 1-5-Busiek & Gregory-s/Godlewski-a. 1-Two covers by Brereton and Salas 4.00

DRACULA VERSUS ZORRO
Topps Comics: Oct, 1993 - No. 2, Nov, 1993 ($2.95, limited series)

1,2: 1-Spot varnish & red foil-c. 2-Polybagged w/16 pg. Zorro #0 4.00

DRACULA VERSUS ZORRO
Dark Horse Comics: Sept, 1998 - No. 2, Oct, 1998 ($2.95, limited series)

1,2 3.00

DRACULA: VLAD THE IMPALER (Also see Bram Stoker's Dracula)
Topps Comics: Feb, 1993 - No. 3, Apr, 1993 ($2.95, limited series)

1-3-Polybagged with 3 trading cards each; Maroto-c/a 4.00

DRAFT, THE
Marvel Comics: 1988 ($3.50, one-shot, squarebound)

1-Sequel to "The Pitt" 4.00

DRAFTED: ONE HUNDRED DAYS
Devil's Due Publishing: June, 2009 ($5.99, one-shot)

1-Barack Obama on a post-galactic-war Earth; Powers-s 6.00

DRAG 'N' WHEELS (Formerly Top Eliminator)
Charlton Comics: No. 30, Sept, 1968 - No. 59, May, 1973

	GD	VG	FN	VF	VF/NM	NM-
30	4	8	12	27	44	60
31-40-Scot Jackson begins	3	6	9	18	28	38
41-50	3	6	9	16	24	32
51-59: Scot Jackson	2	4	6	13	18	22

Modern Comics Reprint 58('78) 5.00

DRAGON, THE (Also see The Savage Dragon)
Image Comics (Highbrow Ent.): Mar, 1996 - No. 5, July, 1996 (99¢, lim. series)

1-5: Reprints Savage Dragon limited series w/new story & art. 5-Youngblood app; includes 5 pg. Savage Dragon story from 1984 3.00

DRAGON AGE (Based on the EA videogame)
IDW Publishing (EA Comics): Mar, 2010 - No. 6, Nov, 2010 ($3.99)

1-6-Orson Scott Card & Aaron Johnston-s; Ramos-c 4.00

DRAGON AGE: MAGEKILLER (Based on the EA videogame)
Dark Horse Comics: Dec, 2015 - No. 5, Apr, 2016 ($3.99, limited series)

1-3-Rucka-s/Carnero-a/Teng-c 4.00

DRAGON AGE: THOSE WHO SPEAK (Based on the EA videogame)
Dark Horse Comics: Aug, 2012 - No. 3, Nov, 2012 ($3.50, limited series)

1-3-Gaider-s/Hardin-a/Palumbo-c 3.50

DRAGON ARCHIVES, THE (Also see The Savage Dragon)
Image Comics: Jun, 1998 - No. 4, Jan, 1999 ($2.95, B&W)

1-4: Reprints early Savage Dragon app. 3.00

DRAGON BALL
Viz Comics: Mar, 1998 - Part 6: #2, Feb, 2003($2.95, B&W, Manga reprints read right to left)

	GD	VG	FN	VF	VF/NM	NM-
Part 1: 1-Akira Toriyama-s/a	2	4	6	8	10	12
2-12						6.00
1-12 (2nd & 3rd printings)						4.00
Part 2: 1-15: 15-($3.50-c)						5.00
Part 3: 1-14						4.00
Part 4: 1-10						4.00
Part 5: 1-7						4.00
Part 6: 1,2						4.00

DRAGON BALL Z
Viz Comics: Mar, 1998 - Part 5: #10, Oct, 2002 ($2.95, B&W, Manga reprints read right to left)

	GD	VG	FN	VF	VF/NM	NM-
Part 1: 1-Akira Toriyama-s/a	2	4	6	8	10	12
2-9						6.00
1-9 (2nd & 3rd printings)						4.00
Part 2: 1-14						5.00
Part 3: 1-10						4.00
Part 4: 1-15						4.00
Part 5: 1-10						4.00

DRAGON, THE: BLOOD & GUTS (Also see The Savage Dragon)
Image Comics (Highbrow Entertainment): Mar, 1995 - No. 3, May, 1995 ($2.50, lim. series)

1-3: Jason Pearson-c/a/scripts 3.00

DRAGON CHIANG
Eclipse Books: 1991 ($3.95, B&W, squarebound, 52 pgs.)

nn-Timothy Truman-c/a(p) 4.00

DRAGONFLIGHT
Eclipse Books: Feb, 1991 - No. 3, 1991 ($4.95, 52 pgs.)

Book One - Three: Adapts 1968 novel 5.00

DRAGONFLY (See Americomics #4)
Americomics: Sum, 1985 - No. 8, 1986 ($1.75/$1.95)

1 4.00
2-8 3.00

DRAGONFORCE
Aircel Publishing: 1988 - No. 13, 1989 ($2.00)

1-Dale Keown-c/a/scripts in #1-12 4.00
2-13: 13-No Keown-a 3.00

Dragon Lines #2 © MAR

Drax #3 © MAR

Dreaming Eagles #1 © Spitfire

	GD 2.0	VG 4.0	FN 6.0	VF 8.0	VF/NM 9.0	NM- 9.2

...Chronicles Book 1-5 ($2.95, B&W, 60 pgs.): Dale Keown-r/Dragonring & Dragonforce 4.00

DRAGONHEART (Movie)
Topps Comics: May, 1996 - No. 2, June, 1996 ($2.95/$4.95, limited series)
1-($2.95, 24 pgs.)-Adaptation of the film; Hildebrandt Bros-c; Lim-a. 3.00
2-($4.95, 64 pgs.) 5.00

DRAGONLANCE (Also see TSR Worlds)
DC Comics: Dec, 1988 - No. 34, Sept, 1991 ($1.25/$1.50, Mando paper)
1-Based on TSR game 4.00
2-34: Based on TSR game. 30-32-Kaluta-c 3.00

DRAGONLANCE: CHRONICLES
Devil's Due Publ.: Aug, 2005 - No. 8, Mar, 2006 ($2.95)
1-8-Dabb-s/Kurth-a 3.00
...: Dragons of Autumn Twilight TPB (2006, $17.95) r/#1-8 18.00

DRAGONLANCE: CHRONICLES (Volume 2)
Devil's Due Publ.: July, 2006 - No. 4, Jan, 2007 ($4.95/$4.99, 48 pgs.)
1-4-Dragons of Winter Night; Dabb-s/Kurth-a 5.00
...: Dragons of Winter Night TPB (3/07, $18.99) r/#1-4; cover gallery 19.00

DRAGONLANCE: CHRONICLES (Volume 3)
Devil's Due Publ.: Mar, 2007 - No. 12, ($3.50)
1-11-Dragons of Spring Dawning; Dabb-s/Cope-a 3.50

DRAGONLANCE: THE LEGEND OF HUMA
Devil's Due Publ.: Jan, 2004 - No. 6, Oct, 2005 ($2.95)
1-6-Mike Miller & Rael-a 3.00

DRAGON LINES
Marvel Comics (Epic Comics/Heavy Hitters): May, 1993 - No. 4, Aug, 1993 ($1.95, limited series)
1-($2.50)-Embossed-c; Ron Lim-c/a in all 4.00
2-4 3.00

DRAGON LINES: WAY OF THE WARRIOR
Marvel Comics (Epic Comics/ Heavy Hitters): Nov, 1993 - No. 2, Jan, 1994 ($2.25, limited series)
1,2-Ron Lim-c/a(p) 3.00

DRAGONQUEST
Silverwolf Comics: Dec, 1986 - No. 2, 1987 ($1.50, B&W, 28 pgs.)
1,2-Tim Vigil-c/a in all 5.00

DRAGONRING
Aircel Publishing: 1986 - V2#15, 1988 ($1.70/$2.00, B&W/color)
1-6: 6-Last B&W issue, V2#1-15($2.00, color) 3.00

DRAGON'S CLAWS
Marvel UK, Ltd.: July, 1988 - No. 10, Apr, 1989 ($1.25/$1.50/$1.75, British)
1-10: 3-Death's Head 1 pg. strip on back-c (1st app.). 4-Silhouette of Death's Head on last pg. 5-1st full app. new Death's Head 3.00

DRAGON'S LAIR: SINGE'S REVENGE (Based on the Don Bluth video game)
CrossGen Comics: Sept, 2003 - No. 3 ($2.95, limited series)
1-3-Mangels-s/Laguna-a 3.00

DRAGONSLAYER (Movie)
Marvel Comics Group: October, 1981 - No. 2, Nov, 1981
1,2-Paramount Disney movie adaptation 4.00

DRAGOON WELLS MASSACRE
Dell Publishing Co.: No. 815, June, 1957

	GD	VG	FN	VF	VF/NM	NM-
Four Color 815-Movie, photo-c	7	14	21	46	86	125

DRAGSTRIP HOTRODDERS (World of Wheels No. 17 on)
Charlton Comics: Sum, 1963; No. 2, Jan, 1965 - No. 16, Aug, 1967

	GD	VG	FN	VF	VF/NM	NM-
1	6	12	18	41	76	110
2-5	4	8	12	25	40	55
6-16	3	6	9	21	33	45

DRAIN
Image Comics: Nov, 2006 - No. 6, Mar, 2008 ($2.99)
1-6: 1-Cebulski-s/Takeda-a; two covers by Takeda and Finch 3.00
Vol. 1 TPB (2008, $16.99) r/#1-6; cover gallery and Takeda sketch art gallery 17.00

DRAKUUN
Dark Horse Comics: Feb, 1997 - No. 25, Mar, 1999 ($2.95, B&W, manga)
1-25; 1-6- Johji Manabe-s/a in all. Rise of the Dragon Princess series. 7-12-Revenge of Gustav. 13-18-Shadow of the Warlock. 19-25-The Hidden War 3.00

DRAMA
Sirius: June, 1994 ($2.95, mature)

	GD	VG	FN	VF	VF/NM	NM-
1-1st full color Dawn app. in comics	1	3	4	6	8	10
1-Limited edition (1400 copies); signed & numbered; fingerprint authenticity	3	6	9	16	23	30

NOTE: *Dawn's 1st full color app. was a pin-up in Amazing Heroes' Swimsuit Special #5.*

DRAMA OF AMERICA, THE
Action Text: 1973 ($1.95, 224 pgs.)

	GD	VG	FN	VF	VF/NM	NM-
1- "Students' Supplement to History"	1	3	4	6	8	10

DRAWING ON YOUR NIGHTMARES
Dark Horse Comics: Oct, 2003 ($2.99, one-shot)
1-Short stories; The Goon, Criminal Macabre, Tales of the Vampires; Templesmith-c 3.00

DRAX (Guardians of the Galaxy)
Marvel Comics: Jan, 2016 - No. 11, Nov, 2016 ($3.99)
1-11-CM Punk & Cullen Bunn-s/Hepburn-a. 1-Guardians app. 4,5-Fin Fang Foom app. 4.00

DRAX THE DESTROYER (Guardians of the Galaxy)
Marvel Comics: Nov, 2005 - No. 4, Feb, 2006 ($2.99, limited series)
1-4-Giffen-s/Breitweiser-a 5.00
...: Earthfall TPB (2006, $10.99) r/#1-4; character design page 11.00

DREADLANDS (Also see Epic)
Marvel Comics (Epic Comics): 1992 - No. 4, 1992 ($3.95, lim. series, 52 pgs.)
1-4: Stiff-c 4.00

DREADSTAR (See Epic Illustrated #3 for 1st app. and Eclipse Graphic Album Series #5)
Marvel Comics (Epic Comics)/First Comics No. 27 on: Nov, 1982 - No. 64, Mar, 1991

	GD	VG	FN	VF	VF/NM	NM-
1	2	4	6	8	10	12
2-5,8-49						4.00
6,7,51-64: 6,7-1st app. Interstellar Toybox; 8pgs. ea.; Wrightson-a. 51-64-Lower print run						5.00
50						6.00
Annual 1 (12/83)-r/The Price (Eclipse Graphic Album Series #5)						5.00

DREADSTAR
Malibu Comics (Bravura): Apr, 1994 - No. 6, Jan, 1995 ($2.50, limited series)
1-6-Peter David scripts: 1,2-Starlin-c 3.00
NOTE: *Issues 1-6 contain Bravura stamps.*

DREADSTAR AND COMPANY
Marvel Comics (Epic Comics): July, 1985 - No. 6, Dec, 1985
1-6: 1,3,6-New Starlin-a: 2-New Wrightson-c; reprints of Dreadstar series 3.00

DREAM BOOK OF LOVE (Also see A-1 Comics)
Magazine Enterprises: No. 106, June-July, 1954 - No. 123, Oct-Nov, 1954

	GD	VG	FN	VF	VF/NM	NM-
A-1 106 (#1)-Powell, Bolle-a; Montgomery Clift, Donna Reed photo-c	18	36	54	105	165	225
A-1-114 (#2)-Guardineer, Bolle-a; Piper Laurie, Victor Mature photo-c	14	28	42	80	115	150
A-1 123 (#3)-Movie photo-c	13	26	39	74	105	135

DREAM BOOK OF ROMANCE (Also see A-1 Comics)
Magazine Enterprises: No. 92, 1954 - No. 124, Oct-Nov, 1954

	GD	VG	FN	VF	VF/NM	NM-
A-1 92 (#5)-Guardineer-a; photo-c	16	32	48	94	147	200
A-1 101 (#6)(4-6/54)-Marlon Brando photo-c; Powell, Bolle, Guardineer-a	34	68	102	199	325	450
A-1 109,110,124: 109 (#7)(7-8/54)-Powell-a; movie photo-c. 110 (#8)(1/54)-Movie photo-c. 124 (#9)(10-11/54)	13	26	39	74	105	135

DREAMER, THE
Kitchen Sink Press: 1986 ($6.95, B&W, graphic novel)
nn-Will Eisner-s/a 15.00
DC Comics Reprint ($7.95, 6/00) 8.00

DREAMERY, THE
Eclipse Comics: Dec, 1986 - No. 14, Feb, 1989 ($2.00, B&W, Baxter paper)
1-14: 2-7-Alice In Wonderland adapt. 3.00

DREAMING, THE (See Sandman, 2nd Series)
DC Comics (Vertigo): June, 1996 - No. 60, May, 2001 ($2.50)
1-McKean-c on all.; LaBan scripts & Snejbjerg-a 4.00
2-30,32-60: 2,3-LaBan scripts & Snejbjerg-a. 4-7-Hogan scripts; Parkhouse-a. 8-Zulli-a. 9-11-Talbot-s/Taylor-a(p). 41-Previews Sandman: The Dream Hunters. 50-Hempel, Fegredo, McManus, Totleben-a 3.00
31-($3.95) Art by various 4.00

Dream Thief #1 © Nitz & Smallwood

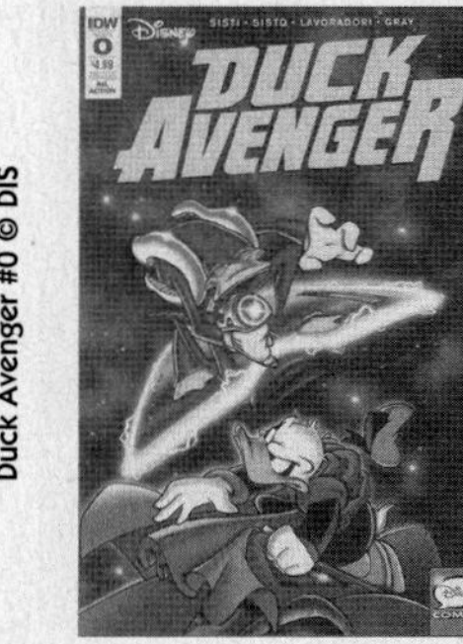

Duck Avenger #0 © DIS

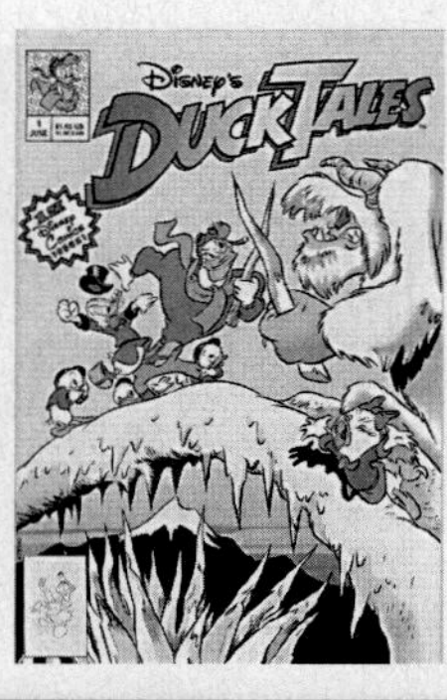

Ducktales #1 © DIS

	GD 2.0	VG 4.0	FN 6.0	VF 8.0	VF/NM 9.0	NM- 9.2

...Beyond The Shores of Night TPB ('97, $19.95) r/#1-8 — 20.00
...Special (7/98, $5.95, one-shot) Trial of Cain — 6.00
...Through The Gates of Horn and Ivory TPB ('99, $19.95) r/#15-19,22-25 — 20.00

DREAMING EAGLES
AfterShock Comics: Dec, 2015 - No. 6, Jun, 2016 ($3.99)

1-6-Ennis-s/Coleby-a; Tuskegee Airmen in WWII — 4.00

DREAM OF LOVE
I. W. Enterprises: 1958 (Reprints)

	GD	VG	FN	VF	VF/NM	NM-
1,2,8: 1-r/Dream Book of Love #1; Bob Powell-a. 2-r/Great Lover's Romances #10. 8-Great Lover's Romances #1; also contains 2 Jon Juan stories by Siegel & Schomburg; Kinstler-c.	3	6	9	14	20	25
9-Kinstler-c; 1pg. John Wayne interview & Frazetta illo from John Wayne Adv. Comics #2	3	6	9	14	20	25

DREAM POLICE
Marvel Comics (Icon): Aug, 2005 ($3.99)

1-Straczynski-s/Deodato-a/c — 4.00

DREAM POLICE
Image Comics (Joe's Comics): Apr, 2014 - No. 12, Sept, 2016 ($2.99)

1-12-Straczynski-s/Kotian-a — 3.00

DREAMS OF THE DARKCHYLDE
Darkchylde Entertainment: Oct, 2000 - No. 6, Sept, 2001 ($2.95)

1-6-Randy Queen-s in all. 1-Brandon Peterson-c/a — 3.00

DREAM TEAM (See Battlezones: Dream Team 2)
Malibu Comics (Ultraverse): July, 1995 ($4.95, one-shot)

1-Pin-ups teaming up Marvel & Ultraverse characters by various artists including Allred, Romita, Darrow, Balent, Quesada & Palmiotti — 5.00

DREAM THIEF
Dark Horse Comics: May, 2013 - No. 5, Sept, 2013 ($3.99, limited series)

1-5-Nitz-s/Smallwood-a. 1-Alex Ross-c. 2-Ryan Sook-c. 4-Dan Brereton-c — 4.00

DREAM THIEF: ESCAPE
Dark Horse Comics: Jun, 2014 - No. 4, Sept, 2014 ($3.99, limited series)

1-4-Nitz-s/Smallwood-c. 1,2-Smallwood-a. 3,4-Galusha-a — 4.00

DREAMWAVE PRODUCTIONS PREVIEW
Dreamwave Productions: May, 2002 ($1.00, one-shot)

nn-Previews Arkanium, Transformers: The War Within and other series — 3.00

DRESDEN FILES (See Jim Butcher's...)

DRIFTER
Image Comics: Nov, 2014 - Present ($3.50/$3.99)

1-17-Ivan Brandon-s/Nic Klein-a; multiple covers on each. 15-Start $3.99-c — 4.00

DRIFT FENCE (See Zane Grey 4-Color 270)

DRIFT MARLO
Dell Publishing Co.: May-July, 1962 - No. 2, Oct-Dec, 1962 (Painted-c)

	GD	VG	FN	VF	VF/NM	NM-
01-232-207 (#1)	5	10	15	30	50	70
2 (12-232-212)	4	8	12	27	44	60

DRISCOLL'S BOOK OF PIRATES
David McKay Publ. (Not reprints): 1934 (B&W, hardcover; 124 pgs, 7x9")

	GD	VG	FN	VF	VF/NM	NM-
nn-"Pieces of Eight" strip by Montford Amory	26	52	78	154	252	350

DRIVER: CROSSING THE LINE (Based on the Ubisoft videogame)
DC Comics: Oct, 2011 ($2.99, one-shot)

1-David Lapham-s/Greg Scott-a/ Jock-c; bonus character design art — 3.00

DROIDS (Based on Saturday morning cartoon) (Also see Dark Horse Comics)
Marvel Comics (Star Comics): April, 1986 - No. 8, June, 1987

	GD	VG	FN	VF	VF/NM	NM-
1-R2D2 & C-3PO from Star Wars app. in all	2	4	6	11	16	20
2-8: 2,5,7,8-Williamson-a(i)	2	4	6	8	10	12

NOTE: *Romita a-3p. Sinnott a-3i.*

DRONES
IDW Publishing: Apr, 2015 - No. 5, Aug, 2015 ($3.99, limited series)

1-5-Chris Lewis-s/Bruno Oliveira-a — 4.00

DROOPY (see Tom & Jerry #60)

DROOPY (Tex Avery's...)
Dark Horse Comics: Oct, 1995 - No. 3, Dec, 1995 ($2.50, limited series)

1-3: Characters created by Tex Avery; painted-c — 3.00

DROPSIE AVENUE: THE NEIGHBORHOOD
Kitchen Sink Press: June, 1995 ($15.95/$24.95, B&W)

nn-Will Eisner (softcover) — 18.00
nn-Will Eisner (hardcover) — 30.00

DROWNED GIRL, THE
DC Comics (Piranha Press): 1990 ($5.95, 52 pgs, mature)

nn — 6.00

DRUG WARS
Pioneer Comics: 1989 ($1.95)

1-Grell-c — 3.00

DRUID
Marvel Comics: May, 1995 - No. 4, Aug, 1995 ($2.50, limited series)

1-4: Warren Ellis scripts. — 3.00

DRUM BEAT
Dell Publishing Co.: No. 610, Jan, 1955

	GD	VG	FN	VF	VF/NM	NM-
Four Color 610-Movie, Alan Ladd photo-c	8	16	24	54	102	150

DRUMS OF DOOM
United Features Syndicate: 1937 (25¢)(Indian)(Text w/color illos.)

	GD	VG	FN	VF	VF/NM	NM-
nn-By Lt. F.A. Methot; Golden Thunder app.; Tip Top Comics ad in comic; nice-c	40	80	120	246	411	575

DRUNKEN FIST
Jademan Comics: Aug, 1988 - No. 54, Jan, 1993 ($1.50/$1.95, 68 pgs.)

1 — 5.00
2-50 — 4.00
51-54 — 4.00

DUCK ALBUM (See Donald Duck Album)
Dell Publishing Co.: No. 353, Oct, 1951 - No. 840, Sept, 1957

	GD	VG	FN	VF	VF/NM	NM-
Four Color 353 (#1)-Barks-c; 1st Uncle Scrooge-c (also appears on back-c).	10	20	30	69	147	225
Four Color 450-Barks-c	8	16	24	51	96	140
Four Color 492,531,560,586,611,649,686,	7	14	21	44	82	120
Four Color 726,782,840	6	12	18	37	66	95

DUCK AVENGER
IDW Publishing: No. 0, Aug, 2016; Oct, 2016 - Present ($4.99/$5.99)

0-Reprints of Italian Donald Duck costumed super-hero stories — 5.00
1,3-($5.99) Three covers. 1-(10/16) Red Raider app. — 6.00
2-($4.99) Three covers; Xadhoom app. — 5.00

DUCKMAN
Dark Horse Comics: Sept, 1990 ($1.95, B&W, one-shot)

1-Story & art by Everett Peck — 4.00

DUCKMAN
Topps Comics: Nov, 1994 - No. 5, May, 1995; No. 0, Feb, 1996 ($2.50)

0 (2/96, $2.95, B&W)-r/Duckman #1 from Dark Horse Comics — 3.00
1-5: 1-w/ coupon #A for Duckman trading card. 2-w/Duckman 1st season episode guide — 3.00

DUCKMAN: THE MOB FROG SAGA
Topps Comics: Nov, 1994 - No. 3, Feb, 1995 ($2.50, limited series)

1-3: 1-w/coupon #B for Duckman trading card, S. Shaw!-c — 3.00

DUCKTALES
Gladstone Publ.: Oct, 1988 - No. 13, May, 1990 (1,2,9-11: $1.50; 3-8: 95¢)

1-Barks-r — 6.00
2-11: 2-7,9-11-Barks-r — 4.00
12,13 ($1.95, 68 pgs.)-Barks-r; 12-r/F.C. #495 — 5.00
Disney Presents Carl Barks' Greatest DuckTales Stories Vol. 1 (Gemstone Publ., 2006, $10.95) r/stories adapted for the animated TV series including "Back to the Klondike" — 11.00
Disney Presents Carl Barks' Greatest DuckTales Stories Vol. 2 (Gemstone Publ., 2006, $10.95) r/stories adapted for the animated TV series; "Robot Robbers" app. — 11.00

DUCKTALES (TV)
Disney Comics: June, 1990 - No. 18, Nov, 1991 ($1.50)

1-All new stories; Marv Wolfman-s — 4.00
2-18 — 3.00
Disney's DuckTales by Marv Wolfman: Scrooge's Quest TPB (Gemstone, 9/07, $15.99) r/#1-7; intro. by Wolfman — 16.00
Disney's DuckTales: The Gold Odyssey TPB (Gemstone, 10/08, $15.99) — 16.00
The Movie nn (1990, $7.95, 68 pgs.)-Graphic novel adapting animated movie — 8.00

DUCKTALES (TV)
Boom Entertainment (KABOOM!): May, 2011 - No. 4, Aug, 2011 ($3.99)

Dumbo FC #668 © DIS

Durango Kid #28 © ME

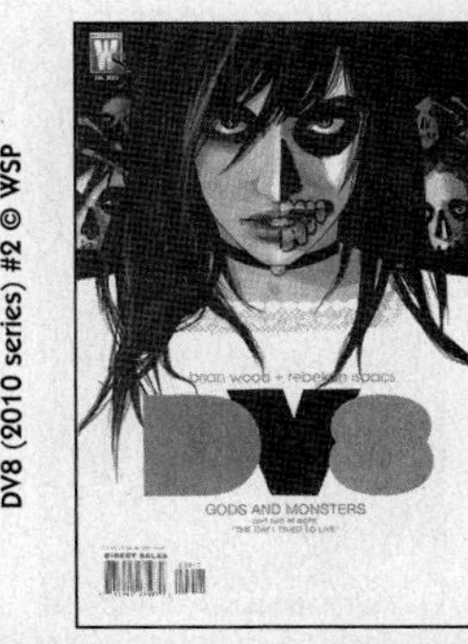

DV8 (2010 series) #2 © WSP

GD 2.0 | VG 4.0 | FN 6.0 | VF 8.0 | VF/NM 9.0 | NM- 9.2

1-6: 1-4-Three covers on each; Spector-s/Massaroli-a. 5,6-Two covers; Crossover with Darkwing Duck #17,18 4.00

DUDLEY (Teen-age)
Feature/Prize Publications: Nov-Dec, 1949 - No. 3, Mar-Apr, 1950

1-By Boody Rogers 19 38 57 111 176 240
2,3 12 24 36 67 94 120

DUDLEY DO-RIGHT (TV)
Charlton Comics: Aug, 1970 - No. 7, Aug, 1971 (Jay Ward)

1 8 16 24 52 99 145
2-7 6 12 18 37 66 95

DUEL MASTERS (Based on a trading card game)
Dreamwave Productions: Nov, 2003 - No. 8, Sept, 2004 ($2.95)

1-8: 1-Bagged with card; Augustyn-s 3.00

DUKE NUKEM: GLORIOUS BASTARD (Based on the video game)
IDW Publishing: Jul, 2011 - No. 4, Nov, 2011 ($3.99)

1-4: 1-Three covers; Waltz-s/Xermanico-a 4.00

DUKE OF THE K-9 PATROL
Gold Key: Apr, 1963

1 (10052-304) 4 8 12 23 37 50

DUMBO (Disney; see Movie Comics, & Walt Disney Showcase #12)
Dell Publishing Co.: No. 17, 1941 - No. 668, Jan, 1958

Four Color 17 (#1)-Mickey Mouse, Donald Duck, Pluto app. 274 548 822 1740 2995 4250
Large Feature Comic 19 ('41)-Part-r 4-Color 17 307 614 921 1950 3350 4750
Four Color 234 ('49) 13 26 39 89 195 300
Four Color 668 (12/55)-1st of two printings. Dumbo on-c with starry sky. Same-c as #234 10 20 30 66 138 210
Four Color 668 (1/58)-2nd printing. Same cover altered with Timothy Mouse added. Same contents 7 14 21 44 82 120

DUMBO COMIC PAINT BOOK (See Dumbo, Large Feature Comic No. 19)

DUNC AND LOO (#1-3 titled "Around the Block with Dunc and Loo")
Dell Publishing Co.: Oct-Dec, 1961 - No. 8, Oct-Dec, 1963

1 5 10 15 35 63 90
2 4 8 12 27 44 60
3-8 3 6 9 21 33 45

NOTE: *Written by* ***John Stanley; Bill Williams*** *art.*

DUNE (Movie)
Marvel Comics: Apr, 1985 - No. 3, June, 1985

1-3-r/Marvel Super Special; movie adaptation 4.00

DUNGEONS & DRAGONS
IDW Publishing: No. 0, Aug, 2010 - No. 15, Jan, 2012($1.00/$3.99)

0-(8/10, $1.00) Five covers; previews D&D series and Dark Sun mini-series 3.00
1-15: 1-(11/10, $3.99) Di Vito-a/Rogers-s; two covers. 2-Two covers 4.00
Annual 2012: Eberron (3/12, $7.99) Crilley-s/Diaz & Rojo-a 8.00
... 100 Page Spectacular (1/12, $7.99) Reprints by various incl. Duursema & Morales 8.00

DUNGEONS & DRAGONS: CUTTER
IDW Publishing: Apr, 2013 - No. 5, Sept, 2013 ($3.99)

1-5-R.A. & Geno Salvatore-s/Baldeon-a; 2 covers on each 4.00

DUNGEONS & DRAGONS: FORGOTTEN REALMS
IDW Publishing: Apr, 2012 - No. 5, Sept, 2012 ($3.99, limited series)

1-5-Greenwood-s/Ferguson-a 4.00
... 100 Page Spectacular (4/12, $7.99) Reprints by various incl. Rags Morales 8.00

DUNGEONS & DRAGONS: FROST GIANT'S FURY
IDW Publishing: Dec, 2016 - Present ($3.99, limited series)

1-Jim Zub-s/Netho Diaz-a 4.00

DUNGEONS & DRAGONS: LEGENDS OF BALDUR'S GATE
IDW Publishing: Oct, 2014 - No. 5, Feb, 2016 ($3.99, limited series)

1-5-Jim Zub-s/Max Dunbar-a 4.00
... #1 Greatest Hits Collection (4/16, $1.00) reprints #1 3.00

DUNGEONS & DRAGONS: SHADOWS OF THE VAMPIRE
IDW Publishing: Apr, 2016 - No. 5, Aug, 2016 ($4.99/$3.99, limited series)

1-($4.99) Jim Zub-s/Nelson Dániel-a; 4 covers 5.00
2-5-($3.99) Three covers on each 4.00

DUNGEONS & DRAGONS: THE LEGEND OF DRIZZT: NEVERWINTER TALES
IDW Publishing: Aug, 2011 - No. 5, Dec, 2011 ($3.99, limited series)

1-5-R.A. & Geno Salvatore-s/Agustin Padilla-a 4.00

DURANGO KID, THE (Also see Best of the West, Great Western & White Indian)
(Charles Starrett starred in Columbia's Durango Kid movies)
Magazine Enterprises: Oct-Nov, 1949 - No. 41, Oct-Nov, 1955 (All 36 pgs.)

1-Charles Starrett photo-c; Durango Kid & his horse Raider begin; Dan Brand & Tipi (origin) begin by Frazetta & continue through #16 74 148 222 470 810 1150
2-Starrett photo-c. 34 68 102 199 325 450
3-5-All have Starrett photo-c. 29 58 87 172 281 390
6-10: 7-Atomic weapon-c/story 16 32 48 94 147 200
11-16-Last Frazetta issue 14 28 42 80 115 150
17-Origin Durango Kid 16 32 48 94 147 200
18-30: 18-Fred Meagher-a on Dan Brand begins.19-Guardineer-c/a(3) begins, end #41. 23-Intro. The Red Scorpion 10 20 30 54 72 90
31-Red Scorpion returns 9 18 27 52 69 85
32-41-Bolle/Frazetta*ish*-a (Dan Brand; true in later issues?) 9 18 27 50 65 80

NOTE: *#6, 8, 14, 15 contain* ***Frazetta*** *art not reprinted in White Indian.* ***Ayers*** *c-18.* ***Guardineer*** *a(3)-19-41; c-19-41.* ***Fred Meagher*** *a-18-29 at least.*

DURANGO KID, THE
AC Comics: 1990 - #2, 1990 ($2.50,$2.75, half-color)

1,2: 1-Starrett photo front/back-c; Guardineer-r. 2-B&W)-Starrett photo-c; White Indian-r by Frazetta; Guardineer-r (50th anniversary of films) 3.00

DUSTCOVERS: THE COLLECTED SANDMAN COVERS 1989-1997
DC Comics (Vertigo): 1997 ($39.95, Hardcover)

Reprints Dave McKean's Sandman covers with Gaiman text 40.00
Softcover (1998, $24.95) 25.00

DUSTY STAR
Image Comics (Desperado Studios): No. 0, Apr, 1997 - No. 1 ($2.95, B&W)

0,1-Pruett-s/Robinson-a 3.00

DUSTY STAR
Image Comics (Desperado Publishing): June, 2006 ($3.50)

1-Pruett-s/Robinson-s/a 3.50

DV8 (See Gen 13)
Image Comics (WildStorm Productions): Aug, 1996 - No. 25, Dec, 1998;
DC Comics (WildStorm Prod.): No. 0, Apr, 1999 - No. 32, Nov, 1999 ($2.50)

1/2 6.00
1-Warren Ellis scripts & Humberto Ramos-c/a(p) 4.00
1-(7-variant covers, w/1 by Jim Lee) ...each 4.00
2-4: 3-No Ramos-a 3.00
5-32: 14-Regular-c, 14-Variant-c by Charest. 26-(5/99)-McGuinness-c 3.00
14-($3.50) Voyager Pack w/Danger Girl preview 5.00
0-(4/99, $2.95) Two covers (Rio and McGuinness) 3.00
Annual 1 (1/98, $2.95) 4.00
Annual 1999 ($3.50) Slipstream x-over with Gen13 4.00
Rave-(7/96, $1.75)-Ramos-c; pinups & interviews 3.00
...: Neighborhood Threat TPB (2002, $14.95) r/#1-6 & #1/2; Ellis intro.; Ramos-c 15.00

DV8: GODS AND MONSTERS
DC Comics (WildStorm): June, 2010 - No. 8, Jan, 2011 ($2.99, limited series)

1-8-Wood-s/Issacs-a 3.00
TPB (2011, $17.99) r/#1-8 18.00

DV8 VS. BLACK OPS
Image Comics (WildStorm): Oct, 1997 - No. 3, Dec, 1997 ($2.50, limited series)

1-3-Bury-s/Norton-a 3.00

DWIGHT D. EISENHOWER
Dell Publishing Co.: December, 1969

01-237-912 - Life story 4 8 12 28 47 65

DYNABRITE COMICS
Whitman Publishing Co.: 1978 - 1979 (69¢, 10x7-1/8", 48 pgs., cardboard-c)
(Blank inside covers)

11350 - Walt Disney's Mickey Mouse & the Beanstalk (4-C 157). 11350-1 - Mickey Mouse Album (4-C 1057, 1151,1246). 11351 - Mickey Mouse & His Sky Adventure (4-C 214, 343). 11354 - Goofy: A Gaggle of Giggles. 11354-1 - Super Goof Meets Super Thief. 11356 - (?). 11359 - Bugs Bunny-r. 11360 - Winnie the Pooh Fun and Fantasy (Disney-r).
each.... 2 4 6 9 12 15

11352 - Donald Duck (4-C 408, Donald Duck 45,52)-Barks-a. 11352-1 - Donald Duck (4-C 318, 10 pg. Barks/ WDC&S 125,128)-Barks-c(r). 11353 - Daisy Duck's Diary (4-C 1055,1150) Barks-a. 11355 - Uncle Scrooge (Barks-a/U.S. 12,33). 11355-1 - Uncle Scrooge (Barks-a/U.S. 13,16) - Barks-c(r). 11357 - Star Trek (r/-Star Trek 33,41). 11358 - Star Trek (r/-Star Trek 34,36). 11361 - Gyro Gearloose & the Disney Ducks (r/4-C 1047,1184)-Barks-c(r)
each.... 2 4 6 10 14 18

Dynamo 5 #10 © Faerber & Asrar

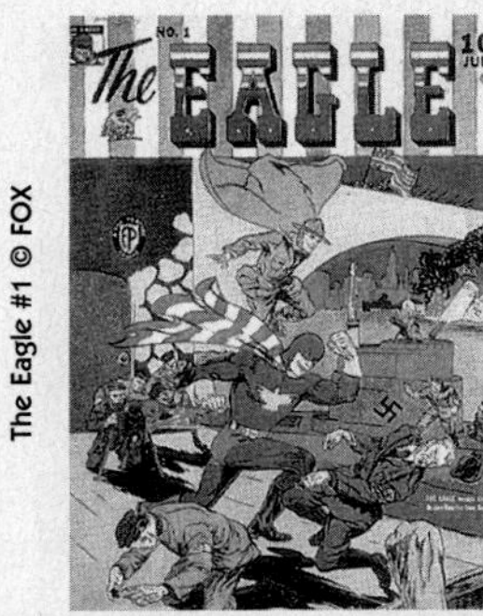

The Eagle #1 © FOX

Earth 2: Society #9 © DC

GD 2.0 VG 4.0 FN 6.0 VF 8.0 VF/NM 9.0 NM- 9.2

GD 2.0 VG 4.0 FN 6.0 VF 8.0 VF/NM 9.0 NM- 9.2

DYNAMIC ADVENTURES
I. W. Enterprises: No. 8, 1964 - No. 9, 1964

8-Kayo Kirby-r by Baker?/Fight Comics 53. 3 6 9 14 20 25
9-Reprints Avon's "Escape From Devil's Island"; Kinstler-c
3 6 9 16 23 30
nn (no date)-Reprints Risks Unlimited with Rip Carson, Senorita Rio; r/Fight #53
3 6 9 16 22 28

DYNAMIC CLASSICS (See Cancelled Comic Cavalcade)
DC Comics: Sept-Oct, 1978 (44 pgs.)

1-Neal Adams Batman, Simonson Manhunter-r 2 4 6 8 10 12

DYNAMIC COMICS (No #4-7)
Harry 'A' Chesler: Oct, 1941 - No. 3, Feb, 1942; No. 8, Mar, 1944 - No. 25, May, 1948

1-Origin Major Victory by Charles Sultan (reprinted in Major Victory #1), Dynamic Man & Hale the Magician; The Black Cobra only app.; Major Victory & Dynamic Man begin
245 490 735 1568 2684 3800
2-Origin Dynamic Boy & Lady Satan; intro. The Green Knight & sidekick Lance Cooper
142 284 426 909 1555 2200
3-1st small logo, resumes with #10 123 246 369 787 1344 1900
8-Classic-c; Dan Hastings, The Echo, The Master Key, Yankee Boy begin; Yankee Doodle Jones app.; hypo story 600 1200 1800 4000 6500 9000
9-Mr. E begins; Mac Raboy-c 116 232 348 742 1271 1800
10-Small logo begins 107 214 321 680 1165 1650
11-Classic-c 258 516 774 1651 2826 4000
12-16: 15-The Sky Chief app. 16-Marijuana story 71 142 213 454 777 1100
17(1/46)-Illustrated in **SOTI**, "The children told me what the man was going to do with the hot poker," but Wertham saw this in Crime Reporter #2
74 148 222 470 810 1150
18-Classic Airplanehead monster-c 71 142 213 454 777 1100
19-Classic puppeteer-c by Gattuso 71 142 213 454 777 1100
20-Bare-breasted woman-c 116 232 348 742 1271 1800
21-Dinosaur-c; new logo 53 106 159 334 567 800
22,25 47 94 141 296 498 700
23,24-(68 pgs.): 23-Yankee Girl app. 43 86 129 271 461 650
I.W. Reprint #1,8('64): 1-r/#23. 8-Exist? 3 6 9 17 26 35
NOTE: ***Kinstler** c-IW #1. **Tuska** art in many issues, #3, 9, 11, 12, 16, 19. Bondage c-16.*

DYNAMITE (Becomes Johnny Dynamite No. 10 on)
Comic Media/Allen Hardy Publ.: May, 1953 - No. 9, Sept, 1954

1-Pete Morisi-a; Don Heck-c; r-as Danger #6 41 82 123 256 428 600
2 22 44 66 132 216 300
3-Marijuana story; Johnny Dynamite (1st app.) begins by Pete Morisi(c/a); Heck text-a; man shot in face at close range 29 58 87 170 278 385
4-Injury-to-eye, prostitution; Morisi-c/a 26 52 78 154 252 350
5-9-Morisi-c/a in all. 7-Prostitute story & reprints 21 42 63 126 206 285

DYNAMO (Also see Tales of Thunder & T.H.U.N.D.E.R. Agents)
Tower Comics: Aug, 1966 - No. 4, June, 1967 (25¢)

1-Crandall/Wood, Ditko/Wood-a; Weed series begins; NoMan & Lightning cameos; Wood-c/a 8 16 24 54 105 150
2-4: Wood-c/a in all 5 10 15 34 60 85
NOTE: ***Adkins/Wood** a-2. **Ditko** a-4?. **Tuska** a-2, 3.*

DYNAMO 5 (See Noble Causes: Extended Family #2 for debut of Captain Dynamo)
Image Comics: Jan, 2007 - No. 25, Oct, 2009 ($3.50/$2.99)

1-Intro. the offspring of Captain Dynamo; Faerber-s/Asrar-a 8.00
2 5.00
3-7,11-24 : 5-Intro. Synergy. 13-Origin of Myriad. 21-Firebird app. 3.50
8-10-($2.99) 3.50
25-($4.99) Back-up short stories of team members 5.00
Annual #1 (4/08, $5.99) r/Captain Dynamo app. in Nobel Causes: Extended Family #2 and three new stories by Faerber & various; pin-up gallery 6.00
#0 (2/09, 99¢) short story leading into #20; text synopsis of story so far 3.00
...: Holiday Special 2010 (12/10, $3.99) Faerber-s/Takara-a 4.00
... Vol. 1: Post-Nuclear Family TPB (2007, $9.99) r/#1-7; Kirkman intro. 10.00
... Vol. 2: Moments of Truth TPB (2008, $14.99) r/#8-13 15.00

DYNAMO 5: SINS OF THE FATHER
Image Comics: Jun, 2010 - No. 5, Oct, 2010 ($3.99, limited series)

1-5-Faerber-s/Brilha-a. 2-4-Invincible app. 4.00

DYNAMO JOE (Also see First Adventures & Mars)
First Comics: May, 1986 - No. 15, Jan, 1988 (#12-15: $1.75)

1-15: 4-Cargonauts begin, Special 1(1/87)-Mostly-r/Mars 3.00

DYNOMUTT (TV)(See Scooby-Doo (3rd series))
Marvel Comics Group: Nov, 1977 - No. 6, Sept, 1978 (Hanna-Barbera)

1-The Blue Falcon, Scooby Doo in all 4 8 12 27 44 60
2-6-All newsstand only 3 6 9 17 26 35

EAGLE, THE (1st Series) (See Science Comics & Weird Comics #8)
Fox Features Syndicate: July, 1941 - No. 4, Jan, 1942

1-The Eagle begins; Rex Dexter of Mars app. by Briefer; all issues feature German war covers 226 452 678 1446 2473 3500
2-The Spider Queen begins (origin) 142 284 426 909 1555 2200
3,4: 3-Joe Spook begins (origin) 129 258 387 826 1413 2000

EAGLE COMICS (2nd Series)
Rural Home Publ.: Feb-Mar, 1945 - No. 2, Apr-May, 1945

1-Aviation stories 77 154 231 493 847 1200
2-Lucky Aces 34 68 102 199 325 450
NOTE: ***L. B. Cole** c/a in each.*

EAGLE RESURGENT
American Mythology: 2016 ($4.99, B&W)

1-New story; Vokes-a/Herman-s; back-up reprint with art by Vokes & Rankin 5.00

EARTH 4 (Also see Urth 4)
Continuity Comics: Dec, 1993 - No. 4, Jan, 1994 ($2.50)

1-4: 1-3 all listed as Dec, 1993 in indicia 3.00

EARTH 4 DEATHWATCH 2000
Continuity Comics: Apr, 1993 - No. 3, Aug, 1993 ($2.50)

1-3 3.00

EARTH MAN ON VENUS (An...) (Also see Strange Planets)
Avon Periodicals: 1951

nn-Wood-a (26 pgs.); Fawcette-c 161 322 483 1030 1765 2500

EARTH 2
DC Comics: Jul, 2012 - No. 32, May, 2015 ($3.99/$2.99)

1-($3.99) James Robinson-s/Nicola Scott-a/Ivan Reis-c; 4.00
1-Variant-c by Hitch 6.00
2-15-($2.99) 2-New Flash. 3-New Green Lantern. 4-New Atom 3.00
15.1, 15.2 (11/13, $2.99, regular covers) 3.00
15.1 (11/13, $3.99, 3-D cover) "Desaad #1" on cover; Levitz-s/Cinar-a 5.00
15.2 (11/13, $3.99, 3-D cover) "Solomon Grundy #1" on cover; Kindt-s/Lopresti-a 5.00
16-24,26-30: 16-Superman returns. 17-Batman returns. 20-Jae Lee-c. 28-Lobo app. 3.00
25-($3.99) New Superman revealed 4.00
#0 (11/12, $2.99) Superman, Batman, Wonder Woman, Terry Sloan app.; Giorello-a 3.00
Annual 1 (7/13, $4.99) Robinson-s/Cafu-a; new Batman app. 5.00
Annual 2 (3/14, $4.99) Taylor-s/Rocha-a; origin of new Batman 5.00
...: Futures End 1 (11/14, $2.99, regular-c) Five years later; Barrows-a 3.00
...: Futures End 1 (11/14, $3.99, 3-D cover) 4.00

EARTH 2: SOCIETY
DC Comics: Aug, 2015 - Present ($2.99)

1-21: 1-Johnny Sorrow app.; Dick Grayson as Batman. 4-Anarky app. 6-Intro. Hourman. 15-Tony Harris-a (8 pgs.) 3.00
Annual 1 (10/16, $4.99) Abnett-s/Redondo & Neves-a; The Ultra-Humanite app. 5.00

EARTH 2: WORLD'S END
DC Comics: Dec, 2014 - No. 26, Jun, 2015 ($2.99, weekly series)

1-25: 1-Prelude to Darkseid's first attack. 3,7,8,10-Constantine app. 3.00
26-($3.99) Andy Kubert-c; leads into Convergence #1 4.00

EARTHWORM JIM (TV, cartoon)
Marvel Comics: Dec, 1995 - No. 3, Feb, 1996 ($2.25)

1-3: Based on video game and toys 3.00

EARTH X
Marvel Comics: No. 0, Mar, 1999 - No. 12, Apr, 2000 ($3.99/$2.99, lim. series)

nn- (Wizard supplement) Alex Ross sketchbook; painted-c 6.00
Sketchbook (2/99) New sketches and previews 6.00
0-(3/99)-Prelude; Leon-a(p)/Ross-c 1 2 3 4 5 7
1-(4/99)-Leon-a(p)/Ross-c 1 2 3 4 5 7
1-2nd printing 4.00
2-12 4.00
#1/2 (Wizard) Nick Fury on cover; Reinhold-a 6.00
#X (6/00, $3.99) 4.00
... Trilogy Companion TPB (2008, $29.99) r/#1/2; artwork and content from the Earth X, Paradise X and Universe X series; gallery of variant covers and promotional art 30.00
HC (2005, $49.99) r/#0,1-12, #1/2, X; foreward by Joss Whedon; Ross sketch pages 50.00

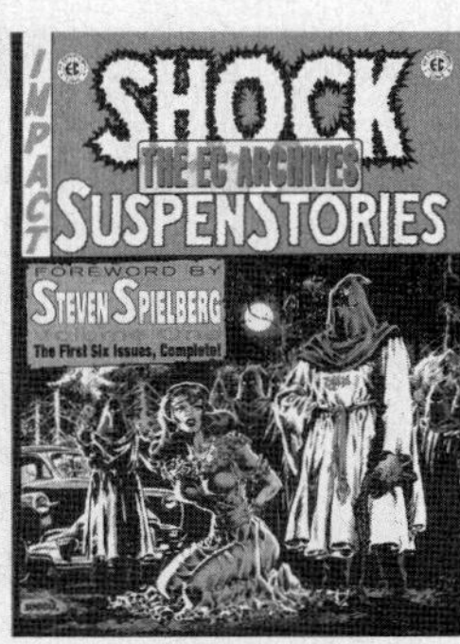

EC Archives Shocking SuspenStories Vol. 1 © WMG

Eclipse Graphic Album #14 © ECL

Eclipso #11 © DC

	GD	VG	FN	VF	VF/NM	NM-
	2.0	4.0	6.0	8.0	9.0	9.2

TPB (12/00, $24.95) r/#0,1-12, X; foreward by Joss Whedon 25.00

EASTER BONNET SHOP (See March of Comics No. 29)

EASTER WITH MOTHER GOOSE
Dell Publishing Co.: No. 103, 1946 - No. 220, Mar, 1949

	GD	VG	FN	VF	VF/NM	NM-
Four Color 103 (#1)-Walt Kelly-a	17	34	51	117	259	400
Four Color 140 ('47)-Kelly-a	13	26	39	91	201	310
Four Color 185 ('48), 220-Kelly-a	12	24	36	82	179	275

EAST MEETS WEST
Innovation Publishing: Apr, 1990 - No. 2, 1990 ($2.50, limited series, mature)

1,2: 1-Stevens part-i; Redondo-c(i). 2-Stevens-c(i); 1st app. Cheech & Chong in comics 3.00

EAST OF WEST
Image Comics: Mar, 2013 - Present ($3.50/$3.99)

1-Hickman-s/Dragotta-a 6.00
2-26-Hickman-s/Dragotta-a 3.50
27-31-($3.99) 4.00
... : The World (12/14, $3.99) Source book for characters, events, settings, timelines 4.00

EC ARCHIVES
Gemstone Publishing/Dark Horse Books: 2006 - Present ($49.95/$49.99, hardcover with dustjacket)

Crime SuspenStories Vol. 1 - Recolored reprints of #1-6; foreward by Max Allan Collins 50.00
Frontline Combat Vol. 1 - Recolored reprints of #1-6; foreward by Henry G. Franke III 50.00
Haunt of Fear Vol. 1 - Recolored reprints of #15-17,4-6; foreward by Robert Englund 50.00
Haunt of Fear Vol. 2 - Recolored reprints of #7-12; foreward by Tim Sullivan 50.00
Panic Vol. 1 - Recolored reprints of #1-6; foreward by Bob Fingerman 50.00
Shock SuspenStories Vol. 1 - Recolored reprints of #1-6; foreward by Steven Spielberg 50.00
Shock SuspenStories Vol. 2 - Recolored reprints of #7-12; foreward by Dean Kamen 50.00
Shock SuspenStories Vol. 3 - Recolored reprints of #13-18; foreward by Brian Bendis 50.00
Tales From the Crypt Vol. 1 - Recolored reprints of Crypt of Terror #17-19 and Tales From the Crypt #20-22; foreward by John Carpenter; Al Feldstein behind-the-scenes info 100.00
Tales From the Crypt Vol. 2 - Recolored reprints of #23-28; foreward by Joe Dante 50.00
Tales From the Crypt Vol. 3 - Recolored reprints of #29-34; foreward by Bob Overstreet 50.00
Tales From the Crypt Vol. 4 - (DH) Recolored reprints of #35-40; foreward by Russ Cochran 50.00
Tales From the Crypt Vol. 5 - (DH) Recolored reprints of #41-46; foreward by Bruce Campbell 50.00
Two-Fisted Tales Vol. 1 - Recolored reprints of #18-23; foreward by Stephen Geppi 50.00
Two-Fisted Tales Vol. 2 - Recolored reprints of #24-29; foreward by Rocco Versaci, Ph.D. 50.00
Two-Fisted Tales Vol. 3 - (DH) Recolored reprints of #30-35; foreward by Joe Kubert 50.00
Vault of Horror Vol. 1 - Recolored reprints of #12-17; foreward by R.L. Stine 50.00
Vault of Horror Vol. 2 - Recolored reprints of #18-23; foreward by John Landis 80.00
Vault of Horror Vol. 3 - (DH) Recolored reprints of #24-29; foreward by Mike Richardson 50.00
Vault of Horror Vol. 4 - (DH) Recolored reprints of #30-35; foreward by Jonathan Maberry 50.00
Weird Fantasy Vol. 1 - (DH) Recolored reprints of #13-17; foreward by Walt Simonson 50.00
Weird Science Vol. 1 - Recolored reprints of #1-6; foreward by George Lucas 75.00
Weird Science Vol. 2 - Recolored reprints of #7-12; foreward by Paul Levitz 50.00
Weird Science Vol. 3 - Recolored reprints of #13-18; foreward by Jerry Weist 50.00

E. C. CLASSIC REPRINTS
East Coast Comix Co.: May, 1973 - No. 12, 1976 (E.C. Comics reprinted in color minus ads)

	GD	VG	FN	VF	VF/NM	NM-
1-The Crypt of Terror #1 (Tales from the Crypt #46)	2	4	6	11	16	20
2-12: 2-Weird Science #15('52). 3-Shock SuspenStories #12. 4-Haunt of Fear #12. 5-Weird Fantasy #13('52). 6-Crime SuspenStories #25. 7-Vault of Horror #26. 8-Shock SuspenStories #6. 9-Two-Fisted Tales #34. 10-Haunt of Fear #23. 11-Weird Science 12(#1). 12-Shock SuspenStories #2	2	4	6	8	11	14

EC CLASSICS
Russ Cochran: Aug, 1985 - No. 12, 1986? (High quality paper; each-r 8 stories in color) (#2-12 were resolicited in 1990)($4.95, 56 pgs., 8x11")

	GD	VG	FN	VF	VF/NM	NM-
1-12: 1-Tales From the Crypt. 2-Weird Science. 3-Two-Fisted Tales (r/31); Frontline Combat (r/9). 4-Shock SuspenStories. 5-Weird Fantasy. 6-Vault of Horror. 7-Weird Science-Fantasy (r/23,24). 8-Crime SuspenStories (r/17,18). 9-Haunt of Fear (r/14,15). 10-Panic (r/1,2). 11-Tales From the Crypt (r/23,24). 12-Weird Science (r/20,22)	1	2	3	4	5	7

ECHO
Image Comics (Dreamwave Prod.): Mar, 2000 - No. 5, Sept, 2000 ($2.50)

1-5: 1-3-Pat Lee-c 3.00
0-(7/00) 3.00

ECHO
Abstract Studio: Mar, 2008 - No. 30, May, 2011 ($3.50)

1-Terry Moore-s/a/c 8.00
2-30 3.50
Terry Moore's Echo: Moon Lake TPB (2008, $15.95) r/#1-5; Moore sketch pages 16.00

ECHO OF FUTUREPAST
Pacific Comics/Continuity Com.: May, 1984 - No. 9, Jan, 1986 ($2.95, 52 pgs.)

1-9: Neal Adams-c/a in all? 6.00
NOTE: ***N. Adams*** *a-1-6,7i,9i; c-1-3, 5p,7i,8,9i.* ***Golden*** *a-1-6 (Bucky O'Hare); c-6.* ***Toth*** *a-6,7.*

ECLIPSE GRAPHIC ALBUM SERIES
Eclipse Comics: Oct, 1978 - 1989 (8-1/2x11") (B&W #1-5)

1-Sabre (10/78, B&W, 1st print.); Gulacy-a; 1st direct sale graphic novel 16.00
1-Sabre (2nd printing, 1/79) 8.00
1-Sabre (3rd printing, $5.95) 6.00
1-Sabre 30th Anniversary Edition (2008, $14.99, 9x6" HC) new McGregor & Gulacy intros. original script with sketch art 15.00
2,6,7: 2-Night Music (11/79, B&W)-Russell-a. 6-I Am Coyote (11/84, color)-Rogers-c/a. 7-The Rocketeer (2nd print, $7.95). 7-The Rocketeer (3rd print, 1991, $8.95) 10.00
3,4: 3-Detectives, Inc. (5/80, B&W, $6.95)-Rogers-a. 4-Stewart The Rat (1980, B&W) -G. Colan-a 10.00
5-The Price (10/81, B&W)-Starlin-a 20.00
7-The Rocketeer (9/85, color)-Dave Stevens-a (r/chapters 1-5)(see Pacific Presents & Starslayer); has 7 pgs. new-a 25.00
7-The Rocketeer, signed & limited HC 90.00
7-The Rocketeer, hardcover (1986, $19.95) 40.00
7-The Rocketeer, unsigned HC (3rd, $32.95) 33.00
8-Zorro In Old California ('86, color) 14.00
8,12-Hardcover 18.00
9,10: 9-Sacred And The Profane ('86)-Steacy-a. 10-Somerset Holmes ('86, $15.95)-Adults, soft-c 16.00
9,10,12-Hardcover ($24.95). 12-signed & #'d 25.00
11-Floyd Farland, Citizen of the Future ('87, $2.95, B&W) Chris Ware-s/a 15.00
12,28,31,35: 12-Silverheels ('87, $7.95, color). 28-Miracleman Book I ($5.95). 31-Pigeons From Hell by R. E. Howard (11/88). 35-Rael: Into The Shadow of the Sun ('88, $7.95) 10.00
13-The Sisterhood of Steel ('87, $8.95, color) 10.00
14,16,18,20,23,24: 14-Samurai, Son of Death ('87, $4.95, B&W). 16,18,20,23-See Airfighters Classics #1-4. 24-Heartbreak ($4.95, B&W) 7.00
14 (2nd pr.),17,21: 14-Samurai, Son of Death ($3.95, 2nd printing). 17-Valkyrie, Prisoner of the Past SC ('88, $3.95, color). 21-XYR-Multiple ending comic ('88, $3.95, B&W) 6.00
15,22,27: 15-Twisted Tales (11/87, color)-Dave Stevens-c. 22-Alien Worlds #1 (5/88, $3.95, 52 pgs.)-Nudity. 27-Fast Fiction (She) ($5.95, B&W) 8.00
17-Valkyrie, Prisoner of the Past S&N Hardcover ('88, $19.95) 25.00
19-Scout: The Four Monsters ('88, $14.95, color)-r/Scout #1-7; soft-c 15.00
25,30,32-34: 25-Alex Toth's Zorro Vol. 1 ,2($10.95, B&W). 30-Brought To Light; Alan Moore scripts ('89). 32-Teenaged Dope Slaves and Reform School Girls. 33-Bogie. 34-Air Fighters Classics #5 12.00
29-Real Love: Best of Simon & Kirby Romance Comics (10/88, $12.95) 15.00
30,31: Limited hardcover ed. ($29.95). 31-signed 30.00
36-Dr. Watchstop: Adventures in Time and Space ('89, $8.95) 10.00

ECLIPSE MAGAZINE (Becomes Eclipse Monthly)
Eclipse Publishing: May, 1981 - No. 8, Jan, 1983 ($2.95, B&W, magazine)

1-8: 1-1st app. Cap'n Quick and a Foozle by Rogers, Ms. Tree by Beatty, and Dope by Trina Robbins. 2-1st app. I Am Coyote by Rogers. 7-1st app. Masked Man by Boyer 4.00
NOTE: ***Colan*** *a-3, 5, 8.* ***Golden*** *c/a-2.* ***Gulacy*** *a-6, c-1, 6.* ***Kaluta*** *c/a-5.* ***Mayerik*** *a-2, 3.* ***Rogers*** *a-1-8.* ***Starlin*** *a-1.* ***Sutton*** *a-6.*

ECLIPSE MONTHLY
Eclipse Comics: Aug, 1983 - No. 10, Jul, 1984 (Baxter paper, $2.00/$1.50/$1.75)

1-10: ($2.00, 52 pgs.)-Cap'n Quick and a Foozle by Rogers, Static by Ditko, Dope by Trina Robbins, Rio by Wildey, The Masked Man by Boyer begin. 3-Ragamuffins begins 4.00
NOTE: ***Boyer*** *c-6.* ***Ditko*** *a-1-3.* ***Rogers*** *a-1-4; c-2, 4, 7.* ***Wildey*** *a-1, 2, 5, 9, 10; c-5, 10.*

ECLIPSO (See Brave and the Bold #64, House of Secrets #61 & Phantom Stranger, 1987)
DC Comics: Nov, 1992 - No. 18, Apr, 1994 ($1.25)

1-18: 1-Giffen plots/breakdowns begin. 10-Darkseid app. Creeper in #3-6,9,11-13. 18-Spectre-c/s 3.00
Annual 1 (1993, $2.50, 68 pgs.)-Intro Prism 4.00
...: The Music of the Spheres TPB (2009, $19.99) r/stories from Countdown to Mystery #1-8 20.00

ECLIPSO: THE DARKNESS WITHIN
DC Comics: July, 1992 - No. 2, Oct, 1992 ($2.50, 68 pgs.)

1,2: 1-With purple gem attached to-c, 1-Without gem; Superman, Creeper app., 2-Concludes Eclipso storyline from annuals 4.00

EC SAMPLER - FREE COMIC BOOK DAY
Gemstone Publishing: May, 2008

Reprinted stories with restored color from Weird Science #6, Two-Fisted Tales #22, Crypt of Terror #17, Shock Suspenstories #6 3.00

E. C. 3-D CLASSICS (See Three Dimensional...)

Eden's Fall #1 © TCOW

Edge of Doom #1 © Niles & Jones

Eerie #17 © AVON

GD VG FN VF VF/NM NM-
2.0 4.0 6.0 8.0 9.0 9.2

GD VG FN VF VF/NM NM-
2.0 4.0 6.0 8.0 9.0 9.2

ECTOKID (See Razorline)
Marvel Comics: Sept, 1993 - No. 9, May, 1994 ($1.75/$1.95)

1-($2.50)-Foil embossed-c; created by C. Barker 4.00
2-9: 2-Origin. 5-Saint Sinner x-over 3.00
...: Unleashed! 1 (10/94, $2.95, 52 pgs.) 4.00

ED "BIG DADDY" ROTH'S RATFINK COMIX (Also see Ratfink)
World of Fandom/ Ed Roth: 1991 - No. 3, 1991 ($2.50)

1-3: Regular Ed., 1-Limited double cover 2 4 6 9 12 15

EDDIE CAMPBELL'S BACCHUS
Eddie Campbell Comics: May, 1995 - No. 60, May, 2001 ($2.95, B&W)

1-Cerebus app. 1 2 3 5 6 8
1-2nd printing (5/97) 3.00
2-10: 9-Alex Ross back-c 5.00
11-60 3.00
Doing The Islands With Bacchus ('97, $17.95) 18.00
Earth, Water, Air & Fire ('98, $9.95) 10.00
King Bacchus ('99, $12.95) 13.00
The Eyeball Kid ('98, $8.50) 8.50

EDDIE STANKY (Baseball Hero)
Fawcett Publications: 1951 (New York Giants)

nn-Photo-c 39 78 117 236 388 540

EDEN'S FALL (Characters from Postal, The Tithe, and Think Tank)
Image Comics (Top Cow): Aug, 2016 - Present ($3.99)

1-3-Matt Hawkins & Bryan Hill-s/Atilio Rojo-a 4.00

EDEN'S TRAIL
Marvel Comics: Jan, 2003 - No. 5, May 2003 ($2.99, unfinished lim. series, printed sideways)

1-5-Chuck Austen-s/Steve Uy-a 3.00

EDGAR ALLAN POE'S MORELLA AND THE MURDERS IN THE RUE MORGUE
Dark Horse Comics: Jun, 2015 ($3.99, one-shot)

1-Adaptation of Poe's poems; story and art by Richard Corben 4.00

EDGAR ALLAN POE'S THE CONQUEROR WORM
Dark Horse Comics: Nov, 2012 ($3.99, one-shot)

1-Adaptation of Poe's poem; story and art by Richard Corben; Corben sketch pages 4.00

EDGAR ALLAN POE'S THE FALL OF THE HOUSE OF USHER
Dark Horse Comics: May, 2013 - No. 2, Jun, 2013 ($3.99, limited series)

1,2-Adaptation of Poe's poem; story and art by Richard Corben; Corben sketch pages 4.00

EDGAR ALLAN POE'S - THE FALL OF THE HOUSE OF USHER AND OTHER TALES OF HORROR
Catlan Communications Pub.: Sept. 1985 (hardcover graphic novel)

nn-Reprints of Poe story issues from Warren comic mags; all Richard Corben-a; numbered edition of 350 signed by Corben; 60 pgs. 130.00
nn-Softcover edition 60.00

EDGAR ALLAN POE'S THE PREMATURE BURIAL
Dark Horse Comics: Apr, 2014 ($3.99, one-shot)

1-Adaptation of The Premature Burial and The Cask of Amontillado; Corben-s/a/c 4.00

EDGAR ALLAN POE'S THE RAVEN AND THE RED DEATH
Dark Horse Comics: Oct, 2013 ($3.99, one-shot)

1-Adaptation of The Raven and The Masque of the Red Death; Corben-s/a/c 4.00

EDGAR BERGEN PRESENTS CHARLIE McCARTHY
Whitman Publishing Co. (Charlie McCarthy Co.): No. 764, 1938 (36 pgs.; 15x10-1/2"; color)

764 84 168 252 538 919 1300

EDGAR RICE BURROUGHS' TARZAN: A TALE OF MUGAMBI
Dark Horse Comics: 1995 ($2.95, one-shot)

1 3.00

EDGAR RICE BURROUGHS' TARZAN: IN THE LAND THAT TIME FORGOT AND THE POOL OF TIME
Dark Horse Comics: 1996 ($12.95, trade paperback)

nn-r/Russ Manning-a 13.00

EDGAR RICE BURROUGHS' TARZAN OF THE APES
Dark Horse Comics: May, 1999 ($12.95, trade paperback)

nn-reprints 13.00

EDGAR RICE BURROUGHS' TARZAN: THE LOST ADVENTURE
Dark Horse Comics: Jan, 1995 - No. 4, Apr, 1995 ($2.95, B&W, limited series)

1-4: ERB's last Tarzan story, adapted by Joe Lansdale 3.00
Hardcover (12/95, $19.95) 20.00
Limited Edition Hardcover ($99.95)-signed & numbered 100.00

EDGAR RICE BURROUGHS' TARZAN: THE RETURN OF TARZAN
Dark Horse Comics: May, 1997 - No. 3, July, 1997 ($2.95, limited series)

1-3 3.00

EDGAR RICE BURROUGHS' TARZAN: THE RIVERS OF BLOOD
Dark Horse Comics: Nov, 1999 - No. 4, Feb, 2000 ($2.95, limited series)

1-4-Kordey-c/a 3.00

EDGE
Malibu Comics (Bravura): July, 1994 - No. 3, Apr, 1995 ($2.50/$2.95, unfinished lim.series)

1,2-S. Grant-story & Gil Kane-c/a; w/Bravura stamp 3.00
3-($2.95-c) 3.00

EDGE (Re-titled as Vector starting with #13)
CrossGeneration Comics: May, 2002 - No. 12, Apr, 2003 ($9.95/$11.95/$7.95, TPB)

1-3: Reprints from various CrossGen titles 10.00
4-8-($11.95) 12.00
9-12-($7.95, 8-1/4" x 5-1/2") digest-sized reprints 8.00

EDGE OF CHAOS
Pacific Comics: July, 1983 - No. 3, Jan, 1984 (Limited series)

1-3-Morrow c/a; all contain nudity 3.00

EDGE OF DOOM (Horror anthology)
IDW Publishing: Oct, 2010 - No. 5, Mar, 2011 ($3.99)

1-5-Steve Niles-s/Kelley Jones-a 4.00

EDGE OF SPIDER-VERSE (See Amazing Spider-Man 2014 series #7-14)
Marvel Comics: Nov, 2014 - No. 5, Dec, 2014 ($3.99, limited series)

1,3-5: 1-Spider-Man Noir; Isanove-a. 3-Weaver-s/a. 5-Gerard Way-s 4.00
2-Gwen Stacy Spider-Woman 1st app.; Robbi Rodriguez-a/c 10.00

EDWARD SCISSORHANDS (Based on the movie)
IDW Publishing: Oct, 2014 - No. 10, Jul, 2015 ($3.99)

1-10-Kate Leth-s/Drew Rausch-a; multiple covers on each 4.00

ED WHEELAN'S JOKE BOOK STARRING FAT & SLAT (See Fat & Slat)

EERIE (Strange Worlds No. 18 on)
Avon Per.: No. 1, Jan, 1947; No. 1, May-June, 1951 - No. 17, Aug-Sept, 1954

1(1947)-1st supernatural comic; Kubert, Fugitani-a; bondage-c
649 1298 1947 4738 8369 12,000
1(1951)-Reprints story from 1947 #1 116 232 348 742 1271 1800
2-Wood-c/a; bondage-c 116 232 348 742 1271 1800
3-Wood-c; Kubert, Wood/Orlando-a 100 200 300 635 1093 1550
4,5-Wood-c 77 154 231 493 847 1200
6,8,13,14: 8-Kinstler-a; bondage-c; Phantom Witch Doctor story
47 94 141 296 498 700
7-Wood/Orlando-c; Kubert-a 60 120 180 381 653 925
9-Kubert-a; Check-c 50 100 150 315 533 750
10,11: 10-Kinstler-a. 11-Kinstlerish-a by McCann 47 94 141 296 498 700
12-Dracula story from novel, 25 pgs. 53 106 159 334 567 800
15-Reprints No. 1('51) minus-c(bondage) 37 74 111 222 361 500
16-Wood-a r-/No. 2 37 74 111 222 361 500
17-Wood/Orlando & Kubert-a; reprints #3 minus inside & outside Wood-c
37 74 111 222 361 500

NOTE: *Hollingsworth a-9-11; c-10, 11.*

EERIE
I. W. Enterprises: 1964

I.W. Reprint #1('64)-Wood-c(r); r-story/Spook #1 3 6 9 21 33 45
I.W. Reprint #2,6,8: 8-Dr. Drew by Grandenetti from Ghost #9
3 6 9 19 30 40
I.W. Reprint #9-r/Tales of Terror #1(Toby); Wood-c 4 8 12 23 37 50

EERIE (Magazine)(See Warren Presents)
Warren Publ. Co.: No. 1, Sept, 1965; No. 2, Mar, 1966 - No. 139, Feb, 1983

1-24 pgs., black & white, small size (5-1/4x7-1/4"), low distribution; cover from inside back cover of Creepy No. 2; stories reprinted from Creepy No. 7, 8. At least three different versions exist.
First Printing - B&W, 5-1/4" wide x 7-1/4" high, evenly trimmed. On page 18, panel 5, in the upper left-hand corner, the large rear view of a bald headed man blends into solid black and is unrecognizable. Overall printing quality is poor. 46 92 138 340 770 1200
Second Printing - B&W, 5-1/4x7-1/4", with uneven, untrimmed edges (if one of these were trimmed evenly, the size would be less than as indicated). The figure of the bald headed man on page 18, panel 5 is clear and discernible. The staples have a 1/4" blue stripe. 15 30 45 103 227 350
Other unauthorized reproductions for comparison's sake would be practically worthless. One known version was

Eerie #60 © WP

Egbert #12 © QUA

80 Page Giant #3 © DC

GD VG FN VF VF/NM NM-
2.0 4.0 6.0 8.0 9.0 9.2

probably shot off a first printing copy with some loss of detail; the finer lines tend to disappear in this version which can be determined by looking at the lower right-hand corner of page one, first story. The roof of the house is shaded with straight lines. These lines are sharp and distinct on original, but broken on this version.

NOTE: ***The Overstreet Comic Book Price Guide*** *recommends that, before buying a 1st issue, you consult an expert.*

2-Frazetta-c; Toth-a; 1st app. host Cousin Eerie 10 20 30 69 147 225
3-Frazetta-c & half pg. ad (rerun in #4); Toth, Williamson, Ditko-a
9 18 27 57 111 165
4,6: 4-Frazetta-a (1/2 pg. ad) 6 12 18 37 66 95
5,7-Frazetta-c. Ditko-a in all 7 14 21 44 82 120
8-Frazetta-c; Ditko-a 8 16 24 51 96 140
9-11,25: 9,10-Neal Adams-a, Ditko-a. 11-Karloff Mummy adapt.-Wood-s/a. 25-Steranko-c
6 12 18 38 69 100
12-16,18-22,24,32-35,40,45: 12,13,20-Poe-s. 12-Bloch-s. 12,15-Jones-a. 13-Lovecraft-s. 14,16-Toth-a. 16,19,24-Stoker-s. 16,32,33,43-Corben-a. 34-Early Boris-c. 35-Early Brunner-a. 35,40-Early Ploog-a. 40-Frankenstein; Ploog-a (6/72, 6 months before Marvel's series) 4 8 12 28 47 65
17-(low distribution) 20 40 60 141 313 485
23-Frazetta-c; Adams-a(reprint) 9 18 27 61 123 185
26-31,36-38,43,44 4 8 12 25 40 55
39,41: 39-1st Dax the Warrior; Maroto-a. 41-(low distribution)
5 10 15 30 50 70
42,51: 42-('73 Annual, 84 pgs.) Spooktacular; Williamson-a. 51-('74 Annual, 76 pgs.) Color poster insert; Toth-a 4 8 12 28 47 65
46,48: 46-Dracula series by Sutton begins; 2pgs. Vampirella. 48-Begin "Mummy Walks" and "Curse of the Werewolf" series (both continue in #49,50,52,53)
4 8 12 25 40 55
47,49,50,52,53: 47-Lilith. 49-Marvin the Dead Thing. 50-Satanna, Daughter of Satan. 52-Hunter by Neary begins. 53-Adams-a 4 8 12 23 37 50
54,55-Color insert Spirit story by Eisner, reprints sections 12/21/47 & 6/16/46
54-Dr. Archaeus series begins 3 6 9 19 30 40
56,57,59,63,69,77,78: All have 8 pg. slick color insert. 56,57,77-Corben-a. 59-(100 pgs.) Summer Special, all Dax issue. 69-Summer Special, all Hunter issue, Neary-a.
78-All Mummy issue 3 6 9 19 30 40
58,60,62,68,72,: 8 pg. slick color insert & Wrightson-a in all. 58,60,62-Corben-a. 60-Summer Giant (9/74, $1.25) 1st Exterminator One; Wood-a. 62-Mummies Walk. 68-Summer Special (84 pgs.) 3 6 9 21 33 45
61,64-67,71: 61-Mummies Walk-s, Wood-a. 64-Corben-a. 64,65,67-Toth-a. 65,66-El Cid.
67-Hunter II. 71-Goblin-c/1st app. 3 6 9 17 26 35
70,73-75 3 6 9 14 20 26
76-1st app. Darklon the Mystic by Starlin-s/a 3 6 9 20 31 42
79,80-Origin Darklon the Mystic by Starlin 3 6 9 17 26 35
81,86,97: 81-Frazetta-c, King Kong; Corben-a. 86-(92 pgs.) All Corben issue. 97-Time Travel/ Dinosaur issue; Corben,Adams-a 3 6 9 16 23 30
82-Origin/1st app. The Rook 3 6 9 18 28 38
83,85,88,89,91-93,98,99: 98-Rook (31 pgs.). 99-1st Horizon Seekers.
2 4 6 10 14 18
84,87,90,96,100: 84,100-Starlin-a. 87-Hunter 3; Nino-a. 87,90-Corben-a. 96-Summer Special (92 pgs.). 100-(92 pgs.) Anniversary issue; Rook (30 pgs.)
2 4 6 13 18 22
94,95-The Rook & Vampirella team-up. 95-Vampirella-c; 1st MacTavish
3 6 9 16 24 32
101,106,112,115,118,120,121,128: 101-Return of Hunter II, Starlin-a. 106-Hard John Nuclear Hit Parade Special, Corben-a. 112-All Maroto issue, Luana-s. 115-All José Ortiz issues. 118-1st Haggarth. 120-1st Zud Kamish. 121-Hunter/Darklon. 128-Starlin-a, Hsu-a
2 4 6 10 14 18
102-105,107-111,113,114,116,117,119,122-124,126,127,129: 103-105,109-111-Gulacy-a. 104-Beast World. 2 4 6 9 13 16
125-(10/81, 84 pgs.) all Neal Adams issue 3 6 9 14 19 24
130-(76 pgs.) Vampirella-c/sty (54 pgs.); Pantha, Van Helsing, Huntress, Dax, Schreck, Hunter, Exterminator One, Rook app. 3 6 9 16 23 30
131-(Lower distr.); all Wood issue 3 6 9 14 20 26
132-134,136: 132-Rook returns. 133-All Ramon Torrents-a issue. 134,136-Color comic insert
2 4 6 10 14 18
135-(Lower distr., 10/82, 100 pgs.) All Ditko issue 3 6 9 14 20 26
137-139 (lower distr.):137-All Super-Hero issue. 138-Sherlock Holmes. 138,139-Color comic insert 2 4 6 13 18 22
Yearbook '70-Frazetta-c 5 10 15 33 57 80
Annual '71, '72-Reprints in both 4 8 12 25 40 55
... Archives - Volume One HC (Dark Horse, 3/09, $49.95, dustjacket) r/#1-5 50.00
... Archives - Volume Two HC (Dark Horse, 9/09, $49.95, dustjacket) r/#6-10; interview with Frank Frazetta from 1985 50.00

NOTE: *The above books contain art by many good artists:* ***N. Adams, Brunner, Corben, Craig (Taycee), Crandall, Ditko, Eisner, Evans, Jeff Jones, Krenkel, McWilliams, Morrow, Orlando, Ploog, Severin, Starlin, Torres, Toth, Williamson, Wood,*** *and* ***Wrightson****; covers by* ***Bode', Corben, Davis, Frazetta, Morrow,*** *and* ***Orlando.*** ***Frazetta*** *c-2, 3, 7, 8, 23. Annuals from 1973-on are included in regular numbering. 1970-74 Annuals are complete reprints. Annuals from 1975-on are in the format of the regular issues.*

EERIE
Dark Horse Comics: Jul, 2012 - Present ($2.99, B&W)
1-8-Sci-fi anthology by various. 2-Allred-a. 3-Wood-a(r). 4,6-Kelley Jones-a 3.00

EERIE ADVENTURES (Also see Weird Adventures)
Ziff-Davis Publ. Co.: Winter, 1951 (Painted-c)
1-Powell-a(2), McCann-a; used in **SOTI**; bondage-c; Krigstein back-c
77 154 231 493 847 1200
NOTE: *Title dropped due to similarity to Avon's Eerie & legal action.*

EERIE TALES (Magazine)
Hastings Associates: 1959 (Black & White)
1-Williamson, Torres, Tuska-a, Powell(2), & Morrow(2)-a
21 42 63 126 206 285

EERIE TALES
Super Comics: 1963-1964
Super Reprint No. 10,11,12,18: 10('63)-r/Spook #27. Purple Claw in #11,12 ('63); #12-r/Avon's Eerie #1('51)-Kida-r 3 6 9 16 24 32
15-Wolverton-a, Spacehawk-r/Blue Bolt Weird Tales #113; Disbrow-a
4 8 12 28 47 65

EFFIGY
DC Comics (Vertigo): Mar, 2015 - No. 7, Sept, 2015 ($2.99/$3.99)
1-5: 1-Tim Seeley-s/Marley Zarcone-a 3.00
6,7-($3.99) 4.00

EGBERT
Arnold Publications/Quality Comics Group: Spring, 1946 - No. 20, Aug, 1950
1-Funny animal; intro Egbert & The Count 21 42 63 122 199 275
2 12 24 36 67 94 120
3-10 9 18 27 52 69 85
11-20 8 16 24 42 54 65

EGYPT
DC Comics (Vertigo): Aug, 1995 - No.7, Feb, 1996 ($2.50, lim. series, mature)
1-7: Milligan scripts in all. 3.00

EH! (...Dig This Crazy Comic) (From Here to Insanity No. 8 on)
Charlton Comics: Dec, 1953 - No. 7, Nov-Dec, 1954 (Satire)
1-Davis-*ish*-c/a by Ayers, Wood-*ish*-a by Giordano; Atomic Mouse app.
40 80 120 246 411 575
2-Ayers-c/a 24 48 72 142 234 325
3,5,7 22 44 66 128 209 290
4,6: Sexual innuendo-c. 6-Ayers-a 26 52 78 154 252 350

EI8GT
Dark Horse Comics: Feb, 2015 - No. 5, Jun, 2015 ($3.50)
1-Rafael Albuquerque-a/c; Mike Johnson-s 3.50

EIGHTBALL (Also see David Boring)
Fantagraphics Books: Oct, 1989 - Present ($2.75/$2.95/$3.95, semi-annually, mature)
1 (1st printing) Daniel Clowes-s/a in all 4 8 12 28 47 65
2,3 2 4 6 13 18 22
4-8 2 4 6 8 11 14
9-19: 17-(8/96) 2 4 6 8 11 14
20-($4.50) 2 4 6 8 10 12
21-($4.95) Concludes David Boring 3-parter 2 4 6 8 10 12
22-($5.95) 29 short stories 2 4 6 8 10 12
23-($7.00, 9" x 12") The Death Ray 2 4 6 9 12 15
Twentieth Century Eightball (2002, $19.00) r/Clowes strips 20.00

EIGHTH WONDER, THE
Dark Horse Comics: Nov, 1997 ($2.95, one-shot)
nn-Reprints stories from Dark Horse Presents #85-87 3.00

EIGHT IS ENOUGH KITE FUN BOOK (See Kite Fun Book 1979 in the Promotional Comics section)

EIGHT LEGGED FREAKS
DC Comics (WildStorm): 2002 ($6.95, one-shot, squarebound)
nn-Adaptation of 2002 mutant spider movie; Joe Phillips-a; intro by Dean Devlin 7.00

18 DAYS (Grant Morrison's...)
Graphic India: 2015 - Present ($1.00/$2.99)
1-19: 1-($1.00) Grant Morrison-s/Jeevan Kang-a. 2-19-($2.99) 3.00

1872 (Secret Wars tie-in)

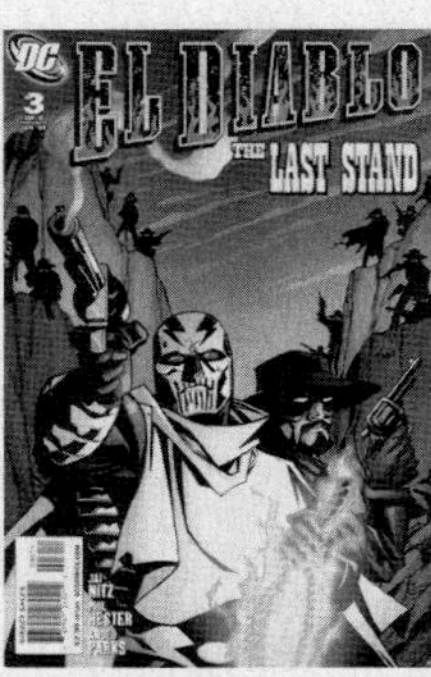

El Diablo (2008 series) #3 © DC

Elektra V2 #4 © MAR

Elektra & Wolverine: The Redeemer #1 © MAR

	GD 2.0	VG 4.0	FN 6.0	VF 8.0	VF/NM 9.0	NM- 9.2

GD VG FN VF VF/NM NM- 2.0 4.0 6.0 8.0 9.0 9.2

Marvel Comics: Sept, 2015 - No. 4, Dec, 2015 ($3.99, limited series)

1-4-Red Wolf in the western town of Timely in 1872. 4-Avengers of the West 4.00

80 PAGE GIANT (...Magazine No. 2-15)
National Periodical Publications: 8/64 - No. 15, 10/65; No. 16, 11/65 - No. 89, 7/71 (25¢)
(All reprints) (#1-56: 84 pgs.; #57-89: 68 pgs.)

	GD 2.0	VG 4.0	FN 6.0	VF 8.0	VF/NM 9.0	NM- 9.2
1-Superman Annual; originally planned as Superman Annual #9 (8/64)	34	68	102	243	542	840
2-Jimmy Olsen	18	36	54	124	275	425
3,4: 3-Lois Lane. 4-Flash-G.A.-r; Infantino-a	15	30	45	100	220	340
5-Batman; has Sunday newspaper strip; Catwoman-r; Batman's Life Story-r (25th anniversary special)	15	30	45	100	220	340
6-Superman	13	26	39	87	191	295
7-Sgt. Rock's Prize Battle Tales; Kubert-c/a	21	42	63	147	324	500
8-More Secret Origins-origins of JLA, Aquaman, Robin, Atom, & Superman; Infantino-a	26	52	78	182	404	625
9-15: 9-Flash (r/Flash #106,117,123 & Showcase #14); Infantino-a. 10-Superboy. 11-Superman; all Luthor issue. 12-Batman; has Sunday newspaper strip. 13-Jimmy Olsen. 14-Lois Lane. 15-Superman and Batman; Joker-c/story	12	24	36	82	179	275

Continued as part of regular series under each title in which that particular book came out, a Giant being published instead of the regular size. Issues No. 16 to No. 89 are listed for your information. See individual titles for prices.
16-JLA #39 (11/65), 17-Batman #176, 18-Superman #183, 19-Our Army at War #164, 20-Action #334, 21-Flash #160, 22-Superboy #129, 23-Superman #187, 24-Batman #182, 25-Jimmy Olsen #95, 26-Lois Lane #68, 27-Batman #185, 28-World's Finest #161, 29-JLA #48, 30-Batman #187, 31-Superman #193, 32-Our Army at War #177, 33-Action #347, 34-Flash #169, 35-Superboy #138, 36-Superman #197, 37-Batman #193, 38-Jimmy Olsen #104, 39-Lois Lane #77, 40-World's Finest #170, 41-JLA #58, 42-Superman #202, 43-Batman #198, 44-Our Army at War #190, 45-Action #360, 46-Flash #178, 47-Superboy #147, 48-Superman #207, 49-Batman #203, 50-Jimmy Olsen #113, 51-Lois Lane #86, 52-World's Finest #179, 53-JLA #67, 54-Superman #212, 55-Batman #208, 56-Our Army at War #203, 57-Action #373, 58-Flash #187, 59-Superboy #156, 60-Superman #217, 61-Batman #213, 62-Jimmy Olsen #122, 63-Lois Lane #95, 64-World's Finest #188, 65-JLA #76, 66-Superman #222, 67-Batman #218, 68-Our Army at War #216, 69-Adventure #390, 70-Flash #196, 71-Superboy #165, 72-Superman #227, 73-Batman #223, 74-Jimmy Olsen #131, 75-Lois Lane #104, 76-World's Finest #197, 77-JLA #85, 78-Superman #232, 79-Batman #228, 80-Our Army at War #229, 81-Adventure #403, 82-Flash #205, 83-Superboy #174, 84-Superman #239, 85-Batman #233, 86-Jimmy Olsen #140, 87-Lois Lane #113, 88-World's Finest #206, 89-JLA #93.

87TH PRECINCT (TV) (Based on the Ed McBain novels)
Dell Publishing Co.: Apr-June, 1962 - No. 2, July-Sept, 1962

	GD 2.0	VG 4.0	FN 6.0	VF 8.0	VF/NM 9.0	NM- 9.2
Four Color 1309(#1)-Krigstein-a	9	18	27	60	120	180
2-Photo-c	7	14	21	43	89	130

E IS FOR EXTINCTION (Secret Wars tie-in)
Marvel Comics: Aug, 2015 - No. 4, Nov, 2015 ($4.99/$3.99, limited series)

1-($4.99) New X-Men in Mutopia; Burnham-s/Villalobos-a 5.00
2-4-($3.99) Cassandra Nova returns 4.00

EL BOMBO COMICS
Standard Comics/Frances M. McQueeny: 1946

	GD 2.0	VG 4.0	FN 6.0	VF 8.0	VF/NM 9.0	NM- 9.2
nn(1946), 1(no date)	17	34	51	98	154	210

EL CAZADOR
CrossGen Comics: Oct, 2003 - No. 6, Jun, 2004 ($2.95)

1-Dixon-s/Epting-a 5.00
2-6: 5-Lady Death preview 3.00
...: The Bloody Ballad of Blackjack Tom 1 (4/04, $2.95, one-shot) Cariello-a 3.00

EL CID
Dell Publishing Co.: No. 1259, 1961

	GD 2.0	VG 4.0	FN 6.0	VF 8.0	VF/NM 9.0	NM- 9.2
Four Color 1259-Movie, photo-c	7	14	21	46	86	125

EL DIABLO (See All-Star Western #2 & Weird Western Tales #12)
DC Comics: Aug, 1989 - No. 16, Jan, 1991 ($1.50-$1.75, color)

1 ($2.50, 52pgs.)-Masked hero 4.00
2-16 3.00

EL DIABLO
DC Comics (Vertigo): Mar, 2001 - No. 4, Jun, 2001 ($2.50, limited series)

1-4-Azzarello-s/Zezelj-a/Sale-c 3.00
TPB (2008, $12.99) r/#1-4 13.00

EL DIABLO
DC Comics: Nov, 2008 - No. 6, Apr, 2009 ($2.99, limited series)

1-6-Nitz-s/Hester-a/c. 4,5-Freedom Fighters app. 3.00

EL DORADO (See Movie Classics)

ELECTRIC ANT
Marvel Comics: Jun, 2010 - No. 5, Oct, 2010 ($3.99, Baxter paper)

1-5-Based on a Philip K. Dick story; David Mack-s/Pascal Alixe-a; Paul Pope-c 4.00

ELECTRIC SUBLIME
IDW Publishing: Oct, 2016 - No. 4, Jan, 2017 ($3.99, limited series)

1-4-W. Maxwell Prince-s/Martin Morazzo-a; two covers on each 4.00

ELECTRIC UNDERTOW (See Strikeforce Morituri: Electric Undertow)

ELECTRIC WARRIOR
DC Comics: May, 1986 - No. 18, Oct, 1987 ($1.50, Baxter paper)

1-18 3.00

ELECTROPOLIS
Image Comics: May, 2001 - No. 4, Jan, 2003 ($2.95/$5.95)

1-3-Dean Motter-s/a. 3-(12/01) 3.00
4-(1/03, $5.95, 72 pages) The Infernal Machine pts. 4-6 6.00

ELEKTRA (Also see Daredevil #319-325)
Marvel Comics: Mar, 1995 - No. 4, June, 1995 ($2.95, limited series)

1-4-Embossed-c; Scott McDaniel-a 4.00

ELEKTRA (Also see Daredevil)
Marvel Comics: Nov, 1996 - No. 19, Jun, 1998 ($1.95)

1-Peter Milligan scripts; Deodato-c/a 4.00
1-Variant-c 6.00
2-19: 4-Dr. Strange-c/app. 10-Logan-c/app. 3.00
#(-1) Flashback (7/97) Matt Murdock-c/app.; Deodato-c/a 3.00
.../Cyblade (Image, 3/97,$2.95) Devil's Reign pt. 7 3.00

ELEKTRA (Vol. 2) (Marvel Knights)
Marvel Comics: Sept, 2001 - No. 35, Jun, 2004 ($3.50/$2.99)

1-Bendis-s/Austen-a/Horn-c 4.00
2-6: 2-Two covers (Sienkiewicz and Horn) 3,4-Silver Samurai app. 3.00
3-Initial printing with panel of nudity; most copies pulped 35.00
7-35: 7-Rucka-s begin. 9,10,17-Bennett-a. 19-Meglia-a. 23-25-Chen-a; Sienkiewicz-c 3.00
...Vol. 1: Introspect TPB (2002, $16.99) r/#10-15; Marvel Knights: Double Shot #3 17.00
...Vol. 2: Everything Old is New Again TPB (2003, $16.99) r/#16-22 17.00
...Vol. 3: Relentless TPB (2004, $14.99) r/#23-28 15.00
...Vol. 4: Frenzy TPB (2004, $17.99) r/#29-35 18.00

ELEKTRA (All-New Marvel Now!)
Marvel Comics: Jun, 2014 - No. 11, May, 2015 ($3.99)

1-11: 1-Blackman-s/Del Mundo-a; multiple covers. 2,6,7-Lady Bullseye app. 4.00

ELEKTRA
Marvel Comics: Apr, 2017 - Present ($3.99)

1-Matt Owens-s/Juann Cabal-a; Arcade app. 4.00

ELEKTRA & WOLVERINE: THE REDEEMER
Marvel Comics: Jan, 2002 - No. 3, Mar, 2002 ($5.95, square-bound, lim. series)

1-3-Greg Rucka-s/Yoshitaka Amano-a/c 6.00
HC (5/02, $29.95, with dustjacket) r/#1-3, interview with Greg Rucka 30.00

ELEKTRA: ASSASSIN (Also see Daredevil)
Marvel Comics (Epic Comics): Aug, 1986 - No. 8, June, 1987 (Limited series, mature)

1,8-Miller scripts in all; Sienkiewicz-c/a. 6.00
2-7 5.00
Signed & numbered hardcover (Graphitti Designs, $39.95, 2000 print run)- reprints 1-8 60.00
TPB (2000, $24.95) 25.00

ELEKTRA: GLIMPSE & ECHO
Marvel Comics: Sept, 2002 - No. 4, Dec, 2002 ($2.99, limited series)

1-4-Scott Morse-s/painted-a 3.00

ELEKTRA LIVES AGAIN (Also see Daredevil)
Marvel Comics (Epic Comics): 1990 ($24.95, oversize, hardcover, 76 pgs.)(Produced by Graphitti Designs)

nn-Frank Miller-c/a/scripts; Lynn Varley painted-a; Matt Murdock & Bullseye app. 40.00
2nd printing (9/02, $24.99) 25.00

ELEKTRA MEGAZINE
Marvel Comics: Nov, 1996 - No. 2, Dec, 1996 ($3.95, 96 pgs., reprints, limited series)

1,2: Reprints Frank Miller's Elektra stories in Daredevil 4.00

ELEKTRA SAGA, THE
Marvel Comics Group: Feb, 1984 - No. 4, June, 1984 ($2.00, limited series, Baxter paper)

1-4-r/Daredevil #168-190; Miller-c/a 5.00

ELEKTRA: THE HAND
Marvel Comics: Nov, 2004 - No. 5, Feb, 2005 ($2.99, limited series)

1-5-Gossett-a/Sienkiewicz-c/Yoshida-s; origin of the Hand in the 16th century 3.00

Elementals #24 © Bill Willingham

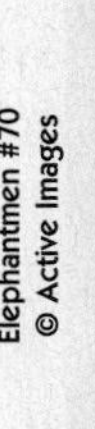
Elephantmen #70 © Active Images

Elfquest V2 #15 © Warp Graphics

	GD 2.0	VG 4.0	FN 6.0	VF 8.0	VF/NM 9.0	NM- 9.2

ELEKTRA: THE MOVIE
Marvel Comics: Feb, 2005 ($5.99)

1-Movie adaptation; McKeever-s/Perkins-a; photo-c 6.00
TPB (2005, $12.95) r/movie adaptation, Daredevil #168, 181 & Elektra #(-1) 13.00

ELEMENTALS, THE (See The Justice Machine & Morningstar Spec.)
Comico The Comic Co. : June, 1984 - No. 29, Sept, 1988; V2#1, Mar, 1989 - No. 28, 1994? ($1.50/$2.50, Baxter paper); V3#1, Dec, 1995 - No. 3 ($2.95)

1-Willingham-c/a, 1-8 5.00
2-29, V2#1-28: 9-Bissette-a(p). 10-Photo-c. V2#6-1st app. Strike Force America. 18-Prelude to Avalon mini-series. 27-Prequel to Strike Force America series 3.00
V3#1-3: 1-Daniel-a(p), bagged w/gaming card 3.00
Lingerie (5/96, $2.95) 3.00
Special 1,2 (3/86, 1/89)-1-Willingham-a(p) 3.00

ELEMENTALS: (Title series), **Comico**

--GHOST OF A CHANCE, 12/95 ($5.95)-graphic novel, nn-Ross-c. 6.00
--HOW THE WAR WAS WON, 6/96 - No. 2, 8/96 ($2.95) 1,2-Tony Daniel-a, & 1-Variant-c; no logo 3.00
--SEX SPECIAL, 1991 - No. 4, Feb, 1993 ($2.95, color) 2 covers for each 3.00
--SEX SPECIAL, 5/97 - No. 2, 6/97 ($2.95, B&W) 1-Tony Daniel, Jeff Moy-a, 2-Robb Phipps, Adam McDaniel-a 3.00
--SWIMSUIT SPECTACULAR 1996, 6/96 ($2.95), 1-pin-ups, 1-Variant-c; no logo 3.00
--THE VAMPIRE'S REVENGE, 6/96 - No. 2 8/96 ($2.95) 1,2-Willingham-s, 1-Variant-c; no logo 3.00

ELEPHANTMEN
Image Comics: July, 2006 - Present ($2.99/$3.50/$3.99) (Flip covers on most)

1-16: 1-Starkings-s/Moritat-a/Ladronn-c. 6-Campbell flip-c. 15-Sale flip-c 4.00
17-30-($3.50) 25-Flip book preview of Marineman 4.00
31-49,51-74-($3.99) 32-Conan/Red Sonja homage. 42-44-Dave Sim-a (5 pgs.) 4.00
50-($5.99) Flip book with reprint of #1; cover gallery 6.00
...: Man and Elephantman 1 (3/11, $3.99) Three covers 4.00
... Shots (5/15, $5.99) Reprints short stories from anthologies; art by Sim, Sale, & others 6.00
...: The Pilot (5/07, $2.99) short stories and pin-ups by various incl. Sale, Jim Lee, Jae Lee 4.00
...: War Toys (11/07 - No. 3, 4/08, $2.99) 1-3-Mappo war; Starkings-s/Moritat-a/Ladronn-c 4.00
... War Toys: Yvette (7/09, $3.50) Starkings-s/Moritat-a 4.00
Giant-Size Elephantmen 1 (10/11, $5.99) r/#31,32 & Man and Elephantman; Campbell-c 6.00

1111 (ELEVEN ELEVEN)
Crusade Entertainment: Oct, 1996 ($2.95, B&W, one-shot)

1-Wrightson-c/a 4.00

ELEVEN OR ONE
Sirius: Apr, 1995 ($2.95)

	GD	VG	FN	VF	VF/NM	NM-
1-Linsner-c/a	1	3	4	6	8	10
1-(6/96) 2nd printing						3.50

ELFLORD
Nightwind Productions: Jun, 1980 - Vol. 2 #1, 1982 (B&W, magazine-size)

	GD	VG	FN	VF	VF/NM	NM-
1-1st Barry Blair-s/c/a in comics; B&W-c; limited print run for all	10	20	30	64	132	200
2-5-B&W-c	5	10	15	31	53	75
6-14: 9-14-Color-c	4	8	12	27	44	60
Vol. 2 #1 (1982)	4	8	12	23	37	50

ELFLORD
Aircel Publ.: 1986 - No. 6, Oct, 1989 ($1.70, B&W); V2#1- V2#31, 1995 ($2.00)

1 4.00
2-4,V2#1-20,22-30: 4-6: Last B&W. V2#1-Color-a begin. 22-New cast. 25-Begin B&W 3.00
1,2-2nd printings 3.00
21-Double size ($4.95) 5.00

ELFLORD
Warp Graphics: Jan, 1997-No.4, Apr, 1997 ($2.95, B&W, mini-series)

1-4 3.00

ELFLORD (CUTS LOOSE) (Vol. 2)
Warp Graphics: Sept, 1997 - No. 7, Apr, 1998 ($2.95, B&W, mini-series)

1-7 3.00

ELFLORD: DRAGON'S EYE
Night Wynd Enterprises: 1993 ($2.50, B&W)

1 3.00

ELFLORD: THE RETURN
Mad Monkey Press: 1996 ($6.95, magazine size)

1 7.00

ELFQUEST (Also see Fantasy Quarterly & Warp Graphics Annual)
Warp Graphics, Inc.: No. 2, Aug, 1978 - No. 21, Feb, 1985 (All magazine size)
No. 1, Apr, 1979

NOTE: **Elfquest** was originally published as one of the stories in **Fantasy Quarterly** #1. When the publisher went out of business, the creative team, Wendy and Richard Pini, formed WaRP Graphics and continued the series, beginning with **Elfquest** #2. **Elfquest** #1, which reprinted the story from **Fantasy Quarterly**, was published about the same time **Elfquest** #4 was released. Thereafter, most issues were reprinted as demand warranted, until Marvel announced it would reprint the entire series under its Epic imprint (Aug., 1985).

	GD	VG	FN	VF	VF/NM	NM-
1(4/79)-Reprints Elfquest story from Fantasy Quarterly No. 1						
1st printing ($1.00-c)	6	12	18	40	73	105
2nd printing ($1.25-c)	2	4	6	9	12	15
3rd printings ($1.50-c)	1	2	3	5	6	8
4th printing; different-c ($1.50-c)						5.00
2(8/78) 1st printing ($1.00-c)	3	6	9	27	44	60
2nd printings ($1.25-c)						6.00
3rd & 4th printings ($1.50-c)(all 4th prints 1989)						5.00
3-5: 1st printings ($1.00-c)	3	6	9	16	23	30
6-9: 1st printings ($1.25-c)	3	6	9	14	20	25
2nd & 3rd printings ($1.50-c)						5.00
10-21: ($1.50-c); 16-8pg. preview of A Distant Soil	2	4	6	11	16	20
10-14: 2nd printings ($1.50)						5.00

ELFQUEST
Marvel Comics (Epic Comics): Aug, 1985 - No. 32, Mar, 1988

1-Reprints in color the Elfquest epic by Warp Graphics 5.00
2-32 4.00

ELFQUEST
DC Comics: 2003 - 2005

Archives Vol. 1 (2003, $49.95, HC) r/#1-5 50.00
Archives Vol. 2 (2005, $49.95, HC) r/#6-10 & Epic Illustrated #1 50.00
25th Anniversary Special (2003, $2.95) r/Elfquest #1 (Apr, 1979); interview w/Pinis 4.00

ELFQUEST (Title series), Warp Graphics
'89 - No. 4, '89 ($1.50, B&W) 1-4: R-original Elfquest series 4.00

ELFQUEST (Volume 2),**Warp Graphics:** V2#1, 5/96 - No. 33, 2/99 ($4.95/$2.95, B&W)
V2#1-31: 1,3,5,8,10,12,13,18,21,23,25-Wendy Pini-c 6.00
32,33-($2.95-c) 4.00

--BLOOD OF TEN CHIEFS, 7/93 - No. 20, 9/95 ($2.00/$2.50)
1-20-By Richard & Wendy Pini 4.00
--HIDDEN YEARS, 5/92 - No. 29, 3/96 ($2.00/$2.25)1-9,9 1/2, 10-29 4.00
--JINK, 11/94 - No. 12, 2/6 ($2.25/$2.50) 1-12-W. Pini/John Byrne-back-c 4.00
--KAHVI, 10/95 - No. 6,3/96 ($2.25, B&W) 1-6 4.00
--KINGS CROSS, 11/97 - No. 2, 12/97 ($2.95, B&W) 1,2 4.00
--KINGS OF THE BROKEN WHEEL, 6/90 - No. 9, 2/92 ($2.00, B&W) (3rd Elfquest saga)
1-9: By R. & W. Pini; 1-Color insert 5.00
1-2nd printing 4.00
--METAMORPHOSIS, 4/96 ($2.95, B&W) 1 4.00
--NEW BLOOD (...Summer Special on-c #1 only), 8/92 - No. 35, 1/96 ($2.00-$2.50, color/B&W) 1-($3.95, 68 pgs.,...Summer Special on-c)-Byrne-a/scripts (16 pgs.) 5.00
2-35: Barry Blair-a in all 4.00
1993 Summer Special ($3.95) Byrne-a/scripts 5.00
--SHARDS, 8/94 - No. 16, 3/96 ($2.25/$2.50) 1-16 4.00
--SIEGE AT BLUE MOUNTAIN, WaRP Graphics/Apple 3/87 - No. 8, 12/88 (1.75/ $1.95, B&W)

	GD	VG	FN	VF	VF/NM	NM-
1-Staton-a(i) in all; 2nd Elfquest saga	1	2	3	5	6	8
1-3-2nd printing						4.00
2-8						5.00

--THE REBELS, 11/94 - No. 12, 3/96 ($2.25/$2.50, B&W/color) 1-12 4.00
--TWO-SPEAR, 10/95 - No. 5, 2/96 ($2.25, B&W) 1-5 4.00
--WAVE DANCERS, 12/93 - No. 6, 3/96, 1-6: 1-Foil-c & poster 4.00
Special 1 ($2.95) 4.00
--WORLDPOOL, 7/97 ($2.95, B&W) 1-Richard Pini-s/Barry Blair-a 4.00

ELFQUEST: THE DISCOVERY
DC Comics: Mar, 2006 - No. 4, Sept, 2006 ($3.99, limited series)

1-4-Wendy Pini-a/Wendy & Richard Pini-s 5.00
TPB (2006, $14.99) r/#1-4 15.00

ELFQUEST: THE FINAL QUEST
Dark Horse Comics: Oct, 2013; No. 1, Jan, 2014 - Present ($3.50/$3.99)

Ellery Queen #1 © Z-D

Elric, Stormbringer #7 © M. Moorcock

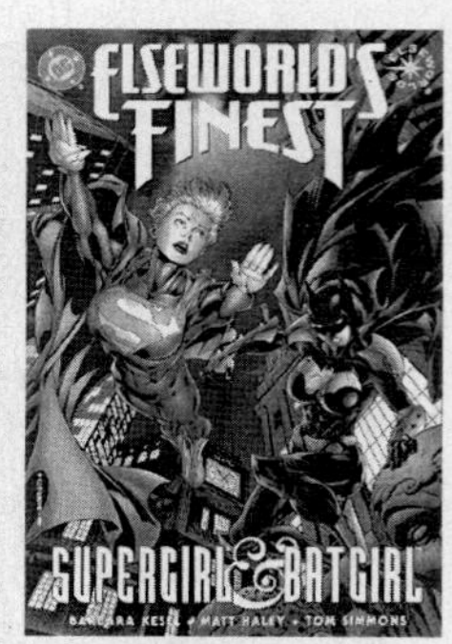

Elseworld's Finest: Supergirl & Batgirl #1 © DC

	GD 2.0	VG 4.0	FN 6.0	VF 8.0	VF/NM 9.0	NM- 9.2

1-14-Wendy Pini-a/Wendy & Richard Pini-s 3.50
15-18-($3.99) 4.00
... Special (10/13, $5.99) Wendy Pini-a/Wendy & Richard Pini-s; prologue to series 6.00

ELFQUEST: THE GRAND QUEST
DC Comics: 2004 - No. 14, 2006 ($9.95/$9.99, B&W, digest-size)

Vol. 1-6 ('04)1-r/Elfquest #1-5; new W. Pini-c. 2-r/#5-8. 3-r/#8-11. 4-r/#11-15. 5-r/#15-18 6-r/#18-20 10.00
Vol. 7-9 ('05) 1-r/Siege At Blue Mountain #1-3. 8-r/SABM #3-5. 9-r/SABM #6-8 10.00
Vol. 10-14 ('05) 10-r/Kings of the Broken Wheel #1-3. 11-KotBW #5-7 & Frazetta Fant. Ill. 12-r/Kings of the Broken Wheel #8&9. 13-r/Elfquest V2 #4-18. 14-r/Hidden Years #4-9½ 10.00

ELFQUEST: THE SEARCHER AND THE SWORD
DC Comics: 2004 ($24.95/$14.99, graphic novel)

HC (2004, $24.95, with dust jacket)-Wendy and Richard Pini-s/a/c 25.00
SC (2004, $14.99) 15.00

ELFQUEST: WOLFRIDER
DC Comics: 2003 - No. 2, 2003 ($9.95, digest-size)

Volume 1 ('03, $9.95, digest-size) r/Elfquest V2#19,21,23,25,27,29,31; Blood of Ten Chiefs #2; Hidden Years #5; New Blood Special #1; New Blood 1993 Special #1; new W. Pini-c 10.00
Volume 2 ('03, $9.95, digest-size) r/Elfquest V2#33; Blood of Ten Chiefs #10,11,19; Warp Graphics Annual #1 10.00

ELF-THING
Eclipse Comics: March, 1987 ($1.50, B&W, one-shot)

1 3.00

ELIMINATOR (Also see The Solution #16 & The Night Man #16)
Malibu Comics (Ultraverse): Apr, 1995 - No. 3, Jul, 1995 ($2.95/$2.50, lim. series)

0-Mike Zeck-a in all 3.00
1-3-($2.50): 1-1st app. Siren 3.00
1-($3.95)-Black cover edition 4.00

ELIMINATOR FULL COLOR SPECIAL
Eternity Comics: Oct, 1991 ($2.95, one-shot)

1-Dave Dorman painted-c 3.00

ELLA CINDERS (See Comics On Parade, Comics Revue #1,4, Famous Comics Cartoon Book, Giant Comics Editions, Sparkler Comics, Tip Top & Treasury of Comics)

ELLA CINDERS
United Features Syndicate: 1938 - 1940

Single Series 3(1938) 42 84 126 267 451 635
Single Series 21(#2 on-c, #21 on inside), 28('40) 37 74 111 222 361 500

ELLA CINDERS
United Features Syndicate: Mar, 1948 - No. 5, Mar, 1949

1-(#2 on cover) 15 30 45 86 133 180
2 11 22 33 60 83 105
3-5 9 18 27 47 61 75

ELLERY QUEEN
Superior Comics Ltd.: May, 1949 - No. 4, Nov, 1949

1-Kamen-c; L.B. Cole-a; r-in Haunted Thrills 52 104 156 328 557 785
2-4: 3-Drug use stories(2) 39 78 117 240 395 550
NOTE: *Iger shop art in all issues.*

ELLERY QUEEN (TV)
Ziff-Davis Publishing Co.: 1-3/52 (Spring on-c) - No. 2, Summer/52 (Saunders painted-c)

1-Saunders-c 47 94 141 296 498 700
2-Saunders bondage, torture-c 39 78 117 231 378 525

ELLERY QUEEN (Also see Crackajack Funnies No. 23)
Dell Publishing Co.: No. 1165, Mar-May, 1961 - No.1289, Apr, 1962

Four Color 1165 (#1) 9 18 27 58 114 175
Four Color 1243 (11/61-1/62), 1289 7 14 21 48 89 130

ELMER FUDD (Also see Camp Comics, Daffy, Looney Tunes #1 & Super Book #10, 22)
Dell Publishing Co.: No. 470, May, 1953 - No. 1293, Mar-May, 1962

Four Color 470 (#1) 10 20 30 64 132 200
Four Color 558,628,689('56) 6 12 18 38 69 100
Four Color 725,783,841,888,938,977,1032,1081,1131,1171,1222,1293('62) 5 10 15 31 53 75

ELMO COMICS
St. John Publishing Co.: Jan, 1948 (Daily strip-r)

1-By Cecil Jensen 12 24 36 67 94 120

ELONGATED MAN (See Flash #112 & Justice League of America #105)
DC Comics: Jan, 1992 - No. 4, Apr, 1992 ($1.00, limited series)

1-4: 3-The Flash app. 3.00

ELRIC (Of Melnibone)(See First Comics Graphic Novel #6 & Marvel Graphic Novel #2)
Pacific Comics: Apr, 1983 - No. 6, Apr, 1984 ($1.50, Baxter paper)

1-6: Russell-c/a(i) in all 3.00

ELRIC
Topps Comics: 1996 ($2.95, one-shot)

0-One Life: Russell-c/a; adapts Neil Gaiman's short story "One Life--Furnished in Early Moorcock." 3.00

ELRIC, SAILOR ON THE SEAS OF FATE
First Comics: June, 1985 - No. 7, June, 1986 ($1.75, limited series)

1-7: Adapts Michael Moorcock's novel 3.00

ELRIC, STORMBRINGER
Dark Horse Comics/Topps Comics: 1997 - No. 7, 1997 ($2.95, limited series)

1-7: Russell-c/s/a; adapts Michael Moorcock's novel 3.00

ELRIC: THE BALANCE LOST
BOOM! Studios: Jul, 2011 - No. 12, Jun, 2012 ($3.99)

1-12: 1-Roberson-s/Biagini-a; four covers. 2-11-Three covers 4.00

ELRIC: THE BANE OF THE BLACK SWORD
First Comics: Aug, 1988 - No. 6, June, 1989 ($1.75/$1.95, limited series)

1-6: Adapts Michael Moorcock's novel 3.00

ELRIC: THE VANISHING TOWER
First Comics: Aug, 1987 - No. 6, June, 1988 ($1.75, limited series)

1-6: Adapts Michael Moorcock's novel 3.00

ELRIC: WEIRD OF THE WHITE WOLF
First Comics: Oct, 1986 - No. 5, June, 1987 ($1.75, limited series)

1-5: Adapts Michael Moorcock's novel 3.00

EL SALVADOR - A HOUSE DIVIDED
Eclipse Comics: March, 1989 ($2.50, B&W, Baxter paper, stiff-c, 52 pgs.)

1-Gives history of El Salvador 4.00

ELSEWHERE PRINCE, THE (Moebius' Airtight Garage)
Marvel Comics (Epic): May, 1990 - No. 6, Oct, 1990 ($1.95, limited series)

1-6: Moebius scripts & back-up-a in all 3.00

ELSEWORLDS 80-PAGE GIANT (See DC Comics Presents: ... for reprint)
DC Comics: Aug, 1999 ($5.95, one-shot)

1-Most copies destroyed by DC over content of the "Superman's Babysitter" story; some UK shipments sold before recall 12 24 36 83 182 280

ELSEWORLD'S FINEST
DC Comics: 1997 - No. 2, 1997 ($4.95, limited series)

1,2: Elseworld's story-Superman & Batman in the 1920's 5.00

ELSEWORLD'S FINEST: SUPERGIRL & BATGIRL
DC Comics: 1998 ($5.95, one-shot)

1-Haley-a 6.00

ELSIE THE COW
D. S. Publishing Co.: Oct-Nov, 1949 - No. 3, July-Aug, 1950

1-(36 pgs.) 29 58 87 170 278 385
2,3 20 40 60 114 182 250

ELSINORE
Alias Entertainment: Apr, 2005 - No. 5, Apr, 2006 (75¢/$2.99/$3.25)

1-5: 1-(75¢-c) Brian Denham-a/Kenneth Lillie-Paetz-s. 2-($2.99-c). 4-($3.25-c) 5-Sparacio-a 3.25

ELSON'S PRESENTS
DC Comics: 1981 (100 pgs., no cover price)

Series 1-6: Repackaged 1981 DC comics; 1-DC Comics Presents #29, Flash #303, Batman #331. 2-Superman #335, Ghosts #96, Justice League of America #186. 3-New Teen Titans #3, Secrets of Haunted House #32, Wonder Woman #275. 4-Secrets of the LSH #1, Brave & the Bold #170, New Adv. of Superboy #13. 5-LSH #271, Green Lantern #136, Super Friends #40. 6-Action #515, Mystery in Space #115, Detective #498 2 4 6 11 16 20

ELTINGVILLE CLUB, THE (Characters from Dork)
Dark Horse Comics: Apr, 2014 - No. 2, Aug, 2015 ($3.99, B&W, limited series)

1,2-Evan Dorkin-s/a 4.00
HC-(2/16, $19.99) Reprints #1,2 and stories from Dork, Instant Piano, DHP 20.00

Elvira #100 © Queen "B" Prods.

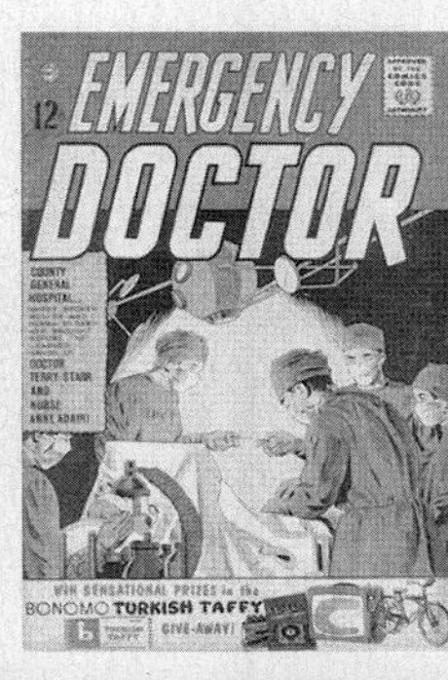

Emergency Doctor #1 © CC

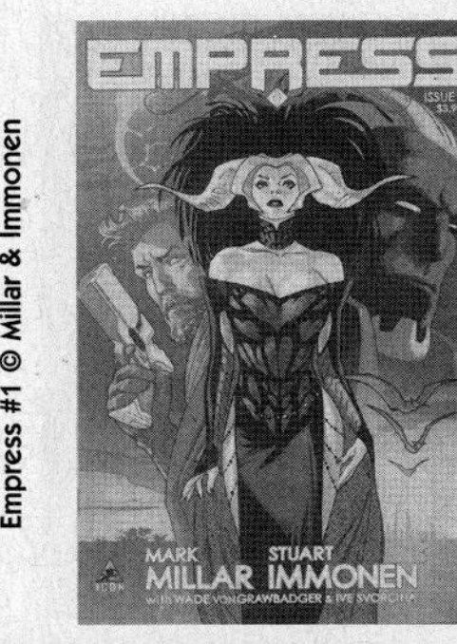

Empress #1 © Millar & Immonen

GD 2.0 | VG 4.0 | FN 6.0 | VF 8.0 | VF/NM 9.0 | NM- 9.2

ELVEN (Also see Prime)
Malibu Comics (Ultraverse): Oct, 1994 - No. 4, Feb, 1995 ($2.50, lim. series)
0 ($2.95)-Prime app. 3.00
1-4: 2,4-Prime app. 3-Primevil app. 3.00
1-Limited Foil Edition- no price on cover 4.00

ELVIRA MISTRESS OF THE DARK
Marvel Comics: Oct, 1988 ($2.00, B&W, magazine size)
1-Movie adaptation 5.00

ELVIRA MISTRESS OF THE DARK
Claypool Comics (Eclipse): May, 1993 - No. 166, Feb, 2007 ($2.50, B&W)
1-Austin-a(i). Spiegle-a 6.00
2-6: Spiegle-a 4.00
7-99,101-166-Photo-c: 3.00
100-(8/01) Kurt Busiek back-up-s; art by DeCarlo and others 4.00
TPB ($12.95) 13.00

ELVIRA'S HOUSE OF MYSTERY
DC Comics: Jan, 1986 - No. 11, Jan, 1987
1,11: 11-Dave Stevens-c 2 4 6 10 14 18
2-10: 9-Photo-c, Special 1 (3/87, $1.25) 6.00

ELVIS MANDIBLE, THE
DC Comics (Piranha Press): 1990 ($3.50, 52 pgs., B&W, mature)
nn 4.00

ELVIS PRESLEY (See Career Girl Romances #32, Go-Go, Howard Chaykin's American Flagg #10, Humbug #8, I Love You #60 & Young Lovers #18)

EL ZOMBO FANTASMA
Dark Horse Comics (Rocket Comics): Apr, 2004 - No. 3, June, 2004 ($2.99)
1-3-Wilkins-s&a/Munroe-s 3.00

E-MAN
Charlton Comics: Oct, 1973 - No. 10, Sept, 1975 (Painted-c No. 7-10)
1-Origin & 1st app. E-Man; Staton c/a in all 3 6 9 16 23 30
2-5: 2,4,5-Ditko-a. 3-Howard-a. 5-Miss Liberty Belle app. by Ditko 2 4 6 9 12 15
6-10: 6,7,9,10-Early Byrne-a (#6 is 1/75). 6-Disney parody. 8-Full-length story; Nova begins as E-Man's partner 2 4 6 11 16 20
1-4,9,10 (Modern Comics reprints, '77) 5.00
NOTE: *Killjoy app.-No. 2, 4. Liberty Belle app.-No. 5. Rog 2000 app.-No. 6, 7, 9, 10. Travis app.-No. 3.* ***Sutton*** *a-1.*

E-MAN
Comico: Sept, 1989 ($2.75, one-shot, no ads, high quality paper)
1-Staton-c/a; Michael Mauser story 3.00

E-MAN
Comico: V4#1, Jan, 1990 - No. 3, Mar, 1990 ($2.50, limited series)
1-3: Staton-c/a 3.00

E-MAN
Alpha Productions: Oct, 1993 ($2.75)
V5#1-Staton-c/a; 20th anniversary issue 3.00

E-MAN COMICS (Also see Michael Mauser & The Original E-Man)
First Comics: Apr, 1983 - No. 25, Aug, 1985 ($1.00/$1.25, direct sales only)
1-25: 2-X-Men satire. 3-X-Men/Phoenix satire. 6-Origin retold. 8-Cutey Bunny app. 10-Origin Nova Kane. 24-Origin Michael Mauser 3.00
NOTE: ***Staton*** *a-1-5, 6-25p; c-1-25.*

E-MAN RETURNS
Alpha Productions: 1994 ($2.75, B&W)
1-Joe Staton-c/a(p) 3.00

EMERALD CITY OF OZ, THE (Dorothy Gale from Wonderful Wizard of Oz)
Marvel Comics: Sept, 2013 - No. 5, Feb, 2014 ($3.99, limited series)
1-5-Eric Shanower-s/Skottie Young-a/c 4.00

EMERALD DAWN
DC Comics: 1991 ($4.95, trade paperback)
nn-Reprints Green Lantern: Emerald Dawn #1-6 1 2 3 5 6 8

EMERALD DAWN II (See Green Lantern...)

EMERGENCY (Magazine)
Charlton Comics: June, 1976 - No. 4, Jan, 1977 (B&W)
1-Neal Adams-c/a; Heath, Austin-a 4 8 12 23 37 50
2,3: 2-N. Adams-c. 3-N. Adams-a. 3 6 9 18 28 38
4-Alcala-a 3 6 9 14 20 25

EMERGENCY (TV)
Charlton Comics: June, 1976 - No. 4, Dec, 1976
1-Staton-c; early Byrne-a (22 pages) 3 6 9 19 30 40
2-4: 2-Staton-c. 2,3-Byrne text illos. 3 6 9 14 20 25

EMERGENCY DOCTOR
Charlton Comics: Summer, 1963 (one-shot)
1 3 6 9 19 30 40

EMIL & THE DETECTIVES (See Movie Comics)

EMISSARY (Jim Valentino's...)
Image Comics (Shadowline): May, 2006 - No. 6 ($3.50)
1-6: 1-Rand-s/Ferreyra-a. 4-6-Long-s 3.50

EMMA (Adaptation of the Jane Austen novel)
Marvel Comics: May, 2011 - No. 5, Sept, 2011 ($3.99)
1-5-Nancy Butler-s/Janet K. Lee-a 4.00

EMMA FROST
Marvel Comics: Aug, 2003 - No. 18, Feb, 2005 ($2.50/$2.99)
1-7-Emma in high school; Bollers-s/Green-a/Horn-c 3.00
8-18-($2.99) 3.00
... Vol. 1: Higher Learning TPB (2004, $7.99, digest size) r/#1-6 8.00
... Vol. 2: Mind Games TPB (2005, $7.99, digest size) r/#7-12 8.00
... Vol. 3: Bloom TPB (2005, $7.99, digest size) r/#13-18 8.00

EMMA PEEL & JOHN STEED (See The Avengers)

EMPEROR'S NEW CLOTHES, THE
Dell Publishing Co.: 1950 (10¢, 68 pgs., 1/2 size, oblong)
nn - (Surprise Books series) 6 12 18 31 38 45

EMPIRE
Image Comics (Gorilla): May, 2000 - No. 2, Sept, 2000 ($2.50)
DC Comics: No. 0, Aug, 2003; Sept, 2003 - No. 6, Feb, 2004 ($4.95/$2.50, limited series)
1,2: 1 (5/00)-Waid-s/Kitson-a; w/Crimson Plague prologue 3.00
0-(8/03) reprints #1,2 5.00
1-6: 1-(9/03) new Waid-s/Kitson-a/c 3.00
TPB (DC, 2004, $14.95) r/series; Kitson sketch pages; Waid intro. 15.00

EMPIRE OF THE DEAD: ACT ONE (George Romero's...)
Marvel Comics: Mar, 2014 - No. 5, Aug, 2014 ($3.99)
1-5-George Romero-s/Alex Maleev-a/c; zombies & vampires 4.00

EMPIRE OF THE DEAD: ACT TWO (George Romero's...)
Marvel Comics: Nov, 2014 - No. 5, Mar, 2015 ($3.99)
1-5-George Romero-s/Dalibor Talajic-a; zombies & vampires 4.00

EMPIRE OF THE DEAD: ACT THREE (George Romero's...)
Marvel Comics: Jun, 2015 - No. 5, Nov, 2015 ($3.99)
1-5-George Romero-s/Andrea Mutti-a; zombies & vampires 4.00

EMPIRE STRIKES BACK, THE (See Marvel Comics Super Special #16 & Marvel Special Edition)

EMPIRE: UPRISING
IDW Publishing: Apr, 2015 - No. 4, Jul, 2015 ($3.99)
1-4: Sequel to the 2003-2004 series; Waid-s/Kitson-a; two covers on each 4.00

EMPRESS
Marvel Comics (Icon): Jun, 2016 - No. 7, Jan, 2017 ($3.99/$5.99)
1-6-Millar-s/Immonen-a 4.00
7-($5.99) 6.00

EMPTY, THE
Image Comics: Feb, 2015 - No. 6, Sept, 2015 ($3.50/$3.99)
1-3-Jimmie Robinson-s/a 3.50
4-6-($3.99) 4.00

EMPTY LOVE STORIES
Slave Labor #1 & 2/Funny Valentine Press: Nov, 1994 - No. 2 ($2.95, B&W)
1,2: Steve Darnall scripts in all. 1-Alex Ross-c. 2-(8/96)-Mike Allred-c 4.00
1,2-2nd printing (Funny Valentine Press) 3.00
... 1999-Jeff Smith-c; Doran-a 3.00
..."Special" (2.95) Ty Templeton-c 3.00

EMPTY ZONE
Image Comics: Jun, 2015 - No. 10, Jul, 2016 ($3.50/$3.99)
1-8-Jason Shawn Alexander-s/a 3.50

Ender in Exile #2 © O.S. Card

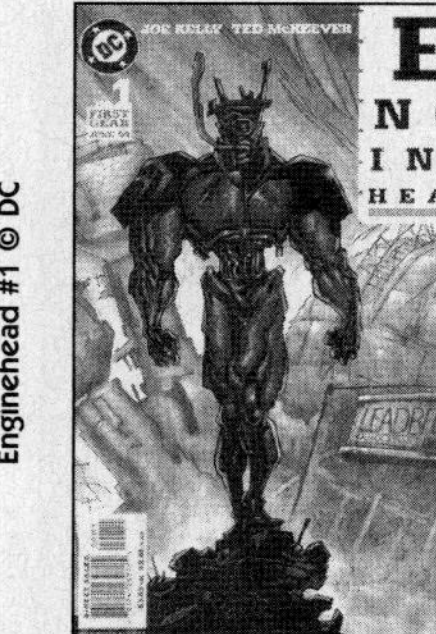

Enginehead #1 © DC

Equilibrium #1 © Miramax

GD 2.0 | VG 4.0 | FN 6.0 | VF 8.0 | VF/NM 9.0 | NM- 9.2

9,10-($3.99) 4.00

ENCHANTED APPLES OF OZ, THE (See First Comics Graphic Novel #5)

ENCHANTED TIKI ROOM
Marvel Comics (Disney Kingdoms): Dec, 2016 - No. 5, Apr, 2017 ($3.99)

1-5-Jon Adams-s/Horacio Domingues-a 4.00

ENCHANTER
Eclipse Comics: Apr, 1987 - No. 3, Aug. 1987 ($2.00, B&W, limited series)

1-3 3.00

ENCHANTING LOVE
Kirby Publishing Co.: Oct, 1949 - No. 6, July, 1950 (All 52 pgs.)

	GD	VG	FN	VF	VF/NM	NM-
1-Photo-c	21	42	63	122	199	275
2-Photo-c; Powell-a	13	26	39	74	105	135
3,4,6: 3-Jimmy Stewart photo-c. 4-Photo-c	13	26	39	72	101	130
5-Ingels-a, 9 pgs.; photo-c	18	36	54	105	165	225

ENCHANTMENT VISUALETTES (Magazine)
World Editions: Dec, 1949 - No. 5, Apr, 1950 (Painted c-1)

	GD	VG	FN	VF	VF/NM	NM-
1-Contains two romance comic strips each	24	48	72	140	230	320
2	15	30	45	90	140	190
3-5	14	28	42	82	121	160

ENDER IN EXILE (Orson Scott Card's...)
Marvel Comics: Aug, 2010 - No. 5, Dec, 2010 ($3.99, limited series)

1-5-Sequel to Ender's Game; Johnston-s/Mhan-a/Fiumara-c 4.00

ENDER'S GAME: BATTLE SCHOOL
Marvel Comics: Dec, 2008 - No. 5, Jun, 2009 ($3.99, limited series)

1-5-Adaptation of Orson Scott Card novel Ender's Game; Yost-s/Ferry-a. 1-Two covers 4.00
Ender's Game: Mazer in Prison Special (4/10, $3.99) Johnston-s/Mhan-a 4.00
Ender's Game: Recruiting Valentine (8/09, $3.99) Timothy Green-a 4.00
Ender's Game: The League War (6/10, $3.99) Aaron Johnston-s/Timothy Green-a 4.00
Ender's Game: War of Gifts Special (2/10, $4.99) Timothy Green-a 5.00

ENDER'S GAME: COMMAND SCHOOL
Marvel Comics: Nov, 2009 - No. 5, Apr, 2010 ($3.99, limited series)

1-5-Adaptation of Orson Scott Card novel Ender's Game; Yost-s/Ferry-a 4.00

ENDER'S SHADOW: BATTLE SCHOOL
Marvel Comics: Feb, 2009 - No. 5, Jun, 2009 ($3.99, limited series)

1-5-Adaptation of O.S. Card novel Ender's Shadow; Carey-s/Fiumara-a. 1-Two covers 4.00

ENDER'S SHADOW: COMMAND SCHOOL
Marvel Comics: Nov, 2009 - No. 5, Apr, 2010 ($3.99, limited series)

1-5-Adaptation of O.S. Card novel Ender's Shadow; Carey-s/Fiumara-a 4.00

END LEAGUE, THE
Dark Horse Comics: Dec, 2007 - No. 9, Nov, 2009 ($2.99/$3.99)

1-8: 1-Broome-c/a; Remender-s. 5,6-Canete-a 3.00
9-($3.99) MacDonald-a/Canete-c 4.00

END OF NATIONS
DC Comics: Jan, 2012 - No. 4, Apr, 2012 ($2.99, limited series)

1-4-Based on the Trion Worlds videogame; Sanchez-s/Guichet-a/Sprouse-c 3.00

END TIMES OF BRAM AND BEN
Image Comics: Jan, 2013 - No. 4, Apr, 2013 ($2.99, limited series)

1-4: 1-Rapture parody; Asmus & Festante-s/Broo-a. 1-Mahfood-c 3.00

ENEMY ACE SPECIAL (Also see Our Army at War #151, Showcase #57, 58 & Star Spangled War Stories #138)
DC Comics: 1990 ($1.00, one-shot)

1-Kubert-r/Our Army #151,153; c-r/Showcase 57 5.00

ENEMY ACE: WAR IDYLL
DC Comics: 1990 (Graphic novel)

Hardcover-George Pratt-s/painted-a/c 30.00
Softcover (1991, $14.95) 15.00

ENEMY ACE: WAR IN HEAVEN
DC Comics: 2001 - No. 2, 2001 ($5.95, squarebound, limited series)

1,2-Ennis-s; Von Hammer in WW2. 1-Weston & Alamy-a. 2-Heath-a 6.00
TPB (2003, $14.95) r/#1,2 & Star Spangled War Stories #139; Jim Dietz-painted-c 15.00

ENGINEHEAD
DC Comics: June, 2004 - No. 6, Nov, 2004 ($2.50, limited series)

1-6-Joe Kelly-s/Ted McKeever-a/c. 6-Metal Men app. 3.00

GD 2.0 | VG 4.0 | FN 6.0 | VF 8.0 | VF/NM 9.0 | NM- 9.2

ENIGMA
DC Comics (Vertigo): Mar, 1993 - No. 8, Oct, 1993 ($2.50, limited series)

1-8: Milligan scripts 3.00
Trade paperback ($19.95)-reprints 20.00

ENO AND PLUM (Also see Cud Comics)
Oni Press: Mar, 1998 ($2.95, B&W)

1-Terry LaBan-s/c/a 3.00

ENSIGN O'TOOLE (TV)
Dell Publishing Co.: Aug-Oct, 1963

	GD	VG	FN	VF	VF/NM	NM-
1	3	6	9	19	30	40

ENSIGN PULVER (See Movie Classics)

ENTER THE HEROIC AGE
Marvel Comics: July, 2010 ($3.99, one-shot)

1-Short stories of Avengers Academy, Atlas, Black Widow, Thunderbolts; Hitch-c 4.00

EPIC
Marvel Comics (Epic Comics): 1992 - Book 4, 1992 ($4.95, lim. series, 52 pgs.)

Book One-Four: 2-Dorman painted-c 5.00
NOTE: *Alien Legion in #3. Cholly & Flytrap by* ***Burden****(scripts) &* ***Suydam****(art) in 3, 4. Dinosaurs in #4. Dreadlands in #1. Hellraiser in #1. Nightbreed in #2. Sleeze Brothers in #2. Stalkers in #1-4. Wild Cards in #1-4.*

EPIC ANTHOLOGY
Marvel Comics (Epic Comics): Apr, 2004 ($5.99)

1-Short stories by various; debut 2nd Sleepwalker by Kirkman-s 6.00

EPIC ILLUSTRATED (Magazine)
Marvel Comics Group: Spring, 1980 - No. 34, Feb, 1986 ($2.00/$2.50, B&W/color, mature)

	GD	VG	FN	VF	VF/NM	NM-
1-Frazetta-c; Silver Surfer/Galactus-sty; Wendy Pini-s/a; Suydam-s/a; Metamorphosis Odyssey begins (thru #9) Starlin-a	3	6	9	16	24	32
2,4-10: 2-Bissette/Veitch-a; Goodwin-s. 4-Ellison 15 pg. story w/Steacy-a; Hempel-s/a; Veitch-s/a. 5-Hildebrandts-c/interview; Jusko-a; Vess-s/a. 6-Ellison-s (26 pgs). 7-Adams-s/a(16 pgs.); BWS interview. 8-Suydam-s/a; Vess-s/a. 9-Conrad-c. 10-Marada the She-Wolf-c/sty(21 pgs.) by Claremont/Bolton	1	3	4	6	8	10
3-1st app. Dreadstar	5	10	15	31	53	75
11-20: 11-Wood-a; Jusko-a. 12-Wolverton Spacehawk-r edited & recolored w/article on him; Muth-a. 13-Blade Runner preview by Williamson. 14-Elric of Melnibone by Russell; Revenge of the Jedi preview. 15-Vallejo-c & interview; 1st Dreadstar solo story (cont'd in Dreadstar #1). 16-B. Smith-c/a(2); Sim-s/a. 17-Starslammers preview. 18-Go Nagai; Williams-a. 19-Jabberwocky w/Hampton-a; Cheech Wizard-s. 20-The Sacred & the Profane begins by Ken Steacy; Elric by Gould; Williams-a	1	3	4	6	8	10
21-30: 21-Vess-s/a. 22-Frankenstein w/Wrightson-a. 26-Galactus series begins (thru #34); Cerebus the Aardvark story by Dave Sim. 27-Groo. 28-Cerebus. 29-1st Sheeva. 30-Cerebus; History of Dreadstar, Starlin-s/a; Williams-a; Vess-a	2	4	6	8	10	12
31-33: 31-Bolton-c/a. 32-Cerebus portfolio.	2	4	6	8	11	14
34-R.E.Howard tribute by Thomas-s/Plunkett-a; Moore-s/Veitch-a; Cerebus; Cholly & Flytrap w/Suydam-a; BWS-a	2	4	6	10	14	18

Sampler (early 1980 8 pg. preview giveaway) same cover as #1 with "Sampler" text 6.00
NOTE: ***N. Adams*** *a-7; c-6.* ***Austin*** *a-15-20i.* ***Bode*** *a-19, 23, 27r.* ***Bolton*** *a-7, 10-12, 15, 18, 22-25; c-10, 18, 22, 23.* ***Boris*** *c/a-15.* ***Brunner*** *c-12.* ***Buscema*** *a-1p, 9p, 11-13p.* ***Byrne/Austin*** *a-26-34.* ***Chaykin*** *a-2; c-8.* ***Conrad*** *a-2-5, 7-9, 25-34; c-17.* ***Corben*** *a-15; c-2.* ***Frazetta*** *c-1.* ***Golden*** *a-3r.* ***Gulacy*** *c/a-3.* ***Jeff Jones*** *c-25.* ***Kaluta*** *a-17r, 21, 24r, 26; c-4, 28.* ***Nebres*** *a-1.* ***Reese*** *a-12.* ***Russell*** *a-2-4, 9, 14, 33; c-14.* ***Simonson*** *a-17.* ***B. Smith*** *c/a-7, 16.* ***Starlin*** *a-1-9, 14, 15, 34.* ***Steranko*** *c-19.* ***Williamson*** *a-13, 27, 34.* ***Wrightson*** *a-13p, 22, 25, 27, 34; c-30.*

EPIC LITE
Marvel Comics (Epic Comics): Sept, 1991 ($3.95, 52 pgs., one-shot)

1-Bob the Alien, Normalman by Valentino 4.00

EPICURUS THE SAGE
DC Comics (Piranha Press): Vol. 1, 1991 - Vol. 2, 1991 ($9.95, 8-1/8x10-7/8")

Volume 1,2-Sam Kieth-c/a; Messner-Loebs-s 12.00
TPB (2003, $19.95) r/ #1,2, Fast Forward Rising the Sun; new story 20.00

EPILOGUE
IDW Publishing: Sept, 2008 - No. 4, Dec, 2008 ($3.99)

1-4-Steve Niles-s/Kyle Hotz-a/c 4.00

EQUILIBRIUM (Based on the 2002 movie)
American Mythology Prods.: 2016 - Present ($3.99)

1,2-Pat Shand-s/Jason Craig-a; multiple covers 4.00

ERADICATOR
DC Comics: Aug, 1996 - No. 3, Oct, 1996 ($1.75, limited series)

1-3: Superman app. 3.00

ERNIE COMICS (Formerly Andy Comics #21; All Love Romances #26 on)

Escape From New York #16 © Studio Canal

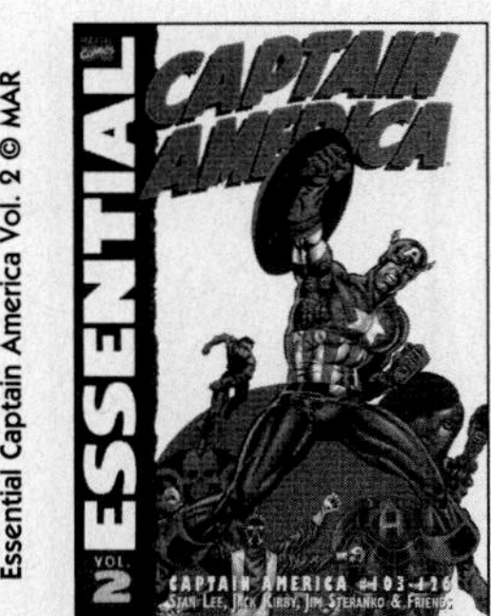

Essential Captain America Vol. 2 © MAR

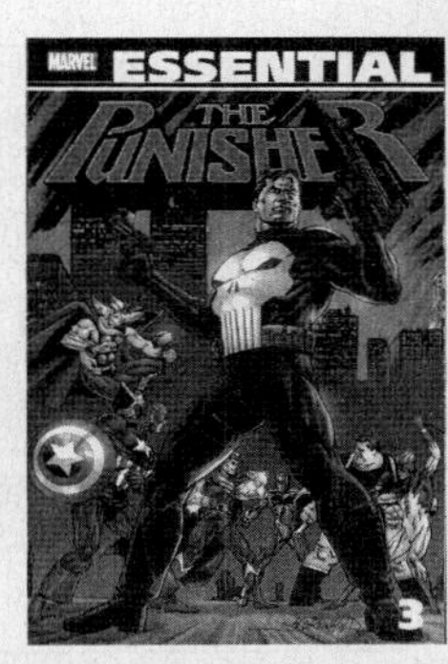

Essential Punisher Vol. 3 © MAR

	GD 2.0	VG 4.0	FN 6.0	VF 8.0	VF/NM 9.0	NM- 9.2

Current Books/Ace Periodicals: No. 22, Sept, 1948 - No. 25, Mar, 1949

nn (9/48,11/48; #22,23)-Teenage humor	10	20	30	58	79	100
24,25	9	18	27	47	61	75

ESCAPADE IN FLORENCE (See Movie Comics)

ESCAPE FROM DEVIL'S ISLAND
Avon Periodicals: 1952

1-Kinstler-c; r/as Dynamic Adventures #9	43	86	129	271	461	650

ESCAPE FROM NEW YORK (Based on the Kurt Russell movie)
BOOM! Studios: Dec, 2014 - No. 16, Apr, 2016 ($3.99)

1-16: 1-8-Christopher Sebela-s/Diego Barreto-a; multiple covers on each. 9-16-Simic-a 4.00

ESCAPE FROM THE PLANET OF THE APES (See Power Record Comics)

ESCAPE TO WITCH MOUNTAIN (See Walt Disney Showcase No. 29)

ESCAPISTS, THE (See Michael Chabon Presents The Amazing Adventures of the Escapist)
Dark Horse Comics: July, 2006 - No. 6, Dec, 2006 ($1.00/$2.99, limited series)

1-($1.00) Frank Miller-c; r/Vaughan story from Michael Chabon... #8 3.00
2-6($2.99) Vaughan-s/Rolston & Alexander-a. 2-James Jean-c. 3-Cassaday-c 3.00

ESPERS (Also see Interface)
Eclipse Comics: July, 1986 - No. 5, Apr, 1987 ($1.25/$1.75, Mando paper)

1-5-James Hudnall story & David Lloyd-a. 3.00

ESPERS
Halloween Comics: V2#1, 1996 - No. 6, 1997 ($2.95, B&W) (1st Halloween Comics series)

V2#1-6: James D. Hudnall scripts 3.00
Undertow TPB ('98, $14.95) r/#1-6 15.00

ESPERS
Image Comics: V3#1, 1997 - Present ($2.95, B&W, limited series)

V3#1-7: James D. Hudnall scripts 3.00
Black Magic TPB ('98, $14.95) r/#1-4 15.00

ESPIONAGE (TV)
Dell Publishing Co.: May-July, 1964

1	3	6	9	19	30	40

ESSENTIAL (Title series), **Marvel Comics**

--ANT-MAN, '02 (B&W- r) V1-Reprints app. from Tales To Astonish #27, #35-69; Kirby-c 15.00

--AVENGERS, '98 (B&W- r) V1-R-Avengers #1-24; new Immonen-c 15.00
V2(6/00)-Reprints Avengers #25-46, King-Size Special #1; Immonen-c 15.00
V3(3/01)-Reprints Avengers #47-68, Annual #2; Immonen-c 15.00
V4('04)-Reprints Avengers #69-97, Incredible Hulk #140; Neal Adams-c 17.00
V5('06)-Reprints Avengers #98-119, Daredevil #99, Defenders #8-11 17.00
V6('08)-Reprints Avengers #120-140, Giant Size #1-4, Capt. Marvel #33 & FF #150 17.00

--CAPTAIN AMERICA, '00 (B&W- r) V1-Reprints stories from Tales of Suspense #59-99, Captain America #100-102; new Romita & Milgrom-c 15.00
V2(1/02)-Reprints #103-126; Steranko-c 15.00
V3('06)-Reprints #127-153 17.00
V4('07)-Reprints #157-186 17.00

--CLASSIC X-MEN, '06 (B&W- r) (See Essential Uncanny X-Men for V1)
V2-($16.99) R-X-Men #25-53 & Avengers #53; Gil Kane-c 17.00

--CONAN, '00 (B&W- r) V1-R-Conan the Barbarian#1-25; new Buscema-c 15.00

--DAREDEVIL, '02 - V4 (B&W-r)
V1-R-Daredevil #1-25 15.00
V2-($16.99) R-Daredevil #26-48, Special #1, Fantastic Four #73 17.00
V3-($16.99) R-Daredevil #49-74, Iron Man #35-38 17.00
V4-($16.99) R-Daredevil #75-101, Avengers #111 17.00

--DAZZLER, '07 (B&W- r) V1-R/#1-21, X-Men #130-131, Amaz. Spider-Man #203 17.00

--DEFENDERS, '05 (B&W-r) V1-Reprints Doctor Strange #183, Sub-Mariner #22,34,35, Incredible Hulk #126, Marvel Feature #1-3, Defenders #1-14, Avengers #115-118 17.00
V2-($16.99) R- Defenders #15-30, Giant-Size Defenders #1-4, Marvel Two-In-One #6,7, Marvel Team-Up #33-35 and Marvel Treasury Edition #12 17.00
V3-($16.99) R- Defenders #31-60 and Annual #1 17.00

--DOCTOR STRANGE, '04 - V3 (B&W-r)
V1-($15.95) Reprints Strange Tales #110,111,114-168 17.00
V1 (2nd printing)-(2006, $16.99) Reprints Strange Tales #110,111,114-168 17.00
V2-($16.99) R-Doctor Strange #169-178,180-183; Avengers #61, Sub-Mariner #22 Marvel Feature #1, Incredible Hulk #126 and Marvel Premiere #3-14 17.00
V3-($16.99) R-Doctor Strange #1-29 & Annual #1;Tomb of Dracula #44,45 17.00

--FANTASTIC FOUR, '98 - V6 (B&W-r)
V1-Reprints FF #1-20, Annual #1; new Alan Davis-c; multiple printings exist 17.00
V2-Reprints FF #21-40, Annual #2; Davis and Farmer-c 15.00
V3-Reprints FF #41-63, Annual #3,4; Davis-c 15.00
V4-Reprints FF #64-83, Annual #5,6 17.00
V5-Reprints FF #84-110 17.00
V6-Reprints FF #111-137 17.00

--GHOST RIDER, '05 (B&W-r) V1-Reprints Marvel Spotlight #5-12, Ghost Rider #1-20 and Daredevil #138 17.00
V2-Reprints Ghost Rider #21-50 17.00

--GODZILLA, '06 (B&W-r) V1-Godzilla #1-24 20.00

--HOWARD THE DUCK, '02 (B&W- r) V1-Reprints #1-27, Annual #1; plus stories from Marvel Treasury Ed. #12, Man-Thing #1, Giant-Size Man-Thing #4,5, Fear #19; Bolland-c 15.00

--HULK, '99 (B&W-r) V1-R-Incred. Hulk #1-6, Tales To Astonish stories; new Timm-c 15.00
V2-Reprints Tales To Astonish #102-117, Annual #1 15.00
V3-Reprints Incredible Hulk #118-142, Capt. Marvel #20&21, Avengers #88 17.00
V4-Reprints Incredible Hulk #143-170 17.00
V5-Reprints Incredible Hulk #171-200, Annual #5 17.00

--HUMAN TORCH, '03 (B&W-r) V1-Strange Tales #101-134 & Ann. 2; Kirby-c 15.00

--IRON MAN, '00 - V3 (B&W-r)
V1-Reprints Tales Of Suspense #39-72; new Timm-c and back-c 15.00
V2-Reprints Tales Of Suspense #73-99, Tales To Astonish #82 & Iron Man #1-11 17.00
V3-Reprints Iron Man #12-38 & Daredevil #73 17.00

--KILLRAVEN, '05 (B&W-r) V1-Reprints Amazing Adventures V2 #18-39, Marvel Team-Up #45, Marvel Graphic Novel #7, Killraven #1 (2001) 17.00

--LUKE CAGE, POWER MAN, '05 (B&W-r) V1-Hero For Hire #1-16 & Power Man #17-27 17.00
V2-Reprints Power Man #28-49 & Annual #1 17.00

--MAN-THING, '06 (B&W-r) V1-Reprints Savage Tales #1, Astonishing Tales #12-13, Adventure Into Fear #10-19, Man-Thing #1-14, Giant-Size Man-Thing #1-2 & Monsters Unleashed #5,8,9 17.00
V2-R/Man-Thing #15-22 & #1-11 ('79 series), Giant-Size Man-Thing #3-5, Rampaging Hulk #7, Marvel Team-Up #68, Marvel Two-In-One #43 & Doctor Strange #41 17.00

--MARVEL HORROR, '06 (B&W-r) V1-R/#Ghost Rider #1-2, Marvel Spotlight #12-24, Son of Satan #1-8, Marvel Two-In-One #14, Marvel Team-Up #32,80,81, Vampire Tales #2-3, Haunt of Horror #2,4,5, Marvel Premiere #27, & Marvel Preview #7 17.00

--MARVEL SAGA, '08 (B&W-r) V1-R/#1-12 17.00

--MARVEL TEAM-UP, '02 - V2 (B&W-r) V1('02, '06)-R/#1-24 17.00
V2-R/#25-51 and Marvel Two-In-One #17 17.00

--MARVEL TWO-IN-ONE, '05 - V2 (B&W-r)
V1-Reprints Marvel Feature #11&12, Marvel Two-In-One #1-20,22-25 & Annual #1, Marvel Team-Up #47 and Fantastic Four Ann. #11 17.00
V2-R/#26-52 & Annual #2,3 17.00

--MONSTER OF FRANKENSTEIN, '04 (B&W-r) V1-Reprints Monster of Frankenstein #1-5, Frankenstein Monster #6-18, Giant-Size Werewolf #2, Monsters Unleashed #2,4-10 & Legion of Monsters #1 17.00

--MOON KNIGHT, '06 (B&W-r) V1-Reprints Moon Knight #1-10 and early apps. 17.00
V2-R/#11-30 17.00

--MS. MARVEL, '07 (B&W-r) V1-Reprints Ms. Marvel #1-23, Marvel Super-Heroes Magazine #10,11, and Avengers Annual #10 17.00

--NOVA, '06 (B&W-r) V1-Reprints Nova #1-25, AS-M #171, Marvel Two-In-One Ann. #3 17.00

--OFFICIAL HANDBOOK OF THE MARVEL UNIVERSE, '06 (B&W-r) V1-Reprints #1-15 profiling Abomination through Zzzax; dead and inactive characters; weapons & hardware; wraparound-c by Byrne 17.00

--OFFICIAL HANDBOOK OF THE MARVEL UNIVERSE - DELUXE EDITION, '06 (B&W-r)
V1-Reprints #1-7 profiling Abomination through Magneto; wraparound-c by Byrne 17.00
V2-Reprints #8-14 profiling Magus through Wolverine; wraparound-c by Byrne 17.00
V3-Reprints #15-20 profiling Wonder Man through Zzzax & Book of the Dead 17.00

--OFFICIAL HANDBOOK OF THE MARVEL UNIVERSE - MASTER EDITION, '08 (B&W-r)
V1-Reprints profiling Abomination through Gargoyle 17.00
V2-Reprints profiles 17.00

--OFFICIAL HANDBOOK OF THE MARVEL UNIVERSE - UPDATE '89, '06 (B&W-r)
V1-Reprints #1-8; wraparound-c by Frenz 17.00

--PETER PARKER, THE SPECTACULAR SPIDER-MAN, '05 (B&W-r) V1-Reprints #1-31 17.00
V2-Reprints #32-53 & Annual #1,2; Amazing Spider-Man Annual #13 17.00
V3-Reprints #54-74 & Annual #3; Frank Miller-c 17.00

--POWER MAN AND IRON FIST, '07 (B&W-r) V1-R/#50-72,74-75 17.00

--PUNISHER, '04, '06 - Present (B&W-r) V1-Reprints early app. in Amazing Spider-Man, Captain America, Daredevil, Marvel Preview and Punisher #1-5 (2 printings) 17.00

Essential Tomb of Dracula Vol. 3 © MAR

Eternals (2006 series) #1 © MAR

Eternal Warrior #11 © VAL

	GD	VG	FN	VF	VF/NM	NM-
	2.0	4.0	6.0	8.0	9.0	9.2

V2-Punisher #1-20, Annual #1 and Daredevil #257 17.00
V3-Punisher #21-40, Annual #2,3 17.00

--RAMPAGING HULK, '08 (B&W-r) V1-R/#1-9, The Hulk! #10-15 & Incredible Hulk #269 17.00

--SAVAGE SHE-HULK, '06 (B&W-r) V1-R/#1-25 17.00

--SILVER SURFER, '98 - Present (B&W-r)
V1-R-material from SS#1-18 and Fantastic Four Ann. #5 15.00
V2-R-SS#1(1982), SS#1-18 & Ann#1(1987), Epic Illustrated #1, Marvel Fanfare #51 17.00

--SPIDER-MAN, '96 - V8 (B&W-r)
V1-R-AF #15, Amaz. S-M #1-20, Ann. #1 (2 printings) 15.00
V2-R-Amaz. Spider-Man #21-43, Annual #2,3 15.00
V3-R-Amaz. Spider-Man #44-68 15.00
V4-R-Amaz. Spider-Man #69-89; Annual #4,5; new Timm-f&b-c 15.00
V5-R-Amaz. Spider-Man #90-113; new Romita-c 15.00
V6-R-Amaz. Spider-Man #114-137, Giant-Size Super-Heroes #1 G-S S-M #1,2 17.00
V7-R-Amaz. Spider-Man #138-160, Annual #10; Giant-Size Spider-Man #3-5 17.00
V8-R-Amaz. Spider-Man #161-185, Annual #11; G-S Spider-Man #6; Nova #12 17.00

--SPIDER-WOMAN, '05 (B&W-r) V1-Reprints Marvel Spotlight #32, Marvel Two-In-One #29-33, Spider-Woman #1-25 17.00
V2-R-Spider-Woman #26-50, Marvel Team-Up #97 & Uncanny X-Men #148 17.00

--SUPER-VILLAIN TEAM-UP, '04 (B&W-r) V1-r/S-V T-U #1-14 & 16-17, Giant-Size S-V T-U #1,2; Avengers #154-156; Champions #16, & Astonishing Tales #1-8 17.00

--TALES OF THE ZOMBIE, '06 (B&W-r) V1-($16.99) r/#1-10 & Dracula Lives #1,2 17.00

--THOR, '01 (B&W-r) V1-R-Journey Into Mystery #83-112 15.00
V2-($16.99) R-Thor #113-136 & Annual #1,2 17.00
V3-($16.99) R-Thor #137-166 17.00

--TOMB OF DRACULA, '03 - V4 (B&W-r) V1-R-Tomb of Dracula #1-25, Werewolf By Night #15, Giant-Size Chillers #1 15.00
V2-($16.99) R-Tomb of Dracula #26-49, Giant-Size Dracula #2-5, Dr. Strange #14 17.00
V3-($16.99) R-Tomb of Dracula #50-70, Tomb of Dracula Magazine #1-4 17.00
V4-($16.99) R/Stories from Tomb of Dracula Magazine #2-6, Dracula Lives! #1-13, and Frankenstein Monster #7-9 17.00

--UNCANNY X-MEN, '99 (B&W reprints) (See Essential Classic X-Men for V2)
V1-Reprints X-Men (1st series) #1-24; Timm-c 15.00

ESSENTIAL VERTIGO: THE SANDMAN
DC Comics (Vertigo): Aug, 1996 - No. 32, Mar, 1999 ($1.95/$2.25, reprints)
1-13,15-31: Reprints Sandman, 2nd series 3.00
14-($2.95) 3.50
32-($4.50) Reprints Sandman Special #1 4.50

ESSENTIAL VERTIGO: SWAMP THING
DC Comics: Nov, 1996 - No. 24, Oct, 1998 ($1.95/$2.25,B&W, reprints)
1-11,13-24: 1-9-Reprints Alan Moore's Swamp Thing stories 3.00
12-($3.50) r/Annual #2 4.00

ESSENTIAL WEREWOLF BY NIGHT
Marvel Comics: 2005 - V2 (B&W reprints)
V1-($16.99) r/Marvel Spotlight #2-4, Werewolf By Night 1-23, Marvel Team-Up #12, Tomb of Dracula #18, Giant-Size Creatures #1 17.00
V2-R/#22-43, Giant-Size Werewolf #2-5 and Marvel Premiere #28 17.00

ESSENTIAL WOLVERINE
Marvel Comics: 1999 - V4 (B&W reprints)
V1-r/#1-23, V2-r/#24-47, V3-R/#48-69, V4-R/#70-90 17.00

ESSENTIAL X-FACTOR
Marvel Comics: 2005 - V2 (B&W reprints)
V1-($16.99) r/X-Factor #1-16 & Annual #1, Avengers #262, Fantastic Four #286, Thor #373&374 and Power Pack #27 17.00
V2-Reprints X-Factor #17-35 & Annual #2, Thor #378 17.00

ESSENTIAL X-MEN
Marvel Comics: 1996 - V8 (B&W reprints)
V1-V4: V1-R/Giant Size X-Men #1, X-Men #94-119. V2-R-X-Men #120-144. V3-R-Uncanny X-Men #145-161, Ann. #3-5. V4-Uncanny X-Men #162-179, Ann. #6 15.00
V5-($16.99) R/Uncanny X-Men #180-198, Ann. #7-8 17.00
V6-($16.99) R/Uncanny X-Men #199-213, Ann. #9, New Mutants Special Edition #1, X-Factor #9-11, New Mutants #46, Thor #373-374 and Power Pack #27 17.00
V7-($16.99) R/Uncanny X-Men #214-228, Ann. #10,11, and F.F. vs. The X-Men #1-4 17.00
V8-($16.99) R/Uncanny X-Men #229-243, Ann. #12 & X-Factor #36-39 17.00

ESTABLISHMENT, THE (Also see The Authority and The Monarchy)
DC Comics (WildStorm): Nov, 2001 - No. 13, Nov, 2002 ($2.50)
1-13-Edginton-s/Adlard-a 3.00

ETERNAL
BOOM! Studios: Dec, 2014 - No. 4, Apr, 2015 ($3.99)
1-4: 1-Harms-s/Valletta-a/Irving-c 4.00

ETERNAL, THE
Marvel Comics (MAX): Aug, 2003 - No. 6, Jan, 2004 ($2.99, mature)
1-6-Austen-s/Walker-a 3.00

ETERNAL BIBLE, THE
Authentic Publications: 1946 (Large size) (16 pgs. in color)
1 16 32 48 94 147 200

ETERNALS, THE
Marvel Comics Group: July, 1976 - No. 19, Jan, 1978
1-(Regular 25¢ edition)-Origin & 1st app. Eternals 3 6 9 21 33 45
1-(30¢-c variant, limited distribution) 5 10 15 31 53 75
2-(Reg. 25¢ edition)-1st app. Ajak & The Celestials 3 6 9 14 20 25
2-(30¢-c variant, limited distribution) 4 8 12 23 37 50
3-19: 14,15-Cosmic powered Hulk-c/story 2 4 6 8 10 12
12-16-(35¢-c variants, limited distribution) 6 12 18 38 69 100
Annual 1(10/77) 2 4 6 9 12 15
Eternals by Jack Kirby HC (2006, $75.00, dust jacket) r/#1-19 & Annual #1; intro by Royer; letter pages from #1,2,Annual #1; afterwords by Robert Greenberger 75.00
NOTE: *Kirby c/a(p) in all.*

ETERNALS, THE
Marvel Comics: Oct, 1985 - No. 12, Sept, 1986 (Maxi-series, mando paper)
1,12 (52 pgs.): 12-Williamson-a(i) 5.00
2-11 4.00

ETERNALS
Marvel Comics: Aug, 2006 - No. 7, Mar, 2007 ($3.99, limited series)
1-7-Neil Gaiman-s/John Romita Jr.-a/Rick Berry-c 4.00
1-7-Variant covers by Romita Jr. 4.00
1-Variant cover by Coipel 4.00
... Sketchbook (2006, $1.99, B&W) character sketches and sketch pages from #1 3.00
HC (2007, $29.99, dustjacket) r/#1-7; gallery of variant covers; sketches, Gaiman interview, Gaiman's original proposal; background essay on Kirby's Eternals 30.00

ETERNALS
Marvel Comics: Aug, 2008 - No. 9, May, 2009 ($2.99)
1-9: 1-6-Acuña-a/c; Knauf-s. 2,4-Iron Man app. 7,8-Nguyen-a; X-Men app. 3.00
Annual 1 (1/09, $3.99) Alixe-a/McGuinness-c; & reprint from Eternals #7 ('77) Kirby-s/a 4.00

ETERNAL SOULFIRE (Also see Soulfire)
Aspen MLT, Inc.: Jul, 2015 - No. 6, Feb, 2016 ($3.99, limited series)
1-6-Multiple covers on each. 1-Krul-s/Konat-a. 3-Tovar & Konat-a 4.00

ETERNALS: THE HEROD FACTOR
Marvel Comics: Nov, 1991 ($2.50, 68 pgs.)
1 4.00

ETERNAL WARRIOR (See Solar #10 & 11)
Valiant/Acclaim Comics (Valiant): Aug, 1992 - No. 50, Mar, 1996 ($2.25/$2.50)
1-Unity x-over; Miller-c; origin Eternal Warrior & Aram (Armstrong) 6.00
1-($2.25-c) Gold logo 2 4 6 13 18 22
1-Gold foil logo on embossed cover; no cover price 3 6 9 17 26 35
2,3,5-8: 2-Unity x-over; Simonson-c. 3-Archer & Armstrong x-over. 5-2nd full app. Bloodshot (12/92; see Rai #0). 6,7: 6-2nd app. Master Darque. 8-Flip book w/Archer & Armstrong #8 4.00
4-1st brief app. Bloodshot (last pg.); see Rai #0 for 1st full app.; Cowan-c 3 6 9 14 20 25
9-25,27-34: 9-1st Book of Geomancer. 14-16-Bloodshot app. 18-Doctor Mirage cameo. 19-Doctor Mirage app. 22-W/bound-in trading card. 25-Archer & Armstrong app.; cont'd from A&A #25 3.00
26-($2.75, 44 pgs.)-Flip book w/Archer & Armstrong 4.00
35-50: 35-Double-c; $2.50-c begins. 50-Geomancer app. 3.00
Special 1 (2/96, $2.50)-Wings of Justice; Art Holcomb script 3.00
Yearbook 1 (1993, $3.95), 2(1994, $3.95) 4.00

ETERNAL WARRIOR (Also see Wrath of the Eternal Warrior)
Valiant Entertainment: Sept, 2013 - No. 8, Apr, 2014 ($3.99)
1-8: 1-Pak-s/Hairsine-a; 2 covers. 2-Hairsine & Crain-a 4.00

ETERNAL WARRIORS: BLACKWORKS
Acclaim Comics (Valiant Heroes): Mar, 1998 ($3.50, one-shot)
1 3.50

Ether #1 © Kindt & Rubin

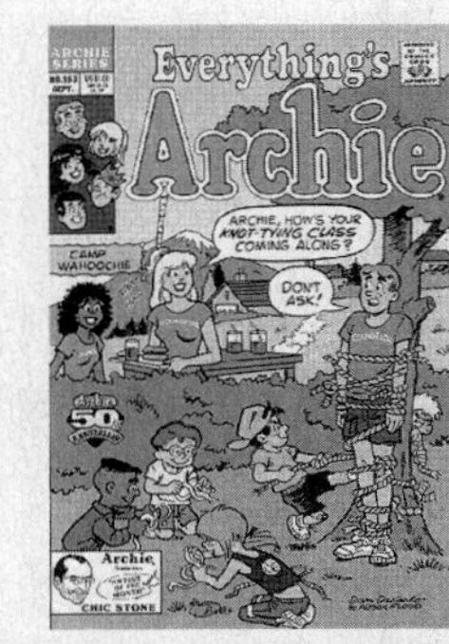

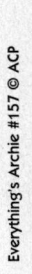

Everything's Archie #157 © ACP

Evil Ernie (1998 series) #1 © Chaos!

	GD 2.0	VG 4.0	FN 6.0	VF 8.0	VF/NM 9.0	NM- 9.2

ETERNAL WARRIOR: DAYS OF STEEL
Valiant Entertainment: Nov, 2014 - No. 3, Jan, 2015 ($3.99)

1-3-Milligan-s/Nord-a						4.00

ETERNAL WARRIORS: DIGITAL ALCHEMY
Acclaim Comics (Valiant Heroes): Vol. 2, Sep, 1997 ($3.95, one-shot, 64 pgs.)

Vol. 2-Holcomb-s/Eaglesham-a(p)						4.00

ETERNAL WARRIORS: FIST AND STEEL
Acclaim Comics (Valiant): May, 1996 - No. 2, June, 1996 ($2.50, lim. series)

1,2: Geomancer app. in both. 1-Indicia reads "June." 2-Bo Hampton-a						3.00

ETERNAL WARRIORS: TIME AND TREACHERY
Acclaim Comics (Valiant Heroes): Vol. 1, Jun, 1997 ($3.95, one-shot, 48 pgs.)

Vol. 1-Reintro Aram, Archer, Ivar the Timewalker, & Gilad the Warmaster; 1st app. Shalla Redburn; Art Holcomb script						4.00

ETERNITY SMITH
Renegade Press: Sept, 1986 - No. 5, May, 1987 ($1.25/$1.50, 36 pgs.)

1-5: 1st app. Eternity Smith. 5-Death of Jasmine						3.00

ETERNITY SMITH
Hero Comics: Sept, 1987 - No. 9, 1988 ($1.95)

V2#1-9: 8-Indigo begins						3.00

ETTA KETT
King Features Syndicate/Standard: No. 11, Dec, 1948 - No. 14, Sept, 1949

11-Teenage	14	28	42	80	115	150
12-14	10	20	30	58	79	100

ETHER
Dark Horse Comics: Nov, 2016 - Present ($3.99)

1-4-Matt Kindt-s/David Rubin-a						4.00

EVA: DAUGHTER OF THE DRAGON
Dynamite Entertainment: 2007 ($4.99, one-shot)

1-Two covers by Jo Chen and Edgar Salazar; Jerwa-s/Salazar-a						5.00

EVANGELINE (Also see Primer)
Comico/First Comics V2#1 on/Lodestone Publ.: 1984 - #2, 6/84; V2#1, 5/87 - V2#12, Mar, 1989 (Baxter paper)

1,2, V2#1 (5/87) - 12, Special #1 (1986, $2.00)-Lodestone Publ.						3.00

EVA THE IMP
Red Top Comic/Decker: 1957 - No. 2, Nov, 1957

1,2	5	10	14	20	24	28

EVEN MORE FUND COMICS (Benefit book for the Comic Book Legal Defense Fund) (Also see More Fund Comics)
Sky Dog Press: Sept, 2004 ($10.00, B&W, trade paperback)

nn-Anthology of short stories and pin-ups by various; Spider-Man-c by Cho						10.00

E.V.E. PROTOMECHA
Image Comics (Top Cow): Mar, 2000 - No. 6, Sept, 2000 ($2.50)

Preview ($5.95) Flip book w/Soul Saga preview	2	4	6	8	10	12
1-6: 1-Covers by Finch, Madureira, Garza. 2-Turner var-c						3.00
1-Another Universe variant-c						5.00
TPB (5/01, $17.95) r/#1-6 plus cover galley and sketch pages						18.00

EVERAFTER (See Fables)
DC Comics (Vertigo): Nov, 2016 - No. 5 ($3.99)

1-7: 1-Justus & Sturges-s/Travis Moore-a; Snow & Bigby app. 7-Buckingham-a						4.00

EVERQUEST: ... (Based on online role-playing game)
DC Comics (WildStorm): 2002 ($5.95, one-shots)

The Ruins of Kunark - Jim Lee & Dan Norton-a; McQuaid & Lee-s; Lee-c						6.00
Transformations - Philip Tan-a; Devin Grayson-s; Portacio-c						6.00

EVERYBODY'S COMICS (See Fox Giants)

EVERYMAN, THE
Marvel Comics (Epic Comics): Nov, 1991 ($4.50, one-shot, 52 pgs.)

1-Mike Allred-a	1	2	3	4	5	7

EVERYTHING HAPPENS TO HARVEY
National Periodical Publications: Sept-Oct, 1953 - No. 7, Sept-Oct, 1954

1	37	74	111	222	361	500
2	19	38	57	111	176	240
3-7	15	30	45	90	140	190

EVERYTHING'S ARCHIE
Archie Publications: May, 1969 - No. 157, Sept, 1991 (Giant issues No. 1-20)

1-(68 pages)	8	16	24	54	102	150
2-(68 pages)	4	8	12	28	47	65
3-5-(68 pages)	4	8	12	25	40	55
6-13-(68 pages)	3	6	9	17	26	35
14-31-(52 pages)	2	4	6	13	18	22
32 (7/74)-50 (8/76)	2	4	6	8	10	12
51-80 (12/79),100 (4/82)	1	2	3	5	6	8
81-99						6.00
101-103,105,106,108-120						5.00
104,107-Cheryl Blossom app.	1	2	3	4	5	7
121-156: 142,148-Gene Colan-a						4.00
157-Last issue						5.00

EVERYTHING'S DUCKY (Movie)
Dell Publishing Co.: No. 1251, 1961

Four Color 1251-Mickey Rooney & Buddy Hackett photo-c	5	10	15	34	60	85

EVE: VALKYRIE (Based on the video game)
Dark Horse Comics: Oct, 2015 - No. 4, Jan, 2016 ($3.99, limited series)

1-4-Brian Wood-s/Eduardo Francisco-a						4.00

EVIL DEAD, THE (Movie)
Dark Horse Comics: Jan, 2008 - No. 4, Apr, 2008 ($2.99, limited series)

1-4-Adaptation of the Sam Raimi/Bruce Campbell movie; Bolton painted-a/c						3.00

EVIL DEAD 2 (Movie)
Space Goat Productions: 2016 ($3.99, one-shots)

...: Revenge of Hitler 1 - Edginton-s/Watts-a						4.00
...: Revenge of Jack the Ripper 1 - Ball-s/Mauriz-a						4.00
...: Revenge of Krampus 1 - Edginton-s/Youkovich-a						4.00

EVIL DEAD 2: BEYOND DEAD BY DAWN (Movie)
Space Goat Productions: 2015 - No. 3 ($3.99, limited series)

1-3-Sequel to the Sam Raimi/Bruce Campbell movie; Hannah-s/Bagenda & Bazaldua-a						4.00

EVIL DEAD 2: CRADLE OF THE DAMNED (Movie)
Space Goat Productions: 2016 - Present ($3.99, limited series)

1-Hannah-s/Bagenda & Bazaldua-a						4.00

EVIL DEAD 2: DARK ONES RISING (Movie)
Space Goat Productions: 2016 - No. 3, 2016 ($3.99, limited series)

1-3-Sequel to the Sam Raimi/Bruce Campbell movie; Hannah-s/Valdes-a						4.00

EVIL ERNIE
Eternity Comics: Dec, 1991 - No. 5, 1992 ($2.50, B&W, limited series)

1-1st app. Lady Death by Steven Hughes (12,000 print run); Lady Death app. in all issues	9	18	27	59	117	175
2-1st Lady Death-c (7,000 print run)	5	10	15	34	60	85
3-(7,000 print run)	4	8	12	28	47	65
4-(8,000 print run)	4	8	12	23	37	50
5	3	6	9	19	30	40
Special Edition 1	3	6	9	17	26	35
Youth Gone Wild! ($9.95, trade paperback)-r/#1-5	2	4	6	8	10	12
Youth Gone Wild! Director's Cut ($4.95)-Limited to 15,000, shows the making of the comic						6.00

EVIL ERNIE (Monthly series)
Chaos! Comics: July, 1998 - No. 10, Apr, 1999 ($2.95)

1-10-Pulido & Nutman-s/Brewer-a						3.00
1-($10.00) Premium Ed.						10.00
... Baddest Battles (1/97, $1.50) Pin-ups; 2 covers						3.00
... Pieces of Me (11/00, $2.95, B&W) Flashback story; Pulido-s/Beck-a						3.00
... Relentless (5/02, $4.99, B&W) Pulido-s/Beck, Bonk, & Brewer-a						5.00
... Returns (10/01, $3.99, B&W) Pulido-s/Beck-a						4.00

EVIL ERNIE
Dynamite Entertainment: 2012 - No. 6, 2013 ($3.99)

1-6: 1-Origin re-told; Snider-s/Craig-a; covers by Brereton, Seeley, Syaf & Bradshaw						4.00

EVIL ERNIE (Volume 2)
Dynamite Entertainment: 2014 - No. 6, 2015 ($3.99)

1-6-Tim & Steve Seeley-s/Rafael Lanhellas-a; multiple covers						4.00

EVIL ERNIE: DEPRAVED
Chaos! Comics: Jul, 1999 - No. 3, Sept, 1999 ($2.95, limited series)

1-3-Pulido-s/Brewer-a						3.00

EVIL ERNIE: DESTROYER

Evil Eye #3 © Richard Sala

Excalibur #125 © MAR

Exciting Comics #13 © STD

	GD 2.0	VG 4.0	FN 6.0	VF 8.0	VF/NM 9.0	NM- 9.2

Chaos! Comics: Oct, 1997 - No. 9, Jun, 1998 ($2.95, limited series)
Preview ($2.50), 1-9-Flip cover 3.00

EVIL ERNIE: GODEATER
Dynamite Entertainment: 2016 - No. 5, 2016 ($3.99)
1-5-Jordan-s/Worley-a; Davidsen-s/Razek-a; multiple covers 4.00

EVIL ERNIE: IN SANTA FE
Devil's Due Publ.: Sept, 2005 - No. 4, Mar, 2006 ($2.95, limited series)
1-4-Alan Grant-s/Tommy Castillo-a/Alex Horley-c 3.00

EVIL ERNIE: REVENGE
Chaos! Comics: Oct, 1994 - No. 4, Feb, 1995 ($2.95, limited series)
1-Glow-in-the-dark-c; Lady Death app. 1-3-flip book w. Kilzone Preview (series of 3) 5.00
1-Commemorative-(4000 print run) 1 3 4 6 8 10
2-4 4.00
Trade paperback (10/95, $12.95) 13.00

EVIL ERNIE: STRAIGHT TO HELL
Chaos! Comics: Oct, 1995 - No. 5, May, 1996 ($2.95, limited series)
1-5: 1-fold-out-c 4.00
1,3:1-($19.95) Chromium Ed. 3-Chastity Chase-c-(4000 printed) 20.00
Special Edition (10,000) 20.00

EVIL ERNIE: THE RESURRECTION
Chaos! Comics: 1993 - No. 4, 1994 (Limited series)
0 5.00
1 2 4 6 8 10 12
1A-Gold 3 6 9 16 23 30
2-4 1 2 3 5 6 8

EVIL ERNIE VS. THE MOVIE MONSTERS
Chaos! Comics: Mar, 1997 ($2.95, one-shot)
1 4.00
1-Variant-"Chaos-Scope•Terror Vision" card stock-c 6.00

EVIL ERNIE VS. THE SUPER HEROES
Chaos! Comics: Aug, 1995; Sept, 1998 ($2.95)
1-Lady Death poster 4.00
1-Foil-c variant (limited to 10,000) 2 4 6 11 16 20
1-Limited Edition (1000) 2 4 6 11 16 20
2-(9/98) Ernie vs. JLA and Marvel parodies 4.00

EVIL ERNIE: WAR OF THE DEAD
Chaos! Comics: Nov, 1999 - No. 3, Jan, 2000 ($2.95, limited series)
1-3-Pulido & Kaminski-s/Brewer-a. 3-End of Evil Ernie 3.00

EVIL EYE
Fantagraphics Books: June, 1998 - No. 12, Jun, 2004 ($2.95/$3.50/$3.95, B&W)
1-7-Richard Sala-s/a 4.00
8-10-($3.50) 4.00
11,12-($3.95) 4.00

EVO (Crossover from Tomb Raider #25 & Witchblade #60)
Image Comics (Top Cow): Feb, 2003 ($2.99, one-shot)
1-Silvestri-c/a(p); Endgame x-over pt. 3; Sara Pezzini & Lara Croft app. 3.00

EWOKS (Star Wars) (TV) (See Star Comics Magazine)
Marvel Comics (Star Comics): June, 1985 - No. 14, Jul, 1987 (75¢/$1.00)
1,10: 10-Williamson-a (From Star Wars) 3 6 9 16 24 32
2-9 2 4 6 8 11 14
11-14: 14-($1.00-c) 2 4 6 10 14 18

EXCALIBUR (Also see Marvel Comics Presents #31)
Marvel Comics: Apr, 1988; Oct, 1988 - No. 125, Oct, 1998 ($1.50/$1.75/$1.99)
Special Edition nn (The Sword is Drawn)(4/88, $3.25)-1st Excalibur comic
1 2 3 5 6 8
Special Edition nn (4/88)-no price on-c 2 4 6 8 10 12
Special Edition nn (2nd & 3rd print, 10/88, 12/89) 5.00
...The Sword is Drawn (Apr, 1992, $4.50) 5.00
1($1.50, 10/88)-X-Men spin-off; Nightcrawler, Shadowcat(Kitty Pryde), Capt. Britain, Phoenix & Meggan begin 6.00
2-4 5.00
5-10 4.00
11-49,51-70,72-74,76: 10,11-Rogers/Austin-a. 21-Intro Crusader X. 22-Iron Man x-over. 24-John Byrne app. in story. 26-Ron Lim-c/a. 27-B. Smith-a(p). 37-Dr. Doom & Iron Man app. 41-X-Men (Wolverine) app.; Cable cameo. 49-Neal Adams c-swipe. 52,57-X-Men (Cyclops, Wolverine) app. 53-Spider-Man-c/story. 58-X-Men (Wolverine, Gambit, Cyclops, etc.)-c/story. 61-Phoenix returns. 68-Starjammers-c/story 3.00
50-($2.75, 56 pgs.)-New logo 4.00
71-($3.95, 52 pgs.)-Hologram on-c; 30th anniversary 5.00
75-($3.50, 52 pgs.)-Holo-grafx foil-c 5.00
75-($2.25, 52 pgs.)-Regular edition 4.00
77-81,83-86: 77-Begin $1.95-c; bound-in trading card sheet. 83-86-Deluxe Editions and Standard Editions. 86-1st app. Pete Wisdom 3.00
82-($2.50)-Newsstand edition 4.00
82-($3.50)-Enhanced edition 5.00
87-89,91-99,101-110: 87-Return from Age of Apocalypse. 92-Colossus-c/app. 94-Days of Future Tense 95-X-Man-c/app. 96-Sebastian Shaw & the Hellfire Club app. 99-Onslaught app. 101-Onslaught tie-in. 102-w/card insert. 103-Last Warren Ellis scripts; Belasco app. 104,105-Hitch & Neary-c/a. 109-Spiral-c/app. 3.00
90,100-($2.95)-double-sized. 100-Onslaught tie-in; wraparound-c 4.00
111-124: 111-Begin $1.99-c, wraparound-c. 119-Calafiore-a 3.00
125-($2.99) Wedding of Capt. Britain and Meggan 4.00
Annual 1,2 ('93, '94, 68 pgs.)-1st app. Khaos. 2-X-Men & Psylocke app. 4.00
#(-1) Flashback (7/97) 3.00
...Air Apparent nn (12/91, $4.95)-Simonson-c 6.00
...Mojo Mayhem nn (12/89, $4.50)-Art Adams/Austin-c/a 6.00
...: The Possession nn (7/91, $2.95, 52 pgs.) 4.00
...: XX Crossing (7/92, 5/92-inside, $2.50)-vs. The X-Men 4.00
...Classic Vol. 1: The Sword is Drawn TPB (2005, $19.99) r/#1-5 & Special Edition nn (The Sword is Drawn) 20.00
...Classic Vol. 2: Two-Edged Sword TPB (2006, $24.99) r/#6-11 25.00
...Classic Vol. 3: Cross-Time Caper Book 1 TPB (2007, $24.99) r/#12-20 25.00
...Classic Vol. 4: Cross-Time Caper Book 2 TPB (2007, $24.99) r/#21-28 25.00
...Classic Vol. 5 TPB (2008, $24.99) r/#29-34 & Marvel GN Excalibur: Weird War III 25.00

EXCALIBUR
Marvel Comics: Feb, 2001 - No. 4, May, 2001 ($2.99)
1-4-Return of Captain Britain; Raimondi-a 3.00

EXCALIBUR (X-Men Reloaded title) (Leads into House of M series, then New Excalibur)
Marvel Comics: July, 2004 - No. 14, July, 2005 ($2.99)
1-14: 1-Claremont-s/Lopresti-a/Park-c; Magneto returns. 6-11-Beast app. 13,14-Prelude to House of M; Dr. Strange app. 3.00
House of M Prelude: Excalibur TPB (2005, $11.99) r/#11-14 12.00
... Vol. 1: Forging the Sword (2004, $9.99) r/#1-4 10.00
... Vol. 2: Saturday Night Fever (2005, $14.99) r/#5-10 15.00

EXCITING COMICS
Nedor/Better Publications/Standard Comics: Apr, 1940 - No. 69, Sept, 1949
1-Origin & 1st app. The Mask, Jim Hatfield, Sgt. Bill King, Dan Williams begin; early Robot-c (see Smash #1) 476 952 1428 3475 6138 8800
2-The Sphinx begins; The Masked Rider app.; Son of the Gods begins, ends #8
239 478 717 1530 2615 3700
3-Classic Science Fiction Robot-c 226 452 678 1446 2473 3500
4-6: All have Sci-Fi covers by Max Plaisted 174 348 522 1114 1907 2700
7,8-Schomburg jungle covers 116 232 348 742 1271 1800
9-Origin/1st app. of The Black Terror & sidekick Tim, begin series (5/41) (Black Terror c-9-21,23-52,54,55) 1350 2700 4050 10,200 19,100 28,000
10-2nd app. Black Terror (6/41) 377 754 1131 2639 4620 6600
11-3rd app. Black Terror (7/41) 226 452 678 1446 2473 3500
12,13-Bondage covers 161 322 483 1030 1765 2500
14-Last Sphinx, Dan Williams 129 258 387 826 1413 2000
15-The Liberator begins (origin); WWII-c 168 336 504 1075 1838 2600
16,19,20: 20-The Mask ends 110 220 330 704 1202 1700
17,18-WWII-c 129 258 387 826 1413 2000
21,23,24 84 168 252 538 919 1300
22-Origin The Eaglet; The American Eagle begins 97 194 291 621 1061 1500
25-Robot-c 142 284 426 909 1555 2200
26-Schomburg-c begin; Nazi WWII-c 194 388 582 1242 2121 3000
27,30-Japanese WWII-c 181 362 543 1158 1979 2800
28-(Scarce) Crime Crusader begins, ends #58; Nazi WWII-c
500 1000 1500 3000 5000 7000
29-Nazi WWII-c 181 362 543 1158 1979 2800
31,35,36-Japanese WWII-c. 35-Liberator ends, not in 31-33
148 296 444 947 1624 2300
32-34,37-Nazi WWII-c 148 296 444 947 1624 2300
38 Gangster-c 103 206 309 659 1130 1600
39-WWII-c; Nazis giving poison candy to kids on cover; origin Kara, Jungle Princess
800 1600 2400 5000 7500 10,000
40,41-Last WWII covers in this title; Japanese WWII-c
142 284 426 909 1555 2200

Executive Assistant: Assassins #16 © Aspen MLT

Exiles #85 © MAR

Ex Machina #26 © Vaughan & Harris

GD 2.0 VG 4.0 FN 6.0 VF 8.0 VF/NM 9.0 NM- 9.2

GD 2.0 VG 4.0 FN 6.0 VF 8.0 VF/NM 9.0 NM- 9.2

42-50: 42-The Scarab begins. 45-Schomburg Robot-c. 49-Last Kara, Jungle Princess.
50-Last American Eagle 74 148 222 470 810 1150
51-Miss Masque begins (1st app.) 97 194 291 621 1061 1500
52,54: 54-Miss Masque ends 68 136 204 435 743 1050
53-Miss Masque-c 116 232 348 742 1271 1800
55-58: 55-Judy of the Jungle begins (origin), ends #69; 1 pg. Ingels-a; Judy of the Jungle
c-56-66. 57,58-Airbrush-c 68 136 204 435 743 1050
59-Frazetta art in Caniff style; signed Frank Frazeta (one t), 9 pgs.
71 142 213 454 777 1100
60-66: 60-Rick Howard, the Mystery Rider begins. 66-Robinson/Meskin-a
65 130 195 416 708 1000
67-69-All western covers 22 44 66 132 216 300
NOTE: ***Schomburg*** *(****Xela****) c-26-68; airbrush c-57-66. Black Terror by* ***R. Moreira****-#65.* ***Roussos*** *a-62. Bondage-c 9, 12, 13, 20, 23, 25, 30, 59.*

EXCITING ROMANCES
Fawcett Publications: 1949 (nd); No. 2, Spring, 1950 - No. 5, 10/50; No. 6 (1951, nd); No. 7, 9/51 -No. 12, 1/53 (Photo-c on #1-3)
1,3: 1(1949). 3-Wood-a 14 28 42 82 121 160
2,4,5-(1950) 10 20 30 56 76 95
6-12 9 18 27 50 65 80
NOTE: ***Powell*** *a-8-10.* ***Marcus Swayze*** *a-5, 6, 9. Photo c-1-7, 10-12.*

EXCITING ROMANCE STORIES (See Fox Giants)

EXCITING WAR (Korean War)
Standard Comics (Better Publ.): No. 5, Sept, 1952 - No. 8, May, 1953; No. 9, Nov, 1953
5 14 28 42 80 115 150
6-Flame thrower/burning body-c 22 44 66 132 216 300
7,9 10 20 30 58 79 100
8-Toth-a 11 22 33 62 86 110

EXCITING X-PATROL
Marvel Comics (Amalgam): June, 1997 ($1.95, one-shot)
1-Barbara Kesel-s/Bryan Hitch-a 3.00

EX-CON
Dynamite Entertainment: 2014 - No. 5, 2015 ($2.99, limited series)
1-5-Swierczynski-s/Burns-a/Bradstreet-c 3.00

EXECUTIONER, THE (Don Pendleton's...)
IDW Publishing: Apr, 2008 - No. 5, Aug, 2008 ($3.99)
1-5-Mack Bolan origin re-told; Gallant-a/Wojtowicz-s 4.00

EXECUTIVE ASSISTANT: ASSASSINS
Aspen MLT: Jul, 2012 - No. 18, Feb, 2014 ($3.99)
1-18: 1-Five covers; Hernandez-s/Gunderson-a 4.00

EXECUTIVE ASSISTANT: IRIS (Also see All New Executive Assistant: Iris)
Aspen MLT: No. 0, Apr, 2009 - No. 6, Nov, 2010 ($2.50/$2.99)
0-($2.50) Wohl-s/Francisco-a; 3 covers 3.00
1-6-($2.99) Multiple covers on each 3.00
Annual 2015 (3/15, $5.99) Three stories by various; Benitez-c 6.00
... Sourcebook 1 (1/16, $4.99) Character profiles & storyline summaries 5.00

EXECUTIVE ASSISTANT: IRIS (Volume 2) (The Hit List Agenda x-over)
Aspen MLT: No. 0, Jul, 2011 - No. 5, Dec, 2011 ($2.50/$2.99/$3.50)
0-($2.50) Wohl-s/Francisco-a; sketch page art; 3 covers 3.00
1-4-($2.99) Multiple covers on each. 1-Francisco-a. 2-4-Odagawa-a 3.00
5-($3.50) Odagawa-a 3.50

EXECUTIVE ASSISTANT: IRIS (Volume 3) (See All New Executive Assistant: Iris for Vol. 4)
Aspen MLT: Dec, 2012 - No. 5, Sept, 2013 ($3.99)
1-5-Multiple covers on each. 1-Wohl-s/Lei-a 4.00

EXECUTIVE ASSISTANT: LOTUS (The Hit List Agenda x-over)
Aspen MLT: Aug, 2011 - No. 3, Oct, 2011 ($2.99, limited series)
1-3-Multiple covers on each. Hernandez-s/Nome-a 3.00

EXECUTIVE ASSISTANT: ORCHID (The Hit List Agenda x-over)
Aspen MLT: Aug, 2011 - No. 3, Oct, 2011 ($2.99, limited series)
1-3: 1-Lobdell-s/Gunnell-a; multiple covers 3.00

EXECUTIVE ASSISTANT: VIOLET (The Hit List Agenda x-over)
Aspen MLT: Aug, 2011 - No. 3, Oct, 2011 ($2.99, limited series)
1-3: 1-Andreyko-s/Mhan-a; multiple covers 3.00

EXILED (Part 1 of x-over with Journey Into Mystery #637,638 & New Mutants #42,43)
Marvel Comics: July, 2012 ($2.99, one-shot)
1-Thor, Loki and New Mutants app.; DiGiandomenico-a 3.00

EXILE ON THE PLANET OF THE APES
BOOM! Studios: Mar, 2012 - No. 4 ($3.99, limited series)
1-3-Bechko & Hardman-s/Laming-a 4.00

EXILES (Also see Break-Thru)
Malibu Comics (Ultraverse): Aug, 1993 - No. 4, Nov, 1993 ($1.95)
1,2,4: 1,2-Bagged copies of each exist. 4-Team dies; story cont'd in Break-Thru #1 3.00
3-($2.50, 40 pgs.)-Rune flip-c/story by B. Smith (3 pgs.) 4.00
1-Holographic-c edition 1 2 3 5 6 8

EXILES (All New, The) (2nd Series) (Also see Black September)
Malibu Comics (Ultraverse): Sept, 1995 - V2#11, Aug, 1996 ($1.50)
Infinity (9/95, $1.50)-Intro new team including Marvel's Juggernaut & Reaper 3.00
Infinity (2000 signed), V2#1 (2000 signed) 1 3 4 6 8 10
V2 #1-(10/95, 64 pgs.)-Reprint of Ultraforce V2#1 follows lead story 4.00
V2#2-4,6-11: 2-1st app. Hellblade. 8-Intro Maxis. 11-Vs. Maxis; Ripfire app.; cont'd in Ultraforce #12 3.00
V2#5-($2.50) Juggernaut returns to the Marvel Universe. 4.00

EXILES (Also see X-Men titles) (Leads into New Exiles series)
Marvel Comics: Aug, 2001 - No. 100, Feb, 2008 ($2.99/$2.25)
1-($2.99) Blink and parallel world X-Men; Winick-s/McKone & McKenna-a
1 2 3 4 5 7
2-10-($2.25) 2-Two covers (McKone & JH Williams III). 5-Alpha Flight app. 4.00
11-24: 22-Blink leaves; Magik joins. 23,24-Walker-a; alternate Weapon-X app. 3.00
25-99: 25-Begin $2.99-c; Inhumans app.; Walker-a. 26-30-Austen-s. 33-Wolverine app. 35-37-Fantastic Four app. 37-Sunfire dies, Blink returns. 38-40-Hyperion app. 69-71-House of M. 77,78-Squadron Supreme app. 85,86-Multiple Wolverines. 90-Claremont-s begin; Psylocke app. 97-Shadowcat joins 3.00
100-($3.99) Last issue; Blink leaves; continues in Exiles (Days of Then and Now); r/#1 4.00
Annual 1 (2/07, $3.99) Bedard-s/Raney-a/c 4.00
Exiles #1 (Days of Then and Now) (3/08, $3.99) short stories by various 4.00

EXILES
Marvel Comics: Jun, 2009 - No. 6, Nov, 2009 ($2.99/$3.99)
1,6-($3.99) Blink and parallel world Scarlet Witch, Beast and others; Bullock-c 4.00
2-5-($2.99) 3.00

EXILES VS. THE X-MEN
Malibu Comics (Ultraverse): Oct, 1995 (one-shot)
0-Limited Super Premium Edition; signed w/certificate; gold foil logo,
0-Limited Premium Edition 1 3 4 6 8 10

EX MACHINA
DC Comics: Aug, 2004 - No. 50, Sept, 2010 ($2.95/$2.99)
1-Intro. Mitchell Hundred; Vaughan-s/Harris-a/c 4.00
1-Special Edition (6/10, $1.00) Reprints #1 with "What's Next?" logo on cover 3.00
2-49: 12-Intro. Automaton. 33-Mitchell meets the Pope 3.00
50-($4.99) Wraparound-c 5.00
...: The Deluxe Edition Book One HC (2008, $29.99, dustjacket) r/#1-11; Vaughan's original proposal, Harris sketch pages; Brad Meltzer intro. 30.00
...: The Deluxe Edition Book Two HC (2009, $29.99, dustjacket) r/#12-20; Special #1,2; script and pencil art for #20; Wachowski Bros. intro. 30.00
...: The Deluxe Edition Book Three HC (2010, $29.99, dustjacket) r/#21-29; Special #3 and Ex Machina: Inside the Machine 30.00
...: The Deluxe Edition Book Four HC (2010, $29.99, dustjacket) r/#30-40; cover gallery 30.00
...: The Deluxe Edition Book Five HC (2011, $29.99, dustjacket) r/#41-50; Special #4 30.00
...: Inside the Machine (4/07, $2.99) script pages and Harris art and cover process 3.00
...: Masquerade Special (#3) (10/07, $3.50) John Paul Leon-a; Harris-c 3.50
... Special 1,2 (6/06 - No. 2, 8/06, $2.99) Sprouse-a; flashback to the Great Machine 3.00
... Special 4 (5/09, $3.99) Leon-a; Great Machine flashback; covers by Harris & Leon 4.00
...: Dirty Tricks TPB (2009, $12.99) r/#35-39 and Masquerade Special #3 13.00
...: Ex Cathedra TPB (2008, $12.99) r/#30-34 13.00
...: March To War TPB (2006, $12.99) r/#17-20 and Special #1,2 13.00
...: Power Down TPB (2008, $12.99) r/#26-29 & ...: Inside the Machine 13.00
...: Ring Out the Old TPB (2010, $14.99) r/#40-44 and Special #4 15.00
...: Smoke Smoke TPB (2007, $12.99) r/#21-25 13.00
...: The First Hundred Days TPB ('05, $9.95) r/#1-5; photo reference and sketch pages 10.00
...: Tag TPB (2005, $12.99) r/#6-10; Harris sketch pages 13.00
...: Term Limits TPB (2010, $14.99) r/#45-50 15.00

EX-MUTANTS
Malibu Comics: Nov, 1992 - No. 18, Apr, 1994 ($1.95/$2.25/$2.50)
1-18: 1-Polybagged w/Skycap; prismatic cover 3.00

EXORCISTS (See The Crusaders)

EXOSQUAD (TV)

Explorers of the Unknown #6 © ACP

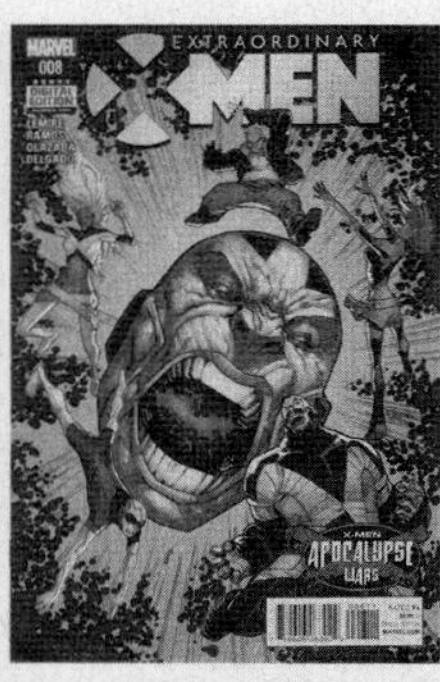

Extraordinary X-Men #8 © MAR

Fables #50 © Bill Willingham & DC

	GD 2.0	VG 4.0	FN 6.0	VF 8.0	VF/NM 9.0	NM- 9.2
Topps Comics: No. 0, Jan, 1994 ($1.00)						
0-($1.00, 20 pgs.)-1st app.; Staton-a(p); wraparound-c						3.00

EXOTIC ROMANCES (Formerly True War Romances)
Quality Comics Group (Comic Magazines): No. 22, Oct, 1955 - No. 31, Nov, 1956

	GD	VG	FN	VF	VF/NM	NM-
22	15	30	45	85	130	175
23-26,29	11	22	33	60	83	105
27,31-Baker-c/a	24	48	72	140	230	320
28,30-Baker-a	17	34	51	98	154	210

EXPENDABLES, THE (Movie)
Dynamite Entertainment: 2010 - No. 4, 2010 ($3.99, limited series)

	GD	VG	FN	VF	VF/NM	NM-
1-4-Chuck Dixon-s/Esteve Polls-a/Lucio Parrillo-c; prelude to the 2010 movie						4.00

EXPLOITS OF DANIEL BOONE
Quality Comics Group: Nov, 1955 - No. 6, Oct, 1956

	GD	VG	FN	VF	VF/NM	NM-
1-All have Cuidera-c(i)	20	40	60	114	182	250
2 (1/56)	14	28	42	82	121	160
3-6	13	26	39	74	105	135

EXPLOITS OF DICK TRACY (See Dick Tracy)

EXPLORER JOE
Ziff-Davis Comic Group (Approved Comics): Win, 1951 - No. 2, Oct-Nov, 1952

	GD	VG	FN	VF	VF/NM	NM-
1-2: Saunders painted covers; 2-Krigstein-a	14	28	42	80	115	150

EXPLORERS OF THE UNKNOWN (See Archie Giant Series #587, 599)
Archie Comics: June, 1990 - No. 6, Apr, 1991 ($1.00)

	GD	VG	FN	VF	VF/NM	NM-
1-6: Featuring Archie and the gang						3.00

EXPOSED (...True Crime Cases; ...Cases in the Crusade Against Crime #5-9)
D. S. Publishing Co.: Mar-Apr, 1948 - No. 9, July-Aug, 1949

	GD	VG	FN	VF	VF/NM	NM-
1	34	68	102	199	325	450
2-Giggling killer story with excessive blood; two injury-to-eye panels; electrocution panel	39	78	117	231	378	525
3,8,9	16	32	48	94	147	200
4-Orlando-a	17	34	51	98	154	210
5-Breeze Lawson, Sky Sheriff by E. Good	17	34	51	98	154	210
6,7: 6-Ingels-a; used in **SOTI**, illo. "How to prepare an alibi" 7-Illo. in **SOTI**, "Diagram for housebreakers;" used by N.Y. Legis. Committee	39	78	117	231	378	525

EXTERMINATION
BOOM! Studios: Jun, 2012 - No. 8, Jan, 2013 ($1.00/$3.99)

	GD	VG	FN	VF	VF/NM	NM-
1-($1.00) Nine covers; Spurrier-s/Jeffrey Edwards-a						3.00
2-8-($3.99)						4.00

EXTERMINATORS, THE
DC Comics (Vertigo): Mar, 2006 - No. 30, Aug, 2008 ($2.99)

	GD	VG	FN	VF	VF/NM	NM-
1-30: Simon Oliver-s/Tony Moore-a in most. 11,12-Hawthorne-a						3.00
...: Bug Brothers TPB (2006, $9.99) r/#1-5; intro. by screenwriter Josh Olson						10.00
...: Bug Brothers Forever TPB (2008, $14.99) r/#24-30; intro. by Simon Oliver						15.00
...: Crossfire and Collateral TPB (2008, $14.99) r/#17-23						15.00
...: Insurgency TPB (2007, $12.99) r/#6-10						13.00
...: Lies of Our Fathers TPB (2007, $14.99) r/#11-16						15.00

EXTINCT!
New England Comics Press: Wint, 1991-92 - No. 2, Fall, 1992 ($3.50, B&W)

	GD	VG	FN	VF	VF/NM	NM-
1,2-Reprints and background info of "perfectly awful" Golden Age stories						4.00

EXTINCTION EVENT
DC Comics (WildStorm): Sept, 2003 - No. 5, Jan, 2004 ($2.50, limited series)

	GD	VG	FN	VF	VF/NM	NM-
1-5-Booth-a/Weinberg-s						3.00

EXTINCTION PARADE, THE
Avatar Press: May, 2013 - Present ($3.99)

	GD	VG	FN	VF	VF/NM	NM-
1-5-Max Brooks-s/Raulo Caceres-a						4.00

EXTRA!
E. C. Comics: Mar-Apr, 1955 - No. 5, Nov-Dec, 1955

	GD	VG	FN	VF	VF/NM	NM-
1-Not code approved	21	42	63	169	270	370
2-5	13	26	39	104	167	230

NOTE: ***Craig, Crandall, Severin** art in all.*

EXTRA!
Gemstone Publishing: Jan, 2000 - No. 5, May, 2000 ($2.50)

	GD	VG	FN	VF	VF/NM	NM-
1-5-Reprints E.C. series						4.00

EXTRA COMICS
Magazine Enterprises: 1948 (25¢, 3 comics in one)

	GD	VG	FN	VF	VF/NM	NM-
1-Giant; consisting of rebound ME comics. Two versions known; (1)-Funnyman by Siegel & Shuster, Space Ace, Undercover Girl, Red Fox by L.B. Cole, Trail Colt & (2)-All Funnyman	66	132	198	419	722	1025

EXTRAORDINARY X-MEN
Marvel Comics: Jan, 2016 - Present ($4.99/$3.99)

	GD	VG	FN	VF	VF/NM	NM-
1-($4.99) Team of Old Man Logan, Storm, Jean Grey & others; Lemire-s/Ramos-a						5.00
2-7,9-19-($3.99) 2-Mister Sinister returns. 6,7,13-16-Ibanez-a. 9-12-Apocalypse Wars						4.00
8-($4.99) Apocalypse Wars x-over; Ramos-a; back-up story with Doctor Strange						5.00
Annual 1 (11/16, $4.99) Masters-s/Barberi-a; Montclare-s/Kämpe-a; Moon Girl app.						5.00

EXTREME
Image Comics (Extreme Studios): Aug, 1993 (Giveaway)

	GD	VG	FN	VF	VF/NM	NM-
0						3.00

EXTREME DESTROYER
Image Comics (Extreme Studios): Jan, 1996 ($2.50)

	GD	VG	FN	VF	VF/NM	NM-
Prologue 1-Polybagged w/card; Liefeld-c, Epilogue 1-Liefeld-c						3.00

EXTREME JUSTICE
DC Comics: No. 0, Jan, 1995 - No. 18, July, 1996 ($1.50/$1.75)

	GD	VG	FN	VF	VF/NM	NM-
0-18						3.00

EXTREMELY YOUNGBLOOD
Image Comics (Extreme Studios): Sept, 1996 ($3.50, one-shot)

	GD	VG	FN	VF	VF/NM	NM-
1						3.50

EXTREME SACRIFICE
Image Comics (Extreme Studios): Jan, 1995 ($2.50, limited series)

	GD	VG	FN	VF	VF/NM	NM-
Prelude (#1)-Liefeld wraparound-c; polybagged w/ trading card						3.00
Epilogue (#2)-Liefeld wraparound-c; polybagged w/trading card						3.00
Trade paperback (6/95, $16.95)-Platt-a						17.00

EXTREME SUPER CHRISTMAS SPECIAL
Image Comics (Extreme Studios): Dec, 1994 ($2.95, one-shot)

	GD	VG	FN	VF	VF/NM	NM-
1						3.00

EXTREMIST, THE
DC Comics (Vertigo): Sept, 1993 - No. 4, Dec, 1993 ($1.95, limited series)

	GD	VG	FN	VF	VF/NM	NM-
1-4-Peter Milligan scripts; McKeever-c/a						3.00
1-Platinum Edition						5.00

EYE OF NEWT
Dark Horse Comics: Jun, 2014 - No. 4, Sept, 2014 ($3.99, limited series)

	GD	VG	FN	VF	VF/NM	NM-
1-4-Michael Hague-s/a/c						4.00

EYE OF THE STORM
Rival Productions: Dec, 1994 - No. 7, June, 1995? ($2.95)

	GD	VG	FN	VF	VF/NM	NM-
1-7: Computer generated comic						3.00

EYE OF THE STORM
DC Comics (WildStorm): Sept, 2003 ($4.95)

	GD	VG	FN	VF	VF/NM	NM-
Annual 1-Short stories by various incl. Portacio, Johns, Coker, Pearson, Arcudi						5.00

FABLES
DC Comics (Vertigo): July, 2002 - Present ($2.50/$2.75/$2.99)

	GD	VG	FN	VF	VF/NM	NM-
1-Willingham-s/Medina-a; two covers by Maleev & Jean						65.00
1: Special Edition (12/06, 25¢) r/#1 with preview of 1001 Nights of Snowfall						3.00
1: Special Edition (9/09, $1.00) r/#1 with preview of Peter & Max						3.00
1-Special Edition (8/10, $1.00) Reprints #1 with "What's Next?" logo on cover						3.00
1-Special Edition (3/16, $3.99) Reprints #1 with new cover by Dave McKean						4.00
2-Medina-a						15.00
3-5						10.00
6-37: 6-10-Buckingham-a. 11-Talbot-a. 18-Medley-a. 26-Preview of The Witching						5.00
6-RRP Edition wraparound variant-c; promotional giveaway for retailers (200 printed)						190.00
38-49,51-74,76-99,101-149: 38-Begin $2.75-c. 49-Begin $2.99-c. 57,58,76-Allred-a. 83-85-X-over with Jack of Fables & The Literals. 101-Shanower-a. 107-Terry Moore-a 113-Back-up art by Russell, Cannon, Hughes. 147-Terry Moore-a (3 pgs.)						3.00
50-($3.99) Wedding of Snow White and Bigby Wolf; preview of Jack of Fables series						5.00
75-($4.99) Geppetto surrenders; pin-up gallery by Powell, Nowlan, Cooke & others						5.00
100-(1/11, $9.99, squarebound) Buckingham-a; short stories art by Hughes & others						10.00
Animal Farm (2003, $12.95, TPB) r/#6-10; sketch pages by Buckingham & Jean						13.00
...: Arabian Nights (And Days) (2006, $14.99, TPB) r/#42-47						15.00
...: Homelands (2005, $14.99, TPB) r/#34-41						15.00
Legends in Exile (2002, $9.95, TPB) r/#1-5; new short story Willingham-s/a						15.00
...: March of the Wooden Soldiers (2004, $17.95, TPB) r/#19-21 & ...: The Last Castle						18.00
...: 1001 Nights of Snowfall HC (2006, $19.99) short stories by Willingham with art by various incl. Bolton, Kaluta, Jean, McPherson, Thompson, Vess, Wheatley, Buckingham						20.00
...: 1001 Nights of Snowfall (2008, $14.99, TPB) short stories with art by various						15.00

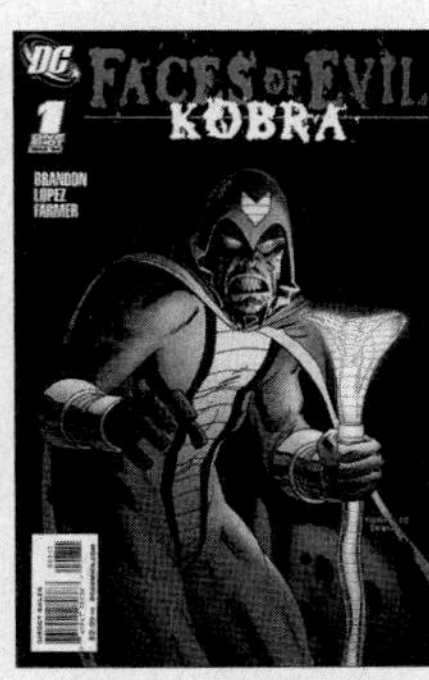

Faces of Evil: Kobra #1 © DC

Fairest #20 © Bill Willingham & DC

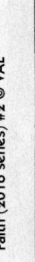

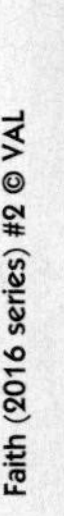
Faith (2016 series) #2 © VAL

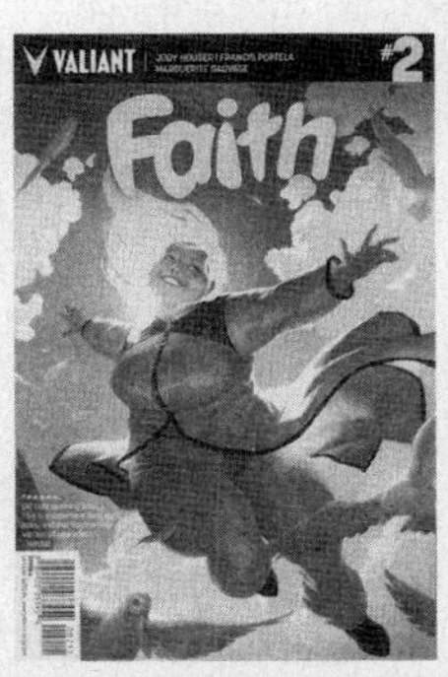

	GD 2.0	VG 4.0	FN 6.0	VF 8.0	VF/NM 9.0	NM- 9.2

...: Rose Red (2011, $17.99, TPB) r/#94-100; Buckingham design and sketch pages 18.00
...: Sons of Empire (2007, $17.99, TPB) r/#52-59 18.00
...: Storybook Love (2004, $14.95, TPB) r/#11-18 15.00
...: The Dark Ages (2009, $17.99, TPB) r/#76-82 18.00
...: The Deluxe Edition Book One HC (2009, $29.99, DJ) r/#1-10; character sketch-a 30.00
...: The Deluxe Edition Book Two HC (2010, $29.99, DJ) r/#11-18 & ...: The Last Castle 30.00
...: The Good Prince (2008, $17.99, TPB) r/#60-69 18.00
...: The Great Fables Crossover (2010, $17.99, TPB) r/#83-85, Jack of Fables #33-35 and The Literals #1-3; sneak preview of Peter & Max: A Fables Novel 18.00
...: The Last Castle (2003, $5.95) Hamilton-a/Willingham-s; prequel to title 6.00
...: The Mean Seasons (2005, $14.99, TPB) r/#22,28-33 15.00
...: War and Pieces (2008, $17.99, TPB) r/#70-75; sketch and pin-up pages 18.00
...: Witches (2010, $17.99, TPB) r/#86-93 18.00
...: Wolves (2006, $17.99, TPB) r/#48-51; script to #50 18.00

FABLES: THE WOLF AMONG US (Based on the Telltale Games video game)
DC Comics (Vertigo): Mar, 2015 - No. 16, Jun, 2016 ($3.99, printing of digital first stories)

1-16-Prequel to Fables; Sturges & Justus-s 4.00

FACE, THE (Tony Trent, the Face No. 3 on) (See Big Shot Comics)
Columbia Comics Group: 1941 - No. 2, 1943

	GD	VG	FN	VF	VF/NM	NM-
1-The Face; Mart Bailey WWII-c	97	194	291	621	1061	1500
2-Bailey WWII-c	68	136	204	435	743	1050

FACES OF EVIL
DC Comics: Mar, 2009 ($2.99, series of one-shots)

...: Deathstroke 1 - Jeanty-a/Ladronn-c; Ravager app. 3.00
...: Kobra 1 - Jason Burr returns; Julian Lopez-a 3.00
...: Prometheus 1 - Gates-s/Dallacchio-a; origin re-told; Anima killed 3.00
...: Solomon Grundy 1 - Johns-s/Kolins-a; leads into Solomon Grundy mini-series 3.00

FACTOR X
Marvel Comics: Mar, 1995 - No. 4, July, 1995 ($1.95, limited series)

1-Age of Apocalypse 4.00
2-4 3.00

FACULTY FUNNIES
Archie Comics: June, 1989 - No. 5, May, 1990 (75¢/95¢ #2 on)

1-5: 1,2,4,5-The Awesome Foursome app. 3.00

FADE FROM GRACE
Beckett Comics: Aug, 2004 - No. 5, Mar, 2005 (99¢/$1.99)

1-(99¢) Jeff Amano-a/c; Gabriel Benson-s; origin of Fade 3.00
2-5-($1.99) 3.00
TPB (2005, $14.99) r/#1-5; cover gallery, afterword by David Mack 15.00

FADE OUT, THE
Image Comics: Aug, 2014 - Present ($3.50/$3.99)

1-12-Ed Brubaker-s/Sean Phillips-a/c. 12-($3.99) 4.00

FAFHRD AND THE GREY MOUSER (Also see Sword of Sorcery & Wonder Woman #202)
Marvel Comics: Oct, 1990 - No. 4, 1991 ($4.50, 52 pgs., squarebound)

1-4: Mignola/Williamson-a; Chaykin scripts 5.00

FAGIN THE JEW
Doubleday: Oct, 2003 ($15.95, softcover graphic novel)

nn-Will Eisner-s/a; story of Fagin from Dickens' Oliver Twist 16.00

FAIREST (Characters from Fables)
DC Comics (Vertigo): May, 2012 - No. 33, Mar, 2015 ($2.99)

1-33: 1-6-Willingham-s/Jimenez-a. 1-Wraparound-c by Hughes & variant-c by Jimenez 3.00
...: In All The Land HC (2013, $24.99, dustjacket) New short stories by various; Hughes-c 25.00

FAIRY QUEST: OUTCASTS
BOOM! Studios: Nov, 2014 - No. 2, Dec, 2014 ($3.99, limited series)

1,2-Jenkins-s/Ramos-a/c 4.00

FAIRY QUEST: OUTLAWS
BOOM! Studios: Feb, 2013 - No. 2, Mar, 2013 ($3.99, limited series)

1,2-Jenkins-s/Ramos-a/c 4.00

FAIRY TALE PARADE (See Famous Fairy Tales)
Dell Publishing Co.: June-July, 1942 - No. 121, Oct, 1946 (Most by Walt Kelly)

	GD	VG	FN	VF	VF/NM	NM-
1-Kelly-a begins	86	172	258	688	1544	2400
2(8-9/42)	38	76	114	285	641	1000
3-5 (10-11/42 - 2-4/43)	29	58	87	196	441	685
6-9 (5-7/43 - 11-1/43-44)	22	44	66	154	340	525
Four Color 50('44), 69('45), 87('45)	21	42	63	147	324	500
Four Color 104, 114('46)-Last Kelly issue	16	32	48	112	249	385
Four Color 121('46)-Not by Kelly	10	20	30	69	147	225

NOTE: *#1-9, 4-Color #50, 69 have **Kelly** c/a; 4-Color #87, 104, 114-**Kelly** art only. #9 has a redrawn version of The Reluctant Dragon. This series contains all the classic fairy tales from Jack In The Beanstalk to Cinderella.*

FAIRY TALES
Ziff-Davis Publ. Co. (Approved Comics): No. 10, Apr-May, 1951 - No. 11, June-July, 1951

	GD	VG	FN	VF	VF/NM	NM-
10,11-Painted-c	22	44	66	128	209	290

FAITH
DC Comics (Vertigo): Nov, 1999 - No. 5, Mar, 2000 ($2.50, limited series)

1-5-Ted McKeever-s/c/a 3.00

FAITH (Zephyr from Harbinger)
Valiant Entertainment: Jan, 2016 - No. 4, Apr, 2016 ($3.99, limited series)

1-4-Houser-s/Portela-a. 3,4-Torque app. 4.00

FAITH (Harbinger)
Valiant Entertainment: Jul, 2016 - Present ($3.99)

1-9: 1-4-Houser-s/Pere Pérez-a. 5-Hillary Clinton app. 7,8-Eisma-a 4.00

FAITHFUL
Marvel Comics/Lovers' Magazine: Nov, 1949 - No. 2, Feb, 1950 (52 pgs.)

	GD	VG	FN	VF	VF/NM	NM-
1,2-Photo-c	15	30	45	85	130	175

FAKER
DC Comics (Vertigo): Sept, 2007 - No. 6, Feb, 2008 ($2.99, limited series)

1-6-Mike Carey-s/Jock-a/c 3.00
TPB (2008, $14.99) r/#1-6; Jock sketch pages 15.00

FALCON (See Marvel Premiere #49, Avengers #181 & Captain America #117 & 133)
Marvel Comics Group: Nov, 1983 - No. 4, Feb, 1984 (Mini-series)

	GD	VG	FN	VF	VF/NM	NM-
1-Paul Smith-c/a(p)	2	4	6	8	10	12

2-4: 2-Paul Smith-c/Mark Bright-a. 3-Kupperberg-c 6.00

FALL AND RISE OF CAPTAIN ATOM, THE
DC Comics: Mar, 2017 - No. 6 ($2.99, limited series)

1-3-Bates-s/Conrad-a 3.00

FALLEN ANGEL
DC Comics: Sept, 2003 - No. 20, July, 2005 ($2.50/$2.95)

1-9-Peter David-s/David Lopez-a/Stelfreeze-c; intro. Lee 3.00
10-20: 10-Begin $2.95-c. 13,17-Kaluta-c. 20-Last issue; Pérez-c 3.00
TPB (2004, $12.95) r/#1-6; intro. by Harlan Ellison 13.00
Down to Earth TPB (2007, $14.99) r/#7-12 15.00

FALLEN ANGEL
IDW Publ.: Dec, 2005 - No. 33, Dec, 2008 ($3.99)

1-33: 1-14-Peter David-s/J.K Woodward-a. Retailer variant-c for each. 15-Donaldson-a. 17-Flip cover with Shi story; Tucci-a. 25-Wraparound-c; character gallery 4.00
... Reborn 1-4 (7/09 - No. 4, 10/09, $3.99) David-s/Woodward-a; Illyria (from Angel) app. 4.00
... Return of the Son 1-4 (1/11 - No. 4, 4/11, $3.99) David-s/Woodward-a; 4.00
...: To Serve in Heaven TPB (8/06, $19.99) r/#1-5; gallery of reg & variant covers 20.00

FALLEN ANGEL ON THE WORLD OF MAGIC: THE GATHERING
Acclaim (Armada): May, 1996 ($5.95, one-shot)

1-Nancy Collins story 6.00

FALLEN ANGELS
Marvel Comics Group: April, 1987 - No. 8, Nov, 1987 (Limited series)

1-8 4.00

FALLEN SON: THE DEATH OF CAPTAIN AMERICA
Marvel Comics: June, 2007 - No. 5, Aug, 2007 ($2.99, limited series)

1-5: Loeb-s in all. 1-Wolverine; Yu-a/c. 2-Avengers; McGuinness-a/c. 3-Captain America; Romita Jr.-a/c; Hawkeye app. 4-Spider-Man; Finch-c/a. 5-Cassaday-c/a 3.00
1-5-Variant covers by Turner 3.00
HC (2007, $19.99, dustjacket) r/#1-5 20.00
TPB (2008, $13.99) r/#1-5 14.00

FALLING IN LOVE
Arleigh Pub. Co./National Per. Pub.: Sept-Oct, 1955 - No. 143, Oct-Nov, 1973

	GD	VG	FN	VF	VF/NM	NM-
1	45	90	135	284	480	675
2	25	50	75	150	245	340
3-10	16	32	48	94	147	200
11-20	14	28	42	82	121	160
21-40	12	24	36	69	97	125
41-47: 47-Last 10¢ issue	11	22	33	62	86	110
48-70	5	10	15	33	57	80
71-99,108: 108-Wood-a (4 pgs., 7/69)	4	8	12	23	37	50

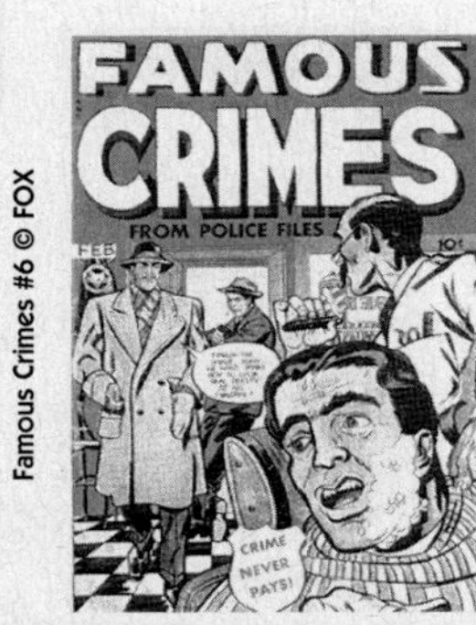
Famous Crimes #6 © FOX

Famous First Edition F-6 © DC

Famous Funnies #21 © EAS

GD VG FN VF VF/NM NM-
2.0 4.0 6.0 8.0 9.0 9.2

100 (7/68) 4 8 12 25 40 55
101-107,109-124 3 6 9 15 22 28
134-143 3 6 9 14 19 24
125-133: 52 pgs. 3 6 9 21 33 45
NOTE: *Colan c/a-75, 81. 52 pgs.-#125-133.*

FALLING MAN, THE
Image Comics: Feb, 1998 ($2.95)
1-McCorkindale-s/Hester-a 3.00

FALL OF THE HOUSE OF USHER, THE (See A Corben Special & Spirit section 8/22/48)

FALL OF THE HULKS (Also see Hulk and Incredible Hulk)
Marvel Comics: Feb, 2010 - July, 2010 ($3.99, one-shots & limited series)
Alpha (2/10) Pelletier-a; The Leader, Dr. Doom, MODOK and The Thinker app. 4.00
Gamma (2/10) Romita Jr. -a; funeral for General Ross 4.00
Red Hulk (3/10 - No. 4, 6/10) 1-4: 1-A-Bomb app. 4.00
Savage She-Hulks (5/10 - No. 3, 7/10) 1-3: Cover tryptich by Campbell; Espin-a 4.00

FALL OF THE ROMAN EMPIRE (See Movie Comics)

FALL OUT TOY WORKS
Image Comics: Sept, 2009 - No. 5, Jun, 2010 ($3.99)
1-5-Co-created by Pete Wentz of the band Fall Out Boy; Basri-a. 5-Lau-c 4.00

FAMILY AFFAIR (TV)
Gold Key: Feb, 1970 - No. 4, Oct, 1970 (25¢)
1-With pull-out poster; photo-c 5 10 15 34 60 85
1-With poster missing 3 6 9 17 26 35
2-4-Photo-c 3 6 9 20 31 42

FAMILY DYNAMIC, THE
DC Comics: Oct, 2008 - No. 3, Dec, 2008 ($2.25)
1-3-J. Torres-s/Tim Levins-a 3.00

FAMILY FUNNIES
Parents' Magazine Institute: No. 9, Aug-Sept, 1946
9 6 12 18 28 34 40

FAMILY FUNNIES (Tiny Tot Funnies No. 9)
Harvey Publications: Sept, 1950 - No. 8, Apr, 1951
1-Mandrake (has over 30 King Feature strips) 10 20 30 58 79 100
2-Flash Gordon, 1 pg. 8 16 24 40 50 60
3-8: 4,5,7-Flash Gordon, 1 pg. 6 12 18 31 38 45

FAMILY GUY (TV)
Devil's Due Publ.: 2006 ($6.95)
nn-101 Ways to Kill Lois; 2-Peter Griffin's Guide to Parenting; 3-Books Don't Taste Very Good 7.00
... A Big Book o' Crap TPB (10/06, $16.95) r/nn,2,3 17.00

FAMILY MATTER
Kitchen Sink Press: 1998 ($24.95/$15.95, graphic novel)
Hardcover ($24.95) Will Eisner-s/a 25.00
Softcover ($15.95) 16.00

FAMOUS AUTHORS ILLUSTRATED (See Stories by...)

FAMOUS CRIMES
Fox Features Syndicate/M.S. Dist. No. 51,52: June, 1948 - No. 19, Sept, 1950; No. 20, Aug, 1951; No. 51, 52, 1953
1-Blue Beetle app. & crime story-r/Phantom Lady #16
77 154 231 493 847 1200
2-Has woman dissolved in acid; lingerie-c/panels 55 110 165 352 601 850
3-Injury-to-eye story used in **SOTI**, pg. 112; has two electrocution stories
61 122 183 390 670 950
4-6 28 56 84 165 270 375
7- "Tarzan, the Wyoming Killer" (**SOTI**, pg. 44) 45 90 135 284 480 675
8-20: 17-Morisi-a. 20-Same cover as #15 21 42 63 122 199 275
51 (nd, 1953) 18 36 54 103 162 220
52 (Exist?) 18 36 54 103 162 220

FAMOUS FEATURE STORIES
Dell Publishing Co.: 1938 (7-1/2x11", 68 pgs.)
1-Tarzan, Terry & the Pirates, King of the Royal Mtd., Buck Jones, Dick Tracy, Smilin' Jack, Dan Dunn, Don Winslow, G-Man, Tailspin Tommy, Mutt & Jeff, Little Orphan Annie reprints - all illustrated text 64 128 192 406 696 985

FAMOUS FIRST EDITION (See Limited Collectors' Edition)
National Periodical Publications/DC Comics: ($1.00, 10x13-1/2", 72 pgs.) (No.6-8, 68 pgs.) 1974 - No. 8, Aug-Sept, 1975; C-61, 1979
(Hardbound editions with dust jackets are from Lyle Stuart, Inc.)
C-26-Action Comics #1; gold ink outer-c 5 10 15 35 63 90
C-26-Hardbound edition w/dust jacket 15 30 45 103 227 350
C-28-Detective #27; silver ink outer-c 5 10 15 35 63 90
C-28-Hardbound edition w/dust jacket 15 30 45 103 227 350
C-30-Sensation #1(1974); bronze ink outer-c 4 8 12 28 47 65
C-30-Hardbound edition w/dust jacket 13 26 39 86 188 290
F-4-Whiz Comics #2(#1)(10-11/74)-Cover not identical to original (dropped "Gangway for Captain Marvel" from cover); gold ink on outer-c 4 8 12 28 47 65
F-4-Hardbound edition w/dust jacket 13 26 39 86 188 290
F-5-Batman #1(F-6 inside); silver ink on outer-c 5 10 15 31 53 75
F-5-Hardbound edition w/dust jacket (exist?) 13 26 39 86 188 290
V2#F-6-Wonder Woman #1 4 8 12 28 47 65
F-6-Wonder Woman #1 Hardbound w/dust jacket 13 26 39 86 188 290
F-7-All-Star Comics #3 4 8 12 28 47 65
F-8-Flash Comics #1(8-9/75) 4 8 12 28 47 65
V8#C-61-Superman #1(1979, $2.00) 4 8 12 25 40 55
V8#C-61 (Whitman variant) 4 8 12 27 44 60
V8#C-61 (Softcover in plain grey slipcase, edition of 250 copies) Each signed by Jerry Siegel and Joe Shuster at the bottom of the inside front cover 550.00
Warning: The above books are almost **exact** reprints of the originals that they represent except for the Giant-Size format. None of the originals are Giant-Size. The first five issues and C-61 were printed with two covers. Reprint information can be found on the outside cover, but not on the inside cover which was reprinted exactly like the original (inside and out).

FAMOUS FUNNIES
Eastern Color: 1934; July, 1934 - No. 218, July, 1955

A Carnival of Comics (See Promotional Comics section)
Series 1-(Very rare)(nd-early 1934)(68 pgs.) No publisher given (Eastern Color PrintingCo.); sold in chain stores for 10¢. 35,000 print run. Contains Sunday strip reprints of Mutt & Jeff, Reg'lar Fellers, Nipper, Hairbreadth Harry, Strange As It Seems, Joe Palooka, Dixie Dugan, The Nebbs, Keeping Up With the Jones, and others. Inside front and back covers and pages 1-16 of Famous Funnies Series 1, #s 49-64 reprinted from **Famous Funnies**, **A Carnival of Comics**, and most of pages 17-48 reprinted from **Funnies on Parade**.
7150 14,300 21,450 43,000 - -
No. 1 (Rare)(7/34-on stands 5/34) - Eastern Color Printing Co. First monthly newsstand comic book. Contains Sunday strip reprints of Toonerville Folks, Mutt & Jeff, Hairbreadth Harry, S'Matter Pop, Nipper, Dixie Dugan, The Bungle Family, Connie, Ben Webster, Tailspin Tommy, The Nebbs, Joe Palooka, & others.
3200 6400 9600 24,000 - -
2 (Rare, 9/34) 800 1600 2400 6000 - -
3-Buck Rogers Sunday strip-r by Rick Yager begins, ends #218; not in #191-208; 1st comic book app. of Buck Rogers; the number of the 1st strip reprinted is pg. 190, Series No. 1
933 1866 2799 7000 - -
4 320 640 960 2400 - -
5-1st Christmas-c on a newsstand comic 347 694 1041 2600 - -
6-10 227 454 681 1700 - -
11,12,18-Four pgs. of Buck Rogers in each issue, completes stories in Buck Rogers #1 which lacks these pages. 18-Two pgs. of Buck Rogers reprinted in Daisy Comics #1
102 204 306 612 1156 1700
13-17,19,20: 14-Has two Buck Rogers panels missing. 17-2nd Christmas-c on a newsstand comic (12/35) 79 158 237 474 937 1400
21,23-30: 27-(10/36)-War on Crime begins (4 pgs.); 1st true crime in comics (reprints); part photo-c. 29-X-Mas-c (12/36) 60 120 180 360 693 1025
22-Four pgs. of Buck Rogers needed to complete stories in Buck Rogers #1
63 126 189 378 714 1050
31,33,34,36,37,39,40: 33-Careers of Baby Face Nelson & John Dillinger traced
42 84 126 252 489 725
32-(3/37) 1st app. the Phantom Magician (costume hero) in Advs. of Patsy
46 92 138 276 526 775
35-Two pgs. Buck Rogers omitted in Buck Rogers #2
46 92 138 276 526 775
38-Full color portrait of Buck Rogers 44 88 132 264 507 750
41-60: 41,53-X-Mas-c. 55-Last bottom panel, pg. 4 in Buck Rogers redrawn in Buck Rogers #3 39 78 117 231 378 525
61,63,64,66,67,69,70 27 54 81 158 259 360
62,65,68,73-78-Two pgs. Kirby-a "Lightnin' & the Lone Rider". 65,77-X-Mas-c
29 58 87 170 278 385
71,79,80: 80-(3/41)-Buck Rogers story continues from Buck Rogers #5
21 42 63 126 206 285
72-Speed Spaulding begins by Marvin Bradley (artist), ends #88. This series was written by Edwin Balmer & Philip Wylie (later appeared as film & book "When Worlds Collide")
24 48 72 140 230 320
81-Origin & 1st app. Invisible Scarlet O'Neil (4/41); strip begins #82, ends #167; 1st non-funny-c (Scarlet O'Neil) 28 56 84 165 270 375
82-Buck Rogers-c 30 60 90 177 289 400
83-87,90: 86-Connie vs. Monsters on the Moon-c (sci/fi). 87 has last Buck Rogers full page-r. 90-Bondage-c 20 40 60 117 189 260

Famous Stars #1 © Z-D

Fanboy #2 © DC

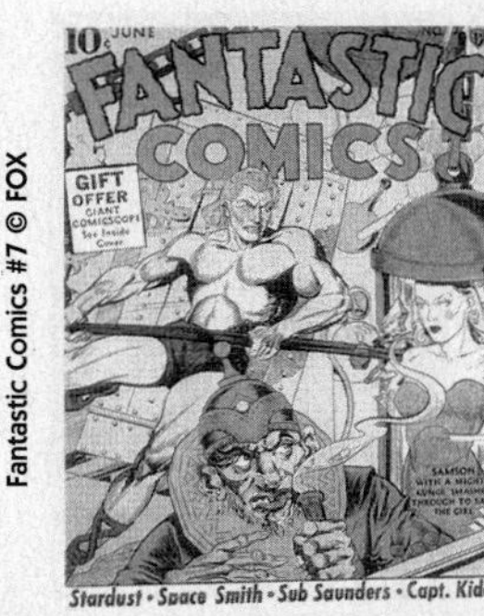

Fantastic Comics #7 © FOX

GD	VG	FN	VF	VF/NM	NM-
2.0	4.0	6.0	8.0	9.0	9.2

88,89: 88-Buck Rogers in "Moon's End" by Calkins, 2 pgs.(not reprints). Beginning with #88, all Buck Rogers pgs. have rearranged panels. 89-Origin & 1st app. Fearless Flint, the Flint Man 20 40 60 120 195 270
91-93,95,96,98-99,101,103-110: 98-Hitler, Tojo and Mussolini on inside back-c. 101-Christmas cover. 105-Series 2 begins (Strip Page #1) 17 34 51 98 154 210
94-Buck Rogers in "Solar Holocaust" by Calkins, 3 pgs.(not reprints) 18 36 54 107 169 230
97-War Bond promotion, Buck Rogers by Calkins, 2 pgs.(not reprints) 18 36 54 107 169 230
100-1st comic to reach #100; 100th Anniversary cover features 11 major Famous Funnies characters, including Buck Rogers 23 46 69 136 223 310
102-Chief Wahoo vs. Hitler,Tojo & Mussolini-c (1/43) 81 162 243 518 884 1250
111-130 (5/45): 113-X-Mas-c 14 28 42 76 108 140
131-150 (1/47): 137-Strip page No. 110 omitted; Christmas-c. 144-(7/46) 12th Anniversary cover 12 24 36 69 97 125
151-162,164-168: 162-New Year's Eve-c 11 22 33 64 90 115
163-St. Valentine's Day-c (2/48) 12 24 36 67 94 120
169,170-Two text illos. by Al Williamson, his 1st comic book work 14 28 42 80 115 150
171-190: 171-Strip pgs. 227,229,230, Series 2 omitted. 172-Strip Pg. 232 omitted. 173-Christmas-c. 190-Buck Rogers ends with start of strip pg. 302, Series 2; Oaky Doaks-c/story 11 22 33 60 83 105
191-197,199,201,203,206-208: No Buck Rogers. 191-Barney Carr, Space detective begins, ends #192. 10 20 30 58 79 100
198,200,202,205-One pg. Frazetta ads; no B. Rogers 11 22 33 60 83 105
204-Used in **POP**, pg. 79,99; war-c begin, end #208 11 22 33 62 86 110
209-216: Frazetta-c. 209-Buck Rogers begins (12/53) with strip pg. 480, Series 2; 211-Buck Rogers ads by Anderson begins, ends #217. #215-Contains B. Rogers strip pg. 515-518, series 2 followed by pgs.179-181, Series 3 181 362 543 1158 1979 2800
217-Buck Rogers 14 28 42 82 121 160
218-Buck Rogers ends with pg. 199, Series 3; Wee Three-c/story 11 22 33 60 83 105

NOTE: ***Rick Yager*** *did the Buck Rogers Sunday strips reprinted in Famous Funnies. The Sundays were formerly done by Russ Keaton and Lt. Dick Calkins did the dailies, but would sometimes assist Yager on a panel or two from time to time. Strip No. 169 is Yager's first full Buck Rogers page. Yager did the strip until 1958 when* ***Murphy Anderson*** *took over.* ***Tuska*** *art from 4/26/59 - 1965. Virtually every panel was rewritten for Famous Funnies. Not identical to the original Sunday page. The Buck Rogers reprints run continuously through Famous Funnies issue No. 190 (Strip No. 302) with no break in story line. The story line has no continuity after No. 190. The Buck Rogers newspaper strips came out in four series: Series 1, 3/30/30 - 9/21/41 (No. 1 - 600); Series 2, 9/28/41 -10/21/51 (No. 1 -525)(Strip No. 110-1/2 (1/2 pg.) published in only a few newspapers); Series 3, 10/28/51 -2/9/58 (No. 100-428)(No No.1-99); Series 4, 2/16/58 - 6/13/65 (No numbers, dates only).* ***Everett*** *c-85, 86.* ***Moulton*** *a-100. Chief Wahoo c-93, 97, 102, 116, 136, 139, 151. Dickie Dare c-83, 88. Fearless Flint c-89. Invisible Scarlet O'Neil c-81, 87, 95, 121(part), 132. Scorchy Smith c-84, 90.*

FAMOUS FUNNIES
Super Comics: 1964

Super Reprint Nos. 15-18:17-r/Double Trouble #1. 18-Space Comics #? 2 4 6 9 12 15

FAMOUS GANGSTERS (Crime on the Waterfront No. 4)
Avon Periodicals/Realistic No. 3: Apr, 1951 - No. 3, Feb, 1952

1-3: 1-Capone, Dillinger; c-/Avon paperback #329. 2-Dillinger Machine Gun Killer; Wood-c/a (1 pg.); r/Saint #7 & retitled "Mike Strong". 3-Lucky Luciano & Murder, Inc; c-/Avon paperback #66 39 78 117 231 378 525

FAMOUS INDIAN TRIBES
Dell Publishing Co.: July-Sept, 1962; No. 2, July, 1972

12-264-209(#1) (The Sioux) 3 6 9 15 21 26
2(7/72)-Reprints above 1 3 4 6 8 10

FAMOUS STARS
Ziff-Davis Publ. Co.: Nov-Dec, 1950 - No. 6, Spring, 1952 (All have photo-c)

1-Shelley Winters, Susan Peters, Ava Gardner, Shirley Temple; Jimmy Stewart & Shelley Winters photo-c; Whitney-a 40 80 120 244 402 560
2-Betty Hutton, Bing Crosby, Colleen Townsend, Gloria Swanson; Betty Hutton photo-c; Everett-a(2) 27 54 81 160 263 365
3-Farley Granger, Judy Garland's ordeal (life story; she died 6/22/69 at the age of 47), Alan Ladd; Farley Granger photo-c; Whitney-a 34 68 102 204 332 460
4-Al Jolson, Bob Mitchum, Ella Raines, Richard Conte, Vic Damone; Jane Russell and Bob Mitchum photo-c; Crandall-a, 6pgs. 24 48 72 142 234 325
5-Liz Taylor, Betty Grable, Esther Williams, George Brent, Mario Lanza; Liz Taylor photo-c; Krigstein-a 52 104 156 322 549 775
6-Gene Kelly, Hedy Lamarr, June Allyson, William Boyd, Janet Leigh, Gary Cooper; Gene Kelly photo-c 22 44 66 128 209 290

FAMOUS STORIES (...Book No. 2)
Dell Publishing Co.: 1942 - No. 2, 1942

1,2: 1-Treasure Island. 2-Tom Sawyer 30 60 90 177 289 400

FAMOUS TV FUNDAY FUNNIES
Harvey Publications: Sept, 1961 (25¢ Giant)

1-Casper the Ghost, Baby Huey, Little Audrey 5 10 15 34 60 85

FAMOUS WESTERN BADMEN (Formerly Redskin)
Youthful Magazines: No. 13, Dec, 1952 - No. 15, Apr, 1953

13-Redskin story 15 30 45 86 133 180
14,15: 15-The Dalton Boys story 11 22 33 62 86 110

FAN BOY
DC Comics: Mar, 1999 - No. 6, Aug, 1999 ($2.50, limited series)

1-6: 1-Art by Aragonés and various in all. 2-Green Lantern-c/a by Gil Kane. 3-JLA. 4-Sgt. Rock art by Heath, Marie Severin. 5-Batman art by Sprang, Adams, Miller, Timm. 6-Wonder Woman; art by Rude, Grell 3.00
TPB (2001, $12.95) r/#1-6 13.00

FANBOYS VS. ZOMBIES
BOOM! Studios: Apr, 2012 - No. 20, Nov, 2013 ($1.00/$3.99)

1-($1.00) Eight covers; Humphries-s/Gaylord-a; zombies at San Diego Comic-Con 3.00
2-20-($3.99) 2-12-Multiple covers on each. 17-Bryan Turner-a 4.00

FANTASTIC (Formerly Captain Science; Beware No. 10 on)
Youthful Magazines: No. 8, Feb, 1952 - No. 9, Apr, 1952

8-Capt. Science by Harrison 45 90 135 284 480 675
9-Harrison-a; decapitation, shrunken head panels 37 74 111 222 361 500

FANTASTIC ADVENTURES
Super Comics: 1963 - 1964 (Reprints)

9,10,12,15,16,18: 9-r/? 10-r/He-Man #2(Toby). 11-Disbrow-a. 12-Unpublished Chesler material? 15-r/Spook #23. 16-r/Dark Shadows #2(Steinway); Briefer-a.18-r/Superior Stories #1 3 6 9 17 26 35
11-Wood-a; r/Blue Bolt #118 4 8 12 23 37 50
17-Baker-a(2) r/Seven Seas #6 4 8 12 23 37 50

FANTASTIC COMICS
Fox Features Syndicate: Dec, 1939 - No. 23, Nov, 1941

1-Intro/origin Samson; Stardust, The Super Wizard, Sub Saunders (by Kiefer), Space Smith, Capt. Kidd begin 649 1298 1947 4738 8369 12,000
2-Powell text illos 314 628 942 2198 3849 5500
3-Classic Lou Fine Robot-c; Powell text illos 5000 10,000 15,000 22,000 29,000 36,000
4-Lou Fine-c 300 600 900 2070 3635 5200
5-Classic Lou Fine-c 423 846 1269 3000 5250 7500
6,7-Simon-c. 6-Bondage/torture-c 290 580 870 1856 3178 4500
8-Bondage/torture-c 194 388 582 1242 2121 3000
9,10: 9-Bondage-c. 10-Intro/origin David, Samson's aide 155 310 465 992 1696 2400
11-17,19,20: 16-Stardust ends 123 246 369 787 1344 1900
18,23: 18-1st app. Black Fury & sidekick Chuck; ends #23. 23-Origin The Gladiator 129 258 387 826 1413 2000
21-The Banshee begins(origin); ends #23; Hitler-c 258 516 774 1651 2826 4000
22-Hitler-c (likeness of Hitler as furnace on cover) 343 686 1029 2400 4200 6000

NOTE: ***Lou Fine*** *c-1-5.* ***Tuska*** *a-3-5, 8. Issue #11 has indicia to Mystery Men Comics #15. All issues feature Samson covers.*

FANTASTIC COMICS (Imagining of a 1941 issue by modern creators in Golden Age style)
Image Comics: No. 24, Jan, 2008 ($5.99, Golden Age sized, one-shot)

24-Samson, Yank Wilson, Stardust, Sub Saunders, Space Smith, Capt. Kidd app.; Larsen-c/a; art by Allred, Sienkiewicz, Yeates, Scioli, Hembeck, Ashley Wood & others 6.00

FANTASTIC COMICS (Fantastic Fears #1-9; Becomes Samson #12)
Ajax/Farrell Publ.: No. 10, Nov-Dec, 1954 - No. 11, Jan-Feb, 1955

10 (#1) 27 54 81 158 259 360
11-Robot-c 34 68 102 199 325 450

FANTASTIC FABLES
Silverwolf Comics: Feb, 1987 - No. 2, 1987 ($1.50, 28 pgs., B&W)

1,2: 1-Tim Vigil-a (6 pgs.). 2-Tim Vigil-a (7 pgs.) 4.00

FANTASTIC FEARS (Formerly Captain Jet) (Fantastic Comics #10 on)
Ajax/Farrell Publ.: No. 7, May, 1953 - No. 9, Sept-Oct, 1954

7(#1, 5/53)-Tales of Stalking Terror 60 120 180 381 653 925
8(#2, 7/53) 43 86 129 271 461 650
3,4 39 78 117 240 395 550
5-(1-2/54)-Ditko story (1st drawn) is written by Bruce Hamilton; r-in Weird V2#8 (1st pro work for Ditko but Daring Love #1 was published 1st) 168 336 504 1075 1838 2600
6-Decapitation-girl's head w/paper cutter (classic) 97 194 291 621 1061 1500
7(5-6/54), 9(9-10/54) 36 72 108 216 351 485
8(7-8/54)-Contains story intended for Jo-Jo; name changed to Kaza; decapitation story

Fantastic Force #2 © MAR

Fantastic Four #48 © MAR

Fantastic Four #113 © MAR

GD 2.0 | VG 4.0 | FN 6.0 | VF 8.0 | VF/NM 9.0 | NM- 9.2

37 74 111 222 361 500

FANTASTIC FIVE
Marvel Comics: Oct, 1999 - No. 5, Feb, 2000 ($1.99)
1-5: 1-M2 Universe; recaps origin; Ryan-a. 2-Two covers 3.00
Spider-Girl Presents Fantastic Five: In Search of Doom (2006, $7.99, digest) r/#1-5 8.00

FANTASTIC FIVE
Marvel Comics: Sept, 2007 - No. 5, Nov, 2007 ($2.99, limited series)
1-5-DeFalco-s/Lim-a; Dr. Doom returns vs. the future Fantastic Five 3.00
...: The Final Doom TPB (2007, $13.99) r/#1-5; cover sketches with inks 14.00

FANTASTIC FORCE
Marvel Comics: Nov, 1994 - No. 18, Apr, 1996 ($1.75)
1-($2.50)-Foil wraparound-c; intro Fantastic Force w/Huntara, Delvor, Psi-Lord & Vibraxas 4.00
2-18: 13-She-Hulk app. 3.00

FANTASTIC FORCE (See Fantastic Four #558, Nu-World heroes from 500 years in the future)
Marvel Comics: Jun, 2009 - No. 4, Sept, 2009 ($3.99/$2.99, limited series)
1-($3.99)-Ahearne-s/Kurth-a/Hitch-c; Fantastic Four app. 4.00
2-4-($2.99) 3,4-Ego the Living Planet app. 3.00

FANTASTIC FOUR (See America's Best TV..., Fireside Book Series, Giant-Size..., Giant Size Super-Stars, Marvel Age..., Marvel Collectors Item Classics, Marvel Knights 4, Marvel Milestone Edition, Marvel's Greatest, Marvel Treasury Edition, Marvel Triple Action, Official Marvel Index to..., Power Record Comics & Ultimate...)

FANTASTIC FOUR (See Volume Three for issues #500-611)
Marvel Comics Group: Nov, 1961 - No. 416, Sept, 1996 (Created by Stan Lee & Jack Kirby)
1-Origin & 1st app. The Fantastic Four (Reed Richards: Mr. Fantastic, Johnny Storm: The Human Torch, Sue Storm: The Invisible Girl, & Ben Grimm: The Thing–Marvel's 1st super-hero group since the G.A.; 1st app. S.A. Human Torch); origin/1st app. The Mole Man. 2300 4600 8800 30,000 85,000 140,000
1-Golden Record Comic Set Reprint (1966)-cover not identical to original 21 42 63 147 324 500
with Golden Record 28 56 84 203 439 750
2-Vs. The Skrulls (last 10¢ issue); (should have a pin-up of The Thing which many copies are missing) 410 820 1230 3700 8850 14,000
3-Fantastic Four don costumes & establish Headquarters; brief 1pg. origin; intro. The Fantasti-Car; Human Torch drawn w/two left hands on-c 350 700 1050 3100 8050 13,000
4-1st S. A. Sub-Mariner app. (5/62) 380 760 1140 3500 8750 14,000
5-Origin & 1st app. Doctor Doom 550 1100 2000 6000 13,000 20,000
6-Sub-Mariner, Dr. Doom team up; 1st Marvel villain team-up (2nd S.A. Sub-Mariner app. 235 470 705 1939 4370 6800
7-10: 7-1st app. Kurrgo. 8-1st app. Puppet-Master & Alicia Masters. 9-3rd Sub-Mariner app. 10-Stan Lee & Jack Kirby app. in story 152 304 456 1254 2827 4300
11-Origin/1st app. The Impossible Man (2/63) 145 290 435 1196 2698 4200
12-Fantastic Four vs. The Hulk (1st meeting); 1st Hulk x-over & ties w/Amazing Spider-Man #1 as 1st Marvel x-over; (3/63) 340 680 1020 3100 8050 13,000
13-Intro. The Watcher; 1st app. The Red Ghost 121 242 363 968 2184 3400
14,15,17,19: 14-Sub-Mariner x-over. 15-1st app. Mad Thinker. 19-Intro. Rama-Tut (Kang) 57 114 171 456 1028 1600
16-1st Ant-Man x-over (7/63); Wasp cameo 75 150 225 600 1350 2100
18-Origin/1st app. The Super Skrull 82 164 246 656 1478 2300
20-Origin/1st app. The Molecule Man 59 118 177 472 1061 1650
21-Intro. The Hate Monger; 1st Sgt. Fury x-over (12/63) 46 92 138 340 770 1200
22-24: 22-Sue Storm gains more powers 36 72 108 259 580 900
25-The Hulk vs. The Thing (their 1st battle); 3rd Avengers x-over (1st time w/Captain America)(cameo, 4/64); 2nd S.A. app. Cap (takes place between Avengers #4 & 5) 71 142 213 568 1284 2000
26-The Hulk vs. The Thing (continued); 4th Avengers x-over 64 128 192 512 1156 1800
27-1st Doctor Strange x-over (6/64) 40 80 120 296 673 1050
28-Early X-Men x-over (7/64); same date as X-Men #6 46 92 138 368 834 1300
29,30: 30-Intro. Diablo 27 54 81 194 435 675
31-35,37-40: 31-Early Avengers x-over (10/64). 33-1st app. Attuma; part photo-c. 35-Intro/1st app. Dragon Man. 39-Wood inks on Daredevil (early x-over) 22 44 66 154 340 525
36-Intro/1st app. Madam Medusa & the Frightful Four (Sandman, Wizard, Paste Pot Pete) 46 92 138 368 834 1300
41-44: 41-43-Frightful Four app. 44-Intro. Gorgon 14 28 42 96 211 325
45-Intro/1st app. The Inhumans (c/story, 12/65); also see Incredible Hulk Special #1 & Thor #146, & 147 111 222 333 888 1994 3100
46-1st Black Bolt-c (Kirby) & 1st full app. 46 92 138 340 770 1200
47-3rd app. The Inhumans 18 36 54 124 275 425
48-Partial origin/1st app. The Silver Surfer & Galactus (3/66) by Lee & Kirby; Galactus brief app. in last panel; 1st of 3 part story 100 200 300 800 1500 2200
49-2nd app./1st cover Silver Surfer & Galactus 46 92 138 340 770 1200
50-Silver Surfer battles Galactus; full S.S.-c 50 100 150 400 900 1400
51-Classic "This Man...This Monster" story 24 48 72 168 372 575
52-1st app. The Black Panther (7/66) 107 214 321 856 1928 3000
53-Origin & 2nd app. The Black Panther; origin/1st app. of Klaw 21 42 63 147 324 500
54-Inhumans cameo 12 24 36 82 179 275
55-Thing battles Silver Surfer; 4th app. Silver Surfer 23 46 69 161 356 550
56-Silver Surfer cameo 12 24 36 79 170 260
57-60: Dr. Doom steals Silver Surfer's powers (also see Silver Surfer: Loftier Than Mortals). 59,60-Inhumans cameo 10 20 30 64 132 200
61-63,68-71: 61-Silver Surfer cameo; Sandman app. (new costume). 62-1st Blastaar; Sandman app. 63-Sandman & Blastaar team-up 8 16 24 54 102 150
64-1st Kree Sentry #459 9 18 27 59 117 175
65-1st app. Ronan the Accuser; 1st Kree Supreme Intelligence 15 30 45 103 227 350
66-Begin 2 part origin of Him (Warlock); does not app. (9/67) 21 42 63 147 324 500
66,67-2nd printings (1994) 2 4 6 11 16 20
67-Origin/1st brief app. Him (Warlock); 1 page; see Thor #165,166 for 1st full app.; white cover scarcer in true high grade 28 56 84 202 451 700
72-Silver Surfer-c/story (pre-dates Silver Surfer #1) 13 26 39 89 195 300
73-Spider-Man, D.D., Thor x-over; cont'd from Daredevil #38 10 20 30 69 147 225
74-77: Silver Surfer app.(#77 is same date/S.S. #1) 9 18 27 62 126 190
78-80: 78-Wizard app. 80-1st Tomazooma, the Living Totem 6 12 18 41 76 110
81,84-88: 81-Crystal joins & dons costume; vs. the Wizard. 84-87-Dr. Doom app. 88-Mole Man app. 6 12 18 40 73 105
82,83-Black Bolt & the Inhumans app.; vs. Maximus 6 12 18 41 80 125
89-98,101: 89-Mole Man app. 91-1st app. Kree disguised as 1930s era gangsters; 1st app. Torgo. 92-The Thing app. as a space gladiator. 93-Thing vs. Torgo. 94-intro Agatha Harkness; Frightful Four app. 95-1st app. the Monocle. 96-Mad-Thinker app. 98-Neil Armstrong Moon landing issue. 101-Last Kirby-a issue 6 12 18 37 66 95
99-Black Bolt & the Inhumans app. 6 12 18 40 73 105
100 (7/70) F.F. vs Thinker and Puppet-Master 9 18 27 62 126 190
102-104: 102-Romita Sr-a; 102-104-Sub-Mariner & Magneto app. 6 12 18 37 66 95
105,106,108,109,111: 108-Features Kirby & Buscema-a; Kirby material produced after issue #101, his last official issue before leaving Marvel. 109-Annihilus app. 111-Hulk cameo 5 10 15 35 63 90
107-Classic Thing transformation-c; 1st John Buscema-a on FF (2/71); 1st app. Janus 6 12 18 40 73 105
110-Initial version w/green Thing and blue faces and pink uniforms on-c 19 38 57 131 291 450
110-Corrected-c w/accurately colored faces and uniforms and orange Thing 6 12 18 38 69 100
112-Hulk Vs. Thing (7/71) 20 40 60 138 307 475
113-115: 113-1st app. The Overmind; Watcher app. 114-vs the Overmind. 115-Origin of the Overmind; plot by Stan Lee, Archie Goodwin script; last 15¢ issue 5 10 15 30 50 70
116 (52 pgs.) FF and Dr. Doom vs. the Overmind; the Stranger app.; Goodwin story 6 12 18 41 76 110
117-119: 117,118-Diablo app; Goodwin-s 119-Black Panther app. vs Klaw; 1st Roy Thomas FF story 4 8 12 28 47 65
120-1st app. Gabriel the Air-Walker (new herald of Galactus); Stan Lee story 5 10 15 31 53 75
121,123: 121-Silver Surfer vs. Gabriel; Galactus app. 123-Silver Surfer & Galactus app. 5 10 15 35 63 90
122-Silver Surfer & Galactus app; black cover, scarcer in higher grade 5 10 15 35 73 105
124,125,127,130,134-140: 125-Last Stan Lee-s. 127-Mole Man & Tyrannus app. 130-vs the new Frightful Four (Thundra, Sandman, Trapster and Wizard; Black Bolt & Inhumans app.). 134,135-Dragon Man app. 134-1st full Gerry Conway issue. 136-Shaper of Worlds app; Dragon Man cameo. 137-Shaper of Worlds app. 138-Return of the Miracle Man. 139-vs. Miracle Man. 140-Annihilus app. 4 8 12 23 37 50
126-Origin FF retold; cover swipe of FF #1; Roy Thomas scripts begin 4 8 12 27 44 60
128-Four page glossy insert of FF Friends & Foes; Mole Man app. 4 8 12 25 40 55

Fantastic Four #244 © MAR

Fantastic Four #249 © MAR

Fantastic Four #309 © MAR

GD	VG	FN	VF	VF/NM	NM-
2.0	4.0	6.0	8.0	9.0	9.2

GD VG FN VF VF/NM NM-
2.0 4.0 6.0 8.0 9.0 9.2

129,131-133: 1st app. Thundra (super-strong Femizon) joins new Frightful Four; Medusa app. 131-Black Bolt, Medusa, Crystal, Quicksilver app; New Frightful Four app; Ross Andru-a; Steranko-c. 132-Black Bolt & Inhumans app.; vs. Maximus; last Roy Thomas-s (returns in issue #158). 133-Thing vs Thundra battle issue; Ramona Fradon-a; Gerry Conway script 5 10 15 31 53 75

141-Franklin Richards 'depowered'; Annihilus app.; FF break-up; last Buscema-a 4 8 12 23 37 50

142-146,148-149: 142-1st Darkoth the Demon; Dr. Doom app; Kirbyish-a by Buckler begins. 143,144-vs. Dr. Doom. 145,146-vs. Ternak the Abominable Snowman. 148-vs. Wizard, Sandman, Trapster. 149-Sub-Mariner app. 3 6 9 21 33 45

147-Thing vs. Sub-Mariner-c/s 4 8 12 27 44 60

150-Crystal & Quicksilver's wedding; Avengers, Ultron-7 and Black Bolt & the Inhumans app; story continued from Avengers #127 5 10 15 31 53 75

151-154,158-160: 151-1st Mahkizmo the Nuclear Man; origin Thundra. 152,153-Thundra & Mahkizmo app. 154-Nick Fury app; part-r issue (Strange Tales #127). 158,159 vs. Xemu; Black Bolt & Inhumans app. 160-Arkon app. 3 6 9 15 22 28

155-157: Silver Surfer & Dr. Doom in all 3 6 9 19 30 40

161-163,168-171: 162,163-Arkon app. 168-Luke Cage, Power Man joins the FF (to replace the Thing). 169-Luke Cage app; 1st app. Thing exoskeleton. 170-Luke Cage leaves the FF; Puppet Master app. 171-1st Gorr the Golden Gorilla; Pérez-a 2 4 6 10 14 18

164,165: 164-Re-intro Marvel Boy (as the Crusader); 1st George Pérez-a on FF. 165-Origin of Marvel Boy & the Crusader; 1st app. Frankie Ray. Pérez-a; death of the Crusader (a new Marvel Boy appears in Captain America #217) 2 4 6 10 15 20

166,167-vs the Hulk; Pérez-a. 167-The Thing loses his powers 3 6 9 17 26 35

169-173-(30¢-c, limited distribution)(4-8/76) 4 8 12 23 37 50

172-175: 172-Galactus & High Evolutionary app. 175-Galactus vs. High Evolutionary; the Thing regains his powers 2 4 6 10 15 20

176-180: 176-Re-intro Impossible Man; Marvel artists app. 177-1st app. the Texas Twister & Captain Ultra; Impossible Man & Brute app. 178-179-Impossible Man, Tigra & Thundra app; Reed loses his stretching ability. 180-r/#101 by Kirby 2 4 6 10 14 18

181-199: 181-183-The Brute, Mad Thinker & Annihilus app; last Roy Thomas-s. 184-1st Eliminator; Len Wein-s begin. (co-plotter in #183-182) 185,186-New Salem Witches app.; part origin Agatha Harkness. 187,188-vs. Klaw & the Molecule Man. 189-G.A Human Torch app.; r-FF Annual #4. 190-1st Marv Wolfman FF. 191-FF break-up; Wolfman/Wein-s. 192-Last Pérez-a; Texas Twister app. 193,194-Diablo & Darkoth the Death Demon app. 195-Sub-Mariner app.; Wolfman begins as full plotter & scripter. 196-1st full app. of the clone of Dr. Doom. 197-vs. the Red Ghost; Reed regains his stretching ability. 198-vs Dr. Doom. 199-Origin & death of the clone of Doom; Dr. Doom app. 2 4 6 8 10 12

200-(11/78 52 pgs)-FF reunited vs. Dr. Doom 2 4 6 10 14 18

201-203,219,222-231: 202-vs. Quasimodo. 219-Sub-Mariner app.; Moench & Sienkiewicz 1st FF work. 222-Agatha Harkness & Gabriel the Devil Hunter app. 224-Contains unused alternate-c for #3 and pin-ups. 225-Thor & Odin app. 226-1st Samurai Destroyer. 229-1st Ebon-Seeker. 230-vs. Ebon Seeker; Avengers app. 231-1st Stygorr of the Negative Zone 6.00

204-1st Nova Corps (cameo); 1st app. Queen Adora of Xandar; 1st app. of Xandar; FF vs. the Skrulls 1 3 4 6 8 10

205-208: 205-1st full app. Nova Corps; Xandarian/Skrull war. 206-Nova app.; story continued from Nova #25; Sphinx app. 207-Spider-Man app. 208-Nova & and the New Champions app. (Powerhouse, Diamondhead, the Comet & Crimebuster); Sphinx app. 1 2 3 5 6 8

209-210,213,214: 209-1st Byrne-a on FF; 1st Herbie the Robot. 210-Galactus app. 213-Galactus vs. the Sphinx; Terrax app. 1 3 4 6 8 10

211-1st app. Terrax (new Herald of Galactus) 3 6 9 14 20 25

212-Byrne-a; Galactus vs. the High Evolutionary 2 4 8 9 12 15

215-218,220-221: Byrne-a in all. 215-Blastaar app; 1st app. the Futurist. 216-Blastaar & Futurist app; last Wolfman-s. 217-Early app. Dazzler (4/80); by Byrne; vs Herbie the Robot (destroyed). 218-Spider-Man app; vs. Frightful Four; continued from Spectacular Spider-Man #42. 220-1st Byrne story on FF; origin retold; Avengers and Vindicator app. 1 2 3 5 6 8

232-Byrne story & art begins (7/81); vs. Diablo; brief Dr. Strange app; re-intro Frankie Raye 1 2 3 5 6 8

233-235,237-241,245-249,251,253-256: 233-Hammerhead app. 234,235-Ego the Living Planet. 238-Origin & 1st app. of Frankie Raye's flame powers, joins the FF. The Thing is 'devolved' into an 'uglier' version. 239-1st app. Aunt Petunia. 240-Black Bolt & the Inhumans app; Attilan (home of the Inhumans) relocated to the Moon. 241-Black Panther app. 245-Thing returns to his rocky-look. 246-Dr. Doom returns. 247-Doom and FF team-up vs. Prince Zorba; Doom regains rule of Latveria; 1st app. Kristoff. 248-Black Bolt & and the Inhumans app. 249-vs Gladiator (of the Sh'iar). 251-FF explore the Negative Zone; Annihilus app. 254-1st Mantracora. 255-Brief Daredevil app; Annihilus app. 256-FF return from the Negative Zone; vs Annihilus; Avengers, Galactus and Nova (Frankie Raye) app. 6.00

236-20th Anniversary issue (11/81, 68 pgs, $1.00)-brief origin FF; Byrne-c(p)/a; new Kirby-a; Marvel Super-Heroes & Stan Lee app. on cover; Dr. Doom and Puppet Master app.; 1st 'Liddleville' 1 2 3 5 6 8

242-vs. Terrax; Thor, Iron Man & Daredevil cameos 1 2 3 5 6 8

243-Classic Galactus-c by Byrne; Thor, Captain America, Dr. Strange, Spider-Man & Daredevil app. 2 4 6 9 12 15

244-Frankie Raye becomes Nova – the new Herald of Galactus 2 4 6 9 12 15

250,257-260: 250-(52 pgs)-Spider-Man x-over; Byrne-a; Skrulls impersonate New X-Men; Gladiator app. 257-Galactus devours the Skrull homeworld; Sue announces pregnancy; Vision & Scarlet Witch cameo. 258-Dr. Doom team-up with Terrax; Kristoff app. 259-Dr. Doom & Terrax. vs FF; Silver Surfer cameo. 260-Terrax, Silver Surfer & Sub-Mariner app.; 'death' of Dr. Doom 1 2 3 5 6 8

252-Reads sideways; Annihilus app. Contains skin 'Tattooz' decals (no 'Tattooz' were included in Canadian editions, also in Amazing Spider-Man #238)

with Tattooz 1 2 3 5 6 8

without Tattooz 6.00

261-262: The Trial of Reed Richards. 261-Silver Surfer & the Watcher app. 262-Origin Galactus; John Byrne writes himself into story; the Watcher, Odin, Eternity app. 6.00

263-285: 263-Mole Man app. Vision cameo. 264-vs Mole Man; swipes-c of FF #1. 265-Secret Wars x-over; She-Hulk replaces the Thing; Vision & Scarlet Witch app. 267-Dr. Octopus, Michael Morbius, Donald Blake & Bruce Banner app; Sue loses her baby. 268-Origin She-Hulk retold; Hulk and Dr. Octopus app. 269-1st app. Terminus; re-intro. Wyatt Wingfoot. 270-vs Terminus. 271-1st Gormuu (flashback story pre-FF #1). 272-1st app. Nathaniel Richards – the Warlord (Reed's father). 273-Nathaniel Richards app. 274-Spider-Man's alien costume app; (4th app. 1/85, 2 pgs.) the Thing app. on Battleword. 275-She-Hulk solo story. 276-Mephisto & Dr. Strange app. 277-Split story format - the Thing returns to Earth and battles Dire Wraiths; FF battle Mephisto; Dr. Strange app. 278-Origin Dr. Doom retold; Kristoff becomes new Dr. Doom. 279-Baxter Building destroyed by Kristoff; new Hate Monger app. 280-New Hate Monger & Psycho Man app.; 1st app. Sue as Malice. 281-New Hate Monger, Malice & Psycho Man app. 282-Power Pack cameo; Secret Wars II x-over; Psycho Man app.; infinity cover. 283,284-vs. Psycho Man. 285-Secret Wars II x-over; Beyonder app. 4.00

286-2nd app. X-Factor 1 3 4 6 8 10

287-295: 287-Return of Dr. Doom. 288-Secret Wars II x-over; Dr. Doom vs. the Beyonder. 289-Blastaar app; Basilisk killed by Scourge; Nick Fury app; Annihilus returns. 290-Blastaar, Annihilus & Nick Fury app. 291-Action Comics #1 cover swipe; Nick Fury app. 292-Hitler-c; Nick Fury app. 293-West Coast Avengers app; last Byrne-a. 294-Byrne plot only (last); Ordway-a; Roger Stern script. 295-Stern-s begin (over brief Byrne plot) 4.00

296-($1.50, 64-pgs)-Barry Smith-c/a (pgs 1-10); Shooter plot; Stan Lee script; Gammil, Frenz, Milgrom, John Buscema, Silvestri and Ordway-p; Sinnott & Colletta-inks; Mole Man app; the Thing returns to the FF 5.00

297-318,321-330: 297-Roger Stern-s begins; John Buscema-a returns. 299-Black costume Spider-Man app. 300-Wedding of Johnny Storm and 'Alicia'- see issue #358. 301-Wizard & Mad-Thinker app. 303-Thundra app. 304-Steve Englehart-s begins; vs. Quicksilver; the Thing becomes leader of the FF. 305-Quicksilver & Kristoff app ; Crystal rejoins FF; Dr. Doom app; leads into FF Annual #20. 306-v.s Diablo; Black Bolt & the Inhumans app; Captain America cameo; Ms. Marvel (Sharon Ventura) app. 307-Ms. Marvel joins the FF. vs. Diablo; Reed and Sue leave the FF. 308-1st Fasaud. 309-vs Fasaud; last Buscema-a. 310-Keith Pollard-a begins; 1st mutated Thing; Ms. Marvel becomes 'She-Thing'. 311-Black Panther & Dr. Doom app. 312-Dr. Doom, Black Panther & X-Factor app. 313-Mole Man app. 314-Belasco & Master Pandemonium app. 315-Master Pandemonium & Comet Man app; Morbius the Living Vampire cameo. 316-Ka-Zar & Shanna the She-Devil app.; origin of the Savage Land. 317-Comet Man app. 318-Molecule Man & Dr. Doom app. 322-Ron Lim guest-a; She-Hulk vs. Ms. Marvel; Dragon Man app; Aron the Renegade Watcher app. 322-Inferno x-over; Graviton, Aron & Dragon Man app. 323-Inferno x-over; Mantis & Kang app. 324-Kang, Mantis & Necrodamus app; Silver Surfer cameo. 325-Mantis, Kang & Silver Surfer app. 326-vs new Frightful Four (Wizard, Hydroman, Klaw and Titania); Reed & Sue return; the Thing becomes human; Englehart-s as 'John Harkness'. 327-vs Frightful Four; Aron the Renegade Watcher & Dragon Man app. 328-1st app. Aron's evil version of the FF; Frightful Four & Dragon Man app. 329-Evil FF vs. Mole Man; Aron app. 3.00

319,320: 319-(Double-size, 39 pgs); Secret Wars III; origin of the Beyonder; Dr. Doom, Molecule Man, Shaper of Worlds, Kubik app. 320-Grey Hulk vs. Thing; Dr. Doom app; x-over w/Incredible Hulk #350 6.00

331-346, 351-357,359,360: 331-Ultron app. in dream sequence; Aron the Renegade Watcher app. 333-Avengers & Dr. Strange app. Evil FF vs real FF; Aron the Renegade Watcher app. 334-Acts of Vengeance x-over; Simonson-s begin; Buckler-a; Thor & Captain America app. 335-Acts of Vengeance x-over; Apocalypse cameo. 336-Acts of Vengeance x-over. 337-Simonson-s and art begin; Thor & Iron Man join FF's mission. 338-Iron Man & Thor app. Death's Head app. Galactus cameo. 339-Thor vs. Gladiator; Galactus & the Black Celestial app. 340-Iron Man, Thor & Galactus app; death of the Black Celestial. 341-Thor, Iron Man & Galactus app. 342-Spider-Man cameo; no Simonson-s or art. 343-President Dan Quale app. 346-T.V.A (Time Variance Authority) app. 351-Kubik &

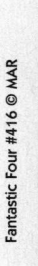

Fantastic Four #389 © MAR

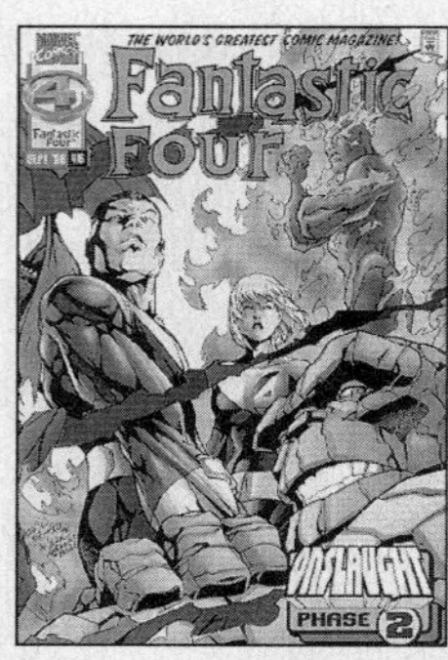

Fantastic Four #416 © MAR

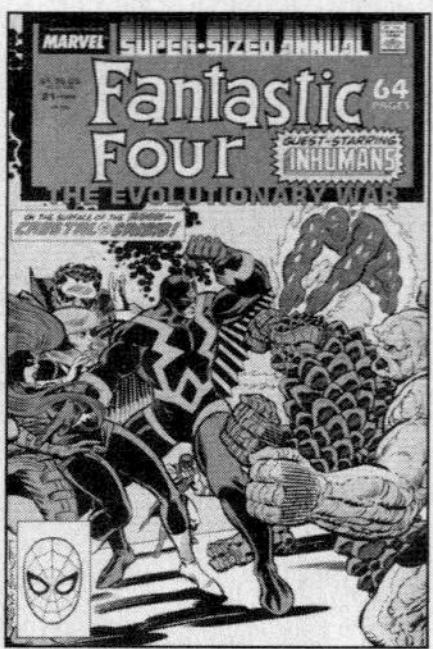

Fantastic Four Annual #21 © MAR

GD VG FN VF VF/NM NM-
2.0 4.0 6.0 8.0 9.0 9.2

Kosmos app; Mark Bagley-a. 352-Reed vs Dr. Doom; Kristof app; Justice Peace & the T.V.A app. 353,354-FF on trial by the T.V.A; Justice Peace and Mark Gruenwald (as Mr. Chairman) app; 354-Last Simonson issue. 355-vs. the Wrecker. 356-1st Tom Defalco-s & Paul Ryan-a (begin four-year run); Puppet Master & New Warriors app. 357-Alicia Masters revealed to be a Skrull (since issue #265); Puppet Master app. 3.00
347-Ghost Rider, Wolverine, Spider-Man, Hulk-c/stories thru #349; Arthur Adams-c/a(p) in each 5.00
347,348-Gold second printings 5.00
348-350: 348-349-Arthur Adams-c/a(p). 350-($1.50, 52 pgs)-The 'real' Dr. Doom returns; Kristoff app. Sharon Ventura becomes human again. Ben becomes the Thing again 5.00
358-(11/91, $2.25, 88 pgs)-30th anniversary issue; gives history of the FF; die-cut-c; Art Adams back-up story-a; origin of Lyja the Skrull as Alicia Masters; 1st app. Paibok the Power Skrull 5.00
361-368, 372-373: 361-Dr. Doom & the Yancy Street gang app. 362-Spider-Man app; 1st app. of the Innerverse. 363-1st app. Occulus. 364,365-vs. Occulus; 365-Sharon Ventura returns. 366-Infinity War x-over; Magus app; Paibok & Devos team-up. 367-Infinity War x-over; Magus app. numerous super-heroes app. 368-Infinity War x-over; Magus app. Human Torch vs. X-Men doppelgangers. 372-Spider-Man, Molecule Man, Puppet Master & Aron the Renegade Watcher app.; Silver Sable & the Wild Pack cameo; Devos, Paibok & Lyja app. 373-Human Torch vs. Silver Sable & the Wild Pack; Molecule Man vs. Aron the Rogue Watcher; Dr. Doom app. (steals the power of Aron) 3.00
369,370-Infinity War x-over. 369-Thanos & Warlock and the Infinity Watch app; Aron the Renegade Watcher app.; the Magus gains the Infinity Gauntlet. 370-Warlock vs. the Magus for the Infinity Gauntlet; 1st app. Lyja the Lazer-fist. 4.00
371-All-white embossed-c ($2.00); 1st new (revealing) Invisible Woman costume; Paibok, Devos & Lyja vs. Human Torch; Aron the Renegade Watcher app; Ms. Marvel (Sharon Ventura) rejoins the FF 4.00
371-All-red 2nd printing ($2.00) 3.00
374,375: 374-vs Wolverine, Dr. Strange, Ghost Rider, the Hulk and Spider-Man (as the Secret Defenders); Thing's face injured by Wolverine; Dr. Doom app; Black Bolt & the Inhumans cameo; Uatu the Watcher app. 375-($2.95, 52 pgs)-Holo-Grafx foil-c; Secret Defenders app.; Black Bolt & the Inhumans app; cosmic powered Dr. Doom app. Uatu app.; re-intro Nathaniel Richards (from issue #273); Lyja changes allegiance to the FF 4.00
376-($2.95)-Variant polybagged w/Dirt Magazine #4 and music tape; harder to find in true NM- 9.2 due to being packaged with a tape cassette 5.00
376-380,382-386: 376-Nathaniel Richards and Dr. Doom app; Franklin becomes an adult (Psi-Lord). 377-1st app. Huntara; origin Devos; Paibok, Dr. Doom & Klaw app. 378-vs. Devos, Paibok & Huntara; Avengers, Spider-Man & Daredevil app. 379-Devos, Paibok, Huntara & Dr. Doom app. 380-Dr. Doom app. 382-Contains a coupon from Kaybee Toys for an exclusive Ghost Rider issue; also has 16-pg Midnight Sons 'Siege of Darkness' insert; Devos vs. the Skrull Empire. 383-Paibok vs. Devos. 384-Scott Lang app. as Ant-Man; Psi-Lord vs. Invisible Woman. 385-Starblast x-over; Ant-Man & Sub-Mariner app.; continues in Namor the Sub-Mariner #48. 386-Starblast x-over; Ant-Man & Sub-Mariner app. 3.00
381-'Death' of Reed Richards (Mr. Fantastic) & Dr. Doom 4.00
387-Newstand ed. ($1.25) 3.00
387-($2.95)-Collectors Ed. w/die-cut foil-c; Ant-Man app; Invisible Woman returns to her regular costume 4.00
388-393,396,397: 388-Bound in trading card sheet; Ant-Man, Sub-Mariner & Avengers app; 1st app. the Dark Raider. 389-Ant-Man, Sub-Mariner and the Collector app. 390- Ant-Man & Sub-Mariner app. Galactus & Silver Surfer app. in flashback to FF #48-50. 391-Ant-Man, Sub-Mariner, Galactus & Silver Surfer app. 392-vs. the Dark Raider. 396-Power Rangers card insert. 397-Aron the Renegade Watcher & the Dark Raider app; return of Kristoff; Ant-Man app. 3.00
394-($2.95)-Collectors Edition-polybagged w/16-pg. Marvel; Action Hour book and acetate print; pink logo; Ant-Man, Wyatt Wingfoot & She-Hulk app. 4.00
394-(Newstand Edition-$1.50; white logo 3.00
395,398,399: 395-Wolverine-c/story; Ant-Man app. 398,399-($2.50)-Rainbow foil-c; Ant-Man, Uatu, Aron & the Dark Raider app. 4.00
400-($3.95, 64-pgs)-Rainbow foil-c; Stan Lee introduction; Celestials vs. the Watchers; Kristoff joins the FF. Ant-Man app.; Avengers & Spider-Man app. in back-up story; origin of the FF retold; Uatu vs. Aron (dies) 5.00
401-404: 401-Atlantis Rising x-over; Sub-Mariner & Thor app; Black Bolt cameo. 402-Atlantis Rising x-over; Sub-Mariner vs. Black Bolt; Thor vs. the FF. 404-1st brief app. Hyperstorm (arm only) 3.00
405-Overpower card insert; scarcer in higher grades due to card indentation; new Ant-Man costume; Zarko the Tomorrow Man app; 2nd app. Hyperstorm (cameo) 4.00
406-Return of Dr. Doom; Hyperstorm revealed, battles FF. 407-Return of Mr. Fantastic; x-over w/FF Unlimited #12; Hyperstorm app. 408-vs Hyperstorm; Dr. Doom app. 409-Dr. Doom & FF vs. Hyperstorm; Thing's facial injury cured (since #374). 410-Gorgon of the Inhumans app. 411-Black Bolt & the Inhumans app. 412-Mr. Fantastic vs. Sub-Mariner. 413-Silver Surfer cameo; x-over w/Doom 2099 #42; Doom 2099 & Hyperstorm app; Franklin returns to being a child (Psi-Lord since #376). 414-Galactus vs. Hyperstorm; last Paul Ryan-a (since #356) 4.00
415-Onslaught tie-in; Pacheco-a; Professor X & Avengers app.; Apocalypse cameo; story continued in X-Men #55 5.00
416-($2.50, 48 pgs)-Onslaught tie-in; Pacheco-a; Dr. Doom app; last issue; story continues in Onslaught Marvel Universe #1; Reed, Ben & Victor Von Doom app. in flashback in back-up story; Uatu the Watcher app. 6.00

#500-up (See Fantastic Four Vol. 3; series resumed original numbering after Vol. 3 #70)

Annual 1('63)-Origin of Sub-Mariner & 1st modern app. of Atlantis & the Atlanteans incl. Lady Dorma; FF origin retold; Spider-Man app. in detailed retelling of his app. from Amazing Spider-Man #1 70 140 210 555 1253 1950
Annual 2('64)-Dr. Doom origin & c/story; FF #5-r in 2nd story; Pharaoh Rama-Tut app. in 3rd story 38 76 114 285 641 1000
Annual 3('65)-Reed & Sue wed; r/#6,11 19 38 57 131 291 450
Special 4(11/66)-G.A. Torch x-over (1st S.A. app.) & origin retold; r/#25,26 (Hulk vs. Thing); Torch vs. Torch battle; Mad-Thinker app; 1st app Quasimodo 12 24 36 80 173 265
Special 5(11/67)-New art; Intro. Psycho-Man; early Black Panther, Inhumans & Silver Surfer (1st solo story); Black Bolt & the Inhumans app; Sue is revealed to be pregnant; Quasimodo app. 12 24 36 83 182 280
Special 6(11/68)-Intro. Annihilus; birth of Franklin Richards; new 48 pg. movie length epic; last non-reprint annual 16 32 48 110 243 375
Special 7(11/69)-all reprint issue; r/FF #1; r/origin of Dr. Doom from FF #5 & Dr. Doom story from FF Annual #2; Marvel staff photos seen in 'Because you Demanded it' featurette; new-c by Kirby 5 10 15 33 57 80
Special 8-10: All reprints. 8(12/70)-F.F. vs. Sub-Mariner plus gallery of F.F. foes. Special 9(12/71)-r/FF #43, Strange Tales #131 & FF Annual #3. Special 10('73)-r/FF Annual #3,4; new-c by John Buscema 3 6 9 21 33 45
Annual 11-14: 11-('76)-New story & art begins; alternate Earth versions of the Invaders app; story continues into Marvel Two-in-One Annual #1; Kirby-c. Annual 12 ('78)-Black Bolt & the Inhumans app; vs. the Sphinx. Annual 13 ('78)-vs the Mole Man; Daredevil app. Annual 14 ('79)-Pérez-a; Avengers cameo; Sandman & Salem's Seven app. 2 4 6 8 10 12
Annual 15-17: 15-(80, 68 pgs.); Perez-a; Captain Marvel & Dr. Doom app. Annual 16-('81)-Ditko-a/c; 1st Dragon lord. Annual 17-('83)-Byrne-c/a; Skrulls app. 6.00
Annual 18-23: 18-('84)-Minor x-over w/X-Men #137; Wolverine cameo; wedding of Black Bolt & Medusa; the Watcher app. Annual 19-('85)-vs the Skrulls; x-over w/Avengers Annual #14. Annual 20-('87)-Dr. Doom & Mephisto app; continued from FF #305. Annual 21-('88, 64 pgs.)-Square bound; Evolutionary War x-over; Black Bolt & the Inhumans app. Aron the Watcher app. (unnamed). Annual 22-('89, 64 pgs.)-Square bound; Atlantis Attacks x-over; Avengers & Dr. Strange app. Annual 23-('90, 64 pgs.)-Squarebound; 'Days of Future Present' Pt. 1; 1st Ahab; story continues in New Mutants Annual #6 (not X-Factor Annual #5 as noted); Dr. Doom app. in back-up feature; Byrne-c 4.00
Annual 24-27 (all square bound editions): Annual 24-('91, 64 pgs.); Korvac Quest Pt.1; Guardians of the Galaxy app; story continues in Thor Annual #16; Molecule Man & Super-Skrull app. in back-up features. Annual 25-('92, 64 pgs.)-Citizen Kang Pt.3; continued from Thor Annual #17; Avengers app.; story continues in Avengers Annual #21; Moondragon vs. Mantis solo story & Kang retrospective. Annual 26-('93, 64 pgs.)-Bagged w/card featuring a new character 'Wildstreak'; vs. Dreadface; Kubik & Kosmos app. in solo story featuring the Celestials. Annual 27-('94, 64 pgs.)-Justice Peace & the T.V.A (Time Variance Authority) app.; featuring the chairman (Mark Gruenwald); Molecule Man vs. Beyonder solo story 4.00
Best of the Fantastic Four Vol. 1 HC (2005, $29.99) oversized reprints of classic stories from FF#1,39,40,51,100,116,176,236,267, Ann.2, V3#56,60 and more; Brevoort intro. 30.00
Maximum Fantastic Four HC (2005, $49.99, dust jacket) r/Fantastic Four #1 with super-sized art; historical background from Walter Mosley and Mark Evanier; dust jacket unfolds to a poster: giant FF#1 cover on one side, gallery of interior pages on other 50.00
...: Monsters Unleashed nn (1992, $5.95)-r/F.F. #347-349 w/new Arthur Adams-c 1 2 3 5 6 8
...: Nobody Gets Out Alive (1994, $15.95) TPB r/ #387-392 16.00
... Omnibus Vol. 1 HC (2005, $99.99) r/#1-30 & Annual 1 plus letter pages; 3 intros. and a 1974 essay by Stan Lee; original plot synopsis for FF #1; essays and Kirby art 100.00
... Omnibus Vol. 2 HC (2007, $99.99) r/#31-60, Annual 2-4 and Not Brand Echh #1 plus letter pages and essays by Stan Lee, Reginald Hudlin, Roy Thomas and others 100.00
Special Edition 1(5/84)-r/Annual #1; Byrne-c/a 5.00
...: The Lost Adventure (4/08, $4.99) Lee & Kirby story partially used in flashback in FF #108 completed with additional art by Frenz & Sinnott; plus reprint of FF #108 5.00
... Visionaries: George Pérez Vol. 1 (2005, $19.99) r/#164-167,170,176-178,184-186 20.00
... Visionaries: George Pérez Vol. 2 (2006, $19.99) r/#187-188,191-192, Annual #14-15, Marvel Two-In-One #60 and back-up story from Adventures of the Thing #3 20.00
... Visionaries (11/01, $19.95) r/#232-240 by John Byrne 20.00
... Visionaries Vol. 2 (2004, $24.99) r/#241-250 by John Byrne 25.00
... Visionaries John Byrne Vol. 3 (2004, $24.99) r/#251-257; Annual #17; Avengers #233 and Thing #2 25.00
... Visionaries John Byrne Vol. 4 (2005, $24.99) r/#258-267; Alpha Flight #4 & Thing #10 25.00
... Visionaries John Byrne Vol. 5 (2005, $24.99) r/#268-275; Annual #18 & Thing #19 25.00

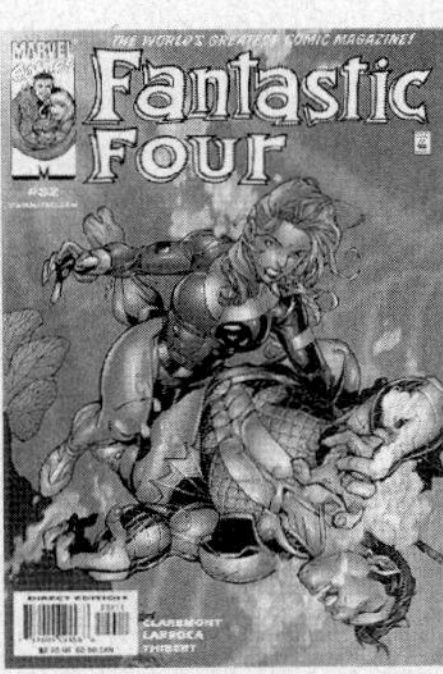

Fantastic Four V3 #32 © MAR

Fantastic Four #611 © MAR

Fantastic Four: Isle De La Muerte! #1 © MAR

	GD 2.0	VG 4.0	FN 6.0	VF 8.0	VF/NM 9.0	NM- 9.2

GD VG FN VF VF/NM NM-
2.0 4.0 6.0 8.0 9.0 9.2

... Visionaries John Byrne Vol. 6 ('06, $24.99) r/#276-284; Secret Wars II #2 & Thing #23 25.00
... Visionaries John Byrne Vol. 7 ('07, $24.99) r/#285,286, Ann. #19, Avengers #263 & Ann. #14, and X-Factor #1 25.00
... Visionaries John Byrne Vol. 8 ('07, $24.99) r/#287-295 25.00
... Visionaries: Walter Simonson Vol. 1 (2007, $19.99) r/#334-341 20.00

*NOTE: **Arthur Adams** c/a-347-349p. **Austin** c(i)-232-236, 238, 240-242, 250i, 286i. **Buckler** c-151, 168. **John Buscema** a(p)-107, 108(w/**Kirby, Sinnott** & **Romita**),109-130, 132, 134-141, 160, 173-175, 202, 296-309p, Annual 11, 13; c(p)-107-122, 124-129, 133-139, 202, Annual 12p, Special 10. **Byrne** a-209-218p, 220p, 221p, 232-265, 266i, 267-273, 274-293p, Annual 17, 19; c-211-214p, 220p, 232-236p, 237, 238p, 239, 240-242p, 243-249, 250p, 251-267, 269-277, 278-281p, 283p, 284, 285, 286p, 288-293, Annual 17, 18. **Ditko** a-13i, 14i(w/**Kirby**-p), Annual 16. **G. Kane** c-145p, 146p, 150p, 160p. **Kirby** a-1-102p, 108p, 180r, 189r, 236p, Special 1-10; c-1-101, 164, 167, 171-177, 180, 181, 190, 200, Annual 11, Special 1-7, 9. **Marcos** a-Annual 14i. **Mooney** a-118i, 152i. **Perez** a(p)-164-167, 170-172, 176-178, 184-188, 191p, 192p. Annual 14p, 15p; c(p)-183-188, 191, 192, 194-197. **Simonson** a-337-341, 343, 344p, 345p, 346, 350p, 352-354; c-212, 334-341, 342p, 343-346, 350, 353, 354. **Steranko** c-130-132p. **Williamson** c-357i.*

FANTASTIC FOUR (Volume Two)
Marvel Comics: V2#1, Nov, 1996 - No. 13, Nov, 1997 ($2.95/$1.95/$1.99) (Produced by WildStorm Productions)

1-($2.95)-Reintro Fantastic Four; Jim Lee-c/a; Brandon Choi scripts; Mole Man app. 5.00
1-($2.95)-Variant-c 1 2 3 4 5 7
2-9: 2-Namor-c/app. 3-Avengers-c/app. 4-Two covers; Dr. Doom cameo 3.00
10,11,13: All $1.99-c. 13-"World War 3"-pt. 1, x-over w/Image 3.00
12-($2.99) "Heroes Reunited"-pt. 1 4.00
...: Heroes Reborn (7/00, $17.95, TPB) r/#1-6 18.00
Heroes Reborn: Fantastic Four (2006, $29.99, TPB) r/#1-12; Jim Lee intro.; pin-ups 30.00

FANTASTIC FOUR (Volume Three)
Marvel Comics: V3#1, Jan, 1998 - No. 588, Apr, 2011 ($2.99/$1.99/$2.25)
No. 600, Jan, 2012 - No. 611, Dec, 2012 (Issues #589-#599 do not exist, see FF series)

1-($2.99)-Heroes Return; Lobdell-s/Davis & Farmer-a 1 2 3 5 6 8
1-Alternate Heroes Return-c 1 3 4 6 8 10
2-4,12: 2-2-covers. 4-Claremont-s/Larroca-a begin; Silver Surfer c/app.
12-($2.99) Wraparound-c by Larroca 5.00
5-11: 6-Heroes For Hire app. 9-Spider-Man-c/app. 11-1st app. Ayesha 4.00
13-24: 13,14-Ronan-c/app. 3.00
25-($2.99) Dr. Doom returns 4.00
26-49: 27-Dr. Doom marries Sue. 30-Begin $2.25-c. 32,42-Namor-c/app. 35-Regular cover; Pacheco-s/a begins. 37-Super-Skrull-c/app. 38-New Baxter Building 3.00
35-($3.25) Variant foil enhanced-c; Pacheco-s/a begins 4.00
50-($3.99, 64 pgs.) BWS-c; Grummett, Pacheco, Rude, Udon-a 4.00
51-53,55-59: 51-53-Bagley-a(p)/Wieringo-c; Inhumans app. 55,56-Immonen-a 57-59-Warren-s/Grant-a 3.00
54-($3.50, 100 pgs.) Birth of Valeria; r/Annual #6 birth of Franklin 4.00
60-(9¢-c) Waid-s/Wieringo-a begin 3.00
60-($2.25 newsstand edition)(also see Promotional Comics section) 3.00
61-70: 62-64-FF vs. Modulus. 65,66-Buckingham-a. 68-70-Dr. Doom app. 3.00
(After #70 [Aug, 2003] numbering reverted back to original Vol. 1 with #500, Sept, 2003)
500-($3.50) Regular edition; concludes Dr. Doom app.; Dr. Strange app.; Rivera painted-c 4.00
500-($4.99) Director's Cut Edition; chromium-c by Wieringo; sketch and script pages 8.00
501-516: 501,502-Casey Jones-a. 503-508-Porter-a. 509-Wieringo-c/a resumes. 512,513-Spider-Man app. 514-516-Ha-c/Medina-a 3.00
517-537: 517-Begin $2.99-c. 519-523-Galactus app. 527-Straczynski-s begins. 537-Dr. Doom. 3.00
527-Variant Edition with different McKone-c 3.00
527-Wizard World Philadelphia Edition with B&W McKone sketch-c 3.00
536-Variant cover by Bryan Hitch 5.00
537-B&W variant cover 5.00
538-542-Civil War. 538-Don Blake reclaims Thor's hammer 4.00
543-45th Anniversary; Black Panther and Storm replace Reed and Sue; Granov-c 4.00
544-553: 544-546-Silver Surfer app.; Turner-c 3.00
554-568-Millar-s/Hitch-a/c. 558-561-Doctor Doom-c/app. 562-Funeral & proposal 3.00
554-Variant-c by Bianchi 6.00
554-Variant Skrull-c by Suydam 30.00
569-($3.99) Wraparound-c; Immonen-a; Dr. Doom app. 4.00
570-586: 570-572,575-578-Eaglesham-a. 574-Spider-Man app. 584-586-Galactus app. 3.00
587-(3/11, $3.99) Death of Human Torch; Epting-a; issue is in black polybag; Davis-c 4.00
587-Variant-c by Cassaday 10.00
588-($3.99) Last issue; Dragotta-a; preview of FF #1; back-up w/Spider-Man; Davis-c 4.00
589-599-**Do not exist**; story continues in FF series
600-(1/12, $7.99) Avengers app.; Human Torch returns, back-up short stories; Dell'Otto-c 8.00
600-Variant-c by John Romita, Jr. 10.00
600-Variant-c by Art Adams 15.00
601-603,605,605.1, 606-611: 601-603-Johnny Storm & Avengers app. 602,603-Galactus app. 605.1-Alternate origin; Choi-a. 607,608-Black Panther app. 611-Doctor Doom app. 3.00
604-($3.99) Future Franklin and Valeria app. 4.00
...'98 Annual ($3.50) Immonen-a 4.00
...'99 Annual ($3.50) Ladronn-a 4.00
...'00 Annual ($3.50) Larocca-a; Marvel Girl back-up story 4.00
...'01 Annual ($2.99) Maguire-a; Thing back-up w/Yu-a 4.00
... Annual 32 (8/10, $4.99) Hitch-a/c 5.00
... Annual 33 (9/12, $4.99) Alan Davis-s/a/c; Dr. Strange & Clan Destine app. 5.00
... : A Death in the Family (7/06, $3.99, one-shot) Weeks-a/c; and r/F.F. #245 4.00
... By J. Michael Straczynski Vol. 1 (2005, $19.99, HC) r/#527-532 20.00
Civil War: Fantastic Four TPB (2007, $17.99) r/#538-543; 45th Anniversary Toasts 18.00
... Cosmic-Size Special 1 (2/09, $4.99) Cary Bates-s/Bing Cansino-a; r/F.F. #237 5.00
Fantastic 4th Voyage of Sinbad (9/01, $5.95) Claremont-s/Ferry-a 6.00
Flesh and Stone (8/01, $12.95, TPB) r/#35-39 13.00
... Giant-Size Adventures 1 (8/09, $3.99) Cifuentes & Coover-a; Egghead app. 4.00
... In...Ataque del M.O.D.O.K.! (11/10, $3.99) English & Spanish editions; Beland-s/Doe-a 4.00
... /Inhumans TPB (2007, $19.99) r/#51-54 and Inhumans ('00) #1-4 20.00
...: Isla De La Muerte! (2/08, $3.99) English & Spanish editions; Beland-s/Doe-a 4.00
... MGC #570 (7/11, $1.00) r/#570 with "Marvel's Greatest Comics" cover banner 3.00
... Presents: Franklin Richards 1 (11/05, $2.99) r/back-up stories from Power Pack #1-4 plus new 5 pg. story; Sumerak-s/Eliopoulos-a (Also see Franklin Richards) 3.00
...Special (2/06, $2.99) McDuffie-s/Casey Jones-a; dinner with Dr. Doom 3.00
...Tales Vol. 1 (2005, $7.99, digest) r/Marvel Age: FF Tales #1, Tales of the Thing #1-3, and Spider-Man Team-Up Special 8.00
...: The Last Stand (8/11, $4.99) r/#574, 587 & 588 (death of Johnny Storm) 5.00
...: The New Fantastic Four HC (2007, $19.99) r/#544-550; variant covers & sketch pgs. 20.00
...: The New Fantastic Four SC (2008, $15.99) r/#544-550; variant covers & sketch pgs. 16.00
... : The Wedding Special 1 (1/06, $5.00) 40th Anniversary new story & r/FF Annual #3 5.00
... Vol. 1 HC (2004, $29.99, dust jacket) oversized reprint /#60-70, 500-502; Mark Waid intro and series proposal; cover gallery 30.00
... Vol. 2 HC (2005, $29.99, d.j.) oversized r/#503-513; Waid intro.; deleted scenes 30.00
... Vol. 3 HC (2005, $29.99, d.j.) oversized r/#514-524; Waid commentaries; cover sketches 30.00
... Vol. 1: Imaginauts (2003, $17.99, TPB) r/#56,60-66; Mark Waid's series proposal 18.00
... Vol. 2: Unthinkable (2003, $17.99, TPB) r/#67-70,500-502; #500 Director's Cut extras 18.00
... Vol. 3: Authoritative Action (2004, $12.99, TPB) r/#503-508 13.00
... Vol. 4: Hereafter (2004, $11.99, TPB) r/#509-513 12.00
... Vol. 5: Disassembled (2004, $14.99, TPB) r/#514-519 15.00
... Vol. 6: Rising Storm (2005, $13.99, TPB) r/#520-524 14.00
...: The Beginning of the End TPB (2008, $14.99) r/#525,526,551-553 & Fantastic Four: Isla De La Muerte! one-shot 15.00
...: The Life Fantastic TPB (2006, $16.99) r/#533-535; The Wedding Special, Special (2/06) and A Death in the Family one-shots 17.00
Wizard #1/2 -Lim-a 10.00

FANTASTIC FOUR (Volume Four) (Marvel NOW!) (Also see FF)
Marvel Comics: Jan, 2013 - No. 16, Mar, 2014 ($2.99)

1-5-Fraction-s/Bagley-a/c 3.00
5AU-(5/13, $3.99) Age of Ultron tie-in; Fraction-s/Araújo-a/Bagley-c 4.00
6-15: 6,7-Blastaar app. 9,13-15-Dr. Doom app. 14,15-Ienco-a 3.00
16-($3.99) Fantastic Four vs. Doom, The Annihilating Conqueror; back-up w/Quinones-a 4.00

FANTASTIC FOUR (Volume Five) (All-New Marvel NOW!)
Marvel Comics: Apr, 2014 - No. 14, Feb, 2015; No. 642, Mar, 2015 - No. 645, Jun, 2015 ($3.99)

1-4-Robinson-s/Kirk-a. 3,4-Frightful Four app. 4.00
5-($4.99) Trial of the Fantastic Four; flashback-a by various incl. Starlin, Allred, Samnee 5.00
6-14: 6-8-Original Sin tie-in. 10,11-Scarlet Witch app. 11,12-Spider-Man app. 4.00
642-(3/15)-644: Heroes Reborn Avengers app. 643,644-Sleepwalker app. 4.00
645-($5.99) Psycho Man & the Frightful Four app.; Kirk-a; bonus back-up stories 6.00
Annual 1 (11/14, $4.99) Sue vs. Doctor Doom in Latveria; Grummett-a 5.00
100th Anniversary Special: Fantastic Four 1 (9/14, $3.99) Van Meter-s/Estep-a 4.00

FANTASTIC FOUR AND POWER PACK
Marvel Comics: Sept, 2007 - No. 4, Dec, 2007 ($2.99, limited series)

1-4-Gurihiru-a/Van Lente-s; the Wizard app. 3.00
...: Favorite Son TPB (2008, $7.99, digest size) r/#1-4 8.00

FANTASTIC FOUR: ATLANTIS RISING
Marvel Comics: June, 1995 - No. 2, July, 1995 ($3.95, limited series)

1,2: Acetate-c 5.00
Collector's Preview (5/95, $2.25, 52 pgs.) 4.00

FANTASTIC FOUR: BIG TOWN
Marvel Comics: Jan, 2001 - No. 4, Apr, 2001 ($2.99, limited series)

1-4:"What If?" story; McKone-a/Englehart-s 3.00

FANTASTIC FOUR: FIREWORKS
Marvel Comics: Jan, 1999 - No. 3, Mar, 1999 ($2.99, limited series)

1-3-Remix; Jeff Johnson-a 3.00

FANTASTIC FOUR: FIRST FAMILY

Fantastic Four 1 2 3 4 #2 © MAR

Fantastic Four Unlimited #7 © MAR

Fantasy Masterpieces #9 © MAR

	GD 2.0	VG 4.0	FN 6.0	VF 8.0	VF/NM 9.0	NM- 9.2

Marvel Comics: May, 2006 - No. 6, Oct, 2006 ($2.99, limited series)

1-6-Casey-s/Weston-a; flashback to the days after the accident 3.00
TPB (2006, $15.99) r/#1-6 16.00

FANTASTIC FOUR: FOES
Marvel Comics: Mar, 2005 - No. 6, Aug, 2005 ($2.99, limited series)

1-6-Kirkman-s/Rathburn-a. 1-Puppet Master app. 3-Super-Skrull app. 4-Mole Man app. 3.00
TPB (2005, $16.99) r/#1-6 17.00

FANTASTIC FOUR: HOUSE OF M (Reprinted in House of M: Fantastic Four/ Iron Man TPB)
Marvel Comics: Sept, 2005 - No. 3, Nov, 2005 ($2.99, limited series)

1-3: Fearsome Four, led by Doom; Scot Eaton-a 3.00

FANTASTIC FOUR INDEX (See Official...)

FANTASTIC FOUR/ IRON MAN: BIG IN JAPAN
Marvel Comics: Dec, 2005 - No. 4, Mar, 2006 ($3.50, limited series)

1-4-Seth Fisher-a/c; Zeb Wells-s; wraparound-c on each 3.50
TPB (2006, $12.99) r/#1-4 and Seth Fisher illustrated story from Spider-Man Unlimited #8 13.00

FANTASTIC FOUR: 1 2 3 4
Marvel Comics: Oct, 2001 - No. 4, Jan, 2002 ($2.99, limited series)

1-4-Morrison-s/Jae Lee-a. 2-4-Namor-c/app. 3.00
TPB (2002, $9.99) r/#1-4 10.00

FANTASTIC FOUR ROAST
Marvel Comics Group: May, 1982 (75¢, one-shot, direct sales)

1-Celebrates 20th anniversary of F.F.#1; X-Men, Ghost Rider & many others cameo; Golden, Miller, Buscema, Rogers, Byrne, Anderson art; Hembeck/Austin-c 5.00

FANTASTIC FOUR: THE END
Marvel Comics: Jan, 2007 - No. 6, May, 2007 ($2.99, limited series)

1-6-Alan Davis-s/a; last adventure of the future FF. 1-Dr. Doom-c/app. 3.00
Roughcut #1 ($3.99) B&W pencil art for full story and text script; B&W sketch cover 4.00
HC (2007, $19.99, dustjacket) r/#1-6 20.00
SC (2008, $14.99) r/#1-6 15.00

FANTASTIC FOUR: THE LEGEND
Marvel Comics: Oct, 1996 ($3.95, one-shot)

1-Tribute issue 4.00

FANTASTIC FOUR: THE MOVIE
Marvel Comics: Aug, 2005 ($4.99/$12.99, one-shot)

1-($4.99) Movie adaptation; Jurgens-a; behind the scenes feature; Doom origin; photo-c 5.00
TPB-($12.99) Movie adaptation, r/Fantastic Four #5 & 190, and FF Vol. 3 #60, photo-c 13.00

FANTASTIC FOUR: TRUE STORY
Marvel Comics: Sept, 2008 - No. 4, Jan, 2009 ($2.99, limited series)

1-4-Cornell-s/Domingues-a/Henrichon-c 3.00

FANTASTIC FOUR 2099
Marvel Comics: Jan, 1996 - No. 8, Aug, 1996 ($3.95/$1.95)

1-($3.95)-Chromium-c; X-Nation preview 4.00
2-8: 4-Spider-Man 2099-c/app. 5-Doctor Strange app. 7-Thibert-c 3.00
NOTE: ***Williamson*** *a-1i; c-1i.*

FANTASTIC FOUR UNLIMITED
Marvel Comics: Mar, 1993 - No. 12, Dec, 1995 ($3.95, 68 pgs.)

1-12: 1-Black Panther app. 4-Thing vs. Hulk. 5-Vs. The Frightful Four. 6-Vs. Namor. 7, 9-12-Wraparound-c 4.00

FANTASTIC FOUR UNPLUGGED
Marvel Comics: Sept, 1995 - No. 6, Aug 1996 (99¢, bi-monthly)

1-6 3.00

FANTASTIC FOUR - UNSTABLE MOLECULES
(Indicia for #1 reads STARTLING STORIES: ... ; #2 reads UNSTABLE MOLECULES)
Marvel Comics: Mar, 2003 - No. 4, June, 2003 ($2.99, limited series)

1-4-Guy Davis-c/a 3.00
Fantastic Four Legends Vol. 1 TPB (2003, $13.99) r/#1-4, origin from FF #1 (1963) 14.00
TPB (2005, $13.99) r/#1-4 14.00

FANTASTIC FOUR VS. X-MEN
Marvel Comics: Feb, 1987 - No. 4, June, 1987 (Limited series)

1-4: 4-Austin-a(i) 4.00

FANTASTIC FOUR: WORLD'S GREATEST COMICS MAGAZINE
Marvel Comics: Feb, 2001 - No. 12 (Limited series)

1-12: Homage to Lee & Kirby era of F.F.; s/a by Larsen & various. 5-Hulk-c/app. 10-Thor app. 3.00

FANTASTIC GIANTS (Formerly Konga #1-23)
Charlton Comics: V2#24, Sept, 1966 (25¢, 68 pgs.)

V2#24-Special Ditko issue; origin Konga & Gorgo reprinted plus two new Ditko stories 6 12 18 38 69 100

FANTASTIC TALES
I. W. Enterprises: 1958 (no date) (Reprint, one-shot)

1-Reprints Avon's "City of the Living Dead" 3 6 9 19 30 40

FANTASTIC VOYAGE (See Movie Comics)
Gold Key: Aug, 1969 - No. 2, Dec, 1969

1 (TV) 4 8 12 27 44 60
2-Cover has the text "Civilian Miniaturized Defense Force" in yellow bar at top; back cover has painted art 3 6 9 19 30 40
2-Variant cover has text "In This Issue Sweepstakes..." along top; ad on back-c 4 8 12 23 37 50

FANTASTIC VOYAGES OF SINDBAD, THE
Gold Key: Oct, 1965 - No. 2, June, 1967

1-Painted-c on both 6 12 18 37 66 95
2 5 10 15 30 50 70

FANTASTIC WORLDS
Standard Comics: No. 5, Sept, 1952 - No. 7, Jan, 1953

5-Toth, Anderson-a 37 74 111 222 361 500
6-Toth-c/a 30 60 90 177 289 400
7 22 44 66 132 216 300

FANTASY FEATURES
Americomics: 1987 - No. 2, 1987 ($1.75)

1,2 3.00

FANTASY ILLUSTRATED
New Media Publ.: Spring 1982 ($2.95, B&W magazine)

1-P. Craig Russell-c/a; art by Ditko, Sekowsky, Sutton; Englehart-s 1 2 3 4 5 7

FANTASY MASTERPIECES (Marvel Super Heroes No. 12 on)
Marvel Comics Group: Feb, 1966 - No. 11, Oct, 1967; V2#1, Dec, 1979 - No. 14, Jan, 1981

1-Photo of Stan Lee (12¢-c #1,2) 9 18 27 58 114 170
2-r/1st Fin Fang Foom from Strange Tales #89 5 10 15 35 63 90
3-8: 3-G.A. Capt. America-r begin, end #11; 1st 25¢ Giant; Colan-r. 3-6-Kirby-c(p). 4-Kirby-c(p)(i). 7-Begin G.A. Sub-Mariner, Torch-r/M. Mystery. 8-Torch battles the Sub-Mariner-r/Marvel Mystery #9 5 10 15 35 63 90
9-Origin Human Torch-r/Marvel Comics #1 6 12 18 37 66 95
10,11: 10-r/origin & 1st app. All Winners Squad from All Winners #19. 11-r/origin of Toro (H.T. #1) & Black Knight #1 5 10 15 34 60 85
V2#1(12/79, 75¢, 52 pgs.)-r/origin Silver Surfer from Silver Surfer #1 with editing plus reprints cover; J. Buscema-a 2 4 6 9 12 15
2-14-Reprints Silver Surfer #2-14 w/covers 6.00
NOTE: ***Buscema*** *c-V2#7-9(in part).* ***Ditko*** *r-1-3, 7, 9.* ***Everett*** *r-1,7-9.* ***Matt Fox*** *r-9i.* ***Kirby*** *r-1-11; c(p)-3, 4i, 5, 6.* ***Starlin*** *r-8-13. Some direct sale V2#14's had a 50¢ cover price. #3-11 contain Capt. America-r/Capt. America #3-10. #7-11 contain G.A.Human Torch & Sub-Mariner-r.*

FANTASY QUARTERLY (Also see Elfquest)
Independent Publishers Syndicate: Spring, 1978 (B&W)

1-1st app. Elfquest; Dave Sim-a (6 pgs.) 8 16 24 54 102 150

FANTOMAN (Formerly Amazing Adventure Funnies)
Centaur Publications: No. 2, Aug, 1940 - No. 4, Dec, 1940

2-The Fantom of the Fair, The Arrow, Little Dynamite-r begin; origin The Ermine by Filchock; Burgos, J. Cole, Ernst, Gustavson-a 142 284 426 909 1555 2200
3,4: Gustavson-r. 4-Red Blaze story 116 232 348 742 1271 1800

FANTOMEX MAX
Marvel Comics: Dec, 2013 - No. 4, Mar, 2014 ($3.99)

1-4-Hope-s/Crystal-a/Francavilla-c 4.00

FAREWELL MOONSHADOW (See Moonshadow)
DC Comics (Vertigo): Jan, 1997 ($7.95, one-shot)

nn-DeMatteis-s/Muth-c/a 8.00

FARGO KID (Formerly Justice Traps the Guilty)(See Feature Comics #47)
Prize Publications: V11#3(#1), June-July, 1958 - V11#5, Oct-Nov, 1958

V11#3(#1)-Origin Fargo Kid, Severin-c/a; Williamson-a(2); Heath-a 18 36 54 105 165 225
V11#4,5-Severin-c/a 13 26 39 74 105 135

FARMER'S DAUGHTER, THE

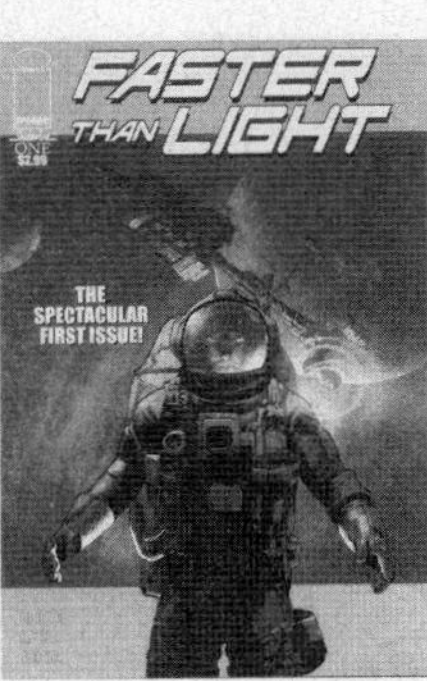

Faster Than Light #1 © Anomaly Prods.

Fatale #21 © Basement Gang

Fathom Blue #3 © Aspen MLT

	GD 2.0	VG 4.0	FN 6.0	VF 8.0	VF/NM 9.0	NM- 9.2

Stanhall Publ./Trojan Magazines: Feb-Mar, 1954 - No. 3, June-July, 1954; No. 4, Oct, 1954

1-Lingerie, nudity panel 84 168 252 538 919 1300
2-4(Stanhall) 55 110 165 352 601 850

FARSCAPE (Based on TV series)
BOOM! Studios: Nov, 2008 - No. 4, Feb, 2009 ($3.99)

1-4-O'Bannon-s/Patterson-a; multiple covers 4.00

FARSCAPE (Based on TV series)
BOOM! Studios: Nov, 2009 - No. 24, Oct, 2011 ($3.99)

1-24-O'Bannon-s/Sliney-a; multiple covers 4.00
...: D'Argo's Lament 1-4 (4/09 - No. 4, 7/09, $3.99) Edwards-a; three covers on each 4.00
...: D'Argo's Quest 1-4 (12/09 - No. 4, 3/10, $3.99) Cleveland-a; three covers on each 4.00
...: D'Argo's Trial 1-4 (8/09 - No. 4, 11/09, $3.99) Cleveland-a; multiple covers on each 4.00
...: Gone and Back 1-4 (7/09 - No. 4, 10/09, $3.99) Patterson-a; multiple covers on each 4.00
...: Scorpius 0-7 (4/10 - No. 7, 2010, $3.99) 0-3-Ruiz-a; multiple-c. 4-7-Purcell-a 4.00
...: Strange Detractors 1-4 (3/09 - No. 4, 6/09, $3.99) Sliney-a; three covers on each 4.00

FARSCAPE: WAR TORN (Based on TV series)
DC Comics (WildStorm): Apr, 2002 - No. 2, May, 2002 ($4.95, limited series)

1,2-Teranishi-a/Wolfman-s; photo-c 5.00

FASHION IN ACTION
Eclipse Comics: Aug, 1986 - Feb, 1987 (Baxter paper)

Summer Special 1 , Winter Special 1, each Snyder III-c/a 3.00

FASTBALL EXPRESS (Major League Baseball)
Ultimate Sports Force: 2000 ($3.95, one-shot)

1-Polybagged with poster; Johnson, Maddux, Park, Nomo, Clemens app. 4.00

FASTER THAN LIGHT
Image Comics (Shadowline): Sept, 2015 - Present ($2.99)

1-10-Brian Haberlin-s/a 3.00

FASTEST GUN ALIVE, THE (Movie)
Dell Publishing Co.: No. 741, Sept, 1956 (one-shot)

Four Color 741-Photo-c 7 14 21 44 82 120

FAST FICTION (...Action) (Stories by Famous Authors Illustrated #6 on)
Seaboard Publ./Famous Authors Ill.: Oct, 1949 - No. 5, Mar, 1950
(All have Kiefer-c)(48 pgs.)

1-Scarlet Pimpernel; Jim Lavery-c/a 28 56 84 135 270 375
2-Captain Blood; H. C. Kiefer-c/a 24 48 72 142 234 325
3-She, by Rider Haggard; Vincent Napoli-a 30 60 90 177 289 400
4-(1/50, 52 pgs.)-The 39 Steps; Lavery-c/a 19 38 57 112 176 240
5-Beau Geste; Kiefer-c/a 19 38 57 112 176 240

NOTE: ***Kiefer** a-2, 5; c-2, 3,5. **Lavery** c/a-1, 4. **Napoli** a-3.*

FAST FORWARD
DC Comics (Piranha Press): 1992 - No. 3, 1993 ($4.95, 68 pgs.)

1-3: 1-Morrison scripts; McKean-c/a. 3-Sam Kieth-a 5.00

FAST WILLIE JACKSON
Fitzgerald Periodicals, Inc.: Oct, 1976 - No. 7, 1977

1 4 8 12 23 37 50
2-7 3 6 9 16 23 30

FAT ALBERT (...& the Cosby Kids) (TV)
Gold Key: Mar, 1974 - No. 29, Feb, 1979

1 4 8 12 25 40 55
2-10 3 6 9 15 22 28
11-29 2 4 6 10 14 18

FATALE (Also see Powers That Be #1 & Shadow State #1,2)
Broadway Comics: Jan, 1996 - No. 6, Aug, 1996 ($2.50)

1-6: J.G. Jones-c/a in all, Preview Edition 1 (11/95, B&W) 3.00

FATALE
Image Comics: Jan, 2012 - No. 24, Jul, 2014 ($3.50)

1-Brubaker-s/Phillips-a/c 5.00
1-Variant-c of Demon with machine gun 8.00
1-Second through Fifth printings 4.00
2-23-Brubaker-s/Phillips-a/c in all 3.50
24-($4.99) Story conclusion; bonus preview of The Fade Out series 5.00

FAT AND SLAT (Ed Wheelan) (Becomes Gunfighter No. 5 on)
E. C. Comics: Summer, 1947 - No. 4, Spring, 1948

1-Intro/origin Voltage, Man of Lightning; "Comics" McCormick, the World's No. 1 Comic Book Fan begins, ends #4 41 82 123 250 418 585
2-4: 4-Comics McCormick-c feature 29 58 87 170 278 385

FAT AND SLAT JOKE BOOK
All-American Comics (William H. Wise): Summer, 1944 (52 pgs., one-shot)

nn-by Ed Wheelan 32 64 96 192 314 435

FATE (See Hand of Fate & Thrill-O-Rama)

FATE
DC Comics: Oct, 1994 - No. 22, Sept, 1996 ($1.95/$2.25)

0,1-22: 8-Begin $2.25-c. 11-14-Alan Scott (Sentinel) app. 10,14-Zatanna app. 21-Phantom Stranger app. 22-Spectre app. 3.00

FATHER'S DAY
Dark Horse Comics: Oct, 2014 - No. 4, Jan, 2015 ($3.99, limited series)

1-4-Mike Richardson-s/Gabriel Guzmán-a 4.00

FATHOM
Comico: May, 1987 - No. 3, July, 1987 ($1.50, limited series)

1-3 3.00

FATHOM
Image Comics (Top Cow Prod.): Aug, 1998 - No. 14, May, 2002 ($2.50)

Preview 12.00
0-Wizard supplement 7.00
0-($6.95) DF Alternate 7.00
1/2 (Wizard) origin of Cannon; Turner-a 6.00
1/2 (3/03, $2.99) origin of Cannon 3.00
1-Turner-s/a; three covers; alternate story pages 6.00
1-Wizard World Ed. 9.00
2-14: 12-14-Witchblade app. 13,14-Tomb Raider app. 3.00
9-Green foil-c edition 15.00
9,12-Holofoil editions 18.00
12,13-DFE alternate-c 6.00
13,14-DFE Gold edition 8.00
14-DFE Blue 15.00
... Collected Edition 1 (3/99, $5.95) r/Preview & all three #1's 6.00
... Collected Edition 2-4 (3-12/99, $5.95) 2-r/#2,3. 3-r/#4,5. 4-r/#6,7 6.00
... Collected Edition 5 (4/00, $5.95) 5-r/#8,9 6.00
... Primer (6/11, $1.00) Comic style summary of Volume 1; text summaries of Vol. 2 & 3 3.00
... Swimsuit Special (5/99, $2.95) Pin-ups by various 3.00
... Swimsuit Special 2000 (12/00, $2.95) Pin-ups by various; Turner-c 3.00
Michael Turner's Fathom HC ('01, $39.95) r/#1-9, black-c w/silver foil 40.00
Michael Turner's Fathom SC ('01, $24.95) r/#1-9, new Turner-c 25.00
Michael Turner's Fathom The Definitive Edition ('08, $49.95) r/Preview, #0,1/2,1-14, Swimsuit Special 1999 & 2000; cover gallery; foreword by Geoff Johns 50.00

FATHOM (MICHAEL TURNER'S...) (Volume 2)
Aspen MLT, Inc.: No. 0, Apr, 2005 - No. 11, Dec, 2006 ($2.50/$2.99)

0-($2.50) Turnbull-a/Turner-c 3.00
1-11-($2.99) 1-Five covers. 2-Two covers. 4-Six covers 3.00
... Beginnings (2005, $1.99) Two covers; Turnbull-a 3.00
...: Killian's Vessel 1 (7/07, $2.99) 3 covers; Odagawa-a 3.00
... Prelude (6/05, $2.99) Seven covers; Garza-a 3.00

FATHOM (MICHAEL TURNER'S...) (Volume 3)
Aspen MLT, Inc.: No. 0, Jun, 2008 - No. 10, Feb, 2010 ($2.50/$2.99)

0-($2.50) Garza-a/c 3.00
1-10-($2.99) Garza-a; multiple covers on each 3.00

FATHOM (MICHAEL TURNER'S...) (Volume 4)
Aspen MLT, Inc.: No. 0, Jun, 2011 - No. 9, May, 2013 ($2.50/$2.99/$3.50)

0-($2.50) Lobdell-s/Konat-a/c; interview with Lobdell; sketch art 3.00
1-3-($2.99) 1-Five covers 3.00
4-9-($3.50) 3.50

FATHOM (MICHAEL TURNER'S...) (Volume 5)
Aspen MLT, Inc.: Jul, 2013 - No. 8, Sept, 2014 ($1.00/$3.99)

1-($1.00) Wohl-s/Konat-a; multiple covers 3.00
2-8-($3.99) Multiple covers on all 4.00
Annual 1 (6/14, $5.99) Turner-c; short stories by Turner, Wohl/Calero, Ruffino & others 6.00

FATHOM (ALL NEW MICHAEL TURNER'S...) (Volume 6)
Aspen MLT, Inc.: Feb, 2017 - Present ($3.99)

1-Northcott-s/Renna-a; multiple covers 4.00

FATHOM BLUE (MICHAEL TURNER'S...)
Aspen MLT, Inc.: Jun, 2015 - No. 6, Dec, 2015 ($3.99, limited series)

1-6-Hernandez-s/Avella-a; multiple covers on all 4.00

Fawcett Movie Comic #19 © FAW

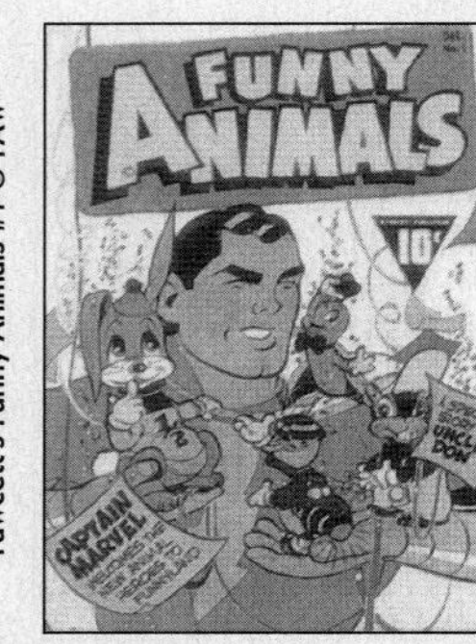

Fawcett's Funny Animals #1 © FAW

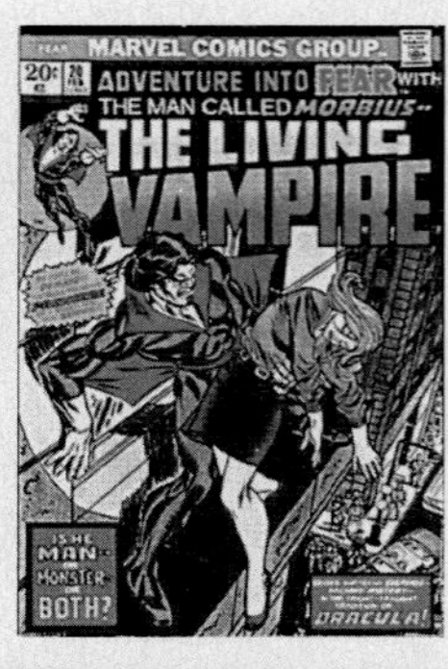

Fear #20 © MAR

	GD 2.0	VG 4.0	FN 6.0	VF 8.0	VF/NM 9.0	NM- 9.2

FATHOM: BLUE DESCENT (MICHAEL TURNER'S...)
Aspen MLT, Inc.: Jun, 2010 - No. 4, Feb, 2012 ($2.50/$2.99, limited series)

0-($2.50) Scott Clark-a; covers by Clark & Benitez 3.00
1-4-($2.99) Alex Sanchez-a. 1-Covers by Clark & Finch 3.00

FATHOM: CANNON HAWKE (MICHAEL TURNER'S...)
Aspen MLT, Inc.: Nov, 2005 - No. 5, Feb, 2006 ($2.99)

1-5-To-a/Turner-c 3.00
... Prelude (11/05, $2.50) Turner-c 3.00

FATHOM: DAWN OF WAR (MICHAEL TURNER'S...)
Aspen MLT, Inc.: Oct, 2004 - No. 3, Dec, 2004 ($2.99, limited series)

0-Caldwell-a 3.00
1-3-Caldwell-a 3.00
...: Cannon Hawke #0 ('04, $2.50) Turner-c 3.00
... The Complete Saga Vol. 1 (2005, $9.99) r/series with cover gallery 10.00

FATHOM: KIANI (MICHAEL TURNER'S...)
Aspen MLT, Inc.: No. 0, Feb, 2007 - No. 4, Dec, 2007 ($2.99, limited series)

0-4-Marcus To-a. 1-Six covers 3.00
Vol. 2 (4/12, $2.50) 0-Four covers 3.00
Vol. 2 (5/12 - No. 4, 11/12, $3.50) 1-4-Hernandez-s/Nome-a; multiple covers on each 3.50
Vol. 3 (3/14 - No. 4, 6/14, $3.99) 1-4-Hernandez-s/Cafaro-a; multiple covers on each 4.00
Vol. 4 (2/15 - No. 4, 5/15, $3.99) 1-4-Hernandez-s/Cafaro-a; multiple covers on each 4.00

FATHOM: KILLIAN'S TIDE
Image Comics (Top Cow Prod.): Apr, 2001 - No. 4, Nov, 2001 ($2.95)

1-4-Caldwell-a(p); two covers by Caldwell and Turner. 2-Flip-book preview of Universe 3.00
1-DFE Blue, 1-Holographic logo 12.00
4-Foil-c 12.00

FATHOM: THE ELITE SAGA (MICHAEL TURNER'S...)
Aspen MLT, Inc.: Jun, 2013 - No. 5, Jul, 2013 ($3.99, weekly limited series)

1-5-Hernandez-s/Marion-a; multiple covers; leads into Fathom Volume 5 4.00

FATIMA...CHALLENGE TO THE WORLD (Also see Our Lady of Fatima)
Catechetical Guild: 1951, 36 pgs. (15¢)

nn (not same as 'Challenge to the World') 6 12 18 29 36 42

FATMAN, THE HUMAN FLYING SAUCER
Lightning Comics(Milson Publ. Co.): April, 1967 - No. 3, Aug-Sept, 1967 (68 pgs.)
(Written by Otto Binder)

1-Origin/1st app. Fatman & Tinman by Beck 5 10 15 35 63 90
2-C. C. Beck-a 4 8 12 25 40 55
3-(Scarce)-Beck-a 6 12 18 37 66 95

FAUNTLEROY COMICS (Super Duck Presents...)
Close-Up/Archie Publications: 1950; No. 2, 1951; No. 3, 1952

1-Super Duck-c/stories by Al Fagaly in all 11 22 33 60 83 105
2,3 7 14 21 35 43 50

FAUST
Northstar Publishing/Rebel Studios #7 on: 1989 - No 13, 1997 ($2.00/$2.25, B&W, mature themes)

1-Decapitation-c; Tim Vigil-c/a in all 3 6 9 14 19 24
1-2nd - 4th printings 4.00
2 2 4 6 8 10 12
2-2nd & 3rd printings, 3,5-2nd printing 4.00
3 1 3 4 6 8 10
4-10: 7-Begin Rebel Studios series 5.00
11-13-Scarce 2 4 6 8 10 12

FAWCETT MOTION PICTURE COMICS (See Motion Picture Comics)

FAWCETT MOVIE COMIC
Fawcett Publications: 1949 - No. 20, Dec, 1952 (All photo-c)

nn- "Dakota Lil"; George Montgomery & Rod Cameron (1949)
20 40 60 114 182 250
nn- "Copper Canyon"; Ray Milland & Hedy Lamarr (1950)
15 30 45 86 133 180
nn- "Destination Moon" (1950) 61 122 183 390 670 950
nn- "Montana"; Errol Flynn & Alexis Smith (1950) 15 30 45 86 133 180
nn- "Pioneer Marshal"; Monte Hale (1950) 15 30 45 86 133 180
nn- "Powder River Rustlers"; Rocky Lane (1950) 20 40 60 114 182 250
nn- "Singing Guns"; Vaughn Monroe, Ella Raines & Walter Brennan (1950)
14 28 42 82 121 160
7- "Gunmen of Abilene"; Rocky Lane; Bob Powell-a (1950)
16 32 48 92 144 195
8- "King of the Bullwhip"; Lash LaRue; Bob Powell-a (1950)
21 42 63 126 206 285
9- "The Old Frontier"; Monte Hale; Bob Powell-a (2/51; mis-dated 2/50)
15 30 45 90 140 190
10- "The Missourians"; Monte Hale (4/51) 15 30 45 90 140 190
11- "The Thundering Trail"; Lash LaRue (6/51) 19 38 57 111 176 240
12- "Rustlers on Horseback"; Rocky Lane (8/51) 15 30 45 90 140 190
13- "Warpath"; Edmond O'Brien & Forrest Tucker (10/51)
14 28 42 80 115 150
14- "Last Outpost"; Ronald Reagan (12/51) 32 64 96 188 307 425
15-(Scarce)- "The Man From Planet X"; Robert Clark; Schaffenberger-a (2/52)
245 490 735 1568 2684 3800
16- "Ten Tall Men"; Burt Lancaster 13 26 39 74 105 135
17- "Rose of Cimarron"; Jack Buetel & Mala Powers 10 20 30 58 79 100
18- "The Brigand"; Anthony Dexter & Anthony Quinn; Schaffenberger-a
10 20 30 58 79 100
19- "Carbine Williams"; James Stewart; Costanza-a; James Stewart photo-c
11 22 33 62 86 110
20- "Ivanhoe"; Robert Taylor & Liz Taylor photo-c 18 36 54 105 165 225

FAWCETT'S FUNNY ANIMALS (No. 1-26, 80-on titled "Funny Animals"; becomes Li'l Tomboy No. 92 on?)
Fawcett Publications/Charlton Comics No. 84 on: 12/42 - #79, 4/53; #80, 6/53 - #83, 12?/53; #84, 4/54 - #91, 2/56

1-Capt. Marvel on cover; intro. Hoppy The Captain Marvel Bunny, cloned from Capt. Marvel; Billy the Kid & Willie the Worm begin 58 116 174 371 636 900
2-Xmas-c 36 72 108 211 343 475
3-5: 3(2/43)-Spirit of '43-c 25 50 75 150 245 340
6,7,9,10 15 30 45 88 137 185
8-Flag-c 16 32 48 92 144 195
11-20: 14-Cover is a 1944 calendar 12 24 36 69 97 125
21-40: 25-Xmas-c. 26-St. Valentine's Day-c 10 20 30 54 72 90
41-86,90,91 9 18 27 47 61 75
87-89(10-54-2/55)-Merry Mailman ish (TV/Radio)-part photo-c
10 20 30 54 72 90

NOTE: *Marvel Bunny in all issues to at least No. 68 (not in 49-54).*

FAZE ONE FAZERS
AC Comics: 1986 - No. 4, Sept, 1986 (Limited series)

1-4 3.00

F.B.I., THE
Dell Publishing Co.: Apr-June, 1965

1-Sinnott-a 3 6 9 17 26 35

F.B.I. STORY, THE (Movie)
Dell Publishing Co.: No. 1069, Jan-Mar, 1960

Four Color 1069-Toth-a; James Stewart photo-c 8 16 24 56 108 160

FBP: FEDERAL BUREAU OF PHYSICS (Titled Collider for issue #1)
DC Comics (Vertigo): Sept, 2013 - No. 24, Nov, 2015 ($2.99/$3.99)

Collider #1- Simon Oliver-s/Robbi Rodriguez-a/Nathan Fox-c 3.00
2-20: 2-(10/13) 3.00
21-24-($3.99) 4.00

FEAR (Adventure into...)
Marvel Comics Group: Nov, 1970 - No. 31, Dec, 1975

1-Fantasy & Sci-Fi-r in early issues; 68 pg. Giant size; Kirby-a(r)
8 16 24 54 102 150
2-6: 2-4-(68 pgs.). 5,6-(52 pgs.) Kirby-a(r) 4 8 12 27 44 60
7-9-Kirby-a(r) 3 6 9 17 26 35
10-Man-Thing begins (10/72, 4th app.), ends #19; see Savage Tales #1 for 1st app.; 1st solo series; Chaykin/Morrow-c/a; 5 10 15 33 57 80
11,12: 11-N. Adams-c. 12-Starlin/Buckler-a 3 6 9 16 23 30
13,14,16-18: 17-Origin/1st app. Wundarr 3 6 9 14 20 26
15-1st full-length Man-Thing story (8/73) 3 6 9 16 24 32
19-Intro. Howard the Duck; Val Mayerik-a (12/73) 9 18 27 59 117 175
20-Morbius, the Living Vampire begins, ends #31; has history recap of Morbius with X-Men & Spider-Man 5 10 15 31 53 75
21-23,25 3 6 9 14 20 26
24-Blade-c/sty 3 6 9 21 33 45
26-31 2 4 6 10 14 18

NOTE: ***Bolle** a-13i. **Brunner** c-15-17. **Buckler** a-11p, 12i. **Chaykin** a-10i. **Colan** a-23r. **Craig** a-10p. **Ditko** a-6-8r. **Evans** a-30. **Everett** a-9, 10i, 21r. **Gulacy** a-20p. **Heath** a-12r. **Heck** a-8r, 13r. **Gil Kane** a-21p; c(p)-20, 21, 23-28, 31. **Kirby** a-1-9r. **Maneely** a-24r. **Mooney** a-11i, 26r. **Morrow** a-11i. **Paul Reinman** a-14r. **Robbins** a(p)-25-27, 31. **Russell** a-23p, 24p. **Severin** c-8. **Starlin** c-12p.*

FEAR AGENT

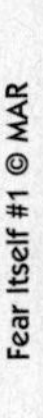
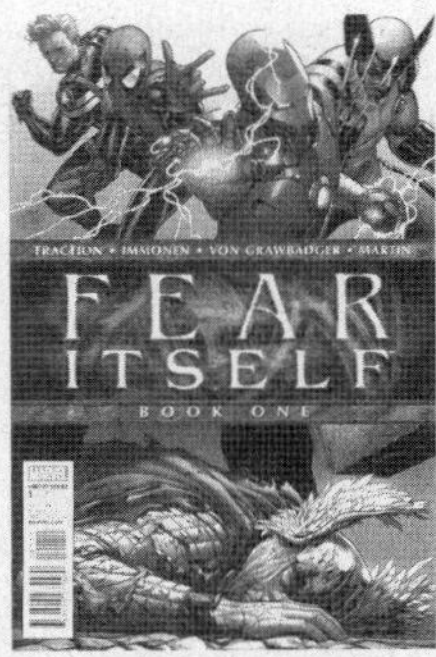

Fear Itself #1 © MAR

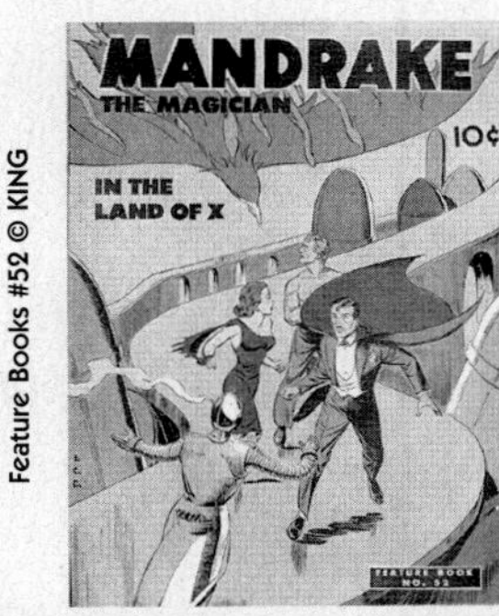

Feature Books #52 © KING

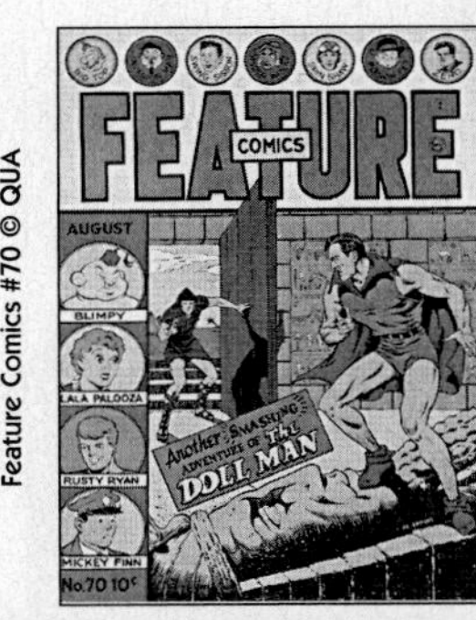

Feature Comics #70 © QUA

GD 2.0 | VG 4.0 | FN 6.0 | VF 8.0 | VF/NM 9.0 | NM- 9.2

Image Comics (#1-11)/Dark Horse Comics.: Oct, 2005 - No. 32, Nov, 2011 ($2.99/$3.50)

1-11: 1-Remender-s/Moore-a. 5-Opeña-a begins. 11-Francavilla-a 3.00
... The Last Goodbye 1-4 (Dark Horse, 6/07 - No. 4, 9/07) (#12-15) 3.00
Tales of the Fear Agent: Twelve Steps in One (#16), 17-27 3.00
28-32-($3.50) Hawthorne & Moore-a/Moore-c 3.50
... Vol 1.: Re-Ignition TPB (2006, $9.99) r/#1-4 10.00
... Vol 2.: My War TPB (Dark Horse Books, 2007, $14.95) r/#5-10; Opeña sketch pages 15.00

FEARBOOK
Eclipse Comics: April, 1986 ($1.75, one-shot, mature)

1-Scholastic Mag-r; Bissette-a 4.00

FEAR EFFECT (Based on the video game)
Image Comics (Top Cow): May, 2000; March, 2001 ($2.95)

Retro Helix 1 (3/01), Special 1 (5/00) 3.00

FEAR IN THE NIGHT (See Complete Mystery No. 3)

FEAR ITSELF
Marvel Comics: Jun, 2011 - No. 7, Dec, 2011 ($3.99/$4.99, limited series)

1-6-Fraction-s/Immonen-a/McNiven-c. 3-Bucky apparently killed 4.00
1-Blank cover 4.00
7-($4.99) Thor perishes; previews of ...: The Fearless, Incredible Hulk #1, Defenders #1 5.00
7.1 Captain America (1/12, $3.99) Brubaker-s/Guice-a; Bucky's fate 4.00
7.2 Thor (1/12, $3.99) Fraction-s/Adam Kubert-a/c; Thor's funeral; Tanarus returns 4.00
7.3 Iron Man (1/12, $3.99) Fraction-s/Larroca-a/c; Odin app. 4.00
...: Black Widow (8/11, $3.99) Peter Nguyen-a; Peregrine app. 4.00
...: Book of the Skull (5/11, $3.99) prequel to series; WWII flashback, Red Skull app. 4.00
...: Fellowship of Fear (10/11, $3.99) profiles of hammer-wielders and fear thrivers 4.00
...: FF (9/11, $2.99) Reed & Sue vs. Ben Grimm; Grummett-a/Dell'Otto-c 3.00
...: Sin's Past (6/11, $4.99) r/Captain America #355-357; Sisters of Sin app. 5.00
... Spotlight (6/11, $3.99) Interviews with Fraction and Immonen; feature articles 4.00
...: The Monkey King (11/11, $2.99) Joshua Fialkov-s/Juan Doe-a 3.00
...: The Worthy (9/11, $3.99) Origins of the hammer wielders; s/a by various 4.00

FEAR ITSELF: DEADPOOL
Marvel Comics: Aug, 2011 - No. 3, Oct, 2011 ($2.99, limited series)

1-3-Hastings-s/Dazo-a 3.00

FEAR ITSELF: FEARSOME FOUR
Marvel Comics: Aug, 2011 - No. 4, Nov, 2011 ($2.99, limited series)

1-4-Art by Bisley and others; Man-Thing, She-Hulk & Howard the Duck app. 3.00

FEAR ITSELF: HULK VS. DRACULA
Marvel Comics: Nov, 2011 - No. 3, Dec, 2011 ($2.99, limited series)

1-3-Gischler-s/Stegman-a; Dell'Otto-c 3.00

FEAR ITSELF: SPIDER-MAN
Marvel Comics: Jul, 2011 - No. 3, Sept, 2011 ($2.99, limited series)

1-3-Yost-s/McKone-a; Vermin app. 3.00

FEAR ITSELF: THE DEEP
Marvel Comics: Aug, 2011 - No. 4, Nov, 2011 ($2.99, limited series)

1-4-Bunn-s/Garbett-a; Sub-Mariner vs. Attuma; Doctor Strange & Silver Surfer app. 3.00

FEAR ITSELF: THE FEARLESS (Follows Fear Itself #7)
Marvel Comics: Dec, 2011 - No. 12, Jun, 2012 ($2.99, limited series)

1-12: 1-Fate of the Hammers; Bagley & Pelletier-a; Art Adams-c. 7-Wolverine app. 3.00

FEAR ITSELF: THE HOME FRONT
Marvel Comics: Jun, 2011 - No. 7, Dec, 2011 ($3.99, limited series)

1-7-Short story anthology; Speedball w/Mayhew-a in all; Chaykin-a; Djurdjevic-c 4.00

FEAR ITSELF: UNCANNY X-FORCE
Marvel Comics: Sept, 2011 - No. 3, Nov, 2011 ($2.99, limited series)

1-3-Bianchi-a/c 3.00

FEAR ITSELF: WOLVERINE
Marvel Comics: Sept, 2011 - No. 3, Nov, 2011 ($2.99, limited series)

1-3-Boschi-a; Wolverine vs. S.T.R.I.K.E. 1-Acuña-c. 2,3-Molina-c 3.00

FEAR ITSELF: YOUTH IN REVOLT
Marvel Comics: Jul, 2011 - No. 6, Dec, 2011 ($2.99, limited series)

1-6-Firestar and The Initiative app.; McKeever-s/Norton-a 3.00

FEARLESS DEFENDERS (Marvel NOW!)
Marvel Comics: Apr, 2013 - No. 12, Feb, 2014 ($2.99/3.99)

1-4,5-7: 1-Valkyrie & Misty Knight team-up; Bunn-s/Sliney-a. 2-Dani Moonstar app. 3.00
4AU-(7/13, $3.99) Age of Ultron tie-in; Dr. Doom & Ares app. 4.00

8-12-($3.99) 4.00

FEARLESS FAGAN
Dell Publishing Co.: No. 441, Dec, 1952 (one-shot)

Four Color 441 5 10 15 31 53 75

FEATHERS
Archaia (BOOM! Studios): Jan, 2015 - No. 6, Jun, 2015 ($3.99, limited series)

1-6-Jorge Corona-s/a 4.00

FEATURE BOOK (Dell) (See Large Feature Comic)

FEATURE BOOKS (Newspaper-r, early issues)
David McKay Publications: May, 1937 - No. 57, 1948 (B&W)
(Full color, 68 pgs. begin #26 on)

Note: See individual alphabetical listings for prices

nn-Popeye & the Jeep (#1, 100 pgs.); reprinted as Feature Books #3(Very Rare; only 3 known copies, 1-VF, 2-in low grade)
nn-Dick Tracy (#1)-Reprinted as Feature Book #4 (100 pgs.) & in part as 4-Color #1 (Rare, less than 10 known copies)
NOTE: *Above books were advertised together with different covers from Feat. Books #3 & 4.*
1-King of the Royal Mtd. (#1)
2-Popeye (6/37) by Segar
3-Popeye (7/37) by Segar; same as nn issue but a new cover added
4-Dick Tracy (8/37)-Same as nn issue but a new cover added
5-Popeye (9/37) by Segar
6-Dick Tracy (10/37)
7-Little Orphan Annie (#1, 11/37) (Rare)-Reprints strips from 12/31/34 to 7/17/35
8-Secret Agent X-9 (12/37) -Not by Raymond
9-Dick Tracy (1/38)
10-Popeye (2/38)
11-Little Annie Rooney (#1, 3/38)
12-Blondie (#1) (4/38) (Rare)
13-Inspector Wade (5/38)
14-Popeye (6/38) by Segar
15-Barney Baxter (#1) (7/38)
16-Red Eagle (8/38)
17-Gangbusters (#1, 9/38) (1st app.)
18,19-Mandrake
20-Phantom (#1, 12/38)
21-Lone Ranger
22-Phantom
23-Mandrake
24-Lone Ranger (1941)
25-Flash Gordon (#1)-Reprints not by Raymond
26-Prince Valiant (1941)-Hal Foster-c/a; newspaper strips reprinted, pgs. 1-28,30-63; color & 68 pg. issues begin; Foster cover is only original comic book artwork by him
27-29,31,34-Blondie
30-Katzenjammer Kids (#1, 1942)
32,35,41,44-Katzenjammer Kids
33(nn)-Romance of Flying; World War II photos
36('43),38,40('44),42,43, 45,47-Blondie
37-Katzenjammer Kids; has photo & biog. of Harold H. Knerr (1883-1949) who took over strip from Rudolph Dirks in 1914
39-Phantom
46-Mandrake in the Fire World-(58 pgs.)
48-Maltese Falcon by Dashiell Hammett('46)
49,50-Perry Mason; based on Gardner novels
51,54-Rip Kirby; Raymond-c/s; origin-#51
52,55-Mandrake
53,56,57-Phantom

NOTE: *All Feature Books through #25 are over-sized 8-1/2x11-3/8" comics with color covers and black and white interiors. The covers are rough, heavy stock. The page counts, including covers, are as follows: nn, #3, 4-100 pgs.; #1, 2-52 pgs.; #5-25 are all 76 pgs. #33 was found in bound set from publisher. Reprints from 1980s exist.*

FEATURE COMICS (Formerly Feature Funnies)
Quality Comics Group: No. 21, June, 1939 - No. 144, May, 1950

21-The Clock, Jane Arden & Mickey Finn continue from Feature Funnies 60 120 180 381 653 925
22-26: 23-Charlie Chan begins (8/39, 1st app.) 43 86 129 271 461 650
26-(nn, nd)-Cover in one color, (10¢, 36 pgs.; issue No. blanked out. Two variations exist, each contain half of the regular #26) 43 86 129 271 461 650
27-(12/39, Rare)-Origin/1st app. Doll Man by Eisner (scripts) & Lou Fine (art); Doll Man begins, ends #139 649 1298 1947 4738 8369 12,000
28-(1/40, Rare)-2nd app. Doll Man by Lou Fine 232 464 696 1485 2543 3600
29-Clock-c 119 238 357 762 1306 1850
30-1st Doll Man-c 210 420 630 1334 2292 3250
31-Last Clock & Charlie Chan issue (4/40); Charlie Chan moves to Big Shot #1 following month (5/40) 79 158 237 502 864 1225
32,34,36: Dollman covers. 32-Rusty Ryan & Samar begin. 34-Captain Fortune app. 79 158 237 502 864 1225
33,35,37: 37-Last Fine Doll Man 50 100 150 315 533 750
NOTE: *A 15¢ Canadian version of Feature Comics #37, made in the US, exists.*
38,40-Dollman covers. 38-Origin the Ace of Space. 40-Bruce Blackburn in costume 57 114 171 362 619 875
39,41: 39-Origin The Destroying Demon, ends #40; X-Mas-c. 40 80 120 242 401 560
42,46,48,50-Dollman covers. 42-USA, the Spirit of Old Glory begins. 46-Intro. Boyville

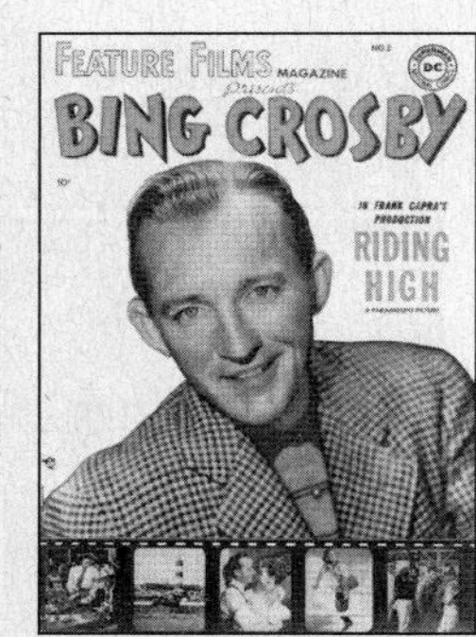

Feature Films #2 © DC

Felicia Hardy: The Black Cat #2 © MAR

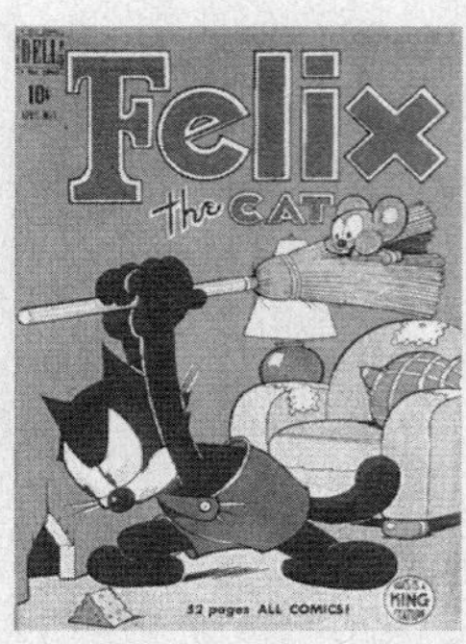

Felix the Cat #14 © KING

	GD 2.0	VG 4.0	FN 6.0	VF 8.0	VF/NM 9.0	NM- 9.2
Brigadiers in Rusty Ryan. 48-USA ends	43	86	129	271	461	650
43,45,47,49: 47-Fargo Kid begins	30	60	90	177	289	400
44-Doll Man by Crandall begins, ends #63; Crandall-a(2)	55	110	165	352	601	850
51,53,55,57,59: 57-Spider Widow begins	22	44	66	128	209	290
52,54,56,58,60-Dollman covers. 56-Marijuana story in Swing Sisson strip. 60-Raven begins, ends #71	32	64	96	188	307	425
61,63,65,67	20	40	60	114	182	250
62,64,66,68-Dollman covers. 68-(5/43)	28	56	84	165	270	375
69,71-Phantom Lady x-over in Spider Widow	22	44	66	128	209	290
70-Dollman-c; Phantom Lady x-over	30	60	90	177	289	400
72,74,77-80,100-Dollman covers. 72-Spider Widow ends	23	46	69	136	223	310
73,75,76	17	34	51	98	154	210
81-99-All Dollman covers	19	38	57	111	176	240
101-144: 139-Last Doll Man & last Doll Man cover. 140-Intro. Stuntman Stetson (Stuntman Stetson c-140-144)	16	32	48	94	147	200

NOTE: ***Celardo*** *a-37-43.* ***Crandall*** *a-44-60, 62, 63-on(most).* ***Gustavson*** *a-(Rusty Ryan)- 32-134.* ***Powell*** *a-34, 64-73. The Clock c-25, 28, 29. Doll Man c-30, 32, 34, 36, 38, 40, 42, 44, 46, 48, 50, 52, 54, 56, 58, 60, 62, 64, 66, 68, 70, 72, 74, 77-139. Joe Palooka c-21, 24, 27.*

FEATURE FILMS
National Periodical Publ.: Mar-Apr, 1950 - No. 4, Sept-Oct, 1950 (All photo-c)

	GD 2.0	VG 4.0	FN 6.0	VF 8.0	VF/NM 9.0	NM- 9.2
1- "Captain China" with John Payne, Gail Russell, Lon Chaney & Edgar Bergen	66	132	198	416	701	985
2- "Riding High" with Bing Crosby	69	138	207	435	735	1035
3- "The Eagle & the Hawk" with John Payne, Rhonda Fleming & D. O'Keefe	66	132	198	416	701	985
4- "Fancy Pants"; Bob Hope & Lucille Ball	72	144	216	454	770	1085

FEATURE FUNNIES (Feature Comics No. 21 on)(Earliest Quality Comics title)
Comic Favorites Inc./Quality Comics Group: Oct, 1937 - No. 20, May, 1939

	GD 2.0	VG 4.0	FN 6.0	VF 8.0	VF/NM 9.0	NM- 9.2
1(V9#1-indicia)-Joe Palooka, Mickey Finn (1st app.), The Bungles, Jane Arden, Dixie Dugan (1st app.), Big Top, Ned Brant, Strange As It Seems, & Off the Record strip reprints begin	280	560	840	1540	2520	3500
2-The Hawk app. (11/37); Goldberg-c	110	220	330	704	1202	1700
3-Hawks of Seas begins by Eisner, ends #12; The Clock begins; Christmas-c	87	174	261	553	952	1350
4,5	63	126	189	403	689	975
6-12: 11-Archie O'Toole by Bud Thomas begins, ends #22	50	100	150	315	533	750
13-Espionage, Starring Black X begins by Eisner, ends #20	53	106	159	334	567	800
14-20	40	80	120	246	411	575

NOTE: *Joe Palooka covers 1, 6, 9, 12, 15, 18.*

FEATURE PRESENTATION, A (Feature Presentations Magazine #6)
(Formerly Women in Love) (Also see Startling Terror Tales #11)
Fox Features Syndicate: No. 5, April, 1950

	GD 2.0	VG 4.0	FN 6.0	VF 8.0	VF/NM 9.0	NM- 9.2
5(#1)-Black Tarantula (scarce)	61	122	183	390	670	950

FEATURE PRESENTATIONS MAGAZINE (Formerly A Feature Presentation #5; becomes Feature Stories Magazine #3 on)
Fox Features Syndicate: No. 6, July, 1950

	GD 2.0	VG 4.0	FN 6.0	VF 8.0	VF/NM 9.0	NM- 9.2
6(#2)-Moby Dick; Wood-c	34	68	102	199	325	450

FEATURE STORIES MAGAZINE (Formerly Feature Presentations Mag. #6)
Fox Features Syndicate: No. 3, Aug, 1950

	GD 2.0	VG 4.0	FN 6.0	VF 8.0	VF/NM 9.0	NM- 9.2
3-Jungle Lil, Zegra stories; bondage-c	41	82	123	256	428	600

FEDERAL MEN COMICS
DC Comics: 1936

nn-Ashcan comic, not distributed to newsstands, only for in house use (no known sales)

FEDERAL MEN COMICS (See Adventure Comics #32, The Comics Magazine, New Adventure Comics, New Book of Comics, New Comics & Star Spangled Comics #91)
Gerard Publ. Co.: No. 2, 1945 (DC reprints from 1930's)

	GD 2.0	VG 4.0	FN 6.0	VF 8.0	VF/NM 9.0	NM- 9.2
2-Siegel/Shuster-a; cover redrawn from Det. #9	37	74	111	222	361	500

FELICIA HARDY: THE BLACK CAT
Marvel Comics: July, 1994 - No. 4, Oct, 1994 ($1.50, limited series)

	GD 2.0	VG 4.0	FN 6.0	VF 8.0	VF/NM 9.0	NM- 9.2
1-4: 1,4-Spider-Man app.						4.00

FELIX'S NEPHEWS INKY & DINKY
Harvey Publications: Sept, 1957 - No. 7, Oct, 1958

	GD 2.0	VG 4.0	FN 6.0	VF 8.0	VF/NM 9.0	NM- 9.2
1-Cover shows Inky's left eye with 2 pupils	11	22	33	60	83	105
2-7	7	14	21	37	46	55

NOTE: ***Messmer*** *art in 1-6.* ***Oriolo*** *a-1-7.*

FELIX THE CAT (See Cat Tales 3-D, The Funnies, March of Comics #24,36,51, New Funnies & Popular Comics)
Dell Publ. No. 1-19/Toby No. 20-61/Harvey No. 62-118/Dell No. 1-12:
1943 - No. 118, Nov, 1961; Sept-Nov, 1962 - No. 12, July-Sept, 1965

	GD 2.0	VG 4.0	FN 6.0	VF 8.0	VF/NM 9.0	NM- 9.2
Four Color 15	75	150	225	600	1350	2100
Four Color 46('44)	38	76	114	285	641	1000
Four Color 77('45)	36	72	108	259	580	900
Four Color 119('46)-All new stories begin	31	62	93	223	499	775
Four Color 135('46)	21	42	63	147	324	500
Four Color 162(9/47)	16	32	48	110	243	375
1(2-3/48)(Dell)	25	50	75	175	388	600
2	12	24	36	81	176	270
3-5	9	18	27	62	126	190
6-19(2-3/51-Dell)	8	16	24	51	96	140
20-30,32,33,36,38-61(6/55)-All Messmer issues.(Toby): 28-(2/52)-Some copies have #29 on cover, #28 on inside (Rare in high grade)	14	28	42	96	211	325
31,34,35-No Messmer-a; Messmer-c only 31,34	8	16	24	51	96	140
37-(100 pgs., 25 ¢, 1/15/53, X-Mas-c, Toby; daily & Sunday-r (rare)	34	68	102	245	548	850
62(8/55)-80,100 (Harvey)	4	8	12	27	44	60
81-99	4	8	12	23	37	50
101-118(11/61): 101-117-Reprints. 118-All new-a	3	6	9	17	26	35
12-269-211(#1, 9-11/62)(Dell)-No Messmer	4	8	12	28	47	65
2-12(7-9/65)(Dell, TV)-No Messmer	4	8	12	23	37	50
3-D Comic Book 1(1953-One Shot, 25¢)-w/glasses	34	68	102	199	325	450
Summer Annual nn ('53, 25¢, 100 pgs., Toby)-Daily & Sunday-r	45	90	135	284	480	675
Winter Annual 2 ('54, 25¢, 100 pgs., Toby)-Daily & Sunday-r	42	84	126	265	445	625

(Special note: Despite the covers on Toby 37 and the Summer Annual above proclaiming "all new stories," they were actually reformatted newspaper strips)

NOTE: ***Otto Messmer*** *went to work for Universal Film as an animator in 1915 and then worked for the Pat Sullivan animation studio in 1916. He created a black cat in the cartoon short, Feline Follies in 1919 that became known as Felix in the early 1920s. The Felix Sunday strip began Aug. 14, 1923 and continued until Sept. 19, 1943 whjen* ***Messmer*** *took the character to Dell (Western Publishing) and began doing Felix comic books, first adapting strips to the comic format. The first all new Felix comic was Four Color #119 in 1946 (#4 in the Dell run). The daily Felix was begun on May 9, 1927 by another artist, but by the following year,* ***Messmer*** *did it too. King Features took the daily away from* ***Messmer*** *in 1954 and he began to do some of his most dynamic art for Toby Press. The daily was continued by* ***Joe Oriolo*** *who drew it until it was discontinued Jan. 9, 1967.* ***Oriolo*** *was* ***Messmer's*** *assistant for many years and inked some of* ***Messmer's*** *pencils through the Toby run, as well as doing some of the stories by himself. Though* ***Messmer*** *continued to work for Harvey, his contirubitons were limited, and no all* ***Messmer*** *stories appeared after the Toby run until some early Toby reprints were published in the 1990s Harvey revival of the title. 4-Color No. 15, 46, 77 and the Toby Annuals are all daily or Sunday newspaper reprints from the 1930's-1940's drawn by* ***Otto Messmer****. #101-r/#64; 102-r/#65; 103-r/#67; 104-117-r/#68-81.* ***Messmer****-a in all Dell/Toby/Harvey issues except #31, 34, 35, 97, 98, 100, 118.* ***Oriolo*** *a-20, 31-on.*

FELIX THE CAT (Also see The Nine Lives of...)
Harvey Comics/Gladstone: Sept, 1991 - No. 7, Jan, 1993 ($1.25/$1.50, bi-monthly)

	GD 2.0	VG 4.0	FN 6.0	VF 8.0	VF/NM 9.0	NM- 9.2
1: 1950s-r/Toby issues by Messmer begins. 1-Inky and Dinky back-up story (produced by Gladstone)						4.00
2-7, Big Book, V2#1 (9/92, $1.95, 52 pgs.)						4.00

FELIX THE CAT AND FRIENDS
Felix Comics: 1992 - No. 5, 1993 ($1.95)

	GD 2.0	VG 4.0	FN 6.0	VF 8.0	VF/NM 9.0	NM- 9.2
1-5: 1-Contains Felix trading cards						3.00

FELIX THE CAT & HIS FRIENDS (Pat Sullivan's...)
Toby Press: Dec, 1953 - No. 3, 1954 (Indicia title for #2&3 as listed)

	GD 2.0	VG 4.0	FN 6.0	VF 8.0	VF/NM 9.0	NM- 9.2
1 (Indicia title, "Felix and His Friends," #1 only)	30	60	90	177	289	400
2-3	18	36	54	107	169	230

FELIX THE CAT DIGEST MAGAZINE
Harvey Comics: July, 1992 ($1.75, digest-size, 98 pgs.)

	GD 2.0	VG 4.0	FN 6.0	VF 8.0	VF/NM 9.0	NM- 9.2
1-Felix, Richie Rich stories						6.00

FELIX THE CAT KEEPS ON WALKIN'
Hamilton Comics: 1991 ($15.95, 8-1/2"x11", 132 pgs.)

	GD 2.0	VG 4.0	FN 6.0	VF 8.0	VF/NM 9.0	NM- 9.2
nn-Reprints 15 Toby Press Felix the Cat and Felix and His Friends stories in new color						16.00

FELL
Image Comics: Sept, 2005 - No. 9, Jan, 2008 ($1.99)

	GD 2.0	VG 4.0	FN 6.0	VF 8.0	VF/NM 9.0	NM- 9.2
1-9-Warren Ellis-s/Ben Templesmith-a						3.00
..., Vol. 1: Feral City TPB (2007, $14.99) r/#1-8						15.00

FELON
Image Comics (Minotaur Press): Nov, 2001 - No. 4, Apr, 2002 ($2.95, B&W)

	GD 2.0	VG 4.0	FN 6.0	VF 8.0	VF/NM 9.0	NM- 9.2
1-4-Rucka-s/Clark-a/c						3.00

FEM FANTASTIQUE
AC Comics: Aug, 1988 ($1.95, B&W)

The Ferret #9 © MAL

FF (2013 series) #1 © MAR

Fight Against Crime #15 © Story

GD 2.0 | VG 4.0 | FN 6.0 | VF 8.0 | VF/NM 9.0 | NM- 9.2

V2#1-By Bill Black; Bettie Page pin-up 4.00

FEMFORCE (Also see Untold Origin of the Femforce)
Americomics: Apr, 1985 - No. 109 (1.75-/2.95, B&W #16-56)

1-Black-a in most; Nightveil, Ms. Victory begin 1 3 4 6 8 10
2-10 4.00
11-43: 25-Origin/1st app. new Ms. Victory. 28-Colt leaves. 29,30-Camilla-r by Mayo from Jungle Comics. 36-(2.95, 52 pgs.) 4.00
44,64: 44-W/mini-comic, Catman & Kitten #0. 64-Re-intro Black Phantom 5.00
45-49,51-63,65-99: 51-Photo-c from movie. 57-Begin color issues. 95-Photo-c 3.00
50 ($2.95, 52 pgs.)-Contains flexi-disc; origin retold; most AC characters app. 4.00
100-($3.95) 5.00
100-($6.90)-Polybagged 1 2 3 5 6 8
101-109-($4.95) 5.00
Special 1 (Fall, '84)(B&W, 52pgs.)-1st app. Ms. Victory, She-Cat, Blue Bulleteer, Rio Rita & Lady Luger 4.00
Bad Girl Backlash-(12/95, $5.00) 5.00
Frightbook 1 ('92, $2.95, B&W)-Halloween special, In the House of Horror 1 ('89, 2.50, B&W), Night of the Demon 1 ('90, 2.75, B&W), Out of the Asylum Special 1 ('87, B&W, $1.95), Pin-Up Portfolio 4.00
Pin-Up Portfolio (5 issues) 4.00

FEMFORCE UP CLOSE
AC Comics: Apr, 1992 - No. 11, 1995 ($2.75, quarterly)

1-11: 1-Stars Nightveil; inside f/c photo from Femforce movie. 2-Stars Stardust. 3-Stars Dragonfly. 4-Stars She-Cat 4.00

FERDINAND THE BULL (See Mickey Mouse Magazine V4#3)(Walt Disney's)
Dell Publishing Co.: 1938 (10¢, large size (9-1/2" x 10"), some color w/rest B&W)

nn 21 42 63 124 202 280

FERRET
Malibu Comics: Sept, 1992; May, 1993 - No. 10, Feb, 1994 ($1.95)

1-(1992, one-shot) 3.00
1-10: 1-Die-cut-c. 2-4-Collector's Ed. w/poster. 5-Polybagged w/Skycap 3.00
2-4-($1.95)-Newsstand Edition w/different-c 3.00

FERRYMAN
DC Comics (WildStorm): Early Dec, 2008 - No. 5, Mar, 2009 ($3.50)

1-5-Andreyko-s/Wayshak-a 3.50

FEVER RIDGE: A TALE OF MACARTHUR'S JUNGLE WAR
IDW Publishing: Feb, 2013 - No. 4, Oct, 2013 ($3.99)

1-4-Heimos-s/Runge-a/DeStefano-I; 1940s War stories on New Guinea 4.00

FF (Fantastic Four after Human Torch's death)
Marvel Comics: May, 2011 - No. 23, Dec, 2012 ($3.99)

1-Hickman-s/Epting-a; Spider-Man joins 4.00
1-Blank variant cover 4.00
1-Variant-c by Daniel Acuña 8.00
1-Variant-c by Stan Goldberg 6.00
2-23-($2.99) 2-Dr. Doom joins. 4,5-Kitson-a. 5-7-Black Bolt returns. 10,11-Avengers app. 3.00
...: Fifty Fantastic Years 1 (11/11, $4.99) Handbook format profiles of heroes and foes 5.00

FF (Marvel NOW!)
Marvel Comics: Jan, 2013 - No. 16, Mar, 2014 ($2.99)

1-15: 1-Fraction-s/Allred-a; new team forms (Ant-Man, She-Hulk, Medusa, Ms. Thing) 6,9-Quinones-a. 7,8,12-15-Dr. Doom app. 11-Impossible Man app. 3.00
16-($3.99) Ant-Man vs. Doom; back-up w/Quinones-a; Uatu & Silver Surfer app. 4.00

F5
Image Comics/Dark Horse: Jan, 2000 - No. 4, Oct, 2000 ($2.50/$2.95)

Preview (1/00, $2.50) Character bios and b&w pages; Daniel-s/a 3.00
1-($2.95, 48 pages) Tony Daniel-s/a 4.00
1-($20.00) Variant bikini-c 20.00
2-4-($2.50) 3.00
F5 Origin (Dark Horse Comics, 11/01, $2.99) w/cover gallery & sketches 3.00

FIBBER McGEE & MOLLY (Radio)(Also see A-1 Comics)
Magazine Enterprises: No. 25, 1949 (one-shot)

A-1 25 13 26 39 74 105 135

FICTION ILLUSTRATED
Byron Preiss Visual Publ./Pyramid: No. 1, Jan, 1975 - No. 4, Jan, 1977 ($1.00, #1,2 are digest size, 132 pgs.; #3,4 are graphic novels for mail order and specialty bookstores only)

1,2: 1-Schlomo Raven; Sutton-a. 2-Starfawn; Stephen Fabian-a. 2 4 6 13 18 22
3-($1.00-c, 4 3/4 x 6 1/2" digest size) Chandler; new Steranko-a 3 6 9 14 20 26
3-($4.95-c, 8 1/2 x 11" graphic novel; low print) same contents and indicia, but "Chandler" is the cover feature title 5 10 15 31 53 75
4-($4.95-c, 8 1/2 x 11" graphic novel; low print) Son of Sherlock Holmes; Reese-a 4 8 12 27 44 60

FICTION SQUAD
BOOM! Studios: Oct, 2014 - No. 6, Mar, 2015 ($3.99, limited series)

1-6-Jenkins-s/Bachs-a 4.00

FIELD, THE
Image Comics: Apr, 2014 - No. 4, Sept, 2014 ($3.50, limited series)

1-4-Brisson-s/Roy-a 3.50

FIERCE
Dark Horse Comics (Rocket Comics): July, 2004 - No. 4, Dec, 2004 ($2.99, limited series)

1-4-Jeremy Love-s/Robert Love-a 3.00

15-LOVE
Marvel Comics: Aug, 2011 - No. 3, Oct, 2011 ($4.99, limited series)

1-3-Tennis academy story; Andi Watson-s/Tommy Ohtsuka-a/c; Sho Murase-c 5.00

50 GIRLS 50
Image Comics: Jun, 2011 - No. 4, Sept, 2011 ($2.99, limited series)

1-4-Frank Cho-c; Cho & Murray-s/Medellin-a 3.00

52 (Leads into Countdown series)
DC Comics: Week One, July, 2006 - Week Fifty-Two, Jul, 2007 ($2.50, weekly series)

1-Chronicles the year after Infinite Crisis; Johns, Morrison, Rucka & Waid-s; JG Jones-c 4.00
2-10: 2-History of the DC Universe back-up thru #11. 6-1st app. The Great Ten. 7-Intro. Kate Kane. 10-Supernova 3.00
11-Batwoman debut (single panel cameo in #9) 4.00
12-52: 12-Isis gains powers; back-up 2 pg. origins begin. 15-Booster Gold killed. 17-Lobo returns. 30-Batman-c/Robin & Nightwing app. 37-Booster Gold returns. 38-The Question dies. 42-Ralph Dibny dies. 44-Isis dies. 48-Renee becomes The Question. 50-World War III. 51-Mister Mind evolves. 52-The Multiverse is re-formed; wraparound-c 3.00
...: The Companion TPB (2007, $19.99) r/solo stories of series' prominent characters 20.00
...: Volume One TPB (2007, $19.99) r/#1-13; sample of page development; cover gallery 20.00
...: Volume Two TPB (2007, $19.99) r/#14-26; creator notes and sketches; cover gallery 20.00
...: Volume Three TPB (2007, $19.99) r/#27-39; notes and sketches; cover gallery 20.00
...: Volume Four TPB (2007, $19.99) r/#40-52; creator commentary; cover gallery 20.00

52 AFTERMATH: THE FOUR HORSEMEN (Takes place during 52 Week Fifty)
DC Comics: Oct, 2007 - No. 6, Mar, 2008 ($2.99, limited series)

1-6-Giffen-s/Olliffe-a; Superman, Batman & Wonder Woman app. 2-4,6-Van Sciver-c 3.00
TPB (2008, $19.99) r/#1-6 20.00

52/WWIII (Takes place during 52 Week Fifty)
DC Comics: Part One, Jun, 2007 - Part Four, Jun, 2007 ($2.50, 4 issues came out same day)

Part One - Part Four: Van Sciver-c; heroes vs. Black Adam. 3-Terra dies 3.00
DC: World War III TPB (2007, $17.99) r/Part One - Four and 52 Week 50 18.00

55 DAYS AT PEKING (See Movie Comics)

FIGHT AGAINST CRIME (Fight Against the Guilty #22, 23)
Story Comics: May, 1951 - No. 21, Sept, 1954

1-True crime stories #1-4 53 106 159 334 567 800
2 32 64 96 188 307 425
3,5: 5-Frazetta-a, 1 pg.; content chan.ge to horror & suspense 32 64 96 188 307 425
4-Drug story "Hopped Up Killers" 34 68 102 199 325 450
6,7: 6-Used in **POP**, pgs. 83,84 30 60 90 177 289 400
8-Last crime format issue 28 56 84 165 270 375

NOTE: *No. 9-21 contain violent, gruesome stories with blood, dismemberment, decapitation, E.C. style plot twists and several E.C. swipes. Bondage c-4, 6, 18, 19.*

9-11,13 54 108 162 343 574 825
12-Morphine drug story "The Big Dope" 58 116 174 371 636 900
14-Tothish art by Ross Andru; electrocution-c 63 126 189 403 689 975
15-B&W & color illos in **POP** 55 110 165 352 601 850
16-E.C. story swipe/Haunt of Fear #19; Tothish-a by Ross Andru; bondage-c 58 116 174 371 636 900
17-Wildey E.C. story swipe/Shock SuspenStories #9; knife through neck-c (1/54) 74 148 222 470 810 1150
18,19: 19-Bondage/torture-c 54 108 162 343 574 825
20-Decapitation cover; contains hanging, ax murder, blood & violence 459 918 1377 3350 5925 8500
21-E.C. swipe 45 90 135 284 480 675

NOTE: ***Cameron*** *a-4, 5, 8.* ***Hollingsworth*** *a-3-7, 9, 10, 13.* ***Wildey*** *a-6, 15, 16.*

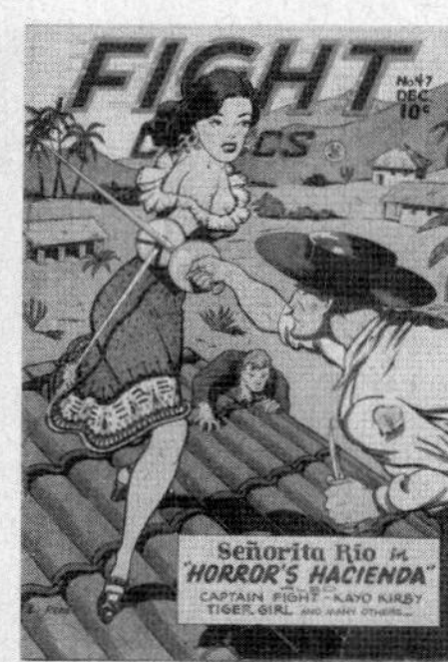

Fight Comics #47 © FH

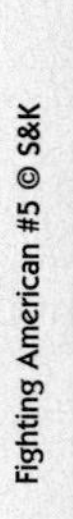
Fighting American #5 © S&K

Fightin' Army #17 © CC

FIGHT AGAINST THE GUILTY (Formerly Fight Against Crime)
Story Comics: No. 22, Dec, 1954 - No. 23, Mar, 1955

	GD 2.0	VG 4.0	FN 6.0	VF 8.0	VF/NM 9.0	NM- 9.2
22-Toth styled art by Ross Andru; Ditko-a; E.C. story swipe; electrocution-c (Last pre-code)	45	90	135	284	480	675
23-Hollingsworth-a	28	56	84	165	270	400

FIGHT CLUB 2 (Sequel to the movie)(Also see Free Comic Book Day 2015)
Dark Horse Comics: May, 2015 - No. 10, Mar, 2016 ($3.99)

	GD 2.0	VG 4.0	FN 6.0	VF 8.0	VF/NM 9.0	NM- 9.2
1-10-Chuck Palahniuk-s/Cameron Stewart-a						4.00

FIGHT COMICS
Fiction House Magazines: Jan, 1940 - No. 83, 11/52; No. 84, Wint, 1952-53; No. 85, Spring, 1953; No. 86, Summer, 1954

	GD 2.0	VG 4.0	FN 6.0	VF 8.0	VF/NM 9.0	NM- 9.2
1-Origin Spy Fighter, Starring Saber; Jack Dempsey life story; Shark Brodie & Chip Collins begin; Fine-c; Eisner-a	389	778	1167	2723	4762	6800
2-Joe Louis life story; Fine/Eisner-c	161	322	483	1030	1765	2500
3-Rip Regan, the Power Man begins (3/40); classic-c	194	388	582	1242	2121	3000
4,5: 4-Fine-c	116	232	348	742	1271	1800
6-10: 6,7-Powell-c	103	206	309	659	1130	1600
11-14: Rip Regan ends	97	194	291	621	1061	1500
15-1st app. Super American plus-c (10/41)	129	258	387	826	1413	2000
16-Captain Fight begins (12/41); Spy Fighter ends	110	220	330	704	1202	1700
17,18: Super American ends	81	162	243	518	884	1250
19-Japanese WWII-c; Captain Fight ends; Senorita Rio begins (6/42, origin & 1st app.); Rip Carson, Chute Trooper begins	90	180	270	576	988	1400
20-Bondage/torture-c	103	206	309	659	1130	1600
21-27,29,30: 21-24,26,27-Japanese WWII-c	77	154	231	493	847	1200
28-Classic Japanese WWII torture-c	116	232	348	742	1271	1800
31-Classic Japanese WWII decapitation-c	314	628	942	2198	3849	5500
32-Tiger Girl begins (6/44, 1st app.?); Nazi WWII-c	129	258	387	826	1413	2000
33,35-39,41,42: 42-Last WWII-c (2/46)	65	130	195	416	708	1000
34-Classic Japanese WWII bondage-c	97	194	291	621	1061	1500
40-Classic Nazi vulture bondage-c	90	180	270	576	988	1400
43,45-50: 48-Used in Love and Death by Legman. 49-Jungle-c begin, end #81	37	74	111	222	361	500
44-Classic bondage/torture-c; Capt. Fight returns	68	136	204	435	743	1050
51-Origin Tiger Girl; Patsy Pin-Up app.	40	80	120	244	402	560
52-60,62-64-Last Baker issue	26	52	78	154	252	350
61-Origin Tiger Girl retold	27	54	81	158	259	360
65-78: 78-Used in **POP**, pg. 99	22	44	66	132	216	300
79-The Space Rangers app.	23	46	69	136	223	310
80-85: 81-Last jungle-c. 82-85-War-c/stories	20	40	60	117	189	260
86-Two Tigerman stories by Evans-r/Rangers Comics #40,41; Moreira-r/Rangers Comics #45	20	40	60	117	189	260

NOTE: *Bondage covers, Lingerie, headlights panels are common. Captain Fight by* ***Kamen****-51-66. Kayo Kirby by* ***Baker****-#43-64, 67(not by Baker). Senorita Rio by* ***Kamen****-#57-64; by* ***Grandenetti****-#65, 66. Tiger Girl by* ***Baker****-#36-60, 62-64;* ***Eisner*** *c-1-3, 5, 10, 11.* ***Kamen*** *a-54?, 57?* ***Tuska*** *a-1, 5, 8, 10, 21, 29, 34.* ***Whitman*** *c-73-84.* ***Zolnerwich*** *c-16, 17, 22. Power Man c-5, 6, 9. Super American c-15-17. Tiger Girl c-49-81.*

FIGHT FOR LOVE
United Features Syndicate: 1952 (no month)

	GD 2.0	VG 4.0	FN 6.0	VF 8.0	VF/NM 9.0	NM- 9.2
nn-Abbie & Slats newspaper-r	9	18	27	52	69	85

FIGHT FOR TOMORROW
DC Comics (Vertigo): Nov, 2002 - No. 6, Apr, 2003 ($2.50, limited series)

	GD 2.0	VG 4.0	FN 6.0	VF 8.0	VF/NM 9.0	NM- 9.2
1-6-Denys Cowan-a/Brian Wood-s. 1-Jim Lee-c. 5-Jo Chen-c						3.00
TPB (2008, $14.99) r/#1-6						15.00

FIGHTING AIR FORCE (See United States Fighting Air Force)

FIGHTIN' AIR FORCE (Formerly Sherlock Holmes?; Never Again? War and Attack #54 on)
Charlton Comics: No. 3, Feb, 1956 - No. 53, Feb-Mar, 1966

	GD 2.0	VG 4.0	FN 6.0	VF 8.0	VF/NM 9.0	NM- 9.2
V1#3	10	20	30	54	72	90
4-10	7	14	21	35	43	50
11(3/58, 68 pgs.)	9	18	27	47	61	75
12 (100 pgs.)-U.S. Nukes Russia	14	28	42	80	115	150
13-30: 13,24-Glanzman-a. 24-Glanzman-c. 27-Area 51, UFO story	3	6	9	19	30	40
31-53: 50-American Eagle begins	3	6	9	15	22	28

FIGHTING AMERICAN
Headline Publ./Prize (Crestwood): Apr-May, 1954 - No. 7, Apr-May, 1955

	GD 2.0	VG 4.0	FN 6.0	VF 8.0	VF/NM 9.0	NM- 9.2
1-Origin & 1st app. Fighting American & Speedboy (Capt. America & Bucky clones); S&K-c/a(3); 1st super hero satire series	194	388	582	1242	2121	3000
2-S&K-a(3)	90	180	270	576	988	1400
3-5: 3,4-S&K-a(3). 5-S&K-a(2); Kirby/?-a	77	154	231	493	847	1200
6-Origin-r (4 pgs.) plus 2 pgs. by S&K	74	148	222	470	810	1150
7-Kirby-a	68	136	204	435	743	1050

NOTE: ***Simon & Kirby*** *covers on all. 6 is last pre-code issue.*

FIGHTING AMERICAN
Harvey Publications: Oct, 1966 (25¢)

	GD 2.0	VG 4.0	FN 6.0	VF 8.0	VF/NM 9.0	NM- 9.2
1-Origin Fighting American & Speedboy by S&K-r; S&K-c/a(3); 1 pg. Neal Adams ad	5	10	15	33	57	80

FIGHTING AMERICAN
DC Comics: Feb, 1994 - No. 6, 1994 ($1.50, limited series)

	GD 2.0	VG 4.0	FN 6.0	VF 8.0	VF/NM 9.0	NM- 9.2
1-6						3.00

FIGHTING AMERICAN (Vol. 3)
Awesome Entertainment: Aug, 1997 - No. 2, Oct, 1997 ($2.50)

	GD 2.0	VG 4.0	FN 6.0	VF 8.0	VF/NM 9.0	NM- 9.2
Preview-Agent America (pre-lawsuit)	1	2	3	5	6	7
1-Four covers by Liefeld, Churchill, Platt, McGuinness						3.00
1-Platinum Edition, 1-Gold foil Edition						10.00
1-Comic Cavalcade Edition, 2-American Ent. Spice Ed.						4.00
2-Platt-c, 2-Liefeld variant-c						3.00

FIGHTING AMERICAN: DOGS OF WAR
Awesome-Hyperwerks: Sept, 1998 - No. 3, May, 1999 ($2.50)

	GD 2.0	VG 4.0	FN 6.0	VF 8.0	VF/NM 9.0	NM- 9.2
Limited Convention Special (7/98, B&W) Platt-a						3.00
1-3-Starlin-s/Platt-a/c						3.00

FIGHTING AMERICAN: RULES OF THE GAME
Awesome Entertainment: Nov, 1997 - No. 3, Mar, 1998 ($2.50, lim. series)

	GD 2.0	VG 4.0	FN 6.0	VF 8.0	VF/NM 9.0	NM- 9.2
1-3: 1-Loeb-s/McGuinness-a/c. 2-Flip book with Swat! preview						3.00
1-Liefeld SPICE variant-c, 1-Dynamic Forces Ed.; McGuinness-c						3.00
1-Liefeld Fighting American & cast variant-c						3.00

FIGHTIN' ARMY (Formerly Soldier and Marine Comics) (See Captain Willy Schultz)
Charlton Comics: No. 16, 1/56 - No. 127, 12/76; No. 128, 9/77 - No. 172, 11/84

	GD 2.0	VG 4.0	FN 6.0	VF 8.0	VF/NM 9.0	NM- 9.2
16	10	20	30	54	72	90
17-19,21-23,25-30	7	14	21	35	43	50
20-Ditko-a	9	18	27	50	65	80
24 (3/58, 68 pgs.)	9	18	27	47	61	75
31-45	3	6	9	18	28	38
46-50,52-60	3	6	9	16	23	30
51-Hitler-c	3	6	9	18	28	38
61-75	3	6	9	14	19	24
76-1st The Lonely War of Willy Schultz	3	6	9	17	26	35
77-80: 77-92-The Lonely War of Willy Schultz. 79-Devil Brigade	3	6	9	14	19	24
81-88,91,93-99: 82,83-Devil Brigade	2	4	6	10	14	18
89,90,92-Ditko-a	3	6	9	14	20	26
100	2	4	6	13	18	22
101-127	2	4	6	8	11	14
128-140	1	2	3	5	7	9
141-165	1	2	3	4	5	7
166-172-Low print run	1	2	3	5	6	8
108 (Modern Comics-1977)-Reprint						5.00

NOTE: ***Aparo*** *c-154.* ***Glanzman*** *a-77-88.* ***Montes/Bache*** *a-48, 49, 51, 69, 75, 76, 170r.*

FIGHTING CARAVANS (See Zane Grey 4-Color 632)

FIGHTING DANIEL BOONE
Avon Periodicals: 1953

	GD 2.0	VG 4.0	FN 6.0	VF 8.0	VF/NM 9.0	NM- 9.2
nn-Kinstler-c/a, 22 pgs.	20	40	60	117	189	260
I.W. Reprint #1-Reprints #1 above; Kinstler-c/a; Lawrence/Alascia-a	3	6	9	14	19	24

FIGHTING DAVY CROCKETT (Formerly Kit Carson)
Avon Periodicals: No. 9, Oct-Nov, 1955

	GD 2.0	VG 4.0	FN 6.0	VF 8.0	VF/NM 9.0	NM- 9.2
9-Kinstler-c	11	22	33	62	86	110

FIGHTIN' FIVE, THE (Formerly Space War) (Also see The Peacemaker)
Charlton Comics: July, 1964 - No. 41, Jan, 1967; No. 42, Oct, 1981 - No. 49, Dec, 1982

	GD 2.0	VG 4.0	FN 6.0	VF 8.0	VF/NM 9.0	NM- 9.2
V2#28-Origin/1st app. Fightin' Five; Montes/Bache-a	5	10	15	35	63	90
29-39-Montes/Bache-a in all	3	6	9	21	33	45
40-Peacemaker begins (1st app.)	6	12	18	37	66	95
41-Peacemaker (2nd app.); Montes/Bache-a	4	8	12	28	47	65
42-49: Reprints						5.00

FIGHTING FRONTS!
Harvey Publications: Aug, 1952 - No. 5, Jan, 1953

	GD 2.0	VG 4.0	FN 6.0	VF 8.0	VF/NM 9.0	NM- 9.2
1	10	20	30	54	72	90
2-Extreme violence; Nostrand/Powell-a	11	22	33	60	83	105

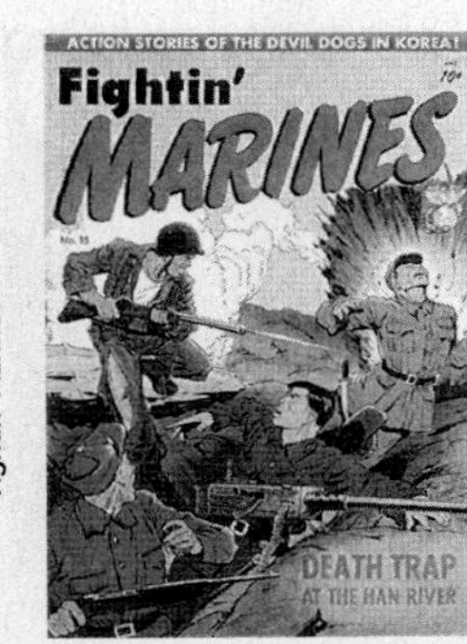

Fightin' Marines #1 © STJ

Fighting Yank #8 © BP

Figment #5 © DIS

	GD 2.0	VG 4.0	FN 6.0	VF 8.0	VF/NM 9.0	NM- 9.2
3-5: 3-Powell-a	7	14	21	37	46	55
FIGHTING INDIAN STORIES (See Midget Comics)						
FIGHTING INDIANS OF THE WILD WEST!						
Avon Periodicals: Mar, 1952 - No. 2, Nov, 1952						
1-Geronimo, Chief Crazy Horse, Chief Victorio, Black Hawk begin; Larsen-a; McCann-a(2)	20	40	60	117	189	260
2-Kinstler-c & inside-c only; Larsen, McCann-a	14	28	42	82	121	160
100 Pg. Annual (1952, 25¢)-Contains three comics rebound; Geronimo, Chief Crazy Horse, Chief Victorio; Kinstler-c	41	82	123	256	428	600
FIGHTING LEATHERNECKS						
Toby Press: Feb, 1952 - No. 6, Dec, 1952						
1- "Duke's Diary"; full pg. pin-ups by Sparling	16	32	48	94	147	200
2-5: 2- "Duke's Diary" full pg. pin-ups. 3-5- "Gil's Gals"; full pg. pin-ups	11	22	33	62	86	110
6-(Same as No. 3-5?)	11	22	33	62	86	110
FIGHTING MAN, THE (War)						
Ajax/Farrell Publications(Excellent Publ.): May, 1952 - No. 8, July, 1953						
1	16	32	48	94	147	200
2	10	20	30	58	79	100
3-8	9	18	27	50	65	80
Annual 1 (1952, 25¢, 100 pgs.)	34	68	102	199	325	450
FIGHTIN' MARINES (Formerly The Texan; also see Approved Comics)						
St. John(Approved Comics)/Charlton Comics No. 14 on: No. 15, 8/51 - No. 12, 3/53; No. 14, 5/55 - No. 132, 11/76; No. 133, 10/77 - No. 176, 9/84 (No #13?) (Korean War #1-3)						
15(#1)-Matt Baker c/a "Leatherneck Jack"; slightly large size; Fightin' Texan No. 16 & 17?	53	106	159	334	567	800
2-1st Canteen Kate by Baker; slightly large size; partial Baker-c	61	122	183	390	670	950
3-9,11-Canteen Kate by Baker; Baker c-#2,3,5-11; 4-Partial Baker-c	37	74	111	222	361	500
10-Matt Baker-c	21	42	63	122	199	275
12-No Baker-a; Last St. John issue?	11	22	33	62	86	110
14 (5/55; 1st Charlton issue; formerly?)-Canteen Kate by Baker; all stories reprinted from #2	21	42	63	122	199	275
15-Baker-c	14	28	42	80	115	150
16,18-20-Not Baker-c. 16-Grey-tone-c	8	16	24	40	50	60
17-Canteen Kate by Baker	16	32	48	94	147	200
21-24	7	14	21	35	43	50
25-(68 pgs.)(3/58)-Check-a?	10	20	30	56	76	95
26-(100 pgs.)(8/58)-Check-a(5)	14	28	42	82	121	160
27-50	3	6	9	18	28	38
51-81: 78-Shotgun Harker & the Chicken series begin	3	6	9	15	22	28
82-85: 85-Last 12¢ issue	3	6	9	14	20	25
86-94: 94-Last 15¢ issue	2	4	6	10	14	18
95-100,122: 122-(1975) Pilot issue for "War" title (Fightin' Marines Presents War)	2	4	6	9	13	16
101-121	2	4	6	8	10	12
123-140: 132 Hitler-c	1	2	3	5	7	9
141-170						6.00
171-176-Low print run	1	2	3	5	6	8
120(Modern Comics reprint, 1977)						5.00

NOTE: *No. 14 & 16 (CC) reprint St. John issues; No. 16 reprints St. John insignia on cover.* ***Colan*** *a-3, 7.* ***Glanzman*** *c/a-92, 94.* ***Montes/Bache*** *a-48, 53, 55, 64, 65, 72-74, 77-83, 176r.*

	GD 2.0	VG 4.0	FN 6.0	VF 8.0	VF/NM 9.0	NM- 9.2
FIGHTING MARSHAL OF THE WILD WEST (See The Hawk)						
FIGHTIN' NAVY (Formerly Don Winslow)						
Charlton Comics: No. 74, 1/56 - No. 125, 4-5/66; No. 126, 8/83 - No. 133, 10/84						
74	5	10	15	34	60	85
75-81	4	8	12	23	37	50
82-Sam Glanzman-a (68 pg. Giant)	5	10	15	31	53	75
83-(100 pgs.)	6	12	18	41	76	110
84-99,101: 101-UFO-c/story	3	6	9	17	26	35
100	3	6	9	18	28	38
102-105,106-125('66)	3	6	9	14	21	26
126-133 (1984)-Low print run	1	2	3	5	6	8

NOTE: ***Montes/Bache*** *a-109.* ***Glanzman*** *a-82, 92, 96, 98, 100, 131r.*

FIGHTING PRINCE OF DONEGAL, THE (See Movie Comics)

FIGHTIN' TEXAN (Formerly The Texan & Fightin' Marines?)
St. John Publishing Co.: No. 16, Sept, 1952 - No. 17, Dec, 1952

	GD 2.0	VG 4.0	FN 6.0	VF 8.0	VF/NM 9.0	NM- 9.2
16,17: Tuska-a each. 17-Cameron-c/a	10	20	30	56	76	95
FIGHTING UNDERSEA COMMANDOS (See Undersea Fighting...)						
Avon Periodicals: May, 1952 - No. 5, April, 1953 (U.S. Navy frogmen)						
1-Cover title is Undersea Fighting... #1 only	17	34	51	98	154	210
2	11	22	33	60	83	105
3-5: 1,3-Ravielli-c. 4-Kinstler-c	10	20	30	54	72	90
FIGHTING WAR STORIES						
Men's Publications/Story Comics: Aug, 1952 - No. 5, 1953						
1	14	28	42	82	121	160
2-5	9	18	27	50	65	80
FIGHTING YANK (See America's Best Comics & Startling Comics)						
Nedor/Better Publ./Standard: Sept, 1942 - No. 29, Aug, 1949						
1-The Fighting Yank begins; Mystico, the Wonder Man app; bondage-c	343	686	1029	2400	4200	6000
2	187	374	561	1197	2049	2900
3,4: Nazi WWII-c. 4-Schomburg-c begin	148	296	444	947	1624	2300
5,8,9: 5-Nazi-c. 8,9-Japan War-c	148	296	444	947	1624	2300
6-Classic Japanese WWII-c	245	490	735	1568	2684	3800
7-Classic Hitler special bomb-c; Grim Reaper app.	271	542	813	1734	2967	4200
10-Nazi bondage/torture/hypo-c	194	388	582	1242	2121	3000
11,14,15: 11-The Oracle app. 15-Bondage/torture-c	81	162	243	518	884	1250
12-Hirohito bondage Japanese WWII-c	155	310	465	992	1696	2400
13-Last War-c (Japanese)	116	232	348	742	1271	1800
16-20: 18-The American Eagle app.	61	122	183	390	670	950
21-Kara, Jungle Princess app.; lingerie-c	155	310	465	993	1696	2400
22-Schomburg Miss Masque dinosaur-c	90	180	270	576	988	1400
23-Classic Schomburg hooded vigilante-c	174	348	522	1114	1907	2700
24-Miss Masque app.	63	126	189	403	689	975
25-Robinson/Meskin-a; strangulation, lingerie panel; The Cavalier app.	61	122	183	390	670	950
26-29: All-Robinson/Meskin-a. 28-One pg. Williamson-a	50	100	150	315	533	750

NOTE: ***Schomburg (Xela)*** *c-4-29; airbrush-c 28, 29. Bondage c-1, 4, 8, 10, 11, 12, 15, 17.*

	GD 2.0	VG 4.0	FN 6.0	VF 8.0	VF/NM 9.0	NM- 9.2
FIGHTMAN						
Marvel Comics: June, 1993 ($2.00, one-shot, 52 pgs.)						
1						4.00
FIGHT THE ENEMY						
Tower Comics: Aug, 1966 - No. 3, Mar, 1967 (25¢, 68 pgs.)						
1-Lucky 7 & Mike Manly begin	4	8	12	27	44	60
2-1st Boris Vallejo comic art; McWilliams-a	3	6	9	21	33	45
3-Wood-a (1/2 pg.); McWilliams, Bolle-a	3	6	9	21	33	45
FIGMENT (Disney Kingdoms) (See Disney Kingdoms: Figment 2 for sequel)						
Marvel Comics: Aug, 2014 - No. 5, Dec, 2014 ($3.99, limited series)						
1-5-Jim Zub-s/Filipe Andrade-a						4.00
FILM FUNNIES						
Marvel Comics (CPC): Nov, 1949 - No. 2, Feb, 1950 (52 pgs.)						
1-Krazy Krow, Wacky Duck	24	48	72	140	230	320
2-Wacky Duck	17	34	51	98	154	210
FILM STARS ROMANCES						
Star Publications: Jan-Feb, 1950 - No. 3, May-June, 1950 (True life stories of movie stars)						
1-Rudy Valentino & Gregory Peck stories; L. B. Cole-c; lingerie panels	44	88	132	277	469	660
2-Liz Taylor/Robert Taylor photo-c & true life story	58	116	174	371	636	900
3-Douglas Fairbanks story; photo-c	27	54	81	158	259	360
FILTH, THE						
DC Comics (Vertigo): Aug, 2002 - No. 13, Oct, 2003 ($2.95, limited series)						
1-13-Morrison-s/Weston & Erskine-a						3.00
TPB (2004, $19.95) r/#1-13						20.00
FINAL CRISIS						
DC Comics: July, 2008 - No. 7, Mar, 2009 ($3.99, limited series)						
1-Grant Morrison-s/J.G. Jones-a/c; Martian Manhunter killed; 2 covers						4.00
1-Director's Cut (10/08, $4.99) B&W printing of #1 with creator commentary						5.00
2-7: 2-Barry Allen-c/cameo; intro Big Science Action; two covers. 6-Batman zapped						4.00
SC (2010, $19.99) r/#1-7, FC: Superman Beyond #1,2, FC: Submit & FC Sketchbook						20.00
...: Rage of the Red Lanterns (12/08, $3.99) Atrocitus app.; intro. Blue Lantern; 3 covers						4.00
...: Requiem (9/08, $3.99) History, death and funeral of the Martian Manhunter; 2 covers						4.00
...: Resist (12/08, $3.99) Checkmate app; Rucka & Trautman-s/Sook-a; 2 covers						4.00
...: Secret Files (2/09, $3.99) origin of Libra; Wein-s/Shasteen-a; JG Jones sketch-a						4.00

Final Crisis: Revelations #1 © DC

Firehair Comics #5 © FH

Fireside Book Series - Bring On the Bad Guys © MAR

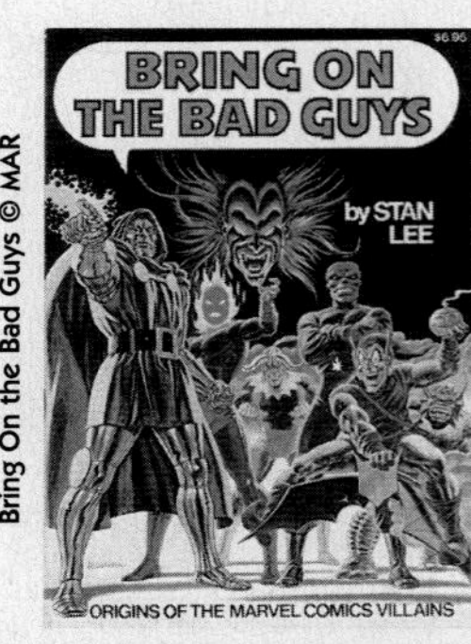

GD 2.0 | VG 4.0 | FN 6.0 | VF 8.0 | VF/NM 9.0 | NM- 9.2

... Sketchbook (7/08, $2.99) Jones development sketches with Morrison commentary 3.00
...: Submit (12/08, $3.99) Black Lightning & Tattooed Man team up; Morrison-s; 2 covers 4.00

FINAL CRISIS: DANCE (Final Crisis Aftermath)
DC Comics: Jul, 2009 - No. 6, Dec, 2009 ($2.99, limited series)
1-6-Super Young Team; Joe Casey-s/Chriscross-a/Stanley Lau-c 3.00
TPB (2009, $17.99) r/#1-6 18.00

FINAL CRISIS: ESCAPE (Final Crisis Aftermath)
DC Comics: Jul, 2009 - No. 6, Dec, 2009 ($2.99, limited series)
1-6-Nemesis & Cameron Chase app.; Ivan Brandon-s/Marco Rudy-a/Scott Hampton-c 3.00
TPB (2010, $17.99) r/#1-6 18.00

FINAL CRISIS: INK (Final Crisis Aftermath)
DC Comics: Jul, 2009 - No. 6, Dec, 2009 ($2.99, limited series)
1-6-The Tattooed Man; Eric Wallace-s/Fabrizio Florentino-a/Brian Stelfreeze-c 3.00
TPB (2010, $17.99) r/#1-6 18.00

FINAL CRISIS: LEGION OF THREE WORLDS
DC Comics: Oct, 2008 - No. 5, Sept, 2009 ($3.99, limited series)
1-Johns-s/Pérez-a; R.J. Brande killed; Time Trapper app.; two covers on each issue 5.00
2-5-Three Legions meet; two covers. 3-Bart Allen returns. 4-Superboy (Conner) returns 4.00
HC (2009, $19.99) r/#1-5; variant covers 20.00
SC (2010, $14.99) r/#1-5; variant covers 15.00

FINAL CRISIS: REVELATIONS
DC Comics: Oct, 2008 - No. 5, Feb, 2009 ($3.99, limited series)
1-5-Spectre and The Question; 2 covers on each. 1-Dr. Light killed; Rucka-s/Tan-a 4.00
HC (2009, $19.99, d.j.) r/#1-5; variant covers 20.00
SC (2010, $14.99) r/#1-5; variant covers 15.00

FINAL CRISIS: ROGUE'S REVENGE
DC Comics: Sept, 2008 - No. 3, Nov, 2008 ($3.99, limited series)
1-3-Johns-s/Kolins-a; Flash's Rogues, Zoom and Inertia app. 4.00
HC (2009, $19.99, d.j.) r/#1-3 & Flash #182,197; variant covers 20.00
SC (2010, $14.99) r/#1-3 & Flash #182,197; variant covers 15.00

FINAL CRISIS: RUN (Final Crisis Aftermath)
DC Comics: Jul, 2009 - No. 6, Dec, 2009 ($2.99, limited series)
1-6-The Human Flame on the run; Sturges-s/Williams-a/Kako-c 3.00
TPB (2010, $17.99) r/#1-6 18.00

FINAL CRISIS: SUPERMAN BEYOND
DC Comics: Oct, 2008 - No. 2, Mar, 2009 ($4.50, limited series)
1,2-Morrison-s/Mahnke-a; parallel-Earth Supermen app.; 3-D pages and glasses 4.50

FINAL NIGHT, THE (See DC related titles and Parallax: Emerald Night)
DC Comics: Nov, 1996 - No. 4, Nov, 1996 ($1.95, weekly limited series)
1-4: Kesel-s/Immonen-a(p) in all. 4-Parallax's final acts 4.00
Preview 3.00
TPB-(1998, $12.95) r/#1-4, Parallax: Emerald Night #1, and preview 13.00

FINALS (See Vertigo Resurrected:... for collected reprint)
DC Comics (Vertigo): Sept, 1999 - No. 4, Dec, 1999 ($2.95, limited series)
1-4-Will Pfeifer-s/Jill Thompson-a 3.00

FINDING NEMO (Based on the Pixar movie)
BOOM! Studios: Jul, 2010 - No. 4, Oct, 2010 ($2.99, limited series)
1-4-Michael Raicht & Brian Smith-s/Jake Myler-a.1-Three covers 3.00

FINDING NEMO: REEF RESCUE (Based on the Pixar movie)
BOOM! Studios: May, 2009 - No. 4, Aug, 2009 ($2.99, limited series)
1-4-Marie Croall-s/Erica Leigh Currey-a; 2 covers 3.00

FIN FANG FOUR RETURN!
Marvel Comics: Jul, 2009 ($3.99, one-shot)
1-Fin Fang Foom, Googam, Elektro, Gorgilla and Doc Samson app. 5.00

FIRE
Caliber Press: 1993 - No. 2, 1993 ($2.95, B&W, limited series, 52 pgs.)
1,2-Brian Michael Bendis-s/a 4.00
TPB (1999, 2001, $9.95) Restored reprints of series 10.00

FIREARM (Also see Codename: Firearm, Freex #15, Night Man #4 & Prime #10)
Malibu Comics (Ultraverse): Sept, 1993 - No. 18, Mar, 1995 ($1.95/$2.50)
0 ($14.95)-Came w/ video containing 1st half of story (comic contains 2nd half); 1st app. Duet 15.00
1,3-6: 1-James Robinson scripts begin; Cully Hamner-a; Chaykin-c; 1st app. Alec Swan. 3-Intro The Sportsmen; Chaykin-c. 4-Break-Thru x-over; Chaykin-c. 5-1st app. Ellen (Swan's girlfriend); 2 pg. origin of Prime. 6-Prime app. (story cont'd in Prime #10); Brereton-c 3.00
1-($2.50)-Newsstand edition polybagged w/card 3.50
1-Ultra Limited silver foil-c 1 2 3 5 6 8
2 ($2.50, 44 pgs.)-Hardcase app.;Chaykin-c; Rune flip-c/story by B. Smith (3 pgs.) 4.00
7-10,12-17: 12-The Rafferty Saga begins, ends #18; 1st app. Rafferty. 15-Night Man & Freex app. 17-Swan marries Ellen 3.00
11-($3.50, 68 pgs.)-Flip book w/Ultraverse Premiere #5 4.00
18-Death of Rafferty; Chaykin-c 4.00
NOTE: *Brereton c-6.* ***Chaykin*** *c-1-4, 14, 16, 18.* ***Hamner*** *a-1-4.* ***Herrera*** *a-12.* ***James Robinson*** *scripts-0-18.*

FIRE BALL XL5 (See Steve Zodiac & The ...)

FIREBIRDS (See Noble Causes)
Image Comics: Nov, 2004 ($5.95)
1-Faerber-s/Ponce-a/c; intro. Firebird 6.00

FIREBRAND (Also see Showcase '96 #4)
DC Comics: Feb, 1996 - No. 9, Oct, 1996 ($1.75)
1-9: Brian Augustyn scripts; Velluto-c/a in all. 9-Daredevil #319-c/swipe 3.00

FIREBREATHER
Image Comics: Jan, 2003 - No. 4, Apr, 2003 ($2.95)
1-4-Hester-s/Kuhn-a 3.00
...: The Iron Saint (12/04, $6.95, squarebound) Hester-s/Kuhn-a 7.00
TPB (7/04, $13.95) r/#1-4; foreword by Brad Meltzer; gallery and sketch pages 14.00

FIREBREATHER
Image Comics: Jun, 2008 - No. 4, Feb, 2009 ($2.99)
1-4-Hester-s/Kuhn-a 3.00

FIREBREATHER (Vol.3): HOLMGANG
Image Comics: Nov, 2010 - No. 4, ($3.99, limited series)
1,2-Hester-s/Kuhn-a 4.00

FIRE FROM HEAVEN
Image Comics (WildStorm Productions): Mar, 1996 ($2.50)
1,2-Moore-s 3.00

FIREHAIR COMICS (Formerly Pioneer West Romances #3-6; also see Rangers Comics)
Fiction House Magazines (Flying Stories): Winter/48-49; No. 2, Wint/49-50; No. 7, Spr/51 - No. 11, Spr/52

	GD	VG	FN	VF	VF/NM	NM-
1-Origin Firehair	34	68	102	199	325	450
2-Continues as Pioneer West Romances for #3-6	18	36	54	105	165	225
7-11	14	28	42	80	115	150
I.W. Reprint 8-(nd)-Kinstler-c; reprints Rangers #57; Dr. Drew story by Grandenetti	3	6	9	16	23	30

FIRESIDE BOOK SERIES (Hard and soft cover editions)
Simon and Schuster: 1974 - 1980 (130-260 pgs.), Square bound, color

		GD	VG	FN	VF	VF/NM	NM-
Amazing Spider-Man, The, 1979,	HC	7	14	21	48	89	130
130 pgs., $3.95, Bob Larkin-c	SC	5	10	15	33	57	80
America At War–The Best of DC War	HC	10	20	30	64	132	200
Comics, 1979, $6.95, 260 pgs, Kubert-c	SC	6	12	18	42	79	115
Best of Spidey Super Stories (Electric	HC	9	18	27	57	111	165
Company) 1978, $3.95,	SC	6	12	18	37	66	95
Bring On The Bad Guys (Origins of the	HC	7	14	21	46	86	125
Marvel Comics Villains) 1976, $6.95, 260 pgs.; Romita-c	SC	5	10	15	31	53	75
Captain America, Sentinel of Liberty,1979,	HC	7	14	21	48	89	130
130 pgs., $12.95, Cockrum-c	SC	5	10	15	33	57	80
Doctor Strange Master of the Mystic	HC	7	14	21	48	89	130
Arts, 1980, 130 pgs.	SC	5	10	15	33	57	80
Fantastic Four, The, 1979, 130 pgs.	HC	7	14	21	46	86	125
	SC	5	10	15	31	53	75
Heart Throbs–The Best of DC Romance	HC	13	26	39	86	188	290
Comics, 1979, 260 pgs., $6.95	SC	8	16	24	56	108	160
Incredible Hulk, The, 1978, 260 pgs.	HC	7	14	21	46	86	125
(8 1/4" x 11")	SC	5	10	15	31	53	75
Marvel's Greatest Superhero Battles,	HC	9	18	27	57	111	165
1978, 260 pgs., $6.95, Romita-c	SC	6	12	18	37	66	95
Mysteries in Space, 1980, $7,95,	HC	8	16	24	52	99	145
Anderson-c. r-DC sci/fi stories	SC	5	10	15	34	60	85
Origins of Marvel Comics, 1974, 260 pgs., $5.95. r-covers & origins of Fantastic Four, Hulk, Spider-Man, Thor,	HC	7	14	21	46	86	125

Firestorm, The Nuclear Man #85 © DC

First Issue Special #13 © DC

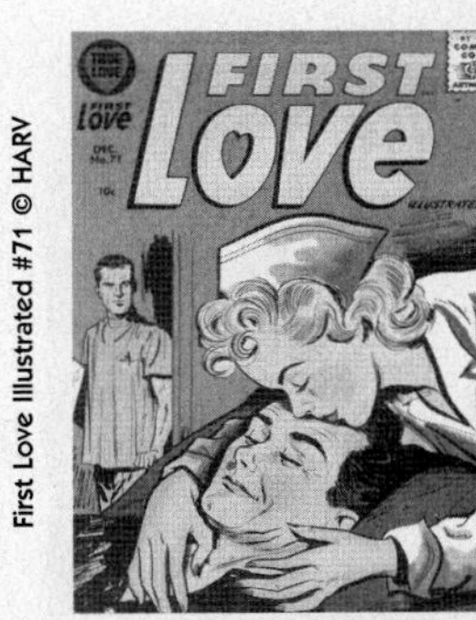

First Love Illustrated #71 © HARV

GD 2.0 VG 4.0 FN 6.0 VF 8.0 VF/NM 9.0 NM- 9.2

& Doctor Strange SC 5 10 15 31 53 75
Silver Surfer, The, 1978, 130 pgs., HC 7 14 21 48 89 130
$4.95, Norem-c SC 5 10 15 34 60 85
Son of Origins of Marvel Comics, 1975, 260 pgs., $6.95, Romita-c. Reprints
covers & origins of X-Men, Iron Man, HC 7 14 21 46 86 125
Avengers, Daredevil, Silver Surfer SC 5 10 15 31 53 75
Superhero Women, The–Featuring the HC 9 18 27 57 111 165
Fabulous Females of Marvel Comics, SC 6 12 18 37 66 95
1977, 260 pgs., $6.95, Romita-c
Note: *Prices listed are for 1st printings. Later printings have lesser value.*

FIRESTAR
Marvel Comics Group: Mar, 1986 - No. 4, June, 1986 (75¢)(From Spider-Man TV series)
1,2: 1-X-Men & New Mutants app. 2-Wolverine-c (not real Wolverine?); Art Adams-a(p) 6.00
3,4: 3-Art Adams/Sienkiewicz-c. 4-B. Smith-c 4.00
X-Men: Firestar Digest (2006, $7.99, digest-size) r/#1-4; profile pages 8.00
1 (Jun, 2010, $3.99) Sean McKeever-s/Emma Rios-a 4.00

FIRESTONE (See Donald And Mickey Merry Christmas)

FIRESTORM (Also see The Fury of Firestorm, Cancelled Comic Cavalcade, DC Comics Presents, Flash #289, & Justice League of America #179)
DC Comics: March, 1978 - No. 5, Oct-Nov, 1978
1-Origin & 1st app. 6 12 18 28 69 100
2,4,5: 2-Origin Multiplex. 4-1st app. Hyena 2 4 6 9 12 15
3-Origin & 1st app. Killer Frost (Crystal Frost) 4 8 12 23 37 50
...: The Nuclear Man TPB (2011, $17.99) r/#1-5 and stories from Flash #289-293, plus story from Cancelled Comic Cavalcade (uncolored) 18.00

FIRESTORM
DC Comics: July, 2004 - No. 35, June, 2007 ($2.50/$2.99)
1-24: 1-Intro. Jason Rusch; Jolley-s/ChrisCross-a. 6-Identity Crisis tie-in. 7-Bloodhound x-over. 8-Killer Frost returns. 9-Ronnie Raymond returns. 17-Villains United tie-in. 21-Infinite Crisis. 24-One Year Later; Killer Frost app. 3.00
25-35: 25-Begin $2.99-c; Mr. Freeze app. 33-35-Mister Miracle & Orion app. 3.00
...: Reborn TPB (2007, $14.99) r/#23-27 15.00

FIRESTORM, THE NUCLEAR MAN (Formerly Fury of Firestorm)
DC Comics: No. 65, Nov, 1987 - No. 100, Aug, 1990
65-99: 66-1st app. Zuggernaut; Firestorm vs. Green Lantern. 67,68-Millennium tie-ins. 71-Death of Capt. X. 83-1st new look 3.00
100-($2.95, 68 pgs.) 4.00
Annual 5 (10/87)-1st app. new Firestorm 4.00

FIRST, THE
CrossGeneration Comics: Jan, 2001 - No. 37, Jan, 2004 ($2.95)
1-3: 1-Barbara Kesel-s/Bart Sears & Andy Smith-a 5.00
4-10 4.00
11-37 3.00
Preview (11/00, free) 8 pg. intro 3.00
Two Houses Divided Vol. 1 TPB (11/01, $19.95) r/#1-7; new Moeller-c 20.00
Magnificent Tension Vol. 2 TPB (2002, $19.95) r/#8-13 20.00
Sinister Motives Vol. 3 TPB (2003, $15.95) r/#14-19 16.00
Vol. 4 Futile Endeavors (2003, $15.95) r/#20-25 16.00
Vol. 5 Liquid Alliances (2003, $15.95) r/#26-31 16.00
Vol. 6 Ragnarok (2004, $15.95) r/#32-37 16.00

FIRST ADVENTURES
First Comics: Dec, 1985 - No. 5, Apr, 1986 ($1.25)
1-5: Blaze Barlow, Whisper & Dynamo Joe in all 3.00

FIRST AMERICANS, THE
Dell Publishing Co.: No. 843, Sept, 1957
Four Color 843-Marsh-a 7 14 21 49 92 135

FIRST BORN (See Witchblade and Darkness titles)
Image Comics (Top Cow): Aug, 2007 - No. 3 ($2.99, limited series)
... First Look (6/07, 99¢) Preview; The Darkness app.; Sejic-a; 2 covers (color & B&W) 3.00
1-3-($2.99) Two covers; Marz-s/Sejic-a. 3-Sara's baby is born 3.00
1-B&W variant Sejic cover 5.00
...: Aftermath (5/08, $3.99) short stories; Magdalena app.; two covers by Sook & Sejic 4.00

FIRST CHRISTMAS, THE (3-D)
Fiction House Magazines (Real Adv. Publ. Co.): 1953 (25¢, 8-1/4x10-1/4", oversize)(Came w/glasses)
nn-(Scarce)-Kelly Freas painted-c; Biblical theme, birth of Christ; Nativity-c
36 72 108 211 343 475

FIRST COMICS GRAPHIC NOVEL
First Comics: Jan, 1984 - No. 21? (52 pgs./176 pgs., high quality paper)
1,2: 1-Beowulf ($5.95)(both printings). 2-Time Beavers 10.00
3($11.95, 100 pgs.)-American Flagg! Hard Times (2nd printing exists) 15.00
4-Nexus ($6.95)-r/B&W 1-3 15.00
5,7: 5-The Enchanted Apples of Oz ($7.95, 52 pgs.)-Intro by Harlan Ellison (1986). 7-The Secret Island Of Oz ($7.95) 10.00
6-Elric of Melnibone ($14.95, 176 pgs.)-Reprints with new color 18.00
8,10,14,18: Teenage Mutant Ninja Turtles Book I -IV ($9.95, 132 pgs.)-8-r/TMNT #1-3 in color w/12 pgs. new-a; origin. 10-r/TMNT #4-6 in color. 14-r/TMNT #7,8 in color plus new 12 pg. story. 18-r/TMNT #10,11 plus 3 pg. fold-out 11.00
9-Time 2: The Epiphany by Chaykin (11/86, $7.95, 52 pgs. - indicia says #8) 15.00
11-Sailor On The Sea of Fate ($14.95) 16.00
nn-Time 2: The Satisfaction of Black Mariah (9/87) 10.00
12-American Flagg! Southern Comfort (10/87, $11.95) 15.00
13,16,17,21: 13-The Ice King Of Oz. 16-The Forgotten Forest of Oz ($8.95). 17-Mazinger (68 pgs., $8.95). 21-Elric, The Weird of the White Wolf; r/#1-5 10.00
15,19: 15-Hex Breaker: Badger ($7.95). 19-The Original Nexus Graphic Novel ($7.95, 104 pgs.)-Reprints First Comics Graphic Novel #4 12.00
20-American Flagg!: State of the Union ($11.95, 96 pgs.); r/A.F. #7-9 15.00
NOTE: *Most or all issues have been reprinted.*

1ST FOLIO (The Joe Kubert School Presents...)
Pacific Comics: Mar, 1984 ($1.50, one-shot)
1-Joe Kubert-c/a(2 pgs.); Adam & Andy Kubert-a 3.00

1ST ISSUE SPECIAL
National Periodical Publications: Apr, 1975 - No. 13, Apr, 1976 (Tryout series)
1,6: 1-Intro. Atlas; Kirby-c/a/script. 6-Dingbats 2 4 6 11 16 20
2,12: 2-Green Team (see Cancelled Comic Cavalcade). 12-Origin/1st app. "Blue" Starman (2nd app. in Starman, 2nd Series #3); Kubert-c 2 4 6 8 11 14
3-Metamorpho by Ramona Fradon 2 4 6 8 11 14
4,10,11: 4-Lady Cop. 10-The Outsiders. 11-Code Name: Assassin; Grell-c
1 3 4 6 8 10
5-Manhunter; Kirby-c/a/script 3 6 9 14 20 26
7,9: 7-The Creeper by Ditko (c/a). 9-Dr. Fate; Kubert-c/Simonson-a.
2 4 6 11 16 20
8-Origin/1st app. The Warlord; Grell-c/a (11/75) 5 10 15 31 53 75
13-Return of the New Gods; Darkseid app.; 1st new costume Orion; predates New Gods #12 by more than a year 3 6 9 19 30 40

FIRST KISS
Charlton Comics: Dec, 1957 - No. 40, Jan, 1965
V1#1 4 8 12 28 47 65
V1#2-10 3 6 9 18 28 38
11-40 3 6 9 14 19 24

FIRST LOVE ILLUSTRATED
Harvey Publications(Home Comics)(True Love): 2/49 - No. 9, 6/50; No. 10, 1/51 - No. 86, 3/58; No. 87, 9/58 - No. 88, 11/58; No. 89, 11/62, No. 90, 2/63
1-Powell-a(2) 20 40 60 114 182 250
2-Powell-a 12 24 36 69 97 125
3-"Was I Too Fat To Be Loved" story 15 30 45 83 124 165
4-10 9 18 27 52 69 85
11,12,14-30: 30-Lingerie panel 8 16 24 42 54 65
13-"I Joined a Teen-age Sex Club" story 11 22 33 62 86 110
31-34,37,39-49: 49-Last pre-code (2/55) 7 14 21 37 46 55
35-Used in **SOTI**, illo "The title of this comic book is First Love"
20 40 60 117 189 260
36-Communism story, "Love Slaves" 12 24 36 69 97 125
38-Nostrand-a 9 18 27 47 61 75
50-66,71-90 6 12 18 31 38 45
67-70-Kirby-c 8 16 24 42 54 65
NOTE: ***Disbrow** a-13. **Orlando** c-87. **Powell** a-1, 3-5, 7, 10, 11, 13-17, 19-24, 26-29, 33,35-41, 43, 45, 46, 50, 54, 55, 57, 58, 61-63, 65, 71-73, 76, 79r, 82, 84, 88.*

FIRST MEN IN THE MOON (See Movie Comics)

FIRST ROMANCE MAGAZINE
Home Comics(Harvey Publ.)/True Love: 8/49 - #6, 6/50; #7, 6/51 - #50, 2/58; #51, 9/58 - #52, 11/58
1 18 36 54 103 162 220
2 11 22 33 62 86 110
3-5 9 18 27 52 69 85
6-10,28: 28-Nostrand-a(Powell swipe) 8 16 24 42 54 65
11-20 7 14 21 37 46 55
21-27,29-32: 32-Last pre-code issue (2/55) 7 14 21 35 43 50

Fish Police #18 © Apple Comics

The Flame #2 © FOX

The Flash #108 © DC

	GD 2.0	VG 4.0	FN 6.0	VF 8.0	VF/NM 9.0	NM- 9.2
33-40,44-52	6	12	18	31	38	45
41-43-Kirby-c	8	16	24	42	54	65

NOTE: *Powell a-1-5, 8-10, 14, 18, 20-22, 24, 25, 28, 36, 46, 48, 51.*

FIRST TRIP TO THE MOON (See Space Adventures No. 20)

FIRST WAVE (Based on Sci-Fi Channel TV series)
Andromeda Entertainment: Dec, 2000 - No. 4, Jun, 2001 ($2.99)

1-4-Kuhoric-s/Parsons-a/Busch-c 3.00

FIRST WAVE (Also see Batman/Doc Savage Special #1)
DC Comics: May, 2010 - No. 6, Mar, 2011 ($3.99, limited series)

1-6-Batman, Doc Savage and The Spirit app.; Azzarello-s/Morales-a/JG Jones-c 4.00
... Special 1 (6/11, $3.99) Winslade-a/Jones-c 4.00
HC (2011, $29.99, dustjacket) r/#1-6 & Batman/Doc Savage Special #1; sketch art 30.00

FIRST X-MEN
Marvel Comics: Oct, 2012 - No. 5, Mar, 2013 ($3.99, limited series)

1-5: 1-Neal Adams-a/c; Adams & Gage-s; Wolverine & Sabretooth 1st meet Xavier 4.00

FISH POLICE (Inspector Gill of the...#2, 3)
Fishwrap Productions/Comico V2#5-17/Apple Comics #18 on:
Dec, 1985 - No. 11, Nov, 1987 ($1.50, B&W); V2#5, April, 1988 - V2#17, May, 1989 ($1.75, color) No. 18, Aug, 1989 - No. 26, Dec, 1990 ($2.25, B&W)

1-11, 1(5/86),2-2nd print, V2#5-17-(Color): V2#5-11. 12-17, new-a, 18-26 ($2.25-c, B&W). 18-Origin Inspector Gill 3.00
Special 1($2.50, 7/87, Comico) 3.00
Graphic Novel: Hairballs (1987, $9.95, TPB) r/#1-4 in color 10.00

FISH POLICE
Marvel Comics: V2#1, Oct, 1992 - No. 6, Mar, 1993 ($1.25)

V2#1-6: 1-Hairballs Saga begins; r/#1 (1985) 3.00

FISTFUL OF BLOOD
IDW Publishing: Oct, 2015 - No. 4, Jan, 2016 ($4.99, limited series)

1-4-Eastman-s/Bisley-a; remastering of series from Heavy Metal magazine 5.00

5 CENT COMICS (Also see Whiz Comics)
Fawcett Publ.: Feb, 1940 (8 pgs., reg. size, B&W)

nn - 1st app. Dan Dare. Ashcan comic, not distributed to newsstands, only for in-house use. A CGC certified 9.6 copy sold for $10,800 in 2003, and a CGC 9.4 sold for $11,500 in 2005.

5 RONIN (Marvel characters in Samurai setting)
Marvel Comics: May, 2011 - No. 5, May, 2011 ($2.99, weekly limited series)

1-Wolverine. 2-Hulk. 3-Punisher. 4-Psylocke; Mack-c. 5-Deadpool 3.00

5-STAR SUPER-HERO SPECTACULAR (See DC Special Series No. 1)

FIVE WEAPONS
Image Comics: Feb, 2013 - No. 10, Jul, 2014 ($3.50)

1-10-Jimmie Robinson-s/a/c 3.50

FIX, THE
Image Comics: Apr, 2016 - Present ($3.99)

1-8-Nick Spencer-s/Steve Lieber-a 4.00

FLAME, THE (See Big 3 & Wonderworld Comics)
Fox Features Synd.: Sum, 1940 - No. 8, Jan, 1942 (#1,2: 68 pgs; #3-8: 44 pgs.)

	GD 2.0	VG 4.0	FN 6.0	VF 8.0	VF/NM 9.0	NM- 9.2
1-Flame stories reprinted from Wonderworld #5-9; origin The Flame; Lou Fine-a (36 pgs.),	389	778	1167	2723	4762	6800
2-Fine-a(2); Wing Turner by Tuska; r/Wonderworld #3,10	142	284	426	909	1555	2200
3-8: 3-Powell-a	107	214	321	680	1165	1650

FLAME, THE (Formerly Lone Eagle)
Ajax/Farrell Publications (Excellent Publ.): No. 5, Dec-Jan, 1954-55 - No. 3, April-May, 1955

	GD 2.0	VG 4.0	FN 6.0	VF 8.0	VF/NM 9.0	NM- 9.2
5(#1)-1st app. new Flame	57	114	171	362	619	875
2,3	37	74	111	222	361	500

FLAMING CARROT COMICS (Also see Junior Carrot Patrol)
Killian Barracks Press: Summer-Fall, 1981 ($1.95, one shot) (Lg size, 8-1/2x11")

	GD 2.0	VG 4.0	FN 6.0	VF 8.0	VF/NM 9.0	NM- 9.2
1-Bob Burden-c/a/scripts; serially #'ed to 6500	5	10	15	34	60	85

FLAMING CARROT COMICS (See Anything Goes, Cerebus, Teenage Mutant Ninja Turtles/Flaming Carrot Crossover & Visions)
Aardvark-Vanaheim/Renegade Press #6-17/Dark Horse #18-31:
May, 1984 - No. 5, Jan, 1985; No. 6, Mar, 1985 - No. 31, Oct, 1994 ($1.70/$2.00, B&W)

	GD 2.0	VG 4.0	FN 6.0	VF 8.0	VF/NM 9.0	NM- 9.2
1-Bob Burden story/art	5	10	15	30	50	70
2	3	6	9	16	23	30
3	2	4	6	10	16	20
4-6	2	4	6	9	12	15
7-9	1	3	4	6	8	10
10-12						6.50
13-15						4.00
15-Variant without cover price						6.00
16-(6/87) 1st app. Mystery Men	1	2	3	5	6	8
17-20: 18-1st Dark Horse issue						4.00
21-23,25: 25-Contains trading cards; TMNT app.						3.00
24-(2.50, 52 pgs.)-10th anniversary issue						4.00
26-28: 26-Begin $2.25-c. 26,27-Teenage Mutant Ninja Turtles x-over. 27-McFarlane-c						3.00
29-31-(2.50-c)						3.00
Annual 1(1/97, $5.00)						5.00
... & Reid Fleming, World's Toughest Milkman (12/02, $3.99) listed as #32 in indicia						4.00
... :Fortune Favors the Bold (1998, $16.95, TPB) r/#19-24						17.00
... :Men of Mystery (7/97, $12.95, TPB) r/#1-3, + new material						13.00
... 's Greatest Hits (4/98, $17.95, TPB) r/#12-18, + new material						18.00
... :The Wild Shall Wild Remain (1997, $17.95, TPB) r/#4-11, + new s/a						18.00

FLAMING CARROT COMICS
Image Comics (Desperado): Dec, 2004 - 2006 ($2.95/$3.50, B&W)

1-3-Bob Burden story/art 3.00
4-($3.50-c) 3.50
... Special #1 (3/06, $3.50) All Photo comic 3.50
... Vol. 6 (2006, $14.99) r/1-4 & Special #1; intro. by Brian Bolland 15.00

FLAMING LOVE
Quality Comics Group (Comic Magazines): Dec, 1949 - No. 6, Oct, 1950 (Photo covers #2-6) (52 pgs.)

	GD 2.0	VG 4.0	FN 6.0	VF 8.0	VF/NM 9.0	NM- 9.2
1-Ward-c/a (9 pgs.)	45	90	135	284	480	675
2	22	44	66	132	216	300
3-Ward-a (9 pgs.); Crandall-a	32	64	96	188	307	425
4-6: 4-Gustavson-a	20	40	60	114	182	250

FLAMING WESTERN ROMANCES (Formerly Target Western Romances)
Star Publications: No. 3, Mar-Apr, 1950

	GD 2.0	VG 4.0	FN 6.0	VF 8.0	VF/NM 9.0	NM- 9.2
3-Robert Taylor, Arlene Dahl photo on-c with biographies inside; L. B. Cole-c	36	72	108	211	343	475

FLARE (Also see Champions for 1st app. & League of Champions)
Hero Comics/Hero Graphics Vol. 2 on: Nov, 1988 - No. 3, Jan, 1989 ($2.75, color, 52 pgs); V2#1, Nov, 1990 - No. 7, Nov, 1991 ($2.95/$3.50, color, mature, 52 pgs.);V2#8, Oct, 1992 - No. 16, Feb, 1994 ($3.50/$3.95, B&W, 36 pgs.)

V1#1-3, V2#1-16: 5-Eternity Smith returns. 6-Intro The Tigress 4.00
Annual 1(1992, $4.50, B&W, 52 pgs.)-Champions-r 4.50

FLARE ADVENTURES
Hero Graphics: Feb, 1992 - No. 12, 1993? ($3.50/$3.95)

1 (90¢, color, 20 pgs.) 4.00
2-12-Flip books w/Champions Classics 4.00

FLASH, THE (See Adventure Comics, The Brave and the Bold, Crisis On Infinite Earths, DC Comics Presents, DC Special, DC Special Series, DC Super-Stars, The Greatest Flash Stories Ever Told, Green Lantern, Impulse, JLA, Justice League of America, Showcase, Speed Force, Super Team Family, Titans & World's Finest)

FLASH, THE (1st Series)(Formerly Flash Comics)(See Showcase #4,8,13,14)
National Periodical Publ./DC: No. 105, Feb-Mar, 1959 - No. 350, Oct, 1985

	GD 2.0	VG 4.0	FN 6.0	VF 8.0	VF/NM 9.0	NM- 9.2
105-(2-3/59)-Origin Flash(retold), & Mirror Master (1st app.)	560	1120	2000	7000	16,500	26,000
106-Origin Grodd & Pied Piper; Flash's 1st visit to Gorilla City; begin Grodd the Super Gorilla trilogy (Scarce)	241	482	723	1988	4494	7000
107-Grodd trilogy, part 2	125	250	375	1000	2250	3500
108-Grodd trilogy ends	104	208	312	832	1866	2900
109-2nd app. Mirror Master	86	172	258	688	1544	2400
110-Intro/origin Kid Flash who later becomes Flash in Crisis On Infinite Earths #12; begin Kid Flash trilogy, ends #112 (also in #114,116,118); 1st app. & origin of The Weather Wizard	190	380	570	1568	3534	5500
111-2nd Kid Flash tryout; Cloud Creatures	61	122	183	488	1094	1700
112-Origin & 1st app. Elongated Man (4-5/60); also apps. in #115,119,130	82	164	246	656	1478	2300
113-Origin & 1st app. Trickster	56	112	168	448	999	1550
114-Captain Cold app. (see Showcase #8)	46	92	138	340	770	1200
115,116,118-120: 119-Elongated Man marries Sue Dearborn. 120-Flash & Kid Flash team-up for 1st time	37	74	111	274	612	950
117-Origin & 1st app. Capt. Boomerang; 1st & only S.A. app. Winky Blinky & Noddy	46	92	138	340	770	1200
121,122: 122-Origin & 1st app. The Top	30	60	90	216	483	750
123-(9/61)-Re-intro. Golden Age Flash; origins of both Flashes; 1st mention of an Earth II where DC G. A. heroes live	207	414	621	1708	3854	6000

The Flash #171 © DC

The Flash #325 © DC

The Flash (2nd series) #200 © DC

	GD 2.0	VG 4.0	FN 6.0	VF 8.0	VF/NM 9.0	NM- 9.2
124-Last 10¢ issue	25	50	75	175	388	600
125-128,130: 127-Return of Grodd-c/story. 128-Origin & 1st app. Abra Kadabra. 130-(7/62)-1st Gauntlet of Super-Villains (Mirror Master, Capt. Cold, The Top, Capt. Boomerang & Trickster)	23	46	69	161	356	550
129-2nd G.A. Flash x-over; J.S.A. cameo in flashback (1st S.A. app. G.A. Green Lantern, Hawkman, Atom, Black Canary & Dr. Mid-Nite. Wonder Woman (1st S.A. app.?) appears)	27	54	81	194	435	675
131-134,136,138: 131-Early Green Lantern x-over (9/62). 136-1st Dexter Miles	17	34	51	117	259	400
135-1st app. of Kid Flash's yellow costume (3/63)	19	38	57	131	291	450
137-G.A. Flash x-over; J.S.A. cameo (1st S.A. app.)(1st real app. since 2-3/51); 1st S.A. app. Vandal Savage & Johnny Thunder; JSA team decides to re-form	38	76	114	281	628	975
139-Origin & 1st app. Prof. Zoom	125	250	375	800	1500	2200
140-Origin & 1st app. Heat Wave	17	34	51	117	259	400
141-146,148-150: 142-Trickster app.	12	24	36	82	179	275
147-2nd Prof. Zoom	16	32	48	110	243	375
151-Engagement of Barry Allen & Iris West; G.A. Flash vs. The Shade.	13	26	39	89	195	300
152-159: 159-Dr. Mid-Nite cameo	10	20	30	64	132	200
160-(80-Pg. Giant G-21); G.A. Flash & Johnny Quick-r	11	22	33	73	157	240
161-164,166,167: 167-New facts about Flash's origin	8	16	24	54	102	150
165-Barry Allen weds Iris West	8	16	24	56	108	160
168,170: 168-Green Lantern-c/app. 170-Dr. Mid-Nite, Dr. Fate, G.A. Flash x-over	8	16	24	54	102	150
169-(80-Pg. Giant G-34)-New facts about origin	9	18	27	57	111	165
171,172,174,176,177,179,180: 171-JLA, Green Lantern, Atom flashbacks. 174-Barry Allen reveals I.D. to wife. 179-(5/68)-Flash travels to Earth-Prime and meets DC editor Julie Schwartz; 1st unnamed app. Earth-Prime (See Justice League of America #123 for 1st named app. & 3rd app. overall)	7	14	21	46	86	125
173-G.A. Flash x-over	8	16	24	54	102	150
175-2nd Superman/Flash race (12/67) (See Superman #199 & World's Finest #198,199); JLA cameo; gold kryptonite used (on J'onn J'onzz impersonating Superman)	17	34	51	117	259	400
178-(80-Pg. Giant G-46)	8	16	24	52	99	145
181-186,188,189: 186-Re-intro. Sargon. 189-Last 12¢-c	5	10	15	34	60	85
187,196: (68-Pg. Giants G-58, G-70)	6	12	18	40	73	105
190-195,197-199: 198-Zatanna 1st solo story	4	8	12	27	44	60
200	5	10	15	30	50	70
201-204,206,207: 201-New G.A. Flash story. 206-Elongated Man begins 207-Last 15¢ issue	3	6	9	21	33	45
205-(68-Pg. Giant G-82)	6	12	18	41	76	110
208-213-(52 pg.): 211-G.A. Flash origin-r/#104; Roller Derby-c. 213-Reprints #137	4	8	12	25	40	55
214-DC 100 Page Super Spectacular DC-11; origin Metal Men-r/Showcase #37; never before published G.A. Flash story	8	16	24	54	102	150
215 (52 pgs.)-Flash-r/Showcase #4; G.A. Flash x-over, continued in #216	4	8	12	27	44	60
216,220: 220-1st app. Turtle since Showcase #4	3	6	9	17	26	35
217-219: Neal Adams-a in all. 217-Green Lantern/Green Arrow series begins (9/72); 2nd G.L. & G.A. team-up series (see Green Lantern #76). 219-Last Green Arrow	5	10	15	30	50	70
221-224,227,228,230,231: 222-G. Lantern x-over. 228-(7-8/74)-Flash writer Cary Bates travels to Earth-One & meets Flash, Iris Allen & Trickster; 2nd unnamed app. Earth-Prime (See Justice League of America #123 for 1st named app. & 3rd app. overall)	3	6	9	14	19	24
225-Professor Zoom-c/app.	5	10	15	31	53	75
226-Neal Adams-p	3	6	9	16	24	32
229,232-(100 pg. issues)-G.A. Flash-r & new-a. 229-G.A. Flash & Rag Doll app. in new story	4	8	12	28	47	65
233-Professor Zoom-c/app.	3	6	9	19	30	40
234-236,238-250: 235-Green Lantern x-over. 243-Death of The Top. 245-Origin The Floronic Man in Green Lantern back-up, ends #246. 246-Last Green Lantern. 247-Jay Garrick app. 250-Intro Golden Glider	2	4	6	10	14	18
237-Professor Zoom-c/app.	3	6	9	16	23	30
251-274: 256-Death of The Top retold. 265-267-(44 pgs.). 267-Origin of Flash's uniform. 270-Intro The Clown	2	4	6	8	10	12
268,273,274,278,283,286-(Whitman variants; low print run; no issue #s shown on covers)	2	4	6	8	11	14
275,276-Iris Allen dies	2	4	6	10	14	18
275,276-(Whitman variants; low print run; no issue #s shown on covers)	2	4	6	11	16	20
277-288,290: 286-Intro/origin Rainbow Raider	1	2	3	5	6	8
289-1st Pérez DC art (Firestorm); new Firestorm back-up series begins (9/80), ends #304	2	3	4	6	8	10
291-299,301-305: 291-1st app. Saber-Tooth (villain). 295-Gorilla Grodd-c/story. 298-Intro & origin new Shade. 301-Atomic bomb-c. 303-The Top returns. 304-Intro/origin Colonel Computron; 305-G.A. Flash x-over						6.00
300-(8/81, 52 pgs.)-25th Anniversary issue; Flash's origin and life story retold; wraparound-c by Infantino; no ads	1	2	3	5	6	8
306-313-Dr. Fate by Giffen. 309-Origin Flash retold						6.00
314-322,325-340: 318-323-Creeper back-ups. 328-Iris West Allen's death retold. 329-JLA app. 340-Trial of the Flash begins						5.00
323,324-Two part Flash vs. Flash story. 323-Creeper back-up. 324-Death of Reverse Flash (Professor Zoom)	3	6	9	17	26	35
341-349: 344-Origin Kid Flash						6.00
350-Double size ($1.25) Final issue	1	2	3	5	6	8
Annual 1 (10-12/63, 84 pgs.)-Origin Elongated Man & Kid Flash-r; origin Grodd; G.A. Flash-r	32	64	96	230	515	800
Annual 1 Replica Edition (2001, $6.95)-Reprints the entire 1963 Annual						7.00
...Chronicles SC Vol. 1 (2009, $14.99)-r/Showcase #4,8,13,14 and Flash #105,106						15.00
...Chronicles SC Vol. 2 (2010, $14.99)-r/Flash #107-112						15.00
The Flash Spectacular (See DC Special Series No. 11)						
The Flash vs. The Rogues TPB (2009, $14.99) r/1st app. of classic rogues in Showcase #8 and Flash #105,106,110,113,117,122,140,155; new Van Sciver-c						15.00
The Life Story of the Flash (1997, $19.95, Hardcover) "Iris Allen's" chronicle of Barry Allen's life; comic panels w/additional text; Waid & Augustyn-s/ Kane & Staton-a/Orbik painted-c						20.00
The Life Story of the Flash (1998, $12.95, Softcover) New Orbik-c						13.00

NOTE: ***N. Adams*** *c-194, 195, 203, 204, 206-208, 211, 213, 215, 226p, 246.* ***M. Anderson*** *c-165, a(i)-195, 200-204, 206-208.* ***Austin*** *a-233i, 234i, 246i.* ***Buckler*** *a-271p, 272p; c(p)-247-250, 252, 253p, 255, 256p, 258, 262, 265-267, 269-271.* ***Giffen*** *a-306-313p; c-310p, 315.* ***Giordano*** *a-226i.* ***Sid Greene*** *a-167-174i, 229i(r).* ***Grell*** *a-237p, 238p, 240-243p; c-236.* ***Heck*** *a-198p.* ***Infantino/Anderson*** *a-135. c-135, 170-174, 192, 200, 201, 328-330.* ***Infantino/Giella*** *c-105-112, 163, 164, 166-168.* ***G. Kane*** *a-195p, 197-199p, 229r, 232r; c-197-199, 312p.* ***Kubert*** *a-108p, 215i(r); c-189-191.* ***Lopez*** *c-272.* ***Meskin*** *a-229r, 232r.* ***Perez*** *a-289-293p; c-293.* ***Starlin*** *a-294-296p.* ***Staton*** *c-263p, 264p. Green Lantern x-over-131, 143, 168, 171, 191.*

FLASH (2nd Series)(See Crisis on Infinite Earths #12 and All Flash #1)
DC Comics: June, 1987 - No. 230, Mar, 2006; No. 231, Oct, 2007 - No. 247, Feb, 2009

	GD 2.0	VG 4.0	FN 6.0	VF 8.0	VF/NM 9.0	NM- 9.2
1-Guice-c/a begins; New Teen Titans app.	2	4	6	11	16	20
2-10: 3-Intro. Kilgore. 5-Intro. Speed McGee. 7-1st app. Blue Trinity. 8,9-Millennium tie-ins. 9-1st app. The Chunk						5.00
11-61: 12-Free extra 16 pg. Dr. Light story. 19-Free extra 16 pg. Flash story. 28-Capt. Cold app. 29-New Phantom Lady app. 40-Dr. Alchemy app. 50-($1.75, 52 pgs.)						4.00
62-78,80: 62-Flash: Year One begins, ends #65. 65-Last $1.00-c. 66-Aquaman app. 69,70-Green Lantern app. 70-Gorilla Grodd story ends. 73-Re-intro Barry Allen & begin saga ("Barry Allen's" true ID revealed in #78). 76-Re-intro of Max Mercury (Quality Comics' Quicksilver), not in uniform until #77. 80-($1.25-c) Regular Edition						4.00
79,80 ($2.50): 79-(68 pgs.) Barry Allen saga ends. 80-Foil-c						5.00
81-91,93,94,0,95-99,101: 81,82-Nightwing & Starfire app. 84-Razer app. 94-Zero Hour. 0-(10/94). 95-"Terminal Velocity" begins, ends #100. 96,98,99-Kobra app. 97-Origin Max Mercury; Chillblaine app.						4.00
92-1st Impulse	3	6	9	16	23	30
100 ($2.50)-Newstand edition; Kobra & JLA app.						4.00
100 ($3.50)-Foil-c edition; Kobra & JLA app.						5.00
102-131: 102-Mongul app.; begin-$1.75-c. 105-Mirror Master app. 107-Shazam app. 108-"Dead Heat" begins; 1st app. Savitar. 109-"Dead Heat" Pt. 2 (cont'd in Impulse #10). 110-"Dead Heat" Pt. 4 (cont'd in Impulse #11). 111-"Dead Heat" finale; Savitar disappears into the Speed Force; John Fox cameo (2nd app.). 112-"Race Against Time" begins, ends #118; re-intro John Fox. 113-Tornado Twins app. 119-Final Night x-over. 127-129-Rogue's Gallery & Neron. 128,129-JLA-app.130-Morrison & Millar-s begin						3.50
132-149: 135-GL & GA app. 142-Wally almost marries Linda; Waid-s return. 144-Cobalt Blue origin. 145-Chain Lightning begins.147-Professor Zoom app. 149-Barry Allen app.						3.00
150-($2.95) Final showdown with Cobalt Blue						4.00
151-162: 151-Casey-s. 152-New Flash-c. 154-New Flash ID revealed. 159-Wally marries Linda. 162-Last Waid-s.						3.00
163-187,189-196,201-206: 163-Begin $2.25-c. 164-186-Bolland-c. 183-1st app of 2nd Trickster (Axel Walker). 196-Winslade-a. 201-Dose-a begins. 205-Batman-c/app.						3.00
188-($2.95) Mirror Master, Weather Wizard, Trickster app.						4.00
197-Origin of Zoom (Hunter Zolomon) (6/03)	4	8	12	23	37	50
198,199-Zoom app.	1	2	3	4	5	7
200-($3.50) Flash vs. Zoom; Barry Allen & Hal Jordan app.; wraparound-c	1	2	3	5	6	8
207-230: 207-211-Turner-c/Porter-a. 209-JLA app. 210-Nightwing app. 212-Origin Mirror Master. 214-216-Identity Crisis x-over. 219-Wonder Woman app. 220-Rogue War 224-Zoom & Prof. Zoom app. 225-Twins born; Barry Allen app.; last Johns-s						3.00
231-247: 231-(10/07) Waid-s/Acuña-a. 240-Grodd app.; "Dark Side Club"						3.00
#1,000,000 (11/98) 853rd Century x-over						3.00

The Flash (2011 series) #21 © DC

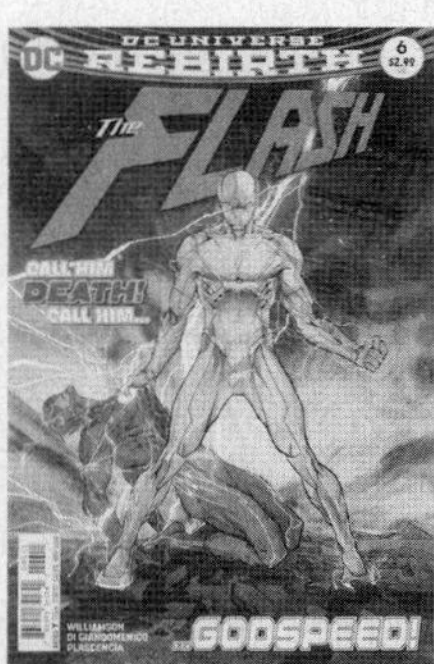

The Flash (2016 series) #6 © DC

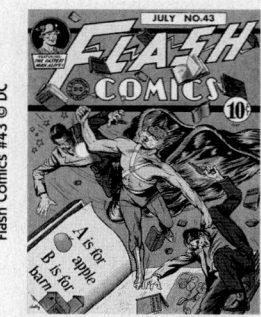

Flash Comics #43 © DC

GD 2.0 | VG 4.0 | FN 6.0 | VF 8.0 | VF/NM 9.0 | NM- 9.2

Annual 1-7,9: 2-('87-'94,'96, 68 pgs), 3-Gives history of G.A.,S.A., & Modern Age Flash in text. 4-Armaggedon 2001. 5-Eclipso-c/story. 7-Elseworlds story. 9-Legends of the Dead Earth story; J.H. Williams-a(p); Mick Gray-a(i) 4.00
Annual 8 (1995, $3.50)-Year One story 4.00
Annual 10 (1997, $3.95)-Pulp Heroes stories 4.00
Annual 11,12 ('98, '99)-11-Ghosts; Wrightson-c. 12-JLApe; Art Adams-c 4.00
Annual 13 ('00, $3.50) Planet DC; Alcatena-c/a 4.00
...: Blitz (2004, $19.95, TPB)-r/#192-200; Kolins-c 20.00
...: Blood Will Run (2002, 2008; $17.95, TPB)-r/#170-176, Secret Files #3, Iron Heights 18.00
...: Crossfire (2004, $17.95, TPB)-r/#183-191 & parts of Flash Secret Files #3 18.00
Dead Heat (2000, $14.95, TPB)-r/#108-111, Impulse #10,11 15.00
...80-Page Giant (8/98, $4.95) Flash family stories by Waid, Millar and others; Mhan-c 5.00
...80-Page Giant 2 (4/99, $4.95) Stories of Flash family, future Kid Flash, original Teen Titans and XS 5.00
...: Emergency Stop (2008, $12.99, TPB)-r/#130-135; Morrison & Millar-s 13.00
...: Ignition (2005, $14.95, TPB)-r/#201-206 15.00
...: Iron Heights (2001, $5.95)-Van Sciver-c/a; 1st app. of the prison; intro. Girder, Murmur, Double Down and Blacksmith 6.00
...: Mercury Falling (2009, $14.99, TPB)-r/Impulse #62-67 15.00
...: Our Worlds at War 1 (10/01, $2.95)-Jae Lee-c; Black Racer app. 3.00
...Plus 1 (1/1997, $2.95)-Nightwing-c/app. 4.00
Race Against Time (2001, $14.95, TPB)-r/#112-118 15.00
...: Rogues (2003, $14.95, TPB)-r/#177-182 15.00
...: Rogue War (2006, $17.99, TPB)-r/#1/2,212,218,220-225; cover gallery 18.00
...Secret Files 1 (11/97, $4.95) Origin-s & pin-ups 5.00
...Secret Files 2 (11/99, $4.95) Origin of Replicant 5.00
...Secret Files 3 (11/01; $4.95) Intro. Hunter Zolomon (who later becomes Zoom) 5.00
Special 1 (1990, $2.95, 84 pgs.)-50th anniversary issue; Kubert-c; 1st Flash story by Mark Waid; 1st app. John Fox (27th Century Flash) 5.00
Terminal Velocity (1996, $12.95, TPB)-r/#95-100. 13.00
...: The Greatest Stories Ever Told (2007, $19.99, TPB) reprints; Ross-c/Waid intro. 20.00
The Return of Barry Allen (1996, $12.95, TPB)-r/#74-79 13.00
The Secret of Barry Allen (2005, $19.99, TPB)-r/#207-211,213-217; Turner sketch page 20.00
...: The Wild Wests HC (2008, $24.99, dustjacket)-r/#231-237 25.00
...: Time Flies (2002, $5.95)-Seth Fisher-c/a; Rozum-s 6.00
TV Special 1 (1991, $3.95, 76 pgs.)-Photo-c plus behind the scenes photos of TV show; Saltares-a, Byrne scripts 5.00
Wizard #1/2 (2005) prelude to Rogue Wars; Justiano-a 10.00
...: Wonderland TPB (2007, $12.99, TPB)-r/#164-169 13.00
NOTE: *Guice a-1-9p, 11p, Annual 1p; c-1-9p, Annual 1p. **Perez** c-15-17, Annual 2i. **Charest** c/a-Annual 5p.*

FLASH, THE (Brightest Day)(Leads into Flashpoint series)
DC Comics: Jun, 2010 - No. 12, Jul, 2011 ($3.99/$2.99)

1-($3.99) Barry Allen vs. the 25th Century Rogues; Johns-s/Manapul-a/c 4.00
1-Variant-c by Tony Harris 10.00
2-12-($2.99) Capt. Boomerang app. 8-Reverse Flash origin retold 3.00
2-12-Variant covers. 2-Sook. 3-Horn. 4-Kolins. 5-Sook. 6-Garza. 7-Cooke 5.00
...: Secret Files and Origins 1 (5/10, $3.99) Johns-s/Kolins-a; profiles of the Rogues 4.00
...: The Dastardly Death of the Rogues HC (2011, $19.99, dj) r/#1-7 & Secret Files 20.00

FLASH (New DC 52)
DC Comics: Nov, 2011 - No. 52, Jul, 2016 ($2.99/$3.99)

1-Manapul & Buccellato-s; Manapul-a/c 1 3 4 6 8 10
1-Special Edition (12/14, $1.00) reprints #1 with Flash TV image above cover logo 3.00
2-24: 6,7-Captain Cold app. 8,9,13-17-Grodd app. 17-24-Reverse Flash app. 18-Takara-a. 21-Kid Flash app. 3.00
23.1, 23.2, 23.3 (11/13, $2.99, regular-c) 3.00
23.1 (11/13, $3.99, 3-D cover) "Grodd #1" on cover; Batista-a/Manapul-c 1 2 3 5 6 8
23.2 (11/13, $3.99, 3-D cover) "Reverse Flash #1" on cover; origin; Hepburn-a/Manapul-c 1 2 3 5 6 8
23.3 (11/13, $3.99, 3-D cover) "The Rogues #1" on cover; Zircher-a/Manapul-c 1 2 3 5 6 8
25-($3.99) Zero Year; Sprouse & Manapul-a; first meeting of Barry and Iris 4.00
26-39: 26-Googe-a. 27-Buccellato-s begin. 28-Deadman app. 3.00
40-49,51,52: 40-($3.99) Professor Zoom cameo. 41-47-Prof. Zoom app. 4.00
50-($4.99) The Rogues and The Riddler app.; back-up Kid Flash story 5.00
#0 (11/12, $2.99) Barry's childhood and origin re-told; Manapul-a/c 3.00
Annual #1 (10/12, $4.99) Continued from #12; origin of Glider; Kolins-a 5.00
Annual #2 (9/13, $4.99) Green Lantern app.; Basri-a 5.00
Annual #3 (6/14, $4.99) Intro. Wally West; Grodd app.; leads into Flash #31 5.00
Annual #4 (9/15, $4.99) Jensen-s/Dazo-a; background on Eobard Thawne; cont'd in #43 5.00
...: Futures End 1 (11/14, $2.99, reg.-c) Five years later; Wally West gains speed power 3.00
...: Futures End 1 (11/14, $3.99, 3-D cover) 4.00

FLASH, THE (DC Rebirth)
DC Comics: Aug, 2016 - Present ($2.99)

1-17: 1-3-Williamson-s/Di Giandomenico-a. 3-Intro Godspeed. 8-Wally becomes the new Kid Flash in costume. 9-Flash of Two Worlds cover swipe; both Wallys app. 10-12-The Shade app. 14-17-Rogues Reloaded 3.00
...: Rebirth (8/16) Williamson-s/Di Giandomenico-a; Wally West & Batman app. 3.00

FLASH, THE (See Tangent Comics/ The Flash)

FLASH AND GREEN LANTERN: THE BRAVE AND THE BOLD
DC Comics: Oct, 1999 - No. 6, Mar, 2000 ($2.50, limited series)

1-6-Waid & Peyer-s/Kitson-a. 4-Green Arrow app.; Grindberg-a(p) 3.00
TPB (2001, $12.95) r/#1-6 13.00

FLASH COMICS
DC Comics:. Dec. 1939

1-Ashcan comic, not distributed to newsstands, only for in-house use. Cover art is Adventure Comics #41 and interior from All-American Comics #8. A CGC certified 9.6 sold for $11,500 in 2004. A CGC certified 9.4 sold for $6,572.50 in 2008. A CGC certified 9.6 sold for $8,513 in 2013.

FLASH COMICS (Whiz Comics No. 2 on)
Fawcett Publications: Jan, 1940 (12 pgs., B&W, regular size)
(Not distributed to newsstands; printed for in-house use)

NOTE: ***Whiz Comics** #2 was preceded by two books, **Flash Comics** and **Thrill Comics**, both dated Jan, 1940, (12 pgs, B&W, regular size) and were not distributed. These two books are identical except for the title, and were sent out to major distributors as ad copies to promote sales. It is believed that the complete 68 page issue of Fawcett's **Flash** and **Thrill Comics** #1 was finished and ready for publication with the January date. Since DC Comics was also about to publish a book with the same date and title, Fawcett hurriedly printed up the black and white version of **Flash Comics** to secure copyright before DC. The inside covers are blank, with the covers and inside pages printed on a high quality uncoated paper stock.The eight page origin story of Captain Thunder is composed of pages 1-7 and 13 of the Captain Marvel story essentially as they appeared in the first issue of **Whiz Comics**. The balloon dialogue on page thirteen was relettered to tie the story into the end of page seven in **Flash** and **Thrill Comics** to produce a shorter version of the origin story for copyright purposes. Obviously, DC acquired the copyright and Fawcett dropped **Flash** as well as **Thrill** and came out with **Whiz Comics** a month later. Fawcett never used the cover to **Flash** and **Thrill** #1, designing a new cover for **Whiz Comics**. Fawcett also must have discovered that Captain Thunder had already been used by another publisher (Captain Terry Thunder by Fiction House). All references to Captain Thunder were relettered to Captain Marvel before appearing in **Whiz**.*

1-(nn on-c, #1 on inside)-Origin & 1st app. Captain Thunder. Cover by C.C. Beck. Eight copies of Flash and three copies of Thrill exist. All 3 copies of Thrill sold in 1986 for between $4,000-$10,000 each. A NM copy of Thrill sold in 1987 for $12,000. A VG copy of Thrill sold in 1987 for $9000 cash. A VF(8.0) copy of Thrill sold in 2003 for $11,400. A CGC certified 9.0 copy of the Flash Comics version sold for $10,117.50 in 2006. A CGC certified 9.4 copy of the Flash Comics version sold for $14,340 in 2008. A CGC certified 9.0 copy of the Thrill Comics version sold for $20,315 in 2008. A CGC certified 8.0 copy sold for $12,999 in 2012.

FLASH COMICS (The Flash No. 105 on) (Also see All-Flash)
National Periodical Publ./All-American: Jan, 1940 - No. 104, Feb, 1949

1-The Flash (origin/1st app.) by Harry Lampert, Hawkman (origin/1st app.) by Gardner Fox, The Whip, & Johnny Thunder (origin/1st app.) by Stan Asch; Cliff Cornwall by Moldoff, Flash Picture Novelets (later Minute Movies w/#12) begin; Moldoff (Shelly) cover; 1st app. Shiera Sanders who later becomes Hawkgirl, #24; reprinted in Famous First Edition (on sale 11/10/39); The Flash-c 15,000 30,000 45,000 110,000 160,000 210,000
1-Reprint, Oversize 13-1/2x10". **WARNING:** This comic is an exact reprint of the original except for its size. DC published it in 1974 with a second cover titling it as a Famous First Edition. There have been many reported cases of the outer cover being removed and the interior sold as the original edition. The reprint with the new outer cover removed is practically worthless. See Famous First Edition for value.

2-Rod Rian begins, ends #11; Hawkman-c 1250 2500 3750 8000 14,000 20,000
3-King Standish begins (1st app.), ends #41 (called The King #16-37,39-41); E.E. Hibbard-a begins on Flash 459 918 1377 3350 5925 8500
4-Moldoff (Shelly) Hawkman begins; The Whip-c 331 662 993 2317 4059 5800
5-The King-c 271 542 813 1734 2967 4200
6-2nd Flash-c (alternates w/Hawkman #6 on) 676 1352 2028 4935 8718 12,500
7-2nd Hawkman-c; 1st Moldoff Hawkman-c 622 1244 1866 4541 8021 11,500
8-New logo begins; classic Moldoff Flash-c 400 800 1200 2800 4900 7000
9,10: 9-Moldoff Hawkman-c; 10-Classic Moldoff Flash-c 411 822 1233 2877 5039 7200
11-13,15-20: 12-Les Watts begins; "Sparks" #16 on. 13-Has full page ad for All Star Comics #3. 17-Last Cliff Cornwall 258 516 774 1651 2826 4000
14-World War II cover 300 600 900 1920 3310 4700
21-Classic Hawkman-c 248 496 744 1575 2713 3850
22,23 232 464 696 1485 2543 3600
24-Shiera becomes Hawkgirl (12/41); see All-Star Comics #5 for 1st app. 258 516 774 1651 2826 4000
25-28,30: 28-Last Les Sparks. 152 304 456 965 1658 2350
29-Ghost Patrol begins (origin/1st app.), ends #104 161 322 483 1030 1765 2500
31-Classic Hawkman dragon-c 174 348 522 1114 1907 2700

Flash Gordon (1988 series) #1 © KING

Flash Gordon: Kings Cross #1 © KING

Flash: Season Zero #9 © DC

	GD 2.0	VG 4.0	FN 6.0	VF 8.0	VF/NM 9.0	NM- 9.2
32,34,35,37-40:	145	290	435	921	1586	2250
33-Classic Hawkman WWII-c; origin The Shade	258	516	774	1651	2826	4000
36-1st app. Rag Doll (see Flash #229)	155	310	465	992	1696	2400
41-50	129	258	387	826	1413	2000
51-61: 52-1st computer in comics, c/s (4/44). 59-Last Minute Movies. 61-Last Moldoff Hawkman	103	206	309	659	1130	1600
62-Hawkman by Kubert begins	126	252	378	806	1378	1950
63-66,68-85: 66,68-Hop Harrigan app. 70-Mutt & Jeff app. 80-Atom begins, ends #104	97	194	291	621	1061	1500
67-Hawkman dinosaur-c; Hop Harrigan app.	116	232	348	742	1271	1800
86-Intro. The Black Canary in Johnny Thunder (8/47); see All-Star #38.	1500	3000	4500	9000	12,000	15,000
87,88,90: 87-Intro. The Foil. 88-Origin Ghost.	142	284	426	909	1555	2200
89-Intro villain The Thorn (scarce)	271	542	813	1734	2967	4200
91,93-99: 98-Atom & Hawkman don new costumes	148	296	444	947	1624	2300
92-1st solo Black Canary plus-c; rare in Mint due to black ink smearing on white-c	432	864	1296	3154	5577	8000
100 (10/48),103(Scarce)-52 pgs. each	300	600	900	1950	3375	4800
101,102(Scarce)	277	554	831	1759	3030	4300
104-Origin The Flash retold (Scarce)	757	1514	2271	5526	9763	14,000

NOTE: ***Irwin Hasen** a-Wheaties Giveaway. c-97, Wheaties Giveaway. **E.E. Hibbard** c-6, 12, 20, 24, 26, 28, 30, 44, 46, 48, 50, 62, 66, 68, 69, 72, 74, 76, 78, 80, 82. **Infantino** a-86p, 90, 93-95, 99-104; c-90, 92, 93, 97, 99, 101, 103. **Kinstler** a-87, 89(Hawkman); c-87. **Chet Kozlak** c-77, 79, 81. **Krigstein** a-94. **Kubert** a-62-76, 83, 85, 86, 88-104; c-63, 65, 67, 70, 71, 73, 75, 83, 85, 86, 88, 89, 91, 94, 96, 98, 100, 104. **Moldoff** a-3; c-3, 7-11, 13-17, plus odd #'s 19-61. **Martin Naydell** c-52, 54, 56, 58, 60, 64, 84.*

FLASH DIGEST, THE (See DC Special Series #24)

FLASH GORDON (See Defenders Of The Earth, Eat Right to Work..., Giant Comic Album, King Classics, King Comics, March of Comics #118, 133, 142, The Phantom #18, Street Comix & Wow Comics, 1st series)

FLASH GORDON
Dell Publishing Co.: No. 25, 1941; No. 10, 1943 - No. 512, Nov, 1953

	GD 2.0	VG 4.0	FN 6.0	VF 8.0	VF/NM 9.0	NM- 9.2
Feature Books 25 (#1)(1941))-r-not by Raymond	161	322	483	1030	1765	2500
Four Color 10(1942)-by Alex Raymond; reprints "The Ice Kingdom"	86	172	258	688	1544	2400
Four Color 84(1945)-by Alex Raymond; reprints "The Fiery Desert"	42	84	126	311	698	1085
Four Color 173	21	42	63	147	324	500
Four Color 190-Bondage-c; "The Adventures of the Flying Saucers"; 5th Flying Saucer story (6/48)- see The Spirit 9/28/47(1st), Shadow Comics V7#10 (2nd, 1/48), Captain Midnight #60 (3rd, 2/48) & Boy Commandos #26 (4th, 3-4/48)	23	46	69	161	356	550
Four Color 204,247	16	32	48	110	243	375
Four Color 424-Painted-c	11	22	33	76	163	250
2(5-7/53-Dell)-Painted-c; Evans-a?	9	18	27	60	120	180
Four Color 512-Painted-c	9	18	27	60	120	180

FLASH GORDON (See Tiny Tot Funnies)
Harvey Publications: Oct, 1950 - No. 4, April, 1951

	GD 2.0	VG 4.0	FN 6.0	VF 8.0	VF/NM 9.0	NM- 9.2
1-Alex Raymond-a; bondage-c; reprints strips from 7/14/40 to 12/8/40	42	84	126	265	445	625
2-Alex Raymond-a; r/strips 12/15/40-4/27/41	27	54	81	158	259	360
3,4-Alex Raymond-a; 3-bondage-c; r/strips 5/4/41-9/21/41. 4-r/strips 10/24/37-3/27/38	26	52	78	154	252	350
5-(Rare)-Small size-5-1/2x8-1/2"; B&W; 32 pgs.; Distributed to some mail subscribers only	84	168	252	538	919	1300

(Also see All-New No. 15, Boy Explorers No. 2, and Stuntman No. 3)

FLASH GORDON
Gold Key: June, 1965

	GD 2.0	VG 4.0	FN 6.0	VF 8.0	VF/NM 9.0	NM- 9.2
1 (1947 reprint)-Painted-c	7	14	21	46	86	125

FLASH GORDON (Also see Comics Reading Libraries in the Promotional Comics section)
King #1-11/Charlton #12-18/Gold Key #19-23/Whitman #28 on:
9/66 - #11, 12/67; #12, 2/69 - #18, 1/70; #19, 9/78 - #37, 3/82 (Painted covers No. 19-30, 34)

	GD 2.0	VG 4.0	FN 6.0	VF 8.0	VF/NM 9.0	NM- 9.2
1-1st S.A. app Flash Gordon; Williamson c/a(2); E.C. swipe/Incredible S.F. #32; Mandrake story	7	14	21	49	92	135
1-Army giveaway(1968)("Complimentary" on cover)(Same as regular #1 minus Mandrake story & back-c)	4	8	12	28	47	65
2-8: 2-Bolle, Gil Kane-c; Mandrake story. 3-Williamson-c. 4-Secret Agent X-9 begins, Williamson-c/a(3). 5-Williamson-c/a(2). 6,8-Crandall-a. 7-Raboy-a (last in comics?). 8-Secret Agent X-9-r	4	8	12	28	47	65
9-13: 9,10-Raymond-r. 10-Buckler's 1st pro work (11/67). 11-Crandall-a. 12-Crandall-c/a. 13-Jeff Jones-a (15 pgs.)	4	8	12	27	44	60
14,15: 15-Last 12¢ issue	3	6	9	19	30	40
16,17: 17-Brick Bradford story	3	6	9	16	24	32
18-Kaluta-a (3rd pro work?)(see Teen Confessions)	3	6	9	21	33	45
19(9/78, G.K.), 20-26	2	4	6	8	10	12
27-29,34-37: 34-37-Movie adaptation	2	4	6	8	11	14
30 (10/80) (scarce, from Whitman 3-pack only, 40¢-c)	4	8	12	27	44	60
30 (7/81; re-issue, 50¢-c), 31-33-single issues	2	4	6	11	16	20
31-33 (Bagged 3-pack): Movie adaptation; Williamson-a.						60.00

NOTE: ***Aparo** a-8. **Bolle** a-21, 22. **Boyette** a-14-18. **Briggs** c-10. **Buckler** a-10. **Crandall** c-6. **Estrada** a-3. **Gene Fawcette** a-29, 30, 34, 37. **McWilliams** a-31-33, 36.*

FLASH GORDON
DC Comics: June, 1988 - No. 9, Holiday, 1988-'89 ($1.25, mini-series)

1-9: 1,5-Painted-c — 4.00

FLASH GORDON
Marvel Comics: June, 1995 - No. 2, July, 1995 ($2.95, limited series)

1,2: Schultz scripts; Williamson-a — 3.00

FLASH GORDON (The Mercy Wars)
Ardden Entertainment: Aug, 2008 - No. 6, Jul, 2009 ($3.99)

1-6: 1-Deneen-s/Green-a; two covers — 4.00
...: The Mercy Wars #0 (4/09, $2.99) — 3.00

FLASH GORDON
Dynamite Entertainment: 2014 ($3.99)

1-8: 1-Parker-s/Shaner-a; six covers. 2-8-Multiple covers on each — 4.00
Annual 2014 ($7.99, squarebound) Short stories of the characters' pasts — 8.00
Holiday Special 2014 ($5.99) Christmas-themed short stories by various — 6.00

FLASH GORDON: INVASION OF THE RED SWORD
Ardden Entertainment: Jan, 2011 - No. 6, Nov, 2011 ($3.99)

1-6-Deneen-s/Garcia-a. 1-Two covers — 4.00

FLASH GORDON: KINGS CROSS
Dynamite Entertainment: 2016 - No. 5, 2017 ($3.99)

1-5-Jeff Parker-s/Jesse Hamm-a; multiple covers on each; Mandrake & Phantom app. — 4.00

FLASH GORDON THE MOVIE
Western Publishing Co.: 1980 (8-1/4 x 11", $1.95, 68 pgs.)

	GD 2.0	VG 4.0	FN 6.0	VF 8.0	VF/NM 9.0	NM- 9.2
11294-Williamson-c/a; adapts movie	2	4	6	10	14	18
13743-Hardback edition	3	6	9	15	21	26

FLASH GORDON: ZEITGEIST
Dynamite Entertainment: 2011 - No. 10, 2013 ($1.00/$3.99)

1-($1.00) Flash, Dale and Zarkov head to Mongo; 4 covers by Ross, Renaud & others — 3.00
2-10-($3.99) 2-8-Three covers. 9,10-Ross-c — 4.00

FLASH/ GREEN LANTERN: FASTER FRIENDS (See Green Lantern/Flash...)
DC Comics: No. 2, 1997 ($4.95, continuation of Green Lantern/Flash: Faster Friends #1)

2-Waid/Augustyn-s — 5.00

FLASHPOINT (Elseworlds Flash)
DC Comics: Dec, 1999 - No. 3, Feb, 2000 ($2.95, limited series)

1-3-Paralyzed Barry Allen; Breyfogle-a/McGreal-s — 3.00

FLASHPOINT (Leads into DC New 52 relaunches)
DC Comics: Jul, 2011 - No. 5, Late Oct, 2011 ($3.99, limited series)

1-5-Johns-s/Andy Kubert-a; 2 covers on each. 2-4-Bonus design art. 5-New timeline — 4.00
...: Abin Sur - The Green Lantern 1-3 (8/11 - No. 3, 10/11, $2.99) Massaferra-a/c — 3.00
...: Batman Knight of Vengeance 1-3 (8/11 - No. 3, 10/11, $2.99) Risso-a/Johnson-c — 5.00
...: Canterbury Cricket, The (8/11, $2.99, one-shot) Carlin-s/Morales-a — 3.00
...: Citizen Cold 1-3 (8/11 - No. 3, 10/11, $2.99) Scott Kolins-s/a/c — 3.00
...: Deadman and the Flying Grayson 1-3 (8/11 - No. 3, 10/11, $2.99) Chiang-c — 3.00
...: Deathstroke & The Curse of the Ravager 1-3 (8/11 - No. 3, 10/11, $2.99) Bennett-a — 3.00
...: Emperor Aquaman 1-3 (8/11 - No. 3, 10/11, $2.99) Bedard-s/Syaf-c — 3.00
...: Frankenstein and the Creatures of the Unknown 1-3 (8/11 - No. 3, 10/11, $2.99) — 3.00
...: Green Arrow Industries (8/11, $2.99, one-shot) Kalvachev-c — 3.00
...: Grodd of War (8/11, $2.99, one-shot) Manapul-c — 3.00
...: Hal Jordan 1-3 (8/11 - No. 3, 10/11, $2.99) 1-Oliver-a. 2,3-Richards-a — 3.00
...: Kid Flash Lost 1-3 (8/11 - No. 3, 10/11, $2.99) Gates-s/Manapul-c; Brainiac app. — 3.00
...: Legion of Doom 1-3 (8/11 - No. 3, 10/11, $2.99) Glass-s/Sepulveda-c — 3.00
...: Lois Lane and the Resistance 1-3 (8/11 - No. 3, 10/11, $2.99) Abnett & Lanning-s — 3.00
...: Outsider, The 1-3 (8/11 - No. 3, 10/11, $2.99) Robinson-s/Nowlan-c — 3.00
...: Project Superman 1-3 (8/11 - No. 3, 10/11, $2.99) Gene Ha-c/a — 3.00
...: Reverse Flash (8/11, $2.99, one-shot) Kolins-s/Gomez-a — 5.00
...: Secret Seven 1-3 (8/11 - No. 3, 10/11, $2.99) Pérez-c on all. 1-Pérez-a. — 3.00
...: Wonder Woman and The Furies 1-3 (8/11 - No. 3, 10/11, $2.99) Aquaman app. — 3.00
...: World of Flashpoint 1-3 (8/11 - No. 3, 10/11, $2.99) Traci 13 app. — 3.00

FLASH: REBIRTH
DC Comics: Jun, 2009 - No. 6, Apr, 2010 ($3.99/$2.99, limited series)

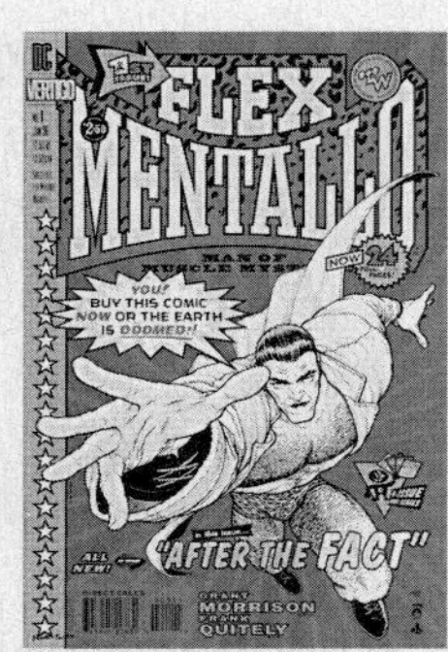

Flex Mentallo #1 © DC

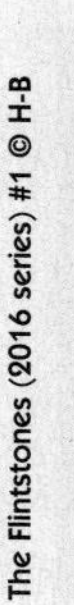
The Flintstones (2016 series) #1 © H-B

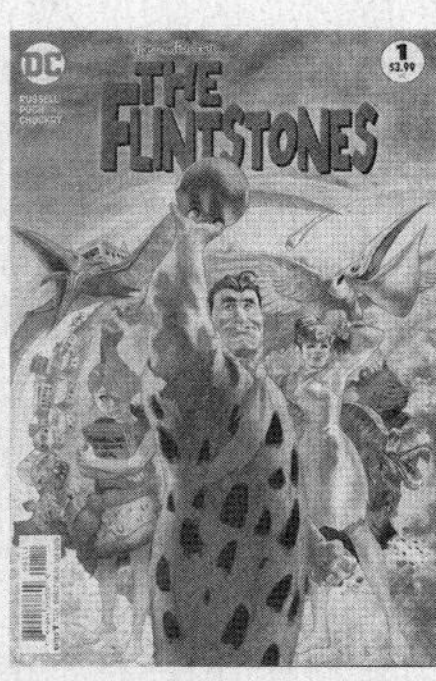

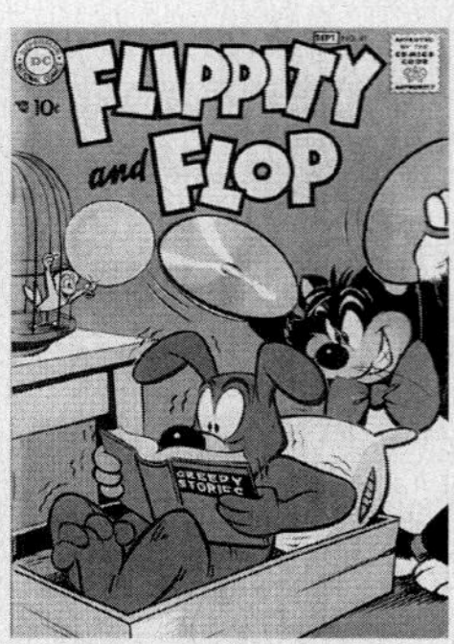

Flippity and Flop #41 © DC

GD 2.0 | VG 4.0 | FN 6.0 | VF 8.0 | VF/NM 9.0 | NM- 9.2

1-($3.99) Barry Allen's return; Johns-s/Van Sciver-a; Flash-c by Van Sciver 5.00
1-Variant Barry Allen-c by Van Sciver 10.00
1-Second thru fourth printings 4.00
1-Special Edition (8/10, $1.00) reprints #1 with "What's Next?" logo on cover 3.00
2-6-($2.99) 3-Max Mercury returns 3.00
2-6-Variant covers by Van Sciver 8.00
HC (2010, $19.99, dustjacket) r/#1-6; Johns original proposal; sketch art; cover gallery 20.00
SC (2011, $14.99) r/#1-6; Johns original proposal; sketch art; cover gallery 15.00

FLASH: SEASON ZERO (Based on the 2014 TV series)
DC Comics: Dec, 2014 - No. 12, Nov, 2015 ($2.99, printings of digital-first stories)
1-12-Photo-c on #1-8. 1-4,6-9-Hester-a. 5-Felicity Smoak app. 7-9-Intro. Suicide Squad 3.00

FLASH: THE FASTEST MAN ALIVE (3rd Series)(See Infinite Crisis)
DC Comics: Aug, 2006 - No. 13, Aug, 2007 ($2.99)
1-Bart Allen becomes the Flash; Lashley-a/Bilson & Demeo-s 3.00
1-Variant-c by Joe and Andy Kubert 5.00
2-12: 5-Cyborg app. 7-Inertia returns. 10-Zoom app. 3.00
13-Bart Allen dies; 2 covers 3.00
13-DC Nation Edition from the 2007 San Diego Comic-Con 8.00
...: Full Throttle TPB (2007, $12.99) r/#7-13, All-Flash #1, DCU Infinite Holiday Spec. story 13.00
...: Lightning in a Bottle TPB (2007, $12.99) r/#1-6 13.00

FLAT-TOP
Mazie Comics/Harvey Publ.(Magazine Publ.) No. 4 on: 11/53 - No. 3, 5/54; No. 4, 3/55 - No. 7, 9/55
1-Teenage; Flat-Top, Mazie, Mortie & Stevie begin 12 24 36 67 94 120
2,3 8 16 24 40 50 60
4-7 6 12 18 31 38 45

FLESH & BLOOD
Brainstorm Comics: Dec, 1995 ($2.95, B&W, mature)
1-Balent-c; foil-c. 3.00

FLESH AND BONES
Upshot Graphics (Fantagraphics Books): June, 1986 - No. 4, Dec, 1986 (Limited series)
1-4: Alan Moore scripts (r) & Dalgoda by Fujitake 3.00

FLESH CRAWLERS
Kitchen Sink Press: Aug, 1993 - No. 3, 1995 ($2.50, B&W, limited series, mature)
1-3 3.00

FLEX MENTALLO (Man of Muscle Mystery) (See Doom Patrol, 2nd Series)
DC Comics (Vertigo): Jun, 1996 - No. 4, Sept, 1996 ($2.50, lim. series, mature)
1-4: Grant Morrison scripts & Frank Quitely-c/a in all; banned from reprints due to Charles Atlas legal action 2 4 6 9 13 16

FLINCH (Horror anthology)
DC Comics (Vertigo): Jun, 1999 - No. 16, Jan, 2001 ($2.50)
1-16: 1-Art by Jim Lee, Quitely, and Corben. 5-Sale-c. 11-Timm-a 3.00

FLINTSTONE KIDS, THE (TV) (See Star Comics Digest)
Star Comics/Marvel Comics #5 on: Aug, 1987 - No. 11, Apr, 1989
1 1 2 3 5 6 8
2-11 5.00

FLINTSTONES, THE (TV)(See Dell Giant #48 for No. 1)
Dell Publ. Co./Gold Key No. 7 (10/62) on: No. 2, Nov-Dec, 1961 - No. 60, Sept, 1970 (Hanna-Barbera)
2-2nd app. (TV show debuted on 9/30/60); 1st app. of Cave Kids; 15¢-c thru #5 9 18 27 59 117 175
3-6(7-8/62): 3-Perry Gunnite begins. 6-1st 12¢-c 6 12 18 38 69 100
7 (10/62; 1st GK) 6 12 18 38 69 100
8-10 5 10 15 33 57 80
11-1st app. Pebbles (6/63) 8 16 24 51 96 140
12-15,17-20 4 8 12 28 47 65
16-1st app. Bamm-Bamm (1/64) 7 14 21 46 86 130
21-23,25-30,33: 26,27-2nd & 3rd app. The Grusomes. 30-1st app. Martian Mopheads (10/65). 33-Meet Frankenstein & Dracula 4 8 12 27 44 60
24-1st app. The Grusomes 5 10 15 35 63 90
31,32,35-40: 31-Xmas-c. 36-Adaptation of "the Man Called Flintstone" movie. 39-Reprints 4 8 12 23 37 50
34-1st app. The Great Gazoo 5 10 15 35 63 90
41-60: 46-Last 12¢ issue 3 6 9 20 31 42
At N. Y. World's Fair ('64)-J.W. Books (25¢)-1st printing; no date on-c (29¢ version exists, 2nd print?) Most H-B characters app.; including Yogi Bear, Top Cat, Snagglepuss and the Jetsons 5 10 15 31 53 75
At N. Y. World's Fair (1965 on-c; re-issue; Warren Pub.)
NOTE: *Warehouse find in 1984.* 2 4 6 10 14 18
Bigger & Boulder 1(#30013-211) (Gold Key Giant, 11/62, 25¢, 84 pgs.) 7 14 21 46 86 125
Bigger & Boulder 2-(1966, 25¢)-Reprints B&B No. 1 4 8 12 23 37 50
...On the Rocks (9/61, $1.00, 6-1/4x9", cardboard-c, high quality paper,116 pgs.) B&W new material 8 16 24 54 102 150
...With Pebbles & Bamm Bamm (100 pgs., G.K.)-30028-511 (paper-c, 25¢) (11/65) 6 12 18 38 69 100
NOTE: *(See Comic Album #16, Bamm-Bamm & Pebbles Flintstone, Dell Giant 48, Golden Comics Digest, March of Comics #229, 243, 271, 289, 299, 317, 327, 341, Pebbles Flintstone, Top Comics #2-4, and Whitman Comic Book.)*

FLINTSTONES, THE (TV)(...& Pebbles)
Charlton Comics: Nov, 1970 - No. 50, Feb, 1977 (Hanna-Barbera)
1 7 14 21 44 82 120
2 4 8 12 27 44 60
3-7,9,10 3 6 9 19 30 40
8- "Flintstones Summer Vacation" (Summer, 1971, 52 pgs.) 5 10 15 31 53 75
11-20,36: 36-Mike Zeck illos (early work) 3 6 9 16 23 30
21-35,38-41,43-45 3 6 9 14 19 24
37-Byrne text illos (early work; see Nightmare #20) 3 6 9 16 23 30
42-Byrne-a (2 pgs.) 3 6 9 16 23 30
46-50 2 4 6 13 18 22
Digest nn (1972, B&W, 100 pgs.) (low print run) 3 6 9 19 30 40
(Also see Barney & Betty Rubble, Dino, The Great Gazoo, & Pebbles & Bamm-Bamm)

FLINTSTONES, THE (TV)(See Yogi Bear, 3rd series) (Newsstand sales only)
Marvel Comics Group: October, 1977 - No. 9, Feb, 1979 (Hanna-Barbera)
1,7-9: 1-(30¢-c). 7-9-Yogi Bear app. 3 6 9 19 30 40
1-(35¢-c variant, limited distribution) 8 16 24 51 96 140
2,3,5,6: Yogi Bear app. 3 6 9 15 22 28
4-The Jetsons app. 3 6 9 16 24 32

FLINTSTONES, THE (TV)
Harvey Comics: Sept, 1992 - No. 13, Jun, 1994 ($1.25/$1.50) (Hanna-Barbera)
V2#1-13 4.00
...Big Book 1,2 (11/92, 3/93; both $1.95, 52 pgs.) 5.00
...Giant Size 1-3 (10/92, 4/93, 11/93; $2.25, 68 pgs.) 5.00

FLINTSTONES, THE (TV)
Archie Publications: Sept, 1995 - No. 22, June, 1997 ($1.50)
1-22 3.00

FLINTSTONES, THE (TV)
DC Comics: Sept, 2016 - Present ($3.99)
1-9: 1-6-Mark Russell-s/Steve Pugh-a; multiple covers. 2-Intro. Dino. 7-Leonardi-a; Great Gazoo app. 4.00

FLINTSTONES AND THE JETSONS, THE (TV)
DC Comics: Aug, 1997 - No. 21, May, 1999 ($1.75/$1.95/$1.99)
1 6.00
2-21: 19-Bizarro Elroy-c 3.00

FLINTSTONES CHRISTMAS PARTY, THE (See The Funtastic World of Hanna-Barbera No. 1)

FLIP
Harvey Publications: April, 1954 - No. 2, June, 1954 (Satire)
1,2-Nostrand-a each. 2-Powell-a 22 44 66 132 216 300

FLIPPER (TV)
Gold Key: Apr, 1966 - No. 3, Nov, 1967 (All have photo-c)
1 6 12 18 38 69 100
2,3 4 8 12 28 47 65

FLIPPITY & FLOP
National Per. Publ. (Signal Publ. Co.): 12-1/51-52 - No. 46, 8-10/59; No. 47, 9-11/60
1-Sam dog & his pets Flippity The Bird and Flop The Cat begin; Twiddle and Twaddle begin 34 68 102 199 325 450
2 17 34 51 98 154 210
3-5 14 28 42 82 121 160
6-10 13 26 39 74 105 135
11-20: 20-Last precode (3/55) 11 22 33 60 83 105
21-47 10 20 30 54 72 90

FLOATERS
Dark Horse Comics: Sept, 1993 - No. 5, Jan, 1994 ($2.50, B&W, lim. series)
1-5 3.00

FLOYD FARLAND (See Eclipse Graphic Album Series #11)

The Fly: Outbreak #3 © 20th Century Fox

Foolkiller (2017 series) #1 © MAR

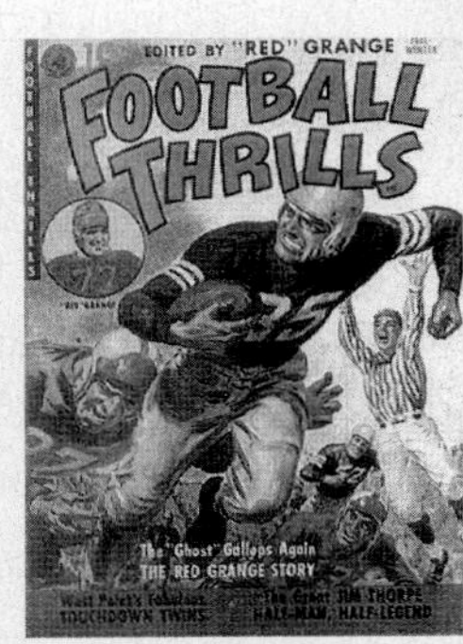

Football Thrills #1 © Z-D

	GD 2.0	VG 4.0	FN 6.0	VF 8.0	VF/NM 9.0	NM- 9.2

FLY, THE (Also see Adventures of…, Blue Ribbon Comics & Flyman)
Archie Enterprises, Inc.: May, 1983 - No. 9, Oct, 1984

1,2: 1-Mr. Justice app; origin Shield; Kirby-a; Steranko-c. 2-Ditko-a; Flygirl app. 6.00
3-5: Ditko-a in all. 4,5-Ditko-c(p) 5.00
6-9: Ditko-a in all. 6-8-Ditko-c(p) 6.00
NOTE: ***Ayers** c-9. **Buckler** a-1, 2. **Kirby** a-1. **Nebres** c-3, 4, 5i, 6, 7i. **Steranko** c-1, 2.*

FLY, THE
Impact Comics (DC): Aug, 1991 - No. 17, Dec, 1992 ($1.00)

1 4.00
2-17: 4-Vs. The Black Hood. 9-Trading card inside 3.00
Annual 1 ('92, $2.50, 68 pgs.)-Impact trading card 4.00

FLYBOY (Flying Cadets)(Also see Approved Comics #5)
Ziff-Davis Publ. Co. (Approved): Spring, 1952 - No. 2, Oct-Nov, 1952

	GD	VG	FN	VF	VF/NM	NM-
1-Saunders painted-c	20	40	60	117	189	260
2-(10-11/52)-Saunders painted-c	14	28	42	82	121	160

FLYING ACES (Aviation stories)
Key Publications: July, 1955 - No. 5, Mar, 1956

	GD	VG	FN	VF	VF/NM	NM-
1	11	22	33	62	86	110
2-5: 2-Trapani-a	7	14	21	37	46	55

FLYING A'S RANGE RIDER, THE (TV)(See Western Roundup under Dell Giants)
Dell Publishing Co.: #404, 6-7/52; #2, June-Aug, 1953 - #24, Aug, 1959 (All photo-c)

	GD	VG	FN	VF	VF/NM	NM-
Four Color 404(#1)-Titled "The Range Rider"	9	18	27	60	120	180
2	5	10	15	35	63	90
3-10	5	10	15	31	53	75
11-16,18-24	4	8	12	28	47	65
17-Toth-a	5	10	15	33	57	80

FLYING CADET (WW II Plane Photos)
Flying Cadet Publ. Co.; Jan, 1943 - V2#8, Nov, 1944 (Half photos, half comics)

	GD	VG	FN	VF	VF/NM	NM-
V1#1-Painted-c	20	40	60	117	189	260
2-Photo-c, P-47 Thunderbolt	13	26	39	72	101	130
3-9 (Two #6's, Sept. & Oct.): 4,5,6a,6b-Photo-c	12	24	36	67	94	120
V2#1-7 (1/44-9/44)(#10-16): 1,2,4-7-Photo-c	11	22	33	62	86	110
7 (#17 on cover)-Bare-breasted woman-c	41	82	123	256	428	600

FLYING COLORS 10th ANNIVERSARY SPECIAL
Flying Colors Comics: Fall 1998 ($2.95, one-shot)

1-Dan Brereton-c; pin-ups by Jim Lee and Jeff Johnson 3.00

FLYIN' JENNY
Pentagon Publ. Co./Leader Enterprises #2: 1946 - No. 2, 1947 (1945 strip-r)

	GD	VG	FN	VF	VF/NM	NM-
nn-Marcus Swayze strip-r (entire insides)	21	42	63	122	199	275
2-Baker-c; Swayze strip reprints	41	82	123	256	428	600

FLYING MODELS
H-K Publ. (Health-Knowledge Publs.): V61#3, May, 1954 (5¢, 16 pgs.)

	GD	VG	FN	VF	VF/NM	NM-
V61#3 (Rare)	9	18	27	50	65	80

FLYING NUN (TV)
Dell Publishing Co.: Feb, 1968 - No. 4, Nov, 1968

	GD	VG	FN	VF	VF/NM	NM-
1-Sally Field photo-c	6	12	18	38	69	100
2-4: 2-Sally Field photo-c	4	8	12	27	44	60

FLYING NURSES (See Sue & Sally Smith…)

FLYING SAUCERS (See The Spirit 9/28/47(1st app.), Shadow Comics V7#10 (2nd, 1/48), Captain Midnight #60 (3rd, 2/48), Boy Commandos #26 (4th, 3-4/48) & Flash Gordon Four Color 190 (5th, 6/48))

FLYING SAUCERS (See Out of This World Adventures #2)
Avon Periodicals/Realistic: 1950; 1952; 1953

	GD	VG	FN	VF	VF/NM	NM-
1(1950)-Wood-a, 21 pgs.; Fawcette-c	110	220	330	704	1202	1700
nn(1952)-Cover altered plus 2 pgs. of Wood-a not in original	55	110	165	352	601	850
nn(1953)-Reprints above (exist?)	55	110	165	352	601	850

FLYING SAUCERS (Comics)
Dell Publishing Co.: April, 1967 - No. 4, Nov, 1967; No. 5, Oct, 1969

	GD	VG	FN	VF	VF/NM	NM-
1-(12¢-c)	4	8	12	27	44	60
2-5: 5-Has same cover as #1, but with 15¢ price	3	6	9	19	30	40

FLY MAN (Formerly Adventures of The Fly; Mighty Comics #40 on)
Mighty Comics Group (Radio Comics) (Archie): No. 32, July, 1965 - No. 39, Sept, 1966 (Also see Mighty Crusaders)

	GD	VG	FN	VF	VF/NM	NM-
32,33-Comet, Shield, Black Hood, The Fly & Flygirl x-over. 33-Re-intro Wizard, Hangman (1st S.A. appearances)	5	10	15	34	60	85
34-39: 34-Shield begins. 35-Origin Black Hood. 36-Hangman x-over in Shield; re-intro. & origin of Web (1st S.A. app.). 37-Hangman, Wizard x-over in Flyman; last Shield issue. 38-Web story. 39-Steel Sterling (1st S.A. app.)	4	8	12	27	44	60

FLY, THE ; OUTBREAK (Sequel to the 1986 and 1989 movies)
IDW Publishing: Mar, 2015 - No. 5, Aug, 2015 ($3.99)

1-5-Martin Brundle's story continues; Brandon Seifert-s/Menton3-a; multiple covers 4.00

FOLLOW THE SUN (TV)
Dell Publishing Co.: May-July, 1962 - No. 2, Sept-Nov, 1962 (Photo-c)

	GD	VG	FN	VF	VF/NM	NM-
01-280-207(No.1)	5	10	15	30	50	70
12-280-211(No.2)	4	8	12	27	44	60

FOODINI (TV)(The Great…; see Jingle Dingle & Pinhead &…)
Continental Publ. (Holyoke): March, 1950 - No. 4, Aug, 1950 (All have 52 pgs.)

	GD	VG	FN	VF	VF/NM	NM-
1-Based on TV puppet show (very early TV comic)	23	46	69	136	223	310
2-Jingle Dingle begins	14	28	42	81	118	155
3,4	11	22	33	60	83	105

FOOEY (Magazine) (Satire)
Scoff Publishing Co.: Feb, 1961 - No. 4, May, 1961

	GD	VG	FN	VF	VF/NM	NM-
1	5	10	15	30	50	70
2-4	3	6	9	21	33	45

FOOFUR (TV)
Marvel Comics (Star Comics)/Marvel No. 5 on: Aug, 1987 - No. 6, Jun, 1988

1-6 5.00

FOOLKILLER (Also see The Amazing Spider-Man #225, The Defenders #73, Man-Thing #3 & Omega the Unknown #8)
Marvel Comics: Oct, 1990 - No. 10, Oct, 1991 ($1.75, limited series)

1-10: 1-Origin 3rd Foolkiller; Greg Salinger app; DeZuniga-a(i) in 1-4. 8-Spider-Man x-over 3.00

FOOLKILLER
Marvel Comics: Dec, 2007 - No. 5, Jul, 2008 ($3.99, limited series)

1-5-Hurwitz-s/Medina-a. 2-Origin 4.00

FOOLKILLER
Marvel Comics: Jan, 2017 - Present ($3.99)

1-4-Max Bemis-s/Dalibor Talajic-a. 4-Deadpool app. 4.00

FOOLKILLER: WHITE ANGELS
Marvel Comics: Sept, 2008 - No. 5, Jan, 2009 ($3.99, limited series)

1-5-Hurwitz-s/Azaceta-a 4.00

FOOM (Friends Of Ol' Marvel)
Marvel Comics: 1973 - No. 22, 1979 (Marvel fan magazine)

	GD	VG	FN	VF	VF/NM	NM-
1	8	16	24	54	102	150
2-Hulk-c by Steranko; Wolverine prototype	10	20	30	64	132	200
3,4	5	10	15	34	60	85
5-9,11: 5-Deathlok preview. 11-Kirby-a & interview	5	10	15	31	53	75
10-Article on new X-Men that came out before Giant-Size X-Men #1; new X-Men cover by Dave Cockrum	10	20	30	69	147	225
12-15: 11-Star-Lord preview. 12-Vision-c. 13-Daredevil-c. 14-Conan. 15-Howard the Duck; preview of Ms. Marvel & Capt. Britain	5	10	15	31	53	75
16-20: 16-Marvel bullpen. 17-Stan Lee issue. 19-Defenders	4	8	12	28	47	65
21-Star Wars	5	10	15	30	50	70
22-Spider-Man-c; low print run final issue	6	12	18	38	69	100

FOOTBALL THRILLS (See Tops In Adventure)
Ziff-Davis Publ. Co.: Fall-Winter, 1951-52 - No. 2, Fall, 1952 (Edited by "Red" Grange)

	GD	VG	FN	VF	VF/NM	NM-
1-Powell a(2); Saunders painted-c; Red Grange, Jim Thorpe stories	27	54	81	158	259	360
2-Saunders painted-c	18	36	54	105	165	225

FOOT SOLDIERS, THE
Dark Horse Comics: Jan, 1996 - No. 4, Apr, 1996 ($2.95, limited series)

1-4: Krueger story & Avon Oeming-a. in all. 1-Alex Ross-c. 4-John K. Snyder, III-c 3.00

FOOT SOLDIERS, THE (Volume Two)
Image Comics: Sept, 1997 - No. 5, May, 1998 ($2.95, limited series)

1-5: 1-Yeowell-a. 2-McDaniel, Hester, Sienkiewicz, Giffen-a 3.00

FOR A NIGHT OF LOVE
Avon Periodicals: 1951

	GD	VG	FN	VF	VF/NM	NM-
nn-Two stories adapted from the works of Emile Zola; Astarita, Ravielli-a; Kinstler-c	37	74	111	222	361	500

FORBIDDEN BRIDES OF THE FACELESS SLAVES IN THE SECRET HOUSE OF THE NIGHT OF DREAD DESIRE (Neil Gaiman's…)

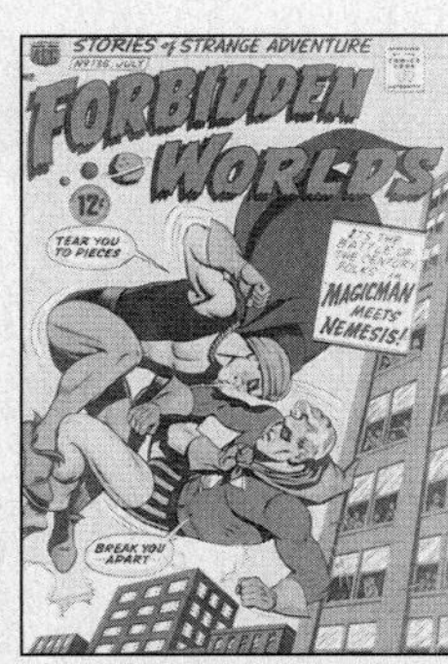

Forbidden Worlds #136 © ACG

Forever Evil #5 © DC

Forever People #3 © DC

GD VG FN VF VF/NM NM-
2.0 4.0 6.0 8.0 9.0 9.2

Dark Horse Books: 2017 ($17.99, HC graphic novel)
HC-Neil Gaiman-s/Shane Oakley-a 18.00

FORBIDDEN KNOWLEDGE: ADVENTURE BEYOND THE DOORWAY TO SOULS WITH RADICAL DREAMER (Also see Radical Dreamer)
Mark's Giant Economy Size Comics: 1996 ($3.50, B&W, one-shot, 48 pgs.)
nn-Max Wrighter app.; Wheatley-c/a/script; painted infinity-c 4.00

FORBIDDEN LOVE
Quality Comics Group: Mar, 1950 - No. 4, Sept, 1950 (52 pgs.)
1-(Scarce)-Classic photo-c; Crandall-a 123 246 369 787 1344 1900
2-(Scarce)-Classic photo-c 84 168 252 538 919 1300
3-(Scarce)-Photo-c 65 130 195 416 708 1000
4-(Scarce)-Ward/Cuidera-a; photo-c 71 142 213 454 777 1100

FORBIDDEN LOVE (See Dark Mansion of...)

FORBIDDEN PLANET
Innovation Publishing: May, 1992 - No. 4, 1992 ($2.50, limited series)
1-4: Adapts movie; painted-c 3.00

FORBIDDEN TALES OF DARK MANSION (Formerly Dark Mansion of Forbidden Love #1-4)
National Periodical Publ.: No. 5, May-June, 1972 - No. 15, Feb-Mar, 1974
5-(52 pgs.) 5 10 15 34 60 85
6-15: 13-Kane/Howard-a 3 6 9 17 26 35
NOTE: ***N. Adams*** *c-9.* ***Alcala*** *a-9-11, 13.* ***Chaykin*** *a-7,15.* ***Evans*** *a-14.* ***Heck*** *a-5.* ***Kaluta*** *a-7i, 8-12; c-7, 8, 13.* ***G. Kane*** *a-13.* ***Kirby*** *a-6.* ***Nino*** *a-8, 12, 15.* ***Redondo*** *a-14.*

FORBIDDEN WORLDS
American Comics Group: 7-8/51 - No. 34, 10-11/54; No. 35, 8/55 - No. 145, 8/67 (No. 1-5: 52 pgs.; No. 6-8: 44 pgs.)
1-Williamson/Frazetta-a (10 pgs.) 181 362 543 1158 1979 2800
2 70 140 210 445 765 1085
3-Williamson/Wood-a (7 pgs.); Frazetta (1 panel) 71 142 213 454 777 1100
4 46 92 138 290 488 685
5-Krenkel/Williamson-a (8 pgs.) 55 110 165 352 601 850
6-Harrison/Williamson-a (8 pgs.) 50 100 150 315 533 750
7,8,10: 7-1st monthly issue 37 74 111 222 361 500
9-A-Bomb explosion story 39 78 117 234 385 535
11-20 26 52 78 154 252 350
21-33: 24-E.C. swipe by Landau 21 42 63 122 199 275
34(10-11/54)(Scarce)(becomes Young Heroes #35 on)-Last pre-code issue;
A-Bomb explosion story 23 46 69 136 223 310
35(8/55)-Scarce 22 44 66 128 209 290
36-62 14 28 42 82 121 160
63,69,76,78-Williamson-a in all; w/Krenkel #69 15 30 45 83 124 165
64,66-68,70-72,74,75,77,79-85,87-90 11 22 33 60 83 105
65- "There's a New Moon Tonight" listed in #114 as holding 1st record fan mail response
15 30 45 83 124 165
73-1st app. Herbie by Ogden Whitney 53 106 159 334 567 800
86-Flying saucer-c by Schaffenberger 12 24 36 67 94 120
91-93,95-100 5 10 15 34 60 85
94-Herbie (2nd app.) 11 22 33 76 163 250
101-109,111-113,115,117-120 4 8 12 28 44 60
110,116-Herbie app. 116-Herbie goes to Hell; Elizabeth Taylor-c
8 16 24 54 102 150
114-1st Herbie-c; contains list of editor's top 20 ACG stories
10 20 30 68 144 220
121-123 3 6 9 21 33 45
124,127-130: 124-Magic Agent app. 4 8 12 23 37 50
125-Magic Agent app.; intro. & origin Magicman series, ends #141; Herbie app.
5 10 15 31 53 75
126-Herbie app. 4 8 12 27 44 60
131-139: 133-Origin/1st app. Dragonia in Magicman (1-2/66); returns in #138.
136-Nemesis x-over in Magicman 3 6 9 21 33 45
140-Mark Midnight app. by Ditko 4 8 12 23 37 50
141-145 3 6 9 19 30 40
NOTE: ***Buscema*** *a-75, 79, 81, 82, 140r.* ***Cameron*** *a-5.* ***Disbrow*** *a-10.* ***Ditko*** *a-137p, 138, 140.* ***Landau*** *a-24, 27-29, 31-34, 48, 86r, 96, 143-45.* ***Lazarus*** *a-18, 23, 24, 57.* ***Moldoff*** *a-27, 31, 139r.* ***Reinman*** *a-93.* ***Whitney*** *a-70, 115, 116, 137; c-40, 46, 57, 60, 68, 70, 78, 79, 90, 93, 94, 100, 102, 103, 106-108, 114, 129.*

FORCE, THE (See The Crusaders)

FORCE MAJEURE: PRAIRIE BAY (Also see Wild Stars)
Little Rocket Publications: May, 2002 ($2.95, B&W)
1-Tierney-s/Gil-c/a 3.00

FORCE OF BUDDHA'S PALM THE
Jademan Comics: Aug, 1988 - No. 55, Feb, 1993 ($1.50/$1.95, 68 pgs.)

GD VG FN VF VF/NM NM-
2.0 4.0 6.0 8.0 9.0 9.2

1,55-Kung Fu stories in all 5.00
2-54 4.00

FORCE WORKS
Marvel Comics: July, 1994 - No. 22, Apr, 1996 ($1.50)
1-($3.95)-Fold-out pop-up-c; Iron Man, Wonder Man, Spider-Woman, U.S. Agent & Scarlet Witch (new costume) 4.00
2-11, 13-22: 5-Blue logo & pink logo versions. 9-Intro Dreamguard. 13-Avengers app. 3.00
5-Pink logo ($2.95)-polybagged w/ 16pg. Marvel Action Hour Preview & acetate print 4.00
12 ($2.50)-Flip book w/War Machine. 4.00

FORD ROTUNDA CHRISTMAS BOOK (See Christmas at the Rotunda)

FOREIGN INTRIGUES (Formerly Johnny Dynamite; becomes Battlefield Action #16 on)
Charlton Comics: No. 14, 1956 - No. 15, Aug, 1956
14,15-Johnny Dynamite continues 8 16 24 44 57 70

FOREMOST BOYS (See 4Most)

FOREVER DARLING (Movie)
Dell Publishing Co.: No. 681, Feb, 1956
Four Color 681-w/Lucille Ball & Desi Arnaz; photo-c 10 20 30 66 138 210

FOREVER EVIL (See Justice League #23 (2013))
DC Comics: Nov, 2013 - No. 7, Jul, 2014 ($3.99, limited series)
1-Earth Three Crime Syndicate takes over; Nightwing unmasked; Johns-s/Finch-a 4.00
1-Director's Cut 1 (12/13, $5.99) Pencil artwork with full script 6.00
2-6: 2-Luthor dons the green battlesuit. 4-Sinestro returns 4.00
7-($4.99) 5.00
... Aftermath: Batman vs. Bane 1 (6/14, $3.99) Tomasi-s/Eaton-a 4.00

FOREVER EVIL: A.R.G.U.S.
DC Comics: Dec, 2013 - No. 6, May, 2014 ($2.99, limited series)
1-6-Gates-s. Steve Trevor in search of missing heroes. 1,2-Deathstroke app. 3.00

FOREVER EVIL: ARKHAM WAR
DC Comics: Dec, 2013 - No. 6, May, 2014 ($2.99, limited series)
1-6-Tomasi-s/Eaton-a; Bane and the Arkham inmates. 4-6-The Talons app. 3.00

FOREVER EVIL: ROGUES REBELLION
DC Comics: Dec, 2013 - No. 6, May, 2014 ($2.99, limited series)
1-6-Buccellato-s/Hepburn-a/Shalvey-c. 2-Deathstorm & Power Ring app. 6-Grodd app. 3.00

FOREVER MAELSTROM
DC Comics: Jan, 2003 - No. 6, Jun, 2003 ($2.95, limited series)
1-6-Chaykin & Tischman-s/Lucas & Barreto-a 3.00

FOREVER PEOPLE, THE
National Periodical Publications: Feb-Mar, 1971 - No. 11, Oct-Nov, 1972 (Fourth World) (#1-3, 10-11 are 36 pgs; #4-9 are 52 pgs.)
1-1st app. Forever People; Superman x-over; Kirby-c/a begins; 1st full app. Darkseid (3rd anywhere, 3 weeks before New Gods #1); Darkseid storyline begins, ends #8 (app. in 1-4,6,8; cameos in 5,11) 14 28 42 96 211 325
2-9: 4-G.A. reprints thru #9. 9,10-Deadman app. 4 8 12 25 40 55
10,11 3 6 9 19 30 40
Jack Kirby's Forever People TPB ('99, $14.95, B&W&Grey) r/#1-11 plus cover gallery 15.00
NOTE: ***Kirby*** *c/a(p)-1-11; #4-9 contain Sandman reprints from Adventure #85, 84, 75, 80, 77, 74 in that order.*

FOREVER PEOPLE
DC Comics: Feb, 1988 - No. 6, July, 1988 ($1.25, limited series)
1-6 4.00

FORGE
CrossGeneration Comics: Feb, 2002 - No. 13, May, 2003 ($9.95/$11.95/$7.95, TPB)
1-3: Reprints from various CrossGen titles 10.00
4-8-($11.95) 12.00
9-13-($7.95, 8-1/4" x 5-1/2") digest-sized reprints 8.00

FOR GIRLS ONLY
Bernard Baily Enterprises: 11/53 - No. 2, 6/54 (100 pgs., digest size, 25¢)
1-25% comic book, 75% articles, illos, games 37 74 111 222 361 500
2-Eddie Fisher photo & story. 30 60 90 177 289 400

FORGOTTEN FOREST OF OZ, THE (See First Comics Graphic Novel #16)

FORGOTTEN REALMS (Also see Avatar & TSR Worlds)
DC Comics: Sept, 1989 - No. 25, Sept, 1991 ($1.50/$1.75)
1, Annual 1 (1990, $2.95, 68 pgs.) 4.00
2-25: Based on TSR role-playing game. 18-Avatar story 3.00

FORGOTTEN REALMS (Based on Wizards of the Coast game)
Devil's Due Publ.: June, 2005 - No. 3, Aug, 2005 ($4.95)

Formic Wars: Burning Earth #1 © MAR

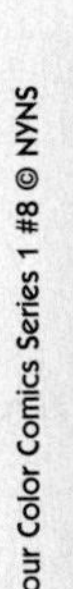
Four Color Comics Series 1 #8 © NYNS

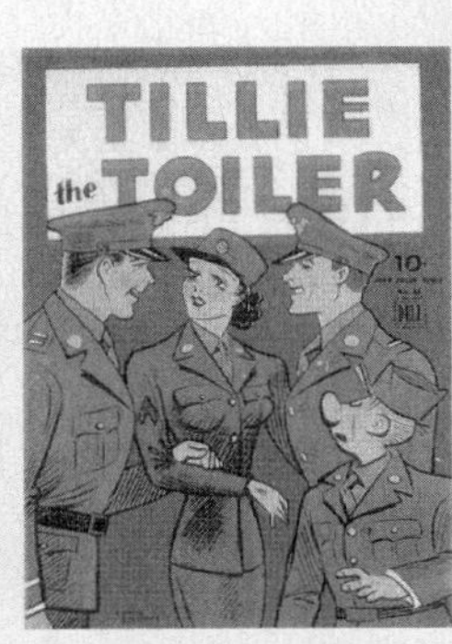

Four Color Comics Series 2 #55 © KING

	GD 2.0	VG 4.0	FN 6.0	VF 8.0	VF/NM 9.0	NM- 9.2
1-3-Salvatore-s/Seeley-a						5.00
...Exile (11/05 - No. 3, 1/06, $4.95) 1-3-Daab-s/Seeley-a. 1-Flip cover						5.00
...: Legacy (2/08 - No. 3, 6/08, $5.50) 1-3-Daab-s/Atkins-a						5.50
The Legend of Drizzt Book II: Exile (2006, $14.95, TPB) r/#1-3						15.00
...Sojourn (3/06 - No. 3, 6/06, $4.95) 1-3-Daab-s/Seeley-a						5.00
...: Streams of Silver (12/06 - No. 3, $5.50) 1-3-Daab-s/Semeiks-a						5.50
...The Crystal Shard (8/06 - No. 3, 12/06, $4.95) 1-3-Daab-s/Semeiks-a						5.00
...The Halfling's Gem (8/07 - No. 3, 12/07, $5.50) 1-3-Daab-s/Seeley-a; two covers						5.50

FORLORN RIVER (See Zane Grey Four Color 395)

FOR LOVERS ONLY (Formerly Hollywood Romances)
Charlton Comics: No. 60, Aug, 1971 - No. 87, Nov, 1976

	GD	VG	FN	VF	VF/NM	NM-
60	3	6	9	19	30	40
61-80,82-87: 67-Morisi-a	2	4	6	11	16	20
81-Psychedelic cover	3	6	9	16	23	30

FORMERLY KNOWN AS THE JUSTICE LEAGUE
DC Comics: Sept, 2003 - No. 6, Feb, 2004 ($2.50, limited series)

	NM-
1-Giffen & DeMatteis-s/Maguire-a; Booster Gold, Blue Beetle, Captain Atom, Mary Marvel, Fire, and Elongated Man app.	4.00
2-6: 3,4-Roulette app. 6-JLA app.	3.00
TPB (2004, $12.95) r/#1-6	13.00

FORMIC WARS: BURNING EARTH
Marvel Comics: Apr, 2011 - No. 7, Sept, 2011 ($3.99, limited series)

	NM-
1-7-Prequel to Orson Scott Card's novel Ender's Game. 1-Covers by Larroca & Hitch	4.00

FORMIC WARS: SILENT STRIKE (Follows Burning Earth limited series)
Marvel Comics: Feb, 2012 - No. 5, Jun, 2012 ($3.99, limited series)

	NM-
1-5-Johnston-s/Caracuzzo-a/Camuncoli-c	4.00

FORT: PROPHET OF THE UNEXPLAINED
Dark Horse Comics: June, 2002 - No. 4, Sept, 2002 ($2.99, B&W, limited series)

	NM-
1-4-Peter Lenkov-s/Frazer Irving-c/a	3.00
TPB (2003, $9.95) r/#1-4	10.00

FORTUNE AND GLORY
Oni Press: Dec, 1999 - No. 3, Apr, 2000 ($4.95, B&W, limited series)

	NM-
1-3-Brian Michael Bendis in Hollywood	5.00
TPB ($14.95)	15.00

40 BIG PAGES OF MICKEY MOUSE
Whitman Publ. Co.: No. 945, Jan, 1936 (10-1/4x12-1/2", 44 pgs., cardboard-c)

	GD	VG	FN	VF	VF/NM	NM-
945-Reprints Mickey Mouse Magazine #1, but with a different cover; ads were eliminated and some illustrated stories had expanded text. The book is 3/4" shorter than Mickey Mouse Mag. #1, but the reprints are same size (Rare)	161	322	483	1030	1765	2500

47 RONIN
Dark Horse Comics: Nov, 2012 - No. 5, Jul, 2013 ($3.99, limited series)

	NM-
1-5-Mike Richardson-s/Stan Sakai-a/c; 18th century samurai legend	4.00

FOR YOUR EYES ONLY (See James Bond...)

FOUNTAIN, THE (Companion graphic novel to the Darren Aronofsky film)
DC Comics (Vertigo): 2005 ($39.99, hardcover with dust jacket)

	NM-
1-Darren Aronofsky-s/Kent Williams-a	40.00

FOUR (Fantastic Four; See Marvel Knights 4 #28-30)

FOUR COLOR
Dell Publishing Co.: Sept?, 1939 - No. 1354, Apr-June, 1962
(Series I are all 68 pgs.)

NOTE: *Four Color only appears on issues #19-25, 1-99,101. Dell Publishing Co. filed these as Series I, #1-25, and Series II, #1-1354. Issues beginning with #710? were printed with and without ads on back cover. Issues without ads are worth more.*

SERIES I:

	GD	VG	FN	VF	VF/NM	NM-
1(nn)-Dick Tracy	1100	2200	3300	8360	15,680	23,000
2(nn)-Don Winslow of the Navy (#1) (Rare) (11/39?)	223	446	669	1416	2433	3450
3(nn)-Myra North (1/40)	103	206	309	659	1130	1600
4-Donald Duck by Al Taliaferro (1940)(Disney)(3/40?)	2000	4000	6000	15,000	27,500	40,000
(Prices vary widely on this book)						
5-Smilin' Jack (#1) (5/40?)	84	168	252	538	919	1300
6-Dick Tracy (Scarce)	258	516	774	1651	2826	4000
7-Gang Busters	58	116	174	371	636	900
8-Dick Tracy	135	270	405	864	1482	2100
9-Terry and the Pirates-r/Super #9-29	77	154	231	493	847	1200
10-Smilin' Jack	69	138	207	442	759	1075
11-Smitty (#1)	53	106	159	334	567	800
12-Little Orphan Annie; reprints strips from 12/19/37 to 6/4/38	63	126	189	403	689	975
13-Walt Disney's Reluctant Dragon('41)-Contains 2 pgs. of photos from film; 2 pg. foreword to Fantasia by Leopold Stokowski; Donald Duck, Goofy, Baby Weems & Mickey Mouse (as the Sorcerer's Apprentice) app. (Disney)	219	438	657	1402	2401	3400
14-Moon Mullins (#1)	48	96	144	302	514	725
15-Tillie the Toiler (#1)	55	110	165	352	601	850
16-Mickey Mouse (#1) (Disney) by Gottfredson	1250	2500	3750	16,500	-	-
17-Walt Disney's Dumbo, the Flying Elephant (#1)(1941)-Mickey Mouse, Donald Duck, & Pluto app. (Disney)	274	548	822	1740	2995	4250
18-Jiggs and Maggie (#1)(1936-38-r)	52	104	156	328	552	775
19-Barney Google and Snuffy Smith (#1)-(1st issue with Four Color on the cover)	52	104	156	323	549	775
20-Tiny Tim	41	82	123	250	418	585
21-Dick Tracy	92	184	276	584	1005	1425
22-Don Winslow	52	104	156	328	552	775
23-Gang Busters	45	90	135	284	480	675
24-Captain Easy	54	108	162	343	574	825
25-Popeye (1942)	107	214	321	680	1165	1650

SERIES II:

	GD	VG	FN	VF	VF/NM	NM-
1-Little Joe (1942)	63	126	189	504	1127	1750
2-Harold Teen	31	62	93	223	499	775
3-Alley Oop (#1)	46	92	138	359	805	1250
4-Smilin' Jack	38	76	114	281	628	975
5-Raggedy Ann and Andy (#1)	46	92	138	350	788	1225
6-Smitty	22	44	66	154	340	525
7-Smokey Stover (#1)	24	48	72	170	378	585
8-Tillie the Toiler	24	48	72	168	372	575
9-Donald Duck Finds Pirate Gold, by Carl Barks & Jack Hannah (Disney) (© 8/17/42)	1000	2000	3000	7600	13,800	20,000
10-Flash Gordon by Alex Raymond; reprinted from "The Ice Kingdom"	86	172	258	688	1544	2400
11-Wash Tubbs	26	52	78	182	404	625
12-Walt Disney's Bambi (#1)	46	92	138	340	770	1200
13-Mr. District Attorney (#1)-See The Funnies #35 for 1st app.	26	52	78	182	404	625
14-Smilin' Jack	30	60	90	216	483	750
15-Felix the Cat (#1)	75	150	225	600	1350	2100
16-Porky Pig (#1)(1942)- "Secret of the Haunted House"	89	178	267	712	1606	2500
17-Popeye	45	90	135	333	754	1175
18-Little Orphan Annie's Junior Commandos; Flag-c; reprints strips from 6/14/42 to 11/21/42	34	68	102	245	548	850
19-Walt Disney's Thumper Meets the Seven Dwarfs (Disney); reprinted in Silly Symphonies	44	88	132	326	738	1150
20-Barney Baxter	24	48	72	170	378	585
21-Oswald the Rabbit (#1)(1943)	38	76	114	285	641	1000
22-Tillie the Toiler	17	34	51	117	259	400
23-Raggedy Ann and Andy	31	62	93	223	499	775
24-Gang Busters	27	54	81	189	420	650
25-Andy Panda (#1) (Walter Lantz)	46	92	138	368	834	1300
26-Popeye	45	90	135	333	754	1175
27-Walt Disney's Mickey Mouse and the Seven Colored Terror	71	142	213	568	1284	2000
28-Wash Tubbs	17	34	51	117	259	400
29-Donald Duck and the Mummy's Ring, by Carl Barks (Disney) (9/43)	795	1590	2385	5804	10,252	14,700
30-Bambi's Children (1943)-Disney	40	80	120	296	673	1050
31-Moon Mullins	15	30	45	105	233	360
32-Smitty	15	30	45	100	220	340
33-Bugs Bunny "Public Nuisance #1"	107	214	321	856	1928	3000
34-Dick Tracy	38	76	114	282	634	985
35-Smokey Stover	14	28	42	96	211	325
36-Smilin' Jack	21	42	63	147	324	500
37-Bringing Up Father	18	36	54	124	275	425
38-Roy Rogers (#1, © 4/44)-1st western comic with photo-c (see Movie Comics #3)	152	304	456	1254	2827	4400
39-Oswald the Rabbit (1944)	27	54	81	189	420	650
40-Barney Google and Snuffy Smith	20	40	60	135	300	465
41-Mother Goose and Nursery Rhyme Comics (#1)-All by Walt Kelly	21	42	63	147	324	500
42-Tiny Tim (1934-r)	16	32	48	110	243	375

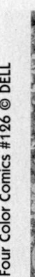

Four Color Comics #88 © WB

Four Color Comics #126 © DELL

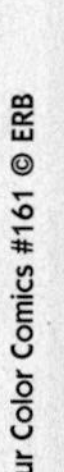
Four Color Comics #161 © ERB

	GD 2.0	VG 4.0	FN 6.0	VF 8.0	VF/NM 9.0	NM- 9.2
43-Popeye (1938-'42-r)	29	58	87	209	467	725
44-Terry and the Pirates (1938-r)	31	62	93	223	499	775
45-Raggedy Ann	25	50	75	175	388	600
46-Felix the Cat and the Haunted Castle	38	76	114	285	641	1000
47-Gene Autry (copyright 6/16/44)	34	68	102	245	548	850
48-Porky Pig of the Mounties by Carl Barks (7/44)	91	182	273	728	1639	2550
49-Snow White and the Seven Dwarfs (Disney)	47	94	141	367	821	1275
50-Fairy Tale Parade-Walt Kelly art (1944)	21	42	63	147	324	500
51-Bugs Bunny Finds the Lost Treasure	35	70	105	252	564	875
52-Little Orphan Annie; reprints strips from 6/18/38 to 11/19/38	24	48	72	168	372	575
53-Wash Tubbs	13	26	39	89	195	300
54-Andy Panda	25	50	75	175	388	600
55-Tillie the Toiler	12	24	36	84	185	285
56-Dick Tracy	34	68	102	247	554	860
57-Gene Autry	29	58	87	209	467	725
58-Smilin' Jack	21	42	63	147	324	500
59-Mother Goose and Nursery Rhyme Comics-Kelly-c/a	17	34	51	117	259	400
60-Tiny Folks Funnies	14	28	42	94	207	329
61-Santa Claus Funnies(11/44)-Kelly art	21	42	63	150	330	510
62-Donald Duck in Frozen Gold, by Carl Barks (Disney) (1/45)	224	448	672	1848	4174	6500
63-Roy Rogers; color photo-all 4 covers	38	76	114	285	641	1000
64-Smokey Stover	12	24	36	79	170	260
65-Smitty	12	24	36	82	179	275
66-Gene Autry	29	58	87	209	467	725
67-Oswald the Rabbit	16	32	48	110	243	375
68-Mother Goose and Nursery Rhyme Comics, by Walt Kelly	17	34	51	117	259	400
69-Fairy Tale Parade, by Walt Kelly	21	42	63	147	324	500
70-Popeye and Wimpy	22	44	66	154	340	525
71-Walt Disney's Three Caballeros, by Walt Kelly (© 4/45)-(Disney)	59	118	177	472	1061	1650
72-Raggedy Ann	20	40	60	141	313	485
73-The Gumps (#1)	11	22	33	76	163	250
74-Marge's Little Lulu (#1)	172	344	516	1419	3210	5000
75-Gene Autry and the Wildcat	23	46	69	164	362	560
76-Little Orphan Annie; reprints strips from 2/28/40 to 6/24/40	19	38	57	131	291	450
77-Felix the Cat	36	72	108	259	580	900
78-Porky Pig and the Bandit Twins	25	50	75	175	388	600
79-Walt Disney's Mickey Mouse in The Riddle of the Red Hat by Carl Barks (8/45)	89	178	267	712	1606	2500
80-Smilin' Jack	13	26	39	89	195	300
81-Moon Mullins	10	20	30	66	138	210
82-Lone Ranger	37	74	111	274	612	950
83-Gene Autry in Outlaw Trail	23	46	69	164	362	560
84-Flash Gordon by Alex Raymond-Reprints from "The Fiery Desert"	42	84	126	311	698	1085
85-Andy Panda and the Mad Dog Mystery	15	30	45	103	227	350
86-Roy Rogers; photo-c	28	56	84	202	451	700
87-Fairy Tale Parade by Walt Kelly; Dan Noonan-c	21	42	63	147	324	500
88-Bugs Bunny's Great Adventure (Sci/fi)	23	46	69	156	348	540
89-Tillie the Toiler	12	24	36	84	185	285
90-Christmas with Mother Goose by Walt Kelly (11/45)	15	30	45	103	227	350
91-Santa Claus Funnies by Walt Kelly (11/45)	16	32	48	110	243	375
92-Walt Disney's The Wonderful Adventures Of Pinocchio (1945); Donald Duck by Kelly, 16 pgs. (Disney)	46	92	138	359	805	1250
93-Gene Autry in The Bandit of Black Rock	19	38	57	133	297	460
94-Winnie Winkle (1945)	12	24	36	79	170	260
95-Roy Rogers Comics; photo-c	28	56	84	202	451	700
96-Dick Tracy	23	46	69	161	356	550
97-Marge's Little Lulu (1946)	64	128	192	512	1156	1800
98-Lone Ranger, The	27	54	81	194	435	675
99-Smitty	10	20	30	66	138	210
100-Gene Autry Comics; 1st Gene Autry photo-c	22	44	66	155	345	535
101-Terry and the Pirates	20	40	60	135	300	465

NOTE: *No. 101 is last issue to carry "Four Color" logo on cover; all issues beginning with No. 100 are marked "...O. S." (One Shot) which can be found in the bottom left-hand panel on the first page; the numbers following "O. S." relate to the year/month issued.*

	GD 2.0	VG 4.0	FN 6.0	VF 8.0	VF/NM 9.0	NM- 9.2
102-Oswald the Rabbit-Walt Kelly art, 1 pg.	13	26	39	89	195	300
103-Easter with Mother Goose by Walt Kelly	17	34	51	117	259	400
104-Fairy Tale Parade by Walt Kelly	16	32	48	112	249	385
105-Albert the Alligator and Pogo Possum (#1) by Kelly (4/46)	50	100	150	400	900	1400
106-Tillie the Toiler (5/46)	10	20	30	64	132	200
107-Little Orphan Annie; reprints strips from 11/16/42 to 3/24/43	17	34	51	117	259	400
108-Donald Duck in The Terror of the River, by Carl Barks (Disney) (© 4/16/46)	148	296	444	1221	2761	4300
109-Roy Rogers Comics; photo-c	21	42	63	147	324	500
110-Marge's Little Lulu	40	80	120	296	673	1050
111-Captain Easy	12	24	36	82	179	275
112-Porky Pig's Adventure in Gopher Gulch	15	30	45	103	227	350
113-Popeye; all new Popeye stories begin	13	26	39	91	201	310
114-Fairy Tale Parade by Walt Kelly	16	32	48	112	249	385
115-Marge's Little Lulu	39	78	117	289	657	1025
116-Mickey Mouse and the House of Many Mysteries (Disney)	27	54	81	184	410	635
117-Roy Rogers Comics; photo-c	17	34	51	117	259	400
118-Lone Ranger, The	27	54	81	194	435	675
119-Felix the Cat; all new Felix stories begin	31	62	93	223	499	775
120-Marge's Little Lulu	34	68	102	245	548	850
121-Fairy Tale Parade-(not Kelly)	10	20	30	69	147	225
122-Henry (#1) (10/46)	15	30	45	100	220	340
123-Bugs Bunny's Dangerous Venture	15	30	45	105	233	360
124-Roy Rogers Comics; photo-c	17	34	51	117	259	400
125-Lone Ranger, The	19	38	57	131	291	450
126-Christmas with Mother Goose by Walt Kelly (1946)	11	22	33	76	163	250
127-Popeye	13	26	39	91	201	310
128-Santa Claus Funnies- "Santa & the Angel" by Gollub; "A Mouse in the House" by Kelly	13	26	39	91	201	310
129-Walt Disney's Uncle Remus and His Tales of Brer Rabbit (#1) (1946)-Adapted from Disney movie "Song of the South"	23	46	69	164	362	560
130-Andy Panda (Walter Lantz)	10	20	30	70	150	230
131-Marge's Little Lulu	34	68	102	245	548	850
132-Tillie the Toiler (1947)	10	20	30	64	132	200
133-Dick Tracy	18	36	54	124	275	425
134-Tarzan and the Devil Ogre; Marsh-c/a	56	112	168	448	999	1550
135-Felix the Cat	21	42	63	147	324	500
136-Lone Ranger, The	19	38	57	131	291	450
137-Roy Rogers Comics; photo-c	17	34	51	117	259	400
138-Smitty	9	18	27	59	117	175
139-Marge's Little Lulu (1947)	32	64	96	230	515	800
140-Easter with Mother Goose by Walt Kelly	13	26	39	91	201	310
141-Mickey Mouse and the Submarine Pirates (Disney)	22	44	66	155	345	535
142-Bugs Bunny and the Haunted Mountain	15	30	45	105	233	360
143-Oswald the Rabbit & the Prehistoric Egg	9	18	27	59	117	175
144-Roy Rogers Comics (1947)-Photo-c	17	34	51	117	259	400
145-Popeye	13	26	39	91	201	310
146-Marge's Little Lulu	32	64	96	230	515	800
147-Donald Duck in Volcano Valley, by Carl Barks (Disney) (5/47)	104	208	312	832	1866	2900
148-Albert the Alligator and Pogo Possum by Walt Kelly (5/47)	38	76	114	282	634	985
149-Smilin' Jack	9	18	27	62	126	190
150-Tillie the Toiler (6/47)	9	18	27	60	120	180
151-Lone Ranger, The	16	32	48	112	249	385
152-Little Orphan Annie; reprints strips from 1/2/44 to 5/6/44	11	22	33	76	163	250
153-Roy Rogers Comics; photo-c	15	30	45	105	233	360
154-Walter Lantz Andy Panda	10	20	30	70	150	230
155-Henry (7/47)	10	20	30	66	138	210
156-Porky Pig and the Phantom	11	22	33	73	157	240
157-Mickey Mouse & the Beanstalk (Disney)	22	44	66	155	345	535
158-Marge's Little Lulu	32	64	96	230	515	800
159-Donald Duck in the Ghost of the Grotto, by Carl Barks (Disney) (8/47)	89	178	267	712	1606	2500
160-Roy Rogers Comics; photo-c	15	30	45	105	233	360
161-Tarzan and the Fires Of Tohr; Marsh-c/a	46	92	138	340	770	1200
162-Felix the Cat (9/47)	16	32	48	110	243	375
163-Dick Tracy	16	32	48	110	243	375
164-Bugs Bunny Finds the Frozen Kingdom	15	30	45	105	233	360
165-Marge's Little Lulu	32	64	96	230	515	800

Four Color Comics #183 © Walter Lantz

Four Color Comics #208 © DIS

Four Color Comics #275 © DIS

	GD 2.0	VG 4.0	FN 6.0	VF 8.0	VF/NM 9.0	NM- 9.2
166-Roy Rogers Comics (52 pgs.)-Photo-c	15	30	45	105	233	360
167-Lone Ranger, The	16	32	48	112	249	385
168-Popeye (10/47)	13	26	39	91	201	310
169-Woody Woodpecker (#1)- "Manhunter in the North"; drug use story	18	36	54	128	284	440
170-Mickey Mouse on Spook's Island (11/47)(Disney)-reprinted in Mickey Mouse #103	19	38	57	133	297	460
171-Charlie McCarthy (#1) and the Twenty Thieves	24	48	72	170	378	585
172-Christmas with Mother Goose by Walt Kelly (11/47)	11	22	33	76	163	250
173-Flash Gordon	21	42	63	147	324	500
174-Winnie Winkle	8	16	24	54	102	150
175-Santa Claus Funnies by Walt Kelly (1947)	13	26	39	91	201	310
176-Tillie the Toiler (12/47)	9	18	27	60	120	180
177-Roy Rogers Comics-(36 pgs.); Photo-c	15	30	45	100	220	340
178-Donald Duck "Christmas on Bear Mountain" by Carl Barks; 1st app. Uncle Scrooge (Disney)(12/47)	136	272	408	1088	2444	3800
179-Uncle Wiggily (#1)-Walt Kelly-c	14	28	42	94	207	320
180-Ozark Ike (#1)	10	20	30	69	147	225
181-Walt Disney's Mickey Mouse in Jungle Magic	19	38	57	133	297	460
182-Porky Pig in Never-Never Land (2/48)	11	22	33	73	157	240
183-Oswald the Rabbit (Lantz)	9	18	27	59	117	175
184-Tillie the Toiler	9	18	27	60	120	180
185-Easter with Mother Goose by Walt Kelly (1948)	12	24	36	82	179	275
186-Walt Disney's Bambi (4/48)-Reprinted as Movie Classic Bambi #3 (1956)	14	28	42	96	211	325
187-Bugs Bunny and the Dreadful Dragon	11	22	33	76	163	250
188-Woody Woodpecker (Lantz, 5/48)	11	22	33	73	157	240
189-Donald Duck in The Old Castle's Secret, by Carl Barks (Disney) (6/48)	79	158	237	632	1416	2200
190-Flash Gordon (6/48); bondage-c; "The Adventures of the Flying Saucers"; 5th Flying Saucer story- see The Spirit 9/28/47(1st), Shadow Comics V7#10 (2nd, 1/48),Captain Midnight #60 (3rd, 2/48) & Boy Commandos #26 (4th, 3-4/48)	23	46	69	161	356	550
191-Porky Pig to the Rescue	11	22	33	73	157	240
192-The Brownies (#1)-by Walt Kelly (7/48)	13	26	39	89	195	300
193-M.G.M. Presents Tom and Jerry (#1)(1948)	23	46	69	164	362	560
194-Mickey Mouse in The World Under the Sea (Disney)-Reprinted in Mickey Mouse #101	19	38	57	133	297	460
195-Tillie the Toiler	8	16	24	51	96	140
196-Charlie McCarthy in The Haunted Hide-Out; part photo-c	15	30	45	105	233	360
197-Spirit of the Border (#1) (Zane Grey) (1948)	11	22	33	73	157	240
198-Andy Panda	10	20	30	70	150	230
199-Donald Duck in Sheriff of Bullet Valley, by Carl Barks; Barks draws himself on wanted poster, last page; used in Love & Death (Disney) (10/48)	84	168	252	672	1511	2350
200-Bugs Bunny, Super Sleuth (10/48)	11	22	33	76	163	250
201-Christmas with Mother Goose by W. Kelly	10	20	30	64	132	200
202-Woody Woodpecker	8	16	24	56	108	160
203-Donald Duck in the Golden Christmas Tree, by Carl Barks (Disney) (12/48)	59	118	177	472	1061	1650
204-Flash Gordon (12/48)	16	32	48	110	243	375
205-Santa Claus Funnies by Walt Kelly	12	24	36	82	179	275
206-Little Orphan Annie; reprints strips from 11/10/40 to 1/11/41	8	16	24	51	96	140
207-King of the Royal Mounted (#1) (12/48)	13	26	39	86	188	290
208-Brer Rabbit Does It Again (Disney) (1/49)	10	20	30	66	138	210
209-Harold Teen	6	12	18	40	73	105
210-Tippie and Cap Stubbs	6	12	18	42	79	115
211-Little Beaver (#1)	9	18	27	59	117	175
212-Dr. Bobbs	6	12	18	38	69	100
213-Tillie the Toiler	8	16	24	51	96	140
214-Mickey Mouse and His Sky Adventure (2/49)(Disney)-Reprinted in Mickey Mouse #105	15	30	45	105	233	360
215-Sparkle Plenty (Dick Tracy-r by Gould)	10	20	30	68	144	220
216-Andy Panda and the Police Pup (Lantz)	8	16	24	55	105	155
217-Bugs Bunny in Court Jester	11	22	33	76	163	250
218-Three Little Pigs and the Wonderful Magic Lamp (Disney) (3/49)(#1)	10	20	30	66	138	210
219-Swee'pea	9	18	27	57	111	165
220-Easter with Mother Goose by Walt Kelly	12	24	36	82	179	275
221-Uncle Wiggily-Walt Kelly cover in part	9	18	27	58	114	170
222-West of the Pecos (Zane Grey)	7	14	21	46	86	125
223-Donald Duck "Lost in the Andes" by Carl Barks (Disney-4/49) (square egg story)	77	154	231	616	1383	2150
224-Little Iodine (#1), by Hatlo (4/49)	12	24	36	81	176	270
225-Oswald the Rabbit (Lantz)	7	14	21	44	82	120
226-Porky Pig and Spoofy, the Spook	9	18	27	61	123	185
227-Seven Dwarfs (Disney)	9	18	27	62	126	190
228-Mark of Zorro, The (#1) (1949)	18	36	54	126	281	435
229-Smokey Stover	6	12	18	40	73	105
230-Sunset Pass (Zane Grey)	7	14	21	46	86	125
231-Mickey Mouse and the Rajah's Treasure (Disney)	15	30	45	105	233	360
232-Woody Woodpecker (Lantz, 6/49)	8	16	24	56	108	160
233-Bugs Bunny, Sleepwalking Sleuth	11	22	33	76	163	250
234-Dumbo in Sky Voyage (Disney)	13	26	39	89	195	300
235-Tiny Tim	6	12	18	41	76	110
236-Heritage of the Desert (Zane Grey) (1949)	7	14	21	46	86	125
237-Tillie the Toiler	8	16	24	51	96	140
238-Donald Duck in Voodoo Hoodoo, by Carl Barks (Disney) (8/49)	57	114	171	456	1028	1600
239-Adventure Bound (8/49)	6	12	18	37	66	95
240-Andy Panda (Lantz)	8	16	24	55	105	155
241-Porky Pig, Mighty Hunter	9	18	27	61	123	185
242-Tippie and Cap Stubbs	5	10	15	31	53	75
243-Thumper Follows His Nose (Disney)	11	22	33	72	154	235
244-The Brownies by Walt Kelly	10	20	30	64	132	200
245-Dick's Adventures (9/49)	6	12	18	37	66	95
246-Thunder Mountain (Zane Grey)	5	10	15	35	63	90
247-Flash Gordon	16	32	48	110	243	375
248-Mickey Mouse and the Black Sorcerer (Disney)	15	30	45	105	233	360
249-Woody Woodpecker in the "Globetrotter" (10/49)	8	16	24	56	108	160
250-Bugs Bunny in Diamond Daze; used in **SOTI**, pg. 309	12	24	36	79	170	260
251-Hubert at Camp Moonbeam	9	18	27	61	123	185
252-Pinocchio (Disney)-not by Kelly; origin	11	22	33	72	154	235
253-Christmas with Mother Goose by W. Kelly	10	20	30	64	132	200
254-Santa Claus Funnies by Walt Kelly; Pogo & Albert story by Kelly (11/49)	12	24	36	82	179	275
255-The Ranger (Zane Grey) (1949)	5	10	15	35	63	90
256-Donald Duck in "Luck of the North" by Carl Barks (Disney) (12/49)-Shows #257 on inside	46	92	138	368	834	1300
257-Little Iodine	8	16	24	55	105	155
258-Andy Panda and the Balloon Race (Lantz)	8	16	24	55	105	155
259-Santa and the Angel (Gollub art-condensed from #128) & Santa at the Zoo (12/49) -two books in one	6	12	18	38	69	100
260-Porky Pig, Hero of the Wild West (12/49)	9	18	27	61	123	185
261-Mickey Mouse and the Missing Key (Disney)	15	30	45	105	233	360
262-Raggedy Ann and Andy	9	18	27	57	111	165
263-Donald Duck in "Land of the Totem Poles" by Carl Barks (Disney) (2/50)-Has two Barks stories	46	92	138	359	805	1250
264-Woody Woodpecker in the Magic Lantern (Lantz)	8	16	24	56	108	160
265-King of the Royal Mounted (Zane Grey)	9	18	27	58	114	170
266-Bugs Bunny on the "Isle of Hercules" (2/50)-Reprinted in Best of Bugs Bunny #1	9	18	27	61	123	185
267-Little Beaver; Harmon-c/a	6	12	18	37	66	95
268-Mickey Mouse's Surprise Visitor (1950)(Disney)	14	28	42	98	217	335
269-Johnny Mack Brown (#1)-Photo-c	18	36	54	124	275	425
270-Drift Fence (Zane Grey) (3/50)	5	10	15	35	63	90
271-Porky Pig in Phantom of the Plains	9	18	27	61	123	185
272-Cinderella (Disney) (4/50)	12	24	36	82	179	275
273-Oswald the Rabbit (Lantz)	7	14	21	44	82	120
274-Bugs Bunny, Hare-brained Reporter	9	18	27	61	123	185
275-Donald Duck in "Ancient Persia" by Carl Barks (Disney) (5/50)	46	92	138	350	788	1225
276-Uncle Wiggily	7	14	21	49	92	135
277-Porky Pig in Desert Adventure (5/50)	9	18	27	61	123	185
278-(Wild) Bill Elliott Comics (#1)-Photo-c	12	24	36	79	170	260
279-Mickey Mouse and Pluto Battle the Giant Ants (Disney); reprinted in Mickey Mouse #102 & 245	12	24	36	79	170	260
280-Andy Panda in The Isle Of Mechanical Men (Lantz)	8	16	24	55	105	155
281-Bugs Bunny in The Great Circus Mystery	9	18	27	61	123	185
282-Donald Duck and the Pixilated Parrot by Carl Barks (Disney) (© 5/23/50)	46	92	138	350	788	1225

Four Color Comics #324 © WP

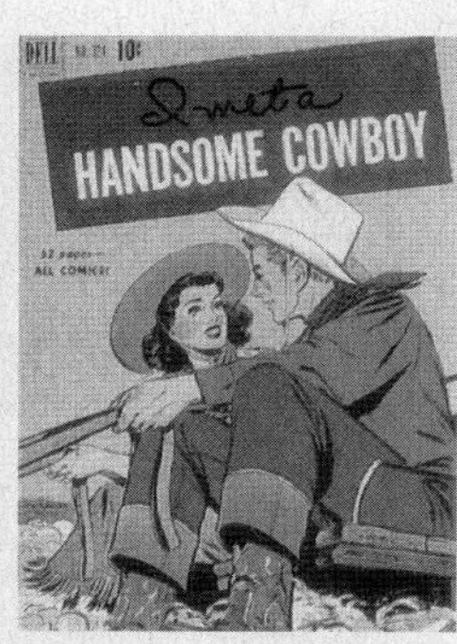

Four Color Comics #361 © WE

Four Color Comics #362 © DIS

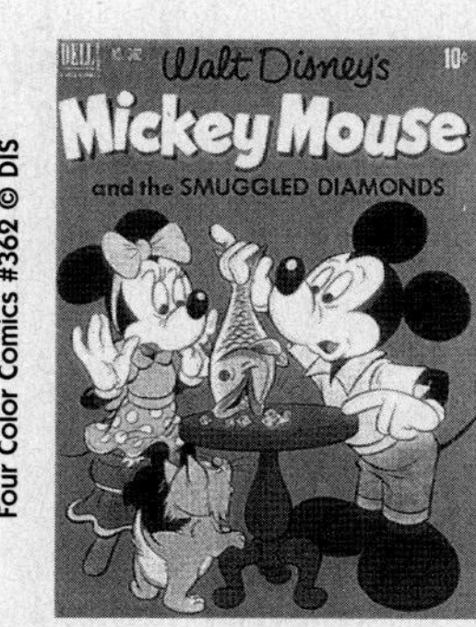

	GD 2.0	VG 4.0	FN 6.0	VF 8.0	VF/NM 9.0	NM- 9.2
283-King of the Royal Mounted (7/50)	9	18	27	58	114	170
284-Porky Pig in The Kingdom of Nowhere	9	18	27	61	123	185
285-Bozo the Clown & His Minikin Circus (#1) (TV)	17	34	51	117	259	400
286-Mickey Mouse in The Uninvited Guest (Disney	12	24	36	79	170	260
287-Gene Autry's Champion in The Ghost Of Black Mountain; photo-c	11	22	33	73	157	240
288-Woody Woodpecker in Klondike Gold (Lantz)	8	16	24	56	108	160
289-Bugs Bunny in "Indian Trouble"	9	18	27	61	123	185
290-The Chief (#1) (8/50)	7	14	21	49	92	135
291-Donald Duck in "The Magic Hourglass" by Carl Barks (Disney) (9/50)	46	92	138	350	788	1225
292-The Cisco Kid Comics (#1)	20	40	60	138	307	475
293-The Brownies-Kelly-c/a	10	20	30	64	132	200
294-Little Beaver	6	12	18	37	66	95
295-Porky Pig in President Porky (9/50)	9	18	27	61	123	185
296-Mickey Mouse in Private Eye for Hire (Disney)	12	24	36	79	170	260
297-Andy Panda in The Haunted Inn (Lantz, 10/50)	8	16	24	55	105	155
298-Bugs Bunny in Sheik for a Day	9	18	27	61	123	185
299-Buck Jones & the Iron Horse Trail (#1)	12	24	36	82	179	275
300-Donald Duck in "Big-Top Bedlam" by Carl Barks (Disney) (11/50)	46	92	138	350	788	1225
301-The Mysterious Rider (Zane Grey)	5	10	15	35	63	90
302-Santa Claus Funnies (11/50)	8	16	24	51	96	140
303-Porky Pig in The Land of the Monstrous Flies	7	14	21	48	89	135
304-Mickey Mouse in Tom-Tom Island (Disney) (12/50)	11	22	33	72	154	235
305-Woody Woodpecker (Lantz)	6	12	18	41	76	110
306-Raggedy Ann	7	14	21	46	86	125
307-Bugs Bunny in Lumber Jack Rabbit	8	16	24	55	105	155
308-Donald Duck in "Dangerous Disguise" by Carl Barks (Disney) (1/51)	44	88	132	326	738	1150
309-Betty Betz' Dollface and Her Gang (1951)	6	12	18	37	66	95
310-King of the Royal Mounted (1/51)	7	14	21	46	86	125
311-Porky Pig in Midget Horses of Hidden Valley	7	14	21	48	89	135
312-Tonto (#1)	11	22	33	73	157	240
313-Mickey Mouse in The Mystery of the Double-Cross Ranch (#1) (Disney) (2/51)	11	22	33	72	154	235

Note: Beginning with the above comic in 1951 Dell/Western began adding #1 in small print on the covers of several long running titles with the evident intention of switching these titles to their own monthly numbers, but when the conversions were made, there was no connection. It is thought that the post office may have stepped in and decreed the sequences should commence as though the first four colors printed had each begun with number one, or the first issues sold by subscription. Since the regular series' numbers don't correctly match to the numbers of earlier issues published, it's not known whether or not the numbering was in error.

	GD 2.0	VG 4.0	FN 6.0	VF 8.0	VF/NM 9.0	NM- 9.2
314-Ambush (Zane Grey)	5	10	15	35	63	90
315-Oswald the Rabbit (Lantz)	6	12	18	40	73	105
316-Rex Allen (#1)-Photo-c; Marsh-a	13	26	39	86	188	290
317-Bugs Bunny in Hair Today Gone Tomorrow (#1)	8	16	24	55	105	155
318-Donald Duck in "No Such Varmint" by Carl Barks (#1)-Indicia shows #317 (Disney, © 1/23/51)	44	88	132	326	738	1150
319-Gene Autry's Champion; painted-c	6	12	18	41	76	110
320-Uncle Wiggily (#1)	7	14	21	49	92	135
321-Little Scouts (#1) (3/51)	6	12	18	37	66	95
322-Porky Pig in Roaring Rockets (#1 on-c)	7	14	21	48	89	135
323-Susie Q. Smith (#1) (3/51)	6	12	18	37	66	95
324-I Met a Handsome Cowboy (3/51)	7	14	21	49	92	135
325-Mickey Mouse in The Haunted Castle (#2) (Disney) (4/51)	11	22	33	72	154	235
326-Andy Panda (#1) (Lantz)	6	12	18	41	76	110
327-Bugs Bunny and the Rajah's Treasure (#2)	8	16	24	55	105	155
328-Donald Duck in Old California (#2) by Carl Barks-Peyote drug use issue (Disney) (5/51)	43	86	129	318	722	1125
329-Roy Roger's Trigger (#1)(5/51)-Painted-c	14	28	42	94	207	320
330-Porky Pig Meets the Bristled Bruiser (#2)	7	14	21	48	89	135
331-Alice in Wonderland (Disney) (1951)	14	28	42	96	211	325
332-Little Beaver	6	12	18	37	66	95
333-Wilderness Trek (Zane Grey) (5/51)	5	10	15	35	63	90
334-Mickey Mouse and Yukon Gold (Disney) (6/51)	11	22	33	72	154	235
335-Francis the Famous Talking Mule (#1, 6/51)-1st Dell non animated movie comic (all issues based on movie)	10	20	30	68	144	220
336-Woody Woodpecker (Lantz)	6	12	18	41	76	110
337-The Brownies-not by Walt Kelly	6	12	18	38	69	100
338-Bugs Bunny and the Rocking Horse Thieves	8	16	24	55	105	155
339-Donald Duck and the Magic Fountain-not by Carl Barks (Disney) (7-8/51)	14	28	42	96	211	325
340-King of the Royal Mounted (7/51)	7	14	21	46	86	125
341-Unbirthday Party with Alice in Wonderland (Disney) (7/51)	14	28	42	96	211	325
342-Porky Pig the Lucky Peppermint Mine; r/in Porky Pig #3	6	12	18	38	69	100
343-Mickey Mouse in The Ruby Eye of Homar-Guy-Am (Disney)-Reprinted in Mickey Mouse #104	9	18	27	62	126	190
344-Sergeant Preston from Challenge of The Yukon (#1) (TV)	12	24	36	81	176	270
345-Andy Panda in Scotland Yard (8-10/51) (Lantz)	6	12	18	41	76	110
346-Hideout (Zane Grey)	5	10	15	35	63	90
347-Bugs Bunny the Frigid Hare (8-9/51)	8	16	24	55	105	155
348-Donald Duck "The Crocodile Collector"; Barks-c only (Disney) (9-10/51)	22	44	66	154	340	525
349-Uncle Wiggily	6	12	18	41	76	110
350-Woody Woodpecker (Lantz)	6	12	18	41	76	110
351-Porky Pig & the Grand Canyon Giant (9-10/51)	6	12	18	38	69	100
352-Mickey Mouse in The Mystery of Painted Valley (Disney)	9	18	27	62	126	190
353-Duck Album (#1)-Barks-c (Disney)	10	20	30	69	147	225
354-Raggedy Ann & Andy	7	14	21	46	86	125
355-Bugs Bunny Hot-Rod Hare	8	16	24	55	105	155
356-Donald Duck in "Rags to Riches"; Barks-c only	22	44	66	154	340	525
357-Comeback (Zane Grey)	5	10	15	33	57	80
358-Andy Panda (Lantz) (11-1/52)	6	12	18	41	76	110
359-Frosty the Snowman (#1)	10	20	30	64	132	200
360-Porky Pig in Tree of Fortune (11-12/51)	6	12	18	38	69	100
361-Santa Claus Funnies	8	16	24	51	96	140
362-Mickey Mouse and the Smuggled Diamonds (Disney)	9	18	27	62	126	190
363-King of the Royal Mounted	6	12	18	40	73	105
364-Woody Woodpecker (Lantz)	6	12	18	37	66	95
365-The Brownies-not by Kelly	6	12	18	38	69	100
366-Bugs Bunny Uncle Buckskin Comes to Town (12-1/52)	8	16	24	55	105	155
367-Donald Duck in "A Christmas for Shacktown" by Carl Barks (Disney) (1-2/52)	34	68	102	245	548	850
368-Bob Clampett's Beany and Cecil (#1)	21	42	63	147	324	500
369-The Lone Ranger's Famous Horse Hi-Yo Silver (#1); Silver's origin	10	20	30	68	144	220
370-Porky Pig in Trouble in the Big Trees	6	12	18	38	69	100
371-Mickey Mouse in The Inca Idol Case (1952) (Disney)	9	18	27	62	126	190
372-Riders of the Purple Sage (Zane Grey)	5	10	15	33	57	80
373-Sergeant Preston (TV)	8	16	24	54	102	150
374-Woody Woodpecker (Lantz)	6	12	18	37	66	95
375-John Carter of Mars (E. R. Burroughs)-Jesse Marsh-a; origin	29	58	87	209	467	725
376-Bugs Bunny, "The Magic Sneeze"	8	16	24	55	105	155
377-Susie Q. Smith	5	10	15	30	50	70
378-Tom Corbett, Space Cadet (#1) (TV)-McWilliams-a	16	32	48	110	243	375
379-Donald Duck in "Southern Hospitality"; Not by Barks (Disney)	14	28	42	96	211	325
380-Raggedy Ann & Andy	7	14	21	46	86	125
381-Marge's Tubby (#1)	18	36	54	126	281	435
382-Snow White and the Seven Dwarfs (Disney)-origin; partial reprint of Four Color #49 (Movie)	10	20	30	64	132	200
383-Andy Panda (Lantz)	5	10	15	35	63	90
384-King of the Royal Mounted (3/52)(Zane Grey)	6	12	18	40	73	105
385-Porky Pig inThe Isle of Missing Ships (3-4/52)	6	12	18	38	69	100
386-Uncle Scrooge (#1)-by Carl Barks (Disney) in "Only a Poor Old Man" (3/52)	179	358	537	1477	3739	6000
387-Mickey Mouse in High Tibet (Disney) (4-5/52)	9	18	27	62	126	190
388-Oswald the Rabbit (Lantz)	6	12	18	40	73	105
389-Andy Hardy Comics (#1)	5	10	15	35	63	90
390-Woody Woodpecker (Lantz)	6	12	18	37	66	95
391-Uncle Wiggily	6	12	18	41	76	110
392-Hi-Yo Silver	6	12	18	41	76	110
393-Bugs Bunny	8	16	24	55	105	155
394-Donald Duck in Malayalaya-Barks-c only (Disney)	22	44	66	154	340	525
395-Forlorn River(Zane Grey)-First Nevada (5/52)	5	10	15	33	57	80

Four Color Comics #444 © M.H. Buell

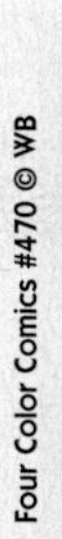
Four Color Comics #470 © WB

Four Color Comics #517 © DIS

	GD 2.0	VG 4.0	FN 6.0	VF 8.0	VF/NM 9.0	NM- 9.2
396-Tales of the Texas Rangers(#1)(TV)-Photo-c	10	20	30	66	138	210
397-Sergeant Preston of the Yukon (TV) (5/52)	8	16	24	54	102	150
398-The Brownies-not by Kelly	6	12	18	38	69	100
399-Porky Pig in The Lost Gold Mine	6	12	18	38	69	100
400-Tom Corbett, Space Cadet (TV)-McWilliams-c/a	10	20	30	64	132	200
401-Mickey Mouse and Goofy's Mechanical Wizard (Disney) (6-7/52)	8	16	24	56	108	160
402-Mary Jane and Sniffles	8	16	24	51	96	140
403-Li'l Bad Wolf (Disney) (6/52)(#1)	7	14	21	46	86	125
404-The Range Rider (#1) (Flying A's...)(TV)-Photo-c	9	18	27	60	120	180
405-Woody Woodpecker (Lantz) (6-7/52)	6	12	18	37	66	95
406-Tweety and Sylvester (#1)	12	24	36	81	176	270
407-Bugs Bunny, Foreign-Legion Hare	7	14	21	48	89	130
408-Donald Duck and the Golden Helmet by Carl Barks (Disney) (7-8/52)	34	68	102	245	548	850
409-Andy Panda (7-9/52)	5	10	15	35	63	90
410-Porky Pig in The Water Wizard (7/52)	6	12	18	38	69	100
411-Mickey Mouse and the Old Sea Dog (Disney) (8-9/52)	8	16	24	56	108	160
412-Nevada (Zane Grey)	5	10	15	33	57	80
413-Robin Hood (Disney-Movie) (8/52)-Photo-c (1st Disney movie Four Color book)	9	18	27	60	120	180
414-Bob Clampett's Beany and Cecil (TV)	12	24	36	84	185	285
415-Rootie Kazootie (#1) (TV)	9	18	27	59	117	175
416-Woody Woodpecker (Lantz)	6	12	18	37	66	95
417-Double Trouble with Goober (#1) (8/52)	5	10	15	33	57	80
418-Rusty Riley, a Boy, a Horse, and a Dog (#1)-Frank Godwin-a (strip reprints) (8/52)	6	12	18	38	69	100
419-Sergeant Preston (TV)	8	16	24	54	102	150
420-Bugs Bunny in The Mysterious Buckaroo (8-9/52)	7	14	21	48	89	130
421-Tom Corbett, Space Cadet(TV)-McWilliams-a	10	20	30	64	132	200
422-Donald Duck and the Gilded Man, by Carl Barks (Disney) (9-10/52) (#423 on inside)	34	68	102	245	548	850
423-Rhubarb, Owner of the Brooklyn Ball Club (The Millionaire Cat) (#1)-Painted cover	7	14	21	44	82	120
424-Flash Gordon-Test Flight in Space (9/52)	11	22	33	76	163	250
425-Zorro, the Return of	10	20	30	69	147	225
426-Porky Pig in The Scalawag Leprechaun	6	12	18	38	69	100
427-Mickey Mouse and the Wonderful Whizzix (Disney) (10-11/52)-Reprinted in Mickey Mouse #100	8	16	24	56	108	160
428-Uncle Wiggily	5	10	15	34	63	90
429-Pluto in "Why Dogs Leave Home" (Disney) (10/52)(#1)	10	20	30	68	144	220
430-Marge's Tubby, the Shadow of a Man-Eater	11	22	33	73	157	240
431-Woody Woodpecker (10/52) (Lantz)	6	12	18	37	66	95
432-Bugs Bunny and the Rabbit Olympics	7	14	21	48	89	130
433-Wildfire (Zane Grey) (11-1/52-53)	5	10	15	33	57	80
434-Rin Tin Tin "In Dark Danger" (#1) (TV) (11/52)-Photo-c	14	28	42	97	214	330
435-Frosty the Snowman (11/52)	6	12	18	40	73	105
436-The Brownies-not by Kelly (11/52)	5	10	15	35	63	90
437-John Carter of Mars (E.R. Burroughs)-Marsh-a	16	32	48	112	249	385
438-Annie Oakley (#1) (TV)	13	26	39	89	195	300
439-Little Hiawatha (Disney) (12/52)j(#1)	7	14	21	44	82	120
440-Black Beauty (12/52)	5	10	15	33	57	80
441-Fearless Fagan	5	10	15	31	53	75
442-Peter Pan (Disney) (Movie)	10	20	30	66	138	210
443-Ben Bowie and His Mountain Men (#1)	9	18	27	58	114	170
444-Marge's Tubby	11	22	33	73	157	240
445-Charlie McCarthy	6	12	18	40	73	105
446-Captain Hook and Peter Pan (Disney)(Movie)(1/53)	9	18	27	58	114	170
447-Andy Hardy Comics	4	8	12	27	44	60
448-Bob Clampett's Beany and Cecil (TV)	12	24	36	84	185	285
449-Tappan's Burro (Zane Grey) (2-4/53)	5	10	15	33	57	80
450-Duck Album; Barks-c (Disney)	8	16	24	51	96	140
451-Rusty Riley-Frank Godwin-a (strip-r) (2/53)	4	8	12	28	47	65
452-Raggedy Ann & Andy (1953)	7	14	21	46	86	125
453-Susie Q. Smith (2/53)	5	10	15	30	50	70
454-Krazy Kat Comics; not by Herriman	5	10	15	35	63	90
455-Johnny Mack Brown Comics(3/53)-Photo-c	6	12	18	40	73	105
456-Uncle Scrooge Back to the Klondike (#2) by Barks (3/53) (Disney)	88	176	264	704	1702	2700
457-Daffy (#1)	12	24	36	79	170	260
458-Oswald the Rabbit (Lantz)	5	10	15	35	63	90

	GD 2.0	VG 4.0	FN 6.0	VF 8.0	VF/NM 9.0	NM- 9.2
459-Rootie Kazootie (TV)	6	12	18	41	76	110
460-Buck Jones (4/53)	6	12	18	41	76	110
461-Marge's Tubby	10	20	30	68	144	220
462-Little Scouts	5	10	15	30	50	70
463-Petunia (4/53)	5	10	15	33	57	80
464-Bozo (4/53)	9	18	27	58	114	170
465-Francis the Famous Talking Mule	6	12	18	41	76	110
466-Rhubarb, the Millionaire Cat; painted-c	6	12	18	37	66	95
467-Desert Gold (Zane Grey) (5-7/53)	5	10	15	33	57	80
468-Goofy (#1) (Disney)	11	22	33	76	163	250
469-Beetle Bailey (#1) (5/53	12	24	36	83	182	280
470-Elmer Fudd	10	20	30	64	132	200
471-Double Trouble with Goober	4	8	12	27	44	60
472-Wild Bill Elliott (6/53)-Photo-c	5	10	15	5	63	90
473-Li'l Bad Wolf (Disney) (6/53)(#2)	5	10	15	34	60	85
474-Mary Jane and Sniffles	6	12	18	42	79	115
475-M.G.M.'s The Two Mouseketeers (#1)	9	18	27	57	111	165
476-Rin Tin Tin (TV)-Photo-c	9	18	27	57	111	165
477-Bob Clampett's Beany and Cecil (TV)	12	24	36	84	185	285
478-Charlie McCarthy	6	12	18	40	73	105
479-Queen of the West Dale Evans (#1)-Photo-c	16	32	48	110	243	375
480-Andy Hardy Comics	4	8	12	27	44	60
481-Annie Oakley And Tagg (TV)	9	18	27	59	117	175
482-Brownies-not by Kelly	5	10	15	35	63	90
483-Little Beaver (7/53)	5	10	15	34	60	85
484-River Feud (Zane Grey) (8-10/53)	5	10	15	33	57	80
485-The Little People-Walt Scott (#1)	8	16	24	51	96	140
486-Rusty Riley-Frank Godwin strip-r	4	8	12	28	47	65
487-Mowgli, the Jungle Book (Rudyard Kipling's)	6	12	18	42	79	115
488-John Carter of Mars (Burroughs)-Marsh-a; painted-c	16	32	48	112	249	385
489-Tweety and Sylvester	7	14	21	49	92	135
490-Jungle Jim (#1)	8	16	24	51	96	140
491-Silvertip (#1) (Max Brand)-Kinstler-a (8/53)	8	16	24	52	99	145
492-Duck Album (Disney)	7	14	21	44	82	120
493-Johnny Mack Brown; photo-c	6	12	18	40	73	105
494-The Little King (#1)	8	16	24	56	108	160
495-Uncle Scrooge (#3) (Disney)-by Carl Barks (9/53)	59	118	177	472	1136	1800
496-The Green Hornet; painted-c	23	46	69	164	362	560
497-Zorro (Sword of…)-Kinstler-a	11	22	33	73	157	240
498-Bugs Bunny's Album (9/53)	6	12	18	38	69	100
499-M.G.M.'s Spike and Tyke (#1) (9/53)	7	14	21	46	86	125
500-Buck Jones	6	12	18	41	76	110
501-Francis the Famous Talking Mule	5	10	15	35	63	90
502-Rootie Kazootie (TV)	6	12	18	41	76	110
503-Uncle Wiggily (10/53)	5	10	15	34	63	90
504-Krazy Kat; not by Herriman	5	10	15	35	63	90
505-The Sword and the Rose (Disney) (10/53)(Movie)-Photo-c	8	16	24	52	99	145
506-The Little Scouts	5	10	15	30	50	70
507-Oswald the Rabbit (Lantz)	5	10	15	35	63	90
508-Bozo (10/53)	9	18	27	58	114	170
509-Pluto (Disney) (10/53)	6	12	18	42	79	115
510-Son of Black Beauty	5	10	15	31	53	75
511-Outlaw Trail (Zane Grey)-Kinstler-a	5	10	15	35	63	90
512-Flash Gordon (11/53)	9	18	27	60	120	180
513-Ben Bowie and His Mountain Men	5	10	15	34	60	85
514-Frosty the Snowman (11/53)	6	12	18	40	73	105
515-Andy Hardy	4	8	12	27	44	60
516-Double Trouble With Goober	4	8	12	27	44	60
517-Chip 'N' Dale (#1) (Disney)	11	22	33	73	157	240
518-Rivets (11/53)	5	10	15	30	50	70
519-Steve Canyon (#1)-Not by Milton Caniff	8	16	24	54	102	150
520-Wild Bill Elliott-Photo-c	5	10	15	5	63	90
521-Beetle Bailey (12/53)	7	14	21	49	92	135
522-The Brownies	5	10	15	35	63	90
523-Rin Tin Tin (TV)-Photo-c (12/53)	9	18	27	57	111	165
524-Tweety and Sylvester	7	14	21	49	92	135
525-Santa Claus Funnies	8	16	24	51	96	140
526-Napoleon	5	10	15	30	50	70
527-Charlie McCarthy	6	12	18	40	73	105
528-Queen of the West Dale Evans; photo-c	9	18	27	60	120	180
529-Little Beaver	5	10	15	34	60	85

Four Color Comics #567 © KING

Four Color Comics #631 © DIS

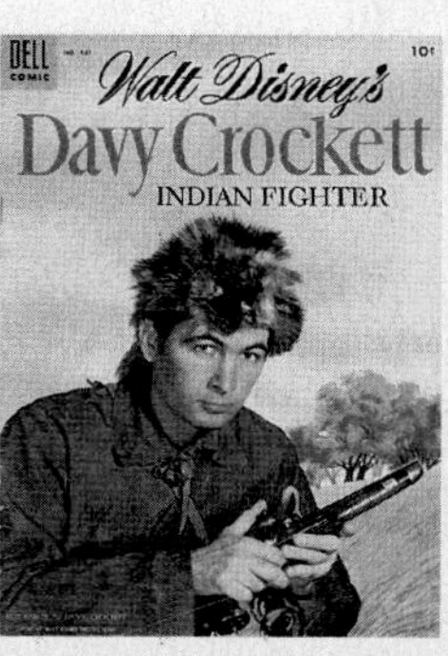

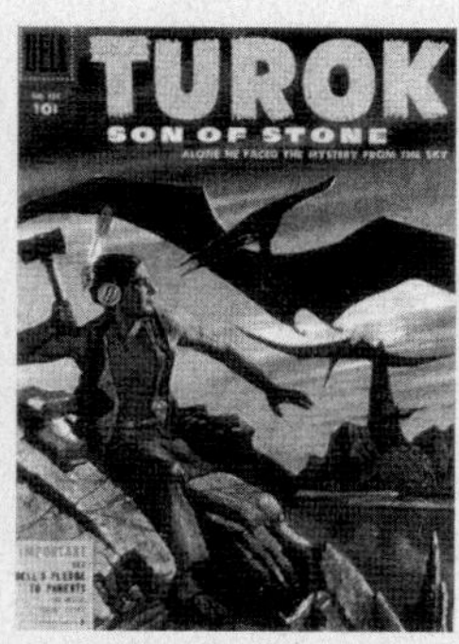

Four Color Comics #656 © WEST

	GD 2.0	VG 4.0	FN 6.0	VF 8.0	VF/NM 9.0	NM- 9.2
530-Bob Clampett's Beany and Cecil (TV) (1/54)	12	24	36	84	185	285
531-Duck Album (Disney)	7	14	21	44	82	120
532-The Rustlers (Zane Grey) (2-4/54)	5	10	15	33	57	80
533-Raggedy Ann and Andy	7	14	21	46	86	125
534-Western Marshal (Ernest Haycox's)-Kinstler-a	6	12	18	38	69	100
535-I Love Lucy (#1) (TV) (2/54)-Photo-c	44	88	132	326	738	1150
536-Daffy (3/54)	7	14	21	48	89	130
537-Stormy, the Thoroughbred… (Disney-Movie) on top 2/3 of each page; Pluto story on bottom 1/3 of each page (2/54)	5	10	15	33	57	80
538-The Mask of Zorro; Kinstler-a	11	22	33	73	157	240
539-Ben and Me (Disney) (3/54)	5	10	15	30	50	70
540-Knights of the Round Table (3/54) (Movie)-Photo-c	6	12	18	41	76	110
541-Johnny Mack Brown; photo-c	6	12	18	40	73	105
542-Super Circus Featuring Mary Hartline (TV) (3/54)	7	14	21	46	86	125
543-Uncle Wiggily (3/54)	5	10	15	34	63	90
544-Rob Roy (Disney-Movie)-Manning-a; photo-c	7	14	21	49	92	135
545-The Wonderful Adventures of Pinocchio-Partial reprint of Four Color #92 (Disney-Movie)	8	16	24	51	96	140
546-Buck Jones	6	12	18	41	76	110
547-Francis the Famous Talking Mule	5	10	15	35	63	90
548-Krazy Kat; not by Herriman (4/54)	5	10	15	31	53	75
549-Oswald the Rabbit (Lantz)	5	10	15	35	63	90
550-The Little Scouts	5	10	15	30	50	70
551-Bozo (4/54)	9	18	27	58	114	170
552-Beetle Bailey	7	14	21	49	92	135
553-Susie Q. Smith	5	10	15	30	50	70
554-Rusty Riley (Frank Godwin strip-r)	4	8	12	28	47	65
555-Range War (Zane Grey)	5	10	15	33	57	80
556-Double Trouble With Goober (5/54)	4	8	12	27	44	60
557-Ben Bowie and His Mountain Men	5	10	15	34	60	85
558-Elmer Fudd (5/54)	6	12	18	38	69	100
559-I Love Lucy (#2) (TV)-Photo-c	27	54	81	189	420	650
560-Duck Album (Disney) (5/54)	7	14	21	44	82	120
561-Mr. Magoo (5/54)	9	18	27	58	114	170
562-Goofy (Disney)(#2)	7	14	21	46	86	125
563-Rhubarb, the Millionaire Cat (6/54)	6	12	18	37	66	95
564-Li'l Bad Wolf (Disney)(#3)	5	10	15	34	60	85
565-Jungle Jim	5	10	15	33	57	80
566-Son of Black Beauty	5	10	15	31	53	75
567-Prince Valiant (#1)-By Bob Fuje (Movie)-Photo-c	10	20	30	64	132	200
568-Gypsy Colt (Movie) (6/54)	5	10	15	35	63	90
569-Priscilla's Pop	5	10	15	31	53	75
570-Bob Clampett's Beany and Cecil (TV)	12	24	36	84	185	285
571-Charlie McCarthy	6	12	18	40	73	105
572-Silvertip (Max Brand) (7/54); Kinstler-a	5	10	15	34	60	85
573-The Little People by Walt Scott	5	10	15	35	63	90
574-The Hand of Zorro; Kinstler-a	11	22	33	73	157	240
575-Annie Oakley and Tagg (TV)-Photo-c	9	18	27	59	117	175
576-Angel (#1) (8/54)	5	10	15	30	50	70
577-M.G.M.'s Spike and Tyke	5	10	15	35	63	90
578-Steve Canyon (8/54)	5	10	15	35	63	90
579-Francis the Famous Talking Mule	5	10	15	35	63	90
580-Six Gun Ranch (Luke Short-8/54)	5	10	15	33	57	80
581-Chip 'N' Dale (#2) (Disney)	6	12	18	42	79	115
582-Mowgli Jungle Book (Kipling) (8/54)	5	10	15	33	57	80
583-The Lost Wagon Train (Zane Grey)	5	10	15	33	57	80
584-Johnny Mack Brown-Photo-c	6	12	18	40	73	105
585-Bugs Bunny's Album	6	12	18	38	69	100
586-Duck Album (Disney)	7	14	21	44	82	120
587-The Little Scouts	5	10	15	30	50	70
588-King Richard and the Crusaders (Movie) (10/54) Matt Baker-a; photo-c	9	18	27	57	111	165
589-Buck Jones	6	12	18	41	76	110
590-Hansel and Gretel; partial photo-c	6	12	18	41	76	110
591-Western Marshal (Ernest Haycox's)-Kinstler-a	5	10	15	34	60	85
592-Super Circus (TV)	6	12	18	37	66	95
593-Oswald the Rabbit (Lantz)	5	10	15	35	63	90
594-Bozo (10/54)	9	18	27	58	114	170
595-Pluto (Disney)	6	12	18	37	66	95
596-Turok, Son of Stone (#1)	79	158	237	632	1416	2200
597-The Little King	5	10	15	34	60	85
598-Captain Davy Jones	5	10	15	35	63	90
599-Ben Bowie and His Mountain Men	5	10	15	34	60	85
600-Daisy Duck's Diary (#1) (Disney) (11/54)	8	16	24	51	96	140
601-Frosty the Snowman	6	12	18	40	73	105
602-Mr. Magoo and Gerald McBoing-Boing	9	18	27	58	114	170
603-M.G.M.'s The Two Mouseketeers	6	12	18	41	76	110
604-Shadow on the Trail (Zane Grey)	5	10	15	33	57	80
605-The Brownies-not by Kelly (12/54)	5	10	15	35	63	90
606-Sir Lancelot (not TV)	6	12	18	42	79	115
607-Santa Claus Funnies	8	16	24	51	96	140
608-Silvertip- "Valley of Vanishing Men" (Max Brand)-Kinstler-a	5	10	15	34	60	85
609-The Littlest Outlaw (Disney-Movie) (1/55)-Photo-c	6	12	18	40	73	105
610-Drum Beat (Movie); Alan Ladd photo-c	8	16	24	54	102	150
611-Duck Album (Disney)	7	14	21	44	82	120
612-Little Beaver (1/55)	5	10	15	33	57	80
613-Western Marshal (Ernest Haycox's) (2/55)-Kinstler-a	5	10	15	34	60	85
614-20,000 Leagues Under the Sea (Disney) (Movie) (2/55)-Painted-c	8	16	24	54	102	150
615-Daffy	7	14	21	48	89	130
616-To the Last Man (Zane Grey)	5	10	15	33	57	80
617-The Quest of Zorro	10	20	30	69	147	225
618-Johnny Mack Brown; photo-c	6	12	18	40	73	105
619-Krazy Kat; not by Herriman	5	10	15	31	53	75
620-Mowgli Jungle Book (Kipling)	5	10	15	33	57	80
621-Francis the Famous Talking Mule (4/55)	5	10	15	33	57	80
622-Beetle Bailey	7	14	21	49	92	135
623-Oswald the Rabbit (Lantz)	5	10	15	33	57	80
624-Treasure Island(Disney-Movie)(4/55)-Photo-c	7	14	21	48	89	130
625-Beaver Valley (Disney-Movie)	6	12	18	37	66	95
626-Ben Bowie and His Mountain Men	5	10	15	34	60	85
627-Goofy (Disney) (5/55)	7	14	21	46	86	125
628-Elmer Fudd	6	12	18	38	69	100
629-Lady and the Tramp with Jock (Disney)	7	14	21	49	92	135
630-Priscilla's Pop	5	10	15	31	53	75
631-Davy Crockett, Indian Fighter (#1) (Disney) (5/55) (TV)-Fess Parker photo-c	14	28	42	96	211	325
632-Fighting Caravans (Zane Grey)	5	10	15	33	57	80
633-The Little People by Walt Scott (6/55)	5	10	15	35	63	90
634-Lady and the Tramp Album (Disney) (6/55)	5	10	15	35	63	90
635-Bob Clampett's Beany and Cecil (TV)	12	24	36	84	185	285
636-Chip 'N' Dale (Disney)	6	12	18	42	79	115
637-Silvertip (Max Brand)-Kinstler-a	5	10	15	34	60	85
638-M.G.M.'s Spike and Tyke (8/55)	5	10	15	35	63	90
639-Davy Crockett at the Alamo (Disney) (7/55) (TV)-Fess Parker photo-c	11	22	33	76	163	260
640-Western Marshal(Ernest Haycox's)-Kinstler-a	5	10	15	34	60	85
641-Steve Canyon (1955)-by Caniff	5	10	15	35	63	90
642-M.G.M.'s The Two Mouseketeers	6	12	18	41	76	110
643-Wild Bill Elliott; photo-c	5	10	15	33	57	80
644-Sir Walter Raleigh (5/55)-Based on movie "The Virgin Queen"; photo-c	6	12	18	42	79	115
645-Johnny Mack Brown; photo-c	6	12	18	40	73	105
646-Dotty Dripple and Taffy (#1)	6	12	18	37	66	95
647-Bugs Bunny's Album (9/55)	6	12	18	38	69	100
648-Jace Pearson of the Texas Rangers (TV)-Photo-c	6	12	18	40	73	105
649-Duck Album (Disney)	7	14	21	44	82	120
650-Prince Valiant; by Bob Fuje	7	14	21	48	89	130
651-King Colt (Luke Short) (9/55)-Kinstler-a	5	10	15	33	57	80
652-Buck Jones	5	10	15	35	63	90
653-Smokey the Bear (#1) (10/55)	10	20	30	64	132	200
654-Pluto (Disney)	6	12	18	37	66	95
655-Francis the Famous Talking Mule	5	10	15	33	57	80
656-Turok, Son of Stone (#2) (10/55)	34	68	102	245	548	850
657-Ben Bowie and His Mountain Men	5	10	15	34	60	85
658-Goofy (Disney)	7	14	21	46	86	125
659-Daisy Duck's Diary (Disney)(#2)	6	12	18	40	73	105
660-Little Beaver	5	10	15	33	57	80
661-Frosty the Snowman	6	12	18	40	73	105
662-Zoo Parade (TV)-Marlin Perkins (11/55)	5	10	15	33	57	80
663-Winky Dink (TV)	8	16	24	51	96	140

Four Color Comics #673 © Tie-Ups

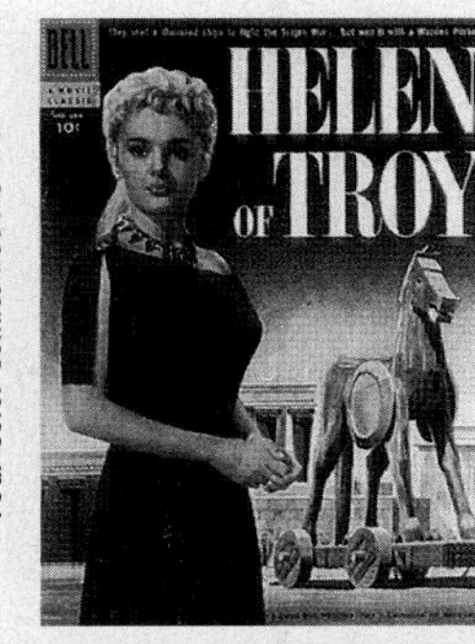

Four Color Comics #684 © WB

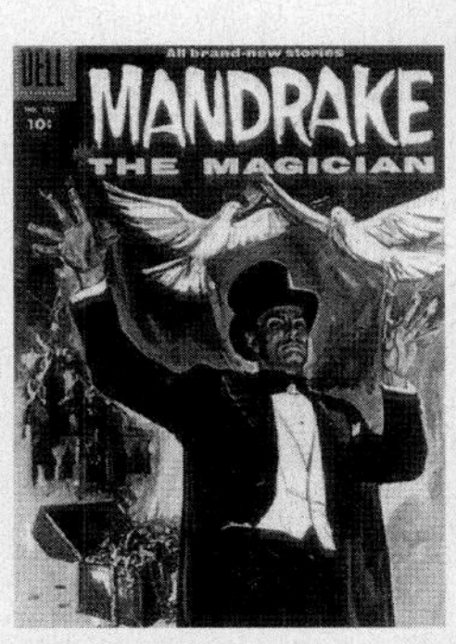

Four Color Comics #752 © KING

	GD 2.0	VG 4.0	FN 6.0	VF 8.0	VF/NM 9.0	NM- 9.2
664-Davy Crockett in the Great Keelboat Race (TV) (Disney) (11/55)-Fess Parker photo-c	11	22	33	75	160	245
665-The African Lion (Disney-Movie) (11/55)	5	10	15	34	60	85
666-Santa Claus Funnies	8	16	24	51	96	140
667-Silvertip and the Stolen Stallion (Max Brand) (12/55)-Kinstler-a	5	10	15	34	60	85
668-Dumbo (Disney) (12/55)-First of two printings. Dumbo on cover with starry sky. Reprints 4-Color #234?; same-c as #234	10	20	30	66	138	210
668-Dumbo (Disney) (1/58)-Second printing. Same cover altered, with Timothy Mouse added. Same contents as above	7	14	21	44	82	120
669-Robin Hood (Disney-Movie) (12/55)-Reprints #413 plus-c; photo-c	5	10	15	35	63	90
670-M.G.M's Mouse Musketeers (#1) (1/56)-Formerly the Two Mouseketeers	6	12	18	38	69	100
671-Davy Crockett and the River Pirates (TV) (Disney) (12/55)-Jesse Marsh-a; Fess Parker photo-c	11	22	33	75	160	245
672-Quentin Durward (1/56) (Movie)-Photo-c	6	12	18	42	79	115
673-Buffalo Bill, Jr. (#1) (TV)-James Arness photo-c	8	16	24	56	108	160
674-The Little Rascals (#1) (TV)	9	18	27	58	114	170
675-Steve Donovan, Western Marshal (#1) (TV)-Kinstler-a; photo-c	7	14	21	48	89	130
676-Will-Yum!	4	8	12	28	47	65
677-Little King	5	10	15	34	60	85
678-The Last Hunt (Movie)-Photo-c	6	12	18	42	79	115
679-Gunsmoke (#1) (TV)-Photo-c	16	32	48	110	243	375
680-Out Our Way with the Worry Wart (2/56)	5	10	15	30	50	70
681-Forever Darling (Movie) with Lucille Ball & Desi Arnaz (2/56)-; photo-c	10	20	30	66	138	210
682-The Sword & the Rose (Disney-Movie)-Reprint of #505; Renamed When Knighthood Was in Flower for the novel; photo-c	6	12	18	40	73	105
683-Hi and Lois (3/56)	5	10	15	34	60	85
684-Helen of Troy (Movie)-Buscema-a; photo-c	9	18	27	59	117	175
685-Johnny Mack Brown; photo-c	6	12	18	40	73	105
686-Duck Album (Disney)	7	14	21	44	82	120
687-The Indian Fighter (Movie)-Kirk Douglas photo-c	7	14	21	48	89	130
688-Alexander the Great (Movie) (5/56)-Buscema-a; photo-c	6	12	18	42	79	115
689-Elmer Fudd (3/56)	6	12	18	38	69	100
690-The Conqueror (Movie) - John Wayne photo-c	15	30	45	103	227	350
691-Dotty Dripple and Taffy	4	8	12	28	47	65
692-The Little People-Walt Scott	5	10	15	33	57	80
693-Song of the South (Disney) (1956)-Partial reprint of #129	7	14	21	49	92	135
694-Super Circus (TV)-Photo-c	6	12	18	37	66	95
695-Little Beaver	5	10	15	33	57	80
696-Krazy Kat; not by Herriman (4/56)	5	10	15	31	53	75
697-Oswald the Rabbit (Lantz)	5	10	15	33	57	80
698-Francis the Famous Talking Mule (4/56)	5	10	15	33	57	80
699-Prince Valiant-by Bob Fuje	7	14	21	48	89	130
700-Water Birds and the Olympic Elk (Disney-Movie) (4/56)	5	10	15	33	57	80
701-Jiminy Cricket (#1) (Disney) (5/56)	8	16	24	51	96	140
702-The Goofy Success Story (Disney)	7	14	21	46	86	125
703-Scamp (#1) (Disney)	8	16	24	56	108	160
704-Priscilla's Pop (5/56)	5	10	15	31	53	75
705-Brave Eagle (#1) (TV)-Photo-c	6	12	18	42	79	115
706-Bongo and Lumpjaw (Disney) (6/56)	6	12	18	37	66	95
707-Corky and White Shadow (Disney) (5/56)-Mickey Mouse Club (TV); photo-c	6	12	18	41	76	110
708-Smokey the Bear	6	12	18	40	73	105
709-The Searchers (Movie) - John Wayne photo-c	23	46	69	161	356	550
710-Francis the Famous Talking Mule	5	10	15	33	57	80
711-M.G.M's Mouse Musketeers	5	10	15	31	53	75
712-The Great Locomotive Chase (Disney-Movie) (9/56)-Photo-c	6	12	18	42	79	115
713-The Animal World (Movie) (8/56)	4	8	12	28	47	65
714-Spin and Marty (#1) (TV) (Disney)-Mickey Mouse Club (6/56); photo-c	11	22	33	72	154	235
715-Timmy (8/56)	5	10	15	35	63	90
716-Man in Space (Disney)(A science feature from Tomorrowland)	7	14	21	49	92	135
717-Moby Dick (Movie)-Gregory Peck photo-c	7	14	21	49	92	135
718-Dotty Dripple and Taffy	4	8	12	28	47	65
719-Prince Valiant; by Bob Fuje (8/56)	7	14	21	48	89	130

	GD 2.0	VG 4.0	FN 6.0	VF 8.0	VF/NM 9.0	NM- 9.2
720-Gunsmoke (TV)-James Arness photo-c	9	18	27	59	117	175
721-Captain Kangaroo (TV)-Photo-c	13	26	39	86	188	290
722-Johnny Mack Brown-Photo-c	6	12	18	40	73	105
723-Santiago (Movie)-Kinstler-a (9/56); Alan Ladd photo-c	8	16	24	54	102	150
724-Bugs Bunny's Album	5	10	15	34	60	85
725-Elmer Fudd (9/56)	5	10	15	31	53	75
726-Duck Album (Disney) (9/56)	6	12	18	37	66	95
727-The Nature of Things (TV) (Disney)-Jesse Marsh-a	5	10	15	33	57	80
728-M.G.M's Mouse Musketeers	5	10	15	31	53	75
729-Bob Son of Battle (11/56)	4	8	12	27	44	60
730-Smokey Stover	5	10	15	33	57	80
731-Silvertip and The Fighting Four (Max Brand)-Kinstler-a	5	10	15	34	60	85
732-Zorro, the Challenge of (10/56)	10	20	30	69	147	225
733-Buck Jones	5	10	15	35	63	90
734-Cheyenne (#1) (TV) (10/56)-Clint Walker photo-c	13	26	39	86	188	290
735-Crusader Rabbit (#1) (TV)	21	42	63	147	324	500
736-Pluto (Disney)	6	12	18	37	66	95
737-Steve Canyon-Caniff-a	5	10	15	35	63	90
738-Westward Ho, the Wagons (Disney-Movie)-Fess Parker photo-c	8	16	24	54	102	150
739-Bounty Guns (Luke Short)-Drucker-a	5	10	15	30	50	70
740-Chilly Willy (#1) (Walter Lantz)	8	16	24	51	96	140
741-The Fastest Gun Alive (Movie)(9/56)-Photo-c	7	14	21	44	82	120
742-Buffalo Bill, Jr. (TV)-Photo-c	5	10	15	35	63	90
743-Daisy Duck's Diary (Disney) (11/56)	6	12	18	40	73	105
744-Little Beaver	5	10	15	33	57	80
745-Francis the Famous Talking Mule	5	10	15	33	57	80
746-Dotty Dripple and Taffy	4	8	12	28	47	65
747-Goofy (Disney)	7	14	21	46	86	125
748-Frosty the Snowman (11/56)	5	10	15	35	63	90
749-Secrets of Life (Disney-Movie)-Photo-c	5	10	15	31	53	75
750-The Great Cat Family (Disney-TV/Movie)-Pinocchio & Alice app.	6	12	18	37	66	95
751-Our Miss Brooks (TV)-Photo-c	7	14	21	48	89	130
752-Mandrake, the Magician	10	20	30	64	132	200
753-Walt Scott's Little People (11/56)	5	10	15	33	57	80
754-Smokey the Bear	6	12	18	40	73	105
755-The Littlest Snowman (12/56)	5	10	15	35	63	90
756-Santa Claus Funnies	8	16	24	51	96	140
757-The True Story of Jesse James (Movie)-Photo-c	8	16	24	54	102	150
758-Bear Country (Disney-Movie)	5	10	15	33	57	80
759-Circus Boy (TV)-The Monkees' Mickey Dolenz photo-c (12/56)	12	24	36	79	170	260
760-The Hardy Boys (#1) (TV) (Disney)-Mickey Mouse Club; photo-c	9	18	27	61	123	185
761-Howdy Doody (TV) (1/57)	9	18	27	61	123	185
762-The Sharkfighters (Movie) (1/57); Buscema-a; photo-c	7	14	21	49	92	125
763-Grandma Duck's Farm Friends (#1) (Disney)	8	16	24	51	96	140
764-M.G.M's Mouse Musketeers	5	10	15	31	53	75
765-Will-Yum!	4	8	12	28	47	65
766-Buffalo Bill, Jr. (TV)-Photo-c	5	10	15	35	63	90
767-Spin and Marty (TV) (Disney)-Mickey Mouse Club (2/57)	8	16	24	56	108	160
768-Steve Donovan, Western Marshal (TV)-Kinstler-a; photo-c	6	12	18	38	69	100
769-Gunsmoke (TV)-James Arness photo-c	9	18	27	59	117	175
770-Brave Eagle (TV)-Photo-c	5	10	15	31	53	75
771-Brand of Empire (Luke Short)(3/57)-Drucker-a	5	10	15	30	50	70
772-Cheyenne (TV)-Clint Walker photo-c	8	16	24	51	96	140
773-The Brave One (Movie)-Photo-c	5	10	15	34	60	85
774-Hi and Lois (3/57)	4	8	12	28	47	65
775-Sir Lancelot and Brian (TV)-Buscema-a; photo-c	9	18	27	59	117	175
776-Johnny Mack Brown; photo-c	6	12	18	40	73	105
777-Scamp (Disney) (3/57)	6	12	18	40	73	105
778-The Little Rascals (TV)	6	12	18	38	69	100
779-Lee Hunter, Indian Fighter (3/57)	6	12	18	37	66	95
780-Captain Kangaroo (TV)-Photo-c	11	22	33	73	157	240
781-Fury (#1) (TV) (3/57)-Photo-c	7	14	21	49	92	135
782-Duck Album (Disney)	6	12	18	37	66	95

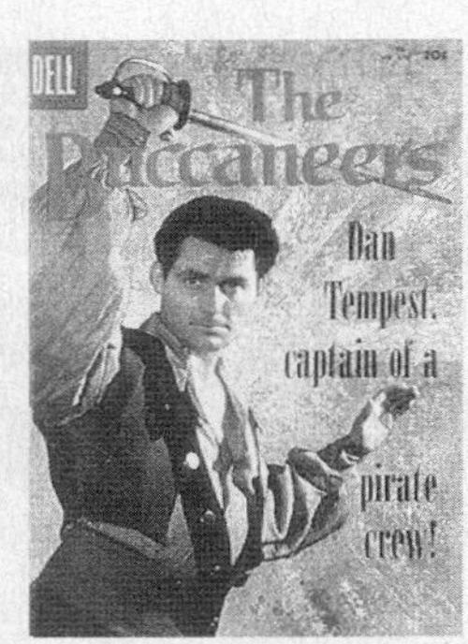

Four Color Comics #800 © DELL

Four Color Comics #854 © DELL

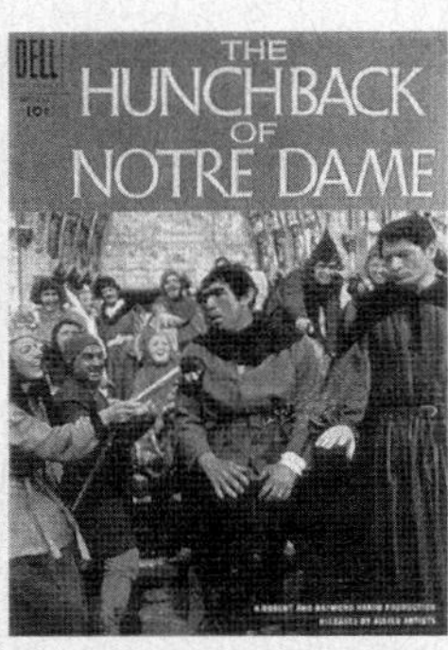

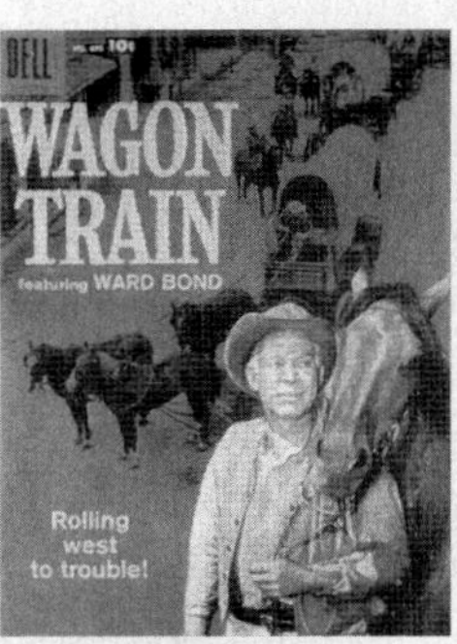

Four Color Comics #895 © Revere

	GD 2.0	VG 4.0	FN 6.0	VF 8.0	VF/NM 9.0	NM- 9.2
783-Elmer Fudd	5	10	15	31	53	75
784-Around the World in 80 Days (Movie) (2/57)-Photo-c	7	14	21	46	86	125
785-Circus Boy (TV) (4/57)-The Monkees' Mickey Dolenz photo-c	9	18	27	62	126	190
786-Cinderella (Disney) (3/57)-Partial-r of #272	6	12	18	41	76	110
787-Little Hiawatha (Disney) (4/57)(#2)	5	10	15	33	57	80
788-Prince Valiant; by Bob Fuje	7	14	21	44	82	120
789-Silvertip-Valley Thieves (Max Brand) (4/57)-Kinstler-a	5	10	15	34	60	85
790-The Wings of Eagles (Movie) (John Wayne)-Toth-a; John Wayne photo-c; 10¢ & 15¢ editions exist	12	24	36	83	182	280
791-The 77th Bengal Lancers (TV)-Photo-c	6	12	18	41	76	110
792-Oswald the Rabbit (Lantz)	5	10	15	33	57	80
793-Morty Meekle	5	10	15	30	50	70
794-The Count of Monte Cristo (5/57) (Movie)-Buscema-a	8	16	24	51	96	140
795-Jiminy Cricket (Disney)(#2)	6	12	18	38	69	100
796-Ludwig Bemelman's Madeleine and Genevieve	5	10	15	30	50	70
797-Gunsmoke (TV)-Photo-c	9	18	27	59	117	175
798-Buffalo Bill, Jr. (TV)-Photo-c	5	10	15	35	63	90
799-Priscilla's Pop	5	10	15	31	53	75
800-The Buccaneers (TV)-Photo-c	6	12	18	42	79	115
801-Dotty Dripple and Taffy	4	8	12	28	47	65
802-Goofy (Disney) (5/57)	7	14	21	46	86	125
803-Cheyenne (TV)-Clint Walker photo-c	8	16	24	51	96	140
804-Steve Canyon-Caniff-a (1957)	5	10	15	35	63	90
805-Crusader Rabbit (TV)	16	32	48	111	246	380
806-Scamp (Disney) (6/57)	6	12	18	40	73	105
807-Savage Range (Luke Short)-Drucker-a	5	10	15	30	50	70
808-Spin and Marty (TV)(Disney)-Mickey Mouse Club; photo-c	8	16	24	56	108	160
809-The Little People (Walt Scott)	5	10	15	33	57	80
810-Francis the Famous Talking Mule	5	10	15	31	53	75
811-Howdy Doody (TV) (7/57)	9	18	27	61	123	185
812-The Big Land (Movie); Alan Ladd photo-c	8	16	24	52	99	145
813-Circus Boy (TV)-The Monkees' Mickey Dolenz photo-c	9	18	27	62	126	190
814-Covered Wagons, Ho! (Disney)-Donald Duck (TV) (6/57); Mickey Mouse app.	5	10	15	34	60	85
815-Dragoon Wells Massacre (Movie)-photo-c	7	14	21	46	86	125
816-Brave Eagle (TV)-photo-c	5	10	15	31	53	75
817-Little Beaver	5	10	15	33	57	80
818-Smokey the Bear (6/57)	6	12	18	40	73	105
819-Mickey Mouse in Magicland (Disney) (7/57)	6	12	18	41	76	110
820-The Oklahoman (Movie)-Photo-c	8	16	24	54	102	150
821-Wringle Wrangle (Disney)-Based on movie "Westward Ho, the Wagons"; Marsh-a; Fess Parker photo-c	7	14	21	46	86	125
822-Paul Revere's Ride with Johnny Tremain (TV) (Disney)-Toth-a	7	14	21	49	92	135
823-Timmy	5	10	15	31	53	75
824-The Pride and the Passion (Movie) (8/57)-Frank Sinatra & Cary Grant photo-c	9	18	27	59	117	175
825-The Little Rascals (TV)	6	12	18	38	69	100
826-Spin and Marty and Annette (TV) (Disney)-Mickey Mouse Club; Annette Funicello photo-c	18	36	54	124	275	425
827-Smokey Stover (8/57)	5	10	15	33	57	80
828-Buffalo Bill, Jr. (TV)-Photo-c	5	10	15	35	63	90
829-Tales of the Pony Express (TV) (8/57)-Painted-c	5	10	15	35	63	90
830-The Hardy Boys (TV) (Disney)-Mickey Mouse Club (8/57); photo-c	8	16	24	54	102	150
831-No Sleep 'Til Dawn (Movie)-Karl Malden photo-c	6	12	18	41	76	110
832-Lolly and Pepper (#1)	6	12	18	37	66	95
833-Scamp (Disney) (9/57)	6	12	18	40	73	105
834-Johnny Mack Brown; photo-c	6	12	18	40	73	105
835-Silvertip-The False Rider (Max Brand)	5	10	15	34	60	85
836-Man in Flight (Disney) (TV) (9/57)	6	12	18	41	76	110
837-Cotton Woods, (All-American Athlete...)	5	10	15	30	50	70
838-Bugs Bunny's Life Story Album (9/57)	5	10	15	34	60	85
839-The Vigilantes (Movie)	7	14	21	44	82	120
840-Duck Album (Disney) (9/57)	6	12	18	37	66	95
841-Elmer Fudd	5	10	15	31	53	75
842-The Nature of Things (Disney-Movie) ('57)-Jesse Marsh-a (TV series)	5	10	15	33	57	80
843-The First Americans (Disney) (TV)-Marsh-a	7	14	21	49	92	135
844-Gunsmoke (TV)-Photo-c	9	18	27	59	117	175
845-The Land Unknown (Movie)-Alex Toth-a	10	20	30	66	138	210
846-Gun Glory (Movie)-by Alex Toth; photo-c	8	16	24	51	96	140
847-Perri (squirrels) (Disney-Movie)-Two different covers published	6	12	18	37	66	95
848-Marauder's Moon (Luke Short)	5	10	15	30	50	70
849-Prince Valiant; by Bob Fuje	7	14	21	44	82	120
850-Buck Jones	5	10	15	35	63	90
851-The Story of Mankind (Movie) (1/58)-Hedy Lamarr & Vincent Price photo-c	7	14	21	44	82	120
852-Chilly Willy (2/58) (Lantz)	5	10	15	34	60	85
853-Pluto (Disney) (10/57)	6	12	18	37	66	95
854-The Hunchback of Notre Dame (Movie)-Photo-c	11	22	33	73	157	240
855-Broken Arrow (TV)-Photo-c	6	12	18	37	66	95
856-Buffalo Bill, Jr. (TV)-Photo-c	5	10	15	35	63	90
857-The Goofy Adventure Story (Disney) (11/57)	7	14	21	46	86	125
858-Daisy Duck's Diary (Disney) (11/57)	5	10	15	35	63	90
859-Topper and Neil (TV) (11/57)	5	10	15	34	60	85
860-Wyatt Earp (#1) (TV)-Manning-a; photo-c	9	18	27	59	117	175
861-Frosty the Snowman	5	10	15	35	63	90
862-The Truth About Mother Goose (Disney-Movie) (11/57)	7	14	21	44	82	120
863-Francis the Famous Talking Mule	5	10	15	31	53	75
864-The Littlest Snowman	5	10	15	35	63	90
865-Andy Burnett (TV) (Disney) (12/57)-Photo-c	8	16	24	52	99	145
866-Mars and Beyond (Disney-TV)(A science feature from Tomorrowland)	7	14	21	49	92	135
867-Santa Claus Funnies	8	16	24	51	96	140
868-The Little People (12/57)	5	10	15	33	57	80
869-Old Yeller (Disney-Movie)-Photo-c	6	12	18	37	66	95
870-Little Beaver (1/58)	5	10	15	33	57	80
871-Curly Kayoe	5	10	15	30	50	70
872-Captain Kangaroo (TV)-Photo-c	11	22	33	73	157	240
873-Grandma Duck's Farm Friends (Disney)	6	12	18	37	66	95
874-Old Ironsides (Disney-Movie with Johnny Tremain) (1/58)	6	12	18	42	79	115
875-Trumpets West (Luke Short) (2/58)	5	10	15	30	50	70
876-Tales of Wells Fargo (#1)(TV)(2/58)-Photo-c	8	16	24	52	99	145
877-Frontier Doctor with Rex Allen (TV)-Alex Toth-a; Rex Allen photo-c	8	16	24	56	108	160
878-Peanuts (#1)-Schulz-c only (2/58)	75	150	225	600	1350	2100
879-Brave Eagle (TV) (2/58)-Photo-c	5	10	15	31	53	75
880-Steve Donovan, Western Marshal-Drucker-a (TV)-Photo-c	5	10	15	31	53	75
881-The Captain and the Kids (2/58)	5	10	15	30	50	70
882-Zorro (Disney)-1st Disney issue; by Alex Toth (TV) (2/58); photo-c	13	26	39	89	195	300
883-The Little Rascals (TV)	5	10	15	35	63	90
884-Hawkeye and the Last of the Mohicans (TV) (3/58); photo-c	7	14	21	44	82	120
885-Fury (TV) (3/58)-Photo-c	5	10	15	35	63	90
886-Bongo and Lumpjaw (Disney) (3/58)	4	8	12	28	47	65
887-The Hardy Boys (Disney) (TV)-Mickey Mouse Club (1/58)-Photo-c	8	16	24	54	102	150
888-Elmer Fudd (3/58)	5	10	15	31	53	75
889-Clint and Mac (Disney) (TV) (3/58)-Alex Toth-a; photo-c	10	20	30	64	132	200
890-Wyatt Earp (TV)-by Russ Manning; photo-c	6	12	18	42	79	115
891-Light in the Forest (Disney-Movie) (3/58)-Fess Parker photo-c	6	12	18	42	79	115
892-Maverick (#1) (TV) (4/58)-James Garner photo-c	18	36	54	124	275	425
893-Jim Bowie (TV)-Photo-c	6	12	18	40	73	105
894-Oswald the Rabbit (Lantz)	5	10	15	33	57	80
895-Wagon Train (#1) (TV) (3/58)-Photo-c	9	18	27	62	126	190
896-The Adventures of Tinker Bell (Disney)	9	18	27	57	111	165
897-Jiminy Cricket (Disney)	6	12	18	38	69	100
898-Silvertip (Max Brand)-Kinstler-a (5/58)	5	10	15	34	60	85
899-Goofy (Disney) (5/58)	5	10	15	35	63	90
900-Prince Valiant; by Bob Fuje	7	14	21	44	82	120
901-Little Hiawatha (Disney)	5	10	15	33	57	80
902-Will-Yum!	4	8	12	28	47	65
903-Dotty Dripple and Taffy	4	8	12	28	47	65

Four Color Comics #919 © Cal Nat

Four Color Comics #924 © WB

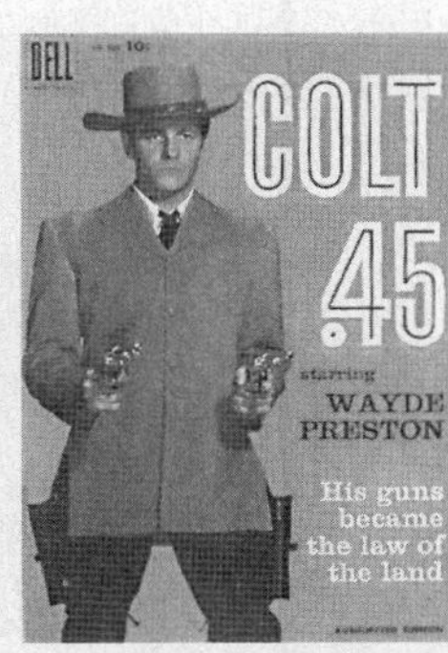

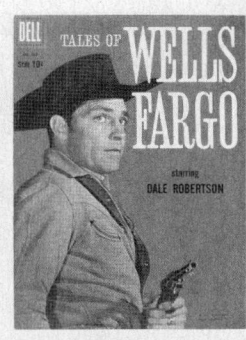

Four Color Comics #968 © DELL

	GD 2.0	VG 4.0	FN 6.0	VF 8.0	VF/NM 9.0	NM- 9.2
904-Lee Hunter, Indian Fighter	5	10	15	30	50	70
905-Annette (Disney) (TV) (5/58)-Mickey Mouse Club; Annette Funicello photo-c	21	42	63	147	324	500
906-Francis the Famous Talking Mule	5	10	15	31	53	75
907-Sugarfoot (#1) (TV)Toth-a; photo-c	10	20	30	67	141	215
908-The Little People and the Giant-Walt Scott (5/58)	5	10	15	33	57	80
909-Smitty	4	8	12	23	37	50
910-The Vikings (Movie)-Buscema-a; Kirk Douglas photo-c	8	16	24	51	96	140
911-The Gray Ghost (TV)-Photo-c	7	14	21	49	92	135
912-Leave It to Beaver (#1) (TV)-Photo-c	13	26	39	91	201	310
913-The Left-Handed Gun (Movie) (7/58); Paul Newman photo-c	9	18	27	57	111	165
914-No Time for Sergeants (Movie)-Andy Griffith photo-c; Toth-a	9	18	27	60	120	180
915-Casey Jones (TV)-Alan Hale photo-c	5	10	15	34	60	85
916-Red Ryder Ranch Comics (7/58)	4	8	12	28	47	65
917-The Life of Riley (TV)-Photo-c	9	18	27	62	126	190
918-Beep Beep, the Roadrunner (#1) (7/58)-Published with two different back covers	12	24	36	81	176	270
919-Boots and Saddles (#1) (TV)-Photo-c	7	14	21	46	86	125
920-Zorro (Disney) (TV) (6/58)Toth-a; photo-c	10	20	30	66	138	210
921-Wyatt Earp (TV)-Manning-a; photo-c	6	12	18	42	79	115
922-Johnny Mack Brown by Russ Manning; photo-c	6	12	18	41	76	110
923-Timmy	5	10	15	31	53	75
924-Colt .45 (#1) (TV) (8/58)-W. Preston photo-c	9	18	27	62	126	190
925-Last of the Fast Guns (Movie) (8/58)-Photo-c	6	12	18	41	76	110
926-Peter Pan (Disney)-Reprint of #442	5	10	15	33	57	80
927-Top Gun (Luke Short) Buscema-a	5	10	15	30	50	70
928-Sea Hunt (#1) (9/58) (TV)-Lloyd Bridges photo-c	10	20	30	66	138	210
929-Brave Eagle (TV)-Photo-c	5	10	15	31	53	75
930-Maverick (TV) (7/58)-James Garner photo-c	9	18	27	62	126	190
931-Have Gun, Will Travel (#1) (TV)-Photo-c	12	24	36	79	170	260
932-Smokey the Bear (His Life Story)	6	12	18	40	73	105
933-Zorro (Disney, 9/58) (TV)-Alex Toth-a; photo-c	10	20	30	66	138	210
934-Restless Gun (#1) (TV)-Photo-c	9	18	27	61	123	185
935-King of the Royal Mounted	5	10	15	31	53	75
936-The Little Rascals (TV)	5	10	15	35	63	90
937-Ruff and Reddy (#1) (9/58) (TV) (1st Hanna-Barbera comic book)	10	20	30	67	141	215
938-Elmer Fudd (9/58)	5	10	15	31	53	75
939-Steve Canyon - not by Caniff	5	10	15	35	63	90
940-Lolly and Pepper (10/58)	4	8	12	28	47	65
941-Pluto (Disney) (10/58)	5	10	15	33	57	80
942-Pony Express (Tales of the ...) (TV)	5	10	15	31	53	75
943-White Wilderness (Disney-Movie) (10/58)	6	12	18	37	66	95
944-The 7th Voyage of Sinbad (Movie) (9/58)-Buscema-a; photo-c	11	22	33	73	157	240
945-Maverick (TV)-James Garner/Jack Kelly photo-c	9	18	27	62	126	190
946-The Big Country (Movie)-Photo-c	6	12	18	42	79	115
947-Broken Arrow (TV)-Photo-c (11/58)	5	10	15	31	53	75
948-Daisy Duck's Diary (Disney) (11/58)	5	10	15	35	63	90
949-High Adventure(Lowell Thomas')(TV)-Photo-c	5	10	15	34	60	85
950-Frosty the Snowman	5	10	15	35	63	90
951-The Lennon Sisters Life Story (TV)-Toth-a, 32 pgs.; photo-c	11	22	33	73	157	240
952-Goofy (Disney) (11/58)	5	10	15	35	63	90
953-Francis the Famous Talking Mule	5	10	15	31	53	75
954-Man in Space-Satellites (TV)	6	12	18	41	76	110
955-Hi and Lois (11/58)	4	8	12	28	47	65
956-Ricky Nelson (#1) (TV)-Photo-c	15	30	45	100	220	340
957-Buffalo Bee (#1) (TV)	8	16	24	52	99	145
958-Santa Claus Funnies	6	12	18	41	76	110
959-Christmas Stories-(Walt Scott's Little People) (1951-56 strip reprints)	5	10	15	33	57	80
960-Zorro (Disney) (TV) (12/58)-Toth art; photo-c	10	20	30	66	138	210
961-Jace Pearson's Tales of the Texas Rangers (TV)-Spiegle-a; photo-c	5	10	15	34	60	85
962-Maverick (TV) (1/59)-James Garner/Jack Kelly photo-c	9	18	27	62	126	190
963-Johnny Mack Brown; photo-c	6	12	18	40	73	105
964-The Hardy Boys (TV) (Disney) (1/59)-Mickey Mouse Club; photo-c	8	16	24	54	102	150

	GD 2.0	VG 4.0	FN 6.0	VF 8.0	VF/NM 9.0	NM- 9.2
965-Grandma Duck's Farm Friends (Disney)(1/59)	5	10	15	34	60	85
966-Tonka (starring Sal Mineo; Disney-Movie)-Photo-c	8	16	24	54	102	150
967-Chilly Willy (2/59) (Lantz)	5	10	15	34	60	85
968-Tales of Wells Fargo (TV)-Photo-c	7	14	21	48	89	130
969-Peanuts (2/59)	27	54	81	189	420	650
970-Lawman (#1) (TV)-Photo-c	10	20	30	69	147	225
971-Wagon Train (TV)-Photo-c	6	12	18	41	76	110
972-Tom Thumb (Movie)-George Pal (1/59)	8	16	24	52	99	145
973-Sleeping Beauty and the Prince(Disney)(5/59)	10	20	30	66	138	210
974-The Little Rascals (TV) (3/59)	5	10	15	35	63	90
975-Fury (TV)-Photo-c	5	10	15	35	63	90
976-Zorro (Disney) (TV)-Toth-a; photo-c	10	20	30	66	138	210
977-Elmer Fudd (3/59)	5	10	15	31	53	75
978-Lolly and Pepper	4	8	12	28	47	65
979-Oswald the Rabbit (Lantz)	5	10	15	33	57	80
980-Maverick (TV) (4-6/59)-James Garner/Jack Kelly photo-c	9	18	27	62	126	190
981-Ruff and Reddy (TV) (Hanna-Barbera)	7	14	21	44	82	120
982-The New Adventures of Tinker Bell (TV) (Disney)	8	16	24	52	99	145
983-Have Gun, Will Travel (TV) (4-6/59)-Photo-c	9	18	27	59	117	175
984-Sleeping Beauty's Fairy Godmothers (Disney)	8	16	24	56	108	160
985-Shaggy Dog (Disney-Movie)-Photo-all four covers; Annette on back-c(5/59)	7	14	21	44	82	120
986-Restless Gun (TV)-Photo-c	7	14	21	46	86	125
987-Goofy (Disney) (7/59)	5	10	15	35	63	90
988-Little Hiawatha (Disney)	5	10	15	33	57	80
989-Jiminy Cricket (Disney) (5-7/59)	6	12	18	38	69	100
990-Huckleberry Hound (#1)(TV)(Hanna-Barbera); 1st app. Huck, Yogi Bear, & Pixie & Dixie & Mr. Jinks	15	30	45	103	227	350
991-Francis the Famous Talking Mule	5	10	15	31	53	75
992-Sugarfoot (TV)-Toth-a; photo-c	9	18	27	63	129	195
993-Jim Bowie (TV)-Photo-c	5	10	15	34	60	85
994-Sea Hunt (TV)-Lloyd Bridges photo-c	7	14	21	48	89	130
995-Donald Duck Album (Disney) (5-7/59)(#1)	6	12	18	42	79	115
996-Nevada (Zane Grey)	5	10	15	33	57	80
997-Walt Disney Presents-Tales of Texas John Slaughter (#1) (TV) (Disney)-Photo-c; photo of W. Disney inside-c	6	12	18	42	79	115
998-Ricky Nelson (TV)-Photo-c	15	30	45	100	220	340
999-Leave It to Beaver (TV)-Photo-c	12	24	36	79	170	260
1000-The Gray Ghost (TV) (6-8/59)-Photo-c	7	14	21	49	92	135
1001-Lowell Thomas' High Adventure (TV) (8-10/59)-Photo-c	5	10	15	33	57	80
1002-Buffalo Bee (TV)	6	12	18	40	73	105
1003-Zorro (TV) (Disney)-Toth-a; photo-c	10	20	30	66	138	210
1004-Colt .45 (TV) (6-8/59)-Photo-c	7	14	21	48	89	130
1005-Maverick (TV)-James Garner/Jack Kelly photo-c	9	18	27	62	126	190
1006-Hercules (Movie)-Buscema-a; photo-c	8	16	24	56	108	160
1007-John Paul Jones (Movie)-Robert Stack photo-c	5	10	15	35	63	90
1008-Beep Beep, the Road Runner (7-9/59)	7	14	21	49	92	135
1009-The Rifleman (#1) (TV)-Photo-c	20	40	60	138	307	475
1010-Grandma Duck's Farm Friends (Disney)-by Carl Barks	11	22	33	73	157	240
1011-Buckskin (#1) (TV)-Photo-c	7	14	21	44	82	120
1012-Last Train from Gun Hill (Movie) (7/59)-Photo-c	8	16	24	52	99	145
1013-Bat Masterson (#1) (TV) (8/59)-Gene Barry photo-c	10	20	30	66	138	210
1014-The Lennon Sisters (TV)-Toth-a; photo-c	10	20	30	69	147	225
1015-Peanuts-Schulz-c	27	54	81	189	420	650
1016-Smokey the Bear Nature Stories	5	10	15	31	53	75
1017-Chilly Willy (Lantz)	5	10	15	34	60	85
1018-Rio Bravo (Movie)(6/59)-John Wayne; Toth-a; John Wayne, Dean Martin & Ricky Nelson photo-c	24	48	72	168	372	575
1019-Wagon Train (TV)-Photo-c	6	12	18	41	76	110
1020-Jungle Jim-McWilliams-a	5	10	15	31	53	75
1021-Jace Pearson's Tales of the Texas Rangers (TV)-Photo-c	5	10	15	34	60	85
1022-Timmy	5	10	15	31	53	75
1023-Tales of Wells Fargo (TV)-Photo-c	7	14	21	48	89	130
1024-Darby O'Gill and the Little People (Disney-Movie)-Toth-a; photo-c	9	18	27	57	111	165
1025-Vacation in Disneyland (8-10/59)-Carl Barks-a(24pgs.) (Disney)						

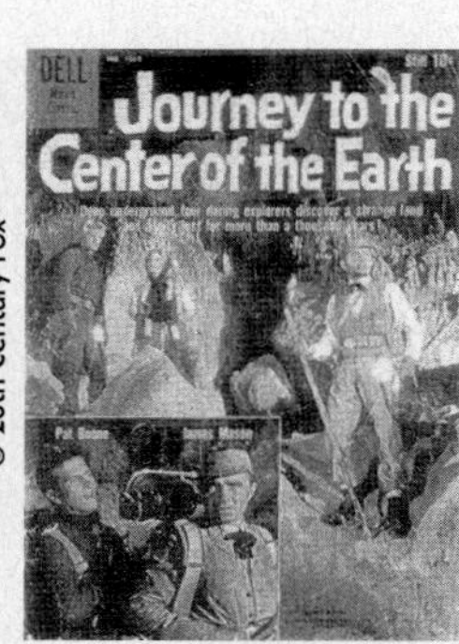

Four Color Comics #1060 © 20th Century Fox

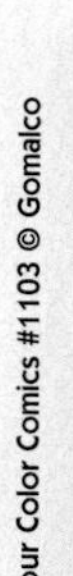
Four Color Comics #1103 © Gomalco

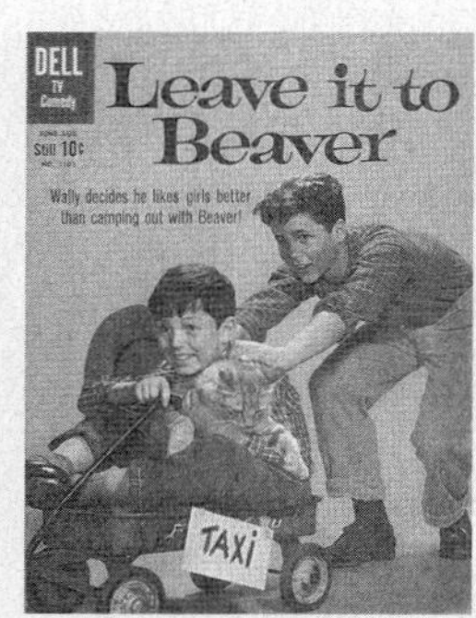

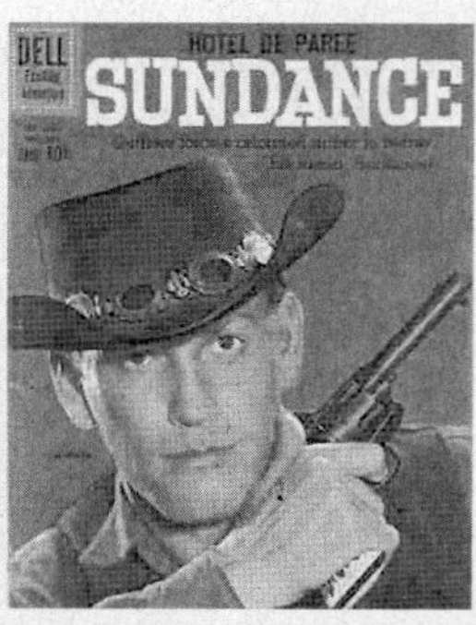

Four Color Comics #1126 © DELL

	GD 2.0	VG 4.0	FN 6.0	VF 8.0	VF/NM 9.0	NM- 9.2
	14	28	42	93	204	315
1026-Spin and Marty (TV) (Disney) (9-11/59)-Mickey Mouse Club; photo-c	7	14	21	44	82	120
1027-The Texan (#1)(TV)-Photo-c	7	14	21	49	92	135
1028-Rawhide (#1) (TV) (9-11/59)-Clint Eastwood photo-c; Tufts-a	21	42	63	147	324	500
1029-Boots and Saddles (TV) (9/59)-Photo-c	5	10	15	33	57	80
1030-Spanky and Alfalfa, the Little Rascals (TV)	5	10	15	35	63	90
1031-Fury (TV)-Photo-c	5	10	15	35	63	90
1032-Elmer Fudd	5	10	15	31	53	75
1033-Steve Canyon-not by Caniff; photo-c	5	10	15	35	63	90
1034-Nancy and Sluggo Summer Camp (9-11/59)	5	10	15	30	50	70
1035-Lawman (TV)-Photo-c	7	14	21	46	86	125
1036-The Big Circus (Movie)-Photo-c	6	12	18	40	73	105
1037-Zorro (Disney) (TV)-Tufts-a; Annette Funicello photo-c	12	24	36	81	176	270
1038-Ruff and Reddy (TV)(Hanna-Barbera)(1959)	7	14	21	44	82	120
1039-Pluto (Disney) (11-1/60)	5	10	15	33	57	80
1040-Quick Draw McGraw (#1) (TV) (Hanna-Barbera) (12-2/60)	12	24	36	83	182	280
1041-Sea Hunt (TV) (10-12/59)-Toth-a; Lloyd Bridges photo-c	7	14	21	48	89	130
1042-The Three Chipmunks (Alvin, Simon & Theodore) (#1) (TV) (10-12/59)	9	18	27	60	120	180
1043-The Three Stooges (#1)-Photo-c	22	44	66	155	345	535
1044-Have Gun, Will Travel (TV)-Photo-c	9	18	27	59	117	175
1045-Restless Gun (TV)-Photo-c	7	14	21	46	86	125
1046-Beep Beep, the Road Runner (11-1/60)	7	14	21	49	92	135
1047-Gyro Gearloose (#1) (Disney)-All Barks-c/a	15	30	45	100	220	340
1048-The Horse Soldiers (Movie) (John Wayne)-Sekowsky-a; painted cover featuring John Wayne	11	22	33	76	163	250
1049-Don't Give Up the Ship (Movie) (8/59)-Jerry Lewis photo-c	9	18	27	58	114	170
1050-Huckleberry Hound (TV) (Hanna-Barbera) (10-12/59)	10	20	30	64	132	200
1051-Donald in Mathmagic Land (Disney-Movie)	8	16	24	56	108	160
1052-Ben-Hur (Movie) (11/59)-Manning-a	9	18	27	61	123	185
1053-Goofy (Disney) (11-1/60)	5	10	15	35	63	90
1054-Huckleberry Hound Winter Fun (TV) (Hanna-Barbera) (12/59)	10	20	30	64	132	200
1055-Daisy Duck's Diary (Disney)-by Carl Barks (11-1/60)	8	16	24	56	108	160
1056-Yellowstone Kelly (Movie)-Clint Walker photo-c	5	10	15	35	63	90
1057-Mickey Mouse Album (Disney)	6	12	18	37	66	95
1058-Colt .45 (TV)-Photo-c	7	14	21	48	89	130
1059-Sugarfoot (TV)-Photo-c	7	14	21	49	92	135
1060-Journey to the Center of the Earth (Movie)-Pat Boone & James Mason photo-c	10	20	30	64	132	200
1061-Buffalo Bee (TV)	6	12	18	40	73	105
1062-Christmas Stories (Walt Scott's Little People strip-r)	5	10	15	33	57	80
1063-Santa Claus Funnies	6	12	18	41	76	110
1064-Bugs Bunny's Merry Christmas (12/59)	5	10	15	34	60	85
1065-Frosty the Snowman	5	10	15	35	63	90
1066-77 Sunset Strip (#1) (TV)-Toth-a (1-3/60)-Efrem Zimbalist, Jr. & Edd "Kookie" Byrnes photo-c	9	18	27	61	123	185
1067-Yogi Bear (#1) (TV) (Hanna-Barbera)	12	24	36	82	179	275
1068-Francis the Famous Talking Mule	5	10	15	31	53	75
1069-The FBI Story (Movie)-Toth-a; James Stewart photo on-c	8	16	24	56	108	160
1070-Solomon and Sheba (Movie)-Sekowsky-a; photo-c	8	16	24	55	105	155
1071-The Real McCoys (#1) (TV) (1-3/60)-Toth-a; Walter Brennan photo-c	8	16	24	51	96	140
1072-Blythe (Marge's)	5	10	15	34	60	85
1073-Grandma Duck's Farm Friends-Barks-c/a (Disney)	11	22	33	73	157	240
1074-Chilly Willy (Lantz)	5	10	15	34	60	85
1075-Tales of Wells Fargo (TV)-Photo-c	7	14	21	48	89	130
1076-The Rebel (#1) (TV)-Sekowsky-a; photo-c	9	18	27	61	123	185
1077-The Deputy (#1) (TV)-Buscema-a; Henry Fonda photo-c	10	20	30	64	132	200
1078-The Three Stooges (2-4/60)-Photo-c	11	22	33	73	157	240
1079-The Little Rascals (TV) (Spanky & Alfalfa)	5	10	15	35	63	90

	GD 2.0	VG 4.0	FN 6.0	VF 8.0	VF/NM 9.0	NM- 9.2
1080-Fury (TV) (2-4/60)-Photo-c	5	10	15	35	63	90
1081-Elmer Fudd	5	10	15	31	53	75
1082-Spin and Marty (Disney) (TV)-Photo-c	7	14	21	44	82	120
1083-Men into Space (TV)-Anderson-a; photo-c	5	10	15	34	60	85
1084-Speedy Gonzales	6	12	18	40	73	105
1085-The Time Machine (H.G. Wells) (Movie) (3/60)-Alex Toth-a; Rod Taylor photo-c	12	24	36	82	179	275
1086-Lolly and Pepper	4	8	12	28	47	65
1087-Peter Gunn (TV)-Photo-c	7	14	21	49	92	135
1088-A Dog of Flanders (Movie)-Photo-c	5	10	15	31	53	75
1089-Restless Gun (TV)-Photo-c	7	14	21	46	86	125
1090-Francis the Famous Talking Mule	5	10	15	31	53	75
1091-Jacky's Diary (4-6/60)	5	10	15	33	57	80
1092-Toby Tyler (Disney-Movie)-Photo-c	6	12	18	38	69	100
1093-MacKenzie's Raiders (Movie/TV)-Richard Carlson photo-c from TV show	6	12	18	37	66	95
1094-Goofy (Disney)	5	10	15	35	63	90
1095-Gyro Gearloose (Disney)-All Barks-c/a	9	18	27	58	114	170
1096-The Texan (TV)-Rory Calhoun photo-c	7	14	21	44	82	120
1097-Rawhide (TV)-Manning-a; Clint Eastwood photo-c	13	26	39	89	195	300
1098-Sugarfoot (TV)-Photo-c	7	14	21	49	92	135
1099-Donald Duck Album (Disney) (5-7/60)-Barks-c	6	12	18	42	79	115
1100-Annette's Life Story (Disney-Movie) (5/60)-Annette Funicello photo-c	17	34	51	117	259	400
1101-Robert Louis Stevenson's Kidnapped (Disney-Movie) (5/60); photo-c	6	12	18	37	66	95
1102-Wanted: Dead or Alive (#1) (TV) (5-7/60); Steve McQueen photo-c	11	22	33	73	157	240
1103-Leave It to Beaver (TV)-Photo-c	12	24	36	79	170	260
1104-Yogi Bear Goes to College (TV) (Hanna-Barbera) (6-8/60)	8	16	24	54	102	150
1105-Gale Storm (Oh! Susanna) (TV)-Toth-a; photo-c	9	18	27	63	129	195
1106-77 Sunset Strip(TV)(6-8/60)-Toth-a; photo-c	7	14	21	49	92	135
1107-Buckskin (TV)-Photo-c	6	12	18	40	73	105
1108-The Troubleshooters (TV)-Keenan Wynn photo-c	6	12	18	37	66	95
1109-This Is Your Life, Donald Duck (Disney) (TV) (8-10/60)-Gyro flashback to WDC&S #141; origin Donald Duck (1st told)	12	24	36	81	176	270
1110-Bonanza (#1) (TV) (6-8/60)-Photo-c	28	56	84	202	451	700
1111-Shotgun Slade (TV)-Photo-c	6	12	18	37	66	95
1112-Pixie and Dixie and Mr. Jinks (#1) (TV) (Hanna-Barbera) (7-9/60)	7	14	21	49	92	135
1113-Tales of Wells Fargo (TV)-Photo-c	7	14	21	48	89	130
1114-Huckleberry Finn (Movie) (7/60)-Photo-c	5	10	15	35	63	90
1115-Ricky Nelson (TV)-Manning-a; photo-c	12	24	36	80	173	265
1116-Boots and Saddles (TV) (8/60)-Photo-c	5	10	15	33	57	80
1117-Boy and the Pirates (Movie)-Photo-c	6	12	18	37	66	95
1118-The Sword and the Dragon (Movie) (6/60)-Photo-c	7	14	21	48	89	130
1119-Smokey the Bear Nature Stories	5	10	15	31	53	75
1120-Dinosaurus (Movie)-Painted-c	8	16	24	51	96	140
1121-Hercules Unchained (Movie) (8/60)-Crandall/Evans-a	8	16	24	56	108	160
1122-Chilly Willy (Lantz)	5	10	15	34	60	85
1123-Tombstone Territory (TV)-Photo-c	7	14	21	49	92	135
1124-Whirlybirds (#1) (TV)-Photo-c	7	14	21	49	92	135
1125-Laramie (#1) (TV)-Photo-c; G. Kane/Heath-a	8	16	24	51	96	140
1126-Hotel Deparee - Sundance (TV) (8-10/60)-Earl Holliman photo-c	6	12	18	40	73	105
1127-The Three Stooges-Photo-c (8-10/60)	11	22	33	73	157	240
1128-Rocky and His Friends (#1) (TV) (Jay Ward) (8-10/60)	25	50	75	175	388	600
1129-Pollyanna (Disney-Movie)-Hayley Mills photo-c	7	14	21	49	92	135
1130-The Deputy (TV)-Buscema-a; Henry Fonda photo-c	8	16	24	54	102	150
1131-Elmer Fudd (9-11/60)	5	10	15	31	53	75
1132-Space Mouse (Lantz) (8-10/60)	5	10	15	33	57	80
1133-Fury (TV)-Photo-c	5	10	15	35	63	90
1134-Real McCoys (TV)-Toth-a; photo-c	8	16	24	51	96	140
1135-M.G.M.'s Mouse Musketeers (9-11/60)	4	8	12	28	47	65
1136-Jungle Cat (Disney-Movie)-Photo-c	6	12	18	37	66	95
1137-The Little Rascals (TV)	5	10	15	35	63	90

Four Color Comics #1179 © DIS

Four Color Comics #1190 © DIS

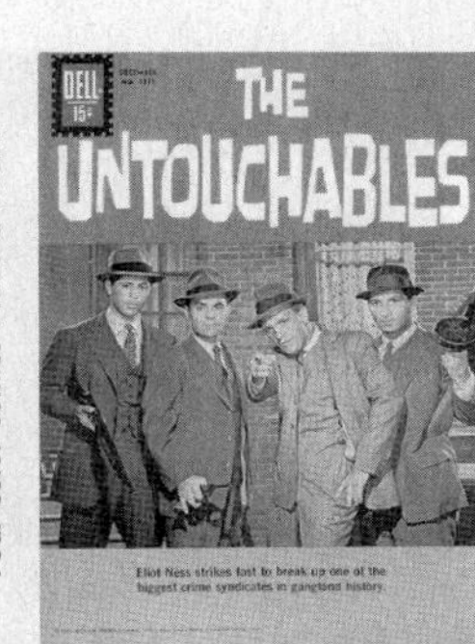

Four Color Comics #1237 © Desilu

	GD 2.0	VG 4.0	FN 6.0	VF 8.0	VF/NM 9.0	NM- 9.2
1138-The Rebel (TV)-Photo-c	8	16	24	51	96	140
1139-Spartacus (Movie) (11/60)-Buscema-a; Kirk Douglas photo-c	10	20	30	69	147	225
1140-Donald Duck Album (Disney)-Barks-c	6	12	18	42	79	115
1141-Huckleberry Hound for President (TV) (Hanna-Barbera) (10/60)	7	14	21	46	86	125
1142-Johnny Ringo (TV)-Photo-c	6	12	18	41	76	110
1143-Pluto (Disney) (11-1/61)	5	10	15	33	57	80
1144-The Story of Ruth (Movie)-Photo-c	8	16	24	54	102	150
1145-The Lost World (Movie)-Gil Kane-a; photo-c; 1 pg. Conan Doyle biography by Torres	9	18	27	57	111	165
1146-Restless Gun (TV)-Photo-c; Wildey-a	7	14	21	46	86	125
1147-Sugarfoot (TV)-Photo-c	7	14	21	49	92	135
1148-I Aim at the Stars-the Werner Von Braun Story (Movie) (11-1/61)-Photo-c	6	12	18	41	76	110
1149-Goofy (Disney) (11-1/61)	5	10	15	35	63	90
1150-Daisy Duck's Diary (Disney) (12-1/61) by Carl Barks	8	16	24	56	108	160
1151-Mickey Mouse Album (Disney) (11-1/61)	6	12	18	37	66	95
1152-Rocky and His Friends (TV) (Jay Ward) (12-2/61)	16	32	48	107	236	365
1153-Frosty the Snowman	5	10	15	35	63	90
1154-Santa Claus Funnies	6	12	18	41	76	110
1155-North to Alaska (Movie)-John Wayne photo-c	15	30	45	100	220	340
1156-Walt Disney Swiss Family Robinson (Movie) (12/60)-Photo-c	7	14	21	46	86	125
1157-Master of the World (Movie) (7/61)	7	14	21	46	86	125
1158-Three Worlds of Gulliver (2 issues exist with different covers) (Movie)-Photo-c	6	12	18	42	79	115
1159-77 Sunset Strip (TV)-Toth-a; photo-c	7	14	21	49	92	135
1160-Rawhide (TV)-Clint Eastwood photo-c	13	26	39	89	195	300
1161-Grandma Duck's Farm Friends (Disney) by Carl Barks (2-4/61)	11	22	33	73	157	240
1162-Yogi Bear Joins the Marines (TV) (Hanna-Barbera) (5-7/61)	8	16	24	54	102	150
1163-Daniel Boone (3-5/61); Marsh-a	5	10	15	35	63	90
1164-Wanted: Dead or Alive (TV)-Steve McQueen photo-c	8	16	24	56	108	160
1165-Ellery Queen (#1) (3-5/61)	9	18	27	58	114	175
1166-Rocky and His Friends (TV) (Jay Ward)	16	32	48	107	236	365
1167-Tales of Wells Fargo (TV)-Photo-c	7	14	21	44	82	120
1168-The Detectives (TV)-Robert Taylor photo-c	9	18	27	61	123	185
1169-New Adventures of Sherlock Holmes	12	24	36	79	170	260
1170-The Three Stooges (3-5/61)-Photo-c	11	22	33	73	157	240
1171-Elmer Fudd	5	10	15	31	53	75
1172-Fury (TV)-Photo-c	5	10	15	35	63	90
1173-The Twilight Zone (#1) (TV) (5/61)-Crandall/Evans-c/a; Crandall tribute to Ingles	18	36	54	128	284	440
1174-The Little Rascals (TV)	5	10	15	33	57	80
1175-M.G.M.'s Mouse Musketeers (3-5/61)	4	8	12	28	47	65
1176-Dondi (Movie)-Origin; photo-c	5	10	15	35	63	90
1177-Chilly Willy (Lantz) (4-6/61)	5	10	15	34	60	85
1178-Ten Who Dared (Disney-Movie) (12/60)-Painted-c; cast member photo on back-c	7	14	21	46	86	125
1179-The Swamp Fox (TV) (Disney)-Leslie Nielsen photo-c	8	16	24	51	96	140
1180-The Danny Thomas Show (TV)-Toth-a; photo-c	13	26	39	89	195	300
1181-Texas John Slaughter (TV) (Walt Disney Presents...) (4-6/61)-Photo-c	5	10	15	35	63	90
1182-Donald Duck Album (Disney) (5-7/61)	5	10	15	34	60	85
1183-101 Dalmatians (Disney-Movie) (3/61)	9	18	27	62	126	190
1184-Gyro Gearloose; All Barks-c/a (Disney) (5-7/61) Two variations exist	9	18	27	58	114	170
1185-Sweetie Pie	5	10	15	34	60	85
1186-Yak Yak (#1) by Jack Davis (2 versions - one minus 3-pg. Davis-c/a)	8	16	24	54	102	150
1187-The Three Stooges (6-8/61)-Photo-c	11	22	33	73	157	240
1188-Atlantis, the Lost Continent (Movie) (5/61)-Photo-c	9	18	27	59	117	175
1189-Greyfriars Bobby (Disney-Movie) (11/61)-Photo-c (scarce)	6	12	18	41	76	110
1190-Donald and the Wheel (Disney-Movie) (11/61); Barks-c	7	14	21	49	92	135

	GD 2.0	VG 4.0	FN 6.0	VF 8.0	VF/NM 9.0	NM- 9.2
1191-Leave It to Beaver (TV)-Photo-c	12	24	36	79	170	260
1192-Ricky Nelson (TV)-Manning-a; photo-c	12	24	36	80	173	265
1193-The Real McCoys (TV) (6-8/61)-Photo-c	7	14	21	48	89	130
1194-Pepe (Movie) (4/61)-Photo-c	5	10	15	30	50	70
1195-National Velvet (#1) (TV)-Photo-c	6	12	18	41	76	110
1196-Pixie and Dixie and Mr. Jinks (TV) (Hanna-Barbera) (7-9/61)	5	10	15	35	63	90
1197-The Aquanauts (TV) (5-7/61)-Photo-c	6	12	18	41	76	110
1198-Donald in Mathmagic Land (Disney-Movie)-Reprint of #1051	6	12	18	37	66	95
1199-The Absent-Minded Professor (Disney-Movie) (4/61)-Photo-c	7	14	21	44	82	120
1199-Shaggy Dog & The Absent-Minded Professor (Disney-Movie) (8/67)-Photo-c	7	14	21	44	82	120
1200-Hennessey (TV) (8-10/61)-Gil Kane-a; photo-c	6	12	18	42	79	115
1201-Goofy (Disney) (8-10/61)	5	10	15	35	63	90
1202-Rawhide (TV)-Clint Eastwood photo-c	13	26	39	89	195	300
1203-Pinocchio (Disney) (3/62)	6	12	18	40	73	105
1204-Scamp (Disney)	4	8	12	27	44	60
1205-David and Goliath (Movie) (7/61)-Photo-c	6	12	18	42	79	115
1206-Lolly and Pepper (9-11/61)	4	8	12	28	47	65
1207-The Rebel (TV)-Sekowsky-a; photo-c	8	16	24	51	96	140
1208-Rocky and His Friends (Jay Ward) (TV)	16	32	48	107	236	365
1209-Sugarfoot (TV)-Photo-c (10-12/61)	7	14	21	49	92	135
1210-The Parent Trap (Disney-Movie) (8/61)-Hayley Mills photo-c	8	16	24	56	108	160
1211-77 Sunset Strip (TV)-Manning-a; photo-c	7	14	21	46	86	125
1212-Chilly Willy (Lantz) (7-9/61)	5	10	15	34	60	85
1213-Mysterious Island (Movie)-Photo-c	7	14	21	49	92	135
1214-Smokey the Bear	5	10	15	31	53	75
1215-Tales of Wells Fargo (TV) (10-12/61)-Photo-c	7	14	21	44	82	120
1216-Whirlybirds (TV)-Photo-c	7	14	21	46	86	125
1218-Fury (TV)-Photo-c	5	10	15	35	63	90
1219-The Detectives (TV)-Robert Taylor & Adam West photo-c	9	18	27	61	123	185
1220-Gunslinger (TV)-Photo-c	7	14	21	49	92	135
1221-Bonanza (TV) (9-11/61)-Photo-c	15	30	45	100	220	340
1222-Elmer Fudd (9-11/61)	5	10	15	31	53	75
1223-Laramie (TV)-Gil Kane-a; photo-c	6	12	18	37	66	95
1224-The Little Rascals (TV) (10-12/61)	5	10	15	33	57	80
1225-The Deputy (TV)-Henry Fonda photo-c	8	16	24	54	102	150
1226-Nikki, Wild Dog of the North (Disney-Movie) (9/61)-Photo-c	5	10	15	33	57	80
1227-Morgan the Pirate (Movie)-Photo-c	6	12	18	42	79	115
1229-Thief of Baghdad (Movie)-Crandall/Evans-a; photo-c	6	12	18	41	76	110
1230-Voyage to the Bottom of the Sea (#1) (Movie)-Photo insert on-c	10	20	30	64	132	200
1231-Danger Man (TV) (9-11/61)-Patrick McGoohan photo-c	10	20	30	66	138	210
1232-On the Double (Movie)	5	10	15	34	60	85
1233-Tammy Tell Me True (Movie) (1961)	6	12	18	38	69	100
1234-The Phantom Planet (Movie) (1961)	6	12	18	42	79	115
1235-Mister Magoo (#1) (12-2/62)	7	14	21	48	89	130
1235-Mister Magoo (3-5/65) 2nd printing; reprint of 12-2/62 issue	5	10	15	35	63	90
1236-King of Kings (Movie)-Photo-c	7	14	21	46	86	125
1237-The Untouchables (#1) (TV)-Not by Toth; photo-c	17	34	51	114	252	390
1238-Deputy Dawg (TV)	9	18	27	63	129	195
1239-Donald Duck Album (Disney) (10-12/61)-Barks-c	6	12	18	42	79	115
1240-The Detectives (TV)-Tufts-a; Robert Taylor photo-c	8	16	24	51	96	140
1241-Sweetie Pie	4	8	12	28	47	65
1242-King Leonardo and His Short Subjects (#1) (TV) (11-1/62)	10	20	30	67	141	215
1243-Ellery Queen	7	14	21	48	89	130
1244-Space Mouse (Lantz) (11-1/62)	5	10	15	33	57	80
1245-New Adventures of Sherlock Holmes	10	20	30	70	150	230
1246-Mickey Mouse Album (Disney)	6	12	18	37	66	95
1247-Daisy Duck's Diary (Disney) (12-2/62)	5	10	15	35	63	90
1248-Pluto (Disney)	5	10	15	33	57	80
1249-The Danny Thomas Show (TV)-Manning-a; photo-c						

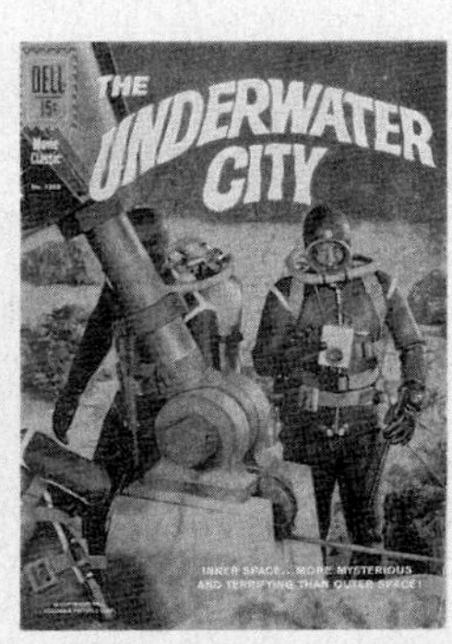

Four Color Comics #1328 © Columbia

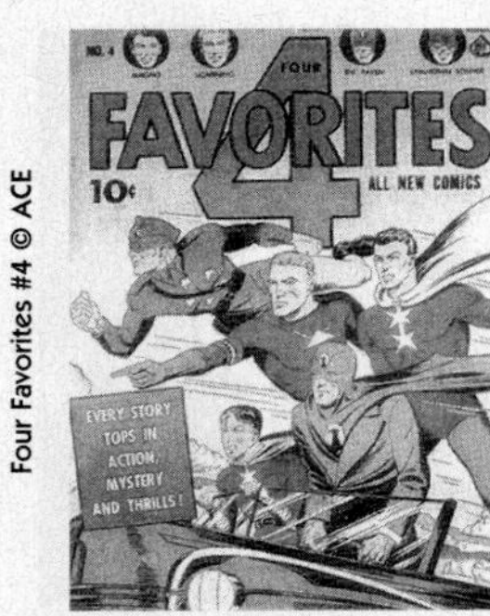

Four Favorites #4 © ACE

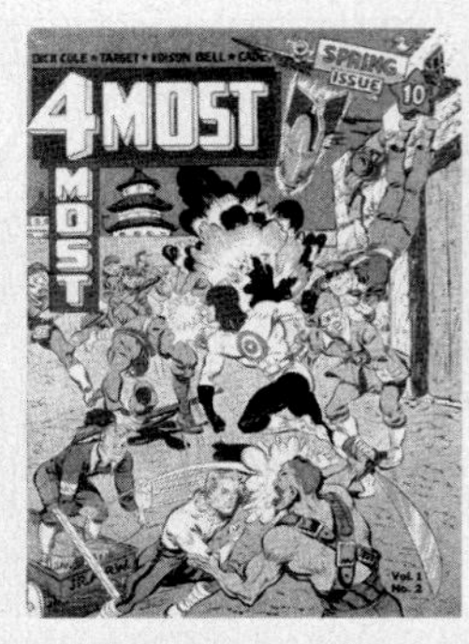

4Most V1 #2 © NOVP

	GD 2.0	VG 4.0	FN 6.0	VF 8.0	VF/NM 9.0	NM- 9.2
	12	24	36	80	173	265
1250-The Four Horsemen of the Apocalypse (Movie)-Photo-c	6	12	18	38	69	100
1251-Everything's Ducky (Movie) (1961)	5	10	15	34	60	85
1252-The Andy Griffith Show (TV)-Photo-c; 1st show aired 10/3/60	36	72	108	259	580	900
1253-Space Man (#1) (1-3/62)	7	14	21	48	89	130
1254- "Diver Dan" (#1) (TV) (2-4/62)-Photo-c	5	10	15	31	53	75
1255-The Wonders of Aladdin (Movie) (1961)	6	12	18	40	73	105
1256-Kona, Monarch of Monster Isle (#1) (2-4/62)-Glanzman-a	9	18	27	61	123	185
1257-Car 54, Where Are You? (#1) (TV) (3-5/62)-Photo-c	8	16	24	54	102	150
1258-The Frogmen (#1)-Evans-a	8	16	24	51	96	140
1259-El Cid (Movie) (1961)-Photo-c	7	14	21	46	86	125
1260-The Horsemasters (TV, Movie) (Disney) (12-2/62)-Annette Funicello photo-c	10	20	30	69	147	225
1261-Rawhide (TV)-Clint Eastwood photo-c	13	26	39	89	195	300
1262-The Rebel (TV)-Photo-c	8	16	24	51	96	140
1263-77 Sunset Strip (TV) (12-2/62)-Manning-a; photo-c	7	14	21	46	86	125
1264-Pixie and Dixie and Mr. Jinks (TV) (Hanna-Barbera)	5	10	15	35	63	90
1265-The Real McCoys (TV)-Photo-c	7	14	21	48	89	130
1266-M.G.M.'s Spike and Tyke (12-2/62)	4	8	12	28	47	65
1267-Gyro Gearloose; Barks-c/a, 4 pgs. (Disney) (12-2/62)	7	14	21	48	89	130
1268-Oswald the Rabbit (Lantz)	5	10	15	33	57	80
1269-Rawhide (TV)-Clint Eastwood photo-c	13	26	39	89	195	300
1270-Bullwinkle and Rocky (#1) (TV) (Jay Ward) (3-5/62)	16	32	48	110	243	375
1271-Yogi Bear Birthday Party (TV) (Hanna-Barbera) (11/61) (Given away for 1 box top from Kellogg's Corn Flakes)	6	12	18	40	73	105
1272-Frosty the Snowman	5	10	15	35	63	90
1273-Hans Brinker (Disney-Movie)-Photo-c (2/62)	6	12	18	37	66	95
1274-Santa Claus Funnies (12/61)	6	12	18	41	76	110
1275-Rocky and His Friends (TV) (Jay Ward)	16	32	48	107	236	365
1276-Dondi	4	8	12	27	44	60
1278-King Leonardo and His Short Subjects (TV)	10	20	30	67	141	215
1279-Grandma Duck's Farm Friends (Disney)	5	10	15	34	60	85
1280-Hennesey (TV)-Photo-c	6	12	18	40	73	105
1281-Chilly Willy (Lantz) (4-6/62)	5	10	15	34	60	85
1282-Babes in Toyland (Disney-Movie) (1/62); Annette Funicello photo-c	12	24	36	83	182	280
1283-Bonanza (TV) (2-4/62)-Photo-c	15	30	45	100	220	340
1284-Laramie (TV)-Heath-a; photo-c	6	12	18	37	66	95
1285-Leave It to Beaver (TV)-Photo-c	12	24	36	79	170	260
1286-The Untouchables (TV)-Photo-c	12	24	36	80	173	265
1287-Man from Wells Fargo (TV)-Photo-c	5	10	15	33	57	80
1288-Twilight Zone (TV) (4/62)-Crandall/Evans-c/a	10	20	30	69	147	225
1289-Ellery Queen	7	14	21	48	89	130
1290-M.G.M.'s Mouse Musketeers	4	8	12	28	47	65
1291-77 Sunset Strip (TV)-Manning-a; photo-c	7	14	21	46	86	125
1293-Elmer Fudd (3-5/62)	5	10	15	31	53	75
1294-Ripcord (TV)	6	12	18	40	73	105
1295-Mister Ed, the Talking Horse (#1) (TV) (3-5/62)-Photo-c	10	20	30	70	150	230
1296-Fury (TV) (3-5/62)-Photo-c	5	10	15	35	63	90
1297-Spanky, Alfalfa and the Little Rascals (TV)	5	10	15	33	57	80
1298-The Hathaways (TV)-Photo-c	5	10	15	31	53	75
1299-Deputy Dawg (TV)	9	18	27	63	129	195
1300-The Comancheros (Movie) (1961)-John Wayne photo-c	14	28	42	94	207	320
1301-Adventures in Paradise (TV) (2-4/62)	6	12	18	37	66	95
1302-Johnny Jason, Teen Reporter (2-4/62)	4	8	12	23	37	50
1303-Lad: A Dog (Movie)-Photo-c	5	10	15	33	57	80
1304-Nellie the Nurse (3-5/62)-Stanley-a	7	14	21	49	92	135
1305-Mister Magoo (3-5/62)	7	14	21	48	89	130
1306-Target: The Corruptors (#1) (TV) (3-5/62)-Photo-c	5	10	15	33	57	80
1307-Margie (TV) (3-5/62)	6	12	18	40	73	105
1308-Tales of the Wizard of Oz (TV) (3-5/62)	11	22	33	73	157	240
1309-87th Precinct (#1) (TV) (4-6/62)-Krigstein-a; photo-c	9	18	27	60	120	180
1310-Huck and Yogi Winter Sports (TV) (Hanna-Barbera) (3/62)	8	16	24	51	96	140
1311-Rocky and His Friends (TV) (Jay Ward)	16	32	48	107	236	365
1312-National Velvet (TV)-Photo-c	4	8	12	27	44	60
1313-Moon Pilot (Disney-Movie)-Photo-c	6	12	18	40	73	105
1328-The Underwater City (Movie) (1961)-Evans-a; photo-c	6	12	18	42	79	115
1329-See Gyro Gearloose #01329-207						
1330-Brain Boy (#1)-Gil Kane-a	10	20	30	64	132	200
1332-Bachelor Father (TV)	6	12	18	42	79	115
1333-Short Ribs (4-6/62)	5	10	15	35	63	90
1335-Aggie Mack (4-6/62)	5	10	15	31	53	75
1336-On Stage; not by Leonard Starr	5	10	15	34	60	85
1337-Dr. Kildare (#1) (TV) (4-6/62)-Photo-c	8	16	24	52	99	145
1341-The Andy Griffith Show (TV) (4-6/62)-Photo-c	33	66	99	238	532	825
1348-Yak Yak (#2)-Jack Davis-c/a	7	14	21	46	86	125
1349-Yogi Bear Visits the U.N. (TV) (Hanna-Barbera) (1/62)-Photo-c	8	16	24	54	102	150
1350-Comanche (Disney-Movie)(1962)-Reprints 4-Color #966 (title change from "Tonka" to "Comanche") (4-6/62)-Sal Mineo photo-c	5	10	15	33	57	80
1354-Calvin & the Colonel (#1) (TV) (4-6/62)	8	16	24	54	102	150

NOTE: *Missing numbers probably do not exist.*

4-D MONKEY, THE (Adventures of... #? on)
Leung's Publications: 1988 - No. 11, 1990 ($1.80/$2.00, 52 pgs.)

	GD 2.0	VG 4.0	FN 6.0	VF 8.0	VF/NM 9.0	NM- 9.2
1-11: 1-Karate Pig, Ninja Flounder & 4-D Monkey (48 pgs., centerfold is a Christmas card). 2-4 (52 pgs.)						4.00

FOUR FAVORITES (Crime Must Pay the Penalty No. 33 on)
Ace Magazines: Sept, 1941 - No. 32, Dec, 1947

	GD 2.0	VG 4.0	FN 6.0	VF 8.0	VF/NM 9.0	NM- 9.2
1-Vulcan, Lash Lightning (formerly Flash Lightning in Sure-Fire), Magno the Magnetic Man & The Raven begin; flag/Hitler-c	290	580	870	1856	3178	4500
2-The Black Ace only app.; WWII flag-c	123	246	369	787	1344	1900
3-Last Vulcan; V For Victory WWII-c	116	232	348	742	1271	1800
4,5: 4-The Raven & Vulcan end; Unknown Soldier begins (see Our Flag), ends #28. 5-Captain Courageous begins (5/42), ends #28 (moves over from Captain Courageous #6); not in #6. 5,6-Bondage/torture-c	116	232	348	742	1271	1800
6-8: 6-The Flag app.; Mr. Risk begins (7/42)	110	220	330	704	1202	1700
9-Kurtzman-a (Lash Lightning); robot-c	116	232	348	742	1271	1800
10-Classic Kurtzman-c/a (Magno & Davey)	161	322	483	1030	1765	2500
11-Kurtzman-a; Hitler, Mussolini, Hirohito-c; L.B. Cole-a; Unknown Soldier by Kurtzman	194	388	582	1242	2121	3000
12-L.B. Cole-a; Japanese WWII-c	110	220	330	704	1202	1700
13-L.B. Cole-c (his first cover?); WWII-c	116	232	348	742	1271	1800
14,16-18,20: 18,20-Palais-c/a	61	122	183	390	670	950
15-Japanese WWII-c	63	126	189	403	689	975
19-Nazi WWII bondage-c	77	154	231	493	847	1200
21-No Unknown Soldier; The Unknown app.	55	110	165	352	601	850
22-27: 22-Captain Courageous drops costume. 23-Unknown Soldier drops costume. 25-29-Hap Hazard app. 26-Last Magno	50	100	150	315	533	750
28,29: Hap Hazard app. in all	37	74	111	222	361	500
30-32: 30-Funny-c begin (teen humor), end #32	18	36	54	103	162	220

NOTE: ***Dave Berg** c-5. **Jim Mooney** a-6; c-1-3. **Palais** a-18-20; c-18-25.*

FOUR HORSEMEN, THE (See The Crusaders)

FOUR HORSEMEN
DC Comics (Vertigo): Feb, 2000 - No. 4, May, 2000 ($2.50, limited series)

	GD 2.0	VG 4.0	FN 6.0	VF 8.0	VF/NM 9.0	NM- 9.2
1-4-Esad Ribic-c/a; Robert Rodi-s						3.00

FOUR HORSEMEN OF THE APOCALYPSE, THE (Movie)
Dell Publishing Co.: No. 1250, Jan-Mar, 1962 (one-shot)

	GD 2.0	VG 4.0	FN 6.0	VF 8.0	VF/NM 9.0	NM- 9.2
Four Color 1250-Photo-c	6	12	18	38	69	100

4MOST (Foremost Boys No. 32-40; becomes Thrilling Crime Cases #41 on)
Novelty Publications/Star Publications No. 37-on:
Winter, 1941-42 - V8#5(#36), 9-10/49; #37, 11-12/49 - #40, 4-5/50

	GD 2.0	VG 4.0	FN 6.0	VF 8.0	VF/NM 9.0	NM- 9.2
V1#1-The Target by Sid Greene, The Cadet & Dick Cole begin with origins retold; produced by Funnies Inc.; quarterly issues begin, end V6#3; German WWII-c	206	412	618	1318	2259	3200
2-Last Target (Spr/42); WWII cover	71	142	213	454	777	1100
3-Dan'l Flannel begins; flag-c	50	100	150	315	533	750
4-1pg. Dr. Seuss (signed) (Aut/42); fish in the face-c	53	106	159	334	567	800
V2#1-3	26	52	78	154	252	350
4-Hitler, Tojo & Mussolini app. as pumpkins on-c	55	110	165	352	601	850

4001 A.D. #1 © VAL

Fox and the Crow #2 © DC

Fox Giant - Burning Romances © FOX

	GD 2.0	VG 4.0	FN 6.0	VF 8.0	VF/NM 9.0	NM- 9.2
V3#1-4	19	38	57	111	176	240
V4#1-4: 2-Walter Johnson-c	15	30	45	83	124	165
V5#1-4: 1-The Target & Targeteers app.	14	28	42	76	108	140
V6#1-4	11	22	33	62	86	110
5-L. B. Cole-c	20	40	60	114	182	250
V7#1,3,5, V8#1, 37	11	22	33	60	83	105
2,4,6-L. B. Cole-c. 6-Last Dick Cole	20	40	60	114	182	250
V8#2,3,5-L. B. Cole-c/a	22	44	66	132	216	300
4-L. B. Cole-a	15	30	45	83	124	165
38-40: 38-Johnny Weismuller (Tarzan) life story & Jim Braddock (boxer) life story. 38-40-L.B. Cole-c. 40-Last White Rider	17	34	51	98	154	210
Accepted Reprint 38-40 (nd): 40-r/Johnny Weismuller life story; all have L.B. Cole-c	10	20	30	56	76	95

411
Marvel Comics: June, 2003 - No. 3 ($3.50, limited series)

1,2-Tributes to peacemakers; s/a by various. 1-Millar, Quitely, Mack, Winslade & others-s/a. 2-Harris, Phillips, Manco, Bruce Jones.						3.50

FOUR POINTS, THE
Aspen MLT Inc.: Apr, 2015 - No. 5, Aug, 2015 ($3.99)

1-5-Lobdell-s/Gunderson-a; multiple covers						4.00

FOUR-STAR BATTLE TALES
National Periodical Publications: Feb-Mar, 1973 - No. 5, Nov-Dec, 1973

1-Reprints begin	3	6	9	16	24	32
2-5	2	4	6	11	16	20

NOTE: ***Drucker** r-1, 3-5. **Heath** r-2, 5; c-1. **Krigstein** r-5. **Kubert** r-4; c-2.*

FOUR STAR SPECTACULAR
National Periodical Publications: Mar-Apr, 1976 - No. 6, Jan-Feb, 1977

1-Includes G.A. Flash story with new art	2	4	6	11	16	20
2-6: Reprints in all. 2-Infinity cover	2	4	6	8	10	12

NOTE: *All contain DC Superhero reprints. #1 has 68 pgs.; #2-6, 52 pgs.. #1, 4-Hawkman app.; #2-Kid Flash app.; #3-Green Lantern app; #2, 4, 5-Wonder Woman, Superboy app; #5-Green Arrow, Vigilante app; #6-Blackhawk G.A.-r.*

FOUR TEENERS (Formerly Crime Must Pay The Penalty; Dotty No. 35 on)
A. A. Wyn: No. 34, April, 1948 (52 pgs.)

34-Teen-age comic; Dotty app.; Curly & Jerry continue from Four Favorites	13	26	39	74	105	135

4001 A.D. (See Valiant 2016 FCBD edition for prelude)
Valiant Entertainment: May, 2016 - No. 4, Aug, 2016 ($3.99, limited series)

1-4-Matt Kindt-s/Clayton Crain-a. 1-David Mack-a (3 pages)						4.00
...: Bloodshot 1 (6/16, $3.99) Lemire-s/Braithwaite-a; Bloodshot reforms in 4001 A.D.						4.00
...: Shadowman 1 (7/16, $3.99) Houser & Roberts-s/Gill-a						4.00
...: War Mother 1 (8/16, $3.99) Van Lente-s/Giorello-a						4.00
...: X-O Manowar 1 (5/16, $3.99) Venditti-s/Henry-a; prelude to main series						4.00

FOURTH WORLD GALLERY, THE (Jack Kirby's...)
DC Comics: 1996 (9/96) ($3.50, one-shot)

nn-Pin-ups of Jack Kirby's Fourth World characters (New Gods, Forever People & Mister Miracle) by John Byrne, Rick Burchett, Dan Jurgens, Walt Simonson & others						4.00

FOUR WOMEN
DC Comics (Homage): Dec, 2001 - No. 5, Apr, 2002 ($2.95, limited series)

1-5-Sam Kieth-s/a						3.00
TPB (2002, $17.95) r/series; foreward by Kieth						18.00

FOX, THE
Archie Comic Publications (Red Circle Comics): Dec, 2013 - No. 5, Apr, 2014 ($2.99)

1-5-Dean Haspiel-a/Haspiel and Mark Waid-s. 1-Three covers. 2-Two covers						3.00

FOX, THE
Archie Comic Publications (Dark Circle Comics): Jun, 2015 - No. 5, Oct, 2015 ($3.99)

1-5-Dean Haspiel-a/Haspiel and Mark Waid-s; multiple covers on each						4.00

FOX AND THE CROW (Stanley & His Monster No. 109 on) (See Comic Cavalcade & Real Screen Comics)
National Periodical Publications: Dec-Jan, 1951-52 - No. 108, Feb-Mar, 1968

1	129	258	387	826	1413	2000
2(Scarce)	57	114	171	362	619	875
3-5	37	74	111	222	361	500
6-10 (6-7/53)	26	52	78	154	252	350
11-20 (10/54)	20	40	60	114	182	250
21-30: 22-Last precode issue (2/55)	15	30	45	83	124	165
31-40	12	24	36	69	97	125
41-60	6	12	18	37	66	95
61-80	5	10	15	31	53	75
81-94: 94-(11/65)-The Brat Finks begin	4	8	12	25	40	55
95-Stanley & His Monster begins (origin & 1st app)	5	10	15	33	57	80
96-99,101-108	3	6	9	19	30	40
100 (10-11/66)	3	6	9	21	33	45

NOTE: *Many later covers by **Mort Drucker.***

FOX AND THE HOUND, THE (Disney)(Movie)
Whitman Publishing Co.: Aug, 1981 - No. 3, Oct, 1981

11292- Golden Press Graphic Novel	2	4	6	8	10	12
1-3-Based on animated movie	1	2	3	5	7	9

FOXFIRE (See The Phoenix Resurrection)
Malibu Comics (Ultraverse): Feb, 1996 - No. 4, May, 1996 ($1.50)

1-4: Sludge, Ultraforce app. 4-Punisher app.						3.00

FOX GIANTS (Also see Giant Comics Edition)
Fox Features Syndicate: 1944 - 1950 (25¢, 132 - 196 pgs.)

Album of Crime nn(1949, 132p)	60	120	180	381	653	925
Album of Love nn(1949, 132p)	65	130	195	416	708	1000
All Famous Crime Stories nn('49, 132p)	60	120	180	381	653	925
All Good Comics 1(1944, 132p)(R.W. Voigt)-The Bouncer, Purple Tigress, Rick Evans, Puppeteer, Green Mask; Infinity-c	74	148	222	470	810	1150
All Great nn(1944, 132p)-Capt. Jack Terry, Rick Evans, Jaguar Man	52	104	156	328	552	775
All Great nn(Chicago Nite Life News)(1945, 132p)-Green Mask, Bouncer, Puppeteer, Rick Evans, Rocket Kelly	50	100	150	315	533	750
All-Great Confession Magazine nn(1949, 132p)	65	130	195	416	708	1000
All-Great Confessions nn(1949, 132p)	65	130	195	416	708	1000
All Great Crime Stories nn('49, 132p)	60	120	180	381	653	925
All Great Jungle Adventures nn('49, 132p)	74	148	222	470	810	1150
All Real Confession Magazine 3 (3/49, 132p)	63	126	189	403	689	975
All Real Confession Magazine 4 (4/49, 132p)	63	126	189	403	689	975
All Your Comics 1(1944, 132p)-The Puppeteer, Red Robbins, & Merciless the Sorcerer	53	106	159	334	567	800
Almanac Of Crime nn(1948, 148p)-Phantom Lady	68	136	204	435	743	1050
Almanac Of Crime 1(1950, 132p)	58	116	174	371	636	900
Book Of Love nn(1950, 132p)	61	122	183	390	670	950
Burning Romances 1(1949, 132p)	71	142	213	454	777	1100
Crimes Incorporated nn(1950, 132p)	55	110	165	352	601	850
Daring Love Stories nn(1950, 132p)	61	122	183	390	670	950
Everybody's Comics 1(1944, 50¢, 196p)-The Green Mask, The Puppeteer, The Bouncer, Rocket Kelly, Rick Evans	63	126	189	403	689	975
Everybody's Comics 1(1946, 196p)-Green Lama, The Puppeteer	52	104	156	328	552	775
Everybody's Comics 1(1946, 196p)-Same as 1945 Ribtickler	40	80	120	246	411	575
Everybody's Comics nn(1947, 132p)-Jo-Jo, Purple Tigress, Cosmo Cat, Bronze Man	52	104	156	328	552	775
Exciting Romance Stories nn(1949, 132p)	65	130	195	416	708	1000
Famous Love nn(1950, 132p)-Photo-c	63	126	189	403	689	975
Intimate Confessions nn(1950, 132p)	61	122	183	390	670	950
Journal Of Crime nn(1949, 132p)	60	120	180	381	653	925
Love Problems nn(1949, 132p)	65	130	195	416	708	1000
Love Thrills nn(1950, 132p)	61	122	183	390	670	950
March of Crime nn('48, 132p)-Female w/rifle-c	61	122	183	390	670	950
March of Crime nn('49, 132p)-Cop w/pistol-c	57	114	171	362	619	875
March of Crime nn(1949, 132p)-Coffin & man w/machine-gun-c	57	114	171	362	619	875
Revealing Love Stories nn(1950, 132p)	61	122	183	390	670	950
Ribtickler nn(1945, 50¢, 196p)-Chicago Nite Life News; Marvel Mutt, Cosmo Cat, Flash Rabbit, The Nebbs app.	47	94	141	296	498	700
Romantic Thrills nn(1950, 132p)	61	122	183	390	670	950
Secret Love Stories nn(1949, 132p)	65	130	195	416	708	1000
Strange Love nn(1950, 132p)-Photo-c	81	162	243	518	884	1250
Sweetheart Scandals nn(1950, 132p)	61	122	183	390	670	950
Teen-Age Love nn(1950, 132p)	61	122	183	390	670	950
Throbbing Love nn(1950, 132p)-Photo-c; used in **POP**, pg. 107	81	162	243	518	884	1250
Truth About Crime nn(1949, 132p)	60	120	180	381	653	925
Variety Comics 1(1946, 132p)-Blue Beetle, Jungle Jo	53	106	159	334	567	800
Variety Comics nn(1950, 132p)-Jungle Jo, My Secret Affair (w/Harrison/Wood-a), Crimes by Women & My Story	50	100	150	315	533	750
Western Roundup nn('50, 132p)-Hoot Gibson; Cody of the Pony Express app.	41	82	123	256	428	600

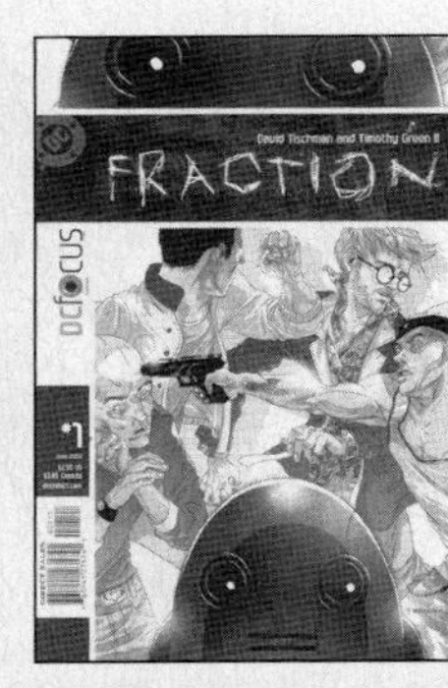

Fraction #1 © Tischman & DC

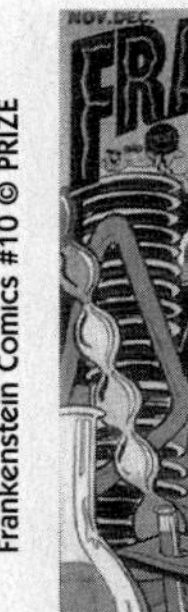
Frankenstein Comics #10 © PRIZE

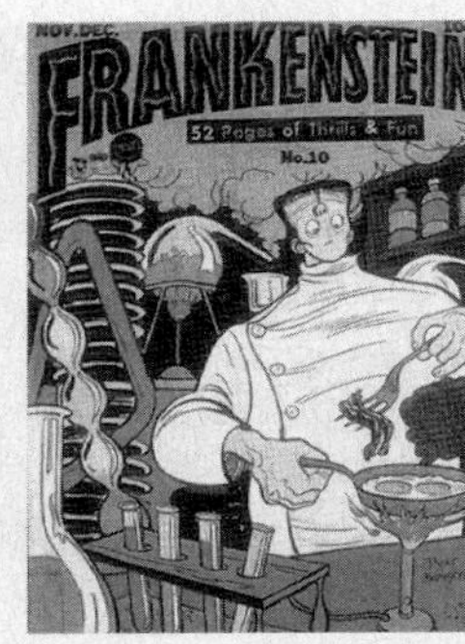

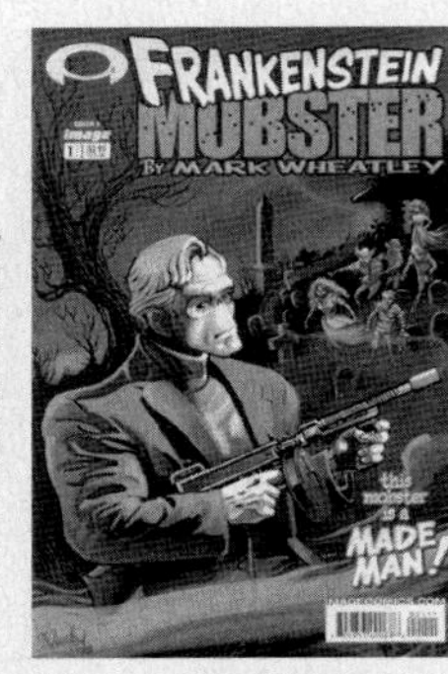

Frankenstein Mobster #1 © Mark Wheatley

	GD	VG	FN	VF	VF/NM	NM-
	2.0	4.0	6.0	8.0	9.0	9.2

NOTE: *Each of the above usually contain four remaindered Fox books minus covers. Since these missing covers often had the first page of the first story, most Giants therefore are incomplete. Approximate values are listed. Books with appearances of Phantom Lady, Rulah, Jo-Jo, etc. could bring more.*

FOXHOLE (Becomes Never Again #8?)
Mainline/Charlton No. 5 on: 9-10/54 - No. 4, 3-4/55; No. 5, 7/55 - No. 7, 3/56

1-Classic Kirby-c	65	130	195	416	708	1000
2-Kirby-c/a(2); Kirby scripts based on his war time experiences						
	41	82	123	256	428	600
3-5-Simon/Kirby-c only	30	60	90	177	289	400
6-Kirby-c/a(2)	39	78	117	231	378	525
7-Simon & Kirby-c	16	32	48	94	147	200
Super Reprints #10,15-17: 10-r/? 15,16-r/United States Marines #5,8.						
17-r/Monty Hall #?	2	4	6	11	16	20
11,12,18-r/Foxhole #1,2,3; Kirby-c	3	6	9	17	26	35

NOTE: ***Kirby** a(r)-Super #11, 12. **Powell** a(r)-Super #15, 16. Stories by actual veterans.*

FOXY FAGAN COMICS (Funny Animal)
Dearfield Publishing Co.: Dec, 1946 - No. 7, Summer, 1948

1-Foxy Fagan & Little Buck begin	14	28	42	80	115	150
2	8	16	24	44	57	70
3-7: 6-Rocket ship-c	8	16	24	40	50	60

FRACTION
DC Comics (Focus): June, 2004 - No. 6, Nov, 2004 ($2.50, limited series)

1-6-David Tischman-s/Timothy Green II-a — 3.00
SC (2011, $17.99) r/#1-6; cover gallery — 18.00

FRACTURED FAIRY TALES (TV)
Gold Key: Oct, 1962 (Jay Ward)

1 (10022-210)-From Bullwinkle TV show	9	18	27	60	120	180

FRAGGLE ROCK (TV)
Marvel Comics (Star Comics)/Marvel V2#1 on: Apr, 1985 - No. 8, Sept, 1986; V2#1, Apr, 1988 - No. 5, Aug, 1988

1-6 (75¢-c) — 5.00
7,8 — 6.00
V2#1-5-($1.00): Reprints 1st series — 3.00

FRAGGLE ROCK: JOURNEY TO THE EVERSPRING, (JIM HENSON'S...)
Archaia: Oct, 2014 - No. 4, Jan, 2015 ($3.99, limited series)

1-4-Kate Leth-s/Jake Myler-a. 1-Multiple covers — 4.00

FRANCIS, BROTHER OF THE UNIVERSE
Marvel Comics Group: 1980 (75¢, 52 pgs., one-shot)

1-John Buscema/Marie Severin-a; story of Francis Bernadone, celebrating his 800th birthday in 1982 — 6.00

FRANCIS THE FAMOUS TALKING MULE (All based on movie)
Dell Publishing Co.: No. 335 (#1), June, 1951 - No. 1090, March, 1960

Four Color 335 (#1)	10	20	30	68	144	220
Four Color 465	6	12	18	41	76	110
Four Color 501,547,579	5	10	15	35	63	90
Four Color 621,655,698,710,745	5	10	15	33	57	80
Four Color 810,863,906,953,991,1068,1090	5	10	15	31	53	75

FRANK
Nemesis Comics (Harvey): Apr (Mar inside), 1994 - No. 4, 1994 ($1.75/$2.50, limited series)

1-4-($2.50, direct sale): 1-Foil-c Edition — 3.50
1-4-($1.75)-Newsstand Editions; Cowan-a in all — 3.00

FRANK
Fantagraphics Books: Sept, 1996 ($2.95, B&W)

1-Woodring-c/a/scripts — 3.00

FRANK BUCK (Formerly My True Love)
Fox Features Syndicate: No. 70, May, 1950 - No. 3, Sept, 1950

70-Wood a(p)(3 stories)-Photo-c	39	78	117	234	385	535
71-Wood-a (9 pgs.); photo/painted-c	20	40	60	118	192	265
3: 3-Photo/painted-c	15	30	45	85	130	175

NOTE: *Based on "Bring 'Em Back Alive" TV show.*

FRANKEN-CASTLE (See The Punisher, 2009 series)

FRANKENSTEIN (See Dracula, Movie Classics & Werewolf)
Dell Publishing Co.: Aug-Oct, 1964; No. 2, Sept, 1966 - No. 4, Mar, 1967

1(12-283-410)(1964)(2nd printing; see Movie Classics for 1st printing)						
	5	10	15	34	60	85
2-Intro. & origin super-hero character (9/66)	5	10	15	30	50	70
3,4	4	8	12	23	37	50

FRANKENSTEIN (The Monster of...; also see Monsters Unleashed #2, Power Record Comics, Psycho & Silver Surfer #7)
Marvel Comics Group: Jan, 1973 - No. 18, Sept, 1975

1-Ploog-c/a begins, ends #6	7	14	21	46	86	125
2	4	8	12	27	44	60
3-5	3	6	9	21	33	45
6,7,10: 7-Dracula cameo	3	6	9	17	26	35
8,9-Dracula c/sty. 9-Death of Dracula	4	8	12	28	47	65
11-17	3	6	9	15	22	28
18-Wrightson-c(i)	3	6	9	16	24	32

NOTE: ***Adkins** c-17i. **Buscema** a-7-10p. **Ditko** a-12r. **G. Kane** c-15p. **Orlando** a-8r. **Ploog** a-1-3, 4p, 5p, 6; c-1-6. **Wrightson** c-18i.*

FRANKENSTEIN (Mary Wollstonecraft Shelley's...; A Marvel Illustrated Novel)
Marvel Pub.: 1983 ($8.95, B&W, 196 pgs., 8x11" TPB)

nn-Wrightson-a; 4 pg. intro. by Stephen King	5	10	15	30	50	70
Limited HC Edition						175.00

FRANKENSTEIN, AGENT OF S.H.A.D.E. (New DC 52)
DC Comics: Nov, 2011 - No. 16, Mar, 2013 ($2.99)

1-16: 1-Lemire-s/Ponticelli-a/J.G. Jones-c; Ray Palmer & The Creature Commandos app. 5-Crossover with OMAC #5. 13-15-Rotworld — 3.00
#0 (11/12, $2.99) Kindt-s/Ponticelli-a; Frankenstein's origin — 3.00

FRANKENSTEIN ALIVE, ALIVE
IDW Publishing: May, 2012 - No. 3, Apr, 2014 ($3.99, B&W)

1-3-Niles-s/Wrightson-a; interview with creators; excerpt from M.W. Shelley writings — 4.00
... Reanimated Edition (4/14, $5.99) r/#1,2; silver foil cover logo — 6.00

FRANKENSTEIN COMICS (Also See Prize Comics)
Prize Publ. (Crestwood/Feature): Sum, 1945 - V5#5(#33), Oct-Nov, 1954

1-Frankenstein begins by Dick Briefer (origin); Frank Sinatra parody						
	300	600	900	2010	3505	5000
2	81	162	243	518	884	1250
3-5	61	122	183	390	670	950
6-10: 7-S&K a(r)/Headline Comics. 8(7-8/47)-Superman satire						
	55	110	165	352	601	850
11-17(1-2/49)-11-Boris Karloff parody-c/story. 17-Last humor issue						
	50	100	150	315	533	750
18(3/52)-New origin, horror series begins	97	194	291	621	1061	1500
19,20(V3#4, 8-9/52)	65	130	195	416	708	1000
21(V3#5), 22(V3#6), 23(V4#1) - #28(V4#6)	58	116	174	371	636	900
29(V5#1) - #33(V5#5)	53	106	159	334	567	800

NOTE: ***Briefer** c/a-all. **Meskin** a-21, 29.*

FRANKENSTEIN/DRACULA WAR, THE
Topps Comics: Feb, 1995 - No. 3, May, 1995 ($2.50, limited series)

1-3 — 3.00

FRANKENSTEIN, JR. (...& the Impossibles) (TV)
Gold Key: Jan, 1966 (Hanna-Barbera)

1-Super hero (scarce)	10	20	30	66	138	210

FRANKENSTEIN MOBSTER
Image Comics: No. 0, Oct, 2003 - No. 7, Dec, 2004 ($2.95)

0-7: 0-Two covers by Wheatley and Hughes; Wheatley-s/a. 1-Variant-c by Wieringo — 3.00

FRANKENSTEIN: OR THE MODERN PROMETHEUS
Caliber Press: 1994 ($2.95, one-shot)

1 — 3.00

FRANKENSTEIN UNDERGROUND (From Hellboy)
Dark Horse Comics: Mar, 2015 - No. 5, Jul, 2015 ($3.50, limited series)

1-5-Mike Mignola-s/c; Ben Stenbeck-a — 3.50

FRANK FRAZETTA FANTASY ILLUSTRATED (Magazine)
Quantum Cat Entertainment: Spring 1998 - No. 8 ($5.95, quarterly)

1-Anthology; art by Corben, Horley, Jusko	1	2	3	4	5	7
1-Linsner variant-c						10.00
2-Battle Chasers by Madureira; Harris-a						8.00
2-Madureira Battle Chasers variant-c						12.00
3-8-Frazetta-c						6.00
3-Tony Daniel variant-c						15.00
5,6-Portacio variant-c, 7,8-Alex Nino variant-c						10.00
8-Alex Ross Chicago Comicon variant-c						10.00

FRANK FRAZETTA'S DEATH DEALER
Image Comics: Mar, 2007 - No. 6, Jan, 2008 ($3.99)

Fray #7 © Joss Whedon

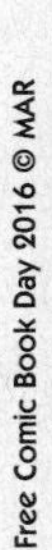
Free Comic Book Day 2016 © MAR

Freedom Fighters #5 © DC

GD 2.0 VG 4.0 FN 6.0 VF 8.0 VF/NM 9.0 NM- 9.2

1-6-Nat Jones-a; 3 covers (Frazetta, Jones, Jones sketch) 4.00

FRANK FRAZETTA'S...
Fantagraphics Books/Image Comics: one-shots

... Creatures 1 (Image Comics, 7/08, $3.99) Bergting-a; covers by Frazetta & Bergting 4.00
... Dark Kingdom 1-4 (Image, 4/08 - No. 4, 1/10, $3.99) Vigil-a; covers by Frazetta & Vigil 4.00
... Dracula Meets the Wolfman 1 (Image, 8/08, $3.99) Francavilla-a; 2 covers 4.00
... Moon Maid 1 (Image, 1/09, $3.99) Tim Vigil-a; covers by Frazetta & Vigil 4.00
... Neanderthal 1 (Image, 4/09, $3.99) Fotos & Vigil-a; covers by Frazetta & Fotos 4.00
... Sorcerer 1 (Image, 8/09, $3.99) Medors-a; covers by Frazetta & Medors 4.00
... Swamp Demon 1 (Image, 7/08, $3.99) Medors-a; covers by Frazetta & Medors 4.00
... Thun'da Tales 1 (Fantagraphics Books, 1987, $2.00) Frazetta-r 6.00
... Untamed Love 1 (Fantagraphics Books, 11/87, $2.00) r/1950's romance comics 6.00

FRANKIE COMICS (...& Lana No. 13-15) (Formerly Movie Tunes; becomes Frankie Fuddle No. 16 on)
Marvel Comics (MgPC): No. 4, Wint, 1946-47 - No. 15, June, 1949

4-Mitzi, Margie, Daisy app. 22 44 66 132 216 300
5-9 15 30 45 83 124 165
10-15: 13-Anti-Wertham editorial 14 28 42 80 115 150

FRANKIE DOODLE (See Sparkler, both series)
United Features Syndicate: No. 7, 1939

Single Series 7 34 68 102 204 332 460

FRANKIE FUDDLE (Formerly Frankie & Lana)
Marvel Comics: No. 16, Aug, 1949 - No. 17, Nov, 1949

16,17 14 28 42 80 115 150

FRANKLIN RICHARDS (Fantastic Four)
Marvel Comics: April, 2006 - Present ($2.99/$3.99, one-shots)

...: April Fools (6/09, $3.99) Eliopoulos-s/a 4.00
...: Collected Chaos (2008, $8.99, digest) reprints various one-shots 9.00
...: Fall Football Fiasco (1/08, $2.99) Eliopoulos-a/Sumerak-s 3.00
...: Happy Franksgiving (1/07, $2.99) Thanksgiving stories by Eliopoulos-a/Sumerak-s 3.00
...: It's Dark Reigning Cats & Dogs (4/09, $3.99) Eliopoulos-s/a 4.00
...: Lab Brat (2007, $7.99, digest) reprints one-shots and Masked Marvel back-ups 8.00
...: March Madness (5/07, $2.99) More science gone wrong by Eliopoulos-a/Sumerak-s 3.00
...: Monster Mash (11/07, $2.99) Science mishaps by Eliopoulos-a/Sumerak-s 3.00
...: Not-So-Secret Invasion (7/08, $2.99) Skrull cover; The Wizard app. 3.00
... One Shot (4/06, $2.99) short stories by Eliopoulos-a/Sumerak-s 3.00
...: School's Out (4/09, $3.99) Eliopoulos-s/a; Katie Power app. 4.00
...: Sons of Geniuses (1/09, $3.99) parallel dimension alternate version hijinks 4.00
...: Spring Break (5/08, $2.99) short stories by Eliopoulos-a/Sumerak-s 3.00
...: Summer Smackdown (10/08, $2.99) short stories by Eliopoulos-a/Sumerak-s 3.00
...: Super Summer Spectacular (9/06, $2.99) short stories by Eliopoulos-a/Sumerak-s 3.00
...: World Be Warned (8/07, $2.99) short stories by Eliopoulos-a/Sumerak-s; Hulk app. 3.00

FRANK LUTHER'S SILLY PILLY COMICS (See Jingle Dingle...)
Children's Comics (Maltex Cereal): 1950 (10¢)

1-Characters from radio, records, & TV 10 20 30 58 79 100
NOTE: *Also printed as a promotional comic for Maltex cereal.*

FRANK MERRIWELL AT YALE (Speed Demons No. 5 on?)
Charlton Comics: June, 1955 - No. 4, Jan, 1956 (Also see Shadow Comics)

1 7 14 21 37 46 55
2-4 5 10 15 24 30 35

FRANTIC (Magazine) (See Ratfink & Zany)
Pierce Publishing Co.: Oct, 1958 - V2#2, Apr, 1959 (Satire)

V1#1 15 30 45 84 127 170
2 10 20 30 58 79 100
V2#1,2: 1-Burgos-a, Severin-c/a; Powell-a? 9 18 27 50 65 80

FRAY (Also see Buffy the Vampire Slayer "season eight" #16-19)
Dark Horse Comics: June, 2001 - No. 8, July, 2003 ($2.99, limited series)

1-Joss Whedon-s/Moline & Owens-a 1 2 3 5 6 8
1-DF Gold edition 2 4 6 9 12 15
2-8: 6-(3/02). 7-(4/03) 4.00
TPB (11/03, $19.95) r/#1-8; intros by Whedon & Loeb; Moline sketch pages 20.00

FREAK FORCE (Also see Savage Dragon)
Image Comics (Highbrow Ent.): Dec, 1993 - No. 18, July, 1995 ($1.95/$2.50)

1-18-Superpatriot & Mighty Man in all; Erik Larsen scripts in all. 4-Vanguard app. 8-Begin $2.50-c. 9-Cyberforce-c & app. 13-Variant-c 3.00

FREAK FORCE (Also see Savage Dragon)
Image Comics: Apr, 1997 - No. 3, July, 1997 ($2.95)

1-3-Larsen-s 3.00

FREAK OUT, USA (See On the Scene Presents...)

FREAK SHOW
Image Comics (Desperado): 2006 ($5.99, B&W, one-shot)

nn-Bruce Jones-s/Bernie Wrightson-c/a 6.00

FREAKS OF THE HEARTLAND
Dark Horse Comics: Jan, 2004 - No. 6, Nov, 2004 ($2.99)

1-6-Steve Niles-s/Greg Ruth-a 3.00

FRECKLES AND HIS FRIENDS (See Crackajack Funnies, Famous Comics Cartoon Book, Honeybee Birdwhistle... & Red Ryder)

FRECKLES AND HIS FRIENDS
Standard Comics/Argo: No. 5, 11/47 - No. 12, 8/49; 11/55 - No. 4, 6/56

5-Reprints 10 20 30 54 72 90
6-12-Reprints. 7-9-Airbrush-c (by Schomburg?). 11-Lingerie panels
8 16 24 40 50 60
NOTE: *Some copies of No. 8 & 9 contain a printing oddity. The negatives were elongated in the engraving process, probably to conform to page dimensions on the filler pages. Those pages only look normal when viewed at a 45 degree angle.*
1(Argo,'55)-Reprints (NEA Service) 6 12 18 28 34 40
2-4 4 8 12 18 22 25

FREDDY (Formerly My Little Margie's Boy Friends) (Also see Blue Bird)
Charlton Comics: V2#12, June, 1958 - No. 47, Feb, 1965

V2#12-Teenage 3 6 9 21 33 45
13-15 3 6 9 15 22 28
16-47 2 4 6 11 16 20

FREDDY
Dell Publishing Co.: May-July, 1963 - No. 3, Oct-Dec, 1964

1 3 6 9 18 28 38
2,3 3 6 9 14 20 26

FREDDY KRUEGER'S A NIGHTMARE ON ELM STREET
Marvel Comics: Oct, 1989 - No. 2, Dec, 1989 ($2.25, B&W, movie adaptation, magazine)

1,2: Origin Freddy Krueger; Buckler/Alcala-a 2 4 6 9 12 15

FREDDY'S DEAD: THE FINAL NIGHTMARE
Innovation Publishing: Oct, 1991 - No. 3, Dec 1991 ($2.50, color mini-series, adapts movie)

1-3: Dismukes (film poster artist) painted-c 3.00

FREDDY VS. JASON VS. ASH (Freddy Krueger, Friday the 13th, Army of Darkness)
DC Comics (WildStorm): Early Jan, 2008 - No. 6, May, 2008 ($2.99, limited series)

1-Three covers by J. Scott Campbell; Kuhoric-s/Craig-a 5.00
1-Second printing with 3 covers combined sideways 4.00
2-6: 2-4-Eric Powell-c. 5,6-Richard Friend-c 4.00
2-4-Second printings with B&W covers 3.00
TPB (2008, $17.99) r/#1-6; creators' interview afterword 18.00

FREDDY VS. JASON VS. ASH: THE NIGHTMARE WARRIORS
DC Comics (WildStorm): Aug, 2009 - No. 6, Jan, 2010 ($3.99, limited series)

1-6-Katz & Kuhoric-s/Craig-a. 1-Suydam-c 4.00
TPB (2010, $17.99) r/#1-6; cover gallery 18.00

FRED HEMBECK DESTROYS THE MARVEL UNIVERSE
Marvel Comics: July, 1989 ($1.50, one-shot)

1-Punisher app.; Staton-i (5 pgs.) 4.00

FRED HEMBECK SELLS THE MARVEL UNIVERSE
Marvel Comics: Oct, 1990 ($1.25, one-shot)

1-Punisher, Wolverine parodies; Hembeck/Austin-c 4.00

FREE COMIC BOOK DAY
Various publishers

2013 (Avengers/Hulk)(Marvel, 5/13) Hulk and Avengers Assemble animated series 3.00
2014 (Guardians of the Galaxy)(Marvel, 5/14) r/#1; Thanos & Spider-Verse back-ups 3.00
2015 (Avengers)(Marvel, 6/15) All-New Avengers and Uncanny Humans 3.00
2015 (Dark Horse, 5/15) Previews Fight Club 2, The Goon, and The Strain 3.00
2015 (Secret Wars #1)(Marvel, 6/15) Prelude to Secret Wars series (#0 on cover); back-up with Avengers/Attack on Titan x-over; Alex Ross wraparound-c 3.00
2016 (Captain America #1)(Marvel, 5/16) Preview of Captain America: Steve Rogers #1 and Amazing Spider-Man "Dead No More" storyline 3.00
2016 (Dark Horse, 5/16) Previews Serenity, Hellboy and Aliens: Defiance 3.00
...: Dark Circle 1 (Archie Comic Pub., 6-7/15) Previews Black Hood, The Fox, The Shield 3.00
...: R.I.P.D. and The True Lives of the Fabulous Killjoys (Dark Horse, 5/13) Flipbook with Mass Effect 3.00

Freshmen #1 © TCOW

The Friendly Ghost, Casper #1 © HARV

Friendly Neighborhood Spider-Man #2 © MAR

GD VG FN VF VF/NM NM-
2.0 4.0 6.0 8.0 9.0 9.2

GD VG FN VF VF/NM NM-
2.0 4.0 6.0 8.0 9.0 9.2

FREEDOM AGENT (Also see John Steele)
Gold Key: Apr, 1963 (12¢)

1 (10054-304)-Painted-c 4 8 12 25 40 55

FREEDOM FIGHTERS (See Justice League of America #107,108)
National Periodical Publ./DC Comics: Mar-Apr, 1976 - No. 15, July-Aug, 1978

1-Uncle Sam, The Ray, Black Condor, Doll Man, Human Bomb, & Phantom Lady begin (all former Quality characters) 3 6 9 16 23 30
2-9: 4,5-Wonder Woman x-over. 7-1st app. Crusaders 2 4 6 9 12 15
10-15: 10-Origin Doll Man; Cat-Man-c/story (4th app; 1st revival since Detective #325). 11-Origin The Ray. 12-Origin Firebrand. 13-Origin Black Condor. 14-Batgirl & Batwoman app. 15-Batgirl & Batwoman app.; origin Phantom Lady 2 4 6 9 13 16
NOTE: *Buckler c-5-11p, 13p, 14p.*

FREEDOM FIGHTERS (Also see "Uncle Sam and the Freedom Fighters")
DC Comics: Nov, 2010 - No. 9, Jul, 2011 ($2.99)

1-9-Travis Moore-a. 1-6-Dave Johnson-c 3.00

FREEDOM FORCE
Image Comics: Jan, 2005 - No. 6, June, 2005 ($2.95)

1-6-Eric Dieter-s/Tom Scioli-a 3.00

FREELANCERS
BOOM! Studios: Oct, 2012 - No. 6, Mar, 2013 ($1.00/$3.99)

1-($1.00) Brill-s/Covey-a; eight covers; back-up origin of Valerie & Cassie 3.00
2-6-($3.99) Multiple covers on each 4.00

FREEMIND
Future Comics: No. 0, Aug, 2002; Nov, 2002 - No. 7, June, 2003 ($3.50)

0-($2.25) Two covers by Giordano & Layton 3.00
1-7 ($3.50) 1-Two covers by Giordano & Layton; Giordano-a thru #3. 4,5-Leeke-a 3.50

FREEREALMS
DC Comics (WildStorm): Sept, 2009 - No. 12, Oct, 2010 ($3.99, limited series)

1-12-Based on the online game; Jon Buran-a 4.00
... Book One TPB (2010, $19.99) r/#1-6 20.00
... Book Two TPB (2010, $19.99) r/#7-12 20.00

FREEX
Malibu Comics (Ultraverse): July, 1993 - No. 18, Mar, 1995 ($1.95)

1-3,5-14,16-18: 1-Polybagged w/trading card. 2-Some were polybagged w/card. 6-Nightman-c/story. 7-2 pg. origin Hardcase by Zeck. 17-Rune app. 3.00
1-Holographic-c edition 8.00
1-Ultra 5,000 limited silver ink-c 5.00
4-($2.50, 48 pgs.)-Rune flip-c/story by B. Smith (3 pgs.); 3 pg. Night Man preview 4.00
15 ($3.50)-w/Ultraverse Premiere #9 flip book; Alec Swan & Rafferty app. 4.00
Giant Size 1 (1994, $2.50)-Prime app. 4.00
NOTE: *Simonson c-1.*

FRENEMY OF THE STATE
Oni Press: May, 2010 - No. 5, Dec, 2011 ($3.99)

1-5-Rashida Jones, Christina Weir & Nunzio DeFilippis-s 4.00

FRENZY (Magazine) (Satire)
Picture Magazine: Apr, 1958 - No. 6, Mar, 1959

1-Painted-c 14 28 42 80 115 150
2-6 9 18 27 47 61 75

FRESHMEN
Image Comics: Jul, 2005 - No. 6, Mar, 2006 ($2.99)

1-Sterbakov-s/Kirk-a; co-created by Seth Green; covers by Pérez, Migliari, Linsner 3.00
2-6-Migliari-c 3.00
... Yearbook (1/06, $2.99) profile pages of characters; art by various incl. Chaykin, Kirk 3.00
... Vol. 1 (3/06, $16.99, TPB) r/#1-6 & Yearbook; cover gallery with concept art 17.00

FRESHMEN (Volume 2)
Image Comics: Nov, 2006 - No. 6, Aug, 2007 ($2.99)

1-6: 1-Sterbakov-s/Conrad-a; 4 covers 3.00
...: Summer Vacation Special (7/08, $4.99) Sterbakov-s; bonus pin-ups by various 5.00
... Vol. 2 Fundamentals of Fear (6/07, $16.99, TPB) r/#1-6; cover gallery, journals 17.00

FRIDAY FOSTER
Dell Publishing Co.: October, 1972

1 4 8 12 28 47 65

FRIDAY THE 13TH (Based on the horror movie franchise)
DC Comics (WildStorm): Feb, 2007 - No. 6, July, 2007 ($2.99, mature)

1-6: 1-Two covers by Sook and Bradstreet; Gray & Palmiotti-s 3.00
...: Abuser and The Abused (6/08, $3.50) Fialkov-s/Andy B. -a 3.50
...: Bad Land 1,2 (3/08 - No. 2, 4/08, $2.99) Marz-s/Huddleston-a/McKone-c 3.00
...: How I Spent My Summer Vacation 1,2 (11/07 - No. 2, 12/07, $2.99) Aaron-s/Archer-a 3.00
...: Pamela's Tale 1,2 (9/07 - No. 2, 10/07, $2.99) Andreyko-s/Moll-a/Nguyen-c 3.00

FRIENDLY GHOST, CASPER, THE (Becomes Casper... #254 on)
Harvey Publications: Aug, 1958 - No. 224, Oct, 1982; No. 225, Oct, 1986 - No. 253, June, 1990

1-Infinity-c 54 108 162 432 966 1500
2 19 38 57 131 291 450
3-6: 6-X-Mas-c 10 20 30 66 138 210
7-10 8 16 24 56 108 160
11-20: 18-X-Mas-c 7 14 21 46 86 125
21-30 5 10 15 31 53 75
31-50 4 8 12 23 37 50
51-70,100: 54-X-Mas-c 3 6 9 19 30 40
71-99 3 6 9 16 23 30
101-131: 131-Last 12¢ issue 3 6 9 14 20 26
132-159 2 4 6 11 16 20
160-163: All 52 pg. Giants 3 6 9 14 20 26
164-199: 173,179,185-Cub Scout Specials 2 4 6 8 10 12
200 2 4 6 8 11 14
201-224 1 2 3 5 7 9
225-237: 230-X-mas-c. 232-Valentine's-c 5.00
238-253: 238-Begin $1.00-c. 238,244-Halloween-c. 243-Last new material 4.00

FRIENDLY NEIGHBORHOOD SPIDER-MAN
Marvel Comics: Dec, 2005 - No. 24, Nov, 2007 ($2.99)

1-Evolve or Die pt. 1; Peter David-s/Mike Wieringo-a; Morlun app. 4.00
1-Variant Wieringo-c with regular costume 5.00
2-4: 2-New Avengers app. 3-Spider-Man dies 3.00
2-4-var-c: 2-Bag-Head Fantastic Four costume. 3-Captain Universe. 4-Wrestler 5.00
5-10: 6-Red & gold costume. 8-10-Uncle Ben app. 3.00
11-23: 17-Black costume; Sandman app. 3.00
24-($3.99) "One More Day" part 2; Quesada-a; covers by Quesada & Djurdjevic 4.00
Annual 1 (7/07, $3.99) Origin of The Sandman; back-up w/Doran-a 4.00
... Vol. 1: Derailed (2006, $14.99) r/#5-10; Wieringo sketch pages 15.00
... Vol. 2: Mystery Date (2007, $13.99) r/#11-16 14.00

FRIENDS OF MAXX (Also see Maxx)
Image Comics (I Before E): Apr, 1996 - No. 3, Mar, 1997 ($2.95)

1-3: Sam Kieth-c/a/scripts. 1-Featuring Dude Japan 3.00

FRIGHT
Atlas/Seaboard Periodicals: June, 1975 (Aug. on inside)

1-Origin/1st app. The Son of Dracula; Frank Thorne-c/a 3 6 9 14 19 24

FRIGHT NIGHT
Now Comics: Oct, 1988 - No. 22, 1990 ($1.75)

1-22: 1,2 Adapts movie. 8, 9-Evil Ed horror photo-c from movie 3.00

FRIGHT NIGHT II
Now Comics: 1989 ($3.95, 52 pgs.)

1-Adapts movie sequel 4.00

FRINGE (Based on the 2008 FOX television series)
DC Comics (WildStorm): Oct, 2008 - No. 6, Aug, 2009 ($2.99, limited series)

1-6-Anthology by various. 1-Mandrake & Coleby-a 3.00
TPB (2009, $19.99) r/#1-6; intro. by TV series co-creators Kurtzman & Orci 20.00

FRINGE: TALES FROM THE FRINGE (Based on the 2008 FOX television series)
DC Comics (WildStorm): Aug, 2010 - No. 6, Jan, 2011 ($3.99, limited series)

1-6-Anthology by various; LaTorre-c. 1-Reg & photo-c 4.00
2-6-Variant covers from parallel world. 2-Death of Batman. 3-Superman/Dark Knight Returns. 4-Crisis #7 Supergirl holding dead Superman. 5-Justice League #1 w/Jonah Hex. 6-Red Lantern/Red Arrow #76 10.00
TPB (2011, $14.99) r/#1-6 with variant cover gallery and sketch art 15.00

FRISKY ANIMALS (Formerly Frisky Fables; Super Cat #56 on)
Star Publications: No. 44, Jan, 1951 - No. 55, Sept, 1953

44-Super Cat; L.B. Cole 20 40 60 114 182 250
45-Classic L. B. Cole-c 28 56 84 165 270 375
46-51,53-55: Super Cat. 54-Super Cat-c begin 19 38 57 109 172 235
52-L. B. Cole-c/a, 3 1/2 pgs.; X-Mas-c 20 40 60 114 182 250
NOTE: *All have **L. B. Cole**-c. No. 47-No Super Cat. **Disbrow** a-49, 52. **Fago** a-51.*

FRISKY ANIMALS ON PARADE (Formerly Parade Comics; becomes Superspook)

From Beyond the Unknown #4 © DC

Frontier Fighters #3 © DC

Frostbite #1 © Williamson & Alexander

	GD 2.0	VG 4.0	FN 6.0	VF 8.0	VF/NM 9.0	NM- 9.2

Ajax-Farrell Publ. (Four Star Comic Corp.): Sept, 1957 - No. 3, Dec-Jan, 1957-1958

	GD	VG	FN	VF	VF/NM	NM-
1-L. B. Cole-c	17	34	51	98	154	210
2-No L. B. Cole-c	10	20	30	56	76	95
3-L. B. Cole-c	15	30	45	85	130	175

FRISKY FABLES (Frisky Animals No. 44 on)
Premium Group/Novelty Publ./Star Publ. V5#4 on: Spring, 1945 - No. 43, Oct, 1950

	GD	VG	FN	VF	VF/NM	NM-
V1#1-Funny animal; Al Fago-c/a #1-38	23	46	69	136	223	310
2,3(Fall & Winter, 1945)	14	28	42	80	115	150
V2#1(#4, 4/46) - 9,11,12(#15, 3/47): 4-Flag-c	11	22	33	60	83	105
10-Christmas-c. 12-Valentine's-c	11	22	33	62	86	110
V3#1(#16, 4/47) - 12(#27, 3/48): 4-Flag-c. 7,9-Infinity-c. 10-X-Mas-c. 12-Washington crossing the Delaware parody-c	10	20	30	54	72	90
V4#1(#28, 4/48) - 7(#34, 2-3/49)	9	18	27	50	65	80
V5#1(#35, 4-5/49) - 4(#38, 10-11/49)	9	18	27	47	61	75
39-43-L. B. Cole-c; 40-Xmas-c	20	40	60	114	182	250
Accepted Reprint No. 43 (nd); L.B. Cole-c	10	20	30	54	72	90

FRITZI RITZ (See Comics On Parade, Single Series #5, 1(reprint), Tip Top & United Comics)

FRITZI RITZ (United Comics No. 8-26) (Also see Tip Topper for early Peanuts by Schulz)
United Features Synd./St. John No. 37-55/Dell No. 56 on:
1939; Fall, 1948; No. 3, 1949 - No. 7, 1949; No. 27, 3-4/53 - No. 36, 9-10/54; No. 37 - No. 55, 9-11/57; No. 56, 12-2/57-58 - No. 59, 9-11/58

	GD	VG	FN	VF	VF/NM	NM-
Single Series #5 (1939)	39	78	117	231	378	525
nn(1948)-Special Fall issue; by Ernie Bushmiller	20	40	60	114	182	250
3(#1)	14	28	42	82	121	160
4-7(1949): 6-Abbie & Slats app.	11	22	33	60	83	105
27(1953)-33,37-50,57-59-Early Peanuts (1-4 pgs.) by Schulz. 29-Five pg. Abbie & Slats; 1 pg. Mamie by Russell Patterson. 38(9/55)-41(4/56)-Low print run	15	30	45	88	137	185
34-36,51-56: 36-1 pg. Mamie by Patterson	9	18	27	50	65	80

NOTE: *Abbie & Slats in #6,7, 27-31. Li'l Abner in #32-36.*

FROGMAN COMICS
Hillman Periodicals: Jan-Feb, 1952 - No. 11, May, 1953

	GD	VG	FN	VF	VF/NM	NM-
1	17	34	51	98	154	210
2	11	22	33	60	83	105
3,4,6-11: 4-Meskin-a	9	18	27	50	65	80
5-Krigstein-a	10	20	30	54	72	90

FROGMEN, THE
Dell Publishing Co.: No. 1258, Feb-Apr, 1962 - No. 11, Nov-Jan, 1964-65 (Painted-c)

	GD	VG	FN	VF	VF/NM	NM-
Four Color 1258(#1)-Evans-a	8	16	24	51	96	140
2,3-Evans-a; part Frazetta inks in #2,3	5	10	15	33	57	80
4,6-11	4	8	12	23	37	50
5-Toth-a	4	8	12	27	44	60

FROM BEYOND THE UNKNOWN
National Periodical Publications: 10-11/69 - No. 25, 11-12/73

	GD	VG	FN	VF	VF/NM	NM-
1	5	10	15	33	57	80
2-6	3	6	9	19	30	40
7-11: (64 pgs.) 7-Intro Col. Glenn Merrit	3	6	9	21	33	45
12-17: (52 pgs.) 13-Wood-a(i)(r). 17-Pres. Nixon-c	3	6	9	17	26	35
18-25: Star Rovers-r begin #18,19. Space Museum in #23-25	2	4	6	13	18	22

NOTE: ***N. Adams** c-3, 6, 8, 9. **Anderson** c-2, 4, 5, 10, 11i, 15-17, 22; reprints-3, 4, 6-8, 10, 11, 13-16, 24, 25. **Infantino** r-1-5, 7-19, 23-25; c-11p. **Kaluta** c-18, 19. **Gil Kane** a-9r. **Kubert** c-1, 7, 12-14. **Toth** a-2r. **Wood** a-13i. Photo c-22.*

FROM DUSK TILL DAWN (Movie)
Big Entertainment: 1996 ($4.95, one-shot)

	GD	VG	FN	VF	VF/NM	NM-
nn-Adaptation of the film; Brereton-c						5.00
nn-($9.95)Deluxe Ed. w/ new material						10.00

FROM HELL
Mad Love/Tundra Publishing/Kitchen Sink: 1991 - No. 11, Sept, 1998 (B&W)

	GD	VG	FN	VF	VF/NM	NM-
1-Alan Moore and Eddie Campbell's Jack The Ripper story collected from the Taboo anthology series	3	6	9	15	22	28
1-(2nd printing)	2	4	6	8	10	12
1-(3rd printing)	1	2	3	4	5	7
2	1	3	4	6	8	10
2-(2nd printing)						6.00
2-(3rd printing)						4.00
3-1st Kitchen Sink Press issue	1	3	4	6	8	10
3-(2nd printing)						5.00
4-10: 10-(8/96)	1	2	3	5	6	8
11-Dance of the Gull Catchers (9/98, $4.95) Epilogue	2	4	6	10	14	18
Tundra Publishing reprintings 1-5 ('92)	1	2	3	4	5	7
HC						125.00
HC Ltd. Edition of 1,000 (signed and numbered)						230.00
TPB-1st printing (11/99)						60.00
TPB-2nd printing (3/00)						50.00
TPB-3rd printing (11/00)						40.00
TPB-4th printing (7/01) Regular and movie covers						35.00
TPB-5th printing - Regular and movie covers						35.00

FROM HERE TO INSANITY (Satire) (Formerly Eh! #1-7) (See Frantic & Frenzy)
Charlton Comics: No. 8, Feb, 1955 - V3#1, 1956

	GD	VG	FN	VF	VF/NM	NM-
8	21	42	63	122	199	275
9	20	40	60	114	182	250
10-Ditko-c/a (3 pgs.)	30	60	90	177	289	400
11-All Kirby except 4 pgs.	39	78	117	240	395	550
12-(Mag. size) Marilyn Monroe, Jackie Gleason-c; all Kirby except 4 pgs.	41	82	123	256	428	600
V3#1(1956)-Ward-c/a(2) (signed McCartney); 5 pgs. Wolverton-a; 3 pgs. Ditko-a; magazine format (cover says "Crazy, Man, Crazy" and becomes Crazy, Man, Crazy with V2#2)	47	94	141	296	498	700

FROM THE PIT
Fantagor Press: 1994 ($4.95, one-shot, mature)

	GD	VG	FN	VF	VF/NM	NM-
1-R. Corben-a; HP Lovecraft back-up story	1	3	4	6	8	10

FRONTIER DOCTOR (TV)
Dell Publishing Co.: No. 877, Feb, 1958 (one-shot)

	GD	VG	FN	VF	VF/NM	NM-
Four Color 877-Toth-a, Rex Allen photo-c	8	16	24	56	108	160

FRONTIER FIGHTERS
National Periodical Publications: Sept-Oct, 1955 - No. 8, Nov-Dec, 1956

	GD	VG	FN	VF	VF/NM	NM-
1-Davy Crockett, Buffalo Bill (by Kubert), Kit Carson begin (Scarce)	55	110	165	352	601	850
2	37	74	111	222	361	500
3-8	34	68	102	199	325	450

NOTE: *Buffalo Bill by **Kubert** in all.*

FRONTIER ROMANCES
Avon Periodicals/I. W.: Nov-Dec, 1949 - No. 2, Feb-Mar, 1950 (Painted-c)

	GD	VG	FN	VF	VF/NM	NM-
1-Used in **SOTI**, pg. 180 (General reference) & illo. "Erotic spanking in a western comic book"	60	120	180	381	653	925
2 (Scarce)-Woodish-a by Stallman	41	82	123	256	428	600
I.W. Reprint #1-Reprints Avon's #1	3	6	9	21	33	45
I.W. Reprint #9-Reprints ?	3	6	9	15	22	28

FRONTIER SCOUT: DAN'L BOONE (Formerly Death Valley; The Masked Raider No. 14 on)
Charlton Comics: No. 10, Jan, 1956 - No. 13, Aug, 1956; V2#14, Mar, 1965

	GD	VG	FN	VF	VF/NM	NM-
10	10	20	30	54	72	90
11-13(1956)	6	12	18	31	38	45
V2#14(3/65)	3	6	9	15	22	28

FRONTIER TRAIL (The Rider No. 1-5)
Ajax/Farrell Publ.: No. 6, May, 1958

	GD	VG	FN	VF	VF/NM	NM-
6	6	12	18	28	34	40

FRONTIER WESTERN
Atlas Comics (PrPI): Feb, 1956 - No. 10, Aug, 1957

	GD	VG	FN	VF	VF/NM	NM-
1-The Pecos Kid rides	22	44	66	132	216	300
2,3,6-Williamson-a, 4 pgs. each	15	30	45	85	130	175
4,7,9,10: 10-Check-a	12	24	36	67	94	120
5-Crandall, Baker, Davis-a; Williamson text illos	15	30	45	83	124	165
8-Crandall, Morrow, & Wildey-a	12	24	36	69	97	125

NOTE: ***Baker** a-9. **Colan** a-2, 6. **Drucker** a-3, 4. **Heath** c-5. **Maneely** c/a-2, 7, 9. **Maurera** a-2. **Romita** a-7. **Severin** c-6, 8, 10. **Tuska** a-2. **Wildey** a-5, 8. Ringo Kid in No. 4.*

FRONTLINE COMBAT
E. C. Comics: July-Aug, 1951 - No. 15, Jan, 1954

	GD	VG	FN	VF	VF/NM	NM-
1-Severin/Kurtzman-a	83	166	249	664	1057	1450
2	41	82	123	328	527	725
3	33	66	99	264	420	575
4-Used in **SOTI**, pg. 257; contains "Airburst" by Kurtzman which is his personal all-time favorite story	33	66	99	264	420	575
5-John Severin and Bill Elder bios.	27	54	81	216	346	475
6-10: 6-Kurtzman bio. 9-Civil War issue	23	46	69	184	292	400
11-15: 11-Civil War issue	18	36	54	144	232	320

NOTE: ***Davis** a-in all; c-11, 12. **Evans** a-10-15. **Heath** a-1. **Kubert** a-14. **Kurtzman** a-1-5; c-1-9. **Severin** a-5-7, 9, 13, 15. **Severin/Elder** a-2-11; c-10. **Toth** a-8, 12. **Wood** a-1-4, 6-10, 12-15; c-13-15. Special issues: No. 7 (Iwo Jima), No. 9 (Civil War), No. 12 (Air Force).*

(Canadian reprints known; see Table of Contents.)

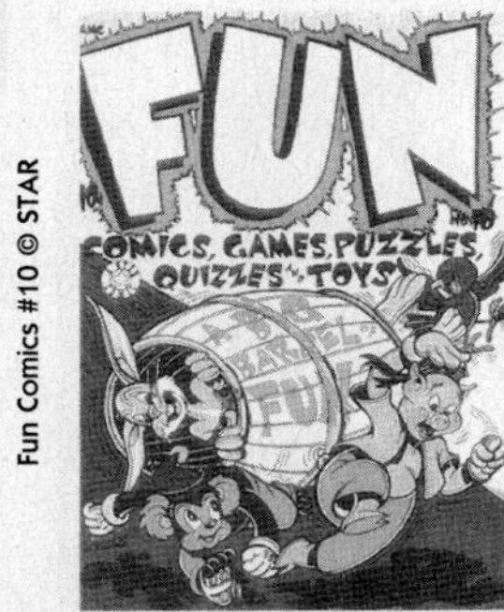

Fun Comics #10 © STAR

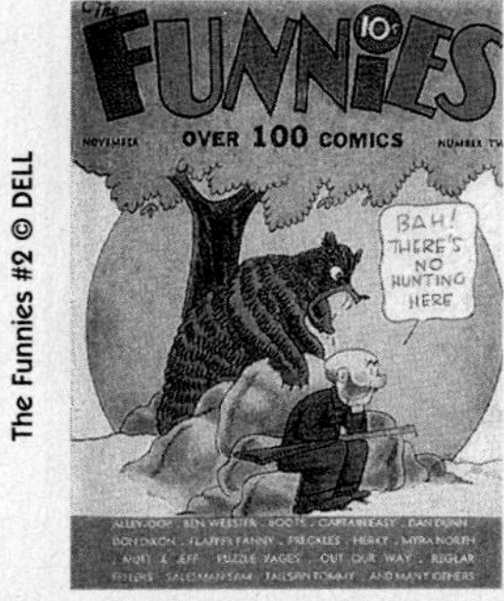

The Funnies #2 © DELL

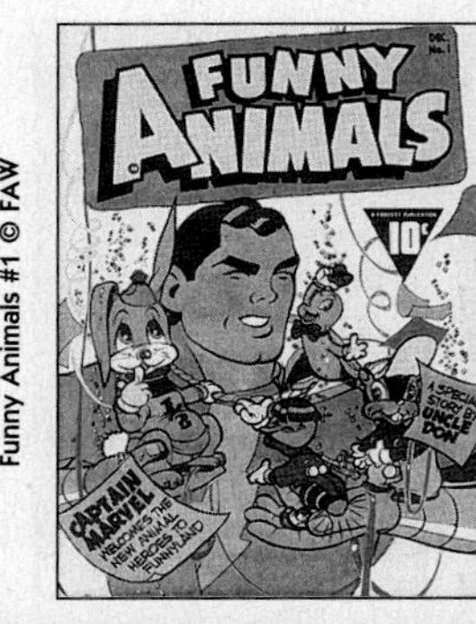

Funny Animals #1 © FAW

FRONTLINE COMBAT
Russ Cochran/Gemstone Publishing: Aug, 1995 - No. 14 ($2.00/$2.50)

	GD 2.0	VG 4.0	FN 6.0	VF 8.0	VF/NM 9.0	NM- 9.2
1-14-E.C. reprints in all						4.00

FRONT PAGE COMIC BOOK
Front Page Comics (Harvey): 1945

	GD 2.0	VG 4.0	FN 6.0	VF 8.0	VF/NM 9.0	NM- 9.2
1-Kubert-a; intro. & 1st app. Man in Black by Powell; Fuje-c	50	100	150	315	533	750

FROST AND FIRE (See DC Science Fiction Graphic Novel)

FROSTBITE
DC Comics (Vertigo): Nov, 2016 - Present ($3.99)

	GD 2.0	VG 4.0	FN 6.0	VF 8.0	VF/NM 9.0	NM- 9.2
1-6-Joshua Williamson-s/Jason Shawn Alexander-a						4.00

FROSTY THE SNOWMAN
Dell Publishing Co.: No. 359, Nov, 1951 - No. 1272, Dec-Feb?/1961-62

	GD 2.0	VG 4.0	FN 6.0	VF 8.0	VF/NM 9.0	NM- 9.2
Four Color 359 (#1)	10	20	30	64	132	200
Four Color 435,514,601,661	6	12	18	40	73	105
Four Color 748,861,950,1065,1153,1272	5	10	15	35	63	90

FROZEN (Disney movie)
Joe Books Ltd.: Jul, 2016 - Present ($2.99)

	GD 2.0	VG 4.0	FN 6.0	VF 8.0	VF/NM 9.0	NM- 9.2
1-5-Georgia Ball-s/Benedetta Barone-a						3.00

FRUITMAN SPECIAL (See Bunny #2 for 1st app.)
Harvey Publications: Dec, 1969 (68 pgs.)

	GD 2.0	VG 4.0	FN 6.0	VF 8.0	VF/NM 9.0	NM- 9.2
1-Funny super hero	4	8	12	23	37	50

F-TROOP (TV)
Dell Publishing Co.: Aug, 1966 - No. 7, Aug, 1967 (All have photo-c)

	GD 2.0	VG 4.0	FN 6.0	VF 8.0	VF/NM 9.0	NM- 9.2
1	8	16	24	55	105	155
2-7	5	10	15	34	60	85

FUGITIVES FROM JUSTICE (True Crime Stories)
St. John Publishing Co.: Feb, 1952 - No. 5, Oct, 1952

	GD 2.0	VG 4.0	FN 6.0	VF 8.0	VF/NM 9.0	NM- 9.2
1	25	50	75	150	245	340
2-Matt Baker-r/Northwest Mounties #2; Vic Flint strip reprints begin	24	48	72	140	230	320
3-Reprints panel from Authentic Police Cases that was used in **SOTI** with changes; Tuska-a	23	46	69	136	223	310
4	14	28	42	80	115	150
5-Last Vic Flint-r; bondage-c	15	30	45	88	137	185

FUGITOID
Mirage Studios: 1985 (B&W, magazine size, one-shot)

	GD 2.0	VG 4.0	FN 6.0	VF 8.0	VF/NM 9.0	NM- 9.2
1-Ties into Teenage Mutant Ninja Turtles #5	3	6	9	14	20	25

FULL OF FUN
Red Top (Decker Publ.)(Farrell)/I. W. Enterprises: Aug, 1957 - No. 2, Nov, 1957; 1964

	GD 2.0	VG 4.0	FN 6.0	VF 8.0	VF/NM 9.0	NM- 9.2
1(1957)-Funny animal; Dave Berg-a	7	14	21	37	46	55
2-Reprints Bingo, the Monkey Doodle Boy	5	10	15	22	26	30
8-I.W. Reprint('64)	2	4	6	9	12	15

FUN AT CHRISTMAS (See March of Comics No. 138)

FUN CLUB COMICS (See Interstate Theatres...)

FUN COMICS (Formerly Holiday Comics #1-8; Mighty Bear #13 on)
Star Publications: No. 9, Jan, 1953 - No. 12, Oct, 1953

	GD 2.0	VG 4.0	FN 6.0	VF 8.0	VF/NM 9.0	NM- 9.2
9-(25¢ Giant)-L. B. Cole X-Mas-c; X-Mas issue	22	44	66	132	216	300
10-12-L. B. Cole-c. 12-Mighty Bear-c/story	18	36	54	105	165	225

FUNDAY FUNNIES (See Famous TV..., and Harvey Hits No. 35,40)

FUN-IN (TV)(Hanna-Barbera)
Gold Key: Feb, 1970 - No. 10, Jan, 1972; No. 11, 4/74 - No. 15, 12/74

	GD 2.0	VG 4.0	FN 6.0	VF 8.0	VF/NM 9.0	NM- 9.2
1-Dastardly & Muttley in Their Flying Machines; Perils of Penelope Pitstop in #1-4; It's the Wolf in all	6	12	18	41	76	110
2-4,6-Cattanooga Cats in 2-4	3	6	9	21	33	45
5,7-Motormouse & Autocat, Dastardly & Muttley in both; It's the Wolf in #7	4	8	12	23	37	50
8,10-The Harlem Globetrotters, Dastardly & Muttley in #10	4	8	12	23	37	50
9-Where's Huddles?, Dastardly & Muttley, Motormouse & Autocat app.	4	8	12	23	37	50
11-Butch Cassidy	3	6	9	19	30	40
12-15: 12,15-Speed Buggy. 13-Hair Bear Bunch. 14-Inch High Private Eye	3	6	9	19	30	40

FUNKY PHANTOM, THE (TV)
Gold Key: Mar, 1972 - No. 13, Mar, 1975 (Hanna-Barbera)

	GD 2.0	VG 4.0	FN 6.0	VF 8.0	VF/NM 9.0	NM- 9.2
1	5	10	15	31	53	75
2-5	3	6	9	18	28	38
6-13	3	6	9	15	22	28

FUNLAND
Ziff-Davis (Approved Comics): No date (1940s) (25¢)

	GD 2.0	VG 4.0	FN 6.0	VF 8.0	VF/NM 9.0	NM- 9.2
nn-Contains games, puzzles, cut-outs, etc.	21	42	63	122	199	275

FUNLAND COMICS
Croyden Publishers: 1945

	GD 2.0	VG 4.0	FN 6.0	VF 8.0	VF/NM 9.0	NM- 9.2
1-Funny animal	17	34	51	98	154	210

FUNNIES, THE (New Funnies No. 65 on)
Dell Publishing Co.: Oct, 1936 - No. 64, May, 1942

	GD 2.0	VG 4.0	FN 6.0	VF 8.0	VF/NM 9.0	NM- 9.2
1-Tailspin Tommy, Mutt & Jeff, Alley Oop (1st app?), Capt. Easy (1st app.), Don Dixon begin	400	800	1200	2300	3650	5000
2 (11/36)-Scribbly by Mayer begins (see Popular Comics #6 for 1st app.)	180	360	540	1035	1643	2250
3	124	248	372	713	1132	1550
4,5: 4(1/37)-Christmas-c	92	184	276	529	840	1150
6-10	70	140	210	403	639	875
11-20: 16-Christmas-c	65	130	195	374	597	820
21-29: 25-Crime Busters by McWilliams(4pgs.)	52	104	156	299	475	650
30-John Carter of Mars (origin/1st app.) begins by Edgar Rice Burroughs; Jim Gary-a Warner Bros.' Bosko-c (4/39)	213	426	639	1363	2332	3300
31-34,36-44: 31,32-Gary-a. 33-John Coleman Burroughs art begins on John Carter. 34-Last funny-c. 40-John Carter of Mars-c	94	188	282	597	1024	1450
35-(9/39)-Mr. District Attorney begins; based on radio show; 1st cover app. John Carter of Mars	148	296	444	947	1624	2300
45-Origin/1st app. Phantasmo, the Master of the World (Dell's 1st super-hero, 7/40) & his sidekick Whizzer McGee	103	206	309	659	1130	1600
46-50: 46-The Black Knight begins, ends #62	58	116	174	371	636	900
51-56-Last ERB John Carter of Mars	47	94	141	296	498	700
57-Intro. & origin Captain Midnight (7/41)	366	732	1098	2562	4481	6400
58-60: 58-Captain Midnight-c begin, end #63	90	180	270	576	988	1400
61-Andy Panda begins by Walter Lantz; WWII-c	123	246	369	787	1344	1900
62,63: 63-Last Captain Midnight-c; bondage-c	71	142	213	454	777	1100
64-Format change; Oswald the Rabbit, Felix the Cat, Li'l Eight Ball app.; origin & 1st app. Woody Woodpecker in Oswald; last Capt. Midnight; Oswald, Andy Panda, Li'l Eight Ball-c	226	452	678	1446	2473	3500

NOTE: ***Mayer** c-26, 48. **McWilliams** art in many issues on "Rex King of the Deep". Alley Oop c-17, 20. Captain Midnight c-57(i/2), 58-63. John Carter c-35-37, 40. Phantasmo c-45-56, 57(1/2), 58-61(part). Rex King c-38, 39, 42. Tailspin Tommy c-41.*

FUNNIES ANNUAL, THE
Avon Periodicals: 1959 ($1.00, approx. 7x10", B&W; tabloid-size)

	GD 2.0	VG 4.0	FN 6.0	VF 8.0	VF/NM 9.0	NM- 9.2
1-(Rare)-Features the best newspaper comic strips of the year: Archie, Snuffy Smith, Beetle Bailey, Henry, Blondie, Steve Canyon, Buz Sawyer, The Little King, Hi & Lois, Popeye, & others. Also has a chronological history of the comics from 2000 B.C. to 1959.	53	106	159	334	567	800

FUNNIES ON PARADE (See Promotional Comics section)

FUNNY ANIMALS (See Fawcett's Funny Animals)
Charlton Comics: Sept, 1984 - No. 2, Nov, 1984

	GD 2.0	VG 4.0	FN 6.0	VF 8.0	VF/NM 9.0	NM- 9.2
1,2-Atomic Mouse-r; low print						6.00

FUNNYBONE (... The Laugh-Book of Comical Comics)
La Salle Publishing Co.: 1944 (25¢, 132 pgs.)

	GD 2.0	VG 4.0	FN 6.0	VF 8.0	VF/NM 9.0	NM- 9.2
nn	32	64	96	188	307	425

FUNNY BOOK (...Magazine for Young Folks) (Hocus Pocus No. 9)
Parents' Magazine Press (Funny Book Publishing Corp.):
Dec, 1942 - No. 9, Aug-Sept, 1946 (Comics, stories, puzzles, games)

	GD 2.0	VG 4.0	FN 6.0	VF 8.0	VF/NM 9.0	NM- 9.2
1-Funny animal; Alice In Wonderland app.	17	34	51	98	154	210
2-Gulliver in Giant-Land	11	22	33	62	86	110
3-9: 4-Advs. of Robin Hood. 9-Hocus-Pocus strip	10	20	30	54	72	90

FUNNY COMICS
Modern Store Publ.: 1955 (7¢, 5x7", 36 pgs.)

	GD 2.0	VG 4.0	FN 6.0	VF 8.0	VF/NM 9.0	NM- 9.2
1-Funny animal	4	8	12	28	47	65

FUNNY COMIC TUNES (See Funny Tunes)

FUNNY FABLES
Decker Publications (Red Top Comics): Aug, 1957 - V2#2, Nov, 1957

	GD 2.0	VG 4.0	FN 6.0	VF 8.0	VF/NM 9.0	NM- 9.2
V1#1	6	12	18	31	38	45
V1#2,V2#1,2: V1#2 (11/57)-Reissue of V1#1	5	10	14	20	24	28

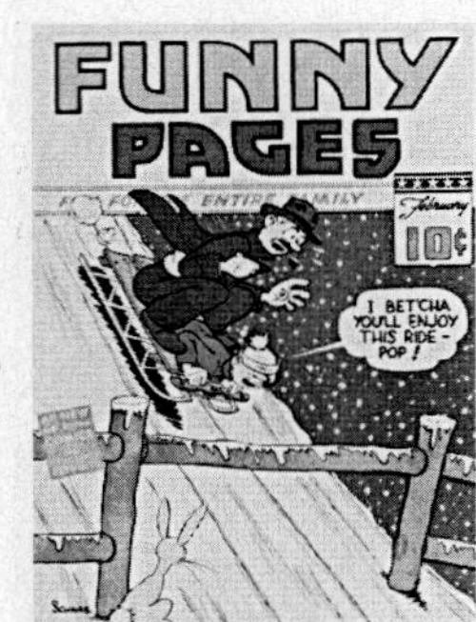

Funny Pages V3 #1 © CM

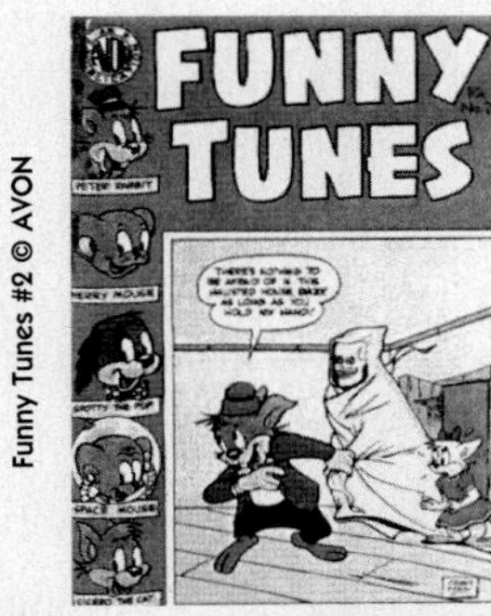

Funny Tunes #2 © AVON

Funtastic World of Hanna-Barbera #3 © H-B

FUNNY FILMS (Features funny animal characters from films)
American Comics Group(Michel Publ./Titan Publ.): Sept-Oct, 1949 - No. 29, May-June, 1954 (No. 1-4: 52 pgs.)

	GD 2.0	VG 4.0	FN 6.0	VF 8.0	VF/NM 9.0	NM- 9.2
1-Puss An' Boots, Blunderbunny begin	18	36	54	107	169	230
2	11	22	33	62	86	110
3-10: 3-X-Mas-c	9	18	27	47	61	75
11-20	7	14	21	35	43	50
21-29	6	12	18	28	34	40

FUNNY FOLKS
DC Comics: Feb, 1946

nn-Ashcan comic, not distributed to newsstands, only for in house use (no known sales)

FUNNY FOLKS (Hollywood... on cover only No. 16-26; becomes Hollywood Funny Folks No. 27 on)
National Periodical Publ.: April-May, 1946 - No. 26, June-July, 1950 (52 pgs., #15 on)

	GD 2.0	VG 4.0	FN 6.0	VF 8.0	VF/NM 9.0	NM- 9.2
1-Nutsy Squirrel begins (1st app.) by Rube Grossman; Grossman-a in most issues	40	80	120	246	411	575
2	20	40	60	117	189	260
3-5: 4-1st Nutsy Squirrel-c	15	30	45	85	130	175
6-10: 6,9-Nutsy Squirrel-c begin	11	22	33	62	86	110
11-26: 15-Begin 52 pg. issues (8-9/48)	10	20	30	54	72	90

NOTE: *Sheldon Mayer a-in some issues. Post a-18. Christmas c-12.*

FUNNY FROLICS
Timely/Marvel Comics (SPI): Summer, 1945 - No. 5, Dec, 1946

	GD 2.0	VG 4.0	FN 6.0	VF 8.0	VF/NM 9.0	NM- 9.2
1-Sharpy Fox, Puffy Pig, Krazy Krow	30	60	90	177	289	400
2-(Fall 1945)	17	34	51	98	154	210
3,4: 3-(Spring 1946)	15	30	45	83	124	165
5-Kurtzman-a	15	30	45	86	133	180

FUNNY FUNNIES
Nedor Publishing Co.: April, 1943 (68 pgs.)

	GD 2.0	VG 4.0	FN 6.0	VF 8.0	VF/NM 9.0	NM- 9.2
1-Funny animals; Peter Porker app.	21	42	63	124	202	280

FUNNYMAN (Also see Cisco Kid Comics & Extra Comics)
Magazine Enterprises: Dec, 1947; No. 1, Jan, 1948 - No. 6, Aug, 1948

nn(12/47)-Prepublication B&W undistributed copy by Siegel & Shuster-(5-3/4x8"), 16 pgs.; Sold at auction in 1997 for $575.00

	GD 2.0	VG 4.0	FN 6.0	VF 8.0	VF/NM 9.0	NM- 9.2
1-Siegel & Shuster-a in all; Dick Ayers 1st pro work (as assistant) on 1st few issues	48	96	144	302	514	725
2	32	64	96	188	307	425
3-6	28	56	84	165	270	375

FUNNY MOVIES (See 3-D Funny Movies)

FUNNY PAGES (Formerly The Comics Magazine)
Comics Magazine Co./Ultem Publ.(Chesler)/Centaur Publications: No. 6, Nov, 1936 - No. 42, Oct, 1940

	GD 2.0	VG 4.0	FN 6.0	VF 8.0	VF/NM 9.0	NM- 9.2
V1#6 (nn, nd)-The Clock begins (2 pgs., 1st app.), ends #11; The Clock is the 1st masked comic book hero	314	628	942	2198	3849	5500
7-11: 11-(6/37)	155	310	465	992	1696	2400
V2#1-V2#5: V2#1 (9/37)(V2#2 on-c; V2#1 in indicia). V2#2 (10/37)(V2#3 on-c; V2#2 in indicia). V2#3(11/37) - 5	123	246	369	787	1344	1900
6(1st Centaur, 3/38)	129	258	387	826	1413	2000
7-9	116	232	348	742	1271	1800
10(Scarce, 9/38)-1st app. of The Arrow by Gustavson (Blue costume)	449	898	1347	3278	5789	8300
11,12	158	316	474	1003	1727	2450
V3#1-Bruce Wayne prototype in "Case of the Missing Heir," by Bob Kane, 3 months before app. Batman (See Det. Pic. Stories #5)	226	452	678	1446	2473	3500
2-6,8: 6,8-Last funny covers	152	304	456	965	1658	2350
7-1st Arrow-c (9/39)	423	846	1269	3000	5250	7500
9-Tarpe Mills jungle-c	165	330	495	1048	1799	2550
10-2nd Arrow-c (Rare)	400	800	1200	2800	4900	7000
V4#1(1/40, Arrow-c)-(Rare)-The Owl & The Phantom Rider app.; origin Mantoka, Maker of Magic by Jack Cole. Mad Ming begins, ends #42; Tarpe Mills-a	400	800	1200	2800	4900	7000
35-Classic Arrow-c (Scarce)	423	846	1269	3000	5250	7500
36-38-Mad Ming-c	226	452	678	1446	2473	3500
39-41-Arrow-c	300	600	900	2010	3505	5000
42 (Scarce,10/40)-Arrow-c	300	600	900	2070	3635	5200

NOTE: *Biro c-V2#9. Burgos c-V3#10. Jack Cole a-V2#3, 7, 8, 10, 11, V3#2, 6, 9, 10, V4#1, 37; c-V3#2, 4. Eisner a-V1#7, 8?, 10. Ken Ernst a-V1#7, 8. Everett a-V2#11 (illos). Filchock c-V2#10, V3#6. Gill Fox a-V2#11. Sid Greene a-39. Guardineer a-V2#2, 3, 5. Gustavson a-V2#5, 11, 12, V3#1-10, 35, 38-42; c-V3#7, 35, 39-42. Bob Kane a-V3#1. McWilliams a-V2#12, V3#1, 3-6. Tarpe Mills a-V3#8-10, V4#1; c-V3#9. Ed Moore Jr. a-V2#12. Schwab c-V3#1. Bob Wood a-V2#2, 3, 8, 11, V3#6, 9, 10; c-V2#6, 7. Arrow c-V3#7, 10, V4#1, 35, 40-42.*

FUNNY PICTURE STORIES (Comic Pages V3#4 on)
Comics Magazine Co./Centaur Publications: Nov, 1936 - V3#3, May, 1939

	GD 2.0	VG 4.0	FN 6.0	VF 8.0	VF/NM 9.0	NM- 9.2
V1#1-The Clock begins (c-feature)(see Funny Pages for 1st app.)	432	864	1296	3154	5577	8000
2	213	426	639	1363	2332	3300
3-6(4/37): 4-Eisner-a	161	322	483	1030	1765	2500
7-(6/37) (Rare) Racial humor-c	400	800	1200	2800	4900	7000
V2#1 (9/37; V1#10 on-c; V2#1 in indicia)-Jack Strand begins	110	220	330	704	1202	1700
2 (10/37; V1#11 on-c; V2#2 in indicia)	110	220	330	704	1202	1700
3-5,7-11(11/38): 4-Christmas-c	103	206	309	659	1130	1600
6-(1st Centaur, 3/38)	113	226	339	718	1234	1750
V3#1(1/39)-3	97	194	291	621	1061	1500

NOTE: *Biro c-V2#1, 8, 9, 11. Guardineer a-V1#11; c-V2#6, V3#5. Bob Wood c/a-V1#11, V2#2; c-V2#3, 5.*

FUNNY STUFF (Becomes The Dodo & the Frog No. 80)
All-American/National Periodical Publications No. 7 on: Summer, 1944 - No. 79, July-Aug, 1954 (#1-7 are quarterly)

	GD 2.0	VG 4.0	FN 6.0	VF 8.0	VF/NM 9.0	NM- 9.2
1-The Three Mouseketeers (ends #28) & The "Terrific Whatzit" begin; Sheldon Mayer-a; Grossman-a in most issues	92	184	276	584	1005	1425
2-Sheldon Mayer-a	43	86	129	271	461	650
3-5: 3-Flash parody. 5-All Mayer-a/scripts issue	32	64	96	188	307	425
6-10 10-(6/46)	20	40	60	117	189	260
11-17,19	15	30	45	90	140	190
18-The Dodo & the Frog (2/47, 1st app?) begin?; X-Mas-c	28	56	84	165	270	375
19-1st Dodo & the Frog-c (3/47)	20	40	60	114	182	250
20-2nd Dodo & the Frog-c (4/47)	14	28	42	82	121	160
21,23-30: 24-Infinity-c. 30-Christmas-c	11	22	33	62	86	110
22-Superman cameo	37	74	111	222	361	500
31-79: 62-Bo Bunny app. by Mayer. 70-Bo Bunny series begins	10	20	30	56	76	95

NOTE: *Mayer a-1-8, 55, ,57, 58, 61, 62, 64, 65, 68, 70, 72, 74-79; c-2, 5, 6, 8.*

FUNNY STUFF STOCKING STUFFER
DC Comics: Mar, 1985 ($1.25, 52 pgs.)

1-Almost every DC funny animal featured 4.00

FUNNY 3-D
Harvey Publications: December, 1953 (25¢, came with 2 pair of glasses)

	GD 2.0	VG 4.0	FN 6.0	VF 8.0	VF/NM 9.0	NM- 9.2
1-Shows cover in 3-D on inside	11	22	33	62	86	110

FUNNY TUNES (Animated Funny Comic Tunes No. 16-22; Funny Comic Tunes No. 23, on covers only; Oscar No. 24 on)
U.S.A. Comics Magazine Corp. (Timely): No. 16, Summer, 1944 - No. 23, Fall, 1946

	GD 2.0	VG 4.0	FN 6.0	VF 8.0	VF/NM 9.0	NM- 9.2
16-Silly Seal, Ziggy Pig, Krazy Krow begin	26	52	78	154	252	350
17 (Fall/44)-Becomes Gay Comics #18 on?	21	42	63	122	199	275
18-22: 21-Super Rabbit app.	20	40	60	114	182	250
23-Kurtzman-a	20	40	60	117	189	260

FUNNY TUNES (Becomes Space Comics #4 on)
Avon Periodicals: July, 1953 - No. 3, Dec-Jan, 1953-54

	GD 2.0	VG 4.0	FN 6.0	VF 8.0	VF/NM 9.0	NM- 9.2
1-Space Mouse, Peter Rabbit, Merry Mouse, Spotty the Pup, Cicero the Cat begin; all continue in Space Comics	12	24	36	69	97	125
2,3	9	18	27	47	61	75

FUNNY WORLD
Marbak Press: 1947 - No. 3, 1948

	GD 2.0	VG 4.0	FN 6.0	VF 8.0	VF/NM 9.0	NM- 9.2
1-The Berrys, The Toodles & other strip-r begin	9	18	27	50	65	80
2,3	6	12	18	31	38	45

FUNTASTIC WORLD OF HANNA-BARBERA, THE (TV)
Marvel Comics Group: Dec, 1977 - No. 3, June, 1978 ($1.25, oversized)

	GD 2.0	VG 4.0	FN 6.0	VF 8.0	VF/NM 9.0	NM- 9.2
1-3: 1-The Flintstones Christmas Party(12/77). 2-Yogi Bear's Easter Parade(3/78). 3-Laff-a-lympics(6/78)	4	8	12	25	40	55

FUN TIME
Ace Periodicals: Spring, 1953; No. 2, Sum, 1953; No. 3(nn), Fall, 1953; No. 4, Wint, 1953-54

	GD 2.0	VG 4.0	FN 6.0	VF 8.0	VF/NM 9.0	NM- 9.2
1-(25¢, 100 pgs.)-Funny animal	21	42	63	124	202	280
2-4 (All 25¢, 100 pgs.)	16	32	48	94	147	200

FUN WITH SANTA CLAUS (See March of Comics No. 11, 108, 325)

FURIOUS
Dark Horse Comics: Jan, 2014 - No. 5, May, 2014 ($3.99)

1-5-Glass-s/Santos-a 4.00

FURTHER ADVENTURES OF CYCLOPS AND PHOENIX (Also see Adventures of Cyclops

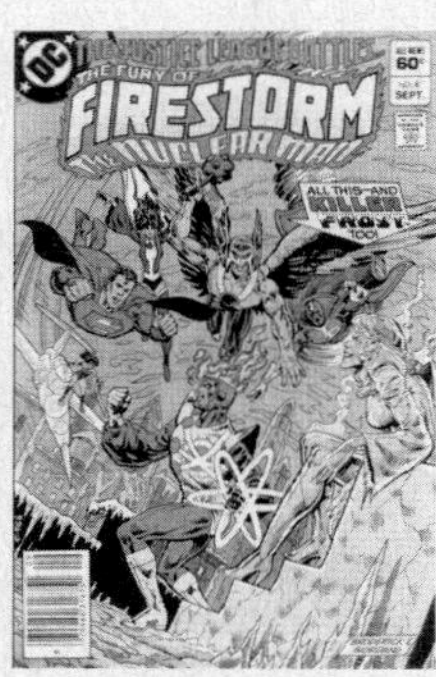

Fury of Firestorm #4 © DC

Futurama Comics #81 © Bongo

Future Quest #1 © H-B

GD 2.0 | VG 4.0 | FN 6.0 | VF 8.0 | VF/NM 9.0 | NM- 9.2

and Phoenix, Uncanny X-Men & X-Men)
Marvel Comics: June, 1996 - No. 4, Sept, 1996 ($1.95, limited series)

1-4: Origin of Mr. Sinister; Milligan scripts; John Paul Leon-c/a(p). 2-4-Apocalypse app. 3.00
Trade Paperback (1997, $14.99) r/1-4 15.00

FURTHER ADVENTURES OF INDIANA JONES, THE (Movie) (Also see Indiana Jones and the Last Crusade & Indiana Jones and the Temple of Doom)
Marvel Comics Group: Jan, 1983 - No. 34, Mar, 1986

1-Byrne/Austin-a; Austin-c 1 2 3 5 6 8
2-34: 2-Byrne/Austin-c/a 4.00

NOTE: ***Austin** a-1i, 2i, 6i, 9i; c-1, 2i, 6i, 9i. **Byrne** a-1p, 2p; c-2p. **Chaykin** a-6p; c-6p, 8p-10p. **Ditko** a-21p, 25-28, 34. **Golden** c-24, 25. **Simonson** c-9. Painted c-14.*

FURTHER ADVENTURES OF NYOKA, THE JUNGLE GIRL, THE (See Nyoka)
AC Comics: 1988 - No. 5, 1989 ($1.95, color; $2.25/$2.50, B&W)

1-5 : 1,2-Bill Black-a plus reprints. 3-Photo-c. 5-(B&W)-Reprints plus movie photos 3.00

FURY (Straight Arrow's Horse...) (See A-1 No. 119)

FURY (TV) (See March Of Comics #200)
Dell Publishing Co./Gold Key: No. 781, Mar, 1957 - Nov, 1962 (All photo-c)

Four Color 781 7 14 21 49 92 135
Four Color 885,975,1031,1080,1133,1172,1218,1296 5 10 15 35 63 90
01292-208(#1-'62), 10020-211(11/62-G.K.) 5 10 15 33 57 80

FURY
Marvel Comics: May, 1994 ($2.95, one-shot)

1-Iron Man, Red Skull, FF, Hatemonger, Logan app.; origin Nick Fury 3.00

FURY (Volume 3)
Marvel Comics (MAX): Nov, 2001 - No. 6, Apr, 2002 ($2.99, mature content)

1-6-Ennis-s/Robertson-a 3.00

FURY/ AGENT 13
Marvel Comics: June, 1998 - No. 2, July, 1998 ($2.99, limited series)

1,2-Nick Fury returns 3.00

FURY MAX (Nick Fury)("My War Gone By" on cover)
Marvel Comics (MAX): Jul, 2012 - No. 13, Aug, 2013 ($3.99, mature content)

1-13: 1-Ennis-s/Parlov-a/Johnson-c; Nick Fury in 1954 Indochina. 7-9-Frank Castle app. 4.00

FURY OF FIRESTORM, THE (Becomes Firestorm The Nuclear Man on cover with #50, in indicia with #65) (Also see Firestorm)
DC Comics: June, 1982 - No. 64, Oct, 1987 (75¢ on)

1-Intro The Black Bison; brief origin 3 6 9 14 20 25
2-6,8-22,25-40,43-64: 4-JLA x-over. 6-Masters of the Universe preview insert. 17-1st app. Firehawk. 21-Death of Killer Frost. 22-Origin. 34-1st app./origin Killer Frost II. 39-Weasel's ID revealed. 48-Intro. Moonbow. 53-Origin & 1st app. Silver Shade. 55,56-Legends x-over. 58-1st app./origin new Parasite 4.00
7-1st app. Plastique 1 3 4 6 8 10
23-(5/84) 1st app. Felicity Smoak (Byte) 2 4 6 11 16 20
24-(6/84)-1st app. Bug (origin); origin Byte; 1st app. Blue Devil in a prevue pull-out 2 4 6 11 16 20
41,42-Crisis x-over 5.00
61-Test cover variant; Superman logo 3 6 9 21 33 45
Annual 1-4: 1(1983), 2(1984), 3(1985), 4(1986) 5.00

NOTE: ***Colan** a-19p, Annual 4p. **Giffen** a-Annual 4p. **Gil Kane** c-30. **Nino** a-37. **Tuska** a-(p)-17, 18, 32, 45.*

FURY OF FIRESTORM: THE NUCLEAR MEN (New DC 52)
DC Comics: Nov, 2011 - No. 20, Jul, 2013 ($2.99)

1-18: 1-Van Sciver & Simone-s/Cinar-a/Van Sciver-c. 7,8-Van Sciver-a. 9-JLI app. 3.00
19,20-Killer Frost app. 5.00
#0 (11/12, #2.99) Cinar-a/c 3.00

FURY OF SHIELD
Marvel Comics: Apr, 1995 - No. 4, July, 1995 ($2.50/$1.95, limited series)

1 ($2.50)-Foil-c 4.00
2-4: 4-Bagged w/ decoder 3.00

FURY: PEACEMAKER
Marvel Comics: Apr, 2006 - No. 6, Sept, 2006 ($3.50, limited series)

1-6-Flashback to WW2; Ennis-s/Robertson-a. 1-Deodato-c. 2-Texeira-c. 5-Dillon-c 3.50
TPB (2006, $17.99) r/#1-6 18.00

FURY: S.H.I.E.L.D. 50TH ANNIVERSARY
Marvel Comics: Nov, 2015 ($3.99, one-shot)

1-Walker-s/Ferguson-a/Deodato-c; Nick Fury Jr. time travels to meet 1965 Nick Fury 4.00

FUSED
Image Comics: Mar, 2002 - No. 4, Jan, 2003 ($2.95)

1-4-Steve Niles-s. 1,2-Paul Lee-a. 3-Brad Rader-a. 4-Templesmith-a 3.00

FUSED
Dark Horse Comics: Dec, 2003 - No. 4, Mar, 2004 ($2.95)

1-4-Steve Niles-s/Josh Medors-a. 1-Powell-c 3.00

FUSION
Eclipse Comics: Jan, 1987 - No. 17, Oct, 1989 ($2.00, B&W, Baxter paper)

1-17: 11-The Weasel Patrol begins (1st app.?) 3.00

FUSION
Image Comics (Top Cow): May, 2009 - No. 3, Jul, 2009 ($2.99, limited series)

1-3-Avengers, Thunderbolts, Cyberforce and Hunter-Killer meet; Kirkham-a 3.00

FUTURAMA (TV)
Bongo Comics: 2000 - No. 81, 2016 ($2.50/$2.99/$3.99, bi-monthly)

1-Based on the FOX-TV animated series; Groening/Morrison-c 3 6 9 16 23 30
1-San Diego Comic-Con Premiere Edition 6 12 18 38 69 100
2-10: 8-CGC cover spoof; X-Men parody 2 4 6 8 10 12
11-30 6.00
31-81: 40,64-Santa app. 50-55-Poster included 4.00
Futurama Adventures TPB (2004, $14.95) r/#5-9 15.00
Futurama Conquers the Universe TPB (2007, $14.95) r/#10-13 15.00
Futurama-O-Rama TPB (2002, $12.95) r/#1-4; sketch pages of Fry's development 15.00
...: The Time Bender Trilogy TPB (2006, $14.95) r/#16-19; cover gallery 15.00

FUTURAMA/SIMPSONS INFINITELY SECRET CROSSOVER CRISIS (TV) (See Simpsons/Futurama Crossover Crisis II for sequel)
Bongo Comics: 2002 - No. 2, 2002 ($2.50, limited series)

1-Evil Brain Spawns put Futurama crew into the Simpsons' Springfield 2 4 6 8 11 14
2 6.00

FUTURE COMICS
David McKay Publications: June, 1940 - No. 4, Sept, 1940

1-(6/40, 64 pgs.)-Origin The Phantom (1st in comics) (4 pgs.); The Lone Ranger (8 pgs.) & Saturn Against the Earth (4 pgs.) begin 300 600 900 2010 3505 5000
2 129 258 387 826 1413 2000
3,4 97 194 291 621 1061 1500

FUTURE COP L.A.P.D. (Electronic Arts video game) (Also see Promotional Comics section)
DC Comics (WildStorm): Jan, 1999 ($4.95, magazine sized)

1-Stories & art by various 5.00

FUTURE IMPERFECT (Secret Wars tie-in)
Marvel Comics: Aug, 2015 - No. 5, Nov, 2015 ($3.99, limited series)

1-5-Peter David-s/Greg Land-a; Maestro (Hulk) and The Thing (Thaddeus Ross) app. 4.00

FUTURE QUEST
DC Comics: Jul, 2016 - Present ($3.99)

1-10: 1-Jonny Quest, Space Ghost, Birdman and Dr. Zin app.; Shaner & Rude-a. 8-Olivetti-a; The Impossibles app. 4.00

FUTURE SHOCK
Image Comics: 2006 (Free Comic Book Day giveaway)

...: FCBD 2006 Edition; Spawn, Invincible, Savage Dragon & others short stories 3.00

FUTURE WORLD COMICS
George W. Dougherty: Summer, 1946 - No. 2, Fall, 1946

1,2: H. C. Kiefer-c; preview of the World of Tomorrow 29 58 87 170 278 385

FUTURE WORLD COMIX (Warren Presents...)
Warren Publications: Sept, 1978 (B&W magazine, 84 pgs.)

1-Corben, Maroto, Morrow, Nino, Sutton-a; Todd-c/a; contains nudity panels 2 4 6 8 11 14

FUTURIANS, THE (See Marvel Graphic Novel #9)
Lodestone Publishing/Eternity Comics: Sept, 1985 - No. 3, 1985 ($1.50)

1-3: Indicia title "Dave Cockrum's..." 3.00
Graphic Novel 1 ($9.95, Eternity)-r/#1-3, plus never published #4 issue 10.00

FX
IDW Publishing: Mar, 2008 - No. 6, Aug, 2008 ($3.99)

1-6-John Byrne-a/c; Wayne Osborne-s 4.00

G-8 (Listed at G-Eight)

GABBY (Formerly Ken Shannon) (Teen humor)

Galactus the Devourer #1 © MAR

Gambit (2012 series) #6 © MAR

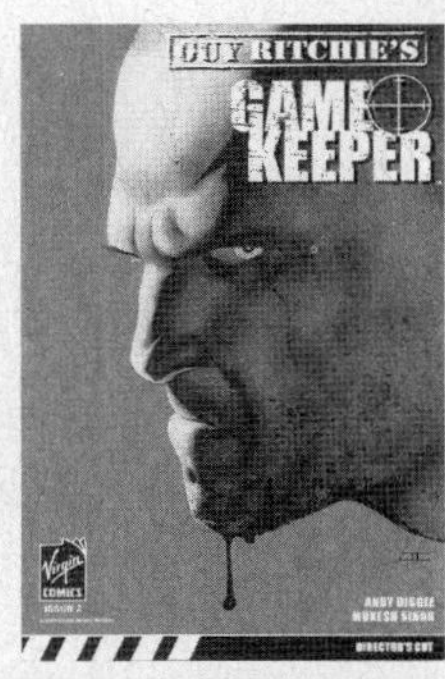

Gamekeeper #2 © Virgin

	GD 2.0	VG 4.0	FN 6.0	VF 8.0	VF/NM 9.0	NM- 9.2

Quality Comics Group: No. 11, Jul, 1953; No. 2, Sep, 1953 - No. 9, Sep, 1954

11(#1)(7/53)	10	20	30	54	72	90
2	7	14	21	35	44	50
3-9	6	12	18	28	34	40

GABBY GOB (See Harvey Hits No. 85, 90, 94, 97, 100, 103, 106, 109)

GABBY HAYES ADVENTURE COMICS
Toby Press: Dec, 1953

1-Photo-c	15	30	45	88	137	185

GABBY HAYES WESTERN (Movie star)(See Monte Hale, Real Western Hero & Western Hero)
Fawcett Publications/Charlton Comics No. 51 on: Nov, 1948 - No. 50, Jan, 1953; No. 51, Dec, 1954 - No. 59, Jan, 1957

1-Gabby & his horse Corker begin; photo front/back-c begin	40	80	120	246	411	575
2	20	40	60	118	192	265
3-5	15	30	45	88	137	185
6-10: 9-Young Falcon begins	14	28	42	78	112	145
11-20: 19-Last photo back-c	11	22	33	64	90	115
21-49: 20,22,24,26,28,29-(52 pgs.)	9	18	27	52	69	85
50-(1/53)-Last Fawcett issue; last photo-c?	10	20	30	58	79	100
51-(12/54)-1st Charlton issue; photo-c	11	22	33	60	83	105
52-59(1955-57): 53,55-Photo-c. 58-Swayze-a	8	16	24	42	54	65

GAGS
United Features Synd./Triangle Publ. No. 9 on: Jul, 1937 - V3#10, Oct, 1944 (13-3/4x10-3/4")

1(7/37)-52 pgs.; 20 pgs. Grin & Bear It, Fellow Citizen	15	30	45	84	127	170
V1#9 (36 pgs.) (7/42)	9	18	27	50	65	80
V3#10	9	18	27	47	61	75

GALACTA: DAUGHTER OF GALACTUS
Marvel Comics: July, 2010 ($3.99, one-shot)

1-Adam Warren-s/Hector Sevilla-a; Warren & Sevilla-c : Wolverine and the FF app. 4.00

GALACTICA 1980 (Based on the Battlestar Galactica TV series)
Dynamite Entertainment: 2009 - No. 4, 2009 ($3.50)

1-4-Guggenheim-s/Razek-a 3.50

GALACTICA: THE NEW MILLENNIUM
Realm Press: Sept, 1999 ($2.99)

1-Stories by Shooter, Braden, Kuhoric 3.00

GALACTIC GUARDIANS
Marvel Comics: July, 1994 - No. 4, Oct, 1994 ($1.50, limited series)

1-4 3.00

GALACTIC WARS COMIX (Warren Presents... on cover)
Warren Publications: Dec, 1978 (B&W magazine, 84 pgs.)

nn-Wood, Williamson-r; Battlestar Galactica/Flash Gordon photo/text stories	2	4	6	8	11	14

GALACTUS THE DEVOURER
Marvel Comics: Sept, 1999 - No. 6, Mar, 2000 ($3.50/$2.50, limited series)

1-($3.50) L. Simonson-s/Muth & Sienkiewicz-a 4.00
2-5-($2.50) Buscema & Sienkiewicz-a 3.00
6-($3.50) Death of Galactus; Buscema & Sienkiewicz-a 4.00

GALAXIA (Magazine)
Astral Publ.: 1981 ($2.50, B&W, 52 pgs.)

1-Buckler/Giordano-c; Texeira/Guice-a; 1st app. Astron, Sojourner, Bloodwing, Warlords; Buckler-s/a	2	4	6	9	13	16

GALAXY QUEST: GLOBAL WARNING! (Based on the 1999 movie)
IDW Publishing: Aug, 2008 - No. 5, Dec, 2008 ($3.99)

1-5-Lobdell-s/Kyriazis-a 4.00

GALAXY QUEST: THE JOURNEY CONTINUES (Based on the 1999 movie)
IDW Publishing: Jan, 2015 - No. 4, Apr, 2015 ($3.99)

1-4-Erik Burnham-s/Nacho Arranz-a 4.00

GALLANT MEN, THE (TV)
Gold Key: Oct, 1963 (Photo-c)

1(1008-310)-Manning-a	3	6	9	21	33	45

GALLEGHER, BOY REPORTER (Disney, TV)
Gold Key: May, 1965

1(10149-505)-Photo-c	3	6	9	17	26	35

	GD 2.0	VG 4.0	FN 6.0	VF 8.0	VF/NM 9.0	NM- 9.2

GAMBIT (See X-Men #266 & X-Men Annual #14)
Marvel Comics: Dec, 1993 - No. 4, Mar, 1994 ($2.00, limited series)

1-($2.50)-Lee Weeks-c/a in all; gold foil stamped-c	2	4	6	10	14	18
1 (Gold)	3	6	9	16	24	32
2-4						6.00

GAMBIT
Marvel Comics: Sept, 1997 - No. 4, Dec, 1997 ($2.50, limited series)

1-4-Janson-a/Mackie & Kavanagh-s 4.00

GAMBIT
Marvel Comics: Feb, 1999 - No. 25, Feb, 2001 ($2.99/$1.99)

1-($2.99) Five covers; Nicieza-a/Skroce-a 5.00
2-11,13-16-($1.99): 2-Two covers (Skroce & Adam Kubert) 3.00
12-($2.99) 4.00
17-24: 17-Begin $2.25-c. 21-Mystique-c/app. 3.00
25-($2.99) Leads into "Gambit & Bishop" 4.00
...1999 Annual ($3.50) Nicieza-s/McDaniel-a 4.00
...2000 Annual ($3.50) Nicieza-s/Derenick & Smith-a 4.00

GAMBIT
Marvel Comics: Nov, 2004 - No. 12, Aug, 2005 ($2.99)

1-12: 1-Jeanty-a/Land-c/Layman-s. 5-Wolverine-c/app. 9-Brother Voodoo-c/app. 3.00
... and the Champions: From the Marvel Vault 1 (10/11, $2.99) George Tuska's last art 3.00
...: Hath No Fury TPB (2005, $14.99) r/#7-12 15.00
...: House of Cards TPB (2005, $14.99) r/#1-6; Land cover sketches; unused covers 15.00

GAMBIT
Marvel Comics: Oct, 2012 - No. 17, Nov, 2013 ($2.99)

1-17: 1-Asmus-s/Mann-a; covers by Mann & Bachalo. 6,7-Pete Wisdom app. 3.00

GAMBIT & BISHOP (**... : Sons of the Atom** on cover)
Marvel Comics: Feb, 2001 - No. 6, May, 2001 ($2.25, bi-weekly limited series)

Alpha (2/01) Prelude to series; Nord-a 3.00
1-6-Jeanty-a/Williams-c 3.00
Genesis (3/01, $3.50) reprints their first apps. and first meeting 4.00

GAMBIT AND THE X-TERNALS
Marvel Comics: Mar, 1995 - No. 4, July, 1995 ($1.95, limited series)

1-4-Age of Apocalypse 4.00

GAMEBOY (Super Mario covers on all)
Valiant: 1990 - No. 5 ($1.95, coated-c)

1-5: 3,4-Layton-c. 4-Morrow-a. 5-Layton-c(i)	1	3	4	6	8	10

GAMEKEEPER (Guy Ritchie's...)
Virgin Comics: Mar, 2007 - No. 5, Sept, 2007; Mar, 2008 - No. 5, Jul, 2008 ($2.99)

1-5-Andy Diggle-s/Mukesh Singh-a; 2 covers on each 3.00
1-Extended Edition (6/07, $2.99) r/#1 with script excerpt and sketch art 3.00
Series 2 (3/08 - No. 5, 7/08) 1-5-Parker-s/Randle-a 3.00
Vol. 1 TPB (10/07, $14.99) r/#1-5; script and sketch pages; Guy Ritchie intro. 15.00

GAME OF THRONES, A (George R.R. Martin's...) (Based on A Song of Fire and Ice)
Dynamite Entertainment: 2011 - Present ($3.99)

1-Covers by Alex Ross and Mike Miller	2	4	6	10	14	18
2-24: 2-Covers by Alex Ross and Mike Miller						4.00

GAMERA
Dark Horse Comics: Aug, 1996 - No. 4, Nov, 1996 ($2.95, limited series)

1-4 3.00

GAMMARAUDERS
DC Comics: Jan, 1989 - No. 10, Dec, 1989 ($1.25/$1.50/$2.00)

1-10-Based on TSR game 3.00

GAMORA (Guardians of the Galaxy)
Marvel Comics: Feb, 2017 - Present ($3.99)

1-3-Perlman-s/Checchetto-a. 1-Thanos & Nebula app. 4.00

GAMORRA SWIMSUIT SPECIAL
Image Comics (WildStorm Productions): June, 1996 ($2.50, one-shot)

1-Campbell wraparound-c; pinups 3.00

GANDY GOOSE (Movies/TV)(See All Surprise, Giant Comics Edition #5A &10, Paul Terry's Comics & Terry-Toons)
St. John Publ. Co./Pines No. 5,6: Mar, 1953 - No. 5, Nov, 1953; No. 5, Fall, 1956 - No. 6, Sum/58

1-All St. John issues are pre-code	12	24	36	67	94	120
2	8	16	24	40	50	60

Gangsters and Gun Molls #4 © AVON

Garfield #7 © PAWS, Inc.

Gay Comics #27 © MAR

	GD 2.0	VG 4.0	FN 6.0	VF 8.0	VF/NM 9.0	NM- 9.2
3-5(1953)(St. John)	7	14	21	35	43	50
5,6(1956-58)(Pines)-CBS Television Presents...	5	10	15	24	30	35

GANG BUSTERS (See Popular Comics #38)
David McKay/Dell Publishing Co.: 1938 - 1943

	GD	VG	FN	VF	VF/NM	NM-
Feature Books 17(McKay)('38)-1st app.	76	152	228	486	831	1175
Large Feature Comic 10('39)-(Scarce)	76	152	228	486	831	1175
Large Feature Comic 17('41)	54	108	162	343	574	825
Four Color 7(1940)	58	116	174	371	636	900
Four Color 23('42)	45	90	135	284	480	675
Four Color 24('43)	27	54	81	189	420	650

GANG BUSTERS (Radio/TV)(Gangbusters #14 on)
National Periodical Publ.: Dec-Jan, 1947-48 - No. 67, Dec-Jan, 1958-59 (No. 1-23: 52 pgs.)

	GD	VG	FN	VF	VF/NM	NM-
1	84	168	252	538	919	1300
2	39	78	117	240	395	550
3-5	28	56	84	165	270	375
6-10: 9-Dan Barry-a. 9,10-Photo-c	21	42	63	122	199	275
11-13-Photo-c	17	34	51	100	158	215
14,17-Frazetta-a, 8 pgs. each. 14-Photo-c	36	72	108	211	343	475
15,16,18-20,26: 26-Kirby-a	15	30	45	85	130	175
21-25,27-30	14	28	42	76	108	140
31-44: 44-Last Pre-code (2-3/55)	12	24	36	67	94	120
45-67	10	20	30	54	72	90

NOTE: ***Barry** a-6, 8, 10. **Drucker** a-51. **Moreira** a-48, 50, 59. **Roussos** a-8.*

GANGLAND
DC Comics (Vertigo): Jun, 1998 - No. 4, Sept, 1998 ($2.95, limited series)

	GD	VG	FN	VF	VF/NM	NM-
1-4:Crime anthology by various. 2-Corben-a						3.00
TPB-(2000, $12.95) r/#1-4; Bradstreet-c						13.00

GANGSTERS AND GUN MOLLS
Avon Per./Realistic Comics: Sept, 1951 - No. 4, June, 1952 (Painted c-1-3)

	GD	VG	FN	VF	VF/NM	NM-
1-Wood-a, 1 pg; c-/Avon paperback #292	61	122	183	390	670	950
2-Check-a, 8 pgs.; Kamen-a; Bonnie Parker story	55	110	165	352	601	850
3-Marijuana mentioned; used in **POP**, pg. 84,85	47	94	141	296	498	700
4-Syd Shores-c	43	86	129	271	461	650

GANGSTERS CAN'T WIN
D. S. Publishing Co.: Feb-Mar, 1948 - No. 9, June-July, 1949 (All 52 pgs?)

	GD	VG	FN	VF	VF/NM	NM-
1-True crime stories	40	80	120	246	411	575
2-Skull-c	28	56	84	165	270	375
3,5,6	20	40	60	120	195	270
4-Acid in face story	26	52	78	154	252	350
7-9	17	34	51	98	154	210

NOTE: ***Ingles** a-5, 6. **McWilliams** a-5, 7, 8. **Reinman** c-6.*

GANG WORLD
Standard Comics: No. 5, Nov, 1952 - No. 6, Jan, 1953

	GD	VG	FN	VF	VF/NM	NM-
5-Bondage-c	20	40	60	117	189	260
6	15	30	45	85	130	175

GARBAGE PAIL KIDS COMIC BOOK (Based on the tranding cards)
IDW Publishing: Dec, 2014 - Feb, 2015 ($3.99, series of one-shots)

	GD	VG	FN	VF	VF/NM	NM-
... Love Stinks (2/15) short stories by various incl. Haspiel, Wheeler, Bagge; 3 covers						4.00
... Puke-tacular (12/14) short stories by various incl. Bagge, Wray, Barta; 3 covers						4.00

GARFIELD (Newspaper/cartoon cat)
Boom Entertainment (KaBOOM!): May, 2012 - No. 36, Apr, 2015 ($3.99)

	GD	VG	FN	VF	VF/NM	NM-
1-24-Evanier-s. 1-Two covers by Barker. 8-Christmas-c. 13,20-Pet Force app.						4.00
1-4-First Appearance Variants by Jim Davis. 1-Garfield. 2-Odie. 3-Jon. 4-Nermal						10.00
25-($4.99) Covers by George Pérez and Barker; bonus pin-ups						5.00
26-36: 30-EC-style horror cover. 33-36-His 9 Lives						4.00
... 2016 Summer Special 1 (7/16, $7.99) Evanier & Nickel-s; Batman spoof	1	2	3	5	6	8
... Cheesy Holiday Special 1 (12/15, $4.99) Christmas stories; Evanier & Nickel-s						5.00
...: Pet Force Special 1 (8/13, $4.99) Cover swipe of Amazing Spider-Man #50						5.00
...: Pet Force 2014 Special (4/14, $4.99) The Pet Force multiverse; bonus sketch art						5.00

GARGOYLE (See The Defenders #94)
Marvel Comics Group: June, 1985 - No. 4, Sept, 1985 (75¢, limited series)

	GD	VG	FN	VF	VF/NM	NM-
1-Wrightson-c; character from Defenders						5.00
2-4						4.00

GARGOYLES (TV cartoon)
Marvel Comics: Feb, 1995 - No. 11, Dec, 1995 ($2.50)

	GD	VG	FN	VF	VF/NM	NM-
1-11: Based on animated series						3.00

GARRISON
DC Comics (WildStorm): Jun, 2010 - No. 6, Nov, 2010 ($2.99)

	GD	VG	FN	VF	VF/NM	NM-
1-6-Mariotte-s/Francavilla-a/c						3.00

GARRISON'S GORILLAS (TV)
Dell Publishing Co.: Jan, 1968 - No. 4, Oct, 1968; No. 5, Oct, 1969 (Photo-c)

	GD	VG	FN	VF	VF/NM	NM-
1	4	8	12	28	47	65
2-5: 5-Reprints #1	3	6	9	19	30	40

GARY GIANNI'S THE MONSTERMEN
Dark Horse Comics: Aug, 1999 ($2.95, one-shot)

	GD	VG	FN	VF	VF/NM	NM-
1-Gianni-s/c/a; back-up Hellboy story by Mignola						4.00

GASM (Sci-Fi, Horror, Fantasy comics magazine)(Mature content)
Stories, Layouts & Press, Inc.: Nov, 1977 - nn (No. 5), Jun, 1978 (B&W/color)

	GD	VG	FN	VF	VF/NM	NM-
1-Mark Wheatley-s/a; Gene Day-s/a; Workman-a	3	6	9	14	19	24
2 (12/77) Wheatley-a; Winnick-s/a; Workman-a	2	4	6	11	16	20
nn(#3, 2/78) Day-s/a; Wheatley-a; Workman-a	2	4	6	10	14	18
nn(#4, 4/78) Day-s/a; Wheatley-a; Corben-a	3	6	9	14	20	26
nn(#5, 6/78) Hempel-a; Howarth-a; Corben-a	3	6	9	15	22	28

GASOLINE ALLEY (Top Love Stories No. 3 on?)
Star Publications: Sept-Oct, 1950 - No. 2, Dec, 1950 (Newspaper-r)

	GD	VG	FN	VF	VF/NM	NM-
1-Contains 1 pg. intro. history of the strip (The Life of Skeezix); reprints 15 scenes of highlights from 1921-1935, plus an adventure from 1935 and 1936 strips; a 2-pg. filler is included on the life of the creator Frank King, with photo of the cartoonist.	20	40	60	115	185	255
2-(1936-37 reprints)-L. B. Cole-c	22	44	66	128	209	290

(See Super Book No. 21)

GASP!
American Comics Group: Mar, 1967 - No. 4, Aug, 1967 (12¢)

	GD	VG	FN	VF	VF/NM	NM-
1	5	10	15	31	53	75
2-4	3	6	9	21	33	45

GATECRASHER
Black Bull Entertainment: Mar, 2000 - No. 4, Jun, 2000 ($2.50, limited series)

	GD	VG	FN	VF	VF/NM	NM-
1,2-Waid-s/Conner & Palmiotti-c/a; 1,2-variant-c by J.G. Jones						3.00
3,4: 3-Jusko var-c. 4-Linsner-c						3.00
... Ring of Fire TPB (11/00, $12.95) r/#1-4; Hughes-c; Ennis intro.						13.00

GATECRASHER (Regular series)
Black Bull Entertainment: Aug, 2000 - No. 6, Jan, 2001 ($2.50, limited series)

	GD	VG	FN	VF	VF/NM	NM-
1-6-Waid-s/Conner & Palmiotti-c/a; 1-3-Variant-c by Fabry. 4-Hildebrandts variant-c. 5-Art Adams var-c. 6-Texeira var-c						3.00

GAY COMICS (Honeymoon No. 41)
Timely Comics/USA Comic Mag. Co. No. 18-24: Mar, 1944 (no month); No. 18, Fall, 1944 - No. 40, Oct, 1949

	GD	VG	FN	VF	VF/NM	NM-
1-Wolverton's Powerhouse Pepper; Tessie the Typist begins; 1st app. Willie (one shot)	74	148	222	470	810	1150
18-(Formerly Funny Tunes #17?)-Wolverton-a	50	100	150	315	533	750
19-29: Wolverton-a in all. 21,24-6 pg., 7 pg. Powerhouse Pepper; additional 2 pg. story in 24). 23-7 pg Wolverton story & 2 two pg stories (total of 11pgs.). 24,29-Kurtzman-a (24-"Hey Look"(2))	47	94	141	296	498	700
30,33,36,37-Kurtzman's "Hey Look"	22	44	66	132	216	300
31-Kurtzman's "Hey Look" (1), Giggles 'N' Grins (1-1/2)	22	44	66	132	216	300
32,35,38-40: 35-Nellie The Nurse begins?	21	42	63	124	202	280
34-Three Kurtzman's "Hey Look"	23	46	69	136	223	310

GAY COMICS (Also see Smile, Tickle, & Whee Comics)
Modern Store Publ.: 1955 (7¢, 5x7-1/4", 52 pgs.)

	GD	VG	FN	VF	VF/NM	NM-
1	4	8	12	28	47	65

GAY PURR-EE (See Movie Comics)

GEARS OF WAR (Based on the video game)
DC Comics (WildStorm): Dec, 2008 - No. 24, Aug, 2012 ($3.99/$2.99)

	GD	VG	FN	VF	VF/NM	NM-
1-15: 1-Liam Sharp-a/Joshua Ortega-s. 1-Two covers						4.00
16-24-($2.99) 16-Traviss-s/Gopez-a. 18-20-Mhan-a. 19-24-Prelude to Gears of War 3						3.00
... Reader (4/09, $3.99) r/#1 & 2 in flipbook						4.00
... Sourcebook (8/09, $3.99) character pin-ups by various; Platt-c						4.00
Book One HC (2009, $19.99, dustjacket) r/#1-6 & Sourcebook						20.00
Book One SC (2010, $14.99) r/#1-6 & Sourcebook						15.00
Book Two HC (2011, $24.99, dustjacket) r/#7-13						25.00

GEAR STATION, THE
Image Comics: Mar, 2000 - No. 5, Nov, 2000 ($2.50)

	GD	VG	FN	VF	VF/NM	NM-
1-Four covers by Ross, Turner, Pat Lee, Fraga						3.00

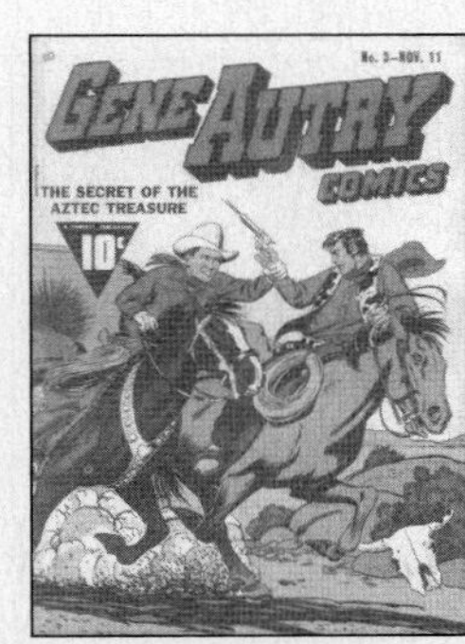
Gene Autry Comics #3 © FAW

Generation Hope #1 © MAR

Generation X #39 © MAR

	GD 2.0	VG 4.0	FN 6.0	VF 8.0	VF/NM 9.0	NM- 9.2

1-($6.95) DF Cover 7.00
2-5: 2-Two covers by Fraga and Art Adams 3.00

GEEK, THE (See Brother Power... & Vertigo Visions)

GEEKSVILLE (Also see 3 Geeks, The)
3 Finger Prints/ Image: Aug, 1999 - No. 6, Mar, 2001 ($2.75/$2.95, B&W)

1,2,4-6-The 3 Geeks by Koslowski; Innocent Bystander by Sassaman 3.00
3-Includes "Babes & Blades" mini-comic 5.00
0-(3/00) First Image issue 3.00
(Vol. 2) 1-4-($2.95) 3-Mini-comic insert by the Geeks. 4-Steve Borock app. 3.00

G-8 AND HIS BATTLE ACES (Based on pulps)
Gold Key: Oct, 1966

1 (10184-610)-Painted-c 4 8 12 25 40 55

G-8 AND HIS BATTLE ACES
Blazing Comics: 1991 ($1.50, one-shot)

1-Glanzman-a; Truman-c 3.00
NOTE: *Flip book format with "The Spider's Web" #1 on other side w/**Glanzman**-a, **Truman**-c.*

GEM COMICS
Spotlight Publishers: Apr, 1945 (52 pgs)

1-Little Mohee, Steve Strong app.; Jungle bondage-c
58 116 174 371 636 900

GEMINAR
Image Comics: July, 2000 ($4.95, B&W)

1-(72-Page Special) Terry Collins-s/Al Bigley-a 5.00

GEMINI BLOOD
DC Comics (Helix): Sept, 1996 - No. 9, May, 1997 ($2.25, limited series)

1-9: 5-Simonson-c 3.00

GEN ACTIVE
DC Comics (WildStorm): May, 2000 - No. 6, Aug, 2001 ($3.95)

1-6: 1-Covers by Campbell and Madureira; Gen 13 & DV8 app. 5-Mahfood-a; Quitely and Stelfreeze-c. 6-Portacio-a/c 4.00

GENE AUTRY (See March of Comics No. 25, 28, 39, 54, 78, 90, 104, 120, 135, 150 in the Promotional Comics section & Western Roundup under Dell Giants)

GENE AUTRY COMICS (Movie, Radio star; singing cowboy)
Fawcett Publications: Jan, 1942 (On sale 12/17/41) - No. 10, 1943 (68 pgs.)
(Dell takes over with No. 11)

1 (Scarce)-Gene Autry & his horse Champion begin; photo back-c
423 846 1269 3000 5250 7500
2-(1942) 90 180 270 576 988 1400
3-5: 3-(11/1/42) 50 100 150 315 533 750
6-10 41 82 123 256 428 600

GENE AUTRY COMICS (...& Champion No. 102 on)
Dell Publishing Co.: No. 11, 1943 - No. 121, Jan-Mar, 1959 (TV - later issues)

11 (1943, 60 pgs.)-Continuation of Fawcett series; photo back-c; first Dell issue
32 64 96 230 515 800
12 (2/44, 60 pgs.) 28 56 84 202 451 700
Four Color 47 (1944, 60 pgs.) 34 68 102 245 548 850
Four Color 57 (11/44), 66('45)(52 pgs. each) 29 58 87 209 467 725
Four Color 75, 83 ('45, 36 pgs. each) 23 46 69 164 362 560
Four Color 93 ('45, 36 pgs.) 19 38 57 133 297 460
Four Color 100 ('46, 36 pgs.) First Gene Autry photo-c
22 44 66 155 345 535
1 (5-6/46, 52 pgs.) 32 64 96 230 515 800
2 (7-8/46)-Photo-c begin, end #111 14 28 42 96 211 325
3-5: 4-Intro Flapjack Hobbs 11 22 33 76 163 250
6-10 10 20 30 64 132 200
11-20: 20-Panhandle Pete begins 9 18 27 60 120 180
21-29 (36 pgs.) 8 16 24 52 99 145
30-40 (52 pgs.) 7 14 21 44 82 120
41-56 (52 pgs.) 6 12 18 38 69 100
57-66 (36 pgs.): 58-X-mas-c 5 10 15 34 60 85
67-80 (52 pgs.): 70-X-mas-c 5 10 15 34 60 85
81-90 (52 pgs.): 82-X-mas-c. 87-Blank inside-c 5 10 15 31 53 75
91-99 (36 pgs. No. 91-on). 94-X-mas-c 4 8 12 28 47 65
100 5 10 15 30 50 70
101-111-Last Gene Autry photo-c 4 8 12 27 44 60
112-121-All Champion painted-c, most by Savitt 4 8 12 25 40 55
NOTE: *Photo back covers 4-18, 20-45, 48-65.* ***Manning*** *a-118.* ***Jesse Marsh*** *art: 4-Color No. 66, 75, 93, 100, No. 1-25, 27-37, 39, 40.*

	GD 2.0	VG 4.0	FN 6.0	VF 8.0	VF/NM 9.0	NM- 9.2

GENE AUTRY'S CHAMPION (TV)
Dell Publ. Co.: No. 287, 8/50; No. 319, 2/51; No. 3, 8-10/51 - No. 19, 8-10/55

Four Color 287(#1)('50, 52 pgs.)-Photo-c 11 22 33 73 157 240
Four Color 319(#2, '51), 3: 2-Painted-c begin, most by Sam Savitt
6 12 18 41 76 110
4-19: 19-Last painted-c 4 8 12 28 47 65

GENE COLAN TRIBUTE BOOK (Produced for The Hero Initiative)
Marvel Comics: 2008 ($9.99, one-shot)

1-Spotlighted stories from Tales of Suspense #89,90, Doctor Strange #174 and others 10.00

GENE DOGS
Marvel Comics UK: Oct, 1993 - No. 4, Jan, 1994 ($1.75, limited series)

1-($2.75)-Polybagged w/4 trading cards 4.00
2-4: 2-Vs. Genetix 3.00

GENE POOL
IDW Publishing: Oct, 2003 ($6.99, squarebound)

nn-Wein & Wolfman-s/Cummings-a 7.00

GENERAL DOUGLAS MACARTHUR
Fox Features Syndicate: 1951

nn-True life story 20 40 60 114 182 250

GENERIC COMIC, THE
Marvel Comics Group: Apr, 1984 (one-shot)

1 3.00

GENERATION HEX
DC Comics (Amalgam): June, 1997 ($1.95, one-shot)

1-Milligan-s/ Pollina & Morales-a 3.00

GENERATION HOPE (See X-Men titles and Cable)
Marvel Comics: Jan, 2011 - No. 17, May, 2012 ($3.99/$2.99)

1-($3.99) Gillen-s/Espin-a; Coipel-c; back-up bio of Hope Summers 4.00
1-Variant-c by Greg Land 8.00
2-17-($2.99) 5,9-McKelvie-a. 10,11-Seeley-a. 11-X-Men: Schism tie-in 3.00

GENERATION M (Follows House of M x-over)
Marvel Comics: Jan, 2006 - No. 5, May, 2006 ($2.99, limited series)

1-5-Jenkins-s/Bachs-a. 1-Chamber app. 2-Jubilee app. 3-Blob-c. 4-Angel-c 3.00
Decimation: Generation M TPB (2006, $13.99) r/#1-5 14.00

GENERATION NEXT
Marvel Comics: Mar, 1995 - No. 4, June, 1995 ($1.95, limited series)

1-4-Age of Apocalypse; Scott Lobdell scripts & Chris Bachalo-c/a 3.00

GENERATION X (See Gen [13]/ Generation X)
Marvel Comics: Oct, 1994 - No. 75, June, 2001 ($1.50/$1.95/$1.99/$2.25)

Collectors Preview ($1.75), "Ashcan" Edition 3.00
-1(7/97) Flashback story 3.00
1/2 (San Diego giveaway) 2 4 6 8 10 12
1-($3.95)-Wraparound chromium-c; Scott Lobdell scripts & Chris Bachalo-a begins 6.00
2-($1.95)-Deluxe edition, Bachalo-a 4.00
3,4-($1.95)-Deluxe Edition; Bachalo-a 4.00
2-10: 2-4-Standard Edition. 5-Returns from "Age of Apocalypse," begin $1.95-c. 6-Bachalo-a(p) ends, returns #17. 7-Roger Cruz-a(p). 10-Omega Red-c/app. 3.00
11-24, 26-28: 13,14-Bishop-app. 17-Stan Lee app. (Stan Lee scripts own dialogue); Bachalo/Buckingham-a; Onslaught update. 18-Toad cameo. 20-Franklin Richards app; Howard the Duck cameo. 21-Howard the Duck app. 22-Nightmare app. 3.00
25-($2.99)-Wraparound-c. Black Tom, Howard the Duck app. 4.00
29-37: 29-Begin $1.99-c, "Operation Zero Tolerance". 33-Hama-s 3.00
38-49: 38-Dodson-a begins. 40-Penance ID revealed. 49-Maggott app. 3.00
50,57-($2.99): 50-Crossover w/X-Man #50 4.00
51-56, 58-62: 59-Avengers & Spider-Man app. 3.00
63-74: 63-Ellis-s begin. 64-Begin $2.25-c. 69-71-Art Adams-c 3.00
75-($2.99) Final issue; Chamber joins the X-Men; Lim-a 4.00
'95 Special-($3.95) 4.00
'96 Special-($2.95)-Wraparound-c; Jeff Johnson-c/a 4.00
'97 Special-($2.99)-Wraparound-c; 4.00
'98 Annual-($3.50)-vs. Dracula 4.00
'99 Annual-($3.50)-Monet leaves 4.00
75¢ Ashcan Edition 3.00
...Holiday Special 1 (2/99, $3.50) Pollina-a 4.00
...Underground Special 1 (5/98, $2.50, B&W) Mahfood-a 3.00

GENERATION X/ GEN [13] (Also see Gen [13]/ Generation X)
Marvel Comics: 1997 ($3.99, one-shot)

Gen 13 #50 © WSP

Gen 13 (2006 series) #13 © WSP

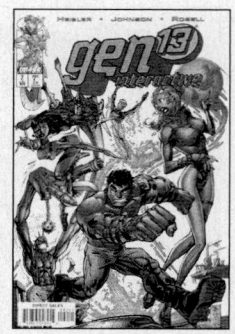

Gen 13 Interactive #2 © WSP

GD VG FN VF VF/NM NM-
2.0 4.0 6.0 8.0 9.0 9.2

1-Robinson-s/Larroca-a(p) 4.00

GENERATION ZERO (see Harbinger Wars)
Valiant Entertainment: Aug, 2016 - Present ($3.99)

1-7: 1-Van Lente-s/Portela-a; multiple covers. 3-Archie-style art by Derek Charm 4.00

GENE RODDENBERRY'S LOST UNIVERSE
Tekno Comix: Apr, 1995 - No. 7, Oct, 1995 ($1.95)

1-7: 1-3-w/ bound-in game piece & trading card. 4-w/bound-in trading card 3.00

GENE RODDENBERRY'S XANDER IN LOST UNIVERSE
Tekno Comix: No. 0, Nov, 1995; No. 1, Dec, 1995 - No. 8, July, 1996 ($2.25)

0,1-8: 1-5-Jae Lee-c. 4-Polybagged. 8-Pt. 5 of The Big Bang x-over 3.00

GENESIS (See DC related titles)
DC Comics: Oct, 1997 - No. 4, Oct, 1997 ($1.95, weekly limited series)

1-4: Byrne-s/Wagner-a(p) in all. 3.00

GENESIS: THE #1 COLLECTION (WildStorm Archives)
WildStorm Productions: 1998 ($9.99, TPB, B&W)

nn-Reprints #1 issues of WildStorm titles and pin-ups 10.00

GENETIX
Marvel Comics UK: Oct, 1993 - No. 6, Mar, 1994 ($1.75, limited series)

1-($2.75)-Polybagged w/4 cards; Dark Guard app. 4.00
2-6: 2-Intro Tektos. 4-Vs. Gene Dogs 3.00

GENEXT (Next generation of X-Men)
Marvel Comics: July, 2008 - No. 5, Nov, 2008 ($3.99, limited series)

1-5: 1-Claremont-s/Scherberger-a; character profile pages 4.00

GENEXT: UNITED
Marvel Comics: July, 2009 - No. 5, Dec, 2009 ($3.99, limited series)

1-5: 1-Claremont-s/Meyers-a; Beast app. 4.00

GENIUS
Image Comics (Top Cow): Aug, 2014 - No. 5, Aug, 2014 ($3.99, limited series)

1-5-Bernardin & Freeman-s/Afua Richardson-a 4.00

GEN 12 (Also see Gen13 and Team 7)
Image Comics (WildStorm Productions): Feb, 1998 - No. 5, June, 1998 ($2.50, lim. series)

1-5: 1-Team 7 & Gen13 app.; wraparound-c 3.00

GEN 13 (Also see Wild C.A.T.S. #1 & Deathmate Black #2)
Image Comics (WildStorm Productions): Feb, 1994 - No. 5, July 1994 ($1.95, limited series)

0 (8/95, $2.50)-Ch. 1 w/Jim Lee-p; Ch. 4 w/Charest-p 4.00
1/2 1 2 3 4 5 7
1-($2.50)-Created by Jim Lee 1 3 4 6 8 10
1-2nd printing 3.00
1-"3-D" Edition (9/97, $4.95)-w/glasses 5.00
2-($2.50) 1 2 3 4 5 7
3-Pitt-c & story 4.00
4-Pitt-c & story; wraparound-c 4.00
5 4.00
5-Alternate Portacio-c; see Deathblow #5 6.00
...Collected Edition ('94, $12.95)-r/#1-5 13.00
...Rave ($1.50, 3/95)-wraparound-c 4.00
...: Who They Are And How They Came To Be... (2006, $14.99) r/#1-5; sketch gallery 15.00

NOTE: *Issues 1-4 contain coupons redeemable for the ashcan edition of Gen 13 #0. Price listed is for a complete book.*

GEN 13
Image Comics (WildStorm Productions): Mar, 1995 - No. 36, Dec, 1998;
DC Comics (WildStorm): No. 37, Mar, 1999 - No. 77, Jul, 2002 ($2.95/$2.50)

1-A (Charge)-Campbell/Garner-c 5.00
1-B (Thumbs Up)-Campbell/Garner-c 5.00
1-C-1-F,1-I-1-M: 1-C (Lil' GEN 13)-Art Adams-c. 1-D (Barbari-GEN)-Simon Bisley-c. 1-E (Your Friendly Neighborhood Grunge)-Cleary-c. 1-F (GEN 13 Goes Madison Ave.)-Golden-c. 1-I (That's the way we became GEN 13)-Campbell/Gibson-c. 1-J (All Dolled Up)-Campbell/McWeeney-c. 1-K (Verti-GEN)-Dunn-c. 1-L (Picto-Fiction). 1-M (Do it Yourself Cover) 1 2 3 4 5 7
1-G (Lin-GEN-re)-Michael Lopez-c 3 6 9 14 20 25
1-H (GEN-et Jackson)-Jason Pearson-c 2 4 6 8 10 12
1-Chromium-c by Campbell 4 8 12 27 44 60
1-Chromium-c by Jim Lee 5 10 15 33 57 80
1-"3-D" Edition (2/98, $4.95)-w/glasses 5.00
2 ($1.95, Newsstand)-WildStorm Rising Pt. 4; bound-in card 3.00
2-12: 2-($2.50, Direct Market)-WildStorm Rising Pt. 4, bound-in card. 6,7-Jim Lee-c/a(p). 9-Ramos-a. 10,11-Fire From Heaven Pt. 3. & Pt.9 4.00

GD VG FN VF VF/NM NM-
2.0 4.0 6.0 8.0 9.0 9.2

11-($4.95)-Special European Tour Edition; chromium-c 2 4 6 10 14 18
13A,13B,13C-($1.30, 13 pgs.): 13A-Archie & Friends app. 13B-Bone-c/app.; Teenage Mutant Ninja Turtles, Madman, Spawn & Jim Lee app. 4.00
14-24: 20-Last Campbell-a 3.00
25-($3.50)-Two covers by Campbell and Charest 4.00
25-($3.50)-Voyager Pack w/Danger Girl preview 5.00
25-Foil-c 10.00
26-32,34: 26-Arcudi-s/Frank-a begins. 34-Back-up story by Art Adams 3.00
33-Flip book w/Planetary preview 4.00
35-49: 36,38,40-Two covers. 37-First DC issue. 41-Last Frank-a 3.00
50-($3.95) Two covers by Lee and Benes; art by various 4.00
51-76: 51-Moy-a; Fairchild loses her powers. 60-Warren-s/a. 66-Art by various incl. Campbell (3 pgs.). 70,75,76-Mays-a. 76-Original team dies 3.00
77-($3.50) Mays, Andrews, Warren-a 4.00
Annual 1 (1997, $2.95) Ellis-s/ Dillon-c/a. 4.00
Annual 1999 ($3.50, DC) Slipstream x-over w/ DV8 4.00
Annual 2000 ($3.50) Devil's Night x-over w/WildStorm titles; Bermejo-c 4.00
...: A Christmas Caper (1/00, $5.95, one-shot) McWeeney-s/a 6.00
... Archives (4/98, $12.99) B&W reprints of mini-series, #0,1/2,1-13ABC; includes cover gallery and sourcebook 13.00
...: Carny Folk (2/00, $3.50) Collect back-up stories 3.50
... European Vacation TPB ($6.95) r/#6,7 7.00
.../ Fantastic Four (2001, $5.95) Maguire-s/c/a(p) 6.00
...: Going West (6/99, $2.50, one-shot) Pruett-s 3.00
...: Grunge Saves the World (5/99, $5.95, one-shot) Altieri-c/a 6.00
... I Love New York TPB ($9.95) r/part #25, 26-29; Frank-c 10.00
... London, New York, Hell TPB ($6.95) r/Annual #1 & Bootleg Ann. #1 7.00
... Lost in Paradise TPB ($6.95) r/#3-5 7.00
.../ Maxx (12/95, $3.50, one-shot) Messner-Loebs-s, 1st Coker-c/a. 4.00
...: Meanwhile (2003, $17.95) r/#43,44,66-70; all Warren-s; art by various 18.00
...: Medicine Song (2001, $5.95) Brent Anderson-c/a(p)/Raab-s 6.00
... Science Friction (2001, $5.95) Haley & Lopresti-a 6.00
... Starting Over TPB ($14.95) r/#1-7 15.00
... Superhuman Like You TPB ($12.95) r/#60-65; Warren-c 13.00
... #13 A,B&C Collected Edition ($6.95, TPB) r/#13A,B&C 7.00
... 3-D Special (1997, $4.95, one-shot) Art Adams-s/a(p) 5.00
...: The Unreal World (7/96, $2.95, one-shot) Humberto Ramos-c/a 3.00
... We'll Take Manhattan TPB ($14.95) r/#45-50; new Benes-c 15.00
...: Wired (4/99, $2.50, one-shot) Richard Bennett-c/a 3.00
... Yearbook 1997 (6/97, $2.50) College-themed stories and pin-ups by various 3.00
...: 'Zine (12/96, $1.95, B&W, digest size) Campbell/Garner-c 3.00
Variant Collection-Four editions (all 13 variants w/Chromium variant-limited, signed) 100.00

GEN 13
DC Comics (WildStorm): No. 0, Sept, 2002 - No. 16, Feb, 2004 ($2.95)

0-(13¢-c) Intro. new team; includes previews of 21 Down & The Resistance 3.00
1-Claremont-s/Garza-c/a; Fairchild app. 3.00
2-16: 8-13-Bachs-a. 16-Original team returns 3.00
...: September Song TPB (2003, $19.95) r/#0-6; Garza sketch pages 20.00

GEN 13 (Volume 4)
DC Comics (WildStorm): Dec, 2006 - No. 39, Feb, 2011 ($2.99)

1-39: 1-Simone-s/Caldwell-a; re-intro the original team; Caldwell-c. 8-The Authority app. 3.00
1-Variant-c by J. Scott Campbell 5.00
...: Armageddon (1/08, $2.99) Gage-s/Meyers-a; future Gen13 app. 3.00
...: Best of a Bad Lot TPB (2007, $14.99) r/#1-6 15.00
...: 15 Minutes TPB (2008, $14.99) r/#14-20 15.00
...: Road Trip TPB (2008, $14.99) r/#7-13 15.00
...: World's End TPB (2009, $17.99) r/#21-26 18.00

GEN 13 BOOTLEG
Image Comics (WildStorm): Nov, 1996 - No. 20, Jul, 1998 ($2.50)

1-Alan Davis-a; alternate costumes-c 3.00
1-Team falling variant-c 4.00
2-7: 2-Alan Davis-a. 5,6-Terry Moore-s. 7-Robinson-s/Scott Hampton-a 3.00
8-10-Adam Warren-s/a 4.00
11-20: 11,12-Lopresti-s/a & Simonson-s. 13-Wieringo-s/a. 14-Mariotte-s/Phillips-a. 15,16-Strnad-s/Shaw-a. 18-Altieri-s/a(p)/c, 18-Variant-c by Bruce Timm 3.00
Annual 1 (2/98, $2.95) Ellis-s/Dillon-c/a 4.00
... Grunge: The Movie (12/97, $9.95) r/#8-10, Warren-c 10.00
...Vol. 1 TPB (10/98, $11.95) r/#1-4 12.00

GEN 13/ GENERATION X (Also see Generation X / Gen 13)
Image Comics (WildStorm Publications): July, 1997 ($2.95, one-shot)

1-Choi-s/ Art Adams-p/Garner-i. Variant covers by Adams/Garner

Georgie Comics #3 © MAR

Ghost #3 © FH

Ghost V2 #1 © DH

GD 2.0 | VG 4.0 | FN 6.0 | VF 8.0 | VF/NM 9.0 | NM- 9.2

and Campbell/McWeeney 3.00
1-($4.95) 3-D Edition w/glasses; Campbell-c 5.00

GEN 13 INTERACTIVE
Image Comics (WildStorm): Oct, 1997 - No. 3, Dec, 1997 ($2.50, lim. series)
1-3-Internet voting used to determine storyline 3.00
... Plus! (7/98, $11.95) r/series & 3-D Special (in 2-D) 12.00

GEN 13 : MAGICAL DRAMA QUEEN ROXY
Image Comics (WildStorm): Oct, 1998 - No. 3, Dec, 1998 ($3.50, lim. series)
1-3-Adam Warren-s/c/a; manga style, 2-Variant-c by Hiroyuki Utatane 3.50
1-($6.95) Dynamic Forces Ed. w/Variant Warren-c 7.00

GEN 13 /MONKEYMAN & O'BRIEN
Image Comics (WildStorm): Jun, 1998 - No. 2, July, 1998 ($2.50, lim. series)
1,2-Art Adams-s/a(p); 1-Two covers 3.00
1-($4.95) Chromium-c 5.00
1-($6.95) Dynamic Forces Ed. 7.00

GEN 13: ORDINARY HEROES
Image Comics (WildStorm Publications): Feb, 1996 - No. 2, July, 1996 ($2.50, lim. series)
1,2-Adam Hughes-c/a/scripts 3.00
TPB (2004, $14.95) r/series, Gen13 Bootleg #1&2 and Wildstorm Thunderbook; new Hughes-c and art pages 15.00

GENTLE BEN (TV)
Dell Publishing Co.: Feb, 1968 - No. 5, Oct, 1969 (All photo-c)
1 4 8 12 25 40 55
2-5: 5-Reprints #1 3 6 9 16 23 30

GEOMANCER (Also see Eternal Warrior: Fist & Steel)
Valiant: Nov, 1994 - No. 8, June, 1995 ($3.75/$2.25)
1 ($3.75)-Chromium wraparound-c; Eternal Warrior app. 4.00
2-8 3.00

GEORGE OF THE JUNGLE (TV)(See America's Best TV Comics)
Gold Key: Feb, 1969 - No. 2, Oct, 1969 (Jay Ward)
1 8 16 24 56 108 160
2 5 10 15 35 63 90

GEORGE PAL'S PUPPETOONS (Funny animal puppets)
Fawcett Publications: Dec, 1945 - No. 18, Dec, 1947; No. 19, 1950
1-Captain Marvel-c 42 84 126 265 445 625
2 23 46 69 136 223 310
3-10 15 30 45 86 133 180
11-19 13 26 39 74 105 135

GEORGE PEREZ'S SIRENS
BOOM! Studios: Sept, 2014 - No. 6, Dec, 2016 ($3.99, limited series)
1-6-George Pérez-s/a; multiple covers 4.00

GEORGIE COMICS (...& Judy Comics #20-35?; see All Teen & Teen Comics)
Timely Comics/GPI No. 1-34: Spr, 1945 - No. 39, Oct, 1952 (#1-3 are quarterly)
1-Dave Berg-a 47 94 141 296 498 700
2 26 52 78 154 252 350
3-5,7,8(11/46) 21 42 63 122 199 275
6-Georgie visits Timely Comics 24 48 72 142 234 325
9,10-Kurtzman's "Hey Look" (1 & ?); Millie the Model & Margie app.
21 42 63 126 206 285
11,12: 11-Margie, Millie app. 18 36 54 103 162 220
13-Kurtzman's "Hey Look", 3 pgs. 18 36 54 107 169 230
14-Wolverton-a(1 pg.); Kurtzman's "Hey Look" 19 38 57 111 176 240
15,16,18-20 17 34 51 98 154 210
17,29-Kurtzman's "Hey Look", 1 pg. 18 36 54 103 162 220
21-24,27,28,30-39: 21-Anti-Wertham editorial. 33-38-Hy Rosen-c
16 32 48 94 147 200
25-Painted-c by classic pin-up artist Peter Driben 53 106 159 334 567 800
26-Logo design swipe from Archie Comics 17 34 51 98 154 210

GERALD McBOING-BOING AND THE NEARSIGHTED MR. MAGOO (TV)
(Mr. Magoo No. 6 on)
Dell Publishing Co.: Aug-Oct, 1952 - No. 5, Aug-Oct, 1953
1 9 18 27 62 126 190
2-5 8 16 24 54 102 150

GERONIMO (See Fighting Indians of the Wild West!)
Avon Periodicals: 1950 - No. 4, Feb, 1952
1-Indian Fighter; Maneely-a; Texas Rangers-r/Cowpuncher #1; Fawcette-c
21 42 63 122 199 275
2-On the Warpath; Kit West app.; Kinstler-c/a 14 28 42 82 121 160
3-And His Apache Murderers; Kinstler-c/a(2); Kit West-r/Cowpuncher #6
14 28 42 82 121 160
4-Savage Raids of; Kinstler-c & inside front-c; Kinstlerish-a by McCann(3)
14 28 42 80 115 150

GERONIMO JONES
Charlton Comics: Sept, 1971 - No. 9, Jan, 1973
1 2 4 6 13 18 22
2-9 2 4 6 8 10 12
Modern Comics Reprint #7('78) 5.00

GETALONG GANG, THE (TV)
Marvel Comics (Star Comics): May, 1985 - No. 6, Mar, 1986
1-6: Saturday morning TV stars 5.00

GET JIRO!
DC Comics (Vertigo): 2012 ($24.99, hardcover graphic novel with dust jacket)
HC - Anthony Bourdain & Joel Rose-s/Langdon Foss-a 25.00
SC - (2013, $14.99) Anthony Bourdain & Joel Rose-s/Langdon Foss-a 15.00

GET JIRO: BLOOD AND SUSHI
DC Comics (Vertigo): 2015 ($22.99, hardcover graphic novel with dust jacket)
HC - Prequel to Get Jiro!; Anthony Bourdain & Joel Rose-s/Alé Garza-a/Dave Johnson-c 23.00

GET LOST
Mikeross Publications/New Comics: Feb-Mar, 1954 - No. 3, June-July, 1954 (Satire)
1-Andru/Esposito-a in all? 37 74 111 222 361 500
2-Andru/Esposito-c; has 4 pg. E.C. parody featuring "The Sewer Keeper"
25 50 75 150 245 340
3-John Wayne 'Hondo' parody 21 42 63 124 202 280
1,2 (10,12/87-New Comics)-B&W r-original 4.00

GET SMART (TV)
Dell Publ. Co.: June, 1966 - No. 8, Sept, 1967 (All have Don Adams photo-c)
1 9 18 27 59 117 175
2,3-Ditko-a 6 12 18 40 73 105
4-8: 8-Reprints #1 (cover and insides) 5 10 15 33 57 80

GHOST (...Comics #9)
Fiction House Magazines: 1951(Winter) - No. 11, Summer, 1954
1-Most covers by Whitman 119 238 357 762 1306 1850
2-Ghost Gallery & Werewolf Hunter stories; classic-c
103 206 309 659 1130 1600
3-9: 3,6,7,9-Bondage-c. 9-Abel, Discount-a 71 142 213 454 777 1100
10,11-Dr. Drew by Grandenetti in each, reprinted from Rangers; 11-Evans-r/ Rangers #39; Grandenetti-r/Rangers #49 53 106 159 334 567 800

GHOST (See Comic's Greatest World)
Dark Horse Comics: Apr, 1995 - No. 36, Apr, 1998 ($2.50/$2.95)
1-Adam Hughes-a 1 2 3 5 6 8
2,3-Hughes-a 4.00
4-24: 4-Barb Wire app. 5,6-Hughes-c. 12-Ghost/Hellboy preview. 15,21-X app. 18,19-Barb Wire app. 3.00
25-($3.50)-48 pgs. special 4.00
26-36: 26-Begin $2.95-c. 29-Flip book w/Timecop. 33-36-Jade Cathedral; Harris painted-c 3.00
Special 1 (7/94, $3.95, 48 pgs.) 1 2 3 4 5 7
Special 2 (6/98, $3.95) Barb Wire app. 4.00
... Black October (1/99, $14.95, trade paperback)-r/#6-9,26,27 15.00
... Nocturnes (1996, $9.95, trade paperback)-r/#1-3 & 5 10.00
... Omnibus Vol. 1 (10/08, $24.95, 9x6") r/#1-12; Special 1 and Decade of Dark Horse #2 25.00
... Stories (1995, $9.95, trade paperback)-r/Early Ghost app. 10.00

GHOST (Volume 2)
Dark Horse Comics: Sept, 1998 - No. 22, Aug, 2000 ($2.95)
1-22: 1-4-Ryan Benjamin-c/Zanier-a 3.00
Handbook (8/99, $2.95) guide to issues and characters 3.00
Special 3 (12/98, $3.95) 4.00

GHOST (3rd series)
Dark Horse Comics: No. 0, Sept, 2012 - No. 4, Mar, 2013 ($2.99)
0-4-DeConnick-s/Noto-a. 0-Frison-c. 1,2-Covers by Noto & Alex Ross 3.00

GHOST (4th series)
Dark Horse Comics: Dec, 2013 - No. 12, Feb, 2015 ($2.99)
1-12: 1,2-DeConnick & Sebela-s/Sook-a/Dodson-c. 3,4-Borges-a 3.00

GHOST AND THE SHADOW
Dark Horse Comics: Dec, 1995 ($2.95, one-shot)

Ghostbusters: International #6 © Columbia Pictures

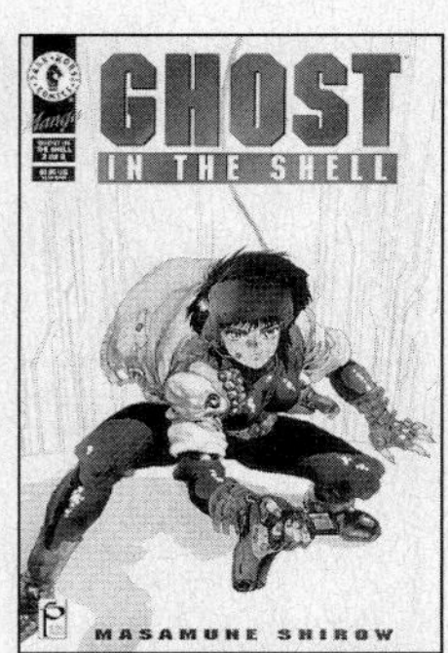

Ghost in the Shell #2 © DH

Ghostly Tales #66 © CC

	GD 2.0	VG 4.0	FN 6.0	VF 8.0	VF/NM 9.0	NM- 9.2
1-Moench scripts						3.00

GHOST/BATGIRL
Dark Horse Comics: Aug, 2000 - No. 4, Dec, 2000 ($2.95, limited series)

	GD 2.0	VG 4.0	FN 6.0	VF 8.0	VF/NM 9.0	NM- 9.2
1-4-New Batgirl; Oracle & Bruce Wayne app.; Benjamin-c/a						3.00

GHOST/HELLBOY
Dark Horse Comics: May, 1996 - No. 2, June, 1996 ($2.50, limited series)

	GD 2.0	VG 4.0	FN 6.0	VF 8.0	VF/NM 9.0	NM- 9.2
1,2: Mike Mignola-c/scripts & breakdowns; Scott Benefiel finished-a						4.00

GHOST BREAKERS (Also see Racket Squad in Action, Red Dragon & (CC) Sherlock Holmes Comics)
Street & Smith Publications: Sept, 1948 - No. 2, Dec, 1948 (52 pgs.)

	GD 2.0	VG 4.0	FN 6.0	VF 8.0	VF/NM 9.0	NM- 9.2
1-Powell-c/a(3); Dr. Neff (magician) app.	42	84	126	267	451	635
2-Powell-c/a(2); Maneely-a	36	72	108	211	343	475

GHOSTBUSTERS (TV) (Also, see Real...and Slimer)
First Comics: Feb, 1987 - No. 6, Aug, 1987 ($1.25)

	GD 2.0	VG 4.0	FN 6.0	VF 8.0	VF/NM 9.0	NM- 9.2
1-6: Based on new animated TV series						4.00

GHOSTBUSTERS
IDW Publishing: Sept, 2011 - No. 16, Dec, 2012 ($3.99)

	GD 2.0	VG 4.0	FN 6.0	VF 8.0	VF/NM 9.0	NM- 9.2
1-16-Burnham-s/Schoening-a; multiple covers						4.00
...: 100-Page Spooktacular (10/12, $7.99) reprints of IDW stories						8.00

GHOSTBUSTERS
IDW Publishing: (one-shots)

	GD 2.0	VG 4.0	FN 6.0	VF 8.0	VF/NM 9.0	NM- 9.2
Annual 2017 (1/17, $7.99) Burnham-s/Schoening-a and short stories by various						8.00
...: Con-Volution (6/10, $3.99) Josh Howard-a						4.00
...: Deviations (3/16, $4.99) What If.. Ghostbusters never crossed the streams						5.00
...: Tainted Love (2/10, $3.99) Salgood Sam-a						4.00
...: What in Samhain Just Happened? (10/10, $3.99) Peter David-s/Dan Schoening-a						4.00

GHOSTBUSTERS
IDW Publishing: Feb, 2013 - No. 20, Sept, 2014 ($3.99)

	GD 2.0	VG 4.0	FN 6.0	VF 8.0	VF/NM 9.0	NM- 9.2
1-20-Janine & the female Ghostbuster crew; Burnham-s/Schoening-a; multiple covers						4.00
Annual 2015 (11/15, $7.99) Burnham-s/Schoening-a and bonus 1-pagers by various						8.00

GHOSTBUSTERS: DISPLACED AGGRESSION
IDW Publishing: Sept, 2009 - No. 4, Dec, 2009 ($3.99)

	GD 2.0	VG 4.0	FN 6.0	VF 8.0	VF/NM 9.0	NM- 9.2
1-3-Lobdell-s/Kyriazis-a						4.00
Hundred Penny Press: Ghostbusters: Displaced Aggression (3/11, $1.00) r/#1						3.00

GHOSTBUSTERS: GET REAL
IDW Publishing: Jun, 2015 - No. 4, Sept, 2015 ($3.99)

	GD 2.0	VG 4.0	FN 6.0	VF 8.0	VF/NM 9.0	NM- 9.2
1-4-Burnham-s/Schoening-a; multiple-c; Real Ghostbusters meet comic Ghostbusters						4.00

GHOSTBUSTERS: INFESTATION (Zombie x-over with Star Trek, G.I. Joe & Transformers)
IDW Publishing: Mar, 2011 - No. 2, Mar, 2011 ($3.99, limited series)

	GD 2.0	VG 4.0	FN 6.0	VF 8.0	VF/NM 9.0	NM- 9.2
1,2-Kyle Hotz-a; covers by Hotz and Snyder III						4.00

GHOSTBUSTERS: INTERNATIONAL
IDW Publishing: Jan, 2016 - No. 11, Nov, 2016 ($3.99)

	GD 2.0	VG 4.0	FN 6.0	VF 8.0	VF/NM 9.0	NM- 9.2
1-11-Burnham-s/Schoening-a; 2 covers on each						4.00

GHOSTBUSTERS: LEGION (Movie)
88 MPH Studios: Feb, 2004 - No. 4, May, 2004 ($2.95/$3.50)

	GD 2.0	VG 4.0	FN 6.0	VF 8.0	VF/NM 9.0	NM- 9.2
1-4-Steve Kurth-a/Andrew Dabb-s						3.00
1-3-($3.50) Brereton variant-c						3.50

GHOSTBUSTERS: THE OTHER SIDE
IDW Publishing: Oct, 2008 - No. 4, Jan, 2009 ($3.99)

	GD 2.0	VG 4.0	FN 6.0	VF 8.0	VF/NM 9.0	NM- 9.2
1-4-Champagne-s/Nguyen-a						4.00

GHOSTBUSTERS II
Now Comics: Oct, 1989 - No. 3, Dec, 1989 ($1.95, mini-series)

	GD 2.0	VG 4.0	FN 6.0	VF 8.0	VF/NM 9.0	NM- 9.2
1-3: Movie Adaptation						3.00

GHOST CASTLE (See Tales of...)

GHOSTED
Image Comics (Skybound): Jul, 2013 - No. 20, May, 2015 ($2.99)

	GD 2.0	VG 4.0	FN 6.0	VF 8.0	VF/NM 9.0	NM- 9.2
1-20: 1-Williamson-s/Sudzuka-a/Phillips-c. 6-10-Gianfelice-a. 16-Ryp-a						3.00

GHOST IN THE SHELL (Manga)
Dark Horse: Mar, 1995 - No. 8, Oct, 1995 ($3.95, B&W/color, lim. series)

	GD 2.0	VG 4.0	FN 6.0	VF 8.0	VF/NM 9.0	NM- 9.2
1	4	8	12	28	47	65
2	3	6	9	16	23	30
3	2	4	6	11	16	20
4-8	2	4	6	8	10	12

GHOST IN THE SHELL 2: MAN-MACHINE INTERFACE (Manga)
Dark Horse Comics: Jan, 2003 - No. 11, Dec, 2003 ($3.50, color/B&W, lim. series)

	GD 2.0	VG 4.0	FN 6.0	VF 8.0	VF/NM 9.0	NM- 9.2
1-11-Masamune Shirow-s/a. 5-B&W						5.00

GHOSTLY HAUNTS (Formerly Ghost Manor)
Charlton Comics: #20, 9/71 - #53, 12/76; #54, 9/77 - #55, 10/77; #56, 1/78 - #58, 4/78

	GD 2.0	VG 4.0	FN 6.0	VF 8.0	VF/NM 9.0	NM- 9.2
20	3	6	9	19	30	40
21	2	4	6	13	18	22
22-25,27,31-34,36-Ditko-c/a. 27-Dr. Graves x-over. 32-New logo. 33-Back to old logo	3	6	9	15	22	28
26,29,30,35-Ditko-c	2	4	6	13	18	22
28,37-40-Ditko-a. 39-Origin & 1st app. Destiny Fox	2	4	6	11	16	20
41,42: 41-Sutton-c; Ditko-a. 42-Newton-c/a	2	4	6	13	18	22
43-46,48,50,52-Ditko-a	2	4	6	10	14	18
47,54,56-Ditko-c/a. 56-Ditko-a(r).	3	6	9	14	19	24
49,51,53,55,57	2	4	6	8	10	12
58 (4/78) Last issue	3	6	9	14	19	24
40,41(Modern Comics-r, 1977, 1978)						6.00

NOTE: ***Ditko** a-22-25, 27, 28, 31-34, 36-41, 43-48, 50, 52, 54, 56r; c-22-27, 29, 30, 33-36, 47, 54, 56. **Glanzman** a-20. **Howard** a-27, 30, 35, 40-43, 48, 54, 57. **Kim** a-38, 41, 57. **Larson** a-48, 50. **Newton** c/a-42. **Staton** a-32, 35; c-28, 46. **Sutton** c-33, 37, 39, 41.*

GHOSTLY TALES (Formerly Blue Beetle No. 50-54)
Charlton Comics: No. 55, 4-5/66 - No. 124, 12/76; No. 125, 9/77 - No. 169, 10/84

	GD 2.0	VG 4.0	FN 6.0	VF 8.0	VF/NM 9.0	NM- 9.2
55-Intro. & origin Dr. Graves; Ditko-a	9	18	27	61	123	185
56-58,60,61,70,71,72,75-Ditko-a. 70-Dr. Graves ends. 75-Last 12¢ issue	5	10	15	30	50	70
59,62-66,68	4	8	12	23	37	50
67,69,73-Ditko-c/a	5	10	15	33	57	80
74,91,98,119,123,124,127-130: 127,130-Sutton-a	2	4	6	13	18	22
76,79-82,85-Ditko-a	3	6	9	16	24	32
77,78,83,84,86-90,92-95,97,99-Ditko-c/a	4	8	12	23	37	50
96-Ditko-c	3	6	9	16	24	32
100-Ditko-c; Sutton-a	3	6	9	17	26	35
101,103-105-Ditko-a	3	6	9	14	19	24
102,109-Ditko-c/a	3	6	9	16	23	30
110,113-Sutton-c; Ditko-a	3	6	9	14	19	24
106-Ditko & Sutton-a; Sutton-c	3	6	9	14	19	24
107-Ditko, Wood, Sutton-a	3	6	9	14	20	26
108,116,117,126-Ditko-a	3	6	9	14	19	24
111,118,120-122,125-Ditko-c/a	3	6	9	16	23	30
112,114,115: 112,114-Ditko, Sutton-a. 114-Newton-a. 115-Newton, Ditko-a.	3	6	9	14	19	24
131-134,151,157,163-Ditko-c/a	2	4	6	13	18	22
135,142,145-150,153,154,156,158-160	1	2	3	5	7	9
136-141,143,144,152,155-Ditko-a	2	4	6	8	10	12
161,162,164-168-Lower print run. 162-Nudity panel	2	4	6	9	12	15
169 (10/84) Last issue; lower print run	2	4	6	11	16	20

NOTE: ***Aparo** a-65, 66, 68, 72, 137, 141r, 142r; c-71, 72, 74-76, 81, 146r, 149. **Ditko** a-55-58, 60, 61, 67, 69-73, 75-90, 92-95, 97, 99-118, 120-122, 125r, 126r, 131-141r, 143r, 144r, 146, 147, 149-152, 154-157, 159-161, 163; c-67, 69, 73, 77, 78, 83, 84, 86-90, 92-97, 99, 102, 109, 111, 118, 120-122, 125, 131-133, 147, 148, 151, 157-160, 163. **Glanzman** a-167. **Howard** a-95, 98, 99, 108, 117, 129, 131; c-98, 107, 120, 121, 161. **Larson** a-117, 119, 136, 159; c-136. **Morisi** a-83, 84, 86. **Newton** a-114; c-115(painted). **Palais** a-61. **Staton** a-161; c-117. **Sutton** a-106, 107, 111-114, 127, 130, 162; c-100, 106, 110, 113(painted). **Wood** a-107.*

GHOSTLY WEIRD STORIES (Formerly Blue Bolt Weird)
Star Publications: No. 120, Sept, 1953 - No. 124, Sept, 1954

	GD 2.0	VG 4.0	FN 6.0	VF 8.0	VF/NM 9.0	NM- 9.2
120-Jo-Jo-r	61	122	183	390	670	950
121-124: 121-Jo-Jo-r. 122-The Mask-r/Capt. Flight #5; Rulah-r; has 1pg. story 'Death and the Devil Pills'-r/Western Outlaws #17. 123-Jo-Jo; Disbrow-a(2). 124-Torpedo Man	55	110	165	352	601	850

NOTE: ***Disbrow** a-120-124. **L. B. Cole** covers-all issues (#122 is a sci-fi cover).*

GHOST MANOR (Ghostly Haunts No. 20 on)
Charlton Comics: July, 1968 - No. 19, July, 1971

	GD 2.0	VG 4.0	FN 6.0	VF 8.0	VF/NM 9.0	NM- 9.2
1	7	14	21	49	92	135
2-7: 7-Last 12¢ issue	4	8	12	27	44	60
8-12,17: 17-Morisi-a	3	6	9	19	30	40
13,14,16-Ditko-a	4	8	12	22	35	48
15,18,19-Ditko-c/a	4	8	12	28	47	65

GHOST MANOR (2nd Series)
Charlton Comics: Oct, 1971-No. 32, Dec, 1976; No. 33, Sept, 1977-No. 77, 11/84

	GD 2.0	VG 4.0	FN 6.0	VF 8.0	VF/NM 9.0	NM- 9.2
1	5	10	15	34	60	85
2,3,5-7,9-Ditko-c	3	6	9	17	26	35
4,10-Ditko-c/a	3	6	9	21	33	45
8-Wood, Ditko-a; Sutton-c	3	6	9	19	30	40

Ghost Rider #5 © ME

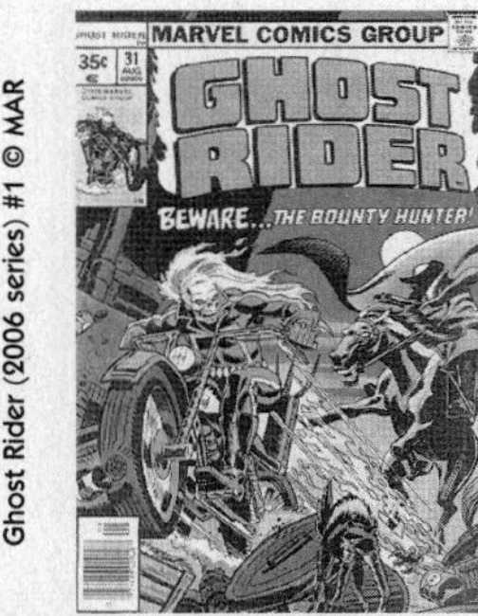

Ghost Rider (2006 series) #1 © MAR

Ghost Rider (2006 series) #1 © MAR

GD VG FN VF VF/NM NM-
2.0 4.0 6.0 8.0 9.0 9.2

11,14-Ditko-c/a 3 6 9 16 24 32
12,17,27,30 2 4 6 9 13 16
13,15,16,23-26,29: 13-Ditko-a. 15,16-Ditko-c. 23-Sutton-a. 24-26,29-Ditko-a. 26-Early Zeck-a; Boyette-c 2 4 6 13 18 22
18-(3/74) Newton 1st pro art; Ditko-a; Sutton-c 3 6 9 15 22 28
19-21: 19-Newton, Sutton-a; nudity panels. 20-Ditko-a. 21-E-Man, Blue Beetle, Capt. Atom cameos; Ditko-a. 2 4 6 13 18 22
22-Newton-c/a; Ditko-a 3 6 9 14 19 24
25,28,31,37,38-Ditko-c/a: 28-Nudity panels 3 6 9 14 19 24
32-36,39,41,45,48-50,53: 34-Black Cat by Kim 2 4 6 8 10 12
40-Ditko-a; torture & drug use 2 4 6 13 18 22
42,43,46,47,51,52,60,62,69-Ditko-c/a 2 4 6 11 16 20
44,54,71-Ditko-a 2 4 6 8 11 14
55,56,58,59,61,63,65-68,70 1 2 3 5 7 9
57-Wood, Ditko, Howard-a 2 4 6 9 12 15
64-Ditko & Newton-a 2 4 6 8 11 14
71-76 (low print) 2 3 4 6 8 10
77-(11/84) Last issue Aparo-r/Space Adventures V3#60 (Paul Mann) 2 4 6 9 13 16
19 (Modern Comics reprint, 1977) 6.00

NOTE: ***Ditko** a-4, 8, 10, 11(2), 13, 14, 18, 20-22, 24-26, 28, 29, 31, 37r, 38r, 40r, 42-44r, 46r, 47, 51r, 52r, 54r, 57, 60, 62(4), 64r, 69, 71; c-2-7, 9-11, 14-16, 28, 31, 37, 38, 42, 43, 46, 47, 51, 52, 60, 62, 64. **Howard** a-4, 8, 12, 17, 19-21, 31, 41, 45, 57. **Newton** a-18-20, 22, 64; c-22. **Staton** a-13, 38, 44, 45. **Sutton** a-19, 23, 25, 45; c-8, 18.*

GHOST RACERS (Secret Wars Battleworld tie-in)
Marvel Comics: Aug, 2015 - No. 4, Nov, 2015 ($3.99, limited series)

1-4-Johnny Blaze, Danny Ketch, Robbie Reyes, Carter Slade app.; Francavilla-c 4.00

GHOST RIDER (See A-1 Comics, Best of the West, Black Phantom, Bobby Benson, Great Western, Red Mask & Tim Holt)
Magazine Enterprises: 1950 - No. 14, 1954

NOTE: *The character was inspired by Vaughn Monroe's "Ghost Riders in the Sky", and Disney's movie "The Headless Horseman".*

1(A-1 #27)-Origin Ghost Rider 116 232 348 742 1271 1800
2-5: 2(A-1 #29), 3(A-1 #31), 4(A-1 #34), 5(A-1 #37)-All Frazetta-c only 90 180 270 576 988 1400
6,7: 6(A-1 #44)-Loco weed story, 7(A-1 #51) 41 82 123 256 428 600
8,9: 8(A-1 #57)-Drug use story, 9(A-1 #69) 36 72 108 211 343 475
10(A-1 #71)-Vs. Frankenstein 39 78 117 231 378 525
11-14: 11(A-1 #75). 12(A-1 #80)-Bondage-c; one-eyed Devil-c. 13(A-1 #84). 14(A-1 #112) 32 64 96 188 307 425

NOTE: ***Dick Ayers** art in all; c-1, 6-14.*

GHOST RIDER, THE (See Night Rider & Western Gunfighters)
Marvel Comics Group: Feb, 1967 - No. 7, Nov, 1967 (Western hero)(12¢)

1-Origin & 1st app. Ghost Rider; Kid Colt-reprints begin 12 24 36 79 170 260
2 7 14 21 44 82 120
3-7: 6-Last Kid Colt-r; All Ayers-c/a(p) 6 12 18 40 73 105

GHOST RIDER (See The Champions, Marvel Spotlight #5, Marvel Team-Up #15, 58, Marvel Treasury Edition #18, Marvel Two-In-One #8, The Original Ghost Rider & The Original Ghost Rider Rides Again)
Marvel Comics Group: Sept, 1973 - No. 81, June, 1983 (Super-hero)

1-Johnny Blaze, the Ghost Rider begins; 1st brief app. Daimon Hellstrom (Son of Satan) 18 36 54 124 275 425
2-1st full app. Daimon Hellstrom; gives glimpse of costume (1 panel); story continues in Marvel Spotlight #12 7 14 21 49 92 135
3-5: 3-Ghost Rider gains power to make cycle of fire; Son of Satan app. 5 10 15 31 53 75
6-10: 10-Hulk on cover; reprints origin/1st app. from Marvel Spotlight #5; Ploog-a 3 6 9 21 33 45
11-16: 11-Hulk app. 3 6 9 14 20 25
17,19-(Reg. 25¢ editions)(4,8/76) 3 6 9 14 20 25
17,19-(30¢-c variants, limited distribution) 4 8 12 28 47 65
18-(Reg. 25¢ edition)(6/76). Spider-Man-c & app. 3 6 9 15 22 28
18-(30¢-c variant, limited distribution) 5 10 15 31 53 75
20-Daredevil x-over; ties into D.D. #138; Byrne-a 3 6 9 17 26 35
21-30: 22-1st app. Enforcer. 29,30-Vs. Dr. Strange 2 4 6 9 12 15
24-26-(35¢-c variants, limited distribution) 5 10 15 31 53 75
31-34,36-49: 40-Nuclear explosion-c 2 3 4 6 8 10
35-Death Race classic; Starlin-c/a/sty 2 4 6 10 14 18
50-Double size 2 4 6 9 12 15
51-76: 55-Werewolf by Night app. 68-Origin retold 6.00
77-80: 77-Origin retold. 80-Brief origin recap 1 2 3 5 6 8
81-Death of Ghost Rider (Demon leaves Blaze) 3 6 9 17 26 35

GD VG FN VF VF/NM NM-
2.0 4.0 6.0 8.0 9.0 9.2

... Team Up TPB (2007, $15.99) r/#27, 50, Marvel Team-Up #91, Marvel Two-In-One #80, Avengers #214 and Marvel Premiere #28; Night Rider app.; cover gallery 16.00

NOTE: ***Anderson** c-64p. **Infantino** a(p)-43, 44, 51. **G. Kane** a-21p; c(p)-1, 2, 4, 5, 8, 9, 11-13, 19, 20, 24, 25. **Kirby** c-21-23. **Mooney** a-2-9p, 30i. **Nebres** c-26i. **Newton** a-23i. **Perez** c-26p. **Shores** a-2i. J. **Sparling** a-62p, 64p, 65p. **Starlin** a(p)-35. **Sutton** a-1p, 44i, 64i, 65i, 66, 67i. **Tuska** a-13p, 14p, 16p.*

GHOST RIDER (Volume 2) (Also see Doctor Strange/Ghost Rider Special, Marvel Comics Presents & Midnight Sons Unlimited)
Marvel Comics (Midnight Sons imprint #44 on): V2#1, May, 1990 - No. 93, Feb, 1998 ($1.50/$1.75/$1.95)

1-($1.95, 52 pgs.)-Origin/1st app. new Ghost Rider; Kingpin app. 2 4 6 11 16 20
1-2nd printing (not gold) 4.00
2-5: 3-Kingpin app. 5-Punisher app.; Jim Lee-c 5.00
5-Gold background 2nd printing 4.00
6-14,16-24,29,30,32-39: 6-Punisher app. 6,17-Spider-Man/Hobgoblin-c/story. 9-X-Factor app. 10-Reintro Johnny Blaze on the last pg. 11-Stroman-c/a(p). 12,13-Dr. Strange x-over cont'd in D.S. #28. 13-Painted-c. 14-Johnny Blaze vs. Ghost Rider; origin recap 1st Ghost Rider (Blaze). 18-Painted-c by Nelson. 29-Wolverine-c/story. 32-Dr. Strange x-over; Johnny Blaze app. 34-Williamson-a(i). 36-Daredevil app. 37-Archangel app. 3.00
15-Glow in the dark-c 4.00
25-27: 25-($2.75)-Double-size; contains pop-up scene insert. 26,27-X-Men x-over; Lee/Williams-c on both 4.00
28,31-($2.50, 52 pgs.)-Polybagged w/poster; part 1 & part 6 of Rise of the Midnight Sons storyline (see Ghost Rider/Blaze #1) 4.00
40-Outer-c is Darkhold envelope made of black parchment w/gold ink; Midnight Massacre; Demogoblin app. 4.00
41-48: 41-Lilith & Centurious app.; begin $1.75-c. 41-43-Neon ink-c. 43-Has free extra 16 pg. insert on Siege of Darkness. 44,45-Siege of Darkness parts 2 & 10. 44-Spot varnish-c. 46-Intro new Ghost Rider. 48-Spider-Man app. 3.00
49,51-60,62-74: 49-Begin $1.95-c; bound-in trading card sheet; Hulk app. 55-Werewolf by Night app. 65-Punisher app. 67,68-Gambit app. 68-Wolverine app. 73,74-Blaze, Vengeance app. 3.00
50,61: 50-($2.50, 52 pgs.)-Regular edition 4.00
50-($2.95, 52 pgs.)-Collectors Ed. die cut foil-c 5.00
75-89: 76-Vs. Vengeance. 77,78-Dr. Strange-app. 78-New costume 3.00
90-92 6.00
93-($2.99)-Last issue; Saltares & Texeira-a 2 4 6 8 10 12
(#94, see Ghost Rider Finale for unpublished story)
#(-1) Flashback (7/97) Saltares-a 3.00
Annual 1,2 ('93, '94, $2.95, 68 pgs.) 1-Bagged w/card 4.00
...And Cable 1 (9/92, $3.95, stiff-c, 68 pgs.)-Reprints Marvel Comics Presents #90-98 w/new Kieth-c 4.00
...:Crossroads (11/95, $3.95) Die cut cover; Nord-a 5.00
... Cycle of Vengeance 1 (3/12, $5.99) r/Marvel Spotlight #5, Ghost Rider (1990) #1 and Ghost Rider (2006) #1; Leinil Yu-c 6.00
... Finale (2007, $3.99) r/#93 and the story meant for the unpublished #94; Saltares-a 4.00
Highway to Hell (2001, $3.50) Reprints origin from Marvel Spotlight #5 3.50
...: Resurrected TPB (2001, $12.95) r/#1-7 13.00

NOTE: ***Andy & Joe Kubert** c/a-28-31. **Quesada** c-21. **Williamson** a(i)-33-35; c-33i.*

GHOST RIDER (Volume 3)
Marvel Comics: Aug, 2001 - No. 6, Jan, 2002 ($2.99, limited series)

1-6-Grayson-s/Kaniuga-a/c 3.00
...: The Hammer Lane TPB (6/02, $15.95) r/#1-6 16.00

GHOST RIDER
Marvel Comics: Nov, 2005 - No. 6, Apr, 2006 ($2.99, limited series)

1-6-Garth Ennis-s/Clayton Crain-a/c. 1-Origin retold 3.00
1 (Director's Cut) (2005, $3.99) r/#1 with Ennis pitch and script and Crain art process 4.00
...: Road to Damnation HC (2006, $19.99, dust jacket) r/#1-6; variant covers & concept-a 20.00
...: Road to Damnation SC (2007, $14.99) r/#1-6; variant covers & concept-a 15.00

GHOST RIDER
Marvel Comics: Sept, 2006 - No. 35, Jul, 2009 ($2.99)

1-11: 1-Daniel Way-s/Saltares & Texeira-a. 2-4-Dr. Strange app. 6,7-Corben-a 3.00
12-27,29-35: 12,13-World War Hulk; Saltares-a/Dell'Otto-c. 23-Danny Ketch returns 3.00
28-($3.99) Silvestri-c/Huat-a; back-up history of Danny Ketch 4.00
Annual 1 (1/08, $3.99) Ben Oliver-a/c/Stuart Moore-s 4.00
Annual 2 (10/08, $3.99) Spurrier-s/Robinson-a; r/Ghost Rider #35 (1979) 4.00
... Vol. 1: Vicious Cycle TPB (2007, $13.99) r/#1-5 14.00
... Vol. 2: The Life and Death of Johnny Blaze TPB (2007, $13.99) r/#6-11 14.00
... Vol. 3: Apocalypse Soon TPB (2008, $10.99) r/#12,13 & Annual #1 11.00
... Vol. 4: Revelations TPB (2008, $14.99) r/#14-19 15.00

GHOST RIDER
Marvel Comics: No. 0.1, Aug, 2011 - No. 9, May 2012 ($2.99/$3.99)

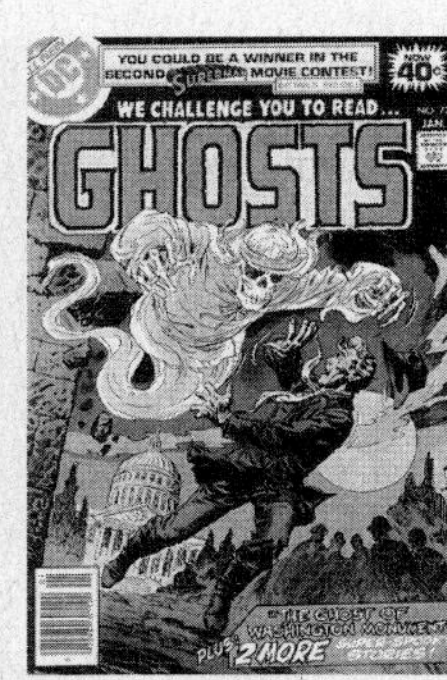

Ghosts #72 © DC

Ghost Stories #32 © DELL

Giant Comics Editions #16 © STJ

	GD 2.0	VG 4.0	FN 6.0	VF 8.0	VF/NM 9.0	NM- 9.2

0.1-($2.99) Johnny Blaze gets rid of the Spirit of Vengeance; Matthew Clark-a 3.00
1-($3.99) Adam Kubert-c; Fear Itself tie-in; new female Ghost Rider; Mephisto app. 4.00
2-9: 2-4-($2.99) Fear Itself tie-in. 5-Garbett-a. 7,8-Hawkeye app. 3.00

GHOST RIDER (Robbie Reyes) (Also see All-New Ghost Rider)
Marvel Comics: Jan, 2017 - No. 5, May, 2017 ($3.99)
1-4-Felipe Smith-s; Hulk (Amadeus Cho) and X-23 app. 1-Intro. Pyston Nitro. 3,4-Silk app. 4.00

GHOST RIDER/BALLISTIC
Marvel Comics: Feb, 1997 ($2.95, one-shot)
1-Devil's Reign pt. 3 3.00

GHOST RIDER/BLAZE: SPIRITS OF VENGEANCE (Also see Blaze)
Marvel Comics (Midnight Sons imprint #17 on): Aug, 1992 - No. 23, June, 1994 ($1.75)
1-($2.75, 52 pgs.)-Polybagged w/poster; part 2 of Rise of the Midnight Sons storyline; Adam Kubert-c/a begins 4.00
2-11,14-21: 4-Art Adams & Joe Kubert-p. 5,6-Spirits of Venom parts 2 & 4 cont'd from Web of Spider-Man #95,96 w/Demogoblin. 14-17-Neon ink-c. 15-Intro Blaze's new costume & power. 17,18-Siege of Darkness parts 8 & 13. 17-Spot varnish-c 3.00
12-($2.95)-Glow-in-the-dark-c 4.00
13-($2.25)-Outer-c is Darkhold envelope made of black parchment w/gold ink; Midnight Massacre x-over 4.00
22,23: 22-Begin $1.95-c; bound-in trading card sheet 3.00
NOTE: *Adam & Joe Kubert c-7, 8. Adam Kubert/Steacy c-6. J. Kubert a-13p(6 pgs.)*

GHOST RIDER/CAPTAIN AMERICA: FEAR
Marvel Comics: Oct, 1992 ($5.95, 52 pgs.)
nn-Wraparound gatefold-c; Williamson inks 6.00

GHOST RIDER: DANNY KETCH
Marvel Comics: Dec, 2008 - No. 5, Apr, 2009 ($3.99, limited series)
1-5-Saltares-a 4.00

GHOST RIDER: HEAVEN'S ON FIRE
Marvel Comics: Oct, 2009 - No. 6, Mar, 2010 ($3.99, limited series)
1-6: 1-Jae Lee-c/Boschi-a/Aaron-s; Hellstorm app.; r/pages from Ghost Rider #1 ('73) 4.00

GHOST RIDER: TRAIL OF TEARS
Marvel Comics: Apr, 2007 - No. 6, Sept, 2007 ($2.99, limited series)
1-6-Garth Ennis-s/Clayton Crain-a/c; Civil War era tale 3.00
HC (2007, $19.99) r/series 20.00
SC (2008, $14.99) r/series 15.00

GHOST RIDER 2099
Marvel Comics: May, 1994 - No. 25, May, 1996 ($1.50/$1.95)
1 ($2.25)-Collector's Edition w/prismatic foil-c 4.00
1 ($1.50)-Regular Edition; bound-in trading card sheet 3.00
2-24: 7-Spider-Man 2099 app. 3.00
2-(Variant; polybagged with Sega Sub-Terrania poster) 5.00
25 ($2.95) 4.00

GHOST RIDER, WOLVERINE, PUNISHER: THE DARK DESIGN
Marvel Comics: Dec, 1994 ($5.95, one-shot)
nn-Gatefold-c 6.00

GHOST RIDER; WOLVERINE; PUNISHER: HEARTS OF DARKNESS
Marvel Comics: Dec, 1991 ($4.95, one-shot, 52 pgs.)
1-Double gatefold-c; John Romita, Jr.-c/a(p) 6.00

GHOSTS (See The World Around Us #24)

GHOSTS (Ghost No. 1)
National Periodical Publications/DC Comics: Sept-Oct, 1971 - No. 112, May, 1982 (No. 1-5: 52 pgs.)

	GD	VG	FN	VF	VF/NM	NM-
1-Aparo-a	11	22	33	76	163	250
2-Wood-a(i)	7	14	21	44	82	120
3-5-(52 pgs.)	6	12	18	38	69	100
6-10	4	8	12	27	44	60
11-20	3	6	9	14	20	25
21-39	2	4	6	9	13	16
40-(68 pgs.)	3	6	9	16	23	30
41-60	2	4	6	8	10	12
61-96	1	2	3	5	6	8
97-99-The Spectre vs. Dr. 13 by Aparo. 97,98-Spectre-c by Aparo.	2	4	6	10	14	18
100-Infinity-c	2	3	4	6	8	10
101-112	1	2	3	5	6	8

NOTE: ***B. Baily** a-77. **Buckler** c-99, 100. **J. Craig** a-108. **Ditko** a-77, 111. **Giffen** a-104p, 106p, 111p. **Glanzman** a-2. **Golden** a-88. **Infantino** a-8. **Kaluta** c-7, 93, 101. **Kubert** a-8; c-89, 105-108, 111. **Mayer** a-111. **McWilliams** a-99. **Win Mortimer** a-89, 91, 94. **Nasser/Netzer** a-97. **Newton** a-92p, 94p. **Nino** a-35, 37, 57. **Orlando** a-74i; c-80. **Redondo** a-8, 13, 45. **Sparling** a(p)-90, 93, 94. **Spiegle** a-103, 105. **Tuska** a-2i. Dr. 13, the Ghostbreaker back-ups in 95-99, 101.*

GHOSTS
DC Comics (Vertigo): Dec, 2012 ($7.99, one-shot)
1-Short stories by various incl. Johns, Lemire, Pope, Lapham; Joe Kubert's last work 8.00

GHOSTS SPECIAL (See DC Special Series No. 7)

GHOST STORIES (See Amazing Ghost Stories)

GHOST STORIES
Dell Publ. Co.: Sept-Nov, 1962; No. 2, Apr-June, 1963 - No. 37, Oct, 1973

	GD	VG	FN	VF	VF/NM	NM-
12-295-211(#1)-Written by John Stanley	6	12	18	38	69	100
2	4	8	12	23	37	50
3-10: Two No. 6's exist with different c/a(12-295-406 & 12-295-503) #12-295-503 is actually #9 with indicia to #6	3	6	9	19	30	40
11-21: 21-Last 12¢ issue	3	6	9	16	23	30
22-37	2	4	6	13	18	22

NOTE: *#21-34, 36, 37 all reprint earlier issues.*

GHOST WHISPERER (Based on the CBS television series)
IDW Publishing: Mar, 2008 - No. 5, July, 2008 ($3.99)
1-5: 1-Two covers by Casagrande & Ho; Casagrande-a 4.00

GHOST WHISPERER: THE MUSE
IDW Publishing: Dec, 2008 - No. 4, Mar, 2009 ($3.99)
1-4-Two covers (photo & art) for each; Barbara Kesel-s/ Adriano Loyola-a 4.00

GHOUL, THE
IDW Publishing: Nov, 2009 - No. 3, Mar, 2010 ($3.99, limited series)
1-3-Niles-s/Wrightson-a 4.00

GHOUL TALES (Magazine)
Stanley Publications: Nov, 1970 - No. 5, July, 1971 (52 pgs.) (B&W)

	GD	VG	FN	VF	VF/NM	NM-
1-Aragon pre-code reprints; Mr. Mystery as host; bondage-c	8	16	24	54	102	150
2,3: 2-(1/71)Reprint/Climax #1. 3-(3/71)	5	10	15	30	50	70
4-(5/71)Reprints story "The Way to a Man's Heart" used in **SOTI**	5	10	15	33	57	80
5-ACG reprints	4	8	12	25	40	55

NOTE: *No. 1-4 contain pre-code Aragon reprints.*

GIANT BOY BOOK OF COMICS (Also see Boy Comics)
Newsbook Publications (Gleason): 1945 (240 pgs., hard-c)

	GD	VG	FN	VF	VF/NM	NM-
1-Crimebuster & Young Robin Hood; Biro-c	107	214	321	680	1165	1650

GIANT COMIC ALBUM
King Features Syndicate: 1972 (59¢, 11x14", 52 pgs., B&W, cardboard-c)

	GD	VG	FN	VF	VF/NM	NM-
Newspaper reprints: Barney Google, Little Iodine, Katzenjammer Kids, Henry, Beetle Bailey, Blondie, & Snuffy Smith each...	3	6	9	19	30	40
Flash Gordon ('68-69 Dan Barry)	4	8	12	25	40	55
Mandrake the Magician ('59 Falk), Popeye	4	8	12	23	37	50

GIANT COMICS
Charlton Comics: Summer, 1957 - No. 3, Winter, 1957 (25¢, 96 pgs., not rebound material)

	GD	VG	FN	VF	VF/NM	NM-
1-Atomic Mouse, Lil Genius, Lil Tomboy app.	24	48	72	142	234	325
2-(Fall '57) Romance	24	48	72	142	234	325
3-Christmas Book; Atomic Mouse, Atomic Rabbit, Li'l Genius, Li'l Tomboy & Atom the Cat stories	19	38	57	111	176	240

GIANT COMICS (See Wham-O Giant Comics)

GIANT COMICS EDITION (See Terry-Toons) (Also see Fox Giants)
St. John Publishing Co.: 1947 - No. 17, 1950 (25¢, 100-164 pgs.)

	GD	VG	FN	VF	VF/NM	NM-
1-Mighty Mouse	58	116	174	371	636	900
2-Abbie & Slats	36	72	108	211	343	475
3-Terry-Toons Album; 100 pgs.	45	90	135	284	480	675
4-Crime comics; contains Red Seal No. 16, used & illo. in **SOTI**	77	154	231	493	847	1200
5-Police Case Book (4/49, 132 pgs.)-Contents varies; contains remaindered St. John books - some volumes contain 5 copies rather than 4, with 160 pages; Matt Baker-c	74	148	222	470	810	1150
5A-Terry-Toons Album (132 pgs.)-Mighty Mouse, Heckle & Jeckle, Gandy Goose & Dinky stories	41	82	123	256	428	600
6-Western Picture Stories; Baker-c/a(3); Tuska-a; The Sky Chief, Blue Monk, Ventrilo app., 132 pgs.	61	122	183	390	670	950
7-Contains a teen-age romance plus 3 Mopsy comics	65	130	195	416	708	1000
8-The Adventures of Mighty Mouse (10/49)	41	82	123	256	428	600

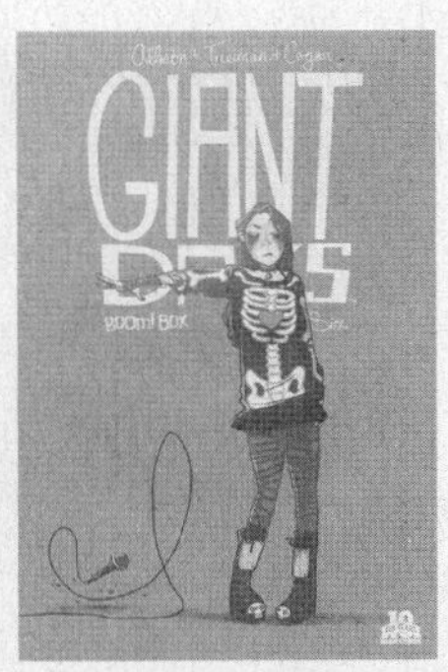

Giant Days #6 © John Allison

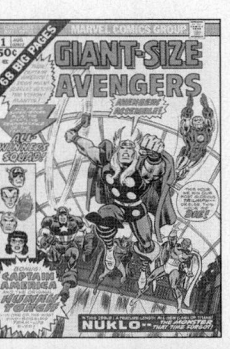

Giant-Size Avengers #1 © MAR

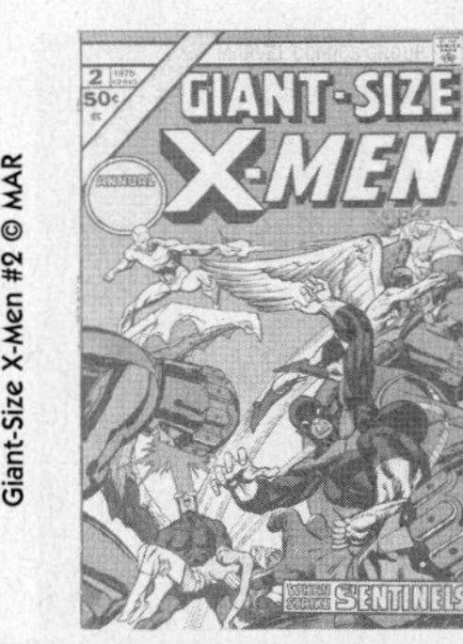

Giant-Size X-Men #2 © MAR

GD 2.0 | VG 4.0 | FN 6.0 | VF 8.0 | VF/NM 9.0 | NM- 9.2

9-Romance and Confession Stories; Kubert-a(4); Baker-a; photo-c (132 pgs.)
161 322 483 1030 1765 2500
10-Terry-Toons Album (132 pgs.)-Mighty Mouse, Heckle & Jeckle, Gandy Goose stories
41 82 123 256 428 600
11-Western Picture Stories-Baker-c/a(4); The Sky Chief, Desperado, & Blue Monk app.; another version with Son of Sinbad by Kubert (132 pgs.)
61 122 183 390 670 950
12-Diary Secrets; Baker prostitute-c; 4 St. John romance comics; Baker-a
1000 2000 3000 6000 9000 12,000
13-Romances; Baker, Kubert-a 155 310 465 992 1696 2400
14-Mighty Mouse Album (132 pgs.) 40 80 120 246 411 575
15-Romances (4 love comics)-Baker-c 181 362 543 1158 1979 2800
16-Little Audrey; Abbott & Costello, Casper 55 110 165 352 601 850
17(nn)-Mighty Mouse Album (nn, no date, but did follow No. 16); 100 pgs. on cover but has 148 pgs. 40 80 120 246 411 575
NOTE: *The above books contain remaindered comics and contents could vary with each issue. No. 11, 12 have part photo magazine insides.*

GIANT COMICS EDITIONS
United Features Syndicate: 1940's (132 pgs.)
1-Abbie & Slats, Abbott & Costello, Jim Hardy, Ella Cinders, Iron Vic, Gordo, & Bill Bumlin 45 90 135 284 480 675
2-Jim Hardy, Ella Cinders, Elmo & Gordo 34 68 102 199 325 450
NOTE: *Above books contain rebound copies; contents can vary.*

GIANT DAYS
BOOM! Studios (BOOM! Box): Mar, 2015 - Present ($3.99)
1-24: 1-6-John Allison-s/Lissa Treiman-a/c. 7-24-Max Sarin-a 4.00
... 2016 Holiday Special #1 (10/16, $7.99) Treiman-a/c; back-up w/Caanan Grall-a 8.00

GIANT GRAB BAG OF COMICS (See Archie All-Star Specials under Archie Comics)

GIANTKILLER
DC Comics: Aug, 1999 - No. 6, Jan, 2000 ($2.50, limited series)
1-6-Story and painted art by Dan Brereton 3.00
...A to Z: A Field Guide to Big Monsters (8/99) 3.00
...Vol. 1 TPB (Image Comics, 2006, $14.99) r/#1-6 & A-Z; gallery of concept art 15.00

GIANTS (See Thrilling True Story of the Baseball...)

GIANT-SIZE ATOM
DC Comics: May, 2011 ($4.99, one-shot)
1-Gary Frank-c; Hawkman app.; Lemire-s/Asrar-a 5.00

GIANT-SIZE...
Marvel Comics Group: May, 1974 - Dec, 1975 (35/50¢, 52/68 pgs.)
(Some titles quarterly) (Scarce in strict NM or better due to defective cutting, gluing and binding; warping, splitting and off-center pages are common)
Avengers 1(8/74)-New-a plus G.A. H. Torch-r; 1st modern app. The Whizzer; 1st modern app. Miss America; 2nd app. Invaders; Kang, Rama-Tut, Mantis app.
6 12 18 37 66 95
Avengers 2,3,5: 2(11/74)-Death of the Swordsman; origin of Rama-Tut. 3(2/75). 5(12/75)-Reprints Avengers Special #1 4 8 12 25 40 55
Avengers 4 (6/75)-Vision marries Scarlet Witch. 5 10 15 35 63 90
Captain America 1(12/75)-r/stories T.O.S. 59-63 by Kirby (#63 reprints origin)
4 8 12 27 44 60
Captain Marvel 1(12/75)-r/Capt. Marvel #17, 20, 21 by Gil Kane (p)
4 8 12 22 35 48
Chillers 1(6/74, 52 pgs)-Curse of Dracula; origin/1st app. Lilith, Dracula's daughter; Heath-r, Colan-c/a(p); becomes Giant-Size Dracula #2 on 5 10 15 35 63 90
Chillers 1(2/75, 50¢, 68 pgs.)-Alcala-a 4 8 12 23 37 50
Chillers 2(5/75)-All-r; Everett-r from Advs. into Weird Worlds
3 6 9 18 28 38
Chillers 3(8/75)-Wrightson-c(new)/a(r); Colan, Kirby, Smith-r
4 8 12 23 37 50
Conan 1(9/74)-B. Smith-r/#3; start adaptation of Howard's "Hour of the Dragon" (ends #4); 1st app. Belit; new-a begins 4 8 12 22 35 48
Conan 2(12/74)-B. Smith-r/#5; Sutton-a(i)(#1 also); Buscema-c
3 6 9 18 28 38
Conan 3-5: 3(4/75)-B. Smith-r/#6; Sutton-a(i). 4(6/75)-B. Smith-r/#7. 5(1975)-B. Smith-r/#14,15; Kirby-c 3 6 9 16 24 32
Creatures 1(5/74, 52 pgs.)-Werewolf app; 1st app. Tigra (formerly Cat); Crandall-r; becomes Giant-Size Werewolf w/#2 6 12 18 38 69 100
Daredevil 1(1975)-Reprints Daredevil Annual #1 3 6 9 20 31 42
Defenders 1(7/74)-Silver Surfer app.; Starlin-a; Ditko, Everett & Kirby reprints
5 10 15 30 50 70
Defenders 2(10/74, 68 pgs.)-New G. Kane-c/a(p); Son of Satan app.; Sub-Mariner-r by Everett; Ditko-r/Strange Tales #119 (Dr. Strange); Maneely-r
4 8 12 22 35 48
Defenders 3(1/75)-1st app. Korvac.; Newton, Starlin-a; Ditko, Everett-r
5 10 15 35 63 90
Defenders 4,5: 4(4/75)-Ditko, Everett-r; G. Kane-c. 5-(7/75)-Guardians 3rd app.
3 6 9 20 31 42
Doc Savage 1(1975, 68 pgs.)-r/#1,2; Mooney-r 3 6 9 16 24 32
Doctor Strange 1(11/75)-Reprints stories from Strange Tales #164-168; Lawrence, Tuska-r 3 6 9 20 31 42
Dracula 2(9/74, 50¢)-Formerly Giant-Size Chillers 4 8 12 22 35 48
Dracula 3(12/74)-Fox-r/Uncanny Tales #6 3 6 9 20 31 42
Dracula 4(3/75)-Ditko-r(2) 3 6 9 20 31 42
Dracula 5(6/75)-1st Byrne art at Marvel 5 10 15 33 57 80
Fantastic Four 2-4: 2(8/74)-Formerly Giant-Size Super-Stars; Ditko-r. 2,4-Buscema-a. 3(11/74)-Buckler-a. 4(2/75)-1st Madrox. 4 8 12 25 40 55
Fantastic Four 5,6: 5(5/75)-All-r; Kirby, G. Kane-r. 6(10/75)-All-r; Kirby-r
3 6 9 20 31 42
Hulk 1(1975) r/Hulk Special #1 4 8 12 22 35 48
Invaders 1(6/75, 50¢, 68 pgs.)-Origin; G.A. Sub-Mariner-r/Sub-Mariner #1; intro Master Man
4 8 12 27 44 60
Iron Man 1(1975)-Ditko reprint 4 8 12 25 40 55
Kid Colt 1-3: 1(1/75). 2(4/75). 3(7/75)-new Ayers-a 7 14 21 48 89 130
Man-Thing 1(8/74)-New Ploog-c/a (25 pgs.); Ditko-r/Amazing Adv. #11; Kirby-r/ Strange Tales Ann. #2 & T.O.S. #15; (#1-5 all have new Man-Thing stories, pre-hero-r & are 68 pgs.) 4 8 12 27 44 60
Man-Thing 2,3: 2(11/74)-Buscema-c/a(p); Kirby, Powell-r. 3(2/75)-Alcala-a; Ditko, Kirby, Sutton-r; Gil Kane-c 3 6 9 20 31 42
Man-Thing 4,5: 4(5/75)-Howard the Duck by Brunner-c/a; Ditko-r. 5(8/75)-Howard the Duck by Brunner (p); Dracula cameo in Howard the Duck; Buscema-a(p); Sutton-a(i); G. Kane-c
4 8 12 27 44 60
Marvel Triple Action 1,2: 1(5/75). 2(7/75) 3 6 9 16 24 32
Master of Kung Fu 1(9/74)-Russell-a; Yellow Claw-r in #1-4; Gulacy-a in #1,2
4 8 12 25 40 55
Master of Kung Fu 2-4: 2-(12/74)-r/Yellow Claw #1. 3(3/75)-Gulacy-a; Kirby-a. 4(6/75)-Kirby-a
3 6 9 20 31 42
Power Man 1(1975) 3 6 9 18 28 38
Spider-Man 1(7/74)-Spider-Man /Human Torch-r by Kirby/Ditko; Byrne-r plus new-a (Dracula-c/story) 6 12 18 41 76 110
Spider-Man 2,3: 2(10/74)-Shang-Chi-c/app. 3(1/75)-Doc Savage-c/app.; Daredevil/ Spider-Man-r w/Ditko-a 4 8 12 27 44 60
Spider-Man 4(4/75)-3rd Punisher app.; Byrne, Ditko-r
10 20 30 66 138 210
Spider-Man 5,6: 5(7/75)-Man-Thing/Lizard-c. 6(9/75) 4 8 12 23 37 50
Super-Heroes Featuring Spider-Man 1(6/74, 35¢, 52 pgs.)-Spider-Man vs. Man-Wolf; Morbius, the Living Vampire app.; Ditko-r; G. Kane-a(p); Spidey villains app.
6 12 18 37 66 95
Super-Stars 1(5/74, 35¢, 52 pgs.)-Fantastic Four; Thing vs. Hulk; Kirbyish-c/a by Buckler/Sinnott; F.F. villains profiled; becomes Giant-Size Fantastic Four #2 on
5 10 15 35 63 90
Super-Villain Team-Up 1(3/75, 68 pgs.)-Craig-r(i) (Also see Fantastic Four #6 for 1st super-villain team-up) 3 6 9 20 31 42
Super-Villain Team-Up 2(6/75, 68 pgs.)-Dr. Doom, Sub-Mariner app.; Spider-Man-r from Amazing Spider-Man #8 by Ditko; Sekowsky-a(p) 3 6 9 17 26 35
Thor 1(7/75) 4 8 12 25 40 55
Werewolf 2(10/74, 68 pgs.)-Formerly Giant-Size Creatures; Ditko-r; Frankenstein app.
3 6 9 19 30 40
Werewolf 3,5: 3(1/75, 68 pgs.). 5(7/75, 68 pgs.) 3 6 9 19 30 40
Werewolf 4(4/75, 68 pgs.)-Morbius the Living Vampire app.
3 6 9 21 33 45
X-Men 1(Summer, 1975, 50¢, 68 pgs.)-1st app. new X-Men; intro. Nightcrawler, Storm, Colossus & Thunderbird; 2nd full app. Wolverine after Incredible Hulk #181
160 320 480 800 1200 1600
X-Men 2 (11/75)-N. Adams-r (51 pgs) 8 16 24 56 108 160
Giant Size Marvel TPB (2005, $24.99) reprints stories from Giant-Size Avengers #1, G-S Fantastic Four #4, G-S Defenders #4, G-S Super-Heroes #1, G-S Invaders #1, G-S X-Men #1 and Giant-Size Creatures #1 25.00

GIANT-SIZE...
Marvel Comics: 2005 - 2014 ($4.99/$3.99)
Astonishing X-Men 1 (7/08, $4.99) Concludes story from Astonishing X-Men #24; Whedon-s/ Cassaday-a/wraparound-c; Spider-Man, FF, Dr. Strange app.; variant cover gallery 5.00
Astonishing X-Men 1 (7/08, $4.99) Variant B&W cover 5.00
Avengers 1 (2/08, $4.99) new short stories and r/Avengers #58, 201; Hitch-c 5.00
Avengers/Invaders 1 ('08, $3.99) r/Avengers #71; Invaders #10, Ann. 1 & G-S #2 4.00
Hulk 1 (8/06, $4.99)-2 new stories; Planet Hulk (David-s/Santacruz-a) & Hulk vs. The Champions (Pak-s/Lopresti-a; r/Incredible Hulk: The End) 5.00

G.I. Combat #87 © DC

Gift Comics #1 © FAW

Gigantic #1 © Remender & Nguyen

GD VG FN VF VF/NM NM-
2.0 4.0 6.0 8.0 9.0 9.2

Incredible Hulk 1 (7/08, $3.99)-1 new story; r/Incredible Hulk Annual #7; Frank-c 4.00
Invaders 2 ('05, $4.99)-new Thomas-s/Weeks-a; r/Invaders #1&2 & All-Winners #1&2 5.00
Marvel Adventures The Avengers (9/07, $3.99) Agents of Atlas and Kang app.; Kirk-a: reprint of 1st Namora app. from Marvel Mystery Comics #82; reprint from Venus #1 4.00
Spider-Man (7/14, $4.99) origin retold, other short stories; Scherberger-c 5.00
Spider-Woman ('05, $4.99)-new Bendis-s/Mays-a; r/Marvel Spotlight #32 & S-W #1,37,38 5.00
Wolverine (12/06, $4.99)-new Lapham-s/Aja-a; r/X-Men #6,7 5.00
X-Men 3 ('05, $4.99)-new Whedon-s/N. Adams-a; r/team-ups; Cockrum & Cassaday-c 5.00

GIANT-SIZE LITTLE MARVEL: AVX (Secret Wars tie-in)
Marvel Comics: Aug, 2015 - No. 4, Nov, 2015 ($3.99, limited series)
1-4-Skottie Young-s/a; all ages kid-version Avengers vs. X-Men spoof. 4-GOTG app. 4.00

GIANT SPECTACULAR COMICS (See Archie All-Star Special under Archie Comics)

GIANT SUMMER FUN BOOK (See Terry-Toons...)

G. I. COMBAT
Quality Comics Group: Oct, 1952 - No. 43, Dec, 1956
1-Crandall-c; Cuidera a-1-43i 142 284 426 909 1555 2200
2 48 96 144 302 514 725
3-5,10-Crandall-c/a 42 84 126 265 445 625
6-Crandall-a 39 78 117 240 395 550
7-9 37 74 111 222 361 500
11-20 29 58 87 170 278 385
21-31,33,35-43: 41-1st S.A. issue 27 54 81 158 259 360
32-Nuclear attack-c/story "Atomic Rocket Assault" 30 60 90 177 289 400
34-Crandall-a 28 56 84 165 270 375

G. I. COMBAT (See DC Special Series #22)
National Periodical Publ./DC Comics: No. 44, Jan, 1957 - No. 288, Mar, 1987
44-Grey tone-c 86 172 258 688 1544 2400
45 37 74 111 274 612 950
46-50 34 68 102 245 548 850
51-Grey tone-c 38 76 114 281 628 975
52-54,59,60 28 56 84 202 451 700
55-Minor Sgt. Rock prototype by Finger 30 60 90 216 483 750
56-Sgt. Rock prototype by Kanigher/Kubert 40 80 120 296 673 1050
57,58-Pre-Sgt. Rock Easy Co. stories 34 68 102 245 548 850
61-65,70-73 22 44 66 154 340 525
66-Pre-Sgt. Rock Easy Co. story 31 62 93 223 499 775
67-1st Tank Killer 40 80 120 296 673 1050
68-(1/59) "The Rock" - Sgt. Rock prototype. Part of lead-up trio to 1st definitive Sgt. Rock. Character named Jimmy referred to as "The Rock" appears as a sergeant on the cover and as a private in the story. In reprint (Our Army at War #242) DC edits Jimmy's name out; also see Our Army at War #81-84 148 296 444 1221 2761 4300
69-Grey tone-c 36 72 108 259 580 900
74-American flag-c 25 50 75 175 388 600
75-80: 75-Grey tone-c begin, end #109 34 68 102 245 548 850
81,82,84-86-Grey tone-c 29 58 87 209 467 725
83-1st Big Al, Little Al, & Charlie Cigar; grey tone-c 37 74 111 274 612 950
87-(4-5/61) 1st Haunted Tank; series begins; classic Heath washtone-c
172 344 516 1419 3210 5000
88-(6-7/61) 2nd Haunted Tank; Grey tone-c 46 92 138 359 805 1250
89,90: 90-Last 10¢ issue; Grey tone-c 29 58 87 209 467 725
91-(12/61-1/62)1st Haunted Tank-c; Grey tone-c 61 122 183 488 1094 1700
92-95,99-Grey tone-c. 94-Panel inspired a famous Roy Lichtenstein painting
25 50 75 175 388 600
96-98-Grey tone-c 19 38 57 131 291 450
100,108: 100-(6-7/63). 108-1st Sgt. Rock x-over; Grey tone-c
20 40 60 141 313 485
101-103,105-107-Grey tone-c 16 32 48 110 243 375
104,109-Grey tone-c 20 40 60 138 307 475
110-112,115-118,120 12 24 36 82 179 275
113-Grey tone-c 16 32 48 112 249 385
114-Origin Haunted Tank 34 68 102 245 548 850
119-Grey tone-c 15 30 45 105 233 360
121-136: 121-1st app. Sgt. Rock's father. 125-Sgt. Rock app. 136-Last 12¢ issue
8 16 24 56 108 160
137,139,140 5 10 15 35 63 90
138-Intro. The Losers (Capt. Storm, Gunner/Sarge, Johnny Cloud) in Haunted Tank (10-11/69)
12 24 36 80 173 265
141-143 4 8 12 25 40 55
144-148 (68 pgs.) 5 10 15 30 50 70
149,151-154 (52 pgs.): 151-Capt. Storm story. 151,153-Medal of Honor series by Maurer
4 8 12 25 40 55
150- (52 pgs.) Ice Cream Soldier story (tells how he got his name); Death of Haunted Tank-c/s
5 10 15 30 50 70
155-167,169,170 3 6 9 14 20 25
168-Neal Adams-c 3 6 9 17 26 35
171-194,196-199 2 4 6 11 16 20
195-(10/76) Haunted Tank meets War That Time Forgot; Dinosaur-c/s; Kubert-a
3 6 9 14 20 25
200-(3/77) Haunted Tank-c/s; Sgt. Rock and the Losers app.; Kubert-c
3 6 9 16 23 30
201,202 ($1.00 size) Neal Adams-c 3 6 9 16 23 30
203-210 ($1.00 size) 3 6 9 14 20 25
211-230 ($1.00 size) 2 4 6 11 16 20
231-259 ($1.00 size).232-Origin Kana the Ninja. 244-Death of Slim Stryker; 1st app. The Mercenaries. 246-(76 pgs., $1.50)-30th Anniversary issue. 257-Intro. Stuart's Raiders
2 4 6 9 13 16
260-281: 260-Begin $1.25, 52 pg. issues, end #281. 264-Intro Sgt. Bullet; origin Kana. 269-Intro. The Bravos of Vietnam. 274-Cameo of Monitor from Crisis on Infinite Earths
2 4 6 8 10 12
282-288 (75¢): 282-New advs. begin 1 2 3 5 7 9

NOTE: ***N. Adams** c-168, 201, 202. **Check** a-168, 173. **Drucker** a-48, 61, 63, 66, 71, 72, 76, 134, 140, 141, 144, 147, 148, 153. **Evans** a-135, 138, 158, 164, 166, 201, 202, 204, 205, 215, 256. Giffen a-267. **Glanzman** a-most issues. **Kubert/Heath** a-most issues; **Kubert** covers most issues. **Morrow** a-159-161(2 pgs.). **Redondo** a-189, 240i, 243i. **Sekowsky** a-162p. **Severin** a-147, 152, 154. **Simonson** c-169. **Thorne** a-152, 156. **Wildey** a-153. Johnny Cloud app.-112, 115, 120. Mlle. Marie app.-123, 132, 200. Sgt. Rock app.-111-113, 115, 120, 125, 141, 146, 147, 149, 200. USS Stevens by **Glanzman**-145, 150-153, 157. **Grandenetti** c-44-48.*

G. I. COMBAT
DC Comics: Nov, 2010 ($3.99, one-shot)
1-Haunted Tank and General J.E.B. Stuart app.; Sturges-s/Winslade-a/Darrow-c 4.00

G. I. COMBAT
DC Comics: Jul, 2012 - No. 7, Feb, 2013 ($3.99)
1-7: 1-War That Time Forgot; Olivetti-a; Unknown Soldier; Panosian-a; two covers 4.00
#0 (11/12, $3.99) Unknown Soldiers through history; War That Time Forgot; Olivetti-a 4.00

GIDGET (TV)
Dell Publishing Co.: Apr, 1966 - No. 2, Dec, 1966
1-Sally Field photo-c 8 16 24 51 96 140
2 6 12 18 37 66 95

GIFT COMICS
Fawcett Publications: 1942 - No. 4, 1949 (50¢/25¢, 324 pgs./152 pgs.)
1-Captain Marvel, Bulletman, Golden Arrow, Ibis the Invincible, Mr. Scarlet, & Spy Smasher begin; not rebound, remaindered comics, printed at same time as originals; 50¢-c & 324 pgs. begin, end #3. 309 618 927 2163 3782 5400
2-Commando Yank, Phantom Eagle, others app. 194 388 582 1242 2121 3000
3-(50¢, 324 pgs.) 142 284 426 909 1555 2200
4-(25¢, 152 pgs.)-The Marvel Family, Captain Marvel, etc.; each issue can vary in contents
84 168 252 538 919 1300

GIFTS FROM SANTA (See March of Comics No. 137)

GIFTS OF THE NIGHT
DC Comics (Vertigo): Feb, 1999 - No. 4, May, 1999 ($2.95, limited series)
1-4-Bolton-c/a; Chadwick-s 3.00

GIGANTIC
Dark Horse Comics: Nov, 2008 - No. 5, Jan, 2010 ($3.50, limited series)
1-5-Remender-s/Nguyen-a; Earth as a reality show 3.50

GIGGLE COMICS (Spencer Spook No. 100) (Also see Ha Ha Comics)
Creston No.1-63/American Comics Group No. 64 on; Oct, 1943 - No. 99, Jan-Feb, 1955
1-Funny animal 41 82 123 256 428 600
2 21 42 63 122 199 275
3-5: Ken Hultgren-a begins? 15 30 45 90 140 190
6-9: 9-1st Superkatt (6/44) 14 28 42 80 115 150
10-Superkatt shoots Japanese plane & fights Nazi robot
15 30 45 84 127 170
11-20 12 24 36 67 94 120
21-40: 22-Spencer Spook 2nd app. 32-Patriotic-c. 37-X-Mas-c. 39-St. Valentine-c
11 22 33 60 83 105
41-54,56-59,62-99: Spencer Spook app. in many. 44-Mussel-Man app. (Superman parody). 45-Witch Hazel 1st app. 46-Bob Hope & Bing Crosby app. 49,69-X-Mas-c.
10 20 30 56 76 95
55,60,61-Milt Gross-a. 61-X-Mas-c 12 24 36 67 94 120

G-I IN BATTLE (G-I No. 1 only)
Ajax-Farrell Publ./Four Star: Aug, 1952 - No. 9, July, 1953; Mar, 1957 - No. 6, May, 1958
1 16 32 48 94 147 200
2 10 20 30 58 79 100

G.I. Jane #5 © Stanhall

G.I. Joe (2001 series) #2 © Hasbro

G.I. Joe, A Real American Hero #2 © Hasbro

	GD 2.0	VG 4.0	FN 6.0	VF 8.0	VF/NM 9.0	NM- 9.2
3-9	9	18	27	52	69	85
Annual 1(1952, 25¢, 100 pgs.)	31	62	93	182	296	410
1(1957-Ajax)	9	18	27	47	61	75
2-6	6	12	18	28	34	40

G. I. JANE
Stanhall/Merit No. 11: May, 1953 - No. 11, Mar, 1955 (Misdated 3/54)

	GD	VG	FN	VF	VF/NM	NM-
1-PX Pete begins; Bill Williams-c/a	34	68	102	199	325	450
2-7(5/54)	22	44	66	133	216	300
8-10(12/54, Stanhall)	20	40	60	114	182	250
11 (3/55, Merit)	20	40	60	114	182	250

G. I. JOE (Also see Advs. of..., Showcase #53, 54 & The Yardbirds)
Ziff-Davis Publ. Co. (Korean War): No. 10, 1950; No. 11, 4-5/51 - No. 51, 6/57(52pgs.: 10-14,6-17?)

	GD	VG	FN	VF	VF/NM	NM-
10(#1, 1950)-Saunders painted-c begin	20	40	60	117	189	260
11-14(#2-5, 10/51): 11-New logo. 12-New logo	14	28	42	76	108	140
V2#6(12/51)-17-(11/52; Last 52 pgs.?)	12	24	36	67	94	120
18-(25¢, 100 pg. Giant, 12-1/52-53)	28	56	84	165	270	375
19-30: 20-22,24,28-31-The Yardbirds app.	10	20	30	56	76	95
31-47,49-51	10	20	30	54	72	90
48-Atom bomb story	10	20	30	56	76	95

NOTE: ***Powell** a-V2#7, 8, 11. **Norman Saunders** painted c-10-14, V2#6-14, 26, 30, 31, 35, 38, 39. **Tuska** a-7. Bondage c-29, 35, 38.*

G. I. JOE (America's Movable Fighting Man)
Custom Comics: 1967 (5-1/8x8-3/8", 36 pgs.)

	GD	VG	FN	VF	VF/NM	NM-
nn-Schaffenberger-a; based on Hasbro toy	3	6	9	21	33	45

G.I. JOE
Dark Horse Comics: Dec, 1995 - No. 4, Apr, 1996 ($1.95, limited series)

1-4: Mike W. Barr scripts. 1-Three Frank Miller covers with title logos in red, white and blue. 2-Breyfogle-c. 3-Simonson-c — 4.00

G.I. JOE
Dark Horse Comics: V2#1, June, 1996 - V2#4, Sept, 1996 ($2.50)

V2#1-4: Mike W. Barr scripts. 4-Painted-c — 4.00

G.I. JOE
Image Comics/Devil's Due Publishing: 2001 - No. 43, May, 2005 ($2.95)

	GD	VG	FN	VF	VF/NM	NM-
1-Campbell-c; back-c painted by Beck; Blaylock-s	2	4	6	8	10	12
1-2nd printing with front & back covers switched						6.00
2,3						5.00
4-($3.50)						5.00
5-20,22-41: 6-SuperPatriot preview. 18-Brereton-c. 31-33-Wraith back-up; Caldwell-a						3.00
21-Silent issue; Zeck-a; two covers by Campbell and Zeck						4.00
42,43-($4.50)-Dawn of the Red Shadows; leads into G.I. Joe Vol. 2						4.50
...: Cobra Reborn (1/04, $4.95) Bradstreet-c/Jenkins-s						5.00
...: G.I. Joe Reborn (2/04, $4.95) Bradstreet-c/Bennett & Saltares-a						5.00
...: Malfunction (2003, $15.95) r/#11-15						16.00
... M. I. A. (2002, $4.95) r/#1&2; Beck back-c from #1 on cover						5.00
...: Players & Pawns (11/04, $12.95) r/#28-33; cover gallery						13.00
...: Reborn (2004, $9.95) r/Cobra Reborn & G.I. Joe Reborn						10.00
...: Reckonings (2002, $12.95) r/#6-9; Zeck-c						13.00
...: Reinstated (2002, $14.95) r/#1-4						15.00
...: The Return of Serpentor (9/04, $12.95) r/#16,22-25; cover gallery						13.00
...Vol. 8: The Rise of the Red Shadows (1/06, $14.95) r/#42,43 & prologue pgs. from #37-41						15.00

G.I. JOE (Volume 2) (Also see Snake Eyes: Declassified)
Devil's Due Publishing: No. 0, June, 2005 - No. 36, June, 2008 (25¢/$2.95/$3.50/$4.50)

	NM-
0-(25¢-c) Casey-s/Caselli-a	3.00
1-4,7-19 ($2.95): 1-Four covers; Casey-s/Caselli-a. 4-R. Black-c	3.00
5,6-($4.50) 6-Wraparound-c	4.50
20-29,31-35-($3.50) 25-Wraparound-c World War III part 1	3.50
30,36-($5.50) 30-Double-sized World War III part 6. 36-Double-sized WW III part 12	5.50
...America's Elite Vol. 1: The Newest War TPB ('06, $14.95) r/#0-5; cover gallery	15.00
...America's Elite Vol. 2: The Ties That Bind TPB (8/06, $15.95) r/#6-12; cover gallery	16.00
...America's Elite Vol. 3: In Sheep's Clothing TPB (2007, $18.99) r/#13-18; cover gallery	19.00
...America's Elite Vol. 4: Truth and Consequences TPB (9/07, $18.99) r/#19-24; covers	19.00
... Data Desk Handbook (10/05, $2.95) character profile pages	3.00
... Data Desk Handbook A-M (10/07, $5.50) character profile pages	5.50
... Data Desk Handbook N-Z (11/07, $3.50) character profile pages	3.50
...: Scarlett: Declassified (7/06, $4.95) Scarlett's childhood and training; Noto-c/a	5.00
... Special Missions (2/06, $4.95) short stories and profile pages by various	5.00
... Special Missions Antarctica (12/06, $4.95) short stories and profile pages by various	5.00
... Special Missions Brazil (4/07, $5.50) short stories and profile pages by various	5.50
... Special Missions: The Enemy (9/07, $5.50) two stories and profile pages by various	5.50
... Special Missions Tokyo (9/06, $4.95) short stories and profile pages by various	5.00
...: The Hunt For Cobra Commander (5/06, 25¢) short story and character profiles	3.00

G.I. JOE
IDW Publishing: No. 0, Oct, 2008; No. 1, Jan, 2009 - No. 27, Feb, 2011 ($1.00/$3.99)

	NM-
0-($1.00) Short stories by Dixon & Hama; creator interviews and character sketches	3.00
1-27-($3.99) 1-Dixon-s/Atkins-a; covers by Johnson, Atkins and Dell'Otto	4.00
...: Cobra Commander Tribute - 100-Page Spectacular 1 (4/11, $7.99) reprints	8.00
...: Special - Helix (8/09, $3.99) Reed-s/Suitor-a	4.00

G.I. JOE, VOLUME 2 (Prelude in G.I. Joe: Cobra Civil War #0) (Season 2 in indicia)
IDW Publishing: May, 2011 - No. 21, Jan, 2013 ($3.99)

1-21: 1-Dixon-s/Saltares-a; three covers by Howard. 9-Cobra Command Part 1 — 4.00

G.I. JOE VOLUME 3
IDW Publishing: Feb, 2013 - No. 15, Apr, 2014 ($3.99)

1-15-Van Lente-s/Kurth-a in most; multiple covers. 6-Igle-a. 12-15-Allor-s — 4.00

G.I. JOE VOLUME 4
IDW Publishing: Sept, 2014 - No. 8, Apr, 2015 ($3.99)

1-4-The Fall of G.I. Joe; Karen Traviss-s/Steve Kurth-a; multiple covers — 4.00

G.I. JOE (Follows the Revolution x-over)
IDW Publishing: Jan, 2017 - Present ($3.99)

	NM-
1,2-Reconstruction; Dreadnoks app.; Milonogiannis-a; multiple covers	4.00
...: Revolution 1 (10/16, $3.99) Tie-in to Revolution x-over; Sitterson-s/Milonogiannis-a	4.00

G.I. JOE AND THE TRANSFORMERS
Marvel Comics Group: Jan, 1987 - No. 4, Apr, 1987 (Limited series)

	GD	VG	FN	VF	VF/NM	NM-
1	2	4	6	9	12	15
2-4	1	2	3	5	6	8

G.I. JOE, A REAL AMERICAN HERO (...Starring Snake-Eyes on-c #135 on)
Marvel Comics Group: June, 1982 - No. 155, Dec, 1994

	GD	VG	FN	VF	VF/NM	NM-
1-Printed on Baxter paper; based on Hasbro toy	4	8	12	27	44	60
2-Printed on regular paper; 1st app. Kwinn	3	6	9	20	31	42
3-10: 6-1st app. Oktober Guard	3	6	9	14	20	25
11-20: 11-Intro Airborne. 13-1st Destro (cameo). 14-1st full app. Destro. 15-1st app. Major Blood. 16-1st app. Cover Girl and Trip-Wire	2	4	6	10	14	18
21-1st app. Storm Shadow; silent issue	5	10	15	34	60	85
22-1st app. Duke and Roadblock	2	4	6	11	16	20
23,24,28-30: 60-Todd McFarlane-a	2	3	4	6	8	10
25-1st full app. Zartan, 1st app of Cutter, Deep Six, Mutt and Junkyard, and The Dreadnoks	3	6	9	16	23	30
26,27-Origin Snake-Eyes parts 1 & 2	3	6	9	14	20	26
31-50: 31-1st Spirit Iron-Knife. 32-1st Blowtorch, Lady J, Recondo, Ripcord. 33-New headquarters. 40-1st app. of Shipwreck, Barbecue. 48-1st app. Sgt. Slaughter. 49-1st app. of Lift-Ticket, Slipstream, Leatherneck, Serpentor						6.00
51-59,61-90						5.00
91,92,94-99: 94-96-Snake Eyes Trilogy						6.00
93-Snake-Eyes' face first revealed	2	4	6	13	18	22
100,135-138: 135-138-($1.75)-Bagged w/trading card. 138-Transformers app.	2	4	6	9	13	16
101-134: 101-New Oktober Guard app. 110-1st Garney-a. 117- Debut G.I. Joe Ninja Force	2	3	4	6	8	10
139-142-New Transformers app.	2	4	6	13	18	22
143,145-149: 145-Intro. G.I. Joe Star Brigade	2	4	6	9	13	16
144-Origin Snake-Eyes	3	6	9	14	19	24
150-Low print thru #155	3	6	9	19	30	40
151-154: 152-30th Anniversary (of doll) issue, original G.I. Joe General Joseph Colton app. (also app. in #151)	3	6	9	18	28	38
155-Last issue	5	10	15	35	63	90
All 2nd printings						4.00
Special #1 (2/95, $1.50) r/#60 w/McFarlane-a. Cover swipe from Spider-Man #1	5	10	15	33	57	80
Special Treasury Edition (1982)-r/#1	3	6	9	19	30	40
Volume 1 TPB (4/02, $24.95) r/#1-10; new cover by Michael Golden						25.00
Volume 2 TPB (6/02, $24.95) r/#11-20; new cover by J. Scott Campbell						25.00
Volume 3 TPB (2002, $24.99) r/#21-30; new cover by J. Scott Campbell						25.00
Volume 4 TPB (2002, $25.99) r/#31-40; new cover by J. Scott Campbell						26.00
Volume 5 TPB (2002, $24.99) r/#42-50; new cover by J. Scott Campbell						25.00
Yearbook 1-4: (3/85-3/88)-r/#1; Golden-c. 2-Golden-c/a						5.00

NOTE: ***Garney** a(p)-110. **Golden** c-23, 29, 34, 36. **Heath** a-24. **Rogers** a(p)-75, 77-82, 84, 86; c-77.*

G. I. JOE, A REAL AMERICAN HERO
IDW Publishing: No. 156, Jul, 2010 - Present ($3.99)

156-199-Continuation of story from Marvel series #155 (1994); Hama-s — 4.00

G.I. Joe, A Real American Hero #227 © Hasbro

G.I. Joe: Reloaded #10 © Hasbro

G.I. Joe vs. The Transformers #1 © Hasbro

	GD	VG	FN	VF	VF/NM	NM-
	2.0	4.0	6.0	8.0	9.0	9.2

200-(3/14, $5.99) Multiple covers; bonus interview with artist SL Gallant 6.00
201-236: 201-214-Hama-s/Gallant-a. 213-Death of Snake Eyes. 216-218-Villanelli-a. 219-225-Cobra World Order 4.00
Annual 2012 (2/12, $7.99) Hama-s; Frenz, Wagner & Trimpe-a 8.00
...: Cobra World Order Prelude (10/15, $3.99) Starts seven-part bi-weekly event 4.00
Hundred Penny Press: G.I. Joe: Real American Hero #1 (3/11, $1.00) r/#1 (1982) 3.00

G.I. JOE: BATTLE FILES
Image Comics: 2002 - No. 3, 2002 ($5.95)
1-3-Profile pages of characters and history; Beck-c 6.00

G.I. JOE: COBRA (#5-on is continuation of G.I. Joe: Cobra II #4, not G.I. Joe: Cobra #4)
IDW Publishing: Mar, 2009 - No. 13, Feb, 2011 ($3.99)
1-4,5-13: 1-4-Gage & Costa-s/Fuso-a/covers by Chaykin & Fuso. 5-8-Carrera-a 4.00
Hundred Penny Press: G.I. Joe: Cobra #1 (4/11, $1.00) r/#1 with Chaykin-c 3.00
... Special (9/09, $3.99) Costa-s/Fuso-a 4.00
... Special 2 - Chameleon (9/10, $3.99) Costa-s/Fuso-a 4.00
... II (1/10 - No. 4, 4/10, $3.99) 1-4-Gage & Costa-s/Fuso-a/covers by Chaykin & Fuso 4.00

G.I. JOE: COBRA CIVIL WAR
IDW Publishing: No. 0, Apr, 2011 ($3.99)
0-Prelude to G.I. Joe, Cobra & Snake Eyes Civil War series; four covers 4.00
0-Muzzle Flash Edition (6/11, price not shown) r/#0 in B&W and partial color 4.00

G.I. JOE: COBRA VOLUME 2 (Prelude in G.I. Joe: Cobra Civil War #0)
IDW Publishing: May, 2011 - No. 9, Jan, 2012 ($3.99)(Re-named Cobra with #10)
1-9: Multiple covers on all. 1-4-Costa-s/Fuso-a 4.00

G. I. JOE COMICS MAGAZINE
Marvel Comics Group: Dec, 1986 - No. 13, 1988 ($1.50, digest-size)
1-G.I. Joe reprints 2 4 6 11 16 20
2-13: G.I. Joe-r 2 4 6 8 10 12

G.I. JOE DECLASSIFIED
Devil's Due Publishing: June, 2006 - No. 3 ($4.95, bi-monthly)
1-3-New "early" adventures of the team; Hama-s; Quinn & DeLandro-a; var-c for each 5.00
TPB (1/07, $18.99) r/#1-3; cover gallery 19.00

G.I. JOE: DEVIATIONS
IDW Publishing: Mar, 2016 ($4.99, one-shot)
1-Paul Allor-s/Corey Lewis-a; What If Cobra defeated G.I. Joe and ruled the world 4.00

G.I. JOE DREADNOKS: DECLASSIFIED
Devil's Due Publishing: Nov, 2006 - No. 3, Mar, 2007 ($4.95/$4.99/$5.50, bi-monthly)
1,2-Secret history of the team; Blaylock-s; var-c for each 5.00
3-($5.50) 5.50

G.I. JOE EUROPEAN MISSIONS (Action Force in indicia) (Series reprints Action Force)
Marvel Comics Ltd. (British): Jun, 1988 - No. 15, Dec, 1989 ($1.50/$1.75)
1,3-Snake Eyes & Storm Shadow-c/s 2 4 6 8 10 12
2,4-15 6.00

G.I. JOE: FRONT LINE
Image Comics: 2002 - No. 18, Dec, 2003 ($2.95)
1-18: 1-Jurgens-a/Hama-s. 1-Two covers by Dorman & Sharpe. 7,8-Harris-c 3.00
...Vol. 1 - The Mission That Never Was TPB (2003, $14.95) r/ #1-4; script pages 15.00
...Vol. 2 - Icebound TPB (3/04, $12.95) r/ #5-8 13.00
...Vol. 3 - History Repeating TPB (4/04, $9.95) r/#11-14 10.00
...Vol. 4 - One-Shots TPB (5/04, $15.95) r/#9,10,15-18 16.00

G.I. JOE: FUTURE NOIR SPECIAL
IDW Publishing: Nov, 2010 - No. 2, Dec, 2010 ($3.99, limited series, greytone art)
1,2-Schmidt-s/Bevilacqua-a 4.00

G. I. JOE: HEARTS & MINDS
IDW Publishing: May, 2010 - No. 5, Sept, 2010 ($3.99)
1-5: Short origin stories; Brooks-s; Chaykin & Fuso-a 4.00

G. I. JOE: INFESTATION (Zombie x-over with Star Trek, Ghostbusters & Transformers)
IDW Publishing: Mar, 2011 - No. 2, Mar, 2011 ($3.99, limited series)
1,2-Timpano-a; covers by Timpano and Snyder III 4.00

G.I. JOE: MASTER & APPRENTICE
Image Comics: May, 2004 - No. 4, Aug, 2004 ($2.95)
1-4-Caselli-a/Jerwa-s 3.00

G.I. JOE: MASTER & APPRENTICE 2
Image Comics: Feb, 2005 - No. 4, May, 2005 ($2.95, limited series)
1-4: Stevens & Vedder-a/Jerwa-s 3.00

	GD	VG	FN	VF	VF/NM	NM-
	2.0	4.0	6.0	8.0	9.0	9.2

G.I. JOE MOVIE PREQUEL...
IDW Publishing: Mar, 2009 - No. 4, June, 2009 ($3.99, limited series)
1-4-Two covers on each: 1-Duke. 2-Destro. 3-The Baroness. 4-SnakeEyes 4.00

G.I. JOE: OPERATION HISS
IDW Publishing: Feb, 2010 - No. 5, Jun, 2010 ($3.99, limited series)
1-5: 1-4-Reed-s/Padilla-a; covers by Corroney & Padilla. 5-Guglotta-a 4.00

G. I. JOE ORDER OF BATTLE, THE
Marvel Comics Group: Dec, 1986 - No. 4, Mar, 1987 (limited series)
1-4 6.00

G.I. JOE: ORIGINS
IDW Publishing: Feb, 2009 - No. 23, Jan, 2011 ($3.99)
1-23: 1-Origin of Snake Eyes; Hama-s. 12-Templesmith-a. 19-Benitez-a 4.00

G.I. JOE: RELOADED
Image Comics: Mar, 2004 -No. 14, Apr, 2005 ($2.95)
1-14: 1-3-Granov-c/Ney Rieber-s. 5,6-Rieber-s/Saltares-a. 8-Origin of the Baroness 3.00
Vol. 1 In the Name of Patriotism (11/04, $12.95) r/#1-6; cover gallery 13.00

G.I. JOE: RISE OF COBRA MOVIE ADAPTATION
IDW Publishing: July, 2009 - No. 4, July, 2009 ($3.99, weekly limited series)
1-4-Tipton-s/Maloney-a; two covers 4.00

G.I. JOE SIGMA 6 (Based on the cartoon TV series)
Devil's Due Publishing: Dec, 2005 - No. 6, May, 2006 ($2.95, limited series)
1-6-Andrew Daab-s 3.00
TPB Vol. 1 (10/06, $10.95, 8-1/4" x 5-3/4") r/#1-6; cover gallery 11.00

G.I. JOE: SNAKE EYES
IDW Publishing: Oct, 2009 - No. 4, Jan, 2010 ($3.99, limited series)
1-4-Ray Park & Kevin VanHook-s/Lee Ferguson-a; two covers 4.00

G.I. JOE: SNAKE EYES, AGENT OF COBRA
IDW Publishing: Jan, 2015 - No. 5, May, 2015 ($3.99, limited series)
1-5-Costa-s/Villanelli-a 4.00

G.I. JOE: SNAKE EYES, VOLUME 2 (Continues as Snake Eyes #8)
IDW Publishing: May, 2011 - No. 7, Nov, 2011 ($3.99)
1-7: 1-Dixon-s/Atkins & Padilla-a; two covers 4.00

G. I. JOE SPECIAL MISSIONS (Indicia title: Special Missions)
Marvel Comics Group: Oct, 1986 - No. 28, Dec, 1989 ($1.00)
1-20 5.00
21-28 6.00

G. I. JOE: SPECIAL MISSIONS
IDW Publishing: Mar, 2013 - No. 14, Apr, 2014($3.99)
1-14: 1-4-Dixon-s/Gulacy-a; covers by Chen and Gulacy. 5-7-Rosado-a. 10-13-Gulacy-a 4.00

G. I. JOE: THE COBRA FILES
IDW Publishing: Apr, 2013 - No. 9, Dec, 2013 ($3.99)
1-9: 1-Costa-s/Fuso-a; multiple covers. 5,6-Dell'edera-a 4.00

G.I. JOE 2 MOVIE PREQUEL...
IDW Publishing: Feb, 2012 - No. 4, Apr, 2012 ($3.99, limited series)
1-4-Barber-s/Navarro & Rojo-a 4.00

G.I. JOE VS. THE TRANSFORMERS
Image Comics: Jun, 2003 - No. 6, Nov, 2003 ($2.95, limited series)
1-Blaylock-s/Mike Miller-a; three covers by Miller, Campbell & Andrews 4.00
1-2nd printing; black cover with logo; back-c by Campbell 3.00
2-6: 2-Two covers by Miller & Brooks 3.00
TPB (3/04, $15.95) r/series; sketch pages 16.00

G.I. JOE VS. THE TRANSFORMERS (Volume 2)
Devil's Due Publ.: Sept, 2004 - No. 4, Dec, 2004 ($4.95/$2.95, limited series)
1-($4.95) Three covers; Jolley-s/Su & Seeley-a 5.00
2-4-($2.95) Two covers by Su & Pollina 3.00
Vol. 2 TPB (4/05, $14.95) r/series; interview with creators; sketch pages and covers 15.00

G.I. JOE VS. THE TRANSFORMERS (Volume 3) THE ART OF WAR
Devil's Due Publ.: Mar, 2006 - No. 5, July, 2006 ($2.95, limited series)
1-5: 1-Three covers; Seeley-s/Ng-a 3.00
TPB (8/06, $14.95) r/series; cover gallery 15.00

G.I. JOE VS. THE TRANSFORMERS (Volume 4) BLACK HORIZON
Devil's Due Publ.: Jan, 2007 - No. 2, Feb, 2007 ($5.50, limited series)
1,2: 1-Three covers; Seeley-s/Wildman-a. 2-Two covers 5.50

Ginger #5 © ACP

Girl Comics #3 © MAR

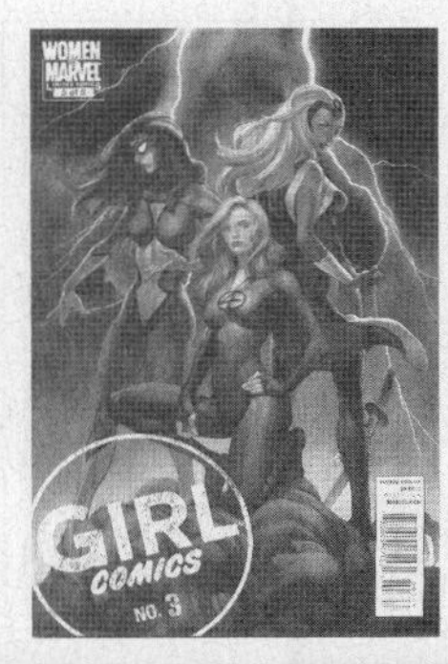

Girls' Romances #20 © DC

G. I. JUNIORS (See Harvey Hits No. 86,91,95,98,101,104,107,110,112,114,116,118,120,122)

GILGAMESH II
DC Comics: 1989 - No. 4, 1989 ($3.95, limited series, prestige format, mature)

	GD 2.0	VG 4.0	FN 6.0	VF 8.0	VF/NM 9.0	NM- 9.2
1-4: Starlin-c/a/scripts						5.00

GIL THORP
Dell Publishing Co.: May-July, 1963

	GD 2.0	VG 4.0	FN 6.0	VF 8.0	VF/NM 9.0	NM- 9.2
1-Caniff-*ish* art	4	8	12	23	37	50

GINGER
Archie Publications: 1951 - No. 10, Summer, 1954

	GD 2.0	VG 4.0	FN 6.0	VF 8.0	VF/NM 9.0	NM- 9.2
1-Teenage humor	28	56	84	165	270	375
2-(1952)	15	30	45	86	133	180
3-6: 6-(Sum/53)	14	28	42	82	121	160
7-10-Katy Keene app.	15	30	45	86	133	180

GINGER FOX (Also see The World of Ginger Fox)
Comico: Sept, 1988 - No. 4, Dec, 1988 ($1.75, limited series)

	GD 2.0	VG 4.0	FN 6.0	VF 8.0	VF/NM 9.0	NM- 9.2
1-4: Part photo-c on all						3.00

GIRL
DC Comics (Vertigo Verite): Jul, 1996 - No. 3, 1996 ($2.50, lim. series, mature)

	GD 2.0	VG 4.0	FN 6.0	VF 8.0	VF/NM 9.0	NM- 9.2
1-3: Peter Milligan scripts; Fegredo-c/a						3.00

GIRL COMICS (Becomes Girl Confessions No. 13 on)
Marvel/Atlas Comics(CnPC): Oct, 1949 - No. 12, Jan, 1952 (#1-4: 52 pgs.)

	GD 2.0	VG 4.0	FN 6.0	VF 8.0	VF/NM 9.0	NM- 9.2
1-Photo-c	28	56	84	168	274	380
2-Kubert-a; photo-c	15	30	45	90	140	190
3-Everett-a; Liz Taylor photo-c	39	78	117	231	378	525
4-11: 4-Photo-c. 10-12-Sol Brodsky-c	14	28	42	82	121	160
12-Krigstein-a; Al Hartley-c	15	30	45	84	127	170

GIRL COMICS
Marvel Comics: May, 2010 - No. 3, Sept, 2010 ($4.99, limited series)

	GD 2.0	VG 4.0	FN 6.0	VF 8.0	VF/NM 9.0	NM- 9.2
1-3-Anthology of short stories by women creators. 1-Conner-c. 2-Thompson-c. 3-Chen-c						5.00

GIRL CONFESSIONS (Formerly Girl Comics)
Atlas Comics (CnPC/ZPC): No. 13, Mar, 1952 - No. 35, Aug, 1954

	GD 2.0	VG 4.0	FN 6.0	VF 8.0	VF/NM 9.0	NM- 9.2
13-Everett-a	15	30	45	88	137	185
14,15,19,20	14	28	42	76	108	140
16-18-Everett-a	14	28	42	82	121	160
21-35: Robinson-a	12	24	36	67	94	120

GIRL CRAZY
Dark Horse Comics: May, 1996 - No. 3, July, 1996 ($2.95, B&W, limited series)

	GD 2.0	VG 4.0	FN 6.0	VF 8.0	VF/NM 9.0	NM- 9.2
1-3: Gilbert Hernandez-a/scripts.						3.00

GIRL FROM U.N.C.L.E., THE (TV) (Also see The Man From...)
Gold Key: Jan, 1967 - No. 5, Oct, 1967

	GD 2.0	VG 4.0	FN 6.0	VF 8.0	VF/NM 9.0	NM- 9.2
1-McWilliams-a; Stephanie Powers photo front/back-c & pin-ups (no ads, 12¢)	7	14	21	46	86	125
2-5-Leonard Swift-Courier No. 5. 4-Back-c pin-up	5	10	15	33	57	80

GIRLS
Image Comics: May, 2005 - No. 24, Apr, 2007 ($2.95/$2.99)

	GD 2.0	VG 4.0	FN 6.0	VF 8.0	VF/NM 9.0	NM- 9.2
1-Luna Brothers-s/a/c						4.00
2-24						3.00
Image Firsts: Girls #1 (4/10, $1.00) r/#1 with "Image Firsts" cover logo						3.00
... Vol. 1: Conception TPB (2005, $14.99) r/#1-6						15.00
... Vol. 2: Emergence TPB (2006, $14.99) r/#7-12						15.00
... Vol. 3: Survival TPB (2006, $14.99) r/#13-18						15.00
... Vol. 4: Extinction TPB (2007, $14.99) r/#19-24						15.00

GIRLS' FUN & FASHION MAGAZINE (Formerly Polly Pigtails)
Parents' Magazine Institute: V5#44, Jan, 1950 - V5#48, Sept., 1950

	GD 2.0	VG 4.0	FN 6.0	VF 8.0	VF/NM 9.0	NM- 9.2
V5#44	8	16	24	40	50	60
45-48	6	12	18	28	34	40

GIRLS IN LOVE
Fawcett Publications: May, 1950 - No. 2, July, 1950

	GD 2.0	VG 4.0	FN 6.0	VF 8.0	VF/NM 9.0	NM- 9.2
1-Photo-c	12	24	36	69	97	125
2-Photo-c	10	20	30	54	72	90

GIRLS IN LOVE (Formerly G. I. Sweethearts No. 45)
Quality Comics Group: No. 46, Sept, 1955 - No. 57, Dec, 1956

	GD 2.0	VG 4.0	FN 6.0	VF 8.0	VF/NM 9.0	NM- 9.2
46	12	24	36	67	94	120
47-53,55,56	9	18	27	52	69	85
54- 'Commie' story	11	22	33	62	86	110
57-Matt Baker-c/a	15	30	45	86	133	180

GIRLS IN WHITE (See Harvey Comics Hits No. 58)

GIRLS' LIFE (Patsy Walker's Own Magazine For Girls!)
Atlas Comics (BFP): Jan, 1954 - No. 6, Nov, 1954

	GD 2.0	VG 4.0	FN 6.0	VF 8.0	VF/NM 9.0	NM- 9.2
1	20	40	60	114	182	250
2-Al Hartley-c	13	26	39	72	101	130
3-6	12	24	36	67	94	120

GIRLS' LOVE STORIES
National Comics(Signal Publ. No. 9-65/Arleigh No. 83-117): Aug-Sept, 1949 - No. 180, Nov-Dec, 1973 (No. 1-13: 52 pgs.)

	GD 2.0	VG 4.0	FN 6.0	VF 8.0	VF/NM 9.0	NM- 9.2
1-Toth, Kinstler-a, 8 pgs. each; photo-c	65	130	195	416	708	1000
2-Kinstler-a?	34	68	102	204	332	460
3-10: 1-9-Photo-c	24	48	72	140	230	320
11-20	19	38	57	111	176	240
21-33: 21-Kinstler-a. 33-Last pre-code (1-2/55)	14	28	42	82	121	160
34-50	11	22	33	62	86	110
51-70	10	20	30	56	76	95
71-99: 83-Last 10¢ issue	5	10	15	31	53	75
100	5	10	15	33	57	80
101-146: 113-117-April O'Day app.	3	6	9	20	31	42
147-151- "Confessions" serial. 150-Wood-a	3	6	9	21	33	45
152-160,171-179	3	6	9	16	23	30
161-170 (52 pgs.)	4	8	12	22	35	48
180 Last issue	3	6	9	20	31	42
Ashcan (8-9/49) not distributed to newsstands	(a FN/VF copy sold for $836.50 in 2012)					

GIRLS' ROMANCES
National Periodical Publ.(Signal Publ. No. 7-79/Arleigh No. 84): Feb-Mar, 1950 - No. 160, Oct, 1971 (No. 1-11: 52 pgs.)

	GD 2.0	VG 4.0	FN 6.0	VF 8.0	VF/NM 9.0	NM- 9.2
1-Photo-c	58	116	174	371	636	900
2-Photo-c; Toth-a	33	66	99	194	317	440
3-10: 3-6-Photo-c	23	46	69	136	223	310
11,12,14-20	16	32	48	94	147	200
13-Toth-c	17	34	51	98	154	210
21-31: 31-Last pre-code (2-3/55)	14	28	42	80	115	150
32-50	6	12	18	40	73	105
51-99: 78-Panel inspired a famous Roy Lichtenstein painting. 80-Last 10¢ issue	5	10	15	31	53	75
100	5	10	15	33	57	80
101-108,110-120: 105-Panel inspired a famous Roy Lichtenstein painting	3	6	9	20	31	42
109-Beatles-c/story	15	30	45	103	227	350
121-133,135-140	3	6	9	18	28	38
134-Neal Adams-c (splash pg. is same as-c)	5	10	15	33	57	80
141-158	3	6	9	16	23	30
159,160-52 pgs.	4	8	12	22	35	48

GIRL WHO KICKED THE HORNETS NEST, THE
DC Comics (Vertigo): 2015 ($29.99, HC graphic novel, dustjacket)

	GD 2.0	VG 4.0	FN 6.0	VF 8.0	VF/NM 9.0	NM- 9.2
HC-Adaptation of the novel; Mina-s/Mutti & Fuso-a/Bermejo-c						30.00

GIRL WHO WOULD BE DEATH, THE
DC Comics (Vertigo): Dec, 1998 - No. 4, March, 1999 ($2.50, lim. series)

	GD 2.0	VG 4.0	FN 6.0	VF 8.0	VF/NM 9.0	NM- 9.2
1-4-Kiernan-s/Ormston-a						3.00

GIRL WITH THE DRAGON TATTOO, THE
DC Comics (Vertigo): Book One, 2012; Book Two, 2013 ($19.99, HC graphic novels)

	GD 2.0	VG 4.0	FN 6.0	VF 8.0	VF/NM 9.0	NM- 9.2
Book One HC-First part of the adaptation of the novel; Mina-s/Manco-a/Bermejo-c						20.00
Book Two HC-Second part of the adaptation; Mina-s/Manco-a/Bermejo-c						20.00

G. I. SWEETHEARTS (Formerly Diary Loves; Girls In Love #46 on)
Quality Comics Group: No. 32, June, 1953 - No. 45, May, 1955

	GD 2.0	VG 4.0	FN 6.0	VF 8.0	VF/NM 9.0	NM- 9.2
32	13	26	39	74	105	135
33-45: 44-Last pre-code (3/55)	10	20	30	54	72	90

G.I. TALES (Formerly Sgt. Barney Barker No. 1-3)
Atlas Comics (MCI): No. 4, Feb, 1957 - No. 6, July, 1957

	GD 2.0	VG 4.0	FN 6.0	VF 8.0	VF/NM 9.0	NM- 9.2
4-Severin-a(4)	13	26	39	74	105	135
5	10	20	30	54	72	90
6-Orlando, Powell, & Woodbridge-a	10	20	30	56	76	95

GIVE ME LIBERTY (Also see Dark Horse Presents Fifth Anniversary Special, Dark Horse Presents #100-4, Happy Birthday Martha Washington, Martha Washington Goes to War, Martha Washington Stranded In Space & San Diego Comicon Comics #2)
Dark Horse Comics: June, 1990 - No. 4, 1991 ($4.95, limited series, 52 pgs.)

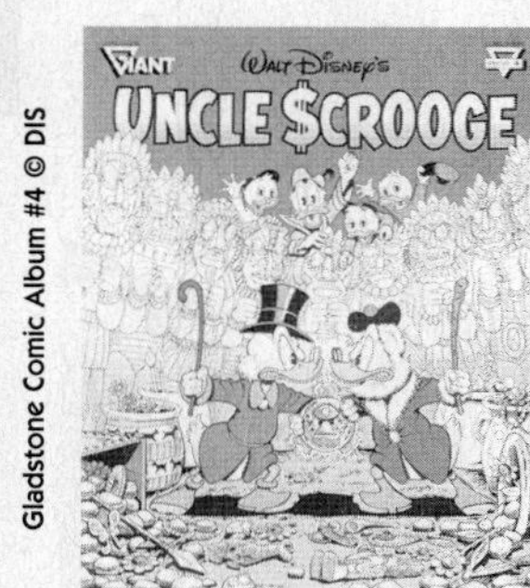

Gladstone Comic Album #4 © DIS

Global Frequency #12 © Ellis & DC

Glory #3 © Rob Liefeld

GD VG FN VF VF/NM NM-
2.0 4.0 6.0 8.0 9.0 9.2

1-4: 1st app. Martha Washington; Frank Miller scripts, Dave Gibbons-c/a in all 6.00

G. I. WAR BRIDES
Superior Publishers Ltd.: Apr, 1954 - No. 8, June, 1955

1 14 28 42 82 121 160
2 10 20 30 56 76 95
3-8: 4-Kamenesque-a; lingerie panels 9 18 27 52 69 85

G. I. WAR TALES
National Periodical Publications: Mar-Apr, 1973 - No. 4, Oct-Nov, 1973

1-Reprints in all; dinosaur-c/s 3 6 9 17 26 35
2-N. Adams-a(r) 2 4 6 13 18 22
3,4: 4-Krigstein-a(r) 2 4 6 11 16 20

NOTE: ***Drucker*** *a-3r, 4r.* ***Heath*** *a-4r.* ***Kubert*** *a-2, 3; c-4r.*

GIZMO (Also see Domino Chance)
Chance Ent.: May-June, 1985 (B&W, one-shot)

1 6.00

GIZMO
Mirage Studios: 1986 - No. 6, July, 1987 ($1.50, B&W)

1-6 4.00

G.L.A. (Great Lakes Avengers)(Also see GLX-Mas Special)
Marvel Comics: June, 2005 - No. 4, Sept, 2005 ($2.99, limited series)

1-4-Slott-s/Pelletier-a 3.00
...: Misassembled TPB (2005, $14.99) r/#1-4, West Coast Avengers #46 (1st app.) and Marvel Super-Heroes #8 (1st app. Squirrel Girl; Ditko-a) 15.00

GLADSTONE COMIC ALBUM
Gladstone: 1987 - No. 28, 1990 ($5.95/$9.95, 8-1/2x11")(All Mickey Mouse albums are by Gottfredson)

1-10: 1-Uncle Scrooge; Barks-r; Beck-c. 2-Donald Duck; r/F.C. #108 by Barks. 3-Mickey Mouse-r by Gottfredson. 4-Uncle Scrooge; r/F.C. #456 by Barks w/unedited story. 5-Donald Duck Advs.; r/F.C. #199. 6-Uncle Scrooge-r by Barks. 7-Donald Duck-r by Barks. 8-Mickey Mouse-r. 9-Bambi; r/F.C. #186? 10-Donald Duck Advs.; r/F.C. #275 1 3 4 6 8 10
11-20: 11-Uncle Scrooge; r/U.S. #4. 12-Donald And Daisy; r/F.C. #1055, WDC&S. 13-Donald Duck Advs.; r/F.C. #408. 14-Uncle Scrooge; Barks-r/U.S #21. 15-Donald And Gladstone; Barks-r. 16-Donald Duck Advs.; r/F.C. #238. 17-Mickey Mouse strip-r (The World of Tomorrow, The Pirate Ghost Ship). 18-Donald Duck and the Junior Woodchucks; Barks-r. 19-Uncle Scrooge; r/U.S. #12; Rosa-c. 20-Uncle Scrooge; r/F.C. #386; Barks-c/a(r) 1 3 4 6 8 10
21-25: 21-Donald Duck Family; Barks-c/a(r). 22-Mickey Mouse strip-r. 23-Donald Duck; Barks-r/D.D. #26 w/unedited story. 24-Uncle Scrooge; Barks-r; Rosa-c. 25-D. Duck; Barks-c/a-r/F.C. #367 1 3 4 6 8 10
26-28: All have $9.95-c. 26-Mickey & Donald; Gottfredson-c/a(r). 27-Donald Duck; r/WDC&S by Barks; Barks painted-c. 28-Uncle Scrooge & Donald Duck; Rosa-c/a (4 stories) 1 3 4 6 8 10
Special 1-7: 1 ('89-'90, $9.95/13.95)-1-Donald Duck Finds Pirate Gold; r/F.C. #9. 2 ('89, $8.95)-Uncle Scrooge and Donald Duck; Barks-r/Uncle Scrooge #5; Rosa-c. 3 ('89, $8.95)-Mickey Mouse strip-r. 4 ('89, $11.95)-Uncle Scrooge; Rosa-c/a-r/Son of the Sun from U.S. #219 plus Barks-r/U.S. 5 ('90, $11.95)-Donald Duck Advs.; Barks-r/F.C. #282 & 422 plus Barks painted-c. 6 ('90, $12.95)-Uncle Scrooge; Barks-c/a-r/Uncle Scrooge. 7 ('90, $13.95)-Mickey Mouse; Gottfredson strip-r 2 4 6 9 11 14

GLADSTONE COMIC ALBUM (2nd Series)(Also see The Original Dick Tracy)
Gladstone Publishing: 1990 ($5.95, 8-1/2 x 11," stiff-c, 52 pgs.)

1,2-The Original Dick Tracy. 2-Origin of the 2-way wrist radio 6.00
3-D Tracy Meets the Mole-r by Gould ($6.95). 1 2 3 5 6 8

GLAMOROUS ROMANCES (Formerly Dotty)
Ace Magazines (A. A. Wyn): No. 41, July, 1949 - No. 90, Oct, 1956 (Photo-c 68-90)

41-Dotty app. 14 28 42 82 121 160
42-72,74-80: 44-Begin 52 pg. issues. 45,50-61-Painted-c. 80-Last pre-code (2/55) 11 22 33 60 83 105
73-L.B. Cole-r/All Love #27 11 22 33 62 86 110
81-90 10 20 30 56 76 95

GLAMOURPUSS
Aardvark-Vanaheim Inc.: Apr, 2008 - No. 26, Jul, 2012 ($3.00, B&W)

1-26: 1-Two covers; Dave Sim-s/a/c. 9,10-Gene Colan-c. 11-Heath-c. 19-Allred-c 3.00
1-Comics Industry Preview Edition (Diamond Dateline supplement) 4.00

GLOBAL FREQUENCY
DC Comics (WildStorm): Dec, 2002 - No. 12, Aug, 2004 ($2.95, limited series)

1-12-Warren Ellis-s. 1-Leach-a. 2-Fabry-a. 3-Dillon-a. 5-Muth-a. 7-Bisley-a. 12-Ha-a 3.00
1-RRP Edition variant-c; promotional giveaway for retailers (200 printed) 10.00

GD VG FN VF VF/NM NM-
2.0 4.0 6.0 8.0 9.0 9.2

...: Detonation Radio TPB (2005, $14.95) r/#7-12 15.00
...: Planet Ablaze TPB (2003, $14.95) r/#1-6 15.00

GLORY
Image Comics (Extreme Studios)/Maximum Press: Mar, 1995 - No. 22, Apr, 1997 ($2.50)

0-Deodato-c/a, 1-(3/95)-Deodato-a 4.00
1A-Variant-c 5.00
2-11,13-22: 4-Variant-c by Quesada & Palmiotti. 5-Bagged w/Youngblood gaming card. 7,8-Deodato-c/a(p). 8-Babewatch x-over. 9-Cruz-c; Extreme Destroyer Pt. 5; polybagged w/card. 10-Angela-c/app. 11-Deodato-c. 3.00
12-($3.50)-Photo-c 4.00
... & Friends Christmas Special (12/95, $2.50) Deodato-c 3.00
... & Friends Lingerie Special (9/95, $2.95) Pin-ups w/photos; photo-c; variant-c exists 3.00
... /Angela: Angels in Hell (4/96, $2.50) Flip book w/Darkchylde #1 4.00
... /Avengelyne (10/95, $3.95) 1-Chromium-c, 1-Regular-c 4.00
Trade Paperback (1995, $9.95)-r/#1-4 10.00

GLORY (Continues numbering from the 1995-1997 series)
Image Comics: Feb, 2012 - No. 34, Apr, 2013 ($2.99/$3.99)

23-28-Joe Keatinge-s/Ross Campbell-a. 23-Supreme app. 3.00
29-34-($3.99) 4.00

GLORY
Awesome Comics: Mar, 1999 ($2.50)

0-Liefeld-c; story and sketch pages 3.00

GLORY (ALAN MOORE'S...)
Avatar Press: Dec, 2001 - No. 2 ($3.50)

Preview-(9/01, $1.99) B&W pages and cover art; Alan Moore-s 3.00
0-Four regular covers 3.50
1,2: 1-Alan Moore-s/Mychaels & Gebbie-a; nine covers by various. 2-Five covers 3.50

GLORY & FRIENDS BIKINI FEST
Image Comics (Extreme): Sept, 1995 - No. 2, Oct, 1995 ($2.50, limited series)

1,2: 1-Photo-c; centerfold photo; pin-ups 4.00

GLORY/CELESTINE: DARK ANGEL
Image Comics/Maximum Press (Extreme Studios): Sept, 1996 - No. 3, Nov, 1996 ($2.50)

1-3 3.00

GLX-MAS SPECIAL (Great Lakes Avengers)
Marvel Comics: Feb, 2006 ($3.99, one-shot)

1-Christmas themed stories by various incl. Haley, Templeton, Grist, Wieringo 4.00

G-MAN: CAPE CRISIS
Image Comics: Aug, 2009 - No. 5, Jan, 2010 ($2.99, limited series)

1-5-Chris Giarrusso-s/a; back-up short strips by various 3.00

GNOME MOBILE, THE (See Movie Comics)

GOBBLEDYGOOK
Mirage Studios: 1984 - No. 2, 1984 (B&W)(1st Mirage comics, published at same time)

1-(24 pgs.)-(distribution of approx. 50) Teenage Mutant Ninja Turtles app. on full page back-c ad; Teenage Mutant Ninja Turtles do not appear inside. 1st app of Fugitoid 207 414 621 1708 3854 6000
2-(24 pgs.)-Teenage Mutant Ninja Turtles on full page back-c ad 82 164 246 656 1478 2300

NOTE: *Counterfeit copies exist. Originals feature both black & white covers and interiors. Signed and numbered copies do not exist.*

GOBBLEDYGOOK
Mirage Studios: Dec, 1986 ($3.50, B&W, one-shot, 100 pgs.)

1-New 8 pg. TMNT story plus a Donatello/Michaelangelo 7 pg. story & a Gizmo story; Corben-i(r)/TMNT #7 2 4 6 11 16 20

GOBLIN, THE
Warren Publishing Co.: June, 1982 - No. 3, Dec, 1982 ($2.25, B&W magazine with 8 pg. color insert comic in all)

1-The Gremlin app. Philo Photon & the Troll Patrol, Micro-Buccaneers & Wizard Wormglow begin & app. in all. Tin Man app. Golden-a(p). Nebres-c/a in all 3 6 9 14 19 24
2,3: 2-1st Hobgoblin. 3-Tin Man app. 2 4 6 10 14 18

NOTE: ***Bermejo*** *a-1-3.* ***Elias*** *a-1-3.* ***Laxamana*** *a-1-3.* ***Nino*** *a-3.*

GOD COMPLEX
Image Comics: Dec, 2009 - No. 7, Jun, 2010 ($2.99)

1-7-Oeming & Berman-s/Broglia-a/Oeming-c 3.00

GODDAMNED, THE
Image Comics: Nov, 2015 - Present ($3.99)

God Is Dead #1 © Avatar

Godland #22 © Casey & Scioli

Godzilla Color Special #1 © Toho

GD 2.0 | VG 4.0 | FN 6.0 | VF 8.0 | VF/NM 9.0 | NM- 9.2

1-5-Jason Aaron-s/r.m. Guéra-a; story of Cain and Noah 4.00

GODDESS
DC Comics (Vertigo): June, 1995 - No. 8, Jan, 1996 ($2.95, limited series)

1-Garth Ennis scripts; Phil Winslade-c/a in all 5.00
2-8 4.00

GODFATHERS, THE (See The Crusaders)

GOD HATES ASTRONAUTS
Image Comics: Sept, 2014 - No. 10, Jul, 2015 ($3.50)

1-10-Ryan Browne-s/a. 1-Covers by Browne & Darrow 3.50

GOD IS
Spire Christian Comics (Fleming H. Revell Co.): 1973, 1975 (35-49¢)

nn-(1973) By Al Hartley 3 6 9 14 19 24
nn-(1975) 2 4 6 10 14 18

GOD IS DEAD
Avatar Press: Aug, 2013 - No. 48, Feb, 2016 ($3.99)

1-24,26-46: 1-5-Hickman & Costa-s/Amorim-a 4.00
25,48-($5.99) 25-Costa-s/DiPascale, Nobile & Urdinola-a. 48-Last issue; cover gallery 6.00
...Book of Acts Alpha (7/14, $5.99) Short stories by Alan Moore and others 6.00
...Book of Acts Omega (7/14, $5.99) Short stories by various 6.00

GODLAND
Image Comics: July, 2005 - Finale, Dec, 2013 ($2.99)

1-15,17-35-Joe Casey-s; Kirby-esque art by Tom Scioli. 13-Var-c by Giffen & Larsen. 33-"Dogland" on cover 3.00
16-(60¢-c) Re-cap/origin issue 3.00
36-($3.99) 4.00
... Finale (12/13, $6.99) Final issue 7.00
Image Firsts: Godland #1 (9/10, $1.00) r/#1 with "Image Firsts" cover logo 3.00
...: Celestial Edition One HC (2007, $34.99) r/#1-12 and story from Image Holiday Special; intro. by Grant Morrison; cover gallery, developmental art and original story pitches 35.00

GOD OF WAR (Based on the Sony videogame)
DC Comics (WildStorm): May, 2010 - No. 6, Mar, 2011 ($3.99/$2.99, limited series)

1-6-Wolfman-s/Sorrentino-a/Park-c. 6-($2.99) 4.00
TPB (2011, $14.99) r/#1-6; cover gallery 15.00

GOD SAVE THE QUEEN
DC Comics (Vertigo): 2007 ($19.99, hardcover with dustjacket, graphic novel)

HC-Mike Carey-s/John Bolton-painted art 20.00
SC-(2008, $12.99) Different painted-c by Bolton 13.00

GOD'S COUNTRY (Also see Marvel Comics Presents)
Marvel Comics: 1994 ($6.95)

nn-P. Craig Russell-a; Colossus story; r/Marvel Comics Presents #10-17 7.00

GOD'S HEROES IN AMERICA
Catechetical Guild Educational Society: 1956 (nn) (25¢/35¢, 68 pgs.)

307 3 6 9 16 23 30

GOD'S SMUGGLER (Religious)
Spire Christian Comics/Fleming H. Revell Co.: 1972 (35¢/39¢/40¢)

1-Three variations exist 3 6 9 14 19 24

GODWHEEL
Malibu Comics (Ultraverse): No. 0, Jan, 1995 - No. 3, Feb, 1995 ($2.50, limited series)

0-3: 0-Flip-c. 1-1st app. Primevil; Thor cameo (1 panel). 3-Pérez-a in Ch. 3, Thor app. 3.00

GODZILLA (Movie)
Marvel Comics : August, 1977 - No. 24, July, 1979 (Based on movie series)

1-(Reg. 30¢ edition)-Moench-s/Trimpe-a/Mooney-i 4 8 12 23 37 50
1-(35¢-c variant, limited distribution) 11 22 33 76 163 250
2-(Reg. 30¢ edition)-Tuska-i. 2 4 6 11 16 20
2,3-(35¢-c variant, limited distribution) 8 16 24 54 102 150
3-(30¢-c) Champions app.(w/o Ghost Rider) 2 4 6 13 18 22
4-10: 4,5-Sutton-a 2 4 6 9 13 16
11-23: 14-Shield app. 20-F.F. app. 21,22-Devil Dinosaur app. 2 4 6 8 11 14
24-Last issue 2 4 6 10 14 18

GODZILLA (Movie)
Dark Horse Comics: May, 1988 - No. 6, 1988 ($1.95, B&W, limited series) (Based on movie series)

1 2 4 6 8 10 12
2-6 1 2 3 5 6 8
...Collection (1990, $10.95)-r/1-6 with new-c 14.00
...Color Special 1 (Sum, 1992, $3.50, color, 44 pgs.)-Arthur Adams wraparound-c/a & part scripts 1 2 3 5 6 8
...King Of The Monsters Special (8/87, $1.50)-Origin; Bissette-c/a 1 2 3 5 6 8
...Vs. Barkley nn (12/93, $2.95, color)-Dorman painted-c 1 2 3 5 6 8

GODZILLA (King of the Monsters) (Movie)
Dark Horse Comics: May, 1995 - No. 16, Sept, 1996 ($2.50) (Based on movies)

0-16: 0-r/Dark Horse Comics #10,11. 1-3-Kevin Maguire scripts. 3-8-Art Adams-c 5.00
...Vs. Hero Zero ($2.50) 5.00

GODZILLA
IDW Publishing: May, 2012 - May, 2013 ($3.99)

1-13: 1-5,7,8,10-Swierczynski-s/Gane-a; multiple covers on each. 6-Wachter-a 4.00
...: The IDW Era (5/14, $3.99) Plot synopses of mini-series and cover galleries 4.00

GODZILLA: CATACLYSM
IDW Publishing: Aug, 2014 - No. 5, Dec, 2014 ($3.99, limited series)

1-5-Bunn-s/Wachter-a; multiple covers on each 4.00

GODZILLA: GANGSTERS AND GOLIATHS
IDW Publishing: Jun, 2011 - No. 5, Oct, 2011 ($3.99, limited series)

1-5-Layman-s/Ponticelli-a; Mothra app. 1-Darrow-c 4.00

GODZILLA IN HELL
IDW Publishing: Jul, 2015 - No. 5, Nov, 2015 ($3.99, limited series)

1-5: Two covers on each. 1-Stokoe-s/a. 5-Wachter-s/a 4.00

GODZILLA: KINGDOM OF MONSTERS
IDW Publishing: Mar, 2011 - No. 12, Feb, 2012 ($3.99)

1-12: 1-Hester-a; covers by Ross & Powell. 2,3-Covers by Hester & Powell 4.00
...: 100 Cover Charity Spectacular (8/11, $7.99) Variant covers for Japan Disaster Relief 8.00

GODZILLA LEGENDS (Spotlight on other monsters)
IDW Publishing: Nov, 2011 - No. 5, Mar, 2012 ($3.99, limited series)

1-5-Art Adams-c. 1-Anguirus. 2-Rodan. 3-Titanosaurus. 4-Hedorah. 5-Kumonga 4.00

GODZILLA: OBLIVION
IDW Publishing: Mar, 2016 - No. 5, Jul, 2016 ($3.99, limited series)

1-5-Fialkov-s/Churilla-a; Mechagodzilla & Ghidorah app. 4.00

GODZILLA: RAGE ACROSS TIME
IDW Publishing: Aug, 2016 - No. 5, Nov, 2016 ($3.99, limited series)

1-5-Story & art by various 4.00

GODZILLA: RULERS OF EARTH
IDW Publishing: Jun, 2013 - No. 25, Jun, 2015 ($3.99, limited series)

1-24: 1-8-Chris Mowry-s/Matt Frank-a 4.00
25-($7.99) Mowry-s/Frank & Zornow-a 8.00

GODZILLA: THE HALF-CENTURY WAR
IDW Publishing: Aug, 2012 - No. 5, Feb, 2013 ($3.99, limited series)

1-5-James Stokoe-s/a 4.00

GOG (VILLAINS) (See Kingdom Come)
DC Comics: Feb, 1998 ($1.95, one-shot)

1-Waid-s/Ordway-a(p)/Pearson-c 3.00

GO GIRL!
Image Comics: Aug, 2000 - No. 5 ($3.50, B&W, quarterly)

1-5-Trina Robbins-s/Anne Timmons-a; pin-up gallery 3.50

GO-GO
Charlton Comics: June, 1966 - No. 9, Oct, 1967

1-Miss Bikini Luv begins; Rolling Stones, Beatles, Elvis, Sonny & Cher, Bob Dylan, Sinatra, parody; Herman's Hermits pin-ups; D'Agostino-c/a in #1-8 7 14 21 49 92 135
2-Ringo Starr, David McCallum & Beatles photos on cover; Beatles story and photos; Blooperman & parody of JLA heroes 7 14 21 49 92 135
3,4: 3-Blooperman, ends #6; 1 pg. Batman & Robin satire; full pg. photo pin-ups Lovin' Spoonful & The Byrds 5 10 15 31 53 75
5,7,9: 5 (2/67)-Super Hero & TV satire by Jim Aparo & Grass Green begins. 6-8-Aparo-a. 7-Photo of Brian Wilson of Beach Boys on-c & Beach Boys photo inside f/b-c. 9-Aparo-c/a 5 10 15 35 55 75
6-Parody of JLA & DC heroes vs. Marvel heroes; Aparo-a; Elvis parody; Petula Clark photo-c; first signed work by Jim Aparo 5 10 15 34 60 85
8-Monkees photo on-c & photo inside f/b-c 6 12 18 37 66 95

The Golden Age #3 © DC

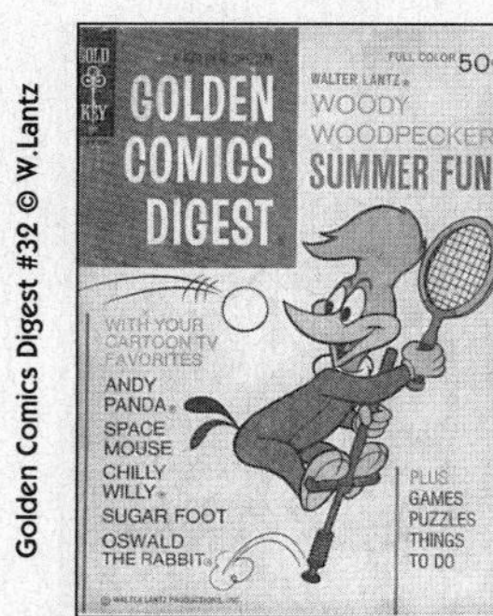

Golden Comics Digest #32 © W.Lantz

Golden Picture Story Book #3 © DIS

	GD 2.0	VG 4.0	FN 6.0	VF 8.0	VF/NM 9.0	NM- 9.2

GD VG FN VF VF/NM NM- 2.0 4.0 6.0 8.0 9.0 9.2

GO-GO AND ANIMAL (See Tippy's Friends...)

GOING STEADY (Formerly Teen-Age Temptations)
St. John Publ. Co.: No. 10, Dec, 1954 - No. 13, June, 1955; No. 14, Oct, 1955

10(1954)-Matt Baker-c/a 71 142 213 454 777 1100
11(2/55, last precode), 12(4/55)-Baker-c 55 110 165 352 601 850
13(6/55)-Baker-c/a 61 122 183 390 670 950
14(10/55)-Matt Baker-c/a, 25 pgs. 81 162 243 518 884 1250

GOING STEADY (Formerly Personal Love)
Prize Publications/Headline: V3#3, Feb, 1960 - V3#6, Aug, 1960; V4#1, Sept-Oct, 1960

V3#3-6, V4#1 4 8 12 27 44 60

GOING STEADY WITH BETTY (Becomes Betty & Her Steady No. 2)
Avon Periodicals: Nov-Dec, 1949 (Teen-age)

1-Partial photo-c 30 60 90 177 289 400

GOLDEN AGE, THE (TPB also reprinted in 2005 as JSA: The Golden Age)
DC Comics (Elseworlds): 1993 - No. 4, 1994 ($4.95, limited series)

1-4: James Robinson scripts; Paul Smith-c/a; gold foil embossed-c 6.00
Trade Paperback (1995, $19.95) intro by Howard Chaykin 20.00

GOLDEN AGE SECRET FILES
DC Comics: Feb, 2001 ($4.95, one-shot)

1-Origins and profiles of JSA members and other G.A. heroes; Lark-c 5.00

GOLDEN ARROW (See Fawcett Miniatures, Mighty Midget & Whiz Comics)

GOLDEN ARROW (...Western No. 6)
Fawcett Publications: Spring, 1942 - No. 6, Spring, 1947 (68 pgs.)

1-Golden Arrow begins 47 94 141 296 498 700
2-(1943) 22 44 66 132 216 300
3-5: 3-(Win/45-46). 4-(Spr/46). 5-(Fall/46) 15 30 45 90 140 190
6-Krigstein-a 16 32 48 94 147 200
Ashcan (1942) not distributed to newsstands, only for in house use. A CGC certified 9.0 sold for $3,734.38 in 2008.

GOLDEN COMICS DIGEST
Gold Key: May, 1969 - No. 48, Jan, 1976

NOTE: *Whitman editions exist of many titles and are generally valued the same.*

1-Tom & Jerry, Woody Woodpecker, Bugs Bunny 5 10 15 33 57 80
2-Hanna-Barbera TV Fun Favorites; Space Ghost, Flintstones, Atom Ant, Jetsons, Yogi Bear, Banana Splits, others app. 6 12 18 41 76 110
3-Tom & Jerry, Woody Woodpecker 3 6 9 16 24 32
4-Tarzan; Manning & Marsh-a 4 8 12 28 47 65
5,8-Tom & Jerry, W. Woodpecker, Bugs Bunny 3 6 9 16 23 30
6-Bugs Bunny 3 6 9 16 23 30
7-Hanna-Barbera TV Fun Favorites 5 10 15 33 57 80
9-Tarzan 4 8 12 28 47 65
10,12-17: 10-Bugs Bunny. 12-Tom & Jerry, Bugs Bunny, W. Woodpecker Journey to the Sun. 13-Tom & Jerry. 14-Bugs Bunny Fun Packed Funnies. 15-Tom & Jerry, Woody Woodpecker, Bugs Bunny. 16-Woody Woodpecker Cartoon Special. 17-Bugs Bunny 3 6 9 16 23 30
11-Hanna-Barbera TV Fun Favorites 5 10 15 34 60 85
18-Tom & Jerry; Barney Bear-r by Barks 3 6 9 16 24 32
19-Little Lulu 4 8 12 25 40 55
20-22: 20-Woody Woodpecker Falltime Funtime. 21-Bugs Bunny Showtime. 22-Tom & Jerry Winter Wingding 3 6 9 16 23 30
23-Little Lulu & Tubby Fun Fling 4 8 12 25 40 55
24-26,28: 24-Woody Woodpecker Fun Festival. 25-Tom & Jerry. 26-Bugs Bunny Halloween Hulla-Boo-Loo; Dr. Spektor article, also #25. 28-Tom & Jerry 3 6 9 14 20 26
27-Little Lulu & Tubby in Hawaii 4 8 12 24 38 52
29-Little Lulu & Tubby 4 8 12 24 38 52
30-Bugs Bunny Vacation Funnies 3 6 9 14 20 26
31-Turok, Son of Stone; r/4-Color #596,656; c-r/#9 4 8 12 27 44 60
32-Woody Woodpecker Summer Fun 3 6 9 14 20 26
33,36: 33-Little Lulu & Tubby Halloween Fun; Dr. Spektor app. 36-Little Lulu & Her Friends 4 8 12 24 38 52
34,35,37-39: 34-Bugs Bunny Winter Funnies. 35-Tom & Jerry Snowtime Funtime. 37-Woody Woodpecker County Fair. 39-Bugs Bunny Summer Fun 3 6 9 14 20 26
38-The Pink Panther 3 6 9 16 24 32
40,43: 40-Little Lulu & Tubby Trick or Treat; all by Stanley. 43-Little Lulu in Paris 4 8 12 24 38 52
41,42,44,47: 41-Tom & Jerry Winter Carnival. 42-Bugs Bunny. 44-Woody Woodpecker Family Fun Festival. 47-Bugs Bunny 3 6 9 14 20 25
45-The Pink Panther 3 6 9 16 24 32
46-Little Lulu & Tubby 4 8 12 21 33 45
48-The Lone Ranger 3 6 9 17 26 35
NOTE: *#1-30, 164 pgs.; #31 on, 132 pgs..*

GOLDEN LAD
Spark/Fact & Fiction Publ.: July, 1945 - No. 5, June, 1946 (#4, 5: 52 pgs.)

1-Origin & 1st app. Golden Lad & Swift Arrow; Sandusky and the Senator begins 60 120 180 381 653 925
2-Mort Meskin-c/a 30 60 90 177 289 400
3,4-Mort Meskin-c/a 27 54 81 158 259 360
5-Origin & 1st app. Golden Girl; Shaman & Flame app. 30 60 90 177 289 400
NOTE: *All have **Robinson**, and **Roussos** art plus **Meskin** covers and art.*

GOLDEN LEGACY
Fitzgerald Publishing Co.: 1966 - 1972 (Black History) (25¢)

1-12,14-16: 1-Toussaint L'Ouverture (1966), 2-Harriet Tubman (1967), 3-Crispus Attucks & the Minutemen (1967), 4-Benjamin Banneker (1968), 5-Matthew Henson (1969), 6-Alexander Dumas & Family (1969), 7-Frederick Douglass, Part 1 (1969), 8-Frederick Douglass, Part 2 (1970), 9-Robert Smalls (1970), 10-J. Cinque & the Amistad Mutiny (1970), 11-Men in Action: White, Marshall J. Wilkins (1970), 12-Black Cowboys (1972), 14-The Life of Alexander Pushkin (1971), 15-Ancient African Kingdoms (1972), 16-Black Inventors (1972) each.... 4 8 12 23 37 50
13-The Life of Martin Luther King, Jr. (1972) 5 10 15 30 50 70
1-10,12,13,15,16(1976)-Reprints 2 4 6 9 12 15

GOLDEN LOVE STORIES (Formerly Golden West Love)
Kirby Publishing Co.: No. 4, April, 1950

4-Powell-a; Glenn Ford/Janet Leigh photo-c 17 34 51 98 154 210

GOLDEN PICTURE CLASSIC, A
Western Printing Co. (Simon & Shuster): 1956-1957 (Text stories w/illustrations in color; 100 pgs. each)

CL-401: Treasure Island 11 22 33 64 90 115
CL-402,403: 402: Tom Sawyer. 403: Black Beauty 10 20 30 54 72 90
CL-404, 405: CL-404: Little Women. CL-405: Heidi 10 20 30 54 72 90
CL-406: Ben Hur 8 16 24 44 57 70
CL-407: Around the World in 80 Days 8 16 24 44 57 70
CL-408: Sherlock Holmes 9 18 27 50 65 80
CL-409: The Three Musketeers 8 16 24 44 57 70
CL-410: The Merry Advs. of Robin Hood 8 16 24 44 57 70
CL-411,412: 411: Hans Brinker. 412: The Count of Monte Cristo 9 18 27 50 65 80
(Both soft & hardcover editions are valued the same)
NOTE: *Recent research has uncovered new information. Apparently #s 1-6 were issued in 1956 and #7-12 in 1957. But they can be found in five different series listings: CL-1 to CL-12 (softbound); CL-401 to CL-412 (also softbound); CL-101 to CL-112 (hardbound); plus two new series discoveries: A Golden Reading Adventure, publ. by Golden Press; edited down to 60 pages and reduced in size to 6x9"; only #s discovered so far are #381 (CL-4), #382 (CL-6) & #387 (CL-3). They have no reorder list and some have covers different from GPC. There have also been found British hardbound editions of GPC with dust jackets. Copies of all five listed series vary from scarce to very rare. Some editions of some series have not yet been found at all.*

GOLDEN PICTURE STORY BOOK
Racine Press (Western): Dec, 1961 (50¢, Treasury size, 52 pgs.) (All are scarce)

ST-1-Huckleberry Hound (TV); Hokey Wolf, Pixie & Dixie, Quick Draw McGraw, Snooper and Blabber, Augie Doggie app. 15 30 45 103 227 350
ST-2-Yogi Bear (TV); Snagglepuss, Yakky Doodle, Quick Draw McGraw, Snooper and Blabber, Augie Doggie app. 15 30 45 103 227 350
ST-3-Babes in Toyland (Walt Disney's...)-Annette Funicello photo-c 19 38 57 131 291 450
ST-4-(...of Disney Ducks)-Walt Disney's Wonderful World of Ducks (Donald Duck, Uncle Scrooge, Donald's Nephews, Grandma Duck, Ludwig Von Drake, & Gyro Gearloose stories) 19 38 57 131 291 450

GOLDEN RECORD COMIC (See Amazing Spider-Man #1, Avengers #4, Fantastic Four #1, Journey Into Mystery #83) (Also see Superman Record Comic and Batman Record Comic in the Promotional section)

GOLDEN STORY BOOKS
Western Printing Co. (Simon & Shuster): 1949-1950 (Heavy covers, digest size, 128 pgs.) (Illustrated text in color)

7-Walt Disney's Mystery in Disneyville, a book-length adventure starring Donald and Nephews, Mickey and Nephews, and with Minnie, Daisy and Goofy. Art by Dick Moores & Manuel Gonzales (scarce) 30 60 90 177 289 400
10-Bugs Bunny's Treasure Hunt, a book-length adventure starring Bugs & Porky Pig, with Petunia Pig & Nephew, Cicero. Art by Tom McKimson (scarce) 21 42 63 122 199 275
11,12-('50): 11-M-G-M's Tom & Jerry. 12-Walt Disney's "So Dear My Heart" 20 40 60 114 182 250

Goldie Vance #1 © Larson & Williams

Gold Key: Alliance #4 © RH

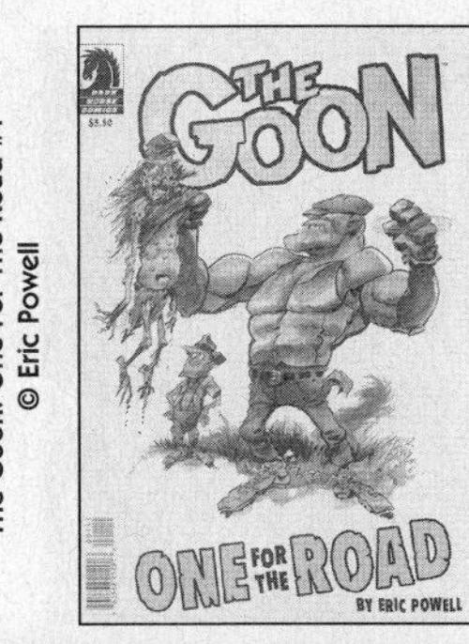

The Goon: One For The Road #1 © Eric Powell

	GD 2.0	VG 4.0	FN 6.0	VF 8.0	VF/NM 9.0	NM- 9.2

GOLDEN WEST LOVE (Golden Love Stories No. 4)
Kirby Publishing Co.: Sept-Oct, 1949 - No. 3, Feb, 1950 (All 52 pgs.)

1-Powell-a in all; Roussos-a; painted-c	22	44	66	128	209	290
2,3: Photo-c	17	34	51	98	154	210

GOLDEN WEST RODEO TREASURY (See Dell Giants)

GOLDFISH (See A.K.A. Goldfish)

GOLDIE VANCE
Boom Entertainment (BOOM! Box): Apr, 2016 - Present ($3.99)

1-10: 1-8-Hope Larson-s/Brittney Williams-a. 1-Five covers. 2-4-Two covers. 9,10-Hayes-a 4.00

GOLDILOCKS (See March of Comics No. 1)

GOLD KEY: ALLIANCE
Dynamite Entertainment: 2016 - No. 5, 2016 ($3.99, limited series)

1-5: 1-Team up of Magnus, Turok, Solar & Samson; Hester-s/Peeples-a 4.00

GOLD KEY CHAMPION
Gold Key: Mar, 1978 - No. 2, May, 1978 (50¢, 52 pgs.)

1,2: 1-Space Family Robinson; half-r. 2-Mighty Samson; half-r	1	3	4	6	8	10

GOLD KEY SPOTLIGHT
Gold Key: May, 1976 - No. 11, Feb, 1978

1-Tom, Dick & Harriet	2	4	6	8	11	14
2-11: 2-Wacky Advs. of Cracky. 3-Wacky Witch. 4-Tom, Dick & Harriet. 5-Wacky Advs. of Cracky. 6-Dagar the Invincible; Santos-a; origin Demonomicon. 7-Wacky Witch & Greta Ghost. 8-The Occult Files of Dr. Spektor, Simbar, Lu-sai; Santos-a. 9-Tragg. 10-O. G. Whiz. 11-Tom, Dick & Harriet	2	4	6	8	10	12

GOLD MEDAL COMICS
Cambridge House: 1945 (25¢, one-shot, 132 pgs.)

nn-Captain Truth by Fujitani as well as Stallman and Howie Post, Crime Detector, The Witch of Salem, Luckyman, others app.	37	74	111	222	361	500

GOMER PYLE (TV)
Gold Key: July, 1966 - No. 3, Oct, 1967

1-Photo front/back-c	7	14	21	46	86	125
2,3-Photo-c	5	10	15	34	60	85

GON
DC Comics (Paradox Press): July, 1996 - No. 4, Oct, 1996; No. 5, 1997 ($5.95, B&W, digest-size, limited series)

1-5: Misadventures of baby dinosaur; 1-Gon. 2-Gon Again. 3-Gon: Here Today, Gone Tomorrow. 4-Gon: Going, Going...Gon. 5-Gon Swimmin'. Tanaka-c/a/scripts in all	1	2	3	5	6	8

GON COLOR SPECTACULAR
DC Comics (Paradox Press): 1998 ($5.95, square-bound)

nn-Tanaka-c/a/scripts	1	2	3	5	6	8

GONERS
Image Comics: Oct, 2014 - No. 6, Mar, 2015 ($2.99)

1-6-Semahn-s/Corona-a 3.00

GON ON SAFARI
DC Comics (Paradox Press): 2000 ($7.95, B&W, digest-size)

nn-Tanaka-c/a/scripts	1	2	3	5	6	8

GON UNDERGROUND
DC Comics (Paradox Press): 1999 ($7.95, B&W, digest-size)

nn-Tanaka-c/a/scripts	1	2	3	5	6	8

GON WILD
DC Comics (Paradox Press): 1997 ($9.95, B&W, digest-size)

nn-Tanaka-c/a/scripts in all. (Rep. Gon #3,4)	1	3	4	6	8	10

GOODBYE, MR. CHIPS (See Movie Comics)

GOOD GIRL ART QUARTERLY
AC Comics: Summer, 1990 - No. 15, Spring, 1994, No. 19, 2001 (B&W/color, 52 pgs.)

1,3-15 ($3.50)-All have one new story (often FemForce) & rest reprints by Baker, Ward & other "good girl" artists 4.00
2 ($3.95), 19 (2001) FX Convention Exclusive 4.00

GOOD GIRL COMICS (Formerly Good Girl Art Quarterly)
AC Comics: No. 16, Summer, 1994 - No. 18, 1995 (B&W)

16-18 4.00

GOOD GUYS, THE
Defiant: Nov, 1993 - No. 9, July, 1994 ($2.50/$3.25/$3.50)

1-($3.50, 52 pgs.)-Glory x-over from Plasm 4.00
2,3,5-9: 3-Chasm app. 9-Pre-Schism issue 3.00
4-($3.25, 52 pgs.) Nudge sends Chasm to Plasm 4.00

GOOD, THE BAD AND THE UGLY, THE (Also see Man With No Name)
Dynamite Entertainment: 2009 - No. 8 ($3.50)

1-8: 1-Character from the 1966 Clint Eastwood movie; Dixon-s/Polls-a; three covers 3.50

GOOD TRIUMPHS OVER EVIL! (Also see Narrative Illustration)
M.C. Gaines: 1943 (12 pgs., 7-1/4"x10", B&W) (not a comic book) (Rare)

nn-A pamphlet, sequel to Narrative Illustration	148	296	444	947	1624	2300

NOTE: ***Print, A Quarterly Journal of the Graphic Arts*** *Vol. 3 No. 3 (64 pg. square bound) features 1st printing of Good Triumphs Over Evil! A VG copy sold for $350 in 2005.*

GOOFY (Disney)(See Dynabrite Comics, Mickey Mouse Magazine V4#7, Walt Disney Showcase #35 & Wheaties)
Dell Publishing Co.: No. 468, May, 1953 - Sept-Nov, 1962

Four Color 468 (#1)	11	22	33	76	163	250
Four Color 562,627,658,702,747,802,857	7	14	21	46	86	125
Four Color 899,952,987,1053,1094,1149,1201	5	10	15	35	63	90
12-308-211(Dell, 9-11/62)	5	10	15	31	53	75

GOOFY ADVENTURES
Disney Comics: June, 1990 - No. 17, 1991 ($1.50)

1-17: Most new stories. 2-Joshua Quagmire-a w/free poster. 7-WDC&S-r plus new-a. 9-Gottfredson-r. 14-Super Goof story. 15-All Super Goof issue. 17-Gene Colan-a(p) 3.00

GOOFY ADVENTURE STORY (See Goofy No. 857)

GOOFY COMICS (Companion to Happy Comics)(Not Disney)
Nedor Publ. Co. No. 1-14/Standard No. 14-48: June, 1943 - No. 48, 1953 (Animated Cartoons)

1-Funny animal; Oriolo-c	37	74	111	222	361	500
2	19	38	57	112	179	240
3-10	15	30	45	85	130	175
11-19	13	26	39	72	101	130
20-35-Frazetta text illos in all	14	28	42	78	112	145
36-48	11	22	33	60	83	105

GOOFY SUCCESS STORY (See Goofy No. 702)

GOON, THE
Avatar Press: Mar, 1999 - No. 3, July, 1999 ($3.00, B&W)

1-Eric Powell-s/a	12	24	36	82	179	275
2,3	5	10	15	35	63	90

...: Rough Stuff (Albatross, 1/03, $15.95) r/Avatar Press series #1-3 20.00
...: Rough Stuff (Dark Horse, 2/04, $12.95) r/Avatar Press series #1-3 newly colored 15.00

GOON, THE (2nd series)
Albatross Exploding Funny Books: Oct, 2002 - No. 4, Feb, 2003 ($2.95)

1-Eric Powell-s/a	5	10	15	34	60	85
2-4	3	6	9	14	20	25
...Color Special 1 (8/02)	3	6	9	16	23	30

...: Nothin' But Misery Vol. 1 (Dark Horse, 7/03, $15.95, TPB) - Reprints The Goon #1-4 (Albatross series), Color Special, and story from DHP #157 18.00

GOON, THE (3rd series) (Also see Dethklok Versus the Goon)
Dark Horse Comics: June, 2003 - No. 44, Nov, 2013 ($2.99/$3.50)

1-Eric Powell-s/a in all	3	6	9	19	30	40
2-4	2	4	6	8	10	12

5-31: 7-Hellboy-c/app; framing seq. by Mignola 14-Two covers 4.00
32-($3.99, 3/09) Tenth Anniversary issue; with sketch pages and pin-ups 5.00
33-44-($3.50) 33-Silent issue. 35-Dorkin-s. 39-Gimmick issue. 41-43-Buckingham-a. 44-Spanish issue 3.50
... 25¢ Edition (9/05, 25¢) 3.00
...: Chinatown and the Mystery of Mr. Wicker HC (11/07, $19.95) original GN; Powell-s/a 20.00
...: Fancy Pants Edition HC (10/05, $24.95, dust jacket) r/#1,2 of 2nd series & #1,3,5,9 of 3rd series; Powell intro.; sketch pages and cover gallery 25.00
...: Heaps of Ruination (5/05, $12.95, TPB) r/#5-8; intro. by Frank Darabont 13.00
...: My Murderous Childhood (And Other Grievous Yarns) (5/04, $13.95, TPB) r/#1-4 and short story from Drawing on Your Nightmares one-shot; intro. by Frank Cho 14.00
...: One For One (8/10, $1.00) r/#1 with red cover frame 3.00
...: One For The Road (6/14, $3.50) Jack Davis-c; EC horror hosts app. 3.50
...: Theater Bizarre (10/15, $3.99) Prelude to The Lords of Misery; Zombo app. 4.00
...: Virtue and the Grim Consequences Thereof (2/06, $16.95) r/#9-13 17.00
...: Wicked Inclinations (12/06, $14.95) r/#14-18; intro. by Mike Allred 15.00

GOON NOIR, THE (Dwight T. Albatross's...)

Gotham Academy #5 © DC

Gotham City Sirens #12 © DC

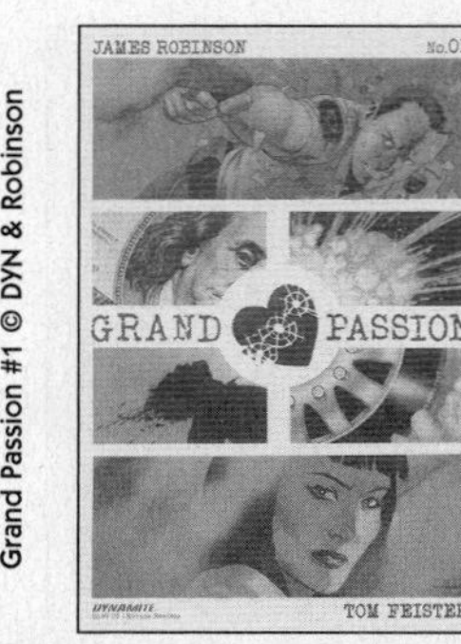

Grand Passion #1 © DYN & Robinson

GD 2.0 | VG 4.0 | FN 6.0 | VF 8.0 | VF/NM 9.0 | NM- 9.2

Dark Horse Comics: Sept, 2006 - No. 3, Jan, 2007 ($2.99, B&W, limited series)
1-3-Anthology 1-Oswalt-s/Ploog-a; Sniegoski-s/Powell-a; Morrison-s/a; Niles-s/Sook-a 3.00

GOON: OCCASION OF REVENGE, THE
Dark Horse Comics: Jul, 2014 - No. 4, Dec, 2014 ($3.50, limited series)
1-4-Powell-s/a. 3-Origin of Kid Gargantuan 3.50

GOON: ONCE UPON A HARD TIME, THE
Dark Horse Comics: Feb, 2015 - No. 4, Oct, 2015 ($3.50, limited series)
1-4-Powell-s/a 3.50

GOOSE (Humor magazine)
Cousins Publ. (Fawcett): Sept, 1976 - No. 3, 1976 (75¢, 52 pgs., B&W)
1-Nudity in all 3 6 9 16 23 30
2,3: 2-(10/76) Fonz-c/s; Lone Ranger story. 3-Wonder Woman, King Kong, Six Million Dollar Man stories 2 4 6 11 16 20

GORDO (See Comics Revue No. 5 & Giant Comics Edition)

GORGO (Based on M.G.M. movie) (See Return of...)
Charlton Comics: May, 1961 - No. 23, Sept, 1965
1-Ditko-a, 22 pgs. 24 48 72 168 372 575
2,3-Ditko-c/a 13 26 39 86 188 290
4-Ditko-c 9 18 27 60 120 180
5-11,13-16: 11,13-16-Ditko-a. 11-Ditko-c 8 16 24 51 96 140
12,17-23: 12-Reptisaurus x-over. 17-23-Montes/Bache-a. 20-Giordano-c 5 10 15 35 63 90
Gorgo's Revenge('62)-Becomes Return of... 6 12 18 42 79 115

GORILLA MAN (From Agents of Atlas)
Marvel Comics: Sept, 2010 - No. 3, Nov, 2010 ($3.99, limited series)
1-3-Parker-s/Caracuzzo-a. 1-Johnson-c. 3-Dell'Otto-c 4.00

GOSPEL BLIMP, THE
Spire Christian Comics (Fleming H. Revell Co.): 1974, 1975 (35¢/39¢, 36 pgs.)
nn-(1974) 3 6 9 14 19 24
nn-(1975) 2 4 6 9 13 16

GOTHAM ACADEMY
DC Comics: Dec, 2014 - No. 18, Jul, 2016 ($2.99)
1-18: 1-Cloonan & Fletcher-s/Kerschl-a. 4-6-Killer Croc. 6,7-Damian Wayne app. 3.00
Annual 1 (10/16, $4.99) Art by Archer, Wildgoose, Dialynas, Msassyk; Blight app. 5.00
...: Endgame 1 (5/15, $2.99) Tie-in to Joker story in Batman titles 3.00

GOTHAM ACADEMY: SECOND SEMESTER
DC Comics: Nov, 2016 - Present ($2.99)
1-6: 1-3-Cloonan, Fletcher & Kerschl-s/Archer-a. 4-Fletcher-s/Jon Lam-a 3.00

GOTHAM BY GASLIGHT (A Tale of the Batman)(See Batman: Master of...)
DC Comics: 1989 ($3.95, one-shot, squarebound, 52 pgs.)
nn-Mignola/Russell-a; intro by Robert Bloch 1 2 3 5 6 8

GOTHAM BY MIDNIGHT
DC Comics: Jan, 2015 - No. 12, Feb, 2016 ($2.99)
1-12: 1-5-Fawkes-s/Templesmith-a/c. 4,5,7-11-The Spectre app. 6-12-Ferreyra-a 3.00
Annual 1 (9/15, $4.99) Fawkes-s/Duce-a; The Gentleman Ghost origin 5.00

GOTHAM CENTRAL
DC Comics: Early Feb, 2003 - No. 40, Apr, 2006 ($2.50)
1-40-Stories of Gotham City Police. 1-Brubaker & Rucka-s/Lark-c/a. 10-Two-Face app. 13,15-Joker-c. 18-Huntress app. 27-Catwoman-c. 32-Poison Ivy app. 34-Teen Titans-c/app. 38-Crispus Allen killed (becomes The Spectre in Infinite Crisis #5) 3.00
... Special Edition 1 (11/14, $1.00) r/#1 with Gotham TV show banner on cover 3.00
... Book One: In the Line of Duty HC (2008, $29.99, dustjacket) r/#1-10; sketch pages 30.00
... Book One: In the Line of Duty SC (2008, $19.99) r/#1-10; sketch pages 20.00
... Book Two: Jokers and Madmen HC (2009, $29.99, dustjacket) r/#11-22 30.00
... Book Two: Jokers and Madmen SC (2011, $19.99) r/#11-22 20.00
... Book Three: On the Freak Beat HC (2010, $29.99, dustjacket) r/#23-31 30.00
... Book Four: Corrigan HC (2011, $29.99, dustjacket) r/#32-40 30.00
...: Dead Robin (2007, $17.99, TPB) r/#33-40; cover gallery 18.00
...: Half a Life (2005, $14.99, TPB) r/#6-10, Batman Chronicles #16 and Detective #747 15.00
...: In The Line of Duty (2004, $9.95, TPB) r/#1-5, cover gallery & sketch pages 10.00
...: The Quick and the Dead TPB (2006, $14.99) r/#23-25,28-31 15.00
...: Unresolved Targets (2006, $14.99, TPB) r/#12-15,19-22, cover gallery 15.00

GOTHAM CITY SIRENS (Batman: Reborn)
DC Comics: Aug, 2009 - No. 26, Oct, 2011 ($2.99)
1-Catwoman, Harley Quinn and Poison Ivy; Dini-s/March-a/c 4 8 12 27 44 60

GD 2.0 | VG 4.0 | FN 6.0 | VF 8.0 | VF/NM 9.0 | NM- 9.2

1-Variant-c by JG Jones 11 22 33 76 163 250
2-4 1 3 4 6 8 10
5-Full Harley Quinn cover 2 4 6 11 16 20
6-10 1 2 3 5 6 8
11-19 5.00
20,23-Joker, Harley Quinn cover 2 4 6 8 10 12
21-Full Harley Quinn cover 2 4 6 8 10 12
22,24-26 5.00
...: Song of the Sirens HC (2010, $19.99, dustjacket) r/#8-13 & Catwoman #83 20.00
...: Union HC (2010, $19.99, dustjacket) r/#1-7 20.00
...: Union SC (2011, $17.99) r/#1-7 18.00

GOTHAM GAZETTE (Battle For The Cowl crossover in Batman titles)
DC Comics: May, 2009; Jul, 2009 ($2.99, one-shots)
1-Short stories of Gotham without Batman; Nguyen, March, ChrisCross & others-a 3.00
...: Batman Alive? (7/09) Vicki Vale app.; Nguyen, March, ChrisCross & others-a 3.00

GOTHAM GIRLS
DC Comics: Oct, 2002 - No. 5, Feb, 2003 ($2.25, limited series)
1-Catwoman, Batgirl, Poison Ivy, Harley Quinn from animated series; Catwoman-c 2 4 6 11 16 20
2,4,5: 2-Poison Ivy-c. 4-Montoya-c. 5-Batgirl-c 2 4 6 8 11 14
3-Harley Quinn-c 4 8 12 23 37 50

GOTHAM NIGHTS (See Batman: Gotham Nights II)
DC Comics: Mar, 1992 - No. 4, June, 1992 ($1.25, limited series)
1-4: Featuring Batman 3.00

GOTHAM UNDERGROUND
DC Comics: Dec, 2007 - No. 9, Aug, 2008 ($2.99, limited series)
1-9-Nine covers interlock for single image; Tieri-s/Calafiore-a/c. 7,8-Vigilante app. 3.00
Batman: Gotham Underground TPB (2008, $19.99) r/#1-9; interlocked image cover 20.00

GOTHIC ROMANCES (Also see My Secrets)
Atlas/Seaboard Publ.: Dec, 1974 (75¢, B&W, magazine, 76 pgs.)
1-Text w/ illos by N. Adams, Chaykin, Heath (2 pgs. ea.); painted cover from Ravenwood Gothic paperback "The Conservatory"(scarce) 27 54 81 189 420 650

GOTHIC TALES OF LOVE (Magazine)
Marvel Comics: Apr, 1975 - No. 3, 1975 (B&W, 76 pgs.)
1-3-Painted-c/a (scarce) 27 54 81 189 420 650

GOVERNOR & J. J., THE (TV)
Gold Key: Feb, 1970 - No. 3, Aug, 1970 (Photo-c)
1 4 8 12 25 40 55
2,3 3 6 9 18 28 38

GRACKLE, THE
Acclaim Comics: Jan, 1997 - No. 4, Apr, 1997 ($2.95, B&W)
1-4: Mike Baron scripts & Paul Gulacy-c/a. 1-4-Doublecross 3.00

GRAFIK MUSIK
Caliber Press: Nov, 1990 - No. 4, Aug, 1991 ($3.50/$2.50)
1-($3.50, 48 pgs., color) Mike Allred-c/a/scripts-1st app. in color of Frank Einstein (Madman) 3 6 9 14 20 25
2-($2.50, 24 pgs., color) 2 4 6 9 12 15
3,4-($2.50, 24 pgs., B&W) 2 4 6 8 10 12

GRANDMA DUCK'S FARM FRIENDS(See Walt Disney's C&S 293 & Wheaties)
Dell Publishing Co.: No. 763, Jan, 1957 - No. 1279, Feb, 1962 (Disney)
Four Color 763 (#1) 8 16 24 51 96 140
Four Color 873 6 12 18 37 66 95
Four Color 965,1279 5 10 15 34 60 85
Four Color 1010,1073,1161-Barks-a; 1073,1161-Barks-c/a 11 22 33 73 157 240

GRAND PASSION
Dynamite Entertainment: 2016 - Present ($3.99)
1-3-James Robinson-s/Tom Feister-a/John Cassaday-c 4.00

GRAND PRIX (Formerly Hot Rod Racers)
Charlton Comics: No. 16, Sept, 1967 - No. 31, May, 1970
16-Features Rick Roberts 3 6 9 21 33 45
17-20 3 6 9 17 26 35
21-31 3 6 9 16 23 30

GRAPHIQUE MUSIQUE
Slave Labor Graphics: Dec, 1989 - No. 3, May, 1990 ($2.95, 52 pgs.)
1-Mike Allred-c/a/scripts 3 6 9 19 30 40

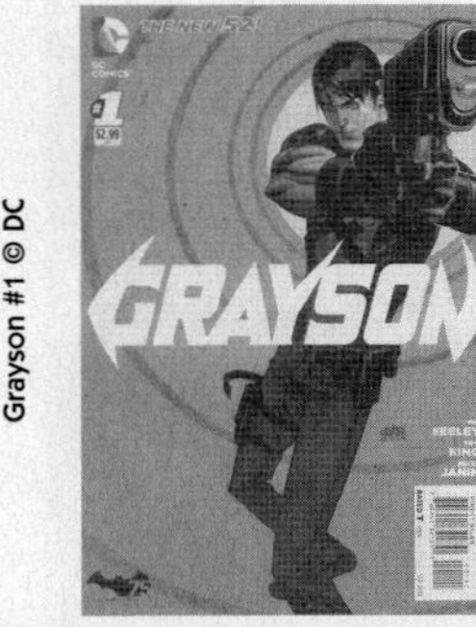

Grayson #1 © DC

The Great Gazoo #3 © H-B

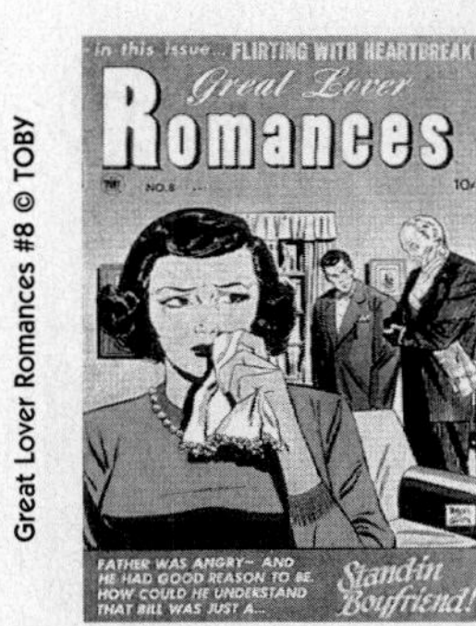

Great Lover Romances #8 © TOBY

GD 2.0 | VG 4.0 | FN 6.0 | VF 8.0 | VF/NM 9.0 | NM- 9.2

2,3 3 6 9 16 23 30

GRAVESLINGER
Image Comics (Shadowline): Oct, 2007 - No. 4, Mar, 2008 ($3.50, limited series)
1-4-Denton & Mariotte-s/Cboins-a 3.50

GRAVE TALES
Hamilton Comics: Oct, 1991 - No. 3, Feb, 1992 ($3.95, B&W, mag., 52 pgs.)
1-Staton-c/a 2 3 4 6 8 10
2,3: 2-Staton-a; Morrow-c 1 2 3 5 6 8

GRAVEYARD SHIFT
Image Comics: Dec, 2014 - No. 4, Apr, 2015 ($3.50)
1-4: 1-Jay Faerber-s/Fran Bueno-a; wraparound-c 3.50

GRAVITY (Also see Beyond! limited series)
Marvel Comics: Aug, 2005 - No. 5, Dec, 2005 ($2.99, limited series)
1-5: 1-Intro. Gravity; McKeever-s/Norton-a. 2-Rhino-c/app. 5-Spider-Man app. 3.00
...: Big-City Super Hero (2005, $7.99, digest) r/#1-5 8.00

GRAY AREA, THE
Image Comics: Jun, 2004 - No. 3, Oct, 2004 ($5.95/$3.95, limited series)
1,3-($5.95) Romita, Jr.-a/Brunswick-s; sketch pages and script pages. 3-Pin-up pages 6.00
2-($3.95) 4.00
...Vol. 1: All Of This Can Be Yours (2005, $14.95) r/series & sketch,script & pin-up pages 15.00

GRAY GHOST, THE
Dell Publishing Co.: No. 911, July, 1958; No. 1000, June-Aug, 1959
Four Color 911 (#1), 1000-Photo-c each 7 14 21 49 92 135

GRAYSON (See Forever Evil) (Leads into Nightwing: Rebirth)
DC Comics: Sept, 2014 - No. 20, Jul, 2016 ($2.99/$3.99)
1-8-Dick Grayson as secret agent; Seeley & King-s/Janin-a. 1,2,6,7-Midnighter app. 3.00
9-20-($3.99): 10-Lex Luthor app. 12-Return to Gotham; Batgirl, Red Robin app. 15-"Robin War" tie-in 4.00
Annual 1 (2/15, $4.99) Mooney-a 5.00
Annual 2 (11/15, $4.99) Superman and Blockbuster app.; Alvaro Martinez-a 5.00
Annual 3 (8/16, $4.99) Harley Quinn, Constantine, Azrael, Simon Baz app. 5.00
...: Futures End 1 (11/14, $2.99, regular-c) Five years later; Mooney-a 3.00
...: Futures End 1 (11/14, $3.99, 3-D cover) 4.00

GREAT ACTION COMICS
I. W. Enterprises: 1958 (Reprints with new covers)
1-Captain Truth reprinted from Gold Medal #1 3 6 9 16 23 30
8,9-Reprints Phantom Lady #15 & 23 6 12 18 41 76 110

GREAT AMERICAN COMICS PRESENTS - THE SECRET VOICE
Peter George 4-Star Publ./American Features Syndicate: 1945 (10¢)
1-Anti-Nazi; "What Really Happened to Hitler" 61 122 183 390 670 950

GREAT AMERICAN WESTERN, THE
AC Comics: 1987 - No. 4, 1990? ($1.75/$2.95/$3.50, B&W with some color)
1-4: 1-Western-r plus Bill Black-a. 2-Tribute to ME comics; Durango Kid photo-c 3-Tribute to Tom Mix plus Roy Rogers, Durango Kid; Billy the Kid-r by Severin; photo-c. 4- ($3.50, 52 pgs., 16 pgs. color)-Tribute to Lash LaRue; photo-c & interior photos; Fawcett-r 4.00
...Presents 1 (1991, $5.00) New Sunset Carson; film history 5.00

GREAT CAT FAMILY, THE (Disney-TV/Movie)
Dell Publishing Co.: No. 750, Nov, 1956 (one-shot)
Four Color 750-Pinocchio & Alice app. 6 12 18 37 66 95

GREAT COMICS
Great Comics Publications: Nov, 1941 - No. 3, Jan, 1942
1-Origin/1st app. The Great Zarro; Madame Strange & Guy Gorham, Wizard of Science & The Great Zarro begin 148 296 444 947 1624 2300
2-Buck Johnson, Jungle Explorer app.; X-Mas-c 74 148 222 470 810 1150
3-Futuro Takes Hitler to Hell-c/s; "The Lost City" movie story (starring William Boyd); continues in Choice Comics #3 (scarce) 1300 2600 3900 6500 9750 13,000

GREAT COMICS
Novack Publishing Co./Jubilee Comics/Knockout/Barrel O' Fun: 1945
1-(Four publ. variations: Barrel O-Fun, Jubilee, Knockout & Novack)-The Defenders, Capt. Power app.; L. B. Cole-c 32 64 96 192 314 435
1-(Jubilee)-Same cover; Boogey Man, Satanas, & The Sorcerer & His Apprentice 29 58 87 170 278 385
1-(Barrel O' Fun)-L. B. Cole-c; Barrel O' Fun overprinted in indicia; Li'l Cactus, Cuckoo Sheriff (humorous) 21 42 63 126 206 285

GREAT DOGPATCH MYSTERY (See Mammy Yokum & the...)

GREATEST AMERICAN HERO (Based on the 1981-1986 TV series)
Catastrophic Comics: Dec, 2008 - No. 3, May, 2009 ($3.50/$3.95)
1-3-Origin re-told; William Katt and others-s. 3-Obama-c/app. 4.00

GREATEST BATMAN STORIES EVER TOLD, THE
DC Comics
Hardcover ($24.95) 50.00
Softcover ($15.95) "Greatest DC Stories Vol. 2" on spine 20.00
Vol. 2 softcover (1992, $16.95) "Greatest DC Stories Vol. 7" on spine 20.00

GREATEST FLASH STORIES EVER TOLD, THE
DC Comics: 1991
nn-Hardcover ($29.95); Infantino-c 45.00
nn-Softcover ($14.95) 20.00

GREATEST GOLDEN AGE STORIES EVER TOLD, THE
DC Comics: 1990 ($24.95, hardcover)
nn-Ordway-c 60.00

GREATEST HITS
DC Comics (Vertigo): Dec, 2008 - No. 6, Apr, 2009 ($2.99, limited series)
1-6-Intro. The Mates superhero team in 1967 England; Tischman-s/Fabry-a/c 3.00

GREATEST JOKER STORIES EVER TOLD, THE (See Batman)
DC Comics: 1983
Hardcover ($19.95)-Kyle Baker painted-c 50.00
Softcover ($14.95) 20.00
Stacked Deck...Expanded Edition (1992, $29.95)-Longmeadow Press Publ. 35.00

GREATEST 1950s STORIES EVER TOLD, THE
DC Comics: 1990
Hardcover ($29.95)-Kubert-c 55.00
Softcover ($14.95) "Greatest DC Stories Vol. 5" on spine 22.00

GREATEST TEAM-UP STORIES EVER TOLD, THE
DC Comics: 1989
Hardcover ($24.95)-DeVries and Infantino painted-c 55.00
Softcover ($14.95) "Greatest DC Stories Vol. 4" on spine; Adams-c 22.00

GREATEST SUPERMAN STORIES EVER TOLD, THE
DC Comics: 1987
Hardcover ($24.95) 50.00
Softcover ($15.95) 22.00

GREAT EXPLOITS
Decker Publ./Red Top: Oct, 1957
1-Krigstein-a(2) (re-issue on cover); reprints Daring Advs. #6 by Approved Comics 6 12 18 31 38 45

GREAT FOODINI, THE (See Foodini)

GREAT GAZOO, THE (The Flintstones)(TV)
Charlton Comics: Aug, 1973 - No. 20, Jan, 1977 (Hanna-Barbera)
1 4 8 12 23 37 50
2-10 3 6 9 14 19 24
11-20 2 4 6 10 14 18

GREAT GRAPE APE, THE (TV)(See TV Stars #1)
Charlton Comics: Sept, 1976 - No. 2, Nov, 1976 (Hanna-Barbera)
1 3 6 9 21 33 45
2 3 6 9 14 20 25

GREAT LAKES AVENGERS (Also see G.L.A.)
Marvel Comics: Dec, 2016 - Present ($3.99)
1-5: 1-Team reunites; Squirrel Girl cameo; Gorman-s/Robson-a 4.00

GREAT LOCOMOTIVE CHASE, THE (Disney)
Dell Publishing Co.: No. 712, Sept, 1956 (one-shot)
Four Color 712-Movie, photo-c 6 12 18 42 79 115

GREAT LOVER ROMANCES (Young Lover Romances #4,5)
Toby Press: 3/51; #2, 1951(nd); #3, 1952 (nd); #6, Oct?, 1952 - No. 22, May, 1955 (Photo-c #1-5, 10 ,13, 15, 17) (no #4, 5)
1-Jon Juan story-r/Jon Juan #1 by Schomburg; Dr. Anthony King app. 22 44 66 132 216 300
2-Jon Juan, Dr. Anthony King app. 14 28 42 80 115 150
3,7,9-14,16-22: 10-Rita Hayworth photo-c. 17-Rita Hayworth & Aldo Ray photo-c 11 22 33 64 90 115
6-Kurtzman-a (10/52) 14 28 42 78 112 145

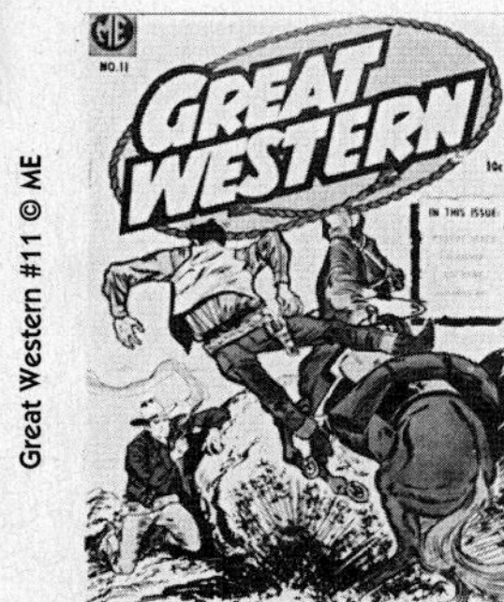

Great Western #11 © ME

Green Arrow (1988 series) #15 © DC

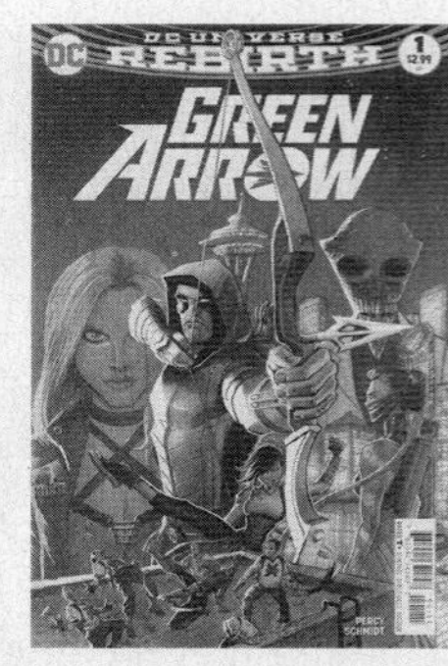

Green Arrow (2016 series) #1 © DC

GD 2.0 | VG 4.0 | FN 6.0 | VF 8.0 | VF/NM 9.0 | NM- 9.2

8-Five pgs. of "Pin-Up Pete" by Sparling 14 28 42 78 112 145
15-Liz Taylor photo-c (scarce) 50 100 150 315 533 750

GREAT RACE, THE (See Movie Classics)

GREAT SCOTT SHOE STORE (See Bulls-Eye)

GREAT SOCIETY COMIC BOOK, THE (Political parody)
Pocket Books Inc./Parallax Pub.: 1966 ($1.00, 36 pgs., 7"x10", one-shot)
nn-Super-LBJ-c/story; 60s politicians app. as super-heroes; Tallarico-a
3 6 9 17 26 35

GREAT TEN, THE (Characters from Final Crisis)
DC Comics: Jan, 2010 - No. 9, Sept, 2010 ($2.99, limited series)
1-9-Super team of China; Bedard-s/McDaniel-a/Stanley Lau-c 3.00

GREAT WEST (Magazine)
M. F. Enterprises: 1969 (B&W, 52 pgs.)
V1#1 2 4 6 10 14 18

GREAT WESTERN
Magazine Enterprises: No. 8, Jan-Mar, 1954 - No. 11, Oct-Dec, 1954
8(A-1 93)-Trail Colt by Guardineer; Powell Red Hawk-r/Straight Arrow begins, ends #11; Durango Kid story 18 36 54 103 162 220
9(A-1 105), 11(A-1 127)-Ghost Rider, Durango Kid app. in each. 9-Red Mask-c, but no app.
15 30 45 83 124 165
10(A-1 113)-The Calico Kid by Guardineer-r/Tim Holt #8; Straight Arrow, Durango Kid app.
12 24 36 69 97 125
I.W. Reprint #1,2 9: 1,2-r/Straight Arrow #36,42. 9-r/Straight Arrow #?
3 6 9 15 22 28
I.W. Reprint #8-Origin Ghost Rider(r/Tim Holt #11); Tim Holt app.; Bolle-a
3 6 9 16 24 32
NOTE: ***Guardineer** c-8. **Powell** a(r)-8-11 (from Straight Arrow).*

GREEK STREET
DC Comics (Vertigo): Sept, 2009 - No. 16, Dec, 2010 ($1.00/$2.99)
1-16: 1-($1.00) Milligan-s/Gianfelice-a. 2: Begin $2.99-c 3.00
...: Blood Calls For Blood SC (2010, $9.99) r/#1-5; Mike Carey intro.; sketch art 10.00
...: Cassandra Complex SC (2010, $14.99) r/#6-11 15.00

GREEN ARROW (See Action #440, Adventure, Brave & the Bold, DC Super Stars #17, Detective #521, Flash #217, Green Lantern #76, Justice League of America #4, Leading Comics, More Fun #73 (1st app.), Showcase '95 #9 & World's Finest Comics)

GREEN ARROW
DC Comics: May, 1983 - No. 4, Aug, 1983 (limited series)
1-Origin; Speedy cameo; Mike W. Barr scripts, Trevor Von Eeden-c/a
2 4 6 10 14 18
2-4 1 3 4 6 8 10

GREEN ARROW
DC Comics: Feb, 1988 - No. 137, Oct, 1998 ($1.00-$2.50) (Painted-c #1-3)
1-Mike Grell scripts begin, ends #80 2 4 6 9 12 15
2-49,51-74,76-86: 27,28-Warlord app. 35-38-Co-stars Black Canary; Bill Wray-i. 40-Grell-a. 47-Begin $1.50-c. 63-No longer has mature readers on-c. 63-66-Shado app. 81-Aparo-a begins, ends #100; Nuklon app. 82-Intro & death of Rival. 83-Huntress-c/story. 84, 85-Deathstroke app. 86-Catwoman-c/story w/Jim Balent layouts 4.00
50,75-($2.50, 52 pgs.): Anniversary issues. 75-Arsenal (Roy Harper) & Shado app. 5.00
0,87-96: 87-$1.95-c begins. 88-Guy Gardner, Martian Manhunter, & Wonder Woman-c/app.; Flash-c. 89-Anarky app. 90-(9/94)-Zero Hour tie-in. 0-(10/94)-1st app. Connor Hawke; Aparo-a(p). 91-(11/94). 93-1st app. Camorouge. 95-Hal Jordan cameo. 96-Intro new Force of July; Hal Jordan (Parallax) app; Oliver Queen learns that Connor Hawke is his son 3.00
97-99,102-109: 97-Begin $2.25-c; no Aparo-a. 97-99-Arsenal app. 102,103-Underworld Unleashed x-over. 104-GL(Kyle Rayner)-c/app. 105-Robin-c/app. 107-109-Thorn app. 109-Lois Lane cameo; Weeks-c. 3.00
100-($3.95)-Foil-c; Superman app. 1 3 4 6 8 10
101-Death of Oliver Queen; Superman app. 3 6 9 16 23 30
110,111-124: 110,111-GL x-over. 110-Intro Hatchet. 114-Final Night. 115-117-Black Canary & Oracle app. 3.00
125-($3.50, 48 pgs)-GL x-over cont. in GL #92 4.00
126-136: 126-Begin $2.50-c. 130-GL & Flash x-over. 132,133-JLA app. 134,135-Brotherhood of the Fist pts. 1,5. 136-Hal Jordan-c/app. 3.00
137-Last issue; Superman app.; last panel cameo of Oliver Queen
2 4 6 9 12 15
#1,000,000 (11/98) 853rd Century x-over 3.00
Annual 1-6 ('88-'94, 68 pgs.)-1-No Grell scripts. 2-No Grell scripts; recaps origin Green Arrow, Speedy, Black Canary & others. 3-Bill Wray-a. 4-50th anniversary issue. 5-Batman, Eclipso app. 6-Bloodlines; Hook app. 4.00
Annual 7-('95, $3.95)-Year One story 4.00
NOTE: ***Aparo** a-0, 81-85, 86 (partial),87p, 88p, 91-95, 96i, 98-100p, 109p; c-81,98-100p. **Austin** c-96i. **Balent** layouts-86. **Burchett** c-91-95. **Campanella** a-100-108i, 110-113i; c-99i, 101-108i,110-113i. **Denys Cowan** a-39p, 41-43p, 47p, 48p, 60p; c-41-43. **Damaggio** a(p)-97p, 100-108p, 110-112p; c-97-99p, 101-108p, 110-113p. **Mike Grell** c-1-4, 10p, 11, 39, 40, 44, 45, 47-80, Annual 4, 5. **Nasser/Netzer** a-89, 96. **Sienkiewicz** a-109i. **Springer** a-67, 68. **Weeks** c-109.*

GREEN ARROW
DC Comics: Apr, 2001 - No. 75, Aug, 2007 ($2.50/$2.99)
1-Oliver Queen returns; Kevin Smith-s/Hester-a/Wagner-painted-c
2 4 6 10 14 18
1-2nd-4th printings 3.00
2-Batman cameo 1 2 3 4 5 7
2-2nd printing 3.00
3-5: 4-JLA app. 5.00
6-15: 7-Barry Allen & Hal Jordan app. 9,10-Stanley & his Monster app. 10-Oliver regains his soul. 12-Hawkman-c/app. 4.00
16-25: 16-Brad Meltzer-s begin; The Shade app. 18-Solomon Grundy-c/app. 19-JLA app. 22-Beatty-s; Count Vertigo app. 23-25-Green Lantern app.; Raab-s/Adlard-a 3.00
26-49: 26-Winick-s begin. 35-37-Riddler app. 43-Mia learns she's HIV+. 45-Mia becomes the new Speedy. 46-Teen Titans app. 49-The Outsiders app. 3.00
50-($3.50) Green Arrow's team and the Outsiders vs. The Riddler and Drakon 4.00
51-59: 51-Anarky app. 52-Zatanna-c/app. 55-59-Dr. Light app. 3.00
60-74: 60-One Year Later starts. 62-Begin $2.99-c; Deathstroke app. 69-Batman app. 3.00
75-($3.50) Ollie proposes to Dinah (see Black Canary mini-series); JLA app. 4.00
...: City Walls SC (2005, $17.95) r/#32, 34-39 18.00
...: Crawling Through the Wreckage SC (2007, $12.99) r/#60-65 13.00
...: Heading Into the Light SC (2006, $12.99) r/#52,54-59 13.00
...: Moving Targets SC (2006, $17.99) r/#40-50 18.00
...: Quiver HC (2002, $24.95) r/#1-10; Smith intro. 25.00
...: Quiver SC (2003, $17.95) r/#1-10; Smith intro. 18.00
...: Road to Jericho SC (2007, $17.99) r/#66-75 18.00
...Secret Files & Origins 1-(12/02, $4.95) Origin stories & profiles; Wagner-c 5.00
...: Sounds of Violence HC (2003, $19.95) r/#11-15; Hester intro. & sketch pages 20.00
...: Sounds of Violence SC (2003, $12.95) r/#11-15; Hester intro. & sketch pages 13.00
...: Straight Shooter SC (2004, $12.95) r/#26-31 13.00
...: The Archer's Quest HC (2003, $19.95) r/#16-21; pitch, script and sketch pages 20.00
...: The Archer's Quest SC (2004, $14.95) r/#16-21; pitch, script and sketch pages 15.00

GREEN ARROW (Brightest Day)
DC Comics: Aug, 2010 - No. 15, Oct, 2011 ($3.99/$2.99)
1-Oliver Queen in the Star City forest; Green Lantern app.; Neves-a/Cascioli-c 5.00
1-Variant-c by Van Sciver 8.00
2-15-($2.99) 2-Green Lantern app. 7-Mayhew-a. 8-11-The Demon app. 12-Swamp Thing 3.00
...: Into the Woods HC (2011, $22.99) r/#1-7; variant cover gallery 23.00

GREEN ARROW (DC New 52)
DC Comics: Nov, 2011 - No. 52, Jul, 2016 ($2.99)
1-Krul-s/Jurgens & Pérez-a/Wilkins-c 1 3 4 6 8 10
2-24: 4,5-Giffen-s. 13,14-Hawkman app. 17-24-Lemire-s/Sorrentino-a/c. 22-Count Vertigo app. 23,24-Richard Dragon app. 3.00
25-($3.99) Zero Year tie-in; Batman app.; back-up with Cowan-a 4.00
26-49: 26-31-Outsiders War; Lemire-s/Sorrentino-a/c. 35-40-Hitch-c; Felicity Smoak app. 3.00
50-($4.99) Kudranski-a; Deathstroke app. 5.00
51,52-Deathstroke app. 3.00
#0 (11/12) Origin story re-told; Nocenti-s/Williams II-a 3.00
Annual 1 (11/15, $4.99) Percy-s/Kudranski-a/Edwards-c 5.00
...: Futures End 1 (11/14, $2.99, regular-c) Five years later; Lemire-s/Sorrentino-a 3.00
...: Futures End 1 (11/14, $3.99, 3-D cover) 4.00

GREEN ARROW (DC Rebirth)
DC Comics: Aug, 2016 - Present ($2.99)
1-18: 1,2-Percy-a/Schmidt-a; Black Canary & Shado app. 3-5-Ferreyra-a. 14-Malcolm Merlyn returns 3.00
...: Rebirth 1 (8/16, $2.99) Percy-a/Schmidt-a; Black Canary app. 3.00

GREEN ARROW/BLACK CANARY (Titled Green Arrow for #30-32)
DC Comics: Dec, 2007 - No. 32, Jun, 2010 ($3.50/$2.99)
1-($3.50) Connor Hawke & Black Canary; follows Wedding Special; Winick-s/Chang-a 4.00
2-21-($2.99) 3-Two covers; Connor shot. 5-Dinah & Ollie's real wedding 3.00
22-30-($3.99) Back-up stories begin. 28-Origin of Cupid. 30-Blackest Night 4.00
30-Variant cover by Mike Grell 8.00
31-32-($2.99) Rise and Fall; Dallocchio-a 3.00
...: A League of Their Own TPB (2009, $17.99) r/#11-14 & G.A. Secret Files & Origins 18.00
...: Big Game TPB (2010, $19.99) r/#21-26 20.00
...: Enemies List TPB (2009, $17.99) r/#15-20 18.00
...: Family Business TPB (2008, $17.99) r/#5-10 18.00
...: Five Stages TPB (2010, $17.99) r/#27-30 18.00
...: Road To The Altar TPB (2008, $17.99) r/proposal pages from Green Arrow #75, Birds of

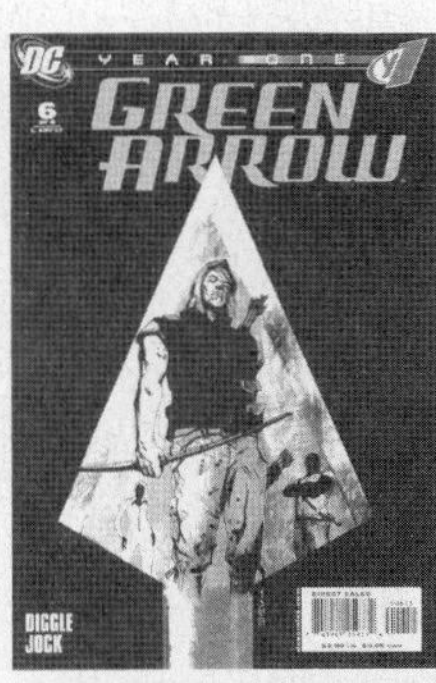

Green Arrow: Year One #6 © DC

Green Hornet (2010 series) #1 © G.H. Inc.

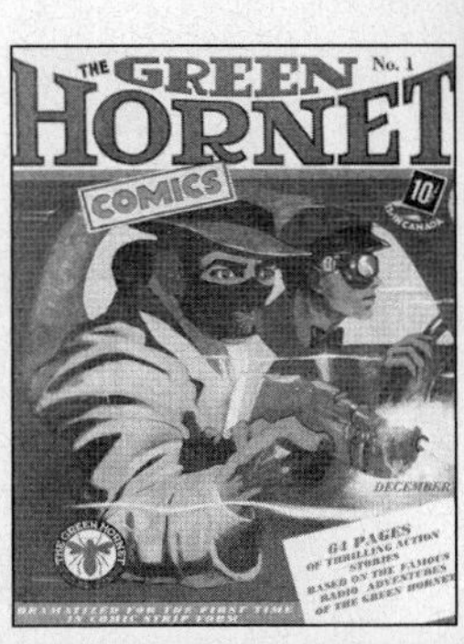

Green Hornet Comics #1 © HOKE

GD VG FN VF VF/NM NM-
2.0 4.0 6.0 8.0 9.0 9.2

Prey #109, Black Canary #1-4 and Black Canary Wedding Planner #1 18.00
...: The Wedding Album HC (2008, $19.99, dustjacket) r/#1-5 & Wedding Special #1 20.00
...: The Wedding Album SC (2009, $17.99) r/#1-5 & Wedding Special #1 18.00
... Wedding Special 1 (11/07, $3.99) Winick-s/Conner-a/c; Dinah & Ollie's "wedding" 5.00
... Wedding Special 1 (11/07, $3.99) 2nd printing with Ryan Sook variant-c 4.00

GREEN ARROW: THE LONG BOW HUNTERS
DC Comics: Aug, 1987 - No. 3, Oct, 1987 ($2.95, limited series, mature)

1-Grell-c/a in all 2 4 6 8 10 12
1,2-2nd printings 4.00
2,3 6.00
Trade paperback (1989, $12.95)-r/#1-3 15.00

GREEN ARROW: THE WONDER YEAR
DC Comics: Feb, 1993 - No. 4, May, 1993 ($1.75, limited series)

1-4: Mike Grell-a(p)/scripts & Gray Morrow-a(i) 4.00

GREEN ARROW: YEAR ONE
DC Comics: Early Sept, 2007 - No. 6, Late Nov, 2007 ($2.99, bi-weekly limited series)

1-6-Origin re-told; Diggle-s/Jock-a 3.00
1-Special Edition (12/14, $1.00) Reprints #1; Arrow TV show banner atop cover 3.00
HC (2008, $24.99) r/#1-6; intro. by Brian K. Vaughan; script and sketch pages 25.00
SC (2009, $14.99) r/#1-6; intro. by Brian K. Vaughan; script and sketch pages 15.00

GREEN BERET, THE (See Tales of...)

GREEN GIANT COMICS (Also see Colossus Comics)
Pelican Publ. (Funnies, Inc.): 1940 (No price on cover; distributed in New York City only)

1-Dr. Nerod, Green Giant, Black Arrow, Mundoo & Master Mystic app.; origin Colossus (Rare)
1350 2700 4050 9700 19,350 29,000

NOTE: *The idea for this book came from George Kapitan. Printed by Moreau Publ. of Orange, N.J. as an experiment to see if they could profitably use the idle time of their 40-page Hoe color press. The experiment failed due to the difficulty of obtaining good quality color registration and Mr. Moreau believes the book never reached the stands. The book has no price or date which lends credence to this. Contains five pages reprinted from Motion Picture Funnies Weekly.*

GREEN GOBLIN
Marvel Comics: Oct, 1995 - No. 13, Oct, 1996 ($2.95/$1.95)

1-($2.95)-Scott McDaniel-c/a begins, ends #7; foil-c 4.00
2-13: 2-Begin $1.95-c. 4-Hobgoblin-c/app; Thing app. 6-Daredevil-c/app. 8-Robertson-a; McDaniel-c. 12,13-Onslaught x-over. 13-Green Goblin quits; Spider-Man app. 3.00

GREENHAVEN
Aircel Publishing: 1988 - No. 3, 1988 ($2.00, limited series, 28 pgs.)

1-3 3.00

GREEN HORNET, THE (TV)
Dell Publishing Co./Gold Key: Sept, 1953; Feb, 1967 - No. 3, Aug, 1967

Four Color 496-Painted-c. 23 46 69 164 362 560
1-Bruce Lee photo-c and back-c pin-up 17 34 51 117 259 400
2,3-Bruce Lee photo-c 10 20 30 70 150 230

GREEN HORNET, THE (Also see Kato of the... & Tales of the...)
Now Comics: Nov, 1989 - No. 14, Feb, 1991 ($1.75)
V2#1, Sept, 1991 - V2#40, Jan, 1995 ($1.95)

1 ($2.95, double-size)-Steranko painted-c; G.A. Green Hornet 6.00
1,2: 1-2nd printing ('90, $3.95)-New Butler-c 4.00
3-14: 5-Death of original ('30s) Green Hornet. 6-Dave Dorman painted-c. 11-Snyder-c 4.00
V2#1-11,13-21,24-26,28-30,32-37: 1-Butler painted-c. 9-Mayerik-c 3.00
12-($2.50)-Color Green Hornet button polybagged inside 4.00
22,23-($2.95)-Bagged w/color hologravure card 4.00
27-($2.95)-Newsstand ed. polybagged w/multi-dimensional card (1993 Anniversary Special on cover), 27-($2.95)-Direct Sale ed. polybagged w/multi-dimensional card; cover variations 4.00
31,38: 31-($2.50)-Polybagged w/trading card 4.00
39,40-Low print run 6.00
1-($2.50)-Polybagged w/button (same as #12) 4.00
2,3-($1.95)-Same as #13 & 14 3.00
Annual 1 (12/92, $2.50), Annual 1994 (10/94, $2.95) 4.00

GREEN HORNET (Becomes Green Hornet: Legacy with #34)
Dynamite Entertainment: 2010 - No. 33, 2013 ($3.99)

1-Kevin Smith-s/Jonathan Lau-a; multiple covers by Alex Ross, Cassaday, Campbell and Segovia 4.00
2-33-Multiple covers by Ross and others on each. 11-Hester-s begins 4.00
Annual 1 (2010, $5.99) Hester-s/Netzer & Rafael-a 6.00
Annual 2 (2012, $4.99) Hester-c/Rahner-s/Cliquet-a; back-up r/G.H. Comics #1 (1940) 5.00
... FCBD Edition; 5 previews of various new Green Hornet series; Cassaday-c 3.00

GREEN HORNET

GD VG FN VF VF/NM NM-
2.0 4.0 6.0 8.0 9.0 9.2

Dynamite Entertainment: 2013 - No. 13, 2014 ($3.99)

1-13: 1-Set in 1941; Mark Waid-s/Daniel Indro-a; 2 covers by Alex Ross & Paolo Rivera 4.00

GREEN HORNET: AFTERMATH
Dynamite Entertainment: 2011 - No. 4, 2011 ($1.99/$3.99, limited series)

1-Nitz-s/Raynor-a; Green Hornet & Kato after the 2011 movie 3.00
2-4-($3.99) 4.00

GREEN HORNET: BLOOD TIES
Dynamite Entertainment: 2010 - No. 4, 2011 ($3.99)

1-4-Ande Parks-s/Johnny Desjardins-a; original Green Hornet & Kato 4.00

GREEN HORNET COMICS (...Racket Buster #44) (Radio, movies)
Helnit Publ. Co.(Holyoke) No. 1-6/Family Comics(Harvey) No. 7-on:
Dec, 1940 - No. 47, Sept, 1949 (See All New #13,14)(Early issues: 68 pgs.)

1-1st app. Green Hornet & Kato; text origin of Green Hornet on inside front-c; intro the Black Beauty (Green Hornet's car); painted-c 815 1630 2445 5950 10,975 16,000
2-(3/41) Early issues based on radio adventures 277 554 831 1759 3030 4300
3 181 362 543 1158 1979 2800
4-6: 6-(8/41) 161 322 483 1030 1765 2500
7 (6/42)-1st app. of the Green Hornet villain The Murdering Clown; origin The Zebra & begins; Robin Hood, Spirit of '76, Blonde Bomber & Mighty Midgets begin; new logo
148 296 444 947 1624 2300
8-Classic horror bondage killer dwarf-c 161 322 483 1030 1765 2500
9-Kirby-c 174 348 522 1114 1907 2700
10-(12/42) Hornet vs. The Murdering Clown-c/sty 129 258 387 826 1413 2000
11-Mr. Q app. 116 232 348 742 1271 1800
12-1st WWII cover for this title; Mr. Q app. 123 246 369 787 1344 1900
13-1st Nazi-c; shows Hitler poster on-c 232 464 696 1485 2543 3600
14-Bondage-c; Mr. Q app. 110 220 330 704 1202 1700
15-Nazi WWII-c 116 232 348 742 1271 1800
16-Nazi WWII prisoner of war cable car cover 123 246 369 787 1344 1900
17-Nazi WWII-c 116 232 348 742 1271 1800
18,19-Japanese WWII-c 116 232 348 742 1271 1800
20-Classic Japanese WWII-c 123 246 369 787 1344 1900
21-23-Japanese WWII-c 87 174 261 553 952 1350
24-Classic Japanese poison rockets Sci-Fi-c 116 232 348 742 1271 1800
25,27,28,30 50 100 150 315 533 750
26-(9/45) Japanese WWII-c 53 106 159 334 567 800
29-Jerry Robinson skull-c 52 104 156 328 552 775
31-The Man in Black Called Fate begins (11-12/45, early app.)
53 106 159 334 567 800
32-36 36 72 108 216 351 485
37,38: Shock Gibson app. by Powell. 37-S&K Kid Adonis reprinted from Stuntman #3. 38-Kid Adonis app. 36 72 108 211 343 475
39-Stuntman story by S&K 39 78 117 236 388 540
40-47: 42-47-Kerry Drake in all. 45-Boy Explorers on-c only. 46- "Case of the Marijuana Racket" cover/story; Kerry Drake app. 27 54 81 160 263 365

NOTE: ***Fuje** a-23, 24, 26. **Henkle** c-7-9. **Kubert** a-20, 30. **Powell** a-7-10, 12, 14, 16-21, 30, 31(2), 32(3), 33, 34(3), 35, 36, 37(2), 38. **Robinson** a-27. **Schomburg** c-17-23. Kirbyish c-7, 15. Bondage c-8, 11, 14, 18, 26, 36.*

GREEN HORNET: DARK TOMORROW
Now Comics: Jun, 1993 - No. 3, Aug, 1993 ($2.50, limited series)

1-3: Future Green Hornet 3.00

GREEN HORNET: GOLDEN AGE RE-MASTERED
Dynamite Entertainment: 2010 - No. 8, 2011 ($3.99)

1-8-Re-colored reprints of 1940's Green Hornet Comics; new Rubenstein-c 4.00

GREEN HORNET: LEGACY (Numbering continues from Green Hornet 2010-2013 series)
Dynamite Entertainment: No. 34, 2013 - No. 42, 2013 ($3.99)

34-42: 34-Jai Nitz-s/Jethro Morales-a 4.00

GREEN HORNET: PARALLEL LIVES
Dynamite Entertainment: 2010 - No. 5, 2010 ($3.99, limited series)

1-5-Jai Nitz-s/Nigel Raynor-a; semi-prequel to the 2011 movie; Kato's origin 4.00

GREEN HORNET: REIGN OF THE DEMON
Dynamite Entertainment: 2016 - No. 4, 2017 ($3.99, limited series)

1-4-David Liss-s/Kewber Baal-a 4.00

GREEN HORNET: SOLITARY SENTINEL, THE
Now Comics: Dec, 1992 - No. 3, 1993 ($2.50, limited series)

1-3 3.00

GREEN HORNET STRIKES!
Dynamite Entertainment: 2010 - No. 10, 2012 ($3.99, limited series)

1-10: 1-Matthews-s/Padilla-a/Cassaday-c; future Green Hornet 4.00

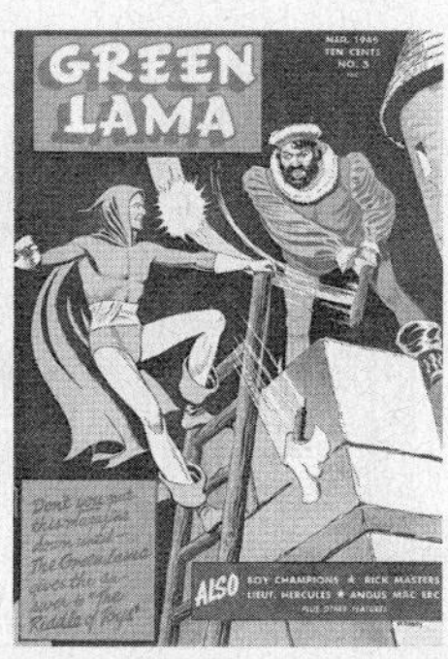

Green Lama #3 © Spark

Green Lantern #19 © DC

Green Lantern (2nd series) #67 © DC

GD VG FN VF VF/NM NM-
2.0 4.0 6.0 8.0 9.0 9.2

GREEN HORNET: YEAR ONE
Dynamite Entertainment: 2010 - No. 12, 2011 ($3.99, limited series)
1-12-Matt Wagner-s/Aaron Campbell-a; 1940s' Green Hornet & Kato. 1-5-Cassaday-c 4.00
...: Special 1 (2013, $4.99) Crosby-s/Menna-a/Chen-c 5.00

GREEN JET COMICS, THE (See Comic Books, Series 1 in the Promotional Comics section)

GREEN LAMA (Also see Comic Books, Series 1, Daring Adventures #17 & Prize Comics #7)
Spark Publications/Prize No. 7 on: Dec, 1944 - No. 8, Mar, 1946
1-Intro. Lt. Hercules & The Boy Champions; Mac Raboy-c/a #1-8
129 258 387 826 1413 2000
2-Lt. Hercules borrows the Human Torch's powers for one panel
71 142 213 454 777 1100
3-5,8: 4-Dick Tracy take-off in Lt. Hercules story by H. L. Gold (science fiction writer); Japanese WWII-c. 5-Nazi WWII-c; Hitler story; Lt. Hercules story; Little Orphan Annie, Smilin' Jack & Snuffy Smith take-off (5/45) 55 110 165 352 601 850
6-Classic Raboy swastika-c 71 142 213 454 777 1100
7-X-mas-c; Raboy craft tint-c/a (note: a small quantity of NM copies surfaced)
34 68 102 199 325 450
... Archives Featuring the Art of Mac Raboy Vol. 1 HC (Dark Horse Books, 4/08, $49.95) r/#1-4 including back-up features; foreward by Chuck Rozanski 50.00
... Archives Featuring the Art of Mac Raboy Vol. 2 HC (Dark Horse Books, 1/09, $49.95) r/#5-8; foreward by Chuck Rozanski 50.00
NOTE: ***Robinson*** *a-3-5, 8.* ***Roussos*** *a-8. Formerly a pulp hero who began in 1940.*

GREEN LANTERN (1st Series) (See All-American, All Flash Quarterly, All Star Comics, The Big All-American & Comic Cavalcade)
National Periodical Publications/All-American: Fall, 1941 - No. 38, May-June, 1949 (#1-18 are quarterly)
1-Origin retold; classic Purcell-c 2700 5400 8100 22,000 39,500 72,000
2-1st book-length story 676 1352 2028 4935 8718 12,500
3-Classic German war-c by Mart Nodell 660 1320 1980 4818 8509 12,200
4-Green Lantern & Doiby Dickles join the Army 400 800 1200 2800 4900 7000
5-WWII-c 326 652 978 2282 3991 5700
6,8: 8-Hop Harrigan begins; classic-c 300 600 900 1920 3310 4700
7-Classic robot-c 303 606 909 2121 3711 5300
9 245 490 735 1568 2684 3800
10-Origin/1st app. Vandal Savage 290 580 870 1856 3178 4500
11,13-15 171 342 513 1086 1868 2650
12-Origin/1st app. Gambler 187 374 561 1197 2049 2900
16-Classic jungle-c (scarce in high grade) 190 380 570 1207 2079 2950
17,19,20 145 290 435 921 1586 2250
18-Christmas-c 190 380 570 1207 2079 2950
21-26 142 284 426 909 1555 2200
27-Origin/1st app. Sky Pirate 174 348 522 1114 1907 2700
28-1st Sportsmaster (Crusher Crock) 158 316 474 1003 1727 2450
29-All Harlequin issue; classic Harlequin-c 213 426 639 1363 2332 3300
30-Origin/1st app. Streak the Wonder Dog by Toth (2-3/48) (Rare)
423 846 1269 3000 5250 7500
31-Harlequin-c/app. 135 270 405 864 1482 2100
32-35: 35-Kubert-c. 35-38-New logo 126 252 378 806 1378 1950
36-38: 37-Sargon the Sorcerer app. 148 296 444 947 1624 2300
NOTE: *Book-length stories #2-7.* ***Mayer/Moldoff*** *c-9.* ***Mayer/Purcell*** *c-8.* ***Purcell*** *c-1.* ***Mart Nodell*** *c-2, 3, 7.* ***Paul Reinman*** *c-11, 12, 15-22.* ***Toth*** *a-28, 30, 31, 34-38; c-28, 30, 34p, 36-38p. Cover to #8 says Fall while the indicia says Summer Issue. Streak the Wonder Dog c-30 (w/Green Lantern), 34, 36, 38.*

GREEN LANTERN (See Action Comics Weekly, Adventure Comics, Brave & the Bold, Day of Judgment, DC Special, DC Special Series, Flash, Guy Gardner, Guy Gardner Reborn, JLA, JSA, Justice League of America, Parallax: Emerald Night, Showcase, Showcase '93 #12 & Tales of The...Corps)

GREEN LANTERN (2nd Series)(Green Lantern Corps #206 on) (See Showcase #22-24)
National Periodical Publ./DC Comics: Jul/Aug. 1960 - No. 89, Apr/May 1972; No. 90, Aug/Sept. 1976 - No. 205, Oct, 1986
1-(7-8/60)-Origin retold; Gil Kane-c/a continues; 1st app. Guardians of the Universe
450 900 1350 4200 10,600 17,000
2-1st Pieface 82 164 246 656 1478 2300
3-Contains readers poll 46 92 138 368 834 1300
4,5: 5-Origin/1st app. Hector Hammond 41 82 123 303 689 1075
6-Intro Tomar-Re the alien G.L. 40 80 120 296 673 1050
7-Origin/1st app. Sinestro (7-8/61) 79 158 237 632 1416 2200
8-1st 5700 A.D. story; grey tone-c 36 72 108 259 580 900
9-1st Sinestro-c; 1st Jordan Brothers; last 10¢-c 34 68 102 245 548 850
10 31 62 93 223 499 775
11,12 21 42 63 147 324 500
13-Flash x-over 32 64 96 230 515 800
14,15,17-20: 14-Origin/1st app. Sonar. 20-Flash x-over
17 34 51 117 259 400

GD VG FN VF VF/NM NM-
2.0 4.0 6.0 8.0 9.0 9.2

16-Origin & 1st app. (Silver Age) Star Sapphire 36 72 108 259 580 900
21,22,25-28,30: 21-Origin & 1st app. Dr. Polaris 12 24 36 81 176 270
23-1st Tattooed Man 14 28 42 96 211 325
24-Origin & 1st app. Shark 15 30 45 100 220 340
29-JLA cameo; 1st Blackhand 13 26 39 91 201 310
31-39: 37-1st app. Evil Star (villain) 10 20 30 69 147 225
40-Origin of Infinite Earths (10/65); 2nd solo G.A. Green Lantern in Silver Age (see Showcase #55); origin The Guardians; Doiby Dickles app. 46 92 138 335 760 1185
41-44,46-50: 42-Zatanna x-over. 43-Flash x-over 9 18 27 60 120 180
45-2nd S.A. app. G.A. Green Lantern in title (6/66) 13 26 39 91 201 310
51,53-58 8 16 24 51 96 140
52-G.A. Green Lantern x-over; Sinestro app. 10 20 30 66 138 210
59-1st app. Guy Gardner (3/68) 21 42 63 147 324 500
60,62-69: 69-Wood inks; last 12¢ issue 6 12 18 38 69 100
61-G.A. Green Lantern x-over 7 14 21 44 82 120
70-75 5 10 15 34 60 85
76-(4/70)-Begin Green Lantern/Green Arrow series (by Neal Adams #76-89) ends #122 (see Flash #217 for 2nd series) 96 192 288 768 1734 2700
77 11 22 33 76 163 250
78-80 10 20 30 66 138 210
81-84: 82-Wrightson-i(1 pg.). 83-G.L. reveals i.d. to Carol Ferris. 84-N. Adams/Wrightson-a (22 pgs.); last 15¢-c; partial photo-c 9 18 27 59 117 175
85,86-(52 pgs.)-Classic anti-drug covers/stories; Speedy as a heroin junkie. 86-G.A. Green Lantern-r; Toth-a 11 22 33 76 163 250
87-(52 pgs.): 2nd app. Guy Gardner (cameo); 1st app. John Stewart (12-1/71-72) (becomes 3rd Green Lantern in #182) 18 36 54 124 275 425
88-(2-3/72, 52 pgs.)-Unpubbed G.A. Green Lantern story; Green Lantern-r/Showcase #23. N. Adams-c/a (1 pg.) 7 14 21 49 92 135
89-(4-5/72, 52 pgs.)-G.A. Green Lantern-r; Green Lantern & Green Arrow move to Flash #217 (2nd team-up series) 8 16 24 56 108 160
90 (8-9/76)-Begin 3rd Green Lantern/Green Arrow team-up series; Mike Grell-c/a begins, ends #111 3 6 9 17 26 35
91-99 2 4 6 10 16 20
100-(1/78, Giant)-1st app. Air Wave II 3 6 9 16 23 30
101-107,111,113-115,117-119: 107-1st Tales of the G.L. Corps story
2 4 6 8 11 14
108-110-(44 pgs)-G.A. Green Lantern back-ups in each. 111-Origin retold; G.A. Green Lantern app. 2 4 6 10 14 18
112-G.A. Green Lantern origin retold 2 4 6 13 18 22
116-1st app. Guy Gardner as a G.L. (5/79) 4 8 12 27 44 60
116-Whitman variant; issue # on cover 5 10 15 31 53 75
117-119,121-(Whitman variants; low print run; none have issue # on cover)
2 4 6 10 14 18
120,121,123-140,142-150: 123-Last Green Lantern/Green Arrow team-up. 130-132-Tales of the G.L. Corps. 132-Adam Strange series begins, ends147. 136,137-1st app. Citadel; Space Ranger app. 142,143-Omega Men app.;Perez-c. 144-Omega Men cameo. 148-Tales of the G.L. Corps begins, ends #173. 150-Anniversary issue, 52 pgs.; no G.L. Corps 1 2 3 5 7 9
122-2nd app. Guy Gardner as Green Lantern; Flash & Hawkman brief app.
3 6 9 14 20 25
141-1st app. Omega Men (6/81) 2 4 6 11 16 20
151-180,183,184,186,187: 159-Origin Evil Star. 160,161-Omega Men app. 172-Gibbons-c/a begins. 175-No issue number shown on cover 6.00
181,182,185,188,191: 181-Hal Jordan resigns as G.L. 182-John Stewart becomes new G.L.; origin recap of Hal Jordan as G.L. 185-Origin new G.L. (John Stewart).188-I.D. revealed; 1st app. Mogo; Alan Moore back-up scripts. 191-Re-intro Star Sapphire (cameo)
1 2 3 5 6 8
189,190,193,196-199,202-205: 194,198-Crisis x-over. 199-Hal Jordan returns as a member of G.L. Corps (3 G.L.s now). 5.00
192-Re-intro & origin of Star Sapphire (1st full app.) 2 4 6 9 13 16
194-Hal Jordan/Guy Gardner battle; Guardians choose Guy Gardner to become new Green Lantern 1 2 3 5 6 8
195-Guy Gardner becomes Green Lantern; Crisis on Infinite Earths x-over
2 4 6 9 13 16
200-Double-size 6.00
201-Green Lantern Corps begins (is cover title, says premiere issue); intro. Kilowog
3 6 9 14 20 25
Annual 1 (Listed as Tales Of The Green Lantern Corps Annual 1)
Annual 2,3 (See Green Lantern Corps Annual #2,3) 5.00
Special 1 (1988), 2 (1989)-(Both $1.50, 52 pgs.) 5.00
... Chronicles TPB (2009, $14.99) r/Showcase #22-24 & Green Lantern #1-3 15.00
... Chronicles Vol. 2 TPB (2009, $14.99) r/Green Lantern #4-9 15.00
... Chronicles Vol. 3 TPB (2010, $14.99) r/Green Lantern #10-14 and Flash #131 15.00
NOTE: ***N. Adams*** *a-76, 77-87p, 89; c-63, 76-89.* ***M. Anderson*** *a-137i.* ***Austin*** *a-93i, 94i, 171i.* ***Chaykin*** *c-196.* ***Greene*** *a-39-49i, 58-63i; c-54-58i.* ***Grell*** *a-90-100, 106, 108-111; c-90-106, 108-112.* ***Heck*** *a-120-122p.* ***Infantino***

Green Lantern (3rd series) #86 © DC

Green Lantern (3rd series) #156 © DC

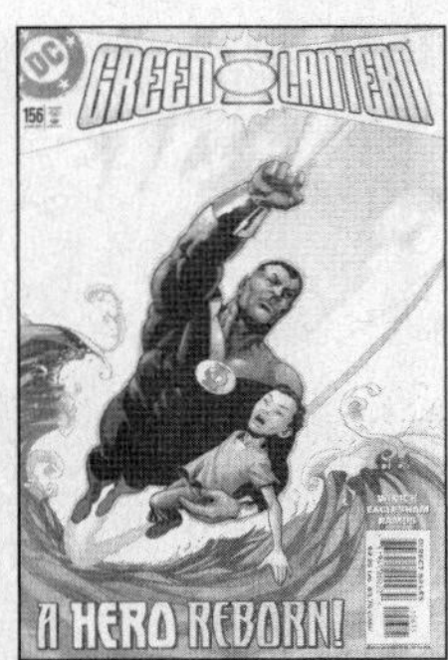

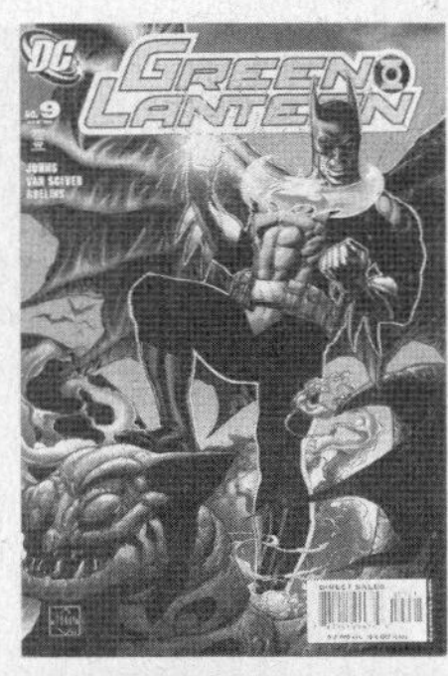

Green Lantern (2005 series) #9 © DC

	GD 2.0	VG 4.0	FN 6.0	VF 8.0	VF/NM 9.0	NM- 9.2

a-137p, 145-147p, 151, 152p. ***Gil Kane*** *a-1-49p, 50-57, 58-61p, 68-75p, 85p(r), 87p(r), 88p(r), 156, 177, 184p; c-1-52, 54-61p, 67-75, 123, 154, 156, 165-171, 177, 184.* ***Newton*** *a-148p, 149p, 181.* ***Perez*** *c-132p, 141-144.* ***Sekowsky*** *a-65p, 170p.* ***Simonson*** *c-200.* ***Sparling*** *a-63p.* ***Starlin*** *c-129, 133.* ***Staton*** *a-117p, 123-127p, 128, 129-131p, 132-139, 140p, 141-146, 147p, 148-150, 151-155p; c-107p, 117p, 135(i), 136p, 145p, 146, 147, 148-152p, 155p.* ***Toth*** *a-86r, 171p.* ***Tuska*** *a-166-168p, 170p.*

GREEN LANTERN (3rd Series)
DC Comics: June, 1990 - No. 181, Nov, 2004 ($1.00/$1.25/$1.50/$1.75/$1.95/$1.99/$2.25)

1-Hal Jordan, John Stewart & Guy Gardner return; Batman & JLA app. 6.00
2-18,20-26: 9-12-Guy Gardner solo story. 13-(52 pgs.). 18-Guy Gardner solo story. 25-($1.75, 52 pgs.)-Hal Jordan/Guy Gardner battle 4.00
19-($1.75, 52 pgs.)-50th anniversary issue; Mart Nodell (original G.A. artist) part-p on G.A. Green Lantern; G. Kane-c 5.00
27-45,47: 30,31-Gorilla Grodd-c/story(see Flash #69). 38,39-Adam Strange-c/story. 42-Deathstroke-c/s. 47-Green Arrow x-over 4.00
46,48,49,50: 46-Superman app. cont'd in Superman #82. 48-Emerald Twilight part 1. 50-($2.95, 52 pgs.)-Glow-in-the-dark-c 6.00
0, 51-62: 51-1st app. New Green Lantern (Kyle Rayner) with new costume. 53-Superman-c/story. 55-(9/94)-Zero Hour. 0-(10/94). 56-(11/94) 4.00
63,64-Kyle Rayner vs. Hal Jordan. 4.00
65-80,82-92: 63-Begin $1.75-c. 65-New Titans app. 66,67-Flash app. 71-Batman & Robin app. 72-Shazam!-c/app. 73-Wonder Woman-c/app. 73-75-Adam Strange app. 76,77-Green Arrow x-over. 80-Final Night. 87-JLA app. 91-Genesis x-over. 92-Green Arrow x-over 3.00
81-(Regular Ed.)-Memorial for Hal Jordan (Parallax); most DC heroes app. 5.00
81-($3.95, Deluxe Edition)-Embossed prism-c 6.00
93-99: 93-Begin $1.95-c; Deadman app. 94-Superboy app. 95-Starlin-a(p). 98,99-Legion of Super-Heroes-c/app. 3.00
100-($2.95) Two covers (Jordan & Rayner); vs. Sinestro 6.00
101-106: 101-106-Hal Jordan-c/app. 103-JLA-c/app. 104-Green Arrow app. 105,106-Parallax app. 3.00
107-126: 107-Jade becomes a Green Lantern. 119-Hal Jordan/Spectre app. 125-JLA app. 3.00
127-149: 127-Begin $2.25-c. 129-Winick-s begin. 134-136-JLA-c/app. 143-Joker: Last Laugh; Lee-c. 145-Kyle becomes The Ion. 149-Superman-c/app. 3.00
150-($3.50) Jim Lee-c; Kyle becomes Green Lantern again; new costume 4.00
151-181: 151-155-Jim Lee-c: 154-Terry attacked. 155-Spectre-c/app. 162-164-Crossover with Green Arrow #23-25. 165-Raab-s begin. 169-Kilowog returns 3.00
#1,000,000 (11/98) 853rd Century x-over; Hitch & Neary-a/c 3.00
Annual 1-3: ('92-'94, 68 pgs.)-1-Eclipso app. 2 -Intro Nightblade. 3-Elseworlds story 4.00
Annual 4 (1995, $3.50)-Year One story 4.00
Annual 5,7,8 ('96, '98, '99, $2.95): 5-Legends of the Dead Earth. 7-Ghosts; Wrightson-c. 8-JLApe; Art Adams-c 4.00
Annual 6 (1997, $3.95)-Pulp Heroes story 5.00
Annual 9 (2000, $3.50) Planet DC 4.00
...80 Page Giant (12/98, $4.95) Stories by various 5.00
...80 Page Giant 2 (6/99, $4.95) Team-ups 5.00
...80 Page Giant 3 (8/00, $5.95) Darkseid vs. the GL Corps 6.00
...: 1001 Emerald Nights (2001, $6.95) Elseworlds; Guay-a/c; LaBan-s 7.00
...3-D #1 (12/98, $3.95) Jeanty-a 4.00
...: A New Dawn TPB (1998, $9.95)-r/#50-55 10.00
...: Baptism of Fire TPB (1999, $12.95)-r/#59,66,67,70-75 13.00
...: Brother's Keeper (2003, $12.95)-r/#151-155; Green Lantern Secret Files #3 13.00
...: Emerald Allies TPB (2000, $14.95)-r/GL/GA team-ups 15.00
...: Emerald Knights TPB (1998, $12.95)-r/Hal Jordan's return 13.00
...: Emerald Twilight nn (1994, $5.95)-r/#48-50 6.00
...: Emerald Twilight/New Dawn TPB (2003, $19.95)-r/#48-55 20.00
...: Ganthet's Tale nn (1992, $5.95, 68 pgs.)-Silver foil logo; Niven scripts; Byrne-c/a 6.00
.../Green Arrow Vol. 1 (2004, $12.95) -r/GL #76-82; intro. by O'Neil 13.00
.../Green Arrow Vol. 2 (2004, $12.95) -r/GL #83-87,89 & Flash #217-219, 226; cover gallery with 1983-84 GL/GA covers #1-7; intro. by Giordano 13.00
.../Green Arrow Collection, Vol. 2-r/GL #84-87,89 & Flash #217-219 & GL/GA #5-7 by O'Neil/Adams/Wrightson 13.00
...: New Journey, Old Path TPB (2001, $12.95)-r/#129-136 13.00
... : Our Worlds at War (8/01, $2.95) Jae Lee-c; prelude to x-over 3.00
...: Passing The Torch (2004, $12.95, TPB) r/#156,158-161 & GL Secret Files #2 13.00
...Plus 1 (12/1996, $2.95)-The Ray & Polaris-c/app. 4.00
...Secret Files 1-3 (7/98-7/02, $4.95)1-Origin stories & profiles. 2-Grell-c 5.00
.../Superman: Legend of the Green Flame (2000, $5.95) 1988 unpub. Neil Gaiman story of Hal Jordan with new art by various; Frank Miller-c 6.00
...: The Power of Ion (2003, $14.95, TPB) r/#142-150 15.00
...The Road Back nn (1992, $8.95)-r/1-8 w/covers 9.00
...: Traitor TPB (2001, $12.95) r/Legends of the DCU #20,21,28,29,37,38 13.00
...: Willworld (2001, $24.95, HC) Seth Fisher-a/J.M. DeMatteis-s; Hal Jordan 25.00
...: Willworld (2003, $17.95, SC) Seth Fisher-a/J.M. DeMatteis-s; Hal Jordan 18.00
NOTE: ***Staton*** *a(p)-9-12; c-9-12.*

GREEN LANTERN (See Tangent Comics/ Green Lantern)

GREEN LANTERN (4th Series) (Follows Hal Jordan's return in Green Lantern: Rebirth)
DC Comics: July, 2005 - No. 67, Aug, 2011 ($3.50/$2.99)

1-($3.50) Two covers by Pacheco and Ross; Johns-s/Van Sciver and Pacheco-a 5.00
2-20-($2.99) 2-4-Manhunters app. 6-Bianchi-a. 7,8-Green Arrow app. 8-Bianchi-c. 9-Batman app.; two covers by Bianchi and Van Sciver. 10,11-Reis-a. 17-19-Star Sapphire returns. 18-Acuna-a; Sinestro Corps back-ups begin 3.00
8-Variant-c by Neal Adams 8.00
21-Sinestro Corps War pt. 2 5.00
21-2nd printing with variant green hued background-c 3.00
22-24: 22-Sinestro Corps War pt. 4; green hued-c. 23-Part 6. 24-Part 8 4.00
22,23-2nd printings. 22-Yellow hued-c. 23-B&W Hal Jordan with colored rings 3.00
25-($4.99) Sinestro Corps War conclusion; Ivan Reis-c 6.00
25-($4.99) Variant cover by Gary Frank; Sinestro Corps War conclusion 8.00
26-28,30-43: 26-Alpha Lanterns. 30-35-Childhood & origin re-told; Sinestro app. 41-Origin Larfleeze. 43-Prologue to Blackest Night, origin of Black Hand; Mahnke-a 3.00
29-Childhood & origin re-told 5.00
29-Special Edition (6/10, $1.00) reprints #29 with "What's Next?" logo on cover 3.00
29-Special Edition (2010 San Diego Comic-Con giveaway) reprints #29 with new Van Sciver cover and Geoff Johns intro on inside front cover 3.00
39-43-Variant covers: 39,40-Migliari. 41-42-Barrows 12.00
44-49,51,52-Blackest Night. 44-Flash app. 46-Sinestro vs. Mongul. 47-Black Lantern Abin Sur. 49-Art by Benes & Ordway; Atom and Mera app. 51-Nekron app. 3.00
44-49,51-Variant covers: 44-Tan. 45-Manapul. 46. Andy Kubert. 47-Benes. 48-Morales. 49-Migliari. 51-Horn. 52-Shane Davis 8.00
50-($3.99)-Black Lantern Spectre & Parallax app.; Mahnke-a/c 4.00
50-Variant-c by Jim Lee 12.00
53-67: 53-62-Brightest Day. 54,55-Lobo app. 58-60-Flash app. 60-Krona returns. 64-67-War of the Green Lanterns x-over. 67-Sinestro becomes a Green Lantern 3.00
FCBD 2011 Green Lantern Flashpoint Special Edition (6/11, giveaway) r/#30 and previews Flashpoint x-over; Andy Kubert-a 3.00
...: Larfleeze Christmas Special 1 (2/11, $3.99) Johns-s/Booth-a/Ha-c 4.00
.../Plastic Man: Weapons of Mass Deception (2/11, $4.99) Brent Anderson-a 5.00
...Secret Files and Origins 2005 (6/05, $4.99) Johns-s/Cooke & Van Sciver-a; profiles with art by various incl. Chaykin, Gibbons, Gleason, Igle; Pacheco-c 5.00
.../Sinestro Corps: Secret Files 1 (2/08, $4.99) Profiles of Green Lanterns and Corps info 5.00
...: Agent Orange HC (2009, $19.99) r/#38-42 & Blackest Night #0; sketch art 20.00
...: Agent Orange SC (2010, $14.99) r/#38-42 & Blackest Night #0; sketch art 15.00
Blackest Night: Green Lantern HC (2010, $24.99) r/#43-52; variant covers; sketch art 25.00
Blackest Night: Green Lantern SC (2011, $19.99) r/#43-52; variant covers; sketch art 20.00
...: Brightest Day HC (2011, $22.99) r/#53-62; variant cover gallery 23.00
...: In Brightest Day SC (2008, $19.99) r/stories selected by Geoff Johns w/commentary 20.00
...: No Fear HC (2006, $24.99) r/#1-6 & Secret Files and Origins 25.00
...: No Fear SC (2008, $12.99) r/#1-6 & Secret Files and Origins 13.00
...: Rage of the Red Lanterns HC (2009, $24.99) r/#26-28,36-38 & Final Crisis: Rage... 25.00
...: Rage of the Red Lanterns SC (2010, $14.99) r/#26-28,36-38 & Final Crisis: Rage... 15.00
...: Revenge of the Green Lanterns HC (2006, $19.99) r/#7-13; variant cover gallery 20.00
...: Revenge of the Green Lanterns SC (2008, $12.99) r/#7-13; variant cover gallery 13.00
...: Secret Origin HC (2008, $19.99) r/#29-35 20.00
...: Secret Origin (New Edition) HC (2010, $19.99) r/#29-35; intro. by Ryan Reynolds 20.00
...: Secret Origin SC (2008, $14.99) r/#29-35 15.00
...: Secret Origin (New Edition) SC (2011, $14.99) r/#29-35; intro. by Ryan Reynolds; photo-c of Reynolds from movie; movie preview photo gallery 15.00
... Super Spectacular (1/12, $7.99, magazine-size) r/Blackest Night #0,1, Green Lantern #76 from 1970 and Brave and the Bold #30 from 2009 8.00
...: Tales of the Sinestro Corps HC (2008, $29.99, d.j.) r/back-up stories from #18-20, Tales of the Sinestro Corps series, Green Lantern: Sinestro Corps Special and Sinestro Corps: Secret Files 30.00
...: Tales of the Sinestro Corps SC (2009, $14.99) same contents as HC 15.00
...: The Sinestro Corps War Vol. 1 HC (2008, $24.99, d.j.) r/#21-23, Green Lantern Corps #14-15 and Green Lantern: Sinestro Corps Special 25.00
...: The Sinestro Corps War Vol. 1 SC (2009, $14.99) same contents as HC 15.00
...: The Sinestro Corps War Vol. 2 HC (2008, $24.99, d.j.) r/#24,25, Green Lantern Corps #16-19; interview with the creators and sketch art 25.00
... - Wanted: Hal Jordan HC (2007, $19.99) r/#14-20 without Sinestro Corps back-ups 20.00
... - Wanted: Hal Jordan SC (2008, $14.99) r/#14-20 without Sinestro Corps back-ups 15.00

GREEN LANTERN (DC New 52)
DC Comics: Nov, 2011 - No. 52, Jul, 2016 ($2.99/$3.99)

1-19: 1-Sinestro as Green Lantern; Johns-s/Mahnke-a/Reis-c (1st & 2nd print). 6-Choi-a. 9-Origin of the Indigo tribe. 14-Justice League app. 17-19-Wrath of the First Lantern 3.00
1-9-Variant-c. 1-Capullo. 2-Finch. 3-Van Sciver. 4-Manapul. 5-Choi. 6-Reis. 8-Keown 4.00
8-Combo pack ($3.99) polybagged with digital code 4.00
20-($7.99, squarebound) Conclusion of "Wrath of the First Lantern"; last Johns-s 8.00
21-23: 21-Venditti-s/Tan-a begin 3.00

Green Lantern (2011 series) #23.1 © DC

Green Lantern Corps #39 © DC

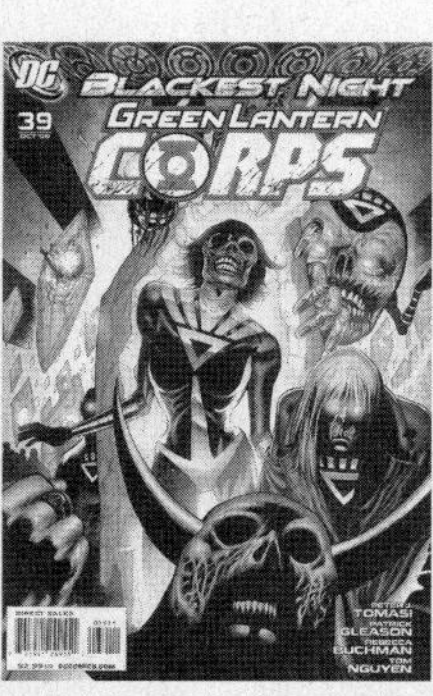

Green Lantern: Mosaic #15 © DC

GD VG FN VF VF/NM NM-
2.0 4.0 6.0 8.0 9.0 9.2

23.1, 23.2, 23.3, 23.4 (11/13, $2.99, regular covers) 3.00
23.1 (11/13, $3.99, 3-D cover) "Relic #1" on cover; origin of Relic; Morales-a 6.00
23.2 (11/13, $3.99, 3-D cover) "Mongul #1" on cover; origin; Starlin-s/Porter-a 5.00
23.3 (11/13, $3.99, 3-D cover) "Black Hand #1" on cover; Soule-s/Ponticelli-a 5.00
23.4 (11/13, $3.99, 3-D cover) "Sinestro #1" on cover; origin; Kindt-s/Eaglesham-a 5.00
24-27,29-34: 24-Lights Out pt. 1; Relic app.; Central Battery destroyed 3.00
28-Flip-book with Red Lanterns #28; Red Lantern Supergirl app. 3.00
35-40: 35-37-Godhead x-over; New Gods, Orion & Metron app. 36,37-Black Hand app. 3.00
41-49,51,52-($3.99) 42,43,45,46-Black Hand app. 43-Relic returns. 47-Parallax app. 4.00
50-($4.99) Parallax app.; Sienkiewicz-c 5.00
#0 (11/12, $2.99) Simon Baz becomes a Green Lantern; Mahnke-a 3.00
Annual 1 (10/12, $4.99) 1st print w/black-c; Rise of the Third Army prologue 5.00
Annual 2 (12/13, $4.99) Lights Out pt. 5; Sean Chen-a 5.00
Annual 3 (2/15, $4.99) Godhead conclusion; Van Sciver-c 5.00
Annual 4 (11/15, $4.99) Venditti-s/Alixe-a 5.00
...: Futures End 1 (11/14, $2.99, regular-c) Five years later; Relic app. 3.00
...: Futures End 1 (11/14, $3.99, 3-D cover) 4.00
.../New Gods: Godhead 1 (12/14, $4.99) Part 1 to Godhead x-over; Highfather app. 5.00

GREEN LANTERN ANNUAL NO. 1, 1963
DC Comics: 1998 ($4.95, one-shot)

1-Reprints Golden Age & Silver Age stories in 1963-style 80 pg. Giant format; new Gil Kane sketch art 5.00

GREEN LANTERN: BRIGHTEST DAY; BLACKEST NIGHT
DC Comics: 2002 ($5.95, squarebound, one-shot)

nn-Alan Scott vs. Solomon Grundy in 1944; Snyder III-c/a; Seagle-s 1 2 3 5 6 8

GREEN LANTERN: CIRCLE OF FIRE
DC Comics: Early Oct, 2000 - No. 2, Late Oct, 2000 (limited series)

1-($4.95) Intro. other Green Lanterns 5.00
2-($3.75) 4.00
Green Lantern (x-overs)- .../Adam Strange; .../Atom; .../Firestorm; ... /Green Lantern, Winick-s; .../Power Girl (all $2.50-c) 3.00
TPB (2002, $17.95) r/#1,2 & x-overs 18.00

GREEN LANTERN CORPS, THE (Formerly Green Lantern; see Tales of...)
DC Comics: No. 206, Nov, 1986 - No. 224, May, 1988

206-223: 212-John Stewart marries Katma Tui. 220,221-Millennium tie-ins 4.00
224-Double-size last issue 5.00
...Corps Annual 2,3- (12/86,8/87) 1-Formerly Tales of ...Annual #1; Alan Moore scripts. 3-Indicia says Green Lantern Annual #3; Moore scripts; Byrne-a 5.00

NOTE: ***Austin*** *a-Annual 3i.* ***Gil Kane*** *a-223, 224p; c-223, 224, Annual 2.* ***Russell*** *a-Annual 3i.* ***Staton*** *a-207-213p, 217p, 221p, 222p, Annual 3; c-207-213p, 217p, 221p, 222p.* ***Willingham*** *a-213p, 219p, 220p, 218p, 219p, Annual 2, 3p; c-218p, 219p.*

GREEN LANTERN CORPS
DC Comics: Aug, 2006 - No. 63, Oct, 2011 ($2.99)

1,14-19: 1-Gibbons-s. 14-19-Sinestro Corps War pts. 3,5,7,9,10, Epilogue 4.00
2-13: 2-6,10,11-Gibbons-s. 9-Darkseid app. 3.00
20-38: 20-Mongul app. 3.00
20-Second printing with sketch-c 3.00
34-38: 34-37-Variant covers by Migliari. 38-Fabry var-c 10.00
39-45-Blackest Night. 43-45-Red Lantern Guy Gardner 3.00
39-45-Variant covers: 39-Jusko. 40-Tucci. 41,42,44-Horn. 43-Ladronn. 45 Bolland 8.00
46,47-($3.99) 46-Blackest Night. 47-Brightest Day 4.00
48-61-($2.99) 48-Migliari-c; Ganthet joins the Corps. 49-52-Cyborg Superman app. 58-60-War of the Green Lanterns x-over. 60-Mogo destroyed 3.00
Blackest Night: Green Lantern Corps HC (2010, $24.99, d.j.) r/#39-47, cover gallery 25.00
Blackest Night: Green Lantern Corps SC (2011, $19.99) r/#39-47, cover gallery 20.00
...: Emerald Eclipse HC (2009, $24.99) r/#33-39; gallery of variant covers 25.00
...: Emerald Eclipse SC (2010, $14.99) r/#33-39; gallery of variant covers 15.00
...: Revolt of the Alpha-Lanterns HC (2011, $22.99) r/#21,22,48-52 23.00
...: Ring Quest TPB (2008, $14.99) r/#19,20,23-26 15.00
...: The Dark Side of Green TPB (2007, $12.99) r/#7-13 13.00
...: To Be a Lantern TPB (2007, $12.99) r/#1-6 13.00

GREEN LANTERN CORPS (DC New 52)
DC Comics: Nov, 2011 - No. 40, May, 2015 ($2.99)

1-23: 1-Tomasi-s/Pasarin-a/Mahnke-c; John Stewart & Guy Gardner. 4-6-Andy Kubert-c 3.00
24-39: 24-Lights Out pt. 2; Oa destroyed. 25-Year Zero. 35-37-Godhead x-over 3.00
40-($3.99) Chang-a 4.00
#0 (11/12, $2.99) Origin of Guy Gardner; Tomasi-s/Pasarin-a 3.00
Annual 1 (3/13, $4.99) Rise of the Third Army conclusion; Mogo returns 5.00
Annual 2 (3/14, $4.99) Villains United; Evil Star, Bolphunga, Kanjar Ro app. 5.00
...: Futures End 1 (11/14, $2.99, regular-c) Five years later; Indigo Tribe app. 3.00
...: Futures End 1 (11/14, $3.99, 3-D cover) 4.00

GREEN LANTERN CORPS: EDGE OF OBLIVION
DC Comics: Mar, 2016 - No. 6, Aug, 2016 ($2.99, limited series)

1-6: 1-3-Taylor-s/Van Sciver-a. 4,5-Syaf-a 3.00

GREEN LANTERN CORPS QUARTERLY
DC Comics: Summer, 1992 - No. 8, Spring, 1994 ($2.50/$2.95, 68 pgs.)

1-G.A. Green Lantern story; Staton-a(p) 5.00
2-8: 2-G.A. G.L.-c/story; Austin-c(i); Gulacy-a(p). 3-G.A. G.L. story. 4-Austin-i. 7-Painted-c; Tim Vigil-a. 8-Lobo-c/s 4.00

GREEN LANTERN CORPS: RECHARGE
DC Comics: Nov, 2005 - No. 5, Mar, 2006 ($3.50/$2.99, limited series)

1-($3.50) Kyle Rayner, Guy Gardner & Kilowog app.; Gleason-a 4.00
2-5-($2.99) 3.00
TPB (2006, $12.99) r/series 13.00

GREEN LANTERN: DRAGON LORD
DC Comics: 2001 - No. 3, 2001 ($4.95, squarebound, limited series)

1-3: A G.L. in ancient China; Moench-s/Gulacy-c/a 5.00

GREEN LANTERN: EMERALD DAWN (Also see Emerald Dawn)
DC Comics: Dec, 1989 - No. 6, May, 1990 ($1.00, limited series)

1-Origin retold; Giffen plots in all 6.00
2-6: 4-Re-intro. Tomar-Re 4.00

GREEN LANTERN: EMERALD DAWN II (Emerald Dawn II #1 & 2)
DC Comics: Apr, 1991 - No. 6, Sept, 1991 ($1.00, limited series)

1-6 3.00
TPB (2003, $12.95) r/#1-6; Alan Davis-c 13.00

GREEN LANTERN: EMERALD WARRIORS
DC Comics: Oct, 2010 - No. 13, Oct, 2011 ($3.99/$2.99)

1-5-($3.99) Guy Gardner's exploits; Migliari-c. 1-Bermejo variant-c. 2-5-Massaferra var-c 4.00
6-13-($2.99) 6,7-Covers by Migliari & Massaferra. 8-10-War of the Green Lanterns x-over 3.00

GREEN LANTERN: EVIL'S MIGHT (Elseworlds)
DC Comics: 2002 - No. 3 ($5.95, squarebound, limited series)

1-3-Kyle Rayner in 19th century NYC; Rogers-a; Chaykin & Tischman-s 6.00

GREEN LANTERN: FEAR ITSELF
DC Comics: 1999 (Graphic novel)

Hardcover ($24.95) Ron Marz-s/Brad Parker painted-a 25.00
Softcover ($14.95) 15.00

GREEN LANTERN/FLASH: FASTER FRIENDS (See Flash/Green Lantern...)
DC Comics: 1997 ($4.95, limited series)

1-Marz-s 5.00

GREEN LANTERN GALLERY
DC Comics: Dec, 1996 ($3.50, one-shot)

1-Wraparound-c; pin-ups by various 3.50

GREEN LANTERN/GREEN ARROW (Also see The Flash #217)
DC Comics: Oct, 1983 - No. 7, April, 1984 (52-60 pgs.)

1-7: r-Green Lantern #76-89 1 3 4 6 8 10

NOTE: ***Neal Adams*** *r-1-7; c-1-4.* ***Wrightson*** *r-4, 5.*

GREEN LANTERN · LEGACY: THE LAST WILL & TESTAMENT OF HAL JORDAN
DC Comics: 2002 ($24.95, hardcover graphic novel)

Hardcover-Anderson & Sienkiewicz-a/c; Kelly-s; Return of Oa 25.00
Softcover (2004, $17.95) 18.00

GREEN LANTERN: LOST ARMY
DC Comics: Aug, 2015 - No. 6, Jan, 2016 ($2.99)

1-6: 1-Bunn-s/Saiz-a; featuring John Stewart, Guy Gardner, Kilowog, Arisia, Krona 3.00

GREEN LANTERN: MOSAIC (Also see Cosmic Odyssey #2)
DC Comics: June, 1992 - No. 18, Nov, 1993 ($1.25)

1-18: Featuring John Stewart. 1-Painted-c by Cully Hamner 3.00

GREEN LANTERN MOVIE PREQUEL (2011 movie)
DC Comics: July, 2011; Oct, 2011 ($2.99, one-shots)

...: Abin Sur 1 - Green-s/Gleason-a; movie photo-c 3.00
...: Hal Jordan 1 - Johns & Berlanti-s/Ordway-a; movie photo-c; Sinestro & Tomar-Re app. 3.00
...: Kilowog 1 - Tomasi-s/Ferreira-a; movie photo-c 3.00
...: Sinestro 1 (10/11) - Johns-s/Tolibao, Richards & Ordway-a; movie photo-c 3.00
...: Tomar-Re 1 - Guggenheim-s/Richards-a; movie photo-c 3.00

GREEN LANTERN: NEW GUARDIANS (DC New 52)

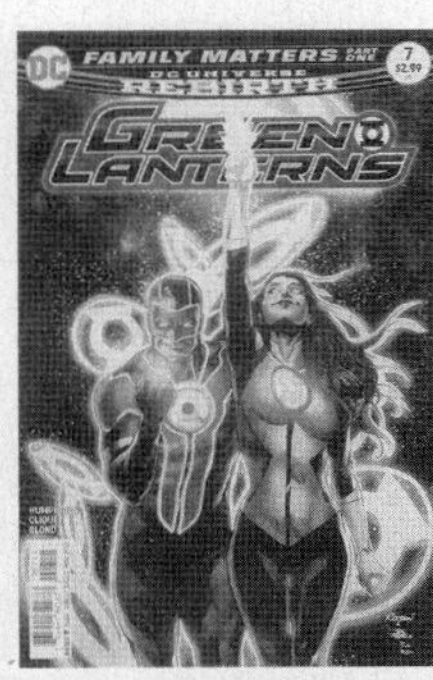

Green Lanterns #7 © DC

Green Mask #7 © FOX

Green Valley #1 © Skybound

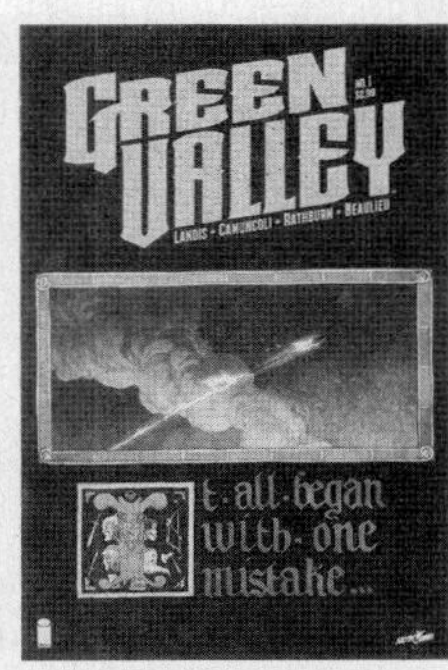

GD 2.0 | VG 4.0 | FN 6.0 | VF 8.0 | VF/NM 9.0 | NM- 9.2

DC Comics: Nov, 2011 - No. 40, May, 2015 ($2.99)
1-Bedard-s/Kirkham-a/c; Kyle origin flashback; Fatality app. 6.00
2-23: 13-16-Third Army. 21-Relic freed. 22,23-Kyle vs. Relic. 23-Blue Lanterns destroyed 3.00
24-34: 24-Lights Out pt. 3. 3.00
35-39: 35-37-Godhead x-over; Highfather app. 38,39-Oblivion returns 3.00
40-($3.99) Oblivion app.; the start of the White Lantern Corps 4.00
#0 (11/12, $2.99) Bedard-s/Kuder-a; Zamarons app. 3.00
Annual 1 (3/13, $4.99) Giffen-s/Kolins-a/c 5.00
Annual 2 (6/14, $4.99) Segovia-a; takes place between #30 & #31 5.00
...: Futures End 1 (11/14, $2.99, regular-c) Five years later; intro. Saysoran 3.00
...: Futures End 1 (11/14, $3.99, 3-D cover) 4.00

GREEN LANTERN: REBIRTH
DC Comics: Dec, 2004 - No. 6, May, 2005 ($2.95, limited series)
1-Johns-s/Van Sciver-a; Hal Jordan as The Spectre on-c 8.00
1-2nd printing; Hal Jordan as Green Lantern on-c 4.00
1-3rd printing; B&W-c version of 1st printing 3.00
1 Special Edition (9/09, $1.00) r/#1 with "After Watchmen" cover frame 3.00
2-Guy Gardner becomes a Green Lantern again; JLA app. 5.00
2-2nd & 3rd printings 3.00
3-6: 3-Sinestro returns. 4-6-JLA & JSA app. 3.00
HC (2005, $24.99, dust jacket) r/series & Wizard preview; intro. by Brad Meltzer 25.00
SC (2007, 2010, $14.99) r/series & Wizard preview; intro. by Brad Meltzer 15.00

GREEN LANTERNS (DC Rebirth) (Also see Hal Jordan and the Green Lantern Corps)
DC Comics: Aug, 2016 - Present ($2.99)
1-18: 1-Simon Baz and Jessica Cruz team up; Humphries-s/Rocha-a. 6-1st app. the Phantom Ring. 8-Dominators app.; Benes-a. 9-14-Phantom Lantern. 16,17-Batman app. 3.00
...: Rebirth 1 (8/16, $2.99) Van Sciver & Benes-a; Hal Jordan & Atrocitus app. 3.00

GREEN LANTERN/SENTINEL: HEART OF DARKNESS
DC Comics: Mar, 1998 - No. 3, May, 1998 ($1.95, limited series)
1-3-Marz-s/Pelletier-a 3.00

GREEN LANTERN/SILVER SURFER: UNHOLY ALLIANCES
DC Comics: 1995 ($4.95, one-shot)(Prelude to DC Versus Marvel)
nn-Hal Jordan app. 6.00

GREEN LANTERN SINESTRO CORPS SPECIAL (Continues in Green Lantern #21)
DC Comics: Aug, 2007 ($4.99, one-shot)
1-Kyle Rayner becomes Parallax; Cyborg Superman & Earth-Prime Superboy app.; Johns-s; Van Sciver-a/c; back-up story origin of Sinestro; Gibbons-a; Sinestro on cover 8.00
1-(2nd printing) Kyle Rayner as Parallax on cover 6.00
1-(3rd printing) Sinestro cover with muted colors 5.00

GREEN LANTERN: THE ANIMATED SERIES (Based on the Cartoon Network series)
DC Comics: No. 0, Jan, 2012 - No. 14, Sept, 2013 ($2.99)
0-14: 0-Baltazar & Franco-s/Brizuela-a; Kilowog and Red Lanterns app. 13-Lobo app. 3.00

GREEN LANTERN: THE GREATEST STORIES EVER TOLD
DC Comics: 2006 ($19.99, TPB)
SC-Reprints Showcase #22; G.L. #1,31,74,87,172; ('90 series) #3, and others; Ross-c 20.00

GREEN LANTERN: THE NEW CORPS
DC Comics: 1999 - No. 2, 1999 ($4.95, limited series)
1,2-Kyle recruits new GLs; Eaton-a 5.00

GREEN LANTERN VS. ALIENS
Dark Horse Comics: Sept, 2000 - No. 4, Dec, 2000 ($2.95, limited series)
1-4: 1-Hal Jordan and GL Corps vs. Aliens; Leonardi-p. 2-4-Kyle Rayner 3.00

GREEN MASK, THE (See Mystery Men)
Summer, 1940 - No. 9, 2/42; No. 10, 8/44 - No. 11, 11/44;
Fox Features Syndicate: V2#1, Spring, 1945 - No. 6, 10-11/46

	GD 2.0	VG 4.0	FN 6.0	VF 8.0	VF/NM 9.0	NM- 9.2
V1#1-Origin The Green Mask & Domino; reprints/Mystery Men #1-3,5-7; Lou Fine-c	300	600	900	1950	3375	4800
2-Zanzibar The Magician by Tuska	116	232	348	742	1271	1800
3-Powell-a; Marijuana story	87	174	261	553	952	1350
4-Navy Jones begins, ends #6	68	136	204	435	743	1050
5	55	110	165	352	601	850
6-The Nightbird begins, ends #9; bondage/torture-c	55	110	165	352	601	850
7-9: 9(2/42)-Becomes The Bouncer #10(nn) on? & Green Mask #10 on	40	80	120	246	411	575
10,11: 10-Origin One Round Hogan & Rocket Kelly	32	64	96	188	307	425
V2#1	24	48	72	142	234	325
2-6	20	40	60	117	189	260

GREEN PLANET, THE
Charlton Comics: 1962 (one-shot) (12¢)

	GD 2.0	VG 4.0	FN 6.0	VF 8.0	VF/NM 9.0	NM- 9.2
nn-Giordano-c; sci-fi	8	16	24	54	102	150

GREEN TEAM (See Cancelled Comic Cavalcade & 1st Issue Special)

GREEN TEAM: TEEN TRILLIONAIRES
DC Comics: Jul, 2013 - No. 8, Mar, 2014 ($2.99)
1-8-Baltazar & Franco-s/Guara-a. 1-3-Conner-c. 3-Deathstroke app. 8-Teen Titans app. 3.00
1-Variant-c by Chiang 3.00

GREEN VALLEY
Image Comics (Skybound): Oct, 2016 - No. 9 ($2.99)
1-5-Max Landis-s/Giuseppe Camuncoli-a 3.00

GREEN WOMAN, THE
DC Comics (Vertigo): 2010 ($24.99, HC graphic novel)
HC-John Bolton-a/Peter Straub & Michael Easton-s 25.00

GREETINGS FROM SANTA (See March of Comics No. 48)

GRENDEL (Also see Primer #2, Mage and Comico Collection)
Comico: Mar, 1983 - No. 3, Feb, 1984 ($1.50, B&W)(#1 has indicia to Skrog #1)

	GD 2.0	VG 4.0	FN 6.0	VF 8.0	VF/NM 9.0	NM- 9.2
1-Origin Hunter Rose	9	18	27	62	126	190
2,3: 2-Origin Argent	7	14	21	46	86	125

GRENDEL
Comico: Oct, 1986 - No. 40, Feb, 1990 ($1.50/$1.95/$2.50, mature)

	GD 2.0	VG 4.0	FN 6.0	VF 8.0	VF/NM 9.0	NM- 9.2
1	1	2	3	5	7	9
1,2: 2nd printings						3.00
2,3,5-15: 13-15-Ken Steacy-c.						4.00
4,16: 4-Dave Stevens-c(i). 16-Re-intro Mage (series begins, ends #19)						6.00
17-40: 24-25,27-28,30-31-Snyder-c/a						3.00
Devil by the Deed (Graphic Novel, 10/86, $5.95, 52 pgs.)-r/Grendel back-ups/ Mage 6-14; Alan Moore intro.	1	3	4	6	8	10
Devil's Legacy ($14.95, 1988, Graphic Novel)	2	4	6	9	12	15
Devil's Vagary (10/87, B&W & red)-No price; included in Comico Collection	2	4	6	8	10	12

GRENDEL (Title series): **Dark Horse Comics**
--ARCHIVES, 5/07 ($14.95, HC) r/1st apps. in Primer #2 and Grendel #1-3; Wagner intro. 15.00
--BEHOLD THE DEVIL, No. 0, 7/07 - No. 8, 6/08 ($3.50/50¢, B&W&Red)
0-(50¢-c) Prelude to series; Matt Wagner-s/a; interview with Wagner 3.00
1-8-Matt Wagner-s/a/c in all 3.50
--BLACK, WHITE, AND RED, 11/98 - No. 4, 2/99 ($3.95, anthology)
1-Wagner-s in all. Art by Sale, Leon and others 5.00
2-4: 2-Mack, Chadwick-a. 3-Allred, Kristensen-a. 4-Pearson, Sprouse-a 4.00
--CLASSICS, 7/95 - 8/95 ($3.95, mature) 1,2-reprints; new Wagner-c 4.00
--CYCLE, 10/95 ($5.95) 1-nn-history of Grendel by M. Wagner & others 6.00
--DEVIL BY THE DEED, 7/93 ($3.95, varnish-c) 1-nn-M. Wagner-c/a/scripts; r/Grendel back-ups from Mage #6-14 6.00
Reprint (12/97, $3.95) w/pin-ups by various 4.00
Hardcover (2007, $12.95) reprint recolored to B&W&red; includes covers and intros from previously reprinted editions 13.00
--DEVIL CHILD, 6/99 - No. 2, 7/99 ($2.95, mature) 1,2-Sale & Kristiansen-a/Schutz-s 3.00
--DEVIL QUEST, 11/95 ($4.95) 1-nn-Prequel to Batman/Grendel II; M. Wagner story & art; r/back-up story from Grendel Tales series. 5.00
--DEVILS AND DEATHS, 10/94 - 11/94 ($2.95, mature) 1,2 3.00
: DEVIL'S LEGACY, 3/00 - No. 12, 2/01 ($2.95, reprints 1986 series, recolored)
1-12-Wagner-s/c; Pander Bros.-a 3.00
: DEVIL'S REIGN, 5/04 - No. 7, 12/04 ($3.50, repr. 1989 series #34-40, recolored)
1-7-Sale-c/a. 3.50
: GOD AND THE DEVIL, No. 0, 1/03 - No. 10, 12/03 ($3.50/$4.99, repr. 1986 series, recolored)
0-9: 0-Sale-c/a; r/#23. 1-9-Snyder-c 3.50
10-($4.99) Double-sized; Snyder-c 5.00
--RED, WHITE & BLACK, 9/02 - No. 4, 12/02 ($4.99, anthology)
1-4-Wagner-s in all. 1-Art by Thompson, Sakai, Mahfood and others. 2-Kelley Jones, Watson, Brereton, Hester & Parks-a. 3-Oeming, Noto, Cannon, Ashley Wood, Huddleston-a 4-Chiang, Dalrymple, Robertson, Snyder III and Zulli-a 5.00
TPB (2005, $19.95) r/#1-4; cover gallery, artist bios 20.00
--TALES: DEVIL'S CHOICES, 3/95 - 6/95 ($2.95, mature) 1-4 3.00

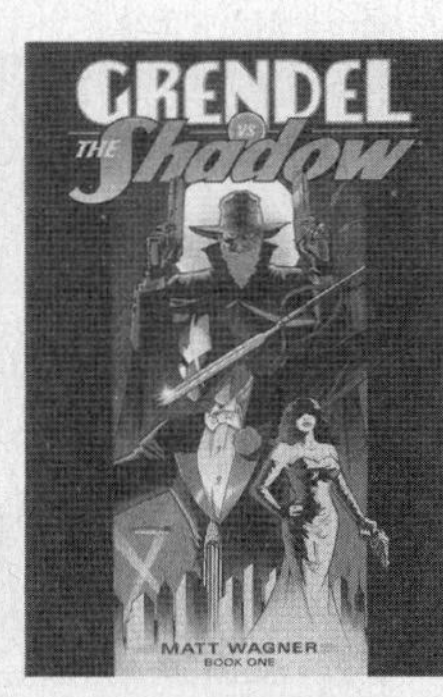

Grendel vs. The Shadow #1 © CN

Grifter #3 © WSP

Grimm Fairy Tales #91 © Zenescope

GD 2.0 | VG 4.0 | FN 6.0 | VF 8.0 | VF/NM 9.0 | NM- 9.2

--TALES: FOUR DEVILS, ONE HELL, 8/93 - 1/94 ($2.95, mature)
1-6-Wagner painted-c 3.00
TPB (12/94, $17.95) r/#1-6 18.00

--TALES: HOMECOMING, 12/94 - 2/95 ($2.95, mature) 1-3 3.00

--TALES: THE DEVIL IN OUR MIDST, 5/94 - 9/95 ($2.95, mature) 1-5-Wagner painted-c 3.00

--TALES: THE DEVIL MAY CARE, 12/95 - No. 6, 5/96 ($2.95, mature)
1-6-Terry LaBan scripts. 5-Batman/Grendel II preview 3.00

--TALES: THE DEVIL'S APPRENTICE, 9/97 - No. 3, 11/97 ($2.95, mature)
1-3 3.00

: THE DEVIL INSIDE, 9/01 - No. 3, 11/01 ($2.99)
1-3-r/#13-15 with new Wagner-c 3.00

VS. THE SHADOW, 9/14 - No. 3, 11/14 ($5.99, squarebound)
Matt Wagner-s/a/c; Grendel time-travels to The Shadow's era 6.00

: WAR CHILD, 8/92 - No. 10, 6/93 ($2.50, lim. series, mature)
1-9: 1-4-Bisley painted-c; Wagner-i & scripts in all 3.00
10-($3.50, 52 pgs.) Wagner-c 4.00
Limited Edition Hardcover ($99.95) 100.00

GREYFRIARS BOBBY (Disney)(Movie)
Dell Publishing Co.: No. 1189, Nov, 1961 (one-shot)
Four Color 1189-Photo-c 6 12 18 41 76 110

GREYLORE
Sirius: 12/85 - No. 5, Sept, 1986 ($1.50/$1.75, high quality paper)
1-5: Bo Hampton-a in all 3.00

GREYSHIRT: INDIGO SUNSET (Also see Tomorrow Stories)
America's Best Comics: Dec, 2001 - No. 6, Aug, 2002 ($3.50, limited series)
1-6-Veitch-s/a. 4-Back-up w/John Severin-a. 6-Cho-a 3.50
TPB (2002, $19.95) r/#1-6; preface by Alan Moore 20.00

GRIDIRON GIANTS
Ultimate Sports Ent.: 2000 - No. 2 ($3.95, cardstock covers)
1,2-NFL players Sanders, Marino, Plummer, T. Davis battle evil 4.00

GRIFFIN, THE
DC Comics: 1991 - No. 6, 1991 ($4.95, limited series, 52 pgs.)
Book 1-6: Matt Wagner painted-c 5.00

GRIFTER (Also see Team 7 & WildC.A.T.S)
Image Comics (WildStorm Prod.): May, 1995 - No. 10, Mar, 1996 ($1.95)
1 ($1.95, Newsstand)-WildStorm Rising Pt. 5 3.00
1-10:1 ($2.50, Direct)-WildStorm Rising Pt. 5, bound-in trading card 3.00
...: One Shot (1/95, $4.95) Flip-c 5.00

GRIFTER
Image Comics (WildStorm Prod.): V2#1, July, 1996 - No. 14, Aug, 1997 ($2.50)
V2#1-14: Steven Grant scripts 3.00

GRIFTER (DC New 52)
DC Comics: Nov, 2011 - No. 16, Mar, 2013 ($2.99)
1-16: 1-Grifter in the new DC universe; Edmonson-s/Cafu-a/c. 4-Green Arrow app. 3.00
#0 (11/12, $2.99) Liefeld-s/c; Clark-a 3.00

GRIFTER & MIDNIGHTER
DC Comics (WildStorm Prod.): May, 2007 - No. 6, Oct, 2007 ($2.99, limited series)
1-6-Dixon-s/Benjamin-a/c. 1,3-The Authority app. 3.00
TPB (2008, $17.99) r/#1-6 18.00

GRIFTER AND THE MASK
Dark Horse Comics: Sept, 1996 - No. 2, Oct, 1996 ($2.50, limited series)
(1st Dark Horse Comics/Image x-over)
1,2: Steve Seagle scripts 3.00

GRIFTER/BADROCK (Also see WildC.A.T.S & Youngblood)
Image Comics (Extreme Studios): Oct, 1995 - No.2, Nov, 1995 ($2.50, unfinished lim. series)
1,2: 2-Flip book w/Badrock #2 3.00

GRIFTER/SHI
Image Comics (WildStorm Productions): Apr, 1996 - No. 2, May, 1996 ($2.95, limited series)
1,2: 1-Jim Lee-c/a(p); Travis Charest-a(p). 2-Billy Tucci-c/a(p); Travis Charest-a(p) 3.00

GRIM GHOST, THE
Atlas/Seaboard Publ.: Jan, 1975 - No. 3, July, 1975
1-3: Fleisher-s in all. 1-Origin. 2-Son of Satan; Colan-a. 3-Heath-c
2 4 6 11 16 20

GRIM GHOST
Ardden Entertainment (Atlas Comics): Mar, 2011 - No. 5 ($2.99)
1-5-Isabella & Susco-s/Kelley Jones-a. 1-Re-intro. Matthew Dunsinane 3.00
... Issue Zero - NY Comicon Edtion (10/10, $2.99) Qing Ping Mui-a; prequel to #1 3.00

GRIMJACK (Also see Demon Knight & Starslayer)
First Comics: Aug, 1984 - No. 81, Apr, 1991 ($1.00/$1.95/$2.25)
1-John Ostrander scripts & Tim Truman-c/a begins. 5.00
2-25: 20-Sutton-c/a begins. 22-Bolland-a. 3.00
26-2nd color Teenage Mutant Ninja Turtles 6.00
27-74,76-81 (Later issues $1.95, $2.25): 30-Dynamo Joe x-over; 31-Mandrake-c/a begins. 73,74-Kelley Jones-a 3.00
75-($5.95, 52 pgs.)-Fold-out map; coated stock 6.00
The Legend of Grimjack Vol. 1 (IDW Publishing, 2004, $19.99) r/Starslayer #10-18; 8 new pages & art 20.00
The Legend of Grimjack Vol. 2 (IDW, 2005, $19.99) r/#1-7; unpublished art 20.00
The Legend of Grimjack Vol. 3 (IDW, 2005, $19.99) r/#8-14; cover gallery 20.00
The Legend of Grimjack Vol. 4 (IDW, 2005, $24.99) r/#15-21; cover gallery 25.00
The Legend of Grimjack Vol. 5 (IDW, 5/06, $24.99) r/#22-30; cover gallery 25.00
The Legend of Grimjack Vol. 6 (IDW, 1/07, $24.99) r/#31-37; cover gallery 25.00
The Legend of Grimjack Vol. 7 (IDW, 4/07, $24.99) r/#38-46; covers; "Rough Trade" 25.00
NOTE: *Truman c/a-1-17.*

GRIMJACK CASEFILES
First Comics: Nov, 1990 - No. 5, Mar, 1991 ($1.95, limited series)
1-5 Reprints 1st stories from Starslayer #10 on 3.00

GRIMJACK: KILLER INSTINCT
IDW Publ.: Jan, 2005 - No. 6, June, 2005 ($3.99, limited series)
1-6-Ostrander-s/Truman-a 4.00

GRIMJACK: THE MANX CAT
IDW Publ.: Aug, 2009 - No. 6, Jan, 2010 ($3.99, limited series)
1-6-Ostrander-s/Truman-a 4.00

GRIMM (Based on the NBC TV series)
Dynamite Entertainment.: 2013 - No. 12, 2014 ($3.99)
1-11: 1-Two covers (Alex Ross & photo). 2-11-Pararillo & photo-c on each 4.00
12-($4.99) Gaffen & McVey-s/Rodolfo-a; Pararillo & photo-c 5.00
#0 (2013, Free Comic Book Day giveaway) Prequel to issue #1; Portacio-c 3.00
... Portland, WU (2014, $7.99) Gaffen & McVey-s/Govar-a/c 8.00
...: The Warlock 1-4 (2013 - No. 4, 2014, $3.99) Nitz-s/Malaga-a 4.00

GRIMM VOLUME 2 (Based on the NBC TV series)
Dynamite Entertainment.: 2016 - Present ($3.99)
1-5-Kittredge-s/Sanapo-a; two covers 4.00

GRIMM FAIRY TALES
Zenescope Entertainment: Jun, 2005 - No. 125, Aug, 2016 ($2.99/$3.99)
1-Al Rio-c; Little Red Riding Hood app.; multiple variant covers
5 10 15 34 60 85
2-Multiple variant covers 3 6 9 17 26 35
3-6-Multiple variant covers 2 4 6 10 14 18
7-12: Multiple covers on each 6.00
13-74,76-84,86-99,101,102: Multiple covers on each 3.00
75-(7/12, $5.99) Covers by Campbell, Sejic, Michaels and others 6.00
85-(5/13, $5.99) Unleashed part 2 6.00
100-(7/14, $5.99) Age of Darkness; covers by Neal Adams and others 6.00
103-124-($3.99) 4.00
125-(8/16, $9.99) Five covers 10.00
#0 Free Comic Book Day Special Edition (4/14, giveaway) Age of Darkness tie-in 3.00
2016 Annual (10/16, $5.99) Spotlight on Skylar; art by various; 4 covers 6.00
... Animated One Shot (10/12, $3.99) Schnepp-c; bonus design art 4.00
Grimm Tales of Terror 2016 Holiday Special (11/16, $5.99) 4 covers 6.00
... Halloween Special 1,2, 2013, 2014, 2015, 2016 (10/09, 10/10, 10/13, 10/14, 9/15, 10/16, $5.99) Multiple covers on each 6.00
... Holiday Edition (11/14, $5.99) The story of Krampus; multiple covers 6.00
... Presents Wounded Warriors (7/13, $6.99) Multiple military-themes covers 7.00
... The Dark Queen One Shot (1/14, $5.99) Sharma-a; 4 covers 6.00

GRIMM FAIRY TALES (Volume 2)
Zenescope Entertainment: Dec, 2016 - Present ($3.99)
1-3-Brusha-s/Silva-a; multiple covers on each 4.00

GRIMM FAIRY TALES PRESENTS ALICE IN WONDERLAND
Zenescope Entertainment: Jan, 2012 - No. 6, May, 2012 ($2.99)
1-Multiple variant covers 3 6 9 14 19 24

Grimmiss Island #4 © Art Baltazar

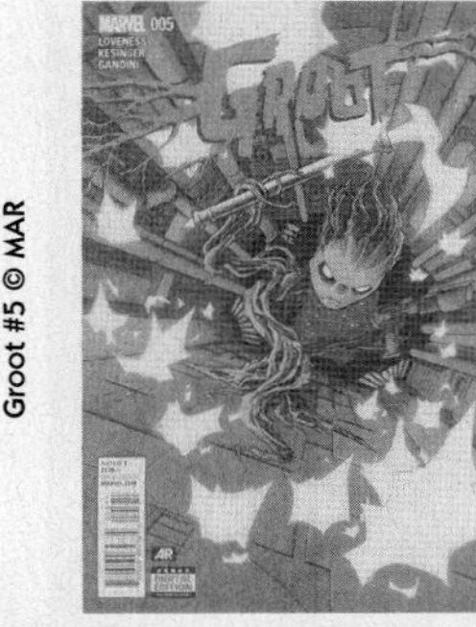

Groot #5 © MAR

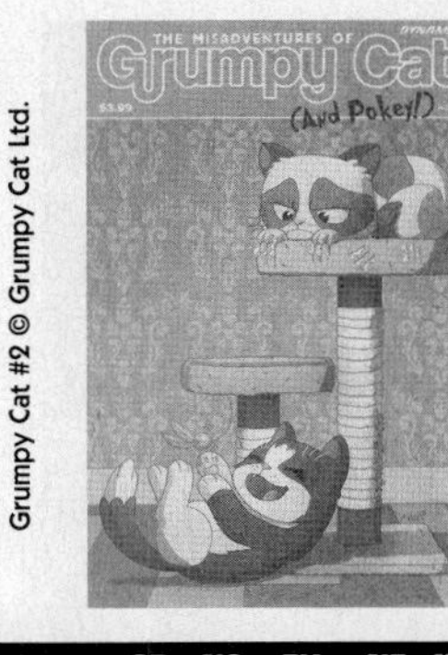

Grumpy Cat #2 © Grumpy Cat Ltd.

GD VG FN VF VF/NM NM-
2.0 4.0 6.0 8.0 9.0 9.2

2-6: Multiple covers on each 1 2 3 5 6 8

GRIMM FAIRY TALES MYTHS & LEGENDS
Zenescope Entertainment: Jan, 2011 - No. 25, Feb, 2013 ($2.99)

1-Campbell-c; multiple variant covers 2 4 6 8 10 12
2-5 5.00
6-24 3.00
25-(2/13, $5.99) Multiple variant covers 6.00

GRIMM FAIRY TALES PRESENTS WONDERLAND (Title changes to Wonderland with #43)
Zenescope Entertainment: Jul, 2012 - Finale, Sept, 2016 ($2.99)

1-Campbell-c; multiple variant covers 1 3 4 6 8 10
2,3 5.00
4-18 3.00
19-24,26-49-($3.99) 4.00
25-(7/14, $5.99) Multiple variant covers 6.00
50-(8/16, $5.99) Multiple variant covers 6.00
... Finale (9/16, $5.99) Last issue; 4 covers; Shand-s/Follini-a 6.00
Free Comic Book Day 2015 Special Edition (5/15, giveaway) Brescini-a 3.00

GRIMMISS ISLAND (Issue #1 titled Itty Bitty Comics #5: Grimmiss Island)
Dark Horse Comics: Mar, 2015 - No. 4, Jun, 2015 ($2.99, limited series)

1-4-All-ages humor story by Art Baltazar & Franco 3.00

GRIMM'S GHOST STORIES (See Dan Curtis)
Gold Key/Whitman No. 55 on: Jan, 1972 - No. 60, June, 1982 (Painted-c #1-42,44,46-56)

1 3 6 9 21 33 45
2-5,8: 5,8-Williamson-a 2 4 6 13 18 22
6,7,9,10 2 4 6 11 16 20
11-20 2 4 6 8 11 14
21-42,45-54: 32,34-Reprints. 45-Photo-c 1 3 4 6 8 10
43,44,55-60: 43,44-(52 pgs.). 43-Photo-c. 58(2/82). 59(4/82)-Williamson-a(r/#8). 60(6/82)
2 4 6 8 11 14
Mini-Comic No. 1 (3-1/4x6-1/2", 1976) 1 3 4 6 8 10

NOTE: *Reprints-#32?, 34?, 39, 43, 44, 47?, 53; 56-60(1/3).* ***Bolle*** *a-8, 17, 22-25, 27, 29(2), 33, 35, 41, 43r, 45(2), 48(2), 50, 52, 57.* ***Celardo*** *a-17, 26, 28p, 30, 31, 43(2), 45.* ***Lopez*** *a-24, 25.* ***McWilliams*** *a-33, 44r, 48, 54(2), 57, 58.* ***Win Mortimer*** *a-31, 33, 49, 51, 55, 56, 58(2), 59, 60.* ***Roussos*** *a-25, 30.* ***Sparling*** *a-23, 24, 28, 30, 31, 33, 43r, 44, 45, 51(2), 52, 56-58, 59(2), 60.* ***Spiegle*** *a-44.*

GRIN (The American Funny Book) (Satire)
APAG House Pubs: Nov, 1972 - No. 3, April, 1973 (Magazine, 52 pgs.)

1-Parodies-Godfather, All in the Family 3 6 9 16 24 32
2,3 2 4 6 11 16 20

GRIN & BEAR IT (See Gags)
Dell Publishing Co.: No. 28, 1941

Large Feature Comic 28 19 38 57 111 176 240

GRINDHOUSE: DOORS OPEN AT MIDNIGHT
Dark Horse Comics: Oct, 2013 - No. 8, May, 2014 ($3.99)

1-8: 1-Francavilla-c/DeCampi-s. 1,2-Bee Vixens From Mars. 3,4-Prison Ship Antares 4.00

GRINDHOUSE: DRIVE IN, BLEED OUT
Dark Horse Comics: Nov, 2014 - No. 8, Aug, 2015 ($3.99)

1-8: 1,2-Slay Ride; DeCampi-s/Guéra-a. 7,8-Nebulina. 8-Manara-c 4.00

GRIPS (Extreme violence)
Silverwolf Comics: Sept, 1986 - No. 4, Dec, 1986 ($1.50, B&W, mature)

1-Tim Vigil-c/a in all 6.00
2-4 4.00

GRIP: THE STRANGE WORLD OF MEN
DC Comics (Vertigo): Jan, 2002 - No. 5, May, 2002 ($2.50, limited series)

1-4-Gilbert Hernandez-s/a 3.00

GRIT GRADY (See Holyoke One-Shot No. 1)

GROO (Also see Sergio Aragonés' Groo...)

GROO (Sergio Aragonés'...)
Image Comics: Dec, 1994 - No. 12, Dec, 1995 ($1.95)

1-12: 2-Indicia reads #1, Jan, 1995; Aragonés-c/a in all 4.00

GROO (Sergio Aragonés'...)
Dark Horse Comics: Jan, 1998 - No. 4, Apr, 1998 ($2.95)

1-4: Aragonés-c/a in all 4.00
...: One For One (9/10, $1.00) reprints #1 with red cover frame 3.00

GROO CHRONICLES, THE (Sergio Aragonés)
Marvel Comics (Epic Comics): June, 1989 - No. 6, Feb, 1990 ($3.50)

Book 1-6: Reprints early Pacific issues 5.00

GD VG FN VF VF/NM NM-
2.0 4.0 6.0 8.0 9.0 9.2

GROO: FRAY OF THE GODS (Sergio Aragonés'...)
Dark Horse Comics: Jul, 2016 - No. 4, Jan, 2017 ($3.99, limited series)

1-4-Aragonés-c/a; Evanier-s 4.00

GROO: FRIENDS AND FOES (Sergio Aragonés'...)
Dark Horse Comics: Jan, 2015 - No. 12, Jan, 2016 ($3.99)

1-12-Aragonés-c/a in all; spotlights on various characters. 1-Spotlight on Captain Ahax 4.00

GROO SPECIAL
Eclipse Comics: Oct, 1984 ($2.00, 52 pgs., Baxter paper)

1-Aragonés-c/a 3 6 9 15 22 28

GROOT (Guardians of the Galaxy)
Marvel Comics: Aug, 2015 - No. 6, Jan, 2016 ($3.99)

1-6: 1-Loveness-s/Kesinger-a; Rocket Raccoon app. 2-Flashback to Groot meeting Rocket. 3-Silver Surfer app. 4.00

GROO THE WANDERER (See Destroyer Duck #1 & Starslayer #5)
Pacific Comics: Dec, 1982 - No. 8, Apr, 1984

1-Aragonés-c/a(p)/Evanier-s in all; Aragonés bio. 3 6 9 16 23 30
2-5: 5-Deluxe paper (1.00-c) 2 4 6 9 13 16
6-8 2 4 6 10 14 18

GROO THE WANDERER (Sergio Aragonés'...) (See Marvel Graphic Novel #32)
Marvel Comics (Epic Comics): March, 1985 - No. 120, Jan, 1995

1-Aragonés-c/a in all 2 4 6 10 14 18
2-10 1 2 3 5 6 8
11-20,50-($1.50, double size) 5.00
21-49,51-99: 87-direct sale only, high quality paper 3.00
100-($2.95, 52 pgs.) 5.00
101-120 4.00
Groo Carnival, The (12/91, $8.95)-r/#9-12 11.00
Groo Garden, The (4/94, $10.95)-r/#25-28 11.00

GROO VS. CONAN (Sergio Aragonés'...)
Dark Horse Comics: Jul, 2014 - No. 4, Oct, 2014 ($3.50, limited series)

1-4: Aragonés & Evanier-s/Aragonés-c/a in all; Thomas Yeates on Conan art 3.50

GROOVY (Cartoon Comics - not CCA approved)
Marvel Comics Group: March, 1968 - No. 3, July, 1968

1-Monkees, Ringo Starr, Sonny & Cher, Mamas & Papas photos
8 16 24 54 102 150
2,3 5 10 15 35 63 90

GROSS POINT
DC Comics: Aug, 1997 - No. 14, Aug, 1998 ($2.50)

1-14: 1-Waid/Augustyn-s 3.00

GROUNDED
Image Comics: July, 2005 - No. 6, May, 2006 ($2.95/$2.99, limited series)

1-6-Mark Sable-s/Paul Azaceta-a. 1-Mike Oeming-c 3.00
Vol. 1: Powerless TPB (2006, $14.99) r/#1-6; sketch pages and creator bios 15.00

GRRL SCOUTS (Jim Mahfood's...) (Also see 40 oz. Collected)
Oni Press: Mar,1999 - No. 4, Dec, 1999 ($2.95, B&W, limited series)

1-4-Mahfood-s/c/a 3.00
TPB (2003, $12.95) r/#1-4; pin-ups by Warren, Winick, Allred, Fegredo and others 13.00

GRRL SCOUTS: WORK SUCKS
Image Comics: Feb, 2003 - No. 4, May, 2003 ($2.95, B&W, limited series)

1-4-Mahfood-s/c/a 3.00
TPB (2004, $12.95) r/#1-4; pin-ups by Oeming, Dwyer, Tennapel and others 13.00

GRUMPY CAT
Dynamite Entertainment: 2015 - No. 3, 2015 ($3.99, limited series)

1-3-Short stories; Ben McCool & Ben Fisher-s/Steve Uy & Michelle Nguyen-a 4.00
..., Free Comic Book Day 2016 (giveaway) Short stories by various 3.00

GRUMPY CAT AND POKEY
Dynamite Entertainment: 2016 - No. 6, 2016 ($3.99, limited series)

1-6-Short stories. 1-McCool & Fisher-s/Uy, Haeser & Garbowska-a; multiple covers 4.00

GUADALCANAL DIARY (See American Library)

GUARDIAN ANGEL
Image Comics: May, 2002 - No. 2, July, 2002 ($2.95)

1,2-Peterson-s/Wiesenfeld-a 3.00

GUARDIANS
Marvel Comics: Sept, 2004 - No. 5, Dec, 2004 ($2.99, limited series)

Guardians of Infinity #1 © MAR

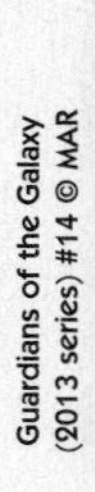
Guardians of the Galaxy (2013 series) #14 © MAR

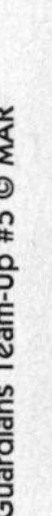
Guardians Team-Up #5 © MAR

	GD	VG	FN	VF	VF/NM	NM-
	2.0	4.0	6.0	8.0	9.0	9.2

1-5-Sumerak-s/Casey Jones-a 3.00

GUARDIANS OF INFINITY
Marvel Comics: Feb, 2016 - No. 8, Sept, 2016 ($4.99)

1-8-Guardians of the Galaxy & 31st century Guardians. 1-Back-up story with The Thing 5.00

GUARDIANS OF KNOWHERE (Secret Wars tie-in)
Marvel Comics: Sept, 2015 - No. 4, Nov, 2015 ($3.99, limited series)

1-4-Bendis-s/Deodato-a; Guardians of the Galaxy, Angela & Mantis app. 4.00
1-Variant Gwenom (Gwen/Venom) cover by Guillory 8.00

GUARDIANS OF METROPOLIS
DC Comics: Nov, 1995 - Feb, 1995 ($1.50, limited series)

1-4: 1-Superman & Granny Goodness app. 3.00

GUARDIANS OF THE GALAXY (Also see The Defenders #26, Marvel Presents #3, Marvel Super-Heroes #18, Marvel Two-In-One #5)
Marvel Comics: June, 1990 - No. 62, July, 1995 ($1.00/$1.25)

1-Valentino-c/a(p) begin; 1st app. Taserface 2 4 6 13 18 22
2-5: 2-Zeck-c(i). 5-McFarlane-c(i) 1 2 3 5 6 8
6-15: 7-Intro Malevolence (Mephisto's daughter); Perez-c(i). 8-Intro Rancor (descendant of Wolverine) in cameo. 9-1st full app. Rancor; Rob Liefeld-c(i). 10-Jim Lee-c(i). 13,14-1st app. Spirit of Vengeance (futuristic Ghost Rider). 14-Spirit of Vengeance vs. The Guardians. 15-Starlin-c(i) 4.00
16-($1.50, 52 pgs.)-Starlin-c(i) 5.00
17-24,26-38,40-47: 17-20-31st century Punishers storyline. 20-Last $1.00-c. 21-Rancor app. 22-Reintro Starhawk. 24-Silver Surfer-c/story; Ron Lim-c. 26-Origin retold. 27-28-Infinity War x-over; 27-Inhumans app. 43-Intro Wooden (son of Thor) 3.00
25-($2.50)-Prism foil-c; Silver Surfer/Galactus-c/s 5.00
25-($2.50)-Without foil-c; newsstand edition 4.00
39-($2.95, 52 pgs.)-Embossed & holo-grafx foil-c; Dr. Doom vs. Rancor 4.00
48,49,51-56: 48-bound-in trading card sheet 4.00
50-($2.00, 52 pgs.)-Newsstand edition 4.00
50-($2.95, 52 pgs.)-Collectors ed. w/foil embossed-c 5.00
57-61 1 2 3 5 6 8
62 2 4 6 9 12 15
Annual 1-4: ('91-'94, 68 pgs.)-1-Origin. 2-Spirit of Vengeance-c/story. 3,4-Bagged w/card 4.00

GUARDIANS OF THE GALAXY (See Annihilation series)
Marvel Comics: July, 2008 - No. 25, Jun, 2010 ($2.99)

1-Continued from Annihilation Conquest #6; origin of the new Guardians: Star-Lord, Drax, Warlock, Rocket Raccoon, Quasar (female version: Phyla-Vell) and Gamora; Mantis and Groot appear but not official members; Cosmo the talking dog and Nova (Richard Rider) app.; Abnett & Lanning-s/Pelletier-a 5 10 15 34 60 85
1-Second printing; variant-c 3 6 9 14 20 25
2,3: 2-Vance Astro (Major Victory) app.; full-size Groot on the cover but still growing (potted plant-size) in story. 3-Starhawk app; Guardians vs. the Universal Church of Truth 2 4 6 10 14 18
3-Variant cover 2 4 6 11 16 20
4,5-Secret Invasion x-overs; Skrulls app. 1 3 4 6 8 10
5-Monkey variant-c by Nic Klein 2 4 6 9 12 15
6-Secret Invasion x-over; Warlock, Gamora, Quasar and Star-Lord leave the team 1 3 4 6 8 10
7-Original Guardians app: Vance Astro, Charlie-27, Martinex & Yondu app; Groot, Mantis and Bug (from the Micronauts) join Rocket Raccoon, Vance Astro (Major Victory) and a re-grown Groot as the Guardians; Blastaar app. 2 4 6 8 10 12
7-Variant-c by Jim Valentino 2 4 6 11 16 20
8-War of Kings x-over; Blastaar & Ronan the Accuser app. 1 3 4 6 8 10
8-Variant-c; Thanos with the Infinity Gauntlet by Brandon Peterson 3 6 9 19 30 40
9,10; 9-War of Kings x-over; Star-Lord and Jack Flagg vs. Blastaar at the super-villain prison in the Negative Zone. 10-War of Kings x-over; Blastaar & Reed Richards app. Star-Lord reunited with the Guardians 1 3 4 6 8 10
11,12: 11-Drax and Quasar (Phyla-Vell) story; Maelstrom & Dragon of the Moon app. 12-Moondragon returns; Quasar (Wendell Vaughn) regains the Quantum-bands becomes Protector of the Universe; Maelstrom & Oblivion app; Phyla-Vell becomes new Avatar of Death 1 3 4 6 8 10
13-War of Kings x-over; Phyla-Vell changes name to 'Martyr'; Moondragon & Jack Flagg join the Guardians; Warlock, Drax & Gamora return to Guardians; Black Bolt & the Inhumans, Vulcan, ruler of the Shi'ar Empire and the Starjammers app.; story continues on War of Kings #3 2 4 6 8 10 12
14-17: 14-War of Kings x-over; Warlock vs. Vulcan; Guardians vs. the Inhumans. 15-War of Kings x-over; Guardians vs. the Sh'iar; Black Bolt & the Inhumans app. 16-War of Kings x-over; Star-Lord, Bug, Jack Flagg, Mantis & Cosmo vs. the Badoon; original Guardians: Martinex, Youndu, Charlie-27, Starhawk and Major Victory app. 17-War of Kings x-over; 'death' of Warlock & Martyr; return of the Magus 1 3 4 6 8 10
17-Variant 70th Anniversary Frame-c by Perkins 2 4 6 11 16 20
18-20: 18-Star-Lord, Mantis, Cosmo, Bug & Jack Flagg in alternate future 3000AD; Killraven & Hollywood (Wonder Man) app.; vs. the Martians; original Guardians app.; Starhawk, Charlie-27 & Nikki. 19-Kang app.; 'death' of Martyr & Warlock again; 'death' of Major Victory, Gamora, Cosmo & Mantis. 20-Realm of Kings x-over; Star-Lord, Groot, Rocket Raccoon, Bug, Jack Flagg, Drax & Moondragon appear as the Guardians 1 3 4 6 8 10
21-Realm of Kings x-over; brief appearance of the Cancerverse 2 4 6 8 10 12
22,23: 23-Realm of Kings x-over; the Magus returns. 23-Martyr, Gamora, Cosmo, Mantis & Major Victory return to life; Magus app. 2 4 6 9 12 15
23-Deadpool Variant-c by Alex Garner 3 6 9 17 26 35
24-Realm of Kings x-over; Thanos returns, kills Martyr; Maelstrom app. 3 6 9 14 20 25
25-Last issue; Guardians vs. Thanos; leads into Thanos Imperative #1 3 6 9 16 23 30
25-Variant-c by Skottie Young 2 4 6 11 16 20

GUARDIANS OF THE GALAXY (Marvel NOW!) (Also see the 2013 Nova series) (See Incredible Hulk #271, Iron Man #55, Marvel Preview #4,7, Strange Tales #180 and Tales to Astonish #13 for 1st app. of 2014 movie characters)
Marvel Comics: No. 0.1, Apr, 2013; No. 1, May, 2013 - No. 27, Jul, 2015 ($3.99)

0.1-(4/13) Origin of Star-Lord; Bendis-s/McNiven-a 5.00
1-Bendis-s/McNiven-a; Iron Man app.; at least 15 variant covers exist 2 4 6 8 10 12
2-4: Iron Man app. 1 2 3 5 6 8
5-Angela & Thanos app. 5.00
6-13: 8,9-Infinity tie-in; Francavilla-a/c. 10-Maguire-a. 11-13-Trial of Jean Grey 4.00
14-($4.99) Venom and Captain Marvel app.; Bradshaw-a; Guardians of 3014 app. 5.00
15-24,26,27: 16,17-Angela app. 18-20-Original Sin tie-in; Thanos app. 23-Origin of the Symbiotes. 24-Black Vortex crossover 4.00
25-($4.99)-Black Vortex crossover; Kree homeworld destroyed 5.00
Annual 1 (2/15, $4.99) Bendis-s/Cho-a; Nick Fury, Dum Dum, Skrulls app. 5.00
...: Best Story Ever 1 (6/15, $3.99) Tim Seeley-s; Nebula & Thanos app. 4.00
...: Galaxy's Most Wanted 1 (9/14, $3.99) Rocket & Groot; DiVito-a; r/Thor #314 Drax app. 4.00
100th Anniversary Special: Guardians of the Galaxy (9/14, $3.99) Future Guardians 4.00
...: Tomorrow's Avengers 1 (9/13, $4.99) Short stories; art by various 5.00
Marvel's Guardians of the Galaxy Prelude 1,2 (6/14 - No. 2, 7/14, $2.99) 1-Gamora & Nebula app. 2-Rocket & Groot 3.00

GUARDIANS OF THE GALAXY
Marvel Comics: Dec, 2015 - Present ($3.99)

1-17: 1-Rocket, Groot, Drax, Venom, The Thing and Kitty Pryde team; Bendis-s. 12,13-Civil War II tie-ins. 12-Avengers app. 14-Spider-Man app.; Maguire-a 4.00

GUARDIANS OF THE GALAXY ADAPTATION ("... Vol. 2 Prelude" on cover)
Marvel Comics: Mar, 2017 - No. 2, Apr, 2017 ($3.99, limited series)

1,2-Adaptation of the 2014 movie; Corona Pilgrim-s/Chris Allen-a 4.00

GUARDIANS OF THE GALAXY & X-MEN: THE BLACK VORTEX
Marvel Comics: Alpha, Apr, 2015 - Omega, Jun, 2015 ($4.99, bookends for crossover)

... Alpha (4/15) Part 1 of crossover; McGuiness-a 5.00
... Omega (6/15) Part 13 of crossover; Ronan app.; McGuinness-a 5.00

GUARDIANS TEAM-UP
Marvel Comics: May, 2015 - No. 10, Oct, 2015 ($3.99)

1-10: 1-Bendis-s/Art Adams-a. 1,2-The Avengers & Nebula app. 3-Black Vortex crossover. 4-Gamora & She-Hulk. 7-Drax & Ant-Man. 9-Spider-Man & Star-Lord; Pulido-s/a. 10-Deadpool & Rocket 4.00

GUARDIANS 3000
Marvel Comics: Dec, 2014 - No. 8, Jul, 2015 ($3.99)

1-8: 1-Abnett-s/Sandoval-a; Alex Ross-c; Guardians vs. Badoon in 3014 A.D. 1-6-Ross-c. 6-Guardians meet the 2015 Guardians 4.00

GUARDING THE GLOBE (See Invincible)
Image Comics: Aug, 2010 - No. 6, Oct, 2011 ($3.50)

1-6-Kirkman & Cereno-s/Getty-a. 1-Back-c swipe of Avengers #4 w/Obama 3.50

GUARDING THE GLOBE (2nd series) (See Invincible Universe)
Image Comics: Sept, 2012 - No. 6, Feb, 2013 ($2.99)

1-6: 1-Wraparound-c; Hester-s/Nauck-a 3.00

GUERRILLA WAR (Formerly Jungle War Stories)
Dell Publishing Co.: No. 12, July-Sept, 1965 - No. 14, Mar, 1966

12-14 3 6 9 15 22 28

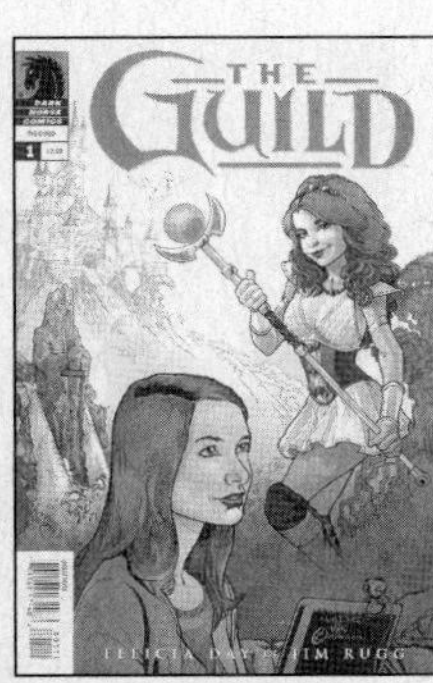

The Guild #1 © The Guild

Gunfighter #8 © WMG

Gun Runner #6 © MAR

GD VG FN VF VF/NM NM-
2.0 4.0 6.0 8.0 9.0 9.2

GUIDEBOOK TO THE MARVEL CINEMATIC UNIVERSE
Marvel Comics: Dec, 2015 - Present ($3.99)

... - Marvel's Agents of S.H.I.E.L.D. Season One (8/16, $3.99) Profile pages 4.00
... - Marvel's Agents of S.H.I.E.L.D. Season Two/Marvel's Agent Carter Season One (12/16, $3.99) Flipbook with character profile pages; both covers by Marcos Martin 4.00
... - Marvel's Agents of S.H.I.E.L.D. Season Three/Marvel's Agent Carter Season Two (2/17, $3.99) Flipbook with character profile pages; covers by Del Mundo & Johnson 4.00
... - Marvel's Avengers: Age of Ultron (11/16, $3.99) Profile pages of characters 4.00
... - Marvel's Captain America: Civil War (3/17, $3.99) Profile pages 4.00
... - Marvel's Captain America: The First Avenger (3/16, $3.99) Profile pages 4.00
... - Marvel's Captain America: The Winter Soldier/Marvel's Ant-Man (7/16, $3.99) Flipbook 4.00
... - Marvel's Guardians of the Galaxy (9/16, $3.99) Profile pages of characters, locations 4.00
... - Marvel's Incredible Hulk/Marvel's Iron Man 2 (1/16, $3.99) Flipbook; profile pages 4.00
... - Marvel's Iron Man (12/15, $3.99) Profile pages of characters, weapons, locations 4.00
... - Marvel's Iron Man 3/Marvel's Thor: The Dark World (6/16, $3.99) Flipbook profiles 4.00
... - Marvel's The Avengers (4/16, $3.99) Profile pages of characters, weapons 4.00
... - Marvel's Thor (2/16, $3.99) Profile pages of characters, weapons, locations 4.00

GUILD, THE (Based on the web-series)
Dark Horse Comics: Mar, 2010 - No. 3, May, 2010 ($3.50, limited series)

1-3-Felicia Day-s/Jim Rugg-a; two covers on each 3.50
... Bladezz 1 (6/11, $3.50) Currie-a/Kerschl-c; variant-c by Dalrymple 3.50
... Clara 1 (9/11, $3.50) Chan-a/Chaykin-c; variant-c by Aronowitz 3.50
... Fawkes 1 (5/12, $3.50) Day & Wheaton-s/McKelvie-a; variant-c by Rios 3.50
... Tink 1 (3/11, $3.50) art by Donaldson, Warren, Seeley & others; variant-c by Bagge 3.50
... Vork 1 (12/10, $3.50) Robertson-a/c; variant-c by Hernandez 3.50
... Zaboo 1 (12/11, $3.50) Cloonan-a/Dorkin-c; variant-c by Jeanty 3.50

GUILTY (See Justice Traps the Guilty)

GULLIVER'S TRAVELS (See Dell Jr. Treasury No. 3)
Dell Publishing Co.: Sept-Nov, 1965

1 5 10 15 31 53 75

GUMBY
Wildcard Ink: July, 2006 - No. 3 ($3.99)

1-3-Bob Burden & Rick Geary-s&a 4.00

GUMBY'S SUMMER FUN SPECIAL
Comico: July, 1987 ($2.50)

1-Art Adams-c/a; B. Burden scripts 5.00

GUMBY'S WINTER FUN SPECIAL
Comico: Dec, 1988 ($2.50, 44 pgs.)

1-Art Adams-c/a 5.00

GUMPS, THE (See Merry Christmas..., Popular & Super Comics)
Dell Publ. Co./Bridgeport Herald Corp.: No. 73, 1945; Mar-Apr, 1947 - No. 5, Nov-Dec, 1947

Four Color 73 (Dell)(1945) 11 22 33 76 163 250
1 (3-4/47) 16 32 48 94 147 200
2-5 11 22 33 62 86 110

GUN CANDY (Also see The Ride)
Image Comics: July, 2005 - No. 2 ($5.99)

1,2-Stelfreeze-c/a; flip book with The Ride (1-Pearson-c. 2-Noto-c) 6.00

GUNFIGHTER (Fat & Slat #1-4) (Becomes Haunt of Fear #15 on)
E. C. Comics (Fables Publ. Co.): No. 5, Sum, 1948 - No. 14, Mar-Apr, 1950

5,6-Moon Girl in each 60 120 180 381 653 925
7-14: 13,14-Bondage-c 43 86 129 271 461 650

NOTE: ***Craig & H. C. Kiefer** art in most issues. **Craig** c-5, 6, 13, 14. **Feldstein/Craig** a-10. **Feldstein** a-7-11. **Harrison/Wood** a-13, 14. **Ingels** a-5-14; c-7-12.*

GUNFIGHTERS, THE
Super Comics (Reprints): 1963 - 1964

10-12,15,16,18: 10,11-r/Billy the Kid #s? 12-r/The Rider #5(Swift Arrow). 15-r/Straight Arrow #42; Powell-r. 16-r/Billy the Kid #?(Toby). 18-r/The Rider #3; Severin-c
2 4 6 10 14 18

GUNFIGHTERS, THE (Formerly Kid Montana)
Charlton Comics: No. 51, 10/66 - No. 52, 10/67; No. 53, 6/79 - No. 85, 7/84

51,52 2 4 6 11 16 20
53,54,56:53,54-Williamson/Torres-r/Six Gun Heroes #47,49. 56-Williamson/Severin-c; Severin-r/Sheriff of Tombstone #1 1 3 4 6 8 10
55,57-80 6.00
81-84-Lower print run 1 2 3 5 6 8
85-S&K-r/1955 Bullseye 1 3 4 6 8 10

GUNFIRE (See Deathstroke Annual #2 & Showcase 94 #1,2)

DC Comics: May, 1994 - No. 13, June, 1995 ($1.75/$2.25)

1-5,0,6-13: 2-Ricochet-c/story. 5-(9/94). 0-(10/94). 6-(11/94) 3.00

GUN GLORY (Movie)
Dell Publishing Co.: No. 846, Oct, 1957 (one-shot)

Four Color 846-Toth-a, photo-c. 8 16 24 51 96 140

GUNHAWK, THE (Formerly Whip Wilson)(See Wild Western)
Marvel Comics/Atlas (MCI): No. 12, Nov, 1950 - No. 18, Dec, 1951
(Also see Two-Gun Western #5)

12 20 40 60 117 189 260
13-18: 13-Tuska-a. 16-Colan-a. 18-Maneely-c 14 28 42 82 121 160

GUNHAWKS (Gunhawk No. 7)
Marvel Comics Group: Oct, 1972 - No. 7, October, 1973

1,6: 1-Reno Jones, Kid Cassidy; Shores-c/a(p). 6-Kid Cassidy dies
3 6 9 17 26 35
2-5,7: 7-Reno Jones solo 2 4 6 11 16 20

GUNMASTER (Becomes Judo Master #89 on)
Charlton Comics: 9/64 - No. 4, 1965; No. 84, 7/65 - No. 88, 3-4/66; No. 89, 10/67

V1#1 3 6 9 21 33 45
2-4, V5#84-86: 84-Formerly Six-Gun Heroes 3 6 9 15 22 28
V5#87-89 2 4 6 11 16 20

NOTE: *Vol. 5 was originally cancelled with #88 (3-4/66). #89 on, became Judo Master, then later in 1967, Charlton issued #89 as a Gunmaster one-shot.*

GUN RUNNER
Marvel Comics UK: Oct, 1993 - No. 6, Mar, 1994 ($1.75, limited series)

1-($2.75)-Polybagged w/4 trading cards; Spirits of Vengeance app. 4.00
2-6: 2-Ghost Rider & Blaze app. 3.00

GUNS AGAINST GANGSTERS (True-To-Life Romances #8 on)
Curtis Publications/Novelty Press: Sept-Oct, 1948 - No. 6, July-Aug, 1949; V2#1, Sept-Oct, 1949

1-Toni & Greg Gayle begins by Schomburg; L.B. Cole-c
43 86 129 271 461 650
2-L.B. Cole-c 32 64 96 188 307 425
3-5 29 58 87 170 278 385
6-Giant shark and Toni Gayle-c by Cole 37 74 111 222 361 500
V2#1 29 58 87 170 278 385

NOTE: ***L. B. Cole** c-1-6, V2#1, 2; a-1, 2, 3(2), 4-6.*

GUNSLINGER
Dell Publishing Co.: No. 1220, Oct-Dec, 1961 (one-shot)

Four Color 1220-Photo-c 7 14 21 49 92 135

GUNSLINGER (Formerly Tex Dawson...)
Marvel Comics Group: No. 2, Apr, 1973 - No. 3, June, 1973

2,3 2 4 6 13 18 22

GUNSLINGERS
Marvel Comics: Feb, 2000 ($2.99)

1-Reprints stories of Two-Gun Kid, Rawhide Kid and Caleb Hammer 3.00

GUNSMITH CATS: (Title series), **Dark Horse Comics**

--BAD TRIP (Manga), 6/98 - No. 6, 11/98 ($2.95, B&W) 1-6 3.00
--BEAN BANDIT (Manga), 1/99 - No. 9 ($2.95, B&W, limited series) 1-9 3.00
--GOLDIE VS. MISTY (Manga), 11/97 - No. 7, 5/98 ($2.95, B&W) 1-7 3.00
--KIDNAPPED (Manga), 11/99 - No. 10, 8/00 ($2.95, B&W) 1-10 3.00
--MISTER V (Manga), 10/00 - No. 11, 8/01 ($3.50/$2.99), B&W) 1-11 3.50
--THE RETURN OF GRAY (Manga), 8/96 - No. 7, 2/97 ($2.95, B&W) 1-7 3.00
--SHADES OF GRAY (Manga), 5/97 - No. 5, 9/97 ($2.95, B&W) 1-5 3.00
--SPECIAL (Manga) Nov, 2001 ($2.99, B&W, one-shot) 3.00

GUNSMOKE (Blazing Stories of the West)
Western Comics (Youthful Magazines): Apr-May, 1949 - No. 16, Jan, 1952

1-Gunsmoke & Masked Marvel begin by Ingels; Ingels bondage-c
52 104 156 328 552 775
2-Ingels-c/a(2) 34 68 102 199 325 450
3-Ingels bondage-c/a 29 58 87 170 278 385
4-6: Ingels-c 23 46 69 136 223 310
7-10 15 30 45 88 137 185
11-16: 15,16-Western/horror stories 15 30 45 85 130 175

NOTE: ***Stallman** a-11, 14. **Wildey** a-15, 16.*

GUNSMOKE (TV)

Gunsmoke #25 © CBS

Gwenpool Special #1 © MAR

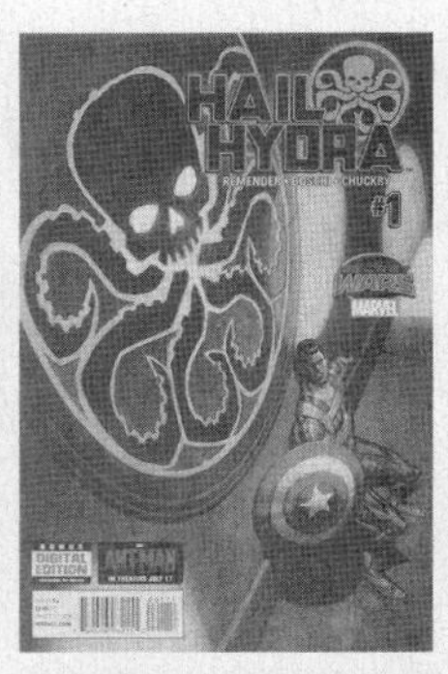

Hail Hydra #1 © MAR

Dell Publishing Co./Gold Key (All have James Arness photo-c): No. 679, Feb, 1956 - No. 27, Feb, 1969 - No. 6, Feb, 1970

	GD 2.0	VG 4.0	FN 6.0	VF 8.0	VF/NM 9.0	NM- 9.2
Four Color 679(#1)	16	32	48	110	243	375
Four Color 720,769,797,844 (#2-5),6(11-1/57-58)	9	18	27	59	117	175
7,8,9,11,12-Williamson-a in all, 4 pgs. each	8	16	24	54	102	150
10-Williamson/Crandall-a, 4 pgs.	8	16	24	54	102	150
13-27	7	14	21	44	82	120
1 (Gold Key)	6	12	18	38	69	100
2-6('69-70)	4	8	12	23	37	50

GUNSMOKE TRAIL
Ajax-Farrell Publ./Four Star Comic Corp.: June, 1957 - No. 4, Dec, 1957

	GD 2.0	VG 4.0	FN 6.0	VF 8.0	VF/NM 9.0	NM- 9.2
1	11	22	33	60	83	105
2-4	7	14	21	35	43	50

GUNSMOKE WESTERN (Formerly Western Tales of Black Rider)
Atlas Comics No. 32-35(CPS/NPI); Marvel No. 36 on: No. 32, Dec, 1955 - No. 77, July, 1963

	GD 2.0	VG 4.0	FN 6.0	VF 8.0	VF/NM 9.0	NM- 9.2
32-Baker & Drucker-a	24	48	72	144	237	330
33,35,36-Williamson-a in each: 5,6 & 4 pgs. plus Drucker-a #33. 33-Kinstler-a?	19	38	57	111	176	240
34-Baker-a, 4 pgs.; Severin-c	19	38	57	111	176	240
37-Davis-a(2); Williamson text illo	15	30	45	90	140	190
38,39: 39-Williamson text illo (unsigned)	14	28	42	82	121	160
40-Williamson/Mayo-a (4 pgs.)	15	30	45	84	127	170
41,42,45,46,48,49,52-54,57,58,60: 49,52-Kid from Texas story. 57-1st Two Gun Kid by Severin. 60-Sam Hawk app. in Kid Colt	13	26	39	74	105	135
43,44-Torres-a	13	26	39	74	105	135
47,51,59,61: 47,51,59-Kirby-a. 61-Crandall-a	14	28	42	80	115	150
50-Kirby, Crandall-a	15	30	45	84	127	170
55,56-Matt Baker-a	15	30	45	84	127	170
62-67,69,71-73,77-Kirby-a. 72-Origin Kid Colt	8	16	24	51	96	140
68,70,74-76: 68-(10¢-c)	7	14	21	46	86	125
68-(10¢ cover price blacked out, 12¢ printed on)	12	24	36	83	182	280

NOTE: *Colan a-35-37, 39, 72, 76.* ***Davis*** *a-37, 52, 54, 55; c-50, 54.* ***Ditko*** *a-66; c-56p.* ***Drucker*** *a-.32-34.* ***Heath*** *c-33.* ***Jack Keller*** *a-34, 35, 40, 51, 53, 55, 56, 60, 61, 65, 68, 69, 71, 72, 74, 75, 77; c-72.* ***Kirby*** *a-47, 50, 51, 59, 62(3), 63-67, 69, 71, 73, 77; c-56(w/****Ditko****), 57, 58, 60, 61(w/****Ayers****), 62, 63, 65, 66, 68, 69, 71-77.* ***Maneely*** *a-53; c-45.* ***Robinson*** *a-35.* ***Severin*** *a-35, 59-61; c-34, 35, 39, 42, 43.* ***Tuska*** *a-34.* ***Wildey*** *a-10, 37, 42, 56, 57. Kid Colt in all. Two-Gun Kid in No. 57, 59, 60-63. Wyatt Earp in No. 45, 48, 49, 51-56, 58.*

GUNS OF FACT & FICTION (Also see A-1 Comics)
Magazine Enterprises: No. 13, 1948 (one-shot)

	GD 2.0	VG 4.0	FN 6.0	VF 8.0	VF/NM 9.0	NM- 9.2
A-1 13-Used in **SOTI**, pg. 19; Ingels & J. Craig-a	29	58	87	170	278	385

GUNS OF THE DRAGON
DC Comics: Oct, 1998 - No. 4, Jan, 1999 ($2.50, limited series)

	GD 2.0	VG 4.0	FN 6.0	VF 8.0	VF/NM 9.0	NM- 9.2
1-4-DCU in the 1920's; Enemy Ace & Bat Lash app.						3.00

GUNWITCH, THE : OUTSKIRTS OF DOOM (See The Nocturnals)
Oni Press: June, 2001 - No. 3, Oct, 2001 ($2.95, B&W, limited series)

	GD 2.0	VG 4.0	FN 6.0	VF 8.0	VF/NM 9.0	NM- 9.2
1-3-Brereton-s/painted-c/Naifeh-s						3.00

GUY GARDNER (Guy Gardner: Warrior #17 on)(Also see Green Lantern #59)
DC Comics: Oct, 1992 - No. 44, July, 1996 ($1.25/$1.50/$1.75)

	GD 2.0	VG 4.0	FN 6.0	VF 8.0	VF/NM 9.0	NM- 9.2
1-Staton-c/a(p) begins						4.00
2-24,0,26-30: 6-Guy vs. Hal Jordan. 8-Vs. Lobo-c/story. 15-JLA x-over, begin $1.50-c. 18-Begin 4-part Emerald Fallout story; splash page x-over GL #50. 18-21-Vs. Hal Jordan. 24-(9/94)-Zero Hour. 0-(10/94)						3.00
25 (11/94, $2.50, 52 pgs.)						4.00
29 ($2.95)-Gatefold-c						4.00
29-Variant-c (Edward Hopper's Nighthawks)						3.00
31-44: 31-$1.75-c begins. 40-Gorilla Grodd-c/app. 44-Parallax-app. (1 pg.)						3.00
Annual 1 (1995, $3.50)-Year One story						4.00
Annual 2 (1996, $2.95)-Legends of the Dead Earth story						4.00

GUY GARDNER: COLLATERAL DAMAGE
DC Comics: 2006 - No. 2 ($5.99, square-bound, limited series)

	GD 2.0	VG 4.0	FN 6.0	VF 8.0	VF/NM 9.0	NM- 9.2
1,2-Howard Chaykin-s/a						6.00

GUY GARDNER REBORN
DC Comics: 1992 - Book 3, 1992 ($4.95, limited series)

	GD 2.0	VG 4.0	FN 6.0	VF 8.0	VF/NM 9.0	NM- 9.2
1-3: Staton-c/a(p). 1-Lobo-c/cameo. 2,3-Lobo-c/s						6.00

GWENPOOL (Also see Unbelievable Gwenpool)
Marvel Comics: Feb, 2016; Feb, 2017 ($5.99, one-shots)

	GD 2.0	VG 4.0	FN 6.0	VF 8.0	VF/NM 9.0	NM- 9.2
... Holiday Special: Merry Mix-Up (2/17, $5.99) 1-Deadpool, Squirrel Girl, Punisher app.						6.00
... Special (2/16, $5.99) 1-Christmas-themed short stories; She-Hulk, Deadpool app.						6.00

GYPSY COLT
Dell Publishing Co.: No. 568, June, 1954 (one-shot)

	GD 2.0	VG 4.0	FN 6.0	VF 8.0	VF/NM 9.0	NM- 9.2
Four Color 568-Movie	5	10	15	35	63	90

GYRO GEARLOOSE (See Dynabrite Comics, Walt Disney's C&S #140 & Walt Disney Showcase #18)
Dell Publishing Co.: No. 1047, Nov-Jan/1959-60 - May-July, 1962 (Disney)

	GD 2.0	VG 4.0	FN 6.0	VF 8.0	VF/NM 9.0	NM- 9.2
Four Color 1047 (No. 1)-All Barks-c/a	15	30	45	100	220	340
Four Color 1095,1184-All by Carl Barks	9	18	27	58	114	170
Four Color 1267-Barks c/a, 4 pgs.	7	14	21	48	89	130
01329-207 (#1, 5-7/62)-Barks-c only (intended as 4-Color 1329?)	5	10	15	35	63	90

HACKER FILES, THE
DC Comics: Aug, 1992 - No. 12, July, 1993 ($1.95)

	GD 2.0	VG 4.0	FN 6.0	VF 8.0	VF/NM 9.0	NM- 9.2
1-12: 1-Sutton-a(p) begins; computer generated-c						3.00

HACK/SLASH
Devil's Due Publishing: Apr. 2004 - No. 32, Mar, 2010 ($3.25/$4.95)

	GD 2.0	VG 4.0	FN 6.0	VF 8.0	VF/NM 9.0	NM- 9.2
1-Seeley-s/Caselli-a/c	3	6	9	21	33	45
...: (The Series) 1-24,26-32 (5/07-No. 32, 3/10, $3.50) Flashack to Cassie's childhood and origin. 12-Milk & Cheese cameo. 15-Re-Animator app.						3.50
25-($5.50) Double sized issue; Baugh-a; two covers						5.50
...: Comic Book Carnage (3/05) Manfredi-a/Seeley-s; Robert Kirkman & Steve Niles app.						5.00
...: First Cut TPB (10/05, $14.95) r/one-shots with sketch pages, designs, interviews						15.00
...: Girls Gone Dead (10/04, $4.95) Manfredi-a/Seeley-s						5.00
...: Land of Lost Toys 1-3 (11/05 - No. 3, 1/06, $3.25) Crossland-a/Seeley-s						3.25
...: New Reader Halloween Treat #1 (10/08, $3.50) origin retold; Cassie's diary pages						3.50
...: The Final Revenge of Evil Ernie (6/05, $4.95) Salman-a/Seeley-s; two covers						5.00
...: Trailers (2/05, $3.25) short stories by Seeley; art by various; three covers						3.25
...: Slice Hard (12/05, $4.95) Seeley-s						5.00
...: Slice Hard Pre-Sliced 25¢ Special (2/06, 25¢) origin story by Seeley; sketch pages						3.00
...: Vs Chucky (3/07, $5.50) Seeley-s/Merhoff-a; 3 covers						5.50
...: Vol. 2 Death By Sequel TPB (1/07, $18.99) r/Land of Lost Toys #1-3, Trailers, Slice Hard						19.00
...: Vol. 3 Friday the 31st TPB (10/07, $18.99) r/The Series #1-4 & ... Vs Chucky						19.00

HACK/SLASH
Image Comics: Jun, 2010 - No. 25, Mar, 2013 ($3.50)

	GD 2.0	VG 4.0	FN 6.0	VF 8.0	VF/NM 9.0	NM- 9.2
1-25: 1-(2/11, $3.50) Seeley-s/Leister-a. 5-Esquejo-c. 9-11-Bomb Queen app.						3.50
... Annual 2010: Murder Messiah (10/10, $5.99) Seeley-s/Morales-a						6.00
... Annual 2011: Hatchet/Slash (11/11, $5.99)						6.00
.../ Eva: Monster's Ball 1-4 (Dynamite Ent., 2011 - No. 4, 2011, $3.99) Jerwa-s/Razek-a						4.00
...: Me Without You (1/11, $3.50) Leister-a/Seeley-s; 2 covers						3.50
...: My First Maniac 1-4 (6/10- No. 4, 9/10) Leister-a/Seeley-s						3.50
.../ Nailbiter 1 (3/15, $4.99) Flip book with Nailbiter / Hack/Slash 1						5.00
...: Son of Samhain 1-5 (7/14- No. 5, 11/14) Laiso-a/Moreci & Seeley-s						3.50
...: Trailers #2 (11/10, $6.99) short stories; story & art by various; Seeley-c						7.00
Image Firsts: Hack/Slash #1 (10/10, $1.00) r/#1 (2004) with "Image Firsts" cover frame						3.00

HACKTIVIST
Archaia Black Label: Jan, 2014 - No. 4, Apr, 2014 ($3.99)

	GD 2.0	VG 4.0	FN 6.0	VF 8.0	VF/NM 9.0	NM- 9.2
1-4-Kelly & Lanzing-s/To-a; created by Alyssa Milano						4.00
... Volume 2 (BOOM! Ent.; 7/15 - No. 6, 12/15, $3.99) 1-6-Kelly & Lanzing-s/To-a						4.00

HAGAR THE HORRIBLE (See Comics Reading Libraries in the Promotional Comics section)

HA HA COMICS (Teepee Tim No. 100 on; also see Giggle Comics)
Scope Mag.(Creston Publ.) No. 1-80/American Comics Group: Oct, 1943 - No. 99, Jan, 1955

	GD 2.0	VG 4.0	FN 6.0	VF 8.0	VF/NM 9.0	NM- 9.2
1-Funny animal	40	80	120	246	411	575
2	21	42	63	122	199	275
3-5: Ken Hultgren-a begins?	15	30	45	88	137	185
6-10	14	28	42	80	115	150
11-20: 14-Infinity-c	12	24	36	69	97	125
21-40	11	22	33	60	83	105
41-43,45-94,97-99: 49,61-X-Mas-c	10	20	30	56	76	95
44-1st Tee-Pee Tim app.; begin series; Little Black Sambo app.	11	22	33	60	83	105
95,96-3-D effect-c/story	17	34	51	98	154	210

HAIL HYDRA (Secret Wars tie-in)
Marvel Comics: Sept, 2015 - No. 4, Jan, 2016 ($3.99, limited series)

	GD 2.0	VG 4.0	FN 6.0	VF 8.0	VF/NM 9.0	NM- 9.2
1-4-Nomad (Ian Rogers) vs. Hydra; Remender-s/Boschi-a; Venom app.						4.00

HAIR BEAR BUNCH, THE (TV) (See Fun-In No. 13)
Gold Key: Feb, 1972 - No. 9, Feb, 1974 (Hanna-Barbera)

	GD 2.0	VG 4.0	FN 6.0	VF 8.0	VF/NM 9.0	NM- 9.2
1	4	8	12	23	37	50
2-9	3	6	9	16	24	32

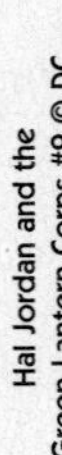

Hal Jordan and the Green Lantern Corps #9 © DC

Halo: Escalation #13 © Microsoft

The Hand of Fate #17 © DC

	GD 2.0	VG 4.0	FN 6.0	VF 8.0	VF/NM 9.0	NM- 9.2

HALCYON
Image Comics: Nov, 2010 - No. 5, May, 2011 ($2.99)
1-5-Guggenheim & Butters-s/Bodenheim-a 3.00

HALF PAST DANGER
IDW Publishing: May, 2013 - No. 6, Oct, 2013 ($3.99, limited series)
1-6: Dinosaurs and Nazis in 1943; Stephen Mooney-s/a/c 4.00

HAL JORDAN AND THE GREEN LANTERN CORPS (DC Rebirth) (Also see Green Lanterns)
DC Comics: Sept, 2016 - Present ($2.99)
1-15: 1-Venditti-s/Sandoval-a; Sinestro app.; GL Corps returns. 4,5-Van Sciver-a. 10-12-Larfleeze app. 3.00
...: Rebirth 1 (9/16, $2.99) Venditti-s/Van Sciver-a; Sinestro & Lyssa app. 3.00

HALLELUJAH TRAIL, THE (See Movie Classics)

HALL OF FAME FEATURING THE T.H.U.N.D.E.R. AGENTS
JC Productions(Archie Comics Group): May, 1983 - No. 3, Dec, 1983
1-3: Thunder Agents-r(Crandall, Kane, Tuska, Wood-a). 2-New Ditko-c 4.00

HALLOWEEN (Movie)
Chaos! Comics: Nov, 2000; Apr, 2001 ($2.95/$2.99, one-shots)
1-Brewer-a; Michael Myers childhood at the Sanitarium 3.00
...II: The Blackest Eyes (4/01, $2.99) Beck-a 3.00
...III: The Devil's Eyes (11/01, $2.99) Justiniano-a 3.00

HALLOWEEN (Halloween Nightdance on cover)(Movie)
Devils Due Publishing: Mar, 2008 - No. 4, May, 2008 ($3.50, limited series)
1-4-Seeley-a/Hutchinson-s; multiple covers on each 3.50
...: 30 Years of Terror (8/08, $5.50) short stories by various incl. Seeley 5.50

HALLOWEEN EVE
Image Comics: Oct, 2012 ($3.99, one-shot)
One-Shot - Brandon Montclare-s/Amy Reeder-a; two covers by Reeder 4.00

HALLOWEEN HORROR
Eclipse Comics: Oct, 1987 (Seduction of the Innocent #7)($1.75)
1-Pre-code horror-r 5.00

HALLOWEEN MEGAZINE
Marvel Comics: Dec, 1996 ($3.95, one-shot, 96 pgs.)
1-Reprints Tomb of Dracula 4.00

HALO GRAPHIC NOVEL (Based on video game)
Marvel Publishing Inc.: 2006 ($24.99, hardcover with dust jacket)
HC-Anthology set in the Halo universe; art by Bisley, Moebius and others; pin-up gallery by various incl. Darrow, Pratt, Williams and Van Fleet; Phil Hale painted-c 25.00

HALO: BLOOD LINE (Based on video game)
Marvel Comics: Feb, 2010 - No. 5, Jul, 2010 ($3.99, limited series)
1-5-Van Lente-s/Portela-a 4.00

HALO: ESCALATION (Based on video game)
Dark Horse Comics: Dec, 2013 - No. 24, Nov, 2015 ($3.99)
1-24: 1-4-Chris Schlerf-s/Sergio Ariño-a 4.00

HALO: FALL OF REACH - BOOT CAMP (Based on video game)
Marvel Comics: Nov, 2010 - No. 4, Apr, 2011 ($3.99, limited series)
1-4-Reed-s/Ruiz-a 4.00

HALO: FALL OF REACH - COVENANT (Based on video game)
Marvel Comics: Jun, 2011 - No. 4, Dec, 2011 ($3.99, limited series)
1-4-Reed-s/Ruiz-a 4.00

HALO: FALL OF REACH - INVASION (Based on video game)
Marvel Comics: Mar, 2012 - No. 4, Aug, 2012 ($3.99, limited series)
1-4-Reed-s/Ruiz-a 4.00

HALO: HELLJUMPER (Based on video game)
Marvel Comics: Sept, 2009 - No. 5, Jan, 2010 ($3.99, limited series)
1-5-Peter David-s/Eric Nguyen-a 4.00

HALO: INITIATION (Based on video game)
Dark Horse Comics: Aug, 2013 - No. 3, Oct, 2013 ($3.99, limited series)
1-3-Brian Reed-s/Marco Castiello-a 4.00

HALO: UPRISING (Based on video game) (Also see Marvel Spotlight: Halo)
Marvel Comics: Oct, 2007 - No. 4, Jun, 2009 ($3.99, limited series)
1-4-Bendis-s/Maleev-a; takes place between the *Halo 2* and *Halo 3* video games 4.00

HALO JONES (See The Ballad of...)

	GD 2.0	VG 4.0	FN 6.0	VF 8.0	VF/NM 9.0	NM- 9.2

HAMMER, THE
Dark Horse Comics: Oct, 1997 - No. 4, Jan, 1998 ($2.95, limited series)
1-4-Kelley Jones-s/c/a, ...: Uncle Alex (8/98, $2.95) 3.00

HAMMER, THE: THE OUTSIDER
Dark Horse Comics: Feb, 1999 - No. 3, Apr, 1999 ($2.95, limited series)
1-3-Kelley Jones-s/c/a 3.00

HAMMERLOCKE
DC Comics: Sept, 1992 - No. 9, May, 1993 ($1.75, limited series)
1-($2.50, 52 pgs.)-Chris Sprouse-c/a in all 4.00
2-9 3.00

HAMMER OF GOD (Also see Nexus)
First Comics: Feb, 1990 - No. 4, May, 1990 ($1.95, limited series)
1-4 3.00

HAMMER OF GOD: BUTCH
Dark Horse Comics: May, 1994 - No. 4, Aug, 1994 ($2.50, limited series)
1-3 3.00

HAMMER OF GOD: PENTATHLON
Dark Horse Comics: Jan, 1994 ($2.50, one shot)
1-Character from Nexus 3.00

HAMMER OF GOD: SWORD OF JUSTICE
First Comics: Feb 1991 - Mar 1991 ($4.95, lim. series, squarebound, 52 pgs.)
V2#1,2 5.00

HAMMER OF THE GODS
Insight Studio Groups: 2001 - No. 5, 2001 ($2.95, limited series)
1-Michael Oeming & Mark Wheatley-s/a; Frank Cho-c 6.00
1-(IDW, 7/11, $1.00) reprints #1 with "Hundred Penny Press" logo on Oeming cover 3.00
2-5: 3-Hughes-c. 5-Dave Johnson-c 3.00
The Color Saga (2002, $4.95) r/"Enemy of the Gods" internet strip 5.00
Mortal Enemy TPB (2002, $18.95) r/#1-5; intro. by Peter David; afterword by Raven 19.00

HAMMER OF THE GODS: HAMMER HITS CHINA
Image Comics: Feb, 2003 - No. 3, Sept, 2003 ($2.95, limited series)
1-3-Oeming & Wheatley-s/a; Oeming-c. 2-Frankenstein Mobster by Wheatley 3.00

HANDBOOK OF THE CONAN UNIVERSE, THE
Marvel Comics: June, 1985; Jan, 1986 ($1.25, one-shot)
1-(6/85) Kaluta-c (2 printings) 6.00
1-(1/86) Kaluta-c 6.00

	GD	VG	FN	VF	VF/NM	NM-
nn-(no date, circa '87-88, B&W, 36 pgs.) reprints '86 with changes; new painted cover	1	2	3	5	6	8

HAND OF FATE (Formerly Men Against Crime)
Ace Magazines: No. 8, Dec, 1951 - No. 25, Dec, 1954 (Weird/horror stories) (Two #25's)

	GD	VG	FN	VF	VF/NM	NM-
8-Surrealistic text story	50	100	150	315	533	750
9,10,21-Necronomicon sty; drug belladonna used	34	68	102	199	325	450
11-18,20,22,23	29	58	87	172	281	390
19-Bondage, hypo needle scenes	31	62	93	182	296	410
24-Electric chair-c	39	78	117	234	385	535
25a(11/54), 25b(12/54)-Both have Cameron-a	24	48	72	142	234	325

NOTE: *Cameron a-9, 10, 19-25a, 25b; c-13.* ***Sekowsky*** *a-8, 9, 13, 14.*

HAND OF FATE
Eclipse Comics: Feb, 1988 - No. 3, Apr, 1988 ($1.75/$2.00, Baxter paper)
1-3; 3-B&W 4.00

HANDS OF THE DRAGON
Seaboard Periodicals (Atlas): June, 1975

	GD	VG	FN	VF	VF/NM	NM-
1-Origin/1st app.; Craig-a(p)/Mooney inks	2	4	6	11	16	20

HANGMAN, THE
Archie Comic Publications: Dec, 2015 - No. 4, Dec, 2016 ($3.99)
1-4-Tieri-s/Ruiz-a; new Hangman recruited; multiple covers 4.00

HANGMAN COMICS (Special Comics No. 1; Black Hood No. 9 on)
(Also see Flyman, Mighty Comics, Mighty Crusaders & Pep Comics)
MLJ Magazines: No. 2, Spring, 1942 - No. 8, Fall, 1943

	GD	VG	FN	VF	VF/NM	NM-
2-The Hangman, Boy Buddies begin	309	618	927	2163	3782	5400
3-Beheading splash pg.; 1st Nazi war-c	309	618	927	2163	3782	5400
4-Classic Nazi WWII hunchback torture-c	300	600	900	2010	3505	5000
5-1st Japan war-c	226	452	678	1446	2473	3500
6-8: 8-2nd app. Super Duck (ties w/Jolly Jingles #11)	206	412	618	1318	2259	3200

Hanna-Barbera All-Stars #2 © H-B

Han Solo #1 © Lucasfilm

Happy Comics #7 © STD

	GD 2.0	VG 4.0	FN 6.0	VF 8.0	VF/NM 9.0	NM- 9.2

NOTE: *Fuje a-7(3), 8(3); c-3.* ***Reinman** c/a-3. Bondage c-3.* ***Sahle** c-6.*

HANK
Pentagon Publishing Co.: 1946

nn-Coulton Waugh's newspaper reprint	10	20	30	54	72	90

HANK JOHNSON, AGENT OF HYDRA (Secret Wars tie-in)
Marvel Comics: Oct, 2015 ($3.99, one-shot)

1-Mandel-s/Walsh-a; Steranko cover swipe by Conner 4.00

HANNA-BARBERA (See Golden Comics Digest No. 2, 7, 11)

HANNA-BARBERA ALL-STARS
Archie Publications: Oct, 1995 - No. 4, Apr, 1996 ($1.50, bi-monthly)

1-4 4.00

HANNA-BARBERA BANDWAGON (TV)
Gold Key: Oct, 1962 - No. 3, Apr, 1963

1-Giant, 84 pgs. 1-Augie Doggie app.; 1st app. Lippy the Lion, Touché Turtle & Dum Dum, Wally Gator, Loopy de Loop,	10	20	30	69	147	225
2-Giant, 84 pgs.; Mr. & Mrs. J. Evil Scientist (1st app.) in Snagglepuss story; Yakky Doodle, Ruff and Reddy and others app.	8	16	24	51	96	140
3-Regular size; Mr. & Mrs. J. Evil Scientist app. (pre-#1), Snagglepuss, Wally Gator and others app.	6	12	18	40	73	105

HANNA-BARBERA GIANT SIZE
Harvey Comics: Oct, 1992 - No. 3 ($2.25, 68 pgs.)

V2#1-3:Flintstones, Yogi Bear, Magilla Gorilla, Huckleberry Hound, Quick Draw McGraw, Yakky Doodle & Chopper, Jetsons & others 6.00

HANNA-BARBERA HI-ADVENTURE HEROES (See Hi-Adventure...)

HANNA-BARBERA PARADE (TV)
Charlton Comics: Sept, 1971 - No. 10, Dec, 1972

1	6	12	18	41	76	110
2,4-10	4	8	12	25	40	55
3-(52 pgs.)- "Summer Picnic"	5	10	15	33	57	80

NOTE: *No. 4 (1/72) went on sale late in 1972 with the January 1973 issues.*

HANNA-BARBERA PRESENTS
Archie Publications: Nov, 1995 - No. 8 ($1.50, bi-monthly)

1-8: 1-Atom Ant & Secret Squirrel. 2-Wacky Races. 3-Yogi Bear. 4-Quick Draw McGraw & Magilla Gorilla. 5-A Pup Named Scooby-Doo. 6-Superstar Olympics. 7-Wacky Races. 8-Frankenstein Jr. & the Impossibles 4.00

HANNA-BARBERA SPOTLIGHT (See Spotlight)

HANNA-BARBERA SUPER TV HEROES (TV)
Gold Key: Apr, 1968 - No. 7, Oct, 1969 (Hanna-Barbera)

1-The Birdman, The Herculoids (ends #6; not in #3), Moby Dick, Young Samson & Goliath (ends #2,4), and The Mighty Mightor begin; Spiegle-a in all	11	22	33	76	163	250
2-The Galaxy Trio app.; Shazzan begins; 12¢ & 15¢ versions exist	8	16	24	56	108	160
3,6,7-The Space Ghost app.	8	16	24	51	96	140
4,5	7	14	21	44	82	120

NOTE: *Birdman in #1,2,4,5. Herculoids in #2,4-7. Mighty Mightor in #1,2,4-7. Moby Dick in all. Shazzan in #2-5. Young Samson & Goliath in #1,3.*

HANNA-BARBERA TV FUN FAVORITES (See Golden Comics Digest #2,7,11)

HANNA-BARBERA (TV STARS) (See TV Stars)

HANS BRINKER (Disney)
Dell Publishing Co.: No. 1273, Feb, 1962 (one-shot)

Four Color 1273-Movie, photo-c	6	12	18	37	66	95

HANS CHRISTIAN ANDERSEN
Ziff-Davis Publ. Co.: 1953 (100 pgs., Special Issue)

nn-Danny Kaye (movie)-Photo-c; fairy tales	18	36	54	105	165	225

HANSEL & GRETEL
Dell Publishing Co.: No. 590, Oct, 1954 (one-shot)

Four Color 590-Partial photo-c	6	12	18	41	76	110

HANSI, THE GIRL WHO LOVED THE SWASTIKA
Spire Christian Comics (Fleming H. Revell Co.): 1973, 1976 (39¢/49¢)

1973 edition with 39¢-c	9	18	27	59	117	175
1976 edition with 49¢-c	7	14	21	49	92	135

HAN SOLO (Star Wars)
Marvel Comics: Aug, 2016 - No. 5, Jan, 2017 ($3.99, limited series)

1-5-Marjorie Liu-s/Mark Brooks-a/Lee Bermejo-c; takes place between Episodes 4 & 5 4.00

HAP HAZARD COMICS (Real Love No. 25 on)
Ace Magazines (Readers' Research): Summer, 1944 - No. 24, Feb, 1949
(#1-6 are quarterly issues)

1	15	30	45	90	140	190
2	10	20	30	54	72	90
3-10	9	18	27	47	61	75
11-13,15-24	8	16	24	42	54	65
14-Feldstein-c (4/47)	10	20	30	56	76	95

HAP HOPPER (See Comics Revue No. 2)

HAPPIEST MILLIONAIRE, THE (See Movie Comics)

HAPPI TIM (See March of Comics No. 182)

HAPPY
Image Comics: Sept, 2012 - No. 4, Feb, 2013 ($2.99, limited series)

1-4-Grant Morrison-s/Darick Robertson-a. 1-Covers by Robertson & Allred 5.00

HAPPY BIRTHDAY MARTHA WASHINGTON (Also see Give Me Liberty, Martha Washington Goes To War, & Martha Washington Stranded In Space)
Dark Horse Comics: Mar, 1995 ($2.95, one-shot)

1-Miller script; Gibbons-c/a 3.00

HAPPY COMICS (Happy Rabbit No. 41 on)
Nedor Publ./Standard Comics (Animated Cartoons): Aug, 1943 - No. 40, Dec, 1950
(Companion to Goofy Comics)

1-Funny animal	34	68	102	199	325	450
2	18	36	54	105	165	225
3-10	14	28	42	80	115	150
11-19	12	24	36	67	94	120
20-31,34-37-Frazetta text illos in all (2 in #34&35, 3 in #27,28,30). 27-Al Fago-a	14	28	42	76	108	140
32-Frazetta-a, 7 pgs. plus 2 text illos; Roussos-a	22	44	66	132	216	300
33-Frazetta-a(2), 6 pgs. each (Scarce)	31	62	93	186	303	420
38-40	11	22	33	60	83	105

HAPPYDALE: DEVILS IN THE DESERT
DC Comics (Vertigo): 1999 - No. 2, 1999 ($6.95, limited series)

1,2-Andrew Dabb-s/Seth Fisher-a 7.00

HAPPY DAYS (TV)(See Kite Fun Book)
Gold Key: Mar, 1979 - No. 6, Feb, 1980

1-Photo-c of TV cast; 35¢-c	3	6	9	16	23	30
2-6-(40¢-c)	2	4	6	9	12	15

HAPPY HOLIDAY (See March of Comics No. 181)

HAPPY HOULIHANS (Saddle Justice No. 3 on; see Blackstone, The Magician Detective)
E. C. Comics: Fall, 1947 - No. 2, Winter, 1947-48

1-Origin Moon Girl (same date as Moon Girl #1)	63	126	189	403	689	975
2	36	72	108	211	343	475

HAPPY JACK
Red Top (Decker): Aug, 1957 - No. 2, Nov, 1957

V1#1,2	5	10	15	22	26	30

HAPPY JACK HOWARD
Red Top (Farrell)/Decker: 1957

nn-Reprints Handy Andy story from E. C. Dandy Comics #5, renamed "Happy Jack"	5	10	15	22	26	30

HAPPY RABBIT (Formerly Happy Comics)
Standard Comics (Animated Cartoons): No. 41, Feb, 1951 - No. 48, Apr, 1952

41-Funny animal	10	20	30	54	72	90
42-48	8	16	24	42	54	65

HARBINGER (Also see Unity)
Valiant: Jan, 1992 - No. 41, June, 1995 ($1.95/$2.50)

0-Prequel to the series; available by redeeming coupons in #1-6; cover image has pink sky; title logo is blue	4	8	12	28	47	65
0-(2nd printing) cover has blue sky & red logo	1	3	4	6	8	10
1-1st app.	7	14	21	46	86	125
2-4: 4-Low print run	2	4	6	13	18	22
5,6: 5-Solar app. 6-Torque dies	2	4	6	9	12	15
7-10: 8,9-Unity x-overs. 8-Miller-c. 9-Simonson-c. 10-1st app. H.A.R.D Corps (10/92)	1	2	3	5	6	8

11-24,26-41: 14-1st app. Stronghold. 18-Intro Screen. 19-1st app. Stunner. 22-Archer & Armstrong app. 24-Cover similar to #1. 26-Intro New Harbingers. 29-Bound-in trading card. 30-H.A.R.D. Corps app. 32-Eternal Warrior app. 33-Dr. Eclipse app. 4.00

Harbinger Wars #4 © VAL

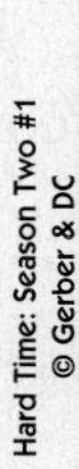

Hard Time: Season Two #1 © Gerber & DC

Harley Quinn (2014 series) #2 © DC

GD VG FN VF VF/NM NM-
2.0 4.0 6.0 8.0 9.0 9.2

25-($3.50, 52 pgs.)-Harada vs. Sting 5.00
...Files 1,2 (8/94,2/95 $2.50) 4.00
...: The Beginning HC (2007, $24.95) recolored reprints #0-7 and Story of Harada from coupons from #1-6; new "Origin of Harada" story by Shooter and Bob Hall 30.00
Trade paperback nn (11/92, $9.95)-Reprints #1-4 & comes polybagged with a copy of Harbinger #0 w/new-c. Price for TPB only 15.00
NOTE: *Issues 1-6 have coupons with origin of Harada and are redeemable for Harbinger #0.*

HARBINGER
Valiant Entertainment: Jun, 2012 - Present ($3.99)(#0 released between #8 & #9)

1-Dysart-s/Khari Evans-a; covers by Lozzi and Suayan (Pullbox variant) 4.00
1-Variant cover by Braithwaite 10.00
1-QR voice variant cover by Jelena Djurdjevic 40.00
2-24-Two covers on each (standard & pullbox). 2-Origin continues. 11-14-Harbinger Wars tie-in. 23-Flamingo dies 4.00
25-($4.99) Back-up story by Tiwary & Larosa; bonus features and cover gallery 5.00
#0 (2/13, $3.99) Origin of Harada; Suayan & Pere Pérez-a; covers by Crain & Suayan 4.00
#0-Variant gatefold-c by Lewis Larosa 15.00
... Bleeding Monk #0 (3/14, $3.99) Dysart-s; art by Evans, Suayan, Segovia & LaRosa 4.00
... Faith #0 (12/14, $3.99) Dysart-s; Robert Gill-a 4.00

HARBINGER: OMEGAS
Valiant Entertainment: Jul, 2014 - No. 3, Oct, 2014 ($3.99, limited series)

1-3-Dysart-s/Sandoval-a 4.00

HARBINGER RENEGADE
Valiant Entertainment: Nov, 2016 - Present ($3.99, limited series)

1-4-Rafer Roberts-s/Darick Robertson-a; intro Alexander Solomon 4.00

HARBINGER WARS
Valiant Entertainment: Apr, 2013 - No. 4, Jul, 2013 ($3.99, limited series)

1-4: 1-Dysart-s/Henry, Crain & Suayan-a; covers by Larosa & Henry (Pullbox) 4.00
1-Variant cover by Crain 10.00
1-Variant cover by Zircher 40.00

HARD BOILED
Dark Horse Comics: Sept, 1990 - No. 3, Mar, 1992 ($4.95/$5.95, 8 1/2x11", lim. series)

1-Frank Miller-s/Darrow-c/a in all; sexually explicit & violent
2 4 6 11 16 20
2,3 2 4 6 8 10 12
TPB (5/93, $15.95) 20.00
Big Damn Hard Boiled (12/97, $29.95, B&W) r/#1-3 30.00

HARDCASE (See Break Thru, Flood Relief & Ultraforce, 1st Series)
Malibu Comics (Ultraverse): June, 1993 - No. 26, Aug, 1995 ($1.95/$2.50)

1-Intro Hardcase; Dave Gibbons-c; has coupon for Ultraverse Premiere #0; Jim Callahan-a(p) begin, ends #3 4.00
1-With coupon missing 2.00
1-Platinum Edition 6.00
1-Holographic Cover Edition; 1st full-c holograph tied w/Prime 1 & Strangers 1 8.00
1-Ultra Limited silver foil-c 6.00
2,3-Callahan-a, 2-($2.50)-Newsstand edition bagged w/trading card 3.00
4,6-15, 17-19: 4-Strangers app. 7-Break-Thru x-over. 8-Solution app. 9-Vs. Turf. 12-Silver foil logo, wraparound-c. 17-Prime app. 3.00
5-($2.50, 48 pgs.)-Rune flip-c/story by B. Smith (3 pgs.) 4.00
16 ($3.50, 68 pgs.)-Rune pin-up 4.00
20-26: 23-Loki app. 3.00
NOTE: ***Perez** a-8(2); c-20i.*

HARDCORE
Image Comics: May, 2012 ($2.99)

1-Kirkman-s/Stelfreeze-a/Silvestri-c 3.00

HARDCORE STATION
DC Comics: July, 1998 - No. 6, Dec, 1998 ($2.50, limited series)

1-6-Starlin-s/a(p). 3-Green Lantern-c/app. 5,6-JLA-c/app. 3.00

H.A.R.D. CORPS, THE (See Harbinger #10)
Valiant: Dec, 1992 - No. 30, Feb, 1995 ($2.25) (Harbinger spin-off)

1-($2.50)-Gatefold-c by Jim Lee & Bob Layton 5.00
1-Gold variant 15.00
2-30: 5-Bloodshot-c/story cont'd from Bloodshot #3. 5-Variant edition; came w/Comic Defense System. 10-Turok app. 17-vs. Armorines. 18-Bound-in trading card. 20-Harbinger app. 3.00

HARD TIME
DC Comics (Focus): Apr, 2004 - No. 12, Mar, 2005 ($2.50)

1-12-Gerber-s/Hurtt-a; 1-Includes previews of other DC Focus series 3.00

GD VG FN VF VF/NM NM-
2.0 4.0 6.0 8.0 9.0 9.2

...: 50 to Life (2004, $9.95, TPB) r/#1-6; cover gallery with sketches 10.00

HARD TIME: SEASON TWO
DC Comics: Feb, 2006 - No. 7, Aug, 2006 ($2.50/$2.99)

1-5-Gerber-s/Hurtt-a 3.00
6,7-($2.99) 7-Ethan paroled in 2053 3.00

HARDWARE
DC Comics (Milestone): Apr, 1993 - No. 50, Apr, 1997 ($1.50/$1.75/$2.50)

1-($2.95)-Collector's Edition polybagged w/poster & trading card (direct sale only) 4.00
1-Platinum Edition 6.00
1-15,17-19: 11-Shadow War x-over. 11,14-Simonson-c. 12-Buckler-a(p). 17-Worlds Collide Pt. 2. 18-Simonson-c; Worlds Collide Pt. 9. 15-1st Humberto Ramos DC work 3.00
16,25: 16-($2.50, 52 pgs.)-Newsstand Ed. 25-($2.95, 52 pgs.) 4.00
16,50-($3.95, 52 pgs.)-16-Collector's Edition w/gatefold 2nd cover by Byrne; new armor; Icon app. 5.00
20-24,26-49: 49-Moebius-c 3.00
...: The Man in the Machine TPB (2010, $19.99) r/#1-8 20.00

HARDY BOYS, THE (Disney
Dell Publ. Co.: No. 760, Dec, 1956 - No. 964, Jan, 1959 (Mickey Mouse Club)

Four Color 760 (#1)-Photo-c 9 18 27 61 123 185
Four Color 830(8/57), 887(1/58), 964-Photo-c 8 16 24 54 102 150

HARDY BOYS, THE (TV)
Gold Key: Apr, 1970 - No. 4, Jan, 1971

1 4 8 12 27 44 60
2-4 3 6 9 17 26 35

HARLAN ELLISON'S DREAM CORRIDOR
Dark Horse Comics: Mar, 1995 - No. 5, July, 1995 ($2.95, anthology)

1-5: Adaptation of Ellison stories. 1-4-Byrne-a. 4.00
Special (1/95, $4.95) 6.00
Trade paperback-(1996, $18.95, 192 pgs)-r/#1-5 & Special #1 19.00

HARLAN ELLISON'S DREAM CORRIDOR QUARTERLY
Dark Horse Comics: V2#1, Aug, 1996 ($5.95, anthology, squarebound)

V2#1-Adaptations of Ellison's stories w/new material; Neal Adams-a 6.00
Volume 2 TPB (3/07, $19.95) r/V2#1 and unpublished material incl. last Swan-a 20.00

HARLEM GLOBETROTTERS (TV) (See Fun-In No. 8, 10)
Gold Key: Apr, 1972 - No. 12, Jan, 1975 (Hanna-Barbera)

1 4 8 12 25 40 55
2-5 3 6 9 15 22 28
6-12 2 4 6 13 18 22
NOTE: *#4, 8, and 12 contain 16 extra pages of advertising.*

HARLEQUIN ROMANCE
Dark Horse Comics: Nov, 2001 ($10.95, hardcover, one-shot)

nn-Neil Gaiman-s; painted-a/c by John Bolton 11.00

HARLEY QUINN (See Batman Adventures #12 for 1st app.)(Also see Gotham City Sirens)
DC Comics: Dec, 2000 - No. 38, Jan, 2004 ($2.95/$2.25/$2.50)

1-Joker and Poison Ivy app.; Terry & Rachel Dodson-a/c
4 8 12 28 47 65
2,3-($2.25): 2-Two-Face-c/app. 3-Slumber party 2 4 6 10 14 18
4-9,11-($2.25). 6,7-Riddler app. 1 2 3 5 6 8
10-Batgirl-c/s 2 4 6 10 14 18
12-($2.95) Batman app. 2 4 6 9 12 15
13,17-19: 13-Joker: Last Laugh. 17,18-Bizarro-c/app. 19-Superman-c
2 4 6 9 12 15
14-16,20-24,26-31,33-37: 23-Begin $2.50-c. 23,24-Martian Manhunter app.
1 2 3 5 6 8
25-Classic Joker-c/s 3 6 9 15 22 28
32-Joker-c/app. 2 4 6 11 16 20
38-Last issue; Adlard-a/Morse-c 3 6 9 14 20 25
Harley & Ivy: Love on the Lam (2001, $5.95) Winick-s/Chiodo-c/a
2 4 6 13 18 22
...: Our Worlds at War (10/01, $2.95) Jae Lee-c; art by various
2 4 6 11 16 20

HARLEY QUINN (DC New 52)
DC Comics: No. 0, Jan, 2014 - No. 30, Sept, 2016 ($2.99/$3.99)

0-Conner & Palmiotti-s; art by Conner & various; Conner-c
2 4 6 9 12 15
0-Variant-c by Stephane Roux 2 4 6 11 16 20
1-(2/14) Chad Hardin-a; Conner-c 2 4 6 13 18 22
1-Variant-c by Adam Hughes 12 24 36 79 170 260

Harley Quinn (2016 series) #13 © DC

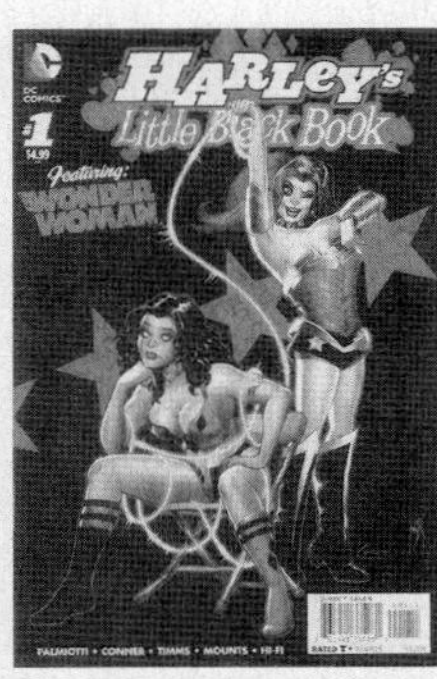

Harley's Little Black Book #1 © DC

Harvey Comics Hits #52 © HARV

GD VG FN VF VF/NM NM-
2.0 4.0 6.0 8.0 9.0 9.2

1-Halloween Fest Special Edition (12/15, free) r/#1 with "Halloween ComicFest" logo 3.00
2-Poison Ivy app. 2 4 6 9 12 15
3-5: 4-Roux-a 1 2 3 5 6 8
6-16: 6,7-Poison Ivy app. 11-13-Power Girl app. 16-Intro. of The Gang of Harleys 4.00
17-30-($3.99) 17-19-Capt Strong app. 20,21-Deadshot app. 25-Joker app.
26-28-Red Tool app. 30-Charretier-a; Poison Ivy app. 4.00
Annual 1 (12/14, $5.99) Polybagged with "Rub 'N Smell" pages 6.00
... & The Suicide Squad April Fools' Special 1 (6/16, $4.99) Rob Williams-s/Jim Lee-a 5.00
...Director's Cut #0 (8/14, $4.99) With commentary by Conner & Palmiotti; cover gallery 5.00
...: Futures End 1 (11/14, $2.99, regular-c) Five years later; Joker app. 3.00
...: Futures End 1 (11/14, $3.99, 3-D cover) 4.00
... Holiday Special (2/15, $4.99) Christmas-themed stories; back-up Darwyn Cooke-a 5.00
... Invades Comic-Con International: San Diego 1 (9/14, $4.99) Wraparound-c 5.00
... Road Trip Special (11/15, $5.99) Harley, Catwoman & Poison Ivy road trip; Conner-c 6.00
... Valentine's Day Special (4/15, $4.99) Bruce Wayne and Poison Ivy app. 5.00

HARLEY QUINN (DC Rebirth)
DC Comics: Oct, 2016 - Present ($2.99)
1-Conner & Palmiotti-s/Hardin-a; Poison Ivy & Red Tool app. 4.00
2-6: 4-Linsner-a. 6-Joker flashback w/Jill Thompson-a (4 pgs.) 3.00
7-15: 9-Kaluta-a (4 pgs.). 10-Linsner & Moritat-a. 15-Power Girl & Atlee app. 3.00
Harley Quinn's Greatest Hits TPB (2016, $9.99) r/Batman Advs. #12 & other stories 10.00

HARLEY QUINN AND HER GANG OF HARLEYS
DC Comics: Jun, 2016 - No. 6, Nov, 2016 ($3.99, limited series)
1-6-Palmiotti & Tieri-s/Mauricet-a/Conner-c; intro. Harley Sinn. 5-Origin of Harley Sinn 4.00

HARLEY QUINN AND POWER GIRL
DC Comics: Aug, 2015 - No. 6, Feb, 2016 ($3.99, limited series)
1-6-Takes place during Harley Quinn #11-13; Vartox app.; Roux-a 4.00

HARLEY'S LITTLE BLACK BOOK (Harley Quinn team-up book)
DC Comics: Feb, 2016 - Present ($4.99, bi-monthly)
1-4: 1-Palmiotti & Conner-s; Wonder Woman app.; Conner-c. 2-Green Lantern app.
3-Zatanna app.; Linsner-a. 4-DC Bombshells app.; Tucci-a 5.00
1-Polybagged variant-c by Campbell (3 versions: sketch, B&W, and color)
1 2 3 5 6 8
5-Neal Adams-a; homage to "Superman vs. Muhammad Ali" 5.00

HAROLD TEEN (See Popular Comics, & Super Comics)
Dell Publishing Co.: No. 2, 1942 - No. 209, Jan, 1949
Four Color 2 31 62 93 223 499 775
Four Color 209 6 12 18 40 73 105

HARROW COUNTY
Dark Horse Comics: May, 2015 - Present ($3.99)
1-20: 1-8-Cullen Bunn-s/Tyler Crook-a. 9,17-Carla Speed McNeil-a 4.00
1-Halloween ComicFest Edition (10/16, no price) r/#1 3.00

HARROWERS, THE (See Clive Barker's...)

HARSH REALM (Inspired 1999 TV series)
Harris Comics: 1993- No. 6, 1994 ($2.95, limited series)
1-6: Painted-c. Hudnall-s/Paquette & Ridgway-a 4.00
TPB (2000, $14.95) r/series 15.00

HARVESTER, THE
Legendary Comics: Feb, 2015 - No. 6, Jul, 2015 ($3.99)
1-6-Brandon Seifert-s/Eric Battle-a/c 4.00

HARVEY
Marvel Comics: Oct, 1970; No. 2, 12/70; No. 3, 6/72 - No. 6, 12/72
1-Teenage 10 20 30 66 138 210
2-6 7 14 21 46 86 125

HARVEY COLLECTORS COMICS (Titled Richie Rich Collectors Comics on cover of #6-on)
Harvey Publ.: Sept, 1975 - No. 15, Jan, 1978; No. 16, Oct, 1979 (52 pgs.)
1-Reprints Richie Rich #1,2 2 4 6 13 18 22
2-10: 7-Splash pg. shows cover to Friendly Ghost Casper #1
2 4 6 8 11 14
11-16: 16-Sad Sack-r 1 2 3 5 7 9
NOTE: *All reprints: Casper-#2, 7, Richie Rich-#1, 3, 5, 6, 8-15, Sad Sack-#16. Wendy-#4.*

HARVEY COMICS HITS (Formerly Joe Palooka #50)
Harvey Publications: No. 51, Oct, 1951 - No. 62, Apr, 1953
51-The Phantom 36 72 108 211 343 475
52-Steve Canyon's Air Power(Air Force sponsored) 13 26 39 72 101 130
53-Mandrake the Magician 20 40 60 114 182 250
54-Tim Tyler's Tales of Jungle Terror 13 26 39 74 105 135
55-Love Stories of Mary Worth 11 22 33 64 90 115
56-The Phantom; bondage-c 27 54 81 158 259 360
57-Rip Kirby Exposes the Kidnap Racket; entire book by Alex Raymond
15 30 45 86 133 180
58-Girls in White (nurses stories) 11 22 33 64 90 115
59-Tales of the Invisible featuring Scarlet O'Neil 12 24 36 69 97 125
60-Paramount Animated Comics #1 (9/52) (3rd app. Baby Huey); 2nd Harvey app. Baby Huey & Casper the Friendly Ghost (1st in Little Audrey #25 (8/52)); 1st app. Herman & Catnip (c/story) & Buzzy the Crow 58 116 174 371 636 900
61-Casper the Friendly Ghost #6 (3rd Harvey Casper, 10/52)-Casper-c
50 100 150 315 533 750
62-Paramount Animated Comics #2; Herman & Catnip, Baby Huey & Buzzy the Crow
18 36 54 105 165 225

HARVEY COMICS LIBRARY
Harvey Publications: Apr, 1952 - No. 2, 1952
1-Teen-Age Dope Slaves as exposed by Rex Morgan, M.D.; drug propaganda story; used in **SOTI**, pg. 27 271 542 813 1734 2967 4200
2-Dick Tracy Presents Sparkle Plenty in "Blackmail Terror"
20 40 60 114 182 250

HARVEY COMICS SPOTLIGHT
Harvey Comics: Sept, 1987 - No. 4, Mar, 1988 (75¢/$1.00)
1-New material; begin 75¢, ends #3; Sad Sack 5.00
2-4: 2,4-All new material. 2-Baby Huey. 3-Little Dot; contains reprints w/5 pg. new story.
4-$1.00-c; Little Audrey 4.00
NOTE: No. 5 was advertised but not published.

HARVEY HITS (Also see Tastee-Freez Comics in the Promotional Comics section)
Harvey Publications: Sept, 1957 - No. 122, Nov, 1967
1-The Phantom 27 54 81 189 420 650
2-Rags Rabbit (10/57) 5 10 15 34 60 85
3-Richie Rich (11/57)-r/Little Dot; 1st book devoted to Richie Rich; see Little Dot for 1st app.
141 282 423 1142 2571 4000
4-Little Dot's Uncles (12/57) 15 30 45 103 227 350
5-Stevie Mazie's Boy Friend (1/58) 4 8 12 28 47 65
6-The Phantom (2/58); 2pg. Powell-a 17 34 51 117 259 400
7-Wendy the Good Little Witch (3/58, pre-dates Wendy #1; 1st book devoted to Wendy)
42 84 126 311 706 1100
8-Sad Sack's Army Life; George Baker-c 8 16 24 51 96 140
9-Richie Rich's Golden Deeds; (2nd book devoted to Richie Rich) reprints Richie Rich story from Tastee-Freez #1 66 132 198 528 1189 1850
10-Little Lotta's Lunch Box 10 20 30 69 147 225
11-Little Audrey Summer Fun (7/58) 8 16 24 54 102 150
12-The Phantom; 2pg. Powell-a (8/58) 14 28 42 96 211 325
13-Little Dot's Uncles (9/58); Richie Rich 1pg. 10 20 30 66 138 210
14-Herman & Katnip (10/58, TV/movies) 4 8 12 28 47 65
15-The Phantom (12/58)-1 pg. origin 14 28 42 96 211 325
16-Wendy the Good Little Witch (1/59); Casper app. 11 22 33 76 163 250
17-Sad Sack's Army Life (2/59) 5 10 15 34 66 85
18-Buzzy & the Crow 4 8 12 25 40 55
19-Little Audrey (4/59) 5 10 15 33 57 80
20-Casper & Spooky 7 14 21 44 82 120
21-Wendy the Witch 7 14 21 44 82 120
22-Sad Sack's Army Life 4 8 12 28 47 65
23-Wendy the Witch (8/59) 7 14 21 44 82 120
24-Little Dot's Uncles (9/59); Richie Rich 1pg. 8 16 24 51 96 140
25-Herman & Katnip (10/59) 3 6 9 21 33 45
26-The Phantom (11/59) 11 22 33 72 154 235
27-Wendy the Good Little Witch (12/59) 6 12 18 42 79 115
28-Sad Sack's Army Life (1/60) 4 8 12 25 40 55
29-Harvey-Toon (No.1)('60); Casper, Buzzy 5 10 15 31 53 75
30-Wendy the Witch (3/60) 6 12 18 42 79 115
31-Herman & Katnip (4/60) 3 6 9 19 30 40
32-Sad Sack's Army Life (5/60) 3 6 9 21 33 45
33-Wendy the Witch (6/60) 6 12 18 40 73 105
34-Harvey-Toon (7/60) 4 8 12 23 37 50
35-Funday Funnies (8/60) 3 6 9 19 30 40
36-The Phantom (1960) 10 20 30 69 147 225
37-Casper & Nightmare 5 10 15 33 57 80
38-Harvey-Toon 4 8 12 23 37 50
39-Sad Sack's Army Life (12/60) 3 6 9 20 31 42
40-Funday Funnies (1/61) 3 6 9 16 24 32
41-Herman & Katnip 3 6 9 16 24 32
42-Harvey-Toon (3/61) 3 6 9 18 28 38
43-Sad Sack's Army Life (4/61) 3 6 9 18 28 38

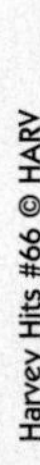
Harvey Hits #66 © HARV

Haunted Mansion #1 © DIS

Haunted Thrills #1 © AJAX

	GD 2.0	VG 4.0	FN 6.0	VF 8.0	VF/NM 9.0	NM- 9.2
44-The Phantom (5/61)	10	20	30	66	138	210
45-Casper & Nightmare	4	8	12	28	47	65
46-Harvey-Toon (7/61)	3	6	9	16	24	32
47-Sad Sack's Army Life (8/61)	3	6	9	16	24	32
48-The Phantom (9/61)	10	20	30	66	138	210
49-Stumbo the Giant (1st app. in Hot Stuff)	8	16	24	56	108	160
50-Harvey-Toon (11/61)	3	6	9	16	23	30
51-Sad Sack's Army Life (12/61)	3	6	9	16	23	30
52-Casper & Nightmare	4	8	12	27	44	60
53-Harvey-Toons (2/62)	3	6	9	16	23	30
54-Stumbo the Giant	5	10	15	31	53	75
55-Sad Sack's Army Life (4/62)	3	6	9	16	23	30
56-Casper & Nightmare	4	8	12	25	40	55
57-Stumbo the Giant	5	10	15	31	53	75
58-Sad Sack's Army Life	3	6	9	16	23	30
59-Casper & Nightmare (7/62)	4	8	12	25	40	55
60-Stumbo the Giant (9/62)	5	10	15	31	53	75
61-Sad Sack's Army Life	3	6	9	15	22	28
62-Casper & Nightmare	4	8	12	22	35	48
63-Stumbo the Giant	4	8	12	27	44	60
64-Sad Sack's Army Life (1/63)	3	6	9	15	22	28
65-Casper & Nightmare	4	8	12	22	35	48
66-Stumbo The Giant (3/63)	4	8	12	27	44	60
67-Sad Sack's Army Life (4/63)	3	6	9	15	22	28
68-Casper & Nightmare	4	8	12	22	35	48
69-Stumbo the Giant (6/63)	4	8	12	27	44	60
70-Sad Sack's Army Life (7/63)	3	6	9	15	22	28
71-Casper & Nightmare (8/63)	3	6	9	20	31	42
72-Stumbo the Giant	4	8	12	27	44	60
73-Little Sad Sack (10/63)	3	6	9	15	22	28
74-Sad Sack's Muttsy… (11/63)	3	6	9	15	22	28
75-Casper & Nightmare	3	6	9	18	28	38
76-Little Sad Sack	3	6	9	15	22	28
77-Sad Sack's Muttsy…	3	6	9	15	22	28
78-Stumbo the Giant (3/64); JFK caricature	4	8	12	28	44	60
79-87: 79-Little Sad Sack (4/64). 80-Sad Sack's Muttsy… (5/64). 81-Little Sad Sack. 82-Sad Sack's Muttsy… 83-Little Sad Sack(8/64). 84-Sad Sack's Muttsy… 85-Gabby Gob (#1) (10/64). 86-G. I. Juniors (#1)(11/64). 87-Sad Sack's Muttsy… (12/64)	3	6	9	15	22	28
88-Stumbo the Giant (1/65)	4	8	12	27	44	60
89-122: 89-Sad Sack's Muttsy… 90-Gabby Gob. 91-G. I. Juniors. 92-Sad Sack's Muttsy… (5/65). 93-Sadie Sack (6/65). 94-Gabby Gob. 95-G. I. Juniors (8/65). 96-Sad Sack's Muttsy… (9/65). 97-Gabby Gob (10/65). 98-G. I. Juniors (11/65). 99-Sad Sack's Muttsy… (12/65). 100-Gabby Gob(1/66). 101-G. I. Juniors (2/66). 102-Sad Sack's Muttsy… (3/66). 103-Gabby Gob. 104- G. I. Juniors. 105-Sad Sack's Muttsy… 106-Gabby Gob (7/66). 107-G. I. Juniors (8/66). 108-Sad Sack's Muttsy…109-Gabby Gob. 110-G. I. Juniors (11/66). 111-Sad Sack's Muttsy… (12/66). 112-G. I. Juniors. 113-Sad Sack's Muttsy… 114-G. I. Juniors. 115-Sad Sack's Muttsy… 116-G. I. Juniors (5/67). 117-Sad Sack's Muttsy… 118-G. I. Juniors. 119-Sad Sack's Muttsy… (8/67). 120-G. I. Juniors (9/67). 121-Sad Sack's Muttsy… (10/67). 122-G. I. Juniors (11/67)	2	4	6	10	14	18

HARVEY HITS COMICS
Harvey Publications: Nov, 1986 - No. 6, Oct, 1987

	GD	VG	FN	VF	VF/NM	NM-
1-Little Lotta, Little Dot, Wendy & Baby Huey	1	2	3	4	5	7
2-6: 3-Xmas-c						4.50

HARVEY POP COMICS (Rock Happening) (Teen Humor)
Harvey Publications: Oct, 1968 - No. 2, Nov, 1969 (Both are 68 pg. Giants)

	GD	VG	FN	VF	VF/NM	NM-
1-The Cowsills	5	10	15	34	60	85
2-Bunny	5	10	15	31	53	75

HARVEY 3-D HITS (See Sad Sack)

HARVEY-TOON (...S) (See Harvey Hits No. 29, 34, 38, 42, 46, 50, 53)

HARVEY WISEGUYS (...Digest #? on)
Harvey Comics: Nov, 1987; #2, Nov, 1988; #3, Apr, 1989 - No. 4, Nov, 1989 (98 pgs., digest-size, $1.25/$1.75)

	GD	VG	FN	VF	VF/NM	NM-
1-Hot Stuff, Spooky, etc.	2	3	4	6	8	10
2-4: 2 (68 pgs.)	1	2	3	4	5	7

HATARI (See Movie Classics)

HATE
Fantagraphics Books: Spr, 1990 - No. 30, 1998 ($2.50/$2.95, B&W/color)

	GD	VG	FN	VF	VF/NM	NM-
1	2	4	6	11	16	20
2-3	1	2	3	5	6	8
4-10						5.00
11-20: 16- color begins						4.00
21-29						3.00
30-($3.95) Last issue						4.00
Annual 1 (2/01, $3.95) Peter Bagge-s/a						5.00
Annual 2-9 (12/01-Present; $4.95) Peter Bagge-s/a						5.00
Buddy Bites the Bullet! (2001, $16.95) r/Buddy stories in color						17.00
Buddy Go Home! (1997, $16.95) r/Buddy stories in color						17.00
Hate-Ball Special Edition ($3.95, giveaway)-reprints						4.00
Hate Jamboree (10/98, $4.50) old & new cartoons						4.50

HATHAWAYS, THE (TV)
Dell Publishing Co.: No. 1298, Feb-Apr, 1962 (one-shot)

	GD	VG	FN	VF	VF/NM	NM-
Four Color 1298-Photo-c	5	10	15	31	53	75

HAUNT
Image Comics: Oct, 2009 - No. 28, Dec, 2012 ($2.99)

	GD	VG	FN	VF	VF/NM	NM-
1-McFarlane & Kirkman-s/Capullo & Ottley-a/McFarlane-a(i)/c; two variant-c						6.00
2-28: 2-Two covers. 13-($1.99). 19-Casey-s/Fox-a begins						3.00
Image Firsts: Haunt #1 (10/10, $1.00) r/#1 with "Image First" cover logo						3.00

HAUNTED (See This Magazine Is Haunted)

HAUNTED (Baron Weirwulf's Haunted Library on-c #21 on)
Charlton Comics: 9/71 - No. 30, 11/76; No. 31, 9/77 - No. 75, 9/84

	GD	VG	FN	VF	VF/NM	NM-
1-All Ditko issue	6	12	18	38	69	100
2-7-Ditko-c/a	3	6	9	21	33	45
8,12,28-Ditko-a	2	4	6	13	18	22
9,19	2	4	6	8	11	14
10,20,15,18: 10,20-Sutton-a. 15-Sutton-c	2	4	6	8	11	14
11,13,14,16-Ditko-c/a	3	6	9	16	23	30
17-Sutton-c/a; Newton-a	2	4	6	9	12	15
21-Newton-c/a; Sutton-a; 1st Baron Weirwulf	3	6	9	16	24	32
22-Newton-c/a; Sutton-a	2	4	6	9	13	16
23,24-Sutton-c; Ditko-a	2	4	6	9	13	16
25-27,29,32,33	1	3	4	6	8	10
30,41,47,49-52,60,74-Ditko-c/a: 51-Reprints #1	2	4	6	11	16	20
31,35,37,38-Sutton-a	1	3	4	6	8	10
34,36,39,40,42,57-Ditko-a	2	4	6	8	10	12
43-46,48,53-56,58,59,61-73: 59-Newton-a. 64-Sutton-c. 71-73-Low print	1	2	3	5	6	8
75-(9/84) Last issue; low print	2	4	6	9	13	16

NOTE: ***Aparo** c-45. **Ditko** a-1-8, 11-16, 18, 23, 24, 28, 30, 34r, 36r, 39-42r, 47r, 49-52r, 57, 60, 74. c-1-7, 11, 13, 14, 16, 30, 41, 47, 49-52, 74. **Howard** a-6, 9, 18, 22, 25, 32. **Kim** a-9, 19. **Morisi** a-13. **Newton** a-17, 21, 59r; c-21, 22(painted). **Staton** a-11, 12, 18, 21, 22, 30, 33, 35, 38; c-18, 33, 38. **Sutton** a-10, 17, 20-22, 31, 35, 37, 38; c-15, 17, 18, 23(painted), 24(painted), 27, 64r. #49 reprints Tales of the Mysterious Traveler #4.*

HAUNTED, THE
Chaos! Comics: Jan, 2002 - No. 4, Apr, 2002 ($2.99, limited series)

	GD	VG	FN	VF	VF/NM	NM-
1-4-Peter David-s/Nat Jones-a						3.00
...: Gray Matters (7/02, $2.99) David-s/Jones-a						3.00

HAUNTED CITY
Aspen MLT: No. 0, Aug, 2011 - Present ($2.50)

	GD	VG	FN	VF	VF/NM	NM-
0-($2.50)-Taylor & Johnson-s/Michael Ryan-a; four covers						3.00
1,2-($3.50) 1-Taylor & Johnson-s/Michael Ryan-a; four covers						3.50

HAUNTED LOVE
Charlton Comics: Apr, 1973 - No. 11, Sept, 1975

	GD	VG	FN	VF	VF/NM	NM-
1-Tom Sutton-a (16 pgs.)	5	10	15	33	57	80
2,3,6,7,10,11	3	6	9	17	26	35
4,5-Ditko-a	3	6	9	21	33	45
8,9-Newton-c	3	6	9	18	28	38
Modern Comics #1(1978)	2	3	4	6	8	10

NOTE: ***Howard** a-8i. **Kim** a-7-9. **Newton** c-8, 9. **Staton** a-1-6. **Sutton** a-1, 3-5, 10, 11.*

HAUNTED MANSION, THE (Disney Kingdoms)
Marvel Comics: May, 2016 - No. 5, Sept, 2016 ($3.99, limited series)

	GD	VG	FN	VF	VF/NM	NM-
1-5-Joshua Williamson-s/Jorge Coelho-a/E.M. Gist-c						4.00
... No. 1 Halloween Comic Fest 2016 (giveaway, 12/16) r/#1						3.00

HAUNTED TANK, THE
DC Comics (Vertigo): Feb, 2009 - No. 5, June, 2009 ($2.99, limited series)

	GD	VG	FN	VF	VF/NM	NM-
1-5-Marraffino-s/Flint-a. 1-Two covers by Flint and Joe Kubert						3.00
TPB (2010, $14.99) r/#1-5						15.00

HAUNTED THRILLS (Tales of Horror and Terror)
Ajax/Farrell Publications: June, 1952 - No. 18, Nov-Dec, 1954

	GD	VG	FN	VF	VF/NM	NM-
1-r/Ellery Queen #1	77	154	231	493	847	1200
2-L. B. Cole-a r-/Ellery Queen #1	47	94	141	296	498	700

Haunt of Fear #19 © WMG

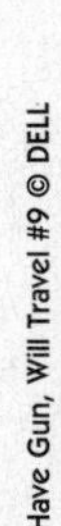
Have Gun, Will Travel #9 © DELL

The Hawk #3 © Z-D

GD VG FN VF VF/NM NM-
2.0 4.0 6.0 8.0 9.0 9.2

3,4: 3-Drug use story 43 86 129 271 461 650
5-Classic skull-c 129 258 387 826 1413 2000
6-8,10,12: 7-Hitler story. 43 86 129 271 461 650
9-Classic decapitated heads-c 81 162 243 518 884 1250
11-Nazi death camp story 50 100 150 315 533 750
13-18: 14-Jesus Christ apps. in story by Webb. 15-Jo-Jo-r. 18-Lingerie panels; skull-c
41 82 123 256 428 600

NOTE: *Kamenish art in most issues.* ***Webb*** *a-12.*

HAUNT OF FEAR (Formerly Gunfighter)
E. C. Comics: No. 15, May-June, 1950 - No. 28, Nov-Dec, 1954

15(#1, 1950)(Scarce) 320 640 960 2560 4080 5600
16-1st app. "The Witches Cauldron" & the Old Witch (by Kamen); begin series as hostess of Haunt of Fear 134 268 402 1072 1711 2350
17-Origin of Crypt of Terror, Vault of Horror, & Haunt of Fear; used in **SOTI**, pg. 43; last pg. Ingels-a used by N.Y. Legis. Comm.; story "Monster Maker" based on Frankenstein. Old Witch by Feldstein 134 268 402 1072 1711 2350
4-Ingels becomes regular artist for Old Witch. 1st Vault Keeper & Crypt Keeper app. in HOF; begin series 86 172 258 688 1094 1500
5-Injury-to-eye panel, pg. 4 of Wood story 77 154 231 616 983 1350
6,7,9,10: 6-Crypt Keeper by Feldstein begins. 9-Crypt Keeper by Davis begins. 10-Ingels biog. 57 114 171 456 728 1000
8-Classic Feldstein Shrunken Head-c 80 160 240 640 1020 1400
11,12: Classic Ingels-c; 11-Kamen biog. 12-Feldstein biog.; "Poetic Justice" story adapted for the 1972 Tales From the Crypt film 51 102 153 408 654 900
13,15,16,20: 16-Ray Bradbury adaptation. 20-Feldstein-r/Vault of Horror #12
47 94 141 376 601 825
14-Origin Old Witch by Ingels; classic-Ingels-c 66 132 198 528 839 1150
17-Classic Ingels-c and "Horror We? How's Bayou?" story, considered ECs best horror story
66 132 198 528 839 1150
18-Old Witch-c; Ray Bradbury adaptation & biography
63 126 189 504 802 1100
19-Used in **SOTI**, ill. "A comic book baseball game" & Senate investigation on juvenile delinq. bondage/decapitation-c 56 112 168 448 712 975
21-27: 22-"Wish You Were Here" story adapted for the 1972 Tales From the Crypt film. 23-EC version of the Hansel and Gretel story; **SOTI**, pg. 241 discusses the original Grimm tale in relation to comics. 24-Used in Senate Investigative Report, pg.8. 26-Contains anti-censorship editorial, 'Are you a Red Dupe?' 27-Cannibalism story; Vault Keeper shown reading **SOTI** 36 72 108 288 457 625
28-Low distribution 49 98 147 392 621 850

NOTE: *(Canadian reprints known; see Table of Contents).* ***Craig*** *a-15-17, 5, 7, 10, 12, 13; c-15-17, 5-7.* ***Crandall*** *a-20, 21, 26, 27.* ***Davis*** *a-4-26, 28.* ***Evans*** *a-15-19, 22-25, 27.* ***Feldstein*** *a-15-17, 20; c-4, 8-10.* ***Ingels*** *a-16, 17, 4-28; c-11-28.* ***Kamen*** *a-16, 4, 6, 7, 9-11, 13-19, 21-28.* ***Krigstein*** *a-28.* ***Kurtzman*** *a-15(#1), 17(#3).* ***Orlando*** *a-9, 12.* ***Wood*** *a-15, 16, 4-6.*

HAUNT OF FEAR, THE
Gladstone Publishing: May, 1991 - No. 2, July, 1991 ($2.00, 68 pgs.)

1,2: 1-Ghastly Ingels-c(r); 2-Craig-c(r) 4.00

HAUNT OF FEAR
Russ Cochran/Gemstone Publ.: Sept, 1991 - No. 5, 1992 ($2.00, 68 pgs.); Nov, 1992 - No. 28, Aug, 1998 ($1.50/$2.00/$2.50)

1-28: 1-Ingels-c(r). 1-3-r/HOF #15-17 with original-c. 4,5-r/HOF #4,5 with original-c 4.00
Annual 1-5: 1- r/#1-5. 2- r/#6-10. 3- r/#11-15. 4- r/#16-20. 5- r/#21-25 14.00
Annual 6-r/#26-28 9.00

HAUNT OF HORROR, THE (Digest)
Marvel Comics: Jun, 1973 - No. 2, Aug, 1973 (164 pgs.; text and art)

1-Morrow painted skull-c; stories by Ellison, Howard, and Leiber; Brunner-a
4 8 12 23 37 50
2-Kelly Freas painted bondage-c; stories by McCaffrey, Goulart, Leiber, Ellison; art by Simonson, Brunner, and Buscema 3 6 9 16 24 32

HAUNT OF HORROR, THE (Magazine)
Cadence Comics Publ. (Marvel): May, 1974 - No. 5, Jan, 1975 (75¢) (B&W)

1,2: 2-Origin & 1st app. Gabriel the Devil Hunter; Satana begins
3 6 9 14 20 26
3-5: 4-Neal Adams-a. 5-Evans-a(2) 3 6 9 17 26 35

NOTE: ***Alcala*** *a-2.* ***Colan*** *a-2p.* ***Heath*** *r-1.* ***Krigstein*** *r-3.* ***Reese*** *a-1.* ***Simonson*** *a-1.*

HAUNT OF HORROR: EDGAR ALLAN POE
Marvel Comics (MAX): July, 2006 - No. 3, Sept, 2006 ($3.99, B&W, limited series)

1-3- Poe-inspired/adapted stories with Richard Corben-a 4.00
HC (2006, $19.99) r/series; cover sketches 20.00

HAUNT OF HORROR: LOVECRAFT
Marvel Comics (MAX): Aug, 2008 - No. 3, Oct, 2008 ($3.99, B&W, limited series)

1-3-Lovecraft-inspired/adapted stories with Richard Corben-a 4.00

HAVE GUN, WILL TRAVEL (TV)
Dell Publishing Co.: No. 931, 8/58 - No. 14, 7-9/62 (All Richard Boone photo-c)

Four Color 931 (#1) 12 24 36 79 170 260
Four Color 983,1044 (#2,3) 9 18 27 59 117 175
4 (1-3/60) - 10 7 14 21 46 86 125
11-14 7 14 21 44 82 120

HAVEN: THE BROKEN CITY (See JLA/Haven: Arrival and JLA/Haven: Anathema)
DC Comics: Feb, 2002 - No. 9, Oct, 2002 ($2.50, limited series)

1-9-Olivetti-c/a: 1- JLA app. Series concludes in JLA/Haven: Anathema 3.00

HAVOK & WOLVERINE - MELTDOWN (See Marvel Comics Presents #24)
Marvel Comics (Epic Comics): Mar, 1989 - No. 4, Oct, 1989 ($3.50, mini-series, squarebound, mature)

1-4: Art by Kent Williams & Jon J. Muth; story by Walt & Louise Simonson 6.00

HAWAIIAN DICK (Also see Aloha, Hawaiian Dick)
Image Comics: Dec, 2002 - No. 3, Feb, 2003 ($2.95, limited series)

1-3-B. Clay Moore-s/Steven Griffin-a 3.00
...: Byrd of Paradise TPB (8/03, $14.95) r/#1-3, script & sketch pages 15.00

HAWAIIAN DICK: SCREAMING BLACK THUNDER
Image Comics: Nov, 2007 - No. 5, Oct, 2008 ($2.99, limited series)

1-5-B. Clay Moore-s/Scott Chantler-a 3.00

HAWAIIAN DICK: THE LAST RESORT
Image Comics: Aug, 2004 - No. 4, June, 2006 ($2.95/$2.99, limited series)

1-4-B. Clay Moore-s/Steven Griffin-a 3.00
Vol. 2 TPB (10/06, $14.99) r/#1-4 & the original series pitch 15.00

HAWAIIAN EYE (TV)
Gold Key: July, 1963 (Troy Donahue, Connie Stevens photo-c)

1 (10073-307) 5 10 15 31 53 75

HAWAIIAN ILLUSTRATED LEGENDS SERIES
Hogarth Press: 1975 (B&W)(Cover printed w/blue, yellow, and green)

1-Kalelealuaka, the Mysterious Warrior 5.00

HAWK, THE (Also see Approved Comics #1, 7 & Tops In Adventure)
Ziff-Davis/St. John Publ. Co. No. 4 on: Wint/51 - No. 3, 11-12/52; No. 4, 1-2/53; No. 8, 9/54 - No. 12, 5/55 (Painted c-1-4)(#5-7 don't exist)

1-Anderson-a 22 44 66 132 216 300
2 (Sum, '52)-Kubert, Infantino-a 14 28 42 80 115 150
3-4 12 24 36 67 94 120
8-12: 8(9/54)-Reprints #3 w/different-c by Baker. 9-Baker-c/a; Kubert-a(r)/#2. 10-Baker-c/a; r/one story from #2. 11-Baker-c; Buckskin Belle & The Texan app. 12-Baker-c/a; Buckskin Belle app. 18 36 54 105 165 225
3-D 1(11/53, 25¢)-Came w/glasses; Baker-c 36 72 108 211 343 475

NOTE: ***Baker*** *c-8-12.* ***Larsen*** *a-10.* ***Tuska*** *a-1, 9, 12. Painted c-1, 4, 7.*

HAWK AND THE DOVE, THE (See Showcase #75 & Teen Titans) (1st series)
National Periodical Publications: Aug-Sept, 1968 - No. 6, June-July, 1969

1-Ditko-c/a 8 16 24 53 89 125
2-6: 5-Teen Titans cameo 5 10 15 32 51 70

NOTE: ***Ditko*** *c/a-1, 2.* ***Gil Kane*** *a-3p, 4p, 5, 6p; c-3-6.*

HAWK AND DOVE (2nd Series)
DC Comics: Oct, 1988 - No. 5, Feb, 1989 ($1.00, limited series)

1-Rob Liefeld-c/a(p) in all; 1st app. Dawn Granger as Dove 4.00
2-5 3.00
Trade paperback ('93, $9.95)-Reprints #1-5 12.00

HAWK AND DOVE
DC Comics: June, 1989 - No. 28, Oct, 1991 ($1.00)

1-28 3.00
Annual 1,2 ('90, '91; $2.00) 1-Liefeld pin-up. 2-Armageddon 2001 x-over 4.00

HAWK AND DOVE
DC Comics: Nov, 1997 - No. 5, Mar, 1998 ($2.50, limited series)

1-5-Baron-s/Zachary & Giordano-a 3.00

HAWK AND DOVE (DC New 52)
DC Comics: Nov, 2011 - No. 8, Jun, 2012 ($2.99)

1-8: 1-Gates-s/Liefeld-a/c; Deadman app. 6-Batman & Robin app.; Liefeld-s/a/c 3.00

HAWK AND WINDBLADE (See Elflord)
Warp Graphics: Aug, 1997 - No.2, Sept, 1997 ($2.95, limited series)

1,2-Blair-s/Chan-c/a 3.00

HAWKEN: MELEE (Based on the computer game Hawken)

Hawkeye (2017 series) #1 © MAR

Hawkgirl #63 © DC

Hawkman V4 #8 © DC

	GD 2.0	VG 4.0	FN 6.0	VF 8.0	VF/NM 9.0	NM- 9.2

Archaia Black Label: Dec, 2013 - No. 5 ($3.99, limited series)
1,2: 1-Abnett-s/Dallocchio-a. 2-Jim Mahfood-s/a 4.00

HAWKEYE (See The Avengers #16 & Tales Of Suspense #57)
Marvel Comics Group: Sept, 1983 - No. 4, Dec, 1983 (limited series)
1-Mark Gruenwald-a/scripts in all; origin Hawkeye 2 4 6 11 16 20
2-4: 3-Origin Mockingbird. 4-Hawkeye & Mockingbird elope 1 3 4 6 8 10

HAWKEYE
Marvel Comics: Jan, 1994 - No. 4, Apr, 1994 ($1.75, limited series)
1-4 5.00

HAWKEYE (Volume 2)
Marvel Comics: Dec, 2003 - No. 8, Aug, 2004 ($2.99)
1-8: 1-6-Nicieza-s/Raffaele-a. 7,8-Bennett-a; Black Widow app. 4.00

HAWKEYE (Also see All-New Hawkeye)
Marvel Comics: Oct, 2012 - No. 22, Sept, 2015 ($2.99)
1-Fraction-s/Aja-a; Kate Bishop app. 3 6 9 14 20 25
2,3 1 3 4 6 8 10
4-8: 7-Lieber & Hamm-a 6.00
9-21: 10,12-Francavilla-a. 11-Dog issue. 16-Released before #15 4.00
22-($4.99) Aja-a 5.00
Annual 1 (9/13, $4.99) Pulido-a; Kate Bishop in L.A.; Madame Mask app. 5.00

HAWKEYE (Kate Bishop as Hawkeye)
Marvel Comics: Feb, 2017 - Present ($3.99)
1-4-Thompson-s/Romero-a 4.00

HAWKEYE AND MOCKINGBIRD (Avengers) (Leads into Widowmaker mini-series)
Marvel Comics: Aug, 2010 - No. 6, Jan, 2011 ($3.99/$2.99)
1-($3.99) Heroic Age; Jim McCann-s/David Lopez-a; history of the characters 4.00
2-6-($2.99) Phantom Rider, Dominic Fortune & Crossfire app. 3.00

HAWKEYE & THE LAST OF THE MOHICANS (TV)
Dell Publishing Co.: No. 884, Mar, 1958 (one-shot)
Four Color 884-Lon Chaney Jr. photo-c 7 14 21 44 82 120

HAWKEYE: BLINDSPOT (Avengers)
Marvel Comics: Apr, 2011 - No. 4, Jul, 2011 ($2.99, limited series)
1-4: 1-McCann-s/Diaz-a; Zemo app. 2-Diaz & Dragotta-a 3.00

HAWKEYE: EARTH'S MIGHTIEST MARKSMAN
Marvel Comics: Oct, 1998 ($2.99, one-shot)
1-Justice and Firestar app.; DeFalco-s 5.00

HAWKEYE VS. DEADPOOL
Marvel Comics: No. 0, Nov, 2014 - No. 4, Mar, 2015 ($4.99/$3.99, limited series)
0-($4.99) Duggan-s/Lolli-a; Black Cat app. 5.00
1-4-($3.99) 1-Covers by Harren & Pearson; Kate Bishop & Typhoid Mary app. 4.00

HAWKGIRL (Title continued from Hawkman #49, Apr, 2006)
DC Comics: No. 50, May, 2006 - No. 66, Sept, 2007 ($2.50/$2.99)
50-66: 50-Chaykin-a/Simonson-s begin; One Year Later. 52-Begin $2.99-c. 57,58-Bennett-a. 59-Blackfire app. 63-Batman app. 64-Superman app. 3.00
...: Hath-Set TPB (2008, $17.99) r/#61-66 18.00
...: Hawkman Returns TPB (2007, $17.99) r/#57-60 & JSA Classified #21,22 18.00
...: The Maw TPB (2007, $17.99) r/#50-56 18.00

HAWKMAN (See Atom & Hawkman, The Brave & the Bold, DC Comics Presents, Detective Comics, Flash Comics, Hawkworld, JSA, Justice League of America #31, Legend of the Hawkman, Mystery in Space, Savage Hawkman, Shadow War Of..., Showcase, & World's Finest #256)

HAWKMAN (1st Series) (Also see The Atom #7 & Brave & the Bold #34-36, 42-44, 51)
National Periodical Publications: Apr-May, 1964 - No. 27, Aug-Sept, 1968
1-(4-5/64)-Anderson-c/a begins, ends #21 53 106 159 424 950 1475
2 20 40 60 141 313 485
3,5: 5-2nd app. Shadow Thief 13 26 39 89 195 300
4-Origin & 1st app. Zatanna (10-11/64) 80 160 320 640 1220 1800
6 10 20 30 66 138 210
7 9 18 27 60 120 180
8-10: 9-Atom cameo; Hawkman & Atom learn each other's I.D.; 3rd app. Shadow Thief 8 16 24 54 102 150
11-15 6 12 18 40 73 105
16-27: 18-Adam Strange x-over (cameo #19). 25-G.A. Hawkman-r by Moldoff. 26-Kirby-a(r). 27-Kubert-c 5 10 15 33 57 80

HAWKMAN (2nd Series)
DC Comics: Aug, 1986 - No. 17, Dec, 1987
1-17: 10-Byrne-c, Special #1 (1986, $1.25) 4.00
Trade paperback (1989, $19.95)-r/Brave and the Bold #34-36,42-44 by Kubert; Kubert-c 20.00

HAWKMAN (4th Series)(See both Hawkworld limited & ongoing series)
DC Comics: Sept, 1993 - No. 33, July, 1996 ($1.75/$1.95/$2.25)
1-($2.50)-Gold foil embossed-c; storyline cont'd from Hawkworld ongoing series; new costume & powers. 4.00
2-13,0,14-33: 2-Green Lantern x-over. 3-Airstryke app. 4,6-Wonder Woman app. 13-(9/94)-Zero Hour. 0-(10/94). 14-(11/94). 15-Aquaman-c & app. 23-Wonder Woman app. 25-Kent Williams-c. 29,30-Chaykin-c. 32-Breyfogle-c 3.00
Annual 1 (1993, $2.50, 68 pgs.)-Bloodlines Earthplague 4.00
Annual 2 (1995, $3.95)-Year One story 4.00

HAWKMAN (Title continues as Hawkgirl #50-on) (See JSA #23 for return)
DC Comics: May, 2002 - No. 49, Apr, 2006 ($2.50)
1-Johns & Robinson-s/Morales-a 5.00
1-2nd printing 3.00
2-40: 2-4-Shadow Thief app. 5,6-Green Arrow-c/app. 8-Atom-c/app. 13-Van Sciver-a. 14-Gentleman Ghost app. 15-Hawkwoman app. 16-Byth returns. 23-25-Black Reign x-over with JSA #56-58. 26-Byrne-c/a. 29,30-Land-c. 37-Golden Eagle returns 3.00
41-49: 41-Hawkman killed. 43-Golden Eagle origin. 46-49-Adam Kubert-c 3.00
...: Allies & Enemies TPB (2004, $14.95) r/#7-14 & pages from Secret Files and Origins 15.00
...: Endless Flight TPB (2003, $12.95) r/#1-6 & Secret Files and Origins 13.00
...: Rise of the Golden Eagle TPB (2006, $17.99) r/#37-45 18.00
... Secret Files and Origins (10/02, $4.95) profiles and pin-ups by various 5.00
... Special 1 (10/08, $3.50) Tie-in to Rann-Thanagar Holy War series; Starlin-s/a(p) 3.50
...: Wings of Fury TPB (2005, $17.99) r/#15-22 18.00

HAWKMOON: THE JEWEL IN THE SKULL
First Comics: May, 1986 - No. 4, Nov, 1986 ($1.75, limited series, Baxter paper)
1-4: Adapts novel by Michael Moorcock 3.00

HAWKMOON: THE MAD GOD'S AMULET
First Comics: Jan, 1987 - No. 4, July, 1987 ($1.75, limited series, Baxter paper)
1-4: Adapts novel by Michael Moorcock 3.00

HAWKMOON: THE RUNESTAFF
First Comics: Jun, 1988 -No. 4, Dec, 1988 ($1.75-$1.95, lim. series, Baxter paper)
1-4: ($1.75) Adapts novel by Michael Moorcock. 3,4 ($1.95) 3.00

HAWKMOON: THE SWORD OF DAWN
First Comics: Sept, 1987 - No. 4, Mar, 1988 ($1.75, lim. series, Baxter paper)
1-4: Dorman painted-c; adapts Moorcock novel 3.00

HAWKS OF THE SEAS (WILL EISNER'S...)
Dark Horse Comics: July, 2003 ($19.95, B&W, hardcover)
nn-Reprints 1937-1939 weekly Pirate serial by Will Eisner; Williamson intro. 20.00

HAWKWORLD
DC Comics: 1989 - No. 3, 1989 ($3.95, prestige format, limited series)
Book 1-3: 1-Tim Truman story & art in all; Hawkman dons new costume; reintro Byth 5.00
TPB (1991, $16.95) r/#1-3 17.00

HAWKWORLD (3rd Series)
DC Comics: June, 1990 - No. 32, Mar, 1993 ($1.50/$1.75)
1-Hawkman spin-off; story cont'd from limited series. 4.00
2-32: 15,16-War of the Gods x-over. 22-J'onn J'onzz app. 3.00
Annual 1-3 ('90-'92, $2.95, 68 pgs.), 2-2nd printing with silver ink-c 4.00
NOTE: *Truman a-30-32; c-27-32, Annual 1.*

HAYWIRE
DC Comics: Oct, 1988 - No. 13, Sept, 1989 ($1.25, mature)
1-13 3.00

HAZARD
Image Comics (WildStorm Prod.): June, 1996 - No. 7, Nov, 1996 ($1.75)
1-7: 1-Intro Hazard; Jeff Mariotte scripts begin; Jim Lee-c(p) 3.00

HEADLINE COMICS
DC Comics: Jan. 1942
nn - Ashcan comic, not distributed to newsstands, only for in-house use. Cover art is More Fun Comics #73, interior being Star Spangled Comics #2 (a FN copy sold for $2270.50 in 2012)

HEADLINE COMICS (...For the American Boy) (...Crime No. 32-39)
Prize Publ./American Boys' Comics: Feb, 1943 - No. 22, Nov-Dec, 1946; No. 23, 1947 - No. 77, Oct, 1956
1-WWII-c/sty.; Junior Rangers-c/stories begin; Yank & Doodle x-over in Junior Rangers (Junior Rangers are Uncle Sam's nephews) 97 194 291 621 1061 1500
2-Japanese WWII-c; Junior Rangers "Nip the Nippons!"-c

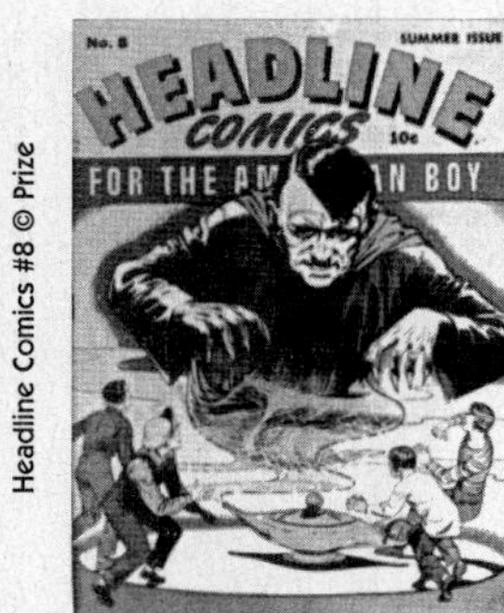

Headline Comics #8 © Prize

Heart Throbs #9 © QUA

Heckle and Jeckle #22 © CBS

	GD 2.0	VG 4.0	FN 6.0	VF 8.0	VF/NM 9.0	NM- 9.2
	58	116	174	371	636	900
3-Junior Rangers vs. Hitler sty.; 1st app. Invisible Boy; German WWII-c; used in **POP**, pg. 84 (scarce)	55	110	165	352	601	850
4-Junior Rangers vs. Hitler, Mussolini, Hirohito & Dr. Schmutz (1st app.); German WWII-c; (scarce)	53	106	159	334	567	800
5-7,9: 5-Junior Rangers invade Italy; WWII-c/sty. 6,7-Nazi WWII-c/sty. 7-1st app. Kinker Kinkaid (ends #12). 9-WWII Halloween-c/sty	50	100	150	315	533	750
8-Classic Hitler-c	1000	2000	3000	6000	8500	11,000
10-Hitler story	43	86	129	271	461	650
11-Classic Mad Japanese scientist WWII-c	103	206	309	659	1130	1600
12,13,15: 13,15-Blue Streak app.	24	48	72	142	234	325
14-Japanese WWII-c	28	56	84	165	270	375
16-Origin & 1st app. Atomic Man (11-12/45)	34	68	102	199	325	450
17,18-Atomic Man-c/sty.	24	48	72	142	234	325
19-Atomic Man-c/sty.; S&K-a	36	72	108	211	343	475
20,21: 21-Atomic Man ends (9-10/46)	20	40	60	117	189	260
22-Last Junior Rangers; Kiefer-c	19	38	57	109	172	235
23,24: (All S&K-a). 23-Valentine's Day Massacre story; content changes to true crime. 24-Dope-crazy killer story	34	68	102	206	336	465
25-35-S&K-c/a. 25-Powell-a	30	60	90	177	289	400
36-S&K-a; photo-c begin	25	50	75	150	245	340
37-1 pg. S&K, Severin-a; rare Kirby photo-c app.	41	82	123	256	428	600
38,40-Meskin-a	14	28	42	82	121	160
39,41-43,46-56: 41-J. Edgar Hoover 26th Anniversary Issue with photo on-c. 43,49-Meskin-a. 48-Meskin-c	14	28	42	76	108	140
44,45-S&K-c; Severin/Elder, Meskin-a	18	36	54	105	165	225
57-77: 70-Roller Derby-c. 72-Meskin-c/a(i)	12	24	36	69	97	125

NOTE: ***Hollingsworth** a-30. Photo c-36-43. **H. C. Kiefer** c-12-16, 22. Atomic Man c-17-19.*

HEAP, THE
Skywald Publications: Sept, 1971 (52 pgs.)

	GD	VG	FN	VF	VF/NM	NM-
1-Kinstler-r/Strange Worlds #8; new-s w/Sutton-a	4	8	12	28	47	65

HEART AND SOUL
Mikeross Publications: April-May, 1954 - No. 2, June-July, 1954

	GD	VG	FN	VF	VF/NM	NM-
1,2	11	22	33	62	86	110

HEARTBREAKERS (Also see Dark Horse Presents)
Dark Horse Comics: Apr, 1996 - No. 4, July, 1996 ($2.95, limited series)

	NM-
1-4: 1-W/paper doll & pin-up. 2-Alex Ross pin-up. 3-Evan Dorkin pin-ups. 4-Brereton-c; Matt Wagner pin-up	3.00
...Superdigest (7/98, $9.95, digest-size) new stories	10.00

HEARTLAND (See Hellblazer)
DC Comics (Vertigo): Mar, 1997 ($4.95, one-shot, mature)

	NM-
1-Garth Ennis-s/Steve Dillon-c/a	5.00

HEART OF EMPIRE
Dark Horse Comics: Apr, 1999 - No. 9, Dec, 1999 ($2.95, limited series)

	NM-
1-9-Bryan Talbot-s/a	3.00

HEART OF THE BEAST, THE
DC Comics (Vertigo): 1994 ($19.95, hardcover, mature)

	NM-
1-Dean Motter scripts	20.00

HEARTS OF DARKNESS (See Ghost Rider; Wolverine; Punisher: Hearts of...)

HEART THROBS (Love Stories No. 147 on)
Quality Comics/National Periodical #47(4-5/57) on (Arleigh #48-101): 8/49 - No. 8, 10/50; No. 9, 3/52 - No. 146, Oct, 1972

	GD	VG	FN	VF	VF/NM	NM-
1-Classic Ward-c, Gustavson-a, 9 pgs.	48	96	144	302	514	725
2-Ward-c/a (9 pgs); Gustavson-a	31	62	93	182	296	410
3-Gustavson-a	15	30	45	88	137	185
4,6,8-Ward-a, 8-9 pgs.	19	38	57	112	179	245
5,7	14	28	42	80	115	150
9-Robert Mitchum, Jane Russell photo-c	15	30	45	90	140	190
10,15-Ward-a	15	30	45	90	140	190
11-14,16-20: 12 (7/52)	12	24	36	69	97	125
21-Ward-c	15	30	45	86	133	180
22,23-Ward-a(p)	13	26	39	74	105	135
24-33: 33-Last pre-code (3/55)	12	24	36	67	94	120
34-39,41-44,46 (12/56; last Quality issue)	11	22	33	62	86	110
40-Ward-a; r-7 pgs./#21	12	24	36	67	94	120
45-Baker-a	7	14	21	48	89	130
47-(4-5/57; 1st DC issue)	20	40	60	135	300	465
48-60, 100	9	18	27	59	117	175
61-70	6	12	18	41	76	110
71-99: 74-Last 10 cent issue	6	12	18	37	66	95
101-The Beatles app. on-c	15	30	45	103	227	350
102-119: 102-123-(Serial)-Three Girls, Their Lives, Their Loves	4	8	12	27	44	60
120-(6-7/69) Neal Adams-c	4	8	12	28	47	65
121-132,143-146	3	6	9	21	33	45
133-142-(52 pgs.)	4	8	12	27	44	60

NOTE: ***Gustavson** a-8. **Tuska** a-128. Photo c-4, 5, 8-10, 15, 17.*

HEART THROBS - THE BEST OF DC ROMANCE COMICS (See Fireside Book Series)

HEART THROBS
DC Comics (Vertigo): Jan, 1999 - No. 4, Apr, 1999 ($2.95, lim. series)

	NM-
1-4-Romance anthology. 1-Timm-c. 3-Corben-a	3.00

HEATHCLIFF (See Star Comics Magazine)
Marvel Comics (Star Comics)/Marvel Comics No. 23 on: Apr, 1985 - No. 56, Feb, 1991 (#16-on, $1.00)

	GD	VG	FN	VF	VF/NM	NM-
1-Post-a most issues	1	2	3	4	5	7
2-10,47: 47-Batman parody (Catman vs. the Soaker)						5.00
11-46,48-56: 43-X-Mas issue						4.00
Annual 1 ('87)						4.00

HEATHCLIFF'S FUNHOUSE
Marvel Comics (Star Comics)/Marvel No. 6 on: May, 1987 - No. 10, 1988

	NM-
1	5.00
2-10	4.00

HEAVEN'S DEVILS
Image Comics: Sept, 2003 - No. 4, July, 2004 ($2.95/$3.50, B&W, limited series)

	NM-
1-3-($2.95) Jai Nitz-s/Zach Howard-a	3.00
4-($3.50) Kevin Sharpe-a	3.50

HEAVY HITTERS
Marvel Comics (Epic Comics): 1993 ($3.75, 68 pgs.)

	NM-
1-Bound w/trading card; Lawdog, Feud, Alien Legion, Trouble With Girls, & Spyke	4.00

HEAVY LIQUID
DC Comics (Vertigo): Oct, 1999 - No. 5, Feb, 2000 ($5.95, limited series)

	NM-
1-5-Paul Pope-s/a; flip covers	6.00
TPB (2001, $29.95) r/#1-5	30.00
TPB (2009, $24.95) r/#1-5; development sketches and cover gallery; new cover	25.00
HC (2008, $39.99, dustjacket) r/#1-5; development sketches and cover gallery	40.00

HECKLE AND JECKLE (Paul Terry's...)(See Blue Ribbon, Giant Comics Edition #5A & 10, Paul Terry's, Terry-Toons Comics)
St. John Publ. Co. No. 1-24/Pines No. 25 on: No. 3, 2/52 - No. 24, 10/55; No. 25, Fall/56 - No. 34, 6/59

	GD	VG	FN	VF	VF/NM	NM-
3(#1)-Funny animal	27	54	81	158	259	360
4(6/52), 5	14	28	42	80	115	150
6-10(4/53)	10	20	30	54	72	90
11-20	8	16	24	40	50	60
21-34: 25-Begin CBS Television Presents on-c	7	14	21	35	43	50

HECKLE AND JECKLE (TV) (See New Terrytoons)
Gold Key/Dell Publ. Co.: 11/62 - No. 4, 8/63; 5/66; No. 2, 10/66; No. 3, 8/67

	GD	VG	FN	VF	VF/NM	NM-
1 (11/62; Gold Key)	6	12	18	37	66	95
2-4	3	6	9	21	33	45
1 (5/66; Dell)	4	8	12	25	40	55
2,3	3	6	9	18	28	38

(See March of Comics No. 379, 472, 484)

HECKLE AND JECKLE 3-D
Spotlight Comics: 1987 - No. 2?, 1987 ($2.50)

	NM-
1,2	5.00

HECKLER, THE
DC Comics: Sept, 1992 - No. 6, Feb, 1993 ($1.25)

	NM-
1-6-T&M Bierbaum-s/Keith Giffen-c/a	3.00

HECTIC PLANET
Slave Labor Graphics 1998 ($12.95/$14.95)

	NM-
Book 1,2-r-Dorkin-s/a from Pirate Corp$ Vol. 1 & 2	15.00

HECTOR COMICS (The Keenest Teen in Town)
Key Publications: Nov, 1953 - No. 3, 1954

	GD	VG	FN	VF	VF/NM	NM-
1-Teen humor	8	16	24	44	57	70
2,3	6	12	18	28	34	40

HECTOR HEATHCOTE (TV)
Gold Key: Mar, 1964

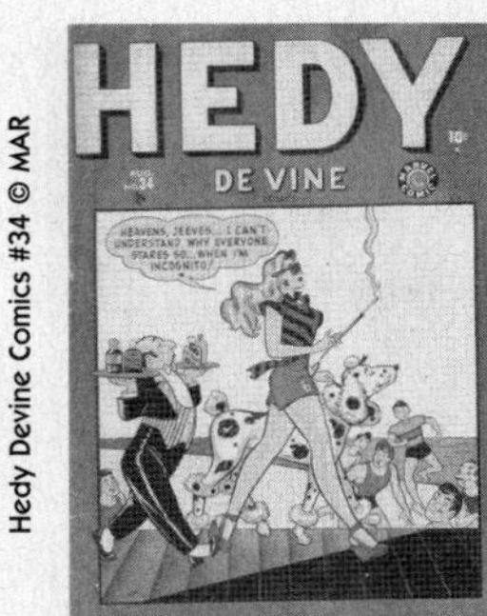

Hedy Devine Comics #34 © MAR

Hellblazer #139 © DC

Hellblazer (2016 series) #1 © DC

	GD 2.0	VG 4.0	FN 6.0	VF 8.0	VF/NM 9.0	NM- 9.2

1 (10111-403) 6 12 18 40 73 105

HECTOR THE INSPECTOR (See Top Flight Comics)

HEDGE KNIGHT, THE
Image Comics: Aug, 2003 - No. 6, Apr, 2004 ($2.95, limited series)

1-6-George R.R. Martin-s/Mike S. Miller-a. 1-Two covers by Kaluta and Miller 3.00
George R.R. Martin's The Hedge Knight HC (Marvel, 2006, $19.99) r/series; 2 covers 20.00
George R.R. Martin's The Hedge Knight SC (Marvel, 2007, $14.99) r/series 15.00
TPB (2004, $14.95) r/series plus new short story 15.00

HEDGE KNIGHT II: SWORN SWORD
Marvel Comics (Dabel Brothers): Jun, 2007 - No. 6, Jun, 2008 ($2.99, limited series)

1-6-George R.R. Martin-s/Mike Miller-a. 1-Two covers by Yu & Miller, plus Miller B&W-c 3.00
... HC (2008, $19.99) r/series; 2 covers 20.00

HEDY DEVINE COMICS (Formerly All Winners #21? or Teen #22?(6/47); Hedy of Hollywood #36 on; also see Annie Oakley, Comedy & Venus)
Marvel Comics (RCM)/Atlas #50: No. 22, Aug, 1947 - No. 50, Sept, 1952

22-1st app. Hedy Devine (also see Joker #32) 58 116 174 371 636 900
23,24,27-30: 23-Wolverton-a, 1 pg; Kurtzman's "Hey Look", 2 pgs. 24,27-30- "Hey Look" by Kurtzman, 1-3 pgs. 37 74 111 222 361 500
25-Classic "Hey Look" by Kurtzman, "Optical Illusion" 39 78 117 240 395 550
26- "Giggles 'n' Grins" by Kurtzman 34 68 102 199 325 450
31-34,36-50: 32-Anti-Wertham editorial 22 44 66 132 216 300
35-Four pgs. "Rusty" by Kurtzman 26 52 78 154 252 350

HEDY-MILLIE-TESSIE COMEDY (See Comedy Comics)

HEDY WOLFE (Also see Patsy & Hedy & Miss America Magazine V1#2)
Atlas Publishing Co. (Emgee): Aug, 1957

1-Patsy Walker's rival; Al Hartley-c 26 52 78 154 252 350

HEE HAW (TV)
Charlton Press: July, 1970 - No. 7, Aug, 1971

1 4 8 12 27 44 60
2-7 3 6 9 18 28 38

HEIDI (See Dell Jr. Treasury No. 6)

HEIDI SAHA (AN ILLUSTRATED HISTORY OF...)
Warren Publishing: 1973 (500 printed)

nn-Photo-c; an early Vampirella model for Warren (a FN/VF copy sold in 2011 for $776.75)

HELEN OF TROY (Movie)
Dell Publishing Co.: No. 684, Mar, 1956 (one-shot)

Four Color 684-Buscema-a, photo-c 9 18 27 59 117 175

HELL
Dark Horse Comics: July, 2003 - No. 4, Mar, 2004 ($2.99, limited series)

1-4-Augustyn-s/Demong-a/Meglia-c 3.00

HELLBLAZER (John Constantine) (See Saga of Swamp Thing #37 & 2013 Constantine title) (Also see Books of Magic limited series)
DC Comics (Vertigo #63 on): Jan, 1988 - No. 300, Apr, 2013 ($1.25-$2.99)

1-(44 pgs.)-John Constantine; McKean-c thru #21; 1st app. Papa Midnite 4 8 12 25 40 55
1-Special Edition (7/10, $1.00) r/#1 with "What's Next?" cover logo 3.00
2-5 1 2 3 5 7 9
6-8,10: 10-Swamp Thing cameo 6.00
9,19: 9-X-over w/Swamp Thing #76. 19-Sandman app. 1 2 3 5 6 8
11-18,20 6.00
21-26,28-30: 22-Williams-c. 24-Contains bound-in Shocker movie poster. 25,26-Grant Morrison scripts. 5.00
27-Neil Gaiman scripts; Dave McKean-a; low print run 2 4 6 10 14 18
31-39: 36-Preview of World Without End. 4.00
40-($2.25, 52 pgs.)-Dave McKean-a & colors; preview of Kid Eternity 5.00
41-Ennis scripts begin; ends #83 5.00
42-49,51-74,76-99,101-119: 44,45-Sutton-a(i). 52-Glenn Fabry painted-c begin. 62-Special Death insert by McKean. 63-Silver metallic ink on-c. 77-Totleben-c. 84-Sean Phillips-c/a begins; Delano story. 85-88-Eddie Campbell story. 89-Paul Jenkins scripts begin 3.50
50,75,100,120: 50-($3.00, 52 pgs.). 75-($2.95, 52 pgs.). 100,120 ($3.50,48 pgs.) 4.00
121-199, 201-249, 251-274,276-299: 129-Ennis-s. 141-Bradstreet-a. 146-150-Corben-a. 151-Azzarello-s begin. 175-Carey-s begin; Dillon-a. 176-Begin $2.75-c. 182,183-Bermejo-a. 216-Mina-s begins. 220-Begin $2.99-c. 229-Carey-s/Leon-a. 234-Initial printing (white title logo) has missing text; corrected printing has lt. blue title logo. 265,266,271-274-Bisley-a.

	GD 2.0	VG 4.0	FN 6.0	VF 8.0	VF/NM 9.0	NM- 9.2

268-271-Shade the Changing Man app. 3.00
200-($4.50) Carey-s/Dillon, Frusin, Manco-a 5.00
250-($3.99) Short stories by various; art by Lloyd, Phillips, Milligan; Bermejo-c 4.00
275-($4.99) Constantine's wedding; Bisley-c 5.00
300-($4.99) Last issue; Bisley-c 5.00
Annual 1 (1989, $2.95, 68 pgs.)-Bryan Talbot's 1st work in American comics 6.00
Annual 1 (Annual 2011 on cover, 2/12, $4.99)-Milligan-s/Bisley-a/c 5.00
Special 1 (1993, $3.95, 68 pgs.)-Ennis story; w/pin-ups. 5.00
...Black Flowers (2005, $14.99, TPB) r/#181-186 15.00
...Bloodlines (2007, $19.99, TPB) r/#47-50,52-55,59-61 20.00
...Damnation's Flame (1999, $16.95, TPB) r/#72-77 17.00
...Dangerous Habits (1997, $14.95, TPB) r/#41-46 15.00
...Fear and Loathing (1997, $14.95, TPB) r/#62-67 18.00
...Fear and Loathing (2nd printing, $17.95) 18.00
...: Freezes Over (2003, $14.95, TPB) r/#157-163 15.00
...Good Intentions (2002, $12.95, TPB) r/#151-156 13.00
...Hard Time (2001, $9.95, TPB) r/#146-150 10.00
...Haunting (2003, $12.95, TPB) r/#134-139 13.00
...Highwater (2004, $19.95, TPB) r/#164-174 20.00
John Constantine Hellblazer: All His Engines HC (2005, $24.95, with dustjacket) new graphic novel; Mike Carey-s/Leonardo Manco-a 25.00
John Constantine Hellblazer: All His Engines SC (2006, $14.99) new graphic novel 15.00
John Constantine Hellblazer: Bloody Carnations SC (2011, $19.99) r/#267-275 20.00
John Constantine Hellblazer: Empathy is the Enemy SC (2006, $14.99) r/#216-222 15.00
John Constantine Hellblazer: Hooked SC (2010, $14.99) r/#256-260 15.00
John Constantine Hellblazer: India SC (2010, $14.99) r/#261-266 15.00
John Constantine Hellblazer: Joyride SC (2008, $14.99) r/#230-237 15.00
John Constantine Hellblazer: Pandemonium HC (2010, $24.99, with dustjacket) new graphic novel; Jamie Delano-s/Jock-a 25.00
John Constantine Hellblazer: Pandemonium SC (2011, $17.99) new graphic novel 18.00
John Constantine Hellblazer: Scab SC (2009, $14.99) r/#250-255 15.00
John Constantine Hellblazer: The Devil You Know SC (2007, $19.99) r/#10-13, Annual #1 and The Horrorist miniseries #1,2 20.00
John Constantine Hellblazer: The Family Man SC (2008, $19.99, TPB) r/#23,24,28-33 20.00
John Constantine Hellblazer: The Fear Machine SC (2008, $19.99, TPB) r/#14-22 20.00
John Constantine Hellblazer: The Red Right Hand SC (2007, $14.99) r/#223-228 15.00
John Const. Hellblazer: The Roots of Coincidence SC ('09, $14.99) r/#243,244,247-249 15.00
...Original Sins (1993, $19.95, TPB) r/#1-9 20.00
...Original Sins (2011, $19.99, TPB) r/#1-9 20.00
...Rake at the Gates of Hell (2003, $19.95, TPB) r/#78-83; Heartland #1 20.00
...: Rare Cuts (2005, $14.95, TPB) r/#11,25,26,35,56,84 & Vertigo Secret Files: Hellblazer 15.00
...: Reasons To Be Cheerful (2007, $14.99, TPB) r/#201-206 15.00
...: Red Sepulchre (2005, $12.99, TPB) r/#175-180 13.00
...: Setting Sun (2004, $12.95, TPB) r/#140-143 13.00
...: Son of Man (2004, $12.95, TPB) r/#129-133 13.00
...: Stations of the Cross (2006, $14.99, TPB) r/#194-200 15.00
...: Staring At The Wall (2005, $14.99, TPB) r/#187-193 15.00
...Tainted Love (1998, $16.95, TPB) r/#68-71, Vertigo Jam #1 and Hellblazer Special #1 17.00
NOTE: *Alcala a-8i, 9i, 18-22i. **Gaiman** scripts-27. **McKean** a-27,40; c-1-21. **Sutton** a-44i, 45i. **Talbot** a-Annual 1.*

HELLBLAZER (DC Rebirth)
DC Comics: Oct, 2016 - Present ($2.99, limited series)

1-7: 1-4-Simon Oliver-s/Moritat-a; Swamp Thing app. 5-7-Cassaday-c 3.00
...: Rebirth 1 (9/16, $2.99) Oliver-s/Moritat-a; Swamp Thing, Wonder Woman app. 3.00

HELLBLAZER: CITY OF DEMONS
DC Comics (Vertigo): Early Dec, 2010 - No. 5, Feb, 2011 ($2.99, limited series)

1-5-Si Spencer-s/Sean Murphy-a/c 3.00
TPB (2011, $14.99) r/#1-5 & story from Vertigo Winter's Edge #3 15.00

HELLBLAZER SPECIAL: BAD BLOOD
DC Comics (Vertigo): Sept, 2000 - No. 4, Dec, 2000 ($2.95, limited series)

1-4-Delano-s/Bond-a; Constantine in 2025 London 3.00

HELLBLAZER SPECIAL: CHAS
DC Comics (Vertigo): Sept, 2008 - No. 5, Jan, 2009 ($2.99, limited series)

1-5-Story of Constantine's cab driver; Oliver-s/Sudzuka-a/Fabry-c 3.00
... - The Knowledge TPB (2009, $14.99) r/#1-5 15.00

HELLBLAZER SPECIAL: LADY CONSTANTINE
DC Comics (Vertigo): Feb, 2003 - No. 4, May, 2003 ($2.95, limited series)

1-4-Story of Johanna Constantine in 1785; Diggle-s/Sudzuka-a/Noto-c 3.00

HELLBLAZER/THE BOOKS OF MAGIC
DC Comics (Vertigo): Dec, 1997 - No. 2, Jan, 1998 ($2.50, limited series)

1,2-John Constantine and Tim Hunter 3.00

Hellboy FCBD 2008 © Mike Mignola

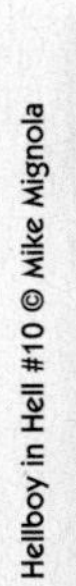
Hellboy in Hell #10 © Mike Mignola

Hellboy: The Storm #3 © Mike Mignola

GD	VG	FN	VF	VF/NM	NM-
2.0	4.0	6.0	8.0	9.0	9.2

HELLBOY (Also see Batman/Hellboy/Starman, Danger Unlimited #4, Dark Horse Presents, Gen[13] #13B, Ghost/Hellboy, John Byrne's Next Men, San Diego Comic Con #2, & Savage Dragon)

HELLBOY
Dark Horse Comics: Apr, 2008

... : Free Comic Book Day; Three short stories; Mignola-c; art by Fegredo, Davis, Azaceta 3.00

HELLBOY: ALMOST COLOSSUS
Dark Horse Comics (Legend): Jun, 1997 - No. 2, Jul, 1997 ($2.95, lim. series)

1,2-Mignola-s/a 5.00

HELLBOY AND THE B.P.R.D.
Dark Horse Comics: Dec, 2014 - No. 5, Apr, 2015 ($3.50, limited series)

1-5-Mignola & Arcudi-s/Maleev-a/c; Hellboy's first mission; set in 1952 3.50
...: 1953 - Beyond the Fences 1-3 (2/16 - No. 3, 4/16, $3.50) Paolo Rivera-a/c 3.50
...: 1953 - The Phantom Hand & The Kelpie (10/15, $3.50) Mignola-s/c; Stenbeck-a 3.50
...: 1953 - The Witch Tree & Rawhead and Bloody Bones (11/15, $3.50) Mignola-s/c; Stenbeck-a 3.50
...: 1954 - Black Sun 1,2 (9/16 - No. 2, 10/16, $3.99) Stephen Green-a/c 4.00
...: 1954 - The Unreasoning Beast (11/16, $3.99) Mignola & Roberson-s/Reynolds-a 4.00

HELLBOY/BEASTS OF BURDEN
Dark Horse Comics: Oct, 2010 ($3.50, one-shot)

... Sacrifice - Evan Dorkin & Mignola-s/Jill Thompson-a 3.50

HELLBOY: BEING HUMAN
Dark Horse Comics: May, 2011 ($3.50, one-shot)

nn-Mignola-s; Richard Corben-a/c; Roger app. 3.50

HELLBOY: BOX FULL OF EVIL
Dark Horse Comics: Aug, 1999 - No. 2, Sept, 1999 ($2.95, lim. series)

1,2-Mignola-s/a; back-up story w/ Matt Smith-a 4.00

HELLBOY: BUSTER OAKLEY GETS HIS WISH
Dark Horse Comics: Apr, 2011 ($3.50, one-shot)

nn-Mignola-s; Kevin Nowlan-a; two covers by Mignola & Nowlan 3.50

HELLBOY CHRISTMAS SPECIAL
Dark Horse Comics: Dec, 1997 ($3.95, one-shot)

nn-Christmas stories by Mignola, Gianni, Darrow, Purcell 6.00

HELLBOY: CONQUEROR WORM
Dark Horse Comics: May, 2001 - No. 4, Aug, 2001 ($2.99, limited series)

1-4-Mignola-s/a/c 4.00

HELLBOY: DARKNESS CALLS
Dark Horse Comics: Apr, 2007 - No. 6, Nov, 2007 ($2.99, limited series)

1-6-Mignola-s/Fegredo-a 3.00

HELLBOY: DOUBLE FEATURE OF EVIL
Dark Horse Comics: Nov, 2010 ($3.50, one-shot)

1-Mignola-s; Corben-a/c 3.50

HELLBOY: HOUSE OF THE LIVING DEAD
Dark Horse Comics: Nov, 2011 ($14.99, hardcover graphic novel)

1-Mignola-s; Corben-a/c; Hellboy and Lucha Libre 15.00

HELLBOY IN HELL (Follows Hellboy's death in Hellboy: The Fury)
Dark Horse Comics: Dec, 2012 - No. 10, Jun, 2016 ($2.99)

1-10-Mignola-s/a/c 3.00
1-Variant "Year in Monsters" cover 10.00

HELLBOY IN MEXICO
Dark Horse Comics: May, 2010 ($3.50, one-shot)

1-Mignola-s; Corben-a/c; Mexican wrestlers vs. monsters 3.50

HELLBOY: IN THE CHAPEL OF MOLOCH
Dark Horse Comics: Oct, 2008 ($2.99, one-shot)

nn-Mignola-s/a/c 3.00

HELLBOY, JR.
Dark Horse Comics: Oct, 1999 - No. 2, Nov, 1999 ($2.95, limited series)

1,2-Stories and art by various 4.00
TPB (1/04, $14.95) r/#1&2, Halloween; sketch pages; intro. by Steve Niles; Bill Wray-c 15.00

HELLBOY, JR., HALLOWEEN SPECIAL
Dark Horse Comics: Oct, 1997 ($3.95, one-shot)

nn-"Harvey" style renditions of Hellboy characters; Bill Wray, Mike Mignola & various-s/a; wraparound-c by Wray 5.00

HELLBOY: MAKOMA, OR A TALE TOLD...
Dark Horse Comics: Feb, 2006 - No. 2, Mar, 2006 ($2.99, lim. series)

1,2-Mignola-s/c; Mignola & Corben-a 3.00

HELLBOY PREMIERE EDITION
Dark Horse Comics (Wizard): 2004 (no price, one-shot)

nn- Two covers by Mignola & Davis; Mignola-s/a; BPRD story w/Arcudi-s/Davis-a 5.00
Wizard World Los Angeles-Movie photo-c; Mignola-s/a; BPRD story w/Arcudi-s/Davis-a 10.00

HELLBOY: SEED OF DESTRUCTION (First Hellboy series)
Dark Horse Comics (Legend): Mar, 1994 - No. 4, Jun, 1994 ($2.50, lim. series)

1-Mignola-c/a w/Byrne scripts; Monkeyman & O'Brien back-up story (origin) by Art Adams. 3 6 9 17 26 35
2-4: 2-1st app. Abe Sapien & Liz Sherman 1 3 4 6 8 10
Hellboy: One for One (8/10, $1.00) r/#1 Hellboy story with red cover frame 3.00
Trade paperback (1994, $17.95)-collects all four issues plus r/Hellboy's 1st app. in San Diego Comic Con #2 & pin-ups 18.00
Limited edition hardcover (1995, $99.95)-includes everything in trade paperback plus additional material. 100.00

HELLBOY STRANGE PLACES
Dark Horse Books: Apr, 2006 ($17.95, TPB)

SC - Reprints Hellboy: The Third Wish #1,2 and Hellboy: The Island #1,2; sketch pages 18.00

HELLBOY: THE BRIDE OF HELL
Dark Horse Comics: Dec, 2009 ($3.50, one-shot)

1-Mignola-s/c; Corben-a; preview of The Marquis: Inferno 3.50

HELLBOY: THE CHAINED COFFIN AND OTHERS
Dark Horse Comics (Legend): Aug, 1998 ($17.95, TPB)

nn-Mignola-c/a/s; reprints out-of-print one shots; pin-up gallery 18.00

HELLBOY: THE COMPANION
Dark Horse Books: May, 2008 ($14.95, 9"x6", TPB)

nn-Overview of Hellboy history, characters, stories, mythology; text with Mignola panels 15.00

HELLBOY: THE CORPSE
Dark Horse Comics: Mar, 2004 (25¢, one-shot)

nn-Mignola-c/a/scripts; reprints "The Corpse" serial from Capitol City's Advance Comics catalog; development sketches and photos of the Corpse from the Hellboy movie 3.00

HELLBOY: THE CORPSE AND THE IRON SHOES
Dark Horse Comics (Legend): Jan, 1996 ($2.95, one-shot)

nn-Mignola-c/a/scripts; reprints "The Corpse" serial w/new story 5.00

HELLBOY: THE CROOKED MAN
Dark Horse Comics: Jul, 2008 - No. 3, Sept, 2008 ($2.99, lim. series)

1-3-Mignola-s/Corben-a/c 3.00

HELLBOY: THE FURY
Dark Horse Comics: Jun, 2011 - No. 3, Aug, 2011 ($2.99, lim. series)

1-3-Mignola-s/c; Fegredo-a. 1-Variant-c by Fegredo. 3-Hellboy dies 3.00
3-Retailer Incentive Variant 26 52 78 130 195 260

HELLBOY: THE GOLDEN ARMY
Dark Horse Comics: Jan, 2008 (no cover price)

nn-Prelude to the 2008 movie; Del Toro & Mignola-s/Velasco-a; 3 photo covers 3.00

HELLBOY: THE ISLAND
Dark Horse Comics: June, 2005 - No. 2, July, 2005 ($2.99, lim. series)

1,2: Mignola-c/a & scripts 4.00

HELLBOY: THE MIDNIGHT CIRCUS
Dark Horse Books: Oct, 2013 ($14.99, hardcover graphic novel)

nn-Mignola-s/c; Fegredo-a; young Hellboy runs away from BPRD in 1948 15.00

HELLBOY: THE RIGHT HAND OF DOOM
Dark Horse Comics (Legend): Apr, 2000 ($17.95, TPB)

nn-Mignola-c/a/s; reprints 18.00

HELLBOY: THE SLEEPING AND THE DEAD
Dark Horse Comics: Dec, 2010 - No. 2, Feb, 2011 ($3.50, lim. series)

1,2-Mignola-s/Scott Hampton-a 3.50

HELLBOY: THE STORM
Dark Horse Comics: Jul, 2010 - No. 3, Sept, 2010 ($2.99, lim. series)

1-3-Mignola-s/Fegredo-a 3.00

HELLBOY: THE THIRD WISH
Dark Horse Comics (Maverick): July, 2002 - No. 2, Aug, 2002 ($2.99, limited series)

1,2-Mignola-c/a/s 4.00

Hello Pal Comics #1 © HARV

Hell's Angel #4 © MAR

He-Man: The Eternity War #10 © Mattel

GD 2.0 | VG 4.0 | FN 6.0 | VF 8.0 | VF/NM 9.0 | NM- 9.2

HELLBOY THE TROLL WITCH AND OTHERS
Dark Horse Books: Nov, 2007 ($17.95, TPB)

SC - Reprints Hellboy: Makoma, Hellboy Premiere Edition and stories from Dark Horse Book of Hauntings, DHB of Witchcraft, DHB of the Dead, DHB of Monsters — 18.00

HELLBOY: THE WILD HUNT
Dark Horse Comics: Dec, 2008 - No. 8, Nov, 2009 ($2.99, lim. series)

1-8: Mignola-c/s; Fegredo-a — 3.00

HELLBOY: THE WOLVES OF ST. AUGUST
Dark Horse Comics (Legend): 1995 ($4.95, squarebound, one-shot)

nn-Mignola--c/a/scripts; r/Dark Horse Presents #88-91 with additional story — 6.00

HELLBOY: WAKE THE DEVIL (Sequel to Seed of Destruction)
Dark Horse Comics (Legend): Jun, 1996 - No. 5, Oct, 1996 ($2.95, lim. series)

1-5: Mignola-c/a & scripts; The Monstermen back-up story by Gary Gianni — 6.00
TPB (1997, $17.95) r/#1-5 — 18.00

HELLBOY: WEIRD TALES
Dark Horse Comics: Feb, 2003 - No. 8, Apr, 2004 ($2.99, limited series, anthology)

1-8-Hellboy stories from other creators. 1-Cassaday-c/s/a; Watson-s/a. 6-Cho-c — 4.00
... Vol. 1 (2004, 17.95) r/#1-4 — 18.00
... Vol. 2 (2004, 17.95) r/#5-8 and Lobster Johnson serial from #1-8 — 18.00

HELLBOY WINTER SPECIAL
Dark Horse Comics: Jan, 2016; Jan, 2017 ($3.99, one-shots)

1-Short stories by Mignola, Sale, Oeming, Allie, Roberson and others; Sale-c — 4.00
nn (1/17)-Short stories; Mignola & Roberson-s, Mitten, Grist & Fiumara-a; Fiumara-c — 4.00

HELLCAT
Marvel Comics: Sept, 2000 - No. 3, Nov, 2000 ($2.99)

1-3-Englehart-s/Breyfogle-a; Hedy Wolfe app. — 3.00

HELLCOP
Image Comics (Avalon Studios): Aug, 1998 - No. 4, Mar, 1999 ($2.50)

1-4: 1-(Oct. on-c) Casey-s — 3.00

HELL ETERNAL
DC Comics (Vertigo Verité): 1998 ($6.95, squarebound, one-shot)

1-Delano-s/Phillips-a — 7.00

HELLGATE: LONDON (Based on the video game)
Dark Horse Comics: No. 0, May 2006 - No. 3, Mar, 2007 ($2.99)

0-3-Edginton-s/Pugh-a/Briclot-c — 3.00

HELLHOUNDS (....: Panzer Cops #3-6)
Dark Horse Comics: 1994 - No. 6, July, 1994 ($2.50, B&W, limited series)

1-6: 1-Hamner-c. 3-(4/94). 2-Joe Phillips-c — 3.00

HELLHOUND, THE REDEMPTION QUEST
Marvel Comics (Epic Comics): Dec, 1993 - No. 4, Mar, 1994 ($2.25, lim. series, coated stock)

1-4 — 3.00

HELLO BUDDIES
Harvey Publications: 1953 (25¢, small size)

1 — 3 | 6 | 9 | 21 | 33 | 45

HELLO, I'M JOHNNY CASH
Spire Christian Comics (Fleming H. Revell Co.): 1976 (39¢/49¢)

nn-(39¢-c) — 3 | 6 | 9 | 16 | 23 | 30
nn-(49¢-c) — 2 | 4 | 6 | 11 | 16 | 20

HELL ON EARTH (See DC Science Fiction Graphic Novel)

HELLO PAL COMICS (Short Story Comics)
Harvey Publications: Jan, 1943 - No. 3, May, 1943 (Photo-c)

1-Rocketman & Rocketgirl begin; Yankee Doodle Jones app.; Mickey Rooney photo-c — 63 | 126 | 189 | 403 | 689 | 975
2-Charlie McCarthy photo-c (scarce) — 56 | 112 | 168 | 349 | 595 | 840
3-Bob Hope photo-c (scarce) — 60 | 120 | 180 | 384 | 660 | 935

HELLRAISER (See Clive Barker's...)

HELLRAISER/NIGHTBREED – JIHAD (Also see Clive Barker's...)
Epic Comics (Marvel Comics): 1991 - Book 2, 1991 ($4.50, 52 pgs.)

Book 1,2 — 5.00

HELL-RIDER (Motorcycle themed magazine)
Skywald Publications: Aug, 1971 - No. 2, Oct, 1971 (B&W, 68 pgs.)

1-Origin & 1st app.; Butterfly & the Wild Bunch begin; 1st Hell-Rider by Andru, Esposito and Friedrich — 5 | 10 | 15 | 35 | 63 | 90
2-Andru, Ayers, Buckler, Shores-a — 4 | 8 | 12 | 27 | 44 | 60

NOTE: *#3 advertised in Psycho #5 but did not come out.* **Buckler** *a-1, 2.* **Rosenbaum** *c-1,2.*

HELL'S ANGEL (Becomes Dark Angel #6 on)
Marvel Comics UK: July, 1992 - No. 5, Nov, 1993 ($1.75)

1-5: X-Men (Wolverine, Cyclops)-c/stories. 1-Origin. 3-Jim Lee cover swipe — 3.00

HELLSHOCK
Image Comics: July, 1994 - No. 4, Nov, 1994 ($1.95, limited series)

1-4-Jae Lee-c/a & scripts. 4-Variant-c. — 3.00

HELLSHOCK
Image Comics: Jan, 1997 - No. 3, Jan, 1998 ($2.95/$2.50, limited series)

1-($2.95)-Jae Lee-c/s/a, Villarrubia-painted-a — 4.00
2-($2.50) — 3.00
Book 3: The Science of Faith (1/98, $2.50) Jae Lee-c/s/a, Villarrubia-painted-a — 3.00
Vol. 1 HC (2006, $49.99) r/#1-3 re-colored, with unpublished 22 pg. conclusion; cover gallery and sketches; alternate opening art; intro. by Jim Lee — 50.00

HELLSPAWN
Image Comics: Aug, 2000 - No. 16, Apr, 2003 ($2.50)

1-Bendis-s/Ashley Wood-c/a; Spawn and Clown app. — 3.00
2-9: 6-Last Bendis-s; Mike Moran (Miracleman app.). 7-Niles-s — 3.00
10-16-Templesmith-a — 3.00
...: The Ashley Wood Collection Vol. 1 (4/06, $24.95, TPB) r/#1-10; sketch & cover gallery — 25.00

HELLSTORM: PRINCE OF LIES (See Ghost Rider #1 & Marvel Spotlight #12)
Marvel Comics: Apr, 1993 - No. 21, Dec, 1994 ($2.00)

1-($2.95)-Parchment-c w/red thermographic ink — 4.00
2-21: 14-Bound-in trading card sheet. 18-P. Craig Russell-c — 3.00

HELLSTORM: SON OF SATAN
Marvel Comics (MAX): Dec, 2006 - No. 5, Apr, 2007 ($3.99, limited series)

1-5-Suydam-c/Irvine-s/Braun & Janson-a — 4.00
... - Equinox TPB (2007, $17.99) r/#1-5; interviews with the creators — 18.00

HELMET OF FATE, THE (Series of one-shots following Doctor Fate's helmet)
DC Comics: Mar, 2007 - May 2007 ($2.99, one-shots)

...: Black Alice (5/07) Simone-s/Rouleau-a/c — 3.00
...: Detective Chimp (3/07) Willingham-s/McManus-a/Bolland-c — 3.00
...: Ibis the Invincible (3/07) Williams-s/Winslade-a; the Ibistick returns — 3.00
...: Sargon the Sorcerer (4/07) Niles-s/Scott Hampton-s; debut new Sargon — 3.00
...: Zauriel (4/07) Gerber-s/Snejbjerg-a/Kaluta-c; leads into new Doctor Fate series — 3.00
TPB (2007, $14.99) r/one-shots — 15.00

HELP US! GREAT WARRIOR
BOOM! Studios (BOOM! Box): Feb, 2015 - No. 6, Jul, 2015 ($3.99)

1-6-Madeleine Flores-s/a — 4.00

HE-MAN (See Masters Of The Universe)

HE-MAN (Also see Tops In Adventure)
Ziff-Davis Publ. Co. (Approved Comics): Fall, 1952

1-Kinstler painted-c; Powell-a — 16 | 32 | 48 | 94 | 147 | 200

HE-MAN
Toby Press: May, 1954 - No. 2, July, 1954 (Painted-c by B. Safran)

1-Gorilla-c — 15 | 30 | 45 | 88 | 137 | 185
2-Shark-c — 15 | 30 | 45 | 85 | 130 | 175

HE-MAN AND THE MASTERS OF THE UNIVERSE
DC Comics: Sept, 2012 - No. 6, Mar, 2013 ($2.99)

1-6: 1-James Robinson-s/Philip Tan-a/c; Skeletor app. 5-Adam gets the sword — 3.00

HE-MAN AND THE MASTERS OF THE UNIVERSE
DC Comics: Jun, 2013 - No. 19, Jan, 2015 ($2.99)

1-19: 1-Giffen-s/Mhan-a/Benes-c. 7,8-Abnett-s/Kayanan-a. 13-18-Origin of She-Ra — 3.00

HE-MAN: THE ETERNITY WAR
DC Comics: Feb, 2015 - No. 15, Apr, 2016 ($2.99)

1-15: 1-Abnett-s/Mhan-a; Hordak invades; origin of Grayskull — 3.00

HE-MAN / THUNDERCATS
DC Comics: Dec, 2016 - No. 6 ($3.99)

1-5-Freddie Williams II-a; Mumm-Ra & Skeletor app. — 4.00

HENNESSEY (TV)
Dell Publishing Co.: No. 1200, Aug-Oct, 1961 - No. 1280, Mar-May, 1962

Four Color 1200-Gil Kane-a, photo-c — 6 | 12 | 18 | 42 | 79 | 115

Herbie #2 © ACG

Hercules (2005 series) #1 © MAR

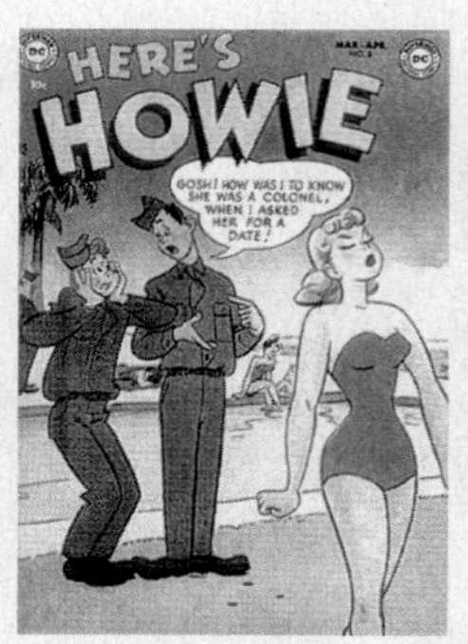

Here's Howie Comics #8 © DC

	GD	VG	FN	VF	VF/NM	NM-
	2.0	4.0	6.0	8.0	9.0	9.2

Four Color 1280-Photo-c 6 12 18 40 73 105

HENRY (Also see Little Annie Rooney)
David McKay Publications: 1935 (52 pgs.) (Daily B&W strip reprints)(10"x10" cardboard-c)
1-By Carl Anderson 40 80 120 246 411 575

HENRY (See King Comics & Magic Comics)
Dell Publishing Co.: No. 122, Oct, 1946 - No. 65, Apr-June, 1961
Four Color 122-All new stories begin 15 30 45 100 220 340
Four Color 155 (7/47), 1 (1-3/48)-All new stories 10 20 30 66 138 210
2 6 12 18 40 73 105
3-10 5 10 15 34 60 85
11-20: 20-Infinity-c 5 10 15 30 50 70
21-30 4 8 12 25 40 55
31-40 3 6 9 21 33 45
41-65 3 6 9 17 26 35

HENRY (See Giant Comic Album and March of Comics No. 43, 58, 84, 101, 112, 129, 147, 162, 178, 189)

HENRY ALDRICH COMICS (TV)
Dell Publishing Co.: Aug-Sept, 1950 - No. 22, Sept-Nov, 1954
1-Part series written by John Stanley; Bill Williams-a
9 18 27 60 120 180
2 5 10 15 35 63 90
3-5 5 10 15 31 53 75
6-10 4 8 12 27 44 60
11-22 4 8 12 23 37 50

HENRY BREWSTER
Country Wide (M.F. Ent.): Feb, 1966 - V2#7, Sept, 1967 (All 25¢ Giants)
1 3 6 9 19 30 40
2-6(12/66), V2#7-Powell-a in most 3 6 9 14 20 25

HEPCATS
Antarctic Press: Nov, 1996 - No. 12 ($2.95, B&W)
0-12-Martin Wagner-c/s/a: 0-color 3.00
0-($9.95) CD Edition 10.00

HERALDS
Marvel Comics: Aug, 2010 - No. 5, Aug, 2010 ($2.99, weelky limited series)
1-5-Kathryn Immonen-s/Zonjic & Harren-a; She-Hulk, Hellcat, Emma Frost, Photon app. 3.00

HERBIE (See Forbidden Worlds #73,94,110,114,116 & Unknown Worlds #20)
American Comics Group: April-May, 1964 - No. 23, Feb, 1967 (All 12¢)
1-Whitney-c/a in most issues 16 32 48 112 249 385
2-4 8 16 24 56 108 160
5-Beatles parody (10 pgs.), Dean Martin, Frank Sinatra app. (10-11/64)
9 18 27 61 123 185
6,7,9,10 7 14 21 48 89 130
8-Origin & 1st app. The Fat Fury 8 16 24 55 105 155
11-23: 14-Nemesis & Magicman app. 17-r/2nd Herbie from Forbidden Worlds #94. 23-r/1st Herbie from F.W. #73 6 12 18 37 66 95
... Archives Volume One HC (Dark Horse, 8/08, $49.95, dust jacket) r/earliest apps. in Forbidden Worlds, Unknown Worlds, and Herbie #1-5; Scott Shaw intro. 50.00

HERBIE
Dark Horse Comics: Oct, 1992 - No. 12, 1993 ($2.50, limited series)
1-Whitney-r plus new-c/a in all; Byrne-c/a & scripts 4.00
2-6: 3-Bob Burden-c/a. 4-Art Adams-c 3.00

HERBIE GOES TO MONTE CARLO, HERBIE RIDES AGAIN (See Walt Disney Showcase No. 24, 41)

HERC (Hercules from the Avengers)
Marvel Comics: Jun, 2011 - No. 10, Jan, 2012 ($2.99)
1-6, (6.1), 7-10: 1-Pak & Van Lente-s; Hobgoblin app. 3-6-Fear Itself tie-in. 6.1-Grell-a 7,8-Spider-Island tie-in; Herc gets Spider-powers. 10-Elektra app. 3.00

HERCULES (See Hit Comics #1-21, Journey Into Mystery Annual, Marvel Graphic Novel #37, Marvel Premiere #26 & The Mighty...)

HERCULES (See Charlton Classics)
Charlton Comics: Oct, 1967 - No. 13, Sept, 1969; Dec, 1968
1-Thane of Bagarth begins; Glanzman-a in all 4 8 12 27 44 60
2-13: 1-5,7-10-Aparo-a. 8-(12¢-c) 4 8 12 23 37 50
4-Magazine format (low distribution) 8 16 24 54 102 150
8-Magazine format (low distribution)(12/68, 35¢, B&W); new Hercules story plus-r story/#1; Thane-r/#1-3 5 10 15 33 57 80
Modern Comics reprint 10('77), 11('78) 6.00

HERCULES (Prince of Power) (Also see The Champions)
Marvel Comics Group: V1#1, Sept, 1982 - V1#4, Dec, 1982;
V2#1, Mar, 1984 - V2#4, Jun, 1984 (color, both limited series)
1-4, V2#1-4: Layton-c/a. 4-Death of Zeus. 4.00
NOTE: *Layton a-1, 2, 3p, 4p, V2#1-4; c-1-4, V2#1-4.*

HERCULES
Marvel Comics: Jun, 2005 - No. 5, Sept, 2005 ($2.99, limited series)
1-5-Texeira-a/c; Tieri-s. 4-Capt. America, Wolverine and New Avengers app. 3.00
...: New Labors of Hercules TPB (2005, $13.99) r/#1-5 14.00

HERCULES
Marvel Comics: Jan, 2016 - Present ($3.99)
1-6: 1-Dan Abnett-s/Luke Ross-a; Gilgamesh app. 4.00

HERCULES: FALL OF AN AVENGER (Continues in Heroic Age: Prince of Power)
Marvel Comics: May, 2010 - No. 2, June, 2010 ($3.99, limited series)
1,2-Follows Hercules' demise in Incredible Hercules #141; Olivetti-c/a 4.00

HERCULES: HEART OF CHAOS
Marvel Comics: Aug, 1997 - No. 3, Oct, 1997 ($2.50, limited series)
1-3-DeFalco-s, Frenz-a 3.00

HERCULES: OFFICIAL COMICS MOVIE ADAPTION
Acclaim Books: 1997 ($4.50, digest size)
nn-Adaptation of the Disney animated movie 4.50

HERCULES: THE LEGENDARY JOURNEYS (TV)
Topps Comics: June, 1996 - No. 5, Oct, 1996 ($2.95)
1-2: 1-Golden-c. 3.00
3-Xena-c/app. 1 2 3 4 5 7
3-Variant-c 2 4 6 9 12 15
4,5: Xena-c/app. 5.00

HERCULES UNBOUND
National Periodical Publications: Oct-Nov, 1975 - No. 12, Aug-Sept, 1977
1-Wood-i begins 2 4 6 9 13 16
2-12: 7-Adams ad. 10-Atomic Knights x-over 2 3 4 6 8 10
NOTE: ***Buckler** c-7p. **Layton** inks-No. 9, 10. **Simonson** a-7-10p, 11, 12; c- 8p, 9-12. **Wood** a-1-8i; c-7i, 8i.*

HERCULES (...Unchained #1121) (Movie)
Dell Publishing Co.: No. 1006, June-Aug, 1959 - No.1121, Aug, 1960
Four Color 1006-Buscema-a, photo-c 8 16 24 56 108 160
Four Color 1121-Crandall/Evans-a 8 16 24 54 102 150

HERCULES: TWILIGHT OF A GOD
Marvel Comics: Aug, 2010 - No. 4, Nov, 2010 ($3.99, limited series)
1-4-Layton-s/a(i); Lim-a; Galactus app. 4.00

HERCULIAN
Image Comics: Mar, 2011 ($4.99, oversized, one-shot)
1-Golden Age style superhero stories and humor pages; Erik Larsen-s/a/c 5.00

HERE COMES SANTA (See March of Comics No. 30, 213, 340)

HERE'S HOWIE COMICS
National Periodical Publications: Jan-Feb, 1952 - No. 18, Nov-Dec, 1954
1 36 72 108 211 343 475
2 19 38 57 109 172 235
3-5: 5-Howie in the Army issues begin (9-10/52) 15 30 45 85 130 175
6-10 14 28 42 80 115 150
11-18 14 28 42 76 108 140
Ashcan (1,2/51) not distributed to newsstands (a FN copy sold for $836.50 in 2012)

HERETIC, THE
Dark Horse (Blanc Noir): Nov, 1996 - No. 4, Mar, 1997 ($2.95, lim. series)
1-4:-w/back-up story 3.00

HERITAGE OF THE DESERT (See Zane Grey, 4-Color 236)

HERMAN & KATNIP (See Harvey Comics Hits #60 & 62, Harvey Hits #14,25,31,41 & Paramount Animated Comics #1)

HERMES VS. THE EYEBALL KID
Dark Horse Comics: Dec, 1994 - No. 3,Feb, 1995 ($2.95, B&W, limited series)
1-3: Eddie Campbell-c/a/scripts 3.00

H-E-R-O (Dial H For HERO)
DC Comics: Apr, 2003 - No. 22, Jan, 2005 ($2.50)
1-Will Pfeiffer-s/Kano-a/Van Fleet-c 3.50
2-22: 2-6-Kano-a. 7,8-Gleason-a. 12-14-Kirk-a. 15-22-Robby Reed app. 3.00
...: Double Feature (6/03, $4.95) r/#1&2 5.00
...: Powers and Abilities (2003, $9.95) r/#1-6; intro. by Geoff Johns 10.00

Hero Comics 2014 © Hero

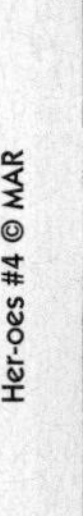
Her-oes #4 © MAR

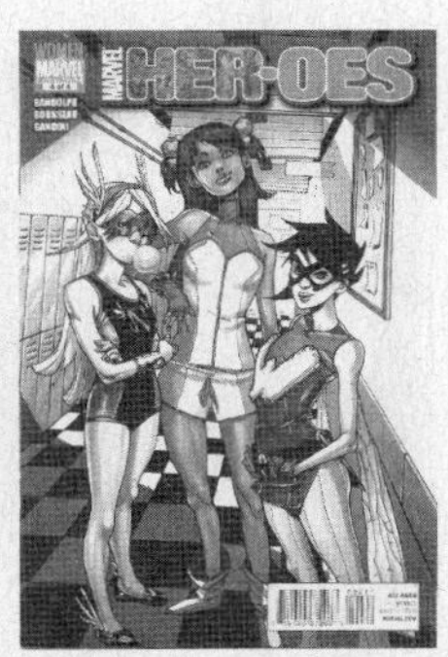

Heroes For Hire (2006 series) #8 © MAR

GD VG FN VF VF/NM NM-
2.0 4.0 6.0 8.0 9.0 9.2

HERO (Warrior of the Mystic Realms)
Marvel Comics: May, 1990 - No. 6, Oct, 1990 ($1.50, limited series)
1-6: 1-Portacio-i 3.00

HERO ALLIANCE, THE
Sirius Comics: Dec, 1985 - No. 2, Sept, 1986 (B&W)
1,2: 2-($1.50), Special Edition 1 (7/86, color) 3.00

HERO ALLIANCE
Wonder Color Comics: May, 1987 ($1.95)
1-Ron Lim-a 3.00

HERO ALLIANCE
Innovation Publishing: V2#1, Sept, 1989 - V2#17, Nov, 1991 ($1.95, 28 pgs.)
V2#1-17: 1,2-Ron Lim-a 3.00
Annual 1 (1990, $2.75, 36 pgs.)-Paul Smith-c/a 3.00
Special 1 (1992, $2.50, 32 pgs.)-Stuart Immonen-a (10 pgs.) 3.00

HERO ALLIANCE: END OF THE GOLDEN AGE
Innovation Publ.: July, 1989 - No. 3, Aug, 1989 ($1.75, bi-weekly lim. series)
1-3: Bart Sears & Ron Lim-c/a; reprints & new-a 3.00

HEROBEAR AND THE KID
Boom Entertainment (KaBOOM!)
... 2013 Annual 1 (10/13, $3.99) Halloween-themed story 4.00
... 2016 Fall Special 1 (10/16, $5.99) Saving Time: Part Two 6.00
... Special (6/13, $3.99) Mike Kunkel-s/a/c 4.00
...: The Inheritance (8/13 - No. 5, 12/13, $3.99) 1-5-Mike Kunkel-s/a/c; origin re-told 4.00

HERO COMICS (Hero Initiative benefit book)
IDW Publishing: 2009 - Present ($3.99)
1-Short story anthology by various incl. Colan, Chaykin; covers by Wagner & Campbell 4.00
2011-Covers by Campbell & Hughes; Gaiman-s/Kieth-a; Chew & Elephantmen app. 4.00
2012-Cover by Campbell; TMNT by Eastman; art by Heath, Sim, Kupperberg, & others 4.00
2014-Covers by Campbell & Kieth; Sable by Grell; art by Kieth, Goldberg & others 4.00
...: A Hero Initiative Benefit Book SC (5/16, $19.99) reprints from previous editions 20.00

HEROES
Marvel Comics: Dec, 2001 ($3.50, magazine-size, one-shot)
1-Pin-up tributes to the rescue workers of the Sept. 11 tragedy; art and text by various; cover by Alex Ross 6.00
1-2nd and 3rd printings 4.00

HEROES (Also see Shadow Cabinet & Static)
DC Comics (Milestone): May, 1996 - No. 6, Nov, 1996 ($2.50, limited series)
1-6: 1-Intro Heroes (Iota, Donner, Blitzen, Starlight, Payback & Static) 3.00

HEROES (Based on the NBC TV series)
DC Comics (WildStorm): 2007; 2009 ($29.99, hardcover with dustjacket)
Vol. 1 - Collects 34 installments of the online graphic novel; art by various; two covers by Jim Lee and Alex Ross; intro. by Masi Oka; Jeph Loeb interview 30.00
Vol. 2 - (2009) Collects 46 installments of the online graphic novel; art by various incl. Gaydos, Grummett, Gunnell, Odagawa; two covers by Tim Sale and Gene Ha 30.00

HER-OES
Marvel Comics: Jun, 2010 - No. 4, Sept, 2010 ($2.99, limited series)
1-4-Randolph-s/Rousseau-a; Wasp, She-Hulk, Namora as teenagers 3.00

HEROES AGAINST HUNGER
DC Comics: 1986 ($1.50; one-shot for famine relief)
1-Superman, Batman app.; Neal Adams-c(p); includes many artists work; Jeff Jones assist (2 pg.) on B. Smith-a; Kirby-a 5.00

HEROES ALL CATHOLIC ACTION ILLUSTRATED
Heroes All Co.: 1943 - V6#5, Mar 10, 1948 (paper covers)

	GD	VG	FN	VF	VF/NM	NM-
V1#1-(16 pgs., 8x11")	24	48	72	142	234	325
V1#2-(16 pgs., 8x11")	19	38	57	111	176	240
V2#1(1/44)-3(3/44)-(16 pgs., 8x11")	15	30	45	94	147	200
V3#1(1/45)-10(12/45)-(16 pgs., 8x11")	15	30	45	85	130	175
V4#1-35 (12/20/46)-(16 pgs.)	14	28	42	80	115	150
V5#1(1/10/47)-8(2/28/47)-(16 pgs.), V5#9(3/7/47)-20(11/25/47)-(32 pgs.), V6#1(1/10/48)-5(3/10/48)-(32 pgs.)	12	24	36	69	97	125

HEROES ANONYMOUS
Bongo Comics: 2003 - No. 6, 2004 ($2.99, limited series)
1-6-($2.99)-Bill Morrison-c. 2-Guerra-a. 3-Pepoy-a 3.00

HEROES FOR HIRE
Marvel Comics: July, 1997 - No. 19, Jan, 1999 ($2.99/$1.99)
1-($2.99)-Wraparound cover 5.00
2-19: 2-Variant cover. 7-Thunderbolts app. 9-Punisher-c/app. 10,11-Deadpool-c/app. 18,19-Wolverine-c/app. 3.00
.../Quicksilver '98 Annual ($2.99) Siege of Wundagore pt.5 4.00

HEROES FOR HIRE
Marvel Comics: Oct, 2006 - No. 15, Dec, 2007 ($2.99)
1-5-Tucci-a/c; Black Cat, Shang-Chi, Tarantula, Humbug & Daughters of the Dragon app. 3.00
6-15: 6-8-Sparacio-c. 9,10-Golden-c. 11-13-World War Hulk x-over. 13-Takeda-c 3.00
... Vol. 1: Civil War (2007, $13.99) r/#1-5 14.00
... Vol. 2: Ahead of the Curve (2007, $13.99) r/#6-10 14.00
... Vol. 3: World War Hulk (2008, $13.99) r/#11-15 14.00

HEROES FOR HIRE
Marvel Comics: Feb, 2011 - No. 12, Nov, 2011 ($3.99/$2.99)
1-($3.99) Abnett & Lanning-s/Walker-a; back-up history of the various teams 4.00
2-12-($2.99) 2-Silver Sable & Ghost Rider app. 5-Punisher app. 9-11-Fear Itself tie-in 3.00

HEROES FOR HOPE STARRING THE X-MEN
Marvel Comics Group: Dec, 1985 ($1.50, one-shot, 52 pgs., proceeds donated to famine relief)
1-Stephen King scripts; Byrne, Miller, Corben-a; Wrightson/J. Jones-a (3 pgs.); Art Adams-c; Starlin back-c 1 3 4 6 8 10

HEROES: GODSEND (Based on the NBC TV series)(Prelude to the 2015 revival)
Titan Comics: Apr, 2016 - No. 5, Aug, 2016 ($3.99, limited series)
1-5: 1-Origin of Farah Nazan; Roy Allan Martinez-a; multiple covers on each 4.00

HEROES, INC. PRESENTS CANNON
Wally Wood/CPL/Gang Publ.: 1969 - No. 2, 1976 (Sold at Army PXs)
nn-Ditko, Wood-a; Wood-c; Reese-a(p) 2 4 6 9 12 15
2-Wood-c; Ditko, Byrne, Wood-a; 8-1/2x10-1/2"; B&W; $2.00 3 6 9 16 23 30

NOTE: *First issue not distributed by publisher; 1,800 copies were stored and 900 copies were stolen from warehouse. Many copies have surfaced in recent years.*

HEROES OF THE WILD FRONTIER (Formerly Baffling Mysteries)
Ace Periodicals: No. 27, Jan, 1956 - No. 2, Apr, 1956
27(#1),2-Davy Crockett, Daniel Boone, Buffalo Bill 6 12 18 29 36 42

HEROES REBORN (one-shots)
Marvel Comics: Jan, 2000 ($1.99)
...:Ashema; ...:Doom; ...:Doomsday; ...:Masters of Evil; ...:Rebel; ...:Remnants; ...:Young Allies 3.00

HEROES REBORN: THE RETURN (Also see Avengers, Fantastic Four, Iron Man & Captain America titles for issues and TPBs)
Marvel Comics: Dec, 1997 - No. 4 ($2.50, weekly mini-series)
1-4-Avengers, Fantastic Four, Iron Man & Captain America rejoin regular Marvel Universe; Peter David-s/Larocca-c/a 4.00
1-4-Variant-c for each 6.00
Wizard 1/2 1 2 3 5 7 9
Return of the Heroes TPB ('98, $14.95) r/#1-4 15.00

HEROES: VENGEANCE (Based on the NBC TV series)(Prelude to the 2015 revival)
Titan Comics: Nov, 2015 - No. 5, Mar, 2016 ($3.99, limited series)
1-5: 1-Origin of El Vengador; Rubine-a; multiple covers on each 4.00

HERO FOR HIRE (Power Man No. 17 on; also see Cage)
Marvel Comics Group: June, 1972 - No. 16, Dec, 1973

	GD	VG	FN	VF	VF/NM	NM-
1-Origin & 1st app. Luke Cage; Tuska-a(p)	46	92	138	340	770	1200
2-Tuska-a(p)	6	12	18	41	76	110
3,4: 3-1st app. Mace. 4-1st app. Phil Fox of the Bugle	5	10	15	31	53	75
5-1st app. Black Mariah	5	10	15	31	53	75
6-10: 8,9-Dr. Doom app. 9-F.F. app.	4	8	12	23	37	50
11-16: 14-Origin retold. 15-Everett Sub-Mariner-r('53). 16-Origin Stilletto; death of Rackham	3	6	9	19	30	40

HERO HOTLINE (1st app. in Action Comics Weekly #637)
DC Comics: April, 1989 - No. 6, Sept, 1989 ($1.75, limited series)
1-6: Super-hero humor; Schaffenberger-i 3.00

HEROIC ADVENTURES (See Adventures)

HEROIC AGE
Marvel Comics: Nov, 2010 ($3.99, limited series)
... Heroes 1 (11/10, $3.99) profile of heroes, bios, pros, cons, "power grid"; Raney-c 4.00
... Villains 1 (1/11, $3.99) profile of villains, bios, pros, cons, "power grid"; Jae Lee-c 4.00

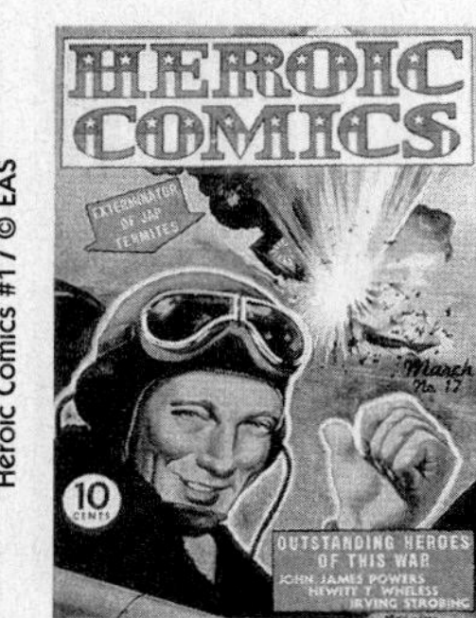

Heroic Comics #17 © EAS

Hickory #1 © QUA

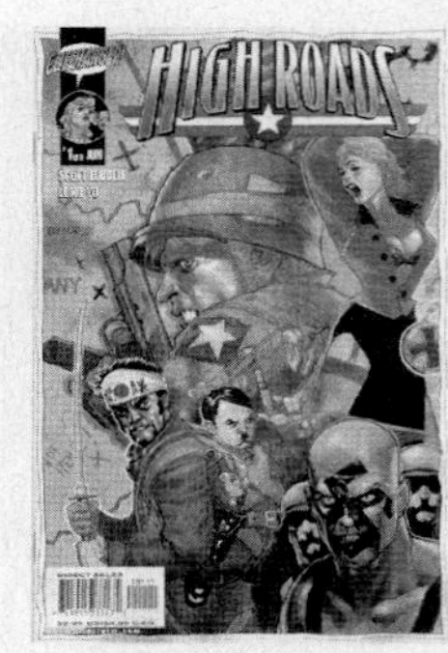

High Roads #1 © Yu

GD 2.0 | VG 4.0 | FN 6.0 | VF 8.0 | VF/NM 9.0 | NM- 9.2

... X-Men 1 (2/11, $3.99) profile of members in Steve Rogers journal entries,; Jae Lee-c 4.00

HEROIC AGE: PRINCE OF POWER (Continued from Hercules: Fall of an Avenger)
Marvel Comics: Jul, 2010 - No. 4, Oct, 2010 ($3.99, limited series)

1-4-Van Lente & Pak-s; Thor app.; leads into Chaos War #1 4.00

HEROIC COMICS (Reg'lar Fellers...#1-15; New Heroic #41 on)
Eastern Color Printing Co./Famous Funnies (Funnies, Inc. No. 1): Aug, 1940 - No. 97, June, 1955

1-Hydroman (origin) by Bill Everett, The Purple Zombie (origin) & Mann of India by Tarpe Mills begins (all 1st apps.) 232 464 696 1485 2543 3600
2 97 194 291 621 1061 1500
3,4 57 114 171 362 619 875
5,6 50 100 150 315 533 750
7-Origin & 1st app. Man O'Metal (1 pg.) 52 104 156 328 552 775
8-10: 10-Lingerie panels 39 78 117 234 385 535
11,13 37 74 111 222 361 500
12-Music Master (origin/1st app.) begins by Everett, ends No. 31; last Purple Zombie & Mann of India 40 80 120 246 411 575
14,15-Hydroman x-over in Rainbow Boy. 14-Origin & 1st app. Rainbow Boy (super hero). 15-1st app. Downbeat 37 74 111 222 361 500
16-20: 16-New logo. 17-Rainbow Boy x-over in Hydroman. 19-Rainbow Boy x-over in Hydroman & vice versa 26 52 78 154 252 350
21-30:25-Rainbow Boy x-over in Hydroman. 28-Last Man O'Metal. 29-Last Hydroman 20 40 60 114 182 250
31,34,38 9 18 27 50 65 80
32,36,37-Toth-a (3-4 pgs. each) 10 20 30 56 76 95
33,35-Toth-a (8 & 9 pgs.) 10 20 30 58 79 100
39-42-Toth, Ingels-a 10 20 30 58 79 100
43,46,47,49-Toth-a (2-4 pgs.). 47-Ingels-a 10 20 30 54 72 90
44,45,50-Toth-a (6-9 pgs.) 10 20 30 56 76 95
48,53,54 9 18 27 47 61 75
51-Williamson-a 10 20 30 56 76 95
52-Williamson-a (3 pg. story) 9 18 27 50 65 80
55-Toth-a 10 20 30 54 72 90
56-60: 60-Everett-a 9 18 27 50 65 80
61-Everett-a 9 18 27 47 61 75
62,64-Everett-c/a 10 20 30 54 72 90
63-Everett-c 9 18 27 52 69 85
65-Williamson/Frazetta-a; Evans-a (2 pgs.) 13 26 39 72 101 130
66,75,94-Frazetta-a (2 pgs. each) 9 18 27 52 69 85
67,73-Frazetta-a (4 pgs. each) 11 22 33 60 83 105
68,74,76-80,84,85,88-93,95-97: 95-Last pre-code 9 18 27 47 61 75
69,72-Frazetta-a (6 & 8 pgs. each); 1st (?) app. Frazetta Red Cross ad 13 26 39 72 101 130
70,71,86,87-Frazetta, 3-4 pgs. each; 1 pg. ad by Frazetta in #70 10 20 30 56 76 95
81,82-Frazetta art (1 pg. each): 81-1st (?) app. Frazetta Boy Scout ad (tied w/ Buster Crabbe #9 9 18 27 50 65 80
83-Frazetta-a (1/2 pg.) 9 18 27 50 65 80

NOTE: ***Evans*** *a-64, 65.* ***Everett*** *a-(Hydroman-c/a-No. 1-9), 44, 60-64; c-1-9, 62-64.* ***Harvey Fuller*** *c-28-35.* ***Sid Greene*** *a-38-43, 46.* ***Guardineer*** *a-42(3), 43, 44, 45(2), 49(3), 50, 60, 61(2), 65, 67(2) 70-72.* ***Ingels*** *c-41.* ***Kiefer*** *a-46, 48; c-19-22, 24, 44, 46, 48, 51-53, 65, 67-69, 71-74, 76, 77, 79, 80, 82, 85, 86, 88, 89, 94, 95.* ***Mort Lawrence*** *a-45.* ***Tarpe Mills*** *a-2(2), 3(2), 10.* ***Ed Moore*** *a-49, 52-54, 56-63, 65-69, 72-74, 76, 77.* ***H.G. Peter*** *a-58-74, 76, 77, 87.* ***Paul Reinman*** *a-49.* ***Rico*** *a-31. Captain Tootsie by* ***Beck****-31, 32. Painted-c #16 on. Hydroman c-1-11. Music Master c-12, 13, 15. Rainbow Boy c-14.*

HERO INITIATIVE: MIKE WIERINGO BOOK (Also see Hero Comics)
Marvel Comics: Aug, 2008 ($4.99)

1-The "What If" Fantastic Four story with Wieringo-a (7 pgs.) finished by other artists after his passing; art by Davis, Immonen, Ramos, Kitson and others; written tributes 5.00

HERO WORSHIP
Avatar Press: Jun, 2012 - No. 6, Nov, 2012 ($3.99)

1-6: 1-Zak Penn & Scott Murphy-s/Michael DiPascale-a; 2 covers 4.00

HERO ZERO (Also see Comics' Greatest World & Godzilla Versus Hero Zero)
Dark Horse Comics: Sept, 1994 ($2.50)

0 3.00

HEX (Replaces Jonah Hex)
DC Comics: Sept, 1985 - No. 18, Feb, 1987 (Story cont'd from Jonah Hex # 92)

1-Hex in post-atomic war world; origin 2 4 6 8 10 12
2-10,14-18: 6-Origin Stiletta 1 2 3 4 5 7
11-13: All contain future Batman storyline. 13-Intro The Dogs of War (origin #15) 1 3 4 6 8 10

NOTE: ***Giffen*** *a(p)-15-18; c(p)-15,17,18.* ***Texeira*** *a-1, 2p, 3p, 5-7p, 9p, 11-14p; c(p)-1, 2, 4-7, 12.*

HEXBREAKER (See First Comics Graphic Novel #15)

HEXED
BOOM! Studios: Aug, 2014 - No. 12, Aug, 2015 ($3.99)

1-12: 1-Michael Alan Nelson-s/Dan Mora-s; 3 covers 4.00

HEY THERE, IT'S YOGI BEAR (See Movie Comics)

HI-ADVENTURE HEROES (TV)
Gold Key: May, 1969 - No. 2, Aug, 1969 (Hanna-Barbera)

1-Three Musketeers, Gulliver, Arabian Knights 5 10 15 30 50 70
2-Three Musketeers, Micro-Venture, Arabian Knights 4 8 12 27 44 60

HI AND LOIS
Dell Publishing Co.: No. 683, Mar, 1956 - No. 955, Nov, 1958

Four Color 683 (#1) 5 10 15 34 60 85
Four Color 774(3/57),955 4 8 12 28 47 65

HI AND LOIS
Charlton Comics: Nov, 1969 - No. 11, July, 1971

1 3 6 9 14 20 25
2-11 2 4 6 9 12 15

HICKORY (See All Humor Comics)
Quality Comics Group: Oct, 1949 - No. 6, Aug, 1950

1-Sahl-c/a in all; Feldstein?-a 26 52 78 154 252 350
2 16 32 48 94 147 200
3-6-Good Girl covers 22 44 66 132 216 300

HIDDEN CREW, THE (See The United States Air Force Presents:...)

HIDE-OUT (See Zane Grey, Four Color No. 346)

HIDING PLACE, THE
Spire Christian Comics (Fleming H. Revell Co.): 1973 (39¢/49¢)

nn 2 4 6 13 18 22

HIGH ADVENTURE
Red Top(Decker) Comics (Farrell): Oct, 1957

1-Krigstein-r from Explorer Joe (re-issue on-c) 5 10 15 23 28 32

HIGH ADVENTURE (TV)
Dell Publishing Co.: No. 949, Nov, 1958 - No. 1001, Aug-Oct, 1959 (Lowell Thomas)

Four Color 949 (#1)-Photo-c 5 10 15 34 60 85
Four Color 1001-Lowell Thomas'...(#2) 5 10 15 33 57 80

HIGH CHAPPARAL (TV)
Gold Key: Aug, 1968 (Photo-c)

1 (10226-808)-Tufts-a 6 12 18 38 69 100

HIGHLANDER
Dynamite Entertainment: No. 0, 2006 - No. 12, 2007 (25¢/$2.99)

0-(25¢-c) Takes place after the first movie; photo-c and Dell'Otto painted-c 3.00
1-12: 1-($2.99) Three covers; Moder-a/Jerwa & Oeming-s. 2-Three covers 3.00
... Origins: The Kurgan 1,2 (2009 - No. 2, 2009, $4.99) Three covers; Rafael-a 5.00
...: Way of the Sword (2007 - No. 4, 2008, $3.50) Two interlocking covers for each 3.50

HIGHLANDER: THE AMERICAN DREAM
IDW Publishing: Feb, 2017 - Present ($3.99)

1-Brian Ruckley-s/Andrea Mutti-a; multiple covers; MacLeod in 1985 New York 4.00

HIGH ROADS
DC Comics (Cliffhanger): June, 2002 - No. 6, Nov, 2002 ($2.95, limited series)

1-6-Leinil Yu-c/a; Lobdell-s 3.00
TPB (2003, $14.95) r/#1-6; sketch pages 15.00

HIGH SCHOOL CONFIDENTIAL DIARY (Confidential Diary #12 on)
Charlton Comics: June, 1960 - No. 11, Mar, 1962

1 4 8 12 27 44 60
2-11 3 6 9 17 26 35

HIGHWAYMEN
DC Comics (WildStorm): Aug, 2007 - No. 5, Dec, 2007 ($2.99)

1-5-Bernardin & Freeman-s/Garbett-a 3.00
TPB (2008, $17.99) r/#1-5 18.00

HIGH WAYS, THE
IDW Publishing: Dec, 2012 - No. 4, Apr, 2013 ($3.99, limited series)

1-4-John Byrne-s/a/c 4.00

HI HI PUFFY AMIYUMI (Based on Cartoon Network animated series)

Hi-Jinx #5 © ACG

Hillbilly #1 © Eric Powell

Hit Comics #26 © QUA

GD VG FN VF VF/NM NM-
2.0 4.0 6.0 8.0 9.0 9.2

DC Comics: Apr, 2006 - No. 3, June, 2006 ($2.25, limited series)
1-3-Phil Moy-a 3.00

HI-HO COMICS
Four Star Publications: nd (2/46?) - No. 3, 1946
1-Funny Animal; L. B. Cole-c 39 78 117 240 395 550
2,3: 2-L. B. Cole-c 22 44 66 132 216 300

HI-JINX (Teen-age Animal Funnies)
La Salle Publ. Co./B&I Publ. Co. (American Comics Group)/Creston: 1945; July-Aug, 1947 - No. 7, July-Aug, 1948
nn-(© 1945, 25 cents, 132 Pgs.)(La Salle) 30 60 90 177 289 400
1-Teen-age, funny animal 20 40 60 117 189 260
2,3 14 28 42 80 115 150
4-7-Milt Gross. 4-X-Mas-c 20 40 60 114 182 250

HI-LITE COMICS
E. R. Ross Publishing Co.: Fall, 1945
1-Miss Shady 21 42 63 126 206 285

HILLBILLY
Albatross Funnybooks: 2016 - Present ($3.99)
1-5-Eric Powell-s/a/c. 2-The Buzzard app. 5-Back-up with Mannion-a 4.00

HILLBILLY COMICS
Charlton Comics: Aug, 1955 - No. 4, July, 1956 (Satire)
1-By Art Gates 12 24 36 69 97 125
2-4 9 18 27 47 61 75

HILLY ROSE'S SPACE ADVENTURES
Astro Comics: May, 1995 - No. 9 ($2.95, B&W)
1 1 2 3 5 7 9
2-9 5.00
Trade Paperback (1996, $12.95)-r/#1-5 13.00

HINTERKIND
DC Comics (Vertigo): Dec, 2013 - No. 18, Jul, 2015 ($2.99)
1-18: 1-Ian Edginton-s/Francesco Trifogli-a/Greg Tocchini-c 3.00

HIP FLASK (Also see Elephantmen)
Active Images/Image Comics
...: Ouroborous (12/12, $4.99) Starkings-s/Ladronn-a 5.00
... Unnatural Selection (9/02, $2.99) Casey & Starkings-s/Ladronn-a; var.-c by Madureira, Campbell, Churchill 3.00

HIP-IT-TY HOP (See March of Comics No. 15)

HIRE, THE (BMWfilms.com's...)
Dark Horse Comics: July, 2004 - No. 6 ($2.99)
1-4: 1-Matt Wagner-s/Wagner & Velasco-a. 2-Bruce Campbell-s/Plunkett-a. 3-Waid-s 3.00
TPB (4/06, $17.95) r/#1-4 18.00

HI-SCHOOL ROMANCE (...Romances No. 41 on)
Harvey Publ./True Love(Home Comics): Oct, 1949 - No. 5, June, 1950; No. 6, Dec, 1950 - No. 73, Mar, 1958; No. 74, Sept, 1958 - No. 75, Nov, 1958
1-Photo-c 15 30 45 90 140 190
2-Photo-c 10 20 30 56 76 95
3-9: 3-5-Photo-c 9 18 27 47 61 75
10-Rape story 10 20 30 56 76 95
11-20 8 16 24 40 50 60
21-31 6 12 18 31 38 45
32- "Unholy passion" story 9 18 27 50 65 80
33-36: 36-Last pre-code (2/55) 6 12 18 29 36 42
37-53,59-72,74,75 5 10 15 24 30 35
54-58,73-Kirby-c 6 12 18 31 38 45
NOTE: *Powell a-1-3, 5, 8, 12-16, 18, 21-23, 25-27, 30-34, 36, 37, 39, 45-48, 50-52, 57, 58, 60, 64, 65, 67, 69.*

HI-SCHOOL ROMANCE DATE BOOK
Harvey Publications: Nov, 1962 - No. 3, Mar, 1963 (25¢ Giants)
1-Powell, Baker-a 5 10 15 35 63 90
2,3 3 6 9 21 33 45

HIS NAME IS SAVAGE (Magazine format)
Adventure House Press: June, 1968 (35¢, 52 pgs.)
1-Gil Kane-a 5 10 15 31 53 75

HI-SPOT COMICS (Red Ryder No. 1 & No. 3 on)
Hawley Publications: No. 2, Nov, 1940
2-David Innes of Pellucidar; art by J. C. Burroughs; written by Edgar Rice Burroughs
161 322 483 1030 1765 2500

HISTORY OF THE DC UNIVERSE (Also see Crisis on Infinite Earths)
DC Comics: Sept, 1986 - No. 2, Nov, 1986 ($2.95, limited series)
1,2: 1-Perez-c/a 5.00
Limited Edition hardcover 4 8 12 26 41 55
Softcover (2002, $9.95) new Alex Ross wraparound-c 13.00
Softcover (2009, $12.99) Alex Ross wraparound-c 13.00

HISTORY OF VIOLENCE, A (Inspired the 2005 movie)
DC Comics (Paradox Press) 1997 ($9.95, B&W graphic novel)
nn-Paperback ($9.95) John Wagner-s/Vince Locke-a 18.00

HIT
BOOM! Studios: Sept, 2013 - No. 4, Dec, 2013 ($3.99, limited series)
1-4-Bryce Carlson-s/Vanesa R. Del Ray-a/Ryan Sook-c 4.00
...: 1957 (3/15 - No. 4, 7/15, $3.99) 1-4-Bryce Carlson-s/Vanesa R. Del Ray-a/c 4.00

HITCHHIKERS GUIDE TO THE GALAXY (See Life, the Universe and Everything & Restaurant at the End of the Universe)
DC Comics: 1993 - No. 3, 1993 ($4.95, limited series)
1-3: Adaptation of Douglas Adams book 5.00
TPB (1997, $14.95) r/#1-3 15.00

HIT COMICS
Quality Comics Group: July, 1940 - No. 65, July, 1950
1-Origin/1st app. Neon, the Unknown & Hercules; intro. The Red Bee; Bob & Swab, Blaze Barton, the Strange Twins, X-5 Super Agent, Casey Jones & Jack & Jill (ends #7) begin
811 1622 2433 5920 10,460 15,000
2-The Old Witch begins, ends #14 (scarce) 343 686 1029 2400 4200 6000
3-Casey Jones ends; transvestism story "Jack & Jill"
343 686 1029 2400 4200 6000
4-Super Agent (ends #17), & Betty Bates (ends #65) begin; X-5 ends
300 600 900 1950 3375 4800
5-Classic Lou Fine cover 838 1676 2514 6117 10,809 15,500
6,8-10: 10-Old Witch by Crandall (4 pgs.); 1st work in comics (4/41)
258 516 774 1651 2826 4000
7-Skull bondage-c 300 600 900 2010 3505 5000
11-Classic cover 300 600 900 2070 3635 5200
12-16: 13-Blaze Barton ends 174 348 522 1114 1907 2700
17-Last Neon; Crandall Hercules in all; last Lou Fine-c; skeleton-c
226 452 678 1446 2473 3500
18-Origin & 1st app. Stormy Foster, the Great Defender (12/41); The Ghost of Flanders begins; Crandall-c 181 362 543 1158 1979 2800
19,20 129 258 387 826 1413 2000
21-24: 21-Last Hercules. 24-Last Red Bee & Strange Twins
123 246 369 787 1344 1900
25-Origin & 1st app. Kid Eternity and begins by Moldoff (12/42); 1st app. The Keeper (Kid Eternity's aide) 226 452 678 1446 2473 3500
26-Blackhawk x-over in Kid Eternity 110 220 330 704 1202 1700
27-29 52 104 156 328 552 775
30,31- "Bill the Magnificent" by Kurtzman, 11 pgs. in each
47 94 141 296 498 700
32-40: 32-Plastic Man x-over. 34-Last Stormy Foster
31 62 93 182 296 410
41-50 22 44 66 128 209 290
51-60-Last Kid Eternity 21 42 63 122 199 275
61-63-Crandall-c/a; 61-Jeb Rivers begins 21 42 63 126 206 285
64,65-Crandall-a 21 42 63 122 199 275
NOTE: *Crandall a-11-17(Hercules), 23, 24(Stormy Foster); c-18-20, 23, 24. Fine c-1-14, 16, 17(most). Ward c-33. Bondage c-7, 64. Hercules c-3, 10-17. Jeb Rivers c-61-65. Kid Eternity c-25-60 (w/Keeper-28-34, 36, 39-43, 45-55). Neon the Unknown c-2, 4, 8, 9. Red Bee c-1, 5-7. Stormy Foster c-18-24.*

HIT-GIRL (Also see Kick-Ass)
Marvel Comics (Icon): Aug, 2012 - No. 5, Apr, 2013 ($2.99, limited series)
1-Takes place between Kick-Ass & Kick Ass 2 series; Millar-s/Romita Jr.-a/c 5.00
2-5 3.00

HITLER'S ASTROLOGER (See Marvel Graphic Novel #35)

HITMAN (Also see Bloodbath #2, Batman Chronicles #4, Demon #43-45 & Demon Annual #2)
DC Comics: May, 1996 - No. 60, Apr, 2001 ($2.25/$2.50)
1-Garth Ennis-s & John McCrea-c/a begin; Batman app.
2 4 6 8 10 12
2-Joker-c;Two Face, Mad Hatter, Batman app. 1 2 3 5 6 8
3-5: 3-Batman-c/app.; Joker app. 4-1st app. Nightfist 5.00
6-20: 8-Final Night x-over. 10-GL cameo. 11-20: 11,12-GL-c/app. 15-20-"Ace of Killers". 16-18-Catwoman app. 17-19-Demon-app. 4.00

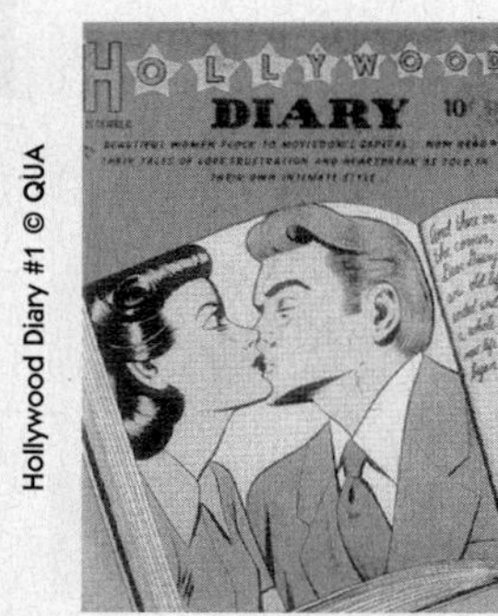

Hollywood Diary #1 © QUA

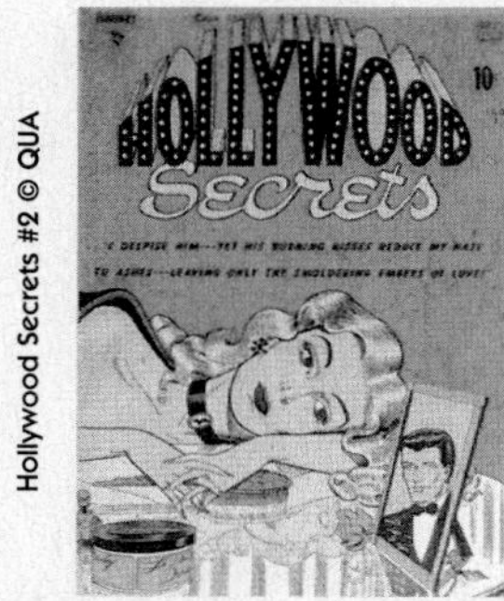

Hollywood Secrets #2 © QUA

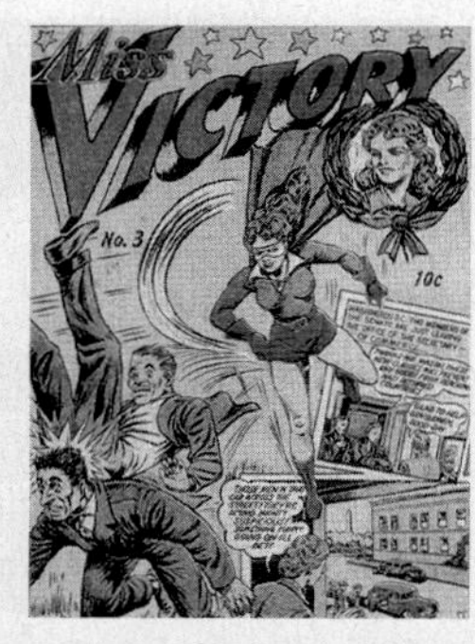

Holyoke One-Shot #3 © HOKE

	GD 2.0	VG 4.0	FN 6.0	VF 8.0	VF/NM 9.0	NM- 9.2

21-59: 34-Superman-c/app. 3.00
60-($3.95) Final issue; includes pin-ups by various 4.00
#1,000,000 (11/98) Hitman goes to the 853rd Century 3.00
Annual 1 (1997, $3.95) Pulp Heroes 5.00
.../Lobo: That Stupid Bastich (7/00, $3.95) Ennis-s/Mahnke-a 4.00
TPB-(1997, $9.95) r/#1-3, Demon Ann. #2, Batman Chronicles #4 10.00
Ace of Killers TPB ('00/'11, $17.95/$17.99) r/#15-22 18.00
Local Heroes TPB ('99, $17.95) r/#9-14 & Annual #1 18.00
10,000 Bullets TPB ('98, $9.95) r/#4-8 10.00
Ten Thousand Bullets TPB ('10, $17.99) r/#4-8 & Annual #1; intro. by Kevin Smith 18.00
Who Dares Wins TPB ('01, $12.95) r/#23-28 13.00

HIT-MONKEY (See Deadpool)
Marvel Comics: Apr, 2010; Sept, 2010 - No. 3, Nov, 2010 ($3.99/$2.99)

1-(4/10, $3.99) Printing of story from Marvel Digital Comics; Frank Cho-c; origin revealed 4.00
1-3-Daniel Way-s/Talajic-a/Johnson-c; Bullseye app. 3.00

HI-YO SILVER (See Lone Ranger's Famous Horse... and The Lone Ranger; and March of Comics No. 215 in the Promotional Comics section)

HOBBIT, THE
Eclipse Comics: 1989 - No. 3, 1990 ($4.95, squarebound, 52 pgs.)

Book 1-3: Adapts novel; Wenzel-a 2 4 6 8 10 12
Book 1-Second printing 5.00
Graphic Novel (1990, Ballantine)-r/#1-3 25.00

HOCUS POCUS (See Funny Book #9)

HOGAN'S HEROES (TV) (Also see Wild!)
Dell Publishing Co.: June, 1966 - No. 8, Sept, 1967; No. 9, Oct, 1969

1: Photo-c on #1-7 7 14 21 48 89 130
2,3-Ditko-a(p) 5 10 15 33 57 80
4-9: 9-Reprints #1 4 8 12 28 47 65

HOKUM & HEX (See Razorline)
Marvel Comics (Razorline): Sept, 1993 - No. 9, May, 1994 ($1.75/$1.95)

1-($2.50)-Foil embossed-c; by Clive Barker 4.00
2-9: 5-Hyperkind x-over 3.00

HOLIDAY COMICS
Fawcett Publications: 1942 (25¢, 196 pgs.)

1-Contains three Fawcett comics plus two page portrait of Captain Marvel; Capt. Marvel, Jungle Girl #1, & Whiz. Not rebound, remaindered comics; printed at the same time as originals (scarce in high grade) 300 600 900 2100 4200 6300

HOLIDAY COMICS (Becomes Fun Comics #9-12)
Star Publications: Jan, 1951 - No. 8, Oct, 1952

1-Funny animal contents (Frisky Fables) in all; L. B. Cole X-Mas-c 34 68 102 199 325 450
2-Classic L. B. Cole-c 32 64 96 188 307 425
3-8: 5,8-X-Mas-c; all L.B. Cole-c 20 40 60 114 182 250
Accepted Reprint 4 (nd)-L.B. Cole-c 10 20 30 58 79 100

HOLIDAY DIGEST
Harvey Comics: 1988 ($1.25, digest-size)

1 1 2 3 5 7 9

HOLIDAY PARADE (Walt Disney's...)
W. D. Publications (Disney): Winter, 1990-91(no year given) - No. 2, Winter, 1990-91 ($2.95, 68 pgs.)

1-Reprints 1947 Firestone by Barks plus new-a 5.00
2-Barks-r plus other stories 4.00

HOLI-DAY SURPRISE (Formerly Summer Fun)
Charlton Comics: V2#55, Mar, 1967 (25¢ Giant)

V2#55 4 8 12 23 37 50

HOLLYWOOD COMICS
New Age Publishers: Winter, 1944 (52 pgs.)

1-Funny animal 20 40 60 114 182 250

HOLLYWOOD CONFESSIONS
St. John Publishing Co.: Oct, 1949 - No. 2, Dec, 1949

1-Kubert-c/a (entire book) 41 82 123 256 428 600
2-Kubert-c/a (entire book) (Scarce) 42 84 126 265 445 625

HOLLYWOOD DIARY
Quality Comics Group: Dec, 1949 - No. 5, July-Aug, 1950

1-No photo-c 27 54 81 158 259 360
2-Photo-c 17 34 51 98 154 210
3-5-Photo-c. 3-Betty Carlin photo-c. 5-June Allyson/Peter Lawford photo-c 15 30 45 88 137 185

HOLLYWOOD FILM STORIES
Feature Publications/Prize: April, 1950 - No. 4, Oct, 1950 (All photo-c; "Fumetti" type movie comic)

1-June Allyson photo-c 21 42 63 124 202 280
2-4: 2-Lizabeth Scott photo-c. 3-Barbara Stanwick photo-c. 4-Betty Hutton photo-c 15 30 45 88 137 185

HOLLYWOOD FUNNY FOLKS (Formerly Funny Folks; Becomes Nutsy Squirrel #61 on)
National Periodical Publ.: No. 27, Aug-Sept, 1950 - No. 60, July-Aug, 1954

27-Nutsy Squirrel continues 14 28 42 76 108 140
28-40 10 20 30 54 72 90
41-60 9 18 27 47 61 75
NOTE: ***Rube Grossman*** *a-most issues.* ***Sheldon Mayer*** *a-27-35, 37-40, 43-46, 48-51, 53, 56, 57, 60.*

HOLLYWOOD LOVE DOCTOR (See Doctor Anthony King...)

HOLLYWOOD PICTORIAL (...Romances on cover)
St. John Publishing Co.: No. 3, Jan, 1950

3-Matt Baker-a; photo-c 37 74 111 222 361 500
(Becomes a movie magazine - Hollywood Pictorial Western with No. 4.)

HOLLYWOOD ROMANCES (Formerly Brides In Love; becomes For Lovers Only #60 on)
Charlton Comics: V2#46, 11/66; #47, 10/67; #48, 11/68;V3#49,11/69-V3#59, 6/71

V2#46-Rolling Stones-c/story 8 16 24 56 108 160
V2#47-V3#59: 56- "Born to Heart Break" begins 3 6 9 14 19 24

HOLLYWOOD SECRETS
Quality Comics Group: Nov, 1949 - No. 6, Sept, 1950

1-Ward-c/a (9 pgs.) 41 82 123 256 428 600
2-Crandall-a, Ward-c/a (9 pgs.) 30 60 90 177 289 400
3-6: All photo-c. 5-Lex Barker (Tarzan)-c 16 32 48 94 147 200
...of Romance, I.W. Reprint #9; r/#2 above w/Kinstler-c 2 4 6 11 16 20

HOLLYWOOD SUPERSTARS
Marvel Comics (Epic Comics): Nov, 1990 - No. 5, Apr, 1991 ($2.25)

1-($2.95, 52 pgs.)-Spiegle-c/a in all; Aragonés-a, inside front-c plus 2-4 pgs. 4.00
2-5 ($2.25) 3.00

HOLO-MAN (See Power Record Comics)

HOLYOKE ONE-SHOT
Holyoke Publishing Co. (Tem Publ.): 1944 - No. 10, 1945 (All reprints)

1,2: 1-Grit Grady (on cover only), Miss Victory, Alias X (origin)-All reprints from Captain Fearless. 2-Rusty Dugan (Corporal); Capt. Fearless (origin), Mr. Miracle (origin) app. 33 66 99 194 317 440
3-Miss Victory; r/Crash #4; Cat Man (origin), Solar Legion by Kirby app.; Miss Victory on cover only (1945) 48 96 144 302 514 725
4,6,8: 4-Mr. Miracle; The Blue Streak app. 6-Capt. Fearless, Alias X, Capt. Stone (splash used as-c to #10); Diamond Jim & Rusty Dugan (splash from cover of #2). 8-Blue Streak, Strong Man (story matches cover to #7)-Crash reprints 28 56 84 165 270 375
5,7: 5-U.S. Border Patrol Comics (Sgt. Dick Carter of the...), Miss Victory (story matches cover to #3), Citizen Smith, & Mr. Miracle app. 7-Secret Agent Z-2, Strong Man, Blue Streak (story matches cover to #8); Reprints from Crash #2 29 58 87 172 281 390
9-Citizen Smith, The Blue Streak, Solar Legion by Kirby & Strongman, the Perfect Human app.; reprints from Crash #4 & 5; Citizen Smith on cover only-from story in #5 (1944-before #3) 32 64 96 188 307 425
10-Captain Stone; r/Crash; Solar Legion by S&K 32 64 96 188 307 425

HOLY TERROR
Legendary Comics: Sept, 2011 ($29.95, HC graphic novel, 12-1/4" wide x 9-1/4" tall)

HC-Frank Miller-s/a/c; B&W art with spot color; The Fixer vs. Al-Qaeda in Empire City 30.00

HOME (Based on the DreamWorks movie)
Titan Comics: Aug, 2015 - No. 4, Nov, 2015 ($3.99)

1-4: 1-Davison-s/Hebb-a 4.00

HOMECOMING
Aspen MLT: Aug, 2012 - No. 4, Sept, 2013 ($3.99)

1-4: 1-Wohl-s/Laiso-a; covers by Michael Turner and Mike DeBalfo 4.00

HOMER COBB (See Adventures of...)

HOMER HOOPER
Atlas Comics: July, 1953 - No. 4, Dec, 1953

Hong on the Range #1 © Flypaper

Hook #1 © MAR

Hopalong Cassidy #3 © FAW

	GD 2.0	VG 4.0	FN 6.0	VF 8.0	VF/NM 9.0	NM- 9.2
1-Teenage humor	14	28	42	82	121	160
2-4	11	22	33	60	83	105

HOMER, THE HAPPY GHOST (See Adventures of...)
Atlas(ACI/PPI/WPI)/Marvel: 3/55 - No. 22, 11/58; V2#1, 11/69 - V2#4, 5/70

	GD 2.0	VG 4.0	FN 6.0	VF 8.0	VF/NM 9.0	NM- 9.2
V1#1-Dan DeCarlo-c/a begins, ends #22	36	72	108	211	343	475
2-1st code approved issue	19	38	57	111	176	240
3-10	18	36	54	105	165	225
11-20,22	16	32	48	94	147	200
21-Sci-fi cover	34	68	102	199	325	450
V2#1 (11/69)	11	22	33	76	163	250
2-4	7	14	21	46	86	125

HOME RUN (Also see A-1 Comics)
Magazine Enterprises: No. 89, 1953 (one-shot)

	GD 2.0	VG 4.0	FN 6.0	VF 8.0	VF/NM 9.0	NM- 9.2
A-1 89 (#3)-Powell-a; Stan Musial photo-c	17	34	51	98	154	210

HOMICIDE (Also see Dark Horse Presents)
Dark Horse Comics: Apr, 1990 ($1.95, B&W, one-shot)

	GD 2.0	VG 4.0	FN 6.0	VF 8.0	VF/NM 9.0	NM- 9.2
1-Detective story						3.00

HOMIES
Dynamite Entertainment: 2016 - No. 4, 2017 ($3.99)

	GD 2.0	VG 4.0	FN 6.0	VF 8.0	VF/NM 9.0	NM- 9.2
1-4-Gonzales & Serrano-s/Huerta-a						4.00

HONEYMOON (Formerly Gay Comics)
A Lover's Magazine(USA) (Marvel): No. 41, Jan, 1950

	GD 2.0	VG 4.0	FN 6.0	VF 8.0	VF/NM 9.0	NM- 9.2
41-Photo-c; article by Betty Grable	15	30	45	85	130	175

HONEYMOONERS, THE (TV)
Lodestone: Oct, 1986 ($1.50)

	GD 2.0	VG 4.0	FN 6.0	VF 8.0	VF/NM 9.0	NM- 9.2
1-Photo-c						6.00

HONEYMOONERS, THE (TV)
Triad Publications: Sept, 1987 - No. 13? ($2.00)

	GD 2.0	VG 4.0	FN 6.0	VF 8.0	VF/NM 9.0	NM- 9.2
1-13						5.00

HONEYMOON ROMANCE
Artful Publications (Canadian): Apr, 1950 - No. 2, July, 1950 (25¢, digest size)

	GD 2.0	VG 4.0	FN 6.0	VF 8.0	VF/NM 9.0	NM- 9.2
1,2-(Rare)	170	340	510	850	1275	1700

HONEY WEST (TV)
Gold Key: Sept, 1966 (Photo-c)

	GD 2.0	VG 4.0	FN 6.0	VF 8.0	VF/NM 9.0	NM- 9.2
1 (10186-609)	9	18	27	57	111	165

HONEY WEST (TV)
Moonstone: 2010 - No. 4 ($5.99/$3.99)

	GD 2.0	VG 4.0	FN 6.0	VF 8.0	VF/NM 9.0	NM- 9.2
1-($5.99) Trina Robbins-s/Cynthia Martin-a; two art covers & two photo covers						6.00
2-4-($3.99)						4.00

HONG KONG PHOOEY (TV)
Charlton Comics: June, 1975 - No. 9, Nov, 1976 (Hanna-Barbera)

	GD 2.0	VG 4.0	FN 6.0	VF 8.0	VF/NM 9.0	NM- 9.2
1	5	10	15	31	53	75
2	3	6	9	18	28	38
3-9	3	6	9	15	22	28

HONG ON THE RANGE
Image/Flypaper Press: Dec, 1997 - No. 3, Feb, 1998 ($2.50, lim. series)

	GD 2.0	VG 4.0	FN 6.0	VF 8.0	VF/NM 9.0	NM- 9.2
1-3: Wu-s/Lafferty-a						3.00

HOOD, THE
Marvel Comics (MAX): Jul, 2002 - No. 6, Dec, 2002 ($2.99, limited series)

	GD 2.0	VG 4.0	FN 6.0	VF 8.0	VF/NM 9.0	NM- 9.2
1-6-Vaughan-s/Hotz-c/a						3.00
Vol. 1 Blood From Stones HC (2007, $19.99, dustjacket) r/#1-6; production sketch art						20.00
Vol. 1 Blood From Stones TPB (2003, $14.99) r/#1-6						15.00

HOODED HORSEMAN, THE (Formerly Blazing West)
American Comics Group (Michel Publ.): No. 21, 1-2/52 - No. 27, 1-2/54; No. 18, 12-1/54-55 - No. 22, 8-9/55

	GD 2.0	VG 4.0	FN 6.0	VF 8.0	VF/NM 9.0	NM- 9.2
21(1-2/52)-Hooded Horseman, Injun Jones cont.	15	30	45	83	124	165
22	10	20	30	56	76	95
23,24,27(1-2/54)	9	18	27	50	65	80
25 (9-10/53)-Cowboy Sahib on cover only; Hooded Horseman i.d. revealed	9	18	27	52	69	85
26-Origin/1st app. Cowboy Sahib by L. Starr	11	22	33	62	86	110
18(12-1/54-55)(Formerly Out of the Night)	10	20	30	54	72	90
19,21,22: 19-Last precode (1-2/55)	8	16	24	44	57	70
20-Origin Johnny Injun	9	18	27	50	65	80

NOTE: *Whitney c/a-21('52), 20-22.*

HOODED MENACE, THE (Also see Daring Adventures)
Realistic/Avon Periodicals: 1951 (one-shot)

	GD 2.0	VG 4.0	FN 6.0	VF 8.0	VF/NM 9.0	NM- 9.2
nn-Based on a band of hooded outlaws in the Pacific Northwest, 1900-1906; reprinted in Daring Advs. #15	58	116	174	371	636	900

HOODS UP (See the Promotional Comics section)

HOOK (Movie)
Marvel Comics: Early Feb, 1992 - No. 4, Late Mar, 1992 ($1.00, limited series)

	GD 2.0	VG 4.0	FN 6.0	VF 8.0	VF/NM 9.0	NM- 9.2
1-4: Adapts movie; Vess-c; 1-Morrow-a(p)						3.00
nn (1991, $5.95, 84 pgs.)-Contains #1-4; Vess-c						6.00
1 (1991, $2.95, magazine, 84 pgs.)-Contains #1-4; Vess-c (same cover as nn issue)						4.00

HOOK JAW
Titan Comics: Jan, 2017 - Present ($3.99)

	GD 2.0	VG 4.0	FN 6.0	VF 8.0	VF/NM 9.0	NM- 9.2
1-3-Inspired by a 1976 British comic strip; Si Spurrier-s/Conor Boyle-a; multiple covers						4.00

HOOT GIBSON'S WESTERN ROUNDUP (See Western Roundup under Fox Giants)

HOOT GIBSON WESTERN (Formerly My Love Story)
Fox Features Syndicate: No. 5, May, 1950 - No. 3, Sept, 1950

	GD 2.0	VG 4.0	FN 6.0	VF 8.0	VF/NM 9.0	NM- 9.2
5,6(#1,2): 5-Photo-c. 6-Photo/painted-c	21	42	63	123	197	270
3-Wood-a; painted-c	22	44	66	131	211	290

HOPALONG CASSIDY (Also see Bill Boyd Western, Master Comics, Real Western Hero, Six Gun Heroes & Western Hero; Bill Boyd starred as Hopalong Cassidy in movies, radio & TV)
Fawcett Publications: Feb, 1943; No. 2, Summer, 1946 - No. 85, Nov, 1953

	GD 2.0	VG 4.0	FN 6.0	VF 8.0	VF/NM 9.0	NM- 9.2
1 (1943, 68 pgs.)-H. Cassidy & his horse Topper begin (on sale 1/8/43)-Captain Marvel app. on-c	290	580	870	1856	3178	4500
2-(Sum, '46)	41	82	123	256	428	600
3,4: 3-(Fall, '46, 52 pgs. begin)	20	40	60	114	182	250
5- "Mad Barber" story mentioned in **SOTI**, pgs. 308,309; photo-c	19	38	57	111	176	240
6-10: 8-Photo-c	16	32	48	94	147	200
11-19: 11,13-19-Photo-c	14	28	42	80	115	150
20-29 (52 pgs.)-Painted/photo-c	12	24	36	69	97	125
30,31,33,34,37-39,41 (52 pgs.)-Painted-c	11	22	33	60	83	105
32,40 (36pgs.)-Painted-c	10	20	30	54	72	90
35,42,43,45-47,49-51,53,54,56 (52 pgs.)-Photo-c	10	20	30	56	76	95
36,44,48 (36 pgs.)-Photo-c	9	18	27	52	69	85
52,55,57-70 (36 pgs.)-Photo-c	9	18	27	47	61	75
71-84-Photo-c	8	16	24	42	54	65
85-Last Fawcett issue; photo-c	9	18	27	52	69	85

NOTE: *Line-drawn c-1-4, 6, 7, 9, 10, 12.*

	GD 2.0	VG 4.0	FN 6.0	VF 8.0	VF/NM 9.0	NM- 9.2
... & The 5 Men of Evil (AC Comics, 1991, $12.95) r/newspaper strips and Fawcett story "Signature of Death"						13.00

HOPALONG CASSIDY
National Periodical Publications: No. 86, Feb, 1954 - No. 135, May-June, 1959 (All-36 pgs.)

	GD 2.0	VG 4.0	FN 6.0	VF 8.0	VF/NM 9.0	NM- 9.2
86-Gene Colan-a begins, ends #117; photo covers continue	36	72	108	216	351	485
87	20	40	60	118	189	260
88-91: 91-1 pg. Superboy-sty (7/54)	15	30	45	83	124	165
92-99 (98 has #93 on-c; last precode issue, 2/55). 95-Reversed photo-c to #52. 98-Reversed photo-c to #61. 99-Reversed photo-c to #60	14	28	42	76	108	140
100-Same cover as #50	15	30	45	83	124	165
101-108: 105-Same photo-c as #54. 107-Same photo-c as #51. 108-Last photo-c	6	12	18	38	69	100
109-130: 118-Gil Kane-a begins. 123-Kubert-a (2 pgs.). 124-Grey tone-c	5	10	15	35	63	90
131-135	6	12	18	37	66	95

HOPELESS SAVAGES (Also see Too Much Hopeless Savages)
Oni Press: Aug, 2001 - No. 4, Nov, 2001 ($2.95, B&W, limited series)

	GD 2.0	VG 4.0	FN 6.0	VF 8.0	VF/NM 9.0	NM- 9.2
1-4-Van Meter-s/Norrie-a/Clugston-Major-a/Watson-c						3.00
Free Comic Book Day giveaway (5/02) r/#1 with "Free Comic Book Day" banner on-c						3.00
TPB (2002, $13.95, 8" x 5.75") r/#1-4; plus color stories; Watson-c						14.00

HOPELESS SAVAGES: GROUND ZERO
Oni Press: June, 2002 - No. 4, Oct, 2002 ($2.95, B&W, limited series)

	GD 2.0	VG 4.0	FN 6.0	VF 8.0	VF/NM 9.0	NM- 9.2
1-4-Van Meter-s/O'Malley-a/Dodson-c. 1-Watson-a						3.00
TPB (2003, $11.95, 8" x 5.75") r/#1-4; Dodson-c						12.00

HOPE SHIP
Dell Publishing Co.: June-Aug, 1963

	GD 2.0	VG 4.0	FN 6.0	VF 8.0	VF/NM 9.0	NM- 9.2
1	3	6	9	15	22	28

HOPPY THE MARVEL BUNNY (See Fawcett's Funny Animals)
Fawcett Publications: Dec, 1945 - No. 15, Sept, 1947

Horrific #12 © Comic Media

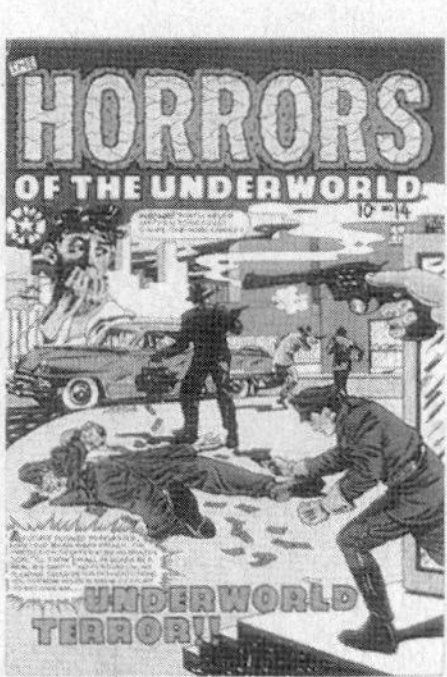

The Horrors #14 © STAR

Hot Rods and Racing Cars #1 © CC

	GD 2.0	VG 4.0	FN 6.0	VF 8.0	VF/NM 9.0	NM- 9.2
1	28	56	84	165	270	375
2	14	28	42	82	121	160
3-15: 7-Xmas-c	12	24	36	67	94	120

HORACE & DOTTY DRIPPLE (Dotty Dripple No. 1-24)
Harvey Publications: No. 25, Aug, 1952 - No. 43, Oct, 1955

	GD 2.0	VG 4.0	FN 6.0	VF 8.0	VF/NM 9.0	NM- 9.2
25-43	4	9	13	18	22	26

HORIZONTAL LIEUTENANT, THE (See Movie Classics)

HOROBI
Viz Premiere Comics: 1990 - No. 8, 1990 ($3.75, B&W, mature readers, 84 pgs.) V2#1, 1990 - No. 7, 1991 ($4.25, B&W, 68 pgs.)

	GD 2.0	VG 4.0	FN 6.0	VF 8.0	VF/NM 9.0	NM- 9.2
1-8: Japanese manga, Part Two, #1-7						5.00

HORRIFIC (Terrific No. 14 on)
Artful/Comic Media/Harwell/Mystery: Sept, 1952 - No. 13, Sept, 1954

	GD 2.0	VG 4.0	FN 6.0	VF 8.0	VF/NM 9.0	NM- 9.2
1	90	180	270	576	988	1400
2	53	106	159	334	567	800
3-Bullet in head-c	174	348	522	1114	1907	2700
4,5,7,9,10: 4-Shrunken head-c. 7-Guillotine-c	48	96	144	302	514	725
6-Jack The Ripper story	50	100	150	315	533	750
8-Origin & 1st app. The Teller (E.C. parody)	53	106	159	334	567	800
11-13: 11-Swipe/Witches Tales #6,27; Devil-c	41	82	123	256	428	600

NOTE: ***Don Heck** a-8; c-3-13. **Hollingsworth** a-4. **Morisi** a-8. **Palais** a-5, 7-12.*

HORRORCIDE
IDW Publishing: Sept, 2004 ($6.99)

	GD 2.0	VG 4.0	FN 6.0	VF 8.0	VF/NM 9.0	NM- 9.2
1-Steve Niles short stories; art by Templesmith, Medors and Chee						7.00

HORROR FROM THE TOMB (Mysterious Stories No. 2 on)
Premier Magazine Co.: Sept, 1954

	GD 2.0	VG 4.0	FN 6.0	VF 8.0	VF/NM 9.0	NM- 9.2
1-Woodbridge/Torres, Check-a; The Keeper of the Graveyard is host	61	122	183	390	670	950

HORRORIST, THE (Also see Hellblazer)
DC Comics (Vertigo): Dec, 1995 - No. 2, Jan, 1996 ($5.95, lim. series, mature)

	GD 2.0	VG 4.0	FN 6.0	VF 8.0	VF/NM 9.0	NM- 9.2
1,2: Jamie Delano scripts, David Lloyd-c/a; John Constantine (Hellblazer) app.						6.00

HORROR OF COLLIER COUNTY
Dark Horse Comics: Oct, 1999 - No. 5, Feb, 2000 ($2.95, B&W, limited series)

	GD 2.0	VG 4.0	FN 6.0	VF 8.0	VF/NM 9.0	NM- 9.2
1-5-Rich Tommaso-s/a						3.00

HORRORS, THE (Formerly Startling Terror Tales #10)
Star Publications: No. 11, Jan, 1953 - No. 15, Apr, 1954

	GD 2.0	VG 4.0	FN 6.0	VF 8.0	VF/NM 9.0	NM- 9.2
11-Horrors of War; Disbrow-a(2)	34	68	102	199	325	450
12-Horrors of War; color illo in **POP**	32	64	96	188	307	425
13-Horrors of Mystery; crime stories	30	60	90	177	289	400
14,15-Horrors of the Underworld; crime stories	32	64	96	188	307	425

NOTE: *All have **L. B. Cole** covers; a-12. **Hollingsworth** a-13. **Palais** a-13r.*

HORROR TALES (Magazine)
Eerie Publications: V1#7, 6/69 - V6#6, 12/74; V7#1, 2/75; V7#2, 5/76 - V8#5, 1977; V9#1-3, 8/78; V10#1(2/79) (V1-V6: 52 pgs.; V7, V8#2: 112 pgs.; V8#4 on: 68 pgs.) (No V5#3, V8#1,3)

	GD 2.0	VG 4.0	FN 6.0	VF 8.0	VF/NM 9.0	NM- 9.2
V1#7	7	14	21	48	89	130
V1#8,9	5	10	15	33	57	80
V2#1-6('70), V3#1-6('71), V4#1-3,5-7('72)	5	10	15	30	50	70
V4#4-LSD story reprint/Weird V3#5	5	10	15	35	63	90
V5#1,2,4,5(6/73),5(10/73),6(12/73),V6#1-6('74),V7#1,2,4('76),V7#3('76)-Giant issue, V8#2,4,5('77)	5	10	15	30	50	70
V9#1-3(11/78, $1.50), V10#1(2/79)	5	10	15	31	53	75

NOTE: *Bondage-c-V6#1, 3, V7#2.*

HORSE FEATHERS COMICS
Lev Gleason Publ.: Nov, 1945 - No. 4, July(Summer on-c), 1948 (52 pgs.) (#2,3 are oversized)

	GD 2.0	VG 4.0	FN 6.0	VF 8.0	VF/NM 9.0	NM- 9.2
1-Wolverton's Scoop Scuttle, 2 pgs.	19	38	57	109	172	235
2	11	22	33	60	83	105
3,4: 3-(5/48)	9	18	27	47	61	75

HORSEMAN
Crusade Comics/Kevlar Studios: Mar, 1996 - No. 3, Nov, 1997 ($2.95)

	GD 2.0	VG 4.0	FN 6.0	VF 8.0	VF/NM 9.0	NM- 9.2
0-1st Kevlar Studios issue, 1-(3/96)-Crusade issue; Shi-c/app., 1-(11/96)-3-(11/97)-Kevlar Studios						3.00

HORSEMASTERS, THE (Disney)(TV, Movie)
Dell Publishing Co.: No. 1260, Dec-Feb, 1961/62

	GD 2.0	VG 4.0	FN 6.0	VF 8.0	VF/NM 9.0	NM- 9.2
Four Color 1260-Annette Funicello photo-c	10	20	30	69	147	225

HORSE SOLDIERS, THE
Dell Publishing Co.: No. 1048, Nov-Jan, 1959/60 (John Wayne movie)

	GD 2.0	VG 4.0	FN 6.0	VF 8.0	VF/NM 9.0	NM- 9.2
Four Color 1048-Painted-c, Sekowsky-a	11	22	33	76	163	250

HORSE WITHOUT A HEAD, THE (See Movie Comics)

HOT DOG
Magazine Enterprises: June-July, 1954 - No. 4, Dec-Jan, 1954-55

	GD 2.0	VG 4.0	FN 6.0	VF 8.0	VF/NM 9.0	NM- 9.2
1(A-1 #107)	9	18	27	47	61	75
2,3(A-1 #115),4(A-1 #136)	6	12	18	31	38	45

HOT DOG (See Jughead's Pal, Hotdog)

HOTEL DEPAREE - SUNDANCE (TV)
Dell Publishing Co.: No. 1126, Aug-Oct, 1960 (one-shot)

	GD 2.0	VG 4.0	FN 6.0	VF 8.0	VF/NM 9.0	NM- 9.2
Four Color 1126-Earl Holliman photo-c	6	12	18	40	73	105

HOT ROD AND SPEEDWAY COMICS
Hillman Periodicals: Feb-Mar, 1952 - No. 5, Apr-May, 1953

	GD 2.0	VG 4.0	FN 6.0	VF 8.0	VF/NM 9.0	NM- 9.2
1	27	54	81	158	259	360
2-Krigstein-a	18	36	54	105	165	225
3-5	13	26	39	72	101	130

HOT ROD COMICS (...Featuring Clint Curtis) (See XMas Comics)
Fawcett Publications: Nov, 1951 (no month given) - V2#7, Feb, 1953

	GD 2.0	VG 4.0	FN 6.0	VF 8.0	VF/NM 9.0	NM- 9.2
nn (V1#1)-Powell-c/a in all	29	58	87	170	278	385
2 (4/52)	15	30	45	90	140	190
3-6, V2#7	13	26	39	72	101	130

HOT ROD KING (Also see Speed Smith the Hot Rod King)
Ziff-Davis Publ. Co.: Fall, 1952

	GD 2.0	VG 4.0	FN 6.0	VF 8.0	VF/NM 9.0	NM- 9.2
1-Giacoia-a; Saunders painted-c	29	58	87	170	278	385

HOT ROD RACERS (Grand Prix No. 16 on)
Charlton Comics: Dec, 1964 - No. 15, July, 1967

	GD 2.0	VG 4.0	FN 6.0	VF 8.0	VF/NM 9.0	NM- 9.2
1	7	14	21	49	92	135
2-5	5	10	15	30	50	70
6-15	4	8	12	23	37	50

HOT RODS AND RACING CARS
Charlton Comics (Motor Mag. No. 1): Nov, 1951 - No. 120, June, 1973

	GD 2.0	VG 4.0	FN 6.0	VF 8.0	VF/NM 9.0	NM- 9.2
1-Speed Davis begins; Indianapolis 500 story	30	60	90	177	289	400
2	15	30	45	88	137	185
3-10	12	24	36	67	94	120
11-20	10	20	30	54	72	90
21-33,36-40	8	16	24	44	57	70
34, 35 (? & 6/58, 68 pgs.)	11	22	33	60	83	105
41-60	7	14	21	37	46	55
61-80	3	6	9	19	30	40
81-100	3	6	9	16	23	30
101-120	3	6	9	14	19	24

HOT SHOT CHARLIE
Hillman Periodicals: 1947 (Lee Elias)

	GD 2.0	VG 4.0	FN 6.0	VF 8.0	VF/NM 9.0	NM- 9.2
1	14	28	42	82	121	160

HOT SHOTS: AVENGERS
Marvel Comics: Oct, 1995 ($2.95, one-shot)

	GD 2.0	VG 4.0	FN 6.0	VF 8.0	VF/NM 9.0	NM- 9.2
nn-pin-ups						3.00

HOTSPUR
Eclipse Comics: Jun, 1987 - No. 3, Sep, 1987 ($1.75, lim. series, Baxter paper)

	GD 2.0	VG 4.0	FN 6.0	VF 8.0	VF/NM 9.0	NM- 9.2
1-3						3.00

HOT STUFF (See Stumbo Tinytown)
Harvey Comics: V2#1, Sept, 1991 - No. 12, June, 1994 ($1.00)

	GD 2.0	VG 4.0	FN 6.0	VF 8.0	VF/NM 9.0	NM- 9.2
V2#1-Stumbo back-up story						5.00
2-12 ($1.50)						4.00
...Big Book 1 (11/92), 2 (6/93) (Both $1.95, 52 pgs.)						5.00

HOT STUFF CREEPY CAVES
Harvey Publications: Nov, 1974 - No. 7, Nov, 1975

	GD 2.0	VG 4.0	FN 6.0	VF 8.0	VF/NM 9.0	NM- 9.2
1	3	6	9	21	33	45
2-7	3	6	9	15	21	26

HOT STUFF DIGEST
Harvey Comics: July, 1992 - No. 5, Nov, 1993 ($1.75, digest-size)

	GD 2.0	VG 4.0	FN 6.0	VF 8.0	VF/NM 9.0	NM- 9.2
V2#1-Hot Stuff, Stumbo, Richie Rich stories						6.00
2-5						4.00

HOT STUFF GIANT SIZE
Harvey Comics: Oct, 1992 - No. 3, Oct, 1993 ($2.25, 68 pgs.)

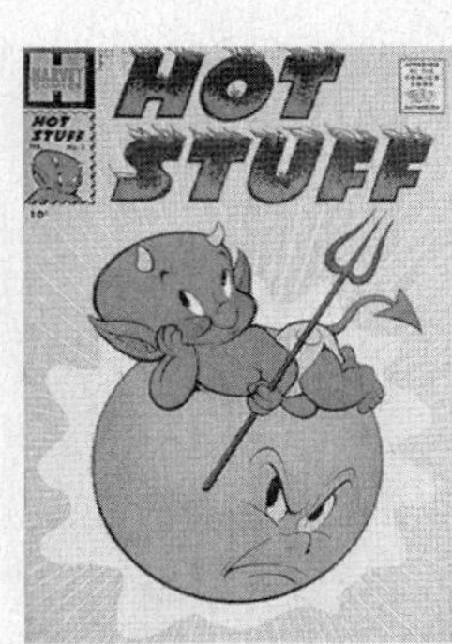

Hot Stuff, The Little Devil #3 © HARV

Hourman #12 © DC

House of Mystery #2 © DC

GD 2.0 VG 4.0 FN 6.0 VF 8.0 VF/NM 9.0 NM- 9.2

V2#1-Hot Stuff & Stumbo stories 5.00
2,3 4.00

HOT STUFF SIZZLERS
Harvey Publications: July, 1960 - No. 59, Mar, 1974; V2#1, Aug, 1992

1- 84 pgs. begin, ends #5; Hot Stuff, Stumbo begin 14 28 42 96 211 325
2-5 7 14 21 49 92 135
6-10: 6-68 pgs. begin, ends #45 5 10 15 35 63 90
11-20 4 8 12 27 44 60
21-45 3 6 9 19 30 40
46-52: 52 pgs. begin 3 6 9 16 23 30
53-59 2 4 6 10 14 18
V2#1-(8/92, $1.25)-Stumbo back-up 5.00

HOT STUFF, THE LITTLE DEVIL (Also see Devil Kids & Harvey Hits)
Harvey Publications (Illustrated Humor): 10/57 - No. 141, 7/77; No. 142, 2/78 - No. 164, 8/82; No. 165, 10/86 - No. 171, 11/87; No. 172, 11/88; No. 173, Sept, 1990 - No. 177, 1/91

1-1st app. Hot Stuff; UFO story 141 282 423 1142 2571 4000
2-Stumbo-like giant 1st app. (12/57) 32 64 96 230 515 800
3-Stumbo the Giant debut (2/58) 19 38 57 133 297 460
4,5 17 34 51 117 259 400
6-10 10 20 30 66 138 210
11-20 8 16 24 51 96 140
21-40 5 10 15 34 60 85
41-60 4 8 12 25 40 55
61-80 3 6 9 19 30 40
81-105 3 6 9 15 22 28
106-112: All 52 pg. Giants 3 6 9 17 26 35
113-125 2 4 6 9 12 15
126-141 1 2 3 5 7 9
142-177: 172-177-($1.00) 6.00
Harvey Comics Classics Vol. 3 TPB (Dark Horse Books, 3/08, $19.95) Reprints Hot Stuff's earliest appearances in this title and Devil Kids, mostly B&W with some color stories; history, early concept drawings; foreword by Mark Arnold 20.00

HOT WHEELS (TV)
National Periodical Publications: Mar-Apr, 1970 - No. 6, Jan-Feb, 1971

1 9 18 27 58 114 170
2,4,5 5 10 15 34 60 85
3-Neal Adams-c 6 12 18 41 76 110
6-Neal Adams-c/a 7 14 21 49 92 135
NOTE: *Toth a-1p, 2-5; c-1p, 5.*

HOURMAN (Justice Society member, see Adventure Comics #48)

HOURMAN (See JLA and DC One Million)
DC Comics: Apr, 1999 - No. 25, Apr, 2001 ($2.50)

1-25: 1-JLA app.; McDaniel-c. 2-Tomorrow Woman-c/app. 6,7-Amazo app. 11-13-Justice Legion A app. 16-Silver Age flashback. 18,19-JSA-c/app. 22-Harris-c/a. 24-Hourman Vs. Rex Tyler 3.00

HOUSE OF FUN
Dark Horse Comics: Dec, 2012 ($3.50)

0-Reprints Evan Dorkin humor strips from Dark Horse Presents #10-12 3.50

HOUSE OF GOLD AND BONES
Dark Horse Comics: Apr, 2013 - No. 4, Jul, 2013 ($3.99, limited series)

1-4-Corey Taylor-s/Richard Clark-a; 2 covers on each 4.00

HOUSE OF HEM
Marvel Comics: 2015 ($7.99, one-shot)

1-Reprints Fred Hembeck's Marvel highlights incl. Fantastic Four Roast; wraparound-c 8.00

HOUSE OF M (Also see miniseries with Fantastic Four, Iron Man and Spider-Man)
Marvel Comics: Aug, 2005 - No. 8, Dec, 2005 ($2.99, limited series)

1-Bendis-s/Coipel-a/Ribic-c; Scarlet Witch changes reality; Quesada variant-c 3.00
2-8-Variant covers for each. 3-Hawkeye returns 3.00
... MGC #1 (6/11, $1.00) r/#1 with "Marvel's Greatest Comics" logo on cover 3.00
Secrets Of The House Of M (2005, $3.99, one-shot) profile pages and background info 4.00
... Sketchbook (6/05) B&W preview sketches by Coipel, Davis, Hairsine, Quesada 3.00
TPB (2006, $24.99) r/#1-8 and The Pulse: House of M Special Edition newspaper 25.00
...: Fantastic Four/ Iron Man TPB (2006, $13.99) r/ both House of M mini-series 14.00
...: World of M Featuring Wolverine TPB (2006, $13.99) r/2005 x-over issues Wolverine #33-35, Black Panther #7, Captain America #10 and The Pulse #10 14.00
HC (2008, $29.99, oversized with d.j.) r/#1-8, The Pulse: House of M Special Edition newspaper and Secrets Of The House Of M one-shot; script pages; cover gallery 30.00

HOUSE OF M (Secret Wars tie-in)
Marvel Comics: Oct, 2015 - No. 4, Dec, 2015 ($3.99, limited series)

GD 2.0 VG 4.0 FN 6.0 VF 8.0 VF/NM 9.0 NM- 9.2

1-4: 1,2-Hopeless & Bunn-s/Failla-a; Magneto & the House of Magnus. 3,4-Anindito-a 4.00

HOUSE OF M: AVENGERS
Marvel Comics: Jan, 2008 - No. 5, Apr, 2008 ($2.99, limited series)

1-5-Gage-s/Perkins-a; Luke Cage, Iron Fist, Hawkeye, Tigra, Misty Knight, Shang-Chi 3.00

HOUSE OF M: MASTERS OF EVIL
Marvel Comics: Oct, 2009 - No. 4, Jan, 2010 ($3.99, limited series)

1-4-Gage-s/Garcia-a/Perkins-c; The Hood app. 4.00

HOUSE OF MYSTERY
DC Comics: Dec/Jan. 1951

nn - Ashcan comic, not distributed to newsstands, only for in-house use. Cover art is Danger Trail #3 with interior being Star Spangled Comics #109. A VG+ copy sold for $2,357.50 in 2002.

HOUSE OF MYSTERY (See Brave and the Bold #93, Elvira's House of Mystery, Limited Collectors' Edition & Super DC Giant)

HOUSE OF MYSTERY, THE
National Periodical Publications/DC Comics: Dec-Jan, 1951-52 - No. 321, Oct, 1983 (No. 194-203: 52 pgs.)

1-DC's first horror comic 284 568 852 1818 3109 4400
2 123 246 369 787 1344 1900
3 74 148 222 470 810 1150
4,5 61 122 183 390 670 950
6-10 55 110 165 352 601 850
11-15 47 94 141 296 498 700
16(7/53)-25 39 78 117 231 378 525
26-35(2/55)-Last pre-code issue; 30-Woodish-a 32 64 96 188 307 425
36-50: 50-Text story of Orson Welles' War of the Worlds broadcast
16 32 48 112 249 385
51-60: 55-1st S.A. issue 14 28 42 96 211 325
61,63,65,66,69,70,72,76,85-Kirby-a 16 32 48 107 236 365
62,64,67,68,71,73-75,77-83,86-99: 92-Grey tone-c 13 26 39 89 195 300
84-Prototype of Negative Man (Doom Patrol) 18 36 54 124 275 425
100 (7/60) 13 26 39 91 201 310
101-116: 109-Toth, Kubert-a. 116-Last 10¢ issue 11 22 33 73 157 240
117-130: 117-Swipes-c to HOS #20. 120-Toth-a 10 20 30 64 132 200
131-142 9 18 27 58 114 170
143-J'onn J'onzz, Manhunter begins (6/64), ends #173; story continues from Detective #326; intro. Idol-Head of Diabolu 17 34 51 117 259 400
144 8 16 24 54 102 150
145-155,157-159: 149-Toth-a. 155-The Human Hurricane app. (12/65), Red Tornado prototype. 158-Origin Diabolu Idol-Head 5 10 15 35 63 90
156-Robby Reed begins (origin/1st app.), ends #173 7 14 21 46 86 125
160-(7/66)-Robby Reed becomes Plastic Man in this issue only; 1st S.A. app. Plastic Man; intro Marco Xavier (Martian Manhunter) & Vulture Crime Organization; ends #173
9 18 27 59 117 175
161-173: 169-Origin/1st app. Gem Girl 4 8 12 28 47 65
174-Mystery format begins. 15 30 45 100 220 340
175-1st app. Cain (House of Mystery host); Adams-c 12 24 36 84 185 285
176,177-Neal Adams-c 9 18 27 58 114 170
178-Neal Adams-c/a (2/69) 9 18 27 61 123 185
179-Neal Adams/Orlando, Wrightson-a (1st pro work, 3 pgs.); Adams-c
12 24 36 82 179 275
180,181,183: Wrightson-a (3,10, & 3 pgs.); Adams-c. 180-Last 12¢ issue; Kane/Wood-a(2). 183-Wood-a 8 16 24 56 108 160
182,184-Adams-c. 182-Toth-a. 184-Kane/Wood, Toth-a 6 12 18 41 76 110
185-Williamson/Kaluta-a; Howard-a (3 pgs.); Adams-c 7 14 21 44 82 120
186-N. Adams-c/a; Wrightson-a (10 pgs.) 9 18 27 59 117 175
187,190: Adams-c. 187-Toth-a. 190-Toth-a(r) 6 12 18 40 73 105
188-Wrightson-a (8 & 3pgs.); Adams-c 7 14 21 49 92 135
189,192,197: Adams-c on all. 189-Wood-a(i). 192-Last 15¢-c
6 12 18 40 73 105
191-Wrightson-a (8 & 3pgs.); Adams-c 7 14 21 49 92 135
193-Wrightson-c 6 12 18 40 73 105
194-Wrightson-c; 52 pgs begin, end #203; Toth,Kirby-a
8 16 24 51 96 140
195: Wrightson-c. Swamp creature story by Wrightson similar to Swamp Thing (10 pgs.)(10/71) 9 18 27 59 117 175
196,198 5 10 15 35 63 90
199-Adams-c; Wood-a(8pgs.); Kirby-a 6 12 18 42 79 115
200-(25¢, 52 pgs.)-One third-r (3/72) 6 12 18 41 76 110
201-203-(25¢, 52 pgs.)-One third-r 5 10 15 33 57 80
204-Wrightson-c/a, 9 pgs. 6 12 18 38 69 100
205,206,208,210,212,215,216,218 4 8 12 23 37 50
207-Wrightson-c/a; Starlin, Redondo-a 6 12 18 38 69 100

House of Mystery (2008 series) #1 © DC

House of Secrets #7 © DC

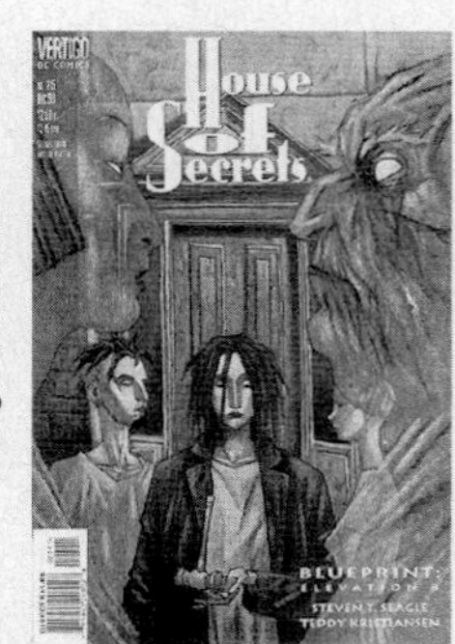

House of Secrets #25 © Seagle & Kristiansen

GD VG FN VF VF/NM NM-
2.0 4.0 6.0 8.0 9.0 9.2

209,211,213,214,217,219-Wrightson-c 5 10 15 31 53 75
220,222,223 3 6 9 21 33 45
221-Wrightson/Kaluta-a(8 pgs.); Wrightson-c 5 10 15 34 60 85
224-229: 224-Wrightson-r from Spectre #9; Dillin/Adams-r from House of Secrets #82; begin 100 pg. issues; Phantom Stranger-r. 225,227-(100 pgs.): 225-Spectre app. 226-Wrightson/Redondo-a Phantom Stranger-r. 228-N. Adams inks; Wrightson-r. 229-Wrightson-a(r); Toth-r; last 100 pg. issue 5 10 15 35 63 90
230,232-235,237-250: 230-UFO-c 3 6 9 15 22 28
231-Classic Wrightson-c 5 10 15 34 60 85
236-Wrightson-c; Ditko-a(p); N. Adams-i 5 10 15 33 57 80
251-254-(84 pgs.)-Adams-c. 251-Wood-a 4 8 12 27 44 60
255,256-(84 pgs.)-Wrightson-c 4 8 12 27 44 60
257-259-(84 pgs.) 3 6 9 18 28 38
260-289: 282-(68 pgs.)-Has extra story "The Computers That Saved Metropolis" Radio Shack giveaway by Jim Starlin 2 4 6 8 10 12
290-1st "I, Vampire" 5 10 15 31 53 75
291-299: 291,293,295-299- "I, Vampire" 2 4 6 10 14 18
300,319-"I, Vampire" 2 4 6 11 16 20
301-318,320: 301-318-"I, Vampire" 2 4 6 10 14 18
321-Death of "I, Vampire" 3 6 9 16 23 30
Welcome to the House of Mystery (7/98, $5.95) reprints stories with new framing story by Gaiman and Aragonés 6.00

NOTE: ***Neal Adams*** *a-236i; c-175-192, 197, 199, 251-254.* ***Alcala*** *a-209, 217, 219, 224, 227.* ***M. Anderson*** *a-212; c/a-37.* ***Aparo*** *a-209.* ***Aragones*** *a-185, 186, 194, 196, 200, 202, 229, 251.* ***Baily*** *a-279p.* ***Cameron*** *a-76, 79.* ***Colan*** *a-202r.* ***Craig*** *a-263, 275, 295, 300.* ***Dillin/Adams*** *r-224.* ***Ditko*** *a-236p, 247, 254, 258, 276; c-277.* ***Drucker*** *a-37.* ***Evans*** *c-218.* ***Fradon*** *a-251.* ***Giffen*** *a-284.* ***Giunta*** *a-199, 227r.* ***Golden*** *a-257, 259.* ***Heath*** *a-194r; c-203.* ***Howard*** *a-182, 185, 187, 196, 229r, 247i, 254, 279i.* ***Kaluta*** *a-195, 200, 250r; c-200-202, 210, 212, 233, 260, 261, 263, 265, 267, 268, 273, 276, 284, 287, 288, 293-295, 300, 302, 304, 305, 309-319, 321.* ***Bob Kane*** *a-84.* ***Gil Kane*** *a-196p, 253p, 300p.* ***Kirby*** *a-194r, 199r; c-65, 76, 78, 79, 85.* ***Kubert*** *c-282, 283, 285, 286, 289-292, 297-299, 301, 303, 306-308.* ***Maneely*** *a-68, 227r.* ***Mayer*** *a-317p.* ***Meskin*** *a-52-144 (most), 195r, 224r, 229r; c-63, 66, 124, 127.* ***Mooney*** *a-24, 159, 160.* ***Moreira*** *a-3, 4, 20-50, 58, 59, 62, 68, 77, 79, 90, 108, 113, 123, 201r, 228; c-4-28, 44, 47, 50, 54, 59, 62, 64, 68, 70, 73.* ***Morrow*** *a-192, 196, 255, 320i.* ***Mortimer*** *a-204(3 pgs.).* ***Nasser*** *a-276.* ***Newton*** *a-259, 272.* ***Nino*** *a-204, 212, 213, 220, 224, 225, 245, 250, 252-256, 283.* ***Orlando*** *a-175(2 pgs.), 178, 240i; c-240, 258p, 262, 264p, 270p, 271, 272, 274, 275, 278, 296i.* ***Redondo*** *a-194, 195, 197, 202, 203, 207, 211, 214, 217, 219, 226, 227, 229, 235, 241, 287(layout), 302p, 303i, 308; c-229.* ***Reese*** *a-195, 200, 205i.* ***Rogers*** *a-254, 274, 277.* ***Roussos*** *a-65, 84, 224i.* ***Sekowsky*** *a-282p.* ***Sparling*** *a-203.* ***Starlin*** *a-207(2 pgs.), 282p; c-281.* ***Leonard Starr*** *a-9.* ***Staton*** *a-300p.* ***Sutton*** *a-189, 271, 290, 291, 293, 295, 297-299, 302, 303, 306-309, 310-313i, 314.* ***Tuska*** *a-293p, 294p, 316p.* ***Wrightson*** *c-193-195, 204, 207, 209, 211, 213, 214, 217, 219, 221, 231, 236, 255, 256; r-224.*

HOUSE OF MYSTERY
DC Comics (Vertigo): Jul, 2008 - No. 42, Dec, 2011 ($2.99)

1-12,14-42: 1-Cain & Abel app.; Rossi-a/Weber-c. 9-Wrightson-a (6 pgs.). 16-Corben-a 3.00
1-Variant-c by Bernie Wrightson 5.00
13-Art by Neal Adams, Ralph Reese, Eric Powell, Sergio Aragonés 3.00
13-Variant-c by Neal Adams 5.00
... Halloween Annual #1 (12/09, $4.99) 1st app. I, Zombie in 7 pg. preview; short stories by various incl. Nowlan, Wagner, Willingham 3 6 9 14 20 25
... Halloween Annual #2 (12/10, $4.99) short stories by various incl. Carey, Allred, Gross 5.00
...: Love Stories for Dead People TPB (2009, $14.99) r/#6-10 15.00
...: Room and Boredom TPB (2008, $9.99) r/#1-5 10.00
...: Safe as Houses TPB (2011, $14.99) r/#26-30 15.00
...: The Beauty of Decay TPB (2010, $17.99) r/#16-20 & Halloween Annual #1 18.00
...: The Space Between TPB (2010, $14.99) r/#11-15; sketch pages 15.00
...: Under New Management TPB (2011, $14.99) r/#20-25 15.00

HOUSE OF NIGHT (Based on the series of novels by P.C. Cast and Kristin Cast)
Dark Horse Comics: Nov, 2011 - No. 5, Mar, 2012 ($1.00/$2.99, limited series)

1-($1.00) Cast, Cast & Dalian-s/Joëlle Jones & Kerschl-a; Frison-c 3.00
1-($1.00) Variant-c by Steve Morris 4.00
2-5-($2.99) Jones-a; two covers by Jones & Ryan Hill on each 3.00

HOUSE OF PENANCE
Dark Horse Comics: Apr, 2016 - Present ($3.99)

1-5: 1-Peter J. Tomasi-s/Ian Bertram-a 4.00

HOUSE OF SECRETS (Combined with The Unexpected after #154)
National Periodical Publications/DC Comics: 11-12/56 - No. 80, 9-10/66; No. 81, 8-9/69 - No. 140, 2-3/76; No. 141, 8-9/76 - No. 154, 10-11/78

1-Drucker-a; Moreira-c 132 264 408 1088 2444 3700
2-Moreira-a 44 88 132 326 738 1150
3-Kirby-c/a 38 76 114 281 628 975
4-Kirby-a 29 58 87 200 467 725
5-7 22 44 66 154 340 525
8-Kirby-a 23 46 69 161 356 550
9-11: 11-Lou Cameron-a (unsigned) 20 40 60 138 307 475
12-Kirby-c/a; Lou Cameron-a 21 42 63 147 324 500
13-15: 14-Flying saucer-c 15 30 45 105 233 360
16-20 14 28 42 98 217 335
21,22,24-30 13 26 39 86 188 290
23-1st app. Mark Merlin & begin series (8/59) 14 28 42 96 211 325
31-50: 48-Toth-a. 50-Last 10¢ issue 11 22 33 76 163 250
51-60: 58-Origin Mark Merlin 9 18 27 59 117 175
61-First Eclipso (7-8/63) and begin series 46 92 138 340 770 1200
62 8 16 24 54 102 150
63-65-Toth-a on Eclipso (see Brave and the Bold #64) 6 12 18 41 76 110
66-1st Eclipso-c (also #67,70,78,79); Toth-a 8 16 24 56 108 160
67,73: 67-Toth-a on Eclipso. 73-Mark Merlin becomes Prince Ra-Man (1st app.) 6 12 18 41 76 110
68-72,74-80: 76-Prince Ra-Man vs. Eclipso. 80-Eclipso, Prince Ra-Man end 6 12 18 37 66 95
81-Mystery format begins; 1st app. Abel (House Of Secrets host); (cameo in DC Special #4) 15 30 45 103 227 350
82-84: 82-Neal Adams-c(i) 7 14 21 49 92 135
85,90: 85-N. Adams-a(i). 90-Buckler (early work)/N. Adams-a(i) 8 16 24 51 96 140
86,88,89,91 7 14 21 44 82 120
87-Wrightson & Kaluta-a 8 16 24 52 99 145
92-1st app. Swamp Thing-c/story (8 pgs.)(6-7/71) by Berni Wrightson(p) w/JeffJones/Kaluta/Weiss ink assists; classic-c. 100 200 400 800 1300 1800
93,94,96-(52 pgs.)-Wrightson-c. 94-Wrightson-a(i); 96-Wood-a 7 14 21 46 86 125
95,97,98-(52 pgs.) 5 10 15 35 63 90
99-Wrightson splash pg. 5 10 15 34 60 85
100-Classic Wrightson-c 7 14 21 49 92 135
101,102,104,105,108-111,113-120 3 6 9 19 30 40
103,106,107-Wrightson-c 5 10 15 33 57 80
112-Grey tone-c 4 8 12 23 37 50
121-133 2 4 6 11 16 20
134-Wrightson-a 3 6 9 17 26 35
135,136,139-Wrightson-a/c 3 6 9 20 31 42
137,138,141-153 2 4 6 8 10 12
140-1st solo origin of the Patchworkman (see Swamp Thing #3) 3 6 9 16 23 30
154 (10-11/78, 44 pgs.) Last issue 2 4 6 9 13 16

NOTE: ***Neal Adams*** *c-81, 82, 84-88, 90, 91.* ***Alcala*** *a-104-107.* ***Anderson*** *a-91. Aparo a-93, 97, 105.* ***B. Bailey*** *a-107.* ***Cameron*** *a-13, 15.* ***Colan*** *a-63.* ***Ditko*** *a-139p, 148.* ***Elias*** *a-58.* ***Evans*** *a-118.* ***Finlay*** *a-7r(Real Fact?).* ***Glanzman*** *a-91.* ***Golden*** *a-151.* ***Heath*** *a-31.* ***Heck*** *a-85.* ***Kaluta*** *a-87, 98, 99; c-98, 99, 101, 102, 105, 149, 151, 154.* ***Bob Kane*** *a-18, 21.* ***G. Kane*** *a-85p.* ***Kirby*** *c-3, 11, 12.* ***Kubert*** *a-39.* ***Meskin*** *a-2-68 (most), 94r; c-55-60.* ***Moreira*** *a-7, 8, 51, 54, 102-104, 106, 108, 113, 116, 118, 121, 123, 127; c-1, 2, 4-10, 13-20.* ***Morrow*** *a-86, 89, 90; c-89, 146-148.* ***Nino*** *a-101, 103, 106, 109, 115, 117, 126, 128, 131, 147, 153.* ***Redondo*** *a-95, 99, 102, 104p, 113, 116, 134, 136, 139, 140.* ***Reese*** *a-85.* ***Severin*** *a-91.* ***Starlin*** *c-150.* ***Sutton*** *a-154.* ***Toth*** *a-63-67, 83, 93r, 94r, 96r-98r, 123.* ***Tuska*** *a-90, 104.* ***Wrightson*** *a-134; c-92-94, 96, 100, 103, 106, 107, 135, 136, 139.*

HOUSE OF SECRETS
DC Comics (Vertigo): Oct, 1996 - No. 25, Dec, 1998 ($2.50) (Creator-owned series)

1-Steven Seagle-s/Kristiansen-c/a. 3.50
2-25: 5,7-Kristiansen-c/a. 6-Fegrado-a 3.00
TPB-(1997, $14.95) r/1-5 15.00

HOUSE OF SECRETS: FACADE
DC Comics (Vertigo): 2001 - No. 2, 2001 ($5.95, limited series)

1,2-Steven Seagle-s/Teddy Kristiansen-c/a. 6.00

HOUSE OF TERROR (3-D)
St. John Publishing Co.: Oct, 1953 (25¢, came w/glasses)

1-Kubert, Baker-a 27 54 81 158 259 360

HOUSE OF YANG, THE (See Yang)
Charlton Comics: July, 1975 - No. 6, June, 1976; 1978

1-Sanho Kim-a in all 2 4 6 13 18 22
2-6 2 4 6 8 10 12
Modern Comics #1,2(1978) 6.00

HOUSE ON THE BORDERLAND
DC Comics (Vertigo): 2000 ($29.95, hardcover, one-shot)

HC-Adaptation of William Hope Hodgson book; Corben-a 30.00
SC (2003, $19.95) 20.00

HOUSE II: THE SECOND STORY
Marvel Comics: Oct, 1987 (One-shot)

1-Adapts movie 4.00

HOWARD CHAYKIN'S AMERICAN FLAGG (See American Flagg!)
First Comics: V2#1, May, 1988 - V2#12, Apr, 1989 ($1.75/$1.95, Baxter paper)

V2#1-9,11,12-Chaykin-c(p) in all 3.00

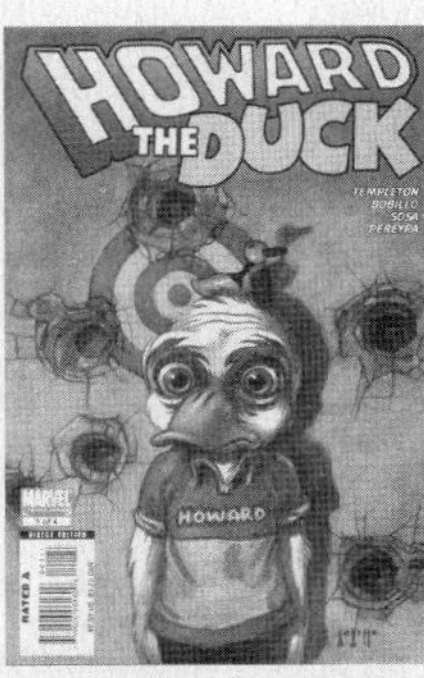

Howard the Duck (2007 series) #1 © MAR

Howdy Doody #3 © CNP

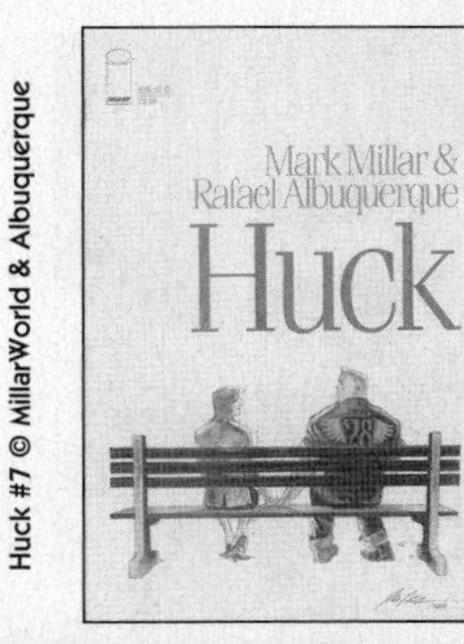

Huck #7 © MillarWorld & Albuquerque

GD 2.0 | VG 4.0 | FN 6.0 | VF 8.0 | VF/NM 9.0 | NM- 9.2

10-Elvis Presley photo-c 4.00

HOWARD THE DUCK (See Bizarre Adventures #34, Crazy Magazine, Fear, Man-Thing, Marvel Treasury Edition & Sensational She-Hulk #14-17)
Marvel Comics Group: Jan, 1976 - No. 31, May, 1979; No. 32, Jan, 1986; No. 33, Sept, 1986

1-Brunner-c/a; Spider-Man x-over (low distr.) 5 10 15 35 63 90
2-Brunner-c/a 2 4 6 11 16 20
3,4-(Regular 25¢ edition). 3-Buscema-a(p), (7/76) 2 4 6 8 11 14
3,4-(30¢-c, limited distribution) 3 6 9 19 30 40
5 2 4 6 8 11 14
6-11: 8-Howard The Duck for president. 9-1st Sgt. Preston Dudley of RCMP. 10-Spider-Man-c/sty 1 2 3 5 7 9
12-1st brief app. Kiss (3/77) 4 8 12 23 37 50
13-(30¢-c) 1st full app. Kiss (6/77); Daimon Hellstrom app. plus cameo of Howard as Son of Satan 4 8 12 27 44 60
13-(35¢-c, limited distribution) 10 20 30 64 132 200
14-32: 14-17-(Regular 30¢-c). 14-Howard as Son of Satan-c/story; Son of Satan app. 16-Album issue; 3 pgs. comics. 22,23-Man-Thing-c/stories; Star Wars parody. 30,32-P. Smith-a 6.00
14-17-(35¢-c, limited distribution) 6 12 18 38 69 100
33-Last issue; low print run 1 2 3 5 6 8
Annual 1(1977, 52 pgs.)-Mayerik-a 2 3 4 6 8 10
... Omnibus HC (2008, $99.99, dustjacket) r/#1-33 & Annual #1, Adventure Into Fear #19, Man-Thing #1, Giant-Size Man-Thing #4&5, Marvel Treasury Ed. #12, Marvel Team-Up #96 and FOOM #15; Gerber foreword; creator interviews; bonus art; 2 covers 100.00

NOTE: ***Austin** c-29i. **Bolland** c-33. **Brunner** a-1p, 2p; c-1, 2. **Buckler** c-3p. **Buscema** a-3p. **Colan** a(p)-4-15, 17-20, 24-27, 30, 31; c(p)-4-31, Annual 1p. **Leialoha** a-1-13i; c(i)-3-5, 8-11. **Mayerik** a-22, 23, 33. **Paul Smith** a-30p, 32. Man-Thing app. in #22, 23.*

HOWARD THE DUCK (Magazine)
Marvel Comics Group: Oct, 1979 - No. 9, Mar, 1981 (B&W, 68 pgs.)

1-Art by Colan, Janson, Golden. Kidney Lady app. 2 4 6 9 12 15
2,3,5-9 (nudity in most): 2-Mayerick-c. 3-Xmas issue; Jack Davis-c; Duck World flashback. 5-Dracula app. 6-1st Street People back-up story. 7-Has pin-up by Byrne; Man-Thing-c/s (46 pgs.). 8-Batman parody w/Marshall Rogers-a; Dave Sim-a (1 pg.). 9-Marie Severin-a; John Pound painted-c 6.00
4-Beatles, John Lennon, Elvis, Kiss & Devo cameos; Hitler app. 2 4 6 9 12 15

NOTE: ***Buscema** a-4p. **Colan** a-1-5p, 7-9p. **Jack Davis** c-3. **Golden** a(p)-1, 5, 6(51pgs.). **Rogers** a-7, 8. **Simonson** a-7.*

HOWARD THE DUCK (Volume 2)
Marvel Comics: Mar, 2002 - No. 6, Aug, 2002 ($2.99)

1-Gerber-s/Winslade-a/Fabry-c 5.00
2-6: 2,4-6-Gerber-s/Winslade-a/Fabry-c. 3-Fabry-a/c 3.00
TPB (9/02, $14.99) r/#1-6 15.00

HOWARD THE DUCK (Volume 3)
Marvel Comics: Dec, 2007 - No. 4, Feb, 2008 ($2.99, limited series)

1-4-Templeton-s/Bobillo-a/c; She-Hulk app. 3.00
...: Media Duckling TPB (2008, $11.99) r/#1-4; Howard the Duck #1 (1/76) and pages from Civil War: Choosing Sides 12.00

HOWARD THE DUCK (Volume 4)
Marvel Comics: May 2015 - No. 5, Oct, 2015 ($3.99)

1-5-Zdarsky-s/Quinones-a. 1-Spider-Man app. 2-Guardians of the Galaxy app. 4.00

HOWARD THE DUCK (Volume 5)
Marvel Comics: Jan, 2016 - No. 11, Dec, 2016 ($4.99/$3.99)

1-3-($4.99): 1-Zdarsky-s/Quinones-a; back-up with Gwenpool in #1-3. 2-Fish-a 5.00
4-11-($3.99) 4,5-Silver Surfer, Galactus & the Guardians of the Galaxy app. 6-Squirrel Girl x-over. 7-Maguire-a. 8-Beverly app. 9-Lea Thompson app. 9-11-Mojo app. 4.00

HOWARD THE DUCK HOLIDAY SPECIAL
Marvel Comics: Feb, 1997 ($2.50, one-shot)

1-Wraparound-c; Hama-s 6.00

HOWARD THE DUCK: THE MOVIE
Marvel Comics Group: Dec, 1986 - No. 3, Feb, 1987 (Limited series)

1-3: Movie adaptation; r/Marvel Super Special 4.00

HOWARD THE HUMAN (Secret Wars tie-in)
Marvel Comics: Oct, 2015 ($3.99, one-shot)

1-Howard the Duck as human in an all-animal world; Skottie Young-s/Jim Mahfood-a 4.00

HOW BOYS AND GIRLS CAN HELP WIN THE WAR
The Parents' Magazine Institute: 1942 (10¢, one-shot)

1-All proceeds used to buy war bonds 34 68 102 199 325 450

HOWDY DOODY (TV)(See Jackpot of Fun-- & Poll Parrot)(Some have stories by John Stanley)
Dell Publishing Co.: 1/50 - No. 38, 7-9/56; No. 761, 1/57; No. 811, 7/57

1-(Scarce)-Photo-c; 1st TV comic 71 142 213 568 1284 2000
2-Photo-c 34 68 102 241 541 840
3-5: All photo-c 19 38 57 133 297 460
6-Used in **SOTI**, pg. 309; classic-c; painted covers begin 21 42 63 147 324 500
7-10 12 24 36 84 185 285
11-20: 13-X-Mas-c 10 20 30 70 150 230
21-38, Four Color 761,811 9 18 27 61 123 185

HOW IT BEGAN
United Features Syndicate: No. 15, 1939 (one-shot)

Single Series 15 34 68 102 204 332 460

HOWLING COMMANDOS OF S.H.I.E.L.D.
Marvel Comics: Dec, 2015 - No. 6, May, 2016 ($3.99)

1-6: 1-Barbiere-s/Schoonover-a; Dum Dum Dugan, Orrgo, Man-Thing, Hit-Monkey app. 4.00

HOW SANTA GOT HIS RED SUIT (See March of Comics No. 2)

HOW THE WEST WAS WON (See Movie Comics)

HOW TO DRAW FOR THE COMICS
Street and Smith: No date (1942?) (10¢, 64 pgs., B&W & color, no ads)

nn-Art by Robert Winsor McCay (recreating his father's art), George Marcoux (Supersnipe artist), Vernon Greene (The Shadow artist), Jack Binder (with biog.), Thorton Fisher, Jon Small, & Jack Farr; has biographies of each artist 39 78 117 231 378 525

H. P. LOVECRAFT'S CTHULHU
Millennium Publications: Dec, 1991 - No. 3, May, 1992 ($2.50, limited series)

1-3: 1-Contains trading cards on thin stock 3.00

H. R. PUFNSTUF (TV) (See March of Comics #360)
Gold Key: Oct, 1970 - No. 8, July, 1972

1-Photo-c 10 20 30 64 132 200
2-8-Photo-c on all. 6-8-Both Gold Key and Whitman editions exist 7 14 21 46 86 125

HUBERT AT CAMP MOONBEAM
Dell Publishing Co.: No. 251, Oct, 1949 (one shot)

Four Color 251 9 18 27 61 123 185

HUCK
Image Comics: Nov, 2015 - No. 6, Apr, 2016($3.50/$3.99)

1-5-MIllar-s/Albuquerque-a; 2 covers on each 3.50
6-($3.99) 4.00

HUCK & YOGI JAMBOREE (TV)
Dell Publishing Co.: Mar, 1961 ($1.00, 6-1/4x9", 116 pgs., cardboard-c, high quality paper) (B&W original material)

nn (scarce) 8 16 24 54 102 150

HUCK & YOGI WINTER SPORTS (TV)
Dell Publishing Co.: No. 1310, Mar, 1962 (Hanna-Barbera) (one-shot)

Four Color 1310 8 16 24 51 96 140

HUCK FINN (See The New Adventures of... & Power Record Comics)

HUCKLEBERRY FINN (Movie)
Dell Publishing Co.: No. 1114, July, 1960

Four Color 1114-Photo-c 5 10 15 35 63 90

HUCKLEBERRY HOUND (See Dell Giant #31,44, Golden Picture Story Book, Kite Fun Book, March of Comics #199, 214, 235, Spotlight #1 & Whitman Comic Books)

HUCKLEBERRY HOUND (TV)
Dell/Gold Key No. 18 (10/62) on: No. 990, 5-7/59 - No. 43, 10/70 (Hanna-Barbera)

Four Color 990(#1)-1st app. Huckleberry Hound, Yogi Bear, & Pixie & Dixie & Mr. Jinks 15 30 45 103 227 350
Four Color 1050,1054 (12/59) 10 20 30 64 132 200
3(1-2/60) - 7 (9-10/60), Four Color 1141 (10/60) 7 14 21 46 86 125
8-10 6 12 18 37 66 95
11,13-17 (6-8/62) 5 10 15 30 50 70
12-1st Hokey Wolf & Ding-a-Ling 5 10 15 33 57 80
18,19 (84pgs.; 18-20 titled ...Chuckleberry Tales) 7 14 21 44 82 120
20-Titled Chuckleberry Tales 4 8 12 28 47 65
21-30: 28-30-Reprints 4 8 12 23 37 50
31-43: 31,32,35,37-43-Reprints 3 6 9 19 30 40

Hulk (1999 series) #1 © MAR

Hulk (2017 series) #1 © MAR

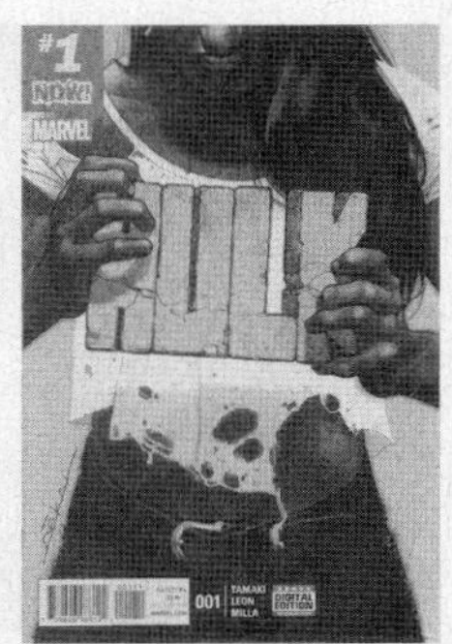

Hulk: Gray #1 © MAR

	GD 2.0	VG 4.0	FN 6.0	VF 8.0	VF/NM 9.0	NM- 9.2

HUCKLEBERRY HOUND (TV)
Charlton Comics: Nov, 1970 - No. 8, Jan, 1972 (Hanna-Barbera)

1	5	10	15	31	53	75
2-8	3	6	9	17	26	35

HUEY, DEWEY, & LOUIE (See Donald Duck, 1938 for 1st app. Also see Mickey Mouse Magazine V4#2, V5#7 & Walt Disney's Junior Woodchucks Limited Series)

HUEY, DEWEY, & LOUIE BACK TO SCHOOL (See Dell Giant #22, 35, 49 & Dell Giants)

HUEY, DEWEY, AND LOUIE JUNIOR WOODCHUCKS (Disney)
Gold Key No. 1-61/Whitman No. 62 on: Aug, 1966 - No. 81, July, 1984
(See Walt Disney's Comics & Stories #125)

1	6	12	18	40	73	105
2,3(12/68)	4	8	12	23	37	50
4,5(4/70)-r/two WDC&S D.Duck stories by Barks	3	6	9	19	30	40
6-17	3	6	9	17	26	35
18,27-30	3	6	9	15	21	26
19-23,25-New storyboarded scripts by Barks, 13-25 pgs. per issue	3	6	9	18	28	38
24,26: 26-r/Barks Donald Duck WDC&S stories	3	6	9	16	23	30
31-57,60,61: 35,41-r/Barks J.W. scripts	2	4	6	8	11	14
58,59: 58-r/Barks Donald Duck WDC&S stories	2	4	6	9	13	16
62-64 (Whitman)	2	4	6	9	13	16
65-(9/80), 66 (Pre-pack? scarce)	4	8	12	25	40	55
67 (1/81),68	2	4	6	9	13	16
67-40¢ cover variant	4	8	12	17	21	24
69-74: 72(2/82), 73(2-3/82), 74(3/82)	2	4	6	8	11	14
75-81 (all #90183; pre-pack; nd, nd code; scarce): 75(4/83), 76(5/83), 77(7/83), 78(8/83), 79(4/84), 80(5/84), 81(7/84)	3	6	9	16	23	30

HUGGA BUNCH (TV)
Marvel Comics (Star Comics): Oct, 1986 - No. 6, Aug, 1987

1-6						5.00

HULK (Magazine)(Formerly The Rampaging Hulk)(Also see The Incredible Hulk)
Marvel Comics: No. 10, Aug., 1978 - No. 27, June, 1981 ($1.50)

10-18: 10-Bill Bixby interview. 11-Moon Knight begins. 12-15,17,18-Moon Knight stories. 12-Lou Ferrigno interview.	2	4	6	10	14	18
19-27: 20-Moon Knight story. 23-Last full color issue; Banner is attacked. 24-Part color, Lou Ferrigno interview. 25-Part color. 26,27-are B&W	2	4	6	9	12	15

NOTE: #10-20 have fragile spines which split easily. ***Alcala*** *a(i)-15, 17-20, 22, 24-27.* ***Buscema*** *a-23; c-26.* ***Chaykin*** *a-21-25.* ***Colan*** *a(p)-11, 19, 24-27.* ***Jusko*** *painted c-12.* ***Nebres*** *a-16.* ***Severin*** *a-19i. Moon Knight by* ***Sienkiewicz*** *in 13-15, 17, 18, 20.* ***Simonson*** *a-27; c-23. Dominic Fortune appears in #21-24.*

HULK (Becomes Incredible Hulk Vol. 2 with issue #12) (Also see Marvel Age Hulk)
Marvel Comics: Apr, 1999 - No. 11, Feb, 2000 ($2.99/$1.99)

1-($2.99) Byrne-s/Garney-a						6.00
1-Variant-c	1	3	4	6	8	10
1-DFE Remarked-c						50.00
1-Gold foil variant						10.00
2-7-($1.99): 2-Two covers. 5-Art by Jurgens, Buscema & Texeira. 7-Avengers app.						4.00
8-Hulk battles Wolverine	1	2	3	5	6	8
9-11: 11-She-Hulk app.						3.00
1999 Annual ($3.50) Chapter One story; Byrne-s/Weeks-a						4.00
Hulk Vs. The Thing (12/99, $3.99, TPB) reprints their notable battles						4.00

HULK (Also see Fall of the Hulks and King-Size Hulk) (Becomes Red She-Hulk with #58)
Marvel Comics: Mar, 2008 - No. 57, Oct, 2012 ($2.99/$3.99)

1-Red Hulk app.; Abomination killed; Loeb-s/McGuinness-a/c	1	3	4	6	8	10
1-Variant-c by Acuña						12.00
1-Variant-c with Incredible Hulk #1 cover swipe by McGuinness						20.00
1,2-2nd printings with wraparound McGuinness variant-c						3.00
2-22: 2-Iron Man app.; Rick Jones becomes the new Abomination. 4,6-Red Hulk vs. green Hulk; two covers (each Hulk); Thor app. 7-9-Art Adams & Cho-a (2 covers) 10-Defenders re-form. 14,15-X-Force, Elektra & Deadpool app. 15-Red She-Hulk app. 19-21-Fall of the Hulks x-over. 19-FF app. 22-World War Hulks						4.00
2-9: 2-Variant-c by Djurdjevic. 3-Var-c by Finch. 5-Var-c by Coipel. 6,7-Var-c by Turner 8-Var-c by Sal Buscema. 9-Two covers w/Hulks as Santa						6.00
23-($4.99) Origin of the Red Hulk; art by Sale, Romita, Deodato, Trimpe, Yu, others						5.00
24-31-($3.99): 24-World war Hulks. 25,26-Iron Man app. 26-Thor app.						4.00
30.1, 32-49 ($2.99): 34-Planet Red Hulk begins. 37-38-Fear Itself tie-in						3.00
50-($3.99) Haunted Hulk; Dr. Strange app.; back-up w/Brereton-a; Pagulayan-c						4.00
50-Variant covers by Art Adams, Humberto Ramos & Walt Simonson						10.00
51-57: 53-57-Eaglesham-a; Alpha Flight app.						3.00
... Family: Green Genes 1 (2/09, $4.99) new She-Hulk, Scorpion, Skaar & Mr. Fixit stories						5.00
... Let the Battle Begin 1 (5/10, $3.99) Snider-s/Kurth-a; Del Mundo-c; McGuinness-a						4.00
... MGC #1 (6/10, $1.00) r/#1 with "Marvel's Greatest Comics" logo on cover						3.00
... Monster-Size Special (12/08, $3.99) monster-themed stories by Niles, David & others						4.00
...: Raging Thunder 1 (8/08, $3.99) Hulk vs. Thundra; Breitweiser-a; r/FF #133; Land-c						4.00
Hulk-Sized Mini-Hulks ('11, $2.99) Red, Green & Blue Hulks all-ages humor; Giarrusso-a						3.00
... Vs. Fin Fang Foom (2/08, $3.99) new re-telling of first meeting; r/Strange Tales #89						4.00
... Vs. Hercules (6/08, $3.99) Djurdjevic-c; new story w/art by various; r/Tales To Ast. #79						4.00
...: Winter Guard (2/10, $3.99) Darkstar, Crimson Dynamo app. Steve Ellis-a/c						4.00
Hulk 100 Project (2008, $10.00, SC, charity book for the HERO Initiative) collection of 100 variant covers by Adams, Romita Sr. & Jr., Cho, McGuinness and more						10.00

	GD 2.0	VG 4.0	FN 6.0	VF 8.0	VF/NM 9.0	NM- 9.2

HULK (Follows Indestructible Hulk series)
Marvel Comics: Jun, 2014 - No. 16, Jul, 2015 ($3.99)

1-15: 1-4-Waid-s/Bagley-a. 3,4-Avengers app. 5-Alex Ross-c. 6-15-Duggan-s. 13,14-Deadpool app. 14-15-Hulk vs. Red Hulk						4.00
16-($4.99) Avengers app.; Duggan-s/Bagley-a; leads into Secret Wars						5.00
Annual 1 (11/14, $4.99) Monty Nero-s; art by Luke Ross, Goddard & Laming						5.00

HULK (Jennifer Walters as Hulk; follows events of Civil War II)
Marvel Comics: Feb, 2017 - Present ($3.99)

1-3-Mariko Tamaki-s/Nico Leon-a. 3-Hellcat app.						4.00

HULK AND POWER PACK (All ages series)
Marvel Comics: May, 2007 - No. 4, Aug, 2007 ($2.99, limited series)

1-4-Sumerak-s. 1,2,4-Williams-a. 1-Absorbing Man app. 3-Kuhn-a; Abomination app.						3.00
...: Pack Smash! (2007, $6.99, digest) r/#1-4						7.00

HULK & THING: HARD KNOCKS
Marvel Comics: Nov, 2004 - No. 4, Feb, 2005 ($3.50, limited series)

1-4-Bruce Jones-s/Jae Lee-a/c						3.50
TPB (2005, $13.99) r/#1-4 and Giant-Size Super-Stars #1						14.00

HULK: BROKEN WORLDS
Marvel Comics: May, 2009 -No. 2, July, 2009 ($3.99, limited series)

1,2-Short stories of alternate world Hulks by various, incl. Trimpe, David, Warren						4.00

HULK CHRONICLES: WWH
Marvel Comics: Oct, 2008 - No. 6, Mar, 2009 ($4.99, limited series)

1-6-Reprints stories from World War Hulk x-over. 1-R/Inc. Hulk #106 & WWH Prologue						5.00

HULK: DESTRUCTION
Marvel Comics: Sept, 2005 - No. 4, Dec, 2005 ($2.99, limited series)

1-4-Origin of the Abomination; Peter David-s/Jim Muniz-a						3.00

HULKED-OUT HEROES
Marvel Comics: Jun, 2010 - No. 2, Jun, 2010 ($3.99, limited series)

1,2-World War Hulks tie-in; Deadpool app.; Ramos-a						4.00

HULK: FUTURE IMPERFECT
Marvel Comics: Jan, 1993 - No. 2, Dec, 1992 (In error) ($5.95, 52 pgs., squarebound, limited series)

1,2: Embossed-c; Peter David story & George Perez-c/a. 1-1st app. Maestro.	1	2	3	5	6	8

HULK: GRAY
Marvel Comics: Dec, 2003 - No. 6, Apr, 2004 ($3.50, limited series)

1-6-Hulk's origin & early days; Loeb-s/Sale-a/c						3.50
HC (2004, $21.99, with dust jacket) oversized r/#1-6						22.00
SC (2005, $19.99) r/#1-6						20.00

HULK: NIGHTMERICA
Marvel Comics: Aug, 2003 - No. 6, May, 2004 ($2.99, limited series)

1-6-Brian Ashmore painted-a/c						3.00

HULK/ PITT
Marvel Comics: 1997 ($5.99, one-shot)

1-David-s/Keown-c/a						6.00

HULK: SEASON ONE
Marvel Comics: 2012 ($24.99, hardcover graphic novel)

HC - Origin and early days; Van Lente-s/Fowler-a/Tedesco painted-c						25.00

HULK SMASH
Marvel Comics: Mar, 2001 - No. 2, Apr, 2001 ($2.99, limited series)

1,2-Ennis-s/McCrea & Janson-a/Nowlan painted-c						3.00

HULK SMASH AVENGERS
Marvel Comics: Jul, 2012 - No. 5, July, 2012 ($2.99, weekly limited series)

1-5-Hulk vs. Avengers from various points in Marvel History. 1-Frenz-a. 5-Oeming-a						3.00

Human Fly #3 © MAR

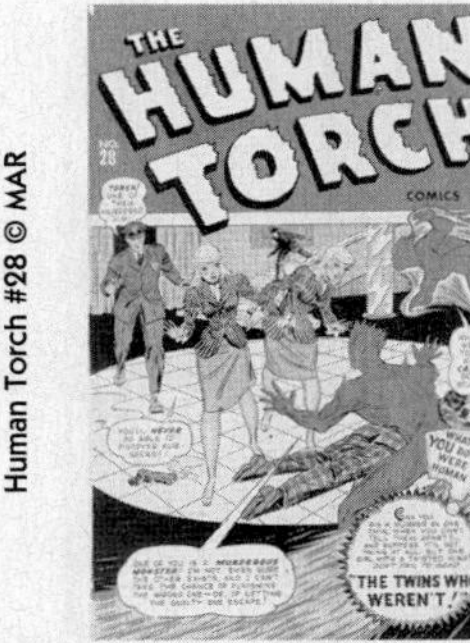

Human Torch #28 © MAR

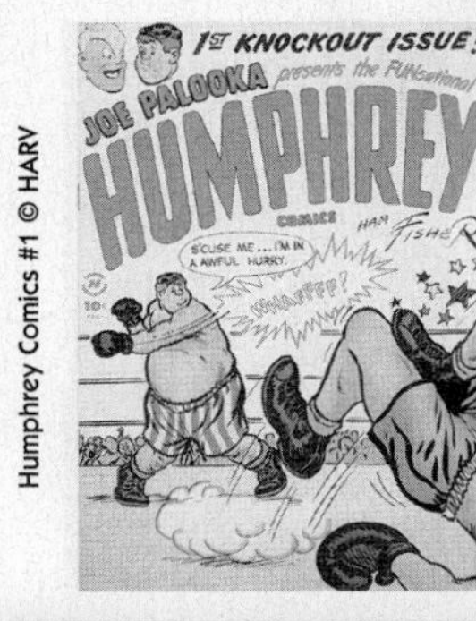

Humphrey Comics #1 © HARV

GD 2.0 VG 4.0 FN 6.0 VF 8.0 VF/NM 9.0 NM- 9.2

HULK: THE MOVIE
Marvel Comics
...Adaptation (8/03, $3.50) Bruce Jones-s/Bagley-a/Keown-c 3.50
TPB (2003, $12.99) r/Adaptation, Ultimates #5, Inc. Hulk #34, Ult. Marvel Team-Up #2&3 13.00

HULK 2099
Marvel Comics: Dec, 1994 - No. 10, Sept, 1995 ($1.50/$1.95)
1-($2.50)-Green foil-c 4.00
2-10: 2-A. Kubert-c 3.00

HULK/WOLVERINE: 6 HOURS
Marvel Comics: Mar, 2003 - No. 4, May, 2003 ($2.99, limited series)
1-4-Bruce Jones-s/Scott Kolins-a; Bisley-c 3.00
Hulk Legends Vol. 1: Hulk/Wolverine: 6 Hours (2003, $13.99, TPB) r/#1-4 & 1st Wolverine app. from Incredible Hulk #181 14.00

HUMAN BOMB
DC Comics: Feb, 2013 - No. 4, May, 2013 ($2.99, limited series)
1-4: 1-Re-intro/origin; Gray & Palmiotti-s/Ordway-a/c 3.00

HUMAN DEFENSE CORPS
DC Comics: Jul, 2003 - No. 6, Dec, 2003 ($2.50, limited series)
1-6-Ty Templeton-s/Sauve, Jr & Vlasco-a. 1-Lois Lane app. 3.00

HUMAN FLY
I.W. Enterprises/Super: 1963 - 1964 (Reprints)
I.W. Reprint #1-Reprints Blue Beetle #44('46) 2 4 6 13 18 22
Super Reprint #10-R/Blue Beetle #46('47) 2 4 6 13 18 22

HUMAN FLY, THE
Marvel Comics Group: Sept, 1977 - No. 19, Mar, 1979
1-(Regular 30¢-c) Origin; Spider-Man x-over 2 4 6 11 16 20
1,2-(35¢-c, limited distribution) 5 10 15 31 53 75
2,9,19: 2-(Regular 30¢-c). 2-Ghost Rider app. 9-Daredevil x-over; Byrne-c(p). 19-Last issue 2 3 4 6 8 10
3-8,10-18 5.00
NOTE: *Austin c-4i, 9i. Elias a-1, 3p, 4p, 7p, 10-12p, 15p, 18p, 19p. Layton c-19.*

HUMANKIND
Image Comics (Top Cow): Sept, 2004 - No. 5, Mar, 2005 ($2.99, limited series)
1-5-Tony Daniel-a. 1-Three covers by Daniel, Silvestri, and Land 3.00

HUMAN RACE, THE
DC Comics: May, 2005 - No. 7, Nov, 2005 ($2.99, limited series)
1-7-Raab-s/Justiniano-a/c 3.00

HUMAN TARGET
DC Comics (Vertigo): Apr, 1999 - No. 4, July, 1999 ($2.95, limited series)
1-4-Milligan-s/Bradstreet-c/Biuković-a 3.00
1-Special Edition (6/10, $1.00) r/#1 with "What's Next?" logo on cover 3.00
TPB (2000, $12.95) new Bradstreet-c 13.00
...: Chance Meetings TPB (2010, $14.99) r/#1-4 and Human Target: Final Cut GN 15.00

HUMAN TARGET
DC Comics (Vertigo): Oct, 2003 - No. 21, June, 2005 ($2.95)
1-21: 1-5-Milligan-s/Pulido-a/c. 6-Chiang-a 3.00
...: Living in Amerika TPB (2004, $14.95) r/#6-10; Chiang sketch pages 15.00
...: Second Chances TPB (2011, $19.99) r/#1-10; Chiang sketch pages 20.00
...: Strike Zones TPB (2004, $9.95) r/#1-5 10.00

HUMAN TARGET (Based on the Fox TV series)
DC Comics: Apr, 2010 - No. 6, Sept, 2010 ($2.99, limited series)
1-6-Wein-s/Redondo-a; back-up stories by various. 1-Bermejo-c. 5-Sook-c 3.00
TPB (2010, $17.99) r/#1-6 18.00

HUMAN TARGET: FINAL CUT
DC Comics (Vertigo): 2002 ($29.95/$19.95, graphic novel)
Hardcover (2002, $29.95) Milligan-s/Pulido-a/c 30.00
Softcover (2003, $19.95) 20.00

HUMAN TARGET SPECIAL (TV)
DC Comics: Nov, 1991 ($2.00, 52 pgs., one-shot)
1 4.00

HUMAN TORCH, THE (Red Raven #1)(See All-Select, All Winners, Marvel Mystery, Men's Adventures, Mystic Comics (2nd series), Sub-Mariner, USA & Young Men)
Timely/Marvel Comics (TP 2,3/TCI 4-9/SePI 10/SnPC 11-25/CnPC 26-35/Atlas Comics (CPC 36-38)): No. 2, Fall, 1940 - No. 15, Spring, 1944; No. 16, Fall, 1944 - No. 35, Mar, 1949 (Becomes Love Tales #36 on); No. 36, April, 1954 - No. 38, Aug, 1954
2(#1)-Intro & Origin Toro; The Falcon, The Fiery Mask, Mantor the Magician, & Microman only app.; Human Torch by Burgos, Sub-Mariner by Everett begin (origin of each in text); WWII-c 2700 5400 8100 19,000 43,500 70,000
3(#2)-40 pg. H.T. story; H.T. & S.M. battle over who is best artist in text-Everett or Burgos 622 1244 1866 4541 8021 11,500
4(#3)-Origin The Patriot in text; last Everett Sub-Mariner; Sid Greene-a 503 1006 1509 3672 6486 9300
5(#4)-The Patriot app; Angel x-over in Sub-Mariner (Summer, 1941); 1st Nazi war-c this title; back-c ad for Young Allies #1 with diff. cover-a 423 846 1269 3088 5444 7800
5-Human Torch battles Sub-Mariner (Fall, '41); 60 pg. story 692 1384 2076 5052 8926 12,800
6-Schomburg hooded villain bondage-c 366 732 1098 2562 4481 6400
7-1st Japanese war-c 400 800 1200 2800 4900 7000
8-Human Torch battles Sub-Mariner; 52 pg. story; Wolverton-a, 1 pg.; Nazi WWII-c 503 1006 1509 3672 6486 9300
9-Classic Human Torch vs. Gen. Rommel, "The Desert Rat"; Nazi WWII-c 400 800 1200 2800 4900 7000
10-Human Torch battles Sub-Mariner, 45 pg. story; Wolverton-a, 1 pg.; Nazi WWII-c 423 846 1269 3067 5384 7700
11,14,15: 11-Nazi WWII-c. 14-Nazi WWII-c; 1st Atlas Globe logo (Winter, 1943-44; see All Winners #11 also) 314 628 942 2198 3849 5500
12-Classic Japanese WWII-c, Torch melts Japanese soldier's arm 811 1622 2433 5920 10,460 15,000
13-Classic Schomburg Japanese WWII bondage-c 343 686 1029 2400 4200 6000
16-20: 16-18,20-Japanese WWII-c. 19-Bondage-c. 20-Last War issue 245 490 735 1568 2684 3800
21,22,24-30: 27-2nd app. (1st-c) Asbestos Lady (see Capt. America Comics #63 for 1st app.) 181 362 543 1158 1979 2800
23 (Sum/46)-Becomes Junior Miss 24? Classic Schomburg Robot-c 271 542 813 1734 2967 4200
31,32: 31-Namora x-over in Sub-Mariner (also #30); last Toro. 32-Sungirl, Namora app.; Sungirl-c 165 330 495 1048 1799 2550
33-Capt. America x-over 168 336 504 1075 1838 2600
34-Sungirl solo 155 310 465 992 1696 2400
35-Captain America & Sungirl app. (1949) 158 316 474 1003 1727 2450
36-38(1954)-Sub-Mariner in all 123 246 369 787 1344 1900
NOTE: *Ayers Human Torch in 36(3). Brodsky c-25, 31-33?, 37, 38. Burgos c-36. Everett a-1-3, 27, 28, 30, 37, 38. Powell a-36(Sub-Mariner). Schomburg c-1-3, 5-8, 10-23. Sekowsky c-28, 34?, 35? Shores c-24, 26, 27, 29, 30. Mickey Spillane text 4-6. Bondage c-2, 12, 19.*

HUMAN TORCH, THE (Also see Avengers West Coast, Fantastic Four, The Invaders, Saga of the Original... & Strange Tales #101)
Marvel Comics Group: Sept, 1974 - No. 8, Nov, 1975
1: 1-8-r/stories from Strange Tales #101-108 5 10 15 30 50 70
2-8: 1st H.T. title since G.A. 7-vs. Sub-Mariner 3 6 9 15 22 28
NOTE: *Golden Age & Silver Age Human Torch-r #1-8. Ayers r-6, 7. Kirby/Ayers r-1-5, 8.*

HUMAN TORCH (From the Fantastic Four)
Marvel Comics: June, 2003 - No. 12, Jun, 2004 ($2.50/$2.99)
1-7-Skottie Young-c/a; Karl Kesel-s 3.00
8-12-($2.99) 8,10-Dodd-a. 9-Young-a. 11-Porter-a. 12-Medina-a 3.00
... Vol. 1: Burn TPB (2005, $7.99, digest size) r/#1-6 8.00

HUMAN TORCH COMICS 70TH ANNIVERSARY SPECIAL
Marvel Comics: July, 2009 ($3.99, one-shot)
1-Covers by Granov and Martin; new story and r/1st app Toro from Human Torch #2 5.00

HUMBUG (Satire by Harvey Kurtzman)
Humbug Publications: Aug, 1957 - No. 9, May, 1958; No. 10, June, 1958; No. 11, Oct, 1958
1-Wood-a (intro pgs. only) 27 54 81 158 259 360
2 15 30 45 85 130 175
3-9: 8-Elvis in Jailbreak Rock 14 28 42 76 108 140
10,11-Magazine format. 10-Photo-c 15 30 45 90 140 190
Bound Volume(#1-9)(extremely rare) 65 130 195 416 708 1000
NOTE: *Davis a-1-11. Elder a-2-4, 6-9, 11. Heath a-2, 4-8, 10. Jaffee a-2, 4-9. Kurtzman a-11.*

HUMDINGER (Becomes White Rider and Super Horse #3 on?)
Novelty Press/Premium Group: May-June, 1946 - V2#2, July-Aug, 1947
1-Jerkwater Line, Mickey Starlight by Don Rico, Dink begin 37 74 111 222 361 500
2 16 32 48 94 147 200
3-6, V2#1,2 12 24 36 69 97 125

HUMONGOUS MAN
Alternative Press (Ikon Press): Sept, 1997 -No. 3 ($2.25, B&W)
1-3-Stepp & Harrison-c/s/a. 3.00

HUMOR (See All Humor Comics)

The Hunger #1 © Speakeasy

Hyperion #1 © MAR

Ibis, The Invincible #5 © FAW

	GD 2.0	VG 4.0	FN 6.0	VF 8.0	VF/NM 9.0	NM- 9.2

HUMPHREY COMICS (Joe Palooka Presents...; also see Joe Palooka)
Harvey Publications: Oct, 1948 - No. 22, Apr, 1952

1-Joe Palooka's pal (r); (52 pgs.)-Powell-a 14 28 42 80 115 150
2,3: Powell-a 9 18 27 47 61 75
4-Boy Heroes app.; Powell-a 9 18 27 50 65 80
5-8,10: 5,6-Powell-a. 7-Little Dot app. 8 16 24 40 50 60
9-Origin Humphrey 9 18 27 47 61 75
11-22 7 14 21 37 46 55

HUNCHBACK OF NOTRE DAME, THE
Dell Publishing Co.: No. 854, Oct, 1957 (one shot)

Four Color 854-Movie, photo-c 11 22 33 73 157 240

HUNGER (See Age of Ultron and Cataclysm titles)
Marvel Comics: Sept, 2013 - No. 4, Dec, 2013 ($3.99, limited series)

1-4-Fialkov-s/Kirk-a/Granov-c; Galactus in the Ultimate Universe. 2-4-Silver Surfer app. 4.00
1-Variant-c by Neal Adams 18.00

HUNGER, THE
Speakeasy Comics: May, 2005 ($2.99)

1-Andy Bradshaw-s/a; Eric Powell-c 3.00

HUNGER DOGS, THE (See DC Graphic Novel #4)

HUNK
Charlton Comics: Aug, 1961 - No. 11, 1963

1 4 8 12 23 37 50
2-11 3 6 9 14 20 25

HUNT, THE
Image Comics (Shadowline): Jul, 2016 - No. 5, Dec, 2016 ($3.99)

1-5-Colin Lorimer-s/a 4.00

HUNTED (Formerly My Love Memoirs)
Fox Features Syndicate: No. 13, July, 1950; No. 2, Sept, 1950

13(#1)-Used in **SOTI**, pg. 42 & illo. "Treating police contemptuously" (lower left);
Hollingsworth bondage-c 43 86 129 271 461 650
2 21 42 63 122 199 275

HUNTER-KILLER
Image Comics (Top Cow): Nov, 2004 - No. 12, Mar, 2007 ($2.99)

0-(11/04, 25¢) Prelude with Silvestri sketch page and Waid afterword 3.00
1-12: 1-(3/05, $2.99) Waid-s/Silvestri-a; four covers. 2-Linsner variant-c 3.00
... Collected Edition Vol. 1 (9/05, $4.99) r/#0-3 5.00
...Dossier 1 (9/05, $2.99) character profiles with art by various; Migliari-c 3.00
... Volume 1 TPB (1/08, $24.99) r/#0-12; Dossier and Script Book; variant covers 25.00

HUNTER: THE AGE OF MAGIC (See Books of Magic)
DC Comics (Vertigo): Sept, 2001 - No. 25, Sept, 2003 ($2.50/$2.75)

1-25: Horrocks-s/Case-a. 1-8-Bolton-c. 14-Begin $2.75-c. 19-Bachalo-c 3.00

HUNTRESS, THE (See All-Star Comics #69, Batman Family, DC Super Stars #17, Detective #652, Infinity, Inc. #1 & Wonder Woman #271)
DC Comics: Apr, 1989 - No. 19, Oct, 1990 ($1.00, mature)

1-Staton-c/a(p) in all 5.00
2-19: 17-19-Batman-c/stories 3.00
...: Darknight Daughter TPB (2006, $19.99) r/origin & early apps. in DC Super Stars #17, Batman Family #18-20 & Wonder Woman #271-287,289,290,294,295; Bolland-c 20.00

HUNTRESS, THE
DC Comics: June, 1994 - No. 4, Sept, 1994 ($1.50, limited series)

1-4-Netzer-c/a: 2-Batman app. 3.00

HUNTRESS (Leads into 2012 World's Finest series)
DC Comics: Dec, 2011 - No. 6, May, 2012 ($2.99, limited series)

1-6-Levitz-s/To-a/March-c 3.00

HUNTRESS: YEAR ONE
DC Comics: Early July, 2008 - No. 6, Late Sept, 2008 ($2.99, limited series)

1-6-Origin re-told; Cliff Richards-a/Ivory Madison-s 3.00
TPB (2009, $17.99) r/#1-6; intro. by Paul Levitz 18.00

HURRICANE COMICS
Cambridge House: 1945 (52 pgs.)

1-(Humor, funny animal) 26 52 78 154 252 350

HUSK
Marvel Comics (Soleil): May, 2010 - No. 2, Jun, 2010 ($5.99, limited series)

1,2-English version of French comic; L'Homme-s/Boudoiron-a 6.00

HYBRIDS
Continunity Comics: Jan, 1994 ($2.50, one-shot)

1-Neal Adams-c(p) & part-a(i); embossed-c. 4.00

HYBRIDS DEATHWATCH 2000
Continuity Comics: Apr, 1993 - No. 3, Aug, 1993 ($2.50)

0-(Giveaway)-Foil-c; Neal Adams-c(i) & plots (also #1,2) 4.00
1-3: 1-Polybagged w/card; die-cut-c. 2-Thermal-c. 3-Polybagged w/card; indestructible-c; Adams plot 4.00

HYBRIDS ORIGIN
Continuity Comics: 1993 - No. 5, Jan, 1994 ($2.50)

1-5: 2,3-Neal Adams-c. 4,5-Valeria the She-Bat app. Adams-c(i) 4.00

HYDE
IDW Publ.: Oct, 2004 ($7.49, one-shot)

1-Steve Niles-s/Nick Stakal 7.50

HYDE-25
Harris Publications: Apr, 1995 ($2.95, one-shot)

0-Coupon for poster; r/Vampirella's 1st app. 3.00

HYDROMAN (See Heroic Comics)

HYPERION (Squadron Supreme)
Marvel Comics: May, 2016 - No. 6, Oct, 2016 ($3.99)

1-6: 1-4,6-Wendig-s/Virella-a. 5-Anindito-a. 5,6-Iron Man & Thundra app. 4.00

HYPERKIND (See Razorline)
Marvel Comics: Sept, 1993 - No. 9, May, 1994 ($1.75/$1.95)

1-($2.50)-Foil embossed-c; by Clive Barker 4.00
2-9 3.00
...Unleashed 1 (8/94, $2.95, 52 pgs., one-shot) 4.00

HYPER MYSTERY COMICS
Hyper Publications: May, 1940 - No. 2, June, 1940 (68 pgs.)

1-Hyper, the Phenomenal begins; Calkins-a 258 516 774 1651 2826 4000
2 142 284 426 909 1555 2200

HYPERNATURALS
BOOM! Studios: Jul, 2012 - No. 12, Jun, 2013 ($3.99)

1-12: 1-Abnett & Lanning-s/Walker & Guinaldo-a; at least eight covers. 2-Two printings 4.00
... Free Comic Book Day Edition (5/12) Prelude to issue #1 3.00

HYPERSONIC
Dark Horse Comics: Nov, 1997 - No. 4, Feb, 1998 ($2.95, limited series)

1-4: Abnett & White-s/Erskine-a 3.00

I AIM AT THE STARS (Movie)
Dell Publishing Co.: No. 1148, Nov-Jan/1960-61 (one-shot)

Four Color 1148-The Werner Von Braun Sty-photo-c 6 12 18 41 76 110

I AM AN AVENGER (See Avengers, Young Avengers and Pet Avengers)
Marvel Comics: Nov, 2010 - No. 5, Mar, 2011 ($3.99, limited series)

1-5-Short stories by various. 1-Yu-c. 2-Land-c. 2-4-Mayhew-a. 3-Noto-c. 4-Acuña-c 4.00

I AM CAPTAIN AMERICA
Marvel Comics: Jan, 2012 ($3.99, one-shot)

1-Collection of Captain America-themed 70th Anniversary covers with artist profiles 4.00

I AM COYOTE (See Eclipse Graphic Album Series & Eclipse Magazine #2)

I AM LEGEND
Eclipse Books: 1991 - No. 4, 1991 ($5.95, B&W, squarebound, 68 pgs.)

1-4: Based on 1954 novel by Richard Matheson 1 2 3 5 6 8

I AM LEGION (English version of French graphic novel Je Suis Légion)
Devils Due Publishing: Jan, 2009 - No. 6, July, 2009 ($3.50)

1-6-John Cassaday-a/Fabien Nury-s; two covers 3.50

IBIS, THE INVINCIBLE (See Fawcett Miniatures, Mighty Midget & Whiz)
Fawcett Publications: 1942 (Fall?); #2, Mar.,1943; #3, Wint, 1945 - #5, Fall, 1946; #6, Spring, 1948

1-Origin Ibis; Raboy-c; on sale 1/2/43 271 542 813 1734 2967 4200
2-Bondage-c (on sale 2/5/43) 113 226 339 718 1234 1750
3-Wolverton-a #3-6 (4 pgs. each) 77 154 231 493 847 1200
4-6: 5-Bondage-c 53 106 159 334 567 800

NOTE: *Mac Raboy c(p)-3-5. Schaffenberger c-6.*

I-BOTS (See Isaac Asimov's I-BOTS)

ICE AGE ON THE WORLD OF MAGIC: THE GATHERING (See Magic The Gathering)

Icon #15 © Milestone

Idolized #1 © David Schwartz

I Hate Fairyland #4 © Skottie Young

	GD 2.0	VG 4.0	FN 6.0	VF 8.0	VF/NM 9.0	NM- 9.2

ICE KING OF OZ, THE (See First Comics Graphic Novel #13)

ICEMAN (Also see The Champions & X-Men #94)
Marvel Comics Group: Dec, 1984 - No. 4, June, 1985 (Limited series)

1,2,4: Zeck covers on all 4.00
3-The Defenders, Champions (Ghost Rider) & the original X-Men x-over 5.00

ICEMAN (X-Men)
Marvel Comics: Dec, 2001 - No. 4, Mar, 2002 ($2.50, limited series)

1-4-Abnett & Lanning-s/Kerschl-a 3.00

ICEMAN AND ANGEL (X-Men)
Marvel Comics: May, 2011 ($2.99, one-shot)

1-Brian Clevinger-s/Juan Doe-a; Goom & Googam app. 3.00

ICON
DC Comics (Milestone): May, 1993 - No. 42, Feb, 1997($1.50/$1.75/$2.50)

1-($2.95)-Collector's Edition polybagged w/poster & trading card (direct sale only) 4.00
1-24,30-42: 9-Simonson-c. 15,16-Worlds Collide Pt. 4 & 11. 15-Superboy app. 16-Superman-c/story. 40-Vs. Blood Syndicate 3.00
25-($2.95, 52 pgs.) 4.00
... A Hero's Welcome SC (2009, $19.99) r/#1-8; intro. by Reginald Hudlin 20.00
...: Mothership Connection SC (2010, $24.99) r/#13,19-22,24-27,30 25.00

IDAHO
Dell Publishing Co.: June-Aug, 1963 - No. 8, July-Sept, 1965

	GD	VG	FN	VF	VF/NM	NM-
1	3	6	9	16	24	32
2-8: 5-7-Painted-c	2	4	6	9	13	16

IDEAL (... a Classical Comic) (2nd Series) (Love Romances No. 6 on)
Timely Comics: July, 1948 - No. 5, March, 1949 (Feature length stories)

	GD	VG	FN	VF	VF/NM	NM-
1-Antony & Cleopatra	37	74	111	222	361	500
2-The Corpses of Dr. Sacotti	31	62	93	186	303	420
3-Joan of Arc; used in **SOTI,** pg. 310 'Boer War'	29	58	87	172	281	390
4-Richard the Lion-hearted; titled "...the World's Greatest Comics"; The Witness story	40	80	120	246	411	575
5-Ideal Love & Romance; change to love; photo-c	20	40	60	117	189	260

IDEAL COMICS (1st Series) (Willie Comics No. 5 on)
Timely Comics (MgPC): Fall, 1944 - No. 4, Spring, 1946

	GD	VG	FN	VF	VF/NM	NM-
1-Funny animal; Super Rabbit in all	39	78	117	240	395	550
2	21	42	63	122	199	275
3,4	19	38	57	111	176	240

IDEAL LOVE & ROMANCE (See Ideal, A Classical Comic)

IDEAL ROMANCE (Formerly Tender Romance)
Key Publ.: No. 3, April, 1954 - No. 8, Feb, 1955 (Diary Confessions No. 9 on)

	GD	VG	FN	VF	VF/NM	NM-
3-Bernard Baily-c	11	22	33	60	83	105
4-8: 4-6-B. Baily-c	8	16	24	44	57	70

IDEALS (Secret Stories)
Ideals Publ., USA: 1981 (68 pgs, graphic novels, 7x10", stiff-c)

	GD	VG	FN	VF	VF/NM	NM-
Captain America - Star Spangled Super Hero	3	6	9	19	30	40
Fantastic Four - Cosmic Quartet	3	6	9	19	30	40
Incredible Hulk - Gamma Powered Goliath	3	6	9	19	30	40
Spider-Man - World Famous Wall Crawler	4	8	12	23	37	50

IDENTITY CRISIS
DC Comics: Aug, 2004 - No. 7, Feb, 2005 ($3.95, limited series)

1-Meltzer-s/Morales-a/Turner-c in all; Sue Dibny murdered 5.00
1-(Second printing) black-c with white sketch lines 5.00
1-(3rd & 4th) 3rd-Bloody broken photo glass image-c by Morales. 4th-Turner red-c 4.00
1-Diamond Retailer Summit Edition with sketch-c 30.00
1-Special Edition (6/09, $1.00) r/#1 with "After Watchmen" cover frame 3.00
2-7: 2-4-Deathstroke app. 5-Firestorm, Jack Drake, Capt. Boomerang killed 4.00
2-(Second printing) new Morales sketch-c 4.00
Final printings for all issues with red background variant covers 4.00
HC (2005, $24.99, dust jacket) r/series; Director's Cut extras; cover gallery; Whedon intro.; 2 covers: Direct Market-c by Turner, Bookstore-c with Morales-a 25.00
SC (2006, $14.99) r/series; Director's Cut extras; cover gallery; Whedon intro 15.00

IDENTITY DISC
Marvel Comics: Aug, 2004 - No. 5, Dec, 2004 ($2.99, limited series)

1-5-Sabretooth, Bullseye, Sandman, Vulture, Deadpool, Juggernaut app.; Higgins-a 4.00
TPB (2004, $13.99) r/#1-5 14.00

IDES OF BLOOD
DC Comics (WildStorm): Oct, 2010 - No. 6, Mar, 2011 ($3.99/$2.99, limited series)

1-6-Stuart Paul-s/Christian Duce-a/Michael Geiger-c; Roman Empire vampires 4.00

I DIE AT MIDNIGHT (Vertigo V2K)
DC Comics (Vertigo): 2000 ($6.95, prestige format, one-shot)

1-Kyle Baker-s/a 7.00

IDOL
Marvel Comics (Epic Comics): 1992 - No. 3, 1992 ($2.95, mini-series, 52 pgs.)

Book 1-3 4.00

IDOLIZED
Aspen MLT: No. 0, Jun, 2012 - No. 5, Apr, 2013 ($2.50/$3.99)

0-($2.50) Schwartz-s/Gunnell-a; regular & photo covers; Superhero Idol background 3.00
1-5-($3.99) 1-Art Adams & photo covers; origin of Joule 4.00

I DREAM OF JEANNIE (TV)
Dell Publishing Co.: Apr, 1965 - No. 2, Dec, 1966 (Photo-c)

	GD	VG	FN	VF	VF/NM	NM-
1-Barbara Eden photo-c, each	12	24	36	79	170	260
2	9	18	27	63	129	195

I FEEL SICK
Slave Labor Graphics: Aug, 1999 - No. 2, May, 2000 ($3.95, limited series)

1,2-Jhonen Vasquez-s/a 4.00

I HATE FAIRYLAND
Image Comics: Oct, 2015 - Present ($3.50)

1-10-Skottie Young-s/a/c; each has variant cover with "F*** Fairyland" title 3.50

I HATE GALLANT GIRL
Image Comics (Shadowline): Nov, 2008 - No. 3, Jan, 2009 ($3.50, limited series)

1-3-Kat Cahill-s/Seth Damoose-a 3.50

I (heart) MARVEL
Marvel Comics: Apr, 2006; May, 2006 ($2.99, one-shots)

...: Marvel AI 1 (4/06) Cebulski-s; manga art by various; Vision, Daredevil, Elektra app. 3.00
...: Masked Intentions 1 (5/06) Squirrel Girl, Speedball, Firestar, Justice app.; Nicieza-s 3.00
...: My Mutant Heart 1 (4/06) Wolverine, Cannonball, Doop app. 3.00
...: Outlaw Love 1 (4/06) Bullseye, The Answer, Ruby Thursday app.; Nicieza-s 3.00
...: Web of Romance 1 (4/06) Spider-Man, Mary Jane, The Avengers app. 3.00

ILLEGITIMATES, THE
IDW Publishing: Dec, 2013 - No. 6, May, 2014 ($3.99)

1-6: 1-Taran Killam & Marc Andreyko-a/Kevin Sharpe-a; covers by Ordway & Willingham 4.00

ILLUMUNATI
Marvel Comics: Jan, 2016 - No. 7, Jul, 2016 ($3.99)

1-7: 1-Williamson-s/Crystal-a; The Hood, Titania and others team. 4-Thor app. 4.00

ILLUMINATOR
Marvel Comics/Nelson Publ.: 1993 - No. 4, 1993 ($4.99/$2.95, 52 pgs.)

1,2-($4.99) Religious themed 5.00
3,4 4.00

ILLUSTRATED GAGS
United Features Syndicate: No. 16, 1940

	GD	VG	FN	VF	VF/NM	NM-
Single Series 16	19	38	57	111	176	240

ILLUSTRATED LIBRARY OF..., AN (See Classics Illustrated Giants)

ILLUSTRATED STORIES OF THE OPERAS
Baily (Bernard) Publ. Co.: 1943 (16 pgs.; B&W) (25 cents) (covers are black,yellow & red, with scarcer editions having B&W with red)

	GD	VG	FN	VF	VF/NM	NM-
nn-(Rare)(4 diff. issues)-Faust (part-r in Cisco Kid #1, 2 cover versions: 25¢ & no price) nn-Aida, nn-Carmen; Baily-a, nn-Rigoletto	69	138	207	442	759	1075

ILLUSTRATED STORY OF ROBIN HOOD & HIS MERRY MEN, THE (See Classics Giveaways, 12/44)

ILLUSTRATED TARZAN BOOK, THE (See Tarzan Book)

I LOVED (Formerly Rulah; Colossal Features Magazine No. 33 on)
Fox Features Syndicate: No. 28, July, 1949 - No. 32, Mar, 1950

	GD	VG	FN	VF	VF/NM	NM-
28	20	40	60	114	182	250
29-32	15	30	45	85	130	175

I LOVE LUCY
Eternity Comics : 6/90 - No. 6, 1990;V2#1, 11/90 - No. 6, 1991 ($2.95, B&W, mini-series)

1-6: Reprints 1950s comic strip; photo-c 4.00
Book II #1-6: Reprints comic strip; photo-c 4.00

	GD	VG	FN	VF	VF/NM	NM-
...In Full Color 1 (1991, $5.95, 52 pgs.)-Reprints I Love Lucy Comics #4,5,8,16; photo-c with embossed logo (2 versions exist, one with pgs. 18 & 19 reversed, the other corrected)	1	2	3	5	6	8

I Love Lucy #24 © Desilu

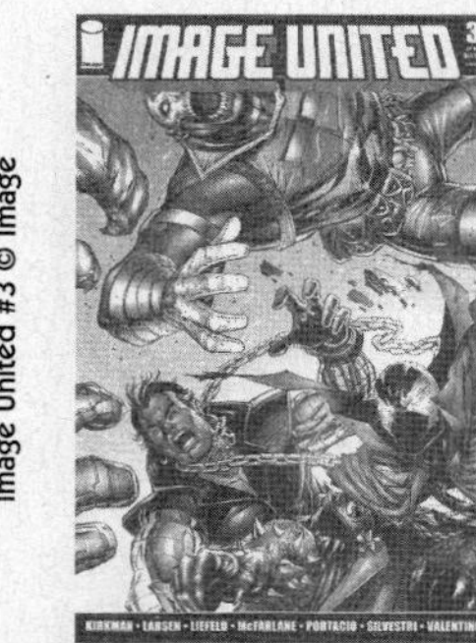

Image United #3 © Image

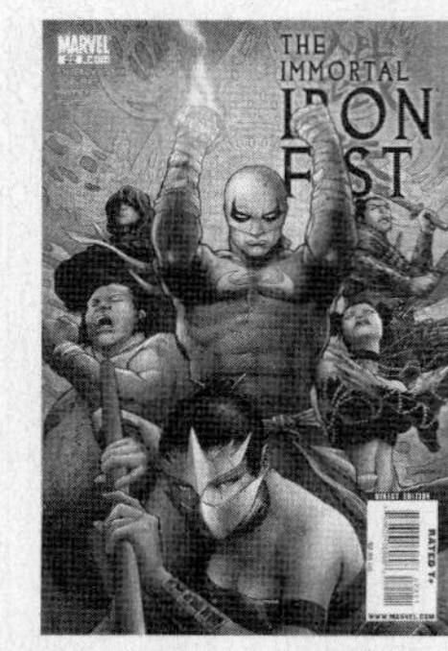

Immortal Iron Fist #22 © MAR

	GD	VG	FN	VF	VF/NM	NM-
	2.0	4.0	6.0	8.0	9.0	9.2

...In 3-D 1 (1991, $3.95, w/glasses)-Reprints I Love Lucy Comics; photo-c; bagged 6.00

I LOVE LUCY COMICS (TV) (Also see The Lucy Show)
Dell Publishing Co.: No. 535, Feb, 1954 - No. 35, Apr-June, 1962 (Lucille Ball photo-c on all)

Four Color 535(#1) 44 88 132 326 738 1150
Four Color 559(#2, 5/54) 27 54 81 189 420 650
3 (8-10/54) - 5 15 30 45 105 233 360
6-10 12 24 36 84 185 285
11-20 10 20 30 66 138 210
21-35 9 18 27 57 111 165

I LOVE NEW YORK
Linsner.com: 2002 ($2.95, B&W, one-shot)

1-Linsner-s/a; benefit book for the Sept. 11 charities 3.00

I LOVE YOU
Fawcett Publications: June, 1950 (one-shot)

1-Photo-c 15 30 45 86 133 180

I LOVE YOU (Formerly In Love)
Charlton Comics: No. 7, 9/55 - No. 121, 12/76; No. 122, 3/79 - No. 130, 5/80

7-Kirby-c; Powell-a 8 16 24 54 102 150
8-10 5 10 15 30 50 70
11-16,18-20 4 8 12 27 44 60
17-(68 pg. Giant) 6 12 18 41 76 110
21-50: 26-No Torres-a 3 6 9 20 31 42
51-59 3 6 9 16 23 30
60-(1/66)-Elvis Presley line drawn c/story 14 28 42 96 211 325
61-85 2 4 6 11 16 20
86-90,92-98,100-110 2 4 6 8 10 12
91-(5/71) Ditko-a (5 pgs.) 2 4 6 13 18 22
99-David Cassidy pin-up 2 4 6 10 14 18
111-113,115-130 1 3 4 6 8 10
114-Psychedelic cover 3 6 9 17 26 35

I, LUSIPHUR (Becomes Poison Elves, 1st series #8 on)
Mulehide Graphics: 1991 - No. 7, 1992 (B&W, magazine size)

1-Drew Hayes-c/a/scripts 4 8 12 25 40 55
2,4,5 3 6 9 14 20 25
3-Low print run 4 8 12 27 44 60
6,7 2 4 6 8 11 14
Poison Elves: Requiem For An Elf (Sirius Ent., 6/96, $14.95, trade paperback)
-Reprints I, Lusiphur #1,2 as text, and 3-6 15.00

I'M A COP
Magazine Enterprises: 1954 - No. 3, 1954

1(A-1 #111)-Powell-c/a in all 15 30 45 88 137 185
2(A-1 #126), 3(A-1 #128) 10 20 30 56 76 95

IMAGE COMICS HARDCOVER
Image Comics: 2005 ($24.99, hardcover with dust jacket)

Vol. 1-New Spawn by McFarlane-s/a; Savage Dragon origin by Larsen; CyberForce by Silvestri; ShadowHawk by Valentino; intro by Marder; Image timeline 25.00

IMAGE COMICS SUMMER SPECIAL
Image Comics: July, 2004 (Free Comic Book Day giveaway)

1-New short stories of Spawn, Invincible, Savage Dragon and Witchblade 3.00

IMAGE FIRST
Image Comics: 2005 ($6.99, TPB)

Vol. 1 (2005) r/Strange Girl #1, Sea of Red #1, The Walking Dead #1 and Girls #1
2 4 6 11 16 20

IMAGE GRAPHIC NOVEL
Image Int.: 1984 ($6.95)(Advertised as Pacific Comics Graphic Novel #1)

1-The Seven Samuroid; Brunner-c/a 12.00

IMAGE HOLIDAY SPECIAL 2005
Image Comics: 2005 ($9.99, TPB)

nn-Holiday-themed short stories by various incl. Larsen, Kurtz, Kirkman, Valentino 10.00

IMAGE INTRODUCES...
Image Comics: Oct, 2001 - June, 2002 ($2.95, anthology)

Believer #1-Schamberger-s/Thurman & Molder-a; Legend of Isis preview 3.00
Cryptopia #1-Raab-s/Quinn-a 3.00
Dog Soldiers #1-Hunter-s/Pachoumis-a 3.00
Legend of Isis #1-Valdez-a 3.00
Primate #1-Two covers; Beau Smith & Bernhardt-s/Byrd-a 3.00

	GD	VG	FN	VF	VF/NM	NM-
	2.0	4.0	6.0	8.0	9.0	9.2

IMAGES OF A DISTANT SOIL
Image Comics: Feb, 1997 ($2.95, B&W, one-shot)

1-Sketches by various 3.00

IMAGES OF SHADOWHAWK (Also see Shadowhawk)
Image Comics: Sept, 1993 - No. 3, 1994 ($1.95, limited series)

1-3: Keith Giffen-c/a; Trencher app. 3.00

IMAGE 20 (FREE COMIC BOOK DAY 2012...)
Image Comics: May, 2012 (giveaway, one-shot)

nn-Previews of Revival, Guarding the Globe, It-Girl and the Atomics, Near Death 3.00

IMAGE TWO-IN-ONE
Image Comics: Mar, 2001 ($2.95, 48 pgs., B&W, one-shot)

1-Two stories; 24 pages produced in 24 hrs. by Larsen and Eliopoulos 4.00

IMAGE UNITED
Image Comics: No. 0, Mar, 2010; Nov, 2009 - No. 6 ($3.99, limited series)

0-(3/10, $2.99) Fortress and Savage Dragon app. 3.00
1-3-($3.99) Image character crossover; Kirkman-s; art by Larsen, Liefeld, McFarlane, Portacio, Silvestri and Valentino; Spawn, Witchblade, Savage Dragon, Youngblood, Cyberforce and Shadowhawk app. Multiple covers on each 4.00
1-Jim Lee variant-c 8.00

IMAGE ZERO
Image Comics: 1993 (Received through mail w/coupons from Image books)

0-Savage Dragon, StormWatch, Shadowhawk, Strykeforce; 1st app. Troll; 1st app. McFarlane's Freak, Blotch, Sweat and Bludd 5.00

IMAGINARIES, THE
Image Comics: Mar, 2005 - No. 4, June, 2005 ($2.95, limited series)

1-4-Mike S. Miller & Ben Avery-s; Miller & Titus-a 3.00

IMAGINE AGENTS
BOOM! Studios: Oct, 2013 - No. 4, Jan, 2014 ($3.99, limited series)

1-4-Brian Joines-s/Bachan-a 4.00

I'M DICKENS - HE'S FENSTER (TV)
Dell Publishing Co.: May-July, 1963 - No. 2, Aug-Oct, 1963 (Photo-c)

1 5 10 15 33 57 80
2 5 10 15 30 50 70

I MET A HANDSOME COWBOY
Dell Publishing Co.: No. 324, Mar, 1951

Four Color 324 7 14 21 49 92 135

IMMORTAL DOCTOR FATE, THE
DC Comics: Jan, 1985 - No. 3, Mar, 1985 ($1.25, limited series)

1-3: 1-Simonson-c/a. 2-Giffen-c/a(p) 4.00

IMMORTAL IRON FIST, THE (Also see Iron Fist)
Marvel Comics: Jan, 2007 - No. 27, Aug, 2009 ($2.99/$3.99)

1-Brubaker & Fraction-s/Aja-c/a; origin retold; intro. Orson Randall
1 3 4 6 8 10
1-Variant-c by Dell'Otto 3 6 9 17 26 35
1-Director's Cut ($3.99) r/#1 and 8-page story from Civil War: Choosing Sides; script excerpt; character designs; sketch and inks art; cover variant and concepts 4.00
2,3 1 2 3 5 6 8
4-13,15-26: 6,17-20-Flashback-a by Heath. 8-1st Immortal weapons. 21-Green-a 3.00
14,27: 14-($3.99) Heroes For Hire app. 27-Last issue; 2 covers; Foreman & Lapham-a 4.00
Annual 1 (11/07, $3.99) Brubaker & Fraction-s/Chaykin, Brereton & J. Djurdjevic-a 4.00
... Orson Randall and the Death Queen of California (11/08, $3.99) art by Camuncoli 4.00
... Orson Randall and the Green Mist of Death (4/08, $3.99) art by Heath and various 4.00
...: The Origin of Danny Rand (2008, $3.99) r/Marvel Premiere #15-16 recolored 4.00
... Vol. 1: The Last Iron Fist Story HC (2007, $19.99, dustjacket) r/#1-6, story from Civil War: Choosing Sides; sketch pages 20.00
... Vol. 1: The Last Iron Fist Story SC (2007, $14.99) same content as HC 15.00
... Vol. 2: The Seven Capital Cities HC (2008, $24.99, dustjacket) r/#8-14 & Annual #1 25.00

IMMORTALIS (See Mortigan Goth: Immortalis)

IMMORTAL II
Image Comics: Apr, 1997 - No. 5, Feb, 1998 ($2.50, B&W&Grey, limited series)

1-5: 1-B&W w/ color pull-out poster 3.00

IMMORTAL WEAPONS (Also see Immortal Iron Fist)
Marvel Comics: Sept, 2009 - No. 5, Jan, 2010 ($3.99, limited series)

1-5: Back-up Iron Fist stories in all. 1-Origin of Fat Cobra. 2-Brereton-a 4.00

IMPACT

Imperium #16 © VAL

Impulse #70 © DC

Incredible Hulk #102 © MAR

GD VG FN VF VF/NM NM-
2.0 4.0 6.0 8.0 9.0 9.2

E. C. Comics: Mar-Apr, 1955 - No. 5, Nov-Dec, 1955

1-Not code approved; classic Holocaust story 21 42 63 168 272 375
1-Variant printed by Charlton. Title logo is white instead of yellow and print quality is inferior. Distributed to newsstands before being destroyed & reprinted (scarce)
29 58 87 232 366 500
2 13 26 39 104 165 225
3-5: 4-Crandall-a 11 22 33 88 139 190

NOTE: ***Crandall** a-1-4. **Davis** a-2-4; c-1-5. **Evans** a-1, 4, 5. **Ingels** a-in all. **Kamen** a-3. **Krigstein** a-1, 5. **Orlando** a-2, 5.*

IMPACT
Gemstone Publishing: Apr, 1999 - No. 5, Aug, 1999 ($2.50)

1-5-Reprints E.C. series 4.00

IMPACT CHRISTMAS SPECIAL
DC Comics (Impact Comics): 1991 ($2.50, 68 pgs.)

1-Gift of the Magi by Infantino/Rogers; The Black Hood, The Fly, The Jaguar, & The Shield stories 4.00

IMPERIAL
Image Comics: Aug, 2014 - No. 4, Nov, 2014 ($2.99, limited series)

1-4-Seagle-s/Dos Santos-a 3.00

IMPERIAL GUARD
Marvel Comics: Jan, 1997 - No. 3, Mar, 1997 ($1.95, limited series)

1-3: Augustyn-s in all; 1-Wraparound-c 3.00

IMPERIUM
Valiant Entertainment: Mar, 2015 - No. 16, May, 2016 ($3.99)

1-16: 1-4-Dysart-s/Braithwaite-a. 5-8-Eaton-a. 9-12-The Vine Imperative; Cafu-a 4.00

IMPOSSIBLE MAN SUMMER VACATION SPECTACULAR, THE
Marvel Comics: Aug, 1990; No. 2, Sept, 1991 ($2.00, 68 pgs.) (See Fantastic Four#11)

1-Spider Man, Quasar, Dr. Strange, She-Hulk, Punisher & Dr. Doom stories; Barry Crain, Guice-a; Art Adams-c(i) 4.00
2-Ka Zar & Thor app.; Cable Wolverine-c app. 4.00

IMPULSE (See Flash #92, 2nd Series for 1st app.) (Also see Young Justice)
DC Comics: Apr, 1995 - No. 89, Oct, 2002 ($1.50/$1.75/$1.95/$2.25/$2.50)

1-Mark Waid scripts & Humberto Ramos-c/a(p) begin; brief retelling of origin 6.00
2-12: 9-XS from Legion (Impulse's cousin) comes to the 20th Century, returns to the 30th Century in #12. 10-Dead Heat Pt. 3 (cont'd in Flash #110). 11-Dead Heat Pt. 4 (cont'd in Flash #111); Johnny Quick dies. 4.00
13-25: 14-Trickster app. 17-Zatanna-c/app. 21-Legion-c/app. 22-Jesse Quick-c/app. 24-Origin; Flash app. 25-Last Ramos-a. 3.00
26-55: 26-Rousseau-a begins. 28-1st new Arrowette (see World's Finest #113). 30-Genesis x-over. 47-Superman-c/app. 50-Batman & Joker-c/app. Van Sciver-a begins 3.00
56-62: 56-Young Justice app. 3.00
63-89: 63-Begin $2.50-c. 66-JLA,JSA-c/app. 68,69-Adam Strange, GL app. 77-Our Worlds at War x-over; Young Justice-c/app. 85-World Without Young Justice x-over pt. 2. 3.00
#1,000,000 (11/98) John Fox app. 3.00
Annual 1 (1996, $2.95)-Legends of the Dead Earth; Parobeck-a 4.00
Annual 2 (1997, $3.95)-Pulp Heroes stories; Orbik painted-c 4.00
.../Atom Double-Shot 1(2/98, $1.95) Jurgens-s/Mhan-a 3.00
...: Bart Saves the Universe (4/99, $5.95) JSA app. 6.00
...Plus (9/97, $2.95) w/Gross Out (Scare Tactics)-c/app. 4.00
...Reckless Youth (1997, $14.95, TPB) r/Flash #92-94, Impulse #1-6 15.00

INCAL, THE
Marvel Comics (Epic): Nov, 1988 - No. 3, Jan, 1989 ($10.95/$12.95, mature)

1-3: Moebius-c/a in all; sexual content 16.00

INCOGNEGRO
DC Comics (Vertigo): 2008 ($19.99, B&W, hardcover graphic novel with dustjacket)

HC-Mat Johnson-s/Warren Pleece-a 20.00

INCOGNITO
Marvel Comics (Icon): Dec, 2008 - No. 6, Aug, 2009 ($3.50/$3.99, limited series)

1-5-Brubaker-s/Phillips-a/c; pulp noir-style 3.50
6-($3.99) Bonus history of the Zeppelin pulps 4.00
...: Bad Influences (10/10 - No. 5, 4/11, $3.50) 1-5 Brubaker-s/Phillips-a/c 3.50

INCOMPLETE DEATH'S HEAD (Also see Death's Head)
Marvel Comics UK: Jan, 1993 - No. 12, Dec, 1993 ($1.75, limited series)

1-($2.95, 56 pgs.)-Die-cut cover 4.00
2-11: 2-Re-intro original Death's Head. 3-Original Death's Head vs. Dragon's Claws 3.00
12-($2.50, 52 pgs.)-She Hulk app. 4.00

INCORRUPTIBLE (Also see Irredeemable)

GD VG FN VF VF/NM NM-
2.0 4.0 6.0 8.0 9.0 9.2

BOOM! Studios: Dec, 2000 - No. 30, May, 2012 ($3.99)

1-30: 1-Waid-s/Diaz-a; 3 covers 4.00
1-Artist Edition (12/11, $3.99) r/#1 in B&W with bonus sketch and design art 4.00

INCREDIBLE HERCULES (Continued from Incredible Hulk #112, Jan, 2008)
Marvel Comics: No. 113, Feb, 2008 - No. 141, Apr, 2010 ($2.99/$3.99)

113-125: 113-Ares and Wonder Man app.; Art Adams-c. 116-Romita Jr-c; Eternals app. 3.00
113-Variant-c by Pham 5.00
126-($3.99) Hercules origin retold; back-up story w/Miyazawa-a 4.00
127-137: 128-Dark Avengers app. 132-Replacement Thor. 136-Thor app. 3.00
138-141-($3.99) Assault on New Olympus; Avengers app. 4.00

INCREDIBLE HULK, THE (See Aurora, The Avengers #1, The Defenders #1, Giant-Size..., Hulk, Marvel Collectors Item Classics, Marvel Comics Presents #26, Marvel Fanfare, Marvel Treasury Edition, Power Record Comics, Rampaging Hulk, She-Hulk, 2099 Unlimited & World War Hulk)

INCREDIBLE HULK, THE
Marvel Comics: May, 1962 - No. 6, Mar, 1963; No. 102, Apr, 1968 - No. 474, Mar, 1999

1-Origin & 1st app. (skin is grey colored); Kirby pencils begin, end #5
4500 9000 16,000 48,000 144,000 240,000
2-1st green skinned Hulk; Kirby/Ditko-a 383 766 1149 3256 7378 11,500
3-Origin retold; 1st app. Ringmaster (9/62) 241 482 723 1988 4494 7000
4,5: 4-Brief origin retold 186 372 558 1535 3468 5400
6-(3/63) Intro. Teen Brigade; all Ditko-a 179 358 537 1477 3339 5200
102-(4/68) (Continued from Tales to Astonish #101)-Origin retold; Hulk in Asgard; Enchantress & Executioner app; Gary Friedrich-s begin 24 48 72 168 372 575
103-1st Space Parasite 10 20 30 64 132 200
104-Hulk vs. the Rhino 10 20 30 64 132 200
105-110: 105-1st Missing Link. 106-vs. Missing Link; Nick Fury & SHIELD app; Trimpe pencils begin (continues through issue #193). 107,108-vs. the Mandarin. 108-Nick Fury & SHIELD app.; Stan Lee-s (continues through issue #120). 109,110-Ka-Zar app.
7 14 21 46 86 125
111-117: 111-Ka-Zar app.; 1st Galaxy Master. 112-Origin of the Galaxy Master. 113-vs. Sandman. 114-Sandman & Mandarin vs. the Hulk. 115-117-vs. the Leader
5 10 15 33 57 80
118-Hulk vs. Sub-Mariner 6 12 18 41 76 110
119,120,123-125: 119-Maximus (of the Inhumans) app. 120-Last Stan Lee plot, Roy Thomas script; Maximus app. 123,124-vs. The Leader. 124-1st Sal Buscema-p (as a fill-in). 125-vs. the Absorbing Man 4 8 12 27 44 60
121-Roy Thomas-s begin; 1st app. and origin of the Glob
5 10 15 33 57 80
122-Hulk battles Thing (12/69); Fantastic Four app. 8 16 24 54 102 150
126-1st Barbara Norriss (becomes Valkyrie in Defenders #4); story continued from Sub-Mariner #22 (see Dr. Strange #183 for pt.1); Dr. Strange gives up being Sorcerer Supreme 5 10 15 35 63 90
127,129,130,132-139: 127-Tryannus & the Mole Man app; 1st app. Mogol. 129-Leader revives the Glob. 130-(story continues from Captain Marvel #21); 132-HYDRA app. 134-1st Golem. 135-Kang & Phantom Eagle app. 136-1st Xeron the Starslayer; Abomination cameo. 137-Xeron app. Hulk vs. Abomination. 138-Sandman app. 139-Leader app; Hulk story continues in Avengers #88 3 6 9 21 33 45
128-Avengers app. 4 8 12 27 44 60
131-1st Jim Wilson; Iron Man app. 5 10 15 30 50 70
140-Writtem by Harlan Ellison; 1st Jarella (Hulk's love); story continues from Avengers #88; battles Psyklop 4 8 12 25 40 55
140-2nd printing 2 4 6 8 10 12
141-1st app. Doc Samson (7/71) 10 20 30 66 138 210
142-2nd Valkyrie app. (Samantha Parrington) (see Avengers #82 for 1st Marvel Valkyrie); Enchantress app. 4 8 12 27 44 60
143,144-Doctor Doom app. 3 6 9 19 30 40
145-(52-pgs)-Origin retold 4 8 12 28 47 65
146-151: 146,147-Richard Nixon & Yhe Leader app. 148-Jarella app. 149-1st app. The Inheritor. 150-Havok app. 151-Has minor Ant-Man app.
3 6 9 17 26 35
152,153: Hulk on trial; Daredevil, Fantastic Four, Avengers app.
3 6 9 19 30 40
154-Ant-Man app; story coincides with Ant-Man's re-intro in Marvel Feature #4; Hydra & the Chameleon app. 3 6 9 19 30 40
155-160: 155-1st Shaper of Worlds. 156-Jarella app. 157,158-the Leader & Rhino app. 158-Counter-Earth & the High Evolutionary app. 159-Steve Englehart-s begin; Hulk vs. Abomination. 160-vs. Tiger Shark app. 3 6 9 17 26 35
161-The Mimic dies; Beast app. 5 10 15 31 53 75
162-1st app. The Wendigo (4/73) Beast app. 8 16 24 54 102 150
163-165,170,173,174,179: 163-1st app. The Gremlin. 164-1st Capt. Omen & Colonel John D. Armbuster. 165-Capt. Omen app; 1st Aquon. 173,174-vs the Cobalt Man. 179-Return of the Missing Link; 1st Len Wein-s 3 6 9 15 22 28
166-169,171: 166-1st Zzzax; Hawkeye app.; story continues into Defenders #7. 167-Hulk vs.

Incredible Hulk #235 © MAR

Incredible Hulk #261 © MAR

Incredible Hulk #386 © MAR

	GD 2.0	VG 4.0	FN 6.0	VF 8.0	VF/NM 9.0	NM- 9.2
MODOK. 168-1st Harpy (transformed Betty Ross; also seen briefly in nudity panels) 169-1st Bi-Beast; MODOK and A.I.M app; Harpy transformed back into Betty. 171-vs. Abomination; last Englehart-s	3	6	9	16	24	32
172-X-Men cameo; origin Juggernaut retold	4	8	12	27	44	60
175-Black Bolt/Inhumans c/story	3	6	9	17	26	35
176-Hulk on Counter-Earth; Man-Beast app; Warlock cameo (2 panels only)	3	6	9	15	22	28
177-1st actual death of Warlock (last panel only); Man-Beast app.	4	8	12	27	44	60
178-Rebirth of Warlock (story continues in Strange Tales #178)	4	8	12	27	44	60
180-(10/74)-1st brief app. Wolverine (last pg.)	27	54	81	194	435	675
181-(11/74)-1st full Wolverine story; Trimpe-a	350	700	1050	1750	2625	3500
182-Wolverine cameo; see Giant-Size X-Men #1 for next app.; 1st Crackajack Jackson	12	24	36	79	170	260
183-192,194-196,199: 183-Zzzax app. 184-vs. Warlord Kraa. 185-Death of Col. Armbuster. 186-1st Devastator. 187-188-vs. the Gremlin, Nick Fury app. 189-Mole Man app. 190-1st Glorian; Shaper of Worlds app. 191-vs. the Toad Men; Glorian & Shaper of Worlds app. 194-vs. the Locust; 1st Sal Buscema-p (through #309). 195-Abomination & Hulk team-up. 196-Hulk vs. Abomination. 199-Hulk vs. SHIELD & Doc Samson; Nick Fury app.	2	4	6	10	14	20
193-vs. Doc Samson c/story; last regular Trimpe-p	2	4	6	10	18	25
197-Collector, Man-Thing & Glob app; Wrightson-c	3	6	9	17	26	35
198-Collector, Man-Thing & Glob app.	3	6	9	16	23	30
198,199, 201,202-(30¢-c variants, lim. distribution)	5	10	15	35	63	90
200-(25¢-c) Silver Surfer app. (illusion only); anniversary issue	3	6	9	21	33	40
200-(30¢-c variant, limited distribution)(6/76)	6	12	18	38	69	100
201-205,208-211,213,215-220: 201-Conan swipe-c/sty (vs. Bronak the Barbarian). 202-Jarella app.; Psyklop cameo. 203-Jarella app.; death of Psyklop. 204-Trimpe-p; alternate Hulk origin. 205-Death of Jarella; vs. the Crypto Man. 208-Absorbing Man app. 209-Hulk vs. Absorbing Man. 210,211-Hulk team-up with Dr. Druid vs. the Maha Yogi. 213-1st Quintronic Man. 215,216-vs. the second Bi-Beast. 218-Doc Samson vs. the Rhino (no Hulk in story). 219-220-vs. Captain Barracuda	2	4	6	8	10	12
206,207-Defenders app.	2	4	6	9	12	15
212,214: 212-1st app. The Constrictor. 214-Hulk vs. Jack of Hearts (1st app. outside of B&W magazines)	2	4	6	9	12	15
212-216-(35¢-c variant, limited distribution)	10	20	30	64	132	200
221-227,230-231: 221-Stingray app. 222-Last Wein-s; Jim Starlin co-plot and (p). 223-The Leader returns; Roger Stern-s begin. 224-225-vs. The Leader. 227-Original Avengers app. (in dream sequence)	1	2	3	5	7	9
228-1st female Moonstone (Karla Sofen) (10/78)	3	6	9	16	23	30
229-2nd app. new Moonstone	2	4	6	8	10	12
232,233: 232-Captain America x-over from Captain America #230; vs. Moonstone, Vamp and 'the Corporation'; Marvel Man (Quasar) app. 233-Marvel Man app. (Quasar)	1	3	4	6	8	10
234-(4/79)-Marvel Man formally changes his name to Quasar	2	4	6	10	18	25
235-249: 235-237-Machine Man app. 238-President Jimmy Carter app. 241-243-vs. Tyrannus. 243-Last Stern-s. 244-vs. It the Living Colossus. 245-1st Mantlo-s (through #313); 1st app. The Super-Mandroid (Col. Talbot); Captain Mar-Vell cameo. 246-Captain Mar-Vell app.; Hulk vs. Super-Mandroid. 247-Minor Captain Mar-Vell app. 248-vs. the Gardener. 249-Steve Ditko-p	1	2	3	5	6	8
250-Giant-Size (square-bound, 48-pgs)-Silver Surfer app.	2	4	6	10	14	18
251-254,256-270: 251-3-D Man app. 252,253-Woodgod app. 254-1st app. the U-Foes (evil versions of the Fantastic Four)256-1st Sabra (Israeli super-hero). 257-1st Arabian Knight. 258,259-Soviet Super-Soldiers, Red Guardian & the Presence app. 260-Death of Col. Talbot. 261-Absorbing Man app. 263-Landslide & Avalanche app. 264-Death of the Night Flyer; Corruptor app. 265-1st app. The Rangers (Firebird, Shooting Star, Night Rider, Red Wolf & Lobo, Texas Tornado); Corruptor app. 266-High Evolutionary app. 267-Glorian & the Shaper of Worlds app. 269-1st Marvel Universe app. of Bereet; 1st Hulk-Hunters (Amphibion, Torgo, Dark Crawler). 270-Hulk Hunters, Bereet & Galaxy Master app.	1	2	3	4	5	7
255-Hulk vs. Thor	1	3	4	6	8	10
271-(5/82)-2nd app. & 1st full app. Rocket Raccoon (see Marvel Preview #7 for debut)	10	20	30	64	132	200
272-3rd app Rocket Raccoon; Sasquatch & Wendigo app; Wolverine & Alpha Flight cameo in flashback; Bruce Banner's mind takes control of the Hulk	2	4	6	11	16	20
273-277,280-299: 273-Sasquatch app. 275-vs. Megalith; U-Foes app. 276,277-U-foes app. 280,281-The Leader returns. 282-She-Hulk app. 283,284-Avengers app; vs. the Leader. 285-Zzzax app. 287-290-MODOK & Abomination app. 292-Circus of Crime & Dragon Man app. 293-Fantastic Four app. (in a dream). 294,295-Boomerang app. 296-Rom app. 297-299-Dr. Strange & Nightmare app.						6.00
278,279-Most Marvel characters app. (Wolverine in both). 279-X-Men & Alpha Flight cameos						6.00
300-(11/84, 52 pgs)-Spider-Man app. in new black costume on-c & 2 pg. cameo; Hulk reverts to savagery; Thor, Daredevil, Power Man & Iron Fist, Human Torch app; Dr. Strange banishes the Hulk from Earth	1	3	4	6	8	10
301-313: 301-Hulk banished to the 'Crossroads' (through #313); Dr. Strange app. 302-Mignola-c. 304-U-Foes cameo; Mignola-c (through issue #309). 305-vs the U-Foes. 306-Return of Xeron the Starslayer. 307-Death of Xeron. 308-vs N'Garia demons. 309-Last Sal Buscema-a. 310-Blevins-a. 311-Mignola-c/a. 312-Secret Wars II x-over; Mignola-c/a; origin retold w/further details regarding physical abuse at the hands of his father. 313-Crossover w/Alpha Flight #29; Mignola-c/a						5.00
314-Byrne-c/a begins; ends #319; Hulk returns to Earth; vs. Doc Samson						6.00
315-319: 315-Hulk & Banner separated. 316-vs Hercules, Sub-Mariner, Wonder Man & Iron Man of the Avengers. 317-1st app. the new Hulkbusters; Hulk vs. Doc Samson. 318-Doc Samson vs. Hulkbusters. 319-Banner and Betty Ross wed						5.00
320,325,327-329: 320-Al Milgrom story & art begin. 325-vs. Zzzax. 327-Zzzax app. 328-1st Peter David-s. 329-1st app. The Outcasts						4.00
321-323: 321-Avengers vs. Hulk. 322-Avengers & West Coast Avengers app. 323-East & West Coast Avengers app.						6.00
324-Return of the Grey Hulk (Banner & Hulk rejoined) first since #1 (c-swipe of #1)	2	4	6	10	18	25
326-Grey vs. Green (Rick Jones) Hulk	1	3	4	6	8	10
330-1st McFarlane-c/p; last Milgrom-s; Thunderbolt Ross 'dies'	3	6	9	17	26	35
331-Peter David begins as regular plotter; McFarlane-p	3	6	9	16	23	30
332-Grey Hulk & Leader vs. Green Hulk (Rick Jones)	2	4	6	8	10	12
333-334,338-339: 338-1st app. Mercy. 339-The Leader app.	1	2	3	4	8	10
335-No McFarlane-a						6.00
336,337-X-Factor app.	1	3	4	6	8	10
340-Classic Hulk vs. Wolverine-c by McFarlane	5	10	15	30	50	70
341-344,346: 341-vs. The Man-Bull; McFarlane begins pencils and inks. 342-The Leader app. 343-1st app. Rock & Redeemer. 344-McFarlane (p) only; vs. The Leader, Rock & Redeemer; Betty revealed to be pregnant. 346-The Leader app. Last McFarlane-p (co-penciled with Erik Larsen)	1	2	3	4	8	12
345-($1.50, 52 pgs) vs. The Leader; Gamma-Bomb explosion; World thinks the Hulk is dead; McFarlane (p) only	1	2	3	4	8	15
347-349,351-366: 347-1st app. The Hulk as 'Mr. Fixit'; relocated to Las Vegas; 1st app. Marlo; Absorbing Man app. 348-vs. Absorbing Man. 349-Spider-Man app; Dr. Doom cameo. 351-How the Hulk survived the Gamma-Bomb is revealed. 355-Glorian app. 356-Glorian & Shaper of Worlds app. 359-Wolverine-c (illusion) by John Byrne. 360-Nightmare & D'spayre app; Betty loses her baby. 361-Iron Man app. 362-Werewolf by Night app. 363-Acts of Vengeance tie-in; Dr. Doom & Grey Gargoyle app. 364-vs Abomination; 1st app. Madman. 365-Fantastic Four app. 366-Leader & Madman app.						4.00
350-Hulk/Thing battle						6.00
367-1st Dale Keown-a on Hulk (3/90) Leader & Madman app.	1	2	3	5	6	8
368-371,373-375: 368-Sam Kieth-c/a; 1st app. Pantheon. 369-Keown-a (becomes regular artist through #398); vs. the Freedom Force. 370,371-Dr. Strange & Namor app. (Defenders reunion). 374,375-vs. the Super-Skrull.						5.00
372-Green Hulk returns	1	2	3	5	6	8
376-Green vs. Grey Hulk; 1st app. Agamemnon of the Pantheon						6.00
377-1st all new Hulk; fluorescent green background-c	1	2	3	5	6	8
377-2nd printing	1	2	3	5	6	8
377-3rd printing	7	14	21	46	86	125
378,380,389-No Keown-a. 380-Doc Samson app.						3.00
379-Contined from issue #377; new direction for the Hulk; 1st app. of Delphi, Ajax, Achilles, Paris & Hector of the Pantheon						4.00
381-392,394-399: 381,382-Pantheon app. 383-Infinity Gauntlet x-over; Abomination app. 384-Infinity Gauntlet tie-in; Abomination app. 385-Infinity Gauntlet tie-in. 386,387-Sabra app. 388-1st app. Speedfreak. 390-X-Factor cameo. 391,392-X-Factor app.394-1st app. Trauma; no Keown-a. 395,396-Punisher app. 397-399; Leader & U-Foes app. 398-Last Keown-a.						3.00
393-($2.50, 72 pgs)						5.00
393-2nd print; silver-ink background						4.00
400-($2.50, 68-pgs)-Holo-grafx foil-c & r/TTA #63						4.00
400-2nd print; yellow logo						4.00
401-403,405-416: 401-U-Foes app. 402-Return of Doc Samson; Juggernaut & Red Skull app. 403-Gary Frank-a begins; Juggernaut & Red Skull app. 405-1st app. Piecemeal. 406-Captain America app. 407-vs. Piecemeal & Madman. 408-vs. Piecemeal & Madman; Motormouth & Killpower (Marvel UK characters) app. 409-vs. Madman; Motormouth & Killpower app. 410-Nick Fury & SHIELD app. 411-Pantheon vs. SHIELD; Nick Fury app.						

Incredible Hulk #418 © MAR

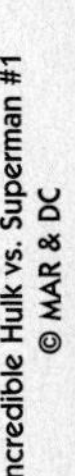
Incredible Hulk vs. Superman #1 © MAR & DC

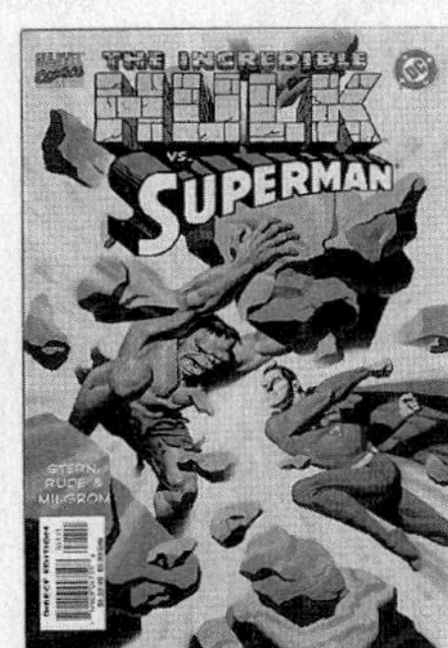

Incredible Hulk V2 #100 © MAR

GD 2.0 | VG 4.0 | FN 6.0 | VF 8.0 | VF/NM 9.0 | NM- 9.2

412-Hulk & She-Hulk vs. Bi-Beast. 413-Trauma app; Pt. 1 (of 4) of the Troyjan War. 414-vs. Trauma; Silver Surfer app. 415-Silver Surfer & Starjammers app. 416-Final of the Troyjan War; death of Trauma. 3.00
404-Avengers vs. Juggernaut & the Hulk; Red Skull app. 4.00
417,419-424: 417-Begins $1.50-c; Rick Jones Bachelor party; many heroes from Avengers & Fantastic Four app; Hulk returns from "Future Imperfect". 419-No Frank-a. 420-Special AIDS awareness issue; death of Jim Wilson. 421-Hulk & the Pantheon in Asgard. 423-Hela app. 3.00
418-($2.50)-Collectors Edition w/Gatefold die-cut-c; the wedding of Rick Jones & Marlo; includes cameo apps. of various Marvel characters as well as DC"s Death & Peter David 4.00
418-($1.50, Regular Edition) 4.00
425-($2.25, 52 pgs); Last Frank-a; Liam Sharp-a begins; death of Achilles 4.00
425-($3.50, 52 pgs)-Holographic-c 5.00
426-433,441,442: 426-Nick Fury app. 427,428-Man-Thing app. 430-Speedfreak app. 431,432-Abomination app. 432-Last Sharp-a. 433-Punisher app; title becomes part of the 'Marvel Edge' titles (through #439) 441-She-Hulk-c/s; "Pulp Fiction" parody-c. 442-She-Hulk & Doc Samson team-up; no Hulk app. 3.00
434-Funeral for Nick Fury; Wolverine, Dr. Strange, Avengers app; Marvel Overpower card insert (harder to find above 9.2 due to card indentations) 4.00
435-($2.50)-Rhino app; excerpt from "What Savage Beast" 4.00
436-439: 436-"Ghosts of the Future" Pt.1 (of 5); Leader app. 439-Maestro app. 4.00
440-"Ghosts of the Future" Pt. 5; Hulk vs. Thor 5.00
443,446-448: 443-Begin $1.50-c; re-app. of Hulk. 446-w/card insert. 447-Begin Deodato-c/a 4.00
444,445: 444-Cable-c/app; Onslaught x-over. 445-Onslaught x-over; Avengers app. 5.00
447-Variant-c 4.00
449-1st app. Thunderbolts (1/97); Citizen V, Songbird, Mach-1, Techno, Atlas & Meteorite 3 6 9 16 23 30
450-($2.95)-Thunderbolts app. 2 stories; Heroes Reborn versions of Hulk, Dr. Strange, Mr. Fantastic & Iron Man app. 5.00
451-453, 458-470: 452-Heroes Reborn Hulk app. 453-Hulk vs. Heroes Reborn Hulk. 458-Mr. Hyde app. 459-Abomination app. 461-Maestro app. 463-Silver Surfer cameo. 464-Silver Surfer app. 465-Mr. Fantastic & Tony Stark app. 466-'Death' of Betty Banner. 467-Last Peter David issue. 468-Casey-s/Puilido-a begin. 469-Super-Adaptoid & Ringmaster app. 470-Ringmaster & the Circus of Crime app. 4.00
454-Wolverine & Ka-Zar app; Adam Kubert-a 5.00
455-Wolverine, Storm, Cannonball & Cyclops of the X-Men app.; Adam Kubert-a 5.00
456-Apocalypse enlists the Hulk as 'War'; Juggernaut app. 6.00
457-Hulk (as Horseman of the Apocalypse 'War' vs. Juggernaut. Apocalypse app. 1 2 3 4 6 8
471-473: 471-Circus of Crime app. 473-Watcher app; Abomination revealed as Betty's killer. 5.00
474-($2.99) Last issue; Abomination app; c-homage to issue #1 1 3 4 6 8 10
#(-1) Flashback (7/97) Kubert-a 3.00
Special 1 (10/68, 25¢, 68 pg.)-New 51 pg. story; Hulk battles the Inhumans (early app) 15 30 45 105 233 360
Special 2 (10/69, 25¢, 68 pg.)-Origin retold (from issue #3) r-TTA #62-66 6 12 18 38 69 100
Special 3,4: 3-(1/71, 25¢, 68 pg.)-r/TTA #70-74. 4-(1/72, 52 pg.)-r/TTA 75-77 & Not Brand Echh #5 4 8 12 23 37 50
Annual 5 (1976) 2nd app. Groot 5 10 15 34 60 85
Annual 6 (1977)-1st app. Paragon (later becomes Her, then later Ayesha); Dr. Strange app. 1 2 3 4 8 12
Annual 7 ('78)-Byrne/Layton-c/a; Iceman & Angel app; vs. the Mastermold 2 4 6 11 16 20
Annual 8 ('79)-Byrne/Stern-s; Hulk vs. Sasquatch 2 4 6 8 10 12
Annual 9,10: 9-('80)-Ditko-p. 10-('81)-Captain Universe app. 6.00
Annual 11 ('82)-Doc Samson back-up by Miller-(p)(5 pg); Spider-Man & Avengers app. 1 2 3 5 6 8
Annual 12-14: 12-('83)-Trimpe-a. 13-('84)-Story takes place at the 'Crossroads' (after Hulk was banished from Earth); takes place between Incredible Hulk #301-302. 14-Byrne-s; takes place between pages of Incredible Hulk #314 5.00
Annual 15-('86)-Zeck-c; Abomination & Tryannus app. 5.00
Annual 16-20: 16-('90, $2.00, 68 pgs. "Lifeform" Pt. 3; continued from Daredevil Annual #6, continued in Silver Surfer Annual #3; She-Hulk app. in back-up story. 17-('91, $2.00)-"Subterranean Wars" Pt. 2; continued from Avengers Annual #20; continued in Namor the Sub-Mariner Annual #1. 18-('92)-"Return of the Defenders" Pt.1; continued in Namor the Sub-Mariner Annual #1. 19-('93)-Bagged w/card; 1st app. Lazarus 4.00
...'97 ($2.99) Pollina-c 4.00
...And Wolverine 1 (10/86, $2.50)-r/1st app. (#180-181) 2 4 6 10 14 18
...: Beauty and the Behemoth ('98, $19.95, TPB) r/Bruce & Betty stories 20.00
...Ground Zero ('95, $12.95) r/#340-346 13.00

GD 2.0 | VG 4.0 | FN 6.0 | VF 8.0 | VF/NM 9.0 | NM- 9.2

...Hercules Unleashed (10/96, $2.50) David-s/Deodato-c/a 4.00
... Omnibus Vol. 1 HC (2008, $99.99, dustjacket) r/#1-6 & 102, Tales To Astonish #59-101 bonus art, cover reprints; afterword by Peter David; Kirby cover from #1 140.00
... Omnibus Vol. 1 HC (2008, $99.99, dustjacket) Variant-c swipe of #1 by Alex Ross 110.00
.../Sub-Mariner '98 Annual ($2.99) 4.00
...Versus Quasimodo 1 (3/83, one-shot)-Based on Saturday morning cartoon 4.00
...Vs. Superman 1 (7/99, $5.95, one-shot)-painted-c by Rude 6.00
...Versus Venom 1 (4/94, $2.50, one-shot)-Embossed-c; red foil logo 4.00
... Visionaries: Peter David Vol. 1 (2005, $19.99) r/#331-339 written by Peter David 20.00
... Visionaries: Peter David Vol. 2 (2005, $19.99) r/#340-348 20.00
... Visionaries: Peter David Vol. 3 (2006, $19.99) r/#349-354, Web of Spider-Man #44, and Fantastic Four #320 20.00
... Visionaries: Peter David Vol. 4 (2007, $19.99) r/#355-363 and Marvel Comics Presents #26,45 20.00
... Visionaries: Peter David Vol. 5 (2008, $19.99) r/#364-372 and Annual #16 20.00
Wizard #1 Ace Edition - Reprints #1 with new Andy Kubert-c 14.00
Wizard #181 Ace Edition - Reprints #181 with new Chen-c 14.00
(Also see titles listed under **Hulk**)

NOTE: ***Adkins*** *a-111-116i.* ***Austin*** *a(i)-350, 351, 353, 354; c-302i, 350i.* ***Ayers*** *a-3-5i.* ***Buckler*** *a-Annual 5; c-252.* ***John Buscema*** *c-202p.* ***Byrne*** *a-314-319p; c-314-316, 318, 319, 359, Annual 14i.* ***Colan*** *c-363.* ***Ditko*** *a-2i, 6, 249, Annual 2r(5), 3r, 9p; c-2i, 6, 235, 249.* ***Everett*** *c-133i.* ***Golden*** *c-248, 251.* ***Kane*** *c(p)-193, 194, 196, 198.* ***Dale Keown*** *a(p)-367, 369-377, 379, 381-388, 390-393, 395-398; c-369-377p, 381, 382p, 384, 385, 386, 387p, 388, 390p, 391-393, 395p, 396, 397p, 398.* ***Kirby*** *a-1-5p, Special 2, 3p, Annual 5p; c-1-5, Annual 5.* ***McFarlane*** *a-330-334p, 336-339p, 340-343, 344-346p; c-330p, 340p, 341-343, 344p, 345, 346p.* ***Mignola*** *c-302, 305, 313.* ***Miller*** *c-258p, 261, 264, 268.* ***Mooney*** *a-230p, 287i, 288i.* ***Powell*** *a-Special 3r(2).* ***Romita*** *a-Annual 17p.* ***Severin*** *a(i)-108-110, 131-133, 141-151, 153-155; c(i)-109, 110, 132, 142, 144-155.* ***Simonson*** *c-283, 364-367.* ***Starlin*** *a-222p; c-217.* ***Staton*** *a(i)-187-189, 191-209.* ***Tuska*** *a-102i, 105i, 106i, 218p.* ***Williamson*** *a-310i; c-310i, 311i.* ***Wrightson*** *c-197.*

INCREDIBLE HULK (Vol. 2) (Formerly Hulk #1-11; becomes Incredible Hercules with #113) (Re-titled Incredible Hulks #612-on)(Also see World War Hulk)
Marvel Comics: No. 12, Mar, 2000 - No. 112, Jan, 2008 ($1.99-$3.50)
No. 600, Sept, 2009 - No. 625, Oct, 2011 ($3.99/$4.99)

12-Jenkins-s/Garney & McKone-a 4.00
13,14-($1.99) Garney & Buscema-a 3.00
15-24,26-32: 15-Begin $2.25-c. 21-Maximum Security x-over. 24-($1.99-c) 3.00
25-($2.99) Hulk vs. The Abomination; Romita Jr.-a 4.00
33-($3.50, 100 pgs.) new Bogdanove-a/Priest-s; reprints 4.00
34-Bruce Jones-s begin; Romita Jr.-a 5.00
35-49,51-54: 35-39-Jones-s/Romita Jr.-a. 40-43-Weeks-a. 44-49-Immonen-a 3.00
50-($3.50) Deodato-a begins; Abomination app. thru #54 4.00
55-74,77-91: 55(25¢-c) Absorbing Man returns; Fernandez-a. 60-65,70-72-Deodato-a. 66-69-Braithwaite-a. 71-74-Iron Man app. 77-($2.99-c) Peter David's-s begin/Weeks-a. 80-Wolverine-c. 82-Jae Lee-c/a. 83-86-House of M x-over. 87-Scorpion app. 3.00
75,76-($3.50) The Leader app. 75-Robertson-a/Frank-c. 76-Braithwaite-a 4.00
92-Planet Hulk begins; Ladronn-c 5.00
92-2nd printing with variant-c by Bryan Hitch 4.00
93-99,101-105 Planet Hulk; Ladronn-c 3.00
100-($3.99) Planet Hulk continues; back-up w/Frank-a; r/#152,153; Ladronn-c 5.00
100-($3.99) Green Hulk variant-c by Michael Turner 10.00
100-($3.99) Gray Hulk variant-c by Michael Turner 30.00
106-World War Hulk begins; Gary Frank-a/c 6.00
106-2nd printing with new cover of Hercules and Angel 3.00
107-112: 107-Hercules vs. Hulk. 108-Rick Jones app. 112-Art Adams-c 3.00
600-(9/09, $4.99) Covers by Ross, Sale and wraparound-c by McGuinness; back-up with Stan Lee-s; r/Hulk: Gray #1; cover gallery 5.00
601-611-($3.99): 601-605-Olivetti-a. 603-Wolverine app. 606-608-Fall of the Hulks 4.00
(Title becomes Incredible Hulks with #612, Nov, 2010)
612-621: 612-617-Dark Son. 618-620-Chaos War. 621-Hercules app. 4.00
622-634-($2.99) 623-625-Ka-Zar app.; Eaglesham-a. 626-629-Grummett-a 3.00
635-($3.99) Fin Fang Foom & Dr. Strange app.; Greg Pak interview 4.00
Annual 2000 ($3.50) Texeira-a/Jenkins-s; Avengers app. 4.00
Annual 2001 ($2.99) Thor-c/app.; Larsen-s/Williams III-c 4.00
Annual 1 (8/11, $3.99) Identity Wars; Spider-Man and Deadpool app.; Barrionuevo-a 4.00
... & The Human Torch: From the Marvel Vault 1 (8/11, $2.99) unpublished story w/Ditko-a 3.00
... : Boiling Point (Volume 2, 2002, $8.99, TPB) r/#40-43; Andrews-c 9.00
Dogs of War (6/01, $19.95, TPB) r/#12-20 20.00
House of M (2006, $13.99) r/House of M tie-in issues Incredible Hulk #83-87 14.00
Hulk: Planet Hulk HC (2007, $39.99, dustjacket) oversized r/#92-105, Planet Hulk: Gladiator Guidebook, stories from Amazing Fantasy (2004) #15 and Giant-Size Hulk #1 40.00
Hulk: Planet Hulk SC (2008, $34.99) same content as HC 35.00
Planet Hulk: Gladiator Guidebook (2006, $3.99) bios of combatants and planet history 4.00
...: Prelude to Planet Hulk (2006, $13.99, TPB) r/#88-91 & Official Handbook: Hulk 2004 14.00
...: Return of the Monster (7/02, $12.99, TPB) r/#34-39 13.00
...: The End (8/02, $5.95) David-s/Keown-a; Hulk in the far future 6.00
...: The End HC (2008, $19.99, dustjacket) r/The End and Hulk: Future Imperfect #1-2 20.00

Incredible Hulk (2011 series) #10 © MAR

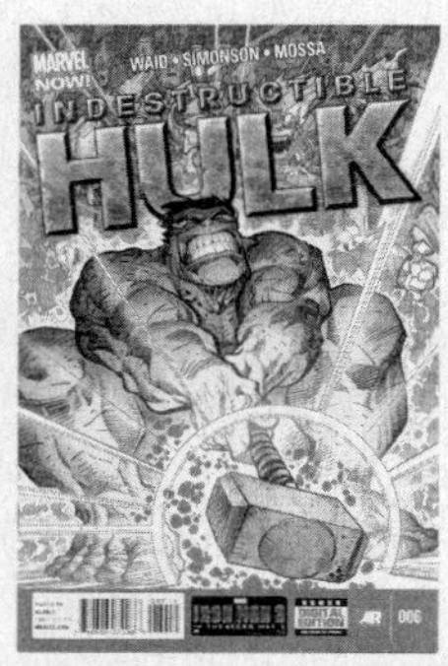

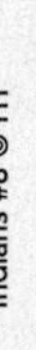
Indestructible Hulk #5 © MAR

Indians #8 © FH

GD VG FN VF VF/NM NM-
2.0 4.0 6.0 8.0 9.0 9.2

GD VG FN VF VF/NM NM-
2.0 4.0 6.0 8.0 9.0 9.2

...Volume 1 HC (2002, $29.99, oversized) r/#34-43 & Startling Stories: Banner #1-4 30.00
...Volume 2 HC (2003, $29.99, oversized) r/#44-54; sketch pages and cover gallery 30.00
Volume 3: Transfer of Power (2003, $12.99, TPB) r/#44-49 13.00
Volume 4: Abominable (2003, $11.99, TPB) r/#50-54; Abomination app.; Deodato-a 12.00
Volume 5: Hide in Plain Sight (2003, $11.99, TPB) r/#55-59; Fernandez-a 12.00
Volume 6: Split Decisions (2004, $12.99, TPB) r/#60-65; Deodato-a 13.00
Volume 7: Dead Like Me (2004, $12.99, TPB) r/#66-69 & Hulk Smash #1&2 13.00
Volume 8: Big Things (2004, $17.99, TPB) r/#70-76; Iron Man app. 18.00
Volume 9: Tempest Fugit (2005, $14.99, TPB) r/#77-82 15.00

INCREDIBLE HULK (Also see Indestructible Hulk)
Marvel Comics: Dec, 2011 - No. 15, Dec, 2012 ($3.99)

1-Aaron-s/Silvestri-a; bonus interview with Aaron; cover by Silvestri 4.00
1-Variant covers by Neal Adams, Whilce Portacio & Ladronn 8.00
2-7: 2-Silvestri, Portacio & Tan-a. 7-Hulk & Banner merge; Portacio-a 4.00
7.1-(7/12, $2.99) Palo-a/Komarck-c; Red She-Hulk app. 3.00
8-15: 8-Punisher app.; Dillon-a. 12-Wolverine & The Thing app. 4.00

INCREDIBLE HULKS: ENIGMA FORCE
Marvel Comics: Nov, 2010 - No. 3, Jan, 2011 ($3.99, limited series)

1-3-Reed-s/Munera-a/Pagulayan-c; Bug app. 4.00

INCREDIBLE MR. LIMPET, THE (See Movie Classics)

INCREDIBLES, THE
Image Comics: Nov, 2004 - No. 4, Feb, 2005 ($2.99, limited series)

1-4-Adaptation of 2004 Pixar movie; Ricardo Curtis-a 3.00
TPB (2005, $12.95) r/#1-4; cover gallery 13.00

INCREDIBLES, THE (Pixar characters)
BOOM! Studios: No. 0, Jul, 2009 - No. 15, Oct, 2010 ($2.99)

0-15: 0-3-City of Incredibles; Waid & Walker-s. 0,1-Wagner-c. 8-15-Walker-s 3.00
...: Family Matters 1-4 (3/09 - No. 4, 6/09) Waid-s/Takara-a. 1-Five covers 3.00

INCREDIBLE SCIENCE FICTION (Formerly Weird Science-Fantasy)
E. C. Comics: No. 30, July-Aug, 1955 - No. 33, Jan-Feb, 1956

	GD 2.0	VG 4.0	FN 6.0	VF 8.0	VF/NM 9.0	NM- 9.2
30-Davis-c begin, end #32	44	88	132	352	564	775
31-Williamson/Krenkel-a, Wood-a(2)	42	84	126	336	538	740
32-"Food For Thought" by Williamson/Krenkel	42	84	126	336	538	740
33-Classic Wood-c; "Judgment Day" story-r/Weird Fantasy #18; final issue & last E.C. comic book	47	94	141	376	601	825

NOTE: ***Davis** a-30, 32, 33; c-30-32. **Krigstein** a-in all. **Orlando** a-30, 32, 33. **Wood** a-30, 31, 33; c-33.*

INCREDIBLE SCIENCE FICTION (Formerly Weird Science-Fantasy)
Russ Cochran/Gemstone Publ.: No. 8, Aug, 1994 - No. 11, May, 1995 ($2.00)

8-11: Reprints #30-33 of E.C. series 4.00

INDEPENDENCE DAY (Movie)
Marvel Comics: No. 0, June, 1996 - No. 2, Aug, 1996 ($1.95, limited series)

0-Special Edition; photo-c 5.00
0-2 3.00

INDEPENDENCE DAY (Movie)
Titan Comics: Mar, 2016 - No. 5, Jul, 2016 ($3.99, limited series)

1-5: 1-Victor Gischler-s/Steve Scott-a; four covers. 2-5-Two covers 4.00

INDESTRUCTIBLE
IDW (Darby Pop): Dec, 2013 - No. 10, Dec, 2014 ($3.99)

1-10: 1-Kline-s/Garron & Garcia-a 4.00
...: Stingray One Shot (5/15, $3.99) Marsick-s/Reguzzoni-a 4.00

INDESTRUCTIBLE HULK (Marvel NOW!)(Follows Incredible Hulk 2011-2012 series)
Marvel Comics: Jan, 2013 - No. 20, May, 2014 ($3.99)

1-Waid-s/Yu-a; Banner hired by SHIELD; Maria Hill app. 4.00
2-20: 2-Iron Man app. 4,5-Attuma app. 6-8-Thor app.; Simonson-a/c. 9,10-Daredevil app. 12-Two-Gun Kid, Kid Colt, and Rawhide Kid app. 17,18-Iron Man app. 4.00
Annual 1 (2/14, $4.99) Parker-s/Asrar-a; Iron Man app. 5.00
... Special 1 (12/13, $4.99) Original X-Men and Superior Spider-Man app. 5.00

INDIANA JONES (Title series), **Dark Horse Comics**

--ADVENTURES, 6/08 ($6.95, digest-sized) Vol. 1 - new all-ages adventures; Beavers-a 7.00
--AND THE ARMS OF GOLD, 2/94 - 5/94 ($2.50) 1-4 3.00
--AND THE FATE OF ATLANTIS, 3/91 - 9/91 ($2.50) 1-4-Dorman painted-c on all; contain trading cards (#1 has a 2nd printing, 10/91) 3.00
--AND THE GOLDEN FLEECE, 6/94 - 7/94 ($2.50) 1,2 3.00
--AND THE IRON PHOENIX, 12/94 - 3/95 ($2.50) 1-4 3.00

INDIANA JONES AND THE KINGDOM OF THE CRYSTAL SKULL
Dark Horse Comics: May, 2008 - No. 2, May, 2008 ($5.99, limited series, movie adaptation)

1,2-Luke Ross-a/John Jackson Miller-adapted-s; two covers by Struzan & Fleming 6.00
TPB (5/08, $12.95) r/#1,2; Struzan-c 13.00

INDIANA JONES AND THE LAST CRUSADE
Marvel Comics: 1989 - No. 4, 1989 ($1.00, limited series, movie adaptation)

1-4: Williamson-i assist 3.00
1-(1989, $2.95, B&W mag., 80 pgs.) 4.00

--AND THE SHRINE OF THE SEA DEVIL: Dark Horse, 9/94 ($2.50, one shot)
1-Gary Gianni-a 3.00
--AND THE SARGASSO PIRATES: Dark Horse, 12/95 - 3/96 ($2.50) 1-4: 1,2-Ross-c 3.00
--AND THE SPEAR OF DESTINY: Dark Horse, 4/95 - 8/95 ($2.50) 1-4 3.00
--AND THE TOMB OF THE GODS, 6/08 - No. 4, 3/09 ($2.99) 1-4: 1-Tony Harris-c 3.00
--THUNDER IN THE ORIENT: Dark Horse, 9/93 - '94 ($2.50)
1-6: Dan Barry story & art in all; 1-Dorman painted-c 3.00

INDIANA JONES AND THE TEMPLE OF DOOM
Marvel Comics Group: Sept, 1984 - No. 3, Nov, 1984 (Movie adaptation)

1-3-r/Marvel Super Special; Guice-a 5.00

INDIANA JONES OMNIBUS
Dark Horse Books: Feb, 2008; June 2008; Feb, 2009 ($24.95, digest-size)

Volume One - Reprints Indiana Jones and the Fate of Atlantis, Indiana Jones: Thunder in the Orient; and Indiana Jones and the Arms of Gold mini-series 25.00
Volume Two - Reprints I.J. and the Golden Fleece, I.J. and the Shrine of the Sea Devil, I.J. and the Iron Phoenix, I.J. and the Spear of Destiny, I.J. and the Sargasso Pirates 25.00
The Further Adventures Volume One - (2/09) r/Raiders of the Lost Ark #1-3 & The Further Adventures of Indiana Jones #1-12 25.00

INDIAN BRAVES (Baffling Mysteries No. 5 on)
Ace Magazines: March, 1951 - No. 4, Sept, 1951

	GD 2.0	VG 4.0	FN 6.0	VF 8.0	VF/NM 9.0	NM- 9.2
1-Green Arrowhead begins, apps. in all	16	32	48	94	147	200
2	10	20	30	54	72	90
3,4	9	18	27	47	61	75
I.W. Reprint #1 (nd)-r/Indian Braves #4	2	4	6	9	13	16

INDIAN CHIEF (White Eagle...) (Formerly The Chief, Four Color 290)
Dell Publ. Co.: No. 3, July-Sept, 1951 - No. 33, Jan-Mar, 1959 (All painted-c)

	GD 2.0	VG 4.0	FN 6.0	VF 8.0	VF/NM 9.0	NM- 9.2
3	5	10	15	33	57	80
4-11: 6-White Eagle app.	4	8	12	28	47	65
12-1st White Eagle (10-12/53)-Not same as earlier character	5	10	15	33	57	80
13-29	4	8	12	23	37	50
30-33-Buscema-a	4	8	12	25	40	55

INDIAN CHIEF (See March of Comics No. 94, 110, 127, 140, 159, 170, 187)

INDIAN FIGHTER, THE (Movie)
Dell Publishing Co.: No. 687, May, 1956 (one-shot)

	GD 2.0	VG 4.0	FN 6.0	VF 8.0	VF/NM 9.0	NM- 9.2
Four Color 687-Kirk Douglas photo-c	7	14	21	48	89	130

INDIAN FIGHTER
Youthful Magazines: May, 1950 - No. 11, Jan, 1952

	GD 2.0	VG 4.0	FN 6.0	VF 8.0	VF/NM 9.0	NM- 9.2
1	19	38	57	111	176	240
2-Wildey-a/c(bondage)	13	26	39	74	105	135
3-11: 3,4-Wildey-a. 6-Davy Crockett story	10	20	30	56	76	95

NOTE: ***Hollingsworth** a-5. **Walter Johnson** c-1, 3, 4, 6. **Palais** a-10. **Stallman** a-5-8. **Wildey** a-2-4; c-2, 5.*

INDIAN LEGENDS OF THE NIAGARA (See American Graphics)

INDIANS
Fiction House Magazines (Wings Publ. Co.): Spring, 1950 - No. 17, Spr, 1953 (1-8: 52 pgs.)

	GD 2.0	VG 4.0	FN 6.0	VF 8.0	VF/NM 9.0	NM- 9.2
1-Manzar The White Indian, Long Bow & Orphan of the Storm begin	30	60	90	177	289	400
2-Starlight begins	15	30	45	90	140	190
3-5: 5-17-Most-c by Whitman	14	28	42	81	118	155
6-10	13	26	39	72	101	130
11-17	11	22	33	64	90	115

INDIANS OF THE WILD WEST
I. W. Enterprises: Circa 1958? (no date) (Reprints)

	GD 2.0	VG 4.0	FN 6.0	VF 8.0	VF/NM 9.0	NM- 9.2
9-Kinstler-c; Whitman-a; r/Indians #?	2	4	6	10	14	18

INDIANS ON THE WARPATH
St. John Publishing Co.: No date (Late 40s, early 50s) (132 pgs.)

	GD 2.0	VG 4.0	FN 6.0	VF 8.0	VF/NM 9.0	NM- 9.2
nn-Matt Baker-c; contains St. John comics rebound. Many combinations possible	42	84	126	265	445	625

INDIAN TRIBES (See Famous Indian Tribes)

Infamous Iron Man #1 © MAR

Infestation 2 #1 © IDW

Infinite Loop #1 © Colinet & Charretier

GD 2.0 | VG 4.0 | FN 6.0 | VF 8.0 | VF/NM 9.0 | NM- 9.2

INDIAN WARRIORS (Formerly White Rider and Super Horse; becomes Western Crime Cases #9)
Star Publications: No. 7, June, 1951 - No. 8, Sept, 1951

7-White Rider & Superhorse continue; "Last of the Mohicans" serial begins; L.B. Cole-c 18 36 54 105 165 225
8-L.B. Cole-c 17 34 51 98 154 210
3-D 1(12/53, 25¢)-Came w/glasses; L.B. Cole-c 34 68 102 199 325 450
Accepted Reprint(nn)(inside cover shows White Rider & Superhorse #11)-r/cover to #7; origin White Rider &...; L.B. Cole-c 8 16 24 40 50 60
Accepted Reprint #8 (nd); L.B. Cole-c (r-cover to #8) 8 16 24 40 50 60

INDOORS-OUTDOORS (See Wisco)

INDOOR SPORTS
National Specials Co.: nd (6x9", 64 pgs., B&W-r, hard-c)

nn-By Tad 5 10 15 24 30 35

INDUSTRIAL GOTHIC
DC Comics (Vertigo): Dec, 1995 - No. 5, Apr, 1996 ($2.50, limited series)

1-5: Ted McKeever-c/a/scripts 3.00

INFAMOUS (Based on the Sony videogame)
DC Comics: Early May, 2011 - No. 6, Late July, 2011 ($2.99, limited series)

1-6: 1-William Harms-s/Eric Nguyen-a/Doug Mahnke-c. 3-6-Benes-c 3.00

INFAMOUS IRON MAN (Doctor Doom as Iron Man)
Marvel Comics: Dec, 2016 - Present ($3.99)

1-5: 1-Bendis-s/Maleev-a; Diablo app. 1-5-The Thing app. 5-Doom's mother returns 4.00

INFERIOR FIVE, THE (Inferior 5 #11, 12) (See Showcase #62, 63, 65)
National Periodical Publications (#1-10: 12¢): 3-4/67 - No. 10, 9-10/68; No. 11, 8-9/72 - No. 12, 10-11/72

1-(3-4/67)-Sekowsky-a(p); 4th app. 5 10 15 34 60 85
2-5: 2-Plastic Man, F.F. app. 4-Thor app. 3 6 9 19 30 40
6-9: 6-Stars DC staff 3 6 9 16 23 30
10-Superman x-over; F.F., Spider-Man & Sub-Mariner app. 3 6 9 18 28 38
11,12: Orlando-c/a; both r/Showcase #62,63 2 4 6 11 16 20

INFERNAL MAN-THING (Sequel to story in Man-Thing #12 [1974])
Marvel Comics: Sept, 2012 - No. 3, Oct, 2012 ($3.99, limited series)

1-3-Gerber-s; painted-a by Nowlan; Art Adams-c. 1,2-Bonus reprint of Man-Thing #12 4.00

INFERNO
Caliber Comics: 1995 - No. 5 ($2.95, B&W)

1-5 3.00

INFERNO (See Legion of Super-Heroes)
DC Comics: Oct, 1997 - No. 4, Feb, 1998 ($2.50, limited series)

1-Immonen-s/c/a in all 4.00
2-4 3.00

INFERNO (Secret Wars tie-in)
Marvel Comics: Jul, 2015 - No. 5, Nov, 2015 ($3.99, limited series)

1-5-Hopeless-s/Garrón-a; Magik, Colossus, Nightcrawler, Madelyne Pryor app. 4.00

INFERNO: HELLBOUND
Image Comics (Top Cow): Jan, 2002 - No. 3 ($2.50/$2.99)

1,2: 1-Seven covers; Silvestri-a/Silvestri and Wohl-s 3.00
3-($2.99) Tan-a 3.00
#0 (7/02, $3.00) Tan-a 3.00
Wizard #0- Previews series; bagged with Wizard Top Cow Special mag 3.00

INFESTATION (Zombie crossover with G.I. Joe, Star Trek, Transformers and Ghostbusters)
IDW Publishing: Jan, 2011 - No. 2, Apr, 2011 ($3.99, limited series)

1,2-Abnett & Lanning-s/Messina-a; two covers by Messina & Snyder III 4.00
...: Outbreak 1-4 (6/11 - No. 4, 9/11, $3.99) Messina-a; Covert Vampiric Operations app. 4.00

INFESTATION 2 (IDW characters vs. H.P. Lovecraft's Elder Gods)
IDW Publishing: Jan, 2012 - No. 2, Apr, 2012 ($3.99, limited series)

1,2-Swierczynski-s/Messina-a; three covers by Garner, Ramondelli & Messina 4.00
...: Dungeons & Dragons 1,2 (2/12 - No. 2, 2/12, $3.99) 3 covers 4.00
...: G.I. Joe 1,2 (3/12 - No. 2, 3/12, $3.99) Raicht-s/De Landro-a; 3 covers 4.00
...: Team-Up 1 (2/12, $3.99) Ryall-s/Robinson-a; covers by Powell & Morrison 4.00
...: Teenage Mutant Ninja Turtles 1,2 (3/12 - No. 2, 3/12, $3.99) Mark Torres-a; 3 covers 4.00
...: 30 Days of Night 1 (4/12, $3.99) Swierczynski-s/Sayger-a; 3 covers 4.00
...: Transformers 1,2 (2/12 - No. 2, 2/12, $3.99) Dixon-s/Guidi-a; 3 covers 4.00

INFINITE, THE
Image Comics (SkyBound): Aug, 2011 - No. 4, Nov, 2011 ($2.99)

1-4: 1-Robert Kirkman-s/Rob Liefeld-a; at least 11 covers. 2-Six covers 3.00

INFINITE CRISIS
DC Comics: Dec, 2005 - No. 7, Jun, 2006 ($3.99, limited series)

1-Johns-s/Jimenez-a; two covers by Jim Lee and George Pérez 5.00
1-RRP Edition with Jim Lee sketch-c 100.00
2-7: 4-New Spectre; Earth-2 returns. 5-Earth-2 Lois dies; new Blue Beetle debut. 6-Superboy killed, new Earth formed. 7-Earth-2 Superman dies 4.00
HC (2006, $24.99, dustjacket) r/#1-7; DiDio intro.; sketch cover gallery; interview/commentary with Johns, Jimenez and editors; sketch art 25.00
... Companion TPB (2006, $14.99) r/Day of Vengeance: Infinite Crisis Special #1, Rann-Thanagar War: ICS #1, The Omac Project: ICS #1, Villains United: ICS #1 15.00
... Secret Files 2006 (4/06, $5.99) tie-in story with Earth-2 Lois and Superman, Earth-Prime Superboy and Alexander Luthor; art by various; profile pages 6.00

INFINITE CRISIS AFTERMATH (See Crisis Aftermath:...)

INFINITE CRISIS: FIGHT FOR THE MULTIVERSE (Based on the video game)
DC Comics: Sept, 2014 - No. 12, Aug, 2015 ($3.99, limited series)

1-12: 1-Abnett-s; art by various. 2-6-Polybagged 4.00

INFINITE LOOP
IDW Publishing: Apr, 2015 - No. 6, Sept, 2015 ($3.99)

1-6-Pierrick Colinet-s/Elsa Charretier-a 4.00

INFINITE VACATION
Image Comics (Shadowline): Jan, 2011 - No. 5, Jan, 2013 ($3.50/$5.99)

1-4-Nick Spencer-s/Christian Ward-a/c 3.50
5-($5.99) Conclusion; gatefold centerfold 6.00

INFINITY (Crossover with the Avengers titles)
Marvel Comics: Oct, 2013 - No. 6, Jan, 2014 ($4.99/$3.99/$5.99, limited series)

1-($4.99) Avengers, Inhumans and Thanos app.; Hickman-s/Cheung-a/Adam Kubert-c 5.00
2-5-($3.99) Opeña-a. 3-Terragen bomb triggered 4.00
6-($5.99) Cheung-a 6.00
Free Comic Book Day 2013 (Infinity) 1 (5/13, giveaway) Previews series; Cheung-a 3.00

INFINITY ABYSS (Also see Marvel Universe: The End)
Marvel Comics: Aug, 2002 - No. 6, Oct, 2002 ($2.99, limited series)

1-5-Starlin-s/a; Thanos, Captain Marvel, Spider-Man, Dr. Strange app. 4.00
6-($3.50) 4.00
Thanos Vol. 2: Infinity Abyss TPB (2003, $17.99) r/ #1-6 25.00

INFINITY CRUSADE
Marvel Comics: June, 1993 - No. 6, Nov, 1993 ($3.50/$2.50, limited series, 52 pgs.)

1-6: By Jim Starlin & Ron Lim. 1-($3.50). 2-6-($2.99) 6.00

INFINITY ENTITY, THE (Concludes in Thanos: The Infinity Entity GN)
Marvel Comics: May, 2016 - No. 4, Jun, 2016 ($3.99, limited series)

1-4: Jim Starlin-s/Alan Davis-a. 1-Rebirth of Adam Warlock. 4-Mephisto app. 4.00

INFINITY GAUNTLET (The... #2 on; see Infinity Crusade, The Infinity War & Warlock & the Infinity Watch)
Marvel Comics: July, 1991 - No. 6, Dec, 1991 ($2.50, limited series)

1-Thanos-c/stories in all; Starlin scripts in all 3 6 9 19 30 40
2-6: 5,6-Ron Lim-c/a 2 4 6 9 12 15
TPB (4/99, $24.95) r/#1-6 30.00
NOTE: *Lim a-3p(part), 5p, 6p; c-5i, 6i.* ***Perez*** *a-1-3p, 4p(part); c-1(painted), 2-4, 5i, 6i.*

INFINITY GAUNTLET (Secret Wars tie-in)
Marvel Comics: Jul, 2015 - No. 5, Jan, 2016 ($3.99, limited series)

1-5-Duggan & Weaver-s/Weaver-a; Thanos & The Guardians of the Galaxy app. 4.00

INFINITY: HEIST (Tie-in to the Infinity crossover)
Marvel Comics: Nov, 2013 - No. 4, Feb, 2014 ($3.99, limited series)

1-4-Tieri-s/Barrionuevo-a; Spymaster, Titanium Man, Whirlwind app. 4.00

INFINITY, INC. (See All-Star Squadron #25)
DC Comics: Mar, 1984 - No. 53, Aug, 1988 ($1.25, Baxter paper, 36 pgs.)

1-Brainwave, Jr., Fury, The Huntress, Jade, Northwind, Nuklon, Obsidian, Power Girl, Silver Scarab & Star Spangled Kid begin 5.00
2-13,38-49,51-53: 2-Dr. Midnite, G.A. Flash, W. Woman, Dr. Fate, Hourman, Green Lantern, Wildcat app. 5-Nudity panels. 13-Re-intro Rose and Thorn. 46,47-Millennium tie-ins 3.00
14-Todd McFarlane-a (5/85, 2nd full story) 2 4 6 8 10 12
15-37-McFarlane-a (20,23,24: 5 pgs. only; 33: 2 pgs.); 18-24-Crisis x-over. 21-Intro new Hourman & Dr. Midnight. 26-New Wildcat app. 31-Star Spangled Kid becomes Skyman. 32-Green Fury becomes Green Flame. 33-Origin Obsidian. 35-1st modern app. G.A. Fury 4.00
50 ($2.50, 52 pgs.) 4.00

The Informer #2 © FTVP

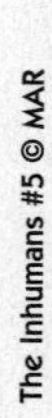

The Inhumans #5 © MAR

Injustice: Gods Among Us #9 © DC

GD VG FN VF VF/NM NM-
2.0 4.0 6.0 8.0 9.0 9.2

GD VG FN VF VF/NM NM-
2.0 4.0 6.0 8.0 9.0 9.2

Annual 1,2: 1(12/85)-Crisis x-over. 2('88, $2.00), Special 1 ('87, $1.50) 4.00
...: The Generations Saga Volume One HC (2011, $39.99) r/#1-4, All-Star Squadron #25,26 & All-Star Squadron Annual #2 40.00
NOTE: ***Kubert*** *r-4.* ***McFarlane*** *a-14-37p, Annual 1p; c(p)-14-19, 22, 25, 26, 31-33, 37, Annual 1.* ***Newton*** *a-12p, 13p(last work 4/85).* ***Tuska*** *a-11p. JSA app. 3-10.*

INFINITY, INC. (See 52)
DC Comics: Nov, 2007 - No. 12, Oct, 2008 ($2.99)

1-12: 1-Milligan-s; Steel app. 3.00
...: Luthor's Monsters TPB (2008, $14.99) r/#1-5 15.00
...: The Bogeyman TPB (2008, $14.99) r/#6-10 15.00

INFINITY MAN AND THE FOREVER PEOPLE
DC Comics: Aug, 2014 - No. 9, May, 2015 ($2.99)

1-9: 1-DiDio-s/Giffen-a. 2,5,6-Grummett-a. 3-Starlin-a. 4-6-Guy Gardner app. 9-Giffen-a 3.00
...: Futures End 1 (11/14, $2.99, regular-c) Five years later; Philip Tan-a 3.00
...: Futures End 1 (11/14, $3.99, 3-D cover) 4.00

INFINITY: THE HUNT (Tie-in to the Infinity crossover)
Marvel Comics: Nov, 2013 - No. 4, Jan, 2014 ($3.99, limited series)

1-4-Kindt-s/Sanders-a; Avengers Academy, Wolverine & She-Hulk app. 4.00

INFINITY WAR, THE (Also see Infinity Gauntlet & Warlock and the Infinity...)
Marvel Comics: June, 1992 - No. 6, Nov, 1992 ($2.50, mini-series)

1-Starlin scripts, Lim-c/a(p), Thanos app. in all 1 2 3 5 6 8
2-6: All have wraparound gatefold covers 6.00
TPB (2006, $29.99) r/#1-6, Marvel Comics Presents #108-111, Warlock and the Infinity Watch #7-10; cover gallery and synopses of Infinity War crossovers 30.00

INFORMER, THE
Feature Television Productions: April, 1954 - No. 5, Dec, 1954

1-Sekowsky-a begins 13 26 39 74 105 135
2 9 18 27 47 61 75
3-5 8 16 24 42 54 65

IN HIS STEPS
Spire Christian Comics (Fleming H. Revell Co.): 1973, 1977 (39/49¢)

nn 2 4 6 11 16 20

INHUMAN (Also see Uncanny Inhumans)
Marvel Comics: Jun, 2014 - No. 14, Jun, 2015 ($3.99)

1-14: 1-3-Soule-s/Madureira-a; Medusa app. 4-7,9-11-Stegman-a. 10-Spider-Man app. 4.00
Annual 1 (7/15, $4.99) Soule-s/Stegman-a; continues from #14; Ms. Marvel app. 5.00
... Special 1 (6/15, $4.99) Crossover with Amaz. Spider-Man & All-New Capt. America 5.00

INHUMANITY
Marvel Comics: Feb, 2014 - No. 2, Mar, 2014 ($3.99)

1,2: 1-After the fall of Attilan, origin of the Inhumans retold; Fraction-s/Coipel-a 4.00
...: Superior Spider-Man 1 (3/14, $3.99) Gage-s/Hans-a/c 4.00
...: The Awakening 1,2 (2/14 - No. 2, 3/14, $3.99) Kindt-s/Davidson-a 4.00

INHUMANOIDS, THE (TV)
Marvel Comics (Star Comics): Jan, 1987 - No. 4, July 1987

1-4: Based on Hasbro toys 4.00

INHUMANS, THE (See Amazing Adventures, Fantastic Four #54 & Special #5, Incredible Hulk Special #1, Marvel Graphic Novel & Thor #146)
Marvel Comics Group: Oct, 1975 - No. 12, Aug, 1977

1: #1-4,6 are 25¢ issues 6 12 18 41 76 110
2-4-Peréz-a 3 6 9 14 20 25
5-12: 9-Reprints Amazing Adventures #1,2('70). 12-Hulk app.
2 4 6 10 14 18
4-(30¢-c variant, limited distribution)(4/76) Pérez-a 4 8 12 23 37 50
6-(30¢-c variant, limited distribution)(8/76) 4 8 12 23 37 50
11,12-(35¢-c variants, limited distribution) 6 12 18 38 69 100
Special 1(4/90, $1.50, 52 pgs.)-F.F. cameo 5.00
...: The Great Refuge (5/95, $2.95) 4.00
NOTE: ***Buckler*** *c-2-4p, 5.* ***Gil Kane*** *a-5-7p; c-1p, 7p, 8p.* ***Kirby*** *a-9r.* ***Mooney*** *a-11i.* ***Perez*** *a-1-4p, 8p.*

INHUMANS (Marvel Knights)
Marvel Comics: Nov, 1998 - No. 12, Oct, 1999 ($2.99, limited series)

1-Jae Lee-c/a; Paul Jenkins-s 3 6 9 14 20 25
1-($6.95) DF Edition; Jae Lee variant-c 3 6 9 19 30 40
2-Two covers by Lee and Darrow 6.00
3-12 4.00
TPB (10/00, $24.95) r/#1-12 25.00

INHUMANS (Volume 3)
Marvel Comics: Jun, 2000 - No. 4, Oct, 2000 ($2.99, limited series)

1-4-Ladronn-c/Pacheco & Marin-s. 1-3-Ladronn-a. 4-Lucas-a 3.00

INHUMANS (Volume 6)
Marvel Comics: Jun, 2003 - No. 12, Jun, 2004 ($2.50/$2.99)

1-12: 1-6-McKeever-s/Clark-a/JH Williams III-c. 7-Begin $2.99-c. 7,8-Teranishi-a 3.00
Vol. 1: Culture Shock (2005, $7.99, digest) r/#1-6; story pitch and sketch pages 8.00

INHUMANS: ATTILAN RISING (Secret Wars tie-in)
Marvel Comics: Jul, 2015 - No. 5, Nov, 2015 ($3.99, limited series)

1-5-Soule-s/Timms-a/Johnson-c 4.00

INHUMANS 2099
Marvel Comics: Nov, 2004 ($2.99, one-shot)

1-Kirkman-s/Rathburn-a/Pat Lee-c 3.00

INHUMANS VS. X-MEN (See IVX)

INJECTION
Image Comics: May, 2015 - Present ($2.99)

1-10-Warren Ellis-s/Declan Shalvey-a 3.00

INJUSTICE: GODS AMONG US (Based on the video game)
DC Comics: Mar, 2013 - No. 12, Feb, 2014 ($3.99)

1-Lois Lane dies; Joker app. 3 6 9 19 30 40
1-Variant-c 3 6 9 21 33 45
1-Second printing 6.00
2-Joker killed 10.00
3-12: 6-Nightwing dies 4.00
Annual 1 (1/14, $4.99) Harley Quinn & Lobo app.; Ryp-c 5.00

INJUSTICE: GODS AMONG US: YEAR THREE (Based on the video game)
DC Comics: Early Dec, 2014 - No. 12, Late May, 2015 ($2.99, printings of digital-first stories)

1-12: 1-Constantine joins the fight. 5-New Deadman app. 3.00
Annual 1 (6/15, $4.99) Prequel to Year Three; Constantine app.; Titans vs. Superman 5.00

INJUSTICE: GODS AMONG US: YEAR FOUR (Based on the video game)
DC Comics: Early Jul, 2015 - No. 12, Late Dec, 2015 ($2.99, printings of digital-first stories)

1-12: 1-The Olympus Gods join the fight. 10-Harley Quinn cover 3.00

INJUSTICE: GODS AMONG US: YEAR FIVE (Based on the video game)
DC Comics: Early Mar, 2016 - No. 20, Late Dec, 2016 ($2.99, printings of digital-first stories)

1-20: 1-Doomsday & Bane app. 6-Solomon Grundy app. 7-Damian becomes Nightwing. 12-Alfred killed by Zsasz. 18-Deathstroke app. 3.00
Annual 1 (1/17, $4.99) Harley Quinn app.; leads into Injustice: Ground Zero 5.00

INJUSTICE: GROUND ZERO (Follows Year Five)
DC Comics: Early Feb, 2016 - Present ($2.99, printings of digital-first stories)

1-7: 1-Mhan & Derenick-a; Harley & Joker app. 3.00

INJUSTICE YEAR TWO (Based on the video game)
DC Comics: Mar, 2014 - No. 12, Late Nov, 2014 ($2.99)

1-12: 1-6,9-12-Sinestro app. 7-11-Harley Quinn app. 3.00
Annual 1 (12/14, $4.99) Stories of Oracle, Green Lantern & Sinestro; Raapack-c 5.00

INKY & DINKY (See Felix's Nephews...)

IN LOVE (...Magazine on-c; I Love You No. 7 on)
Mainline/Charlton No. 5 (5/55)-on: Aug-Sept, 1954 - No. 6, July, 1955 ('Adult Reading' on-c)

1-Simon & Kirby-a; book-length novel in all issues 52 104 156 328 552 775
2,3-S&K-a. 3-Last pre-code (12-1/54-55) 31 62 93 182 296 410
4-S&K-a.(Rare) 34 68 102 199 325 450
5-S&K-c only 18 36 54 107 169 230
6-No S&K-a 11 22 33 64 90 115

INNOVATION SPECTACULAR
Innovation Publishing: 1991 - No. 2, 1991 ($2.95, squarebound, 100 pgs.)

1,2: Contains rebound comics w/o covers 4.00

INNOVATION SUMMER FUN SPECIAL
Innovation Publishing: 1991 ($3.50, B&W/color, squarebound)

1-Contains rebound comics (Power Factory) 4.00

IN SEARCH OF THE CASTAWAYS (See Movie Comics)

INSEXTS
AfterShock Comics: Dec, 2015 - Present ($3.99, mature)

1-9-Marguerite Bennett-s/Ariela Kristantina-a 4.00

INSIDE CRIME (Formerly My Intimate Affair)
Fox Features Syndicate (Hero Books): No. 3, July, 1950 - No. 2, Sept, 1950

3-Wood-a (10 pgs.); L. B. Cole-c 30 60 90 177 289 400

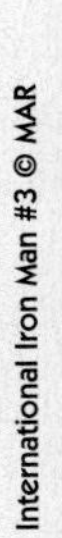
Insufferable #6 © Waid & Krause

International Iron Man #3 © MAR

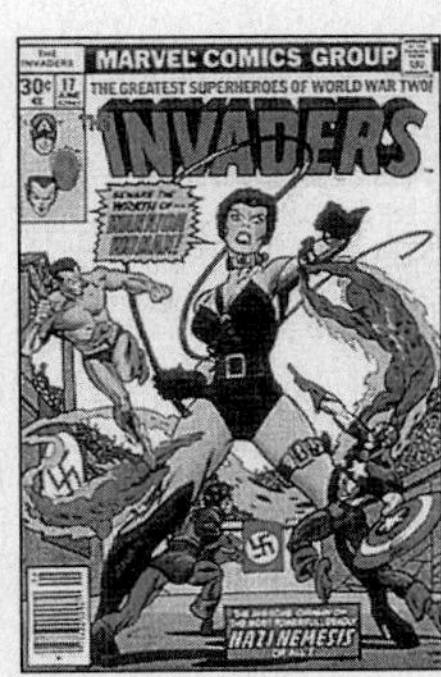

Invaders #17 © MAR

	GD 2.0	VG 4.0	FN 6.0	VF 8.0	VF/NM 9.0	NM- 9.2
2-Used in **SOTI**, pg. 182,183; r/Spook #24	23	46	69	136	223	310
nn (nd, M.S. Dist. Pub.) Wally Wood-c	11	22	33	62	86	110

INSPECTOR, THE (TV) (Also see The Pink Panther)
Gold Key: July, 1974 - No. 19, Feb, 1978

	GD 2.0	VG 4.0	FN 6.0	VF 8.0	VF/NM 9.0	NM- 9.2
1	3	6	9	18	28	38
2-5	2	4	6	13	18	22
6-9	2	4	6	10	14	18
10-19: 11-Reprints	2	4	6	8	10	12

INSPECTOR, THE Volume 2 (The Pink Panther)
American Mythology: 2016 - Present ($3.99)

	GD 2.0	VG 4.0	FN 6.0	VF 8.0	VF/NM 9.0	NM- 9.2
1-The Pink Files; new stories by Fridolfs & Gallagher; reprints						4.00

INSPECTOR GILL OF THE FISH POLICE (See Fish Police)

INSPECTOR WADE
David McKay Publications: No. 13, May, 1938

	GD 2.0	VG 4.0	FN 6.0	VF 8.0	VF/NM 9.0	NM- 9.2
Feature Books 13	33	66	99	194	317	440

INSTANT PIANO
Dark Horse Comics: Aug, 1994 - No. 4, Feb, 1995 ($3.95, B&W, bimonthly, mature)

	GD 2.0	VG 4.0	FN 6.0	VF 8.0	VF/NM 9.0	NM- 9.2
1-4						4.00

INSUFFERABLE
IDW Publishing: May, 2015 - No. 8, Dec, 2015 ($3.99)

	GD 2.0	VG 4.0	FN 6.0	VF 8.0	VF/NM 9.0	NM- 9.2
1-8-Waid-s/Krause-a						4.00

INSUFFERABLE: HOME FIELD ADVANTAGE
IDW Publishing: Oct, 2016 - No. 4, Jan, 2017 ($3.99)

	GD 2.0	VG 4.0	FN 6.0	VF 8.0	VF/NM 9.0	NM- 9.2
1-4-Waid-s/Krause-a						4.00

INSUFFERABLE: ON THE ROAD
IDW Publishing: Feb, 2016 - No. 6, Jul, 2016 ($3.99)

	GD 2.0	VG 4.0	FN 6.0	VF 8.0	VF/NM 9.0	NM- 9.2
1-6-Waid-s/Krause-a						4.00

INSURGENT
DC Comics: Mar, 2013 - No. 3, May, 2013 ($2.99, limited series)

	GD 2.0	VG 4.0	FN 6.0	VF 8.0	VF/NM 9.0	NM- 9.2
1-3-DeSanto & Farmer-s/Dallocchio-a						3.00

INTERFACE
Marvel Comics (Epic Comics): Dec, 1989 - No. 8, Dec, 1990 ($1.95, mature, coated paper)

	GD 2.0	VG 4.0	FN 6.0	VF 8.0	VF/NM 9.0	NM- 9.2
1-8: Cont. from 1st ESPers series; painted-c/a						3.00
Espers: Interface TPB ('98, $16.95) r/#1-6						17.00

INTERNATIONAL COMICS (...Crime Patrol No. 6)
E. C. Comics: Spring, 1947 - No. 5, Nov-Dec, 1947

	GD 2.0	VG 4.0	FN 6.0	VF 8.0	VF/NM 9.0	NM- 9.2
1-Schaffenberger-a begins, ends #4	77	154	231	493	847	1200
2	50	100	150	315	533	750
3-5	45	90	135	284	480	675

INTERNATIONAL CRIME PATROL (Formerly International Comics #1-5; becomes Crime Patrol No. 7 on)
E. C. Comics: No. 6, Spring, 1948

	GD 2.0	VG 4.0	FN 6.0	VF 8.0	VF/NM 9.0	NM- 9.2
6-Moon Girl app.	77	154	231	493	847	1200

INTERNATIONAL IRON MAN
Marvel Comics: May, 2016 - No. 7, Nov, 2016 ($3.99)

	GD 2.0	VG 4.0	FN 6.0	VF 8.0	VF/NM 9.0	NM- 9.2
1-7-Bendis-s/Maleev-a. 1-4-Flashback to college years in London. 5-Intro. Amanda Armstrong. 6,7-Flashback to Stark's real parents meeting						4.00

INTERSECT
Image Comics: Nov, 2014 - No. 6, Apr, 2015 ($3.50)

	GD 2.0	VG 4.0	FN 6.0	VF 8.0	VF/NM 9.0	NM- 9.2
1-6-Ray Fawkes-s/a. 1-Lemire-c. 2-Kindt-c						3.50

IN THE DAYS OF THE MOB (Magazine)
Hampshire Dist. Ltd. (National): Fall, 1971 (B&W)

	GD 2.0	VG 4.0	FN 6.0	VF 8.0	VF/NM 9.0	NM- 9.2
1-Kirby-a; John Dillinger wanted poster inside (1/2 value if poster is missing)	7	14	21	44	82	120

IN THE PRESENCE OF MINE ENEMIES
Spire Christian Comics/Fleming H. Revell Co.: 1973 (35/49¢)

	GD 2.0	VG 4.0	FN 6.0	VF 8.0	VF/NM 9.0	NM- 9.2
nn	2	4	6	10	14	18

IN THE SHADOW OF EDGAR ALLAN POE
DC Comics (Vertigo): 2002 (Graphic novel)

	GD 2.0	VG 4.0	FN 6.0	VF 8.0	VF/NM 9.0	NM- 9.2
Hardcover (2002, $24.95) Fuqua-s/Phillips and Parke photo-a						25.00
Softcover (2003, $17.95)						18.00

INTIMATE
Charlton Comics: Dec, 1957 - No. 3, May, 1958

	GD 2.0	VG 4.0	FN 6.0	VF 8.0	VF/NM 9.0	NM- 9.2
1	6	12	18	28	34	40
2,3	4	8	12	18	22	25

INTIMATE CONFESSIONS (See Fox Giants)

INTIMATE CONFESSIONS
Country Press Inc.: 1942

nn-Ashcan comic, not distributed to newsstands, only for in house use. A VF copy sold for $1,000 in 2007, and a VF+ copy sold for $1,525 in 2007.

INTIMATE CONFESSIONS
Realistic Comics: July-Aug, 1951 - No. 7, Aug, 1952; No. 8, Mar, 1953 (All painted-c)

	GD 2.0	VG 4.0	FN 6.0	VF 8.0	VF/NM 9.0	NM- 9.2
1-Kinstler-a; c/Avon paperback #222	194	388	582	1242	2121	3000
2	43	86	129	271	461	650
3-c/Avon paperback #250; Kinstler-c/a	47	94	141	296	498	700
4-8: 4-c/Avon paperback #304; Kinstler-c. 6-c/Avon paperback #120. 8-c/Avon paperback #375; Kinstler-a	42	84	126	265	445	625

INTIMATE CONFESSIONS
I. W. Enterprises/Super Comics: 1964

	GD 2.0	VG 4.0	FN 6.0	VF 8.0	VF/NM 9.0	NM- 9.2
I.W. Reprint #9,10, Super Reprint #10,12,18	2	4	6	13	18	22

INTIMATE LOVE
Standard Comics: No. 5, 1950 - No. 28, Aug, 1954

	GD 2.0	VG 4.0	FN 6.0	VF 8.0	VF/NM 9.0	NM- 9.2
5-8: 6-8-Severin/Elder-a	14	28	42	76	108	140
9	10	20	30	56	76	95
10-Jane Russell, Robert Mitchum photo-c	15	30	45	88	137	185
11-18,20,23,25,27,28	10	20	30	54	72	90
19,21,22,24,26-Toth-a	11	22	33	60	83	105

NOTE: ***Celardo** a-8, 10. **Colletta** a-23. **Moreira** a-13(2). Photo-c-6, 7, 10, 12, 14, 15, 18-20, 24, 26, 27.*

INTIMATES, THE
DC Comics (WildStorm): Jan, 2005 - No. 12, Dec, 2005 ($2.95/$2.99)

	GD 2.0	VG 4.0	FN 6.0	VF 8.0	VF/NM 9.0	NM- 9.2
1-12: 1-Joe Casey-s/Jim Lee-c/Lee and Giuseppe Camuncoli-a						3.00

INTIMATE SECRETS OF ROMANCE
Star Publications: Sept, 1953 - No. 2, Apr, 1954

	GD 2.0	VG 4.0	FN 6.0	VF 8.0	VF/NM 9.0	NM- 9.2
1,2-L. B. Cole-c	20	40	60	118	192	265

INTRIGUE
Quality Comics Group: Jan, 1955

	GD 2.0	VG 4.0	FN 6.0	VF 8.0	VF/NM 9.0	NM- 9.2
1-Horror; Jack Cole reprint/Web of Evil	36	72	108	216	351	485

INTRIGUE
Image Comics: Aug, 1999 - No. 3, Feb, 2000 ($2.50/$2.95)

	GD 2.0	VG 4.0	FN 6.0	VF 8.0	VF/NM 9.0	NM- 9.2
1,2: 1-Two covers (Andrews, Wieringo); Shum-s/Andrews-a						3.00
3-($2.95)						3.00

INTRUDER
TSR, Inc.: 1990 - No. 10, 1991 ($2.95, 44 pgs.)

	GD 2.0	VG 4.0	FN 6.0	VF 8.0	VF/NM 9.0	NM- 9.2
1-10						4.00

INVADERS, THE (TV)(Aliens From a Dying Planet)
Gold Key: Oct, 1967 - No. 4, Oct, 1968 (All have photo-c)

	GD 2.0	VG 4.0	FN 6.0	VF 8.0	VF/NM 9.0	NM- 9.2
1-Spiegle-a in all	8	16	24	51	96	140
2-4: 2-Pin-up on back-c. 3-Has variant 15¢-c with photo back-c	5	10	15	35	63	90

INVADERS, THE (Also see The Avengers #71, Giant-Size Invaders, and All-New Invaders)
Marvel Comics Group: August, 1975 - No. 40, May, 1979; No. 41, Sept, 1979

	GD 2.0	VG 4.0	FN 6.0	VF 8.0	VF/NM 9.0	NM- 9.2
1-Captain America & Bucky, Human Torch & Toro, & Sub-Mariner begin; cont'd. from Giant Size Invaders #1; #1-7 are 25¢ issues	6	12	18	37	66	95
2-5: 2-1st app. Brain-Drain. 3-Battle issue; Cap vs. Namor vs. Torch; intro U-Man	3	6	9	17	26	35
6-10: 6,7-(Regular 25¢ edition). 6-(7/76) Liberty Legion app. 7-Intro Baron Blood & intro/1st app. Union Jack; Human Torch origin retold. 8-Union Jack-c/story. 9-Origin Baron Blood. 10-G.A. Capt. America-r/C.A #22	2	4	6	11	16	20
6,7-(30¢-c variants, limited distribution)	5	10	15	30	50	70
11-19: 11-Origin Spitfire; intro The Blue Bullet. 14-1st app. The Crusaders. 16-Re-intro The Destroyer. 17-Intro Warrior Woman. 18-Re-intro The Destroyer w/new origin. 19-Hitler-c/story	2	4	6	8	11	14
17-19,21-(35¢-c variants, limited distribution)	9	18	27	59	117	175
20-(Regular 30¢-c) Reprints origin/1st app. Sub-Mariner from Motion Picture Funnies Weekly with color added & brief write-up about MPFW; 1st app. new Union Jack II	2	4	6	10	14	18
20-(35¢-c variant, limited distribution)	10	20	30	64	132	200
21-(Regular 30¢ edition)-r/Marvel Mystery #10 (battle issue)	2	4	6	9	13	16

22-30,34-40: 22-New origin Toro. 24-r/Marvel Mystery #17 (team-up issue; all-r). 25-All new-a

Invader Zim #8 © Viacom

Invincible #89 © Kirkman & Walker

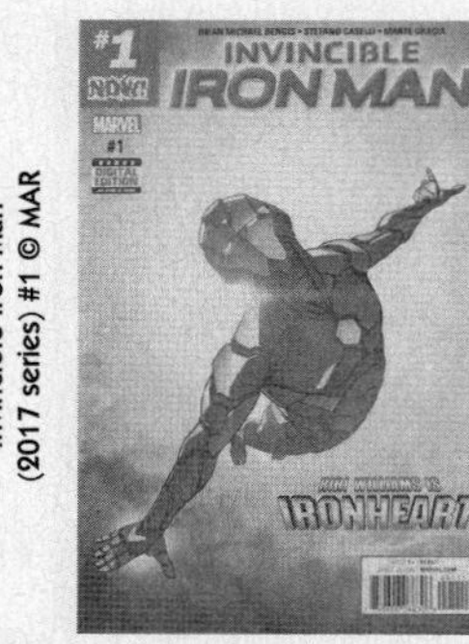

Invincible Iron Man (2017 series) #1 © MAR

	GD 2.0	VG 4.0	FN 6.0	VF 8.0	VF/NM 9.0	NM- 9.2
begins. 28-Intro new Human Top & Golden Girl. 29-Intro Teutonic Knight. 34-Mighty Destroyer joins. 35-The Whizzer app.	1	2	3	5	7	9
31-33: 31-Frankenstein-c/sty. 32,33-Thor app.	2	4	6	8	11	14
41-Double size last issue	3	6	9	14	19	24
Annual 1 (9/77)-Schomburg, Rico stories (new); Schomburg-c/a (1st for Marvel in 30 years); Avengers app.; re-intro The Shark & The Hyena	5	10	15	31	53	75

... Classic Vol. 1 TPB (2007, $24.99) r/#1-9, Giant-Size Invaders #1 and Marvel Premiere #29,30; cover pencils and cover inks 25.00

NOTE: ***Buckler** a-5. **Everett** r-20('39), 21(1940), 24, Annual 1. **Gil Kane** c(p)-13, 17, 18, 20-27. **Kirby** c(p)-3-12, 14-16, 32, 33. **Mooney** a-5i, 16, 22. **Robbins** a-1-4, 6-9, 10(3 pg.), 11-15, 17-21, 23, 25-28; c-28.*

INVADERS (See Namor, the Sub-Mariner #12)
Marvel Comics Group: May, 1993 - No. 4, Aug, 1993 ($1.75, limited series)

1-4 3.00

INVADERS (2004 title - see New Invaders)

INVADERS FROM HOME
DC Comics (Piranha Press): 1990 - No. 6, 1990 ($2.50, mature)

1-6 3.00

INVADERS NOW! (See Avengers/Invaders and The Torch series)
Marvel Comics: Nov, 2010 - No. 5, Mar, 2011 ($3.99, limited series)

1-5-Alex Ross-c; Steve Rogers, Bucky, Human Torch & Toro, Sub-Mariner app. 4.00

INVADER ZIM
Oni Press: Jul, 2015 - Present ($3.99)

1-Jhonen Vasquez-s/Aaron Alexovich-a; multiple covers 4.00
2-17 4.00
... #1 Square One Edition (2/17, $1.00) r/#1 3.00

INVASION
DC Comics: Holiday, 1988-'89 - No. 3, Jan, 1989 ($2.95, lim. series, 84 pgs.)

1-3:1-McFarlane/Russell-a. 2-McFarlane/Russell & Giffen/Gordon-a 5.00
Invasion! TPB (2008, $24.99) r/#1-3 25.00

INVINCIBLE (Also see The Pact #4)
Image Comics: Jan, 2003 - Present ($2.95/$2.99)

	GD	VG	FN	VF	VF/NM	NM-
1-Kirkman-s/Walker-a	9	18	27	59	117	175
2,3-Kirkman-s/Walker-a	3	6	9	21	33	45
4-8: 4-Preview of The Moth	2	4	6	10	14	18
9-14: 11-Origin of Omni-Man. 14-Cho-c	1	2	3	5	6	8

15-24,26-41,43-49: 33-Tie-in w/Marvel Team-Up #14 5.00
25-($4.95) Science Dog app.; back-up stories w/origins of Science Dog and teammates 6.00
42-($1.99) Includes re-cap of the entire series 5.00
50-(6/08, $4.99) Two covers; back-up origin of Cecil Stedman; Science Dog app. 6.00
51-59,61-74: 51-Jim Lee-c; new costumes. 57-Continues in Astounding Wolf-Man #11. 71-74-Viltrumite War 4.00
76-99,101-109,111-117: 89-Intro. Zandale. 97-Origin of Bulletproof. 112-Baby born 3.00

	GD	VG	FN	VF	VF/NM	NM-
60-($3.99) Invincible War; Witchblade, Savage Dragon, Spawn, Youngblood app.	1	2	3	5	6	8
75-($5.99) Viltrumite War; Science Dog back-up; 2 covers	1	2	3	4	5	7

100-(1/13, $3.99) "The Death of Everyone" conclusion; multiple covers 5.00
110-Rape issue 6.00
118-133: 118-(25¢-c). 124-126-Reboot. 132-Oliver dies. 133-(25¢-c) Mark & Eve wedding 3.00
#0-(4/05, 50¢) Origin of Invincible; Ottley-a 3.00
Image Firsts: Invincible #1 (4/10, $1.00) r/#1 with "Image Firsts" cover logo 3.00
Official Handbook of the Invincible Universe 1,2 (11/06, 1/07, $4.99) profile pages 5.00
Official Handbook of the Invincible Universe Vol. 1 (2007, $12.99) r/#1-2; sketch pages 13.00
... Presents Atom Eve 1,2 (12/07, 3/08, $2.99) origin of Atom Eve; Bellegarde-a 3.00
... Presents Atom Eve & Rex Splode 1-3 (10/09 - 2/10, $2.99) origin of Rex 3.00
... Returns (4/10, $3.99) Leads into Viltrumite War in #71; 4 covers 4.00
... Universe Primer 1 (5/08, $5.99) r/Invincible #1, Brit #1, Astounding Wolf-Man #1 6.00
The Complete Invincible Library Vol. 1 Slipcase HC (2006, $125.00) oversized r/#1-24, #0 and story from Image Comics Summer Special (FCBD 2004); sketch pages; script for #1 125.00
..., Ultimate Collection Vol. 1 HC (2005, $34.95) oversized r/#1-13; sketch pages 35.00
..., Ultimate Collection Vol. 2 HC (2006, $34.99) oversized r/#14-24, #0 and story from Image Comics Summer Special (FCBD 2004); sketch pages and script for #23; intro by Damon Lindelof; afterword by Robert Kirkman 35.00
..., Ultimate Collection Vol. 3 HC (2007, $34.95) oversized r/#25-35 & The Pact #4; sketch pages and script for #28; afterword by Robert Kirkman 35.00
..., Ultimate Collection Vol. 4 HC (2008, $34.99) oversized r/#36-47; sketch & script pgs. 35.00
Vol. 1: Family Matters TPB (8/03, $12.95) r/#1-4; intro. by Busiek; sketch pages 13.00
Vol. 2: Eight in Enough TPB (3/04, $12.95) r/#5-8; intro. by Larsen; sketch pages 13.00
Vol. 3: Perfect Strangers TPB (2004, $12.95) r/#9-12; intro. by Brevoort; sketch pages 13.00
Vol. 4: Head of the Class TPB (1/05, $14.95) r/#14-19; intro. by Waid; sketch pages 15.00
Vol. 5: The Facts of Life TPB (2005, $14.99) r/#0,20-24; intro. by Wieringo; sketch pages 15.00
Vol. 6: A Different World TPB (2006, $14.99) r/#25-30; intro. by Brubaker; sketch pages 15.00
Vol. 7: Three's Company TPB (2006, $14.99) r/#31-35 & The Pact #4; sketch pages 15.00
Vol. 8: My Favorite Martian TPB (2007, $14.99) r/#36-41; sketch pages 15.00
Vol. 9: Out of This World TPB (2008, $14.99) r/#42-47; sketch pages 15.00

INVINCIBLE FOUR OF KUNG FU & NINJA
Leung Publications: April, 1988 - No. 6, 1989 ($2.00)

1-($2.75) 4.00
2-6: 2-Begin $2.00-c 3.00

INVINCIBLE IRON MAN
Marvel Comics: July, 2008 - No. 33, Feb, 2011;
No. 500, Mar, 2011 - No. 527, Dec, 2012 ($2.99/$3.99)

1-Fraction-s/Larroca-a; covers by Larroca & Quesada 4.00
1-Downey movie photo wraparound 5.00
1-Secret Movie Variant white-c with movie cast 30.00
2-18: 2-War Machine and Thor app. 7-Spider-Man app. 8-10-Dark Reign. 11-War Machine app.; Pepper gets her armor suit. 12-Namor app. 3.00
19,20-($3.99) 20-Stark Disassembled starts; back-up synopsis of recent storylines 4.00
21-24-Covers by Larocca and Zircher: 21-Thor & Capt. America app. 22-Dr. Strange app. 3.00
25-($3.99) Fraction-s/Larroca-a; new armor 4.00
26-31-($2.99) 29-New Rescue armor 3.00
32,33-($3.99)-War Machine app.; back-up w/McKelvie-a 4.00
(After #33, numbering reverts to original Vol. 1 as #500)
500-(3/11, $4.99) Two covers by Larroca; Mandarin & Spider-Man app.; cover gallery 5.00
500-Variant-c by Romita Jr. 10.00
500.1 (4/11, $2.99) History re-told; Fraction-s/Larroca-a/c 3.00
501-527-($3.99) 501-503-Doctor Octopus app. 503-Back-up w/Chaykin-a. 504-509-Fear Itself tie-in; Grey Gargoyle app. 517-New War Machine armor 4.00
Annual 1 (8/10, $4.99) Larroca-c; history of the Mandarin; Di Giandomenico-a 5.00
...MGC #1 (4/10, free) r/#1 with "Marvel's Greatest Comics" cover logo 3.00

INVINCIBLE IRON MAN
Marvel Comics: Dec, 2015 - No. 14, Dec, 2016 ($3.99)

1-6,8-14: 1-Bendis-s/Marquez-a; Doctor Doom & Madame Masque app. 6-14-Deodato-a. 8-Spider-Man app. 11-14-Civil War II tie-in 4.00
7-1st app. Riri Williams; Spider-Man app. 10.00

INVINCIBLE IRON MAN (Riri Williams as Ironheart)
Marvel Comics: Jan, 2017 - Present ($3.99)

1-4: 1-Bendis-s/Caselli-a; Riri Williams childhood origin; Animax app. 4.00

INVINCIBLE UNIVERSE (Characters from Invincible)
Image Comics: Apr, 2013 - No. 12, Apr, 2014 ($2.99)

1-12-Hester-s/Nauck-a. 1-Wraparound-c 3.00

INVISIBLE BOY (See Approved Comics)

INVISIBLE MAN, THE (See Superior Stories #1 & Supernatural Thrillers #2)

INVISIBLE PEOPLE
Kitchen Sink Press: 1992 (B&W, lim. series)

Book One: Sanctum; Book Two: "The Power": Will Eisner-s/a in all 4.00
Book Three: "Mortal Combat" 4.00
Hardcover ($34.95) 35.00
TPB (DC Comics, 9/00, $12.95) reprints series 13.00

INVISIBLE REPUBLIC
Image Comics: Feb, 2015 - Present ($2.99/$3.99)

1-10-Hardman & Bechko-s/Hardman-a 3.00
11-15-($3.99) 4.00

INVISIBLES, THE (1st Series)
DC Comics (Vertigo): Sept, 1994 - No. 25, Oct, 1996 ($1.95/$2.50, mature)

1-($2.95, 52 pgs.)-Intro King Mob, Ragged Robin, Boy, Lord Fanny & Dane (Jack Frost); Grant Morrison scripts in all 6.00
2-8: 4-Includes bound-in trading cards. 5-1st app. Orlando; brown paper-c 4.00
9-25: 10-Intro Jim Crow. 13-15-Origin Lord Fanny. 19-Origin King Mob; polybagged. 20-Origin Boy. 21-Mister Six revealed. 25-Intro Division X 3.00
Apocalipstick (2001, $19.95, TPB)-r/#9-16; Bolland-c 20.00
Entropy in the U.K. (2001, $19.95, TPB)-r/#17-25; Bolland-c 20.00
Say You Want A Revolution (1996, $17.50, TPB)-r/#1-8 18.00

NOTE: ***Buckingham** a-25p. **Rian Hughes** c-1, 5. **Phil Jimenez** a-17p-19p. **Paul Johnson** a-16, 21. **Sean Phillips** c-2-4, 6-25. **Weston** a-10p. **Yeowell** a-1p-4p, 22p-24p.*

INVISIBLES, THE (2nd Series)
DC Comics (Vertigo): V2#1, Feb, 1997 - No. 22, Feb, 1999 ($2.50, mature)

1-Intro Jolly Roger; Grant Morrison scripts, Phil Jimenez-a, & Brian Bolland-c begins 4.00

Iron Fist #2 © MAR

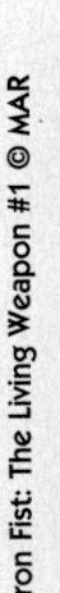

Iron Fist: The Living Weapon #1 © MAR

Iron Man #109 © MAR

GD 2.0 | VG 4.0 | FN 6.0 | VF 8.0 | VF/NM 9.0 | NM- 9.2

2-22: 9,14-Weston-a 3.00
Bloody Hell in America TPB ('98, $12.95) r/#1-4 13.00
Counting to None TPB ('99, $19.95) r/#5-13 20.00
Kissing Mr. Quimper TPB ('00, $19.95) r/#14-22 20.00

INVISIBLES, THE (3rd Series) (Issue #'s go in reverse from #12 to #1)
DC Comics (Vertigo): V3#12, Apr, 1999 - No. 1, June, 2000 ($2.95, mature)

1-12-Bolland-c; Morrison-s on all. 1-Quitely-a. 2-4-Art by various. 5-8-Phillips-a. 9-12-Phillip Bond-a. 3.00
The Invisible Kingdom TPB ('02, $19.95) r/#12-1; new Bolland-c 20.00

INVISIBLE SCARLET O'NEIL (Also see Famous Funnies #81 & Harvey Comics Hits #59)
Famous Funnies (Harvey): Dec, 1950 - No. 3, Apr, 1951 (2-3 pgs. of Powell-a in each issue.)

1 15 30 45 88 137 185
2,3 12 24 36 67 94 120

ION (Green Lantern Kyle Rayner) (See Countdown)
DC Comics: Jun, 2006 - No. 12, May, 2007 ($2.99)

1-12: 1-Marz-s/Tocchini-a. 3-Mogo app. 9,10-Tangent Green Lantern app. 12-Monitor app. 3.00
...: The Torchbearer TPB (2007, $14.99) r/#1-6 15.00

I, PAPARAZZI
DC Comics (Vertigo): 2001 ($29.95, HC, digitally manipulated photographic art)

nn-Pat McGreal-s/Steven Parke-digital-a/Stephen John Phillips-photos 30.00

IRON AGE
Marvel Comics: Aug, 2011 - No. 3, Oct, 2011 ($4.99, limited series)

1-3-Iron Man time travels. 1-Avengers. 2-Fantastic Four. 3-Dazzler & X-Men 5.00
...: Alpha (8/11, $2.99) First part of the series; Dark Phoenix app.; Issacs-a 3.00
...: Omega (10/11, $2.99) Conclusion of the series; Olivetti-c/Issacs-a 3.00

IRON AND THE MAIDEN
Aspen MLT: Sept, 2007 - No. 4, Dec, 2007 ($3.99)

1-4: 1-Two covers by Manapul and Madureira/Matsuda; Jason Rubin-s 4.00
...: Brutes, Bims and the City (2/08, $2.99) character backgrounds/development art 3.00

IRON CORPORAL, THE (See Army War Heroes #22)
Charlton Comics: No. 23, Oct, 1985 - No. 25, Feb, 1986

23-25: Glanzman-a(r); low print 6.00

IRON FIST (See Immortal Iron Fist, Deadly Hands of Kung Fu, Marvel Premiere & Power Man)
Marvel Comics: Nov, 1975 - No. 15, Sept, 1977

1-Iron Fist battles Iron Man (#1-6: 25¢) 9 18 27 59 117 175
2 4 8 12 27 44 60
3-10: 4-6-(Regular 25¢ edition)(4-6/76). 8-Origin retold
3 6 9 19 30 40
4-6-(30¢-c variant, limited distribution) 5 10 15 35 63 90
11,13: 13-(30¢-c) 3 6 9 16 24 32
12-Capt. America app. 4 8 12 23 37 50
13-(35¢-c variant, limited distribution) 13 26 39 89 195 300
14-1st app. Sabretooth (8/77)(see Power Man) 17 34 51 117 259 400
14-(35¢-c variant, limited distribution) 141 282 423 1142 2571 4000
15-(Regular 30¢ ed.) X-Men app., Byrne-a 6 12 18 41 76 110
15-(35¢-c variant, limited distribution) 46 92 138 340 770 1200

NOTE: *Adkins a-8p, 10i, 13i; c-8i.* ***Byrne*** *a-1-15p; c-8p, 15p.* ***G. Kane*** *c-4-6p.* ***McWilliams*** *a-1i.*

IRON FIST
Marvel Comics: Sept, 1996 - No. 2, Oct, 1996 ($1.50, limited series)

1,2 4.00

IRON FIST
Marvel Comics: Jul, 1998 - No. 3, Sept, 1998 ($2.50, limited series)

1-3: Jurgens-s/Guice-a 4.00

IRON FIST (Also see Immortal Iron Fist)
Marvel Comics: May, 2004 - No. 6, Oct, 2004 ($2.99)

1-6: 1-4,6-Kevin Lau-c/a. 5-Mays-c/a 4.00

IRON FIST: THE LIVING WEAPON
Marvel Comics: Jun, 2014 - No. 12, Jul, 2015 ($3.99)

1-12-Kaare Andrews-s/a/c; origin re-told in flashbacks 4.00

IRON FIST: WOLVERINE
Marvel Comics: Nov, 2000 - No. 4, Feb, 2001 ($2.99, limited series)

1-4-Igle-c/a; Kingpin app. 2-Iron Man app. 3,4-Capt. America app. 4.00

IRON GHOST
Image Comics: Apr, 2005 - No. 6, Mar, 2006 ($2.95/$2.99, limited series)

1-6-Chuck Dixon-s/Sergio Cariello-a; flip cover on each 3.00

GD 2.0 | VG 4.0 | FN 6.0 | VF 8.0 | VF/NM 9.0 | NM- 9.2

IRONHAND OF ALMURIC (Robert E. Howard's...)
Dark Horse Comics: Aug, 1991 - No. 4, 1991 ($2.00, B&W, mini-series)

1-4: 1-Conrad painted-c 3.00

IRON HORSE (TV)
Dell Publishing Co.: March, 1967 - No. 2, June, 1967

1-Dale Robertson photo covers on both 3 6 9 17 26 35
2 3 6 9 15 21 26

IRONJAW (Also see The Barbarians)
Atlas/Seaboard Publ.: Jan, 1975 - No. 4, July, 1975

1,2-Neal Adams-c. 1-1st app. Iron Jaw; Sekowsky-a(p); Fleisher-s
3 6 9 14 20 25
3,4-Marcos. 4-Origin 2 4 6 9 13 16

IRON LANTERN
Marvel Comics (Amalgam): June, 1997 ($1.95, one-shot)

1-Kurt Busiek-s/Paul Smith & Al Williamson-a 3.00

IRON MAN (Also see The Avengers #1, Giant-Size..., Marvel Collectors Item Classics, Marvel Double Feature, Marvel Fanfare, Tales of Suspense #39 & Uncanny Tales #52)
Marvel Comics: May, 1968 - No. 332, Sept, 1996

1-Origin; Colan-c/a(p); story continued from Iron Man & Sub-Mariner #1
110 220 330 650 1025 1400
2 13 26 39 89 195 300
3-Iron Man vs. The Freak 10 20 30 64 132 200
4,5: 4-Unicorn app. 8 16 24 56 108 160
6-10: 7,8-Gladiator app. 9-Iron Man battles green Hulk-like android. 9,10-The Mandarin app.
7 14 21 46 86 125
11-15: 10,11-Mandarin app. 13-1st app. Controller. 15-Last 12c issue; vs Unicorn and the Red Ghost 6 12 18 38 69 100
16,18-20: 16-Vs. Unicorn and the Red Ghost. 18-Avengers app. 19-Captain America app. 5 10 15 31 53 75
17-1st Madame Masque & Midas (Mordecai Midas) 6 12 18 38 69 100
21-24,26-30: 21-Crimson Dynamo app. 22-Death of Janice Cord; Crimson Dynamo app. 27-Intro Firebrand. 28-Controller app. 4 8 12 25 40 55
25-Iron Man battles Sub-Mariner 4 8 12 28 47 65
31-42: 33-1st app. Spymaster. 35-Daredevil & Nick Fury vs. Zodiak; x-over w/Daredevil #73. 36-Daredevil & Nick Fury vs Zodiak. 39-Avengers app. 42-Last 15c issue
3 6 9 21 33 45
43-Intro the Guardsman (25¢ Giant, 52 pgs); Giant-Man back-up (r) from TTA #52
5 10 15 35 63 90
44-46,48-53: 44-Capt. America app; back-up Ant-Man w/Andru-a. 46-The Guardsman dies. 48-Firebrand app. 49-Super-Adaptoid app. 50-Princess Python app. 53-1st Black Lama; Starlin part pencils 3 6 9 18 30 40
47-Origin retold; Barry Smith-a(p) 6 12 18 38 69 100
54-Iron Man battles Sub-Mariner; 1st app. Moondragon (1/73) as Madame MacEvil; Everett part-c 11 22 33 76 163 250
55-1st app. Thanos, Drax the Destroyer, Mentor, Starfox & Kronos (2/73); Starlin-c/a
110 220 330 650 1025 1400
56-Starlin-a 5 10 15 33 57 80
57-63: 57,58-Mandarin and Unicorn app. 59-Firebrand app. 60,61-Vs. the Masked Marauder. 62-Whiplash app. 63-Vs. Dr. Spectrum 3 6 9 16 24 32
64,65,67-70: 64,65-Dr. Spectrum app; origin is #65; Thor brief app. 67-Last 20c issue. 68-Sunfire, Mandarin and Unicorn app. 69,70-Mandarin, Yellow Claw & Ultimo app.
3 6 9 14 20 25
66-Iron Man vs. Thor. 4 8 12 27 44 60
71-84: 71-Yellow Claw & Black Lama app. 72-Black Lama app; Iron Man at the San Diego Comic Con. 73-Vs. Crimson Dynamo & Radioactive Man; Stark Industries renamed Stark International. 74-Modok vs. Mad-Thinker; Black Lama app in "War of the Super-Villains". 75-Black Lama & Yellow Claw app. 76-r/#9. 77-Conclusion of the "War of the Super-Villains"; Black Lama app. 80-Origin of Black Lama. 81-Black Lama & Firebrand app. 82,83-Red Ghost app. 2 4 6 10 14 18
85-89-(Regular 25¢ editions): 86-1st app. Blizzard. 87-Origin Blizzard. 88-Brief Thanos cameo. 89-Daredevil app.; last 25¢-c 2 4 6 10 14 18
85-89-(30¢-c variants, limited distribution)(4-8/76) 5 10 15 31 53 75
90-99: 90,91-Blood Brothers & Controller app. 92-Vs. Melter. 95-Ultimo app. 96-1st new Guardsman (Michael O' Brien). 98,99-Mandarin & Sunfire app.
2 4 6 9 12 15
99,101-103-(35¢-c variants, limited dist.) 10 20 30 69 147 225
100-(7/77)-Starlin-c; Iron Man vs. The Mandarin 4 8 12 25 40 55
100-(35¢-c variant, limited dist.) 17 34 51 117 259 400
101-117: 101-Intro DreadKnight; Frankenstein app. 103-Jack of Hearts app; guest stars through issue #113. 104-107-Vs. Midas. 109-1st app. New Crimson Dynamo; 1st app. Vanguard. 110-Origin Jack of Hearts retold; death of Count Nefaria. 113,114-Unicorn and

Iron Man #125 © MAR

Iron Man #261 © MAR

Iron Man V2 #8 © MAR

GD VG FN VF VF/NM NM-
2.0 4.0 6.0 8.0 9.0 9.2

Titanium Man app. 114,115-Avengers app; 1st John Romita Jr. pencils on Iron Man (10/78). 116-1st David Michelinie & Bob Layton issue 2 4 6 8 10 12
118-Byrne-a(p); 1st app. Jim Rhodes 4 8 12 28 47 65
119,122-124,127: 122-Origin. 123-128-Tony treated for alcohol problem. 123,124-Vs. Blizzard, Melter & Whiplash; Justin Hammer app. 127-Vs. Justin Hammer's "Super-Villain army" 2 4 6 11 16 20
120,121,126: 120,121-Sub-Mariner app. 126-Classic Tony becoming Iron Man-c 2 4 6 13 19 25
125-Avengers & Ant-Man (Scott Lang) app. 3 6 9 16 23 30
128-(11/79) Classic Tony Stark alcoholism cover 5 10 15 35 63 90
129,130,134-149: 134,135-Titanium Man app. 137-139-Spymaster app. 142-Intro. Space Armor. 143-1st app. Sunturion. 146 Backlash app. (formally Whiplash). 148-Captain America app. 149-Dr. Doom app. 1 2 3 5 7 9
131,132-Hulk x-over 2 4 6 8 10 12
133-Hulk/Ant Man-c 2 4 6 9 12 15
150-Double size; Dr. Doom; Merlin & Camelot 2 4 6 10 14 18
151-168: 151-Ant-Man (Scott Lang) app. 152-1st app stealth armor. 153-Living Laser app; last Layton co-plot (returns in #215). 154-Unicorn app. 156-Intro the Mauler; last Michelinie plot (returns in issue #215); last Romita Jr. art (p). 159-Paul Smith-a(p); Fantastic Four app. 160-Serpent Squad app. 161-Moon Knight app. 163-Intro. Obadiah Stane (hand only). 166-1st full app. Obadiah Stane. 167-Tony Stark alcohol problem resurfaces. 168-Machine Man app. 6.00
169-New Iron Man (Jim Rhodes replaces Tony Stark) 2 4 6 9 12 15
170,171 6.00
172-199: 172-Captain America x-over. 173-Stark International becomes Stane International. 179-Radioactive Man app. 180-181-Vs. Mandarin. 186-Intro. Vibro. 188-Brother Grimm app. 189-Intro. Termite. 190-Scarlet Witch app. 191-198-Tony Stark returns as original Iron Man. 191-192-Vibro app. 192-Tony Stark Iron Man vs. James Rhodes Iron Man. 193-West Coast Avengers app; unofficial 'Godzilla' app. 194-Intro. Scourge; kills the Enforcer. 195-West Coast Avengers & Shaman from Alpha Flight app. 197-Secret Wars II x-over; Byrne-c 5.00
200-(11/85, $1.25, 52 pgs.)-Tony Stark returns as new Iron Man (red & white armor) thru #230 2 4 6 8 10 12
201-213,215-224: 206-Hawkeye & Mockingbird app. 211-Vs. the Melter. 213-Intro. New Dominic Fortune. 215-Return of Michelinie/Layton creative team; James Rhodes app. (as Iron Man – also in #216). 219-Intro. The Ghost. 220-Spymaster & Ghost app. 221-Vs. Ghost. 222-Force app. 223-Intro. new Blizzard (Donald Gil). 224-Vs. Beetle, Backlash, Blizzard & Justin Hammer 4.00
214-Spider-Woman (Julia Carpenter) app. in new black costume (1/87) 6.00
225-(12/87, $1.25, 40 pgs)- Armor Wars begins; Ant-Man app. 1 3 4 6 8 10
226-227,229-230: Armor Wars in all. 226-West Coast Avengers app. 227-Beetle app.; Iron Man vs SHIELD Mandroids. 229-Vs. Crimson Dynamo & Titanium Man. 230-Armor Wars conclusion; vs Firepower 5.00
228-Armor Wars; Iron Man vs. Captain America (as the Captain) 6.00
231,234,247: 231-Intro. new Iron Man armor. 234-Spider-Man x-over. 247-Hulk x-over 5.00
232,233,235-243,245,246,248,249: 232-Barry Windsor Smith co-plot and (p). 233-Ant-Man app. 235,236-Vs. Grey Gargoyle. 238-Rhino & Capt. America app. 239,240-Vs. Justin Hammer. 241,242-Mandarin app. 243-Tony Stark loses use of legs. 249-Dr. Doom app. 3.00
244-($1.50, 52 pgs.)-New Armor makes him walk 4.00
250-($1.50, 52 pgs.)-Dr. Doom-c/story; Acts of Vengeance x-over; last Michelinie/Layton issue 4.00
251-274,276-281,283,285-287,289,292-299: 251,252-Acts of Vengeance x-over. 255-Intro new Crimson Dynamo (Valenyine Shatalov). 258-Byrne script & Romita Jr.-a(p) begins. 259-Armor Wars II begins; ends #266. 260-Vs. Living Laser. 261-Fin Fang Foom app. 261-264-Mandarin & Fin Fang Foom app. 266-Last Romita Jr.-a(p). 267,268-Origin expanded; Mandarin added to origin. 270-275-Dragon seed story w/Mandarin and Fin Fang Foom. 276-Black Widow app. 277-Last Byrne-s. 278-279-Operation Galactic Storm x-overs. 281-Intro. Masters of Silence; 1st cameo app. War Machine. 285,286-Beetle, Backlash & Blizzard app. 287-West Coast Avengers app. 287-Intro Atom Smasher. 289-Vs. Living Laser. 290-James Rhodes retains the War Machine armor. 292-Capt. America app. 295-Infinity Crusade x-over. 296,297-Omega Red app. 298,299-Return of Ultimo 3.00
275-($1.50, 52 pgs.) Mandarin & Fin Fang Foom app. 4.00
282-1st full app. War Machine (7/92) 4 8 12 23 37 50
284-Death of Iron Man (Tony Stark); James Rhodes becomes War Machine 6.00
288-($2.50, 52pg.)-Silver foil stamped-c; Iron Man's 350th app. in comics 5.00
290-($2.95, 52pg.)-Gold foil stamped-c; 30th ann. 5.00
291-Iron Man & War Machine team-up 5.00
300-($3.95, 68 pgs.)-Collector's Edition w/embossed foil-c; anniversary issue; War Machine-c/story 5.00
300-($2.50, 68 pgs.)-Newsstand Edition 4.00
301,303: 301-Venom cameo. 303-Captain America app. 4.00
302-Venom-c/story; Captain America app. 6.00
304-Thunderstrike app; begin $1.50-c; bound-in-trading card sheet 2 4 6 10 14 18

GD VG FN VF VF/NM NM-
2.0 4.0 6.0 8.0 9.0 9.2

305-Hulk-c/story 2 4 6 10 14 18
306-309-Mandarin app. 309-War Machine app. 3.00
310-($2.95) Polybagged w/16 pg Marvel Action Hour preview & acetate print 6.00
310-($1.50) Regular edition; white logo; "Hands of the Mandarin" x-over w/Force Works and War Machine 4.00
311,312- "Hands of the Mandarin" x-over w/Force Works and War Machine. 312-w/bound-in Power Ranger card 4.00
313,315,316,318: 315-316-Black Widow app. 316-Crimson Dynamo & Titanium Man app. 5.00
314-Crossover w/Captain America; Henry Pym app. 6.00
317-($2.50)-Flip book; Black Widow app; death of Titanium Man; Hawkeye, War Machine & USAgent app. 6.00
319-Intro. new Iron Man armor; Force Works app; prologue to "The Crossing" story 6.00
320,321: 321-w/Overpower card insert 5.00
322-324-Avengers app; x-over w/Avengers and Force Works 1 2 3 5 6 8
325-($2.95)-Wraparound-c; Tony Stark Iron Man vs "Teen" Tony Iron Man; Avengers & Force Works x-over; continued in Avengers #395 1 2 3 5 7 9
326- "Teen" Tony app. as Iron Man thru #332; Avengers, Thor & Cap America x-over 6.00
327-330: 330-War Machine & Stockpile app; return of Morgan Stark 4.00
331-War Machine app; leads into the "Onslaught" x-over 5.00
332-(9/96) Onslaught x-over; last issue 6.00

Special 1 (8/70)-Sub-Mariner x-over; Everett-c 5 10 15 34 60 85
Special 2 (11/71, 52 pgs.)-r/TOS #81,82,91 (all-r) 3 6 9 19 30 40
Annual 3 (1976)-Man-Thing app. 3 6 9 14 20 25
King Size 4 (8/77)-The Champions (w/Ghost Rider) app.; Newton-a(i) 2 4 6 11 16 20
Annual 5 ('82) Black Panther & Mandarin app. 1 3 4 6 8 10
Annual 6-9: ('83-'86) 6-New Iron Man (J. Rhodes) app. 8-X-Factor app. 5.00
Annual 10 ('89) Atlantis Attacks x-over; P. Smith-a; Layton/Guice-a; Sub-Mariner app. 4.00
Annual 11-14 ('90-'93): 11-Terminus Factor pt. 2; origin of Mrs. Arbogast by Ditko (p&i). 12-1 pg. origin recap; Ant-Man back-up-s; Subterranean Wars Pt. 4. 13-Darkhawk & Avengers West Coast app.; Colan/Williamson-a. 14-Bagged w/card; 1st app. Face Thief 4.00
Annual 15 ('94)- Iron Man vs. the Controller 4.00
...: Armor Wars TPB (2007, $24.99) r/#225-232; Michelinie intro. 25.00
Manual 1 (1993, $1.75)-Operations handbook 3.00
Graphic Novel: Crash (1988, $12.95, Adults, 72 pgs.)-Computer generated art & color; violence & nudity 13.00
...Collector's Preview 1(11/94, $1.95)-wraparound-c; text & illos-no comics 3.00
...: Demon in a Bottle HC (2008, $24.99) r/#120-128; two covers 25.00
...: Demon in a Bottle TPB (2006, $24.99) r/#120-128 25.00
...: Many Armors of Iron Man (2008, $24.99) r/#47, 142-144, 152-153, 200, 218 25.00
...Vs. Dr. Doom (12/94, $12.95)-r/#149-150, 249,250. Julie Bell-c 13.00
...Vs. Dr. Doom: Doomquest HC (2008, $19.99, dustjacket)-r/#149-150, 249,250; new Michelinie intro.; bonus art 20.00
...: War Machine TPB (2008, $29.99) r/#280-291 30.00
The Invincible Iron Man Omnibus Vol. 1 HC (2008, $99.99, dustjacket) r/Iron Man stories from Tales of Suspense #39-83 & Tales To Astonish #82; 1992 intro. by Stan Lee; 1975 essay by Lee; 2008 essay by Layton; gallery of original art and covers; creator bios 100.00

NOTE: ***Austin*** *c-105i, 109-111i, 151i.* ***Byrne*** *a-118p; c-109p, 197, 253.* ***Colan*** *a-1p, 253, Special 1p(3); c-1p.* ***Craig*** *a-1i, 2-4, 5-13i, 14, 15-19i, 24p, 25p, 26-28i; c-2-4.* ***Ditko*** *a-160p.* ***Everett*** *c-29.* ***Guice*** *a-233-241p.* ***G. Kane*** *c(p)-52-54, 63, 67, 72-75, 77-79, 88, 98.* ***Kirby*** *a-Special 1p; 80p, 90, 92-95.* ***Mooney*** *a-40i, 43i, 47i.* ***Perez*** *c-103p.* ***Simonson*** *c-Annual 8.* ***B. Smith*** *a-232p, 243i; c-232.* ***P. Smith*** *a-159p, 245p, Annual 10p; c-159.* ***Starlin*** *a-53p(part), 55p, 56p; c-55p, 160, 163.* ***Tuska*** *a-5-13p, 15-23p, 24i, 32p, 38-46p, 48-54p, 57-61p, 63-69p, 70-72p, 78p, 86-92p, 95-106p, Annual 4p.* ***Wood*** *a-Special 1i.*

IRON MAN (The Invincible...) (Volume Two)
Marvel Comics: Nov, 1996 - No. 13, Nov, 1997 ($2.95/$1.95/$1.99)
(Produced by WildStorm Productions)

V2#1-3-Heroes Reborn begins; Scott Lobdell scripts & Whilce Portacio-c/a begin; new origin Iron Man & Hulk. 2-Hulk app. 3-Fantastic Four app. 4.00
1-Variant-c 5.00
4-11: 4-Two covers. 6-Fantastic Four app.; Industrial Revolution; Hulk app. 7-Return of Rebel. 11-($1.99) Dr. Doom-c/app. 3.00
12-($2.99) "Heroes Reunited"-pt. 3; Hulk-c/app. 4.00
13-($1.99) "World War 3"-pt. 3, x-over w/Image 3.00
Heroes Reborn: Iron Man (2006, $29.99, TPB) r/#1-12; Heroes Reborn #1/2; pin-ups 30.00

IRON MAN (The Invincible...) (Volume Three)
Marvel Comics: Feb, 1998 - No. 89, Dec, 2004 ($2.99/$1.99/$2.25)

V3#1-($2.99)-Follows Heroes Return; Busiek scripts & Chen-c/a begin; Deathsquad app. 6.00
1-Alternate Ed. 1 2 3 5 7 9
2-12: 2-Two covers. 6-Black Widow-c/app. 7-Warbird-c/app. 8-Black Widow app. 9-Mandarin returns 4.00
13-($2.99) battles the Controller 5.00
14-24: 14-Fantastic Four-c/app. 3.00

Iron Man V3 #50 © MAR

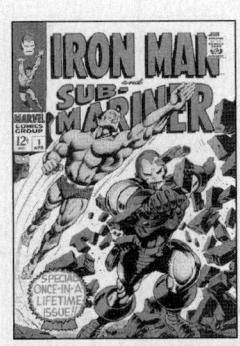

Iron Man and Sub-Mariner #1 © MAR

Iron Man: Legacy #6 © MAR

	GD 2.0	VG 4.0	FN 6.0	VF 8.0	VF/NM 9.0	NM- 9.2

25-($2.99) Iron Man and Warbird battle Ultimo; Avengers app. 4.00
26-30-Quesada-s. 28-Whiplash killed. 29-Begin $2.25-c. 3.00
31-45,47-49,51-54: 35-Maximum Security x-over; FF-c/app. 41-Grant-a begins. 44-New armor debut. 48-Ultron-c/app. 3.00
46-($3.50, 100 pgs.) Sentient armor returns; r/V1#78,140,141 4.00
50-($3.50) Grell-s begin; Black Widow app. 4.00
55-($3.50) 400th issue; Asamiya-c; back-up story Stark reveals ID; Grell-a 4.00
56-66: 56-Reis-a. 57,58-Ryan-a. 59-61-Grell-c/a. 62,63-Ryan-a. 64-Davis-a; Thor-c/app. 3.00
67-89: 67-Begin $2.99-c; Gene Ha-c. 75-83-Granov-c. 84-Avengers Disassembled prologue 85-89-Avengers Disassembled. 85-88-Harris-a. 86-89-Pat Lee-c. 87-Rumiko killed 3.00
.../Captain America '98 Annual ($3.50) vs. Modok 4.00
1999, 2000 Annual ($3.50) 4.00
2001 Annual ($2.99) Claremont-s/Ryan-a 4.00
Avengers Disassembled: Iron Man TPB (2004, $14.99) r/#84-89 15.00
Mask in the Iron Man (5/01, $14.95, TPB) r/#26-30, #1/2 15.00

IRON MAN (The Invincible...)
Marvel Comics: Jan, 2005 - No. 35, Jan, 2009 ($3.50/$2.99)

1-($3.50-c) Warren Ellis-s/Adi Granov-c/a; start of Extremis storyline 5.00
2-6-($2.99): 5-Flashback to origin; Stark gets new abilities 4.00
7-14: 7-Knauf-s/Zircher-a. 13,14-Civil War 3.00
15-24,26,27,29-35: 15-Stark becomes Director of S.H.I.E.L.D. 19,20-World War Hulk. 33-Secret Invasion; War Machine app. 34,35-War Machine title logo 3.00
25,28-($3.99) 25-Includes movie preview & armor showcase. 28-Red & white armor 4.00
All-New Iron Manual (2/08, $4.99) Handbook-style guide to characters & armor suits 5.00
... By Design 1 (11/10, $3.99) Gallery of 2010 variant covers with artist commentary 4.00
.../Captain America: Casualities of War (2/07, $3.99) two covers; flashbacks 4.00
...: Director of S.H.I.E.L.D. Annual 1 (1/08, $3.99) Madame Hydra app.; Cheung-c 4.00
Free Comic Book Day 2010 (Iron Man: Supernova) #1 (5/10, 9-1/2" x 6-1/4") Nova app. 3.00
Free Comic Book Day 2010 (Iron Man/Thor) #1 (5/10, 9-1/2" x 6-1/4") Romita Jr.-a/c 3.00
...Golden Avenger 1 (11/08, $2.99) Santacruz-a; movie photo-c 3.00
.../Hulk/Fury 1 (2/09, $3.99) crossover of movie-version characters 4.00
Indomitable Iron Man (4/10, $3.99) B&W stories; Chaykin-s/a; Rosado-a; Parrillo-c 4.00
Iron Manual Mark 3 (6/10, $3.99) Handbook-format profiles of characters 4.00
...: Iron Protocols (12/09, $3.99) Olivetti-c/Nelson-a 4.00
...: Kiss and Kill (8/10, $3.99) Black Widow and Wolverine app. 4.00
Marvel Halloween Ashcan 2007 (8-1/2" x 5-3/8") updated origin; Michael Golden-c 3.00
...: Requiem (2009, $4.99) r/TOS #39, Iron Man #144 (1981); armor profiles 5.00
...: The End (1/09, $4.99) future Tony Stark retires; Michelinie-s/Chang & Layton-a 5.00
...: Titanium! 1 (12/10, $4.99) short stories by various; Yardin-c 5.00
Civil War: Iron Man TPB (2007, $11.99) r/#13,14, .../Captain America: Casualities of War, and Civil War: The Confession 12.00
HC (2006, $19.99, dust jacket) r/#1-6 and Granov covers from Iron Man V3 #75-83 20.00
...: Director of S.H.I.E.L.D. TPB (2007, $14.99) r/#15-18; Strange Tales #135 (1965) and Iron Man #129; profile pages for Iron Man and S.H.I.E.L.D.; creator interviews 15.00
...: Extremis SC (2007, $14.99) r/#1-6 and Granov covers from Iron Man V3 #75-83 15.00
...: Execute Program SC (2007, $14.99) r/#7-12; cover layouts and sketches 15.00

IRON MAN (Marvel Now!)(Leads into Superior Iron Man)
Marvel Comics: Jan, 2013 - No. 28, Aug, 2014 ($3.99)

1-28: 1-8-Gillen-s/Land-c/a. 5-Stark heads out to space. 9-17-Secret Origin of Tony Stark. 9-12-Eaglesham-a. 17-Arno Stark revealed. 23-26-Malekith app. 4.00
20.INH (3/12, $3.99) Inhumanity tie-in; origin The Exile; Padilla-a 4.00
Annual 1 (4/14, $4.99) Gillen-s/Martinez, Padilla & Marz-a 5.00
... Special 1 (9/14, $4.99) Cont'd from Uncanny X-Men Special #1; Ryan-s/Handoko-a 5.00

IRON MAN (The Armor Wars)
Marvel Comics: No. 258.1, Jul, 2013 - No. 258.4, Jul, 2013 ($3.99, weekly limited series)

258.1-258.4 - Set after Iron Man #258 (1990); Michelinie-s/Dave Ross & Bob Layton-a 4.00

IRON MAN AND POWER PACK
Marvel Comics: Jan, 2008 - No. 4, Apr, 2008 ($2.99, limited series)

1-4-Gurihiru-c/Sumerak-s; Puppet Master app.; Mini Marvels back-ups in each 3.00
...: Armored and Dangerous TPB (2008, $7.99, digest size) r/series 8.00

IRON MAN & SUB-MARINER
Marvel Comics Group: Apr, 1968 (12¢, one-shot) (Pre-dates Iron Man #1 & Sub-Mariner #1)

1-Iron Man story by Colan/Craig continued from Tales of Suspense #99 & continued in Iron Man #1; Sub-Mariner story by Colan continued from Tales to Astonish #101 & continued in Sub-Mariner #1; Colan/Everett-c 17 34 51 117 259 400

IRON MAN AND THE ARMOR WARS
Marvel Comics: Oct, 2009 - No. 4, Jan, 2010 ($2.99, limited series)

1-4-Rousseau-a; Crimson Dynamo & Omega Red app. 3.00

IRON MAN: ARMORED ADVENTURES
Marvel Comics: Sept, 2009 ($3.99, one-shot)

1-Based on the 2009 cartoon; Brizuela-a; Nick Fury & Living Laser app. 4.00

IRON MAN: BAD BLOOD
Marvel Comics: Sept, 2000 - No. 4, Dec, 2000 ($2.99, limited series)

1-4-Micheline-s/Layton-a 3.00

IRON MAN: ENTER THE MANDARIN
Marvel Comics: Nov, 2007 - No. 6, Apr, 2008 ($2.99, limited series)

1-6-Casey-s/Canete-a; retells first meeting 3.00
TPB (2008, $14.99) r/#1-6 15.00

IRON MAN: EXTREMIS DIRECTOR'S CUT
Marvel Comics: Jun, 2010 - No. 6, Sept, 2010 ($3.99, limited series)

1-6-Reprints Iron Man #1-6 (2005 series) with script pages and design art 4.00

IRON MAN: FATAL FRONTIER
Marvel Comics: 2014 ($34.99, hardcover)

HC - Printing of digital comic #1-13 and r/Iron Man Annual #1 (4/14) 35.00

IRON MAN: HOUSE OF M (Also see House of M and related x-overs)
(Reprinted in House of M: Fantastic Four/ Iron Man TPB)
Marvel Comics: Sept, 2005 - No. 3, Nov, 2005 ($2.99, limited series)

1-3-Pat Lee-a/c; Greg Pak-s 3.00

IRON MAN: HYPERVELOCITY
Marvel Comics: Mar, 2007 - No. 6, Aug, 2007 ($2.99, limited series)

1-6-Adam Warren-s/Brian Denham-a/c 3.00
TPB (2007, $14.99) r/#1-6; layout pages and armor design sketches 15.00

IRON MAN: I AM IRON MAN
Marvel Comics: Mar, 2010 - No. 2, Apr, 2010 ($3.99, limited series)

1,2-Adaptation of the first movie; Peter David-s/Sean Chen-a/Adi Granov-c 4.00

IRON MAN: INEVITABLE
Marvel Comics: Feb, 2006 - No. 6, July, 2006 ($2.99, limited series)

1-6-Joe Casey-s/Frazer Irving; Spymaster and the Living Laser app. 3.00
TPB (2006, $14.99) r/#1-6; cover sketches 15.00

IRON MAN: LEGACY
Marvel Comics: Jun, 2010 - No. 11, Apr, 2011 ($3.99/$2.99)

1-Van Lente-s/Kurth-a; Dr. Doom app.; back-up r/debut in Tales of Suspense #39 4.00
2-11-($2.99) 4-Titanium Man & Crimson Dynamo app. 6-The Pride app. 3.00

IRON MAN: LEGACY OF DOOM
Marvel Comics: Jun, 2008 - No. 4, Sept, 2008 ($2.99, limited series)

1-4-Michelinie-s/Lim & Layton-a; Dr. Doom app. 3.00

IRON MAN NOIR
Marvel Comics: Jun, 2010 - No. 4, Sept, 2010 ($3.99, limited series)

1-4-Pulp-style set in 1939; Snyder-s/Garcia-a 4.00

IRON MAN: RAPTURE
Marvel Comics: Jan, 2011 - No. 4, Feb, 2011 ($3.99, limited series)

1-4-Irvine-s/Medina-a/Bradstreet-c. 3,4-War Machine app. 4.00

IRON MAN: SEASON ONE
Marvel Comics: 2013 ($24.99, hardcover graphic novel)

HC - Origin story and early days; Chaykin-s/Parel-a/Tedesco painted-c 25.00

IRON MAN: THE COMING OF THE MELTER
Marvel Comics: Jul, 2013 ($3.99, one-shot)

1-Movie version; Ron Lim-a; back-up reprint of Iron Man #72 (1/75); 3 covers 4.00

IRON MAN: THE IRON AGE
Marvel Comics: Aug, 1998 - No. 2, Sept, 1998 ($5.99, limited series)

1,2-Busiek-s; flashback story from gold armor days 6.00

IRON MAN: THE LEGEND
Marvel Comics: Sept, 1996 ($3.95, one-shot)

1-Tribute issue 5.00

IRON MAN/ THOR
Marvel Comics: Jan, 2011 - No. 4, Apr, 2011 ($3.99, limited series)

1-4-Eaton-a; Crimson Dynamo & Diablo app. 4.00

IRON MAN 2: ... (Follows the first movie)
Marvel Comics: Jun, 2010 - Nov, 2010 ($3.99, limited series)

Agents of S.H.I.E.L.D. 1 (11/10, $3.99) Nick Fury, Agent Coulson & Black Widow app. 4.00
Public Identity (6/10 - No. 3, 7/10, $3.99) 1-3-Kitson & Lim-a/Granov-c 4.00
Spotlight (4/10, $3.99) Interviews with Granov, Guggenheim, Fraction, Ellis, Michelinie 4.00

Iron Man 2.0 #1 © MAR

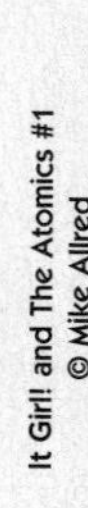
It Girl! and The Atomics #1 © Mike Allred

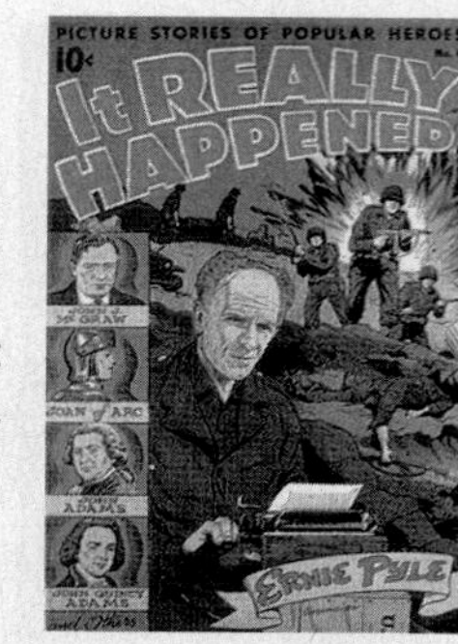

It Really Happened #6 © STD

	GD	VG	FN	VF	VF/NM	NM-
	2.0	4.0	6.0	8.0	9.0	9.2

IRON MAN 2 ADAPTATION, (MARVEL'S...)
Marvel Comics: Jan, 2013 - No. 2, Feb, 2013 ($2.99, limited series)
1,2-Photo-c; Rosanas-a 3.00

IRON MAN 2.0
Marvel Comics: Apr, 2011 - No. 12, Feb, 2012 ($3.99/$2.99)
1-($3.99) Spencer-s/Kitson-c; back-up history of War Machine 4.00
1-Variant-c by Djurdjevic 6.00
2-7,(7.1),8-12-($2.99) 2,3-Kitson, Kano & Di Giandomenico-a. 5-7-Fear Itself tie-in 3.00
...: Modern Warfare 1 (10/11, $4.99) r/#1-3 with variant covers 5.00

IRON MAN 3 PRELUDE, (MARVEL'S...)
Marvel Comics: Mar, 2013 - No. 2, Apr, 2013 ($2.99, limited series)
1,2-Photo-c; Gage-s/Kurth-a; War Machine app. 3.00

IRON MAN 2020 (Also see Machine Man limited series)
Marvel Comics: June, 1994 ($5.95, one-shot)
nn 6.00

IRON MAN: VIVA LAS VEGAS
Marvel Comics: Jul, 2008 - No. 2 ($3.99, unfinished limited series)
1,2-Jon Favreau-s/Adi Granov-a/c 4.00

IRON MAN VS WHIPLASH
Marvel Comics: Jan, 2010 - No. 4, Apr, 2010 ($3.99, limited series)
1-4-Briones-a/Peterson-c; origin of new Whiplash 4.00

IRON MAN/X-O MANOWAR: HEAVY METAL (See X-O Manowar/Iron Man: In Heavy Metal)
Marvel Comics: Sept, 1996 ($2.50, one-shot) (1st Marvel/Valiant x-over)
1-Pt. II of Iron Man/X-O Manowar x-over; Fabian Nicieza scripts; 1st app. Rand Banion 4.00

IRON MARSHALL
Jademan Comics: July, 1990 - No. 32, Feb, 1993 ($1.75, plastic coated-c)
1,32: Kung Fu stories. 1-Poster centerfold 4.00
2-31-Kung Fu stories in all 3.00

IRON PATRIOT (Marvel Now!)
Marvel Comics: May, 2014 - No. 5, Sept, 2014 ($3.99)
1-5-James Rhodes in the armor; Ales Kot-s/Garry Brown-a/c 4.00

IRON VIC (See Comics Revue No. 3 & Giant Comics Editions)
United Features Syndicate/St. John Publ. Co.: 1940

	GD	VG	FN	VF	VF/NM	NM-
Single Series 22	34	68	102	204	332	460

IRONWOLF
DC Comics: 1986 ($2.00, one shot)
1-r/Weird Worlds #8-10; Chaykin story & art 4.00

IRONWOLF: FIRES OF THE REVOLUTION (See Weird Worlds #8-10)
DC Comics: 1992 ($29.95, hardcover)
nn-Chaykin/Moore story, Mignola-a w/Russell inks. 30.00

IRREDEEMABLE (Also see Incorruptible)
BOOM! Studios: Apr, 2009 - No. 37, May, 2012 ($3.99)
1-37: 1-Waid-s/Krause-a; 3 covers; Grant Morrison afterword. 2-32-Three covers 4.00
1-Artist Edition (12/11, $3.99) r/#1 in B&W with bonus sketch and design art 4.00
... Special 1 (4/10, $3.99) Art by Azaceta, Rios & Chaykin; three covers 4.00

IRREDEEMABLE ANT-MAN, THE
Marvel Comics: Dec, 2006 - No. 12, Nov, 2007 ($2.99)
1-12-Kirkman-s/Hester-a/c; intro. Eric O'Grady as the new Ant-Man. 7-Ms. Marvel app. 10-World War Hulk x-over 3.00
... Vol. 1: Lowlife (2007, $9.99, digest) r/#1-6 10.00
... Vol. 2: Small-Minded (2007, $9.99, digest) r/#7-12 10.00

ISAAC ASIMOV'S I-BOTS
Tekno Comix: Dec, 1995 - No. 7, May, 1996 ($1.95)
1-7: 1-6-Perez-c/a. 2-Chaykin variant-c exists. 3-Polybagged. 7-Lady Justice-c/app. 3.00

ISAAC ASIMOV'S I-BOTS
BIG Entertainment: V2#1, June, 1996 - No. 9, Feb, 1997 ($2.25)
V2#1-9: 1-Lady Justice-c/app. 6-Gil Kane-c 3.00

ISIS (TV) (Also see Shazam)
National Per.l Publ./DC Comics: Oct-Nov, 1976 - No. 8, Dec-Jan, 1977-78

	GD	VG	FN	VF	VF/NM	NM-
1-Wood inks	3	6	9	14	20	25
2-8: 5-Isis new look. 7-Origin	2	3	4	6	8	10

ISLAND AT THE TOP OF THE WORLD (See Walt Disney Showcase #27)

ISLAND OF DR. MOREAU, THE (Movie)
Marvel Comics Group: Oct, 1977 (52 pgs.)

	GD	VG	FN	VF	VF/NM	NM-
1-Gil Kane-c	1	2	3	5	6	8

I SPY (TV)
Gold Key: Aug, 1966 - No. 6, Sept, 1968 (All have photo-c)

	GD	VG	FN	VF	VF/NM	NM-
1-Bill Cosby, Robert Culp photo covers	10	20	30	66	138	210
2-6: 3,4-McWilliams-a. 5-Last 12¢-c	6	12	18	38	69	100

IT! (See Astonishing Tales No. 21-24 & Supernatural Thrillers No. 1)

ITCHY & SCRATCHY COMICS (The Simpsons TV show)
Bongo Comics: 1993 - No. 3, 1993 ($1.95)

	GD	VG	FN	VF	VF/NM	NM-
1-3: 1-Bound-in jumbo poster. 3-w/decoder screen trading card	2	4	6	8	10	12
Holiday Special ('94, $1.95)	1	3	4	6	8	10

IT GIRL (Also see Atomics, and Madman Comics)
Oni Press: May, 2002 ($2.95, one-shot)
1-Allred-s/Clugston-Major-c/a; Atomics and Madman app. 3.00

IT GIRL! AND THE ATOMICS (Also see Atomics, and Madman Comics)
Image Comics: Aug, 2012 - No. 12, Jul, 2013 ($2.99)
1-12: 1-Rich-s/Norton-a/Allred-c. 2-Two covers (Allred & Cooke). 6-Clugston Flores-a 3.00

IT REALLY HAPPENED
William H. Wise No. 1,2/Standard (Visual Editions): 1944 - No. 11, Oct, 1947

	GD	VG	FN	VF	VF/NM	NM-
1-Kit Carson & Ben Franklin stories	26	52	78	154	252	350
2,3-Nazi WWII-c	15	30	45	85	130	175
4,6,9,11: 4-D-Day story. 6-Ernie Pyle WWII-c; Joan of Arc story. 9-Captain Kidd & Frank Buck stories	14	28	42	76	108	140
5-Lou Gehrig & Lewis Carroll stories	18	36	54	107	169	230
7-Teddy Roosevelt story	15	30	45	83	124	165
8-Story of Roy Rogers	17	34	51	98	154	210
10-Honus Wagner & Mark Twain stories	15	30	45	90	140	190

NOTE: *Guardineer a-7(2), 8(2), 10, 11.* ***Schomburg*** *c-1-7, 9-11.*

IT RHYMES WITH LUST (Also see Bold Stories & Candid Tales)
St. John Publishing Co.: 1950 (Digest size, 128 pgs., 25¢)

	GD	VG	FN	VF	VF/NM	NM-
nn (Rare)-Matt Baker & Ray Osrin-a	284	568	852	1818	3109	4400

IT'S A BIRD...
DC Comics: 2004 ($24.95, hardcover with dust jacket)
HC-Semi-autobiographical story of Steven Seagle writing Superman; Kristiansen-a 25.00
SC-($17.95) 18.00

IT'S ABOUT TIME (TV)
Gold Key: Jan, 1967

	GD	VG	FN	VF	VF/NM	NM-
1 (10195-701)-Photo-c	4	8	12	27	44	60

IT'S A DUCK'S LIFE
Marvel Comics/Atlas(MMC): Feb, 1950 - No. 11, Feb, 1952

	GD	VG	FN	VF	VF/NM	NM-
1-Buck Duck, Super Rabbit begin	19	38	57	111	176	240
2	12	24	36	67	94	120
3-11	11	22	33	60	83	105

IT'S GAMETIME
National Periodical Publications: Sept-Oct, 1955 - No. 4, Mar-Apr, 1956

	GD	VG	FN	VF	VF/NM	NM-
1-(Scarce)-Infinity-c; Davy Crockett app. in puzzle	100	200	300	635	1093	1550
2,3 (Scarce): 2-Dodo & The Frog	69	138	207	442	759	1075
4 (Rare)	73	146	219	467	796	1125

IT'S LOVE, LOVE, LOVE
St. John Publishing Co.: Nov, 1957 - No. 2, Jan, 1958 (10¢)

	GD	VG	FN	VF	VF/NM	NM-
1,2	8	16	24	44	57	70

IT! THE TERROR FROM BEYOND SPACE
IDW Publishing: Jul, 2010 - No. 3, Sept, 2010 ($3.99, limited series)
1-3-Naraghi-s/Dos Santos-a/Mannion-c 4.00

ITTY BITTY COMICS (Issue #5, see Grimmiss Island; title changes to Grimmiss Island)
Dark Horse Comics: Nov, 2014 - No. 4, Feb, 2015 ($2.99, limited series)
1-4-All-ages humor stories of kid-version Mask by Art Baltazar & Franco 3.00

ITTY BITTY COMICS: THE MASK
Dark Horse Comics: Nov, 2014 - No. 4, Feb, 2015 ($2.99, limited series)
1-4-All-ages humor stories of kid-version Mask by Art Baltazar & Franco 3.00

ITTY BITTY HELLBOY
Dark Horse Comics: Aug, 2013 - No. 5, Dec, 2013 ($2.99, limited series)

I, Vampire #19 © DC

IVX #1 © MAR

Jack Kirby's Fourth World #10 © DC

	GD	VG	FN	VF	VF/NM	NM-
	2.0	4.0	6.0	8.0	9.0	9.2

1-5-All-ages humor stories of kid-version Hellboy characters by Art Baltazar & Franco 3.00

ITTY BITTY HELLBOY: THE SEARCH FOR THE WERE-JAGUAR
Dark Horse Comics: Nov, 2015 - No. 4, Feb, 2016 ($2.99, limited series)

1-4-All-ages humor stories of kid-version Hellboy characters by Art Baltazar & Franco 3.00

I, VAMPIRE (DC New 52)
DC Comics: Nov, 2011 - No. 19, Jun, 2013 ($2.99)

1-19: 1-Fialkov-s/Sorrentino-a/Frison-c. 4-Constantine app. 5-7-Batman app. 7,8-Crossover with Justice League Dark #7,8. 12-Stormwatch app. 16-19-Constantine app. 3.00
#0-(11/12, $2.99) Origin of Andrew Bennett; Fialkov-s/Sorrentino-a/Crain-c 3.00

IVANHOE (See Fawcett Movie Comics No. 20)

IVANHOE
Dell Publishing Co.: July-Sept, 1963

	GD	VG	FN	VF	VF/NM	NM-
1 (12-372-309)	3	6	9	20	31	42

IVAR, TIMEWALKER
Valiant Entertainment: Jan, 2015 - No. 12, Dec, 2015 ($3.99)

1-12: 1-4-Fred Van Lente-s/Clayton Henry-a. 5-8-Portela-a. 9-Pere Perez-a 4.00

IVX (Inhumans vs X-Men) (Also see Death of X)
Marvel Comics: No. 0, Jan, 2017 - No. 6 ($3.99/$4.99/$5.99)

0-($4.99) Soule-s/Rocafort-a; Beast, Medusa, Emma Frost, Magneto app. 5.00
1-($5.99) Soule & Lemire-s/Yu-a; multiple covers 6.00
2-5-($3.99) 2-Yu-a. 3-5-Garrón-a 4.00

IWO JIMA (See Spectacular Features Magazine)

IXTH GENERATION (See Ninth Generation)

I, ZOMBIE (Inspired the 2015 TV show)(See House of Mystery Halloween Annual #1 for 1st app.)
DC Comics (Vertigo): July, 2010 - No. 28, Oct, 2012 ($1.00/$2.99)

1-($1.00) Allred-a/Roberson-s; 2 covers by Allred & Cooke

	GD	VG	FN	VF	VF/NM	NM-
	3	6	9	16	23	30

2-28-($2.99) Allred-c/a in most. 12-Gilbert Hernandez-a. 18-Jay Stephens-a. 25-Rugg-a 3.00
... Special Edition 1 (5/15, $1.00) r/#1; new inteview with Allred 3.00
...: Dead to the World TPB (2011, $14.99) r/#1-5 & House of Mystery Hall. Ann. #1 15.00

JACE PEARSON OF THE TEXAS RANGERS (Radio/TV)(4-Color #396 is titled Tales of the Texas Rangers; ...'s Tales of ... #11-on)(See Western Roundup under Dell Giants)
Dell Publishing Co.: No. 396, 5/52 - No. 1021, 8-10/59 (No #10) (All-Photo-c)

	GD	VG	FN	VF	VF/NM	NM-
Four Color 396 (#1)	10	20	30	66	138	210
2(5-7/53) - 9(2-4/55)	6	12	18	40	73	105
Four Color 648(#10, 9/55)	6	12	18	40	73	105
11(11-2/55-56) - 14,17-20(6-8/58)	5	10	15	33	57	80
15,16-Toth-a	5	10	15	34	60	85
Four Color 961,1021: 961-Spiegle-a	5	10	15	34	60	85

NOTE: *Joel McCrea photo c-1-9, F.C. 648 (starred on radio show only); Willard Parker photo c-11-on (starred on TV series).*

JACK ARMSTRONG (Radio)(See True Comics)
Parents' Institute: Nov, 1947 - No. 9, Sept, 1948; No. 10, Mar, 1949 - No. 13, Sept, 1949

nn (6/47) Ashcan edition; full color slick cover (a FN/VF sold for $485 in 2011)
1-(Scarce) (odd size) Cast intro. inside front-c; Vic Hardy's Crime Lab begins

	GD	VG	FN	VF	VF/NM	NM-
	47	94	141	296	498	700
2	21	42	63	122	199	275
3-5	15	30	45	88	137	185
6-13	14	28	42	80	115	150

JACK AVARICE IS THE COURIER
IDW Publishing: Nov, 2012 - No. 5, Nov, 2012 ($3.99, weekly limited series)

1-5-Chriss Madden-s/a/c 4.00

JACK CROSS
DC Comics: Oct, 2005 - No. 4, Jan, 2006 ($2.50)

1-4-Warren Ellis-s/Gary Erskine-a 3.00
DC Comics Presents: Jack Cross #1 (12/10, $7.99, squarebound) r/#1-4 8.00

JACKED
DC Comics (Vertigo): Jan, 2016 - No. 6, Jun, 2016 ($3.99)

1-6-Eric Kripke-s/John Higgins-a/Glenn Fabry-c 4.00

JACK HUNTER
Blackthorne Publishing: July, 1987 - No. 3 ($1.25)

1-3 3.00

JACKIE CHAN'S SPARTAN X
Topps Comics: May, 1997 - No. 3 ($2.95, limited series)

1-3-Michael Golden-s/a; variant photo-c 3.00

JACKIE CHAN'S SPARTAN X: HELL BENT HERO FOR HIRE
Image Comics (Little Eva Ink): Mar, 1998 - No. 3 ($2.95, B&W)

1-3-Michael Golden-s/a: 1-variant photo-c 3.00

JACKIE GLEASON (TV) (Also see The Honeymooners)
St. John Publishing Co.: Sept, 1955 - No. 4, Dec, 1955?

	GD	VG	FN	VF	VF/NM	NM-
1(1955)(TV)-Photo-c	74	148	222	470	810	1150
2-4	48	96	144	302	514	725

JACKIE GLEASON AND THE HONEYMOONERS (TV)
National Periodical Publications: June-July, 1956 - No. 12, Apr-May, 1958

	GD	VG	FN	VF	VF/NM	NM-
1-1st app. Ralph Kramden	129	258	387	826	1413	2000
2	63	126	189	403	689	975
3-11: 8-Statue of Liberty-c	50	100	150	315	533	750
12 (Scarce)	69	138	207	442	759	1075

JACKIE JOKERS (Became Richie Rich &...)
Harvey Publications: March, 1973 - No. 4, Sept, 1973 (#5 was advertised, but not published)

	GD	VG	FN	VF	VF/NM	NM-
1-1st app.	3	6	9	16	22	28
2-4: 2-President Nixon app.	2	4	6	8	11	14

JACKIE ROBINSON (Famous Plays of...) (Also see Negro Heroes #2 & Picture News #4)
Fawcett Publications: May, 1950 - No. 6, 1952 (Baseball hero) (All photo-c)

	GD	VG	FN	VF	VF/NM	NM-
nn	97	194	291	621	1061	1500
2	55	110	165	352	601	850
3-6	47	94	141	296	498	700

JACK IN THE BOX (Formerly Yellowjacket Comics #1-10; becomes Cowboy Western Comics #17 on)
Frank Comunale/Charlton Comics No. 11 on: Feb, 1946; No. 11, Oct, 1946 - No. 16, Nov-Dec, 1947

	GD	VG	FN	VF	VF/NM	NM-
1-Stitches, Marty Mouse & Nutsy McKrow	22	44	66	132	216	300
11-Yellowjacket (early Charlton comic)	24	48	72	142	234	325
12,14,15	15	30	45	85	130	175
13-Wolverton-a	23	46	69	136	223	310
16-12 pg. adapt. of Silas Marner; Kiefer-a	15	30	45	88	137	185

JACK KIRBY OMNIBUS, THE
DC Comics: 2011; 2013 ($49.99, hardcover with dustjacket)

Vol. 1 ('11) Recolored reprints of Kirby's DC work from 1946, 1957-1959; Evanier intro. 50.00
Vol. 2 ('13) Recolored reprints of Kirby's DC work from 1973-1987; Morrow intro. 50.00

JACK KIRBY'S FOURTH WORLD (See Mister Miracle & New Gods, 3rd Series)
DC Comics: Mar, 1997 - No. 20, Oct, 1998 ($1.95/$2.25)

1-20: 1-Byrne-a/scripts & Simonson-c begin; story cont'd from New Gods, 3rd Series #15; retells "The Pact" (New Gods, 1st Series #7); 1st brief DC app. Thor. 2-Thor vs. Big Barda; "Apokolips Then" back-up begins; Kirby-c/swipe (Thor #126) 8-Genesis x-over. 10-Simonson-s/a 13-Simonson back-up story. 20-Superman-c/app. 3.00

JACK KIRBY'S FOURTH WORLD OMNIBUS
DC Comics: 2007 - Vol. 4, 2008 ($49.99, hardcovers with dustjackets)

Vol. 1 ('07) Recolored reprints in chronological order of Superman's Pal, Jimmy Olsen #133-139, Forever People #1-3, New Gods #1-3, and Mister Miracle #1-3; Morrison intro, bonus art 50.00
Vol. 2 ('07) r/Jimmy Olsen #141-145, F.P. #4-6, N.G. #4-6 & M.M. #4-6; bonus art 50.00
Vol. 3 ('07) r/Jimmy Olsen #146-148, F.P. #7-10, N.G. #7-10 & M.M. #7-9; bonus art 50.00
Vol. 4 ('08) r/F.P. #11, M.M. #10-18, N.G. #11 & reprint series #6, & DC Graphic Novel #6 (The Hunger Dogs); Levitz intro.; Evanier afterword; character profile pages 50.00

JACK KIRBY'S GALACTIC BOUNTY HUNTERS
Marvel Comics (Icon): July, 2006 - No. 6, Nov, 2007 ($3.99)

1-6-Based on a Kirby concept; Mike Thibodeaux-a; Lisa Kirby, Thibodeaux and others-s 4.00
HC (2007, $24.99) r/series; pin-ups and supplemental art and interviews 25.00

JACK KIRBY'S SECRET CITY SAGA
Topps Comics (Kirbyverse): No. 0, Apr, 1993; No. 1, May, 1993 - No. 4, Aug, 1993 ($2.95, limited series)

0-(No cover price, 20 pgs.)-Simonson-c/a 3.00
0-Red embossed-c (limited ed.) 5.00
1-4-Bagged w/3 trading cards; Ditko-c/a: 1-Ditko/Art Adams-c. 2-Ditko/Byrne-c; has coupon for Pres. Clinton holo-foil trading card. 3-Dorman poster; has coupon for Gore holo-foil trading card. 4-Ditko/Perez-c 3.00
NOTE: *Issues #1-4 contain coupons redeemable for Kirbychrome version of #1*

JACK KIRBY'S SILVER STAR (Also see Silver Star)
Topps Comics (Kirbyverse): Oct, 1993 ($2.95)(Intended as a 4-issue limited series)

1-Silver ink-c; Austin-c/a(i); polybagged w/3 cards 3.00

JACK KIRBY'S TEENAGENTS (See Satan's Six)
Topps Comics (Kirbyverse): Aug, 1993 - No. 4, Nov, 1993 ($2.95, limited series)

Jack of Fables #39 © Willingham & DC

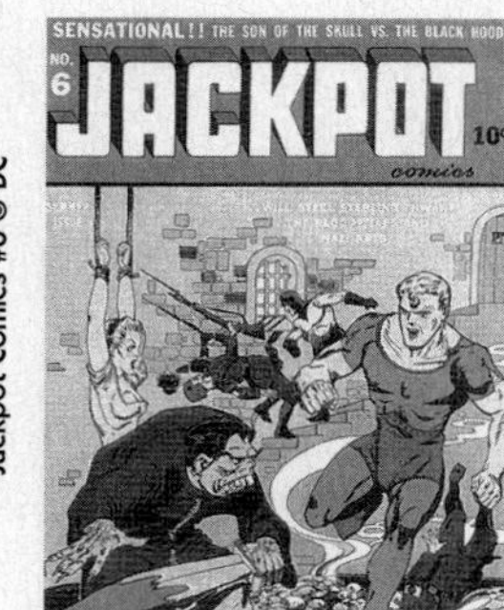

Jackpot Comics #6 © DC

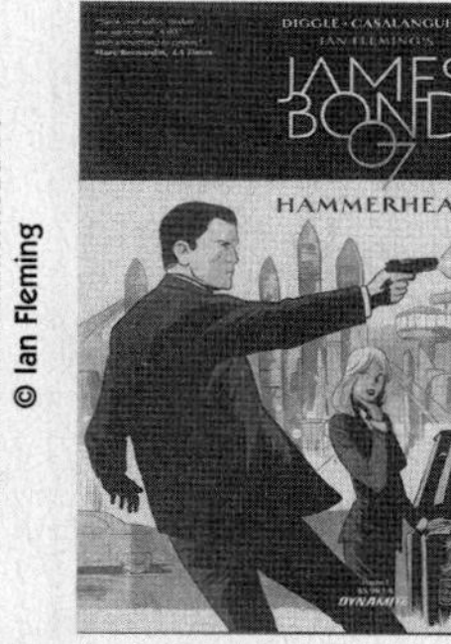

James Bond: Hammerhead #1 © Ian Fleming

GD VG FN VF VF/NM NM-
2.0 4.0 6.0 8.0 9.0 9.2

1-4: Bagged with/3 trading cards; Busiek-s/Austin-c(i): 3-Liberty Project app. 3.00

JACK KRAKEN
Dark Horse Comics: May, 2014 ($3.99, one-shot)
1-Tim Seeley-s; art by Ross Campbell & Jim Terry 4.00

JACK OF FABLES (See Fables)
DC Comics (Vertigo): Sept, 2006 - No. 50, Apr, 2011 ($2.99)
1-49: 1-Willingham & Sturges-s/Akins-a. 33-35-Crossover with Fables and The Literals 3.00
50-($4.99) Akins & Braun-a; Bolland-c 5.00
1-Special Edition (8/10, $1.00) r/#1 with "What's Next?" logo on cover 3.00
...: Americana TPB (2008, $14.99) r/#17-21 15.00
...: Jack of Hearts TPB (2007, $14.99) r/#6-11 15.00
...: The Bad Prince TPB (2008, $14.99) r/#12-16 15.00
...: The Big Book of War TPB (2009, $14.99) r/#28-32 15.00
...: The End TPB (2011, $17.99) r/#46-50 18.00
...: The Fulminate Blade TPB (2011, $14.99) r/#41-45 15.00
...: The (Nearly) Great Escape TPB (2007, $14.99) r/#1-5; Akins sketch pages 15.00
...: The New Adventures of Jack and Jack TPB (2010, $14.99) r/#36-40 15.00
...: Turning Pages TPB (2009, $14.99) r/#22-27 15.00

JACK OF HEARTS (Also see The Deadly Hands of Kung Fu #22 & Marvel Premiere #44)
Marvel Comics Group: Jan, 1984 - No. 4, Apr, 1984 (60¢, limited series)
1-4 4.00

JACKPOT
AfterShock Comics: Apr, 2016 - Present ($3.99)
1-4-Ray Fawkes-s/Marco Failla-a/Brian Stelfreeze-c 4.00

JACKPOT COMICS (Jolly Jingles #10 on)
MLJ Magazines: Spring, 1941 - No. 9, Spring, 1943
1-The Black Hood, Mr. Justice, Steel Sterling & Sgt. Boyle begin; Biro-c
331 662 993 2317 4059 5800
2-S. Cooper-c 161 322 483 1030 1765 2500
3-Hubbell-c 126 252 378 806 1378 1950
4-Archie begins; (his face appears on cover in small circle) (Win/41; on sale 12/41)-(also see Pep Comics #22); 1st app. Mrs. Grundy, the principal; Novick-c
3500 7000 10,500 20,000 26,000 32,000
5-Hitler, Tojo, Mussolini-c by Montana; 1st definitive Mr. Weatherbee; 1st brief app. Reggie in 1 panel 486 972 1458 3550 6275 9000
6-9: 6,7-Bondage-c by Novick. 8,9-Sahle-c 226 452 678 1446 2473 3500

JACK Q FROST (See Unearthly Spectaculars)

JACK STAFF (Vol. 2; previously published in Britain)
Image Comics: Feb, 2003 - No. 20, May, 2009 ($2.95/$3.50)
1-5-Paul Grist-s/a 3.50
6-20-($3.50) 6-Flashback to the WW2 Freedom Fighters 3.50
... Special 1 (1/08, $3.50) Molachi the Immortal app. 3.50
The Weird World of Jack Staff King Size Special 1 (7/07, $5.99, B&W) r/story serialized in Comics International magazine; afterword by Grist 6.00
Vol. 1: Everything Used to Be Black and White TPB (12/03, $19.95) r/British issues 20.00
Vol. 2: Soldiers TPB (2005, $15.95) r/#1-5; cover gallery 16.00
Vol. 3: Echoes of Tomorrow TPB (2006, $16.99) r/#6-12; cover gallery 17.00

JACK THE GIANT KILLER (See Movie Classics)

JACK THE GIANT KILLER (New Adventures of...)
Bimfort & Co.: Aug-Sept, 1953
V1#1-H. C. Kiefer-c/a 28 56 84 165 270 375

JACKY'S DIARY
Dell Publishing Co.: No. 1091, Apr-June, 1960 (one-shot)
Four Color 1091 5 10 15 33 57 80

JADEMAN COLLECTION
Jademan Comics: Dec, 1989 - No. 3, 1990 ($2.50, plastic coated-c, 68 pgs.)
1-3: 1-Wraparound-c w/fold-out poster 4.00

JADEMAN KUNG FU SPECIAL
Jademan Comics: 1988 ($1.50, 64 pgs.)
1 4.00

JADE WARRIORS (Mike Deodato's...)
Image Comics (Glass House Graphics): Nov, 1999 - No. 3, 2000 ($2.50)
1-3-Deodato-a 3.00
1-Variant-c 3.00

JAGUAR, THE (Also see The Adventures of...)
Impact Comics (DC): Aug, 1991 - No. 14, Oct, 1992 ($1.00)
1-14: 4-The Black Hood x-over. 7-Sienkiewicz-c. 9-Contains Crusaders trading card 3.00
Annual 1 (1992, $2.50, 68 pgs.)-With trading card 4.00

JAGUAR GOD
Verotik: Mar, 1995 - No. 7, June, 1997 ($2.95, mature)
0 (2/96, $3.50)-Embossed Frazetta-c; Bisley-a; w/pin-ups. 5.00
1-Frazetta-c. 5.00
2-7: 2-Frazetta-c. 3-Bisley-c. 4-Emond-c. 7-($2.95)-Frazetta-c 4.00

JAKE THRASH
Aircel Publishing: 1988 - No. 3, 1988 ($2.00)
1-3 3.00

JAM, THE (...Urban Adventure)
Slave Labor Nos. 1-5/Dark Horse Comics Nos. 6-8/Caliber Comics No. 9 on:
Nov, 1989 - No. 14, 1997 ($1.95/$2.50/$2.95, B&W)
1-14: Bernie Mireault-c/a/scripts. 6-1st Dark Horse issue. 9-1st Caliber issue 3.00

JAMBOREE COMICS
Round Publishing Co.: Feb, 1946(no month given) - No. 3, Apr, 1946
1-Funny animal 21 42 63 122 199 275
2,3 15 30 45 85 130 175

JAMES BOND
Dynamite Entertainment: 2015 - No. 12, 2016 ($3.99)
1-12-Warren Ellis-s/Jason Masters-a; multiple covers on each. 1-6-Vargr. 7-12-Eidolon 4.00

JAMES BOND (Volume 2)
Dynamite Entertainment: 2017 - Present ($3.99)
1-Black Box; Percy-s/Lobosco-a; five covers 4.00

JAMES BOND 007: A SILENT ARMAGEDDON
Dark Horse Comics/Acme Press: Mar, 1993 - Apr 1993 (limited series)
1,2 4.00

JAMES BOND 007: GOLDENEYE (Movie)
Topps Comics: Jan, 1996 ($2.95, unfinished limited series of 3)
1-Movie adaptation; Stelfreeze-c 3.00

JAMES BOND 007: SERPENT'S TOOTH
Dark Horse Comics/Acme Press: July 1992 - Aug 1992 ($4.95, limited series)
1-3-Paul Gulacy-c/a 5.00

JAMES BOND 007: SHATTERED HELIX
Dark Horse Comics: Jun 1994 - July 1994 ($2.50, limited series)
1,2 3.00

JAMES BOND 007: THE QUASIMODO GAMBIT
Dark Horse Comics: Jan 1995 - May 1995 ($3.95, limited series)
1-3 4.50

JAMES BOND: FELIX LEITER
Dynamite Entertainment: 2017 - No. 12, 2016 ($3.99)
1,2-James Robinson-s/Aaron Campbell-a 4.00

JAMES BOND FOR YOUR EYES ONLY
Marvel Comics Group: Oct, 1981 - No. 2, Nov, 1981
1,2-Movie adapt.; r/Marvel Super Special #19 6.00

JAMES BOND: HAMMERHEAD
Dynamite Entertainment: 2016 - Present ($3.99)
1-5-Diggle-s/Casalanguida-a. 1-Three covers 4.00

JAMES BOND JR. (TV)
Marvel Comics: Jan, 1992 - No. 12, Dec, 1992 (#1: $1.00, #2-on: $1.25)
1-12: Based on animated TV show 3.00

JAMES BOND: LICENCE TO KILL (See Licence To Kill)

JAMES BOND: PERMISSION TO DIE
Eclipse Comics/ACME Press: 1989 - No. 3, 1991 ($3.95, lim. series, squarebound, 52 pgs.)
1-3: Mike Grell-c/a/scripts in all. 3-($4.95) 5.00

JAM, THE: SUPER COOL COLOR INJECTED TURBO ADVENTURE #1 FROM HELL!
Comico: May, 1988 ($2.50, 44 pgs., one-shot)
1 4.00

JANE ARDEN (See Feature Funnies & Pageant of Comics)
St. John (United Features Syndicate): Mar, 1948 - No. 2, June, 1948
1-Newspaper reprints 15 30 45 88 137 185

Jeanie Comics #15 © MAR

Jem and the Holograms #6 © Hasbro

Jesse James #1 © AVON

	GD 2.0	VG 4.0	FN 6.0	VF 8.0	VF/NM 9.0	NM- 9.2
2	12	24	36	67	94	120

JANE WIEDLIN'S LADY ROBOTIKA
Image Comics: Jul, 2010 - No. 2, Aug, 2010 ($3.50, unfinished limited series)

	GD	VG	FN	VF	VF/NM	NM-
1,2-Wiedlin & Bill Morrison-s. 1-Morrison & Rodriguez-a. 2-Moy-a						3.50

JANN OF THE JUNGLE (Jungle Tales No. 1-7)
Atlas Comics (CSI): No. 8, Nov, 1955 - No. 17, June, 1957

	GD	VG	FN	VF	VF/NM	NM-
8(#1)	42	84	126	267	451	635
9,11-15	26	52	78	154	252	350
10-Williamson/Colletta-c	27	54	81	158	259	360
16,17-Williamson/Mayo-a(3), 5 pgs. each	27	54	81	162	266	370

NOTE: ***Everett** c-15-17. **Heck** a-8, 15, 17. **Maneely** c-11. **Shores** a-8.*

JASON & THE ARGOBOTS
Oni Press: Aug, 2002 - No. 4, Dec, 2002 ($2.95, B&W, limited series)

	GD	VG	FN	VF	VF/NM	NM-
1-4-Torres-s/Norton-c/a						3.00
Vol. 1 Birthquake TPB (6/03, $11.95, digest size) r/#1-4, Sunday comic strips						12.00
Vol. 2 Machina Ex Deus TPB (9/03, $11.95, digest size) new story						12.00

JASON & THE ARGONAUTS (See Movie Classics)

JASON GOES TO HELL: THE FINAL FRIDAY (Movie)
Topps Comics: July, 1993 - No. 3, Sept, 1993 ($2.95, limited series)

	GD	VG	FN	VF	VF/NM	NM-
1-3: Adaptation of film. 1-Glow-in-the-dark-c						3.00

JASON'S QUEST (See Showcase #88-90)

JASON VS. LEATHERFACE
Topps Comics: Oct, 1995 - No. 3, Jan, 1996 ($2.95, limited series)

	GD	VG	FN	VF	VF/NM	NM-
1-3: Collins scripts; Bisley-c						5.00

JAWS 2 (See Marvel Comics Super Special, A)

JAY & SILENT BOB (See Clerks, Oni Double Feature, and Tales From the Clerks)
Oni Press: July, 1998 - No. 4, Oct, 1999 ($2.95, B&W, limited series)

	GD	VG	FN	VF	VF/NM	NM-
1-Kevin Smith-s/Fegredo-a; photo-c & Quesada/Palmiotti-c						8.00
1-San Diego Comic Con variant covers (2 different covers, came packaged with action figures)						10.00
1-2nd & 3rd printings, 2-4: 2-Allred-c. 3-Flip-c by Jaime Hernandez						3.00
Chasing Dogma TPB (1999, $11.95) r/#1-4; Alanis Morissette intro.						13.00
Chasing Dogma TPB (2001, $12.95) r/#1-4 in color; Morissette intro.						13.00
Chasing Dogma HC (1999, $69.95, S&N) r/#1-4 in color; Morissette intro.						70.00

JCP FEATURES
J.C. Productions (Archie): Feb, 1982-c; Dec, 1981-indicia ($2.00, one-shot, B&W magazine)

	GD	VG	FN	VF	VF/NM	NM-
1-T.H.U.N.D.E.R. Agents; Black Hood by Morrow & Neal Adams; Texeira-a; 2 pgs. S&K-a from Fly #1	2	4	6	8	10	12

JEANIE COMICS (Formerly All Surprise; Cowgirl Romances #28)
Marvel Comics/Atlas(CPC): No. 13, April, 1947 - No. 27, Oct, 1949

	GD	VG	FN	VF	VF/NM	NM-
13-Mitzi, Willie begin	32	64	96	188	307	425
14,15	21	42	63	126	206	285
16-Used in Love and Death by Legman; Kurtzman's "Hey Look"	24	48	72	142	234	325
17-19,21,22-Kurtzman's "Hey Look" (1-3 pgs. each)	18	36	54	105	165	225
20,23-27	17	34	51	98	154	210

JEEP COMICS (Also see G.I. Comics and Overseas Comics)
R. B. Leffingwell & Co.: Winter, 1944, No. 2, Spring, 1945 - No. 3, Mar-Apr, 1948

	GD	VG	FN	VF	VF/NM	NM-
1-Capt. Power, Criss Cross & Jeep & Peep (costumed) begin	76	152	228	486	831	1175
2- Jeep & Peep-c	47	94	141	296	498	700
3-L. B. Cole dinosaur-c	58	116	174	371	636	900

JEFF JORDAN, U.S. AGENT
D. S. Publishing Co.: Dec, 1947 - Jan, 1948

	GD	VG	FN	VF	VF/NM	NM-
1	18	36	54	103	162	220

JEFF STEINBERG: CHAMPION OF EARTH
Oni Press: Aug, 2016 - No. 6, MAr, 2017 ($4.99)

	GD	VG	FN	VF	VF/NM	NM-
1-6: 1-Fialkov-s/Fleecs-a; covers by Fleecs & Burnham						5.00

JEM & THE HOLOGRAMS
IDW Publishing: Mar, 2015 - Present ($3.99)

	GD	VG	FN	VF	VF/NM	NM-
1-23: 1-Origin re-told; multiple covers						4.00
Annual 2017 (1/17, $7.99) Thompson-s; art by Lagace and others; 2 covers						8.00
... Holiday Special (12/15, $3.99) Mebberson-a						4.00
IDW Greatest Hits: Jem and the Holograms #1 (7/16, $1.00) r/#1						3.00
... Valentine Special (2/16, $3.99) Thompson-s/Bartel-a						4.00

JEMM, SON OF SATURN
DC Comics: Sept, 1984 - No. 12, Aug, 1985 (Maxi-series, mando paper)

	GD	VG	FN	VF	VF/NM	NM-
1-12: 3-Origin						4.00

NOTE: ***Colan** a-1-12p; c-1-5, 7-12p.*

JEM: THE MISFITS (From Jem and the Holograms)
IDW Publishing: Dec, 2016 - Present ($3.99)

	GD	VG	FN	VF	VF/NM	NM-
1,2-Kelly Thompson-s/Jenn St-Onge-a						4.00

JENNIFER BLOOD
Dynamite Entertainment: 2011 - No. 36, 2014 ($3.99)

	GD	VG	FN	VF	VF/NM	NM-
1-36: 1-3-Garth Ennis-s/Adriano Batista-a; four covers on each. 4-The Ninjettes app.						4.00
Annual 1 (2012, $4.99) Al Ewing-s/Igor Vitorino-a/Sean Chen-c; origin						5.00

JENNIFER BLOOD: BORN AGAIN
Dynamite Entertainment: 2014 - No. 5, 2014 ($3.99)

	GD	VG	FN	VF	VF/NM	NM-
1-5-Steven Grant-s/Kewber Baal-a/Stephen Segovia-c						4.00

JENNIFER BLOOD: FIRST BLOOD
Dynamite Entertainment: 2011 - No. 6, 2013 ($3.99)

	GD	VG	FN	VF	VF/NM	NM-
1-6-Mike Carroll-s/Igor Vitorino-a/Mike Mayhew-c; origin & training						4.00

JENNIFER'S BODY (Based on the 2009 movie)
BOOM! Studios: Aug, 2009 ($24.99, hardcover graphic novel)

	GD	VG	FN	VF	VF/NM	NM-
HC-Short stories of Jennifer and her victims; Spears-s/art by various; pin-up art						25.00

JENNY FINN
Oni Press: June, 1999 - No. 2, Sept, 1999 ($2.95, B&W, unfinished lim. series)

	GD	VG	FN	VF	VF/NM	NM-
1,2-Mignola & Nixey-s/Nixey-a/Mignola-c						3.00
...: Doom (Atomeka, 2005, $6.99, TPB) r/#1 & 2 with new supplemental material						7.00

JENNY SPARKS: THE SECRET HISTORY OF THE AUTHORITY
DC Comics (WildStorm): Aug, 2000 - No. 5, Mar, 2001 ($2.50, limited series)

	GD	VG	FN	VF	VF/NM	NM-
1-Millar-s/McCrea & Hodgkins-a/Hitch & Neary-c						4.00
1-Variant-c by McCrea	1	3	4	6	8	10
2-5: 2-Apollo & Midnighter. 3-Jack Hawksmoor. 4-Shen. 5-Engineer						3.00
TPB (2001, $14.95) r/#1-5; Ellis intro.						15.00

JERICHO (Based on the TV series)
Devil's Due Publishing/IDW Publishing: Oct, 2009 - Present ($3.99)

	GD	VG	FN	VF	VF/NM	NM-
... Redux (IDW, 2/11, $7.99) r/Season 3: Civil War #1-3						8.00
... Season 3: Civil War 1-4: 1-Story by the show's writing staff						4.00
... Season 4: 1-5: 1-(7/12) Photo-c & Bradstreet-c						4.00

JERRY DRUMMER (Boy Heroes of the Revolutionary War) (Formerly Soldier & Marine V2#9)
Charlton Comics: V3#10, Apr, 1957 - V3#12, Oct, 1957

	GD	VG	FN	VF	VF/NM	NM-
V3#10-12: 11-Whitman-c/a	6	12	18	29	36	42

JERRY IGER'S... (All titles, Blackthorne/First)(Value: cover or less)

JERRY LEWIS (See The Adventures of...)

JERSEY GODS
Image Comics: Feb, 2009 - No. 12, May, 2010 ($3.50)

	GD	VG	FN	VF	VF/NM	NM-
1-11: 1-Brunswick-s/McDaid-a; two covers by McDaid and Allred						3.50
12-($4.99) Wraparound cover swipe of Superman #252 by Allred						5.00

JESSE JAMES (The True Story Of..., also seeThe Legend of...)
Dell Publishing Co.: No. 757, Dec, 1956 (one shot)

	GD	VG	FN	VF	VF/NM	NM-
Four Color 757-Movie, photo-c	8	16	24	54	102	150

JESSE JAMES (See Badmen of the West & Blazing Sixguns)
Avon Periodicals: 8/50 - No. 9, 11/52; No. 15, 10/53 - No. 29, 8-9/56

	GD	VG	FN	VF	VF/NM	NM-
1-Kubert Alabam-r/Cowpuncher #1	20	40	60	118	192	265
2-Kubert-a(3)	15	30	45	88	137	185
3-Kubert Alabam-r/Cowpuncher #2	15	30	45	85	130	175
4,9-No Kubert	11	22	33	60	83	105
5,6-Kubert Jesse James-a(3); 5-Wood-a(1pg.)	15	30	45	85	130	175
7-Kubert Jesse James-a(2)	14	28	42	81	118	155
8-Kinstler-a(3)	11	22	33	64	90	115
15-Kinstler-r/#3	10	20	30	56	76	95
16-Kinstler-r/#3 & story-r/Butch Cassidy #1	10	20	30	58	79	100
17-19,21: 17-Jesse James-r/#4; Kinstler-c idea from Kubert splash in #6. 18-Kubert Jesse James-r/#5. 19-Kubert Jesse James-r/#6. 21-Two Jesse James-r/#4, Kinstler-r/#4	10	20	30	54	72	90
20-Williamson/Frazetta-a; r/Chief Vic. Apache Massacre; Kubert Jesse James-r/#6; Kit West story by Larsen	15	30	45	88	137	185

22-29: 22,23-No Kubert. 24-New McCarty strip by Kinstler; Kinstler-r. 25-New McCarty Jesse James strip by Kinstler; Jesse James-r/#7,9. 26,27-New McCarty Jesse James strip plus a Kinstler/McCann Jesse James-r. 28-Reprints most of Red Mountain, Featuring Quantrells

Jessica Jones #1 © MAR

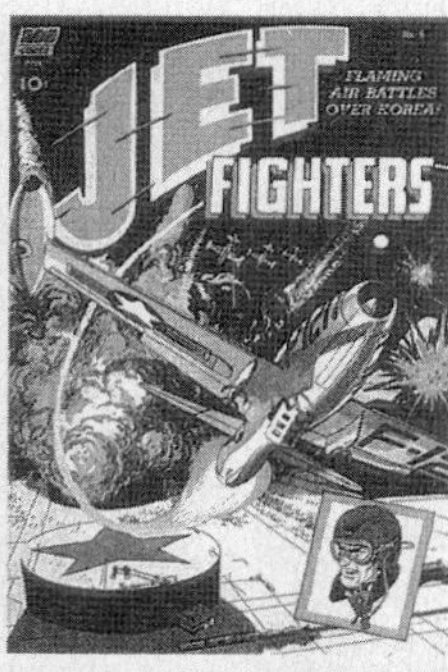

Jet Fighters #5 © STD

Jiggs and Maggie #19 © STD

GD 2.0 VG 4.0 FN 6.0 VF 8.0 VF/NM 9.0 NM- 9.2

Raiders 10 20 30 54 72 90
Annual nn (1952; 25¢, 100 pgs.)- "...Brings Six-Gun Justice to the West"- 3 earlier issues rebound; Kubert, Kinstler-a(3) 34 68 102 199 325 450
NOTE: *Mostly reprints #10 on.* **Fawcette** *c-1, 2.* **Kida** *a-5.* **Kinstler** *a-3, 4, 7-9, 15r, 16r(2), 21-27; c-3, 4, 9, 17-27. Painted c-5-8. 22 has 2 stories r/Sheriff Bob Dixon's Chuck Wagon #1 with name changed to Sheriff Bob Trent.*

JESSE JAMES
Realistic Publications: July, 1953
nn-Reprints Avon's #1; same-c, colors different 11 22 33 60 83 105

JESSICA JONES (Also see Alias)
Marvel Comics: Dec, 2016 - Present ($3.99)
1-5-Bendis-s/Gaydos-a; Luke Cage app. 1-Misty Knight app. 4.00

JEST (Formerly Snap; becomes Kayo #12)
Harry 'A' Chesler: No. 10, 1944; No. 11, 1944
10-Johnny Rebel & Yankee Boy app. in text 22 44 66 132 216 300
11-Little Nemo in Adventure Land 21 42 63 122 199 275

JESTER
Harry 'A' Chesler: No. 10, 1945
10 20 40 60 117 189 260

JESUS
Spire Christian Comics (Fleming H. Revell Co.): 1979 (49¢)
nn 2 4 6 11 16 20

JET (See Jet Powers)

JET (Crimson from Wildcore & Backlash)
DC Comics (WildStorm): Nov, 2000 - No. 4, Feb, 2001 ($2.50, limited series)
1-4-Nguyen-a/Abnett & Lanning-s 3.00

JET ACES
Fiction House Magazines: 1952 - No. 4, 1953
1- Sky Advs. of American War Aces (on sale 6/20/52) 20 40 60 114 182 250
2-4 12 24 36 69 97 125

JETCAT CLUBHOUSE (Also see Land of Nod, The)
Oni Press: Apr, 2001 - No. 3, Aug, 2001 ($3.25)
1-3-Jay Stephens-s/a. 1-Wraparound-c 3.25
TPB (8/02, $10.95, 8 3/4" x 5 3/4") r/#1-3 & stories from Nickelodeon mag. & other 11.00

JET DREAM (...and Her Stunt-Girl Counterspies)(See The Man from Uncle #7)
Gold Key: June, 1968 (12¢)
1-Painted-c 3 6 9 21 33 45

JET FIGHTERS (Korean War)
Standard Magazines: No. 5, Nov, 1952 - No. 7, Mar, 1953
5,7-Toth-a. 5-Toth-c 15 30 45 83 124 165
6-Celardo-a 11 22 33 60 83 105

JET POWER
I.W. Enterprises: 1963
I.W. Reprint 1,2-r/Jet Powers #1,2 3 6 9 16 24 32

JET POWERS (American Air Forces No. 5 on)
Magazine Enterprises: 1950 - No. 4, 1951
1(A-1 #30)-Powell-c/a begins 38 76 114 226 368 510
2(A-1 #32) Classic Powell dinosaur-c/a 38 76 114 226 368 510
3(A-1 #35)-Williamson/Evans-a 40 80 120 244 407 570
4(A-1 #38)-Williamson/Wood-a; "The Rain of Sleep" drug story 40 80 120 244 407 570

JET PUP (See 3-D Features)

JETSONS, THE (TV) (See March of Comics #276, 330, 348 & Spotlight #3)
Gold Key: Jan, 1963 - No. 36, Oct, 1970 (Hanna-Barbera)
1-1st comic book app. 24 48 72 168 372 575
2 10 20 30 66 138 210
3-10: 9-Flintstones x-over 8 16 24 51 96 140
11-22 6 12 18 40 73 105
23-36-Reprints: 23-(7/67) 4 8 12 27 44 60

JETSONS, THE (TV) (Also see Golden Comics Digest)
Charlton Comics: Nov, 1970 - No. 20, Dec, 1973 (Hanna-Barbera)
1 8 16 24 54 102 150
2 4 8 12 28 47 65
3-10: Flintstones x-over 3 6 9 20 31 42
11-20 3 6 9 16 24 32

GD 2.0 VG 4.0 FN 6.0 VF 8.0 VF/NM 9.0 NM- 9.2

nn (1973, digest, 60¢, 100 pgs.) B&W one page gags 4 8 12 23 37 50

JETSONS, THE (TV)
Harvey Comics: V2#1, Sept, 1992 - No. 5, Nov, 1993 ($1.25/$1.50) (Hanna-Barbera)
V2#1-5 5.00
...Big Book V2#1,2,3 ($1.95, 52 pgs.): 1-(11/92). 2-(4/93). 3-(7/93) 5.00
...Giant Size 1,2,3 ($2.25, 68 pgs): 1-(10/92). 2-(4/93). 3-(10/93) 5.00

JETSONS, THE (TV)
Archie Comics: Sept, 1995 - No. 8, Apr, 1996 ($1.50)
1-8 3.00

JETTA OF THE 21ST CENTURY
Standard Comics: No. 5, Dec, 1952 - No. 7, Apr, 1953 (Teen-age Archie type)
5-Dan DeCarlo-a 30 60 90 177 289 400
6-Robot-c 37 74 111 222 361 500
7 20 40 60 114 182 250
TPB (Airwave Publ., 2006, $9.99) B&W reprint of series; Bill Morrison intro./back-c 10.00

JEW GANGSTER
DC Comics: 2005 ($14.99, SC graphic novel)
SC-Joe Kubert-s/a 15.00

JEZEBEL JADE (Hanna-Barbara)
Comico: Oct, 1988 - No. 3, Dec, 1988 ($2.00, mini-series)
1-3: Johnny Quest spin-off; early Adam Kubert-a 3.00

JEZEBELLE (See Wildstorm 2000 Annuals)
DC Comics (WildStorm): Mar, 2001 - No. 6, Aug, 2001 ($2.50, limited series)
1-6-Ben Raab-s/Steve Ellis-a 3.00

JIGGS & MAGGIE
Dell Publishing Co.: No. 18, 1941 (one shot)
Four Color 18 (#1)-(1936-38-r) 52 104 156 328 552 775

JIGGS & MAGGIE
Standard Comics/Harvey Publications No. 22 on: No. 11, 1949 (June) - No. 21, 2/53; No. 22, 4/53 - No. 27, 2-3/54
11 20 40 60 114 182 250
12-15,17-21 14 28 42 76 108 140
16-Wood text illos. 14 28 42 78 112 145
22-24-Little Dot app. 12 24 36 69 97 125
25,27 11 22 33 60 83 105
26-Four pgs. partially in 3-D 15 30 45 83 124 165
NOTE: *Sunday page reprints by McManus loosely blended into story continuity. Based on Bringing Up Father strip. Advertised on covers as "All New."*

JIGSAW (Big Hero Adventures)
Harvey Publ. (Funday Funnies): Sept, 1966 - No. 2, Dec, 1966 (36 pgs.)
1-Origin & 1st app.; Crandall-a (5 pgs.) 3 6 9 21 33 45
2-Man From S.R.A.M. 3 6 9 15 22 28

JIGSAW OF DOOM (See Complete Mystery No. 2)

JIM BOWIE (Formerly Danger?; Black Jack No. 20 on)
Charlton Comics: No. 16, Mar, 1956 - No. 19, Apr, 1957
16 8 16 24 42 54 65
17-19: 18-Giordano-c 6 12 18 29 36 42

JIM BOWIE (TV, see Western Tales)
Dell Publishing Co.: No. 893, Mar, 1958 - No. 993, May-July, 1959
Four Color 893 (#1) 6 12 18 40 73 105
Four Color 993-Photo-c 5 10 15 34 60 85

JIM BUTCHER'S THE DRESDEN FILES: DOWN TOWN (Based on the Dresden Files novels)
Dynamite Entertainment: 2015 - No. 6, 2015 ($3.99, limited series)
1-6: 1-Jim Butcher & Mark Powers-s/Carlos Gomez-a/Stjepan Sejic-c 4.00

JIM BUTCHER'S THE DRESDEN FILES: FOOL MOON
Dynamite Entertainment: 2011 - No. 8, 2012 ($3.99, limited series)
1-8: 1-Jim Butcher & Mark Powers-s/Chase Conley-a/Brett Booth-c 4.00

JIM BUTCHER'S THE DRESDEN FILES: GHOUL GOBLIN
Dynamite Entertainment: 2012 - No. 6, 2013 ($3.99, limited series)
1-6: 1-Jim Butcher & Mark Powers-s/Joseph Cooper-a; Syaf-c 4.00

JIM BUTCHER'S THE DRESDEN FILES: STORM FRONT (Based on the Dresden Files novels)
Dabel Bros. Productions: Oct, 2008 (Nov. on-c) - No. 4, Apr, 2009 ($3.99, limited series)
1-4-Jim Butcher & Mark Powers-s/Ardian Syaf-a; covers by Syaf & Tsai 4.00
Vol. 2: 1,2 (7/09 - No. 4) 4.00

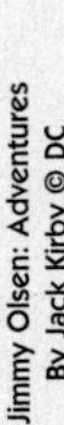

Jimmy Olsen: Adventures By Jack Kirby © DC

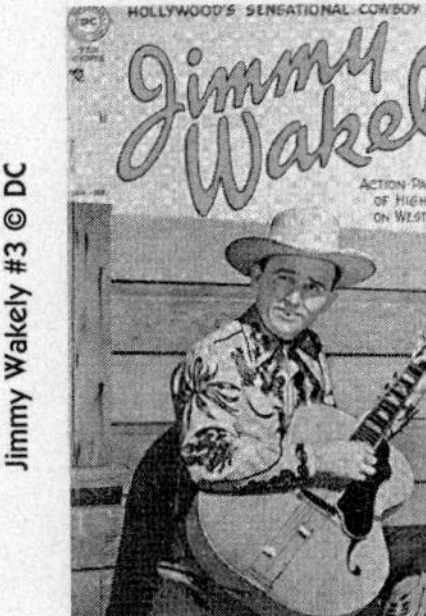

Jimmy Wakely #3 © DC

Jingle Jangle Comics #4 © EAS

GD VG FN VF VF/NM NM-
2.0 4.0 6.0 8.0 9.0 9.2

JIM BUTCHER'S THE DRESDEN FILES: WAR CRY
Dynamite Entertainment: 2014 - No. 5, 2014 ($3.99/$4.99, limited series)

1-4: 1-Jim Butcher & Mark Powers-s/Carlos Gomez-a; Sejic-c 4.00
5-($4.99) Wraparound-c by Sejic 5.00

JIM BUTCHER'S THE DRESDEN FILES: WELCOME TO THE JUNGLE
Dabel Bros. Productions: Mar, 2008 (Apr. on-c) - No. 4, Jul, 2008 ($3.99, limited series)

1-Jim Butcher-s/Ardian Syaf-a; Ardian Syaf-c 5.00
1-Variant-c by Chris McGrath 8.00
1-New York Comic-Con 2008 variant-c 15.00
1-Second printing 4.00
2-4-Two covers on each 4.00
HC (2008, $19.95, dustjacket) r/#1-4; Butcher intro.; concept art pages 20.00

JIM BUTCHER'S THE DRESDEN FILES: WILD CARD
Dynamite Entertainment: 2016 - No. 6, 2016 ($3.99, limited series)

1-6-Jim Butcher & Mark Powers-s/Carlos Gomez-a/c 4.00

JIM DANDY
Dandy Magazine (Lev Gleason): May, 1956 - No. 3, Sept, 1956 (Charles Biro)

1-Jim Dandy adventures w/Cup, an alien & his flying saucer (both invisible) from the planet Zikalug begins; ends #3. Biro-c. 1,2-Bammy Boozle app.
12 24 36 67 94 120
2,3: 2-Two pg. actual flying saucer reports 8 16 24 44 57 70

JIM HARDY (See Giant Comics Eds., Sparkler & Treasury of Comics #2 & 5)
United Features Syndicate/Spotlight Publ.: 1939; 1942; 1947 - No. 2, 1947

Single Series 6 ('39) 42 84 126 265 445 625
Single Series 27('42) 36 72 108 211 343 475
1('47)-Spotlight Publ. 15 30 45 85 130 175
2 10 20 30 54 72 90

JIM HARDY
Spotlight/United Features Synd.: 1944 (25¢, 132 pgs.) (Tip Top, Sparkler-r)

nn-Origin Mirror Man; Triple Terror app. 39 78 117 231 378 525

JIM HENSON'S THE STORYTELLER: DRAGONS (Also see The Storyteller)
BOOM! Studios (Archaia): Dec, 2015 - No. 4, Mar, 2016 ($3.99, limited series)

1-4: 2-Pride-s/a 4.00

JIM HENSON'S THE STORYTELLER: WITCHES
BOOM! Studios (Archaia): Sept, 2014 - No. 4, Dec, 2014 ($3.99, limited series)

1-4: 1-Vidaurri-s/a. 2-Vanderklugt-s/a. 3-Matthew Dow Smith-s/a. 4-Stokely-s/a 4.00

JIMINY CRICKET (Disney,, see Mickey Mouse Mag. V5#3 & Walt Disney Showcase #37)
Dell Publishing Co.: No. 701, May, 1956 - No. 989, May-July, 1959

Four Color 701 8 16 24 51 96 140
Four Color 795, 897, 989 6 12 18 38 69 100

JIM LEE SKETCHBOOK
DC Comics (WildStorm): 2002 (no price, 16 pgs.)

nn-Various DC and WildStorm character sketches by Lee 8.00

JIMMY CORRIGAN (See Acme Novelty Library)

JIMMY DURANTE (Also see A-1 Comics)
Magazine Enterprises: No. 18, Oct, 1949 - No. 20, Winter 1949-50

A-1 18,20-Photo-c (scarce) 52 104 156 328 552 775

JIMMY OLSEN (See Superman's Pal...)

JIMMY OLSEN
DC Comics: May, 2011 ($5.99, one-shot)

1-Reprints back-up feature from Action Comics #893-896 plus new material; Conner-c 6.00

JIMMY OLSEN: ADVENTURES BY JACK KIRBY
DC Comics: 2003, 2004 ($19.95, TPB)

nn-(2003) Reprints Jack Kirby's early issues of Superman's Pal Jimmy Olsen #133-139,141; Mark Evanier intro.; cover by Kirby and Steve Rude 20.00
Vol. 2 (2004) Reprints #142-148; Evanier intro.; cover gallery and sketch pages 20.00

JIMMY WAKELY (Cowboy movie star)
National Per. Publ.: Sept-Oct, 1949 - No. 18, July-Aug, 1952 (1-13: 52pgs.)

1-Photo-c, 52 pgs. begin; Alex Toth-a; Kit Colby Girl Sheriff begins
41 82 123 256 428 600
2-Toth-a 18 36 54 105 165 225
3,4,6,7-Frazetta-a in all, 3 pgs. each; Toth-a in all. 7-Last photo-c. 4-Kurtzman "Pot-Shot Pete", 1 pg; Toth-a 21 42 63 122 199 275
5,8-15-Toth-a; 12,14-Kubert-a (3 & 2 pgs.) 16 32 48 94 147 200
16-18 15 30 45 83 124 165

NOTE: *Gil Kane c-10-18p.*

JIM RAY'S AVIATION SKETCH BOOK
Vital Publishers: Mar-Apr, 1946 - No. 2, May-June, 1946 (15¢)

1-Picture stories of planes and pilots; atomic explosion panel
39 78 117 231 378 525
2-Story of General "Nap" Arnold 25 50 75 147 241 335

JIM SOLAR (See Wisco/Klarer in the Promotional Comics section)

JINGLE BELLE (Paul Dini's...)
Oni Press/Top Cow: Nov, 1999 - No. 2, Dec, 1999 ($2.95, B&W, limited series)

1,2-Paul Dini-s. 2-Alex Ross flip-c 3.00
Jingle Belle: Dash Away All (12/03, $11.95, digest-size) Dini-s/Garibaldi-a 12.00
Jingle Belle: Gift-Wrapped (Top Cow, 12/11, $3.99) Dini-s/Gladden-a 4.00
Jingle Belle: Santa Claus vs. Frankenstein (Top Cow, 12/08, $2.99) Dini-s/Gladden-a 3.00
Jingle Belle's Cool Yule (11/02, $13.95,TPB) r/All-Star Holiday Hullabaloo, The Mighty Elves, and Jubilee; internet strips and a color section w/DeStefano-a 14.00
Paul Dini's Jingle Belle Jubilee (11/01, $2.95) Dini-s; art by Rolston, DeCarlo, Morrison and Bone; pin-ups by Thompson and Aragonés 3.00
Paul Dini's Jingle Belle's All-Star Holiday Hullabaloo (11/00, $4.95) stories by various including Dini, Aragonés, Jeff Smith, Bill Morrison; Frank Cho-c 5.00
Paul Dini's Jingle Belle: The Fight Before Christmas (12/05, $2.99) Dini-s/Bone & others-a 3.00
Paul Dini's Jingle Belle: The Mighty Elves (7/01, $2.95) Dini-s/Bone-a 3.00
Paul Dini's Jingle Belle Winter Wingding (11/02, $2.95) Dini-s/Clugston-Major-c 3.00
The Bakers Meet Jingle Belle (12/06, $2.99) Dini-s/Kyle Baker-a 3.00
TPB (10/00, $8.95) r/#1&2, and app. from Oni Double Feature #13 9.00

JINGLE BELLE (Paul Dini's...)
Dark Horse Comics: Nov, 2004 - No. 4, Apr, 2005 ($2.99, limited series)

1-4-Paul Dini-s/Jose Garibaldi-a 3.00
TPB (9/05, $12.95) r/#1-4 13.00

JINGLE BELLS (See March of Comics No. 65)

JINGLE DINGLE CHRISTMAS STOCKING COMICS (See Foodini #2)
Stanhall Publications: V2#1, 1951 (no date listed) (25¢, 100 pgs.; giant-size) (Publ. annually)

V2#1-Foodini & Pinhead, Silly Pilly plus games & puzzles
22 44 66 132 216 300

JINGLE JANGLE COMICS (Also see Puzzle Fun Comics)
Eastern Color Printing Co.: Feb, 1942 - No. 42, Dec, 1949

1-Pie-Face Prince of Old Pretzleburg, Jingle Jangle Tales by George Carlson, Hortense, & Benny Bear begin 46 92 138 287 486 685
2-4: 2,3-No Pie-Face Prince. 4-Pie-Face Prince-c 21 42 63 122 199 275
5 (10/42) 19 38 57 111 176 240
6-10: 8-No Pie-Face Prince 15 30 45 85 130 175
11-15 12 24 36 69 97 125
16-30: 17,18-No Pie-Face Prince. 24,30-XMas-c 10 20 30 56 76 95
31-42: 36,42-Xmas-c 9 18 27 52 69 85

NOTE: *George Carlson a-(2) in all except No. 2, 3, 8; c-1-6. Carlson 1 pg. puzzles in 9, 10, 12-15, 18, 20. Carlson illustrated a series of Uncle Wiggily books in 1930's.*

JING PALS
Victory Publishing Corp.: Feb, 1946 - No. 4, Aug?, 1946 (Funny animal)

1-Wishing Willie, Puggy Panda & Johnny Rabbit begin
17 34 51 98 154 210
2-4 11 22 33 60 83 105

JINKS, PIXIE, AND DIXIE (See Kite Fun Book & Whitman Comic Books)

JINX
Caliber Press: 1996 - No. 7, 1996 ($2.95, B&W, 32 pgs.)

1-7: Brian Michael Bendis-c/a/scripts. 2-Photo-c 3.00

JINX (Volume 2)
Image Comics: 1997 - No. 5, 1998 ($2.95, B&W, bi-monthly)

1-4: Brian Michael Bendis-c/a/scripts. 3.00
5-($3.95) Brereton-c 4.00
...Buried Treasures ('98, $3.95) short stories, ...Confessions ('98, $3.95) short stories, ...Pop Culture Hoo-Hah ('98, $3.95) humor shorts 4.00
TPB (1997, $10.95) r/Vol 1,#1-4 11.00
...: The Definitive Collection ('01, $24.95) remastered #1-5, sketch pages, art gallery, script excerpts, Mack intro. 25.00

JINX: TORSO
Image Comics: 1998 - No. 6, 1999 ($3.95/$4.95, B&W)

1-6-Based on Eliot Ness' pursuit of America's first serial killer; Brian Michael Bendis & Marc Andreyko-s/Bendis-a. 3-6-($4.95) 5.00

JLA #18 © DC

JLA #50 © DC

JLA / Avengers #3 © DC / MAR

	GD 2.0	VG 4.0	FN 6.0	VF 8.0	VF/NM 9.0	NM- 9.2

Softcover (2000, $24.95) r/#1-6; intro. by Greg Rucka; photo essay of the actual murders and police documents 25.00
Hardcover (2000, $49.95) signed & numbered 50.00

JIRNI
Aspen MLT: Apr, 2013 - No. 5, Oct, 2013 ($1.00/$3.99)

1-($1.00) J.T. Krul-s/Paolo Pantalena-a; multiple covers 3.00
2-5-($3.99) Multiple covers on each 4.00
Vol. 2 #1 (6/14, $3.99) Krul-s/Pantalena-a 4.00
Vol. 2 #1-5 (8/15 - No. 5, 12/15, $3.99) Krul-s/Marion-a; multiple covers on each 4.00

JLA (See Justice League of America and Justice Leagues)
DC Comics: Jan, 1997 - No. 125, Apr, 2006 ($1.95/$1.99/$2.25/$2.50)

	GD	VG	FN	VF	VF/NM	NM-
1-Morrison-s/Porter & Dell-a. The Hyperclan app.	2	4	6	9	12	15
2	1	3	4	6	8	10
3,4	1	2	3	5	7	9

5-Membership drive; Tomorrow Woman app. 6.00
6-9: 6-1st app. Zauriel. 8-Green Arrow joins. 6.00
10-21: 10-Rock of Ages begins. 11-Joker and Luthor-c/app. 14-Darkseid app. 15-($2.95) Rock of Ages concludes. 16-New members join; Prometheus app. 17,20-Jorgensen-a. 18-21-Waid-s. 20,21-Adam Strange c/app. 5.00
22-40: 22-Begin $1.99-c; Sandman (Daniel) app. 27-Amazo app. 28-31-JSA app. 35-Hal Jordan/Spectre app. 36-40-World War 3 3.00
41-($2.99) Conclusion of World War 3; last Morrison-s 4.00
42-46: 43-Waid-s; Ra's al Ghul app. 44-Begin $2.25-c. 46-Batman leaves 3.00
47-49: 47-Hitch & Neary-a begins; JLA battles Queen of Fables 3.00
50-($3.75) JLA vs. Dr. Destiny; art by Hitch & various 4.00
51-74: 52-55-Hitch-a. 59-Joker: Last Laugh. 61-68-Kelly-s/Mahnke-a. 69-73-Hunt for Aquaman; bi-monthly with alternating art by Mahnke and Guichet 3.00
75-(1/03, $3.95) leads into Aquaman (4th series) #1 4.00
76-93: 76-Firestorm app. 77-Banks-a. 79-Kanjar Ro app. 91-93-O'Neil-s/Huat-a 3.00
94-99-Byrne & Ordway-a/Claremont-s; Doom Patrol app. 3.00
100-($3.50) Intro. Vera Black; leads into Justice League Elite #1 4.00
101-114: 101-106-Austen-s/Garney-a/c. 107-114-Crime Syndicate app.; Busiek-s 3.00
115-125: 115-Begin $2.50-c; Johns & Heinberg-s; Secret Society of Super-Villains app. 3.00
#1,000,000 (11/98) 853rd Century x-over 3.00
Annual 1 (1997, $3.95) Pulp Heroes; Augustyn-s/Olivetti & Ha-a 4.00
Annual 2 (1998, $2.95) Ghosts; Wrightson-c 4.00
Annual 3 (1999, $2.95) JLApe; Art Adams-c 4.00
Annual 4 (2000, $3.50) Planet DC x-over; Steve Scott-c/a 4.00
... American Dreams (1998, $7.95, TPB) r/#5-9 8.00
...: Crisis of Conscience TPB (2006, $12.99) r/#115-119 13.00
.../ Cyberforce (DC/Top Cow, 2005, $5.99) Kelly-s/Mahnke-a/Silvestri-c 6.00
Divided We Fall (2001, $17.95, TPB) r/#47-54 18.00
...80-Page Giant 1 (7/98, $4.95) stories & art by various 6.00
...80-Page Giant 2 (11/99, $4.95) Green Arrow & Hawkman app. Hitch-c 6.00
...80-Page Giant 3 (10/00, $5.95) Pariah & Harbinger; intro. Moon Maiden 6.00
...Foreign Bodies (1999, $5.95, one-shot) Kobra app.; Semeiks-a 6.00
...Gallery (1997, $2.95) pin-ups by various; Quitely-c 3.00
...God & Monsters (2001, $6.95, one-shot) Benefiel-a/c 7.00
Golden Perfect (2003, $12.95, TPB) r/#61-65 13.00
.../ Haven: Anathema (2002, $6.95) Concludes the Haven: The Broken City series 7.00
.../ Haven: Arrival (2001, $6.95) Leads into the Haven: The Broken City series 7.00
...In Crisis Secret Files 1 (11/98, $4.95) recap of JLA in DC x-overs 5.00
...: Island of Dr. Moreau, The (2002, $6.95, one-shot) Elseworlds; Pugh-c/a; Thomas-s 7.00
.../ JSA Secret Files & Origins (1/03, $4.95) prelude to JLA/JSA: Virtue & Vice; short stories and pin-ups by various; Pacheco-c 5.00
.../ JSA: Virtue and Vice HC (2002, $24.95) Teams battle Despero & Johnny Sorrow; Goyer & Johns-s/Pacheco-a/c 25.00
.../ JSA: Virtue and Vice SC (2003, $17.95) 18.00
Justice For All (1999, $14.95, TPB) r/#24-33 15.00
New World Order (1997, $5.95, TPB) r/#1-4 6.00
...: Obsidian Age Book One, The (2003, $12.95) r/#66-71 13.00
...: Obsidian Age Book Two, The (2003, $12.95) r/#72-76 13.00
One Million (2004, $19.95, TPB) r/#DC One Million #1-4 and other #1,000,000 x-overs 20.00
...: Our Worlds at War (9/01, $2.95) Jae Lee-c; Aquaman presumed dead 3.00
...: Pain of the Gods (2005, $12.99) r/#101-106 13.00
...Primeval (1999, $5.95, one-shot) Abnett & Lanning-s/Olivetti-a 6.00
...: Riddle of the Beast HC (2001, $24.95) Grant-s/painted-a by various; Sweet-c 25.00
...: Riddle of the Beast SC (2003, $14.95) Grant-s/painted-a by various; Kaluta-c 15.00
Rock of Ages (1998, $9.95, TPB) r/#10-15 10.00
Rules of Engagement (2004, $12.95, TPB) r/#77-82 13.00
...: Seven Caskets (2000, $5.95, one-shot) Brereton-s/painted-c/a 6.00
...: Shogun of Steel (2002, $6.95, one-shot) Elseworlds; Justiniano-c/a 7.00
...Showcase 80-Page Giant (2/00, $4.95) Hitch-c 5.00
Strength in Numbers (1998, $12.95, TPB) r/#16-23, Secret Files #2 and Prometheus #1 13.00
...Superpower (1999, $5.95, one-shot) Arcudi-s/Eaton-a; Mark Antaeus joins 6.00
Syndicate Rules (2005, $17.99, TPB) r/#107-114, Secret Files #4 18.00
Terror Incognita (2002, $12.95, TPB) r/#55-60 13.00
...: The Deluxe Edition Vol. 1 HC (2008, $29.99, dustjacket) oversized r/#1-9 and JLA Secret Files #1 30.00
...: The Deluxe Edition Vol. 2 HC (2009, $29.99, dustjacket) oversized r/#10-17, JLA/Wildcats, and Prometheus #1 30.00
...: The Deluxe Edition Vol. 3 HC (2010, $29.99, dustjacket) oversized r/#22-26, 28-31 & #1,000,000 30.00
...: The Deluxe Edition Vol. 4 HC (2010, $34.99, dustjacket) oversized r/#34, 36-41, JLA Classified #1-3 and JLA: Earth 2 GN 35.00
The Tenth Circle (2004, $12.95, TPB) r/#94-99 13.00
...: The Greatest Stories Ever Told TPB (2006, $19.99) r/Justice League of America #19,71,122, 166-168,200, Justice League #1, JLA Secret Files #1 and JLA #61; Alex Ross-c 20.00
Tower of Babel (2001, $12.95, TPB) r/#42-46, Secret Files #3, 80-Page Giant #1 13.00
Trial By Fire (2004, $12.95, TPB) r/#84-89 13.00
...Vs. Predator (DC/Dark Horse, 2000, $5.95, one-shot) Nolan-c/a 6.00
...: Welcome to the Working Week (2003, $6.95, one-shot) Patton Oswalt-s 7.00
...: World War III (2000, $12.95, TPB) r/#34-41 13.00
...: World Without a Justice League (2006, $12.99, TPB) r/#120-125 13.00
...: Zatanna's Search (2003, $12.95, TPB) rep. Zatanna's early app. & origin; Bolland-c 13.00

JLA: ACT OF GOD
DC Comics: 2000 - No. 3, 2001 ($4.95, limited series)

1-3-Elseworlds; metahumans lose their powers; Moench-s/Dave Ross-a 5.00

JLA: AGE OF WONDER
DC Comics: 2003 - No. 2, 2003 ($5.95, limited series)

1,2-Elseworlds; Superman and the League of Science during the Industrial Revolution 6.00

JLA: A LEAGUE OF ONE
DC Comics: 2000 (Graphic novel)

Hardcover ($24.95) Christopher Moeller-s/painted-a 25.00
Softcover (2002, $14.95) 15.00

JLA/AVENGERS (See Avengers/JLA for #2 & #4)
Marvel Comics: Sept, 2003; No. 3, Dec, 2003 ($5.95, limited series)

1-Busiek-s/Pérez-a; wraparound-c; Krona, Starro, Grandmaster, Terminus app. 6.00
3-Busiek-s/Pérez-a; wraparound-c; Phantom Stranger app. 6.00
SC (2008, $19.99) r/4-issue series; cover gallery; intros by Stan Lee & Julius Schwartz 20.00

JLA: BLACK BAPTISM
DC Comics: May, 2001 - No. 4, Aug, 2001 ($2.50, limited series)

1-4-Saiz-a(p)/Bradstreet-c; Zatanna app. 3.00

JLA: CLASSIFIED
DC Comics: Jan, 2005 - No. 54, May, 2008 ($2.95/$2.99)

1-3-Morrison-s/McGuinness-a/c; Ultramarines app. 3.00
4-9-"I Can't Believe It's Not The Justice League," Giffen & DeMatteis-s/Maguire-a 3.00
10-31,33-54: 10-15-New Maps of Hell; Ellis-s/Guice-a. 16-21-Garcia-Lopez-a. 22-25-Detroit League & Royal Flush Gang app.; Englehart-s. 26-28-Chaykin-s. 37-41-Kid Amazo. 50-54-Byrne-a/Middleston-c 3.00
32-($3.99) Dr. Destiny app.; Jurgens-a 4.00
I Can't Believe It's Not The Justice League TPB (2005, $12.99) r/#4-9 13.00
...: Kid Amazo TPB (2007, $12.99) r/#37-41 13.00
...: New Maps of Hell TPB (2006, $12.99) r/#10-15 13.00
...: That Was Now, This Is Then TPB (2008, $14.99) r/#50-54 15.00
...: The Hypothetical Woman TPB (2008, $12.99) r/#16-21 13.00
...: Ultramarine Corps TPB (2007, $14.99) r/#1-3, JLA/WildC.A.T.s #1 and JLA Secret Files 2004 #1 15.00

JLA CLASSIFIED: COLD STEEL
DC Comics: 2005 - No. 2, 2006 ($5.99, limited series, prestige format)

1,2-Chris Moeller-s/a; giant robot Justice League 6.00

JLA: CREATED EQUAL
DC Comics: 2000 - No. 2, 2000 ($5.95, limited series, prestige format)

1,2-Nicieza-s/Maguire-a; Elseworlds-Superman as the last man on Earth 6.00

JLA: DESTINY
DC Comics: 2002 - No. 4, 2002 ($5.95, prestige format, limited series)

1-4-Elseworlds; Arcudi-s/Mandrake-a 6.00

JLA: EARTH 2
DC Comics: 2000 (Graphic novel)

Hardcover ($24.95) Morrison-s/Quitely-a; Crime Syndicate app. 25.00
Softcover ($14.95) 15.00

JLA: Year One #12 © DC

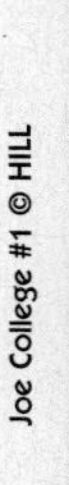
Joe College #1 © HILL

Joe Palooka #18 © HARV

GD 2.0 | VG 4.0 | FN 6.0 | VF 8.0 | VF/NM 9.0 | NM- 9.2

JLA: GATEKEEPER
DC Comics: 2001 - No. 3, 2001 ($4.95, prestige format, limited series)
1-3-Truman-s/a 5.00

JLA: HEAVEN'S LADDER
DC Comics: 2000 ($9.95, Treasury-size one-shot)
nn-Bryan Hitch & Paul Neary-c/a; Mark Waid-s 10.00

JLA/HITMAN (Justice League/Hitman in indicia)
DC Comics: Nov, 2007 - No. 2, Dec, 2007 ($3.99, limited series)
1,2-Ennis-s/McCrea-a; Bloodlines creatures return 4.00

JLA: INCARNATIONS
DC Comics: Jul, 2001 - No. 7, Feb, 2002 ($3.50, limited series)
1-7-Ostrander-s/Semeiks-a; different eras of the Justice League 4.00

JLA: LIBERTY AND JUSTICE
DC Comics: Nov, 2003 ($9.95, Treasury-size one-shot)
nn-Alex Ross-c/a; Paul Dini-s; story of the classic Justice League 10.00

JLA PARADISE LOST
DC Comics: Jan, 1998 - No. 3, Mar, 1998 ($1.95, limited series)
1-3-Millar-s/Olivetti-a 3.00

JLA: SCARY MONSTERS
DC Comics: May, 2003 - No. 6, Oct, 2003 ($2.50, limited series)
1-6-Claremont-s/Art Adams-c 3.00

JLA SECRET FILES
DC Comics: Sept, 1997 - 2004 ($4.95)
1-Standard Ed. w/origin-s & pin-ups 5.00
1-Collector's Ed. w/origin-s & pin-ups; cardstock-c 6.00
2,3: 2-(8/98) origin-s of JLA #16's newer members. 3-(12/00) 5.00
... 2004 (11/04) Justice League Elite app.; Mahnke & Byrne-a; Crime Syndicate app. 5.00

JLA: SECRET ORIGINS
DC Comics: Nov, 2002 ($7.95, Treasury-size one-shot)
nn-Alex Ross 2-page origins of Justice League members; text by Paul Dini 8.00

JLA: SECRET SOCIETY OF SUPER-HEROES
DC Comics: 2000 - No. 2, 2000 ($5.95, limited series, prestige format)
1,2-Elseworlds JLA; Chaykin and Tischman-s/McKone-a 6.00

JLA /SPECTRE: SOUL WAR
DC Comics: 2003 - No. 2, 2003 ($5.95, limited series, prestige format)
1,2-DeMatteis-s/Banks & Neary-a 6.00

JLA: THE NAIL (Elseworlds) (Also see Justice League of America: Another Nail)
DC Comics: Aug, 1998 - No. 3, Oct, 1998 ($4.95, prestige format)
1-3-JLA in a world without Superman; Alan Davis-s/a(p) 5.00
TPB ('98, $12.95) r/series w/new Davis-c 13.00

JLA / TITANS
DC Comics: Dec, 1998 - No. 3, Feb, 1999 ($2.95, limited series)
1-3-Grayson-s; P. Jimenez-c/a 3.00
...:The Technis Imperative ('99, $12.95, TPB) r/#1-3; Titans Secret Files 13.00

JLA: TOMORROW WOMAN (Girlfrenzy)
DC Comics: June, 1998 ($1.95, one-shot)
1-Peyer-s; story takes place during JLA #5 3.00

JLA / WILDC.A.T.S
DC Comics: 1997 ($5.95, one-shot, prestige format)
1-Morrison-s/Semeiks & Conrad-a 6.00

JLA /WITCHBLADE
DC Comics/Top Cow: 2000 ($5.95, prestige format, one-shot)
1-Pararillo-c/a 6.00

JLA / WORLD WITHOUT GROWN-UPS (See Young Justice)
DC Comics: Aug, 1998 - No. 2, Sept, 1998 ($4.95, prestige format)
1,2-JLA, Robin, Impulse & Superboy app.; Ramos & McKone-a 6.00
TPB ('98, $9.95) r/series & Young Justice: The Secret #1 10.00

JLA: YEAR ONE
DC Comics: Jan, 1998 - No. 12, Dec, 1998 ($2.95/$1.95, limited series)
1-($2.95)-Waid & Augustyn-s/Kitson-a 5.00
1-Platinum Edition 10.00
2-8-($1.95): 5-Doom Patrol-c/app. 7-Superman app. 4.00
9-12 3.00
TPB ('99,'09; $19.95/$19.99) r/#1-12; Busiek intro. 20.00

JLA-Z
DC Comics: Nov, 2003 - No. 3, Jan, 2004 ($2.50, limited series)
1-3-Pin-ups and info on current and former JLA members and villains; art by various 3.00

JLX
DC Comics (Amalgam): Apr, 1996 ($1.95, one-shot)
1-Mark Waid scripts 3.00

JLX UNLEASHED
DC Comics (Amalgam): June, 1997 ($1.95, one-shot)
1-Priest-s/ Oscar Jimenez & Rodriquez/a 3.00

JOAN OF ARC (Also see A-1 Comics, Classics Illustrated #78, and Ideal a Classical Comic)
Magazine Enterprises: No. 21, 1949 (one shot)
A-1 21-Movie adaptation; Ingrid Bergman photo-covers & interior photos; Whitney-a 29 58 87 170 278 385

JOE COLLEGE
Hillman Periodicals: Fall, 1949 - No. 2, Wint, 1950 (Teen-age humor, 52 pgs.)
1-Powell-a; Briefer-a 14 28 42 82 121 160
2-Powell-a 10 20 30 56 76 95

JOE FRANKENSTEIN
IDW Publishing: Feb, 2015 - No. 4, May, 2015 ($3.99)
1-4-Chuck Dixon & Graham Nolan-s/Graham Nolan-a 4.00

JOE GOLEM
Dark Horse Comics: Nov, 2015 - No. 5, Mar, 2016 ($3.50)
1-5-Mignola & Golden-s/Reynolds-a 4.00

JOE JINKS
United Features Syndicate: No. 12, 1939
Single Series 12 31 62 93 186 303 420

JOE KUBERT PRESENTS
DC Comics: Dec, 2012 - No. 6, May, 2013 ($4.99, limited series)
1-6: Anthology of short stories by Kubert, Buniak & Glanzman. 1-Hawkman app. 5.00

JOE LOUIS (See Fight Comics #2, Picture News #6 & True Comics #5)
Fawcett Publications: Sept, 1950 - No. 2, Nov, 1950 (Photo-c) (Boxing champ) (See Dick Cole #10)
1-Photo-c; life story 55 110 165 352 601 850
2-Photo-c 39 78 117 240 395 550

JOE PALOOKA (1st Series)(Also see Big Shot Comics, Columbia Comics & Feature Funnies)
Columbia Comic Corp. (Publication Enterprises): 1942 - No. 4, 1944
1-1st to portray American president; gov't permission required 129 258 387 826 1413 2000
2 (1943)-Hitler-c 97 194 291 621 1061 1500
3-Nazi Sub-c 48 96 144 302 514 725
4 39 78 117 231 378 525

JOE PALOOKA (2nd Series) (Battle Adv. #68-74; ...Advs. #75, 77-81, 83-85, 87; Champ of the Comics #76, 82, 86, 89-93) (See All-New)
Harvey Publications: Nov, 1945 - No. 118, Mar, 1961
1-By Ham Fisher 53 106 159 334 567 800
2 26 52 78 154 252 350
3,4,6,7-1st Flyin' Fool, ends #25 16 32 48 94 147 200
5-Boy Explorers by S&K (7-8/46) 21 42 63 122 199 275
8-10 14 28 42 80 115 150
11-14,16,18-20: 14-Black Cat text-s(2). 18-Powell-a.; Little Max app. 19-Freedom Train-c 11 22 33 64 90 115
15-Origin & 1st app. Humphrey (12/47); Super-heroine Atoma app. by Powell 15 30 45 90 140 190
17-Humphrey vs. Palooka-c/s; 1st app. Little Max 15 30 45 90 140 190
21-26,29,30: 22-Powell-a. 30-Nude female painting 10 20 30 56 76 95
27-Little Max app.; Howie Morenz-s 10 20 30 58 79 100
28-Babe Ruth 4 pg. sty. 10 20 30 58 79 100
31,39,51: 31-Dizzy Dean 4 pg. sty. 39-(12/49) Humphrey & Little Max begin; Sonny Baugh football-s; Sherlock Max-s. 51-Babe Ruth 2 pg. sty; Jake Lamotta 1/2 pg. sty 9 18 27 50 65 80
32-38,40-50,52-61: 35-Little Max-c/story(4 pgs.); Joe Louis 1 pg. sty. 36-Humphrey story. 41-Bing Crosby photo on-c. 44-Palooka marries Ann Howe. 50-(11/51)-Becomes Harvey Comics Hits #51 8 16 24 44 57 70
62-S&K Boy Explorers-r 9 18 27 50 65 80
63-65,73-80,100: 79-Story of 1st meeting with Ann 8 16 24 40 50 60

Joe the Barbarian #4 © Morrison & DC

John Byrne's Next Men #29 © John Byrne

John Carter, Warlord of Mars #1 © ERB

	GD 2.0	VG 4.0	FN 6.0	VF 8.0	VF/NM 9.0	NM- 9.2

66,67-'Commie' torture story "Drug-Diet Horror" 13 26 39 72 101 130
68,70-72: 68,70-Joe vs. "Gooks"-c. 71-Bloody bayonets-c. 72-Tank-c
12 24 36 69 97 125
69-1st "Battle Adventures" issue; torture & bondage 13 26 39 74 105 135
81-99,101-115: 104,107-Humphrey & Little Max-s 7 14 21 37 46 55
116-S&K Boy Explorers-r (Giant, '60) 9 18 27 47 61 75
117-(84 pg. Giant) r/Commie issues #66,67; Powell-a 9 18 27 52 69 85
118-(84 pg. Giant) Jack Dempsey 2 pg. sty, Powell-a 9 18 27 47 61 75
...Visits the Lost City nn (1945)(One Shot)(50¢)-164 page continuous story strip reprint. Has biography & photo of Ham Fisher; possibly the single longest comic book story published in that era (159 pgs.?) (scarce) 232 464 696 1485 2543 3600

NOTE: ***Nostrand/Powell** a-73. **Powell** a-7, 8, 10, 12, 14, 17, 19, 26-45, 47-53, 70, 73 at least. Black Cat text stories #8, 12, 13, 19.*

JOE PALOOKA
IDW Publishing: Dec, 2012 - No. 6, May, 2013 ($3.99, limited series)
1-6: 1-Bullock-s/Peniche-a; Joe Palooka updated as a MMA fighter 4.00

JOE PSYCHO & MOO FROG
Goblin Studios: 1996 - No. 5, 1997 ($2.50, B&W)
1-5: 4-Two covers 3.00
...Full Color Extravagarbonzo ($2.95, color) 3.00

JOE THE BARBARIAN
DC Comics (Vertigo): Mar, 2010 - No. 8, May, 2011 ($1.00/$2.99/$3.99)
1-($1.00) Grant Morrison-s/Sean Murphy-a 3.00
2-7-($2.99) 3.00
8-($3.99) 4.00

JOE YANK (Korean War)
Standard Comics (Visual Editions): No. 5, Mar, 1952 - No. 16, 1954
5-Toth, Celardo, Tuska-a 11 22 33 60 83 105
6-Toth, Severin/Elder-a 10 20 30 58 79 100
7-Pinhead Perkins by Dan DeCarlo (in all?) 9 18 27 47 61 75
8-Toth-c 9 18 27 52 69 85
9-16: 9-Andru-c. 12-Andru-a 8 16 24 44 57 70

JOHN BOLTON'S HALLS OF HORROR
Eclipse Comics: June, 1985 - No. 2, June, 1985 ($1.75, limited series)
1,2-British-r; Bolton-c/a 4.00

JOHN BOLTON'S STRANGE WINK
Dark Horse Comics: Mar, 1998 - No. 3, May, 1998 ($2.95, B&W, limited series)
1-3-Anthology; Bolton-s/c/a 3.00

JOHN BYRNE'S NEXT MEN (See Dark Horse Presents #54)
Dark Horse Comics (Legend imprint #19 on): Jan, 1992 - No. 30, Dec, 1994 ($2.50, mature)
1-Silver foil embossed-c; Byrne-c/a/scripts in all 4.00
1-4: 1-2nd printing with gold ink logo 3.00
0-(2/92)-r/chapters 1-4 from DHP w/new Byrne-c 3.00
5-20,22-30: 7-10-MA #1-4 mini-series on flip side. 16-Origin of Mark IV. 17-Miller-c. 19-22-Faith storyline. 23-26-Power storyline. 27-30-Lies storyline Pt. 1-4 3.00
21-(12/93) 2nd Hellboy; cover and Hellboy pages by Mike Mignola; Byrne other pages (see San Diego Comic Con Comics #2 for 1st app.) 5 10 15 30 50 70
...Parallel, Book 2 ($16.95)-TPB; r/#7-12 17.00
...Fame, Book 3($16.95)-TPB r/#13-18 17.00
...Faith, Book 4($14.95)-TPB r/#19-22 15.00

NOTE: *Issues 1 through 6 contain certificates redeemable for an exclusive Next Men trading card set by Byrne. Prices are for complete books. **Cody** painted c-23-26. **Mignola** a-21(part); c-21.*

JOHN BYRNE'S NEXT MEN (Continues in Next Men: Aftermath #40)
IDW Publishing: Dec, 2010 - No. 9, Aug, 2011 ($3.99)
1-9-John Byrne-s/a/c in all. 1-Origin retold. 6,7-Abraham Lincoln app. 4.00

JOHN BYRNE'S 2112
Dark Horse Comics (Legend): Oct, 1991 ($9.95, TPB)
1-Byrne-c/a/s 10.00

JOHN CARTER OF MARS (See The Funnies & Tarzan #207)
Dell Publishing Co.: No. 375, Mar-May, 1952 - No. 488, Aug-Oct, 1953 (Edgar Rice Burroughs)
Four Color 375 (#1)-Origin; Jesse Marsh-a 29 58 87 209 467 725
Four Color 437, 488-Painted-c 16 32 48 112 249 385

JOHN CARTER OF MARS
Gold Key: Apr, 1964 - No. 3, Oct, 1964
1(10104-404)-r/4-Color #375; Jesse Marsh-a 6 12 18 40 73 105
2(407), 3(410)-r/4-Color #437 & 488; Marsh-a 5 10 15 30 50 70

JOHN CARTER OF MARS
House of Greystroke: 1970 (10-1/2x16-1/2", 72 pgs., B&W, paper-c)
1941-42 Sunday strip-r; John Coleman Burroughs-a 4 8 12 23 37 50

JOHN CARTER OF MARS: A PRINCESS OF MARS
Marvel Comics: Nov, 2011 - No. 5, Mar, 2012 ($2.99, limited series)
1-5: 1-Langridge-s/Andrade-a; covers by Young and Andrade. 2-4-Young-c 3.00

JOHN CARTER: THE END
Dynamite Entertainment: 2017 - Present ($3.99)
1-Brian Wood-s/Alex Cox-a; multiple covers 4.00

JOHN CARTER: THE GODS OF MARS
Marvel Comics: May, 2012 - No. 5, Sept, 2012 ($3.99, limited series)
1-5-Sam Humphries-s/Ramón Pérez-a; Carter's 2nd trip to Mars 4.00

JOHN CARTER: THE WORLD OF MARS
Marvel Comics: Dec, 2011 - No. 4, Mar, 2012 ($3.99, limited series)
1-4-Movie prequel; Peter David-s/Luke Ross-a. 1-Ribic-c. 4-Olivetti-c 4.00

JOHN CARTER, WARLORD OF MARS (Also see Tarzan #207-209 and Weird Worlds)
Marvel Comics: June, 1977 - No. 28, Oct, 1979
1,18: 1-Origin. 18-Frank Miller-a(p)(1st publ. Marvel work)
3 6 9 17 26 35
1-(35¢-c variant, limited dist.) 9 18 27 59 117 175
2-5-(35¢-c variants, limited dist.) 6 12 18 38 69 100
2-17,19-28: 11-Origin Dejah Thoris 1 3 4 6 8 10
Annuals 1-3: 1(1977). 2(1978). 3(1979)-All 52 pgs. with new book-length stories
1 3 4 6 8 10
Edgar Rice Burroughs' John Carter of Mars: Weird Worlds TPB (Dark Horse Books, Jan. 2011, $14.99) r/stories from Tarzan #207-209 and Weird Worlds #1-7; Marv Wolfman intro. 15.00

NOTE: ***Austin** c-24i. **Gil Kane** a-1-10p; c-1p, 2p, 3, 4-9p, 10, 15p, Annual 1p. **Layton** a-17i. **Miller** c-25, 26p. **Nebres** a-2-4i, 8-16i; c(i)-6-9, 11-22, 25, Annual 1. **Perez** c-24p. **Simonson** a-15p. **Sutton** a-7i.*

JOHN CARTER, WARLORD OF MARS
Dynamite Entertainment: 2014 - No. 14, 2015 ($3.99)
1-14: 1-5-Marz-s/Malsuni-a; multiple covers on all 4.00
... 2015 Special ($4.99) Napton-s/Rodolfo-a/Parillo-c 5.00

JOHN CONSTANTINE - HELLBLAZER SPECIAL: PAPA MIDNITE
DC Comics (Vertigo): April, 2005 - No. 5, Aug, 2005 ($2.95/$2.99, limited series)
1-5-Origin of Papa Midnite; Akins-a/Johnson-s 3.00

JOHN F. KENNEDY, CHAMPION OF FREEDOM
Worden & Childs: 1964 (no month) (25¢)
nn-Photo-c 8 16 24 52 99 145

JOHN F. KENNEDY LIFE STORY
Dell Publishing Co.: Aug-Oct, 1964; Nov, 1965; June, 1966 (12¢)
12-378-410-Photo-c 7 14 21 49 92 135
12-378-511 (reprint, 11/65) 3 6 9 21 33 45
12-378-606 (reprint, 6/66) 3 6 9 19 30 40

JOHN FORCE (See Magic Agent)

JOHN HIX SCRAP BOOK, THE
Eastern Color Printing Co. (McNaught Synd.): Late 1930's (no date) (10¢, 68 pgs., regular size)
1-Strange As It Seems (resembles Single Series books)
41 82 123 250 418 585
2-Strange As It Seems 28 56 84 165 270 375

JOHN JAKES' MULLKON EMPIRE
Tekno Comix: Sept, 1995 - No. 6, Feb, 1996 ($1.95)
1-6 3.00

JOHN LAW DETECTIVE (See Smash Comics #3)
Eclipse Comics: April, 1983 ($1.50, Baxter paper)
1-Three Eisner stories originally drawn in 1948 for the never published John Law #1; original cover pencilled in 1948 & inked in 1982 by Eisner 4.00

JOHN McCAIN (See Presidential Material: John McCain)

JOHNNY APPLESEED (See Story Hour Series)

JOHNNY CASH (See Hello, I'm...)

JOHNNY DANGER (See Movie Comics, 1946)
Toby Press: 1950 (Based on movie serial)
1-Photo-c; Sparling-a 22 44 66 132 216 300

JOHNNY DANGER PRIVATE DETECTIVE

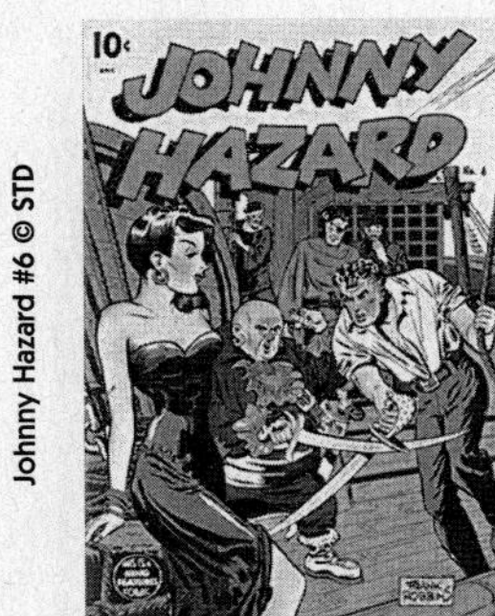

Johnny Hazard #6 © STD

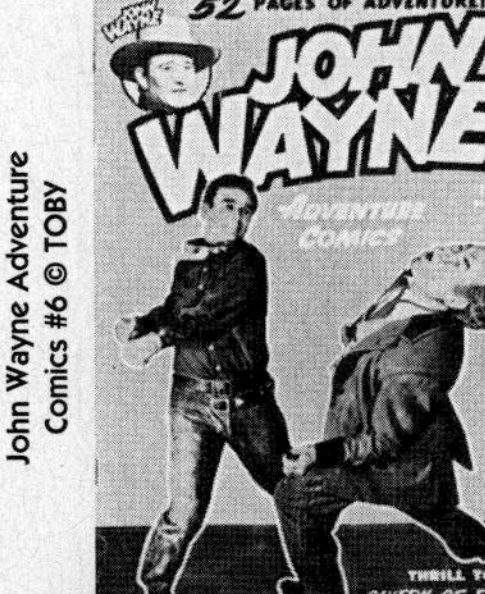

John Wayne Adventure Comics #6 © TOBY

The Joker #6 © DC

Toby Press: Aug, 1954 (Reprinted in Danger #11 by Super)

	GD 2.0	VG 4.0	FN 6.0	VF 8.0	VF/NM 9.0	NM- 9.2
1-Photo-c; Opium den story	20	40	60	114	182	250

JOHNNY DYNAMITE (Formerly Dynamite #1-9; Foreign Intrigues #14 on)
Charlton Comics: No. 10, June, 1955 - No. 12, Oct, 1955

	GD 2.0	VG 4.0	FN 6.0	VF 8.0	VF/NM 9.0	NM- 9.2
10-12	14	28	42	76	108	140

JOHNNY DYNAMITE
Dark Horse Comics: Sept, 1994 - Dec, 1994 ($2.95, B&W & red, limited series)

	GD 2.0	VG 4.0	FN 6.0	VF 8.0	VF/NM 9.0	NM- 9.2
1-4: Max Allan Collins scripts in all; Terry Beatty-a						3.00
...: Underworld GN (AiT/Planet Lar, 3/03, $12.95, B&W) r/#1-4 in B&W without red						13.00

JOHNNY HAZARD
Best Books (Standard Comics) (King Features): No. 5, Aug, 1948 - No. 8, May, 1949; No. 35, date?

	GD 2.0	VG 4.0	FN 6.0	VF 8.0	VF/NM 9.0	NM- 9.2
5-Strip reprints by Frank Robbins (c/a)	18	36	54	105	165	225
6,8-Strip reprints by Frank Robbins	15	30	45	88	137	185
7,35: 7-New art, not Robbins	12	24	36	67	94	120

JOHNNY JASON (...Teen Reporter)
Dell Publishing Co.: Feb-Apr, 1962 - No. 2, June-Aug, 1962

	GD 2.0	VG 4.0	FN 6.0	VF 8.0	VF/NM 9.0	NM- 9.2
Four Color 1302, 2(01380-208)	4	8	12	23	37	50

JOHNNY LAW, SKY RANGER
Good Comics (Lev Gleason): Apr, 1955 - No. 3, Aug, 1955; No. 4, Nov, 1955

	GD 2.0	VG 4.0	FN 6.0	VF 8.0	VF/NM 9.0	NM- 9.2
1-Edmond Good-c/a	10	20	30	58	79	100
2-4	7	14	21	35	43	50

JOHNNY MACK BROWN (Western star; see Western Roundup under Dell Giants)
Dell Publishing Co.: No. 269, Mar, 1950 - No. 963, Feb, 1959 (All Photo-c)

	GD 2.0	VG 4.0	FN 6.0	VF 8.0	VF/NM 9.0	NM- 9.2
Four Color 269(#1)(3/50, 52pgs.)-Johnny Mack Brown & his horse Rebel begin; photo front/back-c begin; Marsh-a in #1-9	18	36	54	124	275	425
2(10-12/50, 52pgs.)	10	20	30	64	132	200
3(1-3/51, 52pgs.)	8	16	24	54	102	150
4-10 (9-11/52)(36pgs.), Four Color 455,493,541,584,618,645,685,722,776,834,963	6	12	18	40	73	105
Four Color 922-Manning-a	6	12	18	41	76	110

JOHNNY NEMO
Eclipse Comics: Sept, 1985 - No. 3, Feb, 1986 (Mini-series)

	GD 2.0	VG 4.0	FN 6.0	VF 8.0	VF/NM 9.0	NM- 9.2
1-3						4.00

JOHNNY PERIL (See Comic Cavalcade #15, Danger Trail #5, Sensation Comics #107 & Sensation Mystery)

JOHNNY RINGO (TV)
Dell Publishing Co.: No. 1142, Nov-Jan, 1960/61 (one shot)

	GD 2.0	VG 4.0	FN 6.0	VF 8.0	VF/NM 9.0	NM- 9.2
Four Color 1142-Photo-c	6	12	18	41	76	110

JOHNNY STARBOARD (See Wisco)

JOHNNY THE HOMICIDAL MANIAC (Also see Squee)
Slave Labor Graphics: Aug, 1995 - No. 7, Jan, 1997 ($2.95, B&W, lim. series)

	GD 2.0	VG 4.0	FN 6.0	VF 8.0	VF/NM 9.0	NM- 9.2
1-Jhonen Vasquez-c/s/a (1995)	6	12	18	38	69	100
1-Special Signed & numbered edition of 2,000 (1996)	3	6	9	17	26	35
2,3: 2-(11/95). 3-(2/96)	1	2	3	5	6	8
4-7: 4-(5-96). 5-(8/96)						4.00
Hardcover-($29.95) r/#1-7						35.00
TPB-($19.95)						25.00

JOHNNY THUNDER
National Periodical Publications: Feb-Mar, 1973 - No. 3, July-Aug, 1973

	GD 2.0	VG 4.0	FN 6.0	VF 8.0	VF/NM 9.0	NM- 9.2
1-Johnny Thunder & Nighthawk-r. in all	2	4	6	13	18	22
2,3: 2-Trigger Twins app.	2	4	6	8	11	14

NOTE: *All contain 1950s DC reprints from All-American Western.* ***Drucker*** *r-2, 3.* ***G. Kane*** *r-2, 3.* ***Moreira*** *r-1.* ***Toth*** *r-1, 3; c-1r, 3r. Also see All-American, All-Star Western, Flash Comics, Western Comics, World's Best & World's Finest.*

JOHN PAUL JONES
Dell Publishing Co.: No. 1007, July-Sept, 1959 (one-shot)

	GD 2.0	VG 4.0	FN 6.0	VF 8.0	VF/NM 9.0	NM- 9.2
Four Color 1007-Movie, Robert Stack photo-c	5	10	15	35	63	90

JOHN ROMITA JR. 30TH ANNIVERSARY SPECIAL
Marvel Comics: 2006 ($3.99, one-shot)

	GD 2.0	VG 4.0	FN 6.0	VF 8.0	VF/NM 9.0	NM- 9.2
nn-r/1st story in Amazing Spider-Man Annual #11; timeline, sketch pages, interviews						4.00

JOHN STEED & EMMA PEEL (See The Avengers, Gold Key series)

JOHN STEELE SECRET AGENT (Also see Freedom Agent)
Gold Key: Dec, 1964

	GD 2.0	VG 4.0	FN 6.0	VF 8.0	VF/NM 9.0	NM- 9.2
1-Freedom Agent	5	10	15	33	57	80

JOHN WAYNE ADVENTURE COMICS (Movie star; See Big Tex, Oxydol-Dreft, Tim McCoy, & With The Marines...#1)
Toby Press: Winter, 1949-50 - No. 31, May, 1955 (Photo-c: 1-12,17,25-on)

	GD 2.0	VG 4.0	FN 6.0	VF 8.0	VF/NM 9.0	NM- 9.2
1 (36pgs.)-Photo-c begin (1st time in comics on-c)	252	504	756	1613	2757	3900
2-4: 2-(4/50, 36pgs.)-Williamson/Frazetta-a(2) 6 & 2 pgs. (one story-r/Billy the Kid #1); photo back-c. 3-(36pgs.)-Williamson/Frazetta-a(2), 16 pgs. total; photo back-c. 4-(52pgs.)-Williamson/Frazetta-a(2), 16 pgs. total	82	164	246	528	902	1275
5 (52pgs.)-Kurtzman-a-(Alfred "L" Newman in Potshot Pete)	61	122	183	390	670	950
6 (52pgs.)-Williamson/Frazetta-a (10 pgs.); Kurtzman-a "Pot-Shot Pete", (5 pgs.); & "Genius Jones", (1 pg.)	73	146	219	467	796	1125
7 (52pgs.)-Williamson/Frazetta-a (10 pgs.)	63	126	189	403	689	975
8 (36pgs.)-Williamson/Frazetta-a(2) (12 & 9 pgs.)	76	152	228	486	831	1175
9-11: Photo western-c	43	86	129	268	454	640
12,14-Photo war-c. 12-Kurtzman-a(2 pg.) "Genius"	43	86	129	271	461	650
13,15: 13,15-Line-drawn-c begin, end #24	39	78	117	236	388	540
16-Williamson/Frazetta-r/Billy the Kid #1	40	80	120	248	414	580
17-Photo-c	40	80	120	248	414	580
18-Williamson/Frazetta-a (r/#4 & 8, 19 pgs.)	43	86	129	268	454	640
19-24: 23-Evans-a?	36	72	108	214	347	480
25-Photo-c resume; end #31; Williamson/Frazetta-r/Billy the Kid #3	43	86	129	268	454	640
26-28,30-Photo-c	39	78	117	236	388	540
29,31-Williamson/Frazetta-a in each (r/#4, 2)	41	82	123	256	428	600

NOTE: *Williamsonish art in later issues by* ***Gerald McCann.***

JO-JO COMICS (...Congo King #7-29; My Desire #30 on)(Also see Fantastic Fears and Jungle Jo)
Fox Feature Syndicate: 1945 - No. 29, July, 1949 (Two No.7's; no #13)

	GD 2.0	VG 4.0	FN 6.0	VF 8.0	VF/NM 9.0	NM- 9.2
nn(1945)-Funny animal, humor	22	44	66	132	216	300
2(Sum,'46)-6(4-5/47): Funny animal. 2-Ten pg. Electro story (Fall/46)	15	30	45	88	137	185
7(7/47)-Jo-Jo, Congo King begins (1st app.); Bronze Man & Purple Tigress app.	97	194	291	621	1061	1500
7(#8) (9/47)	71	142	213	454	777	1100
8(#9) Classic Kamen mountain of skulls-c; Tanee begins	90	180	270	576	988	1400
9,10(#10,11)	61	122	183	390	670	950
11,12(#12,13),14,16: 11,16-Kamen bondage-c	54	108	162	343	574	825
15-Cited by Dr. Wertham in 5/47 Saturday Review of Literature	55	110	165	352	601	850
17-Kamen bondage-c	65	130	195	416	708	1000
18-20	53	106	159	334	567	800
21-24,26-29: 21-Hollingsworth-a (4 pgs.; 23-1 pg.)	43	86	129	271	461	650
25-Bondage-c	77	154	231	493	847	1200

NOTE: *Many bondage-c/a by* ***Baker/Kamen/Feldstein/Good.*** *No. 7's have Princesses Gwenna, Geesa, Yolda, & Safra before settling down on Tanee.*

JOKEBOOK COMICS DIGEST ANNUAL (...Magazine No. 5 on)
Archie Publications: Oct, 1977 - No. 13, Oct, 1983 (Digest Size)

	GD 2.0	VG 4.0	FN 6.0	VF 8.0	VF/NM 9.0	NM- 9.2
1(10/77)-Reprints; Neal Adams-a	2	4	6	13	18	22
2(4/78)-5	2	4	6	9	12	15
6-13	1	3	4	6	8	10

JOKER
DC Comics: 2008 ($19.99, hardcover graphic novel with dustjacket)

	GD 2.0	VG 4.0	FN 6.0	VF 8.0	VF/NM 9.0	NM- 9.2
HC-Joker is released from Arkham; Azzarello-s/Bermejo-a						20.00

JOKER, THE (See Batman #1, Batman: The Killing Joke, Brave & the Bold, Detective, Greatest Joker Stories & Justice League Annual #2)
National Periodical Publications: May, 1975 - No. 9, Sept-Oct, 1976

	GD 2.0	VG 4.0	FN 6.0	VF 8.0	VF/NM 9.0	NM- 9.2
1-Two-Face app.	6	12	18	40	73	105
2-4: 3-The Creeper app. 4-Green Arrow-c/sty	4	8	12	23	37	50
5-9: 6-Sherlock Holmes-c/sty. 7-Lex Luthor-c/story. 8-Scarecrow-c/story. 9-Catwoman-c/story	3	6	9	19	30	40
...: The Greatest Stories Ever Told TPB (2008, $19.99) r/Batman #1 and other apps.						20.00

JOKER, THE (See Tangent Comics/ The Joker)

JOKER COMICS (Adventures Into Terror No. 43 on)
Timely/Marvel Comics No. 36 on (TCI/CDS): Apr, 1942 - No. 42, Aug, 1950

	GD 2.0	VG 4.0	FN 6.0	VF 8.0	VF/NM 9.0	NM- 9.2
1-(Rare)-Powerhouse Pepper (1st app.) begins by Wolverton; Stuporman app. from Daring Comics	314	628	942	2198	3849	5500
2-Wolverton-a; 1st app. Tessie the Typist & begin series	123	246	369	787	1344	1900
3-5-Wolverton-a	71	142	213	454	777	1100
6-10-Wolverton-a. 6-Tessie-c begin	50	100	150	315	533	750

Jolly Jingles #12 © MLJ

Jonah Hex (2006 series) #50 © DC

Jonesy #6 © Humphries & Boyle

GD VG FN VF VF/NM NM-
2.0 4.0 6.0 8.0 9.0 9.2

11-20-Wolverton-a 45 90 135 284 480 675
21,22,24-27,29,30-Wolverton cont'd. & Kurtzman's "Hey Look" in #23-27
40 80 120 246 411 575
23-1st "Hey Look" by Kurtzman; Wolverton-a 41 82 123 256 428 600
28,32,34,37-41: 28-Millie the Model begins. 32-Hedy begins. 41-Nellie the Nurse app.
22 44 66 128 209 290
31-Last Powerhouse Pepper; not in #28 37 74 111 218 354 490
33,35,36-Kurtzman's "Hey Look" 22 44 66 132 216 300
42-Only app. 'Patty Pinup,' clone of Millie the Model 22 44 66 132 216 300

JOKER: DEVIL'S ADVOCATE
DC Comics: 1996 ($24.95/$12.95, one-shot)
nn-(Hardcover)-Dixon scripts/Nolan & Hanna-a 30.00
nn-(Softcover) 15.00

JOKER: LAST LAUGH (See Batman: The Joker's Last Laugh for TPB)
DC Comics: Dec, 2001 - No. 6, Jan, 2002 ($2.95, weekly limited series)
1-6: 1,6-Bolland-c 3.00
...Secret Files (12/01, $5.95) Short stories by various; Simonson-c 6.00

JOKER / MASK
Dark Horse Comics: May, 2000 - No. 4, Aug, 2000 ($2.95, limited series)
1-4-Batman, Harley Quinn, Poison Ivy app. 1 3 4 6 8 10

JOKER'S ASYLUM
DC Comics: Sept, 2008 ($2.99, weekly limited series of one-shots)
...: Joker - Andy Kubert-c, Sanchez-a; ...: Penguin - Pearson-c/a; ...: Poison Ivy - Guillem March-c/a; ...: Scarecrow - Juan Doe-c/a; ...: Two-Face - Andy Clarke-c/a 3.00
Batman: The Joker's Asylum TPB (2008, $14.99) r/one-shots 15.00

JOKER'S ASYLUM II
DC Comics: Aug, 2010 ($2.99, weekly limited series of one-shots)
...: Clayface - Kelley Jones-c/a; ; ...: Killer Croc - Mattina-c; Mad Hatter - Giffen & Sienkiewicz-a, Sienkiewicz-c; ...: Riddler - Van Sciver-c 3.00
...: Harley Quinn - Quinones-a 2 4 6 11 16 20
Batman: The Joker's Asylum Volume 2 TPB (2011, $14.99) r/one-shots 15.00

JOLLY CHRISTMAS, A (See March of Comics No. 269)

JOLLY COMICS: **Four Star Publishing Co.:** 1947 (Advertised, not published)

JOLLY COMICS
No publisher: No date (1930s-40s)(10¢, cover is black/red ink on yellow paper, blank inside-c)
nn-Snuffy Smith & Katzenjamer Kids on-c only. Buck Rogers, Dickey Dare, Napoleon & others app. Reprints Ace Comics #8-c. A GD copy sold in 2014 for $358.50
213 426 639 1363 2332 3300

JOLLY JINGLES (Formerly Jackpot Comics)
MLJ Magazines: No. 10, Sum, 1943 - No. 16, Wint, 1944/45
10-Super Duck begins (origin & 1st app.); Woody The Woodpecker begins (not same as Lantz character) 58 116 174 371 636 900
11 (Fall, '43)-2nd Super Duck (see Hangman #8) 30 60 90 177 289 400
12-Hitler-c 77 154 231 493 847 1200
13-16: 13-Sahle-c. 15,16-Vigoda-c 21 42 63 122 199 275

JONAH HEX (See All-Star Western, Hex and Weird Western Tales)
National Periodical Pub./DC Comics: Mar-Apr, 1977 - No. 92, Aug, 1985
1-Garcia-Lopez-c/a 10 20 30 69 147 225
2-1st app. El Papagayo 6 12 18 38 69 100
3,4,9: 9-Wrightson-c. 5 10 15 33 57 80
5,6,10: 5-Rep 1st app. from All-Star Western #10 5 10 15 30 50 70
7,8-Explains Hex's face disfigurement (origin) 5 10 15 35 63 90
11-20: 12-Starlin-c 3 6 9 19 30 40
21-32: 23-Intro. Mei Ling. 31,32-Origin retold 2 4 6 13 18 22
33-50 2 4 6 8 11 14
51-80 1 2 3 5 7 9
81-91: 89-Mark Texeira-a. 91-Cover swipe from Superman #243 (hugging a mystery woman)
2 4 6 8 10 12
92-Story cont'd in Hex #1 3 6 9 19 30 40
NOTE: ***Ayers*** *a(p)-35-37, 40, 41, 44-53, 56, 58-82.* ***Buckler*** *a-11; c-11, 13-16.* ***Kubert*** *c-43-46.* ***Morrow*** *a-90-92; c-10.* ***Spiegle(Tothish)*** *a-34, 38, 40, 49, 52.* ***Texeira*** *a-89p. Batlash back-ups in 49, 52. El Diablo back-ups in 48, 56-60, 73-75. Scalphunter back-ups in 40, 41, 45-47.*

JONAH HEX (Also see All Star Western [2011 DC New 52 title])
DC Comics: Jan, 2006 - No. 70, Oct, 2011 ($2.99)
1-Justin Gray & Jimmy Palmiotti-s/Luke Ross-a/Quitely-c 5.00
1-Special Edition (7/10, $1.00) r/#1 with "What's Next?" logo on cover 3.00
2-49,51-70: 3-Bat Lash app. 10,16,17,19,20,22-Noto-a. 11-El Diablo app.; Beck-a. 13-15-Origin retold. 21,23,27,30,32,37,38,42,52,54,57,59,61,63,67-Bernet-a. 33-Darwyn Cooke-a/c. 34-Sparacio-a. 51-Giordano-c. 53-Tucci-c/a. 62-Risso-a 3.00
50-($3.99) Darwyn Cooke-a/c 4.00
...: Bullets Don't Lie TPB (2009, $14.99) r/#31-36 15.00
...: Counting Corpses TPB (2010, $14.99) r/#43,50-54 15.00
...: Face Full of Violence TPB (2006, $12.99) r/#1-6 13.00
...: Guns of Vengeance TPB (2007, $12.99) r/#7-12 13.00
...: Lead Poisoning TPB (2009, $14.99) r/#37-42 15.00
...: Luck Runs Out TPB (2008, $12.99) r/#25-30 13.00
...: No Way Back HC (2010, $19.99) new GN; Gray & Palmiotti-s/DeZuniga-a 20.00
...: No Way Back SC (2011, $14.99) new GN; Gray & Palmiotti-s/DeZuniga-a 15.00
...: Only the Good Die Young TPB (2008, $12.99) r/#19-24 13.00
...: Origins TPB (2007, $12.99) r/#13-18 13.00
...: Tall Tales TPB (2011, $14.99) r/#55-60 15.00
...: The Six Gun War TPB (2010, $14.99) r/#44-49 15.00
...: Welcome to Paradise TPB (2010, $17.99) r/debut in All-Star Western #10 plus early apps. in Weird Western Tales and Jonah Hex #2,4 (1977 series) 18.00

JONAH HEX AND OTHER WESTERN TALES (Blue Ribbon Digest)
DC Comics: Sept-Oct, 1979 - No. 3, Jan-Feb, 1980 (100 pgs.)
1-3: 1-Origin Scalphunter-r, Ayers/Evans, Neal Adams-a.; painted-c. 2-Weird Western Tales-r; Neal Adams, Toth, Aragones-a. 3-Outlaw-r, Scalphunter-r; Gil Kane, Wildey-a
2 4 6 11 16 20

JONAH HEX: RIDERS OF THE WORM AND SUCH
DC Comics (Vertigo): Mar, 1995 - No. 5, July, 1995 ($2.95, limited series)
1-5-Lansdale story, Truman -a 4.00

JONAH HEX: SHADOWS WEST
DC Comics (Vertigo): Feb, 1999 - No. 3, Apr, 1999 ($2.95, limited series)
1-3-Lansdale-s/Truman -a 4.00

JONAH HEX SPECTACULAR (See DC Special Series No. 16)

JONAH HEX: TWO-GUN MOJO
DC Comics (Vertigo): Aug, 1993 - No. 5, Dec, 1993 ($2.95, limited series)
1-Lansdale scripts in all; Truman/Glanzman-a in all w/Truman-c 6.00
1-Platinum edition with no price on cover 20.00
2-5 4.00
TPB-(1994, $12.95) r/#1-5 13.00

JONESY (Formerly Crack Western)
Comic Favorite/Quality Comics Group: No. 85, Aug, 1953; No. 2, Oct, 1953 - No. 8, Oct, 1954
85(#1)-Teen-age humor 10 20 30 54 72 90
2 6 12 18 31 38 45
3-8 6 12 18 28 34 40

JONESY
BOOM! Studios (BOOM! Box): Feb, 2016 - Present ($3.99, originally a 4-part series)
1-10-Sam Humphries-s/Caitlin Rose Boyle-a. 1-Multiple covers 4.00

JON JUAN (Also see Great Lover Romances)
Toby Press: Spring, 1950
1-All Schomburg-a (signed Al Reid on-c); written by Siegel; used in **SOTI**, pg. 38 (Scarce)
77 154 231 493 847 1200

JONNI THUNDER (...A.K.A. Thunderbolt)
DC Comics: Feb, 1985 - No. 4, Aug, 1985 (75¢, limited series)
1-4: 1-Origin & 1st app. 4.00

JONNY DOUBLE
DC Comics (Vertigo): Sept, 1998 - No. 4, Dec, 1998 ($2.95, limited series)
1-4-Azzarello-s 3.00
TPB (2002, $12.95) r/#1-4; Chiarello-c 13.00

JONNY QUEST (TV)
Gold Key: Dec, 1964 (Hanna-Barbera)
1 (10139-412) 32 64 96 230 515 800

JONNY QUEST (TV)
Comico: June 1986 - No. 31, Dec, 1988 ($1.50/$1.75)(Hanna-Barbera)
1,3,5: 3,5-Dave Stevens-c 6.00
2,4,6-31: 30-Adapts TV episode 4.00
Special 1(9/88, $1.75), 2(10/88, $1.75) 4.00
NOTE: ***M. Anderson*** *a-9.* ***Mooney*** *a-Special 1.* ***Pini*** *a-2.* ***Quagmire*** *a-31p.* ***Rude*** *a-1; c-2i.* ***Sienkiewicz*** *c-11.* ***Spiegle*** *a-7, 12, 21; c-21* ***Staton*** *a-2i, 11p.* ***Steacy*** *c-8.* ***Stevens*** *a-4i; c-3,5.* ***Wildey*** *a-1, c-1, 7, 12.* ***Williamson*** *a-4i; c-4i.*

JONNY QUEST CLASSICS (TV)
Comico: May, 1987 - No. 3, July, 1987 ($2.00) (Hanna-Barbera)
1-3: Wildey-c/a; 3-Based on TV episode 4.00

Josie and the Pussycats V2 #1 © ACP

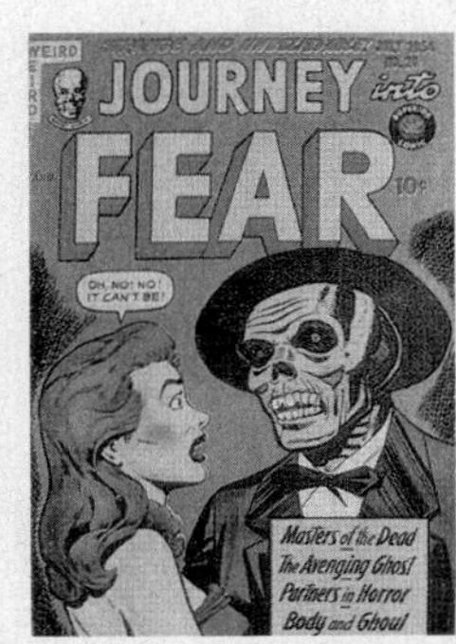

Journey Into Fear #20 © SUPR

Journey Into Mystery #67 © MAR

	GD 2.0	VG 4.0	FN 6.0	VF 8.0	VF/NM 9.0	NM- 9.2

JON SABLE, FREELANCE (Also see Mike Grell's Sable & Sable)
First Comics: 6/83 - No. 56, 2/88 (#1-17, $1; #18-33, $1.25, #34-on, $1.75)

1-Mike Grell-c/a/scripts 5.00
2-56: 3-5-Origin, parts 1-3. 6-Origin, part 4. 11-1st app. of Maggie the Cat. 14-Mando paper begins. 16-Maggie the Cat. app. 25-30-Shatter app. 34-Deluxe format begins ($1.75) 3.00
The Complete Jon Sable, Freelance: Vol. 1 (IDW, 2005, $19.99) r/#1-6 20.00
The Complete Jon Sable, Freelance: Vol. 2 (IDW, 2005, $19.99) r/#7-11 20.00
The Complete Jon Sable, Freelance: Vol. 3 (IDW, 2005, $19.99) r/#12-16 20.00
The Complete Jon Sable, Freelance: Vol. 4 (IDW, 2005, $19.99) r/#17-21 20.00
NOTE: *Aragones a-33; c-33(part). Grell a-1-43;c-1-52, 53p, 54-56.*

JON SABLE, FREELANCE
IDW Publ.: (Limited series)

...: Ashes of Eden 1-5 (2009 - No. 5, 2/10, $3.99) Mike Grell-c/a/scripts 4.00
...: Bloodtrail 1-6 (4/05 - No. 6, 11/05, $3.99) Mike Grell-c/a/scripts 4.00
...: Bloodtrail TPB (4/06, $19.99) r/#1-6; cover gallery 20.00

JOSEPH & HIS BRETHREN (See The Living Bible)

JOSIE (She's... #1-16) (...& the Pussycats #45 on) (See Archie's Pals 'n' Gals #23 for 1st app.) (Also see Archie Giant Series Magazine #528, 540, 551, 562, 571, 584, 597, 610, 622)
Archie Publ./Radio Comics: Feb, 1963; No. 2, Aug, 1963 - No. 106, Oct, 1982

	GD	VG	FN	VF	VF/NM	NM-
1	38	76	114	285	641	1000
2	11	22	33	76	163	250
3-5	8	16	24	54	102	150
6-10: 6-(5/64) Book length Haunted Mansion-c/s. 7-(8/64) 1st app. Alexandra Cabot?	5	10	15	35	63	90
11-20	4	8	12	28	47	65
21, 23-30	4	8	12	23	37	50
22 (9/66)-Mighty Man & Mighty (Josie Girl) app.	4	8	12	27	44	60
31-44	3	6	9	19	30	40
45 (12/69)-Josie and the Pussycats begins (Hanna Barbera TV cartoon); 1st app. of the Pussycats	25	50	75	175	388	600
46-2nd app./1st cover Pussycats	10	20	30	64	132	200
47-3rd app. of the Pussycats	6	12	18	41	76	110
48,49-Pussycats band-c/s	7	14	21	44	82	120
50-J&P-c; go to Hollywood, meet Hanna & Barbera	7	14	21	49	92	135
51-54	3	6	9	19	30	40
55-74 (2/74)(52 pg. issues). 73-Pussycats band-c	3	6	9	19	30	40
75-90(8/76)	2	4	6	13	18	22
91-99	2	4	6	10	14	18
100 (10/79)	2	4	6	13	18	22
101-106: 103-Pussycats band-c	2	4	6	11	16	20

JOSIE & THE PUSSYCATS (TV)
Archie Comics: 1993 - No. 2, 1994 ($2.00, 52 pgs.)(Published annually)

1,2-Bound-in pull-out poster in each. 2-(Spr/94) 5.00

JOSIE AND THE PUSSYCATS
Archie Comic Publications: Nov, 2016 - Present ($3.99)

1-4-Bennett & Deordio-s/Audrey Mok-a; multiple covers; back-up classic reprints 4.00

JOURNAL OF CRIME (See Fox Giants)

JOURNEY
Aardvark-Vanaheim #1-14/Fantagraphics Books #15-on: 1983 - No. 14, Sept, 1984; No. 15, Apr, 1985 - No. 27, July, 1986 (B&W)

1 4.00
2-27: 20-Sam Kieth-a 3.00

JOURNEY INTO FEAR
Superior-Dynamic Publications: May, 1951 - No. 21, Sept, 1954

	GD	VG	FN	VF	VF/NM	NM-
1-Baker-r(2)	77	154	231	493	847	1200
2	52	104	156	328	552	775
3,4	43	86	129	271	461	650
5-10,15: 15-Used in **SOTI**, pg. 389	39	78	117	231	378	525
11-14,16-21	37	74	111	222	361	500

NOTE: *Kamenish 'headlight'-a most issues.* ***Robinson*** *a-10.*

JOURNEY INTO MYSTERY (1st Series) (Thor Nos. 126-502)
Atlas(CPS No. 1-48/AMI No. 49-68/Marvel No. 69 (6/61) on): 6/52 - No. 48, 8/57; No. 49, 11/58 - No. 125, 2/66; 503, 11/96 - No. 521, June, 1998

	GD	VG	FN	VF	VF/NM	NM-
1-Weird/horror stories begin	1000	2000	3000	7000	10,500	14,000
2	219	438	657	1402	2401	3400
3,4	174	348	522	1114	1907	2700
5-11	161	322	483	1030	1765	2500
12-20,22: 15-Atomic explosion panel. 22-Davis*esque*-a; last pre-code issue (2/55)	108	216	324	686	1181	1675
21-Kubert-a; Tothish-a by Andru	110	220	330	704	1202	1700
23-32,35-38,40: 24-Torres?-a. 38-Ditko-a	81	162	243	518	884	1250
33-Williamson-a; Ditko-a (his 1st for Atlas?)	87	174	261	553	952	1350
34,39: 34-Krigstein-a. 39-1st S.A. issue; Wood-a	82	164	246	528	902	1275
41-Crandall-a; Frazetta*esque*-a by Morrow	40	80	120	296	673	1050
42,46,48: 42,48-Torres-a. 46-Torres & Krigstein-a	38	76	114	285	641	1000
43,44-Williamson/Mayo-a in both. 43-Invisible Woman prototype	40	80	120	296	673	1050
45,47	38	76	114	282	634	985
49-Matt Fox, Check-a	40	80	120	296	673	1050
50,52-54: Ditko/Kirby-a. 50-Davis-a. 54-Williamson-a	46	92	138	359	805	1250
51-Kirby/Wood-a	46	92	138	368	834	1300
55-61,63-65,67-69,71,72,74,75: 74-Contents change to Fantasy. 75-Last 10¢ issue	38	76	114	285	641	1000
62-Prototype ish. (The Hulk); 1st app. Xemnu (Titan) called "The Hulk"	75	150	225	600	1350	2100
66-Prototype ish. (The Hulk)-Return of Xemnu "The Hulk"	54	108	162	432	966	1500
70-Prototype ish. (The Sandman)(7/61); similar to Spidey villain	40	80	120	296	673	1050
73-Story titled "The Spider" where a spider is exposed to radiation & gets powers of a human and shoots webbing; a reverse prototype of Spider-Man's origin	61	122	183	488	1094	1700
76,77,80,81: 80-Anti-communist propaganda story	32	64	96	230	515	800
76-(10¢ cover price blacked out, 12¢ printed on)	46	92	138	368	834	1300
78-The Sorceror (Dr. Strange prototype) app. (3/62)	42	84	126	311	706	1100
79-Prototype issue. (Mr. Hyde)	36	72	108	259	580	900
82-Prototype ish. (Scorpion)	35	70	105	252	564	875
83-Origin & 1st app. The Mighty Thor by Kirby (8/62) and begin series; Thor-c also begin	1600	3200	5600	16,000	40,000	75,000
83-Reprint from the Golden Record Comic Set	18	36	54	122	271	420
With the record (1966)	26	52	78	183	407	630
84-2nd app. Thor	259	518	777	2137	4819	7500
85-1st app. Loki & Heimdall; 1st brief app. Odin (1 panel); 1st app. Asgard	252	504	756	2079	4690	7300
86-1st full app. Odin	93	186	279	744	1672	2600
87-89: 89-Origin Thor retold	79	158	237	632	1416	2200
90-No Kirby-a	59	118	177	472	1061	1650
91,92,94,96-Sinnott-a	46	92	138	350	788	1225
93,97-Kirby-a; Tales of Asgard series begins #97 (origin which concludes in #99); origin & 1st app. Lava Man. 97-1st app. Surtur (1 panel)	49	98	147	382	854	1325
95-Sinnott-a; Thor vs. Thor	50	100	150	400	900	1400
98,99-Kirby/Heck-a. 98-Origin/1st app. The Human Cobra. 99-1st app. Mr. Hyde; Surtur app.	37	74	111	274	612	950
100-Kirby/Heck-a; Thor battles Mr. Hyde	36	72	108	259	580	900
101,108: 101-(2/64)-2nd Avengers x-over (w/o Capt. America); see Tales Of Suspense #49 for 1st x-over. 108-(9/64)-Early Dr. Strange & Avengers x-over; ten extra pgs. Kirby-a	25	50	75	175	388	600
102-(3/64) 1st app. Sif	38	76	114	285	641	1000
103-1st app. Enchantress	61	122	183	488	1094	1700
104-107,110: 105-109-Ten extra pgs. Kirby-a in each. 107-1st app. Grey Gargoyle. 110,111-Two part battle vs. The Human Cobra & Mr. Hyde	23	46	69	161	356	550
109-Magneto-c & app. (1st x-over, 10/64)	45	90	135	333	754	1175
111,113: 113-Origin Loki	18	36	54	124	275	425
112-Thor Vs. Hulk (1/65); Origin Loki	56	112	168	448	999	1550
114-Origin/1st app. Absorbing Man	27	54	81	189	420	650
115-Detailed origin of Loki	20	40	60	138	307	475
116,117,120-123,125	14	28	42	96	211	325
118-1st app. Destroyer	23	46	69	161	356	550
119-Intro Hogun, Fandral, Volstagg; 2nd Destroyer	19	38	57	131	291	450
124-Hercules-c/story	15	30	45	100	220	340

503-521: 503-(11/96, $1.50)-The Lost Gods begin; Tom DeFalco scripts & Deodato Studios-c/a. 505-Spider-Man-c/app. 509-Loki-c/app. 514-516-Shang-Chi 3.00
#(-1) Flashback (7/97) Tales of Asgard Donald Blake app. 3.00

	GD	VG	FN	VF	VF/NM	NM-
Annual 1(1965, 25¢, 72 pgs.)-New Thor vs. Hercules(1st app.)-c/story (see Incredible Hulk #3); Kirby-c/a; r/#85,93,95,97	29	58	87	209	467	725

NOTE: ***Ayers*** *a-14, 39, 64i, 71i, 74i, 80i.* ***Bailey*** *a-43.* ***Briefer*** *a-5, 12.* ***Cameron*** *a-35.* ***Check*** *a-17.* ***Colan*** *a-23, 81; c-14.* ***Ditko*** *a-33, 38, 50-96; c-58, 67, 71, 88i.* ***Kirby/Ditko*** *a-50-83.* ***Everett*** *a-20, 48; c-4-7, 9, 36, 37, 39-42, 44, 45, 47.* ***Forte*** *a-19, 35, 40, 53.* ***Heath*** *a-4-6, 11, 14; c-1, 8, 11, 15, 51.* ***Heck*** *a-53, 73.* ***Kirby*** *a(p)-51, 52, 56, 57-60, 62-64, 66, 67, 69-89, 93, 97, 98, 100(w/Heck), 101-125; c-50-57, 59-66, 68-70, 72-82, 88(w/Ditko), 83 & 84(w/Sinnott), 85-96(w/Ayers), 97-125p.* ***Leiber/Fox*** *a-93, 98-102.* ***Maneely*** *c-20-22.* ***Morisi*** *a-42.* ***Morrow*** *a-41, 42.* ***Orlando*** *a-30, 45, 57.* ***Mac Pakula*** *(Tothish) a-9, 35, 41.* ***Powell*** *a-20, 27, 34.* ***Reinman*** *a-39, 70, 87, 92, 96i.* ***Robinson*** *a-9.* ***Roussos*** *a-39.* ***Robert Sale*** *a-14.* ***Severin*** *a-27; c-30.* ***Sinnott*** *a-41; c-50.* ***Tuska*** *a-11.* ***Wildey*** *a-16.*

Journey Into Mystery #622 © MAR

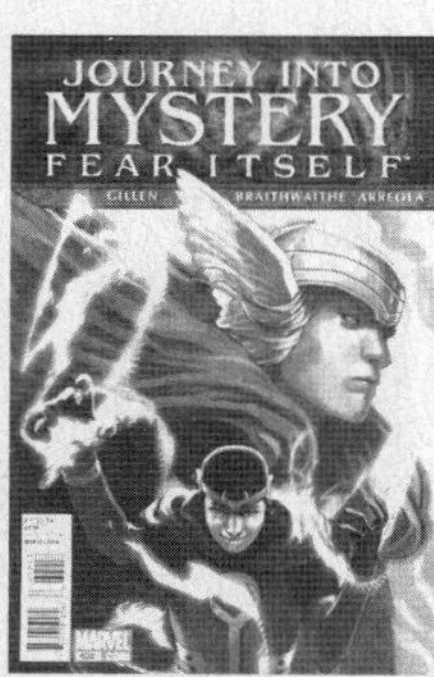

Joyride #1 © Lanzing, Kelly & To

JSA #77 © DC

	GD	VG	FN	VF	VF/NM	NM-
	2.0	4.0	6.0	8.0	9.0	9.2

GD VG FN VF VF/NM NM-
2.0 4.0 6.0 8.0 9.0 9.2

JOURNEY INTO MYSTERY (Series and numbering continue from Thor #621)
Marvel Comics: No. 622, Jun, 2011 - No. 655, Oct, 2013 ($3.99/$2.99)

622-Reincarnated young Loki; Thor app.; Braithwaite-a; Hans-c 4.00
622-Variant covers by Art Adams and Lee Weeks 6.00
623-626, 626.1, 627-630-($2.99) Fear Itself tie-in. 628,629-Portacio-a 3.00
631-655: 631-Portacio-a; Aftermath. 632-Hellstrom app. 637,638-Exiled x-over with New Mutants #41-43. 642-644-Crossover with Mighty Thor #19-21. 646-Features Sif 3.00

JOURNEY INTO MYSTERY (2nd Series)
Marvel Comics: Oct, 1972 - No. 19, Oct, 1975

1-Robert Howard adaptation; Starlin/Ploog-a 4 8 12 28 47 65
2-5: 2,3,5-Bloch adapt. 4-H. P. Lovecraft adapt. 3 6 9 17 26 35
6-19: Reprints 3 6 9 16 23 30

NOTE: ***N. Adams*** *a-2i.* ***Ditko*** *r-7, 10, 12, 14, 15, 19; c-10.* ***Everett*** *r-9, 14.* ***G. Kane*** *a-1p, 2p; c-1-3p.* ***Kirby*** *r-7, 13, 15, 18, 19; c-7.* ***Mort Lawrence*** *r-2.* ***Maneely*** *r-3.* ***Orlando*** *r-16.* ***Reese*** *a-1, 2i.* ***Starlin*** *a-1p, 3p.* ***Torres*** *r-16.* ***Wildey*** *r-9, 14.*

JOURNEY INTO UNKNOWN WORLDS (Formerly Teen)
Atlas Comics (WFP): No. 36, Sept, 1950 - No. 38, Feb, 1951;
No. 4, Apr, 1951 - No. 59, Aug, 1957

36(#1)-Science fiction/weird; "End Of The Earth" c/story
275 550 825 1750 3275 4800
37(#2)-Science fiction; "When Worlds Collide" c/story; Everett-c/a; Hitler story
123 246 369 787 1344 1900
38(#3)-Science fiction 103 206 309 659 1130 1600
4-6,8,10-Science fiction/weird 65 130 195 416 708 1000
7-Wolverton-a "Planet of Terror", 6 pgs; electric chair c-inset/story
103 206 309 659 1130 1600
9-Giant eyeball story 90 180 270 576 988 1400
11,12-Krigstein-a 50 100 150 315 533 750
13,16,17,20 43 86 129 271 461 650
14-Wolverton-a "One of Our Graveyards Is Missing", 4 pgs; Tuska-a
77 154 231 493 847 1200
15-Wolverton-a "They Crawl by Night", 5 pgs.; 2 pg. Maneely s/f story
77 154 231 493 847 1200
18,19-Matt Fox-a 50 100 150 315 533 750
21-33: 21-Decapitation-c. 24-Sci/fic story. 26-Atom bomb panel. 27-Sid Check-a.
33-Last pre-code (2/55) 39 78 117 236 388 540
34-Kubert, Torres-a 33 66 99 194 317 440
35-Torres-a 30 60 90 177 289 400
36-45,48,50,53,55,59: 43-Krigstein-a. 44-Davis-a. 45,55,59-Williamson-a in all; with Mayo #55,59. 55-Crandall-a. 48,53-Crandall-a (4 pgs. #48). 48-Check-a. 50-Davis, Crandall-a
29 58 87 170 278 385
46,47,49,52,54,56-58: 54-Torres-a 27 54 81 158 259 360
51-Ditko, Wood-a 31 62 93 182 296 410

NOTE: ***Ayers*** *a-24, 43.* ***Berg*** *a-38(#3), 43.* ***Lou Cameron*** *a-33.* ***Colan*** *a-37(#2), 6, 17, 19, 20, 23, 39.* ***Ditko*** *a-45, 51.* ***Drucker*** *a-35, 58.* ***Everett*** *a-37(#2), 11, 14, 41, 55, 56; c-37(#2), 11, 13, 14, 17, 22, 47, 48, 50, 53-55, 59.* ***Forte*** *a-49.* ***Fox*** *a-21i.* ***Heath*** *a-36(#1), 4, 6-8, 17, 20, 22, 36i; c-18.* ***Keller*** *a-15.* ***Mort Lawrence*** *a-38, 39.* ***Maneely*** *a-7, 8, 15, 16, 22, 49, 58; c-8, 19, 25, 52.* ***Morrow*** *a-48.* ***Orlando*** *a-44, 57.* ***Pakula*** *a-36.* ***Powell*** *a-42, 53, 54.* ***Reinman*** *a-8.* ***Rico*** *a-21.* ***Robert Sale*** *a-24, 49.* ***Sekowsky*** *a-4, 5, 9.* ***Severin*** *a-38, 51; c-38, 48i, 56.* ***Sinnott*** *a-9, 21, 24.* ***Tuska*** *a-38(#3), 14.* ***Wildey*** *a-25, 43, 44.*

JOURNEY TO STAR WARS: THE FORCE AWAKENS - SHATTERED EMPIRE
Marvel Comics: Nov, 2015 - No. 4, Dec, 2015 ($3.99, weekly limited series)

1-4-Rucka-s; takes place just after Episode 6 Battle of Endor; multiple covers on each 4.00

JOURNEY TO THE CENTER OF THE EARTH (Movie)
Dell Publishing Co.: No. 1060, Nov-Jan, 1959/60 (one-shot)

Four Color 1060-Pat Boone & James Mason photo-c 10 20 30 64 132 200

JOYRIDE
BOOM! Studios: Apr, 2016 - Present ($3.99, originally planned as a 4-part series)

1-10-Jackson Lanzing & Collin Kelly-s/Marcus To-a. 1-Multiple covers 4.00

JSA (Justice Society of America) (Also see All Star Comics)
DC Comics: Aug, 1999 - No. 87, Sept, 2006 ($2.50/$2.99)

1-Robinson and Goyer-s; funeral of Wesley Dodds 2 4 6 8 10 12
2-5: 4-Return of Dr. Fate 6.00
6-24: 6-Black Adam-c/app. 11,12-Kobra. 16-20-JSA vs. Johnny Sorrow. 19,20-Spectre app. 22-Hawkgirl origin. 23-Hawkman returns 4.00
25-($3.75) Hawkman rejoins the JSA 1 2 3 5 7 9
26-36, 38-49: 27-Capt. Marvel app. 29-Joker: Last Laugh. 31,32-Snejbjerg-a. 33-Ultra-Humanite. 34-Intro. new Crimson Avenger and Hourman. 42-G.A. Mr. Terrific and the Freedom Fighters app. 46-Eclipso returns 3.00
37-($3.50) Johnny Thunder merges with the Thunderbolt; origin new Crimson Avenger 4.00
50-($3.95) Wraparound-c by Pacheco; Sentinel becomes Green Lantern again 4.00
51-74,76-82: 51-Kobra killed. 54-JLA app. 55-Ma Hunkle (Red Tornado) app. 56-58-Black Reign x-over with Hawkman #23-25. 64-Sand returns. 67-Identity Crisis tie-in; Gibbons-a. 68,69,72-81-Ross-c. 73,74-Day of Vengeance tie-in. 76-OMAC tie-in. 82-Infinite Crisis x-over; Levitz-s/Pérez-a 3.00
75-($2.99) Day of Vengeance tie-in; Alex Ross Spectre-c 4.00
83-87: One Year Later; Pérez-c. 83-85,87-Morales-a; Gentleman Ghost app. 85-Begin $2.99-c; Earth-2 Batman, Atom, Sandman, Mr. Terrific app. 86,87-Ordway-a. 3.00
Annual 1 (10/00, $3.50) Planet DC; intro. Nemesis 4.00
...: Black Reign TPB (2005, $12.99) r/#56-58, Hawkman #23-25; Watson cover gallery 13.00
...: Black Vengeance TPB (2006, $19.99) r/#66-75 20.00
...: Darkness Falls TPB (2002, $19.95) r/#6-15 20.00
...: Fair Play TPB (2003, $14.95) r/#26-31 & Secret Files #2 15.00
...: Ghost Stories TPB (2006, $14.99) r/#82-87 15.00
...: Justice Be Done TPB (2000, $14.95) r/Secret Files & #1-5 15.00
...: Lost TPB (2005, $19.99) r/#59-67 20.00
...: Mixed Signals TPB (2006, $14.99) r/#76-81 15.00
...: Our Worlds at War 1 (9/01, $2.95) Jae Lee-c; Saltares-a 3.00
... Presents Green Lantern TPB (2008, $14.99) r/JSA Classified #25,32,33 and Green Lantern: Brightest Day, Blackest Night 15.00
...: Princes of Darkness TPB (2005, $19.95) r/#46-55 20.00
...: Savage Times TPB (2004, $14.95) r/#39-45 15.00
... Secret Files 1 (8/99, $4.95) Origin stories and pin-ups; death of Wesley Dodds (G.A. Sandman); intro new Hawkgirl 5.00
... Secret Files 2 (9/01, $4.95) Short stories and profile pages 5.00
...: Stealing Thunder TPB (2003, $14.95) r/#32-38; JSA vs. The Ultra-Humanite 15.00
...: The Golden Age TPB (2005, $19.99) r/"The Golden Age" Elseworlds mini-series 20.00
...: The Return of Hawkman TPB (2002, $19.95) r/#16-26 & Secret Files #1 20.00

JSA: ALL STARS
DC Comics: July, 2003 - No. 8, Feb, 2004 ($2.50/$3.50, limited series, back-up stories in Golden Age style)

1-3,5,6,8-Goyer & Johns-s/Cassaday-c. 1-Velluto-a; intro. Legacy. 2-Hawkman by Loeb/Sale 3-Dr. Fate by Cooke. 5-Hourman by Chaykin. 6-Dr. Mid-nite by Azzarello/Risso 3.00
4-Starman by Robinson/Harris; 1st app. Courtney Whitmore as Stargirl 3.00
7-($3.50) Mr. Terrific back-up story by Chabon; Lark-a 4.00
TPB (2004, $14.95) r/#1-8 15.00

JSA: ALL STARS
DC Comics: Feb, 2010 - No. 18, Jul, 2011 ($3.99/$2.99)

1-13-Younger JSA members form team. 1-Covers by Williams and Sook 4.00
14-18-($2.99) 3.00
...: Constellations TPB (2010, $14.99) r/#1-6 and sketch art 15.00
...: Glory Days TPB (2011, $17.99) r/#7-13 18.00

JSA: CLASSIFIED (Issues #1-4 reprinted in Power Girl TPB)
DC Comics: Sept, 2005 - No. 39, Aug, 2008 ($2.50/$2.99)

1-(1st printing) Conner-c/a; origin of Power Girl 4.00
1-(1st printing) Adam Hughes variant-c 5.00
1-(2nd & 3rd printings) 2nd-Hughes B&W sketch-c. 3rd-Close-up of Conner-c 3.00
2-11: 2-LSH app. 4-Leads into Infinite Crisis #2. 5-7-Injustice Society app. 10-13-Vandal Savage origin retold; Gulacy-a/c 3.00
12-39: 12-Begin $2.99-c. 17,18-Bane app. 19,20-Morales-a. 21,22-Simonson-s/a 3.00
...: Honor Among Thieves TPB (2007, $14.99) r/#5-9 15.00

JSA LIBERTY FILES: THE WHISTLING SKULL
DC Comics: Feb, 2013 - No. 6, Jul, 2013 ($2.99, limited series)

1-6-Dr. Mid-Nite and Hourman in 1940; B. Clay Moore-s/Tony Harris-c/a 3.00

JSA STRANGE ADVENTURES
DC Comics: Oct, 2004 - No. 6, Mar, 2005 ($3.50, limited series)

1-6-Johnny Thunder as pulp writer; Kitson-a/Watson-c/ Kevin Anderson-s 3.50
TPB (2010, $14.99) r/#1-6 15.00

JSA: THE LIBERTY FILE (Elseworlds)
DC Comics: Feb, 2000 - No. 2, Mar, 2000 ($6.95, limited series)

1,2-Batman, Dr. Mid-Nite and Hourman vs. WW2 Joker; Tony Harris-c/a 7.00
JSA: The Liberty Files TPB (2004, $19.95) r/The Liberty File and The Unholy Three series 20.00

JSA: THE UNHOLY THREE (Elseworlds)(Sequel to JSA: The Liberty File)
DC Comics: 2003 - No. 2, 2003 ($6.95, limited series)

1,2-Batman, Superman and Hourman; Tony Harris-c/a 7.00

JSA VS. KOBRA
DC Comics: Aug, 2009 - No. 6, Jan, 2010 ($2.99, limited series)

1-6-Kramer-a/Ha-c; Jason Burr app. 3.00
TPB (2010, $14.99) r/#1-6; cover gallery 15.00

J2 (Also see A-Next and Juggernaut)
Marvel Comics: Oct, 1998 - No. 12, Sept, 1999 ($1.99)

Jubilee #1 © MAR

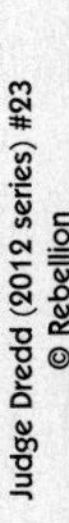
Judge Dredd (2012 series) #23 © Rebellion

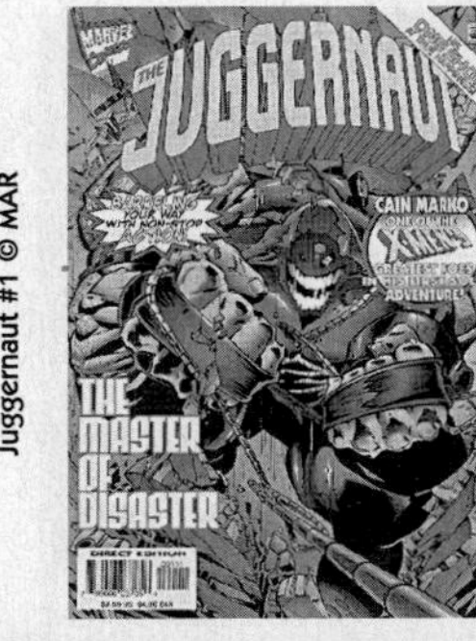

Juggernaut #1 © MAR

1-12:1-Juggernaut's son; Lim-a. 2-Two covers; X-People app. 3-J2 battles the Hulk 3.00
Spider-Girl Presents Juggernaut Jr. Vol.1: Secrets & Lies (2006, $7.99, digest) r/#1-6 8.00

JUBILEE (X-Men)
Marvel Comics: Nov, 2004 - No. 6, Apr, 2005 ($2.99)
1-6: 1-Jubilee in a Los Angeles high school; Kirkman-s; Casey Jones-c 3.00

JUDAS COIN, THE
DC Comics: 2012 ($22.99, hardcover graphic novel with dust jacket)
HC-Walt Simonson-s/a/c; Batman, Two-Face, Golden Gladiator, Viking Prince, Captain Fear, Bat Lash, Manhunter 2070 app.; bonus sketch gallery 23.00

JUDENHASS
Aardvark-Vanaheim Press: 2008 ($4.00, B&W, squarebound)
nn-Dave Sim-writer/artist; The Shoah and Jewish persecution through history 4.00

JUDE, THE FORGOTTEN SAINT
Catechetical Guild Education Soc.: 1954 (16 pgs.; 8x11"; full color; paper-c)
nn 6 12 18 28 34 40

J.U.D.G.E.: THE SECRET RAGE
Image Comics: Mar, 2000 - No. 3, May, 2000 ($2.95)
1-3-Greg Horn-s/c/a 3.00

JUDGE COLT
Gold Key: Oct, 1969 - No. 4, Sept, 1970 (Painted cover)
1 3 6 9 16 23 30
2-4 2 4 6 9 13 16

JUDGE DREDD (...Classics #62 on; also see Batman - Judge Dredd, The Law of Dredd & 2000 A.D. Monthly)
Eagle Comics/IPC Magazines Ltd./Quality Comics #34-35, V2#1-37/ Fleetway #38 on: Nov, 1983 - No. 35, 1986; V2#1, Oct, 1986 - No. 77, 1993
1-Bolland-c/a 3 6 9 17 26 35
2-5 1 3 4 6 8 10
6-35 5.00
V2#1-('86)-New look begins 5.00
2-10 4.00
11-77: 20-Begin $1.50-c. 21/22, 23/24-Two issue numbers in one. 28-1st app. Megaman (super-hero). 39-Begin $1.75-c. 51-Begin $1.95-c. 53-Bolland-a. 57-Reprints 1st published Judge Dredd story 3.00
Special 1 5.00
NOTE: ***Bolland** a-1-6, 8, 10; c-1-10, 15. **Guice** c-V2#23/24, 26, 27.*

JUDGE DREDD (3rd Series)
DC Comics: Aug, 1994 - No. 18, Jan, 1996 ($1.95)
1-18: 12-Begin $2.25-c 3.00
nn ($5.95)-Movie adaptation, Sienkiewicz-c 6.00

JUDGE DREDD
IDW Publishing: Nov, 2012 - No. 30, May, 2015 ($3.99)
1-30: 1-Swierczynski-s; six covers 4.00

JUDGE DREDD
IDW Publishing: Dec, 2015 - No. 12, Nov, 2016 ($3.99)
1-12: 1-Farinas & Freitas-s/McDaid-a; multiple covers 4.00
Annual 1 (2/17, $7.99) Farinas & Freitas-s/McDaid-a; two covers 8.00

JUDGE DREDD: ANDERSON, PSI-DIVISION
IDW Publishing: Aug, 2014 - No. 4, Dec, 2014 ($3.99)
1-4-Matt Smith-s/Carl Critchlow-a; three covers on each 4.00

JUDGE DREDD CLASSICS (Reprints)
IDW Publishing: Jul, 2013 - Present ($3.99)
1-6-Wagner & Grant-s 4.00
Free Comic Book Day 2013 (5/13, free) Judge Death app.; Walter the Wobot back-ups 3.00
...: The Dark Judges 1-5 (1/15 - No. 5, 5/15, $3.99) Wagner & Grant-s/Bolland-a 4.00

JUDGE DREDD: LEGENDS OF THE LAW
DC Comics: Dec, 1994 - No. 13, Dec, 1995 ($1.95)
1-13: 1-5-Dorman-c 3.00

JUDGE DREDD: MEGA-CITY TWO
IDW Publishing: Jan, 2014 - No. .5, May, 2014 ($3.99)
1-5-Wolk-s/Farinas-a 4.00

JUDGE DREDD'S CRIME FILE
Eagle Comics: Aug, 1985 - No. 6, Feb, 1986 ($1.25, limited series)
1-6: 1-Byrne-a 5.00

JUDGE DREDD: THE EARLY CASES
Eagle Comics: Feb, 1986 - No. 6, Jul, 1986 ($1.25, Mega-series, Mando paper)
1-6: 2000 A.D.-r 5.00

JUDGE DREDD: THE JUDGE CHILD QUEST (Judge Child in indicia)
Eagle Comics: Aug, 1984 - No. 5, Oct, 1984 ($1.25, Lim. series, Baxter paper)
1-5: 2000A.D.-r; Bolland-c/a 6.00

JUDGE DREDD: THE MEGAZINE
Fleetway/Quality: 1991 - No. 3 ($4.95, stiff-c, squarebound, 52 pgs.)
1-3 5.00

JUDGE DREDD VS. ALIENS: INCUBUS
Dark Horse Comics: March, 2003 - No. 4, June, 2003 ($2.99, limited series)
1-4-Flint-a/Wagner & Diggle-s 3.00

JUDGE DREDD: YEAR ONE
IDW Publishing: Mar, 2013 - No. 4, Jul, 2013 ($3.99)
1-4-Matt Smith-s/Simon Coleby-a 4.00

JUDGE PARKER
Argo: Feb, 1956 - No. 2, 1956
1-Newspaper strip reprints 7 14 21 35 43 50
2 5 10 15 24 30 35

JUDGMENT DAY
Awesome Entertainment: June, 1997 - No. 3, Oct, 1997 ($2.50, limited series)
1-3: 1 Alpha-Moore-s/Liefeld-c/a(p) flashback art by various in all. 2 Omega. 3 Final Judgment. All have a variant cover by Dave Gibbons 3.00
...Aftermath-($3.50) Moore-s/Kane-a; Youngblood, Glory, New Men, Maximage, Allies and Spacehunter short stories. Also has a variant cover by Dave Gibbons 4.00
TPB (Checker Books, 2003, $16.95) r/series 17.00

JUDO JOE
Jay-Jay Corp.: Aug, 1953 - No. 3, Dec, 1953 (Judo lessons in each issue)
1-Drug ring story 14 28 42 78 112 145
2,3: 3-Hypo needle story 9 18 27 52 69 85

JUDOMASTER (Gun Master #84-89) (Also see Crisis on Infinite Earths, Sarge Steel #6, Special War Series, & Thunderbolt)
Charlton Comics: No. 89, May-June, 1966 - No. 98, Dec, 1967 (Two No. 89's)
89-3rd app. Judomaster 4 8 12 25 40 55
90-Origin of Thunderbolt 4 8 12 23 37 50
91-Sarge Steel begins 3 6 9 21 33 45
92-98: 93-Intro. Tiger 3 6 9 20 31 42
93,94,96,98 (Modern Comics reprint, 1977) 6.00
NOTE: ***Morisi** Thunderbolt #90. #91 has 1 pg. biography on writer/artist Frank McLaughlin.*

JUDY CANOVA (Formerly My Experience) (Stage, screen, radio)
Fox Features Syndicate: No. 23, May, 1950 - No. 3, Sept, 1950
23(#1)-Wood-c,a(p)? 26 52 78 154 252 350
24-Wood-a(p) 24 48 72 144 237 330
3-Wood-c; Wood/Orlando-a 27 54 81 158 259 360

JUDY GARLAND (See Famous Stars)

JUDY JOINS THE WAVES
Toby Press: 1951 (For U.S. Navy)
nn 7 14 21 37 46 55

JUGGERNAUT (See X-Men)
Marvel Comics: Apr, 1997, Nov, 1999 ($2.99, one-shots)
1-(4/97) Kelly-s/ Rouleau-a 3.00
1-(11/99) Casey-s; Eighth Day x-over; Thor, Iron Man, Spidey app. 3.00

JUGHEAD (Formerly Archie's Pal...)
Archie Publications: No. 127, Dec, 1965 - No. 352, June, 1987
127-130: 129-LBJ on cover 3 6 9 17 26 35
131,133,135-160(9/68) 3 6 9 15 22 28
132,134: 132-Shield-c; The Fly & Black Hood app.; Shield cameo. 134-Shield-c 4 8 12 27 44 60
161-180 2 4 6 13 18 22
181-199 2 4 6 9 13 16
200(1/'72) 2 4 6 11 16 20
201-240(5/75) 2 4 6 8 10 12
241-270(11/77) 1 2 3 5 7 9
271-299 1 2 3 4 5 7
300(5/80)-Anniversary issue; infinity-c 1 2 3 5 6 8
301-320(1/82) 5.00

Jughead V3 #11 © ACP

Jughead with Archie Digest #171 © ACP

Juice Squeezers #1 © David Lapham

	GD 2.0	VG 4.0	FN 6.0	VF 8.0	VF/NM 9.0	NM- 9.2
321-324,326-352						4.00
325-(10/82) Cheryl Blossom app. (not on cover); same month as intro. (cover & story) in Archie's Girls, Betty & Veronica #320; Jason Blossom app.; DeCarlo-a	8	16	24	54	102	150

JUGHEAD (2nd Series)(Becomes Archie's Pal Jughead Comics #46 on)
Archie Enterprises: Aug, 1987 - No. 45, May, 1993 (.75/$1.00/$1.25)

	GD	VG	FN	VF	VF/NM	NM-
1	1	2	3	4	5	7
2-10						4.00
11-45: 4-X-Mas issue. 17-Colan-c/a						3.00

JUGHEAD (Volume 3)
Archie Comic Publications: Nov, 2015 - Present ($3.99)

1-13-Multiple covers and classic back-up reprints. 1-6-Chip Zdarsky-s/Erica Henderson-a. 5,6-Jughead as Captain Hero. 7-13-Derek Charm-a. 9-13-Ryan North-s; Sabrina app. 4.00

JUGHEAD AND ARCHIE DOUBLE DIGEST (Becomes Jughead & Archie Comics Digest)
Archie Comic Publ.: Jun, 2014 - Present ($3.99-$6.99, digest-size)

	NM-
1-3: 1-Reprints; That Wilkin Boy app.	4.00
4,7-9,11-14,16,19-($4.99)	5.00
5,10,15,21,23,25-($6.99, 320 pgs.) Titled Jughead & Archie Jumbo Comics Digest	7.00
6,17,18,20,22,24-($5.99, 192 pgs.) Titled Jughead & Archie Comics Annual. 24-Winter Annual	6.00

JUGHEAD & FRIENDS DIGEST MAGAZINE
Archie Publ.: June, 2005 - No. 38, Aug, 2010 ($2.39/$2.49/$2.69, digest-size)

1-38: 1-That Wilkin Boy app. 3.00

JUGHEAD AS CAPTAIN HERO (See Archie as Pureheart the Powerful, Archie Giant Series Magazine #142 & Life With Archie)
Archie Publications: Oct, 1966 - No. 7, Nov, 1967

	GD	VG	FN	VF	VF/NM	NM-
1-Super hero parody	7	14	21	46	86	125
2	5	10	15	30	50	70
3-7	4	8	12	27	44	60

JUGHEAD COMICS. NIGHT AT GEPPI'S ENTERTAINMENT MUSEUM
Archie Comic Publ. Inc: 2008

Free Comic Book Day giveaway - New story; Archie gang visits GEM; Steve Geppi app. 3.00

JUGHEAD JONES COMICS DIGEST, THE (...Magazine No. 10-64; Jughead Jones Digest Magazine #65)
Archie Publ.: June, 1977 - No. 100, May, 1996 ($1.35/$1.50/$1.75, digest-size, 128 pgs.)

	GD	VG	FN	VF	VF/NM	NM-
1-Neal Adams-a; Capt. Hero-r	3	6	9	20	31	42
2(9/77)-Neal Adams-a	3	6	9	15	22	28
3-6,8-10	2	4	6	11	16	20
7-Origin Jaguar-r; N. Adams-a.	2	4	6	13	18	22
11-20: 13-r/1957 Jughead's Folly	2	4	6	8	10	12
21-50	1	2	3	4	5	7
51-70						5.00
71-100						3.00

JUGHEAD'S BABY TALES
Archie Comics: Spring, 1994 - No. 2, Wint. 1994 ($2.00, 52 pgs.)

1,2: 1-Bound-in pull-out poster 4.00

JUGHEAD'S DINER
Archie Comics: Apr, 1990 - No. 7, Apr, 1991 ($1.00)

	NM-
1	4.00
2-7	3.00

JUGHEAD'S DOUBLE DIGEST (...Magazine #5)
Archie Comics: Oct, 1989 - No. 200, Apr, 2014 ($2.25 - $3.99/$5.99)

	GD	VG	FN	VF	VF/NM	NM-
1	2	4	6	8	10	12
2-10: 2,5-Capt. Hero stories	1	2	3	5	6	8
11-25						5.00
26-195: 58-Begin $2.99-c. 66-Begin $3.19-c. 91-Begin $3.59-c. 138-Reprints entire Jughead #1 (1949). 139-142-"New Look" Jughead; Staton-a. 148-Begin $3.99-c						4.00
196-200-($5.99) Titled "Jughead's Double Double Digest"						6.00
Archie New Look Series Book 2, Jughead "The Matchmakers" TPB (2009, $10.95) r/new look series in #139-142; new cover by Staton & Milgrom						11.00

JUGHEAD'S EAT-OUT COMIC BOOK MAGAZINE (See Archie Giant Series Magazine No. 170)

JUGHEAD'S FANTASY
Archie Publications: Aug, 1960 - No. 3, Dec, 1960

	GD	VG	FN	VF	VF/NM	NM-
1	18	36	54	124	275	425
2	11	22	33	76	163	250
3	10	20	30	64	132	200

JUGHEAD'S FOLLY
Archie Publications (Close-Up): 1957 (36 pgs.)(one-shot)

	GD	VG	FN	VF	VF/NM	NM-
1-Jughead a la Elvis (Rare) (1st reference to Elvis in comics?)	68	136	204	435	743	1050

JUGHEAD'S JOKES
Archie Publications: Aug, 1967 - No. 78, Sept, 1982
(No. 1-8, 38 on: reg. size; No. 9-23: 68 pgs.; No. 24-37: 52 pgs.)

	GD	VG	FN	VF	VF/NM	NM-
1	6	12	18	37	66	95
2	4	8	12	23	37	50
3-8	3	6	9	16	24	32
9,10 (68 pgs.)	3	6	9	18	28	38
11-23(4/71) (68 pgs.)	3	6	9	16	23	30
24-37(1/74) (52 pgs.)	2	4	6	11	16	20
38-50(9/76)	1	3	4	6	8	10
51-78						6.00

JUGHEAD'S PAL HOT DOG (See Laugh #14 for 1st app.)
Archie Comics: Jan, 1990 - No. 5, Oct, 1990 ($1.00)

	NM-
1	4.00
2-5	3.00

JUGHEAD'S SOUL FOOD
Spire Christian Comics (Fleming H. Revell Co.): 1979 (49¢/59¢)

	GD	VG	FN	VF	VF/NM	NM-
nn-Low print run	3	6	9	15	22	28

JUGHEAD'S TIME POLICE
Archie Comics: July, 1990 - No. 6, May, 1991 ($1.00, bi-monthly)

	NM-
1	4.00
2-6: Colan a-3-6p; c-3-6	3.00

JUGHEAD WITH ARCHIE DIGEST (...Plus Betty & Veronica & Reggie Too No. 1,2; ...Magazine #33-?, 101-on; ...Comics Digest Mag.)
Archie Pub.: Mar, 1974 - No. 200, May, 2005 ($1.00-$2.39)

	GD	VG	FN	VF	VF/NM	NM-
1	5	10	15	31	53	75
2	3	6	9	21	33	45
3-10	3	6	9	17	26	35
11-13,15-17,19,20: Capt. Hero-r in #14-16; Capt. Pureheart #17,19	2	4	6	10	14	18
14,18,21,22-Pureheart the Powerful in #18,21,22	2	4	6	11	16	20
23-30: 29-The Shield-r. 30-The Fly-r	1	3	4	6	8	10
31-50,100	1	2	3	5	6	8
51-99	1	2	3	4	5	7
101-121						4.00
122-200: 156-Begin $2.19-c. 180-Begin $2.39-c						3.00

JUICE SQUEEZERS
Dark Horse Comics: Jan, 2014 - No. 4, Apr, 2014 ($3.99, limited series)

1-4-David Lapham-s/a/c 4.00

JUKE BOX COMICS
Famous Funnies: Mar, 1948 - No. 6, Jan, 1949

	GD	VG	FN	VF	VF/NM	NM-
1-Toth-c/a; Hollingsworth-a	37	74	111	222	361	500
2-Transvestism story	22	44	66	132	216	300
3-6: 3-Peggy Lee story. 4-Jimmy Durante line drawn-c. 6-Features Desi Arnaz plus Arnaz line drawn-c	18	36	54	105	165	225

JUMBO COMICS (Created by S.M. Iger)
Fiction House Magazines (Real Adv. Publ. Co.): Sept, 1938 - No. 167, Mar, 1953 (No. 1-3: 68 pgs.; No. 4-8: 52 pgs.)(No. 1-8 oversized-10-1/2x14-1/2"; black & white)

	GD	VG	FN	VF	VF/NM	NM-
1-(Rare)-Sheena Queen of the Jungle(1st app.) by Meskin, Hawks of the Seas (The Hawk #10 on; see Feature Funnies #3) by Eisner, The Hunchback by Dick Briefer (ends #8), Wilton of the West (ends #24), Inspector Dayton (ends #67) & ZX-5 (ends #140) begin; 1st comic art by Jack Kirby (Count of Monte Cristo & Wilton of the West); Mickey Mouse appears (1 panel) with brief biography of Walt Disney; 1st app. Peter Pupp by Bob Kane. Note: Sheena was created by Iger for publication in England as a newspaper strip. The early issues of Jumbo contain Sheena strip-r; multiple panel-c 1,2,7	3750	7500	11,250	30,000	-	-
2-(Rare)-Origin Sheena. Diary of Dr. Hayward by Kirby (also #3) plus 2 other stories; contains strip from Universal Film featuring Edgar Bergen & Charlie McCarthy plus-c (preview of film)	1300	2600	3900	10,400	-	-
3-Last Kirby issue	925	1850	2775	7400	-	-
4-(Scarce)-Origin The Hawk by Eisner; Wilton of the West by Fine (ends #14)(1st comic work); Count of Monte Cristo by Fine (ends #15); The Diary of Dr. Hayward by Fine (cont'd #8,9)	875	1750	2625	7000	-	-
5-Christmas-c	800	1600	2400	6400	-	-

6-8-Last B&W issue. #8 was a 1939 N. Y. World's Fair Special Edition; Frank

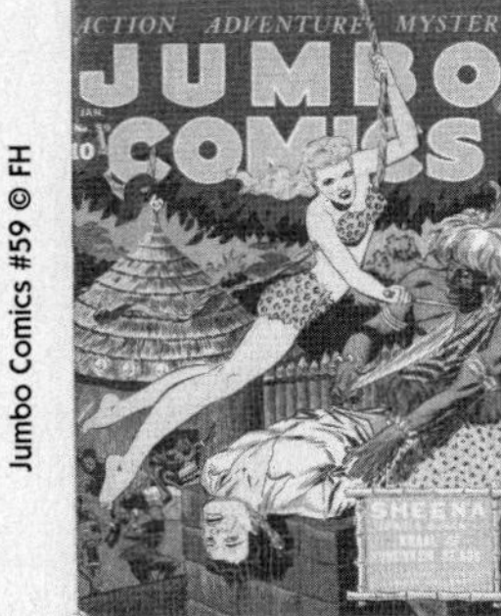

Jumbo Comics #59 © FH

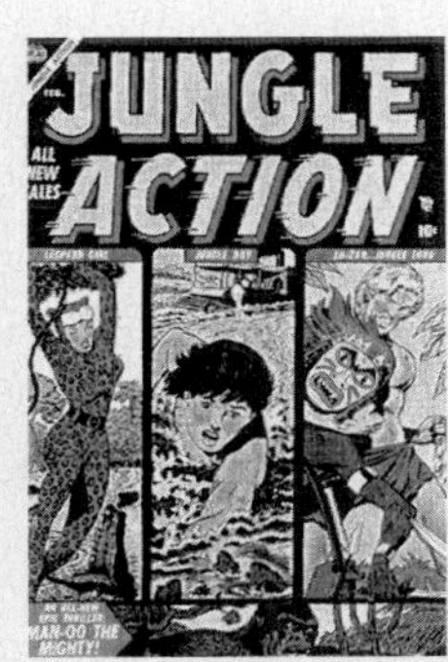

Jungle Action #3 © MAR

Jungle Comics #413 © FH

GD VG FN VF VF/NM NM-
2.0 4.0 6.0 8.0 9.0 9.2

Buck's Jungleland story 700 1400 2100 5600 - -
9-Stuart Taylor begins by Fine (ends #140); Fine-c; 1st color issue (8-9/39)-1st Sheena (jungle) cover; 8-1/4x10-1/4" (oversized in width only) 825 1650 2475 6600 - -
10-Regular size 68 pg. issues begin; Sheena dons new costume w/origin costume; Stuart Taylor sci/fi-c; classic Lou Fine-c. 432 864 1296 3154 5577 8000
11-13: 12-The Hawk-c by Eisner. 13-Eisner-c 206 412 618 1318 2259 3200
14-Intro. Lightning (super-hero) on-c only 219 438 657 1402 2401 3400
15-1st Lightning story and begins, ends #41 155 310 465 992 1696 2400
16-Lightning-c 168 336 504 1075 1838 2600
17,18,20: 17-Lightning part-c 123 246 369 787 1344 1900
19-Classic Sheena Giant Ape-c by Powell 155 310 465 992 1696 2400
21-30: 22-1st Tom, Dick & Harry; origin The Hawk retold. 25-Midnight the Black Stallion begins, ends #65 90 180 270 576 988 1400
31-(9/41)-1st app. Mars God of War in Stuart Taylor story (see Planet Comics #15.) (scarce) 258 516 774 1651 2826 4000
32-40: 35-Shows V2#11 (correct number does not appear) 71 142 213 454 777 1100
41-50: 42-Ghost Gallery begins, ends #167 47 94 141 296 498 700
51-60: 52-Last Tom, Dick & Harry 40 80 120 246 411 575
61-70: 68-Sky Girl begins, ends #130; not in #79 36 72 108 211 343 475
71-93,95-99: 89-ZX5 becomes a private eye. 28 56 84 165 270 375
94-Used in Love and Death by Legman 30 60 90 177 289 400
100 30 60 90 177 289 400
101-121 24 48 72 142 234 325
121-140,150-158: 155-Used in **POP**, pg. 98 22 44 66 128 209 290
141-149-Two Sheena stories. 141-Long Bow, Indian Boy begins, ends #160 22 44 66 132 216 300
159-163: Space Scouts serial in all. 160-Last jungle-c (6/52). 161-Ghost Gallery covers begin, end #167. 163-Suicide Smith app. 24 48 72 142 234 325
164-The Star Pirate begins, ends #165 24 48 72 142 234 325
165-167: 165,167-Space Rangers app. 24 48 72 142 234 325

NOTE: *Bondage covers, negligee panels, torture, etc. are common in this series. Hawks of the Seas, Inspector Dayton, Spies in Action, Sports Shorts, & Uncle Otto by Eisner, #1-7. Hawk by* ***Eisner****-#10-15.* ***Eisner*** *c-1-8, 12-14. 1pg. Patsy pin-ups in 92-97, 99-101. Sheena by* ***Meskin****-#1, 4; by* ***Powell****-#2, 3, 5-28;* ***Powell*** *c-14, 16, 17, 19.* ***Powell/Eisner*** *c-15. Sky Girl by* ***Matt Baker****-#69-78, 80-130. ZX-5 & Ghost Gallery by* ***Kamen****-#90-130.* ***Bailey*** *a-3-8.* ***Briefer*** *a-1-8, 10.* ***Fine*** *a-14; c-9-11.* ***Kamen*** *a-101, 105, 123, 132; c-105, 121-145.* ***Bob Kane*** *a-1-8.* ***Whitman*** *c-146-167(most). Jungle c-9, 13, 15, 17 on.*

JUMPER: JUMPSCARS
Oni Press: Jan, 2008 ($14.95, graphic novel)

SC-Prelude to 2008 movie Jumper; Brian Hurtt-a/c 15.00

JUNGLE ACTION
Atlas Comics (IPC): Oct, 1954 - No. 6, Aug, 1955

1-Leopard Girl begins by Al Hartley (#1,3); Jungle Boy by Forte; Maneely-a in all 48 96 144 302 514 725
2-(3-D effect cover) 42 84 126 265 445 625
3-6: 3-Last precode (2/55) 30 60 90 177 289 400

NOTE: ***Maneely*** *c-1, 2, 5, 6.* ***Romita*** *a-3, 6.* ***Shores*** *a-3, 6; c-3, 4?.*

JUNGLE ACTION (...& Black Panther #18-21?)
Marvel Comics Group: Oct, 1972 - No. 24, Nov, 1976

1-Lorna, Jann-r (All reprints in 1-4) 3 6 9 21 33 45
2-4 3 6 9 14 20 25
5-Black Panther begins (r/Avengers #62) 11 22 33 76 163 250
6-New solo Black Panther stories begin 8 16 24 54 102 150
7,9,10: 9-Contains pull-out centerfold ad by Mark Jewelers 3 6 9 19 30 40
8-Origin Black Panther 5 10 15 33 57 80
11-20,23,24: 19-23-KKK x-over. 23-r/#22. 24-1st Wind Eagle; story contd in Marvel Premiere #51-#53 3 6 9 14 20 25
21,22-(Regular 25¢ edition)(5,7/76) 3 6 9 14 20 25
21,22-(30¢-c variant, limited distribution) 7 14 21 46 86 125

NOTE: ***Buckler*** *a-6-9p, 22; c-8p, 12p.* ***Buscema*** *a-5p; c-22.* ***Byrne*** *c-23.* ***Gil Kane*** *a-8p; c-2, 4, 10p, 11p, 13-17, 19, 24.* ***Kirby*** *c-18.* ***Maneely*** *r-1.* ***Russell*** *a-13i.* ***Starlin*** *c-3p.*

JUNGLE ADVENTURES
Super Comics: 1963 - 1964 (Reprints)

10,12,15,17,18: 10-r/Terrors of the Jungle #4 & #10(Rulah). 12-r/Zoot #14(Rulah).15-r/Kaanga from Jungle #152 & Tiger Girl. 17-All Jo-Jo-r. 18-Reprints/White Princess of the Jungle #1; no Kinstler-a; origin of both White Princess & Cap'n Courage 3 6 9 18 28 38

JUNGLE ADVENTURES
Skywald Comics: Mar, 1971 - No. 3, June, 1971 (25¢, 52 pgs.) (Pre-code reprints & new-s)

1-Zangar origin; reprints of Jo-Jo, Blue Gorilla(origin)/White Princess #3, Kinstler-r/White Princess #2 3 6 9 19 30 40
2,3: 2-Zangar, Sheena-r/Sheena #17 & Jumbo #162, Jo-Jo, origin Slave Girl-r. 3-Zangar, Jo-Jo, White Princess, Rulah-r 3 6 9 15 22 28

JUNGLE BOOK (See King Louie and Mowgli, Movie Comics, Mowgli..., Walt Disney Showcase #45 & Walt Disney's The Jungle Book)

JUNGLE CAT (Disney)
Dell Publishing Co.: No. 1136, Sept-Nov, 1960 (one shot)

Four Color 1136-Movie, photo-c 6 12 18 37 66 95

JUNGLE COMICS
Fiction House Magazines: 1/40 - No. 157, 3/53; No. 158, Spr, 1953 - No. 163, Summer, 1954

1-Origin The White Panther, Kaanga, Lord of the Jungle, Tabu, Wizard of the Jungle; Wambi, the Jungle Boy, Camilla & Capt. Terry Thunder begin (all 1st app.). Lou Fine-c 622 1244 1866 4541 8021 11,500
2-Fantomah, Mystery Woman of the Jungle begins, ends #51; The Red Panther begins, ends #26 206 412 618 1318 2259 3200
3,4 155 310 465 992 1696 2400
5-Classic Eisner-c 187 374 561 1197 2049 2900
6-10: 7,8-Powell-c 94 188 282 597 1024 1450
11-Classic dinosaur-c 97 194 291 621 1061 1500
12-20: 13-Tuska-c 63 126 189 403 689 975
21-30: 25-Shows V2#1 (correct number does not appear). #27-New origin Fantomah, Daughter of the Pharoahs; Camilla dons new costume 52 104 156 328 557 785
31-40 41 82 123 250 418 585
41,43-50 37 74 111 222 361 500
42-Kaanga by Crandall, 12 pgs. 39 78 117 231 378 525
51-60 33 66 99 194 317 440
61-70: 67-Cover swipes Crandall splash pg. in #42 29 58 87 170 278 385
71-80: 79-New origin Tabu 25 50 75 147 241 335
81-97,99 24 48 72 140 230 320
98-Used in **SOTI**, pg. 185 & illo "In ordinary comic books, there are pictures within pictures for children who know how to look;" used by N.Y. Legis. Comm. 36 72 108 216 351 485
100 28 56 84 165 270 375
101-110: 104-In Camilla story, villain is Dr. Wertham 23 46 69 136 223 310
111-120: 118-Clyde Beatty app. 22 44 66 128 209 290
121-130 21 42 63 122 199 275
131-163: 135-Desert Panther begins in Terry Thunder (origin), not in #137; ends (dies) #138. 139-Last 52 pg. issue. 141-Last Tabu. 143,145-Used in **POP**, pg. 99. 151-Last Camilla & Terry Thunder. 152-Tiger Girl begins. 158-Last Wambi; Sheena app. 20 40 60 114 182 250
I.W. Reprint #1,9: 1-r/? 9-r/#151 3 6 9 16 24 32

NOTE: *Bondage covers, negligee panels, torture, etc. are common to this series. Camilla by* ***Fran Hopper****-#70-92; by* ***Baker****-#69, 100-113, 115, 116; by* ***Lubbers****-#97-99 by* ***Tuska****-#63, 65. Kaanga by* ***John Celardo****-#80-113; by* ***Larsen****-#71, 75-79; by* ***Moreira****-#58, 60, 61, 63-70, 72-74; by* ***Tuska****-#37, 62; by* ***Whitman****-#114-163. Tabu by* ***Larsen****-#59-75, 82-92; by* ***Whitman****-#93-115. Terry Thunder by* ***Hopper****-#71, 72; by* ***Celardo****-#78, 79; by* ***Lubbers****-#80-85. Tiger Girl-r by* ***Baker****-#152, 153, 155-157, 159. Wambi by* ***Baker****-#62-67, 74.* ***Astarita*** *c-45, 46.* ***Celardo*** *a-78; c-98-113.* ***Crandall*** *c-67 from splash pg.* ***Eisner*** *c-2, 5, 6.* ***Fine*** *c-1.* ***Larsen*** *a-65, 66, 71, 72, 74, 75, 79, 83, 84, 87-90.* ***Moreira*** *c-43, 44.* ***Morisi*** *a-51.* ***Powell*** *c-7, 8.* ***Sultan*** *c-3, 4.* ***Tuska*** *c-13.* ***Whitman*** *c-132-163(most).* ***Zolnerowich*** *c-11, 12, 18-41.*

JUNGLE COMICS
Blackthorne Publishing: May, 1988 - No. 4 ($2.00, B&W/color)

1-Dave Stevens-c; B. Jones scripts in all 2 4 6 13 18 22
2-4: 2-B&W-a begins 5.00

JUNGLE GIRL (See Lorna, the...)

JUNGLE GIRL (Nyoka, Jungle Girl No. 2 on)
Fawcett Publications: Fall, 1942 (one-shot)(No month listed)

1-Bondage-c; photo of Kay Aldridge who played Nyoka in movie serial app. on-c. Adaptation of the classic Republic movie serial Perils of Nyoka. 1st comic to devote entire contents to a movie serial adaptation 139 278 417 883 1517 2150

JUNGLE GIRL
Dynamite Entertainment: No. 0, 2007 - 2009 (25¢/$2.99/$3.50)

0-(25¢-c) Eight page preview; preview of Superpowers w/Alex Ross-a 3.00
1-5-Frank Cho-plot/cover; Batista-a/variant-c 3.00
... Season 2 ($3.50) 1-5-Two covers by Cho & Batista 3.50
... Season 3 ($3.99) 1-4-Cho-c/Jadson-a/Murray-s 4.00

JUNGLE GIRLS
AC Comics: 1989 - No. 16, 1993 (B&W)

1-16: 1-4,10,13-16-New story & "good girl" reprints. 5-9,11,12-All g.g. reprints (Baker, Powell, Lubbers, others) 3.00

JUNGLE JIM (Also see Ace Comics)
Standard Comics (Best Books): No. 11, Jan, 1949 - No. 20, Apr, 1951

Jungle Tales #5 © MAR

Junior Comics #13 © FOX

Jupiter's Circle #5 © MillarWorld & Quitely

	GD 2.0	VG 4.0	FN 6.0	VF 8.0	VF/NM 9.0	NM- 9.2

11 12 24 36 69 97 125
12-20 9 18 27 47 61 75

JUNGLE JIM
Dell Publishing Co.: No. 490, 8/53 - No. 1020, 8-10/59 (Painted-c)

Four Color 490(#1) 8 16 24 51 96 140
Four Color 565(#2, 6/54) 5 10 15 33 57 80
3(10-12/54)-5 4 8 12 27 44 60
6-19(1-3/59) 4 8 12 25 40 55
Four Color 1020(#20) 5 10 15 31 53 75

JUNGLE JIM
King Features Syndicate: No. 5, Dec, 1967

5-Reprints Dell #5; Wood-c 2 4 6 10 14 18

JUNGLE JIM (Continued from Dell series)
Charlton Comics: No. 22, Feb, 1969 - No. 28, Feb, 1970 (#21 was an overseas edition only)

22-Dan Flagg begins; Ditko/Wood-a 3 6 9 20 31 42
23-26: 23-Last Dan Flagg; Howard-c. 24-Jungle People begin 3 6 9 15 21 26
27,28: 27-Ditko/Howard-a. 28-Ditko-a 3 6 9 16 24 32

NOTE: *Ditko cover of #22 reprints story panels*

JUNGLE JO
Fox Feature Syndicate (Hero Books): Mar, 1950 - No. 3, Sept, 1950

nn-Jo-Jo blanked out in titles of interior stories, leaving Congo King; came out after Jo-Jo #29 (intended as Jo-Jo #30?) 60 120 180 381 653 925
1-Tangi begins; part Wood-a 63 126 189 403 689 975
2,3 48 96 144 302 514 725

JUNGLE LIL (Dorothy Lamour #2 on; also see Feature Stories Magazine)
Fox Feature Syndicate (Hero Books): April, 1950

1 52 104 156 328 552 775

JUNGLE TALES (Jann of the Jungle No. 8 on)
Atlas Comics (CSI): Sept, 1954 - No. 7, Sept, 1955

1-Jann of the Jungle 45 90 135 284 480 675
2-7: 3-Last precode (1/55) 34 68 102 199 325 450

NOTE: *Heath c-5.* **Heck** *a-6, 7.* **Maneely** *a-2; c-1, 3.* **Shores** *a-5-7; c-4, 6.* **Tuska** *a-2.*

JUNGLE TALES OF TARZAN
Charlton Comics: Dec, 1964 - No. 4, July, 1965

1 5 10 15 33 57 80
2-4 4 8 12 22 37 50

NOTE: **Giordano** *c-3p.* **Glanzman** *a-1-3.* **Montes/Bache** *a-4.*

JUNGLE TERROR (See Harvey Comics Hits No. 54)

JUNGLE THRILLS (Formerly Sports Thrills; Terrors of the Jungle #17 on)
Star Publications: No. 16, Feb, 1952; Dec, 1953; No. 7, 1954

16-Phantom Lady & Rulah story-reprint/All Top No. 15; used in **POP**, pg. 98,99; L. B. Cole-c 53 106 159 334 567 800
3-D 1(12/53, 25¢)-Came w/glasses; Jungle Lil & Jungle Jo appear; L. B. Cole-c 53 106 159 334 567 800
7-Titled 'Picture Scope Jungle Adventures;' (1954, 36 pgs, 15¢)-3-D effect c/stories; story & coloring book; Disbrow-a/script; L.B. Cole-c 53 106 159 334 567 800

JUNGLE TWINS, THE (Tono & Kono)
Gold Key/Whitman No. 18: Apr, 1972 - No. 17, Nov, 1975; No. 18, May, 1982

1-All painted covers 3 6 9 16 23 30
2-5 2 4 6 9 12 15
6-18: 18(Whitman, 5/82)-Reprints 1 3 4 6 8 10

NOTE: *UFO c/story No. 13. Painted-c No. 1-17.* **Spiegle** *c-18.*

JUNGLE WAR STORIES (Guerrilla War No. 12 on)
Dell Publishing Co.: July-Sept, 1962 - No. 11, Apr-June, 1965 (Painted-c)

01-384-209 (#1) 4 8 12 23 37 50
2-11 3 6 9 16 24 32

JUNIE PROM (Also see Dexter Comics)
Dearfield Publishing Co.: Winter, 1947-48 - No. 7, Aug, 1949

1-Teen-age 22 44 66 132 216 300
2 18 36 54 105 165 225
3-7 17 34 51 98 154 210

JUNIOR
Fantagraphics Books: June, 2000 - No. 5, Jan, 2001 ($2.95, B&W)

1-5-Peter Bagge-s/a 3.00

JUNIOR CARROT PATROL (Jr. Carrot Patrol #2)
Dark Horse Comics: May, 1989; No. 2, Nov, 1990 ($2.00, B&W)

1,2-Flaming Carrot spin-off. 1-Bob Burden-c(i) 3.00

JUNIOR COMICS (Formerly Li'l Pan; becomes Western Outlaws with #17)
Fox Feature Syndicate: No. 9, Sept, 1947 - No. 16, July, 1948

9-Feldstein-c/a; headlights-c 161 322 483 1030 1765 2500
10-16: 10-12,14-16-Feldstein-c/a; headlights-c 148 296 444 947 1624 2300

JUNIOR FUNNIES (Formerly Tiny Tot Funnies No. 9)
Harvey Publ. (King Features Synd.): No. 10, Aug, 1951 - No. 13, Feb, 1952

10-Partial reprints in all; Blondie, Dagwood, Daisy, Henry, Popeye, Felix, Katzenjammer Kids 6 12 18 28 34 40
11-13 5 10 15 24 30 35

JUNIOR HOPP COMICS
Stanmor Publ.: Feb, 1952 - No. 3, July, 1952

1-Teenage humor 17 34 51 98 154 210
2,3: 3-Dave Berg-a 12 24 36 69 97 125

JUNIOR MEDICS OF AMERICA, THE
E. R. Squire & Sons: No. 1359, 1957 (15¢)

1359 4 8 12 17 21 24

JUNIOR MISS
Timely/Marvel (CnPC): Wint, 1944; No. 24, Apr, 1947 - No. 39, Aug, 1950

1-Frank Sinatra & June Allyson life story 40 80 120 246 411 575
24-Formerly The Human Torch #23? 20 40 60 118 192 265
25-38: 29,31,34-Cindy-c/stories (others?) 14 28 42 80 115 150
39-Kurtzman-a 15 30 45 84 127 170

NOTE: *Painted-c 35-37. 35, 37-all romance. 36, 38-mostly teen humor.* **Louise Alston** *c-36.*

JUNIOR PARTNERS (Formerly Oral Roberts' True Stories)
Oral Roberts Evangelistic Assn.: No. 120, Aug, 1959 - V3#12, Dec, 1961

120(#1) 4 8 12 23 37 50
2(9/59) 3 6 9 16 24 32
3-12(7/60) 2 4 6 13 18 22
V2#1(8/60)-5(12/60) 2 4 6 9 13 16
V3#1(1/61)-12 2 4 6 8 10 12

JUNIOR TREASURY (See Dell Junior...)

JUNIOR WOODCHUCKS GUIDE (Walt Disney's...)
Danbury Press: 1973 (8-3/4"x5-3/4", 214 pgs., hardcover)

nn-Illustrated text based on the long-standing J.W. Guide used by Donald Duck's nephews Huey, Dewey & Louie by Carl Barks. The guidebook was a popular plot device to enable the nephews to solve problems facing their uncle or Scrooge McDuck (scarce) 5 10 15 31 53 75

JUNIOR WOODCHUCKS LIMITED SERIES (Walt Disney's...)
W. D. Publications (Disney): July, 1991 - No. 4, Oct, 1991 ($1.50, limited series; new & reprint-a)

1-4: 1-The Beagle Boys app.; Barks-r 3.00

JUNIOR WOODCHUCKS (See Huey, Dewey & Louie...)

JUPITER'S CIRCLE (Prequel to Jupiter's Legacy)
Image Comics: Apr, 2015 - No. 6, Sept, 2015 ($3.50/$3.99)

1-6-Mark Millar-s/Frank Quitely-a/c. 1-Three covers. 1-3,6-Torres-a. 4,5-Gianfelice-a 4.00
Volume 2 (11/15 - No. 6, 5/16) 1-6-Covers by Quitely & Sienkiewicz. 1,2,6-Torres-a. 3-5-Spouse-a 4.00

JUPITER'S LEGACY
Image Comics: Apr, 2013 - No. 5, Jan, 2015 ($2.99/$4.99)

1-4-Mark Millar-s/Frank Quitely-a/c 3.00
1-Variant-c by Hitch 4.00
5-($4.99) Covers by Hitch and Fegredo; bonus pin-ups and cosplay photos 5.00
1-Studio Edition (12/13, $4.99) Quitely's B&W art and Millar's script; design art 5.00

JUPITER'S LEGACY 2
Image Comics: Jan, 2016 - No. 5 ($3.99)

1-4-Mark Millar-s/Frank Quitely-a/c 4.00

JURASSIC PARK
Topps Comics: June, 1993 - No. 4, Aug, 1993; No. 5, Oct, 1994 - No. 10, Feb, 1995

1-($2.50)-Newsstand Edition; Kane/Perez-a in all; 1-4: movie adaptation 4.00
1-($2.95)-Collector's Ed.; polybagged w/3 cards 5.00
1-Amberchrome Edition w/no price or ads 1 2 3 5 6 8
2-4-($2.50)-Newsstand Edition 3.00
2,3-($2.95)-Collector's Ed.; polybagged w/3 cards 4.00
4-10: 4-($2.95)-Collector's Ed.; polybagged w/1 of 4 different action hologram trading card;

Justice #12 © DC

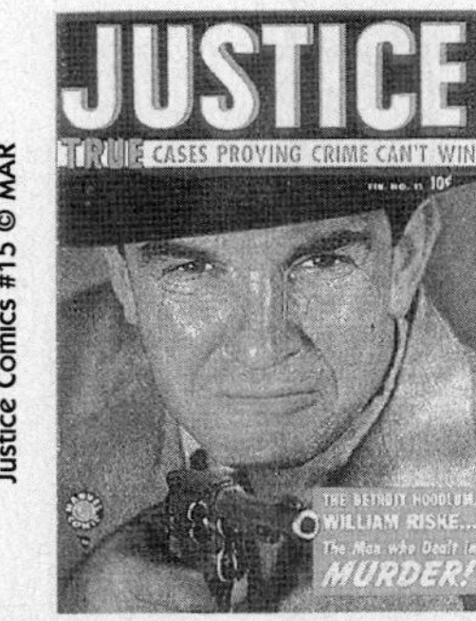

Justice Comics #15 © MAR

Justice League America #34 © DC

GD 2.0 | VG 4.0 | FN 6.0 | VF 8.0 | VF/NM 9.0 | NM- 9.2

Gil Kane/Perez-a. 5-becomes Advs. of 3.00
Annual 1 ($3.95, 5/95) 4.00
Trade paperback (1993, $9.95)-r/#1-4; bagged w/#0 10.00

JURASSIC PARK
IDW Publishing: Jun, 2010 - No. 5, Oct, 2010 ($3.99, limited series)
1-5: Takes place 13 years after the first movie; Schreck-s. 1-Covers by Yeates & Miller 4.00

JURASSIC PARK: DANGEROUS GAMES
IDW Publishing: Sept, 2011 - No. 5, Jan, 2012 ($3.99, limited series)
1-5-Erik Bear-s/Jorge Jimenez-a, 1-Covers by Darrow & Zornow 4.00

JURASSIC PARK: RAPTOR
Topps Comics: Nov, 1993 - No. 2, Dec, 1993 ($2.95, limited series)
1,2: 1-Bagged w/3 trading cards & Zorro #0; Golden c-1,2 4.00

JURASSIC PARK: RAPTORS ATTACK
Topps Comics: Mar, 1994 - No. 4, June, 1994 ($2.50, limited series)
1-4-Michael Golden-c/frontispiece 3.00

JURASSIC PARK: RAPTORS HIJACK
Topps Comics: July, 1994 - No. 4, Oct, 1994 ($2.50, limited series)
1-4: Michael Golden-c/front piece 3.00

JURASSIC PARK: THE DEVILS IN THE DESERT
IDW Publishing: Jan, 2011 - No. 4, Apr, 2011 ($3.99, limited series)
1-4-John Byrne-s/a/c 4.00

JUST A PILGRIM
Black Bull Entertainment: May, 2001 - No. 5, Sept, 2001 ($2.99)
Limited Preview Edition (12/00, $7.00) Ennis & Ezquerra interviews 7.00
1-Ennis-s/Ezquerra-a; two covers by Texeira & JG Jones 3.00
2-5: 2-Fabry-c. 3-Nowlan-c. 4-Sienkiewicz-c 3.00
TPB (11/01, $12.99) r/#1-5; Waid intro. 13.00

JUST A PILGRIM: GARDEN OF EDEN
Black Bull Entertainment: May, 2002 - No. 4, Aug, 2002 ($2.99, limited series)
Limited Preview Ed. (1/02, $7.00) Ennis & Ezquerra interviews; Jones-c 7.00
1-4-Ennis-s/Ezquerra-a 3.00
TPB (11/02, $12.99) r/#1-4; Gareb Shamus intro. 13.00

JUSTICE
Marvel Comics Group (New Universe): Nov, 1986 - No. 32, June, 1989
1-32: 26-32-$1.50-c (low print run) 3.00

JUSTICE
DC Comics: Oct, 2005 - No. 12, Aug, 2007 ($2.99/$3.50/$3.99, bi-monthly maxi-series)
1-Classic Justice League vs. The Legion of Doom; Alex Ross & Doug Braithwaite-a; Jim Krueger-s; two covers by Ross; Ross sketch pages 5.00
1-2nd & 3rd printings 4.00
2-($3.50) 4.00
2 (2nd printing), 3-11-($3.50) 3.50
12-($3.99) Two covers (Heroes & Villains) 4.00
Absolute Justice HC (2009, $99.99, slipcased book with dustjacket) oversized r/#1-12; afterwords by creators; Ross sketch and design art; photo gallery of action figures 100.00
HC (2011, $39.99, dustjacket) r/#1-12 40.00
... Volume One HC (2006, $19.99, dustjacket) r/#1-4; Krueger intro.; sketch pages 20.00
... Volume One SC (2008, $14.99) r/#1-4; Krueger intro.; sketch pages 15.00
... Volume Two HC (2007, $19.99, dustjacket) r/#5-8; Krueger intro.; sketch pages 20.00
... Volume Two SC (2008, $14.99) r/#5-8; Krueger intro.; sketch pages 15.00
... Volume Three HC (2007, $19.99, dustjacket) r/#9-12; Ross intro.; sketch pages 20.00
... Volume Three SC (2007, $14.99) r/#9-12; Ross intro.; sketch pages 15.00

JUSTICE COMICS (Formerly Wacky Duck; Tales of Justice #53 on)
Marvel/Atlas Comics (NPP 7-9,4-19/CnPC 20-23/MjMC 24-38/Male 39-52:
No. 7, Fall/47 - No. 9, 6/48; No. 4, 8/48 - No. 52, 3/55

	GD	VG	FN	VF	VF/NM	NM-
7(#1, 1947)	34	68	102	206	336	465
8(#2)-Kurtzman-a "Giggles 'n' Grins" (3)	22	44	66	132	216	300
9(#3, 6/48)	20	40	60	117	189	260
4	18	36	54	105	165	225
5(9/48)-9: 8-Anti-Wertham editorial	15	30	45	90	140	190
10-15-Photo-c	14	28	42	80	115	150
16-30	13	26	39	74	105	135
31-40,42-52: 35-Gene Colan-a. 48-Last precode; Pakula & Tuska-a. 50-Ayers-a	12	24	36	69	97	125
41-Electrocution-c	20	40	60	114	182	250

NOTE: ***Hartley*** *a-48.* ***Heath*** *a-24.* ***Maneely*** *c-44, 52.* ***Pakula*** *a-43, 45, 47, 48.* ***Louis Ravielli*** *a-39, 47.* ***Robinson*** *a-22, 25, 41.* ***Sale*** *c-45.* ***Shores*** *c-7(#1), 8(#2)?* ***Tuska*** *a-41, 48.* ***Wildey*** *a-52.*

JUSTICE: FOUR BALANCE
Marvel Comics: Sept, 1994 - No. 4, Dec, 1994 ($1.75, limited series)
1-4: 1-Thing & Firestar app. 3.00

JUSTICE, INC. (The Avenger) (Pulp)
National Periodical Publications: May-June, 1975 - No. 4, Nov-Dec, 1975

	GD	VG	FN	VF	VF/NM	NM-
1-McWilliams-a, Kubert-c; origin	2	4	6	11	16	20
2-4: 2-4-Kirby-a(p), c-2,3p. 4-Kubert-c	2	4	6	11	16	20

NOTE: *Adapted from Kenneth Robeson novel, creator of Doc Savage.*

JUSTICE, INC. (Pulp)
DC Comics: 1989 - No. 2, 1989 ($3.95, 52 pgs., squarebound, mature)
1,2: Re-intro The Avenger; Andrew Helfer scripts & Kyle Baker-c/a 5.00

JUSTICE, INC. (Pulp)
Dynamite Entertainment: 2014 - No. 6, 2015 ($3.99/$5.99)
1-5-The Shadow, Doc Savage and The Avenger app; Uslan-s/Timpano-a; multiple covers 4.00
6-($5.99) Covers by Ross, Francavilla, Hardman and Syaf 6.00

JUSTICE, INC.: THE AVENGER (Pulp)
Dynamite Entertainment: 2015 - No. 6, 2015 ($3.99)
1-6: 1-Waid-s/Freire-a; multiple covers incl. 1975 series #1 cover swipe by Ross 4.00

JUSTICE LEAGUE (...International #7-25; ...America #26 on)
DC Comics: May, 1987 - No. 113, Aug, 1996 (Also see Legends #6)

	GD	VG	FN	VF	VF/NM	NM-
1-Batman, Green Lantern (Guy Gardner), Blue Beetle, Mr. Miracle, Capt. Marvel & Martian Manhunter begin; 1st app. Maxwell Lord	2	4	6	11	16	20
2,3: 3-Regular-c (white background)						5.00
3-Limited-c (yellow background, Superman logo)	4	8	12	25	40	55

4-6,8-10: 4-Booster Gold joins. 5-Origin Gray Man; Batman vs. Guy Gardner; Creeper app. 9,10-Millennium x-over 4.00
7-($1.25, 52 pgs.)-Capt. Marvel & Dr. Fate resign; Capt. Atom & Rocket Red join 5.00
11-17,22,23,25-49,51-68,71-82: 16-Bruce Wayne-c/story. 31,32-J. L. Europe x-over. 58-Lobo app. 61-New team begins; swipes-c to J.L. of A. #1('60). 70-Newsstand version w/o outer-c. 71-Direct sales version w/black outer-c. 71-Newsstand version w/o outer-c. 80-Intro new Booster Gold. 82,83-Guy Gardner-c/stories 3.00
18-21,24,50: 18-21-Lobo app. 24-($1.50)-1st app. Justice League Europe. 50-($1.75, 52 pgs.) 4.00
69-Doomsday tie-in; takes place between Superman: The Man of Steel #18 & Superman #74 6.00
69,70-2nd printings 3.00
70-Funeral for a Friend part 1; red 3/4 outer-c 5.00
83-99,101-113: 92-(9/94)-Zero Hour x-over; Triumph app. 113-Green Lantern, Flash & Hawkman app. 3.00
100 ($3.95)-Foil-c; 52 pgs. 5.00
100 ($2.95)-Newstand 4.00
#0-(10/94) Zero Hour (publ between #92 & #93); new team begins (Hawkman, Flash, Wonder Woman, Metamorpho, Nuklon, Crimson Fox, Obsidian & Fire) 3.00
Annual 1-8,10 ('87-'94, '96, 68 pgs.): 2-Joker-c/story; Batman cameo. 5-Armageddon 2001 x-over; Silver ink 2nd print. 7-Bloodlines x-over. 8-Elseworlds story. 10-Legends of the Dead Earth 4.00
Annual 9 (1995, $3.50)-Year One story 4.00
Special 1,2 ('90,'91, 52 pgs.): 1-Giffen plots. 2-Staton-a(p) 4.00
Spectacular 1 (1992, $1.50, 52 pgs.)-Intro new JLI & JLE teams; ties into JLI #61 & JLE #37; two interlocking covers by Jurgens 4.00
A New Beginning Trade Paperback (1989, $12.95)-r/#1-7 13.00
... International Vol. 1 HC (2008, $24.99) r/#1-7; new intro. by Giffen 25.00
... International Vol. 1 SC (2009, $17.99) r/#1-7; new intro. by Giffen 18.00
... International Vol. 2 HC (2008, $24.99) r/#8-13, Annual #1 and Suicide Squad #13 25.00
... International Vol. 2 SC (2009, $17.99) r/#8-13, Annual #1 and Suicide Squad #13 18.00
... International Vol. 3 SC (2009, $19.99) r/#14-22 20.00
... International Vol. 4 SC (2010, $17.99) r/#23-30 18.00
... International Vol. 5 SC (2011, $19.99) r/#Annual #2,3 & Justice League Europe #1-6 20.00
... International Vol. 6 SC (2011, $24.99) r/#31-35 & Justice League Europe #7-11 25.00

NOTE: ***Anderson*** *c-61i.* ***Austin*** *a-1i, 60i; c-1i.* ***Giffen*** *a-13; c-21p.* ***Guice*** *a-62i.* ***Maguire*** *a-1-12, 16-19, 22, 23.* ***Russell*** *a-Annual 1i; c-54i.* ***Willingham*** *a-30p, Annual 2.*

JUSTICE LEAGUE (DC New 52)
DC Comics: Oct, 2011 - No. 52, Aug, 2016 ($3.99)

	GD	VG	FN	VF	VF/NM	NM-
1-Johns-s/Jim Lee-a/c; Batman, Green Lantern & Superman app.; orange background-c	2	4	6	11	16	20
1-Combo-Pack edition ($4.99) polybagged with digital download code; blue background-c	1	3	4	6	8	10
1-Variant-c by Finch						25.00
1-Second printing						25.00

2-11,13-23: 3-Wonder Woman & Aquaman arrive. 4-Darkseid arrives. 6-Pandora back-up. 7-Gene Ha-a; back-up Shazam origin begins; Frank-a. 8-D'Anda-a. 13,14-Cheetah app.

Justice League (2011 series) #50 © DC

Justice League Dark #37 © DC

Justice League of America #13 © DC

GD VG FN VF VF/NM NM-
2.0 4.0 6.0 8.0 9.0 9.2

15-17-Throne of Atlantis. 22,23-Trinity War. 23-Crime Syndicate arrives 4.00

12-Superman/Wonder Woman kiss-c 4.00

23.1, 23.2, 23.3, 23.4 (11/13, $2.99, regular-c) 3.00

23.1 (11/13, $3.99, 3-D cover) "Darkseid #1" on cover; origin; Kaiyo app.; Reis-c 5.00

23.2 (11/13, $3.99, 3-D cover) "Lobo #1" on cover; Bennett-s/Oliver-a/Kuder-c 5.00

23.3 (11/13, $3.99, 3-D cover) "Dial E #1" on cover; Miéville-s; art by various 5.00

23.4 (11/13, $3.99, 3-D cover) "Secret Society #1" on cover; Owlman app.; Kudranski-a 5.00

24-29-Forever Evil. 24-Origin of Ultraman. 25-Origin of Owlman. 27-Cyborg upgraded. 28,29-Metal Men return 4.00

30-39: 30-Lex Luthor app.; intro Jessica Cruz. 31-33-Doom Patrol app. 33-Luthor joins. 35-Amazo virus unleashed; intro Lena Luthor 4.00

40-Darkseid War prologue, continues in DC's 2015 FCBD edition; intro. Grail (cameo) 4.00

41-($4.99) Darkseid War pt 1; Mister Miracle & the Anti-Monitor app.; intro Myrina Black 5.00

42-49-Darkseid War; Darkseid vs. the Anti-Monitor. 45,46-Manapul-a 4.00

48-Coloring Book variant-c by Kolins 4.00

50-($5.99) Conclusion to Darkseid War; Jessica Cruz becomes a Green Lantern 6.00

51,52: 51-Flashback with Robin; Pelletier-a. Lex Luthor as Superman; Grummett-a 4.00

#0-(11/12, $3.99) Origin of Shazam; back-up with Pandora 4.00

...: Darkseid War: Batman (12/15, $3.99) Pasarin-a; Batman on Mobius chair; Joe Chill app. 4.00

...: Darkseid War: Flash (1/16, $3.99) Merino-a; Flash vs. the Black Racer 4.00

...: Darkseid War: Green Lantern (1/16, $3.99) Shaner-a; Hal Jordan becomes God of Light 4.00

...: Darkseid War: Lex Luthor (2/16, $3.99) Dazo-a; The God of Apocalypse 4.00

...: Darkseid War: Shazam (1/16, $3.99) Kolins-a 4.00

...: Darkseid War Special (6/16, $3.99) Reis, Jimenez & Pelletier-a; Grail's origin 4.00

...: Darkseid War: Superman (1/16, $3.99) Dazo-a; The God of Steel 4.00

...: Futures End 1 (11/14, $2.99, regular-c) Cont'd from Justice League United: FE #1 3.00

...: Futures End 1 (11/14, $3.99, 3-D cover) 4.00

...: Trinity War Director's Cut 1 (10/13, $5.99) r/#22 pencil art and script 6.00

JUSTICE LEAGUE (DC Rebirth)
DC Comics: Sept, 2016 - Present ($2.99)

1-11: 1-Hitch-s/Daniel-a. 4-Merino-a. Clark & Derenick-a. 11-Amazo app. 3.00

1 Director's Cut (12/16, $5.99) r/#1 with B&W art; original script; variant cover gallery 6.00

12-16: 12,13: Justice League vs. Suicide Squad tie-ins. 12-Max Lord returns 3.00

...: Rebirth 1 (9/16, $2.99) Hitch-s/a; pre-New 52 Superman joins 3.00

JUSTICE LEAGUE ADVENTURES (Based on Cartoon Network series)
DC Comics: Jan, 2002 - No. 34, Oct, 2004 ($1.99/$2.25)

1-Timm & Ross-c 4.00

2-32: 3-Nicieza-s. 5-Starro app. 10-Begin $2.25-c. 14-Includes 16 pg. insert for VERB with Haberlin CG-art. 15,29-Amancio-a. 16-McCloud-s. 20-Psycho Pirate app. 25,26-Adam Strange-c/app. 28-Legion of Super-Heroes app. 30-Kamandi app. 3.00

Free Comic Book Day giveaway - (5/02) r/#1 with "Free Comic Book Day" banner on-c 3.00

TPB (2003, $9.95) r/#1,3,6,10-13; Timm/Ross-c from #1 10.00

...Vol. 1: The Magnificent Seven (2004, $6.95) digest-size reprints #3,6,10-12 7.00

...Vol. 2: Friends and Foes (2004, $6.95) digest-size reprints #13,14,16,19,20 7.00

JUSTICE LEAGUE: A MIDSUMMER'S NIGHTMARE
DC Comics: Sept, 1996 - No. 3, Nov, 1996 ($2.95, limited series, 38 pgs.)

1-3: Re-establishes Superman, Batman, Green Lantern, The Martian Manhunter, Flash, Aquaman & Wonder Woman as the Justice League; Mark Waid & Fabian Nicieza co-scripts; Jeff Johnson & Darick Robertson-a(p); Kevin Maguire-c 5.00

TPB-(1997, $8.95) r/1-3 9.00

JUSTICE LEAGUE: CRY FOR JUSTICE
DC Comics: Sept, 2009 - No. 7, Apr, 2010 ($3.99, limited series)

1-7-James Robinson-s/Mauro Cascioli-a/c. 1-Two covers; Congorilla origin 4.00

HC (2010, $24.99, d.j.) r/#1-7, Face of Evil: Prometheus 25.00

SC (2011, $19.99) r/#1-7, Face of Evil: Prometheus 20.00

JUSTICE LEAGUE DARK (DC New 52)
DC Comics: Nov, 2011 - No. 40, May, 2015 ($2.99/$3.99)

1-23: 1-Milligan-s; Deadman, Madame Xanadu, Zatanna, Shade, John Constantine app. 7,8-Crossover with I,Vampire #6,7. 7-Batgirl app. 9-Black Orchid joins. 11,12-Tim Hunter app. 13-Leads into J.L. Dark Annual #1. 19-21-Flash app. 22,23-Trinity War 3.00

23.1, 23.2 (11/13, $2.99, regular-c) 3.00

23.1 (11/13, $3.99, 3-D cover) "The Creeper #1" on cover; origin; Nocenti-s/Janin-c 5.00

23.2 (11/13, $3.99, 3-D cover) "Eclipso #1" on cover; origin; Tan-a/Janin-c 5.00

24-40: 24-29-Forever Evil tie-ins. 40-Constantine returns 4.00

#0-(11/12, $2.99) Constantine and Zatanna's 1st meeting; Garbett-a/Sook-c 3.00

Annual #1 (12/12, $4.99) Continued from #13; Frankenstein & Amethyst app. 5.00

Annual #2 (12/14, $4.99) Janson-a/March-c; House of Wonders app. 5.00

...: Futures End 1 (11/14, $2.99, regular-c) Five years later; Etrigan app. 3.00

...: Futures End 1 (11/14, $3.99, 3-D cover) 4.00

JUSTICE LEAGUE ELITE (See JLA #100 and JLA Secret Files 2004)
DC Comics: Sept, 2004 - No. 12, Aug, 2005 ($2.50)

GD VG FN VF VF/NM NM-
2.0 4.0 6.0 8.0 9.0 9.2

1-12-Flash, Green Arrow, Vera Black and others; Kelly-s/Mahnke-a. 5,6-JSA app. 3.00

JL Elite TPB (2005, $19.99) r/#1-4, Action #775, JLA #100, JLA Secret Files 2004 20.00

... Vol. 2 TPB (2007, $19.99) r/#5-12 20.00

JUSTICE LEAGUE EUROPE (Justice League International #51 on)
DC Comics: Apr, 1989 - No. 68, Sept., 1994 (75¢/ $1.00/$1.25/$1.50)

1-Giffen plots in all, breakdowns in #1-8,13-30; Justice League #1-c/swipe 4.00

2-10: 7-9-Batman app. 7,8-JLA x-over. 8,9-Superman app. 3.00

11-49: 12-Metal Men app. 20-22-Rogers-c/a(p). 33,34-Lobo vs. Despero. 37-New team begins; swipes-c to JLA #9; see JLA Spectacular 3.00

50-($2.50, 68 pgs.)-Battles Sonar 4.00

51-68: 68-Zero Hour x-over; Triumph joins Justice League Task Force (See JLTF #17) 3.00

Annual 1-5 ('90-'94, 68 pgs.)-1-Return of the Global Guardians; Giffen plots/breakdowns. 2-Armageddon 2001; Giffen-a(p); Rogers-a(p); Golden-a(i). 5-Elseworlds story 4.00

NOTE: *Phil Jimenez a-68p. Rogers c/a-20-22. Sears a-1-12, 14-19, 23-29; c-1-10, 12, 14-19, 23-29.*

JUSTICE LEAGUE: GENERATION LOST (Brightest Day)
DC Comics: Early July, 2010 - No. 24, Early Jun, 2011 ($2.99, bi-weekly limited series)

1-23: 1-Maxwell Lord's return; Winick & Giffen-s. 1-5,7-Harris-c. 13-Magog killed 3.00

24-($4.99) Wonder Woman vs. Omac Prime; Lopresti-a/Nguyen-c 5.00

... Volume One HC (2010, $39.99, dustjacket) r/#1-12; cover gallery 40.00

JUSTICE LEAGUE: GODS & MONSTERS (Tie-in to 2015 animated film)
DC Comics: Oct, 2015 - No. 3, Oct, 2015 ($3.99, weekly limited series)

1-3-DeMatteis & Timm-/Silas-a; alternate Superman, Batman & Wonder Woman 4.00

... - Batman 1 (9/15, $3.99) origin of the Kirk Langstrom Batman; Matthew Dow Smith-a 4.00

... - Superman 1 (9/15, $3.99) origin of the Hernan Guerra Superman; Moritat-a 4.00

... - Wonder Woman 1 (9/15, $3.99) origin of Bekka of New Genesis; Leonardi-a 4.00

JUSTICE LEAGUE INTERNATIONAL (See Justice League Europe)

JUSTICE LEAGUE INTERNATIONAL (DC New 52)
DC Comics: Nov, 2011 - No. 12, Oct, 2012 ($2.99)

1-12: 1-Jurgens-s/Lopresti-a/c; Batman, Booster Gold, Guy Gardner, Vixen, Fire, Ice. 8-Batwing joins; OMAC app. 3.00

Annual 1 (10/12, $4.99) Fabok-a/c; JLI vs. OMAC; Blue Beetle joins 5.00

JUSTICE LEAGUE OF AMERICA (See Brave & the Bold #28-30, Mystery In Space #75 & Official... Index) (See Crisis on Multiple Earths TPBs for reprints of JLA/JSA crossovers)
National Periodical Publ./DC Comics: Oct-Nov, 1960 - No. 261, Apr, 1987 (#91-99,139-157: 52 pgs.)

	GD 2.0	VG 4.0	FN 6.0	VF 8.0	VF/NM 9.0	NM- 9.2
1-(10-11/60)-Origin & 1st app. Despero; Aquaman, Batman, Flash, Green Lantern, J'onn J'onzz, Superman & Wonder Woman continue from Brave and the Bold	525	1050	2100	6300	16,150	26,000
2	114	228	342	912	2056	3200
3-Origin/1st app. Kanjar Ro (see Mystery in Space #75)(scarce in high grade due to black-c)	107	214	321	856	1928	3000
4-Green Arrow joins JLA	70	140	210	560	1255	1950
5-Origin & 1st app. Dr. Destiny	56	112	168	448	999	1550
6-8,10: 6-Origin & 1st app. Prof. Amos Fortune. 7-(10-11/61)-Last 10¢ issue. 10-(3/62)-Origin & 1st app. Felix Faust; 1st app. Lord of Time	43	86	129	318	722	1125
9-(2/62)-Origin JLA (1st origin)	50	100	150	390	870	1350
11-15: 12-(6/62)-Origin & 1st app. Dr. Light. 13-(8/62)-Speedy app. 14-(9/62)-Atom joins JLA.	28	56	84	196	428	660
16-20: 17-Adam Strange flashback	23	46	69	164	362	560
21-(8/63)-"Crisis on Earth-One"; re-intro. of JSA in this title (see Flash #129) (1st S.A. app. Hourman & Dr. Fate)	43	86	129	318	722	1125
22- "Crisis on Earth-Two"; JSA x-over (story continued from #21)	34	68	102	245	548	850
23-28: 24-Adam Strange app. 27-Robin app.	16	32	48	112	249	385
29-"Crisis on Earth-Three"; JSA x-over; 1st app. Crime Syndicate of America (Ultraman, Owlman, Superwoman, Power Ring, Johnny Quick); 1st S.A. app. Starman	22	44	66	154	340	525
30-JSA x-over; Crime Syndicate app.	19	38	57	131	291	450
31-Hawkman joins JLA, Hawkgirl cameo (11/64)	13	26	39	91	201	310
32,34: 32-Intro & Origin Brain Storm. 34-Joker-c/sty	10	20	30	69	147	225
33,35,36,40,41: 40-3rd S.A. Penguin app. 41-Intro & origin The Key	10	20	30	66	138	210
37-39: 37,38-JSA x-over. 37-1st S.A. app. Mr. Terrific; Batman cameo. 38-"Crisis on Earth-A". 39-Giant G-16; r/B&B #28,30 & JLA #5	12	24	36	81	176	270
42-45: 42-Metamorpho app. 43-Intro. Royal Flush Gang	8	16	24	56	108	160
46-JSA x-over; 1st S.A. app. Sandman; 3rd S.A. app. of G.A. Spectre (8/66)	12	24	36	82	179	275
47-JSA x-over; 4th S.A. app of G.A. Spectre.	10	20	30	64	132	200
48-Giant G-29; r/JLA #2,3 & B&B #29	9	18	27	58	114	170
49-54,57,59,60: 51-Zatanna app.	7	14	21	46	86	125

Justice League of America #195 © DC

Justice League of America #217 © DC

Justice League of America (2006 series) #41 © DC

	GD 2.0	VG 4.0	FN 6.0	VF 8.0	VF/NM 9.0	NM- 9.2
55-Intro. Earth 2 Robin (1st G.A. Robin in S.A.)	9	18	27	60	120	180
56-JLA vs. JSA (1st G.A. Wonder Woman in S.A.)	8	16	24	54	102	150
58-Giant G-41; r/JLA #6,8,1	8	16	24	52	99	145
61-63,66,68-72: 69-Wonder Woman quits. 71-Manhunter leaves. 72-Last 12¢ issue	5	10	15	35	63	90
64,65-JSA story. 64-(8/68)-Origin/1st app. S.A. Red Tornado	6	12	18	37	66	95
67-Giant G-53; r/JLA #4,14,31	7	14	21	48	89	130
73-1st S.A. app. of G.A. Superman	6	12	18	40	73	105
74-Black Canary joins; Larry Lance dies; 1st meeting of G.A. & S.A. Superman; Neal Adams-c	8	16	24	54	102	150
75-2nd app. Green Arrow in new costume (see Brave & the Bold #85)	15	30	45	103	227	350
76-Giant G-65	6	12	18	38	69	100
77-80: 78-Re-intro Vigilante (1st S.A. app?)	4	8	12	28	47	65
81-84,86-90: 82-1st S.A. app. of G.A. Batman (cameo). 83-Apparent death of The Spectre. 87-Zatanna app. 90-Last 15¢ issue	4	8	12	27	44	60
85,93-(Giant G-77,G-89; 68 pgs.)	5	10	15	31	53	75
91,92: 91-1st meeting of the G.A. & S.A. Robin; begin 25¢, 52 pgs. issues, ends #99. 92-S.A. Robin tries on costume that is similar to that of G.A. Robin in All Star Comics #58	4	8	12	28	47	65
94-1st app. Merlyn (Green Arrow villain); reprints 1st Sandman story (Adv. #40) & origin/1st app. Starman (Adv. #61); Deadman x-over; N. Adams-a (4 pgs.)	8	16	24	52	99	145
95,96: 95-Origin Dr. Fate & Dr. Midnight -r/ More Fun #67, All-American #25). 96-Origin Hourman (Adv. #48); Wildcat-r	5	10	15	30	50	70
97-99: 97-Origin JLA retold; Sargon, Starman-r. 98-G.A. Sargon, Starman-r. 99-G.A. Sandman, Atom-r; last 52 pg. issue	4	8	12	27	44	60
100-(8/72)-1st meeting of G.A. & S.A. W. Woman	6	12	18	37	66	95
101,102: JSA x-overs. 102-Red Tornado destroyed	4	8	12	27	44	60
103-106,109: 103-Rutland Vermont Halloween x-over; Phantom Stranger joins. 105-Elongated Man joins. 106-New Red Tornado joins. 109-Hawkman resigns	3	6	9	19	30	40
107,108-JSA x-over; 1st revival app. of G.A. Uncle Sam, Black Condor, The Ray, Dollman, Phantom Lady & The Human Bomb	4	8	12	23	37	50
110,112-116: All 100 pgs. 112-Amazo app; Crimson Avenger, Vigilante-r; origin Starman-r/ Adv. #81. 115-Martian Manhunter app.	5	10	15	31	53	75
111-JLA vs. Injustice Gang; intro. Libra (re-appears in 2008's Final Crisis); Shining Knight, Green Arrow-r	5	10	15	34	60	85
117-122,125-134: 117-Hawkman rejoins. 120,121-Adam Strange app. 125,126-Two-Face-app. 128-Wonder Woman rejoins. 129-Destruction of Red Tornado	3	6	9	16	23	30
123-(10/75),124: JLA/JSA x-over. DC editor Julie Schwartz & JLA writers Cary Bates & Elliot S! Maggin appear in story as themselves. 1st named app. Earth-Prime (3rd app. after Flash; 1st Series #179 & 228)	3	6	9	17	26	35
135-136: 135-137-G.A. Bulletman, Bulletgirl, Spy Smasher, Mr. Scarlet, Pinky & Ibis x-over, 1st appearances since G.A.	3	6	9	17	26	35
137-(12/76) Superman battles G.A. Captain Marvel	4	8	12	23	37	50
138-Adam Strange app. w/c by Neal Adams; 1st app. Green Lantern of the 73rd Century	3	6	9	19	30	40
139-157: 139-157-(52 pgs.): 139-Adam Strange app. 144-Origin retold; origin J'onn J'onzz. 145-Red Tornado resurrected. 147,148-Legion of Super-Heroes x-over	2	4	6	10	14	18
158-160-(44 pgs.)	2	4	6	8	11	14
158,160-162,169,171,172,173,176,179,181-(Whitman variants; low print run, none show issue # on cover)	2	4	6	10	14	18
161-165,169-182: 161-Zatanna joins & new costume. 171,172-JSA x-over. 171-Mr. Terrific murdered. 178-Cover similar to #1; J'onn J'onzz app. 179-Firestorm joins. 181-Green Arrow leaves JLA	1	2	3	5	6	8
166-168- "Identity Crisis (2004)" precursor; JSA app. vs. Secret Society of Super-Villains	3	6	9	16	23	30
166-168-Whitman variants (no issue # on covers)	4	8	12	23	37	50
183-185-JSA/New Gods/Darkseid/Mr. Miracle x-over	2	4	6	10	14	18
186-194,198,199: 192,193-Real origin Red Tornado. 193-1st app. All-Star Squadron as free 16 pg. insert						6.00
195-197-JSA app. vs. Secret Society of Super-Villains	1	2	3	5	6	8
200 ($1.50, Anniversary issue, 76 pgs.)-JLA origin retold; Green Arrow rejoins; Bolland, Aparo, Giordano, Gil Kane, Infantino, Kubert-a; Pérez-c/a	1	3	4	6	8	10
201-206,209-243,246-259: 203-Intro/origin new Royal Flush Gang. 219,220-True origin Black Canary. 228-Re-intro Martian Manhunter. 228-230-War of the Worlds storyline; JLA Satellite destroyed by Martians. 233-Story cont'd from Annual #2. 243-Aquaman leaves. 250-Batman rejoins. 253-Origin Despero. 258-Death of Vibe. 258-261-Legends x-over						5.00
207,208-JSA, JLA, & All-Star Squadron team-up	1	2	3	4	5	7
244,245-Crisis x-over						6.00
260-Death of Steel	1	2	3	4	5	7
261-Last issue	1	3	4	6	8	10
Annual 1-3 ('83-'85), 2-Intro new J.L.A. (Aquaman, Martian Manhunter, Steel, Gypsy, Vixen, Vibe, Elongated Man & Zatanna). 3-Crisis x-over						5.00
... Hereby Elects (2006, $14.99, TPB) reprints issues where new members joined; JLofA #4,75,105,106,146,161,173 &174; roster of various incarnations; Ordway-c						15.00

NOTE: ***Neal Adams*** *c-63, 66, 67, 70, 74, 79, 81, 82, 86-89, 91, 92, 94, 96-98, 138, 139.* ***M. Anderson*** *c-1-4, 6, 7, 10, 12-14.* ***Aparo*** *a-200.* ***Austin*** *a-200i.* ***Baily*** *a-96r.* ***Bolland*** *a-200.* ***Buckler*** *c-158, 163, 164.* ***Burnley*** *r-94, 98, 99.* ***Greene*** *a-46-61i, 64-73i, 110i(r).* ***Grell*** *c-117, 122.* ***Kaluta*** *c-154p.* ***Gil Kane*** *a-200.* ***Krigstein*** *a-96(r/Sensation #84).* ***Kubert*** *a-200; c-72, 73.* ***Nino*** *a-228i, 230i.* ***Orlando*** *c-151i.* ***Perez*** *a-184-186p, 192-197p, 200p; c-184p, 186, 192-195, 196p, 197p, 199, 200, 201p, 202, 203-205p, 207-209, 212-215, 217, 219, 220.* ***Reinman*** *r-97.* ***Roussos*** *a-62i.* ***Sekowsky*** *a-37, 38, 44-63p, 110-112p(r); c-46-48p, 51p.* ***Sekowsky/Anderson*** *c-5, 8, 9, 11, 15.* ***B. Smith*** *c-185i.* ***Starlin*** *c-178-180, 183, 185p.* ***Staton*** *a-244p; c-157p, 244p.* ***Toth*** *r-110.* ***Tuska*** *a-153, 228p, 241-243p. JSA x-overs-21, 22, 29, 30, 37, 38, 46, 47, 55, 56, 64, 65, 73, 74, 82, 83, 91, 92, 100, 101, 102, 107, 108, 110, 113, 115, 123, 124, 135-137, 147, 148, 159, 160, 171, 172, 183-185, 195-197, 207-209, 219, 220, 231, 232, 244.*

JUSTICE LEAGUE OF AMERICA
DC Comics: No. 0, Sept, 2006 - No. 60, Oct, 2011 ($2.99/$3.99)

	NM- 9.2
0-Meltzer-s; history of the JLA; art by various incl. Lee, Giordano, Benes; Turner-c	5.00
0-Variant-c by Campbell	15.00
1-($3.99) Two interlocking covers by Benes; Benes-a	5.00
1-Variant-c by Turner	8.00
1-RRP Edition; sideways composite of both Benes covers	50.00
1-Second printing; Benes cover image between black bars	4.00
2-5-($2.99) Turner-c	4.00
2-5: Variant-c: 2-Jimenez. 3-Sprouse. 4-JG Jones. 5-Art Adams	5.00
6,7-($3.50) 6-JLA vs. Amazo; covers by Turner and Hughes. 7-Roster picked, new HQs; two Benes covers and Turner cover.	4.00
8-11,13-24,26-38-($2.99) 8-11-JLA/JSA team-up; covers by Turner & Jimenez. 10-Wally West returns. 13-Two covers. 13-15-Injustice Gang. 16-Tangent Flash. 20-Queen Bee app. 21-Libra app.; leads into Final Crisis #1. 35,36-Royal Flush Gang app. 38-Bagley-a begins	3.00
12-($3.50) Two Ross covers; origin retold with Wight-a; Benes-a	4.00
25-($3.99) McDuffie-s/art by various; Benes-c	4.00
39-49,51,52-($3.99) 39,40-Blackest Night. 41-New team; 2 covers. 44-48-Justice Society app. 44-Jade returns.	4.00
50-($4.99) Crime Syndicate app.; Bagley-a; wraparound-c by Van Sciver	5.00
50-Variant-c by Bagley, swipe of Quitely's JLA: Earth 2 cover	8.00
50-Variant-c by Jim Lee; swipe of Brave and the Bold #28 Starro cover	120.00
53-60-($2.99) 54-Booth-a; Eclipso returns. 55-Doomsday app.	3.00
... 80 Page Giant (11/09, $5.99) Anacleto-c; short stories by various; Ra's al Ghul app.	6.00
... 80 Page Giant 2011 (6/11, $5.99) Lau-c; chapters by various; JLA goes to Hell	6.00
Free Comic Book Day giveaway - (2007) r/#0 with "Free Comic Book Day" banner on-c	3.00
Justice League Wedding Special 1 (11/07, $3.99) McKone-a; Injustice League forms	4.00
...: Dark Things HC (2011, $24.99, dustjacket) r/#44-48 & J.S.A. #41,42	25.00
...: The Injustice Gang HC (2008, $19.99, dustjacket) r/#13-16; Wedding Special	20.00
...: The Lightning Saga HC (2008, $24.99, dustjacket) r/#0,8-12 & Justice Society of America #5,6; intro. by Patton Oswalt	25.00
...: The Lightning Saga SC (2008, $17.99) r/#0,8-12 & J.S.A. #5,6; intro. by Oswalt	18.00
...: Sanctuary SC (2009, $14.99) r/#17-21	15.00
...: Second Coming HC (2009, $19.99, dustjacket) r/#22-26	20.00
...: Second Coming SC (2010, $17.99) r/#22-26	18.00
...: Team History HC (2010, $19.99, dustjacket) r/#38-43	20.00
...: The Tornado's Path HC (2007, $24.99, dustjacket) r/#1-7; variant cover gallery; Lindelof intro.; commentary by Meltzer & Benes	25.00
...: The Tornado's Path SC (2008, $17.99) r/#1-7; variant cover gallery; Lindelof intro.; commentary by Meltzer & Benes	18.00
...: When Worlds Collide HC (2009, $24.99, dustjacket) r/#27,28,30-34	25.00
...: When Worlds Collide SC (2010, $14.99) r/#27,28,30-34	15.00

JUSTICE LEAGUE OF AMERICA (DC New 52)(Leads into Justice League United)
DC Comics: Apr, 2013 - No. 14, Jul, 2014 ($3.99)

	NM- 9.2
1-Johns-s/Finch-a/c; Green Arrow, Catwoman, Martian Manhunter, Katana & others team; variants covers with U.S. flag and each of the 50 state flags plus DC and Puerto Rico	4.00
2-Covers by Finch and Ryp	4.00
3-7: 3-5-Martian Manhunter back-up. 4,5-Shaggy Man app. 6,7-Trinity War	4.00
7.1, 7.2, 7.3, 7.4 (11/13, $2.99, regular-c)	3.00
7.1 (11/13, $3.99, 3-D cover) "Deadshot #1" on cover; origin; Kindt-s/Daniel-c	5.00
7.2 (11/13, $3.99, 3-D cover) "Killer Frost #1" on cover; origin; Gates-s/Santacruz-a	5.00
7.3 (11/13, $3.99, 3-D cover) "Shadow Thief #1" on cover; origin; Hardin-a/Daniel-c	5.00
7.4 (11/13, $3.99, 3-D cover) "Black Adam #1" on cover; Black Adam returns	5.00
8-14-Forever Evil. 10-Stargirl origin. 11,12-Despero app.	4.00

JUSTICE LEAGUE OF AMERICA
DC Comics: Aug, 2015 - No. 10, Jan, 2017 ($5.99/$3.99)

Justice League of America (2017 series) #1 © DC

Justice League United #0 © DC

Justice Society of America #13 © DC

GD 2.0 | VG 4.0 | FN 6.0 | VF 8.0 | VF/NM 9.0 | NM- 9.2

GD 2.0 | VG 4.0 | FN 6.0 | VF 8.0 | VF/NM 9.0 | NM- 9.2

1-($5.99) Bryan Hitch-s/a; the Parasite app. 6.00
2-10-($3.99) 2-4-Hitch-s/a. 5-Martian Manhunter spotlight; Kindt & Williams-s/Tan-a 4.00

JUSTICE LEAGUE OF AMERICA (DC Rebirth)
DC Comics: Apr, 2017 - Present ($2.99)

1-Orlando-s/Reis-a; team of Batman, Black Canary, Lobo, Vixen, Killer Frost, The Atom & The Ray; Lord Havok app. 3.00
...: Killer Frost - Rebirth 1 (3/17, $2.99) Orlando-s/Andolfo-a; Amanda Waller app. 3.00
...: Rebirth 1 (4/17, $2.99) Orlando-s/Reis-a; team assembles 3.00
...: The Atom - Rebirth 1 (3/17, $2.99) Orlando-s; Ryan Choi as the new Atom 3.00
...: The Ray - Rebirth 1 (3/17, $2.99) Orlando-s; Stephen Byrne-a; origin 3.00
...: Vixen - Rebirth 1 (3/17, $2.99) Orlando & Houser-s; Jamal Campbell-a; origin retold 3.00

JUSTICE LEAGUE OF AMERICA : ANOTHER NAIL (Elseworlds) (Also see JLA: The Nail)
DC Comics: 2004 - No. 3, 2004 ($5.95, prestige format)

1-3-Sequel to JLA: The Nail; Alan Davis-s/a(p) 6.00
TPB (2004, $12.95) r/series 13.00

JUSTICE LEAGUE OF AMERICA SUPER SPECTACULAR
DC Comics: 1999 ($5.95, mimics format of DC 100 Page Super Spectaculars)

1-Reprints Silver Age JLA and Golden Age JSA 6.00

JUSTICE LEAGUE OF AMERICA'S VIBE (DC New 52)
DC Comics: Apr, 2013 - No. 10, Feb, 2014 ($2.99)

1-10: 1,2-Johns & Kreisberg-s/Woods-a/Finch-c; origin. 5-Suicide Squad app. 3.00

JUSTICE LEAGUE OF AMERICA/ THE 99
DC Comics: Dec, 2010 - No. 6, May, 2011 ($3.99/$2/99, limited series)

1-3-($3.99) Derenick-a/Massaferra-c; JLA meets Teshkeel Comics characters 4.00
4-6-($2.99) Starro app. 3.00

JUSTICE LEAGUE/ POWER RANGERS
DC Comics: Mar, 2017 - No. 6, ($3.99, limited series)

1,2-Tom Taylor-s/Stephen Byrne-a; Lord Zedd app.; Power Rangers in JLA dimension 4.00

JUSTICE LEAGUE QUARTERLY (...International Quarterly #6 on)
DC Comics: Winter, 1990-91 - No. 17, Winter, 1994 ($2.95/$3.50, 84 pgs.)

1-12,14-17: 1-Intro The Conglomerate (Booster Gold, Praxis, Gypsy, Vapor, Echo, Maxi-Man, & Reverb); Justice League #1-c/swipe. 1,2-Keith Giffen plots/breakdowns. 3-Giffen plot; 72 pg. story. 4-Rogers/Russell-a in back-up. 5,6-Mark Waid scripts. 8,17-Global Guardians app. 4.00
13-Linsner-c 6.00
NOTE: *Phil Jimenez a-17p. Sprouse a-1p.*

JUSTICE LEAGUE: RISE AND FALL
DC Comics: 2010, 2011

Justice League: The Rise and Fall Special #1 (5/10, $3.99) Hunt for Green Arrow 4.00
HC-(2011, $24.99) Reprints Justice League of America #43, Justice League: The Rise and Fall Special #1, Green Arrow #31,32 and Justice League: The Rise of Arsenal #1-4 25.00

JUSTICE LEAGUES...
DC Comics: Mar, 2001 ($2.50, limited series)

JL?, Justice League of Amazons, Justice League of Atlantis, Justice League of Arkham, Justice League of Aliens, JLA: JLA split by the Advance Man; Perez-c in all; s&a by various 3.00

JUSTICE LEAGUE TASK FORCE
DC Comics: June, 1993 - No. 37, Aug, 1996 ($1.25/$1.50/$1.75)

1-16,0,17-37: Aquaman, Nightwing, Flash, J'onn J'onzz, & Gypsy form team. 5,6-Knight-quest tie-ins (new Batman cameo #5, 1 pg.). 15-Triumph cameo. 16-(9/94)-Zero Hour x-over; Triumph app. 0-(10/94). 17-(11/94)-Triumph becomes part of Justice League Task Force (See JLE #68). 26-Impulse app. 35-Warlord app. 37-Triumph quits team 3.00

JUSTICE LEAGUE: THE NEW FRONTIER SPECIAL (Also see DC: The New Frontier)
DC Comics: May, 2008 ($4.99, one-shot)

1-Short stories by Darwyn Cooke, J. Bone and Dave Bullock; bonus storyboards from the movie 5.00

JUSTICE LEAGUE: THE RISE OF ARSENAL (Follows Justice League: Cry For Justice)
DC Comics: May, 2010 - No. 4, Aug, 2010 ($3.99, limited series)

1-4-Horn-c/Borges-a/Krul-s. 2,3-Cheshire app. 4.00

JUSTICE LEAGUE 3000
DC Comics: Feb, 2014 - No. 15, May, 2015 ($2.99)

1-15-Justice League of the 31st century. 1-Giffen & DeMatteis-s/Porter-a/c. 10-Etrigan app. 11-Blue Beetle and Booster Gold cameo. 12-14-Blue Beetle and Booster Gold app. 14-Kamandi app.; Kuhn-a 14,15-Etrigan app. 15-Fire returns 3.00

JUSTICE LEAGUE 3001
DC Comics: Aug, 2015 - No. 12, Jul, 2016 ($2.99)

1-12: 1-Giffen & DeMatteis-s/Porter-a/c; Supergirl app. 4-Kolins-a. 5,6-Harley Quinn app. 3.00

JUSTICE LEAGUE UNITED (DC New 52)
DC Comics: No. 0, Jun, 2014 - No. 16, Feb, 2016 ($3.99)

0-16: 0-Lemire-s/McKone-a; Adam Strange, Lobo & Byth app. 3-Hawkman killed. 6-10-Legion of Super-Heroes app. 11-13,15-Harris-c. 13-15-Sgt Rock app. 4.00
Annual #1 (12/14, $4.99) Legion of Super-Heroes app.; continued in #6 5.00
...: Futures End 1 (11/14, $2.99, reg-c) 5 years later; 2-parter with Justice League: FE #1 3.00
...: Futures End 1 (11/14, $3.99, 3-D cover) 4.00

JUSTICE LEAGUE UNLIMITED (Based on Cartoon Network animated series)
DC Comics: Nov, 2004 - No. 46, Aug, 2008 ($2.25)

1-46: 1-Zatanna app. 2,23,42-Royal Flush Gang app. 4-Adam Strange app. 10-Creeper app. 17-Freedom Fighters app. 18-Space Cabby app. 27-Black Lightning app. 34-Zod app. 41-Harley Quinn-c/app. 3.00
Free Comic Book Day giveaway (5/06) r/#1 with "Free Comic Book Day" banner on-c 3.00
Jam Packed Action (2005, $7.99, digest) adaptations of two TV episodes 8.00
... Vol. 1: United They Stand (2005, $6.99, digest) r/#1-5 7.00
... Vol. 2: World's Greatest Heroes (2006, $6.99, digest) r/#6-10 7.00
... Vol. 3: Champions of Justice (2006, $6.99, digest) r/#11-15 7.00
...: Heroes (2009, $12.99, full-size) r/#23-29 13.00
...: The Ties That Bind (2008, $12.99, full-size) r/#16-22 13.00

JUSTICE LEAGUE VS. SUICIDE SQUAD (Leads into Justice League of America '17 series)
DC Comics: Feb, 2017 - No. 6, Mar, 2017 ($3.99, weekly limited series)

1-6: 1-Max Lord & Lobo app.; Fabok-a. 2-Daniel-a. 4-6-Eclipso app. 6-Porter-a 4.00

JUSTICE MACHINE, THE
Noble Comics: June, 1981 - No. 5, Nov, 1983 ($2.00, nos. 1-3 are mag. size)

	GD	VG	FN	VF	VF/NM	NM-
1-Byrne-c(p)	3	6	9	15	21	26
2-Austin-c(i)	2	4	6	9	12	15
3	1	3	4	6	8	10

4,5, Annual 1: Ann. 1-(1/84, 68 pgs.)(published by Texas Comics); 1st app. The Elementals; Golden-c(p); new Thunder Agents story (43 pgs.) 6.00

JUSTICE MACHINE (Also see The New Justice Machine)
Comico/Innovation Publishing: Jan, 1987 - No. 29, May 1989 ($1.50/$1.75)

1-29 3.00
Annual 1(6/89, $2.50, 36 pgs.)-Last Comico ish. 3.00
Summer Spectacular 1 ('89, $2.75)-Innovation Publ.; Byrne/Gustovich-c 3.00

JUSTICE MACHINE, THE
Innovation Publishing: 1990 - No. 4, 1990 ($1.95/$2.25, deluxe format, mature)

1-4: Gustovich-c/a in all 3.00

JUSTICE MACHINE FEATURING THE ELEMENTALS
Comico: May, 1986 - No. 4, Aug, 1986 ($1.50, limited series)

1-4 3.00

JUSTICE RIDERS
DC Comics: 1997 ($5.95, one-shot, prestige format)

1-Elseworlds; Dixon-s/Williams & Gray-a 6.00

JUSTICE SOCIETY
DC Comics: 2006; 2007 ($14.99, TPB)

Vol. 1 - Rep. from 1976 revival in All Star Comics #58-67 & DC Special #29; Bolland-c 15.00
Vol. 2 - R/All Star Comics #68-74 & Adventure Comics #461-466; new Bolland-c 15.00

JUSTICE SOCIETY OF AMERICA (See Adventure #461 & All-Star #3)
DC Comics: April, 1991 - No. 8, Nov, 1991 ($1.00, limited series)

1-8: 1-Flash. 2-Black Canary. 3-Green Lantern. 4-Hawkman. 5-Flash/Hawkman. 6-Green Lantern/Black Canary. 7-JSA 3.00

JUSTICE SOCIETY OF AMERICA (Also see Last Days of the... Special)
DC Comics: Aug, 1992 - No. 10, May, 1993 ($1.25)

1-10: 1-1st app. Jesse Quick 3.00

JUSTICE SOCIETY OF AMERICA (Follows JSA series)
DC Comics: Feb, 2007 - No. 54, Oct, 2011 ($3.99/$2.99)

1-($3.99) New team selected; intro. Maxine Hunkle; Alex Ross-c 4.00
1-Variant-c by Eaglesham 6.00
2-22,24-49,51-54: 1-Covers by Ross & Eaglesham. 3,4-Vandal Savage app. 5,6-JLA/JSA team-up. 9-22-Kingdom Come Superman app.18-Magog app. 22-Superman returns to Kingdom Come Earth; Ross partial art. 23-25-Ordway-a. 26-Triptych cover by Ross. 33-Team splits. 34,35-Mordru app. 41,42-Justice League x-over. 52-54-Challengers of the Unknown app. 54-Darwyn Cooke-c 3.00
23-Black Adam-c/app. 6.00
50-($4.99) Degaton app.; art by Derenick, Chaykin, Williams II, and Pérez; Massafera-c 5.00

Just Image Stan Lee with Chris Bachalo Creating Catwoman #1 © DC

Ka'anga Comics #9 © FH

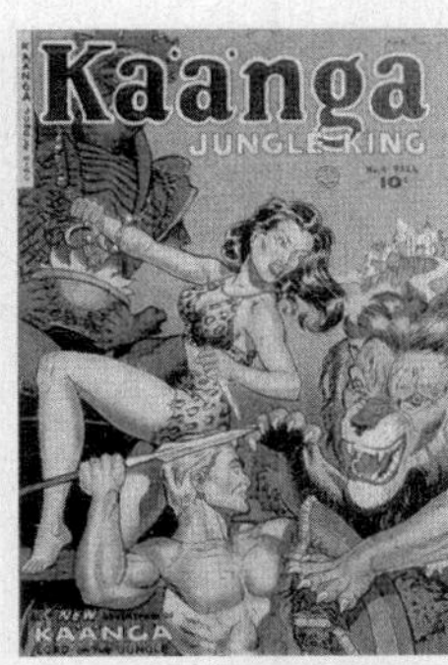

kaboom! Summer Blast FCBD 2013 © kaboom!

	GD 2.0	VG 4.0	FN 6.0	VF 8.0	VF/NM 9.0	NM- 9.2
JSA Annual 1 (9/08, $3.99) Power Girl on Earth-2; Ross-c/Ordway-a						5.00
JSA Annual 2 (4/10, $4.99) All Star team app.; Magog quits; Williams-a						5.00
... 80 Page Giant (1/10, $5.99) short stories by various incl. Ordway, S. Hampton						6.00
... 80 Page Giant 2010 (12/10, $5.99) short stories by various						6.00
... 80 Page Giant 2011 (8/11, $5.99) short stories by various incl. Chaykin, Hampton						6.00
... Special (11/10, $4.99) Scott Kolins-s/a; spotlight on Magog						5.00
...: Axis of Evil SC (2010, $14.99) r/#34-40						15.00
...: Black Adam and Isis HC (2009, $19.99, d.j.) r/#23-28						20.00
...: Black Adam and Isis SC (2010, $14.99) r/#23-28						15.00
... Kingdom Come Special: Magog (1/09, $3.99) Pasarin-a; origin re-told; 2 covers						4.00
... Kingdom Come Special: Superman (1/09, $3.99) Lois' death re-told; Alex Ross-s/a/c; thumbnails, photo references, sketch art						4.00
... Kingdom Come Special: Superman (1/09, $3.99) Eaglesham variant cover						8.00
... Kingdom Come Special: The Kingdom (1/09, $3.99) Pasarin-a; 2 covers						4.00
...: The Bad Seed SC (2010, $14.99) r/#29-33						15.00
...: The Next Age SC (2008, $14.99) r/#1-4; Ross and Eaglesham sketch pages						15.00
...: Thy Kingdom Come Part One HC (2008, $19.99, d.j.) r/#7-12; Ross sketch pages						20.00
...: Thy Kingdom Come Part One SC (2009, $14.99) r/#7-12; Ross sketch pages						15.00
...: Thy Kingdom Come Part Two HC (2008, $24.99, d.j.) r/#13-18 & Annual #1; Ross sketch pages						25.00
...: Thy Kingdom Come Part Two SC (2009, $19.99) r/#13-18 & Ann. #1; Ross sketch-a						20.00
...: Thy Kingdom Come Part Three HC (2009, $24.99, d.j.) r/#19-22 & K.C. Specials - Superman, Magog and The Kingdom; Ross sketch pages						25.00
...: Thy Kingdom Come Part Three SC (2010, $19.99) same contents as HC						20.00

JUSTICE SOCIETY OF AMERICA 100-PAGE SUPER SPECTACULAR
DC Comics: 2000 ($6.95, mimics format of DC 100 Page Super Spectaculars)

1-"1975 Issue" reprints Flash team-up and Golden Age JSA 7.00

JUSTICE SOCIETY RETURNS, THE (See All Star Comics (1999) for related titles)
DC Comics: 2003 ($19.95, TPB)

TPB-Reprints 1999 JSA x-over from All-Star Comics #1,2 and related one-shots 20.00

JUSTICE TRAPS THE GUILTY (Fargo Kid V11#3 on)
Prize/Headline Publications: Oct-Nov, 1947 - V11#2(#92), Apr-May, 1958 (True FBI Cases)

	GD 2.0	VG 4.0	FN 6.0	VF 8.0	VF/NM 9.0	NM- 9.2
V2#1-S&K-c/a; electrocution-c	68	136	204	435	743	1050
2-S&K-c/a	37	74	111	222	361	500
3-5-S&K-c/a	34	68	102	204	332	460
6-S&K-c/a; Feldstein-a	36	72	108	216	351	485
7,9-S&K-c/a. 7-9-V2#1-3 in indicia; #7-9 on-c	31	62	93	182	296	410
8-Krigstein-a; S&K-c; electric chair-c	28	56	84	165	270	375
10-Krigstein-a; S&K-c/a	31	62	93	182	296	410
11,18,19-S&K-c	18	36	54	103	162	220
12,14-17,20-No S&K. 14-Severin/Elder-a (8pg.)	12	24	36	67	94	120
13-Used in **SOTI**, pg. 110-111	14	28	42	78	112	145
21,30-S&K-c/a	18	36	54	107	169	230
22,23-S&K-c	14	28	42	81	118	155
24-26,27,29,31-50: 32-Meskin story	11	22	33	62	86	110
28-Kirby-c	14	28	42	76	108	140
51-55,57,59-70	10	20	30	56	76	95
56-Ben Oda, Joe Simon, Joe Genola, Mort Meskin & Jack Kirby app. in police line-up on classic-c	20	40	60	114	182	250
58-Illo. in **SOTI**, "Treating police contemptuously" (top left); text on heroin	28	56	84	165	270	375
71-92: 76-Orlando-a	9	18	27	47	61	75

NOTE: ***Bailey** a-12, 13. **Elder** a-8. **Kirby** a-19p. **Meskin** a-22, 27, 63, 64; c-45, 46. **Robinson/Meskin** a-5, 19. **Severin** a-8, 11p. Photo c-12, 15-17.*

JUST IMAGINE STAN LEE WITH... (Stan Lee re-invents DC icons)
DC Comics: 2001 - 2002 ($5.95, prestige format, one-shots)
(Adam Hughes back-c on all)(Michael Uslan back-up stories in all, diff. artists)

	NM- 9.2
Scott McDaniel Creating **Aquaman**- Back-up w/Fradon-a	6.00
Joe Kubert Creating **Batman**- Back-up w/Kaluta-a	6.00
Chris Bachalo Creating **Catwoman**- Back-up w/Cooke & Allred-a	6.00
John Cassaday Creating **Crisis**- no back-up story	6.00
Kevin Maguire Creating **The Flash**- Back-up w/Aragonés-a	6.00
Dave Gibbons Creating **Green Lantern**- Back-up w/Giordano-a	6.00
Jerry Ordway Creating **JLA**	6.00
John Byrne Creating **Robin**- Back-up w/John Severin-a	6.00
Walter Simonson Creating **Sandman**- Back-up w/Corben-a	6.00
Gary Frank Creating **Shazam!**- Back-up w/Kano-a	6.00
John Buscema Creating **Superman**- Back-up w/Kyle Baker-a	6.00
Jim Lee Creating **Wonder Woman**- Back-up w/Gene Colan-a	6.00
Secret Files and Origins #1 (3/02, $4.95) Crisis prologue; Jurgens-a	5.00
TPB -Just Imagine Stan Lee Creating the DC Universe: Book One (2002, $19.95) r/Batman, Wonder Woman, Superman, Green Lantern	20.00
TPB -Just Imagine Stan Lee Creating the DC Universe: Book Two (2003, $19.95) r/Flash, JLA, Secret Files and Origins, Robin, Shazam; sketch pages	20.00
TPB -Just Imagine Stan Lee Creating the DC Universe: Book Three (2004, $19.95) r/Aquaman, Catwoman, Sandman, Crisis; profile pages	20.00

JUST MARRIED
Charlton Comics: January, 1958 - No. 114, Dec, 1976

	GD 2.0	VG 4.0	FN 6.0	VF 8.0	VF/NM 9.0	NM- 9.2
1	5	10	15	35	63	90
2	3	6	9	21	33	45
3-10	3	6	9	17	26	35
11-30	3	6	9	14	20	26
31-50	2	4	6	11	16	20
51-70	2	4	6	9	13	16
71-78,80-89	2	4	6	8	11	14
79-Ditko-a (7 pages)	2	4	6	10	14	18
90-Susan Dey and David Cassidy full page poster	2	4	6	11	16	20
91-114	2	4	6	8	10	12

KA'A'NGA COMICS (...Jungle King)(See Jungle Comics)
Fiction House Magazines (Glen-Kel Publ. Co.): Spring, 1949 - No. 20, Summer, 1954

	GD 2.0	VG 4.0	FN 6.0	VF 8.0	VF/NM 9.0	NM- 9.2
1-Ka'a'nga, Lord of the Jungle begins	57	114	171	362	619	875
2 (Winter, '49-'50)	32	64	96	188	307	425
3,4	24	48	72	142	234	325
5-Camilla app.	22	44	66	132	216	300
6-10: 7-Tuska-a. 9-Tabu, Wizard of the Jungle app. 10-Used in **POP**, pg. 99	16	32	48	94	147	200
11-15: 15-Camilla-r by Baker/Jungle #106	14	28	42	80	115	150
16-Sheena app.	14	28	42	82	121	160
17-20	13	26	39	74	105	135
I.W. Reprint #1,8: 1-r/#18; Kinstler-c. 8-r/#10	3	6	9	14	20	25

NOTE: ***Celardo** c-1. **Whitman** c-8-20(most).*

KABOOM
Awesome Entertainment: Sept, 1997 - No. 3, Nov, 1997 ($2.50)

1-3: 1-Matsuda-a/Loeb-s; 4 covers exist (Matsuda, Sale, Pollina and McGuinness), 1-Dynamic Forces Edition, 2-Regular, 2-Alicia Watcher variant-c, 2-Gold logo variant-c, 3-Two covers by Liefeld & Matsuda, 3-Dynamic Forces Ed., Prelude Ed. 3.00
Prelude Gold Edition 4.00

KABOOM (2nd series)
Awesome Entertainment: July, 1999 - No. 3, Dec, 1999 ($2.50)

1-3: 1-Grant-a(p); at least 4 variant covers 3.00

KABOOM! SUMMER BLAST FREE COMIC BOOK DAY EDITION
Boom Entertainment (KaBOOM!): May 2013; May 2014 (free giveaways)

nn-(5/13) Short stories of Adventure Time, Regular Show, Herobear, Garfield, Peanuts 3.00
nn-(5/14) Adventure TIme, Regular Show, Steven Universe, Uncle Grandpa and others 3.00

KABUKI
Caliber: Nov, 1994 ($3.50, B&W, one-shot)

	GD 2.0	VG 4.0	FN 6.0	VF 8.0	VF/NM 9.0	NM- 9.2
nn-(Fear The Reaper) 1st app.; David Mack-c/a/s	1	2	3	5	6	8
Color Special (1/96, $2.95)-Mack-c/a/scripts; pin-ups by Tucci, Harris & Quesada						4.00
Gallery (8/95, $2.95)- pinups from Mack, Bradstreet, Paul Pope & others						3.00

KABUKI
Image Comics: Oct, 1997 - No. 9, Mar, 2000 ($2.95, color)

	GD 2.0	VG 4.0	FN 6.0	VF 8.0	VF/NM 9.0	NM- 9.2
1-David Mack-c/s/a						5.00
1-($10.00)-Dynamic Forces Edition	1	3	4	6	8	10
2-5						4.00
6-9						3.00
#1/2 (9/01, $2.95) r/Wizard 1/2; Eklipse Mag. article; bio						3.00
...Classics (2/99, $3.95) Reprints Fear the Reaper						4.00
...Classics 2 (3/99, $3.95) Reprints Dance of Dance						4.00
...Classics 3-5 (3-6/99, $4.95) Reprints Circle of Blood-Acts 1-3						5.00
...Classics 6-12 (7/99-3/00, $3.25) Various reprints						3.25
...Images (6/98, $4.95) r/#1 with new pin-ups						5.00
...Images 2 (1/99, $4.95) r/#1 with new pin-ups						5.00
...Metamorphosis TPB (10/00, $24.95) r/#1-9; Sienkiewicz intro.; 2nd printing exists						25.00
...Reflections 1-4 (7/98-5/02; $4.95) new story plus art techniques						5.00
... The Ghost Play (11/02, $2.95) new story plus interview						3.00

KABUKI
Marvel Comics (Icon): July, 2004 - Present ($2.99, color)

1-9: 1-David Mack-c/s/a in all; variant-c by Alex Maleev. 4-Variant-c by Adam Hughes. 6-Variant-c by Mignola. 8-Variant-c by Kent Williams. 9-Allred var-c 3.00
...: The Alchemy HC (2008, $29.99, dust jacket) oversized r/#1-9; bonus art & content 30.00
... Reflections 5-15 (7/05-10/09, $5.99) paintings & sketches of recent work; photos 6.00

Kabuki Agents (Scarab) #8 © David Mack

Kamandi Challenge #1 © DC

Katana #1 © DC

GD 2.0 | VG 4.0 | FN 6.0 | VF 8.0 | VF/NM 9.0 | NM- 9.2

GD 2.0 | VG 4.0 | FN 6.0 | VF 8.0 | VF/NM 9.0 | NM- 9.2

KABUKI AGENTS (SCARAB)
Image Comics: Aug, 1999 - No. 8, Aug, 2001 ($2.95, B&W)
1-8-David Mack-s/Rick Mays-a 3.00
Lost in Translation HC (3/02, $29.95) r/#1-8; intro. by Paul Pope 30.00
Lost in Translation SC (3/02, $19.95) r/#1-8; intro. by Paul Pope 20.00

KABUKI: CIRCLE OF BLOOD
Caliber Press: Jan, 1995 - No. 6, Nov, 1995 ($2.95, B&W)
1-David Mack story/a in all 5.00
2-6: 3-#1 on inside indicia. 3.00
6-Variant-c 3.00
TPB ($16.95) r/#1-6, intro. by Steranko 17.00
TPB (1997, $17.95) Image Edition-r/#1-6, intro. by Steranko 18.00
TPB ($24.95) Deluxe Edition 25.00

KABUKI: DANCE OF DEATH
London Night Studios: Jan, 1995 ($3.00, B&W, one-shot)
1-David Mack-c/a/scripts 1 2 3 5 6 8

KABUKI: DREAMS
Image Comics: Jan, 1998 ($4.95, TPB)
nn-Reprints Color Special & Dreams of the Dead 5.00

KABUKI: DREAMS OF THE DEAD
Caliber: July, 1996 ($2.95, one-shot)
nn-David Mack-c/a/scripts 3.00

KABUKI FAN EDITION
Gemstone Publ./Caliber: Feb, 1997 (mail-in offer, one-shot)
nn-David Mack-c/a/scripts 4.00

KABUKI: MASKS OF THE NOH
Caliber: May, 1996 - No. 4, Feb, 1997 ($2.95, limited series)
1-4: 1-Three-c (1A-Quesada, 1B-Buzz, &1C-Mack). 3-Terry Moore pin-up 3.00
TPB-(4/98, $10.95) r/#1-4; intro by Terry Moore 11.00

KABUKI: SKIN DEEP
Caliber Comics: Oct, 1996 - No. 3, May, 1997 ($2.95)
1-3:David Mack-c/a/scripts. 2-Two-c (1-Mack, 1-Ross) 3.00
TPB-(5/98, $9.95) r/#1-3; intro by Alex Ross 10.00

KAMANDI: AT EARTH'S END
DC Comics: June, 1993 - No. 6, Nov, 1993 ($1.75, limited series)
1-6: Elseworlds storyline 3.00

KAMANDI CHALLENGE, THE (Commemoration for Jack Kirby's 100th birthday)
DC Comics: Mar, 2017 - No. 12 ($4.99/$3.99, limited series)
1-($4.99) DiDio-s/Giffen-a; Abnett-s/Eaglesham-a; Timm-c 5.00
2-($3.99) Neal Adams-a; Tomasi-s; covers by Adams & Rocafort 4.00
... Special 1 (3/17, $7.99) r/#1,32 and unpubl'd #60,61 from Cancelled Comic Cavalcade 8.00

KAMANDI, THE LAST BOY ON EARTH (Also see Alarming Tales #1, Brave and the Bold #120 & 157, Cancelled Comic Cavalcade & Wednesday Comics)
National Periodical Publ./DC Comics: Oct-Nov, 1972 - No. 59, Sept-Oct, 1978
1-Origin & 1st app. Kamandi; intro Ben Boxer 7 14 21 46 86 125
2,3 4 8 12 28 47 65
4,5: 4-Intro. Prince Tuftan of the Tigers 4 8 12 25 40 55
6-10 3 6 9 18 28 38
11-20 3 6 9 15 22 28
21-28,30,31,33-40: 24-Last 20¢ issue. 31-Intro Pyra. 2 4 6 13 18 22
29,32: 29-Superman x-over. 32-(68 pgs.)-r/origin from #1 plus one new story; 4 pg. biog. of Jack Kirby with B&W photos 3 6 9 14 20 26
41-57 2 4 6 10 14 18
58-Karate Kid x-over from LSH (see Karate Kid #15) 3 6 9 14 19 24
59-(44 pgs.)-Story cont'd in Brave and the Bold #157; The Return of Omac back-up by Starlin-c/a(p) 3 6 9 16 23 30
NOTE: ***Ayers** a(p)-48-59 (most). **Giffen** a-44p, 45p. **Kirby** a-1-40p; c-1-33. **Kubert** c-34-41. **Nasser** a-45p, 46p. **Starlin** a-59p; c-57, 59p.*

KAMUI (Legend Of...#2 on)
Eclipse Comics/Viz Comics: May 12, 1987 - No. 37, Nov. 15, 1988 ($1.50, B&W, bi-weekly)
1-37: 1-3 have 2nd printings 3.00

KANAN - THE LAST PADAWAN (Star Wars)
Marvel Comics: Jun, 2015 - No. 12, May, 2016 ($3.99)
1-12: 1-Weisman-s/Larraz-a; takes place after Episode 3; flashbacks to the Clone Wars. 9-11-General Grievous app. 4.00

KANE & LYNCH (Based on the video games)
DC Comics (WildStorm): Oct, 2010 - No. 6, Apr, 2011 ($3.99/$2.99, limited series)
1-4-($3.99) Templesmith-c/Edginton-s/Mitten-a 4.00
5,6-($2.99) 3.00
TPB (2011, $17.99) r/#1-6; cover gallery 18.00

KAOS MOON (Also see Negative Burn #34)
Caliber Comics: 1996 - No. 4, 1997 ($2.95, B&W)
1-4-David Boller-s/a 3.00
3,4-Limited Alternate-c 4.00
3,4-Gold Alternate-c, Full Circle TPB ($5.95) r/#1,2 6.00

KAPTARA
Image Comics: Apr, 2015 - No. 5, Nov, 2015 ($3.50)
1-5-Chip Zdarsky-s/Kagan McLeod-a 3.50

KARATE KID (See Action, Adventure, Legion of Super-Heroes, & Superboy)
National Periodical Publications/DC Comics: Mar-Apr, 1976 - No. 15, July-Aug, 1978 (Legion of Super-Heroes spin-off)
1-Meets Iris Jacobs; Estrada/Staton-a 3 6 9 17 26 35
2-14: 2-Major Disaster app. 14-Robin x-over 2 3 4 6 8 10
15-Continued into Kamandi #58 2 4 6 11 16 20
NOTE: ***Grell** c-1-4, 7, 8, 5p, 6p, **Staton** a-1-9i. Legion x-over-No. 1, 2, 4, 6, 10, 12, 13. Princess Projectra x-over-#8, 9.*

KARNAK (Inhumans)
Marvel Comics: Dec, 2015 - No. 6, Apr, 2017 ($3.99)
1-6: 1,2-Warren Ellis-s/Gerardo Zaffino-a. 3-6-Roland Boschi-a 4.00

KATANA (DC New 52) (From Justice League Of America 2013 series)
DC Comics: Apr, 2013 - No. 10, Feb, 2014 ($2.99)
1-10: 1,2-Nocenti-s/Sanchez-a/Finch-c; origin. 2-Steve Trevor app. 3-6-Creeper app. 3.00

KATHY
Standard Comics: Sept, 1949 - No. 17, Sept, 1955
1-Teen-age 19 38 57 111 176 240
2-Schomburg-c 14 28 42 82 121 160
3-5 11 22 33 62 86 110
6-17: 17-Code approved 10 20 30 56 76 95

KATHY (The Teenage Tornado)
Atlas Comics/Marvel (ZPC): Oct, 1959 - No. 27, Feb, 1964 (most issues contain paper dolls and pin-up pages)
1-The Teen-age Tornado; Goldberg-c/a in all 22 44 66 132 216 300
2 15 30 45 83 124 165
3-15 14 28 42 80 115 150
16-23,25,27 12 24 36 67 94 120
24-(8/63) Frank Sinatra, Cary Grant, Ed Sullivan & Liz Taylor-c 16 32 48 94 147 200
26-(12/63) Kathy becomes a model; Millie app. 13 26 39 74 105 135

KAT KARSON
I. W. Enterprises: No date (Reprint)
1-Funny animals 2 4 6 10 12 15

KATO (Also see The Green Hornet)
Dynamite Entertainment: 2010 - No. 14, 2011 ($3.99)
1-14: 1-Kato and daughter origin; Garza-a/Parks-s. 2-10 Bernard-a 4.00
Annual 1 (2011, $4.99) Parks-s/Salazar-a 5.00

KATO OF THE GREEN HORNET (Also see The Green Hornet)
Now Comics: Nov, 1991 - No. 4, Feb, 1992 ($2.50, mini-series)
1-4: Brent Anderson-c/a 3.00

KATO OF THE GREEN HORNET II (Also see The Green Hornet)
Now Comics: Nov, 1992 - No. 2, Dec, 1993 ($2.50, mini-series)
1,2-Baron-s/Mayerik & Sherman-a 3.00

KATO ORIGINS (Also see The Green Hornet: Year One)
Dynamite Entertainment: 2010 - No. 11, 2011 ($3.99)
1-11-Kato in 1942; Jai Nitz-s/Colton Worley-a; covers by Worley & Francavilla 4.00

KATY KEENE (Also see Kasco Komics, Laugh, Pep, Suzie, & Wilbur)
Archie Publ./Close-Up/Radio Comics: 1949 - No. 4, 1951; No. 5, 3/52 - No. 62, Oct, 1961 (50-53-Adventures of...on-c) (Cut and missing pages are common)
1-Bill Woggon-c/a begins; swipes-c to Mopsy #1 213 426 639 1363 2332 3300
2-(1950) 68 136 204 435 743 1050
3-5: 3-(1951). 4-(1951). 5-(3/52) 53 106 159 334 567 800
6-10 39 78 117 240 395 550
11,13-21: 21-Last pre-code issue (3/55) 33 66 99 194 317 440
12-(Scarce) 39 78 117 240 395 550

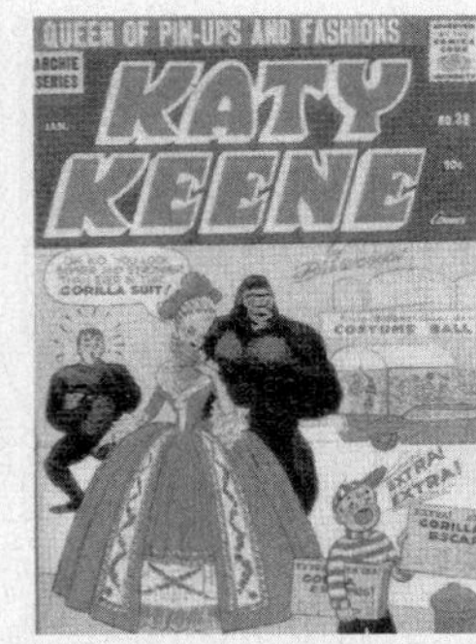

Katy Keene #38 © ACP

Ka-Zar V2 #16 © MAR

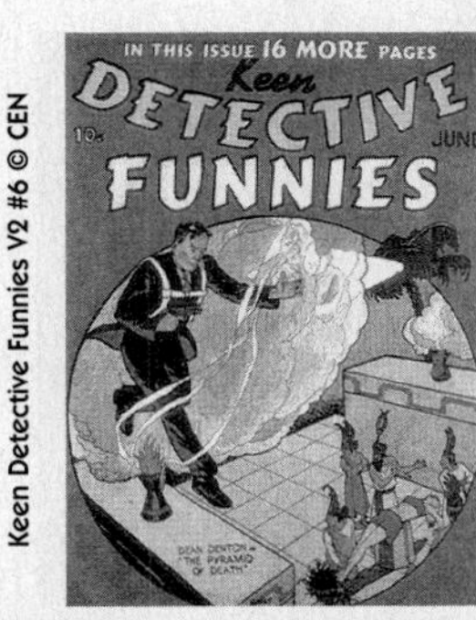

Keen Detective Funnies V2 #6 © CEN

	GD 2.0	VG 4.0	FN 6.0	VF 8.0	VF/NM 9.0	NM- 9.2
22-40	23	46	69	136	223	310
41-60: 54-Wedding Album plus wedding pin-up	19	38	57	109	172	235
61-Sci-fi-c	22	44	66	132	216	300
62-Classic Robot-c	34	68	102	199	325	450
Annual 1('54, 25¢)-All new stories; last pre-code	55	110	165	352	601	850
Annual 2-6('55-59, 25¢)-All new stories	32	64	96	188	307	425
3-D 1(1953, 25¢, large size)-Came w/glasses	39	78	117	231	378	525
Charm 1(9/58)-Woggon-c/a; new stories, and cut-outs	29	58	87	170	278	385
Glamour 1(1957)-Puzzles, games, cut-outs	29	58	87	170	278	385
Spectacular 1('56)	30	60	90	177	289	400

NOTE: *Debby's Diary in #45, 47-49, 52, 57.*

KATY KEENE COMICS DIGEST MAGAZINE
Close-Up, Inc. (Archie Ent.): 1987 - No. 10, July, 1990 ($1.25/$1.35/$1.50, digest size)

	GD 2.0	VG 4.0	FN 6.0	VF 8.0	VF/NM 9.0	NM- 9.2
1	2	4	6	10	14	18
2-10	1	3	4	6	8	10

NOTE: *Many used copies are cut-up inside.*

KATY KEENE FASHION BOOK MAGAZINE
Radio Comics/Archie Publications: 1955 - No. 13, Sum, '56 - N. 23, Wint, '58-59 (nn 3-10) (no #11,12)

	GD 2.0	VG 4.0	FN 6.0	VF 8.0	VF/NM 9.0	NM- 9.2
1-Bill Woggon-c/a	54	108	162	343	574	825
2	31	62	93	182	296	410
13-18: 18-Photo Bill Woggon	23	46	69	136	223	310
19-23	20	40	60	114	182	250

KATY KEENE HOLIDAY FUN (See Archie Giant Series Magazine No. 7, 12)

KATY KEENE MODEL BEHAVIOR
Archie Comic Publications: 2008 ($10.95, TPB)

	GD 2.0	VG 4.0	FN 6.0	VF 8.0	VF/NM 9.0	NM- 9.2
Vol. 1 - New story and reprinted apps./pin-ups from Archie & Friends #101-112						11.00

KATY KEENE PINUP PARADE
Radio Comics/Archie Publications: 1955 - No. 15, Summer, 1961 (25¢)
(Cut-out & missing pages are common)

	GD 2.0	VG 4.0	FN 6.0	VF 8.0	VF/NM 9.0	NM- 9.2
1-Cut-outs in all?; last pre-code issue	54	108	162	343	574	825
2-(1956)	31	62	93	182	296	410
3-5: 3-(1957). 5-(1959)	26	52	78	154	252	350
6-10,12-14: 8-Mad parody. 10-Bill Woggon photo	22	44	66	128	209	290
11-Story of how comics get CCA approved, narrated by Katy	27	54	81	158	259	360
15(Rare)-Photo artist & family	41	82	123	251	418	585

KATY KEENE SPECIAL (Katy Keene #7 on; see Laugh Comics Digest)
Archie Ent.: Sept, 1983 - No. 33, 1990 (Later issues published quarterly)

	GD 2.0	VG 4.0	FN 6.0	VF 8.0	VF/NM 9.0	NM- 9.2
1-10: 1-Woggon-r; new Woggon-c. 3-Woggon-r						5.00
11-25: 12-Spider-Man parody						6.00
26-32-(Low print run)	1	2	3	5	7	9
33	2	4	6	8	10	12

KATZENJAMMER KIDS, THE (See Captain & the Kids & Giant Comic Album)
David McKay Publ./Standard No. 12-21(Spring/'50 - 53)/Harvey No. 22, 4/53 on: 1945-1946; Summer, 1947 - No. 27, Feb-Mar, 1954

	GD 2.0	VG 4.0	FN 6.0	VF 8.0	VF/NM 9.0	NM- 9.2
Feature Books 30	21	42	63	122	199	275
Feature Books 32,35('45),41,44('46)	19	38	57	109	172	235
Feature Book 37-Has photos & biography of Harold Knerr	20	40	60	114	182	250
1(1947)-All new stories begin	20	40	60	114	182	250
2-5	12	24	36	69	97	125
6-11	10	20	30	56	76	95
12-14(Standard)	9	18	27	47	61	75
15-21(Standard)	8	16	24	44	57	70
22-25,27(Harvey): 22-24-Henry app.	7	14	21	35	43	50
26-Half in 3-D	16	32	48	94	147	200

KAYO (Formerly Bullseye & Jest; becomes Carnival Comics)
Harry 'A' Chesler: No. 12, Mar, 1945

	GD 2.0	VG 4.0	FN 6.0	VF 8.0	VF/NM 9.0	NM- 9.2
12-Green Knight, Capt. Glory, Little Nemo (not by McCay)	22	44	66	132	216	300

KA-ZAR (Also see Marvel Comics #1, Savage Tales #6 & X-Men #10)
Marvel Comics Group: Aug, 1970 - No. 3, Mar, 1971 (Giant-Size, 68 pgs.)

	GD 2.0	VG 4.0	FN 6.0	VF 8.0	VF/NM 9.0	NM- 9.2
1-Reprints earlier Ka-Zar stories; Avengers x-over in Hercules; Daredevil, X-Men app.; hidden profanity-c	4	8	12	27	44	60
2,3-Daredevil-r. 2-r/Daredevil #13 w/Kirby layouts; Ka-Zar origin, Angel-r from X-Men by Tuska. 3-Romita & Heck-a (no Kirby)	3	6	9	17	26	35

NOTE: ***Buscema** r-2. **Colan** a-1p(r). **Kirby** c/a-1, 2. #1-Reprints X-Men #10 & Daredevil #24.*

KA-ZAR
Marvel Comics Group: Jan, 1974 - No. 20, Feb, 1977 (Regular Size)

	GD 2.0	VG 4.0	FN 6.0	VF 8.0	VF/NM 9.0	NM- 9.2
1	3	6	9	14	19	24
2-10	2	4	6	8	10	12
11-14,16,18-20: 16-Only a 30 ¢ edition exists	1	2	3	5	6	8
15,17-(Regular 25¢ edition)(8/76)	1	2	3	5	6	8
15,17-(30¢-c variants, limited distribution)	3	6	9	17	26	35

NOTE: ***Alcala** a-6i, 8i. **Brunner** c-4. **J. Buscema** a-6-10p; c-1, 5, 7. **Heath** a-12. **G. Kane** c(p)-3, 5, 8-11, 15, 20. **Kirby** c-12p. **Reinman** a-1p.*

KA-ZAR (Volume 2)
Marvel Comics: May, 1997 - No. 20, Dec, 1998 ($1.95/$1.99)

	GD 2.0	VG 4.0	FN 6.0	VF 8.0	VF/NM 9.0	NM- 9.2
1-Waid-s/Andy Kubert-c/a. thru #4						4.00
1-2nd printing; new cover						3.00
2,4: 2-Two-c						3.00
3-Alpha Flight #1 preview						4.00
5-13,15-20: 8-Includes Spider-Man Cybercomic CD-ROM. 9-11-Thanos app. 15-Priest-s/Martinez & Rodriguez-a begin; Punisher app.						3.00
14-($2.99) Last Waid/Kubert issue; flip book with 2nd story previewing new creative team of Priest-s/Martinez & Rodriguez-a						4.00
'97 Annual ($2.99)-Wraparound-c						4.00

KA-ZAR
Marvel Comics: Aug, 2011 - No. 5, Dec, 2011 ($2.99, limited series)

	GD 2.0	VG 4.0	FN 6.0	VF 8.0	VF/NM 9.0	NM- 9.2
1-5-Jenkins-s/Alixe-a/c						3.00

KA-ZAR OF THE SAVAGE LAND
Marvel Comics: Feb, 1997 ($2.50, one-shot)

	GD 2.0	VG 4.0	FN 6.0	VF 8.0	VF/NM 9.0	NM- 9.2
1-Wraparound-c						4.00

KA-ZAR: SIBLING RIVALRY
Marvel Comics: July, 1997 ($1.95, one-shot)

	GD 2.0	VG 4.0	FN 6.0	VF 8.0	VF/NM 9.0	NM- 9.2
(# -1) Flashback story w/Alpha Flight #1 preview						3.00

KA-ZAR THE SAVAGE (See Marvel Fanfare)
Marvel Comics Group: Apr, 1981 - No. 34, Oct, 1984 (Regular size)(Mando paper #10 on)

	GD 2.0	VG 4.0	FN 6.0	VF 8.0	VF/NM 9.0	NM- 9.2
1						5.00
2-20,24,27,28,30-34: 11-Origin Zabu. 12-One of two versions with panel missing on pg. 10. 20-Kraven the Hunter-c/story (also apps. in #21)						3.00
12-Version with panel on pg. 10 (1600 printed)	1	2	3	5	6	8
21-23, 25,26-Spider-Man app. 26-Photo-c.						4.00
29-Double size; Ka-Zar & Shanna wed						4.00

NOTE: ***B. Anderson** a-1-15p, 18, 19; c-1-17, 18p, 20(back). **G. Kane** a(back-up)-11, 12, 14.*

KEEN DETECTIVE FUNNIES (Formerly Detective Picture Stories?)
Centaur Publications: No. 8, July, 1938 - No. 24, Sept, 1940

	GD 2.0	VG 4.0	FN 6.0	VF 8.0	VF/NM 9.0	NM- 9.2
V1#8-The Clock continues-r/Funny Picture Stories #1; Roy Crane-a (1st?)	343	686	1029	2400	4200	6000
9-Tex Martin by Eisner; The Gang Buster app.	258	516	774	1651	2826	4000
10,11: 11-Dean Denton story (begins?)	226	452	678	1446	2473	3500
V2#1,2-The Eye Sees by Frank Thomas begins; ends #23(Not in V2#3&5). 2-Jack Cole-a	135	270	405	864	1482	2100
3-6: 3-TNT Todd begins. 4-Gabby Flynn begins. 5,6-Dean Denton story	129	258	387	826	1413	2000
7-The Masked Marvel by Ben Thompson begins (7/39, 1st app.)(scarce)	300	600	900	1950	3375	4800
8-Nudist ranch panel w/four girls	135	270	405	864	1482	2100
9-11	116	232	348	742	1271	1800
12(12/39)-Origin The Eye Sees by Frank Thomas; death of Masked Marvel's sidekick ZL	142	284	426	909	1555	2200
V3#1	113	226	339	718	1234	1750
18-Bondage/torture-c	148	296	444	947	1624	2300
19,21,22	113	226	339	718	1234	1750
20-Classic Eye Sees-c by Thomas	226	452	678	1446	2473	3500
23-Air Man begins (intro); Air Man-c	155	310	465	992	1696	2400
24-(scarce) Air Man-c	161	322	483	1030	1765	2500

NOTE: ***Burgos** a-V2#2. **Jack Cole** a-V2#2. **Eisner** a-10, V2#6r. **Ken Ernst** a-V2#4-7, 9, 10, 19, 21; c-V2#4. **Everett** a-V2#6, 7, 9, 11, 12, 20. **Guardineer** a-V2#5, 66. **Gustavson** a-V2#4-6. **Simon** c-V3#1. **Thompson** c-V2#7, 9, 10, 22.*

KEEN KOMICS
Centaur Publications: V2#1, May, 1939 - V2#3, Nov, 1939

	GD 2.0	VG 4.0	FN 6.0	VF 8.0	VF/NM 9.0	NM- 9.2
V2#1(Large size)-Dan Hastings (s/f), The Big Top, Bob Phantom the Magician, The Mad Goddess app.	226	452	678	1446	2473	3500
V2#2(Reg. size)-The Forbidden Idol of Machu Picchu; Cut Carson by Burgos begins	97	194	291	621	1061	1500
V2#3-Saddle Sniffl by Jack Cole, Circus Pays, Kings Revenge app.						

Ken Shannon #7 © QUA

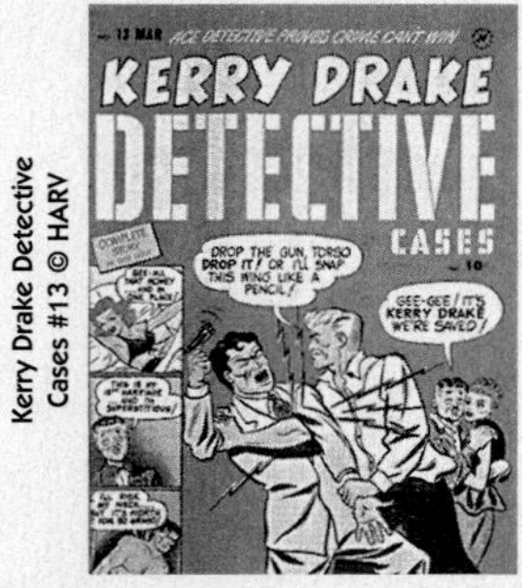

Kerry Drake Detective Cases #13 © HARV

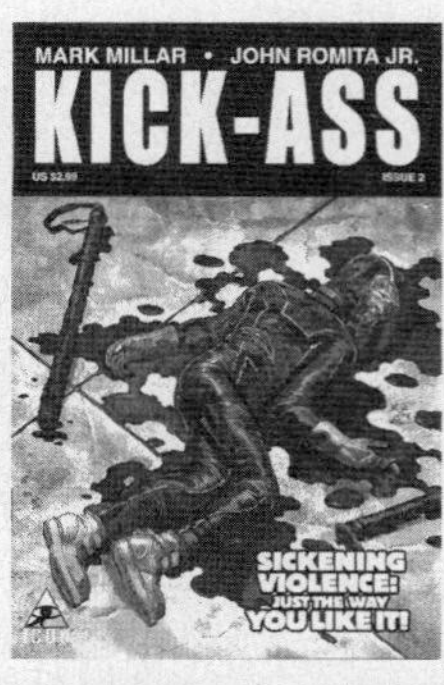

Kick-Ass #2 © MM & JR,Jr.

	GD 2.0	VG 4.0	FN 6.0	VF 8.0	VF/NM 9.0	NM- 9.2

84 168 252 538 919 1300
NOTE: *Binder a-V2#2. Burgos a-V2#2, 3. Ken Ernst a-V2#3. Gustavson a-V2#2. Jack Cole a-V2#3.*

KEEN TEENS (Girls magazine)
Life's Romances Publ./Leader/Magazine Ent.: 1945; nn, 1946; No. 3, Feb-Mar, 1947 - No. 6, Aug-Sept, 1947
nn (#1)-14 pgs. Claire Voyant (cont'd. in other nn issue) movie photos, Dotty Dripple, Gertie O'Grady & Sissy; Van Johnson, Sinatra photo-c 45 90 135 284 480 675
nn (#2, 1946)-16 pgs. Claire Voyant & 16 pgs. movie photos 34 68 102 199 325 450
3-6: 4-Glenn Ford photo-c. 5-Perry Como-c 17 34 51 98 154 210

KELLYS, THE (Formerly Rusty Comics; Spy Cases No. 26 on)
Marvel Comics (HPC): No. 23, Jan, 1950 - No. 25, June, 1950 (52 pgs.)
23-Teenage 16 32 48 94 147 200
24,25: 24-Margie app. 12 24 36 67 94 120

KEN MAYNARD WESTERN (Movie star)(See Wow Comics, 1936)
Fawcett Publ.: Sept, 1950 - No. 8, Feb, 1952 (All 36 pgs; photo front/back-c)
1-Ken Maynard & his horse Tarzan begin 28 56 84 165 270 375
2 17 34 51 98 154 210
3-8: 6-Atomic bomb explosion panel 14 28 42 76 108 140

KENNEL BLOCK BLUES
BOOM! Studios: Feb, 2016 - No. 4, May, 2016 ($3.99, limited series)
1-4-Ryan Ferrier-s/Daniel Bayliss-a 4.00

KEN SHANNON (Becomes Gabby #11 on) (Also see Police Comics #103)
Quality Comics Group: Oct, 1951 - No. 10, Apr, 1953 (A private eye)
1-Crandall-a 45 90 135 284 480 675
2-Crandall c/a(2) 40 80 120 244 355 465
3-Horror-c; Crandall-a 39 78 117 240 395 550
4,5-Crandall-a 26 52 78 154 252 350
6-Crandall-c/a; "The Weird Vampire Mob"-c/s 41 82 123 256 428 600
7-"The Ugliest Man Alive"-c; Crandall-a 37 74 111 222 361 500
8,9: 8-Opium den drug use story 22 44 66 128 209 290
10-Crandall-c 22 44 66 132 216 300
NOTE: *Crandall/Cuidera c-1-10. Jack Cole a-1-9. #1-15 published after title change to Gabby.*

KEN STUART
Publication Enterprises: Jan, 1949 (Sea Adventures)
1-Frank Borth-c/a 11 22 33 62 86 110

KENT BLAKE OF THE SECRET SERVICE (Spy)
Marvel/Atlas Comics (20CC): May, 1951 - No. 14, July, 1953
1-Injury to eye, bondage, torture; Brodsky-c 27 54 81 158 259 360
2-Drug use w/hypo scenes; Brodsky-c 18 36 54 105 165 225
3-14: 8-R.Q. Sale-a (2 pgs.) 13 26 39 74 105 135
NOTE: *Heath c-5, 7, 8. Infantino c-12. Maneely c-3. Sinnott a-2(3). Tuska a-8(3pg.).*

KENTS, THE
DC Comics: Aug, 1997 - No. 12, July, 1998 ($2.50, limited series)
1-12-Ostrander-s/art by Truman and Bair (#1-8), Mandrake (#9-12) 3.00
TPB ($19.95) r/#1-12 20.00

KERRY DRAKE (Also see A-1 Comics)
Argo: Jan, 1956 - No. 2, March, 1956
1,2-Newspaper-r 8 16 24 44 57 70

KERRY DRAKE DETECTIVE CASES (...Racket Buster No. 32,33)
(Also see Chamber of Clues & Green Hornet Comics #42-47)
Life's Romances/Com/Magazine Ent. No.1-5/Harvey No.6 on: 1944 - No. 5, 1944; No. 6, Jan, 1948 - No. 33, Aug, 1952
nn(1944)(A-1 Comics)(slightly over-size) 31 62 93 186 303 420
2 19 38 57 111 176 240
3-5(1944) 15 30 45 90 140 190
6,8(1948): Lady Crime by Powell. 8-Bondage-c 12 24 36 67 94 120
7-Kubert-a; biog of Andriola (artist) 13 26 39 74 105 135
9,10-Two-part marijuana story; Kerry smokes marijuana in #10 15 30 45 88 137 185
11-15 10 20 30 58 79 100
16-33 9 18 27 50 65 80
NOTE: *Andiola c-6-9. Berg a-5. Powell a-10-23, 28, 29.*

KEVIN KELLER (Also see Veronica #202 for 1st app. & #207-210 for first mini-series)
Archie Comics Publications: Apr, 2012 - No. 15, Nov, 2014 ($2.99)
1-14-Two covers on each. 5-Action #1 swipe-c. 6-George Takei app. 3.00
15-($3.99) The Equalizer app.; 3 covers incl. Sensation #1 and X-Men #141 swipes 4.00

KEWPIES
Will Eisner Publications: Spring, 1949
1-Feiffer-a; Kewpie Doll ad on back cover; used in **SOTI**, pg. 35 58 116 174 371 636 900

KEY COMICS
Consolidated Magazines: Jan, 1944 - No. 5, Aug, 1946
1-The Key, Will-O-The-Wisp begin 48 96 144 302 514 725
2 (3/44) 27 54 81 158 259 360
3,4: 3 (Winter 45/46). 4-(5/46)-Origin John Quincy The Atom (begins); Walter Johnson c-3-5 23 46 69 136 223 310
5-4pg. Faust Opera adaptation; Kiefer-a; back-c advertises "Masterpieces Illustrated" by Lloyd Jacquet after he left Classic Comics (no copies of Masterpieces Illustrated known) 30 60 90 177 289 400

KEY OF Z
BOOM! Studios: Oct, 2011 - No. 4, Jan, 2012 ($3.99, limited series)
1-4: 1-Claudio Sanchez & Chondra Echert-s/Aaron Kuder-a; covers by Fox & Moore 4.00

KEY RING COMICS
Dell Publishing Co.: 1941 (16 pgs.; two colors) (sold 5 for 10¢)
1-Sky Hawk, 1-Features Sleepy Samson, 1-Origin Greg Gilday; r/War Comics #2 14 28 42 82 121 160
1-Radior (Super hero) 16 32 48 94 147 200
1-Viking Carter (WWII Nazi-c) 16 32 48 94 147 200
NOTE: *Each book has two holes in spine to put in binder.*

KICK-ASS
Marvel Comics (Icon): April, 2008 - No. 8, Mar, 2010 ($2.99)
1-Mark Millar-s/John Romita Jr.-a/c 20.00
1-Red variant cover by McNiven 25.00
1-2nd printing 4.00
1-Director's Cut (8/08, $3.99) r/#1 with script and sketch pages; Millar afterword 5.00
2 8.00
3-8: 3-1st app. Hit-Girl. 5-Intro. Red Mist 4.00
NOTE: *Multiple printings exist for most issues.*

KICK-ASS 2
Marvel Comics (Icon): Dec, 2010 - No. 7, May, 2012 ($2.99/$4.99)
1-6-Mark Millar-s/John Romita Jr.-a/c. 1-Five printings 3.00
1-6-Variant covers. 1-Edwards. 2-Yu. 5-Photo & Hitch. 6-Photo-c 5.00
7-($4.99) Extra-sized finale; bonus preview of Secret Service #1 5.00
7-($4.99) Variant photo-c 7.00

KICK-ASS 3
Marvel Comics (Icon): Jul, 2013 - No. 8, Oct, 2014 ($2.99/$3.99/$4.99/$5.99)
1-5-($2.99) Mark Millar-s/John Romita Jr.-a/c 3.00
1-5-Variant covers. 1-Hughes. 2-Fegredo. 3-Mack. 5-Bond 5.00
6-($4.99) Secret origin of Hit-Girl 5.00
7-($3.99) 4.00
8-($5.99) 6.00

KID CARROTS
St. John Publishing Co.: September, 1953
1-Funny animal 10 20 30 54 72 90

KID COLT ONE-SHOT
Marvel Comics: Sept, 2009 ($3.99)
1-DeFalco-s/Burchett-a/Luke Ross-c 4.00

KID COLT OUTLAW (Kid Colt #1-4; ...Outlaw #5-on)(Also see All Western Winners, Best Western, Black Rider, Giant-Size..., Two-Gun Kid, Two-Gun Western, Western Winners, Wild Western, Wisco)
Marvel Comics(LCC) 1-16; Atlas(LMC) 17-102; Marvel 103-on: 8/48 - No. 139, 3/68; No. 140, 11/69 - No. 229, 4/79
1-Kid Colt & his horse Steel begin. 181 362 543 1158 1979 2800
2 79 158 237 502 864 1225
3-5: 4-Anti-Wertham editorial; Tex Taylor app. 5-Blaze Carson app. 60 120 180 381 653 925
6-8: 6-Tex Taylor app; 7-Nimo the Lion begins, ends #10 39 78 117 240 395 550
9,10 (52 pgs.) 39 78 117 240 395 550
11-Origin (10/50) 42 84 126 265 445 625
12-20 27 54 81 160 263 365
21-32 22 44 66 132 216 300
33-45: Black Rider in all 20 40 60 114 182 250
46,47,49,50 18 36 54 105 165 225

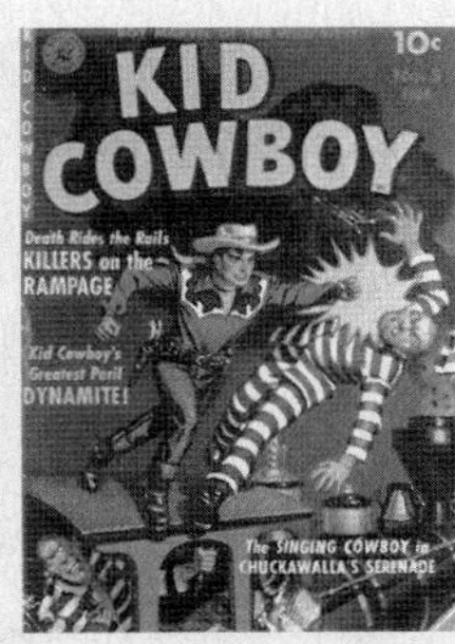

Kid Cowboy #5 © Z-D

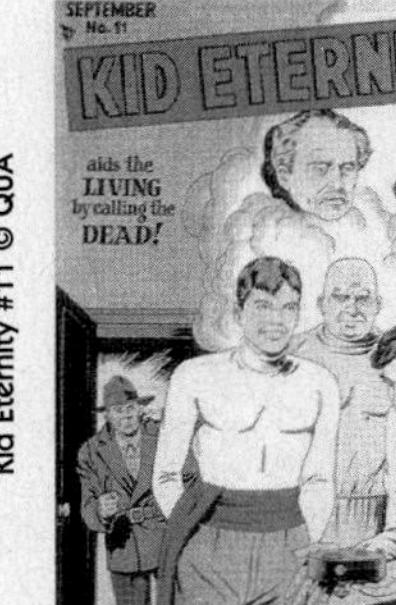

Kid Eternity #11 © QUA

Kid Movie Komics #11 © MAR

GD VG FN VF VF/NM NM-
2.0 4.0 6.0 8.0 9.0 9.2

48-Kubert-a 19 38 57 109 172 235
51-53,55,56 16 32 48 94 147 200
54-Williamson/Maneely-c 17 34 51 98 154 210
57-60,66: 4-pg. Williamson-a in all 10 20 30 66 138 210
61-63,67-78,80-86: 70-Severin-c. 69,73-Maneely-c. 86-Kirby-a(r).
10 20 30 64 132 200
64,65-Crandall-a 10 20 30 66 138 210
79,87: 79-Origin retold. 87-Davis-a(r) 10 20 30 66 138 210
88,89-Williamson-a in both (4 pgs.). 89-Redrawn Matt Slade #2
10 20 30 66 138 210
90-99,101-106,108,109: 91-Kirby/Ayers-c. 95-Kirby/Ayers-c/story. 102-Last 10¢ issue
11 22 33 76 163 250
100 13 26 39 89 195 300
107-Only Kirby sci-fi cover of title 36 72 108 259 580 900
110-(5/63)-1st app. Iron Mask (Iron Man type villain) 13 26 39 89 195 300
111-113,115-120 8 16 24 56 108 160
114-(1/64)-2nd app. Iron Mask 10 20 30 64 132 200
121-129,133-139: 121-Rawhide Kid x-over. 125-Two-Gun Kid x-over. 139-Last 12¢ issue
5 10 15 35 63 90
130-132 (68 pgs.)-one new story each. 130-Origin 6 12 18 41 76 110
140-155: 140-Reprints begin (later issues mostly-r). 155-Last 15¢ issue
3 6 9 16 23 30
156-Giant; reprints (52 pgs.) 3 6 9 20 31 42
157-180,200: 170-Origin retold. 3 6 9 14 20 25
181-199 2 4 6 11 16 20
201-229: 201-New material w/Rawhide Kid app; Kane-c. 229-Rawhide Kid-r
2 4 6 10 14 18
205-209-(30¢-c variants, limited dist.) 10 20 30 64 132 200
218-220-(35¢-c variants, limited dist.) 19 38 57 131 291 450
...Album (no date; 1950's; Atlas Comics)-132 pgs.; cardboard cover,
B&W stories; (Rare) 155 310 465 992 1696 2400

NOTE: ***Ayers** a-many. **Colan** a-52, 53, 84, 112, 114; c(p)-223, 228, 229. **Crandall** a-140r, 167r. **Everett** a-90, 137i, 225i(r). **Heath** a-8(2); c-34, 35, 39, 44, 46, 48, 49, 57, 64. **Heck** a-135, 139. **Jack Keller** a-25(2), 26-68(3-4), 73, 78, 84, 85, 88, 92, 94p, 98, 99, 101, 102, 106-108, 110-112, 114, 115, 117-127, 129, 130, 132, 140-150r. **Kirby** a-86r, 93, 96, 119, 176(part); c-87, 92-95, 97, 99-112, 114-117, 121-123, 197r; w/**Ditko** c-89. **Maneely** a-12, 68, 81; c-17, 19, 40-43, 47, 52, 53, 62, 65, 68, 73, 78, 81, 142r, 150r. **Morrow** a-173r, 216r. **Rico** a-13, 18. **Severin** c-55, 58, 59, 84, 143, 148, 149i. **Shores** a-39, 41-43, 143r; c-1-10(most), 24. **Sutton** a-136, 137p, 225p(r). **Wildey** a-47, 54, 82, 144r. **Williamson** r-147, 170, 172, 216. **Woodbridge** a-64, 81. Black Rider in #33-45, 74, 86. Iron Mask in #110, 114, 121, 127. Sam Hawk in #80, 84, 101, 111, 121, 146, 174, 181, 188.*

KID COWBOY (Also see Approved Comics #4 & Boy Cowboy)
Ziff-Davis Publ./St. John (Approved Comics) #11,14: 1950 - No. 11, Wint, '52-'53; No. 13, April 1953; No. 14, June, 1954 (No #12) (Painted covers #1-10,13,14)

1-Lucy Belle & Red Feather begin 20 40 60 114 182 250
2-Maneely-c 14 28 42 76 108 140
3-11,13,14: (#3, spr. '51). 5-Berg-a. 14-Code approved
12 24 36 69 97 125

KID DEATH & FLUFFY HALLOWEEN SPECIAL
Event Comics: Oct, 1997 ($2.95, B&W, one-shot)

1-Variant-c by Cebollero & Quesada/Palmiotti 3.00

KID DEATH & FLUFFY SPRING BREAK SPECIAL
Event Comics: July, 1996 ($2.50, B&W, one-shot)

1-Quesada & Palmiotti-c/scripts 3.00

KIDDIE KAPERS
Kiddie Kapers Co., 1945/Decker Publ. (Red Top-Farrell): 1945?(nd); Oct, 1957; 1963 - 1964

1(nd, 1945-46?, 36 pgs.)-Infinity-c; funny animal 11 22 33 60 83 105
1(10/57)(Decker)-Little Bit-r from Kiddie Karnival 5 10 15 22 26 30
Super Reprint #7, 10('63), 12, 14('63), 15,17('64), 18('64): 10, 14-r/Animal Adventures #1. 15-Animal Advs. #? 17-Cowboys 'N' Injuns #? 2 4 6 8 11 14

KIDDIE KARNIVAL
Ziff-Davis Publ. Co. (Approved Comics): 1952 (25¢, 100 pgs.) (One Shot)

nn-Rebound Little Bit #1,2; painted-c 36 72 108 216 351 485

KID ETERNITY (Becomes Buccaneers) (See Hit Comics)
Quality Comics Group: Spring, 1946 - No. 18, Nov, 1949

1 90 180 270 576 988 1400
2 39 78 117 240 395 550
3-Mac Raboy-a 40 80 120 246 411 575
4-10 25 50 75 147 241 335
11-18 19 38 57 112 179 245

KID ETERNITY
DC Comics: 1991 - No. 3, Nov, 1991 ($4.95, limited series)

1-3: Grant Morrison scripts/Duncan Fegredo-a/c 6.00
TPB (2006, $14.99) r/#1-3 15.00

KID ETERNITY
DC Comics (Vertigo): May, 1993 - No. 16, Sept, 1994 ($1.95, mature)

1-16: 1-Gold ink-c. 6-Photo-c. All Sean Phillips-c/a except #15 (Phillips-c/i only) 3.00

KID FROM DODGE CITY, THE
Atlas Comics (MMC): July, 1957 - No. 2, Sept, 1957

1-Don Heck-c 14 28 42 80 115 150
2-Everett-c 10 20 30 58 79 100

KID FROM TEXAS, THE (A Texas Ranger)
Atlas Comics (CSI): June, 1957 - No. 2, Aug, 1957

1-Powell-a; Severin-c 14 28 42 76 108 140
2 9 18 27 52 69 85

KID KOKO
I. W. Enterprises: 1958

Reprint #1,2-(r/M.E.'s Koko & Kola #4, 1947) 2 4 6 8 11 14

KID KOMICS (Kid Movie Komics No. 11)
Timely Comics (USA 1,2/FCI 3-10): Feb, 1943 - No. 10, Spring, 1946

1-Origin Captain Wonder & sidekick Tim Mullrooney, & Subbie; intro the Sea-Going Lad, Pinto Pete, & Trixie Trouble; Knuckles & Whitewash Jones (from Young Allies) app.; Wolverton-a (7 pgs.) 595 1190 1785 4350 7925 11,500
2-The Young Allies, Red Hawk, & Tommy Tyme begin; last Captain Wonder & Subbie; Schomburg Japanese WWII bondage-c 290 580 870 1856 3178 4500
3-The Vision, Daredevils & Red Hawk app. 194 388 582 1242 2121 3000
4-The Destroyer begins; Sub-Mariner app.; Red Hawk & Tommy Tyme end; classic Schomburg WWII human meat grinder-c 245 490 735 1568 2684 3800
5,6: 5-Tommy Tyme begins, ends #10 123 246 369 787 1344 1900
7-10: 7,10-The Whizzer app. Destroyer not in #7,8. 10-Last Destroyer, Young Allies & Whizzer 107 214 321 680 1165 1650

NOTE: ***Brodsky** c-5. **Schomburg** c-2-4, 6-10. **Shores** c-1. Captain Wonder c-1, 2. The Young Allies c-3-10.*

KID MONTANA (Formerly Davy Crockett Frontier Fighter; The Gunfighters No. 51 on)
Charlton Comics: V2#9, Nov, 1957 - No. 50, Mar, 1965

V2#9 (#1) 4 8 12 27 44 60
10 3 6 9 19 30 40
11,12,14-20 3 6 9 15 22 28
13-Williamson-a 3 6 9 19 30 40
21-35: 25,31-Giordano-c. 32-Origin Kid Montana. 34-Geronimo-c/s. 35-Snow Monster-c/s
2 4 6 11 16 20
36-50: 36-Dinosaur-c/s. 37,48-Giordano-c 2 4 6 9 12 15

NOTE: *Title change to Montana Kid on cover only #44 & 45; remained Kid Montana on inside. **Chasal** a-29,30. **Giordano** c-25,31,37,48. **Giordano/Alascia** c-12. **Mastroserio** a-9,11,13,14,22; c-11,14. **Masulli/Mastroserio** c-13. **Montes/Bache** c-42. **Morisi** c-16,32-34,36?,40,41,44,46; a-13,15;16,31-50. **Nicholas/Alascia** a-44,48.*

KID MOVIE KOMICS (Formerly Kid Komics; Rusty Comics #12 on)
Timely Comics: No. 11, Summer, 1946

11-Silly Seal & Ziggy Pig; 2 pgs. Kurtzman "Hey Look" plus 6 pg. "Pigtales" story 30 60 90 177 289 400

KIDNAPPED (See Marvel Illustrated: Kidnapped)

KIDNAPPED (Robert Louis Stevenson's...also see Movie Comics)(Disney)
Dell Publishing Co.: No. 1101, May, 1960

Four Color 1101-Movie, photo-c 6 12 18 37 66 95

KIDNAP RACKET (See Harvey Comics Hits No. 57)

KID SLADE, GUNFIGHTER (Formerly Matt Slade...)
Atlas Comics (SPI): No. 5, Jan, 1957 - No. 8, July, 1957

5-Maneely, Roth, Severin-a in all; Maneely-c 14 28 42 82 121 160
6,8-Severin-c 10 20 30 56 76 95
7-Williamson/Mayo-a, 4 pgs.; Maneely-c 12 24 36 67 94 120

KID SUPREME (See Supreme)
Image Comics (Extreme Studios): Mar, 1996 - No. 3, July, 1996 ($2.50)

1-3: Fraga-a/scripts. 3-Glory-c/app. 3.00

KID TERRIFIC
Image Comics: Nov, 1998 ($2.95, B&W)

1-Snyder & Diliberto-s/a 3.00

KID ZOO COMICS
Street & Smith Publications: July, 1948 (52 pgs.)

1-Funny Animal 32 64 96 188 307 425

KILL ALL PARENTS

Kill or Be Killed #1 © Basement Gang

Killraven (2002 series) #1 © MAR

King Comics #35 © KFS

GD VG FN VF VF/NM NM-
2.0 4.0 6.0 8.0 9.0 9.2

Image Comics: June, 2008 ($3.99, one-shot)
1-Marcelo Di Chiara-a/Mark Andrew Smith-s 4.00

KILLAPALOOZA
DC Comics (WildStorm): July, 2009 - No. 6, Dec, 2009 ($2.99, limited series)
1-6: 1-Beechen-s/Hairsine-a/c 3.00
TPB (2010, $19.99) r/#1-6 20.00

KILLER (...Tales By Timothy Truman)
Eclipse Comics: March, 1985 ($1.75, one-shot, Baxter paper)
1-Timothy Truman-c/a 3.00

KILLER INSTINCT (Video game)
Acclaim Comics: June, 1996 - No. 6 ($2.50, limited series)
1-6: 1-Bart Sears-a(p). 4-Special #1. 5-Special #2. 6-Special #3 3.00

KILLERS, THE
Magazine Enterprises: 1947 - No. 2, 1948 (No month)
1-Mr. Zin, the Hatchet Killer; mentioned in **SOTI**, pgs. 179,180; used by N.Y. Legis. Comm.;
L. B. Cole-c 148 296 444 947 1624 2300
2-(Scarce)-Hashish smoking story; "Dying, Dying, Dead" drug story; Whitney, Ingels-a;
Whitney hanging-c 123 246 369 787 1344 1900

KILLING GIRL
Image Comics: Aug, 2007 - No. 5, Dec, 2007 ($2.99, limited series)
1-5: 1-Frank Espinosa-a/Glen Brunswick-s; covers by Espinosa and Frank Cho 3.00

KILLING JOKE, THE (See Batman: The Killing Joke under Batman one-shots)

KILL OR BE KILLED
Image Comics: Aug, 2016 - Present ($3.99)
1-6-Ed Brubaker-s/Sean Phillips-a 4.00

KILLPOWER: THE EARLY YEARS
Marvel Comics UK: Sept, 1993 - No. 4, Dec, 1993 ($1.75, mini-series)
1-($2.95)-Foil embossed-c 4.00
2-4: 2-Genetix app. 3-Punisher app. 3.00

KILLRAVEN (See Amazing Adventures #18 (5/73))
Marvel Comics: Feb, 2001 ($2.99, one-shot)
1-Linsner-s/a/c 3.00

KILLRAVEN
Marvel Comics: Dec, 2002 - No. 6, May, 2003 ($2.99, limited series)
1-6-Alan Davis-s/a(p)/Mark Farmer-i 3.00
HC (2007, $19.99) r/#1-6; cover gallery, pencil art; foreward by Alan Davis 20.00

KILLRAZOR
Image Comics (Top Cow Productions): Aug, 1995 ($2.50, one-shot)
1 3.00

KILL YOUR BOYFRIEND
DC Comics (Vertigo): June, 1995 ($4.95, one-shot)
1-Grant Morrison story 6.00
1 ($5.95, 1998) 2nd printing 6.00

KILROY (Volume 2)
Caliber Press: 1998 ($2.95, B&W)
1-Pruett-s 3.00

KILROY IS HERE
Caliber Press: 1995 ($2.95, B&W)
1-10 3.00

KILROYS, THE
B&I Publ. Co. No. 1-19/American Comics Group: June-July, 1947 - No. 54, June-July, 1955

	GD	VG	FN	VF	VF/NM	NM-
1	26	52	78	154	252	350
2	15	30	45	85	130	175
3-5: 5-Gross-a	14	28	42	80	115	150
6-10: 8-Milt Gross's Moronica (1st app.)	11	22	33	62	86	110
11-20: 14-Gross-a	10	20	30	56	76	95
21-30	9	18	27	52	69	85
31-47,50-54	9	18	27	47	61	75
48,49-(3-D effect-c/stories)	18	36	54	105	165	225

KILROY: THE SHORT STORIES
Caliber Press: 1995 ($2.95, B&W)
1 3.00

KIN
Image Comics (Top Cow): Mar, 2000 - No. 6, Sept, 2000 ($2.95)
1-5-Gary Frank-s/c/a 3.00
1-($6.95) DF Alternate footprint cover 7.00
6-($3.95) 4.00
... Descent of Man TPB (2002, $19.95) r/ #1-6 20.00

KINDRED, THE
Image Comics (WildStorm Productions): Mar, 1994 - No. 4, July, 1995 ($1.95, lim. series)
1-($2.50)-Grifter & Backlash app. in all; bound-in trading card 4.00
2-4 3.00
2,3: 2-Variant-c. 3-Alternate-c by Portacio, see Deathblow #5 4.00
Trade paperback (2/95, $9.95) 10.00
NOTE: *Booth c/a-1-4. The first four issues contain coupons redeemable for a Jim Lee Grifter/Backlash print.*

KINDRED II, THE
DC Comics (WildStorm): Mar, 2002 - No. 4, June, 2002 ($2.50, limited series)
1-4-Booth-s/Booth & Regla-a 3.00

KINETIC
DC Comics (Focus): May, 2004 - No. 8, Dec, 2004 ($2.50)
1-8-Puckett-s/Pleece-a/c 3.00
TPB (2005, $9.99) r/#1-8; cover gallery and sketch pages 10.00

KING (Magazine)
Skywald Publ.: Mar, 1971 - No. 2, July, 1971

	GD	VG	FN	VF	VF/NM	NM-
1-Violence; semi-nudity; Boris Vallejo-a (2 pgs.)	5	10	15	31	53	75
2-Photo-c	3	6	9	21	33	45

KING ARTHUR AND THE KNIGHTS OF JUSTICE
Marvel Comics UK: Dec, 1993 - No. 3, Feb, 1994 ($1.25, limited series)
1-3: TV adaptation 3.00

KING CLASSICS
King Features : 1977 (36 pgs., cardboard-c) (Printed in Spain for U.S. distr.)
1-Connecticut Yankee, 2-Last of the Mohicans, 3-Moby Dick, 4-Robin Hood, 5-Swiss Family Robinson, 6-Robinson Crusoe, 7-Treasure Island, 8-20,000 Leagues, 9-Christmas Carol, 10-Huck Finn, 11-Around the World in 80 Days, 12-Davy Crockett, 13-Don Quixote, 14-Gold Bug, 15-Ivanhoe, 16-Three Musketeers, 17-Baron Munchausen, 18-Alice in Wonderland, 19-Black Arrow, 20-Five Weeks in a Balloon, 21-Great Expectations, 22-Gulliver's Travels, 23-Prince & Pauper, 24-Lawrence of Arabia (Originals, 1977-78)

	GD	VG	FN	VF	VF/NM	NM-
each....	2	4	6	10	14	18
Reprints (1979; HRN-24)	2	4	6	8	10	12

NOTE: *The first eight issues were not numbered. Issues No. 25-32 were advertised but not published. The 1977 originals have HRN 32a; the 1978 originals have HRN 32b.*

KING COLT (See Luke Short's Western Stories)

KING COMICS (Strip reprints)
David McKay Publications/Standard #156-on: 4/36 - No. 155, 11-12/49; No. 156, Spr/50 - No. 159, 2/52 (Winter on-c)

	GD	VG	FN	VF	VF/NM	NM-
1-1st app. Flash Gordon by Alex Raymond; Brick Bradford (1st app.), Popeye, Henry (1st app.) & Mandrake the Magician (1st app.) begin; Popeye-c begin	1400	2800	4200	11,200	-	-
2	360	720	1080	1980	2990	4000
3	245	490	735	1348	2074	2800
4	190	380	570	1045	1623	2200
5	140	280	420	770	1185	1600
6-10: 9-X-Mas-c	95	190	285	523	812	1100
11-20	75	150	225	413	607	800
21-30: 21-X-Mas-c	55	110	165	303	452	600
31-40: 33-Last Segar Popeye	45	90	135	248	387	525
41-50: 46-Text illos by Marge Buell contain characters similar to Lulu, Alvin & Tubby. 50-The Lone Ranger begins	36	72	108	211	343	475
51-60: 52-Barney Baxter begins?	34	68	102	199	325	450
61-The Phantom begins	34	68	102	204	332	460
62-80: 76-Flag-c. 79-Blondie begins	20	40	60	114	182	250
81-99	15	30	45	85	130	175
100	18	36	54	103	162	220
101-114: 114-Last Raymond issue (1 pg.); Flash Gordon by Austin Briggs begins, ends #155	14	28	42	76	108	140
115-145: 117-Phantom origin retold	10	20	30	56	76	95
146,147-Prince Valiant in both	9	18	27	50	65	80
148-155: 155-Flash Gordon ends (11-12/49)	9	18	27	50	65	80
156-159: 156-New logo begins (Standard)	9	18	27	47	61	75

NOTE: *Marge Buell text illos in No. 24-46 at least.*

KING CONAN (Conan The King No. 20 on)
Marvel Comics Group: Mar, 1980 - No. 19, Nov, 1983 (52 pgs.)

	GD	VG	FN	VF	VF/NM	NM-
1	2	4	6	9	12	15
2-19: 4-Death of Thoth Amon. 7-1st Paul Smith-a, 1 pg. pin-up (9/81)						5.00

NOTE: ***J. Buscema** a-1-9p, 17p; c(p)-1-5, 7-9, 14, 17. **Kaluta** c-19. **Nebres** a-17i, 18, 19i. **Severin** c-18. **Simonson** c-6.*

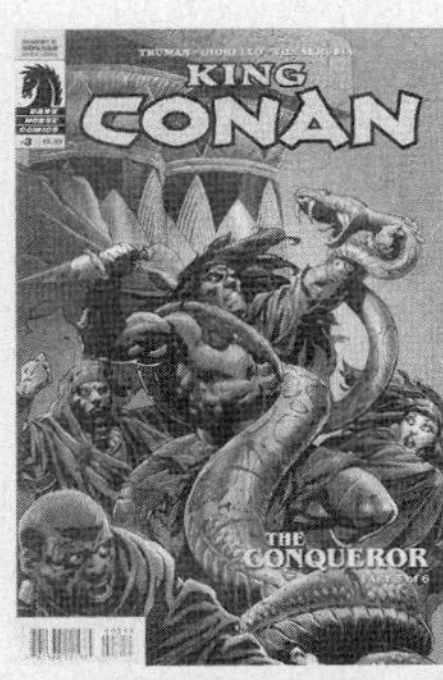

King Conan: The Conqueror #3 © CPI

King: Flash Gordon #1 © KFS

Kingpin (2017 series) #1 © MAR

	GD 2.0	VG 4.0	FN 6.0	VF 8.0	VF/NM 9.0	NM- 9.2

KING CONAN: THE CONQUEROR
Dark Horse Comics: Feb, 2014 - No. 6, Jul, 2014 ($3.50, limited series)
1-6-Truman-s/Giorello-a/c 3.50

KING CONAN: THE HOUR OF THE DRAGON
Dark Horse Comics: May, 2013 - No. 6, Oct, 2013 ($3.50, limited series)
1-6-Truman-s/Giorello-a/Parel-c 3.50

KING CONAN: THE PHOENIX ON THE SWORD
Dark Horse Comics: Jan, 2012 - No. 4, Apr, 2012 ($3.50, limited series)
1-4-Truman-s/Giorello-a/Robinson-c. 1-Variant-c by Parel 3.50

KING CONAN: THE SCARLET CITADEL
Dark Horse Comics: Feb, 2011 - No. 4, May, 2011 ($3.50, limited series)
1-4-Truman-s/Giorello-a/Robertson-c. 1-Variant-c by Parel 3.50

KING CONAN: WOLVES BEYOND THE BORDER
Dark Horse Comics: Dec, 2015 - No. 4, Mar, 2016 ($3.99, limited series)
1-4-Truman-s/Giorello-a/c. 1-Kull app. 4-Bran Mak Morn app. 4.00

KING DAVID
DC Comics (Vertigo): 2002 ($19.95, 8 1/2" x 11")
nn-Story of King David; Kyle Baker-s/a 20.00

KINGDOM, THE
DC Comics: Feb, 1999 - No. 2, Feb, 1999 ($2.95/$1.99, limited series)
1,2-Waid-s; sequel to Kingdom Come; introduces Hypertime 4.00
...: Kid Flash 1 (2/99, $1.99) Waid-s/Pararillo-a, ...: Nightstar 1 (2/99, $1.99) Waid-s/Haley-a, ...: Offspring 1 (2/99, $1.99) Waid-s/Quitely-a, ...: Planet Krypton 1 (2/99, $1.99) Waid-s/Kitson-a, ...: Son of the Bat 1 (2/99, $1.99) Waid-s/Apthorp-a 3.00

KINGDOM COME (Also see Justice Society of America #9-22)
DC Comics: 1996 - No. 4, 1996 ($4.95, painted limited series)

	GD	VG	FN	VF	VF/NM	NM-
1-Mark Waid scripts & Alex Ross-painted c/a in all; tells the last days of the DC Universe; 1st app. Magog	2	4	6	8	10	12
2-Superman forms new Justice League	1	2	3	5	6	8
3-Return of Captain Marvel	1	2	3	5	6	8
4-Final battle of Superman and Captain Marvel	1	3	4	6	8	10

Deluxe Slipcase Edition-($89.95) w/Revelations companion book, 12 new story pages, foil stamped covers, signed and numbered 120.00
Hardcover Edition-($29.95)-Includes 12 new story pages and artwork from Revelations, new cover artwork with gold foil inlay 40.00
Hardcover 2nd printing 30.00
Softcover Ed.-($14.95)-Includes 12 new story pgs. & artwork from Revelations, new c-artwork 20.00
Softcover Ed.-(2008, $17.99)-New wraparound gatefold cover by Ross 18.00

KING: FLASH GORDON
Dynamite Entertainment: 2015 - No. 4, 2015 ($3.99)
1-4: 1-Acker & Blacker-s/Ferguson-a/Cooke-c; variant-c by Liefeld. 2-Zdarsky-c 4.00

KING: JUNGLE JIM
Dynamite Entertainment: 2015 - No. 4, 2015 ($3.99)
1-4: 1-Tobin-s/Jarrell-a/Cooke-c; variant-c by Liefeld. 2-Zdarsky-c 4.00

KING KONG (See Movie Comics)

KING KONG: THE 8TH WONDER OF THE WORLD (Adaptation of 2005 movie)
Dark Horse Comics: Dec, 2005 ($3.99, planned limited series completed in TPB)
1-Photo-c; Dustin Weaver-a/Christian Gossett-s 4.00
TPB (11/06, $12.95) r/#1 and unpublished parts 2&3; photo-c; Dorman paintings 13.00

KING LEONARDO & HIS SHORT SUBJECTS (TV)
Dell Publishing Co./Gold Key: Nov-Jan, 1961-62 - No. 4, Sept, 1963

	GD	VG	FN	VF	VF/NM	NM-
Four Color 1242,1278	10	20	30	67	141	215
01390-207(5-7/62)(Dell)	8	16	24	52	99	145
1 (10/62)	9	18	27	60	120	180
2-4	7	14	21	48	89	130

KING LOUIE & MOWGLI (See Jungle Book under Movie Comics)
Gold Key: May, 1968 (Disney)

	GD	VG	FN	VF	VF/NM	NM-
1 (#10223-805)-Characters from Jungle Book	3	6	9	19	30	40

KING: MANDRAKE THE MAGICIAN
Dynamite Entertainment: 2015 - No. 4, 2015 ($3.99)
1-4: 1-Langridge-s/Treece-a/Cooke-c; variant-c by Liefeld. 2-Zdarsky-c 4.00

KING OF DIAMONDS (TV)
Dell Publishing Co.: July-Sept, 1962

	GD	VG	FN	VF	VF/NM	NM-
01-391-209-Photo-c	4	8	12	25	40	55

KING OF KINGS (Movie)
Dell Publishing Co.: No. 1236, Oct-Nov, 1961

	GD	VG	FN	VF	VF/NM	NM-
Four Color 1236-Photo-c	7	14	21	46	86	125

KING OF THE BAD MEN OF DEADWOOD
Avon Periodicals: 1950 (See Wild Bill Hickok #16)

	GD	VG	FN	VF	VF/NM	NM-
nn-Kinstler-c; Kamen/Feldstein-r/Cowpuncher #2	19	38	57	111	176	240

KING OF THE ROYAL MOUNTED (See Famous Feature Stories, King Comics, Red Ryder #3 & Super Book #2, 6)

KING OF THE ROYAL MOUNTED (Zane Grey's...)
David McKay/Dell Publishing Co.: No. 1, May, 1937; No. 9, 1940; No. 207, Dec, 1948 - No. 935, Sept-Nov, 1958

	GD	VG	FN	VF	VF/NM	NM-
Feature Books 1 (5/37)(McKay)	110	220	330	704	1202	1700
Large Feature Comic 9 (1940)	53	106	159	334	567	800
Four Color 207(#1, 12/48)	13	26	39	86	188	290
Four Color 265,283	9	18	27	58	114	170
Four Color 310,340	7	14	21	46	86	125
Four Color 363,384, 8(6-8/52)-10	6	12	18	40	73	105
11-20	5	10	15	31	53	75
21-28(3-5/58)	4	8	12	27	44	60
Four Color 935(9-11/58)	5	10	15	31	53	75

NOTE: *4-Color No. 207, 265, 283, 310, 340, 363, 384 are all newspaper reprints with* ***Jim Gary*** *art. No. 8 on are all Dell originals. Painted c-No. 9-on.*

KINGPIN
Marvel Comics: Nov, 1997 ($5.99, squarebound, one-shot)
nn-Spider-Man & Daredevil vs. Kingpin; Stan Lee-s/ John Romita Sr.-a 6.00

KINGPIN
Marvel Comics: Aug, 2003 - No. 7, Jan, 2004 ($2.50/$2.99, limited series)
1-6-Bruce Jones-s/Sean Phillips & Klaus Janson-a 3.00
7-($2.99) 3.00

KINGPIN
Marvel Comics: Apr, 2017 - Present ($3.99)
1-Wilson Fisk goes legit; Matthew Rosenberg-s/Ben Torres-a 4.00

KING: PRINCE VALIANT
Dynamite Entertainment: 2015 - No. 4, 2015 ($3.99)
1-4: 1-Cosby-s/Salasl-a/Cooke-c; variant-c by Liefeld. 2-Zdarsky-c 4.00

KING RICHARD & THE CRUSADERS
Dell Publishing Co.: No. 588, Oct, 1954

	GD	VG	FN	VF	VF/NM	NM-
Four Color 588-Movie, Matt Baker-a, photo-c	9	18	27	57	111	165

KING-SIZE CABLE SPECTACULAR (Takes place between Cable (2008 series) #6 & #7)
Marvel Comics: Nov, 2008 ($4.99, one-shot)
1-Lashley-a; Deadpool #1 preview; cover gallery of variants from 2008 series 5.00

KING-SIZE HULK (Takes place between Hulk (2008 series) #3 & #4)
Marvel Comics: July, 2008 ($4.99, one-shot)
1-Art Adams, Frank Cho, & Herb Trimpe-a; double-c by Cho & Adams; Red Hulk, She-Hulk & Wendigo app.; origin Abomination; r/Incr. Hulk #180,181 & Avengers #83 5.00

KING-SIZE SPIDER-MAN SUMMER SPECIAL
Marvel Comics: Oct, 2008 ($4.99, one-shot)
1-Short stories by various; Falcon app.; Burchett, Giarrusso & Coover-a 5.00

KINGS OF THE NIGHT
Dark Horse Comics: 1990 - No. 2, 1990 ($2.25, limited series)
1,2-Robert E. Howard adaptation; Bolton-c 3.00

KING SOLOMON'S MINES (Movie)
Avon Periodicals: 1951

	GD	VG	FN	VF	VF/NM	NM-
nn (#1 on 1st page)	43	86	129	271	461	650

KINGS QUEST
Dynamite Entertainment: 2016 - No. 5, 2016 ($3.99, limited series)
1-5-Flash Gordon, Mandrake, Prince Valiant, The Phantom team; multiple-c on each 4.00

KING'S ROAD
Dark Horse Comics: Feb, 2016 - No. 3, Apr, 2016 ($3.99, limited series)
1-3-Peter Hogan-s/Phil Winslade & Staz Johnson-a; Johnson-c 4.00

KINGS WATCH
Dynamite Entertainment: 2013 - No. 5, 2014 ($3.99)
1-5-Flash Gordon, Mandrake and The Phantom team up; Parker-s/Laming-a 4.00

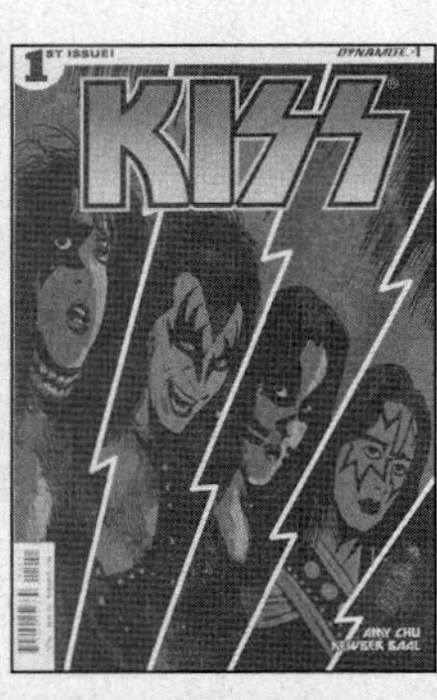

KISS (2016 series) #1 © KISS Catalog

The Kitchen #4 © Masters & Doyle

Klaus #1 © Grant Morrison

	GD	VG	FN	VF	VF/NM	NM-
	2.0	4.0	6.0	8.0	9.0	9.2

KINGSWAY WEST
Dark Horse Comics: Aug, 2016 - No. 4, Feb, 2017 ($3.99)
1-4-Greg Pak-s/Mirko Colak-a/c 4.00

KING: THE PHANTOM
Dynamite Entertainment: 2015 - No. 4, 2015 ($3.99)
1-4: 1-Clevinger-s/Schoonover-a/Cooke-c; var-c by Liefeld; Mandrake app. 2-Zdarsky-c 4.00

KING TIGER
Dark Horse Comics: Aug, 2015 - No. 4, Nov, 2015 ($3.99, limited series)
1-4-Randy Stradley-s/Doug Wheatley-a/c 4.00

KIPLING, RUDYARD (See Mowgli, The Jungle Book)

KIRBY: GENESIS
Dynamite Entertainment: No. 0, 2011 - No. 8, 2012 ($1.00/$3.99)
0-($1.00) Busiek-s; art by Alex Ross & Jack Herbert; series preview, sketch-a 3.00
1-8-($3.99) Ross & Herbert-a. 1-Seven covers. 2-8-Covers by Ross & Sook 4.00

KIRBY: GENESIS - CAPTAIN VICTORY
Dynamite Entertainment: 2011 - No. 6, 2012 ($3.99)
1-6: 1-Origin retold; four covers; Sterling Gates-s/Wagner Reis-a 4.00

KIRBY: GENESIS - DRAGONSBANE
Dynamite Entertainment: 2012 - No. 4, 2013 ($3.99, unfinished limited series)
1-4-Rodi & Ross-s/Casas-a; covers by Ross and Herbert 4.00

KIRBY: GENESIS - SILVER STAR
Dynamite Entertainment: 2011 - No. 6, 2012 ($3.99)
1-6-Jai Nitz-s/Johnny Desjardins-a. 1-Four covers. 2-6-Three covers 4.00

KISS (See Crazy Magazine, Howard the Duck #12, 13, Marvel Comics Super Special #1, 5, Rock Fantasy Comics #10 & Rock N' Roll Comics #9)

KISS
Dark Horse Comics: June, 2002 - No. 13, Sept, 2003 ($2.99, limited series)
1-Photo-c and J. Scott Campbell-c; Casey-s 5.00
2-13: 2-Photo-c and J. Scott Campbell-c. 3-Photo-c and Leinil Yu-c 4.00
...: Men and Monsters TPB (9/03, $12.95) r/#7-10 13.00
...: Rediscovery TPB (2003, $9.95) r/#1-3 10.00
...: Return of the Phantom TPB (2003, $9.95) r/#4-6 10.00
...: Unholy War TPB (2004, $9.95) r/#11-13 10.00

KISS
IDW Publishing: June, 2012 - No. 8, Jan, 2013 ($3.99)
1-8-Multiple covers on each. 1,2-Ryall-s/Igle-a 4.00

KISS (Volume 1)
Dynamite Entertainment: 2016 - Present ($3.99)
1-5-Amy Chu-s/Kewber Baal-a; multiple covers 4.00
...: The Demon 1,2 (2017, $3.99) prequel to 2016 series; Chu & Burnham-s/Casallos-a 4.00

KISS 4K
Platinum Studios Comics: May, 2007 - No. 6, Apr, 2008 ($3.99/$2.99)
1-Sprague-s/Crossley & Campos-a/Migliari-c 4.00
1-B&W sketch-c 6.00
1-Destroyer Edition ($50.00, 30"x18", edition of 5000) 50.00
2-6-($2.99) 3.00
KISSMAS (12/07, $4.99) Christmas-themed issue; re-cap of issues #1-4 5.00

KISS KIDS
IDW Publishing: Aug, 2013 - No. 4, Nov, 2013 ($3.99, limited series)
1-4-Short stories of KISS members as grade-school kids; Ryall & Waltz-s 4.00

KISS SOLO
IDW Publishing: Mar, 2013 - No. 4, Jun, 2013 ($3.99, limited series)
1-4-Multiple covers on each. 1-Ryall-s/Medina-a. 2-Waltz-s/Rodriguez-a 4.00

KISS: THE PSYCHO CIRCUS
Image Comics: Aug, 1997 - No. 31, June, 2000 ($1.95/$2.25/$2.50)
1-Holguin-s/Medina-a(p) 1 3 4 6 8 10
1-2nd & 3rd printings 3.00
2 6.00
3,4: 4-Photo-c 5.00
5-8: 5-Begin $2.25-c 4.00
9-29 4.00
30,31: 30-Begin $2.50-c 4.00
Book 1 TPB ('98, $12.95) r/#1-6 13.00
Book 2 Destroyer TPB (8/99, $9.95) r/#10-13 10.00
Book 3 Whispered Scream TPB ('00, $9.95) r/#7-9,18 10.00
...Magazine 1 ($6.95) r/#1-3 plus interviews 7.00
...Magazine 2-5 ($4.95) 2-r/#4,5 plus interviews. 3-r/#6,7. 4-r/#8,9 5.00
Wizard Edition ('98, supplement) Bios, tour preview and interviews 3.00

	GD	VG	FN	VF	VF/NM	NM-
	2.0	4.0	6.0	8.0	9.0	9.2

KISSING CHAOS
Oni Press: Sept, 2001 - No. 8, Mar, 2002 ($2.25, B&W, 6" x 9", limited series)
1-8-Arthur Dela Cruz-s/a 3.00
...: Nine Lives (12/03, $2.99, regular comic-sized) 3.00
...: 1000 Words (7/03, $2.99, regular comic-sized) 3.00
TPB (9/02, $17.95) r/#1-8 18.00

KISSING CHAOS: NONSTOP BEAUTY
Oni Press: Oct, 2002 - No. 4, March, 2003 ($2.95, B&W, 6" x 9", limited series)
1-4-Arthur Dela Cruz-s/a 3.00
TPB (9/03, $11.95) r/#1-4 12.00

KISS KISS BANG BANG
CrossGen Comics: Feb, 2004 - No. 5, Jun, 2004 ($2.95)
1-5-Bedard-s/Perkins-a 3.00

KISS ME, SATAN
Dark Horse Comics: Sept, 2013 - No. 5, Jan, 2014 ($3.99, limited series)
1-5-Gischler-s/Ferreyra-a; Dave Johnson-c 4.00

KISSYFUR (TV)
DC Comics: 1989 (Sept.) ($2.00, 52 pgs., one-shot)
1-Based on Saturday morning cartoon 4.00

KIT CARSON (Formerly All True Detective Cases No. 4; Fighting Davy Crockett No. 9; see Blazing Sixguns & Frontier Fighters)
Avon Periodicals: 1950; No. 2, 8/51 - No. 3, 12/51; No. 5, 11-12/54 - No. 8, 9/55 (No #4)
nn(#1) (1950)- "...Indian Scout" ; r-Cowboys 'N' Injuns #? 15 30 45 86 133 180
2(8/51) 11 22 33 64 90 115
3(12/51)- "...Fights the Comanche Raiders" 10 20 30 58 79 100
5-6,8(11-12/54-9/55): 5-Formerly All True Detective Cases (last pre-code); titled "...and the Trail of Doom" 10 20 30 54 72 90
7-McCann-a? 10 20 30 54 72 90
I.W. Reprint #10('63)-r/Kit Carson #1; Severin-c 2 4 6 11 16 20
NOTE: *Kinstler c-1-3, 5-8.*

KIT CARSON & THE BLACKFEET WARRIORS
Realistic: 1953
nn-Reprint; Kinstler-c 10 20 30 56 76 95

KITCHEN, THE
DC Comics (Vertigo): Jan, 2015 - No. 8, Aug, 2015 ($2.99, limited series)
1-8-Masters-s/Doyle-a/Cloonan-c 3.00

KIT KARTER
Dell Publishing Co.: May-July, 1962
1 3 6 9 18 28 38

KITTY
St. John Publishing Co.: Oct, 1948
1-Teenage; Lily Renee-c/a 18 36 54 105 165 225

KITTY PRYDE, AGENT OF S.H.I.E.L.D. (Also see Excalibur and Mekanix)
Marvel Comics: Dec, 1997 - No. 3, Feb, 1998 ($2.50, limited series)
1-3-Hama-s 3.00

KITTY PRYDE AND WOLVERINE (Also see Uncanny X-Men & X-Men)
Marvel Comics Group: Nov, 1984 - No. 6, Apr, 1985 (Limited series)
1-6: Characters from X-Men 5.00
X-Men: Kitty Pryde and Wolverine HC (2008, $19.99) r/series 20.00

KLARER GIVEAWAYS (See Wisco in the Promotional Comics section)

KLARION (The Witchboy)
DC Comics: Dec, 2014 - No. 6, May, 2015 ($2.99)
1-6: 1-3-Nocenti-s/McCarthy-a. 4-Fiorentino-a 3.00

KLAUS
BOOM! Studios: Nov, 2015 - No. 7, Aug, 2016 ($3.99)
1-7: 1-Origin of Santa Claus; Grant Morrison-s/Dan Mora-a; multiple covers 4.00
... and the Witch of Winter 1 (12/16, $7.99) Morrison-s/Mora-a; Geppetto app. 8.00

KLAWS OF THE PANTHER (Also see Black Panther)
Marvel Comics: Dec, 2010 - No. 4, Feb, 2011 ($3.99, limited series)
1-4-Maberry-s/Gugliotta-a/Del Mundo-c. 1-Ka-Zar & Shanna app. 3-Spider-Man app. 4.00

Knight and Squire #1 © DC

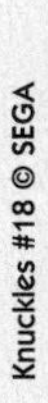
Knuckles #18 © SEGA

Kong of Skull Island #1 © DeVito Artworks

	GD 2.0	VG 4.0	FN 6.0	VF 8.0	VF/NM 9.0	NM- 9.2

KNIGHT AND SQUIRE (Also see Batman #667-669)
DC Comics: Dec, 2010 - No. 6, May, 2011 ($2.99, limited series)
1-6-Cornell-s/Broxton-a. 1-Two covers by Paquette & Tucci. 5,6-Joker app. 3.00
TPB (2011, $14.99) r/#1-6; sketch and design art 15.00

KNIGHTHAWK
Acclaim Comics (Windjammer): Sept, 1995 - No. 6, Nov, 1995 ($2.50, lim. series)
1-6: 6-origin 3.00

KNIGHTMARE
Antarctic Press: July, 1994 - May, 1995 ($2.75, B&W, mature readers)
1-6 3.00

KNIGHTMARE
Image Comics (Extreme Studios): Feb, 1995 - No. 5, June, 1995 ($2.50)
0 ($3.50) 4.00
1-5: 4-Quesada & Palmiotti variant-c, 5-Flip book w/Warcry 3.00

KNIGHTS 4 (See Marvel Knights 4)

KNIGHTS OF PENDRAGON, THE (Also see Pendragon)
Marvel Comics Ltd.: July, 1990 - No. 18, Dec, 1991 ($1.95)
1-18: 1-Capt. Britain app. 2,8-Free poster inside. 9,10-Bolton-c. 11,18-Iron Man app. 3.00

KNIGHTS OF THE ROUND TABLE
Dell Publishing Co.: No. 540, Mar, 1954
Four Color 540-Movie, photo-c 6 12 18 41 76 110

KNIGHTS OF THE ROUND TABLE
Pines Comics: No. 10, April, 1957
10-Features Sir Lancelot 5 10 15 24 30 35

KNIGHTS OF THE ROUND TABLE
Dell Publishing Co.: Nov-Jan, 1963-64
1 (12-397-401)-Painted-c 3 6 9 20 31 42

KNIGHTSTRIKE (Also see Operation: Knightstrike)
Image Comics (Extreme Studios): Jan, 1996 ($2.50)
1-Rob Liefeld & Eric Stephenson story; Extreme Destroyer Part 6. 3.00

KNIGHT WATCHMAN (See Big Bang Comics & Dr. Weird)
Image Comics: June, 1998 - No. 4, Oct, 1998 ($2.95/$3.50, B&W, lim. series)
1-3-Ben Torres-c/a in all 3.00
4-($3.50) 3.50

KNIGHT WATCHMAN: GRAVEYARD SHIFT
Caliber Press: 1994 ($2.95, B&W)
1,2-Ben Torres-a 3.00

KNOCK KNOCK (...Who's There?)
Dell Publ./Gerona Publications: No. 801, 1936 (52 pgs.) (8x9", B&W)
801-Joke book; Bob Dunn-a 14 28 42 82 121 160

KNOCKOUT ADVENTURES
Fiction House Magazines: Winter, 1953-54
1-Reprints Fight Comics #53 w/Rip Carson-c/s 14 28 42 76 108 140

KNUCKLES (Spin-off of Sonic the Hedgehog)
Archie Publications: Apr, 1997 - No. 32, Feb, 2000 ($1.50/$1.75/$1.79)
1-32 4.00

KNUCKLES' CHAOTIX
Archie Publications: Jan, 1996 ($2.00, annual)
1 5.00

KOBALT
DC Comics (Milestone): June, 1994 - No. 16, Sept, 1995 ($1.75/$2.50)
1-16: 1-Byrne-c. 4-Intro Page. 16-Kent Williams-c 3.00

KOBRA (Unpublished #8 appears in DC Special Series No. 1)
National Periodical Publications: Feb-Mar, 1976 - No. 7, Mar-Apr, 1977
1-1st app.; Kirby-a redrawn by Marcos; only 25¢-c 3 6 9 14 20 25
2-7: (All 30¢ issues) 3-Giffen-a 1 3 4 6 8 10
...: Resurrection TPB (2010, $19.99) r/#1, DC Special Series No. 1 and later apps. in Checkmate #23-25, Faces of Evil: Kobra #1 and various Who's Who issues 20.00
NOTE: ***Austin** a-3i. **Buckler** a-5p; c-5p. **Kubert** c-4. **Nasser** a-6p, 7; c-7.*

KOKEY KOALA (...and the Magic Button)
Toby Press: May, 1952
1-Funny animal 14 28 42 82 121 160

KOKO AND KOLA (Also see A-1 Comics #16 & Tick Tock Tales)
Com/Magazine Enterprises: Fall, 1946 - No. 5, May, 1947; No. 6, 1950
1-Funny animal 15 30 45 86 133 180
2-X-Mas-c 11 22 33 60 83 105
3-6: 6(A-1 28) 10 20 30 54 72 90

KO KOMICS
Gerona Publications: Oct, 1945 (scarce)
1-The Duke of Darkness & The Menace (hero); Kirby-c 97 194 291 621 1061 1500

KOLCHAK: THE NIGHT STALKER (TV)
Moonstone: 2002 - Present ($6.50/$6.95)
1-($6.50) Jeff Rice-s/Gordon Purcell-a 6.50
... Black & White & Read All Over (2005, $4.95) short stories by various; 2 covers 5.00
... Devil in the Details (2003, $6.95) Trevor Von Eeden-a 7.00
... Eve of Terror (2005, $5.95) Gentile-s/Figueroa-a/Beck-c 6.00
... Fever Pitch (2002, $6.95) Christopher Jones-a 7.00
... Get of Belial (2002, $6.95) Art Nichols-a 7.00
... Lambs to the Slaughter (2003, $6.95) Trevor Von Eeden-a 7.00
... Pain Most Human (2004, $6.95) Greg Scott-a 7.00
... Tales: The Frankenstein Agenda 1 (2007 - No. 3, $3.50) Michelinie-s 3.50
... Tales of the Night Stalker 1-7 (2003-Present, $3.50) two covers by Moore & Ulanski 3.50
TPB (2004, $17.95) r/#1, Get of Belial & Fever Pitch 18.00
Vol. 2: Terror Within TPB (2006, $16.95) r/Pain Most Human, Pain Without Tears & Devil in the Details 17.00

KOMIC KARTOONS
Timely Comics (EPC): Fall, 1945 - No. 2, Winter, 1945
1,2-Andy Wolf, Bertie Mouse 31 62 93 182 296 410

KOMIK PAGES (Formerly Snap; becomes Bullseye #11)
Harry 'A' Chesler, Jr. (Our Army, Inc.): Apr, 1945 (All reprints)
10(#1 on inside)-Land O' Nod by Rick Yager (2 pgs.), Animal Crackers, Foxy GrandPa, Tom, Dick & Mary, Cheerio Minstrels, Red Starr plus other 1-2 pg. strips; Cole-a 24 48 72 142 234 325

KONA (...Monarch of Monster Isle)
Dell Publishing Co.: Feb-Apr, 1962 - No. 21, Jan-Mar, 1967 (Painted-c)
Four Color 1256 (#1) 9 18 27 61 123 185
2-10: 4-Anak begins. 6-Gil Kane-c 5 10 15 33 57 80
11-21 4 8 12 28 47 65
NOTE: ***Glanzman** a-all issues.*

KONGA (Fantastic Giants No. 24) (See Return of...)
Charlton Comics: 1960; No. 2, Aug, 1961 - No. 23, Nov, 1965
1(1960)-Based on movie; Giordano-c 23 46 69 161 356 550
2-5: 2-Giordano-c; no Ditko-a 10 20 30 66 138 210
6-9-Ditko-c/a 9 18 27 58 114 170
10-15 8 16 24 54 102 150
16-23 5 10 15 35 63 90
NOTE: ***Ditko** a-1, 3-15; c-4, 6-9, 11. **Glanzman** a-12. **Montes & Bache** a-16-23.*

KONGA'S REVENGE (Formerly Return of...)
Charlton Comics: No. 2, Summer, 1963 - No. 3, Fall, 1964; Dec, 1968
2,3: 2-Ditko-c/a 7 14 21 44 82 120
1(12/68)-Reprints Konga's Revenge #3 3 6 9 16 24 32

KONG OF SKULL ISLAND
BOOM! Studios: Jul, 2016 - Present ($3.99, limited series)
1-8-James Asmus-s/Carlos Magno-a; multiple covers on each 4.00

KONG THE UNTAMED
National Periodical Publications: June-July, 1975 - V2#5, Feb-Mar, 1976
1-1st app. Kong; Wrightson-c; Alcala-a 2 4 6 13 18 22
2-Wrightson-c; Alcala-a 2 4 6 10 14 18
3-5: 3-Alcala-a 1 3 4 6 8 10

KOOKABURRA K
Marvel Comics (Soleil): 2009 - No. 3, 2010 ($5.99, limited series)
1-3-Humbertos Ramos-a/c 6.00

KOOKIE
Dell Publishing Co.: Feb-Apr, 1962 - No. 2, May-July, 1962 (15 cents)
1-Written by John Stanley; Bill Williams-a 7 14 21 46 86 125
2 6 12 18 41 76 110

KOOSH KINS

Krampus #5 © Joines & Kotz

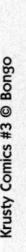

Krusty Comics #3 © Bongo

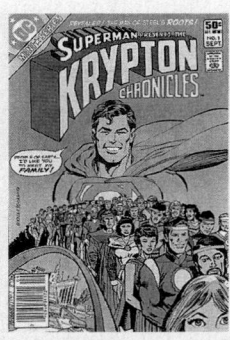

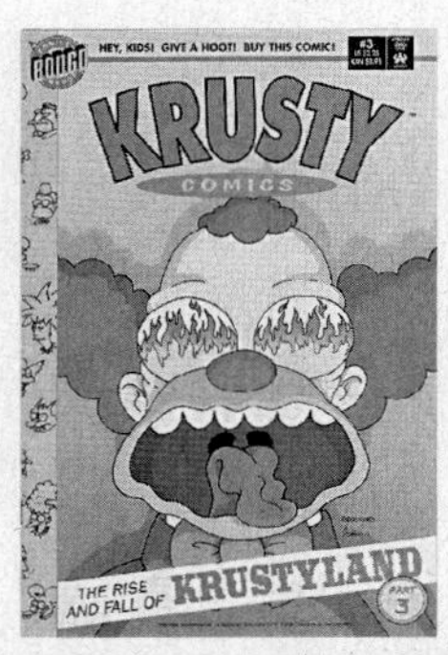

Krypton Chronicles #1 © DC

Archie Comics: Oct, 1991 - No. 3, Feb, 1992 ($1.00, bi-monthly, limited series)

	GD 2.0	VG 4.0	FN 6.0	VF 8.0	VF/NM 9.0	NM- 9.2
1-3						4.00

NOTE: *No. 4 was planned, but cancelled.*

KORAK, SON OF TARZAN (Edgar Rice Burroughs)(See Tarzan #139)
Gold Key: Jan, 1964 - No. 45, Jan, 1972 (Painted-c No. 1-?)

	GD 2.0	VG 4.0	FN 6.0	VF 8.0	VF/NM 9.0	NM- 9.2
1-Russ Manning-a	8	16	24	56	108	160
2-5-Russ Manning-a	5	10	15	33	57	80
6-11-Russ Manning-a	5	10	15	30	50	70
12-23: 12,13-Warren Tufts-a. 14-Jon of the Kalahari ends. 15-Mabu, Jungle Boy begins. 21-Manning-a. 23-Last 12¢ issue	4	8	12	27	44	60
24-30	3	6	9	21	33	45
31-45	3	6	9	17	26	35

KORAK, SON OF TARZAN (Tarzan Family #60 on; see Tarzan #230)
National Periodical Publications: V9#46, May-June, 1972 - V12#56, Feb-Mar, 1974; No. 57, May-June, 1975 - No. 59, Sept-Oct, 1975 (Edgar Rice Burroughs)

	GD 2.0	VG 4.0	FN 6.0	VF 8.0	VF/NM 9.0	NM- 9.2
46-(52 pgs.)-Carson of Venus begins (origin), ends #56; Pellucidar feature; Weiss-a	3	6	9	15	22	28
47-59: 49-Origin Korak retold	2	4	6	8	11	14

NOTE: *All have covers by* ***Joe Kubert. Manning*** *strip reprints-No. 57-59.* ***Murphy Anderson*** *a-52,56.* ***Michael Kaluta*** *a-46-56.* ***Frank Thorne*** *a-46-51.*

KORE
Image Comics: Apr, 2003 - No. 5, Sept, 2003 ($2.95)

	GD 2.0	VG 4.0	FN 6.0	VF 8.0	VF/NM 9.0	NM- 9.2
1-5: 1-Two covers by Capullo and Seeley; Seeley-a (p)						3.00

KORG: 70,000 B. C. (TV)
Charlton Publications: May, 1975 - No. 9, Nov, 1976 (Hanna-Barbera)

	GD 2.0	VG 4.0	FN 6.0	VF 8.0	VF/NM 9.0	NM- 9.2
1,2: 1-Boyette-c/a. 2-Painted-c; Byrne text illos	2	4	6	11	16	20
3-9	2	4	6	8	11	14

KORNER KID COMICS: Four Star Publications: 1947 (Advertised, not pub.)

KORVAC SAGA (Secret Wars tie-in)
Marvel Comics: Aug, 2015 - No. 4, Nov, 2015 ($3.99, limited series)

	GD 2.0	VG 4.0	FN 6.0	VF 8.0	VF/NM 9.0	NM- 9.2
1-4-Guardians 3000, Avengers and Wonder Man app.; Abnett-s/Schmidt-a						4.00

KRAMPUS
Image Comics: Dec, 2013 - No. 5, May, 2014 ($2.99)

	GD 2.0	VG 4.0	FN 6.0	VF 8.0	VF/NM 9.0	NM- 9.2
1-5-Sinterklaas' assistant; Joines-s/Kotz-a						3.00

KRAZY KAT
Holt: 1946 (Hardcover)

	GD 2.0	VG 4.0	FN 6.0	VF 8.0	VF/NM 9.0	NM- 9.2
Reprints daily & Sunday strips by Herriman	55	110	165	352	601	850
dust jacket only	42	84	126	265	450	635

KRAZY KAT (See Ace Comics & March of Comics No. 72, 87)

KRAZY KAT COMICS (...& Ignatz the Mouse early issues)
Dell Publ. Co./Gold Key: May-June, 1951 - F.C. #696, Apr, 1956; Jan, 1964 (None by Herriman)

	GD 2.0	VG 4.0	FN 6.0	VF 8.0	VF/NM 9.0	NM- 9.2
1(1951)	9	18	27	59	117	175
2-5 (#5, 8-10/52)	5	10	15	34	60	85
Four Color 454,504	5	10	15	35	63	90
Four Color 548,619,696 (4/56)	5	10	15	31	53	75
1(10098-401)(1/64-Gold Key)(TV)	4	8	12	25	40	55

KRAZY KOMICS (1st Series) (Cindy Comics No. 27 on) (Also see Ziggy Pig)
Timely Comics (USA No. 1-21/JPC No. 22-26): July, 1942 - No. 26, Spr, 1947

	GD 2.0	VG 4.0	FN 6.0	VF 8.0	VF/NM 9.0	NM- 9.2
1-Toughy Tomcat, Ziggy Pig (by Jaffee) & Silly Seal begin	135	270	405	864	1482	2100
2	47	94	141	296	498	700
3-8,10	36	72	108	211	343	475
9-Hitler parody-c	61	122	183	390	670	950
11,13,14	24	48	72	142	234	325
12-Timely's entire art staff drew themselves into a Creeper story	37	74	111	222	361	500
15-(8-9/44)-Has "Super Soldier" by Pfc. Stan Lee	25	50	75	150	245	340
16-24,26: 16-(10-11/44). 26-Super Rabbit-c/story	21	42	63	122	199	275
25-Wacky Duck-c/story & begin; Kurtzman-a (6pgs.)	24	48	72	142	234	325

KRAZY KOMICS (2nd Series)
Timely/Marvel Comics: Aug, 1948 - No. 2, Nov, 1948

	GD 2.0	VG 4.0	FN 6.0	VF 8.0	VF/NM 9.0	NM- 9.2
1-Wolverton (10 pgs.) & Kurtzman (8 pgs.)-a; Eustice Hayseed begins (Li'l Abner swipe)	54	108	162	343	574	825
2-Wolverton-a (10 pgs.); Powerhouse Pepper cameo	39	78	117	231	378	525

KRAZY KROW (Also see Dopey Duck, Film Funnies, Funny Frolics & Movie Tunes)
Marvel Comics (ZPC): Summer, 1945 - No. 3, Wint, 1945/46

	GD 2.0	VG 4.0	FN 6.0	VF 8.0	VF/NM 9.0	NM- 9.2
1	30	60	90	177	289	400
2,3	19	38	57	111	176	240
I.W. Reprint #1('57), 2('58), 7	2	4	6	11	16	20

KRAZYLIFE (Becomes Nutty Life #2)
Fox Feature Syndicate: 1945 (no month)

	GD 2.0	VG 4.0	FN 6.0	VF 8.0	VF/NM 9.0	NM- 9.2
1-Funny animal	28	56	84	165	270	375

KREE/SKRULL WAR STARRING THE AVENGERS, THE
Marvel Comics: Sept, 1983 - No. 2, Oct, 1983 ($2.50, 68 pgs., Baxter paper)

	GD 2.0	VG 4.0	FN 6.0	VF 8.0	VF/NM 9.0	NM- 9.2
1,2						6.00

NOTE: ***Neal Adams*** *p-1r, 2.* ***Buscema*** *a-1r, 2r.* ***Simonson*** *a-1p; c-1p.*

KROFFT SUPERSHOW (TV)
Gold Key: Apr, 1978 - No. 6, Jan, 1979

	GD 2.0	VG 4.0	FN 6.0	VF 8.0	VF/NM 9.0	NM- 9.2
1-Photo-c	3	6	9	17	26	35
2-6: 6-Photo-c	3	6	9	14	19	24

KRULL
Marvel Comics Group: Nov, 1983 - No. 2, Dec, 1983

	GD 2.0	VG 4.0	FN 6.0	VF 8.0	VF/NM 9.0	NM- 9.2
1,2-Adaptation of film; r/Marvel Super Special. 1-Photo-c from movie						4.00

KRUSTY COMICS (TV)(See Simpsons Comics)
Bongo Comics: 1995 - No. 3, 1995 ($2.25, limited series)

	GD 2.0	VG 4.0	FN 6.0	VF 8.0	VF/NM 9.0	NM- 9.2
1-3						4.00

KRYPTON CHRONICLES
DC Comics: Sept, 1981 - No. 3, Nov, 1981

	GD 2.0	VG 4.0	FN 6.0	VF 8.0	VF/NM 9.0	NM- 9.2
1-3: 1-Buckler-c(p)						4.00

KRYPTO THE SUPERDOG (TV)
DC Comics: Nov, 2006 - No. 6, Apr, 2007 ($2.25)

	GD 2.0	VG 4.0	FN 6.0	VF 8.0	VF/NM 9.0	NM- 9.2
1-6-Based on Cartoon Network series. 1-Origin retold						3.00

KULL
Dark Horse Comics: Nov, 2008 - No. 6, May, 2009 ($2.99)

	GD 2.0	VG 4.0	FN 6.0	VF 8.0	VF/NM 9.0	NM- 9.2
1-6: 1-Nelson-s/Conrad-a; two covers by Andy Brase and Joe Kubert						3.00

KULL AND THE BARBARIANS
Marvel Comics: May, 1975 - No. 3, Sept, 1975 ($1.00, B&W, magazine)

	GD 2.0	VG 4.0	FN 6.0	VF 8.0	VF/NM 9.0	NM- 9.2
1-(84 pgs.) Andru/Wood-r/Kull #1; 2 pgs. Neal Adams; Gil Kane(p), Marie & John Severin-a(r); Krenkel text illo.	3	6	9	16	24	32
2,3: 2-(84 pgs.) Red Sonja by Chaykin begins; Solomon Kane by Weiss/Adams; Gil Kane-a; Solomon Kane pin-up by Wrightson. 3-(76 pgs.) Origin Red Sonja by Chaykin; Adams-a; Solomon Kane app.	3	6	9	14	19	24

KULL: THE CAT AND THE SKULL
Dark Horse Comics: Oct, 2011 - No. 4, Jan, 2012 ($3.50, limited series)

	GD 2.0	VG 4.0	FN 6.0	VF 8.0	VF/NM 9.0	NM- 9.2
1-4-Lapham-s/Guzman-a/Chen-c. 1-Variant-c by Hans						3.50

KULL THE CONQUEROR (...the Destroyer #11 on; see Conan #1, Creatures on the Loose #10, Marvel Preview, Monsters on the Prowl)
Marvel Comics Group: June, 1971 - No. 2, Sept, 1971; No. 3, July, 1972 - No. 15, Aug, 1974; No. 16, Aug, 1976 - No. 29, Oct, 1978

	GD 2.0	VG 4.0	FN 6.0	VF 8.0	VF/NM 9.0	NM- 9.2
1-Andru/Wood-a; 2nd app. & origin Kull; 15¢ issue	6	12	18	37	66	95
2-5: 2-3rd Kull app. Last 15¢ iss. 3-13: 20¢ issues. 3-Thulsa Doom-c/app.	3	6	9	17	26	35
6-10: 7-Thulsa Doom-c/app	2	4	6	10	14	18
11-15: 11-15-Ploog-a. 14,15: 25¢ issues	2	4	6	8	11	14
16-(Regular 25¢ edition)(8/76)	2	3	4	6	8	10
16-(30¢-c variant, limited distribution)	3	6	9	17	26	35
17-29: 21-23-(Reg. 30¢ editions)	2	3	4	6	8	10
21-23-(35¢-c variants, limited distribution)	10	20	30	64	132	200

NOTE: *No. 1, 2, 7-9, 11 are based on Robert E. Howard stories.* ***Alcala*** *a-17p, 18-20i; c-24.* ***Ditko*** *a-12r, 15r.* ***Gil Kane*** *c-15p, 21.* ***Nebres*** *a-22i-27i; c-25i, 27i.* ***Ploog*** *c-11, 12p, 13.* ***Severin*** *a-2-9i; c-2-10i, 19.* ***Starlin*** *c-14.*

KULL THE CONQUEROR
Marvel Comics Group: Dec, 1982 - No. 2, Mar, 1983 (52 pgs., Baxter paper)

	GD 2.0	VG 4.0	FN 6.0	VF 8.0	VF/NM 9.0	NM- 9.2
1,2: 1-Buscema-a(p)						4.00

KULL THE CONQUEROR (No. 9,10 titled "Kull")
Marvel Comics Group: 5/83 - No. 10, 6/85 (52 pgs., Baxter paper)

	GD 2.0	VG 4.0	FN 6.0	VF 8.0	VF/NM 9.0	NM- 9.2
V3#1-10: Buscema-a in #1-3,5-10						4.00

NOTE: *Bolton a-4. Golden painted c-3-8. Guice a-4p. Sienkiewicz a-4; c-2.*

KULL: THE HATE WITCH
Dark Horse Comics: Nov, 2010 - No. 4, Feb, 2011 ($3.50)

	GD 2.0	VG 4.0	FN 6.0	VF 8.0	VF/NM 9.0	NM- 9.2
1-4-Lapham-s/Guzman-a/Fleming-c						3.50

Kurt Busiek's Astro City V2 #16 © Jukebox

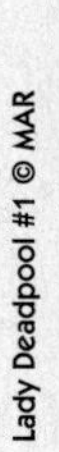
Lady Deadpool #1 © MAR

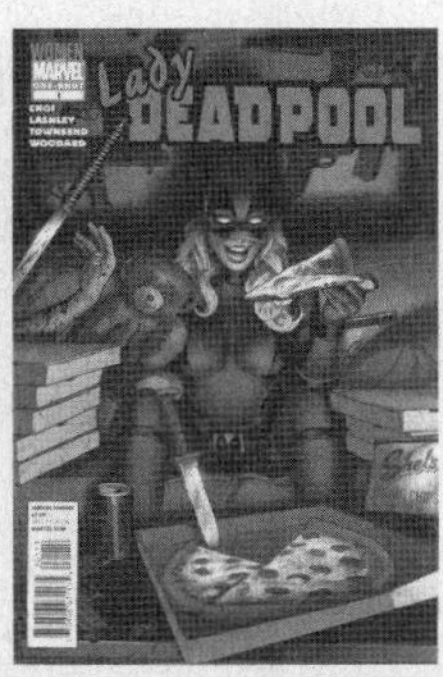

Lady Death: A Medieval Tale #2 © CRO

	GD 2.0	VG 4.0	FN 6.0	VF 8.0	VF/NM 9.0	NM- 9.2

KUNG FU (See Deadly Hands of..., & Master of...)

KUNG FU FIGHTER (See Richard Dragon...)

KUNG FU PANDA
Titan Comics: Nov, 2015 -No. 4, Jan, 2016 ($3.99, limited series)

1-4-Simon Furman-s. 1,2-Lee Robinson-a 4.00

KUNG FU PANDA 2
Ape Entertainment: 2011 - No. 6, 2012 ($3.95/$3.99, limited series)

1-6-Short stories by various 4.00

KURT BUSIEK'S ASTRO CITY (Limited series) (Also see Astro City: Local Heroes)
Image Comics (Juke Box Productions): Aug, 1995 - No. 6, Jan, 1996 ($2.25)

1-Kurt Busiek scripts, Brent Anderson-a & Alex Ross front & back-c begins; 1st app. Samaritan & Honor Guard (Cleopatra, MHP, Beautie, The Black Rapier, Quarrel & N-Forcer) 2 4 6 8 10 12
2-6: 2-1st app. The Silver Agent, The Old Soldier, & the "original" Honor Guard (Max O'Millions, Starwoman, the "original" Cleopatra, the "original" N-Forcer, the Bouncing Beatnik, Leopardman & Kitkat). 3-1st app. Jack-in-the-Box & The Deacon. 4-1st app. Winged Victory (cameo), The Hanged Man & The First Family. 5-1st app. Crackerjack, The Astro City Irregulars, Nightingale & Sunbird. 6-Origin Samaritan; 1st full app. Winged Victory 1 3 4 6 8 10
Life In The Big City-(8/96, $19.95, trade paperback)-r/Image Comics limited series w/sketchbook & cover gallery; Ross-c 20.00
Life In The Big City-(8/96, $49.95, hardcover, 1000 print run)-r/Image Comics limited series w/sketchbook & cover gallery; Ross-c 50.00

KURT BUSIEK'S ASTRO CITY (1st Homage Comics series)
Image Comics (Homage Comics): V2#1, Sept, 1996 - No. 15, Dec, 1998;
DC Comics (Homage Comics): No. 16, Mar, 1999 - No. 22, Aug, 2000 ($2.50)

1/2-(10/96)-The Hanged Man story; 1st app. The All-American & Slugger, The Lamplighter, The Time-Keeper & Eterneon 1 3 4 6 8 10
1/2-(1/98) 2nd printing w/new cover 3.00
1- Kurt Busiek scripts, Alex Ross-c, Brent Anderson-p & Will Blyberg-i begin; intro The Gentleman, Thunderhead & Helia. 1 2 3 5 6 8
1-(12/97, $4.95) "3-D Edition" w/glasses 5.00
2-Origin The First Family; Astra story 1 2 3 4 5 7
3-5: 4-1st app. The Crossbreed, Ironhorse, Glue Gun & The Confessor (cameo) 6.00
6-10 5.00
11-22: 14-20-Steeljack story arc. 16-(3/99) First DC issue 3.00
TPB-($19.95) Ross-c, r/#4-9, #1/2 w/sketchbook 20.00
Family Album TPB ($19.95) r/#1-3,10-13 20.00
The Tarnished Angel HC ($29.95) r/#14-20; new Ross dust jacket; sketch pages by Anderson & Ross; cover gallery with reference photos 30.00
The Tarnished Angel SC ($19.95) r/#14-20; new Ross-c 20.00

LABMAN
Image Comics: Nov, 1996 ($3.50, one-shot)

1-Allred-c 4.00

LAB RATS
DC Comics: June, 2002 - No. 8, Jan, 2003 ($2.50)

1-8-John Byrne-s/a. 5,6-Superman app. 3.00

LABYRINTH
Marvel Comics Group: Nov, 1986 - No. 3, Jan, 1987 (Limited series)

1-3: David Bowie movie adaptation; r/Marvel Super Special #40 2 4 6 13 18 22

LABYRINTH 30TH ANNIVERSARY SPECIAL (Jim Henson's...)
Boom Entertainment (Archaia): Aug, 2016 ($9.99, one-shot)

1-Short stories by various; multiple covers 10.00

LA COSA NOSTROID (See Scud: The Disposible Assassin)
Fireman Press: Mar, 1996 - No. 9, 1998 ($2.95, B&W)

1-9-Dan Harmon-s/Rob Schrab-c/a 3.00

LAD: A DOG (Movie)
Dell Publishing Co.: 1961 - No. 2, July-Sept, 1962

Four Color 1303 5 10 15 33 57 80
2 4 8 12 23 37 50

LADY AND THE TRAMP (Disney, See Dell Giants & Movie Comics)
Dell Publishing Co.: No. 629, May, 1955 - No. 634, June, 1955

Four Color 629 (#1)-..with Jock 7 14 21 49 92 135
Four Color 634-...Album 5 10 15 35 63 90

LADY CASTLE
BOOM! Studios: Jan, 2017 - No. 4 ($3.99, limited series)

1-Delilah Dawson-s/Ashley Woods-a 4.00

LADY COP (See 1st Issue Special)

LADY DEADPOOL
Marvel Comics: Sept, 2010 ($3.99, one-shot)

1-Land-c/Lashley-a 2 4 6 9 12 15

LADY DEATH (See Evil Ernie)
Chaos! Comics: Jan, 1994 - No. 3, Mar, 1994 ($2.75, limited series)

1/2-S. Hughes-c/a in all, 1/2 Velvet 1 2 3 4 5 7
1/2 Gold 1 3 4 6 8 10
1/2 Signed Limited Edition 2 4 6 8 10 12
1-($3.50)-Chromium-c 2 4 6 11 16 20
1-Commemorative 2 4 6 9 13 16
1-(9/96, $2.95) "Encore Presentation"; r/#1 3.00
2 1 2 3 5 6 8
3 5.00
... And Jade (4/02, $2.99) Augustyn-s/Reis-a 3.00
...And The Women of Chaos! Gallery #1 (11/96, $2.25) pin-ups by various 3.00
.../Bad Kitty (9/01, $2.99) Mota-c/a 3.00
.../Bedlam (6/02, $2.99) Augustyn-s/Reis-c 3.00
...By Steven Hughes (6/00, $2.95) Tribute issue to Steven Hughes 3.00
...By Steven Hughes Deluxe Edition(6/00, $15.95) 16.00
.../Chastity (1/02, $2.99) Mota-c/a; Augustyn-s 3.00
...Death Becomes Her #0 (11/97, $2.95) Hughes-c/a 3.00
...FAN Edition: All Hallow's Eve #1 (1/97, mail-in) 5.00
...In Lingerie #1 (8/95, $2.95) pin-ups, wraparound-c 3.00
...In Lingerie #1-Leather Edition (10,000) 12.00
...In Lingerie #1-Micro Premium Edition; Lady Demon-c (2,000) 35.00
...: Love Bites (3/01, $2.99) Kaminski-s/Luke Ross-a 3.00
.../Medieval Witchblade (8/01, $3.50) covers by Molenaar and Silvestri 3.50
.../Medieval Witchblade Preview Ed. (8/01, $1.99) Molenaar-c 3.00
...: Mischief Night (11/01, $2.99) Ostrander-s/Reis-a 3.00
...: Re-Imagined (7/02, $2.99) Gossett-c 3.00
...: River of Fear (4/01, $2.99) Bennett-a(p)/Cleavenger-c 3.00
...Swimsuit Special #1-($2.50)-Wraparound-c 3.00
...Swimsuit Special #1-Red velvet-c 14.00
...Swimsuit 2001 #1-(2/01, $2.99)-Reis-c; art by various 3.00
....: The Reckoning (7/94, $6.95)-r/#1-3 7.00
...: The Reckoning (8/95, $12.95)- new printing including Lady Death 1/2 & Swimsuit Special #1 13.00
.../Vampirella (3/99, $3.50) Hughes-c/a 3.50
.../Vampirella 2 (3/00, $3.50) Deodato-c/a 3.50
... Vs. Purgatori (12/99, $3.50) Deodato-a 3.50
... Vs. Vampirella Preview (2/00, $1.00) Deodato-a/c 3.00

LADY DEATH (Ongoing series)
Chaos! Comics: Feb, 1998 - No. 16, May, 1999 ($2.95)

1-16: 1-4: Pulido-s/Hughes-c/a. 5-8,13-16-Deodato-a. 9-11-Hughes-a 3.00
...Retribution (8/98, $2.95) Jadsen-a 3.00
...Retribution Premium Ed. 6.00

LADY DEATH
Boundless Comics: No. 0, Nov, 2010 - No. 26 ($3.99)

0-26-Pulido & Wolfer-s/Mueller-a on most; multiple covers on all. 25-Borstel-a 4.00
... Free Comic Book Day 2012 (5/12, free) "The Beginning" on cover; Mueller-a 3.00
... Origins Annual 1 (8/11, $4.99) Martin-a/Pulido-s 5.00
... Premiere (7/10, free) previews series; five covers 3.00

LADY DEATH...
Coffin Comics (One-shots)

... Chaos Rules 1 (5/16, $7.99) Pulido & Augustyn-s/Verma-a 8.00
... Revelations 1 (2/17, $3.99) Pin-up gallery of covers 4.00
... Zodiac 1 (12/16, $3.99) 12 pin-up images of the 12 zodiac signs by Nei Ruffino 4.00

LADY DEATH: ALIVE
Chaos! Comics: May, 2001 - No. 4, Aug, 2001 ($2.99, limited series)

1-4-Ivan Reis-a; Lady Death becomes mortal 3.00

LADY DEATH: A MEDIEVAL TALE (Brian Pulido's...)
CG Entertainment: Mar, 2003 - No. 12, Apr, 2004 ($2.95)

1-12: 1-Brian Pulido-s/Ivan Reis-a; Lady Death in the CrossGen Universe 3.00
Vol.1 TPB (2003, $9.95) digest-sized reprint of #1-6 10.00

LADY DEATH: APOCALYPSE
Boundless Comics: Jan, 2015 - No. 6, Jun, 2015 ($4.99)

Lady Demon (2014 series) #4 © DYN

Lady Killer #4 © Jones & Rich

Lady Pendragon V3 #2 © Matt Hawkins

GD 2.0 | VG 4.0 | FN 6.0 | VF 8.0 | VF/NM 9.0 | NM- 9.2

1-6: 1-4-Wolfer-s/Borstel-a; multiple covers. 5,6-Wickline-s/Mueller-a 5.00
#0 (8/15, $6.99) Pulido-s/Valenzuela-a; bonus art gallery 7.00

LADY DEATH: DARK ALLIANCE
Chaos! Comics: July, 2002 - No. 5, ($2.99, limited series)
1-3-Reis-a/Ostrander-s 3.00

LADY DEATH: DARK MILLENNIUM
Chaos! Comics: Feb, 2000 - No. 3, Apr, 2000 ($2.95, limited series)
Preview (6/00, $5.00) 5.00
1-3-Ivan Reis-a 3.00

LADY DEATH: GODDESS RETURNS
Chaos! Comics: Jun, 2002 - No. 2, Aug, 2002 ($2.99, limited series)
1,2-Mota-a/Ostrander-s 3.00

LADY DEATH: HEARTBREAKER
Chaos! Comics: Mar, 2002 - No. 4, ($2.99, limited series)
1-Molenaar-a/Ostrander-s 3.00

LADY DEATH: JUDGEMENT WAR
Chaos! Comics: Nov, 1999 - No. 3, Jan, 2000 ($2.95, limited series)
Prelude (10/99) two covers 3.00
1-3-Ivan Reis-a 3.00

LADY DEATH: LAST RITES
Chaos! Comics: Oct, 2001 - No. 4, Feb, 2001 ($2.99, limited series)
1-4-Ivan Reis-a/Ostrander-s 3.00

LADY DEATH ORIGINS: CURSED
Boundless Comics: Mar, 2012 - No. 3, May, 2012 ($4.99/$3.99, limited series)
1-($4.99)-Pulido-s/Guzman-a; multiple covers 5.00
2,3-($3.99) 4.00

LADY DEATH: THE CRUCIBLE
Chaos! Comics: Nov, 1996 - No. 6, Oct, 1997 ($3.50/$2.95, limited series)
1/2 4.00
1/2 Cloth Edition 8.00
1-Wraparound silver foil embossed-c 4.00
2-6-($2.95) 3.00

LADY DEATH: THE GAUNTLET
Chaos! Comics: Apr, 2002 - No. 2, May, 2002 ($2.99, limited series)
1,2: 1-J. Scott Campbell-c/redesign of Lady Death's outfit; Mota-a 3.00

LADY DEATH: THE ODYSSEY
Chaos! Comics: Apr, 1996 - No. 4, Aug, 1996 ($3.50/$2.95)
1-($1.50)-Sneak Peek Preview 3.00
1-($1.50)-Sneak Peek Preview Micro Premium Edition (2500 print run) 2 4 6 8 10 12
1-($3.50)-Embossed, wraparound goil foil-c 5.00
1-Black Onyx Edition (200 print run) 5 10 15 33 57 80
1-($19.95)-Premium Edition (10,000 print run) 20.00
2-4-($2.95) 3.00

LADY DEATH: THE RAPTURE
Chaos! Comics: Jun, 1999 - No. 4, Sept, 1999 ($2.95, limited series)
1-4-Ivan Reis-c/a; Pulido-s 3.00

LADY DEATH: THE WILD HUNT (Brian Pulido's...)
CG Entertainment: Apr, 2004 - No. 2, May, 2005 ($2.95)
1-2: 1-Brian Pulido-s/Jim Cheung-a 3.00

LADY DEATH: TRIBULATION
Chaos! Comics: Dec, 2000 - No. 4, Mar, 2001 ($2.95, limited series)
1-4-Ivan Reis-a; Kaminski-s 3.00

LADY DEATH II: BETWEEN HEAVEN & HELL
Chaos! Comics: Mar, 1995 - No. 4, July, 1995 ($3.50, limited series)
1-Chromium wraparound-c; Evil Ernie cameo 5.00
1-Commemorative (4,000), 1-Black Velvet-c 2 4 6 10 14 18
1-Gold 1 3 4 6 8 10
1-"Refractor" edition (5,000) 2 4 6 11 16 20
2-4 3.50
4-Lady Demon variant-c 1 2 3 5 7 9
Trade paperback-($12.95)-r/#1-4 13.00

LADY DEMON
Chaos! Comics: Mar, 2000 - No. 3, May, 2000 ($2.95, limited series)
1-3-Kaminski-s/Brewer-a 3.00

LADY DEMON
Dynamite Entertainment: 2014 - No. 4, 2015 ($3.99)
1-4: 1-3-Gillespie-s/Andolfo-a; multiple covers. 1-Origin retold. 4-Ramirez-a 4.00

LADY FOR A NIGHT (See Cinema Comics Herald)

LADY JUSTICE (See Neil Gaiman's...)

LADY KILLER
Dark Horse Comics: Jan, 2015 - No. 5, May, 2015 ($3.50)
1-5-Joëlle Jones-a/Jones and Jamie Rich-s 3.50

LADY KILLER 2
Dark Horse Comics: Aug, 2016 - Present ($3.99)
1-3-Joëlle Jones-s/a 4.00

LADY LUCK (Formerly Smash #1-85) (Also see Spirit Sections #1)
Quality Comics Group: No. 86, Dec, 1949 - No. 90, Aug, 1950
86(#1) 97 194 291 621 1061 1500
87-90 66 132 198 419 722 1025

LADY MECHANIKA
Aspen MLT: No. 0, Oct, 2010 - No. 5, Mar, 2015 ($2.50/$2.99)
0-Joe Benitez-s/a; two covers; Benitez interview and sketch pages 3.00
0-(Benitez Productions, 8/15, $1.00) 3.00
1-(1/11, $2.99) Multiple covers 10.00
2-5-Multiple covers on each. 5-($4.99) 5.00
... FCBD Vol. 1 Issue 1 (5/16, giveaway) r/#0; excerpt from mini-series 3.00

LADY MECHANIKA: LA DAMA DE LA MUERTE
Benitez Productions: Sept, 2016 - No. 3, Dec, 2016 ($3.99)
1-3-Joe Benitez-a/s; M.M. Chen-s; multiple covers on each 4.00

LADY MECHANIKA: THE LOST BOYS OF WEST ABBEY
Benitez Productions: May, 2016 - No. 2, Jun, 2016 ($3.99)
1,2-Joe Benitez-a/M.M. Chen-s; multiple covers on each 4.00

LADY MECHANIKA: THE TABLET OF DESTINIES
Benitez Productions: Apr, 2015 - No. 6, Oct, 2015 ($3.99)
1-6-Joe Benitez-s/a; multiple covers on each 4.00

LADY PENDRAGON
Maximum Press: Mar, 1996 ($2.50)
1-Matt Hawkins script 3.00

LADY PENDRAGON
Image Comics: Nov, 1998 - No. 3, Jan, 1999 ($2.50, mini-series)
Preview (6/98) Flip book w/ Deity preview 3.00
1-3: 1-Matt Hawkins-s/Stinsman-a 3.00
1-($6.95) DF Ed. with variant-c by Jusko 7.00
2-($4.95)Variant edition 5.00
0-(3/99) Origin; flip book 3.00

LADY PENDRAGON (Volume 3)
Image Comics: Apr, 1999 - No. 9, Mar, 2000 ($2.50, mini-series)
1,2,4-6,8-10: 1-Matt Hawkins-s/Stinsman-a. 2-Peterson-c 3.00
3-Flip book w/Alley Cat preview (1st app.) 4.00
7-($3.95) Flip book; Stinsman-a/Cleavenger painted-a 4.00
Gallery Edition (10/99, $2.95) pin-ups 3.00
...Merlin (1/00, $2.95) Stinsman-a 3.00
.../ More Than Mortal (5/99, $2.50) Scott-s/Norton-a; 2 covers by Norton & Finch 3.00
.../ More Than Mortal Preview (2/99) Diamond Dateline supplement 3.00
Pilot Season: Lady Pendragon (5/08, $3.99) Hawkins-s/Eru-a; wraparound-c by Struzan 4.00

LADY RAWHIDE
Topps Comics: July, 1995 - No. 5, Mar, 1996 ($2.95, bi-monthly, limited series)
1-5: Don McGregor scripts & Mayhew-a. in all. 2-Stelfreeze-c. 3-Hughes-c. 4-Golden-c. 5-Julie Bell-c. 3.00
It Can't Happen Here TPB (8/99, $16.95) r/#1-5 17.00
Mini Comic 1 (7/95) Maroto-a; Zorro app. 3.00
Special Edition 1 (6/95, $3.95)-Reprints 4.00

LADY RAWHIDE (Volume 2)
Topps Comics: Oct, 1996 -No. 5, June, 1997 ($2.95, limited series)
1-5: 1-Julie Bell-c. 3.00

LADY RAWHIDE (Volume 1)
Dynamite Entertainment: 2013 - No. 5, 2014 ($3.99)

Lady Rawhide / Lady Zorro #1 © Zorro Prods.

Lana #7 © MAR

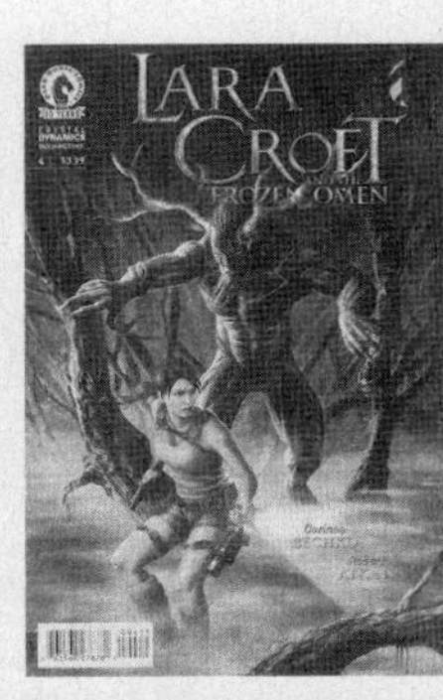

Lara Croft and the Frozen Omen #4 © Square Enix

	GD 2.0	VG 4.0	FN 6.0	VF 8.0	VF/NM 9.0	NM- 9.2

1-5-Trautmann-s/Estevam-a/Linsner-c 4.00

LADY RAWHIDE / LADY ZORRO
Dynamite Entertainment: 2015 - No. 4, 2015 ($3.99, limited series)
1-4-Denton-s/Villegas-a. 1-Mayhew-c. 2-4-Chin-c 4.00

LADY RAWHIDE OTHER PEOPLE'S BLOOD (ZORRO'S ...)
Image Comics: Mar, 1999 - No. 5, July, 1999 ($2.95, B&W)
1-5-Reprints Lady Rawhide series in B&W 3.00

LADY SUPREME (See Asylum)(Also see Supreme & Kid Supreme)
Image Comics (Extreme): May, 1996 - No. 2, June, 1996 ($2.50, limited series)
1,2-Terry Moore -s: 1-Terry Moore-c. 2-Flip book w/Newmen preview 3.00

LADY ZORRO
Dynamite Entertainment: 2014 - No. 4, 2014 ($3.99, limited series)
1-4-de Campi-s/Villegas-a/Linsner-c 4.00

LAFF-A-LYMPICS (TV)(See The Funtastic World of Hanna-Barbera)
Marvel Comics: Mar, 1978 - No. 13, Mar, 1979 (Newsstand sales only)
1-Yogi Bear, Scooby Doo, Pixie & Dixie, etc. 3 6 9 19 30 40
2-8 3 6 9 14 19 24
9-13: 11-Jetsons x-over; 1 pg. illustrated bio of Mighty Mightor, Herculoids, Shazzan, Galaxy Trio & Space Ghost 3 6 9 16 23 30

LAFFY-DAFFY COMICS
Rural Home Publ. Co.: Feb, 1945 - No. 2, Mar, 1945
1-Funny animal 14 28 42 76 108 140
2-Funny animal 11 22 33 62 86 110

LAKE OF FIRE
Image Comics: Aug, 2016 - No. 5, Dec, 2016 ($3.99)
1-5-Nathan Fairbairn-s/Matt Smith-a 4.00

LA MUERTA...
Coffin Comics (One-shots)
...: Descent 1 (7/16, $7.99) Maclean-s/Gomez-a; origin 8.00
...: Last Rites 1 (9/16, $7.99) Maclean-s/Gomez-a; origin 8.00

LANA (Little Lana No. 8 on)
Marvel Comics (MjMC): Aug, 1948 - No. 7, Aug, 1949 (Also see Annie Oakley)
1-Rusty, Millie begin 53 106 159 334 567 800
2-Kurtzman's "Hey Look" (1); last Rusty 26 52 78 154 252 350
3-7: 3-Nellie begins 20 40 60 114 182 250

LANCELOT & GUINEVERE (See Movie Classics)

LANCELOT LINK, SECRET CHIMP (TV)
Gold Key: Apr, 1971 - No. 8, Feb, 1973 (All photo-c)
1 5 10 15 35 63 90
2-8 4 8 12 23 37 50

LANCELOT STRONG (See The Shield)

LANCE O'CASEY (See Mighty Midget & Whiz Comics)
Fawcett Publications: Spring, 1946 - No. 3, Fall, 1946; No. 4, Summer, 1948
1-Captain Marvel app. on-c 26 52 78 154 252 350
2 16 32 48 94 147 200
3,4 14 28 42 80 115 150
NOTE: *The cover for the 1st issue was done in 1942 but was not published until 1946. The cover shows 68 pages but actually has only 36 pages.*

LANCER (TV)(Western)
Gold Key: Feb, 1969 - No. 3, Sept, 1969 (All photo-c)
1 4 8 12 23 37 50
2,3 3 6 9 17 26 35

LANDO (Star Wars)
Marvel Comics: Sept, 2015 - No. 5, Dec, 2015 ($3.99, limited series)
1-5-Soule-s/Maleev-a; Lobot & Emperor Palpatine app. 4.00

LAND OF NOD, THE
Dark Horse Comics: July, 1997 - No. 3, Feb, 1998 ($2.95, B&W)
1-3-Jetcat; Jay Stephens-s/a 3.00

LAND OF OZ
Arrow Comics: 1998 - No. 9 ($2.95, B&W)
1-9-Bishop-s/Bryan-s/a 3.00

LAND OF THE DEAD (George A. Romaro's...)
IDW Publishing: Aug, 2005 - No. 5 ($3.99, limited series)
1-4-Adaptation of 2005 movie; Ryall-s/Rodriguez-a 4.00
TPB (3/06, $19.99) r/#1-5; cover gallery 20.00

LAND OF THE GIANTS (TV)
Gold Key: Nov, 1968 - No. 5, Sept, 1969 (All have photo-c)
1 6 12 18 37 66 95
2-5 4 8 12 25 40 55

LAND OF THE LOST COMICS (Radio)
E. C. Comics: July-Aug, 1946 - No. 9, Spring, 1948
1 41 82 123 256 428 600
2 26 52 78 154 252 350
3-9 22 44 66 132 216 300

LAND UNKNOWN, THE (Movie)
Dell Publishing Co.: No. 845, Sept, 1957
Four Color 845-Alex Toth-a 10 20 30 66 138 210

LANTERN CITY (TV)
BOOM! Studios (Archaia): May, 2015 - No. 12, Apr, 2016 ($3.99)
1-12: 1-Jenkins & Daley-s/Magno-a. 3-Daley & Scott-s 4.00

LA PACIFICA
DC Comics (Paradox Press): 1994/1995 ($4.95, B&W, limited series, digest size, mature)
1-3 5.00

LARA CROFT AND THE FROZEN OMEN (Also see Tomb Raider titles)
Dark Horse Comics: Oct, 2015 - No. 5, Feb, 2016 ($3.99)
1-5: 1-Corinna Bechko-s/Randy Green-a 4.00

LARAMIE (TV)
Dell Publishing Co.: Aug, 1960 - July, 1962 (All photo-c)
Four Color 1125-Gil Kane/Heath-a 8 16 24 51 96 140
Four Color 1223,1284, 01-418-207 (7/62) 6 12 18 37 66 95

LAREDO (TV)
Gold Key: June, 1966
1 (10179-606)-Photo-c 3 6 9 21 33 45

LARFLEEZE (Orange Lantern) (Story continued from back-ups in Threshold #1-5)
DC Comics: Aug, 2013 - No. 12, Aug, 2014 ($2.99)
1-12: 1-Giffen & DeMatteis-s/Kolins-a/Porter-c; origin told 3.00

LARGE FEATURE COMIC (Formerly called Black & White in previous guides)
Dell Publishing Co.: 1939 - No. 13, 1943

Note: See individual alphabetical listings for prices

1 (Series I)-Dick Tracy Meets the Blank
3-Heigh-Yo Silver! The Lone Ranger (text & ill.)(76 pgs.); also exists as a Whitman #710; based on radio
6-Terry & the Pirates & The Dragon Lady; reprints dailies from 1936
8-Dick Tracy the Racket Buster
9-King of the Royal Mounted (Zane Grey's...)
10-(Scarce)-Gang Busters (No. appears on inside front cover); first slick cover (based on radio program)
13-Dick Tracy and Scottie of Scotland Yard
15-Dick Tracy and the Kidnapped Princes
17-Gang Busters (1941)
18-Phantasmo (see The Funnies #45)
20-Donald Duck Comic Paint Book (rarer than #16) (Disney)
21,22: 21-Private Buck. 22-Nuts & Jolts
24-Popeye in "Thimble Theatre" by Segar
26-Smitty
28-Grin and Bear It
30-Tillie the Toiler
2-Winnie Winkle (#1)
3-Dick Tracy
4-Tiny Tim (#1)
6-Terry and the Pirates; Caniff-a
8-Bugs Bunny (#1)('42)
9-Bringing Up Father
10-Popeye (Thimble Theatre)
11-Barney Google and Snuffy Smith
2-Terry and the Pirates (#1)
4-Dick Tracy Gets His Man
5-Tarzan of the Apes (#1) by Harold Foster (origin); reprints 1st Tarzan dailies from 1929
7-(Scarce, 52 pgs.)-Hi-Yo Silver the Lone Ranger to the Rescue; also exists as a Whitman #715, based on radio program
11-Dick Tracy Foils the Mad Doc Hump
12-Smilin' Jack; no number on-c
14-Smilin' Jack Helps G-Men Solve a Case!
16-Donald Duck; 1st app. Daisy Duck on back cover (6/41-Disney)
19-Dumbo Comic Paint Book (Disney); partial-r from 4-Color #17
23-The Nebbs
25-Smilin' Jack-1st issue to show title on-c
27-Terry and the Pirates; Caniff-c/a
29-Moon Mullins
1 (Series II)-Peter Rabbit by Harrison Cady; arrival date-3/27/42
5-Toots and Casper
7-Pluto Saves the Ship (#1) (Disney)-Written by Carl Barks, Jack Hannah, & Nick George (Barks' 1st comic book work)
12-Private Buck

Lash LaRue Western #46 © FAW

Lassie #17 © MGM

Last Gang in Town #1 © Oliver & Dayglo

GD VG FN VF VF/NM NM-
2.0 4.0 6.0 8.0 9.0 9.2

13-(nn)-1001 Hours Of Fun; puzzles & games; by A. W. Nugent. This book was bound as #13 with Large Feature Comics in publisher's files

NOTE: *The Black & White Feature Books are oversized 8-1/2x11-3/8" comics with color covers and black and white interiors. The first nine issues all have rough, heavy stock covers and, except for #7, all have 76 pages, including covers. #7 and #10-on all have 52 pages. Beginning with #10 the covers are slick and thin and, because of their size, are difficult to handle without damaging. For this reason, they are seldom found in fine to mint condition. The paper stock, unlike Wow #1 and Capt. Marvel #1, is itself not unstable ...just thin. Many issues were reprinted in the early 1980s, identical except for the copyright notice on the first page.*

LARRY DOBY, BASEBALL HERO
Fawcett Publications: 1950 (Cleveland Indians)

nn-Bill Ward-a; photo-c 81 162 243 518 884 1250

LARRY HARMON'S LAUREL AND HARDY (...Comics)
National Periodical Publ.: July-Aug, 1972 (Digest advertised, not published)

1-Low print run 9 18 27 59 117 175

LARS OF MARS
Ziff-Davis Publishing Co.: No. 10, Apr-May, 1951 - No. 11, July-Aug, 1951 (Painted-c) (Created by Jerry Siegel, editor)

10-Origin; Anderson-a(3) in each; classic robot-c 107 214 321 680 1165 1650
11-Gene Colan-a; classic-c 87 174 261 553 952 1350

LARS OF MARS 3-D
Eclipse Comics: Apr, 1987 ($2.50)

1-r/Lars of Mars #10,11 in 3-D plus new story 5.00
2-D limited edition (B&W, 100 copies) 20.00

LASER ERASER & PRESSBUTTON (See Axel Pressbutton & Miracle Man 9)
Eclipse Comics: Nov, 1985 - No. 6, 1987 (95¢/$2.50, limited series)

1-6: 5,6-(95¢) 3.00
...In 3-D 1 (8/86, $2.50) 4.00
2-D 1 (B&W, limited to 100 copies signed & numbered) 20.00

LASH LARUE WESTERN (Movie star; King of the bullwhip)(See Fawcett Movie Comic, Motion Picture Comics & Six-Gun Heroes)
Fawcett Publications: Sum, 1949 - No. 46, Jan, 1954 (36 pgs., 1-6,9,13,16-on)

1-Lash & his horse Black Diamond begin; photo front/back-c begin
58 116 174 371 636 900
2(11/49) 28 56 84 165 270 375
3-5 21 42 63 126 206 285
6,9: 6-Last photo back-c; intro. Frontier Phantom (Lash's twin brother)
19 38 57 109 172 235
7,8,10 (52pgs.) 20 40 60 114 182 250
11,12,14,15 (52pgs.) 15 30 45 84 127 170
13,16-20 (36pgs.) 14 28 42 80 115 150
21-30: 21-The Frontier Phantom app. 12 24 36 69 97 125
31-45 11 22 33 60 83 105
46-Last Fawcett issue & photo-c 11 22 33 64 90 115

LASH LARUE WESTERN (Continues from Fawcett series)
Charlton Comics: No. 47, Mar-Apr, 1954 - No. 84, June, 1961

47-Photo-c 14 28 42 80 115 150
48 11 22 33 60 83 105
49-60, 67,68-(68 pgs.). 68-Check-a 9 18 27 52 69 85
61-66,69,70: 52-r/#8; 53-r/#22 9 18 27 47 61 75
71-83 8 16 24 40 50 60
84-Last issue 9 18 27 47 61 75

LASH LARUE WESTERN
AC Comics: 1990 ($3.50, 44 pgs) (24 pgs. of color, 16 pgs. of B&W)

1-Photo covers; r/Lash #6; r/old movie posters 4.00
Annual 1 (1990, $2.95, B&W, 44 pgs.)-Photo covers 4.00

LASSIE (TV)(M-G-M's... #1-36; see Kite Fun Book)
Dell Publ. Co./Gold Key No. 59 (10/62) on: June, 1950 - No. 70, July, 1969

1 (52 pgs.)-Photo-c; inside lists One Shot #282 in error
23 46 69 161 356 550
2-Painted-c begin 8 16 24 54 102 150
3-10 6 12 18 37 66 95
11-19: 12-Rocky Langford (Lassie's master) marries Gerry Lawrence. 15-1st app. Timbu
5 10 15 30 50 70
20-22-Matt Baker-a 5 10 15 33 57 80
23-38: 33-Robinson-a. 4 8 12 28 47 65
39-1st app. Timmy as Lassie picks up her TV family; photo-c
5 10 15 35 63 90

GD VG FN VF VF/NM NM-
2.0 4.0 6.0 8.0 9.0 9.2

40-50-Photo-c on all 4 8 12 28 47 65
51-58-Photo-c on all 4 8 12 27 44 60
59 (10/62)-1st Gold Key 4 8 12 28 47 65
60-70: 63-Last Timmy (10/63). 64-r/#19. 65-Forest Ranger Corey Stuart begins, ends #69. 70-Forest Rangers Bob Ericson & Scott Turner app. (Lassie's new masters)
4 8 12 25 40 55
11193(1978, $1.95, 224 pgs., Golden Press)-Baker-r (92 pgs.)
4 8 12 25 40 55

NOTE: *Also see March of Comics #210, 217, 230, 254, 266, 278, 296, 308, 324,334, 346, 358, 370, 381, 394, 411, 432.*

LAST AMERICAN, THE
Marvel Comics (Epic): Dec, 1990 - No. 4, March, 1991 ($2.25, mini-series)

1-4: Alan Grant scripts 3.00

LAST AVENGERS STORY, THE (Last Avengers #1)
Marvel Comics: Nov, 1995 - No. 2, Dec, 1995 ($5.95, painted, limited series) (Alterniverse)

1,2: Peter David story; acetate-c in all. 1-New team (Hank Pym, Wasp, Human Torch, Cannonball, She-Hulk, Hotshot, Bombshell, Tommy Maximoff, Hawkeye & Mockingbird) forms to battle Ultron 59, Kang the Conqueror, The Grim Reaper & Oddball 6.00

LAST BATTLE, THE
Image Comics: Dec, 2011 ($7.99, square-bound, one-shot)

1-Facari-s/Brereton-painted art/c; Roman gladiator story; bonus Brereton sketch pages 8.00

LAST CHRISTMAS, THE
Image Comics: May, 2006 - No. 5, Oct, 2006 ($2.99, limited series)

1-5-Gerry Duggan & Brian Posehn-s/Rick Remender & Hilary Barta-a 3.00
TPB (2006, $14.99) r/#1-5; Patton Oswalt intro.; sketch pages and art 15.00

LAST CONTRACT, THE
BOOM! Studios: Jan, 2016 - No. 4, Apr, 2016 ($3.99, limited series)

1-4-Brisson-s/Estherren-a/c 4.00

LAST DAY IN VIETNAM
Dark Horse Books: July, 2000 ($10.95, graphic novel)

nn-Will Eisner-s/a/c 11.00

LAST DAYS OF ANIMAL MAN, THE
DC Comics: July, 2009 - No. 6, Dec, 2009 ($2.99, limited series)

1-6: 1-Conway-s/Batista-a/Bolland-c. 3,4-Starfire app. 5,6-Future Justice League app. 3.00
TPB (2010, $17.99) r/#1-6 18.00

LAST DAYS OF THE JUSTICE SOCIETY SPECIAL
DC Comics: 1986 ($2.50, one-shot, 68 pgs.)

1-62 pg. JSA story plus unpubbed G.A. pg. 2 4 6 8 10 12

LAST DEFENDERS, THE
Marvel Comics: May, 2008 - No. 6, Oct, 2008 ($2.99, limited series)

1-6-Nighthawk, She-Hulk, Colossus, and Blazing Skull; Muniz-a. 2-Deodato-c 3.00

LAST FANTASTIC FOUR STORY, THE
Marvel Comics: Oct, 2007 ($4.99, one-shot)

1-Stan Lee-s/John Romita, Jr.-a/c; Galactus app. 5.00

LAST GANG IN TOWN
DC Comics (Vertigo): Feb, 2016 - No. 6, Aug, 2016 ($3.99, limited series)

1-6: 1-Simon Oliver-s/Rufus Dayglo-a/Rob Davis-c 4.00

LAST GENERATION, THE
Black Tie Studios: 1986 - No. 5, 1989 ($1.95, B&W, high quality paper)

1-5 3.00
Book 1 (1989, $6.95)-By Caliber Press 7.00

LAST HERO STANDING (Characters from Spider-Girl's M2 universe)
Marvel Comics: Aug, 2005 - No. 5, Aug, 2005 ($2.99, weekly limited series)

1-5: 1-DeFalco-s/Olliffe-a. 4-Thor app. 5-Capt. America dies 3.00
TPB (2005, $13.99) r/#1-5 14.00

LAST HUNT, THE
Dell Publishing Co.: No. 678, Feb, 1956

Four Color 678-Movie, photo-c 6 12 18 42 79 115

LAST KISS
ACME Press (Eclipse): 1988 ($3.95, B&W, squarebound, 52 pgs.)

1-One story adapts E.A. Poe's The Black Cat 4.00

LAST OF THE COMANCHES (Movie) (See Wild Bill Hickok #28)
Avon Periodicals: 1953

nn-Kinstler-c/a, 21pgs.; Ravielli-a 18 36 54 103 162 220

The Last Phantom #1 © KFS

Laugh Comics #35 © ACP

Laurel and Hardy #3 © DELL

GD 2.0 | VG 4.0 | FN 6.0 | VF 8.0 | VF/NM 9.0 | NM- 9.2

LAST OF THE ERIES, THE (See American Graphics)

LAST OF THE FAST GUNS, THE
Dell Publishing Co.: No. 925, Aug, 1958

Four Color 925-Movie, photo-c 6 12 18 41 76 110

LAST OF THE MOHICANS (See King Classics & White Rider and...)

LAST OF THE VIKING HEROES, THE (Also see Silver Star #1)
Genesis West Comics: Mar, 1987 - No. 12 ($1.50/$1.95)

1-4,5A,5B,6-12: 4-Intro The Phantom Force, 1-Signed edition ($1.50), 5A-Kirby/Stevens-c. 5B,6 ($1.95). 7-Art Adams-c. 8-Kirby back-c. 4.00
Summer Special 1-3: 1-(1988)-Frazetta-c & illos. 2 (1990, $2.50)-A TMNT app. 3 (1991, $2.50)-Teenage Mutant Ninja Turtles 4.00
Summer Special 1-Signed edition (sold for $1.95) 4.00
NOTE: *Art Adams c-7.* ***Byrne*** *c-3.* ***Kirby*** *c-1p, 5p.* ***Perez*** *c-2i.* ***Stevens*** *c-5Ai.*

LAST ONE, THE
DC Comics (Vertigo): July, 1993 - No. 6, Dec, 1993 ($2.50, lim. series, mature)

1-6 3.00

LAST PHANTOM, THE (Lee Falk's Phantom)
Dynamite Entertainment: 2010 - No. 12, 2012 ($3.99)

1-12-Beatty-s/Ferigato-a; 1-Two covers by Alex Ross; Neves & Prado var. covers 4.00
Annual 1 (2011, $4.99) Beatty-s/Desjardins-a; two covers by Desjardins & Ross 5.00

LAST PLANET STANDING
Marvel Comics: July, 2006 - No. 5, Sept, 2006 ($2.99, limited series)

1-5-Galactus threatens Spider-Girl & Fantastic Five's M2 Earth; Avengers app.; Olliffe-a 3.00
TPB (2006, $13.99) r/series 14.00

LAST SHOT
Image Comics: Aug, 2001 - No. 4, Mar, 2002 ($2.95, limited series)

1-4: 1-Wraparound-c; by Studio XD 3.00
...: First Draw (5/01, $2.95) Introductory one-shot 3.00

LAST SONS OF AMERICA
BOOM! Studios: Nov, 2015 - No. 4, Apr, 2016 ($3.99, limited series)

1-4-Phillip Johnson-s/Matthew Dow Smith-a 4.00

LAST STARFIGHTER, THE
Marvel Comics Group: Oct, 1984 - No. 3, Dec, 1984 (75¢, movie adaptation)

1-3: r/Marvel Super Special; Guice-c 4.00

LAST TEMPTATION, THE
Marvel Comics: 1994 - No. 3, 1994 ($4.95, limited series)

1-3-Alice Cooper story; Neil Gaiman scripts; McKean-c; Zulli-a: 1-Two covers 5.00
HC (Dark Horse Comics, 2005, $14.95) r/#1-3; Gaiman intro. 15.00

LAST TRAIN FROM GUN HILL
Dell Publishing Co.: No. 1012, July, 1959

Four Color 1012-Movie, photo-c 8 16 24 52 99 145

LAST TRAIN TO DEADSVILLE: A CAL McDONALD MYSTERY (See Criminal Macabre)
Dark Horse Comics: May, 2004 - No. 4, Sept, 2004 ($2.99, limited series)

1-4-Steve Niles-s/Kelley Jones-a/c 3.00
TPB (2005, $14.95) r/series 15.00

LATEST ADVENTURES OF FOXY GRANDPA (See Foxy Grandpa)

LATEST COMICS (Super Duper No. 3?)
Spotlight Publ./Palace Promotions (Jubilee): Mar, 1945 - No. 2, 1945?

1-Super Duper 19 38 57 111 176 240
2-Bee-29 (nd); Jubilee in indicia blacked out 14 28 42 82 121 160

LAUGH
Archie Enterprises: June, 1987 - No. 29, Aug, 1991 (75¢/$1.00)

V2#1 5.00
2-10,14,24: 5-X-Mas issue. 14-1st app. Hot Dog. 24-Re-intro Super Duck 4.00
11-13,15-23,25-29: 19-X-Mas issue 3.00

LAUGH COMICS (Teenage) (Formerly Black Hood #9-19) (Laugh #226 on)
Archie Publications (Close-Up): No. 20, Fall, 1946 - No. 400, Apr, 1987

20-Archie begins; Katy Keene & Taffy begin by Woggon; Suzie & Wilbur also begin; Archie covers begin 155 310 465 992 1696 2400
21-23,25 60 120 180 381 803 925
24- "Pipsy" by Kirby (6 pgs.) 61 122 183 390 670 950
26-30 40 80 120 246 411 575
31-40 32 64 96 188 307 425
41-60: 41,54-Debbi by Woggon 22 44 66 132 216 300
61-80: 67-Debbi by Woggon 15 30 45 85 130 175
81-99 8 16 24 54 102 150
100 8 16 24 56 108 160
101-105,110,112,114-126: 125-Debbi app. 6 12 18 38 69 100
106-109,111,113-Neal Adams-a (1 pg.) in each 6 12 18 40 73 105
127-144: Super-hero app. in all (see note) 7 14 21 44 82 120
145-(4/63) Josie by DeCarlo begins 7 14 21 44 82 120
146-149-early Josie app. by DeCarlo 5 10 15 33 57 80
150,162,163,165,167,169,170-No Josie 3 6 9 21 33 45
151-161,164,168-Josie app. by DeCarlo 4 8 12 27 44 60
166-Beatles-c (1/65) 6 12 18 42 79 115
171-180, 200 (12/67) 3 6 9 17 26 35
181-199 3 6 9 15 22 28
201-240(3/71) 2 4 6 11 16 20
241-280(7/74) 2 4 6 9 13 16
281-299 2 4 6 8 10 12
300(3/76) 2 4 6 8 11 14
301-340 (7/79) 1 2 3 5 7 9
341-370 (1/82) 1 2 3 4 5 7
371-379,385-399 5.00
380-Cheryl Blossom app. 2 4 6 9 12 15
381-384,400: 381-384-Katy Keene app.; by Woggon-381,382 6.00
NOTE: *The Fly app. in 128, 129, 132, 134, 138, 139. Flygirl app. in 136, 137, 143. Flyman app. in 137. The Jaguar app. in 127, 130, 131, 133, 135, 140-142, 144. Josie app. in 145-149, 151-161, 164, 168. Katy Keene app. in 20-125, 129, 130, 133. Horror/Sci-Fi covers on 128-135, 137, 139. Many issues contain paper dolls.* ***Al Fagaly*** *c-20-29.* ***Montana*** *c-33, 36, 37, 42.* ***Bill Vigoda*** *c-30, 50.*

LAUGH COMICS DIGEST (...Magazine #23-89; Laugh Digest Mag. #90 on)
Archie Publ. (Close-Up No. 1, 3 on): 8/74; No. 2, 9/75; No. 3, 3/76 - No. 200, Apr, 2005 (Digest-size) (Josie and Sabrina app. in most issues)

1-Neal Adams-a 5 10 15 31 53 75
2,7,8,19-Neal Adams-a 3 6 9 19 30 40
3-6,9,10 3 6 9 15 22 28
11-18,20 2 4 6 11 16 20
21-40 2 4 6 9 13 16
41-60 1 3 4 6 8 10
61-80 1 2 3 5 6 8
81-99 5.00
100 6.00
101-138 4.00
139-200: 139-Begin $1.95-c. 148-Begin $1.99-c. 156-Begin $2.19-c. 180-Begin $2.39-c 3.00
NOTE: *Katy Keene in 23, 25, 27, 32-38, 40, 45-48, 50. The Fly-r in 19, 20. The Jaguar-r in 25, 27. Mr. Justice-r in 21. The Web-r in 23.*

LAUGH COMIX (Laugh Comics inside)(Formerly Top Notch Laugh; Suzie Comics No. 49 on)
MLJ Magazines: No. 46, Summer, 1944 - No. 48, Winter, 1944-45

46-Wilbur & Suzie in all; Harry Sahle-c 34 68 102 199 325 450
47,48: 47-Sahle-c. 48-Bill Vigoda-c 22 44 66 132 216 300

LAUGH-IN MAGAZINE (TV)(Magazine)
Laufer Publ. Co.: Oct, 1968 - No. 12, Oct, 1969 (50¢) (Satire)

V1#1 5 10 15 30 50 70
2-12 3 6 9 21 33 45

LAUREL & HARDY (See Larry Harmon's... & March of Comics No. 302, 314)

LAUREL AND HARDY (...Comics)
St. John Publ. Co.: 3/49 - No. 3, 9/49; No. 26, 11/55 - No. 28, 3/56 (No #4-25)

1 84 168 253 538 919 1300
2 42 84 126 265 445 625
3 36 72 108 211 343 475
26-28 (Reprints) 17 34 51 98 154 210

LAUREL AND HARDY (TV)
Dell Publishing Co.: Oct, 1962 - No. 4, Sept-Nov, 1963

12-423-210 (8-10/62) 6 12 18 38 69 100
2-4 (Dell) 4 8 12 27 44 60

LAUREL AND HARDY (Larry Harmon's...)
Gold Key: Jan, 1967 - No. 2, Oct, 1967

1-Photo back-c 4 8 12 27 44 60
2 4 8 12 21 33 45

L.A.W., THE (LIVING ASSAULT WEAPONS)
DC Comics: Sept, 1999 - No. 6, Feb, 2000 ($2.50, limited series)

1-6-Blue Beetle, Question, Judomaster, Capt. Atom app.; Giordano-a. 5-JLA app. 3.00

LAW AGAINST CRIME (Law-Crime on cover)
Essenkay Publishing Co.: April, 1948 - No. 3, Aug, 1948 (Real Stories from Police Files)

1-(#1-3 are half funny animal, half crime stories)-L. B. Cole-c/a in all; electrocution-c

Lawbreakers Suspense Stories #15 © CC

Lazarus #4 © Rucka & Lark

Leading Comics #5 © DC

	GD	VG	FN	VF	VF/NM	NM-
	2.0	4.0	6.0	8.0	9.0	9.2

	90	180	270	576	988	1400
2-L. B. Cole-c/a	63	126	189	403	689	975
3-Used in **SOTI**, pg. 180,181 & illo "The wish to hurt or kill couples in lovers' lanes;" reprinted in All-Famous Crime #9	82	164	246	528	902	1275

LAW AND ORDER
Maximum Press: Sept, 1995 - No. 2, 1995 ($2.50, unfinished limited series)

1,2 — 3.00

LAWBREAKERS (...Suspense Stories No. 10 on)
Law and Order Magazines (Charlton): Mar, 1951 - No. 9, Oct-Nov, 1952

1	43	86	129	271	461	650
2	26	52	78	154	252	350
3,5,6,8,9: 6-Anti-Wertham editorial	21	42	63	126	206	285
4- "White Death" junkie story	32	64	96	188	307	425
7- "The Deadly Dopesters" drug story	32	64	96	188	307	425

LAWBREAKERS ALWAYS LOSE!
Marvel Comics (CBS): Spring, 1948 - No. 10, Oct, 1949

1-2pg. Kurtzman-a, "Giggles 'n' Grins"	40	80	120	244	402	560
2	21	42	63	122	199	275
3-5: 4-Vampire story	17	34	51	98	154	210
6(2/49)-Has editorial defense against charges of Dr. Wertham	19	38	57	109	172	235
7-Used in **SOTI**, illo "Comic-book philosophy"	34	68	102	199	325	450
8-10: 9,10-Photo-c	15	30	45	88	137	185

NOTE: ***Brodsky** c-4, 5. **Shores** c-1-3, 6-8.*

LAWBREAKERS SUSPENSE STORIES (Formerly Lawbreakers; Strange Suspense Stories No. 16 on)
Capitol Stories/Charlton Comics: No. 10, Jan, 1953 - No. 15, Nov, 1953

10	48	96	144	302	514	725
11 (3/53)-Severed tongues-c/story & woman negligee scene	284	568	852	1818	3109	4400
12-14: 13-Giordano-c begin, end #15	36	72	108	211	343	475
15-Acid-in-face-c/story; hands dissolved in acid story	74	148	222	470	810	1150

LAW-CRIME (See Law Against Crime)

LAWDOG
Marvel Comics (Epic Comics): May, 1993 - No. 10, Feb, 1993

1-10 — 3.00

LAWDOG/GRIMROD: TERROR AT THE CROSSROADS
Marvel Comics (Epic Comics): Sept, 1993 ($3.50)

1 — 4.00

LAWMAN (TV)
Dell Publishing Co.: No. 970, Feb, 1959 - No. 11, Apr-June, 1962 (All photo-c)

Four Color 970(#1) John Russell, Peter Brown photo-c	10	20	30	69	147	225
Four Color 1035('60), 3(2-4/60)-Toth-a	7	14	21	46	86	125
4-11	6	12	18	37	66	95

LAW OF DREDD, THE (Also see Judge Dredd)
Quality Comics/Fleetway #8 on: 1989 - No. 33, 1992 ($1.50/$1.75)

1-33: Bolland a-1-6,8,10-12,14(2 pg),15,19 — 3.00

LAWRENCE (See Movie Classics)

LAZARUS
Image Comics: Jun, 2013 - Present ($2.99/$3.50/$3.99)

1-9-Rucka-s/Lark-a/c — 3.50
10-21-($3.50) 19-Bonus preview of Black Magic #1 — 3.50
22-25-($3.99) — 4.00
Image Firsts Lazarus #1 (11/15, $1.00) reprints #1; afterword by Rucka; Lark sketch art — 3.00
... Sourcebook, Volume 1: Carlyle (4/16, $3.99) Dossier of politics, locations, weapons — 4.00

LAZARUS CHURCHYARD
Tundra Publishing: June, 1992 - No. 3, 1992 ($3.95/$4.50, 44 pgs., coated stock)

1-3 — 5.00
The Final Cut (Image, 1/01, $14.95, TPB) Reprints Ellis/D'Israeli strips — 15.00

LAZARUS FIVE
DC Comics: July, 2000 - No. 5, Nov, 2000 ($2.50, limited series)

1-5-Harris-c/Abell-a(p) — 3.00

LEADING COMICS
DC Comics: Jan. 1942

nn - Ashcan comic, not distributed to newsstands, only for in-house use. Cover art is Detective Comics #57, interior of Star Spangled Comics #2 (a FN+ copy sold for $1015.75 in 2012)

LEADING COMICS (...Screen Comics No. 42 on)
National Periodical Publications: Winter, 1941-42 - No. 41, Feb-Mar, 1950

	GD	VG	FN	VF	VF/NM	NM-
	2.0	4.0	6.0	8.0	9.0	9.2

1-Origin The Seven Soldiers of Victory; Green Arrow & Speedy, Crimson Avenger, Shining Knight, The Vigilante, Star Spangled Kid & Stripesy begin; The Dummy (Vigilante villain) 1st app.; 1st Green Arrow-c	389	778	1167	2723	4762	6800
2-Meskin-a; Fred Ray-c	119	238	357	762	1306	1850
3	94	188	282	597	1024	1450
4,5	68	136	204	435	743	1050
6-10	52	104	156	328	552	775
11,12,14(Spring, 1945)	40	80	120	246	411	575
13-Classic robot-c	103	206	309	659	1130	1600
15-(Sum,'45)-Contents change to funny animal	26	52	78	154	252	350
16-22,24-30: 16-Nero Fox-c begin, end #22	14	28	42	80	115	150
23-1st app. Peter Porkchops by Otto Feuer & begins	26	52	78	154	252	350
31,32,34-41: 34-41-Leading Screen... on-c only	12	24	36	67	94	120
33-(Scarce)	20	40	60	114	182	250

NOTE: ***Otto Feuer**-a most #15-on; **Rube Grossman**-a most #15-on;c-15-41. **Post** a-23-37, 39, 41.*

LEADING MAN
Image Comics: June, 2006 - No. 5, Feb, 2007 ($3.50, limited series)

1-5-B. Clay Moore-s/Jeremy Haun-a — 3.50
TPB (2/07, $14.95) r/#1-5; sketch gallery — 15.00

LEADING SCREEN COMICS (Formerly Leading Comics)
National Periodical Publ.: No. 42, Apr-May, 1950 - No. 77, Aug-Sept, 1955

42-Peter Porkchops-c/stories continue	12	24	36	67	94	120
43-77	11	22	33	60	83	105

NOTE: ***Grossman** a-most. **Mayer** a-45-48, 50, 54-57, 60, 62-74, 75(3), 76, 77.*

LEAGUE OF CHAMPIONS, THE (Also see The Champions)
Hero Graphics: Dec, 1990 - No. 12, 1992 ($2.95, 52 pgs.)

1-12: 1-Flare app. 2-Origin Malice — 4.00

LEAGUE OF EXTRAORDINARY GENTLEMEN, THE
America's Best Comics: Mar, 1999 - No. 6, Sept, 2000 ($2.95, limited series)

1-Alan Moore-s/Kevin O'Neill-a	2	4	6	10	14	18
1-DF Edition ($10.00) O'Neill-c	3	6	9	14	20	25
2,3						6.00
4-6: 5-Revised printing with "Amaze 'Whirling Spray' Syringe" parody ad						4.00
5-Initial printing recalled because of "Marvel Co. Syringe" parody ad	12	24	36	83	182	280
... Compendium 1,2: 1-r/#1,2. 2-r/#3,4						6.00
Hardcover (2000, $24.95) r/#1-6 plus cover gallery						25.00

LEAGUE OF EXTRAORDINARY GENTLEMEN, THE (Volume 2)
America's Best Comics: Sept, 2002 - No. 6, Nov, 2003 ($3.50, limited series)

1-6-Alan Moore-s/Kevin O'Neill-a — 5.00
... Bumper Compendium 1,2: 1-r/#1,2. 2-r/#3,4 — 6.00
... Black Dossier (HC, 2007, $29.99) new graphic novel; 3-D section with glasses; extras 30.00

LEAGUE OF EXTRAORDINARY GENTLEMEN
Top Shelf Productions/Knockabout Comics: 2009; 2011; 2012 ($7.95/$9.95, squarebound)

... Century: 1910 (2009, $7.95) Alan Moore-s/Kevin O'Neill-a — 8.00
... Century #2 "1969" (2011, $9.95) Alan Moore-s/Kevin O'Neill-a — 10.00
... Century #3 "2009" (2012, $9.95) Alan Moore-s/Kevin O'Neill-a — 10.00

LEAGUE OF JUSTICE
DC Comics (Elseworlds): 1996 - No. 2, 1996 ($5.95, 48 pgs., squarebound)

1,2: Magic-based alternate DC Universe story; Giordano-i — 6.00

LEATHERFACE
Arpad Publishing: May (April on-c), 1991 - No. 4, May, 1992 ($2.75, painted-c)

1-4-Based on Texas Chainsaw movie; Dorman-c	1	2	3	5	7	9

LEATHERNECK THE MARINE (See Mighty Midget Comics)

LEAVE IT TO BEAVER (TV)
Dell Publishing Co.: No. 912, June, 1958; May-July, 1962 (All photo-c)

Four Color 912	13	26	39	91	201	310
Four Color 999,1103,1191,1285, 01-428-207	12	24	36	79	170	260

LEAVE IT TO BINKY (Binky No. 72 on) (Super DC Giant) (No. 1-22: 52 pgs.)
National Periodical Publs.: 2-3/48 - #60, 10/58; #61, 6-7/68 - #71, 2-3/70 (Teen-age humor)

1-Lucy wears Superman costume	42	84	126	265	445	625
2	21	42	63	126	206	285
3,4	15	30	45	88	137	185

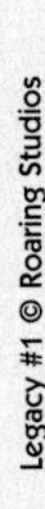
Legacy #1 © Roaring Studios

Legendary Star-Lord #4 © MAR

Legend of Wonder Woman #6 © DC

	GD 2.0	VG 4.0	FN 6.0	VF 8.0	VF/NM 9.0	NM- 9.2
5-Superman cameo	20	40	60	114	182	250
6-10	14	28	42	76	108	140
11-14,16-22: Last 52 pg. issue	12	24	36	67	94	120
15-Scribbly story by Mayer	14	28	42	76	108	140
23-28,30-45: 45-Last pre-code (2/55)	10	20	30	56	76	95
29-Used in **POP**, pg. 78	10	20	30	58	79	100
46-60: 60-(10/58)	5	10	15	35	63	90
61 (6-7/68) 1950's reprints with art changes	5	10	15	34	60	85
62-69: 67-Last 12¢ issue	4	8	12	27	44	60
70-7pg. app. Bus Driver who looks like Ralph from Honeymooners	5	10	15	30	50	70
71-Last issue	4	8	12	28	47	65

NOTE: *Aragones-a-61, 62, 67. Drucker a-28. Mayer a-1, 2, 15. Created by Mayer.*

LEAVE IT TO CHANCE
Image Comics (Homage Comics): Sept, 1996 - No. 11, Sept, 1998; No. 13, July, 2002
DC Comics (Homage Comics): No. 12, Jun, 1999 ($2.50/$2.95/$4.95)

1-3: 1-Intro Chance Falconer & St. George; James Robinson scripts & Paul Smith-c/a 5.00
4-12: 12-(6/99) 3.00
13-(7/02, $4.95) includes sketch pages and pin-ups 5.00
Free Comic Book Day Edition (2003) - James Robinson-s/Paul Smith-a 3.00
Shaman's Rain TPB (1997, $9.95) r/#1-4 10.00
Shaman's Rain HC (2002, $14.95, over-sized 8 1/4" x 12") r/#1-4 15.00
Trick or Threat TPB (1997, $12.95) r/#5-8 13.00
Trick or Threat HC (2002, $14.95, over-sized 8 1/4" x 12") r/#5-8 15.00
Vol. 3: Monster Madness and Other Stories HC (2003, $14.95, 8 1/4" x 12") r/#9-11 15.00

LEAVING MEGALOPOLIS: SURVIVING MEGALOPOLIS
Dark Horse Comics: Jan, 2016 - No. 6, Sept, 2016 ($3.99)

1-6-Gail Simone-s/Jim Calafiore-a 4.00

LEE HUNTER, INDIAN FIGHTER
Dell Publishing Co.: No. 779, Mar, 1957; No. 904, May, 1958

	GD	VG	FN	VF	VF/NM	NM-
Four Color 779 (#1)	6	12	18	37	66	95
Four Color 904	5	10	15	30	50	70

LEFT-HANDED GUN, THE (Movie)
Dell Publishing Co.: No. 913, July, 1958

	GD	VG	FN	VF	VF/NM	NM-
Four Color 913-Paul Newman photo-c	9	18	27	57	111	165

LEGACY
Majestic Entertainment: Oct, 1993 - No. 2, Nov, 1993; No. 0, 1994 ($2.25)

1-2,0: 1-Glow-in-the-dark-c. 0-Platinum 3.00

LEGACY
Image Comics: May, 2003 - No. 4, Feb, 2004 ($2.95)

1-4: 1-Francisco-a/Treffiletti-s 3.00

LEGACY OF KAIN (Based on the Eidos video game)
Top Cow Productions: Oct, 1999; Jan, 2004 ($2.99)

...Defiance 1 (1/04, $2.99) Cha-c; Kirkham-a 3.00
...Soul Reaver 1 (10/99, Diamond Dateline supplement) Benitez-c 3.00

LEGACY OF LUTHER STRODE, THE (Also see Legend of Luther Strode)
Image Comics: Apr, 2015 - Present ($3.99/$3.50)

1-($3.99) Justin Jordan-s/Tradd Moore-a 4.00
2-6-($3.50) 3.50

LEGEND
DC Comics (WildStorm): Apr, 2005 - No. 4, July, 2005 ($5.95/$5.99, limited series)

1-4-Howard Chaykin-s/Russ Heath-a; inspired by Philip Wylie's novel "Gladiator" 6.00

LEGENDARY STAR-LORD (Guardians of the Galaxy)
Marvel Comics: Sept, 2014 - No. 12, Jul, 2015 ($3.99)

1-12: 1-Humphries-s/Medina-a. 4-Thanos app. 9-11-Black Vortex x-over 4.00

LEGENDARY TALESPINNERS
Dynamite Entertainment: 2010 - No. 3, 2010 ($3.99)

1-3-Kuhoric-s/Bond-a; two covers 4.00

LEGENDERRY: A STEAMPUNK ADVENTURE
Dynamite Entertainment: 2014 - No. 7, 2014 ($3.99)

1-7-Willingham-s/Davila-a/Benitez-c. 4.00

LEGENDERRY: GREEN HORNET
Dynamite Entertainment: 2015 - No. 5, 2015 ($3.99)

1-5-Gregory-s/Peeples-a; multiple covers 4.00

LEGENDERRY: RED SONJA
Dynamite Entertainment: 2015 - No. 5, 2015 ($3.99)

1-5: 1-Andreyko-s/Aneke-a; multiple covers; Steampunk Sonja; Bride of Frankenstein app. 4.00

LEGENDERRY: VAMPIRELLA
Dynamite Entertainment: 2015 - No. 5, 2015 ($3.99)

1-5-Avallone-s/Cabrera-a; Steampunk Vampirella 4.00

LEGEND OF CUSTER, THE (TV)
Dell Publishing Co.: Jan, 1968

	GD	VG	FN	VF	VF/NM	NM-
1-Wayne Maunder photo-c	3	6	9	17	26	35

LEGEND OF ISIS
Alias Entertainment: May, 2005 - No. 5 ($2.99)

1-5: 1-Three covers; Ottney-s/Fontana-a 3.00
...: Beginnings TPB (5/05, $9.99) Ottney-s 10.00

LEGEND OF JESSE JAMES, THE (TV)
Gold Key: Feb, 1966

	GD	VG	FN	VF	VF/NM	NM-
10172-602-Photo-c	3	6	9	17	26	35

LEGEND OF KAMUI, THE (See Kamui)

LEGEND OF LOBO, THE (See Movie Comics)

LEGEND OF LUTHER STRODE, THE (Sequel to Strange Talent of Luther Strode)
Image Comics: Dec, 2012 - No. 6, Aug, 2013 ($3.50, limited series)

1-5: Justin Jordan-s/Tradd Moore-a 3.50

LEGEND OF OZ: TIK-TOK AND THE KALIDAH
Aspen MLT: Apr, 2016 - No. 3, Jul, 2016 ($3.99)

1-3-Rob Anderson-s/Renato Rei-a. 1-Three covers. 2,3-Two covers 4.00

LEGEND OF OZ: THE WICKED WEST
Big Dog Press: Oct, 2011 - No. 6, Aug, 2012; Oct, 2012 - No. 18, May 2014 ($3.50)

1-6-Multiple covers on all 3.50
Vol. 2 1-18-Multiple covers on all 3.50

LEGEND OF OZ: THE WICKED WEST
Aspen MLT: Oct, 2015 - No. 6, Mar, 2016 ($3.99)

1-6-Reprints 2011 series 4.00

LEGEND OF SUPREME
Image Comics (Extreme): Dec, 1994 - No. 3, Feb, 1995 ($2.50, limited series)

1-3 3.00

LEGEND OF THE ELFLORD
DavDez Arts: July, 1998 - No. 2, Sept, 1998 ($2.95)

1,2-Barry Blair & Colin Chin-s/a 3.00

LEGEND OF THE HAWKMAN
DC Comics: 2000 - No. 3, 2000 ($4.95, limited series)

1-3-Raab-s/Lark-c/a 5.00

LEGEND OF THE SHADOW CLAN
Aspen MLT: Feb, 2013 - No. 5, Jul, 2013 ($1.00/$3.99)

1-($1.00) David Wohl-s/Cory Smith-a; mutiple covers 3.00
2-5-($3.99) 4.00

LEGEND OF THE SHIELD, THE
DC Comics (Impact Comics): July, 1991 - No. 16, Oct, 1992 ($1.00)

1-16: 6,7-The Fly x-over. 12-Contains trading card 4.00
Annual 1 (1992, $2.50, 68 pgs.)-Snyder-a; w/trading card 4.00

LEGEND OF WONDER WOMAN, THE
DC Comics: May, 1986 - No. 4, Aug, 1986 (75¢, limited series)

1-4 4.00

LEGEND OF WONDER WOMAN, THE (Printing of digital-first stories)
DC Comics: Mar, 2016 - No. 9, Oct, 2016 ($3.99)

1-9: Childhood/origin flashbacks of Diana; Renae de Liz-s/a. 2-Steve Trevor app. 4.00

LEGEND OF YOUNG DICK TURPIN, THE (Disney)(TV)
Gold Key: May, 1966

	GD	VG	FN	VF	VF/NM	NM-
1 (10176-605)-Photo/painted-c	3	6	9	17	26	35

LEGEND OF ZELDA, THE (Link: The Legend... in indicia)
Valiant Comics: 1990 - No. 4, 1990 ($1.95, coated stiff-c) V2#1, 1990 - No. 5, 1990 ($1.50)

	GD	VG	FN	VF	VF/NM	NM-
1-4: 4-Layton-c(i)	2	4	6	10	14	18
V2#1-5	1	3	4	6	8	10

LEGENDS
DC Comics: Nov, 1986 - No. 6, Apr, 1987 (75¢, limited series)

1-Byrne-c/a(p) in all; 1st app. Amanda Waller and the new Captain Marvel

Legends of the DC Universe #5 © DC

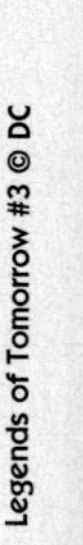
Legends of Tomorrow #3 © DC

The Legion #27 © DC

	GD 2.0	VG 4.0	FN 6.0	VF 8.0	VF/NM 9.0	NM- 9.2
	2	4	6	8	10	12
2,4,5						6.00
3-1st app. new Suicide Squad; death of Blockbuster	3	6	9	16	23	30
6-1st app. new Justice League	2	4	6	8	10	12

LEGENDS OF DANIEL BOONE, THE (...Frontier Scout)
National Periodical Publications: Oct-Nov, 1955 - No. 8, Dec-Jan, 1956-57

	GD	VG	FN	VF	VF/NM	NM-
1 (Scarce)-Nick Cardy c-1-8	54	108	162	346	591	835
2 (Scarce)	40	80	120	246	411	575
3-8 (Scarce)	34	68	102	199	325	450

LEGENDS OF NASCAR, THE
Vortex Comics: Nov, 1990 - No. 14, 1992? (#1 3rd printing (1/91) says 2nd printing inside)

1-Bill Elliott biog.; Trimpe-a ($1.50) 5.00
1-2nd printing (11/90, $2.00) 3.00
1-3rd print; contains Maxx racecards ($3.00) 3.00
2-14: 2-Richard Petty. 3-Ken Schrader (7/91). 4-Bobby Allison; Spiegle-a(p); Adkins part-i. 5-Sterling Marlin. 6-Bill Elliott. 7-Junior Johnson; Spiegle-c/a. 8-Benny Parsons; Heck-a 3.00
1-13-Hologram cover versions. 2-Hologram shows Bill Elliott's car by mistake (all are numbered & limited) 5.00
2-Hologram corrected version 5.00
Christmas Special ($5.95) 6.00

LEGENDS OF RED SONJA
Dynamite Entertainment: 2013 - No. 5, 2014 ($3.99)

1-5-Short stories by various incl. Simone, Grayson; covers by Anacleto & Thorne 4.00

LEGENDS OF THE DARK CLAW
DC Comics (Amalgam): Apr, 1996 ($1.95)

1-Jim Balent-c/a 3.00

LEGENDS OF THE DARK KNIGHT (See Batman: ...)

LEGENDS OF THE DARK KNIGHT
DC Comics: Dec, 2012 - Present ($3.99, printings of stories first released online)

1-13: 1-Lindelof-s. 2-4-Joker app. 5-Hester-a 4.00
... 100 Page Super Spectacular 1-5 (2/14 - Present, quarterly, $9.99) 1-(2/14) 10.00

LEGENDS OF THE DC UNIVERSE
DC Comics: Feb, 1998 - No. 41, June, 2001 ($1.95/$1.99/$2.50)

1-13,15-21: 1-3-Superman; Robinson-s/Semeiks-a/Orbik-painted-c. 4,5-Wonder Woman; Deodato-a/Rude painted-c. 8-GL/GA, O'Neil-s. 10,11-Batgirl; Dodson-a. 12,13-Justice League. 15-17-Flash. 18-Kid Flash; Guice-a. 19-Impulse; prelude to JLApe Annuals. 20,21-Abin Sur 4.00
14-($3.95) Jimmy Olsen; Kirby-esque-c by Rude 5.00
22-27,30: 22,23-Superman; Rude-c/Ladronn-a. 26,27-Aquaman/Joker 3.00
28,29: Green Lantern & the Atom; Gil Kane-a; covers by Kane and Ross 3.00
31,32: 32-Begin $2.50-c; Wonder Woman; Texeira-c 3.00
33-36-Hal Jordan as The Spectre; DeMatteis-s/Zulli-a; Hale painted-c 3.00
37-41: 37,38-Kyle Rayner. 39-Superman. 40,41-Atom; Harris-c 3.00
... Crisis on Infinite Earths 1 (2/99, $4.95) Untold story during and after Crisis on Infinite Earths #4; Wolfman-s/Ryan-a/Orbik-c 5.00
... 80 Page Giant 1 (9/98, $4.95) Stories and art by various incl. Ditko, Perez, Gibbons, Mumy; Joe Kubert-c 5.00
... 80 Page Giant 2 (1/00, $4.95) Stories and art by various incl. Challengers by Art Adams; Sean Phillips-c 5.00
... 3-D Gallery (12/98, $2.95) Pin-ups w/glasses 3.00

LEGENDS OF THE LEGION (See Legion of Super-Heroes)
DC Comics: Feb, 1998 - No. 4, May, 1998 ($2.25, limited series)

1-4:1-Origin-s of Ultra Boy. 2-Spark. 3-Umbra. 4-Star Boy 3.00

LEGENDS OF THE STARGRAZERS (See Vanguard Illustrated #2)
Innovation Publishing: Aug, 1989 - No. 6, 1990 ($1.95, limited series, mature)

1-6: 1-Redondo part inks 3.00

LEGENDS OF THE WORLD'S FINEST (See World's Finest)
DC Comics: 1994 - No. 3, 1994 ($4.95, squarebound, limited series)

1-3: Simonson scripts; Brereton-c/a; embossed foil logos 6.00
TPB-(1995, $14.95) r/#1-3 15.00

LEGENDS OF TOMORROW
DC Comics: May, 2016 - Present ($7.99, squarebound)

1-6: Short stories of Firestorm, Metal Men, Metamorpho and Sugar & Spike. 6-Legion of Super-Heroes app. 8.00

L.E.G.I.O.N. (The # to right of title represents year of print)(Also see Lobo & R.E.B.E.L.S.)
DC Comics: Feb, 1989 - No. 70, Sept, 1994 ($1.50/$1.75)

1-Giffen plots/breakdowns in #1-12,28 5.00
2-22,24-47: 3-Lobo app. #3 on. 4-1st Lobo-c this title. 5-Lobo joins L.E.G.I.O.N. 13-Lar Gand app. 16-Lar Gand joins L.E.G.I.O.N., leaves #19. 31-Capt. Marvel app. 35-L.E.G.I.O.N. '92 begins 3.00
23,70-($2.50, 52 pgs.)-L.E.G.I.O.N. '91 begins. 70-Zero Hour 4.00
48,49,51-69: 48-Begin $1.75-c. 63-L.E.G.I.O.N. '94 begins; Superman x-over 3.00
50-($3.50, 68 pgs.) 4.00
Annual 1-5 ('90-94, 68 pgs.): 1-Lobo, Superman app. 2-Alan Grant scripts. 5-Elseworlds story; Lobo app. 4.00
NOTE: *Alan Grant scripts in #1-39, 51, Annual 1, 2.*

LEGION, THE (Continued from Legion Lost & Legion Worlds)
DC Comics: Dec, 2001 - No. 38, Oct, 2004 ($2.50)

1-Abnett & Lanning-s; Coipel & Lanning-c/a 4.00
2-24: 3-8-Ra's al Ghul app. 5-Snejbjerg-a. 9-DeStefano-a. 12-Legion vs. JLA. 16-Fatal Five app.; Walker-a 17,18-Ra's al Ghul app. 20-23-Universo app. 3.00
25-($3.95) Art by Harris, Cockrum, Rivoche; teenage Clark Kent app.; Harris-c 4.00
26-38-Superboy in classic costume. 26-30-Darkseid app. 31-Giffen-a. 35-38-Jurgens-a 3.00
...Secret Files 3003 (1/04, $4.95) Kirk-a, Harris-c/a; Superboy app. 5.00
...Foundations TPB (2004, $19.95) r/#25-30 & Secret Files 3003; Harris-c 20.00

LEGION LOST (Continued from Legion of Super-Heroes [4th series] #125)
DC Comics: May, 2000 - No. 12, Apr, 2001 ($2.50, limited series)

	GD	VG	FN	VF	VF/NM	NM-
1-Abnett & Lanning-s. Coipel & Lanning-c/a	1	2	3	4	5	7

2-12-Abnett & Lanning-s. Coipel & Lanning-c/a in most. 4,9-Alixe-a 3.00
HC (2011, $39.99, dustjacket) r/#1-12 40.00

LEGION LOST (DC New 52)
DC Comics: Nov, 2011 - No. 16, Mar, 2013 ($2.99)

1-16: 1-Nicieza-s/Woods/a/c; Legionnaires trapped in the 21st century. 7,8-DeFalco-s. 8-Prelude to The Culling; Ravagers app. 9-The Culling x-over with Teen Titans. 14-16-Superboy & the Ravagers app. 3.00
#0 (11/12, $2.99) Origin of Timber Wolf; DeFalco-s/Woods-a 3.00

LEGIONNAIRES (See Legion of Super-Heroes #40, 41 & Showcase 95 #6)
DC Comics: Apr, 1992 - No. 81, Mar, 2000 ($1.25/$1.50/$2.25)

0-(10/94)-Zero Hour restart of Legion; released between #18 & #19 3.00
1-49,51-77: 1-(4/92)-Chris Sprouse-c/a; polybagged w/SkyBox trading card. 11-Kid Quantum joins. 18-(9/94)-Zero Hour. 19(11/94). 37-Valor (Lar Gand) becomes M'onel (5/96). 43-Legion tryouts; reintro Princess Projectra, Shadow Lass & others. 47-Forms one cover image with LSH #91. 60-Karate Kid & Kid Quantum join. 61-Silver Age & 70's Legion app. 76-Return of Wildfire. 79,80-Coipel-c/a; Legion vs. the Blight 3.00
50-($3.95) Pullout poster by Davis/Farmer 4.00
#1,000,000 (11/98) Sean Phillips-a 3.00
Annual 1,3 ('94,'96 $2.95)-1-Elseworlds-s. 3-Legends of the Dead Earth-s 4.00
Annual 2 (1995, $3.95)-Year One-s 4.50

LEGIONNAIRES THREE
DC Comics: Jan, 1986 - No. 4, May, 1986 (75¢, limited series)

1-4 4.00

LEGION OF MONSTERS (Also see Marvel Premiere #28 & Marvel Preview #8)
Marvel Comics Group: Sept, 1975 ($1.00, B&W, magazine, 76 pgs.)

	GD	VG	FN	VF	VF/NM	NM-
1-Origin & 1st app. Legion of Monsters; Neal Adams-c; Morrow-a; origin & only app. The Manphibian; Frankenstein by Mayerik; Bram Stoker's Dracula adaptation; Reese-a; painted-c (#2 was advertised with Morbius & Satana, but was never published)	5	10	15	34	60	85

LEGION OF MONSTERS (One-shots)
Marvel Comics: Apr, 2007 - Sept, 2007 ($2.99)

... Man-Thing (5/07) Huston-s/Janson-a/Land-c; Simon Garth: Zombie by Ted McKeever 3.00
... Morbius (9/07) Cahill-s/Gaydos-a/Land-c; Dracula w/Finch-a/Cebulski-s 3.00
... Satana (8/07) Furth-s/Andrasofszky-a/Land-c; Living Mummy by Hickman 3.00
... Werewolf By Night (4/07) Carey-s/Land-a/c; Monster of Frankenstein by Skottie Young 3.00
HC (2007, $24.99, dustjacket) oversized r/series and classic stories; sketch pages 25.00

LEGION OF MONSTERS
Marvel Comics: Dec, 2011 - No. 4, Mar, 2012 ($3.99, limited series)

1-4-Hopeless-s/Doe-a/c; Morbius, Manphibian, Elsa Bloodstone app. 4.00

LEGION OF NIGHT, THE
Marvel Comics: Oct, 1991 - No. 2, Oct, 1991 ($4.95, 52 pgs.)

1,2-Whilce Portacio-c/a(p) 5.00

LEGION OF SUBSTITUTE HEROES SPECIAL (See Adventure Comics #306)
DC Comics: July, 1985 ($1.25, one-shot, 52 pgs.)

1-Giffen-c/a(p) 4.00

LEGION OF SUPER-HEROES (See Action Comics, Adventure, All New Collectors Edition, Legionnaires, Legends of the Legion, Limited Collectors Edition, Secrets of the..., Superboy &

Legion of Super-Heroes (3rd series) #45 © DC

Legion of Super-Heroes (4th series) #122 © DC

Legion of Super-Heroes (6th series) #45 © DC

	GD 2.0	VG 4.0	FN 6.0	VF 8.0	VF/NM 9.0	NM- 9.2

Superman)
National Periodical Publications: Feb, 1973 - No. 4, July-Aug, 1973

1-Legion & Tommy Tomorrow reprints begin 3 6 9 17 26 35
2-4: 2-Forte-r. 3-r/Adv. #340. Action #240. 4-r/Adv. #341, Action #233; Mooney-r 2 4 6 11 16 20

LEGION OF SUPER-HEROES, THE (Formerly Superboy and...; Tales of The Legion #314 on)
DC Comics: No. 259, Jan, 1980 - No. 313, July, 1984

259(#1)-Superboy leaves Legion 2 4 6 8 11 14
260-270,285-289: 265-Contains 28 pg. insert "Superman & the TRS-80 computer"; origin Tyroc; Tyroc leaves Legion 6.00
261,263,264,266-(Whitman variants; low print run; no cover #'s) 2 4 6 8 11 14
271-284: 272-Blok joins; origin; 20 pg. insert-Dial 'H' For Hero. 277-Intro. Reflecto. 280-Superboy re-joins Legion. 282-Origin Reflecto. 283-Origin Wildfire 6.00
290-294-Great Darkness saga. 294-Double size (52 pgs.) 1 2 3 5 7 9
295-299,301-313: 297-Origin retold. 298-Free 16 pg. Amethyst preview. 306-Brief origin Star Boy (Swan art). 311-Colan-a 4.00
300-(68 pgs., Mando paper)-Anniversary issue; has c/a by almost everyone at DC 5.00
Annual 1-3(82-84, 52 pgs.)-1-Giffen-c/a; 1st app./origin new Invisible Kid who joins Legion. 2-Karate Kid & Princess Projectra wed & resign 4.00
...The Great Darkness Saga (1989, $17.95, 196 pgs.)-r/LSH #287,290-294 & Annual #3; Giffen-c/a 2 4 6 10 14 18
...The Great Darkness Saga The Deluxe Edition HC (2010, $39.99, dj)-r/LSH #284-296 & Annual #1; new intro. by Levitz, script for #290, Giffen design sketches 40.00
NOTE: ***Aparo*** *c-282, 283, 300(part).* ***Austin*** *c-268i.* ***Buckler*** *c-273p, 274p, 276p.* ***Colan*** *a-311p.* ***Ditko*** *a(p)-267, 268, 272, 274, 276, 281.* ***Giffen*** *a-285-313p, Annual 1p; c-287p, 288p, 289, 290p, 291p, 292, 293, 294-299p, 300, 301-313p, Annual 1p, 2p.* ***Perez*** *c-268p, 277-280, 281p.* ***Starlin*** *a-265.* ***Staton*** *a-259p, 260p, 280.* ***Tuska*** *a-308p.*

LEGION OF SUPER-HEROES (3rd Series) (Reprinted in Tales of the Legion)
DC Comics: Aug, 1984 - No. 63, Aug, 1989 ($1.25/$1.75, deluxe format)

1-Silver ink logo 6.00
2-36,39-44,46-49,51-62: 4-Death of Karate Kid. 5-Death of Nemesis Kid. 12-Cosmic Boy, Lightning Lad, & Saturn Girl resign. 14-Intro new members: Tellus, Sensor Girl, Quislet. 15-17-Crisis tie-ins. 18-Crisis x-over. 25-Sensor Girl i.d. revealed as Princess Projectra. 35-Saturn Girl rejoins. 42,43-Millennium tie-ins. 44-Origin Quislet 3.00
37,38-Death of Superboy 2 4 6 9 13 16
45,50: 45 ($2.95, 68 pgs.)-Anniversary ish. 50-Double size ($2.50-c) 4.00
63-Final issue 4.00
Annual 1-4 (10/85-'88, 52 pgs.)-1-Crisis tie-in 4.00
....: An Eye For An Eye TPB (2007, $17.99)-r/#1-6; intro by Paul Levitz; cover gallery 18.00
....: The More Things Change TPB (2008, $17.99)-r/#7-13; cover gallery 18.00
NOTE: ***Byrne*** *c-36p.* ***Giffen*** *a(p)-1, 2, 50-55, 57-63, Annual 1p, 2; c-1-5p, 54p, Annual 1.* ***Orlando*** *a-6p.* ***Steacy*** *c-45-50, Annual 3.*

LEGION OF SUPER-HEROES (4th Series)
DC Comics: Nov, 1989 - No. 125, Mar, 2000 ($1.75/$1.95/$2.25)

0-(10/94)-Zero Hour restart of Legion; released between #61 & #62 3.00
1-Giffen-c/a(p)/scripts begin (4 pg.-a only #18) 6.00
2-20,26-49,51-53,55-58: 4-Mon-El (Lar Gand) destroys Time Trapper, changes reality. 5-Alt. reality story where Mordru rules all; Ferro Lad app. 6-1st app. of Laurel Gand (Lar Gand's cousin). 8-Origin. 13-Free poster by Giffen showing new costumes. 15-(2/91)-1st reference of Lar Gand as Valor. 17-Tornado Twins app. 26-New map of headquarters. 34-Six pg. preview of Timber Wolf mini-series. 40-Minor Legionnaires app. 41-(3/93)-SW6 Legion renamed Legionnaires w/new costumes and some new code-names 4.00
21-25: 21-24-Lobo & Darkseid storyline. 24-Cameo SW6 younger Legion duplicates. 25-SW6 Legion full intro. 5.00
50-($3.50, 68 pgs.) 5.00
54-($2.95)-Die-cut & foil stamped-c 5.00
59-99: 61-(9/94)-Zero Hour. 62-(11/94). 75-XS travels back to the 20th Century (cont'd in Impulse #9). 77-Origin of Brainiac 5. 81-Reintro Sun Boy. 85-Half of the Legion sent to the 20th century, Superman-c/app. 86-Final Night. 87-Deadman-c/app. 88-Impulse-c/app. Adventure Comics #247 cover swipe. 91-Forms one cover image with Legionnaires #47. 96-Wedding of Ultra Boy and Apparition. 99-Robin, Impulse, Superboy app. 3.00
100-($5.95, 96 pgs.)-Legionnaires return to the 30th Century; gatefold-c; 5 stories-art by Simonson, Davis and others 1 2 3 4 5 7
101-121: 101-Armstrong-a(p) begins. 105-Legion past & present vs. Time Trapper. 109-Moder-a. 110-Thunder joins. 114,115-Bizarro Legion. 120,121-Fatal Five. 3.00
122-124: 122,123-Coipel-c/a. 124-Coipel-c 4.00
125-Leads into "Legion Lost" maxi-series; Coipel-c 5.00
#1,000,000 (11/98) Giffen-a 3.00
Annual 1-5 (1990-1994, $3.50, 68 pgs.): 4-Bloodlines. 5-Elseworlds story 4.00
Annual 6 (1995,$3.95)-Year One story 4.00
Annual 7 (1996, $3.50, 48 pgs.)-Legends of the Dead Earth story; intro 75th Century Legion of Super-Heroes; Wildfire app. 4.00
Legion: Secret Files 1 (1/98, $4.95) Retold origin & pin-ups 5.00
Legion: Secret Files 2 (6/99, $4.95) Story and profile pages 5.00
The Beginning of Tomorrow TPB ('99, $17.95) r/post-Zero Hour reboot 18.00
NOTE: ***Giffen*** *a-1-24; breakdowns-26-32, 34-36; c-1-7, 8(part), 9-24.* ***Brandon Peterson*** *a(p)-15(1st for DC), 16, 18, Annual 2(54 pgs.); c-Annual 2p.* ***Swan/Anderson*** *c-8(part).*

LEGION OF SUPER-HEROES (5th Series) (Title becomes Supergirl and the Legion of Super-Heroes #16-36) (Intro. in Teen Titans/Legion Special)
DC Comics: Feb, 2005 - No. 15, Apr, 2006; No. 37, Feb, 2008 - No. 50, Mar, 2009 ($2.95/$2.99)

1-15: 1-Waid-s/Kitson-a/c. 4-Kirk & Gibbons-a. 9-Jeanty-a. 15-Dawnstar, Tyroc, Blok-c 3.00
37-50: 37-Shooter-s/Manapul-a begin; two interlocking covers. 50-Wraparound cover 3.00
44-Variant-c by Neal Adams 5.00
... Death of a Dream TPB ('06, $14.99) r/#7-13 15.00
... Enemy Manifest HC ('09, $24.99, dustjacket) r/#45-50 25.00
... Enemy Manifest SC ('10, $14.99) r/#45-50 15.00
... Enemy Rising HC ('08, $19.99, dustjacket) r/#37-44 20.00
... Enemy Rising SC ('09, $14.99) r/#37-44 15.00
...: 1050 Years of the Future TPB ('08, $19.99) r/greatest tales of their 50 year history 20.00
... Teenage Revolution TPB ('05, $14.99) r/#1-6 & Teen Titans/Legion Spec.; sketch pages 15.00

LEGION OF SUPER-HEROES (6th Series)
DC Comics: Jul, 2010 - No. 16, Oct, 2011 ($3.99/$2.99)

1-9: 1-Earth-Man app.; Titan destroyed; Levitz-s/Cinar-a/c. 6-Jimenez back-up-a 4.00
1-6-Variant covers by Jim Lee 8.00
10-16-($2.99) 12-16-Legion of Super-Villains app. 3.00
Annual 1 (2/11, $4.99) New Emerald Empress; Levitz-s/Giffen-a 5.00
...: The Choice HC (2011, $24.99, dustjacket) r/#1-6; variant-c gallery and Cinar art 25.00

LEGION OF SUPER-HEROES (DC New 52)(Also see Legion Lost)
DC Comics: Nov, 2011 - No. 23, Oct, 2013 ($2.99)

1-23: 1-4-Levitz-s/Portela-a. 5-Simonson-c/a. 8-Lightle-a. 17-Giffen-a. 23-Maguire-a 3.00
#0 (11/12, $2.99) Story of Brainiac 5 joining the Legion; Levitz-s/Kolins-a 3.00

LEGION OF SUPER-HEROES IN THE 31ST CENTURY (Based on the animated series)
DC Comics: June, 2007 - No. 20, Jan, 2009 ($2.25)

1-20: 1-Chynna Clugston-a; Fatal Five app. 6-Green Lantern Corps app. 15-Impulse app. 3.00
1-(6/07) Free Comic Book Day giveaway 3.00
...: Tomorrow's Heroes (2008, $14.99) r/#1-7; cover gallery 15.00

LEGION OF SUPER-VILLAINS
DC Comics: May, 2011 ($4.99, one-shot)

1-Levitz-s/Portela-a; Saturn Queen, Lightning Lord, Sun-Killer, Micro Lad app. 5.00

LEGION: PROPHETS (Prelude to 2010 movie)
IDW Publishing: Nov, 2009 - No. 4, Dec, 2009 ($3.99, limited series)

1-4: Stewart & Waltz-s. 1-Muriel-a. 2-Holder-a. 3-Paronzini-a. 4-Gaydos-a 4.00

LEGION: SCIENCE POLICE (See Legion of Super-Heroes)
DC Comics: Aug, 1998 - No. 4, Nov, 1998 ($2.25, limited series)

1-4-Ryan-a 3.00

LEGION: SECRET ORIGIN (Legion of Super-Heroes)
DC Comics: Dec, 2011 - No. 6, May, 2012 ($2.99, limited series)

1-6-Levitz-s/Batista-a; formation of the Legion retold 3.00

LEGION WORLDS (Follows Legion Lost series)
DC Comics: Jun, 2001 - No. 6, Nov, 2001 ($3.95, limited series)

1-6-Abnett & Lanning-s; art by various. 5-Dillon-a. 6-Timber Wolf app. 4.00

LEMONADE KID, THE (See Bobby Benson's B-Bar-B Riders)
AC Comics: 1990 ($2.50, 28 pgs.)

1-Powell-c(r); Red Hawk-r by Powell; Lemonade Kid-r/Bobby Benson by Powell (2 stories) 3.00

LENNON SISTERS LIFE STORY, THE
Dell Publishing Co.: No. 951, Nov, 1958 - No. 1014, Aug, 1959

Four Color 951 (#1)-Toth-a, 32pgs, photo-c 11 22 33 73 157 240
Four Color 1014-Toth-a, photo-c 10 20 30 69 147 225

LENORE
Slave Labor Graphics/Titan Comics: Feb, 1998 - Present ($2.95/$3.95, B&W, color #13-on)

1-12: 1-Roman Dirge-s/a, 1,2-2nd printing 4.00
13-($3.95, color) 4.00
Vol. 2 (8/09 - Present) 1-11: 1-1st and 2nd printings; Lenore's origin 4.00
...: Cooties TPB (3/06, $13.95) r/#9-12; pin-ups by various 14.00
...: Noogies TPB ($11.95) r/#1-4 12.00
...: Pink Bellies HC (Titan, 3/15, $17.99) Vol. 2 #8-11 18.00
...: Purple Nurples HC (8/13, $17.95) Vol. 2 #4-7 18.00

Leonard Nimoy's Primortals #3 © Tekno

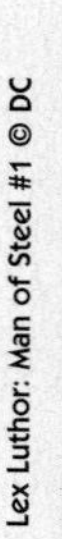
Lex Luthor: Man of Steel #1 © DC

Liberty Meadows #9 © Creators Synd.

GD 2.0 | VG 4.0 | FN 6.0 | VF 8.0 | VF/NM 9.0 | NM- 9.2

...: Swirlies HC (8/12, $17.95) r/#13 & Vol. 2 #1-3 — 18.00
...: Wedgies TPB (2000, $13.95) r/#5-8 — 14.00

LEONARD NIMOY'S PRIMORTALS
Tekno Comix: Mar, 1995 - No. 15, May, 1996 ($1.95)

1-15: Concept by Leonard Nimoy & Isaac Asimov 1-3-w/bound-in game piece & trading card. 4-w/Teknophage Steel Edition coupon. 13,14-Art Adams-c. 15-Simonson-c — 3.00

LEONARD NIMOY'S PRIMORTALS
BIG Entertainment: V2#0, June, 1996 - No. 8, Feb, 1997 ($2.25)

V2#0-8: 0-Includes Pt. 9 of "The Big Bang" x-over. 0,1-Simonson-c. 3-Kelley Jones-c — 3.00

LEONARD NIMOY'S PRIMORTALS ORIGINS
Tekno Comix: Nov, 1995 - No. 2, Dec, 1995 ($2.95, limited series)

1,2: Nimoy scripts; Art Adams-c; polybagged — 3.00

LEONARDO (Also see Teenage Mutant Ninja Turtles)
Mirage Studios: Dec, 1986 ($1.50, B&W, one-shot)

1 — 2 4 6 10 14 18

LEO THE LION
I. W. Enterprises: No date(1960s) (10¢)

1-Reprint — 2 4 6 9 13 16

LEROY (Teen-age)
Standard Comics: Nov, 1949 - No. 6, Nov, 1950

1 — 18 36 54 103 162 220
2-Frazetta text illo. — 12 24 36 67 94 120
3-6: 3-Lubbers-a — 11 22 33 60 83 105

LETHAL (Also see Brigade)
Image Comics (Extreme Studios): Feb, 1996 ($2.50, unfinished limited series)

1-Marat Mychaels-c/a. — 3.00

LETHAL FOES OF SPIDER-MAN (Sequel to Deadly Foes of Spider-Man)
Marvel Comics: Sept, 1993 - No. 4, Dec, 1993 ($1.75, limited series)

1-4 — 3.00

LETHARGIC LAD
Crusade Ent.: June, 1996 - No. 3, Sept, 1996 ($2.95, B&W, limited series)

1,2 — 3.00
3-Alex Ross-c/swipe (Kingdom Come) — 4.00
...Jumbo Sized Annual #1 (Summer 2002, $3.99) prints comic stories from internet — 4.00

LETHARGIC LAD ADVENTURES
Crusade Ent./Destination Ent.#3 on: Oct, 1997 - No. 12, Sept./Oct. 1999 ($2.95, B&W)

1-12-Hyland-s/a. 9-Alex Ross sketch page & back-c — 3.00

LET ME IN: CROSSROADS (Based on the 2010 movie Let Me In)
Dark Horse Comics: Dec, 2010 - No. 4, Mar, 2011 ($3.99, limited series)

1-4-Prelude to the film; Andreyko-s/Reynolds-a/Phillips-c — 4.00
1-4 Variant photo-c — 8.00

LET'S PRETEND (CBS radio)
D. S. Publishing Co.: May-June, 1950 - No. 3, Sept-Oct, 1950

1 — 18 36 54 105 165 225
2,3 — 14 28 42 82 121 160

LET'S READ THE NEWSPAPER
Charlton Press: 1974

nn-Features Quincy by Ted Sheares — 1 3 4 6 8 10

LET'S TAKE A TRIP (TV) (CBS Television Presents)
Pines Comics: Spring, 1958

1-Marv Levy-c/a — 5 10 15 23 28 32

LETTER 44
Oni Press: Oct, 2013 - Present ($1.00/$3.99)

1-($1.00)-Soule-a/Alberto Alburquerque-a — 5.00
2-30-($3.99) 7-Joëlle Jones-a. 14-Drew Moss-a. 28-Gluskova-a — 4.00
... #1 Square One Edition (2/17, $1.00) r/#1 — 3.00

LETTERS TO SANTA (See March of Comics No. 228)

LEX LUTHOR: MAN OF STEEL
DC Comics: May, 2005 - No. 5, Sept, 2005 ($2.99, limited series)

1-5: 1-Azzarello-s/Bermejo-a/c in all. 3-Batman-c/app. — 3.00
TPB (2005, $12.99) r/series — 13.00
Luthor HC (2010, $19.99, d.j.) r/#1-5 with 10 new story pages; cover gallery & sketch-a — 20.00

LEX LUTHOR: THE UNAUTHORIZED BIOGRAPHY
DC Comics: 1989 ($3.95, 52 pgs., one-shot, squarebound)

1-Painted-c; Clark Kent app. — 6.00

LIBERTY COMICS (Miss Liberty No. 1)
Green Publishing Co.: No. 5, May, 1945 - No. 15, July, 1946 (MLJ & other-r)

5 (5/45)-The Prankster app; Starr-a — 26 52 78 154 252 350
10-Hangman & Boy Buddies app.; reprints 3 Hangman stories, incl. Hangman #8 — 24 48 72 142 234 325
11 (V2#2, 1/46)-Wilbur in women's clothes — 18 36 54 105 165 225
12 (V2#4)-Black Hood & Suzie app.; classic Skull-c — 65 130 195 416 708 1000
14,15-Patty of Airliner; Starr-a in both — 21 42 63 120 199 275

LIBERTY COMICS (The CBLDF Presents...)
Image Comics: July, 2008; Oct, 2009 ($3.99/$4.99, Comic Book Legal Defense Fund benefit)

1-Two covers by Campbell & Mignola; art by Cooke, Aragones, A. Adams & others — 4.00
1-(12/08) Second printing with Thor-c by Simonson — 4.00
2-(10/09, $4.99) two covers by Romita Jr. & Sale; art by Allred, Templesmith, Jim Lee — 5.00
Liberty Annual 2010 (10/10, $4.99) Covers by Gibbons & Robertson — 5.00
Liberty Annual 2011 (10/11, $4.99) Covers by Wagner & Cassaday — 5.00
Liberty Annual 2012 (10/12, $4.99) Covers by Dodson & Bá; Walking Dead story — 5.00
Liberty Annual 2013 (10/13, $4.99) Covers by Corben & Marquez — 5.00
Liberty Annual 2014 (10/14, $4.99) Covers by Allred, Simonson, & Charm — 5.00
Liberty Annual 2015 (10/15, $4.99) Covers by Fegredo, Fowler & Del Rey — 5.00
Liberty Annual 2016 (11/16, $4.99) Stories by Guinan, Pope, Wimberly, Schkade & others — 5.00

LIBERTY COMICS
Heroic Publishing: Sept, 2007 ($4.50)

1-Mark Sparacio-c — 4.50

LIBERTY GIRL
Heroic Publishing: Aug, 2006 - No. 3, May, 2007 ($3.25/$2.99)

1-3-Mark Sparacio-c/a — 3.25

LIBERTY GUARDS
Chicago Mail Order: No date (1946?)

nn-Reprints Man of War #1 with cover of Liberty Scouts #1; Gustavson-c — 41 82 123 256 428 600

LIBERTY MEADOWS
Insight Studios Group/Image Comics #27 on: 1999 - No. 37 ($2.95, B&W)

1-Frank Cho-s/a; reprints newspaper strips — 3 6 9 14 20 25
1-2nd & 3rd printings — 1 2 3 4 5 7
2,3 — 2 4 6 8 11 14
4-10 — 1 2 3 4 5 7
11-25,27-37: 20-Adam Hughes-c. 22-Evil Brandy vs. Brandy. 27-1st Image issue, printed sideways — 3.00
..., Cover Girl HC (Image, 2006, $24.99, with dustjacket) r/color covers of #1-19,21-37 along with B&W inked versions, sketches and pin-up art — 25.00
...: Eden Book 1 SC (Image, 2002, $14.95) r/#1-9; sketch gallery — 15.00
...: Eden Book 1 SC 2nd printing (Image, 2004, $19.95) r/#1-9; sketch gallery — 20.00
...: Eden Book 1 HC (Image, 2003, $24.95, with dustjacket) r/#1-9; sketch gallery — 25.00
...: Creature Comforts Book 2 HC (Image, 2004, $24.95, with d.j.) r/#10-18; sketch gallery — 25.00
...: Creature Comforts Book 2 SC (Image, 12/04, $14.95) r/#10-18; sketch gallery — 15.00
...Book 3: Summer of Love HC (Image, 12/04, $24.95) r/#19-27; sketch gallery — 25.00
...Book 3: Summer of Love SC (Image, 7/05, $14.95) r/#19-27; sketch gallery — 15.00
...Book 4: Cold, Cold Heart HC (Image, 9/05, $24.95) r/#28-36; sketch gallery — 25.00
...Book 4: Cold, Cold Heart SC (Image, 2006, $14.99) r/#28-36; sketch gallery — 15.00
Image Firsts: Liberty Meadows #1 (9/10, $1.00) r/#1 — 3.00
... Sourcebook (5/04, $4.95) character info and unpublished strips — 5.00
... Wedding Album (#26) (2002, $2.95) — 3.00

LIBERTY PROJECT, THE
Eclipse Comics: June, 1987 - No. 8, May, 1988 ($1.75, color, Baxter paper)

1-8: 6-Valkyrie app. — 3.00

LIBERTY SCOUTS (See Liberty Guards & Man of War)
Centaur Publications: No. 2, June, 1941 - No. 3, Aug, 1941

2(#1)-Origin The Fire-Man, Man of War; Vapo-Man & Liberty Scouts begin; intro Liberty Scouts; Gustavson-c/a in both — 148 296 444 947 1624 2300
3(#2)-Origin & 1st app. The Sentinel — 103 206 309 659 1130 1600

LICENCE TO KILL (James Bond 007) (Movie)
Eclipse Comics: 1989 ($7.95, slick paper, 52 pgs.)

nn-Movie adaptation; Timothy Dalton photo-c — 1 2 3 5 6 8
Limited Hardcover ($24.95) — 25.00

LIDSVILLE (TV)
Gold Key: Oct, 1972 - No. 5, Oct, 1973

Life of Captain Marvel #1 © MAR

Life Story #2 © FAW

Life With Archie #2 © ACP

	GD 2.0	VG 4.0	FN 6.0	VF 8.0	VF/NM 9.0	NM- 9.2
1-Photo-c on all	5	10	15	31	53	75
2-5	3	6	9	21	33	45

LIEUTENANT, THE (TV)
Dell Publishing Co.: April-June, 1964

	GD 2.0	VG 4.0	FN 6.0	VF 8.0	VF/NM 9.0	NM- 9.2
1-Photo-c	3	6	9	17	26	35

LIEUTENANT BLUEBERRY (Also see Blueberry)
Marvel Comics (Epic Comics): 1991 - No. 3, 1991 (Graphic novel)

	GD 2.0	VG 4.0	FN 6.0	VF 8.0	VF/NM 9.0	NM- 9.2
1,2 ($8.95)-Moebius-a in all	2	4	6	11	16	20
3 ($14.95)	3	6	9	15	22	28

LT. ROBIN CRUSOE, U.S.N. (See Movie Comics & Walt Disney Showcase #26)

LIFE EATERS, THE
DC Comics (WildStorm): 2003 ($29.95, hardcover with dust jacket)

	GD 2.0	VG 4.0	FN 6.0	VF 8.0	VF/NM 9.0	NM- 9.2
HC-David Brin-s; Scott Hampton-painted-a/c; Norse Gods team with the Nazis						30.00
SC-(2004, $19.95)						20.00

LIFE OF CAPTAIN MARVEL, THE
Marvel Comics Group: Aug, 1985 - No. 5, Dec, 1985 ($2.00, Baxter paper)

	GD 2.0	VG 4.0	FN 6.0	VF 8.0	VF/NM 9.0	NM- 9.2
1-5: 1-All reprint Starlin issues of Iron Man #55, Capt. Marvel #25-34 plus Marvel Feature #12 (all with Thanos). 4-New Thanos back-c by Starlin						6.00

LIFE OF CHRIST, THE
Catechetical Guild Educational Society: No. 301, 1949 (35¢, 100 pgs.)

	GD 2.0	VG 4.0	FN 6.0	VF 8.0	VF/NM 9.0	NM- 9.2
301-Reprints from Topix(1949)-V5#11,12	9	18	27	50	65	80

LIFE OF CHRIST: THE CHRISTMAS STORY, THE
Marvel Comics/Nelson: Feb, 1993 ($2.99, slick stock)

	GD 2.0	VG 4.0	FN 6.0	VF 8.0	VF/NM 9.0	NM- 9.2
nn						5.00

LIFE OF CHRIST: THE EASTER STORY, THE
Marvel Comics/Nelson: 1993 ($2.99, slick stock)

	GD 2.0	VG 4.0	FN 6.0	VF 8.0	VF/NM 9.0	NM- 9.2
nn						5.00

LIFE OF CHRIST VISUALIZED
Standard Publishers: 1942 - No. 3, 1943

	GD 2.0	VG 4.0	FN 6.0	VF 8.0	VF/NM 9.0	NM- 9.2
1-3: All came in cardboard case, each...	9	18	27	50	65	80
Case only.....	10	20	30	54	72	90

LIFE OF CHRIST VISUALIZED
The Standard Publ. Co.: 1946? (48 pgs. in color)

	GD 2.0	VG 4.0	FN 6.0	VF 8.0	VF/NM 9.0	NM- 9.2
nn	7	14	21	37	46	55

LIFE OF ESTHER VISUALIZED
The Standard Publ. Co.: No. 2062, 1947 (48 pgs. in color)

	GD 2.0	VG 4.0	FN 6.0	VF 8.0	VF/NM 9.0	NM- 9.2
2062	7	14	21	37	46	55

LIFE OF JOSEPH VISUALIZED
The Standard Publ. Co.: No. 1054, 1946 (48 pgs. in color)

	GD 2.0	VG 4.0	FN 6.0	VF 8.0	VF/NM 9.0	NM- 9.2
1054	7	14	21	37	46	55

LIFE OF PAUL (See The Living Bible)

LIFE OF POPE JOHN PAUL II, THE
Marvel Comics Group: Jan, 1983 ($1.50/$1.75)

	GD 2.0	VG 4.0	FN 6.0	VF 8.0	VF/NM 9.0	NM- 9.2
1	2	4	6	8	10	12

LIFE OF RILEY, THE (TV)
Dell Publishing Co.: No. 917, July, 1958

	GD 2.0	VG 4.0	FN 6.0	VF 8.0	VF/NM 9.0	NM- 9.2
Four Color 917-William Bendix photo-c	9	18	27	62	126	190

LIFE ON ANOTHER PLANET
Kitchen Sink Press: 1978 (B&W, graphic novel, magazine size)

	GD 2.0	VG 4.0	FN 6.0	VF 8.0	VF/NM 9.0	NM- 9.2
nn-Will Eisner-s/a						20.00
Reprint (DC Comics, 5/00, $12.95)						13.00

LIFE'S LIKE THAT
Croyden Publ. Co.: 1945 (25¢, B&W, 68 pgs.)

	GD 2.0	VG 4.0	FN 6.0	VF 8.0	VF/NM 9.0	NM- 9.2
nn-Newspaper Sunday strip-r by Neher	7	14	21	35	43	50

LIFE STORIES OF AMERICAN PRESIDENTS (See Dell Giants)

LIFE STORY
Fawcett Publications: Apr, 1949 - V8#46, Jan, 1953; V8#47, Apr, 1953 (All have photo-c?)

	GD 2.0	VG 4.0	FN 6.0	VF 8.0	VF/NM 9.0	NM- 9.2
V1#1	17	34	51	98	154	210
2	11	22	33	60	83	105
3-6, V2#7-12 (3/50)	10	20	30	54	72	90
V3#13-Wood-a (4/50)	15	30	45	90	140	190
V3#14-18, V4#19-24, V5#25-30, V6#31-35	9	18	27	50	65	80
V6#36- "I sold drugs" on-c	14	28	42	82	121	160
V7#37,40-42, V8#44,45	9	18	27	47	61	75
V7#38, V8#43-Evans-a	9	18	27	50	65	80
V7#39-Drug Smuggling & Junkie story	12	24	36	69	97	125
V8#46,47 (Scarce)	10	20	30	56	76	100

NOTE: *Powell a-13, 23, 24, 26, 28, 30, 32, 39.* ***Marcus Swayze*** *a-1-3, 10-12, 15, 16, 20, 21, 23-25, 31, 35, 37, 40, 44, 46.*

LIFE, THE UNIVERSE AND EVERYTHING (See Hitchhikers Guide to the Galaxy & Restaurant at the End of the Universe)
DC Comics: 1996 - No. 3, 1996 ($6.95, squarebound, limited series)

	GD 2.0	VG 4.0	FN 6.0	VF 8.0	VF/NM 9.0	NM- 9.2
1-3: Adaptation of novel by Douglas Adams.	1	2	3	4	5	7

LIFE WITH ARCHIE
Archie Publications: Sept, 1958 - No. 286, Sept, 1991

	GD 2.0	VG 4.0	FN 6.0	VF 8.0	VF/NM 9.0	NM- 9.2
1	50	100	150	400	900	1400
2-(9/59)	19	38	57	131	291	450
3-5: 3-(7/60)	13	26	39	89	195	300
6-8,10	10	20	30	69	147	225
9,11-Horror/SciFi-c	13	26	39	89	195	300
12-20	7	14	21	46	86	125
21(7/63)-30	6	12	18	40	73	105
31-34,36-38,40,41	5	10	15	33	57	80
35,39-Horror/Sci-Fi-c	8	16	24	54	102	150
42-Pureheart begins (1st app.-c/s, 10/65)	10	20	30	64	132	200
43,44	6	12	18	38	69	100
45(1/66) 1st Man From R.I.V.E.R.D.A.L.E.	7	14	21	46	86	125
46-Origin Pureheart	6	12	18	40	73	105
47-49	5	10	15	33	57	80
50-United Three begin: Pureheart (Archie), Superteen (Betty), Captain Hero (Jughead)	6	12	18	41	76	110
51-59: 59-Pureheart ends	5	10	15	30	50	70
60-Archie band begins, ends #66	5	10	15	34	60	85
61-66: 61-Man From R.I.V.E.R.D.A.L.E.-c/s	4	8	12	25	40	55
67-80	3	6	9	17	26	35
81-99	3	6	9	16	23	30
100 (8/70), 113-Sabrina & Salem app.	3	6	9	19	30	40
101-112, 114-130(2/73), 139(11/73)-Archie Band c/s	2	4	6	11	16	20
131,134-138,140-146,148-161,164-170(6/76)	2	4	6	9	12	15
132,133,147,163-all horror-c/s	3	6	9	14	20	26
162-UFO c/s	3	6	9	14	19	24
171,173-175,177-184,186,189,191-194,196	2	3	4	6	8	10
172,185,197 : 172-(9/77)-Bi-Cent. spec. ish, 185-2nd 24th cent.-c/s, 197-Time machine/SF-c/s	2	4	6	8	10	12
176(12/76)-1st app. Capt. Archie of Starship Rivda, in 24th century c/s; 1st app. Stella the Robot	3	6	9	14	19	24
187,188,195,198,199-all horror-c/s	2	4	6	9	13	16
190-1st Dr. Doom-c/s	2	4	6	9	13	16
200 (12/78) Maltese Pigeon-s	2	4	6	8	11	14
201-203,205-237,239,240(1/84): 208-Reintro Veronica	1	2	3	5	6	8
204-Flying saucer-c/s	2	3	4	6	8	10
238-(9/83)-25th anniversary issue; Ol' Betsy (jalopy) replaced	1	2	3	5	7	9
241-278,280-285: 250-Comic book convention-s						5.00
279,286: 279-Intro Mustang Sally ($1.00, 7/90)						6.00

NOTE: ***Gene Colan*** *a-272-279, 285, 286. Horror/Sci-Fi-c 9, 11, 35, 39, 162.*

LIFE WITH ARCHIE (The Married Life) (Magazine)
Archie Publications: Sept, 2010 - No. 37, Sept, 2014 ($3.99, magazine-size)

	GD 2.0	VG 4.0	FN 6.0	VF 8.0	VF/NM 9.0	NM- 9.2
1-15,17-34: Continuation of Married Life stories from Archie #600-605; articles/interviews						4.00
16-Kevin Keller gay wedding						10.00
36-($4.99, comic-size) Death of Archie; 5 covers by Allred, Francavilla, Hughes, Ramon Perez & Staples	1	2	3	5	6	8
37-($4.99, comic-size) One Year Later aftermath; 5 covers by Chiang, Edwards, Alex Ross, Simonson & Thompson						5.00
...: The Death of Archie: A Life Celebrated Commemorative Issue (2014, $9.99) reprints #36 & #37 in magazine size; afterword by Jon Goldwater; cover gallery w/artist quotes						10.00

LIFE WITH MILLIE (Formerly A Date With Millie) (Modeling With Millie #21 on)
Atlas/Marvel Comics Group: No. 8, Dec, 1960 - No. 20, Dec, 1962

	GD 2.0	VG 4.0	FN 6.0	VF 8.0	VF/NM 9.0	NM- 9.2
8-Teenage	10	20	30	69	147	225
9-11	8	16	24	54	102	150
12-20	7	14	21	49	92	135

LIFE WITH SNARKY PARKER (TV)
Fox Feature Syndicate: Aug, 1950

	GD 2.0	VG 4.0	FN 6.0	VF 8.0	VF/NM 9.0	NM- 9.2
1-Early TV comic; photo-c from TV puppet show	31	62	93	182	296	410

Lightning Comics V2 #5 © ACE

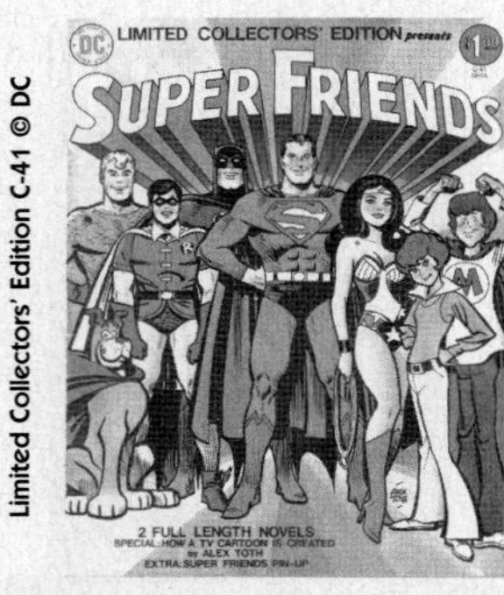

Limited Collectors' Edition C-41 © DC

Linda #2 © AJAX

GD VG FN VF VF/NM NM-
2.0 4.0 6.0 8.0 9.0 9.2

GD VG FN VF VF/NM NM-
2.0 4.0 6.0 8.0 9.0 9.2

LIGHT AND DARKNESS WAR, THE
Marvel Comics (Epic Comics): Oct, 1988 - No. 6, Dec, 1989 ($1.95, lim. series)
1-6 3.00

LIGHT BRIGADE, THE
DC Comics: 2004 - No. 4, 2004 ($5.95, limited series)
1-4-Archangels in World War II; Tomasi-s/Snejbjerg-a 6.00
TPB (2005, 2009, $19.99) r/series; cover galery 20.00

LIGHT FANTASTIC, THE (Terry Pratchett's)
Innovation Publishing: June, 1992 - No. 4, Sept, 1992 ($2.50, mini-series)
1-4: Adapts 2nd novel in Discworld series 3.00

LIGHT IN THE FOREST (Disney)
Dell Publishing Co.: No. 891, Mar, 1958
Four Color 891-Movie, Fess Parker photo-c 6 12 18 42 79 115

LIGHTNING COMICS (Formerly Sure-Fire No. 1-3)
Ace Magazines: No. 4, Dec, 1940 - No. 13(V3#1), June, 1942
4-Characters continue from Sure-Fire 181 362 543 1158 1979 2800
5,6: 6-Dr. Nemesis begins 116 232 348 742 1271 1800
V2#1-6: 2- "Flash Lightning" becomes "Lash..." 97 194 291 621 1061 1500
V3#1-Intro. Lightning Girl & The Sword 97 194 291 621 1061 1500
NOTE: *Anderson a-V2#6. Mooney c-V1#5, 6, V2#1-6, V3#1. Bondage c-V2#6. Lightning-c on all.*

LIGHTNING COMICS PRESENTS
Lightning Comics: May, 1994 ($3.50)
1-Red foil-c distr. by Diamond Distr., 1-Black/yellow/blue-c distrib. by Capital Distr., 1-Red/yellow-c distributed by H. World, 1-Platinum 3.50

LI'L ... (These titles are listed under Little ...)

LILI
Image Comics: No. 0, 1999 ($4.95, B&W)
0-Bendis & Yanover-s 5.00

LILLITH (See Warrior Nun...)
Antarctic Press: Sept, 1996 - No. 3, Feb, 1997 ($2.95, limited series)
1-3: 1-Variant-c 3.00

LIMITED COLLECTORS' EDITION (See Famous First Edition, Marvel Treasury #28, Rudolph The Red-Nosed Reindeer, & Superman Vs. The Amazing Spider-Man; becomes All-New Collectors' Edition)
National Periodical Publications/DC Comics:
(#21-34,51-59: 84 pgs.; #35-41: 68 pgs.; #42-50: 60 pgs.)
C-21, Summer, 1973 - No. C-59, 1978 ($1.00) (10x13-1/2")
(Rudolph...C-20 (implied), 12/72)-See Rudolph The Red-Nosed Reindeer
C-21: Shazam (TV); r/Captain Marvel Jr. #11 by Raboy; C.C. Beck-c, biog. & photo 3 6 9 19 30 40
C-22: Tarzan; complete origin reprinted from #207-210; all Kubert-c/a; Joe Kubert biography & photo inside 3 6 9 16 24 32
C-23: House of Mystery; Wrightson, N. Adams/Orlando, G. Kane/Wood, Toth, Aragones, Sparling reprints 4 8 12 23 37 50
C-24: Rudolph The Red-Nosed Reindeer 6 12 18 38 69 100
C-25: Batman; Neal Adams-c/a(r); G.A. Joker-r; Batman/Enemy Ace-r; Novick-a(r); has photos from TV show 4 8 12 25 40 55
C-26: See Famous First Edition C-26 (same contents)
C-27,C-29,C-31: C-27: Shazam (TV); G.A. Capt. Marvel & Mary Marvel-r; Beck-r. C-29: Tarzan; reprints "Return of Tarzan" from #219-223 by Kubert; Kubert-c. C-31: Superman; origin-r; Giordano-a; photos of George Reeves from 1950s TV show on inside b/c; Burnley, Boring-r 3 6 9 16 23 30
C-32: Ghosts (new-a) 3 6 9 21 33 45
C-33: Rudolph The Red-Nosed Reindeer(new-a) 5 10 15 35 63 90
C-34: Christmas with the Super-Heroes; unpublished Angel & Ape story by Oksner & Wood; Batman & Teen Titans-r 3 6 9 16 23 30
C-35: Shazam (TV); photo cover features TV's Captain Marvel, Jackson Bostwick; Beck-r; TV photos inside b/c 3 6 9 15 22 28
C-36: The Bible; all new adaptation beginning with Genesis by Kubert, Redondo & Mayer; Kubert-c 3 6 9 15 22 28
C-37: Batman; r-1946 Sundays; inside b/c photos of Batman TV show villains (all villain issue; r/G.A. Joker, Catwoman, Penguin, Two-Face, & Scarecrow stories plus 1946 Sundays-r) 3 6 9 17 26 35
C-38: Superman; 1 pg. N. Adams; part photo-c; photos from TV show on inside back-c 3 6 9 15 22 28
C-39: Secret Origins of Super-Villains; N. Adams-i(r); collection reprints 1950's Joker origin, Luthor origin from Adv. Comics #271, Captain Cold origin from Showcase #8 among others; G.A. Batman-r; Beck-r 3 6 9 15 22 28
C-40: Dick Tracy by Gould featuring Flattop; newspaper-r from 12/21/43 - 5/17/44; biog. of Chester Gould 3 6 9 15 22 28
C-41: Super Friends (TV); JLA-r(1965); Toth-c/a 3 6 9 16 23 30
C-42: Rudolph 4 8 12 27 44 60
C-43-C-47: C-43: Christmas with the Super-Heroes; Wrightson, S&K, Neal Adams-a. C-44: Batman; N. Adams-p(r) & G.A.-r; painted-c. C-45: More Secret Origins of Super-Villains; Flash-r/#105; G.A. Wonder Woman & Batman/Catwoman-r. C-46: Justice League of America(1963-r); 3 pgs. Toth-a C-47: Superman Salutes the Bicentennial (Tomahawk interior); 2 pgs. new-a 3 6 9 14 20 26
C-48,C-49: C-48: Superman Vs. The Flash (Superman/Flash race); swipes-c to Superman #199; r/Superman #199 & Flash #175; 6 pgs. Neal Adams-a. C-49: Superboy & the Legion of Super-Heroes 3 6 9 16 23 30
C-50: Rudolph The Red-Nosed Reindeer; contains poster attached at the centerfold with a cardstock flap (1/2 price if poster is missing) 4 8 12 27 44 60
C-51: Batman; Neal Adams-c/a 3 6 9 16 24 32
C-52,C-57: C-52: The Best of DC; Neal Adams-c/a; Toth, Kubert-a. C-57: Welcome Back, Kotter-r(TV)(5/78) includes unpublished #11 3 6 9 15 22 28
C-53 thru C-56, C-58, C-60 thru C-62 (See All-New Collectors' Edition)
C-59: Batman's Strangest Cases; N. Adams-r; Wrightson-r/Swamp Thing #7; N. Adams/Wrightson-c 3 6 9 15 22 28
NOTE: *All-r with exception of some special features and covers. Aparo a-52r; c-37. Grell c-49. Infantino a-25, 39, 44, 45, 52. Bob Kane r-25. Robinson r-25, 44. Sprang r-44. Issues #21-31, 35-39, 45, 48 have back cover cut-outs.*

LINDA (Everybody Loves...) (Phantom Lady No. 5 on)
Ajax-Farrell Publ. Co.: Apr-May, 1954 - No. 4, Oct-Nov, 1954
1-Kamenish-a 16 32 48 94 147 200
2-Lingerie panel 13 26 39 72 101 130
3,4 11 22 33 60 83 105

LINDA CARTER, STUDENT NURSE (Also see Night Nurse)
Atlas Comics (AMI): Sept, 1961 - No. 9, Jan, 1963
1-Al Hartley-c 77 154 231 493 847 1200
2-9 18 36 54 105 165 225

LINDA LARK
Dell Publishing Co.: Oct-Dec, 1961 - No. 8, Aug-Oct, 1963
1 3 6 9 18 28 38
2-8 3 6 9 14 19 24

LINE OF DEFENSE 3000AD (Based on the video game)
DC Comics: No. 0, 2012 (no price)
0-Brian Ching-a 3.00

LINUS, THE LIONHEARTED (TV)
Gold Key: Sept, 1965
1 (10155-509) 6 12 18 38 69 100

LION, THE (See Movie Comics)

LIONHEART
Awesome Comics: Sept, 1999 - No. 2, Dec, 1999 ($2.99/$2.50)
1-Ian Churchill-story/a, Jeph Loeb-s; Coven app. 3.50
2-Flip book w/Coven #4 3.00

LION OF SPARTA (See Movie Classics)

LIPPY THE LION AND HARDY HAR HAR (TV)
Gold Key: Mar, 1963 (12¢) (See Hanna-Barbera Band Wagon #1)
1 (10049-303) 7 14 21 46 86 125

LISA COMICS (TV)(See Simpsons Comics)
Bongo Comics: 1995 ($2.25)
1-Lisa in Wonderland 4.00

LITERALS, THE (See Fables and Jack of Fables)
DC Comics (Vertigo): June, 2009 - No. 3, Aug, 2009 ($2.99)
1-3-Crossover with Fables #83-85 and Jack of Fables #33-35; Buckingham-c/a 3.00

LI'L ABNER (See Comics on Parade, Sparkle, Sparkler Comics, Tip Top Comics & Tip Topper)
United Features Syndicate: 1939 - 1940
Single Series 4 ('39) 89 178 267 565 970 1375
Single Series 18 ('40) (#18 on inside, #2 on-c) 65 130 195 416 708 1000

LI'L ABNER (Al Capp's; continued from Comics on Parade #58)
Harvey Publ. No. 61-69 (2/49)/Toby Press No. 70 on: No. 61, Dec, 1947 - No. 97, Jan, 1955 (See Oxydol-Dreft in Promotional Comics section)
61(#1)-Wolverton & Powell-a 23 46 69 136 223 310
62-65: 63-The Wolf Girl app. 65-Powell-a 15 30 45 85 130 175
66,67,69,70 14 28 42 82 121 160
68-Full length Fearless Fosdick-c/story 15 30 45 88 137 185

Li'l Abner #62 © TOBY

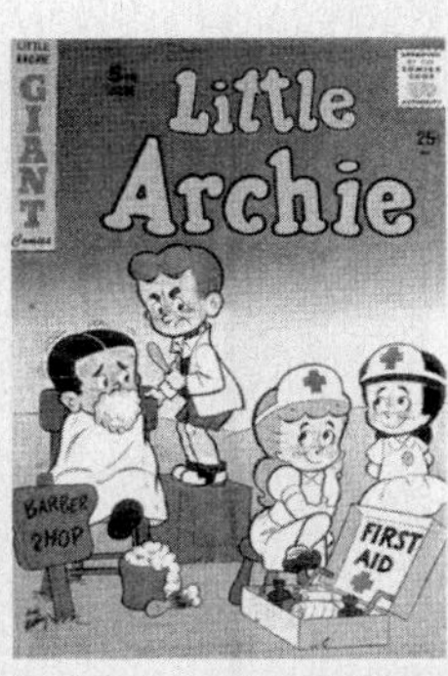

Little Archie #5 © ACP

Little Audrey and Melvin #1 © HARV

	GD 2.0	VG 4.0	FN 6.0	VF 8.0	VF/NM 9.0	NM- 9.2
71-74,76,80	13	26	39	74	105	135
75,77-79,86,91-All with Kurtzman art; 86-Sadie Hawkins Day. 91-r/#77	15	30	45	83	124	165
81-85,87-90,92-94,96,97: 83-Evil-Eye Fleegle & Double Whammy app. 88-Cousin Weakeyes goes hunting. 94-Six lessons from Adam Lazonga. 96-Football issue	12	24	36	69	97	125
95-Full length Fearless Fosdick story	14	28	42	76	108	140

LI'L ABNER
Toby Press: 1951

	GD	VG	FN	VF	VF/NM	NM-
1	18	36	54	103	162	220

LI'L ABNER'S DOGPATCH (See Al Capp's...)

LITTLE AL OF THE F.B.I.
Ziff-Davis Publications: No. 10, 1950 (no month) - No. 11, Apr-May, 1951 (Saunders painted-c)

	GD	VG	FN	VF	VF/NM	NM-
10(1950)	18	36	54	105	165	225
11(1951)	14	28	42	80	115	150

LITTLE AL OF THE SECRET SERVICE
Ziff-Davis Publications: No. 10, 7-8/51; No, 2, 9-10/51; No. 3, Winter, 1951 (Saunders painted-c)

	GD	VG	FN	VF	VF/NM	NM-
10(#1)	17	34	51	98	154	210
2,3	14	28	42	76	108	140

LITTLE AMBROSE
Archie Publications: September, 1958

	GD	VG	FN	VF	VF/NM	NM-
1-Bob Bolling-c	17	34	51	98	154	210

LITTLE ANGEL
Standard (Visual Editions)/Pines: No. 5, Sept, 1954; No. 6, Sept, 1955 - No. 16, Sept, 1959

	GD	VG	FN	VF	VF/NM	NM-
5-Last pre-code issue	8	16	24	42	54	65
6-16	6	12	18	28	34	40

LITTLE ANNIE ROONEY (Also see Henry)
David McKay Publ.: 1935 (25¢, B&W dailies, 48 pgs.)(10"x10", cardboard-c)

	GD	VG	FN	VF	VF/NM	NM-
Book 1-Daily strip-r by Darrell McClure	38	76	114	226	368	510

LITTLE ANNIE ROONEY (See King Comics & Treasury of Comics)
David McKay/St. John/Standard: 1938; Aug, 1948 - No. 3, Oct, 1948

	GD	VG	FN	VF	VF/NM	NM-
Feature Books 11 (McKay, 1938)	39	78	117	231	378	525
1 (St. John)	15	30	45	88	137	185
2,3	10	20	30	54	72	90

LITTLE ARCHIE (The Adventures of... #13-on) (See Archie Giant Series Mag. #527, 534, 538, 545, 549, 556, 560, 566, 570, 583, 594, 596, 607, 609, 619)
Archie Publications: 1956 - No. 180, Feb, 1983 (Giants No. 3-84)

	GD	VG	FN	VF	VF/NM	NM-
1-(Scarce)	114	228	342	912	2056	3200
2 (1957)	38	76	114	285	641	1000
3-5: 3-(1958)-Bob Bolling-c & giant issues begin	21	42	63	147	324	500
6-10	15	30	45	103	227	350
11-17,19,21 (84 pgs.)	11	22	33	73	157	240
18,20,22 (84 pgs.)-Horror/Sci-Fi-c	15	30	45	103	227	350
23-39 (68 pgs.)	7	14	21	46	86	125
40 (Fall/66)-Intro. Little Pureheart-c/s (68 pgs.)	8	16	24	51	96	140
41,44-Little Pureheart (68 pgs.)	6	12	18	37	66	95
42-Intro The Little Archies Band, ends #66 (68 pgs.)	6	12	18	40	73	105
43-1st Boy From R.I.V.E.R.D.A.L.E. (68 pgs.)	6	12	18	38	69	100
45-58 (68 pgs.)	5	10	15	31	53	75
59 (68 pgs.)-Little Sabrina begins	7	14	21	48	89	130
60-66 (68 pgs.)	4	8	12	27	44	60
67(9/71)-84: 84-Last 52pg. Giant-Size (2/74)	3	6	9	17	26	35
85-99	2	4	6	10	14	18
100	2	4	6	13	18	22
101-112,114-116,118-129	2	4	6	8	10	12
113,117,130: 113-Halloween Special issue(12/76). 117-Donny Osmond-c cameo 130-UFO cover (5/78)	2	4	6	9	13	16
131-150(1/80), 180(Last issue, 2/83)	1	2	3	5	7	9
151-179						5.00
...In Animal Land 1 (1957)	27	54	81	189	420	650
...In Animal Land 17 (Winter, 1957-58)-19 (Summer,1958)-Formerly Li'l Jinx	10	20	30	66	138	210
Archie Classics - The Adventures of Little Archie Vol. 1 TPB (2004, $10.95) reprints						11.00
Vol. 2 TPB (2008, $9.95) reprints plus new 22 pg. story with Bolling-s/a						10.00

NOTE: *Little Archie Band app. 42-66. Little Sabrina in 59-78,80-180*

LITTLE ARCHIE CHRISTMAS SPECIAL (See Archie Giant Series #581)

LITTLE ARCHIE COMICS DIGEST ANNUAL (...Magazine #5 on)
Archie Publications: 10/77 - No. 48, 5/91 (Digest-size, 128 pgs., later issues $1.35-$1.50)

	GD	VG	FN	VF	VF/NM	NM-
1(10/77)-Reprints	3	6	9	19	30	40
2(4/78,3(11/78)-Neal Adams-a. 3-The Fly-r by S&K	3	6	9	14	20	26
4(4/79) - 10	2	4	6	10	14	18
11-20	2	4	6	8	10	12
21-30: 28-Christmas-c	1	2	3	5	6	8
31-48: 40,46-Christmas-c						5.00

NOTE: *Little Archie, Little Jinx, Little Jughead & Little Sabrina in most issues.*

LITTLE ARCHIE DIGEST MAGAZINE
Archie Comics: July, 1991 - No. 21, Mar, 1998 ($1.50/$1.79/$1.89, digest size, bi-annual)

	GD	VG	FN	VF	VF/NM	NM-
V2#1						6.00
2-10						4.00
11-21						3.00

LITTLE ARCHIE MYSTERY
Archie Publications: Aug, 1963 - No. 2, Oct, 1963 (12¢ issues)

	GD	VG	FN	VF	VF/NM	NM-
1	13	26	39	89	195	300
2	8	16	24	51	96	140

LITTLE ASPIRIN (See Little Lenny & Wisco)
Marvel Comics (CnPC): July, 1949 - No. 3, Dec, 1949 (52 pgs.)

	GD	VG	FN	VF	VF/NM	NM-
1-Oscar app.; Kurtzman-a (4 pgs.)	20	40	60	117	189	260
2-Kurtzman-a (4 pgs.)	13	26	39	72	101	130
3-No Kurtzman-a	10	20	30	58	79	100

LITTLE AUDREY (Also see Playful...)
St. John Publ.: Apr, 1948 - No. 24, May, 1952

	GD	VG	FN	VF	VF/NM	NM-
1-1st app. Little Audrey	135	270	405	864	1482	2100
2	40	80	120	246	411	575
3-5	26	52	78	154	252	350
6-10	19	38	57	111	176	240
11-20: 16-X-Mas-c	14	28	42	82	121	160
21-24	13	26	39	74	105	135

LITTLE AUDREY (See Harvey Hits #11, 19)
Harvey Publications: No. 25, Aug, 1952 - No. 53, April, 1957

	GD	VG	FN	VF	VF/NM	NM-
25-(Paramount Pictures Famous Star... on-c); 1st Harvey Casper and Baby Huey (1 month earlier than Harvey Comic Hits #60(9/52))	25	50	75	175	388	600
26-30: 26-28-Casper app.	8	16	24	54	102	150
31-40: 32-35-Casper app.	6	12	18	40	73	105
41-53	5	10	15	31	53	75
...Clubhouse 1 (9/61, 68 pg. Giant)-New stories & reprints	8	16	24	51	96	140

LITTLE AUDREY
Harvey Comics: Aug, 1992 - No. 8, July, 1994 ($1.25/$1.50)

	GD	VG	FN	VF	VF/NM	NM-
V2#1						4.00
2-8						3.00

LITTLE AUDREY (...Yearbook)
St. John Publishing Co.: 1950 (50¢, 260 pgs.)

Contains 8 complete 1949 comics rebound; Casper, Alice in Wonderland, Little Audrey, Abbott & Costello, Pinocchio, Moon Mullins, Three Stooges (from Jubilee), Little Annie Rooney app. (Rare)

	GD	VG	FN	VF	VF/NM	NM-
	181	362	543	1158	1979	2800

(Also see All Good & Treasury of Comics)

NOTE: *This book contains remaindered St. John comics; many variations possible.*

LITTLE AUDREY & MELVIN (Audrey & Melvin No. 62)
Harvey Publications: May, 1962 - No. 61, Dec, 1973

	GD	VG	FN	VF	VF/NM	NM-
1	9	18	27	61	123	185
2-5	4	8	12	25	40	55
6-10	3	6	9	21	33	45
11-20	3	6	9	16	23	30
21-40: 22-Richie Rich app.	2	4	6	13	18	22
41-50,55-61	2	4	6	9	13	16
51-54: All 52 pg. Giants	2	4	6	13	18	22

LITTLE AUDREY TV FUNTIME
Harvey Publ.: Sept, 1962 - No. 33, Oct, 1971 (#1-31: 68 pgs.; #32,33: 52 pgs.)

	GD	VG	FN	VF	VF/NM	NM-
1-Richie Rich app.	9	18	27	62	126	190
2,3: Richie Rich app.	4	8	12	27	44	60
4,5: 5-25¢ & 35¢ issues exist	4	8	12	23	37	50
6-10	3	6	9	17	26	35
11-20	3	6	9	14	19	24
21-33	2	4	6	11	16	20

LITTLE BAD WOLF (Disney; see Walt Disney's C&S #52, Walt Disney Showcase #21 &

Little Dot #13 © HARV

Little Eva #2 © STJ

Little Giant Movie Funnies #2 © CEN

Wheaties)
Dell Publishing Co.: No. 403, June, 1952 - No. 564, June, 1954

	GD 2.0	VG 4.0	FN 6.0	VF 8.0	VF/NM 9.0	NM- 9.2
Four Color 403 (#1)	7	14	21	46	86	125
Four Color 473 (6/53), 564	5	10	15	34	60	85

LI'L BATTLESTAR GALACTICA (Classic 1978 TV series)
Dynamite Entertainment: 2014 ($3.99, one-shot)

	GD 2.0	VG 4.0	FN 6.0	VF 8.0	VF/NM 9.0	NM- 9.2
1-Kid version spoof by Franco & Art Baltazar; covers by Baltazar & Garbowska						4.00

LITTLE BEAVER
Dell Publishing Co.: No. 211, Jan, 1949 - No. 870, Jan, 1958 (All painted-c)

	GD 2.0	VG 4.0	FN 6.0	VF 8.0	VF/NM 9.0	NM- 9.2
Four Color 211('49)-All Harman-a	9	18	27	59	117	175
Four Color 267,294,332(5/51)	6	12	18	37	66	95
3(10-12/51)-8(1-3/53)	5	10	15	30	50	70
Four Color 483(8-10/53),529	5	10	15	34	60	85
Four Color 612,660,695,744,817,870	5	10	15	33	57	80

LI'L BIONIC KIDS (Six Million Dollar Man and Bionic Woman)
Dynamite Entertainment: 2014 ($3.99, one-shot)

	GD 2.0	VG 4.0	FN 6.0	VF 8.0	VF/NM 9.0	NM- 9.2
1-Kid version spoof; Bigfoot app.; Jerwa-s/McGinty-a; covers by Baltazar & Garbowska						4.00

LITTLE BIT
Jubilee/St. John Publishing Co.: Mar, 1949 - No. 2, June, 1949

	GD 2.0	VG 4.0	FN 6.0	VF 8.0	VF/NM 9.0	NM- 9.2
1-Kid humor	12	24	36	69	97	125
2	9	18	27	50	65	80

LI'L DEPRESSED BOY
Image Comics: Feb, 2011 - No. 16, Apr, 2013 ($2.99/$3.99)

	GD 2.0	VG 4.0	FN 6.0	VF 8.0	VF/NM 9.0	NM- 9.2
1-12-S. Steven Struble-s/Sina Grace-a. 5-Guillory-c. 6-Adlard-c. 10-Childish Gambino app.						3.00
13-16-($3.99)						4.00
Vol. 0 (12/11, $9.99) reprints earlier stories from webcomics & anthologies; various-a						10.00

LI'L DEPRESSED BOY: SUPPOSED TO BE THERE TOO
Image Comics: Oct, 2014 - No. 5, Jun, 2015 ($3.99)

	GD 2.0	VG 4.0	FN 6.0	VF 8.0	VF/NM 9.0	NM- 9.2
1-5-S. Steven Struble-s/Sina Grace-a						4.00

LITTLE DOT (See Humphrey, Li'l Max, Sad Sack, and Tastee-Freez Comics)
Harvey Publications: Sept, 1953 - No. 164, Apr, 1976

	GD 2.0	VG 4.0	FN 6.0	VF 8.0	VF/NM 9.0	NM- 9.2
1-Intro./1st app. Richie Rich & Little Lotta	676	1352	2028	4935	8718	12,500
2-1st app. Freckles & Pee Wee (Richie Rich's poor friends)	161	322	483	1030	1765	2500
3	90	180	270	576	988	1400
4	84	168	252	538	919	1300
5-Origin dots on Little Dot's dress	87	174	261	553	952	1350
6-Richie Rich, Little Lotta, & Little Dot all on cover; 1st Richie Rich cover featured	194	388	582	1242	2121	3000
7-10: 9-Last pre-code issue (1/55)	61	122	183	390	670	950
11-20	36	72	108	211	343	475
21-30	18	36	54	105	165	225
31-40	14	28	42	80	115	150
41-50	11	22	33	62	86	110
51-60	9	18	27	52	69	85
61-80	4	8	12	27	44	60
81-100	3	6	9	19	30	40
101-141	3	6	9	16	23	30
142-145: All 52 pg. Giants	3	6	9	17	26	35
146-164	2	4	6	11	16	20

NOTE: *Richie Rich & Little Lotta in all.*

LITTLE DOT
Harvey Comics: Sept, 1992 - No. 7, June, 1994 ($1.25/$1.50)

	GD 2.0	VG 4.0	FN 6.0	VF 8.0	VF/NM 9.0	NM- 9.2
V2#1-Little Dot, Little Lotta, Richie Rich in all						4.00
2-7 ($1.50)						3.00

LITTLE DOT DOTLAND (Dot Dotland No. 62, 63)
Harvey Publications: July, 1962 - No. 61, Dec, 1973

	GD 2.0	VG 4.0	FN 6.0	VF 8.0	VF/NM 9.0	NM- 9.2
1-Richie Rich begins	12	24	36	81	176	270
2,3	7	14	21	44	82	120
4,5	5	10	15	35	63	90
6-10	5	10	15	30	50	70
11-20	4	8	12	23	37	50
21-30	3	6	9	17	26	35
31-50	3	6	9	16	23	30
51-54: All 52 pg. Giants	3	6	9	17	26	35
55-61	2	4	6	11	16	20

LITTLE DOT'S UNCLES & AUNTS (See Harvey Hits No. 4, 13, 24)
Harvey Enterprises: Oct, 1961; No. 2, Aug, 1962 - No. 52, Apr, 1974

	GD 2.0	VG 4.0	FN 6.0	VF 8.0	VF/NM 9.0	NM- 9.2
1-Richie Rich begins; 68 pgs. begin	13	26	39	91	201	310
2,3	8	16	24	51	96	140
4,5	5	10	15	35	63	90
6-10	5	10	15	31	53	75
11-20	4	8	12	23	37	50
21-37: Last 68 pg. issue	3	6	9	18	28	38
38-52: All 52 pg. Giants	3	6	9	16	23	30

LITTLE DRACULA
Harvey Comics: Jan, 1992 - No. 3, May, 1992 ($1.25, quarterly, mini-series)

	GD 2.0	VG 4.0	FN 6.0	VF 8.0	VF/NM 9.0	NM- 9.2
1-3						3.00

LITTLE ENDLESS STORYBOOK, THE (See The Sandman titles and Delirium's Party)
DC Comics: 2001 ($5.95, Prestige format, one-shot)

	GD 2.0	VG 4.0	FN 6.0	VF 8.0	VF/NM 9.0	NM- 9.2
nn-Jill Thompson-s/painted-a/c; puppy Barnabas searches for Delirium						20.00
HC (2011, $14.99) r/story plus original character sketches and merchandise design						15.00

LI'L ERNIE (Evil Ernie)
Dynamite Entertainment: 2014 ($3.99, one-shot)

	GD 2.0	VG 4.0	FN 6.0	VF 8.0	VF/NM 9.0	NM- 9.2
1-Kid version spoof; Roger Langridge-s/a; covers by Baltazar & Garbowska						4.00

LITTLE EVA
St. John Publishing Co.: May, 1952 - No. 31, Nov, 1956

	GD 2.0	VG 4.0	FN 6.0	VF 8.0	VF/NM 9.0	NM- 9.2
1	19	38	57	111	176	240
2	12	24	36	67	94	120
3-5	10	20	30	54	72	90
6-10	9	18	27	47	61	75
11-31	8	16	24	42	54	65
3-D 1,2(10/53, 11/53, 25¢)-Both came w/glasses. 1-Infinity-c	18	36	54	107	169	230
I.W. Reprint #1-3,6-8: 1-r/Little Eva #28. 2-r/Little Eva #29. 3-r/Little Eva #24	2	4	6	8	11	14
Super Reprint #10,12('63),14,16,18('64): 18-r/Little Eva #25.	2	4	6	8	11	14

LI'L GENIUS (Formerly Super Brat; Summer Fun No. 54) (See Blue Bird & Giant Comics #3)
Charlton Comics: No. 6, 1954 - No. 52, 1/65; No. 53, 10/65; No. 54, 10/85 - No. 55, 1/86

	GD 2.0	VG 4.0	FN 6.0	VF 8.0	VF/NM 9.0	NM- 9.2
6 (#1)	11	22	33	62	86	110
7-10	7	14	21	37	46	55
11-1st app. Li'l Tomboy (10/56); same month as 1st issue of Li'l Tomboy (V14#92)	8	16	24	40	50	60
12-15,19,20	6	12	18	29	36	42
16,17-(68 pgs.)	8	16	24	40	50	60
18-(100 pgs., 10/58)	11	22	33	60	83	105
21-35: 34-Atomic bomb explosion	3	6	9	15	22	28
36-53	2	4	6	10	14	18
54,55 (Low print)						6.00

LI'L GHOST
St. John Publ. Co./Fago No. 1 on: 2/58; No. 2,1/59 - No. 3, Mar, 1959

	GD 2.0	VG 4.0	FN 6.0	VF 8.0	VF/NM 9.0	NM- 9.2
1(St. John)	11	22	33	62	86	110
2,3	7	14	21	37	46	55

LITTLE GIANT COMICS
Centaur Publications: 7/38 - No. 3, 10/38; No. 4, 2/39 (132 pgs.) (6-3/4x4-1/2")

	GD 2.0	VG 4.0	FN 6.0	VF 8.0	VF/NM 9.0	NM- 9.2
1-B&W with color-c; stories, puzzles, magic	213	426	639	1363	2332	3300
2,3-B&W with color-c	142	284	426	909	1555	2200
4 (6-5/8x9-3/8")(68 pgs., B&W inside)	142	284	426	909	1555	2200

NOTE: *Filchock c-2, 4. **Gustavson** a-1. **Pinajian** a-4. **Bob Wood** a-1.*

LITTLE GIANT DETECTIVE FUNNIES
Centaur Publ.: Oct, 1938; No. 4, Jan, 1939 (6-3/4x4-1/2", 132 pgs., B&W)

	GD 2.0	VG 4.0	FN 6.0	VF 8.0	VF/NM 9.0	NM- 9.2
1-B&W with color-c	213	426	639	1363	2332	3300
4(1/39, B&W; color-c; 68 pgs., 6-1/2x9-1/2")-Eisner-r	142	284	426	909	1555	2200

LITTLE GIANT MOVIE FUNNIES
Centaur Publ.: Aug, 1938 - No. 2, Oct, 1938 (6-3/4x4-1/2", 132 pgs., B&W)

	GD 2.0	VG 4.0	FN 6.0	VF 8.0	VF/NM 9.0	NM- 9.2
1-Ed Wheelan's "Minute Movies" reprints	213	426	639	1363	2332	3300
2-Ed Wheelan's "Minute Movies" reprints	142	284	426	909	1555	2200

LITTLE GROUCHO (...the Red-Headed Tornado; ...Grouchy No. 2)
Reston Publ. Co.: No. 16; Feb-Mar, 1955 - No. 2, June-July, 1955 (See Tippy Terry)

	GD 2.0	VG 4.0	FN 6.0	VF 8.0	VF/NM 9.0	NM- 9.2
16, 1 (2-3/55)	9	18	27	50	65	80
2(6-7/55)	7	14	21	35	43	50

LITTLE HIAWATHA (Disney; see Walt Disney's C&S #143)

Little Lizzie #2 © MAR

Little Lotta #1 © HARV

Little Max Comics #50 © HARV

Dell Publishing Co.: No. 439, Dec, 1952 - No. 988, May-July, 1959

	GD 2.0	VG 4.0	FN 6.0	VF 8.0	VF/NM 9.0	NM- 9.2
Four Color 439 (#1)	7	14	21	44	82	120
Four Color 787 (4/57), 901 (5/58), 988	5	10	15	33	57	80

LITTLE IKE
St. John Publishing Co.: April, 1953 - No. 4, Oct, 1953

	GD 2.0	VG 4.0	FN 6.0	VF 8.0	VF/NM 9.0	NM- 9.2
1-Kid humor	12	24	36	67	94	120
2	8	16	24	40	50	60
3,4	7	14	21	35	43	50

LITTLE IODINE (See Giant Comic Album)
Dell Publ. Co.: No. 224, 4/49 - No. 257, 1949; 3-5/50 - No. 56, 4-6/62 (1-4-52pgs.)

	GD 2.0	VG 4.0	FN 6.0	VF 8.0	VF/NM 9.0	NM- 9.2
Four Color 224-By Jimmy Hatlo	12	24	36	81	176	270
Four Color 257	8	16	24	55	105	155
1(3-5/50)	10	20	30	64	132	200
2-5	5	10	15	35	63	90
6-10	5	10	15	30	50	70
11-20	4	8	12	27	44	60
21-30: 27-Xmas-c	4	8	12	23	37	50
31-40	3	6	9	21	33	45
41-56	3	6	9	19	30	40

LITTLE JACK FROST
Avon Periodicals: 1951

	GD 2.0	VG 4.0	FN 6.0	VF 8.0	VF/NM 9.0	NM- 9.2
1	14	28	42	80	115	150

LI'L JINX (Little Archie in Animal Land #17) (Also see Pep Comics #62)
Archie Publications: No. 1(#11), Nov, 1956 - No. 16, Sept, 1957

	GD 2.0	VG 4.0	FN 6.0	VF 8.0	VF/NM 9.0	NM- 9.2
1(#11)-By Joe Edwards; "First Issue" on cover	15	30	45	88	137	185
12(1/57)-16	11	22	33	62	86	110

LI'L JINX (See Archie Giant Series Magazine No. 223)

LI'L JINX CHRISTMAS BAG (See Archie Giant Series Mag. No. 195, 206, 219)

LI'L JINX GIANT LAUGH-OUT (See Archie Giant Series Mag. No. 176, 185)
Archie Publications: No. 33, Sept, 1971 - No. 43, Nov, 1973 (52 pgs.)

	GD 2.0	VG 4.0	FN 6.0	VF 8.0	VF/NM 9.0	NM- 9.2
33-43 (52 pgs.)	2	4	6	13	18	22

LITTLE JOE (See Popular Comics & Super Comics)
Dell Publishing Co.: No. 1, 1942

	GD 2.0	VG 4.0	FN 6.0	VF 8.0	VF/NM 9.0	NM- 9.2
Four Color 1	63	126	189	504	1127	1750

LITTLE JOE
St. John Publishing Co.: Apr, 1953

	GD 2.0	VG 4.0	FN 6.0	VF 8.0	VF/NM 9.0	NM- 9.2
1	8	16	24	42	54	65

LI'L KIDS (Also see Li'l Pals)
Marvel Comics Group: 8/70 - No. 2, 10/70; No. 3, 11/71 - No. 12, 6/73

	GD 2.0	VG 4.0	FN 6.0	VF 8.0	VF/NM 9.0	NM- 9.2
1	8	16	24	54	102	150
2-9	4	8	12	28	47	65
10-12-Calvin app.	5	10	15	30	50	70

LITTLE KING
Dell Publishing Co.: No. 494, Aug, 1953 - No. 677, Feb, 1956

	GD 2.0	VG 4.0	FN 6.0	VF 8.0	VF/NM 9.0	NM- 9.2
Four Color 494 (#1)	8	16	24	56	108	160
Four Color 597, 677	5	10	15	34	60	85

LITTLE LANA (Formerly Lana)
Marvel Comics (MjMC): No. 8, Nov, 1949; No. 9, Mar, 1950

	GD 2.0	VG 4.0	FN 6.0	VF 8.0	VF/NM 9.0	NM- 9.2
8,9	18	36	54	105	165	225

LITTLE LENNY
Marvel Comics (CDS): June, 1949 - No. 3, Nov, 1949

	GD 2.0	VG 4.0	FN 6.0	VF 8.0	VF/NM 9.0	NM- 9.2
1-Little Aspirin app.	15	30	45	86	133	180
2,3	10	20	30	56	76	95

LITTLE LIZZIE
Marvel Comics (PrPI)/Atlas (OMC): 6/49 - No. 5, 4/50; 9/53 - No. 3, Jan, 1954

	GD 2.0	VG 4.0	FN 6.0	VF 8.0	VF/NM 9.0	NM- 9.2
1-Kid humor	17	34	51	98	154	210
2-5	11	22	33	60	83	105
1 (9/53, 2nd series by Atlas)-Howie Post-c	13	26	39	74	105	135
2,3	10	20	30	54	72	90

LITTLE LOTTA (See Harvey Hits No. 10)
Harvey Publications: 11/55 - No. 110, 11/73; No. 111, 9/74 - No. 120, 5/76
V2#1, Oct, 1992 - No. 4, July, 1993 ($1.25)

	GD 2.0	VG 4.0	FN 6.0	VF 8.0	VF/NM 9.0	NM- 9.2
1-Richie Rich (r) & Little Dot begin	50	100	150	400	900	1400
2,3	16	32	48	110	243	375
4,5	10	20	30	69	147	225
6-10	7	14	21	46	86	125
11-20	5	10	15	35	63	90
21-40	4	8	12	23	37	50
41-60	3	6	9	18	28	38
61-80: 62-1st app. Nurse Jenny	3	6	9	15	22	28
81-99	2	4	6	11	16	20
100-103: All 52 pg. Giants	3	6	9	14	19	24
104-120	2	4	6	8	10	12
V2#1-4 (1992-93)						4.00

NOTE: *No. 121 was advertised, but never released.*

LITTLE LOTTA FOODLAND
Harvey Publications: 9/63 - No. 14, 10/67; No. 15, 10/68 - No. 29, Oct, 1972

	GD 2.0	VG 4.0	FN 6.0	VF 8.0	VF/NM 9.0	NM- 9.2
1-Little Lotta, Little Dot, Richie Rich, 68 pgs. begin	11	22	33	73	157	240
2,3	6	12	18	38	69	100
4,5	5	10	15	30	50	70
6-10	4	8	12	23	37	50
11-20	3	6	9	16	23	30
21-26: 26-Last 68 pg. issue	3	6	9	14	20	25
27,28: Both 52 pgs.	2	4	6	11	16	20
29-(36 pgs.)	2	4	6	8	11	14

LITTLE LULU (Formerly Marge's Little Lulu)
Gold Key 207-257/Whitman 258 on: No. 207, Sept, 1972 - No. 268, Mar, 1984

	GD 2.0	VG 4.0	FN 6.0	VF 8.0	VF/NM 9.0	NM- 9.2
207,209,220-Stanley-r. 207-1st app. Henrietta	2	4	6	13	18	22
208,210-219: 208-1st app. Snobbly, Wilbur's butler	2	4	6	9	13	16
221-240,242-249, 250(r/#166), 251-254(r/#206)	2	4	6	8	10	12
241,263-Stanley-r	2	4	6	8	11	14
255-257(Gold Key): 256-r/#212	1	3	4	6	8	10
258,259,262(50¢-c),264(2/82),265(3/82) (Whitman)	2	4	6	11	16	20
260-(9/80)(Whitman pre-pack only - low distribution)	15	30	45	103	227	350
261-(11/80)(Whitman pre-pack only)	7	14	21	44	82	120
262-(1/81) Variant 40¢-c price error (reg. ed. 50¢-c)	3	6	9	15	22	28
266-268 (All #90028 on-c; no date, no date code; 3-pack): 266(7/83). 267(8/83). 268(3/84)-Stanley-r	3	6	9	17	26	35

LITTLE MARY MIXUP (See Comics On Parade)
United Features Syndicate: No. 10, 1939, - No. 26, 1940

	GD 2.0	VG 4.0	FN 6.0	VF 8.0	VF/NM 9.0	NM- 9.2
Single Series 10, 26	34	68	102	206	336	465

LITTLE MAX COMICS (Joe Palooka's Pal; see Joe Palooka)
Harvey Publications: Oct, 1949 - No. 73, Nov, 1961

	GD 2.0	VG 4.0	FN 6.0	VF 8.0	VF/NM 9.0	NM- 9.2
1-Infinity-c; Little Dot begins; Joe Palooka on-c	25	50	75	150	245	340
2-Little Dot app.; Joe Palooka on-c	14	28	42	82	121	160
3-Little Dot app.; Joe Palooka on-c	10	20	30	58	79	100
4-10: 5-Little Dot app., 1pg.	9	18	27	47	61	75
11-20	8	16	24	40	50	60
21-40: 23-Little Dot app. 38-r/#20	6	12	18	31	38	45
41-62,66	3	6	9	17	26	35
63-65,67-73-Include new five pg. Richie Rich stories. 70-73-Little Lotta app.	3	6	9	18	28	38

LI'L MENACE
Fago Magazine Co.: Dec, 1958 - No. 3, May, 1959

	GD 2.0	VG 4.0	FN 6.0	VF 8.0	VF/NM 9.0	NM- 9.2
1-Peter Rabbit app.	9	18	27	50	65	80
2-Peter Rabbit (Vincent Fago's)	7	14	21	35	43	50
3	6	12	18	28	34	40

LITTLE MERMAID, THE (Walt Disney's...; also see Disney's...)
W. D. Publications (Disney): 1990 (no date given)($5.95, no ads, 52 pgs.)

	GD 2.0	VG 4.0	FN 6.0	VF 8.0	VF/NM 9.0	NM- 9.2
nn-Adapts animated movie	1	2	3	4	5	7
nn-Comic version ($2.50)						4.00

LITTLE MERMAID, THE
Disney Comics: 1992 - No. 4, 1992 ($1.50, mini-series)

	GD 2.0	VG 4.0	FN 6.0	VF 8.0	VF/NM 9.0	NM- 9.2
1-4: Based on movie						4.00
1-4: 2nd printings sold at Wal-Mart w/different-c						4.00

LITTLE MISS MUFFET
Best Books (Standard Comics)/King Features Synd.: No. 11, Dec, 1948 - No. 13, March, 1949

	GD 2.0	VG 4.0	FN 6.0	VF 8.0	VF/NM 9.0	NM- 9.2
11-Strip reprints; Fanny Cory-c/a	10	20	30	54	72	90
12,13-Strip reprints; Fanny Cory-c/a	8	16	24	40	50	60

LITTLE MISS SUNBEAM COMICS
Magazine Enterprises/Quality Bakers of America: June-July, 1950 - No. 4, Dec-Jan, 1950-51

	GD 2.0	VG 4.0	FN 6.0	VF 8.0	VF/NM 9.0	NM- 9.2
1	17	34	51	98	154	210
2-4	10	20	30	58	79	100

Little Orphan Annie #1 © NS

Little Roquefort Comics #2 © Pines

Little Sad Sack #14 © HARV

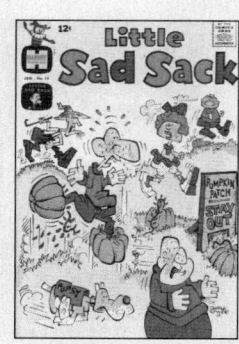

	GD 2.0	VG 4.0	FN 6.0	VF 8.0	VF/NM 9.0	NM- 9.2
...Advs. In Space ('55)	7	14	21	35	43	50

LITTLE MONSTERS, THE (See March of Comics #423, Three Stooges #17)
Gold Key: Nov, 1964 - No. 44, Feb, 1978

	GD 2.0	VG 4.0	FN 6.0	VF 8.0	VF/NM 9.0	NM- 9.2
1	5	10	15	33	57	80
2	3	6	9	19	30	40
3-10	3	6	9	16	24	32
11-20	3	6	9	15	21	26
21-30: 19-21-Reprints	2	4	6	11	16	20
31-44: 34-39,43-Reprints	2	4	6	8	11	14

LITTLE MONSTERS (Movie)
Now Comics: 1989 - No. 6, June, 1990 ($1.75)

	GD 2.0	VG 4.0	FN 6.0	VF 8.0	VF/NM 9.0	NM- 9.2
1-6: Photo-c from movie						3.00

LITTLE NEMO (See Cocomalt, Future Comics, Help, Jest, Kayo, Punch, Red Seal, & Superworld; most by Winsor McCay Jr., son of famous artist) (Other McCay books: see Little Sammy Sneeze & Dreams of the Rarebit Fiend)

LITTLE NEMO (...in Slumberland)
McCay Features/Nostalgia Press('69): 1945 (11x7-1/4", 28 pgs., B&W)

	GD 2.0	VG 4.0	FN 6.0	VF 8.0	VF/NM 9.0	NM- 9.2
1905 & 1911 reprints by Winsor McCay	10	20	30	56	76	95
1969-70 (Exact reprint)	2	4	6	9	12	15

LITTLE NEMO: RETURN TO SLUMBERLAND
IDW Publishing: Aug, 2014 - No. 4, Feb, 2015 ($3.99)

	GD 2.0	VG 4.0	FN 6.0	VF 8.0	VF/NM 9.0	NM- 9.2
1-4-New stories in McCay style; Shanower-s/Rodriguez-a in all. 1-Multiple covers						4.00

LITTLE ORPHAN ANNIE (See Annie, Famous Feature Stories, Marvel Super Special, Merry Christmas..., Popular Comics, Super Book #7, 11, 23 & Super Comics)

LITTLE ORPHAN ANNIE
David McKay Publ./Dell Publishing Co.: No. 7, 1937 - No. 3, Sept-Nov, 1948; No. 206, Dec, 1948

	GD 2.0	VG 4.0	FN 6.0	VF 8.0	VF/NM 9.0	NM- 9.2
Feature Books(McKay) 7-(1937) (Rare)	110	220	330	704	1202	1700
Four Color 12(1941)	63	126	189	403	689	975
Four Color 18(1943)-Flag-c	34	68	102	245	548	850
Four Color 52(1944)	24	48	72	168	372	575
Four Color 76(1945)	19	38	57	131	291	450
Four Color 107(1946)	17	34	51	117	259	400
Four Color 152(1947)	11	22	33	76	163	250
1(3-5/48)-r/strips from 5/7/44 to 7/30/44	11	22	33	73	157	240
2-r/strips from 7/21/40 to 9/9/40	8	16	24	54	102	150
3-r/strips from 9/10/40 to 11/9/40	8	16	24	54	102	150
Four Color 206(12/48)	8	16	24	51	96	140

LI'L PALS (Also see Li'l Kids)
Marvel Comics Group: Sept, 1972 - No. 5, May, 1973

	GD 2.0	VG 4.0	FN 6.0	VF 8.0	VF/NM 9.0	NM- 9.2
1	7	14	21	49	92	135
2-5	5	10	15	30	50	70

LI'L PAN (Formerly Rocket Kelly; becomes Junior Comics with #9)(Also see Wotalife Comics)
Fox Features Syndicate: No. 6, Dec-Jan, 1946-47 - No. 8, Apr-May, 1947

	GD 2.0	VG 4.0	FN 6.0	VF 8.0	VF/NM 9.0	NM- 9.2
6	14	28	42	76	108	140
7,8: 7-Atomic bomb story; robot-c	11	22	33	62	86	110

LITTLE PEOPLE (Also see Darby O'Gill & the...)
Dell Publishing Co.: No. 485, Aug-Oct, 1953 - No. 1062, Dec, 1959 (Walt Scott's)

	GD 2.0	VG 4.0	FN 6.0	VF 8.0	VF/NM 9.0	NM- 9.2
Four Color 485 (#1)	8	16	24	51	96	140
Four Color 573(7/54), 633(6/55)	5	10	15	35	63	90
Four Color 692(3/56),753(11/56),809(7/57),868(12/57),908(5/58),959(12/58),1062	5	10	15	33	57	80

LITTLE RASCALS
Dell Publishing Co.: No. 674, Jan, 1956 - No. 1297, Mar-May, 1962

	GD 2.0	VG 4.0	FN 6.0	VF 8.0	VF/NM 9.0	NM- 9.2
Four Color 674 (#1)	9	18	27	58	114	170
Four Color 778(3/57),825(8/57)	6	12	18	38	69	100
Four Color 883(3/58),936(9/58),974(3/59),1030(9/59),1079(2-4/60),1137(9-11/60)	5	10	15	35	63	90
Four Color 1174(3-5/61),1224(10-12/61),1297	5	10	15	33	57	80

LI'L RASCAL TWINS (Formerly Nature Boy)
Charlton Comics: No. 6, 1957 - No. 18, Jan, 1960

	GD 2.0	VG 4.0	FN 6.0	VF 8.0	VF/NM 9.0	NM- 9.2
6-Li'l Genius & Tomboy in all	6	12	18	29	36	42
7-18: 7-Timmy the Timid Ghost app.	4	8	12	18	22	25

LITTLE RED HOT: (CHANE OF FOOLS)
Image Comics: Feb, 1999 - No. 3, Apr, 1999 ($2.95/$3.50, B&W, limited series)

	GD 2.0	VG 4.0	FN 6.0	VF 8.0	VF/NM 9.0	NM- 9.2
1-3-Dawn Brown-s/a. 2,3-($3.50-c)						3.50
The Foolish Collection TPB ($12.95) r/#1-3						13.00

LITTLE RED HOT: BOUND
Image Comics: July, 2001 - No. 3, Nov, 2001 ($2.95, color, limited series)

	GD 2.0	VG 4.0	FN 6.0	VF 8.0	VF/NM 9.0	NM- 9.2
1-3-Dawn Brown-s/a.						3.00

LITTLE ROQUEFORT COMICS (See Paul Terry's Comics #105)
St. John Publishing Co.(all pre-code)/Pines No. 10: June, 1952 - No. 9, Oct, 1953; No. 10, Summer, 1958

	GD 2.0	VG 4.0	FN 6.0	VF 8.0	VF/NM 9.0	NM- 9.2
1-By Paul Terry; Funny Animal	12	24	36	67	94	120
2	8	16	24	40	50	60
3-10: 10-CBS Television Presents on-c	7	14	21	35	43	50

LITTLE SAD SACK (See Harvey Hits No. 73, 76, 79, 81, 83)
Harvey Publications: Oct, 1964 - No. 19, Nov, 1967

	GD 2.0	VG 4.0	FN 6.0	VF 8.0	VF/NM 9.0	NM- 9.2
1-Richie Rich app. on cover only	5	10	15	31	53	75
2-10	3	6	9	17	26	35
11-19	3	6	9	15	22	28

LITTLE SCOUTS
Dell Publishing Co.: No. 321, Mar, 1951 - No. 587, Oct, 1954

	GD 2.0	VG 4.0	FN 6.0	VF 8.0	VF/NM 9.0	NM- 9.2
Four Color 321 (#1, 3/51)	6	12	18	37	66	95
2(10-12/51) - 6(10-12/52)	4	8	12	25	40	55
Four Color 462,506,550,587	5	10	15	30	50	70

LITTLE SHOP OF HORRORS SPECIAL (Movie)
DC Comics: Feb, 1987 ($2.00, 68 pgs.)

	GD 2.0	VG 4.0	FN 6.0	VF 8.0	VF/NM 9.0	NM- 9.2
1-Colan-c/a						5.00

LI'L SONJA (Red Sonja)
Dynamite Entertainment: 2014 ($3.99, one-shot)

	GD 2.0	VG 4.0	FN 6.0	VF 8.0	VF/NM 9.0	NM- 9.2
1-Kid version spoof; Jim Zub-s/Joel Carroll-a; covers by Baltazar & Garbowska						4.00

LITTLE SPUNKY
I. W. Enterprises: No date (1958) (10¢)

	GD 2.0	VG 4.0	FN 6.0	VF 8.0	VF/NM 9.0	NM- 9.2
1-r/Frisky Fables #1	2	4	6	8	11	14

LITTLE STAR
Oni Press: Feb, 2005 - No. 6, Dec, 2005 ($2.99, B&W, limited series)

	GD 2.0	VG 4.0	FN 6.0	VF 8.0	VF/NM 9.0	NM- 9.2
1-6-Andi Watson-s/a						3.00
TPB (4/06, $19.95) r/#1-6						20.00

LITTLE STOOGES, THE (The Three Stooges' Sons)
Gold Key: Sept, 1972 - No. 7, Mar, 1974

	GD 2.0	VG 4.0	FN 6.0	VF 8.0	VF/NM 9.0	NM- 9.2
1-Norman Maurer cover/stories in all	3	6	9	18	28	38
2-7	2	4	6	13	18	22

LITTLEST OUTLAW (Disney)
Dell Publishing Co.: No. 609, Jan, 1955

	GD 2.0	VG 4.0	FN 6.0	VF 8.0	VF/NM 9.0	NM- 9.2
Four Color 609-Movie, photo-c	6	12	18	40	73	105

LITTLEST PET SHOP (Based on the Hasbro toys)
IDW Publishing: May, 2014 - No. 5, Sept, 2014 ($3.99)

	GD 2.0	VG 4.0	FN 6.0	VF 8.0	VF/NM 9.0	NM- 9.2
1-5: 1-Ball-s/Peña-a; multiple covers. 2-5-Two covers on each						4.00
... Spring Cleaning (4/15, $7.99) Four short stories; Ball-s; art by various						8.00

LITTLEST SNOWMAN, THE
Dell Publishing Co.: No. 755, 12/56; No. 864, 12/57; 12-2/1963-64

	GD 2.0	VG 4.0	FN 6.0	VF 8.0	VF/NM 9.0	NM- 9.2
Four Color 755,864, 1(1964)	5	10	15	35	63	90

LI'L TOMBOY (Formerly Fawcett's Funny Animals; see Giant Comics #3)
Charlton Comics: V14#92, Oct, 1956; No. 93, Mar, 1957 - No. 107, Feb, 1960

	GD 2.0	VG 4.0	FN 6.0	VF 8.0	VF/NM 9.0	NM- 9.2
V14#92-Ties as 1st app. with Li'l Genius #11	6	12	18	27	33	38
93-107: 97-Atomic Bunny app.	5	10	14	20	24	28

LI'L VAMPI (Vampirella)
Dynamite Entertainment: 2014 ($3.99, one-shot)

	GD 2.0	VG 4.0	FN 6.0	VF 8.0	VF/NM 9.0	NM- 9.2
1-Kid version spoof; Trautmann-s/Garbowska-a; covers by Baltazar & Garbowska						4.00

LI'L WILLIE COMICS (Formerly & becomes Willie Comics #22 on)
Marvel Comics (MgPC): No. 20, July, 1949 - No. 21, Sept, 1949

	GD 2.0	VG 4.0	FN 6.0	VF 8.0	VF/NM 9.0	NM- 9.2
20,21: 20-Little Aspirin app.	16	32	48	94	147	200

LITTLE WOMEN (See Power Record Comics)

LIVE IT UP
Spire Christian Comics (Fleming H. Revell Co.): 1973, 1974,1976 (39-49 cents)

	GD 2.0	VG 4.0	FN 6.0	VF 8.0	VF/NM 9.0	NM- 9.2
nn-1973 Edition	2	4	6	13	18	22
nn-1974,1976 Editions	2	4	6	8	11	14

LIVEWIRES
Marvel Comics: Apr, 2005 - No. 6, Sept, 2005 ($2.99, limited series)

Lobo #15 © DC

Lobster Johnson: The Glass Mantis #1 © Mike Mignola

Locke & Key: Small World #1 © Hill & IDW

	GD 2.0	VG 4.0	FN 6.0	VF 8.0	VF/NM 9.0	NM- 9.2

1-6-Adam Warren-s/c; Rick Mays-a 3.00
...: Clockwork Thugs, Yo (2005, $7.99, digest) r/#1-6 8.00

LIVING BIBLE, THE
Living Bible Corp.: Fall, 1945 - No. 3, Spring, 1946

	GD 2.0	VG 4.0	FN 6.0	VF 8.0	VF/NM 9.0	NM- 9.2
1-The Life of Paul; all have L. B. Cole-c	41	82	123	250	418	585
2-Joseph & His Brethren; Jonah & the Whale	29	58	87	170	278	385
3-Chaplains At War (classic-c)	42	84	126	267	451	635

LIVING WITH THE DEAD
Dark Horse Comics: Oct, 2007 - No. 3, Nov, 2007 ($2.99, limited series)

1-3-Zombies; Mike Richardson-s/Ben Stenbeck-a/Richard Corben-c 3.00

LOADED BIBLE
Image Comics: Apr, 2006; May, 2007; Feb, 2008 ($4.99)

...: Jesus vs. Vampires (4/06) Tim Seeley-s/Nate Bellegarde-a 5.00
...2: Blood of Christ (5/07) Seeley-s/Mike Norton-a. ...3: Communion (2/08) 5.00

LOBO
Dell Publishing Co.: Dec, 1965; No. 2, Oct, 1966

	GD 2.0	VG 4.0	FN 6.0	VF 8.0	VF/NM 9.0	NM- 9.2
1-1st black character to have his own title	21	42	63	147	324	500
2	11	22	33	76	163	250

LOBO (Also see Action #650, Adventures of Superman, Demon (2nd series), Justice League, L.E.G.I.O.N., Mister Miracle, Omega Men #3 & Superman #41)
DC Comics: Nov, 1990 - No. 4, Feb, 1991 ($1.50, color, limited series)

	GD 2.0	VG 4.0	FN 6.0	VF 8.0	VF/NM 9.0	NM- 9.2
1-(99¢)-Giffen plots/Breakdowns in all	1	3	4	6	8	10

1-2nd printing 4.00
2-4: 2-Legion '89 spin-off. 1-4 have Bisley painted covers & art 5.00
...: Blazing Chain of Love 1 (9/92, $1.50)-Denys Cowan-c/a; Alan Grant scripts, ...Convention Special 1 (1993, $1.75), ...: Portrait of a Victim 1 (1993, $1.75) 3.00
... Paramilitary Christmas Special 1 (1991, $2.39, 52 pgs.) Bisley-c/a 4.00
...: Portrait of a Bastich TPB (2008, $19.99) r/#1-4 & Lobo's Back #1-4 20.00

LOBO (Also see Showcase '95 #9)
DC Comics: Dec, 1993 - No. 64, Jul, 1999 ($1.75/$1.95/$2.25/$2.50, mature)

1 ($2.95)-Foil enhanced-c; Alan Grant scripts begin 4.00
2-9,0,10-64: 2-7-Alan Grant scripts. 9-(9/94). 0-(10/94)-Origin retold. 50-Lobo vs. the DCU. 58-Giffen-a 3.00
#1,000,000 (11/98) 853rd Century x-over 3.00
Annual 1 (1993, $3.50, 68 pgs.)-Bloodlines x-over 4.00
Annual 2 (1994, $3.50)-21 artists (20 listed on-c); Alan Grant script; Elseworlds story 4.00
Annual 3 (1995, $3.95)-Year One story 4.00
.../Authority: Holiday Hell TPB (2006, $17.99) r/Lobo Paramilitary Christmas Special; Authority/Lobo: Jingle Hell and Spring Break Massacre; WildStorm Winter Special 18.00
...Big Babe Spring Break Special (Spr, '95, $1.95)-Balent-a 3.00
...Bounty Hunting for Fun and Profit ('95)-Bisley-c 5.00
... Chained (5/97, $2.50)-Alan Grant story 3.00
.../Deadman: The Brave And The Bald (2/95, $3.50) 4.00
.../Demon: Helloween (12/96, $2.25)-Giarrano-a 3.00
...Fragtastic Voyage 1 ('97, $5.95)-Mejia painted-c/a 6.00
...Gallery (9/95, $3.50)-pin-ups. 3.50
...In the Chair 1 (8/94, $1.95, 36 pgs.), ...I Quit-(12/95, $2.25) 3.00
.../Judge Dredd ('95, $4.95). 5.00
...Lobocop 1 (2/94, $1.95)-Alan Grant scripts; painted-c 3.00

LOBO (Younger version from New 52 Justice League #23.2)
DC Comics: Dec, 2014 - No. 13, Feb, 2016 ($2.99)

1-13: 1-5-Bunn-s/Brown-a. 4-Superman app. 10,11-Sinestro app. 13-Hal Jordan app. 3.00
Annual 1 (9/15, $4.99) Bunn-s/Rocha-a; the Sinestro Corps app.; leads into Lobo #10 5.00

LOBO: (Title Series), DC Comics

--A CONTRACT ON GAWD, 4/94 - 7/94 (mature) 1-4: Alan Grant scripts. 3-Groo cameo 3.00
--DEATH AND TAXES, 10/96 - No. 4, 1/97, 1-4-Giffen/Grant scripts 3.00
--GOES TO HOLLYWOOD, 8/96 ($2.25), 1-Grant scripts 3.00
--HIGHWAY TO HELL, 1/10 - No. 2, 2/10 ($6.99), 1,2-Scott Ian-s/Sam Kieth-a/c 7.00
TPB (2010, $19.99) r/#1,2; intro. by Scott Ian; Kieth B&W art pages 20.00
--INFANTICIDE, 10/92 - 1/93 ($1.50, mature), 1-4-Giffen-c/a; Grant scripts 3.00
--/ MASK, 2/97 - No. 2, 3/97 ($5.95), 1,2 6.00
--'S BACK, 5/92 - No. 4, 11/92 ($1.50, mature), 1-4: 1-Has 3 outer covers. Bisley painted-c 1,2; a-1-3. 3-Sam Kieth-c; all have Giffen plots/breakdown & Grant scripts 4.00
Trade paperback (1993, $9.95)-r/1-4 10.00
--THE DUCK, 6/97 ($1.95), 1-A. Grant-s/V. Semeiks & R. Kryssing-a 3.00
--UNAMERICAN GLADIATORS, 6/93 - No. 4, 9/93 ($1.75, mature), 1-4-Mignola-c; Grant/Wagner scripts 4.00
--UNBOUND, 8/03 - No. 6, 5/04 ($2.95), 1-6-Giffen-s/Horley-c/a. 4-6-Ambush Bug app. 3.00

LOBSTER JOHNSON (One-shots) (See B.P.R.D. and Hellboy titles)
Dark Horse Comics

...: A Chain Forged in Life (7/15, $3.50) Mignola & Arcudi-s; Nixey & Nowlan-a 3.50
...: Caput Mortuum (9/12, $3.50) Mignola & Arcudi-s; Zonjic-c/a 3.50
...: Garden of Bones (1/17, $3.99) Mignola & Arcudi-s; Stephen Green-a/Zonjic-c 4.00
...: Satan Smells a Rat (5/13, $3.50) Mignola & Arcudi-s; Nowlan-c/a 3.50
...: The Forgotten Man (4/16, $3.50) Mignola & Arcudi-s; Snejbjerg-a/Zonjic-c 3.50
...: The Glass Mantis (12/15, $3.50) Mignola & Arcudi-s; Fejzula-a/Zonjic-c 3.50

LOBSTER JOHNSON: A SCENT OF LOTUS (See B.P.R.D. and Hellboy titles)
Dark Horse Comics: Jul, 2013 - No. 2, Aug, 2013 ($3.50, limited series)

1,2-Mignola & Arcudi-s; Fiumara-a/Zonjic-c 3.50

LOBSTER JOHNSON: GET THE LOBSTER
Dark Horse Comics: Feb, 2014 - No. 5, Aug, 2014 ($3.99, limited series)

1-5-Mignola & Arcudi-s; Zonjic-a/c 4.00

LOBSTER JOHNSON: METAL MONSTERS OF MIDTOWN
Dark Horse Comics: May, 2016 - No. 3, Jul, 2016 ($3.50/$3.99, limited series)

1-3-Mignola & Arcudi-s; Zonjic-a/c. 1-$3.50. 2,3-$3.99 4.00

LOBSTER JOHNSON: THE BURNING HAND
Dark Horse Comics: Jan, 2012 - No. 5, May, 2012 ($3.50, limited series)

1-5-Mignola & Arcudi-s; Zonjic-a. 1-Two covers by Dave Johnson & Mignola 3.50

LOBSTER JOHNSON: THE IRON PROMETHEUS
Dark Horse Comics: Sept, 2007 - No. 5, Jan, 2008 ($2.99, limited series)

1-Mignola-s/c; Armstrong-a 6.00
2-5-Mignola-s/c; Armstrong-a 4.00

LOCKE & KEY
IDW Publ.: Feb, 2008 - No. 6, July, 2008 ($3.99, limited series)

1-Joe Hill-s/Gabriel Rodriguez-a 40.00
1-Second printing 5.00
2 10.00
3-6 5.00
...: Free Comic Book Day Edition (5/11) r/story from Crown of Shadows 3.00
...: Grindhouse (8/12, $3.99) EC-style; Hill-s/Rodriguez-a; bonus Guide to the Keyhouse 4.00
...: Guide to the Known Keys (1/12, $3.99) Key to the Moon; bonus Guide to the Keys 4.00
...: Welcome to Lovecraft Legacy Edition #1 (8/10, $1.00) r/#1; synopsis of later issues 3.00
...: Welcome to Lovecraft Special Edition #1 SC (9/09, $5.99) Hill-s/Rodriguez-a; script; back-up story with final art from Seth Fisher 6.00

LOCKE & KEY: ALPHA
IDW Publ.: Aug, 2013 - No. 2, Oct, 2013 ($7.99, limited series)

1,2-Series conclusion; Joe Hill-s/Gabriel Rodriguez-a 8.00

LOCKE & KEY: CLOCKWORKS
IDW Publ.: Jun, 2011 - No. 6, Apr, 2012 ($3.99, limited series)

1-6: 1-Hill-s/Rodriguez-a; set in 1776 4.00

LOCKE & KEY: CROWN OF SHADOWS
IDW Publ.: Nov, 2009 - No. 6, Apr, 2010 ($3.99, limited series)

1-6-Joe Hill-s/Gabriel Rodriguez-a 4.00

LOCKE & KEY: HEAD GAMES
IDW Publ.: Jan, 2009 - No. 6, Jun, 2009 ($3.99, limited series)

1-6-Joe Hill-s/Gabriel Rodriguez-a. 3-EC style-c 4.00

LOCKE & KEY: KEYS TO THE KINGDOM
IDW Publ.: Sept, 2010 - No. 6, Mar, 2011 ($3.99, limited series)

1-6-Joe Hill-s/Gabriel Rodriguez-a 4.00

LOCKE & KEY: OMEGA
IDW Publ.: Nov, 2012 - No. 5, May, 2013 ($3.99, limited series)

1-5-Next to Final series; Joe Hill-s/Gabriel Rodriguez-a 4.00

LOCKE & KEY: SMALL WORLD
IDW Publ.: Dec, 2016 ($4.99, one-shot)

1-Set in early 1900s; Joe Hill-s/Gabriel Rodriguez-a; multiple covers 5.00

LOCKJAW AND THE PET AVENGERS (Also see Tails of the Pet Avengers)
Marvel Comics: July, 2009 - No. 4, Oct, 2009 ($2.99, limited series)

1-4-Lockheed, Frog Thor, Zabu, Lockjaw and Redwing team up; 2 covers on each 3.00

LOCKJAW AND THE PET AVENGERS UNLEASHED
Marvel Comics: May, 2010 - No. 4, Aug, 2010 ($2.99, limited series)

Logan: Shadow Society #1 © MAR

Lone Eagle #4 © AJAX

Lone Ranger #39 © Lone Ranger Inc.

GD 2.0 | VG 4.0 | FN 6.0 | VF 8.0 | VF/NM 9.0 | NM- 9.2

1-4-Eliopoulos-s/Guara-a; 2 covers on each 3.00

LOCO (Magazine) (Satire)
Satire Publications: Aug, 1958 - V1#3, Jan, 1959
V1#1-Chic Stone-a 9 18 27 47 61 75
V1#2,3-Severin-a, 2 pgs. Davis; 3-Heath-a 7 14 21 35 43 50

LOGAN (Wolverine)
Marvel Comics: May, 2008 - No. 3, Jul, 2008 ($3.99, limited series)
1-3-Vaughan-s/Risso-a/c; regular & B&W editions for each 4.00

LOGAN: PATH OF THE WARLORD
Marvel Comics: Feb, 1996 ($5.95, one-shot)
1-John Paul Leon-a 6.00

LOGAN: SHADOW SOCIETY
Marvel Comics: 1996 ($5.95, one-shot)
1 6.00

LOGAN'S RUN
Marvel Comics Group: Jan, 1977 - No. 7, July, 1977
1: 1-5-Based on novel & movie 2 4 6 9 12 15
2-5,7: 6,7-New stories adapted from novel 1 3 4 6 8 10
6-1st Thanos solo story (back-up) by Zeck (6/77)(See Iron Man #55 for debut) 4 8 12 27 44 60
6-(35¢-c variant, limited distribution) 13 26 39 89 195 300
7-(35¢-c variant, limited distribution) 10 20 30 64 132 200
NOTE: ***Austin** a-6i. **Gulacy** c-6. **Kane** c-7p. **Perez** a-1-5p; c-1-5p. **Sutton** a-6p, 7p.*

LOIS & CLARK, THE NEW ADVENTURES OF SUPERMAN
DC Comics: 1994 ($9.95, one-shot)
1-r/Man of Steel #2, Superman Ann. 1, Superman #9 & 11, Action #600 & 655, Adventures of Superman #445, 462 & 466 1 3 4 6 8 10

LOIS LANE (Also see Daring New Adventures of Supergirl, Showcase #9,10 & Superman's Girlfriend...)
DC Comics: Aug, 1986 - No. 2, Sept, 1986 ($1.50, 52 pgs.)
1,2-Morrow-c/a in each 4.00

LOKI (Thor)
Marvel Comics: Sept, 2004 - No. 4, Nov, 2004 ($3.50)
1-4-Rodi-s/Ribic-a/c 3.50
HC (2005, $17.99, with dustjacket) oversized r/#1-4; original proposal and sketch pages 18.00
SC (2007, $12.99) r/#1-4; original proposal and sketch pages 13.00

LOKI (Thor)
Marvel Comics: Dec, 2010 - No. 4, May, 2011 ($3.99, limited series)
1-4-Aguirre-Sacasa-s/Fiumara-a. 2-Balder dies 4.00

LOKI: AGENT OF ASGARD (Thor)
Marvel Comics: Apr, 2014 - No. 17, Oct, 2015 ($2.99/$3.99)
1-5: 1-Ewing-s/Garbett-a/Frison-c; Avengers app. 3.00
6-17-($3.99) 6-9-Axis tie-ins. 6,7-Doctor Doom app. 14-17-Secret Wars tie-ins 4.00

LOKI: RAGNAROK AND ROLL (not the character from Thor)
BOOM! Studios: Feb, 2014 - No. 4, Jun, 2014 ($3.99, limited series)
1,2-Esquivel-s/Gaylord-a/Ziritt-c 4.00

LOLA XOXO
Aspen MLT: Apr, 2014 - No. 6, Mar, 2015 ($3.99)
1-6-Siya Oum-s/a; multiple covers 4.00
The Art of Lolo XOXO 1 (9/16, $5.99) Siya Oum sketch pages and cover gallery 6.00

LOLA XOXO: WASTELAND MADAM
Aspen MLT: Apr, 2015 - No. 4, Feb, 2016 ($3.99)
1-4-Vince Hernandez-s/Siya Oum-a; multiple covers 4.00

LOLLY AND PEPPER
Dell Publishing Co.: No. 832, Sept, 1957 - July, 1962
Four Color 832(#1) 6 12 18 37 66 95
Four Color 940,978,1086,1206 4 8 12 28 47 65
01-459-207 (7/62) 3 6 9 17 26 35

LOMAX (See Police Action)

LONDON'S DARK
Escape/Titan: 1989 ($8.95, B&W, graphic novel)
nn-James Robinson script; Paul Johnson-c/a 1 2 3 5 7 9

LONE
Dark Horse Comics: Sept, 2003 - No. 6, Mar, 2004 ($2.99)
1-6-Stuart Moore-s/Jerome Opeña-a/Templesmith-c 3.00

LONE EAGLE (The Flame No. 5 on)
Ajax/Farrell Publications: Apr-May, 1954 - No. 4, Oct-Nov, 1954
1 14 28 42 78 112 145
2-4: 3-Bondage-c 9 18 27 50 65 80

LONE GUNMEN, THE (From the X-Files)
Dark Horse Comics: June, 2001 ($2.99, one-shot)
1-Paul Lee-a; photo-c 3.00

LONELY HEART (Formerly Dear Lonely Hearts; Dear Heart #15 on)
Ajax/Farrell Publ. (Excellent Publ.): No. 9, Mar, 1955 - No. 14, Feb, 1956
9-Kamen-*esque*-a; (Last precode) 14 28 42 80 115 150
10-14 10 20 30 54 72 90

LONE RANGER, THE (See Ace Comics, Aurora, Dell Giants, Future Comics, Golden Comics Digest #48, King Comics, Magic Comics & March of Comics #165, 174, 193, 208, 225, 238, 310, 322, 338, 350)

LONE RANGER, THE
Dell Publishing Co.: No. 3, 1939 - No. 167, Feb, 1947
Large Feature Comic 3(1939)-Heigh-Yo Silver; text with illus. by Robert Weisman; also exists as a Whitman #710 (scarce) 271 542 813 1734 2967 4200
Large Feature Comic 7(1939)-Illustr. by Henry Vallely; Hi-Yo Silver the Lone Ranger to the Rescue; also exists as Whitman #715 (scarce) 258 516 774 1651 2826 4000
Feature Book 21(1940), 24(1941) 103 206 309 659 1130 1600
Four Color 82(1945) 37 74 111 274 612 950
Four Color 98(1945),118(1946) 27 54 81 194 435 675
Four Color 125(1946),136(1947) 19 38 57 131 291 450
Four Color 151,167(1947) 16 32 48 112 249 385

LONE RANGER, THE (Movie, radio & TV; Clayton Moore starred as Lone Ranger in the movies; No. 1-37: strip reprints)(See Dell Giants)
Dell Publishing Co.: Jan-Feb, 1948 - No. 145, May-July, 1962
1 (36 pgs.)-The Lone Ranger, his horse Silver, companion Tonto & his horse Scout begin 63 126 189 504 1127 1750
2 (52 pgs. begin, end #41) 27 54 81 189 420 650
3-5 22 44 66 154 340 525
6,7,9,10 16 32 48 112 249 385
8-Origin retold; Indian back-c begin, end #35 19 38 57 131 291 450
11-20: 11- "Young Hawk" Indian boy serial begins, ends #145 12 24 36 80 173 265
21,22,24-31: 51-Reprint. 31-1st Mask logo 10 20 30 64 132 200
23-Origin retold 12 24 36 80 173 265
32-37: 32-Painted-c begin. 36-Animal photo back-c begin, end #49. 37-Last newspaper-r issue; new outfit; red shirt becomes blue; most known copies show the blue shirt on-c & inside 9 18 27 58 114 170
37-Variant issue; Long Ranger wears a red shirt on-c and inside. A few copies of the red shirt outfit were printed before catching the mistake and changing the color to blue (rare) 16 32 48 110 243 375
38-41 (All 52 pgs.) 38-Paul S. Newman-s (wrote most of the stories #38-on) 8 16 24 54 102 150
42-50 (36 pgs.) 7 14 21 46 86 125
51-74 (52 pgs.): 56-One pg. origin story of Lone Ranger & Tonto. 71-Blank inside-c 6 12 18 42 79 115
75,77-99: 79-X-mas-c 6 12 18 40 73 105
76-Classic flag-c 6 12 18 42 79 115
100 7 14 21 46 86 125
101-111: Last painted-c 6 12 18 37 66 95
112-Clayton Moore photo-c begin, end #145 15 30 45 103 227 350
113-117: 117-10¢ &15¢-c exist 9 18 27 60 120 180
118-Origin Lone Ranger, Tonto, & Silver retold; Dan Reid origin; Special Silver anniversary issue 19 38 57 131 291 450
119-140: 139-Fran Striker-s 8 16 24 56 108 160
141-145 9 18 27 58 114 170
NOTE: ***Hank Hartman** painted c(signed)-65, 66, 70, 75, 82; unsigned-64?, 67-69?, 71, 72, 73?, 74?, 76-78, 80, 81, 83-91, 92?, 93-111. **Ernest Nordli** painted c(signed)-42, 50, 52, 53, 56, 59, 60; unsigned-39-41, 44-49, 51, 54, 55, 57, 58, 61-63?*

LONE RANGER, THE
Gold Key (Reprints in #13-20): 9/64 - No. 16, 12/69; No. 17, 11/72; No. 18, 9/74 - No. 28, 3/77
1-Retells origin 5 10 15 35 63 90
2 3 6 9 21 33 45
3-10: Small Bear-r in #6-12. 10-Last 12¢ issue 3 6 9 19 30 40
11-17 3 6 9 15 22 28
18-28 2 4 6 11 16 20
Golden West 1(30029-610, 10/66)-Giant; r/most Golden West #3 including Clayton Moore photo front/back-c 6 12 18 38 69 100

Lone Ranger #2 © Classic Media Inc.

Lone Rider #8 © SUPR

Lone Wolf 2100: Chase the Setting Sun #1 © DH

	GD 2.0	VG 4.0	FN 6.0	VF 8.0	VF/NM 9.0	NM- 9.2

LONE RANGER
Dynamite Entertainment: 2006 - No. 25, 2011 ($2.99/$3.50/$3.99)

1-Retells origin; Carriello-a/Matthews-s; badge cover by Cassaday 4.00
1-Variant mask cover by Cassaday 5.00
1-Baltimore Comic-Con 2006 variant cover with masked face and horse silhouette 12.00
1-Directors' Cut ($4.99) r/#1 with comments at page bottoms, script and sketches 5.00
2-23: 2-Origin continues; Tonto app. 3.50
24-($3.99) 4.00
25-($4.99) Carriello-a 5.00
... and Tonto 1-4 (200-2010, $4.99) Cassaday-c 5.00
... Volume 1: Now and Forever TPB (2007, $19.99) r/#1-6; sketch pages 20.00

LONE RANGER, THE (Volume 2)
Dynamite Entertainment: 2012 - No. 25, 2014 ($3.99)

1-25: 1-Parks-s/Polls-a; two covers by Ross & Francavilla. 2-21-Francavilla-c 4.00
Annual 2013 ($4.99) Denton-s/Triano-a/Worley-c 5.00

LONE RANGER AND TONTO, THE
Topps Comics: Aug, 1994 - No. 4, Nov, 1994 ($2.50, limited series)

1-4: 3-Origin of Lone Ranger; Tonto leaves; Lansdale story, Truman-c/a in all. 3.00
1-4: Silver logo. 1-Signed by Lansdale and Truman 6.00
Trade paperback (1/95, $9.95) 10.00

LONE RANGER AND ZORRO: THE DEATH OF ZORRO, THE
Dynamite Entertainment: 2011 - No. 5, 2011 ($3.99, limited series)

1-5: 1-Four covers by Alex Ross and others; Parks-s/Polls-a 4.00

LONE RANGER GREEN HORNET
Dynamite Entertainment: 2016 - No. 5, 2016 ($3.99, limited series)

1-5-Uslan-s/Timpano-a. 3-Jesse Owens as the new Lone Ranger 4.00

LONE RANGER'S COMPANION TONTO, THE (TV)
Dell Publishing Co.: No. 312, Jan, 1951 - No. 33, Nov-Jan/58-59 (All painted-c)

	GD	VG	FN	VF	VF/NM	NM-
Four Color 312(#1, 1/51)	11	22	33	73	157	240
2(8-10/51),3: (#2 titled "Tonto")	6	12	18	41	76	110
4-10	5	10	15	35	63	90
11-20	5	10	15	31	53	75
21-33	4	8	12	28	47	65

NOTE: ***Ernest Nordli*** *painted c(signed)-2, 7; unsigned-3-6, 8-11, 12?, 13, 14, 18?, 22-24? See Aurora Comic Booklets.*

LONE RANGER'S FAMOUS HORSE HI-YO SILVER, THE (TV)
Dell Publishing Co.: No. 369, Jan, 1952 - No. 36, Oct-Dec, 1960 (All painted-c, most by Sam Savitt) (Lone Ranger appears in most issues)

	GD	VG	FN	VF	VF/NM	NM-
Four Color 369(#1)-Silver's origin as told by The Lone Ranger	10	20	30	68	144	220
Four Color 392(#2, 4/52)	6	12	18	41	76	110
3(7-9/52)-10(4-6/52)	5	10	15	31	53	75
11-36	4	8	12	27	44	60

LONE RANGER, THE : SNAKE OF IRON
Dynamite Entertainment: 2012 - No. 4, 2013 ($3.99, limited series)

1-4: 1-Dixon-s/Polls-a/Calero-c 4.00

LONE RANGER, THE : VINDICATED
Dynamite Entertainment: 2014 - No. 4, 2015 ($3.99, limited series)

1-4-Justin Gray-s/Rey Villegas-a. 1-Cassaday-c. 2-4-Laming-c 4.00

LONE RIDER (Also see The Rider)
Superior Comics(Farrell Publ.): Apr, 1951 - No. 26, Jul, 1955 (#3-on: 36 pgs.)

	GD	VG	FN	VF	VF/NM	NM-
1 (52 pgs.)-The Lone Rider & his horse Lightnin' begin; Kamen-*ish*-a begins	32	64	96	188	307	425
2 (52 pgs.)-The Golden Arrow begins (origin)	20	40	60	120	195	220
3-6: 6-Last Golden Arrow	17	34	51	98	154	210
7-Golden Arrow becomes Swift Arrow; origin of his shield	20	40	60	120	195	220
8-Origin Swift Arrow	18	36	54	107	169	230
9,10	12	24	36	69	97	125
11-14	10	20	30	54	72	90
15-Golden Arrow origin-r from #2, changing name to Swift Arrow	10	20	30	58	79	100
16-20,22-26: 23-Apache Kid app.	9	18	27	50	65	80
21-3-D effect-c	16	32	48	94	147	200

LONERS, THE
Marvel Comics: June, 2007 - No. 6, Jan, 2008 ($2.99, limited series)

1-6-Cebulski-s/Moline-a/Pearson-c; Lightspeed, Spider-Woman, Ricochet app. 3.00
...: The Secret Lives of Super Heroes TPB (2008, $14.99) r/#1-6; sketch pages 15.00

LONE WOLF AND CUB
First Comics: May, 1987 - No. 45, Apr, 1991 ($1.95-$3.25, B&W, deluxe size)

	GD	VG	FN	VF	VF/NM	NM-
1-Frank Miller-c & intro.; reprints manga series by Koike & Kojima	1	2	3	6	8	10
1-2nd print, 3rd print, 2-2nd print						4.00
2-12: 6-72 pgs. origin issue						6.00
13-38,40: 40-Ploog-c						4.00
39-($5.95, 120 pgs.)-Ploog-c	1	2	3	4	5	7
41-44: 41-($3.95, 84 pgs.)-Ploog-c. 42-Ploog-c						6.00
45-Last issue; low print	2	4	6	8	10	12
Deluxe Edition ($19.95, B&W)						20.00

NOTE: ***Sienkiewicz*** *c-13-24.* ***Matt Wagner*** *c-25-30.*

LONE WOLF AND CUB (Trade paperbacks)
Dark Horse Comics: Aug, 2000 - No. 28 ($9.95, B&W, 4" x 6", approx. 300 pgs.)

1-Collects First Comics reprint series; Frank Miller-c 18.00
1-(2nd printing) 12.00
1-(3rd-5th printings) 10.00
2,3-(1st printings) 12.00
2,3-(2nd printings) 10.00
4-28 10.00

LONE WOLF 2100 (Also see Reveal)
Dark Horse Comics: May, 2002 - No. 11, Dec, 2003 ($2.99, color)

1-New homage to Lone Wolf and Cub; Kennedy-s/Velasco-a 4.00
2-11 3.00
...: The Red File (1/03, $2.99) character and story background files 3.00
... Vol. 1 - Shadows on Saplings TPB (2003, $12.95, 6" x 9") r/#1-4 13.00
... Vol. 2 - The Language of Chaos TPB (2003, $12.95, 6" x 9") r/#5-8, Dirty Tricks short story from Reveal 13.00

LONE WOLF 2100: CHASE THE SETTING SUN
Dark Horse Comics: Jan, 2016 - No. 4, Apr, 2016 ($3.99, color)

1-4-Heisserer-s/Sepulveda-a 4.00

LONG BOW (...Indian Boy)(See Indians & Jumbo Comics #141)
Fiction House Mag. (Real Adventures Publ.): 1951 - No. 8, Fall, 1952; No. 9, Spring, 1953

	GD	VG	FN	VF	VF/NM	NM-
1-Most covers by Maurice Whitman	18	36	54	107	169	230
2	11	22	33	62	86	110
3-9	10	20	30	56	76	95

LONG HOT SUMMER, THE
DC Comics (Milestone): Jul, 1995 - No. 3, Sept, 1995 ($2.95/$2.50, lim. series)

1-3: 1-($2.95-c). 2,3-($2.50-c) 3.00

LONG JOHN SILVER & THE PIRATES (Formerly Terry & the Pirates)
Charlton Comics: No. 30, Aug, 1956 - No. 32, March, 1957 (TV)

	GD	VG	FN	VF	VF/NM	NM-
30-32: Whitman-c	10	20	30	54	72	90

LONGSHOT (Also see X-Men, 2nd Series #10)
Marvel Comics: Sept, 1985 - No. 6, Feb, 1986 (60¢, limited series)

	GD	VG	FN	VF	VF/NM	NM-
1-Art Adams/Whilce Portacio-c/a in all	3	6	9	16	23	30
2-5: 4-Spider-Man app.	2	4	6	9	12	15
6-Double size	2	4	6	11	16	20
Trade Paperback (1989, $16.95)-r/#1-6						17.00

LONGSHOT
Marvel Comics: Feb, 1998 ($3.99, one-shot)

1-DeMatteis-s/Zulli-a 4.00

LONGSHOT SAVES THE MARVEL UNIVERSE
Marvel Comics: Jan, 2014 - No. 4, Feb, 2014 ($2.99, limited series)

1-4-Hastings-s/Camagni-a/Nakayama-c. 3,4-Superior Spider-Man app. 3.00

LOOKING GLASS WARS: HATTER M
Image Comics (Desperado): Dec, 2005 - No. 4, Nov, 2006 ($3.99)

1-4-Templesmith-a/c 4.00

LOONEY TUNES (2nd Series) (TV)
Gold Key/Whitman: April, 1975 - No. 47, June, 1984

	GD	VG	FN	VF	VF/NM	NM-
1-Reprints	3	6	9	21	33	45
2-10: 2,4-reprints	2	4	6	13	18	22
11-20: 16-reprints	2	4	6	9	12	15
21-30	2	3	4	6	8	10
31,32,36-42(2/82)	1	2	3	5	6	8
33-(8/80)-35 (Whitman pre-pack only, scarce)	3	6	9	21	33	45
43(4/82),44(6/83) (low distribution)	2	4	6	9	13	16

45-47 (All #90296 on-c; nd, nd code, pre-pack) 45(8/83), 46(3/84), 47(6/84)

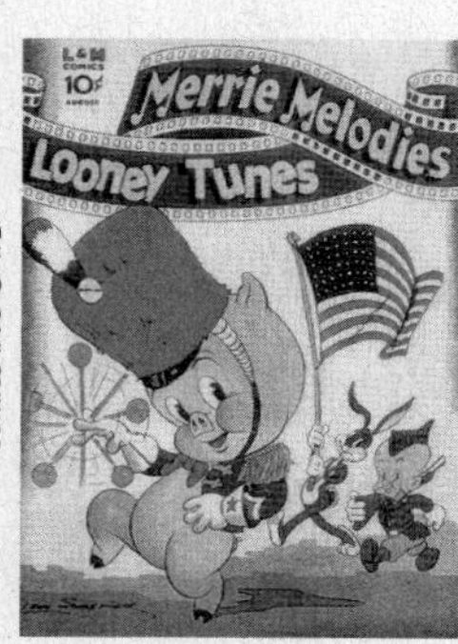

Looney Tunes and Merrie Melodies Comics #10 © WB

Lorna the Jungle Girl #7 © MAR

Lost in Space (1998 series) #2 © New Line

GD VG FN VF VF/NM NM-
2.0 4.0 6.0 8.0 9.0 9.2

	GD 2.0	VG 4.0	FN 6.0	VF 8.0	VF/NM 9.0	NM- 9.2
	3	6	9	14	20	26

LOONEY TUNES (3rd Series) (TV)
DC Comics: Apr, 1994 - Present ($1.50/$1.75/$1.95/$1.99/$2.25/$2.50/$2.99)

1-10,120: 1-Marvin Martian-c/sty; Bugs Bunny, Roadrunner, Daffy begin. 120-($2.95-C) 4.00
11-119,121-187: 23-34-($1.75-c). 35-43-($1.95-c). 44-Begin $1.99-c. 93-Begin $2.25-c. 100-Art by various incl. Kyle Baker, Marie Severin, Darwyn Cooke, Jill Thompson 3.00
188-235: 188-Begin $2.99-c; Scooby-Doo spoof. 193-Christmas-c 3.00
...Back In Action Movie Adaptation (12/03, $3.95) photo-c 4.00

LOONEY TUNES AND MERRIE MELODIES COMICS ("Looney Tunes" #166(8/55) on)
(Also see Porky's Duck Hunt)
Dell Publishing Co.: 1941 - No. 246, July-Sept, 1962

	GD	VG	FN	VF	VF/NM	NM-
1-Porky Pig, Bugs Bunny, Daffy Duck, Elmer Fudd, Mary Jane & Sniffles, Pat Patsy and Pete begin (1st comic book app. of each). Bugs Bunny story by Win Smith (early Mickey Mouse artist)	1150	2300	3450	8800	17,900	27,000
2 (11/41)	179	358	537	1477	3339	5200
3-Kandi the Cave Kid begins by Walt Kelly; also in #4-6,8,11,15	118	236	354	944	2122	3300
4-Kelly-a	118	236	354	944	2122	3300
5-Bugs Bunny The Super-Duper Rabbit story (1st funny animal super hero, 3/42; also see Coo Coo); Kelly-a	86	172	258	688	1544	2400
6,8: 8-Kelly-a	64	128	192	512	1156	1800
7,9,10: 9-Painted-c. 10-Flag-c	50	100	150	390	870	1350
11,15-Kelly-a; 15-Christmas-c	50	100	150	390	870	1350
12-14,16-19	37	74	111	274	612	950
20-25: Pat, Patsy & Pete by Walt Kelly in all. 20-War Bonds-c	30	60	90	219	490	760
26-30	23	46	69	161	356	550
31-40: 33-War Bonds-c. 39-Christmas-c	18	36	54	128	284	440
41-50: 45-War Bonds-c	14	28	42	96	211	325
51-60: 51-Christmas-c	11	22	33	76	163	250
61-80	8	16	24	56	108	160
81-99: 87,99-Christmas-c	7	14	21	49	92	135
100-New Year's-c	8	16	24	52	99	145
101-120	6	12	18	40	73	105
121-150: 124-New Year's-c. 133-Tattoo-c	5	10	15	35	63	90
151-200: 159-Christmas-c	5	10	15	33	57	80
201-240	5	10	15	31	53	75
241-246	5	10	15	33	57	80

LOONY SPORTS (Magazine)
3-Strikes Publishing Co.: Spring, 1975 (68 pgs.)

	GD	VG	FN	VF	VF/NM	NM-
1-Sports satire	2	4	6	8	11	14

LOOSE CANNON (Also see Action Comics Annual #5 & Showcase '94 #5)
DC Comics: June, 1995 - No. 4, Sept, 1995 ($1.75, limited series)

1-4: Adam Pollina-a. 1-Superman app. 3.00

LOOY DOT DOPE
United Features Syndicate: No. 13, 1939

	GD	VG	FN	VF	VF/NM	NM-
Single Series 13	32	64	96	192	314	435

LORD JIM (See Movie Comics)

LORD OF THE JUNGLE
Dynamite Entertainment: 2012 - No. 15, 2013 ($1.00/$3.99)

1-($1.00) Retelling of Tarzan's origin; Nelson-s/Castro-a; four covers 3.00
2-15-($3.99) 2-6-Three covers. 7-13-Two covers 4.00
Annual 1 (2012, $4.99) Rahner-s/Davila-a/Parrillo-c 5.00

LORD PUMPKIN
Malibu Comics (Ultraverse): Oct, 1994 ($2.50, one-shot)

0-Two covers 3.00

LORD PUMPKIN/NECROMANTRA
Malibu Comics (Ultraverse): Apr, 1995 - No. 4, July, 1995 ($2.95, limited series, flip book)

1-4 3.00

LORDS OF AVALON: KNIGHT OF DARKNESS
Marvel Comics: Jan, 2008 - No. 6, July, 2009 ($3.99, limited series)

1-6-($3.99)-Kenyon & Furth-s; Ohtsuka-a/c 4.00

LORDS OF AVALON: SWORD OF DARKNESS
Marvel Comics: Apr, 2008 - No. 6, Sept, 2008 ($3.99/$2.99, limited series)

1-($3.99)-Adaptation of Sherrilyn Kenyon's Arthurian fantasy; Ohtsuka-a/c 4.00
2-6-($2.99) 3.00
HC (2008, $19.99) r/#1-6; two covers 20.00

LORDS OF MARS
Dynamite Entertainment: 2013 - No. 6, 2014 ($3.99, limited series)

1-6-Tarzan and Jane meet John Carter on Mars; Nelson-s/Castro-a; multiple covers 4.00

LORDS OF THE JUNGLE
Dynamite Entertainment: 2016 - No. 6, 2016 ($3.99, limited series)

1-6-Tarzan and Sheena app.; Bechko-s/Castro-a; covers by Castro & Massafera 4.00

LORNA, RELIC WRANGLER
Image Comics: Mar, 2011 ($3.99, one-shot)

1-Micah Harris-s; J. Bone-c 4.00

LORNA THE JUNGLE GIRL (...Jungle Queen #1-5)
Atlas Comics (NPI 1/OMC 2-11/NPI 12-26): July, 1953 - No. 26, Aug, 1957

	GD	VG	FN	VF	VF/NM	NM-
1-Origin & 1st app.	53	106	159	334	567	800
2-Intro. & 1st app. Greg Knight	29	58	87	170	278	385
3-5	25	50	75	147	241	335
6-11: 11-Last pre-code (1/55)	21	42	63	126	206	285
12-17,19-26: 14-Colletta & Maneely-c	20	40	60	114	182	250
18-Williamson/Colletta-c	20	40	60	117	189	260

NOTE: ***Brodsky** c-1-3, 5, 9. **Everett** c-21, 23-26. **Heath** c-6, 7. **Maneely** c-12, 15. **Romita** a-18, 20, 22, 24, 26. **Shores** a-14-16, 18, 24, 26; c-11, 13, 16. **Tuska** a-6.*

LOSERS (Inspired the 2010 movie)
DC Comics (Vertigo): Aug, 2003 - No. 32, Mar, 2006 ($2.95/$2.99)

1-Andy Diggle-s/Jock-a 4.00
1-Special Edition (6/10, $1.00) r/#1 with "What's Next?" logo on cover 3.00
2-32: 15-Bagged with Sky Captain CD. 20-Oliver-a. 27-Wilson-a 3.00
...: Ante Up TPB (2004, $9.95) r/#1-6 10.00
...: Book Two TPB (2010, $24.99) r/#13-32; Ian Rankin intro.; preliminary art pages 25.00
...: Close Quarters TPB (2005, $14.99) r/#20-25 15.00
...: Double Down TPB (2004, $12.95) r/#7-12 13.00
...: Endgame TPB (2006, $14.99) r/#26-32 15.00
...: Trifecta TPB (2005, $14.99) r/#13-19 15.00
...: Volumes One and Two TPB (2010, $19.99) r/#1-12; new intro. by Diggle 20.00

LOSERS SPECIAL (See Our Fighting Forces #123)(Also see G.I. Combat & Our Fighting Forces)
DC Comics: Sept, 1985 ($1.25, one-shot)

1-Capt. Storm, Gunner & Sarge; Crisis on Infinite Earths x-over 6.00

LOST, THE
Chaos! Comics: Dec, 1997 - No. 3 ($2.95, B&W, unfinished limited series)

1-3-Andreyko-script: 1-Russell back-c 3.00

LOST BOYS, THE (Sequel to the 1987 vampire movie)
DC Comics (Vertigo): Dec, 2016 - No. 6 ($3.99)

1-5-Tim Seeley-s/Scott Godlewski-a/Tony Harris-c; Frog Bros. app. 4.00

LOST BOYS: REIGN OF FROGS (Based on the 1987 vampire movie)
DC Comics (WildStorm): Jul, 2008 - No. 4, Oct, 2008 ($3.50, limited series)

1-4-Rodionoff-s/Gomez-a; Edgar Frog app. 3.50
TPB (2009, $12.99) r/#1-4 13.00

LOST CONTINENT
Eclipse Int'l: Sept, 1990 - No. 6, 1991 ($3.50, B&W, squarebound, 60 pgs.)

1-6: Japanese story translated to English 4.00

LOST IN SPACE (Movie)
Dark Horse Comics: Apr, 1998 - No. 3, July, 1998 ($2.95, limited series)

1-3-Continuation of 1998 movie; Erskine-c 3.00

LOST IN SPACE (TV)(Also see Space Family Robinson)
Innovation Publishing: Aug, 1991 - No. 12, Jan, 1993 ($2.50, limited series)

1-12: Bill Mumy (Will Robinson) scripts in #1-9. 9-Perez-c 3.00
1,2-Special Ed.; r/#1,2 plus new art & new-c 3.00
Annual 1,2 (1991, 1992, $2.95, 52 pgs.) 4.00
...: Project Robinson (11/93, $2.50) 1st & only part of intended series 3.00

LOST IN SPACE: THE LOST ADVENTURES (IRWIN ALLEN'S...) (TV)
American Gothic Press: Mar, 2016 - No. 6, Nov, 2016 ($3.99, limited series)

1-6-Adaptation of unused scripts. 1-3-The Curious Galactics. 4-6-Malice in Wonderland 4.00

LOST IN SPACE: VOYAGE TO THE BOTTOM OF THE SOUL
Innovation Publishing: No. 13, Aug, 1993 - No. 18, 1994 ($2.50, limited series)

13(V1#1, $2.95)-Embossed silver logo edition; Bill Mumy scripts begin; painted-c 3.00
13(V1#1, $4.95)-Embossed gold logo edition bagged w/poster 5.00
14-18: Painted-c 3.00

NOTE: *Originally intended to be a 12 issue limited series.*

Love and Marriage #2 © SUPR

Love Confessions #4 © QUA

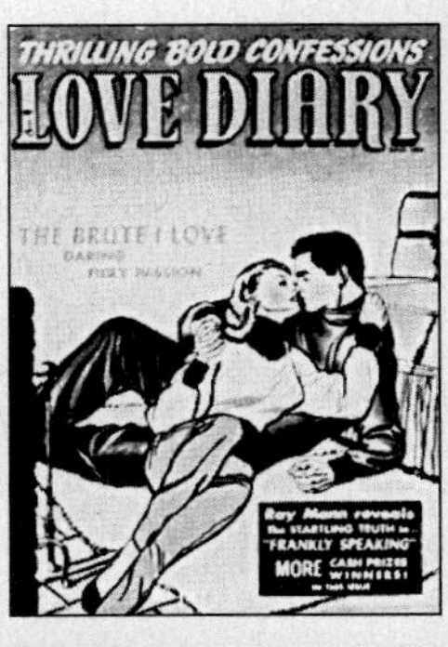

Love Diary #34 © CC

	GD 2.0	VG 4.0	FN 6.0	VF 8.0	VF/NM 9.0	NM- 9.2

LOST ONES, THE
Image Comics: Mar, 2000 ($2.95)

1-Ken Penders-s/a						3.00

LOST PLANET
Eclipse Comics: 5/87 - No. 5, 2/88; No. 6, 3/89 (Mini-series, Baxter paper)

1-6-Bo Hampton-c/a in all						3.00

LOST WAGON TRAIN, THE (See Zane Grey Four Color 583)

LOST WORLD, THE
Dell Publishing Co.: No. 1145, Nov-Jan, 1960-61

Four Color 1145-Movie, Gil Kane-a, photo-c; 1pg. Conan Doyle biography by Torres	9	18	27	57	111	165

LOST WORLD, THE (See Jurassic Park)
Topps Comics: May, 1997 - No. 4, Aug, 1997 ($2.95, limited series)

1-4-Movie adaption						3.00

LOST WORLDS (Weird Tales of the Past and Future)
Standard Comics: No. 5, Oct, 1952 - No. 6, Dec, 1952

5- "Alice in Terrorland" by Alex Toth; J. Katz-a	49	98	147	305	520	735
6-Toth-a	40	80	120	244	402	560

LOTS 'O' FUN COMICS
Robert Allen Co.: 1940s? (5¢, heavy stock, blue covers)

nn-Contents can vary; Felix, Planet Comics known; contents would determine value. Similar to Up-To-Date Comics. Remainders - re-packaged.

LOT 13
DC Comics: Dec, 2012 - No. 5, Apr, 2013 ($2.99, limited series)

1-5-Niles-s/Fabry-a/c						3.00

LOU GEHRIG (See The Pride of the Yankees)

LOVE ADVENTURES (Actual Confessions #13)
Marvel (IPS)/Atlas Comics (MPI): Oct, 1949; No. 2, Jan, 1950; No. 3, Feb, 1951 - No. 12, Aug, 1952

1-Photo-c	25	50	75	150	245	340
2-Powell-a; Tyrone Power, Gene Tierney photo-c	18	36	54	107	169	230
3-8,10-12: 8-Robinson-a	14	28	42	78	112	145
9-Everett-a	14	28	42	80	115	150

LOVE AND MARRIAGE
Superior Comics Ltd. (Canada): Mar, 1952 - No. 16, Sept, 1954

1	20	40	60	117	189	260
2	12	24	36	69	97	125
3-10	11	22	33	62	86	110
11-16	10	20	30	56	76	95
I.W. Reprint #1,2,8,11,14: 8-r/Love and Marriage #3. 11-r/Love and Marriage #11	2	4	6	10	14	18
Super Reprint #10('63),15,17('64):15-Love and Marriage #?	2	4	6	10	14	18

NOTE: *All issues have* **Kamenish** *art.*

LOVE AND ROCKETS
Fantagraphics Books: 1981 - No. 50, May, 1996 ($2.95/$2.50/$4.95, B&W, mature)

1-B&W-c (1981, $1.00; publ. by Hernandez Bros.)(800 printed)	8	16	24	54	102	150
1 (Fall '82; Fantagraphics, color-c)	4	8	12	27	44	60
1-2nd & 3rd printing, 2-11,29-31: 2nd printings						4.00
2	3	6	9	16	23	30
3-10	2	4	6	8	10	12
11-49: 30 ($2.95, 52 pgs.)						5.00
50-($4.95)						6.00

LOVE AND ROCKETS (Volume 2)
Fantagraphics Books: Spring, 2001 - Present ($3.95-$7.99, B&W, mature)

1-9-Gilbert, Jaime and Mario Hernandez-s/a						5.00
10-($5.95)						6.00
11-19-($4.50)						4.50
20-($7.99)						8.00
...: Stories • Free Comic Book Day 2016 Edition (giveaway)						3.00

LOVE AND ROMANCE
Charlton Comics: Sept, 1971 - No. 24, Sept, 1975

1	3	6	9	17	26	35
2-5,7-10	2	4	6	10	14	18
6-David Cassidy pin-up; grey-tone cover	3	6	9	14	19	24
11,13-24	2	4	6	8	10	12
12-Susan Dey poster	2	4	6	10	14	18

LOVE AT FIRST SIGHT
Ace Magazines (RAR Publ. Co./Periodical House): Oct, 1949 - No. 43, Nov, 1956 (Photo-c: 18-42)

1-Painted-c	28	56	84	165	270	375
2-Painted-c	15	30	45	85	130	175
3-10: 4,7-Painted-c	14	28	42	80	115	150
11-20	14	28	42	76	108	140
21-33: 33-Last pre-code	13	26	39	72	101	130
34-43	11	22	33	62	86	110

LOVE BUG, THE (See Movie Comics)

LOVEBUNNY AND MR. HELL
Devil's Due Publ./Image Comics: 2002 - 2004 ($2.95, B&W, one-shots)

1-Tim Seeley-s						3.00
...: A Day in the Lovelife (Image, 2003) Blaylock-a						3.00
...: Savage Love (Image, 2003) Seeley-s/a; Savage Dragon app.; Seeley & Larsen-c						3.00
TPB (4/04, $9.95, digest-sized) reprints						10.00

LOVE CLASSICS
A Lover's Magazine/Marvel: Nov, 1949 - No. 2, Feb, 1950 (Photo-c, 52 pgs.)

1,2: 2-Virginia Mayo photo-c; 30 pg. story "I Turned Into a Small-Town Flirt"	21	42	63	124	202	275

LOVE CONFESSIONS
Quality Comics: Oct, 1949 - No. 54, Dec, 1956 (Photo-c: 3,4,6,7,9,11-18,21,24,25)

1-Ward-c/a, 9 pgs; Gustavson-a	40	80	120	246	411	575
2-Gustavson-a; Ward-c	21	42	63	122	199	275
3	15	30	45	85	130	175
4-Crandall-a	15	30	45	90	140	190
5-Ward-a, 7 pgs.	17	34	51	98	154	210
6,7,9,11-13,15,16,18: 7-Van Johnson photo-c. 8-Robert Mitchum & Jane Russell photo-c	14	28	42	76	108	140
8,10-Ward-a (2 stories in #10)	16	32	48	94	147	200
14,17,19,22-Ward-a; 17-Faith Domerque photo-c	15	30	45	90	140	190
20-Ward-a(2)	16	32	48	94	147	200
21,23-28,30-38,40-42: Last precode, 4/55	12	24	36	67	94	120
29-Ward-a	15	30	45	85	130	175
39,53-Matt Baker-a	14	28	42	82	121	160
43,44,46,47,50-52,54: 47-Ward-c?	11	22	33	62	86	110
45,48-Ward-a	13	26	39	74	105	135
49-Baker-c/a	18	36	54	103	162	220

LOVECRAFT
DC Comics: 2003 (graphic novel)

Hardcover ($24.95) Rodionoff & Giffen-s/Breccia-a; intro. by John Carpenter						25.00
Softcover ($17.95)						18.00

LOVE DIARY
Our Publishing Co./Toytown/Patches: July, 1949 - No. 48, Oct, 1955 (Photo-c: 1-24,27-29) (52 pgs. #1-11?)

1-Krigstein-a	29	58	87	172	281	390
2,3-Krigstein & Mort Leav-a in each	18	36	54	105	165	225
4-8	15	30	45	83	124	165
9,10-Everett-a	15	30	45	85	130	175
11-15,17-20	14	28	42	80	115	150
16- Mort Leav-a, 3 pg. Baker-sty. Leav-a	14	28	42	82	121	160
21-30,32-48: 45-Leav-a. 47-Last precode(12/54)	14	28	42	76	108	140
31-John Buscema headlights-c	18	36	54	105	165	225

LOVE DIARY (Diary Loves #2 on; title change due to previously published title)
Quality Comics Group: Sept, 1949

1-Ward-c/a, 9 pgs.	40	80	120	246	411	575

LOVE DIARY
Charlton Comics: July, 1958 - No. 102, Dec, 1976

1	11	22	33	62	86	110
2	8	16	24	40	50	60
3-5,7-10: 10-Photo-c	7	14	21	35	43	50
6-Torres-a	7	14	21	37	46	55
11-20: 20-Photo-c	3	6	9	17	26	35
21-40	3	6	9	15	22	28
41-60	2	4	6	13	18	22
61-78,80,100-102	2	4	6	9	13	16
79-David Cassidy pin-up	2	4	6	13	18	22

Love Experiences #6 © ACE

Love is Love TPB

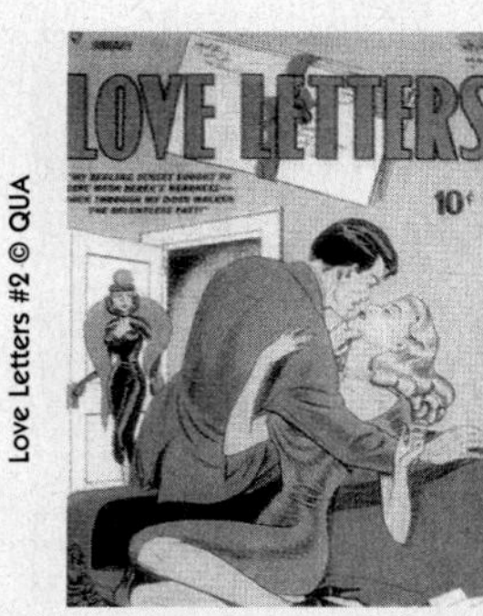

Love Letters #2 © QUA

	GD 2.0	VG 4.0	FN 6.0	VF 8.0	VF/NM 9.0	NM- 9.2
81,83,84,86-99	2	4	6	8	10	12
82,85: 82-Partridge Family poster. 85-Danny poster	2	4	6	10	14	18

LOVE DOCTOR (See Dr. Anthony King...)

LOVE DRAMAS (True Secrets No. 3 on?)
Marvel Comics (IPS): Oct, 1949 - No. 2, Jan, 1950

	GD 2.0	VG 4.0	FN 6.0	VF 8.0	VF/NM 9.0	NM- 9.2
1-Jack Kamen-a; photo-c	24	48	72	140	230	320
2-Photo-c	17	34	51	98	154	210

LOVE EXPERIENCES (Challenge of the Unknown No. 6)
Ace Periodicals (A.A. Wyn/Periodical House): Oct, 1949 - No. 5, June, 1950; No. 6, Apr, 1951 - No. 38, June, 1956

	GD 2.0	VG 4.0	FN 6.0	VF 8.0	VF/NM 9.0	NM- 9.2
1-Painted-c	25	50	75	150	245	340
2	15	30	45	84	127	170
3-5: 5-Painted-c	14	28	42	80	115	150
6-10	13	26	39	74	105	135
11-30: 30-Last pre-code (2/55)	12	24	36	69	97	125
31-38: 38-Indicia date-6/56; c-date-8/56	11	22	33	62	86	110

NOTE: ***Anne Brewster** a-15. Photo c-4, 15-35, 38.*

LOVE FIGHTS
Oni Press: June, 2003 - No. 12, Aug, 2004 ($2.99, B&W)

	GD 2.0	VG 4.0	FN 6.0	VF 8.0	VF/NM 9.0	NM- 9.2
1-12-Andi Watson-s/a						3.00
Vol. 1 TPB (4/04, $14.95, digest-size) r/#1-6						15.00

LOVE IS LOVE
IDW Publishing/DC Comics: 2016 ($9.99, TPB)

	GD 2.0	VG 4.0	FN 6.0	VF 8.0	VF/NM 9.0	NM- 9.2
SC-Anthology to benefit the survivors of the Orlando Pulse shooting; Charretier-c						10.00

LOVE JOURNAL
Our Publishing Co.: No. 10, Oct, 1951 - No. 25, July, 1954

	GD 2.0	VG 4.0	FN 6.0	VF 8.0	VF/NM 9.0	NM- 9.2
10	24	48	72	142	234	325
11-15,17-25: 19-Mort Leav-a	15	30	45	84	127	170
16-Buscema headlight-c	18	36	54	105	165	225

LOVELAND
Mutual Mag./Eye Publ. (Marvel): Nov, 1949 - No. 2, Feb, 1950 (52 pgs.)

	GD 2.0	VG 4.0	FN 6.0	VF 8.0	VF/NM 9.0	NM- 9.2
1,2-Photo-c	16	32	48	94	147	200

LOVELESS
DC Comics: Dec, 2005 - No. 24, Jun, 2008 ($2.99)

	GD 2.0	VG 4.0	FN 6.0	VF 8.0	VF/NM 9.0	NM- 9.2
1-24: 1-Azzarello-s/Frusin-a. 6-8,15,22,23,24-Zezelj-a. 11,12,16-21-Dell'Edera-a						3.00
...: A Kin of Homecoming TPB (2006, $9.99) r/#1-5						10.00
...: Blackwater Falls TPB (2008, $19.99) r/#13-24						20.00
...: Thicker Than Blackwater TPB (2007, $14.99) r/#6-12						15.00

LOVE LESSONS
Harvey Comics/Key Publ. No. 5: Oct, 1949 - No. 5, June, 1950

	GD 2.0	VG 4.0	FN 6.0	VF 8.0	VF/NM 9.0	NM- 9.2
1-Metallic silver-c printed over the cancelled covers of Love Letters #1; indicia title is "Love Letters"	15	30	45	88	137	185
1-Non-metallic version	15	30	45	88	137	185
2-Powell-a; photo-c	9	18	27	52	69	85
3-5: 3,4-Photo-c	8	16	24	42	54	65

LOVE LETTERS (10/49, Harvey; advertised but never published; covers were printed before cancellation and were used as the cover to Love Lessons #1)

LOVE LETTERS (Love Secrets No. 32 on)
Quality Comics: 11/49 - #6, 9/50; #7, 3/51 - #31, 6/53; #32, 2/54 - #51, 12/56

	GD 2.0	VG 4.0	FN 6.0	VF 8.0	VF/NM 9.0	NM- 9.2
1-Ward-c, Gustavson-a	32	64	96	188	307	425
2-Ward-c, Gustavson-a	23	46	69	136	223	310
3-Gustavson-a	17	34	51	98	154	210
4-Ward-a, 9 pgs.; photo-c	20	40	60	120	195	270
5-8,10	14	28	42	76	108	140
9-One pg. Ward "Be Popular with the Opposite Sex"; Robert Mitchum photo-c	14	28	42	81	118	155
11-Ward-r/Broadway Romances #2 & retitled	14	28	42	81	118	155
12-15,18-20	12	24	36	69	97	125
16,17-Ward-a; 16-Anthony Quinn photo-c. 17-Jane Russell photo-c	16	32	48	94	147	200
21-29	12	24	36	67	94	120
30,31(6/53)-Ward-a	14	28	42	76	108	140
32(2/54)-39: 37-Ward-a. 38-Crandall-a. 39-Last precode (4/55)	11	22	33	62	86	110
40-48	10	20	30	56	76	95
49-51: 49,50-Baker-a. 51-Baker-c	15	30	45	88	137	185

NOTE: *Photo-c on most 3-28.*

LOVE LIFE
P. L. Publishing Co.: Nov, 1951

	GD 2.0	VG 4.0	FN 6.0	VF 8.0	VF/NM 9.0	NM- 9.2
1	14	28	42	82	121	160

LOVELORN (Confessions of the Lovelorn #52 on)
American Comics Group (Michel Publ./Regis Publ.): Aug-Sept, 1949 - No. 51, July, 1954 (No. 1-26: 52 pgs.)

	GD 2.0	VG 4.0	FN 6.0	VF 8.0	VF/NM 9.0	NM- 9.2
1	21	42	63	124	202	280
2	14	28	42	76	108	140
3-10	11	22	33	64	90	115
11-20,22-48: 18-Drucker-a(2 pgs.). 46-Lazarus-a	10	20	30	58	79	100
21-Prostitution story	14	28	42	82	121	160
49-51-Has 3-D effect-c/stories	19	38	57	109	172	235

LOVE MEMORIES
Fawcett Publications: 1949 (no month) - No. 4, July, 1950 (All photo-c)

	GD 2.0	VG 4.0	FN 6.0	VF 8.0	VF/NM 9.0	NM- 9.2
1	17	34	51	98	154	210
2-4: 2-(Win/49-50)	11	22	33	60	83	105

LOVE ME TENDERLOIN: A CAL McDONALD MYSTERY
Dark Horse Comics: Jan, 2004 ($2.99, one-shot)

	GD 2.0	VG 4.0	FN 6.0	VF 8.0	VF/NM 9.0	NM- 9.2
1-Niles-s/Templesmith-a/c						3.00

LOVE MYSTERY
Fawcett Publications: June, 1950 - No. 3, Oct, 1950 (All photo-c)

	GD 2.0	VG 4.0	FN 6.0	VF 8.0	VF/NM 9.0	NM- 9.2
1-George Evans-a	22	44	66	128	209	290
2,3-Evans-a. 3-Powell-a	16	32	48	94	147	200

LOVE PROBLEMS (See Fox Giants)

LOVE PROBLEMS AND ADVICE ILLUSTRATED (see True Love...)

LOVE ROMANCES (Formerly Ideal #5)
Timely/Marvel/Atlas(TCI No. 7-71/Male No. 72-106): No. 6, May, 1949 - No. 106, July, 1963

	GD 2.0	VG 4.0	FN 6.0	VF 8.0	VF/NM 9.0	NM- 9.2
6-Photo-c	24	48	72	140	230	320
7-Photo-c; Kamen-a	15	30	45	85	130	175
8-Kubert-a; photo-c	15	30	45	85	130	175
9-20: 9-12-Photo-c	14	28	42	82	121	160
21,24-Krigstein-a	15	30	45	83	124	165
22,23,25-35,37,39,40	14	28	42	80	115	150
36,38-Krigstein-a	14	28	42	81	118	155
41-44,46,47: Last precode (2/55)	14	28	42	78	112	145
45,57-Matt Baker-a	15	30	45	86	133	180
48,50-52,54-56,58-74	7	14	21	48	89	130
49,53-Toth-a, 6 & ? pgs.	8	16	24	51	96	140
75,77,82-Matt Baker-a	9	18	27	58	114	170
76,78-81,86,88-90,92-95: 80-Heath-c. 95-Last 10¢-c?	9	18	27	57	111	165
83,84,87,91,106-Kirby-c. 83-Severin-a	10	20	30	69	147	225
85,96,99-105-Kirby-c/a	12	24	36	82	179	275
97-10¢ cover price blacked out, 12¢ printed on cover; Kirby-c/a	19	38	57	131	291	450
98-Kirby-c/a	12	24	36	82	179	275

NOTE: ***Anne Brewster** a-67, 72. **Colletta** a-37, 40, 42, 44, 46, 67(2); c-42, 44, 46, 49, 54, 80. **Everett** c-70. **Hartley** c-20, 21, 30, 31. **Heath** a-87. **Kirby** c-80, 85, 88. **Robinson** a-29.*

LOVERS (Formerly Blonde Phantom)
Marvel Comics No. 23,24/Atlas No. 25 on (ANC): No. 23, May, 1949 - No. 86, Aug?, 1957

	GD 2.0	VG 4.0	FN 6.0	VF 8.0	VF/NM 9.0	NM- 9.2
23-Photo-c begin, end #29	24	48	72	140	230	320
24-Toth-*ish* plus Robinson-a	15	30	45	83	124	165
25,30-Kubert-a; 7, 10 pgs.	15	30	45	84	127	170
26-29,31-36,39,40: 35-Maneely-c	14	28	42	80	115	150
37,38-Krigstein-a	15	30	45	83	124	165
41-Everett-a(2)	15	30	45	83	124	165
42,44-65: 65-Last pre-code (1/55)	13	26	39	72	101	130
43-Frazetta 1 pg. ad	13	26	39	74	105	135
66,68-80,82-86	12	24	36	69	97	125
67-Toth-a	13	26	39	74	105	135
81-Baker-a	14	28	42	80	115	150

NOTE: ***Anne Brewster** a-86. **Colletta** a-54, 59, 62, 64, 65, 69, 85; c-61, 64, 65, 75. **Hartley** c-37, 53, 54. **Heath** a-61. **Maneely** a-57. **Powell** a-27, 30. **Robinson** a-42, 54, 56.*

LOVERS' LANE
Lev Gleason Publications: Oct, 1949 - No. 41, June, 1954 (No. 1-18: 52 pgs.)

	GD 2.0	VG 4.0	FN 6.0	VF 8.0	VF/NM 9.0	NM- 9.2
1-Biro-c	19	38	57	111	176	240
2-Biro-c	12	24	36	67	94	120
3-20: 3,4-Painted-c. 20-Frazetta 1 pg. ad	11	22	33	60	83	105
21-38,40,41	10	20	30	54	72	90
39-Story narrated by Frank Sinatra	12	24	36	67	94	120

NOTE: ***Briefer** a-6, 13, 21. **Esposito** a-5. **Fuje** a-4, 16; c-many. **Guardineer** a-1, 3. **Kinstler** c-41. **Sparling** a-3.*

Love Scandals #2 © QUA

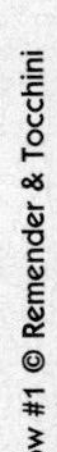
Low #1 © Remender & Tocchini

Lucifer (2016 series) #5 © DC

	GD 2.0	VG 4.0	FN 6.0	VF 8.0	VF/NM 9.0	NM- 9.2
Tuska a-6. Painted c-3-18. Photo c-19-22, 26-28.						
LOVE SCANDALS						
Quality Comics: Feb, 1950 - No. 5, Oct, 1950 (Photo-c #2-5) (All 52 pgs.)						
1-Ward-c/a, 9 pgs.	34	68	102	199	325	450
2,3: 2-Gustavson-a	15	30	45	88	137	185
4-Ward-a, 18 pgs; Gil Fox-a	24	48	72	140	230	320
5-C. Cuidera-a; tomboy story "I Hated Being a Woman"	19	38	57	109	172	235
LOVE SECRETS						
Marvel Comics(IPC): Oct, 1949 - No. 2, Jan, 1950 (52 pgs., photo-c)						
1	20	40	60	120	195	270
2	15	30	45	84	127	170
LOVE SECRETS (Formerly Love Letters #31)						
Quality Comics Group: No. 32, Aug, 1953 - No. 56, Dec, 1956						
32	15	30	45	86	133	180
33,35-39	12	24	36	67	94	120
34-Ward-a	15	30	45	84	127	170
40-Matt Baker-c	15	30	45	86	133	180
41-43: 43-Last precode (3/55)	12	24	36	67	94	120
44,47-50,53,54	11	22	33	60	83	105
45-Ward-a	14	28	42	76	108	140
46-Ward-a; Baker-a	15	30	45	83	124	165
51,52-Ward(r). 52-r/Love Confessions #17	12	24	36	67	94	120
55,56: 55-Baker-a. 56-Baker-c	14	28	42	81	118	155
LOVE STORIES (See Top Love Stories)						
LOVE STORIES (Formerly Heart Throbs)						
National Periodical Publ.: No. 147, Nov, 1972 - No. 152, Oct-Nov, 1973						
147-152	3	6	9	14	20	26
LOVE STORIES OF MARY WORTH (See Harvey Comics Hits #55 & Mary Worth)						
Harvey Publications: Sept, 1949 - No. 5, May, 1950						
1-1940's newspaper reprints-#1-4	9	18	27	47	61	75
2-5: 3-Kamen/Baker-a?	6	12	18	31	38	45
LOVE TALES (Formerly The Human Torch #35)						
Marvel/Atlas Comics (ZPC No. 36-50/MMC No. 67-75): No. 36, 5/49 - No. 58, 8/52; No. 59, date? - No. 75, Sept, 1957						
36-Photo-c	24	48	72	140	230	320
37	14	28	42	82	121	160
38-44,46-50: 39-41-Photo-c	14	28	42	80	115	150
45,51,52,69: 45-Powell-a. 51,69-Everett-a. 52-Krigstein-a	14	28	42	81	118	155
53-60: 60-Last pre-code (2/55)	13	26	39	72	101	130
61-68,70-75: 75-Brewster, Cameron, Colletta-a	12	24	36	67	94	120
LOVE THRILLS (See Fox Giants)						
LOVE TRAILS (Western romance)						
A Lover's Magazine (CDS)(Marvel): Dec, 1949 - No. 2, Mar, 1950 (52 pgs.)						
1,2: 1-Photo-c	18	36	54	103	162	220
LOW						
Image Comics: Aug, 2014 - Present ($3.99/$3.50)						
1,11-15-($3.99) Remender-s/Tocchini-a						4.00
2-10-($3.50) Remender-s/Tocchini-a						3.50
LOWELL THOMAS' HIGH ADVENTURE (See High Adventure)						
LT. (See Lieutenant)						
LUCAS STAND						
BOOM! Studios: Jun, 2016 - No. 6, Nov, 2016 ($3.99, limited series)						
1-6-Kurt Sutter & Caitlin Kittredge-s/Jesús Hervás-a. 1-Multiple covers						4.00
LUCIFER (See The Sandman #4)						
DC Comics (Vertigo): Jun, 2000 - No. 75, Aug, 2006 ($2.50/$2.75)						
1-Carey-s/Weston-a/Fegredo-c	4	8	12	25	40	55
2,3-Carey-s/Weston-a/Fegredo-c	1	2	3	5	6	8
4-10: 4-Pleece-a. 5-Gross-a						4.00
11-49,51-73: 16-Moeller-c begin. 25,26-Death app. 45-Naifeh-a. 53-Kaluta-c begin. 62-Doran-a. 63-Begin $2.75-c						3.00
50-($3.50) P. Craig Russell-a; Mazikeen app.						4.00
74-($2.99) Kaluta-c						3.00
75-($3.99) Last issue; Lucifer's origins retold; Morpheus app.; Gross-a/Moeller-c						4.00
Preview-16 pg. flip book w/Swamp Thing Preview						3.00
Vertigo Essentials: Lucifer #1 Special Edition (3/16, $1.00) Flipbook with GN promos						3.00

	GD 2.0	VG 4.0	FN 6.0	VF 8.0	VF/NM 9.0	NM- 9.2
...: A Dalliance With the Damned TPB ('02, $14.95) r/#14-20						15.00
...: Children and Monsters TPB ('01, $17.95) r/#5-13						18.00
...: Crux TPB (2006, $14.99) r/#55-61						15.00
...: Devil in the Gateway TPB ('01, $14.95) r/#1-4 & Sandman Presents:..#1-3						15.00
...: Evensong TPB (2007, $14.99) r/#70-75 & Lucifer: Nirvana one-shot						15.00
...: Exodus TPB (2005, $14.95) r/#42-44,46-49						15.00
...: Inferno TPB (2003, $14.95) r/#29-35						15.00
...: Mansions of the Silence TPB (2004, $14.95) r/#36-41						15.00
...: Morningstar TPB (2006, $14.99) r/#62-69						15.00
...: Nirvana (2002, $5.95) Carey-s/Muth-painted-c/a; Daniel app.						6.00
...: The Divine Comedy TPB (2003, $17.95) r/#21-28						18.00
...: The Wolf Beneath the Tree TPB (2005, $14.99) r/#45,50-54						15.00
LUCIFER (See The Sandman #4)						
DC Comics (Vertigo): Feb, 2016 - Present ($3.99)						
1-15: 1-Holly Black-s/Lee Garbett-a/Dave Johnson-c. 6-Stephanie Hans-a						4.00
LUCIFER'S HAMMER (Larry Niven & Jerry Pournelle's...)						
Innovation Publishing: Nov, 1993 - No. 6, 1994 ($2.50, painted, limited series)						
1-6: Adaptatin of novel, painted-c & art						3.00
LUCKY COMICS						
Consolidated Magazines: Jan, 1944; No. 2, Sum, 1945 - No. 5, Sum, 1946						
1-Lucky Starr & Bobbie begin	34	68	102	199	325	450
2-4	18	36	54	105	165	225
5-Devil-c by Walter Johnson	22	44	66	132	216	300
LUCKY DUCK						
Standard Comics (Literary Ent.): No. 5, Jan, 1953 - No. 8, Sept, 1953						
5-Funny animal; Irving Spector-a	11	22	33	64	90	115
6-8-Irving Spector-a	10	20	30	54	72	90
NOTE: *Harvey Kurtzman tried to hire Spector for Mad #1.*						
LUCKY "7" COMICS						
Howard Publishers Ltd.: 1944 (No date listed)						
1-Pioneer, Sir Gallagher, Dick Royce, Congo Raider, Punch Powers; bondage-c	50	100	150	315	533	750
LUCKY STAR (Western)						
Nation Wide Publ. Co.: 1950 - No. 7, 1951; No. 8, 1953 - No. 14, 1955 (5x7-1/4"; full color, 5¢)						
nn (#1)-(5¢, 52 pgs.)-Davis-a	20	40	60	120	195	270
2,3-(5¢, 52 pgs.)-Davis-a	14	28	42	80	115	150
4-7-(5¢, 52 pgs.)-Davis-a	14	28	42	76	108	140
8-14-(36 pgs.)(Exist?)	14	28	42	76	108	140
Given away with Lucky Star Western Wear by the Juvenile Mfg. Co.	7	14	21	35	43	50
LUCY SHOW, THE (TV) (Also see I Love Lucy)						
Gold Key: June, 1963 - No. 5, June, 1964 (Photo-c: 1,2)						
1	10	20	30	70	150	230
2	6	12	18	41	76	110
3-5: Photo back c-1,2,4,5	6	12	18	37	66	95
LUCY, THE REAL GONE GAL (Meet Miss Pepper #5 on)						
St. John Publishing Co.: June, 1953 - No. 4, Dec, 1953						
1-Negligee panels	34	68	102	199	325	450
2	18	36	54	105	165	225
3,4: 3-Drucker-a	16	32	48	94	147	200
LUDWIG BEMELMAN'S MADELEINE & GENEVIEVE						
Dell Publishing Co.: No. 796, May, 1957						
Four Color 796	5	10	15	30	50	70
LUDWIG VON DRAKE (TV)(Disney)(See Walt Disney's C&S #256)						
Dell Publishing Co.: Nov-Dec, 1961 - No. 4, June-Aug, 1962						
1	6	12	18	38	69	100
2-4	5	10	15	30	50	70
LUFTWAFFE: 1946 (Volume 1)						
Antarctic Press: July, 1996 - No. 4, Jan, 1997 ($2.95, B&W, limited series)						
1-4-Ben Dunn & Ted Nomura-s/a, ...Special Ed.						3.00
LUFTWAFFE: 1946 (Volume 2)						
Antarctic Press: Mar, 1997 - No. 18 ($2.95/$2.99, B&W, limited series)						
1-18: 8-Reviews Tigers of Terra series						3.00
Annual 1 (4/98, $2.95)-Reprints early Nomura pages						4.00
...Color Special (4/98)						3.00
...Technical Manual 1,2 (2/98, 4/99)						4.00

Lumberjanes #9 © BOOM

Lynch Mob #2 © Chaos!

Machine Man #1 © MAR

GD 2.0 | VG 4.0 | FN 6.0 | VF 8.0 | VF/NM 9.0 | NM- 9.2

LUGER
Eclipse Comics: Oct, 1986 - No. 3, Feb, 1987 ($1.75, miniseries, Baxter paper)
1-3: Bruce Jones scripts; Yeates-c/a 3.00

LUKE CAGE (See Cage & Hero for Hire)

LUKE CAGE NOIR
Marvel Comics: Oct, 2009 - No. 4, Jan, 2010 ($3.99, limited series)
1-4-Glass & Benson-a/Martinbrough-a; covers by Bradstreet and Calero 4.00

LUKE SHORT'S WESTERN STORIES
Dell Publishing Co.: No. 580, Aug, 1954 - No. 927, Aug, 1958
Four Color 580(8/54), 651(9/55)-Kinstler-a 5 10 15 33 57 80
Four Color 739,771,807,848,875,927 5 10 15 30 50 70

LUMBERJANES
BOOM! Box: Apr, 2014 - Present ($3.99)
1-Noelle Stevenson & Grace Ellis-s/Brooke Allen-a; multiple covers 10.00
2 6.00
3-24,26-35 4.00
25-($4.99) Two covers by Allen & Wiedle; preview of Lumberjanes/Gotham Academy 5.00
...: Beyond Bay Leaf (10/15, $4.99) Faith Erin Hicks-s/Rosemary Valero-O'Connell-a 5.00
...: Making the Ghost of It 2016 Special 1 (5/16, $7.99) Wang-s/Norrie-a; Ganucheau-a 8.00

LUMBERJANES / GOTHAM ACADEMY
BOOM! Box: Jun, 2016 - No. 6, Nov, 2016 ($3.99)
1-6: 1-Chynna Clugston Flores-s/Rosemary Valero-O'Connell-a; multiple covers 4.00

LUNA MOON-HUNTER
WaterWalker Studios: Jul, 2012 - No. 2, Aug, 2012 ($5.95, limited series)
1,2-Rob Hughes-s/Jeff Slemons-a. 1-Posada-c. 2-Buzz-c 6.00
SC-($24.95, 180 pgs.) Painted-c by Buzz & Parrillo; art by Slemons, Buzz & LaRocque 25.00
HC-($49.95, limited edition of 1000) Signed by Hughes & Slemons; 2 bonus articles 50.00

LUNATIC FRINGE, THE
Innovation Publishing: July, 1989 - No. 2, 1989 ($1.75, deluxe format)
1,2 3.00

LUNATICKLE (Magazine) (Satire)
Whitstone Publ.: Feb, 1956 - No. 2, Apr, 1956
1,2-Kubert-a (scarce) 9 18 27 47 61 75

LUNATIK
Marvel Comics: Dec, 1995 - No. 3, Feb, 1996 ($1.95, limited series)
1-3 3.00

LURKERS, THE
IDW Publ.: Oct, 2004 - No. 4, Jan, 2005 ($3.99)
1-4-Niles-s/Casanova-a 4.00

LUST FOR LIFE
Slave Labor Graphics: Feb, 1997 - No. 4, Jan, 1998 ($2.95, B&W)
1-4: 1-Jeff Levin-s/a 3.00

LUTHOR (See Lex Luthor: Man of Steel)

LYCANTHROPE LEO
Viz Communications: 1994 - No. 7($2.95, B&W, limited series, 44 pgs.)
1-7 4.00

LYNCH (See Gen [13])
Image Comics (WildStorm Productions): May, 1997 ($2.50, one-shot)
1-Helmut-c/app. 3.00

LYNCH MOB
Chaos! Comics: June, 1994 - No. 4, Sept, 1994 ($2.50, limited series)
1-4 5.00
1-Special edition full foil-c 1 2 3 5 6 8

LYNDON B. JOHNSON
Dell Publishing Co.: Mar, 1965
12-445-503-Photo-c 3 6 9 19 30 40

M
Eclipse Books: 1990 - No. 4, 1991 ($4.95, painted, 52 pgs.)
1-Adapts movie; contains flexi-disc ($5.95) 6.00
2-4 5.00

MACE GRIFFIN BOUNTY HUNTER (Based on video game)
Image Comics (Top Cow): May, 2003 ($2.99, one-shot)
1-Nocon-a 3.00

MACGYVER: FUGITIVE GAUNTLET (Based on TV series)
Image Comics: Oct, 2012 - No. 5, Feb, 2013 ($3.50, limited series)
1-5-Lee Zlotoff & Tony Lee-s/Will Sliney-a 3.50

MACHETE (Based on the Robert Rodriguez movie)
IDW Publishing: No. 0, Sept, 2010 ($3.99)
0-Origin story; Rodriguez & Kaufman-s/Sayger-a; 3 covers 4.00

MACHINE, THE
Dark Horse Comics: Nov, 1994 - No. 4, Feb, 1995 ($2.50, limited series)
1-4 3.00

MACHINE MAN (Also see 2001, A Space Odyssey)
Marvel Comics Group: Apr, 1978 - No. 9, Dec, 1978; No. 10, Aug, 1979 - No. 19, Feb, 1981
1-Jack Kirby-c/a/scripts begin; end #9 3 6 9 19 30 40
2-9-Kirby-c/a/s. 9-(12/78) 2 4 6 9 12 15
10-17: 10-(8/79) Marv Wolfman scripts & Ditko-a begins
1 3 4 6 8 10
18-Wendigo, Alpha Flight-ties into X-Men #140 3 6 9 16 23 30
19-Intro/1st app. Jack O'Lantern (Macendale), later becomes 2nd Hobgoblin
3 6 9 16 23 30
NOTE: *Austin c-7i, 19i.* ***Buckler*** *c-17p, 18p.* ***Byrne*** *c-14p.* ***Ditko*** *a-10-19; c-10-13, 14i, 15, 16.* ***Kirby*** *a-1-9p; c-1-5, 7-9p.* ***Layton*** *c-7i.* ***Miller*** *c-19p.* ***Simonson*** *c-6.*

MACHINE MAN (Also see X-51)
Marvel Comics Group: Oct, 1984 - No. 4, Jan, 1985 (limited series)
1-4-Barry Smith-c/a(i) & colors in all. 1-3-Trimpe-a(p). 2-1st app. Arno Stark 5.00
TPB (1988, $6.95) r/ #1-4; Barry Smith-c 10.00
.../Bastion '98 Annual ($2.99) wraparound-c 4.00

MACHINE MAN 2020
Marvel Comics: Aug, 1994 - No. 2, Sept, 1994 ($2.00, 52 pgs., limited series)
1,2: Reprints Machine Man limited series; Barry Windsor-Smith-c/i(r) 4.00

MACHINE TEEN
Marvel Comics: July, 2005 - No. 5, Nov, 2005 ($2.99, limited series)
1-5-Sumerak-s/Hawthorne-a. 1-James Jean-c 3.00
...: History (2005, $7.99, digest) r/#1-5 8.00

MACK BOLAN: THE EXECUTIONER (Don Pendleton's...)
Innovation Publishing: July, 1993 ($2.50)
1-3-($2.50) 3.00
1-($3.95)-Indestructible Cover Edition 4.00
1-($2.95)-Collector's Gold Edition; foil stamped 4.00
1-($3.50)-Double Cover Edition; red foil outer-c 4.00

MACKENZIE'S RAIDERS (Movie, TV)
Dell Publishing Co.: No. 1093, Apr-June, 1960
Four Color 1093-Richard Carlson photo-c from TV show
6 12 18 37 66 95

MACROSS (Becomes Robotech: The Macross Saga #2 on)
Comico: Dec, 1984 ($1.50)(Low print run)
1-Early manga app. 4 8 12 28 47 65

MACROSS II
Viz Select Comics: 1992 - No. 10, 1993 ($2.75, B&W, limited series)
1-10: Based on video series 4.00

MAD (Tales Calculated to Drive You...)
E. C. Comics (Educational Comics): Oct-Nov, 1952 - Present (No. 24-on are magazine format) (Kurtzman editor No. 1-28, Feldstein No. 29 - No. ?)
1-Wood, Davis, Elder start as regulars 429 858 1287 3432 5466 7500
2-Dick Tracy cameo 114 228 342 912 1456 2000
3,4: 3-Stan Lee mentioned. 4-Reefer mention story "Flob Was a Slob" by Davis;
Superman parody 83 166 249 664 1057 1450
5-W.M. Gaines biog. 163 326 489 1304 2077 2850
6-11: 6-Popeye cameo. 7,8- "Hey Look" reprints by Kurtzman. 11-Wolverton-a;
Davis story was-r/Crime Suspenstories #12 w/new Kurtzman dialogue
60 120 180 480 765 1050
12-15: 12-Archie parody. 15,18-Pot Shot Pete-r by Kurtzman
48 96 144 384 612 840
16-23(5/55): 18-Alice in Wonderland by Jack Davis. 21-1st app. Alfred E. Neuman on-c in fake ad. 22-All by Elder plus photo-montages by Kurtzman.
23-Special cancel announcement 40 80 120 320 510 700
24(7/55)-1st magazine issue (25¢); Kurtzman logo & border on-c; 1st "What? Me Worry?" on-c; 2nd printing exists 94 188 282 752 1201 1650
25-Jaffee starts as regular writer 44 88 132 352 564 775

Mad #41 © EC Pub.

Mad #343 © EC Pub.

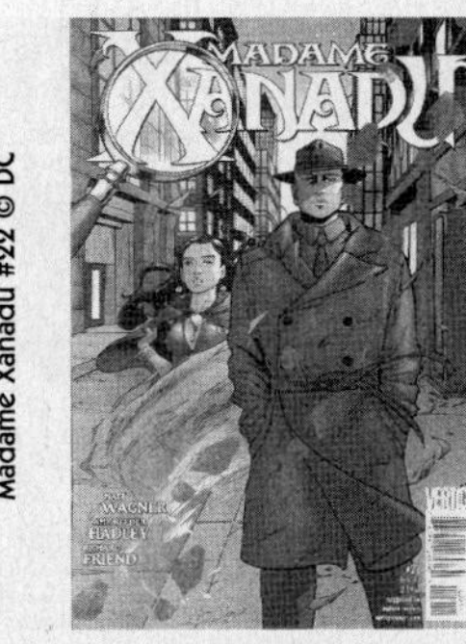

Madame Xanadu #22 © DC

	GD 2.0	VG 4.0	FN 6.0	VF 8.0	VF/NM 9.0	NM- 9.2
26,27: 27-Jaffee starts as story artist; new logo	39	78	117	312	499	685
28-Last issue edited by Kurtzman; (three cover variations exist with different wording on contents banner on lower right of cover; value of each the same)	36	72	108	216	351	485
29-Kamen-a; Don Martin starts as regular; Feldstein editing begins	36	72	108	216	351	485
30-1st A. E. Neuman cover by Mingo; last Elder-a; Bob Clarke starts as regular; Disneyland & Elvis Presley spoof	51	102	153	321	541	760
31-Freas starts as regular; last Davis-a until #99	32	64	96	192	314	435
32,33: 32-Orlando, Drucker, Woodbridge start as regulars; Wood back-c. 33-Orlando back-c	27	54	81	162	266	370
34-Berg starts as regular	22	44	66	132	216	300
35-Mingo wraparound-c; Crandall-a	22	44	66	132	216	300
36-40 (7/58): 39-Beall-c	18	36	54	105	165	225
41-50: 42-Danny Kaye-s. 44-Xmas-c. 47-49-Sid Caesar-s. 48-Uncle Sam-c. 50 (10/59)-Peter Gunn-s	15	30	45	90	140	190
51-59: 52-Xmas-c; 77 Sunset Strip. 53-Rifleman-s. 54-Jaffee-a begins. 55-Sid Caesar-s. 59-Strips of Superman, Flash Gordon, Donald Duck & others. 59-Halloween/Headless Horseman-c	14	28	42	80	115	150
60 (1/61)-JFK/Nixon flip-c; 1st Spy vs. Spy by Prohias, who starts as regular	15	30	45	86	133	180
61-70: 64-Rickard starts as regular. 65-JFK-s. 66-JFK-c. 68-Xmas-c by Martin. 70-Route 66-s	6	12	18	41	76	110
71-75,77-80 (7/63): 72-10th Anniv. special; 1/3 pg. strips of Superman, Tarzan & others. 73-Bonanza-s. 74-Dr. Kildare-s	5	10	15	31	53	75
76-Aragonés starts as regular	5	10	15	34	60	85
81-85: 81-Superman strip. 82-Castro-c. 85-Lincoln-c	4	8	12	28	47	65
86-1st Fold-in; commonly creased back covers makes these and later issues scarcer in NM	5	10	15	33	57	80
87,88	5	10	15	31	53	75
89,90: 89-One strip by Walt Kelly; Frankenstein-c; Fugitive-s. 90-Ringo back-c by Frazetta; Beatles app.	5	10	15	33	57	80
91,94,96,100: 94-King Kong-c. 96-Man From U.N.C.L.E. 100-(1/66)-Anniversary issue	4	8	12	28	47	65
92,93,95,97-99: 99-Davis-a resumes	4	8	12	27	44	60
101,104,106,108,114,115,119,121: 101-Infinity-c; Voyage to the Bottom of the Sea-s. 104-Lost in Space-s. 106-Tarzan back-c by Frazetta; 2 pg. Batman by Aragonés. 108-Hogan's Heroes by Davis. 114-Rat Patrol-s. 115-Star Trek. 119-Invaders (TV). 121-Beatles-c; Ringo pin-up; flip-c of Sik-Teen; Flying Nun-s	3	6	9	20	31	42
102,103,107,109-113,116-118,120(7/68): 118-Beatles cameo	3	6	9	18	28	38
105-Batman-c/s, TV show parody (9/66)	4	8	12	23	37	50
122,124,126,128,129,131-134,136,137,139,140: 122-Ronald Reagan photo inside; Drucker & Mingo-c. 126-Family Affair-s. 128-Last Orlando. 131-Reagan photo back-c. 132-Xmas-c. 133-John Wayne/True Grit. 136-Room 222	3	6	9	15	22	28
123-Four different covers	3	6	9	16	23	30
125,127,130,135,138: 125-2001 Space Odyssey; Hitler back-c. 127-Mod Squad-c/s. 130-Land of the Giants-s; Torres begins as reg. 135-Easy Rider-c by Davis. 138-Snoopy-c; MASH-s	3	6	9	16	24	32
141-149,151-156,158-165,167-170: 141-Hawaii Five-0. 147-All in the Family-s. 153-Dirty Harry-s. 155-Godfather-c/s. 156-Columbo-s. 159-Clockwork Orange-c/s. 161-Tarzan-s. 164-Kung Fu (TV)-s. 165-James Bond-s; Dean Martin-c. 169-Drucker-c; McCloud-s. 170-Exorcist-s	3	6	9	14	19	24
150-(4/72) Partridge Family-s	3	6	9	15	21	26
157-(3/73) Planet of the Apes-c/s	3	6	9	16	23	30
166-(4/74) Classic finger-c	3	6	9	16	23	30
171-185,187,189-192,194,195,198,199: 172-Six Million Dollar Man-s; Hitler back-c. 178-Godfather II-c/s. 180-Jaws-c/s (1/76). 182-Bob Jones starts as regular.185-Starsky & Hutch-s. 187-Fonz/Happy Days-c/s; Harry North starts as regular. 189-Travolta/Kotter-c/s. 190-John Wayne-c/s. 192-King Kong-c/s. 194-Rocky-c/s; Laverne & Shirley-s. 199-James Bond-s	2	4	6	10	14	18
186,188,197,200: 186-Star Trek-c/s. 188-Six Million Dollar Man/ Bionic Woman. 197-Spock-s; Star Wars-s. 200-Close Encounters	2	4	6	13	18	22
193,196: 193-Farrah/Charlie's Angels-c/s. 196-Star Wars-c/s	3	6	9	14	19	24
201,203,205,220: 201-Sat. Night Fever-c/s. 203-Star Wars. 205-Travolta/Grease. 220-Yoda-c, Empire Strikes Back-s	2	4	6	9	13	16
202,204,206,207,209,211-219,221-227,229,230: 204-Hulk TV show. 206-Tarzan. 208-Superman movie. 209-Mork & Mindy. 212-Spider-Man-s; Alien (movie)-s. 213-James Bond, Dracula, Rocky II-s 216-Star Trek. 219-Martin-c. 221-Shining-s. 223-Dallas-c/s. 225-Popeye. 226-Superman II. 229-James Bond. 230-Star Wars	1	3	4	6	8	10
208,228: 208-Superman movie-c/s; Battlestar Galactica-s. 228-Raiders of the Lost Ark-c/s	2	4	6	9	12	15
210-Lord of the Rings	2	4	6	9	13	16
231-235,237-241,243-249,251-260: 233-Pac-Man-c. 234-MASH-c/s. 235-Flip-c with Rocky III & Conan; Boris-a. 239-Mickey Mouse-c. 241-Knight Rider-s. 243-Superman III. 245- Last Rickard-a. 247-Seven Dwarfs-c. 253-Supergirl movie-s; Prince/Purple Rain-s. 254-Rock stars-s. 255-Reagan-c; Cosby-s. 256-Last issue edited by Feldstein; Dynasty, Bev. Hills Cop. 259-Rambo. 260-Back to the Future-c/s; Honeymooners-s	1	2	3	5	6	8
236,242,250: 236-E.T.-c/s;Star Trek II-s. 242-Star Wars/A-Team-c/s. 250-Temple of Doom-c/s; Tarzan-s	1	2	3	5	7	9
261-267,269-276,278-288,290-297: 261-Miami Vice. 262-Rocky IV-c/s, Leave It To Beaver-s. 263-Young Sherlock Holmes-s. 264-Hulk Hogan-c; Rambo-s. 267-Top Gun. 271-Star Trek IV-c/s. 272-ALF-c; Get Smart-s. 273-Pee Wee Herman-c/s. 274-Last Martin-a. 281-California Raisins-c. 282-Star Trek:TNG-s; ALF-s. 283-Rambo III-c/s. 284-Roger Rabbit-c/s. 285-Hulk Hogan-c. 287-3 pgs. Eisner-a. 291-TMNT-c; Indiana Jones-s. 292-Super Mario Bros.-c; Married with Children-s. 295-Back to the Future II. 297-Mike Tyson-c	1	2	3	4	5	7
268,277,289,298-300: 268-Aliens-c/s. 277-Michael Jackson-c/s; Robocop-s. 289-Batman movie parody. 298-Gremlins II-c/s; Robocop II. Batman-s. 299-Simpsons-c/story; Total Recall-s. 300(1/91) Casablanca-s, Dick Tracy-s, Wizard of Oz-s, Gone With The Wind-s	1	2	3	5	6	8
300-303 (1/91-6/91)-Special Hussein Asylum Editions; only distributed to the troops in the Middle East (see Mad Super Spec.)	2	4	6	13	18	22
301-310,312,313,315-320,322,324,326-334,337-349: 303-Home Alone-c/s. 305-Simpsons-s. 306-TMNT II movie. 308-Terminator II. 315-Tribute to William Gaines. 316-Photo-c. 319-Dracula-c/s. 320-Disney's Aladdin-s. 322-Batman Animated series. 327-Seinfeld-s; X-Men-s. 331-Flintstones-c/s. 332-O.J. Simpson-c/s; Simpsons app. in Lion King. 334-Frankenstein-c/s. 338-Judge Dredd-c by Frazetta. 341-Pocahontas-s. 345-Beatles app. (1 pg.) 347-Broken Arrow & Mission Impossible						5.00
311,314,321,323,325,335,336,350,354,358: 311-Addams Family-c/story, Home Improvement-s. 314-Batman Returns-c/story. 321-Star Trek DS9-c/s. 323-Jurassic Park-c/s. 325,336-Beavis & Butthead-c/s. 335-X-Files-s; Pulp Fiction-s; Interview with the Vampire-s. 336-Lois & Clark-s. 350-Polybagged w/CD Rom. 354-Star Wars; Beavis & Butthead-s. 358-X-Files						6.00
351-353,355-357,359-500						5.00
501-539-($5.99)						6.00
Mad About Super Heroes (2002, $9.95) r/super hero app.; Alex Ross-c						10.00

NOTE: ***Aragones*** *c-210, 293.* ***Beall*** *c-39.* ***Davis*** *c-2, 27, 135, 139, 173, 178, 212, 213, 219, 246, 260, 296, 308.* ***Drucker*** *a-35-62; c-122, 169, 176, 225, 234, 264, 266, 274, 280, 285, 297, 299, 303, 314, 315, 321.* ***Elder*** *c-5, 259, 261, 268.* ***Elder/Kurtzman*** *a-258-274.* ***Jules Feiffer*** *a(r)-42.* ***Freas*** *c-40-59, 62-67, 69-70, 72, 74.* ***Heath*** *a-14, 27.* ***Jaffee*** *c-199, 217, 224, 258.* ***Kamen*** *a-29.* ***Krigstein*** *a-12, 17, 24, 26.* ***Kurtzman*** *c-1, 3, 4, 6-10, 13, 16, 18.* ***Martin*** *a-29-62; c-68, 165, 229.* ***Mingo*** *c-30-37, 61, 71, 75-80, 82-114, 117-124, 126, 129, 131, 133, 134, 136, 140, 143-148, 150-162, 164, 166-168, 171, 172, 174, 175, 177, 179, 181, 183, 185, 198, 206, 209, 211, 214, 218, 221, 222, 300.* ***John Severin*** *a-1-6, 9, 10.* ***Wolverton*** *c-11; a-11, 17, 29, 31, 36, 40, 82, 137.* ***Wood*** *a-1-21, 23-62; c-26, 28, 29.* ***Woodbridge*** *a-35-62. Issues 1-23 are 36 pgs.; 24-28 are 58 pgs.; 29 on are 52 pgs.*

MAD (See Mad Follies, ...Special, More Trash from..., and The Worst from...)

MAD ABOUT MILLIE (Also see Millie the Model)
Marvel Comics Group: April, 1969 - No. 16, Nov, 1970

	GD	VG	FN	VF	VF/NM	NM-
1-Giant issue	9	18	27	61	123	185
2,3 (Giants)	6	12	18	40	73	105
4-10	5	10	15	31	53	75
11-16: 16-r	5	10	15	30	50	70
Annual 1(11/71, 52 pgs.)	5	10	15	31	53	75

MADAME FRANKENSTEIN
Image Comics: May, 2014 - No. 7, Nov, 2014 ($2.99, B&W, limited series)

1-7-Jamie Rich-s/Megan Levens-a/Joëlle Jones-c. 1-Variant-c by Mittens 3.00

MADAME MIRAGE
Image Comics (Top Cow): June, 2007 - No. 6, May, 2008 ($2.99)

1-6: 1-Paul Dini-s/Kenneth Rocafort-a; two covers by Horn and Rocafort 3.00
... First Look (5/07, 99¢) preview of series; Dini interview; cover gallery 3.00
Volume 1 TPB (7/08, $14.99) r/#1-6; cover gallery; cover and design sketches 15.00

MADAME XANADU
DC Comics: July, 1981 ($1.00, no ads, 36 pgs.)

	GD	VG	FN	VF	VF/NM	NM-
1-Marshall Rogers-a (25 pgs.); Kaluta-c/a (2pgs.); pin-up	1	2	3	5	6	8

MADAME XANADU (Also see Doorway to Nightmare)
DC Comics (Vertigo): Aug, 2008 - No. 29, Jan, 2011 ($2.99)

1-Matt Wagner-s/Amy Reeder Hadley-a/c; Phantom Stranger app. 4.00
1,2-Variant covers. 1-Wagner. 2-Kaluta 5.00
2-29: 2-10-Amy Reeder Hadley-a/c; Phantom Stranger app. 6-Death (from The Sandman) app.; covers by Hadley & Quitely. 9-Zatara app. 10-Jim Corrigan becomes The Spectre. 11-15-Kaluta-a. 14,15-Sandman (Wesley Dodds) app. 16-18-Hadley-a; Det. Jones app. 3.00
...: Broken House of Cards TPB (2011, $17.99) r/#16-23 and story from House of Mystery Halloween Annual #1 18.00

Mad Follies #1 © EC Pub.

Madman Comics #1 © Mike Allred

Mad Max: Fury Road: Furiosa #1 © WB

	GD 2.0	VG 4.0	FN 6.0	VF 8.0	VF/NM 9.0	NM- 9.2
...: Disenchanted TPB (2009, $12.99) r/#1-10; James Robinson intro.; Hadley sketch-a						13.00
...: Exodus TPB (2010, $12.99) r/#11-15; Chris Roberson intro.						13.00
...: Extra-Sensory TPB (2011, $17.99) r/#24-29						18.00

MADBALLS
Star Comics/Marvel Comics #9 on: Sept, 1986 - No. 3, Nov, 1986; No. 4, June, 1987 - No. 10, June, 1988

	GD	VG	FN	VF	VF/NM	NM-
1-10: Based on toys. 9-Post-a						5.00

MAD DISCO
E.C. Comics: 1980 (one-shot, 36 pgs.)

	GD	VG	FN	VF	VF/NM	NM-
1-Includes 30 minute flexi-disc of Mad disco music	2	4	6	11	16	20

MAD-DOG
Marvel Comics: May, 1993 - No. 6, Oct, 1993 ($1.25)

	GD	VG	FN	VF	VF/NM	NM-
1-6-Flip book w/2nd story "created" by Bob Newhart's character from his TV show "Bob" set at a comic book company; actual s/a-Ty Templeton						3.00

MAD DOGS
Eclipse Comics: Feb, 1992 - No. 3, July, 1992 ($2.50, B&W, limited series)

	GD	VG	FN	VF	VF/NM	NM-
1-3						3.00

MAD 84 (Mad Extra)
E.C. Comics: 1984 (84 pgs.)

	GD	VG	FN	VF	VF/NM	NM-
1	1	3	4	6	8	10

MAD FOLLIES (Special)
E. C. Comics: 1963 - No. 7, 1969

	GD	VG	FN	VF	VF/NM	NM-
nn(1963)-Paperback book covers	19	38	57	129	287	445
2(1964)-Calendar	15	30	45	100	220	340
3(1965)-Mischief Stickers	11	22	33	76	163	250
4(1966)-Mobile; Frazetta-r/back-c Mad #90	9	18	27	57	111	165
5,6: 5(1967)-Stencils. 6(1968)-Mischief Stickers	7	14	21	44	82	120
7(1969)-Nasty Cards	7	14	21	44	82	120

(If bonus is missing, issue is half price)
NOTE: ***Clarke** c-4. **Frazetta** r-4, 6 (1 pg. ea.). **Mingo** c-1-3. **Orlando** a-5.*

MAD HATTER, THE (Costumed Hero)
O. W. Comics Corp.: Jan-Feb, 1946; No. 2, Sept-Oct, 1946

	GD	VG	FN	VF	VF/NM	NM-
1-Freddy the Firefly begins; Giunta-c/a	77	154	231	493	847	1200
2-Has ad for E.C.'s Animal Fables #1	40	80	120	246	411	575

MADHOUSE
Ajax/Farrell Publ. (Excellent Publ./4-Star): 3-4/54 - No. 4, 9-10/54; 6/57 - No. 4, Dec?, 1957

	GD	VG	FN	VF	VF/NM	NM-
1(1954)	39	78	117	231	378	525
2,3	20	40	60	120	195	270
4-Surrealistic-c	27	54	81	162	266	370
1(1957, 2nd series)	15	30	45	90	140	190
2-4 (#4 exist?)	11	22	33	62	86	110

MAD HOUSE (Formerly Madhouse Glads; ...Comics #104? on)
Red Circle Productions/Archie Publications: No. 95, 9/74 - No. 97, 1/75; No. 98, 8/75 - No. 130, 10/82

	GD	VG	FN	VF	VF/NM	NM-
95,96-Horror stories through #97; Morrow-c	2	4	6	11	16	20
97-Intro. Henry Hobson; Morrow-a/c, Thorne-a	2	4	6	10	14	18
98,99,101-120-Satire/humor stories. 110-Sabrina app.,1pg.	1	3	4	6	8	10
100	2	4	6	8	10	12
121-129	2	4	6	8	10	12
130	2	4	6	9	13	16
Annual 8(1970-71)-Formerly Madhouse Ma-ad Annual; Sabrina app. (6 pgs.)	4	8	12	27	44	60
Annual 9-12(1974-75): 11-Wood-a(r)	3	6	9	14	20	25
...Comics Digest 1('75-76) r/1st & 2nd Sabrina app.	2	4	6	10	14	18
2-8(8/82)(...Mag. #5 on)-Sabrina in many	2	4	6	8	11	14

NOTE: ***B. Jones** a-96. **McWilliams** a-97. **Wildey** a-95, 96. See Archie Comics Digest #1, 13.*

MADHOUSE GLADS (Formerly ...Ma-ad; Madhouse #95 on)
Archie Publ.: No. 73, May, 1970 - No. 94, Aug, 1974 (No. 78-92: 52 pgs.)

	GD	VG	FN	VF	VF/NM	NM-
73-77,93,94: 74-1 pg. Sabrina	2	4	6	9	13	16
78-92 (52 pgs.)	2	4	6	11	16	20

MADHOUSE MA-AD (...Jokes #67-70; ...Freak-Out #71-74)
(Formerly Archie's Madhouse) (Becomes Madhouse Glads #73 on)
Archie Publications: No. 67, April, 1969 - No. 72, Jan, 1970

	GD	VG	FN	VF	VF/NM	NM-
67-71: 70-1 pg. Sabrina	3	6	9	15	22	28
72-6 pgs. Sabrina	4	8	12	27	44	60
...Annual 7(1969-70)-Formerly Archie's Madhouse Annual; becomes Madhouse Annual; 6 pgs. Sabrina	4	8	12	28	47	65

MADMAN (See Creatures of the Id #1)
Tundra Publishing: Mar, 1992 - No. 3, 1992 ($3.95, duotone, high quality, lim. series, 52 pgs.)

	GD	VG	FN	VF	VF/NM	NM-
1-Mike Allred-c/a in all	2	4	6	8	10	12
1-2nd printing						4.00
2,3						6.00

MADMAN ADVENTURES
Tundra Publishing: 1992 - No. 3, 1993 ($2.95, limited series)

	GD	VG	FN	VF	VF/NM	NM-
1-Mike Allred-c/a in all	1	3	4	6	8	10
2,3						5.00
TPB (Oni Press, 2002, $14.95) r/#1-3 & first app. of Frank Einstein from Creatures of the Id in color; gallery pages						15.00

MADMAN ATOMIC COMICS (Also see The Atomics)
Image Comics: Apr, 2007 - Present ($2.99/$3.50)

	GD	VG	FN	VF	VF/NM	NM-
1-12-Mike Allred-s/c/a. 1-Origin re-told; pin-ups by Rivoche and Powell. 3-Sale back-c						3.50
13-17-($3.50) Wraparound-c. 14-Back up w/Darwyn Cooke-a						3.50
All-New Giant-Size Super Ginchy Special (4/11, $5.99) Allred-s/a; back-ups/pin-ups						6.00
Madman In Your Face 3D Special (11/14, $9.99) Classic stories converted to 3D plus a new short story by Mike Allred and pin-ups by various; glasses included						10.00
... Vol. 1 (2008, $19.99) r/#1-7; bonus art; Jamie Rich intro.						20.00

MADMAN COMICS (Also see The Atomics)
Dark Horse Comics (Legend No. 2 on): Apr, 1994 - No. 20, Dec, 2000 ($2.95/$2.99)

	GD	VG	FN	VF	VF/NM	NM-
1-Allred-c/a; F. Miller back-c.	1	2	3	5	6	8
2-3: 3-Alex Toth back-c.						5.00
4-11: 4-Dave Stevens back-c. 6,7-Miller/Darrow's Big Guy app. 6-Bruce Timm back-c. 7-Darrow back-c. 8-Origin?; Bagge back-c. 10-Allred/Ross-c; Ross back-c. 11-Frazetta back-c						4.00
12-16: 12-(4/99)						3.50
17-20: 17-The G-Men From Hell #1 on cover; Brereton back-c. 18-(#2). 19,20-($2.99-c). 20-Clowes back-c						3.50
... Boogaloo TPB (6/99, $8.95) r/Nexus Meets Madman & Madman/The Jam						9.00
... Gargantua! (2007, $125.00, HC with dustjacket) r/Madman#1-3, Madman Adventures #1-3, Madman Comics #1-20 and Madman King-Size Super Groovy Special; pin-ups						125.00
Image Firsts: Madman #1 (10/10, $1.00) r/#1						3.00
Ltd. Ed. Slipcover (1997, $99.95, signed and numbered) w/Vol.1 & Vol. 2. Vol.1- reprints #1-5; Vol. 2- reprints #6-10						100.00
The Complete Madman Comics: Vol. 2 (11/96, $17.95, TPB) r/#6-10 plus new material						18.00
Madman King-Size Super Groovy Special (Oni Press, 7/03, $6.95) new short stories by Allred, Derington, Krall and Weissman						7.00
Madman Picture Exhibition No. 1-4 (4-7/02, $3.95) pin-ups by various						4.00
Madman Picture Exhibition Limited Edition (10/02, $29.95) Hardcover collects MPE #1-4						30.00
... Volume 2 SC (2007, $17.99) r/#1-11; Erik Larsen intro.						18.00
... Volume 3 SC (2007, $17.99) r/#12-20 and story from King-Size Groovy; Allred intro.						18.00
Yearbook '95 (1996, $17.95, TPB)-r/#1-5, intro by Teller						18.00

MADMAN / THE JAM
Dark Horse Comics: Jul, 1998 - No. 2, Aug, 1998 ($2.95, mini-series)

	GD	VG	FN	VF	VF/NM	NM-
1,2-Allred & Mireault-s/a						4.00

MAD MAX: FURY ROAD (Based on the 2015 movie)
DC Comics (Vertigo): Jul, 2015 - Oct, 2015 ($4.99, series of one-shots)

	GD	VG	FN	VF	VF/NM	NM-
... :Furiosa (8/15, $4.99) Origin of Furiosa; Tristan Jones-a; Edwards-c						5.00
...: Max 1,2 (9/15, 10/15, $4.99) Recap of Max's history & prelude to movie						5.00
...: Nux & Immortan Joe (7/15, $4.99) Origins of Nux & Immortan Joe; Edwards-c						5.00

MAD MONSTER PARTY (See Movie Classics)

MADNESS IN MURDERWORLD
Marvel Comics: 1989 (Came with computer game from Paragon Software)

	GD	VG	FN	VF	VF/NM	NM-
V1#1-Starring The X-Men						5.00

MADRAVEN HALLOWEEN SPECIAL
Hamilton Comics: Oct, 1995 ($2.95, one-shot)

	GD	VG	FN	VF	VF/NM	NM-
nn-Morrow-a						3.00

MADROX (from X-Factor)
Marvel Comics (Marvel Knights): Nov, 2004 - No. 5, Mar, 2005 ($2.99)

	GD	VG	FN	VF	VF/NM	NM-
1-5-Peter David-s/Pablo Raimondi-a; Strong Guy app.						3.00
...: Multiple Choice TPB (2005, $13.99) r/#1-5						14.00
X-Factor: Madrox - Multiple Choice HC (2008, $19.99) r/#1-5						20.00

MAD SPECIAL (...Super Special)
E. C. Publications, Inc.: Fall, 1970 - No. 141, Nov, 1999 (84 - 116 pgs.)
(If bonus is missing, issue is one half price)

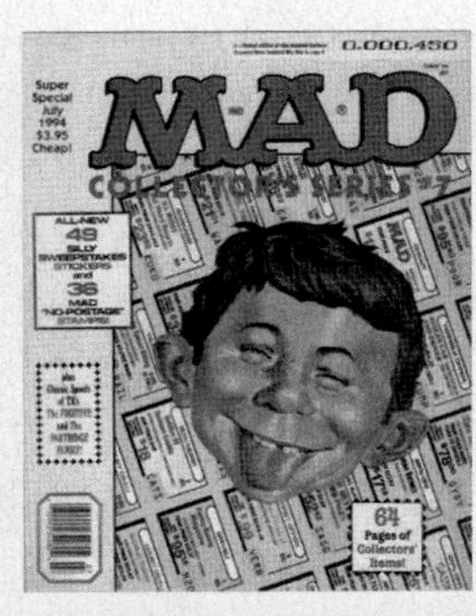

Mad Super Special #94 © EC Pub.

Mae #1 © Gene Ha

Magic Comics #19 © KFS

	GD 2.0	VG 4.0	FN 6.0	VF 8.0	VF/NM 9.0	NM- 9.2
Fall 1970(#1)-Bonus-Voodoo Doll; contains 17 pgs. new material	9	18	27	58	114	170
Spring 1971(#2)-Wall Nuts; 17 pgs. new material	5	10	15	33	57	80
3-Protest Stickers	5	10	15	33	57	80
4-8: 4-Mini Posters. 5-Mad Flag. 6-Mad Mischief Stickers. 7-Presidential candidate posters, Wild Shocking Message posters. 8-TV Guise	5	10	15	30	50	70
9(1972)-Contains Nostalgic Mad #1 (28 pgs.)	4	8	12	25	40	55
10-13: 10-Nonsense Stickers (Don Martin). 13-Sickie Stickers; 3 pgs. Wolverton-r/Mad #137. 11-Contains 33-1/3 RPM record. 12-Contains Nostalgic Mad #2 (36 pgs.); Davis, Wolverton-a	3	6	9	19	30	40
14,16-21,24: 4-Vital Message posters & Art Depreciation paintings. 16-Mad-hesive Stickers. 17-Don Martin posters. 20-Martin Stickers. 18-Contains Nostalgic Mad #4 (36 pgs.). 21,24-Contains Nostalgic Mad #5 (28 pgs.) & #6 (28 pgs.)	3	6	9	16	23	30
15-Contains Nostalgic Mad #3 (28 pgs.)	3	6	9	16	24	32
22,23,25,27-29,30: 22-Diplomas. 23-Martin Stickers. 25-Martin Posters. 27-Mad Shock-Sticks. 28-Contains Nostalgic Mad #7 (36 pgs.). 29-Mad Collectable-Connectables Posters. 30-The Movies	2	4	6	9	13	16
26-Has 33-1/3 RPM record	2	4	6	13	18	22
31,33-35,37-50	2	4	6	8	11	14
32-Contains Nostalgic Mad #8. 36-Has 96 pgs. of comic book & comic strip spoofs: titles "The Comics" on-c	2	4	6	9	13	16
51-70	1	3	4	6	8	10
71-88,90-100: 71-Batman parodies-r by Wood, Drucker. 72-Wolverton-c r-from 1st panel in Mad #11; Wolverton-s r/new dialogue. 83-All Star Trek spoof issue	1	2	3	5	6	8
76-(Fall, 1991)-Special Hussein Asylum Edition; distributed only to the troops in the Middle East (see Mad #300-303)	2	4	6	13	18	22
89-($3.95)-Polybagged w/1st of 3 Spy vs. Spy hologram trading cards (direct sale only issue) (other cards came w/card set)	1	3	4	6	8	10
101-141: 117-Sci-Fi parodies-r.						4.00

NOTE: *#28-30 have no number on cover.* ***Freas*** *c-76.* ***Mingo*** *c-9, 11, 15, 19, 23.*

MAE
Dark Horse Comics: May, 2016 - Present ($3.99)

1-Gene Ha-s/a/c; intro. by Bill Willingham; bonus pin-ups by Graham & Conner 5.00
2-6: 2-5-Gene Ha-s/a/c. 3-Bonus pin-up by Katie Cook. 6-Ha-s/Ganucheau-a 4.00

MAGDALENA, THE (See The Darkness #15-18)
Image Comics (Top Cow): Apr, 2000 - No. 3, Jan, 2001 ($2.50)

Preview Special ('00, $4.95) Flip book w/Blood Legacy preview 5.00
1-Benitez-c/a; variant covers by Silvestri & Turner 3.00
2,3: 2-Two covers 3.00
.../Angelus #1/2 (11/01, $2.95) Benitez-c/Ching-a 3.00
...Blood Divine (2002, $9.95) r/#1-3 & #1/2; cover gallery 10.00
.../Vampirella (7/03, $2.99) Wohl-s/Benitez-a; two covers 3.00

MAGDALENA, THE (Volume 2)
Image Comics (Top Cow): Aug, 2003 - No. 4, Dec, 2003 ($2.99)

Preview (6/03) B&W preview; Wizard World East logo on cover 3.00
1-4-Holguin-s/Basaldua-a 3.00
1-Variant-c by Jim Silke benefitting ACTOR charity 5.00
TPB Volume 1 (12/06, $19.99) r/both series, Darkness #15-18 & Magdalena/Angelus 20.00
.../Daredevil (5/08, $3.99) Phil Hester-s/a; Hester & Sejic-c 4.00
.../Vampirella (12/04, $2.99) Kirkman-s/Manapul-a; two covers by Manapul and Bachalo 3.00
... Vs. Dracula Monster War 2005 (6/05, $2.99) four covers; Joyce Chin-a 3.00

MAGDALENA, THE (Volume 3)
Image Comics (Top Cow): Apr, 2010 - No. 12, May, 2012 ($3.99)

1-12: 1-Marz-s/Blake-a/Sook-c. 7,8-Keu Cha-a 4.00
... Seventh Sacrament 1 (12/14, $3.99) Tini Howard-s/Aileen Oracion-a 4.00

MAGE (The Hero Discovered…; also see Grendel #16)
Comico: Feb, 1984 (no month) - No. 15, Dec, 1986 ($1.50, Mando paper)

	GD	VG	FN	VF	VF/NM	NM-
1-Comico's 1st color comic	2	4	6	8	11	14
2-5: 3-Intro Edsel						6.00
6-Grendel begins (1st in color)	3	6	9	14	20	25
7-1st new Grendel story	2	4	6	8	10	12
8-14: 13-Grendel dies. 14-Grendel story ends						6.00
15-($2.95) Double size w/pullout poster	1	2	3	5	6	8

Image Firsts: Mage - The Hero Discovered #1 (10/10, $1.00) r/#1 w/"Image Firsts" logo 3.00
TPB Volume 1-4 (Image, $5.95) 1- r/#1,2. 2- r/#3,4. 3- r/#5,6. 4- r/#7,8 7.00
TPB Volume 5-7 (Image, $6.95) 5- r/#9,10. 6- r/#11,12. 7- r/#13,14 7.00
TPB Volume 8 (Image, 9/99, $7.50) r/#15 7.50
..., Vol. 1 TPB (Image, 2004, $29.99) r/#1-15; cover gallery, promo artwork, bonus art 30.00

MAGE (The Hero Defined) (Volume 2)
Image Comics: July, 1997 - No. 15, Oct, 1999 ($2.50)

0-(7/97, $5.00) American Ent. Ed. 5.00
1-14:Matt Wagner-c/s/a in all. 13-Three covers 3.00
1-"3-D Edition" (2/98, $4.95) w/glasses 5.00
15-($5.95) Acetate cover 6.00
Volume 1,2 TPB ('98,'99, $9.95) 1- r/#1-4. 2-r/#5-8 10.00
Volume 3 TPB ('00, $12.95) r/#9-12 13.00
Volume 4 TPB ('01, $14.95) r/#13-15 15.00
Hardcover Vol. 2 (2005, $49.95) r/#1-15; cover gallery, character design & sketch pages 50.00

MAGE KNIGHT: STOLEN DESTINY (Based on the fantasy game Mage Knight)
Idea + Design Works: Oct, 2002 - No. 5, Feb, 2003 ($3.50, limited series)

1-5: 1-J. Scott Campbell-c; Cabrera-a/Dezago-s, 2-Dave Johnson-c 3.50

MAGGIE AND HOPEY COLOR SPECIAL (See Love and Rockets)
Fantagraphics Books: May, 1997 ($3.50, one-shot)

1 4.00

MAGGIE THE CAT (Also see Jon Sable, Freelance #11 & Shaman's Tears #12)
Image Comics (Creative Fire Studio): Jan, 1996 - No. 2, Feb, 1996 ($2.50, unfinished limited series)

1,2: Mike Grell-c/a/scripts 3.00

MAGICA DE SPELL (See Walt Disney Showcase #30)

MAGIC AGENT (See Forbidden Worlds & Unknown Worlds)
American Comics Group: Jan-Feb, 1962 - No. 3, May-June, 1962

	GD	VG	FN	VF	VF/NM	NM-
1-Origin & 1st app. John Force	4	8	12	25	40	55
2,3	3	6	9	18	28	38

MAGICAL POKÉMON JOURNEY
Viz Comics: 2000 - Present ($4.95, B&W, magazine-size)

1-4 5.00
Part 2: 1-3; Part 3: 1-4: 1-Includes color poster; Part 4: 1-4; Part 5: 1-4; Part 6: 1-4 5.00

MAGIC COMICS
David McKay Publications: Aug, 1939 - No. 123, Nov-Dec, 1949

	GD	VG	FN	VF	VF/NM	NM-
1-Mandrake the Magician, Henry, Popeye , Blondie, Barney Baxter, Secret Agent X-9 (not by Raymond), Bunky by Billy DeBeck & Thornton Burgess text stories illustrated by Harrison Cady begin; Henry covers begin	359	718	1077	2118	3659	5200
2	128	256	384	755	1303	1850
3	93	186	279	549	950	1350
4	76	152	228	448	774	1100
5	64	128	192	378	652	925
6-11: 8-11-Mandrake/Henry funny covers	50	100	150	315	533	750
12-16,18,20: 12-20,22-24-Serious Mandrake mystery covers	68	136	204	435	743	1050
17-The Lone Ranger begins (scarce)	90	180	270	576	988	1400
19-Classic robot-c (scarce)	155	310	465	992	1696	2400
21-Mandrake/Henry funny cover	39	78	117	240	395	550
22-24	50	100	150	315	533	750
25-1st Blondie-c	39	78	117	240	395	550
26-30: 26-Dagwood-c begin	30	60	90	177	289	400
31-40: 36-Flag-c	21	42	63	122	199	275
41-50	16	32	48	94	147	200
51-60	14	28	42	80	115	150
61-70	12	24	36	67	94	120
71-99, 107,108-Flash Gordon app; not by Raymond	10	20	30	54	72	90
100	11	22	33	60	83	105
101-106,109-123: 123-Last Dagwood-c	9	18	27	50	65	80

MAGIC FLUTE, THE (See Night Music #9-11)

MAGICIAN: APPRENTICE
Dabel Brothers/Marvel Comics (Dabel Brothers) #3 on: Mar, 2007 - No. 12, Dec, 2007 ($2.95/$2.99)

1-12-Adaptation of the Raymond E. Feist Riftwar Saga series 3.00
1,2-($5.95) 1-Wraparound variant-c by Maitz. 2-Wraparound variant-c by Booth 6.00
Collected Edition (10/06, $3.99) r/#1&2 4.00
Vol. 1 HC (2007, $19.99, dustjacket) r/#1-6; foreword by Feist 20.00
Vol. 1 SC (2007, $15.99) r/#1-6; foreword by Feist 16.00
Vol. 2 HC (2008, $19.99, dustjacket) r/#7-12 20.00

MAGIC PICKLE
Oni Press: Sept, 2001 - No. 4, Dec, 2001 ($2.95, limited series)

1-4-Scott Morse-s/a; Mahfood-a (2 pgs.) 3.00

MAGIC SWORD, THE (See Movie Classics)

Magilla Gorilla #1 © H-B

Magneto (2011 series) #1 © MAR

Magnus, Robot Fighter #27 © RH

	GD	VG	FN	VF	VF/NM	NM-
	2.0	4.0	6.0	8.0	9.0	9.2

MAGIC THE GATHERING (Title Series), **Acclaim Comics (Armada)**
...ANTIQUITIES WAR,11/95 - 2/96 ($2.50), 1-4-Paul Smith-a(p) 3.00
...ARABIAN NIGHTS, 12/95 - 1/96 ($2.50), 1,2 3.00
...COLLECTION ,'95 ($4.95), 1,2-polybagged 5.00
...CONVOCATIONS, '95 ($2.50), 1-nn-pin-ups 3.00
...ELDER DRAGONS ,'95 ($2.50), 1,2-Doug Wheatley-a 3.00
...FALLEN ANGEL ,'95 ($5.95), nn 6.00
...FALLEN EMPIRES ,9/95 - 10/95 ($2.75), 1,2 3.00
...Collection ($4.95)-polybagged 5.00
...HOMELANDS ,'95 ($5.95), nn-polybagged w/card; Hildebrandts-c 6.00
... ICE AGE (On The World of...) ,7/5 -11/95 ($2.50), 1-4: 1,2-bound-in Magic Card. 3,4-bound-in insert 3.00
...LEGEND OF JEDIT OJANEN, '96 ($2.50), 1,2 3.00
...NIGHTMARE, '95 ($2.50, one shot), 1 3.00
...THE SHADOW MAGE, 7/95 - 10/95 ($2.50), 1-4-bagged w/Magic The Gathering card 3.00
...Collection 1,2 (1995, $4.95)-Trade paperback; polybagged 5.00
...SHANDALAR ,'96 ($2.50), 1,2 3.00
...WAYFARER ,11/95 - 2/96 ($2.50), 1-5 3.00

MAGIC: THE GATHERING
IDW Publishing: Dec, 2011 - No. 4, Mar, 2012 ($3.99, limited series)
1-4-Forbeck-s/Cóccolo-a 4.00

MAGIC: THE GATHERING: GERRARD'S QUEST
Dark Horse Comics: Mar, 1998 - No. 4, June, 1998 ($2.95, limited series)
1-4: Grell-s/Mhan-a 3.00

MAGIC: THE GATHERING - PATH OF VENGEANCE
IDW Publishing: Oct, 2012 - No. 4, Feb, 2013 ($4.99, limited series, bagged with card)
1-4-Forbeck-s/Cóccolo-a 5.00

MAGIC: THE GATHERING - THEROS
IDW Publishing: Oct, 2013 - Present ($4.99, limited series, bagged with card)
1-5-Ciaramella-s/Cóccolo-a 5.00

MAGIC: THE GATHERING - THE SPELL THIEF
IDW Publishing: May, 2012 - No. 4, Aug, 2012 ($4.99, limited series, bagged with card)
1-4-Forbeck-s/Cóccolo-a 5.00

MAGIK (Illyana and Storm Limited Series)
Marvel Comics Group: Dec, 1983 - No. 4, Mar, 1984 (60¢, limited series)
1-4: 1-Characters from X-Men; Inferno begins; X-Men cameo (Buscema pencils in #1,2; c-1p. 2-4: 2-Nightcrawler app. & X-Men cameo 5.00

MAGIK (See Black Sun mini-series)
Marvel Comics: Dec, 2000 - No. 4, Mar, 2001 ($2.99, limited series)
1-4-Liam Sharp-a/Abnett & Lanning-s; Nightcrawler app. 3.00

MAGILLA GORILLA (TV) (See Kite Fun Book)
Gold Key: May, 1964 - No. 10, Dec, 1968 (Hanna-Barbera)
1-1st comic app. 9 18 27 59 117 175
2-4: 3-Vs. Yogi Bear for President. 4-1st Punkin Puss & Mushmouse, Ricochet Rabbit & Droop-a-Long 5 10 15 33 57 80
5-10: 10-Reprints 4 8 12 28 47 65

MAGILLA GORILLA (TV)(See Spotlight #4)
Charlton Comics: Nov, 1970 - No. 5, July, 1971 (Hanna-Barbera)
1 5 10 15 34 60 85
2-5 3 6 9 21 33 45

MAGNETIC MEN FEATURING MAGNETO
Marvel Comics (Amalgam): June, 1997 ($1.95, one-shot)
1-Tom Peyer-s/Barry Kitson & Dan Panosian-a 3.00

MAGNETO (See X-Men #1)
Marvel Comics: nd (Sept, 1993) (Giveaway) (one-shot)
0-Embossed foil-c by Sienkiewicz; r/Classic X-Men #19 & 12 by Bolton 5.00

MAGNETO
Marvel Comics: Nov, 1996 - No. 4, Feb, 1997 ($1.95, limited series)
1-4: Peter Milligan scripts & Kelley Jones-a(p) 3.00

MAGNETO
Marvel Comics: Mar, 2011 ($2.99, one-shot)
1-Howard Chaykin-s/a; Roger Cruz-c 3.00

MAGNETO
Marvel Comics: May, 2014 - No. 21, Oct, 2015 ($3.99)
1-21: 1-Bunn-s/Walta-a/Rivera-c. 9-12-AXIS tie-ins. 18-21-Secret Wars tie-ins 4.00

MAGNETO AND THE MAGNETIC MEN
Marvel Comics (Amalgam): Apr, 1996 ($1.95, one-shot)
1-Jeff Matsuda-a(p) 3.00

MAGNETO ASCENDANT
Marvel Comics: May, 1999 ($3.99, squarebound one-shot)
1-Reprints early Magneto appearances 4.00

MAGNETO: DARK SEDUCTION
Marvel Comics: Jun, 2000 - No. 4, Sept, 2000 ($2.99, limited series)
1-4: Nicieza-s/Cruz-a. 3,4-Avengers-c/app. 3.00

MAGNETO: NOT A HERO (X-Men Regenesis)
Marvel Comics: Jan, 2012 - No. 4, Apr, 2012 ($2.99, limited series)
1-4-Skottie Young-s/Clay Mann-a; Joseph returns 3.00

MAGNETO REX
Marvel Comics: Apr, 1999 - No. 3, July, 1999 ($2.50, limited series)
1-3-Rogue, Quicksilver app.; Peterson-a(p) 3.00

MAGNUS, ROBOT FIGHTER (...4000 A.D.)(See Doctor Solar)
Gold Key: Feb, 1963 - No. 46, Jan, 1977 (All painted covers except #5,30,31)
1-Origin & 1st app. Magnus; Aliens (1st app.) series begins 50 100 150 400 900 1400
2,3 11 22 33 76 163 250
4-10: 10-Simonson fan club illo (5/65, 1st-a?) 7 14 21 49 92 135
11-20 5 10 15 33 57 80
21,24-28: 28-Aliens ends 4 8 12 25 40 55
22,23: 22-Origin-r/#1; last 12¢ issue 4 8 12 27 44 60
29-46-Mostly reprints 3 6 9 14 20 25
...: One For One (Dark Horse Comics, 9/10, $1.00) r/#1 3.00
Russ Manning's Magnus Robot Fighter - Vol. 1 HC (Dark Horse, 2004, $49.95) r/#1-7 70.00
Russ Manning's Magnus Robot Fighter - Vol. 2 HC (DH, 6/05, $49.95) r/#8-14; forward by Steve Rude 50.00
Russ Manning's Magnus Robot Fighter - Vol. 3 HC (Dark Horse, 10/06, $49.95) r/#15-21 50.00
NOTE: ***Manning*** *a-1-22, 28-43(r).* ***Spiegle*** *a-23, 44r.*

MAGNUS ROBOT FIGHTER (Also see Vintage Magnus)
Valiant/Acclaim Comics: May, 1991 - No. 64, Feb, 1996 ($1.75/$1.95/$2.25/$2.50)
1-Nichols/Layton-c/a; 1-8 have trading cards 2 4 6 10 14 18
2-4,6,8: 4-Rai cameo. 6-1st Solar x-over. 1 3 4 6 8 10
5-Origin & 1st full app. Rai (10/91); #5-8 are in flip book format and back-c & half of book are Rai #1-4 mini-series 3 6 9 16 23 30
7-Magnus vs. Rai-c/story; 1st X-O Armor 2 4 6 11 16 20
0-Origin issue; Layton-a; ordered through mail w/coupons from 1st 8 issues plus 50¢; B. Smith trading card 3 6 9 18 28 38
0-Sold thru comic shops without trading card 3 6 9 14 19 24
9-11 6.00
12-(3.25, 44 pgs.)-Turok-c/story (1st app. in Valiant universe, 5/92); has 8 pg. Magnus story insert 3 6 9 17 26 35
13-24,26-48: 14-1st app. Isak. 15,16-Unity x-overs. 15-Miller-c. 16-Birth of Magnus. 21-New direction & new logo.24-Story cont'd in Rai & the Future Force #9. 33-Timewalker app. 36-Bound-in trading cards. 37-Rai, Starwatchers & Psi-Lords app. 44-Bound-in sneak peek card 4.00
21-Gold ink variant 2 4 6 9 12 15
25-($2.95)-Embossed silver foil-c; new costume 5.00
49-63 4.00
64-($2.50): 64-Magnus dies? 2 4 6 9 12 15
...Invasion (1994, $9.95)-r/Rai #1-4 & Magnus #5-8 12.00
Magnus Steel Nation (1994, $9.95) r/#1-4 12.00
Yearbook (1994, $3.95, 52 pgs.) 5.00
NOTE: ***Ditko/Reese*** *a-18.* ***Layton*** *a(i)-5; c-6-9i, 25; back(i)-5-8.* ***Reese*** *a(i)-22, 25, 28; c(i)-22, 24, 28.* ***Simonson*** *c-16. Prices for issues 1-8 are for trading cards and coupons intact.*

MAGNUS ROBOT FIGHTER
Acclaim Comics (Valiant Heroes): V2#1, May, 1997 - No. 18, Jun, 1998 ($2.50)
1-18: 1-Reintro Magnus; Donavon Wylie (X-O Manowar) cameo; Tom Peyer scripts & Mike McKone-c/a begin; painted variant-c exists 3.00

MAGNUS ROBOT FIGHTER
Dark Horse Comics: Aug, 2010 - No. 4, May, 2011 ($3.50)
1-4: 1-Shooter-s/Reinhold-a; covers by Swanland & Reinhold; back-up r/#1 (1963) 3.50

Magog #5 © DC

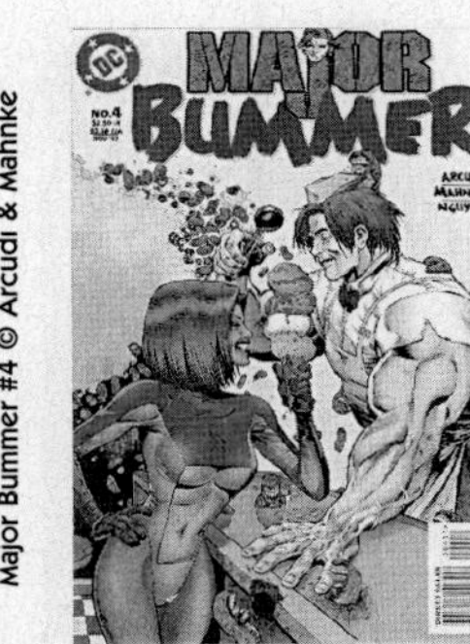

Major Bummer #4 © Arcudi & Mahnke

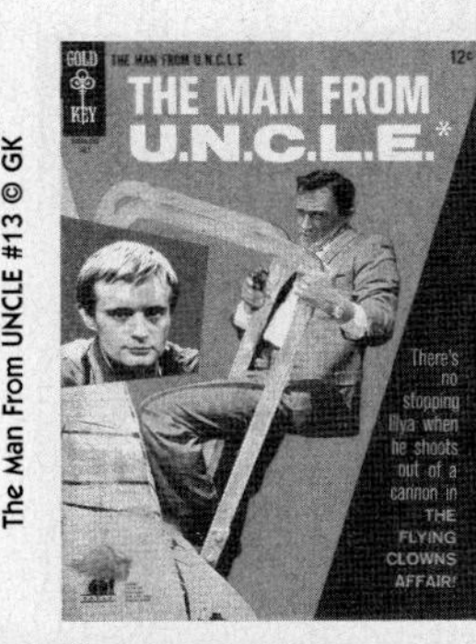

The Man From UNCLE #13 © GK

	GD 2.0	VG 4.0	FN 6.0	VF 8.0	VF/NM 9.0	NM- 9.2

MAGNUS ROBOT FIGHTER
Dynamite Entertainment: 2014 - No. 12, 2015 ($3.99)

1-12: 1-8-Fred Van Lente-s/Cory Smith-a; multiple covers on each 4.00
#0 (2014, $3.99) Takes place between #2 & #3; Roberto Castro-a 4.00

MAGNUS ROBOT FIGHTER/NEXUS
Valiant/Dark Horse Comics: Dec, 1993 - No. 2, Apr, 1994 ($2.95, lim. series)

1,2: Steve Rude painted-c & pencils in all 4.00

MAGOG (See Justice Society of America 2007 series)(Continues in Justice Society Special #1)
DC Comics: Nov, 2009 - No.12, Ot. 2010 ($2.99)

1-12: 1-Giffen-s/Porter-a/Fabry-c; variant-c by Porter. 7-Zatanna app. 3.00
...: Lethal Force TPB (2010, $14.99) r/#1-5 15.00

MAID OF THE MIST (See American Graphics)

MAI, THE PSYCHIC GIRL
Eclipse Comics: May, 1987 - No. 28, July, 1989 ($1.50, B&W, bi-weekly, 44pgs.)

1-28, 1,2-2nd print 4.00

MAJESTIC (Mr. Majestic from WildCATS)
DC Comics: Oct, 2004 - No. 4, Jan, 2005 ($2.95, limited series)

1-4-Kerschl-a/Abnett & Lanning-s. 1-Superman app.; Superman #1 cover swipe 3.00
...: Strange New Visitor TPB (2005, $14.99) r/#1-4 & Action #811, Advs. of Superman #624 & Superman #201 15.00

MAJESTIC (Mr. Majestic from WildCATS)
DC Comics (WildStorm): Mar, 2005 - No. 17, July, 2006 ($2.95/$2.99)

1-17: 1-Googe-a/Abnett & Lanning-s; Superman app. 9-Jeanty-a; Zealot app. 3.00
...: Meanwhile, Back on Earth... TPB (2006, $14.99) r/#8-12 15.00
...: The Final Cut TPB (2007, $14.99) r/#13-17 & story fro WildStorm Winter Special 15.00
...: While You Were Out TPB (2006, $12.99) r/#1-7 13.00

MAJOR BUMMER
DC Comics: Aug, 1997 - No. 15, Oct, 1998 ($2.50)

1-15: 1-Origin and 1st app. Major Bummer 3.00

MAJOR HOOPLE COMICS (See Crackajack Funnies)
Nedor Publications: nd (Jan, 1943)

	GD	VG	FN	VF	VF/NM	NM-
1-Mary Worth, Phantom Soldier app. by Moldoff	37	74	111	222	361	500

MAJOR VICTORY COMICS (Also see Dynamic Comics)
H. Clay Glover/Service Publ./Harry 'A' Chesler: 1944 - No. 3, Summer, 1945

	GD	VG	FN	VF	VF/NM	NM-
1-Origin Major Victory (patriotic hero) by C. Sultan (reprint from Dynamic #1); 1st app. Spider Woman; Nazi WWII-c	84	168	252	538	919	1300
2-Dynamic Boy app.; WWII-c	53	106	159	334	567	800
3-Rocket Boy app.; WWII-c	50	100	150	315	533	750

MALIBU ASHCAN: RAFFERTY (See Firearm #12)
Malibu Comics (Ultraverse): Nov, 1994 (99¢, B&W w/color-c; one-shot)

1-Previews "The Rafferty Saga" storyline in Firearm; Chaykin-c 3.00

MALTESE FALCON
David McKay Publications: No. 48, 1946

	GD	VG	FN	VF	VF/NM	NM-
Feature Books 48-by Dashiell Hammett	97	194	291	621	1061	1500

MALU IN THE LAND OF ADVENTURE
I. W. Enterprises: 1964 (See White Princess of Jungle #2)

	GD	VG	FN	VF	VF/NM	NM-
1-r/Avon's Slave Girl Comics #1; Severin-c	5	10	15	30	50	70

MAMMOTH COMICS
Whitman Publishing Co.(K. K. Publ.): 1938 (84 pgs.) (B&W, 8-1/2x11-1/2")

	GD	VG	FN	VF	VF/NM	NM-
1-Alley Oop, Terry & the Pirates, Dick Tracy, Little Orphan Annie, Wash Tubbs, Moon Mullins, Smilin' Jack, Tailspin Tommy, Don Winslow, Dan Dunn, Smokey Stover & other reprints (scarce)	239	478	717	1530	2615	3700

MAN AGAINST TIME
Image Comics (Motown Machineworks): May, 1996 - No. 4, Aug, 1996 ($2.25, lim. series)

1-4: 1-Simonson-c. 2,3-Leon-c. 4-Barreto & Leon-c 3.00

MAN-BAT (See Batman Family, Brave & the Bold, & Detective #400)
National Periodical Publ./DC Comics: Dec-Jan, 1975-76 - No. 2, Feb-Mar, 1976; Dec, 1984

	GD	VG	FN	VF	VF/NM	NM-
1-Ditko-a(p); Aparo-c; Batman app.; 1st app. She-Bat?; 1st app. Baron Tyme	3	6	9	16	23	30
2-Aparo-c	2	4	6	10	14	18

1 (12/84)-N. Adams-r(3)/Det.(Vs. Batman on-c) 6.00

MAN-BAT
DC Comics: Feb, 1996 - No. 3, Apr, 1996 ($2.25, limited series)

1-3: Dixon scripts in all. 2-Killer Croc-c/app. 3.00

MAN-BAT
DC Comics: Jun, 2006 - No. 5, Oct, 2006 ($2.99, limited series)

1-5: Bruce Jones-s/Mike Huddleston-a/c. 1-Hush app. 3.00

MAN CALLED A-X, THE
Malibu Comics (Bravura): Nov, 1994 - No. 4, Jun, 1995 ($2.95, limited series)

0-4: Marv Wolfman scripts & Shawn McManus-c/a. 0-(2/95). 1-"1A" on cover 3.00

MAN CALLED A-X, THE
DC Comics: Oct, 1997 - No. 8, May, 1998 ($2.50)

1-8: Marv Wolfman scripts & Shawn McManus-c/a. 3.00

MAN CALLED KEV, A (See The Authority)
DC Comics (WildStorm): Sept, 2006 - No. 5, Feb, 2007 ($2.99, limited series)

1-5-Ennis-s/Ezquerra-a/Fabry-c 3.00
TPB (2007, $14.99) r/#1-5; cover gallery 15.00

MAN COMICS
Marvel/Atlas Comics (NPI): Dec, 1949 - No. 28, Sept, 1953 (#1-6: 52 pgs.)

	GD	VG	FN	VF	VF/NM	NM-
1-Tuska-a	34	68	102	199	325	450
2-Tuska-a	18	36	54	105	165	225
3-6	15	30	45	85	130	175
7,8	15	30	45	83	124	165
9-13,15: 9-Format changes to war	15	30	45	83	124	165
14-Henkel (3 pgs.); Pakula-a	15	30	45	84	127	170
16-21,23-28: 28-Crime issue (Bob Brant)	14	28	42	81	118	155
22-Krigstein-a, 5 pgs.	15	30	45	85	130	175

NOTE: ***Berg*** *a-14, 15, 19.* ***Colan*** *a-9, 21, 23.* ***Everett*** *a-8, 22; c-22, 25.* ***Heath*** *a-11, 13, 16, 17, 21.* ***Kubertish*** *a-by* ***Bob Brown****-3.* ***Maneely*** *a-11-13; c-10, 11, 16.* ***Reinman*** *a-11.* ***Robinson*** *a-7, 10, 14.* ***Robert Sale*** *a-9, 11.* ***Sinnott*** *a-22, 23.* ***Tuska*** *a-14, 23.*

MANDRAKE THE MAGICIAN (See Defenders Of The Earth, 123, 46, 52, 55, Giant Comic Album, King Comics, Magic Comics, The Phantom #21, Tiny Tot Funnies & Wow Comics, '36)

MANDRAKE THE MAGICIAN (See Harvey Comics Hits #53)
David McKay Publ./Dell/King Comics (All 12¢): 1938 - 1948; Sept, 1966 - No. 10, Nov, 1967

	GD	VG	FN	VF	VF/NM	NM-
Feature Books 18,19,23 (1938)	97	194	291	621	1061	1500
Feature Books 46	55	110	165	352	601	850
Feature Books 52,55	50	100	150	315	533	750
Four Color 752 (11/56)	10	20	30	64	132	200
1-Begin S.O.S. Phantom, ends #3	6	12	18	37	66	95
2-7,9: 4-Girl Phantom app. 5-Flying Saucer-c/story. 5,6-Brick Bradford app. 7-Origin Lothar. 9-Brick Bradford app.	3	6	9	21	33	45
8-Jeff Jones-a (4 pgs.)	4	8	12	23	37	50
10-Rip Kirby app.; Raymond-a (14 pgs.)	4	8	12	27	44	60

MANDRAKE THE MAGICIAN
Marvel Comics: Apr, 1995 - No. 2, May, 1995 ($2.95, unfinished limited series)

1,2: Mike Barr scripts 3.00

MAN-EATING COW (See Tick #7,8)
New England Comics: July, 1992 - No. 10, 1994? ($2.75, B&W, limited series)

1-10 3.00
Man-Eating Cow Bonanza (6/96, $4.95, 128 pgs.)-r/#1-4. 5.00

MAN FROM ATLANTIS (TV)
Marvel Comics: Feb, 1978 - No. 7, Aug, 1978

	GD	VG	FN	VF	VF/NM	NM-
1-(84 pgs.)-Sutton-a(p), Buscema-c; origin & cast photos	2	4	6	8	12	15

2-7 6.00

MAN FROM PLANET X, THE
Planet X Productions: 1987 (no price; probably unlicensed)

1-Reprints Fawcett Movie Comic 3.00

MAN FROM U.N.C.L.E., THE (TV) (Also see The Girl From Uncle)
Gold Key: Feb, 1965 - No. 22, Apr, 1969 (All photo-c)

	GD	VG	FN	VF	VF/NM	NM-
1	12	24	36	83	182	280
2-Photo back c-2-8	7	14	21	44	82	120
3-10: 7-Jet Dream begins (1st app., also see Jet Dream) (all new stories)	5	10	15	33	57	80
11-22: 19-Last 12¢ issue. 21,22-Reprint #10 & 7	5	10	15	30	50	70

MAN FROM U.N.C.L.E., THE (TV)
Entertainment Publishing: 1987 - No. 11 ($1.50/$1.75, B&W)

1-7 ($1.50), 8-11 ($1.75) 4.00

MAN FROM WELLS FARGO (TV)
Dell Publishing Co.: No. 1287, Feb-Apr, 1962 - May-July, 1962 (Photo-c)

	GD	VG	FN	VF	VF/NM	NM-
Four Color 1287, #01-495-207	5	10	15	33	57	80

Manhattan Projects #11 © Hickman & Pitarra

Manhunter (2004 series) #21 © DC

The Man of Steel #5 © DC

GD 2.0 | VG 4.0 | FN 6.0 | VF 8.0 | VF/NM 9.0 | NM- 9.2

GD 2.0 | VG 4.0 | FN 6.0 | VF 8.0 | VF/NM 9.0 | NM- 9.2

MANGA DARKCHYLDE (Also see Darkchylde titles)
Dark Horse Comics: Feb, 2005 - No. 5 ($2.99, limited series)
1,2-Randy Queen-s/a; manga-style pre-teen Ariel Chylde 3.00

MANGA SHI (See Tomoe)
Crusade Entertainment: Aug, 1996 ($2.95)
1-Printed back to front (manga-style) 3.00

MANGA SHI 2000
Crusade Entertainment: Feb, 1997 - No. 3, June, 1997 ($2.95, mini-series)
1-3: 1-Two covers 3.00

MANGA ZEN (Also see Zen Intergalactic Ninja)
Zen Comics (Fusion Studios): 1996 - No. 3, 1996 ($2.50, B&W)
1-3 3.00

MANGAZINE
Antarctic Press: Aug, 1985 - No. 5, Dec, 1986 (B&W)
1-5: 1-Soft paper-c 3.00

MANHATTAN PROJECTS, THE
Image Comics: Mar, 2012 - No. 25, Nov, 2014 ($3.50)
1-Hickman-s/Pitarra-a; intro. Robert and Joseph Oppenheimer 40.00
2 20.00
3 10.00
4-6 8.00
7-25: 10,15,19-Browne-a 4.00

MANHATTAN PROJECTS, THE : THE SUN BEYOND THE STARS
Image Comics: Mar, 2015 - No. 4, Feb, 2016 ($3.50)
1-4-Hickman-s/Pitarra-a 3.50

MANHUNT! (Becomes Red Fox #15 on)
Magazine Enterprises: 10/47 - No. 11, 8/48; #13,14, 1953 (no #12)
1-Red Fox by L. B. Cole, Undercover Girl by Whitney, Space Ace begin (1st app.); negligee panels 71 142 213 454 777 1100
2-Electrocution-c 77 154 231 493 847 1200
3-6: 6-Bondage-c 41 82 123 256 428 600
7-10: 7-Space Ace ends. 8-Trail Colt begins (intro/1st app., 5/48) by Guardineer; Trail Colt-c. 10-G. Ingels-a 37 74 111 222 361 500
11(8/48)-Frazetta-a, 7 pgs.; The Duke, Scotland Yard begin 50 100 150 315 533 750
13(A-1 #63)-Frazetta, r-/Trail Colt #1, 7 pgs. 40 80 120 246 411 575
14(A-1 #77)-Bondage/hypo-c; last L. B. Cole Red Fox; Ingels-a 129 258 387 826 1413 2000

NOTE: *Guardineer a-1-5; c-8. Whitney a-2-14; c-1-6, 10. Red Fox by L. B. Cole-#1-14. #15 was advertised but came out as Red Fox #15.*

MANHUNTER (See Adventure #58, 73, Brave & the Bold, Detective Comics, 1st Issue Special, House of Mystery #143 and Justice League of America)
DC Comics: 1984 ($2.50, 76 pgs; high quality paper)
1-Simonson-c/a(r)/Detective; Batman app. 5.00

MANHUNTER
DC Comics: July, 1988 - No. 24, Apr, 1990 ($1.00)
1-24: 8,9-Flash app. 9-Invasion. 17-Batman-c/sty 3.00

MANHUNTER
DC Comics: No. 0, Nov, 1994 - No. 12, Nov, 1995 ($1.95/$2.25)
0-12 3.00

MANHUNTER (Also see Batman: Streets of Gotham)
DC Comics: Oct, 2004 - No. 38, Mar, 2009 ($2.50/$2.99)
1-21: 1-Intro. Kate Spencer; Saiz-a/Jae Lee-c/Andreyko-s. 2,3 Shadow Thief app. 13,14-Omac x-over. 20-One Year Later 3.00
22-30: 22-Begin $2.99-c. 23-Sandra Knight app. 27-Chaykin-c. 28-Batman app. 3.00
31-38: 31-(8/08) Gaydos-a. 33,34-Suicide Squad app. 3.00
...: Forgotten (2009, $17.99) r/#31-38 18.00
...: Origins (2007, $17.99) r/#15-23 18.00
...: Street Justice (2005, $12.99) r/#1-5; Andreyko intro. 13.00
...: Trial By Fire (2007, $17.99) r/#6-14 18.00
...: Unleashed (2008, $17.99) r/#24-30 18.00

MANHUNTER: ...
DC Comics: 1979, 1999
The Complete Saga TPB (1979) Reprints stories from Detective Comics #437-443 by Goodwin and Simonson 40.00
The Special Edition TPB (1999, $9.95) r/stories from Detective Comics #437-443 12.00

MANIFEST DESTINY
Image Comics (Skybound): Nov, 2013 - Present ($2.99)
1-Lewis & Clark in 1804 American Frontier encountering zombies & other creatures; Chris Dingess-s/Matthew Roberts-a 3 6 9 16 24 32
2 1 3 4 6 8 10
3-26: 25-Back-up Sacagawea story 3.00

MANIFEST ETERNITY
DC Comics: Aug, 2006 - No. 6, Jan, 2007 ($2.99)
1-6-Lobdell-s/Nguyen-a/c 3.00

MAN IN BLACK (See Thrill-O-Rama) (Also see All New Comics, Front Page, Green Hornet #31, Strange Story & Tally-Ho Comics)
Harvey Publications: Sept, 1957 - No. 4, Mar, 1958
1-Bob Powell-c/a 18 36 54 105 165 225
2-4: Powell-c/a 14 28 42 80 115 150

MAN IN BLACK
Lorne-Harvey Publications (Recollections): 1990 - No. 2, July, 1991 (B&W)
1,2 4.00

MAN IN FLIGHT (Disney, TV)
Dell Publishing Co.: No. 836, Sept, 1957
Four Color 836 6 12 18 41 76 110

MAN IN SPACE (Disney, TV, see Dell Giant #27)
Dell Publishing Co.: No. 716, Aug, 1956 - No. 954, Nov, 1958
Four Color 716-A science feat. from Tomorrowland 7 14 21 49 92 135
Four Color 954-Satellites 6 12 18 41 76 110

MANKIND (WWF Wrestling)
Chaos Comics: Sept, 1999 ($2.95, one-shot)
1-Regular and photo-c 3.00
1-Premium Edition ($10.00) Dwayne Turner & Danny Miki-c 10.00

MANN AND SUPERMAN
DC Comics: 2000 ($5.95, prestige format, one-shot)
nn-Michael T. Gilbert-s/a 6.00

MAN OF STEEL, THE (Also see Superman: The Man of Steel)
DC Comics: 1986 (June release) - No. 6, 1986 (75¢, limited series)
1-6: 1-Silver logo; Byrne-c/a/scripts in all; origin, 1-Alternate-c for newsstand sales,1-Distr. to toy stores by So Much Fun, 2-6: 2-Intro. Lois Lane, Jimmy Olsen. 3-Intro/origin Magpie; Batman-c/story. 4-Intro. new Lex Luthor 1 2 3 5 6 8
1-6-Silver Editions (1993, $1.95)-r/1-6 3.00
...The Complete Saga nn (SC)-Contains #1-6, given away in contest; limited edition 4 8 12 28 47 65

NOTE: *Issues 1-6 were released between Action #583 (9/86) & Action #584 (1/87) plus Superman #423 (9/86) & Advs. of Superman #424 (1/87).*

MAN OF THE ATOM (See Solar, Man of the Atom Vol. 2)

MAN OF WAR (See Liberty Guards & Liberty Scouts)
Centaur Publications: Nov, 1941 - No. 2, Jan, 1942
1-The Fire-Man, Man of War, The Sentinel, Liberty Guards, & Vapo-Man begin; Gustavson-c/a; Flag-c 206 412 618 1318 2259 3200
2-Intro The Ferret; Gustavson-c/a 148 296 444 947 1624 2300

MAN OF WAR
Eclipse Comics: Aug, 1987 - No. 3, Feb, 1988 ($1.75, Baxter paper)
1-3: Bruce Jones scripts 3.00

MAN OF WAR (See The Protectors)
Malibu Comics: 1993 - No, 8, Feb, 1994 ($1.95/$2.50/$2.25)
1-5 ($1.95)-Newsstand Editions w/different-c 3.00
1-8: 1-5-Collector's Edi. w/poster. 6-8 ($2.25): 6-Polybagged w/Skycap. 8-Vs. Rocket Rangers 4.00

MAN O' MARS
Fiction House Magazines: 1953; 1964
1-Space Rangers; Whitman-c 71 142 213 454 777 1100
I.W. Reprint #1-r/Man O'Mars #1 & Star Pirate; Murphy Anderson-a 6 12 18 41 76 110

MANTECH ROBOT WARRIORS
Archie Enterprises, Inc.: Sept, 1984 - No. 4, Apr, 1985 (75¢)
1-4: Ayers-c/a(p). 1-Buckler-c(i) 4.00

MAN-THING (See Fear, Giant-Size..., Marvel Comics Presents, Marvel Fanfare, Monsters Unleashed, Power Record Comics & Savage Tales)

Man-Thing #14 © MAR

The Mantle #1 © Brisson & Level

The Many Ghosts of Dr. Graves #41 © CC

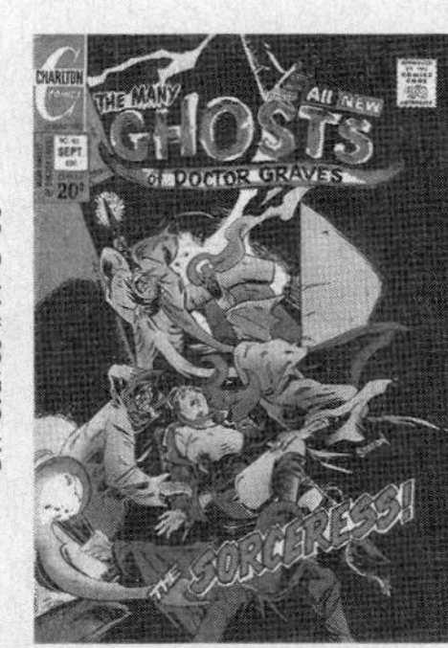

	GD 2.0	VG 4.0	FN 6.0	VF 8.0	VF/NM 9.0	NM- 9.2

Marvel Comics Group: Jan, 1974 - No. 22, Oct, 1975; V2#1, Nov, 1979 - V2#11, July, 1981

1-Howard the Duck(2nd app.) cont'd/Fear #19	7	14	21	46	86	125
2	3	6	9	17	26	35
3-1st app. original Foolkiller	3	6	9	15	22	28
4-Origin Foolkiller; last app. 1st Foolkiller	3	6	9	14	20	26
5-11-Ploog-a. 11-Foolkiller cameo (flashback)	3	6	9	14	20	26
12-22: 19-1st app. Scavenger. 20-Spidey cameo. 21-Origin Scavenger, Man-Thing. 22-Howard the Duck cameo	2	4	6	9	13	16
V2#1(1979)	2	4	6	9	12	15
V2#2-11: 4-Dr. Strange-c/app. 11-Mayerik-a						6.00

NOTE: *Alcala a-14. **Brunner** c-1. J. **Buscema** a-12p, 13p, 16p. **Gil Kane** c-4p, 10p, 12-20p, 21. **Mooney** a-17, 18, 19p, 20-22, V2#1-3p. **Ploog** Man-Thing-5p, 6p, 7, 8, 9-11p; c-5, 6, 8, 9, 11. **Sutton** a-13i. No. 19 says #10 in indicia.*

MAN-THING (Volume Three, continues in Strange Tales #1 (9/98))
Marvel Comics: Dec, 1997 - No. 8, July, 1998 ($2.99)

1-8-DeMatteis-s/Sharp-a. 2-Two covers. 6-Howard the Duck-c/app. 3.00

MAN-THING (Prequel to 2005 movie)
Marvel Comics: Sept, 2004 - No. 3, Nov, 2004 ($2.99, limited series)

1-3-Hans Rodionoff-s/Kyle Hotz-a 3.00
...: Whatever Knows Fear... (2005, $12.99, TPB) r/#1-3, Savage Tales #1, Adv. Into Fear #16 13.00

MANTLE
Image Comics: May, 2015 - No. 5, Sept, 2015 ($3.99, limited series)

1-5-Brisson-s/Level-a 4.00

MANTRA
Malibu Comics (Ultraverse): July, 1993 - No. 24, Aug, 1995 ($1.95/$2.50)

1-Polybagged w/trading card & coupon						5.00
1-Newsstand edition w/o trading card or coupon						3.00
1-Full cover holographic edition	2	4	6	8	10	12
1-Ultra-limited silver foil-c	1	2	3	5	6	8
2,3,5-9,11-24: 2-($2.50-Newsstand edition bagged w/card. 3-Intro Warstrike & Kismet. 6-Break-Thru x-over. 7-Prime app.; origin Prototype by Jurgens/Austin (2 pgs.). 11-New costume. 17-Intro NecroMantra & Pinnacle; prelude to Godwheel						3.00
4-($2.50, 48 pgs.)-Rune flip-c/story by B. Smith (3 pgs.)						4.00
10-($3.50, 68 pgs.)-Flip-c w/Ultraverse Premiere #2						4.00
Giant Size 1 (7/94, $2.50, 44 pgs.)						4.00
...Spear of Destiny 1,2 (4/95, $2.50, 36pgs.)						3.00

MANTRA (2nd Series) (Also See Black September)
Malibu Comics (Ultraverse): Infinity, Sept, 1995 - No. 7, Apr, 1996 ($1.50)

Infinity (9/95, $1.50)-Black September x-over, Intro new Mantra 3.00
1-7: 1-(10/95). 5-Return of Eden (original Mantra). 6,7-Rush app. 3.00

MAN WITH NO NAME, THE (Based on the Clint Eastwood gunslinger character)
Dynamite Entertainment: 2008 - No. 11, 2009 ($3.50)

1-11: 1-Gage-s/Dias-a/Isanove-c. 7-Bernard-a 3.50

MAN WITH THE SCREAMING BRAIN (Based on screenplay by Bruce Campbell & David Goodman)
Dark Horse Comics: Apr, 2005 - No. 4, July, 2005 ($2.99, limited series)

1-4-Campbell & Goodman-s; Remender-a/c. 1-Variant-c by Noto. 3-Powell var-c. 4-Mignola var-c 3.00
TPB (11/05, $13.95) r/#1-4; David Goodman intro.; cover gallery 14.00

MAN WITH THE X-RAY EYES, THE (See X,... under Movie Comics)

MANY GHOSTS OF DR. GRAVES, THE (Doctor Graves #73 on)
Charlton Comics: 5/67 - No. 60, 12/76; No. 61, 9/77 - No. 62, 10/77; No. 63, 2/78 - No. 65, 4/78; No. 66, 6/81 - No. 72, 5/82

1-Ditko-a; Palais-a; early issues 12¢-c	7	14	21	49	92	135
2-6,8,10	3	6	9	19	30	40
7,9-Ditko-a	4	8	12	23	37	50
11-13,16-18-Ditko-c/a	3	6	9	19	30	40
14,19,23,25	2	4	6	10	14	18
15,20,21-Ditko-a	3	6	9	14	20	25
22,24,26,27,29-35,38,40-Ditko-c/a	3	6	9	15	22	28
28-Ditko-c	3	6	9	14	20	25
36,46,56,57,59,61,66,67,69,71	2	4	6	8	10	12
37,41,43,51,60-Ditko-a	2	4	6	9	13	16
39,58-Ditko-c. 39-Sutton-a. 58-Ditko-a	2	4	6	9	13	16
42,44,53-Sutton-c; Ditko-a. 42-Sutton-a	2	4	6	9	13	16
45-(5/74) 2nd Newton comic work (8 pgs.); new logo; Sutton-c	2	4	6	11	16	20
47-Newton, Sutton, Ditko-a	2	4	6	10	14	18
48-Ditko, Sutton-a	2	4	6	9	13	16
49-Newton-c/a; Sutton-a.	2	4	6	8	11	14
50-Sutton-a	2	4	6	8	10	12
52-Newton-c; Ditko-a	2	4	6	9	13	16
54-Early Byrne-c; Ditko-a	2	4	6	10	14	18
55-Ditko-c; Sutton-a	2	4	6	9	13	16
62-65,68-Ditko-c/a. 65-Sutton-a	2	4	6	11	16	20
70,72-Ditko-a	2	4	6	10	14	18
Modern Comics Reprint 12,25 (1978)						6.00

NOTE: ***Aparo** a-4, 5, 7, 8, 66r, 69r; c-8, 14, 19, 66r, 67r. **Byrne** c-54. **Ditko** a-1, 7, 9, 11-13, 15-18, 20-22, 24, 26, 27, 29, 30-35, 37, 38, 40-44, 47, 48, 51-54, 58, 60r-65r, 70, 72; c-11-13, 16-18, 22, 24, 26-35, 38, 40, 55, 58, 62-65. **Howard** a-38, 39, 45i, 65; c-48. **Kim** a-36, 46, 52. **Larson** a-58. **Morisi** a-13, 14, 23, 26. **Newton** a-45, 47p, 49p; c-49, 52. **Staton** a-36, 37, 41, 43. **Sutton** a-39, 42, 47-50, 55, 65; c-42, 44, 45; painted c-53. **Zeck** a-56, 59.*

MANY LOVES OF DOBIE GILLIS (TV)
National Periodical Publications: May-June, 1960 - No. 26, Oct, 1964

1-Most covers by Bob Oskner	24	48	72	168	372	575
2-5	13	26	39	89	195	300
6-10: 10-Last 10¢-c	10	20	30	64	132	200
11-26: 20-Drucker-a. 24-(3-4/64). 25-(9/64)	9	18	27	59	117	175

MANY WORLDS OF TESLA STRONG, THE (Also see Tom Strong)
America's Best Comics: July, 2003 ($5.95, one-shot)

1-Two covers by Timm & Art Adams; art by various incl. Campbell, Cho, Noto, Hughes 6.00

MARA
Image Comics: Dec, 2012 - No. 6, Oct, 2013 ($2.99)

1-6-Brian Wood-s/Ming Doyle-a 3.00

MARAUDER'S MOON (See Luke Short, Four Color #848)

MARCH OF COMICS (See Promotional Comics section)

MARCH OF CRIME (Formerly My Love Affair #1-6) (See Fox Giants)
Fox Features Synd.: No. 7, July, 1950 - No. 2, Sept, 1950; No. 3, Sept, 1951

7(#1)(7/50)-True crime stories; Wood-a	44	88	132	277	469	660
2(9/50)-Wood-a (exceptional)	42	84	126	267	451	635
3(9/51)	23	46	69	136	223	310

MARCO POLO (Also see Classic Comics #27
Charlton Comics Group: 1962 (Movie classic)

nn (Scarce)-Glanzman-c/a (25 pgs.)	10	20	30	66	138	210

MARC SILVESTRI SKETCHBOOK
Image Comics (Top Cow): Jan, 2004 ($2.99, one-shot)

1-Character sketches, concept artwork, storyboards of Witchblade, Darkness & others 3.00

MARC SPECTOR: MOON KNIGHT (Also see Moon Knight)
Marvel Comics: June, 1989 - No. 60, Mar, 1994 ($1.50/$1.75, direct sales)

1	1	2	3	5	6	8
2-24,26-49,51-54,58,59: 4-Intro new Midnight. 8,9-Punisher app. 15-Silver Sable app. 19-21-Spider-Man & Punisher app. 32,33-Hobgoblin II (Macendale) & Spider-Man (in black costume) app. 35-38-Punisher story. 42-44-Infinity War x-over. 46-Demogoblin app. 51,53-Gambit app. 55-New look. 57-Spider-Man-c/story. 60-Moon Knight dies						3.00
25,50: 25-(52 pgs.)-Ghost Rider app. 50-(56 pgs.)-Special die-cut-c						4.00
55-New look; Platt-c/a	3	6	9	16	23	30
56,60-Platt-c/a	1	3	4	6	8	10
57-Spider-Man-c/app.; Platt-c/a	3	6	9	17	26	35
58,59-Platt-c						6.00
...: Divided We Fall ($4.95, 52 pgs.)						5.00
Special 1 (1992, $2.50)						4.00

NOTE: *Cowan c(p) 20-23. **Guice** c-20. **Heath** c/a-4. **Platt**-a 55-57,60; c-55-60.*

MARGARET O'BRIEN (See The Adventures of...)

MARGE'S LITTLE LULU (Continues as Little Lulu from #207 on)
Dell Publishing Co./Gold Key #165-206: No. 74, 6/45 - No. 164, 7-9/62; No. 165, 10/62 - No. 206, 8/72

Marjorie Henderson Buell, born in Philadelphia, Pa., in 1904, created Little Lulu, a cartoon character that appeared weekly in the Saturday Evening Post from Feb. 23, 1935 through Dec. 30, 1944. She was not responsible for any of the comic books. **John Stanley** did pencils only on all Little Lulu comics through at least #135 (1959). He did pencils and inks on Four Color #74 & 97. **Irving Tripp** began inking stories from #1 on, and remained the comic's illustrator throughout its entire run. **Stanley** did storyboards (layouts), pencils, and scripts in all cases and inking only on covers. His word balloons were written in cursive. **Tripp** and occasionally other artists at Western Publ. in Poughkeepsie, N.Y. blew up the pencilled pages, inked the blowups, and lettered them. **Arnold Drake** did storyboards, pencils and scripts starting with #197 (1970) on, amidst reprinted issues. **Buell** sold her rights exclusively to Western Publ. in Dec., 1971. The earlier issues had to be approved by **Buell** prior to publication.

Four Color 74('45)-Intro Lulu, Tubby & Alvin	172	344	516	1419	3210	5000
Four Color 97(2/46)	64	128	192	512	1156	1800
(Above two books are all John Stanley - cover, pencils, and inks.)						
Four Color 110('46)-1st Alvin Story Telling Time; 1st app. Willy; variant cover exists	40	80	120	296	673	1050
Four Color 115-1st app. Boys' Clubhouse	39	78	117	289	657	1025

Marge's Little Lulu #25 © M. Buell

Margie Comics #40 © MAR

Marineman #1 © Ian Churchill

	GD 2.0	VG 4.0	FN 6.0	VF 8.0	VF/NM 9.0	NM- 9.2
Four Color 120, 131: 120-1st app. Eddie	34	68	102	245	548	850
Four Color 139('47),146,158	32	64	96	230	515	800
Four Color 165 (10/47)-Smokes doll hair & has wild hallucinations. 1st Tubby detective story	32	64	96	230	515	800
1(1-2/48)-Lulu's Diary feature begins	71	142	213	568	1284	2000
2-1st app. Gloria; 1st app. Miss Feeny	31	62	93	223	499	775
3-5	27	54	81	194	435	675
6-10: 7-1st app. Annie; Xmas-c	21	42	63	150	330	510
11-20: 18-X-Mas-c. 19-1st app. Wilbur. 20-1st app. Mr. McNabbem	17	34	51	114	252	390
21-30: 26-r/F.C. 110. 30-Xmas-c	15	30	45	100	220	340
31-38,40: 35-1st Mumday story	12	24	36	81	176	270
39-Intro. Witch Hazel in "That Awful Witch Hazel"	12	24	36	82	179	275
41-60: 42-Xmas-c. 45-2nd Witch Hazel app. 49-Gives Stanley & others credit	10	20	30	69	147	225
61-80: 63-1st app. Chubby (Tubby's cousin). 68-1st app. Prof. Cleff. 78-Xmas-c. 80-Intro. Little Itch (2/55)	9	18	27	57	111	165
81-99: 90-Xmas-c	7	14	21	46	86	125
100	7	14	21	49	92	135
101-130: 123-1st app. Fifi	6	12	18	37	66	95
131-164: 135-Last Stanley-p	5	10	15	33	57	80
165-Giant; ...in Paris ('62)	9	18	27	61	123	185
166-Giant; ...Christmas Diary (1962 - '63)	9	18	27	61	123	185
167-169	4	8	12	28	47	65
170,172,175,176,178-196,198-200-Stanley-r. 182-1st app. Little Scarecrow Boy	3	6	9	17	26	35
171,173,174,177,197	3	6	9	16	23	30
201,203,206-Last issue to carry Marge's name	3	6	9	14	20	26
202,204,205-Stanley-r	3	6	9	16	23	30
...Summer Camp 1(8/67-G.K.-Giant) '57-58-r	5	10	15	35	63	90
...Trick 'N' Treat 1(12¢)(12/62-Gold Key)	6	12	18	40	73	105
Marge's Lulu and Tubby in Japan (15¢)(5-7/62) 01476-207	7	14	21	44	82	120

NOTE: *See Dell Giant Comics #23, 29, 36, 42, 50, & Dell Giants for annuals. All Giants not by Stanley from L.L. on Vacation (7/54) on. Irving Tripp a-#1-on. Christmas c-7, 18, 30, 42, 78, 90, 126, 166, 250. Summer Camp issues #173, 177, 181, 189, 197, 201, 206.*

MARGE'S LITTLE LULU (See Golden Comics Digest #19, 23, 27, 29, 33, 36, 40, 43, 46, & March of Comics #251, 267, 275, 293, 307, 323, 335, 349, 355, 369, 385, 406, 417, 427, 439, 456, 468, 475, 488)

MARGE'S TUBBY (Little Lulu)(See Dell Giants)
Dell Publishing Co./Gold Key: No. 381, Aug, 1952 - No. 49, Dec-Feb, 1961-62

	GD	VG	FN	VF	VF/NM	NM-
Four Color 381(#1)-Stanley script; Irving Tripp-a	18	36	54	126	281	435
Four Color 430,444-Stanley-a	11	22	33	73	157	240
Four Color 461 (4/53)-1st Tubby & Men From Mars story; Stanley-a	10	20	30	68	144	220
5 (7-9/53)-Stanley-a	8	16	24	54	102	150
6-10	7	14	21	44	82	120
11-20	5	10	15	34	60	85
21-30	5	10	15	30	50	70
31-49	4	8	12	27	44	60
...& the Little Men From Mars No. 30020-410(10/64-G.K.)-25¢, 68 pgs.	7	14	21	44	82	120

NOTE: ***John Stanley** did all storyboards & scripts through at least #35 (1959). **Lloyd White** did all art except F.C. 381, 430, 444, 461 & #5.*

MARGIE (See My Little...)

MARGIE (TV)
Dell Publ. Co.: No. 1307, Mar-May, 1962 - No. 2, July-Sept, 1962 (Photo-c)

	GD	VG	FN	VF	VF/NM	NM-
Four Color 1307(#1)	6	12	18	40	73	105
2	4	8	12	28	47	65

MARGIE COMICS (Formerly Comedy Comics; Reno Browne #50 on)
(Also see Cindy Comics & Teen Comics)
Marvel Comics (ACI): No. 35, Winter, 1946-47 - No. 49, Dec, 1949

	GD	VG	FN	VF	VF/NM	NM-
35	26	52	78	154	252	350
36-38,42,45,47-49	15	30	45	88	137	185
39,41,43(2),44,46-Kurtzman's "Hey Look"	16	32	48	94	147	200
40-Three "Hey Looks", three "Giggles 'n' Grins" by Kurtzman	18	36	54	103	162	220

MARINEMAN (Ian Churchill's...)
Image Comics: Dec, 2010 - No. 6, Jun, 2011 ($3.99/$4.99)

	NM-
1-5-Ian Churchill-s/a/c	4.00
6-($4.99) Origin revealed	5.00

MARINES (See Tell It to the...)

MARINES ATTACK
Charlton Comics: Aug, 1964 - No. 9, Feb-Mar, 1966

	GD	VG	FN	VF	VF/NM	NM-
1-Glanzman-a begins	4	8	12	23	37	50
2-9: 8-1st Vietnam war-c/story	3	6	9	16	23	30

MARINES AT WAR (Formerly Tales of the Marines #4)
Atlas Comics (OPI): No. 5, Apr, 1957 - No. 7, Aug, 1957

	GD	VG	FN	VF	VF/NM	NM-
5-7	14	28	42	82	121	160

NOTE: ***Colan** a-5. **Drucker** a-5. **Everett** a-5. **Maneely** a-5. **Orlando** a-7. **Severin** c-5.*

MARINES IN ACTION
Atlas News Co.: June, 1955 - No. 14, Sept, 1957

	GD	VG	FN	VF	VF/NM	NM-
1-Rock Murdock, Boot Camp Brady begin	20	40	60	117	189	260
2-14	14	28	42	82	121	160

NOTE: ***Berg** a-2, 8, 9, 11, 14. **Heath** c-2, 9. **Maneely** c-1, 3. **Severin** a-4; c-7-11, 14.*

MARINES IN BATTLE
Atlas Comics (ACI No. 1-12/WPI No. 13-25): Aug, 1954 - No. 25, Sept, 1958

	GD	VG	FN	VF	VF/NM	NM-
1-Heath-c; Iron Mike McGraw by Heath; history of U.S. Marine Corps. begins	36	72	108	211	343	475
2-Heath-c	18	36	54	107	169	230
3-6,8-10: 4-Last precode (2/55); Romita-a	15	30	45	85	130	175
7-Kubert/Moskowitz-a (6 pgs.)	15	30	45	86	133	180
11-16,18-21,24	15	30	45	83	124	165
17-Williamson-a (3 pgs.)	15	30	45	88	137	185
22,25-Torres-a	15	30	45	83	124	165
23-Crandall-a; Mark Murdock app.	15	30	45	84	127	170

NOTE: ***Berg** a-22. **G. Colan** a-22, 23. **Drucker** a-6. **Everett** a-4, 15; c-21. **Heath** c-1, 2, 4. **Maneely** c-23, 24. **Orlando** a-14. **Pakula** a-6, 23. **Powell** a-16. **Severin** a-22; c-12. **Sinnott** a-23. **Tuska** a-15.*

MARINE WAR HEROES (Charlton Premiere #19 on)
Charlton Comics: Jan, 1964 - No. 18, Mar, 1967

	GD	VG	FN	VF	VF/NM	NM-
1-Montes/Bache-c/a	4	8	12	23	37	50
2-16,18: 11-Vietnam sty w/VC tunnels & moles.14,18-Montes/Bache-a	3	6	9	16	23	30
17-Tojo's plan to bomb Pearl Harbor & 1st Atomic bomb blast on Japan	3	6	9	21	33	45

MARK, THE (Also see Mayhem)
Dark Horse Comics: Dec, 1993 - No. 4, Mar, 1994 ($2.50, limited series)

	NM-
1-4	3.00

MARK HAZZARD: MERC
Marvel Comics Group: Nov, 1986 - No. 12, Oct, 1987 (75¢)

	NM-
1-12: Morrow-a	3.00
Annual 1 (11/87, $1.25)	4.00

MARK OF CHARON (See Negation)
CG Entertainment: Apr, 2003 - No. 5, Aug, 2003 ($2.95, limited series)

	NM-
1-5-Bedard-s/Bennett-a	3.00

MARK OF ZORRO (See Zorro, Four Color #228)

MARK 1 COMICS (Also see Shaloman)
Mark 1 Comics: Apr, 1988 - No. 3, Mar, 1989 ($1.50)

	NM-
1-3: Early Shaloman app. 2-Origin	3.00

MARKSMAN, THE (Also see Champions)
Hero Comics: Jan, 1988 - No. 5, 1988 ($1.95)

	NM-
1-5: 1-Rose begins. 1-3-Origin The Marksman	3.00
Annual 1 ('88, $2.75, 52 pgs.)-Champions app.	4.00

MARK TRAIL
Standard Magazines (Hall Syndicate)/Fawcett Publ. No. 5: Oct, 1955; No. 5, Summer, 1959

	GD	VG	FN	VF	VF/NM	NM-
1(1955)-Sunday strip-r	7	14	21	37	46	55
5(1959) By Ed Dodd	5	10	15	22	26	30
...Adventure Book of Nature 1 (Summer, 1958, 25¢, Pines)-100 pg. Giant; Special Camp Issue; contains 78 Sunday strip-r by Ed Dodd	9	18	27	52	69	85

MARMADUKE MONK
I. W. Enterprises/Super Comics: No date; 1963 (10¢)

	GD	VG	FN	VF	VF/NM	NM-
I.W. Reprint 1 (nd)	2	4	6	8	11	14
Super Reprint 14 (1963)-r/Monkeyshines Comics #?	2	4	6	8	10	12

MARMADUKE MOUSE
Quality Comics Group (Arnold Publ.): Spring, 1946 - No. 65, Dec, 1956 (Early issues: 52 pgs.)

	GD	VG	FN	VF	VF/NM	NM-
1-Funny animal	20	40	60	114	182	250
2	12	24	36	69	97	125
3-10	10	20	30	56	76	95

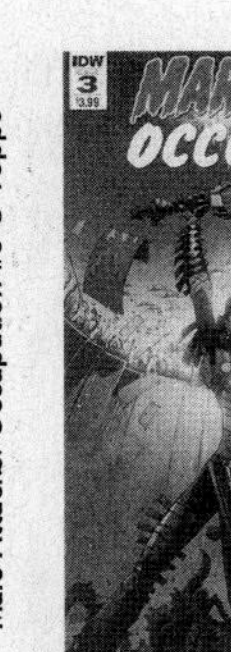
Marmaduke Mouse #41 © QUA

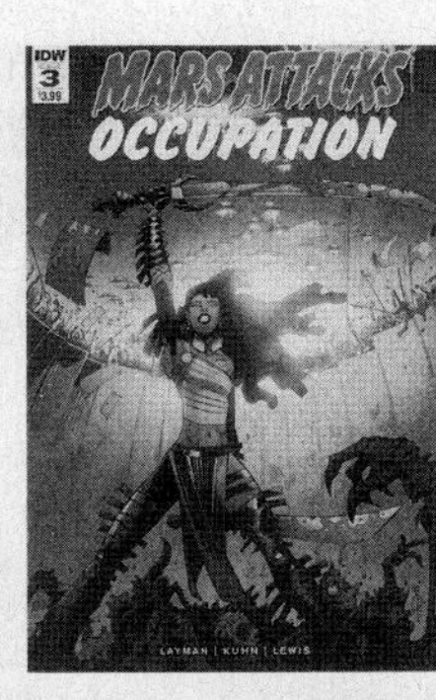
Mars Attacks: Occupation #3 © Topps

Martian Manhunter (2015 series) #7 © DC

GD VG FN VF VF/NM NM-
2.0 4.0 6.0 8.0 9.0 9.2

11-30 8 16 24 42 54 65
31-65: Later issues are 36 pgs. 7 14 21 35 43 50
Super Reprint #14(1963) 2 4 6 9 12 15

MARQUIS, THE
Oni Press
...: A Sin of One ($2.99, 5/03) Guy Davis-s/a; Michael Gaydos-c 3.00
...: Intermezzo TPB ($11.95, 12/03) r/A Sin of One and Hell's Courtesan #1,2 12.00

MARQUIS, THE: DANSE MACABRE
Oni Press: May, 2000 - No. 5, Feb, 2001 ($2.95, B&W, limited series)
1-5-Guy Davis-s/a. 1-Wagner-c. 2-Mignola-c. 3-Vess-c. 5-K. Jones-c 3.00
TPB (8/2001, $18.95) r/1-5 & Les Preludes; Seagle intro. 19.00

MARQUIS, THE: DEVIL'S REIGN: HELL'S COURTESAN
Oni Press: Feb, 2002 - No. 2, Apr, 2002 ($2.95, B&W, limited series)
1,2-Guy Davis-s/a 3.00

MARRIAGE OF HERCULES AND XENA, THE
Topps Comics: July, 1998 ($2.95, one-shot)
1-Photo-c; Lopresti-a; Alex Ross pin-up, 1-Alex Ross painted-c 3.00
1-Gold foil logo-c 5.00

MARRIED ... WITH CHILDREN (TV)(Based on Fox TV show)
Now Comics: June, 1990 - No. 7, Feb, 1991(12/90 inside) ($1.75)
V2#1, Sept, 1991 - No. 7, Apr, 1992 ($1.95)
1-7: 2-Photo-c, 1,2-2nd printing, V2#1-7: 1,4,6-Photo-c 3.00
...Buck's Tale (6/94, $1.95) 3.00
...1994 Annual nn (2/94, $2.50, 52 pgs.)-Flip book format 4.00
Special 1 (7/92, $1.95)-Kelly Bundy photo-c/poster 3.00

MARRIED ... WITH CHILDREN: KELLY BUNDY
Now Comics: Aug, 1992 - No. 3, Oct, 1992 ($1.95, limited series)
1-3: Kelly Bundy photo-c & poster in each 3.00

MARRIED ... WITH CHILDREN: QUANTUM QUARTET
Now Comics: Oct, 1993 - No. 4, 1994, ($1.95, limited series)
1-4: Fantastic Four parody 3.00

MARRIED ... WITH CHILDREN: 2099
Now Comics: June, 1993 - No. 3, Aug, 1993 ($1.95, limited series)
1-3 3.00

MARS
First Comics: Jan, 1984 - No. 12, Jan, 1985 ($1.00, Mando paper)
1-12: Marc Hempel & Mark Wheatley story & art. 2-The Black Flame begins. 10-Dynamo Joe begins 3.00
TPB (IDW Publ., 8/05, $39.99) r/#1-12, creator commentary; bonus art; new Hempel-c 40.00

MARS & BEYOND (Disney, TV)
Dell Publishing Co.: No. 866, Dec, 1957
Four Color 866-A Science feat. from Tomorrowland 7 14 21 49 92 135

MARS ATTACKS
Topps Comics: May, 1994 - No. 5, Sept, 1994 ($2.95, limited series)
1-5-Giffen story; flip books 2 4 6 8 10 12
Special Edition 2 4 6 9 12 15
Trade paperback (12/94, $12.95)-r/limited series plus new 8 pg. story 15.00

MARS ATTACKS
Topps Comics: V2#1, 8/95 - V2#3, 10/95; V2#4, 1/96 - No. 7, 5/96($2.95, bi-monthly #6 on)
V2#1-7: 1-Counterstrike storyline begins. 4-(1/96). 5-(1/96). 5,7-Brereton-c. 6-(3/96)-Simonson-c. 7-Story leads into Baseball Special #1 5.00
Baseball Special 1 (6/96, $2.95)-Bisley-c. 5.00

MARS ATTACKS
IDW Publishing: Jun, 2012 - No. 10, May, 2013 ($3.99, issues #6-10 polybagged with card)
1-10: 1-Layman-s/McCrea-a; 58 covers including all 54 cards from 1962 set 4.00
... #1 IDW's Greatest Hits Edition (3/16, $1.00) reprints #1 3.00
... Art Gallery (9/14, $3.99) Trading card style art by various 4.00
...: Classics Obliterated (6/13, $7.99) Spoofs of Moby Dick, Jeckll & Hyde, Robinson Crusoe 8.00
... KISS (1/13, $3.99) Ryall-s/Robinson-a; 2 variant-c with Judge Dredd & Star Slammers 4.00
... Popeye (1/13, $3.99) Beatty-a; 2 variant-c with Miss Fury & Opus 4.00
... The Holidays (10/12, $7.99) short stories for Halloween-Christmas; 5 covers 8.00
... The Real Ghostbusters (1/13, $3.99) Holder-a; 2 variant-c with Chew & Madman 4.00
... : The Transformers (1/13, $3.99) 2 variant-c with Spike & Strangers in Paradise 4.00
... Zombie vs. Robots (1/13, $3.99) Ryall-s; 2 variant-c with Rog-2000 & Cerebus 4.00

MARS ATTACKS FIRST BORN
IDW Publishing: May, 2014 - No. 4, Aug, 2014 ($3.99, limited series)
1-4-Chris Ryall-s/Sam Kieth-a; multiple covers on each 4.00

MARS ATTACKS HIGH SCHOOL
Topps Comics: May, 1997 - No. 2, Sept, 1997 ($2.95, B&W, limited series)
1,2-Stelfreeze-c 4.00

MARS ATTACKS JUDGE DREDD
IDW Publishing: Sept, 2013 - No. 4, Dec, 2013 ($3.99, limited series)
1-4-Al Ewing-s/John McCrea-a/Greg Staples-c 4.00

MARS ATTACKS IMAGE
Topps Comics: Dec, 1996 - No. 4, Mar, 1997 ($2.50, limited series)
1-4-Giffen-s/Smith & Sienkiewicz-a 4.00

MARS ATTACKS: OCCUPATION
IDW Publishing: Mar, 2016 - No. 5, Jul, 2016 ($3.99, limited series)
1-5-John Layman-s/Andy Kuhn-a; multiple covers 4.00

MARS ATTACKS THE SAVAGE DRAGON
Topps Comics: Dec, 1996 - No. 4, Mar, 1997 ($2.95, limited series)
1-4: 1-w/bound-in card 4.00

MARSHAL BLUEBERRY (See Blueberry)
Marvel Comics (Epic Comics): 1991 ($14.95, graphic novel)
1-Moebius-a 3 6 9 16 23 30

MARSHAL LAW (Also see Crime And Punishment: Marshall Law...)
Marvel Comics (Epic Comics): Oct, 1987 - No. 6, May, 1989 ($1.95, mature)
1-6 3.00

M.A.R.S. PATROL TOTAL WAR (Formerly Total War #1,2)
Gold Key: No. 3, Sept, 1966 - No. 10, Aug, 1969 (All-Painted-c except #7)
3-Wood-a; aliens invade USA 5 10 15 35 63 90
4-10 4 8 12 23 37 50
Wally Wood's M.A.R.S. Patrol Total War TPB (Dark Horse, 9/04, $12.95) r/#3 & Total War #1&2; foreward by Batton Lash; afterword by Dan Adkins 13.00

MARTHA WASHINGTON (Also see Dark Horse Presents Fifth Anniversary Special, Dark Horse Presents #100-4, Give Me Liberty, Happy Birthday Martha Washington & San Diego Comicon Comics #2)

MARTHA WASHINGTON... (one-shots)
Dark Horse Comics (Legend): ($2.95/$3.50, one-shots)
... Dies (7/07, $3.50) Miller-s/Gibbons-a; r/Miller's original outline for Give Me Liberty 4.00
... Stranded in Space (11/95, $2.95) Miller-s/Gibbons-a; Big Guy app. 5.00

MARTHA WASHINGTON GOES TO WAR
Dark Horse Comics (Legend): May, 1994 - No. 5, Sep, 1994 ($2.95, lim. series)
1-5-Miller scripts; Gibbons-c/a 5.00
TPB ($17.95) r/#1-5 18.00

MARTHA WASHINGTON SAVES THE WORLD
Dark Horse Comics: Dec, 1997 - No. 3, Feb, 1998 ($2.95/$3.95, lim. series)
1,2-Miller scripts; Gibbons-c/a in all 5.00
3-($3.95) 5.00

MARTHA WAYNE (See The Story of...)

MARTIAN MANHUNTER (See Detective Comics & Showcase '95 #9)
DC Comics: May, 1988 - No. 4, Aug,. 1988 ($1.25, limited series)
1-4: 1,4-Batman app. 2-Batman cameo 4.00
Special 1-(1996, $3.50) 4.00

MARTIAN MANHUNTER (See JLA)
DC Comics: No. 0, Oct, 1998 - No. 36, Nov, 2001 ($1.99)
0-(10/98) Origin retold; Ostrander-s/Mandrake-c/a 3.00
1-36: 1-(12/98). 6-9-JLA app. 18,19-JSA app. 24-Mahnke-a 3.00
#1,000,000 (11/98) 853rd Century x-over 3.00
Annual 1,2 (1998,1999; $2.95) 1-Ghosts; Wrightson-c. 2-JLApe 4.00

MARTIAN MANHUNTER (See DCU Brave New World)
DC Comics: Oct, 2006 - No. 8, May, 2007 ($2.99, limited series)
1-8-Lieberman-s/Barrionuevo-a/c 3.00
...: The Others Among Us TPB (2007, $19.99) r/#1-8 & story from DCU Brave New World 20.00

MARTIAN MANHUNTER
DC Comics: Aug, 2015 - No. 12, Jul, 2016 ($2.99)
1-12: 1-Rob Williams-s/Eddy Barrows-a. 1-3-JLA app. 10-Origin 3.00

MARTIAN MANHUNTER: AMERICAN SECRETS
DC Comics: 1992 - Book Three, 1992 ($4.95, limited series, prestige format)

Marvel Adventures Hulk #14 © MAR

Marvel Adventures Spider-Man #15 © MAR

Marvel Age Fantastic Four #1 © MAR

	GD 2.0	VG 4.0	FN 6.0	VF 8.0	VF/NM 9.0	NM- 9.2

1-3: Barreto-a 5.00

MARTIN KANE (William Gargan as... Private Eye)(Stage/Screen/Radio/TV)
Fox Features Syndicate (Hero Books): No. 4, June, 1950 - No. 2, Aug, 1950 (Formerly My Secret Affair)

	GD	VG	FN	VF	VF/NM	NM-
4(#1)-True crime stories; Wood-c/a(2); used in **SOTI**, pg. 160; photo back-c	37	74	111	222	361	500
2-Wood/Orlando story, 5 pgs; Wood-a(2)	26	52	78	154	252	350

MARTIN LUTHER KING AND THE MONTGOMERY STORY (See Promotional Comics section)

MARTIN MYSTERY
Dark Horse (Bonelli Comics): Mar, 1999 - No. 6, Aug, 1999 ($4.95, B&W, digest size)

1-6-Reprints Italian series in English; Gibbons-c on #1-3 5.00

MARTY MOUSE
I. W. Enterprises: No date (1958?) (10¢)

	GD	VG	FN	VF	VF/NM	NM-
1-Reprint	2	4	6	9	12	15

MARVEL ACTION HOUR FEATURING IRON MAN (TV cartoon)
Marvel Comics: Nov, 1994 - No. 8, June, 1995 ($1.50/$2.95)

1-8: Based on cartoon series 3.00
1 ($2.95)-Polybagged w/16 pg Marvel Action Hour Preview & acetate print 4.00

MARVEL ACTION HOUR FEATURING THE FANTASTIC FOUR (TV cartoon)
Marvel Comics: Nov, 1994 - No. 8, June, 1995 ($1.50/$2.95)

1-8: Based on cartoon series 3.00
1-($2.95)-Polybagged w/ 16 pg. Marvel Action Hour Preview & acetate print 4.00

MARVEL ACTION UNIVERSE (TV cartoon)
Marvel Comics: Jan, 1989 ($1.00, one-shot)

1-r/Spider-Man And His Amazing Friends 4.00

MARVEL ADVENTURES
Marvel Comics: Apr, 1997 - No. 18, Sept, 1998 ($1.50)

1-18-"Animated style": 1,4,7-Hulk-c/app. 2,11-Spider-Man. 3,8,15-X-Men. 5-Spider-Man & X-Men. 6-Spider-Man & Human Torch. 9,12-Fantastic Four. 10,16-Silver Surfer. 13-Spider-Man & Silver Surfer. 14-Hulk & Dr. Strange. 18-Capt. America 3.00

MARVEL ADVENTURES...
Marvel Comics: 2007, 2008 (Free Comic Book Day giveaways)

... Free Comic Book Day 2007 (6/07) 1-Iron Man, Hulk and Franklin Richards app. 3.00
... Free Comic Book Day 2008 - Iron Man, Hulk, Ant-Man and Spider-Man app. 3.00

MARVEL ADVENTURES FANTASTIC FOUR (All ages title)
Marvel Comics: No. 0, July, 2005 - No. 48, July, 2009 ($1.99/$2.50/$2.99)

0-($1.99) Movie version characters; Dr. Doom app.; Eaton-a 3.00
1-10-($2.50) 1-Skrulls app.; Pagulayan-a. 7-Namor app. 3.00
11-48-($2.99) 12,42-Dr. Doom app. 24-Namor app. 26,28-Silver Surfer app. 3.00
... Vol. 1: Family of Heroes (2005, $6.99, digest) r/#1-4 7.00
... Vol. 2: Fantastic Voyages (2006, $6.99, digest) r/#5-8 7.00
... Vol. 3: World's Greatest (2006, $6.99, digest) r/#9-12 7.00
... Vol. 4: Cosmic Threats (2006, $6.99, digest) r/#13-16 7.00
... Vol. 5: All 4 One, 4 For All (2007, $6.99, digest) r/#17-20 7.00
... Vol. 6: Monsters & Mysteries (2007, $6.99, digest) r/#21-24 7.00
... Vol. 7: The Silver Surfer (2007, $6.99, digest) r/#25-28 7.00
... Vol. 8: Monsters, Moles, Cowboys & Coupons (2008, $7.99, digest) r/#29-32 8.00

MARVEL ADVENTURES FLIP MAGAZINE (All ages title)
Marvel Comics: Aug, 2005 - No. 26, Sept, 2007 ($3.99/$4.99)

1-11: 1-10-Rep. Marvel Advs. Fantastic Four and Marvel Advs. Spider-Man in flip format 4.00
12-14-($4.99) Reprints Marvel Advs. Spider-Man & X-Men/Power Pack in flip format 5.00
15-26-Rep. Marvel Advs. Fantastic Four and Marvel Advs. Spider-Man in flip format 5.00

MARVEL ADVENTURES HULK (All ages title)
Marvel Comics: Sept, 2007 - No. 16, Dec, 2008 ($2.99)

1-16: 1-New version of Hulk's origin; Pagulayan-c. 2-Jamie Madrox app. 13-Mummies 3.00
... Vol. 1: Misunderstood Monster (2007, $6.99, digest) r/#1-4 7.00

MARVEL ADVENTURES IRON MAN (All ages title)
Marvel Comics: July, 2007 - No. 13, Jul, 2008 ($2.99)

1-13: 1-4-Michael Golden-c. 1-New version of Iron Man's origin. 2-Intro. the Mandarin 3.00
... Vol. 1: Heart of Steel (2007, $6.99, digest) r/#1-4 7.00
... Vol. 2: Iron Armory (2008, $7.99, digest) r/#5-8 8.00

MARVEL ADVENTURES SPIDER-MAN (All ages title)
Marvel Comics: May, 2005 - No. 61, May, 2010 ($2.50/$2.99)

1-13-Lee & Ditko stories retold with new art. 13-Conner-c 3.00
14-48: 14-Begin $2.99-c. 14-16-Conner-c. 22,23-Black costume. 35-Venom app. 3.00
50-($3.99) Sinister Six app.; back-up w/Sonny Liew-a 4.00
51-61: 53-Emma Frost becomes a regular; intro. Chat; Skottie Young-c begin 3.00
... Vol. 1 HC (2006, $19.99, with dustjacket) r/#1-8; plot for #7; sketch pages from #6,8 20.00
... Vol. 1: The Sinister Six (2005, $6.99, digest) r/#1-4 7.00
... Vol. 2: Power Struggle (2005, $6.99, digest) r/#5-8 7.00
... Vol. 3: Doom With a View (2006, $6.99, digest) r/#9-12 7.00
... Vol. 4: Concrete Jungle (2006, $6.99, digest) r/#13-16 7.00
... Vol. 5: Monsters on the Prowl (2007, $6.99, digest) r/#17-20 7.00
... Vol. 6: The Black Costume (2007, $6.99, digest) r/#21-24 7.00
... Vol. 7: Secret Identity (2007, $6.99, digest) r/#25-28 7.00
... Vol. 8: Forces of Nature (2008, $7.99, digest) r/#29-32 8.00
... Vol. 9: Fiercest Foes (2008, $7.99, digest) r/#33-36 8.00

MARVEL ADVENTURES SPIDER-MAN (All ages title)
Marvel Comics: June, 2010 - No. 24, May, 2012 ($3.99/$2.99)

1-($3.99) Tobin-s; Franklin Richards back-up 4.00
2-23-($2.99): 3,7-Wolverine app. 3,4-Bullseye app. 6-Doctor Octopus app. 3.00

MARVEL ADVENTURES STARRING DAREDEVIL (...Adventure #3 on)
Marvel Comics Group: Dec, 1975 - No. 6, Oct, 1976

	GD	VG	FN	VF	VF/NM	NM-
1	2	4	6	13	18	22
2-6-r/Daredevil #22-27 by Colan. 3-5-(25¢-c)	1	3	4	6	8	10
3-5-(30¢-c variants, limited distribution)(4,6,8/76)	5	10	15	31	53	75

MARVEL ADVENTURES SUPER HEROES (All ages title)
Marvel Comics: Sept, 2008 - No. 21, May, 2010 ($2.99)

1-21: 1-4: Spider-Man, Hulk and Iron Man team-ups. 1-Hercules app. 5-Dr. Strange app. 6-Ant-Man origin re-told. 7-Thor. 8,12-Capt. America. 17-Avengers begin 3.00

MARVEL ADVENTURES SUPER HEROES (All ages title)
Marvel Comics: June, 2010 - No. 24, May, 2012 ($3.99/$2.99)

1-($3.99) Iron Man and Avengers vs. Magneto 4.00
2-24-($2.99) 4-Deadpool app. 5-Rhino app. 11,12,22-Hulk app. 13,14,19-Thor 3.00

MARVEL ADVENTURES THE AVENGERS (All ages title)
Marvel Comics: July, 2006 - No. 39, Oct, 2009 ($2.99)

1-39-Spider-Man, Wolverine, Hulk, Iron Man, Capt. America, Storm, Giant-Girl app. 3.00
... Vol. 1: Heroes Assembled (2006, $6.99, digest) r/#1-4 7.00
... Vol. 2: Mischief (2007, $6.99, digest) r/#5-8 7.00
... Vol. 3: Bizarre Adventures (2007, $6.99, digest) r/#9-12 7.00
... Vol. 4: The Dream Team (2007, $6.99, digest) r/#13-15 & Giant-Size #1 7.00
... Vol. 5: Some Assembling Required (2008, $7.99, digest) r/#16-19 8.00

MARVEL ADVENTURES TWO-IN-ONE
Marvel Comics: Oct, 2007 - No. 18 ($4.99, bi-weekly)

1-18: 1-9-Reprints Marvel Adventures Spider-Man and Fantastic Four stories. 10-Hulk 5.00

MARVEL AGE FANTASTIC FOUR (All ages title)
Marvel Comics: Jun, 2004 - No. 12, Mar, 2005 ($2.25)

1-12-Lee & Kirby stories retold with new art by various. 11-Impossible Man app. 3.00
...Tales (4/05, $2.25) retells first meeting with the Black Panther; O'Hare & Lim-a 3.00
Vol. 1: All For One TPB (2004, $5.99, digest size) r/#1-4 6.00
Vol. 2: Doom TPB (2004, $5.99, digest size) r/#5-8 6.00
Vol. 3: The Return of Doctor Doom TPB (2005, $5.99, digest size) r/#9-12 6.00

MARVEL AGE HULK (All ages title)
Marvel Comics: Nov, 2004 - No. 4, Feb, 2005 ($1.75)

1-3-Lee & Kirby stories retold with new art by various 3.00
Vol. 1: Incredible TPB (2005, $5.99, digest size) r/#1-4 6.00
Vol. 2: Defenders (2008, $7.99, digest) r/#5-8 8.00

MARVEL AGE SPIDER-MAN (All ages title)
Marvel Comics: May, 2004 - No. 20, Mar, 2005 ($2.25)

1-20-Lee & Ditko stories retold with new art. 4-Doctor Doom app. 5-Lizard app. 3.00
1-(Free Comic Book Day giveaway, 8/04) Spider-Man vs. The Vulture; Brooks-a 3.00
Vol. 1 TPB (2004, $5.99, digest) 1-r/#1-4 6.00
Vol. 2: Everyday Hero TPB (2004, $5.99, digest) r/#5-8 6.00
Vol. 3: Swingtime TPB (2004, $5.99, digest) r/#9-12 6.00
Spidey Strikes Back TPB (2005, 5.99, digest) r/#17-20 6.00

MARVEL AGE SPIDER-MAN TEAM-UP (Marvel Adventures on cover)
Marvel Comics: June, 2005 (Free Comic Book Day giveaway)

1-Spider-Man meets the Fantastic Four 3.00

MARVEL AGE TEAM-UP (All ages Spider-Man team-ups) (Also see Free Comic Book Day edition in the Promotional Comics section)
Marvel Comics: Nov, 2004 - No. 5, Apr, 2005 ($1.75)

1-5-Stories retold with new art by various. 1-Fantastic Four app. 3-Kitty Pryde app. 3.00

Marvel Boy #2 © MAR

Marvel Collectible Classics #4 © MAR

Marvel Comics Presents #3 © MAR

GD VG FN VF VF/NM NM-
2.0 4.0 6.0 8.0 9.0 9.2

GD VG FN VF VF/NM NM-
2.0 4.0 6.0 8.0 9.0 9.2

... Vol. 1: A Little Help From My Friends (2005, $7.99, digest) r/#1-5 8.00

MARVEL AND DC PRESENT FEATURING THE UNCANNY X-MEN AND THE NEW TEEN TITANS
Marvel Comics/DC Comics: 1982 ($2.00, 68 pgs., one-shot, Baxter paper)

1-3rd app. Deathstroke the Terminator; Darkseid app.; Simonson/Austin-c/a 3 6 9 15 22 28

MARVEL APES
Marvel Comics: Nov, 2008 - No. 4, Dec, 2008 ($3.99, limited series)

1-4: 1-Kesel-s/Bachs-a; back-up history story with Peyer-s/Kitson-a; two covers 4.00
1-($10.00) Hero Initiative edition with Daredevil gorilla cover by Mike Wieringo 10.00
#0-(2008, $3.99) r/Amazing Spider-Man #110,111; gallery of Marvel Apes variant covers 4.00
...: Amazing Spider-Monkey Special 1 (6/09, $3.99) Sandmonk and the Apevengers app. 4.00
...: Grunt Line 1 (7/09, $3.99) Kesel-s; Charles Darwin app. 4.00
...: Speedball Special 1 (5/09, $3.99) Bachs & Hardin-a 4.00

MARVEL ASSISTANT-SIZED SPECTACULAR
Marvel Comics: Jun, 2009 - No. 2, Jun, 2009 ($3.99, limited series)

1,2-Short stories by various incl. Isanove, Giarrusso, Nauck, Wyatt Cenak, Warren 4.00

MARVEL ATLAS (Styled after the Official Marvel Handbooks)
Marvel Comics: 2007 - No. 2, 2008 ($3.99, limited series)

1,2-Profiles and maps of countries in the Marvel Universe 4.00

MARVEL BOY (Astonishing #3 on; see Marvel Super Action #4)
Marvel Comics (MPC): Dec, 1950 - No. 2, Feb, 1951

1-Origin Marvel Boy by Russ Heath 142 284 426 909 1555 2200
2-Everett-a; Washington DC under attack 97 194 291 621 1061 1500

MARVEL BOY (Marvel Knights)
Marvel Comics: Aug, 2000 - No. 6, Mar, 2001 ($2.99, limited series)

1-Intro. Marvel Boy; Morrison-s/J.G. Jones-c/a 4.00
1-DF Variant-c 5.00
2-6 3.00
TPB (6/01, $15.95) 16.00

MARVEL BOY: THE URANIAN (Agents of Atlas)
Marvel Comics: Mar, 2010 - No. 3, May, 2010 ($3.99, limited series)

1-3-Origin re-told; back-up reprints from 1950s; Heath & Everett-a 4.00

MARVEL CHILLERS (Also see Giant-Size Chillers)
Marvel Comics Group: Oct, 1975 - No. 7, Oct, 1976 (All 25¢ issues)

1-Intro. Modred the Mystic, ends #2; Kane-c(p) 3 6 9 16 23 30
2,4,5,7: 4-Kraven app. 5,6-Red Wolf app. 7-Kirby-c; Tuska-p 2 4 6 9 12 15
3-Tigra, the Were-Woman begins (origin), ends #7 (see Giant-Size Creatures #1). Chaykin/Wrightson-c. 5 10 15 30 50 70
4-6-(30¢-c variants, limited distribution)(4-8/76) 4 8 12 27 44 60
6-Byrne-a(p); Buckler-c(p) 2 4 6 11 16 20
NOTE: *Bolle a-1. Buckler c-2. Kirby c-7.*

MARVEL CLASSICS COMICS SERIES FEATURING...
(Also see Pendulum Illustrated Classics)
Marvel Comics Group: 1976 - No. 36, Dec, 1978 (52 pgs., no ads)

1-Dr. Jekyll and Mr. Hyde 2 4 6 10 14 18
2-10,28: 28-1st Golden-c/a; Pit and the Pendulum 2 4 6 8 10 12
11-27,29-36 1 2 3 5 7 9
NOTE: *Adkins c-1i, 4i, 12i. Alcala a-34i; c-34. Bolle a-35. Buscema c-17p, 19p, 26p. Golden c/a-28. Gil Kane c-1-16p, 21p, 22p, 24p, 32p. Nebres a-5; c-24i. Nino a-2, 8, 12. Redondo a-1, 9. No. 1-12 were reprinted from Pendulum Illustrated Classics.*

MARVEL COLLECTIBLE CLASSICS: AVENGERS
Marvel Comics: 1998 ($10.00, reprints with chromium wraparound-c)

1-Reprints Avengers Vol.3, #1; Perez-c 3 6 9 16 23 30

MARVEL COLLECTIBLE CLASSICS: SPIDER-MAN
Marvel Comics: 1998 ($10.00, reprints with chromium wraparound-c)

1-Reprints Amazing Spider-Man #300; McFarlane-c 40 80 120 200 280 360
2-Reprints Spider-Man #1; McFarlane-c 20 40 60 100 140 180

MARVEL COLLECTIBLE CLASSICS: X-MEN
Marvel Comics: 1998 ($10.00, reprints with chromium wraparound-c)

1-Reprints (Uncanny) X-Men #1 & 2; Adam Kubert-c 3 6 9 17 26 35
2-6: 2-Reprints Uncanny X-Men #141 & 142; Byrne-c. 3-Reprints (Uncanny) X-Men #137; Larroca-c. 4-Reprints X-Men #25; Andy Kubert-c. 5-Reprints Giant Size X-Men #1; Gary Frank-c. 6-Reprints X-Men V2#1; Ramos-c 3 6 9 16 23 30

MARVEL COLLECTOR'S EDITION
Marvel Comics: 1992 (Ordered thru mail with Charleston Chew candy wrapper)

1-Flip-book format; Spider-Man, Silver Surfer, Wolverine (by Sam Kieth), & Ghost Rider stories; Wolverine back-c by Kieth 1 2 3 5 6 8

MARVEL COLLECTORS' ITEM CLASSICS (Marvel's Greatest #23 on)
Marvel Comics Group(ATF): Feb, 1965 - No. 22, Aug, 1969 (25¢, 68 pgs.)

1-Fantastic Four, Spider-Man, Thor, Hulk, Iron Man-r begin 11 22 33 76 163 250
2 (4/66) 6 12 18 41 76 110
3,4 5 10 15 35 63 90
5-10 5 10 15 33 57 80
11-22: 22-r/The Man in the Ant Hill/TTA #27 4 8 12 28 47 65
NOTE: *All reprints; **Ditko, Kirby** art in all.*

MARVEL COMICS (Marvel Mystery Comics #2 on)
Timely Comics (Funnies, Inc.): Oct, Nov, 1939

NOTE: The first issue was originally dated October 1939. Most copies have a black circle stamped over the date (on cover and inside) with "November" printed over it. However, some copies do not have the November overprint and could have a higher value. Most No. 1's have printing defects, i.e., tilted pages which caused trimming into the panels usually on right side and bottom. Covers exist with and without gloss finish.

1-Origin Sub-Mariner by Bill Everett(1st newsstand app.); 1st 8 pgs. were produced for Motion Picture Funnies Weekly #1 which was probably not distributed outside of advance copies; intro Human Torch by Carl Burgos, Kazar the Great (1st Tarzan clone), & Jungle Terror(only app.); intro. The Angel by Gustavson, The Masked Raider & his horse Lightning (ends #12); cover by sci/fi pulp illustrator Frank R. Paul 28,000 56,000 84,000 190,000 320,000 625,000

MARVEL COMICS
Marvel Comics: 1990 ($17.95, hardcover)

1-Reprint of entire Marvel Comics #1 3 6 9 16 23 30

MARVEL COMICS
Marvel Comics

... No. 1 Halloween Comic Fest 2014 (giveaway) Re-colored reprint of Human Torch and Sub-Mariner stories from Marvel Comics #1; cover swipe by Jelena Djurdjevic 3.00
... 70th Anniversary Special (10/09, $4.99) Re-colored reprint of entire Marvel Comics #1; cover swipe by Jelena Djurdjevic 6.00

MARVEL COMICS PRESENTS
Marvel Comics (Midnight Sons imprint #143 on): Early Sept, 1988 - No. 175, Feb, 1995 ($1.25/$1.50/$1.75, bi-weekly)

1-Wolverine by Buscema in #1-10 1 3 4 6 8 10
2-5 6.00
6-10: 6-Sub-Mariner app. 10-Colossus begins 4.00
11-18,20-47,51-71: 17-Cyclops begins. 24-Havok begins. 25-Origin/1st app. Nth Man. 26-Hulk begins by Rogers. 29-Quasar app. 31-Excalibur begins by Austin (i). 32-McFarlane-a(p). 33-Capt. America; Jim Lee-a. 37-Devil-Slayer app. 38-Wolverine begins by Buscema; Hulk app. 39-Spider-Man app. 46-Liefeld Wolverine-c. 51-53-Wolverine by Rob Liefeld. 54-61-Wolverine/Hulk story: 54-Werewolf by Night begins; The Shroud by Ditko. 58-Iron Man by Ditko. 59-Punisher. 62-Deathlok & Wolverine stories 63-Wolverine. 64-71-Wolverine/Ghost Rider 8-part story. 70-Liefeld Ghost Rider/Wolverine-c 3.00
19-1st app. Damage Control 1 3 4 6 8 10
48-50-Wolverine & Spider-Man team-up by Erik Larsen-c/a. 48-Wasp app. 49,50-Savage Dragon prototype app. by Larsen. 50-Silver Surfer. 50-53-Comet Man; Mumy scripts 5.00
72-Begin 13-part Weapon-X story (Wolverine origin) by B. Windsor-Smith (prologue) 2 4 6 9 12 15
73-Weapon-X part 1; Black Knight, Sub-Mariner 5.00
74-84: 74-Weapon-X part 2; Black Knight, Sub-Mariner. 76-Death's Head story. 77-Mr. Fantastic story. 78-Iron Man by Steacy. 80,81-Capt. America by Ditko/Austin. 81-Daredevil by Rogers/Williamson. 82-Power Man. 83-Human Torch by Ditko(a&scripts); $1.00-c direct, $1.25 newsstand. 84-Last Weapon-X (24 pg. conclusion) 3.00
85-Begin 8-part Wolverine story by Sam Kieth (c/a); 1st Kieth-a on Wolverine; begin 8-part Beast story by Jae Lee(p) with Liefeld part pencils #85,86; 1st Jae Lee-a (assisted w/Liefeld, 1991) 4.00
86-90: 86-89-Wolverine, Beast stories continue. 90-Begin 8-part Ghost Rider & Cable story, ends #97; begin flip book format w/two-c 3.00
91-174: 93-Begin 6-part Wolverine story, ends #98. 98-Begin 2-part Ghost Rider story. 99-Spider-Man story. 100-Full-length Ghost Rider/Wolverine story by Sam Kieth w/Tim Vigil assists; anniversary issue, non flip-book. 101-Begin 6-part Ghost Rider/Dr. Strange story & begin 8-part Wolverine/Nightcrawler story by Colan/Williamson; Punisher story. 107-Begin 6-part Ghost Rider/Werewolf by Night story. 109-Begin 8 part Wolverine/Typhoid Mary story. 111-Iron Fist. 113-Begin 6-part Giant-Man & begin 6-part Ghost Rider/Iron Fist stories. 117-Preview of Ravage 2099 (1st app.); begin 6 part Wolverine/Venom story w/Kieth-a. 118-Preview of Doom 2099 (1st app.). 119-Begin Ghost Rider/Cloak & Dagger by Colan. 120,136,138-Spider-Man. 123-Begin 8-part Ghost Rider/Typhoid Mary story; begin 4-part She Hulk story; begin 8-part Wolverine/Lynx story. 125-Begin 6-part Iron Fist

Marvel Comics Presents (2007 series) #2 © MAR

Marvel Divas #1 © MAR

Marvel Family #13 © FAW

	GD 2.0	VG 4.0	FN 6.0	VF 8.0	VF/NM 9.0	NM- 9.2

story. 130-Begin 6-part Ghost Rider/ Cage story. 136-Daredevil. 137-Begin 6-part Wolverine story & 6-part Ghost Rider story. 147-Begin 2-part Vengeance-c/story w/new Ghost Rider. 149-Vengeance-c/story w/new Ghost Rider. 150-Silver ink-c; begin 2-part Bloody Mary story w/Typhoid Mary,Wolverine, Daredevil, new Ghost Rider; intro Steel Raven. 152-Begin 4-part Wolverine, 4-part War Machine, 4-part Vengeance, 3-part Moon Knight stories; same date as War Machine #1. 143-146: Siege of Darkness parts 3,6,11,14; all have spot-varnished-c. 143-Ghost Rider/Scarlet Witch; intro new Werewolf. 144-Begin 2-part Morbius story. 145-Begin 2-part Nightstalkers story. 153-155-Bound-in Spider-Man trading card sheet 3.00
175-Flip-book with New Genix-c 2 4 6 9 12 15
...Colossus: God's Country (1994, $6.95) r/#10-17 1 2 3 4 5 7
...: Wolverine Vol. 1 TPB (2005, $12.99) r/Wolverine stories from #1-10 13.00
...: Wolverine Vol. 2 TPB (2006, $12.99) r/from #39-50 and Marvel Age Annual #4 13.00
...: Wolverine Vol. 3 TPB (2006, $12.99) r/from #51-61 13.00
...: Wolverine Vol. 4 TPB (2006, $12.99) r/from #62-71 13.00

NOTE: ***Austin** a-31-37i; c(i)-48, 50, 99, 122. **Buscema** a-1-10, 38-47; c-6. **Byrne** a-79; c-71. **Colan** a(p)-36, 37. **Colan/Williamson** a-101-108. **Ditko** a-7p, 10, 56p, 58, 80, 81, 83. **Guice** a-62. **Sam Kieth** a-85-92, 117-122; c-85-98, 99p, 100-108, 117, 118, 120-122; back c-109-113, 117. **Jae Lee** c-129(back). **Liefeld** a-51, 52, 53p(2), 85p; c-46, 70. **McFarlane** c-32. **Mooney** a-73. **Rogers** a-26, 38, 46i, 81p. **Russell** a-10-14,16,17i; c-4,19, 30,31i. **Saltares** a-8p(early), 38-45p. **Simonson** c-1. **B. Smith** a-72-84; c-72-84. **P. Smith** c-34. **Sparling** a-33. **Starlin** a-89i. **Staton** a-74. **Steacy** a-78. **Sutton** a-101-105. **Williamson** c-62i. Two Gun Kid by **Gil Kane** in #116, 122.*

MARVEL COMICS PRESENTS
Marvel Comics: Nov, 2007 - No. 12, Oct, 2008 ($3.99)

1-12-Short stories by various. 1-Wraparound-c by Campbell 4.00

MARVEL COMICS SUPER SPECIAL, A (Marvel Super Special #5 on)
Marvel Comics: Sept, 1977 - No. 41(?), Nov, 1986 (nn 7) ($1.50, magazine)

1-Kiss, 40 pgs. comics plus photos & features; John Buscema-a(p); also see Howard the Duck #12; ink contains real KISS blood; Dr. Doom, Spider-Man, Avengers, Fantastic Four, Mephisto app. 12 24 36 82 179 275
2-Conan (1978) 3 6 9 14 20 25
3-Close Encounters of the Third Kind (1978); Simonson-a 2 4 6 11 16 20
4-The Beatles Story (1978)-Perez/Janson-a; has photos & articles 6 12 18 38 69 100
5-Kiss (1978)-Includes poster 12 24 36 82 179 275
6-Jaws II (1978) 2 4 6 9 13 16
7-Sgt. Pepper; Beatles movie adaptation; withdrawn from U.S. distribution (French ed. exists)
8-Battlestar Galactica; tabloid size ($1.50, 1978); adapts TV show 2 4 6 13 18 20
8-Modern-r of tabloid size 2 4 6 10 14 18
8-Battlestar Galactica; publ. in regular magazine format; low distribution ($1.50, 8-1/2x11") 3 6 9 14 20 25
9-Conan 2 4 6 11 16 20
10-Star-Lord (1st color story) 4 8 12 28 47 65
11-13-Weirdworld begins #11; 25 copy special press run of each with gold seal and signed by artists (Proof quality), Spring-June, 1979 8 16 24 55 105 155
11-14: 11-13-Weirdworld (regular issues): 11-Fold-out centerfold. 14-Miller-c(p); adapts movie "Meteor." 1 3 4 6 8 10
15-Star Trek with photos & pin-ups ($1.50-c) 2 4 6 11 16 20
15-With $2.00 price; the price was changed at tail end of a 200,000 press run 3 6 9 14 20 25
16-Empire Strikes Back adaptation; Williamson-a 4 8 12 23 37 50
17-20 (Movie adaptations): 17-Xanadu. 18-Raiders of the Lost Ark. 19-For Your Eyes Only (James Bond). 20-Dragonslayer 6.00
21,23,25,26,28-30 (Movie adaptations): 21-Conan. 23-Annie. 25-Rock and Rule-w/photos; artwork is from movie. 26-Octopussy (James Bond). 28-Krull; photo-c. 29-Tarzan of the Apes (Greystoke movie). 30-Indiana Jones and the Temple of Doom 1 2 3 4 5 7
22-Blade Runner; Williamson-a/Steranko-c 3 6 9 14 20 25
24-The Dark Crystal 2 4 6 9 12 15
27-Return of the Jedi 2 4 6 9 12 15
31-39,41: 31-The Last Star Fighter. 32-The Muppets Take Manhattan. 33-Buckaroo Banzai. 34-Sheena. 35-Conan The Destroyer. 36-Dune. 37-2010. 38-Red Sonja. 39-Santa Claus:The Movie. 41-Howard The Duck 1 2 3 5 7 9
40-Labyrinth 3 6 9 19 30 40

NOTE: ***J. Buscema** a-1, 2, 9, 11-13, 18p, 21, 35, 40; c-11(part), 12. **Chaykin** a-9, 19p; c-18, 19. **Colan** a(p)-6, 10, 14. **Morrow** a-34; c-1i, 34. **Nebres** a-11. **Spiegle** a-29. **Stevens** a-27. **Williamson** a-27. #22-28 contain photos from movies.*

MARVEL COMICS: 2001
Marvel Comics: 2001 (no cover price, one-shot)

1-Previews new titles for Fall 2001; Wolverine-c 3.00

MARVEL DABEL BROTHERS SAMPLER
Marvel Comics: Dec, 2006 (no cover price, one-shot)

1-Profiles and sample pages of Anita Blake, Magician: Apprentice, Red Prophet, Ptolus 3.00

MARVEL DIVAS
Marvel Comics: Sept, 2009 - No. 4, Dec, 2009 ($3.99, limited series)

1-4-Black Cat, Firestar, Hellcat and Photon app. 1-Campbell-c 4.00

MARVEL DOUBLE FEATURE
Marvel Comics Group: Dec, 1973 - No. 21, Mar, 1977

1-Capt. America, Iron Man-r/T.O.S. begin 3 6 9 16 23 30
2-10: 3-Last 20¢ issue 2 4 6 8 10 12
11-17,20,21:17-Story-r/Iron Man & Sub-Mariner #1; last 25¢ issue 1 2 3 5 7 9
15-17-(30¢-c variants, limited distribution)(4,6,8/76) 3 6 9 19 30 40
18,19-Colan/Craig-r from Iron Man #1 in both 2 4 6 8 10 12

NOTE: ***Colan** r-1-19p. **Craig** r-17-19i. **G. Kane** r-15p; c-15p. **Kirby** r-1-16p, 20, 21; c-17-20.*

MARVEL DOUBLE SHOT
Marvel Comics: Jan, 2003 - No. 4, April, 2003 ($2.99, limited series)

1-4: 1-Hulk by Haynes; Thor w/Asamiya-a; Jusko-c. 2-Dr. Doom by Rivera; Simpsons-style Avengers by Bill Morrison 3.00

MARVEL FAMILY (Also see Captain Marvel Adventures No. 18)
Fawcett Publications: Dec, 1945 - No. 89, Jan, 1954

1-Origin Captain Marvel, Captain Marvel Jr., Mary Marvel, & Uncle Marvel retold; origin/1st app. Black Adam 600 1200 1800 4000 6500 9000
2-The 3 Lt. Marvels & Uncle Marvel app. 77 154 231 493 847 1200
3 54 108 162 346 591 835
4,5 45 90 135 284 480 675
6-10: 7-Shazam app. 39 78 117 231 378 525
11-20 31 62 93 182 296 410
21-30 27 54 81 158 259 360
31-40 23 46 69 136 223 310
41-46,48-50 22 44 66 128 209 290
47-Flying Saucer-c/story (5/50) 29 58 87 170 278 385
51-76 20 40 60 120 195 270
77-Communist Threat-c 36 72 108 211 343 475
78,81-Used in **POP**, pg. 92,93. 23 46 69 136 223 310
79,80,82-88: 79-Horror satire-c 22 44 66 132 216 300
89-Last issue; last Fawcett Captain Marvel app. (low distribution) 34 68 102 199 325 450

MARVEL FANFARE (1st Series)
Marvel Comics Group: Mar, 1982 - No. 60, Jan, 1992 ($1.25/$2.25, slick paper, direct sales)

1-Spider-Man/Angel team-up; 1st Paul Smith-a (1st full story; see King Conan #7); Daredevil app. (many copies were printed missing the centerfold) 1 3 4 6 8 10
2-Spider-Man, Ka-Zar, The Angel. F.F. origin retold 1 2 3 5 6 8
3,4-X-Men & Ka-Zar. 4-Deathlok, Spidey app. 6.00
5-14: 5-Dr. Strange, Capt. America. 6-Spider-Man, Scarlet Witch. 7-Incredible Hulk; D.D. back-up(also 15). 8-Dr. Strange; Wolf Boy begins. 9-Man-Thing. 10-13-Black Widow. 14-The Vision 4.00
15,24,33: 15-The Thing by Barry Smith, c/a. 24-Weirdworld; Wolverine back-up. 33-X-Men, Wolverine app.; Punisher pin-up 5.00
16-23,25-32,34-44,46-50: 16,17-Skywolf. 16-Sub-Mariner back-up. 17-Hulk back-up. 18-Capt. America by Miller. 19-Cloak and Dagger. 20-Thing/Dr. Strange. 21-Thing/Dr. Strange /Hulk. 22,23-Iron Man vs. Dr. Octopus. 25,26-Weirdworld. 27-Daredevil/Spider-Man. 28-Alpha Flight. 29-Hulk. 30-Moon Knight. 31,32-Captain America. 34-37-Warriors Three. 38-Moon Knight/Dazzler. 39-Moon Knight/Hawkeye. 40-Angel/Rogue & Storm. 41-Dr. Strange. 42-Spider-Man. 43-Sub-Mariner/Human Torch. 44-Iron Man vs. Dr. Doom by Ken Steacy. 46-Fantastic Four. 47-Hulk. 48-She-Hulk/Vision. 49-Dr. Strange/Nick Fury. 50-X-Factor 3.00
45-All pin-up issue by Steacy, Art Adams & others 5.00
51-($2.95, 52 pgs.)-Silver Surfer; Fantastic Four & Capt. Marvel app.; 51,52-Colan/Williamson back-up (Dr. Strange) 4.00
52,53,56-60: 52,53-Black Knight; 53-Iron Man back up. 56-59-Shanna the She-Devil. 58-Vision & Scarlet Witch back-up. 60-Black Panther/Rogue/Daredevil stories 3.00
54,55-Wolverine back-ups. 54-Black Knight. 55-Power Pack 4.00
... Vol. 1 TPB (2008, $24.99) r/#1-7 25.00

NOTE: ***Art Adams** c-13. **Austin** a-1i, 4i, 33i, 38i; c-8i, 33i. **Buscema** a-51p. **Byrne** a-1p, 29, 48; c-29. **Chiodo** painted c-56-59. **Colan** a-51p. **Cowan/Simonson** c/a-60. **Golden** a-1, 2, 4p, 47; c-1, 2, 47. **Infantino** c/a(p)-8. **Gil Kane** a-8-11p. **Miller** a-18; c-1(Back-c), 18. **Perez** a-10, 11p, 12, 13p; c-10-13p. **Rogers** a-5p; c-5p. **Russell** a-5i, 6i, 8-11i, 43i; c-5i, 6. **Paul Smith** a-1p, 4p, 32, 60; c-4p. Staton c/a-50(p). **Williamson** a-30i, 51i.*

MARVEL FANFARE (2nd Series)
Marvel Comics: Sept, 1996 - No. 6, Feb, 1997 (99¢)

1-6: 1-Capt. America & The Falcon-c/story; Deathlok app. 2-Wolverine & Hulk-c/app. 3-Ghost Rider & Spider-Man-c/app. 5-Longshot-c/app. 6-Sabretooth, Power Man, &

Marvel Feature (2nd series) #6 © MAR

Marvel Graphic Novel #6 © Walt Simonson

Marvel Holiday Special 1994 © MAR

GD VG FN VF VF/NM NM-
2.0 4.0 6.0 8.0 9.0 9.2

Iron Fist-c/app 3.00

MARVEL FEATURE (See Marvel Two-In-One)
Marvel Comics Group: Dec, 1971 - No. 12, Nov, 1973 (1,2: 25¢, 52 pg. giants) (#1-3: quarterly)

1-Origin/1st app. The Defenders (Sub-Mariner, Hulk & Dr. Strange); see Sub-Mariner #34,35 for prequel; Dr. Strange solo story (predates Dr. Strange #1) plus 1950s Sub-Mariner-r; Neal Adams-c 20 40 60 138 307 475
2-2nd app. Defenders; 1950s Sub-Mariner-r. Rutland, Vermont Halloween x-over 9 18 27 57 111 165
3-Defenders ends 6 12 18 40 73 105
4-Re-intro Antman (1st app. since 1960s), begin series; brief origin; Spider-Man app. 8 16 24 54 102 150
5-7,9,10: 6-Wasp app. & begins team-ups. 9-Iron Man app. 10-Last Antman 3 6 9 21 33 45
8-Origin Antman & Wasp-r/TTA #44; Kirby-a 4 8 12 23 37 50
11-Thing vs. Hulk; 1st Thing solo book (9/73); origin Fantastic Four retold 7 14 21 49 92 135
12-Thing/Iron Man; early Thanos app.; occurs after Capt. Marvel #33; Starlin-a(p) 5 10 15 34 60 85

NOTE: ***Bolle*** *a-9i.* ***Everett*** *a-1i, 3i.* ***Hartley*** *r-10.* ***Kane*** *c-3p, 7p.* ***Russell*** *a-7-10p.* ***Starlin*** *a-8, 11, 12; c-8.*

MARVEL FEATURE (Also see Red Sonja)
Marvel Comics: Nov, 1975 - No. 7, Nov, 1976 (Story cont'd in Conan #68)

1-Red Sonja begins (pre-dates Red Sonja #1); adapts Howard short story; Adams-r/Savage Sword of Conan #1 3 6 9 16 23 30
2-6: Thorne-c/a in #2-7. 4,5-(Regular 25¢ edition)(5,7/76) 1 3 4 6 8 10
4,5-(30¢-c variants, limited distribution) 4 8 12 27 44 60
7-Red Sonja battles Conan 2 4 6 13 18 22

MARVEL FRONTIER COMICS UNLIMITED
Marvel Frontier Comics: Jan, 1994 ($2.95, 68 pgs.)

1-Dances with Demons, Immortalis, Children of the Voyager, Evil Eye, The Fallen stories 4.00

MARVEL FUMETTI BOOK
Marvel Comics Group: Apr, 1984 ($1.00, one-shot)

1-All photos; Stan Lee photo-c; Art Adams touch-ups 5.00

MARVEL FUN & GAMES
Marvel Comics Group: 1979/80 (color comic for kids)

1,11: 1-Games, puzzles, etc. 11-X-Men-c 2 4 6 8 10 12
2-10,12,13: (beware marked pages) 1 2 3 4 5 7

MARVEL GIRL
Marvel Comics: Apr, 2011 ($2.99, one-shot)

1-Early X-Men days of Jean Grey; Fialkov-s/Plati-a/Cruz-c 3.00

MARVEL GRAPHIC NOVEL
Marvel Comics Group (Epic Comics): 1982 - No. 38, 1990? ($5.95/$6.95)

1-Death of Captain Marvel (2nd Marvel graphic novel); Capt. Marvel battles Thanos by Jim Starlin (c/a/scripts) 5 10 15 31 53 75
1 (2nd & 3rd printings) 2 4 6 11 16 20
2-Elric: The Dreaming City 2 4 6 10 14 18
3-Dreadstar; Starlin-c/a, 52 pgs. 3 6 9 14 20 25
4-Origin/1st app. The New Mutants (1982) 7 14 21 46 86 125
4,5-2nd printings 2 4 6 10 14 18
5-X-Men; book-length story (1982) 3 6 9 21 33 45
6-15,20,25,30,31: 6-The Star Slammers. 7-Killraven. 8-Super Boxers; Byrne scripts. 9-The Futurians. 10-Heartburst. 11-Void Indigo. 12-Dazzler. 13-Starstruck. 14-The Swords Of The Swashbucklers. 15-The Raven Banner (a Tale of Asgard). 20-Greenberg the Vampire. 25-Alien Legion. 30-A Sailor's Story. 31-Wolfpack 2 4 6 8 10 12
16,17,21,29: 16-The Aladdin Effect (Storm, Tigra, Wasp, She-Hulk). 17-Revenge Of The Living Monolith (Spider-Man, Avengers, FF app.). 21-Marada the She-Wolf. 29-The Big Chance (Thing vs. Hulk) 2 4 6 9 12 15
18,19,26-28: 18-She Hulk. 19-Witch Queen of Acheron (Conan). 26-Dracula. 27-Avengers (Emperor Doom). 28-Conan the Reaver 2 4 6 10 14 18
22-Amaz. Spider-Man in Hooky by Wrightson 2 4 6 13 18 22
23-Dr. Strange 2 4 6 11 16 20
24-Love and War (Daredevil); Miller scripts 2 4 6 11 16 20
32-Death of Groo 2 4 6 11 16 20
32-2nd printing ($5.95) 2 4 6 8 10 12
33,34,36,37: 33-Thor. 34-Predator & Prey (Cloak & Dagger). 36-Willow (movie adapt.). 37-Hercules 2 4 6 8 10 12
35-Hitler's Astrologer (The Shadow, $12.95, HC) 2 4 6 11 16 20
35-Soft-c reprint (1990, $10.95) 2 4 6 9 12 15
38-Silver Surfer (Judgement Day)($14.95, HC) 2 4 6 13 18 22
38-Soft-c reprint (1990, $10.95) 2 4 6 9 12 15
nn-Abslom Daak: Dalek Killer (1990, $8.95) Dr. Who 2 4 6 9 12 15
nn-Arena by Bruce Jones (1989, $5.95) Dinosaurs 2 4 6 8 10 12
nn- A-Team Storybook Comics Illustrated (1983) r/ A-Team mini-series #1-3 2 4 6 8 10 12
nn-Ax (1988, $5.95) Ernie Colan-s/a 2 4 6 8 10 12
nn-Black Widow Coldest War (4/90, $9.95) 2 4 6 9 12 15
nn-Chronicles of Genghis Grimtoad (1990, $8.95)-Alan Grant-s 2 4 6 8 10 12
nn-Conan the Barbarian in the Horn of Azoth (1990, $8.95) 2 4 6 8 11 16
nn-Conan of Isles ($8.95) 2 4 6 8 11 16
nn-Conan Ravagers of Time (1992, $9.95) Kull & Red Sonja app. 2 4 6 8 11 16
nn-Conan -The Skull of Set 2 4 6 8 11 16
nn-Doctor Strange and Doctor Doom Triumph and Torment (1989, $17.95, HC) 2 4 6 13 18 22
nn-Dreamwalker (1989, $6.95)-Morrow-a 2 4 6 8 10 12
nn-Excalibur Weird War III (1990, $9.95) 2 4 6 8 10 12
nn-G.I. Joe - The Trojan Gambit (1983, 68 pgs.) 2 4 6 9 12 15
nn-Harvey Kurtzman Strange Adventures (Epic, $19.95, HC) Aragonés, Crumb 3 6 9 14 20 25
nn-Hearts and Minds (1990, $8.95) Heath-a 2 4 6 8 10 12
nn-Inhumans (1988, $7.95)-Williamson-i 3 6 9 14 20 25
nn-Jhereg (Epic, 1990, $8.95) 2 4 6 8 10 12
nn-Kazar-Guns of the Savage Land (7/90, $8.95) 2 4 6 8 10 12
nn-Kull-The Vale of Shadow ('89, $6.95) 2 4 6 8 10 12
nn-Last of the Dragons (1988, $6.95) Austin-a(i) 2 4 6 8 10 12
nn-Nightraven: House of Cards (1991, $14.95) 2 4 6 10 14 18
nn-Nightraven: The Collected Stories (1990, $9.95) Bolton-r/British Hulk mag.; David Lloyd-c/a 2 4 6 8 10 12
nn-Original Adventures of Cholly and Flytrap (Epic, 1991, $9.95) Suydam-s/c/a 2 4 6 10 14 18
nn-Rick Mason Agent (1989, $9.95) 2 4 6 8 10 12
nn-Roger Rabbit In The Resurrection Of Doom (1989, $8.95) 2 4 6 9 12 15
nn-A Sailor's Story Book II: Winds, Dreams and Dragons ('86, $6.95, softcover) Glansman-s/c/a 2 4 6 8 10 12
nn-Squadron Supreme: Death of a Universe (1989, $9.95) Gruenwald-s; Ryan & Williamson-a 3 6 9 14 20 25
nn-Who Framed Roger Rabbit (1989, $6.95) 2 4 6 9 12 15

NOTE: ***Aragones*** *a-27, 32.* ***Buscema*** *a-38.* ***Byrne*** *c/a-18.* ***Heath*** *a-35i.* ***Kaluta*** *a-13, 35p; c-13.* ***Miller*** *a-24p.* ***Simonson*** *a-6; c-6.* ***Starlin*** *c/a-1,3.* ***Williamson*** *a-34.* ***Wrightson*** *c-29i.*

MARVEL HEARTBREAKERS
Marvel Comics: Apr, 2010 ($3.99, one-shot)

1-Romance short stories; Spider-Man, MJ & Gwen app.; Casagrande-a; Beast app. 4.00

MARVEL - HEROES & LEGENDS
Marvel Comics: Oct, 1996; 1997 ($2.95)

nn-Wraparound-c, ...1997 ($2.99) -Original Avengers story 3.00

MARVEL HEROES FLIP MAGAZINE
Marvel Comics: Aug, 2005 - No. 26, Sept, 2007 ($3.99/$4.99)

1-11-Reprints New Avengers and Captain America (2005 series) in flip format thru #13 4.00
12-26: 14-19-Reprints New Avengers and Young Avengers in flip format. 20-Ghost Rider 5.00

MARVEL HOLIDAY SPECIAL
Marvel Comics: No. 1, 1991 ($2.25, 84 pgs.) - Present

1-X-Men, Fantastic Four, Punisher, Thor, Capt. America, Ghost Rider, Capt. Ultra, Spidey stories; Art Adams-c/a 4.00
nn (1/93)-Wolverine, Thanos (by Starlin/Lim/Austin) 4.00
nn (1994)-Capt. America, X-Men, Silver Surfer 4.00
... 1996-Spider-Man by Waid & Olliffe; X-Men, Silver Surfer 4.00
... 2004-Spider-Man by DeFalco & Miyazawa; X-Men, Fantastic Four 4.00
... 2004 TPB ($15.99) r/M.H.S. 2004 & past Christmas-themed stories 16.00
1 (1/06, $3.99) new Christmas-themed stories by various; Immonen-c 4.00
... 2006 (2/07, $3.99) Fin Fang Foom, Hydra, AIM app.; gallery of past covers; Irving-c 4.00
... 2007 (2/08, $3.99) Spider-Man & Wolverine stories; Hembeck-a 4.00
... 2011 (2/12, $3.99) Seeley-c; Spider-Man, Wolverine, Nick Fury, The Thing app. 4.00
Marvel Holiday (2006, $7.99, digest) reprints from M.H.S. 2004, 2006 & TPB 8.00
Marvel Holiday Spectacular Magazine (2009, $9.99, magazine) reprints from M.H.S. '93, '94, & Amazing Spider-Man #166; and new material w/Doe, Semeiks & Nauck-a 10.00

NOTE: ***Art Adams*** *c-'93.* ***Golden*** *a-'93.* ***Perez*** *c-'94.*

MARVEL ILLUSTRATED...
Marvel Comics: 2007 ($2.99)

Marvel Knights 4 #1 © MAR

Marvel Knights Spider-Man #1 © MAR

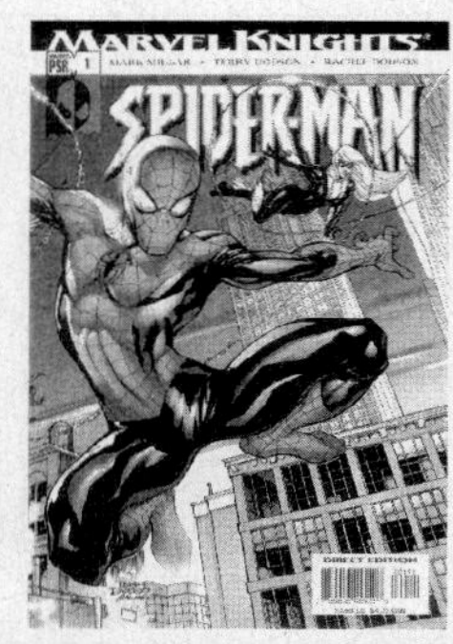

Marvel Masterpieces Collection #4 © MAR

	GD 2.0	VG 4.0	FN 6.0	VF 8.0	VF/NM 9.0	NM- 9.2

...Jungle Book - reprints from Marvel Fanfare #8-11; Gil Kane-s/a(p); P. Craig Russell-i 3.00

MARVEL ILLUSTRATED: KIDNAPPED (Title changes to Kidnapped with #5)
Marvel Comics: Jan, 2009 - No. 5, May, 2009 ($3.99, limited series)

1-5-Adaptation of the Stevenson novel; Roy Thomas-s/Mario Gully-a/Parel-c 4.00

MARVEL ILLUSTRATED: LAST OF THE MOHICANS
Marvel Comics: July, 2007 - No. 6, Dec, 2007 ($2.99, limited series)

1-6-Adaptation of the Cooper novel; Roy Thomas-s/Steve Kurth-a. 1-Jo Chen-c 3.00
HC (2008, $19.99) r/#1-6 20.00

MARVEL ILLUSTRATED: MOBY DICK
Marvel Comics: Apr, 2008 - No. 6, Sept, 2008 ($2.99, limited series)

1-6-Adaptation of the Melville novel; Roy Thomas-s/Alixe-a/Watson-c 3.00

MARVEL ILLUSTRATED: PICTURE OF DORIAN GRAY
Marvel Comics: Jan, 2008 - No. 6, July, 2008 ($2.99, limited series)

1-6-Adaptation of the Wilde novel; Roy Thomas-s/Fiumara-a. 1-Parel-c 3.00

MARVEL ILLUSTRATED: SWIMSUIT ISSUE (Also see Marvel Swimsuit Special)
Marvel Comics: 1991 ($3.95, magazine, 52 pgs.)

V1#1-Parody of Sports Illustrated swimsuit issue; Mary Jane Parker centerfold pin-up by Jusko; 2nd print exists 1 3 4 6 8 10

MARVEL ILLUSTRATED: THE ILIAD
Marvel Comics: Feb, 2008 - No. 8, Sept, 2008 ($2.99, limited series)

1-8-Adaptation of Homer's Epic Poem; Roy Thomas-s/Sepulveda-a/Rivera-c 3.00

MARVEL ILLUSTRATED: THE MAN IN THE IRON MASK
Marvel Comics: Sept, 2007 - No. 6, Feb, 2008 ($2.99, limited series)

1-6-Adaptation of the Dumas novel; Roy Thomas-s/Hugo Petrus-a. 1-Djurdjevic-c 3.00
HC (2008, $19.99) r/#1-6 20.00

MARVEL ILLUSTRATED: THE ODYSSEY (Title changes to The Odyssey with #7)
Marvel Comics: Nov, 2008 - No. 8, June, 2009 ($3.99, limited series)

1-8-Adaptation of Homer's Epic Poem; Roy Thomas-s/Greg Tocchini-a/c 4.00

MARVEL ILLUSTRATED: THE THREE MUSKETEERS
Marvel Comics: Aug, 2008 - No. 6, Jan, 2009 ($3.99, limited series)

1-6-Adaptation of the Dumas novel; Roy Thomas-s/Hugo Petrus-a/Parel-c 4.00

MARVEL ILLUSTRATED: TREASURE ISLAND
Marvel Comics: Aug, 2007 - No. 6, Jan, 2008 ($2.99, limited series)

1-6-Adaptation of the Stevenson novel; Roy Thomas-s/Mario Gully-a/Greg Hildebrandt-c 3.00
HC (2008, $19.99) r/#1-6 20.00

MARVEL KNIGHTS (See Black Panther, Daredevil, Inhumans, & Punisher)
Marvel Comics: 1998 (Previews for upcoming series)

Sketchbook-Wizard suppl.; Quesada & Palmiotti-c 3.00
Tourbook-($2.99) Interviews and art previews 3.00

MARVEL KNIGHTS
Marvel Comics: July, 2000 - No. 15, Sept, 2001 ($2.99)

1-Daredevil, Punisher, Black Widow, Shang-Chi, Dagger app. 4.00
2-15: 2-Two covers by Barreto & Quesada 3.00
.../Marvel Boy Genesis Edition (6/00) Sketchbook preview 3.00
...: Millennial Visions (2/02, $3.99) Pin-ups by various; Harris-c 4.00

MARVEL KNIGHTS (Volume 2)
Marvel Comics: May, 2002 - No. 6, Oct, 2002 ($2.99)

1-6-Daredevil, Punisher, Black Widow app.; Ponticelli-a 3.00

MARVEL KNIGHTS: DOUBLE SHOT
Marvel Comics: June, 2002 - No. 4, Sept, 2002 ($2.99, limited series)

1-4: 1-Punisher by Ennis & Quesada; Daredevil by Haynes; Fabry-c 3.00

MARVEL KNIGHTS 4 (Fantastic Four) (Issues #1&2 are titled **Knights 4**) (#28-30 titled **Four**)
Marvel Comics: Apr, 2004 - No. 30, July, 2006 ($2.99)

1-30: 1-7-McNiven-c/a; Aguirre-Sacasa-a. 8,9-Namor app. 13-Cho-c. 14-Land-c. 21-Flashback meeting with Black Panther. 30-Namor app. 3.00
...Vol. 1: The Wolf at the Door (2004, $16.99, TPB) r/#1-7 17.00
...Vol. 2: The Stuff of Nightmares (2005, $13.99, TPB) r/#8-12 14.00
...Vol. 3: Divine Time (2005, $14.99, TPB) r/#13-18 15.00
...Vol. 4: Impossible Things Happen Every Day (2006, $14.99, TPB) r/#19-24 15.00
Fantastic Four: The Resurrection of Nicholas Scratch TPB (2006, $14.99) r/#25-30 15.00

MARVEL KNIGHTS: HULK
Marvel Comics: Feb, 2014 - No. 4, May, 2104 ($3.99, limited series)

1-4-Keatinge-s/Kowalski-a; Banner in Paris 4.00

MARVEL KNIGHTS MAGAZINE
Marvel Comics: May, 2001 - No. 6, Oct, 2001 ($3.99, magazine size)

1-6-Reprints of recent Daredevil, Punisher, Black Widow, Inhumans 4.00

MARVEL KNIGHTS SPIDER-MAN (Title continues in Sensational Spider-Man #23)
Marvel Comics: Jun, 2004 - No. 22, Mar, 2006 ($2.99)

1-Wraparound-c by Dodson; Millar-s/Dodson-a; Green Goblin app. 4.00
2-12: 2-Avengers app. 2,3-Vulture & Electro app. 5,8-Cho-c/a. 6-8-Venom app. 3.00
13-18-Reginald Hudlin-s/Billy Tan-a. 13,14,18-New Avengers app. 15-Punisher app. 3.00
19-22-The Other x-over pts. 2,5,8,11; Pat Lee-a 3.00
19-22-var-c: 19-Black costume. 20-Scarlet Spider. 21-Spider-Armor. 22-Peter Parker 5.00
... Vol. 1 HC (2005, $29.99, over-sized with d.j.) r/#1-12; Stan Lee intro.; Dodson & Cho sketch pages 30.00
... Vol. 1: Down Among the Dead Men (2004, $9.99, TPB) r/#1-4 10.00
... Vol. 2: Venomous (2005, $9.99, TPB) r/#5-8 10.00
... Vol. 3: The Last Stand (2005, $9.99, TPB) r/#9-12 10.00
... Vol. 4: Wild Blue Yonder (2005, $14.99, TPB) r/#13-18 15.00

MARVEL KNIGHTS: SPIDER-MAN
Marvel Comics: Dec, 2013 - No. 5, Apr, 2014 ($3.99, limited series)

1-5-Matt Kindt-s/Marco Rudy-a; Arcade app. 4.00

MARVEL KNIGHTS 2099
Marvel Comics: 2005 ($13.99, TPB)

nn-Reprints one shots: Daredevil 2099, Punisher 2099, Black Panther 2099, Inhumans 2099 and Mutant 2099; Pat Lee-c 14.00

MARVEL KNIGHTS: X-MEN
Marvel Comics: Jan, 2014 - No. 5, May, 2014 ($3.99, limited series)

1-4-Brahm Revel-s/Cris Peter-a; Sabretooth app. 4.00

MARVEL LEGACY: ...
Marvel Comics: 2006, 2007 ($4.99, one-shots)

... The 1960s Handbook - Profiles of 1960s iconic and minor characters; info thru 1969 5.00
... The 1970s Handbook - Profiles of 1970s iconic and minor characters; info thru 1979 5.00
... The 1980s Handbook - Profiles of 1980s iconic and minor characters; info thru 1989 5.00
... The 1990s Handbook - Profiles of 1990s iconic and minor characters; Lim-c 5.00
...: The 1960s-1990s Handbook TPB (2007, $19.99) r/one-shots 20.00

MARVELMAN CLASSIC
Marvel Comics: 2010 ($34.99, B&W)

HC-(2010, $34.99) Reprints of 1950s British Marvelman stories; character history 35.00
... Primer (8/10, $3.99) Character history; Mick Anglo interview; Quesada-c 4.00

MARVELMAN FAMILY'S FINEST
Marvel Comics: 2010 - No. 6, Jan, 2011 ($3.99, B&W, limited series)

1-6-Reprints of 1950s Marvelman, Young Marvelman and Marvelman Family stories 4.00

MARVEL MANGAVERSE:... (one-shots)
Marvel Comics: March, 2002 ($2.25, manga-inspired one-shots)

Avengers Assemble! - Udon Studio-s/a 3.00
Eternity Twilight ($3.50) - Ben Dunn-s/a/wrap-around-c 4.00
Fantastic Four - Adam Warren-s/Keron Grant-a 3.00
Ghost Riders - Chuck Austen-s/a 3.00
Punisher - Peter David-s/Lea Hernandez-a 3.00
Spider-Man - Kaare Andrews-s/a 3.00
X-Men - C.B. Cebulski-s/Jeff Matsuda-a 3.00

MARVEL MANGAVERSE (Manga series)
Marvel Comics: June, 2002 - No. 6, Nov., 2002 ($2.25)

1-6: 1-Ben Dunn-s/a; intro. manga Captain Marvel 3.00
Vol. 1 TPB (2002, $24.95) r/one-shots 25.00
Vol. 2 TPB (2002, $12.99) r/#1-6 13.00
Vol. 3: Spider-Man-Legend of the Spider-Clan (2003, $11.99, TPB) r/series 12.00

MARVEL MASTERPIECES COLLECTION, THE
Marvel Comics: May, 1993 - No. 4, Aug, 1993 ($2.95, coated paper, lim. series)

1-4-Reprints Marvel Masterpieces trading cards w/ new Jusko paintings in each; Jusko painted-c/a 3.00

MARVEL MASTERPIECES 2 COLLECTION, THE
Marvel Comics: July, 1994 - No. 3, Sept, 1994 ($2.95, limited series)

1-3: 1-Kaluta-c; r/trading cards; new Steranko centerfold 3.00

MARVEL MILESTONE EDITION
Marvel Comics: 1991 - 1999 ($2.95, coated stock)(r/originals with original ads w/silver ink-c)

...: Amazing Fantasy #15 (3/92); ....:Hulk #181 (8/99, $2.99) 2 4 6 11 16 20

Marvel Milestones: Iron Man, Ant-Man & Captain America © MAR

Marvel Must Haves: NYX #4-5 © MAR

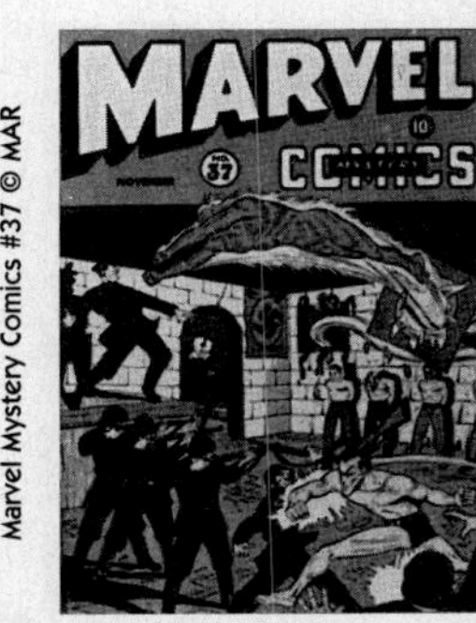

Marvel Mystery Comics #37 © MAR

GD VG FN VF VF/NM NM-
2.0 4.0 6.0 8.0 9.0 9.2

...: Amazing Spider-Man #1 (1/93), ...: Amazing Spider-Man #1 (1/93) variation- no price on-c, ...: Amazing Spider-Man #3 (3/95, $2.95), ...: Amazing Spider-Man #129 (11/92), ...: Avengers #1 (9/93), ...:Avengers #4 (3/95, $2.95), ...: Captain America #1 (3/95, $3.95), ...: Fantastic Four #1 (11/91), ...: Fantastic Four #5 (11/92), ...: Giant Size X-Men #1 (1991, $3.95, 68 pgs.), ...: Incredible Hulk #1 (3/92, says 3/91 by error), ...: Iron Man #55 (11/92), ...: Strange Tales-r/Dr. Strange stories from #110, 111, 114, & 115; ...: Tales of Suspense #39 (3/93), ...: X-Men #1-Reprints X-Men #1 (1991)
2 4 6 8 10 12
...: Amazing Spider-Man #149 (11/94, $2.95), ...: Avengers #16 (10/93), ...: X-Men #9 (10/93), ...:X-Men #28 (11/94, $2.95) 6.00
...: Iron Fist #14 (11/92) 1 3 4 6 8 10

MARVEL MILESTONES
Marvel Comics: 2005 - 2006 ($3.99, coated stock)(r/originals w/silver ink-c)

...: Beast & Kitty Pryde-r/from Amazing Adventures #11 & Uncanny X-Men #153 5.00
...: Black Panther, Storm & Ka-Zar-r/from Black Panther #26, Marvel Team-Up #100 and Marvel Mystery Comics #7 5.00
...: Blade, Man-Thing & Satana-r/from Tomb of Dracula #10, Adv. Into Fear #16 and Vampire Tales #2 5.00
...: Captain Britain, Psylocke & Sub-Mariner-r/from Spect. Spidey #114, Uncanny X-Men #213 and Human Torch #2 5.00
...: Doom, Sub-Mariner & Red Skull -r/from FF Ann. #2, Sub-Mariner Comics #1, Captain America Comics #1 5.00
...: Dragon Lord, Speedball and The Man in the Sky -r/from Marvel Spotlight #5, Speedball #1 and Amazing Adult Fantasy #14; Ditko-a on all 5.00
...: Dr. Strange, Silver Surfer, Sub-Mariner, & Hulk -r/from Marvel Premiere #3, FF Ann. #5, Marvel Comics #1, Incredible Hulk #3 5.00
...: Ghost Rider, Black Widow & Iceman -r/from Marvel Spotlight #5, Daredevil #81, X-Men #47 5.00
...: Iron Man, Ant-Man & Captain America -r/from TOS #39,40, TTA #27, Capt. America #1 5.00
...: Legion of Monsters, Spider-Man and Brother Voodoo -r/Marvel Premiere #28 & others 5.00
...: Millie the Model & Patsy Walker-r/from Millie the Model #100, Defenders #65 5.00
...: Onslaught -r/Onslaught: Marvel; wraparound-c 5.00
...: Rawhide Kid & Two-Gun Kid-r/Two-Gun Kid #60 and Rawhide Kid #17 5.00
...: Special: Bloodstone, X-51 & Captain Marvel II ($4.99) -r/from Marvel Presents #1, Machine Man #1, Amazing Spider-Man Ann. #19, and Bloodstone #1 6.00
...: Star Brand & Quasar -r/from Star Brand #1 & Quasar #1 5.00
...: Ultimate Spider-Man, Ult. X-Men, Microman & Mantor -r/from Ultimate Spider-Man #1/2, Ultimate X-Men #1/2 and Human Torch #2 5.00
...: Venom & Hercules -r/Marvel S-H Secret Wars #8, Journey Into Mystery Ann. #1 5.00
...: Wolverine, X-Men & Tuk: Caveboy -r/from Marvel Comics Presents #1, Uncanny X-Men #201, Capt. America Comics #1,2 5.00
...: (Jim Lee and Chris Claremont) X-Men and the Starjammers Pt. 1 -r/Unc. X-Men #275 5.00
...: X-Men and the Starjammers Pt. 2 -r/Unc. X-Men #276,277 5.00

MARVEL MINI-BOOKS (See Promotional Comics section)

MARVEL MONSTERS:... (one-shots)
Marvel Comics: Dec, 2005 ($3.99)

...Devil Dinosaur 1 - Hulk app.; Eric Powell-c/a; Sniegoski-s; r/Journey Into Mystery #62 5.00
...Fin Fang Four 1 - FF app.; Powell-c; Langridge-s/Gray-a; r/Strange Tales #89 5.00
...From the Files of Ulysses Bloodstone 1 - Guide to classic Marvel monsters; Powell-c 5.00
...Monsters on the Prowl 1 - Niles-s/Fegredo-a/Powell-c; Thing, Hulk, Giant-Man & Beast app. 5.00
...Where Monsters Dwell 1 - Giffen-s/a; David-s/Pander-a; Parker-s/Braun-s; Powell-c 5.00
HC (2006, $20.99, dust jacket) r/one-shots 21.00

MARVEL MOVIE PREMIERE (Magazine)
Marvel Comics Group: Sept, 1975 (B&W, one-shot)

1-Burroughs' "The Land That Time Forgot" adapt. 2 4 6 9 13 16

MARVEL MOVIE SHOWCASE FEATURING STAR WARS
Marvel Comics Group: Nov, 1982 - No. 2, Dec, 1982 ($1.25, 68 pgs.)

1-Star Wars movie adaptation; reprints Star Wars #1-3 by Chaykin; reprints-c to Star Wars #1
3 6 9 21 33 45
2-Reprints Star Wars #4-6; Stevens-r 3 6 9 15 22 28

MARVEL MOVIE SPOTLIGHT FEATURING RAIDERS OF THE LOST ARK
Marvel Comics Group: Nov, 1982 ($1.25, 68 pgs.)

1-Edited-r/Raiders of the Lost Ark #1-3; Buscema-c/a(p); movie adapt. 6.00

MARVEL MUST HAVES (Reprints of recent sold-out issues)
Marvel Comics: Dec, 2001 - Present ($2.99/$3.99/$4.99)

1,2,4-6: 1-r/Wolverine: Origin #1, Startling Stories: Banner #1, Tangled Web #4 and Cable #97. 2-Amazing Spider-Man #36 and others. 4-Truth #1, Capt. America V4 #1, and The Ultimates #1. 5-r/Ultimate War #1, Ult. X-Men #26, Ult Spider-Man #33. 6-Ult. Spider-Man #33-36 4.00
3-r/Call of Duty: The Brotherhood #1 & Daredevil #32,33 3.00
Amazing Spider-Man #30-32; Incredible Hulk #34-36; The Ultimates #1-3; Ultimate Spider-Man #1-3; Ultimate X-Men #1-3; (New) X-Men #114-116 each.... 4.00
NYX #1-3; NYX #4-5 with sketch & cover gallery; Ultimates 2 #1-3 each... 5.00
Spider-Man and the Black Cat #1-3; preview of #4 5.00

MARVEL MYSTERY COMICS (Formerly Marvel Comics) (Becomes Marvel Tales No. 93 on)
Timely /Marvel Comics (TP #2-17/TCI #18-54/MCI #55-92): No. 2, Dec, 1939 - No. 92, June, 1949 (Some material from #8-10 reprinted in 2004's Marvel 65th Anniversary Special #1)

2-(Rare)-American Ace begins, ends #3; Human Torch (blue costume) by Burgos, Sub-Mariner by Everett continue; 2 pg. origin recap of Human Torch; Angel-c
3850 7700 11,550 29,000 62,000 95,000
3-New logo from Marvel pulp begins; 1st app. of television in comics? in Human Torch story (1/40); Angel-c 2400 4800 7200 18,500 36,750 55,000
4-Intro. Electro, the Marvel of the Age (ends #19), The Ferret, Mystery Detective (ends #9); 1st Sub-Mariner-c by Schomburg; 2nd German swastika on-c of a comic (2/40); one month after Top-Notch Comics #2 2700 5400 8100 20,000 40,000 60,000
5 Classic Schomburg Torch-c, his 1st ever (Scarce)
3400 6800 10,200 25,000 52,500 80,000
6-Angel-c; Gustavson Angel story 1000 2000 3000 7500 13,750 20,000
7-Sub-Mariner attacks N.Y. city & Torch joins police force setting up battle in #8-10. Classic Schomburg Torch-c, his 2nd ever 1200 2400 3600 8400 16,200 24,000
8-1st Human Torch & Sub-Mariner battle(6/40) 1500 3000 4500 11,200 23,100 35,000
9-(Scarce)-Human Torch & Sub-Mariner battle (cover/story); classic-c by Everett
5000 10,000 15,000 37,000 71,000 105,000
10-Human Torch & Sub-Mariner battle, conclusion, 1 pg.; Terry Vance, the Schoolboy Sleuth begins, ends #57 1300 2600 3900 9700 19,850 30,000
11-Schomburg Torch-c, his 3rd ever 486 972 1458 3550 6275 9000
12-Classic Angel-c by Kirby 514 1028 1542 3750 6625 9500
13-Intro. of The Vision by S&K (11/40); Sub-Mariner dons new costume, ends #15; Schomburg's 4th Human Torch-c 730 1460 2190 5329 9415 13,500
14-16: 14-Shows-c to Human Torch #1 on-c (12/40). 15-S&K Vision, Gustavson Angel story
423 846 1269 3000 5250 7500
17-Human Torch/Sub-Mariner team-up by Burgos/Everett; Human Torch pin-up on back-c; shows-c to Human Torch #2 on-c 423 846 1269 3088 5444 7800
18-1st app. villain "The Cat's Paw" 389 778 1167 2723 4762 6800
19,20: 19-Origin Toro in text; shows-c to Sub-Mariner #1 on-c. 20-Origin The Angel in text
400 800 1200 2800 4900 7000
21-The Patriot begins, (intro. in Human Torch #4 (#3)); not in #46-48; Sub-Mariner pin-up on back-c (7/41) 423 846 1269 3000 5250 7500
22-25: 23-Last Gustavson Angel; origin The Vision in text. 24-Injury-to-eye story
400 800 1200 2800 4900 7000
26-29: 27-Ka-Zar ends; last S&K Vision who battles Satan. 28-Jimmy Jupiter in the Land of Nowhere begins, ends #48; Sub-Mariner vs. The Flying Dutchman
389 778 1167 2723 4762 6800
30-"Remember Pearl Harbor" Japanese war-c 432 864 1296 3154 5577 8000
31,32-"Remember Pearl Harbor" Japanese war-c. 31-Sub-Mariner by Everett ends, resumes #84. 32-1st app. The Boboes 389 778 1167 2723 4762 6800
33,35,36,38,39: 36-Nazi invasion of NYC cover. 39-WWI Nazi-c
371 742 1113 2600 4550 6500
34-Everett, Burgos, Martin Goodman, Funnies, Inc. office appear in story & battles Hitler; last Burgos Human Torch 383 766 1149 2681 3191 6700
37-Classic Hitler-c 417 834 1251 2919 5110 7300
40-Classic Zeppelin-c 811 1622 2433 5920 10,460 15,000
41-Hirohito & Tojo-c 411 822 1233 2877 5639 7200
42,43,47 360 720 1080 2520 4410 6300
44-Classic Super Plane-c 975 1950 2919 7100 12,550 18,000
45-Red Skull, Nazi hooded Vigilante war-c 432 864 1296 3154 5577 8000
46-Classic Hitler-c 1100 2200 3300 8360 15,180 22,000
48-Last Vision; flag-c 371 742 1113 2600 4550 6500
49-Origin Miss America 371 742 1113 2600 4550 6500
50-Mary becomes Miss Patriot (origin) 343 686 1029 2400 4200 6000
51-60: 54-Bondage-c 300 600 900 1920 3310 4700
61,62,64-Last German war-c 271 542 813 1734 2967 4200
63-Classic Hitler War-c; The Villainess Cat-Woman only app.
423 846 1269 3000 5250 7500
65,66-Last Japanese War-c 271 542 813 1734 2967 4200
67-78: 74-Last Patriot. 75-Young Allies begin. 76-Ten Chapter Miss America serial begins, ends #85 155 310 465 992 1696 2400
79-New cover format; Super Villains begin on cover; last Angel
177 354 531 1124 1937 2750
80-1st app. Capt. America in Marvel Comics 187 374 561 1197 2049 2900
81-Captain America app. 158 316 474 1003 1727 2450
82-Origin & 1st app. Namora (5/47); 1st Sub-Mariner/Namora team-up; Captain America app.
314 628 942 2198 3849 5500
83,85: 83-Last Young Allies. 85-Last Miss America; Blonde Phantom app.
148 296 444 947 1624 2300

Marvel 1985 #6 © MAR

Marvelous Land of Oz #1 © MAR

Marvel Premiere #50 © MAR

GD VG FN VF VF/NM NM-
2.0 4.0 6.0 8.0 9.0 9.2

84-Blonde Phantom begins (on-c of #84,88,89); Sub-Mariner by Everett begins;
Captain America app.; Everett-c 187 374 561 1197 2049 2900
86-Blonde Phantom i.d. revealed; Captain America app.; last Bucky app.
155 310 465 992 1696 2400
87-1st Capt. America/Golden Girl team-up; last Toro app. (8/48)
161 322 483 1030 1765 2500
88-Golden Girl, Namora, & Sun Girl (1st in Marvel Comics) x-over; Captain America,
Blonde Phantom app. 158 316 474 1003 1727 2450
89-1st Human Torch/Sun Girl team-up; 1st Captain America solo; Blonde Phantom app.
155 310 465 992 1696 2400
90,91: 90-Blonde Phantom un-masked; Captain America app. 91-Capt. America app.;
Blonde Phantom & Sub-Mariner end; early Venus app. (4/49) (scarce)
213 426 639 1363 2332 3300
92-Feature story on the birth of the Human Torch and the death of Professor Horton
(his creator); 1st app. The Witness in Marvel Comics; Captain America app. (scarce)
400 800 1200 2800 4900 7000
132 Pg. issue, B&W, 25¢ (1943-44)-printed in N. Y.; square binding, blank inside covers); has
Marvel No. 33-c in color; contains Capt. America #18 & Marvel Mystery Comics #33;
same contents as Captain America Annual 7000 14,000 21,500 43,500 - -
132 Pg. issue (with variant contents), B&W, 25¢ (1942-'43)- square binding, blank inside
covers; has same Marvel No. 33-c in color but contains Capt. America #22 & Marvel
Mystery Comics #41 instead 7000 14,000 21,500 43,500 - -

NOTE: *Brodsky c-49, 72, 86, 88-92. Crandall a-26i. Everett c-9, 27, 84. Gabrielle c-30-32. Schomburg c-3-11, 13-29, 33-36, 39-48, 50-59, 63-69, 74, 76, 132 pg. issue. Shores c-37, 38, 75p, 77, 78p, 79p, 80, 81p, 82-84, 85p, 87p. Sekowsky c-73. Bondage covers-3, 4, 7, 12, 28, 29, 49, 50, 52, 56, 57, 58, 59, 65. Angel c-2, 3, 8, 12. Remember Pearl Harbor issues-#30-32.*

MARVEL MYSTERY COMICS
Marvel Comics: Dec, 1999 ($3.95, reprints)

1-Reprints original 1940s stories; Schomburg-c from #74 5.00

MARVEL MYSTERY COMICS 70th ANNIVERARY SPECIAL
Marvel Comics: Jul, 2009 ($3.99, one-shot)

1-Rivera-c; new Sub-Mariner/Human Torch team-up set in 1941; reps. from #4 & 5 5.00

MARVEL MYSTERY HANDBOOK: 70th ANNIVERARY SPECIAL
Marvel Comics: 2009 ($4.99, one-shot)

1-Official Handbook-style profile pages of characters from Marvel's first year 5.00

MARVEL NEMESIS: THE IMPERFECTS (EA Games characters)
Marvel Comics: July, 2005 - No. 6, Dec, 2005 ($2.99, limited series)

1-6-Jae Lee-c/Greg Pak-s/Renato Arlem-a; Spider-Man, Thing, Wolverine, Elektra app 3.00
Digest (2005, $7.99) r/#1-6 8.00

MARVEL 1985
Marvel Comics: July, 2008 - No. 6, Dec, 2008 ($3.99, limited series)

1-6: 1-Marvel villains come to the real world; Millar-s/Edwards-a; three covers 4.00
HC (2009, $24.99) r/#1-6; intro. by Lindelof; Edwards production art 25.00

MARVEL NO-PRIZE BOOK, THE (The Official... on-c)
Marvel Comics Group: Jan, 1983 (one-shot, direct sales only)

1-Golden-c; Kirby-a 5.00

MARVEL NOW! POINT ONE
Marvel Comics: Dec, 2012 ($5.99, one-shot)

1-Short story lead-ins to new Marvel Now! series; Nick Fury, Nova, Star-Lord, Ant-Man &
others app.; s/a by various; Granov-c and baby variant-c by Skottie Young 6.00

MARVEL: NOW WHAT?!
Marvel Comics: Dec, 2013 ($3.99, one-shot)

1-Short story spoofs; Doct. Octopus, X-Men, Avengers; s/a by various; Skottie Young-c 4.00

MARVELOUS ADVENTURES OF GUS BEEZER
Marvel Comics: May, 2003; Feb, 2004 ($2.99, one-shots)

...: Gus Beezer & Spider-Man 1 - (5/03) Gurihiru-a 3.00
...: Hulk 1 - (5/03) Simone-s/Lethcoe-a; She-Hulk app. 3.00
...: Spider-Man 1 - (5/03) Simone-s/Lethcoe-a; The Lizard & Dr. Doom app. 3.00
...: X-Men 1 - (5/03) Simone-s/Lethcoe-a 3.00

MARVELOUS LAND OF OZ (Sequel to Wonderful Wizard of Oz)
Marvel Comics: Jan, 2010 - No. 8, Sept, 2010 ($3.99, limited series)

1-8-Eric Shanower-a/Skottie Young-a/c. 1-Two covers by Young 4.00
1-Variant Pumpkinhead/Saw-Horse cover by McGuinness 6.00

MARVEL PETS HANDBOOK (Also see "Lockjaw and the Pet Avengers")
Marvel Comics: 2009 ($3.99, one-shot)

1-Official Handbook-style profile pages of animal characters 4.00

MARVEL PREMIERE

GD VG FN VF VF/NM NM-
2.0 4.0 6.0 8.0 9.0 9.2

Marvel Comics Group: April, 1972 - No. 61, Aug, 1981 (A tryout book for new characters)

1-Origin Warlock (pre-#1) by Gil Kane/Adkins; origin Counter-Earth; Hulk & Thor cameo
(#1-14 are 20¢-c) 13 26 39 89 195 300
2-Warlock ends; Kirby Yellow Claw-r 4 8 12 28 47 65
3-Dr. Strange series begins (pre #1, 7/72), B. Smith-c/a(p)
8 16 24 56 108 160
4-Smith/Brunner-a 4 8 12 25 40 55
5-9: 8-Starlin-c/a(p) 3 6 9 17 26 35
10-Death of the Ancient One 3 6 9 21 33 45
11-14: 11-Dr. Strange origin-r by Ditko. 14-Last Dr. Strange (3/74), gets own title
3 months later 3 6 9 14 20 25
15-Origin/1st app. Iron Fist (5/74), ends #25 25 50 75 175 388 600
16,25: 16-2nd app. Iron Fist; origin cont'd from #15; Hama's 1st Marvel-a. 25-1st Byrne
Iron Fist (moves to own title next) 5 10 15 34 60 85
17,18,20,22-24: Iron Fist in all 3 6 9 21 33 45
19-1st app. Colleen Wing; Iron Fist app. 6 12 18 38 69 100
21-1st app. Misty Knight; Iron Fist app. 5 10 15 35 63 90
26-Hercules. 2 4 6 8 10 12
27-Satana 2 4 6 11 16 20
28-Legion of Monsters (Ghost Rider, Man-Thing, Morbius, Werewolf)
5 10 15 31 53 75
29-46: 29,30-The Liberty Legion. 29-1st modern app. Patriot. 31-1st app. Woodgod; last
25¢ issue. 32-1st app. Monark Starstalker. 33,34-1st color app. Solomon Kane (Robert E.
Howard adaptation "Red Shadows".) 35-Origin/1st app. 3-D Man. 36,37-3-D Man.
38-1st Weirdworld. 39,40-Torpedo. 41-1st Seeker 3000! 42-Tigra. 43-Paladin. 44-Jack of
Hearts (1st solo book, 10/78). 45,46-Man-Wolf 1 2 3 5 6 8
29-31-(30¢-c variants, limited distribution)(4,6,8/76) 4 8 12 23 37 50
36-38-(35¢-c variants, limited distribution)(6,8,10/77) 6 12 18 38 69 100
47-Origin/1st app. new Ant-Man (Scott Lang); Byrne-a
8 16 24 56 108 160
48-Ant-Man; Byrne-a 4 8 12 23 37 50
49-The Falcon (1st solo book, 8/79) 2 4 6 11 16 20
50-1st app. Alice Cooper; co-plotted by Alice 3 6 9 16 23 30
51-53-Black Panther 2 4 6 9 12 15
54-56: 54-1st Caleb Hammer. 55-Wonder Man. 56-1st color app. Dominic Fortune 6.00
57-Dr. Who (2nd U.S. app.-see Movie Classics) 3 6 9 19 30 40
58-60-Dr. Who 1 3 4 6 8 10
61-Star Lord 2 4 6 9 12 15

NOTE: *N. Adams (Crusty Bunkers) part inks-10, 12, 13. Austin a-50i, 56i; c-46i, 50i, 56i, 58. Brunner a-4i, 6p, 9-14p; c-9-14. Byrne a-47p, 48p. Chaykin a-32-34; c-32, 33, 56. Giffen a-31p, 44p; c-44. Gil Kane a(p)-1, 2, 15; c(p)-1, 2, 15, 16, 22-24, 27, 36, 37. Kirby c-26, 29-31, 35. Layton a-47i, 48i; c-47. McWilliams a-25i. Miller c-49p, 53p, 58p. Nebres a-44i; c-38i. Nino a-38i. Perez c/a-38p, 45p, 46p. Ploog a-38; c-5-7. Russell a-7p. Simonson a-60(2pgs.); c-57. Starlin a-8p; c-8. Sutton a-41, 43, 50p, 61; c-50p, 61. #57-60 publ'd w/two different prices on-c.*

MARVEL PRESENTS
Marvel Comics: October, 1975 - No. 12, Aug, 1977 (#1-6 are 25¢ issues)

1-Origin & 1st app. Bloodstone 3 6 9 14 20 25
2-Origin Bloodstone continued; Buckler-c 2 3 4 6 8 10
3-Guardians of the Galaxy (1st solo book, 2/76) begins, ends #12
4 8 12 28 47 65
4-7,9-12: 9,10-Origin Starhawk 2 4 6 8 10 12
4-6-(30¢-c variants, limited distribution)(4-8/76) 4 8 12 23 37 50
8-r/story from Silver Surfer #2 plus 4 pgs. new-a 2 4 6 8 10 12
11,12-(35¢-c variants, limited distribution)(6,8/77) 7 14 21 44 82 120

NOTE: *Austin a-6i. Buscema r-8p. Chaykin a-5p. Kane c-1p. Starlin layouts-10.*

MARVEL PREVIEW (Magazine) (Bizarre Adventures #25 on)
Marvel Comics: Feb (no month), 1975 - No. 24, Winter, 1980 (B&W) ($1.00)

1-Man-Gods From Beyond the Stars; Crusty Bunkers (Neal Adams)-a(i) & cover; Nino-a
3 6 9 19 30 40
2-1st origin The Punisher (see Amaz. Spider-Man #129 & Classic Punisher);
1st app. Dominic Fortune; Morrow-c 10 20 30 66 138 210
3,8,10: 3-Blade the Vampire Slayer. 8-Legion of Monsters; Morbius app. 10-Thor the Mighty;
Starlin frontispiece 3 6 9 17 26 35
4-Star-Lord & Sword in the Star (origins & 1st app.); Morrow-c
16 32 48 112 249 385
5-Sherlock Holmes 3 6 9 14 19 24
6,9: 6-Sherlock Holmes; N. Adams frontispiece. 9-Man-God; origin Star Hawk, ends #20
2 4 6 11 16 20
7-(Summer/76) Debut of Rocket Raccoon (called Rocky Raccoon) in Sword in the Star story
(see Incredible Hulk #271 (5/82) for next app.); Satana on cover
30 60 90 216 483 750
11,14,15,18-Star-Lord. 11-Byrne-a; Starlin frontispiece; 2 versions: with and w/o white Heinlein
text at lower right corner of front-c; 1st app. Spartax. 14-Starlin painted-c. 18-Sienkiewicz-a;
Veitch & Bissette-a 5 10 15 31 53 75

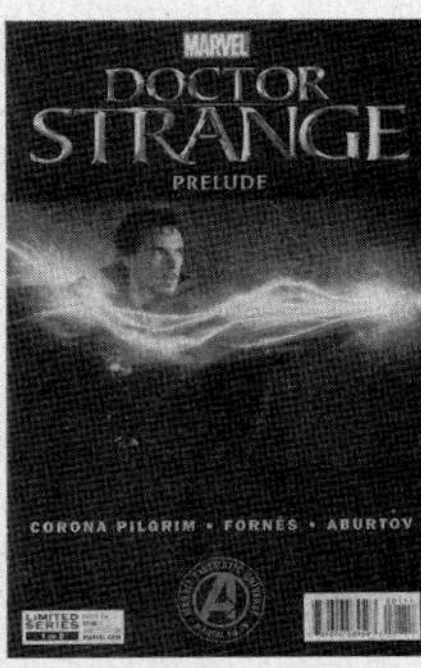

Marvel's Doctor Strange Prelude #1 © MAR

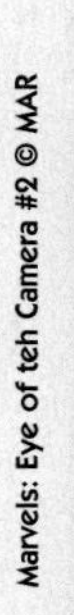

Marvels: Eye of teh Camera #2 © MAR

Marvels of Science #2 © CC

GD 2.0 | VG 4.0 | FN 6.0 | VF 8.0 | VF/NM 9.0 | NM- 9.2

12,16,19,21,23: 12-Haunt of Horror. 16-Masters of Terror. 19-Kull. 21-Moon Knight (Spr/80)-Predates Moon Knight #1; The Shroud by Ditko. 23-Bizarre Advs.; Miller-a 2 4 6 8 10 12
13,17,20,22,24: 17-Blackmark by G. Kane (see Savage Sword of Conan #1-3). 20-Bizarre Advs. 22-King Arthur. 24-Debut Paradox 1 2 3 5 6 8
NOTE: ***N. Adams*** *(C. Bunkers) r-20i.* ***Buscema*** *a-22, 23.* ***Byrne*** *a-11.* ***Chaykin*** *a-20r; c-20 (new).* ***Colan*** *a-8, 16p(3), 18p, 23p; c-16p.* ***Elias*** *a-18.* ***Giffen*** *a-7.* ***Infantino*** *a-14p.* ***Kaluta*** *a-12; c-15.* ***Miller*** *a-23.* ***Morrow*** *a-8i; c-2-4.* ***Perez*** *a-20p.* ***Ploog*** *a-8.* ***Starlin*** *c-13, 14. Nudity in some issues.*

MARVEL RIOT
Marvel Comics: Dec, 1995 ($1.95, one-shot)
1-"Age of Apocalypse" spoof; Lobdell script 3.00

MARVEL ROMANCE
Marvel Comics: 2006 ($19.99, TPB)
nn-Reprints romance stories from 1960-1972; art by Kirby, Buscema, Colan, Romita 20.00

MARVEL ROMANCE REDUX (Humor stories using art reprinted from Marvel romance comics)
Marvel Comics: Apr, 2006 - Aug, 2006 ($2.99, one-shots)
...: But I Thought He Loved Me Too (4/06) art by Kirby, Colan, Buscema & Romita; Giffen-c 3.00
...: Guys & Dolls (5/06) art by Starlin, Heck, Colan & Buscema; Conner-c 3.00
...: I Should Have Been a Blonde (7/06) art by Brodsky Colletta & Colan; Cho-c 3.00
...: Love is a Four Letter Word (8/06) art by Kirby, Buscema, Colan & Heck; Land-c 3.00
...: Restraining Orders are For Other Girls (6/06) art by Giordano, Kirby; Baker-c 3.00
...: Another Kind of Love TPB (2007, $13.99) r/one-shots 14.00

MARVELS (Also see Marvels: Eye of the Camera)
Marvel Comics: Jan, 1994 - No. 4, Apr, 1994 ($5.95, painted lim. series)
No. 1 (2nd Printing), Apr, 1996 - No. 4 (2nd Printing), July, 1996 ($2.95)
1-4: Kurt Busiek scripts & Alex Ross painted-c/a in all; double-c w/acetate overlay 1 2 3 5 6 8
Marvel Classic Collectors Pack ($11.90)-Issues #1 & 2 boxed (1st printings). 2 4 6 9 13 16
0-(8/94, $2.95)-no acetate overlay. 5.00
1-4-(2nd printing): r/original limited series w/o acetate overlay 3.00
Hardcover (1994, $59.95)-r/#0-4; w/intros by Stan Lee, John Romita, Sr., Kurt Busiek & Scott McCloud. 60.00
...: 10th Anniversary Edition (2004, $49.99, hardcover w/dustjacket) r/#0-4; scripts and commentaries; Ross sketch pages, cover gallery, behind the scenes art 50.00
Trade paperback ($19.95) 20.00

MARVEL SAGA, THE
Marvel Comics Group: Dec, 1985 - No. 25, Dec, 1987
1-25 4.00
NOTE: ***Williamson*** *a(i)-9, 10; c(i)-7, 10-12, 14, 16.*

MARVEL'S ANT-MAN PRELUDE (For the 2015 movie)
Marvel Comics: Apr, 2015 - No. 2, May, 2015 ($2.99, limited series)
1,2-Will Corona Pilgrim-s/Sepulveda-a; photo-c on both; Agent Carter app. 4.00

MARVEL'S CAPTAIN AMERICA: CIVIL WAR PRELUDE (For the 2016 movie)
Marvel Comics: Feb, 2016 - No. 4, Mar, 2016 ($2.99, limited series)
1-4: 1,2-Adaptation of Iron Man 3 movie; Pilgrim-s/Kudranski-a. 3,4-Adapts Captain America: The Winter Soldier movie; Ferguson-a 3.00

MARVELS COMICS: ... (Marvel-type comics read in the Marvel Universe)
Marvel Comics: Jul, 2000 ($2.25, one-shots)
...Captain America #1 -Frenz & Sinnott-a; ...Daredevil #1 -Isabella-s/Newell-a; ...Fantastic Four #1 -Kesel-s/Paul Smith-a; Spider-Man #1 -Oliff-a; ...Thor #1 -Templeton-s/Aucoin-a 3.00
...X-Men #1 -Millar-s/ Sean Phillips & Duncan Fegredo-a 3.00
The History of Marvels Comics (no cover price)-Faux history; previews titles 3.00

MARVEL'S DOCTOR STRANGE PRELUDE (2016 movie)
Marvel Comics: Sept, 2016 - No. 2, Oct, 2016 ($3.99, limited series)
1,2-Corona Pilgrim-s/Fornés-a; photo-c 4.00

MARVEL SELECT FLIP MAGAZINE
Marvel Comics: Aug, 2005 - No. 24 ($3.99/$4.99)
1-11-Reprints Astonishing X-Men and New X-Men: Academy X in flip format 4.00
12-24-($4.99) Reprints recent X-Men mini-series in flip format 5.00

MARVEL SELECTS:
Marvel Comics: Jan, 2000 - No. 6, June, 2000 ($2.75/$2.99, reprints)
...Fantastic Four 1-6: Reprints F.F. #107-112; new Davis-c 3.00
...Spider-Man 1,2,4-6: Reprints AS-M #100,101,103,104,93; Wieringo-c 3.00
...Spider-Man 3 ($2.99): Reprints AS-M #102; new Wieringo-c 3.00

MARVEL 75TH ANNIVERSARY CELEBRATION
Marvel Comics: Dec, 2014 ($5.99, one-shot)
1-Short stories by various incl. Stan Lee, Timm, Bendis, Stan Goldberg; Rivera-c 6.00

MARVELS: EYE OF THE CAMERA (Sequel to Marvels)
Marvel Comics: Feb, 2009 - No. 6, Apr, 2010 ($3.99, limited series)
1-6-Kurt Busiek-s/Jay Anacleto-a; continuing story of photographer Phil Sheldon 4.00
1-6-B&W edition 4.00

MARVEL'S GREATEST COMICS (Marvel Collectors' Item Classics #1-22)
Marvel Comics Group: No. 23, Oct, 1969 - No. 96, Jan, 1981
23-34 (Giants). Begin Fantastic Four-r/#30s?-116 3 6 9 17 26 35
35-37-Silver Surfer-r/Fantastic Four #48-50 2 4 6 9 12 15
38-50: 42-Silver Surfer-r/F.F.(others?) 1 2 3 5 7 9
51-70: 63,64-(25¢ editions) 6.00
63,64-(30¢-c variants, limited distribution)(5,7/76) 3 6 9 19 30 40
71-96: 71-73-(30¢ editions) 5.00
71-73-(35¢-c variants, limited distribution)(7,9-10/77) 5 10 15 33 57 80
...: Fantastic Four #52 (2006, $2.99) reprints entire comic with ads and letter column 6.00
NOTE: *Dr. Strange, Fantastic Four, Iron Man, Watcher-#23, 24. Capt. America, Dr. Strange, Iron Man, Fantastic Four-#25-28. Fantastic Four-#38-96.* ***Buscema*** *r-85-92; c-87-92r.* ***Ditko*** *r-23-28.* ***Kirby*** *r-23-82; c-75, 77p, 80p. #81 reprints Fantastic Four #100.*

MARVEL'S GREATEST SUPERHERO BATTLES (See Fireside Book Series)

MARVEL: SHADOWS AND LIGHT
Marvel Comics: Feb, 1997 ($2.95, B&W, one-shot)
1-Tony Daniel-c 3.00

MARVEL 1602
Marvel Comics: Nov, 2003 - No. 8, June, 2004 ($3.50/$3.99, limited series)
1-7-Neil Gaiman-s; Andy Kubert & Richard Isanove-a 3.50
8-($3.99) 4.00
... MGC #1 (7/10, $1.00) r/#1 with "Marvel's Greatest Comics" logo on cover 3.00
HC (2004, $24.99) r/series; script pages for #1, sketch pages and Gaiman afterword 25.00
SC (2005, $19.99) 20.00

MARVEL 1602: FANTASTICK FOUR
Marvel Comics: Nov, 2006 - No. 5, Mar, 2007s ($3.50, limited series)
1-5-Peter David-s/Pascal Alixe-a/Leinil Yu-c 3.50
TPB (2007, $14.99) r/#1-5; sketch page 15.00

MARVEL 1602: NEW WORLD
Marvel Comics: Oct, 2005 - No. 5, Jan, 2006 ($3.50, limited series)
1-5-Greg Pak-s/Greg Tocchini-a; "Hulk" and "Iron Man" app. 3.50
TPB (2006, $14.99) r/#1-5 15.00

MARVEL 65TH ANNIVERSARY SPECIAL
Marvel Comics: 2004 ($4.99, one-shot)
1-Reprints Sub-Mariner & Human Torch battle from Marvel Mystery Comics #8-10 6.00

MARVELS OF SCIENCE
Charlton Comics: March, 1946 - No. 4, June, 1946
1-A-Bomb story 24 48 72 142 234 325
2-4 14 28 42 82 121 160

MARVEL SPECIAL EDITION FEATURING... (Also see Special Collectors' Ed.)
Marvel Comics Group: 1975 - 1978 (84 pgs.) (Oversized)
1-The Spectacular Spider-Man ($1.50); r/Amazing Spider-Man #6,35, Annual 1; Ditko-a(r) 3 6 9 19 30 40
1,2-Star Wars ('77,'78) r/Star Wars #1-3 & #4-6; regular edition 2 4 6 11 16 20
1,2-Star Wars ('77,'78) Whitman variant 3 6 9 16 23 30
3-Star Wars ('78, $2.50, 116 pgs.); r/S. Wars #1-6; regular edition and Whitman variant exist 3 6 9 14 20 26
3-Close Encounters of the Third Kind (1978, $1.50, 56 pgs.)-Movie adaptation; Simonson-a(p) 2 4 6 10 14 18
V2#2(Spring, 1980, $2.00, oversized)- "Star Wars: The Empire Strikes Back"; r/Marvel Comics Super Special #16 3 6 9 16 23 30
NOTE: ***Chaykin*** *c/a(r)-1(1977), 2, 3.* ***Stevens*** *a(r)-2i, 3i.* ***Williamson*** *a(r)-V2#2.*

MARVEL SPECTACULAR
Marvel Comics Group: Aug, 1973 - No. 19, Nov, 1975
1-Thor-r from mid-sixties begin by Kirby 3 6 9 14 20 25
2-19 1 3 4 6 8 10

MARVELS: PORTRAITS
Marvel Comics: Mar, 1995 - No. 4, June, 1995 ($2.95, limited series)
1-4: Different artists renditions of Marvel characters 3.00

MARVEL SPOTLIGHT (...& Son of Satan #19, 20, 23, 24)
Marvel Comics Group: Nov, 1971 - No. 33, Apr, 1977; V2#1, July, 1979 - V2#11, Mar, 1981

Marvel Spotlight #32 © MAR

Marvel Spotlight: Dark Reign © MAR

Marvel Super-Heroes #12 © MAR

GD VG FN VF VF/NM NM-
2.0 4.0 6.0 8.0 9.0 9.2

(A try-out book for new characters)
1-Origin Red Wolf (western hero)(1st solo book, pre-#1); Wood inks, Neal Adams-c;
only 15¢ issue 5 10 15 35 63 90
2-(25¢, 52 pgs.)-Venus-r by Everett; origin/1st app. Werewolf By Night (begins) by Ploog;
N. Adams-c 18 36 54 126 281 435
3,4: 4-Werewolf By Night ends (6/72); gets own title 9/72
6 12 18 40 73 105
5-Origin/1st app. Ghost Rider (8/72) & begins 44 88 132 326 738 1150
6-8: 6-Origin G.R. retold. 8-Last Ploog issue 8 16 24 54 102 150
9-11-Last Ghost Rider (gets own title next mo.) 6 12 18 38 69 100
12-Origin & 2nd full app. The Son of Satan (10/73); story cont'd from Ghost Rider #2 & into
#3; series begins, ends #24 5 10 15 30 50 70
13-24: 13-Partial origin Son of Satan. 14-Last 20¢ issue. 22-Ghost Rider-c & cameo
(5 panels). 24-Last Son of Satan (10/75); gets own title 12/75
2 4 6 9 12 15
25,27,30,31: 27-(Regular 25¢-c), Sub-Mariner app. 30-The Warriors Three. 31-Nick Fury
1 2 3 5 6 8
26-Scarecrow 2 4 6 8 10 12
27-(30¢-c variant, limited distribution) 4 8 12 23 37 50
28-(Regular 25¢-c) 1st solo Moon Knight app. 7 14 21 46 86 125
28-(30¢-c variant, limited distribution) 13 26 39 89 195 300
29-(Regular 25¢-c) (8/76) Moon Knight app.; last 25¢ issue
3 6 9 19 30 40
29-(30¢-c variant, limited distribution) 7 14 21 44 82 120
32-1st app./partial origin Spider-Woman (2/77); Nick Fury app.
7 14 21 49 92 135
33-Deathlok; 1st app. Devil-Slayer 2 4 6 9 12 15
V2#1-Captain Marvel & Drax app. 2 4 6 8 10 12
1-Variant copy missing issue #1 on cover 3 6 9 19 30 40
2-5,9-11: 2-4-Captain Marvel. 2-Drax app. 4-Ditko-c/a. 5-Dragon Lord. 9-11-Captain
Universe (see Micronauts #8) 6.00
6-Star-Lord origin 4 8 12 27 44 60
7-Star-Lord; Miller-c 4 8 12 23 37 50
8-Capt. Marvel; Miller-c/a(p) 2 4 6 8 10 12

NOTE: ***Austin*** *c-V2#2i, 8.* ***J. Buscema*** *c/a-30p.* ***Chaykin*** *a-31; c-26, 31.* ***Colan*** *a-18p, 19p.* ***Ditko*** *a-V2#4, 5, 9-11; c-V2#4, 9-11.* ***Kane*** *c-21p, 32p.* ***Kirby*** *c-29p.* ***McWilliams*** *a-20i.* ***Miller*** *a-V2#8p; c(p)-V2#2, 5, 7, 8.* ***Mooney*** *a-8i, 10i, 14p, 15, 16p, 17p, 24p, 27, 32i.* ***Nasser*** *a-33p.* ***Ploog*** *a-2-5, 6-8p; c-3-9.* ***Romita*** *c-13.* ***Sutton*** *a-9-11p, V2#6, 7. #29-25¢ & 30¢ issues exist.*

MARVEL SPOTLIGHT (Most issues spotlight one Marvel artist and one Marvel writer)
Marvel Comics: 2005 - Present ($2.99/$3.99)

...Brian Bendis/Mark Bagley; Daniel Way/Olivier Coipel; David Finch/Roberto Aguirre-Sacasa;
Ed Brubaker/Billy Tan; John Cassaday/Sean McKeever; Joss Whedon/Michael Lark;
Laurell K. Hamilton/George R.R. Martin; Neil Gaiman/Salvador Larroca; Robert Kirkman/
Greg Land; Stan Lee/Jack Kirby; Warren Ellis/Jim Cheung each... 3.00
...Steve McNiven/Mark Millar - Civil War 10.00
...: Captain America (2009) interviews with Brubaker & Hitch; Reborn preview 3.00
...: Captain America Remembered (2007) character features; creator interviews 3.00
...: Civil War Aftermath (2007) Top 10 Moments, casualty list, previews of upcoming series 3.00
...: Dark Reign (2009) features on the Avengers, Fury and others; creator interview 4.00
...: Dark Tower (2007) previews the Stephen King adaptation; creator interviews 5.00
...: Deadpool (2009) character features; interviews with Kelly, Way, Medina & Benson 3.00
...: Fantastic Four and Silver Surfer (2007) character features; creator interviews 3.00
...: Ghost Rider (2007) character and movie features; creator interviews 3.00
...: Halo (2007) a World of Halo feature; Bendis & Maleev interviews 3.00
...: Heroes Reborn/Onslaught Reborn (2006) 3.00
...: Hulk Movie (2008) character and movie features; comic & movie creator interviews 3.00
...: Iron Man Movie (2008) character and movie features; Terrence Howard interview 3.00
...: Iron Man 2 (4/10) movie preview; Granov, Fraction interviews; Whiplash profile 4.00
...: Marvel Knights 10th Anniversary (2008) Quesada interview; series synopsies 3.00
...: Marvel Zombies/Mystic Arcana (2008) character features; creator interviews 3.00
...: Marvel Zombies Return (2009) character features; creator interviews 3.00
...: New Mutants (2009) character features; Claremont & McLeod interviews 3.00
...: Punisher Movie (2008) character and movie features; creator interviews 3.00
...: Secret Invasion (2008) features on the Skrulls; Bendis, Reed & Yu interviews 3.00
...: Secret Invasion Aftermath (2008) Skrull profiles; Bendis, Reed & Diggle interviews 4.00
...: Spider-Man (2007) character features; creator interviews; Ditko art showcase 3.00
...: Spider-Man - Brand New Day (2008) storyline features; Romitas interviews 3.00
...: Spider-Man-One More Day/Brand New Day (2008) storyline features; interviews 3.00
...: Summer Events (2009, $3.99) 2009 title previews; creator interviews 4.00
...: Thor (2007) character features; Straczynski interview; Romita Jr. art showcase 3.00
...: Ultimates 3 (2008) character features; Loeb & Madureira interviews 3.00
...: Ultimatum (2008) previews the limited series; Loeb & Bendis interviews 3.00
...: Uncanny X-Men 500 Issues Celebration (2008) creator interviews; timeline 3.00
...: War of Kings (2009) character features; Abnett, Lanning, Pelletier interviews 3.00

GD VG FN VF VF/NM NM-
2.0 4.0 6.0 8.0 9.0 9.2

...: Wolverine (2009, $3.99) preview of 2009 Wolverine stories; creator interviews 4.00
...: World War Hulk (2007) character features; creator interviews; early art showcase 3.00
...: X-Men: Messiah Complex (2008) X-Men crossover features; creator interviews 3.00

MARVELS PROJECT, THE
Marvel Comics: Oct, 2009 - No. 8, July, 2010 ($3.99, limited series)

1-8-Emergence of Marvel heroes in 1939-40; Brubaker-s/Epting-a; Epting & McNiven-c 4.00
1-8-Variant covers by Parel 5.00

MARVEL'S SPIDER-MAN: HOMECOMING PRELUDE
Marvel Comics: May, 2017 - No. 2 ($3.99, limited series)

1-Adaptation of Captain America: Civil War movie; Pilgrim-s/Nauck-a; photo cover 4.00

MARVEL'S THE AVENGERS
Marvel Comics: Feb, 2015 - No. 2, Mar, 2015 ($2.99, limited series)

1,2-Adaptation of 2012 movie; Pilgrim-s/Bennett-a; photo covers 3.00

MARVEL'S THE AVENGERS: BLACK WIDOW STRIKES
Marvel Comics: Jul, 2012 - No. 3, Aug, 2012 ($2.99, limited series)

1-3-Prelude to 2012 movie; Van Lente-s. 1,3-Photo-c. 2-Granov-c 3.00

MARVEL'S THE AVENGERS PRELUDE
Marvel Comics: May, 2012 - No. 4, Jun, 2012 ($2.99, limited series)

1-4: 1-Prelude to 2012 movie; Luke Ross & Daniel HDR-a 3.00

MARVEL'S THE AVENGERS: THE AVENGERS INITIATIVE
Marvel Comics: Jul, 2012 ($2.99, one-shot)

1-Prelude to 2012 movie; Van Lente-s/Lim-a 3.00

MARVEL SUPER ACTION (Magazine)
Marvel Comics Group: Jan, 1976 (B&W, 76 pgs.)

1-2nd app. Dominic Fortune (see Marvel Preview); early Punisher app.; Weird World &
The Huntress; Evans, Ploog-a 8 16 24 54 102 150

MARVEL SUPER ACTION
Marvel Comics Group: May, 1977 - No. 37, Nov, 1981

1-Reprints Capt. America #100 by Kirby 3 6 9 14 20 25
2-13: 2,3,5-13 reprint Capt. America #101,102,103-111. 4-Marvel Boy-r(origin)/M. Boy #1.
11-Origin-r. 12,13-Classic Steranko-c/a(r). 2 4 6 8 10 12
2,3-(35¢-c variants, limited distribution)(6,8/77) 9 18 27 59 117 175
14-20: r/Avengers #55,56, Annual 2, others 1 2 3 5 6 8
21-37: 30-r/Hulk #6 from U.K. 6.00

NOTE: ***Buscema*** *a(r)-14p, 15p; c-18-20, 22, 35r-37.* ***Everett*** *a-4.* ***Heath*** *a-4r.* ***Kirby*** *r-1-3, 5-11.* ***B. Smith*** *a-27r, 28r.* ***Steranko*** *a(r)-12p, 13p; c-12r, 13r.*

MARVEL SUPER HERO CONTEST OF CHAMPIONS
Marvel Comics Group: June, 1982 - No. 3, Aug, 1982 (Limited series)

1-Features nearly all Marvel characters currently appearing in their comics;
1st Marvel limited series 2 4 6 13 18 22
2,3 2 4 6 9 12 15

MARVEL SUPER HEROES
Marvel Comics Group: October, 1966 (25¢, 68 pgs.) (1st Marvel one-shot)

1-r/origin Daredevil from D.D. #1; r/Avengers #2; G.A. Sub-Mariner-r/Marvel Mystery #8
(Human Torch app.). Kirby-a 12 24 36 79 170 260

MARVEL SUPER-HEROES (Formerly Fantasy Masterpieces #1-11)
(Also see Giant-Size Super Heroes) (#12-20: 25¢, 68 pgs.)
Marvel Comics: No. 12, 12/67 - No. 31, 11/71; No. 32, 9/72 - No. 105, 1/82

12-Origin & 1st app. Capt. Marvel of the Kree; G.A. Human Torch, Destroyer, Capt. America,
Black Knight, Sub-Mariner-r (#12-20 all contain new stories and reprints)
25 50 75 175 388 600
13-2nd app. Capt. Marvel; 1st app. of Carol Danvers (later becomes Ms. Marvel);
Golden Age Black Knight, Human Torch, Vision, Capt. America, Sub-Mariner-r
50 100 150 400 900 1400
14-Amazing Spider-Man (5/68, new-a by Andru/Everett); G.A. Sub-Mariner, Torch, Mercury
(1st Kirby-a at Marvel), Black Knight, Capt. America reprints
10 20 30 65 135 200
15-Black Bolt cameo in Medusa (new-a); Black Knight, Sub-Mariner, Black Marvel,
Capt. America-r 6 12 18 41 76 110
16,17: 16-Origin & 1st app. S. A. Phantom Eagle; G.A. Torch, Capt. America, Black Knight,
Patriot, Sub-Mariner-r. 17-Origin Black Knight (new-a); G.A. Torch, Sub-Mariner-r;
reprint from All-Winners Squad #21 (cover & story)
5 10 15 31 53 75
18-Origin/1st app. Guardians of the Galaxy (1/69); G.A. Sub-Mariner, All-Winners Squad-r
38 76 114 285 641 1000
19-Ka-Zar (new-a); G.A. Torch, Marvel Boy, Black Knight, Sub-Mariner reprints; Smith-c(p);
Tuska-a(r) 4 8 12 27 44 60

Marvel Super-Heroes #86 © MAR

Marvel Tales #120 © MAR

Marvel Tales (2nd series) #91 © MAR

	GD 2.0	VG 4.0	FN 6.0	VF 8.0	VF/NM 9.0	NM- 9.2
20-Doctor Doom (5/69); r/Young Men #24 w/-c	5	10	15	35	63	90
21-31: All-r issues. 21-X-Men, Daredevil, Iron Man-r begin, end #31. 31-Last Giant issue	3	6	9	17	26	35
32-50: 32-Hulk/Sub-Mariner-r begin from TTA.	1	2	3	6	8	10
51-70,100: 56-r/origin Hulk/Inc. Hulk #102; Hulk-r begin	1	2	3	5	6	8
57,58-(30¢-c variants, limited distribution)(5,7/76)	4	8	12	27	44	60
65,66-(35¢-c variants, limited distribution)(7,9/77)	6	12	18	38	69	100
71-99,101-105						6.00

NOTE: ***Austin** a-104. **Colan** a(p)-12, 13, 15, 18; c-12, 13, 15, 18. **Everett** a-14i(new); r-14, 15i, 18, 19, 33; c-85(r). New **Kirby** c-22, 27, 54. **Maneely** r-14, 15, 19. **Severin** r-83-85i, 100-102; c-100-102r. **Starlin** c-47. **Tuska** a-19p. Black Knight-r by **Maneely** in 12-16, 19. Sub-Mariner-r by **Everett** in 12-20.*

MARVEL SUPER-HEROES
Marvel Comics: May, 1990 - V2#15, Oct, 1993 ($2.95/$2.50, quart., 68-84 pgs.)

	GD	VG	FN	VF	VF/NM	NM-
1-Moon Knight, Hercules, Black Panther, Magik, Brother Voodoo, Speedball (by Ditko) & Hellcat; Hembeck-a						5.00
2,4,5,V2#3,6,7,9,13-15: 2-Summer Special(7/90); Rogue, Speedball (by Ditko), Iron Man, Falcon, Tigra & Daredevil. 4-Spider-Man/Nick Fury, Daredevil,Speedball, Wonder Man, Spitfire & Black Knight; Byrne-c. 5-Thor, Dr. Strange, Thing & She-Hulk; Speedball by Ditko(p). V2#3-Retells origin Capt. America w/new facts; Blue Shield, Capt. Marvel, Speedball, Wasp; Hulk by Ditko/Rogers V2#6-9: 6,7-($2.25-c) X-Men, Cloak & Dagger, The Shroud (by Ditko) & Marvel Boy in each. 9-West Coast Avengers, Iron Man app.; Kieth-c(p). V2#13-15 ($2.75, 84 pgs.): 13-All Iron Man 30th anniversary. 15-Iron Man/Thor/Volstagg/Dr. Druid						4.00
V2#8-1st app. Squirrel Girl; X-Men, Namor & Iron Man (by Ditko); Larsen-c	4	8	12	28	47	65
V2#10-Ms. Marvel/Sabretooth-c/story (intended for Ms. Marvel #24; shows-c to #24); Namor, Vision, Scarlet Witch stories; $2.25-c	1	3	4	6	8	10
V2#11-Original Ghost Rider-c/story; Giant-Man, Ms. Marvel stories	2	4	6	8	10	12
V2#12-Dr. Strange, Falcon, Iron Man						4.00

MARVEL SUPER-HEROES MEGAZINE
Marvel Comics: Oct, 1994 - No. 6, Mar, 1995 ($2.95, 100 pgs.)

	GD	VG	FN	VF	VF/NM	NM-
1-6: 1-r/FF #232, DD #159, Iron Man #115, Incred. Hulk #314						4.00

MARVEL SUPER-HEROES SECRET WARS (See Secret Wars II)
Marvel Comics Group: May, 1984 - No. 12, Apr, 1985 (limited series)

	GD	VG	FN	VF	VF/NM	NM-
1	3	6	9	14	20	25
1-3-(2nd printings, sold in multi-packs)						4.00
2-6,9-11: 6-The Wasp dies	1	3	4	6	8	10
7,12: 7-Intro. new Spider-Woman. 12-($1.00, 52 pgs.)	2	4	6	9	12	15
8-Spider-Man's new black costume explained as alien costume (1st app. Venom as alien costume)	5	10	15	30	50	70
Secret Wars Omnibus HC (2008, $99.99, dustjacket) r/#1-12, Thor #383, She-Hulk (2004) #10 and What If? (1989) #4 & #114; photo gallery of related toys; pencil-a from #1						100.00

NOTE: ***Zeck** a-1-12; c-1,3,8-12. Additional artists (John Romita Sr., Art Adams and others) had uncredited art in #12.*

MARVEL SUPER HERO SPECTACULAR (All ages)
Marvel Comics: Dec, 2015 ($3.99, one-shot)

	GD	VG	FN	VF	VF/NM	NM-
1-Avengers, Guardians of the Galaxy and Spider-Man app.; bonus puzzle pages						4.00

MARVEL SUPER HERO SQUAD (All ages)
Marvel Comics: Mar, 2009; Nov, 2009 - No. 4, Feb, 2010 ($3.99/$2.99)

	GD	VG	FN	VF	VF/NM	NM-
1-4-Based on the animated series; back-up humor strips and pin-ups						3.00
...Hero Up! (3/09, $3.99) Collects humor strips from MarvelKids.com; 2 covers						4.00

MARVEL SUPER HERO SQUAD (All ages)
Marvel Comics: Mar, 2010 - No. 12, Feb, 2011 ($2.99)

	GD	VG	FN	VF	VF/NM	NM-
1-12-Based on the animated series. 1-Wraparound-c						3.00
Super Hero Squad Spectacular 1 (4/11, $3.99) The Beyonder app.						4.00

MARVEL SUPER SPECIAL, A (See Marvel Comics Super...)

MARVEL SWIMSUIT SPECIAL (Also see Marvel Illustrated...)
Marvel Comics: 1992 - No. 4, 1995 ($3.95/$4.50, magazine, 52 pgs.)

	GD	VG	FN	VF	VF/NM	NM-
1-4-Silvestri-c; pin-ups by diff. artists. 2-Jusko-c. 3-Hughes-c	1	3	4	6	8	10

MARVEL TAILS STARRING PETER PORKER THE SPECTACULAR SPIDER-HAM
(Also see Peter Porker...)
Marvel Comics Group: Nov, 1983 (one-shot)

	GD	VG	FN	VF	VF/NM	NM-
1-Peter Porker, the Spectacular Spider-Ham, Captain Americat, Goose Rider, Hulk Bunny app.						4.00

MARVEL TALES (Formerly Marvel Mystery Comics #1-92)
Marvel/Atlas Comics (MCI): No. 93, Aug, 1949 - No. 159, Aug, 1957

	GD 2.0	VG 4.0	FN 6.0	VF 8.0	VF/NM 9.0	NM- 9.2
93-Horror/weird stories begin	245	490	735	1568	2684	3800
94-Everett-a	142	284	426	909	1555	2200
95-New logo	116	232	348	742	1271	1800
96,99,101,103,105	71	142	213	454	777	1100
97-Sun Girl, 2 pgs; Kirbyish-a; one story used in N.Y. State Legislative document	94	188	282	597	1024	1450
98,100: 98-Krigstein-a	73	146	219	467	796	1125
102-Wolverton-a "The End of the World", (6 pgs.)	90	180	270	576	988	1400
104-Wolverton-a "Gateway to Horror", (6 pgs.)	94	188	282	597	1024	1450
106,107-Krigstein-a. 106-Decapitation story	58	116	174	371	636	900
108-120: 116-(7/53) Werewolf By Night story. 118-Hypo-c/panels in End of World story. 120-Jack Katz-a	53	106	159	334	567	800
121,123-131: 128-Flying Saucer-c. 131-Last precode (2/55)	42	84	126	265	445	625
122-Kubert-a	42	84	126	267	451	635
132,133,135-141,143,145	37	74	111	222	361	500
134-Krigstein, Kubert-a; flying saucer-c	39	78	117	236	388	540
142-Krigstein-a	38	76	114	228	369	510
144-Williamson/Krenkel-a, 3 pgs.	38	76	114	228	369	510
146,148-151,154-156,158: 150-1st S.A. issue. 156-Torres-a	32	64	96	188	307	425
147,152: 147-Ditko-a. 152-Wood, Morrow-a	34	68	102	204	332	460
153-Everett End of World c/story	38	76	114	228	369	510
157,159-Krigstein-a	33	66	99	194	317	440

NOTE: ***Andru** a-103. **Briefer** a-118. **Check** a-147. **Colan** a-102, 105, 107, 118, 120, 121, 127, 131. **Drucker** a-127, 135, 141, 146, 150. **Everett** a-98, 104, 106(2), 108(2), 131, 148, 151, 153, 155; c-107, 109, 111, 112, 114, 117, 127, 143, 147-151, 153, 155, 156. **Forte** a-119, 125, 130, 158. **Heath** a-110, 113, 118, 119; c-104-106, 110, 130. **Gil Kane** a-117. **Lawrence** a-130. **Maneely** a-111, 126, 129; c-108, 116, 120, 129, 152. **Mooney** a-114. **Morisi** a-153. **Morrow** a-150, 152, 156. **Orlando** a-149, 151, 157. **Pakula** a-119, 121, 133, 135, 144, 150, 152, 156. **Powell** a-136, 137, 150, 154. **Ravielli** a-117, 123. **Rico** a-97, 99. **Romita** a-108. **Sekowsky** a-96-98. **Shores** a-110; c-96. **Sinnott** a-105, 116, 144. **Tuska** a-114. **Whitney** a-107. **Wildey** a-126, 138.*

MARVEL TALES (...Annual #1,2; ...Starring Spider-Man #123 on)
Marvel Comics Group (NPP earlier issues): 1964 - No. 291, Nov, 1994 (No. 1-32: 72 pgs.)
(#1-3 have Canadian variants; back & inside-c are blank, same value)

	GD	VG	FN	VF	VF/NM	NM-
1-Reprints origins of Spider-Man/Amazing Fantasy #15, Hulk/Inc. Hulk#1, Ant-Man/T.T.A. #35, Giant Man/T.T.A. #49, Iron Man/T.O.S. #39,48, Thor/J.I.M. #83 & r/Sgt. Fury #1	32	64	96	230	515	800
2 ('65)-r/X-Men #1(origin), Avengers #1(origin), origin Dr. Strange-r/Strange Tales #115 & origin Hulk(Hulk #3)	10	20	30	66	138	210
3 (7/66)-Spider-Man, Strange Tales (H. Torch), Journey into Mystery (Thor), Tales to Astonish (Ant-Man)-r begin (r/Strange Tales #101)	6	12	18	40	73	105
4,5	5	10	15	30	50	70
6-8,10: 10-Reprints 1st Kraven/Amaz. S-M #15	3	6	9	21	33	45
9-r/Amazing Spider-Man #14 w/cover	4	8	12	23	37	50
11-33: 11-Spider-Man battles Daredevil-r/Amaz. Spider-Man #16. 13-Origin Marvel Boy-r from M. Boy #1. 22-Green Goblin-c/story-r/Amaz. Spider-Man #27. 30-New Angel story (x-over w/Ka-Zar #2,3). 32-Last 72 pg. iss. 33-(52 pgs.) Kraven-r	3	6	9	16	23	30
34-50: 34-Begin regular size issues	2	3	4	6	8	10
51-65	1	2	3	5	6	8
66-70-(Regular 25¢ editions)(4-8/76)	1	2	3	5	6	8
66-70-(30¢-c variants, limited distribution)	4	8	12	27	44	60
71-105: 75-Origin Spider-Man-r. 77-79-Drug issues-r/Amaz. Spider-Man #96-98. 98-Death of Gwen Stacy-r/Amaz. Spider-Man #121 (Green Goblin). 99-Death Green Goblin-r/Amaz. Spider-Man #122. 100-(52 pgs.)-New Hawkeye/Two Gun Kid story. 101-105-All Spider-Man-r						6.00
80-84-(35¢-c variants, limited distribution)(6-10/77)	5	10	15	35	63	90
106-r/1st Punisher-Amazing Spider-Man #129	2	4	6	9	12	15
107-136: 107-133-All Spider-Man-r. 111,112-r/Spider-Man #134,135 (Punisher). 113,114-r/Spider-Man #136,137(Green Goblin). 126-128-r/clone story from Amazing Spider-Man #149-151. 134-136-Dr. Strange-r begin; SpM stories continue. 134-Dr. Strange-r/Strange Tales #110						5.00
137-Origin-r Dr. Strange; shows original unprinted-c & origin Spider-Man/Amazing Fantasy #15	2	4	6	9	12	15
137-Nabisco giveaway	2	4	6	9	12	15
138-Reprints all Amazing Spider-Man #1; begin reprints of Spider-Man with covers similar to originals	1	3	4	6	8	10
139-144: r/Amazing Spider-Man #2-7						6.00
145-149,151-190,193-199: Spider-Man-r continue w/#8 on. 149-Contains skin "Tattooz" decals. 153-r/1st Kraven/Spider-Man #15. 155-r/2nd Green Goblin/Spider-Man #17. 161,164,165-Gr. Goblin-c/stories-r/Spider-Man #23,26,27. 178,179-Green Goblin-c/story-r/Spider-Man #39,40. 187,189-Kraven-r. 193-Byrne-r/Marvel Team-Up begin w/scripts						5.00
150,191,192,200: 150-($1.00, 52pgs.)-r/Spider-Man Annual #1(Kraven app.). 191-($1.50, 68 pgs.)-r/Spider-Man #96-98. 192-($1.25, 52 pgs.)-r/Spider-Man #121,122. 200-Double size ($1.25)-Miller-c & r/Annual #14						6.00

Marvel Tales (2nd series) #289 © MAR

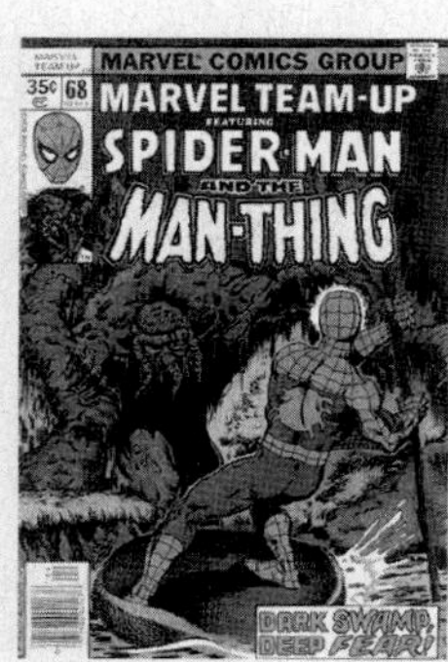

Marvel Team-Up #68 © MAR

Marvel Team-Up #148 © MAR

GD VG FN VF VF/NM NM-
2.0 4.0 6.0 8.0 9.0 9.2

201-249,251,252,254-257: 208-Last Byrne-r. 210,211-r/Spidey #134,135. 212,213-r/Giant-Size Spidey #4. 213-r/1st solo Silver Surfer story/F.F. Annual #5. 214,215-r/Spidey #161,162. 222-Reprints origin Punisher/Spect. Spider-Man #83; last Punisher reprint. 209-Reprints 1st app. The Punisher/Amazing Spider-Man #129; Punisher reprints begin, end #222. 223-McFarlane-c begins, end #239. 233-Spider-Man/X-Men team-ups begin; r/X-Men #35. 234-r/Marvel Team-Up #4. 235,236-r/M. Team-Up Annual #1. 237,238-r/M. Team-Up #150. 239,240-r/M. Team-Up #38,90(Beast). 242-r/M.Team-Up #89. 243-r/M. Team-Up #117 (Wolverine). 251-r/Spider-Man #100 (Green Goblin-c/story). 252-r/1st app. Morbius/Amaz. Spider-Man #101. 254-r/M. Team-Up #15(Ghost Rider); new painted-c. 255,256-Spider-Man & Ghost Rider-r/Marvel Team-Up #58,91. 257-Hobgoblin-r begin (r/ASM #238) 3.00
250.253: 250-($1.50, 52 pgs.)-r/1st Karma/M. Team-Up #100. 253-($1.50, 52 pgs.) -r/Amaz. S-M #102 4.00
258-291: 258-261-r/A. Spider-Man #239,249-251(Hobgoblin). 262,263-r/Marv. Team-Up #53,54. 262-New X-Men vs. Sunstroke story. 263-New Woodgod origin story. 264,265-r/Amazing Spider-Man Annual 5. 266-273-Reprints alien costume stories/A. S-M 252-259. 277-r/1st Silver Sable/A. S-M 265. 283-r/A. S-M 275 (Hobgoblin). 284-r/A. S-M 276 (Hobgoblin) 3.00
285-variant w/Wonder-Con logo on c-no price-giveaway 3.00
286-($2.95)-p/bagged w/16 page insert & animation print 4.00

NOTE: *All contain reprints; some have new art. #89-97-r/Amazing Spider-Man #110-118; #98-136-r/#121-159; #137-150-r/Amazing Fantasy #15, #1-12 & Annual 1; #151-167-r/#13-28 & Annual 2; #168-186-r/#29-46.* **Austin** *a-100i; c-272i, 273i.* **Byrne** *a(r)-193-198p, 201-208p.* **Ditko** *a-1-30, 83, 100, 137-155.* **G. Kane** *a-71, 81, 98-101p, 249r; c-125-127p, 130p, 137-155.* **Sam Kieth** *c-255, 262, 263.* **Ron Lim** *c-266p-281p, 283p-285p.* **McFarlane** *c-223-239.* **Mooney** *a-63, 95-97i, 103(i).* **Nasser** *a-100p.* **Nebres** *a-242i.* **Perez** *c-259-261.* **Rogers** *c-240, 241, 243-252.*

MARVEL TALES FLIP MAGAZINE
Marvel Comics: Sept, 2005 - No. 25, Sept, 2007 ($3.99/$4.99)

1-6-Reprints Amazing Spider-Man #30-up and Amazing Fantasy (2004) in flip format 4.00
7-10-Reprints Amazing Spider-Man #36-up and Runaways Vol. 2 in flip format 4.00
11-25-($4.99) Reprints Amazing Spider-Man #36-up and Runaways Vol. 2 in flip format 5.00

MARVEL TAROT, THE
Marvel Comics: 2007 ($3.99, one-shot)

1-Marvel characters featured in Tarot deck images; Djurdjevic-c 4.00

MARVEL TEAM-UP (See Marvel Treasury Edition #18 & Official Marvel Index To...)
(Replaced by Web of Spider-Man)
Marvel Comics Group: March, 1972 - No. 150, Feb, 1985
NOTE: *Spider-Man team-ups in all but Nos. 18, 23, 26, 29, 32, 35, 97, 104, 105, 137.*

1-Human Torch 12 24 36 84 185 285
2-Human Torch 5 10 15 35 63 90
3-Spider-Man/Human Torch vs. Morbius (part 1); 3rd app. of Morbius (7/72) 6 12 18 41 76 110
4-Spider-Man/X-Men vs. Morbius (part 2 of story); 4th app. of Morbius 6 12 18 41 76 110
5-10: 5-Vision. 6-Thing. 7-Thor. 8-The Cat (4/73, came out between The Cat #3 & 4). 9-Iron Man. 10-Human Torch 3 6 9 20 31 42
11-Inhumans 3 6 9 16 23 30
12-Werewolf (By Night) (8/73) 3 6 9 19 30 40
13,14,16-20: 13-Capt. America. 14-Sub-Mariner. 16-Capt. Marvel. 17-Mr. Fantastic. 18-Human Torch/Hulk. 19-Ka-Zar. 20-Black Panther; last 20¢ issue 2 4 6 13 18 22
15-1st Spider-Man/Ghost Rider team-up (11/73) 4 8 12 23 37 50
21,23-30: 21-Dr. Strange. 23-H-T/Iceman (X-Men cameo). 24-Brother Voodoo. 25-Daredevil. 26-H-T/Thor. 27-Hulk. 28-Hercules. 29-H-T/Iron Man. 30-Falcon 2 4 6 8 10 12
22-Hawkeye 2 4 6 11 16 20
31-45,47-50: 31-Iron Fist. 32-H-T/Son of Satan. 33-Nighthawk. 34-Valkyrie. 35-H-T/Dr. Strange. 36-Frankenstein. 37-Man-Wolf. 38-Beast. 39-H-T. 40-Sons of the Tiger/H-T. 41-Scarlet Witch. 42-The Vision. 43-Dr. Doom; retells origin. 44-Moondragon. 45-Killraven. 47-Thing. 48-Iron Man; last 25¢ issue. 49-Dr. Strange; Iron Man app. 50-Iron Man; Dr. Strange app. 1 2 3 5 6 8
44-48-(30¢-c variants, limited distribution)(4-8/76) 5 10 15 33 57 80
46-Spider-Man/Deathlok team-up 1 2 3 5 7 9
51,52,56,57: 51-Iron Man; Dr. Strange app. 52-Capt. America. 56-Daredevil. 57-Black Widow; 2nd app. Silver Samurai 1 2 3 4 5 7
53-Hulk; Woodgod & X-Men app., 1st Byrne-a on X-Men (1/77) 3 6 9 21 33 45
54,55,58-60: 54,59,60: 54-Hulk; Woodgod app. 59-Yellowjacket/The Wasp. 60-The Wasp (Byrne-a in all). 55-Warlock-c/story; Byrne-a. 58-Ghost Rider 2 3 4 6 8 10
58-62-(35¢-c variants, limited distribution)(6-10/77) 8 16 24 54 102 150
61-64,67-70: All Byrne-a; 61-H-T. 62-Ms. Marvel; last 30¢ issue. 63-Iron Fist. 64-Daughters of the Dragon. 67-Tigra; Kraven the Hunter app. 68-Man-Thing. 69-Havok (from X-Men). 70-Thor 1 2 3 5 7 9
65-Capt. Britain (1st U.S. app.) 4 8 12 25 40 55
66-Capt. Britain; 1st app. Arcade 2 4 6 11 16 20

GD VG FN VF VF/NM NM-
2.0 4.0 6.0 8.0 9.0 9.2

71-74,76-78,80: 71-Falcon. 72-Iron Man. 73-Daredevil. 74-Not Ready for Prime Time Players (Belushi). 76-Dr. Strange. 77-Ms. Marvel. 78-Wonder Man. 80-Dr. Strange/Clea; last 35¢ issue 6.00
75,79,81: Byrne-a(p). 75-Power Man; Cage app. 79-Mary Jane Watson as Red Sonja; Clark Kent cameo (1 panel, 3/79). 81-Death of Satana 1 2 3 5 6 8
82-85,87-94,96-99: 82-Black Widow. 83-Nick Fury. 84-Shang-Chi. 89-Nightcrawler (X-Men). 91-Ghost Rider. 92-Hawkeye. 93-Werewolf by Night. 94-Spider-Man vs. The Shroud. 96-Howard the Duck; last 40¢ issue. 97-Spider-Woman/ Hulk. 98-Black Widow. 99-Machine Man. 85-Shang-Chi/Black Widow/Nick Fury. 87-Black Panther. 88-Invisible Girl. 90-Beast 5.00
86-Guardians of the Galaxy 1 3 4 6 8 10
95-Mockingbird (intro.); Nick Fury app. 4 8 12 28 47 65
100-(Double-size)-Spider-Man & Fantastic Four story with origin/1st app. Karma, one of the New Mutants; X-Men & Professor X cameo; Miller-c/a(p); Storm & Black Panther story; brief origins; Byrne-a(p) 2 4 6 9 12 15
101,102,104-116: 101-Nighthawk(Ditko-a). 102-Doc Samson. 104-Hulk/Ka-Zar. 105-Hulk/Power Man/Iron Fist. 106-Capt. America. 107-She-Hulk. 108-Paladin; Dazzler cameo. 109-Dazzler; Paladin app. 110-Iron Man. 111-Devil-Slayer. 112-King Kull; last 50¢ issue. 113-Quasar. 114-Falcon. 115-Thor. 116-Valkyrie 4.00
103-Ant-Man 2 4 6 9 12 15
117-Wolverine-c/story 2 4 6 8 10 12
118-140,142-149: 118-Professor X; Wolverine app. (4 pgs.); X-Men cameo. 119-Gargoyle. 120-Dominic Fortune. 121-Human Torch. 122-Man-Thing. 123-Daredevil. 124-The Beast. 125-Tigra. 126-Hulk & Powerman/Son of Satan. 127-The Watcher. 128-Capt. America; Spider-Man/Capt. America photo-c. 129-The Vision. 130-Scarlet Witch. 131-Frogman. 132-Mr. Fantastic. 133-Fantastic Four. 134-Jack of Hearts. 135-Kitty Pryde; X-Men cameo. 136-Wonder Man. 137-Aunt May/Franklin Richards. 138-Sandman. 139-Nick Fury. 140-Black Widow. 142-Capt. Marvel. 143-Starfox. 144-Moon Knight. 145-Iron Man. 146-Nomad. 147-Human Torch; Spider-Man back to old costume. 148-Thor. 149-Cannonball 4.00
141-Daredevil; SpM/Black Widow app. (Spidey in new black costume; ties w/ Amazing Spider-Man #252 for 1st black costume) 4 8 12 25 40 55
150-X-Men ($1.00, double-size); B. Smith-c 1 2 3 5 6 8
Annual 1 (1976)-Spider-Man/X-Men (early app.) 3 6 9 21 33 45
Annual 2 (1979)-Spider-Man/Hulk 1 3 4 6 8 10
Annuals 3,4: 3 (1980)-Hulk/Power Man/Machine Man/Iron Fist; Miller-c(p). 4 (1981)-Spider-Man /Daredevil/Moon Knight/Power Man/Iron Fist; brief origins of each; Miller-c; Miller scripts on Daredevil 1 2 3 4 5 7
Annuals 5-7: 5 (1982)-SpM/The Thing/Scarlet Witch/Dr. Strange/Quasar. 6 (1983)-Spider-Man/ New Mutants (early app.), Cloak & Dagger. 7(1984)-Alpha Flight; Byrne-c(i) 6.00

NOTE: **Art Adams** *c-141p.* **Austin** *a-79i; c-76i, 79i, 96i, 101i, 112i, 130i.* **Bolle** *a-9i.* **Byrne** *a(p)-53-55, 59-70, 75, 79, 100; c-68p, 70p, 72p, 75, 76p, 79p, 129i, 133i.* **Colan** *a-87p.* **Ditko** *a-101.* **Kane** *a(p)-4-6, 13, 14, 16-19, 23; c(p)-4, 13, 14, 17-19, 23, 25, 26, 32-35, 37, 41, 44, 45, 47, 53, 54.* **Miller** *a-100p; c-95p, 99p, 100p, 102p, 106.* **Mooney** *a-2i, 7i, 8, 10p, 11p, 16i, 24-31p, 72, 93i, Annual 5i.* **Nasser** *a-89p; c-101p.* **Simonson** *c-99i, 148.* **Paul Smith** *c-131, 132.* **Starlin** *c-27.* **Sutton** *a-93p. "H-T" means Human Torch; "SpM" means Spider-Man; "S-M" means Sub-Mariner.*

MARVEL TEAM-UP (2nd Series)
Marvel Comics: Sept, 1997 - No. 11, July, 1998 ($1.99)

1-11: 1-Spider-Man team-ups begin, Generation x-app. 2-Hercules-c/app.; two covers. 3-Sandman. 4-Man-Thing. 7-Blade. 8-Namor team-ups begin, Dr. Strange app. 9-Capt. America. 10-Thing. 11-Iron Man 3.00

MARVEL TEAM-UP
Marvel Comics: Jan, 2005 - No. 25, Dec, 2006 ($2.25/$2.99)

1-7,9: 1,2-Spider-Man & Wolverine; Kirkman-s/Kolins-a. 5,6-X-23 app. 3.00
8,10-25 ($2.99-c) 10-Spider-Man & Daredevil. 12-Origin of Titannus. 14-Invincible app. 15-2nd app. of 2nd Sleepwalker 3.00
... Vol. 1: The Golden Child TPB (2005, $12.99) r/#1-6 13.00
... Vol. 2: Master of the Ring TPB (2005, $17.99) r/#7-13 18.00
... Vol. 3: League of Losers TPB (2006, $13.99) r/#14-18 14.00
... Vol. 4: Freedom Ring TPB (2007, $17.99) r/#19-25 18.00

MARVEL: THE LOST GENERATION
Marvel Comics: No. 12, Mar, 2000 - No. 1, Feb, 2001 ($2.99, issue #s go in reverse)

1-12-Stern-s/Byrne-s/a; untold story of The First Line. 5-Thor app. 3.00

MARVEL/ TOP COW CROSSOVERS
Image Comics (Top Cow): Nov, 2005 ($24.99, TPB)

Vol. 1-Reprints crossovers with Wolverine, Witchblade, Hulk, Darkness; Devil's Reign 25.00

MARVEL TREASURY EDITION
Marvel Comics Group/Whitman #17,18: 1974; #2, Dec, 1974 - #28, 1981 ($1.50/$2.50, 100 pgs., oversized, new-a &-r)(Also see Amazing Spider-Man, The, Marvel Spec. Ed. Feat.--, Savage Fists of Kung Fu, Superman Vs. , & 2001, A Space Odyssey)

1-Spectacular Spider-Man; story-r/Marvel Super-Heroes #14; Romita-c/a(r); G. Kane,

Marvel Treasury Edition #21 © MAR

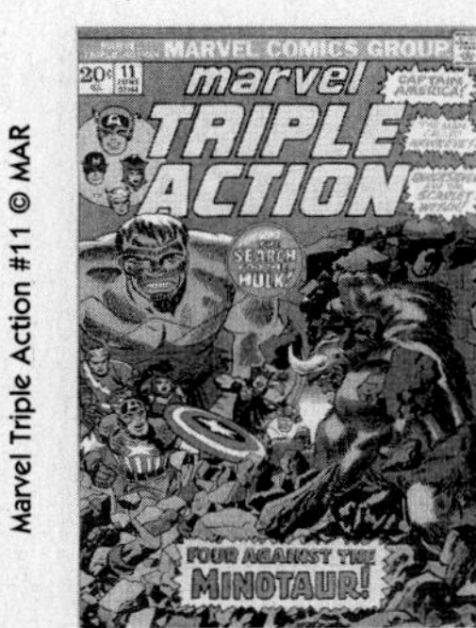

Marvel Triple Action #11 © MAR

Marvel Tsum Tsum #1 © MAR

GD 2.0 VG 4.0 FN 6.0 VF 8.0 VF/NM 9.0 NM- 9.2

GD 2.0 VG 4.0 FN 6.0 VF 8.0 VF/NM 9.0 NM- 9.2

Ditko-r; Green Goblin/Hulk-r 5 10 15 33 57 80
1-1,000 numbered copies signed by Stan Lee & John Romita on front-c & sold thru mail for $5.00; these were the 1st 1,000 copies off the press
11 22 33 72 154 235
2-10: 2-Fantastic Four-r/F.F. 6,11,48-50(Silver Surfer). 3-The Mighty Thor-r/Thor #125-130. 4-Conan the Barbarian; Barry Smith-c/a(r)/Conan #11. 5-The Hulk (origin-r/Hulk #3). 6-Dr. Strange. 7-Mighty Avengers. 8-Giant Superhero Holiday Grab-Bag; Spider-Man, Hulk, Nick Fury. 9-Giant; Super-hero Team-up. 10-Thor; r/Thor #154-157
3 6 9 17 26 35
11-20: 11-Fantastic Four. 12-Howard the Duck (r/#H. the Duck #1 & G.S. Man-Thing #4,5) plus new Defenders story. 13-Giant Super-Hero Holiday Grab-Bag. 14-The Sensational Spider-Man; r/1st Morbius from Amazing S-M #101,102 plus #100 & r/Not Brand Echh #6. 15-Conan; B. Smith, Neal Adams-i; r/Conan #24. 16-The Defenders (origin) & Valkyrie; r/Defenders #1,4,13,14. 17-Incredible Hulk; Blob, Havok, Rhino and The Leader app. 18-The Astonishing Spider-Man; r/Spider-Man's 1st team-ups with Iron Fist, The X-Men, Ghost Rider & Werewolf by Night; inside back-c has photos from 1978 Spider-Man TV show. 19-Conan the Barbarian. 20-Hulk 3 6 9 14 20 25
21-24,27: 21-Fantastic Four. 22-Spider-Man. 23-Conan. 24-Rampaging Hulk. 27-Spider-Man
3 6 9 14 20 25
25-Spider-Man vs. The Hulk new story 3 6 9 16 24 32
26-The Hulk; 6 pg. new Wolverine/Hercules-s 3 6 9 16 23 30
28-Spider-Man/Superman; (origin of each) 5 10 15 31 53 75

NOTE: *Reprints-2, 3, 5, 7-9, 13, 14, 16, 17.* ***Neal Adams*** *a(i)-6, 15.* ***Brunner*** *a-6, 12; c-6.* ***Buscema*** *a-15, 19, 28; c-28.* ***Colan*** *a-6r; c-12p.* ***Ditko*** *a-1, 6.* ***Gil Kane*** *c-16p.* ***Kirby*** *a-1-3, 5, 7, 9-11; c-7.* ***Perez*** *a-26.* ***Romita*** *c-1, 5.* ***B. Smith*** *a-4, 15, 19; c-4, 19.*

MARVEL TREASURY OF OZ FEATURING THE MARVELOUS LAND OF OZ
Marvel Comics Group: 1975 ($1.50, oversized) (See MGM's Marvelous...)

1-Roy Thomas-s/Alfredo Alcala-a; Romita-c & bk-c 3 6 9 16 23 30

MARVEL TREASURY SPECIAL (Also see 2001: A Space Odyssey)
Marvel Comics Group: 1974; 1976 ($1.50, oversized, 84 pgs.)

Vol. 1-Spider-Man, Torch, Sub-Mariner, Avengers "Giant Superhero Holiday Grab-Bag"; Wood, Colan/Everett, plus 2 Kirby-r; reprints Hulk vs. Thing from Fantastic Four #25,26
3 6 9 16 24 32
Vol. 1-... Featuring Captain America's Bicentennial Battles (6/76)-Kirby-a; B. Smith inks, 11 pgs. 3 6 9 17 26 35

MARVEL TRIPLE ACTION (See Giant-Size...)
Marvel Comics Group: Feb, 1972 - No. 24, Mar, 1975; No. 25, Aug, 1975 - No. 47, Apr, 1979

1-(25¢ giant, 52 pgs.)-Dr. Doom, Silver Surfer, The Thing begin, end #4 ('66 reprints from Fantastic Four) 4 8 12 23 37 50
2-5 2 4 6 10 14 18
6-10 1 3 4 6 8 10
11-47: 45-r/X-Men #45. 46-r/Avengers #53(X-Men) 1 2 3 5 6 8
29,30-(30¢-c variants, limited distribution)(5,7/76) 4 8 12 23 37 50
36,37-(35¢-c variants, limited distribution)(7,9/77) 6 12 18 38 69 100

NOTE: *#5-44, 46, 47 reprint Avengers #11 thru ?. #40-r/Avengers #48(1st Black Knight).* ***Buscema*** *a(r)-35p, 36p, 38p, 39p, 41, 42, 43p, 44p, 46p, 47p.* ***Ditko*** *a-2r; c-47.* ***Kirby*** *a(r)-1-4p; c-9-19, 22, 24, 29.* ***Starlin*** *c-7.* ***Tuska*** *a(r)-40p, 43i, 46i, 47i. #2 through #17 are 20¢-c.*

MARVEL TRIPLE ACTION
Marvel Comics: May, 2009 - No. 2, Jun, 2009 ($5.99, limited series)

1,2-Reprints stories from Wolverine First Class, Marvel Adventures Avengers & Marvel Super Heroes 6.00

MARVEL TSUM TSUM
Marvel Comics: Oct, 2016 - No. 4, Jan, 2017 ($3.99, limited series)

1-4-Based on Japanese stackable plush toys. 1-Spider-Man and the Avengers app. 4.00

MARVEL TV: GALACTUS - THE REAL STORY
Marvel Comics: Apr, 2009 ($3.99, one-shot)

1-The "hoax" of Galactus, Tieri-s/Santacruz-a; r/Fantastic Four #50 4.00

MARVEL TWO-IN-ONE (...Featuring ... #82 on; also see The Thing)
Marvel Comics Group: January, 1974 - No. 100, June, 1983

1-Thing team-ups begin; Man-Thing 7 14 21 46 86 125
2,3: 2-Sub-Mariner; last 20¢ issue. 3-Daredevil 3 6 9 20 31 42
4,6: 4-Capt. America. 6-Dr. Strange (11/74) 3 6 9 15 22 28
5-Guardians of the Galaxy (9/74, 2nd app.) 4 8 12 25 40 55
7,9,10 2 4 6 10 14 18
8-Early Ghost Rider app. (3/75) 3 6 9 16 23 30
11-14,19,20: 13-Power Man. 14-Son of Satan (early app.)
1 3 4 6 8 10
15-18-(Regular 25¢ editions)(5-7/76) 17-Spider-Man 1 3 4 6 8 10
15-18-(30¢-c variants, limited distribution) 4 8 12 23 37 50
21-29: 27-Deathlok. 29-Master of Kung Fu; Spider-Woman cameo
1 2 3 5 6 8
28,29,31-(35¢-c variants, limited distribution) 5 10 15 31 53 75
30-2nd full app. Spider-Woman (see Marvel Spotlight #32 for 1st app.)
2 4 6 9 13 16
30-(35¢-c variant, limited distribution)(8/77) 7 14 21 46 86 125
31-33-Spider-Woman app. 1 3 4 6 8 10
34-40: 39-Vision 1 2 3 4 5 7
41,42,44,45,47-49: 42-Capt. America. 45-Capt. Marvel 6.00
43,50,53,55-Byrne-a(p). 53-Quasar(7/79, 2nd app.) 1 2 3 5 7 9
46-Thing battles Hulk-c/story 2 4 6 8 10 12
51-The Beast, Nick Fury, Ms. Marvel; Miller-a/c 1 2 3 5 7 9
52-Moon Knight app.; 1st app. Crossfire 2 4 6 8 10 12
54-Death of Deathlok; Byrne-a 2 4 6 10 14 18
56-60,64-68,70-74,76-79,81,82: 60-Intro. Impossible Woman. 68-Angel. 71-1st app. Maelstrom. 76-Iceman 4.00
61-63: 61-Starhawk (from Guardians); "The Coming of Her" storyline begins, ends #63; cover similar to F.F. #67 (Him-c). 62-Moondragon; Thanos & Warlock cameo in flashback; Starhawk app. 63-Warlock revived shortly; Starhawk & Moondragon app.
1 3 4 6 8 10
69-Guardians of the Galaxy 1 3 4 6 8 10
75-Avengers (52 pgs.) 5.00
80,90,100: 80-Ghost Rider. 90-Spider-Man. 100-Double size, Byrne-s 5.00
83-89,91-99: 83-Sasquatch. 84-Alpha Flight app. 93-Jocasta dies. 96-X-Men-c & cameo 4.00
Annual 1 (1976, 52 pgs.)-Thing/Liberty Legion; Kirby-c 2 4 6 10 14 18
Annual 2 (1977, 52 pgs.)-Thing/Spider-Man; 2nd death of Thanos; end of Thanos saga; Warlock app.; Starlin-c/a 6 12 18 38 69 100
Annual 3,4 (1978-79, 52 pgs.): 3-Nova. 4-Black Bolt 1 2 3 4 5 7
Annual 5-7 (1980-82, 52 pgs.): 5-Hulk. 6-1st app. American Eagle. 7-The Thing/Champion; Sasquatch, Colossus app.; X-Men cameo (1 pg.) 5.00

NOTE: ***Austin*** *c(i)-42, 54, 56, 58, 61, 63, 66.* ***John Buscema*** *a-30p, 45; c-30p.* ***Byrne*** *(p)-43, 50, 53-55; c-43, 53p, 56p, 98i, 99i.* ***Gil Kane*** *a-1p, 2p; c(p)-1-3, 9-11, 14, 28.* ***Kirby*** *c-12, 19p, 20, 25, 27.* ***Mooney*** *a-18i, 38i, 90i.* ***Nasser*** *a-70p.* ***Perez*** *a(p)-56-58, 60, 64, 65; c(p)-32, 33, 42, 50-52, 54, 55, 57, 58, 61-66, 70.* ***Roussos*** *a-Annual 1i.* ***Simonson*** *c-43i, 97p, Annual 6i.* ***Starlin*** *c-6, Annual 1.* ***Tuska*** *a-6p.*

MARVEL TWO-IN-ONE
Marvel Comics: Sept, 2007 - No. 17, Jan, 2009 ($4.99, 64 pgs.)

1-8,13-16-Reprints Marvel Adventures Avengers and X-Men: First Class stories 5.00
9-12,17-Reprints Marvel Adventures Iron Man and Avengers stories 5.00

MARVEL UNIVERSE (See Official Handbook Of The...)

MARVEL UNIVERSE (Title on variant covers for newsstand editions of some 2001 Marvel titles. See indicia for actual titles and issue numbers)

MARVEL UNIVERSE
Marvel Comics: June, 1998 - No. 7, Dec, 1998 ($2.99/$1.99)

1-($2.99)-Invaders stories from WW2; Stern-s 4.00
2-7-($1.99): 2-Two covers. 4-7-Monster Hunters; Manley-a/Stern-s 3.00

MARVEL UNIVERSE AVENGERS AND ULTIMATE SPIDER-MAN
Marvel Comics: 2012 (no price, Halloween giveaway)

1-Reprints from Marvel Universe Ultimate Spider-Man #1 & Avengers E.M.H #1 3.00

MARVEL UNIVERSE AVENGERS ASSEMBLE (Based on the Disney XD animated series) (Titled Avengers Assemble for #1,2)
Marvel Comics: Dec, 2013 - No. 12, Nov, 2014 ($3.99/$2.99)

1-($3.99) Red Skull app.; bonus Lego-style story 4.00
2-12-($2.99) 5-Dracula app. 7-Hyperion app. 12-Impossible Man app. 3.00

MARVEL UNIVERSE AVENGERS ASSEMBLE: CIVIL WAR
Marvel Comics: May, 2016 - No. 4, Aug, 2016 ($2.99)

1-4: 1,2,4-Ultron app. 3.00

MARVEL UNIVERSE AVENGERS ASSEMBLE SEASON TWO
Marvel Comics: Jan, 2015 - No. 16, Apr, 2016 ($3.99/$2.99)

1-($3.99) Red Skull & Thanos app. 4.00
2-16-($2.99) 2-Thanos & The Watcher app. 4-Winter Soldier app. 9-Ant-Man joins 3.00

MARVEL UNIVERSE AVENGERS: ULTRON REVOLUTION
Marvel Comics: Sept, 2016 - Present ($2.99)

1-9-Ultron returns; A.I.M. app. 3.00

MARVEL UNIVERSE GUARDIANS OF THE GALAXY (Disney XD animated series)
Marvel Comics: Apr, 2015 - No. 4, Jul, 2015 ($2.99)

1-4: 1-Back-up story with Star-Lord origin 3.00

MARVEL UNIVERSE GUARDIANS OF THE GALAXY (Disney XD animated series)
Marvel Comics: Dec, 2015 - Present ($3.99/$2.99)

1-($3.99) Cosmo & Korath app.; bonus Lego story 4.00
2-17-($2.99) 3-Fin Fang Foom app. 4-Grandmaster app. 13-Loki app. 3.00

Marvel Universe vs. The Punisher #1 © MAR

Marvel Zombies Halloween #1 © MAR

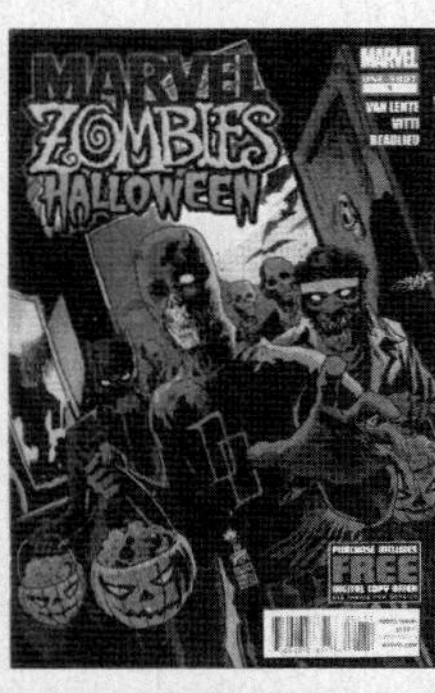

Marvel Zombies 5 #3 © MAR

GD	VG	FN	VF	VF/NM	NM-
2.0	4.0	6.0	8.0	9.0	9.2

GD VG FN VF VF/NM NM-
2.0 4.0 6.0 8.0 9.0 9.2

MARVEL UNIVERSE HULK: AGENTS OF S.M.A.S.H (Disney XD animated series)
Marvel Comics: Dec, 2013 - No. 4, Mar, 2014 ($2.99)

1-4: 1-Hulk, A-Bomb, She-Hulk, Red Hulk and Skaar team-up 3.00

MARVEL UNIVERSE: MILLENNIAL VISIONS
Marvel Comics: Feb, 2002 ($3.99, one-shot)

1-Pin-ups by various; wraparound-c by JH Williams & Gray 4.00

MARVEL UNIVERSE: THE END (Also see Infinity Abyss)
Marvel Comics: May, 2003 - No. 6, Aug, 2003 ($3.50/$2.99, limited series)

1-($3.50)-Thanos, X-Men, FF, Avengers, Spider-Man, Daredevil app.; Starlin-s/a(p) 4.00
2-6-($2.99) Akhenaten, Eternity, Living Tribunal app. 3.00
Thanos Vol. 3: Marvel Universe - The End (2003, $16.99) r/#1-6 17.00

MARVEL UNIVERSE ULTIMATE SPIDER-MAN (Based on the animated series)
Marvel Comics: Jun, 2012 - No. 31, Dec, 2014 ($2.99)

1-31: 1-Agent Coulson app. 13-Iron Man app. 16,19-Venom app. 29-Spider-Ham app. 3.00

MARVEL UNIVERSE ULTIMATE SPIDER-MAN: CONTEST OF CHAMPIONS
Marvel Comics: May, 2016 - No. 4, Aug, 2016 ($2.99, limited series)

1-4-The Collector & Grandmaster app. 1-Iron Man, Hulk & Kraven app. 3.00

MARVEL UNIVERSE ULTIMATE SPIDER-MAN SPIDER-VERSE
Marvel Comics: Jan, 2016 - No. 4, Apr, 2016 ($3.99/$2.99)

1-($3.99) 1-Spider-Man 2099 and Spider-Girl app. 4.00
2-4-($2.99) 3,4-Miles Morales app. 3.00

MARVEL UNIVERSE ULTIMATE SPIDER-MAN VS. THE SINISTER SIX
Marvel Comics: Sept, 2016 - Present ($2.99)

1-8: 1,2-Doctor Octopus & Scarlet Spider app. 3-Dr. Strange app. 6-Venom app. 3.00

MARVEL UNIVERSE ULTIMATE SPIDER-MAN: WEB WARRIORS
Marvel Comics: Jan, 2015 - No. 12, Dec, 2015 ($3.99/$2.99)

1-($3.99) Captain America & Doctor Doom app.; back-up with Iron Spider 4.00
2-12-($2.99) 2-Hawkeye app. 3-Iron Man app. 8-Deadpool app. 12-Howling Commandos 3.00
.../Avengers Assemble Halloween ComicFest 2015 #1 (giveaway) reprints 3.00

MARVEL UNIVERSE VS. THE AVENGERS
Marvel Comics: Dec, 2012 - No. 4, Mar, 2013 ($3.99, limited series)

1-4-Avengers vs. Marvel Zombies; Maberry-s/Fernandez-a/Kuder-c 4.00

MARVEL UNIVERSE VS. THE PUNISHER
Marvel Comics: Oct, 2010 - No. 4, Nov, 2010 ($3.99, limited series)

1-4-Punisher vs. Marvel Zombies; Maberry-s/Parlov-a/c 4.00

MARVEL UNIVERSE VS. WOLVERINE
Marvel Comics: Aug, 2011 - No. 4, Nov, 2011 ($3.99, limited series)

1-4-Wolverine vs. Marvel Zombies; Maberry-s/Laurence Campbell-a/c 4.00

MARVEL UNLIMITED (Title on variant covers for newsstand editions of some 2001 Daredevil issues. See indicia for actual titles and issue numbers)

MARVEL VALENTINE SPECIAL
Marvel Comics: Mar, 1997 ($2.99, one-shot)

1-Valentine stories w/Spider-Man, Daredevil, Cyclops, Phoenix 3.00

MARVEL VERSUS DC (See DC Versus Marvel) (Also see Amazon, Assassins, Bruce Wayne: Agent of S.H.I.E.L.D., Bullets & Bracelets, Doctor Strangefate, JLX, Legend of the Dark Claw, Magneto & The Magnetic Men, Speed Demon, Spider-Boy, Super Soldier, & X-Patrol)
Marvel Comics: No. 2, 1996 - No. 3, 1996 ($3.95, limited series)

2,3: 2-Peter David script. 3-Ron Marz script; Dan Jurgens-a(p). 1st app. of Super Soldier, Spider-Boy, Dr. Doomsday, Doctor Strangefate, The Dark Claw, Nightcreeper, Amazon, Wraith & others. Storyline continues in Amalgam books. 5.00

MARVEL VISIONARIES
Marvel Comics: 2002 - 2007 (various prices, HC and TPB)

...: Chris Claremont (2005, $29.99) r/X-Men #137, Uncanny X-Men #153,205,268 & Ann. #12, Iron Fist #14, Wolverine #3, New Mutants #21 and other highlights 30.00
...: Gil Kane (8/02, $24.95) r/Amazing Spider-Man #99, Marvel Premiere #1,#15, TOA #76 & others; plus sketch pages and a cover gallery 25.00
...: Jack Kirby HC (2004, $29.99) r/career highlights- Red Raven Comics #1 (1st work), Captain America Comics #1, Avengers #4, Fantastic Four #48-50 and more 30.00
...: Jack Kirby Vol. 2 HC (2006, $34.99) r/career highlights- Captain America, Two-Gun Kid, Fantastic Four, Thor, Fin Fang Foom, Devil Dinosaur, romance and more 35.00
...: Jim Steranko (9/02, $14.95) r/Captain America #110,111,113; X-Men #50,51 and stories from Tower of Shadows #1 and Our Love Story #5; plus a cover gallery 15.00
...: John Buscema (2007, $34.99) r/career highlights-Avengers, Silver Surfer, Thor, FF, Hulk, Wolverine and others; Roy Thomas intro.; sketch pages and pin-up art 35.00
...: John Romita Jr. (2005, $29.99) r/various stories 1977-2002; debut in AS-M Ann. #11; Iron Man #128, AS-M V2 #36, issues of Hulk, Daredevil: The Man Without Fear, Punisher; sketch pages; intro. by John Romita Sr. 30.00
...: John Romita Sr. (2005, $29.99) r/various stories 1951-1997 including Young Men #24&26, Daredevil #16, ASM #39,42,50; sketch pages; intro. by John Romita Jr. 30.00
...: Roy Thomas (2006, $34.99) r/career highlights; intro. by Stan Lee 35.00
...: Steve Ditko (2005, $29.99) r/various stories 1961-1992; intro. by Blake Bell 30.00
...: Stan Lee HC (2005, $29.99) r/career highlights- Captain America Comics #3 (1st work), and various Spider-Man, FF, Thor, Daredevil stories; 1940-1995; Roy Thomas intro. 30.00

MARVEL WEDDINGS
Marvel Comics: 2005 ($19.99, TPB)

TPB-Reprints weddings of Peter & Mary Jane, Reed & Sue, Scott & Jean, and others 20.00

MARVEL WESTERNS: ...
Marvel Comics: 2006 ($3.99, one-shots)

... Kid Colt and the Arizona Girl 1 (9/06) 2 short stories & 3 Kirby/Ayers reps.; Powell-c 4.00
... Outlaw Files-Profiles and essays about Marvel western characters 4.00
... Strange Westerns Starring The Black Rider 1 (10/06) Englehart-s/Rogers-a & 2 Kirby Rawhide Kid reprints; Rogers-c 4.00
... The Two-Gun Kid 1 (8/06) 2 short stories & a Kirby/Ayers reprint; Powell-c 4.00
... Western Legends 1 (9/06) 2 short stories & r/Rawhide Kid origin by Kirby; Powell-c 4.00
HC (2006, $20.99, dustjacket) r/one-shots 21.00

MARVEL X-MEN COLLECTION, THE
Marvel Comics: Jan, 1994 - No. 3, Mar, 1994 ($2.95, limited series)

1-3-r/X-Men trading cards by Jim Lee 3.00

MARVEL - YEAR IN REVIEW (Magazine)
Marvel Comics: 1989 - No. 3, 1991 (52 pgs.)

1-3: 1-Spider-Man-c by McFarlane. 2-Capt. America-c. 3-X-Men/Wolverine-c 5.00

MARVEL: YOUR UNIVERSE
Marvel Comics: 2008; May, 2009 - No. 3, July, 2009 ($5.99)

1-3-Reprints of 5 recent comics (Ms. Marvel, Nova, Immortal Iron Fist & others) 6.00
...Saga (2008, no cover price) - Re-caps of crossovers (Secret War thru Secret Invasion) 3.00

MARVEL ZOMBIES (See Ultimate Fantastic Four #21-23, 30-32)
Marvel Comics: Feb, 2006 - No. 5, June, 2006 ($2.99, limited series)

1-Zombies vs. Magneto; Kirkman-s/Phillips-a/Suydam-c swipe of A.F. #15 38.00
1-(2nd-4th printings) Variant Suydam-c swipes of Spider-Man #1, Amazing Spider-Man #50 and Incredible Hulk #1 6.00
2-Avengers #4 cover swipe by Suydam 10.00
3-5: 3-Inc. Hulk #340 c-swipe. 4-X-Men #1 c-swipe. 5-AS-M Ann. #21 c-swipe 6.00
3-5-(2nd printings) 3-Daredevil #179 c-swipe. 4-AS-M #39 c-swipe. 5-Silver Surfer #1 4.00
...: Dead Days (7/07, $3.99) Early days of the plaque; Kirkman-s/Phillips-a/Suydam-c 5.00
...: Dead Days HC (2008, $29.99, oversized) r/Dead Days one-shot, Ultimate Fantastic Four #21-23, 30-32, and Black Panther #28-30 30.00
...: Evil Evolution (1/10, $4.99) Apes vs. Zombies; Marcos Martin-c 5.00
... Halloween (12/12, $3.99) Van Lente-s/Vitti-a/Francavilla-c 4.00
... MGC #1 (7/10, $1.00) r/#1 with "Marvel's Greatest Comics" logo on cover 3.00
...: The Book of Angels, Demons and Various Monstrosities (2007, $3.99) profile pages 5.00
...: The Covers HC (2007, $19.99, d.j.) Suydam's covers with originals and commentary 20.00
HC (2006, $19.99) r/#1-5; Kirkman foreword; cover gallery with variants 20.00

MARVEL ZOMBIES 2
Marvel Comics: Dec, 2007 - No. 5, Apr, 2008 ($2.99, limited series)

1-5-Kirkman-s/Phillips-a/Suydam zombie-fied cover swipes 5.00
HC (2008, $19.99) r/#1-5; cover swipe gallery 20.00

MARVEL ZOMBIES 3
Marvel Comics: Dec, 2008 - No. 4, Mar, 2009 ($3.99, limited series)

1-4-Van Lente-s/Walker-a/Land-c; Machine Man, Jocasta and Morbius app. 5.00

MARVEL ZOMBIES 4
Marvel Comics: Jun, 2009 - No. 4, Sept, 2009 ($3.99, limited series)

1-4-Van Lente-s/Walker-a/Land-c; Zombie Deadpool head app. 4.00

MARVEL ZOMBIES 5
Marvel Comics: Jun, 2010 - No. 5, Sept, 2010 ($3.99, limited series)

1-5-Van Lente-s; Machine Man and Howard the Duck app. 3-Kaluta-a 4.00

MARVEL ZOMBIES (Secret Wars tie-in)
Marvel Comics: Aug, 2015 - No. 4, Dec, 2015 ($3.99, limited series)

1-4-Spurrier-s/Walker-a; Elsa Bloodstone vs. zombies. 2,3-Deadpool app. 4.00

MARVEL ZOMBIES / ARMY OF DARKNESS
Marvel Comics/Dynamite Entertainment: May, 2007 - No. 5, Aug, 2007($2.99, limited series)

1-Zombies vs. Ash during the start of the plaque; Layman-s/Neves-a/Suydam-c 7.00

Mary Jane #1 © DC

Mary Marvel Comics #16 © FAW

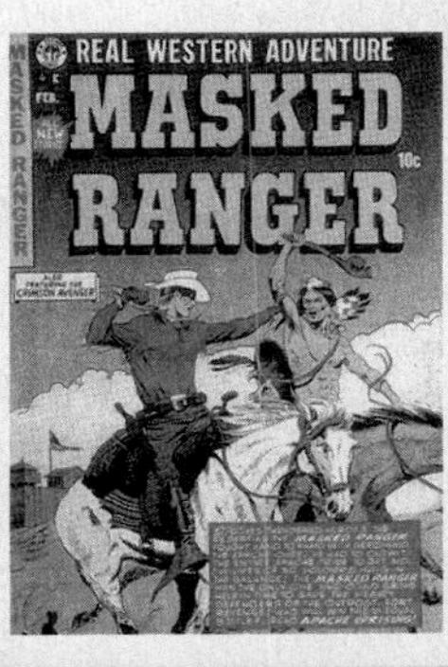

Masked Ranger #6 © CC

	GD 2.0	VG 4.0	FN 6.0	VF 8.0	VF/NM 9.0	NM- 9.2

1-Second printing with Suydam zombie-fied Captain America Comics #1 cover swipe 4.00
2-5-Suydam zombie-fied cover swipes on all 5.00
HC (2007, $19.99) r/#1-5; cover gallery with variants and non-zombied original covers 20.00

MARVEL ZOMBIES CHRISTMAS CAROL ("Zombies Christmas Carol" on cover)
Marvel Comics: Aug, 2011 - No. 5, Oct, 2011 ($3.99, limited series)
1-5-Adaptation of the Dickens classic with zombies; Kaluta-c/Baldeon-a 4.00

MARVEL ZOMBIES DESTROY!
Marvel Comics: Jul, 2012 - No. 5, Sept, 2012 ($3.99, limited series)
1-5-Howard the Duck, Dum Dum Dugan vs. zombies; Del Mundo-c 4.00

MARVEL ZOMBIES RETURN
Marvel Comics: Nov, 2009 - No. 5, Nov, 2009 ($3.99, weekly limited series)
1-5-Suydam-c. 1-Zombie Spider-Man eats the Earth-Z Sinister Six; Dragotta-a. 4.00

MARVEL ZOMBIES SUPREME
Marvel Comics: May, 2011 - No. 5, Aug, 2011 ($3.99, limited series)
1-5-Zombies in Squadron Supreme dimension; Blanco-a/Komarck-c; Jack of Hearts app. 4.00

MARVILLE
Marvel Comics: Nov, 2002 - No. 7, Jul, 2003 ($2.25, limited series)
1-6-Satire on DC/AOL-Time-Warner; Jemas-a/Bright-a/Horn-c 3.00
1-($3.95) Variant foil cover by Udon Studios; bonus sketch pages and Jemas afterword 4.00
7-($2.99) Intro. to Epic Comics line with submission guidelines 3.00

MARVIN MOUSE
Atlas Comics (BPC): September, 1957
1-Everett-c/a; Maneely-a 16 32 48 94 147 200

MARY JANE (Spider-Man) (Also see Spider-Man Loves Mary Jane)
Marvel Comics: Aug, 2004 - No. 4, Nov, 2004 ($2.25, limited series)
1-4-Marvel Age series with teen-age MJ Watson; Miyazawa-c/a; McKeever-s 3.00
... Vol. 1: Circle of Friends (2004, $5.99, digest-size) r/#1-4 6.00

MARY JANE & SNIFFLES (See Looney Tunes)
Dell Publishing Co.: No. 402, June, 1952 - No. 474, June, 1953
Four Color 402 (#1) 8 16 24 51 96 140
Four Color 474 6 12 18 42 79 115

MARY JANE: HOMECOMING (Spider-Man)
Marvel Comics: May, 2005 - No. 4, Aug, 2005 ($2.99, limited series)
1-4-Teen-age MJ Watson in high school; Miyazawa-c/a; McKeever-s 3.00
... Vol. 2 (2005, $6.99, digest-size) r/#1-4 7.00

MARY MARVEL COMICS (Monte Hale #29 on) (Also see Captain Marvel #18, Marvel Family, Shazam, & Wow Comics)
Fawcett Publications: Dec, 1945 - No. 28, Sept, 1948
1-Captain Marvel introduces Mary on-c; intro/origin Georgia Sivana
161 322 483 1030 1765 2500
2 71 142 213 454 777 1100
3,4: 3-New logo 50 100 150 315 533 750
5-8: 8-Bulletgirl x-over in Mary Marvel; X-Mas-c 40 80 120 246 411 575
9,10 37 74 111 222 361 500
11-20 27 54 81 158 259 360
21-28: 28-Western-c 24 48 72 140 230 320

MARY POPPINS (See Movie Comics & Walt Disney Showcase No. 17)

MARY SHELLEY'S FRANKENSTEIN
Topps Comics: Oct, 1994 - Jan, 1995 ($2.95, limited series)
1-4-polybagged w/3 trading cards 4.00
1-4 ($2.50)-Newstand ed. 3.00

MARY WORTH (See Harvey Comics Hits #55 & Love Stories of...)
Argo: March, 1956 (Also see Romantic Picture Novelettes)
1 8 16 24 42 54 65

MASK (TV)
DC Comics: Dec, 1985 - No. 4, Mar, 1986; Feb, 1987 - No. 9, Oct, 1987
1-4; 1-9 (2nd series)-Sat. morning TV show. 4.00

MASK, THE (Also see Mayhem)
Dark Horse Comics: Aug, 1991 - No. 4, Oct, 1991; No. 0, Dec, 1991 ($2.50, 36 pgs., limited series)
1-4: 1-1st app. Lt. Kellaway as The Mask (see Dark Horse Presents #10 for 1st app.) 5.00
0-(12/91, B&W, 56 pgs.)-r/Mayhem #1-4 4.00
...Omnibus Vol. 1 (8/08, $24.95) r/#1-4, Mask Returns and Mask Strikes Back series 25.00
...Omnibus Vol. 2 (4/09, $24.95) r/#1-4, The Hunt For Green October, World Tour, Southern Discomfort, Toys in the Attic series and short stories from DHP 25.00

...: HUNT FOR GREEN OCTOBER July, 1995 - Oct, 1995 ($2.50, lim. series)
1-4-Evan Dorkin scripts 3.00

.../ MARSHAL LAW Feb, 1998 - No. 2, Mar, 1998 ($2.95, lim. series)
1,2-Mills-s/O'Neill-a 3.00

...: OFFICIAL MOVIE ADAPTATION July, 1994 - Aug, 1994 ($2.50, lim. series)
1,2 3.00

... RETURNS Oct, 1992 - No. 4, Mar, 1993 ($2.50, limited series)
1-4 4.00

... SOUTHERN DISCOMFORT Mar, 1996 - No. 4, July, 1996 ($2.50, lim. series)
1-4 3.00

... STRIKES BACK Feb, 1995 - No. 5, Jun, 1995 ($2.50, limited series)
1-5 3.00

... SUMMER VACATION July, 1995 ($10.95, one shot, hard-c)
1-nn-Rick Geary-c/a 11.00

... TOYS IN THE ATTIC Aug, 1998 - No. 4, Nov, 1998 ($2.95, limited series)
1-4-Fingerman-s 3.00

... VIRTUAL SURREALITY July, 1997 ($2.95, one shot)
nn-Mignola, Aragonés, and others-s/a 3.00

... WORLD TOUR Dec, 1995 - No. 4, Mar, 1996 ($2.50, limited series)
1-4: 3-X & Ghost-c/app. 3.00

MASK COMICS
Rural Home Publ.: Feb-Mar, 1945 - No. 2, Apr-May, 1945; No. 2, Fall, 1945
1-Classic L. B. Cole Satan-c/a; Palais-a 400 800 1200 2800 4900 7000
2-(Scarce)-Classic L. B. Cole Satan-c; Black Rider, The Boy Magician, & The Collector app.
290 580 870 1856 3178 4500
2-(Fall, 1945)-No publ.-same as regular #2; L. B. Cole-c
226 452 678 1446 2473 3500

MASKED BANDIT, THE
Avon Periodicals: 1952
nn-Kinstler-a 19 38 57 111 176 240

MASKED MAN, THE
Eclipse Comics: 12/84 - #10, 4/86; #11, 10/87; #12, 4/88 ($1.75/$2.00, color/B&W #9 on, Baxter paper)
1-12: 1-Origin retold. 3-Origin Aphid-Man; begin $2.00-c 3.00

MASKED MARVEL (See Keen Detective Funnies)
Centaur Publications: Sept, 1940 - No. 3, Dec, 1940
1-The Masked Marvel begins 187 374 561 1197 2049 2900
2,3: 2-Gustavson, Tarpe Mills-a 129 258 387 826 1413 2000

MASKED RAIDER, THE (Billy The Kid #9 on; Frontier Scout, Daniel Boone #10-13) (Also see Blue Bird)
Charlton Comics: June, 1955 - No. 8, July, 1957; No. 14, Aug, 1958 - No. 30, June, 1961
1-Masked Raider & Talon the Golden Eagle begin; painted-c
13 26 39 72 101 130
2 8 16 24 42 54 65
3-8,15: 8-Billy The Kid app. 15-Williamson-a, 7 pgs. 6 12 18 31 38 45
14,16-30: 22-Rocky Lane app. 5 10 15 24 30 35

MASKED RANGER
Premier Magazines: Apr, 1954 - No. 9, Aug, 1955
1-The Masked Ranger, his horse Streak, & The Crimson Avenger (origin) begin, end #9; Woodbridge/Frazetta-a 41 82 123 256 428 600
2,3 16 32 48 94 147 200
4-8-All Woodbridge-a. 5-Jesse James by Woodbridge. 6-Billy The Kid by Woodbridge. 7-Wild Bill Hickok by Woodbridge. 8-Jim Bowie's Life Story
17 34 51 98 154 210
9-Torres-a; Wyatt Earp by Woodbridge; Says Death of Masked Ranger on-c
18 36 54 107 169 230
NOTE: *Check a-1. Woodbridge c/a-1, 4-9.*

M.A.S.K.: MOBILE ARMORED STRIKE KOMMAND (Hasbro toy)
IDW Publishing: Nov, 2016 - Present ($3.99)
1-3: 1,2-Easton-s/Vargas-a. 3-Samu-a 4.00
...: Revolution 1 (9/16, $3.99) Easton-s/Vargas-a 4.00

MASK OF DR. FU MANCHU, THE (See Dr. Fu Manchu)
Avon Periodicals: 1951
1-Sax Rohmer adapt.; Wood-c/a (26 pgs.); Hollingsworth-a
116 232 348 742 1271 1800

MASK OF ZORRO, THE

The Massive #1 © Brian Wood

Master Comics #12 © FAW

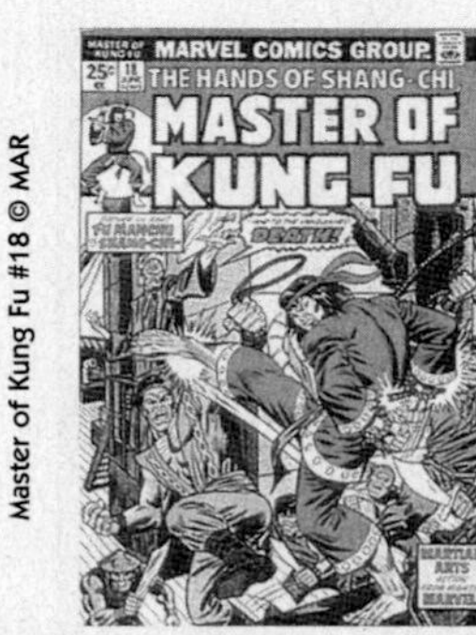

Master of Kung Fu #18 © MAR

GD 2.0 | VG 4.0 | FN 6.0 | VF 8.0 | VF/NM 9.0 | NM- 9.2

Image Comics: Aug, 1998 - No. 4, Dec, 1998 ($2.95, limited series)
1-4-Movie adapt. Photo variant-c 3.00

MASKS
Dynamite Entertainment: 2012 - No. 8, 2013 ($3.99)
1-Team-up of the Shadow, Green Hornet, Spider; Alex Ross-a; multiple covers 5.00
2-8: 2-Miss Fury and Green Lama app.; Calero-a. 3-Black Terror app. 4.00

MASKS 2
Dynamite Entertainment: 2015 - No. 8, 2015 ($3.99)
1-8-Pulp hero team-up; Bunn-s/Casallos-a; multiple covers on each 4.00

MASKS: TOO HOT FOR TV!
DC Comics (WildStorm): Feb, 2004 ($4.95)
1-Short stories by various incl. Thompson, Brubaker, Mahnke, Conner; Fabry-c 5.00

MASQUE OF THE RED DEATH (See Movie Classics)

MASQUERADE (See Project Superpowers)
Dynamite Entertainment: 2009 - No. 4, 2009 ($3.50, limited series)
1-4-Alex Ross & Phil Hester-s/Carlos Paul-a; covers by Ross & others 3.50

MASS EFFECT: EVOLUTION (2nd series based on the EA video game)
Dark Horse Comics: Jan, 2011 - No. 4, Apr, 2011 ($3.50, limited series)
1-4-Walters & Jackson Miller-s/Carnevale-c 3.50

MASS EFFECT: FOUNDATION (Based on the EA video game)
Dark Horse Comics: Jul, 2013 - No. 13, Jul, 2014 ($3.99, limited series)
1-13: 1-Walters-s/Francia-a. 2-4-Parker-a 4.00

MASS EFFECT: HOMEWORLDS (Based on the EA video game)
Dark Horse Comics: Apr, 2012 - No. 4, Aug, 2012 ($3.50, limited series)
1-4: 1-Walters-s/Francisco-a 3.50

MASS EFFECT: INVASION (3rd series based on the EA video game)
Dark Horse Comics: Oct, 2011 - No. 4, Jan, 2012 ($3.50, limited series)
1-4-Walters & Jackson Miller-s/Carnevale-c 3.50

MASS EFFECT: REDEMPTION (Based on the EA video game)
Dark Horse Comics: Jan, 2010 - No. 4, Apr, 2010 ($3.50, limited series)
1-4-Walters & Jackson Miller-s/Francia-a 3.50

MASSIVE, THE
Dark Horse Comics: Jun, 2012 - No. 30, Dec, 2014 ($3.50)
1-30: 1-Brian Wood-s/Kristian Donaldson-a. 4-9,25-30-Brown-a. 10-Erskine-a 3.50
...: Ninth Wave 1-6 ($3.99, 12/15 - No. 6, 5/16) Prequel to series; Wood-s/Brown-a 4.00

MASTER COMICS (Combined with Slam Bang Comics #7 on)
Fawcett Publications: Mar, 1940 - No. 133, Apr, 1953 (No. 1-6: oversized issues) (#1-3: 15¢, 52 pgs.; #4-6: 10¢, 36 pgs.; #7-Begin 68 pg. issues)

	GD 2.0	VG 4.0	FN 6.0	VF 8.0	VF/NM 9.0	NM- 9.2
1-Origin & 1st app. Master Man; The Devil's Dagger, El Carim, Master of Magic, Rick O'Say, Morton Murch, White Rajah, Shipwreck Roberts, Frontier Marshal, Streak Sloan, Mr. Clue begin (all features end #6)	946	1892	2838	6906	12,203	17,500
2 (Rare)	300	600	900	1950	3375	4800
3-6: 6-Last Master Man (Rare)	232	464	696	1485	2543	3600

NOTE: *#1-6 rarely found in near mint or very fine condition due to large-size format.*

	GD 2.0	VG 4.0	FN 6.0	VF 8.0	VF/NM 9.0	NM- 9.2
7-(10/40)-Bulletman, Zoro, the Mystery Man (ends #22), Lee Granger, Jungle King, & Buck Jones begin; only app. The War Bird & Mark Swift & the Time Retarder; Zoro, Lee Granger, Jungle King & Mark Swift all continue from Slam Bang; Bulletman moves from Nickel	300	600	900	1950	3375	4800
8-The Red Gaucho (ends #13), Captain Venture (ends #22) & The Planet Princess begin	161	322	483	1030	1765	2500
9,10: 10-Lee Granger ends	129	258	387	826	1413	2000
11-Origin & 1st app. Minute-Man (2/41)	277	554	831	1759	3030	4300
12	129	258	387	826	1413	2000
13-Origin & 1st app. Bulletgirl; Hitler-c	258	516	774	1651	2826	4000
14-16: 14-Companions Three begins, ends #31	116	232	348	742	1271	1800
17-20: 17-Raboy-a on Bulletman begins. 20-Captain Marvel cameo app. in Bulletman	110	220	330	704	1202	1700
21-(12/41; Scarce)-Captain Marvel & Bulletman team up against Capt. Nazi; origin & 1st app. Capt. Marvel Jr's most famous nemesis Captain Nazi who will cause creation of Capt. Marvel Jr. in Whiz #25. Part I of trilogy origin of Capt. Marvel Jr.; 1st Mac Raboy-c for Fawcett; Capt. Nazi-c	703	1406	2109	5132	9066	13,000
22-(1/42)-Captain Marvel Jr. moves over from Whiz #25 & teams up with Bulletman against Captain Nazi; part III of trilogy origin of Capt. Marvel Jr. & his 1st cover and adventure	622	1244	1866	4541	8021	11,500
23-Capt. Marvel Jr. c/stories begin (1st solo story); fights Capt. Nazi by himself.	300	600	900	2070	3635	5200
24,25	135	270	405	864	1482	2100
26,28,30-Captain Marvel Jr. vs. Capt. Nazi. 28-Liberty Bell-c. 30-Flag-c	129	258	387	826	1413	2000
27-Captain Marvel Jr. "V For Victory"-c; Capt. Nazi app.	161	322	483	1030	1765	2500
29-Hitler & Hirohito-c	245	490	735	1568	2684	3800
31,32,35: 32-Last El Carim & Buck Jones; intro Balbo, the Boy Magician in El Carim story; classic Eagle-c by Raboy	110	220	330	704	1202	1700
33-Capt. Marvel Jr. smashing swastika-c; Balbo, the Boy Magician (ends #47), Hopalong Cassidy (ends #49) begins	142	284	426	909	1555	2200
34-Capt. Marvel Jr. vs. Capt. Nazi-c/story; 1st mention of Capt. Nippon	129	258	387	826	1413	2000
36-Statue of Liberty-c	97	194	291	621	1061	1500
37-39	84	168	252	538	919	1300
40-Classic flag-c	135	270	405	864	1482	2100
41-(8/43)-Bulletman, Capt. Marvel Jr. & Bulletgirl x-over in Minute-Man; only app. Crime Crusaders Club (Capt. Marvel Jr., Minute-Man, Bulletman & Bulletgirl)	84	168	252	538	919	1300
42-47,49: 46-Hitler story. 47-Hitler becomes Corpl. Hitler Jr. 49-Last Minute-Man	54	108	162	343	574	825
48-Intro. Bulletboy; Capt. Marvel cameo in Minute-Man	57	114	171	362	619	875
50-Intro Radar & Nyoka the Jungle Girl & begin series (5/44); Radar also intro in Captain Marvel #35 (same date); Capt. Marvel x-over in Radar; origin Radar; Capt. Marvel & Capt. Marvel, Jr. introduce Radar on-c	54	108	162	346	591	835
51-58	31	62	93	182	296	410
59-62: Nyoka serial "Terrible Tiara" in all; 61-Capt. Marvel Jr. 1st meets Uncle Marvel	32	64	96	192	314	435
63-80	24	48	72	140	230	320
81,83-87,89-91,95-99: 88-Hopalong Cassidy begins (ends #94). 95-Tom Mix begins (cover only in #123, ends #133)	22	44	66	128	209	290
82,88,92-94-Krigstein-a	22	44	66	132	216	300
100	22	44	66	132	216	300
101-106-Last Bulletman (not in #104)	21	42	63	124	202	280
107-120: 118-Mary Marvel	20	40	60	120	195	270
121-131-(lower print run): 123-Tom Mix-c only	22	44	66	128	209	290
132-B&W and color illos in **POP**; last Nyoka	22	44	66	132	216	300
133-Bill Battle app.	28	56	84	165	270	375

NOTE: ***Mac Raboy** a-15-39, 40(part), 42, 58. c-21-49, 51, 52, 54, 56, 58, 68(part), 69(part). Bulletman c-7-11, 13(half), 15, 18(part), 19, 20, 21(w/Capt. Marvel & Capt. Nazi), 22(w/Capt. Marvel, Jr.). Capt. Marvel, Jr. c-23-133. Master Man c-1-6. Minute Man c-12, 13(half), 14, 16, 17, 18(part).*

MASTER DARQUE
Acclaim Comics (Valiant): Feb, 1998 ($3.95)
1-Manco-a/Christina Z.-s 4.00

MASTER DETECTIVE
Super Comics: 1964 (Reprints)

	GD 2.0	VG 4.0	FN 6.0	VF 8.0	VF/NM 9.0	NM- 9.2
17-r/Criminals on the Loose V4 #2; r/Young King Cole #?; McWilliams-r	2	4	6	8	11	14

MASTER OF KUNG FU (Formerly Special Marvel Edition; see Deadly Hands of Kung Fu & Giant-Size...)
Marvel Comics Group: No. 17, April, 1974 - No. 125, June, 1983

	GD 2.0	VG 4.0	FN 6.0	VF 8.0	VF/NM 9.0	NM- 9.2
17-Starlin-a; intro Black Jack Tarr; 3rd Shang-Chi (ties w/Deadly Hands #1)	4	8	12	27	44	60
18,20	3	6	9	16	23	30
19-Man-Thing-c/story	3	6	9	18	28	38
21-23,25-30	2	4	6	10	14	18
24-Starlin, Simonson-a	2	4	6	11	16	20
31-50: 33-1st Leiko Wu. 43-Last 25¢ issue	1	3	4	6	8	10
39-43-(30¢-c variants, limited distribution)(5-7/76)	5	10	15	33	57	80
51-75						6.00
53-57-(35¢-c variants, limited distribution)(6-10/77)	6	12	18	38	69	100
76-99						5.00
100,118,125-Double size						6.00
101-117,119-124						4.00
Annual 1(4/76)-Iron Fist app.	3	6	9	19	30	40

NOTE: ***Austin** c-63i, 74i. **Buscema** c-44p. **Gulacy** a(p)-18-20, 22, 25, 29-31, 33-35, 38, 39, 40(p&i), 42-50, 53r(#20); c-51, 55, 64, 67. **Gil Kane** c(p)-20, 38, 39, 42, 45, 59, 63. **Nebres** c-73i. **Starlin** a-17p, 24; c-54. **Sutton** a-42i. #53 reprints #20.*

MASTER OF KUNG FU (Secret Wars tie-in)
Marvel Comics: Jul, 2015 - No. 4, Oct, 2015 ($3.99, limited series)
1-4-Blackman-s/Talajic-a/Francavilla-c; Shang-Chi & Iron Fist app. 4.00

MASTER OF KUNG-FU: BLEEDING BLACK
Marvel Comics: Feb, 1991 ($2.95, 84 pgs., one-shot)

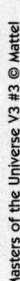

Masters of the Universe V3 #3 © Mattel

Maximage #6 © Rob Liefeld

Max Ride: Final Flight #5 © James Patterson

GD 2.0 VG 4.0 FN 6.0 VF 8.0 VF/NM 9.0 NM- 9.2

1-The Return of Shang-Chi 4.00

MASTER OF KUNG-FU, SHANG-CHI:... (2002 series, see Shang Chi:...)

MASTER OF THE WORLD
Dell Publishing Co.: No. 1157, July, 1961

Four Color 1157-Movie based on Jules Verne's "Master of the World" and "Robur the Conqueror" novels; with Vincent Price & Charles Bronson 7 14 21 46 86 125

MASTERS OF TERROR (Magazine)
Marvel Comics Group: July, 1975 - No. 2, Sept, 1975 (B&W) (All reprints)

1-Brunner, Barry Smith-a; Morrow/Steranko-c; Starlin-a(p); Gil Kane-a 3 6 9 17 26 35
2-Reese, Kane, Mayerik-a; Adkins/Steranko-c 2 4 6 13 18 22

MASTERS OF THE UNIVERSE (See DC Comics Presents #47 for 1st app.)
DC Comics: Dec, 1982 - No. 3, Feb, 1983 (Mini-series)

1 3 6 9 15 22 28
2,3: 2-Origin He-Man & Ceril 2 4 6 9 12 15

NOTE: *Alcala a-1i,, 2i. Tuska a-1-3p; c-1-3p. #2 has 75 & 95 cent cover price.*

MASTERS OF THE UNIVERSE (Comic Album)
Western Publishing Co.: 1984 (8-1/2x11", $2.95, 64 pgs.)

11362-Based on Mattel toy & cartoon 2 4 6 11 16 20

MASTERS OF THE UNIVERSE
Star Comics/Marvel #7 on: May 1986 - No. 13, May, 1988 (75¢/$1.00)

1 3 6 9 15 22 28
2-11: 8-Begin $1.00-c 1 2 3 5 6 8
12-Death of He-Man (1st Marvel app.) 4 8 12 22 35 48
13-Return of He-Man & death of Skeletor 4 8 12 22 35 48
The Motion Picture (11/87, $2.00)-Tuska-p 2 4 6 9 12 15

MASTERS OF THE UNIVERSE
Image Comics: Nov, 2002 - No. 4, March, 2003 ($2.95, limited series)

1-($2.95) Two covers by Santalucia and Campbell; Santalucia-a 4.00
1-($5.95) Variant-c by Norem w/gold foil logo 6.00
2-4($2.95) 2-Two covers by Santalucia and Manapul. 3,4-Two covers 3.00
TPB (CrossGen, 2003, $9.95, 8-1/4" x 5-1/2") digest-sized reprints #1-4 10.00

MASTERS OF THE UNIVERSE (Volume 2)
Image Comics: March, 2003 - No. 6, Aug, 2003 ($2.95)

1-6-($2.95) 1-Santalucia-c. 2-Two covers by Santalucia & JJ Kirby 3.00
1-($5.95) Wraparound variant-c by Struzan w/silver foil logo 6.00
3,4-($5.95) Wraparound variant holofoil-c. 3-By Edwards 4-By Boris Vallejo & Julie Bell 6.00
Volume 2 Dark Reflections TPB (2004, $18.95) r/#1-6 19.00

MASTERS OF THE UNIVERSE (Volume 3)
MVCreations: Apr, 2004 - No. 8, Dec, 2004 ($2.95)

1-8: 1-Santalucia-c 3.00

MASTERS OF THE UNIVERSE...
CrossGen Comics

...Rise of the Snake-Men (Nov, 2003 - No. 3, $2.95) Meyers-a 3.00
...The Power of Fear (12/03, $2.95, one-shot) Santalucia-a 3.00

MASTERS OF THE UNIVERSE, ICONS OF EVIL
Image Comics/CrossGen Comics: 2003 ($4.95, one-shots)

...Beastman -(Image) Origin of Beast Man; Tony Moore-a 5.00
...Mer-Man -(CrossGen) 5.00
...Trapjaw -(CrossGen) 5.00
...Tri-Klops -(CrossGen) Walker-c 5.00
TPB (3/04, $18.95, MVCreations) r/one-shots; sketch pages 19.00

MASTERS OF THE UNIVERSE: ...
DC Comics: Dec, 2012; Mar, 2013; Jul, 2013 ($2.99, one-shots)

... Origin Of He-Man (3/13) Fialkov-s; Ben Oliver-a/c; Prince Adam finds the sword 3.00
... Origin Of Hordak (7/13) Giffen & Keene-s/Giffen-a/c 3.00
... The Origin Of Skeletor (12/12) Fialkov-s; Fraser Irving-a/c; Keldor becomes Skeletor 3.00

MASTERWORKS SERIES OF GREAT COMIC BOOK ARTISTS, THE
Sea Gate Dist./DC Comics: May, 1983 - No. 3, Dec, 1983 (Baxter paper)

1-3: 1,2-Shining Knight by Frazetta r-/Adventure. 2-Tomahawk by Frazetta-r. 3-Wrightson-c/a(r) 6.00

MATADOR
DC Comics (WildStorm): July, 2005 - No. 6, May, 2006 ($2.99, limited series)

1-6-Devin Grayson-s/Brian Stelfreeze-a/c 3.00

MATRIX COMICS, THE (Movie)
Burlyman Entertainment: 2003; 2004 ($21.95, trade paperback)

nn-Short stories by various incl. Wachowskis, Darrow, Gaiman, Sienkiewicz, Bagge 22.00
...Volume One Preview (7/03, no cover price) bios of creators; Chadwick-s/a 3.00
Volume 2-(2004) Short stories by various incl. Wachowskis, Sale, McKeever, Dorman 22.00

MATT SLADE GUNFIGHTER (Kid Slade Gunfighter #5 on; See Western Gunfighters)
Atlas Comics (SPI): May, 1956 - No. 4, Nov, 1956

1-Intro Matt & horse Eagle; Williamson/Torres-a 22 44 66 132 216 300
2-Williamson-a 15 30 45 85 130 175
3,4 12 24 36 69 97 125

NOTE: *Maneely a-1, 3, 4; c-1, 2, 4. Roth a-2-4. Severin a-1, 3, 4. Maneely c/a-1. Issue #s stamped on cover after printing.*

MAUS: A SURVIVOR'S TALE (First graphic novel to win a Pulitzer Prize)
Pantheon Books: 1986, 1991 (B&W)

Vol. 1-(...: My Father Bleeds History)(1986) Art Spiegelman-s/a; recounts stories of Spiegelman's father in 1930s-40s Nazi-occupied Poland; collects first six stories serialized in Raw Magazine from 1980-1985 30.00
Vol. 2-(...: And Here My Troubles Began)(1991) 25.00
Complete Maus Survivor's Tale -HC Vols. 1& 2 w/slipcase 35.00
Hardcover Vol. 1 (1991) 30.00
Hardcover Vol. 2 (1991) 30.00
TPB (1992, $14.00) Vols. 1& 2 18.00

MAVERICK (TV)
Dell Publishing Co.: No. 892, 4/58 - No. 19, 4-6/62 (All have photo-c)

Four Color 892 (#1)-James Garner photo-c begin 18 36 54 124 275 425
Four Color 930,945,962,980,1005 (6-8/59): 945-James Garner/Jack Kelly photo-c begin 9 18 27 62 126 190
7 (10-12/59) - 14: 11-Variant edition has "Time For Change" comic strip on back-c. 14-Last Garner/Kelly-c 8 16 24 54 102 150
15-18: Jack Kelly/Roger Moore photo-c 7 14 21 44 82 120
19-Jack Kelly photo-c (last issue) 7 14 21 46 86 125

MAVERICK (See X-Men)
Marvel Comics: Jan, 1997 ($2.95, one-shot)

1-Hama-s 4.00

MAVERICK (See X-Men)
Marvel Comics: Sept, 1997 - No. 12, Aug, 1998 ($2.99/$1.99)

1,12: 1-($2.99)-Wraparound-c. 12-($2.99) Battles Omega Red 4.00
2-11: 2-Two covers. 4-Wolverine app. 6,7-Sabretooth app. 3.00

MAVERICK MARSHAL
Charlton Comics: Nov, 1958 - No. 7, May, 1960

1 6 12 18 33 41 48
2-7 5 10 15 23 28 32

MAVERICKS
Daggar Comics Group: Jan, 1994 - No. 5, 1994 (#1-$2.75, #2-5-$2.50)

1-5: 1-Bronze. 1-Gold. 1-Silver 3.00

MAX BRAND (See Silvertip)

MAX HAMM FAIRY TALE DETECTIVE
Nite Owl Comix: 2002 - 2004 ($4.95, B&W, 6 1/2" x 8")

1-(2002) Frank Cammuso-s/a 5.00
Vol. 2 #1-3 (2003-2004) Frank Cammuso-s/a 5.00

MAXIMAGE
Image Comics (Extreme Studios): Dec, 1995 - No. 7, June 1996 ($2.50)

1-7: 1-Liefeld-c. 2-Extreme Destroyer Pt. 2; polybagged w/card. 4-Angela & Glory-c/app. 3.00

MAXIMO
Dreamwave Prods.: Jan, 2004 ($3.95, one-shot)

1-Based on the Capcom video game 4.00

MAXIMUM SECURITY (Crossover)
Marvel Comics: Oct, 2000 - No. 3, Jan, 2001 ($2.99)

1-3-Busiek-s/Ordway-a; Ronan the Accuser, Avengers app. 3.00
...Dangerous Planet 1: Busiek-s/Ordway-a; Ego, the Living Planet 3.00
Thor vs. Ego (11/00, $2.99) Reprints Thor #133,160,161; Kirby-a 3.00

MAX RIDE: FINAL FLIGHT (Based on the James Patterson novel Maximum Ride)
Marvel Comics: Nov, 2016 - No. 5, Mar, 2017 ($3.99, limited series)

1-5-Jody Houser-s/Marco Failla-a. 1-Two covers (Nakamura & Oum) 4.00

MAX RIDE: FIRST FLIGHT (Based on the James Patterson novel Maximum Ride)
Marvel Comics: Jun, 2015 - No. 5, Oct, 2015 ($3.99, limited series)

The Maxx: Maxximized #5 © Sam Kieth

MD #5 © WMG

Mechanism #1 © Ienco & TCOW

GD VG FN VF VF/NM NM-
2.0 4.0 6.0 8.0 9.0 9.2

1-5-Marguerite Bennett-s/Alex Sanchez-a. 1-Three covers 4.00

MAX RIDE: ULTIMATE FLIGHT (Based on the James Patterson novel Maximum Ride)
Marvel Comics: Jan, 2016 - No. 5, May, 2016 ($3.99, limited series)

1-5-Jody Houser-s/RB Silva-a. 1-Two covers 4.00

MAXX (Also see Darker Image, Primer #5, & Friends of Maxx)
Image Comics (I Before E): Mar, 1993 - No. 35, Feb, 1998 ($1.95)

1/2 1 3 4 6 8 10
1/2 (Gold) 20.00
1-Sam Kieth-c/a/scripts 5.00
1-Glow-in-the-dark variant 2 4 6 8 10 12
1-"3-D Edition" (1/98, $4.95) plus new back-up story 5.00
2-12: 6-Savage Dragon cameo(1 pg.). 7,8-Pitt-c & story 3.00
13-16 3.00
17-35: 21-Alan Moore-s 3.00
Volume 1 TPB (DC/WildStorm, 2003, $17.95) r/#1-6 18.00
Volume 2 TPB (DC/WildStorm, 2004, $17.95) r/#7-13 18.00
Volume 3 TPB (DC/WildStorm, 2004, $17.95) r/#14-20 18.00
Volume 4 TPB (DC/WildStorm, 2005, $17.95) r/#21-27 18.00
Volume 5 TPB (DC/WildStorm, 2005, $19.99) r/#28-35 20.00
Volume 6 TPB (DC/WildStorm, 2006, $19.99) r/Friends of Maxx #1-3 & The Maxx 3-D 20.00

MAXX: MAXXIMIZED
IDW Publishing: Nov, 2013 - No. 35, Sept, 2016 ($3.99)

1-35-Remastered, recolored reprint of the original Maxx issues 4.00

MAYA (See Movie Classics)
Gold Key: Mar, 1968

1 (10218-803)(TV) Photo-c 3 6 9 16 24 32

MAYDAY
Image Comics: Nov, 2016 - No. 5 ($3.99, limited series)

1-4-Alex de Campi-s/Tony Parker-a 4.00

MAYHEM
Dark Horse Comics: May, 1989 - No. 4, Sept, 1989 ($2.50, B&W, 52 pgs.)

1-Four part Stanley Ipkiss/Mask story begins; Mask-c
1 3 4 6 8 10
2-4: 2-Mask 1/2 back-c. 4-Mask-c 1 2 3 5 7 9

MAYHEM (Tyrese Gibson's...)
Image Comics: Aug, 2009 - No. 3, Oct, 2009 ($2.99, limited series)

1-3-Tyrese Gibson co-writer; Tone Rodriguez-a/c 3.00

MAZE AGENCY, THE
Comico/Innovation Publ. #8 on: Dec, 1988 - No. 20, 1991 ($1.95-$2.50, color)

1-20: 9-Ellery Queen app. 7 ($2.50)-Last Comico issue 3.00
Annual 1 (1990, $2.75)-Ploog-c; Spirit tribute ish 4.00
Special 1 (1989, $2.75)-Staton-p (Innovation) 4.00
TPB (IDW Publ., 11/05, $24.99) r/#1-5 25.00

MAZE AGENCY, THE (Vol. 2)
Caliber Comics: July, 1997 - No. 3, 1998 ($2.95, B&W)

1-3: 1-Barr-s/Gonzales-a(p). 3-Hughes-c 3.00

MAZE AGENCY, THE
Caliber Comics: Nov, 2005 - No. 3, Jan, 2006 ($3.99, limited series)

1-3-Barr-s/Padilla-a(p)/c 4.00

MAZE RUNNER: THE SCORCH TRIALS (Based on the Maze Runner movies)
BOOM! Studios: Jun, 2015 ($14.99, squarebound SC)

...Official Graphic Novel Prelude - Short stories about the characters; s/a by various 15.00

MAZIE (...& Her Friends) (See Flat-Top, Mortie, Stevie & Tastee-Freez)
Mazie Comics(Magazine Publ.)/Harvey Publ. No. 13-on: 1953 - #12, 1954; #13, 12/54 - #22, 9/56; #23, 9/57 - #28, 8/58

1-(Teen-age)-Stevie's girlfriend 14 28 42 76 108 140
2 8 16 24 44 57 70
3-10 8 16 24 40 50 60
11-28 7 14 21 35 43 50

MAZIE
Nation Wide Publishers: 1950 - No. 7, 1951 (5¢) (5x7-1/4"-miniature)(52 pgs.)

1-Teen-age 21 42 63 122 199 275
2-7 15 30 45 85 130 175

MAZINGER (See First Comics Graphic Novel #17)

'MAZING MAN
DC Comics: Jan, 1986 - No. 12, Dec, 1986

1-11: 7,8-Hembeck-a 3.00
12-Dark Knight part-c by Miller 4.00
Special 1 ('87), 2 (4/88), 3 ('90)-All $2.00, 52pgs. 4.00

McCANDLESS & COMPANY
Mandalay Books/American Mythology

...: Dead Razor (2001, $7.95) J.C. Vaughn-s/Busch & Sheehan-a; 3 covers 8.00
...: Insecurituies (American Myth., 10/16, $4.99) Vaughn-s/Gonzales-a/Oeming-c 5.00
Crime Scenes: A McCandless & Company Reader TPB (Spring 2006, $17.95) Vaughn-s 18.00

McHALE'S NAVY (TV) (See Movie Classics)
Dell Publ. Co.: May-July, 1963 - No. 3, Nov-Jan, 1963-64 (All have photo-c)

1 6 12 18 38 69 100
2,3 5 10 15 30 50 70

McKEEVER & THE COLONEL (TV)
Dell Publishing Co.: Feb-Apr, 1963 - No. 3, Aug-Oct, 1963

1-Photo-c 5 10 15 34 60 85
2,3-Photo-c 4 8 12 28 47 65

McLINTOCK (See Movie Comics)

MD
E. C. Comics: Apr-May, 1955 - No. 5, Dec-Jan, 1955-56

1-Not approved by code; Craig-c 19 38 57 152 239 325
2-5 11 22 33 88 144 200

NOTE: ***Crandall, Evans, Ingels, Orlando*** *art in all issues;* ***Craig*** *c-1-5.*

MD
Russ Cochran/Gemstone Publishing: Sept, 1999 - No. 5, Jan, 2000 ($2.50)

1-5-Reprints original EC series 4.00
Annual 1 (1999, $13.50) r/#1-5 14.00

MEASLES
Fantagraphics Books: Christmas 1998 - No. 8 ($2.95, B&W, quarterly)

1-8-Anthology: 1-Venus-s by Hernandez 3.00

MECHA (Also see Mayhem)
Dark Horse Comics: June, 1987 - No. 6, 1988 ($1.50/$1.95, color/B&W)

1-6: 1,2 ($1.95, color), 3,4-($1.75, B&W), 5,6-($1.50, B&W) 3.00

MECHANIC, THE
Image Comics: 1998 ($5.95, one-shot, squarebound)

1-Chiodo-painted art; Peterson-s 6.00
1-($10.00) DF Alternate Cover Ed. 10.00

MECHANISM
Image Comics (Top Cow): Jul, 2016 - No. 5, Nov, 2016 ($3.99)

1-5-Raffaele Ienco-s/a 4.00

MECHA SPECIAL
Dark Horse Comics: May, 1995 ($2.95, one-shot)

1 3.00

MECH DESTROYER
Image Comics: Apr, 2001 - No. 4, Sept, 2001 ($2.95, limited series)

1-4-Jae Kim-c/a; Robert Chong-s 3.00

MEDAL FOR BOWZER, A (See Promotional Comics section)

MEDAL OF HONOR COMICS
A. S. Curtis: Spring, 1946

1-War stories 15 30 45 88 137 185

MEDAL OF HONOR SPECIAL
Dark Horse Comics: 1994 ($2.50, one-shot)

1-Kubert-c/a (first story) 3.00

MEDIA STARR
Innovation Publ.: July, 1989 - No. 3, Sept, 1989 ($1.95, mini-series, 28 pgs.)

1-3: Deluxe format 3.00

MEDIEVAL SPAWN/WITCHBLADE
Image Comics (Top Cow Productions): May, 1996 - No. 3, June, 1996 ($2.95, limited series)

1-3-Garth Ennis scripts in all 6.00
1-Platinum foil-c (500 copies from Pittsburgh Con) 35.00
1-Gold 10.00
1-ETM Exclusive Edition; gold foil logo 7.00
TPB ($9.95) r/#1-3 10.00

Megamind #1 © Dreamworks

Megaton #5 © Gary Carlson

Menace #11 © MARV

GD 2.0 | VG 4.0 | FN 6.0 | VF 8.0 | VF/NM 9.0 | NM- 9.2

MEET ANGEL (Formerly Angel & the Ape)
National Periodical Publications: No. 7, Nov-Dec, 1969
7-Wood-a(i) 3 6 9 19 30 40

MEET CORLISS ARCHER (Radio/Movie)(My Life #4 on)
Fox Features Syndicate: Mar, 1948 - No. 3, July, 1948
1-(Teen-age)-Feldstein-c/a; headlight-c 113 226 339 718 1234 1750
2 58 116 174 371 636 900
3 54 108 162 343 574 825
NOTE: *No. 1-3 used in Seduction of the Innocent, pg. 39.*

MEET HERCULES (See Three Stooges)

MEET MERTON
Toby Press: Dec, 1953 - No. 4, June, 1954
1-(Teen-age)-Dave Berg-c/a 20 40 60 114 182 250
2-Dave Berg-c/a 12 24 36 69 97 125
3,4-Dave Berg-c/a 11 22 33 62 86 110
I.W. Reprint #9, Super Reprint #11('63), 18 2 4 6 8 11 14

MEET MISS BLISS (Becomes Stories Of Romance #5 on)
Atlas Comics (LMC): May, 1955 - No. 4, Nov, 1955
1-Al Hartley-c/a 22 44 66 132 216 300
2-4 15 30 45 85 130 175

MEET MISS PEPPER (Formerly Lucy, The Real Gone Gal)
St. John Publishing Co.: No. 5, April, 1954 - No. 6, June, 1954
5-Kubert/Maurer-a 30 60 90 177 289 400
6-Kubert/Maurer-a; Kubert-c 26 52 78 154 252 350

MEGACITY909
Devil's Due Publ.: Sept, 2004 - No. 8, Aug, 2005 ($2.95)
1-8-Kano Kang & Zack Suh-a 3.00

MEGA DRAGON & TIGER
Image Comics: Mar, 1999 - No. 5 ($2.95)
1-5-Tony Wong-s/a 3.00

MEGALITH (Megalith Deathwatch 2000 #1,2 of second series)
Continuity: 1989 - No. 9, Mar, 1992; No, 0, Apr, 1993 - No. 7, Jan, 1994
1-9-($2.00-c) 1-Neal Adams & Mark Texiera-c/Texiera & Nebres-a 3.00
2nd series: 0-(4/93)-Foil-c; no c-price, giveaway; Adams plot 3.00
1-7: 1-3-Bagged w/card: 1-Gatefold-c by Nebres; Adams plot. 2-Fold-out-c; Adams plot. 3-Indestructible-c. 4-7-Embossed-c: 4-Adams/Nebres-c; Adams part-i. 5-Sienkiewicz-i. 6-Adams part-i. 7-Adams-c(p); Adams plot 3.00

MEGAMAN
Dreamwave Productions: Sept, 2003 - No. 4, Dec, 2003 ($2.95)
1-4-Brian Augustyn-s/Mic Fong-a 3.00
1-($5.95) Chromium wraparound variant-c 6.00

MEGA MAN (Based on the Capcom video game character)
Archie Comics Publications: Jul, 2011 - Present ($2.99/$3.99)
1-39 1-Spaziante-a. 20-39-Multiple covers. 24-Worlds Collide x-over begins 3.00
40-49,51-55 ($3.99) Two covers on most. 51,52-Three covers 4.00
50-($4.99) Six covers; "Worlds Unite" Sonic/Mega Man x-over pt. 4 5.00
Free Comic Book Day Edition (2012, giveaway) Origin re-told 3.00
...: Worlds Unite Battles 1 (8/15, $3.99) Sonic/Mega Man x-over; 3 wraparound covers 4.00

MEGAMIND: BAD. BLUE. BRILLIANT (DreamWorks'...) (Based on the 2010 movie)
Ape Entertainment: 2010 - No. 4, 2011 ($3.95, limited series)
1-4: 1-High school flashback 4.00
nn-($6.95, 9x6") Prequel to the movie; Joe Kelly-s 7.00

MEGA MORPHS
Marvel Comics: Oct, 2005 - No. 4, Dec, 2005 ($2.99, limited series)
1-4-Giant robots based on action figures; McKeever-s; Kang-a 3.00
Digest (2006, $7.99) r/#1-4 plus mini-comics 8.00

MEGATON (A super hero)
Megaton Publ.: Nov, 1983; No. 2, Oct, 1985 - No. 8, Aug, 1987 (B&W)
1-($2.00, 68 pgs.)-Erik Larsen's 1st pro work; Vanguard by Larsen begins (1st app.), ends #4; 1st app. Megaton, Berzerker, & Ethrian; Guice-c/a(p); Gustovich-a(p) in #1,2 2 4 6 11 16 20
2-($2.00, 68 pgs.)-1st brief app. The Dragon (1 pg.) by Larsen (later The Savage Dragon in Image Comics); Guice-c/a(p) 2 4 6 9 12 15
3-(44 pgs.)-1st full app. Savage Dragon-c/story by Larsen; 1st comic book work by Angel Medina (pin-up) 3 6 9 19 30 40
4-(52 pgs.)-2nd full app. Savage Dragon by Larsen; 4,5-Wildman by Grass Green 2 4 6 8 10 12
5-1st Liefeld published-a (inside f/c, 6/86) 1 2 3 5 7 9
6,7: 6-Larsen-c 1 2 3 4 5 7
8-1st Liefeld story-a (7 pg. super hero story) plus 1 pg. Youngblood ad 1 3 4 6 8 10
...Explosion (6/87, 16 pg. color giveaway)-1st app. Youngblood by Rob Liefeld (2 pg. spread); shows Megaton heroes 5 10 15 33 57 75
...Holiday Special 1 (1994, $2.95, color, 40 pgs., publ. by Entity Comics)-Gold foil logo; bagged w/Kelley Jones card; Vanguard, Megaton plus shows unpublished-c to 1987 Youngblood #1 by Liefeld/Ordway 5.00
NOTE: *Copies of Megaton Explosion were also released in early 1992 all signed by Rob Liefeld and were made available to retailers.*

MEGATON MAN (See Don Simpson's Bizarre Heroes)
Kitchen Sink Enterprises: Nov, 1984 - No. 10, 1986
1-10, 1-2nd printing (1989) 3.00
...Meets The Uncategorizable X-Thems 1 (4/89, $2.00) 3.00

MEGATON MAN: BOMB SHELL
Image Comics: Jul, 1999 - No. 2 ($2.95, B&W, mini-series)
1-Reprints stories from Megaton Man internet site 3.00

MEGATON MAN: HARD COPY
Image Comics: Feb, 1999 - No. 2, Apr, 1999 ($2.95, B&W, mini-series)
1,2-Reprints stories from Megaton Man internet site 3.00

MEGATON MAN VS. FORBIDDEN FRANKENSTEIN
Fiasco Comics: Apr, 1996 ($2.95, B&W, one-shot)
1-Intro The Tomb Team (Forbidden Frankenstein, Drekula, Bride of the Monster, & Moon Wolf). 3.00

MEK (See Reload/Mek flipbook for TPB reprint)
DC Comics (Homage): Jan, 2003 - No. 3, Mar, 2003 ($2.95, limited series)
1-3-Warren Ellis-s/Steve Rolston-a 3.00

MEKANIX (See X-Men titles) (See X-Treme X-Men Vol. 4 for TPB)
Marvel Comics: Dec, 2002 - No. 6, May, 2003 ($2.99, limited series)
1-6-Kitty Pryde in college; Claremont-s/Bobillo & Sosa-a 3.00

MEL ALLEN SPORTS COMICS (The Voice of the Yankees)
Standard Comics: No. 5, Nov, 1949; No. 6, June, 1950
5(#1 on inside)-Tuska-a 23 46 69 136 223 310
6(#2)-Lou Gehrig story 16 32 48 94 147 200

MELVIN MONSTER
Dell Publishing Co.: Apr-June, 1965 - No. 10, Oct, 1969
1-By John Stanley 6 12 18 40 73 105
2-10-All by Stanley. #10-r/#1 5 10 15 30 50 70

MELVIN THE MONSTER (See Peter, the Little Pest & Dexter The Demon #7)
Atlas Comics (HPC): July, 1956 - No. 6, July, 1957
1-Maneely-c/a 16 32 48 94 147 200
2-6: 4-Maneely-c/a 12 24 36 67 94 120

MENACE
Atlas Comics (HPC): Mar, 1953 - No. 11, May, 1954
1-Horror & sci/fi stories begin; Everett-c/a 161 322 483 1030 1765 2500
2-Post-atom bomb disaster by Everett; anti-Communist propaganda/torture scenes; Sinnott sci/fi story "Rocket to the Moon" 103 206 309 659 1130 1600
3,4,6-Everett-a. 4-Sci/fi story "Escape to the Moon". 6-Romita sci/fi story "Science Fiction" 77 154 231 493 847 1200
5-Origin & 1st app. The Zombie by Everett (reprinted in Tales of the Zombie #1)(7/53); 5-Sci/fi story "Rocket Ship" 142 284 426 909 1555 2200
7,8,10,11: 7-Frankenstein story. 8-End of world story; Heath 3-D art(3 pgs.). 10-H-Bomb panels 61 122 183 390 670 950
9-Everett-a r-in Vampire Tales #1 77 154 231 493 847 1200
NOTE: ***Brodsky** c-7, 8, 11. **Colan** a-6; c-9. **Everett** a-1-6, 9; c-1-6. **Heath** a-1-8; c-10. **Katz** a-11. **Maneely** a-3, 5, 7-9. **Powell** a-11. **Romita** a-3, 6, 8, 11. **Shelly** a-10. **Shores** a-7. **Sinnott** a-2, 7. **Tuska** a-1, 2, 5.*

MENACE
Awesome-Hyperwerks: Nov, 1998 ($2.50)
1-Jada Pinkett Smith-s/Fraga-a 3.00

MEN AGAINST CRIME (Formerly Mr. Risk; Hand of Fate #8 on)
Ace Magazines: No. 3, Feb, 1951 - No. 7, Oct, 1951
3-Mr. Risk app. 12 24 36 69 97 125
4-7: 4-Colan-a; entire book-r as Trapped! #4. 5-Meskin-a 9 18 27 50 65 80

MEN, GUNS, & CATTLE (See Classics Illustrated Special Issue)

Men in Action #6 © MAR

Men's Adventures #21 © MAR

Meridian #1 © CRO

MEN IN ACTION (Battle Brady #10 on)
Atlas Comics (IPS): April, 1952 - No. 9, Dec, 1952 (War stories)

	GD 2.0	VG 4.0	FN 6.0	VF 8.0	VF/NM 9.0	NM- 9.2
1-Berg, Reinman-a	28	56	84	165	270	375
2,3: 3-Heath-c/a	15	30	45	88	137	185
4-6,8,9	15	30	45	84	127	170
7-Krigstein-a; Heath-c	15	30	45	88	137	185

NOTE: ***Brodsky** a-3; c-1, 4-6. **Maneely** c-5. **Pakula** a-1, 6. **Robinson** c-8. **Shores** c-9. **Sinnott** a-6.*

MEN IN ACTION
Ajax/Farrell Publications: Apr, 1957 - No. 6, Jun, 1958

	GD 2.0	VG 4.0	FN 6.0	VF 8.0	VF/NM 9.0	NM- 9.2
1	12	24	36	67	94	120
2	8	16	24	42	54	65
3-6	7	14	21	37	46	55

MEN IN BLACK, THE (1st series)
Aircel Comics (Malibu): Jan, 1990 - No. 3 Mar, 1990 ($2.25, B&W, lim. series)

	GD 2.0	VG 4.0	FN 6.0	VF 8.0	VF/NM 9.0	NM- 9.2
1-Cunningham-s/a in all	6	12	18	37	66	95
2,3	3	6	9	17	26	35
Graphic Novel (Jan, 1991) r/#1-3	3	6	9	16	23	30

MEN IN BLACK (2nd series)
Aircel Comics (Malibu): May, 1991 - No. 3, Jul, 1991 ($2.50, B&W, lim. series)

	GD 2.0	VG 4.0	FN 6.0	VF 8.0	VF/NM 9.0	NM- 9.2
1-Cunningham-s/a in all	3	6	9	19	30	40
2,3	2	4	6	11	16	20

MEN IN BLACK: FAR CRY
Marvel Comics: Aug, 1997 ($3.99, color, one-shot)

	GD 2.0	VG 4.0	FN 6.0	VF 8.0	VF/NM 9.0	NM- 9.2
1-Cunningham-s						4.00

MEN IN BLACK: RETRIBUTION
Marvel Comics: Dec, 1997 ($3.99, color, one-shot)

	GD 2.0	VG 4.0	FN 6.0	VF 8.0	VF/NM 9.0	NM- 9.2
1-Cunningham-s; continuation of the movie						4.00

MEN IN BLACK: THE MOVIE
Marvel Comics: Oct, 1997 ($3.99, one-shot, movie adaptation)

	GD 2.0	VG 4.0	FN 6.0	VF 8.0	VF/NM 9.0	NM- 9.2
1-Cunningham-s						4.00

MEN INTO SPACE
Dell Publishing Co.: No. 1083, Feb-Apr, 1960

	GD 2.0	VG 4.0	FN 6.0	VF 8.0	VF/NM 9.0	NM- 9.2
Four Color 1083-Anderson-a, photo-c	5	10	15	34	60	85

MEN OF BATTLE (Also see New Men of Battle)
Catechetical Guild: V1#5, March, 1943 (Hardcover)

	GD 2.0	VG 4.0	FN 6.0	VF 8.0	VF/NM 9.0	NM- 9.2
V1#5-Topix reprints	6	12	18	28	34	40

MEN OF WAR
DC Comics, Inc.: August, 1977 - No. 26, March, 1980 (#9,10: 44 pgs.)

	GD 2.0	VG 4.0	FN 6.0	VF 8.0	VF/NM 9.0	NM- 9.2
1-Enemy Ace, Gravedigger (origin #1,2) begin	3	6	9	16	23	30
2-4,8-10,12-14,19,20: All Enemy Ace stories. 4-1st Dateline Frontline. 9-Unknown Soldier app.	2	4	6	10	14	18
5-7,11,15-18,21-25: 17-1st app. Rosa	2	4	6	8	11	14
26-Sgt. Rock & Easy Co.-c/s	3	6	9	14	19	24

NOTE: ***Chaykin** a-9, 10, 12-14, 19, 20. **Evans** c-25. **Kubert** c-2-23, 24p, 26.*

MEN OF WAR (DC New 52)
DC Comics: Nov, 2011 - No. 8, Jun, 2012 ($3.99)

	GD 2.0	VG 4.0	FN 6.0	VF 8.0	VF/NM 9.0	NM- 9.2
1-8: 1-Sgt. Rock's grandson in modern times; Derenick-a; Navy Seals back-up; Winslade-a 6-Back-up w/Corben-a. 8-Frankenstein & G.I. Robot app.						4.00

MEN OF WRATH
Marvel Comics (ICON): Oct, 2014 - No. 5, Feb, 2015 ($3.50, limited series)

	GD 2.0	VG 4.0	FN 6.0	VF 8.0	VF/NM 9.0	NM- 9.2
1-5-Jason Aaron-s/Ron Garney-a; two covers on each. 5-Alex Ross var-c						3.50

MEN'S ADVENTURES (Formerly True Adventures)
Marvel/Atlas Comics (CCC): No. 4, Aug, 1950 - No. 28, July, 1954

	GD 2.0	VG 4.0	FN 6.0	VF 8.0	VF/NM 9.0	NM- 9.2
4(#1)(52 pgs.)	39	78	117	231	378	525
5-Flying Saucer story	26	52	78	154	252	350
6-8: 7-Buried alive story. 8-Sci/fic story	24	48	72	140	230	320
9-20: All war format	18	36	54	105	165	225
21,22,24,26: All horror format	39	78	117	231	378	525
23-Crandall-a; Fox-a(i); horror format	39	78	117	240	395	550
25-Shrunken head-c	61	122	183	390	670	950
27,28-Human Torch & Toro-c/stories; Captain America & Sub-Mariner stories in each (also see Young Men #24-28)	155	310	465	992	1696	2400

NOTE: ***Ayers** a-20, 27(H. Torch). **Berg** a-15, 16. **Brodsky** c-4-9, 11, 12, 16-18, 24. **Burgos** c-27, 28 (Human Torch). **Colan** a-13, 14, 19. **Everett** a-10, 14, 22, 25, 28; c-14, 21-23. **Hartley** a-12. **Heath** a-8, 11, 24; c-13, 20, 26. **Lawrence** a-23; 27(Captain America). **Maneely** a-24; c-10, 15. **Mac Pakula** a-15, 25. **Post** a-23. **Powell** a-27(Sub-Mariner). **Reinman** a-11, 12, 16. **Robinson** c-19. **Romita** a-22. **Sale** a-12, 14. **Shores** c-25. **Sinnott** a-13, 21. **Tuska** a-24. Adventure-#4-8; War-#9-20; Weird/Horror-#21-26.*

MENZ INSANA
DC Comics (Vertigo): 1997 ($7.95, one-shot)

	GD 2.0	VG 4.0	FN 6.0	VF 8.0	VF/NM 9.0	NM- 9.2
nn-Fowler-s/Bolton painted art	1	2	3	5	6	8

MEPHISTO VS... (See Silver Surfer #3)
Marvel Comics Group: Apr, 1987 - No. 4, July, 1987 ($1.50, mini-series)

	GD 2.0	VG 4.0	FN 6.0	VF 8.0	VF/NM 9.0	NM- 9.2
1-4: 1-Fantastic Four; Austin-i. 2-X-Factor. 3-X-Men. 4-Avengers						4.00

MERC (See Mark Hazzard: Merc)

MERCENARIES (Based on the Pandemic video game)
Dynamite Entertainment: 2007 - No. 3, 2008 ($3.99, limited series)

	GD 2.0	VG 4.0	FN 6.0	VF 8.0	VF/NM 9.0	NM- 9.2
1-3-Michael Turner-c; Brian Reed-s/Edgar Salazar-a						4.00

MERCHANTS OF DEATH
Acme Press (Eclipse): Jul, 1988 - No. 4, Nov, 1988 ($3.50, B&W/16 pgs. color, 44 pg. mag.)

	GD 2.0	VG 4.0	FN 6.0	VF 8.0	VF/NM 9.0	NM- 9.2
1-4: 4-Toth-c						4.00

MERCILESS: THE RISE OF MING (Also see Flash Gordon: Zeitgeist)
Dynamite Entertainment: 2012 - No. 4, 2012 ($3.99, limited series)

	GD 2.0	VG 4.0	FN 6.0	VF 8.0	VF/NM 9.0	NM- 9.2
1-4 Ming the Merciless' rise to power; Alex Ross-c; Beatty-c/Adrian-a						4.00

MERCY THOMPSON (Patricia Briggs'...)
Dynamite Entertainment: 2014 - No. 6, 2015 ($3.99, limited series)

	GD 2.0	VG 4.0	FN 6.0	VF 8.0	VF/NM 9.0	NM- 9.2
1-6-Patricia Briggs & Rik Hoskin-s/Tom Garcia-a						4.00

MERIDIAN
CrossGeneration Comics: Jul, 2000 - No. 44, Apr, 2004 ($2.95)

	GD 2.0	VG 4.0	FN 6.0	VF 8.0	VF/NM 9.0	NM- 9.2
1-44: Barbara Kesel-s						3.00
Flying Solo Vol. 1 TPB (2001, $19.95) r/#1-7; cover by Steve Rude						20.00
Going to Ground Vol. 2 TPB (2002, $19.95) r/#8-14						20.00
Taking the Skies Vol. 3 TPB (2002, $15.95) r/#15-20						16.00
Vol. 4: Coming Home (12/02, $15.95) r/#21-26						16.00
Vol. 5: Minister of Cadador (7/03, $15.95) r/#27-32						16.00
Vol. 6: Changing Course (1/04, $15.95) r/#33-38						16.00
Traveler Vol. 1-4 ($9.95): Digest-size reprints of TPBs						10.00

MERLIN JONES AS THE MONKEY'S UNCLE (See Movie Comics and The Misadventures of... under Movie Comics)

MERRILL'S MARAUDERS (See Movie Classics)

MERRY CHRISTMAS (See A Christmas Adventure, Donald Duck..., Dell Giant #39, & March of Comics #153 in the Promotional Comics section)

MERRY COMICS
Carlton Publishing Co.: Dec, 1945 (10¢)

	GD 2.0	VG 4.0	FN 6.0	VF 8.0	VF/NM 9.0	NM- 9.2
nn-Boogeyman app.	21	42	63	124	202	280

MERRY COMICS: Four Star Publications: 1947 (Advertised, not published)

MERRY-GO-ROUND COMICS
LaSalle Publ. Co./Croyden Publ./Rotary Litho.: 1944 (25¢, 132 pgs.); 1946; 9-10/47 - No. 2, 1948

	GD 2.0	VG 4.0	FN 6.0	VF 8.0	VF/NM 9.0	NM- 9.2
nn(1944)(LaSalle)-Funny animal; 29 new features	20	40	60	120	195	270
21 (Publisher?)	10	20	30	56	76	95
1(1946)(Croyden)-Al Fago-c; funny animal	13	26	39	72	101	130
V1#1,2(1947-48; 52 pgs.)(Rotary Litho. Co. Ltd., Canada); Ken Hultgren-a	10	20	30	56	76	95

MERRY MAILMAN (See Fawcett's Funny Animals #87-89)

MERRY MOUSE (Also see Funny Tunes & Space Comics)
Avon Periodicals: June, 1953 - No. 4, Jan-Feb, 1954

	GD 2.0	VG 4.0	FN 6.0	VF 8.0	VF/NM 9.0	NM- 9.2
1-1st app.; funny animal; Frank Carin-c/a	11	22	33	64	90	115
2-4	8	16	24	40	50	60

MERV PUMPKINHEAD, AGENT OF D.R.E.A.M. (See The Sandman)
DC Comics (Vertigo): 2000 ($5.95, one-shot)

	GD 2.0	VG 4.0	FN 6.0	VF 8.0	VF/NM 9.0	NM- 9.2
1-Buckingham-a(p); Nowlan painted-c						6.00

META-4
First Comics: Feb, 1991 - No. 4, 1991 ($2.25)

	GD 2.0	VG 4.0	FN 6.0	VF 8.0	VF/NM 9.0	NM- 9.2
1-($3.95, 52pgs.)						4.00
2-4						3.00

METAL GEAR SOLID (Based on the video game)
IDW Publ.: Sept, 2004 - No. 12, Aug, 2005 ($3.99)

	GD 2.0	VG 4.0	FN 6.0	VF 8.0	VF/NM 9.0	NM- 9.2
1-12: 1-Two covers; Ashley Wood-a/Kris Oprisko-s						4.00
1-Retailer edition with foil cover						15.00

METAL GEAR SOLID: SONS OF LIBERTY
IDW Publ.: Sept, 2005 - No. 12, Sept, 2007 ($3.99)

Metal Men (2007 series) #3 © DC

Metamorpho #2 © DC

Miami Vice Remix #4 © Universal Stus.

GD VG FN VF VF/NM NM-
2.0 4.0 6.0 8.0 9.0 9.2

#0 (9/05) profile pages on characters; Ashley Wood-a 4.00
1-12: 1-Two covers; Ashley Wood-a/Alex Garner-s 4.00

METALLIX
Future Comics: Dec, 2002 - No. 6, June, 2003 ($3.50)

0-6-Ron Lim-a. 0-(6/03) Origin. 1-Layton-c 3.50
1-Collector's Edition with variant cover by Lim 3.50
1-Free Comic Book Day Edition (4/03) Layton-c 3.00

METAL MEN (See Brave & the Bold, DC Comics Presents, and Showcase #37-40)
National Periodical Publications/DC Comics: 4-5/63 - No. 41, 12-1/69-70; No. 42, 2-3/73 - No. 44, 7-8/73; No. 45, 4-5/76 - No. 56, 2-3/78

1-(4-5/63)-5th app. Metal Men 54 108 162 432 966 1500
2 20 40 60 135 300 465
3-5 13 26 39 89 195 300
6-10 9 18 27 59 117 175
11-20: 12-Beatles cameo (2-3/65) 7 14 21 46 86 125
21-Batman, Robin & Flash x-over 6 12 18 37 66 95
22-26,28-30 5 10 15 34 60 85
27-Origin Metal Men retold 6 12 18 42 79 115
31-41(1968-70): 38-Last 12¢ issue. 41-Last 15¢ 5 10 15 31 53 75
42-44(1973)-Reprints 2 4 6 10 14 18
45('76)-49-Simonson-a in all: 48,49-Re-intro Eclipso 2 4 6 10 14 18
50-56: 50-Part-r. 54,55-Green Lantern x-over 2 4 6 9 12 15

NOTE: ***Andru/Esposito** c-1-30. **Aparo** c-53-56. **Giordano** c-45, 46. **Kane/Esposito** a-30, 31; c-31. **Simonson** a-45-49; c-47-52. **Staton** a-50-56.*

METAL MEN (Also see Tangent Comics/ Metal Men)
DC Comics: Oct, 1993 - No. 4, Jan, 1994 ($1.25, mini-series)

1-($2.50)-Multi-colored foil-c 4.00
2-4: 2-Origin 3.00

METAL MEN (Also see 52)
DC Comics: Oct, 2007 - No. 8, Jul, 2008 ($2.99, limited series)

1-8-Duncan Rouleau-s/a; origin re-told. 3-Chemo returns 3.00
HC (2008, $24.99, dustjacket) r/#1-8; cover gallery and sketch pages 25.00
SC (2009, $14.99) r/#1-8; cover gallery and sketch pages 15.00

METAMORPHO (See Action Comics #413, Brave & the Bold #57,58, 1st Issue Special, & World's Finest #217)
National Periodical Publications: July-Aug, 1965 - No. 17, Mar-Apr, 1968 (All 12¢ issues)

1-(7-8/65)-3rd app. Metamorpho 13 26 39 89 195 300
2,3 7 14 21 46 86 125
4-6,10:10-Origin & 1st app. Element Girl (1-2/67) 6 12 18 37 66 95
7-9 5 10 15 33 57 80
11-17: 17-Sparling-c/a 5 10 15 30 50 70

NOTE: ***Ramona Fradon** a-B&B 57, 58, 1-4. **Orlando** a-5, 6; c-5-9, 11. **Trapani** a(p)-7-16; i-16.*

METAMORPHO
DC Comics: Aug, 1993 - No. 4, Nov, 1993 ($1.50, mini-series)

1-4 3.00

METAMORPHO: YEAR ONE
DC Comics: Early Dec, 2007 - No. 6, Late Feb, 2008 ($2.99, limited series)

1-6-Origin re-told; Jurgens-s/Jurgens & Delperdang-a/Nowlan-c. 6-Justice League app. 3.00
TPB ('08, $14.99) r/#1-6 15.00

METAPHYSIQUE
Malibu Comics (Bravura): Apr, 1995 - No. 6, Oct, 1995 ($2.95, limited series)

1-6: Norm Breyfogle-c/a/scripts 3.00

METEOR COMICS
L. L. Baird (Croyden): Nov, 1945

1-Captain Wizard, Impossible Man, Race Wilkins app.; origin Baldy Bean, Capt. Wizard's sidekick; bare-breasted mermaids story 43 86 129 271 461 650

METEOR MAN
Marvel Comics: Aug, 1993 - No. 6, Jan, 1994 ($1.25, limited series)

1-6: 1-Regular unbagged. 4-Night Thrasher-c/story. 6-Terry Austin-c(i) 3.00
1-Polybagged w/button & rap newspaper 4.00
...: The Movie (4/93 [7/93 on cover], $2.25) movie adaptation 3.00

METROPOL (See Ted McKeever's...)

METROPOL A.D. (See Ted McKeever's...)

METROPOLIS S.C.U. (Also see Showcase '96 #1)
DC Comics: Nov, 1995 - No. 4, Feb, 1996 ($1.50, limited series)

1-4:1-Superman-c & app. 3.00

MEZZ: GALACTIC TOUR 2494 (Also See Nexus)

GD VG FN VF VF/NM NM-
2.0 4.0 6.0 8.0 9.0 9.2

Dark Horse Comics: May, 1994 ($2.50, one-shot)

1 3.00

MGM'S MARVELOUS WIZARD OF OZ (See Marvel Treasury of Oz)
Marvel Comics Group/National Periodical Publications: 1975 ($1.50, 84 pgs.; oversize)

1-Adaptation of MGM's movie; J. Buscema-a 3 6 9 16 23 30

M.G.M'S MOUSE MUSKETEERS (Formerly M.G.M.'s The Two Mouseketeers)
Dell Publishing Co.: No. 670, Jan, 1956 - No. 1290, Mar-May, 1962

Four Color 670 (#4) 6 12 18 38 69 100
Four Color 711,728,764 5 10 15 31 53 75
8 (4-6/57) - 21 (3-5/60) 4 8 12 27 44 60
Four Color 1135,1175,1290 4 8 12 28 47 65

M.G.M.'S SPIKE AND TYKE (also see Tom & Jerry #79)
Dell Publishing Co.: No. 499, Sept, 1953 - No. 1266, Dec-Feb, 1961-62

Four Color 499 (#1) 7 14 21 46 86 125
Four Color 577,638 5 10 15 35 63 90
4(12-2/55-56)-10 4 8 12 27 44 60
11-24(12-2/60-61) 4 8 12 23 37 50
Four Color 1266 4 8 12 28 47 65

M.G.M.'S THE TWO MOUSKETEERS
Dell Publishing Co.: No. 475, June, 1953 - No. 642, July, 1955

Four Color 475 (#1) 9 18 27 57 111 165
Four Color 603 (11/54), 642 6 12 18 41 76 110

MIAMI VICE REMIX
IDW Publishing (Lion Forge): Mar, 2015 - No. 5, Jul, 2015 ($3.99, limited series)

1-5-Joe Casey-s/Jim Mahfood-a; re-imagined Crockett & Tubbs 4.00

MICE TEMPLAR, THE
Image Comics: Sept, 2007 - No. 6, Oct, 2008 ($3.99/$2.99)

1-($3.99)-Bryan Glass-s/Michael Avon Oeming-a/c 4.00
2-6-($2.99) 3.00

MICE TEMPLAR, THE , VOLUME 2: DESTINY
Image Comics: July, 2009 - No. 9, May, 2010 ($3.99/$2.99/$4.99)

1,2-($3.99) 1-Bryan Glass-s/Oeming & Santos-a; 2 covers. 2-Santos-a 4.00
3-8-($2.99)-Santos-a; 2 covers by Oeming & Santos 3.00
9-($4.99) 5.00

MICE TEMPLAR, THE , VOLUME 3: A MIDWINTER NIGHT'S DREAM
Image Comics: Dec, 2010 - No. 8, Mar, 2012 ($3.99/$2.99)

1,8-($3.99) 1-Bryan Glass-s/Oeming & Santos-a; 2 covers 4.00
2-7-($2.99)-Santos-a; 2 covers by Oeming & Santos 3.00

MICE TEMPLAR, THE , VOLUME 4: LEGEND
Image Comics: Mar, 2013 - No. 14, Oct, 2014 ($3.99/$2.99/$4.99)

1-($3.99)-Bryan Glass-s/Victor Santos-a; 2 covers 4.00
2-7-($2.99)-Santos-a; 2 covers by Oeming & Santos 3.00
8-($4.99) 5.00
9-13-($3.99) 4.00
14-($5.99) Bonus back-up Hammer of the Gods by Oeming & Wheatley 6.00

MICE TEMPLAR, THE , VOLUME 5: NIGHT'S END
Image Comics: Mar, 2015 - No. 5, Sept, 2015 ($3.99/$5.99)

1,3,5-($3.99)-Bryan Glass-s/Victor Santos-a; 2 covers by Oeming & Santos 4.00
2,4-($5.99)-Bonus back-up Hammer of the Gods 6.00

MICHAELANGELO CHRISTMAS SPECIAL (See Teenage Mutant Ninja Turtles Christmas Special)

MICHAELANGELO, TEENAGE MUTANT NINJA TURTLE
Mirage Studios: 1986 (One shot) ($1.50, B&W)

1-Christmas-c/story 3 6 9 16 23 30
1-2nd printing ('89, $1.75)-Reprint plus new-a 6.00

MICHAEL CHABON PRESENTS THE AMAZING ADVENTURES OF THE ESCAPIST
Dark Horse Comics: Feb, 2004 - No. 8, Nov, 2005 ($8.95, squarebound)

1-5,7,8-Short stories by Chabon and various incl. Chaykin, Starlin, Brereton, Baker 9.00
6-Includes 6 pg. Spirit & Escapist story (Will Eisner's last work); Spirit on cover 9.00
... Vol. 1 (5/04, $17.95, digest-size) r/#1&2; wraparound-c by Chris Ware 18.00
... Vol. 2 (11/04, $17.95, digest-size) r/#3&4; wraparound-c by Matt Kindt 18.00
... Vol. 3 (4/06, $14.95, digest-size) r/#5&6; Tim Sale-c 15.00

MICHAEL MOORCOCK'S ELRIC: THE MAKING OF A SORCEROR
DC Comics: 2004 - No. 4, 2006 ($5.95, prestige format, limited series)

1-4-Moorcock-s/Simonson-a 6.00
TPB (2007, $19.99) r/#1-4 20.00

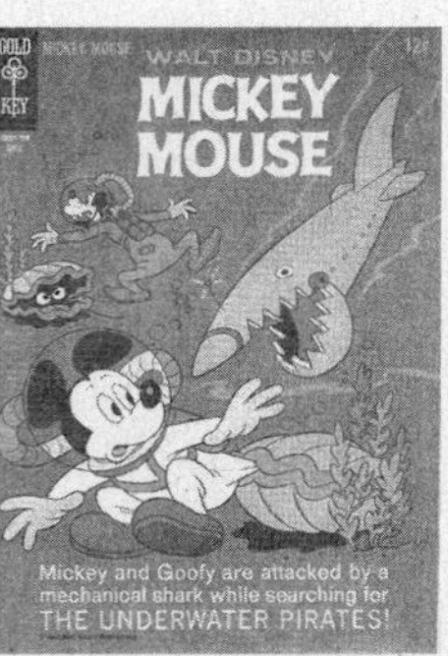

GOLD KEY
WALT DISNEY
MICKEY MOUSE
Mickey and Goofy are attacked by a mechanical shark while searching for THE UNDERWATER PIRATES!

Mickey Mouse #112 © DIS

Mickey Mouse (2015 series) #7 © DIS

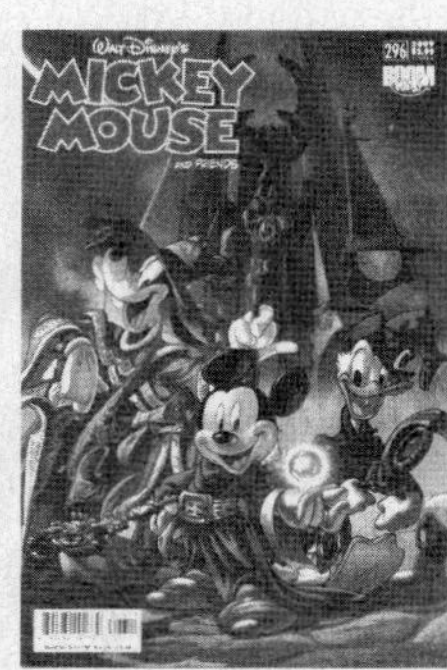

Mickey Mouse and Friends #296 © DIS

MICHAEL MOORCOCK'S MULTIVERSE
DC Comics (Helix): Nov, 1997 - No. 12, Oct, 1998 ($2.50, limited series)

	GD 2.0	VG 4.0	FN 6.0	VF 8.0	VF/NM 9.0	NM- 9.2
1-12: Simonson, Reeve & Ridgway-a						3.00
TPB (1999, $19.95) r/#1-12						20.00

MICHAEL TURNER, A TRIBUTE TO...
Aspen MLT: 2008 ($8.99, squarebound)

	GD 2.0	VG 4.0	FN 6.0	VF 8.0	VF/NM 9.0	NM- 9.2
nn-Pin-ups and tributes from Turner's colleagues and friends; Turner & Ross-c						9.00

MICHAEL TURNER PRESENTS: ASPEN (See Aspen)

MICKEY AND DONALD (See Walt Disney's...)

MICKEY AND DONALD CHRISTMAS PARADE
IDW Publishing: Dec, 2015; Dec, 2016 ($5.99, squaredbound)

	GD 2.0	VG 4.0	FN 6.0	VF 8.0	VF/NM 9.0	NM- 9.2
1,2-English translations of Dutch, Italian and Swedish Disney Christmas stories						6.00

MICKEY AND DONALD IN VACATIONLAND (See Dell Giant No. 47)

MICKEY & THE BEANSTALK (See Story Hour Series)

MICKEY & THE SLEUTH (See Walt Disney Showcase #38, 39, 42)

MICKEY FINN (Also see Big Shot Comics #74 & Feature Funnies)
Eastern Color 1-4/McNaught Synd. #5 on (Columbia)/Headline V3#2:
Nov?, 1942 - V3#2, May, 1952

	GD 2.0	VG 4.0	FN 6.0	VF 8.0	VF/NM 9.0	NM- 9.2
1	30	60	90	177	289	400
2	15	30	45	90	140	190
3-Charlie Chan story	12	24	36	69	97	125
4	10	20	30	56	76	95
5-10	9	18	27	47	61	75
11-15(1949): 12-Sparky Watts app.	8	16	24	40	50	60
V3#1,2(1952)	6	12	18	31	38	45

MICKEY MALONE
Hale Nass Corp.: 1936 (Color, punchout-c) (B&W-a on back)

	GD 2.0	VG 4.0	FN 6.0	VF 8.0	VF/NM 9.0	NM- 9.2
nn - 1pg. of comics	300	600	1200	-	-	-

MICKEY MANTLE (See Baseball's Greatest Heroes #1)

MICKEY MOUSE (See Adventures of Mickey Mouse, The Best of Walt Disney Comics, Cheerios giveaways, Donald and ..., Dynabrite Comics, 40 Big Pages..., Gladstone Comic Album, Merry Christmas From..., Walt Disney's Mickey and Donald, Walt Disney's Comics & Stories, Walt Disney's..., & Wheaties)

MICKEY MOUSE (...Secret Agent #107-109; Walt Disney's... #148-205?)
(See Dell Giants for annuals) (#204 exists from both G.K. & Whitman)
Dell Publ. Co./Gold Key #85-204/Whitman #204-218/Gladstone #219 on:
#16, 1941 - #84, 7-9/62; #85, 11/62 - #218, 6/84; #219, 10/86 - #256, 4/90

	GD 2.0	VG 4.0	FN 6.0	VF 8.0	VF/NM 9.0	NM- 9.2
Four Color 16(1941)-1st Mickey Mouse comic book; "...vs. the Phantom Blot" by Gottfredson	1250	2500	3750	16,500	-	-
Four Color 27(1943)- "7 Colored Terror"	71	142	213	568	1284	2000
Four Color 79(1945)-By Carl Barks (1 story)	89	178	267	712	1606	2500
Four Color 116(1946)	27	54	81	184	410	635
Four Color 141,157(1947)	22	44	66	155	345	535
Four Color 170,181,194('48)	19	38	57	133	297	460
Four Color 214('49),231,248,261	15	30	45	105	233	360
Four Color 268-Reprints/WDC&S #22-24 by Gottfredson ("Surprise Visitor")	14	28	42	98	217	335
Four Color 279,286,296	12	24	36	79	170	260
Four Color 304,313(#1),325(#2),334	11	22	33	72	154	235
Four Color 343,352,362,371,387	9	18	27	62	126	190
Four Color 401,411,427(10-11/52)	8	16	24	56	108	160
Four Color 819-Mickey Mouse in Magicland	6	12	18	41	76	110
Four Color 1057,1151,1246(1959-61)-Album; #1057 has 10¢ & 12¢ editions; back covers are different	6	12	18	37	66	95
28(12-1/52-53)-32,34	6	12	18	40	73	105
33-(Exists with 2 dates, 10-11/53 & 12-1/54)	6	12	18	40	73	105
35-50	5	10	15	35	63	90
51-73,75-80	5	10	15	31	53	75
74-Story swipe "The Rare Stamp Search" from 4-Color #422- "The Gilded Man"	5	10	15	33	57	80
81-105: 93,95-titled "Mickey Mouse Club Album". 100-105: Reprint 4-Color #427,194,279, 170,343,214 in that order	4	8	12	25	40	55
106-120	3	6	9	19	30	40
121-130	3	6	9	16	23	30
131-146	3	6	9	14	20	25
147,148: 147-Reprints "The Phantom Fires" from WDC&S #200-202.148-Reprints "The Mystery of Lonely Valley" from WDC&S #208-210	3	6	9	14	20	25
149-158	2	4	6	10	14	18
159-Reprints "The Sunken City" from WDC&S #205-207	2	4	6	10	14	18
160-178: 162-165,167-170-r	2	4	6	10	14	18
167-Whitman edition	2	4	6	10	14	18
179-(52 pgs.)	2	4	6	11	16	20
180-203: 200-r/Four Color #371	2	4	6	8	10	12
204-(Whitman or G.K.), 205,206	2	4	6	9	13	16
207(8/80), 209(pre-pack?)	5	10	15	35	63	90
208-(8-12/80)-Only distr. in Whitman 3-pack	10	20	30	66	138	210
210(2/81),211-214	2	4	6	9	13	16
215-218: 215(2/82), 216(4/82), 217(3/84), 218(misdated 8/82; actual date 7/84)	2	4	6	10	14	18
219-1st Gladstone issue; The Seven Ghosts serial-r begins by Gottfredson	2	4	6	11	16	20
220,221	2	3	4	6	8	10
222-225: 222-Editor-in Grief strip-r						5.00
226-230						5.00
231-243,246-254: 240-r/March of Comics #27. 245-r/F.C. #279. 250-r/F.C. #248						4.00
244 (1/89, $2.95, 100 pgs.)-Squarebound 60th anniversary issue; gives history of Mickey						5.00
245, 256: 245-r/F.C. #279. 256-$1.95, 68 pgs.						5.00
255 ($1.95, 68 pgs.)						5.00

NOTE: *Reprints #195-197, 198(2/3), 199(1/3), 200-208, 211(1/2), 212, 213, 215(1/3), 216-on.* ***Gottfredson*** *Mickey Mouse serials in #219-239, 241-244, 246-249, 251-253, 255.*

	GD 2.0	VG 4.0	FN 6.0	VF 8.0	VF/NM 9.0	NM- 9.2
Album 01-518-210(Dell), 1(10082-309)(9/63-Gold Key)	3	6	9	21	33	45
...Club 1(1/64-Gold Key)(TV)	4	8	12	22	35	48
Mini Comic 1(1976)(3-1/4x6-1/2")-Reprints 158	1	2	3	5	6	8
Surprise Party 1(30037-901, G.K.)(1/69)-40th Anniversary (see Walt Disney Showcase #47)	3	6	9	20	31	42
Surprise Party 1(1979)-r/1969 issue	1	2	3	5	6	8

MICKEY MOUSE (Continued from Mickey Mouse and Friends)
BOOM! Studios: No. 304, Jan, 2011 - No. 309, Jun, 2011 ($3.99)

	GD 2.0	VG 4.0	FN 6.0	VF 8.0	VF/NM 9.0	NM- 9.2
304-309: 304-Peg-Leg Pete app. 309-Continues in Walt Disney's C&S #720						4.00

MICKEY MOUSE
IDW Publishing: Jun, 2015 - Present ($3.99)

	GD 2.0	VG 4.0	FN 6.0	VF 8.0	VF/NM 9.0	NM- 9.2
1-Legacy numbered #310; art by Cavazzano and others; multiple covers						4.00
2-17-Classic Disney and foreign reprints; multiple covers on each						4.00

MICKEY MOUSE ADVENTURES
Disney Comics: June, 1990 - No. 18, Nov, 1991 ($1.50)

	GD 2.0	VG 4.0	FN 6.0	VF 8.0	VF/NM 9.0	NM- 9.2
1,8,9: 1-Bradbury, Murry-r/M.M. #45,73 plus new-a. 8-Byrne-c. 9-Fantasia 50th ann. issue w/new adapt. of movie						4.00
2-7,10-18: 2-Begin all new stories. 10-r/F.C. #214						3.00

MICKEY MOUSE AND FRIENDS (Continued from Walt Disney's Mickey Mouse and Friends)
(Title continues as Mickey Mouse #304-on)
BOOM! Studios: No. 296, Sept, 2009 - No. 303, Dec, 2010 ($2.99/$3.99)

	GD 2.0	VG 4.0	FN 6.0	VF 8.0	VF/NM 9.0	NM- 9.2
296-299,301-303: 296-299-Wizards of Mickey stories. 301-Conclusion to story in #300						3.00
300-($3.99, 9/10) Petrucha-s/Pelaez-a; back-up Tanglefoot story w/Gottfredson-a						4.00
300 Deluxe Edition ($6.99) Variant cover by Daan Jippes						7.00

MICKEY MOUSE CLUB FUN BOOK
Golden Press: 1977 (1.95, 228 pgs.)(square bound)

	GD 2.0	VG 4.0	FN 6.0	VF 8.0	VF/NM 9.0	NM- 9.2
11190-1950s-r; 20,000 Leagues, M. Mouse Silly Symphonys, The Reluctant Dragon, etc.	4	8	12	27	44	60

MICKEY MOUSE CLUB MAGAZINE (See Walt Disney...)

MICKEY MOUSE COMICS DIGEST
Gladstone: 1986 - No. 5, 1987 (96 pgs.)

	GD 2.0	VG 4.0	FN 6.0	VF 8.0	VF/NM 9.0	NM- 9.2
1 ($1.25-c)	1	2	3	5	6	8
2-5: 3-5 ($1.50-c)						5.00

MICKEY MOUSE IN COLOR
Another Rainbow/Pantheon: 1988 (Deluxe, 13"x17", hard-c, $250.00)
(Trade, 9-7/8"x11-1/2", hard-c, $39.95)

	GD 2.0	VG 4.0	FN 6.0	VF 8.0	VF/NM 9.0	NM- 9.2
Deluxe limited edition of 3,000 copies signed by Floyd Gottfredson and Carl Barks, designated as the "Official Mickey Mouse 60th Anniversary" book. Mickey Sunday and daily reprints, plus Barks "Riddle of the Red Hat" from Four Color #79. Comes with 45 r.p.m. record interview with Gottfredson and Barks. 240 pgs.	12	24	36	82	179	275
Deluxe, limited to 100 copies, as above, but with a unique colored pencil original drawing of Mickey Mouse by Carl Barks.						800.00
Pantheon trade edition, edited down & without Barks, 192 pgs.	3	6	9	19	30	40

MICKEY MOUSE MAGAZINE (Becomes Walt Disney's Comics & Stories)(Also see 40 Big Pages of Mickey Mouse)
K. K. Publ./Western Publishing Co.: Summer, 1935 (June-Aug, indicia) - V5#12, Sept, 1940;

Mickey Mouse Magazine V4 #7 © DIS

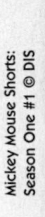

Mickey Mouse Shorts: Season One #1 © DIS

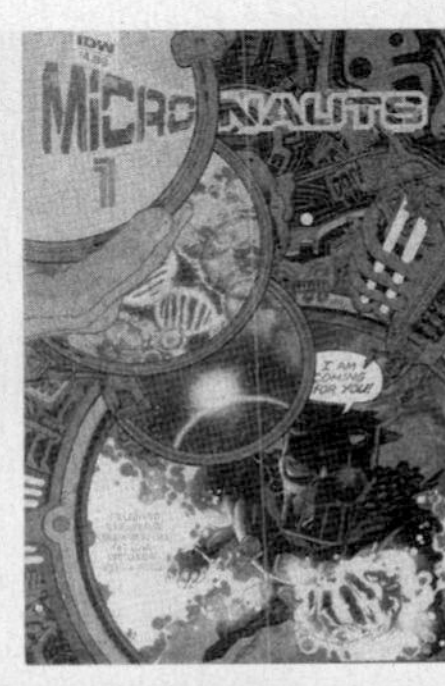

Micronauts (2016 series) #1 © Hasbro

GD 2.0 | VG 4.0 | FN 6.0 | VF 8.0 | VF/NM 9.0 | NM- 9.2

V1#1-5, V3#11,12, V4#1-3 are 44 pgs; V2#3-100 pgs; V5#12-68 pgs; rest are 36 pgs.(No V3#1, V4#6)

V1#1 (Large size, 13-1/4x10-1/4"; 25¢)-Contains puzzles, games, cels, stories & comics of Disney characters. Promotional magazine for Disney cartoon movies and paraphernalia 1425 2850 4275 9200 19,000 -

Note: *Some copies were autographed by the editors & given away with all early one year subscriptions.*

2 (Size change, 11-1/2x8-1/2"; 10/35; 10¢)-High quality paper begins; Messmer-a 306 612 918 2600 - -

3,4: 3-Messmer-a 176 352 528 1500 - -

5-1st Donald Duck solo-c; 2nd cover app. ever; last 44 pg. & high quality paper issue 353 706 1059 3000 - -

6-9: 6-36 pg. issues begin; Donald becomes editor. 8-2nd Donald solo-c. 9-1st Mickey/Minnie-c 159 318 477 1350 - -

10-12, V2#1,2: 11-1st Pluto/Mickey-c; Donald fires himself and appoints Mickey as editor 147 294 441 1250 - -

V2#3-Special 100 pg. Christmas issue (25¢); Messmer-a; Donald becomes editor of Wise Quacks 471 942 1413 4000 - -

4-Mickey Mouse Comics & Roy Ranger (adventure strip) begin; both end V2#9; Messmer-a 129 258 387 1100 - -

5-9: 5-Ted True (adventure strip, ends V2#9) & Silly Symphony Comics (ends V3#3) begin. 6-1st solo Minnie-c. 6-9-Mickey Mouse Movies cut-out in each 60 120 180 381 653 925

10-1st full color issue; Mickey Mouse (by Gottfredson; ends V3#12) & Silly Symphony (ends V3#3) full color Sunday-r, Peter The Farm Detective (ends V5#8) & Ole Of The North (ends V3#3) begins 90 180 270 576 988 1400

11-13: 12-Hiawatha-c & feature story 57 114 171 362 619 875

V3#2-Big Bad Wolf Halloween-c 65 130 195 416 708 1000

3 (12/37)-1st app. Snow White & The Seven Dwarfs (before release of movie) (possibly 1st in print); Mickey X-Mas-c 116 232 348 742 1271 1800

4 (1/38)-Snow White & The Seven Dwarfs serial begins (on stands before release of movie); Ducky Symphony (ends V3#11) begins 95 190 285 608 1042 1475

5-1st Snow White & Seven Dwarfs-c (St. Valentine's Day) 111 222 333 710 1218 1725

6-Snow White serial ends; Lonesome Ghosts app. (2 pp.) 66 132 198 419 722 1025

7-Seven Dwarfs Easter-c 61 122 183 390 670 950

8-10: 9-Dopey-c. 10-1st solo Goofy-c 52 104 156 328 552 775

11,12 (44 pgs; 8 more pgs. color added). 11-Mickey the Sheriff serial (ends V4#3) & Donald Duck strip-r (ends V3#12) begin. Color feature on Snow White's Forest Friends 55 110 165 352 601 850

V4#1 (10/38; 44 pgs.)-Brave Little Tailor-c/feature story, nominated for Academy Award; Bobby & Chip by Otto Messmer (ends V4#2) & The Practical Pig (ends V4#2) begin 54 108 162 343 574 825

2 (44 pgs.)-1st Huey, Dewey & Louie-c 58 116 174 371 636 900

3 (12/38, 44 pgs.)-Ferdinand The Bull-c/feature story, Academy Award winner; Mickey Mouse & The Whalers serial begins, ends V4#12 54 108 162 343 574 825

4-Spotty, Mother Pluto strip-r begin, end V4#8 52 104 156 328 552 775

5-St. Valentine's day-c. 1st Pluto solo-c 57 114 171 362 619 875

7 (3/39)-The Ugly Duckling-c/feature story, Academy Award winner 54 108 162 343 574 825

7 (4/39)-Goofy & Wilbur The Grasshopper classic-c/feature story from 1st Goofy solo cartoon movie; Timid Elmer begins, ends V5#5 57 114 171 362 619 875

8-Big Bad Wolf-c from Practical Pig movie poster; Practical Pig feature story 54 108 162 343 574 825

9-Donald Duck & Mickey Mouse Sunday-r begin; The Pointer feature story, nominated for Academy Award 54 108 162 343 574 825

10-Classic July 4th drum & fife-c; last Donald Sunday-r 74 148 222 470 810 1150

11-1st slick-c; last over-sized issue 53 106 159 334 567 800

12 (9/39; format change, 10-1/4x8-1/4")-1st full color, cover to cover issue; Donald's Penguin-c/feature story 58 116 174 371 636 900

V5#1-Black Pete-c; Officer Duck-c/feature story; Autograph Hound feature story; Robinson Crusoe serial begins 68 136 204 435 743 1050

2-Goofy-c; 1st brief app. Pinocchio 74 148 222 470 810 1150

3 (12/39)-Pinocchio Christmas-c (Before movie release). 1st app. Jiminy Cricket; Pinocchio serial begins 90 180 270 576 988 1400

4,5: 5-Jiminy Cricket-c; Pinocchio serial ends; Donald's Dog Laundry feature story 58 116 174 371 636 900

6,7: 6-Tugboat Mickey feature story; Rip Van Winkle feature begins, ends V5#8. 7-2nd Huey, Dewey & Louie-c 57 114 171 362 619 875

8-Last magazine size issue; 2nd solo Pluto-c; Figaro & Cleo feature story 58 116 174 371 636 900

9-11: 9 (6/40; change to comic book size)-Jiminy Cricket feature story; Donald-c & Sunday-r begin. 10-Special Independence Day issue. 11-Hawaiian Holiday & Mickey's Trailer feature stories; last 36 pg. issue 63 126 189 403 689 975

12 (Format change)-The transition issue (68 pgs.) becoming a comic book. With only a title change to follow, becomes Walt Disney's Comics & Stories #1 with the next issue 476 952 1428 3475 6138 8800

NOTE: ***Otto Messmer**-a is in many issues of the first two-three years. The following story titles and issues have gags created by **Carl Barks:** V4#3(12/38)-'Donald's Better Self' & 'Donald's Golf Game;' V4#4(1/39)-'Donald's Lucky Day;' V4#7(3/39)-'Hockey Champ;' V4#7(4/39)-'Donald's Cousin Gus;' V4#9(6/39)-'Sea Scouts;' V4#12(9/39)-'Donald's Penguin;' V5#9 (6/40)-'Donald's Vacation;' V5#10(7/40)-'Bone Trouble;' V5#12(9/40)-'Window Cleaners.'*

MICKEY MOUSE MAGAZINE (Russian Version)
May 16, 1991 (1st Russian printing of a modern comic book)

1-Bagged w/gold label commemoration in English 10.00

MICKEY MOUSE MARCH OF COMICS (See March of Comics #8,27,45,60,74)

MICKEY MOUSE SHORTS: SEASON ONE
IDW Publishing: Jul, 2016 - No. 4, Oct, 2016 ($3.99, limited series)

1-4-Adaptations of new Disney cartoon shorts 4.00

MICKEY MOUSE'S SUMMER VACATION (See Story Hour Series)

MICKEY MOUSE SUMMER FUN (See Dell Giants)

MICKEY SPILLANE'S MIKE DANGER
Tekno Comix: Sept, 1995 - No. 11, May, 1996 ($1.95)

1-11: 1-Frank Miller-c. 7-polybagged; Simonson-c. 8,9-Simonson-c 3.00

MICKEY SPILLANE'S MIKE DANGER
Big Entertainment: V2#1, June, 1996 - No. 10, Apr, 1997 ($2.25)

V2#1-10: Max Allan Collins scripts 3.00

MICKEY'S TWICE UPON A CHRISTMAS (Disney)
Gemstone Publishing: 2004 ($3.95, square-bound, one-shot)

nn-Christmas short stories with Mickey, Minnie, Donald, Uncle Scrooge, Goofy and others 4.00

MICROBOTS, THE
Gold Key: Dec, 1971 (one-shot)

1 (10271-112) Painted-c 3 6 9 15 22 28

MICRONAUTS (Toys)
Marvel Comics Group: Jan, 1979 - No. 59, Aug, 1984 (Mando paper #53 on)

1-Intro/1st app. Baron Karza 2 4 6 9 12 15

2-7,9,10,35,37,57: 7-Man-Thing app.9-1st app. Cilicia. 35-Double size; origin Microverse; intro Death Squad; Dr. Strange app. 37-Nightcrawler app.; X-Men cameo (2 pgs.). 57-(52 pgs.) 5.00

8-1st app. Capt. Universe (8/79) 3 6 9 17 26 35

11-34,36,38-56,58,59: 13-1st app. Jasmine. 15-Death of Microtron. 15-17-Fantastic Four app. 17-Death of Jasmine. 20-Ant-Man app. 21-Microverse series begins. 25-Origin Baron Karza. 25-29-Nick Fury app. 27-Death of Biotron. 34-Dr. Strange app. 38-First direct sale. 40-Fantastic Four app. 48-Early Guice-a begins. 59-Golden painted-c 4.00

Annual 1,2 (12/79,10/80)-Ditko-c/a 5.00

NOTE: *#38-on distributed only through comic shops. **N. Adams** c-7i. **Chaykin** a-13-18p. **Ditko** a-39p. **Giffen** a-36p, 37p(part). **Golden** a-1-12p; c-2-7p, 8-23, 24p, 38, 39, 59. **Guice** a-48-58p; c-49-58. **Gil Kane** a-38, 40-45p; c-40-45. **Layton** c-33-37. **Miller** c-31.*

MICRONAUTS (Micronauts: The New Voyages on cover)
Marvel Comics Group: Oct, 1984 - No. 20, May, 1986

V2#1-20 4.00

NOTE: ***Kelley Jones** a-1; c-1, 6. **Guice** a-4p; c-2p.*

MICRONAUTS
Image Comics: 2002 - No. 11, Sept, 2003 ($2.95)

2002 Convention Special (no cover price, B&W) previews series 3.00

1-11: 1-3-Hanson-a; Dave Johnson-c. 4-Su-a; 2 covers by Linsner & Hanson 3.00

...Vol. 1: Revolution (2003, $12.95, digest size) r/#1-5 13.00

MICRONAUTS (Volume 2)
Devil's Due Publishing: Mar, 2004 - No. 3, May, 2004 ($2.95)

1-3-Jolley-s/Broderick-a 3.00

MICRONAUTS
IDW Publishing: Apr, 2016 - Present ($4.99/$3.99)

1-($4.99) Cullen Bunn-s/David Baldeón-a; multiple covers; Baron Karza app. 5.00

2-9-($3.99) Max Dunbar-a. 5-Revolution tie-in 4.00

Annual #1 (1/17, $7.99) Bunn-s/Ferreira-a; future Micronauts app. 8.00

...: Revolution 1 (9/16, $3.99) Tie-in w/Transformers, G.I. Joe, M.A.S.K.,Action Man, Rom 4.00

MICRONAUTS: KARZA

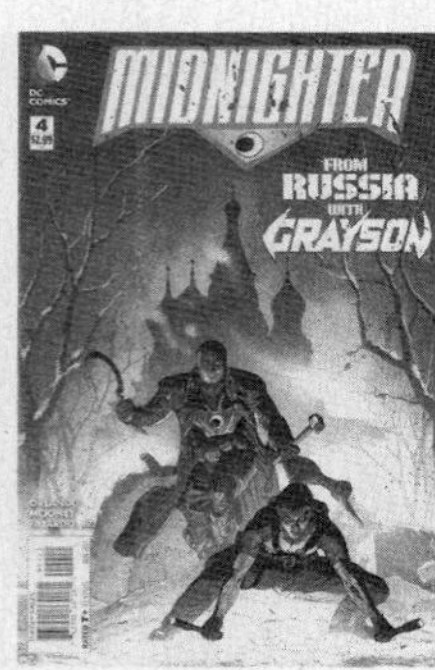

Midnighter (2015 series) #4 © DC

Midnight Tales #12 © CC

Mighty Avengers (2013 series) #13 © MAR

GD VG FN VF VF/NM NM-
2.0 4.0 6.0 8.0 9.0 9.2

Image Comics: Feb, 2003 - No. 4, May, 2003 ($2.95)
1-4-Krueger-s/Kurth-a 3.00

MICRONAUTS SPECIAL EDITION
Marvel Comics Group: Dec, 1983 - No. 5, Apr, 1984 ($2.00, limited series, Baxter paper)
1-5: r-/original series 1-12; Guice-c(p)-all 4.00

MIDGET COMICS (Fighting Indian Stories)
St. John Publishng Co.: Feb, 1950 - No. 2, Apr, 1950 (5-3/8x7-3/8", 68 pgs.)
1-Fighting Indian Stories; Matt Baker-c 32 64 96 188 307 425
2-Tex West, Cowboy Marshal (also in #1) 15 30 45 83 124 165

MIDNIGHT (See Smash Comics #18)

MIDNIGHT
Ajax/Farrell Publ. (Four Star Comic Corp.): Apr, 1957 - No. 6, June, 1958
1-Reprints from Voodoo & Strange Fantasy with some changes
18 36 54 105 165 225
2-6 12 24 36 69 97 125

MIDNIGHTER (See The Authority)
DC Comics (WildStorm): Jan, 2007 - No. 20, Aug, 2008 ($2.99)
1-20: 1-Ennis-s/Sprouse-a/c. 6-Fabry-a. 7-Vaughan-s. 8-Gage-s. 9-Stelfreeze-a 3.00
1-4-Variant covers. 1-Michael Golden. 2-Art Adams 3-Jason Pearson. 4-Glenn Fabry 4.00
...: Anthem TPB (2008, $14.99) r/#7,10-15 15.00
...: Armageddon (12/07, $2.99) Gage-s/Coleby-a/McKone-c 3.00
...: Assassin8 TPB (2009, $14.99) r/#16-20 15.00
...: Killing Machine TPB (2008, $14.99) r/#1-6 15.00

MIDNIGHTER (See The Authority)
DC Comics: Aug, 2015 - No. 12, Jul, 2016 ($2.99)
1-12: 1-Orlando-s/Aco-a. 3-5-Grayson app. 9-12-Harley Quinn & Suicide Squad app. 3.00

MIDNIGHTER AND APOLLO (The Authority)
DC Comics: Dec, 2016 - No. 6, May, 2017 ($3.99, limited series)
1-6-Orlando-s/Blanco-a. 1,2-Henry Bendix app. 2-6-Neron app. 4.00

MIDNIGHT MASS
DC Comics (Vertigo): Jun, 2002 - No. 8, Jan, 2003 ($2.50)
1-8-Rozum-s/Saiz & Palmiotti-a 3.00

MIDNIGHT MASS: HERE THERE BE MONSTERS
DC Comics (Vertigo): March, 2004 - No. 6, Aug, 2004 ($2.95, limited series)
1-6-Rozum-s/Paul Lee-a 3.00

MIDNIGHT MEN
Marvel Comics (Epic Comics/Heavy Hitters): June, 1993 - No. 4, Sept, 1993 ($2.50/$1.95, limited series)
1-($2.50)-Embossed-c; Chaykin-c/a & scripts in all 4.00
2-4 3.00

MIDNIGHT MYSTERY
American Comics Group: Jan-Feb, 1961 - No. 7, Oct, 1961
1-Sci/Fi story 8 16 24 51 96 140
2-7: 7-Gustavson-a 5 10 15 30 50 70
NOTE: *Reinman a-1, 3. Whitney a-1, 4-6; c-1-3, 5, 7.*

MIDNIGHT NATION
Image Comics (Top Cow): Oct, 2000 - No. 12, July, 2002 ($2.50/$2.95)
1-Straczynski-s/Frank-a; 2 covers 3.50
2-11: 9-Twin Towers cover 3.00
12-($2.95) Last issue 3.00
Wizard #1/2 (2001) Michael Zulli-a; two covers by Frank 3.00
Vol. 1 ('03, $29.99, TPB) r/#1-12 & Wizard #1/2; cover gallery; afterword by Straczynski 30.00

MIDNIGHT OF THE SOUL
Image Comics: Jun, 2016 - No. 5, Oct, 2016 ($3.50, limited series)
1-5-Howard Chaykin-s/a/c; set in 1950s New York City 3.50

MIDNIGHT SOCIETY: THE BLACK LAKE
Dark Horse Comics: Jun, 2015 - No. 4, Oct, 2015 ($3.99)
1-4-Drew Johnson-s/a/c 4.00

MIDNIGHT SONS UNLIMITED
Marvel Comics (Midnight Sons imprint #4 on): Apr, 1993 - No. 9, May, 1995 ($3.95, 68 pgs.)
1-9: Blaze, Darkhold (by Quesada #1), Ghost Rider, Morbius & Nightstalkers in all. 1-Painted-c. 3-Spider-Man app. 4-Siege of Darkness part 17; new Dr. Strange & new Ghost Rider app.; spot varnish-c 4.00
NOTE: *Sears a-2.*

MIDNIGHT TALES
Charlton Press: Dec, 1972 - No. 18, May, 1976
V1#1 3 6 9 16 23 30
2-10 2 4 6 10 14 18
11-18: 11-14-Newton-a(p) 2 4 6 8 11 14
12,17(Modern Comics reprint, 1977) 6.00
NOTE: ***Adkins** a-12i, 13i. **Ditko** a-12. **Howard** (Wood imitator) a-1-15, 17, 18; c-1-18. **Don Newton** a-11-14p. **Staton** a-1, 3-11, 13. **Sutton** a-3-10.*

MIGHTY, THE
DC Comics: Apr, 2009 - No. 12, Mar, 2010 ($2.99)
1-12: Tomasi & Champagne-s/Dave Johnson-c. 1-4-Snejbjerg-a. 5-12-Samnee-a 3.00
...: Volume 1 TPB (2009, $17.99) r/#1-6 18.00
...: Volume 2 TPB (2010, $17.99) r/#7-12 18.00

MIGHTY ATOM, THE (...& the Pixies #6) (Formerly The Pixies #1-5)
Magazine Enterprises: No. 6, 1949; Nov, 1957 - No. 6, Aug-Sept, 1958
6(1949-M.E.)-no month (1st Series) 7 14 21 35 43 50
1-6(2nd Series)-Pixies-r 4 8 12 18 22 25
I.W. Reprint #1(nd) 2 4 6 8 11 14

MIGHTY AVENGERS
Marvel Comics: May, 2007 - No. 36, Jun, 2010 ($3.99/$2.99)
1-($3.99) Iron Man, Ms. Marvel select new team; Bendis-s/Cho-a/c; Mole Man app. 5.00
2-6-($2.99) Ultron returns 3.00
7-15: 7-Bagley-a begins; Venom on-c. 9-11-Dr. Doom app. 3.00
12-20-Secret Invasion: 12,13-Maleev-a. 15-Romita Jr.-a. 16-Elektra. 20-Wasp funeral 3.00
21-($3.99) Dark Reign; Scarlet Witch returns; new team assembled; Pham-a 4.00
22-36: 25,26-Fantastic Four app. 35,36-Siege; Ultron returns 3.00
...: Most Wanted Files (2007, $3.99) profiles of members, accomplices & adversaries 4.00
... Vol. 1: The Ultron Initiative HC (2008, $19.99) r/#1-6; variant covers and sketch art 20.00
... Vol. 2: Venom Bomb HC (2008, $19.99) r/#7-11; B&W cover art 20.00

MIGHTY AVENGERS (Continues in Captain America and the Mighty Avengers)
Marvel Comics: Nov, 2013 - No. 14, Nov, 2014 ($3.99)
1-14: 1-Luke Cage, White Tiger, Power Man, Spectrum & Superior Spider-Man team; Land-a. 4-Falcon app. 5-She-Hulk app. 6-8-Schiti-a. 9-Ronin unmasked. 10-12-Original Sin 4.00

MIGHTY BEAR (Formerly Fun Comics; becomes Unsane #15)
Star Publ. No. 13,14/Ajax-Farrell (Four Star): No. 13, Jan, 1954 - No. 14, Mar, 1954; 9/57 - No. 3, 2/58
13,14-L. B. Cole-c 18 36 54 105 165 225
1-3('57-58)Four Star; becomes Mighty Ghost #4 7 14 21 37 46 55

MIGHTY CAPTAIN MARVEL, THE (Follows events of Civil War II))
Marvel Comics: No. 0, Feb, 2017 - Present ($3.99)
0-Stohl-s/Laiso-a; Alpha Flight app. 4.00
1-(3/17) Stohl-s/Rosanas-a 4.00

MIGHTY COMICS (...Presents) (Formerly Flyman)
Radio Comics (Archie): No. 40, Nov, 1966 - No. 50, Oct, 1967 (All 12¢ issues)
40-Web 5 10 15 30 50 70
41-50: 41-Shield, Black Hood. 42-Black Hood. 43-Shield, Web & Black Hood. 44-Black Hood, Steel Sterling & The Shield. 45-Shield & Hangman; origin Web retold. 46-Steel Sterling, Web & Black Hood. 47-Black Hood & Mr. Justice. 48-Shield & Hangman; Wizard x-over in Shield. 49-Steel Sterling & Fox; Black Hood x-over in Steel Sterling. 50-Black Hood & Web; Inferno x-over in Web 4 8 12 28 47 65
NOTE: *Paul Reinman a-40-50.*

MIGHTY CRUSADERS, THE (Also see Adventures of the Fly, The Crusaders & Fly Man)
Mighty Comics Group (Radio Comics): Nov, 1965 - No. 7, Oct, 1966 (All 12¢)
1-Origin The Shield 7 14 21 44 82 120
2-Origin Comet 4 8 12 28 47 65
3,5-7: 3-Origin Fly-Man. 5-Intro. Ultra-Men (Fox, Web, Capt. Flag) & Terrific Three (Jaguar, Mr. Justice, Steel Sterling). 7-Steel Sterling feature; origin Fly-Girl
4 8 12 27 44 60
4-1st S.A. app. Fireball, Inferno & Fox; Firefly, Web, Bob Phantom, Blackjack, Hangman, Zambini, Kardak, Steel Sterling, Mr. Justice, Wizard, Capt. Flag, Jaguar x-over
4 8 12 28 47 65
Volume 1: Origin of a Super Team TPB (2003, $12.95) r/#1 & Fly Man #31-33 13.00
NOTE: *Reinman a-6.*

MIGHTY CRUSADERS, THE (All New Advs. of...#2)
Red Circle Prod./Archie Ent. No. 6 on: Mar, 1983 - No. 13, Sept, 1985 ($1.00, 36 pgs, Mando paper)
1-Origin Black Hood, The Fly, Fly Girl, The Shield, The Wizard, The Jaguar, Pvt. Strong & The Web. 1 2 3 4 5 7
2-10: 2-Mister Midnight begins. 4-Darkling replaces Shield. 5-Origin Jaguar, Shield begins.

Mighty Crusaders (2010 series) #1 © ACP

Mighty Marvel Western #1 © MAR

Mighty Morphin Power Rangers: Pink #2 © SCGPR

	GD 2.0	VG 4.0	FN 6.0	VF 8.0	VF/NM 9.0	NM- 9.2
7-Untold origin Jaguar. 10-Veitch-a						5.00
11-13-Lower print run						6.00

NOTE: ***Buckler** a-1-3, 4i, 5p, 7p, 8i, 9i; c-1-10p.*

MIGHTY CRUSADERS, THE (Also see The Shield, The Web and The Red Circle)
DC Comics: Sept, 2010 - No. 6, Feb, 2011 ($3.99, limited series)

	GD	VG	FN	VF	VF/NM	NM-
1-6-The Shield, The Web, Fly-Girl, Inferno, War Eagle & The Comet team-up						4.00
... Special 1 (7/10, $4.99) Prequel to series; Pina-a/Lau-c						5.00

MIGHTY GHOST (Formerly Mighty Bear #1-3)
Ajax/Farrell Publ.: No. 4, June, 1958

	GD	VG	FN	VF	VF/NM	NM-
4	7	14	21	37	46	55

MIGHTY HERCULES, THE (TV)
Gold Key: July, 1963 - No. 2, Nov, 1963

	GD	VG	FN	VF	VF/NM	NM-
1 (10072-307)	11	22	33	77	166	255
2 (10072-311)	11	22	33	73	157	240

MIGHTY HEROES, THE (TV) (Funny)
Dell Publishing Co.: Mar, 1967 - No. 4, July, 1967

	GD	VG	FN	VF	VF/NM	NM-
1-Also has a 1957 Heckle & Jeckle-r	10	20	30	64	132	200
2-4: 4-Has two 1958 Mighty Mouse-r	7	14	21	44	82	120

MIGHTY HEROES
Spotlight Comics: 1987 (B&W, one-shot)

	GD	VG	FN	VF	VF/NM	NM-
1-Heckle & Jeckle backup						5.00

MIGHTY HEROES
Marvel Comics: Jan, 1998 ($2.99, one-shot)

	GD	VG	FN	VF	VF/NM	NM-
1-Origin of the Mighty Heroes						3.00

MIGHTY LOVE
DC Comics: 2003 ($24.99/$17.95, graphic novel)

	GD	VG	FN	VF	VF/NM	NM-
HC-($24.95) Howard Chaykin-s/a; intro. Skylark and the Iron Angel						25.00
SC-($17.95)						18.00

MIGHTY MAN (From Savage Dragon titles)
Image Comics: Dec, 2004 ($7.95, one-shot)

	GD	VG	FN	VF	VF/NM	NM-
1-Reprints seriaizedl back-up from Savage Dragon #109-118						8.00

MIGHTY MARVEL TEAM-UP THRILLERS
Marvel Comics: 1983 ($5.95, trade paperback)

	GD	VG	FN	VF	VF/NM	NM-
1-Reprints team-up stories	3	6	9	18	28	38

MIGHTY MARVEL WESTERN, THE
Marvel Comics Group (LMC earlier issues): Oct, 1968 - No. 46, Sept, 1976 (#1-14: 68 pgs.; #15,16: 52 pgs.)

	GD	VG	FN	VF	VF/NM	NM-
1-Begin Kid Colt, Rawhide Kid, Two-Gun Kid-r	7	14	21	44	82	120
2-5: (2-14 are 68 pgs.)	4	8	12	27	44	60
6-16: (15,16 are 52 pgs.)	3	6	9	21	33	45
17-20	2	4	6	13	18	22
21-30,32,37: 24-Kid Colt-r end. 25-Matt Slade-r begin. 32-Origin-r/Rawhide Kid #23; Williamson-r/Kid Slade #7. 37-Williamson, Kirby-r/Two-Gun Kid 51	2	4	6	9	13	16
31,33-36,38-46: 31-Baker-r.	2	4	6	8	11	14
45-(30¢-c variant, limited distribution)(6/76)	8	16	24	54	102	150

NOTE: ***Jack Davis** a(r)-21-24. **Keller** r-1-13, 22. **Kirby** a(r)-1-3, 6, 9, 12-14, 16, 25-29, 32-38, 40, 41, 43-46; c-29. **Maneely** a(r)-22. **Severin** c-3i, 9. No Matt Slade-#43.*

MIGHTY MIDGET COMICS, THE (Miniature)
Samuel E. Lowe & Co.: No date; circa 1942-1943 (Sold 2 for 5¢, B&W and red, 36 pgs, approx. 5x4")

	GD	VG	FN	VF	VF/NM	NM-
Bulletman #11(1943)-r/cover/Bulletman #3	16	32	48	94	147	200
Captain Marvel Adventures #11	16	32	48	94	147	200
Captain Marvel #11 (Same as above except for full color ad on back cover; this issue was glued to cover of Captain Marvel #20 and is not found in fine-mint condition)	340	680	1020	-	-	-
Captain Marvel Jr. #11 (Same-c as Master #27	16	32	48	94	147	200
Captain Marvel Jr. #11 (Same as above except for full color ad on back-c; this issue was glued to cover of Captain Marvel #21 and is not found in fine-mint condition)	340	680	1020	-	-	-
Golden Arrow #11	15	30	45	86	133	180
Golden Arrow #11 (Same as above except for full color ad on back-c; this issue was glued to cover of Captain Marvel #21 and is not found in fine-mint condition)	280	560	840	-	-	-
Ibis the Invincible #11(1942)-Origin; reprints cover to Ibis #1 (Predates Fawcett's Ibis the Invincible #1).	16	32	48	94	147	200
Spy Smasher #11(1942)	16	32	48	94	147	200

NOTE: *The above books came in a box called "box full of books" and was distributed with other Samuel Lowe puzzles, paper dolls, coloring books, etc. They are not titled Mighty Midget Comics. All have a war bond seal on back cover which is otherwise blank. These books came in a "Mighty Midget" flat cardboard counter display rack.*

	GD	VG	FN	VF	VF/NM	NM-
Balbo, the Boy Magician #12 (1943)-1st book devoted entirely to character.	10	20	30	54	72	90
Bulletman #12	12	24	36	69	97	125
Commando Yank #12 (1943)-Only comic devoted entirely to character.	10	20	30	56	76	95
Dr. Voltz the Human Generator (1943)-Only comic devoted entirely to character.	10	20	30	54	72	90
Lance O'Casey #12 (1943)-1st comic devoted entirely to character (Predates Fawcett's Lance O'Casey #1).	10	20	30	54	72	90
Leatherneck the Marine (1943)-Only comic devoted entirely to character.	10	20	30	54	72	90
Minute Man #12	12	24	36	67	94	120
Mister "Q" (1943)-Only comic devoted entirely to character.	10	20	30	54	72	90
Mr. Scarlet and Pinky #12 (1943)-Only comic devoted entirely to character.	10	20	30	58	79	100
Pat Wilton and His Flying Fortress (1943)-1st comic devoted entirely to character.	10	20	30	54	72	90
The Phantom Eagle #12 (1943)-Only comic devoted entirely to character.	10	20	30	54	72	90
State Trooper Stops Crime (1943)-Only comic devoted entirely to character.	10	20	30	54	72	90
Tornado Tom (1943)-Origin, r/from Cyclone #1-3; only comic devoted entirely to character.	10	20	30	54	72	90

MIGHTY MORPHIN POWER RANGERS (Also see Saban's Mighty Morphin' Power Rangers)
BOOM! Studios: No. 0, Jan, 2016; Mar, 2016 - Present ($3.99)

	GD	VG	FN	VF	VF/NM	NM-
0-Higgins-s/Prasetya-a; Rita Repulsa & Scorpina app.; multiple covers						4.00
1-11: 1-4,6-9,11-Higgins-s/Prasetya-a. 5-Silas-a. 10-Lam-a						4.00
2016 Annual 1 (8/16, $7.99) Short stories; art by Guillory, Terry Moore, Kochalka						8.00

MIGHTY MORPHIN POWER RANGERS: PINK
BOOM! Studios: Jun, 2016 - No. 6, Jan, 2017 ($3.99, limited series)

	GD	VG	FN	VF	VF/NM	NM-
1-6-Fletcher & Thompson-s/DiNicuolo-a; multiple covers						4.00

MIGHTY MORPHIN' POWER RANGERS: THE MOVIE (Also see Saban's Mighty Morphin' Power Rangers)
Marvel Comics: Sept, 1995 ($3.95, one-shot)

	GD	VG	FN	VF	VF/NM	NM-
nn-Adaptation of movie						5.00

MIGHTY MOUSE (See Adventures of..., Dell Giant #43, Giant Comics Edition, March of Comics #205, 237, 247, 257, 447, 459, 471, 483, Oxydol-Dreft, Paul Terry's, & Terry-Toons Comics)

MIGHTY MOUSE (1st Series)
Timely/Marvel Comics (20th Century Fox): Fall, 1946 - No. 4, Summer, 1947

	GD	VG	FN	VF	VF/NM	NM-
1	200	400	600	1280	2190	3100
2	76	152	228	486	831	1175
3,4	48	96	144	302	514	725

MIGHTY MOUSE (2nd Series) (Paul Terry's... #62-71)
St. John Publishing Co./Pines No. 68 (3/56) on (TV issues #72 on): Aug, 1947 - No. 67, 11/55; No. 68, 3/56 - No. 83, 6/59

	GD	VG	FN	VF	VF/NM	NM-
5(#1)	58	116	174	371	636	900
6-10: 10-Over-sized issue	24	48	72	142	234	325
11-19	15	30	45	88	137	185
20 (11/50) - 25-(52 pg. editions)	13	26	39	74	105	135
20-25-(36 pg. editions)	11	22	33	64	90	115
26-37: 35-Flying saucer-c	11	22	33	60	83	105
38-45-(100 pgs.)	20	40	60	117	189	260
46-83: 62-64,67-Painted-c. 82-Infinity-c	10	20	30	56	76	95
Album nn (nd, 1952/53?, St. John)(100 pgs.)(Rebound issues w/new cover)	27	54	81	158	259	360
Album 1(10/52, 25¢, 100 pgs., St. John)-Gandy Goose app.	34	68	102	199	325	450
Album 2,3(11/52 & 12/52, St. John) (100 pgs.)	26	52	78	154	252	350
Fun Club Magazine 1(Fall, 1957-Pines, 25¢, 100 pgs.) (CBS TV)-Tom Terrific, Heckle & Jeckle, Dinky Duck, Gandy Goose	20	40	60	114	182	250
Fun Club Magazine 2-6(Winter, 1958-Pines)	12	24	36	67	94	120
3-D 1-(1st printing-9/53, 25¢)(St. John)-Came w/glasses; stiff covers; says World's First! on-c; 1st 3-D comic	28	56	84	165	270	375
3-D 1-(2nd printing-10/53, 25¢)-Came w/glasses; slick, glossy covers, slightly smaller	20	40	60	114	182	250
3-D 2,3(11/53, 12/53, 25¢)-(St. John)-With glasses	20	40	60	114	182	250

MIGHTY MOUSE (TV)(3rd Series)(Formerly Adventures of Mighty Mouse)
Gold Key/Dell Publ. Co. No. 166-on: No. 161, Oct, 1964 - No. 172, Oct, 1968

Mighty Samson (2010 series) #1 © RH

Mighty Thor #15 © MAR

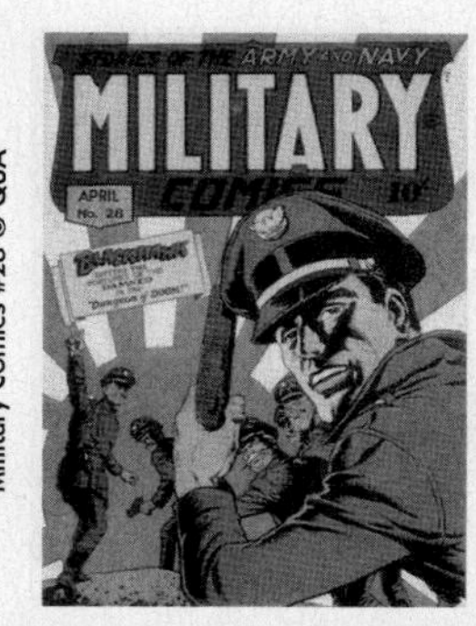

Military Comics #28 © QUA

GD 2.0 | VG 4.0 | FN 6.0 | VF 8.0 | VF/NM 9.0 | NM- 9.2

161(10/64)-165(9/65)-(Becomes Adventures of... No. 166 on)
4 8 12 28 47 65
166(3/66), 167(6/66)-172 3 6 9 20 31 42

MIGHTY MOUSE (TV)
Spotlight Comics: 1987 - No. 2, 1987 ($1.50, color)
1,2-New stories 4.00
...And Friends Holiday Special (11/87, $1.75) 4.00

MIGHTY MOUSE (TV)
Marvel Comics: Oct, 1990 - No. 10, July, 1991 ($1.00)(Based on Sat. cartoon)
1-10: 1-Dark Knight-c parody. 2-10: 3-Intro Bat-Bat; Byrne-c. 4,5-Crisis-c/story parodies w/Perez-c. 6-Spider-Man-c parody. 7-Origin Bat-Bat 3.00

MIGHTY MOUSE ADVENTURE MAGAZINE
Spotlight Comics: 1987 ($2.00, B&W, 52 pgs., magazine size, one-shot)
1-Deputy Dawg, Heckle & Jeckle backup stories 5.00

MIGHTY MOUSE ADVENTURES (Adventures of... #2 on)
St. John Publishing Co.: November, 1951
1 40 80 120 244 402 560

MIGHTY MOUSE ADVENTURE STORIES (Paul Terry's... on-c only)
St. John Publishing Co.: 1953 (50¢, 384 pgs.)
nn-Rebound issues 57 114 171 362 619 875

MIGHTY MUTANIMALS (See Teenage Mutant Ninja Turtles Adventures #19)
May, 1991 - No. 3, July, 1991 ($1.00, limited series)
Archie Comics: Apr, 1992 - No. 8, June, 1993 ($1.25)
1-3: 1-Story cont'd from TMNT Advs. #19. 1 2 3 5 6 8
1-4 (1992) 1 2 3 5 6 8
5-8: 7-1st app. Merdude 2 4 6 8 10 12

MIGHTY SAMSON (Also see Gold Key Champion)
Gold Key/Whitman #32: July, 1964 - No. 20, Nov, 1969; No. 21, Aug, 1972; No. 22, Dec, 1973 - No. 31, Mar, 1976; No. 32, Aug, 1982 (Painted-c #1-31)
1-Origin/1st app.; Thorne-a begins 8 16 24 51 96 140
2-5 4 8 12 28 47 65
6-10: 7-Tom Morrow begins, ends #20 3 6 9 20 30 40
11-20 3 6 9 16 23 30
21-31: 21,22-r 2 4 6 11 16 20
32(Whitman, 8/82)-r 2 4 6 8 10 12

MIGHTY SAMSON
Dark Horse Comics: Dec, 2010 - No. 4, Oct, 2011 ($3.50)
1-4: 1-Origin retold; Shooter & Vaughn-s/Olliffe-a/Swanland-c; r/1st app. from 1964 3.50
1-Variant-c by Olliffe 4.00

MIGHTY THOR, THE (Continues in Thor; God of Thunder)
Marvel Comics: Jun, 2011 - No. 22, Dec, 2012 ($3.99)
1-Fraction-s/Coipel-a; Silver Surfer app.; bonus concept art from the movie 4.00
1-Variant-c by Charest 6.00
1-Variant-c by Simonson 10.00
2-22: 3-6-Galactus app. 7-Fear Itself tie-in; Odin's 1st battle vs. the Serpent. 8-Tanarus. 13-17-Simonson-c. 18-21-Alan Davis-a 4.00
12.1 (6/12, $2.99) Kitson-a/Coipel-c; flashbacks from Volstagg & Sif 3.00
Annual 1 (8/12, $4.99) Silver Surfer & Galactus app.; DeMatteis-s/Elson-a 5.00

MIGHTY THOR (Jane Foster as Thor)
Marvel Comics: Jan, 2016 - Present ($4.99/$3.99)
1-($4.99) Tri-fold cover; Aaron-s/Dauterman-a; Loki app. 5.00
2-16-($3.99) 3-Multiple Lokis app. 12-Origin of Mjolnir; Frazer Irving-a. 14-Epting-a 4.00

MIKE BARNETT, MAN AGAINST CRIME (TV)
Fawcett Publications: Dec, 1951 - No. 6, Oct, 1952
1 20 40 60 117 189 260
2 14 28 42 76 108 140
3,4,6 11 22 33 62 86 110
5- "Market for Morphine" cover/story 15 30 45 85 130 175

MIKE DANGER (See Mickey Spillane's...)

MIKE DEODATO'S...
Caliber Comics: 1996, ($2.95, B&W)
...FALLOUT 3000 #1, **...JONAS** (mag. size) #1,**...PRIME CUTS** (mag. size) #1, **...PROTHEUS** #1,2, **...RAMTHAR** #1,**...RAZOR NIGHTS** #1 3.00

MIKE GRELL'S SABLE (Also see Jon Sable & Sable)
First Comics: Mar, 1990 - No. 10, Dec, 1990 ($1.75)

GD 2.0 | VG 4.0 | FN 6.0 | VF 8.0 | VF/NM 9.0 | NM- 9.2

1-10: r/Jon Sable Freelance #1-10 by Grell 3.00

MIKE MIST MINUTE MIST-ERIES (See Ms. Tree/Mike Mist in 3-D)
Eclipse Comics: April, 1981 ($1.25, B&W, one-shot)
1 3.00

MIKE SHAYNE PRIVATE EYE
Dell Publishing Co.: Nov-Jan, 1962 - No. 3, Sept-Nov, 1962
1 4 8 12 23 37 50
2,3 3 6 9 16 24 32

MILES MORALES: ULTIMATE SPIDER-MAN
Marvel Comics: Jul, 2014 - No. 12, Jun, 2015 ($3.99)
1-11: 1-Bendis-s/Marquez-a; Peter Parker & Norman Osborn return. 11-Dr. Doom app. 4.00
12-Dr. Doom and the Ultimates app.; leads into Secret Wars #1 4.00

MILESTONE FOREVER
DC Comics: Apr, 2010 - No. 2, May, 2010 ($5.99, squarebound, limited series)
1,2-McDuffie-s/Leon & Bright-a; Icon, Blood Syndicate, Hardware and Static app. 6.00

MILITARY COMICS (Becomes Modern Comics #44 on)
Quality Comics Group: Aug, 1941 - No. 43, Oct, 1945
1-Origin/1st app. Blackhawk by C. Cuidera (Eisner scripts); Miss America, The Death Patrol by Jack Cole (also #2-7,27-30), & The Blue Tracer by Guardineer; X of the Underground, The Yankee Eagle, Q-Boat & Shot & Shell, Archie Atkins, Loops & Banks by Bud Ernest (Bob Powell)(ends #13) begin 432 864 1296 3154 5577 8000
2-Secret War News begins (by McWilliams #2-16); Cole-a; new uniform with yellow circle & hawk's head for Blackhawk 135 270 405 864 1482 2100
3-Origin/1st app. Chop Chop (9/41) 116 232 348 742 1271 1800
4 103 206 309 659 1130 1600
5-The Sniper begins; Miss America in costume #4-7
90 180 270 576 988 1400
6-9: 8-X of the Underground begins (ends #13). 9-The Phantom Clipper begins (ends #16)
71 142 213 454 777 1100
10-Classic Eisner-c 90 180 270 576 988 1400
11-Flag-c 68 136 204 435 743 1050
12-Blackhawk by Crandall begins, ends #22 71 142 213 454 777 1100
13-15: 14-Private Dogtag begins (ends #83) 58 116 174 371 636 900
16-20: 16-Blue Tracer ends. 17-P.T. Boat begins 53 106 159 334 567 800
21-31: 22-Last Crandall Blackhawk. 23-Shrunken head-c. 27-Death Patrol revived. 28-True story of Mussolini 47 94 141 296 498 700
32-43 41 82 123 256 428 600
NOTE: ***Berg** a-6. **Al Bryant** c-31-34, 38, 40-43. **J. Cole** a-1-3, 27-32. **Crandall** a-12-22; c-13-20. **Cuidera** c-2-9. **Eisner** c-1, 2(part), 9, 10. **Kotsky** c-21-29, 35, 37, 39. **McWilliams** a-2-16. **Powell** a-1-13. **Ward** Blackhawk-30, 31(15 pgs. each); c-30.*

MILK AND CHEESE (Also see Cerebus Bi-Weekly #20)
Slave Labor: 1991 - Present ($2.50, B&W)
1-Evan Dorkin story & art in all 4 8 12 27 44 60
1-2nd-6th printings 4.00
2-"Other #1" 3 6 9 16 24 32
2-reprint 3.00
3-"Third #1" 2 4 6 11 16 20
4-"Fourth #1", 5-"First Second Issue" 1 3 4 6 8 10
6,7: 6-"#666" 5.00
NOTE: *Multiple printings of all issues exist and are worth cover price unless listed here.*

MILKMAN MURDERS, THE
Dark Horse Comics: Jun, 2004 - No. 4, Aug, 2004 ($2.99, limited series)
1-4-Casey-s/Parkhouse-a 3.00

MILLARWORLD (Mark Millar characters)
Image Comics: Jul, 2016 ($2.99, one-shot)
...Annual 2016 1 (7/16) Short stories of Kick-Ass, Hit-Girl, Chrononauts and others 3.00

MILLENNIUM
DC Comics: Jan, 1988 - No. 8, Feb, 1988 (Weekly limited series)
1-Englehart-s/Staton c/a(p) 4.00
2-8 3.00
TPB (2008, $19.99) r/#1-8 20.00

MILLENNIUM (TV, spin-off from The X-Files)
IDW Publishing: Jan, 2015 - No. 5, May, 2015 ($3.99, limited series)
1-5: 1-Frank Black & Agent Mulder app.; Joe Harris-s/Colin Lorimer-a; three covers 4.00

MILLENNIUM EDITION:... (Reprints of classic DC issues, plus some WildStorm and non-DC issues with characters now published by DC)
DC Comics: Feb, 2000 - Feb, 2001 (gold foil cover stamps)
Action Comics #1, Adventure Comics #61, All Star Comics #3, All Star Comics #8, Batman #1,

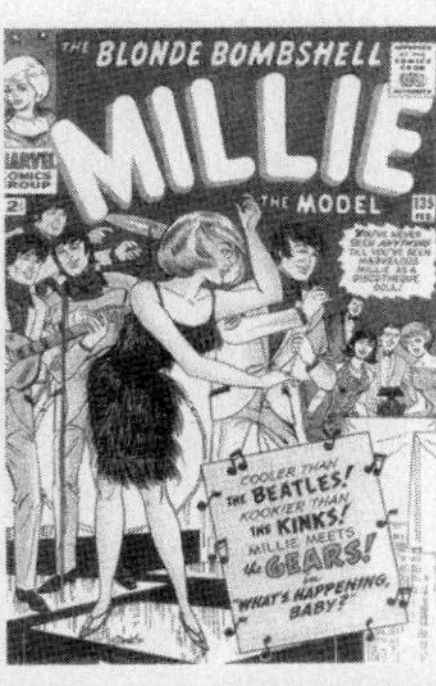

Millie the Model #135 © MAR

Mind Mgmt #28 © Matt Kindt

Minimum Wage: So Many Bad Decisions #6 © Bob Fingerman

	GD 2.0	VG 4.0	FN 6.0	VF 8.0	VF/NM 9.0	NM- 9.2
Detective Comics #1, Detective Comics #27, Detective Comics #38, Flash Comics #1, Military Comics #1, More Fun Comics #73, Police Comics #1, Sensation Comics #1, Superman #1, Whiz Comics #2, Wonder Woman #1 -($3.95-c)						5.00
Action Comics #252, Adventure Comics #247, Brave and the Bold #28, Brave and the Bold #85, Crisis on Infinite Earths #1, Detective #225, Detective #327, Detective #359, Detective #395, Flash #123, Gen13 #1, Green Lantern #76, House of Mystery #1, House of Secrets #92, JLA #1, Justice League #1, Mad #1, Man of Steel #1, Mysterious Suspense #1, New Gods, #1, New Teen Titans #1, Our Army at War #81, Plop! #1, Saga of the Swamp Thing #21, Shadow #1, Showcase #4, Showcase #9, Showcase #22, Superman #233, Superman (2nd) #75, Superman's Pal Jimmy Olsen #1, Watchmen #1, WildC.A.T.s #1, Wonder Woman (2nd) #1, World's Finest #71 -($2.50-c)						4.00
All-Star Western #10, Hellblazer #1, More Fun Comics #101, Preacher #1, Sandman #1, Spirit #1, Superboy #1, Superman #76, Young Romance #1-($2.95-c)						4.00
Batman: The Dark Knight Returns #1, Kingdom Come #1 -($5.95-c)						6.00
All Star Comics #3, Batman #1, Justice League #1: Chromium cover						12.00
Crisis on Infinite Earths #1 Chromium cover						20.00

MILLENNIUM FEVER
DC Comics (Vertigo): Oct, 1995 - No.4, Jan, 1996 ($2.50, limited series)

	GD	VG	FN	VF	VF/NM	NM-
1-4: Duncan Fegredo-c/a						3.00

MILLENNIUM 2.5 A.D.
ACG Comics: No. 1, 2000 ($2.95)

	GD	VG	FN	VF	VF/NM	NM-
1-Reprints 1934 Buck Rogers daily strips #1-48						3.00

MILLIE, THE LOVABLE MONSTER
Dell Publishing Co.: Sept-Nov, 1962 - No. 6, Jan, 1973

	GD	VG	FN	VF	VF/NM	NM-
12-523-211-Bill Woggon c/a in all	5	10	15	31	53	75
2(8-10/63)	4	8	12	28	47	65
3(8-10/64)	4	8	12	25	40	55
4(7/72), 5(10/72), 6(1/73)	3	6	9	14	19	24

NOTE: ***Woggon** a-3-6; c-3-6. 4 reprints 1; 5 reprints 2; 6 reprints 3.*

MILLIE THE MODEL (See Comedy Comics, A Date With..., Joker Comics #28, Life With..., Mad About..., Marvel Mini-Books, Misty & Modeling With...)
Marvel/Atlas/Marvel Comics(CnPC #1)(SPI/Male/VPI):1945 - No. 207, Dec, 1973

	GD	VG	FN	VF	VF/NM	NM-
1-Origin	194	388	582	1242	2121	3000
2 (10/46)-Millie becomes The Blonde Phantom to sell Blonde Phantom perfume; a pre-Blonde Phantom app. (see All-Select #11, Fall, 1946)	55	110	165	352	601	850
3-8,10: 4-7-Willie app. 7-Willie smokes extra strong tobacco. 8,10-Kurtzman's "Hey Look". 8-Willie & Rusty app.	45	90	135	284	480	675
9-Powerhouse Pepper by Wolverton, 4 pgs.	47	94	141	296	498	700
11-Kurtzman-a, "Giggles 'n' Grins"	32	64	96	188	307	425
12,15,17,19,20: 12-Rusty & Hedy Devine app.	27	54	81	160	263	365
13,14,16,18: 13,14,16-Kurtzman's "Hey Look". 13-Hedy Devine app. 18-Dan DeCarlo-a begins	28	56	84	165	270	375
21-30	27	54	81	160	263	360
31-40	15	30	45	103	227	350
41-60	15	30	45	100	220	340
61-80	13	26	39	89	195	300
81-99: 93-Last DeCarlo issue?	10	20	30	66	138	210
100	10	20	30	69	147	225
101-106,108-130	6	12	18	40	73	105
107-Jack Kirby app. in story	6	12	18	42	79	115
131-134,136,138-153: 141-Groovy Gears-c/s	4	8	12	28	47	65
135-(2/66) 1st app. Groovy Gears	5	10	15	35	57	80
137-2nd app. Groovy Gears	5	10	15	30	50	70
154-New Millie begins (10/67)	6	12	18	38	69	100
155-190	4	8	12	28	47	65
191,193-199,201-206	4	8	12	25	40	55
192-(52 pgs.)	4	8	12	28	47	65
200,207(Last issue)	4	8	12	28	47	65
(Beware: cut-up pages are common in all Annuals)						
Annual 1(1962)-Early Marvel annual (2nd?)	30	60	90	216	483	750
Annual 2(1963)	15	30	45	103	227	350
Annual 3-5 (1964-1966)	8	16	24	54	102	150
Annual 6-10(1967-11/71)	6	12	18	41	76	110
Queen-Size 11(9/74), 12(1975)	6	12	18	37	66	95

NOTE: ***Dan DeCarlo** a-18-93.*

MILLION DOLLAR DIGEST (Richie Rich... #23 on; also see Richie Rich...)
Harvey Publications: 11/86 - No. 7, 11/87; No. 8, 4/88 - No. 34, Nov, 1994 ($1.25/$1.75, digest size)

	GD	VG	FN	VF	VF/NM	NM-
1	1	2	3	5	6	8
2-8: 8-(68 pgs.)						6.00
9-20: 9-Begin $1.75-c. 14-May not exist	1	2	3	4	5	7
21-34	1	3	4	6	8	10

MILT GROSS FUNNIES (Also see Picture News #1)
Milt Gross, Inc. (ACG?): Aug, 1947 - No. 2, Sept, 1947

	GD	VG	FN	VF	VF/NM	NM-
1	26	52	78	154	252	350
2	18	36	54	105	165	225

MILTON THE MONSTER & FEARLESS FLY (TV)
Gold Key: May, 1966

	GD	VG	FN	VF	VF/NM	NM-
1 (10175-605)	8	16	24	54	102	150

MINDFIELD
Aspen MLT: No. 0, May, 2010 - No. 6, Sept, 2011 ($2.50/$2.99)

	GD	VG	FN	VF	VF/NM	NM-
0-($2.50) Krul-s/Konat-a; 3 covers						3.00
1-6-($2.99) Multiples covers on each						3.00

MIND MGMT
Dark Horse Comics: May, 2012 - No. 35, Jul, 2015 ($3.99)

	GD	VG	FN	VF	VF/NM	NM-
1-Matt Kindt-s/a/c						30.00
2-6						10.00
7-35						4.00
#0 (11/12, $2.99) Prints background stories from Mind MGMT Secret Files digital site						3.00
New MGMT#1/Mind Mgmt #36 (8/15, $3.99) Series conclusion						4.00

MIND THE GAP
Image Comics: May, 2012 - No. 17, May, 2014 ($2.99)

	GD	VG	FN	VF	VF/NM	NM-
1-17: 1-8,10-McCann-s/Esquejo-a/c. 9-McDaid-a. 11,12-Basri-a						3.00

MINIMUM CARNAGE
Marvel Comics: Dec, 2012 - Jan, 2013 ($3.99, limited series)

	GD	VG	FN	VF	VF/NM	NM-
...: Alpha (12/12) Venom, Carnage and Scarlet Spider app.; Medina-a/Crain-c						4.00
...: Omega (1/13) The Enigma Force in the Microverse app.						4.00

MINIMUM WAGE
Fantagraphics Books: V1#1, July, 1995 ($9.95, B&W, graphic novel, mature)
V2#1, 1995 - 1997 ($2.95, B&W, mature)

	GD	VG	FN	VF	VF/NM	NM-
V1#1-Bob Fingerman story & art	1	3	4	6	8	10
V2#1-9($2.95): Bob Fingerman story & art. 2-Kevin Nowlan back-c. 4-w/pin-ups. 5-Mignola back-c						3.00
Book Two TPB ('97, $12.95) r/V2#1-5						13.00

MINIMUM WAGE
Image Comics: Jan, 2014 - No. 6, Jun, 2014 ($3.50, B&W&Green, mature)

	GD	VG	FN	VF	VF/NM	NM-
1-6-Bob Fingerman story & art; story resumes in May 2000						3.50

MINIMUM WAGE: SO MANY BAD DECISIONS
Image Comics: May, 2015 - No. 6, Oct, 2015 ($3.99, B&W&Green/color pages, mature)

	GD	VG	FN	VF	VF/NM	NM-
1-6-Bob Fingerman story & art. 3-Marc Maron app.						4.00

MINIONS (From Despicable Me movies)
Titan Comics: Jul, 2015 - No. 2, Aug, 2015 ($3.99, limited series)

	GD	VG	FN	VF	VF/NM	NM-
1,2-Short stories and one-page gags; Ah-Koon-s/Collin-a						4.00

MINISTRY OF SPACE
Image Comics: Apr, 2001 - No. 3, Apr, 2004 ($2.95, limited series)

	GD	VG	FN	VF	VF/NM	NM-
1-3-Warren Ellis-s/Chris Weston-a						3.00
...Vol. 1 Omnibus (3/04, $4.95) r/1&2						5.00
TPB (12/04, $12.95) r/series; sketch & design pages; intro by Mark Millar						13.00

MINOR MIRACLES
DC Comics: 2000 ($12.95, B&W, squarebound)

	GD	VG	FN	VF	VF/NM	NM-
nn-Will Eisner-s/a						13.00

MINUTE MAN (See Master Comics & Mighty Midget Comics)
Fawcett Publications: Summer, 1941 - No. 3, Spring, 1942 (68 pgs.)

	GD	VG	FN	VF	VF/NM	NM-
1	213	426	639	1363	2332	3300
2-Japanese invade NYC Statue of Liberty WWII-c	155	310	465	992	1696	2400
3	123	246	369	787	1344	1900

MINX, THE
DC Comics (Vertigo): Oct, 1998 - No. 8, May, 1999 ($2.50, limited series)

	GD	VG	FN	VF	VF/NM	NM-
1-8-Milligan-s/Phillips-c/a						3.00

MIRACLE COMICS
Hillman Periodicals: Feb, 1940 - No. 4, Mar, 1941

	GD	VG	FN	VF	VF/NM	NM-
1-Sky Wizard Master of Space, Dash Dixon, Man of Might, Pinkie Parker, Dusty Doyle, The Kid Cop, K-7, Secret Agent, The Scorpion, & Blandu, Jungle Queen begin; Masked Angel only app. (all 1st app.)	258	516	774	1651	2826	4000
2	135	270	405	864	1482	2100

Miracleman (2014 series) #2 © MAR

Mirror's Edge #4 © EA

Miss Fury #10 © DYN

3,4: 3-Devil-c; Bill Colt, the Ghost Rider begins. 4-The Veiled Prophet & Bullet Bob (by Burnley) app. 116 232 348 742 1271 1800

MIRACLEMAN
Eclipse Comics: Aug, 1985 - No. 15, Nov, 1988; No. 16, Dec, 1989 - No. 24, Aug, 1993

1-r/British Marvelman series; Alan Moore scripts in #1-16 2 4 6 8 10 12
1-Gold variant (edition of 400, same as regular comic, but signed by Alan Moore, came with signed & #'d gold certificate of authenticity) 54 108 162 432 966 1500
1-Blue variant (edition of 600, comic came with signed blue certificate of authenticity) 34 68 102 245 548 850
2-8,10: 8-Airboy preview. 6,9,10-Origin Miracleman. 10-Snyder-c 1 2 3 5 6 8
9-Shows graphic scenes of childbirth 2 4 6 8 10 12
11-14(5/87-4/88) Totleben-a 2 4 6 11 16 20
15-($1.75-c, low print) end of Kid Miracleman 6 12 18 41 76 110
16-Last Alan Moore-s; 1st $1.95-c (low print) 3 6 9 16 24 32
17-22: 17-"The Golden Age" begins, ends #22. Dave McKean-c begins, end #22; Neil Gaiman scripts in #17-24 2 4 6 11 16 20
23-"The Silver Age" begins; Barry W. Smith-c 3 6 9 16 23 30
24-Last issue; Smith-c 3 6 9 19 30 40
3-D #1 (12/85) 2 4 6 8 10 12
3-D #1 Blue variant (edition of 99) 3 6 9 21 33 45
3-D #1 Gold variant (edition of 199) 3 6 9 16 23 30

NOTE: *Miracleman 3-D #1 (12/85) (2D edition) Interior is the same as the 3-D version except in non 3-D format. Indicia are the same for both versions of the book with only the non 3-D art distinguishing this book from the standard 3-D version. Standard 3-D edition has house ad mentioning the non 3-D edition. Two known copies exist, one in the Michigan State University Special Collection Department. (No known sales)*

Book One: A Dream of Flying (1988, $9.95, TPB) r/#1-5; Leach-c 25.00
Book One: A Dream of Flying-Hardcover (1988, $29.95) r/#1-5 70.00
Book Two: The Red King Syndrome (1990, $12.95, TPB) r/#6-10; Bolton-c 30.00
Book Two: The Red King Syndrome-Hardcover (1990, $30.95) r/#6-10 85.00
Book Three: Olympus (1990, $12.95, TPB) r/#11-16 130.00
Book Three: Olympus-Hardcover (1990, $30.95) r/#11-16 250.00
Book Four: The Golden Age (1992, $15.95, TPB) r/#17-22 30.00
Book Four: The Golden Age Hardcover (1992, $33.95) r/#17-22 50.00
Book Four: The Golden Age (1993, $12.99, TPB) new McKean-c 15.00

NOTE: *Eclipse archive copies exist for #4,5,8,17,23. Each has a small Miracleman image foil-stamped on the cover.* ***Chaykin** c-3. **Gulacy** c-7. **McKean** c-17-22. **B. Smith** c-23, 24. **Starlin** c-4. **Totleben** a-11-13; c-9, 11-13. **Truman** c-6.*

MIRACLEMAN
Marvel Comics: Mar, 2014 - No. 16, May, 2015 ($5.99/$4.99)

1-($5.99) Remastered reprints of Miracleman #1 and stories from Warrior #1&2; interview with Mick Anglo; reprints of 1950s Marvelman stories; Quesada-c 6.00
2-15: 2-($4.99) R/Warrior #3-5 and Kid Marvelman debut (1955) 5.00
16-($5.99) End of Book Three; bonus pencil art and design sketches 6.00
All-New Miracleman Annual 1 (2/15, $4.99) New stories; Morrison-s/Quesada-a and Milligan-s/Allred-a; bonus script and art pages 5.00

MIRACLEMAN: APOCRYPHA
Eclipse Comics: Nov, 1991 - No. 3, Feb, 1992 ($2.50, limited series)

1-3: 1-Stories by Neil Gaiman, Mark Buckingham, Alex Ross & others. 3-Stories by James Robinson, Kelley Jones, Matt Wagner, Neil Gaiman, Mark Buckingham & others 1 2 3 4 5 7
TPB (12/92, $15.95) r/#1-3; Buckingham-c 20.00

MIRACLEMAN BY GAIMAN & BUCKINGHAM (The Golden Age)
Marvel Comics: Nov, 2015 - No. 6, Mar, 2016 ($4.99)

1-6-Remastered reprints of Miracleman #17-22 with bonus script and art pages 5.00

MIRACLEMAN FAMILY
Eclipse Comics: May, 1988 - No. 2, Sept, 1988 ($1.95, lim. series, Baxter paper)

1,2: 2-Gulacy-c 5.00

MIRACLE OF THE WHITE STALLIONS, THE (See Movie Comics)

MIRROR'S EDGE (Based on the EA video game)
DC Comics (WildStorm): Dec, 2008 - No. 6, Jun, 2009 ($3.99, limited series)

1-6: 1-Origin of Faith; Rhianna Pratchett-s/Matthew Dow Smith-a 4.00
TPB (2009, $19.99) r/#1-6 20.00

MIRROR'S EDGE: EXORDIUM (Based on the EA video game)
Dark Horse Comics: Sept, 2015 - No. 6, Feb, 2016 ($3.99, limited series)

1-6: 1-Emgård-s/Häggström & Sammelin-a 4.00

MISADVENTURES OF ADAM WEST, THE
Bluewater Comics: Jul, 2011 - Feb, 2012 ($3.99)

1-4: 1-Two covers; co-created by Adam West 4.00

GD VG FN VF VF/NM NM-
2.0 4.0 6.0 8.0 9.0 9.2

Second series 1-3 (1/12 - No. 3, 2/12) 4.00

MISADVENTURES OF MERLIN JONES, THE (See Movie Comics & Merlin Jones as the Monkey's Uncle under Movie Comics)

MISPLACED
Image Comics: May, 2003 - No. 4, Dec, 2004 ($2.95)

1-4: 1-Three covers by Blaylock, Green and Clugston-Major; Blaylock-s/a 3.00
... @17 (12/04, $4.95) Nara from "Dead @17 " app.; Blaylock-s/a 5.00

MISS AMERICA COMICS (Miss America Magazine #2 on; also see Blonde Phantom & Marvel Mystery Comics)
Marvel Comics (20CC): 1944 (one-shot)

1-2 pgs. pin-ups 284 568 852 1818 3109 4400

MISS AMERICA COMICS 70th ANNIVERARY SPECIAL
Marvel Comics: Aug, 2009 ($3.99, one-shot)

1-Eaglesham-c; new Miss America & Whizzer story; reps. from All Winners #9-11 5.00

MISS AMERICA MAGAZINE (Formerly Miss America; Miss America #51 on)
Miss America Publ. Corp./Marvel/Atlas (MAP): V1#2, Nov, 1944 - No. 93, Nov, 1958

V1#2-Photo-c of teenage girl in Miss America costume; Miss America, Patsy Walker (intro.) comic stories plus movie reviews & stories; intro. Buzz Baxter & Hedy Wolfe; 1 pg. origin Miss America 271 542 813 1734 2967 4200
3-5-Miss America & Patsy Walker stories 90 180 270 576 988 1400
6-Patsy Walker only 53 106 159 334 567 800
V2#1(4/45)-6(9/45)-Patsy Walker continues 21 42 63 122 199 275
V3#1(10/45)-6(4/46) 17 34 51 98 154 210
V4#1(5/46),2,5(9/46) 15 30 45 88 137 185
V4#3(7/46)-Liz Taylor photo-c 39 78 117 231 378 525
V4#4 (8/46; 68 pgs.), V4#6 (10/46; 92 pgs.) 15 30 45 83 124 165
V5#1(11/46)-6(4/47), V6#1(5/47)-3(7/47) 14 28 42 82 121 160
V7#1(8/47)-23(#56, 6/49) 14 28 42 81 118 155
V7#24(#57, 7/49)-Kamen-a (becomes Best Western #58 on?) 14 28 42 82 121 160
V7#25(8/49), 27-44(3/52), VII,nn(5/52) 14 28 42 80 115 150
V7#26(9/49)-All comics 15 30 45 83 124 165
V1,nn(7/52)-V1,nn(1/53)(#46-49), V7#50(Spring '53), V1#51-V7?#54(7/53), 55-93 14 28 42 76 108 140

NOTE: *Photo-c #1, 4, V2#1, 4, 5, V3#5, V4#3, 4, 6, V7#15, 16, 24, 26, 34, 37, 38. Painted c-3.* ***Powell** a-V7#31.*

MISS BEVERLY HILLS OF HOLLYWOOD (See Adventures of Bob Hope)
National Periodical Publ.: Mar-Apr, 1949 - No. 9, July-Aug, 1950 (52 pgs.)

1 (Meets Alan Ladd) 60 120 180 381 653 925
2-William Holden photo on-c 43 86 129 271 461 650
3-5: 2-9-Part photo-c. 5-Bob Hope photo on-c 39 78 117 236 388 540
6,7,9: 6-Lucille Ball photo on-c 36 72 108 214 347 480
8-Reagan photo on-c 40 80 120 244 402 560

NOTE: *Beverly meets Alan Ladd in #1, Eve Arden #2, Betty Hutton #4, Bob Hope #5.*

MISS CAIRO JONES
Croyden Publishers: 1945

1-Bob Oksner daily newspaper-r (1st strip story); lingerie panels 21 42 63 126 206 285

MISS FURY
Adventure Comics: 1991 - No. 4, 1991 ($2.50, limited series)

1-4: 1-Origin; granddaughter of original Miss Fury 3.00
1-Limited ed. ($4.95) 5.00

MISS FURY
Dynamite Entertainment: 2013 - No. 11, 2014 ($3.99)

1-11: 1-Multiple covers on all; Herbert-a; origin 4.00

MISS FURY (VOLUME 2)
Dynamite Entertainment: 2016 - No. 5, 2016 ($3.99, limited series)

1-5-Corinna Bechko-s/Jonathan Lau-a; covers by Lotay & Lau 4.00

MISS FURY COMICS (Newspaper strip reprints)
Timely Comics (NPI 1/CmPI 2/MPC 3-8): Winter, 1942-43 - No. 8, Winter, 1946 (Published twice a year)

1-Origin Miss Fury by Tarpe' Mills (68 pgs.) in costume w/paper dolls with cut-out costumes 432 864 1296 3154 5577 8000
2-(60 pgs.)-In costume w/paper dolls; hooded Nazi-c 239 478 717 1530 2615 3700
3-(60 pgs.)-In costume w/paper dolls; Hitler-c 194 388 582 1242 2121 3000
4-(52 pgs.)-Classic Nazi WWII-c with giant swastika, Tojo & Hitler photo on wall; in costume, 2 pgs. w/paper dolls 168 336 504 1075 1838 2600
5-(52 pgs.)-In costume w/paper dolls; Japanese WWII-c

Mission: Impossible #4 © DELL

Mr. District Attorney #2 © DC

Mister Miracle #19 © DC

	GD 2.0	VG 4.0	FN 6.0	VF 8.0	VF/NM 9.0	NM- 9.2
	129	258	387	826	1413	2000
6-(52 pgs.)-Not in costume in inside stories, w/paper dolls	108	216	324	686	1181	1675
7,8-(36 pgs.)-In costume 1 pg. each; no paper dolls	86	172	258	546	936	1325

NOTE: *Schomburg c-1, 5, 6.*

MISS FURY DIGITAL FIRST
Dynamite Entertainment: 2013 - No. 2, 2013 ($3.99, limited series)

	GD	VG	FN	VF	VF/NM	NM-
1,2-Prints online stories. 1-Reis, Desjardins, Casas-a. 2-Casas-a						4.00

MISSION IMPOSSIBLE (TV) (Also see Wild!)
Dell Publ. Co.: May, 1967 - No. 4, Oct, 1968; No. 5, Oct, 1969 (All have photo-c)

	GD	VG	FN	VF	VF/NM	NM-
1	7	14	21	49	92	135
2-5: 5-Reprints #1	5	10	15	35	63	90

MISSION IMPOSSIBLE (Movie) (1st Paramount Comics book)
Marvel Comics (Paramount Comics): May, 1996 ($2.95, one-shot)

	GD	VG	FN	VF	VF/NM	NM-
1-Liefeld-c & back-up story						3.00

MISS LIBERTY (Becomes Liberty Comics)
Burten Publishing Co.: 1945 (MLJ reprints)

	GD	VG	FN	VF	VF/NM	NM-
1-The Shield & Dusty, The Wizard, & Roy, the Super Boy app.; r/Shield-Wizard #13	36	72	108	211	343	475

MISS MELODY LANE OF BROADWAY (See The Adventures of Bob Hope)
National Periodical Publ.: Feb-Mar, 1950 - No. 3, June-July, 1950 (52 pgs.)

	GD	VG	FN	VF	VF/NM	NM-
1-Movie stars photos app. on all-c.	61	122	183	390	670	950
2,3: 3-Ed Sullivan photo on-c.	39	78	117	235	385	535

MISS PEACH
Dell Publishing Co.: Oct-Dec, 1963; 1969

	GD	VG	FN	VF	VF/NM	NM-
1-Jack Mendelsohn-a/script	7	14	21	44	82	120
...Tells You How to Grow (1969; 25¢)-Mel Lazarus-a; also given away (36 pgs.)	5	10	15	30	50	70

MISS PEPPER (See Meet Miss Pepper)

MISS SUNBEAM (See Little Miss...)

MISS VICTORY (See Captain Fearless #1,2, Holyoke One-Shot #3, Veri Best Sure Fire & Veri Best Sure Shot Comics)

MISTER AMERICA
Endeavor Comics: Apr, 1994 - No. 2, May, 1994 ($2.95, limited series)

	GD	VG	FN	VF	VF/NM	NM-
1,2						3.00

MR. & MRS. BEANS
United Features Syndicate: No. 11, 1939

	GD	VG	FN	VF	VF/NM	NM-
Single Series 11	34	68	102	204	332	460

MR. & MRS. J. EVIL SCIENTIST (TV)(See The Flintstones & Hanna-Barbera Band Wagon #3)
Gold Key: Nov, 1963 - No. 4, Sept, 1966 (Hanna-Barbera, all 12¢)

	GD	VG	FN	VF	VF/NM	NM-
1	5	10	15	35	63	90
2-4	4	8	12	23	37	50

MR. ANTHONY'S LOVE CLINIC (Based on radio show)
Hillman Periodicals: Nov, 1949 - No. 5, Apr-May, 1950 (52 pgs.)

	GD	VG	FN	VF	VF/NM	NM-
1-Photo-c on all	20	40	60	114	182	250
2	14	28	42	76	108	140
3-5	12	24	36	67	94	120

MISTER BLANK
Amaze Ink: No. 0, Jan, 1996 - No. 14, May, 2000 ($1.75/$2.95, B&W)

	GD	VG	FN	VF	VF/NM	NM-
0-($1.75, 16 pgs.) Origin of Mr. Blank						3.00
1-14-($2.95) Chris Hicks-s/a						3.00

MR. DISTRICT ATTORNEY (Radio/TV)
National Per. Publ.: Jan-Feb, 1948 - No. 67, Jan-Feb, 1959 (1-23: 52 pgs.)

	GD	VG	FN	VF	VF/NM	NM-
1-Howard Purcell c-5-23 (most)	87	174	261	553	952	1350
2	41	82	123	256	428	600
3-5	29	58	87	170	278	385
6-10: 8-Rise & fall of Lucky Lynn	22	44	66	132	216	300
11-20	17	34	51	98	154	210
21-43: 43-Last pre-code (1-2/55)	14	28	42	76	108	140
44-67: 55-UFO story	11	22	33	62	86	110

MR. DISTRICT ATTORNEY (SeeThe Funnies #35)
Dell Publishing Co.: No. 13, 1942

	GD	VG	FN	VF	VF/NM	NM-
Four Color 13-See The Funnies #35 for 1st app.	26	52	78	182	404	625

MISTER E (Also see Books of Magic limited series)
DC Comics: Jun, 1991- No. 4, Sept, 1991($1.75, limited series)

	GD	VG	FN	VF	VF/NM	NM-
1-4-Snyder III-c/a; follow-up to Books of Magic limited series						3.00

MISTER ED, THE TALKING HORSE (TV)
Dell Publishing Co./Gold Key: Mar-May, 1962 - No. 6, Feb, 1964 (All photo-c; photo back-c: 1-6)

	GD	VG	FN	VF	VF/NM	NM-
Four Color 1295	10	20	30	70	150	230
1(11/62) (Gold Key)-Photo-c	8	16	24	51	96	140
2-6: Photo-c	5	10	15	33	57	80

(See March of Comics #244, 260, 282, 290)

MR. GUM (From The Atomics)
Oni Press: April, 2003 ($2.99, one-shot)

	GD	VG	FN	VF	VF/NM	NM-
1-Mike Allred-s/J. Bone-a; Madman & The Atomics app.						3.00

MR. HERO, THE NEWMATIC MAN (See Neil Gaiman's...)

MR. MAGOO (TV) (The Nearsighted..., ...& Gerald McBoing Boing 1954 issues; formerly Gerald McBoing-Boing And ...)
Dell Publishing Co.: No. 6, Nov-Jan, 1953-54; 5/54 - 3-5/62; 9-11/63 - 3-5/65

	GD	VG	FN	VF	VF/NM	NM-
6	9	18	27	58	114	170
Four Color 561(5/54),602(11/54)	9	18	27	58	114	170
Four Color 1235(#1, 12-2/62),1305(#2, 3-5/62)	7	14	21	48	89	130
3(9-11/63) - 5	6	12	18	42	79	115
Four Color 1235(12-536-505)(3-5/65)-2nd Printing	5	10	15	35	63	90

MR. MAJESTIC (See WildC.A.T.S.)
DC Comics (WildStorm): Sept, 1999 - No. 9, May, 2000 ($2.50)

	GD	VG	FN	VF	VF/NM	NM-
1-9: 1-McGuinness-a/Casey & Holguin-s. 2-Two covers						3.00
TPB (2002, $14.95) r/#1-6 & Wildstorm Spotlight #1						15.00

MISTER MIRACLE (1st series) (See Cancelled Comic Cavalcade)
National Periodical Publications/DC Comics: 3-4/71 - V4#18, 2-3/74; V5#19, 9/77 - V6#25, 8-9/78; 1987 (Fourth World)

	GD	VG	FN	VF	VF/NM	NM-
1-1st app. Mr. Miracle (#1-3 are 15¢)	8	16	24	56	108	160
2,3: 2-Intro. Granny Goodness. 3-Last 15¢ issue	4	8	12	28	47	65
4-8: 4-Intro. Barda; Boy Commandos-r begin; all 52 pgs.	4	8	12	28	47	65
9-18: 9-Origin Mr. Miracle; Darkseid cameo. 15-Intro/1st app. Shilo Norman. 18-Barda & Scott Free wed; New Gods app. & Darkseid cameo; Last Kirby issue.	3	6	9	16	23	30
19-25 (1977-78)	2	4	6	8	10	12
Special 1(1987, $1.25, 52 pgs.)						5.00
Jack Kirby's Fourth World TPB ('01, $12.95) B&W&Grey-toned reprint of #11-18; Mark Evanier intro.						13.00
Jack Kirby's Mister Miracle TPB ('98, $12.95) B&W&Grey-toned reprint of #1-10; David Copperfield intro.						13.00

NOTE: *Austin a-19i.* ***Ditko*** *a-6r.* ***Golden*** *a-23-25p; c-25p.* ***Heath*** *a-24i, 25i; c-25i.* ***Kirby*** *a(p)/c-1-18.* ***Nasser*** *a-19i.* ***Rogers*** *a-19-22p; c-19, 20p, 21p, 22-24. 4-8 contain* ***Simon & Kirby*** *Boy Commandos reprints from Detective 82,76, Boy Commandos 1, 3 & Detective 64 in that order.*

MISTER MIRACLE (2nd Series) (See Justice League)
DC Comics: Jan, 1989 - No. 28, June, 1991 ($1.00/$1.25)

	GD	VG	FN	VF	VF/NM	NM-
1-28: 13,14-Lobo app. 22-1st new Mr. Miracle w/new costume						3.00

MISTER MIRACLE (3rd Series)
DC Comics: Apr, 1996 - No. 7, Oct, 1996 ($1.95)

	GD	VG	FN	VF	VF/NM	NM-
1-7: 2-Vs. JLA. 6-Simonson-c						3.00

MR. MIRACLE (See Capt. Fearless #1 & Holyoke One-Shot #4)

MR. MONSTER (1st Series)(Doc Stearn... #7 on; See Airboy-Mr. Monster Special, Dark Horse Presents, Super Duper Comics & Vanguard Illustrated #7)
Eclipse Comics: Jan, 1985 - No. 10, June, 1987 ($1.75, Baxter paper)

	GD	VG	FN	VF	VF/NM	NM-
1,3: 1-1st story-r from Vanguard Ill. #7(1st app.). 3-Alan Moore scripts; Wolverton-r/Weird Mysteries #5.						5.00
2-Dave Stevens-c	1	3	4	6	8	10
4-10: 6-Ditko-r/Fantastic Fears #5 plus new Giffen-a. 10- "6-D" issue						4.00

MR. MONSTER
Dark Horse Comics: Feb, 1988 - No. 8, July, 1991 ($1.75, B&W)

	GD	VG	FN	VF	VF/NM	NM-
1-7						3.00
8-($4.95, 60 pgs.)-Origins conclusion						5.00

MR. MONSTER ATTACKS! (Doc Stearn...)
Tundra Publ.: Aug, 1992 - No. 3, Oct, 1992 ($3.95, limited series, 32 pgs.)

	GD	VG	FN	VF	VF/NM	NM-
1-3: Michael T. Gilbert-a/scripts; Gilbert/Dorman painted-c						4.00

MR. MONSTER PRESENTS (CRACK-A-BOOM!)
Caliber Comics: 1997 - No. 3, 1997 ($2.95, B&W&Red, limited series)

	GD	VG	FN	VF	VF/NM	NM-
1-3: Michael T. Gilbert-a/scripts: 1-Wraparound-c						3.00

Mister Mystery #15 © Media Pub.

Mister X: Eviction #2 © Dean Motter

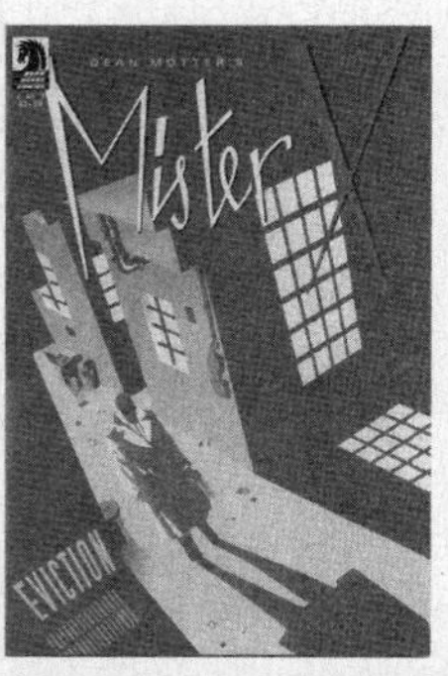

Mitzi's Romances #8 © MAR

GD VG FN VF VF/NM NM-
2.0 4.0 6.0 8.0 9.0 9.2

MR. MONSTER'S GAL FRIDAY...KELLY!
Image Comics: Jan, 2000 - No. 3, May, 2004 ($3.50, B&W)
1-3-Michael T. Gilbert-c; story & art by various. 3-Alan Moore-s 3.50

MR. MONSTER'S SUPER-DUPER SPECIAL
Eclipse Comics: May, 1986 - No. 8, July, 1987
1-(5/86)...3-D High Octane Horror #1 5.00
1-(5/86)...2-D version, 100 copies 2 4 6 11 16 20
2-(8/86)...High Octane Horror #1, 3-(9/86)...True Crime #1, 4-(11/86)...True Crime #2, 5-(1/87)...Hi-Voltage Super Science #1, 6-(3/87)...High Shock Schlock #1, 7-(5/87)...High Shock Schlock #2, 8-(7/87)...Weird Tales Of The Future #1 4.00
NOTE: ***Jack Cole** r-3, 4. **Evans** a-2r. **Kubert** a-1r. **Powell** a-5r. **Wolverton** a-2r, 7r, 8r.*

MR. MONSTER VS. GORZILLA
Image Comics: July, 1998 ($2.95, one-shot)
1-Michael T. Gilbert-a 3.00

MR. MONSTER: WORLDS WAR TWO
Atomeka Press: 2004 ($6.99, one-shot)
nn-Michael T. Gilbert-s/George Freeman-a; two covers by Horley & Dorman 7.00

MR. MUSCLES (Formerly Blue Beetle #18-21)
Charlton Comics: No. 22, Mar, 1956; No. 23, Aug, 1956
22,23 9 18 27 50 65 80

MR. MXYZPTLK (VILLAINS)
DC Comics: Feb, 1998 ($1.95, one-shot)
1-Grant-s/Morgan-a/Pearson-c 3.00

MISTER MYSTERY (Tales of Horror and Suspense)
Mr. Publ. (Media Publ.) No. 1-3/SPM Publ./Stanmore (Aragon): Sept, 1951 - No. 19, Oct, 1954
1-Kurtzman-*esque* horror story 116 232 348 742 1271 1800
2,3-Kurtzman-*esque* story. 3-Anti-Wertham edit. 68 136 204 435 743 1050
4-Bondage-c 90 180 270 576 988 1400
5,8,10 65 130 195 416 708 1000
6-Classic torture-c 181 362 543 1158 1979 2800
7- "The Brain Bats of Venus" by Wolverton; partially re-used in Weird Tales of the Future #7 181 362 543 1158 1979 2800
9-Nostrand-a 65 130 195 416 708 1000
11-Wolverton "Robot Woman" story/Weird Mysteries #2, cut up, rewritten & partially redrawn 148 296 444 947 1624 2300
12-Classic injury to eye-c 371 742 1113 2600 4550 6500
13-16,19: 15- "Living Dead" junkie story. 16-Bondage-c. 19-Reprints 55 110 165 352 601 850
17-Severed heads-c 97 194 291 621 1061 1500
18- "Robot Woman" by Wolverton reprinted from Weird Mysteries #2; decapitation, bondage-c 110 220 330 704 1202 1700
NOTE: ***Andru** a-1, 2p, 3p. **Andru/Esposito** c-1-3. **Baily** c-10-18(most). **Mortellaro** c-5-7. Bondage c-7, 16. Some issues have graphic dismemberment scenes.*

MR. PEABODY AND SHERMAN (Based on the 2014 Dreamworks movie)
IDW Publishing: Nov, 2013 - No. 4, Jan, 2014 ($3.99)
1-4: 1-Fisch-s/Monlongo-a; 3 covers. 2-Three covers. 3,4-Two covers 4.00

MR. PUNCH
DC Comics (Vertigo): 1994 ($24.95, one-shot)
nn (Hard-c)-Gaiman scripts; McKean-c/a 40.00
nn (Soft-c) 18.00

MISTER Q (See Mighty Midget Comics & Our Flag Comics #5)

MR. RISK (Formerly All Romances; Men Against Crime #3 on)(Also see Our Flag Comics & Super-Mystery Comics)
Ace Magazines: No. 7, Oct, 1950; No. 2, Dec, 1950
7,2 13 26 39 74 105 135

MR. SCARLET & PINKY (See Mighty Midget Comics)

MR. T
APComics: May, 2005 ($3.50)
1-Chris Bunting-s/Neil Edwards-a 3.50

MR. T AND THE T-FORCE
Now Comics: June, 1993 - No. 10, May, 1994 ($1.95, color)
1-10-Newsstand editions: 1-7-polybagged with photo trading card in each. 1,2-Neal Adams-c/a(p). 3-Dave Dorman painted-c 3.00
1-10-Direct Sale editions polybagged w/line drawn trading cards. 1-Contains gold foil trading card by Neal Adams 3.00

GD VG FN VF VF/NM NM-
2.0 4.0 6.0 8.0 9.0 9.2

MISTER TERRIFIC (DC New 52)(Leads into Earth 2 series)
DC Comics: Nov, 2011 - No. 8, Jun, 2012 ($2.99)
1-8: 1-Wallace-s/Gugliotta-a/JG Jones-c; origin re-told. 2-Intro. Brainstorm 3.00

MISTER UNIVERSE (Professional wrestler)
Mr. Publications Media Publ. (Stanmor, Aragon): July, 1951; No. 2, Oct, 1951 - No. 5, April, 1952
1 23 46 69 136 223 310
2- "Jungle That Time Forgot", (24 pg. story); Andru/Esposito-c 15 30 45 83 124 165
3-Marijuana story 15 30 45 83 124 165
4,5-"Goes to War" cover/stories (Korean War) 12 24 36 67 94 120

MISTER X (See Vortex)
Mr. Publications/Vortex Comics/Caliber V3#1 on: 6/84 - No. 14, 8/88 ($1.50/$2.25, direct sales, coated paper);V2#1, Apr, 1989 - V2#12, Mar, 1990 ($2.00/$2.50, B&W, newsprint) V3#1, 1996 - No. 4, 1996 ($2.95, B&W)
1-14: 11-Dave McKean story & art (6 pgs.) 4.00
V2 #1-12: 1-11 (Second Coming, B&W): 1-Four diff.-c. 10-Photo-c 3.00
V3 #1-4 3.00
Return of... ($11.95, graphic novel)-r/V1#1-4 12.00
Return of... ($34.95, hardcover limited edition)-r/1-4 35.00
Special (no date, 1990?) 3.00

MISTER X
Dark Horse Comics: Mar, 2013 ($2.99, one-shot)
...: Hard Candy (3/13) Dean Motter-s/a 3.00

MISTER X: CONDEMNED
Dark Horse Comics: Dec, 2008 - No. 4, Mar, 2009 ($3.50, limited series)
1-4-Dean Motter-s/a 3.50

MISTER X: EVICTION
Dark Horse Comics: May, 2013 - No. 3, Jul, 2013 ($3.99, limited series)
1-3-Dean Motter-s/a 4.00

MISTER X: RAZED
Dark Horse Comics: Feb, 2015 - No. 4, May, 2015 ($3.99, limited series)
1-4-Dean Motter-s/a 4.00

MISTY
Marvel Comics (Star Comics): Dec, 1985 - No. 6, May, 1986 (Limited series)
1-6: Millie The Model's niece 4.00

MITZI COMICS (Becomes Mitzi's Boy Friend #2-7)(See All Teen)
Timely Comics: Spring, 1948 (one-shot)
1-Kurtzman's "Hey Look" plus 3 pgs. "Giggles 'n' Grins" 47 94 141 296 498 700

MITZI'S BOY FRIEND (Formerly Mitzi Comics; becomes Mitzi's Romances)
Marvel Comics (TCI): No. 2, June, 1948 - No. 7, April, 1949
2 25 50 75 150 245 340
3-7 18 36 54 105 165 225

MITZI'S ROMANCES (Formerly Mitzi's Boy Friend)
Timely/Marvel Comics (TCI): No. 8, June, 1949 - No. 10, Dec, 1949
8-Becomes True Life Tales #8 (10/49) on? 19 38 57 109 172 235
9,10: 10-Painted-c 16 32 48 94 147 200

MNEMOVORE
DC Comics (Vertigo): Jun, 2005 - No. 6, Nov, 2005 ($2.99, limited series)
1-6-Rodionoff & Fawkes-s/Huddleston-a/c 3.00

MOBY DICK (See Feature Presentations #6, King Classics, and Classic Comics #5)
Dell Publishing Co.: No. 717, Aug, 1956
Four Color 717-Movie, Gregory Peck photo-c 7 14 21 49 92 135

MOBY DUCK (See Donald Duck #112 & Walt Disney Showcase #2,11)
Gold Key (Disney): Oct, 1967 - No. 11, Oct, 1970; No. 12, Jan, 1974 - No. 30, Feb, 1978
1-Three Little Pigs app. 3 6 9 20 31 42
2-5: 2-Beagle Boys app. 5-Captain Hook app. 2 4 6 11 16 20
6-11: 6-Huey, Dewey & Louie app. 2 4 6 9 13 16
12-30: 21,30-r 1 3 4 6 8 10

MOCKINGBIRD (From S.H.I.E.L.D.)
Marvel Comics: May, 2016 - No. 8, Dec, 2016 ($3.99)
1-8: 1-4-Chelsea Cain-s/Kate Niemczyk-a/Joëlle Jones-c. 5-Moustafa-a. 6-Civil War II tie-in 4.00
... S.H.I.E.L.D. 50th Anniversary (11/15, $3.99) Joëlle Jones-a; back-up with Red Widow 4.00

Modern Comics #60 © QUA

Mod Wheels #17 © GK

The Monarchy #1 © DC

GD VG FN VF VF/NM NM-
2.0 4.0 6.0 8.0 9.0 9.2

MOCKING DEAD, THE
Dynamite Entertainment: 2013 - No. 5, 2014 ($3.99, B&W, limited series)
1-5: 1-Fred Van Lente-s/Max Dunbar-a 4.00

MODEL FUN (With Bobby Benson)
Harle Publications: No. 2, Fall, 1954 - No. 5, July, 1955
2-Bobby Benson 7 14 21 35 43 50
3-5-Bobby Benson 5 10 15 23 28 32

MODELING WITH MILLIE (Formerly Life With Millie)
Atlas/Marvel Comics (Male Publ.): No. 21, Feb, 1963 - No. 54, June, 1967
21 8 16 24 56 108 160
22-30 5 10 15 34 60 85
31-53 5 10 15 30 50 70
54-Last issue; Gears-c & 6 pg. story; Beatles swipe imitators; FF #63 comic appears in story; "Millie the Marvel" 6 pg. story as super-hero 5 10 15 33 57 80

MODELS, INC.
Marvel Comics: Oct, 2009 - No. 4, Jan, 2010 ($3.99, limited series)
1-4-Millie the Model, Patsy Walker, Mary Jane Watson app.; Land-c. 1-Tim Gunn app. 4.00

MODERN COMICS (Formerly Military Comics #1-43)
Quality Comics Group: No. 44, Nov, 1945 - No. 102, Oct, 1950
44-Blackhawk continues 54 108 162 343 574 825
45-52: 49-1st app. Fear, Lady Adventuress 38 76 114 228 369 510
53-Torchy by Ward begins (9/46) 42 84 126 265 445 625
54-60: 55-J. Cole-a 32 64 96 192 314 435
61-Classic-c 39 78 117 231 378 525
62-64,66-77,79,80: 73-J. Cole-a 31 62 93 182 296 410
65-Classic Grim Reaper Skull-c 61 122 183 390 670 950
78-1st app. Madame Butterfly 34 68 102 204 332 460
81-99,101: 82,83-One pg. J. Cole-a. 83-Last 52 pg. issue 99-Blackhawks on the moon-c/story 31 62 93 182 296 410
100 32 64 96 192 314 435
102-(Scarce)-J. Cole-a; Spirit by Eisner app. 39 78 117 234 385 535
NOTE: ***Al Bryant** c-44-51, 54, 55, 66, 69. **Jack Cole** a-55, 73. **Crandall** Blackhawk-#46, 47, 50, 51, 54, 56, 58-60, 64, 67-70, 73, 74, 76-78, 80-83; c-60-65, 67, 68, 70-95. **Crandall/Cuidera** c-56-59, 96-102. **Gustavson** a-47, 49. **Ward** Blackhawk-#52, 53, 55 (15 pgs. each). Torchy in #53-102; by **Ward** only in #53-89(9/49); by **Gil Fox** #92, 93, 102.*

MODERN LOVE
E. C. Comics: June-July, 1949 - No. 8, Aug-Sept, 1950
1-Feldstein, Ingels-a 103 206 309 659 1130 1600
2-Craig/Feldstein-c/s 71 142 213 454 777 1100
3 61 122 183 390 670 950
4-6 (Scarce): 4-Bra/panties panels 84 168 252 538 919 1300
7,8 61 122 183 390 670 950
NOTE: ***Craig** a-3. **Feldstein** a-in most issues; c-1, 2i, 3-8. **Harrison** a-4. **Iger** a-6-8. **Ingels** a-1, 2, 4-7. **Palais** a-5. **Wood** a-7. **Wood/Harrison** a-5-7. (Canadian reprints known; see Table of Contents.)*

MODERN WARFARE 2: GHOST (Based on the videogame)
DC Comics (WildStorm): Jan, 2010 - No. 6, Sept, 2010 ($3.99, limited series)
1-6: 1-Two covers; Lapham-s/West-a 4.00
TPB (2010, $17.99) r/#1-6; cover sketches and sketch art 18.00

MOD LOVE
Western Publishing Co.: 1967 (50¢, 36 pgs.)
1-(Low print) 7 14 21 46 86 125

MODNIKS, THE
Gold Key: Aug, 1967 - No. 2, Aug, 1970
10206-708(#1) 3 6 9 21 33 45
2 3 6 9 15 22 28

M.O.D.O.K. ASSASSIN (Secret Wars tie-in)
Marvel Comics: Jul, 2015 - No. 5, Nov, 2015 ($3.99, limited series)
1-5-Yost-s/Pinna-a; Angela app. 1-Bullseye, Baron Mordo & Clea app. 4.00

M.O.D.O.K.: REIGN DELAY
Marvel Comics: Nov, 2009 ($3.99, one-shot)
1-M.O.D.O.K. cartoony humor stories from Marvel Digital Comics; Ryan Dunlavey-s/a 4.00

MOD SQUAD (TV)
Dell Publishing Co.: Jan, 1969 - No. 3, Oct, 1969 - No. 8, April, 1971
1-Photo-c 6 12 18 38 69 100
2-4: 2-4-Photo-c 4 8 12 27 44 60
5-8: 8-Photo-c; Reprints #2 4 8 12 23 37 50

MOD WHEELS
Gold Key: Mar, 1971 - No. 19, Jan, 1976
1 4 8 12 25 40 55
2-9 3 6 9 16 23 30
10-19: 11,15-Extra 16 pgs. ads 3 6 9 14 19 24

MOE & SHMOE COMICS
O. S. Publ. Co.: Spring, 1948 - No. 2, Summer, 1948
1 10 20 30 58 79 100
2 7 14 21 37 46 55

MOEBIUS (Graphic novel)
Marvel Comics (Epic Comics): Oct, 1987 - No. 6, 1988; No. 7, 1990; No. 8, 1991 ($9.95, 8x11", mature)
1,2,4-6,8: (#2, 2nd printing, $9.95) 3 6 9 17 26 35
3,7,0: 3-(1st & 2nd printings, $12.95). 0 (1990, $12.95) 3 6 9 19 30 40
Moebius I-Signed & #'d hard-c ($45.95, Graphitti Designs, 1,500 copies printed)-r/#1-3 7 14 21 46 86 125

MOEBIUS COMICS
Caliber: May, 1996 - No. 6 ($2.95, B&W)
1-6: Moebius-c/a. 1-William Stout-a 4.00

MOEBIUS: THE MAN FROM CIGURI
Dark Horse Comics: 1996 ($7.95, digest-size)
nn-Moebius-c/a 2 4 6 10 14 18

MOLLY MANTON'S ROMANCES (Romantic Affairs #3)
Marvel Comics (SePI): Sept, 1949 - No. 2, Dec, 1949 (52 pgs.)
1-Photo-c (becomes Blaze the Wonder Collie #2 (10/49) on? & Molly Manton's Romances #2 22 44 66 132 216 300
2-Titled "Romances of…"; photo-c 15 30 45 88 137 185

MOLLY O'DAY (Super Sleuth)
Avon Periodicals: February, 1945 (1st Avon comic)
1-Molly O'Day, The Enchanted Dagger by Tuska (r/Yankee #1), Capt'n Courage, Corporal Grant app. 68 136 204 435 743 1050

MOMENT OF SILENCE
Marvel Comics: Feb, 2002 ($3.50, one-shot)
1-Tributes to the heroes and victims of Sept. 11; s/a by various 3.50

MONARCHY, THE (Also see The Authority and StormWatch)
DC Comics (WildStorm): Apr, 2001 - No. 12, May, 2002 ($2.50)
1-12: 1-McCrea & Leach-a/Young-s 3.00
Bullets Over Babylon TPB (2001, $12.95) r/#1-4, Authority #21 13.00

MONKEES, THE (TV)(Also see Circus Boy, Groovy, Not Brand Echh #3, Teen-Age Talk, Teen Beam & Teen Beat)
Dell Publishing Co.: March, 1967 - No. 17, Oct, 1969
1-Photo-c 9 18 27 60 120 180
2-17: All photo-c. 17-Reprints #1 6 12 18 37 66 95

MONKEY AND THE BEAR, THE
Atlas Comics (ZPC): Sept, 1953 - No. 3, Jan, 1954
1-Howie Post-c/a in all; funny animal 13 26 39 74 105 135
2,3 9 18 27 52 69 85

MONKEYMAN AND O'BRIEN (Also see Dark Horse Presents #80, 100-5, Gen[13]/…, Hellboy: Seed of Destruction, & San Diego Comic Con #2)
Dark Horse Comics (Legend): Jul, 1996 - No. 3, Sept, 1996 ($2.95, lim. series)
1-3: New stories; Art Adams-c/a/scripts 4.00
nn-(2/96, $2.95)-r/back-up stories from Hellboy: Seed of Destruction; Adams-c/a/scripts 4.00

MONKEYSHINES COMICS
Ace Periodicals/Publishers Specialists/Current Books/Unity Publ.: Summer, 1944 - No. 27, July, 1949
1-Funny animal 16 32 48 94 147 200
2-(Aut/44) 10 20 30 58 79 100
3-10: 3-(Win/44) 10 20 30 54 72 90
11-18,20-27: 23,24-Fago-c/a 8 16 24 44 57 70
19-Frazetta-a 10 20 30 54 72 90

MONKEY'S UNCLE, THE (See Merlin Jones As… under Movie Comics)

MONOLITH, THE
DC Comics: Apr, 2004 - No. 12, Mar, 2005 ($3.50/$2.95)
1-($3.50) Palmiotti & Gray-s/Winslade-a 3.50
2-12-($2.95): 6-8-Batman app.; Coker-a 3.00

Monster Hunters #16 © CC

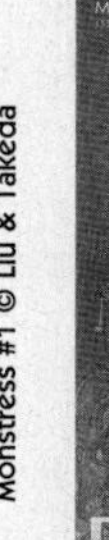
Monstress #1 © Liu & Takeda

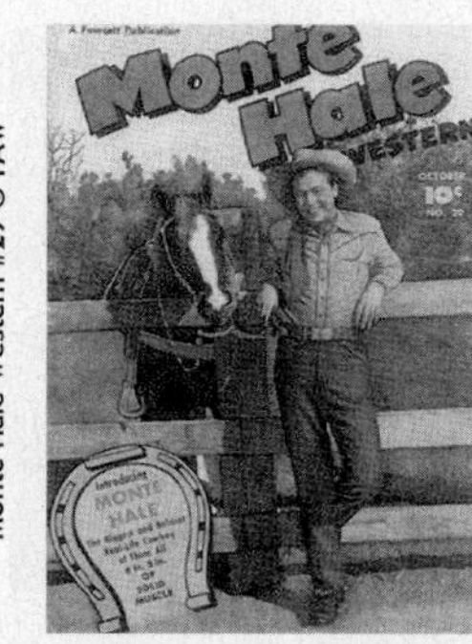

Monte Hale Western #29 © FAW

	GD 2.0	VG 4.0	FN 6.0	VF 8.0	VF/NM 9.0	NM- 9.2

...: Volume One HC (Image Comics, 2012, $17.99) r/#1-4; intro. by Jim Steranko 18.00

MONROES, THE (TV)
Dell Publishing Co.: Apr, 1967

1-Photo-c 3 6 9 17 26 35

MONSTER
Fiction House Magazines: 1953 - No. 2, 1953

1-Dr. Drew by Grandenetti; reprint from Rangers Comics #48; Whitman-c
68 136 204 435 743 1050
2-Whitman-c 47 94 141 296 498 700

MONSTER CRIME COMICS (Also see Crime Must Stop)
Hillman Periodicals: Oct, 1952 (15¢, 52 pgs.)

1 (Scarce) 213 426 639 1363 2332 3300

MONSTER HOUSE (Companion to the 2006 movie)
IDW Publishing: June, 2006 ($7.99, one-shot)

nn-Two stories about Bones and Skull by Joshua Dysart and Simeon Wilkins 8.00

MONSTER HOWLS (Magazine)
Humor-Vision: December, 1966 (Satire) (35¢, 68 pgs.)

1-John Severin-a 5 10 15 34 60 85

MONSTER HUNTERS
Charlton Comics: Aug, 1975 - No. 9, Jan, 1977; No. 10, Oct, 1977 - No. 18, Feb, 1979

1-Howard-a; Newton-c; 1st Countess Von Bludd and Colonel Whiteshroud
3 6 9 17 26 35
2-Sutton-c/a; Ditko-a 3 6 9 14 19 24
3,4,5,7: 4-Sutton-c/a 2 4 6 9 12 15
6,8,10: 6,8,10-Ditko-a 2 4 6 10 14 18
9,11,12 1 3 4 6 8 10
13,15,18-Ditko-c/a. 18-Sutton-a 2 4 6 10 14 18
14-Special all-Ditko issue 3 6 9 16 24 32
16,17-Sutton-a 2 3 4 6 8 10
1,2 (Modern Comics reprints, 1977) 6.00
NOTE: ***Ditko** a-2, 6, 8, 10, 13-15r, 18r; c-13-15, 18. **Howard** a-1, 3, 17; r-13. **Morisi** a-1. **Staton** a-1, 13. **Sutton** a-2, 4; c-2, 4; r-16-18. **Zeck** a-4-9. Reprints in #12-18.*

MONSTER MADNESS (Magazine)
Marvel Comics: 1972 - No. 3, 1973 (60¢, B&W)

1-3: Stories by "Sinister" Stan Lee. 1-Frankenstein photo-c. 2-Son of Frankenstein photo-c. 3-Bride of Frankenstein photo-c 4 8 12 27 44 60

MONSTER MAN
Image Comics (Action Planet): Sept, 1997 ($2.95, B&W)

1-Mike Manley-c/s/a 3.00

MONSTER MASTERWORKS
Marvel Comics: 1989 ($12.95, TPB)

nn-Reprints 1960's monster stories; art by Kirby, Ditko, Ayers, Everett 20.00

MONSTER MATINEE
Chaos! Comics: Oct, 1997 - No. 3, Oct, 1997 ($2.50, limited series)

1-3: pin-ups 3.00

MONSTER MENACE
Marvel Comics: Dec, 1993 - No. 4, Mar, 1994 ($1.25, limited series)

1-4: Pre-code Atlas horror reprints. 6.00
NOTE: ***Ditko**-r & **Kirby**-r in all.*

MONSTER OF FRANKENSTEIN (See Frankenstein and Essential Monster of Frankenstein)

MONSTER PILE-UP
Image Comics: Aug, 2008 ($1.99)

1-New short stories of Astounding Wolf-Man, Firebreather, Perhapanauts, Proof 3.00

MONSTERS ATTACK (Magazine)
Globe Communications Corpse: Sept, 1989 - No. 5, Dec, 1990 (B&W)

1-5-Ditko, Morrow, J. Severin-a. 5-Toth, Morrow-a 1 2 3 4 5 7

MONSTERS, INC. (Based on the Disney/Pixar movie)
BOOM! Studios: Jun, 2009 - No. 4, Nov, 2009 ($2.99, limited series)

...: Laugh Factory 1-4: 1,3-Three covers. 2,4-Two covers 3.00

MONSTERS, INC. (Based on the Disney/Pixar movie)
Marvel Worldwide Inc.: Feb, 2013 - No. 2 ($2.99, limited series)

1,2-Movie adaptation 3.00
...: A Perfect Date (2013, $2.99) 3.00
...: The Humanween Party (4/13, $2.99) 3.00

MONSTERS ON THE PROWL (Chamber of Darkness #1-8)
Marvel Comics Group (No. 13,14: 52 pgs.): No. 9, 2/71 - No. 27, 11/73; No. 28, 6/74 - No. 30, 10/74

9-Barry Smith inks 5 10 15 31 53 75
10-12,15: 12-Last 15¢ issue 3 6 9 19 30 40
13,14-(52 pgs.) 4 8 12 22 35 48
16-(4/72)-King Kull 4th app.; Severin-c 4 8 12 22 35 48
17-30 3 6 9 16 24 32
NOTE: ***Ditko** r-9, 14, 16. **Kirby** r-10-17, 21, 23, 25, 27, 28, 30; c-9, 25. **Kirby/Ditko** r-14, 17-20, 22, 24, 26, 29. **Marie/John Severin** a-16(Kull). 9-13, 15 contain one new story. Woodish art by **Reese**-11. King Kull created by Robert E. Howard.*

MONSTERS TO LAUGH WITH (Magazine) (Becomes Monsters Unlimited #4)
Marvel Comics Group: 1964 - No. 3, 1965 (B&W)

1-Humor by Stan Lee 7 14 21 46 86 125
2,3: 3-Frankenstein photo-c 5 10 15 31 53 75

MONSTERS UNLEASHED (Magazine)
Marvel Comics Group: July, 1973 - No. 11, Apr, 1975; Summer, 1975 (B&W)

1-Soloman Kane sty; Werewolf app. 4 8 12 28 47 65
2-4: 2-The Frankenstein Monster begins, ends #10. 3-Neal Adams-c/a; The Man-Thing begins (origin-r); Son of Satan preview. 4-Werewolf app. 4 8 12 23 37 50
5-7: Werewolf in all. 5-Man-Thing. 7-Williamson-a(r) 3 6 9 17 26 35
8-11: 8-Man-Thing; N. Adams-r. 9-Man-Thing; Wendigo app. 10-Origin Tigra
3 6 9 18 28 38
Annual 1 (Summer,1975, 92 pgs.)-Kane-a 3 6 9 17 26 35
NOTE: ***Boris** c-2, 6. **Brunner** a-2; c-11. **J. Buscema** a-2p, 4p, 5p. **Colan** a-1, 4r. **Davis** a-3r. **Everett** a-2r. **G. Kane** a-3. **Krigstein** r-4. **Morrow** a-3; c-1. **Perez** a-8. **Ploog** a-6. **Reese** a-1, 2. **Tuska** a-3p. **Wildey** a-1r.*

MONSTERS UNLEASHED
Marvel Comics: Mar, 2017 - No. 5 ($4.99, limited series with tie-ins)

1-4: 1-Cullen Bunn-s/Steve McNiven-a; Avengers, X-Men, Guardians of the Galaxy, Inhumans & Champions app. 2-Greg Land-a. 3-Leinil Yu-a. 4-Salvador Larroca-a 5.00

MONSTERS UNLIMITED (Magazine) (Formerly Monsters To Laugh With)
Marvel Comics Group: No. 4, 1965 - No. 7, 1966 (B&W)

4-7: 4,7-Frankenstein photo-c 5 10 15 31 53 75

MONSTER WORLD
DC Comics (WildStorm): Jul, 2001 - No. 4, Oct, 2001 ($2.50, limited series)

1-4-Lobdell-s/Meglia-c/a 3.00

MONSTER WORLD
American Gothic Press: Dec, 2015 - No. 4, May, 2016 ($3.99)

1-4-Philip Kim & Steve Niles-s/Piotr Kowalski-a 4.00

MONSTRESS
Image Comics: Nov, 2015 - Present ($4.99/$3.99)

1-($4.99) Marjorie Liu-s/Sana Tekeda-a 5.00
2-10-($3.99) 4.00

MONTANA KID, THE (See Kid Montana)

MONTE HALE WESTERN (Movie star; Formerly Mary Marvel #1-28; also see Fawcett Movie Comic, Motion Picture Comics, Picture News #8, Real Western Hero, Six-Gun Heroes, Western Hero & XMas Comics)
Fawcett Publ./Charlton No. 83 on: No. 29, Oct, 1948 - No. 88, Jan, 1956

29-(#1, 52 pgs.)-Photo-c begin, end #82; Monte Hale & his horse Pardner begin
26 52 78 154 252 350
30-(52 pgs.)-Big Bow and Little Arrow begin, end #34; Captain Tootsie by Beck
14 28 42 80 115 150
31-36,38-40-(52 pgs.): 34-Gabby Hayes begins, ends #80. 39-Captain Tootsie by Beck
12 24 36 67 94 120
37,41,45,49-(36 pgs.) 10 20 30 54 72 90
42-44,46-48,50-(52 pgs.): 47-Big Bow & Little Arrow app.
10 20 30 58 79 100
51,52,54-56,58,59-(52 pgs.) 9 18 27 52 69 85
53,57-(36 pgs.): 53-Slim Pickens app. 8 16 24 44 57 70
60-81: 36 pgs. #60-on. 80-Gabby Hayes ends 8 16 24 42 54 65
82-Last Fawcett issue (6/53) 9 18 27 52 69 85
83-1st Charlton issue (2/55); B&W photo back-c begin. Gabby Hayes returns, ends #86
10 20 30 58 79 100
84 (4/55) 8 16 24 44 57 70
85-86 8 16 24 42 54 65
87,88: 87-Wolverton-r, 1/2 pg. 88-Last issue 8 16 24 44 57 70
NOTE: ***Gil Kane** a-33?, 34? **Rocky Lane** -1 pg. (Carnation ad)-38, 40, 41, 43, 44, 46, 55.*

MONTY HALL OF THE U.S. MARINES (See With the Marines...)
Toby Press: Aug, 1951 - No. 11, Apr, 1953

Moon Girl and Devil Dinosaur #4 © MAR

Moon Knight (2011 series) #12 © MAR

Moonshine #1 © Azzarello & Risso

	GD 2.0	VG 4.0	FN 6.0	VF 8.0	VF/NM 9.0	NM- 9.2
1	14	28	42	80	115	150
2	9	18	27	50	65	80
3-5	8	16	24	44	57	70
6-11	8	16	24	40	50	60

NOTE: *Full page pin-ups (Pin-Up Pete) by* ***Jack Sparling*** *in #1-9.*

MOON, A GIRL...ROMANCE, A (Becomes Weird Fantasy #13 on; formerly Moon Girl #1-8)
E. C. Comics: No. 9, Sept-Oct, 1949 - No. 12, Mar-Apr, 1950

	GD 2.0	VG 4.0	FN 6.0	VF 8.0	VF/NM 9.0	NM- 9.2
9-Moon Girl cameo	97	194	291	621	1061	1500
10,11	84	168	252	538	919	1300
12-(Scarce)	94	188	282	597	1024	1450

NOTE: ***Feldstein, Ingels*** *art in all.* ***Feldstein*** *c-9-12.* ***Wood/Harrison*** *a-10-12. Canadian reprints known; see Table of Contents.*

MOON GIRL AND DEVIL DINOSAUR
Marvel Comics: Jan, 2016 - Present ($3.99)

	GD 2.0	VG 4.0	FN 6.0	VF 8.0	VF/NM 9.0	NM- 9.2
1-16: 1-Reeder & Montclare-s/Bustos-a; intro. Lunella Lafayette. 4-Hulk app. 9-11-Ms. Marvel app. 14-Thing & Hulk (Cho) app. 15-Ironheart app.						4.00

MOON GIRL AND THE PRINCE (#1) (Moon Girl #2-6; Moon Girl Fights Crime #7, 8; becomes A Moon, A Girl, Romance #9 on)(Also see Animal Fables #7, Int. Crime Patrol #6, Happy Houlihans & Tales From The Crypt #22)
E. C. Comics: Fall, 1947 - No. 8, Summer, 1949

	GD 2.0	VG 4.0	FN 6.0	VF 8.0	VF/NM 9.0	NM- 9.2
1-Origin Moon Girl (see Happy Houlihans #1). Intro Santana, Queen of the Underworld	135	270	405	864	1482	2100
2-Moon Girl battles Futureman	77	154	231	493	847	1200
3,4: 3-Santana, Queen of the Underworld returns. 4-Moon Girl vs. a vampire	71	142	213	454	777	1100
5-E.C.'s 1st horror story, "Zombie Terror"	174	348	522	1114	1907	2700
6-8 (Scarce): 7-Origin Star (Moongirl's sidekick)	84	168	252	538	919	1300

NOTE: ***Craig*** *a-2, 5; c-1, 2.* ***Moldoff*** *a-1-8; c-3-8 (Shelly).* ***Wheelan's*** *Fat and Slat app. in #3, 4, 6. #2 & #3 are 52 pgs., #4 on, 36 pgs. Canadian reprints known; (see Table of Contents.)*

MOON KNIGHT (Also see The Hulk, Marc Spector…, Marvel Preview #21, Marvel Spotlight & Werewolf by Night #32)
Marvel Comics Group: Nov, 1980 - No. 38, Jul, 1984 (Mando paper #33 on)

	GD 2.0	VG 4.0	FN 6.0	VF 8.0	VF/NM 9.0	NM- 9.2
1-Origin resumed in #4	3	6	9	17	26	35
2-15,25,35: 4-Intro Midnight Man. 25-Double size. 35-($1.00, 52 pgs.)-X-Men app.; F.F. cameo						5.00
16-24,26-28,31-34,36-38: 16-The Thing app.						4.00
29,30-Werewolf By Night app.						6.00

NOTE: ***Austin*** *c-27i, 31i.* ***Cowan*** *a-16; c-16, 17.* ***Kaluta*** *c-36-38; back c-35.* ***Miller*** *c-9, 12p, 13p, 15p, 27p.* ***Ploog*** *back c-35.* ***Sienkiewicz*** *a-1-15, 17-20, 22-26, 28-30, 33i, 36(4), 37; c-1-5, 7, 8, 10, 11, 14-16, 18-26, 28-30, 31p, 33, 34.*

MOON KNIGHT
Marvel Comics Group: June, 1985 - V2#6, Dec, 1985

	GD 2.0	VG 4.0	FN 6.0	VF 8.0	VF/NM 9.0	NM- 9.2
V2#1-Double size; new costume						5.00
V2#2-6: 6-Sienkiewicz painted-c						3.00

MOON KNIGHT
Marvel Comics: Jan, 1998 - No. 4, Apr, 1998 ($2.50, limited series)

	GD 2.0	VG 4.0	FN 6.0	VF 8.0	VF/NM 9.0	NM- 9.2
1-4-Moench-s/Edwards-c/a						3.00

MOON KNIGHT (Volume 3)
Marvel Comics: Jan, 1999 - No. 4, Feb, 1999 ($2.99, limited series)

	GD 2.0	VG 4.0	FN 6.0	VF 8.0	VF/NM 9.0	NM- 9.2
1-4-Moench-s/Texeira-a(p)						3.00

MOON KNIGHT (Fourth series) (Leads into Vengeance of the Moon Knight)
Marvel Comics: June, 2006 - No. 30, Jul, 2009 ($2.99)

	GD 2.0	VG 4.0	FN 6.0	VF 8.0	VF/NM 9.0	NM- 9.2
1-Finch-a/c; Huston-s						4.00
1-B&W sketch variant-c						6.00
2-19,21-26: 7-Spider-Man app. 9,10-Punisher app. 13-Suydam-c begin. 23-25-Bullseye						3.00
20-($3.99) Deodato-a; back-up r/1st app. in Werewolf By Night #32,33						4.00
Annual 1 (1/08, $3.99) Swierczynski-s/Palo-a						4.00
...: Saga (2009, free) synopsis of origin and major storylines						3.00
...: Silent Knight 1 (1/09, $3.99) Milligan-s/Laurence Campbell-a/Crain-c						4.00

MOON KNIGHT (Fifth series)
Marvel Comics: Jul, 2011 - No. 12, Jun, 2012 ($3.99, limited series)

	GD 2.0	VG 4.0	FN 6.0	VF 8.0	VF/NM 9.0	NM- 9.2
1-Bendis-s/Maleev-a/c; Wolverine, Spider-Man and Capt. America "app."						4.00
2-12: 2-Echo returns. 3-Bullseye-c						4.00

MOON KNIGHT (Sixth series)
Marvel Comics: May, 2014 - No. 17, Sept, 2015 ($3.99)

	GD 2.0	VG 4.0	FN 6.0	VF 8.0	VF/NM 9.0	NM- 9.2
1-17: 1-6-Ellis-s/Shalvey-a. 7-12-Wood-s/Smallwood-a. 13-17-Bunn						4.00

MOON KNIGHT (Seventh series)
Marvel Comics: Jun, 2016 - Present ($4.99/$3.99)

	GD 2.0	VG 4.0	FN 6.0	VF 8.0	VF/NM 9.0	NM- 9.2
1-($4.99)-Lemire-s/Smallwood-a						5.00
2-12-($3.99) 5-9-Art by Smallwood, Stokoe, Torres, and Francavilla						4.00

MOON KNIGHT: DIVIDED WE FALL
Marvel Comics: 1992 ($4.95, 52 pgs.)

	GD 2.0	VG 4.0	FN 6.0	VF 8.0	VF/NM 9.0	NM- 9.2
nn-Denys Cowan-c/a(p)						5.00

MOON KNIGHT SPECIAL
Marvel Comics: Oct, 1992 ($2.50, 52 pgs.)

	GD 2.0	VG 4.0	FN 6.0	VF 8.0	VF/NM 9.0	NM- 9.2
1-Shang Chi, Master of Kung Fu-c/story						4.00

MOON KNIGHT SPECIAL EDITION
Marvel Comics Group: Nov, 1983 - No. 3, Jan, 1984 ($2.00, limited series, Baxter paper)

	GD 2.0	VG 4.0	FN 6.0	VF 8.0	VF/NM 9.0	NM- 9.2
1-3: Reprints from Hulk mag. by Sienkiewicz						4.00

MOON MULLINS (See Popular Comics, Super Book #3 & Super Comics)
Dell Publishing Co.: 1941 - 1945

	GD 2.0	VG 4.0	FN 6.0	VF 8.0	VF/NM 9.0	NM- 9.2
Four Color 14(1941)	48	96	144	302	514	725
Large Feature Comic 29(1941)	36	72	108	216	351	485
Four Color 31(1943)	15	30	45	105	233	360
Four Color 81(1945)	10	20	30	66	138	210

MOON MULLINS
Michel Publ. (American Comics Group)#1-6/St. John #7,8: Dec-Jan, 1947-48 - No. 8, Mar-May, 1949 (52 pgs)

	GD 2.0	VG 4.0	FN 6.0	VF 8.0	VF/NM 9.0	NM- 9.2
1-Alternating Sunday & daily strip-r	24	48	72	142	234	325
2	15	30	45	84	127	170
3-8: 7,8-St. John Publ. 7,8-…Featuring Kayo on-c	14	28	42	82	121	160

NOTE: ***Milt Gross*** *a-2-6, 8.* ***Frank Willard*** *r-all.*

MOON PILOT
Dell Publishing Co.: No. 1313, Mar-May, 1962

	GD 2.0	VG 4.0	FN 6.0	VF 8.0	VF/NM 9.0	NM- 9.2
Four Color 1313-Movie, photo-c	6	12	18	40	73	105

MOONSHADOW (Also see Farewell, Moonshadow)
Marvel Comics (Epic Comics): 5/85 - #12, 2/87 ($1.50/$1.75, mature)
(1st fully painted comic book)

	GD 2.0	VG 4.0	FN 6.0	VF 8.0	VF/NM 9.0	NM- 9.2
1-Origin; J. M. DeMatteis scripts & Jon J. Muth painted-c/a.						6.00
2-12: 11-Origin						4.00
Trade paperback (1987?)-r/#1-12						14.00
Signed & #ed HC ($39.95, 1,200 copies)-r/#1-12	4	8	12	27	44	60

MOONSHADOW
DC Comics (Vertigo): Oct, 1994 - No. 12, Aug, 1995 ($2.25/$2.95)

	GD 2.0	VG 4.0	FN 6.0	VF 8.0	VF/NM 9.0	NM- 9.2
1-11: Reprints Epic series.						3.00
12 ($2.95)-w/expanded ending						4.00
The Complete Moonshadow TPB ('98, $39.95) r/#1-12 and Farewell Moonshadow; new Muth painted-c						40.00

MOONSHINE
Image Comics: Oct, 2016 - Present ($3.99)

	GD 2.0	VG 4.0	FN 6.0	VF 8.0	VF/NM 9.0	NM- 9.2
1-5-Brian Azzarello-s/Eduardo Risso-a. 1-Covers by Risso & Frank Miller						4.00

MOON-SPINNERS, THE (See Movie Comics)

MOONSTONE MONSTERS
Moonstone: 2003 - 2005 ($2.95, B&W)

	GD 2.0	VG 4.0	FN 6.0	VF 8.0	VF/NM 9.0	NM- 9.2
...: Demons ($2.95) - Short stories by various; Frenz-c						3.00
...: Ghosts ($2.95) - Short stories by various; Frenz-c						3.00
...: Sea Creatures ($2.95) - Short stories by various; Frenz-c						3.00
...: Witches ($2.95) - Short stories by various; Frenz-c						3.00
...: Zombies ($2.95) - Short stories by various; Frenz-c						3.00
Volume 1 (2004, $16.95, TPB) r/short stories from series; Wolak-c						17.00

MOONSTONE NOIR
Moonstone: 2003 - 2004 ($2.95/$4.95/$5.50, B&W)

	GD 2.0	VG 4.0	FN 6.0	VF 8.0	VF/NM 9.0	NM- 9.2
...: Bulldog Drummond (2004, $4.95) - Messner-Loebs-s/Barkley-a						5.00
...: Johnny Dollar ($4.95) - Gallaher-s/Theriault-a						5.00
...: Mr. Keen, Tracer of Lost Persons 1,2 ($2.95, limited series) - Ferguson-a						3.00
...: Mysterious Traveler (2003, $5.50) - Trevor Von Eeden-a/Joe Gentile-s						5.50
...: Mysterious Traveler Returns (2004, $4.95) - Trevor Von Eeden-a/Joe Gentile-s						5.00
...: The Lone Wolf ($4.95) - Jolley-s/Croall-a						5.00

MOPSY (See Pageant of Comics & TV Teens)
St. John Publ. Co.: Feb, 1948 - No. 19, Sept, 1953

	GD 2.0	VG 4.0	FN 6.0	VF 8.0	VF/NM 9.0	NM- 9.2
1-Part-r; reprints "Some Punkins" by Neher	37	74	111	222	361	500
2	15	30	45	85	130	175
3-10(1953): 8-Lingerie panels	14	28	42	82	121	160
11-19: 19-Lingerie-c	14	28	42	76	108	140

NOTE: *#1-7, 13, 18, 19 have paper dolls.*

Morbius: The Living Vampire #25 © MAR

More Fun Comics #80 © DC

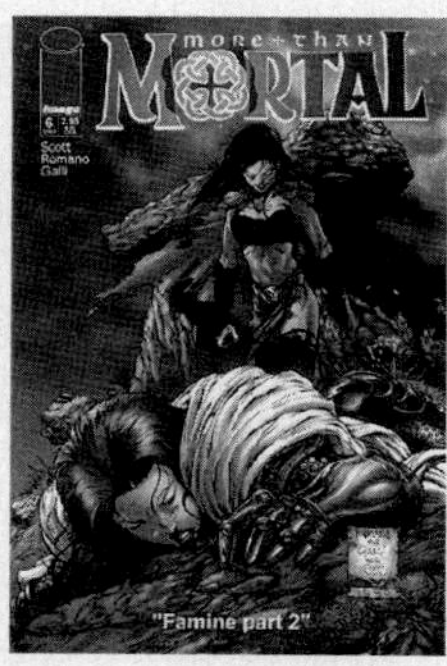

More Than Mortal #6 © Sharon Scott

GD 2.0 | VG 4.0 | FN 6.0 | VF 8.0 | VF/NM 9.0 | NM- 9.2

MORBIUS REVISITED
Marvel Comic: Aug, 1993 - No. 5, Dec, 1993 ($1.95, mini-series)

1-5-Reprints Fear #27-31 3.00

MORBIUS: THE LIVING VAMPIRE (Also see Amazing Spider-Man #101,102, Fear #20, Marvel Team-Up #3, 4, Midnight Sons Unl. & Vampire Tales)
Marvel Comics (Midnight Sons imprint #16 on): Sep, 1992 - No. 32, Apr, 1995 ($1.75/$1.95)

1-($2.75, 52 pgs.)-Polybagged w/poster; Ghost Rider & Johnny Blaze x-over (part 3 of Rise of the Midnight Sons) 4.00
2-11,13-24,26-32: 3,4-Vs. Spider-Man-c/s.15-Ghost Rider app. 16-Spot varnish-c. 16,17-Siege of Darkness, parts 5 &13. 18-Deathlok app. 21-Bound-in Spider-Man trading card sheet; Spider-Man app. 3.00
12-($2.25)-Outer-c is a Darkhold envelope made of black parchment w/gold ink; Midnight Massacre x-over 4.00
25-($2.50, 52 pgs.)-Gold foil logo 4.00

MORBIUS: THE LIVING VAMPIRE (Marvel NOW!)
Marvel Comics: Mar, 2013 - No. 9, Nov, 2013 ($2.99)

1-9: 1-Keatinge-s/Elson-a/Dell'Otto-c. 6,7-Superior Spider-Man app. 3.00

MORE FUN COMICS (Formerly New Fun Comics #1-6)
National Periodical Publs: No. 7, Jan, 1936 - No. 127, Nov-Dec, 1947 (No. 7,9-11: paper-c)

7(1/36)-Oversized, paper-c; 1 pg. Kelly-a 1000 2000 3000 8000 - -
8(2/36)-Oversized (10x12"), paper-c; 1 pg. Kelly-a; Sullivan-c 1000 2000 3000 8000 - -
9(3-4/36)(Very rare, 1st standard-sized comic book with original material)-Last multiple panel-c 1375 2750 4125 11,000 - -
10,11(7/36): 10-Last Henri Duval by Siegel & Shuster. 11-1st "Calling All Cars" by Siegel & Shuster; new classic logo begins 725 1450 2175 5800 - -
12(8/36)-Slick-c begin 550 1100 1650 4400 - -
V2#1(9/36, #13) 1 pg. Fred Astaire photo/bio 500 1000 1500 4000 - -
2(10/36, #14)-Dr. Occult in costume (1st in color)(Superman prototype; 1st DC appearance) continues from The Comics Magazine, ends #17 2000 4000 6000 16,000 - -
V2#3(11/36, #15), 17(V2#5) 825 1650 2475 6600 - -
16(V2#4)-Cover numbering begins; ties with New Comics #11 as 1st DC Christmas-c; last Superman tryout issue 900 1800 2700 7200 - -
18-20(V2#8, 5/37) 375 750 1125 3000 - -
21(V2#9)-24(V2#12, 9/37) 239 478 717 1530 2615 3700
25(V3#1, 10/37)-27(V3#3, 12/37): 27-Xmas-c 239 478 717 1530 2615 3700
28-30: 30-1st non-funny cover 232 464 696 1485 2543 3600
31-Has ad for Action Comics #1 290 580 870 1856 3178 4500
32-35: 32-Last Dr. Occult 206 412 618 1318 2259 3200
36-40: 36-(10/38)-The Masked Ranger & sidekick Pedro begins; Ginger Snap by Bob Kane (2 pgs.; 1st-a?). 39-Xmas-c 214 428 642 1284 2142 3000
41-50: 41-Last Masked Ranger. 43-Beany (1 pg.) and Ginger Snap centerfold by Bob Kane 187 374 561 1197 2049 2900
51-The Spectre app. (in costume) in one panel ad at end of Buccaneer story 530 1060 1590 3180 5840 8500
52-(2/40)-Origin/1st app. The Spectre (in costume splash panel only), part 1 by Bernard Baily (parts 1 & 2 written by Jerry Siegel; Spectre's costume changes color from purple & blue to green & grey; last Wing Brady; Spectre-c 10,000 20,000 30,000 70,000 125,000 180,000
53-Origin The Spectre (in costume at end of story), part 2; Capt. Desmo begins; Spectre-c 3300 6600 9900 23,000 53,500 84,000
54-The Spectre in costume; last King Carter; classic-Spectre-c 2000 4000 6000 14,000 27,000 40,000
55-(Scarce, 5/40)-Dr. Fate begins (1st app.); last Bulldog Martin; Spectre-c 1900 3800 5700 14,000 26,000 38,000
56-1st Dr. Fate-c (classic), origin continues. Congo Bill begins (6/40), 1st app.; 946 1892 2838 6906 12,203 17,500
57-60-All Spectre-c 486 972 1458 3550 6275 9000
61,65: 61-Classic Dr. Fate-c. 65-Classic Spectre-c 459 918 1377 3350 5925 8500
62-64,66: 63-Last Lt. Bob Neal. 64-Lance Larkin begins; all Spectre-c 343 686 1029 2400 4200 6000
67-(5/41)-Origin (1st) Dr. Fate; last Congo Bill & Biff Bronson (Congo Bill continues in Action Comics #37, 6/41)-Spectre-c 676 1352 2028 4935 8718 12,500
68-70: 68-Clip Carson begins. 70-Last Lance Larkin; all Dr. Fate-c 300 600 900 1950 3375 4800
71-Origin & 1st app. Johnny Quick by Mort Weisinger (9/41); classic sci/fi Dr. Fate-c 443 886 1329 3234 5717 8200
72-Dr. Fate's new helmet; last Sgt. Carey, Sgt. O'Malley & Captain Desmo; German submarine-c (Nazi war-c) 300 600 900 1920 3310 4700
73-Origin & 1st app. Aquaman (11/41) by Paul Norris; intro. Green Arrow & Speedy; Dr. Fate-c 10,000 20,000 30,000 65,000 90,000 115,000
74-2nd Aquaman; 1st Percival Popp, Supercop; Dr. Fate-c 649 1298 1947 4738 8369 12,000
75,76: 75-New origin Spectre; Nazi spy ring cover w/Hitler's photo. 76-Last Dr. Fate-c; Johnny Quick (by Meskin #76-97) begins, ends #107; last Clip Carson 300 600 900 1950 3375 4800
77-Green Arrow-c begin 226 452 678 1446 2473 3500
78-80 174 348 522 1114 1907 2700
81-83,85,88,90: 81-Last large logo. 82-1st small logo. 116 232 348 742 1271 1800
84-Green Arrow Japanese war-c 123 246 369 787 1344 1900
86,87-Johnny Quick-c. 87-Last Radio Squad 116 232 348 742 1271 1800
89-Origin Green Arrow & Speedy Team-up 129 258 387 826 1413 2000
91-97,99: 91-1st bi-monthly issue. 93-Dover & Clover begin (1st app., 9-10/43). 97-Kubert-a 87 174 261 553 952 1350
98-Last Dr. Fate (scarce) 100 200 300 635 1093 1550
100 (11-12/44)-Johnny Quick-c 94 188 282 597 1024 1450
101-Origin & 1st app. Superboy (1-2/45)(not by Siegel & Shuster); last Spectre issue; Green Arrow-c 838 1676 2514 6117 10,809 15,500
102-2nd Superboy app; 1st Dover & Clover-c 152 304 456 965 1658 2350
103-3rd Superboy app; last Green Arrow-c 110 220 330 704 1202 1700
104-1st Superboy-c w/Dover & Clover 97 194 291 621 1061 1500
105,106-Superboy-c 86 172 258 546 936 1325
107-Last Johnny Quick & Superboy 84 168 252 538 919 1300
108-120: 108-Genius Jones begins; 1st c-app. (3-4/46; cont'd from Adventure Comics #102) 28 56 84 165 270 375
121-124,126: 121-123,126-Post funny animal (Jimminy & the Magic Book)-c 26 52 78 154 252 350
125-Superman c-app.w/Jimminy 94 188 282 597 1024 1450
127-(Scarce)-Post-c/a 42 84 126 265 445 625

NOTE: *All issues are scarce to rare. Cover features: The Spectre-#52-55, 57-60, 62-67. Dr. Fate-#56, 61, 68-76. The Green Arrow & Speedy-#77-85, 88-97, 99, 101 (w/Dover & Clover-#98, 103). Johnny Quick-#86, 87, 100. Dover & Clover-#102, (104, 106 w/Superboy), 107, 108(w/Genius Jones), 110, 112, 114, 117, 119. Genius Jones-#109, 111, 113, 115, 116, 118, 120.* ***Baily*** *a-45, 52-on; c-52-55, 57-60, 62-67.* ***Al Capp*** *a-45(signed Koppy).* ***Ellsworth*** *c-7.* ***Creig Flessel*** *c-30, 31, 35-48(most).* ***Guardineer*** *c-47, 49, 50.* ***Kiefer*** *a-20.* ***Meskin*** *c-86, 87, 100?* ***Moldoff*** *c-51.* ***George Papp*** *c-77-85.* ***Post*** *c-121-127.* ***Vincent Sullivan*** *c-8-28, 32-34.*

MORE FUND COMICS (Benefit book for the Comic Book Legal Defense Fund)
(Also see Even More Fund Comics)
Sky Dog Press: Sept, 2003 ($10.00, B&W, trade paperback)

nn-Anthology of short stories and pin-ups by various; Hulk-c by Pérez 10.00

MORE SEYMOUR (See Seymour My Son)
Archie Publications: Oct, 1963

1-DeCarlo-a? 3 6 9 21 33 45

MORE THAN MORTAL (Also see Lady Pendragon/...)
Liar Comics: June, 1997 - No. 4, Apr, 1998 ($2.95, limited series)
Image Comics: No. 5, Dec, 1999 - No. 6, Mar, 2000 ($2.95)

1-Blue forest background-c, 1-Variant-c 4.00
1-White-c 6.00
1-2nd printing; purple sky cover 3.00
2-4: 3-Silvestri-c, 4-Two-c, one by Randy Queen 3.00
5,6: 5-1st Image Comics issue 3.00

MORE THAN MORTAL: OTHERWORLDS
Image Comics: July, 1999 - No. 4, Dec, 1999 ($2.95, limited series)

1-4-Firchow-a. 1-Two covers 3.00

MORE THAN MORTAL SAGAS
Liar Comics: Jun, 1998 - No. 3, Dec, 1998 ($2.95, limited series)

1,2-Painted art by Romano. 2-Two-c, one by Firchow 3.00
1-Variant-c by Linsner 5.00

MORE THAN MORTAL TRUTHS AND LEGENDS
Liar Comics: Aug, 1998 - No. 6, Apr, 1999 ($2.95)

1-6-Firchow-a(p) 3.00
1-Variant-c by Dan Norton 4.50

MORE TRASH FROM MAD (Annual)
E. C. Comics: 1958 - No. 12, 1969
(Note: Bonus missing = half price)

nn(1958)-8 pgs. color Mad reprint from #20 16 32 48 112 249 385
2(1959)-Market Product Labels 11 22 33 76 163 250
3(1960)-Text book covers 10 20 30 69 147 225
4(1961)-Sing Along with Mad booklet 10 20 30 69 147 225
5(1962)-Window Stickers; r/from Mad #39 8 16 24 54 102 150
6(1963)-TV Guise booklet 8 16 24 54 102 150
7(1964)-Alfred E. Neuman commemorative stamps 7 14 21 44 82 120
8(1965)-Life size poster-Alfred E. Neuman 5 10 15 35 63 90

Morning Glories #50 © Spencer & Eisma

Mosaic #2 © MAR

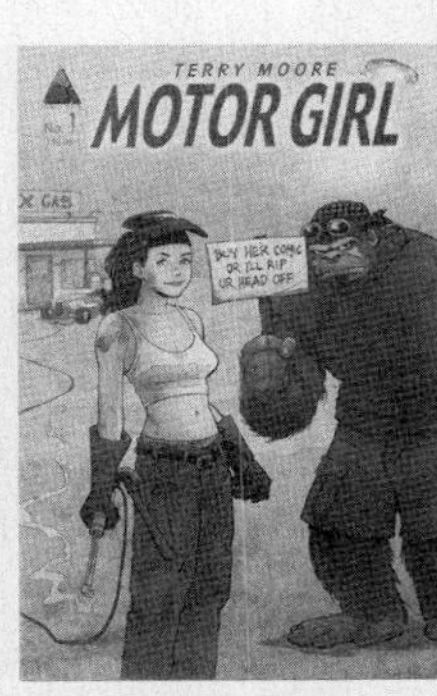

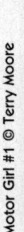

Motor Girl #1 © Terry Moore

GD 2.0 | VG 4.0 | FN 6.0 | VF 8.0 | VF/NM 9.0 | NM- 9.2

9-12: 9,10(1966-67)-Mischief Sticker. 11(1968)-Campaign poster & bumper sticker.
12(1969)-Pocket medals 5 10 15 35 63 90
NOTE: *Kelly Freas c-1, 2, 4. Mingo c-3, 5-9, 12.*

MORGAN THE PIRATE (Movie)
Dell Publishing Co.: No. 1227, Sept-Nov, 1961
Four Color 1227-Photo-c 6 12 18 42 79 115

MORLOCKS
Marvel Comics: June, 2002 - No. 4, Sept, 2002 ($2.50, limited series)
1-4-Johns-s/Martinbrough-c/a. 1-1st app. Angel Dust 3.00

MORLOCK 2001
Atlas/Seaboard Publ.: Feb, 1975 - No. 3, July, 1975
1,2: 1-(Super-hero)-Origin & 1st app.; Milgrom-c 2 4 6 11 16 20
3-Ditko/Wrightson-a; origin The Midnight Man & The Mystery Men
3 6 9 15 22 28

MORNING GLORIES
Image Comics: Aug, 2010 - Present ($3.99/$3.50/$2.99)
1-($3.99) Nick Spencer-s/Joe Eisma-a/Rodin Esquejo-c; group cover 10.00
1-Second-Fourth printings 4.00
2-($3.50) Regular cover and white background 2nd printing 5.00
3-6-Regular covers and white background 2nd printings 4.00
7-23-($2.99) 3.00
24,25,27,28-($3.99) 4.00
26-($1.00) Start of Season Two 3.00
29-48-($3.50) 3.50
49-($4.99) Spencer-s/Eisma-a 5.00
50-(7/16, $5.99) 6.00
...Vol. 1 TPB (2/11, $9.99) r/#1-6 10.00

MORNINGSTAR SPECIAL
Comico: Apr, 1990 ($2.50)
1-From the Elementals; Willingham-c/a/scripts 3.00

MORTAL KOMBAT
Malibu Comics: July, 1994 - No. 6, Dec, 1994 ($2.95)
1-6: 1-Two diff. covers exist 3.00
1-Limited edition gold foil embossed-c 4.00
0 (12/94), Special Edition 1 (11/94) 3.00
Tournament Edition I12/94, $3.95), II('95)($3.95) 4.00
...: **BARAKA** ,June, 1995 ($2.95, one-shot) #1; ...**BATTLEWAVE** ,2/95 - No. 6, 7/95 , #1-6; ...**GORO, PRINCE OF PAIN** ,9/94 - No. 3, 11/94, #1-3; ...**KITANA AND MILEENA** ,8/95 , ...**KUNG LAO** ,7/95 , #1; ... **RAYDON & KANO** ,3/95 - No. 3, 5/95, #1-3: ...(all $2.95-c) 3.00
...: **U.S. SPECIAL FORCES** ,1/95 - No. 2, ($3.50), #1,2 3.50

MORTAL KOMBAT X
DC Comics: Mar, 2015 - No. 12, Jan, 2016 ($3.99, printings of digital-first stories)
1-12: 1-Kittelsen-s/Soy-a/Reis-c. 9-12-Jae Lee-c 4.00

MORTIE (Mazie's Friend; also see Flat-Top)
Magazine Publishers: Dec, 1952 - No. 4, June, 1953?
1 11 22 33 62 86 110
2-4 7 14 21 37 46 55

MORTIGAN GOTH: IMMORTALIS (See Marvel Frontier Comics Unlimited)
Marvel Comics: Sept, 1993 - No. 4, Mar, 1994 ($1.95, mini-series)
1-($2.95)-Foil-c 4.00
2-4 3.00

MORT THE DEAD TEENAGER
Marvel Comics: Nov, 1993 - No. 4, Mar, 1994 ($1.75, mini-series)
1-4 3.00

MORTY MEEKLE
Dell Publishing Co.: No. 793, May, 1957
Four Color 793 5 10 15 30 50 70

MOSAIC
Marvel Comics: Dec, 2016 - Present ($4.99/$3.99)
1-($4.99) Geoffrey Thorne-s/Khary Randolph-a; intro. Morris Sackett 5.00
2-5-($3.99) 3,4-Spider-Man app. 4.00

MOSES & THE TEN COMMANDMENTS (See Dell Giants)

MOSTLY WANTED
DC Comics (WildStorm): Jul, 2000 - No. 4, Nov, 2000 ($2.50, limited series)
1-4-Lobdell-s/Flores-a 3.00

MOTEL HELL (Based on the 1980 movie)
IDW Publishing: Oct, 2010 - No. 3, Dec, 2010 ($3.99, limited series)
1-3-Matt Nixon-s/Chris Moreno-a. 1,2-Bradstreet-c. 3-Moreno-c 4.00

MOTH, THE
Dark Horse Comics: Apr, 2004 - No. 4, Aug, 2004 ($2.99)
1-4-Steve Rude-c/a; Gary Martin-s 3.00
... Special (3/04, $4.95) 5.00
TPB (5/05, $12.95) r/#1-4 and Special; gallery of extras 13.00

MOTH, THE
Rude Dude Productions: May 2008 (Free Comic Book Day giveaway)
... Special Edition - Steve Rude-s/a; sketch pages 3.00

MOTHER GOOSE AND NURSERY RHYME COMICS (See Christmas With Mother Goose)
Dell Publishing Co.: No. 41, 1944 - No. 862, Nov, 1957
Four Color 41-Walt Kelly-c/a 21 42 63 147 324 500
Four Color 59, 68-Kelly c/a 17 34 51 117 259 400
Four Color 862-The Truth About..., Movie (Disney) 7 14 21 44 82 120

MOTHER PANIC
DC Comics (Young Animal): Jan, 2017 - Present ($3.99)
1-3: 1-Houser-s/Edwards-a; Batman cameo. 3-Batman & Batwoman app. 4.00

MOTHER TERESA OF CALCUTTA
Marvel Comics Group: 1984
1-(52 pgs.) No ads 1 3 4 6 8 10

MOTION PICTURE COMICS (See Fawcett Movie Comics)
Fawcett Publications: No. 101, 1950 - No. 114, Jan, 1953 (All-photo-c)
101- "Vanishing Westerner"; Monte Hale (1950) 15 30 45 90 140 190
102- "Code of the Silver Sage"; Rocky Lane (1/51) 15 30 45 83 124 165
103- "Covered Wagon Raid"; Rocky Lane (3/51) 15 30 45 83 124 165
104- "Vigilante Hideout"; Rocky Lane (5/51)-Book length Powell-a
15 30 45 83 124 165
105- "Red Badge of Courage"; Audie Murphy; Bob Powell-a (7/51)
18 36 54 105 165 225
106- "The Texas Rangers"; George Montgomery (9/51)
15 30 45 83 124 165
107- "Frisco Tornado"; Rocky Lane (11/51) 14 28 42 80 115 150
108- "Mask of the Avenger"; John Derek 12 24 36 69 97 125
109- "Rough Rider of Durango"; Rocky Lane 14 28 42 80 115 150
110- "When Worlds Collide"; George Evans-a (5/52); Williamson & Evans drew themselves in story; (also see Famous Funnies No. 72-88) 77 154 231 493 847 1200
111- "The Vanishing Outpost"; Lash LaRue 15 30 45 90 140 190
112- "Brave Warrior"; Jon Hall & Jay Silverheels 12 24 36 67 94 120
113- "Walk East on Beacon"; George Murphy; Schaffenberger-a
10 20 30 54 72 90
114- "Cripple Creek"; George Montgomery (1/53) 10 20 30 58 79 100

MOTION PICTURE FUNNIES WEEKLY (See Promotional Comics section)

MOTOR CRUSH
Image Comics: Dec, 2016 - Present ($3.99)
1-3-Fletcher & Stewart-s/Tarr-a; covers by Tarr & Stewart 4.00

MOTOR GIRL
Abstract Studio: 2016 - Present ($3.99)
1-4-Terry Moore-s/a/c 4.00

MOTORHEAD (See Comic's Greatest World)
Dark Horse Comics: Aug, 1995 - No. 6, Jan, 1996 ($2.50)
1-6: Bisley-c on all. 1-Predator app. 3.00
Special 1 (3/94, $3.95, 52pgs.)-Jae Lee-c; Barb Wire, The Machine & Wolf Gang app. 4.00

MOTORMOUTH (... & Killpower #7? on)
Marvel Comics UK: June, 1992 - No. 12, May, 1993 ($1.75)
1-13: 1,2-Nick Fury app. 3-Punisher-c/story. 5,6-Nick Fury & Punisher app. 6-Cable cameo. 7-9-Cable app. 3.00

MOUNTAIN MEN (See Ben Bowie)

MOUSE MUSKETEERS (See M.G.M.'s...)

MOUSE ON THE MOON, THE (See Movie Classics)

MOVEMENT, THE
DC Comics: Jul, 2013 - No. 12, Jul. 2014 ($2.99)
1-12: 1-Gail Simone-s/Freddie Williams-a/Amanda Conner-c. 2-4-Rainmaker app. 9,10-Batgirl app. 3.00

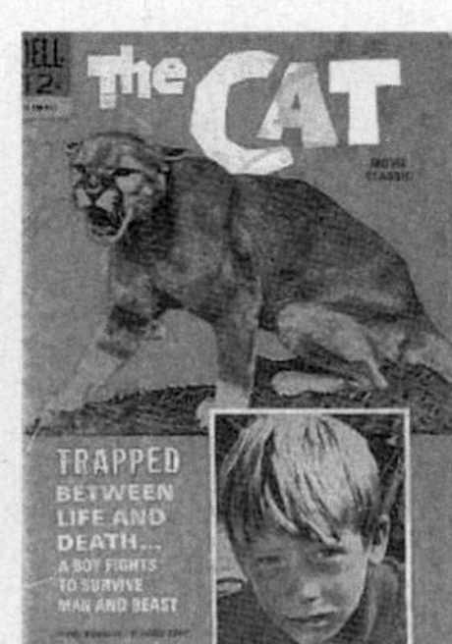

Movie Classics - The Cat © DELL

Movie Classics - Mad Monster Party © DELL

Movie Comics #6 © DC

	GD 2.0	VG 4.0	FN 6.0	VF 8.0	VF/NM 9.0	NM- 9.2

MOVIE CARTOONS
DC Comics: Dec, 1944 (cover only ashcan)

nn-Ashcan comic, not distributed to newsstands, only for in house use. Covers were produced, but not the rest of the book. A copy sold in 2006 for $500.

MOVIE CLASSICS
Dell Publishing Co.: Apr, 1956; May-Jul, 1962 - Dec, 1969

(Before 1963, most movie adaptations were part of the 4-Color series)
(Disney movie adaptations after 1970 are in Walt Disney Showcase)

Title	GD	VG	FN	VF	VF/NM	NM-
Around the World Under the Sea 12-030-612 (12/66)	3	6	9	19	30	40
Bambi 3(4/56)-Disney; r/4-Color #186	4	8	12	23	37	50
Battle of the Bulge 12-056-606 (6/66)	3	6	9	20	31	42
Beach Blanket Bingo 12-058-509	6	12	18	40	73	105
Bon Voyage 01-068-212 (12/62)-Disney; photo-c	3	6	9	21	33	45
Castilian, The 12-110-401	3	6	9	19	30	40
Cat, The 12-109-612 (12/66)	3	6	9	18	28	38
Cheyenne Autumn 12-112-506 (4-6/65)	5	10	15	31	53	75
Circus World, Samuel Bronston's 12-115-411; John Wayne app.; John Wayne photo-c	9	18	27	58	114	170
Countdown 12-150-710 (10/67)-James Caan photo-c	3	6	9	20	31	42
Creature, The 1 (12-142-302) (12-2/62-63)	9	18	27	58	114	170
Creature, The 12-142-410 (10/64)	5	10	15	30	50	70
David Ladd's Life Story 12-173-212 (10-12/62)-Photo-c	6	12	18	40	73	105
Die, Monster, Die 12-175-603 (3/66)-Photo-c	5	10	15	33	57	80
Dirty Dozen 12-180-710 (10/67)	4	8	12	27	44	60
Dr. Who & the Daleks 12-190-612 (12/66)-Peter Cushing photo-c; 1st U.S. app. of Dr. Who	11	22	33	76	163	250
Dracula 12-231-212 (10-12/62)	8	16	24	56	108	160
El Dorado 12-240-710 (10/67)-John Wayne; photo-c	10	20	30	66	138	210
Ensign Pulver 12-257-410 (8-10/64)	3	6	9	18	28	38
Frankenstein 12-283-305 (3-5/63)(see Frankenstein 8-10/64 for 2nd printing)	9	18	27	57	111	165
Great Race, The 12-299-603 (3/66)-Natallie Wood, Tony Curtis photo-c	4	8	12	27	44	60
Hallelujah Trail, The 12-307-602 (2/66) (Shows 1/66 inside); Burt Lancaster, Lee Remick photo-c	5	10	15	30	50	70
Hatari 12-340-301 (1/63)-John Wayne	7	14	21	44	82	120
Horizontal Lieutenant, The 01-348-210 (10/62)	3	6	9	18	28	38
Incredible Mr. Limpet, The 12-370-408; Don Knotts photo-c	5	10	15	30	50	70
Jack the Giant Killer 12-374-301 (1/63)	7	14	21	44	82	120
Jason & the Argonauts 12-376-310 (8-10/63)-Photo-c	8	16	24	54	102	150
Lancelot & Guinevere 12-416-310 (10/63)	5	10	15	30	50	70
Lawrence 12-426-308 (8/63)-Story of Lawrence of Arabia; movie ad on back-c; not exactly like movie	5	10	15	30	50	70
Lion of Sparta 12-439-301 (1/63)	3	6	9	21	33	45
Mad Monster Party 12-460-801 (9/67)-Based on Kurtzman's screenplay	8	16	24	51	96	140
Magic Sword, The 01-496-209 (9/62)	5	10	15	31	53	75
Masque of the Red Death 12-490-410 (8-10/64)-Vincent Price photo-c	5	10	15	35	63	90
Maya 12-495-612 (12/66)-Clint Walker & Jay North part photo-c	4	8	12	23	37	50
McHale's Navy 12-500-412 (10-12/64)	4	8	12	27	44	60
Merrill's Marauders 12-510-301 (1/63)-Photo-c	3	6	9	18	28	38
Mouse on the Moon, The 12-530-312 (10/12/63)-Photo-c	3	6	9	21	33	45
Mummy, The 12-537-211 (9-11/62) 2 versions with different back-c	9	18	27	58	114	170
Music Man, The 12-538-301 (1/63)	3	6	9	19	30	40
Naked Prey, The 12-545-612 (12/66)-Photo-c	5	10	15	31	53	75
Night of the Grizzly, The 12-558-612 (12/66)-Photo-c	3	6	9	21	33	45
None But the Brave 12-565-506 (4-6/65)	5	10	15	31	53	75
Operation Bikini 12-597-310 (10/63)-Photo-c	3	6	9	19	30	40
Operation Crossbow 12-590-512 (10-12/65)	3	6	9	19	30	40
Prince & the Pauper, The 01-654-207 (5-7/62)-Disney	3	6	9	21	33	45
Raven, The 12-680-309 (9/63)-Vincent Price photo-c	6	12	18	37	66	95
Ring of Bright Water 01-701-910 (10/69) (inside shows #12-701-909)	3	6	9	21	33	45
Runaway, The 12-707-412 (10-12/64)	3	6	9	18	28	38
Santa Claus Conquers the Martians #? (1964)-Photo-c	9	18	27	58	114	170
Santa Claus Conquers the Martians 12-725-603 (3/66, 12¢)-Reprints 1964 issue; photo-c	6	12	18	40	73	105
Another version given away with a Golden Record, SLP 170, nn, no price (3/66)-Complete with record	10	20	30	69	147	225
Six Black Horses 12-750-301 (1/63)-Photo-c	3	6	9	19	30	40
Ski Party 12-743-511 (9-11/65)-Frankie Avalon photo-c; photo inside-c; Adkins-a	4	8	12	28	47	65
Smoky 12-746-702 (2/67)	3	6	9	18	28	38
Sons of Katie Elder 12-748-511 (9-11/65); John Wayne app.; photo-c	10	20	30	66	138	210
Tales of Terror 12-793-302 (2/63)-Evans-a	5	10	15	31	53	75
Three Stooges Meet Hercules 01-828-208 (8/62)-Photo-c	8	16	24	51	96	140
Tomb of Ligeia 12-830-506 (4-6/65)	5	10	15	31	53	75
Treasure Island 01-845-211 (7-9/62)-Disney; r/4-Color #624	3	6	9	19	30	40
Twice Told Tales (Nathaniel Hawthorne) 12-840-401 (11-1/63-64); Vincent Price photo-c	5	10	15	33	57	80
Two on a Guillotine 12-850-506 (4-6/65)	3	6	9	21	33	45
Valley of Gwangi 01-880-912 (12/69)	8	16	24	52	99	145
War Gods of the Deep 12-900-509 (7-9/65)	3	6	9	19	30	40
War Wagon, The 12-533-709 (9/67); John Wayne app.	7	14	21	48	89	130
Who's Minding the Mint? 12-924-708 (8/67)	3	6	9	18	28	38
Wolfman, The 12-922-308 (6-8/63)	8	16	24	56	108	160
Wolfman, The 1(12-922-410)(8-10/64)-2nd printing; r/#12-922-308	4	8	12	22	35	48
Zulu 12-950-410 (8-10/64)-Photo-c	6	12	18	41	76	110

MOVIE COMICS (See Cinema Comics Herald & Fawcett Movie Comics)

MOVIE COMICS
National Periodical Publications/Picture Comics: April, 1939 - No. 6, Sept-Oct, 1939 (Most all photo-c)

Issue	GD	VG	FN	VF	VF/NM	NM-
1- "Gunga Din", "Son of Frankenstein", "The Great Man Votes", "Fisherman's Wharf", & "Scouts to the Rescue" part 1; Wheelan "Minute Movies" begin	366	732	1098	2562	4481	6400
2- "Stagecoach", "The Saint Strikes Back", "King of the Turf","Scouts to the Rescue" part 2, "Arizona Legion", Andy Devine photo-c	258	516	774	1651	2826	4000
3- "East Side of Heaven", "Mystery in the White Room", "Four Feathers", "Mexican Rose" with Gene Autry, "Spirit of Culver", "Many Secrets", "The Mikado" (1st Gene Autry photo cover)	194	388	582	1242	2121	3000
4- "Captain Fury", Gene Autry in "Blue Montana Skies", "Streets of N.Y." with Jackie Cooper, "Oregon Trail" part 1 with Johnny Mack Brown, "Big Town Czar" with Barton MacLane, & "Star Reporter" with Warren Hull	148	296	444	947	1624	2300
5- "The Man in the Iron Mask", "Five Came Back", "Wolf Call", "The Girl & the Gambler", "The House of Fear", "The Family Next Door", "Oregon Trail" part 2	161	322	483	1030	1765	2500
6- "The Phantom Creeps", "Chumps at Oxford", & "The Oregon Trail" part 3; 2nd Robot-c	226	452	678	1446	2473	3500

NOTE: *Above books contain many original movie stills with dialogue from movie scripts. All issues are scarce.*

MOVIE COMICS
Fiction House Magazines: Dec, 1946 - No. 4, 1947

Issue	GD	VG	FN	VF	VF/NM	NM-
1-Big Town (by Lubbers), Johnny Danger begin; Celardo-a; Mitzi of the Movies by Fran Hopper	41	82	123	256	428	600
2-(2/47)- "White Tie & Tails" with William Bendix; Mitzi of the Movies begins; Matt Baker-a	31	62	93	186	303	420
3-(6/47)-Andy Hardy starring Mickey Rooney	31	62	93	186	303	420
4-Mitzi In Hollywood by Matt Baker; Merton of the Movies with Red Skelton; Yvonne DeCarlo & George Brent in "Slave Girl"	39	78	117	231	378	525

MOVIE COMICS
Gold Key/Whitman: Oct, 1962 - 1984

Title	GD	VG	FN	VF	VF/NM	NM-
Alice in Wonderland 10144-503 (3/65)-Disney; partial reprint of 4-Color #331	3	6	9	21	33	45
Alice In Wonderland #1 (Whitman pre-pack, 3/84)	2	4	6	10	14	18
Aristocats, The 1 (30045-103)(3/71)-Disney; with pull-out poster (25¢) (No poster = half price)	6	12	18	40	73	105
Bambi 1 (10087-309)(9/63)-Disney; r/4-C #186	4	8	12	23	37	50
Bambi 2 (10087-607)(7/66)-Disney; r/4-C #186	3	6	9	19	30	40
Beneath the Planet of the Apes 30044-012 (12/70)-with pull-out poster; photo-c (No poster = half price)	8	16	24	54	102	150
Big Red 10026-211 (11/62)-Disney; photo-c	3	6	9	19	30	40
Big Red 10026-503 (3/65)-Disney; reprints 10026-211; photo-c						

Movie Comics - Bullwhip Griffin © DIS

Movie Comics - Lt. Robin Crusoe © DIS

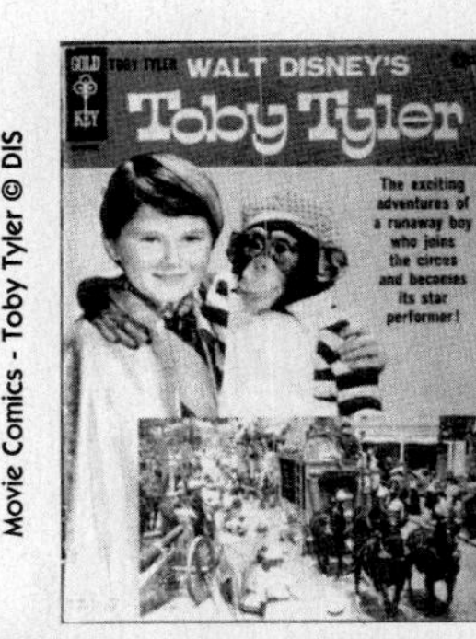

Movie Comics - Toby Tyler © DIS

GD 2.0 | VG 4.0 | FN 6.0 | VF 8.0 | VF/NM 9.0 | NM- 9.2

3 6 9 16 23 30
Blackbeard's Ghost 10222-806 (6/68)-Disney 3 6 9 18 28 38
Bullwhip Griffin 10181-706 (6/67)-Disney; Spiegle-a; photo-c
3 6 9 21 33 45
Captain Sindbad 10077-309 (9/63)-Manning-a; photo-c
5 10 15 35 63 90
Chitty Chitty Bang Bang 1 (30038-902)(2/69)-with pull-out poster; Disney; photo-c
(No poster = half price) 6 12 18 37 66 95
Cinderella 10152-508 (8/65)-Disney; r/4-C #786 4 8 12 25 40 55
Darby O'Gill & the Little People 10251-001(1/70)-Disney; reprints 4-Color #1024 (Toth-a); photo-c 4 8 12 28 47 65
Dumbo 1 (10090-310)(10/63)-Disney; r/4-C #668 3 6 9 20 31 42
Emil & the Detectives 10120-502 (11/64)-Disney; photo-c & back-c photo pin-up
3 6 9 19 30 40
Escapade in Florence 1 (10043-301)(1/63)-Disney; starring Annette Funicello
7 14 21 44 82 120
Fall of the Roman Empire 10118-407 (7/64); Sophia Loren photo-c
4 8 12 23 37 50
Fantastic Voyage 10178-702 (2/67)-Wood/Adkins-a; photo-c
5 10 15 33 57 80
55 Days at Peking 10081-309 (9/63)-Photo-c 3 6 9 19 30 40
Fighting Prince of Donegal, The 10193-701 (1/67)-Disney
3 6 9 18 28 38
First Men in the Moon 10132-503 (3/65)-Fred Fredericks-a; photo-c
4 8 12 23 37 50
Gay Purr-ee 30017-301(1/63, 84 pgs.) 5 10 15 30 50 70
Gnome Mobile, The 10207-710 (10/67)-Disney; Walter Brennan photo-c & back-c photo pin-up
4 8 12 21 33 45
Goodbye, Mr. Chips 10246-006 (6/70)-Peter O'Toole photo-c
3 6 9 19 30 40
Happiest Millionaire, The 10221-804 (4/68)-Disney 3 6 9 21 33 45
Hey There, It's Yogi Bear 10122-409 (9/64)-Hanna-Barbera
6 12 18 37 66 95
Horse Without a Head, The 10109-401 (1/64)-Disney 3 6 9 18 28 38
How the West Was Won 10074-307 (7/63)-Based on the L'Amour novel; Tufts-a
4 8 12 27 44 60
In Search of the Castaways 10048-303 (3/63)-Disney; Hayley Mills photo-c
6 12 18 37 66 95
Jungle Book, The 1 (6022-801)(1/68-Whitman)-Disney; large size (10x13-1/2"); 59¢
6 12 18 37 66 95
Jungle Book, The 1 (30033-803)(3/68, 68 pgs.)-Disney; same contents as Whitman #1
4 8 12 23 37 50
Jungle Book, The 1 (6/78, $1.00 tabloid) 3 6 9 16 23 30
Jungle Book (7/84)-r/Giant; Whitman pre-pack 2 4 6 10 14 18
Kidnapped 10080-306 (6/63)-Disney; reprints 4-Color #1101; photo-c
3 6 9 19 30 40
King Kong 30036-809(9/68-68 pgs.)-painted-c 4 8 12 25 40 55
King Kong nn-Whitman Treasury($1.00, 68 pgs.,1968), same cover as Gold Key issue
5 10 15 31 53 75
King Kong 11299(#1-786, 10x13-1/4", 68 pgs., $1.00, 1978)
3 6 9 17 26 35
Lady and the Tramp 10042-301 (1/63)-Disney; r/4-Color #629
3 6 9 20 31 42
Lady and the Tramp 1 (1967-Giant; 25¢)-Disney; reprints part of Dell #1
5 10 15 31 53 75
Lady and the Tramp 2 (10042-203)(3/72)-Disney; r/4-Color #629
3 6 9 16 23 30
Legend of Lobo, The 1 (10059-303)(3/63)-Disney; photo-c
3 6 9 16 23 30
Lt. Robin Crusoe, U.S.N. 10191-610 (10/66)-Disney; Dick Van Dyke photo-c & back-c photo pin-up 3 6 9 17 26 35
Lion, The 10035-301 (1/63)-Photo-c 3 6 9 16 24 32
Lord Jim 10156-509 (9/65)-Photo-c 3 6 9 16 24 32
Love Bug, The 10237-906 (6/69)-Disney; Buddy Hackett photo-c
4 8 12 21 33 45
Mary Poppins 10136-501 (1/65)-Disney; photo-c 5 10 15 30 50 70
Mary Poppins 30023-501 (1/65-68 pgs.)-Disney; photo-c
6 12 18 41 76 110
McLintock 10110-403 (3/64); John Wayne app.; John Wayne & Maureen O'Hara photo-c
10 20 30 66 138 210
Merlin Jones as the Monkey's Uncle 10115-510 (10/65)-Disney; Annette Funicello front/back photo-c 5 10 15 34 60 85
Miracle of the White Stallions, The 10065-306 (6/63)-Disney
3 6 9 18 28 38

GD 2.0 | VG 4.0 | FN 6.0 | VF 8.0 | VF/NM 9.0 | NM- 9.2

Misadventures of Merlin Jones, The 10115-405 (5/64)-Disney; Annette Funicello photo front/back-c 5 10 15 34 60 85
Moon-Spinners, The 10124-410 (10/64)-Disney; Hayley Mills photo-c
6 12 18 37 66 95
Mutiny on the Bounty 1 (10040-302)(2/63)-Marlon Brando photo-c
3 6 9 21 33 45
Nikki, Wild Dog of the North 10141-412 (12/64)-Disney; reprints 4-Color #1226
3 6 9 16 23 30
Old Yeller 10168-601 (1/66)-Disney; reprints 4-Color #869; photo-c
3 6 9 16 23 30
One Hundred & One Dalmations 1 (10247-002) (2/70)-Disney; reprints Four Color #1183
3 6 9 17 26 35
Peter Pan 1 (10086-309)(9/63)-Disney; reprints Four Color #442
3 6 9 20 31 42
Peter Pan 2 (10086-909)(9/69)-Disney; reprints Four Color #442
3 6 9 16 23 30
Peter Pan 1 (3/84)-r/4-Color #442; Whitman pre-pack 2 4 6 11 16 20
P.T. 109 10123-409 (9/64)-John F. Kennedy 4 8 12 28 47 65
Rio Conchos 10143-503(3/65) 3 6 9 21 33 45
Robin Hood 10163-506 (6/65)-Disney; reprints Four Color #413
3 6 9 16 24 32
Shaggy Dog & the Absent-Minded Professor 30032-708 (8/67-Giant, 68 pgs.) Disney; reprints 4-Color #985,1199 5 10 15 30 50 70
Sleeping Beauty 1 (30042-009)(9/70)-Disney; reprints Four Color #973; with pull-out poster
(No poster = half price) 6 12 18 37 66 95
Snow White & the Seven Dwarfs 1 (10091-310)(10/63)-Disney; reprints Four Color #382
3 6 9 19 30 40
Snow White & the Seven Dwarfs 10091-709 (9/67)-Disney; reprints Four Color #382
3 6 9 16 23 30
Snow White & the Seven Dwarfs 90091-204 (2/84)-Reprints Four Color #382; Whitman pre-pack 2 4 6 11 16 20
Son of Flubber 1 (10057-304)(4/63)-Disney; sequel to "The Absent-Minded Professor"
3 6 9 21 33 45
Summer Magic 10076-309 (9/63)-Disney; Hayley Mills photo-c; Manning-a
6 12 18 37 66 95
Swiss Family Robinson 10236-904 (4/69)-Disney; reprints Four Color #1156; photo-c
3 6 9 17 26 35
Sword in the Stone, The 30019-402 (2/64-Giant, 68 pgs.)-Disney (see March of Comics #258 & Wart and the Wizard 6 12 18 37 66 95
That Darn Cat 10171-602 (2/66)-Disney; Hayley Mills photo-c
6 12 18 37 66 95
Those Magnificent Men in Their Flying Machines 10162-510 (10/65); photo-c
3 6 9 19 30 40
Three Stooges in Orbit 30016-211 (11/62-Giant, 32 pgs.)-All photos from movie; stiff-photo-c
8 16 24 56 108 160
Tiger Walks, A 10117-406 (6/64)-Disney; Torres?, Tufts-a; photo-c
4 8 12 23 37 50
Toby Tyler 10142-502 (2/65)-Disney; reprints Four Color #1092; photo-c
3 6 9 17 26 35
Treasure Island 1 (10200-703)(3/67)-Disney; reprints Four Color #624; photo-c
3 6 9 16 23 30
20,000 Leagues Under the Sea 1 (10095-312)(12/63)-Disney; reprints Four Color #614
3 6 9 17 26 35
Wonderful Adventures of Pinocchio, The 1 (10089-310)(10/63)-Disney; reprints Four Color #545 (see Wonderful Advs. of...) 3 6 9 20 31 42
Wonderful Adventures of Pinocchio, The 10089-109 (9/71)-Disney; reprints Four Color #545
3 6 9 16 23 30
Wonderful World of the Brothers Grimm 1 (10008-210)(10/62)
4 8 12 27 44 60
X, the Man with the X-Ray Eyes 10083-309 (9/63)-Ray Milland photo on-c
6 12 18 41 76 110
Yellow Submarine 35000-902 (2/69-Giant, 68 pgs.)-With pull-out poster;
The Beatles cartoon movie; Paul S. Newman-s 23 46 69 161 356 550
Without poster 10 20 30 64 132 200

MOVIE FABLES
DC Comics: Dec, 1944 (cover only ashcan)
nn-Ashcan comic, not distributed to newsstands, only for in house use. Covers were produced, but not the rest of the book. A copy sold in 2006 for $500.

MOVIE GEMS
DC Comics: Dec, 1944 (cover only ashcan)
nn-Ashcan comic, not distributed to newsstands, only for in house use. Covers were produced, but not the rest of the book. A copy sold in 2006 for $500.

MOVIE LOVE (Also see Personal Love)

Movie Love #17 © FF

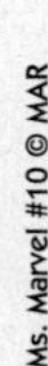
Ms. Marvel #10 © MAR

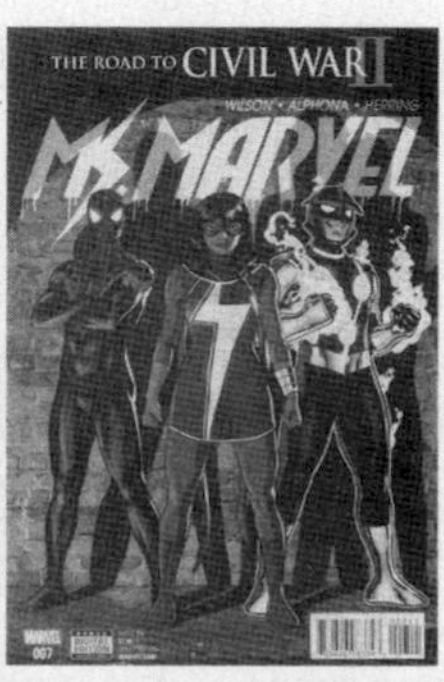

Ms. Marvel (2016 series) #7 © MAR

	GD 2.0	VG 4.0	FN 6.0	VF 8.0	VF/NM 9.0	NM- 9.2

Famous Funnies: Feb, 1950 - No. 22, Aug, 1953 (All photo-c)

1-Dick Powell, Evelyn Keyes, & Mickey Rooney photo-c	22	44	66	132	216	300
2-Myrna Loy photo-c	14	28	42	80	115	150
3-7,9: 6-Ricardo Montalban photo-c. 9-Gene Tierney, John Lund, Glenn Ford, & Rhonda Fleming photo-c.	14	28	42	76	108	140
8-Williamson/Frazetta-a, 6 pgs.	52	104	156	322	549	775
10-Frazetta-a, 6 pgs.	52	104	156	328	557	785
11,14-16: 14-Janet Leigh photo-c	13	26	39	74	105	135
12-Dean Martin & Jerry Lewis photo-c (12/51, pre-dates Advs. of Dean Martin & Jerry Lewis comic)	24	48	72	142	234	325
13-Ronald Reagan photo-c with 1 pg. biog.	32	64	96	188	307	425
17-Leslie Caron & Ralph Meeker photo-c; 1 pg. Frazetta ad	14	28	42	76	108	140
18-22: 19-John Derek photo-c. 20-Donald O'Connor & Debbie Reynolds photo-c. 21-Paul Henreid & Patricia Medina photo-c. 22-John Payne & Coleen Gray photo-c	13	26	39	72	101	130

NOTE: *Each issue has a full-length movie adaptation with photo covers.*

MOVIE MONSTERS (Magazine)
Atlas/Seaboard: Dec, 1974 - No. 4, Aug, 1975 (B&W; Film, photo & article magazine)

1-(84 pages) Planet of the Apes, King Kong, Sindbad & Harryhausen, Christopher Lee Dracula, Star Trek, Werewolf, Creature from the Black Lagoon, Hammer's Mummy, Gorgo, & Exorcist	4	8	12	23	37	50
2-(2/1975) 2001: Planet of the Apes-c; 2001: A Space Odyssey; Doc Savage; Frankenstein; Rodan; One Million Years BC; (lower print run)	4	8	12	23	37	50
3-(4/1975) Phantom of the Opera-c; Wolfman, Godzilla, Boris Karloff, Batman, Forbidden Planet, Jack the Giant Killer	4	8	12	23	37	50
4-(8/1975) Thing, Flash Gordon, Lon Chaney Jr., Lost Worlds, Loch Ness Monster, Day the Earth Stood Still, Star Trek	4	8	12	23	37	50

MOVIE THRILLERS (Movie)
Magazine Enterprises: 1949

1-Adaptation of "Rope of Sand" w/Burt Lancaster; Burt Lancaster photo-c	28	56	84	165	270	375

MOVIE TOWN ANIMAL ANTICS (Formerly Animal Antics; becomes Raccoon Kids #52 on)
National Periodical Publ.: No. 24, Jan-Feb, 1950 - No. 51, July-Aug, 1954

24-Raccoon Kids continue	12	24	36	67	94	120
25-51	10	20	30	54	72	90

NOTE: ***Sheldon Mayer** a-28-33, 35, 37-41, 43, 44, 47, 49-51.*

MOVIE TUNES COMICS (Formerly Animated...; Frankie No. 4 on)
Marvel Comics (MgPC): No. 3, Fall, 1946

3-Super Rabbit, Krazy Krow, Silly Seal & Ziggy Pig	20	40	60	114	182	250

MOWGLI JUNGLE BOOK (Rudyard Kipling's...)
Dell Publ. Co.: No. 487, Aug-Oct, 1953 - No. 620, Apr, 1955

Four Color 487 (#1)	6	12	18	42	79	115
Four Color 582 (8/54), 620	5	10	15	33	57	80

MPH
Image Comics: May, 2014 - No. 5, Feb, 2015 ($2.99/$4.99)

1-4-($2.99) Mark Millar-s/Duncan Fegredo-a; multiple covers on each 3.00
5-($4.99) Two covers 5.00

MR. (See Mister)

MRS. DEADPOOL AND THE HOWLING COMMANDOS (Secret Wars tie-in)
Marvel Comics: Aug, 2015 - No. 4, Nov, 2015 ($3.99, limited series)

1-4-Duggan-s/Espin-a; Dracula and Ghost Deadpool app. 4.00

M. REX
Image Comics: July, 1999 - No. 2, Dec, 1999 ($2.95)

Preview ($5.00) B&W pages and sketchbook; Rouleau-a 5.00
1,2-($2.95) 1-Joe Kelly-s/Rouleau-a/Anacleto-c. 2-Rouleau-c 3.00

MS. MARVEL (Also see The Avengers #183)
Marvel Comics Group: Jan, 1977 - No. 23, Apr, 1979

1-1st app. Ms. Marvel; Scorpion app. in #1,2	8	16	24	56	108	160
2-Origin	3	6	9	16	23	30
3-10: 5-Vision app. 6-10-(Reg. 30¢-c). 9-1st Deathbird. 10-Last 30¢ issue	2	4	6	11	16	20
6-10-(35¢-c variants, limited dist.)(6/77)	13	26	39	89	195	300
11-15,19-22: 19-Capt. Marvel app. 20-New costume	2	4	6	9	12	15
16-1st brief app. Mystique (Raven Darkholme)	5	10	15	35	63	90
17-Brief app. Mystique, disguised as Nick Fury	4	8	12	27	44	60
18-1st full app. Mystique; Avengers x-over	8	16	24	54	102	150
23-Vance Astro (leader of the Guardians) app.	3	6	9	14	20	25

NOTE: ***Austin** c-14i, 16i, 17i, 22i. **Buscema** a-1-3p; c(p)-2, 4, 6, 7, 15. **Infantino** a-14p, 19p. **Gil Kane** c-8. **Mooney** a-4-8p, 13p, 15-18p. **Starlin** c-12.*

MS. MARVEL (Also see New Avengers)
Marvel Comics: May, 2006 - No. 50, Apr, 2010 ($2.99)

1-Cho-c/Reed-s/De La Torre-a; Stilt-Man app.	2	4	6	9	12	15
1-Variant cover by Michael Turner	3	6	9	17	26	35

2-24: 4,5-Dr. Strange app. 6,7-Araña app. 3.00
25-($3.99) Two covers by Horn and Dodson; Secret Invasion 4.00
26-49: 26-31-Secret Invasion. 34-Spider-Man app. 35-Dark Reign. 37-Carol explodes. 39,40,46,48,49-Takeda-a. 40-Deadpool app. 41-Carol returns. 47-Spider-Man app. 3.00
50-($3.99) Mystique and Captain Marvel app.; Takeda & Oliver-a 4.00
... Annual 1 (11/08, $3.99) Spider-Man app.; Horn-c 4.00
... Special (3/07, $2.99) Reed-s/Camuncoli-a/c 3.00
... Storyteller (1/09, $2.99) Reed-s/Camuncoli-a/c 3.00
... Vol. 1: Best of the Best HC (2006, $19.99) r/#1-5 & Giant-Size Ms. Marvel #1 20.00
... Vol. 1: Best of the Best SC (2007, $14.99) r/#1-5 & Giant-Size Ms. Marvel #1 15.00
... Vol. 2: Civil War HC (2007, $19.99) r/#6-10 & Ms. Marvel Special #1 20.00
... Vol. 2: Civil War SC (2007, $14.99) r/#6-10 & Ms. Marvel Special #1 15.00
... Vol. 3: Operation Lightning Storm HC (2007, $19.99) r/#11-17 20.00
... Vol. 4: Monster Smash HC (2008, $19.99) r/#18-24 20.00

MS. MARVEL (Kamala Khan)(See Captain Marvel [2012-2014] #14&17 for cameo 1st apps.)
Marvel Comics: Apr, 2014 - No. 19, Dec, 2015 ($2.99)

1-Intro. Kamala Khan; G. Willow Wilson-s/Adrian Alphona-a; Pichelli-c	3	6	9	14	19	24
2-McKelvie-c	1	3	4	6	8	10

3-7: 3-5-Alphona-a. 3-McKelvie-c. 6,7-Wolverine app.; Wyatt-a 5.00
8-15: 8-11-Alphona-a. 9-Medusa app. 12-Loki app.; Bondoc-a. 13-15-Miyazawa-a 3.00
16-19-Secret Wars tie-ins; Captain Marvel app.; Alphona-a 3.00

MS. MARVEL (Kamala Khan)(Follows events of Secret Wars)
Marvel Comics: Jan, 2016 - Present ($4.99/$3.99)

1-($4.99) Wilson-s/Miyazawa & Alphona-a; Chiang-c 5.00
2-11,13-15-($3.99) 2,3-Dr. Faustus app. 4-6-Nico Leon-a. 8-11-Civil War II tie-in 4.00
12-($4.99) Andolfo-a; back-up Red Widow story 5.00

MS. MYSTIC
Pacific Comics: Oct, 1982 - No. 2, Feb, 1984 ($1.00/$1.50)

1,2: Neal Adams-c/a/script. 1-Origin; intro Erth, Ayre, Fyre & Watr 5.00

MS. MYSTIC
Continuity Comics: 1988 - No. 9, May, 1992 ($2.00)

1-9: 1,2-Reprint Pacific Comics issues 3.00

MS. MYSTIC
Continunity Comics: V2#1, Oct, 1993 - V2#4, Jan, 1994 ($2.50)

V2#1-4: 1-Adams-c(i)/part-i. 2-4-Embossed-c. 2-Nebres part-i. 3-Adams-c(i)/plot. 4-Adams-c(p)/plot 3.00

MS. MYSTIC DEATHWATCH 2000 (Ms. Mystic #3)
Continuity: May, 1993 - No. 3, Aug, 1993 ($2.50)

1-3-Bagged w/card; Adams plots 3.00

MS. TREE QUARTERLY / SPECIAL
DC Comics: Summer, 1990 -No. 10, 1992 ($3.95/$3.50, 84 pgs, mature)

1-10: 1-Midnight story; Batman text story, Grell-a. 2,3-Midnight stories; The Butcher text stories 4.00

NOTE: ***Cowan** c-2. **Grell** c-1, 6. **Infantino** a-8.*

MS. TREE'S THRILLING DETECTIVE ADVENTURES (Ms. Tree #4 on; also see The Best of Ms. Tree)(Baxter paper #4-9) (See Eclipse Magazine #1 for 1st app.)
Eclipse Comics/Aardvark-Vanaheim 10-18/Renegade Press 19 on:
2/83 - #9, 7/84; #10, 8/84 - #18, 5/85; #19, 6/85 - #50, 6/89

1 4.00
2-49: 2-Schythe begins. 9-Last Eclipse & last color issue. 10,11-two-tone 3.00
50-Contains flexi-disc ($3.95, 52 pgs.) 4.00
Ms. Tree 3-D 1 (Renegade, 8/85)-With glasses; Mike Mist app. 3.00
Summer Special 1 (8/86) 3.00
1950s Three-Dimensional Crime (7/87, no glasses)-Johnny Dynamite in 3-D 3.00

NOTE: ***Miller** pin-up 1-4. Johnny Dynamite-r begin #36 by **Morisi**.*

MS. VICTORY SPECIAL(Also see Capt. Paragon & Femforce)
Americomics: Jan, 1985 (nd)

1 3.00

MUCHA LUCHA (Based on Kids WB animated TV show)
DC Comics: Jun, 2003 - No. 3, Aug, 2003 ($2.25, limited series)

Multiversity #2 © DC

Muppet King Arthur #1 © Muppet Studios

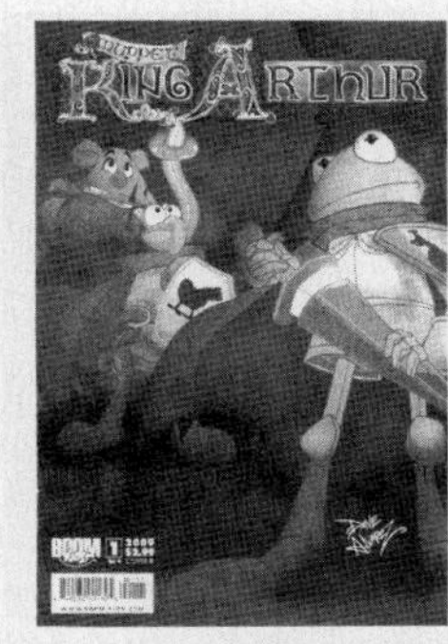

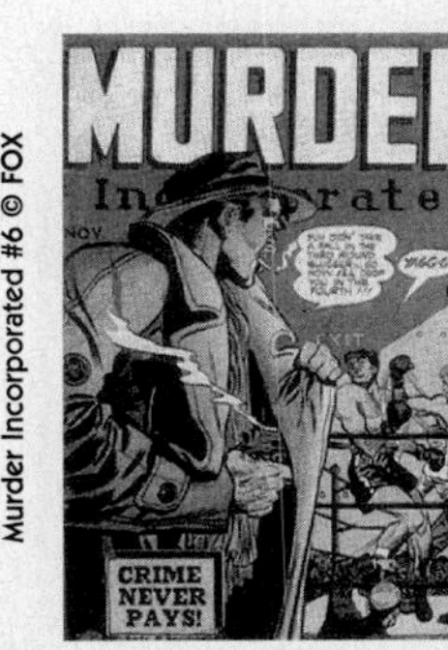

Murder Incorporated #6 © FOX

	GD 2.0	VG 4.0	FN 6.0	VF 8.0	VF/NM 9.0	NM- 9.2

1-3-Rikochet, Buena Girl and The Flea app. 3.00

MUDMAN
Image Comics: Nov, 2011 - No. 6 ($3.50)

1-6-Paul Grist-s/a 3.50

MUGGSY MOUSE (Also see Tick Tock Tales)
Magazine Enterprises: 1951 - No. 3, 1951; No. 4, 1954 - No. 5, 1954; 1963

	GD	VG	FN	VF	VF/NM	NM-
1(A-1 #33)	12	24	36	69	97	125
2(A-1 #36)-Racist-c	17	34	51	98	154	210
3(A-1 #39), 4(A-1 #95), 5(A-1 #99)	9	18	27	47	61	75
Super Reprint #14(1963), I.W. Reprint #1,2 (nd)	2	4	6	8	11	14

MUGGY-DOO, BOY CAT
Stanhall Publ.: July, 1953 - No. 4, Jan, 1954

	GD	VG	FN	VF	VF/NM	NM-
1-Funny animal; Irving Spector-a	10	20	30	58	79	100
2-4	7	14	21	35	43	50
Super Reprint #12('63), 16('64)	2	4	6	8	11	14

MULAN: REVELATIONS
Dark Horse Comics: Jun, 2015 - No. 4, Nov, 2015 ($3.99)

1-4-Andreyko-s/Kaneshiro-a; Mulan in 2125 Shanghai 4.00

MULLKON EMPIRE (See John Jake's...)

MULTIVERSITY, THE
DC Comics: Oct, 2014 - No. 2, Jun, 2015 ($4.99/$5.99)

1-($4.99) Morrison-s/Reis-a; Earth-23 Superman, Capt. Carrot, alternate Earth heroes gather 5.00
2-($5.99) Morrison-s/Reis-a/c 6.00
... 1&2 Director's Cut (2/16, $7.99, squarebound) reprints #1&2 with original B&W pencil art plus Morrison's original story proposals 8.00
...: Guidebook (3/15, $7.99) Legion of Sivanas, Kamandi app.; Multiverse map 8.00
...: Mastermen (4/15, $4.99) Earth-10 Overman & The Freedom Fighters; Jim Lee-a 5.00
...: Pax Americana 1 (1/15, $4.99) Earth-4 Charlton heroes; Quitely-a 5.00
...: Pax Americana Director's Cut 1 (7/15, $9.99) Quitely pencil art and Morrison's script excerpts; polybagged with large folded Multiverse map 10.00
...: The Just 1 (12/14, $4.99) Earth-16 Super-Sons and Justice League offspring; Oliver-a 5.00
...: The Society of Super-Heroes: Conquerors of the Counter-World 1 (11/14, $4.99) Earth-40 Dr. Fate, Green Lantern, Blackhawks, The Atom vs. Vandal Savage; Sprouse-a 5.00
...: Thunderworld Adventures 1 (2/15, $4.99) Earth-5 Shazam Family; Cam Stewart-c 5.00
...: Ultra Comics 1 (5/15, $4.99) Earth-33 Ultra; Mahnke-a 5.00

MUMMY, THE (See Universal Presents... under Dell Giants & Movie Classics)

MUMMY, THE: PALIMPSEST
Titan Comics (Hammer Comics): Dec, 2016 - Present ($3.99)

1-3-Peter Milligan-s/Ronilson Freire-a 4.00

MUMMY, THE: THE RISE AND FALL OF XANGO'S AX (Based on the Brendan Fraser movies)
IDW Publishing: Apr, 2008 - No. 4, July, 2008 ($3.99, limited series)

1-4-Prequel to '08 movie The Mummy: Tomb of the Dragon Emperor; Stephen Mooney-a 4.00

MUNCHKIN
BOOM! Studios (BOOM! Box): Jan, 2015 - No. 25, Jan, 2017 ($3.99)

1-24-Short stories of characters from the card game; each issue contains a card 4.00
25-($4.99) Covers by McGinty & Fridolfs 5.00
...: Deck the Dungeons (12/15, $4.99) Katie Cook-s/Mike Luckas-a; 2 covers 5.00

MUNDEN'S BAR ANNUAL
First Comics: Apr, 1988; 1989 ($2.95/$5.95)

1-($2.95)-r/from Grimjack; Fish Police story; Ordway-c 3.00
2-($5.95)-Teenage Mutant Ninja Turtles app. 6.00

MUNSTERS, THE (TV)
Gold Key: Jan, 1965 - No. 16, Jan, 1968 (All photo-c)

	GD	VG	FN	VF	VF/NM	NM-
1 (10134-501)	20	40	60	138	307	475
2	10	20	30	66	138	210
3-5	8	16	24	56	108	160
6-16	8	16	24	51	96	140

MUNSTERS, THE (TV)
TV Comics!: Aug, 1997 - No. 4 ($2.95, B&W)

1-4-All have photo-c 3.00
1,4-($7.95)-Variant-c 8.00
2-Variant-c w/Beverly Owens as Marilyn 3.00
Special Comic Con Ed. (7/97, $9.95) 10.00

MUPPET... (TV)
BOOM! Studios

... King Arthur 1-4 (12/09 - No. 4, 3/10, $2.99) Benjamin & Storck-s/Alvarez-a; 2 covers 3.00
... Peter Pan 1-4 (8/09 - No. 4, 11/09, $2.99) Randolph-s/Mebberson-a; multiple covers 3.00
... Robin Hood 1-4 (4/09 - No. 4, 7/09, $2.99) Beedle-s/Villavert Jr.-a; multiple covers 3.00
... Sherlock Holmes 1-4 (8/10 - No. 4, 11/10, $2.99) Storck-s/Mebberson-a/c 3.00
... Snow White 1-4 (4/10 - No. 4, 7/10, $2.99) Snider & Storck-s/Paroline-a; 2 covers 3.00

MUPPET BABIES, THE (TV)(See Star Comics Magazine)
Marvel Comics (Star Comics)/Marvel #18 on: Aug, 1985 - No. 26, July, 1989 (Children's book)

1-26 5.00

MUPPETS (The Four Seasons)
Marvel Worldwide: Sept, 2012 - No. 4, Dec, 2012 ($2.99, limited series)

1-4-Roger Landridge-s/a 3.00

MUPPET SHOW, THE (TV)
BOOM! Studios: Mar, 2009 - No. 4, Jun, 2009 ($2.99, limited series)

1-4-Roger Landridge-s/a; multiple covers 3.00
...: The Treasure of Peg Leg Wilson (7/09 - No. 4, 10/09) 1-4-Landridge-s/a; multiple-c 3.00

MUPPET SHOW COMIC BOOK, THE (TV)
BOOM! Studios: No. 0, Nov, 2009 - No. 11, Oct, 2010 ($2.99)

0-11: 0-3-Roger Landridge-s/a; multiple covers. 0-Paroline-a; Pigs in Space 3.00

MUPPETS TAKE MANHATTAN, THE
Marvel Comics (Star Comics): Nov, 1984 - No. 3, Jan, 1985

1-3-Movie adapt. r-/Marvel Super Special 4.00

MURCIELAGA, SHE-BAT
Heroic Publishing: Jan, 1993 - No. 2, 1993 (B&W)

1-($1.50, 28 pgs.) 3.00
2-($2.95, 36 pgs.)-Coated-c 3.00

MURDER CAN BE FUN
Slave Labor Graphics: Feb, 1996 - No. 12 ($2.95, B&W)

1-12: 1-Dorkin-c. 2-Vasquez-c. 3.00

MURDER INCORPORATED (My Private Life #16 on)
Fox Feature Syndicate: 1/48 - No. 15, 12/49; (2 No.9's); 6/50 - No. 3, 8/51

	GD	VG	FN	VF	VF/NM	NM-
1 (1st Series); 1,2 have 'For Adults Only' on-c	65	130	195	416	708	1000
2-Electrocution story	43	86	129	271	461	650
3,5-7,9(4/49),10(5/49),11-15	32	64	96	188	307	425
4-Classic lingerie-c	53	106	159	334	567	800
8-Used in **SOTI**, pg. 160	36	72	108	211	343	475
9(3/49)-Possible use in **SOTI**, pg. 145; r/Blue Beetle #56('48)	32	64	96	188	307	425
5(#1, 6/50)(2nd Series)-Formerly My Desire #4; bondage-c.	25	50	75	150	245	340
2(8/50)-Morisi-a	22	44	66	132	216	300
3(8/51)-Used in **POP**, pg. 81; Rico-a; lingerie-c/panels	30	60	90	177	289	400

MURDERLAND
Image Comics: Aug, 2010 - No. 3, Nov, 2010 ($2.99)

1-3-Stephen Scott-s/David Haun-a 3.00

MURDER ME DEAD
El Capitán Books: July, 2000 - No. 9, Oct, 2001 ($2.95/$4.95, B&W)

1-8-David Lapham-s/a 3.00
9-($4.95) 5.00

MURDEROUS GANGSTERS
Avon Per./Realistic No. 3 on: Jul, 1951; No. 2, Dec, 1951 - No. 4, Jun, 1952

	GD	VG	FN	VF	VF/NM	NM-
1-Pretty Boy Floyd, Leggs Diamond; 1 pg. Wood-a	68	136	204	435	743	1050
2-Baby-Face Nelson; 1 pg. Wood-a; classic painted-c	65	130	195	416	708	1000
3-Painted-c	39	78	117	240	395	550
4- "Murder by Needle" drug story; Mort Lawrence-a; Kinstler-c	41	82	123	256	428	600

MURDER MYSTERIES (Neil Gaiman's...)
Dark Horse Comics: 2002 ($13.95, HC, one-shot)

HC-Adapts Gaiman story; P. Craig Russell-script/art 14.00

MURDER TALES (Magazine)
World Famous Publications: V1#10, Nov, 1970 - V1#11, Jan, 1971 (52 pgs.)

	GD	VG	FN	VF	VF/NM	NM-
V1#10-One pg. Frazetta ad	4	8	12	28	47	65
11-Guardineer-r; bondage-c	4	8	12	25	40	55

MUSHMOUSE AND PUNKIN PUSS (TV)

Mutant Chronicles #3 © Target Games

Mutopia X #1 © MAR

Mutt & Jeff #49 © DC

GD 2.0 | VG 4.0 | FN 6.0 | VF 8.0 | VF/NM 9.0 | NM- 9.2

GD 2.0 | VG 4.0 | FN 6.0 | VF 8.0 | VF/NM 9.0 | NM- 9.2

Gold Key: September, 1965 (Hanna-Barbera)
1 (10153-509) 7 14 21 49 92 135

MUSIC BOX (Jennifer Love Hewitt's...)
IDW Publishing: Nov, 2009 - No. 5, Apr, 2010 ($3.99, lim. series)
1-5-Anthology; Scott Lobdell-s/art by various. 1-Gaydos-a. 3-Archer-a 4.00

MUSIC MAN, THE (See Movie Classics)

MUTANT CHRONICLES (Video game)
Acclaim Comics (Armada): May, 1996 - No. 4, Aug, 1996 ($2.95, lim. series)
1-4: Simon Bisley-c on all, Sourcebook (#5) 3.00

MUTANT EARTH (Stan Winston's...)
Image Comics: April, 2002 - No. 4, Jan, 2003 ($2.95)
1-4-Flip book w/Realm of the Claw 3.00
Trakk...His Adventures in Mutant Earth TPB (2003, $16.95) r/#1-4; Winston interview 17.00

MUTANT MISADVENTURES OF CLOAK AND DAGGER, THE
(Becomes Cloak and Dagger #14 on)
Marvel Comics: Oct, 1988 - No. 19, Aug, 1991 ($1.25/$1.50)
1-8,10-15: 1-X-Factor app. 10-Painted-c. 12-Dr. Doom app. 14-Begin new direction 3.00
9,16-19: 9-(52 pgs.) The Avengers x-over; painted-c. 16-18-Spider-Man x-over. 18-Infinity Gauntlet x-over; Thanos cameo; Ghost Rider app. 19-(52 pgs.) Origin Cloak & Dagger 4.00
NOTE: ***Austin** a-12i; c(i)-4, 12, 13; scripts-all. **Russell** a-2i. **Williamson** a-14i-16i; c-15i.*

MUTANTS & MISFITS
Silverline Comics (Solson): 1987 - No. 3, 1987 ($1.95)
1-3 3.00

MUTANTS VS. ULTRAS
Malibu Comics (Ultraverse): Nov, 1995 ($6.95, one-shot)
1-r/Exiles vs. X-Men, Night Man vs. Wolverine, Prime vs. Hulk 7.00

MUTANT, TEXAS: TALES OF SHERIFF IDA RED (Also see Jingle Belle)
Oni Press: May, 2002 - No. 4, Nov, 2002 ($2.95, B&W, limited series)
1-4-Paul Dini-s/J. Bone-c/a 3.00
TPB (2003, $11.95) r/#1-4; intro. by Joe Lansdale 12.00

MUTANT 2099
Marvel Comics (Marvel Knights): Nov, 2004 ($2.99, one-shot)
1-Kirkman-s/Pat Lee-c 3.00

MUTANT X (See X-Factor)
Marvel Comics: Nov, 1998 - No. 32, June, 2001 ($2.99/$1.99/$2.25)
1-($2.99) Alex Summers with alternate world's X-Men 4.00
2-11,13-19-($1.99): 2-Two covers. 5-Man-Spider-c/app. 3.00
12,25-($2.99): 12-Pin-up gallery by Kaluta, Romita, Byrne 4.00
20-24,26-32: 20-Begin $2.25-c. 28-31-Logan-c/app. 32-Last issue 3.00
Annual '99, '00 (5/99,'00, $3.50) '00-Doran-a(p) 4.00
Annual 2001 ($2.99) Story occurs between #31 & #32; Dracula app. 4.00

MUTANT X (Based on TV show)
Marvel Comics: May, 2002; June, 2002 ($3.50)
...: Dangerous Decisions (6/02) -Kuder-s/Immonen-a 3.50
...: Origin (5/02) -Tischman & Chaykin-s/Ferguson-a 3.50

MUTATIS
Marvel Comics (Epic Comics): 1992 - No. 3, 1992 ($2.25, mini-series)
1-3: Painted-c 3.00

MUTIES
Marvel Comics: Apr, 2002 - No. 6, Sept, 2002 ($2.50)
1-6: 1-Bollars-s/Ferguson-a. 2-Spaziante-a. 3-Haspiel-a. 4-Kanuiga-a 3.00

MUTINY (Stormy Tales of the Seven Seas)
Aragon Magazines: Oct, 1954 - No. 3, Feb, 1955
1 17 34 51 98 154 210
2,3: 2-Capt. Mutiny. 3-Bondage-c 14 28 42 76 108 140

MUTINY ON THE BOUNTY (See Classics Illustrated #100 & Movie Comics)

MUTOPIA X (Also see House of M and related titles)
Marvel Comics: Sept, 2005 - No. 5, Jan, 2006 ($2.99, limited series)
1-5-Medina-a/Hine-s 3.00
House of M: Mutopia X (2006, $13.99, TPB) r/series 14.00

MUTT AND JEFF (See All-American, All-Flash #18, Cicero's Cat, Comic Cavalcade, Famous Feature Stories, The Funnies, Popular & Xmas Comics)
All American/National 1-103(6/58)/Dell 104(10/58)-115 (10-12/59)/ Harvey 116(2/60)-148: Summer, 1939 (nd) - No. 148, Nov, 1965
1(nn)-Lost Wheels 194 388 582 1242 2121 3000
2(nn)-Charging Bull (Summer, 1940, nd; on sale 6/20/40) 84 168 252 538 919 1300
3(nn)-Bucking Broncos (Summer, 1941, nd) 57 114 171 362 619 875
4(Winter, '41), 5(Summer, '42) 54 108 162 343 574 825
6-10: 6-Includes Minute Man Answers the Call 32 64 96 188 307 425
11-20: 20-X-Mas-c 21 42 63 126 206 285
21-30 16 32 48 94 147 200
31-50: 32-X-Mas-c 14 28 42 82 121 160
51-75-Last Fisher issue. 53-Last 52 pgs. 12 24 36 67 94 120
76-99,101-103: 76-Last pre-code issue(1/55) 5 10 15 35 63 90
100 6 12 18 37 66 95
104-115,132-148 5 10 15 30 48 65
116-131-Richie Rich app. 5 10 15 32 51 70
...Jokes 1-3(8/60-61, Harvey)-84 pgs.; Richie Rich in all; Little Dot in #2,3; Lotta in #2 5 10 15 30 48 65
...New Jokes 1-4(10/63-11/65, Harvey)-68 pgs.; Richie Rich in #1-3; Stumbo in #1 4 8 12 24 37 50
NOTE: *Most all issues by **Al Smith**. Issues from 1963 on have **Fisher** reprints. Clarification: early issues signed by Fisher are mostly drawn by Smith.*

MY BROTHERS' KEEPER
Spire Christian Comics (Fleming H. Revell Co.): 1973 (35/49¢, 36 pgs.)
nn 2 4 6 13 18 22

MY CONFESSIONS (My Confession #7&8; formerly Western True Crime; A Spectacular Feature Magazine #11)
Fox Feature Syndicate: No. 7, Aug, 1949 - No. 10, Jan-Feb, 1950
7-Wood-a (10 pgs.) 58 116 174 371 636 900
8,9: 8-Harrison/Wood-a (19 pgs.). 9-Wood-a 34 68 102 199 325 450
10 21 42 63 122 199 275

MYCROFT HOLMES AND THE APOCALYPSE HANDBOOK
Titan Comics: Sept, 2016 - No. 5, Mar, 2017 ($3.99)
1-5-Sherlock Holmes' older brother; Kareem Abdul-Jabbar & Raymond Obstfeld-s 4.00

MY DATE COMICS (Teen-age)
Hillman Periodicals: July, 1947 - V1#4, Jan, 1948 (2nd Romance comic; see Young Romance)
1-S&K-c/a 42 84 126 265 445 625
2-4-S&K-c/a; Dan Barry-a 30 60 90 177 289 400

MY DESIRE (Formerly Jo-Jo Comics; becomes Murder, Inc. #5 on)
Fox Feature Syndicate: No. 30, Aug, 1949 - No. 4, April, 1950
30 (#1) 26 52 78 154 252 350
31 (#2, 10/49),3(2/50),4 19 38 57 111 176 240
31 (Canadian edition) 12 24 36 67 94 120
32(12/49)-Wood-a 30 60 90 177 289 400

MY DIARY (Becomes My Friend Irma #3 on?)
Marvel Comics (A Lovers Mag.): Dec, 1949 - No. 2, Mar, 1950
1,2-Photo-c 20 40 60 114 182 250

MY EXPERIENCE (Formerly All Top; becomes Judy Canova #23 on)
Fox Feature Syndicate: No. 19, Sept, 1949 - No. 22, Mar, 1950
19,21: 19-Wood-a. 21-Wood-a(2) 33 66 99 194 317 440
20 18 36 54 105 165 225
22-Wood-a (9 pgs.) 30 60 90 177 289 400

MY FAITH IN FRANKIE
DC Comics (Vertigo): March, 2004 - No. 4, June, 2004 ($2.95, limited series)
1-4-Mike Carey-s/Sonny Liew & Marc Hempel-a 3.00
TPB (2004, $6.95, digest-size) r/series in B&W; Dead Boy Detectives preview 7.00

MY FAVORITE MARTIAN (TV)
Gold Key: 1/64; No.2, 7/64 - No. 9, 10/66 (No. 1,3-9 have photo-c)
1-Russ Manning-a 10 20 30 69 147 225
2 6 12 18 41 76 110
3-9 5 10 15 35 63 90

MY FRIEND IRMA (Radio/TV) (Formerly My Diary? and/or Western Life Romances?)
Marvel/Atlas Comics (BFP): No. 3, June, 1950 - No. 47, Dec, 1954; No. 48, Feb, 1955
3-Dan DeCarlo-a in all; 52 pgs. begin, end ? 50 100 150 315 533 750
4-Kurtzman-a (10 pgs.) 24 48 72 142 234 325
5- "Egghead Doodle" by Kurtzman (4 pgs.) 20 40 60 114 182 250
6,8-10: 9-Paper dolls, 1 pg; Millie app. (5 pgs.) 16 32 48 94 147 200
7-One pg. Kurtzman-a 17 34 51 98 154 210
11-23: 23-One pg. Frazetta-a 14 28 42 80 115 150
24-48: 41,48-Stan Lee & Dan DeCarlo app. 13 26 39 74 105 135

My Greatest Adventure #3 © DC

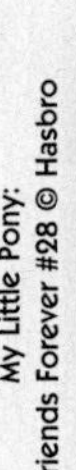

My Little Pony: Friends Forever #28 © Hasbro

My Love (2nd series) #10 © MAR

	GD 2.0	VG 4.0	FN 6.0	VF 8.0	VF/NM 9.0	NM- 9.2

MY GIRL PEARL
Atlas Comics: 4/55 - #4, 10/55; #5, 7/57 - #6, 9/57; #7, 8/60 - #11, ?/61

	GD	VG	FN	VF	VF/NM	NM-
1-Dan DeCarlo-c/a in #1-6	37	74	111	222	361	500
2	15	30	45	85	130	175
3-6	14	28	42	76	108	140
7-11	6	12	18	40	73	105

MY GREATEST ADVENTURE (Doom Patrol #86 on)
National Periodical Publications: Jan-Feb, 1955 - No. 85, Feb, 1964

	GD	VG	FN	VF	VF/NM	NM-
1-Before CCA	141	282	423	1142	2571	4000
2	50	100	150	390	870	1350
3-5	36	72	108	259	580	900
6-10: 6-Science fiction format begins	29	58	87	209	467	725
11-14: 12-1st S.A. issue	22	44	66	155	345	535
15-17: Kirby-a in all	24	48	72	168	372	575
18-Kirby-c/a	27	54	81	184	410	635
19,23-25	19	38	57	131	291	450
20,21,28-Kirby-a	22	44	66	155	345	535
22-Space Ranger prototype (7-8/58)(see Showcase #15 for Space Ranger debut)	20	40	60	140	310	480
26,27,29,30	15	30	45	103	227	350
31-40	12	24	36	84	185	285
41,42,44-57,59	11	22	33	75	160	245
43-Kirby-a	12	24	36	79	170	260
58,60,61-Toth-a; Last 10¢ issue	11	22	33	76	163	250
62-76,78,79: 79-Promotes "Legion of the Strange" for next issue; renamed Doom Patrol for #80	9	18	27	62	126	190
77-Toth-a; Robotman prototype	10	20	30	64	132	200
80-(6/63)-Intro/origin Doom Patrol and begin series; origin & 1st app. Negative Man, Elasti-Girl & S.A. Robotman	100	200	300	800	1800	2800
81,85-Toth-a	20	40	60	138	307	475
82-84	19	38	57	131	291	450

NOTE: ***Anderson** a-42. **Cameron** a-24. **Colan** a-77. **Meskin** a-25, 26, 32, 39, 45, 50, 56, 57, 61, 64, 70, 73, 74, 76, 79; c-76. **Moreira** a-11, 12, 15, 17, 20, 23, 25, 27, 37, 40-43, 46, 48, 55-57, 59, 60, 62-65, 67, 69, 70; c-1-4, 7-10. **Roussos** c/a-71-73. **Wildey** a-32.*

MY GREATEST ADVENTURE (Also see 2011 Weird Worlds series)
DC Comics: Dec, 2011 - No. 6, May, 2012 ($3.99, limited series)

	GD	VG	FN	VF	VF/NM	NM-
1-6-Short stories of Tanga, Robotman, and Garbage Man; Lopresti-s/a, Maguire-s/a						4.00

MY GREAT LOVE (Becomes Will Rogers Western #5)
Fox Feature Syndicate: Oct, 1949 - No. 4, Apr, 1950

	GD	VG	FN	VF	VF/NM	NM-
1	25	50	75	150	245	340
2-4	15	30	45	85	130	175

MY INTIMATE AFFAIR (Inside Crime #3)
Fox Feature Syndicate: Mar, 1950 - No. 2, May, 1950

	GD	VG	FN	VF	VF/NM	NM-
1	26	52	78	154	252	350
2	15	30	45	85	130	175

MY LIFE (Formerly Meet Corliss Archer)
Fox Feature Syndicate: No. 4, Sept, 1948 - No. 15, July, 1950

	GD	VG	FN	VF	VF/NM	NM-
4-Used in **SOTI**, pg. 39; Kamen/Feldstein-a	52	104	156	328	552	775
5-Kamen-a	32	64	96	188	307	425
6-Kamen/Feldstein-a	36	72	108	211	343	475
7-Wood-a; wash cover	37	74	111	222	361	500
8,9,11-15	18	36	54	105	165	225
10-Wood-a	28	56	84	168	274	380

MY LITTLE MARGIE (TV)
Charlton Comics: July, 1954 - No. 54, Nov, 1964

	GD	VG	FN	VF	VF/NM	NM-
1-Photo front/back-c	37	74	111	222	361	500
2-Photo front/back-c	19	38	57	109	172	235
3-7,10	12	24	36	69	97	125
8,9-Infinity-c	13	26	39	72	101	130
11-14: Part-photo-c (#13, 8/56). 14-UFO cover	10	20	30	58	79	100
15-19	10	20	30	54	72	90
20-(25¢, 100 pg. issue)	15	30	45	86	133	180
21-40: 40-Last 10¢ issue	5	10	15	30	50	70
41-53	4	8	12	27	44	60
54-(11/64) Beatles on cover; lead story spoofs the Beatle haircut craze of the 1960's; Beatles app. (scarce)	16	32	48	110	243	375

NOTE: *Doll cut-outs in 32, 33, 40, 45, 50.*

MY LITTLE MARGIE'S BOY FRIENDS (TV) (Freddy V2#12 on)
Charlton Comics: Aug, 1955 - No. 11, Apr?, 1958

	GD	VG	FN	VF	VF/NM	NM-
1-Has several Archie swipes	15	30	45	88	137	185
2	10	20	30	54	72	90
3-11	9	18	27	47	61	75

MY LITTLE MARGIE'S FASHIONS (TV)
Charlton Comics: Feb, 1959 - No. 5, Nov, 1959

	GD	VG	FN	VF	VF/NM	NM-
1	14	28	42	80	115	150
2-5	9	18	27	47	61	75

MY LITTLE PHONY: A BRONY ADVENTURE
Dynamite Entertainment: 2014 ($5.99, one-shot)

	GD	VG	FN	VF	VF/NM	NM-
1-My Little Pony fandom parody; Moreci & Seeley-a/Haeser & Baal-a; 2 covers						6.00

MY LITTLE PONY
IDW Publishing

	GD	VG	FN	VF	VF/NM	NM-
... Annual #1: Equestria Girls (10/13, $7.99) Price & Fleecs-a; multiple covers						8.00
... Annual 2014 (9/14, $7.99) Anderson-s/Bates-a; two covers						8.00
... Annual 2017 (2/17, $7.99) Short stories by Whitley, Rice, Price & others; two covers						8.00
... Art Gallery (11/13, $3.99) Pin-ups by Sara Richard & others						4.00
... Cover Gallery (8/13, $3.99) Gallery of regular and variant covers						4.00
... Halloween Comicfest 2016 (10/16, giveaway) reprints Friends Forever #4						3.00
... Holiday Special (12/15, $3.99) Cook-s/Hickey, Garbowska, Price, Cook-a; 3 covers						4.00

MY LITTLE PONY: FIENDS FOREVER
IDW Publishing: Apr, 2015 - No. 5, May, 2015 ($3.99, weekly mini-series)

	GD	VG	FN	VF	VF/NM	NM-
1-5-Spotlight on Equestria's villains. 1-Whitley-s/Hickey-a. 3-Garbowska-a						4.00

MY LITTLE PONY: FRIENDS FOREVER
IDW Publishing: Jan, 2014 - Present ($3.99)

	GD	VG	FN	VF	VF/NM	NM-
1-37: 1-de Campi-s/McNeil-a; multiple covers. 3,6,10,13,14,21,27,30,34,37-Garbowska-a. 8-Katie Cook-s						4.00
... - Halloween Fest 2014 (10/14, giveaway) reprints #2						3.00

MY LITTLE PONY: FRIENDSHIP IS MAGIC
IDW Publishing: Nov, 2012 - Present ($3.99)

	GD	VG	FN	VF	VF/NM	NM-
1-Katie Cook-s/Andy Price-a; 7 covers						5.00
1-Subscription variant cover by Jill Thompson						5.00
2-49,51-Multiple covers on each. 18,19-Interlocking covers						4.00
50-($5.99) Anderson-s/Price-a; Whitley-s/Fosgitt-a						6.00
... #1 Greatest Hits (8/16, $1.00) reprints #1						3.00
... #1 Hundred Penny Press (2/14, $1.00) reprints #1						3.00

MY LITTLE PONY MICRO-SERIES
IDW Publishing: Feb, 2013 - No. 10, Dec, 2013 ($3.99)

	GD	VG	FN	VF	VF/NM	NM-
1-Twilight Sparkle - Zahler-s/a						5.00
2-10: 2-Rainbow Dash. 3-Rarity. 4-Fluttershy						4.00

MY LOVE (Becomes Two Gun Western #5 (11/50) on?)
Marvel Comics (CLDS): July, 1949 - No. 4, Apr, 1950 (All photo-c)

	GD	VG	FN	VF	VF/NM	NM-
1	21	42	63	126	206	285
2,3	15	30	45	85	130	175
4-Bettie Page photo-c (see Cupid #2)	50	100	150	315	533	750

MY LOVE
Marvel Comics Group: Sept, 1969 - No. 39, Mar, 1976

	GD	VG	FN	VF	VF/NM	NM-
1	9	18	27	57	111	165
2-9: 4-6-Colan-a	5	10	15	31	53	75
10-Williamson-r/My Own Romance #71; Kirby-a	5	10	15	33	57	80
11-13,15-19	4	8	12	27	44	60
14-(52 pgs.)-Woodstock-c/sty; Morrow-c/a; Kirby/Colletta-r	7	14	21	46	86	125
20-Starlin-a	4	8	12	28	47	65
21,22,24-27,29-38: 38-Reprints	4	8	12	23	37	50
23-Steranko-r/Our Love Story #5	4	8	12	27	44	60
28-Kirby-a	4	8	12	25	40	55
39-Last issue; reprints	4	8	12	25	40	55
Special 1 (12/71)(52 pgs.)	5	10	15	34	60	85

NOTE: ***John Buscema** a-1-7, 10, 18-21, 22r(2), 24r, 25r, 29r, 34r, 36r, 37r, Spec. (r)(4); c-13, 15, 25, 27, Spec. **Colan** a-4, 5, 6, 8, 9, 16, 17, 20, 21, 22, 24r, 27r, 30r, 35r, 39r. **Colan/Everett** a-13, 15, 16, 27(r#13). **Kirby** a-(r)-14, 26, 28. **Romita** a-1-3, 19, 20, 25, 34, 38; c-1-3, 15.*

MY LOVE AFFAIR (March of Crime #7 on)
Fox Feature Syndicate: July, 1949 - No. 6, May, 1950

	GD	VG	FN	VF	VF/NM	NM-
1	25	50	75	150	245	340
2	15	30	45	85	130	175
3-6-Wood-a. 5-(3/50)-Becomes Love Stories #6	27	54	81	158	259	360

MY LOVE LIFE (Formerly Zegra)
Fox Feature Synd.: No. 6, June, 1949 - No. 13, Aug, 1950; No. 13, Sept, 1951

	GD	VG	FN	VF	VF/NM	NM-
6-Kamenish-a	24	48	72	142	234	325

My Love Story #2 © FOX

My Only Love #8 © CC

My Secret Confession #1 © Sterling

	GD 2.0	VG 4.0	FN 6.0	VF 8.0	VF/NM 9.0	NM- 9.2
7-13	15	30	45	85	130	175
13 (9/51)(Formerly My Story #12)	14	28	42	82	121	160

MY LOVE MEMOIRS (Formerly Women Outlaws; Hunted #13 on)
Fox Feature Syndicate: No. 9, Nov, 1949 - No. 12, May, 1950

	GD 2.0	VG 4.0	FN 6.0	VF 8.0	VF/NM 9.0	NM- 9.2
9,11,12-Wood-a	27	54	81	158	259	360
10	15	30	45	85	130	175

MY LOVE SECRET (Formerly Phantom Lady; Animal Crackers #31)
Fox Feature Syndicate/M. S. Distr.: No. 24, June, 1949 - No. 30, June, 1950; No. 53, 1954

	GD 2.0	VG 4.0	FN 6.0	VF 8.0	VF/NM 9.0	NM- 9.2
24-Kamen/Feldstein-a	28	56	84	165	270	375
25-Possible caricature of Wood on-c?	18	36	54	105	165	225
26,28-Wood-a	27	54	81	158	259	360
27,29,30: 30-Photo-c	16	32	48	94	147	200
53-(Reprint, M.S. Distr.) 1954? nd given; formerly Western Thrillers; becomes Crimes by Women #54; photo-c	10	20	30	58	79	100

MY LOVE STORY (Hoot Gibson Western #5 on)
Fox Feature Syndicate: Sept, 1949 - No. 4, Mar, 1950

	GD 2.0	VG 4.0	FN 6.0	VF 8.0	VF/NM 9.0	NM- 9.2
1	24	48	72	142	234	325
2	15	30	45	85	130	175
3,4-Wood-a	27	54	81	158	259	360

MY LOVE STORY
Atlas Comics (GPS): April, 1956 - No. 9, Aug, 1957

	GD 2.0	VG 4.0	FN 6.0	VF 8.0	VF/NM 9.0	NM- 9.2
1	18	36	54	103	162	220
2	11	22	33	64	90	115
3,7: Matt Baker-a. 7-Toth-a	15	30	45	83	124	165
4-6,8,9	11	22	33	60	83	105

NOTE: ***Brewster** a-3. **Colletta** a-1(2), 3, 4(2), 5; c-3.*

MYLO XYLOTO COMICS
Bongo Comics: 2013 - No. 6, 2013 ($3.99, limited series)

	GD 2.0	VG 4.0	FN 6.0	VF 8.0	VF/NM 9.0	NM- 9.2
1-6-Mark Osborne & Coldplay-s/Fuentes-a						4.00

MY NAME IS BRUCE
Dark Horse Comics: Sept, 2008 ($3.50, one-shot)

	GD 2.0	VG 4.0	FN 6.0	VF 8.0	VF/NM 9.0	NM- 9.2
nn-Adaptation of the Bruce Campbell movie; Cliff Richards-a/Bart Sears-c						3.50

MY NAME IS HOLOCAUST
DC Comics: May, 1995 - No. 5, Sept, 1995 ($2.50, limited series)

	GD 2.0	VG 4.0	FN 6.0	VF 8.0	VF/NM 9.0	NM- 9.2
1-5						3.00

MY ONLY LOVE
Charlton Comics: July, 1975 - No. 9, Nov, 1976

	GD 2.0	VG 4.0	FN 6.0	VF 8.0	VF/NM 9.0	NM- 9.2
1	3	6	9	14	19	24
2,4-9	2	4	6	9	13	16
3-Toth-a	2	4	6	11	16	20

MY OWN ROMANCE (Formerly My Romance; Teen-Age Romance #77 on)
Marvel/Atlas (MjPC/RCM No. 4-59/ZPC No. 60-76): No. 4, Mar, 1949 - No. 76, July, 1960

	GD 2.0	VG 4.0	FN 6.0	VF 8.0	VF/NM 9.0	NM- 9.2
4-Photo-c	21	42	63	124	202	280
5-10: 5,6,8-10-Photo-c	14	28	42	80	115	150
11-20: 14-Powell-a	13	26	39	74	105	135
21-42,55: 42-Last precode (2/55). 55-Toth-a	12	24	36	69	97	125
43-54,56-60	6	12	18	41	76	110
61-70,72,73,75,76	6	12	18	38	69	100
71-Williamson-a	6	12	18	42	79	115
74-Kirby-a	6	12	18	42	79	115

NOTE: ***Brewster** a-59. **Colletta** a-45(2), 48, 50, 55, 57(2), 59; c-58i, 59, 61. **Everett** a-25; c-58p. **Kirby** c-71, 75, 76. **Morisi** a-18. **Orlando** a-61. **Romita** a-36. **Tuska** a-10.*

MY PAL DIZZY (See Comic Books, Series I)

MY PAST (...Confessions) (Formerly Western Thrillers)
Fox Feature Syndicate: No. 7, Aug, 1949 - No. 11, Apr, 1950 (Crimes Inc. #12)

	GD 2.0	VG 4.0	FN 6.0	VF 8.0	VF/NM 9.0	NM- 9.2
7	26	52	78	154	252	350
8-10	15	30	45	85	130	175
11-Wood-a	27	54	81	158	259	360

MY PERSONAL PROBLEM
Ajax/Farrell/Steinway Comic: 11/55; No. 2, 2/56; No. 3, 9/56 - No. 4, 11/56; 10/57 - No. 3, 5/58

	GD 2.0	VG 4.0	FN 6.0	VF 8.0	VF/NM 9.0	NM- 9.2
1	11	22	33	62	86	110
2-4	8	16	24	40	50	60
1-3('57-'58)-Steinway	6	12	18	31	38	45

MY PRIVATE LIFE (Formerly Murder, Inc.; becomes Pedro #18)
Fox Feature Syndicate: No. 16, Feb, 1950 - No. 17, April, 1950

	GD 2.0	VG 4.0	FN 6.0	VF 8.0	VF/NM 9.0	NM- 9.2
16,17	18	36	54	105	165	225

MYRA NORTH (See The Comics, Crackajack Funnies & Red Ryder)
Dell Publishing Co.: No. 3, Jan, 1940

	GD 2.0	VG 4.0	FN 6.0	VF 8.0	VF/NM 9.0	NM- 9.2
Four Color 3	103	206	309	659	1130	1600

MY REAL LOVE
Standard Comics: No. 5, June, 1952 (Photo-c)

	GD 2.0	VG 4.0	FN 6.0	VF 8.0	VF/NM 9.0	NM- 9.2
5-Toth-a, 3 pgs.; Tuska, Cardy, Vern Greene-a	15	30	45	85	130	175

MY ROMANCE (Becomes My Own Romance #4 on)
Marvel Comics (RCM): Sept, 1948 - No. 3, Jan, 1949

	GD 2.0	VG 4.0	FN 6.0	VF 8.0	VF/NM 9.0	NM- 9.2
1	24	48	72	140	230	320
2,3: 2-Anti-Wertham editorial (11/48)	15	30	45	88	137	185

MY ROMANTIC ADVENTURES (Formerly Romantic Adventures)
American Comics Group: No. 68, 8/56 - No. 115, 12/60; No. 116, 7/61 - No. 138, 3/64

	GD 2.0	VG 4.0	FN 6.0	VF 8.0	VF/NM 9.0	NM- 9.2
68	9	18	27	47	61	75
69-85	7	14	21	35	43	50
86-Three pg. Williamson-a (2/58)	8	16	24	44	57	70
87-100	3	6	9	19	30	40
101-138	3	6	9	16	23	30

NOTE: ***Whitney** art in most issues.*

MY SECRET (Becomes Our Secret #4 on)
Superior Comics, Ltd.: Aug, 1949 - No. 3, Oct, 1949

	GD 2.0	VG 4.0	FN 6.0	VF 8.0	VF/NM 9.0	NM- 9.2
1	20	40	60	117	189	260
2,3	15	30	45	85	130	175

MY SECRET AFFAIR (Becomes Martin Kane #4)
Hero Book (Fox Feature Syndicate): Dec, 1949 - No. 3, April, 1950

	GD 2.0	VG 4.0	FN 6.0	VF 8.0	VF/NM 9.0	NM- 9.2
1-Harrison/Wood-a (10 pgs.)	34	68	102	204	332	460
2,3-Wood-a	28	56	84	168	274	380

MY SECRET CONFESSION
Sterling Comics: September, 1955

	GD 2.0	VG 4.0	FN 6.0	VF 8.0	VF/NM 9.0	NM- 9.2
1-Sekowsky-a	11	22	33	60	83	105

MY SECRET LIFE (Formerly Western Outlaws; Romeo Tubbs #26 on)
Fox Feature Syndicate: No. 22, July, 1949 - No. 27, July, 1950; No. 27, 9/51

	GD 2.0	VG 4.0	FN 6.0	VF 8.0	VF/NM 9.0	NM- 9.2
22	20	40	60	114	182	250
23,26-Wood-a, 6 pgs.	28	56	84	165	270	375
24,25,27	15	30	45	90	140	190
27 (9/51)	14	28	42	82	121	160

NOTE: *The title was changed to Romeo Tubbs after #25 even though #26 & 27 did come out.*

MY SECRET LIFE (Formerly Young Lovers; Sue & Sally Smith #48)
Charlton Comics: No. 19, Aug, 1957 - No. 47, Sept, 1962

	GD 2.0	VG 4.0	FN 6.0	VF 8.0	VF/NM 9.0	NM- 9.2
19	4	8	12	25	40	55
20-35	3	6	9	16	23	30
36-47: 44-Last 10¢ issue. 47-1st app. Sue & Sally Smith	3	6	9	14	20	26

MY SECRET MARRIAGE
Superior Comics, Ltd.: May, 1953 - No. 24, July, 1956 (Canadian)

	GD 2.0	VG 4.0	FN 6.0	VF 8.0	VF/NM 9.0	NM- 9.2
1	18	36	54	103	162	220
2	11	22	33	62	86	110
3-24	10	20	30	56	76	95
I.W. Reprint #9	2	4	6	8	11	14

NOTE: *Many issues contain **Kamen-ish** art.*

MY SECRET ROMANCE (Becomes A Star Presentation #3)
Hero Book (Fox Feature Syndicate): Jan, 1950 - No. 2, March, 1950

	GD 2.0	VG 4.0	FN 6.0	VF 8.0	VF/NM 9.0	NM- 9.2
1	22	44	66	132	216	300
2-Wood-a	27	54	81	158	259	360

MY SECRETS (Magazine) (Also see Gothic Romances)
Atlas/Seaboard: Feb, 1975 (B&W, 68 pgs.)

	GD 2.0	VG 4.0	FN 6.0	VF 8.0	VF/NM 9.0	NM- 9.2
Vol. 1 #1	15	30	45	105	233	360

MY SECRET STORY (Formerly Captain Kidd #25; Sabu #30 on)
Fox Feature Syndicate: No. 26, Oct, 1949 - No. 29, April, 1950

	GD 2.0	VG 4.0	FN 6.0	VF 8.0	VF/NM 9.0	NM- 9.2
26	20	40	60	117	189	260
27-29	15	30	45	85	130	175

MYSPACE DARK HORSE PRESENTS
Dark Horse Books: Sept, 2008 - Feb, 2011 ($19.95/$19.99, TPB)

	GD 2.0	VG 4.0	FN 6.0	VF 8.0	VF/NM 9.0	NM- 9.2
Vol. 1 - Short stories previously appearing on Dark Horse's MySpace.com webpage; s/a by various incl. Whedon, Bá, Bagge, Mignola, Moon, Nord, Trimpe, Warren, Way						20.00
Vol. 2 - Collects stories from online #7-12; s/a by Way, Niles, Dorkin, Hotz & others						20.00
Vol. 3 - Collects stories from online #13-19; s/a by Mignola, Cloonan & others						20.00

Mysteries #3 © SUPR

Mystery Comics #1 © WHW

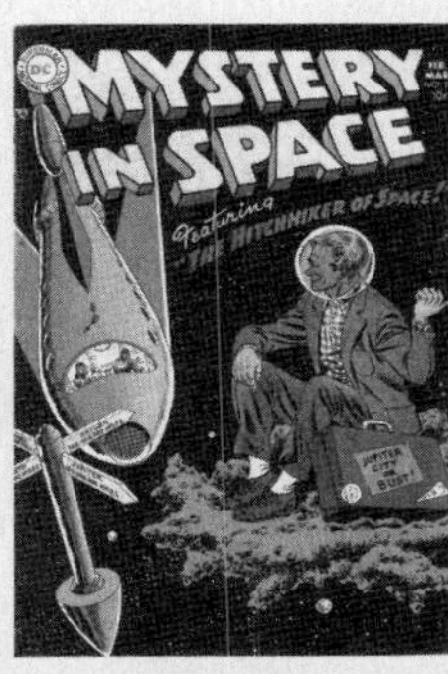

Mystery in Space #24 © DC

	GD 2.0	VG 4.0	FN 6.0	VF 8.0	VF/NM 9.0	NM- 9.2
Vol. 4 - Collects stories from online #20-24; s/a by Whedon, Chen & others						20.00
Vol. 5 - Collects stories from online #25-30; s/a by Thompson, Aragonés & others						20.00
Vol. 6 - Collects stories from online #31-36; s/a by Sakai, Dorkin & others						20.00

MYSTERIES (...Weird & Strange)
Superior/Dynamic Publ. (Randall Publ. Ltd.): May, 1953 - No. 11, Jan, 1955

	GD 2.0	VG 4.0	FN 6.0	VF 8.0	VF/NM 9.0	NM- 9.2
1-All horror stories	50	100	150	315	533	750
2-A-Bomb blast story	32	64	96	192	314	435
3-11: 10-Kamenish-c/a reprinted from Strange Mysteries #2; cover is from a panel in Strange Mysteries #2	29	58	87	170	278	385

MYSTERIES IN SPACE (See Fireside Book Series)

MYSTERIES OF SCOTLAND YARD (Also see A-1 Comics)
Magazine Enterprises: No. 121, 1954 (one shot)

	GD 2.0	VG 4.0	FN 6.0	VF 8.0	VF/NM 9.0	NM- 9.2
A-1 121-Reprinted from Manhunt (5 stories)	15	30	45	85	130	175

MYSTERIES OF UNEXPLORED WORLDS (See Blue Bird)(Becomes Son of Vulcan V2#49 on)
Charlton Comics: Aug, 1956; No. 2, Jan, 1957 - No. 48, Sept, 1965

	GD 2.0	VG 4.0	FN 6.0	VF 8.0	VF/NM 9.0	NM- 9.2
1	37	74	111	222	361	500
2-No Ditko	16	32	48	94	147	200
3,4,8,9 Ditko-a. 3-Diko c/a (4). 4-Ditko c/a (2).	30	60	90	177	289	400
5,6,10,11: 5,6-Ditko-c/a (all). 10-Ditko-c/a(4). 11-Ditko-c/a(3); signed J. Kotdi	31	62	93	186	303	420
7-(2/58, 68 pgs.) 4 stories w/Ditko-a	34	68	102	204	332	460
12-Ditko sty (3); Baker story "The Charm Bracelet"	30	60	90	177	289	400
13-18,20	10	20	30	56	76	95
19,21-24,26-Ditko-a	23	46	69	136	223	310
25,27-30: 28-Communist A-bomb story w/Khrushchev	5	10	15	31	53	75
31-45: 43-Atomic bomb panel	4	8	12	25	40	55
46(5/65)-Son of Vulcan begins (origin/1st app.)	4	8	12	27	44	60
47,48	4	8	12	21	33	45

NOTE: *Ditko c-3-6, 10, 11, 19, 21-24. Covers to #19, 21-24 reprint story panels.*

MYSTERIOUS ADVENTURES
Story Comics: Mar, 1951 - No. 24, Mar, 1955; No. 25, Aug, 1955

	GD 2.0	VG 4.0	FN 6.0	VF 8.0	VF/NM 9.0	NM- 9.2
1-All horror stories	90	180	270	576	988	1400
2-(6/51)	50	100	150	315	533	750
3,4,6,10	47	94	141	296	498	700
5-Severed heads/bondage-c	53	106	159	334	567	800
7-Dagger in eye panel; dismemberment stories	57	114	171	362	619	875
8-Eyeball story	58	116	174	371	636	900
9-Extreme violence (8/52)	53	106	159	334	567	800
11-(12/52)-Used in **SOTI**, pg. 84	50	100	150	315	533	750
12,14: 14-E.C. Old Witch swipe	47	94	141	296	498	700
13-Classic skull-c	90	180	270	576	988	1400
15-21: 18-Used in Senate Investigative report, pgs. 5,6; E.C. swipe/TFTC #35; The Coffin-Keeper & Corpse (hosts). 20-Electric chair-c; used by Wertham in the Senate hearings. 21-Bondage/beheading-c; extreme violence	71	142	213	454	777	1100
22- "Cinderella" parody	50	100	150	315	533	750
23-Disbrow-a (6 pgs.); E.C. swipe "The Mystery Keeper's Tale" (host) and "Mother Ghoul's Nursery Tale"	45	90	135	284	480	675
24,25	39	78	117	231	378	525

NOTE: ***Tothish** art by **Ross Andru**-#22, 23. **Bache** a-8. **Cameron** a-5-7. **Harrison** a-12. **Hollingsworth** a-3-8, 12. **Schaffenberger** a-24, 25. **Wildey** a-15, 17.*

MYSTERIOUS ISLAND (Also see Classic Comics #34)
Dell Publishing Co.: No. 1213, July-Sept, 1961

	GD 2.0	VG 4.0	FN 6.0	VF 8.0	VF/NM 9.0	NM- 9.2
Four Color 1213-Movie, photo-c	7	14	21	49	92	135

MYSTERIOUS ISLE
Dell Publishing Co.: Nov-Jan, 1963/64 (Jules Verne)

	GD 2.0	VG 4.0	FN 6.0	VF 8.0	VF/NM 9.0	NM- 9.2
1-Painted-c	3	6	9	21	33	45

MYSTERIOUS RIDER, THE (See Zane Grey, 4-Color 301)

MYSTERIOUS STORIES (Formerly Horror From the Tomb #1)
Premier Magazines: No. 2, Dec-Jan, 1954-1955 - No. 7, Dec, 1955

	GD 2.0	VG 4.0	FN 6.0	VF 8.0	VF/NM 9.0	NM- 9.2
2-Woodbridge-c; last pre-code issue	53	106	159	334	567	800
3-Woodbridge-c/a	39	78	117	231	378	525
4-7: 5-Cinderella parody. 6-Woodbridge-c	36	72	108	211	343	475

NOTE: ***Hollingsworth** a-2, 4.*

MYSTERIOUS STRANGER
DC Comics: Aug/Sept. 1952

nn-Ashcan comic, not distributed to newsstands, only for in-house use. Cover art is All Star Western #60 with interior being Sensation Comics #100. A FN/VF copy sold for $2,357.50 in 2002.

MYSTERIOUS SUSPENSE (Also see Blue Beetle #1 (1967))
Charlton Comics: Oct, 1968 (12¢)

	GD 2.0	VG 4.0	FN 6.0	VF 8.0	VF/NM 9.0	NM- 9.2
1-Return of the Question by Ditko (c/a)	6	12	18	41	76	110

MYSTERIOUS TRAVELER (See Tales of the...)

MYSTERIOUS TRAVELER COMICS (Radio)
Trans-World Publications: Nov, 1948

	GD 2.0	VG 4.0	FN 6.0	VF 8.0	VF/NM 9.0	NM- 9.2
1-Powell-c/a(2); Poe adaptation, "Tell Tale Heart"	68	136	204	435	743	1050

MYSTERIUS
DC Comics (WildStorm): Mar, 2009 - No. 6, Aug, 2009 ($2.99, limited series)

	GD 2.0	VG 4.0	FN 6.0	VF 8.0	VF/NM 9.0	NM- 9.2
1-6-Jeff Parker-a/Tom Fowler-a						3.00
TPB (2010, $17.99) r/#1-6						18.00

MYSTERY COMICS
William H. Wise & Co.: 1944 - No. 4, 1944 (No months given)

	GD 2.0	VG 4.0	FN 6.0	VF 8.0	VF/NM 9.0	NM- 9.2
1-The Magnet, The Silver Knight, Brad Spencer, Wonderman, Dick Devins, King of Futuria, & Zudo the Jungle Boy begin (all 1st app.); Schomburg-c on all	168	336	504	1075	1838	2600
2-Bondage-c	103	206	309	659	1130	1600
3,4: 3-Lance Lewis, Space Detective begins (1st app.); Robot-c. 4-(V2#1 inside); KKK-c	97	194	291	621	1061	1500

MYSTERY COMICS DIGEST
Gold Key/Whitman?: Mar, 1972 - No. 26, Oct, 1975

	GD 2.0	VG 4.0	FN 6.0	VF 8.0	VF/NM 9.0	NM- 9.2
1-Ripley's Believe It or Not; reprint of Ripley's #1 origin Ra-Ka-Tep the Mummy; Wood-a	4	8	12	26	41	55
2-9: 2-Boris Karloff Tales of Mystery; Wood-a; 1st app. Werewolf Count Wulfstein. 3-Twilight Zone (TV); Crandall, Toth & George Evans-a; 1st app. Tragg & Simbar the Lion Lord; (2) Crandall/Frazetta-r/Twilight Zone #1 4-Ripley's Believe It or Not; 1st app. Baron Tibor, the Vampire. 5-Boris Karloff Tales of Mystery; 1st app. Dr. Spektor. 6-Twilight Zone (TV); 1st app. U.S. Marshal Reid & Sir Duane; Evans-r. 7-Ripley's Believe It or Not; origin The Lurker in the Swamp; 1st app. Duroc. 8-Boris Karloff Tales of Mystery; McWilliams-r; Orlando-r. 9-Twilight Zone (TV); Williamson, Crandall, McWilliams-a; 2nd Tragg app.;Torres, Evans, Heck/Tuska-r	3	6	9	20	30	40
10-26: 10,13-Ripley's Believe It or Not: 13-Orlando-r. 11,14-Boris Karloff Tales of Mystery. 14-1st app. Xorkon. 12,15-Twilight Zone (TV). 16,19,22,25-Ripley's Believe It or Not. 17-Boris Karloff Tales of Mystery; Williamson-r; Orlando-r. 18,21,24-Twilight Zone (TV). 20,23,26-Boris Karloff Tales of Mystery	3	6	9	16	23	30

NOTE: *Dr. Spektor app.-#5, 10-12, 21. Durak app.-#15. Duroc app.-#14 (later called Durak). King George 1st app.-#8.*

MYSTERY GIRL
Dark Horse Comics: Dec, 2015 - No. 4, Mar, 2016 ($3.99)

	GD 2.0	VG 4.0	FN 6.0	VF 8.0	VF/NM 9.0	NM- 9.2
1-4-Tobin-s/Albuquereque-a						4.00

MYSTERY IN SPACE (Also see Fireside Book Series and Pulp Fiction Library: ...)
National Periodical Pub.: 4-5/51 - No. 110, 9/66; No. 111, 9/80 - No. 117, 3/81 (#1-3: 52 pgs.)

	GD 2.0	VG 4.0	FN 6.0	VF 8.0	VF/NM 9.0	NM- 9.2
1-Frazetta-a, 8 pgs.; Knights of the Galaxy begins, ends #8	248	496	744	2046	4623	7200
2	88	176	264	704	1577	2450
3	63	126	187	504	1127	1750
4,5	50	100	150	400	900	1400
6-10: 7-Toth-a	40	80	120	296	673	1050
11-15	33	66	99	240	538	835
16-18,20-25: Interplanetary Insurance feature by Infantino in all. 21-1st app. Space Cabbie. 24-Last pre-code issue	30	60	90	211	473	735
19-Virgil Finlay-a	31	62	93	225	505	785
26-40: 26-Space Cabbie feature begins. 34-1st S.A. issue. 36,40-Grey-tone-c	23	46	69	164	362	560
41-52: 45,46-Grey-tone-c. 47-Space Cabbie ends	17	34	51	119	265	410
53-Adam Strange begins (8/59, 10pg. sty); robot-c	155	310	465	1279	2890	4500
54	43	86	129	318	722	1125
55-Grey tone-c	41	82	123	304	690	1075
56-60: 59-Kane/Anderson-a	23	46	69	164	362	560
61-71: 61-1st app. Adam Strange foe Ulthoon. 62-1st app. A.S. foe Mortan. 63-Origin Vandor. 66-Star Rovers begin (1st app.). 68-1st app. Dust Devils (6/61). 69-1st Mailbag. 70-2nd app. Dust Devils. 71-Last 10¢ issue	18	36	54	128	284	440
72-74,76-80	13	26	39	86	188	290
75-JLA x-over in Adam Strange (5/62)(sequel to J.L.A. #3, 2nd app. of Kanjar Ro)	22	44	66	152	336	520
81-86	10	20	30	64	132	200
87-(11/63)-Adam Strange/Hawkman double feat begins; 3rd Hawkman tryout series	15	30	45	100	220	340
88-Adam Strange & Hawkman stories	13	26	39	89	195	300
89-Adam Strange & Hawkman stories	13	26	39	86	188	290

Mystery Men Comics #15 © FOX

Mystery Society #1 © Niles

Mystical Tales #1 © MAR

GD VG FN VF VF/NM NM-
2.0 4.0 6.0 8.0 9.0 9.2

90-Book-length Adam Strange & Hawkman story; 1st team-up (3/64); Hawkman moves to own title next month; classic-c 15 30 45 100 220 340
91-102: 91-End Infantino art on Adam Strange; double-length Adam Strange story. 92-Space Ranger begins (6/64), ends #103. 92-94,96,98-Space Ranger-c. 94,98-Adam Strange/Space Ranger team-up. 102-Adam Strange ends (no Space Ranger) 7 14 21 44 82 120
103-Origin Ultra, the Multi-Alien; last Space Ranger 5 10 15 35 63 90
104-110: 110-(9/66)-Last 12¢ issue 5 10 15 30 50 70
V17#111(9/80)-117: 117-Newton-a(3 pgs.) 2 4 6 8 11 14

NOTE: ***Anderson*** *a-2, 4, 8-10, 12-17, 19, 45-48, 51, 57, 59i, 61-64, 70, 76, 87-91; c-9, 10, 15-25, 87, 89, 105-108, 110.* ***Aparo*** *a-111.* ***Austin*** *a-112i.* ***Bolland*** *a-115.* ***Craig*** *a-114, 116.* ***Ditko*** *a-111, 114-116.* ***Drucker*** *a-13, 14.* ***Elias*** *a-98, 102, 103.* ***Golden*** *a-113p.* ***Sid Greene*** *a-78, 91.* ***Infantino*** *a-1-8, 11, 14-25, 27-46, 48, 49, 51, 53-91, 103, 117; c-60-86, 88, 90, 91, 105, 107.* ***Gil Kane*** *a-14p, 15p, 18p, 19p, 26p, 29-59p(most), 100-102; c-52, 101.* ***Kubert*** *a-113; c-111-115.* ***Moreira*** *c-27, 28.* ***Rogers*** *a-111.* ***Sekowsky*** *a-52.* ***Simon & Kirby*** *a-4(2 pgs.).* ***Spiegle*** *a-111, 114.* ***Starlin*** *c-116.* ***Sutton*** *a-112.* ***Tuska*** *a-115p, 117p.*

MYSTERY IN SPACE
DC Comics: Nov, 2006 - No. 8, Jul, 2007 ($3.99, limited series)

1-8: 1-Captain Comet's rebirth; Starlin-s/Shane Davis-a; The Weird by Starlin 4.00
1-Variant cover by Neal Adams 10.00
Volume One TPB (2007, $17.99) r/#1-5 18.00
Volume Two TPB (2007, $17.99) r/#6-8 and The Weird from #1-4 18.00

MYSTERY IN SPACE
DC Comics (Vertigo): Jul, 2012 ($7.99, one-shot)

1-Short sci-fi stories by various incl. Kaluta, Allred, Baker, Diggle, Gianfelice; Sook-c 8.00

MYSTERY MEN
Marvel Comics: Aug, 2011 - No. 5, Nov, 2011 ($2.99, limited series)

1-5-Zircher-a/c; Liss-s; Pulp-era characters in 1932 3.00

MYSTERY MEN COMICS
Fox Features Syndicate: Aug, 1939 - No. 31, Feb, 1942

1-Intro. & 1st app. The Blue Beetle, The Green Mask, Rex Dexter of Mars by Briefer, Zanzibar by Tuska, Lt. Drake, D-13-Secret Agent by Powell, Chen Chang, Wing Turner, & Captain Denny Scott 1350 2700 4050 10,000 17,500 25,000
2-Robot & sci/fi-c (2nd Robot-c w/Movie #6) 423 846 1269 3000 5250 7500
3 (10/39)-Classic Lou Fine-c 622 1244 1866 4541 8021 11,500
4,5: 4-Capt. Savage begins (11/39) 331 662 993 2317 4059 5800
6-Tuska-c 300 600 900 1950 3375 4800
7-1st Blue Beetle-c app. 343 686 1029 2400 4200 6000
8-Lou Fine bondage-c 314 628 942 2198 3849 5500
9-The Moth begins; Lou Fine-c 219 438 657 1402 2401 3400
10-12: All Joe Simon-c. 10-Wing Turner by Kirby; Simon bondage-c. 11-Intro. Domino 213 426 639 1363 2332 3300
13-Intro. Lynx & sidekick Blackie (8/40) 142 284 426 909 1555 2200
14-18 135 270 405 864 1482 2100
19-Intro. & 1st app. Miss X (ends #21) 142 284 426 909 1555 2200
20-31: 26-The Wraith begins 129 258 387 826 1413 2000

NOTE: ***Briefer*** *a-1-15, 20, 24; c-9.* ***Cuidera*** *a-22.* ***Lou Fine*** *c-1-5,8,9.* ***Powell*** *a-1-15, 24.* ***Simon*** *c-10-12.* ***Tuska*** *a-1-16, 22, 24, 27; c-6. Bondage-c 1, 3, 7, 8, 10, 25, 27-29, 31. Blue Beetle c-7, 8, 10-31. D-13 Secret Agent c-6. Green Mask c-1, 3-5. Rex Dexter of Mars c-2, 9.*

MYSTERY MEN MOVIE ADAPTION
Dark Horse Comics: July, 1999 - No. 2, Aug, 1999 ($2.95, mini-series)

1,2-Fingerman-s; photo-c 3.00

MYSTERY PLAY, THE
DC Comics (Vertigo): 1994 ($19.95, one-shot)

nn-Hardcover-Morrison-s/Muth-painted art 25.00
Softcover ($9.95)-New Muth cover 10.00

MYSTERY SOCIETY
IDW Publishing: May, 2010 - No. 5, Oct, 2010 ($3.99, limited series)

1-5-Niles-s/Staples-a 4.00
... Special (3/13, $3.99) Niles-s/Ritchie-a/c 4.00

MYSTERY TALES
Atlas Comics (20CC): Mar, 1952 - No. 54, Aug, 1957

1-Horror/weird stories in all 181 362 543 1158 1979 2800
2-Krigstein-a 103 206 309 659 1130 1600
3-10: 6-A-Bomb panel. 10-Story similar to "The Assassin" from Shock SuspenStories 84 168 252 538 919 1300
11,13-21: 14-Maneely s/f story. 20-Electric chair issue. 21-Matt Fox-a; decapitation story 57 114 171 362 619 875
12,22: 12-Matt Fox-a. 22-Forte/Matt Fox-c; a(i) 60 120 180 381 653 925
23-26 (2/55)-Last precode issue 52 104 156 328 552 775
27,29-35,37,38,41-43,48,49: 43-Morisi story contains Frazetta art swipes from Untamed Love 41 82 123 256 428 600

GD VG FN VF VF/NM NM-
2.0 4.0 6.0 8.0 9.0 9.2

28,36,39,40,45: 28-Jack Katz-a. 36,39-Krigstein-a. 40,45-Ditko-a (#45 is 3 pgs. only) 41 82 123 260 435 610
44,51-Williamson/Krenkel-a 42 84 126 265 445 625
46-Williamson/Krenkel-a; Crandall text illos 42 84 126 265 445 625
47-Crandall, Ditko, Powell-a 42 84 126 265 445 625
50,52,53: 50-Torres, Morrow-a 41 82 123 256 428 600
54-Crandall, Check-a 41 82 123 260 435 610

NOTE: ***Ayers*** *a-18, 49, 52.* ***Berg*** *a-17, 51.* ***Colan*** *a-1, 3, 18, 35, 43.* ***Colletta*** *a-18.* ***Drucker*** *a-41.* ***Everett*** *a-2, 29, 33, 35, 41; c-8-11, 14, 38, 39, 41, 43, 44, 46, 48-51, 53.* ***Fass*** *a-16.* ***Forte*** *a-21, 22, 45, 46.* ***Matt Fox*** *a-12?, 21, 22; c-22.* ***Heath*** *a-3; c-3, 15, 17, 26.* ***Heck*** *a-25.* ***Kinstler*** *a-15.* ***Mort Lawrence*** *a-26, 32, 34.* ***Maneely*** *a-1, 9, 14, 22; c-12, 23, 24, 27.* ***Mooney*** *a-3, 40.* ***Morisi*** *a-43, 49, 52.* ***Morrow*** *a-50.* ***Orlando*** *a-51.* ***Pakula*** *a-16.* ***Powell*** *a-21, 29, 37, 38, 47.* ***Reinman*** *a-1, 14, 17.* ***Robinson*** *a-7p, 42.* ***Romita*** *a-37.* ***Roussos*** *a-4, 44.* ***R.Q. Sale*** *a-45, 46, 49.* ***Severin*** *c-52.* ***Shores*** *a-17, 45.* ***Tuska*** *a-10, 12, 14.* ***Whitney*** *a-2.* ***Wildey*** *a-37.*

MYSTERY TALES
Super Comics: 1964

Super Reprint #16,17('64): 16-r/Tales of Horror #2. 17-r/Eerie #14(Avon), 18-Kubert-r/Strange Terrors #4 3 6 9 14 20 25

MYSTERY TRAIL
DC Comics: Feb/Mar 1950

nn - Ashcan comic, not distributed to newsstands, only for in-house use. Cover art is Danger Trail #3 with interior being Star Spangled Comics #109. A FN/VF copy sold for $2,357.50 in 2002.

MYSTIC (3rd Series)
Marvel/Atlas Comics (CLDS 1/CSI 2-21/OMC 22-35/CSI 35-61): March, 1951 - No. 61, Aug, 1957

1-Atom bomb panels; horror/weird stories in all 135 270 405 864 1482 2100
2 66 132 198 419 722 1025
3-Eyes torn out 58 116 174 371 636 900
4- "The Devil Birds" by Wolverton (6 pgs.) 95 190 285 603 1039 1475
5,7-10 47 94 141 298 504 710
6- "The Eye of Doom" by Wolverton (7 pgs.) 95 190 285 603 1039 1475
11-17,19,20: 16-Bondage/torture c/story 41 82 123 256 428 600
18-Classic Everett skeleton-c 65 130 195 416 708 1000
21-25,27-36-Last precode (3/55). 25-E.C. swipe 38 76 114 228 369 510
26-Atomic War story; severed head story/cover 42 84 126 265 450 635
37-51,53-56,61 31 62 93 182 296 410
52-Wood-a; Crandall-a? 32 64 96 192 314 435
57-Story "Trapped in the Ant-Hill" (1957) is very similar to "The Man in the Ant Hill" in TTA #27 41 82 123 256 428 600
58,59-Krigstein-a 32 64 96 188 307 425
60-Williamson/Mayo-a (4 pgs.) 32 64 96 192 314 435

NOTE: ***Andru*** *a-23, 25.* ***Ayers*** *a-35, 53; c-8.* ***Berg*** *a-49.* ***Cameron*** *a-49, 51.* ***Check*** *a-31, 60.* ***Colan*** *a-3, 7, 12, 21, 37, 60.* ***Colletta*** *a-29.* ***Drucker*** *a-46, 52, 56.* ***Everett*** *a-8, 9, 17, 40, 44, 57; c-13, 18, 21, 42, 47, 49, 51-55, 57-59, 61.* ***Forte*** *a-35, 52, 58.* ***Fox*** *a-24i.* ***Al Hartley*** *a-35.* ***Heath*** *a-10; c-10, 20, 22, 23, 25, 30.* ***Infantino*** *a-12.* ***Kane*** *a-8, 24p.* ***Jack Katz*** *a-31, 33.* ***Mort Law.rence*** *a-19, 37.* ***Maneely*** *a-22, 24, 58; c-7, 15, 28, 29, 31.* ***Moldoff*** *a-29.* ***Morisi*** *a-48, 49, 52.* ***Morrow*** *a-51.* ***Orlando*** *a-57, 61.* ***Pakula*** *a-52, 57, 59.* ***Powell*** *a-52, 54-56.* ***Robinson*** *a-5.* ***Romita*** *a-11, 15.* ***R.Q. Sale*** *a-35, 53, 58.* ***Sekowsky*** *a-1, 2, 4, 5.* ***Severin*** *c-56, 60.* ***Tuska*** *a-15.* ***Whitney*** *a-33.* ***Wildey*** *a-28, 30.* ***Ed Win*** *a-17, 20. Canadian reprints known-title 'Startling.'*

MYSTIC (Also see CrossGen Chronicles)
CrossGeneration Comics: Jul, 2000 - No. 43, Jan, 2004 ($2.95)

1-43: 1-Marz-s/Peterson & Dell-a. 15-Cameos by DC & Marvel characters 3.00

MYSTIC (CrossGen characters)
Marvel Comics: Oct, 2011 - No. 4, Jan, 2012 ($2.99, limited series)

1-4-G. Willow Wilson-s/David López-a/Amanda Conner-c 3.00

MYSTICAL TALES
Atlas Comics (CCC 1/EPI 2-8): June, 1956 - No. 8, Aug, 1957

1-Everett-c/a 60 120 180 381 653 925
2-4: 2-Berg-a. 3,4-Crandall-a. 34 68 102 204 332 460
5-Williamson-a (4 pgs.) 36 72 108 216 351 485
6-Torres, Krigstein-a 34 68 102 199 325 450
7-Bolle, Forte, Torres, Orlando-a 32 64 96 192 314 435
8-Krigstein, Check-a 34 68 102 199 325 450

NOTE: ***Everett*** *a-1; c-1-4, 6, 7.* ***Orlando*** *a-1, 2, 7.* ***Pakula*** *a-3.* ***Powell*** *a-1, 4.*

MYSTIC ARCANA
Marvel Comics: Aug, 2007 - Jan, 2008 ($2.99)

1-Magik on-c; art by Scott and Nguyen; Ian McNee and Dani Moonstar app. 3.00
(#2)...: Black Knight 1 (9/07, $2.99) Djurdjevic-c/Grummett & Hanna-a; origin retold 3.00
3-("Scarlet Witch" on cover)(10/07, $2.99) Djurdjevic-c/Santacruz-a; childhood 3.00
(#4)...: Sister Grimm 1 (1/08, $2.99) Nico Minoru from Runaways; Djurdjevic-c/Noto-a 3.00
...: The Book of Marvel Magic ('07, $3.99) Official Handbook profiles of the magic-related 4.00
HC (2007, $24.99, d.j.) r/series and ...: The Book of Marvel Magic 25.00

MYSTIC COMICS (1st Series)

Mythos: Fantastic Four #1 © MAR

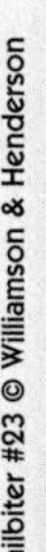
Mythos: The Final Tour #1 © DC

Nailbiter #23 © Williamson & Henderson

GD 2.0 | VG 4.0 | FN 6.0 | VF 8.0 | VF/NM 9.0 | NM- 9.2

Timely Comics (TPI 1-5/TCI 8-10): March, 1940 - No. 10, Aug, 1942

1-Origin The Blue Blaze, The Dynamic Man, & Flexo the Rubber Robot; Zephyr Jones, 3X's & Deep Sea Demon app.; The Magician begins (all 1st app.); c-from Spider pulp V18#1, 6/39 — 1500 3000 4500 12,000 25,000 38,000
2-The Invisible Man & Master Mind Excello begin; Space Rangers, Zara of the Jungle, Taxi Taylor app. (scarce) — 703 1406 2109 5132 9066 13,000
3-Origin Hercules, who last appears in #4 — 459 918 1377 3350 5925 8500
4-Origin The Thin Man & The Black Widow; Merzak the Mystic app.; last Flexo, Dynamic Man, Invisible Man & Blue Blaze (some issues have date sticker on cover; others have July w/August overprint in silver color); Roosevelt assassination-c — 649 1298 1947 4738 8369 12,000
5-(3/41)-Origin The Black Marvel, The Blazing Skull, The Sub-Earth Man, Super Slave & The Terror; The Moon Man & Black Widow app.; 5-German war-c begin, end #10 — 423 846 1269 3000 5250 7500
6-(10/41)-Origin The Challenger & The Destroyer (1st app.?; also see All-Winners #2, Fall, 1941) — 524 1048 1572 3825 6763 9700
7-The Witness begins (12/41, origin & 1st app.); origin Davey & the Demon; last Black Widow; Hitler opens his trunk of terror-c by Simon & Kirby (classic-c) — 703 1406 2109 5132 9066 13,000
8,10: 10-Father Time, World of Wonder, & Red Skeleton app.; last Challenger & Terror — 486 972 1458 3550 6275 9000
9-Gary Gaunt app.; last Black Marvel, Mystic & Blazing Skull; Hitler-c — 622 1244 1866 4541 8021 11,500

NOTE: ***Gabrielle** c-8-10. **Rico** a-9(2). **Schomburg** a-1-4; c-1-6. **Sekowsky** a-9. **Sekowsky/Klein** a-8 (Challenger). Bondage c-1, 2, 9.*

MYSTIC COMICS (2nd Series)
Timely Comics (ANC): Oct, 1944 - No. 3, Win, 1944-45; No. 4, Mar, 1945

1-The Angel, The Destroyer, The Human Torch, Terry Vance the Schoolboy Sleuth, & Tommy Tyme begin — 300 600 900 1920 3310 4700
2-(Fall/44)-Last Human Torch & Terry Vance; bondage/hypo-c — 181 362 543 1158 1979 2800
3-Last Angel (two stories) & Tommy Tyme — 142 284 426 909 1555 2200
4-The Young Allies-c & app.; Schomburg-c — 135 270 405 864 1482 2100

MYSTIC COMICS 70th ANNIVERARY SPECIAL
Marvel Comics: Oct, 2009 ($3.99, one-shot)

1-New story of The Vision; r/G.A. Vision app. from Marvel Myst. Comics #13 & 16 — 5.00

MYSTIC HANDS OF DR. STRANGE
Marvel Comics: May, 2010 ($3.99, B&W, one-shot)

1-Short stories; art by Irving, Brunner, McKeever & Marcos Martin; Parrillo-c — 4.00

MYSTIQUE (See X-Men titles)
Marvel Comics: June, 2003 - No. 24, Apr, 2005 ($2.99)

1-24: 1-6-Linsner-c/Vaughan-s/Lucas-a. 7-Ryan-a begins. 8-Horn-c. 9-24-Mayhew-c 23-Wolverine & Rogue app. — 3.00
... Vol. 1: Drop Dead Gorgeous TPB (2004, $14.99) r/#1-6 — 15.00
... Vol. 2: Tinker, Tailor, Mutant, Spy TPB (2004, $17.99) r/#7-13 — 18.00
... Vol. 3: Unnatural TPB (2004, $13.99) r/#14-18 — 14.00

MYSTIQUE & SABRETOOTH (Sabretooth and Mystique on-c)
Marvel Comics: Dec, 1996 - No. 4, Mar, 1997 ($1.95, limited series)

1-4: Characters from X-Men — 3.00

MY STORY (...True Romances in Pictures #5,6; becomes My Love Life #13) (Formerly Zago)
Hero Books (Fox Features Syndicate): No. 5, May, 1949 - No. 12, Aug, 1950

5-Kamen/Feldstein-a — 30 60 90 177 289 400
6-8,11,12: 12-Photo-c — 17 34 51 98 154 210
9,10-Wood-a — 27 54 81 158 259 360

MYTHIC
Image Comics: May, 2015 - Present ($1.99/$2.99/$3.99)

1-3: 1-($1.99) Phil Hester-s/John McCrea-a. 2,3-($2.99) — 3.00
4-8-($3.99) — 4.00

MYTHOS
Marvel Comics: Mar, 2006 - Dec, 2007 ($3.99)

1-Retelling of X-Men #1 with painted-a by Paolo Rivera; Paul Jenkins-s — 4.00
...: Captain America 1 (8/08) Retelling of origin; painted-a by Rivera; Jenkins-s — 4.00
...: Fantastic Four 1 (12/07) Retelling of Fantastic Four #1; painted-a by Rivera; Jenkins-s — 4.00
...: Ghost Rider 1 (3/07) Retelling of Marvel Spotlight #5; painted-a by Rivera; Jenkins-s — 4.00
...: Hulk 1 (10/06) Retelling of Incredible Hulk #1; painted-a by Rivera; Jenkins-s — 4.00
...: Spider-Man 1 (8/07) Retelling of Amazing Fantasy #15; painted-a by Rivera; Jenkins-s — 4.00

MYTHOS: THE FINAL TOUR
DC Comics/Vertigo: Dec, 1996 - No. 3, Feb, 1997 ($5.95, limited series)

GD 2.0 | VG 4.0 | FN 6.0 | VF 8.0 | VF/NM 9.0 | NM- 9.2

1-3: 1-Ney Rieber-s/Amaro-a. 2-Snejbjerg-a; Constantine-app. 3-Kristiansen-a; Black Orchid-app. — 6.00

MYTHSTALKERS
Image Comics: Mar, 2003 - No. 8, Mar, 2004 ($2.95)

1-8-Jiro-a — 3.00

MY TRUE LOVE (Formerly Western Killers #64; Frank Buck #70 on)
Fox Features Syndicate: No. 65, July, 1949 - No. 69, March, 1950

65 — 24 48 72 142 234 325
66,68,69: 69-Morisi-a — 17 34 51 98 154 210
67-Wood-a — 27 54 81 158 259 360

NAIL, THE
Dark Horse Comics: June, 2004 - No. 4, Oct, 2004 ($2.99, limited series)

1-4-Rob Zombie & Steve Niles-s/Nat Jones-a/Simon Bisley-c — 3.00
TPB (2005, $12.95) r/series — 13.00

NAILBITER
Image Comics: May, 2014 - No. 30, Mar, 2017 ($2.99)

1-29: 1-Williamson-s/Henderson-a. 7-Brian Bendis appears as a character. 13-Archie style cover — 3.00
30-($3.99) Final issue — 4.00
.../ Hack/Slash 1 (3/15, $4.99) Flip book with Hack/Slash / Nailbiter 1 — 5.00

NAKED BRAIN (Marc Hempel's...)
Insight Studios Group: 2002 - No. 3, 2002 ($2.95, B&W, limited series)

1-3-Marc Hempel cartoons and sketches; Tug & Buster app. — 3.00

NAKED PREY, THE (See Movie Classics)

'NAM, THE (See Savage Tales #1, 2nd series & Punisher Invades...)
Marvel Comics Group: Dec, 1986 - No. 84, Sept, 1993

1-Golden a(p)/c begins, ends #13 — 1 2 3 5 6 8
1 (2nd printing) — 3.00
2-7,9-25,27-66,70-74: 7-Golden-a (2 pgs.). 32-Death R. Kennedy. 52,53-Frank Castle (The Punisher) app. 52,53-Gold 2nd printings. 58-Silver logo. 65-Heath-c/a. 70-Lomax scripts begin — 3.00
8-1st app. Fudd Verzyl, Tunnel Rat — 5.00
26-2nd app. Fudd Verzyl, Tunnel Rat — 4.00
67-69-Punisher 3 part story — 4.00
75-($2.25, 52 pgs.) — 6.00
76-84 — 3.00
Trade Paperback 1,2: 1-r/#1-4. 2-r/#5-8 — 1 2 3 5 6 8
TPB ('99, $14.95) r/#1-4; recolored — 15.00

'NAM MAGAZINE, THE
Marvel Comics: Aug, 1988 - No. 10, May, 1989 ($2.00, B&W, 52pgs.)

1-10: Each issue reprints 2 issues of the comic — 4.00

NAMELESS
Image Comics: Feb, 2015 - No. 6, Dec, 2015 ($2.99)

1-6-Morrison-s/Burnham-a — 3.00

NAMELESS, THE
Image Comics: May, 1997 - No. 5, Sept, 1997 ($2.95, B&W)

1-5: Pruett/Hester-s/a — 3.00
...: The Director's Cut TPB (2006, $15.99) r/#1-5; original proposal by Pruett — 16.00

NAMES, THE
DC Comics (Vertigo): Nov, 2014 - No. 9, Jul, 2015 ($2.99, limited series)

1-9-Peter Milligan-s/Leandro Fernandez-a — 3.00

NAMESAKE
BOOM! Studios: Nov, 2016 - No. 4, Feb, 2017 ($3.99, limited series)

1-4-Orlando-s/Rebelka-a — 4.00

NAMES OF MAGIC, THE (Also see Books of Magic)
DC Comics (Vertigo): Feb, 2001 - No. 5, June, 2001 ($2.50, limited series)

1-5: Bolton painted-c on all; Case-a; leads into Hunter: The Age of Magic — 3.00
TPB (2002, $14.95) r/#1-5 — 15.00

NAME OF THE GAME, THE
DC Comics: 2001 ($29.95, graphic novel)

Hardcover ($29.95) Will Eisner-s/a — 30.00

NAMOR (Volume 2)
Marvel Comics: June, 2003 - No. 12, May, 2004 (25¢/$2.25/$2.99)

1-(25¢-c)Young Namor in the 1920s; Larroca-c/a — 3.00
2-6-($2.25) Larroca-a — 3.00

Namora #1 © MAR

Nathaniel Dusk #2 © DC

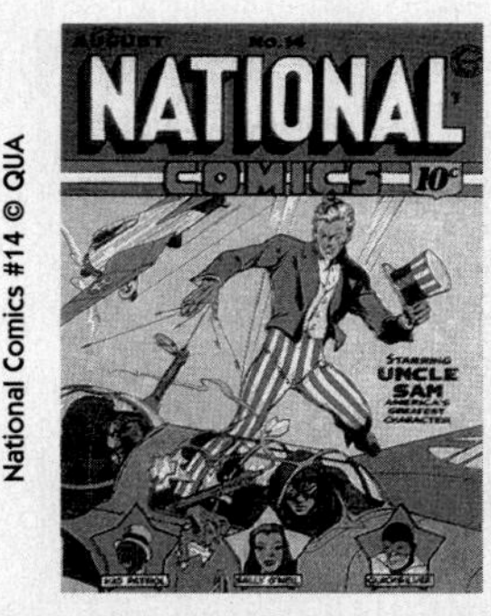

National Comics #14 © QUA

GD VG FN VF VF/NM NM-
2.0 4.0 6.0 8.0 9.0 9.2

GD VG FN VF VF/NM NM-
2.0 4.0 6.0 8.0 9.0 9.2

7-12-($2.99): 7-Olliffe-a begins 3.00

NAMORA (See Marvel Mystery Comics #82 & Sub-Mariner Comics)
Marvel Comics (PrPl): Fall, 1948 - No. 3, Dec, 1948

1-Sub-Mariner x-over in Namora; Namora by Everett(2), Sub-Mariner by Rico (10 pgs.) 300 600 900 2010 3505 5000
2-The Blonde Phantom & Sub-Mariner story; Everett-a 206 412 618 1318 2259 3200
3-(Scarce)-Sub-Mariner app.; Everett-a 239 478 717 1530 2615 3700

NAMORA (See Agents of Atlas)
Marvel Comics: Aug, 2010 ($3.99, one-shot)

1-Parker-s/Pichelli-a 4.00

NAMOR: THE FIRST MUTANT (Curse of the Mutants x-over with X-Men titles)
Marvel Comics: Oct, 2010 - No. 11, Aug, 2011 ($3.99/$2.99)

1-($3.99) Olivetti-a/Stuart Moore-s/Jae Lee-c; back-up retelling of origin and history 4.00
2-11-($2.99) 2-Emma Frost app. 5-Mayhew-c. 6-10-Noto-c 3.00
... Annual 1 (7/11, $3.99) Part 3 of "Escape From the Negative Zone" x-over; Fiumara-a 4.00

NAMOR, THE SUB-MARINER (See Prince Namor & Sub-Mariner)
Marvel Comics: Apr, 1990 - No. 62, May, 1995 ($1.00/$1.25/$1.50)

1-Byrne-c/a/scripts in 1-25 (scripts only #26-32) 1 2 3 5 6 8
2-5: 5-Iron Man app. 4.00
6-11,13-23,25,27-36,38-49,51-62: 16-Re-intro Iron Fist (8-cameo only). 18-Punisher cameo (1 panel); 21-23,25-Wolverine cameos. 22,23-Iron Fist app. 28-Iron Fist-c/story. 31-Dr. Doom-c/story. 33,34-Iron Fist cameo. 35-New Tiger Shark-c/story. 48-The Thing app. 3.00
12,24: 12-(52pgs.)-Re-intro. The Invaders. 24-Namor vs. Wolverine 4.00
26-Namor w/new costume; 1st Jae Lee-c/a this title (5/92) & begins 5.00
37-Aqua holografx foil-c 4.00
50-($1.75, 52 pgs.)-Newsstand ed.; w/bound-in S-M trading card sheet (both versions) 4.00
50-($2.95, 52 pgs.)-Collector edition w/foil-c 5.00
Annual 1-4 ('91-94, 68 pgs.): 1-3 pg. origin recap. 2-Return/Defenders. 3-Bagged w/card. 4-Painted-c 4.00

NOTE: *Jae Lee a-26-30p, 31-37, 38p, 39, 40; c-26-40.*

NANCY AND SLUGGO (See Comics On Parade & Sparkle Comics)
United Features Syndicate: No. 16, 1949 - No. 23, 1954

16(#1) 10 20 30 58 79 100
17-23 8 16 24 40 50 60

NANCY & SLUGGO (Nancy #146-173; formerly Sparkler Comics)
St. John/Dell #146-187/Gold Key #188 on: No. 121, Apr, 1955-No. 192, Oct, 1963

121(4/55)(St. John) 10 20 30 54 72 90
122-145(7/57)(St. John) 8 16 24 44 57 70
146(9/57)-Peanuts begins, ends #192 (Dell) 8 16 24 56 108 160
147-161 (Dell) Peanuts in all 8 16 24 51 86 120
162-165,177-180-John Stanley-a 7 14 21 44 82 120
166-176-Oona & Her Haunted House series; Stanley-a 7 14 21 49 92 135
181-187(3-5/62)(Dell) 5 10 15 35 63 90
188(10/62)-192 (Gold Key) 5 10 15 35 63 90
Four Color 1034(9-11/59)-Summer Camp 5 10 15 30 50 70
(See Dell Giant #34, 45 & Dell Giants)

NANNY AND THE PROFESSOR (TV)
Dell Publishing Co.: Aug, 1970 - No. 2, Oct, 1970 (Photo-c)

1-(01-546-008) 5 10 15 30 50 70
2 4 8 12 25 40 55

NAPOLEON
Dell Publishing Co.: No. 526, Dec, 1953

Four Color 526 5 10 15 30 50 70

NAPOLEON & SAMANTHA (See Walt Disney Showcase No. 10)

NAPOLEON & UNCLE ELBY (See Clifford McBride's...)
Eastern Color Printing Co.: July, 1942 (68 pgs.) (One Shot)

1 43 86 129 271 461 650
1945-American Book-Strafford Press (128 pgs.) (8x10-1/2"; B&W reprints; hardcover) 15 30 45 83 124 165

NARRATIVE ILLUSTRATION, THE STORY OF THE COMICS (Also see Good Triumphs Over Evil!)
M.C. Gaines: Summer, 1942 (32 pgs., 7-1/4"x10", B&W w/color inserts)

nn-16 pgs. text with illustrations of ancient art, strips and comic covers; 4 pg. WWII War Bond promo, "The Minute Man Answers the Call" color comic drawn by Shelly and a special 8-page color comic insert of "The Story of Saul" (from Picture Stories from the Bible #10 or soon to appear in PS #10) or "Noah and His Ark" or "The Story of Ruth". Insert has special title page indicating it was part of a Sunday newspaper supplement insert series that had already run in a New England "Sunday Herald." Another version exists with insert from Picture Stories from the Bible #7. (very rare) Estimated value... 1500.00

NOTE: ***Print, A Quarterly Journal of the Graphic Arts** Vol. 3 No. 2 (88 pg., square bound) features the 1st printing of Narrative Illustration, The Story of The Comics. A VG+ copy sold for $750 in 2005.*

NASCAR HEROES
Starbridge Media: 2007 - No. 3 ($3.95)

1-3: 1-Origin of fictional racer Jimmy Dash. 3-Origin of the Daytona 500; DeStefano-s 4.00
nn-(2008, Free Comic Book Day giveaway) The Mystery of Driver Z 3.00

NASH (WCW Wrestling)
Image Comics: July, 1999 - No. 2, July, 1999 ($2.95)

1,2-Regular and photo-c 3.00
1-($6.95) Photo-split-cover Edition 7.00

NATHANIEL DUSK
DC Comics: Feb, 1984 - No. 4, May, 1984 ($1.25, mini-series, direct sales, Baxter paper)

1-4: 1-Intro/origin; Gene Colan-c/a in all 3.00

NATHANIEL DUSK II
DC Comics: Oct, 1985 - No. 4, Jan, 1986 ($2.00, mini-series, Baxter paper)

1-4: Gene Colan-c/a in all 3.00

NATIONAL COMICS
Quality Comics Group: July, 1940 - No. 75, Nov, 1949

1-Uncle Sam begins (1st app.); origin sidekick Buddy by Eisner; origin Wonder Boy & Kid Dixon; Merlin the Magician (ends #45); Cyclone, Kid Patrol, Sally O'Neil Policewoman, Pen Miller (by Klaus Nordling; ends #22), Prop Powers (ends #26), & Paul Bunyan (ends #22) begin 649 1299 1947 4738 8369 12,000
2 274 548 822 1740 2995 4250
3-Last Eisner Uncle Sam 203 406 609 1289 2220 3150
4-Last Cyclone 152 304 456 965 1658 2350
5-(11/40)-Quicksilver begins (1st app.; 3rd w/lightning speed?; re-intro'd by DC in 1993 as Max Mercury in Flash #76, 2nd series); origin Uncle Sam; bondage-c 181 362 543 1158 1979 2800
6,8-11: 8-Jack & Jill begins (ends #22). 9-Flag-c 145 290 435 921 1586 2250
7-Classic Lou Fine-c 309 618 927 2163 3782 5400
12-15-Lou Fine-a 113 226 339 718 1234 1750
16-Classic skeleton-c; Lou Fine-a 181 362 543 1158 1979 2800
17,19-22: 21-Classic Nazi swastika cover. 22-Last Pen Miller (moves to Crack #23) 87 174 261 553 952 1350
18-(12/41)-Shows Asians attacking Pearl Harbor; on stands one month before actual event 174 348 522 1114 1907 2700
23-The Unknown & Destroyer 171 begin 87 174 261 553 952 1350
24-Japanese War-c 90 180 270 576 988 1400
25-30: 25-Nazi drug usage/hypodermic needle in story. 26-Wonder Boy ends. 27- G-2 the Unknown begins (ends #46). 29-Origin The Unknown 61 122 183 390 670 950
31-33: 33-Chic Carter begins (ends #47) 57 114 171 362 619 875
34-37,40: 35-Last Kid Patrol 52 104 156 328 552 775
38-Hitler, Tojo, Mussolini-c 90 180 270 576 988 1400
39-Hitler-c 92 184 276 584 1005 1425
41-Classic Uncle Sam American Eagle WWII-c 50 100 150 315 533 750
42-The Barker begins (1st app?, 5/44); The Barker covers begin 41 82 123 256 428 600
43-50: 48-Origin The Whistler 28 56 84 165 270 375
51-Sally O'Neil by Ward, 8 pgs. (12/45) 30 60 90 117 289 400
52-60 20 40 60 118 192 265
61-67: 67-Format change; Quicksilver app. 15 30 45 90 140 190
68-75: The Barker ends 15 30 45 83 124 165

NOTE: ***Cole** Quicksilver-13; Barker-43; c-43, 46, 47, 49-51. **Crandall** Uncle Sam-11-13 (with **Fine**), 25, 26; c-24-26, 30-33, 43. **Crandall** Paul Bunyan-10-13. **Fine** Uncle Sam-13 (w/**Crandall**), 17, 18; c-1-14, 16, 18, 21. **Gill Fox** c-69-74. **Guardineer** Quicksilver-27, 35. **Gustavson** Quicksilver-14-26. **McWilliams** a-23-28, 55, 57. Uncle Sam c-1-41. Barker c-42-75.*

NATIONAL COMICS (Also see All Star Comics 1999 crossover titles)
DC Comics: May, 1999 ($1.99, one-shot)

1-Golden Age Flash and Mr. Terrific; Waid-s/Lopresti-a 3.00

NATIONAL COMICS
DC Comics: Sept, 2012 ($3.99, one-shots)

... Eternity 1 (9/12) Re-intro of Kid Eternity; Lemire-s/Hamner-a/c 4.00
... Looker 1 (10/12) Vampire supermodel; Edginton-s/Mike S. Miller-a/March-c 4.00
... Madame X 1 (12/12) Rob Williams-s/Trevor Hairsine-a/Fiona Staples-c 4.00
... Rose & Thorn 1 (11/12) Taylor-s/Googe-a/Sook-c 4.00

National Velvet FC #1312 © DELL

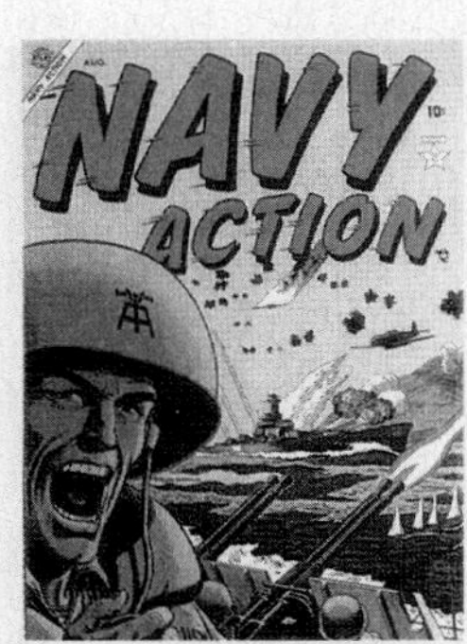

Navy Action #1 © MAR

Negative Burn #48 © Caliber

NATIONAL CRUMB, THE (Magazine-Size)
Mayfair Publications: August, 1975 (52 pgs., B&W) (Satire)

	GD 2.0	VG 4.0	FN 6.0	VF 8.0	VF/NM 9.0	NM- 9.2
1-Grandenetti-c/a, Ayers-a	2	4	6	11	16	20

NATIONAL VELVET (TV)
Dell Publishing Co./Gold Key: May-July, 1961 - No. 2, Mar, 1963 (All photo-c)

	GD 2.0	VG 4.0	FN 6.0	VF 8.0	VF/NM 9.0	NM- 9.2
Four Color 1195 (#1)	6	12	18	41	76	110
Four Color 1312, 01-556-207, 12-556-210 (Dell)	4	8	12	27	44	60
1,2: 1(12/62) (Gold Key). 2(3/63)	4	8	12	27	44	60

NATION OF SNITCHES
Piranha Press (DC): 1990 ($4.95, color, 52 pgs.)

	GD 2.0	VG 4.0	FN 6.0	VF 8.0	VF/NM 9.0	NM- 9.2
nn						5.00

NATION X (X-Men on the Utopia island)
Marvel Comics: Feb, 2010 - No. 4, May, 2010 ($3.99, limited series)

	GD 2.0	VG 4.0	FN 6.0	VF 8.0	VF/NM 9.0	NM- 9.2
1-4-Short stories by various. 1,4-Allred-a. 2-Choi, Cloonan-a. 4-Doop app.						4.00
...: X-Factor (3/10, $3.99) David-s/DeLandro-a						4.00

NATURE BOY (Formerly Danny Blaze; Li'l Rascal Twins #6 on)
Charlton Comics: No. 3, March, 1956 - No. 5, Feb, 1957

	GD 2.0	VG 4.0	FN 6.0	VF 8.0	VF/NM 9.0	NM- 9.2
3-1st app./origin; Blue Beetle story (last Golden Age app.); Buscema-c/a	22	44	66	132	216	300
4,5	16	32	48	94	147	200

NOTE: ***John Buscema** a-3, 4p, 5; c-3. **Powell** a-4.*

NATURE OF THINGS (Disney, TV/Movie)
Dell Publishing Co.: No. 727, Sept, 1956 - No. 842, Sept, 1957

	GD 2.0	VG 4.0	FN 6.0	VF 8.0	VF/NM 9.0	NM- 9.2
Four Color 727 (#1), 842-Jesse Marsh-a	5	10	15	33	57	80

NAUSICAA OF THE VALLEY OF WIND
Viz Comics: 1988 - No. 7, 1989; 1989 - No. 4, 1990 ($2.50, B&W, 68pgs.)

	GD 2.0	VG 4.0	FN 6.0	VF 8.0	VF/NM 9.0	NM- 9.2
Book 1-7: 1-Contains Moebius poster						5.00
Part II, Book 1-4 ($2.95)						5.00

NAVY ACTION (Sailor Sweeney #12-14)
Atlas Comics (CDS): Aug, 1954 - No. 11, Apr, 1956; No. 15, 1/57 - No. 18, 8/57

	GD 2.0	VG 4.0	FN 6.0	VF 8.0	VF/NM 9.0	NM- 9.2
1-Powell-a	39	78	117	240	395	550
2-Lawrence-a; RQ Sale-a	21	42	63	122	199	275
3-11: 4-Last precode (2/55)	18	36	54	105	165	225
15-18	16	32	48	94	147	200

NOTE: ***Berg** a-7, 9. **Colan** a-8. **Drucker** a-7, 17. **Everett** a-3, 7, 16; c-16, 17. **Heath** c-1, 2, 5, 6. **Maneely** a-5, 7, 8, 18; c-9, 11. **Pakula** a-2, 3, 9. **Reinman** a-17.*

NAVY COMBAT
Atlas Comics (MPI): June, 1955 - No. 20, Oct, 1958

	GD 2.0	VG 4.0	FN 6.0	VF 8.0	VF/NM 9.0	NM- 9.2
1-Torpedo Taylor begins by Don Heck; Heath-c	37	74	111	222	361	500
2	20	40	60	117	189	260
3-10	18	36	54	105	165	225
11,13-16,18-20: 14-Torres-a	16	32	48	94	147	200
12-Crandall-a	17	34	51	98	154	210
17-Williamson-a, 4 pgs.; Torres-a	17	34	51	98	154	210

NOTE: ***Ayers** a-15. **Berg** a-10, 11. **Colan** a-11. **Drucker** a-7. **Everett** a-3, 20; c-8 & 9 w/**Tuska**, 10, 13-16. **Forte** a-15, 18. **Heck** a-11(2), 15, 19. **Maneely** c-1, 6, 11, 17. **Morisi** a-8. **Pakula** a-7, 18. **Powell** a-20. **Reinman** a-18.*

NAVY HEROES
Almanac Publishing Co.: 1945

	GD 2.0	VG 4.0	FN 6.0	VF 8.0	VF/NM 9.0	NM- 9.2
1-Heavy in propaganda	16	32	48	94	147	200

NAVY PATROL
Key Publications: May, 1955 - No. 4, Nov, 1955

	GD 2.0	VG 4.0	FN 6.0	VF 8.0	VF/NM 9.0	NM- 9.2
1	10	20	30	56	76	95
2-4	8	16	24	40	50	60

NAVY TALES
Atlas Comics (CDS): Jan, 1957 - No. 4, July, 1957

	GD 2.0	VG 4.0	FN 6.0	VF 8.0	VF/NM 9.0	NM- 9.2
1-Everett-c; Berg, Powell-a	34	68	102	199	325	450
2-Williamson/Mayo-a(5 pgs); Crandall-a	20	40	60	114	182	250
3,4-Reinman-a; Severin-c. 4-Crandall-a	17	34	51	98	154	210

NOTE: ***Colan** a-4. **Maneely** c-2. **Reinman** a-2-4. **Sinnott** a-4.*

NAVY TASK FORCE
Stanmor Publications/Aragon Mag. No. 4-8: Feb, 1954 - No. 8, April, 1956

	GD 2.0	VG 4.0	FN 6.0	VF 8.0	VF/NM 9.0	NM- 9.2
1	12	24	36	67	94	120
2	8	16	24	44	57	70
3-8: 8-r/Navy Patrol #1; defeat of the Japanese Navy	8	16	24	40	50	60

NAVY WAR HEROES
Charlton Comics: Jan, 1964 - No. 7, Mar-Apr, 1965

	GD 2.0	VG 4.0	FN 6.0	VF 8.0	VF/NM 9.0	NM- 9.2
1	4	8	12	23	37	50
2-7	3	6	9	15	22	28

NAZA (Stone Age Warrior)
Dell Publishing Co.: Nov-Jan, 1963-64 - No. 9, March, 1966

	GD 2.0	VG 4.0	FN 6.0	VF 8.0	VF/NM 9.0	NM- 9.2
12-555-401 (#1)-Painted-c	5	10	15	31	53	75
2-9: 2-4-Painted-c	4	8	12	23	37	50

NEBBS, THE (Also see Crackajack Funnies)
Dell Publishing Co./Croydon Publishing Co.: 1941; 1945

	GD 2.0	VG 4.0	FN 6.0	VF 8.0	VF/NM 9.0	NM- 9.2
Large Feature Comic 23(1941)	22	44	66	132	216	300
1(1945, 36 pgs.)-Reprints	14	28	42	76	108	140

NECESSARY EVIL
Desperado Publishing: Oct, 2007 - No. 9, Nov, 2008 ($3.99)

	GD 2.0	VG 4.0	FN 6.0	VF 8.0	VF/NM 9.0	NM- 9.2
1-9: 1-Joshua Williamson-s/Marcus Harris-a/Dustin Nguyen-c						4.00

NECROMANCER
Image Comics (Top Cow): Sept, 2005 - No. 6, July 2006 ($2.99)

	GD 2.0	VG 4.0	FN 6.0	VF 8.0	VF/NM 9.0	NM- 9.2
1-6: 1-Manapul-a/Ortega-s; three covers by Manapul, Horn & Bachalo						3.00
... Pilot Season Vol. 1 #1 (11/07, $2.99) Ortega-s/Meyers-a/Manapul-c						3.00

NECROMANCER: THE GRAPHIC NOVEL
Marvel Comics (Epic Comics): 1989 ($8.95)

	GD 2.0	VG 4.0	FN 6.0	VF 8.0	VF/NM 9.0	NM- 9.2
nn						9.00

NECROWAR
Dreamwave Productions: July, 2003 - No. 3, Sept, 2003 ($2.95)

	GD 2.0	VG 4.0	FN 6.0	VF 8.0	VF/NM 9.0	NM- 9.2
1-3-Furman-s/Granov-digital art						3.00

NEGATION
CrossGeneration Comics: Dec, 2001 - No. 27, Mar, 2004 ($2.95)

	GD 2.0	VG 4.0	FN 6.0	VF 8.0	VF/NM 9.0	NM- 9.2
Prequel (12/01)						3.00
1-27: 1-(1/02) Pelletier-a/Bedard & Waid-s						3.00
... Lawbringer (11/02, $2.95) Nebres-a						3.00
Vol. 1: Bohica! (10/02, $19.95, TPB) r/ Prequel & #1-6						20.00
Vol. 2: Baptism of Fire (5/03, $15.95, TPB) r/#7-12						16.00
Vol. 3: Hounded (12/03, $15.95, TPB) r/#13-18						16.00

NEGATION WAR
CrossGeneration Comics: Apr, 2004 - No. 6 ($2.95)

	GD 2.0	VG 4.0	FN 6.0	VF 8.0	VF/NM 9.0	NM- 9.2
1-4-Bedard-s/Pelletier-a						3.00

NEGATIVE BURN
Caliber: 1993 - No. 50, 1997 ($2.95, B&W, anthology)

	GD 2.0	VG 4.0	FN 6.0	VF 8.0	VF/NM 9.0	NM- 9.2
1,2,4-12,14-47: Anthology by various including Bolland, Burden, Doran, Gaiman, Moebius, Moore, & Pope						4.00
3,13: 3-Bone story. 13-Strangers in Paradise story	2	4	6	8	10	12
48,49-($4.95)						5.00
50-($6.95, 96 pgs.)-Gaiman, Robinson, Bolland						7.00
...Summer Special 2005 (Image, 2005, $9.99) new short stories by various						10.00
...: The Best From 1993-1998 (Image, 1/05, $19.95) r/short stories by various						20.00
...Winter Special 2005 (Image, 2005, $9.95) new short stories by various						10.00

NEGATIVE BURN
Image Comics (Desperado): May, 2006 - No. 21 ($5.99, B&W, anthology)

	GD 2.0	VG 4.0	FN 6.0	VF 8.0	VF/NM 9.0	NM- 9.2
1-21: 1-Art by Bolland, Powell, Luna, Smith, Hester. 2-Milk & Cheese by Dorkin						6.00

NEGRO (See All-Negro)

NEGRO HEROES (Calling All Girls, Real Heroes, & True Comics reprints)
Parents' Magazine Institute: Spring, 1947 - No. 2, Summer, 1948

	GD 2.0	VG 4.0	FN 6.0	VF 8.0	VF/NM 9.0	NM- 9.2
1	155	310	465	992	1696	2400
2-Jackie Robinson-c/story	155	310	465	992	1696	2400

NEGRO ROMANCE (Negro Romances #4)
Fawcett Publications: June, 1950 - No. 3, Oct, 1950 (All photo-c)

	GD 2.0	VG 4.0	FN 6.0	VF 8.0	VF/NM 9.0	NM- 9.2
1-Evans-a (scarce)	219	438	657	1402	2401	3400
2,3 (scarce)	181	362	543	1158	1979	2800

NEGRO ROMANCES (Formerly Negro Romance; Romantic Secrets #5 on)
Charlton Comics: No. 4, May, 1955

	GD 2.0	VG 4.0	FN 6.0	VF 8.0	VF/NM 9.0	NM- 9.2
4-Reprints Fawcett #2 (scarce)	161	322	483	1030	1765	2500

NEIL GAIMAN AND CHARLES VESS' STARDUST
DC Comics (Vertigo): 1997 - No. 4, 1998 ($5.95/$6.95, square-bound, lim. series)

	GD 2.0	VG 4.0	FN 6.0	VF 8.0	VF/NM 9.0	NM- 9.2
1-4: Gaiman text with Vess paintings in all						7.00
Hardcover (1998, $29.95) r/series with new sketches						35.00
Softcover (1999, $19.95) oversized; new Vess-c						20.00

Neil Young's Greendale HC © Neil Young

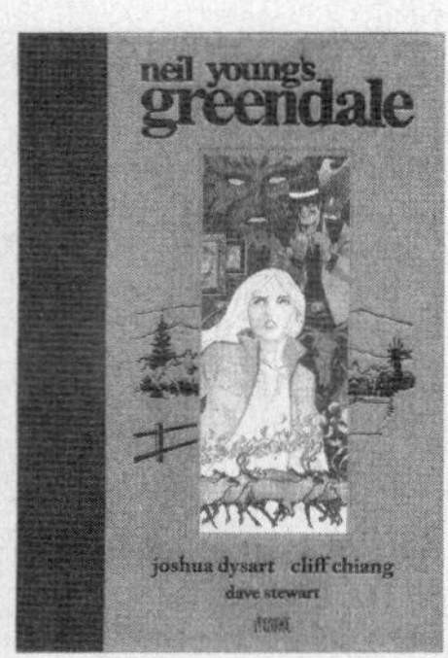

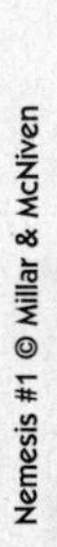

Nemesis #1 © Millar & McNiven

New Adventure Comics #17 © DC

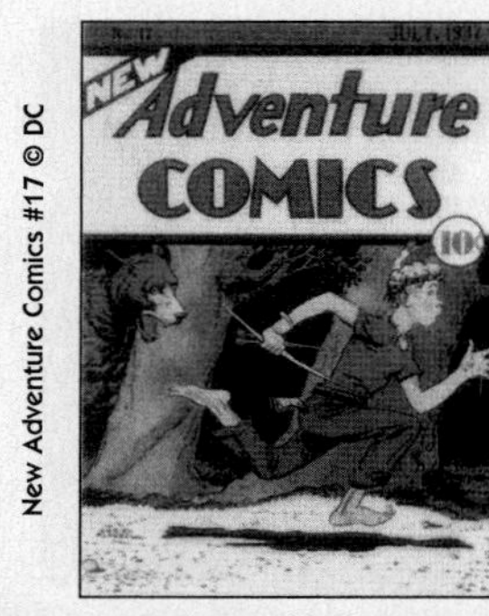

	GD 2.0	VG 4.0	FN 6.0	VF 8.0	VF/NM 9.0	NM- 9.2

NEIL GAIMAN'S LADY JUSTICE
Tekno Comix: Sept, 1995 - No. 11, May, 1996 ($1.95/$2.25)

1-11: 1-Sienkiewicz-c; pin-ups. 1-5-Brereton-c. 7-Polybagged. 11-The Big Bang Pt. 7 3.00
Free Comic Book Day (Super Genius, 2015, giveaway) r/#1 3.00

NEIL GAIMAN'S LADY JUSTICE
BIG Entertainment: V2#1, June, 1996 - No. 9, Feb, 1997 ($2.25)

V2#1-9: Dan Brereton-c on all. 6-8-Dan Brereton script 3.00

NEIL GAIMAN'S MIDNIGHT DAYS
DC Comics (Vertigo): 1999 ($17.95, trade paperback)

nn-Reprints Gaiman's short stories; new Swamp Thing w/ Bissette-a 18.00

NEIL GAIMAN'S MR. HERO-THE NEWMATIC MAN
Tekno Comix: Mar, 1995 - No. 17, May, 1996 ($1.95/$2.25)

1-17: 1-Intro Mr. Hero & Teknophage; bound-in game piece and trading card. 4-w/Steel edition Neil Gaiman's Teknophage #1 coupon. 13-Polybagged 3.00

NEIL GAIMAN'S MR. HERO-THE NEWMATIC MAN
BIG Entertainment: V2#1, June, 1996 ($2.25)

V2#1-Teknophage destroys Mr. Hero; includes The Big Bang Pt. 10 3.00

NEIL GAIMAN'S NEVERWHERE
DC Comics (Vertigo): Aug, 2005 - No. 9, Sept, 2006 ($2.99, limited series)

1-9-Adaptation of Gaiman novel; Carey-s/Fabry-a/c 3.00
TPB (2007, $19.99) r/series; intro. by Carey 20.00

NEIL GAIMAN'S PHAGE-SHADOWDEATH
BIG Entertainment: June, 1996 - No. 6, Nov, 1996 ($2.25, limited series)

1-6: Bryan Talbot-c & scripts in all. 1-1st app. Orlando Holmes 3.00

NEIL GAIMAN'S TEKNOPHAGE
Tekno Comix: Aug, 1995 - No. 10, Mar, 1996 ($1.95/$2.25)

1-6-Rick Veitch scripts & Bryan Talbot-c/a. 3.00
1-Steel Edition 4.00
7-10: Paul Jenkins scripts in all. 8-polybagged 3.00

NEIL GAIMAN'S WHEEL OF WORLDS
Tekno Comix: Apr, 1995 - No. 1, May, 1996 ($2.95/$3.25)

0-1st app. Lady Justice; 48 pgs.; bound-in poster 5.00
0-Regular edition 4.00
1 ($3.25, 5/96)-Bruce Jones scripts; Lady Justice & Teknophage app.; CGI photo-c 4.00

NEIL THE HORSE (See Charlton Bullseye #2)
Aardvark-Vanaheim #1-10/Renegade Press #11 on: 2/83 - No. 10, 12/84; No. 11, 4/85 - #15, 1985 (B&W)

1($1.40) 4.00
1-2nd print 3.00
2-12: 11-w/paperdolls 3.00
13-15: Double size ($3.00). 13-w/paperdolls. 15 is a flip book(2-c) 4.00

NEIL YOUNG'S GREENDALE
DC Comics (Vertigo): 2010 ($19.99, hardcover graphic novel)

HC-Story based on the Neil Young album; Dysart-s/Chiang-a; intro. by Neil Young 20.00

NELLIE THE NURSE (Also see Gay Comics & Joker Comics)
Marvel/Atlas Comics (SPI/LMC): 1945 - No. 36, Oct, 1952; 1957

	GD	VG	FN	VF	VF/NM	NM-
1-(1945)	90	180	270	576	988	1400
2-(Spring/46)	37	74	111	222	361	500
3,4: 3-New logo (9/46)	28	56	84	165	270	375
5-Kurtzman's "Hey Look" (3); Georgie app.	29	58	87	172	281	390
6-8,10: 7,8-Georgie app. 10-Millie app.	24	48	72	142	234	325
9-Wolverton-a (1 pg.); Mille the Model app.	24	48	72	144	237	330
11,14-16,18-Kurtzman's "Hey Look"	25	50	75	147	241	335
12- "Giggles 'n' Grins" by Kurtzman	24	48	72	142	234	325
13,17,19,20: 17-Annie Oakley app.	20	40	60	120	195	270
21-30: 28-Mr. Nexdoor-r (3 pgs.) by Kurtzman/Rusty #22	18	36	54	105	165	225
31-36: 36-Post-c	16	32	48	94	147	200
1('57)-Leading Mag. (Atlas)-Everett-a, 20 pgs	30	60	90	177	289	400

NELLIE THE NURSE
Dell Publishing Co.: No. 1304, Mar-May, 1962

	GD	VG	FN	VF	VF/NM	NM-
Four Color 1304-Stanley-a	7	14	21	49	92	135

NEMESIS (Millar & McNiven's...)
Marvel Comics (Icon): May, 2010 - No. 4, Feb, 2011 ($2.99)

1-4-Millar-s/McNiven-a 3.00
1,2-Variant covers: 1-Yu. 2-Cassaday 8.00

NEMESIS ARCHIVES (Listed with Adventures Into the Unknown)

NEMESIS: THE IMPOSTERS
DC Comics: May, 2010 - No. 4, Aug, 2010 ($2.99, limited series)

1-4-Richards-a/Luvisi-c. 1-Joker app. 2-4-Batman app. 3.00

NEMESIS THE WARLOCK (Also see Spellbinders)
Eagle Comics: Sept, 1984 - No. 7, Mar, 1985 (limited series, Baxter paper)

1-7: 2000 A.D. reprints 3.00

NEMESIS THE WARLOCK
Quality Comics/Fleetway Quality #2 on: 1989 - No. 19, 1991 ($1.95, B&W)

1-19 3.00

NEMO (The League of Extraordinary Gentlemen)
Top Shelf Productions: ($14.95, hardcover, one-shots)

...: Heart of Ice HC (2/13) Alan Moore-s/Kevin O'Neill-a 15.00
...: River of Ghosts HC (2015) Alan Moore-s/Kevin O'Neill-a 15.00
...: Roses of Berlin HC (3/14) Alan Moore-s/Kevin O'Neill-a 15.00

NEON JOE, WEREWOLF HUNTER (Based on Adult Swim TV series)
DC Comics: 2015 (no price, one-shot)

nn - Origin of Neon Joe; Glaser-s/Mandrake & Duursema-a/Panosian-c 3.00

NEUTRO
Dell Publishing Co.: Jan, 1967

	GD	VG	FN	VF	VF/NM	NM-
1-Jack Sparling-c/a (super hero); UFO-s	4	8	12	25	40	55

NEVADA (See Zane Grey's Four Color 412, 996 & Zane Grey's Stories of the West #1)

NEVADA (Also see Vertigo Winter's Edge #1)
DC Comics (Vertigo): May, 1998 - No. 6, Oct, 1998 ($2.50, limited series)

1-6-Gerber-s/Winslade-c/a 3.00
TPB-(1999, $14.95) r/#1-6 & Vertigo Winter's Edge preview 15.00

NEVER AGAIN (War stories; becomes Soldier & Marine V2#9)
Charlton Comics: Aug, 1955; No. 8, July, 1956 (No #2-7)

	GD	VG	FN	VF	VF/NM	NM-
1-WWII	11	22	33	60	83	105
8-(Formerly Foxhole?)	7	14	21	35	43	50

NEVERBOY
Dark Horse Comics: Mar, 2015 - No. 6, Aug, 2015 ($3.99)

1-6-Shaun Simon-s/Tyler Jenkins-a 4.00

NEVERMEN, THE (See Dark Horse Presents #148-150)
Dark Horse Comics: May, 2000 - No. 4, Aug, 2000 ($2.95, limited series)

1-4-Phil Amara-s/Guy Davis-a 3.00

NEVERMEN, THE: STREETS OF BLOOD
Dark Horse Comics: Jan, 2003 - No. 3, Apr, 2003 ($2.99, limited series)

1-3-Phil Amara-s/Guy Davis-a 3.00
TPB (7/03, $9.95) r/#1-3; Paul Jenkins intro.; Davis sketch pages 10.00

NEW ADVENTURE COMICS (Formerly New Comics; becomes Adventure Comics #32 on; V1#12 indicia says NEW COMICS #12)
National Periodical Publications: V1#12, Jan, 1937 - No. 31, Oct, 1938

	GD	VG	FN	VF	VF/NM	NM-
V1#12-Federal Men by Siegel & Shuster continues; Jor-L mentioned; Whitney Ellsworth-c begin, end #14	650	1300	1950	5200	-	-
V2#1(2/37, #13)-(Rare)	650	1300	1950	5200	-	-
V2#2 (#14)	563	1126	1689	4500	-	-
15(V2#3)-20(V2#8): 15-1st Adventure logo; Creig Flessel-c begin, end #31. 16-1st non-funny cover. 17-Nadir, Master of Magic begins, ends #30	424	848	1272	2332	3916	5500
21(V2#9),22(V2#10, 2/37): 22-X-Mas-c	368	736	1104	2024	3412	4800
23-25,28-31	336	672	1008	1848	3124	4400
26(5/38) (rare) has house ad for Action Comics #1 showing B&W image of cover (early published image of Superman)(prices vary widely on this book)	4400	8800	13,200	32,000	-	-
27(6/38) has house ad for Action Comics #1 showing B&W image of cover (rare) (early published image of Superman)	1400	2800	4200	8000	12,000	16,000

NEW ADVENTURES OF ABRAHAM LINCOLN, THE
Image Comics (Homage): 1998 ($19.95, one-shot)

1-Scott McCloud-s/computer art 20.00

NEW ADVENTURES OF CHARLIE CHAN, THE (TV)
National Periodical Publications: May-June, 1958 - No. 6, Mar-Apr, 1959

	GD	VG	FN	VF	VF/NM	NM-
1 (Scarce)-John Broome-s/Sid Greene-a in all	92	184	276	584	1005	1425

New Adventures of Superboy #5 © DC

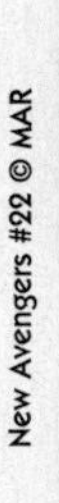
New Avengers #22 © MAR

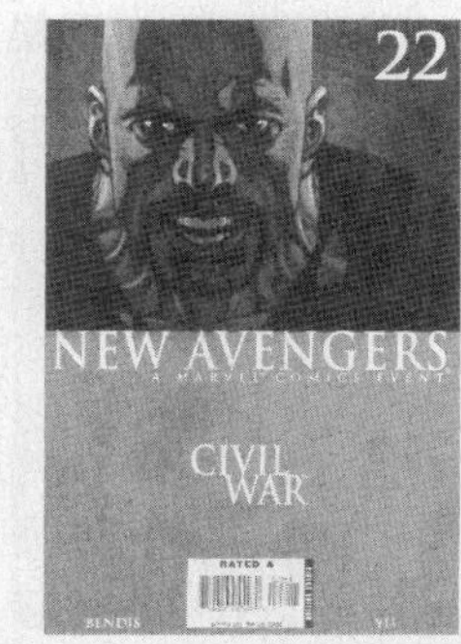

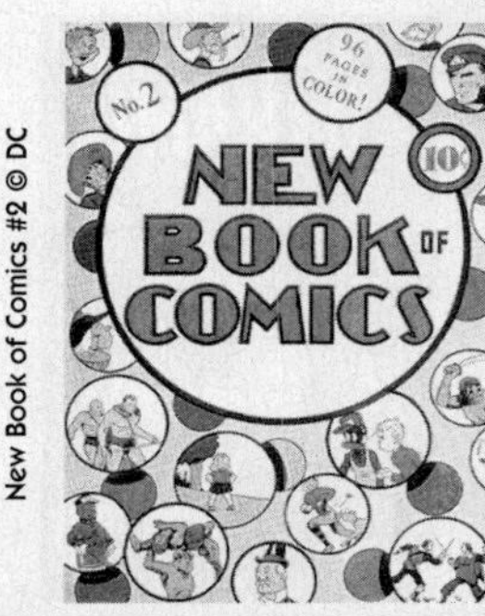

New Book of Comics #2 © DC

GD 2.0 | VG 4.0 | FN 6.0 | VF 8.0 | VF/NM 9.0 | NM- 9.2

2 (Scarce) 57 114 171 362 619 875
3-6 (Scarce)-Greene/Giella-a 50 100 150 315 533 750

NEW ADVENTURES OF CHOLLY AND FLYTRAP, THE
Epic Comics: Dec, 1990 - No. 3, Feb, 1991 ($4.95, limited series)
1-3-Arthur Suydam-s/a/c; painted covers 5.00

NEW ADVENTURES OF HUCK FINN, THE (TV)
Gold Key: December, 1968 (Hanna-Barbera)
1- "The Curse of Thut"; part photo-c 3 6 9 21 33 45

NEW ADVENTURES OF PINOCCHIO (TV)
Dell Publishing Co.: Oct-Dec, 1962 - No. 3, Sept-Nov, 1963
12-562-212(#1) 7 14 21 48 89 130
2,3 6 12 18 38 69 100

NEW ADVENTURES OF ROBIN HOOD (See Robin Hood)

NEW ADVENTURES OF SHERLOCK HOLMES (Also see Sherlock Holmes)
Dell Publishing Co.: No. 1169, Mar-May, 1961 - No. 1245, Nov-Jan, 1961/62
Four Color 1169(#1) 12 24 36 79 170 260
Four Color 1245 10 20 30 70 150 230

NEW ADVENTURES OF SPEED RACER
Now Comics: Dec, 1993 - No. 7, 1994? ($1.95)
1-7 3.00
0-(Premiere)-3-D cover 3.00

NEW ADVENTURES OF SUPERBOY, THE (Also see Superboy)
DC Comics: Jan, 1980 - No. 54, June, 1984
1 1 3 4 6 8 10
2-6,8-10 4.00
11-49,51-54: 11-Superboy gets new power. 14-Lex Luthor app. 15-Superboy gets new parents. 28-Dial "H" For Hero begins, ends #49. 45-47-1st app. Sunburst. 48-Begin 75¢-c. 3.00
1,2,5,6,8 (Whitman variants; low print run; no issue # shown on cover) 2 4 6 11 16 20
7,50: 7-Has extra story "The Computers That Saved Metropolis" by Starlin (Radio Shack giveaway w/indicia). 50-Legion app. 5.00
NOTE: *Buckler a-9p; c-36p. Giffen a-50; c-50. 40i. Gil Kane c-32p, 33p, 35, 39, 41-49. Miller c-51. Starlin a-7. Krypto back-ups in 17, 22. Superbaby in 11, 14, 19, 24.*

NEW ADVENTURES OF THE PHANTOM BLOT, THE (See The Phantom Blot)

NEW AMERICA
Eclipse Comics: Nov, 1987 - No. 4, Feb, 1988 ($1.75, Baxter paper)
1-4: Scout limited series 3.00

NEW ARCHIES, THE (TV)
Archie Comic Publications: Oct, 1987 - No. 22, May, 1990 (75¢)
1 5.00
2-10: 3-Xmas issue 4.00
11-22: 17-22 (95¢-$1.00): 21-Xmas issue 3.00

NEW ARCHIES DIGEST (TV)(...Comics Digest Magazine #4?-10; ...Digest Magazine #11 on)
Archie Comics: May, 1988 - No. 14, July, 1991 ($1.35/$1.50, quarterly)
1 6.00
2-14: 6-Begin $1.50-c 3.50

NEW AVENGERS, THE (Also see Promotional section for military giveaway)
Marvel Comics: Jan, 2005 - No. 64, Jun, 2010 ($2.25/$2.50/$2.99/$3.99)
1-Bendis-s/Finch-a; Spider-Man app.; re-intro The Sentry; 4 covers by McNiven, Quesada & Finch; variants from #1-6 combine for one team image 5.00
1-Director's Cut ($3.99) includes alternate covers, script, villain gallery 4.00
1-MGC (6/10 $1.00) r/#1 with "Marvel's Greatest Comics" cover logo 3.00
2-20: 2-6-Finch-a. 4-1st app. Maria Hill. 5-Wolverine app. 7-10-Origin of the Sentry; McNiven-a. 11-Debut of Ronin. 14,15-Cho-c/a. 17-20-Deodato-a 3.00
21-48: 21-26-Civil War. 21-Chaykin-a/c. 26-Maleev-a. 27-31-Yu-a; Echo & "Elektra" app. 33-37-The Hood app. 38-Gaydos-a. 39-Mack-a. 40-47-Secret Invasion 3.00
49-($3.99) Dark Reign 4.00
50-($4.99) Dark Reign; Tan, Hitch, McNiven, Yu, Horn & others-a; Tan wraparound-c 5.00
50-($4.99) Adam Kubert variant-c 6.00
51-64-($3.99) Dark Reign. 51,52-Tan & Bachalo-a. 54-Brother Voodoo becomes Sorceror Supreme. 56-Wrecking Crew app. 61-64-Siege; Steve Rogers app. 4.00
51-54-Variant covers by Bachalo 7.00
56,57-Variant covers. 56-70th Anniversary frame. 57-Super Hero Squad 6.00
Annual 1 (6/06, $3.99) Wedding of Luke Cage and Jessica Jones; Bendis-s/Coipel-a 4.00
Annual 2 (2/08, $3.99) Avengers vs. The Hood's gang; Bendis-s/Pagulayan-a 4.00
Annual 3 (2/10, $4.99) Mayhew-c/a; Dark Avengers app.; Siege preview 5.00
... Finale (6/10, $4.99) Follows Siege #4; Bendis-s/Hitch-a/c; Count Nefaria app. 5.00
...: Illuminati (5/06, $3.99) Bendis-s/Maleev-a; leads into Planet Hulk; Civil War preview 4.00
... Most Wanted Files (2006, $3.99) profile pages of Avenger villains 4.00
... Volume 1 HC (2007, $29.99) oversized r/#1-10, ... Most Wanted Files, and ... Guest Starring the Fantastic Four (militiary giveaway); new intro. by Bendis; script & sketch pages 30.00
... Volume 2 HC (2008, $29.99) oversized r/#11-20, ... Annual #1, and story from Giant-Size Spider-Woman; variant covers & sketch pages 30.00

NEW AVENGERS (The Heroic Age)
Marvel Comics: Aug, 2010 - No. 34, Jan, 2013 ($3.99)
1-Bendis-s/Immonen-a/c; Luke Cage forms new team; back-up text Avengers history 4.00
1-Variant-c by Djurdjevic 6.00
2-16: Hellstrom & Doctor Voodoo app.; back-up text Avengers history. 6-Doctor Voodoo killed. 9-13-Nick Fury flashback w/Chaykin-a. 10-Intro. Avengers 1959. 14-16-Fear Itself. 16-Daredevil joins 4.00
16.1 (11/11, $2.99) Neal Adams-a/c; Bendis-s; Norman Osborn app. 3.00
17-23-($3.99) 17-Norman Osborn attacks; Iron Man app.; Deodato-a 4.00
24-33: 24-30-Avengers vs. X-Men tie-in. 26,27-DaVinci app. 31-Gaydos-a. 32-Pacheco-a 4.00
34-($4.99) Dr. Strange become Sorcerer Supreme again; Deodato-a; gallery of Bendis-era Avengers covers 5.00
Annual 1 (11/11, $4.99) Dell'Otto-a; Wonder Man app.; continues in Avengers Annual #1 5.00

NEW AVENGERS (Marvel NOW!)
Marvel Comics: Mar, 2013 - No. 33, Jun, 2015 ($3.99)
1-7: 1-Hickman-s/Epting-a; Black Panther and the Illuminati. 4-Galactus app. 4.00
8-23: 8-12-Infinity tie-ins; Deodato-a. 13-Inhumanity; Bianchi-a. 17-21-Great Society app. 4.00
24-($4.99) Doctor Doom, Thanos and the Cabal app. 5.00
25-32: 27-Kudranski-a. 28,32-Deodato-a 4.00
33-($4.99) Doctor Doom & Molecule Man app.; leads into Secret Wars x-over; Deodato-a 5.00
Annual 1 (8/14, $4.99) Spotlight on Doctor Strange; Marco Rudy-a 5.00

NEW AVENGERS (Follows events of Secret Wars)(See U.S.Avengers)
Marvel Comics: Dec, 2015 - No. 18, Jan, 2017 ($3.99)
1-18: 1-Ewing-s/Sandoval-a; Squirrel Girl app. 5,6-Avengers of 20XX app. 8-10-Standoff tie-in; Marcus To-a. 12-17-Civil War II tie-in. 12-16-Interlocking covers 4.00

NEW AVENGERS: ILLUMINATI (Also see Civil War and Secret Invasion)
Marvel Comics: Feb, 2007 - No. 5, Jan, 2008 ($2.99, limited series)
1-5-Bendis & Reed-s/Cheung-a. 3-Origin of The Beyonder. 5-Secret Invasion 3.00
HC (2008, $19.99, dustjacket) r/#1-5; cover sketch art 20.00
SC (2008, $14.99) r/#1-5; cover sketch art 15.00

NEW AVENGERS: LUKE CAGE
Marvel Comics: Jun, 2010 - No. 3, Aug, 2010 ($3.99, limited series)
1-3-Arcudi-s/Canete-a; Spider-Man & Ronin app. 4.00

NEW AVENGERS: THE REUNION
Marvel Comics: May, 2009 - No. 4, Aug, 2009 ($3.99, limited series)
1-4-Mockingbird and Ronin (Hawkeye); McCann-s/López-a/Jo Chen-c 4.00

NEW AVENGERS/TRANSFORMERS
Marvel Comics: Sept, 2007 - No. 4, Dec, 2007 ($2.99, limited series)
1-4-Kirkham-a; Capt. America app. 1-Cheung-c. 2-Pearson-c 3.00
TPB (2008, $10.99) r/#1-4 11.00

NEW AVENGERS: ULTRON FOREVER
Marvel Comics: Jun, 2015 ($4.99)(Continues in Uncanny Avengers: Ultron Forever)
1-Part 2 of 3-part crossover with Avengers and Uncanny Avengers; Ewing-s/Alan Davis-a; team-up of past, present and future Avengers vs. Ultron 5.00

NEW BOOK OF COMICS (Also see Big Book Of Fun)
National Periodical Publ.: 1937; No. 2, Spring, 1938 (100 pgs. each) (Reprints)
1(Rare)-1st regular size comic annual; 2nd DC annual; contains r/New Comics #1-4 & More Fun #9; r/Federal Men (8 pgs.), Henri Duval (1 pg.), & Dr. Occult in costume (1 pg.) by Siegel & Shuster; Moldoff, Sheldon Mayer (15 pgs.)-a 1850 3700 5550 12,000 21,000 30,000
2-Contains-r/More Fun #15 & 16; r/Dr. Occult in costume (a Superman prototype), & Calling All Cars (4 pgs.) by Siegel & Shuster 950 1900 2850 6175 11,088 16,000

NEW COMICS (New Adventure #12 on)
National Periodical Publ.: 12/35 - No. 11, 12/36 (No. 1-6: paper cover) (No. 1-5: 84 pgs.)
V1#1-Billy the Kid, Sagebrush 'n' Cactus, Jibby Jones, Needles, The Vikings, Sir Loin of Beef, Now-When I Was a Boy, & other 1-2 pg. strips; 2 pgs. Kelly art(1st)-(Gulliver's Travels); Sheldon Mayer-a(1st)(2 2pg. strips); Vincent Sullivan-c(1st) 2333 4666 7000 14,700 – –
2-1st app. Federal Men by Siegel & Shuster & begins (also see The Comics Magazine #2); Mayer, Kelly-a (Rare)(1/36) 1300 2600 3900 8200 – –
3-6: 3,4-Sheldon Mayer-a which continues in The Comics Magazine #1. 3-Vincent Sullivan-c.

New Dynamix #1 © WSP

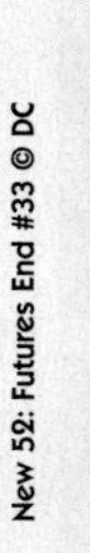
New 52: Futures End #33 © DC

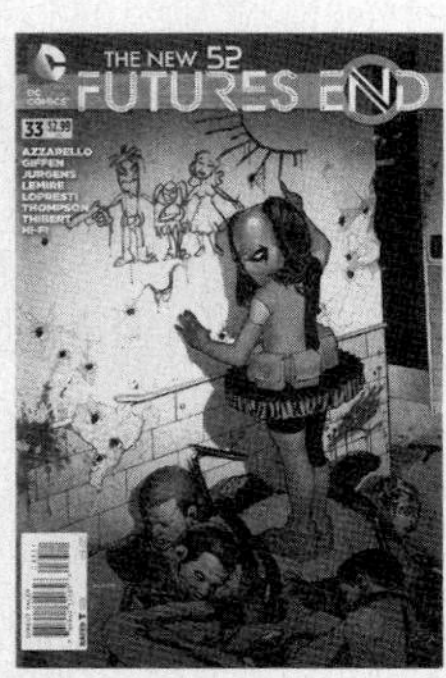

New Gods #5 © DC

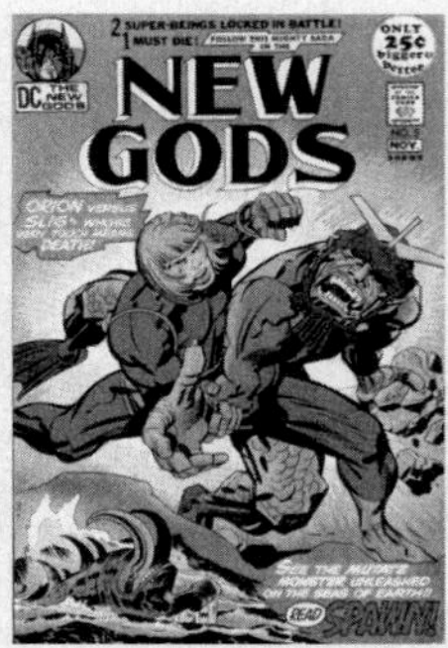

	GD 2.0	VG 4.0	FN 6.0	VF 8.0	VF/NM 9.0	NM- 9.2

4-Dickens' "A Tale of Two Cities" adaptation begins. 5-Junior Federal Men Club; Kiefer-a.

6- "She" adaptation begins	800	1600	2400	5600	–	–
7-10	514	1028	1542	3600	–	–
11-Ties with More Fun #16 as DC's 1st Christmas-c	570	1140	1710	4000	–	–

NOTE: *#1-6 rarely occur in mint condition.* ***Whitney Ellsworth** c-4-11.*

NEW CRUSADERS (Rise of the Heroes)
Archie Comics (Red Circle Comics): Oct, 2012 - Present ($2.99)

1-6-The Shield and the offspring of the Mighty Crusaders 3.00

NEW DEADWARDIANS, THE
DC Comics (Vertigo): May, 2012 - No. 8, Dec, 2012 ($2.99, limited series)

1-8-Abnett-s/Culbard-a 3.00

NEW DEFENDERS (See Defenders)

NEW DNAGENTS, THE (Formerly DNAgents)
Eclipse Comics: V2#1, Oct, 1985 - V2#17, Mar, 1987 (Whole #s 25-40; Mando paper)

V2#1-17: 1-Origin recap. 7-Begin 95 cent-c. 9,10-Airboy preview 3.00
3-D 1 (1/86, $2.25) 3.00
2-D 1 (1/86)-Limited ed. (100 copies) 10.00

NEW DYNAMIX
DC Comics (WildStorm): May, 2008 - No. 5, Sept, 2008 ($2.99, limited series)

1-5-Warner-s/J.J. Kirby-a/c. 1-Variant-c by Jim Lee. 1-Convention Ed. with Lee-c 3.00

NEW ETERNALS: APOCALYPSE NOW (Also see Eternals, The)
Marvel Comics: Feb, 2000 ($3.99, one-shot)

1-Bennett & Hanna-a; Ladronn-c 4.00

NEW EXCALIBUR
Marvel Comics: Jan, 2006 - No. 24, Dec, 2007 ($2.99)

1-24: 1-Claremont-s/Ryan-a; Dazzler app. 3-Juggernaut app. 4-Lionheart app. 3.00
... Vol. 1: Defenders of the Realm TPB (2006, $17.99) r/#1-7 18.00
... Vol. 2: Last Days of Camelot TPB (2007, $19.99) r/#8-15 20.00
... Vol. 3: Battle for Eternity TPB (2007, $24.99) r/#16-24; sketch pages 25.00

NEW EXILES (Continued from Exiles #100 and Exiles - Days of Then and Now)
Marvel Comics: Mar, 2008 - No. 18, Apr, 2009 ($2.99)

1-18: 1-Claremont-s/Grummett-a; 2 covers by Land & Golden; new team 3.00
1-2nd printing with Grummett-c 3.00
Annual 1 (2/09, $3.99) Claremont-s/Grummett-a 4.00

NEW 52: FUTURE'S END
DC Comics: No 0, Jun, 2014 - No. 48, Jun, 2015 ($2.99, weekly limited series)

... FCBD Special Edition #0 (6/14, giveaway) Part 1; 35 years in the future 3.00
1-36: 1-Set 5 years in the future; Azzarello, Lemire, Jurgens & Giffen-s. 29-New Firestorm. 33-Kid Deathstroke-c. 44-Brainiac steals New York (Convergence) 3.00

NEWFORCE (Also see Newmen)
Image Comics (Extreme Studios): Jan, 1996-No. 4, Apr, 1996 ($2.50, lim. series)

1-4: 1-"Extreme Destroyer" Pt. 8; polybagged w/gaming card. 4-Newforce disbands 3.00

NEW FUN COMICS (More Fun #7 on; see Big Book of Fun Comics)
National Periodical Publications: Feb, 1935 - No. 6, Oct, 1935 (10x15", No. 1-4,: slick-c) (No. 1-5: 36 pgs; 40 pgs. No. 6)

V1#1 (1st DC comic); 1st app. Oswald The Rabbit; Jack Woods (cowboy) begins	8286	16,572	24,858	58,000	–	–
2(3/35)-(Very Rare)	3857	7714	11,571	27,000	–	–
3-5(8/35): 3-Don Drake on the Planet Soro-c/story (sci/fi, 4/35); early (maybe 1st) DC letter column. 5-Soft-c	2571	5142	7713	18,000	–	–
6(10/35)-1st Dr. Occult by Siegel & Shuster (Leger & Reuths); last "New Fun" title. "New Comics" #1 begins in Dec. which is reason for title change to More Fun; Henri Duval (ends #10) by Siegel & Shuster begins; paper-c	4143	8286	12,429	29,000	–	–

NEW FUNNIES (The Funnies #1-64; Walter Lantz...#109 on; New TV... #259, 260, 272, 273; TV Funnies #261-271)
Dell Publishing Co.: No. 65, July, 1942 - No. 288, Mar-Apr, 1962

65(#1)-Andy Panda in a world of real people, Raggedy Ann & Andy, Oswald the Rabbit (with Woody Woodpecker x-overs), Li'l Eight Ball & Peter Rabbit begin; Bugs Bunny and Elmer app.	89	178	267	712	1606	2500
66-70: 66-Felix the Cat begins. 67-Billy & Bonny Bee by Frank Thomas begins. 69-Kelly-a (2 pgs.); The Brownies begin (not by Kelly); Halloween-c	30	60	90	216	483	750
71-75: 71-Christmas-c. 72-Kelly illos. 75-Brownies by Kelly?	21	42	63	146	311	475
76-Andy Panda (Carl Barks & Pabian-a); Woody Woodpecker x-over in Oswald ends	50	100	150	400	900	1400
77,78: 77-Kelly-c. 78-Andy Panda in a world with real people ends	15	30	45	103	227	350
79-81	10	20	30	69	147	225
82-Brownies by Kelly begins	11	22	33	73	157	240
83-85-Brownies by Kelly in ea. 83-X-mas-c; Homer Pigeon begins. 85-Woody Woodpecker, 1 pg. strip begins	11	22	33	72	154	235
86-90: 87-Woody Woodpecker stories begin	9	18	27	57	111	165
91-99	8	16	24	51	96	140
100 (6/45)	8	16	24	54	102	150
101-120: 119-X-Mas-c	7	14	21	46	86	125
121-150: 131,143-X-Mas-c	6	12	18	40	73	105
151-200: 155-X-Mas-c. 167-X-Mas-c. 182-Origin & 1st app. Knothead & Splinter. 191-X-Mas-c	5	10	15	35	63	90
201-240	5	10	15	35	57	80
241-288: 270,271-Walter Lantz c-app. 281-1st story swipes/WDC&S #100	5	10	15	30	50	70

NOTE: *Early issues written by* ***John Stanley.***

NEW GODS, THE (1st Series)(New Gods #12 on)(See Adventure #459, DC Graphic Novel #4, 1st Issue Special #13 & Super-Team Family)
National Periodical Publications/DC Comics: 2-3/71 - V2#11, 10-11/72; V3#12, 7/77 - V3#19, 7-8/78 (Fourth World)

1-Intro/1st app. Orion; 4th app. Darkseid (cameo; 3 weeks after Forever People #1) (#1-3 are 15¢ issues)	9	18	27	61	123	185
2-Darkseid-c/story (2nd full app., 4-5/71)	5	10	15	35	63	90
3-1st app. Black Racer; last 15¢ issue	4	8	12	23	37	50
4-6,8,9: (25¢, 52 pg. giants): 4-Darkseid cameo; origin Manhunter-r. 5,8-Young Gods feature. 9-1st app. Forager	4	8	12	23	37	50
7-1st app. Steppenwolf (2-3/72); Darkseid app.; origin Orion; 1st origin of all New Gods as a group; Young Gods feature	11	22	33	76	163	250
10,11: 11-Last Kirby issue.	3	6	9	19	30	40
12-19: Darkseid storyline w/minor apps. 12-New costume Orion (see 1st Issue Special #13 for 1st new costume). 19-Story continued in Adventure Comics #459,460	2	4	6	8	10	12

Jack Kirby's New Gods TPB ('98, $11.95, B&W&Grey) r/#1-11 plus cover gallery of original series and "84 reprints 12.00

NOTE: *#4-9(25¢, 52 pgs.) contain Manhunter-r by* ***Simon*** *&* ***Kirby*** *from Adventure #73, 74, 75, 76, 77, 78 with covers in that order.* ***Adkins*** *i-12-14, 17-19.* ***Buckler*** *a(p)-15.* ***Kirby*** *c/a-1-11p.* ***Newton*** *a(p)-12-14, 16-19.* ***Starlin*** *c-17.* ***Staton*** *c-19p.*

NEW GODS (Also see DC Graphic Novel #4)
DC Comics: June, 1984 - No. 6, Nov, 1984 ($2.00, Baxter paper)

1-5: New Kirby-c; r/New Gods #1-10. 5.00

6-Reprints New Gods #11 w/48 pgs of new Kirby story & art; leads into DC Graphic Novel #4	2	4	6	8	10	12

NEW GODS (2nd Series)
DC Comics: Feb, 1989 - No. 28, Aug, 1991 ($1.50)

1-28 3.00

NEW GODS (3rd Series) (Becomes Jack Kirby's Fourth World) (Also see Showcase '94 #1 & Showcase '95 #7)
DC Comics: Oct, 1995 - No. 15, Feb, 1997 ($1.95)

1-11,13-15: 9-Giffen-a(p). 10,11-Superman app. 13-Takion, Mr. Miracle & Big Barda app. 13-15-Byrne-a(p)/scripts & Simonson-c. 15-Apokolips merged w/ New Genesis; story cont'd in Jack Kirby's Fourth World 3.00
12-(11/96, 99¢)-Byrne-a(p)/scripts & Simonson-c begin; Takion cameo; indicia reads October 1996 3.00
...Secret Files 1 (9/98, $4.95) Origin-s 5.00

NEW GUARDIANS, THE
DC Comics: Sept, 1988 - No. 12, Sept, 1989 ($1.25)

1-($2.00, 52 pgs)-Staton-c/a in #1-9 4.00
2-12 3.00

NEW HEROIC (See Heroic)

NEW INVADERS (Titled Invaders for #0 & #1) (See Avengers V3#83,84)
Marvel Comics: No. 0, Aug, 2004 - No. 9, June, 2005 ($2.99)

0-9-Roster of U.S. Agent, Sub-Mariner, Blazing Skull and others. 0-Avengers app. 3.00

NEW JUSTICE MACHINE, THE (Also see The Justice Machine)
Innovation Publishing: 1989 - No. 3, 1989 ($1.95, limited series)

1-3 3.00

NEW KIDS ON THE BLOCK, THE (Also see Richie Rich and...)
Harvey Comics: Dec, 1990 - No. 8, Dec, 1991 ($1.25)

1-8 4.00

Newmen #3 © Image

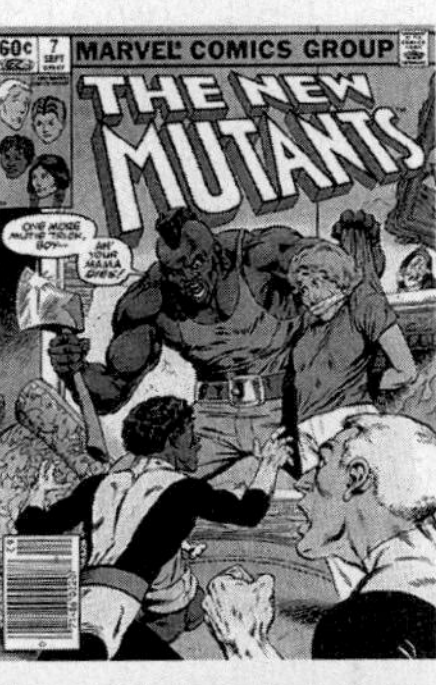

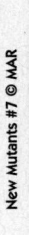

New Mutants #7 © MAR

New Romances #7 © STD

GD 2.0 | VG 4.0 | FN 6.0 | VF 8.0 | VF/NM 9.0 | NM- 9.2

...**Back Stage Pass** 1(12/90) - 7(11/91) **Chillin'** 1(12/90) - 7(12/91): 1-Photo-c
...**Comic Tour** '90/91 1 (12/90) - 7(12/91) **Digest** 1(1/91) - 5(1/92) **Hanging Tough** 1 (2/91)
Magic Summer Tour 1 (Fall/90) **Magic Summer Tour** nn (Fall/90, sold at concerts)
Step By Step 1 (Fall/90, one-shot) **Valentine Girl** 1 (Fall/90, one-shot)-Photo-c 4.00

NEW LINE CINEMA'S TALES OF HORROR (Anthology)
DC Comics (WildStorm): Nov, 2007 ($2.99, one-shot)
1-Freddy Krueger and Leatherface app.; Darick Robertson-c 3.00

NEW LOVE (See Love & Rockets)
Fantagraphics Books: Aug, 1996 - No. 6, Dec, 1997 ($2.95, B&W, lim. series)
1-6: Gilbert Hernandez-s/a 3.00

NEWMAN
Image Comics (Extreme Studios): Jan, 1996 - No. 4, Apr, 1996 ($2.50, lim. series)
1-4: 1-Extreme Destroyer Pt. 3; polybagged w/card. 4-Shadowhunt tie-in; Eddie Collins becomes new Shadowhawk 3.00

NEW MANGVERSE (Also see Marvel Mangaverse)
Marvel Comics: Mar, 2006 - No. 5, July, 2006 ($2.99, lim. series)
1-5: Cebulski-s/Ohtsuka-a; The Hand and Elektra app. 3.00
...: The Rings of Fate (2006, $7.99, digest) r/#1-5 8.00

NEWMEN (becomes The Adventures Of The...#22)
Image Comics (Extreme Studios): Apr, 1994 - No. 20, Nov, 1995; No. 21, Nov, 1996 ($1.95/$2.50)
1-21: 1-5: Matsuda-c/a. 10-Polybagged w/trading card. 11-Polybagged. 20-Has a variant-c; Babewatch! x-over. 21-(11/96)-Series relaunch; Chris Sprouse-a begins; pin-up. 16-Has a variant-c by Quesada & Palmiotti 3.00
TPB-(1996, $12.95) r/#1-4 w/pin-ups 13.00

NEW MEN OF BATTLE, THE
Catechetical Guild: 1949 (nn) (Carboard-c)
nn(V8#1-3,5,6)-192 pgs.; contains 6 issues of Topix rebound 10 20 30 54 72 90
nn(V8#7-V8#11)-160 pgs.; contains 5 iss. of Topix 9 18 27 50 65 80

NEW MGMT (See Mind MGMT)

NEW MUTANTS, THE (See Marvel Graphic Novel #4 for 1st app.)(Also see X-Force & Uncanny X-Men #167)
Marvel Comics Group: Mar, 1983 - No. 100, Apr, 1991
1-Claremont-s/McLeod-a 2 4 6 11 16 20
2-10: 3,4-Ties into X-Men #167. 10-1st app. Magma 5.00
11-15,17,19,20: 13-Kitty Pryde app. 4.00
16-1st app. Warpath (w/out costume); see Uncanny X-Men #193 2 4 6 11 16 20
18-Intro. new Warlock 2 4 6 8 10 12
21-Double size; origin new Warlock; newsstand version has cover price written in by Sienkiewicz 5.00
22-24,27-30: 23-25-Cloak & Dagger app. 4.00
25-1st brief app. Legion (David Haller) 3 6 9 16 23 30
26-1st full Legion app. 3 6 9 19 30 40
31-49,51-58: 35-Magneto intro'd as new headmaster. 43-Portacio-i. 58-Contains pull-out mutant registration form 4.00
50,73: 50-Double size. 73-(52 pgs.). 5.00
59-61: Fall of The Mutants series. 60-(52 pgs.) 5.00
62-72,74-85: 68-Intro Spyder. 63-X-Men & Wolverine clones app. 76-X-Factor & X-Terminator app. 85-Liefeld-c begin 4.00
86-Rob Liefeld-a begins; McFarlane-c(i) swiped from Ditko splash pg.; 1st brief app. Cable (last page teaser) 2 4 6 10 14 18
87-1st full app. Cable (3/90) 8 16 24 56 108 160
87-2nd printing; gold metallic ink-c ($1.00) 2 4 6 10 14 18
88-2nd app. Cable 1 3 4 6 8 10
92-No Liefeld-a; Liefeld-c 5.00
89,90,91,93-97,99: 89-3rd app. Cable. 90-New costumes. 90,91-Sabretooth app. 93,94-Cable vs. Wolverine. 95-97-X-Tinction Agenda x-over. 95-Death of new Warlock. 97-Wolverine & Cable-c, but no app. 99-1st app. of Feral (of X-Force); Byrne-c/swipe (X-Men, 1st Series #138) 6.00
95,100-Gold 2nd printing. 100-Silver ink 3rd printing 6.00
98-1st app. Deadpool, Gideon & Domino (2/91); 2nd Shatterstar (cameo); Liefeld-c/a 13 26 39 91 201 310
100-(52 pgs.)-1st brief app. X-Force 2 4 6 11 16 20
Annual 1 (1984) 1 3 4 6 8 10
Annual 2 (1986, $1.25)-1st Psylocke 4 8 12 27 44 60
Annual 3,4,6,7 ('87, '88,'90,'91, 68 pgs.): 4-Evolutionary War x-over. 6-1st new costumes by Liefeld (3 pgs.); 1st brief app. Shatterstar (of X-Force). 7-Liefeld pin-up only; X-Terminators back-up story; 2nd app. X-Force (cont'd in New Warriors Annual #1) 5.00
Annual 5 (1989, $2.00, 68 pgs.)-Atlantis Attacks; 1st Liefeld-a on New Mutants 6.00
... Classic Vol. 1 TPB (2006, $24.99) r/#1-7, Marvel Graphic Novel #4, Uncanny X-Men #167 25.00
... Classic Vol. 2 TPB (2007, $24.99) r/#8-17 25.00
... Classic Vol. 3 TPB (2008, $24.99) r/#18-25 & Annual #1 25.00
Special 1-Special Edition ('85, 68 pgs.)-Ties in w/X-Men Alpha Flight limited series; cont'd in X-Men Annual #9; Art Adams/Austin-a 1 3 4 6 8 10
Summer Special 1(Sum/90, $2.95, 84 pgs.) 5.00
NOTE: ***Art Adams** c-38, 39. **Austin** c-57i. **Byrne** c/a-75p. **Liefeld** a-86-91p, 93-96p, 98-100, Annual 5p, 6(3 pgs.); c-85-91p, 92, 93p, 94, 95, 96p, 97-100, Annual 5, 6p. **McFarlane** c-85-89i, 93i. **Portacio** a(i)-43. **Russell** a-48i. **Sienkiewicz** a-18-31, 35-38i; c-17-31, 35i, 37i, Annual 1. **Simonson** c-11p. **B. Smith** c-36, 40-48. **Williamson** a(i)-69, 71-73, 78-80, 82, 83; c(i)-69, 72, 73, 78i.*

NEW MUTANTS (Continues as New X-Men (Academy X))
Marvel Comics: July, 2003 - No. 13, June, 2004 ($2.50/$2.99)
1-13: 1-6-Josh Middleton-c. 7-11-Bachalo-c. 8-Begin $2.99 3.00
... Vol. 1: Back To School TPB (2005, $16.99) r/#1-6; new Middleton-c 17.00

NEW MUTANTS
Marvel Comics: July, 2009 - No. 50, Dec, 2012 ($3.99/$2.99)
1-($3.99) Neves-a; Legion app.; covers by Ross, Adam Kubert, McLeod, Benjamin 4.00
2-24-($2.99) 2-10-Adam Kubert-c. 11-Siege; Dodson-c. 12-14-Second Coming 3.00
25-($3.99) Fernandez-a; wraparound-c by Djurdjevic; Nate Grey returns 4.00
26-50: 29-32-Fear Itself tie-in. 33-Regenesis. 34-Blink returns. 42,43-Exiled x-over with Exiled #1 & Journey Into Mystery #637,638 3.00
... Saga (2009, giveaway) New Mutants character profiles and story synopsies; Neves-c 3.00

NEW MUTANTS FOREVER
Marvel Comics: Oct, 2010 - No. 5, Feb, 2011 ($3.99, limited series)
1-5-Claremont-s/Rio & McLeod-a; Red Skull app. 1-Back-up history of New Mutants 4.00

NEW MUTANTS, THE: TRUTH OR DEATH
Marvel Comics: Nov, 1997 - No. 3, Jan, 1998 ($2.50, limited series)
1-3-Raab-s/Chang-a(p) 3.00

NEW PEOPLE, THE (TV)
Dell Publishing Co.: Jan, 1970 - No. 2, May, 1970
1 3 6 9 16 24 32
2-Photo-c 3 6 9 15 21 26

NEW ROMANCER
DC Comics (Vertigo): Feb, 2016 - No. 6, Jul, 2016 ($3.99, limited series)
1-6-Milligan-s/Parson-a; Lord Byron & Casanova in present day 4.00

NEW ROMANCES
Standard Comics: No. 5, May, 1951 - No. 21, May, 1954
5-Photo-c 19 38 57 111 176 240
6-9: 6-Barbara Bel Geddes, Richard Basehart "Fourteen Hours" photo-c. 7-Ray Milland & Joan Fontaine photo-c. 9-Photo-c from '50s movie 13 26 39 74 105 135
10,14,16,17-Toth-a 14 28 42 78 112 145
11-Toth-a; Liz Taylor, Montgomery Clift photo-c 36 72 108 211 343 475
12,13,15,18-21 12 24 36 67 94 120
NOTE: ***Celardo** a-9. **Moreira** a-6. **Tuska** a-7, 20. Photo c-5-16.*

NEWSBOY LEGION BY JOE SIMON AND JACK KIRBY, THE
DC Comics: 2010 ($49.99, hardcover with dustjacket)
Vol. 1 - Reprints apps. in Star Spangled Comics #7-32; new intro. by Joe Simon 50.00

NEW SHADOWHAWK, THE (Also see Shadowhawk & Shadowhunt)
Image Comics (Shadowline Ink): June, 1995 - No. 7, Mar, 1996 ($2.50)
1-7: Kurt Busiek scripts in all 3.00

NEW STATESMEN, THE
Fleetway Publications (Quality Comics): 1989 - No. 5, 1990 ($3.95, limited series, mature readers, 52pgs.)
1-5: Futuristic; squarebound; 3-Photo-c 4.00

NEWSTRALIA
Innovation Publ.: July, 1989 - No. 5, 1989 ($1.75, color)(#2 on, $2.25, B&W)
1-5: 1,2: Timothy Truman-c/a; Gustovich-i 3.00

NEW SUICIDE SQUAD (DC New 52)
DC Comics: Sept, 2014 - No. 22, Sept, 2016 ($2.99)
1-New team of Harley Quinn, Joker's Daughter, Black Manta, Deathstroke, Deadshot 3 6 9 17 26 35
2,3 1 2 3 5 6 8
4-10 4.00
11-22: 22-Cliquet-a 3.00

New Super-Man #1 © DC

New Teen Titans #28 © DC

New Warriors #10 © MAR

GD VG FN VF VF/NM NM-
2.0 4.0 6.0 8.0 9.0 9.2

Annual 1 (11/15, $4.99) Continues story from #12; Briones-a 5.00
...: Futures End 1 (11/14, $2.99, regular-c) Five years later; Coelho-a 3.00
...: Futures End 1 (11/14, $3.99, 3-D cover) 4.00

NEW SUPERMAN (DC Rebirth)(See Batman/Superman #32 for 1st app.)
DC Comics: Sept, 2016 - Present ($2.99)

1-8: 1-Kong Kenan as China's Superman; origin; Gene Luen Yang-a/Bogdanovic-a. 7,8-Master I-Ching app. 8-Ching Lung (from Detective Comics #1) app. 3.00

NEW TALENT SHOWCASE (Talent Showcase #16 on)
DC Comics: Jan, 1984 - No. 19, Oct, 1985 (Direct sales only)

1-19: Features new strips & artists. 18-Williamson-c(i) 3.00

NEW TALENT SHOWCASE
DC Comics: Jan, 2017 ($7.99, one-shot)

1-Janson-c; short stories by various; Wonder Woman, Harley Quinn, Deadman app. 8.00

NEW TEEN TITANS, THE (See DC Comics Presents #26, Marvel and DC Present & Teen Titans; Tales of the Teen Titans #41 on)
DC Comics: Nov, 1980 - No. 40, Mar, 1984

1-Robin, Kid Flash, Wonder Girl, The Changeling (1st app.), Starfire, The Raven, Cyborg begin; partial origin 4 8 12 28 47 65
2-1st app. Deathstroke the Terminator 9 18 27 57 111 165
3-9: 3-Origin Starfire; Intro The Fearsome Five. 4-Origin continues; J.L.A. app. 6-Origin Raven. 7-Cyborg origin. 8-Origin Kid Flash retold. 9-Minor app. Deathstroke on last pg. 2 4 6 8 11 14
10-2nd app. Deathstroke the Terminator (see Marvel & DC Present for 3rd app.); origin Changeling retold 2 4 6 11 16 20
11-20: 13-Return of Madame Rouge & Capt. Zahl; Robotman revived. 14-Return of Mento; origin Doom Patrol. 15-Death of Madame Rouge & Capt. Zahl; intro. new Brotherhood of Evil. 16-1st app. Captain Carrot (free 16 pg. preview). 18-Return of Starfire. 19-Hawkman teams-up 1 2 3 4 5 7
21-Intro Night Force in free 16 pg. insert; intro Brother Blood 1 3 4 6 8 10
22-25,27-33,35-40: 22-1st app. Bethany Snow. 23-1st app. Vigilante (not in costume), & Blackfire; bondage-c. 24-Omega Men app. 25-Omega Men cameo; free 16 pg. preview Masters of the Universe. 27-Free 16 pg. preview Atari Force. 29-The New Brotherhood of Evil & Speedy app. 30-Terra joins the Titans. 37-Batman & The Outsiders x-over. 38-Origin Wonder Girl. 39-Last Dick Grayson as Robin; Kid Flash quits 5.00
26-1st app. Terra 2 4 6 8 10 12
34-4th app. Deathstroke the Terminator 2 4 6 8 10 12
Annual 1(11/82)-Omega Men app. 1 3 4 6 8 10
Annual V2#2(9/83)-1st app. Vigilante in costume; 1st app. Lyla 3 6 9 17 26 35
Annual 3 (See Tales of the Teen Titans Annual #3)
...: Games GN (2011, $24.99, HC) Wolfman-s/Pérez-a/c; original GN started in 1988, finished in 2011; '80s NTT roster; afterword by Pérez; Wolfman's original plot 25.00
...: Games GN (2013, $16.99, SC) same contents as HC 17.00
...: Terra Incognito TPB (2006, $19.99) r/#26,28-34 & Annual #2 20.00
...: The Judas Contract TPB (2003, $19.95) r/#39,40 plus Tales of the Teen Titans #41-44 & Annual #3 20.00
...: Who is Donna Troy? TPB (2005, $19.99) r/#38,Tales of the Teen Titans #50, New Titans #50-55 and Teen Titans/Outsiders Secret Files 2003 20.00

NOTE: ***Pérez*** *a-1-4p, 6-34p, 37-40p, Annual 1p, 2p; c-1-12, 13-17p, 18-21, 22p, 23p, 24-37, 38, 39(painted), 40, Annual 1, 2.*

NEW TEEN TITANS, THE (Becomes The New Titans #50 on)
DC Comics: Aug, 1984 - No. 49, Nov, 1988 ($1.25/$1.75; deluxe format)

1-New storyline; Pérez-c/a begins 2 4 6 8 10 12
2,3: 2-Re-intro Lilith 6.00
4-10: 5-Death of Trigon. 7-9-Origin Lilith. 8-Intro Kole. 10-Kole joins 5.00
11-49: 13,14-Crisis x-over. 20-Robin (Jason Todd) joins; original Teen Titans return. 38-Infinity, Inc. x-over. 47-Origin of all Titans; Titans (East & West) pin-up by Pérez 4.00
Annual 1-4 (9/85-'88): 1-Intro. Vanguard. 2-Byrne c/a(p); origin Brother Blood; intro new Dr. Light. 3-Intro. Danny Chase. 4-Pérez-c 4.00
...: The Terror of Trigon TPB (2003, $17.95) r/#1-5; new cover by Phil Jimenez 18.00

NOTE: ***Buckler*** *c-10.* ***Kelley Jones*** *a-47, Annual 4.* ***Erik Larsen*** *a-33.* ***Orlando*** *c-33p.* ***Perez*** *a-1-5; c-1-7, 19-23, 43.* ***Steacy*** *c-47.*

NEW TERRYTOONS (TV)
Dell Publishing Co./Gold Key: 6-8/60 - No. 8, 3-5/62; 10/62 - No. 54, 1/79

1(1960-Dell)-Deputy Dawg, Dinky Duck & Hashimoto-San begin (1st app. of each) 10 20 30 64 132 200
2-8(1962) 6 12 18 41 76 110
1(30010-210)(10/62-Gold Key, 84 pgs.)-Heckle & Jeckle begins 9 18 27 58 114 170
2(30010-301)-84 pgs. 7 14 21 49 92 135

GD VG FN VF VF/NM NM-
2.0 4.0 6.0 8.0 9.0 9.2

3-5 4 8 12 27 44 60
6-10 4 8 12 21 33 45
11-20 3 6 9 15 22 28
21-30 2 4 6 9 13 16
31-43 1 3 4 6 8 10
44-54: Mighty Mouse-c/s in all 2 4 6 8 11 14

NOTE: *Reprints: #4-12, 38, 40, 47. (See March of Comics #379, 393, 412, 435)*

NEW TESTAMENT STORIES VISUALIZED
Standard Publishing Co.: 1946 - 1947

"New Testament Heroes–Acts of Apostles Visualized, Book I"
"New Testament Heroes–Acts of Apostles Visualized, Book II"
"Parables Jesus Told" Set.... 17 34 51 98 154 210

NOTE: *All three are contained in a cardboard case, illustrated on front and info about the set.*

NEW THUNDERBOLTS (Continues in Thunderbolts #100)
Marvel Comics: Jan, 2005 - No. 18, Apr, 2006 ($2.99)

1-18: 1-Grummett-a/Nicieza-s. 1-Captain Marvel app. 2-Namor app. 4-Wolverine app. 3.00
... Vol. 1: One Step Forward (2005, $14.99) r/#1-6 15.00
... Vol. 2: Modern Marvels (2005, $14.99) r/#7-12 15.00
... Vol. 3: Right of Power (2006, $17.99) r/#13-18 & Thunderbolts #100 18.00

NEW TITANS, THE (Formerly The New Teen Titans)
DC Comics: No. 50, Dec, 1988 - No. 130, Feb, 1996 ($1.75/$2.25)

50-Perez-c/a begins; new origin Wonder Girl 6.00
51-59: 50-55-Painted-c. 55-Nightwing (Dick Grayson) forces Danny Chase to resign; Batman app. in flashback, Wonder Girl becomes Troia 4.00
60,61: 60-A Lonely Place of Dying Part 2 continues from Batman #440; new Robin tie-in; Timothy Drake app. 61-A Lonely Place of Dying Part 4 4.00
62-70,72-99,101-124,126-130: 62-65: Deathstroke the Terminator app. 65-Tim Drake (Robin) app. 70-1st Deathstroke solo cover/sty. 72-79-Deathstroke in all: 74-Intro. Pantha. 79-Terra brought back to life; 1 panel cameo Team Titans (1st app.). Deathstroke in #80-84,86. 80-2nd full app. Team Titans. 83,84-Deathstroke kills his son, Jericho. 85-Team Titans app. 86-Deathstroke vs. Nightwing-c/story; last Deathstroke app. 87-New costume Nightwing. 90-92-Parts 2,5,8 Total Chaos (Team Titans). 99-1st app. Arsenal. 115-(11/94) 3.00
71-(44 pgs.)-10th anniversary issue; Deathstroke cameo 4.00
100-($3.50, 52 pgs.)-Holo-grafx foil-c 4.00
125 (3.50)-wraparound-c 4.00
#0-(10/94) Zero Hour, released between #114 & 115 3.00
Annual 5-10 ('89-'94, 68 pgs.. 7-Armageddon 2001 x-over; 1st full app. Teen (Team) Titans (new group). 8-Deathstroke app.; Eclipso app. (minor). 10-Elseworlds story 4.00
Annual 11 (1995, $3.95)-Year One story 4.00

NOTE: ***Perez*** *a-50-55p, 57,60p, 58,59,61(layouts); c-50-61, 62-67i, Annual 5i; co-plots-66.*

NEW TV FUNNIES (See New Funnies)

NEW TWO-FISTED TALES, THE
Dark Horse Comics/Byron Preiss:1993 ($4.95, limited series, 52 pgs.)

1-Kurtzman-r & new-a 5.00

NOTE: ***Eisner*** *c-1i.* ***Kurtzman*** *c-1p, 2.*

NEWUNIVERSAL
Marvel Comics: Feb, 2007 - No. 6, July, 2007 ($2.99)

1-6-Warren Ellis-s/Salvador Larroca-a. 1,2-Variant covers by Ribic 3.00
...: 1959 (9/08, $3.99) Aftermath of the White Event of 1953; Tony Stark app. 4.00
...: Conqueror (10/08, $3.99) The White Event of 2689 B.C.; Eric Nguyen-a 4.00
... : Everything Went White HC (2007, $19.99) r/#1-6; sketch pages 20.00
... : Everything Went White SC (2008, $14.99) r/#1-6; sketch pages 15.00

NEWUNIVERSAL: SHOCKFRONT
Marvel Comics: Jul, 2008 - Present ($2.99)

1,2-Warren Ellis-s/Steve Kurth-a 3.00

NEW WARRIORS, THE (See Thor #411,412)
Marvel Comics: July, 1990 - No. 75, 1996 ($1.00/$1.25/$1.50)

1-Williamson-i; Bagley-c/a(p) in 1-13, Annual 1 2 4 6 9 12 15
1-Gold 2nd printing (7/91) 4.00
2-5: 1,3-Guice-c(i). 2-Williamson-c/a(i). 4.00
6-24,26-49,51-75: 7-Punisher cameo (last pg.). 8,9-Punisher app. 14-Darkhawk & Namor x-over. 17-Fantastic Four & Silver Surfer x-over. 19-Gideon (of X-Force) app. 28-Intro Turbo & Cardinal. 31-Cannonball & Warpath app. 42-Nova vs. Firelord. 46-Photo-c. 47-Bound-in S-M trading card sheet. 52-12 pg. ad insert. 62-Scarlet Spider-c/app. 70-Spider-Man-c/app. 72-Avengers-c/app. 3.00
25-($2.50, 52 pgs.)-Die-cut cover 4.00
40,60: 40-($2.25)-Gold foil collector's edition 4.00
50-($2.95, 52 pgs.)-Glow in the dark-c 4.00
Annual 1-4('91-'94,68 pgs.)-1-Origins all members; 3rd app. X-Force (cont'd from New Mutants

The New West #1 © Black Bull

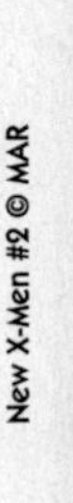
New X-Men #2 © MAR

Nexus #99 © Rude Dude Prods.

GD 2.0 | VG 4.0 | FN 6.0 | VF 8.0 | VF/NM 9.0 | NM- 9.2

Ann. #7 & cont'd in X-Men Ann. #15); x-over before X-Force #1. 3-Bagged w/card 4.00

NEW WARRIORS, THE
Marvel Comics: Oct, 1999 - No. 10, July, 2000 ($2.99/$2.50)

0-Wizard supplement; short story and preview sketchbook 3.00
1-($2.99) 4.00
2-10: 2-Two covers. 5-Generation X app. 9-Iron Man-c 3.00

NEW WARRIORS (See Civil War #1)
Marvel Comics: Aug, 2005 - No. 6, Feb, 2006 ($2.99, limited series)

1-6-Scottie Young-a 3.00
...: Reality Check TPB (2006, $14.99) r/#1-6 15.00

NEW WARRIORS (The Initiative)
Marvel Comics: Aug, 2007 - No. 20, Mar, 2009 ($2.99)

1-19: 1-Medina-a; new team is formed. 2-Jubilee app. 14-16-Secret Invasion 3.00
20-($3.99) 4.00
...: Defiant TPB (2008, $14.99) r/#1-6 15.00

NEW WARRIORS (All-New Marvel Now)
Marvel Comics: Apr, 2014 - No. 12, Jan, 2015 ($3.99)

1-12: 1-Nova, Speedball, Justice, Sun Girl, Scarlet Spider team; Yost-s/To-a 4.00

NEW WAVE, THE
Eclipse Comics: 6/10/86 - No. 13, 3/87 (#1-8: bi-weekly, 20pgs; #9-13: monthly)

1-13:1-Origin, concludes #5. 6-Origin Megabyte. 8,9-The Heap returns. 13-Snyder-c 3.00
...Versus the Volunteers 3-D #1,2(4/87): 1-Snyder-c 3.00

NEW WEST, THE
Black Bull Comics: Mar, 2005 - No. 2, Jun, 2005 ($4.99, limited series)

1,2-Phil Noto-a/c; Jimmy Palmiotti-s 5.00

NEW WORLD (See Comic Books, series I)

NEW WORLDS
Caliber: 1996 - No. 6 ($2.95/$3.95, 80 pgs., B&W, anthology)

1-6: 1-Mister X & other stories 4.00

NEW X-MEN (See X-Men *2nd series* #114-156)

NEW X-MEN (Academy X) (Continued from New Mutants)
Marvel Comics: July, 2004 - No. 46, Mar, 2008 ($2.99)

1-46: 1,2-Green-c/a. 16-19-House of M. 20,21-Decimation. 40-Endangered Species back-ups begin. 44-46-Messiah Complex x-over; Ramos-a 3.00
Yearbook 1 (12/05, $3.99) new story and profile pages 4.00
...: Childhood's End Vol. 1 TPB (2006, $10.99) r/#20-23 11.00
...: Childhood's End Vol. 2 TPB (2006, $10.99) r/#24-27 11.00
...: Childhood's End Vol. 3 TPB (2006, $10.99) r/#28-32 11.00
...: Childhood's End Vol. 4 TPB (2007, $10.99) r/#33-36 11.00
...: Childhood's End Vol. 5 TPB (2007, $17.99) r/#37-43 18.00
House of M: New X-Men TPB (2006, $13.99) r/#16-19 and selections from Secrets Of The House of M one-shot 14.00
... Vol. 1: Choosing Sides TPB (2004, $14.99) r/#1-6 15.00
... Vol. 2: Haunted TPB (2005, $14.99) r/#7-12 15.00
... Vol. 3: X-Posed TPB (2006, $14.99) r/#12-15 & Yearbook Special 15.00

NEW X-MEN: HELLIONS
Marvel Comics: July, 2005 - No. 4, Oct, 2005 ($2.99, limited series)

1-4-Henry-a/Weir & DeFilippis-s 3.00
TPB (2006, $9.99) r/#1-4 10.00

NEW YORK FIVE, THE
DC Comics (Vertigo): Mar, 2011 - No. 4, Jun, 2011 ($2.99, B&W, limited series)

1-4-Brian Wood-s/Ryan Kelly-a 3.00

NEW YORK GIANTS (See Thrilling True Story of the Baseball Giants)

NEW YORK STATE JOINT LEGISLATIVE COMMITTEE TO STUDY THE PUBLICATION OF COMICS, THE
N.Y. State Legislative Document: 1951, 1955

This document was referenced by Wertham for **Seduction of the Innocent.** Contains numerous repros from comics showing violence, sadism, torture, and sex. 1955 version (196p, No. 37, 2/23/55) - Sold for $180 in 1986.

NEW YORK, THE BIG CITY
Kitchen Sink Press: 1986 ($10.95, B&W); **DC Comics:** July, 2000 ($12.95, B&W)

nn-(1986, $10.95) Will Eisner-s/a 25.00
nn-(2000, $12.95) new printing 13.00

NEW YORK WORLD'S FAIR (Also see Big Book of Fun & New Book of Fun)
National Periodical Publ.: 1939, 1940 (100 pgs.; cardboard covers)
(DC's 4th & 5th annuals)

1939-Scoop Scanlon, Superman (blond haired Superman on-c), Sandman, Zatara, Slam Bradley, Ginger Snap by Bob Kane begin; 1st published app. The Sandman (see Adventure #40 for his 1st drawn story); Vincent Sullivan-c; cover background by Guardineer
1800 3600 5400 13,000 30,000 –
1940-Batman, Hourman, Johnny Thunderbolt, Red, White & Blue & Hanko (by Creig Flessel) app.; Superman, Batman & Robin-c (1st time they all appear together); early Robin app.; 1st Burnley-c/a (per Burnley) 950 1900 2850 7000 16,000 –

NOTE: *The 1939 edition was published 4/29/39 and released 4/30/39, the day the fair opened, at 25¢, and was first sold only at the fair. Since all other comics were 10¢, it didn't sell. Remaining copies were advertised beginning in the August issues of most DC comics for 25¢, but soon the price was dropped to 15¢. Everyone that sent a quarter through the mail for it received a free Superman #1 or a #2 to make up the dime difference. 15¢ stickers were placed over the 25¢ price. Four variations on the 15¢ stickers are known. The 1940 edition was published 5/11/40 and was priced at 15¢. It was a precursor to World's Best #1.*

NEW YORK: YEAR ZERO
Eclipse Comics: July, 1988 - No. 4, Oct, 1988 ($2.00, B&W, limited series)

1-4 3.00

NEXT, THE
DC Comics: Sept, 2006 - No. 6, Feb, 2007 ($2.99, limited series)

1-6-Tad Williams-s/Dietrich Smith-a; Superman app. 3.00

NEXT MEN (See John Byrne's...)

NEXT MEN: AFTERMATH (Continued from John Byrne's Next Men 2010-2011 series)
IDW Publishing: No. 40, Feb, 2012 - No. 44, Jun, 2012 ($3.99)

40-44-John Byrne-s/a/c 4.00

NEXT NEXUS, THE
First Comics: Jan, 1989 - No. 4, April, 1989 ($1.95, limited series, Baxter paper)

1-4: Mike Baron scripts & Steve Rude-c/a. 3.00
TPB (10/89, $9.95) r/series 10.00

NEXTWAVE: AGENTS OF H.A.T.E
Marvel Comics: Mar, 2006 - No. 12, Mar, 2007 ($2.99)

1-12-Warren Ellis-s/Stuart Immonen-a. 2-Fin Fang Foom app. 12-Devil Dinosaur app. 3.00
Vol. 1 - This Is What They Want HC (2006, $19.99) r/#1-6; Ellis original pitch 20.00
Vol. 1 - This Is What They Want SC (2007, $14.99) r/#1-6; Ellis original pitch 15.00
Vol. 2 - I Kick Your Face HC (2007, $19.99) r/#7-12 20.00
Vol. 2 - I Kick Your Face SC (2008, $14.99) r/#7-12 15.00

NEXUS (See First Comics Graphic Novel #4, 19 & The Next Nexus)
Capital Comics/First Comics No. 7 on: June, 1981 - No. 6, Mar, 1984; No. 7, Apr, 1985 - No. 80?, May, 1991 (Direct sales only, 36 pgs.; V2#1('83)-printed on Baxter paper)

1-B&W version; mag. size; w/double size poster 3 6 9 17 26 35
1-B&W 1981 limited edition; 500 copies printed and signed; same as above except this version has a 2-pg. poster & a pencil sketch on paperboard by Steve Rude
6 12 18 38 69 100
2-B&W, magazine size 2 4 6 11 16 20
3-B&W, magazine size; Brunner back-c; contains 33-1/3 rpm record ($2.95 price)
2 4 6 9 13 16
V2#1-Color version 5.00
2-49,51-80: 2-Nexus' origin begins. 67-Snyder-c/a 3.00
50-($3.50, 52 pgs.) 4.00
Hardcover Volume One (Dark Horse Books, 11/05, $49.95) r/#1-3 & V2 #1-4; creator bios 50.00
HC Volume Two (Dark Horse Books, 3/06, $49.95) r/V2 #5-11; creator bios 50.00
HC Volume Three (Dark Horse Books, 5/06, $49.95) r/V2 #12-18; Marz forward 50.00
HC Volume Four (Dark Horse Books, 8/06, $49.95) r/V2 #19-25; Powell forward 50.00
HC Volume Five (Dark Horse Books, 2/07, $49.95) r/V2 #26-32; Brubaker forward 50.00
HC Volume Six (Dark Horse Books, 2/07, $49.95) r/V2 #33-39; Evanier forward 50.00
HC Volume Seven (Dark Horse Books, 2/08, $49.95) r/V2 #40-46; Brunning forward 50.00
HC Volume Eight (Dark Horse Books, 1/09, $49.95) r/V2 #47-52 and The Next Nexus #1; interview with original publishers John Davis and Milton Griepp 50.00
HC Volume Nine (Dark Horse Books, 8/09, $49.95) r/V2 #53-57 & The Next Nexus #2-4 50.00

NOTE: ***Bissette** c-V2#29. **Giffen** c/a-V2#23. **Gulacy** c-1 (B&W), 2(B&W). **Mignola** c/a-V2#28. **Rude** c-3(B&W), V2#1-22, 24-27, 33-36, 39-42, 45-48, 50, 58-60, 75; a-1-3, V2#1-7, 8-16p, 18-22p, 24-27p, 33-36p, 39-42p, 45-48p, 50, 58, 59p, 60. **Paul Smith** a-V2#37, 38, 43, 44, 51-55p; c-V2#37, 38, 43, 44, 51-55.*

NEXUS
Rude Dude Productions: No. 99, July, 2007 - No. 102, Jun, 2009 ($2.99)

99-Mike Baron scripts & Steve Rude-c/a 3.00
100-($4.99) Part 2 of Space Opera; back-up feature: History of Nexus 5.00
101/102-(6/09, $4.95) Combined issue 5.00
..., Free Comic Book Day 2007 - Excerpts from previous issues and preview of #99 3.00
... Greatest Hits (8/07, $1.99) same content as Free Comic Book Day 2007 3.00
...: The Origin (11/07, $3.99) reprints the 7/96 one-shot 4.00

NEXUS: ALIEN JUSTICE
Dark Horse Comics: Dec, 1992 - No. 3, Feb, 1993 ($3.95, limited series)

Nickel Comics #2 © FAW

Nick Fury, Agent of SHIELD #16 © MAR

Nightcrawler (2014 series) #8 © MAR

	GD 2.0	VG 4.0	FN 6.0	VF 8.0	VF/NM 9.0	NM- 9.2

1-3: Mike Baron scripts & Steve Rude-c/a 4.00

NEXUS: EXECUTIONER'S SONG
Dark Horse Comics: June, 1996 - No. 4, Sept, 1996 ($2.95, limited series)
1-4: Mike Baron scripts & Steve Rude-c/a 3.00

NEXUS FILES
First Comics: 1989 ($4.50, color/16pgs. B&W, one-shot, squarebound, 52 pgs.)
1-New Rude-a; info on Nexus 4.50

NEXUS: GOD CON
Dark Horse Comics: Apr, 1997 - No. 2, May, 1997 ($2.95, limited series)
1,2-Baron-s/Rude-c/a 3.00

NEXUS LEGENDS
First Comics: May, 1989 - No. 23, Mar, 1991 ($1.50, Baxter paper)
1-23: R/1-3(Capital) & early First Comics issues w/new Rude covers #1-6,9,10 3.00

NEXUS MEETS MADMAN (...Special)
Dark Horse Comics: May, 1996 ($2.95, one-shot)
nn-Mike Baron & Mike Allred scripts, Steve Rude-c/a. 3.00

NEXUS: NIGHTMARE IN BLUE
Dark Horse Comics: July, 1997 - No. 4, Oct, 1997 ($2.95, limited series)
1-4: 1,2,4-Adam Hughes-c 3.00

NEXUS: THE LIBERATOR
Dark Horse Comics: Aug, 1992 - No. 4, Nov, 1992 ($2.95, limited series)
1-4 3.00

NEXUS: THE ORIGIN
Dark Horse Comics: July, 1996 ($3.95, one-shot)
nn-Mike Baron- scripts, Steve Rude-c/a. 4.00

NEXUS: THE WAGES OF SIN
Dark Horse Comics: Mar, 1995 - No. 4, June, 1995 ($2.95, limited series)
1-4 3.00

NFL RUSH ZONE: SEASON OF THE GUARDIANS
Action Lab Comics: Feb, 2013 - No. 4 ($3.99)
1-4: 1-Matt Ryan & Roddy White app. 4.00
Free Comic Book Day edition (2013, giveaway) 3.00

NFL SUPERPRO
Marvel Comics: Oct, 1991 - No. 12, Sept, 1992 ($1.00)
1-12: 1-Spider-Man-c/app. 3.00
Special Edition (9/91, $2.00) Jusko painted-c 4.00
Super Bowl Edition (3/91, squarebound) Jusko painted-c 4.00

NICKEL COMICS
Dell Publishing Co.: 1938 (Pocket size - 7-1/2x5-1/2")(68 pgs.)
1- "Bobby & Chip" by Otto Messmer, Felix the Cat artist. Contains some English reprints
86 172 258 546 936 1325

NICKEL COMICS
Fawcett Publications: Feb 1940
nn - Ashcan comic, not distributed to newsstands, only for in-house use. A CGC certified 9.6 copy sold for $7,200 in 2003. In 2008, a CGC certified 8.5 sold for $2,390 and an uncertified Near Mint copy sold for $3,100.

NICKEL COMICS
Fawcett Publications: May, 1940 - No. 8, Aug, 1940 (36 pgs.; Bi-Weekly; 5¢)

	GD	VG	FN	VF	VF/NM	NM-
1-Origin/1st app. Bulletman	389	778	1167	2723	4762	6800
2	119	238	357	762	1306	1850
3	87	174	261	553	952	1350
4-The Red Gaucho begins	73	146	219	467	796	1125
5-7	71	142	213	454	777	1100
8-World's Fair-c; Bulletman moved to Master Comics #7 in October (scarce)	90	180	270	576	988	1400

NOTE: *Beck c-5-8. Jack Binder c-1-4. Bondage c-5. Bulletman c-1-8.*

NICK FURY, AGENT OF SHIELD (See Fury, Marvel Spotlight #31 & Shield)
Marvel Comics Group: 6/68 - No. 15, 11/69; No. 16, 11/70 - No. 18, 3/71

	GD	VG	FN	VF	VF/NM	NM-
1	14	28	42	96	211	325
2-4: 4-Origin retold	8	16	24	51	96	140
5-Classic-c	8	16	24	56	108	160
6,7: 7-Salvador Dali painting swipe	7	14	21	46	86	125
8-11,13: 9-Hate Monger begins, ends #11. 10-Smith layouts/pencil. 11-Smith-c. 13-1st app. Super-Patriot; last 12¢ issue	4	8	12	28	47	65
12-Smith-c/a	5	10	15	30	50	70
14-Begin 15¢ issues	4	8	12	25	40	55
15-1st app. & death of Bullseye-c/story(11/69); Nick Fury shot & killed; last 15¢ issue	7	14	21	48	89	130
16-18-(25¢, 52 pgs.)-r/Str. Tales #135-143	3	6	9	20	31	42

TPB (May 2000, $19.95) r/ Strange Tales #150-168 20.00
...: Who is Scorpio? TPB (11/00, $12.95) r/#1-3,5; Steranko-c 13.00
NOTE: *Adkins a-3i. Craig a-10i. Sid Greene a-12i. Kirby a-16-18r. Springer a-4, 6, 7, 8p, 9, 10p, 11; c-8, 9. Steranko a(p)-1-3, 5; c-1-7.*

NICK FURY AGENT OF SHIELD (Also see Strange Tales #135)
Marvel Comics: Dec, 1983 - No. 2, Jan, 1984 (2.00, 52 pgs., Baxter paper)
1,2-r/Nick Fury #1-4; new Steranko-c 1 2 3 5 6 8

NICK FURY, AGENT OF S.H.I.E.L.D.
Marvel Comics: Sept, 1989 - No. 47, May, 1993 ($1.50/$1.75)
V2#1 5.00
2-26,30-47: 10-Capt. America app. 13-Return of The Yellow Claw. 15-Fantastic Four app. 30,31-Deathlok app. 36-Cage app. 37-Woodgod c/story. 38-41-Flashes back to pre-Shield days after WWII. 44-Capt. America-c/s. 45-Viper-c/s. 46-Gideon x-over 3.00
27-29-Wolverine-c/stories 4.00
NOTE: *Alan Grant scripts-11. Guice a(p)-20-23, 25, 26; c-20-28.*

NICK FURY'S HOWLING COMMANDOS
Marvel Comics: Dec, 2005 - No. 6, May, 2006 ($2.99)
1-6: 1-Giffen-s/Francisco-a 3.00
1-Director's Cut ($3.99) r/#1 with original script and sketch design pages 4.00

NICK FURY VS. S.H.I.E.L.D.
Marvel Comics: June, 1988 - No. 6, Nov, 1988 ($3.50, 52 pgs, deluxe format)
1,2: 1-Steranko-c. 2-(Low print run) Sienkiewicz-c 6.00
3-6 5.00

NICK HALIDAY (Thrill of the Sea)
Argo: May, 1956
1-Daily & Sunday strip-r by Petree 9 18 27 50 65 80

NIGHT AND THE ENEMY (Graphic Novel)
Comico: 1988 (8-1/2x11") ($11.95, color, 80 pgs.)
1-Harlan Ellison scripts/Ken Steacy-c/a; r/Epic Illustrated & new-a (1st & 2nd printings) 12.00
1-Limited edition ($39.95) 40.00

NIGHT BEFORE CHRISTMAS, THE (See March of Comics No. 152 in the Promotional Comics section)

NIGHT BEFORE CHRISTMASK, THE
Dark Horse Comics: Nov, 1994 ($9.95, one-shot)
nn-Hardcover book; The Mask; Rick Geary-c/a 10.00

NIGHTBREED (See Clive Barker's Nightbreed)

NIGHT CLUB
Image Comics: Apr, 2005 - No. 4, Dec, 2006 ($2.95/$2.99, limited series)
1-4: 1-Mike Baron-s/Mike Norton-a 3.00

NIGHTCRAWLER (X-Men)
Marvel Comics Group: Nov, 1985 - No. 4, Feb, 1986 (Mini-series from X-Men)
1-4: 1-Cockrum-c/a 6.00

NIGHTCRAWLER (Volume 2)
Marvel Comics: Feb, 2002 - No. 4, May, 2002 ($2.50, limited series)
1-4-Matt Smith-a 3.00

NIGHTCRAWLER
Marvel Comics: Nov, 2004 - No. 12, Jan, 2006 ($2.99)
1-12: 1-6-Robertson-a/Land-c. 2-Magik app. 8-Wolverine app. 10-Man-Thing app. 3.00
...: The Devil Inside TPB (2005, $14.99) r/#1-6 15.00
...: The Winding Way TPB (2006, $14.99) r/#7-12 15.00

NIGHTCRAWLER
Marvel Comics: Jun, 2014 - No. 12, May, 2015 ($3.99)
1-12: 1-Claremont-s/Nauck-a. 7-Death of Wolverine tie-in 4.00

NIGHTFALL: THE BLACK CHRONICLES
DC Comics (Homage): Dec, 1999 - No. 3, Feb, 2000 ($2.95, limited series)
1-3-Coker-a/Gilmore-s 3.00

NIGHT FORCE, THE (See New Teen Titans #21)
DC Comics: Aug, 1982 - No. 14, Sept, 1983 (60¢)
1 4.00
2-14: 13-Origin Baron Winter. 14-Nudity panels 3.00
NOTE: *Colan c/a-1-14p. Giordano c-1i, 2i, 4i, 5i, 7i, 12i.*

NIGHT FORCE

Nighthawk (2016 series) #1 © MAR

The Night Man #8 © MAL

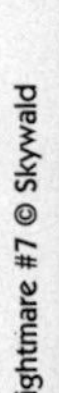
Nightmare #7 © Skywald

	GD 2.0	VG 4.0	FN 6.0	VF 8.0	VF/NM 9.0	NM- 9.2

DC Comics: Dec, 1996 - No. 12, Nov, 1997 ($2.25)

1-12: 1-3-Wolfman-s/Anderson-a(p). 8-"Convergence" part 2 3.00

NIGHT FORCE
DC Comics: May, 2012 - No. 7, Nov, 2012 ($2.99, limited series)

1-7-Wolfman-s/Mandrake-a/Manco-c 3.00

NIGHT GLIDER
Topps Comics (Kirbyverse): April, 1993 ($2.95, one-shot)

1-Kirby c-1, Heck-a; polybagged w/Kirbychrome trading card 4.00

NIGHTHAWK
Marvel Comics: Sept, 1998 - No. 3, Nov, 1998 ($2.99, mini-series)

1-3-Krueger-s; Daredevil app. 3.00

NIGHTHAWK (From Squadron Supreme)
Marvel Comics: Jul, 2016 - No. 6, Dec, 2016 ($3.99)

1-6: 1-Walker-s/Villalobos-a/Cowan-c. 3-Morazzo-a 4.00

NIGHTINGALE, THE
Henry H. Stansbury Once-Upon-A-Time Press, Inc.: 1948 (10¢, 7-1/4x10-1/4", 14 pgs., 1/2 B&W)

(Very Rare)-Low distribution; distributed to Westchester County & Bronx, N.Y. only; used in **Seduction of the Innocent**, pg. 312,313 as the 1st and only "good" comic book ever published. Ill. by Dong Kingman; 1,500 words of text, printed on high quality paper & no word balloons. Copyright registered 10/22/48, distributed week of 12/5/48. Only 5000 copies printed, 6 currently known to still exist. (By Hans Christian Andersen)
Estimated value........ 250.00

NIGHT MAN, THE (See Sludge #1)
Malibu Comics (Ultraverse): Oct, 1993 - No. 23, Aug, 1995 ($1.95/$2.50)

1-($2.50, 48 pgs.)-Rune flip-c/story by B. Smith (3 pgs.) 4.00
1-Ultra-Limited silver foil-c 8.00
2-15, 17: 3-Break-Thru x-over; Freex app. 4-Origin Firearm (2 pgs.) by Chaykin. 6-TNTNT app. 8-1st app. Teknight 3.00
16 ($3.50)-flip book (Ultraverse Premiere #11) 4.00
...:The Pilgrim Conundrum Saga (1/95, $3.95, 68 pgs.)-Strangers app. 4.00
18-23: 22-Loki-c/app. 3.00
Infinity ($1.50) 3.00
...Vs. Wolverine #0-Kelley Jones-c; mail in offer 1 3 4 6 8 10
NOTE: Zeck a-16.

NIGHT MAN, THE
Malibu Comics (Ultraverse): Sept, 1995 - No.4, Dec, 1995 ($1.50, lim. series)

1-4: Post Black September storyline 3.00

NIGHT MAN, THE /GAMBIT
Malibu Comics (Ultraverse): Mar, 1996 - No. 3, May, 1996 ($1.95, lim. series)

0-Limited Premium Edition 4.00
1-3: David Quinn scripts in all. 3-Rhiannon discovered to be The Night Man's mother 3.00

NIGHTMARE
Ziff-Davis (Approved Comics)/St. John No. 3: Summer, 1952 - No. 3, Winter, 1952, 53 (Painted-c)

1-1 pg. Kinstler-a; Tuska-a(2) 65 130 195 416 708 1000
2-Kinstler-a-Poe's "Pit & the Pendulum" 45 90 135 284 480 675
3-Kinstler-a 41 82 123 256 428 600

NIGHTMARE (Weird Horrors #1-9) (Amazing Ghost Stories #14 on)
St. John Publishing Co.: No. 10, Dec, 1953 - No. 13, Aug, 1954

10-Reprints Ziff-Davis Weird Thrillers #2 w/new Kubert-c plus 2 pgs. Kinstler-a; Anderson, Colan & Toth-a 60 120 180 381 653 925
11-Krigstein-a; painted-c; Poe adapt., "Hop Frog" 45 90 135 284 480 675
12-Kubert bondage-c; adaptation of Poe's "The Black Cat"; Cannibalism story 43 86 129 271 461 650
13-Reprints Z-D Weird Thrillers #3 with new cover; Powell-a(2), Tuska-a; Baker-c 39 78 117 231 378 525

NIGHTMARE (Magazine) (Also see Psycho)
Skywald Publishing Corp.: Dec, 1970 - No. 23, Feb, 1975 (B&W, 68 pgs.)

1-Everett-a; Heck-a; Shores-a 10 20 30 66 138 210
2-5,8,9: 2,4-Decapitation story. 5-Nazi-s; Boris Karloff 4 pg. photo/text-s. 8-Features E.C. movie "Tales From the Crypt"; reprints some E.C. comics panels. 9-Wrightson-a; bondage-c; 1st Lovecraft Saggoth Chronicles/Cthulhu 6 12 18 37 66 95
6-Kaluta-a; Jeff Jones-c, photo & interview; 1st Living Gargoyle; Love Witch-s w/nudity; Boris Karloff-s 6 12 18 40 73 105
7 5 10 15 33 57 80
10-Wrightson-a (1 pg.); Princess of Earth-c/s; Edward & Mina Sartyros, the Human Gargoyles series continues from Psycho #8 6 12 18 38 69 100
11-19: 12-Excessive gore, severed heads. 13-Lovecraft-s. 15-Dracula-c/s. 17-Vampires issue; Autobiography of a Vampire series begins 4 8 12 28 47 65
20-John Byrne's 1st artwork (2 pgs.)(8/74); severed head-c; Hitler app. 8 16 24 54 102 150
21-23: 21-(1974 Summer Special)-Kaluta-a. 22-Tomb of Horror issue. 23-(1975 Winter Special) 5 10 15 31 53 75
Annual 1(1972)-Squarebound; B. Jones-a 5 10 15 31 53 75
Winter Special 1(1973)-All new material 4 8 12 28 47 65
Yearbook nn(1974)-B. Jones, Reese, Wildey-a 4 8 12 28 47 65
*NOTE: **Adkins** a-5. **Boris** c-2, 3, 5 (#4 is not by Boris). **Buckler** a-3, 15. **Byrne** a-20p. **Everett** a-1, 2, 4, 5, 12. **Jeff Jones** a-6, 21r(Psycho #6); c-6. **Katz** a-3, 5, 21. **Reese** a-4, 5. **Wildey** a-4, 5, 6, 21, '74 Yearbook. **Wrightson** a-9, 10.*

NIGHTMARE (Alex Nino's)
Innovation Publishing: 1989 ($1.95)

1-Alex Nino-a 3.00

NIGHTMARE
Marvel Comics: Dec, 1994 - No. 4, Mar, 1995 ($1.95, limited series)

1-4 3.00

NIGHTMARE & CASPER (See Harvey Hits #71) (Casper & Nightmare #6 on) (See Casper The Friendly Ghost #19)
Harvey Publications: Aug, 1963 - No. 5, Aug, 1964 (25¢)

1-All reprints? 7 14 21 46 86 125
2-5: All reprints? 5 10 15 30 50 70

NIGHTMARE ON ELM STREET, A (Also see Freddy Krueger's...)
DC Comics (WildStorm): Dec, 2006 - Present ($2.99)

1-8: 1-Two covers by Harris & Bradstreet; Dixon-s/West-a 3.00

NIGHTMARES (See Do You Believe in Nightmares)

NIGHTMARES
Eclipse Comics: May, 1985 - No. 2, May, 1985 ($1.75, Baxter paper)

1,2 3.00

NIGHTMARE THEATER
Chaos! Comics: Nov, 1997 - No. 4, Nov, 1997 ($2.50, mini-series)

1-4-Horror stories by various; Wrightson-a 3.00

NIGHTMASK
Marvel Comics Group: Nov, 1986 - No. 12, Oct, 1987

1-12 3.00

NIGHT MASTER
Silverwolf: Feb, 1987 ($1.50, B&W)

1-Tim Vigil-c/a 3.00

NIGHTMASTER (See Shadowpact)
DC Comics: Jan, 2011 ($2.99, one-shot)

1-Wrightson-c/Beechen-s/Dwyer-a; Shadowpact app. 3.00

NIGHT MUSIC (See Eclipse Graphic Album Series, The Magic Flute)
Eclipse Comics: Dec, 1984 - No. 11, 1990 ($1.75/$3.95/$4.95, Baxter paper)

1-7: 3-Russell's Jungle Book adapt. 4,5-Pelleas And Melisande (double titled) 6-Salomé (double titled). 7-Red Dog #1 3.00
8-($3.95) Ariane and Bluebeard 4.00
9-11-($4.95) The Magic Flute; Russell adapt. 5.00

NIGHT NURSE
Marvel Comics Group: Nov, 1972 - No. 4, May, 1973

1 21 42 63 147 324 500
2-4 9 18 27 61 123 185

NIGHT NURSE
Marvel Comics: Jul, 2015 ($7.99, one-shot)

1-Reprints 1972 series #1-4 and Daredevil V2 #80; Siya Oum-c 8.00

NIGHT OF MYSTERY
Avon Periodicals: 1953 (no month) (one-shot)

nn-1 pg. Kinstler-a, Hollingsworth-c 65 130 195 416 708 1000

NIGHT OF THE GRIZZLY, THE (See Movie Classics)

NIGHT OF THE LIVING DEADPOOL
Marvel Comics: Mar, 2014 - No. 4, May, 2014 ($3.99, limited series)

1-4-Bunn-s/Rosanas-a; Deadpool in a zombie apocalypse 4.00

NIGHTRAVEN (See Marvel Graphic Novel)

NIGHT RIDER (Western)
Marvel Comics Group: Oct, 1974 - No. 6, Aug, 1975

Nightstalkers #11 © MAR

Night Thrasher #14 © MAR

Nightwing (2016 series) #1 © DC

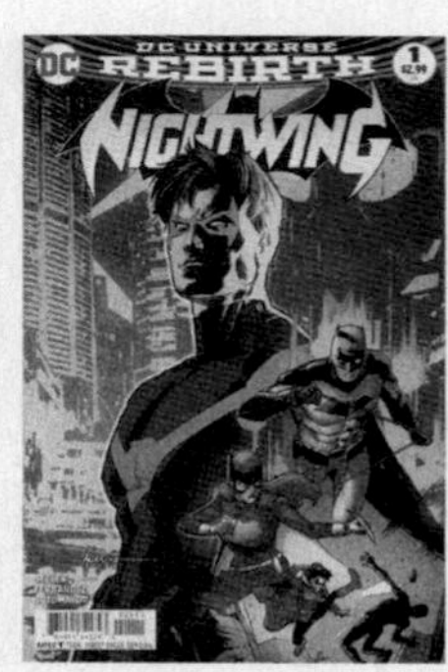

GD 2.0 | VG 4.0 | FN 6.0 | VF 8.0 | VF/NM 9.0 | NM- 9.2

1: 1-6 reprint Ghost Rider #1-6 (#1-origin) 3 6 9 19 30 40
2-6 2 4 6 11 16 20

NIGHT'S CHILDREN: THE VAMPIRE
Millenium: July, 1995 - No. 2, Aug, 1995 ($2.95, B&W)
1,2: Wendy Snow-Lang story & art 3.00

NIGHTSIDE
Marvel Comics: Dec, 2001 - No. 4, Mar, 2002 ($2.99)
1-4: 1-Weinberg-s/Derenick-a; intro Sydney Taine 3.00

NIGHTS INTO DREAMS (Based on video game)
Archie Comics: Feb, 1998 -No. 6, Oct, 1998 ($1.75, limited series)
1-6 3.00

NIGHTSTALKERS (Also see Midnight Sons Unlimited)
Marvel Comics (Midnight Sons #14 on): Nov, 1992 - No. 18, Apr, 1994 ($1.75)
1-($2.75, 52 pgs.)-Polybagged w/poster; part 5 of Rise of the Midnight Sons storyline; Garney/Palmer-c/a begins; Hannibal King, Blade & Frank Drake begin 4.00
2-9,11-18: 5-Punisher app. 7-Ghost Rider app. 8,9-Morbius app. 14-Spot varnish-c. 14,15-Siege of Darkness Pts 1 & 9 3.00
10-($2.25)-Outer-c is a Darkhold envelope made of black parchment w/gold ink; Midnight Massacre part 1 4.00

NIGHT TERRORS,THE
Chanting Monks Studios: 2000 ($2.75, B&W)
1-Bernie Wrightson-c; short stories, one by Wrightson-s/a 3.00

NIGHT THRASHER (Also see The New Warriors)
Marvel Comics: Aug, 1993 - No. 21, Apr, 1995 ($1.75/$1.95)
1-($2.95, 52 pgs.)-Red holo-grafx foil-c; origin 4.00
2-21: 2-Intro Tantrum. 3-Gideon (of X-Force) app. 10-Bound-in trading card sheet; Iron Man app. 15-Hulk app. 3.00

NIGHT THRASHER: FOUR CONTROL
Marvel Comics: Oct, 1992 - No. 4, Jan, 1993 ($2.00, limited series)
1-4: 2-Intro Tantrum. 3-Gideon (of X-Force) app. 3.00

NIGHT TRIBES
DC Comics (WildStorm): July, 1999 ($4.95, one-shot)
1-Golden & Sniegoski-s/Chin-a 5.00

NIGHTVEIL (Also see Femforce)
Americomics/AC Comics: Nov, 1984 - No. 7, 1987 ($1.75)
1-7 3.00
...'s Cauldron Of Horror 1 (1989, B&W)-Kubert, Powell, Wood-r plus new Nightveil story 3.00
...'s Cauldron Of Horror 2 (1990, $2.95, B&W)-Pre-code horror-r by Kubert & Powell 3.00
...'s Cauldron Of Horror 3 (1991) 3.00
Special 1 ('88, $1.95)-Kaluta-c 3.00
One Shot ('96, $5.95)-Flip book w/ Colt 6.00

NIGHTWATCH
Marvel Comics: Apr, 1994 - No. 12, Mar, 1995 ($1.50)
1-($2.95)-Collectors edition; foil-c; Ron Lim-c/a begins; Spider-Man app. 4.00
1-12-Regular edition. 2-Bound-in S-M trading card sheet; 5,6-Venom-c & app. 7,11-Cardiac app. 3.00

NIGHTWING (Also see New Teen Titans, New Titans, Showcase '93 #11,12, Tales of the New Teen Titans & Teen Titans Spotlight)
DC Comics: Sept, 1995 - No. 4, Dec, 1995 ($2.25, limited series)
1-Dennis O'Neil story/Greg Land-a in all 1 3 4 6 8 10
2-4 4.00
...: Alfred's Return (7/95, $3.50) Giordano-a 4.00
...Ties That Bind (1997, $12.95, TPB) r/mini-series & Alfred's Return 13.00

NIGHTWING
DC Comics: Oct, 1996 - No. 153, Apr, 2009 ($1.95/$1.99/$2.25/$2.50/$2.99)
1-Chuck Dixon scripts & Scott McDaniel-c/a 3 6 9 17 26 35
2,3 1 2 3 5 6 8
4-10: 6-Robin-c/app. 5.00
11-20: 13-15-Batman app. 19,20-Cataclysm pts. 2,11 4.00
21-49,51-64: 23-Green Arrow app. 26-29-Huntress-c/app. 30-Superman-c/app. 35-39-No Man's Land. 41-Land/Geraci-a begins. 46-Begin $2.25-c. 47-Texiera-c. 52-Catwoman-c/app. 54-Shrike app. 3.00
50-($3.50) Nightwing battles Torque 4.00
65-74,76-99: 65,66-Bruce Wayne: Murderer x-over pt. 3,9. 68,69: B.W.: Fugitive pt. 6,9. 70-Last Dixon-s. 71-Devin Grayson-s begin. 81-Batgirl vs. Deathstroke. 93-Blockbuster killed. 94-Copperhead app. 96-Bagged w/CD. 96-98-War Games 3.00
75-(1/03, $2.95) Intro. Tarantula 4.00
100-(2/05, $2.95) Tarantula app. 4.00
101-117: 101-Year One begins. 103-Jason Todd & Deadman app. 107-110-Hester-a. 109-Begin $2.50-c. 109,110-Villains United tie-ins. 112-Deathstroke app. 3.00
118-149,151-153: 118-One Year Later; Jason Todd as 2nd Nightwing. 120-Begin $2.99-c. 138,139-Resurrection of Ra's al Ghul x-over. 138-2nd printing. 147-Two-Face app. 3.00
150-($3.99) Batman R.I.P. x-over; Nightwing vs. Two-Face; Tan-c 4.00
#1,000,000 (11/98) teams with future Batman 3.00
Annual 1(1997, $3.95) Pulp Heroes 4.00
Annual 2 (6/07, $3.99) Dick Grayson and Barbara Gordon's shared history 4.00
...Eighty Page Giant 1 (12/00, $5.95) Intro. of Hella; Dixon-s/Haley-c 6.00
...: Big Guns (2004, $14.95, TPB) r/#47-50; Secret Files 1, Eighty Page Giant 1 15.00
...: Brothers in Blood (2007, $14.99, TPB) r/#118-124 15.00
...: A Darker Shade of Justice (2001, $19.95, TPB) r/#30-39, Secret Files #1 20.00
...: Freefall (2008, $17.99, TPB) r/#140-146 18.00
...: A Knight in Blüdhaven (1998, $14.95, TPB) r/#1-8 15.00
...: Love and Bullets (2000, $17.95, TPB) r/#1/2, 19,21,22,24-29 18.00
...: Love and War (2007, $14.99, TPB) r/#125-132 15.00
...: On the Razor's Edge (2005, $14.99, TPB) r/#52,54-60 15.00
...: Our Worlds at War (9/01, $2.95) Jae Lee-c 3.00
...: Renegade TPB (2006, $17.95) r/#112-117 18.00
...: Rough Justice (1999, $17.95, TPB) r/#9-18 18.00
Secret Files 1 (10/99, $4.95) Origin-s and pin-ups 5.00
...: The Great Leap (2009, $19.99) r/#147-153 20.00
...: The Hunt for Oracle (2003, $14.95, TPB) r/#41-46 & Birds of Prey #20,21 15.00
...: The Lost Year (2008, $14.99) r/#133-137 & Annual #2 15.00
...: The Target (2001, $5.95) McDaniel-c/a 6.00
Wizard 1/2 (Mail offer) 5.00
...: Year One (2005, $14.99) r/#101-106 15.00

NIGHTWING (DC New 52)(Leads into Grayson series)
DC Comics: Nov, 2011 - No. 30, Jul, 2014 ($2.99)
1-Dick Grayson in black/red costume; Higgins-s/Barrows-a/c 20.00
1-2nd printing with red background-c 10.00
2-7,10-14: 2-4-Batgirl app. 13,14-Lady Shiva app. 14-Joker cameo 4.00
8,9: 8-Night of the Owls prelude. 9-Night of the Owls x-over 5.00
15-Die-cut cover with Joker mask; Death of the Family tie-in 5.00
16-18: 16-Death of the Family tie-in. 18-Requiem; Tony Zucco returns 4.00
19-24,26-29: 19-24-Prankster app. 26,27-Mad Hatter app. 28,29-Mr. Zsasz app. 3.00
25-($3.99) Zero Year flashback to Haly's Circus days; Higgins-s/Conrad & Richards-a 4.00
30-($3.99) Aftermath of Forever Evil series; Grayson joins Spyral 4.00
#0-(11/12, $2.99) Origin re-told/updated; Lady Shiva app.; DeFalco-s/Barrows-a 4.00
Annual #1 (12/13, $4.99) Batgirl Wanted! tie-in; Firefly app. 5.00

NIGHTWING (DC Rebirth)
DC Comics: Sept, 2016 - Present ($2.99)
1-16: 1-Seeley-s/Fernandez-a. 1-Intro. Raptor. 5,6-Night of the Monster Men x-over 3.00
...: Rebirth (9/16, $2.99) Seeley-s/Paquette-a; Damian app.; back in Nightwing costume 3.00

NIGHTWING (See Tangent Comics/ Nightwing)

NIGHTWING AND HUNTRESS
DC Comics: May, 1998 - No. 4, Aug, 1998 ($1.95, limited series)
1-4-Grayson-s/Land & Sienkiewicz-a 3.00
TPB (2003, $9.95) r/#1/4; cover gallery 10.00

NIGHTWINGS (See DC Science Fiction Graphic Novel)

NIGHTWORLD
Image Comics: Aug, 2014 - No. 4, Nov, 2014 ($3.99, limited series)
1-4-McGovern-s/Leandri-a/c 4.00

NIKKI, WILD DOG OF THE NORTH (Disney, see Movie Comics)
Dell Publishing Co.: No. 1226, Sept, 1961
Four Color 1226-Movie, photo-c 5 10 15 33 57 80

9-11 - ARTISTS RESPOND
Dark Horse Comics: 2002 ($9.95, TPB, proceeds donated to charities)
Volume 1-Short stories about the September 11 tragedies by various Dark Horse, Chaos! and Image writers and artists; Eric Drooker-c 10.00

9-11: EMERGENCY RELIEF
Alternative Comics: 2002 ($14.95, TPB, proceeds donated to the Red Cross)
nn-Short stories by various inc. Pekar, Eisner, Hester, Oeming, Noto; Cho-c 15.00

9-11 - THE WORLD'S FINEST COMIC BOOK WRITERS AND ARTISTS TELL STORIES TO REMEMBER
DC Comics: 2002 ($9.95, TPB, proceeds donated to charities)

Ninjak (2015 series) #9 © VAL

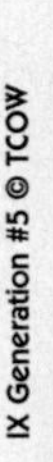
IX Generation #5 © TCOW

Nocturnals: Carnival of Beasts © Dan Brereton

Volume 2-Short stories about the September 11 tragedies by various DC, MAD, and WildStorm writers and artists ; Alex Ross-c 10.00

NINE RINGS OF WU-TANG
Image Comics: July, 1999 - No. 5, July, 2000 ($2.95)

Preview (7/99, $5.00, B&W) 5.00
1-5: 1-(11/99, $2.95) Clayton Henry-a 3.00
Tower Records Variant-c 5.00
Wizard #0 Prelude 3.00
TPB (1/01, $19.95) r/#1-5, Preview & Prelude; sketchbook & cover gallery 20.00

1963
Image Comics (Shadowline Ink): Apr, 1993 - No. 6, Oct, 1993 ($1.95, lim. series)

1-6: Alan Moore scripts; Veitch, Bissette & Gibbons-a(p) 3.00
1-Gold 4.00
*NOTE: **Bissette** a-2-4; **Gibbons** a-1i, 2i, 6i; c-2.*

1984 (Magazine) (1994 #11 on)
Warren Publishing Co.: June, 1978 - No. 10, Jan, 1980 ($1.50, B&W with color inserts, mature content with nudity; 84 pgs. except #4 has 92 pgs.)

1-Nino-a in all; Mutant World begins by Corben 3 6 9 14 19 24
2-10: 4-Rex Havoc begins. 7-1st Ghita of Alizarr by Thorne. 9-1st Starfire 2 4 6 9 13 16
NOTE: ***Alcala** a-1-3,5,7i. **Corben** a-1-8; c-1,2. **Nebres** a-1-8,10. **Thorne** a-7,8,10. **Wood** a-1,2,5i.*

1994 (Formerly 1984) (Magazine)
Warren Publishing Co.: No. 11, Feb, 1980 - No. 29, Feb, 1983 (B&W with color; mature; #11-(84 pgs.); #12-16,18-21,24-(76 pgs.); #17,22,23,25-29-(68 pgs.)

11,17,18,20,22,23,29: 11,17-8 pgs. color insert. 18-Giger-c. 20-1st Diana Jacklighter Manhuntress by Maroto. 22-1st Sigmund Pavlov by Nino; 1st Ariel Hart by Hsu. 23-All Nino issue 2 4 6 8 11 14
12-16,19,21,24-28: 21-1st app. Angel by Nebres. 27-The Warhawks return 1 3 4 6 8 10
NOTE: ***Corben** c-26. **Maroto** a-20, 21, 24-28. **Nebres** a-11-13, 15, 16, 18, 21, 22, 25, 28. **Nino** a-11-19, 20(2), 21, 25, 26, 28; c-21. **Redondo** c-20. **Thorne** a-11-14, 17-21, 24-26, 28, 29.*

NINJA BOY
DC Comics (WildStorm): Oct, 2001 - No. 6, Mar, 2002 ($3.50/$2.95)

1-($3.50) Ale Garza-a/c 3.50
2-6-($2.95) 3.00
...: Faded Dreams TPB (2003, $14.95) r/#1-6; sketch pages 15.00

NINJA HIGH SCHOOL (1st series)
Antarctic Press: 1986 - No. 3, Aug, 1987 (B&W)

1-Ben Dunn-s/c/a; early Manga series 2 4 6 9 12 15
2,3 1 3 4 6 8 10

NINJAK (See Bloodshot #6, 7 & Deathmate)
Valiant/Acclaim Comics (Valiant) No. 16 on: Feb, 1994 - No. 26, Nov. 1995 ($2.25/$2.50)

1 ($3.50)-Chromium-c; Quesada-c/a(p) in #1-3 6.00
1-Gold 2 4 6 11 16 20
2-13: 3-Batman, Spawn & Random (from X-Factor) app. as costumes at party (cameo). 4-w/bound-in trading card. 5,6-X-O app. 4.00
0,00,14-26: 14-(4/95)-Begin $2.50-c. 0-(6/95, $2.50). 00-(6/95, $2.50) 3.00
... Black Water HC (2013, $24.99) r/#1-6, #0, #00; bonus Quesada sketch-a 25.00
Yearbook 1 (1994, $3.95) 4.00

NINJAK
Acclaim Comics (Valiant Heroes): V2#1, Mar, 1997 -No. 12, Feb, 1998 ($2.50)

V2#1-12: 1-Intro new Ninjak; 1st app. Brutakon; Kurt Busiek scripts begin; painted variant-c exists. 2-1st app. Karnivor & Zeer. 3-1st app. Gigantik, Shurikai, & Nixie. 4-Origin; 1st app. Yasuiti Motomiya; intro The Dark Dozen; Colin King cameo. 9-Copycat-c 3.00

NINJAK
Valiant Entertainment: Mar, 2015 - Present ($3.99)

1-24-Multiple covers on each: 1-Kindt-s/Guice and Mann-a. 4-Origin of Roku; Ryp-a 4.00

NINJA SCROLL
DC Comics (WildStorm): Nov, 2006 - No. 12, Oct, 2007 ($2.99)

1-12: 1-J. Torres-s/Michael Chang Ting Yu-a/c. 11-Puckett-s/Meyers-a 3.00
1-3-Variant covers by Jim Lee 5.00
TPB (2007, $19.99) r/#1-3,5-7 20.00

NINJETTES (See Jennifer Blood #4)
Dynamite Entertainment: 2012 - No. 6, 2012 ($3.99, limited series)

1-6-Origin of the team; Ewing-s/Casallos-a. 6-Jennifer Blood app. 4.00

NINTENDO COMICS SYSTEM (Also see Adv. of Super Mario Brothers)
Valiant Comics: Feb, 1990 - No. 9, Oct, 1991 ($4.95, card stock-c, 68 pgs.)

1-9: 1-Featuring Game Boy, Super Mario, Clappwall. 3-Layton-c. 5-8-Super Mario Bros. 9-Dr. Mario 1st app. 2 4 6 8 10 12

(Ninth) **IXTH GENERATION** (See Aphrodite IX & Poseidon IX)
Image Comics (Top Cow): Jan, 2015 - No. 8, Mar, 2016 ($3.99)

1-8: 1-4-Hawkins-s/Sejic-a; Aphrodite IX app. 5-7-Atilio Rojo-a 4.00
... Hidden Files 1 (4/15, $3.99) Short story and guide to the cities; Hawkins-s/Rojo-a 4.00

NOAH (Adaptation of the 2014 movie)
Image Comics: Mar, 2014 (HC, $29.99, 8-3/4" x 11-1/2")

HC-Darren Aronofsky & Ari Handel-s/Niko Henrichon-a 30.00

NOAH'S ARK
Spire Christian Comics/Fleming H. Revell Co.: 1973,1975 (35/49¢)

nn-By Al Hartley 2 4 6 11 16 20

NOBLE CAUSES
Image Comics: July, 2001; Jan, 2002 - No. 4, May, 2002 ($2.95)

...First Impressions (7/01) Intro. the Noble family; Faerber-s 3.00
1-4: 1-(1/02) Back-up-s with Conner-a. 2-Igle back-up-a. 2-4-Two covers 3.00
...: Extended Family (5/03, $6.95) short stories by various 7.00
...: Extended Family 2 (6/04, $7.95) short stories by various 8.00
Vol. 1: In Sickness and in Health (2003, $12.95) r/#1-4 & ...First Impresssions 13.00

NOBLE CAUSES (Volume 3)
Image Comics: July, 2004 - No. 40, Mar, 2009 ($3.50)

1-24,26-40-Faerber-s. 1-Two covers. 2-Venture app. 5-Invincible app. 3.50
25-($4.99) Art by various; Randolph-c 5.00
Vol. 4: Blood and Water (2005, $14.95) r/#1-6 15.00
Vol. 5: Betrayals (2006, $14.99) r/#7-12 & The Pact V2 #2 15.00
Vol. 6: Hidden Agendas (2006, $15.99) r/#13-18 and Image Holiday Spec. 2005 story 16.00
Vol. 7: Powerless (2007, $15.99) r/#19-25; Wieringo sketch page 16.00

NOBLE CAUSES: DISTANT RELATIVES
Image Comics: Jul, 2003 - No. 4, Oct, 2003 ($2.95, B&W, limited series)

1-4-Faerber-s/Richardson & Ponce-a 3.00
Vol. 3: Distant Relatives (1/05, $12.95) r/#1-4; intro. by Joe Casey 13.00

NOBLE CAUSES: FAMILY SECRETS
Image Comics: Oct, 2002 - No. 4, Jan, 2003 ($2.95, limited series)

1-4-Faerber-s/Oeming-c. 1-Variant cover by Walker. 2,3-Valentino var-c. 4-Hester var-c 3.00
Vol. 2: Family Secrets (2004, $12.95) r/#1-4; sketch pages 13.00

NOBODY (Amado, Cho & Adlard's...)
Oni Press: Nov, 1998 - No. 4, Feb, 1999 ($2.95, B&W, mini-series)

1-4 3.00

NOCTURNALS, THE
Malibu Comics (Bravura): Jan, 1995 - No. 6, Aug, 1995 ($2.95, limited series)

1-6: Dan Brereton painted-c/a & scripts 3.00
1-Glow-in-the-Dark premium edition 5.00

NOCTURNALS, THE
Dark Horse Comics/Image Comics/Oni Press: one-shots and trade paperbacks

Black Planet TPB (Oni Press, 1998, $19.95) r/#1-6 (Malibu Comics series) 20.00
Black Planet and Other Stories HC (Olympian Publ.; 7/07, $39.95) r/Black Planet & Witching Hour contents; cover & sketch gallery with Brereton interviews 40.00
Carnival of Beasts (Image, 7/08, $6.99) short stories; Brereton-s/Brereton & others-a 7.00
Troll Bridge (Oni Press, 2000, $4.95, B&W & orange) Brereton-s/painted-c; art by Brereton, Chin, Art Adams, Sakai, Timm, Warren, Thompson, Purcell, Stephens and others 5.00
Unhallowed Eve TPB (Oni Press, 10/02, $9.95) r/Witching Hour & Troll Bridge one-shots 10.00
Witching Hour (Dark Horse, 5/98, $4.95) Brereton-s/a; reprints DHP stories + 8 new pgs. 5.00

NOCTURNALS: THE DARK FOREVER
Oni Press: Jul, 2001 -No. 3, Feb, 2002 ($2.95, limited series)

1-3-Brereton-s/painted-a/c 3.00
TPB (5/02, $9.95) r/#1-3; afterword & pin-ups by Alex Ross 10.00

NOCTURNE
Marvel Comics: June, 1995 - No. 4, Sept. 1995 ($1.50, limited series)

1-4 3.00

NO ESCAPE (Movie)
Marvel Comics: June, 1994 - No. 3, Aug, 1994 ($1.50)

1-3: Based on movie 3.00

NO HONOR
Image Comics (Top Cow): Feb, 2001 - No. 4, July, 2001 ($2.50)

Preview (12/00, B&W) Silvestri-c 3.00

Noman #2 © Tower

No Mercy #6 © de Campi & McNeil

Nova #20 © MAR

	GD	VG	FN	VF	VF/NM	NM-
	2.0	4.0	6.0	8.0	9.0	9.2

1-4-Avery-s/Crain-a 3.00
TPB (8/03, $12.99) r/#1-4; intro. by Straczynski 13.00

NOIR
Dynamite Entertainment: 2013 - No. 5, 2014 ($3.99, limited series)
1-5: 1-Miss Fury, Black Sparrow & The Shadow app.; Gischler-s/Mutti-a 4.00

NOMAD (See Captain America #180)
Marvel Comics: Nov, 1990 - No. 4, Feb, 1991 ($1.50, limited series)
1-4: 1,4-Captain America app. 3.00

NOMAD
Marvel Comics: V2#1, May, 1992 - No. 25, May, 1994 ($1.75)
V2#1-25: 1-Has gatefold-c w/map/wanted poster. 4-Deadpool x-over. 5-Punisher vs. Nomad-c/story. 6-Punisher & Daredevil-c/story cont'd in Punisher War Journal #48. 7-Gambit-c/story. 10-Red Wolf app. 21-Man-Thing-c/story. 25-Bound-in trading card sheet 3.00

NOMAD: GIRL WITHOUT A WORLD (Rikki Barnes from Captain America V2 Heroes Reborn)
Marvel Comics: Nov, 2009 - No. 4, Feb, 2010 ($3.99, limited series)
1-4-McKeever-s. 2-Falcon app. 4-Young Avengers app. 4.00

NOMAN (See Thunder Agents)
Tower Comics: Nov, 1966 - No. 2, March, 1967 (25¢, 68 pgs.)
1-Wood/Williamson-c; Lightning begins; Dynamo cameo; Kane-a(p) & Whitney-a
8 16 24 54 102 150
2-Wood-c only; Dynamo x-over; Whitney-a 5 10 15 34 60 85

NO MERCY
Image Comics: Apr, 2015 - Present ($2.99/$3.99)
1-4-Alex de Campi-s/Carla Speed McNeil-a 3.00
5-13-($3.99) 6-EC-style cover 4.00

NONE BUT THE BRAVE (See Movie Classics)

NON-HUMANS
Image Comics: Oct, 2012 - No. 4, Jul, 2013 ($2.99)
1-4-Brunswick-s/Portacio-a/c 3.00

NOODNIK COMICS (See Pinky the Egghead)
Comic Media/Mystery/Biltmore: Dec, 1953; No. 2, Feb, 1954 - No. 5, Aug, 1954
3-D(1953, 25¢; Comic Media)(#1)-Came w/glasses 30 60 90 177 289 400
2-5 10 20 30 58 79 100

NORMALMAN (See Cerebus the Aardvark #55, 56)
Aardvark-Vanaheim/Renegade Press #6 on: Jan, 1984 - No. 12, Dec, 1985 ($1.70/$2.00)
1-12: 1-Jim Valentino-c/a in all. 6-12 ($2.00, B&W): 10-Cerebus cameo; Sim-a (2 pgs.) 3.00
...- Megaton Man Special 1 (Image Comics, 8/94, $2.50) 3.00
...3-D 1 (Annual, 1986, $2.25) 3.00
...Twentieth Anniversary Special (7/04, $2.95) 3.00

NORTHANGER ABBEY (Adaptation of the Jane Austen novel)
Marvel Comics: Jan, 2012 - No. 5, May, 2012 ($3.99, mini-series)
1-5-Nancy Butler-s/Janet K. Lee-a/Julian Tedesco-c 4.00

NORTH AVENUE IRREGULARS (See Walt Disney Showcase #49)

NORTH 40
DC Comics (WildStorm): Sept, 2009 - No. 6, Feb, 2010 ($2.99)
1-6-Aaron Williams-s/Fiona Staples-a 3.00
TPB (2010, $17.99) r/#1-6 18.00

NORTHGUARD (See Captain Canuck)
Chapterhouse Comics Group: Aug, 2016 - Present ($3.99)
1-4: 1,2-Falcone-s/Salas-a 4.00

NORTHLANDERS
DC Comics (Vertigo): Feb, 2008 - No. 50, Jun, 2012 ($2.99)
1-50: 1-Vikings in 980 A.D.; Wood-s/Gianfelice-a; covers by Carnivale. 35-Cloonan-a 3.00
1-3-Variant covers. 1-Adam Kubert. 2-Andy Kubert. 3-Dave Gibbons 5.00
...: Blood in the Snow TPB (2010, $14.99) r/#9,10,17-20 15.00
...: Metal and Other Stories TPB (2011, $17.99) r/#29-36 18.00
...: Sven the Returned TPB (2008, $9.99) r/#1-8; cover gallery 10.00
...: The Cross + The Hammer TPB (2009, $14.99) r/#11-16 15.00
...: The Plague Widow TPB (2010, $16.99) r/#21-28 17.00

NORTHSTAR
Marvel Comics: Apr, 1994 - No. 4, July, 1994 ($1.75, mini-series)
1-4: Character from Alpha Flight 3.00

NORTH TO ALASKA
Dell Publishing Co.: No. 1155, Dec, 1960
Four Color 1155-Movie, John Wayne photo-c 15 30 45 100 220 340

NORTHWEST MOUNTIES (Also see Approved Comics #12)
Jubilee Publications/St. John: Oct, 1948 - No. 4, July, 1949
1-Rose of the Yukon by Matt Baker; Walter Johnson-a; Lubbers-c
50 100 150 315 533 750
2-Baker-a; Lubbers-c. Ventrilo app. 40 80 120 244 402 560
3-Bondage-c, Baker-a; Sky Chief, K-9 app. 41 82 123 250 418 585
4-Baker-c/a(2 pgs.); Blue Monk & The Desperado app.
44 88 132 277 469 660

NOSFERATU WARS
Dark Horse Comics: Mar, 2014 ($3.99, one-shot)
1-Reprints serial story from Dark Horse Presents #26-29; Niles-s/Menton3-a 4.00

NO SLEEP 'TIL DAWN
Dell Publishing Co.: No. 831, Aug, 1957
Four Color 831-Movie, Karl Malden photo-c 6 12 18 41 76 110

NOSTALGIA ILLUSTRATED
Marvel Comics: Nov, 1974 - V2#8, Aug, 1975 (B&W, 76 pgs.)
V1#1 3 6 9 21 33 45
V1#2, V2#1-8 3 6 9 15 22 28

NOT BRAND ECHH (Brand Echh #1-4; See Crazy, 1973)
Marvel Comics Group (LMC): Aug, 1967 - No. 13, May, 1969
(1st Marvel parody book)
1: 1-8 are 12¢ issues 7 14 21 48 89 130
2-8: 3-Origin Thor, Hulk & Capt. America; Monkees, Alfred E. Neuman cameo. 4-X-Men app. 5-Origin/intro. Forbush Man. 7-Origin Fantastical-4 & Stuporman. 8-Beatles cameo; X-Men satire; last 12¢-c 4 8 12 25 40 55
9-13 (25¢, 68 pgs., all Giants) 9-Beatles cameo. 10-All-r; The Old Witch, Crypt Keeper & Vault Keeper cameos. 12,13-Beatles cameo 5 10 15 30 50 70
NOTE: *Colan a(p)-4, 5, 8, 9, 13.* ***Everett*** *a-1i.* ***Kirby*** *a(p)-1, 3, 5-7, 10r; c-1p.* ***J. Severin*** *a-1; c-3, 6-8, 11.* ***M. Severin*** *a-1-13; c-2, 9, 10, 12, 13.* ***Sutton*** *a-3, 4, 5i, 6i, 8, 9, 10r, 11-13; c-5. Archie satire in #9. Avengers satire in #8, 12.*

NOTHING CAN STOP THE JUGGERNAUT
Marvel Comics: 1989 ($3.95)
1-r/Amazing Spider-Man #229 & 230 5.00

NO TIME FOR SERGEANTS (TV)
Dell Publ. Co.: No. 914, July, 1958; Feb-Apr, 1965 - No. 3, Aug-Oct, 1965
Four Color 914 (Movie)-Toth-a; Andy Griffith photo-c 9 18 27 60 120 180
1(2-4/65) (TV): Photo-c 5 10 15 34 60 85
2,3 (TV): Photo-c 4 8 12 28 47 65

NOVA (The Man Called... No. 22-25)(See New Warriors)
Marvel Comics Group: Sept, 1976 - No. 25, May, 1979
1-Origin/1st app. Nova (Richard Rider) Marv Wolfman-s; John Buscema-a
6 12 18 41 76 110
2,3: 2-1st app. Condor & Powerhouse. 3-1st app. Diamondhead; Sal Buscema-p begin
2 4 6 9 12 15
4,12: 4-Thor x-over; 1st app. The Corrupter; Kirby-c. 12-Spider-Man x-over w/Amazing Spider-Man #171 2 4 6 10 14 18
5-11: 5-Nova vs. Tyrannus; Kirby-c; Marvel Bullpen app (incl. Stan Lee) 6-1st app. The Sphinx & Megaman. 7-Sphinx, Condor, Powerhouse & Diamondhead app. 8-Origin Megaman. 9-Megaman app. 10-Sphinx, Condor, Powerhouse & Diamondhead app. 11-vs. Sphinx 1 3 4 6 8 10
10,11-(35¢-c variants, limited distribution)(6,7/77) 8 16 24 54 102 150
12-(35¢-c variant, limited distribution)(8/77) 10 20 30 64 132 200
13,14-(Regular 30¢ editions)(9/77) 13-Intro Crime-Buster; Sandman app. 14-vs. Sandman
1 2 3 5 6 8
13,14-(35¢-c variants, limited distribution) 8 16 24 54 102 150
15-24: 15-Infantino-a begins. 16-18-vs. Yellow Claw; Nick Fury and SHIELD app. 19-Wally West (Kid Flash) cameo; 1st app Blackout. 20-1st Project X (Sherlock Holmes robot). 21-Richard reveals his Nova I.D to parents; vs Corrupter. 22-1st app the Comet (in costume). 23-Dr. Sun app. (origin) from Tomb of Dracula; Sphinx cameo. 24-Origin Powerhouse, Diamondhead, Crime-Buster, Comet Man, Sphinx & Dr. Sun app.
1 2 3 5 6 8
25-Last issue; Powerhouse, Diamondhead, Crime-Buster, Comet Man, Sphinx & Dr. Sun app. story continues in Fantastic Four #204-214 2 4 6 10 14 18
NOTE: ***Austin*** *c-21i, 23i.* ***John Buscema*** *a(p)-1-3, 8, 21; c-1p, 2, 15.* ***Infantino*** *a(p)-15-20, 22-25; c-17-20, 21p, 23p, 24p.* ***Kirby*** *c-4p, 5, 7.* ***Nebres*** *c-25i.* ***Simonson*** *a-23i.*

NOVA
Marvel Comics: Jan, 1994 - June, 1995 ($1.75/$1.95) (Started as 4-part mini-series)
1-($2.95, 52 pgs.)-Collector's Edition w/gold foil-c; new Nova costume; Nicieza-s/Marrinan-a;

Nova V2 #1 © MAR

Nova (2016 series) #7 © MAR

Number of the Beast #2 © WSP

GD VG FN VF VF/NM NM-
2.0 4.0 6.0 8.0 9.0 9.2

GD VG FN VF VF/NM NM-
2.0 4.0 6.0 8.0 9.0 9.2

continued from New Warriors #42; re-intro Richard Rider's supporting cast – Ginger Jaye, Bernie Dillon & Roger 'Caps' Cooper; origin & history recap; vs. Gladiator of the Shi'ar Imperial Guard; Queen Adora app. 6.00
1-($2.25, 52 pgs.)-Newsstand Edition w/o foil-c 4.00
2-5: 2-1st app. Tailhook; Speedball app. 3-vs. Spider-Man; Corrupter app; 1st app Nova 00. 4-Vs. Nova 00; contains Rock Video Monthly insert (centerfold). 5-Re-intro Condor; Sphinx cameo; leads into New Warriors #47; contains centerfold insert for Marvel 'Masterprints' 3.00
6,7: 6-'Time and Time Again', pt.3; story continued from Night Thrasher #11; Rage & Firestar solo stories; continues in New Warriors #48. 7- 'Time and Time Again' pt.6; continued from Night Thrasher #12; Rage & Firestar solo stories; Cloak and Dagger app; continues in New Warriors #49; last Nicieza-s 4.00
8-12: 8-1st app. Shatterforce. 9-Vs. Shatterforce. 10-Vs. Diamondhead & Rhino; New Warriors and Corrupter app. 11-She-Hulk, the Thing & Ant-Man guest star; Nick Fury cameo; contains two inserts – a Marvel Subscription offer and a centerfold insert for a personalized X-Men/Captain Universe comic. 12-Vs. Nova 00; Nick Fury, Black Bolt & the Inhumans app. 13-'Deathstorm' T-Minus 3; Firestar, Night Thrasher & Nick Fury app. 14-'Deathstorm' T-Minus 2; Nova 00, Darkhawk & the New Warriors app. 15-'Deathstorm' T-Minus 1; 1st app. Kraa (brother of Zorr from Nova #1, 1976) 3.00
16-18: 16-'Deathstorm' conclusion; vs. Kraa; Nova-Corps app; death of Nova 00. 17-vs. Supernova (Garthan Saal); Richard is stripped of his rank; Queen Adora app. 18-Last issue; Richard Rider de-powered; Supernova becomes Nova-Prime; Dire Wraith Queen app; story continues in New Warriors #60 6.00

NOVA
Marvel Comics: May, 1999 - No. 7, Nov, 1999 ($2.99/$1.99)

1-($2.99, 38 pgs.) –Larsen-s/Bennett-a; wraparound-c by Larsen; origin retold; Nebula app; reveals her father to be Zorr (from issue #1, 1976); She-Hulk, Spider-Man, Speedball, Namorita app. 5.00
2-6: 2-Two covers; vs. Diamondhead; Captain America app.; Namorita's skin returns to normal. 3-Savage Dragon app.; (as a Skrull); New Warriors, Thor, Fantastic Four & the Condor app.; return of the Sphinx. 4-vs. Condor; Fantastic Four app; Red Raven cameo. 5-Spider-Man app. 6-vs. the Sphinx; Venom cameo 3.00
7-Last issue; Red Raven & Bi-Beast app. vs. Venom 4.00

NOVA (See Secret Avengers and The Thanos Imperative)
Marvel Comics: June, 2007 - No. 36, Jun, 2010 ($2.99)

1-Abnett/Lanning-s; Chen-a; Granov-c; continued from Annihilation #6; brief Iron Man app. 3 6 9 16 23 30
2-The Initiative x-over; Nova returns to Earth; vs. Diamondhead; Iron Man & the Thunderbolts (Penance, Radioactive Man, Venom & Moonstone) app. 1 3 4 6 8 10
3-The Initiative x-over; vs. the Thunderbolts; Iron Man app.; Nova leaves Earth 1 2 3 5 6 8
4-7,9: Annihilation Conquest x-overs. 4-Phalanx and Gamora app. 5-Nova infected with the Phalanx virus; Gamora app. 6-Gamora-c by Granov; Drax app. 7-Gamora and Drax app; last Chen-a. 9-Cosmo, Gamora and Drax app. 7.00
8-1st app. Cosmo - the Russian telepathic dog; 1st app. Knowhere – a space station formed out of the severed head of a Celestial (as seen in the GOTG movie); 1st app. of the Luminals; 1st Wellington Alves-a; brief Peter Quill (Starlord) app. 3 6 9 16 23 30
10-14: 10-Nova and Gamora solo story; Drax app.; leads into Nova Annual #1. 11-Gamora, Drax & Warlock of the New Mutants app; Pelletier-a begins. 12-Warlock of the New Mutants app. Nova, Gamora & Drax cured of the Phalanx virus; leads into Annihilation Conquest #6. 13-Galactus & Silver Surfer app.; contains 5-pg preview of the new Eternals series; Alves-a. 14-Galactus app.; Nova vs. Silver Surfer. 15-Galactus & Silver Surfer app. 6.00
16-18: Secret Invasion x-over. 16-Super-Skrull app.; Nova returns to Earth. 17-Team up w/Darkhawk at Project Pegasus vs. the Skrulls; Quasar (Wendell Vaughn) returns. 18-Quasar & Darkhawk app; vs. the Skrulls; return of the Nova Corps 5.00
18-Zombie 1:10 variant-c by Wellington Alves 6.00
19-Darkhawk app.; Robbie Rider joins the Nova-Corps; Serpent Society app. 20-New Warriors flashback; Justice & Firestar app; Ego the Living Planet app. 21-Fantastic Four app; Ego the Living Planet becomes new base for the Nova Corps; Nova's powers are taken away. 22-Quasar app.; Andrea Divito-a begins 4.00
20-Villain 'Sphinx' variant-c by Mike Deodato Jr. 1 2 3 5 6 8
23-28: War of Kings x-over. 23-Richard Rider dons the Quantum Bands – becomes the new Quasar. 24-Gladiator & the Shi'ar Imperial Guard app. 25-Richard regains his Nova powers; Wendell Vaughn (Quasar) regains the Quantum Bands; Emperor Vulcan app. 26-Lord Ravenous app. 27-Blastaar & Lord Ravenous app. 28-War of Kings ends; Robbie Rider officially joins the Nova Corps. Quasar app. 6.00
25-'Dirty Dancing' 1980s decade 1:10 variant by Alina Urusov 5.00
28-Marvel Comics 70th Anniversary frame variant 6.00
29,30: 'Starstalker' parts 1-2. 29-1st Marvel Universe app. of Monark Starstalker (previously from Marvel Premiere #32). 30-vs. Ego the Living Planet 3.00
31-Darkhawk app. 5.00
32-34: Realm of Kings x-over; 32,33-Reed Richards, Black Bolt, Darkhawk, Namorita & the Sphinx app. 33-Moonstone, Man-Wolf, Bloodstone, Basilisk app. 34-'Death' of Black Bolt; Nova vs. Moonstone, Reed Richards vs. Bloodstone, Namorita vs. Man-Wolf, Darkhawk vs. Gyre the Raptor; contains 6 pg. preview of the New Ultimates series 1 2 3 5 6 8
34-Deadpool variant-c 2 4 6 8 12 15
35-Realm of Kings x-over; Reed Richards, Darkhawk, Namorita vs. Sphinx; Namorita brought back to current continuity 1 3 4 6 8 10
36-Last issue; Darkhawk & Quasar app.; leads into Thanos Imperative Ignition 2 4 6 8 12 15
Annual #1 (4/08, $3.99); Slightly altered origin retold; Annihilation Conquest tie-in; Quasar app.; takes place between Nova issues #10-11 1 2 3 5 6 8
...: Origin of Richard Rider (2009, $4.99) origin retold from Nova #1 & 4 ('76) 5.00
... Vol. 1: Annihilation - Conquest TPB (2007, $17.99) r/#1-7; cover sketches 18.00

NOVA (Marvel NOW!)
Marvel Comics: Apr, 2013 - No. 31, Jul, 2015 ($3.99)

1-Loeb-s/McGuinness-a/c; Rocket Raccoon & Gamora app.; multiple variant covers 6.00
2-9: 2,3-Rocket Raccoon & Gamora app. 7-Superior Spider-Man app. 8,9-Infinity tie-in 4.00
10-($4.99) "Issue #100"; Speedball & Justice app.; cover gallery 5.00
11-24,26-31: 12-16-Beta Ray Bill app. 18-20-Original Sin tie-in. 19,20-Rocket Raccoon app. 23,24-Axis tie-in. 28-Black Vortex crossover 4.00
25-($4.99) Axis tie-in; Sam joins the Avengers 5.00
Annual 1 (5/15, $4.99) The Hulk app.; Duggan-s/Baldeon-a 5.00
... Special 1 (10/14, $4.99) Part 3 of x-over with Iron Man & Uncanny X-Men 5.00

NOVA
Marvel Comics: Jan, 2016 - No. 11, Nov, 2016 ($3.99)

1-11: 1-Sean Ryan-s/Cory Smith-a. 3,4-Ms. Marvel & Spider-Man (Miles) app. 8,9-Civil War II tie-in. 10,11-Richard Rider returns 4.00

NOVA
Marvel Comics: Feb, 2017 - Present ($3.99)

1-3: 1-Ramón Pérez-a; Richard Rider & Ego app. 4.00

NOW AGE ILLUSTRATED (See Pendulum Illustrated Classics)

NOW AGE BOOKS ILLUSTRATED (See Pendulum Illustrated Classics)

NOWHERE MAN
Dynamite Entertainment: 2011 - No. 4, 2011 ($3.99)

1-4-Marc Guggenheim-s/Jeevan J. Kang-a 4.00

NOWHERE MEN
Image Comics: Nov, 2012 - Present ($2.99)

1-Stephenson-s/Bellegarde-a 25.00
1-2nd thru 5th printings 4.00
2 10.00
3-11 4.00

NTH MAN THE ULTIMATE NINJA (See Marvel Comics Presents #25)
Marvel Comics: Aug, 1989 - No. 16, Sept, 1990 ($1.00)

1-16-Ninja mercenary. 8-Dale Keown's 1st Marvel work (1/90, pencils) 3.00

NUCLEUS (Also see Cerebus)
Heiro-Graphic Publications: May, 1979 ($1.50, B&W, adult fanzine)

1-Contains "Demonhorn" by Dave Sim; early app. of Cerebus The Aardvark (4 pg. story) 5 10 15 34 60 85

NUKLA
Dell Publishing Co.: Oct-Dec, 1965 - No. 4, Sept, 1966

1-Origin & 1st app. Nukla (super hero) 4 8 12 28 47 65
2,3 3 6 9 19 30 40
4-Ditko-a, c(p) 4 8 12 23 37 50

NUMBER OF THE BEAST
DC Comics (WildStorm): June, 2008 - No. 8, Sept, 2008 ($2.99, limited series)

1-8-Beatty-s/Sprouse-a/c. 1-Variant-c by Mahnke. 6-The Authority app. 3.00
TPB (2008, $19.99) r/#1-8; character dossiers 20.00

NURSE BETSY CRANE (Formerly Teen Secret Diary) (Also see Registered Nurse for reprints)
Charlton Comics: V2#12, Aug, 1961 - V2#27, Mar, 1964 (See Soap Opera Romances)

V2#12-27 3 6 9 19 30 40

NURSE HELEN GRANT (See The Romances of...)

NURSE LINDA LARK (See Linda Lark)

NURSERY RHYMES
Ziff-Davis Publ. Co. (Approved Comics): No. 10, July-Aug, 1951 - No. 2, Winter, 1951

The Nurses #3 © GK

NYX #1 © MAR

Obi-Wan and Anakin #4 © Lucasfilm

	GD 2.0	VG 4.0	FN 6.0	VF 8.0	VF/NM 9.0	NM- 9.2
(Painted-c)						
10 (#1), 2: 10-Howie Post-a	19	38	57	109	172	235
NURSES, THE (TV)						
Gold Key: April, 1963 - No. 3, Oct, 1963 (Photo-c: #1,2)						
1	4	8	12	27	44	60
2,3	3	6	9	17	26	35
NUTS! (Satire)						
Premiere Comics Group: March, 1954 - No. 5, Nov, 1954						
1-Hollingsworth-a	36	72	108	211	343	475
2,4,5: 5-Capt. Marvel parody	22	44	66	132	216	300
3-Drug "reefers" mentioned; Marilyn Monroe & Joe DiMaggio parody-c	24	48	72	142	234	325
NUTS (Magazine) (Satire)						
Health Knowledge: Feb, 1958 - No. 2, April, 1958						
1	10	20	30	54	72	90
2	7	14	21	37	46	55
NUTS & JOLTS						
Dell Publishing Co.: No. 22, 1941						
Large Feature Comic 22	20	40	60	117	189	260
NUTSY SQUIRREL (Formerly Hollywood Funny Folks)(See Comic Cavalcade)						
National Periodical Publications: #61, 9-10/54 - #69, 1-2/56; #70, 8-9/56 - #71, 10-11/56; #72, 11/57						
61-Mayer-a; Grossman-a in all	14	28	42	76	108	140
62-72: Mayer a-62,65,67-72	10	20	30	54	72	90
NUTTY COMICS						
Fawcett Publications: Winter, 1946						
1-Capt. Kidd story; 1 pg. Wolverton-a	14	28	42	80	115	150
NUTTY COMICS						
Home Comics (Harvey Publications): 1945; No. 4, May-June, 1946 - No. 8, June-July, 1947 (No #2,3)						
nn-Helpful Hank, Bozo Bear & others (funny animal)	9	18	27	50	65	80
4	7	14	21	37	46	55
5-Rags Rabbit begins(1st app.); infinity-c	8	16	24	42	54	65
6-8	6	12	18	31	38	45
NUTTY LIFE (Formerly Krazy Life #1; becomes Wotalife Comics #3 on)						
Fox Features Syndicate: No. 2, Summer, 1946						
2	21	42	63	122	199	275
NYOKA, THE JUNGLE GIRL (Formerly Jungle Girl; see The Further Adventures of..., Master Comics #50 & XMas Comics)						
Fawcett Publications: No. 2, Winter, 1945 - No. 77, June, 1953 (Movie serial)						
2	65	130	195	416	708	1000
3	36	72	108	216	351	485
4,5	31	62	93	182	296	410
6-11,13,14,16-18-Krigstein-a: 17-Sam Spade ad by Lou Fine	20	40	60	118	192	265
12,15,19,20	19	38	57	111	176	240
21-30: 25-Clayton Moore photo-c?	14	28	42	78	112	145
31-40	11	22	33	64	90	115
41-50	10	20	30	58	79	100
51-60	9	18	27	52	69	85
61-77	9	18	27	47	61	75
NOTE: *Photo-c from movies 25, 30-70, 72, 75-77. Bondage c-4, 5, 7, 8, 14, 24.*						
NYOKA, THE JUNGLE GIRL (Formerly Zoo Funnies; Space Adventures #23 on)						
Charlton Comics: No. 14, Nov, 1955 - No. 22, Nov, 1957						
14	11	22	33	64	90	115
15-22	10	20	30	54	72	90
NYX (Also see X-23 title)						
Marvel Comics: Nov, 2003 - No. 7, Oct, 2005 ($2.99)						
1,2: 1-Quesada-s/Middleton-a/c; intro. Kiden Nixon	2	4	6	8	10	12
3-1st app. X-23	15	30	45	103	227	350
4-2nd app X-23	3	6	9	21	33	45
5,6-Teranishi-a	2	4	6	8	10	12
7-($3.99) Teranishi-a	1	2	3	5	6	8
NYX X-23 (2005, $34.99, oversized with d.j.) r/X-23 #1-6 & NYX #1-7; intro by Craig Kyle; sketch pages, development art and unused covers						45.00
...: Wannabe TPB (2006, $19.99) r/#1-7; development art and unused covers						20.00
NYX: NO WAY HOME						
Marvel Comics: Oct, 2008 - No. 6, Apr, 2009 ($3.99)						
1-6: 1-Andrasofszky-a/Liu-s/Urusov-c; sketch pages, character and cover design art						5.00
OAKLAND PRESS FUNNYBOOK, THE						
The Oakland Press: 9/17/78 - 4/13/80 (16 pgs.) (Weekly)						
Full color in comic book form; changes to tabloid size 4/20/80-on						
Contains Tarzan by Manning, Marmaduke, Bugs Bunny, etc. (low distribution); 9/23/79 - 4/13/80 contain Buck Rogers by Gray Morrow & Jim Lawrence						3.00
OAKY DOAKS (See Famous Funnies #190)						
Eastern Color Printing Co.: July, 1942 (One Shot)						
1	34	68	102	204	332	460
OBERGEIST: RAGNAROK HIGHWAY						
Image Comics (Top Cow/Minotaur): May, 2001 - No. 6, Nov, 2001 ($2.95, limited series)						
Preview ('01, B&W, 16 pgs.) Harris painted-c						3.00
1-6-Harris-c/a/Jolley-s. 1-Three covers						3.00
... :The Directors' Cut (2002, $19.95, TPB) r/#1-6; Bruce Campbell intro.						20.00
... :The Empty Locket (3/02, $2.95, B&W) Harris & Snyder-a						3.00
OBIE						
Store Comics: 1953 (6¢)						
1	8	16	24	40	50	60
OBI-WAN AND ANAKIN (Star Wars)						
Marvel Comics: Mar, 2016 - No. 5, Jul, 2016 ($3.99)						
1-5-Takes place a few years after Episode One; Soule-s/Checchetto-a/c						4.00
OBJECTIVE FIVE						
Image Comics: July, 2000 - No. 6, Jan, 2001($2.95)						
1-6-Lizalde-a						3.00
OBLIVION						
Comico: Aug, 1995 - No. 3, May, 1996 ($2.50)						
1-3: 1-Art Adams-c. 2-(1/96)-Bagged w/gaming card. 3-(5/96)-Darrow-c						3.00
OBNOXIO THE CLOWN (Character from Crazy Magazine)						
Marvel Comics Group: April, 1983 (one-shot)						
1-Vs. the X-Men						5.00
OCCULT CRIMES TASKFORCE						
Image Comics: July, 2006 - No. 4, May, 2007 ($2.99, limited series)						
1-4-Rosario Dawson & David Atchison-s/Tony Shasteen-a						3.00
... Vol. 1 TPB (2007, $14.99) r/#1-4; sketch and cover development art						15.00
OCCULTIST, THE						
Dark Horse Comics: Dec, 2010 ($3.50, one-shot)						
1-Richardson & Seeley-s/Drujiniu-a/Morris-c						3.50
OCCULTIST, THE						
Dark Horse Comics: Nov, 2011 - No. 3, Jan, 2012 ($3.50, limited series)						
1-3-Seeley-s/Drujiniu-a/Morris-c. 1-Variant-c by Frison						3.50
OCCULTIST, THE						
Dark Horse Comics: Oct, 2013 - No. 5, Feb, 2014 ($3.50, limited series)						
1-5-Seeley-s/Norton-a/Morris-c. 1-Variant-c by Rivera						3.50
OCCULT FILES OF DR. SPEKTOR, THE						
Gold Key/Whitman No. 25: Apr, 1973 - No. 24, Feb, 1977; No. 25, May, 1982 (Painted-c #1-24)						
1-1st app. Lakota; Baron Tibor begins	5	10	15	33	57	80
2-5: 3-Mummy-c/s. 5-Jekyll & Hyde-c/s	3	6	9	19	30	40
6-10: 6,9-Frankenstein. 8,9-Dracula c/s. 9.-Jekyll & Hyde c/s. 9,10-Mummy-c/s	3	6	9	15	22	28
11-13,15-17,19-22,24: 11-1st app. Spektor as Werewolf. 11-13-Werewolf-c/s. 12,16-Frankenstein c/s. 17-Zombie/Voodoo-c. 19-Sea monster-c/s. 20-Mummy-s. 21-Swamp monster-c/s. 24-Dragon-c/s	2	4	6	11	16	20
14-Dr. Solar app.	3	6	9	16	24	32
18,23-Dr. Solar cameo	2	4	6	13	18	22
22-Return of the Owl-c/s	2	4	6	13	18	22
25(Whitman, 5/82)-r/#1 with line drawn-c	2	4	6	9	13	16
NOTE: *Also see Dan Curtis, Golden Comics Digest 33, Gold Key Spotlight, Mystery Comics Digest 5, & Spine Tingling Tales.*						
OCCUPY AVENGERS (Follows Civil War II)						
Marvel Comics: Jan, 2017 - Present ($3.99)						
1-4-Hawkeye and Red Wolf team; Pacheco-a. 3,4-Nighthawk & Nick Fury LMD app.						4.00
OCCUPY COMICS						
Black Mask Studios: 2013 - No. 3, 2013 ($3.50)						

October Faction #11 © IDW, Niles & Worm

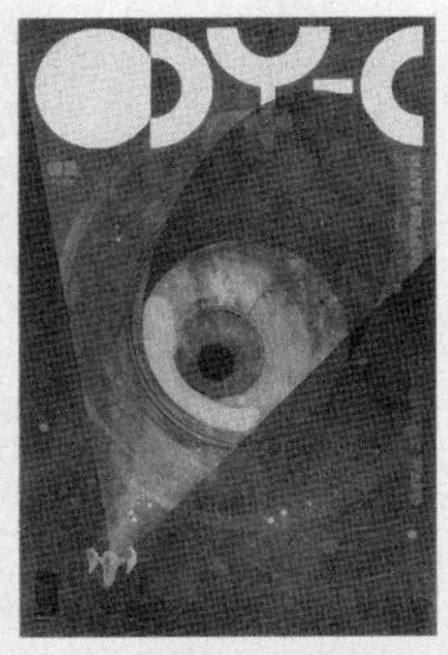

ODY-C #8 © Milkfed & Ward

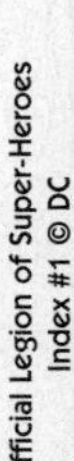

Official Legion of Super-Heroes Index #1 © DC

	GD 2.0	VG 4.0	FN 6.0	VF 8.0	VF/NM 9.0	NM- 9.2

1-3-Short stories and essays about the Occupy movement; s/a by various. 1-Allred-c 3.50

OCEAN
DC Comics (WildStorm): Dec, 2005 - No. 6, Sept, 2005 ($2.95/$2.99/$3.99, limited series)
1-5-Warren Ellis-s/Chris Sprouse-a 3.00
6-($3.99) Conclusion 4.00

OCTOBER FACTION, THE
IDW Publishing: Oct, 2014 - No. 18, Jul, 2016 ($3.99)
1-18-Steve Niles-s/Damien Worm-a/c 4.00

OCTOBER FACTION, THE: DEADLY SEASON
IDW Publishing: Oct, 2016 - No. 5, Feb, 2017 ($3.99)
1-5-Steve Niles-s/Damien Worm-a/c 4.00

ODDLY NORMAL
Image Comics: Sept, 2014 - No. 10, Sept, 2015 ($2.99)
1-10-Otis Frampton-s/a 3.00

ODELL'S ADVENTURES IN 3-D (See Adventures in 3-D)

ODY-C
Image Comics: Nov, 2014 - Present ($3.99)
1-12: 1-Matt Fraction-s/Christian Ward-a; 8-page gatefold 4.00

ODYSSEY, THE (See Marvel Illustrated: The Odyssey)

ODYSSEY OF THE AMAZONS
DC Comics: Mar, 2017 - No. 6 ($3.99, limited series)
1,2-Eearly history of the Amazons; Kevin Grevioux-s/Ryan Benjamin-a 4.00

OFFCASTES
Marvel Comics (Epic Comics/Heavy Hitters): July, 1993 - No. 3, Sept, 1993 ($1.95, limited series)
1-3: Mike Vosburg-c/a/scripts in all 3.00

OFFICIAL CRISIS ON INFINITE EARTHS INDEX, THE
Independent Comics Group (Eclipse): Mar, 1986 ($1.75)
1 5.00

OFFICIAL CRISIS ON INFINITE EARTHS CROSSOVER INDEX, THE
Independent Comics Group (Eclipse): July, 1986 ($1.75)
1-Pérez-c. 5.00

OFFICIAL DOOM PATROL INDEX, THE
Independent Comics Group (Eclipse): Feb, 1986 - No. 2, Mar, 1986 ($1.50, limited series)
1,2: Byrne-c. 4.00

OFFICIAL HANDBOOK OF THE CONAN UNIVERSE (See Handbook of...)

OFFICIAL HANDBOOK OF THE MARVEL UNIVERSE, THE
Marvel Comics Group: Jan, 1983 - No. 15, May, 1984 (Limited series)
1-Lists Marvel heroes & villains (letter A) 6.00
2-15: 2 (B-C, 3-(C-D). 4-(D-G). 5-(H-J), 6-(K-L). 7-(M). 8-(N-P); Punisher-c. 9-(Q-S), 10-(S). 11-(S-U). 12-(V-Z); Wolverine-c. 13,14-Book of the Dead. 15-Weaponry catalogue 5.00
NOTE: ***Bolland** a-8. **Byrne** c/a(p)-1-14; c-15p. **Grell** a-6, 9. **Kirby** a-1, 3. **Layton** a-2, 5, 7. **Mignola** a-3, 4, 5, 6, 8, 12. **Miller** a-4-6, 8, 10. **Nebres** a-3, 4, 8. **Redondo** a-3, 4, 8, 13, 14. **Simonson** a-1, 4, 6-13. **Paul Smith** a-1-12. **Starlin** a-5, 7, 8, 10, 13, 14. **Steranko** a-8p. **Zeck**-2-14.*

OFFICIAL HANDBOOK OF THE MARVEL UNIVERSE, THE
Marvel Comics Group: Dec, 1985 - No. 20, Feb, 1988 ($1.50, maxi-series)
V2#1-Byrne-c 5.00
2-20: 2,3-Byrne-c 4.00
Trade paperback Vol. 1-10 ($6.95) 1 3 4 6 8 10
NOTE: ***Art Adams** a-7, 8, 11, 12, 14. **Bolland** a-8, 10, 13. **Buckler** a-1, 3, 5, 10. **Buscema** a-1, 5, 8, 9, 10, 13, 14. **Byrne** a-1-14; c-1-11. **Ditko** a-1, 2, 4, 6, 7, 11, 13. a-7, 11. **Mignola** a-2, 4, 9, 11, 13. **Miller** a-2, 4, 12. **Simonson** a-1, 2, 4-13, 15. **Paul Smith** a-1-5, 7-12, 14. **Starlin** a-6, 8, 9, 12, 16. **Zeck** a-1-4, 6, 7, 9-14, 16.*

OFFICIAL HANDBOOK OF THE MARVEL UNIVERSE, THE
Marvel Comics: July, 1989 - No. 8, Mid-Dec, 1990 ($1.50, lim. series, 52 pgs.)
V3#1-8: 1-McFarlane-a (2 pgs.) 4.00

OFFICIAL HANDBOOK OF THE MARVEL UNIVERSE, THE (Also see Spider-Man)
Marvel Comics: 2004 - Present ($3.99, one-shots)
...: Alternate Universes 2005 - Profile pages of 1602, MC2, 2099, Earth X, Mangaverse, Days of Future Past, Squadron Supreme, Spider-Ham's Larval Earth and others 4.00
...: Avengers 2004 - Profile pages; art by various; lists of character origins and 1st apps. 4.00
...: Avengers 2005 - Profile pages and info for New Avengers, Young Avengers & others 4.00
...: Book of the Dead 2004 - Profile pages of deceased Marvel characters; art by various; 4.00
...: Daredevil 2004 - Profile pages; art by various; lists of character origins and 1st apps. 4.00
...: Fantastic Four 2005 - Profile pages of members, friends & enemies 4.00
...: Golden Age 2005 - Profile pages; art by various; lists of character origins and 1st apps. 4.00
...: Horror 2005 - Profile pages; art by various; lists of character origins and 1st apps. 4.00
...: Hulk 2004 - Profile pages; art by various; lists of character origins and 1st apps. 4.00
...: Marvel Knights 2005 - Profile pages of characters from Marvel Knights line 4.00
...: Spider-Man 2004 - Profile pages; art by various; lists of character origins and 1st apps. 4.00
...: Spider-Man 2005 - Profile pages of Spidey's friends and foes, emphasizing the recent 4.00
...: Wolverine 2004 - Profile pages; art by various; lists of character origins and 1st apps. 4.00
...: Teams 2005 - Profile pages of Avengers, X-Men and other teams 4.00
...: Women of Marvel 2005 - Profile pages; art by various; Greg Land-c 4.00
...: X-Men 2004 - Profile pages; art by various; lists of character origins and 1st apps. 4.00
...: X-Men 2005 - Profile pages; art by various; lists of character origins and 1st apps. 4.00
...: X-Men - The Age of Apocalypse 2005 - Profile pages of characters plus Exiles 4.00

OFFICIAL HANDBOOK OF THE MARVEL UNIVERSE A-Z UPDATE
Marvel Comics: Apr, 2010 - No. 5, 2010 ($3.99, limited series)
1-5-Profile pages; Andrasofszky-c 4.00

OFFICIAL HANDBOOK OF THE ULTIMATE MARVEL UNIVERSE, THE
Marvel Comics: 2005 ($3.99, one-shots)
... 2005: The Fantastic Four and Spider-Man - Profile pages; art by various 4.00
... The Ultimates and X-Men 2005 - Profile pages; art by various; Bagley-c 4.00

OFFICIAL HAWKMAN INDEX, THE
Independent Comics Group: Nov, 1986 - No. 2, Dec, 1986 ($2.00)
1,2 4.00

OFFICIAL INDEX TO THE MARVEL UNIVERSE (Also see "Avengers, Thor...")
Marvel Comics: 2009 - No. 14, April, 2010 ($3.99)
1-14-Each issue has chronological synopsies, creator credits, character lists for 40-50 issues of apps. for Iron Man, Spider-Man and the X-Men starting with 1st apps. in issue #1 4.00

OFFICIAL JUSTICE LEAGUE OF AMERICA INDEX, THE
Independent Comics Group (Eclipse): April, 1986 - No. 8, Mar, 1987 ($2.00, Baxter paper)
1-8: 1,2-Perez-c. 6.00

OFFICIAL LEGION OF SUPER-HEROES INDEX, THE
Independent Comics Group (Eclipse): Dec, 1986 - No. 5, 1987 ($2.00, limited series) (No Official in Title #2 on)
1-5: 4-Mooney-c 6.00

OFFICIAL MARVEL INDEX TO MARVEL TEAM-UP
Marvel Comics Group: Jan, 1986 - No. 6, 1987 ($1.25, limited series)
1-6 4.00

OFFICIAL MARVEL INDEX TO THE AMAZING SPIDER-MAN
Marvel Comics Group: Apr, 1985 - No. 9, Dec, 1985 ($1.25, limited series)
1 ($1.00)-Byrne-c. 5.00
2-9: 5,6,8,9-Punisher-c. 4.00

OFFICIAL MARVEL INDEX TO THE AVENGERS, THE
Marvel Comics: Jun, 1987 - No. 7, Aug, 1988 ($2.95, limited series)
1-7 5.00

OFFICIAL MARVEL INDEX TO THE AVENGERS, THE
Marvel Comics: V2#1, Oct, 1994 - V2#6, 1995 ($1.95, limited series)
V2#1-#6 4.00

OFFICIAL MARVEL INDEX TO THE FANTASTIC FOUR
Marvel Comics Group: Dec, 1985 - No. 12, Jan, 1987 ($1.25, limited series)
1-12: 1-Byrne-c. 1,2-Kirby back-c (unpub. art) 4.00

OFFICIAL MARVEL INDEX TO THE X-MEN, THE
Marvel Comics: May, 1987 - No. 7, July, 1988 ($2.95, limited series)
1-7 5.00

OFFICIAL MARVEL INDEX TO THE X-MEN, THE
Marvel Comics: V2#1, Apr, 1994 - V2#5, 1994 ($1.95, limited series)
V2#1-5: 1-Covers X-Men #1-51. 2-Covers #52-122,Special #1,2,Giant-Size #1,2. 3-Byrne-c; covers #123-177, Annuals 3-7, Spec. Ed. #1. 4-Covers Uncanny X-Men #178-234, Annuals 8-12. 5-Covers #235-287, Annuals 13-15 4.00

OFFICIAL SOUPY SALES COMIC (See Soupy Sales)

OFFICIAL TEEN TITANS INDEX, THE
Indep. Comics Group (Eclipse): Aug, 1985 - No. 5, 1986 ($1.50, lim. series)
1-5 4.00

OFFICIAL TRUE CRIME CASES (Formerly Sub-Mariner #23; All-True Crime Cases #26 on)
Marvel Comics (OCI): No. 24, Fall, 1947 - No. 25, Winter, 1947-48

	GD 2.0	VG 4.0	FN 6.0	VF 8.0	VF/NM 9.0	NM- 9.2
24(#1)-Burgos-a; Syd Shores-c	26	52	78	154	252	350
25-Syd Shores-c; Kurtzman's "Hey Look"	20	40	60	114	182	250

Oh My Goddess pt. 6 #3 © Fujishima

Okay Comics #1 © UFS

Old Man Logan #15 © MAR

GD VG FN VF VF/NM NM-
2.0 4.0 6.0 8.0 9.0 9.2

OF SUCH IS THE KINGDOM
George A. Pflaum: 1955 (15¢, 36 pgs.)

nn-Reprints from 1951 Treasure Chest 4 7 10 14 17 20

O.G. WHIZ (See Gold Key Spotlight #10)
Gold Key: 2/71 - No. 6, 5/72; No. 7, 5/78 - No. 11, 1/79 (No. 7: 52 pgs.)

1-John Stanley script 5 10 15 31 53 75
2-John Stanley script 4 8 12 23 37 50
3-6(1972) 3 6 9 17 26 35
7-11(1978-79)-Part-r: 9-Tubby issue 2 4 6 9 12 15

OH, BROTHER! (Teen Comedy)
Stanhall Publ.: Jan, 1953 - No. 5, Oct, 1953

1-By Bill Williams 15 30 45 85 130 175
2-5 11 22 33 60 83 105

OH MY GODDESS! (Manga)
Dark Horse Comics: Aug, 1994 - No. 112 ($2.50-$3.99, B&W)

1-6-Kosuke Fujishima-s/a in all 3.00
... **PART II** 2/95 - No. 9, 9/95 ($2.50, B&W, lim.series) #1-9 3.00
... **PART III** 11/95 - No. 11, 9/96 ($2.95, B&W, lim. series) #1-11 3.00
... **PART IV** 12/96 - No. 8, 7/97 ($2.95, B&W, lim. series) #1-8 3.00
... **PART V** 9/97 - No. 12, 8/98 ($2.95, B&W, lim. series)
1,2,5,8: 5-Ninja Master pt. 1 3.00
3,4,6,7,10-12-($3.95, 48 pgs.) 10-Fallen Angel. 11-Play The Game 4.00
9-($3.50) "It's Lonely At The Top" 3.50
... **PART VI** 10/98 - No. 5, 3/99 ($3.50/$2.95, B&W, lim. series)
1-($3.50) 3.50
2-6-($2.95)-6-Super Urd one-shot 3.00
... **PART VII** 5/99 - No. 8, 12/99 ($2.95, B&W, lim. series) #1-3 3.00
4-8-($3.50) 3.50
... **PART VIII** 1/00 - No. 6, 6/00 ($3.50, B&W, lim. series) #1-3,5,7 3.50
4-($2.95) "Hail To The Chief" begins 3.00
... **PART IX** 7/00 - No. 7, 1/01 ($3.50/$2.99) #1-4: 3-Queen Sayoko 3.50
5-7-($2.99) 3.00
... **PART X** 2/01 - No. 5, 6/01 ($3.50) #1-5 3.50
... **PART XI** 10/01 - No. 10, 3/02 ($3.50) #1,2,7,8 3.50
3-6,9-($2.99) Mystery Child 3.00
10-($3.99) 4.00
(Series adapts new numbering) 88-90-($3.50) Learning to Love 3.50
91-94,96-103,105,107-110: 91-94 ($2.99) Traveler. 96-98-The Phantom Racer 3.00
95,104,106-($3.50) 95-Traveler pt. 5 3.50
111,112-($3.99) 4.00

OH SUSANNA (TV)
Dell Publishing Co.: No. 1105, June-Aug, 1960 (Gale Storm)

Four Color 1105-Toth-a, photo-c 9 18 27 63 129 195

OKAY COMICS
United Features Syndicate: July, 1940

1-Captain & the Kids & Hawkshaw the Detective reprints
45 90 135 284 480 675

O.K. COMICS
Hit Publications: May, 1940 (ashcan)

nn-Ashcan comic, not distributed to newsstands, only for in house use. A CGC certified 8.0 copy sold in 2003 for $1,000.

O.K. COMICS
United Features Syndicate/Hit Publications: July, 1940 - No. 2, Oct, 1940

1-Little Giant (w/super powers), Phantom Knight, Sunset Smith, & The Teller Twins begin 81 162 243 518 884 1250
2 (Rare)-Origin Mister Mist by Chas. Quinlan 84 168 252 538 919 1300

OKLAHOMA KID
Ajax/Farrell Publ.: June, 1957 - No. 4, 1958

1 11 22 33 62 86 110
2-4 7 14 21 37 46 55

OKLAHOMAN, THE
Dell Publishing Co.: No. 820, July, 1957

Four Color 820-Movie, photo-c 8 16 24 54 102 150

OKTANE
Dark Horse Comics: Aug, 1995 - Nov, 1995 ($2.50, color, limited series)

1-4-Gene Ha-a 3.00

OKTOBERFEST COMICS
Now & Then Publ.: Fall 1976 (75¢, Canadian, B&W, one-shot)

1-Dave Sim-s/a; Gene Day-a; 1st app. Uncle Hans & Natter P. Bombast; The Beavers sty; 1st Cap'n Riverrat, Sim-s/Day-a 3 6 9 16 23 30

OLD GLORY COMICS
DC Comics: 1941

nn - Ashcan comic, not distributed to newsstands, only for in-house use. Cover art is Flash Comics #12 with interior being Action Comics #37 (no known sales)

OLD GUARD, THE
Image Comics: Feb, 2017 - Present ($3.99)

1-Greg Rucka-s/Leandro Fernández-a 4.00

OLD IRONSIDES (Disney)
Dell Publishing Co.: No. 874, Jan, 1958

Four Color 874-Movie w/Johnny Tremain 6 12 18 42 79 115

OLD MAN LOGAN (Secret Wars tie-in)
Marvel Comics: Jul, 2015 - No. 5, Dec, 2015 ($4.99/$3.99, limited series)

1-($4.99) Bendis-s/Sorrentino-a; future Logan from Wolverine V3 #66; Emma Frost app. 5.00
2-5-($3.99) 2-Sabretooth app. 3-Apocalypse app. 5-X-Men app. 4.00

OLD MAN LOGAN (Follows Secret Wars)
Marvel Comics: Mar, 2016 - Present ($4.99/$3.99)

1-($4.99) Lemire-s/Sorrentino-a; future Logan in current Marvel Universe 5.00
2-18-($3.99) 2-Amadeus Cho Hulk app. 4-Steve Rogers app. 7-Lady Deathstrike app. 14,15-Dracula app.; Andrade-a 4.00

OLD YELLER (Disney, see Movie Comics, and Walt Disney Showcase #25)
Dell Publishing Co.: No. 869, Jan, 1958

Four Color 869-Movie, photo-c 6 12 18 37 66 95

OMAC (One Man Army; ...Corps. #4 on; also see Kamandi #59 & Warlord) (See Cancelled Comic Cavalcade)
National Periodical Publications: Sept-Oct, 1974 - No. 8, Nov-Dec, 1975

1-Origin 5 10 15 33 57 80
2-8: 8-2 pg. Neal Adams ad 3 6 9 17 26 35
Jack Kirby's Omac: One Man Army Corps HC (2008, $24.99, d.j.) r/#1-8; Evanier intro. 25.00
NOTE: *Kirby a-1-8p; c-1-7p. Kubert c-8.*

OMAC (See DCU Brave New World)
DC Comics: Sept, 2006 - No. 8, Apr, 2007 ($2.99, limited series)

1-8: 1-Bruce Jones-s/Renato Guedes-a. 1-3-Firestorm & Cyborg app. 8-Superman app. 3.00

O.M.A.C. (DC New 52)
DC Comics: Nov, 2011 - No. 8, Jun, 2012 ($2.99)

1-8: 1-DiDio-s/Giffen-a/c; Dubbilex and Brother Eye app. 2-Max Lord & Sarge Steel app. 5-Crossover with Frankenstein, Agent of SHADE #5. 6-Kolins-a 3.00

OMAC: ONE MAN ARMY CORPS
DC Comics: 1991 - No. 4, 1991 ($3.95, B&W, mini-series, mature, 52 pgs.)

Book One - Four: John Byrne-c/a & scripts 5.00

OMAC PROJECT, THE
DC Comics: June, 2005 - No. 6, Nov, 2005 ($2.50, limited series)

1-6-Prelude to Infinite Crisis x-over; Rucka-s/Saiz-a 3.00
...: Infinite Crisis Special 1 (5/06, $4.99) Rucka-s/Saiz-a; follows destruction of satellite 5.00
TPB (2005, $14.99) r/#1-6, Countdown to Infinite Crisis, Wonder Woman #219 15.00

O'MALLEY AND THE ALLEY CATS
Gold Key: April, 1971 - No. 9, Jan, 1974 (Disney)

1 3 6 9 16 23 30
2-9 2 4 6 9 13 16

OMEGA ELITE
Blackthorne Publishing: 1987 ($1.25)

1-Starlin-c 3.00

OMEGA FLIGHT
Marvel Comics: Jun, 2007 - No. 5, Oct, 2007 ($2.99, limited series)

1-Oeming-s/Kolins-a; Wrecking Crew app. 4.00
1-Second printing with Sasquatch variant-c 3.00
2-5: 5-Beta Ray Bill app. 3.00
...: Alpha to Omega TPB ('07, $13.99) r/#1-5, USAgent story/Civil War: Choosing Sides 14.00

OMEGA MEN, THE (See Green Lantern #141)
DC Comics: Dec, 1982 - No. 38, May, 1986 ($1.00/$1.25/$1.50; Baxter paper)

1,20: 20-2nd full Lobo story 5.00
2,4-9,11-19,21-25,28-30,32,33,36,38: 2-Origin Broot. 5,9-2nd & 3rd app. Lobo (cameo, 2 pgs.

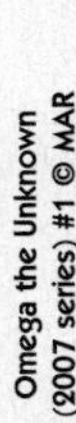
Omega the Unknown (2007 series) #1 © MAR

100 Bullets #100 © Azzarello, Risso & DC

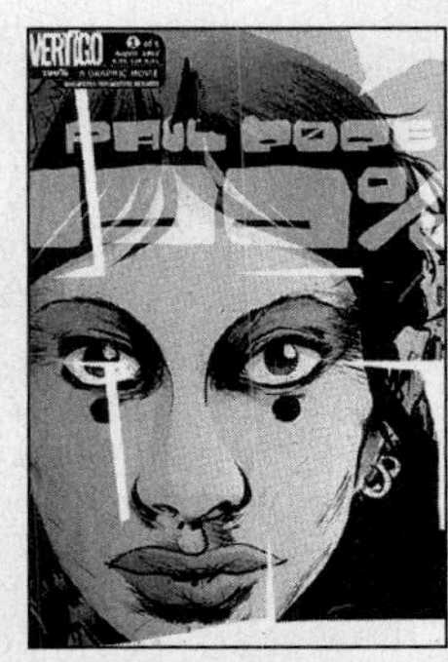

100% #1 © Paul Pope

	GD 2.0	VG 4.0	FN 6.0	VF 8.0	VF/NM 9.0	NM- 9.2

each). 7-Origin The Citadel. 19-Lobo cameo. 30-Intro new Primus 3.00
3-1st app. Lobo (5 pgs.)(6/83); Lobo-c 4 8 12 27 44 60
10-1st full Lobo story 6.00
26,27,31,34,35: 26,27-Alan Moore scripts. 31-Crisis x-over. 34,35-Teen Titans x-over 4.00
37-1st solo Lobo story (8 pg. back-up by Giffen) 6.00
Annual 1(11/84, 52 pgs.), 2(11/85) 4.00
NOTE: ***Giffen** c/a-1-6p. **Morrow** a-24r. **Nino** c/a-16, 21; a-Annual 1i.*

OMEGA MEN, THE
DC Comics: Dec, 2006 - No. 6, May, 2007 ($2.99, limited series)
1-6: 1-Superman, Wonder Girl, Green Lantern app.; Flint-a/Gabrych-s 3.00

OMEGA MEN, THE
DC Comics: Aug, 2015 - No. 12, Jul, 2016 ($2.99)
1-12: 1-Tom King-s/Barnaby Bagenda-a; Kyle Rayner app. 4-Cypress-a 3.00

OMEGA THE UNKNOWN
Marvel Comics Group: March, 1976 - No. 10, Oct, 1977
1-1st app. Omega 3 6 9 16 23 30
2,3-(Regular 25¢ editions). 2-Hulk-c/story. 3-Electro-c/story.
2 3 4 6 8 10
2,3-(30¢-c variants, limited distribution) 3 6 9 19 30 40
4-10: 8-1st brief app. 2nd Foolkiller (Greg Salinger), 1 panel only. 9,10-(Reg. 30¢ editions). 9-1st full app. 2nd Foolkiller 1 2 3 5 6 8
9,10-(35¢-c variants, limited distribution) 6 12 18 38 69 100
... Classic TPB (2005, $29.99) r/#1-10 30.00
NOTE: ***Kane** c(p)-3, 5, 8, 9. **Mooney** a-1-3, 4p, 5, 6p, 7, 8i, 9, 10.*

OMEGA: THE UNKNOWN
Marvel Comics: Dec, 2007 - No. 10, Sept, 2008 ($2.99, limited series)
1-10-Jonathan Lethem-s/Farel Dalrymple-a 3.00

OMEN
Northstar Publishing: 1989 - No. 3, 1989 ($2.00, B&W, mature)
1-Tim Vigil-c/a in all 1 2 3 5 7 9
1, (2nd printing) 3.00
2,3 6.00

OMEN, THE
Chaos! Comics: May, 1998 - No. 5, Sept, 1998 ($2.95, limited series)
1-5: 1-Six covers, ...: Vexed (10/98, $2.95) Chaos! characters appear 3.00

OMNI MEN
Blackthorne Publishing: 1987 - No. 3, 1987 ($1.25)
1-3 3.00
Graphic Novel (1989, $3.50) 4.00

ONCE UPON A TIME: OUT OF THE PAST (TV)
Marvel Comics: 2015 ($24.99, hardcover with dustjacket)
HC-Sequel to Shadow of the Queen HC; Bechko & Vazquez-s; Stacy Lee-c 25.00

ONCE UPON A TIME: SHADOW OF THE QUEEN (TV)
Marvel Comics: 2013 ($19.99, hardcover with dustjacket)
HC-Regina and the Huntsman; Bechko-s; art by Del Mundo, Lolos, Henderson, & Kaluta 20.00

ONE, THE
Marvel Comics (Epic Comics): July, 1985 - No. 6, Feb, 1986 (Limited series, mature)
1-6: Post nuclear holocaust super-hero. 2-Intro The Other 3.00

ONE-ARM SWORDSMAN, THE
Victory Prod./Lueng's Publ. #4 on: 1987 - No. 12, 1990 ($2.75/$1.80, 52 pgs.)
1-3 ($2.75) 4.00
4-12: 4-6-$1.80-c. 7-12-$2.00-c 4.00

ONE-HIT WONDER
Image Comics: Feb, 2014 - No. 5, Apr, 2015 ($3.50)
1-5: 1-4-Sapolsky-s/Olivetti-a/c. 5-Thompson & Fiorelli-a/Roux-a 3.50

ONE HUNDRED AND ONE DALMATIANS (Disney, see Cartoon Tales, Movie Comics, and Walt Disney Showcase #9, 51)
Dell Publishing Co.: No. 1183, Mar, 1961
Four Color 1183-Movie 9 18 27 62 126 190

101 DALMATIONS (Movie)
Disney Comics: 1991 (52 pgs., graphic novel)
nn-($4.95, direct sales)-r/movie adaptation & more 5.00
1-($2.95, newsstand edition) 3.00

101 WAYS TO END THE CLONE SAGA (See Spider-Man)
Marvel Comics: Jan, 1997 ($2.50, one-shot)
1 3.00

100 BULLETS
DC Comics (Vertigo): Aug, 1999 - No. 100, Jun, 2009 ($2.50/$2.75/$2.99)
1-Azzarello-s/Risso-a/Dave Johnson-c 3 6 9 21 33 45
2-5 6.00
6-49,51-61: 26-Series summary; art by various. 45-Preview of Losers 4.00
50-($3.50) History of the Trust 5.00
62-71: 62-Begin $2.75-c. 64-Preview of Loveless 3.00
72-99: 72-Begin $2.99-c 3.00
100-($4.99) Final issue 6.00
...#1/Crime Line Sampler Flip-Book (9/09, $1.00) r/#1 with previews of upcoming GNs 3.00
...: A Foregone Tomorrow TPB (2002, $17.95) r/#20-30 18.00
...: Decayed TPB (2006, $14.99) r/#68-75; Darwyn Cooke intro. 15.00
...: First Shot, Last Call TPB (2000, $9.95) r/#1-5, Vertigo Winter's Edge #3 10.00
...: Hang Up on the Hang Low TPB (2001, $9.95) r/#15-19; Jim Lee intro. 10.00
...: Once Upon a Crime TPB (2007, $12.99) r/#76-83 13.00
...: Samurai TPB (2003, $12.95) r/#43-49 13.00
...: Six Feet Under the Gun TPB (2003, $12.95) r/#37-42 13.00
...: Split Second Chance TPB (2001, $14.95) r/#6-14 15.00
...: Strychnine Lives TPB (2006, $14.99) r/#59-67; Manuel Ramos intro. 15.00
...: The Counterfifth Detective TPB (2003, $12.95) r/#31-36 13.00
...: The Hard Way TPB (2005, $14.99) r/#50-58 15.00
...: Wilt TPB (2009, $19.99) r/#89-100; Azzarello intro. 20.00

100 BULLETS: BROTHER LONO
DC Comics (Vertigo): Aug, 2013 - No. 8, Apr, 2014 ($3.99/$2.99, limited series)
1-($3.99) Azzarello-s/Risso-a/Dave Johnson-c 4.00
2-8-($2.99) Azzarello-s/Risso-a/Dave Johnson-c on all 3.00

100 GREATEST MARVELS OF ALL TIME
Marvel Comics: Dec, 2001 ($7.50/$3.50, limited series)
1-5-Reprints top #6-#25 stories voted by poll for Marvel's 40th ann. 7.50
6-($3.50) (#5 on-c) Reprints X-Men (2nd series) #1 4.00
7-($3.50) (#4 on-c) Reprints Giant-Size X-Men #1 4.00
8-($3.50) (#3 on-c) Reprints (Uncanny) X-Men #137 (Death of Jean Grey) 4.00
9-($3.50) (#2 on-c) Reprints Fantastic Four #1 4.00
10-($3.50) (#1 on-c) Reprints Amazing Fantasy #15 (1st app. Spider-Man) 4.00

100 PAGES OF COMICS
Dell Publishing Co.: 1937 (Stiff covers, square binding)
101(Found on back cover)-Alley Oop, Wash Tubbs, Capt. Easy, Og Son of Fire, Apple Mary, Tom Mix, Dan Dunn, Tailspin Tommy, Doctor Doom
161 322 483 1030 1765 2500

100 PAGE SUPER SPECTACULAR (See DC 100 Page Super Spectacular)

100%
DC Comics (Vertigo): Aug, 2002 - No. 5, July, 2003 ($5.95, B&W, limited series)
1-5-Paul Pope-s/a 6.00
HC (2009, $39.99, dustjacket) r/#1-5; sketch pages and background info 40.00
TPB (2005, $24.99) r/#1-5; sketch pages and background info 25.00
TPB (2009, $29.99) r/#1-5; sketch pages and background info 30.00

100% TRUE?
DC Comics (Paradox Press): Summer 1996 - No. 2 ($4.95, B&W)
1,2-Reprints stories from various Paradox Press books. 5.00

$1,000,000 DUCK (See Walt Disney Showcase #5)

ONE MILLION YEARS AGO (Tor #2 on)
St. John Publishing Co.: Sept, 1953
1-Origin & 1st app. Tor; Kubert-c/a; Kubert photo inside front cover
21 42 63 126 206 285

ONE MONTH TO LIVE ("Heroic Age: ..." in indicia)
Marvel Comics: Nov, 2010 - No. 5, Nov, 2010 ($2.99, weekly limited series)
1-5-Remender-s; Spider-Man and the Fantastic Four app. 3.00

ONE PLUS ONE
Oni Press: Sept, 2002 - No. 5, March, 2003 ($2.95, B&W, limited series)
1-5-Shaffer-s/Krall-a 3.00
TPB (9/03, $14.95, digest-size) r/#1-5 & story from Oni Press Color Special 2002 15.00

ONE SHOT (See Four Color...)

1001 HOURS OF FUN
Dell Publishing Co.: No. 13, 1943
Large Feature Comic 13 (nn)-Puzzles & games; by A.W. Nugent. This book was bound as #13 w/Large Feature Comics in publisher's files 32 64 96 192 314 435

Onslaught Reborn #2 © MAR

Operation Peril #2 © ACG

Optimus Prime #1 © Hasbro

	GD	VG	FN	VF	VF/NM	NM-
	2.0	4.0	6.0	8.0	9.0	9.2

ONE TRICK RIP OFF, THE (See Dark Horse Presents)

ONI (Adaption of video game)
Dark Horse Comics: Feb, 2001 - No. 3, Apr, 2001 ($2.99, limited series)
1-3-Sunny Lee-a(p) 3.00

ONIBA: SWORDS OF THE DEMON
Aspen MLT: No. 0, Oct, 2015 ($2.50)
0-Hernandez-s/Pantalena-a; two covers 3.00

ONI DOUBLE FEATURE (See Clerks: The Comic Book and Jay & Silent Bob)
Oni Press: Jan, 1998 - No. 13, Sept, 1999 ($2.95, B&W)
1-Jay & Silent Bob; Kevin Smith-s/Matt Wagner-a 1 3 4 6 8 10
1-2nd printing 3.00
2-11,13: 2,3-Paul Pope-s/a. 3,4-Nixey-s/a. 4,5-Sienkewicz-s/a. 6,7-Gaiman-s. 9-Bagge-c. 13-All Paul Dini-s; Jingle Belle 3.00
12-Jay & Silent Bob as Bluntman & Chronic; Smith-s/Allred-a 5.00

ONI PRESS COLOR SPECIAL
Oni Press: Jun, 2001; Jul, 2002 ($5.95, annual)
...2001-Oeming "Who Killed Madman?" cover; stories & art by various 6.00
...2002-Allred wraparound-c; stories & art by various 6.00

ONSLAUGHT: EPILOGUE
Marvel Comics: Feb, 1997 ($2.95, one-shot)
1-Hama-s/Green-a; Xavier-c; Bastion-app. 4.00

ONSLAUGHT: MARVEL
Marvel Comics: Oct, 1996 ($3.95, one-shot)
1-Conclusion to Onslaught x-over; wraparound-c 1 2 3 4 5 7

ONSLAUGHT REBORN
Marvel Comics: Jan, 2007 - No. 5, Feb, 2008 ($2.99, limited series)
1-5-Loeb-s/Liefeld-a; female Bucky app. 2-Variant-c by Joe Madureira. 3-McGuiness var-c. 4-Campbell var-c. 5-Bianchi var-c; female Bucky goes to regular Marvel Universe 3.00
1-Variant-c by Michael Turner 4.00
HC (2008, $19.99) r/#1-5; sketch pages; foreword by Liefeld 20.00

ONSLAUGHT UNLEASHED
Marvel Comics: Apr, 2011 - No. 4, Jul, 2011 ($3.99, limited series)
1-4-McKeever-s/Andrade-a/Ramos-c; Secret Avengers & Young Allies app. 4.00

ONSLAUGHT: X-MEN
Marvel Comics: Aug, 1996 ($3.95, one-shot)
1-Waid & Lobdell script; Fantastic Four & Avengers app.; Xavier as Onslaught 5.00
1-Variant-c 2 4 6 8 10 12

ON STAGE
Dell Publishing Co.: No. 1336, Apr-June, 1962
Four Color 1336-Not by Leonard Starr 5 10 15 34 60 85

ON THE DOUBLE (Movie)
Dell Publishing Co.: No. 1232, Sept-Nov, 1961
Four Color 1232 5 10 15 34 60 85

ON THE ROAD TO PERDITION (Movie)
DC Comics (Paradox Press): 2003 - Book 3, 2004 ($7.95, 8"x5 1/2", B&W, limited series)
...: Oasis, Book 1-Max Allan Collins-s/José Luis García-López-a/David Beck-c 8.00
...: Sanctuary, Book 2-Max Allan Collins-s/Steve Lieber-a/José Luis García-López-c 8.00
...: Detour, Book 3-Max Allan Collins-s/José Luis García-López-a/Steve Lieber-c/a(i) 8.00
Road to Perdition 2: On the Road (2004, $14.95) r/series; Collins intro. 15.00

ON THE ROAD WITH ANDRAE CROUCH
Spire Christian Comics (Fleming H. Revell): 1973, 1974 (39¢)
nn-1973 Edition 2 4 6 13 18 22
nn-1974 Edition 2 4 6 9 13 16

ON THE SCENE PRESENTS:...
Warren Publishing Co.: Oct, 1966 - No. 2, 1967 (B&W magazine, two #1 issues)
#1 "Super Heroes" (68 pgs.) Batman 1966 movie photo-c/s; has articles/photos/comic art from serials on Superman, Flash Gordon, Capt. America, Capt. Marvel and The Phantom 4 8 12 28 47 65
#1 "Freak Out, USA" (Fall/1966, 60 pgs.) (lower print run) articles on musicians like Zappa, Jefferson Airplane, Supremes 5 10 15 30 50 70
#2 "Freak Out, USA" (2/67, 52 pgs.) Beatles, Country Joe, Doors/Jim Morrison, Bee Gees 5 10 15 30 50 70

ON THE SPOT (Pretty Boy Floyd...)
Fawcett Publications: Fall, 1948
nn-Pretty Boy Floyd photo on-c; bondage-c 34 68 102 199 325 450

ONYX
IDW Publishing: Jul, 2015 - No. 4, Oct, 2015 ($3.99)
1-4-Gabriel Rodriguez & Chris Ryall-s&a. 1-Three covers 4.00

ONYX OVERLORD
Marvel Comics (Epic): Oct, 1992 - No. 4, Jan, 1993 ($2.75, mini-series)
1-4: Moebius scripts 3.00

OPEN SPACE
Marvel Comics: Mid-Dec, 1989 - No. 4, Aug, 1990 ($4.95, bi-monthly, 68 pgs.)
1-4: 1-Bill Wray-a; Freas-c 5.00
0-(1999) Wizard supplement; unpubl. early Alex Ross-a; new Ross-c 3.00

OPERATION BIKINI (See Movie Classics)

OPERATION: BROKEN WINGS, 1936
BOOM! Studios: Nov, 2011 - No. 3, Jan, 2012 ($3.99, limited series)
1-3-Hanna-s/Hairsine-a; English translation of French comic 4.00

OPERATION BUCHAREST (See The Crusaders)

OPERATION CROSSBOW (See Movie Classics)

OPERATION: KNIGHTSTRIKE (See Knightstrike)
Image Comics (Extreme Studios): May, 1995 - No.3, July, 1995 ($2.50)
1-3 3.00

OPERATION PERIL
American Comics Group (Michel Publ.): Oct-Nov, 1950 - No. 16, Apr-May, 1953 (#1-5: 52 pgs.)
1-Time Travelers, Danny Danger (by Leonard Starr) & Typhoon Tyler (by Ogden Whitney) begin 41 82 123 250 418 585
2-War-c 23 46 69 136 223 310
3-War-c; horror story 21 42 63 126 206 285
4,5-Sci/fi-c/story 23 46 69 136 223 310
6-10: 6,8,9,10-Sci/fi-c. 6-Tank vs. T-Rex-c. 7-Sabretooth-c 21 42 63 122 199 275
11,12-War-c; last Time Travelers 14 28 42 80 115 150
13-16: All war format 10 20 30 56 76 95
NOTE: *Starr a-2, 5. Whitney a-1, 2, 5-10, 12; c-1, 3, 5, 8, 9.*

OPERATION: S.I.N.
Marvel Comics: Mar, 2015 - No. 5, Jul, 2015 ($3.99, limited series)
1-5-Peggy Carter & Howard Stark in 1952; Kathryn Immonen-s/Rich Ellis-a 4.00

OPERATION: STORMBREAKER
Acclaim Comics (Valiant Heroes): Aug, 1997 ($3.95, one-shot)
1-Waid/Augustyn-s, Braithwaite-a 4.00

OPTIC NERVE
Drawn and Quarterly: Apr, 1995 - Present ($2.95-$3.95, bi-annual)
1-7: Adrian Tomine-c/a/scripts in all 3.00
8-11: 8-($3.50). 9-11-($3.95) 4.00
12,13-($5.95) Half front-c. 12-Amber Sweet story 6.00
14-($6.95) Half front-c 7.00
32 Stories-($9.95, trade paperback)-r/Optic Nerve mini-comics 10.00
32 Stories-($29.95, hardcover)-r/Optic Nerve mini-comics; signed & numbered 30.00

OPTIMUS PRIME (Transformers)
IDW Publishing: Nov, 2016 - Present ($3.99)
1-4-Follows Revolution x-over. 1-3-Barber-s/Zama-a; multiple covers on each. 4-Milne-a 4.00

ORACLE: THE CURE
DC Comics: May, 2009 - No. 3, Jul, 2009 ($2.99, limited series)
1-3-Guillem March-c; Calculator app. 3.00
TPB (2010, $17.99) r/#1-3 and Birds of Prey #126,127 18.00

ORAL ROBERTS' TRUE STORIES (Junior Partners #120 on)
TelePix Publ. (Oral Roberts' Evangelistic Assoc./Healing Waters): 1956 (no month) - No. 119, 7/59 (15¢)(No. 102: 25¢)
V1#1(1956)-(Not code approved)- "The Miracle Touch" 19 38 57 109 172 235
102-(Only issue approved by code, 10/56) "Now I See" 13 26 39 74 105 135
103-119: 115-(114 on inside) 10 20 30 54 72 90
NOTE: *Also see Happiness & Healing For You.*

ORANGE BIRD, THE
Walt Disney Educational Media Co.: No date (1980) (36 pgs.; in color; slick cover)
nn-Included with educational kit on foods, ...in Nutrition Adventures nn (1980)

Orbiter HC © Ellis & Doran

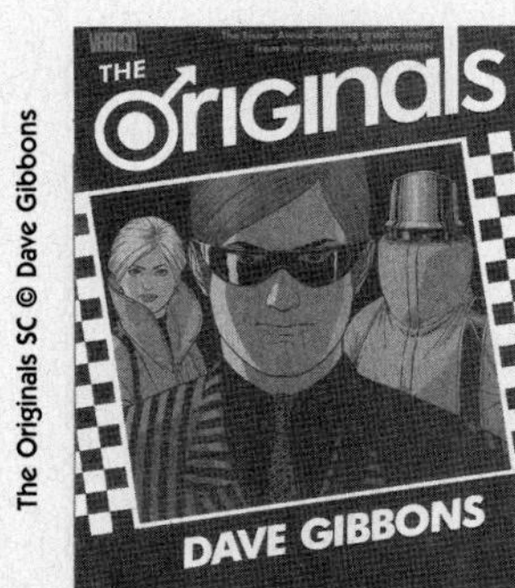

The Originals SC © Dave Gibbons

Orion #13 © DC

	GD 2.0	VG 4.0	FN 6.0	VF 8.0	VF/NM 9.0	NM- 9.2

...and the Nutrition Know-How Revue nn (1983) 3.00

ORB (Magazine)
Orb Publishing: 1974 - No. 6, Mar/Apr 1976 (B&W/color)

	GD 2.0	VG 4.0	FN 6.0	VF 8.0	VF/NM 9.0	NM- 9.2
1-1st app. Northern Light & Kadaver, both series begin	5	10	15	30	50	70
2,3 (72 pgs.)	3	6	9	16	23	30
4-6 (60 pgs.): 4,5-origin Northern Light	2	4	6	10	14	18

NOTE: ***Allison** a-1-3. **Gene Day** a-1-6. **P. Hsu** a-4-6. **Steacy** s/a-3,4.*

ORBIT
Eclipse Books: 1990 - No. 3, 1990 ($4.95, 52 pgs., squarebound)
1-3: Reprints from Isaac Asimov's Science Fiction Magazine; 1-Dave Stevens-c, Bolton-a. 3-Bolton-c/a, Yeates-a 5.00

ORBITER
DC Comics (Vertigo): 2003 ($24.95, hardcover with dust jacket)
HC-Warren Ellis-s/Colleen Doran-a 25.00
SC-(2004, $17.95) Warren Ellis-s/Colleen Doran-a 18.00

ORCHID
Dark Horse Comics: Oct, 2011 - No. 12, Jan, 2013 ($1.00/$3.50)
1-Tom Morello-s/Scott Hepburn-a; covers by Carnevale & Fairey 3.00
2-12-($3.50) Carnevale-c 3.50

ORDER, THE (cont'd from Defenders V2#12)
Marvel Comics: Apr, 2002 - No. 6, Sept, 2002 ($2.25, limited series)
1-6: 1-Haley-a/Duffy & Busiek-s. 3-Avengers-c/app. 4-Jurgens-a 3.00

ORDER, THE (The Initiative following Civil War)
Marvel Comics: Sept, 2007 - No. 10, Jun, 2008 ($2.99)
1-10-California's Initiative team; Fraction-s/Kitson-a/c 3.00
... Vol. 1: The Next Right Thing TPB (2008, $14.99) r/#1-7 15.00

ORIENTAL HEROES
Jademan Comics: Aug, 1988 - No. 55, Feb, 1993 ($1.50/$1.95, 68 pgs.)
1,55 5.00
2-54 4.00

ORIGINAL ADVENTURES OF CHOLLY & FLYTRAP, THE
Image Comics: Feb, 2006 - No. 2, June, 2006 ($5.99, limited series)
1,2-Arthur Suydam-s/a; interview with Suydam and art pages 6.00

ORIGINAL ASTRO BOY, THE
Now Comics: Sept, 1987 - No. 20, Jun, 1989 ($1.50/$1.75)
1-20-All have Ken Steacy painted-c/a 4.00

ORIGINAL BLACK CAT, THE
Recollections: Oct. 6, 1988 - No. 9, 1992 ($2.00, limited series)
1-9: Elias-r; 1-Bondage-c. 2-Murphy Anderson-c 4.00

ORIGINAL DICK TRACY, THE
Gladstone Publishing: Sept, 1990 - No. 5, 1991 ($1.95, bi-monthly, 68pgs.)
1-5: 1-Vs. Pruneface. 2-& the Evil influence; begin $2.00-c 4.00
NOTE: *#1 reprints strips 7/16/43 - 9/30/43. #2 reprints strips 12/1/46 - 2/2/47. #3 reprints 8/31/46 - 11/14/46. #4 reprints 9/17/45 - 12/23/45. #5 reprints 6/10/46 - 8/28/46.*

ORIGINAL DOCTOR SOLAR, MAN OF THE ATOM, THE
Valiant: Apr, 1995 ($2.95, one-shot)
1-Reprints Doctor Solar, Man of the Atom #1,5; Bob Fugitani-r; Paul Smith-c; afterword by Seaborn Adamson 4.00

ORIGINAL E-MAN AND MICHAEL MAUSER, THE
First Comics: Oct, 1985 - No. 7, April, 1986 ($1.75/$2.00, Baxter paper)
1-6: 1-Has r-/Charlton's E-Man, Vengeance Squad. 2-Shows #4 in indicia by mistake 3.00
7-($2.00, 44 pgs.)-Staton-a 4.00

ORIGINAL GHOST RIDER, THE
Marvel Comics: July, 1992 - No. 20, Feb, 1994 ($1.75)
1-20: 1-7-r/Marvel Spotlight #5-11 by Ploog w/new-c. 3-New Phantom Rider (former Night Rider) back-ups begin by Ayers. 4-Quesada-c(p). 8-Ploog-c. 8,9-r/Ghost Rider #1,2. 10-r/Marvel Spotlight #12. 11-18,20-r/Ghost Rider #3-12. 19-r/Marvel Two-in-One #8 3.00

ORIGINAL GHOST RIDER RIDES AGAIN, THE
Marvel Comics: July, 1991 - No. 7, Jan, 1992, ($1.50, limited series, 52 pgs.)
1-7: 1-r/Ghost Rider #68(origin),69 w/covers. 2-7: R/ G.R. #70-81 w/covers 4.00

ORIGINAL MAGNUS ROBOT FIGHTER, THE
Valiant: Apr, 1995 ($2.95, one-shot)
1-Reprints Magnus, Robot Fighter 4000 #2; Russ Manning-r; Rick Leonardi-c; afterword by Seaborn Adamson 4.00

ORIGINAL NEXUS GRAPHIC NOVEL (See First Comics Graphic Novel #19)

ORIGINALS, THE
DC Comics (Vertigo): 2004 ($24.95/$17.99, B&W graphic novel)
HC (2004, $24.95) Dave Gibbons-s/a 25.00
SC (2005, $17.99) 18.00

ORIGINAL SHIELD, THE
Archie Enterprises, Inc.: Apr, 1984 - No. 4, Oct, 1984
1-4: 1,2-Origin Shield; Ayers p-1-4, Nebres c-1,2 5.00

ORIGINAL SIN
Marvel Comics: No. 0, Jun, 2014 - No. 8, Nov, 2014 ($4.99/$3.99, limited series)
0-($4.99) Origin of the Watcher re-told; Nova (Sam Alexander) app.; Waid-s/Cheung-a 5.00
1-($4.99) The Watcher is murdered; Aaron-s/Deodato-a 5.00
2-7-($3.99) 5-Nick Fury's origin. 7-Thor loses use of his hammer 4.00
8-($4.99) Murderer revealed; new Watcher begins 5.00
Annual 1 (12/14, $4.99) Fury and Howard Stark in 1958; Cisic-a/Tedesco-c 5.00
#3.1 - #3.4 (Hulk vs. Iron Man) ($3.99, 8/14 - 10/14) Flashback to the Gamma bomb 4.00
#5.1 - #5.5 (Thor & Loki: The Tenth Realm) ($3.99, 9/14 - 11/14) Angela revealed as Thor's sister; Aaron & Ewing-s 4.00

ORIGINAL SINS (Secrets from the Watcher's Eyes unleashed in Original Sin #3)
Marvel Comics: Aug, 2014 - No. 5, Oct, 2014 ($3.99, limited series)
1-5-Short stories; Young Avengers in all issue; The Hood apps. 1-Deathlok prelude. 5-Secret of Dum Dum Dugan 4.00

ORIGINAL SWAMP THING SAGA, THE (See DC Special Series #2, 14, 17, 20)

ORIGINAL TUROK, SON OF STONE, THE
Valiant: Apr, 1995 - No. 2, May, 1995 ($2.95, limited series)
1,2: 1-Reprints Turok, Son of Stone #24,25,42; Alberto Gioletti-r; Rags Morales-c; afterword by Seaborn Adamson. 2-Reprints Turok, Son of Stone #24,33; Gioletti-r; McKone-c 4.00

ORIGIN OF GALACTUS (See Fantastic Four #48-50)
Marvel Comics: Feb, 1996 ($2.50, one-shot)
1-Lee & Kirby reprints w/pin-ups 4.00

ORIGIN OF THE DEFIANT UNIVERSE, THE
Defiant Comics: Feb, 1994 ($1.50, 20 pgs., one-shot)
1-David Lapham, Adam Pollina & Alan Weiss-a; Weiss-c 5.00
NOTE: *The comic was originally published as Defiant Genesis and was distributed at the 1994 Philadelphia ComicCon.*

ORIGINS OF MARVEL COMICS (Also see Fireside Book Series)
Marvel Comics: July, 2010 ($3.99, one-shot)
1-Single page origins of prominent Marvel characters; text and art by various 4.00
...: X-Men (11/10, $3.99) single page origins of X-Men and other mutants; s/a-various 4.00

ORIGIN II (Sequel to Wolverine: The Origin)
Marvel Comics: Feb, 2014 - No. 5, Jun, 2014 ($4.99/$3.99, limited series)
1-($4.99) Gillen-s/Adam Kubert-a/c; acetate overlay on cover; set in 1907 5.00
2-5-($3.99) Sabretooth app. 4.00

ORION (Manga)
Dark Horse Comics: Sept, 1992 - No. 6, July, 1993 ($2.95/$3.95, B&W, bimonthly, lim. series)
1-6:1,2,6-Squarebound): 1-Masamune Shirow-c/a/s in all 4.00

ORION (See New Gods)
DC Comics: June, 2000 - No. 25, June, 2002 ($2.50)
1-14-Simonson-s/a. 3-Back-up story w/Miller-a. 4-Gibbons-a back-up. 7-Chaykin back-up. 8-Loeb/Liefeld back-up. 10-A. Adams back-up-a 12-Jim Lee back-up-a. 13-JLA-c/app.; Byrne-a 3.00
15-($3.95) Black Racer app.; back-up story w/J.P. Leon-a 4.00
16-24-Simonson-s/a: 19-Joker: Last Laugh x-over 3.00
25-($3.95) Last issue; Mister Miracle-c/app. 4.00
The Gates of Apocalypse (2001, $12.95, TPB) r/#1-5 & various short-s 13.00

ORORO: BEFORE THE STORM (Storm from X-Men)
Marvel Comics: Aug, 2005 - No. 4, Nov, 2005 ($2.99, limited series)
1-4-Barberi-a/Sumerak-s; young Storm in Egypt 3.00
... Digest (2006, $6.99) r/#1-4 7.00

ORPHAN BLACK (Based on the BBC TV show)
IDW Publishing: Feb, 2015 - No. 5, Jun, 2015 ($3.99)
1-6: Multiple covers on all. 1-Kudranski-a; spotlight on Sarah. 2-Spotlight on Helena. 3-Alison. 4-Cosima. 5-Rachel 4.00

ORPHAN BLACK: HELSINKI

Oscar Comics #3 © MAR

Otherworld #1 © Phil Jimenez

Our Army at War #152 © DC

GD 2.0 | VG 4.0 | FN 6.0 | VF 8.0 | VF/NM 9.0 | NM- 9.2

IDW Publishing: Nov, 2015 - No. 5, Mar, 2016 ($3.99)
1-5: Multiple covers on all. 1-Alan Quah-a

OSBORN (Green Goblin)
Marvel Comics: Jan, 2011 - No. 5, Jun, 2011 ($3.99, limited series)
1-5-Deconnick-s/Rios-a/Oliver-c 4.00

OSBORN JOURNALS (See Spider-Man titles)
Marvel Comics: Feb, 1997 ($2.95, one-shot)
1-Hotz-c/a 3.00

OSCAR COMICS (Formerly Funny Tunes; Awful...#11 & 12) (Also see Cindy Comics)
Marvel Comics: No. 24, Spring, 1947 - No. 10, Apr, 1949; No. 13, Oct, 1949
24(#1, Spring, 1947) 26 52 78 154 252 350
25(#2, Sum, 1947)-Wolverton-a plus Kurtzman's "Hey Look"
27 54 81 158 259 360
26(#3)-Same as regular #3 except #26 was printed over in black ink with #3 appearing on-c below the over print 18 36 54 105 165 225
3-9,13: 8-Margie app. 18 36 54 105 165 225
10-Kurtzman's "Hey Look" 20 40 60 114 182 250

OSWALD THE RABBIT (Also see New Fun Comics #1)
Dell Publishing Co.: No. 21, 1943 - No. 1268, 12-2/61-62 (Walter Lantz)
Four Color 21(1943) 38 76 114 285 641 1000
Four Color 39(1943) 27 54 81 189 420 650
Four Color 67(1944) 16 32 48 110 243 375
Four Color 102(1946)-Kelly-a, 1 pg. 13 26 39 89 195 300
Four Color 143,183 9 18 27 59 117 175
Four Color 225,273 7 14 21 44 82 120
Four Color 315,388 6 12 18 40 73 105
Four Color 458,507,549,593 5 10 15 35 63 90
Four Color 623,697,792,894,979,1268 5 10 15 33 57 80

OSWALD THE RABBIT (See The Funnies, March of Comics #7, 38, 53, 67, 81, 95, 111, 126, 141, 156, 171, 186, New Funnies & Super Book #8, 20)

OTHER DEAD, THE
IDW Publishing: Sept, 2013 - No. 6, Feb, 2014 ($3.99)
1-6-Zombie animals; Ortega-s/Mui-a. 1-Variant-c by Dorman. 2-6-Pres. Obama app. 4.00

OTHER SIDE, THE
DC Comics (Vertigo): Dec, 2006 - No. 5, Apr, 2007 ($2.99, limited series)
1-5-Soldiers from both sides of the Vietnam War; Aaron-s/Stewart-a/c 3.00
TPB (2007, $12.99) r/#1-5; sketch pages, Stewart's travelogue to Saigon 13.00

OTHERWORLD
DC Comics (Vertigo): May, 2005 - No. 7, Nov, 2005 ($2.99)
1-7-Phil Jimenez-s/a(p) 3.00
...: Book One TPB (2006, $19.99) r/#1-7; cover gallery 20.00

OUR ARMY AT WAR (Becomes Sgt. Rock #302 on; also see Army At War)
National Periodical Publications: Aug, 1952 - No. 301, Feb, 1977
1 231 462 693 1906 4303 6700
2 96 192 288 768 1734 2700
3,4: 4-Krigstein-a 75 150 225 600 1350 2100
5-7 54 108 162 432 966 1500
8-11,14-Krigstein-a 52 104 156 408 917 1425
12,15-20 46 92 138 340 770 1200
13-Krigstein-c/a; flag-c 53 106 159 416 933 1450
21-31: Last precode (2/55) 32 64 96 230 515 800
32-40 28 56 84 202 451 700
41-60: 51-1st S.A. issue. 57,60-Grey tone-c 25 50 75 175 388 600
61-70: 61-(8/57) Pre-Sgt. Rock Easy Co.-c/s. 67-Minor Sgt. Rock prototype
23 46 69 161 356 550
71-80 21 42 63 147 324 500
81-(4/59) "The Rock of Easy" - Sgt. Rock prototype. Part of lead-up trio to 1st definitive Sgt. Rock. Story features a character named "Sgt. Rocky" as a "4th grade rate" sergeant (three stripes/chevrons) who is referred to as "The Rock of Easy". Editor also promises more stories of "...Rock-like Sergeant". Andru & Esposito-a/Haney-s
333 666 1000 2831 6416 10,000
82-(5/59) "Hold up Easy"- 1st app. of a Sgt. Rock. Part of lead-up trio to 1st definitive Sgt. Rock. Character named Sgt. Rock appears in a supporting "motivator" role as a "4th grade rate" sergeant (three stripes/chevrons) in six panels in six page story; Haney-s/Drucker-a 129 258 387 1032 2316 3600
83-(6/59) "The Rock and Wall" - 1st true appearance of Sgt. Rock. Sgt. Rock finally introduced as a Master Sergeant (three chevrons and three rockers) and is main character of story. 1st specific narration that defines the "Rock of Easy" as Sgt. Rock. 1st actual "Sgt. Rock" collaboration between creators Robert Kanigher and Joe Kubert
800 1600 2400 6800 15,400 24,000
84-(7/59) "Laughter on Snakehead Hill" - 2nd appearance of Sgt. Rock. Story advances true Sgt. Rock continuity in 13-page title story featuring Sgt. Rock and Easy Co.; Kanigher-s/Novick-a/Kubert-c 66 132 198 528 1189 1850
85-Origin & 1st app. Ice Cream Soldier 66 132 198 528 1189 1850
86,87-Early Sgt. Rock; Kubert-a 50 100 150 400 900 1400
88-1st Sgt. Rock-c; Kubert-c/a 66 132 198 528 1189 1850
89-"No Shot From Easy!" story; Heath-c 42 84 126 311 706 1100
90-Kubert-c/a; How Rock got his stripes 71 142 213 568 1284 2000
91-All-Sgt. Rock issue; Grandenetti-c/Kubert-a 121 242 363 968 2184 3400
92,94,96-99: 97-Regular Kubert-c begin 32 64 96 230 515 800
93-1st Zack Nolan 36 72 108 259 580 900
95-1st app. Bulldozer 40 80 120 296 673 1050
100 46 92 138 340 770 1200
101,108,113: 101-1st app. Buster. 113-1st app. Wildman & Jackie Johnson
26 52 78 182 404 625
102-104,106,107,109,110,114,116-120: 104-Nurse Jane-c/s. 109-Pre Easy Co. Sgt. Rock-s. 118-Sunny injured 23 46 69 161 356 550
105-1st app. Junior 28 56 84 202 451 700
111-1st app. Wee Willie & Sunny 32 64 96 230 515 800
112-Classic Easy Co. roster-c 68 136 204 544 1222 1900
115-Rock revealed as orphan; 1st x-over Mlle. Marie. 1st Sgt. Rock's battle family
29 58 87 209 467 725
121-125 16 32 48 112 249 385
126-1st app. Canary; grey tone-c 25 50 75 175 388 600
127-2nd all-Sgt. Rock issue; 1st app. Little Sure Shot 27 54 81 189 420 650
128-Training & origin Sgt. Rock; 1st Sgt. Krupp 38 76 114 285 641 1000
129-139: 138-1st Sparrow. 141-1st Shaker 15 30 45 103 227 350
140-3rd all-Sgt. Rock issue 17 34 51 117 259 400
141-150: 147,148-Rock becomes a General 11 22 33 76 163 250
151-Intro. Enemy Ace by Kubert (2/65), black-c 44 88 132 326 738 1150
152-4th all-Sgt. Rock issue 14 28 42 96 211 325
153-2nd app. Enemy Ace (4/65) 20 40 60 138 307 475
154,156,157,159-161,165-167: 157-2 pg. centerfold spread pin-up as part of story. 159-1st Nurse Wendy Winston-c/s. 165-2nd Iron Major 10 20 30 64 132 200
155-3rd app. Enemy Ace (6/65)(see Showcase) 14 28 42 96 211 325
158-Book-length Sgt. Rock story; origin & 1st app. Iron Major(9/65), formerly Iron Captain; flashback to death of Rock's brother Josh 11 22 33 72 154 235
162,163-Viking Prince x-over in Sgt. Rock 10 20 30 69 147 225
164-Giant G-19 15 30 45 103 227 350
168-1st Unknown Soldier app.; referenced in Star-Spangled War Stories #157; (Sgt. Rock x-over) (6/66) 17 34 51 117 259 400
169,170 8 16 24 56 108 160
171-176,178-181: 171-1st Mad Emperor 8 16 24 51 96 140
177-(80 pg. Giant G-32) 10 20 30 64 132 200
182,183,186-Neal Adams-a. 186-Origin retold 9 18 27 57 111 165
184-Wee Willie dies 9 18 27 61 123 185
185,187,188,193-195,197-199 6 12 18 41 76 110
189,191,192,196: 189-Intro. The Teen-age Underground Fighters of Unit 3. 196-Hitler cameo
6 12 18 42 79 115
190-(80 pg. Giant G-44) 8 16 24 54 102 150
200-12 pg. Rock story told in verse; Evans-a 7 14 21 44 82 120
201,202,204-207: 201-Krigstein-r/#14. 204,205-All reprints; no Sgt. Rock. 207-Last 12¢ cover
5 10 15 34 60 85
203-(80 pg. Giant G-56)-All-r, Sgt. Rock story 7 14 21 48 89 130
208-215 4 8 12 27 44 60
216,229-(80 pg. Giants G-68, G-80): 216-Has G-58 on-c by mistake
6 12 18 40 73 105
217-219: 218-1st U.S.S. Stevens 4 8 12 25 40 55
220-Classic dinosaur/Sgt. Rock-c/s 4 8 12 28 47 65
221-228,230-234: 231-Intro/death Rock's brother. 234-Last 15¢ issue
3 6 9 21 33 45
235-239,241: 52 pg. Giants 4 8 12 27 44 60
240-Neal Adams-a; 52 pg. Giant 5 10 15 31 53 75
242-Also listed as DC 100 Page Super Spectacular #9
9 18 27 58 114 170
243-246: (All 52 pgs.) 244-No Adams-a 4 8 12 25 40 55
247-250,254-268,270: 247-Joan of Arc 3 6 9 15 22 28
251-253-Return of Iron Major 3 6 9 16 24 32
269,275-(100 pgs.) 5 10 15 31 53 75
271,272,274,276-279 3 6 9 14 19 24
273-Crucifixion-c 3 6 9 16 24 32
280-(68 pgs.)-200th app. Sgt. Rock; reprints Our Army at War #81,83
4 8 12 22 35 48

Our Fighting Forces #3 © DC

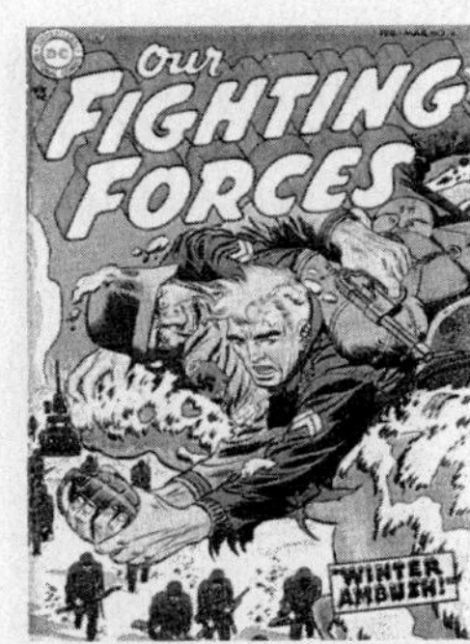

Our Flag Comics #1 © ACE

Our Love #1 © MAR

	GD 2.0	VG 4.0	FN 6.0	VF 8.0	VF/NM 9.0	NM- 9.2
281-299,301: 295-Bicentennial cover	2	4	6	13	18	22
300-Sgt. Rock-s by Kubert (2/77)	3	6	9	15	22	28

NOTE *Alcala a-251. **Drucker** a-27, 67, 68, 79, 82, 83, 96, 164, 177, 203, 212, 243r, 244, 269r, 275r, 280r. **Evans** a-165-175, 200, 266, 269, 270, 274, 276, 278, 280. **Glanzman** a-218, 220, 222, 223, 225, 227, 230-232, 238-241, 244, 247, 248, 256-259, 261, 265-267, 271, 282, 283, 298. **Grandenetti** c-91,120. **Grell** a-287. **Heath** a-50, 164, & most 176-281. **Kubert** a-38, 59, 67, 68 & most issues from 83-165, 171, 233, 236, 267, 275, 300; c-84, 280. **Maurer** a-233, 237, 239, 240, 45, 280, 284, 288, 290, 291, 295. **Severin** a-236, 252, 265, 267, 269r, 272. **Toth** a-235, 241, 254. **Wildey** a-283-285, 287p. **Wood** a-249.*

OUR ARMY AT WAR
DC Comics: Nov, 2010 ($3.99, one-shot)

	GD 2.0	VG 4.0	FN 6.0	VF 8.0	VF/NM 9.0	NM- 9.2
1-Joe Kubert-c; Mike Marts-s/Victor Ibáñez-a						4.00
TPB (2011, $14.99) r/#1 and other 2010 war one-shots Weird War Tales #1, Our Fighting Forces #1, G.I. Combat #1 and Star-Spangled War Stories #1						15.00

OUR FIGHTING FORCES
National Per. Publ./DC Comics: Oct-Nov, 1954 - No. 181, Sept-Oct, 1978

	GD 2.0	VG 4.0	FN 6.0	VF 8.0	VF/NM 9.0	NM- 9.2
1-Grandenetti-c/a	136	272	408	1088	2444	3800
2	51	102	153	392	884	1375
3-Kubert-c; last precode issue (3/55)	43	86	129	318	722	1125
4,5	36	72	108	259	580	900
6-9: 7-1st S.A. issue	31	62	93	223	479	735
10-Wood-a	30	60	90	219	490	760
11-19	25	50	75	175	388	600
20-Grey tone-c (4/57)	32	64	96	230	515	800
21-30	20	40	60	141	313	485
31-40	18	36	54	122	271	420
41-Unknown Soldier tryout	21	42	63	147	324	500
42-44	17	34	51	117	259	400
45-1st app. of Gunner & Sarge, app. thru #94	54	108	162	432	966	1500
46	24	48	72	168	372	575
47	18	36	54	124	275	425
48,50	15	30	45	103	227	350
49-1st Pooch	26	52	78	182	404	625
51-Grey tone-c	23	46	69	161	356	550
52-64: 64-Last 10¢ issue	12	24	36	82	179	275
65-70: 66-Panel inspired a famous Roy Lichtenstein painting	10	20	30	64	132	200
71-Classic grey tone-c; Pooch fires machine gun; panel inspired a famous Roy Lichtenstein painting	21	42	63	147	324	500
72-80	8	16	24	56	108	160
81-90	7	14	21	44	82	120
91-98: 95-Devil-Dog begins, ends #98.	6	12	18	37	66	95
99-Capt. Hunter begins, ends #106	6	12	18	41	76	110
100	6	12	18	38	69	100
101-105,107-120: 116-Mlle. Marie app. 120-Last 12¢ issue	5	10	15	30	50	70
106-Hunters Hellcats begin	5	10	15	31	53	75
121,122: 121-Intro. Heller	4	8	12	27	44	60
123-The Losers (Capt. Storm, Gunner & Sarge, Johnny Cloud) begin	9	18	27	57	111	165
124-132: 132-Last 15¢ issue	4	8	12	23	37	50
133-137 (Giants). 134-Toth-a	4	8	12	27	44	60
138-145,147-150	3	6	9	16	23	30
146-Classic "Burma Sky" story; Toth-a/Goodwin-s	3	6	9	17	26	35
151-162-Kirby a(p)	3	6	9	18	28	38
163-180	3	6	9	14	19	24
181-Last issue	3	6	9	16	23	30
... (War One-Shot) 1 (11/10, $3.99) The Losers app.; B. Clay Moore-s/Chad Hardin-a						4.00

NOTE: ***N. Adams** c-147. **Drucker** a-28, 37, 39, 42-44, 49, 53, 133r. **Evans** a-149, 164-174, 177-181. **Glanzman** a-125-128, 132, 134, 138-141, 143, 144. **Heath** a-2, 16, 18, 28, 41, 44, 49, 50, 59, 64, 114, 135-138r; c-51. **Kirby** a-151-162p; c-152-159. **Kubert** c/a in many issues. **Maurer** a-135. **Redondo** a-166. **Severin** a-123-130, 131i, 132-150.*

OUR FIGHTING MEN IN ACTION (See Men In Action)

OUR FLAG COMICS
Ace Magazines: Aug, 1941 - No. 5, April, 1942

	GD 2.0	VG 4.0	FN 6.0	VF 8.0	VF/NM 9.0	NM- 9.2
1-Captain Victory, The Unknown Soldier (intro.) & The Three Cheers begin	271	542	813	1734	2967	4200
2-Origin The Flag (patriotic hero); 1st app?	155	310	465	992	1696	2400
3-5: 5-Intro & 1st app. Mr. Risk	142	284	426	909	1555	2200

NOTE: ***Anderson** a-1, 4. **Mooney** a-1, 2; c-2.*

OUR GANG COMICS (With Tom & Jerry #39-59; becomes Tom & Jerry #60 on; based on film characters)
Dell Publishing Co.: Sept-Oct, 1942 - No. 59, June, 1949

	GD 2.0	VG 4.0	FN 6.0	VF 8.0	VF/NM 9.0	NM- 9.2
1-Our Gang & Barney Bear by Kelly, Tom & Jerry, Pete Smith, Flip & Dip, The Milky Way begin (all 1st app.)	93	186	279	744	1672	2600
2-Benny Burro begins (#2 by Kelly)	36	72	108	259	580	900
3-5	22	44	66	154	340	525
6-Bumbazine & Albert only app. by Kelly	29	58	87	209	467	725
7-No Kelly story	16	32	48	110	243	375
8-Benny Burro begins by Barks	38	76	114	281	628	975
9-Barks-a(2): Benny Burro & Happy Hound; no Kelly story	34	68	102	242	541	840
10-Benny Burro by Barks	25	50	75	175	388	600
11-1st Barney Bear & Benny Burro by Barks (5-6/44); Happy Hound by Barks	34	68	102	242	541	840
12-20	16	32	48	107	236	365
21-30: 30-X-Mas-c	11	22	33	77	166	255
31-36-Last Barks issue	9	18	27	63	129	195
37-40	7	14	21	44	82	120
41-50	6	12	18	38	69	100
51-57	5	10	15	35	63	90
58,59-No Kelly art or Our Gang stories	5	10	15	33	57	80
Our Gang Volume 1 (Fantagraphics Books, 2006, $12.95, TPB) r/Our Gang stories written and by Walt Kelly from #1-8; Leonard Maltin intro.; Jeff Smith-c						13.00
Our Gang Volume 2 (Fantagraphics Books, 2007, $12.95, TPB) r/Our Gang stories written and by Walt Kelly from #9-15; Steve Thompson intro.; Jeff Smith-c						13.00
Our Gang Volume 3 (Fantagraphics Books, 2008, $14.99, TPB) r/Our Gang stories written and by Walt Kelly from #16-23; Steve Thompson intro.; Jeff Smith-c						15.00

NOTE: ***Barks** art in part only. **Barks** did not write Barney Bear stories #30-34. (See March of Comics #3, 26). Early issues have photo back-c.*

OUR LADY OF FATIMA (Also see Fatima...)
Catechetical Guild Educational Society: 3/11/55 (15¢) (36 pgs.)

	GD 2.0	VG 4.0	FN 6.0	VF 8.0	VF/NM 9.0	NM- 9.2
395	6	12	18	28	34	40

OUR LOVE (True Secrets #3 on? or Romantic Affairs #3 on?)
Marvel Comics (SPC): Sept, 1949 - No. 2, Jan, 1950

	GD 2.0	VG 4.0	FN 6.0	VF 8.0	VF/NM 9.0	NM- 9.2
1-Photo-c	24	48	72	142	234	325
2-Photo-c	15	30	45	85	130	175

OUR LOVE STORY
Marvel Comics Group: Oct, 1969 - No. 38, Feb, 1976

	GD 2.0	VG 4.0	FN 6.0	VF 8.0	VF/NM 9.0	NM- 9.2
1	9	18	27	59	117	175
2-4,6-8,10,11	5	10	15	33	57	80
5-Steranko-a	10	20	30	70	150	230
9,12-Kirby-a	5	10	15	34	60	85
13-(10/71, 52 pgs.)	6	12	18	37	66	95
14-New story by Gary Fredrich & Tarpe' Mills	5	10	15	33	57	80
15-20,27:27-Colan/Everett-a(r?); Kirby/Colletta-r	4	8	12	25	40	55
21-26,28-37	4	8	12	23	37	50
38-Last issue	4	8	12	27	44	60

NOTE: ***J. Buscema** a-1-3, 5-7, 9, 13r, 16r, 19r(2), 21r, 22r(2), 23r, 34r, 35r; c-11, 13, 16, 22, 23, 24, 27, 35. **Colan** a-3-6, 21r(#6), 22r, 23r(#3), 24r(#4), 27; c-19. **Katz** a-17. **Maneely** a-13r. **Romita** a-13r; c-1, 2, 4-6. **Weiss** a-16, 17, 29r(#17).*

OUR MEN AT WAR
DC Comics: Aug/Sept 1952

nn - Ashcan comic, not distributed to newsstands, only for in-house use. Cover art is All Star Western #60, interior being Detective Comics #181 (a FN/VF copy sold for $1195 in 2012)

OUR MISS BROOKS
Dell Publishing Co.: No. 751, Nov, 1956

	GD 2.0	VG 4.0	FN 6.0	VF 8.0	VF/NM 9.0	NM- 9.2
Four Color 751-Photo-c	7	14	21	48	89	130

OUR SECRET (Exciting Love Stories)(Formerly My Secret)
Superior Comics Ltd.: No. 4, Nov, 1949 - No. 8, Jun, 1950

	GD 2.0	VG 4.0	FN 6.0	VF 8.0	VF/NM 9.0	NM- 9.2
4-Kamen-a; spanking scene	22	44	66	132	216	300
5,6,8	14	28	42	81	118	155
7-Contains 9 pg. story intended for unpublished Ellery Queen #5; lingerie panels	15	30	45	83	124	165

OUTBREED 999
Blackout Comics: May, 1994 - No. 6, 1994 ($2.95)

	GD 2.0	VG 4.0	FN 6.0	VF 8.0	VF/NM 9.0	NM- 9.2
1-6: 4-1st app. of Extreme Violet in 7 pg. backup story						3.00

OUTCAST, THE
Valiant: Dec, 1995 ($2.50, one-shot)

	GD 2.0	VG 4.0	FN 6.0	VF 8.0	VF/NM 9.0	NM- 9.2
1-Breyfogle-a.						3.00

OUTCAST BY KIRKMAN & AZACETA
Image Comics: Jun, 2014 - Present ($2.99)

	GD 2.0	VG 4.0	FN 6.0	VF 8.0	VF/NM 9.0	NM- 9.2
1-Kirkman-s/Azaceta-a/c						10.00

Outer Limits #17 © DELL

Outlaw Kid (2nd series) #8 © MAR

Out of the Shadows #5 © STD

	GD 2.0	VG 4.0	FN 6.0	VF 8.0	VF/NM 9.0	NM- 9.2
2						5.00
3-25: 25-(25¢-c)						3.00

OUTCASTS
DC Comics: Oct, 1987 - No. 12, Sept, 1988 ($1.75, limited series)

	GD 2.0	VG 4.0	FN 6.0	VF 8.0	VF/NM 9.0	NM- 9.2
1-12: John Wagner & Alan Grant scripts in all						3.00

OUTER LIMITS, THE (TV)
Dell Publishing Co.: Jan-Mar, 1964 - No. 18, Oct, 1969 (Most painted-c)

	GD 2.0	VG 4.0	FN 6.0	VF 8.0	VF/NM 9.0	NM- 9.2
1	11	22	33	73	157	240
2-5	6	12	18	41	76	110
6-10	5	10	15	35	63	90
11-18: 17-Reprints #1. 18-r/#2	5	10	15	31	53	75

OUTER SPACE (Formerly This Magazine Is Haunted, 2nd Series)
Charlton Comics: No. 17, May, 1958 - No. 25, Dec, 1959; Nov, 1968

	GD 2.0	VG 4.0	FN 6.0	VF 8.0	VF/NM 9.0	NM- 9.2
17-Williamson/Wood-a	14	28	42	80	115	150
18-20-Ditko-a	23	46	69	136	223	310
21-Ditko-c	20	40	60	114	182	250
22-25	14	28	42	80	115	150
V2#1(11/68)-Ditko-a, Boyette-c	5	10	15	30	50	70

OUT FOR BLOOD
Dark Horse: Sept, 1999 - No. 4, Dec, 1999 ($2.95, B&W, limited series)

	GD 2.0	VG 4.0	FN 6.0	VF 8.0	VF/NM 9.0	NM- 9.2
1-4-Kelley Jones-c; Erskine-a						3.00

OUTLANDERS (Manga)
Dark Horse Comics: Dec, 1988 - No. 33, Sept,1991 ($2.00-$2.50, B&W, 44 pgs.)

	GD 2.0	VG 4.0	FN 6.0	VF 8.0	VF/NM 9.0	NM- 9.2
1-33: Japanese Sci-fi manga						4.00

OUTLAW (See Return of the...)

OUTLAW FIGHTERS
Atlas Comics (IPC): Aug, 1954 - No. 5, Apr, 1955

	GD 2.0	VG 4.0	FN 6.0	VF 8.0	VF/NM 9.0	NM- 9.2
1-Tuska-a	15	30	45	85	130	175
2-5: 5-Heath-c/a, 7 pgs.	11	22	33	60	83	105

NOTE: ***Hartley** a-3. **Heath** c/a-5. **Maneely** c-2. **Pakula** a-2. **Reinman** a-2. **Tuska** a-1-3.*

OUTLAW KID, THE (1st Series; see Wild Western)
Atlas Comics (CCC No. 1-11/EPI No. 12-29): Sept, 1954 - No. 19, Sept, 1957

	GD 2.0	VG 4.0	FN 6.0	VF 8.0	VF/NM 9.0	NM- 9.2
1-Origin; The Outlaw Kid & his horse Thunder begin; Black Rider app.	34	68	102	199	325	450
2-Black Rider app.	15	30	45	88	137	185
3-7,9: 3-Wildey-a(3)	14	28	42	80	115	150
8-Williamson/Woodbridge-a, 4 pgs.	14	28	42	82	121	160
10-Williamson-a	14	28	42	82	121	160
11-17,19: 13-Baker text illo. 15-Williamson text illo (unsigned)	11	22	33	62	86	110
18-Williamson/Mayo-a	12	24	36	67	94	120

NOTE: ***Berg** a-4, 7, 13. **Maneely** c-1-3, 5-8, 11-13, 15, 16, 18. **Pakula** a-3. **Severin** c-10, 17, 19. **Shores** a-1. **Wildey** a-1(3), 2-8, 10, 11, 12(4), 13(4), 15-19(4 each); c-4.*

OUTLAW KID, THE (2nd Series)
Marvel Comics Group: Aug, 1970 - No. 30, Oct, 1975

	GD 2.0	VG 4.0	FN 6.0	VF 8.0	VF/NM 9.0	NM- 9.2
1-Reprints; 1-Orlando-r, Wildey-r(3)	3	6	9	19	30	40
2,3,9: 2-Reprints. 3,9-Williamson-a(r)	2	4	6	13	18	22
4-7: 7-Last 15¢ issue	2	4	6	11	16	20
8-Double size (52 pgs.); Crandall-r	3	6	9	16	24	32
10-Origin	3	6	9	19	30	40
11-20: new-a in #10-16	2	4	6	13	18	22
21-30: 27-Origin-r/#10	2	4	6	9	13	16

NOTE: ***Ayers** a-10, 27r. **Berg** a-7, 25r. **Everett** a-2(2 pgs.). **Gil Kane** c-10, 11, 15, 27r, 28. **Roussos** a-10i, 27i(r). **Severin** c-1, 9, 20, 25. **Wildey** r-1-4, 6-9, 19-22, 25, 26. **Williamson** a-28r. **Woodbridge/Williamson** a-9r.*

OUTLAW NATION
DC Comics (Vertigo): Nov, 2000 - No. 19, May, 2002 ($2.50)

	GD 2.0	VG 4.0	FN 6.0	VF 8.0	VF/NM 9.0	NM- 9.2
1-19-Fabry painted-c/Delano-s/Sudzuka-a						3.00
TPB (Image Comics, 11/06, $15.99) B&W reprint of #1-19; Delano intro.						16.00

OUTLAW PRINCE, THE
Dark Horse Books: 2011 ($12.99, SC, 80 pgs.)

	GD 2.0	VG 4.0	FN 6.0	VF 8.0	VF/NM 9.0	NM- 9.2
SC-Adaptation of ERB's The Outlaw of Torn; Rob Hughes-s/Thomas Yeates painted-a; origin/1st app. Norman of Torn; intro. & death of Lady Maud						13.00
Deluxe HC Limited Edition ($49.99, 112 pgs.) Bonus 2 articles (approx. 200 signed)						50.00

OUTLAWS
D. S. Publishing Co.: Feb-Mar, 1948 - No. 9, June-July, 1949

	GD 2.0	VG 4.0	FN 6.0	VF 8.0	VF/NM 9.0	NM- 9.2
1-Violent & suggestive stories	34	68	102	204	332	460
2-Ingels-a; Baker-a	34	68	102	204	332	460
3,5,6: 3-Not Frazetta. 5-Sky Sheriff by Good app. 6-McWilliams-a	17	34	51	98	154	210
4-Orlando-a	18	36	54	103	162	220
7,8-Ingels-a in each	24	48	72	142	234	325
9-(Scarce)-Frazetta-a (7 pgs.)	48	96	144	302	514	725

NOTE: *Another #3 was printed in Canada with **Frazetta** art "Prairie Jinx," 7 pgs.*

OUTLAWS, THE (Formerly Western Crime Cases)
Star Publishing Co.: No. 10, May, 1952 - No. 13, Sep, 1953; No. 14, Apr, 1954

	GD 2.0	VG 4.0	FN 6.0	VF 8.0	VF/NM 9.0	NM- 9.2
10-L.B. Cole-c	22	44	66	132	216	300
11-14-L.B. Cole-c. 14-Reprints Western Thrillers #4 (Fox) w/new L.B. Cole-c; Kamen, Feldstein-r	18	36	54	103	162	220

OUTLAWS
DC Comics: Sept, 1991 - No. 8, Apr, 1992 ($1.95, limited series)

	GD 2.0	VG 4.0	FN 6.0	VF 8.0	VF/NM 9.0	NM- 9.2
1-8: Post-apocalyptic Robin Hood.						3.00

OUTLAWS OF THE WEST (Formerly Cody of the Pony Express #10)
Charlton Comics: No. 11, 7/57 - No. 81, 5/70; No. 82, 7/79 - No. 88, 4/80

	GD 2.0	VG 4.0	FN 6.0	VF 8.0	VF/NM 9.0	NM- 9.2
11	8	16	24	44	57	70
12,13,15-17,19,20	6	12	18	27	33	38
14-(68 pgs., 2/58)	9	18	27	50	65	80
18-Ditko-a	10	20	30	56	76	95
21-30	3	6	9	16	23	30
31-50: 34-Gunmaster app.	2	4	6	13	18	22
51-63,65,67-70: 54-Kid Montana app.	2	4	6	10	14	18
64,66: 64-Captain Doom begins (1st app.). 68-Kid Montana series begins	2	4	6	13	18	22
71-79: 73-Origin & 1st app. The Sharp Shooter, last app. #74. 75-Last Capt. Doom	2	4	6	9	12	15
80,81-Ditko-a	2	4	6	13	18	22
82-88						6.00
64,79(Modern Comics-r, 1977, '78)						6.00

OUTLAWS OF THE WILD WEST
Avon Periodicals: 1952 (25¢, 132 pgs.) (4 rebound comics)

	GD 2.0	VG 4.0	FN 6.0	VF 8.0	VF/NM 9.0	NM- 9.2
1-Wood back-c; Kubert-a (3 Jesse James-r)	39	78	117	240	395	550

OUTLAW TRAIL (See Zane Grey 4-Color 511)

OUT OF SANTA'S BAG (See March of Comics #10 in the Promotional Comics section)

OUT OF THE NIGHT (The Hooded Horseman #18 on)
Amer. Comics Group (Creston/Scope): Feb-Mar, 1952 - No. 17, Oct-Nov, 1954

	GD 2.0	VG 4.0	FN 6.0	VF 8.0	VF/NM 9.0	NM- 9.2
1-Williamson/LeDoux-a (9 pgs.); ACG's 1st editor's page	77	154	231	493	847	1200
2-Williamson-a (5 pgs.)	54	108	162	343	574	825
3,5-10: 9-Sci/Fic story	34	68	102	206	336	465
4-Williamson-a (7 pgs.)	43	86	129	271	461	650
11-17: 13-Nostrand-a? 17-E.C. Wood swipe	27	54	81	160	263	365

NOTE: ***Landau** a-14, 16, 17. **Shelly** a-12.*

OUT OF THE SHADOWS
Standard Comics/Visual Editions: No. 5, July, 1952 - No. 14, Aug, 1954

	GD 2.0	VG 4.0	FN 6.0	VF 8.0	VF/NM 9.0	NM- 9.2
5-Toth-p; Moreira, Tuska-a; Roussos-c	60	120	180	381	653	925
6-Toth/Celardo-a; Katz-a(2)	42	84	126	265	445	625
7,9: 7-Jack Katz-c/a(2). 9-Crandall-a(2)	39	78	117	236	388	540
8-Katz shrunken head-c	81	162	243	518	884	1250
10-Spider-c; Sekowsky-a	41	82	123	250	418	585
11-Toth-a, 2 pgs.; Katz-a; Andru-c	39	78	117	240	395	550
12-Toth/Peppe-a(2); Katz-a	43	86	129	271	461	650
13-Cannabalism story; Sekowsky-a; Roussos-c	45	90	135	284	480	675
14-Toth-a	39	78	117	231	378	525

OUT OF THE VORTEX (Comics' Greatest World:... #1-4)
Dark Horse Comics: Oct., 1993 - No. 12, Oct, 1994 ($2.00, limited series)

	GD 2.0	VG 4.0	FN 6.0	VF 8.0	VF/NM 9.0	NM- 9.2
1-12: 1-Foil logo. 4-Dorman-c(p). 6-Hero Zero x-over. 12-$2.50-c						3.00

NOTE: ***Art Adams** c-7. **Golden** c-8. **Mignola** c-2. **Simonson** c-3. **Zeck** c-10.*

OUT OF THIS WORLD
Charlton Comics: Aug, 1956 - No. 16, Dec, 1959

	GD 2.0	VG 4.0	FN 6.0	VF 8.0	VF/NM 9.0	NM- 9.2
1	32	64	96	188	307	425
2	17	34	51	98	154	210
3-6-Ditko-c/a (3) each	36	72	108	211	343	475
7-(2/58, 15¢, 68 pgs.)-Ditko-c/a(4)	37	74	111	222	361	500
8-(5/58, 15¢, 68 pgs.)-Ditko-a(2)	34	68	102	199	325	450
9,10,12,16-Ditko-a	26	52	78	154	252	350
11-Ditko c/a (3)	31	62	93	182	296	410
13,15	14	28	42	81	118	155
14-Matt Baker-a, 7 pg. story	15	30	45	84	127	170

Outsiders (2003 series) #2 © DC

Over the Garden Wall (2016 series) #1 © CN

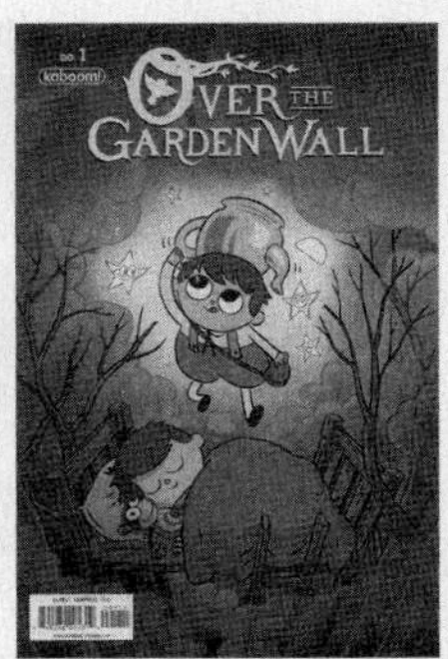

Ozma of Oz #8 © MAR

	GD 2.0	VG 4.0	FN 6.0	VF 8.0	VF/NM 9.0	NM- 9.2

NOTE: *Ditko c-3-12, 16. Reinman a-10.*

OUT OF THIS WORLD
Avon Periodicals: June, 1950; Aug, 1950

	GD 2.0	VG 4.0	FN 6.0	VF 8.0	VF/NM 9.0	NM- 9.2
1-Kubert-a(2) (one reprinted/Eerie #1, 1947) plus Crom the Barbarian by Gardner Fox & John Giunta (origin); Fawcette-c	129	258	387	826	1413	2000
1-(8/50) Reprint; no month on cover	77	154	231	493	847	1200

OUT OF THIS WORLD ADVENTURES
Avon Periodicals: July, 1950 - No. 2, Apr, 1951 (25¢ sci-fi pulp magazine with 32-page color comic insert)

	GD 2.0	VG 4.0	FN 6.0	VF 8.0	VF/NM 9.0	NM- 9.2
1-Kubert-a(2); Crom the Barbarian by Fox & Giunta; text stories by Cummings, Van Vogt, del Rey, Chandler	90	180	270	576	988	1400
2-Kubert-a plus The Spider God of Akka by Gardner Fox & John Giunta pulp magazine w/comic insert; Wood-a (21 pgs.); mentioned in **SOTI,** page 120	58	116	174	371	636	900

OUT OUR WAY WITH WORRY WART
Dell Publishing Co.: No. 680, Feb, 1956

	GD 2.0	VG 4.0	FN 6.0	VF 8.0	VF/NM 9.0	NM- 9.2
Four Color 680	5	10	15	30	50	70

OUTPOSTS
Blackthorne Publishing: June, 1987 - No. 4, 1987 ($1.25)

1-4: 1-Kaluta-c(p) 3.00

OUTSIDERS, THE
DC Comics: Nov, 1985 - No. 28, Feb, 1988

1 4.00
2-28: 18-26-Batman returns. 21-Intro. Strike Force Kobra; 1st app. Clayface IV 22-E.C. parody; Orlando-a. 21- 25-Atomic Knight app. 27,28-Millennium tie-ins 3.00
Annual 1 (12/86, $2.50), Special 1 (7/87, $1.50) 4.00
NOTE: *Aparo a-1-7, 9-14, 17-22, 25, 26; c-1-7, 9-14, 17, 19-26. **Byrne** a-11. **Bolland** a-6, 18; c-16. **Ditko** a-13p. **Erik Larsen** a-24, 27 28; c-27, 28. **Morrow** a-12.*

OUTSIDERS
DC Comics: Nov, 1993 - No. 24, Nov, 1995 ($1.75/$1.95/$2.25)

1-11,0,12-24: 1-Alpha; Travis Charest-c. 1-Omega; Travis Charest-c. 5-Atomic Knight app. 8-New Batman-c/story. 11-(9/94)-Zero Hour. 0-(10/94).12-(11/94). 21-Darkseid cameo. 22-New Gods app. 3.00

OUTSIDERS (See Titans/Young Justice: Graduation Day)(Leads into Batman and the Outsiders)
DC Comics: Aug, 2003 - No. 50, Nov, 2007 ($2.50/$2.99)

1-Nightwing, Arsenal, Metamorpho app.; Winick-s/Raney-a 5.00
2-Joker and Grodd app. 4.00
3-33: 3-Joker-c. 5,6-ChrisCross-a. 8-Huntress app. 9,10-Capt. Marvel Jr. app. 24,25-X-over with Teen Titans. 26,27-Batman & old Outsiders 3.00
34-50: 34-One Year Later. 36-Begin $2.99-c. 37-Superman app. 44-Red Hood app. 3.00
Annual 1 (6/07, $3.99) McDaniel-a; Black Lightning app. 4.00
.../Checkmate: Checkout TPB (2008, $14.99) r/#47-49 & Checkmate #13-15 15.00
... Double Feature (10/03, $4.95) r/#1,2 5.00
...: Crisis Intervention TPB (2006, $12.99) r/#29-33 13.00
...: Looking For Trouble TPB (2004, $12.95) r/#1-7 & Teen Titans/Outsiders Secret Files & Origins 2003; intro. by Winick 13.00
...: Pay As You Go TPB (2007, $14.99) r/#42-46 & Annual #1 15.00
...: Sum of All Evil TPB (2004, $14.95) r/#8-15 15.00
...: The Good Fight TPB (2006, $14.99) r/#34-41 15.00
...: Wanted TPB (2005, $14.99) r/#16-23 15.00

OUTSIDERS, THE (See Batman and the Outsiders for #1-14 and #40)
DC Comics: No. 15, Apr, 2009 - No. 39, Jun, 2011 ($2.99)

15-23,26-39: 15-Alfred assembles a new team; Garbett-a. 17-19-Deathstroke app. 3.00
24,25-($3.99) Blackest Night; Terra rises as a Black Lantern 4.00
...: The Deep TPB (2009, $14.99) r/#15-20 & Batman and the Outsiders Special #1 15.00
...: The Great Divide TPB (2011, $17.99) r/#32-40; cover gallery 18.00
...: The Hunt TPB (2010, $14.99) r/#21-25 15.00
...: The Road to Hell TPB (2010, $14.99) r/#26-31 15.00

OUTSIDERS: FIVE OF A KIND (Bridges Outsiders #49 & 50)
DC Comics: Oct, 2007 ($2.99, weekly limited series)

...Katana/Shazam! (part 2 of 5) - Barr-s/Sharpe-a 3.00
...Metamorpho/Aquaman (part 4 of 5) - Wilson-s/Middleton-a 3.00
...Nightwing/Captain Boomerang (part 1 of 5) - DeFilippis & Weir-s/Willams-a 3.00
...Thunder/Martian Manhunter (part 3 of 5) - Bedard-s/Turnbull-a; Grayven app. 3.00
...Wonder Woman/Grace (part 5 of 5) - Andreyko-s/Richards-a 3.00
TPB (2008, $14.99) r/series & Outsiders #50 15.00

OUT THERE
DC Comics(Cliffhanger): July, 2001 - No. 18, Aug, 2003 ($2.50/$2.95)

1-Humberto Ramos-c/a; Brian Augustyn-s 3.00
1-Variant-c by Carlos Meglia 4.00
2-18: 3-Variant-c by Bruce Timm. 9-Begin $2.95-c 3.00
...: The Evil Within TPB (2002, $12.95) r/#1-6; Ramos sketch pages 13.00

OVERKILL: WITCHBLADE/ ALIENS/ DARKNESS/ PREDATOR
Image Comics/Dark Horse Comics: Dec, 2000 - No. 2, 2001 ($5.95)

1,2-Jenkins-s/Lansing, Ching & Benitez-a 6.00

OVERTAKEN
Aspen/MLT: Aug, 2013 - Present ($1.00/$3.99)

1,2-Mastromauro-s/Lorenzana-a; multiple covers on each. 1-($1.00-c). 2-(3/16) 4.00

OVER THE EDGE
Marvel Comics: Nov, 1995 - No. 10, Aug, 1996 (99¢)

1-10: 1,6,10-Daredevil-c/story. 2,7-Dr. Strange-c/story. 3-Hulk-c/story. 4,9-Ghost Rider-c/story. 5-Punisher-c/story. 8-Elektra-c/story 3.00

OVER THE GARDEN WALL (Based on the Cartoon Network mini-series)
Boom Entertainment (KaBOOM!): Aug, 2015 - No. 4, Nov, 2015 ($3.99, limited series)

1-4-Pat McHale-s/Jim Campbell-a; multiple covers on each 4.00
Special 1 (11/14, $4.99)-Prequel to the Cartoon Network mini-series; McHale-s/Campbell-a 5.00

OVER THE GARDEN WALL ONGOING (Based on the Cartoon Network mini-series)
Boom Entertainment (KaBOOM!): Apr, 2016 - Present ($3.99, limited series)

1-11: 1-4-Two stories in each; Campbell-s/Burgos-a & Levari-s/McGee-a; multiple covers 4.00

OWL, THE (See Crackajack Funnies #25, Popular Comics #72 and Occult Files of Dr. Spektor #22)
Gold Key: April, 1967; No. 2, April, 1968

	GD 2.0	VG 4.0	FN 6.0	VF 8.0	VF/NM 9.0	NM- 9.2
1-Written by Jerry Siegel; '40s super hero	5	10	15	34	60	85
2	4	8	12	28	47	65

OWL, THE (See Project Superpowers)
Dynamite Entertainment: 2013 - No. 4, 2013 ($3.99, limited series)

1-4-Golden Age hero in modern times; Krul-s/H.K. Michael-a; covers by Ross & Syaf 4.00

OZ (See First Comics Graphic Novel, Marvel Treaury Of Oz & MGM's Marvelous...)

OZ
Caliber Press: 1994 - 1997 ($2.95, B&W)

0-20: 0-Released between #10 & #11 3.00
1 ($5.95)-Limited Edition; double-c 6.00
...Specials: Freedom Fighters. Lion. Scarecrow. Tin Man 3.00

OZARK IKE
Dell Publishing Co./Standard Comics B11 on: Feb, 1948; Nov, 1948 - No. 24, Dec, 1951; No. 25, Sept, 1952

	GD 2.0	VG 4.0	FN 6.0	VF 8.0	VF/NM 9.0	NM- 9.2
Four Color 180(1948-Dell)	10	20	30	69	147	225
B11, B12, 13-15	12	24	36	69	97	125
16-25	11	22	33	60	83	105

OZ: DAEMONSTORM
Caliber Press: 1997 ($3.95, B&W, one-shot)

1 4.00

OZMA OF OZ (Dorothy Gale from Wonderful Wizard of Oz)
Marvel Comics: Jan, 2011 - No. 8, Sept, 2011 ($3.99, limited series)

1-6-Eric Shanower-s/Skottie Young-a/c 4.00
Oz Primer (5/11, $3.99) creator interviews and character profiles 4.00

OZ: ROMANCE IN RAGS
Caliber Press: 1996 ($2.95, B&W, limited series)

1-3, ..Special 3.00

OZ SQUAD
Brave New Worlds/Patchwork Press: 1992 - No. 4, 1994 ($2.50/$2.75, B&W)

1-4-Patchwork Press 3.00

OZ SQUAD
Patchwork Press: Dec, 1995 - No. 10, 1996 ($3.95/$2.95, B&W)

1-($3.95) 4.00
2-10 3.00

OZ: STRAW AND SORCERY
Caliber Press: 1997 ($2.95, B&W, limited series)

1-3 3.00

OZ-WONDERLAND WARS, THE
DC Comics: Jan, 1986 - No. 3, March, 1986 (Mini-series)(Giants)

Ozzie and Harriet #2 © DC

Painkiller Jane #2 © Q&P

Panic #2 © WMG

GD 2.0 | VG 4.0 | FN 6.0 | VF 8.0 | VF/NM 9.0 | NM- 9.2

1-3-Capt. Carrot app.; funny animals 4.00

OZZIE & BABS (TV Teens #14 on)
Fawcett Publications: Dec, 1947 - No. 13, Fall, 1949

1-Teen-age 14 28 42 80 115 150
2 9 18 27 47 61 75
3-13 8 16 24 40 50 60

OZZIE AND HARRIET (The Adventures of... on cover) (Radio)
National Periodical Publications: Oct-Nov, 1949 - No. 5, June-July, 1950

1-Photo-c 100 200 300 635 1093 1550
2 48 96 144 302 514 725
3-5 40 80 120 246 411 575

OZZY OSBOURNE (Todd McFarlane Presents)
Image Comics (Todd McFarlane Prod.): June, 1999 ($4.95, magazine-sized)

1-Bio, interview and comic story; Ormston painted-a; Ashley Wood-c 5.00

PACIFIC COMICS GRAPHIC NOVEL (See Image Graphic Novel)

PACIFIC PRESENTS (Also see Starslayer #2, 3)
Pacific Comics: Oct, 1982 - No. 2, Apr, 1983; No. 3, Mar, 1984 - No. 4, Jun, 1984

1-Chapter 3 of The Rocketeer; Stevens-c/a; Bettie Page model
2 4 6 10 14 18
2-Chapter 4 of The Rocketeer (4th app.); nudity; Stevens-c/a
2 4 6 10 14 18
3,4: 3-1st app. Vanity 3.00
NOTE: ***Conrad** a-3, 4; c-3.* ***Ditko** a-1-3; c-1(1/2).* ***Dave Stevens** a-1, 2; c-1(1/2), 2.*

PACIFIC RIM: TALES FROM THE DRIFT
Legendary Comics: Nov, 2015 - No. 4, Apr, 2016 ($3.99)

1-4-Beachum & Fialkov-s/Marz-a 4.00

PACIFIC RIM: TALES FROM YEAR ZERO
Legendary Comics: Jun, 2013 ($24.99, HC graphic novel)

HC - Prequel to the 2013 movie; Beacham-s/Alex Ross-c; art by various 25.00

PACT, THE
Image Comics: Feb, 1994 - No. 3, June, 1994 ($1.95, limited series)

1-3: Valentino co-scripts & layouts 3.00

PACT, THE
Image Comics: Apr, 2005 - No. 4, Jan, 2006 ($2.99/$2.95)

1-4: Invincible, Shadowhawk, Firebreather & Zephyr team-up. 1-Valentino-s/a 3.00

PAGEANT OF COMICS (See Jane Arden & Mopsy)
Archer St. John: Sept, 1947 - No. 2, Oct, 1947

1-Mopsy strip-r 20 40 60 114 182 250
2-Jane Arden strip-r 12 24 36 69 97 125

PAINKILLER JANE
Event Comics: June, 1997 - No. 5, Nov, 1997 ($3.95/$2.95)

1-Augustyn/Waid-s/Leonardi/Palmiotti-a, variant-c 4.00
2-5: Two covers (Quesada, Leonardi) 3.00
0-(1/99, $3.95) Retells origin; two covers 4.00
Essential Painkiller Jane TPB (2007, $19.99) r/#0-5; cover gallery and pin-ups 20.00

PAINKILLER JANE
Dynamite Entertainment: 2006 - No. 3, 2006 ($2.99)

1-3-Quesada & Palmiotti-s/Moder-a. 1-Four covers by Q&P, Moder, Tan and Conner 3.00
Volume #1 TPB (2007, $9.99) r/#1-3; cover gallery and Palmiotti interview 10.00

PAINKILLER JANE
Dynamite Entertainment: No. 0, 2007 - No. 5, 2007 ($3.50)

0-(25¢) Quesada & Palmiotti-s/Moder-a 3.00
1-5-($3.50) 1-Continued from #0; 5 covers. 4,5-Crossover with Terminator 2 #6,7 3.50
Volume #2 TPB (2007, $11.99) r/#0-3; cover gallery 12.00

PAINKILLER JANE / DARKCHYLDE
Event Comics: Oct, 1998 ($2.95, one-shot)

Preview-($6.95) DF Edition, 1-($6.95) DF Edition 7.00
1-Three covers; J.G. Jones-a 3.00

PAINKILLER JANE / HELLBOY
Event Comics: Aug, 1998 ($2.95, one-shot)

1-Leonardi & Palmiotti-a 3.00

PAINKILLER JANE: THE PRICE OF FREEDOM
Marvel Comics (ICON): Nov, 2013 - No. 4, Jan, 2014 ($3.99/$2.99, limited series)

1-($3.99) Palmiotti-s/Santacruz & Lotfi-a; covers by Amanda Conner & Dave Johnson 4.00
2-4-($2.99) Santacruz-a/Conner-c 3.00

PAINKILLER JANE: THE 22 BRIDES
Marvel Comics (ICON): May, 2014 - No. 3, Oct, 2014 ($4.99/$3.99, limited series)

1-($4.99) Palmiotti-s/Santacruz & Fernandez-a; covers by Christian & Conner 5.00
2,3-($3.99) Santacruz-a2-Photo-c. 3-Conner-c 4.00

PAINKILLER JANE VS. THE DARKNESS
Event Comics: Apr, 1997 ($2.95, one-shot)

1-Ennis-s; four variant-c (Conner, Hildebrandts, Quesada, Silvestri) 3.50

PAKKINS' LAND
Caliber Comics (Tapestry): Oct, 1996 - No. 6, July, 1997 ($2.95, B&W)

1-Gary and Rhoda Shipman-s/a 6.00
2,3 4.00
1-3-2nd printing 3.00
4-6 3.00
0-(6/97, $1.95) 3.00

PAKKINS' LAND
Alias Enterprises: Apr, 2005 - No. 2 ($2.99)

1,2-Gary Shipman-s/a 3.00

PAKKINS' LAND: FORGOTTEN DREAMS
Caliber Comics/Image Comics #4: Apr, 1998 - No. 4, Mar, 2000 ($2.95, B&W)

1-4-Gary and Rhoda Shipman-s/a 3.00

PAKKINS' LAND: QUEST FOR KINGS
Caliber Comics: Aug, 1997 - No. 6, Mar, 1998 ($2.95, B&W)

1-6: 1-Gary and Rhoda Shipman-s/a; Jeff Smith var-c 3.00

PANCHO VILLA
Avon Periodicals: 1950

nn-Kinstler-c 26 52 78 154 252 350

PANHANDLE PETE AND JENNIFER (TV) (See Gene Autry #20)
J. Charles Laue Publishing Co.: July, 1951 - No. 3, Nov, 1951

1 11 22 33 60 83 105
2,3: 2-Interior photo-cvrs 8 16 24 40 50 60

PANIC (Companion to Mad)
E. C. Comics (Tiny Tot Comics): Feb-Mar, 1954 - No. 12, Dec-Jan, 1955-56

1-Used in Senate Investigation hearings; Elder draws entire E. C. staff; Santa Claus & Mickey Spillane parody 40 80 120 320 510 700
2-Atomic bomb-c 19 38 57 148 237 325
3,4: 3-Senate Subcommittee parody; Davis draws Gaines, Feldstein & Kelly, 1 pg.; Old King Cole smokes marijuana. 4-Infinity-c; John Wayne parody
16 32 48 128 202 275
5-11: 8-Last pre-code issue (5/55). 9-Superman, Smilin' Jack & Dick Tracy app. on-c; has photo of Walter Winchell on-c. 11-Wheedies cereal box-c
14 28 42 112 181 250
12 (Low distribution; thousands were destroyed) 19 38 57 152 246 340
NOTE: ***Davis** a-1-12; c-12.* ***Elder** a-1-12.* ***Feldstein** c-1-3, 5.* ***Kamen** a-1.* ***Orlando** a-1-9.* ***Wolverton** c-4, panel-3.* ***Wood** a-2-9, 11, 12.*

PANIC (Magazine) (Satire)
Panic Publ.: July, 1958 - No. 6, July, 1959; V2#10, Dec, 1965 - V2#12, 1966

1 14 28 42 76 108 140
2-6 9 18 27 50 65 80
V2#10-12: Reprints earlier issues 3 6 9 17 26 35
NOTE: ***Davis** a-3(2 pgs.), 4, 5, 10; c-10.* ***Elder** a-5.* ***Powell** a-V2#10, 11.* ***Torres** a-1-5.* ***Tuska** a-V2#11.*

PANIC
Gemstone Publishing: March, 1997 - No. 12, Dec, 1999 ($2.50, quarterly)

1-12: E.C. reprints 4.00

PANTHA (See Vampirella-The New Monthly #16,17)

PANTHA (Also see Prophecy)
Dynamite Entertainment: 2012 - No. 6, 2013 ($3.99)

1-6: 1-Jerwa-s/Rodrix-a; covers by Sean Chen & Texiera. 2-6-Texiera-c 4.00

PANTHA: HAUNTED PASSION (Also see Vampirella Monthly #0)
Harris Comics: May, 1997 ($2.95, B&W, one-shot)

1-r/Vampirella #30,31 3.00

PANTHEON
IDW Publishing: Apr, 2010 - No. 5, Aug, 2010 ($3.99)

1-5-Andreyko-s/Molnar-a; co-created by Michael Chiklis 4.00

PAPA MIDNITE (See John Constantine - Hellblazer Special:...)

Paper Girls #4 © Vaughan & Chiang

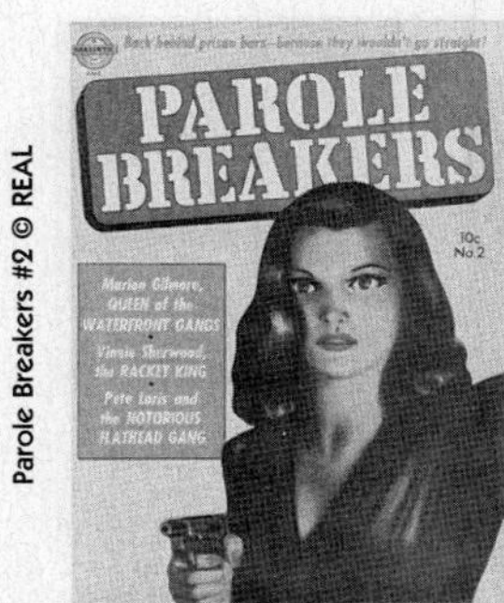

Parole Breakers #2 © REAL

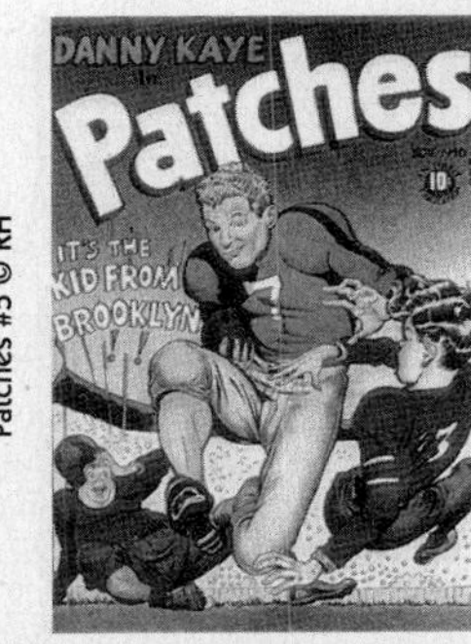

Patches #5 © RH

	GD 2.0	VG 4.0	FN 6.0	VF 8.0	VF/NM 9.0	NM- 9.2

PAPER GIRLS
Image Comics: Oct, 2015 - Present ($2.99)
1-12-Brian K. Vaughn-s/Cliff Chiang-a 3.00

PARADE (See Hanna-Barbera...)

PARADE COMICS (See Frisky Animals on Parade)

PARADE OF PLEASURE
Derric Verschoyle Ltd., London, England: 1954 (192 pgs.) (Hardback book)
By Geoffrey Wagner. Contains section devoted to the censorship of American comic books with illustrations in color and black and white. (Also see **Seduction of the Innocent**).
Distributed in USA by Library Publishers, N. Y. 138 276 414 552 689 825
with dust jacket.... 258 516 774 1109 1330 1550

PARADISE TOO!
Abstract Studios: 2000 - No. 14, 2003 ($2.95, B&W)
1-14-Terry Moore's unpublished newspaper strips and sketches 3.00
Complete Paradise Too TPB (2010, $29.95) r/#1-14 with bonus material 30.00
...: Checking For Weirdos TPB (4/03, $14.95) r/#8-12 15.00
...: Drunk Ducks! TPB (7/02, $15.95) r/#1-7 16.00

PARADISE X (Also see Earth X and Universe X)
Marvel Comics: Apr, 2002 - No. 12, Aug, 2003 ($4.50/$2.99)
0-Ross-c; Braithwaite-a 4.50
1-12-($2.99) Ross-c; Braithwaite-a. 7-Punisher on-c. 10-Kingpin on-c 3.00
...:A (10/03, $2.99) Braithwaite-a; Ross-c 3.00
...:Devils (11/02, $4.50) Sadowski-a; Ross-c 4.50
...:Ragnarok 1,2 (3/02, 4/03; $2.99) Yeates-a; Ross-c 3.00
...:X (11/03, $2.99) Braithwaite-a; Ross-c; conclusion of story 3.00
...:Xen (7/02, $4.50) Yeowell & Sienkiewicz-a; Ross-c 4.50
Earth X Vol. 4: Paradise X Book 1 (2003, $29.99, TPB) r/#0,1-5, ...: Xen; Heralds #1-3 30.00
Vol. 5: Paradise X Book 2 (2004, $29.99, TPB) r/#6-12, Ragnarok #1&2; Devils, A & X 30.00

PARADISE X: HERALDS (Also see Earth X and Universe X)
Marvel Comics: Dec, 2001 - No. 3, Feb, 2002 ($3.50)
1-3-Prelude to Paradise X series; Ross-c; Pugh-a 3.50
Special Edition (Wizard preview) Ross-c 3.00

PARADOX
Dark Visions Publ: June, 1994 - No. 2, Aug, 1994 ($2.95, B&W, mature)
1,2: 1-Linsner-c. 2-Boris-c. 3.00

PARALLAX: EMERALD NIGHT (See Final Night)
DC Comics: Nov, 1996 ($2.95, one-shot, 48 pgs.)
1-Final Night tie-in; Green Lantern (Kyle Rayner) app. 4.00

PARAMOUNT ANIMATED COMICS (See Harvey Comics Hits #60, 62)
Harvey Publications: No. 3, Jun, 1953 - No. 22, Jul, 1956
3-Baby Huey, Herman & Katnip, Buzzy the Crow begin
28 56 84 165 270 375
4-6 14 28 42 80 115 150
7-Baby Huey becomes permanent cover feature; cover title becomes Baby Huey with #9
24 48 72 142 234 325
8-10: 9-Infinity-c 12 24 36 69 97 125
11-22 10 20 30 54 72 90

PARENT TRAP, THE (Disney)
Dell Publishing Co.: No. 1210, Oct-Dec, 1961
Four Color 1210-Movie, Hayley Mills photo-c 8 16 24 56 108 160

PARIAH (Aron Warner's...)
Dark Horse Comics: Feb, 2014 - No. 8, Sept, 2014 ($3.99)
1-8-Aron Warner & Philip Gelatt-s/Brett Weldele-a 4.00

PARLIAMENT OF JUSTICE
Image Comics: Mar, 2003 ($5.95, B&W, one-shot, square-bound)
1-Michael Avon Oeming-c/s; Neil Vokes-a 6.00

PARODY
Armour Publishing: Mar, 1977 - No. 3, Aug, 1977 (B&W humor magazine)
1 3 6 9 14 19 24
2,3: 2-King Kong, Happy Days. 3-Charlie's Angels, Rocky
2 4 6 10 14 18

PAROLE BREAKERS
Avon Periodicals/Realistic #2 on: Dec, 1951 - No. 3, July, 1952
1(#2 on inside)-r-c/Avon paperback #283 (painted-c)
55 110 165 352 601 850
2-Kubert-a; r-c/Avon paperback #114 (photo-c) 41 82 123 256 428 600
3-Kinstler-c 37 74 111 222 361 500

PARTRIDGE FAMILY, THE (TV)(Also see David Cassidy)
Charlton Comics: Mar, 1971 - No. 21, Dec, 1973
1-(2 versions: B&W photo-c & tinted color photo-c) 6 12 18 41 76 110
2-4,6-10 4 8 12 25 40 55
5-Partridge Family Summer Special (52 pgs.); The Shadow, Lone Ranger, Charlie McCarthy, Flash Gordon, Hopalong Cassidy, Gene Autry & others app.
7 14 21 46 86 125
11-21 3 6 9 21 33 45

PARTS OF A HOLE
Caliber Press: 1991 ($2.50, B&W)
1-Short stories & cartoons by Brian Michael Bendis 3.00

PARTS UNKNOWN
Eclipse Comics/FX: July, 1992 - No. 4, Oct, 1992 ($2.50, B&W, mature)
1-4: All contain FX gaming cards 3.00

PARTS UNKNOWN
Image Comics: May, 2000 - Sept, 2000 ($2.95, B&W)
...: Killing Attractions 1 (5/00) Beau Smith-s/Brad Gorby-a 3.00
...: Hostile Takeover 1-4 (6-9/00) 3.00

PASSION, THE
Catechetical Guild: No. 394, 1955
394 6 12 18 31 38 45

PASSOVER (See Avengelyne)
Maximum Press: Dec, 1996 ($2.99, one-shot)
1 3.00

PAST AWAYS
Dark Horse Comics: Mar, 2015 - No. 9, Mar, 2016 ($3.99)
1-9: 1-Matt Kindt-s/Scott Kolins-a; two covers by Kolins & Kindt 4.00

PAT BOONE (TV)(Also see Superman's Girlfriend Lois Lane #9)
National Per. Publ.: Sept-Oct, 1959 - No. 5, May-Jun, 1960 (All have photo-c)
1 42 84 126 265 445 625
2-5: 3-Fabian, Connie Francis & Paul Anka photos on-c. 4-Previews "Journey To The Center Of The Earth". 4-Johnny Mathis & Bobby Darin photos on-c. 5-Dick Clark & Frankie Avalon photos on-c 34 68 102 199 325 450

PATCHES
Rural Home/Patches Publ. (Orbit): Mar-Apr, 1945 - No. 11, Nov, 1947
1-L. B. Cole-c 41 82 123 256 428 600
2 16 32 48 94 147 200
3,4,6,8-11: 6-Henry Aldrich story. 8-Smiley Burnette-c/s (6/47); pre-dates Smiley Burnette #1. 9-Mr. District Attorney story (radio). Leav/Keigstein-a (16 pgs.). 9-11-Leav-c. 10-Jack Carson (radio) c/story; Leav-c. 11-Red Skelton story 15 30 45 88 137 185
5-Danny Kaye-c/story; L.B. Cole-c. 20 40 60 118 192 265
7-Hopalong Cassidy-c/story 18 36 54 107 169 230

PATH, THE (Also see Negation War)
CrossGeneration Comics: Apr, 2002 - No. 23, Apr, 2004 ($2.95)
1-23: 1-Ron Marz-s/Bart Sears-a. 13-Matthew Smith-a begins 3.00

PATHFINDER (Based on the Pathfinder roleplaying game)
Dynamite Entertainment: 2012 - No. 12, 2013 ($3.99)
1-12: 1-Jim Zub-s/Andrew Huerta-a; four covers. 2-12-Multiple covers on each 4.00
... Special 2013 ($4.99, 40 pgs.) Jim Zub-s/Kevin Stokes-a 5.00

PATHFINDER: CITY OF SECRETS (Based on the Pathfinder roleplaying game)
Dynamite Entertainment: 2014 - No. 6, 2014 ($4.99)
1-6-Zub-s/Oliveira-a; Bound-in poster; multiple covers on each 5.00

PATHFINDER: GOBLINS! (Based on the Pathfinder roleplaying game)
Dynamite Entertainment: 2013 - No. 5, 2013 ($3.99)
1-5: Short stories by various; multiple covers on each 4.00

PATHFINDER: HOLLOW MOUNTAIN (Based on the Pathfinder roleplaying game)
Dynamite Entertainment: 2015 - No. 6, 2016 ($4.99)
1-6: 1-Sutter-s/Garcia-a; multiple covers 5.00

PATHFINDER: ORIGINS (Based on the Pathfinder roleplaying game)
Dynamite Entertainment: 2015 - No. 6, 2015 ($4.99)
1-6: 1-Spotlight on Valeros; multiple-c. 2-Kyra. 3-Seoni. 4-Merisiel. 5-Harsk. 6-Ezren 5.00

PATHFINDER: WORLDSCAPE (Based on the Pathfinder roleplaying game)

The Patriots #2 © WSP

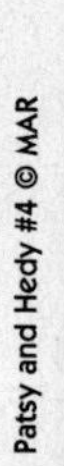
Patsy and Hedy #4 © MAR

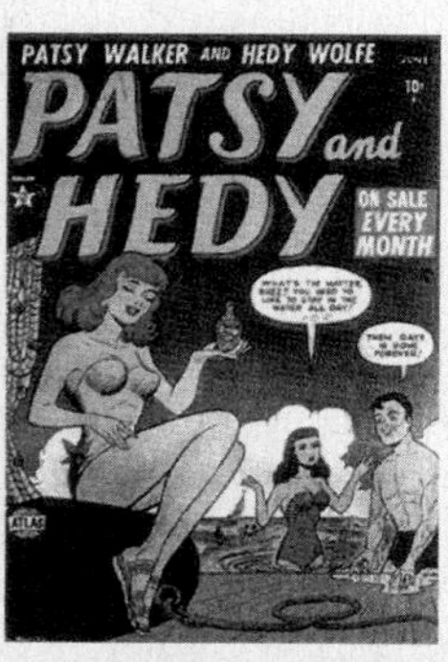

Patsy Walker, AKA Hellcat #7 © MAR

	GD 2.0	VG 4.0	FN 6.0	VF 8.0	VF/NM 9.0	NM- 9.2

Dynamite Entertainment: 2016 - Present ($4.99)

1-5-Red Sonja, John Carter and Tarzan app.; Jonathan Lau-a						5.00

PATHWAYS TO FANTASY
Pacific Comics: July, 1984

1-Barry Smith-c/a; Jeff Jones-a (4 pgs.)						4.00

PATORUZU (See Adventures of...)

PATRIOTS, THE
DC Comics (WildStorm): Jan, 2000 - No. 10, Oct, 2000 ($2.50)

1-10-Choi and Peterson-s/Ryan-a						3.00

PATSY & HEDY (Teenage)(Also see Hedy Wolfe)
Atlas Comics/Marvel (GPI/Male): Feb, 1952 - No. 110, Feb, 1967

1-Patsy Walker & Hedy Wolfe; Al Jaffee-c	50	100	150	315	533	750
2	21	42	63	122	199	275
3-10: 3,7,8,9-Al Jaffee-c	18	36	54	105	165	225
11-20: 17,19,20-Al Jaffee-c	15	30	45	88	137	185
21-40	14	28	42	80	115	150
41-50	7	14	21	44	82	120
51-60	6	12	18	41	76	110
61-80,100: 88-Lingerie panel	6	12	18	38	69	100
81-87,89-99,101-110	6	12	18	37	66	95
Annual 1(1963)-Early Marvel annual	10	20	30	64	132	200

PATSY & HER PALS (Teenage)
Atlas Comics (PPI): May, 1953 - No. 29, Aug, 1957

1-Patsy Walker	37	74	111	222	361	500
2	18	36	54	105	165	225
3-10	15	30	45	88	137	185
11-29: 24-Everett-c	14	28	42	80	115	150

PATSY WALKER (See All Teen, A Date With Patsy, Girls' Life, Miss America Magazine, Patsy & Hedy, Patsy & Her Pals & Teen Comics)
Marvel/Atlas Comics (BPC): 1945 (no month) - No. 124, Dec, 1965

1-Teenage	226	452	678	1446	2473	3500
2	41	82	123	256	428	600
3,4,6-10	34	68	102	199	325	450
5-Injury-to-eye-c	37	74	111	222	361	500
11,12,15,16,18	22	44	66	128	209	290
13,14,17,19-22-Kurtzman's "Hey Look"	22	44	66	132	216	300
23,24	20	40	60	114	182	250
25-Rusty by Kurtzman; painted-c	22	44	66	132	216	300
26-29,31: 26-31: 52 pgs.	17	34	51	98	154	210
30(52 pgs.)-Egghead Doodle by Kurtzman (1 pg.)	18	36	54	103	162	220
32-57: Last precode (3/55)	15	30	45	90	140	190
58-80,100	8	16	24	54	102	150
81-98: 92,98-Millie x-over	7	14	21	48	89	130
99-Linda Carter x-over	10	20	30	64	132	200
101-124	6	12	18	38	69	100
Fashion Parade 1(1966, 68 pgs.) (Beware cut-out & marked pages)	9	18	27	59	117	175

NOTE: Painted c-25-28. Anti-Wertham editorial in #21. Georgie app. in #8, 11, 17. Millie app. in #10, 92, 98. Mitzi app. in #11. Rusty app. in #12, 25. Willie app. in #12. ***Al Jaffee*** *c-44, 47, 49, 51, 57, 58.*

PATSY WALKER, A.K.A. HELLCAT
Marvel Comics: Feb, 2016 - Present ($3.99)

1-15: 1-Kate Leth-s/Brittney Williams-a; She-Hulk and Tom Hale app. 2-Hedy Wolfe app. 6-Natasha Allegri-a. 6,7-Jessica Jones app. 8-Civil War II tie-in						4.00

PATSY WALKER: HELLCAT
Marvel Comics: Sept, 2008 - No. 5, Feb, 2009 ($2.99, limited series)

1-5-Lafuente-a/Kathryn Immonen-s/Stuart Immonen-c; Hellcat joins The Initiative						3.00

PAT THE BRAT (Adventures of Pipsqueak #34 on)
Archie Publications (Radio): June, 1953; Summer, 1955 - No. 4, 5/56; No. 15, 7/56 - No. 33, 7/59

nn(6/53)	16	32	48	94	147	200
1(Summer, 1955)	15	30	45	85	130	175
2-4-(5/56) (#5-14 not published). 3-Early Bolling-a	9	18	27	50	65	80
15-(7/56)-33: 18-Early Bolling-a	4	8	12	28	47	65

PAT THE BRAT COMICS DIGEST MAGAZINE
Archie Publications: October, 1980 (95¢)

1-Li'l Jinx & Super Duck app.	2	4	6	9	13	16

PATTY CAKE
Permanent Press: Mar, 1995 - No. 9, Jul, 1996 ($2.95, B&W)

1-9: Scott Roberts-s/a						3.00

PATTY CAKE
Caliber Press (Tapestry): Oct, 1996 - No. 3, Apr, 1997 ($2.95, B&W)

1-3: Scott Roberts-s/a, ...Christmas (12/96)						3.00

PATTY CAKE & FRIENDS
Slave Labor Graphics: Nov, 1997 - Nov, 2000 ($2.95, B&W)

Here There Be Monsters (10/97), 1-14: Scott Roberts-s/a						3.00
Volume 2 #1 (11/00, $4.95)						5.00

PATTY POWERS (Formerly Della Vision #3)
Atlas Comics: No. 4, Oct, 1955 - No. 7, Oct, 1956

4	16	32	48	94	147	200
5-7	14	28	42	76	108	140

PAT WILTON (See Mighty Midget Comics)

PAUL
Spire Christian Comics (Fleming H. Revell Co.): 1978 (49¢)

nn	2	4	6	10	14	18

PAULINE PERIL (See The Close Shaves of...)

PAUL REVERE'S RIDE (TV, Disney, see Walt Disney Showcase #34)
Dell Publishing Co.: No. 822, July, 1957

Four Color 822-w/Johnny Tremain, Toth-a	7	14	21	49	92	135

PAUL TERRY (See Heckle and Jeckle)

PAUL TERRY'S ADVENTURES OF MIGHTY MOUSE (See Adventures of...)

PAUL TERRY'S COMICS (Formerly Terry-Toons Comics; becomes Adventures of Mighty Mouse No. 126 on)
St. John Publishing Co.: No. 85, Mar, 1951 - No. 125, May, 1955

85,86-Same as Terry-Toons #85, & 86 with only a title change; published at same time?; Mighty Mouse, Heckle & Jeckle & Gandy Goose continue from Terry-Toons	12	24	36	69	97	125
87-99	9	18	27	52	69	85
100	10	20	30	56	76	95
101-104,107-125: 121,122,125-Painted-c	9	18	27	50	65	80
105,106-Giant Comics Edition (25¢, 100 pgs.) (9/53 & ?). 105-Little Roquefort-c/story	19	38	57	109	172	235

PAUL TERRY'S MIGHTY MOUSE (See Mighty Mouse)

PAUL TERRY'S MIGHTY MOUSE ADVENTURE STORIES (See Mighty Mouse Adventure Stories)

PAUL THE SAMURAI (See The Tick #4)
New England Comics: July, 1992 - No. 6, July, 1993 ($2.75, B&W)

1-6						3.00

PAWNEE BILL
Story Comics (Youthful Magazines?): Feb, 1951 - No. 3, July, 1951

1-Bat Masterson, Wyatt Earp app.	14	28	42	80	115	150
2,3: 3-Origin Golden Warrior; Cameron-a	9	18	27	47	61	75

PAYBACKS, THE
Dark Horse Comics: Sept, 2015 - No. 4, Dec, 2015 ($3.99)

1-4: 1-Cates & Rahal-s/Shaw-a						4.00

PAY-OFF (This Is the..., ...Crime, ...Detective Stories)
D. S. Publishing Co.: July-Aug, 1948 - No. 5, Mar-Apr, 1949 (52 pgs.)

1-True Crime Cases #1,2	31	62	93	186	303	420
2	18	36	54	103	162	220
3-5-Thrilling Detective Stories	15	30	45	85	130	175

PEACEMAKER, THE (Also see Fightin' Five)
Charlton Comics: V3#1, Mar, 1967 - No. 5, Nov, 1967 (All 12¢ cover price)

1-Fightin' Five begins	5	10	15	33	57	80
2,3,5	3	6	9	20	31	42
4-Origin The Peacemaker	4	8	12	25	40	55
1,2(Modern Comics reprint, 1978)						6.00

PEACEMAKER (Also see Crisis On Infinite Earths & Showcase '93 #7,9,10)
DC Comics: Jan, 1988 - No. 4, Apr, 1988 ($1.25, limited series)

1-4						4.00

PEANUTS (Charlie Brown) (See Fritzi Ritz, Nancy & Sluggo, Sparkle & Sparkler, Tip Top, Tip Topper & United Comics)
United Features Syndicate/Dell Publishing Co./Gold Key: 1953-54; No. 878, 2/58 - No. 13, 5-7/62; 5/63 - No. 4, 2/64

1(U.F.S.)(1953-54)-Reprints United Features' Strange As It Seems, Willie, Ferdnand

Peanuts V2 #24 © Peanuts WW

Pebbles and Bamm-Bamm #33 © H-B

Penny Dreadful #5 © SHO

	GD 2.0	VG 4.0	FN 6.0	VF 8.0	VF/NM 9.0	NM- 9.2
(scarce)	649	1298	1947	4738	8369	12,000
Four Color 878(#1) (Dell) Schulz-s/a, with assistance from Dale Hale and Jim Sasseville thru #4	75	150	225	600	1350	2100
Four Color 969,1015('59)	27	54	81	189	420	650
4(2-4/60) Schulz-s/a; one story by Anthony Pocrnich, Schulz's assistant cartoonist	15	30	45	100	220	340
5-13-Schulz-c only; s/a by Pocrnich	12	24	36	84	185	285
1(Gold Key, 5/63)	27	54	81	194	435	675
2-4	11	22	33	76	163	250

PEANUTS (Charlie Brown)
BOOM! Entertainment: No. 0, Nov, 2011 - No. 4, Apr, 2012; V2 No. 1, Aug, 2012 - No. 32, Apr, 2016 ($1.00/$3.99)

0-(11/11, $1.00) New short stories and Sunday page reprints 3.00
1-4: 1-(1/12, $3.99) New short stories and Sunday page reprints; Snoopy sled cover 4.00
1-4-Variant-c with first appearance image. 1-Charlie Brown. 2-Lucy. 3-Linus. 4-Snoopy 6.00
(Volume 2)
1-32: 1-(8/12, "#1 of 4" on-c) 4.00
1-12-Variant-c with first appearance image. 1-Schroeder. 2-Pig-Pen. 4-Woodstock 10.00
... Free Comic Book Day Edition (5/12) Giveaway flip book with Adventure Time 3.00
...: Friends Forever 2016 Special (7/16, $7.99) New and classic short stories 8.00
Happiness is a Warm Blanket, Charlie Brown HC (Boom Entertainment, 3/2011, $19.99) adaptation of new animated special 20.00
It's Tokyo, Charlie Brown (10/12, $13.99, squarebound GN) Vicki Scott-s/a; bonus art 14.00
...: The Snoopy Special 1 (11/15, $4.99) New and classic Snoopy short stories 5.00
...: Where Beagles Dare! GN (9/15, $9.99, SC) Jason Cooper-s/Vicki Scott-a 10.00

PEANUTS HALLOWEEN
Fantagraphics Books: Sept, 2008 (8-1/2" x 5-3/8" ashcan giveaway)

nn-Halloween themed reprints in color and B&W 2.00

PEBBLES & BAMM BAMM (TV) (See Cave Kids #7, 12)
Charlton Comics: Jan, 1972 - No. 36, Dec, 1976 (Hanna-Barbera)

	GD 2.0	VG 4.0	FN 6.0	VF 8.0	VF/NM 9.0	NM- 9.2
1-From the Flintstones; "Teen Age..." on cover	4	8	12	28	47	65
2-10	3	6	9	16	24	32
11-20	2	4	6	13	18	22
21-36	2	4	6	9	13	16
nn (1973, digest, 100 pgs.) B&W one page gags	3	6	9	17	26	35

PEBBLES & BAMM BAMM (TV)
Harvey Comics: Nov, 1993 - No. 3, Mar, 1994 ($1.50) (Hanna-Barbera)

V2#1-3 3.00
...Giant Size 1 (10/93, $2.25, 68 pgs.)("Summer Special" on-c) 4.00

PEBBLES FLINTSTONE (TV) (See The Flintstones #11)
Gold Key: Sept, 1963 (Hanna-Barbera)

	GD 2.0	VG 4.0	FN 6.0	VF 8.0	VF/NM 9.0	NM- 9.2
1 (10088-309)-Early Pebbles app.	8	16	24	51	96	140

PEDRO (Formerly My Private Life #17; also see Romeo Tubbs)
Fox Features Syndicate: No. 18, June, 1950 - No. 2, Aug, 1950?

	GD 2.0	VG 4.0	FN 6.0	VF 8.0	VF/NM 9.0	NM- 9.2
18(#1)-Wood-c/a(p)	24	48	72	142	234	325
2-Wood-a?	16	32	48	94	147	200

PEE-WEE PIXIES (See The Pixies)

PELLEAS AND MELISANDE (See Night Music #4, 5)

PENALTY (See Crime Must Pay the...)

PENANCE: RELENTLESS (See Civil War, Thunderbolts and related titles)
Marvel Comics: Nov, 2007 - No. 5 ($2.99)

1-5-Speedball/Penance; Jenkins-s/Gulacy-a. 3-Wolverine app. 3.00
TPB (2008, $13.99) r/#1-5 14.00

PENDRAGON (Knights of... #5 on; also see Knights of...)
Marvel Comics UK, Ltd.: July, 1992 - No. 15, Sept, 1993 ($1.75)

1-15: 1-4-Iron Man app. 6-8-Spider-Man app. 3.00

PENDULUM ILLUSTRATED BIOGRAPHIES
Pendulum Press: 1979 (B&W)

19-355x-George Washington/Thomas Jefferson, 19-3495-Charles Lindbergh/Amelia Earhart, 19-3509-Harry Houdini/Walt Disney, 19-3517-Davy Crockett/Daniel Boone-Redondo-a, 19-3525-Elvis Presley/Beatles, 19-3533-Benjamin Franklin/Martin Luther King Jr, 19-3541-Abraham Lincoln/Franklin D. Roosevelt, 19-3568-Marie Curie/Albert Einstein-Redondo-a, 19-3576-Thomas Edison/Alexander Graham Bell-Redondo-a, 19-3584-Vince Lombardi/Pele, 19-3592-Babe Ruth/Jackie Robinson, 19-3606-Jim Thorpe/Althea Gibson

	GD 2.0	VG 4.0	FN 6.0	VF 8.0	VF/NM 9.0	NM- 9.2
Softback						5.00
Hardback	1	2	3	4	5	7

PENDULUM ILLUSTRATED CLASSICS (Now Age Illustrated)
Pendulum Press: 1973 - 1978 (75¢, 62pp, B&W, 5-3/8x8")
(Also see Marvel Classics)

64-100x(1973)-Dracula-Redondo art, 64-131x-The Invisible Man-Nino art, 64-0968-Dr. Jekyll and Mr. Hyde-Redondo art, 64-1005-Black Beauty, 64-1010-Call of the Wild, 64-1020-Frankenstein, 64-1025-Hucklebury Finn, 64-1030-Moby Dick-Nino-a, 64-1040-Red Badge of Courage, 64-1045-The Time Machine-Nino-a, 64-1050-Tom Sawyer, 64-1055-Twenty Thousand Leagues Under the Sea, 64-1069-Treasure Island, 64-1328(1974)-Kidnapped, 64-1336-Three Musketeers-Nino art, 64-1344-A Tale of Two Cities, 64-1352-Journey to the Center of the Earth, 64-1360-The War of the Worlds-Nino-a, 64-1379-The Greatest Advs. of Sherlock Holmes-Redondo art, 64-1387-Mysterious Island, 64-1395-Hunchback of Notre Dame, 64-1409-Helen Keller-story of my life, 64-1417-Scarlet Letter, 64-1425-Gulliver's Travels, 64-2618(1977)-Around the World in Eighty Days, 64-2626-Captains Courageous, 64-2634-Connecticut Yankee, 64-2642-The Hound of the Baskervilles, 64-2650-The House of Seven Gables, 64-2669-Jane Eyre, 64-2677-The Last of the Mohicans, 64-2685-The Best of O'Henry, 64-2693-The Best of Poe-Redondo-a, 64-2707-Two Years Before the Mast, 64-2715-White Fang, 64-2723-Wuthering Heights, 64-3126(1978)-Ben Hur-Redondo art, 64-3134-A Christmas Carol, 64-3142-The Food of the Gods, 64-3150-Ivanhoe, 64-3169-The Man in the Iron Mask, 64-3177-The Prince and the Pauper, 64-3185-The Prisoner of Zenda, 64-3193-The Return of the Native, 64-3207-Robinson Crusoe, 64-3215-The Scarlet Pimpernel, 64-3223-The Sea Wolf, 64-3231-The Swiss Family Robinson, 64-3851-Billy Budd, 64-386x-Crime and Punishment, 64-3878-Don Quixote, 64-3886-Great Expectations, 64-3894-Heidi, 64-3908-The Iliad, 64-3916-Lord Jim, 64-3924-The Mutiny on Board H.M.S. Bounty, 64-3932-The Odyssey, 64-3940-Oliver Twist, 64-3959-Pride and Prejudice, 64-3967-The Turn of the Screw

	GD 2.0	VG 4.0	FN 6.0	VF 8.0	VF/NM 9.0	NM- 9.2
Softback						6.00
Hardback	1	2	3	5	6	8

NOTE: *All of the above books can be ordered from the publisher; some were reprinted as Marvel Classic Comics #1-12. In 1972 there was another brief series of 12 titles which contained Classics Ill. artwork. They were entitled* ***Now Age Books*** *Illustrated, but can be easily distinguished from later series by the small Classics Illustrated logo at the top of the front cover. The format is the same as the later series. The 48 pg. C.I. art was stretched out to make 62 pgs. After Twin Circle Publ. terminated the Classics Ill. series in 1971, they made a one year contract with Pendulum Press to print these twelve titles of C.I. art. Pendulum was unhappy with the contract, and at the end of 1972 began their own art series, utilizing the talents of the Filipino artist group. One detail which makes this rather confusing is that when they redid the art in 1973, they gave it the same identifying no. as the 1972 series. All 12 of the 1972 C.I. editions have new covers, taken from internal art panels. In spite of their recent age, all of the 1972 C.I. series are very rare. Mint copies would fetch at least $50. Here is a list of the 1972 series, with C.I. title no. counterpart:*

64-1005 (CI#60-A2) 64-1010 (CI#91) 64-1015 (CI-Jr #503) 64-1020 (CI#26)
64-1025 (CI#19-A2) 64-1030 (CI#5-A2) 64-1035 (CI#169) 64-1040 (CI#98)
64-1045 (CI#133) 64-1050 (CI#50-A2) 64-1055 (CI#47) 64-1060 (CI-Jr#535)

PENDULUM ILLUSTRATED ORIGINALS
Pendulum Press: 1979 (In color)

94-4254-Solarman: The Beginning (See Solarman) 6.00

PENDULUM'S ILLUSTRATED STORIES
Pendulum Press: 1990 - No. 72, 1990? (No cover price ($4.95), squarebound, 68 pgs.)

1-72: Reprints Pendulum Ill. Classics series 5.00

PENGUIN: PAIN & PREJUDICE (Batman)
DC Comics: Dec, 2011 - No. 5, Apr, 2012 ($2.99, limited series)

1-5-Hurwitz-s/Kudranski-a/c; Penguin's childhood and rise to power 3.00

PENGUINS OF MADAGASCAR (Based on the DreamWorks movie and TV series)
Ape Entertainment: 2010 - No. 4, 2011 ($3.95, limited series)

1-4-Skipper, Kowalski, Private and Rico app. 4.00

PENGUINS OF MADAGASCAR (Based on the DreamWorks movie and TV series)
Titan Comics: Dec, 2014 - No. 4, Mar, 2015 ($3.99, limited series)

1-4-Skipper, Kowalski, Private and Rico app. 4.00

PENNY
Avon Comics: 1947 - No. 6, Sept-Oct, 1949 (Newspaper reprints)

	GD 2.0	VG 4.0	FN 6.0	VF 8.0	VF/NM 9.0	NM- 9.2
1-Photo & biography of creator	30	60	90	177	289	400
2-5	15	30	45	85	130	175
6-Perry Como photo on-c	15	30	45	88	137	185

PENNY CENTURY (See Love and Rockets)
Fantagraphics Books: Dec, 1997 - No. 7, Jul, 2000 ($2.95, B&W, mini-series)

1-7-Jaime Hernandez-s/a 3.00

PENNY DORA AND THE WISHING BOX
Image Comics: Nov, 2014 - No. 5, Jun, 2015 ($2.99)

1-5-Michael Stock-s/Sina Grace-a 3.00

PENNY DREADFUL (Based on the Showtime TV series)
Titan Comics: Jun, 2016 - Present ($3.99)

1-5: 1-Wilson-Cairns-s/De Martinis-a; multiple covers 4.00

PEP COMICS (See Archie Giant Series #576, 589, 601, 614, 624)
MLJ Magazines/Archie Publications No. 56 (3/46) on: Jan, 1940 - No. 411, Mar, 1987

	GD 2.0	VG 4.0	FN 6.0	VF 8.0	VF/NM 9.0	NM- 9.2
1-Intro. The Shield (1st patriotic hero) by Irving Novick; origin & 1st app. The Comet by Jack Cole, The Queen of Diamonds & Kayo Ward; The Rocket, The Press Guardian (The Falcon #1 only), Sergeant Boyle, Fu Chang, & Bentley of of Scotland Yard; Robot-c; Shield-c begin	946	1892	2838	6906	12,203	17,500
2-Origin The Rocket	300	600	900	2010	3505	5000
3	245	490	735	1568	2684	3800

Pep Comics #39 © ACP

The Perfect Crime #28 © Cross

Perfect Love #3 © Z-D

	GD 2.0	VG 4.0	FN 6.0	VF 8.0	VF/NM 9.0	NM- 9.2
4-Wizard cameo; early robot-s	213	426	639	1363	2332	3300
5-Wizard cameo in Shield story	213	426	639	1363	2332	3300
6-10: 8-Last Cole Comet; no Cole-a in #6,7	174	348	522	1114	1907	2700
11-Dusty, Shield's sidekick begins (1st app.); last Press Guardian, Fu Chang	181	362	543	1158	1979	2800
12-Origin & 1st app. Fireball (2/41); last Rocket & Queen of Diamonds; Danny in Wonderland begins	206	412	618	1318	2259	3200
13-15	155	310	465	992	1696	2400
16-Origin Madam Satan; blood drainage-c	245	490	735	1568	2684	3800
17-Origin/1st app. The Hangman (7/41); death of The Comet; Comet is revealed as Hangman's brother	497	994	1491	3628	6414	9200
18,19,21: 21-Last Madam Satan	155	310	465	992	1696	2400
20-Classic Nazi swastika-c; last Fireball	300	600	900	2070	3635	5200
22-Intro. & 1st app. Archie, Betty, & Jughead (12/41); (on sale 10/41)(also see Jackpot)	25,000	50,000	75,000	170,000	245,000	320,000
23-Statue of Liberty-c (1/42; on sale 11/41)	2000	4000	6000	12,000	17,000	22,000
24-Coach Kleats app. (unnamed until Archie #94); bondage/torture-c	703	1406	2109	5132	9066	13,000
25-1st app. Archie's jalopy; 1st skinny Mr. Weatherbee prototype	459	918	1377	3350	5925	8500
26-1st app. Veronica Lodge (4/42); "Remember Pearl Harbor!" cover caption	811	1622	2433	5920	10,460	15,000
27-Bill of Rights-c	371	742	1113	2600	4550	6500
28-Classic swastika/Hangman-c	354	708	1062	2478	4339	6200
29,30: 29-Origin Shield retold; 30-Capt. Commando begins; bondage/torture-c; 1st Miss Grundy (definitive version); see Jackpot #4	343	686	1029	2400	4200	6000
31-33,35: 31-MLJ offices & artists are visited in Sgt. Boyle story; 1st app. Mr. Lodge. 32-Shield dons new costume. 33-Pre-Moose tryout (see Jughead #1)	300	600	900	2070	3635	5200
34-Classic Bondage/Hypo-c	1400	2800	4200	9400	14,700	20,000
36-1st full Archie-c in Pep (2/43) w/Shield & Hangman (see Jackpot #4 where Archie's face appears in a small circle)	1600	3200	4800	11,000	18,500	26,000
37-40	245	490	735	1568	2684	3800
41-Archie-c begin	300	600	900	2010	3505	5000
42-45	194	388	582	1242	2121	3000
46,47,49,50: 47-Last Hangman issue; infinity-c	168	336	504	1075	1838	2600
48-Black Hood begins (5/44); ends #51,59,60; Archie fish-c	206	412	618	1318	2259	3200
51-60: 52-Suzie begins; 1st Mr Weatherbee-c. 56-Last Capt. Commando. 59-Black Hood not in costume; lingerie panels; Archie dresses as his aunt; Suzie ends. 60-Katy Keene begins(3/47), ends #154	81	162	243	518	884	1250
61-65-Last Shield. 62-1st app. Li'l Jinx (7/47)	65	130	195	416	708	1000
66-80: 66-G-Man Club becomes Archie Club (2/48); Nevada Jones by Bill Woggon. 76-Katy Keene story. 78-1st app. Dilton	39	78	117	231	378	525
81-99	23	46	69	136	223	310
100	27	54	81	158	259	360
101-130	15	30	45	88	137	185
131(2/59)-137	6	12	18	41	76	110
138-140-Neal Adams-a (1 pg.) in each	7	14	21	44	82	120
141-149(9/61)	5	10	15	35	63	90
150-160-Super-heroes app. in each (see note). 150 (10/61?)-2nd or 3rd app. The Jaguar? 151-154,156-158-Horror/Sci/Fi-c. 157-Li'l Jinx. 159-Both 12¢ and 15¢ covers exist	8	16	24	51	96	140
161(3/63)-167,169-180: 161-3rd Josie app.; early Josie stories w/DeCarlo-a begin (see Note for others)	4	8	12	27	44	60
168,200: 168-(1/64)-Jaguar app. 200-(12/66)	4	8	12	28	47	65
181(5/65)-199: 187-Pureheart try-out story. 192-UFO-c. 198-Giantman-c(only)	3	6	9	21	33	45
201-217,219-226,228-240(4/70): 224-(12/68) 1st app. Archie's pet, Hot Dog (later becomes Jughead's pet)	3	6	9	16	23	30
218,227-Archies Band-c only	3	6	9	17	26	35
241-270(10/72)	2	4	6	13	18	22
271-297,299	2	4	6	9	12	15
298, 300: 298-Josie and the Pussycats-c. 300(4/75)	2	4	6	13	18	22
301-340(8/78)	1	3	4	6	8	10
341-382	1	2	3	4	5	7
383(4/82),393(3/84): 383-Marvelous Maureen begins (Sci/fi). 393-Thunderbunny begins	1	2	3	5	6	8
384-392,394,395,397-399,401-410						5.00
396-Early Cheryl Blossom-c	2	4	6	9	12	15
400(5/85),411: 400-Story featuring Archie staff (DeCarlo-a)	1	2	3	4	5	7

NOTE: ***Biro** a-2, 4, 5. **Jack Cole** a-1-5, 8. **Al Fagaly** c-55-72. **Fuje** a-39, 45, 47; c-34. **Meskin** a-2, 4, 5, 11(2). **Montana** c-30, 32, 33, 36, 73-87(most). **Novick** c-1-28, 29(w/**Schomburg**), 31i. **Harry Sahle** c-35, 39-50. **Schomburg** c-38. **Bob Wood** a-2, 4-6, 11. The Fly app. in 151, 154, 160. Flygirl app. in 153, 155, 156, 158. Jaguar app. in 150, 152, 157, 159, 168. Josie by **DeCarlo** in 161-166, 168-171, 173, 175-177, 179, 181. Katy Keene by **Bill Woggon** in 73-126. Bondage c-7, 12, 13, 15, 18, 21, 31, 32. Cover features: Shield #1-16; Shield/Hangman #17-27, 29-41; Hangman #28. Archie #36, 41-on.*

PEP COMICS FEATURING BETTY AND VERONICA
Archie Comic Publications: May, 2011 (Giveaway)

	GD	VG	FN	VF	VF/NM	NM-
Free Comic Book Day Edition - Little Archie flashback						3.00

PEPE
Dell Publishing Co.: No. 1194, Apr, 1961

	GD	VG	FN	VF	VF/NM	NM-
Four Color 1194-Movie, photo-c	5	10	15	30	50	70

PERFECT CRIME, THE
Cross Publications: Oct, 1949 - No. 33, May, 1953 (#2-14, 52 pgs.)

	GD	VG	FN	VF	VF/NM	NM-
1-Powell-a(2)	43	86	129	271	461	650
2 (4/50)	24	48	72	144	237	330
3-10: 7-Steve Duncan begins, ends #30. 10-Flag-c	22	44	66	128	209	290
11-Used in **SOTI**, pg. 159	24	48	72	142	234	325
12-14	20	40	60	120	195	270
15- "The Most Terrible Menace" 2 pg. drug editorial (8/51)	22	44	66	132	216	300
16,17,19-25,27-29,31-33	18	36	54	103	162	220
18-Drug cover, heroin drug propaganda story, plus 2 pg. anti-drug editorial (11/51)	39	78	117	231	378	525
26-Drug-c with hypodermic needle; drug propaganda story (7/52)	39	78	117	240	395	550
30-Strangulation cover (11/52)	39	78	117	231	378	525

NOTE: ***Powell** a-No. 1, 2, 4. **Wildey** a-1, 5. Bondage c-11.*

PERFECT LOVE
Ziff-Davis(Approved Comics)/St. John No. 9 on: #10, 8-9/51 (cover date; 5-6/51 indicia date); #2, 10-11/51 - #10, 12/53

	GD	VG	FN	VF	VF/NM	NM-
10(#1)(8-9/51)-Painted-c	27	54	81	158	259	360
2(10-11/51)	18	36	54	105	165	225
3,5-7: 3-Painted-c. 5-Photo-c	15	30	45	86	133	180
4,8 (Fall, 1952)-Kinstler-a; last Z-D issue	15	30	45	88	137	185
9,10 (10/53, 12/53, St. John): 9-Painted-c. 10-Photo-c	15	30	45	85	130	175

PERHAPANAUTS, THE
Dark Horse Comics: Nov, 2005 - No. 4, Feb, 2006 ($2.99, limited series)

	GD	VG	FN	VF	VF/NM	NM-
1-4-Todd Dezago-s/Craig Rousseau-a/c						3.00
... Annual #1 (2/08, $3.50) Two covers by Rousseau and Allred						3.50
...: Danger Down Under! 1-5 (11/12 - No. 5, 6/13, $3.50) Two covers on each						3.50
... Halloween Spooktacular 1 (10/09, $3.50) Hembeck, Rousseau and others-a						3.50
,,, - Molly's Story (2/10, $3.50) Copland-a						3.50
(2nd series) (4/08 - No. 6, $3.50) 1-6: 1-Two covers by Art Adams and Rousseau						3.50

PERHAPANAUTS: SECOND CHANCES, THE
Dark Horse Comics: Oct, 2006 - No. 4, Jan, 2007 ($2.99, limited series)

	GD	VG	FN	VF	VF/NM	NM-
1-4-Todd Dezago-s/Craig Rousseau-a/c						3.00

PERRI (Disney)
Dell Publishing Co.: No. 847, Jan, 1958

	GD	VG	FN	VF	VF/NM	NM-
Four Color 847-Movie, w/2 diff-c publ.	6	12	18	37	66	95

PERRY MASON
David McKay Publications: No. 49, 1946 - No. 50, 1946

	GD	VG	FN	VF	VF/NM	NM-
Feature Books 49, 50-Based on Gardner novels	40	80	120	244	402	560

PERRY MASON MYSTERY MAGAZINE (TV)
Dell Publishing Co.: June-Aug, 1964 - No. 2, Oct-Dec, 1964

	GD	VG	FN	VF	VF/NM	NM-
1-Raymond Burr painted-c	6	12	18	41	76	120
2-Raymond Burr photo-c	5	10	15	33	57	80

PERSONAL LOVE (Also see Movie Love)
Famous Funnies: Jan, 1950 - No. 33, June, 1955

	GD	VG	FN	VF	VF/NM	NM-
1-Photo-c	24	48	72	140	230	320
2-Kathryn Grayson & Mario Lanza photo-c	15	30	45	83	124	165
3-7,10: 7-Robert Walker & Joanne Dru photo-c. 10-Loretta Young & Joseph Cotton photo-c	14	28	42	80	115	150
8,9: 8-Esther Williams & Howard Keel photo-c. 9-Debra Paget & Louis Jourdan photo-c	14	28	42	81	118	155
11-Toth-a; Glenn Ford & Gene Tierney photo-c	15	30	45	86	133	180
12,16,17-One pg. Frazetta each. 17-Rock Hudson & Yvonne DeCarlo photo-c	14	28	42	81	118	155

13-15,18-23: 12-Jane Greer & William Lundigan photo-c. 14-Kirk Douglas photo-c. 15-Dale Robertson & Joanne Dru photo-c. 18-Gregory Peck & Susan Hayworth photo-c.

Peter Cannon: Thunderbolt #10 © DYN

Peter Panda #7 © DC

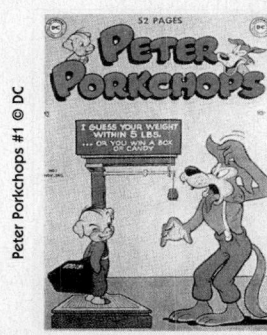

Peter Porkchops #1 © DC

GD VG FN VF VF/NM NM-
2.0 4.0 6.0 8.0 9.0 9.2

19-Anthony Quinn & Suzan Ball photo-c. 20-Robert Wagner & Kathleen Crowley photo-c.
21-Roberta Peters & Byron Palmer photo-c. 22-Dale Robertson photo-c.
23-Rhonda Fleming-c 14 28 42 76 108 140
24,27,28-Frazetta-a in each (8,8&6 pgs.). 27-Rhonda Fleming & Fernando Lamas photo-c.
28-Mitzi Gaynor photo-c 55 110 165 352 601 850
25-Frazetta-a (tribute to Bettie Page, 7 pg. story); Tyrone Power/Terry Moore
photo-c from "King of the Khyber Rifles" 77 154 231 493 847 1200
26,29,30,33: 26-Constance Smith & Byron Palmer photo-c. 29-Charlton Heston & Nicol Morey photo-c. 30-Johnny Ray & Mitzi Gaynor photo-c. 33-Dana Andrews & Piper Laurie photo-c
14 28 42 76 108 140
31-Marlon Brando & Jean Simmons photo-c; last pre-code (2/55)
16 32 48 94 147 200
32-Classic Frazetta-a (8 pgs.); Kirk Douglas & Bella Darvi photo-c
74 148 222 470 810 1150

NOTE: *All have photo-c. Many feature movie stars.* ***Everett*** *a-5, 9, 10, 24.*

PERSONAL LOVE (Going Steady V3#3 on)
Prize Publ. (Headline): V1#1, Sept, 1957 - V3#2, Nov-Dec, 1959

V1#1 14 28 42 78 112 145
2 9 18 27 52 69 85
3-6(7-8/58) 8 16 24 44 57 70
V2#1(9-10/58)-V2#6(7-8/59) 8 16 24 40 50 60
V3#1-Wood?/Orlando-a 8 16 24 42 54 65
2 7 14 21 37 46 55

PETER CANNON - THUNDERBOLT (See Crisis on Infinite Earths)(Also see Thunderbolt)
DC Comics: Sept, 1992 - No. 12, Aug, 1993 ($1.25)

1-12 3.00

PETER CANNON: THUNDERBOLT
Dynamite Entertainment: 2012 - No. 13, 2013 ($3.99)

1-10: 1-Darnell & Ross-s/Lau-a; back-up unpublished '80s Thunderbolt story; Pete Morisi-s/a.
1-3-Four covers on each. 4-7-Covers by Ross & Segovia 4.00

PETER COTTONTAIL
Key Publications: Jan, 1954; Feb, 1954 - No. 2, Mar, 1954 (Says 3/53 in error)

1(1/54)-Not 3-D 9 18 27 52 69 85
1(2/54)-(3-D, 25¢)-Came w/glasses; written by Bruce Hamilton
21 42 63 122 199 275
2-Reprints 3-D #1 but not in 3-D 6 12 18 31 38 45

PETER GUNN (TV)
Dell Publishing Co.: No. 1087, Apr-June, 1960

Four Color 1087-Photo-c 7 14 21 49 92 135

PETE ROSE: HIS INCREDIBLE BASEBALL CAREER
Masstar Creations Inc.: 1995

1-John Tartaglione-a 4.00

PETER PAN (Disney) (See Hook, Movie Classics & Comics, New Adventures of... & Walt Disney Showcase #36)
Dell Publishing Co.: No. 442, Dec, 1952 - No. 926, Aug, 1958

Four Color 442 (#1)-Movie 10 20 30 66 138 210
Four Color 926-Reprint of 442 5 10 15 33 57 80

PETER PAN
Disney Comics: 1991 ($5.95, graphic novel, 68 pgs.)(Celebrates video release)

nn-r/Peter Pan Treasure Chest from 1953 7.00

PETER PANDA
National Periodical Publications: Aug-Sept, 1953 - No. 31, Aug-Sept, 1958

1-Grossman-c/a in all 57 114 171 362 619 875
2 29 58 87 170 278 385
3,4,6-8,10 23 46 69 136 223 310
5-Classic-c (scarce) 97 194 291 621 1061 1500
9-Robot-c 36 72 108 216 351 485
11-31 17 34 51 98 154 210

PETER PAN RECORDS (See Power Records)

PETER PAN TREASURE CHEST (See Dell Giants)

PETER PANZERFAUST
Image Comics (Shadowline): Feb, 2012 - No. 25, Dec, 2016 ($3.50/$3.99)

1-Kurtis Wiebe-s/Tyler Jenkins-a/c; Peter Pan-type character in WWII Europe
7 14 21 46 86 125
1-Second printing 3 6 9 16 23 30
2 4 8 12 23 37 50
3 2 4 6 11 16 20

GD VG FN VF VF/NM NM-
2.0 4.0 6.0 8.0 9.0 9.2

4-8 1 2 3 5 6 8
9-1st full app. Kapitan Haken 2 4 6 8 10 12
10-24 4.00
25-Last issue; bonus preview of Rat Queens v2 5.00

PETER PARKER (See The Spectacular Spider-Man)

PETER PARKER
Marvel Comics: May, 2010 - No. 5, Sept, 2010 ($3.99/$2.99)

1-($3.99) Prints material from Marvel Digital Comics; Olliffe-a; back-up w/Hembeck-s/a 4.00
2-5-($2.99): 2-4-Olliffe-a. 3-Braithwaite-c. 5-Nauck-a; Thing app. 3.00

PETER PARKER: SPIDER-MAN
Marvel Comics: Jan, 1999 - No. 57, Aug, 2003 ($2.99/$1.99/$2.25)

1-Mackie-s/Romita Jr.-a; wraparound-c 1 2 3 5 6 8
1-($6.95) DF Edition w/variant-c by the Romitas 2 4 6 8 10 12
2-11,13-17-($1.99): 2-Two covers; Thor app. 3-Iceman-c/app. 4-Marrow-c/app.
5-Spider-Woman app. 7,8-Blade app. 9,10-Venom app. 11-Iron Man & Thor-c/app. 3.00
12-($2.99) Sinister Six and Venom app. 4.00
18-24,26-43: 18-Begin $2.25-c. 20-Jenkins-s/Buckingham-a start. 23-Intro Typeface.
24-Maximum Security x-over. 29-Rescue of MJ. 30-Ramos-c. 42,43-Mahfood-a 3.00
25-($2.99) Two covers; Spider-Man & Green Goblin 4.00
44-47-Humberto Ramos-c/a; Green Goblin-c/app. 3.00
48,49,51-57: 48,49-Buckingham-c/a. 51,52-Herrera-a. 56,57-Kieth-a; Sandman returns 3.00
50-($3.50) Buckingham-c/a 4.00
#156.1 (10/12, $2.99, 50th Anniversary one-shot) Stern-s/De La Torre-a/Romita Jr.-c 3.00
...'99 Annual (8/99, $3.50) Man-Thing app. 4.00
...'00 Annual ($3.50) Bounty app.; Joe Bennett-a; Black Cat back-up story 4.00
...'01 Annual ($2.99) Avery-s 4.00
...: A Day in the Life TPB (5/01, $14.95) r/#20-22,26; Webspinners #10-12 15.00
...: One Small Break TPB (2002, $16.95) r/#27,28,30-34; Andrews-c 17.00
Spider-Man: Return of the Goblin TPB (2002, $8.99) r/#44-47; Ramos-c 9.00
...Vol. 4: Trials & Tribulations TPB (2003, $11.99) r/#35,37,48-50; Cho-c 12.00

PETER PAT
United Features Syndicate: No. 8, 1939

Single Series 8 36 72 108 216 351 485

PETER PAUL'S 4 IN 1 JUMBO COMIC BOOK
Capitol Stories (Charlton): No date (1953)

1-Contains 4 comics bound; Space Adventures, Space Western, Crime & Justice,
Racket Squad in Action 42 84 126 265 445 625

PETER PIG
Standard Comics: No. 5, May, 1953 - No. 6, Aug, 1953

5,6 7 14 21 35 43 50

PETER PORKCHOPS (See Leading Comics #23) (Also see Capt. Carrot)
National Periodical Publications: 11-12/49 - No. 61, 9-11/59; No. 62, 10-12/60 (1-11: 52 pgs.)

1 34 68 102 199 325 450
2 15 30 45 90 140 190
3-10: 6- "Peter Rockets to Mars!" c/story 13 26 39 74 105 135
11-30 10 20 30 56 76 95
31-62 9 18 27 47 61 75

NOTE: ***Otto Feuer*** *a-all.* ***Rube Grossman****-a most issues.* ***Sheldon Mayer*** *a-30-38, 40-44, 46-52, 61.*

PETER PORKER, THE SPECTACULAR SPIDER-HAM
Star Comics (Marvel): May, 1985 - No. 17, Sept, 1987 (Also see Marvel Tails)

1-Michael Golden-c 5.00
2-17: 12-Origin/1st app. Bizarro Phil. 13-Halloween issue 4.00

NOTE: *Back-up features: 2-X-Bugs. 3-Iron Mouse. 4-Croctor Strange. 5-Thrr, Dog of Thunder.*

PETER POTAMUS (TV)
Gold Key: Jan, 1965 (Hanna-Barbera)

1-1st app. Peter Potamus & So-So, Breezly & Sneezly
8 16 24 56 108 160

PETER RABBIT (See New Funnies #65 & Space Comics)
Dell Publishing Co.: No. 1, 1942

Large Feature Comic 1 74 148 222 470 810 1150

PETER RABBIT (Adventures of...; New Advs. of... #9 on)(Also see Funny Tunes & Space Comics)
Avon Periodicals: 1947 - No. 34, Aug-Sept, 1956

1(1947)-Reprints 1943-44 Sunday strips; contains a biography & drawing of Cady
36 72 108 216 351 485
2 (4/48) 24 48 72 144 237 330
3 ('48) - 6(7/49)-Last Cady issue 21 42 63 126 206 285
7-10(1950-8/51): 9-New logo 11 22 33 64 90 115

Petticoat Junction #2 © DELL

The Phantom #16 © KFS

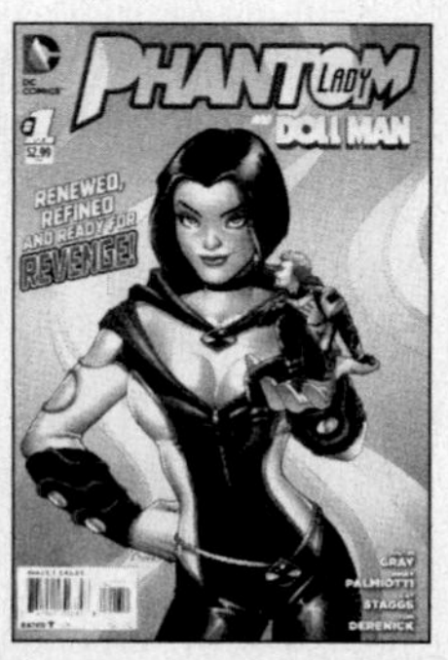

Phantom Lady (2012 series) #1 © DC

GD 2.0 | VG 4.0 | FN 6.0 | VF 8.0 | VF/NM 9.0 | NM- 9.2

11(11/51)-34('56)-Avon's character 10 20 30 54 72 90
...Easter Parade (1952, 25¢, 132 pgs.) 21 42 63 124 202 280
...Jumbo Book (1954-Giant Size, 25¢)-Jesse James by Kinstler (6 pgs.); space ship-c 25 50 75 150 245 340

PETER RABBIT 3-D
Eternity Comics: April, 1990 ($2.95, with glasses; sealed in plastic bag)
1-By Harrison Cady (reprints) 3.00

PETER, THE LITTLE PEST (#4 titled Petey)
Marvel Comics Group: Nov, 1969 - No. 4, May, 1970
1 6 12 18 42 79 115
2-4-r-Dexter the Demon & Melvin the Monster 5 10 15 30 50 70

PETE'S DRAGON (See Walt Disney Showcase #43)

PETE THE PANIC
Stanmor Publications: November, 1955
nn-Code approved 8 16 24 40 50 60

PETEY (See Peter, the Little Pest)

PETTICOAT JUNCTION (TV, inspired Green Acres)
Dell Publ. Co.: Oct-Dec, 1964 - No. 5, Oct-Dec, 1965 (#1-3, 5 have photo-c)
1 6 12 18 40 73 105
2-5 5 10 15 30 50 70

PETUNIA (Also see Looney Tunes and Porky Pig)
Dell Publishing Co.: No. 463, Apr, 1953
Four Color 463 5 10 15 33 57 80

PHAGE (See Neil Gaiman's Teknophage & Neil Gaiman's Phage-Shadowdeath)

PHANTACEA
McPherson Publishing Co.: Sept, 1977 - No. 6, Summer, 1980 (B&W)
1-Early Dave Sim-a (32 pgs.) 4 8 12 28 47 65
2-Dave Sim-a(10 pgs.) 3 6 9 14 19 24
3-6: 3-Flip-c w/Damnation Bridge. 4-Gene Day-a 2 4 6 10 14 18

PHANTASMO (See The Funnies #45)
Dell Publishing Co.: No. 18, 1941
Large Feature Comic 18 40 80 120 246 411 575

PHANTOM, THE
David McKay Publishing Co.: 1939 - 1949
Feature Books 20 155 310 465 992 1696 2400
Feature Books 22 86 172 258 546 936 1325
Feature Books 39 65 130 195 416 708 1000
Feature Books 53,56,57 50 100 150 315 533 750

PHANTOM, THE (See Ace Comics, Defenders Of The Earth, Eat Right to Work and Win, Future Comics, Harvey Comics Hits #51,56, Harvey Hits #1, 6, 12, 15, 26, 36, 44, 48, & King Comics)

PHANTOM, THE (nn (#29)-Published overseas only) (Also see Comics Reading Libraries in the Promotional Comics section)
Gold Key(#1-17)/King(#18-28)/Charlton(#30 on): Nov, 1962 - No. 17, Jul, 1966; No. 18, Sept, 1966 - No. 28, Dec, 1967; No. 30, Feb, 1969 - No. 74, Jan, 1977
1-Origin revealed on inside-c & back-c 21 42 63 147 324 500
2-King, Queen & Jack begins, ends #11 10 20 30 66 138 210
3-5 8 16 24 56 108 160
6-10 7 14 21 44 82 120
11-17: 12-Track Hunter begins 6 12 18 37 66 95
18-Flash Gordon begins; Wood-a 5 10 15 30 50 70
19-24: 20-Flash Gordon ends (both by Gil Kane). 21-Mandrake begins. 20,24-Girl Phantom app. 4 8 12 27 44 60
25-28: 25-Jeff Jones-a(4 pgs.); 1 pg. Williamson ad. 26-Brick Bradford app. 28-Brick Bradford app. 3 6 9 21 33 45
30-33: 33-Last 12¢ issue 3 6 9 16 24 32
34-40: 36,39-Ditko-a 3 6 9 16 23 30
41-66,72: 46-Intro. The Piranha. 51-Grey tone-c. 62-Bolle-c 3 6 9 14 19 24
67-Origin retold; Newton-c/a; Humphrey Bogart, Lauren Bacall & Peter Lorre app. 3 6 9 16 24 32
68,70,71,73-Newton-c/a 2 4 6 13 18 22
69-Newton-c only 2 4 6 13 18 22
74-Classic flag-c by Newton; Newton-a; 3 6 9 16 23 30
NOTE: *Aparo a-31-34, 36-38; c-31-38, 60, 61. Painted c-1-17.*

PHANTOM, THE
DC Comics: May, 1988 - No. 4, Aug, 1988 ($1.25, mini-series)
1-4: Orlando-c/a in all 4.00

PHANTOM, THE
DC Comics: Mar, 1989 - No. 13, Mar, 1990 ($1.50)
1-13: 1-Brief origin 4.00

PHANTOM, THE
Wolf Publishing: 1992 - No. 8, 1993 ($2.25)
1-8 3.00

PHANTOM, THE
Moonstone: 2003 - No. 26, Dec, 2008 ($3.50/$3.99)
1-26: 1-Cassaday-c/Raab-s/Quinn-a 4.00
... Annual #1 (2007, $6.50) Blevins-c; stroy and art by various incl. Nolan 6.50
... - Captain Action 1 (2010, $3.99) covers by Thibert, Sparacio, and Gilbert 4.00

PHANTOM, THE
Hermes Press: 2014 - Present ($3.99)
1-4: 1-Peter David-s/Sal Velluto-a; four covers 4.00

PHANTOM BLOT, THE (#1 titled New Adventures of...)
Gold Key: Oct, 1964 - No. 7, Nov, 1966 (Disney)
1 (Meets The Mysterious Mr. X) 5 10 15 35 63 90
2-1st Super Goof 5 10 15 31 53 75
3-7 3 6 9 21 33 45

PHANTOM EAGLE (See Mighty Midget, Marvel Super Heroes #16 & Wow #6)

PHANTOM FORCE
Image Comics/Genesis West #0, 3-7: 12/93 - #2, 1994; #0, 3/94; #3, 5/94 - #8, 10/94 ($2.50/$3.50, limited series)
0 (3/94, $2.50)-Kirby/Jim Lee-c; Kirby-p pgs. 1,5,24-29. 4.00
1 (12/93, $2.50)-Polybagged w/trading card; Kirby/Liefeld-c; Kirby plots/pencils w/inks by Liefeld, McFarlane, Jim Lee, Silvestri, Larsen, Williams, Ordway & Miki 4.00
2 ($3.50)-Kirby-a(p); Kirby/Larson-c 5.00
3-8: 3-(5/94, $2.50)-Kirby/McFarlane-c 4-(5/94)-Kirby-c(p). 5-(6/94) 4.00

PHANTOM GUARD
Image Comics (WildStorm Productions): Oct, 1997 - No. 6, Mar, 1998 ($2.50)
1-6: 1-Two covers 3.00
1-($3.50)-Voyager Pack w/Wildcore preview 4.00

PHANTOM JACK
Image Comics: Mar, 2004 - No. 5, July, 2004 ($2.95)
1-5-Mike San Giacomo-s/Mitchell Breitweiser-a. 4-Initial printings with errors exist 3.00
The Collected Edition (Speakeasy Comics, 2005, $17.99) r/series; Bendis intro 18.00

PHANTOM LADY (1st Series) (My Love Secret #24 on) (Also see All Top, Daring Adventures, Freedom Fighters, Jungle Thrills, & Wonder Boy)
Fox Features Syndicate: No. 13, Aug, 1947 - No. 23, Apr, 1949
13(#1)-Phantom Lady by Matt Baker begins (see Police Comics #1 for 1st app.); Blue Beetle story 432 864 1296 3154 5577 8000
14-16: 14(#2)-Not Baker-c. 15-P.L. injected with experimental drug. 16-Negligee-c, panels; true crime stories begin 300 600 900 1920 3310 4700
17-Classic bondage cover; used in **SOTI**, illo "Sexual stimulation by combining 'headlights' with the sadist's dream of tying up a woman" 1300 2600 3900 10,000 17,500 25,000
18,19 258 516 774 1651 2826 4000
20-22 226 452 678 1446 2473 3500
23-Classic bondage-c 541 1082 1623 3950 6975 10,000
NOTE: ***Matt Baker** a-in all; c-13, 15-21. **Kamen** a-22, 23.*

PHANTOM LADY (2nd Series) (See Terrific Comics) (Formerly Linda)
Ajax/Farrell Publ.: V1#5, Dec-Jan, 1954/1955 - No. 4, June, 1955
V1#5(#1)-By Matt Baker 155 310 465 992 1696 2400
V1#2-Last pre-code 107 214 321 680 1165 1650
3,4-Red Rocket. 3-Heroin story 87 174 261 553 952 1350

PHANTOM LADY
Verotik Publications: 1994 ($9.95)
1-Reprints G. A. stories from Phantom Lady and All Top Comics; Adam Hughes-c 12.00

PHANTOM LADY
DC Comics: Oct, 2012 - No. 4, Jan, 2013 ($2.99, limited series)
1-4-Gray and Palmiotti-s/Staggs-a. 1-Re-intro with Doll Man; Conner-c 3.00

PHANTOM PLANET, THE
Dell Publishing Co.: No. 1234, 1961
Four Color 1234-Movie 6 12 18 42 79 115

PHANTOM STRANGER, THE (1st Series)(See Saga of Swamp Thing)
National Periodical Publications: Aug-Sept, 1952 - No. 6, June-July, 1953

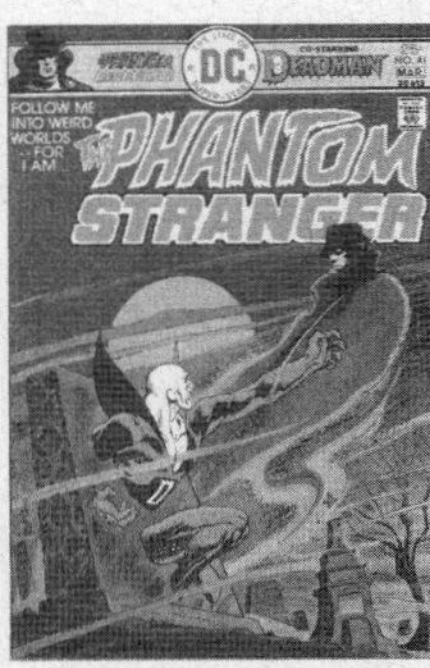

Phantom Stranger #41 © DC

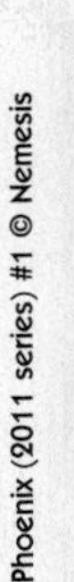

Phoenix (2011 series) #1 © Nemesis

Pictorial Romances #4 © STJ

	GD 2.0	VG 4.0	FN 6.0	VF 8.0	VF/NM 9.0	NM- 9.2
1(Scarce)-1st app.	343	686	1029	2400	4200	6000
2 (Scarce)	239	478	717	1530	2615	3700
3-6 (Scarce)	232	464	696	1485	2543	3600

Ashcan (8,9/52) Not distributed to newsstands, only for in house use (no known sales)

PHANTOM STRANGER, THE (2nd Series) (See Showcase #80) (See Showcase Presents for B&W reprints)
National Periodical Publs.: May-June, 1969 - No. 41, Feb-Mar, 1976; No. 42, Mar, 2010

	GD	VG	FN	VF	VF/NM	NM-
1-2nd S.A. app. P. Stranger; only 12¢ issue	11	22	33	73	157	240
2,3	6	12	18	38	69	100
4-1st new look Phantom Stranger; N. Adams-a	6	12	18	41	76	110
5-7	5	10	15	31	53	75
8-14: 14-Last 15¢ issue	4	8	12	23	37	50
15-19: All 25¢ giants (52 pgs.)	4	8	12	25	40	55
20-Dark Circle begins, ends #24.	3	6	9	16	24	32
21,22	3	6	9	14	20	25
23-Spawn of Frankenstein begins by Kaluta	4	8	12	25	40	55
24,25,27-30-Last Spawn of Frankenstein	3	6	9	19	30	40
26- Book-length story featuring Phantom Stranger, Dr. 13 & Spawn of Frankenstein	3	6	9	21	33	45
31-The Black Orchid begins (6-7/74).	3	6	9	18	28	38
32,34-38: 34-Last 20¢ issue (#35 on are 25¢)	2	4	6	13	18	22
33,39-41: 33-Deadman-c/story. 39-41-Deadman app.	3	6	9	14	20	25
42-(3/10, $2.99) Blackest Night one-shot; Syaf-a; Spectre, Deadman and Blue Devil app.						3.00

NOTE: ***N. Adams** a-4; c-3-19. **Anderson** a-4, 5i. **Aparo** a-7-17, 19-26; c-20-24, 33-41. **B. Bailey** a-27-30. **DeZuniga** a-12-16, 18, 19, 21, 22, 31, 34. **Grell** a-33. **Kaluta** a-23-25; c-26. **Meskin** r-15, 16, 18, 19. **Redondo** a-32, 35, 36. **Sparling** a-20. **Starr** a-17r. **Toth** a-15r. Black Orchid by **Carrilo**-38-41. Dr. 13 solo in-13, 18, 19, 20, 21, 34. Frankenstein by **Kaluta**-23-25; by **Baily**-27-30. No Black Orchid-33, 34, 37.*

PHANTOM STRANGER (See Justice League of America #103)
DC Comics: Oct, 1987 - No. 4, Jan, 1988 (75¢, limited series)

1-4-Mignola/Russell-c/a & Eclipso app. in all. 3,4-Eclipso-c 5.00

PHANTOM STRANGER (See intro. in DC Comics - The New 52 FCBD Special Edition) (Title changes to Trinity of Sin: The Phantom Stranger with #9 (Aug, 2013))
DC Comics: No. 0, Nov, 2012 - No. 22, Oct, 2015 ($2.99)

0-22: 0-Origin retold; Spectre app.; DiDio-s/Anderson-a. 2-Pandora app. 4,5-Jae Lee-c; Justice League Dark app. 6,7-Gene Ha-a/c; The Question app. 11-Trinity War. 12-17-Forever Evil tie-in. 18-Superman app. 20-The Spectre app. 3.00

...: Future's End (11/14, $3.99) 3-D lenticular cover; five years later; Winslade-a 4.00

...: Future's End (11/14, $2.99) regular cover; five years later 3.00

PHANTOM STRANGER (See Vertigo Visions-The Phantom Stranger)

PHANTOM: THE GHOST WHO WALKS
Marvel Comics: Feb, 1995 - No. 3, Apr, 1995 ($2.95, limited series)

1-3 4.00

PHANTOM: THE GHOST WHO WALKS
Moonstone: 2003 ($16.95, TPB)

nn-Three new stories by Raab, Goulart, Collins, Blanco and others; Klauba painted-c 17.00

PHANTOM 2040 (TV cartoon)
Marvel Comics: May, 1995 - No. 4, Aug, 1995 ($1.50)

1-4-Based on animated series; Ditko-a(p) in all 4.00

PHANTOM WITCH DOCTOR (Also see Durango Kid #8 & Eerie #8)
Avon Periodicals: 1952

1-Kinstler-c/a (7 pgs.) 71 142 213 454 777 1100

PHANTOM ZONE, THE (See Adventure #283 & Superboy #100, 104)
DC Comics: January, 1982 - No. 4, April, 1982

1-4-Superman app. in all. 2-4: Batman, Green Lantern app. 4.00

NOTE: ***Colan** a-1-4p; c-1-4p. **Giordano** c-1-4i.*

PHAZE
Eclipse Comics: Apr, 1988 - No. 2, Oct, 1988 ($2.25)

1,2: 1-Sienkiewicz-c. 2-Gulacy painted-c 3.00

PHIL RIZZUTO (Baseball Hero)(See Sport Thrills, Accepted reprint)
Fawcett Publications: 1951 (New York Yankees)

nn-Photo-c 71 142 213 454 777 1100

PHOENIX
Atlas/Seaboard Publ.: Jan, 1975 - No. 4, Oct, 1975

1-Origin; Rovin-s/Amendola-a 2 4 6 11 16 20

2-4: 3-Origin & only app. The Dark Avenger. 4-New origin/costume The Protector (formerly Phoenix) 2 4 6 9 13 16

NOTE: ***Infantino** appears in #1, 2. **Austin** a-3i. **Thorne** c-3.*

PHOENIX
Ardden Entertainment (Atlas Comics): Mar, 2011 - No. 6, May, 2012 ($2.99)

1-6-Krueger & Deneen-s/Zachary-a; origin re-told 3.00

... Issue Zero - NY Comicon Edtion (10/10, $2.99) Dorien-a; origin prequel to #1 3.00

PHOENIX (...The Untold Story)
Marvel Comics Group: April, 1984 ($2.00, one-shot)

1-Byrne/Austin-r/X-Men #137 with original unpublished ending 2 4 6 8 10 12

PHOENIX RESURRECTION, THE
Malibu Comics (Ultraverse): 1995 - 1996 ($3.95)

Genesis #1 (12/95)-X-Men app; wraparound-c, Revelations #1 (12/95)-X-Men app; wraparound-c, Aftermath #1 (1/96)-X-Men app. 5.00

0-($1.95)-r/series 3.00

0-American Entertainment Ed. 4.00

PHOENIX WITHOUT ASHES
IDW Publishing: Aug, 2010 - No. 4, Nov, 2010 ($3.99, limited series)

1-4-Harlan Ellison-s/Alan Robinson-a 4.00

PHONOGRAM
Image Comics: Aug, 2006 - No. 6, May, 2007 ($3.50, limited series)

1-Gillen-s/McKelvie-a 15.00

2-6 5.00

PHONOGRAM: THE SINGLES CLUB (Volume 2)
Image Comics: Dec, 2008 - No. 7, Feb, 2010 ($3.50, limited series)

1-7-Gillen-s/McKelvie-a. 5-Recalled for bar-code error 4.00

PHONOGRAM (Volume 3)(The Immaterial Girl)
Image Comics: Aug, 2015 - No. 6, Jan, 2016 ($3.99, limited series)

1-6-Gillen-s/McKelvie-a 4.00

PICNIC PARTY (See Dell Giants)

PICTORIAL CONFESSIONS (Pictorial Romances #4 on)
St. John Publishing Co.: Sept, 1949 - No. 3, Dec, 1949

	GD	VG	FN	VF	VF/NM	NM-
1-Baker-c/a(3)	65	130	195	416	708	1000
2-Baker-a; photo-c	39	78	117	231	378	525
3-Kubert, Baker-a; part Kubert-c	40	80	120	246	411	575

PICTORIAL LOVE STORIES (Formerly Tim McCoy)
Charlton Comics: No. 22, Oct, 1949 - No. 26, July, 1950 (all photo-c)

22-26: All have "Me-Dan Cupid". 25-Fred Astaire-c 21 42 63 122 199 275

PICTORIAL LOVE STORIES
St. John Publishing Co.: October, 1952

1-Baker-c 41 82 123 256 428 600

PICTORIAL ROMANCES (Formerly Pictorial Confessions)
St. John Publ. Co.: No. 4, Jan, 1950; No. 5, Jan, 1951 - No. 24, Mar, 1954

	GD	VG	FN	VF	VF/NM	NM-
4-Baker-a; photo-c	45	90	135	284	480	675
5,10-All Matt Baker issues. 5-Reprints all stories from #4 w/new Baker-c	50	100	150	315	533	750
6-9,12,13,15,16-Baker-c, 2-3 stories	48	96	144	302	514	725
11-Baker-c/a(3); Kubert-r/Hollywood Confessions #1	50	100	150	315	533	750
14,21-24: Baker-c/a each. 21,24-Each has signed story by Estrada	53	106	159	334	567	800
17-20(7/53, 25¢, 100 pgs.): Baker-c/a; each has two signed stories by Estrada	97	194	291	621	1061	1500

NOTE: ***Matt Baker** art in most issues. **Estrada** a-17-20(2), 21, 24.*

PICTURE CRIMES
David McKay Publ.: June, 1937

1 (a GD+ copy sold in 2012 for $478)

PICTURE NEWS
Lafayette Street Corp.: Jan, 1946 - No. 10, Jan-Feb, 1947

	GD	VG	FN	VF	VF/NM	NM-
1-Milt Gross begins, ends No. 6; 4 pg. Kirby-a; A-Bomb-c/story	48	96	144	302	514	725
2-Atomic explosion panels; Frank Sinatra/Perry Como story	25	50	75	150	245	340
3-Atomic explosion panels; Frank Sinatra, June Allyson, Benny Goodman stories	22	44	66	132	216	300
4-Atomic explosion panels; "Caesar and Cleopatra" movie adapt. w/Claude Raines & Vivian Leigh; Jackie Robinson story	25	50	75	147	241	335

5-7: 5-Hank Greenberg story; Atomic explosion panel. 6-Joe Louis-c/story

The Pilgrim #2 © Ryan & Grell

Pinhead #2 © Clive Barker

Pinky and the Brain #20 © WB

GD 2.0 | VG 4.0 | FN 6.0 | VF 8.0 | VF/NM 9.0 | NM- 9.2

20 40 60 114 182 250

8,10: 8-Monte Hale story (9-10/46; 1st?). 10-Dick Quick; A-Bomb story; Krigstein, Gross-a 20 40 60 117 189 260

9-A-Bomb story; "Crooked Mile" movie adaptation; Joe DiMaggio story. 22 44 66 128 209 290

PICTURE PARADE (Picture Progress #5 on)
Gilberton Company (Also see A Christmas Adventure): Sept, 1953 - V1#4, Dec, 1953 (28 pgs.)

V1#1-Andy's Atomic Adventures; A-bomb blast-c; (Teachers version distributed to schools exists) 20 40 60 114 182 250
2-Around the World with the United Nations 12 24 36 69 97 125
3-Adventures of the Lost One(The American Indian), 4-A Christmas Adventure (r-under same title in 1969) 12 24 36 69 97 125

PICTURE PROGRESS (Formerly Picture Parade)
Gilberton Corp.: V1#5, Jan, 1954 - V3#2, Oct, 1955 (28-36 pgs.)

V1#5-9,V2#1-9: 5-News in Review 1953. 6-The Birth of America. 7-The Four Seasons. 8-Paul Revere's Ride. 9-The Hawaiian Islands(5/54). V2#1-The Story of Flight(9/54). 2-Vote for Crazy River (The Meaning of Elections). 3-Louis Pasteur. 4-The Star Spangled Banner. 5-News in Review 1954. 6-Alaska: The Great Land. 7-Life in the Circus. 8-The Time of the Cave Man. 9-Summer Fun(5/55) 9 18 27 50 65 80
V3#1,2: 1-The Man Who Discovered America. 2-The Lewis & Clark Expedition 9 18 27 47 61 75

PICTURE SCOPE JUNGLE ADVENTURES (See Jungle Thrills)

PICTURE STORIES FROM AMERICAN HISTORY
National/All-American/E. C. Comics: 1945 - No. 4, Sum, 1947 (#1,2: 10¢, 56 pgs.; #3,4: 15¢, 52 pgs.)

1 30 60 90 177 289 400
2-4 24 48 72 140 230 320

PICTURE STORIES FROM SCIENCE
E.C. Comics: Spring, 1947 - No. 2, Fall, 1947

1-(15¢) 30 60 90 177 289 400
2-(10¢) 24 48 72 140 230 320

PICTURE STORIES FROM THE BIBLE (See Narrative Illustration, the Story of the Comics by M.C. Gaines)
National/All-American/E.C. Comics: 1942 - No. 4, Fall, 1943; 1944-46

1-4('42-Fall, '43)-Old Testament (DC) 24 48 72 142 234 325
Complete Old Testament Edition, (12/43-DC, 50¢, 232 pgs.);-1st printing; contains #1-4; 2nd - 8th (1/47) printings exist; later printings by E.C. some with 65¢-c 32 64 96 192 314 435
Complete Old Testament Edition (1945-publ. by Bible Pictures Ltd.)-232 pgs., hardbound, in color with dust jacket 32 64 96 192 314 435

NOTE: *Both Old and New Testaments published in England by Bible Pictures Ltd. in hardback, 1943, in color, 376 pgs. (2 vols.: O.T. 232 pgs. & N.T. 144 pgs.), and were also published by Scarf Press in 1979 (Old Test., $9.95) and in 1980 (New Test., $7.95)*

1-3(New Test.; 1944-46, DC)-52 pgs. ea. 20 40 60 114 182 250
The Complete Life of Christ Edition (1945, 25¢, 96 pgs.)-Contains #1&2 of the New Testament Edition 32 64 96 192 314 435
1,2(Old Testament-r in comic book form)(E.C., 1946; 52 pgs.) 20 40 60 114 182 250
1(DC),2(AA),3(EC)(New Testament-r in comic book form)(E.C., 1946; 52 pgs.) 20 40 60 114 182 250
Complete New Testament Edition (1945-E.C., 40¢, 144 pgs.)-Contains #1-3 1946 printing has 50¢-c 32 64 96 192 314 435

NOTE: *Another British series entitled **The Bible Illustrated** from 1947 has recently been discovered, with the same internal artwork. This eight edition series (5-OT, 3-NT) is of particular interest to Classics Ill. collectors because it exactly copied the C.I. logo format. The British publisher was Thorpe & Porter, who in 1951 began publishing the British Classics Ill. series. All editions of The Bible Ill. have new British painted covers. While this market is still new, and not all editions have as yet been found, current market value is about the same as the first U.S. editions of Picture Stories From The Bible.*

PICTURE STORIES FROM WORLD HISTORY
E.C. Comics: Spring, 1947 - No. 2, Summer, 1947 (52, 48 pgs.)

1-(15¢) 30 60 90 177 289 400
2-(10¢) 24 48 72 140 230 320

PIGS
Image Comics: Sept, 2011 - No. 8, Aug, 2012 ($2.99)

1-8: 1-Cosby & McCool-s/Tamura-a/Jock-c. 3-Conner-c. 5-Gibbons-c. 7-Ramos-c 3.00

PILGRIM, THE
IDW Publishing: Apr, 2010 - No. 2, Jun, 2010 ($3.99, limited series)

1,2-Mike Grell-a/c; Mark Ryan-s 4.00

PILOT SEASON...
Image Comics (Top Cow): 2008 - 2011 ($1.00/$2.99/$3.99, one-shots)

...: Asset (9/10, $3.99) Sablik-s/Marquez-a/Frison-c 4.00
...: City of Refuge (10/11, $3.99) Foehl-s/Calero-a/c 4.00
...: Crosshair (10/10, $3.99) Katz-s/Jefferson-a/Silvestri-c 4.00
...: Declassified (10/09, $1.00) Preview of one-shots with covers, script and sketch pgs. 3.00
...: Demonic (1/10, $2.99) Kirkman-s/Benitez-a; two covers by Silvestri 3.00
...: Fleshdigger (10/11, $3.99) Denton & Keene-s; Sanchez-a; Francavilla-c 4.00
...: Forever (10/10, $3.99) Inglesby-s/Nachlik-a/Hutomo-c 4.00
...: Murdered (11/09, $2.99) Kirkman-s/Blake-a; two covers by Silvestri 3.00
...: 7 Days From Hell (10/10, $3.99) Noto-a/Hill & Levin-s/Stelfreeze-c 4.00
...: Stellar (7/10, $2.99) Kirkman-s/Chang-a/Silvestri-c 3.00
...: The Beauty (10/11, $3.99) Haun & Hurley-s/Haun-a/c (becomes a 2015 series) 10.00
...: The Test (10/10, $3.99) Fialkov-s/Ekedal-a/Hutomo-c 4.00
...: 39 Minutes (9/10, $3.99) Harms-s/Lando-a/Albuquerque-c 4.00
...: Twilight Guardian (5/08, $3.99) Hickman-s 4.00

PINHEAD
Marvel Comics (Epic Comics): Dec, 1993 - No. 6, May, 1994 ($2.50)

1-($2.95)-Embossed foil-c by Kelley Jones; Intro Pinhead & Disciples (Snakeoil, Hangman, Fan Dancer & Dixie) 4.00
2-6 3.00

PINHEAD & FOODINI (TV)(Also see Foodini & Jingle Dingle Christmas...)
Fawcett Publications: July, 1951 - No. 4, Jan, 1952 (Early TV comic)

1-(52 pgs.)-Photo-c; based on TV puppet show 32 64 96 188 307 425
2,3-Photo-c 16 32 48 94 147 200
4 14 28 42 80 115 150

PINHEAD VS. MARSHALL LAW (Law in Hell)
Marvel Comics (Epic): Nov, 1993 - No. 2, Dec, 1993 ($2.95, lim. series)

1,2: 1-Embossed red foil-c. 2-Embossed silver foil-c 4.00

PINK DUST
Kitchen Sink Press: 1998 ($3.50, B&W, mature)

1-J. O'Barr-s/a 3.50

PINK PANTHER, THE (TV)(See The Inspector & Kite Fun Book)
Gold Key #1-70/Whitman #71-87: April, 1971 - No. 87, Mar, 1984

1-The Inspector begins 5 10 15 34 60 85
2-5 3 6 9 17 26 35
6-10 3 6 9 14 19 24
11-30: Warren Tufts-a #16-on 2 4 6 9 13 16
31-60 2 4 6 8 11 14
61-70 1 2 3 5 7 9
71-74,81-83: 81(2/82), 82(3/82), 83(4/82) 2 4 6 8 10 12
75(8/80)-77 (Whitman pre-pack) (scarce) 4 8 12 25 40 55
78(1/81)-80 (Whitman pre-pack) (not as scarce) 2 4 6 10 14 18
78 (1/81, 40¢-c) Cover price error variant 3 6 9 14 20 26
84-87(All #90266 on-c, no date or date code): 84(6/83), 85(8/83), 87(3/84) 3 6 9 14 20 26
Mini-comic No. 1(1976)(3-1/4x6-1/2") 1 3 4 6 8 10

NOTE: *Pink Panther began as a movie cartoon. (See Golden Comics Digest #38, 45 and March of Comics #376, 384, 390, 409, 418, 429, 441, 449, 461, 473, 486); #37, 72, 80-85 contain reprints.*

PINK PANTHER SUPER SPECIAL (TV)
Harvey Comics: Oct, 1993 ($2.25, 68 pgs.)

V2#1-The Inspector & Wendy Witch stories also 4.00

PINK PANTHER, THE
Harvey Comics: Nov, 1993 - No. 9, July, 1994 ($1.50)

V2#1-9 3.00

PINK PANTHER, THE (Volume 3)
American Mythology Productions: 2016 - Present ($3.99)

1-4-New and classic short stories by various; multiple covers on each. 4-Trick or Pink 4.00
...: Cartoon Hour Special (2017, $4.99) Short stories by various; 3 covers 5.00
...: Snow Day (2017, $3.99) New short stories by S.A. Check and reprint; 3 covers 4.00

PINKY & THE BRAIN (See Animaniacs)
DC Comics: July, 1996 - No. 27, Nov, 1998 ($1.75/$1.95/$1.99)

1-27, ...Christmas Special (1/96, $1.50) 3.00

PINKY LEE (See Adventures of...)

PINKY THE EGGHEAD
I.W./Super Comics: 1963 (Reprints from Noodnik)

I.W. Reprint #1,2(nd) 2 4 6 8 11 14

Pioneer Picture Stories #2 © CNast

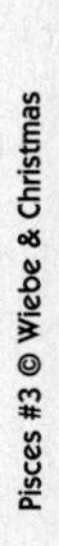

Pisces #3 © Wiebe & Christmas

Planetary #5 © WSP

	GD 2.0	VG 4.0	FN 6.0	VF 8.0	VF/NM 9.0	NM- 9.2

Super Reprint #14-r/Noodnik Comics #4 2 4 6 8 11 14

PINOCCHIO (See 4-Color #92, 252, 545, 1203, Mickey Mouse Mag. V5#3, Movie Comics under Wonderful Advs. of..., New Advs. of..., Thrilling Comics #2, Walt Disney Showcase, Walt Disney's..., Wonderful Advs. of..., & World's Greatest Stories #2)
Dell Publishing Co.: No. 92, 1945 - No. 1203, Mar, 1962 (Disney)

Four Color 92-The Wonderful Adventures of...; 16 pg. Donald Duck story ; entire book by Kelly 46 92 138 359 805 1250
Four Color 252 (10/49)-Origin, not by Kelly 11 22 33 72 154 235
Four Color 545 (3/54)-The Wonderful Advs. of...; part-r of 4-Color #92; Disney-movie 8 16 24 51 96 140
Four Color 1203 (3/62) 6 12 18 40 73 105

PINOCCHIO AND THE EMPEROR OF THE NIGHT
Marvel Comics: Mar, 1988 ($1.25, 52 pgs.)

1-Adapts film 4.00

PINOCCHIO LEARNS ABOUT KITES (See Kite Fun Book)

PIN-UP PETE (Also see Great Lover Romances & Monty Hall...)
Toby Press: 1952

1-Jack Sparling pin-ups 21 42 63 124 202 280

PIONEER MARSHAL (See Fawcett Movie Comics)

PIONEER PICTURE STORIES
Street & Smith Publications: Dec, 1941 - No. 9, Dec, 1943

1-The Legless Air Ace begins; WWII-c 52 104 156 328 552 775
2 -True life story of Errol Flynn 24 48 72 142 234 325
3-5,7-9 21 42 63 122 199 275
6-Classic Japanese WWII "Remember Pearl Harbor"-c 77 154 231 493 847 1200

PIONEER WEST ROMANCES (Firehair #1,2,7-11)
Fiction House Magazines: No. 3, Spring, 1950 - No. 6, Winter, 1950-51

3-(52 pgs.)-Firehair continues 19 38 57 109 172 235
4-6 19 38 57 109 172 235

PIPSQUEAK (See The Adventures of...)

PIRACY
E. C. Comics: Oct-Nov, 1954 - No. 7, Oct-Nov, 1955

1-Williamson/Torres-a 31 62 93 248 392 535
2-Williamson/Torres-a 20 40 60 160 255 350
3-7: 5-7-Comics Code symbol on cover 16 32 48 128 202 275

NOTE: ***Crandall** a-in all; c-2-4. **Davis** a-1, 2, 6. **Evans** a-3-7; c-7. **Ingels** a-3-7. **Krigstein** a-3-5, 7; c-5, 6. **Wood** a-1, 2; c-1.*

PIRACY
Gemstone Publishing: March, 1998 - No. 7, Sept, 1998 ($2.50)

1-7: E.C. reprints 4.00
Annual 1 ($10.95) Collects #1-4 11.00
Annual 2 ($7.95) Collects #5-7 8.00

PIRANA (See The Phantom #46 & Thrill-O-Rama #2, 3)

PIRATE CORP$, THE (See Hectic Planet)
Eternity Comics/Slave Labor Graphics: 1987 - No. 4, 1988 ($1.95)

1-4: 1,2-Color. 3,4-B&W 3.00
Special 1 ('89, B&W)-Slave Labor Publ. 3.00

PIRATE CORP$, THE (Volume 2)
Slave Labor Graphics: 1989 - No. 6, 1992 ($1.95)

1-6-Dorkin-s/a 3.00

PIRATE OF THE GULF, THE (See Superior Stories #2)

PIRATES COMICS
Hillman Periodicals: Feb-Mar, 1950 - No. 4, Aug-Sept, 1950 (All 52 pgs.)

1 26 52 78 154 252 350
2-Dave Berg-a 17 34 51 98 154 210
3,4-Berg-a 15 30 45 88 137 185

PIRATES OF CONEY ISLAND, THE
Image Comics: Oct, 2006 - No. 8 ($2.99)

1-6-Rick Spears-s/Vasilis Lolos-a; two covers. 2-Cloonan var-c 3.00

PIRATES OF DARK WATER, THE (Hanna Barbera)
Marvel Comics: Nov, 1991 - No. 9, Aug, 1992 ($1.95)

1-9: 9-Vess-c 3.00

PISCES
Image Comics: Apr, 2015 - No. 3, Jul, 2015 ($3.50/$3.99, unfinished series)

1-3-Kurtis Wiebe-s/Johnnie Christmas-a 4.00

P.I.'S: MICHAEL MAUSER AND MS. TREE, THE
First Comics: Jan, 1985 - No. 3, May, 1985 ($1.25, limited series)

1-3: Staton-c/a(p) 3.00

PITT, THE (Also see The Draft & The War)
Marvel Comics: Mar, 1988 ($3.25, 52 pgs., one-shot)

1-Ties into Starbrand, D.P.7 4.00

PITT (See Youngblood #4 & Gen 13 #3,#4)
Image Comics #1-9/Full Bleed #1/2,10-on: Jan, 1993 - No. 20 ($1.95, intended as a four part limited series)

1/2-(12/95)-1st Full Bleed issue 4.00
1-Dale Keown-c/a. 1-1st app. The Pitt 5.00
2-13: All Dale Keown-c/a. 3 (Low distribution). 10 (1/96)-Indicia reads "January 1995" 3.00
14-20: 14-Begin $2.50-c, pullout poster 3.00
TPB-(1997, $9.95) r/#1/2, 1-4 12.00
TPB 2-(1999, $11.95) r/#5-9 12.00

PITT CREW
Full Bleed Studios: Aug, 1998 - No. 5, Dec, 1999 ($2.50)

1-5: 1-Richard Pace-s/Ken Lashley-a. 2-4-Scott Lee-a 3.00

PITT IN THE BLOOD
Full Bleed Studios: Aug, 1996 ($2.50, one-shot)

nn-Richard Pace-a/script 3.00

PIXIE & DIXIE & MR. JINKS (TV)(See Jinks, Pixie, and Dixie & Whitman Comic Books)
Dell Publishing Co./Gold Key: July-Sept, 1960 - Feb, 1963 (Hanna-Barbera)

Four Color 1112 7 14 21 49 92 135
Four Color 1196,1264, 01-631-207 (Dell, 7/62) 5 10 15 35 63 90
1(2/63-Gold Key) 6 12 18 37 66 95

PIXIE PUZZLE ROCKET TO ADVENTURELAND
Avon Periodicals: Nov, 1952

1 21 42 63 122 199 275

PIXIES, THE (Advs. of...)(The Mighty Atom and ...#6 on)(See A-1 Comics #16)
Magazine Enterprises: Winter, 1946 - No. 4, Fall?, 1947; No. 5, 1948

1-Mighty Atom 10 20 30 58 79 100
2-5-Mighty Atom 7 14 21 35 43 50
I.W. Reprint #1(1958), 8-(Pee-Wee Pixies), 10-I.W. on cover, Super on inside 2 4 6 8 11 14

PIZZAZZ
Marvel Comics: Oct, 1977 - No. 16, Jan, 1979 (slick-color kids mag. w/puzzles, games, comics)

1-Star Wars photo-c/article; origin Tarzan; KISS photos/article; Iron-On bonus; 2 pg. pin-up calendars thru #8 3 6 9 19 30 40
2-Spider-Man-c; Beatles pin-up calendar 2 4 6 13 18 22
3-8: 3-Close Encounters-s; Bradbury-s. 4-Alice Cooper, Travolta; Charlie's Angels/Fonz/Hulk/Spider-Man-c. 5-Star Trek quiz. 6-Asimov-s. 7-James Bond; Spock/Darth Vader-c. 8-TV Spider-Man photo-c/article 2 4 6 11 16 20
9-14: 9-Shaun Cassidy-c. 10-Sgt. Pepper-c/s. 12-Battlestar Galactica-s; Spider-Man app. 13-TV Hulk-c/s. 14-Meatloaf-c/s 2 4 6 10 14 18
15,16: 15-Battlestar Galactica-s. 16-Movie Superman photo-c/s, Hulk. 2 4 6 11 16 20

NOTE: ***Star Wars** comics in all (1-6:Chaykin-a, 7-9: DeZuniga-a, 10-13:Simonson/Janson-a. 14-16:Cockrum-a). **Tarzan** comics, 1pg.-#1-8. 1pg. "Hey Look" by Kurtzman #12-16.*

PLANETARY (See Preview in flip book Gen13 #33)
DC Comics (WildStorm Prod.): Apr, 1999 - No. 27, Dec, 2009 ($2.50/$2.95/$2.99)

1-Ellis-s/Cassaday-a/c 2 4 6 8 10 12
1-Special Edition (6/09, $1.00) r/#1 with "After Watchmen" cover frame 3.00
2-5 6.00
6-10 5.00
11-15: 12-Fourth Man revealed 4.00
16-26: 16-Begin $2.95-c. 23-Origin of The Drummer 3.00
27-($3.99) Wraparound gatefold-c 4.00
...: All Over the World and Other Stories (2000, $14.95) r/#1-6 & Preview 15.00
...: All Over the World and Other Stories-Hardcover (2000, $24.95) r/#1-6 & Preview; with dustjacket 25.00
.../Batman: Night on Earth 1 (8/03, $5.95) Ellis-s/Cassaday-a 6.00
...: Crossing Worlds (2004, $14.95) r/Batman, JLA, and The Authority x-overs 15.00
.../JLA: Terra Occulta (11/02, $5.95) Elseworlds; Ellis-s/Ordway-a 6.00
...: Leaving the 20th Century -HC (2004, $24.95) r/#13-18 25.00
...: Leaving the 20th Century -SC (2004, $14.99) r/#13-18 15.00

Planet Comics #14 © FH

Planet Hulk #5 © MAR

Plastic Man #31 © QUA

GD VG FN VF VF/NM NM-
2.0 4.0 6.0 8.0 9.0 9.2

...: Spacetime Archaeology -HC (2010, $24.99) r/#19-27 25.00
...: Spacetime Archaeology -SC (2010, $17.99) r/#19-27 18.00
.../The Authority: Ruling the World (8/00, $5.95) Ellis-s/Phil Jimenez-a 6.00
...: The Fourth Man -Hardcover (2001, $24.95) r/#7-12 25.00
...: The Planetary Reader (8/03, $5.95) r/#13-15 6.00

PLANETARY BRIGADE (Also see Hero Squared)
BOOM! Studios: Feb, 2006 - No. 2, Mar, 2006 ($2.99)

1-3-Giffen & DeMatteis-s/art by various; Haley-c 3.00
... Origins 1-3 (10/06-4/07, $3.99) Giffen & DeMatteis-s/Julia Bax-a 4.00

PLANET COMICS
Fiction House Magazines: 1/40 - No. 62, 9/49; No. 63, Wint, 1949-50; No. 64, Spring, 1950; No. 65, 1951(nd); No. 66-68, 1952(nd); No. 69, Wint, 1952-53; No. 70-72, 1953(nd); No. 73, Winter, 1953-54

1-Origin Auro, Lord of Jupiter by Briefer (ends #61); Flint Baker & The Red Comet begin; Eisner/Fine-c 1275 2550 3825 9500 17,750 26,000
2-Lou Fine-c (Scarce) 568 1136 1704 4146 7323 10,500
3-Eisner-c 389 778 1167 2723 4762 6800
4-Gale Allen and the Girl Squadron begins 331 662 993 2317 4059 5800
5,6-(Scarce): 5-Eisner/Fine-c 354 708 1062 2478 4339 6200
7-12: 8-Robot-c. 12-The Star Pirate begins 284 568 852 1818 3109 4400
13,14: 13-Reff Ryan begins 245 490 735 1568 2684 3800
15-(Scarce)-Mars, God of War begins (11/41); see Jumbo Comics #31 for 1st app. 649 1298 1947 4738 8369 12,000
16-20,22 174 348 522 1114 1907 2700
21-The Lost World & Hunt Bowman begin 181 362 543 1158 1979 2800
23-26: 26-Space Rangers begin (9/43), end #71 155 310 465 992 1696 2400
27-30 123 246 369 787 1344 1900
31-35: 33-Origin Star Pirates Wonder Boots, reprinted in #52. 35-Mysta of the Moon begins, ends #62 110 220 330 704 1202 1700
36-45: 38-1st Mysta of the Moon-c. 41-New origin of "Auro, Lord of Jupiter". 42-Last Gale Allen. 43-Futura begins 97 194 291 621 1061 1500
46-60: 48-Robot-c. 53-Used in **SOTI**, pg. 32 81 162 243 518 884 1250
61-68,70: 64,70-Robot-c. 65-70-All partial-r of earlier issues. 70-r/stories from #41 66 132 198 419 722 1025
69-Used in **POP**, pgs. 101,102 68 136 204 435 743 1050
71-73-No series stories. 71-Space Rangers strip 58 116 174 371 636 900
I.W. Reprint 1,8,9: 1(nd)-r/#70; cover-r from Attack on Planet Mars. 8 (r/#72), 9-r/#73 8 16 24 54 102 150

NOTE: ***Anderson*** *a-33-38, 40-51 (Star Pirate).* ***Matt Baker*** *a-53-59 (Mysta of the Moon).* ***Celardo*** *c-12.* ***Bill Discount*** *a-71 (Space Rangers).* ***Elias*** *c-70.* ***Evans*** *a-46-49 (Auro, Lord of Jupiter), 50-64 (Lost World).* ***Fine*** *c-2, 5.* ***Hopper*** *a-31, 35 (Gale Allen), 41, 42, 48, 49 (Mysta of the Moon).* ***Ingels*** *a-24-31 (Lost World), 56-61 (Auro, Lord of Jupiter).* ***Lubbers*** *a-44-47 (Space Rangers); c-40, 41.* ***Moreira*** *a-43, 44 (Mysta of the Moon).* ***Renee*** *a-40-49 (Lost World); c-33, 35, 39.* ***Tuska*** *a-30 (Star Pirate).* ***M. Whitman*** *a-50-52 (Mysta of the Moon), 53-58 (Star Pirate); c-71-73.* ***Starr*** *a-59.* ***Zolnerwich*** *c-10. 13-25. Bondage c-53.*

PLANET COMICS
Pacific Comics: 1984 ($5.95)

1-Reprints Planet Comics #1(1940) 1 2 3 5 6 8

PLANET COMICS
Blackthorne Publishing: Apr, 1988 - No. 3 ($2.00, color/B&W #3)

1-New stories; Dave Stevens-c 2 4 6 13 18 22
2,3: New stories 6.00

PLANET HULK (See Incredible Hulk and Giant-Size Hulk #1 (2006))

PLANET HULK (Secret Wars tie-in)
Marvel Comics: Jul, 2015 - No. 5, Nov, 2015 ($4.99/$3.99, limited series)

1-($4.99) Humphries-s/Laming-a; Steve Rogers app.; back-up Pak-s//Miyazawa-a 5.00
2-5-($3.99) Doc Green & Devil Dinosaur app. 4.00

PLANET OF THE APES (Magazine) (Also see Adventures on the... & Power Record Comics)
Marvel Comics Group: Aug, 1974 - No. 29, Feb, 1977 (B&W) (Based on movies)

1-Ploog-a 4 8 12 25 40 55
2-Ploog-a 3 6 9 16 24 32
3-10 3 6 9 14 20 26
11-20 3 6 9 15 22 28
21-28 (low distribution) 3 6 9 19 30 40
29 (low distribution) 5 10 15 33 57 80

NOTE: ***Alcala*** *a-7-11, 17-22, 24.* ***Ploog*** *a-1-4, 6, 8, 11, 13, 14, 19.* ***Sutton*** *a-11, 12, 15, 17, 19, 20, 23, 24, 29.* ***Tuska*** *a-1-6.*

PLANET OF THE APES
Adventure Comics: Apr, 1990 - No. 24, 1992 ($2.50, B&W)

1-New movie tie-in; comes w/outer-c (3 colors) 4.00
1-Limited serial numbered edition ($5.00) 1 2 3 5 6 8
1-2nd printing (no outer-c, $2.50) 3.00

GD VG FN VF VF/NM NM-
2.0 4.0 6.0 8.0 9.0 9.2

2-24 3.00
Annual 1 ($3.50) 4.00
...Urchak's Folly 1-4 ($2.50, mini-series) 3.00

PLANET OF THE APES (The Human War)
Dark Horse Comics: Jun, 2001 - No. 3, Aug, 2001 ($2.99, limited series)

1-3-Follows the 2001 movie; Edginton-s 3.00

PLANET OF THE APES
Dark Horse Comics: Sept, 2001 - No. 6, Feb, 2002 ($2.99, ongoing series)

1-6: 1-3-Edginton-s. 1-Photo & Wagner covers. 2-Plunkett & photo-c 3.00

PLANET OF THE APES
BOOM! Studios: Apr, 2011 - No. 15, Jun, 2012 ($3.99)

1-4,6-15-Takes place 1200 years before Taylor's arrival; Magno-a; three covers 4.00
5-($1.00) Three covers 3.00
Annual 1 (8/12, $4.99) Short stories by various; six covers 5.00
Giant 1 (9/13, $4.99) Gregory-s/Barreto-a 5.00
Special 1 (2/13, $4.99) Continued from #15; Diego Barreto-a 5.00
Spectacular 1 (7/13, $4.99) Gregory-s/Barreto-a 5.00

PLANET OF THE APES: CATACLYSM
BOOM! Studios: Sept, 2012 - No. 12, Aug, 2013 ($3.99)

1-12-Takes place 8 years before Taylor's arrival; Couceiro-a. 1-Multiple covers 4.00

PLANET OF THE APES/ GREEN LANTERN
BOOM! Studios: Feb, 2017 - No. 6 ($3.99, limited series)

1-Bagenda-a; Hal Jordan & Sinestro on the POTA; Cornelius app.; multiple covers 4.00

PLANET OF VAMPIRES
Seaboard Publications (Atlas): Feb, 1975 - No. 3, July, 1975

1-Neal Adams-c(i); 1st Broderick-c/a(p); Hama-s 3 6 9 15 22 28
2,3: 2-Neal Adams-c. 3-Heath-c/a 2 4 6 10 14 18

PLANET TERRY
Marvel Comics (Star Comics)/Marvel: April, 1985 - No. 12, March, 1986 (Children's comic)

1-12 5.00
1-Variant with "Star Chase" game on last page & inside back-c 15.00

PLANTS VS. ZOMBIES (Based on the Electronic Arts game)
Dark Horse Comics: Jun, 2015 - No. 12, Jun, 2016 ($2.99)

1-12: 1-3-Bully For You; Tobin-s/Chan-a. 4-6-Grown Sweet Home. 7-9-Petal to the Metal 3.00
...: Garden Warfare 1-3 (10/15 - No. 3, 12/15, $2.99) Tobin-s/Chabot-a 3.00

PLASM (See Warriors of Plasm)
Defiant Comics: June, 1993

0-Came bound into Diamond Previews V3#6 (6/93); price is for complete Previews with comic still attached 5.00
0-Comic only removed from Previews 3.00

PLASMER
Marvel Comics UK: Nov, 1993 - No. 4, Feb, 1994 ($1.95, limited series)

1-($2.50)-Polybagged w/4 trading cards 4.00
2-4: Capt. America & Silver Surfer app. 3.00

PLASTIC FORKS
Marvel Comis (Epic Comics): 1990 - No. 5, 1990 ($4.95, 68 pgs., limited series, mature)

Book 1-5: Squarebound 5.00

PLASTIC MAN (Also see Police Comics & Smash Comics #17)
Vital Publ. No. 1,2/Quality Comics No. 3 on: Sum, 1943 - No. 64, Nov, 1956

nn(#1)- "In The Game of Death"; Skull-c; Jack Cole-c/a begins; ends-#64? 454 908 1362 3314 5857 8400
nn(#2, 2/44)- "The Gay Nineties Nightmare" 181 362 543 1158 1979 2800
3 (Spr, '46) 118 236 354 749 1287 1825
4 (Sum, '46) 89 178 267 565 970 1375
5 (Aut, '46) 73 146 219 467 796 1125
6-10 60 120 180 381 653 925
11-15,17-20 53 106 159 334 567 800
16-Classic-c 61 122 183 390 670 950
21-30: 26-Last non-r issue? 41 82 123 256 428 600
31-40: 40-Used in POP, pg. 91 34 68 102 199 325 450
41-64: 53-Last precode issue. 54-Robot-c. 64-Sci-fi-c 28 56 84 165 270 375
Super Reprint 11,16,18: 11('63)-r/#16. 16-r/#18 & #21; Cole-a. 18('64)-Spirit-r by Eisner from Police #95 4 8 12 24 37 50

NOTE: ***Cole*** *r-44, 49, 56, 58, 59 at least.* ***Cuidera*** *c-32-64i.*

PLASTIC MAN (See DC Special #15 & House of Mystery #160)

Plop! #19 © DC

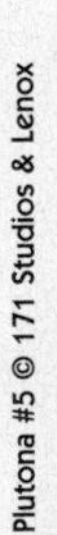

Plutona #5 © 171 Studios & Lenox

Poe Dameron #1 © Lucasfilm

National Periodical Publications/DC Comics: 11-12/66 - No. 10, 5-6/68; V4#11, 2-3/76 - No. 20, 10-11/77

	GD 2.0	VG 4.0	FN 6.0	VF 8.0	VF/NM 9.0	NM- 9.2
1-Real 1st app. Silver Age Plastic Man (House of Mystery #160 is actually tryout); Gil Kane-c/a; 12¢ issues begin	10	20	30	68	144	220
2-5: 4-Infantino-c; Mortimer-a	5	10	15	31	53	75
6-10('68): 7-G.A. Plastic Man & Woozy Winks (1st S.A. app.) app.; origin retold. 10-Sparling-a; last 12¢ issue	4	8	12	27	44	60
V4#11('76)-20: 11-20-Fradon-p. 17-Origin retold	2	4	6	8	11	14
...80-Page Giant (2003, $6.95) reprints origin and other stories in 80-Pg. Giant format						7.00
...Special 1 (8/99, $3.95)						4.00

PLASTIC MAN
DC Comics: Nov, 1988 - No. 4, Feb, 1989 ($1.00, mini-series)

1-4: 1-Origin; Woozy Winks app. 4.00

PLASTIC MAN
DC Comics: Feb, 2004 - No. 20, Mar, 2006 ($2.95/$2.99)

1-20-Kyle Baker-s/a in most. 1-Retells origin. 7,12-Scott Morse-s/a. 8-JLA cameo 3.00
...: On the Lam TPB (2004, $14.95) r/#1-6 15.00
...: Rubber Bandits TPB (2005, $14.99) r/#8-11,13,14 15.00

PLASTRON CAFE
Mirage Studios: Dec, 1992 - No. 4, July, 1993 ($2.25, B&W)

1-4: 1-Teenage Mutant Ninja Turtles app.; Kelly Freas-c. 2-Hildebrandt painted-c. 4-Spaced & Alien Fire stories 3.00

PLAYFUL LITTLE AUDREY (TV)(Also see Little Audrey #25)
Harvey Publications: 6/57 - No. 110, 11/73; No. 111, 8/74 - No. 121, 4/76

	GD 2.0	VG 4.0	FN 6.0	VF 8.0	VF/NM 9.0	NM- 9.2
1	27	54	81	189	420	650
2	11	22	33	76	163	250
3-5	8	16	24	54	102	150
6-10	6	12	18	40	73	105
11-20	5	10	15	31	53	75
21-40	4	8	12	25	40	55
41-60	3	6	9	19	30	40
61-84: 84-Last 12¢ issue	3	6	9	15	22	28
85-99	2	4	6	11	16	20
100-52 pg. Giant	3	6	9	16	23	30
101-103: 52 pg. Giants	3	6	9	14	20	25
104-121	1	3	4	6	8	10
...In 3-D (Spring, 1988, $2.25, Blackthorne #66)						4.00

PLOP! (Also see The Best of DC #60,63 digests)
National Periodical Publications: Sept-Oct, 1973 - No. 24, Nov-Dec, 1976

	GD 2.0	VG 4.0	FN 6.0	VF 8.0	VF/NM 9.0	NM- 9.2
1-Sergio Aragonés-a begins; Wrightson-a	4	8	12	23	37	50
2-4,6-20	3	6	9	14	20	26
5-Wrightson-a	3	6	9	15	22	28
21-24 (52 pgs.). 23-No Aragonés-a; Lord of the Rings parody with Wally Wood-s/a	3	6	9	16	23	30

NOTE: ***Alcala*** *a-1-3.* ***Anderson*** *a-5.* ***Aragonés*** *a-1-22, 24.* ***Ditko*** *a-16p.* ***Evans*** *a-1.* ***Mayer*** *a-1.* ***Orlando*** *a-21, 22; c-21.* ***Sekowsky*** *a-5, 6p.* ***Toth*** *a-11.* ***Wolverton*** *r-4, 22-24(1 pg.ea.); c-1-12, 14, 17, 18.* ***Wood*** *a-14, 16i, 18-24; c-13, 15, 16, 19.*

PLUTO (See Cheerios Premiums, Four Color #537, Mickey Mouse Magazine, Walt Disney Showcase #4, 7, 13, 20, 23, 33 & Wheaties)
Dell Publ. Co.: No. 7, 1942; No. 429, 10/52 - No. 1248, 11-1/61-62 (Disney)

	GD 2.0	VG 4.0	FN 6.0	VF 8.0	VF/NM 9.0	NM- 9.2
Large Feature Comic 7(1942)-Written by Carl Barks, Jack Hannah, & Nick George (Barks' 1st comic book work)	200	400	600	1280	2190	3100
Four Color 429 (#1)	10	20	30	68	144	220
Four Color 509	6	12	18	42	79	115
Four Color 595,654,736,853	6	12	18	37	66	95
Four Color 941,1039,1143,1248	5	10	15	33	57	80

PLUTONA
Image Comics: Sept, 2015 - No. 5 ($2.99)

1-4-Lemire-s/Lenox-a 3.00

POCKET CLASSICS
Academic Inc. Publications: 1984 (B&W, 4 1/4" x 6 3/4", 68 pages)

C1(Black Beauty. C2(The Call of the Wild). C3(Dr. Jekyll and Mr. Hyde). C4(Dracula). C5(Frankenstein). C6(Huckleberry Finn). C7(Moby Dick). C8(The Red Badge of Courage). C9(The Time Machine). C10(Tom Sawyer). C11(Treasure Island). C12(20,000 Leagues Under the Sea). C13(The Great Adventures of Sherlock Holmes). C14(Gulliver's Travels). C15(The Hunchback of Notre Dame). C16(The Invisible Man). C17(Journey to the Center of the Earth). C18(Kidnapped). C19(The Mysterious Island). C20(The Scarlet Letter). C21(The Story of My Life). C22(A Tale of Two Cities). C23(The Three Musketeers). C24(The War of the Worlds). C25(Around the World in Eighty Days). C26(Captains Courageous). C27 (A Connecticut Yankee in King Arthur's Court). C28(Sherlock Holmes - The Hound of the Baskervilles). C29(The House of the Seven Gables). C30(Jane Eyre). C31(The Last of the Mohicans). C32(The Best of O. Henry). C33(The Best of Poe). C34(Two Years Before the Mast). C35(White Fang). C36(Wuthering Heights). C37(Ben Hur). C38(A Christmas Carol). C39(The Food of the Gods). C40(Ivanhoe). C41(The Man in the Iron Mask). C42(The Prince and the Pauper). C43(The Prisoner of Zenda). C44(The Return of the Native). C45(Robinson Crusoe). C46(The Scarlet Pimpernel). C47(The Sea Wolf). C48(The Swiss Family Robinson). C49(Billy Budd). C50(Crime and Punishment). C51(Don Quixote). C52(Great Expectations). C53(Heidi). C54(The Illiad). C55(Lord Jim). C56(The Mutiny on Board H.M.S. Bounty). C57(The Odyssey). C58(Oliver Twist). C59(Pride and Prejudice). C60(The Turn of the Screw) each... 8.00

Shakespeare Series:
S1(As You Like It). S2(Hamlet). S3(Julius Caesar). S4(King Lear). S5(Macbeth). S6(The Merchant of Venice). S7(A Midsummer Night's Dream). S8(Othello). S9(Romeo and Juliet). S10(The Taming of the Shrew). S11(The Tempest). S12(Twelfth Night) each... 9.00

POCKET COMICS (Also see Double Up)
Harvey Publications: Aug, 1941 - No. 4, Jan, 1942 (Pocket size; 100 pgs.)
(Tied with Spitfire Comics #1 for earliest Harvey comic)

	GD 2.0	VG 4.0	FN 6.0	VF 8.0	VF/NM 9.0	NM- 9.2
1-Origin & 1st app. The Black Cat, Cadet Blakey the Spirit of '76, The Red Blazer, The Phantom, Sphinx, & The Zebra; Phantom Ranger, British Agent #99, Spin Hawkins, Satan, Lord of Evil begin (1st app. of each); classic Simon horror cover showing an army battling a gigantic monster with the Statue of Liberty in its claws; Simon-c/a in #1-3	258	516	774	1651	2826	4000
2 (9/41)-Black Cat & Nazi WWII-c by Simon	174	348	522	1114	1907	2700
3,4-Black Cat & Nazi WWII-c. 3-Simon-c	168	336	504	1075	1838	2600

POE DAMERON (Star Wars)
Marvel Comics: Jun, 2016 - Present ($4.99/$3.99)

1-($4.99) Soule-s/Noto-a/c; prelude to The Force Awakens; back-up w/Eliopoulos-a 5.00
2-6,8-11-($3.99) Black Squadron app. 4.00
7-($4.99) Anzueta-a; Leia cameo 5.00

POGO PARADE (See Dell Giants)

POGO POSSUM (Also see Animal Comics & Special Delivery)
Dell Publishing Co.: No. 105, 4/46 - No. 148, 5/47; 10-12/49 - No. 16, 4-6/54

	GD 2.0	VG 4.0	FN 6.0	VF 8.0	VF/NM 9.0	NM- 9.2
Four Color 105(1946)-Kelly-c/a	50	100	150	400	900	1400
Four Color 148-Kelly-c/a	38	76	114	282	634	985
1-(10-12/49)-Kelly-c/a in all	35	70	105	252	564	875
2	22	44	66	154	340	525
3-5	15	30	45	105	233	360
6-10: 10-Infinity-c	13	26	39	91	201	310
11-16: 11-X-Mas-c	10	20	30	69	147	225

NOTE: *#1-4, 9-13: 52 pgs.; #5-8, 14-16: 36 pgs.*

POINT BLANK (See Wildcats)
DC Comics (WildStorm): Oct, 2002 - No. 5, Feb, 2003 ($2.95, limited series)

1-5-Brubaker-s/Wilson-a/Bisley-c. 1-Variant-c by Wilson; Grifter and John Lynch app. 3.00
TPB (2003, $14.95), (2009, $14.99) r/#1-5; afterword by Brubaker 15.00

POINT ONE
Marvel Comics: Jan, 2012 ($5.99, one-shot)

1-Short story preludes to Marvel's event storylines for 2012; s/a by various 6.00

POISON ELVES (Formerly I, Lusiphur)
Mulehide Graphics: No. 8, 1993- No. 20, 1995 (B&W, magazine/comic size, mature readers)

	GD 2.0	VG 4.0	FN 6.0	VF 8.0	VF/NM 9.0	NM- 9.2
8-Drew Hayes-c/a/scripts.	2	4	6	8	10	12
9-11: 11-1st comic size issue	2	4	6	8	10	12
12,14,16	1	2	3	5	6	8
13,15-(low print)	2	4	6	8	11	14
15-2nd print						4.00
17-20	1	2	3	5	6	8
...Desert of the Third Sin-(1997, $14.95, TPB)-r/#13-18						15.00
...Patrons-($4.95, TPB)-r/#19,20						5.00
...Traumatic Dogs-(1996, $14.95,TPB)-Reprints I, Lusiphur #7, Poison Elves #8-12						15.00

POISON ELVES (See I, Lusiphur)
Sirius Entertainment: June, 1995 - No. 79, Sept, 2004 ; No. 80, Nov, 2007 ($2.50/$2.95, B&W, mature readers)

1-Linsner-c; Drew Hayes-a/scripts in all. 6.00
1-2nd print 3.00
2-25: 12-Purple Marauder-c/app. 3.00
26-45, 47-49 3.00
46,50-79: 61-Fillbäch Brothers-s/a. 74-Art by Crilley (3 pgs.) 3.00
80-($3.50) Tribute issue to Drew Hayes; sketchbook and notebook art with commentary 3.50
... Baptism By Fire-(2003, $19.95, TPB)-r/#48-59 20.00
... Color Special #1 (12/98, $2.95) 5.00

Poison Elves Ventures #2 © Sirius

Police Action #3 © Seaboard

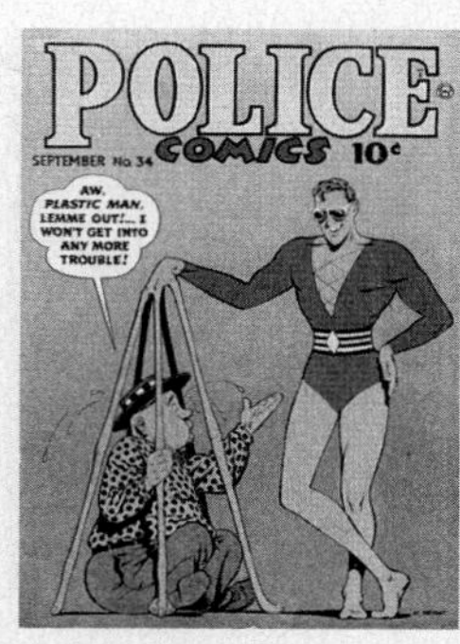

Police Comics #34 © QUA

GD 2.0 | VG 4.0 | FN 6.0 | VF 8.0 | VF/NM 9.0 | NM- 9.2

... Companion (12/02, $3.50) Back-story and character bios 3.50
... : Dark Wars TPB Vol. 1 (2005, $15.95) r/#60,62-68 16.00
... FAN Edition #1 mail-in offer; Drew Hayes-c/s/a 1 2 3 5 6 8
... Rogues-(2002, $15.95, TPB)-r/#40-47 16.00
...Salvation-(2001, $19.95, TPB)-r/#26-39 20.00
...Sanctuary-(1999, $14.95, TPB)-r/#1-12 15.00

POISON ELVES
Ape Entertainment: 2013 - Present ($2.99, B&W)
1-3: 1-Horan-s/Montos-a; Davidsen-s/Ritchie-a; 3 covers by Robertson, Montos & Moore 3.00

POISON ELVES: DOMINION
Sirius Entertainment: Sept, 2005 - No. 6, Sept, 2006 ($3.50, B&W, limited series)
1-6-Keith Davidsen-s/Scott Lewis-a 3.50

POISON ELVES: HYENA
Sirius Entertainment: Sept, 2004 - No. 4, Feb, 2005 ($2.95, B&W, limited series)
1-4-Keith Davidsen-s/Scott Lewis-a 3.00
Ventures TPB Vol. 1: The Hyena Collection (2006, $14.95) r/#1-4 & 2 short stories 15.00

POISON ELVES: LOST TALES
Sirius Entertainment: Jan, 2006 - No. 11 ($2.95, B&W, limited series)
1-11-Aaron Bordner-a; Bordner & Davidsen-s 3.00

POISON ELVES: LUSIPHUR & LIRILITH
Sirius Entertainment: 2001 - No. 4, 2001 ($2.95, B&W, limited series)
1-4-Drew Hayes-s/Jason Alexander-a 3.00
TPB (2002, $11.95) r/#1-4 12.00

POISON ELVES: PARINTACHIN
Sirius Entertainment: 2001 - No. 3, 2002 ($2.95, B&W, limited series)
1-3-Drew Hayes-c/Fillbäch Brothers-s/a 3.00
TPB (2003, $8.95) r/#1-3 9.00

POISON ELVES VENTURES
Sirius Entertainment: May, 2005 - No. 4, Apr, 2006 ($3.50, B&W, limited series)
... #1: Cassanova; ...#2: Lynn; ...#3: The Purple Marauder; #4: Jace - Bordner-a 3.50

POISON IVY: CYCLE OF LIFE AND DEATH
DC Comics: Mar, 2016 - No. 6 ($2.99, limited series)
1-6: 1-Amy Chu-s/Clay Mann-a; covers by Mann & Dodson; Harley Quinn app. 3.00

POKÉMON (TV) (Also see Magical Pokémon Journey)
Viz Comics: Nov, 1998 - 2000 ($3.25/$3.50, B&W)
...Part 1: The Electric Tale of Pikachu
1-Toshiro Ono-s/a 2 4 6 8 10 12
1-4 (2nd through current printings) 4.00
2 6.00
3,4 5.00
TPB ($12.95) 13.00
...Part 2: Pikachu Strikes Back
1 6.00
2-4 5.00
TPB 13.00
...Part 3: Electric Pikachu Boogaloo
1 6.00
2-4 ($2.95-c) 5.00
TPB 13.00
...Part 4: Surf's Up Pikachu
1,3,4 5.00
2 ($2.95-c) 5.00
TPB 13.00
NOTE: Multiple printings exist for most issues

POKÉMON ADVENTURES
Viz Comics: Sept, 1999 - No. 4 ($5.95, B&W, magazine-size)
1-4-Includes stickers bound in 6.00

POKÉMON ADVENTURES
Viz Comics: 2000 - 2002 ($2.95/$4.95, B&W)
Part 2 (2/00-7/00) 1-6-Includes stickers bound in 5.00
Part 3 (8/00-2/01) 1-7 5.00
Part 4 (3/00-6/01) 1-4 5.00
Part 5 (7/01-10/01) 1-4 5.00
Part 6: 1-4, Part 7 1-5 5.00

POKÉMON: THE FIRST MOVIE
Viz Comics: 1999 ($3.95)
Mewtwo Strikes Back 1-4 5.00
Pikachu's Vacation 5.00

POKÉMON: THE MOVIE 2000
Viz Comics: 2000 ($3.95)
1-Official movie adaption 5.00
Pikachu's Rescue Adventure 5.00
...:The Power of One (mini-series) 1-3 5.00

POLARITY
BOOM! Studios: Apr, 2013 - No. 4 ($3.99, limited series)
1-4: 1-Bemis-s/Coelho-a; 3 covers 4.00

POLICE ACADEMY (TV)
Marvel Comics: Nov, 1989 - No. 6, Feb, 1990 ($1.00)
1-6: Based on TV cartoon; Post-c/a(p) in all 4.00

POLICE ACTION
Atlas News Co.: Jan, 1954 - No. 7, Nov, 1954
1-Violent-a by Robert Q. Sale 29 58 87 170 278 385
2 15 30 45 86 133 180
3-7: 7-Powell-a 14 28 42 82 121 160
NOTE: *Ayers a-4, 5. Colan a-1. Forte a-1, 2. Mort Lawrence a-5. Maneely a-3; c-1, 5. Reinman a-6, 7.*

POLICE ACTION
Atlas/Seaboard Publ.: Feb, 1975 - No. 3, June, 1975
1-3: 1-Lomax, N.Y.P.D., Luke Malone begin; McWilliams-a. 2-Origin Luke Malone, Manhunter; Ploog-a 2 4 6 10 14 18
NOTE: *Ploog art in all. Sekowsky/McWilliams a-1-3. Thorne c-3.*

POLICE AGAINST CRIME
Premiere Magazines: April, 1954 - No. 9, Aug, 1955
1-Disbrow-a; extreme violence (man's face slashed with knife); Hollingsworth-a 43 86 129 271 461 650
2-Hollingsworth-a 24 48 72 142 234 325
3-9 21 42 63 122 199 275

POLICE BADGE #479 (Formerly Spy Thrillers #1-4)
Atlas Comics (PrPI): No. 5, Sept, 1955
5-Maneely-c/a (6 pgs.); Heck-a 14 28 42 80 115 150

POLICE CASE BOOK (See Giant Comics Editions)

POLICE CASES (See Authentic... & Record Book of...)

POLICE COMICS
Quality Comics Group (Comic Magazines): Aug, 1941 - No. 127, Oct, 1953
1-Origin/1st app. Plastic Man by Jack Cole (r-in DC Special #15), The Human Bomb by Gustavson, & No. 711; intro. The Firebrand by Reed Crandall, The Mouthpiece by Guardineer, Phantom Lady, & The Sword; Chic Carter by Eisner app.; Firebrand-c 1-4 975 1950 2919 7100 12,550 18,000
2-Plastic Man smuggles opium 320 640 960 2240 3920 5600
3 245 490 735 1568 2684 3800
4 210 420 630 1334 2292 3250
5-Plastic Man covers begin, end #102; Plastic Man forced to smoke marijuana 343 686 1029 2400 4200 6000
6,7 177 354 531 1124 1937 2750
8-Manhunter begins (origin/1st app.) (3/42) 200 400 600 1280 2190 3100
9,10 139 278 417 883 1517 2150
11-The Spirit strip reprints begin by Eisner (origin-strip #1); 1st comic book app. The Spirit & 1st cover app. (9/42) 383 766 1149 2681 4691 6700
12-Intro. Ebony 184 368 552 1168 2009 2850
13-Intro. Woozy Winks; last Firebrand 194 388 582 1242 2121 3000
14-19: 15-Last No. 711; Destiny begins 77 154 231 493 847 1200
20-The Raven x-over in Phantom Lady; features Jack Cole himself 77 154 231 493 847 1200
21,22: 21-Raven & Spider Widow x-over in Phantom Lady (cameo in #22) 65 130 195 416 708 1000
23-30: 23-Last Phantom Lady. 24-26-Flatfoot Burns by Kurtzman in all 58 116 174 371 636 900
31-41: 37-1st app. Candy by Sahle & begins (12/44). 41-Last Spirit-r by Eisner 50 100 150 315 533 750
42,43-Spirit-r by Eisner/Fine 41 82 123 256 428 600
44-Fine Spirit-r begin, end #88,90,92 41 82 123 256 428 600
45-50: 50-(#50 on-c, #49 on inside, 1/46) 36 72 108 214 347 480
51-60: 58-Last Human Bomb 30 60 90 177 289 400
61-88,90,92: 63-(Some issues have #65 printed on cover, but #63 on inside) Kurtzman-a, 6 pgs. 90,92-Spirit by Fine 25 50 75 150 245 340
89,91,93-No Spirit stories 23 46 69 136 223 310

Police Line-up #4 © AVON

Polly Pigtails #36 © PMI

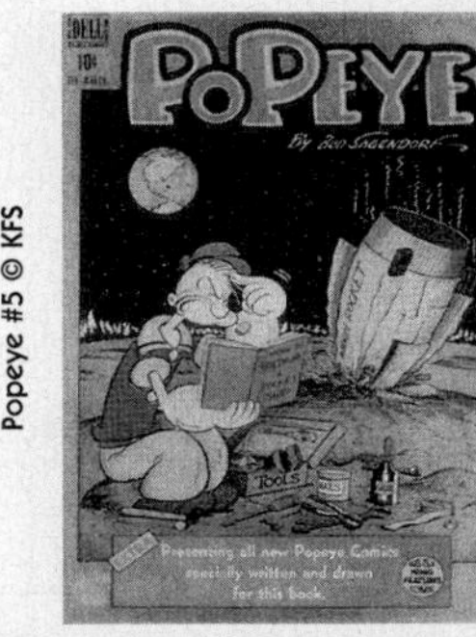

Popeye #5 © KFS

GD 2.0 VG 4.0 FN 6.0 VF 8.0 VF/NM 9.0 NM- 9.2

94-99,101,102: Spirit by Eisner in all; 101-Last Manhunter. 102-Last Spirit & Plastic Man by Jack Cole 32 64 96 192 314 435
100 39 78 117 231 378 525
103-Content change to crime; Ken Shannon & T-Man begin (1st app. of each, 12/50) 37 74 111 222 361 500
104-112,114-127: Crandall-a most issues (not in 104,105,122,125-127). 109-Atomic bomb story. 112-Crandall-a 22 44 66 132 216 300
113-Crandall-c/a(2), 9 pgs. each 25 50 75 147 241 335

NOTE: *Most Spirit stories signed by Eisner are not by him; all are reprints.* ***Crandall*** *Firebrand-1-8. Spirit by* ***Eisner*** *1-41, 94-102; by* ***Eisner/Fine****-42, 43; by* ***Fine****-44-88, 90, 92, 103, 109.* ***Al Bryant*** *c-33, 34.* ***Cole*** *c-17-32, 35-102(most).* ***Crandall*** *c-13, 14.* ***Crandall/Cuidera*** *c-105-127.* ***Eisner*** *c-4i.* ***Gill Fox*** *c-1-3, 4p, 5-12, 15. Bondage c-103, 109, 125.*

POLICE LINE-UP
Avon Periodicals/Realistic Comics #3,4: Aug, 1951 - No. 4, July, 1952 (Painted-c #1-3)

1-Wood-a, 1 pg. plus part-c; spanking panel-r/Saint #5 45 90 135 284 480 675
2-Classic story "The Religious Murder Cult", drugs, perversion; r/Saint #5; c-r/Avon paperback #329 36 72 108 211 343 475
3,4: 3-Kubert-a(r?)/part-c; Kinstler-a (inside-c only) 24 48 72 142 234 325

POLICE TRAP (Public Defender In Action #7 on)
Mainline #1-4/Charlton #5,6: 8-9/54 - No. 4, 2-3/55; No. 5, 7/55 - No. 6, 9/55

1-S&K covers-all issues; Meskin-a; Kirby scripts 37 74 111 222 361 500
2-4 22 44 66 128 209 290
5,6-S&K-c/a 27 54 81 162 266 370

POLICE TRAP
Super Comics: No. 11, 1963; No. 16-18, 1964

Reprint #11,16-18: 11-r/Police Trap #3. 16-r/Justice Traps the Guilty #? 17-r/Inside Crime #3 & r/Justice Traps The Guilty #83; 18-r/Inside Crime #3 2 4 6 9 13 16

POLLY & HER PALS (See Comic Monthly #1)

POLLY & THE PIRATES
Oni Press: Sept, 2005 - No. 6, June, 2006 ($2.99, B&W, limited series)

1-6-Ted Naifeh-s/a; Polly is shanghaied by the pirate ship Titania 3.00
TPB (7/06, $11.95, digest) r/#1-6 12.00

POLLYANNA (Disney)
Dell Publishing Co.: No. 1129, Aug-Oct, 1960

Four Color 1129-Movie, Hayley Mills photo-c 7 14 21 49 92 135

POLLY PIGTAILS (Girls' Fun & Fashion Magazine #44 on)
Parents' Magazine Institute/Polly Pigtails: Jan, 1946 - V4#43, Oct-Nov, 1949

1-Infinity-c; photo-c 20 40 60 117 189 260
2-Photo-c 13 26 39 72 101 130
3-5: 3,4-Photo-c 11 22 33 62 86 110
6-10: 7-Photo-c 10 20 30 54 72 90
11-30: 22-Photo-c 9 18 27 47 61 75
31-43: 38-Natalie Wood photo-c 8 16 24 40 50 60

PONY EXPRESS (See Tales of the...)

PONYTAIL (Teen-age)
Dell Publishing Co./Charlton No. 13 on: 7-9/62 - No. 12, 10-12/65; No. 13, 11/69 - No. 20, 1/71

12-641-209(#1) 4 8 12 23 37 50
2-12 3 6 9 17 26 35
13-20 3 6 9 14 19 24

POP
Dark Horse Comics: Aug, 2014 - No. 4, Nov, 2014 ($3.99, limited series)

1-4-Curt Pires-s/Jason Copland-a 4.00

POP COMICS
Modern Store Publ.: 1955 (36 pgs.; 5x7"; in color) (7¢)

1-Funny animal 8 16 24 40 50 60

POPEYE (See Comic Album #7, 11, 15, Comics Reading Libraries *in the Promotional Comics section,* Eat Right to Work and Win, Giant Comic Album, King Comics, Kite Fun Book, Magic Comics, March of Comics #37,52, 66, 80, 96, 117, 134, 148, 157, 169, 194, 246, 264, 274, 294, 453, 465, 477 & Wow Comics, 1st series)

POPEYE
David McKay Publications: 1937 - 1939 (All by Segar)

Feature Books nn (100 pgs.) (Very Rare) 975 1950 2919 7100 12,550 18,000
Feature Books 2 (52 pgs.) 139 278 417 1015 1583 2150
Feature Books 3 (100 pgs.)-r/nn issue with new-c 107 214 321 680 1165 1650
Feature Books 5,10 (76 pgs.) 97 194 291 621 1061 1500
Feature Books 14 (76 pgs.) (Scarce) 110 220 330 704 1202 1700

POPEYE (Strip reprints through 4-Color #70)
Dell #1-65/Gold Key #66-80/King #81-92/Charlton #94-138/Gold Key #139-155/Whitman #156 on: 1941 - 1947; #1, 2-4/48 - #65, 7-9/62; #66, 10/62 - #80, 5/66; #81, 8/66 - #92, 12/67; #94, 2/69 - #138, 1/77; #139, 5/78 - #171, 6/84 (no #93,160,161)

Large Feature Comic 24('41)-Half by Segar 94 188 282 597 1024 1450
Four Color 25('41)-by Segar 107 214 321 680 1165 1650
Large Feature Comic 10('43) 69 138 207 442 759 1075
Four Color 17('43),26('43)-by Segar 45 90 135 333 754 1175
Four Color 43('44) 29 58 87 209 467 725
Four Color 70('45)-Title: ...& Wimpy 22 44 66 154 340 525
Four Color 113('46-original strips begin),127,145('47),168 13 26 39 91 201 310
1(2-4/48)(Dell)-All new stories continue 30 60 90 216 483 750
2 14 28 42 98 217 335
3-10: 5-Popeye on moon w/rocket-c 11 22 33 76 163 250
11-20 9 18 27 60 120 180
21-40,46: 46-Origin Swee' Pee 8 16 24 51 96 140
41-45,47-50 6 12 18 40 73 105
51-60 5 10 15 35 63 90
61-65 (Last Dell issue) 5 10 15 31 53 75
66(10/62),67-Both 84 pgs. (Gold Key) 6 12 18 40 73 105
68-80 4 8 12 25 40 55
81-92,94-97 (no #93): 97-Last 12¢ issue 3 6 9 20 31 42
98,99,101-107,109-138: 123-Wimpy beats Neil Armstrong to the moon. 130-1st app. Superstuff 3 6 9 14 19 24
100 3 6 9 17 26 35
108-Traces Popeye's origin from 1929 3 6 9 15 27 28
139-155: 144-50th Anniversary issue 2 4 6 8 10 12
156,157,162-167(Whitman)(no #160,161).167(3/82) 2 4 6 10 14 18
158(9/80),159(11/80)-pre-pack only 5 10 15 30 50 70
168-171:(All #90069 on-c; pre-pack) 168(6/83). 169(#168 on-c)(8/83). 170(3/84). 171(6/84) 3 6 9 17 26 35

NOTE: *Reprints-#145, 147, 149, 151, 153, 155, 157, 163-168(1/3), 170.*

POPEYE
Harvey Comics: Nov, 1993 - No. 7, Aug, 1994 ($1.50)

V2#1-7 3.00
...Summer Special V2#1-(10/93, $2.25, 68 pgs.)-Sagendorf-r & others 4.00

POPEYE
IDW Publishing: Apr, 2012 - No. 12, Apr, 2013 ($3.99)

1-12-New stories in classic style; Langridge-s. 1-Action #1 cover swipe. 12-Barney Google and Spark Plug app. 4.00

POPEYE (CLASSIC...)
IDW Publishing: Aug, 2012 - Present ($3.99/$4.99)

1-43-Reprints of Bud Sagendorf's classic stories 4.00
44-55-($4.99) 5.00

POPEYE SPECIAL
Ocean Comics: Summer, 1987 - No. 2, Sept, 1988 ($1.75/$2.00)

1,2: 1-Origin 4.00

POPPLES (TV, movie)
Star Comics (Marvel): Dec, 1986 - No. 4, Jun, 1987

1-4-Based on toys 5.00

POPPO OF THE POPCORN THEATRE
Fuller Publishing Co. (Publishers Weekly): 10/29/55 - No. 13, 1956 (weekly)

1 10 20 30 54 72 90
2-5 7 14 21 37 46 55
6-13 6 12 18 31 38 45

NOTE: *By* ***Charles Biro.*** *10¢ cover, given away by supermarkets such as IGA.*

POP-POP COMICS
R. B. Leffingwell Co.: No date (Circa 1945) (52 pgs.)

1-Funny animal 15 30 45 86 133 180

POPULAR COMICS
Dell Publishing Co.: Feb, 1936 - No. 145, July-Sept, 1948

1-Dick Tracy (1st comic book app.), Little Orphan Annie, Terry & the Pirates, Gasoline Alley, Don Winslow (1st app.), Harold Teen, Little Joe, Skippy, Moon Mullins, Mutt & Jeff, Tailspin Tommy, Smitty, Smokey Stover, Winnie Winkle & The Gumps begin (all strip-r) 900 1800 2700 6300 - -
2 264 528 792 1850 - -
3 200 400 600 1400 - -
4-6(7/36): 5-Tom Mix begins. 6-1st app. Scribbly 157 314 471 1100 - -

Popular Comics #77 © DELL

Porky Pig #45 © WB

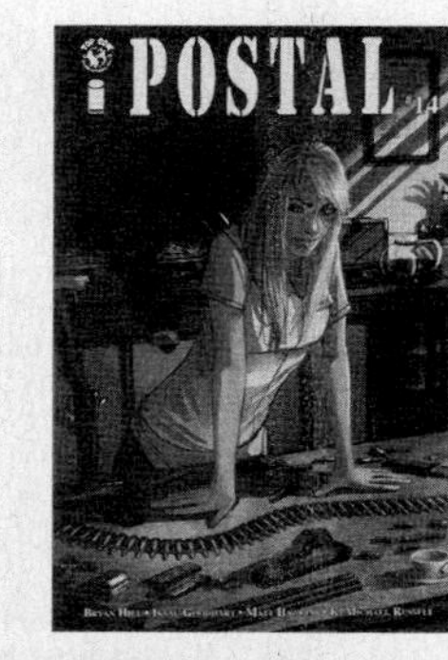

Postal #14 © Hawkins & TCOW

	GD 2.0	VG 4.0	FN 6.0	VF 8.0	VF/NM 9.0	NM- 9.2
7-10: 8,9-Scribbly & Reglar Fellers app.	129	258	387	900	-	-
11-20: 12-X-Mas-c	83	166	249	477	739	1000
21-27: 27-Last Terry & the Pirates, Little Orphan Annie, & Dick Tracy	63	126	189	362	556	750
28-37: 28-Gene Autry app. 31,32-Tim McCoy app. 35-Christmas-c; Tex Ritter app.	49	98	147	282	434	585
38-43: Tarzan in text only. 38-(4/39)-Gang Busters (Radio, 2nd app.) & Zane Grey's Tex Thorne begins? 43-The Masked Pilot app.; 1st non-funny-c?	47	94	141	270	415	560
44,45: 45-Hurricane Kid-c	40	80	140	230	353	475
46-Origin/1st app. Martan, the Marvel Man(12/39)	50	100	175	288	444	600
47-49-Martan, the Marvel Man-c	44	88	154	253	389	525
50-Gang Busters-c	38	76	133	219	335	450
51-Origin The Voice (The Invisible Detective) strip begins (5/40)	40	80	140	230	353	475
52-Classic Martan blasting robots-c/sty	63	126	221	362	556	750
53-56: 55-End of World story	35	70	123	201	313	425
57-59-Martan, the Marvel Man-c	42	84	147	242	371	500
60-Origin/1st app. Professor Supermind and Son (2/41)	40	80	140	230	358	485
61-64,66-Professor Supermind-c. 63-Smilin' Jack begins	33	66	116	190	295	400
65-Classic Professor Supermind WWII-c	42	84	147	242	371	500
67-71	23	46	69	136	223	310
72-The Owl & Terry & the Pirates begin (2/42); Smokey Stover reprints begin	42	84	126	242	371	500
73-75	29	58	87	167	259	350
76-78-Capt. Midnight in all (see The Funnies #57)	40	80	120	230	358	485
79-85-Last Owl	27	54	81	155	238	320
86-99: 86-Japanese WWII-c. 98-Felix the Cat, Smokey Stover-r begin	18	36	54	104	157	210
100	20	40	60	115	175	235
101-130	10	20	30	58	89	120
131-145: 142-Last Terry & the Pirates	9	18	27	52	79	105

NOTE: *Martan, the Marvel Man c-47-49, 52, 57-59. Professor Supermind c-60-63, 64(1/2), 65, 66. The Voice c-53.*

POPULAR FAIRY TALES (See March of Comics #6, 18)

POPULAR ROMANCE
Better-Standard Publications: No. 5, Dec, 1949 - No. 29, July, 1954

	GD 2.0	VG 4.0	FN 6.0	VF 8.0	VF/NM 9.0	NM- 9.2
5	18	36	54	103	162	220
6-9: 7-Palais-a; lingerie panels	14	28	42	78	112	145
10-Wood-a (2 pgs.)	15	30	45	84	127	170
11,12,14-16,18-21,28,29	12	24	36	69	97	125
13,17-Severin/Elder-a (3&8 pgs.)	13	26	39	74	105	135
22-27-Toth-a	14	28	42	80	115	150

NOTE: *All have photo-c. **Tuska** art in most issues.*

POPULAR TEEN-AGERS (Secrets of Love) (School Day Romances #1-4)
Star Publications: No. 5, Sept, 1950 - No. 23, Nov, 1954

	GD 2.0	VG 4.0	FN 6.0	VF 8.0	VF/NM 9.0	NM- 9.2
5-Toni Gay, Midge Martin & Eve Adams continue from School Day Romances; Ginger Bunn (formerly Ginger Snapp & becomes Honey Bunn #6 on) begins; all features end #8	41	82	123	256	428	600
6-8 (7/51)-Honey Bunn begins; all have L. B. Cole-c; 6-Negligee panels	37	74	111	222	361	500
9-(...Romances; 1st romance issue, 10/51)	32	64	96	188	307	425
10-(...Secrets of Love thru #23)	30	60	90	177	289	400
11,16,18,19,22,23	26	52	78	154	252	350
12,13,17,20,21-Disbrow-a	28	56	84	165	270	375
14-Harrison/Wood-a	36	72	108	211	343	475
15-Wood?, Disbrow-a	29	58	87	172	281	390
Accepted Reprint 5,6 (nd); L.B. Cole-c	9	18	27	52	69	85

NOTE: *All have **L. B. Cole** covers.*

PORKY PIG (See Bugs Bunny &..., Kite Fun Book, Looney Tunes, March of Comics #42, 57, 71, 89, 99, 113, 130, 143, 164, 175, 192, 209, 218, 367, and Super Book #6, 18, 30)

PORKY PIG (...& Bugs Bunny #40-69)
Dell Publishing Co./Gold Key No. 1-93/Whitman No. 94 on: No. 16, 1942 - No. 81, Mar-Apr, 1962; Jan, 1965 - No. 109, June, 1984

	GD 2.0	VG 4.0	FN 6.0	VF 8.0	VF/NM 9.0	NM- 9.2
Four Color 16(#1, 1942)	89	178	267	712	1606	2500
Four Color 48(1944)-Carl Barks-a	91	182	273	728	1639	2550
Four Color 78(1945)	25	50	75	175	388	600
Four Color 112(7/46)	15	30	45	103	227	350
Four Color 156,182,191('49)	11	22	33	73	157	240
Four Color 226,241('49),260,271,277,284,295	9	18	27	61	123	185
Four Color 303,311,322,330: 322-Sci/fi-c/story	7	14	21	48	89	135
Four Color 342,351,360,370,385,399,410,426	6	12	18	38	69	100
25 (11-12/52)-30	5	10	15	33	57	80
31-40	5	10	15	30	50	70
41-60	4	8	12	25	40	55
61-81(3-4/62)	3	6	9	21	33	45
1(1/65-Gold Key)(2nd Series)	5	10	15	31	53	75
2,4,5-r/4-Color 226,284 & 271 in that order	3	6	9	19	30	40
3,6-10: 3-r/Four Color #342	3	6	9	16	24	32
11-30	3	6	9	14	19	24
31-54	2	4	6	10	14	18
55-70	2	4	6	8	11	14
71-93(Gold Key)	2	3	4	6	8	10
94-96	2	4	6	8	10	12
97(9/80),98-pre-pack only (99 known not to exist)	4	8	12	27	44	60
100	2	4	6	10	14	18
101-105: 104(2/82). 105(4/82)	2	4	6	8	11	14
106-109 (All #90140 on-c, no date or date code): 106(7/83), 107(8/83), 108(2/84), 109(6/84) low print run	3	6	9	14	20	26

NOTE: *Reprints-#1-8, 9-35(2/3); 36-46(1/4-1/2), 58, 67, 69-74, 76, 78, 102-109(1/3-1/2).*

PORKY PIG'S DUCK HUNT
Saalfield Publishing Co.: 1938 (12pgs.)(large size)(heavy linen-like paper)

	GD 2.0	VG 4.0	FN 6.0	VF 8.0	VF/NM 9.0	NM- 9.2
2178-1st app. Porky Pig & Daffy Duck by Leon Schlesinger. Illustrated text story book written in verse. 1st book ever devoted to these characters. (see Looney Tunes #1 for their 1st comic book app.)	73	146	219	467	796	1125

PORTENT, THE
Image Comics: Feb, 2006 - No. 4, Aug, 2006 ($2.99)

	NM- 9.2
1-4-Peter Bergting-s/a	3.00
Vol. 1: Duende TPB (2006, 12.99) r/#1-4; pin-up art; intro. by Kaluta	13.00

PORTIA PRINZ OF THE GLAMAZONS
Eclipse Comics: Dec, 1986 - No. 6, Oct, 1987 ($2.00, B&W, Baxter paper)

	NM- 9.2
1-6	3.00

POSEIDON IX (Also see Aphrodite IX and (Ninth) IX Generation)
Image Comics (Top Cow): Sept, 2015 ($3.99, one-shot)

	NM- 9.2
1-Howard-s/Sevy-a; story continues in IX Generation #5	4.00

POSSESSED, THE
DC Comics (Cliffhanger): Sept, 2003 - No. 6, March, 2004 ($2.95, limited series)

	NM- 9.2
1-6-Johns & Grimminger-s/Sharp-a	3.00
TPB (2004, $14.95) r/#1-6; promo art and sketch pages	15.00

POSTAL (Also see Eden's Fall)
Image Comics (Top Cow): Feb, 2015 - Present ($3.99)

	NM- 9.2
1-18: 1-Matt Hawkins & Bryan Hill-s/Issac Goodheart-a	4.00
...: Dossier 1 (11/15, $3.99) Ryan Cady-a; background on Eden and character profiles	4.00

POST GAZETTE (See Meet the New... in the Promotional Comics section)

POWDER RIVER RUSTLERS (See Fawcett Movie Comics)

POWER & GLORY (See American Flagg! & Howard Chaykin's American Flagg!
Malibu Comics (Bravura): Feb, 1994 - No. 4, May, 1994 ($2.50, limited series, mature)

	NM- 9.2
1A, 1B-By Howard Chaykin; w/Bravura stamp	3.00
1-Newsstand ed. (polybagged w/children's warning on bag), Gold ed., Silver-foil ed., Blue-foil ed.(print run of 10,000), Serigraph ed. (print run of 3,000)($2.95)-Howard Chaykin-c/a begin	4.00
2-4-Contains Bravura stamp	3.00
Holiday Special (Win '94, $2.95)	3.00

POWER COMICS
Holyoke Publ. Co./Narrative Publ.: 1944 - No. 4, 1945

	GD 2.0	VG 4.0	FN 6.0	VF 8.0	VF/NM 9.0	NM- 9.2
1-L. B. Cole-c	194	388	582	1242	2121	3000
2-Hitler, Hirohito-c (scarce)	206	412	618	1318	2259	3200
3-Classic L.B. Cole-c; Dr. Mephisto begins?	206	412	618	1318	2259	3200
4-L.B. Cole-c; Miss Espionage app. #3,4; Leav-a	142	284	426	909	1555	2200

POWER COMICS
Power Comics Co.: 1977 - No. 5, Dec, 1977 (B&W)

	GD 2.0	VG 4.0	FN 6.0	VF 8.0	VF/NM 9.0	NM- 9.2
1- "A Boy And His Aardvark" by Dave Sim; first Dave Sim aardvark (not Cerebus)	3	6	9	17	26	35
1-Reprint (3/77, black-c)	1	2	3	5	6	8
2-Cobalt Blue by Gustovich	1	3	4	6	8	10
3-5: 3-Nightwitch. 4-Northern Light. 5-Bluebird	1	3	4	6	8	10

POWER COMICS
Eclipse Comics (Acme Press): Mar, 1988 - No. 4, Sept, 1988 ($2.00, B&W, mini-series)

Power Girl #10 © DC

Power Man and Iron Fist #54 © MAR

The Power of Shazam! #1 © DC

GD 2.0 VG 4.0 FN 6.0 VF 8.0 VF/NM 9.0 NM- 9.2

1-4: Bolland, Gibbons-r in all 3.00

POWER COMPANY, THE
DC Comics: Apr, 2002 - No. 18, Sep, 2003 ($2.50/$2.75)

1-6-Busiek-s/Grummett-a. 6-Green Arrow & Black Canary-c/app. 3.00
7-18: 7:Begin $2.75-c. 8,9-Green Arrow app. 11-Firestorm joins. 15-Batman app. 3.00
...Bork (3/02) Busiek-s/Dwyer-a; Batman & Flash (Barry Allen) app. 3.00
...Josiah Power (3/02) Busiek-s/Giffen-a; Superman app. 3.00
...Manhunter (3/02) Busiek-s/Jurgens-a; Nightwing app. 3.00
...Sapphire (3/02) Busiek-s/Bagley-a; JLA & Kobra app. 3.00
...Skyrocket (3/02) Busiek-s/Staton-a; Green Lantern (Hal Jordan) app. 3.00
...Striker Z (3/02) Busiek-s/Bachs-a; Superboy app. 3.00
...Witchfire (3/02) Busiek-s/Haley-a; Wonder Woman app. 3.00

POWER CUBED
Dark Horse Comics: Sept, 2015 - No. 4, Jan, 2016 ($3.99, limited series)

1-4-Aaron Lopresti-s/a 4.00

POWER FACTOR
Wonder Color Comics #1/Pied Piper #2: May, 1987 - No. 2, 1987 ($1.95)

1,2: Super team. 2-Infantino-c 3.00

POWER FACTOR
Innovation Publishing: Oct, 1990 - No. 3, 1991 ($1.95/$2.25)

1-3: 1-R-/1st story + new-a, 2-r/2nd story + new-a. 3-Infantino-a 3.00

POWER GIRL (See All-Star #58, Infinity, Inc., JSA Classified, Showcase #97-99)
DC Comics: June, 1988 - No. 4, Sept, 1988 ($1.00, color, limited series)

1 2 4 6 8 10 12
2-4 5.00
TPB (2006, $14.99) r/Showcase #97-99; Secret Origins #11; JSA Classified #1-4 and pages from JSA #32,39; cover gallery 15.00

POWER GIRL
DC Comics: Jul, 2009 - No. 27, Oct, 2011 ($2.99)

1-Amanda Conner-a; covers by Conner and Hughes; Ultra-Humanite app. 3 6 9 15 22 28
2-Conner-a; covers by Conner and Hughes 1 3 4 6 8 10
3-10: 3-6-Covers by Conner and March 5.00
11-26: 13-23-Winick-s/Basri-a. 20,21-Crossover with Justice League: Generation Lost #18-22 23-Zatanna app. 24,25-Batman app.; Prasetya-a 4.00
27-Cyclone app. 3 6 9 17 26 35
...: Aliens and Apes SC (2010, $17.99) r/#7-12 18.00
...: A New Beginning SC (2010, $17.99) r/#1-6; gallery of variant covers 18.00
...: Bomb Squad SC (2011, $14.99) r/#13-18 15.00

POWERHOUSE PEPPER COMICS (See Gay Comics, Joker Comics & Tessie the Typist)
Marvel Comics (20CC): No. 1, 1943; No. 2, May, 1948 - No. 5, Nov, 1948

1-(60 pgs.)-Wolverton-a in all; c-2,3 232 464 696 1485 2543 3600
2 100 200 300 635 1093 1550
3,4 94 188 282 597 1024 1450
5-(Scarce) 107 214 321 680 1165 1650

POWERLESS
Marvel Comics: Aug, 2004 - No. 6, Jan, 2005 ($2.99, limited series)

1-6-Peter Parker, Matt Murdock and Logan without powers; Gaydos-a 3.00
TPB (2005, $14.99) r/series; sketch page by Gaydos 15.00

POWER LINE
Marvel Comics (Epic Comics): May, 1988 - No. 8, Sept, 1989 ($1.25/$1.50)

1-8: 2-Williamson-i. 3-Dr. Zero app. 4-7-Morrow-a. 8-Williamson-i 3.00

POWER LINES
Image Comics: Mar, 2016 - Present ($3.50/$3.99)

1-3-Jimmie Robinson-s/a. 1-($3.50-c). 2-Begin $3.99-c 4.00

POWER LORDS
DC Comics: Dec, 1983 - No. 3, Feb, 1984 (Limited series, Mando paper)

1-3: Based on Revell toys 4.00

POWER MAN (Formerly Hero for Hire; ...& Iron Fist #50 on; see Cage & Giant-Size...)
Marvel Comics Group: No. 17, Feb, 1974 - No. 125, Sept, 1986

17-Luke Cage continues; Iron Man app. 4 8 12 27 44 60
18-20: 18-Last 20¢ issue; intro. Wrecking Crew 3 6 9 16 23 30
21-23,25-30 2 4 6 9 12 15
24-Intro. Black Goliath 6 12 18 38 69 100
30-(30¢-c variant, limited distribution)(4/76) 4 8 12 25 40 55
31-46: 31-Part Neal Adams-i. 34-Last 25¢ issue. 36-r/Hero For Hire #12. 41-1st app. Thunderbolt. 45-Starlin-c. 1 3 4 6 8 10
31-34-(30¢-c variants, limited distribution)(5-8/76) 4 8 12 25 40 55
44-46-(35¢-c variants, limited distribution)(6-8/77) 8 16 24 56 108 160
47-Barry Smith-a 2 4 6 8 10 12
47-(35¢-c variant, limited distribution)(10/77) 8 16 24 56 108 160
48-Power Man/Iron Fist 1st meet; Byrne-a(p) 5 10 15 35 63 90
49-Byrne-a(p) 3 6 9 14 20 25
50-Iron Fist joins Cage; Byrne-a(p) 5 10 15 30 50 70
51-56,58-65,67-77: 58-Intro El Aguila. 75-Double size. 77-Daredevil app. 6.00
57-New X-Men app. (6/79) 4 8 12 25 40 55
66-2nd app. Sabretooth (see Iron Fist #14) 5 10 15 35 63 90
78,84: 78-3rd app. Sabretooth (cameo under cloak). 84-4th app. Sabretooth 4 8 12 25 40 55
79-83,85-99,101-124: 87-Moon Knight app. 109-The Reaper app. 4.00
100-Double size; Origin K'un L'un 6.00
125-Double size; Death of Iron Fist 2 4 6 9 12 15
Annual 1(1976)-Punisher cameo in flashback 3 6 9 14 20 25

NOTE: ***Austin*** *c-102i.* ***Byrne*** *a-48-50; c-102, 104, 106, 107, 112-116.* ***Kane*** *c(p)-24, 25, 28, 48.* ***Miller*** *a-68, 76(2 pgs.); c-66-68, 70-74, 80i.* ***Mooney*** *a-38i, 53i, 55i.* ***Nebres*** *a-76p.* ***Nino*** *a-42i, 43i.* ***Perez*** *a-27.* ***B. Smith*** *a-47i.* ***Tuska*** *a(p)-17, 20, 24, 26, 28, 29, 36, 47. Painted c-75, 100.*

POWER MAN AND IRON FIST
Marvel Comics: Apr, 2011 - No. 5, Jul, 2011 ($2.99, limited series)

1-5-Van Lente-s/Alves-a; Victor Alvarez as Power Man 3.00

POWER MAN AND IRON FIST
Marvel Comics: Apr, 2016 - Present ($3.99)

1-13: 1-Luke Cage and Danny Rand; David Walker-s/Sanford Greene-a; Tombstone app. 6-9-Civil War II tie-in 4.00
...: Sweet Christmas Annual 1 (2/17, $4.99) Walker-s/Hepburn-a; Daimon Hellstrom app. 5.00

POWER OF PRIME
Malibu Comics (Ultraverse): July, 1995 - No. 4, Nov, 1995 ($2.50, lim. series)

1-4 3.00

POWER OF SHAZAM!, THE (See SHAZAM!)
DC Comics: 1994 (Painted graphic novel) (Prequel to new series)

Hardcover-($19.95)-New origin of Shazam!; Ordway painted-c/a & script 3 6 9 14 20 25
Softcover-($7.50), Softcover-($9.95)-New-c. 2 4 6 8 10 12

POWER OF SHAZAM!, THE
DC Comics: Mar, 1995 - No. 47, Mar, 1999; No. 48, Mar, 2010 ($1.50/$1.75/$1.95/$2.50)

1-Jerry Ordway scripts begin 1 2 3 5 6 8
2-20: 4-Begin $1.75-c. 6:Re-intro of Capt. Nazi. 8-Re-intro of Spy Smasher, Bulletman & Minuteman; Swan-a (7 pgs.). 11-Re-intro of Ibis, Swan-a(2 pgs.). 14-Gil Kane-a(p). 20-Superman-c/app.; "Final Night" 3.00
21-47: 21-Plastic Man-c/app. 22-Batman-c/app. 35,36-X-over w/Starman #39,40. 38-41-Mr. Mind. 43-Bulletman app. 45-JLA-c/app. 3.00
48-(3/10, $2.99) Blackest Night one-shot; Osiris rises as a Black Lantern; Kramer-a 3.00
#1,000,000 (11/98) 853rd Century x-over; Ordway-c/s/a 3.00
Annual 1 (1996, $2.95)-Legends of the Dead Earth story; Jerry Ordway-c; Mike Manley-a 4.00

POWER OF STRONGMAN, THE (Also see Strongman)
AC Comics: 1989 ($2.95)

1-Powell G.A.-r 3.00

POWER OF THE ATOM (See Secret Origins #29)
DC Comics: Aug, 1988 - No. 18, Nov, 1989 ($1.00)

1-18: 6-Chronos returns; Byrne-p. 9-JLI app. 3.00

POWER OF THE DARK CRYSTAL (Jim Henson)
BOOM! Studios (Archaia): Feb, 2017 - No. 12 ($3.99)

1-Simon Spurrier-s/Kelly & Nichole Matthews-a; multiple covers 4.00

POWER PACHYDERMS
Marvel Comics: Sept, 1989 ($1.25, one-shot)

1-Elephant super-heroes; parody of X-Men, Elektra, & 3 Stooges 3.00

POWER PACK
Marvel Comics Group: Aug, 1984 - No. 62, Feb, 1991

1-($1.00, 52 pgs.)-Origin & 1st app. Power Pack 5.00
2-18,20-26,28,30-45,47-62 3.00
19-(52 pgs.)-Cloak & Dagger, Wolverine app. 4.00
27-Mutant massacre; Wolverine & Sabretooth app. 5.00
29,46: 29-Spider-Man & Hobgoblin app. 46-Punisher app. 4.00
Graphic Novel: Power Pack & Cloak & Dagger: Shelter From the Storm ('89, SC, $7.95) Velluto/Farmer-a 10.00

Powerpuff Girls #16 © CN

Powers (2015 series) #2 © Jinxworld

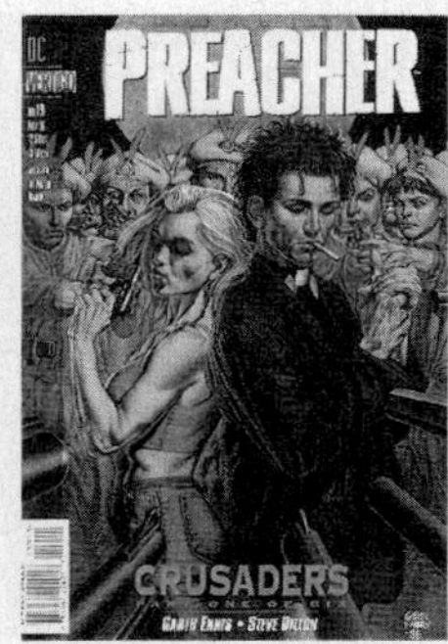

Preacher #19 © Ennis & Dillon

	GD 2.0	VG 4.0	FN 6.0	VF 8.0	VF/NM 9.0	NM- 9.2

GD 2.0 VG 4.0 FN 6.0 VF 8.0 VF/NM 9.0 NM- 9.2

...Holiday Special 1 (2/92, $2.25, 68 pgs.) 4.00
NOTE: ***Austin** scripts-53. **Mignola** c-20. **Morrow** a-51. **Spiegle** a-55i. **Williamson** a(i)-43, 50, 52.*

POWER PACK (Volume 2)
Marvel Comics: Aug, 2000 - No. 4, Nov, 2000 ($2.99, limited series)
1-4-Doran & Austin-c/a 3.00

POWER PACK
Marvel Comics: June, 2005 - No. 4, Aug, 2005 ($2.99, limited series)
1-4-Sumerak-s/Gurihiru-a; back-up Franklin Richards story. 3-Fantastic Four app. 3.00
... Digest (2006, $6.99) r/#1-4 7.00

POWER PACK: DAY ONE
Marvel Comics: May, 2008 - No. 4, Aug, 2008($2.99, limited series)
1-4-Van Lente-s/Gurihiru-a; origin retold; Coover-a back-ups. 1-Fantastic Four cameo 3.00

POWERPUFF GIRLS, THE (Also see Cartoon Network Starring... #1)
DC Comics: May, 2000 - No. 70, Mar, 2006 ($1.99/$2.25)
1 1 3 4 6 8 10
2-10 5.00
11-55,57-70: 25-Pin-ups by Allred, Byrne, Baker, Mignola, Hernandez, Warren 4.00
56-($2.95) Bonus pages; Mojo Jojo-c 5.00
...Double Whammy (12/00, $3.95) r/#1,2 & a Dexter's Lab story 5.00
...Movie: The Comic (9/02, $2.95) Movie adaptation; Phil Moy & Chris Cook-a 4.00

POWERPUFF GIRLS
IDW Publishing: Sept, 2013 - No. 10, Jun, 2014 ($3.99)
1-10: 1-Five covers; Troy Little-s/a; Mojo Jojo app. 2-10-Multiple covers on each 4.00

POWERPUFF GIRLS (Based on the 2016 TV reboot)
IDW Publishing: Jul, 2016 - Present ($3.99)
1-6: 1-4-Derek Charm-a; multiple covers on each. 1-Mojo Jojo app. 4.00

POWERPUFF GIRLS: SUPER SMASH-UP!
IDW Publishing: Jan, 2015 - No. 5, May, 2015 ($3.99, limited series)
1-5-Dexter's Laboratory's Dexter & Dee-Dee app.; multiple covers on each 4.00

POWER RANGERS ZEO (TV)(Saban's...)(Also see Saban's Mighty Morphin Power Rangers)
Image Comics (Extreme Studios): Aug, 1996 ($2.50)
1-Based on TV show 4.00

POWER RECORD COMICS (Named Peter Pan Record Comics for #33-47)
Marvel Comics/Power Records: 1974 - 1978 ($1.49, 7x10" comics, 20 pgs. with 45 R.P.M. record) (Clipped corners - reduce value 20%) (Comic alone - 50%; record alone - 50%) (Some copies significantly warped by shrinkwrapping - reduce value 20%) (PR22, PR23, PR38, PR43, PR44 do not exist)
PR10-Spider-Man-r/from #124,125; Man-Wolf app. PR18-Planet of the Apes-r. PR19-Escape From the Planet of the Apes-r. PR20-Beneath the Planet of the Apes-r. PR21-Battle for the Planet of the Apes-r. PR24-Spider-Man II-New-a begins. PR27-Batman "Stacked Cards"; N. Adams-a(p). PR30-Batman "Robin Meets Man-Bat"; N. Adams-r/Det.(7 pgs.).
With record; each... 5 10 15 35 63 90
PR11-Incredible Hulk-r/#171. PR12-Captain America-r/#168. PR13-Fantastic Four-r/#126. PR14-Frankenstein-Ploog-r/#1. PR15-Tomb of Dracula-Colan-r/#2. PR16-Man-Thing-Ploog-r/#5. PR17-Werewolf By Night-Ploog-r/Marvel Spotlight #2. PR28-Superman "Alien Creatures". PR29-Space: 1999 "Breakaway". PR31-Conan-N. Adams-a; reprinted in Conan #116. PR32-Space: 1999 "Return to the Beginning". PR33-Superman-G.A. origin, Buckler-a(p). PR34-Superman. PR35-Wonder Woman-Buckler-a(p)
With record; each... 5 10 15 31 53 75
PR11, PR24-(1981 Peter Pan records re-issues) PR11-New Abomination & Rhino-c
With record; each... 5 10 15 33 57 80
PR25-Star Trek "Passage to Moauv". PR26-Star Trek "Crier in Emptiness." PR36-Holo-Man. PR37-Robin Hood. PR39-Huckleberry Finn. PR40-Davy Crockett. PR41-Robinson Crusoe. PR42-20,000 Leagues Under the Sea. PR47-Little Women
With record; each... 4 8 12 28 47 65
PR25, PR26 (Peter Pan records re-issues with photo covers). PR45-Star Trek "Dinosaur Planet". PR46-Star Trek "The Robot Masters" 4 8 12 28 47 65
NOTE: *Peter Pan re-issues exist for #25-32 and are valued the same.*

POWERS
Image Comics: 2000 - No. 37, Feb, 2004 ($2.95)
1-Bendis-s/Oeming-a; murder of Retro Girl 3 6 9 16 23 30
2-6: 6-End of Retro Girl arc. 1 3 4 6 8 10
7-14: 7-Warren Ellis app. 12-14-Death of Olympia 4.00
15-37: 31-36-Origin of the Powers 3.00
Annual 1 (2001, $3.95) 4.00
...: Anarchy TPB (11/03, $14.95) r/#21-24; interviews, sketchbook, cover gallery 15.00
...Coloring/Activity Book (2001, $1.50, B&W, 8 x 10.5") Oeming-a 3.00
... Firsts 1 (6/15, $1.00) r/#1 3.00
...: Forever TPB (2005, $19.95) r/#31-37; script for #31, sketchbook, cover gallery 20.00
...: Little Deaths TPB (2002, $19.95) r/#7,12-14, Ann. #1, Coloring/Activity Book; sketch pages, cover gallery 20.00
...: Roleplay TPB (2001, $13.95) r/#8-11; sketchbook, cover gallery 14.00
... Scriptbook (2001, $19.95) scripts for #1-11; Oeming sketches 20.00
...: Supergroup TPB (2003, $19.95) r/#15-20; sketchbook, cover gallery 20.00
...: The Definitive Collection Vol. 1 HC (2006, $29.99, dust jacket) r/#1-11 & Coloring/Activity Book, script for #1, sketch pages and covers, interviews, letter column highlights 30.00
...: The Definitive Collection Vol. 2 HC (2009, $29.99, dust jacket) r/#12-24 & Annual #1; cover gallery; 1st Bendis/Oeming Jinx story; interviews, letter column highlights 30.00
...: Who Killed Retro Girl TPB (2000, $21.95) r/#1-6; sketchbook, cover gallery, and promotional strips from Comic Shop News 22.00

POWERS
Marvel Comics (Icon): Jul, 2004 - No. 30, Sept, 2008 ($2.95/$3.95)
1-11,13-24-Bendis-s/Oeming-a. 14-Cover price error 3.00
12-($3.95, 64 pages) 2 covers; Bendis & Oeming interview 4.00
25-30-($3.95, 40 pages) 25-Two covers; Bendis interview 4.00
Annual 2008 (5/08, $4.95) Bendis-s/Oeming-a; interview with Brubaker, Simone, others 5.00
...: Legends TPB (2005, $17.95) r/#1-6; sketchbook, cover gallery 18.00
...: Psychotic TPB (1/06, $19.95) r/#7-12; Bendis & Oeming interview, cover gallery 20.00
...: Cosmic TPB (10/07, $19.95) r/#13-18; script and sketch pages 20.00
...: Secret Identity TPB (12/07, $19.95) r/#19-24; script pages 20.00

POWERS (Volume 3)
Marvel Comics (Icon): Nov, 2009 - No. 11, Jul, 2012 ($3.95)
1-11-Bendis-s/Oeming-a 4.00

POWERS (Volume 5)
Marvel Comics (Icon): Jan, 2015 - Present ($3.99)
1-7-Bendis-s/Oeming-a. 1-Bonus photo spread of TV show cast 4.00

POWERS: BUREAU (Follows Volume 3)
Marvel Comics (Icon): Feb, 2013 - No. 12, Nov, 2014 ($3.95)
1-12-Bendis-s/Oeming-a 4.00

POWERS THAT BE (Becomes Star Seed No.7 on)
Broadway Comics: Nov, 1995 - No. 6, June, 1996 ($2.50)
1-6: 1-Intro of Fatale & Star Seed. 6-Begin $2.95-c. 3.00
Preview Editions 1-3 (9/95 - 11/95, B&W) 3.00

POWER UP
BOOM! Studios: Jul, 2015 - No. 6, Dec, 2015 ($3.99)
1-6-Katie Leth-s/Matt Cummings-a. 1-Multiple covers 4.00

POW MAGAZINE (Bob Sproul's) (Satire Magazine)
Humor-Vision: Aug, 1966 - No. 3, Feb, 1967 (30¢)
1,2: 2-Jones-a 4 8 12 28 47 65
3-Wrightson-a 5 10 15 34 60 85

PREACHER
DC Comics (Vertigo): Apr, 1995 - No. 66, Oct, 2000 ($2.50, mature)
nn-Preview 10 20 30 69 147 225
1 ($2.95)-Ennis scripts, Dillon-a & Fabry-c in all; 1st app. Jesse, Tulip, & Cassidy
10 20 30 69 147 225
1-Retailer Incentive Edition (5/16, $3.99) r/#1 with new cover by Steve Dillon 4.00
1-Special Edition (6/09, $1.00) r/#1 with "After Watchmen" cover frame 4.00
2-1st app. Saint of Killers. 4 8 12 28 47 65
3 3 6 9 20 31 42
4,5 3 6 9 16 23 30
6-10 2 4 6 10 14 18
11,12,14,15: 12-Polybagged w/videogame w/Ennis text
1 3 4 6 8 10
13-Hunters storyline begins; ends #17; 1st app. Herr Starr
3 6 9 21 33 45
16-20: 19-Saint of Killers app.; begin "Crusaders", ends #24 6.00
21-25: 21-24-Saint of Killers app. 25-Origin of Cassidy. 4.00
26-49,52-64: 52-Tulip origin 3.00
50-($3.75) Pin-ups by Jim Lee, Bradstreet, Quesada and Palmiotti 4.00
51-Includes preview of 100 Bullets; Tulip origin 1 3 4 6 8 10
65,66-($3.75) 65-Almost everyone dies. 66-Final issue
1 3 4 6 8 10
Alamo (2001, $17.95, TPB) r/#59-66; Fabry-c 18.00
All Hell's a-Coming (2000, $17.95, TPB)-r/#51-58, ...:Tall in the Saddle 18.00
... Book One HC (2009, $39.99, d.j.) r/#1-12; new Ennis intro.; pin-ups from #50,66 40.00
... Book Two HC (2010, $39.99, d.j.) r/#13-26; new Stuart Moore intro. 40.00

Predators #3 © 20th Century Fox

Pretty Deadly #8 © Milkfed & Rios

Prez (2015 series) #4 © DC

	GD 2.0	VG 4.0	FN 6.0	VF 8.0	VF/NM 9.0	NM- 9.2

... Book Three HC (2010, $39.99, d.j.) r/#27-33, ...Special: Saint of Killers #1-4 & ...Special: Cassidy: Blood & Whiskey #1; new Ennis intro. 40.00
... Book Four HC (2011, $39.99, d.j.) r/#34-40, ...Special: One Man's War, ...Special: The Story of You-Know-Who, & ...Special: The Good Old Boys; new Dillon intro. 40.00
...: Dead or Alive HC (2000, $29.95) Gallery of Glenn Fabry's cover paintings for every Preacher issue; commentary by Fabry & Ennis 30.00
...: Dead or Alive SC (2003, $19.95) 20.00
Dixie Fried (1998, $14.95, TPB)-r/#27-33, Special: Cassidy 15.00
Gone To Texas (1996, $14.95, TPB)-r/#1-7; Fabry-c 15.00
Proud Americans (1997, $14.95, TPB)-r/#18-26; Fabry-c 15.00
Salvation (1999, $14.95, TPB)-r/#41-50; Fabry-c 15.00
Until the End of the World (1996, $14.95, TPB)-r/#8-17; Fabry-c 15.00
War in the Sun (1999, $14.95, TPB)-r/#34-40 15.00

PREACHER SPECIAL: CASSIDY: BLOOD & WHISKEY
DC Comics (Vertigo): 1998 ($5.95, one-shot)
1-Ennis-scripts/Fabry-c/Dillon-a 6.00

PREACHER SPECIAL: ONE MAN'S WAR
DC Comics (Vertigo): Mar, 1998 ($4.95, one-shot)
1-Ennis-scripts/Fabry-c /Snejbjerg-a 5.00

PREACHER SPECIAL: SAINT OF KILLERS
DC Comics (Vertigo): Aug, 1996 - No. 4, Nov, 1996 ($2.50, lim. series, mature)
1-4: Ennis-scripts/Fabry-c. 1,2-Pugh-a. 3,4-Ezquerra-a 4.00
1-Signed & numbered 20.00

PREACHER SPECIAL: THE GOOD OLD BOYS
DC Comics (Vertigo): Aug, 1997 ($4.95, one-shot, mature)
1-Ennis-scripts/Fabry-c /Esquerra-a 5.00

PREACHER SPECIAL: THE STORY OF YOU-KNOW-WHO
DC Comics (Vertigo): Dec, 1996 ($4.95, one-shot, mature)
1-Ennis-scripts/Fabry-c/Case-a 5.00

PREACHER: TALL IN THE SADDLE
DC Comics (Vertigo): 2000 ($5.95, one-shot)
1-Ennis-scripts/Fabry-c/Dillon-a; early romance of Tulip and Jesse 6.00

PRECINCT, THE
Dynamite Entertainment: 2015 - No. 5, 2016 ($3.99)
1-5-Barbarie-s/Zamora-a. 1-Covers by Benitez & Robertson 4.00

PREDATOR (Also see Aliens Vs. ..., Batman vs. ..., Dark Horse Comics, & Dark Horse Presents)
Dark Horse Comics: June, 1989 - No. 4, Mar, 1990 ($2.25, limited series)

	GD	VG	FN	VF	VF/NM	NM-
1-Based on movie; 1st app. Predator	3	6	9	19	30	40
1-2nd printing	1	3	4	6	8	10
2	1	3	4	6	8	10
3,4	1	2	3	5	6	8

Trade paperback (1990, $12.95)-r/#1-4 15.00
... Omnibus Volume 1 (8/07, $24.95, 6" x 9") r/#1-4, ... Cold War, ... Dark River, ...Bloody Sands of Time mini-series and stories from Dark Horse Comics #1,2,4-7,10-12 25.00
... Omnibus Volume 2 (2/08, $24.95, 6" x 9") r/ ... Big Game, ... Race War, ...Invaders From The, Fourth Dimension mini-series and stories from Dark Horse Comics #16-18,20,21; Dark Horse Presents #46 and A Decade of Dark Horse 25.00
... Omnibus Volume 3 (6/08, $24.95, 6" x 9") r/ ... Bad Blood, ... Kindred, ...Hell and Hot Water, ... Strange Roux mini-series and stories from Dark Horse Comics #12-14 and Dark Horse Presents #119 & 124 25.00

PREDATOR
Dark Horse Comics: June, 2009 - No. 4, Jan, 2010 ($3.50, limited series)
1-4-Arcudi-s/Saltares-a/Swanland-c; variant-c by Warner 3.50

PREDATOR: (title series) **Dark Horse Comics**
--BAD BLOOD, 12/93 - No. 4, 1994 ($2.50) 1-4 4.00
--BIG GAME, 3/91 - No. 4, 6/91 ($2.50) 1-4: 1-3-Contain 2 Dark Horse trading cards 4.00
--BLOODY SANDS OF TIME, 2/92 - No. 2, 2/92 ($2.50) 1,2-Dan Barry-c/a(p)/scripts 4.00
--CAPTIVE, 4/98 ($2.95, one-shot) 1 4.00
--COLD WAR, 9/91 - No. 4, 12/91 ($2.50) 1-4: All have painted-c 4.00
--DARK RIVER, 7/96 - No.4, 10/96 ($2.95)1-4: Miran Kim-c 4.00
--HELL & HOT WATER, 4/97 - No. 3, 6/97 ($2.95) 1-3 4.00
--HELL COME A WALKIN', 2/98 - No. 2, 3/98 ($2.95) 1,2-In the Civil War 4.00
--HOMEWORLD, 3/99 - No. 4, 6/99 ($2.95) 1-4 4.00
--INVADERS FROM THE FOURTH DIMENSION, 7/94 ($3.95, one-shot, 52 pgs.) 1 4.00
--JUNGLE TALES. 3/95 ($2.95t) 1-r/Dark Horse Comics 4.00
--KINDRED, 12/96 - No. 4, 3/97 ($2.50) 1-4 4.00
--NEMESIS, 12/97 - No. 2, 1/98 ($2.95) 1,2-Predator in Victorian England; Taggart-c 4.00
--PRIMAL, 7/97 - No. 2, 8/97 ($2.95) 1,2 4.00
--RACE WAR (See Dark Horse Presents #67), 2/93 - No. 4,10/93 ($2.50, color) 1-4,0: 1-4-Dorman painted-c #1-4, 0(4/93) 4.00
--STRANGE ROUX, 11/96 ($2.95, one-shot) 1 4.00
--XENOGENESIS (Also see Aliens Xenogenesis), 8/99 - No. 4, 11/99 ($2.95) 1,2-Edginton-s 4.00

PREDATOR: FIRE AND STONE (Crossover with Aliens, AvP, and Prometheus)
Dark Horse Comics: Oct, 2014 - No. 4, Jan, 2015 ($3.50, limited series)
1-4-Williamson-s/Mooneyham-a 3.50

PREDATOR: LIFE AND DEATH (Continues in Prometheus: Life and Death)
Dark Horse Comics: Mar, 2016 - No. 4, Jun, 2016 ($3.99, limited series)
1-4-Abnett-s/Thies-a 4.00

PREDATORS (Based on the 2010 movie)
Dark Horse Comics: Jun, 2010 - No. 4, Jun, 2010 ($2.99, weekly limited series)
1-4-Prequel to the 2010 movie; stories by Andreyko and Lapham; Paul Lee-c 3.00
... Film Adaptation (7/10, $6.99) Tobin-s/Drujiniu-s/photo-c 7.00
...: Preserve the Game (7/10, $3.50) Sequel to the movie; Lapham-s/Jefferson-a 3.50

PREDATOR 2
Dark Horse Comics: Feb, 1991 - No. 2, June, 1991 ($2.50, limited series)
1,2: 1-Adapts movie; both w/trading cards & photo-c 4.00

PREDATOR VS. JUDGE DREDD
Dark Horse Comics: Oct, 1997 - No. 3 ($2.50, limited series)
1-3-Wagner-s/Alcatena-a/Bolland-c 4.00

PREDATOR VS. JUDGE DREDD VS. ALIENS
Dark Horse Comics/IDW: Jul, 2016 - Present ($3.99, limited series)
1-3-Layman-s/Mooneyham-a/Fabry-c 4.00

PREDATOR VS. MAGNUS ROBOT FIGHTER
Dark Horse/Valiant: Oct, 1992 - No. 2, 1993 ($2.95, limited series)
(1st Dark Horse/Valiant x-over)
1,2: (Reg.)-Barry Smith-c; Lee Weeks-a. 2-w/trading cards 4.00
1 (Platinum edition, 11/92)-Barry Smith-c 10.00

PREHISTORIC WORLD (See Classics Illustrated Special Issue)

PRELUDE TO DEADPOOL CORPS (Leads into Deadpool Corps #1)
Marvel Comics: May, 2010 - No. 5, May, 2010 ($3.99/$2.99, weekly limited series)
1-($3.99) Deadpool & Lady Deadpool vs. alternate dimension Capt. America; Liefeld-a 4.00
2-5-($2.99) Alternate reality Deadpools team-up; Dave Johnson interlocking covers 3.00

PRELUDE TO INFINITE CRISIS
DC Comics: 2005 ($5.99, squarebound)
nn-Reprints stories and panels with commentary leading into Infinite Crisis series 6.00

PREMIERE (See Charlton Premiere)

PRESIDENTIAL MATERIAL
IDW Publishing: Oct, 2008 ($3.99/$7.99)
...: Barack Obama - Biography of the candidate; Mariotte-s/Morgan-a/Campbell-c 4.00
...: John McCain - Biography of the candidate; Helfer-s/Thompson-a/Campbell-c 4.00
Flipbook ($7.99) Both issues in flipbook format 8.00

PRESTO KID, THE (See Red Mask)

PRETTY BOY FLOYD (See On the Spot)

PRETTY DEADLY
Image Comics: Oct, 2013 - Present ($3.50)
1-10-DeConnick-s/Rios-a/c 3.50

PREZ (See Cancelled Comic Cavalcade, Sandman #54 & Supergirl #10)
National Periodical Publications: Aug-Sept, 1973 - No. 4, Feb-Mar, 1974

	GD	VG	FN	VF	VF/NM	NM-
1-Origin; Joe Simon scripts	3	6	9	17	26	35
2-4	2	4	6	13	18	22

PREZ
DC Comics: Aug, 2015 - No. 6, Feb, 2016 ($2.99)
1-6: 1-Intro. Beth Ross; Mark Russell-s/Ben Caldwell-a 3.00

PRICE, THE (See Eclipse Graphic Album Series)

PRIDE & JOY

Primal Force #7 © DC

Princess Ugg #8 © Ted Naifeh

Prison Break! #3 © AVON

	GD 2.0	VG 4.0	FN 6.0	VF 8.0	VF/NM 9.0	NM- 9.2

DC Comics (Vertigo): July, 1997 - No. 4, Oct, 1997 ($2.50, limited series)

1-4-Ennis-s 3.00
TPB (2004, $14.95) r/#1-4 15.00

PRIDE & PREJUDICE
Marvel Comics: June, 2009 - No. 5, Oct, 2009 ($3.99, limited series)

1-5-Adaptation of the Jane Austen novel; Nancy Butler-s/Hugo Petrus-a 4.00

PRIDE AND THE PASSION, THE
Dell Publishing Co.: No. 824, Aug, 1957

Four Color 824-Movie, Frank Sinatra & Cary Grant photo-c
9 18 27 59 117 175

PRIDE OF BAGHDAD
DC Comics (Vertigo): 2006 ($19.99, hardcover with dustjacket)

HC-A pride of lions escaping from the Baghdad zoo in 2003; Vaughan-s/Henrichon-a 20.00
SC-(2007, $12.99) 13.00

PRIDE OF THE YANKEES, THE (See Real Heroes & Sport Comics)
Magazine Enterprises: 1949 (The Life of Lou Gehrig)

nn-Photo-c; Ogden Whitney-a 84 168 252 538 919 1300

PRIEST (Also see Asylum)
Maximum Press: Aug, 1996 - No. 2, Oct, 1996 ($2.99)

1,2 3.00

PRIMAL FORCE
DC Comics: No. 0, Oct, 1994 - No. 14, Dec, 1995 ($1.95/$2.25)

0-14: 0- Teams Red Tornado, Golem, Jack O'Lantern, Meridian & Silver Dragon. 9-begin $2.25-c 3.00

PRIMAL MAN (See The Crusaders)

PRIMAL RAGE
Sirius Entertainment: 1996 ($2.95)

1-Dark One-c; based of video game 3.00

PRIME (See Break-Thru, Flood Relief & Ultraforce)
Malibu Comics (Ultraverse): June, 1993 - No. 26, Aug, 1995 ($1.95/$2.50)

1-1st app. Prime; has coupon for Ultraverse Premiere #0 4.00
1-With coupon missing 2.00
1-Full cover holographic edition; 1st of kind w/Hardcase #1 & Strangers #1 10.00
1-Ultra 5,000 edition w/silver ink-c 6.00
2-4,6-11,14-26: 2-Polybagged w/card & coupon for U. Premiere #0. 3,4-Prototype app. 4-Direct sale w/o card.4-($2.50)-Newsstand ed. polybagged w/card. 6-Bill & Chelsea Clinton app.115-Intro Papa Verite; Pérez-c/a. 16-Intro Turbo Charge 3.00
5-($2.50, 48 pgs.)-Rune flip-c/story part B by Barry Smith; see Sludge #1 for 1st app. Rune; 3-pg. Night Man preview 4.00
12-($3.50, 68 pgs.)-Flip book w/Ultraverse Premiere #3; silver foil logo 4.00
13-($2.95, 52 pgs.)-Variant covers 4.00
...: Gross and Disgusting 1 (10/94, $3.95)-Boris-c; "Annual" on cover, published monthly in indicia 4.00
...Month "Ashcan" (8/94, 75¢)-Boris-c 3.00
... Time: A Prime Collection (1994, $9.95)-r/1-4 10.00
...Vs. The Incredible Hulk (1995)-mail away limited edition 10.00
...Vs. The Incredible Hulk Premium edition 10.00
...Vs. The Incredible Hulk Super Premium edition 15.00
NOTE: *Perez a-15; c-15, 16.*

PRIME (Also see Black September)
Malibu Comics (Ultraverse): Infinity, Sept, 1995 - V2#15, Dec, 1996 ($1.50)

Infinity, V2#1-15: Post Black September storyline. 6-8-Solitaire app. 9-Breyfogle-c/a. 10-12-Ramos-c. 15-Lord Pumpkin app. 3.00
Infinity Signed Edition (2,000 printed) 1 2 3 5 6 8

PRIME/CAPTAIN AMERICA
Malibu Comics: Mar, 1996 ($3.95, one-shot)

1-Norm Breyfogle-a 5.00

PRIME8: CREATION
Two Morrows Publishing: July, 2001 ($3.95, B&W)

1-Neal Adams-c 4.00

PRIMER (Comico...)
Comico: Oct (no month), 1982 - No. 6, Feb, 1984 (B&W)

1 (52 pgs.) 2 4 6 13 18 22
2-1st app. Grendel & Argent by Wagner 9 18 27 62 126 190
3,4 2 4 6 9 12 15
5-1st Sam Kieth art in comics ('83) & 1st The Maxx 6 12 18 37 66 95
6-Intro & 1st app. Evangeline 2 4 6 13 18 22

PRIMORTALS (Leonard Nimoy's...)

PRIMUS (TV)
Charlton Comics: Feb, 1972 - No. 7, Oct, 1972

1-Staton-a in all 2 4 6 11 16 20
2-7: 6-Drug propaganda story 2 4 6 8 11 14

PRINCE NAMOR, THE SUB-MARINER (Also see Namor ...)
Marvel Comics Group: Sept, 1984 - No. 4, Dec, 1984 (Limited-series)

1-4 5.00

PRINCE OF PERSIA: BEFORE THE SANDSTORM (Based on the 2010 movie)
Dynamite Entertainment: 2010 - No. 4, 2010 ($3.99, limited series)

1-4-Art by Fowler and various. 1-Chang-a. 2-Lopez-a. 3-Edwards-a 5.00

PRINCESS LEIA (Star Wars)
Marvel Comics: May, 2015 - No. 5, Sept, 2015 ($3.99)

1-5-Mark Waid-s/Terry Dodson-a; story follows the ending of Episode IV 4.00

PRINCESS SALLY (Video game)
Archie Publications: Apr, 1995 - No. 3, June, 1995 ($1.50, limited series)

1-3: Spin-off from Sonic the Hedgehog 4.00

PRINCESS UGG
Oni Press: Jun, 2014 - No. 8, Mar, 2015 ($3.99)

1-8-Ted Naifeh-s/a 4.00

PRINCE VALIANT (See Ace Comics, Comics Reading Libraries *in the Promotional Comics section*, & King Comics #146, 147)
David McKay Publ./Dell: No. 26, 1941; No. 67, June, 1954 - No. 900, May, 1958

Feature Books 26 ('41)-Harold Foster-c/a; newspaper strips reprinted, pgs. 1-28,30-63; color & 68 pgs; Foster cover is only original comic book artwork by him
170 340 510 1080 1815 2550
Four Color 567 (6/54)(#1)-By Bob Fuje-Movie, photo-c
10 20 30 64 132 200
Four Color 650 (9/55), 699 (4/56), 719 (8/56),-Fuje-a 7 14 21 48 89 130
Four Color 788 (4/57), 849 (1/58), 900-Fuje-a 7 14 21 44 82 120

PRINCE VALIANT
Marvel Comics: Dec, 1994 - No. 4, Mar, 1995 ($3.95, limited series)

1-4: Kaluta-c in all 4.00

PRINCE VANDAL
Triumphant Comics: Nov, 1993 - Apr?, 1994 ($2.50)

1-6: 1,2-Triumphant Unleashed x-over 3.00

PRIORITY: WHITE HEAT
AC Comics: 1986 - No. 2, 1986 ($1.75, mini-series)

1,2-Bill Black-a 3.00

PRISCILLA'S POP
Dell Publishing Co.: No. 569, June, 1954 - No. 799, May, 1957

Four Color 569 (#1), 630 (5/55), 704 (5/56),799 5 10 15 31 53 75

PRISON BARS (See Behind...)

PRISON BREAK!
Avon Per./Realistic No. 3 on: Sept, 1951 - No. 5, Sept, 1952 (Painted c-3)

1-Wood-c & 1 pg.; has-r/Saint #7 retitled Michael Strong Private Eye
55 110 165 352 601 850
2-Wood-c; Kubert-a; Kinstler inside front-c 43 86 129 271 461 650
3-Orlando, Check-a; c-/Avon paperback #179 34 68 102 199 325 450
4,5: 4-Kinstler-c & inside f/c; Lawrence, Lazarus-a. 5-Kinstler-c; Infantino-a
30 60 90 177 289 400

PRISONER, THE (TV)
DC Comics: 1988 - No. 4, 1989 ($3.50, squarebound, mini-series)

1-4 (Books a-d) 5.00

PRISON RIOT
Avon Periodicals: 1952

1-Marijuana Murders-1 pg. text; Kinstler-c; 2 Kubert illos on text pages
41 82 123 256 428 600

PRISON TO PRAISE
Logos International: 1974 (35¢) (Religious, Christian)

nn-True Story of Merlin R. Carothers 2 4 6 13 18 22

PRIVATE BUCK
Dell Publishing Co./Rand McNally: No. 21, 1941 - No. 12, 1942 (4-1/2" x 5-1/2", 1942)

Prize Comics #2 © PRIZE

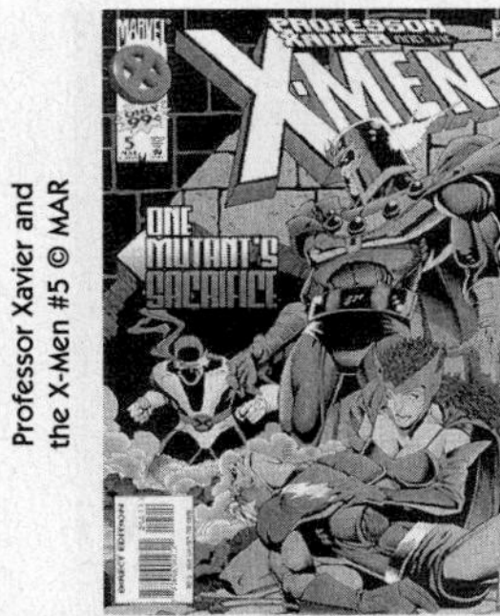

Professor Xavier and the X-Men #5 © MAR

Project Superpowers: Blackcross #4 © DYN

	GD 2.0	VG 4.0	FN 6.0	VF 8.0	VF/NM 9.0	NM- 9.2

Large Feature Comic 21 (#1)(1941)(Series I), 22 (1941)(Series I), 12 (1942)(Series II)
20 40 60 114 182 250
382-Rand McNally, one panel per page; small size 10 20 30 58 79 100

PRIVATE EYE (Cover title: Rocky Jorden...#6-8)
Atlas Comics (MCI): Jan, 1951 - No. 8, March, 1952

1-Cover title: Crime Cases... #1-5 24 48 72 144 237 330
2,3-Tuska c/a(3) 14 28 42 82 121 160
4-8 13 26 39 72 101 130

NOTE: *Henkel a-6(3), 7; c-7.* ***Sinnott*** *a-6.*

PRIVATE EYE (See Mike Shayne...)

PRIVATE SECRETARY
Dell Publishing Co.: Dec-Feb, 1962-63 - No. 2, Mar-May, 1963

1 3 6 9 20 31 42
2 3 6 9 16 24 32

PRIVATE STRONG (See The Double Life of...)

PRIZE COMICS (...Western #69 on) (Also see Treasure Comics)
Prize Publications: March, 1940 - No. 68, Feb-Mar, 1948

1-Origin Power Nelson, The Futureman & Jupiter, Master Magician; Ted O'Neil, Secret Agent M-11, Jaxon of the Jungle, Bucky Brady & Storm Curtis begin (1st app. of each)
314 628 942 2198 3849 5500
2-The Black Owl begins (1st app.) 206 412 618 1318 2259 3200
3-Classic sci-fi-c 194 388 582 1242 2121 3000
4-Classic robot-c 232 464 696 1485 2543 3600
5-Dr. Dekkar, Master of Monsters app. 148 296 444 947 1624 2300
6-Classic sci-fi-c; Dr. Dekkar app. 174 348 522 1114 1907 2700
7-(Scarce)-1st app. The Green Lama (12/40); Black Owl by S&K; origin/1st app. Dr. Frost & Frankenstein; Capt. Gallant, The Great Voodini & Twist Turner begin;
649 1298 1947 4738 8369 12,000
8,9-Black Owl & Ted O'Neil by S&K 168 336 504 1075 1838 2600
10-12,14,15: 11-Origin Bulldog Denny. 14-War-c 129 258 387 826 1413 2000
13-Yank & Doodle begin (8/41, origin/1st app.) 155 310 465 992 1676 2400
16-19: 16-Spike Mason begins 119 238 357 762 1306 1850
20-(Rare) Frankenstein, Black Owl, Green Lama, Yank and Doodle WWII parade-c
314 628 942 2198 3849 5500
21,25,27,28,31-All WWII covers 97 194 291 621 1061 1500
22-24,26: 22-Statue of Liberty Japanese attack war-c. 23-Uncle Sam patriotic war-c. 24-Lincoln statue patriotic-c. 26-Liberty Bell-c 129 258 387 826 1413 2000
29,30,32 81 162 243 518 884 1250
33-Classic bondage/torture-c 161 322 483 1030 1765 2500
34-Origin Airmale, Yank & Doodle; The Black Owl joins army, Yank & Doodle's father assumes Black Owl's role 58 116 174 371 636 900
35-36,38-39: 35-Flying Fist & Bingo begin 53 106 159 334 567 800
37-Intro. Stampy, Airmale's sidekick; Hitler-c 226 452 678 1446 2473 3500
40-Nazi WWII-c 55 110 165 352 601 850
41-45,47-50: 45-Yank & Doodle learn Black Owl's I.D. (their father). 48-Prince Ra begins
47 94 141 296 498 700
46-Classic Zombie Horror-c/story 103 206 309 659 1130 1600
51-62,64,67,68: 53-Transvestism story. 55-No Frankenstein. 57-X-Mas-c. 64-Black Owl retires 34 68 102 199 325 450
63-Simon & Kirby c/a 37 74 111 222 361 500
65,66-Frankenstein-c by Briefer 39 78 117 240 395 550

NOTE: ***Briefer*** *a 7-on; c-65, 66.* ***J. Binder*** *a-16; c-21-29.* ***Guardineer*** *a-62.* ***Kiefer*** *c-62.* ***Palais*** *c-68.* ***Simon & Kirby*** *c-63, 75, 83.*

PRIZE COMICS WESTERN (Formerly Prize Comics #1-68)
Prize Publications (Feature): No. 69(V7#2), Apr-May, 1948 - No. 119, Nov-Dec, 1956 (No. 69-84: 52 pgs.)

69(V7#2) 15 30 45 86 133 180
70-75: 74-Kurtzman-a (8 pgs.) 14 28 42 80 115 150
76-Randolph Scott photo-c; "Canadian Pacific" movie adaptation
14 28 42 82 121 160
77-Photo-c; Severin/Elder, Mart Bailey-a; "Streets of Laredo" movie adaptation
14 28 42 80 115 150
78-Photo-c; S&K-a, 10 pgs.; Severin, Mart Bailey-a; "Bullet Code", & "Roughshod" movie adaptations 18 36 54 103 162 220
79-Photo-c; Kurtzman-a, 8 pgs.; Severin/Elder, Severin, Mart Bailey-a; "Stage To Chino" movie adaptation w/George O'Brien 18 36 54 103 162 220
80-82-Photo-c; 80,81-Severin/Elder-a(2). 82-1st app. The Preacher by Mart Bailey; Severin/Elder-a(3) 14 28 42 82 121 160
83,84 13 26 39 72 101 130
85-1st app. American Eagle by John Severin & begins (V9#6, 1-2/51)
20 40 60 120 195 270
86,101-105, 109-Severin/Williamson-a 14 28 42 78 112 145
87-99,110,111-Severin/Elder-a(2-3) each 14 28 42 81 110 155
100 15 30 45 85 124 165
106-108,112 10 20 30 56 76 95
113-Williamson/Severin-a(2)/Frazetta? 14 28 42 81 118 155
114-119: Drifter series in all; by Mort Meskin #114-118
9 18 27 52 69 85

NOTE: ***Fass*** *a-81.* ***Severin & Elder*** *c-84-99.* ***Severin*** *a-72, 75, 77-79, 83-86, 96, 97, 100-105; c-92,100-109(most), 110-119.* ***Simon & Kirby*** *c-75, 83.*

PRIZE MYSTERY
Key Publications: May, 1955 - No. 3, Sept, 1955

1 12 24 36 69 97 125
2,3 9 18 27 47 61 75

PRO, THE
Image Comics: July, 2002 ($5.95, squarebound, one-shot)

1-Ennis-s/Conner & Palmiotti-a; prostitute gets super-powers 8.00
1-Second printing with different cover 6.00
Hardcover Edition (10/04, $14.95) oversized reprint plus new 8 pg. story; sketch pages 15.00

PROFESSIONAL FOOTBALL (See Charlton Sport Library)

PROFESSOR COFFIN
Charlton Comics: No. 19, Oct, 1985 - No. 21, Feb, 1986

19-21: Wayne Howard-a(r); low print run 1 2 3 5 6 8

PROFESSOR OM
Innovation Publishing: May, 1990 - No. 2, 1990 ($2.50, limited series)

1,2-East Meets West spin-off 3.00

PROFESSOR XAVIER AND THE X-MEN (Also see X-Men, 1st series)
Marvel Comics: Nov, 1995 - No. 18 (99¢)

1-18: Stories featuring the Original X-Men. 2-vs. The Blob. 5-Vs. the Original Brotherhood of Evil Mutants. 10-Vs. The Avengers 3.00

PROGRAMME, THE
DC Comics (WildStorm): Sept, 2007 - No. 12, Aug, 2008 ($2.99, limited series)

1-12: 1-Milligan-s/C.P. Smith-a; covers by Smith & Van Sciver 3.00
Book One TPB (2008, $17.99) r/#1-6; cover sketches 18.00
Book Two TPB (2008, $17.99) r/#7-12; cover sketches 18.00

PROJECT A-KO (Manga)
Malibu Comics: Mar, 1994 - No. 4, June, 1994 ($2.95)

1-4-Based on anime film 3.00

PROJECT A-KO 2 (Manga)
CPM Comics: May, 1995 - No. 3, Aug, 1995 ($2.95, limited series)

1-3 3.00

PROJECT A-KO VERSUS THE UNIVERSE (Manga)
CPM Comics: Oct, 1995 - No. 5, June, 1996 ($2.95, limited series, bi-monthly)

1-5 3.00

PROJECT BLACK SKY
Dark Horse Comics

... Sampler (10/14, $4.99) 1-Reprints The Occultist (2013) #1, Brain Boy (2013) #0, Ghost (2013) #1, Blackout #1 5.00
Free Comic Book Day: Project Black Sky (5/14, giveaway) Capt. Midnight & Brain Boy app. 3.00

PROJECT SUPERPOWERS
Dynamite Entertainment: 2008 - No. 7, 2008 ($1.00/$3.50/$2.99)

0-($1.00) Two connecting covers by Alex Ross; re-intro of Golden Age heroes 3.00
0-($1.00) Variant cover by Michael Turner 5.00
1-($3.50) Covers by Ross and Turner; Jim Krueger-s/Carlos Paul-a 3.50
2-7-($2.99) 3.00
... Chapter One HC (2008, $29.99, dustjacket) r/#0-7; Ross sketch pages; layout art 30.00

PROJECT SUPERPOWERS: BLACKCROSS
Dynamite Entertainment: 2015 - No. 6, 2015 ($3.99)

1-6-Warren Ellis-s/Colton Worley-a; multiple covers on each 4.00

PROJECT SUPERPOWERS: CHAPTER TWO
Dynamite Entertainment: 2009 - No. 12, 2010 ($1.00/$2.99)

... Chapter Two Prelude (2008, $1.00) Ross sketch pages and mini-series previews 3.00
0-($1.00) Three connecting covers by Alex Ross; The Inheritors assemble 3.00
1-12-($2.99) 1-Krueger & Ross-s/Salazar-a; Ross sketch pages; 2 Ross covers 3.00
... X-Mas Carol (2010, $5.99) Berkenkotter-a/Ross-c 6.00

PROJECT SUPERPOWERS: MEET THE BAD GUYS
Dynamite Entertainment: 2009 - No. 4, 2009 ($2.99)

Promethea #27 © ABC

Prophet #45 © Rob Liefeld

Psi-Lords #2 © VAL

	GD 2.0	VG 4.0	FN 6.0	VF 8.0	VF/NM 9.0	NM- 9.2

1-4: Ross & Casey-s. 1-Bloodlust. 2-The Revolutionary. 3-Dagon. 4-Supremacy 3.00

PROMETHEA
America's Best Comics: Aug, 1999 - No. 32, Apr, 2005 ($3.50/$2.95)

1-Alan Moore-s/Williams III & Gray-a; Alex Ross painted-c 4.00
1-Variant-c by Williams III & Gray 4.00
2-31-($2.95): 7-Villarrubia photo-a. 10-"Sex, Stars & Serpents". 26-28-Tom Strong app. 27-Cover swipe of Superman vs. Spider-Man treasury ed. 3.00
32-($3.95) Final issue; pages can be cut & assembled into a 2-sided poster 2 4 6 9 12 15
32-Limited edition of 1000; variant issue printed as 2-sided poster, signed by Moore and Williams; each came with a 48 page book of Promethea covers 120.00
Book 1 Hardcover ($24.95, dust jacket) r/#1-6 25.00
Book 1 TPB ($14.95) r/#1-6 15.00
Book 2 Hardcover ($24.95, dust jacket) r/#7-12 25.00
Book 2 TPB ($14.95) r/#7-12 15.00
Book 3 Hardcover ($24.95, dust jacket) r/#13-18 25.00
Book 3 TPB ($14.95) r/#13-18 15.00
Book 4 Hardcover ($24.95, dust jacket) r/#19-25 25.00
Book 4 TPB ($14.99) r/#19-25 15.00
Book 5 Hardcover ($24.95, d.j.) r/#26-32; includes 2-sided poster image from #32 25.00
Book 5 TPB ($14.99) r/#26-32; includes 2-sided poster image from #32 15.00

PROMETHEUS: FIRE AND STONE (Crossover with Aliens, AvP, and Predator)
Dark Horse Comics: Sept, 2014 - No. 4, Dec, 2014 ($3.50, limited series)

1-4-Tobin-s/Ferreyra-a 3.50
... – Omega (2/15, $4.99) DeConnick-s/Alessio-a; finale to the crossover 4.00

PROMETHEUS: LIFE AND DEATH (Continues in Aliens: Life and Death)
Dark Horse Comics: Jun, 2016 - No. 4, Sept, 2016 ($3.99, limited series)

1-4-Abnett-s/Mutti-a 4.00

PROMETHEUS (VILLAINS) (Leads into JLA #16,17)
DC Comics: Feb, 1998 ($1.95, one-shot)

1-Origin & 1st app.; Morrison-s/Pearson-c 3.00

PROPELLERMAN
Dark Horse Comics: Jan, 1993 - No. 8, Mar, 1994 ($2.95, limited series)

1-8: 2,4,8-Contain 2 trading cards 3.00

PROPHECY
Dynamite Entertainment: 2012 - No. 7, 2013 ($3.99, limited series)

1-7: 1-Marz-s/Geovani-a; Vampirella,Red Sonja, Dracula & Pantha app. 4-Ash app. 4.00

PROPHET (See Youngblood #2)
Image Comics (Extreme Studios): Oct, 1993 - No. 10, 1995 ($1.95)

1-($2.50)-Liefeld/Panosian-c/a; 1st app. Mary McCormick; Liefeld scripts in 1-4; #1-3 contain coupons for Prophet #0 4.00
1-Gold foil embossed-c edition rationed to dealers 6.00
2-10: 2-Liefeld-c(p). 3-1st app. Judas. 4-1st app. Omen; Black and White Pt. 3 by Thibert. 4-Alternate-c by Stephen Platt. 5,6-Platt-c/a. 7-(9/94, $2.50)-Platt-c/a. 8-Bloodstrike app. 10-Polybagged w/trading card; Platt-c. 3.00
0-(7/94, $2.50)-San Diego Comic Con ed. (2200 copies) 4.00

PROPHET
Image Comics (Extreme Studios): V2#1, Aug, 1995 - No. 8 ($3.50)

V2#1-8: Dixon scripts in all. 1-4-Platt-a. 1-Boris-c; F. Miller variant-c. 4-Newmen app. 5,6-Wraparound-c 3.50
Annual 1 (9/95, $2.50)-Bagged w/Youngblood gaming card; Quesada-c 3.00
Babewatch Special 1 (12/95, $2.50)-Babewatch tie-in 3.00
1995 San Diego Edition-B&W preview of V2#1. 3.00
TPB-(1996, $12.95) r/#1-7 13.00

PROPHET (Volume 3)
Awesome Comics: Mar, 2000 ($2.99)

1-Flip-c by Jim Lee and Liefeld 3.00

PROPHET
Image Comics: No. 21, Jan, 2012 - No. 45, Jul, 2014 ($2.99/$3.99)

21-27-($2.99): 21-Two covers; Graham-s 3.00
28-45-($3.99): 29-Dalrymple-a 4.00

PROPHET/CABLE
Image Comics (Extreme): Jan, 1997 - No. 2, Mar, 1997 ($3.50, limited series)

1,2-Liefeld-c/a: 2-#1 listed on cover 4.00

PROPHET/CHAPEL: SUPER SOLDIERS
Image Comics (Extreme): May, 1996 - No. 2, June, 1996 ($2.50, limited series)

1,2: 1-Two covers exist 3.00
1-San Diego Edition; B&W-c 3.00

PROPHET EARTHWAR
Image Comics: Jan, 2016 - No. 6, Nov, 2016 ($3.99)

1-6: 1-Graham & Roy-s/Milonogiannis & Roy-a 4.00

PROPHET: STRIKEFILE
Image Comics: Sept, 2014 - No. 2, Nov, 2015 ($3.99)

1,2-Short stories and profile pages by various 4.00

PROPOSITION PLAYER
DC Comics (Vertigo): Dec, 1999 - No. 6, May, 2000 ($2.50, limited series)

1-6-Willingham-s/Guinan-a/Bolton-c 3.00
TPB (2003, $14.95) r/#1-6; intro. by James McManus 15.00

PROTECTORS (Also see The Ferret)
Malibu Comics: Sept, 1992 - No. 20, May, 1994 ($1.95-$2.95)

1-20 ($2.50, direct sale)-With poster & diff-c: 1-Origin; has 3/4 outer-c. 3-Polybagged w/Skycap 3.50
1-12 ($1.95, newsstand)-Without poster 3.00

PROTECTORS, INC.
Image Comics: Nov, 2013 - No. 10, Nov, 2014 ($2.99)

1-10-Straczynski-s/Purcell-a; multiple covers on #1-7 3.00

PROTOTYPE (Also see Flood Relief & Ultraforce)
Malibu Comics (Ultraverse): Aug, 1993 - No. 18, Feb, 1995 ($1.95/$2.50)

1-Holo-c 1 2 3 5 6 8
1-Ultra Limited silver foil-c 6.00
1,3: 3-($2.50, 48 pgs.)-Rune flip-c/story by B. Smith (3 pgs.) 4.00
2,4-12,14-18: 4-Intro Wrath. 5-Break-Thru & Strangers x-over. 6-Arena cameo. 7,8-Arena-c/story. 12-(7/94). 14 (10/94) 3.00
13 (8/94, $3.50)-Flip book (Ultraverse Premiere #6) 4.00
#0-(8/94, $2.50, 44 pgs.) 4.00
Giant Size 1 (10/94, $2.50, 44 pgs.) 4.00

PROTOTYPE (Based on the Activision video game)
DC Comics (WildStorm): Jun, 2009 - No. 6, Nov, 2009 ($3.99, limited series)

1-6-Darick Robertson-c/a 4.00
TPB (2010, $19.99) r/#1-6 20.00

PROWLER (Also see Clone Conspiracy and Amazing Spider-Man)
Marvel Comics: Dec, 2016 - Present ($3.99)

1-5-Sean Ryan-s/Javier Saltares-a 4.00

PRUDENCE & CAUTION (Also see Dogs of War & Warriors of Plasm)
Defiant: May, 1994 - No. 2, June, 1994 ($3.50/$2.50)(Spanish versions exist)

1-($3.50, 52 pgs.)-Chris Claremont scripts in all 4.00
2-($2.50) 3.00

PRYDE AND WISDOM (Also see Excalibur)
Marvel Comics: Sept, 1996 - No. 3, Nov, 1996 ($1.95, limited series)

1-3: Warren Ellis scripts; Terry Dodson & Karl Story-c/a 3.00

PSI-FORCE
Marvel Comics Group: Nov, 1986 - No. 32, June, 1989 (75¢/$1.50)

1-25: 11-13-Williamson-i 3.00
26-32 3.00
Annual 1 (10/87) 4.00
... Classic Vol. 1 TPB (2008, $24.99) r/#1-9 25.00

PSI-JUDGE ANDERSON
Fleetway Publications (Quality): 1989 - No. 15, 1990 ($1.95, B&W)

1-15 4.00

PSI-LORDS
Valiant: Sept, 1994 - No. 10, June, 1995 ($2.25)

1-($3.50)-Chromium wraparound-c 5.00
1-Gold 8.00
2-10: 3-Chaos Effect Epsilon Pt. 2 3.00

PSYBA-RATS (Also see Showcase '94 #3,4)
DC Comics: Apr, 1995-No. 3, June, 1995 ($2.50, limited series)

1-3 3.00

PSYCHO (Magazine) (Also see Nightmare)
Skywald Publ. Corp.: Jan, 1971 - No. 24, Mar, 1975 (68 pgs.; B&W)

1-All reprints 8 16 24 54 102 150

Psycho #3 © Skywald

The Pulse #11 © MAR

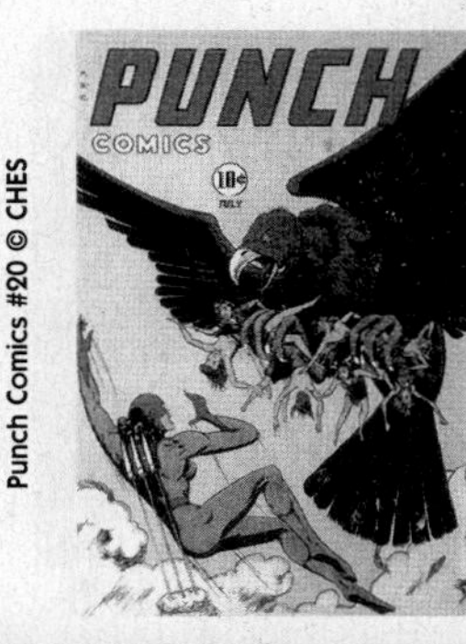

Punch Comics #20 © CHES

	GD 2.0	VG 4.0	FN 6.0	VF 8.0	VF/NM 9.0	NM- 9.2
2-Origin & 1st app. The Heap, series begins	6	12	18	37	68	95
3-Frankenstein series by Adkins begins	5	10	15	35	63	90
4-7,9,10: 4-7-Squarebound. 4-1st Out of Chaos/Satan-c/s	5	10	15	33	57	80
8-(Squarebound)1st app. Edward & Mina Sartyros, the Human Gargoyles	5	10	15	35	63	90
11-17: 13-Cannabalism; 3 pgs of Christopher Lee as Dracula photos	4	8	12	27	44	60
18-Injury to eye-c	5	10	15	31	53	75
19-Origin Dracula.	4	8	12	28	47	65
20-Severed Head-c	5	10	15	33	57	80
21-24: 22-1974 Fall Special; Reese, Wildey-a(r). 24-1975 Winter Special; Dave Sim scripts (1st pro work)	5	10	15	30	50	70
Annual 1 (1972)(68 pgs.) Dracula & the Heap app.	5	10	15	30	50	70
Yearbook (1974-nn)-Everett, Reese-a	4	8	12	27	44	60

NOTE: ***Boris** c-3, 5. **Buckler** a-2, 4, 5. **Gene Day** a-21, 23, 24. **Everett** a-3-6. **B. Jones** a-4. **Jeff Jones** a-6, 7, 9; c-12. **Kaluta** a-13. **Katz/Buckler** a-3. **Kim** a-24. **Morrow** a-1. **Reese** a-5. **Dave Sim** s-24. **Sutton** a-3. **Wildey** a-5.*

PSYCHO, THE
DC Comics: 1991 - No. 3, 1991 ($4.95, squarebound, limited series)

1-3-Hudnall-s/Brereton painted-a/c 5.00
TPB (Image Comics, 2006, $17.99) r/series; Brereton sketch pages; Hudnall afterword 18.00

PSYCHOANALYSIS
E. C. Comics: Mar-Apr, 1955 - No. 4, Sept-Oct, 1955

	GD	VG	FN	VF	VF/NM	NM-
1-All Kamen-c/a; not approved by code	23	46	69	184	292	400
2-4-Kamen-c/a in all	15	30	45	120	193	265

PSYCHOANALYSIS
Gemstone Publishing: Oct, 1999 - No. 4, Jan, 2000 ($2.50)

1-4-Reprints E.C. series 4.00
Annual 1 (2000, $10.95) r/#1-4 11.00

PSYCHOBLAST
First Comics: Nov, 1987 - No. 9, July, 1988 ($1.75)

1-9 3.00

PSYCHO BONKERS
Aspen MLT: May, 2015 - No. 4, Sept, 2015 ($3.99)

1-4-Vince Hernandez-s/Adam Archer-a 4.00

PSYCHONAUTS
Marvel Comics (Epic Comics): Oct, 1993 - No. 4, Jan, 1994 ($4.95, lim. series)

1-4: American/Japanese co-produced comic 5.00

PSYLOCKE
Marvel Comics: Jan, 2010 - No. 4, Apr, 2010 ($3.99, limited series)

	GD	VG	FN	VF	VF/NM	NM-
1-Finch-c/Yost-s/Tolibao-a in all	4	8	12	23	37	50
2	2	4	6	10	14	18
3,4-Wolverine app.	2	4	6	8	10	12

PSYLOCKE & ARCHANGEL CRIMSON DAWN
Marvel Comics: Aug, 1997 - No. 4, Nov, 1997 ($2.50, limited series)

1-4-Raab-s/Larroca-a(p) 4.00

PTOLUS: CITY BY THE SPIRE
Dabel Brothers Productions/Marvel Comics (Dabel Brothers) #2 on: June, 2006 - No. 6, Mar, 2007 ($2.99)

1-(1st printing, Dabel) Adaptation of the Monte Cook novel; Cook-s 4.00
1-(2nd printing, Marvel), 2-6 3.00
Monte Cooke's Ptolus: City By the Spire TPB (2007, $14.99) r/#1-6 15.00

P.T. 109 (See Movie Comics)

PUBLIC DEFENDER IN ACTION (Formerly Police Trap)
Charlton Comics: No. 7, Mar, 1956 - No. 12, Oct, 1957

	GD	VG	FN	VF	VF/NM	NM-
7	12	24	36	69	97	125
8-12	9	18	27	47	61	75

PUBLIC ENEMIES
D. S. Publishing Co.: 1948 - No. 9, June-July, 1949

	GD	VG	FN	VF	VF/NM	NM-
1-True Crime Stories	34	68	102	199	325	450
2-Used in **SOTI**, pg. 95	26	52	78	154	252	350
3-5: 5-Arrival date of 10/1/48	18	36	54	107	169	230
6,8,9	18	36	54	103	162	220
7-McWilliams-a; injury to eye panel	18	36	54	107	169	230

PUBLIC RELATIONS
Devil's Due/1First Comics: 2015 - Present ($3.99)

1-13: 1-3-Sturges & Justus-s/Hahn-a; Annie Wu-c 4.00

PUBO
Dark Horse Comics: Dec, 2002 - No. 3, Mar, 2003 ($3.50, B&W, limited series)

1-3-Leland Purvis-s/a 3.50

PUDGY PIG
Charlton Comics: Sept, 1958 - No. 2, Nov, 1958

	GD	VG	FN	VF	VF/NM	NM-
1,2	3	6	9	17	26	35

PUFFED
Image Comics: Jul, 2003 - No. 3, Sept, 2003 ($2.95, B&W)

1-3-Layman-s/Crosland-a. 1-Two covers by Crosland & Quitely 3.00

PULP FANTASTIC (Vertigo V2K)
DC Comics (Vertigo): Feb, 2000 - No. 3, Apr, 2000 ($2.50, limited series)

1-3-Chaykin & Tischman-s/Burchett-a 3.00

PULP FICTION LIBRARY: MYSTERY IN SPACE
DC Comics: 1999 ($19.95, TPB)

nn-Reprints classic sci-fi stories from Mystery in Space, Strange Adventures, Real Fact Comics and My Greatest Adventure 20.00

PULSE, THE (Also see Alias and Deadline)
Marvel Comics: Apr, 2004 - No. 14, May, 2006 ($2.99)

1-Jessica Jones, Ben Urich, Kat Farrell app.; Bendis-s/Bagley-a 5.00
2-14: 2-5-Bendis-s/Bagley-a. 3-5-Green Goblin app. 6,7-Brent Anderson-a 9-Wolverine app. 10-House of M. 11-14-Gaydos-a 3.00
...: House of M Special (9/05, 50¢) tabloid newspaper format; Mayhew- "photos" 3.00
Vol. 1: Thin Air (2004, $13.99) r/#1-5, gallery of cover layouts and sketches 14.00
Vol. 2: Secret War (2005, $11.99) r/#6-9 12.00
Vol. 3: Fear (2006, $14.99) r/#11-14 and New Avengers Annual #1 15.00

PUMA BLUES
Aardvark One International/Mirage Studios #21 on: 1986 - No. 26, 1990 ($1.70-$1.75, B&W)

1-19, 21-26: 1-1st & 2nd printings. 25,26-$1.75-c 3.00
20 ($2.25)-By Alan Moore, Miller, Grell, others 5.00
Trade Paperback (12/88, $14.95) 15.00

PUMPKINHEAD: THE RITES OF EXORCISM (Movie)
Dark Horse Comics: 1993 - No. 2, 1993 ($2.50, limited series)

1,2: Based on movie; painted-c by McManus 3.00

PUNCH & JUDY COMICS
Hillman Per.: 1944; No. 2, Fall, 1944 - V3#2, 12/47; V3#3, 6/51 - V3#9, 12/51

	GD	VG	FN	VF	VF/NM	NM-
V1#1-(60 pgs.)	27	54	81	158	259	360
2	14	28	42	82	121	160
3-12(7/46)	12	24	36	69	97	125
V2#1(8/49),3-9	10	20	30	54	72	90
V2#2,10-12, V3#1-Kirby-a(2) each	21	42	63	126	206	285
V3#2-Kirby-a	20	40	60	114	182	250
3-9	9	18	27	50	65	80

PUNCH COMICS
Harry 'A' Chesler: 12/41; #2, 2/42; #9, 7/44 - #19, 10/46; #20, 7/47 - #23, 1/48

	GD	VG	FN	VF	VF/NM	NM-
1-Mr. E, The Sky Chief, Hale the Magician, Kitty Kelly begin	181	362	543	1158	1979	2800
2-Captain Glory app.	116	232	348	742	1271	1800
9-Rocketman & Rocket Girl & The Master Key begin; classic-c	290	580	870	1856	3178	4500
10-Sky Chief app.; J. Cole-a; Master Key-r/Scoop #3	71	142	213	454	777	1100
11-Origin Master Key-r/Scoop #1; Sky Chief, Little Nemo app.; Jack Cole-a; Fine-*ish* art by Sultan	74	148	222	470	810	1150
12-Rocket Boy & Capt. Glory app; classic Skull-c	2800	5600	8400	15,000	21,500	28,000
13-Cover has list of 4 Chesler artists' names on tombstone	103	206	309	659	1130	1600
14,15,21: 21-Hypo needle story	71	142	213	454	777	1100
16,17-Gag-c	39	78	117	240	395	550
18-Bondage-c; hypodermic panels	74	148	222	470	810	1150
19-Giant bloody hands-c	142	284	426	909	1555	2200
20-Unique cover with bare-breasted women. Rocket Girl-c	168	336	504	1075	1838	2600
22,23-Little Nemo-not by McCay. 22-Intro Baxter (teenage)(68 pgs.)	25	50	75	150	245	340

PUNCHY AND THE BLACK CROW
Charlton Comics: No. 10, Oct, 1985 - No. 12, Feb, 1986

The Punisher #21 © MAR

The Punisher (1998 series) #1 © MAR

The Punisher (2009 series) #5 © MAR

	GD 2.0	VG 4.0	FN 6.0	VF 8.0	VF/NM 9.0	NM- 9.2

10-12: Al Fago funny animal-r; low print run 6.00

PUNISHER (See Amazing Spider-Man #129, Blood and Glory, Born, Captain America #241, Classic Punisher, Daredevil #182-184, 257, Daredevil and the..., Ghost Rider V2#5, 6, Marc Spector #8 & 9, Marvel Preview #2, Marvel Super Action, Marvel Tales, Power Pack #46, Spectacular Spider-Man #81-83, 140, 141, 143 & new Strange Tales #13 & 14)

PUNISHER (The...)
Marvel Comics Group: Jan, 1986 - No. 5, May, 1986 (Limited series)

	GD	VG	FN	VF	VF/NM	NM-
1-Double size	5	10	15	30	50	70
2-5	2	4	6	11	16	20

Trade Paperback (1988)-r/#1-5 16.00
Circle of Blood TPB (8/01, $15.95) Zeck-c 16.00
Circle of Blood HC (2008, $19.99) two covers 20.00
NOTE: *Zeck a-1-4; c-1-5.*

PUNISHER (The...) (Volume 2)
Marvel Comics: July, 1987 - No. 104, July, 1995

	GD	VG	FN	VF	VF/NM	NM-
1	3	6	9	17	26	35
2-9: 8-Portacio/Williams-c/a begins, ends #18. 9-Scarcer, low dist.						6.00
10-Daredevil app; ties in w/Daredevil #257	2	4	6	11	16	20

11-25,50: 13-18-Kingpin app. 19-Stroman-c/a. 20-Portacio-c(p). 24-1st app. Shadowmasters. 25,50:($1.50,52 pgs.). 25-Shadowmasters app. 4.00
26-49,51-74,76-85,87-89: 57-Photo-c; came w/outer-c (newsstand ed. w/o outer-c). 59-Punisher is severely cut & has skin grafts (has black skin). 60-62-Luke Cage app. 62-Punisher back to white skin. 68-Tarantula-c/story. 85-Prequel to Suicide Run Pt. 0. 87,88-Suicide Run Pt. 6 & 9 3.00
75-($2.75, 52 pgs.)-Embossed silver foil-c 4.00
86-($2.95, 52 pgs.)-Embossed & foil stamped-c; Suicide Run part 3 4.00
90-99: 90-bound-in cards. 99-Cringe app. 3.00
100,104: 100-($2.95, 68 pgs.). 104-Last issue 4.00
100-($3.95, 68 pgs.)-Foil cover 5.00
101-103: 102-Bullseye 3.50
"Ashcan" edition (75¢)-Joe Kubert-c 3.00
Annual 1-7 ('88-'94, 68 pgs.) 1-Evolutionary War x-over. 2-Atlantis Attacks x-over; Jim Lee-a(p) (back-up story, 6 pgs.); Moon Knight app. 4-Golden-c(p). 6-Bagged w/card. 4.00
...: A Man Named Frank (1994, $6.95, TPB) 7.00
...and Wolverine in African Saga nn (1989, $5.95, 52 pgs.)-Reprints Punisher War Journal #6 & 7; Jim Lee-c/a(r) 6.00
... Assassin Guild ('88, $6.95, graphic novel) 10.00
Back to School Special 1-3 (11/92-10/94, $2.95, 68 pgs.) 4.00
.../Batman: Deadly Knights (10/94, $4.95) 6.00
.../Black Widow: Spinning Doomsday's Web (1992, $9.95, graphic novel) 12.00
...Bloodlines nn (1991, $5.95, 68 pgs.) 6.00
...: Die Hard in the Big Easy nn ('92, $4.95, 52 pgs.) 6.00
...: Empty Quarter nn ('94, $6.95) 7.00
...G-Force nn (1992, $4.95, 52 pgs.)-Painted-c 6.00
...Holiday Special 1-3 (1/93-1/95,, 52 pgs.,68pgs.)-1-Foil-c 4.00
...Intruder Graphic Novel (1989, $14.95, hardcover) 20.00
...Intruder Graphic Novel (1991, $9.95, softcover) 12.00
...Invades the 'Nam: Final Invasion nn (2/94, $6.95)-J. Kubert-c & chapter break art; reprints The 'Nam #84 & unpublished #85,86 10.00
...Kingdom Gone Graphic Novel (1990, $16.95, hardcover) 20.00
...Meets Archie (8/94, $3.95, 52 pgs.)-Die cut-c; no ads; same contents as Archie Meets The Punisher 5.00
...Movie Special 1 (6/90, $5.95, squarebound, 68 pgs.) painted-c; Brent Anderson-a; contents intended for a 3 issue series which was advertised but not published 6.00
...: No Escape nn (1990, $4.95, 52 pgs.)-New-a 6.00
...Return to Big Nothing Graphic Novel (Epic, 1989, $16.95, hardcover) 25.00
...Return to Big Nothing Graphic Novel (Marvel, 1989, $12.95, softcover) 15.00
...The Prize nn (1990, $4.95, 68 pgs.)-New-a 6.00
Summer Special 1-4(8/91-7/94, 52 pgs.):1-No ads. 2-Bisley-c; Austin-a(i). 3-No ads 4.00
NOTE: ***Austin** c(i)-47, 48. **Cowan** c-39. **Golden** c-50, 85, 86, 100. **Heath** a-26, 27, 89, 90, 91; c-26, 27. **Quesada** c-56p, 62p. **Sienkiewicz** c-Back to School 1.**Stroman** a-76p(9 pgs.). **Williamson** a(i)-25, 60-62i, 64-70, 74, Annual 5; c(i)-62, 65-68.*

PUNISHER (Also see Double Edge)
Marvel Comics: Nov, 1995 - No. 18, Apr, 1997 ($2.95/$1.95/$1.50)

1 ($2.95)-Ostrander scripts begin; foil-c. 4.00
2-18: 7-Vs. S.H.I.E.L.D. 11-"Onslaught." 12-17-X-Cutioner-c/app. 17-Daredevil, Spider-Man-c/app. 3.00

PUNISHER (Marvel Knights)
Marvel Comics: Nov, 1998 - No. 4, Feb, 1999 ($2.99, limited series)

1-4: 1-Wrightson-a; Wrightson & Jusko-c 3.00
1-($6.95) DF Edition; Jae Lee variant-c 7.00

PUNISHER (Marvel Knights) (Volume 3)
Marvel Comics: Apr, 2000 - No. 12, Mar, 2001 ($2.99, limited series)

	GD	VG	FN	VF	VF/NM	NM-
1-Ennis-s/Dillon & Palmiotti-a/Bradstreet-c	1	3	4	6	8	10
1-Bradstreet white variant-c	2	4	6	8	10	12
1-($6.95) DF Edition; Jurgens & Ordway variant-c	2	4	6	9	12	15

2-Two covers by Bradstreet & Dillon 3.00
3-($3.99) Bagged with Marvel Knights Genesis Edition; Daredevil app. 4.00
4-12: 9-11-The Russian app. 3.00
HC (6/02, $34.95) r/#1-12, Punisher Kills the Marvel Universe, and Marvel Knights Double Shot #1 35.00
... By Garth Ennis Omnibus (2008, $99.99) oversized r/#1-12, #1-7 & #13-37 of 2001 series, Punisher Kills the Marvel Universe, and Marvel Knights Double Shot #1; extras 100.00
.../Painkiller Jane (1/01, $3.50) Jusko-c; Ennis-s/Jusko and Dave Ross-a(p) 3.50
...: Welcome Back Frank TPB (4/01, $19.95) r/#1-12 20.00

PUNISHER (Marvel Knights) (Volume 4)
Marvel Comics: Aug, 2001 - No. 37, Feb, 2004 ($2.99)

1-Ennis-s/Dillon & Palmiotti-a/Bradstreet-c; The Russian app. 4.00
2-Two covers (Dillon & Bradstreet) Spider-Man-c/app. 3.00
3-37: 3-7-Ennis-s/Dillon-a. 9-12-Peyer-s/Gutierrez-a. 13,14-Ennis-s/Dilllon-a. 16,17-Wolverine app.; Robertson-a. 18-23,32-Dillon-a. 24-27-Mandrake-a. 27-Elektra app. 33-37-Spider-Man, Daredevil, & Wolverine app. 36,37-Hulk app. 3.00
...Army of One TPB (2/02, $15.95) r/#1-7; Bradstreet-c 16.00
Vol. 2 HC (2003, $29.95) r/#1-7,13-18; intro. by Mike Millar 30.00
Vol. 3 HC (2004, $29.95) r/#19-27; script pages for #19 30.00
Vol. 3: Business as Usual TPB (2003, $14.99) r/#13-18; Bradstreet-c 15.00
Vol. 4: Full Auto TPB (2003, $17.99) r/#20-26; Bradstreet-c 18.00
Vol. 5: Streets of Laredo TPB (2003, $17.99) r/#19,27-32 18.00
Vol. 6: Confederacy of Dunces TPB (2004, $13.99) r/#33-37 14.00

PUNISHER (Marvel MAX)(Title becomes "Punisher: Frank Castle MAX" with #66)
Marvel Comics: Mar, 2004 - No. 75, Dec, 2009 ($2.99/$3.99)

1-49,51-60: 1-Ennis-s/LaRosa-a/Bradstreet-c; flashback to his family's murder; Micro app. 6-Micro killed. 7-12,19-25-Fernandez-a. 13-18-Braithwaite-a. 31-36-Barracuda. 43-49-Medina-a. 51-54-Barracuda app. 60-Last Ennis-s/Bradstreet-c 3.00
50-($3.99) Barracuda returns; Chaykin-a 4.00
61-65-Gregg Hurwitz-s/Dave Johnson-c/Laurence Campbell-a 3.00
66-73-($3.99) 66-70-Six Hours to Kill; Swierczynski-s. 71-73-Parlov-a 4.00
74,75-($4.99) 74-Parlov-a. 75-Short stories; art by Lashley, Coker, Parlov & others 5.00
Annual (11/07, $3.99) Mike Benson-s/Laurence Campbell-a 4.00
...: Bloody Valentine (4/06, $3.99) Palmiotti & Gray-s/Gulacy & Palmiotti-a; Gulacy-c 4.00
...: Force of Nature (4/08, $4.99) Swierczynski-s/Lacombe-a/Deodato-c 5.00
...: MAX MGC #1 (5/10, $1.00) reprints #1 with "Marvel's Greatest Comics" cover logo 3.00
...: MAX: Naked Kill (8/09, $3.99) Campbell-a/Bradstreet-c 4.00
...: MAX Special: Little Black Book (8/08, $3.99) Gischler-s/Palo-a/Johnson-c 4.00
...: MAX X-Mas Special (2/09, $3.99) Aaron-s/Boschi-a/Bachalo-c 4.00
...: Red X-Mas (2/05, $3.99) Palmiotti & Gray-s/Texeira & Palmiotti-a; Texeira-c 4.00
...: Silent Night (2/06, $3.99) Diggle-s/Hotz-a/Deodato-c 4.00
...: The Cell (7/05, $4.99) Ennis-s/LaRosa-a/Bradstreet-c 5.00
...: The Tyger (2/06, $4.99) Ennis-s/Severin-a/Bradstreet-c; Castle's childhood 5.00
...: Very Special Holidays TPB ('06, $12.99) r/Red X-Mas, Bloody Valentine and Silent Night 13.00
...: X-Mas Special (1/07, $3.99) Stuart Moore-s/CP Smith-a 4.00
... MAX: From First to Last HC (2006, $19.99) r/The Tyger, The Cell and The End 1-shots 20.00
... MAX Vol. 1 (2005, $29.99) oversized r/#1-12; gallery of Fernandez art from #7 shown from layout to colored pages 30.00
... MAX Vol. 2 (2006, $29.99) oversized r/#13-24; gallery of Fernandez pencil art 30.00
... MAX Vol. 3 (2007, $29.99) oversized r/#25-36; gallery of Fernandez & Parlov art 30.00
... MAX Vol. 4 (2008, $29.99) oversized r/#37-49; gallery of Fernandez & Medina art 30.00
Vol. 1: In the Beginning TPB (2004, $14.99) r/#1-6 15.00
Vol. 2: Kitchen Irish TPB (2004, $14.99) r/#7-12 15.00
Vol. 3: Mother Russia TPB (2005, $14.99) r/#13-18 15.00
Vol. 4: Up is Down and Black is White TPB (2005, $14.99) r/#19-24 15.00
Vol. 5: The Slavers TPB (2006, $15.99) r/#25-30; Fernandez pencil pages 16.00
Vol. 6: Barracuda TPB (2006, $15.99) r/#31-36; Parlov sketch page 16.00
Vol. 7: Man of Stone TPB (2007, $15.99) r/#37-42 16.00
Vol. 8: Widowmaker TPB (2007, $17.99) r/#43-49 18.00
Vol. 9: Long Cold Dark TPB (2008, $15.99) r/#50-54 16.00

PUNISHER (Frank Castle in the Marvel Universe after Secret Invasion)
(Title changes to Franken-Castle for #17-21)
Marvel Comics: Mar, 2009 - No. 21, Nov, 2010 ($3.99/$2.99)

1-($3.99) Dark Reign; Sentry app.; Remender-s/Opena-a; character history; 2 covers 4.00
2-5,7-10($2.99) 2-7-The Hood app. 4-Microchip returns. 5-Daredevil #183 cover swipe 3.00
6-($3.99) Huat-a/McKone-c; profile pages of resurrected villains 4.00
11-Follows Dark Reign: The List - Punisher; Franken-Castle begins; Tony Moore-a 4.00
12-16-Franken-Castle continues; Legion of Monsters app. 14-Brereton & Moore-a 3.00

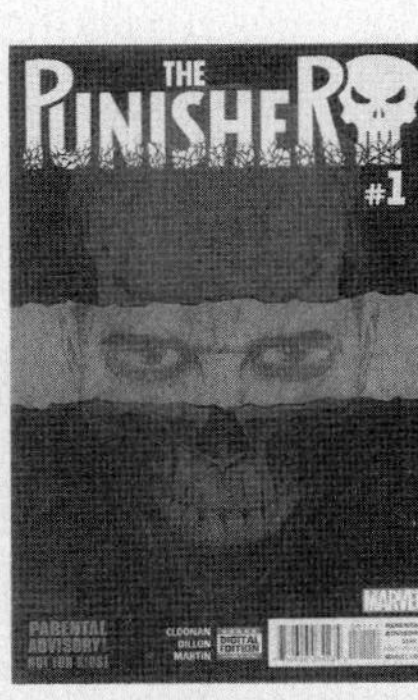

The Punisher (2016 series) #1 © MAR

The Punisher: The End #1 © MAR

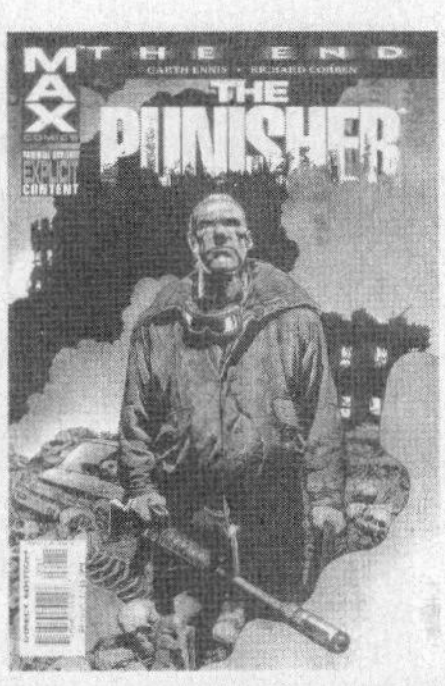

Punisher War Journal (2007 series) #10 © MAR

GD 2.0 VG 4.0 FN 6.0 VF 8.0 VF/NM 9.0 NM- 9.2

Franken-Castle 17-20: 19, 20-Wolverine & Daken app. 3.00
Franken-Castle 21-($3.99) Brereton-a/c; Legion of Monsters app.; Frank gets body back 4.00
Annual 1 (11/09, $3.99) Pearson-a/c; Spider-Man app. 4.00
...: Franken-Castle - The Birth of the Monster 1 (7/10, $4.99) r/#11 & Dark Reign: The List 5.00

PUNISHER (Frank Castle in the Marvel Universe)(Continues in Punisher: War Zone [2012])
Marvel Comics: Oct, 2011 - No. 16, Nov, 2012 ($3.99/$2.99)

1-($3.99) Rucka-s/Checchetto-a/Hitch-c 4.00
1-Variant-c by Sal Buscema 6.00
1-Variant-c by Neal Adams 10.00
2-16-($2.99): 2,3-Vulture app. 10-Spider-Man & Daredevil app. 3.00
..., Moon Knight & Daredevil: The Big Shots (10/11, $3.99) Previews new series for Punisher, Moon Knight & Daredevil; creator interviews and production art 4.00

PUNISHER, THE
Marvel Comics: Apr, 2014 - No. 20, Sept, 2015 ($3.99)

1-20: 1-Edmonson-s/Gerads-a; Howling Commandos app. 2-6-Electro app. 16,17-Captain America (Falcon) app. 19,20-Secret Wars tie-ins 4.00

PUNISHER, THE
Marvel Comics: Jul, 2016 - Present ($3.99)

1-9: 1-Becky Cloonan-s/Steve Dillon-a. 7-Steve Dillon's last work 4.00
Annual 1 (12/16, $4.99) Gerry Conway-s/Felix Ruiz-a 5.00

PUNISHER AND WOLVERINE: DAMAGING EVIDENCE (See Wolverine and...)

PUNISHER ARMORY, THE
Marvel Comics: 7/90 ($1.50); No. 2, 6/91; No. 3, 4/92 - 10/94($1.75/$2.00)

1-10: 1-r/weapons pgs. from War Journal. 1,2-Jim Lee-c. 3-10-All new material. 3-Jusko painted-c 4.00

PUNISHER: IN THE BLOOD (Marvel Universe Frank Castle)
Marvel Comics: Jan, 2011 - No. 5, May, 2011 ($3.99, limited series)

1-5-Remender-s/Boschi-a; Jigsaw & Microchip app. 4.00

PUNISHER KILLS THE MARVEL UNIVERSE
Marvel Comics: Nov, 1995 ($5.95, one-shot)

1-Garth Ennis script/Doug Braithwaite-a 3 6 9 21 33 45
1-2nd printing (3/00) Steve Dillon-c 6.00
1-3rd printing (2008, $4.99) original 1995 cover 5.00

PUNISHER MAGAZINE, THE
Marvel Comics: Oct, 1989 - No. 16, Nov, 1990 ($2.25, B&W, Magazine, 52 pgs.)

1-16: 1-r/Punisher #1('86). 2,3-r/Punisher 2-5. 4-16: 4-7-r/Punisher V2#1-8. 4-Chiodo-c. 8-r/Punisher #10 & Daredevil #257; Portacio & Lee-r. 14-r/Punisher War Journal #1,2 w/new Lee-c. 16-r/Punisher W. J. #3,8 4.00
NOTE: *Chiodo painted c-4, 7, 16. Jusko painted c-6, 8. Jim Lee r-8, 14-16; c-14. Portacio/Williams r-7-12.*

PUNISHERMAX
Marvel Comics (MAX): Jan, 2010 - No. 22, Apr, 2012 ($3.99)

1-22-Aaron-s/Dillon-a/Johnson-c. 1-5-Rise of the Kingpin. 6-11-Bullseye. 17-20-Elektra app. 21-Castle dies. 22-Afterword by Aaron 4.00
...: Butterfly (5/10, $4.99) Valerie D'Orazio-s/Laurence Campbell-a/c 5.00
...: Get Castle (3/10, $4.99) Rob Williams-s/Laurence Campbell-a/Bradstreet-c 5.00
...: Happy Ending (10/10, $3.99) Milligan-s/Ryp-a/c 4.00
...: Hot Rods of Death (11/10, $4.99) Huston-s/Martinbrough-a/Bradstreet-c 5.00
...: Tiny Ugly World (12/10, $4.99) Lapham-s/Talajic-a/Bradstreet-c 5.00

PUNISHER: NIGHTMARE
Marvel Comics: Mar, 2013 - No. 5, Mar, 2013 ($3.99, weekly limited series)

1-5-Texeira-a/c; Gimple-s 4.00

PUNISHER NOIR
Marvel Comics: Oct, 2009 - No. 4, Jan, 2010 ($3.99, limited series)

1-4-Pulp-style set in 1935; Tieri-s/Azaceta-a 4.00

PUNISHER: OFFICIAL MOVIE ADAPTATION
Marvel Comics: May, 2004 - No. 3, May, 2004 ($2.99, limited series)

1-3-Photo-c of Thomas Jane; Milligan-s/Olliffe-a 3.00

PUNISHER: ORIGIN OF MICRO CHIP, THE
Marvel Comics: July, 1993 - No. 2, Aug, 1993 ($1.75, limited series)

1,2 4.00

PUNISHER: P.O.V.
Marvel Comics: 1991 - No. 4, 1991 ($4.95, painted, limited series, 52 pgs.)

1-4: Starlin scripts & Wrightson painted-c/a in all. 2-Nick Fury app. 6.00

PUNISHER PRESENTS: BARRACUDA MAX
Marvel Comics (MAX): Apr, 2007 - No. 5, Aug, 2007 ($3.99, limited series)

1-5-Ennis-s/Parlov-a/c 4.00
SC (2007, $17.99) r/series; sketch pages 18.00

PUNISHER: THE END
Marvel Comics: June, 2004 ($4.50, one-shot)

1-Ennis-s/Corben-a/c 4.50

PUNISHER: THE GHOSTS OF INNOCENTS
Marvel Comics: Jan, 1993 - No. 2, Jan, 1993 ($5.95, 52 pgs.)

1,2-Starlin scripts 6.00

PUNISHER: THE MOVIE
Marvel Comics: 2004 ($12.99,TPB)

nn-Reprints Amazing Spider-Man #129; Official Movie Adaptation and Punisher V3 #1 13.00

PUNISHER: THE TRIAL OF THE PUNISHER
Marvel Comics: Nov, 2013 - No. 2, Dec, 2013 ($3.99, limited series)

1-Guggenheim-s/Yu-a/c. 2-Suayan-a; Matt Murdock app. 4.00

PUNISHER 2099 (See Punisher War Journal #50)
Marvel Comics: Feb, 1993 - No. 34, Nov, 1995 ($1.25/$1.50/$1.95)

1-Foil stamped-c 4.00
1-(Second printing) 3.00
2-24,26-34: 13-Spider-Man 2099 x-over; Ron Lim-c(p). 16-bound-in card sheet 3.00
25 ($2.95, 52 pgs.)-Deluxe edition; embossed foil-cover 5.00
25 ($2.25, 52 pgs.) 4.00
(Marvel Knights) #1 (11/04, $2.99) Kirkman-s/Mhan-a/Pat Lee-c 3.00

PUNISHER VS. BULLSEYE
Marvel Comics: Jan, 2006 - No. 5, May, 2006 ($2.99, limited series)

1-5-Daniel Way-s/Steve Dillon-a 3.00
TPB (2006, $13.99) r/#1-5; cover sketch pages 14.00

PUNISHER VS. DAREDEVIL
Marvel Comics: Jun, 2000 ($3.50, one-shot)

1-Reprints Daredevil #183,#184 & #257 4.00

PUNISHER WAR JOURNAL, THE
Marvel Comics: Nov, 1988 - No. 80, July, 1995 ($1.50/$1.75/$1.95)

1-Origin The Punisher; Matt Murdock cameo; Jim Lee inks begin
2 4 6 8 10 12
2-7: 2,3-Daredevil x-over; Jim Lee-c(i). 4-Jim Lee c/a begins. 6-Two part Wolverine story begins. 7-Wolverine-c, story ends 4.00
8-49,51-60,62,63,65: 13-16,20-22: No Jim Lee-a. 13-Lee-c only. 13-15-Heath-i. 14,15-Spider-Man x-over. 19-Last Jim Lee-c/a.29,30-Ghost Rider app. 31-Andy & Joe Kubert art. 36-Photo-c. 47,48-Nomad/Daredevil-c/stories; see Nomad. 57,58-Daredevil & Ghost Rider-c/stories. 62,63-Suicide Run Pt. 4 & 7 3.00
50,61,64($2.95, 52 pgs.): 50-Preview of Punisher 2099 (1st app.); embossed-c. 61-Embossed foil cover; Suicide Run Pt. 1. 64-Die-cut-c; Suicide Run Pt. 10 4.00
64-($2.25, 52 pgs.)-Regular cover edition 4.00
66-74,76-80: 66-Bound-in card sheet 3.00
75 ($2.50, 52 pgs.) 4.00
NOTE: *Golden c-25-30, 40, 61, 62. Jusko painted c-31, 32. Jim Lee a-1i-3i, 4p-13p, 17p-19p; c-2i, 3i, 4p-15p, 17p, 18p, 19p. Painted c-40.*

PUNISHER WAR JOURNAL (Frank Castle back in the regular Marvel Universe)
Marvel Comics: Jan, 2007 - No. 26, Feb, 2009 ($2.99)

1-Civil War tie-in; Spider-Man app; Fraction-s/Olivetti-a 5.00
1-B&W edition (11/06) 5.00
2-5: 2,3-Civil War tie-in. 4-Deodato-a 4.00
6-11,13-24,26: 6-10-Punisher dons Captain America-*esque* outfit. 7-Two covers. 11-Winter Soldier app. 16-23-Chaykin-a. 18-23-Jigsaw app. 24-Secret Invasion 3.00
12,25-($3.99) 12-World War Hulk x-over; Fraction-s/Olivetti-a. 25-Secret Invasion 4.00
... Annual 1 (1/09, $3.99) Spurrier-s/Dell'edera-a 4.00
... Vol. 1: Civil War HC (2007, $19.99) r/#1-4 and #1 B&W edition; Olivetti sketch pages 20.00
... Vol. 1: Civil War SC (2007, $14.99) r/#1-4 and #1 B&W edition; Olivetti sketch pages 15.00
... Vol. 2: Goin' Out West HC (2007, $24.99) r/#5-11; Olivetti sketch page 25.00
... Vol. 2: Goin' Out West SC (2008, $17.99) r/#5-11; Olivetti sketch page 18.00
... Vol. 3: Hunter Hunted HC (2008, $19.99) r/#12-17 20.00

PUNISHER: WAR ZONE, THE
Marvel Comics: Mar, 1992 - No. 41, July, 1995 ($1.75/$1.95)

1-($2.25, 40 pgs.)-Die cut-c; Romita, Jr.-c/a begins 6.00
2-22,24,26,27-41: 8-Last Romita, Jr.-c/a. 19-Wolverine app. 24-Suicide Run Pt. 5. 27-Bound-in card sheet. 31-36-Joe Kubert-a 3.00
23-($2.95, 52 pgs.)-Embossed foil-c; Suicide Run part 2; Buscema-a(part) 4.00
25-($2.25, 52 pgs.)-Suicide Run part 8; painted-c 4.00
Annual 1,2 ('93, 94, $2.95, 68 pgs.)-1-Bagged w/card; John Buscema-a 4.00

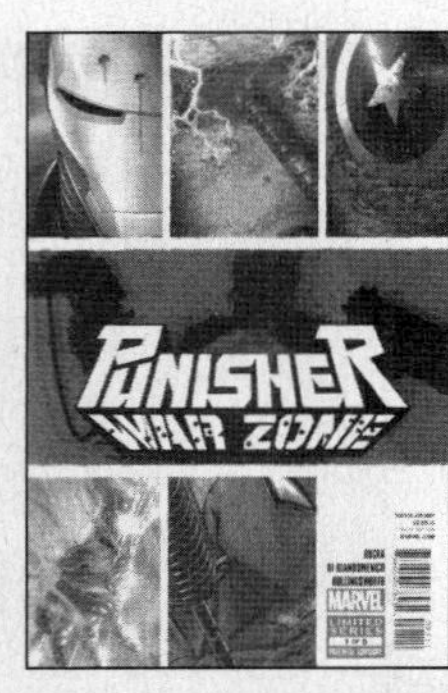

Punisher War Zone (2012 series) #1 © MAR

The Purple Claw #1 © Minoan

Quantum & Woody #12 © VAL

GD	VG	FN	VF	VF/NM	NM-
2.0	4.0	6.0	8.0	9.0	9.2

GD VG FN VF VF/NM NM-
2.0 4.0 6.0 8.0 9.0 9.2

...: River Of Blood TPB (2006, $15.99) r/#31-36; Joe Kubert-a 16.00
NOTE: *Golden c-23. Romita, Jr. c/a-1-8.*

PUNISHER: WAR ZONE
Marvel Comics: Feb, 2009 - No. 6, Mar, 2009 ($3.99, weekly limited series)
1-6-Ennis-s/Dillon-a/c; return of Ma Gnucci 4.00
1-Variant cover by John Romita, Jr. 6.00

PUNISHER: WAR ZONE (Follows Punisher 2011-2012 series)
Marvel Comics: Dec, 2012 - No. 5, Apr, 2013 ($3.99, limited series)
1-5: Rucka-s; Spider-Man and The Avengers app. 4.00

PUNISHER: YEAR ONE
Marvel Comics: Dec, 1994 - No. 4, Apr, 1995 ($2.50, limited series)
1-4 3.00

PUNK MAMBO
Valiant Entertainment: No. 0, Nov, 2014 ($3.99, one-shot)
0-Milligan-s/Gill-a; bonus preview of The Valiant #1 4.00

PUNK ROCK JESUS
DC Comics (Vertigo): Sept, 2012 - No. 6, Feb, 2013 ($2.99, B&W, limited series)
1-6-Sean Murphy-s/a/c; cloning of Jesus 3.00

PUNX
Acclaim (Valiant): Nov, 1995 - No. 3, Jan, 1996 ($2.50, unfinished lim. series)
1-3: Giffen story & art in all. 2-Satirizes Scott McCloud's Understanding Comics 3.00
(Manga) Special 1 (3/96, $2.50)-Giffen scripts 3.00

PUPPET COMICS
George W. Dougherty Co.: Spring, 1946 - No. 2, Summer, 1946
1-Funny animal in both 22 44 66 132 216 300
2 15 30 45 85 130 175

PUPPETOONS (See George Pal's...)

PUREHEART (See Archie as...)

PURGATORI
Chaos! Comics: Prelude #-1, 5/96 ($1.50, 16 pgs.); 1996 - No. 3 Dec, 1996 ($3.50/$2.95, limited series)
Prelude #-1-Pulido story; Balent-c/a; contains sketches & interviews 3.00
0-(2/01, $2.99) Prelude to "Love Bites"; Rio-c/a 3.00
1/2 (12/00, $2.95) Al Rio-c/a 3.00
1-($3.50)-Wraparound cover; red foil embossed-c; Jim Balent-a 5.00
1-($19.95)-Premium Edition (1000 print run) 20.00
2-($3.00)-Wraparound-c 3.00
2-Variant-c 5.00
...: Heartbreaker 1 (3/02, $2.99) Jolley-s 3.00
...: Love Bites 1 (3/01, $2.99) Turnbull-a/Kaminski-s 3.00
...: Mischief Night 1 (11/01, $2.99) 3.00
...: Re-Imagined 1 (7/02, $2.99) Jolley-s/Neves-a 3.00
...The Dracula Gambit-($2.95) 3.00
...The Dracula Gambit Sketchbook-($2.95) 3.00
...The Vampire's Myth 1-($19.95) Premium Ed. (10,000) 20.00
...Vs. Chastity (7/00, $2.95) Two versions (Alpha and Omega) with different endings; Rio-a 3.00
...Vs. Lady Death (1/01, $2.95) Kaminski-s 3.00
...Vs. Vampirella (4/00, $2.95) Zanier-a; Chastity app. 3.00

PURGATORI
Chaos! Comics: Oct, 1998 - No. 7, Apr, 1999 ($2.95)
1-7-Quinn-s/Rio-c/a. 2-Lady Death-c 3.00

PURGATORI
Dynamite Entertainment: 2014 - Present ($3.99)
1-5: 1-Gillespie-s; multiple covers. 2-4-Jade app. 4.00

PURGATORI: DARKEST HOUR
Chaos! Comics: Sept, 2001 - No. 2, Oct, 2001 ($2.99, limited series)
1,2 3.00

PURGATORI: EMPIRE
Chaos! Comics: May, 2000 - No. 3, July, 2000 ($2.95, limited series)
1-3-Cleavenger-c 3.00

PURGATORI: GODDESS RISING
Chaos! Comics: July, 1999 - No. 4, Oct, 1999 ($2.95, limited series)
1-4-Deodato-c/a 3.00

PURGATORI: GOD HUNTER
Chaos! Comics: Apr, 2002 - No. 2, May, 2002 ($2.99, limited series)
1,2-Molenaar-a/Jolley-s 3.00

PURGATORI: GOD KILLER
Chaos! Comics: Jun, 2002 - No. 2, July, 2002 ($2.99, limited series)
1,2-Molenaar-a/Jolley-s 3.00

PURGATORI: THE HUNTED
Chaos! Comics: Jun, 2001 - No. 2, Aug, 2001 ($2.99, limited series)
1,2 3.00

PURPLE CLAW, THE (Also see Tales of Horror)
Minoan Publishing Co./Toby Press: Jan, 1953 - No. 3, May, 1953
1-Origin; horror/weird stories in all 39 78 117 240 395 550
2,3: 1-3 r-in Tales of Horror #9-11 27 54 81 158 259 360
I.W. Reprint #8-Reprints #1 3 6 9 16 23 30

PUSH (Based on the 2009 movie)
DC Comics (WildStorm): Early Jan, 2009 - No. 6, Apr, 2009 ($3.50, limited series)
1-6-Movie prequel; Bruno Redondo-a. 1-Jock-c 3.50
TPB (2009, $19.99) r/#1-6 20.00

PUSSYCAT (Magazine)
Marvel Comics Group: Oct, 1968 (B&W reprints from Men's magazines)
1-(Scarce)-Ward, Everett, Wood-a; Everett-c 32 64 96 230 515 800

PUZZLE FUN COMICS (Also see Jingle Jangle)
George W. Dougherty Co.: Spring, 1946 - No. 2, Summer, 1946 (52 pgs.)
1-Gustavson-a 26 52 78 154 252 350
2 16 32 48 94 147 200
NOTE: *#1 & 2('46) each contain a **George Carlson** cover plus a 6 pg. story "Alec in Fumbleland"; also many puzzles in each.*

PvP (Player vs. Player)
Image Comics: Mar, 2003 - No. 45, Mar, 2010 ($2.95/$2.99/$3.50, B&W, reads sideways)
1-34,36-Scott Kurtz-s/a in all. 1,16-Frank Cho-c. 11-Savage Dragon-c/app. 14-Invincible app. 19-Jonathan Luna-c. 25-Cho-a (2 pgs.) 3.00
35,37-45 ($3.50): 45-Brandy from Liberty Meadows app. 3.50
#0 (7/05, 50¢) Secret Origin of Skull 3.00
...: At Large TPB (7/04, $11.95) r/#1-6 12.00
... Vol. 2: Reloaded TPB (12/04, $11.95) r/#7-12 12.00
... Vol. 3: Rides Again TPB (2005, $11.99) r/#13-18 12.00
... Vol. 4: PVP Goes Bananas TPB (2007, $12.99) r/#19-24 13.00
... Vol. 5: PVP Treks On TPB (2008, $14.99) r/#25-31 15.00
...: The Dork Ages TPB (2/04, $11.95) r/#1-6 from Dork Storm Press 12.00

Q2: THE RETURN OF QUANTUM & WOODY
Valiant Entertainment: Oct, 2014 - No. 5, Feb, 2015 ($3.99, limited series)
1-5: 1-Priest-s/Bright-a; multiple covers 4.00

QUACK!
Star Reach Productions: July, 1976 - No. 6, 1977? ($1.25, B&W)
1-Brunner-c/a on Duckaneer (Howard the Duck clone); Dave Stevens, Gilbert, Shaw-a 2 4 6 10 14 18
1-2nd printing (10/76) 5.00
2-6: 2-Newton the Rabbit Wonder by Aragonés/Leialoha; Gilbert, Shaw-a; Leialoha-c. 3-The Beavers by Dave Sim begin, end #5; Gilbert, Shaw-a; Sim/Leialoha-c. 6-Brunner-a (Duckeneer); Gilbert-a 2 4 6 8 10 12

QUADRANT
Quadrant Publications: 1983 - No. 8, 1986 (B&W, nudity, adults)
1-Peter Hsu-c/a in all 2 4 6 10 14 18
2-8 2 3 4 6 8 10

QUAKE: S.H.I.E.L.D. 50TH ANNIVERSARY
Marvel Comics: Nov, 2015 ($3.99, one-shot)
1-Spotlight on Daisy Johnson; Daniel Johnson-a/Nakayama-c; Avengers app. 4.00

QUANTUM & WOODY
Acclaim Comics: June, 1997 - No. 17, No. 32 (9/99), No. 18 - No. 21, Feb, 2000 ($2.50)
1-17: 1-1st app.; two covers. 6-Copycat-c. 9-Troublemakers app. 3.00
32-(9/99); 18-(10/99),19-21 3.00
The Director's Cut TPB ('97, $7.95) r/#1-4 plus extra pages 8.00

QUANTUM & WOODY
Valiant Entertainment: Jul, 2013 - Present ($3.99)
1-12: 1-Asmus-s/Fowler-a; covers by Ryan Sook & Marcos Martin; origin re-told 4.00
#0 -(3/14, $3.99) Story of the goat; Asmus-s/Fowler-a/c 4.00
... Valiant-Sized #1 (12/14, $4.99) Thomas Edison app. 5.00

QUANTUM & WOODY: MUST DIE

Quasar #15 © MAR

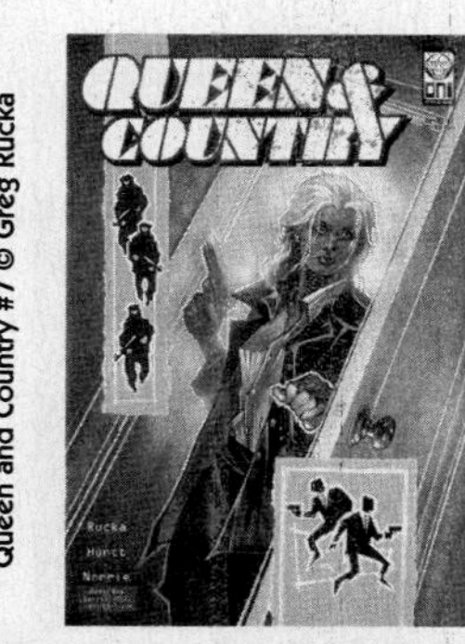

Queen and Country #7 © Greg Rucka

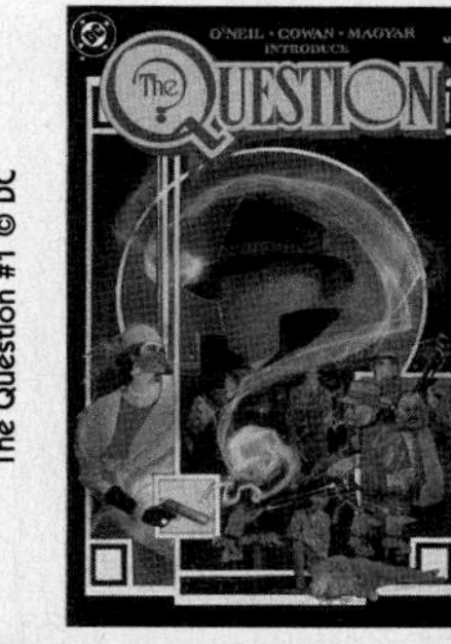

The Question #1 © DC

	GD 2.0	VG 4.0	FN 6.0	VF 8.0	VF/NM 9.0	NM- 9.2

Valiant Entertainment: Jan, 2015 - No. 4, Apr, 2015 ($3.99, limited series)

1-4: 1-James Asmus-s/Steve Lieber-a; multiple covers on each 4.00

QUANTUM LEAP (TV) (See A Nightmare on Elm Street)
Innovation Publishing: Sept, 1991 - No. 12, Jun, 1993 ($2.50, painted-c)

1-12: Based on TV show; all have painted-c. 8-Has photo gallery 4.00
Special Edition 1 (10/92)-r/#1 w/8 extra pgs. of photos & articles 4.00
Time and Space Special 1 (#13) ($2.95)-Foil logo 4.00

QUANTUM TUNNELER, THE
Revolution Studio: Oct, 2001 (no cover price, one-shot)

1-Prequel to "The One" movie; Clayton Henry-a 3.00

QUARANTINE ZONE
DC Comics: Apr, 2016 ($22.99, HC graphic novel)

HC - Daniel Wilson-s/Fernando Pasarin-a 23.00

QUASAR (See Avengers #302, Captain America #217, Incredible Hulk #234, Marvel Team-Up #113 & Marvel Two-in-One #53)
Marvel Comics: Oct, 1989 - No. 60, Jul, 1994 ($1.00/$1.25, Direct sales #17 on)

1-Gruenwald-s/Paul Ryan-c/a begin; Origin of Wendell Vaughn from Marvel Man to Quasar; Marvel Boy & Fantastic Four app. 6.00
2-6: 2-Origin of the Quantum-Bands; Deathurge & Eon app; Quasar becomes 'Protector of the Universe'. 3-Human Torch app. 4-Aquarian app. 5,6-Acts of Vengeance tie-in. 5-Absorbing Man & Loki app. 6-Red Ghost, Living Laser, Uatu the Watcher app; Venom cameo (2pgs); last Ryan-a(p) 3.00
7-Spider-Man & Quasar vs. Terminus 4.00
8-14,18: 8-Secret Wars x-over; Mike Manley-a begins. 9-Modam (female Modok) app. 10-Dr. Minerva app. 11-Excalibur & Mordred app; first Moondragon as 'H.D Steckley'. 12-Eternals app.; death of Quasar's father (Gilbert). 13-Squadron Supreme & Overmind app. 14-McFarlane-c; Squadron Supreme, Overmind app. 18-1st app. Origin & Unbeing; new Quasar costume; 1st Greg Capullo-a 3.00
15,16: 15-Mignola-c; Squadron Supreme, Overmind, the Stranger & the Watchers app. 16-($1.50, 52 pgs.) Squadron Supreme, Overmind, Stranger & the Watchers app. 4.00
17-Features Marvel's speedsters: Quicksilver, Makkari, Captain Marvel (Monica Rambeau), Speed Demon, Black Racer, Super Sabre & the Runner; Flash parody 'Buried Alien' 5.00
19-(2/91)-Re-intro Jack of Hearts & Maelstrom (neither one seen since 1984); Dr. Strange app. 6.00
20,21: 20-Fantastic Four & the Presence app. 21-Maelstrom revealed as the 'Cosmic Assassin' 5.00
22,23,27,29: 22-Quasar dies; Deathurge app. 'H.D Steckley' revealed to be Moondragon. 23-Ghost Rider app. 27-Original Marvel Boy app. 29-Kismet (Her) app; Vanity Fair Demi Moore pregnancy parody-c 3.00
24-Brief Infinity Gauntlet reference; Thanos & Mephisto app.; vs. Maelstrom; 1st app. Infinity (the female aspect of Eternity) 1 2 3 5 6 8
25-($1.50)-New costume Quasar (returns to life); Eternity, Infinity, Oblivion, Death, Celestials, Galactus, Watchers app.; 'death' of Maelstrom 4.00
26-Infinity Gauntlet tie-in; Thanos & Moondragon app. 5.00
28,30-33: 28-Kismet (Her) app.; Avengers; Warlock, Moondragon, Jack of Hearts app. 30-What If..? issue; Watcher, Thanos, Maelstrom app. 31-Quasar in the New Universe; gains the power of the Starbrand. 32-Operation Galactic Storm Pt. 3; continued from Avengers West Coast #80; Shi'ar Imperial Guard app.; 1st app. Korath the Pursuer. 33-Operation Galactic Storm Pt.10; continued from Avengers West Coast #81; story continues in Wonder Man #8 4.00
34-39,41-49,51-53: 34-Opertation Galactic Storm Pt. 17; continued from Captain America #400; continued in Avengers West Coast #82. 35-Operation Galactic Storm aftermath; Quasar quits the Avengers. 38-Infinity War x-over; Quasar & the Avengers vs. Warlock, Thanos & the Infinity Watch; last Capullo-a. 39-Infinity War x-over; Thanos & Deathurge app. 41-Avengers app. 42-Punisher app. 43-Quasar returns to life. 47,48-Thunderstrike app. 49-Kismet app. 51,52: 52-Squadron Supreme app. 53-Warlock & the Infinity Watch app. 3.00
40,50: 40-Infinity War x-over; Quasar uses the Ultimate Nullifier and dies; Thanos app. 50-($2.95, 52 pgs.)-Holo-grafix foil-c Silver Surfer, Man-Thing, Ren & Stimpy app. 4.00
54,55: 53-Warlock & the Infinity Watch app. 54-Starblast tie-in; continued from Starblast #1; Hyperion vs. Gladiator. 55-Starblast tie-in; continued from Starblast #2; Black Bolt app; continued in Starblast #3 4.00
56-57: 56-Starblast tie-in; continued from Starblast #4; New Universe app.; continued in Starblast #4. 57-Living Tribunal & the New Universe app. 5.00
58,59: 58-w/bound-in card sheet; Makkari wins the Galactic Race; DC Comics Flash (as Fastforward) app. 59-Thanos & Starfox app. 6.00
60-Last issue; Avengers, New Warriors & Fantastic Four app; Quasar leaves Earth 1 2 3 5 6 8
Special #1-3 ($1.25, newsstand)-Same as #32-34 3.00

QUEEN & COUNTRY (See Whiteout)
Oni Press: Mar, 2001 - No. 32, Aug, 2007 ($2.95/$2.99, B&W)

1-Rucka-s in all. Rolston-a/Sale-c 1 2 3 4 5 7
2-5: 2-4-Rolston-a/Sale-c. 5-Snyder-c/Hurtt-a 4.00
6-24,26-32: 6,7-Snyder-c/Hurtt-a. 13-15-Alexander-a. 16-20-McNeil-a. 21-24-Hawthorne-a. 26-28-Norton-a 3.00
25-($5.99) Rolston-a 6.00
Free Comic Book Day giveaway (5/02) r/#1 with "Free Comic Book Day" banner on-c 3.00
Operation: Blackwall (10/03, $8.95, TPB) r/#13-15; John Rogers intro. 9.00
Operation: Broken Ground (2002, $11.95, TPB) r/#1-4; Ellis intro. 12.00
Operation: Crystal Ball (1/03, $14.95, TPB) r/#8-12; Judd Winick intro. 15.00
Operation: Dandelion HC (8/04, $25.00) r/#21-24; Jamie S. Rich intro. 25.00
Operation: Dandelion (8/04, $11.95, TPB) r/#21-24; Jamie S. Rich intro. 12.00
Operation: Morningstar (9/02, $8.95, TPB) r/#5-7; Stuart Moore intro. 9.00
Operation: Storm Front (3/04, $14.95, TPB) r/#16-20; Geoff Johns intro. 15.00

QUEEN & COUNTRY: DECLASSIFIED
Oni Press: Nov, 2002 - No. 3, Jan, 2003 ($2.95, B&W, limited series)

1-3-Rucka-s/Hurtt-a/Morse-c 3.00
TPB (7/03, $8.95) r/#1-3; intro. by Micah Wright 9.00

QUEEN & COUNTRY: DECLASSIFIED (Volume 2)
Oni Press: Jan, 2005 - No. 3, Feb, 2006 ($2.95/$2.99, B&W, limited series)

1-3-Rucka-s/Burchett-a/c 3.00
TPB (3/06, $8.95) r/#1-3 9.00

QUEEN & COUNTRY: DECLASSIFIED (Volume 3)
Oni Press: Jun, 2005 - No. 3, Aug, 2005 ($2.95, B&W, limited series)

1-3- "Sons & Daughters;" Johnston-s/Mitten-a/c 3.00
TPB (3/06, $8.95) r/#1-3 9.00

QUEEN OF THE WEST, DALE EVANS (TV)(See Dale Evans Comics, Roy Rogers & Western Roundup under Dell Giants)
Dell Publ. Co.: No. 479, 7/53 - No. 22, 1-3/59 (All photo-c; photo back c-4-8,15)

	GD 2.0	VG 4.0	FN 6.0	VF 8.0	VF/NM 9.0	NM- 9.2
Four Color 479(#1, '53)	16	32	48	110	243	375
Four Color 528(#2, '54)	9	18	27	60	120	180
3,4: 3(4-6/54)-Toth-a. 4-Toth, Manning-a	7	14	21	46	86	125
5-10-Manning-a. 5-Marsh-a	6	12	18	40	73	105
11,19,21-No Manning 21-Tufts-a	5	10	15	31	53	75
12-18,20,22-Manning-a	5	10	15	34	60	85

QUEEN SONJA (See Red Sonja)
Dynamite Entertainment: 2009 - No. 35, 2013 ($2.99/$3.99)

1-10: 1-Rubi-a/Ortega-s; 3 covers; back-up r/Marvel Feature #1 4.00
11-35-($3.99) 16-Thulsa Doom returns 4.00

QUENTIN DURWARD
Dell Publishing Co.: No. 672, Jan, 1956

Four Color 672-Movie, photo-c 6 12 18 42 79 115

QUESTAR ILLUSTRATED SCIENCE FICTION CLASSICS
Golden Press: 1977 (224 pgs.) ($1.95)

11197-Stories by Asimov, Sturgeon, Silverberg & Niven; Starstream-r 3 6 9 20 30 40

QUEST FOR CAMELOT
DC Comics: July, 1998 ($4.95)

1-Movie adaption 5.00

QUEST FOR DREAMS LOST (Also see Word Warriors)
Literacy Volunteers of Chicago: July 4, 1987 ($2.00, B&W, 52 pgs.)(Proceeds donated to help fight illiteracy)

1-Teenage Mutant Ninja Turtles by Eastman/Laird, Trollords, Silent Invasion, The Realm, Wordsmith, Reacto Man, Eb'nn, Aniverse 4.00

QUESTION, THE (See Americomics, Blue Beetle (1967), Charlton Bullseye & Mysterious Suspense)

QUESTION, THE (Also see Showcase '95 #3)
DC Comics: Feb, 1987 - No. 36, Mar, 1990; No. 37, Mar, 2010 ($1.50)

1-36: Denny O'Neil scripts in all 3.00
37-(3/10, $2.99) Blackest Night one-shot; Victor Sage rises; Shiva app.; Cowan-a 3.00
Annual 1 (1988, $2.50) 4.00
Annual 2 (1989, $3.50) 4.00
...: Epitaph For a Hero TPB (2008, $19.99) r/#13-18 20.00
...: Peacemaker TPB (2010, $19.99) r/#31-36 20.00
...: Pipeline TPB (2011, $14.99) r/stories from Detective Comics #854-865; sketch-a 15.00
...: Poisoned Ground TPB (2008, $19.99) r/#7-12 20.00
...: Riddles TPB (2009, $19.99) r/#25-30 20.00
...: Welcome to Oz TPB (2009, $19.99) r/#19-24 20.00
...: Zen and Violence TPB (2007, $19.99) r/#1-6 20.00

Quick Draw McGraw #3 © H-B

Race to the Moon #1 © HARV

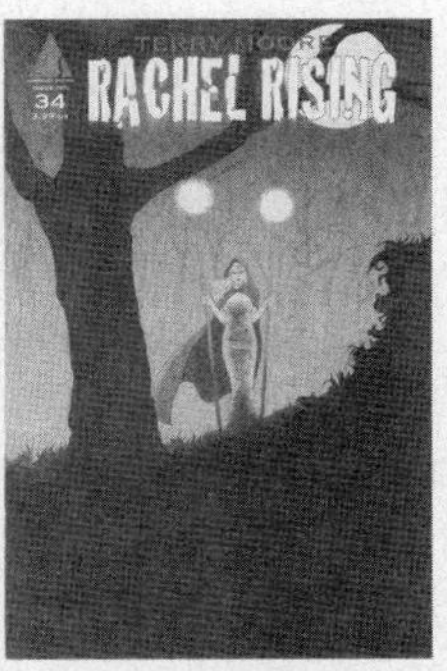

Rachel Rising #34 © Terry Moore

GD 2.0 | VG 4.0 | FN 6.0 | VF 8.0 | VF/NM 9.0 | NM- 9.2

GD 2.0 | VG 4.0 | FN 6.0 | VF 8.0 | VF/NM 9.0 | NM- 9.2

QUESTION, THE (Also see Crime Bible and 52)
DC Comics: Jan, 2005 - No. 6, Jun, 2005 ($2.95, limited series)
1-6-Rick Veitch-s/Tommy Lee Edwards-a. 4,6-Superman app. 3.00

QUESTION QUARTERLY, THE
DC Comics: Summer, 1990 - No. 5, Spring, 1992 ($2.50/$2.95, 52pgs.)
1-5 4.00
NOTE: ***Cowan** a-1, 2, 4, 5; c-1-3, 5. **Mignola** a-5i. **Quesada** a-3-5.*

QUESTION RETURNS, THE
DC Comics: Feb, 1997 ($3.50, one-shot)
1-Brereton-c 4.00

QUESTPROBE
Marvel Comics: 8/84; No. 2, 1/85; No. 3, 11/85 (lim. series)
1-3: 1-The Hulk app. by Romita. 2-Spider-Man; Mooney-a(i). 3-Human Torch & Thing 4.00

QUICK DRAW McGRAW (TV) (Hanna-Barbera)(See Whitman Comic Books)
Dell Publishing Co./Gold Key No. 12 on: No. 1040, 12-2/59-60 - No. 11, 7-9/62; No. 12, 11/62; No. 13, 2/63; No. 14, 4/63; No. 15, 6/69 (1st show aired 9/29/59)

Issue	GD	VG	FN	VF	VF/NM	NM-
Four Color 1040(#1) 1st app. Quick Draw & Baba Looey, Augie Doggie & Doggie Daddy and Snooper & Blabber	12	24	36	83	182	280
2(4-6/60)-4,6: 2-Augie Doggie & Snooper & Blabber stories (8 pgs. each); pre-dates both of their #1 issues. 4-Augie Doggie & Snooper & Blabber stories.	5	10	15	35	63	90
5-1st Snagglepuss app.; last 10¢ issue	6	12	18	38	69	100
7-11	5	10	15	30	50	70
12,13-Title change to ...Fun-Type Roundup (84pgs.)	6	12	18	38	69	100
14,15: 15-Reprints	4	8	12	27	44	60

QUICK DRAW McGRAW (TV)(See Spotlight #2)
Charlton Comics: Nov, 1970 - No. 8, Jan, 1972 (Hanna-Barbera)

Issue	GD	VG	FN	VF	VF/NM	NM-
1	5	10	15	30	50	70
2-8	3	6	9	18	28	38

QUICKSILVER (See Avengers)
Marvel Comics: Nov, 1997 - No. 13, Nov, 1998 ($2.99/$1.99)
1-($2.99)-Peyer-s/Casey Jones-a; wraparound-c 4.00
2-11: 2-Two covers-variant by Golden. 4-6-Inhumans app. 3.00
12-($2.99) Siege of Wundagore pt. 4 4.00
13-Magneto-c/app.; last issue 3.00

QUICK-TRIGGER WESTERN (...Action #12; Cowboy Action #5-11)
Atlas Comics (ACI #12/WPI #13-19): No. 12, May, 1956 - No. 19, Sept, 1957

Issue	GD	VG	FN	VF	VF/NM	NM-
12-Baker-a	20	40	60	120	195	270
13-Williamson-a, 5 pgs.	18	36	54	103	162	220
14-Everett, Crandall, Torres-a; Heath-c	16	32	48	94	147	200
15,16: 15-Torres, Crandall-a. 16-Orlando, Kirby-a	15	30	45	84	127	170
17,18: 18-Baker-a	15	30	45	83	124	165
19	13	26	39	74	105	135

NOTE: ***Ayers** a-17. **Colan** a-16. **Maneely** a-15, 17; c-15, 18. **Morrow** a-18. **Powell** a-14. **Severin** a-19; c-12, 13, 16, 17, 19. **Shores** a-16. **Tuska** a-17.*

QUINCY (See Comics Reading Libraries in the Promotional Comics section)

QUITTER, THE
DC Comics (Vertigo): 2005 ($19.99, B&W graphic novel)
HC ($19.99) Autobiography of Harvey Pekar; Pekar-s/Daen Haspiel-a 20.00
SC (2006, $12.99) 13.00

RACCOON KIDS, THE (Formerly Movietown Animal Antics)
National Periodical Publications (Arleigh No. 63,64): No. 52, Sept-Oct, 1954 - No. 62, Oct-Nov, 1956; No. 63, Sept, 1957; No. 64, Nov, 1957

Issue	GD	VG	FN	VF	VF/NM	NM-
52-Doodles Duck by Mayer	15	30	45	83	124	165
53-64: 53-62-Doodles Duck by Mayer	11	22	33	62	86	110

NOTE: ***Otto Feuer**-a most issues. **Rube Grossman**-a most issues.*

RACE FOR THE MOON
Harvey Publications: Mar, 1958 - No. 3, Nov, 1958

Issue	GD	VG	FN	VF	VF/NM	NM-
1-Powell-a(5); 1/2-pg. S&K-a; cover redrawn from Galaxy Science Fiction pulp (5/53)	18	36	54	105	165	225
2-Kirby/Williamson-c(r)/a(3); Kirby-p 7 more stys	27	54	81	158	259	360
3-Kirby/Williamson-c/a(4); Kirby-p 6 more stys	29	58	87	170	278	385

RACER-X
Now Comics: 8/88 - No. 11, 8/89; V2#1, 9/89 - V2#10, 1990 ($1.75)
0-Deluxe ($3.50) 5.00
1 (9/88) - 11, V2#1-10 4.00

RACER X (See Speed Racer)

RACHEL RISING
DC Comics (WildStorm): Oct, 2000 - No. 3, Dec, 2000 ($2.95, limited series)
1-3: 1-Tommy Yune-s/Jo Chen-a; 2 covers by Yune. 2,3-Kabala app. 4.00

RACHEL RISING
Abstract Studio: 2011 - No. 42, 2016 ($3.99, B&W)
1-Terry Moore-s/a/c; back cover by Fabio Moon; green background on cover 80.00
1-(2nd printing) Red background on cover 35.00
1-(3rd printing) Red background on cover 35.00
2 35.00
3-6 10.00
7-42: 42-Final issue 4.00
Halloween ComicFest Edition (2014, giveaway) Reprints #1 with orange bkgd on cover 5.00

RACING PETTYS
STP Corp.: 1980 ($2.50, 68 pgs., 10 1/8" x 13 1/4")

Issue	GD	VG	FN	VF	VF/NM	NM-
1-Bob Kane-a. Kane bio on inside back-c.	2	4	6	8	10	12

RACK & PAIN
Dark Horse Comics: Mar, 1994 - No. 4, June, 1994 ($2.50, limited series)
1-4: Brian Pulido scripts in all. 1-Greg Capullo-c 3.00

RACK & PAIN: KILLERS
Chaos! Comics: Sept, 1996 - No. 4, Jan, 1997 ($2.95, limited series)
1-4: Reprints Dark Horse series; Jae Lee-c 3.00

RACKET SQUAD IN ACTION
Capitol Stories/Charlton Comics: May-June, 1952 - No. 29, Mar, 1958

Issue	GD	VG	FN	VF	VF/NM	NM-
1	34	68	102	199	325	450
2-4,6: 3,4,6-Dr. Neff, Ghost Breaker app.	18	36	54	103	162	220
5-Dr. Neff, Ghost Breaker app; headlights-c	47	94	141	296	498	700
7-10: 10-Explosion-c	15	30	45	90	140	190
11-Ditko-c/a	39	78	117	231	378	525
12-Ditko explosion-c (classic); Shuster-a(2)	61	122	183	390	670	950
13-Shuster-c(p)/a.	14	28	42	81	118	155
14-Marijuana story "Shakedown"; Giordano-c	18	36	54	107	169	230
15-28: 15,20,22,23-Giordano-c	13	26	39	74	105	135
29-(15¢, 68 pgs.)	15	30	45	85	130	175

RADIANT LOVE (Formerly Daring Love #1)
Gilmor Magazines: No. 2, Dec, 1953 - No. 6, Aug, 1954

Issue	GD	VG	FN	VF	VF/NM	NM-
2	21	42	63	122	199	275
3-6	15	30	45	88	137	185

RADICAL DREAMER
Blackball Comics: No. 0, May, 1994 - No. 4, Nov, 1994 ($1.99, bi-monthly) (1st poster format comic)
0-4: 0-2-($1.99, poster format): 0-1st app. Max Wrighter. 3,4-($2.50-c) 3.00

RADICAL DREAMER
Mark's Giant Economy Size Comics: V2#1, June, 1995 - V2#6, Feb, 1996 ($2.95, B&W, limited series)
V2#1-6 3.00
Prime (5/96, $2.95) 3.00
Dreams Cannot Die!-(1996, $20.00, softcover)-Collects V1#0-4 & V2#1-6; intro by Kurt Busiek; afterward by Mark Waid 20.00
Dreams Cannot Die!-(1996, $60.00, hardcover)-Signed & limited edition; collects V1#0-4 & V2#1-6; intro by Kurt Busiek; afterward by Mark Waid 60.00

RADIOACTIVE MAN (Simpsons TV show)
Bongo Comics: 1993 - No. 6, 1994 ($1.95/$2.25, limited series)

Issue	GD	VG	FN	VF	VF/NM	NM-
1-($2.95)-Glow-in-the-dark-c; bound-in jumbo poster; origin Radioactive Man; (cover dated Nov. 1952)	1	3	4	6	8	10

2-6: 2-Says #88 on-c & inside & dated May 1962; cover parody of Atlas Kirby monster-c; Superior Squad app.; origin Fallout Boy. 3-($1.95)-Cover "dated" Aug 1972 #216. 4-($2.25)-Cover "dated" Oct 1980 #412; w/trading card. 5-Cover "dated" Jan 1986 #679; w/trading card. 6-(Jan 1995 #1000) 4.00
Colossal #1-($4.95) 7.00
#4 (2001, $2.50) Faux 1953 issue; Murphy Anderson-i (6 pgs.) 3.00
#100 (2000, $2.50) Comic Book Guy-c/app.; faux 1963 issue inside 3.00
#136 (2001, $2.50) Dan DeCarlo-c/a 3.00
#222 (2001, $2.50) Batton Lash-s; Radioactive Man in 1972-style 3.00
#575 (2002, $2.50) Chaykin-c; Radioactive Man in 1984-style 3.00
1963-106 (2002, $2.50) Radioactive Man in 1960s Gold Key-style; Groening-c 3.00
#7 Bongo Super Heroes Starring... (2003, $2.50) Marvel Silver Age-style Superior Squad 3.00
#8 Official Movie Adaptation (2004, $2.99) starring Rainier Wolfcastle and Milhouse 3.00
#9 (#197 on-c) (2004, $2.50) Kirby-esque New Gods spoof; Golden Age Radio Man app. 3.00

RADIO FUNNIES

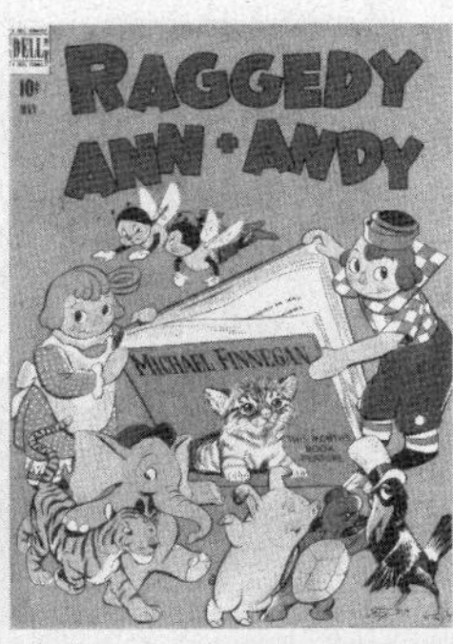

Raggedy Ann and Andy #24 © DELL

Ragnarok #1 © Walt Simonson

Rampaging Hulk #5 © MAR

GD VG FN VF VF/NM NM-
2.0 4.0 6.0 8.0 9.0 9.2

DC Comics: Mar. 1939; undated variant

nn-(3/39) Ashcan comic, not distributed to newsstands, only for in-house use. Cover art is Adventure Comics #39 with interior being Detective Comics #19 (no known sales)
nn - Ashcan comic. No date. Cover art is Detective #26 with interior from Detective #17; one copy, graded at GD/VG, sold at auction for $4481.25 in Nov, 2009. Another copy graded at GD/VG sold at auction for $3346 in Feb, 2010.

RAGAMUFFINS
Eclipse Comics: Jan, 1985 ($1.75, one shot)

1-Eclipse Magazine-r, w/color; Colan-a 3.00

RAGE (Based on the id video game)
Dark Horse Comics: Jun, 2011 - No. 3, Aug, 2011 ($3.50, limited series)

1-3-Nelson-s/Mutti-a/Fabry-c. 1-Variant-c by Martiniere 3.50

RAGEMOOR
Dark Horse Comics: Mar, 2012 - No. 4, Jun, 2012 ($3.50, B&W, limited series)

1-4-Richard Corben-a/c; Jan Strnad-s 3.50

RAGGEDY ANN AND ANDY (See Dell Giants, March of Comics #23 & New Funnies)
Dell Publishing Co.: No. 5, 1942 - No. 533, 2/54; 10-12/64 - No. 4, 3/66

Four Color 5(1942) 46 92 138 350 788 1225
Four Color 23(1943) 31 62 93 223 499 775
Four Color 45(1943) 25 50 75 175 388 600
Four Color 72(1945) 20 40 60 141 313 485
1(6/46)-Billy & Bonnie Bee by Frank Thomas 29 58 87 209 467 725
2,3: 3-Egbert Elephant by Dan Noonan begins 15 30 45 100 220 340
4-Kelly-a, 16 pgs. 15 30 45 105 233 360
5,6,8-10 12 24 36 80 173 265
7-Little Black Sambo, Black Mumbo & Black Jumbo only app; Christmas-c
14 28 42 94 207 320
11-20 10 20 30 64 132 200
21-Alice In Wonderland cover/story 12 24 36 80 173 265
22-27,29-39(8/49), Four Color 262 (1/50): 34-"...In Candyland"
9 18 27 57 111 165
28-Kelly-c 9 18 27 59 117 175
Four Color 306,354,380,452,533 7 14 21 46 86 125
1(10-12/64-Dell) 4 8 12 23 37 50
2,3(10-12/65), 4(3/66) 3 6 9 16 23 30
NOTE: *Kelly art ("Animal Mother Goose")-#1-34, 36, 37; c-28. Peterkin Pottle by* ***John Stanley*** *in 32-38.*

RAGGEDY ANN AND ANDY
Gold Key: Dec, 1971 - No. 6, Sept, 1973

1 3 6 9 18 28 38
2-6 3 6 9 15 21 26

RAGGEDY ANN & THE CAMEL WITH THE WRINKLED KNEES (See Dell Jr. Treasury #8)

RAGMAN (See Batman Family #20, The Brave & The Bold #196 & Cancelled Comic Cavalcade)
National Per. Publ./DC Comics No. 5: Aug-Sept, 1976 - No. 5, Jun-Jul, 1977

1-Origin & 1st app. 3 6 9 16 23 30
2-5: 2-Origin ends; Kubert-c. 4-Drug use story 2 4 6 8 10 12
NOTE: ***Kubert*** *a-4, 5; c-1-5.* ***Redondo*** *studios a-1-4.*

RAGMAN (2nd Series)
DC Comics: Oct, 1991 - No. 8, May, 1992 ($1.50, limited series)

1-8: 1-Giffen plots/breakdowns. 3-Origin. 8-Batman-c/story 3.00

RAGMAN: CRY OF THE DEAD
DC Comics: Aug, 1993 - No. 6, Jan, 1994 ($1.75, limited series)

1-6: Joe Kubert-c 3.00

RAGMAN: SUIT OF SOULS
DC Comics: Dec, 2010 ($3.99, one-shot)

1-Gage-s/Segovia-a/Saiz-c; origin retold 4.00

RAGNAROK
IDW Publishing: Jul, 2014 - Present ($3.99/$4.99)

1-7-Walt Simonson-s/a; two covers on each 4.00
8-11-($4.99) 5.00

RAGS RABBIT (Formerly Babe Ruth Sports #10 or Little Max #10?; also see Harvey Hits #2, Harvey Wiseguys & Tastee Freez)
Harvey Publications: No. 11, June, 1951 - No. 18, March, 1954 (Written & drawn for little folks)

11-(See Nutty Comics #5 for 1st app.) 6 12 18 31 38 45
12-18 5 10 15 24 30 35

RAI (Rai and the Future Force #9-23) (See Magnus #5-8)
Valiant: Mar, 1992 - No. 0, Oct, 1992; No. 9, May, 1993 - No. 33, Jun, 1995 ($1.95/$2.25)

1-Valiant's 1st original character 2 4 6 11 16 20
2-5: 4-Low print run 2 4 6 9 12 15
6-10: 6,7-Unity x-overs. 7-Death of Rai. 9-($2.50)-Gatefold-c; story cont'd from Magnus #24; Magnus, Eternal Warrior & X-O app. 6.00
11-33: 15-Manowar Armor app. 17-19-Magnus x-over. 21-1st app. The Starwatchers (cameo); trading card. 22-Death of Rai. 26-Chaos Effect Epsilon Pt. 3 4.00
#0-(11/92)-Origin/1st app. new Rai (Rising Spirit) & 1st full app. & partial origin Bloodshot; also see Eternal Warrior #4; tells future of all characters
2 4 6 13 18 22
NOTE: ***Layton*** *c-2i, 9i.* ***Miller*** *c-6.* ***Simonson*** *c-7.*

RAI
Valiant Entertainment: May, 2014 - Present ($3.99)

1-16: 1-Kindt-s/Crain-s; Rai in Japan in the year 4001. 15,16-4001 AD tie-ins 4.00

RAIDERS OF THE LOST ARK (Movie)
Marvel Comics Group: Sept, 1981 - No. 3, Nov, 1981 (Movie adaptation)

1-r/Marvel Comics Super Special #18 2 4 6 8 10 12
2,3 1 2 3 5 6 8
NOTE: ***Buscema*** *a(p)-1-3; c(p)-1.* ***Simonson*** *a-3i; scripts-1-3.*

RAINBOW BRITE AND THE STAR STEALER
DC Comics: 1985

nn-Movie adaptation 2 4 6 8 10 12

RAISE THE DEAD
Dynamite Entertainment: 2007 - No. 4, Aug, 2007 ($3.50)

1-4-Arthur Suydam-c/Leah Moore & John Reppion-s/Petrus-a; Phillips var-c on all 4.00
... Vol. 1 HC (2007, $19.99) r/#1-4; script, interview & sketch pages; cover gallery 20.00

RAISE THE DEAD 2
Dynamite Entertainment: 2010 - No. 4, 2011 ($3.99)

1-4-Leah Moore & John Reppion-s/Vilanova-a 4.00

RALPH KINER, HOME RUN KING
Fawcett Publications: 1950 (Pittsburgh Pirates)

nn-Photo-c; life story 60 120 180 381 658 935

RALPH SNART ADVENTURES
Now Comics: June, 1986 - V2#9, 1987; V3#1 - #26, Feb, 1991; V4#1, 1992 - #4, 1992

1-3, V2#1-7,V3#1-23,25,26:1-($1.00, B&W)-1(B&W),V2#1(11/86), B&W), 8,9-color. V3#1(9/88)-Color begins 3.00
V3#24-($2.50)-3-D issue, V4#1-3-Direct sale versions w/cards 3.00
V4#1-3-Newsstand versions w/random cards 3.00
Book 1 1 2 3 5 6 8
3-D Special (11/92, $3.50)-Complete 12-card set w/3-D glasses 4.00

RAMAR OF THE JUNGLE (TV)
Toby Press No. 1/Charlton No. 2 on: 1954 (no month); No. 2, Sept, 1955 - No. 5, Sept, 1956

1-Jon Hall photo-c; last pre-code issue 24 48 72 142 234 325
2-5: 2-Jon Hall photo-c 17 34 51 98 154 210

RAMAYAN 3392 A.D.
Virgin Comics: Sept, 2006 - No. 8, Aug, 2008 ($2.99)

1-8: 1-Alex Ross-c; re-imagining of the Indian myth of Ramayana; poster of cover inside 3.00
... Reloaded (8/07 - No. 7, 7/08, $2.99) 1-7: 1-Two covers by Kang and Oeming 3.00
... Reloaded Guidebook (4/08, $2.99) Profiles of characters and weapons 3.00

RAMM
Megaton Comics: May, 1987 - No. 2, Sept, 1987 ($1.50, B&W)

1,2-Both have 1 pg. Youngblood ad by Liefeld 3.00

RAMPAGING HULK (The Hulk #10 on; also see Marvel Treasury Edition)
Marvel Comics Group: Jan, 1977 - No. 9, June, 1978 ($1.00, B&W magazine)

1-Bloodstone story w/Buscema & Nebres-a. Origin re-cap w/Simonson-a; Gargoyle, UFO story; Ken Barr-c 3 6 9 18 28 38
2-Old X-Men app; origin old w/Simonson-a & new X-Men in text w/Cockrum illos; Bloodstone story w/Brown & Nebres-a 3 6 9 15 22 28
3-9: 3-Iron Man app.; Norem-c. 4-Gallery of villains w/Giffen-a. 5,6-Hulk vs. Sub-Mariner. 7-Man-Thing story. 8-Original Avengers app. 9-Thor vs. Hulk battle; Shanna the She-Devil story w/DeZuniga-a 2 4 6 13 18 22
NOTE: ***Alcala*** *a-1-3i, 5i, 8i.* ***Buscema*** *a-1.* ***Giffen*** *a-4.* ***Nino*** *a-4i.* ***Simonson*** *a-1-3p.* ***Starlin*** *a-4(w/Nino), 7; c-4, 5, 7.*

RAMPAGING HULK
Marvel Comics: Aug, 1998 - No. 6, Jan, 1999 ($2.99/$1.99)

1-($2.99) Flashback stories of Savage Hulk; Leonardi-a 4.00
2-6-($1.99): 2-Two covers 3.00

Rangers Comics #41 © FH

Rasl #1 © Jeff Smith

Rat Queens #1 © Wiebe & Upchurch

GD 2.0 | VG 4.0 | FN 6.0 | VF 8.0 | VF/NM 9.0 | NM- 9.2

RAMPAGING WOLVERINE
Marvel Comics: June, 2009 ($3.99, B&W, one-shot)
1-Short stories by Fialkov, Luque, Ted McKeever, Yost, Santolouco, Firth, Nelson 4.00

RANDOLPH SCOTT (Movie star)(See Crack Western #67, Prize Comics Western #76, Western Hearts #8, Western Love #1 & Western Winners #7)

RANGE BUSTERS
Fox Features Syndicate: Sept, 1950 (One shot)
1 (Exist?) 20 40 60 117 189 260

RANGE BUSTERS (Formerly Cowboy Love?; Wyatt Earp, Frontier Marshall #11 on)
Charlton Comics: No. 8, May, 1955 - No. 10, Sept, 1955
8 8 16 24 42 54 65
9,10 6 12 18 28 34 40

RANGELAND LOVE
Atlas Comics (CDS): Dec, 1949 - No. 2, Mar, 1950 (52 pgs.)
1-Robert Taylor & Arlene Dahl photo-c 20 40 60 114 182 250
2-Photo-c 15 30 45 84 127 170

RANGER, THE (See Zane Grey, Four Color #255)

RANGE RIDER, THE (TV)(See Flying A's...)

RANGE ROMANCES
Comic Magazines (Quality Comics): Dec, 1949 - No. 5, Aug, 1950 (#5: 52 pg)
1-Gustavson-c/a 27 54 81 158 259 360
2-Crandall-c/a 26 52 78 154 252 350
3-Crandall, Gustavson-a; photo-c 22 44 66 132 216 300
4-Crandall-a; photo-c 20 40 60 117 189 260
5-Gustavson-a; Crandall-a(p); photo-c 20 40 60 117 189 260

RANGERS COMICS (...of Freedom #1-7)
Fiction House Magazines: 10/41 - No. 67, 10/52; No. 68, Fall, 1952; No. 69, Winter, 1952-53 (Flying stories)
1-Intro. Ranger Girl & The Rangers of Freedom; ends #7, cover app. only #5
541 1082 1623 3950 6975 10,000
2 194 388 582 1242 2121 3000
3 135 270 405 864 1482 2100
4,5 97 194 291 621 1061 1500
6-10-All Japanese war covers. 8-U.S. Rangers begin
77 154 231 493 847 1200
11,12-Commando Rangers app. 74 148 222 470 810 1150
13-Commando Ranger begins-not same as Commando Rangers; Nazi war-c
81 162 243 518 884 1250
14-Classic Japanese bondage/torture WWII-c 97 194 291 621 1061 1500
15-20: 15,17,19-Japanese war-c. 18-Nazi war-c 61 122 183 390 670 950
21-Intro/origin Firehair (begins, 2/45) 81 162 243 518 884 1250
22-25,27,29-Japanese war-c. 23-Kazanda begins, ends #28
47 94 141 296 498 700
26-Classic Japanese WWII good girl-c 77 154 231 493 847 1200
28,30: 28-Tiger Man begins (origin/1st app., 4/46), ends #46. 30-Crusoe Island begins, ends #40 40 80 120 246 411 575
31-40: 33-Hypodermic panels 36 72 108 211 343 475
41-46: 41-Last Werewolf Hunter 26 52 78 154 252 350
47-56- "Eisnerish" Dr. Drew by Grandenetti. 48-Last Glory Forbes. 53-Last 52 pg. issue. 55-Last Sky Rangers 24 48 72 142 234 325
57-60-Straight run of Dr. Drew by Grandenetti 18 36 54 105 165 225
61-69: 64-Suicide Smith begins. 63-Used in **POP**, pgs. 85, 99. 67-Space Rangers begin, end #69 15 30 45 90 140 190

NOTE: *Bondage, discipline covers, lingerie panels are common. Crusoe Island by* ***Larsen-#30-36.*** *Firehair by* ***Lubbers-#30-49.*** *Glory Forbes by* ***Baker-#36-45, 47;*** *by* ***Whitman-#34, 35.*** *I Confess in #41-53. Jan of the Jungle in #42-58. King of the Congo in #49-53. Tiger Man by* ***Celardo-#30-39. M. Anderson*** *a-30?* ***Baker*** *a-36-38, 42, 44.* ***John Celardo*** *a-34, 36-39.* ***Lee Elias*** *a-21-28.* ***Evans*** *a-19, 38-46, 48-52.* ***Hopper*** *a-25, 26.* ***Ingels*** *a-13-16.* ***Larsen*** *a-34.* ***Bob Lubbers*** *a-30-38, 40-44; c-40-45.* ***Moreira*** *a-41-47.* ***Tuska*** *a-16, 17, 19, 22.* ***M. Whitman*** *c-61-66.* ***Zolnerwich*** *c-1-17.*

RANGO (TV)
Dell Publishing Co.: Aug, 1967
1-Photo-c of comedian Tim Conway 4 8 12 28 47 65

RANN-THANAGAR HOLY WAR (Also see Hawkman Special #1)
DC Comics: July, 2008 - No. 8, Feb, 2009 ($3.50, limited series)
1-8-Adam Strange & Hawkman app.; Starlin-s/Lim-a. 1-Two covers by Starlin & Lim 3.50
Volume One TPB (2009, $19.99) r/#1-4 & Hawkman Special #1 20.00
Volume Two TPB (2009, $19.99) r/#5-8 & Adam Strange Special #1 20.00

RANN-THANAGAR WAR (See Adam Strange 2004 mini-series)(Prelude to Infinite Crisis)
DC Comics: July, 2005 - No. 6, Dec, 2005 ($2.50, limited series)
1-6-Adam Strange, Hawkman and Green Lantern (Kyle Rayner) app.; Gibbons-s/Reis-a 3.00
...: Infinite Crisis Special (4/06, $4.99) Kyle Rayner becomes Ion again; Jade dies 5.00
TPB (2005, $12.99) r/#1-6; cover gallery; new Bolland-c 13.00

RAPHAEL (See Teenage Mutant Ninja Turtles)
Mirage Studios: 1985 ($1.50, 7-1/2x11", B&W w/2 color cover, one-shot)
1-1st Turtles one-shot spin-off; contains 1st drawing of the Turtles as a group from 1983
7 14 21 49 92 135
1-2nd printing (11/87); new-c & 8 pgs. art 2 4 6 8 11 14

RAPHAEL BAD MOON RISING (See Teenage Mutant Ninja Turtles)
Mirage Publishing: July, 2007 - No. 4, Oct, 2007 ($3.25, B&W, limited series)
1-4-Continued from Tales of the TMNT #7; Lawson-a 3.25

RAPTURE
Dark Horse Comics: May, 2009 - No. 6, Jan, 2010 ($2.99, limited series)
1-6-Taki Soma & Michael Avon Oeming-s/a/c. 1-Maleev var-c. 2-Mack var-c 3.00

RASCALS IN PARADISE
Dark Horse Comics: Aug, 1994 - No. 3, Dec, 1994 ($3.95, magazine size)
1-3-Jim Silke-a/story 4.00
Trade paperback-($16.95)-r/#1-3 17.00

RASL
Cartoon Books: Mar, 2008 - No. 15, Jul, 2012 ($3.50/$4.99, B&W)
1-14-Jeff Smith-s/a/c 3.50
15-($4.99) Conclusion 5.00

RATCHET & CLANK (Based on the Sony videogame)
DC Comics (WildStorm thru #4): Nov, 2010 - No. 6, Apr, 2011 ($3.99/$2.99, limited series)
1-4-Fixman-s/Archer-a 4.00
5,6-($2.99) 3.00
TPB (2011, $17.99) r/#1-6 18.00

RATFINK (See Frantic and Zany)
Canrom, Inc.: Oct, 1964
1-Woodbridge-a 9 18 27 59 117 175

RAT GOD
Dark Horse Comics: Feb, 2015 - No. 5, Jun, 2015 ($3.99, limited series)
1-5-Richard Corben-s/a/c 4.00

RAT PATROL, THE (TV) (Also see Wild!)
Dell Publishing Co.: Mar, 1967 - No. 5, Nov, 1967; No. 6, Oct, 1969
1-Christopher George photo-c 6 12 18 40 73 105
2-6: 3-6-Photo-c 4 8 12 27 44 60

RAT QUEENS
Image Comics (Shadowline): Sept, 2013 - No. 16, May, 2016 ($3.50/$3.99)
1-Kurtis Wiebe-s/Roc Upchurch-a/c 1 3 4 6 8 10
1-Variant-c by Fiona Staples 40.00
2-10: 2-8-Two covers on each. 9,10-Sejic-a. 9-Frison-c 3.50
11-16-($3.99) Fowler-a 4.00
... Special: Braga #1 (1/15, $3.50) Wiebe-s/Tess Fowler-a; origin of Braga the Orc 3.50

RAT QUEENS (Volume 2)
Image Comics (Shadowline): Mar, 2017 - Present ($3.99)
1-Kurtis Wiebe-s/Owen Gieni-a/c 4.00

RAVAGERS, THE (See Teen Titans and Superboy New 52 series)
DC Comics: Jul, 2012 - No. 12, Jul, 2013 ($2.99)
1-12: 1-Fairchild, Beast Boy, Terra, Thunder, Lightning, Ridge team; Churchill-a 3.00
#0 (11/12, $2.99) Churchill-a; origin of Beast Boy & Terra 3.00

RAVAGE 2099 (See Marvel Comics Presents #117)
Marvel Comics: Dec, 1992 - No. 33, Aug, 1995($1.25/$1.50)
1-($1.75)-Gold foil stamped-c; Stan Lee scripts 4.00
1-($1.75)-2nd printing 3.00
2-24,26-33: 5-Last Ryan-c. 6-Last Ryan-a. 14-Punisher 2099 x-over. 15-Ron Lim-c(p). 18-Bound-in card sheet 3.00
25 ($2.25, 52 pgs.) 4.00
25 ($2.95, 52 pgs.)-Silver foil embossed-c 5.00

RAVEN (See DC Special: Raven and Teen Titans titles)

RAVEN (From Teen Titans)
DC Comics: Nov, 2016 - No. 6, Apr, 2017 ($2.99, limited series)
1-6: 1-3-Wolfman-s/Borges-a. 4-6-Neves-a 3.00

RAVEN, THE (See Movie Classics)

Rawhide Kid #45 © MAR

The Ray (1994 series) #1 © DC

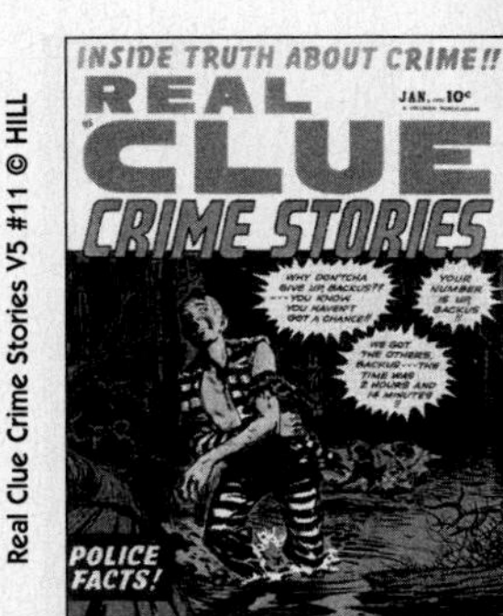

Real Clue Crime Stories V5 #11 © HILL

RAVEN CHRONICLES
Caliber (New Worlds): 1995 - No. 16 ($2.95, B&W)

	GD 2.0	VG 4.0	FN 6.0	VF 8.0	VF/NM 9.0	NM- 9.2
1-16: 10-Flip book w/Wordsmith #6. 15-Flip book w/High Caliber #4						3.00

RAVENS AND RAINBOWS
Pacific Comics: Dec, 1983 (Baxter paper)(Reprints fanzine work in color)

	GD 2.0	VG 4.0	FN 6.0	VF 8.0	VF/NM 9.0	NM- 9.2
1-Jeff Jones-c/a(r); nudity scenes						3.00

RAWHIDE (TV)
Dell Publishing Co./Gold Key: Sept-Nov, 1959 - June-Aug, 1962; July, 1963 - No. 2, Jan, 1964

	GD 2.0	VG 4.0	FN 6.0	VF 8.0	VF/NM 9.0	NM- 9.2
Four Color 1028 (#1)	21	42	63	147	324	500
Four Color 1097,1160,1202,1261,1269	13	26	39	89	195	300
01-684-208 (8/62, Dell)	10	20	30	70	150	230
1(10071-307) (7/63, Gold Key)	10	20	30	70	150	230
2-(12¢)	10	20	30	64	132	200

NOTE: *All have Clint Eastwood photo-c.* ***Tufts*** *a-1028.*

RAWHIDE KID
Atlas/Marvel Comics (CnPC No. 1-16/AMI No. 17-30): Mar, 1955 - No. 16, Sept, 1957; No. 17, Aug, 1960 - No. 151, May, 1979

	GD 2.0	VG 4.0	FN 6.0	VF 8.0	VF/NM 9.0	NM- 9.2
1-Rawhide Kid, his horse Apache & sidekick Randy begin; Wyatt Earp app.; #1 was not code approved; Maneely splash pg.	181	362	543	1158	1979	2800
2	50	100	150	315	533	750
3-5	39	78	117	240	395	550
6-10: 7-Williamson-a (4 pgs.)	32	64	96	188	307	425
11-16: 16-Torres-a	26	52	78	154	252	350
17-Origin by Jack Kirby; Kirby-a begins	116	232	348	742	1271	1800
18-21,24-30	25	50	75	175	388	600
22-Monster-c/story by Kirby/Ayers	28	56	84	202	451	700
23-Origin retold by Jack Kirby	38	76	114	285	641	1000
31-35,40: 31,32-Kirby-a. 33-35-Davis-a. 34-Kirby-a. 35-Intro & death of The Raven. 40-Two-Gun Kid x-over.	13	26	39	89	195	300
36,37,39,41,42-No Kirby. 42-1st Larry Lieber issue	10	20	30	69	147	225
38-Red Raven-c/story; Kirby-c (2/64); Colan-a	14	28	42	96	211	325
43-Kirby-a (beware: pin-up often missing)	13	26	39	91	201	310
44,46: 46-Toth-a. 46-Doc Holliday-c/s	9	18	27	62	126	190
45-Origin retold, 17 pgs.	12	24	36	79	170	260
47-49,51-60	7	14	21	44	82	120
50-Kid Colt x-over; vs. Rawhide Kid	7	14	21	48	89	130
61-70: 64-Kid Colt story. 66-Two-Gun Kid story. 67-Kid Colt story. 70-Last 12¢ issue	5	10	15	33	57	80
71-78,80-83,85	3	6	9	20	31	42
79,84,86,95: 79-Williamson-a(r). 84,86: Kirby-a. 86-Origin-r; Williamson-r/Ringo Kid #13 (4 pgs.)	3	6	9	21	33	45
87-91: 90-Kid Colt app. 91-Last 15¢ issue	3	6	9	18	28	38
92,93 (52 pg.Giants). 92-Kirby-a	4	8	12	25	40	55
94,96-99	3	6	9	16	24	32
100 (6/72)-Origin retold & expanded	3	6	9	21	33	45
101-120: 115-Last new story	3	6	9	14	19	24
121-151	2	4	6	10	14	18
133,134-(30¢-c variants, limited distribution)(5,7/76)	6	12	18	38	69	100
140,141-(35¢-c variants, limited distribution)(7,9/77)	13	26	39	89	195	300
Special 1(9/71, 25¢, 68 pgs.)-All Kirby/Ayers-r	5	10	15	31	53	75

NOTE: ***Ayers*** *a-13, 14, 16, 29, 37-39, 61.* ***Colan*** *a-5, 35, 37, 38; c-145p, 148p, 149p.* ***Davis*** *a-125r.* ***Everett*** *a-54i, 65, 66, 88, 96i, 148i(r).* ***Gulacy*** *c-147.* ***Heath*** *c-4.* ***G. Kane*** *c-101, 144.* ***Keller*** *a-5, 39, 41, 144r.* ***Kirby*** *a-17-32, 34, 42, 43, 84, 86, 92, 109r, 112r, 116r, 117r, 137r, Spec. 1; c-17-35, 37, 38, 40, 41, 43-47, 137r.* ***Maneely*** *c-1, 2, 5, 6, 14.* ***Morisi*** *a-13.* ***Morrow/Williamson*** *r-111.* ***Roussos*** *r-146i, 147i, 149-151i.* ***Severin*** *a-16; c-8, 13.* ***Sutton*** *a-61, 93.* ***Torres*** *a-99r.* ***Tuska*** *a-14.* ***Wildey*** *r-146-151(Outlaw Kid).* ***Williamson*** *r-79, 86, 95.*

RAWHIDE KID
Marvel Comics Group: Aug, 1985 - No. 4, Nov, 1985 (Mini-series)

	GD 2.0	VG 4.0	FN 6.0	VF 8.0	VF/NM 9.0	NM- 9.2
1-4						5.00

RAWHIDE KID
Marvel Comics (MAX): Apr, 2003 - No. 5, June, 2003 ($2.99, limited series)

	GD 2.0	VG 4.0	FN 6.0	VF 8.0	VF/NM 9.0	NM- 9.2
1-John Severin-a/Ron Zimmerman-s; Dave Johnson-c						3.00
2-5: 3-Dodson-c. 4-Darwyn Cooke-c. 5-J. Scott Campbell-c						3.00
Vol. 1: Slap Leather TPB (2003, $12.99) r/#1-5						13.00

RAWHIDE KID (The Sensational Seven)
Marvel Comics: Aug, 2010 - No. 4, Nov, 2010 ($3.99, limited series)

	GD 2.0	VG 4.0	FN 6.0	VF 8.0	VF/NM 9.0	NM- 9.2
1-4-Chaykin-a/Zimmerman-s. 1-Cassaday-c. 2-Dave Johnson-c. 4-Suydam-c						4.00

RAY, THE (See Freedom Fighters & Smash Comics #14)
DC Comics: Feb, 1992 - No. 6, July, 1992 ($1.00, mini-series)

	GD 2.0	VG 4.0	FN 6.0	VF 8.0	VF/NM 9.0	NM- 9.2
1-Sienkiewicz-c; Joe Quesada-a(p) in 1-5						5.00
2-6: 3-6-Quesada-c(p). 6-Quesada layouts only						3.00
...In a Blaze of Power (1994, $12.95)-r/#1-6 w/new Quesada-c						13.00

RAY, THE
DC Comics: May, 1994 - No. 28, Oct, 1996 ($1.75/$1.95/$2.25)

	GD 2.0	VG 4.0	FN 6.0	VF 8.0	VF/NM 9.0	NM- 9.2
1-Quesada-c(p); Superboy app.						3.00
1-($2.95)-Collectors Edition w/diff. Quesada-c; embossed foil-c						4.00
2-5,0,6-24,26-28: 2-Quesada-c(p); Superboy app. 5-(9/94). 0-(10/94)						3.00
25-($3.50)-Future Flash (Bart Allen)-c/app; double size						4.00
Annual 1 ($3.95, 68 pgs.)-Superman app.						4.00

RAY, THE
DC Comics: Feb, 2012 - No. 4, May, 2012 ($2.99, limited series)

	GD 2.0	VG 4.0	FN 6.0	VF 8.0	VF/NM 9.0	NM- 9.2
1-4: 1-Igle-a/Palmiotti & Gray-s; origin of the new Ray; intro. Lucien Gates						3.00

RAY BRADBURY COMICS
Topps Comics: Feb, 1993 - V4#1, June, 1994 ($2.95)

	GD 2.0	VG 4.0	FN 6.0	VF 8.0	VF/NM 9.0	NM- 9.2
1-5-Polybagged w/3 trading cards each. 1-All dinosaur issue; Corben-a; Williamson/Torres/Krenkel-r/Weird Science-Fantasy #25. 3-All dinosaur issue; Steacy painted-c; Stout-a						3.00
Special Edition 1 (1994, $2.95)-The Illustrated Man						3.00
...Special: Tales of Horror #1 ($2.50), ...Trilogy of Terror V3#1 (5/94, $2.50), ...Martian Chronicles V4#1 (6/94, $2.50)-Steranko-c						3.00

NOTE: ***Kelley Jones*** *a-Trilogy of Terror V3#1.* ***Kaluta*** *a-Martian Chronicles V4#1.* ***Kurtzman/Matt Wagner*** *c-2.* ***McKean*** *c-4.* ***Mignola*** *a-4.* ***Wood*** *a-Trilogy of Terror V3#1r.*

RAZORLINE
Marvel Comics: Sept, 1993 (75¢, one-shot)

	GD 2.0	VG 4.0	FN 6.0	VF 8.0	VF/NM 9.0	NM- 9.2
1-Clive Barker super-heroes: Ectokid, Hokum & Hex, Hyperkind & Saint Sinner						3.00

RAZOR'S EDGE, THE
DC Comics (WildStorm): Dec, 2004 - No. 5, Apr, 2005 ($2.95)

	GD 2.0	VG 4.0	FN 6.0	VF 8.0	VF/NM 9.0	NM- 9.2
1-5-Warblade; Bisley-c/a; Ridley-s						3.00

REAL ADVENTURE COMICS (Action Adventure #2 on)
Gillmor Magazines: Apr, 1955

	GD 2.0	VG 4.0	FN 6.0	VF 8.0	VF/NM 9.0	NM- 9.2
1	10	20	30	58	79	100

REAL ADVENTURES OF JONNY QUEST, THE
Dark Horse Comics: Sept, 1996 - No. 12, Sept, 1997 ($2.95)

	GD 2.0	VG 4.0	FN 6.0	VF 8.0	VF/NM 9.0	NM- 9.2
1-12						3.00

REAL CLUE CRIME STORIES (Formerly Clue Comics)
Hillman Periodicals: V2#4, June, 1947 - V8#3, May, 1953

	GD 2.0	VG 4.0	FN 6.0	VF 8.0	VF/NM 9.0	NM- 9.2
V2#4(#1)-S&K c/a(3); Dan Barry-a	49	98	147	309	522	735
5-7-S&K c/a(3-4). 7-Iron Lady app.	39	78	117	240	395	550
8-12	14	28	42	81	118	155
V3#1-8,10-12, V4#1-3,5-8,11,12	13	26	39	72	101	130
V3#9-Used in **SOTI**, pg. 102	15	30	45	83	124	165
V4#4-S&K-a	15	30	45	84	127	170
V4#9,10-Krigstein-a	13	26	39	74	105	135
V5#1-5,7,8,10,12	10	20	30	56	76	95
6,9,11(1/54)-Krigstein-a	11	22	33	60	83	105
V6#1-5,8,9,11	9	18	27	52	69	85
6,7,10,12-Krigstein-a. 10-Bondage-c	11	22	33	60	83	105
V7#1-3,5-11, V8#1-3: V7#6-1 pg. Frazetta ad "Prayer" - 1st app.?	10	20	30	56	76	95
4,12-Krigstein-a	11	22	33	60	83	105

NOTE: ***Barry*** *a-9, 10; c-V2#8.* ***Briefer*** *a-V6#6.* ***Fuje*** *a- V2#7(2), 8, 11.* ***Infantino*** *a-V2#8; c-V2#11.* ***Lawrence*** *a-V3#8, V5#7.* ***Powell*** *a-V4#11, 12. V5#4, 5, 7 are 68 pgs.*

REAL EXPERIENCES (Formerly Tiny Tessie)
Atlas Comics (20CC): No. 25, Jan, 1950

	GD 2.0	VG 4.0	FN 6.0	VF 8.0	VF/NM 9.0	NM- 9.2
25-Virginia Mayo photo-c from movie "Red Light"	15	30	45	83	124	165

REAL FACT COMICS
National Periodical Publications: Mar-Apr, 1946 - No. 21, July-Aug, 1949

	GD 2.0	VG 4.0	FN 6.0	VF 8.0	VF/NM 9.0	NM- 9.2
1-S&K-c/a; Harry Houdini story; Just Imagine begins (not by Finlay); Fred Ray-a	47	94	141	296	498	700
2-S&K-a; Rin-Tin-Tin & P. T. Barnum stories	28	56	84	165	270	375
3-H.G. Wells, Lon Chaney stories; early DC letter column (New Fun Comics #3 from 1935 may be the 1st)	26	52	78	154	252	350
4-Virgil Finlay-a on 'Just Imagine' begins, ends #12 (2 pgs. each); Jimmy Stewart & Jack London stories; Joe DiMaggio 1 pg. biography	29	58	87	172	281	390
5-Batman/Robin-c taken from cover of Batman #9; 5 pg. story about creation of Batman & Robin; Tom Mix story	155	310	465	992	1696	2400
6-Origin & 1st app. Tommy Tomorrow by Weisinger and Sherman (1-2/47); Flag-c; 1st writing by Harlan Ellison (letter column, non-professional); "First Man to Reach Mars" epic-c/story	84	168	252	538	919	1300
7-(No. 6 on inside)-Roussos-a; D. Fairbanks sty.	15	30	45	94	147	200

Real Heroes #2 © Bryan Hitch

Real Life Comics #13 © Nedor

Realm of Kings: Inhumans #3 © MAR

GD 2.0 | VG 4.0 | FN 6.0 | VF 8.0 | VF/NM 9.0 | NM- 9.2

8-2nd app. Tommy Tomorrow by Finlay (5-6/47) 48 96 144 302 514 725
9-S&K-a; Glenn Miller, Indianapolis 500 stories 21 42 63 122 199 275
10-Vigilante by Meskin (based on movie serial); 4 pg. Finlay s/f story
20 40 60 118 192 265
11,12: 11-Annie Oakley, G-Men stories; Kinstler-a 14 28 42 82 121 160
13-Dale Evans and Tommy Tomorrow-c/stories 37 74 111 222 361 500
14,17,18: 14-Will Rogers story 14 28 42 80 115 150
15-Nuclear explosion part-c ("Last War on Earth" story); Clyde Beatty story
15 30 45 94 147 200
16-Tommy Tomorrow app.; 1st Planeteers? 36 72 108 211 343 475
19-Sir Arthur Conan Doyle story 15 30 45 83 124 165
20-Kubert-a, 4 pgs; Daniel Boone story 15 30 45 88 137 185
21-Kubert-a, 2 pgs; Kit Carson story 14 28 42 80 115 150
Ashcan (2/46) nn-Not distributed to newsstands, only for in house use. Covers were produced, but not the rest of the book. A copy sold in 2008 for $500.
NOTE: ***Barry*** *c-16.* ***Virgil Finlay*** *c-6, 8.* ***Meskin*** *c-10.* ***Roussos*** *a-1-4, 6.*

REAL FUNNIES
Nedor Publishing Co.: Jan, 1943 - No. 3, June, 1943
1-Funny animal, humor; Black Terrier app. (clone of The Black Terror)
34 68 102 206 336 465
2,3 18 36 54 105 165 225

REAL GHOSTBUSTERS, THE (Also see Slimer)
Now Comics: Aug, 1988 - No. 28, Feb, 1991 ($1.75/$1.95)
1-Based on Ghostbusters movie 2 4 6 10 14 18
2 1 2 3 5 6 8
3-28 4.00

REAL HEROES
Image Comics: Mar, 2014 - No. 4, Nov, 2014 ($3.99)
1-3-Bryan Hitch-s/a 4.00
4-($4.99) 5.00

REAL HEROES COMICS
Parents' Magazine Institute: Sept, 1941 - No. 16, Oct, 1946
1-Roosevelt-c/story 32 64 96 188 307 425
2-J. Edgar Hoover-c/story 15 30 45 83 124 165
3-5,7-10: 4-Churchill, Roosevelt stories 14 28 42 76 108 140
6-Lou Gehrig-c/story 19 38 57 112 179 245
11-16: 13-Kiefer-a 10 20 30 54 72 90

REALISTIC ROMANCES
Realistic Comics/Avon Periodicals: July-Aug, 1951 - No. 17, Aug-Sept, 1954 (No #9-14)
1-Kinstler-a; c-/Avon paperback #211 40 80 120 246 411 575
2 21 42 63 126 206 285
3,4 21 42 63 122 199 275
5,8-Kinstler-a 21 42 63 124 202 280
6-c-/Diversey Prize Novels #6; Kinstler-a 21 42 63 126 206 285
7-Evans-a?; c-/Avon paperback #360 21 42 63 126 206 285
15,17: 17-Kinstler-c 20 40 60 118 192 265
16-Kinstler marijuana story-r/Romantic Love #6 21 42 63 124 202 280
I.W. Reprint #1,8,9: #1-r/Realistic Romances #4; Astarita-a. 9-r/Women To Love #1 3 6 9 14 20 25
NOTE: ***Astarita*** *a-2-4, 7, 8, 17. Photo c-1, 2. Painted c-3, 4.*

REALITY CHECK
Image Comics: Sept, 2013 - No. 4, Dec, 2013 ($2.99)
1-4-Brunswick-s/Bogdanovic-a 3.00

REAL LIFE COMICS
Nedor/Better/Standard Publ./Pictorial Magazine No. 13: Sept, 1941 - No. 59, Sept, 1952
1-Uncle Sam-c/story; Daniel Boone story 73 146 219 467 796 1125
2-Woodrow Wilson-c/story 37 74 111 222 361 500
3-Classic Schomburg Hitler-c with "Emperor of Hate" emblazoned in blood behind him. Cover shows world at war, concentration camps and Nazis killing civilians; Hitler 10 pg. bio
595 1190 1785 4350 7675 11,000
4,5: 4-Story of American flag "Old Glory" 31 62 93 182 296 410
6-10: 6-Wild Bill Hickok story 26 52 78 154 252 350
11-14,16-20: 17-Albert Einstein story 22 44 66 128 209 290
15-Japanese WWII-c by Schomburg 27 54 81 158 259 360
21-23,25,26,28-30: 29-A-Bomb story. 28-Japanese WWII-c
20 40 60 114 182 250
24-Story of Baseball (Babe Ruth); Japanese WWII-c
26 52 78 154 252 350
27-Schomburg A-Bomb-c; story of A-Bomb 25 50 75 150 245 340
31-33,35,36,42-44,48,49: 32-Frank Sinatra story. 49-Baseball issue
17 34 51 98 154 210
34,37-41,45-47: 34-Jimmy Stewart story. 37-Story of motion pictures; Bing Crosby story. 38-Jane Froman story. 39-"1,000,000 A.D." story. 40-Bob Feller. 41-Jimmie Foxx story ("Jimmy" on-c); "Home Run" Baker story. 45-Story of Olympic games; Burl Ives & Kit Carson story. 46-Douglas Fairbanks Jr. & Sr. story. 47-George Gershwin story
18 36 54 103 162 220
50-Frazetta-a (5 pgs.) 31 62 93 182 296 410
51-Jules Verne "Journey to the Moon" by Evans; Severin/Elder-a
22 44 66 128 209 290
52-Frazetta-a (4 pgs.); Severin/Elder-a(2); Evans-a 34 68 102 199 325 450
53-57-Severin/Elder-a. 54-Bat Masterson-c/story 18 36 54 103 162 220
58-Severin/Elder-a(2) 18 36 54 105 165 225
59-1 pg. Frazetta; Severin/Elder-a 18 36 54 105 165 225
NOTE: ***Guardineer*** *a-40(2), 44.* ***Meskin*** *a-52.* ***Roussos*** *a-50.* ***Schomburg*** *c-1-5, 7, 11, 13-21, 23, 24, 26-28, 30-32-40, 42, 44-50, 54, 55.* ***Tuska*** *a-53. Photo-c 5, 6.*

REAL LIFE SECRETS (Real Secrets #2 on)
Ace Periodicals: Sept, 1949 (one-shot)
1-Painted-c 16 32 48 94 147 200

REAL LIFE STORY OF FESS PARKER (Magazine)
Dell Publishing Co.: 1955
1 8 16 24 54 102 150

REAL LIFE TALES OF SUSPENSE (See Suspense)

REAL LOVE (Formerly Hap Hazard)
Ace Periodicals (A. A. Wyn): No. 25, April, 1949 - No. 76, Nov, 1956
25 18 36 54 103 162 220
26 14 28 42 78 112 145
27-L. B. Cole-a 14 28 42 82 121 160
28-35 13 26 39 72 101 130
36-66: 66-Last pre-code (2/55) 12 24 36 67 94 120
67-76 11 22 33 60 83 105
NOTE: *Photo c-50-76. Painted c-46.*

REALM, THE
Arrow Comics/WeeBee Comics #13/Caliber Press #14 on: Feb, 1986 - No. 21, 1991 (B&W)
1-3,5-21 3.00
4-1st app. Deadworld (9/86) 4.00
Book 1 ($4.95, B&W) 5.00

REAL McCOYS, THE (TV)
Dell Publ. Co.: No. 1071, 1-3/60 - 5-7/1962 (All have Walter Brennan photo-c)
Four Color 1071,1134-Toth-a in both 8 16 24 51 96 140
Four Color 1193,1265 7 14 21 48 89 130
01-689-207 (5-7/62) 6 12 18 42 79 115

REALM OF KINGS (Also see Guardians of the Galaxy and Nova)
Marvel Comics: Jan, 2010 ($3.99, one-shot)
1-Abnett & Lanning-s/Manco & Asrar-a; Guardians of the Galaxy app. 4.00

REALM OF KINGS: IMPERIAL GUARD
Marvel Comics: Jan, 2010 - No. 5, May, 2010 ($3.99, limited series)
1-5-Abnett & Lanning-s/Walker-a; Starjammers app. 4.00

REALM OF KINGS: INHUMANS
Marvel Comics: Jan, 2010 - No. 5, May, 2010 ($3.99, limited series)
1-5-Abnett & Lanning-s/Raimondi-a; Mighty Avengers app. 4.00

REALM OF KINGS: SON OF HULK
Marvel Comics: Apr, 2010 - No. 4, July, 2010 ($3.99, limited series)
1-4-Reed-s/Munera-a; leads into Incredible Hulk #609 4.00

REALM OF THE CLAW (Also see Mutant Earth as part of a flipbook)
Image Comics: Oct, 2003 - No. 2 ($2.95)
0-(7/03, $5.95) Convention Special; cover has gold-foil title logo 6.00
1,2-Two covers by Yardin 3.00
Vol. 1 TPB (2006, $16.99) r/series; concept art & sketch pages 17.00

REAL SCREEN COMICS (#1 titled Real Screen Funnies; TV Screen Cartoons #129-138)
National Periodical Publications: Spring, 1945 - No. 128, May-June, 1959 (#1-40: 52 pgs.)
1-The Fox & the Crow, Flippity & Flop, Tito & His Burrito begin
113 226 339 718 1234 1750
2 47 94 141 296 498 700
3-5 32 64 96 188 307 425
6-10 (2-3/47) 21 42 63 122 199 275
11-20 (10-11/48): 13-The Crow x-over in Flippity & Flop
16 32 48 94 147 200

Realworlds: Wonder Woman © DC

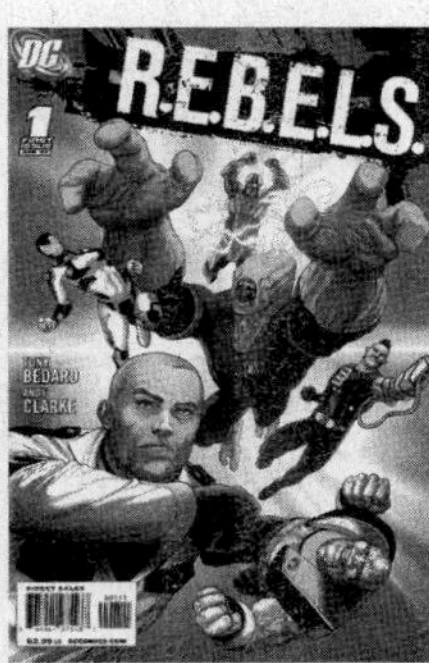

R.E.B.E.L.S. #1 © DC

Red Arrow #3 © P.L. Pub.

	GD 2.0	VG 4.0	FN 6.0	VF 8.0	VF/NM 9.0	NM- 9.2
21-30 (6-7/50)	14	28	42	76	108	140
31-50	11	22	33	60	83	105
51-99	10	20	30	54	72	90
100	10	20	30	56	76	95
101-128	8	16	24	44	57	70

REAL SCREEN FUNNIES
DC Comics: Spring 1945

1-Ashcan comic, not distributed to newsstands, only for in-house use. Cover art is Real Screen Funnies #1 with interior being Detective Comics #92. Only ashcan cover to be produced using the regular production first issue art and only using the color yellow. A copy sold in 2008 for $3,000. A FN/VF copy sold for $1314.50 in 2012.

REAL SECRETS (Formerly Real Life Secrets)
Ace Periodicals: No. 2, Nov, 1950 - No. 5, May, 1950

	GD	VG	FN	VF	VF/NM	NM-
2-Painted-c	14	28	42	76	108	140
3-5: 3-Photo-c	11	22	33	60	83	105

REAL SPORTS COMICS (All Sports Comics #2 on)
Hillman Periodicals: Oct-Nov, 1948 (52 pgs.)

	GD	VG	FN	VF	VF/NM	NM-
1-Powell-a (12 pgs.)	39	78	117	240	395	550

REAL WAR STORIES
Eclipse Comics: July, 1987; No. 2, Jan, 1991 ($2.00, 52 pgs.)

1-Bolland-a(p), Bissette-a, Totleben-a(i); Alan Moore scripts (2nd printing exists, 2/88) 5.00
2-($4.95) 5.00

REAL WESTERN HERO (Formerly Wow #1-69; Western Hero #76 on)
Fawcett Publications: No. 70, Sept, 1948 - No. 75, Feb, 1949 (All 52 pgs.)

	GD	VG	FN	VF	VF/NM	NM-
70(#1)-Tom Mix, Monte Hale, Hopalong Cassidy, Young Falcon begin	22	44	66	132	216	300
71-75: 71-Gabby Hayes begins. 71,72-Captain Tootsie by Beck. 75-Big Bow and Little Arrow app.	15	30	45	85	130	175

NOTE: *Painted/photo c-70-73; painted c-74, 75.*

REAL WEST ROMANCES
Crestwood Publishing Co./Prize Publ.: 4-5/49 - V1#6, 3/50; V2#1, Apr-May, 1950 (All 52 pgs. & photo-c)

	GD	VG	FN	VF	VF/NM	NM-
V1#1-S&K-a(p)	26	52	78	154	252	350
2-Gail Davis and Rocky Shahan photo-c	14	28	42	80	115	150
3-Kirby-a(p) only	14	28	42	82	121	160
4-S&K-a; Whip Wilson, Reno Browne photo-c	19	38	57	111	176	240
5-Audie Murphy, Gale Storm photo-c; S&K-a	17	34	51	98	154	210
6-Produced by S&K, no S&K-a; Robert Preston & Cathy Downs photo-c	13	26	39	74	105	135
V2#1-Kirby-a(p)	13	26	39	74	105	135

NOTE: ***Meskin** a-V1#5, 6. **Severin/Elder** a-V1#3-6, V2#1. **Meskin** a-V1#6. **Leonard Starr** a-1-3. Photo-c V1#1-6, V2#1.*

REALWORLDS :...
DC Comics: 2000 ($5.95, one-shots, prestige format)

Batman - Marshall Rogers-a/Golden & Sniegoski-s; Justice League of America -Dematteis-s/Barr-painted art; Superman - Vance-s/García-López & Rubenstein-a; Wonder Woman - Hanson & Neuwirth-s/Sam-a 6.00

REANIMATOR (Based on the 1985 horror movie)
Dynamite Entertainment: 2015 - No. 4, 2015 ($3.99, mini-series)

1-4-Further exploits of Herbert West; Davidsen-s/Valiente-a; four covers on each 4.00

RE-ANIMATOR IN FULL COLOR
Adventure Comics: Oct, 1991 - No. 3, 1992 ($2.95, mini-series)

1-3: Adapts horror movie. 1-Dorman painted-c 3.00

REAP THE WILD WIND (See Cinema Comics Herald)

REBEL, THE (TV)(Nick Adams as Johnny Yuma)
Dell Publishing Co.: No. 1076, Feb-Apr, 1960 - No. 1262, Dec-Feb, 1961-62

	GD	VG	FN	VF	VF/NM	NM-
Four Color 1076 (#1)-Sekowsky-a, photo-c	9	18	27	61	123	185
Four Color 1138 (9-11/60), 1207 (9-11/61), 1262-Photo-c	8	16	24	51	96	140

REBELS
Dark Horse Comics: Apr, 2015 - Present ($3.99)

1-Set in Revolutionary War 1775 Vermont; Brian Wood-s/Andrea Mutti-a/Tula Lotay-c 5.00
2-10: 4-General Washington app. 4.00

R.E.B.E.L.S.
DC Comics: Apr, 2009 - No. 28, Jul, 2011 ($2.99)

1-9,12-28: 1-Bedard-s/Clarke-a; Vril Dox returns; Supergirl app.; 2 covers. 15-Starfire app. 19-28-Lobo app. 3.00
10,11-($3.99) Blackest Night x-over; Vril Dox joins the Sinestro Corps 4.00
Annual 1 (12/09, $4.99) Origin on Starro the Conqueror; Despero app. 5.00
...: Sons of Brainiac TPB (2011, $14.99) r/#15-20 15.00
...: Strange Companions TPB (2010, $14.99) r/#7-9 & Annual #1 15.00
...: The Coming of Starro TPB (2010, $17.99) r/#1-6 18.00
...: The Son and the Stars TPB (2010, $17.99) r/#10-14 18.00

R.E.B.E.L.S. '94 (Becomes R.E.B.E.L.S. '95 & R.E.B.E.L.S. '96)
DC Comics: No. 0, Oct, 1994 - No. 17, Mar, 1996 ($1.95/$2.25)

0-17: 8-$2.25-c begins. 15-R.E.B.E.L.S '96 begins. 3.00

REBORN
Image Comics: Oct, 2016 - Present ($3.99)

1-Mark Millar-s/Greg Capullo-a 5.00
2-4 4.00

RECORD BOOK OF FAMOUS POLICE CASES
St. John Publishing Co.: 1949 (25¢, 132 pgs.)

	GD	VG	FN	VF	VF/NM	NM-
nn-Kubert-a(3); r/Son of Sinbad; Baker-c	53	106	159	334	567	800

RED (Inspired the 2010 Bruce Willis movie)
DC Comics (Homage): Sept, 2003 - No. 3, Feb, 2004 ($2.95, limited series)

1-3-Warren Ellis-s/Cully Hamner-a/c 5.00
Red/Tokyo Storm Warning TPB (2004, $14.95) Flip book r/both series 15.00
Red: Eyes Only (2/11, $4.99) comic prequel; Hamner-s/a/c 5.00
Red: Frank (11/10, $3.99) movie prequel; Noveck-s/Masters-a/Hamner & photo-c 4.00
Red: Joe (11/10, $3.99) movie prequel; Wagner-s/Redondo-a/Hamner & photo-c 4.00
Red: Marvin (11/10, $3.99) movie prequel; Hoeber-s/Olmos-a/Hamner & photo-c 4.00
Red: Victoria (11/10, $3.99) movie prequel; Hoeber-s/Hahn-a/Hamner & photo-c 4.00
...: Better R.E.D. Than Dead TPB (2011, $14.99) r/movie prequel issues; sketch-a 15.00

RED ARROW
P. L. Publishing Co.: May-June, 1951 - No. 3, Oct, 1951

	GD	VG	FN	VF	VF/NM	NM-
1-Bondage-c	14	28	42	82	121	160
2,3	10	20	30	56	76	95

RED BAND COMICS
Enwil Associates: Nov, 1944, No. 2, Jan, 1945 - No. 4, May, 1945

	GD	VG	FN	VF	VF/NM	NM-
1-Bogeyman-c/intro. (The Spirit swipe)	47	94	141	296	498	700
2-Origin Bogeyman & Santanas; c-reprint/#1	34	68	102	199	325	450
3,4-Captain Wizard app. in both (1st app.); each has identical contents/cover	32	64	96	188	307	425

REDBLADE
Dark Horse Comics: Apr, 1993 - No. 3, July, 1993 ($2.50, mini-series)

1-3: 1-Double gatefold-c 3.00

RED CIRCLE, THE (Re-introduction of characters from MLJ/Archie publications)
DC Comics: Oct, 2009 ($2.99, series of one-shots)

...Inferno 1 - Hangman app.; Straczynski-s/Greg Scott-a 5.00
...The Hangman 1 - Origin retold; Straczynski-s/Derenick & Sienkiewicz-a 5.00
...The Shield 1 - Origin retold; Straczynski-s/McDaniel-a 5.00
...The Web 1 - Straczynski-s/Robinson-a 5.00

RED CIRCLE COMICS (Also see Blazing Comics & Blue Circle Comics)
Rural Home Publications (Enwil): Jan, 1945 - No. 4, April, 1945

	GD	VG	FN	VF	VF/NM	NM-
1-The Prankster & Red Riot begin	71	142	213	454	777	1100
2-Starr-a; The Judge (costumed hero) app.	37	74	111	222	361	500
3,4-Starr-c/a. 3-The Prankster not in costume	30	60	90	177	289	400
4-(Dated 4/45)-Leftover covers to #4 were later restapled over early 1950s coverless comics; variations in the coverless comics used are endless; Woman Outlaws, Dorothy Lamour, Crime Does Not Pay, Sabu, Diary Loves, Love Confessions & Young Love V3#3 known	20	40	60	118	192	265

RED CIRCLE SORCERY (Chilling Adventures in Sorcery #1-5)
Red Circle Prod. (Archie): No. 6, Apr, 1974 - No. 11, Feb, 1975 (All 25¢ iss.)

	GD	VG	FN	VF	VF/NM	NM-
6,8,9,11: 6-Early Chaykin-a. 7-Pino-a. 8-Only app. The Cobra	2	4	6	9	13	16
7-Bruce Jones-a with Wrightson, Kaluta, Jeff Jones	3	6	9	14	19	24
10-Wood-a(i)	2	4	6	10	14	18

NOTE: ***Chaykin** a-6, 10. **McWilliams** a-10(2 & 3 pgs.). **Mooney** a-11p. **Morrow** a-6-8, 9(text illos), 10, 11i; c-6-11. **Thorne** a-8, 10. **Toth** a-8, 9.*

RED CITY
Image Comics: Jun, 2014 - No. 4, Sept, 2014 ($2.99)

1-4-Corey-s. 1,2-Dos Santos-a. 3,4-Diecidue-a 3.00

RED DOG (See Night Music #7)

RED DRAGON

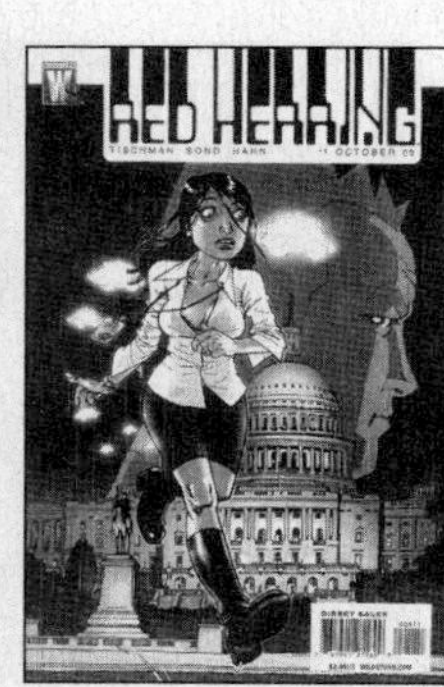

Red Herring #1 © Tischman & Bond

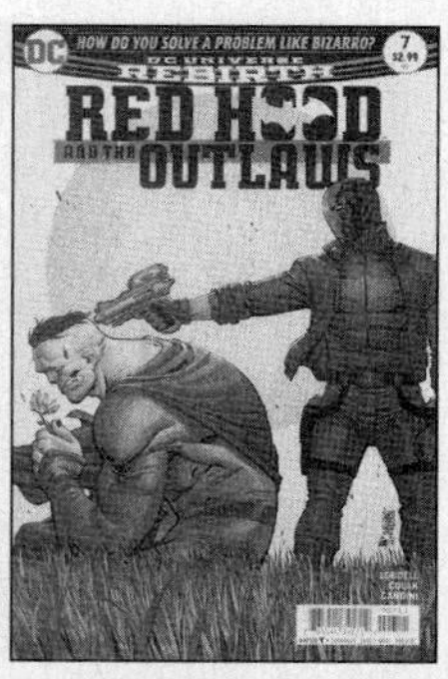

Red Hood and the Outlaws (2016 series) #7 © DC

Red Robin #4 © DC

	GD	VG	FN	VF	VF/NM	NM-
	2.0	4.0	6.0	8.0	9.0	9.2

Comico: June, 1996 ($2.95)
1-Bisley-c 3.00

RED DRAGON COMICS (1st Series) (Formerly Trail Blazers; see Super Magician V5#7, 8)
Street & Smith Publications: No. 5, Jan, 1943 - No. 9, Jan, 1944

	GD	VG	FN	VF	VF/NM	NM-
5-Origin Red Rover, the Crimson Crimebuster; Rex King, Man of Adventure, Captain Jack Commando, & The Minute Man begin; text origin Red Dragon; Binder-c	90	180	270	576	988	1400
6-Origin The Black Crusader & Red Dragon (3/43); 1st story app. Red Dragon & 1st cover (classic-c)	258	516	774	1651	2826	4000
7-Classic Japanese exploding soldier WWII-c	314	628	942	2198	3849	5500
8-The Red Knight app.	61	122	183	390	670	950
9-Origin Chuck Magnon, Immortal Man	61	122	183	390	670	950

RED DRAGON COMICS (2nd Series)(See Super Magician V2#8)
Street & Smith Publications: Nov, 1947 - No. 6, Jan, 1949; No. 7, July, 1949

	GD	VG	FN	VF	VF/NM	NM-
1-Red Dragon begins; Elliman, Nigel app.; Edd Cartier-c/a	116	232	348	742	1271	1800
2-Cartier-c	58	116	174	371	636	900
3-1st app. Dr. Neff Ghost Breaker by Powell; Elliman, Nigel app.	45	90	135	284	480	675
4-Cartier c/a	60	120	180	381	653	925
5-7	36	72	108	211	343	475

NOTE: *Maneely a-5, 7. **Powell** a-2-7; c-3, 5, 7.*

RED EAGLE
David McKay Publications: No. 16, Aug, 1938

	GD	VG	FN	VF	VF/NM	NM-
Feature Books 16	34	68	102	199	325	450

REDEYE (See Comics Reading Libraries in the Promotional Comics section)

RED FOX (Formerly Manhunt! #1-14; also see Extra Comics)
Magazine Enterprises: No. 15, 1954

	GD	VG	FN	VF	VF/NM	NM-
15(A-1 #108)-Undercover Girl story; L.B. Cole-c/a (Red Fox); r-from Manhunt; Powell-a	19	38	57	109	172	235

RED GOOSE COMIC SELECTIONS (See Comic Selections)

RED HAWK (See A-1 Comics, Bobby Benson's ..#14-16 & Straight Arrow #2)
Magazine Enterprises: No. 90, 1953

	GD	VG	FN	VF	VF/NM	NM-
11-(A-1 Comics #90)-Powell-c/a	13	26	39	72	101	130

RED HERRING
DC Comics (WildStorm): Oct, 2009 - No. 6, Mar, 2010 ($2.99, limited series)
1-6-Tischman-s/Bond-a 3.00

RED HOOD AND THE OUTLAWS (DC New 52)
DC Comics: Nov, 2011 - No. 40, May, 2015 ($2.99)

	GD	VG	FN	VF	VF/NM	NM-
1-Jason Todd, Starfire, Roy Harper team; Lobdell-s/Rocafort-a/c	2	4	6	8	10	12

2-4 6.00
5-8 4.00
9-Night of the Owls tie-in; Mr. Freeze vs. Talon 5.00
10-14 3.00
15-(2/13) Death of the Family tie-in; die-cut cover; Joker app. 5.00
16-18: 16,17-Death of the Family tie-in 4.00
19-24,26-40: 24,26,27-Ra's al Ghul app. 30,31-Lobo app. 37-Arsenal's origin 3.00
25-($3.99) Zero Year tie-in; Talia and the Red Hood Gang app.; Haun-a 4.00
#0-(11/12, $2.99) Jason Todd's origin re-told; Joker app. 6.00
Annual 1 (7/13, $4.99) Takes place between #20 & 21; Green Arrow app.; Barrionuevo-a 5.00
Annual 2 (2/15, $4.99) Christmas-themed; Derenick-a 5.00
...: Futures End 1 (11/14, $2.99, regular-c) Five years later; Lobdell-s/Kolins-a 3.00
...: Futures End 1 (11/14, $3.99, 3-D cover) 4.00

RED HOOD AND THE OUTLAWS (DC Rebirth)
DC Comics: Oct, 2016 - Present ($2.99)
1-7: 1-Jason Todd, Artemis & Bizarro team; Lobdell-s/Soy-a; Blask Mask app. 3.00
...: Rebirth (9/16, $2.99) Jason Todd origin re-told; Batman app. 3.00

RED HOOD / ARSENAL
DC Comics: Aug, 2015 - No. 13, Aug, 2016 ($2.99)
1-13: 1-Jason Todd & Roy Harper team; Lobdell-s/Medri. 3-5-Batman (Gordon) app. 6-13-Joker's Daughter app. 7-"Robin War" tie-in. 13-Bonus flashback 1st meeting 3.00

RED HOOD: THE LOST DAYS
DC Comics: Aug, 2010 - No. 6, Jan, 2011 ($2.99, limited series)
1-6-The Return of Jason Todd; Winick-s/Raimondi-a/Tucci-c. 6-Joker & Hush app. 4.00
TPB (2011, $14.99) r/#1-6 15.00

RED LANTERNS (DC New 52)
DC Comics: Nov, 2011 - No. 40, May, 2015 ($2.99)
1-34: 1-Milligan-s/Benes-a/c; Atrocitus, Dex-Starr & Bleez app. 6-8,11-Guy Gardner app. 10-Stormwatch app. 13-15-Rise of the Third Army. 17-First Lantern app. 24-Lights Out pt. 4. 28-Flipbook with Green Lantern #28; Supergirl app. 29-Superman app. 3.00
35-40: 35-37-Godhead x-over; Simon Baz app. 3.00
#0-(11/12, $2.99) Origin of Atrocitus, the 1st Red Lantern; Syaf-a 3.00
Annual 1 (9/14, $4.99) Story occurs between #33 & 34; Batman cameo 5.00
...: Futures End 1 (11/14, $2.99, regular-c) Five years later; Soule-s/Calafiore-a 3.00
...: Futures End 1 (11/14, $3.99, 3-D cover) 4.00

RED MASK (Formerly Tim Holt; see Best Comics, Blazing Six-Guns)
Magazine Enterprises No. 42-53/Sussex No. 54 (M.E. on-c): No. 42, June-July, 1954 - No. 53, May, 1956; No. 54, Sept, 1957

	GD	VG	FN	VF	VF/NM	NM-
42-Ghost Rider by Ayers continues, ends #50; Black Phantom continues; 3-D effect c/stories begin	21	42	63	122	199	275
43- 3-D effect-c/stories	19	38	57	109	172	235
44-52: 3-D effect stories only. 47-Last pre-code issue. 50-Last Ghost Rider. 51-The Presto Kid begins by Ayers (1st app.); Presto Kid-c begins; last 3-D effect story. 52-Origin The Presto Kid	17	34	51	98	154	210
53,54-Last Black Phantom; last Presto Kid-c	15	30	45	83	124	165
I.W. Reprint #1 (r-/#52). 2 (nd, r/#51 w/diff.-c). 3, 8 (nd; Kinstler-c); 8-r/Red Mask #52	3	6	9	16	22	28

NOTE: ***Ayers** art on Ghost Rider & Presto Kid. **Bolle** art in all (Red Mask); c-43, 44, 49. **Guardineer** a-52. Black Phantom in #42-44, 47-50, 53, 54.*

REDMASK OF THE RIO GRANDE
AC Comics: 1990 ($2.50, 28pgs.)(Has photos of movie posters)
1-Bolle-c/a(r); photo inside-c 3.00

RED MENACE
DC Comics (WildStorm): Jan, 2007 - No. 6, Jun, 2007 ($2.99, limited series)
1-6-Ordway-a/c; Bilson, DeMeo & Brody-s 3.00
TPB (2007, $17.99) r/series, sketch pages & variant covers 18.00

RED MOUNTAIN FEATURING QUANTRELL'S RAIDERS (Movie)(Also see Jesse James #28)
Avon Periodicals: 1952

	GD	VG	FN	VF	VF/NM	NM-
nn-Alan Ladd; Kinstler-c	32	64	96	192	314	435

RED ONE
Image Comics: Mar, 2015 - Present ($2.99)
1-4-Xavier Dorison-s/Terry Dodson-a/c 3.00

RED PROPHET: THE TALES OF ALVIN MAKER
Dabel Brothers Prods./Marvel Comics (Dabel Brothers): Mar, 2006 - No. 12, Mar, 2008 ($2.99)
1-12-Adaptation of Orson Scott Card novel. 1-Miguel Montenegro-a 3.00
... Vol. 1 HC (2007, $19.99, dustjacket) r/#1-6 20.00
... Vol. 1 SC (2007, $15.99) r/#1-6 16.00
... Vol. 2 HC (2008, $19.99, dustjacket) r/#7-12 20.00

"RED" RABBIT COMICS
Dearfield Comic/J. Charles Laue Publ. Co.: Jan, 1947 - No. 22, Aug-Sep, 1951

	GD	VG	FN	VF	VF/NM	NM-
1	15	30	45	90	140	190
2	10	20	30	56	76	95
3-10	9	18	27	50	65	80
11-17,19-22	8	16	24	42	54	65
18-Flying Saucer-c (1/51)	10	20	30	56	76	95

RED RAVEN COMICS (Human Torch #2 on)(Also see X-Men #44 & Sub-Mariner #26, 2nd series)
Timely Comics: August, 1940

	GD	VG	FN	VF	VF/NM	NM-
1-Origin & 1st app. Red Raven; Comet Pierce & Mercury by Kirby, The Human Top & The Eternal Brain; intro. Magar, the Mystic & only app.; Kirby-c (his 1st signed work)	1900	3800	5700	14,500	26,250	38,000

RED ROBIN (Batman: Reborn)
DC Comics: Aug, 2009 - No. 26, Oct, 2011 ($2.99)
1-26-Tim (Drake) Wayne in the Kingdom Come costume; Bachs-a. 1-Two covers 3.00

RED ROCKET 7
Dark Horse Comics: Aug, 1997 - No. 7, June, 1998 ($3.95, square format, limited series)
1-7-Mike Allred-c/s/a 4.00

RED RYDER COMICS (Hi Spot #2)(Movies, radio)(See Crackajack Funnies & Super Book of Comics)
Hawley Publ. No. 1/Dell Publishing Co.(K.K.) No. 3 on: 9/40; No. 3, 8/41 - No. 5, 12/41; No. 6, 4/42 - No. 151, 4-6/57 (Beware of almost identical reprints of #1 made in the late 1980s)
1-Red Ryder, his horse Thunder, Little Beaver & his horse Papoose strip reprints begin by Fred Harman; 1st meeting of Red & Little Beaver; Harman line-drawn-c #1-85

Red Ryder Comics #8 © DELL

Red She-Hulk #66 © MAR

Red Sonja (Volume 2) #7 © Red Sonja LLC

	GD 2.0	VG 4.0	FN 6.0	VF 8.0	VF/NM 9.0	NM- 9.2
	245	490	735	1568	2684	3800
3-(Scarce)-Alley Oop, Capt. Easy, Dan Dunn, Freckles & His Friends, King of the Royal Mtd., Myra North strip-r begin	50	100	150	400	900	1400
4-6: 6-1st Dell issue (4/42)	25	50	75	175	388	600
7-10	21	42	63	147	324	500
11-20	15	30	45	103	227	350
21-32-Last Alley Oop, Dan Dunn, Capt. Easy, Freckles	10	20	30	69	147	225
33-40 (52 pgs.): 40-Photo back-c begin, end #57	9	18	27	58	114	170
41 (52 pgs.)-Rocky Lane photo back-c	9	18	27	60	120	180
42-46 (52 pgs.): 46-Last Red Ryder strip-r	7	14	21	49	92	135
47-53 (52 pgs.): 47-New stories on Red Ryder begin. 49,52-Harmon photo back-c	6	12	18	41	76	110
54-92: 54-73 (36 pgs.). 59-Harmon photo back-c. 73-Last King of the Royal Mtd; strip-r by Jim Gary. 74-85 (52 pgs.)-Harman line-drawn-c. 86-92 (52 pgs.)-Harman painted-c	6	12	18	37	66	95
93-99,101-106: 94-96 (36 pgs.)-Harman painted-c. 97,98,(36 pgs.)-Harman line-drawn-c. 99,101-106 (36 pgs.)-Jim Bannon Photo-c	5	10	15	33	57	80
100 (36 pgs.)-Bannon photo-c	5	10	15	34	60	85
107-118 (52 pgs.)-Harman line-drawn-c	5	10	15	31	53	75
119-129 (52 pgs.): 119-Painted-c begin, not by Harman, end #151	5	10	15	30	50	70
130-151 (36 pgs.): 145-Title change to Red Ryder Ranch Magazine 149-Title change to Red Ryder Ranch Comics	4	8	12	28	47	65
Four Color 916 (7/58)	4	8	12	28	47	65

NOTE: ***Fred Harman** a-1-99; c-1-98, 107-118. Don Red Barry, Allan Rocky Lane, Wild Bill Elliott & Jim Bannon starred as Red Ryder in the movies. Robert Blake starred as Little Beaver.*

RED RYDER PAINT BOOK
Whitman Publishing Co.: 1941 (8-1/2x11-1/2", 148 pgs.)

	GD	VG	FN	VF	VF/NM	NM-
nn-Reprints 1940 daily strips	76	152	228	479	810	1140

RED SEAL COMICS (Formerly Carnival Comics, and/or Spotlight Comics?)
Harry 'A' Chesler/Superior Publ. No. 19 on: No. 14, 10/45 - No. 18, 10/46; No. 19, 6/47 - No. 22, 12/47

	GD	VG	FN	VF	VF/NM	NM-
14-The Black Dwarf begins (continued from Spotlight?); Little Nemo app; bondage/hypo-c; Tuska-a	94	188	282	597	1024	1450
15-Torture story; funny-c	41	82	123	256	428	600
16-Used in **SOTI**, pg. 181, illo "Outside the forbidden pages of de Sade, you find draining a girl's blood only in children's comics;" drug club story r-later in Crime Reporter #1; Veiled Avenger & Barry Kuda app; Tuska-a; funny-c	63	126	189	403	689	975
17,18,20: Lady Satan, Yankee Girl & Sky Chief app; 17-Tuska-a	60	120	180	381	653	925
19-No Black Dwarf (on-c only); Zor, El Tigre app.	58	116	174	371	636	900
21-Lady Satan & Black Dwarf app.	36	72	108	211	343	475
22-Zor, Rocketman app. (68 pgs.)	36	72	108	211	343	475

RED SHE-HULK (Title continues from Hulk (2008 series) #57)
Marvel Comics: No. 58, Dec, 2012 - No. 67, Sept, 2013 ($2.99)

58-67-Betty Ross character; Pagulayan-a/c. 59,60-Avengers app. 66-Man-Thing app. 3.00

REDSKIN (Thrilling Indian Stories)(Famous Western Badmen #13 on)
Youthful Magazines: Sept, 1950 - No. 12, Oct, 1952

	GD	VG	FN	VF	VF/NM	NM-
1-Walter Johnson-a (7 pgs.)	20	40	60	117	189	260
2	14	28	42	76	108	140
3-12: 3-Daniel Boone story. 6-Geronimo story	11	22	33	62	86	110

NOTE: ***Walter Johnson** c-3, 4. **Palais** a-11. **Wildey** a-5, 11. Bondage c-6, 12.*

RED SKULL
Marvel Comics: Sept, 2011 - No. 5, Jan, 2012 ($2.99, limited series)

1-5-Pak-s/Colak-a/Aja-c; Red Skull's childhood and origin 3.00

RED SKULL (Secret Wars Battleworld tie-in)
Marvel Comics: Sept, 2015 - No. 3, Nov, 2015 ($3.99, limited series)

1-3-Joshua Williamson-s/Luca Pizzari-a; Crossbones, Magneto & Bucky app. 4.00

RED SONJA (Also see Conan #23, Kull & The Barbarians, Marvel Feature & Savage Sword Of Conan #1)
Marvel Comics Group: 1/77 - No. 15, 5/79; V1#1, 2/83 - V2#2, 3/83; V3#1, 8/83 - V3#4, 2/84; V3#5, 1/85 - V3#13, 5/86

	GD	VG	FN	VF	VF/NM	NM-
1-Created by Robert E. Howard	3	6	9	21	33	45
2-10: 5-Last 30¢ issue	2	4	6	8	10	12
4,5-(35¢-c variants, limited distribution)(7,9/77)	8	16	24	54	102	150
11-15, V2#1,V2#2: 14-Last 35¢ issue	1	3	4	6	8	10
V3#1 ($1.00, 52 pgs.)	1	3	4	6	8	10
V3#2-13: #2-4 ($1.00, 52 pgs.)						5.00

NOTE: ***Brunner** c-12-14. **J. Buscema** a(p)-12, 13, 15; c-V#1. **Nebres** a-V3#3i(part). **N. Redondo** a-8i, V3#2i, 3i. **Simonson** a-V3#1. **Thorne** c/a-1-11.*

RED SONJA (Continues in Queen Sonja) (Also see Classic Red Sonja)
Dynamite Entertainment: No. 0, Apr, 2005 - No. 80, 2013 (25¢/$2.99/$3.99)

0-(4/05, 25¢) Greg Land-c/Mel Rubi-a/Oeming & Carey-s 4.00
1-(6/05, $2.99) Five covers by Ross, Linsner, Cassaday, Turner, Rivera; Rubi-a 10.00
2-46-Multiple covers on all. 29-Sonja dies. 34-Sonja reborn 3.00
5-RRP Edition with Red Foil logo and Isanove-a 15.00
50-('10, $4.99) new stories and reprints; Marcos, Chin, Desjardins-a; 4 covers 5.00
51-79-($3.99): 51-56-Geovani-a; multiple covers on each 4.00
80-($4.99) Red Sonja vs. Dracula; bonus interview with Gail Simone 5.00
Annual #1 (2007, $3.50) Oeming-s/Sadowski-a; Red Sonja Comics Chronology 4.00
Annual #2 (2009, $3.99) Gage-s/Marcos-a; wraparound Prado-c & Marcos-c 4.00
Annual #3 (2010, $5.99) Brereton-s/c/a; Batista-a 6.00
Annual #4 (2013, $4.99) Beatty-s/Mena-a 5.00
... Blue (2011, $4.99) Brett-s/Geovani-a; covers by Geovani & Rubi 5.00
... Break the Skin (2011, $4.99) Winslade-c/Van Meter-s/Salazar-a 5.00
... Cover Showcase Vol. 1 (2007, $5.99) gallery of variant covers; Cho sketches 6.00
... Deluge (2011, $4.99) Brereton-s/c; Bolson-a/var-c; reprint from Conan #48 ('74) 5.00
Giant Size Red Sonja #1 (2007, $4.99) Chaykin-c; new story and reprints and pin-ups 5.00
Giant Size Red Sonja #2 (2008, $4.99) Segovia-c; new story and reprints and pin-ups 5.00
... Goes East ($4.99) three covers; Joe Ng-a 5.00
...: Monster Isle ($4.99) two covers; Pablo Marcos-a/Roy Thomas-s 5.00
... One More Day ($4.99) two covers; Liam Sharp-a 5.00
... Raven ('12, $4.99) Antonio-a/Martin-c; bonus pin-up gallery 5.00
...: Revenge of the Gods 1-5 (2011 - No. 5, 2011, $3.99) Sampare-a/Lieberman-s 4.00
... Vacant Shell ($4.99) two covers; Remender-s/Renaud-a 5.00
...: Wrath of the Gods 1-5 (2010 - No. 5, 2010, $3.99) Geovani-a 4.00
The Adventures of Red Sonja TPB (2005, $19.99) r/Marvel Feature #1-7 20.00
The Adventures of Red Sonja Vol. 2 TPB (2007, $19.99) r/#1-7 of '77 Marvel series 20.00
... Vol. 1 TPB (2006, $19.99) r/#0-6; gallery of covers and variants; creators interview 20.00
... Vol. 2 Arrowsmith TPB (2007, $19.99) r/#7-12; gallery of covers and variants 20.00
... Vol. 3 The Rise of Gath TPB (2007, $19.99) r/#13-18; gallery of covers and variants 20.00
... Vol. 4 Animals & More TPB (2007, $24.99) r/#19-24; gallery of covers and variants 25.00

RED SONJA (Volume 2)
Dynamite Entertainment: 2013 - No. 18, 2015 ($3.99)

1-18: 1-Gail Simone-s/Walter Geovani-a; six covers. 2-18-Multiple covers 4.00
#0 (2014, $3.99) Simone-s/Salonga-a/Hardman-c 4.00
#100 (2015, $7.99) Five short stories by various incl. Simone, Oeming, Marcos; 5 covers 8.00
#1973 (2015, $7.99) Five short stories by various incl. Simone, Bunn, Thomas & others 8.00
...: and Cub (2014, $4.99) Nancy Collins-s/Fritz Casas-a/J.M. Linsner-c 5.00
...: Berserker (2014, $4.99) Jim Zub-s/Jonathan Lau-a/Jeffrey Cruz-c 5.00
...: Sanctuary (2014, $4.99) Mason-s/Salonga-a/Davila-c; includes full script 5.00

RED SONJA (Volume 3)
Dynamite Entertainment: 2016 - No. 6, 2016 ($3.99)

1-6: 1-Marguerite Bennett-s/Aneke-a; multiple covers 4.00

RED SONJA (Volume 4)
Dynamite Entertainment: No. 0, 2016 - Present ($3.99)

0-(25¢) Sonja transported to present day New York City; Amy Chu-s/Carlos Gomez-a 3.00
1,2-($3.99) Amy Chu-s/Carlos Gomez-a; multiple covers 4.00

RED SONJA: ATLANTIS RISES
Dynamite Entertainment: 2012 - No. 4, 2012 ($3.99, limited series)

1-4-Lieberman-s/Dunbar-a/Parrillo-c 4.00

RED SONJA/CLAW: THE DEVIL'S HANDS (See Claw the Unconquered)
DC Comics (WildStorm)/Dynamite Ent.: May, 2006 - No. 4, Aug, 2006 ($2.99, limited series)

1-4-Covers by Jim Lee & Dell'Otto; Andy Smith-a 1-Alex Ross var-c. 2-Dell'Otto var-c. 3-Bermejo var-c. 4-Andy Smith var-c 3.00
TPB (2007, $12.99) r/#1-4; cover gallery 13.00

RED SONJA/ CONAN
Dynamite Entertainment: 2015 - No. 4, 2015 ($3.99, limited series)

1-4-Gischler-s/Castro-a; multiple covers 4.00

RED SONJA: SCAVENGER HUNT
Marvel Comics: Dec, 1995 ($2.95, one-shot)

1 4.00

RED SONJA: THE BLACK TOWER
Dynamite Entertainment: 2014 - No. 4, 2015 ($3.99, limited series)

1-4-Tieri-s/Razek-a/Conner-c 4.00

RED SONJA: THE MOVIE
Marvel Comics Group: Nov, 1985 - No. 2, Dec, 1985 (Limited series)

Red Thorn #2 © Baillie & Hetrick

Red Wolf (2016 series) #1 © MAR

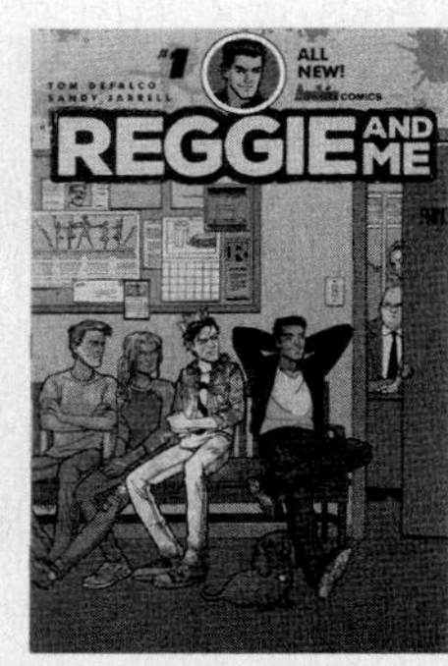

Reggie and Me (2017 series) #1 © ACP

	GD 2.0	VG 4.0	FN 6.0	VF 8.0	VF/NM 9.0	NM- 9.2

1,2-Movie adapt-r/Marvel Super Spec. #38 — 4.00

RED SONJA: UNCHAINED
Dynamite Entertainment: 2013 - No. 4, 2013 ($3.99, limited series)

1-4-Follows the Red Sonja: Blue one-shot; Jadsen-a — 4.00

RED SONJA: VULTURE'S CIRCLE
Dynamite Entertainment: 2015 - No. 5, 2015 ($3.99, limited series)

1-5-Collins & Lieberman-s/Casas-a; three covers on each — 4.00

RED SONJA VS. THULSA DOOM
Dynamite Entertainment: 2005 - No. 4, 2006 ($3.50)

1-4-Conrad-a; Conrad & Dell'Otto covers — 3.50
..., Volume 1 TPB (2006, $14.99) r/series; cover gallery — 15.00

RED STAR, THE
Image Comics/Archangel Studios: June, 2000 - No. 9, June, 2002 ($2.95)

1-Christian Gossett-s/a(p) — 4.00
2-9: 9-Beck-c — 3.00
#(7.5) Reprints Wizard #1/2 story with new pages — 3.00
Annual 1 (Archangel Studios, 11/02, $3.50) "Run Makita Run" — 4.00
TPB (4/01, $24.95, 9x12") oversized r/#1-4; intro. by Bendis — 25.00
Nokgorka TPB (8/02, $24.95, 9x12") oversized r/#6-9; w/sketch pages — 25.00
Wizard 1/2 (mail order) — 10.00

RED STAR, THE (Volume 2)
CrossGen #1,2/Archangel Studios #3 on: Feb, 2003 - No. 5, July, 2004 ($2.95/$2.99)

1-5-Christian Gossett-s/a(p) — 3.00
Prison of Souls TPB (8/04, $24.95, 9x12") oversized r/#1-5; w/sketch pages — 25.00

RED STAR, THE: SWORD OF LIES
Archangel Studios: Aug, 2006 ($4.50)

1-Christian Gossett-s/a(p); origin of the Red Star team — 4.50

RED TEAM
Dynamite Entertainment: 2013 - No. 7, 2014 ($3.99)

1-7: 1-Ennis-s/Cermak-a; covers by Chaykin & Sook — 4.00

RED TEAM, VOLUME 2: DOUBLE TAP, CENTER MASS
Dynamite Entertainment: 2016 - Present ($3.99)

1-7: 1-Ennis-s/Cermak-a/Panosian-c — 4.00

RED THORN
DC Comics (Vertigo): Jan, 2016 - No. 13, Feb, 2017 ($3.99)

1-13: 1-6-David Baillie-s/Meghan Hetrick-a. 7-Steve Pugh-a — 4.00

RED TORNADO (See All-American #20 & Justice League of America #64)
DC Comics: July, 1985 - No. 4, Oct, 1985 (Limited series)

1-4: Kurt Busiek scripts in all. 1-3-Superman & Batman cameos — 4.00

RED TORNADO
DC Comics: Nov, 2009 - No. 6, Apr, 2010 ($2.99, limited series)

1-6: 1-3-Benes-c. 5,6-Vixen app. — 3.00
...: Family Reunion TPB (2010, $17.99) r/#1-6 — 18.00

RED WARRIOR
Marvel/Atlas Comics (TCI): Jan, 1951 - No. 6, Dec, 1951

	GD	VG	FN	VF	VF/NM	NM-
1-Red Warrior & his horse White Wing; Tuska-a	20	40	60	114	182	250
2-Tuska-c	12	24	36	69	97	125
3-6: 4-Origin White Wing. 6-Maneely-c	10	20	30	58	79	100

RED, WHITE & BLUE COMICS
DC Comics: 1941

nn - Ashcan comic, not distributed to newsstands, only for in-house use. Cover art is All-American Comics #20 with interior being Flash Comics #17 (no known sales)

RED WING
Image Comics: Jul, 2011 - No. 4, Oct, 2011 ($3.50, limited series)

1-4-Hickman-s/Pitarra-a — 3.50

RED WOLF (See Avengers #80 & Marvel Spotlight #1)
Marvel Comics Group: May, 1972 - No. 9, Sept, 1973

	GD	VG	FN	VF	VF/NM	NM-
1-(Western hero); Gil Kane/Severin-c; Shores-a	4	8	12	23	37	50
2-9: 2-Kane-c; Shores-a. 6-Tuska-r in back-up. 7-Red Wolf as super hero begins. 9-Origin sidekick, Lobo (wolf)	3	6	9	16	23	30

RED WOLF (From the Secret Wars tie-in series 1872)
Marvel Comics: Feb, 2016 - No. 6, Jul, 2016 ($3.99)

1-6: 1-Edmondson-s/Talajic-a. 2-Red Wolf in the present — 4.00

REESE'S PIECES
Eclipse Comics: Oct, 1985 - No.2, Oct, 1985 ($1.75, Baxter paper)

1,2-B&W-r in color — 3.00

REFORM SCHOOL GIRL!
Realistic Comics: 1951

	GD	VG	FN	VF	VF/NM	NM-
nn-Used in **SOTI**, pg. 358, & cover ill. with caption "Comic books are supposed to be like fairy tales"; classic photo-c	1000	2000	3000	7600	13,800	20,000

(Prices vary widely on this book)

NOTE: *The cover and title originated from a digest-sized book published by Diversey Publishing Co. of Chicago in 1948. The original book "House of Fury", Doubleday, came out in 1941. The girl's real name which appears on the cover of the digest and comic is Marty Collins, Canadian model and ice skating star who posed for this special color photograph for the Diversey novel.*

REGENTS ILLUSTRATED CLASSICS
Prentice Hall Regents, Englewood Cliffs, NJ 07632: 1981 (Plus more recent reprintings) (48 pgs., B&W-a with 14 pgs. of teaching helps)

NOTE: *This series contains Classics Ill. art, and was produced from the same illegal source as* ***Cassette Books.*** *But when Twin Circle sued to stop the sale of the Cassette Books, they decided to permit this series to continue. This series was produced as a teaching aid. The 20 title series is divided into four levels based upon number of basic words used therein. There is also a teacher's manual for each level. All of the titles are still available from the publisher for about $5 each retail. The number to call for mail order purchases is (201)767-5937. Almost all of the issues have new covers taken from some interior art panel. Here is a list of the series by Regents ident. no. and the Classics Ill. counterpart.*

16770(Cl#24-A2)18333(Cl#3-A2)21668(Cl#13-A2)32224(Cl#21)33051(Cl#26)35788(Cl#84)37153(Cl#16)44460(Cl#19-A2)44808(Cl#18-A2)52395(Cl#4-A2)58627(Cl#5-A2)60067(Cl#30)68405(Cl#23A1)70302(Cl#29)78192(Cl#7-A2)78193(Cl#10-A2)79679(Cl#85)92046(Cl#1-A2)93062(Cl#64)93512(Cl#25)

RE: GEX
Awesome-Hyperwerks: Jul, 1998 - No. 0, Dec, 1998; ($2.50)

Preview (7/98) Wizard Con Edition — 3.00
0-(12/98) Loeb-s/Liefeld-a/Pat Lee-c, 1-(9/98) Loeb-s/Liefeld-a/c — 3.00

REGGIE (Formerly Archie's Rival...; Reggie & Me #19 on)
Archie Publications: No. 15, Sept, 1963 - No. 18, Nov, 1965

	GD	VG	FN	VF	VF/NM	NM-
15(9/63), 16(10/64), 17(8/65), 18(11/65)	5	10	15	30	50	70

NOTE: *Cover title No. 15 & 16 is Archie's Rival Reggie.*

REGGIE AND ME (Formerly Reggie)
Archie Publ.: No. 19, Aug, 1966 - No. 126, Sept, 1980 (No. 50-68: 52 pgs.)

	GD	VG	FN	VF	VF/NM	NM-
19-Evilheart app.	4	8	12	23	37	50
20-23-Evilheart app.; with Pureheart #22	3	6	9	19	30	40
24-40(3/70)	3	6	9	14	20	26
41-49(7/71)	2	4	6	11	16	20
50(9/71)-68 (1/74, 52 pgs.)	3	6	9	14	19	24
69-99	2	4	6	8	10	12
100(10/77)	2	4	6	9	12	15
101-126	1	2	3	5	7	9

REGGIE AND ME (Volume 2)
Archie Comic Publications: Jan, 2017 - No. 5 ($3.99)

1,2-Multiple covers and classic back-up reprints. Tom DeFalco-s/Sandy Jarrell-a — 4.00

REGGIE'S JOKES (See Reggie's Wise Guy Jokes)

REGGIE'S REVENGE!
Archie Comic Publications, Inc.: Spring, 1994 - No. 3 ($2.00, 52 pgs.) (Published semi-annually)

1-Bound-in pull-out poster — 5.00
2,3 — 4.00

REGGIE'S WISE GUY JOKES
Archie Publications: Aug, 1968 - No. 55, 1980 (#5-28 are Giants)

	GD	VG	FN	VF	VF/NM	NM-
1	4	8	12	27	44	60
2-4	3	6	9	14	20	26
5-16 (1/71)(68 pg. Giants)	3	6	9	16	24	32
17-28 (52 pg. Giants)	2	4	6	13	18	22
29-40(1/77)	1	3	4	6	8	10
41-55	1	2	3	5	6	8

REGISTERED NURSE
Charlton Comics: Summer, 1963

	GD	VG	FN	VF	VF/NM	NM-
1-r/Nurse Betsy Crane & Cynthia Doyle	3	6	9	19	30	40

REG'LAR FELLERS
Visual Editions (Standard): No. 5, Nov, 1947 - No. 6, Mar, 1948

	GD	VG	FN	VF	VF/NM	NM-
5,6	9	18	27	50	65	80

REG'LAR FELLERS HEROIC (See Heroic Comics)

REGULAR SHOW (Based on Cartoon Network series)
Boom Entertainment (kaBOOM!): Apr, 2013 - No. 40, Oct, 2016 ($3.99)

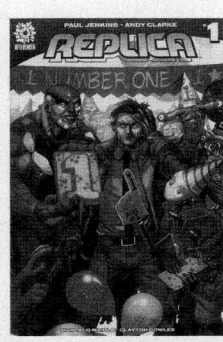

Regular Show: Skips #4 © Cartoon Nework

Replica #1 © Paul Jenkins

Rescue #1 © MAR

GD 2.0 VG 4.0 FN 6.0 VF 8.0 VF/NM 9.0 NM- 9.2

1-40-Multiple covers on all 4.00
2014 Annual 1 (6/14, $4.99) Four short stories by various; three covers 5.00
2015 Special 1 (3/15, $4.99) Four short stories by various; two covers 5.00

REGULAR SHOW: SKIPS (Based on Cartoon Network series)
Boom Entertainment (kaBOOM!): Nov, 2013 - No. 6, Apr, 2014 ($3.99)

1-6-Mad Rupert-s/a; multiple covers on all 4.00

REID FLEMING, WORLD'S TOUGHEST MILKMAN
Eclipse Comics/ Deep Sea Comics: 1980; 8/86; V2#1, 12/86 - V2#3, 12/88; V2#4, 11/89; V2#5, 11/90 - V2#9, 4/98 (B&W)

1-(1980, self-published) David Boswell-s/a 5.00
1-2nd, 4th & 5th printings ($2.50); (3rd print, large size, 8/86, $2.50) 3.00
V2#1 (10/86, regular size, $2.00), 1-2nd print, 3rd print ($2.00, 2/89) 3.00
2-9 , V2#2-2nd & 3rd printings, V2#4-2nd printing, V2#5 ($2.00), V2#6 (Deep Sea, r/V2#5)
7-9-New stories 3.00

REIGN IN HELL
DC Comics: Sept, 2008 - No. 8, Apr, 2009 ($3.50, limited series)

1-8-Neron, Shadowpact app.; Giffen-s; Dr. Occult back-up w/Segovia-a. 1-Two covers 3.50
TPB (2009, $19.99) r/#1-8 20.00

REIGN OF THE ZODIAC
DC Comics: Oct, 2003 - No. 8, May, 2004 ($2.75)

1-8: 1-6,8-Giffen-s/Doran-a/Harris-c. 7-Byrd-a 3.00

RELATIVE HEROES
DC Comics: Mar, 2000 - No. 6, Aug, 2000 ($2.50, limited series)

1-6-Grayson-s/Guichet & Sowd-a. 6-Superman-c/app. 3.00

RELOAD
DC Comics (Homage): May, 2003 - No. 3, Sept, 2003 ($2.95, limited series)

1-3-Warren Ellis-s/Paul Gulacy & Jimmy Palmiotti-a 3.00
.../Mek TPB (2004, $14.95, flip book) r/Reload #1-3 & Mek #1-3 15.00

RELUCTANT DRAGON, THE (Walt Disney's...)
Dell Publishing Co.: No. 13, 1940

Four Color 13-Contains 2 pgs. of photos from film; 2 pg. foreword to Fantasia by Leopold Stokowski; Donald Duck, Goofy, Baby Weems & Mickey Mouse (as the Sorcerer's Apprentice) app. 219 438 657 1402 2401 3400

REMAINS
IDW Publishing: May, 2004 - No. 5, Sept, 2004 ($3.99)

1-5-Steve Niles-s/Kieron Dwyer-a 4.00

REMARKABLE WORLDS OF PROFESSOR PHINEAS B. FUDDLE, THE
DC Comics (Paradox Press): 2000 - No. 4, 2000 ($5.95, limited series)

1-4-Boaz Yakin-s/Erez Yakin-a 6.00
TPB (2001, $19.95) r/series 20.00

REMEMBER PEARL HARBOR
Street & Smith Publications: 1942 (68 pgs.) (Illustrated story of the battle)

nn-Uncle Sam-c; Jack Binder-a 77 154 231 493 847 1200

REN & STIMPY SHOW, THE (TV) (Nickelodeon cartoon characters)
Marvel Comics: Dec, 1992 - No. 44, July, 1996 ($1.75/$1.95)

1-($2.25)-Polybagged w/scratch & sniff Ren or Stimpy air fowler (equal numbers of each were made) 1 3 4 6 8 10
1-2nd & 3rd printing; different dialogue on-c 4.00
2-6: 4-Muddy Mudskipper back-up. 5-Bill Wray painted-c. 6-Spider-Man vs. Powdered Toast Man 5.00
7-17: 12-1st solo back-up story w/Tank & Brenner 4.00
18-44: 18-Powered Toast Man app. 4.00
25 ($2.95) Deluxe edition w/die cut cover 5.00
...Don't Try This at Home (3/94, $12.95, TPB)-r/#9-12 13.00
...Eenteractive Special ('95, $2.95) 4.00
...Holiday Special 1994 (2/95, $2.95, 52 pgs.) 4.00
...Mini Comic (1995) 5.00
...Pick of the Litter nn (1993, $12.95, TPB)-r/#1-4 13.00
...Radio Daze (11/95, $1.95) 4.00
...Running Joke nn (1993, $12.95, TPB)-r/#1-4 plus new-a 13.00
...Seeck Little Monkeys (1/95, $12.95)-r/#17-20 13.00
...Special 2 (7/94, $2.95, 52 pgs.), ...Special 3 (10/94, $2.95, 52 pgs.)-Choose adventure, ...Special: Around the World in a Daze ($2.95), ...Special: Four Swerks (1/95, $2.95, 52 pgs.)-FF #1 cover swipe; cover reads "Four Swerks w/5 pg. coloring book.", ...Special: Powdered Toast Man 1 (4/94, $2.95, 52 pgs.), ...Special: Powdered Toast Man's Cereal Serial (4/95, $2.95), ...Special: Sports (10/95, $2.95) 4.00
...Tastes Like Chicken nn (11/93,$12.95,TPB)-r/#5-8 13.00
...Your Pals (1994, $12.95, TPB)-r/#13-16 13.00

RENATO JONES: THE ONE %
Image Comics: May, 2016 - Present ($3.99)

1-5-Kaare Andrews-s/a/c 4.00

RENFIELD
Caliber Press: 1994 - No. 3, 1995 ($2.95, B&W, limited series)

1-3 3.00

RENO BROWNE, HOLLYWOOD'S GREATEST COWGIRL (Formerly Margie Comics; Apache Kid #53 on; also see Western Hearts, Western Life Romances & Western Love)
Marvel Comics (MPC): No. 50, April, 1950 - No. 52, Sept, 1950 (52 pgs.)

50-Reno Browne photo-c on all 29 58 87 170 278 385
51,52 24 48 72 142 234 325

REPLICA
AfterShock Comics: Dec, 2015 - No. 5, Apr, 2016 ($3.99)

1-5-Paul Jenkins-s/Andy Clarke-a 4.00

REPTILICUS (Becomes Reptisaurus #3 on)
Charlton Comics: Aug, 1961 - No. 2, Oct, 1961

1 (Movie) 20 40 60 141 313 485
2 10 20 30 69 147 225

REPTISAURUS (Reptilicus #1,2)
Charlton Comics: V2#3, Jan, 1962 - No. 8, Dec, 1962; Summer, 1963

V2#3-8: 3-Flying saucer-c/s. 8-Montes/Bache-c/a 5 10 15 35 63 90
Special Edition 1 (Summer, 1963) 5 10 15 34 60 85

REQUIEM FOR DRACULA
Marvel Comics: Feb, 1993 ($2.00, 52 pgs.)

nn-r/Tomb of Dracula #69,70 by Gene Colan 4.00

RESCUE (Pepper Potts in Iron Man armor)
Marvel Comics: July, 2010 ($3.99, one-shot)

1-DeConnick-s/Mutti-a/Foreman-c 4.00

RESCUERS, THE (See Walt Disney Showcase #40)

RESIDENT ALIEN
Dark Horse Comics: No. 0, Apr, 2012 - No. 3, Jul, 2012 ($3.50, limited series)

0-3-Hogan-s/Parkhouse-a: 0-Reprints chapters from Dark Horse Presents #4-6 3.50

RESIDENT ALIEN: THE MAN WITH NO NAME
Dark Horse Comics: Sept, 2016 - No. 4, Dec, 2016 ($3.99, limited series)

1-4-Hogan-s/Parkhouse-a 4.00

RESIDENT ALIEN: THE SAM HAIN MYSTERY
Dark Horse Comics: No. 0, Apr, 2015 - No. 3, Jul, 2015 ($3.99, limited series)

0-3-Hogan-s/Parkhouse-a: 0-Reprints chapters from Dark Horse Presents V3 #1-3 4.00

RESIDENT ALIEN: THE SUICIDE BLONDE
Dark Horse Comics: No. 0, Aug, 2013 - No. 3, Nov, 2013 ($3.99, limited series)

0-3-Hogan-s/Parkhouse-a: 0-Reprints chapters from Dark Horse Presents #18-20 4.00

RESIDENT EVIL (Based on video game)
Image Comics (WildStorm): Mar, 1998 - No. 5 ($4.95, quarterly magazine)

1 3 6 9 16 23 30
2-5 2 4 6 10 14 18
...Code: Veronica 1-4 (2002, $14.95) English reprint of Japanese comics 15.00
...Collection One ('99, $14.95, TPB) r/#1-4 15.00

RESIDENT EVIL (Volume 2)
DC Comics (WildStorm): May, 2009 - No. 6, Feb, 2011 ($3.99)

1-6: 1,2-Liam Sharpe-a. 1-Two covers 4.00
...: Volume 2 TPB (2011, $19.99) r/#1-6 20.00

RESIDENT EVIL: FIRE AND ICE
DC Comics (WildStorm): Dec, 2000 - No. 4, May, 2001 ($2.50, limited series)

1-4-Bermejo-c 4.00
TPB (2009, $24.99) r/#1-4 plus short stories from Resident Evil magazine 25.00

RESISTANCE (Based on the video game)
DC Comics (WildStorm): Early Mar, 2009 - No. 6, Jul, 2009 ($3.99, limited series)

1-6-Ramón Pérez-a/C.P. Smith-c 4.00
TPB (2010, $19.99) r/#1-6 20.00

RESISTANCE, THE
DC Comics (WildStorm): Nov, 2002 - No. 8, June, 2003 ($2.95)

1-8-Palmiotti & Gray-s/Santacruz-a 3.00

Resurrection Man #16 © DC

Return of the Gremlins #2 © DIS

Revival #7 © Seeley & Norton

	GD 2.0	VG 4.0	FN 6.0	VF 8.0	VF/NM 9.0	NM- 9.2

REST (Milo Ventimiglia Presents...)
Devil's Due Publ.: No. 0, Aug, 2008 - No. 2 (99¢/$3.50)

0-(99¢) Prelude to series; Powers-s/McManus-a 3.00
1,2-($3.50) 1-Two covers (Tim Sale art & Milo Ventimiglia photo) 3.50

RESTAURANT AT THE END OF THE UNIVERSE, THE (See Hitchhiker's Guide to the Galaxy & Life, the Universe & Everything)
DC Comics: 1994 - No. 3, 1994 ($6.95, limited series)

1-3 7.00

RESTLESS GUN (TV)
Dell Publishing Co.: No. 934, Sept, 1958 - No. 1146, Nov-Jan, 1960-61

	GD	VG	FN	VF	VF/NM	NM-
Four Color 934 (#1)-Photo-c	9	18	27	61	123	185
Four Color 986 (5/59), 1045 (11-1/60), 1089 (3/60), 1146-Wildey-a; all photo-c	7	14	21	46	86	125

RESURRECTIONISTS
Dark Horse Comics: Nov, 2014 - Present ($3.50)

1-4-Van Lente-s/Rosenzweig-a 3.50

RESURRECTION MAN
DC Comics: May, 1997 - No. 27, Aug, 1999 ($2.50)

1-Lenticular disc on cover 5.00
2-5: 2-JLA app. 4.00
6-10: 6-Genesis-x-over. 7-Batman app. 10-Hitman-c/app. 3.00
11-27: 16,17-Supergirl x-over. 18-Deadman & Phantom Stranger-c/app. 21-JLA-c/app. 3.00
#1,000,000 (11/98) 853rd Century x-over 3.00

RESURRECTION MAN (DC New 52)
DC Comics: Nov, 2011 - No. 12, Oct, 2012; No. 0, Nov, 2012 ($2.99)

1-12: 1-Abnett & Lanning-s/Dagnino-a/Reis-c; Body Doubles app. 9-Suicide Squad app. 3.00
#0 (11/12) Origin of Mitch Shelley and the Body Doubles; Bachs-a/Francavilla-c 3.00

RETIEF (Keith Laumer's)
Adventure Comics (Malibu): Dec, 1989 - Vol. 2, No.6, ($2.25, B&W)

1-6,Vol. 2, #1-6,Vol. 3 (...of The CDT) #1-6 3.00
...and The Warlords #1-6, ...: Diplomatic Immunity #1 (4/91), ...: Giant Killer #1 (9/91), ...: Crime & Punishment #1 (11/91) 3.00

RETROVIRUS
Image Comics: Nov, 2012 ($12.99, hardcover GN)

HC-Gray & Palmiotti-s/Fernandez-a/Conner-c 13.00

RETURN FROM WITCH MOUNTAIN (See Walt Disney Showcase #44)

RETURNING, THE
BOOM! Studios: Mar, 2014 - No. 4, Jun, 2014 ($3.99, limited series)

1-4-Jason Starr-s/Andrea Mutti-a/Frazer Irving-c 4.00

RETURN OF ALISON DARE: LITTLE MISS ADVENTURES, THE (Also see Alison Dare: Little Miss Adventures)
Oni Press: Apr, 2001 - No. 3, Sept, 2001 ($2.95, B&W, limited series)

1-3-J. Torres-s/J.Bone-c/a 3.00

RETURN OF GORGO, THE (Formerly Gorgo's Revenge)
Charlton Comics: No. 2, Aug, 1963; No. 3, Fall, 1964 (12¢)

	GD	VG	FN	VF	VF/NM	NM-
2,3-Ditko-c/a; based on M.G.M. movie	7	14	21	49	92	135

RETURN OF KONGA, THE (Konga's Revenge #2 on)
Charlton Comics: 1962

	GD	VG	FN	VF	VF/NM	NM-
nn	7	14	21	49	92	135

RETURN OF MEGATON MAN
Kitchen Sink Press: July, 1988 - No. 3, 1988 ($2.00, limited series)

1-3: Simpson-c/a 3.00

RETURN OF THE GREMLINS (The Roald Dahl characters)
Dark Horse Comics: Mar, 2008 - No. 3, May, 2008 ($2.99, limited series)

1-3-Richardson-s/Yeagle-a. 1-Back-up reprint of intro. from 1943. 2-Back-up reprints of three Gremlin Gus 2-pagers from 1943. 3-Back-up reprints 3.00

RETURN OF THE LIVING DEADPOOL
Marvel Comics: Apr, 2015 - No. 4, Jul, 2015 ($3.99, limited series)

1-4-Cullen Bunn-s/Nik Virella-a 6.00

RETURN OF THE OUTLAW
Toby Press (Minoan): Feb, 1953 - No. 11, 1955

	GD	VG	FN	VF	VF/NM	NM-
1-Billy the Kid	10	20	30	58	79	100
2	7	14	21	37	46	55
3-11	7	14	21	35	43	50

RETURN TO JURASSIC PARK
Topps Comics: Apr, 1995 - No. 9, Feb, 1996 ($2.50/$2.95)

1-9: 3-Begin $2.95-c. 9-Artist's Jam issue 3.00

RETURN TO THE AMALGAM AGE OF COMICS: THE MARVEL COMICS COLLECTION
Marvel Comics: 1997 ($12.95, TPB)

nn-Reprints Amalgam one-shots: Challengers of the Fantastic #1, The Exciting X-Patrol #1, Iron Lantern #1, The Magnetic Men Featuring Magneto #1, Spider-Boy Team-Up #1 & Thorion of the New Asgods #1 13.00

REVEAL
Dark Horse Comics: Nov, 2002 ($6.95, squarebound)

1-Short stories of Dark Horse characters by various; Lone Wolf 2100, Buffy, Spyboy app. 7.00

REVEALING LOVE STORIES (See Fox Giants)

REVEALING ROMANCES
Ace Magazines: Sept, 1949 - No. 6, Aug, 1950

	GD	VG	FN	VF	VF/NM	NM-
1	18	36	54	103	162	220
2	11	22	33	62	86	110
3-6	10	20	30	56	76	95

REVELATIONS
Dark Horse Comics: Aug, 2005 - No. 6, Jan, 2006 ($2.99, limited series)

1-6-Paul Jenkins-s/Humberto Ramos-a/c 3.00
1-6-(BOOM! Studios, 1/14 - No. 6, 6/14, $3.99) reprints original series 4.00

REVENGE
Image Comics: Feb, 2014 - No. 4, Jun, 2014 ($2.99)

1-4-Jonathan Ross-s/Ian Churchill-a 3.00

REVENGE OF THE PROWLER (Also see The Prowler)
Eclipse Comics: Feb, 1988 - No. 4, June, 1988 ($1.75/$1.95)

1,3,4: 1-$1.75. 3,4-$1.95-c; Snyder III-a(p) 3.00
2 ($2.50)-Contains flexi-disc 4.00

REVISIONIST, THE
AfterShock Comics: Jun, 2016 - No. 6, Nov, 2016 ($3.99)

1-6: 1-Frank Barbiere-s/Garry Brown-a 4.00

REVIVAL
Image Comics: Jul, 2012 - No. 47, Feb, 2017 ($2.99/$3.99)

1-Tim Seeley-s/Mike Norton-a/Jenny Frison-c 12.00
1-Variant-c by Craig Thompson 18.00
1-Second-fourth printings 4.00
2-26 3.00
27-47-($3.99) 4.00

REVOLUTION
IDW Publishing: Sept, 2016 - No. 5, Nov, 2016 ($3.99, limited series)

1-5-Barber & Bunn-s/Ossio-a; multiple covers on each; G.I. Joe, Transformers, Rom, Micronauts, and M.A.S.K. app. 2-5-Bonus character profile pages 4.00

REVOLUTIONARIES (Follows the Revolution x-over)
IDW Publishing: Dec, 2016 - Present ($3.99)

1,2-Barber-s/Ossio-a; multiple covers on each; G.I. Joe, Transformers, Rom app. 4.00

REVOLUTIONARY WAR
Marvel Comics: Mar, 2014 - May, 2014 ($3.99)

...: Alpha 1 (3/14) Part 1; Lanning & Cowsill-s/Elson-a; Capt. Britain & Pete Wisdom app. 4.00
...: Dark Angel 1 (3/14) Part 2; Gillen-s/Dietrich Smith-a; Mephisto app. 4.00
...: Death's Head II 1 (4/14) Part 4; Lanning & Cowsill-s/Roche-a 4.00
...: Knights of Pendragon 1 (3/14) Part 3; Williams-s/Sliney-a; Union Jack app. 4.00
...: Motormouth 1 (5/14) Part 6; Dakin-s/Cliquet-a; Killpower app. 4.00
...: Omega 1 (5/14) Part 8; conclusion; Lanning & Cowsill-s/Elson-a 4.00
...: Supersoldiers 1 (4/14) Part 5; Williams-s/Brent Anderson-a 4.00
...: Warheads 1 (5/14) Part 7; Lanning & Cowsill-s/Erskine-a 4.00

REVOLUTION ON THE PLANET OF THE APES
Mr. Comics: Dec, 2005 - No. 6, Aug, 2006 ($3.95)

1-6: 1,2-Salgood Sam-a 4.00

REX ALLEN COMICS (Movie star)(Also see Four Color #877 & Western Roundup under Dell Giants)
Dell Publ. Co.: No. 316, Feb, 1951 - No. 31, Dec-Feb, 1958-59 (All-photo-c)

	GD	VG	FN	VF	VF/NM	NM-
Four Color 316(#1)(52 pgs.)-Rex Allen & his horse Koko begin; Marsh-a	13	26	39	86	188	290
2 (9-11/51, 36 pgs.)	8	16	24	55	105	150
3-10	6	12	18	38	69	100

Reyn #1 © Symons & Stockman

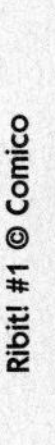

Ribit! #1 © Comico

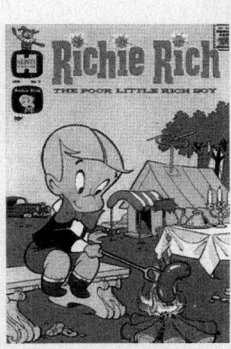

Richie Rich #2 © HARV

	GD 2.0	VG 4.0	FN 6.0	VF 8.0	VF/NM 9.0	NM- 9.2
11-20	5	10	15	34	60	85
21-23,25-31	5	10	15	31	53	75
24-Toth-a	5	10	15	34	60	85

NOTE: ***Manning*** *a-20, 27-30. Photo back-c F.C. #316, 2-12, 20, 21.*

REX DEXTER OF MARS (See Mystery Men Comics)
Fox Features Syndicate: Fall, 1940 (68 pgs.)

1-Rex Dexter, Patty O'Day, & Zanzibar (Tuska-a) app.; Briefer-c/a
245 490 735 1568 2684 3800

REX HART (Formerly Blaze Carson; Whip Wilson #9 on)
Timely/Marvel Comics (USA): No. 6, Aug, 1949 - No. 8, Feb, 1950 (All photo-c)

6-Rex Hart & his horse Warrior begin; Black Rider app; Captain Tootsie by Beck; Heath-a
26 52 78 154 252 350
7,8: 18 pg. Thriller in each. 7-Heath-a. 8-Blaze the Wonder Collie app. in text
18 36 54 105 165 225

REX MORGAN, M.D. (Also see Harvey Comics Library)
Argo Publ.: Dec, 1955 - No. 3, Apr?, 1956

1-r/Rex Morgan daily newspaper strips & daily panel-r of "These Women" by D'Alessio & "Timeout" by Jeff Keate 14 28 42 80 115 150
2,3 10 20 30 56 76 95

REX MUNDI (Latin for "King of the World")
Image Comics: No. 0, Aug, 2002 - No. 18, Apr, 2006 ($2.95/$2.99)

0-18-Arvid Nelson-s. 0-13-Eric Johnson-a. 14,15-Jim DiBartolo-a. 18-Ramos-c 3.00
Vol. 1: The Guardian of the Temple TPB (1/04, $14.95) r/#0-5 15.00
Book 1: The Guardian of the Temple TPB (Dark Horse, 11/06, $16.95) r/#0-5 & Brother Matthew web comic; Dysart intro. 17.00
Vol. 2: The River Underground TPB (4/05, $14.95) r/#6-11 15.00
Book 2: The River Underground (Dark Horse, 2006, $16.95) r/#6-11 17.00
Vol. 3: The Lost Kings TPB (Dark Horse, 9/06, $16.95) r/#12-17 17.00
Book Four: Crowd and Sword TPB (Dark Horse, 12/07, $16.95) r/#18 plus V2 #1-5 and story from Dark Horse Book of Monsters 17.00

REX MUNDI (Volume 2)
Dark Horse Comics: July, 2006 - No. 19, Aug, 2009 ($2.99)

1-19-Arvid Nelson-s. 1-JH Williams-c. 16-Chen-c. 18-Linsner-c 3.00
Book Five: The Valley at the End of the World TPB (11/08, $17.95) r/#6-12 18.00

REX THE WONDER DOG (See The Adventures of...)

REYN
Image Comics: Jan, 2015 - No. 10, Nov, 2015 ($2.99)

1-10-Symons-s/Stockman-a 3.00

RHUBARB, THE MILLIONAIRE CAT
Dell Publishing Co.: No. 423, Sept-Oct, 1952 - No. 563, June, 1954

	GD	VG	FN	VF	VF/NM	NM-
Four Color 423 (#1)	7	14	21	44	82	120
Four Color 466(5/53),563	6	12	18	37	66	95

RIB
Dilemma Productions: Oct, 1995 - April, 1996 ($1.95, B&W)

Ashcan, 1 3.00

RIB
Bookmark Productions: 1996 ($2.95, B&W)

1-Sakai-c; Andrew Ford-s/a 3.00

RIB
Caliber Comics: May, 1997 - No. 5, 1998 ($2.95, B&W)

1-5: 1-"Beginnings" pts. 1 & 2 3.00

RIBIT! (Red Sonja imitation)
Comico: Jan, 1989 - No. 4, April?, 1989 ($1.95, limited series)

1-4: Frank Thorne-c/a/scripts 3.00

RIBTICKLER (Also see Fox Giants)
Fox Feature Synd./Green Publ. (1957)/Norlen (1959): 1945, No. 2, 1946, No. 3, Jul-Aug, 1946 - No. 9, Jul-Aug, 1947; 1957; 1959

	GD	VG	FN	VF	VF/NM	NM-
1-Funny animal	20	40	60	117	189	260
2-(1946)	12	24	36	69	97	125
3-9: 3,5,7-Cosmo Cat app.	11	22	33	60	83	105
3,7,8 (Green Publ.-1957), 3,7,8 (Norlen Mag.-1959)	3	6	9	16	23	30

RICHARD DRAGON
DC Comics: July, 2004 - No. 12, Jun, 2005 ($2.50)

1-12: 1-Dixon-s/McDaniel-a/c; Ben Turner app. 2,3-Nightwing app. 4-6,11,12-Lady Shiva 3.00

RICHARD DRAGON, KUNG-FU FIGHTER (See The Batman Chronicles #5, Brave & the Bold, & The Question)
National Periodical Publ./DC Comics: Apr-May, 1975 - No. 18, Nov-Dec, 1977

1-Intro Richard Dragon, Ben Stanley & O-Sensei; 1st app. Barney Ling; adaptation of Jim Dennis novel "Dragon's Fists" begins, ends #4 3 6 9 19 30 40
2,3: 2-Intro Carolyn Woosan; Starlin/Weiss-c/a; bondage-c. 3-Kirby-a(p); Giordano bondage-c 2 4 6 9 12 15
4,6-8-Wood inks. 4-Carolyn Woosan dies 2 4 6 8 10 12
5-1st app. Lady Shiva; Wood inks 6 12 18 38 69 100
9-13,15-17: 9-Ben Stanley becomes Ben Turner; intro Preying Mantis. 16-1st app. Prof Ojo.
1 3 4 6 8 10
14-"Spirit of Bruce Lee" 3 6 9 14 20 26
18-1st app. Ben Turner as The Bronze Tiger 2 4 6 9 12 15

NOTE: ***Buckler*** *a-14. c-15, 18.* ***Chua*** *c-13.* ***Estrada*** *a-9, 13-18.* ***Estrada/Abel*** *a-10-12.* ***Estrada/Wood*** *a-4-8.* ***Giordano*** *c-1, 3-11.* ***Weiss*** *a-2(partial) c-2i.*

RICHARD THE LION-HEARTED (See Ideal a Classical Comic)

RICHIE RICH (See Harvey Collectors Comics, Harvey Hits, Little Dot, Little Lotta, Little Sad Sack, Million Dollar Digest, Mutt & Jeff, Super Richie & 3-D Dolly; also Tastee-Freez Comics in the Promotional Comics section)

RICHIE RICH (...the Poor Little Rich Boy) (See Harvey Hits #3, 9)
Harvey Publ.: Nov, 1960 - #218, Oct, 1982; #219, Oct, 1986 - #254, Jan, 1991

	GD	VG	FN	VF	VF/NM	NM-
1-(See Little Dot #1 for 1st app.)	300	600	900	2550	5775	9000
2	86	172	258	688	1544	2400
3-5	46	92	138	340	770	1200
6-10: 8-Christmas-c	27	54	81	189	420	650
11-20	16	32	48	112	249	385
21-30	11	22	33	76	163	250
31-40	9	18	27	61	123	185
41-50: 42(2/66)-X-mas-c	7	14	21	49	92	135
51-55,57-60: 59-Buck, prototype of Dollar the Dog	5	10	15	35	63	90
56-1st app. Super Richie	6	12	18	41	76	110
61-64,66-80: 71-Nixon & Robert Kennedy caricatures; outer space-c	4	8	12	28	47	65
65-Buck the Dog (Dollar prototype) on cover	6	12	18	37	66	95
81-99	3	6	9	21	33	45
100(12/70)-1st app. Irona the robot maid	4	8	12	25	40	55
101-111,117-120	3	6	9	14	20	26
112-116: All 52 pg. Giants	3	6	9	16	24	32
121-140: 137-1st app. Mr. Cheepers and Professor Keenbean	2	4	6	9	13	16
141-160: 145-Infinity-c. 155-3rd app. The Money Monster	2	4	6	8	10	12
161-180	1	3	4	6	8	10
181-199	1	2	3	5	6	8
200	1	3	4	6	8	10
201-218: 210-Stone-Age Riches app	1	2	3	4	5	7
219-254: 237-Last original material						6.00

Harvey Comics Classics Vol. 2 TPB (Dark Horse Books, 10/07, $19.95) Reprints Richie Rich's early appearances in this title, Little Dot and Richie Rich Success Stories, mostly B&W with some color stories; history and interview with Ernie Colón 20.00

RICHIE RICH
Harvey Comics: Mar, 1991 - No. 28, Nov, 1994 ($1.00, bi-monthly)

1-28: Reprints best of Richie Rich 3.00
Giant Size 1-4 (10/91-10/93, $2.25, 68 pgs.) 4.00

RICHIE RICH ADVENTURE DIGEST MAGAZINE
Harvey Comics: 1992 - No. 7, Sept, 1994 ($1.25, quarterly, digest-size)

1-7 4.00

RICHIE RICH AND...
Harvey Comics: Oct, 1987 - No. 11, May, 1990 ($1.00)

1-Professor Keenbean 4.00
2-11: 2-Casper. 3-Dollar the Dog. 4-Cadbury. 5 Mayda Munny. 6-Irona. 7-Little Dot. 8-Professor Keenbean. 9-Little Audrey. 10-Mayda Munny. 11-Cadbury 3.00

RICHIE RICH AND BILLY BELLHOPS
Harvey Publications: Oct, 1977 (52 pgs., one-shot)

1 2 4 6 11 16 20

RICHIE RICH AND CADBURY
Harvey Publ.: 10/77; #2, 9/78 - #23, 7/82; #24, 7/90 - #29, 1/91 (1-10: 52pgs.)

	GD	VG	FN	VF	VF/NM	NM-
1-(52 pg. Giant)	2	4	6	11	16	20
2-10-(52 pg. Giant)	2	4	6	8	10	12
11-23						6.00
24-29: 24-Begin $1.00-c						4.00

RICHIE RICH AND CASPER

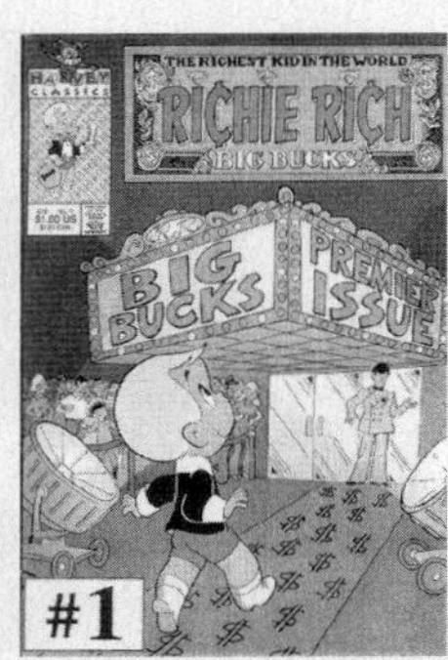

Richie Rich Big Bucks #1 © HARV

Richie Rich Diamonds #1 © HARV

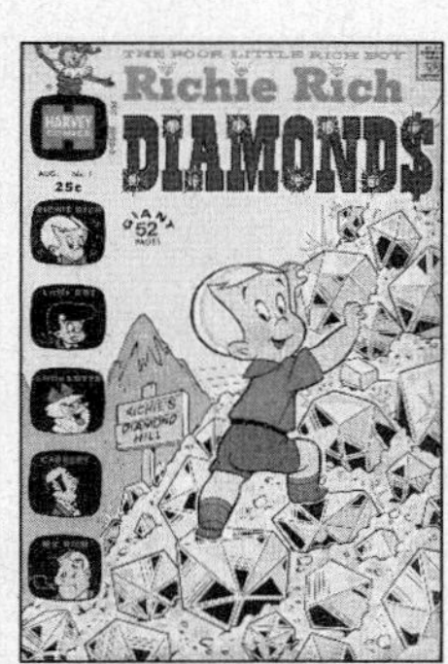

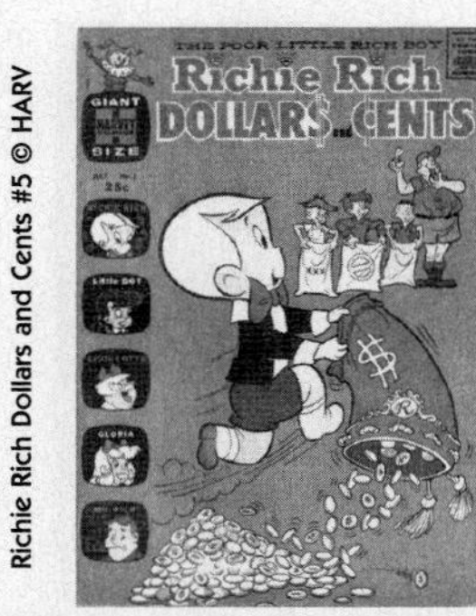

Richie Rich Dollars and Cents #5 © HARV

Harvey Publications: Aug, 1974 - No. 45, Sept, 1982

	GD 2.0	VG 4.0	FN 6.0	VF 8.0	VF/NM 9.0	NM- 9.2
1	3	6	9	19	30	40
2-5	2	4	6	13	18	22
6-10: 10-Xmas-c	2	4	6	9	13	16
11-20	1	3	4	6	8	10
21-45: 22-Xmas-c						6.00

RICHIE RICH AND DOLLAR THE DOG (See Richie Rich #65)
Harvey Publications: Sept, 1977 - No. 24, Aug, 1982 (#1-10: 52 pgs.)

	GD 2.0	VG 4.0	FN 6.0	VF 8.0	VF/NM 9.0	NM- 9.2
1-(52 pg. Giant)	2	4	6	11	16	20
2-10-(52 pg. Giant)	2	4	6	8	10	12
11-24						6.00

RICHIE RICH AND DOT
Harvey Publications: Oct, 1974 (one-shot)

	GD 2.0	VG 4.0	FN 6.0	VF 8.0	VF/NM 9.0	NM- 9.2
1	3	6	9	15	22	28

RICHIE RICH AND GLORIA
Harvey Publications: Sept, 1977 - No. 25, Sept, 1982 (#1-11: 52 pgs.)

	GD 2.0	VG 4.0	FN 6.0	VF 8.0	VF/NM 9.0	NM- 9.2
1-(52 pg. Giant)	2	4	6	11	16	20
2-11-(52 pg. Giant)	2	4	6	8	10	12
12-25						6.00

RICHIE RICH AND HIS GIRLFRIENDS
Harvey Publications: April, 1979 - No. 16, Dec, 1982

	GD 2.0	VG 4.0	FN 6.0	VF 8.0	VF/NM 9.0	NM- 9.2
1-(52 pg. Giant)	2	4	6	9	13	16
2-(52 pg. Giant)	1	3	4	6	8	10
3-10	1	2	3	5	6	8
11-16						6.00

RICHIE RICH AND HIS MEAN COUSIN REGGIE
Harvey Publications: April, 1979 - No. 3, 1980 (50¢) (#1,2: 52 pgs.)

	GD 2.0	VG 4.0	FN 6.0	VF 8.0	VF/NM 9.0	NM- 9.2
1	2	4	6	9	13	16
2-3:	1	3	4	6	8	10

NOTE: *No. 4 was advertised, but never released.*

RICHIE RICH AND JACKIE JOKERS (Also see Jackie Jokers)
Harvey Publications: Nov, 1973 - No. 48, Dec, 1982

	GD 2.0	VG 4.0	FN 6.0	VF 8.0	VF/NM 9.0	NM- 9.2
1: 52 pg. Giant; contains material from unpublished Jackie Jokers #5	4	8	12	23	37	50
2,3-(52 pg. Giants). 2-R.R. & Jackie 1st meet	3	6	9	15	22	28
4,5	2	4	6	13	18	22
6-10	2	4	6	9	13	16
11-20,26: 11-1st app. Kool Katz. 26-Star Wars parody	1	3	4	6	8	10
21-25,27-40	1	2	3	4	5	7
41-48						6.00

RICHIE RICH AND PROFESSOR KEENBEAN
Harvey Comics: Sept, 1990 - No. 2, Nov, 1990 ($1.00)

	GD 2.0	VG 4.0	FN 6.0	VF 8.0	VF/NM 9.0	NM- 9.2
1,2						3.00

RICHIE RICH AND THE NEW KIDS ON THE BLOCK
Harvey Publications: Feb, 1991 - No. 3, June, 1991 ($1.25, bi-monthly)

	GD 2.0	VG 4.0	FN 6.0	VF 8.0	VF/NM 9.0	NM- 9.2
1-3: 1,2-New Richie Rich stories						4.00

RICHIE RICH AND TIMMY TIME
Harvey Publications: Sept, 1977 (50¢, 52 pgs, one-shot)

	GD 2.0	VG 4.0	FN 6.0	VF 8.0	VF/NM 9.0	NM- 9.2
1	2	4	6	11	16	20

RICHIE RICH BANK BOOK
Harvey Publications: Oct, 1972 - No. 59, Sept, 1982

	GD 2.0	VG 4.0	FN 6.0	VF 8.0	VF/NM 9.0	NM- 9.2
1	4	8	12	28	47	65
2-5: 2-2nd app. The Money Monster	3	6	9	16	23	30
6-10	2	4	6	11	16	20
11-20: 18-Super Richie app.	2	4	6	8	10	12
21-30	1	2	3	5	7	9
31-40	1	2	3	4	5	7
41-59						6.00

RICHIE RICH BEST OF THE YEARS
Harvey Publications: Oct, 1977 - No. 6, June, 1980 (128 pgs., digest-size)

	GD 2.0	VG 4.0	FN 6.0	VF 8.0	VF/NM 9.0	NM- 9.2
1(10/77)-Reprints	2	4	6	9	12	15
2-6(11/79-6/80, 95¢). #2(10/78)-Rep.. #3(6/79, 75¢)	1	2	3	5	7	9

RICHIE RICH BIG BOOK
Harvey Publications: Nov, 1992 - No. 2, May, 1993 ($1.50, 52 pgs.)

	GD 2.0	VG 4.0	FN 6.0	VF 8.0	VF/NM 9.0	NM- 9.2
1,2						4.00

RICHIE RICH BIG BUCKS
Harvey Publications: Apr, 1991 - No. 8, July, 1992 ($1.00, bi-monthly)

	GD 2.0	VG 4.0	FN 6.0	VF 8.0	VF/NM 9.0	NM- 9.2
1-8						3.00

RICHIE RICH BILLIONS
Harvey Publications: Oct, 1974 - No. 48, Oct, 1982 (#1-33: 52 pgs.)

	GD 2.0	VG 4.0	FN 6.0	VF 8.0	VF/NM 9.0	NM- 9.2
1	3	6	9	21	33	45
2-5: 2-Christmas issue	3	6	9	14	20	25
6-10	2	4	6	10	14	18
11-20	2	4	6	8	10	12
21-33	1	2	3	5	6	8
34-48: 35-Onion app.						6.00

RICHIE RICH CASH
Harvey Publications: Sept, 1974 - No. 47, Aug, 1982

	GD 2.0	VG 4.0	FN 6.0	VF 8.0	VF/NM 9.0	NM- 9.2
1-1st app. Dr. N-R-Gee	3	6	9	19	30	40
2-5	2	4	6	13	18	22
6-10	2	4	6	9	13	16
11-20	1	3	4	6	8	10
21-30	1	2	3	4	5	7
31-47: 33-Dr. Blemish app.						6.00

RICHIE RICH CASH MONEY
Harvey Comics: May, 1992 - No. 2, Aug, 1992 ($1.25)

	GD 2.0	VG 4.0	FN 6.0	VF 8.0	VF/NM 9.0	NM- 9.2
1,2						3.00

RICHIE RICH, CASPER AND WENDY - NATIONAL LEAGUE
Harvey Comics: June, 1976 (50¢)

	GD 2.0	VG 4.0	FN 6.0	VF 8.0	VF/NM 9.0	NM- 9.2
1-Newsstand version of the baseball giveaway	2	4	6	13	18	22

RICHIE RICH COLLECTORS COMICS (See Harvey Collectors Comics)

RICHIE RICH DIAMONDS
Harvey Publications: Aug, 1972 - No. 59, Aug, 1982 (#1, 23-45: 52 pgs.)

	GD 2.0	VG 4.0	FN 6.0	VF 8.0	VF/NM 9.0	NM- 9.2
1-(52 pg. Giant)	5	10	15	30	50	70
2-5	3	6	9	16	23	30
6-10	2	4	6	11	16	20
11-22	2	4	6	8	10	12
23-30-(52 pg. Giants)	2	4	6	8	11	14
31-45: 39-r/Origin Little Dot	1	2	3	5	7	9
46-50	1	2	3	4	5	7
51-59						6.00

RICHIE RICH DIGEST MAGAZINE
Harvey Publications: Oct, 1986 - No. 42, Oct, 1994 ($1.25/$1.75, digest-size)

	GD 2.0	VG 4.0	FN 6.0	VF 8.0	VF/NM 9.0	NM- 9.2
1	1	2	3	5	6	8
2-10						5.00
11-20						4.00
21-42						4.00

RICHIE RICH DIGEST STORIES (...Magazine #?-on)
Harvey Publications: Oct, 1977 - No., 17, Oct, 1982 (75¢/95¢, digest-size)

	GD 2.0	VG 4.0	FN 6.0	VF 8.0	VF/NM 9.0	NM- 9.2
1-Reprints	2	4	6	9	12	15
2-10: Reprints	1	2	3	5	7	9
11-17: Reprints						6.00

RICHIE RICH DIGEST WINNERS
Harvey Publications: Dec, 1977 - No. 16, Sept, 1982 (75¢/95¢, 132 pgs., digest-size)

	GD 2.0	VG 4.0	FN 6.0	VF 8.0	VF/NM 9.0	NM- 9.2
1	2	4	6	9	12	15
2-5	1	2	3	5	7	9
6-16						6.00

RICHIE RICH DOLLARS & CENTS
Harvey Publications: Aug, 1963 - No. 109, Aug, 1982 (#1-43: 68 pgs.; 44-60, 71-94: 52 pgs.)

	GD 2.0	VG 4.0	FN 6.0	VF 8.0	VF/NM 9.0	NM- 9.2
1: (#1-64 are all reprint issues)	17	34	51	117	259	400
2	9	18	27	60	120	180
3-5: 5-r/1st app. of R.R. from Little Dot #1	8	16	24	54	102	150
6-10	6	12	18	40	73	105
11-20	4	8	12	28	47	65
21-30: 25-r/1st app. Nurse Jenny (Little Lotta #62)	3	6	9	21	33	45
31-43: 43-Last 68 pg. issue	3	6	9	17	26	35
44-60: All 52 pgs.	3	6	9	14	19	25
61-71	1	3	4	6	8	10
72-94: All 52 pgs.	2	4	6	8	10	12
95-99,101-109						6.00
100-Anniversary issue	1	2	3	5	7	9

RICHIE RICH FORTUNES
Harvey Publications: Sept, 1971 - No. 63, July, 1982 (#1-15: 52 pgs.)

	GD 2.0	VG 4.0	FN 6.0	VF 8.0	VF/NM 9.0	NM- 9.2
1	5	10	15	34	60	85

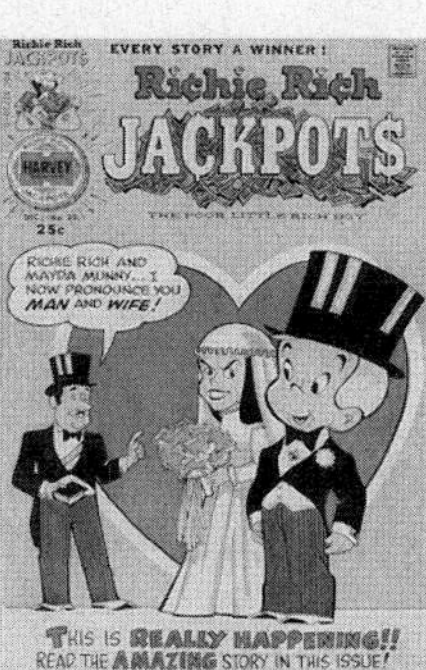

Richie Rich Jackpots #20 © HARV

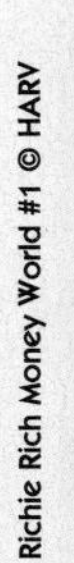

Richie Rich Money World #1 © HARV

Richie Rich Success Stories #66 © HARV

	GD 2.0	VG 4.0	FN 6.0	VF 8.0	VF/NM 9.0	NM- 9.2
2-5	3	6	9	19	30	40
6-10	2	4	6	13	18	22
11-15: 11-r/1st app. The Onion	2	4	6	9	12	15
16-30	1	2	3	5	7	9
31-40	1	2	3	4	5	7
41-63: 62-Onion app.						6.00

RICHIE RICH GEMS
Harvey Publications: Sept, 1974 - No. 43, Sept, 1982

	GD 2.0	VG 4.0	FN 6.0	VF 8.0	VF/NM 9.0	NM- 9.2
1	3	6	9	19	30	40
2-5	2	4	6	13	18	22
6-10	2	4	6	9	13	16
11-20	1	3	4	6	8	10
21-30	1	2	3	4	5	7
31-43: 36-Dr. Blemish, Onion app. 38-1st app. Stone-Age Riches						6.00
44-48 (Ape Entertainment, 2011-2012, $3.99) new stories w/Colon-a & reprints						4.00
... Special Collection (Ape Entertainment, 2012, $6.99) r/Valentine & Winter Specials						7.00
... Valentines Special (Ape Entertainment, 2012, $3.99) new story w/Colon-a & reprints						4.00
... Winter Special (Ape Entertainment, 2011, $3.99) new story w/Colon-a & reprints						4.00

RICHIE RICH GOLD AND SILVER
Harvey Publications: Sept, 1975 - No. 42, Oct, 1982 (#1-27: 52 pgs.)

	GD 2.0	VG 4.0	FN 6.0	VF 8.0	VF/NM 9.0	NM- 9.2
1	3	6	9	17	26	35
2-5	2	4	6	11	16	20
6-10	2	4	6	8	11	14
11-27	1	2	3	5	7	9
28-42: 34-Stone-Age Riches app.						6.00

RICHIE RICH GOLD NUGGETS DIGEST
Harvey Publications: Dec., 1990 - No. 4, June, 1991 ($1.75, digest-size)

	GD 2.0	VG 4.0	FN 6.0	VF 8.0	VF/NM 9.0	NM- 9.2
1-4						4.00

RICHIE RICH HOLIDAY DIGEST MAGAZINE (...Digest #4)
Harvey Publications: Jan, 1980 - #3, Jan, 1982; #4, 3/88; #5, 2/89 (annual)

	GD 2.0	VG 4.0	FN 6.0	VF 8.0	VF/NM 9.0	NM- 9.2
1-X-Mas-c	1	3	4	6	8	10
2-5: 2,3: All X-Mas-c. 4-(3/88, $1.25), 5-(2/89, $1.75)	1	2	3	4	5	7

RICHIE RICH INVENTIONS
Harvey Publications: Oct, 1977 - No. 26, Oct, 1982 (#1-11: 52 pgs.)

	GD 2.0	VG 4.0	FN 6.0	VF 8.0	VF/NM 9.0	NM- 9.2
1	2	4	6	11	16	20
2-5	2	4	6	8	10	12
6-11	1	2	3	5	6	8
12-26						6.00

RICHIE RICH JACKPOTS
Harvey Publications: Oct, 1972 - No. 58, Aug, 1982 (#41-43: 52 pgs.)

	GD 2.0	VG 4.0	FN 6.0	VF 8.0	VF/NM 9.0	NM- 9.2
1-Debut of Cousin Jackpots	4	8	12	28	47	65
2-5	3	6	9	16	23	30
6-10	2	4	6	11	16	20
11-15,17-20	2	4	6	8	10	12
16-Super Richie app.	2	4	6	9	12	15
21-30	1	2	3	5	7	9
31-40,44-50: 37-Caricatures of Frank Sinatra, Dean Martin, Sammy Davis, Jr. 45-Dr. Blemish app.	1	2	3	4	5	7
41-43 (52 pgs.)	1	3	4	6	8	10
51-58						6.00

RICHIE RICH MILLION DOLLAR DIGEST (...Magazine #?-on)(See Million Dollar Digest)
Harvey Publications: Oct, 1980 - No. 10, Oct, 1982 ($1.50)

	GD 2.0	VG 4.0	FN 6.0	VF 8.0	VF/NM 9.0	NM- 9.2
1	1	3	4	6	8	10
2-10						7.00

RICHIE RICH MILLIONS
Harvey Publ.: 9/61; #2, 9/62 - #113, 10/82 (#1-48: 68 pgs.; 49-64, 85-97: 52 pgs.)

	GD 2.0	VG 4.0	FN 6.0	VF 8.0	VF/NM 9.0	NM- 9.2
1: (#1-3 are all reprint issues)	21	42	63	147	324	500
2	10	20	30	66	138	210
3-5: All other giants are new & reprints. 5-1st 15 pg. Richie Rich story	8	16	24	56	108	160
6-10	7	14	21	49	92	135
11-20	5	10	15	35	63	90
21-30	4	8	12	27	44	60
31-48: 31-1st app. The Onion. 48-Last 68 pg. Giant	3	6	9	19	30	40
49-64: 52 pg. Giants	3	6	9	14	20	25
65-67,69-73,75-84	2	4	6	8	10	12
68-1st Super Richie-c (11/74)	2	4	6	13	18	22
74-1st app. Mr. Woody; Super Richie app.	2	4	6	8	11	14
85-97: 52 pg. Giants	2	4	6	8	11	14
98,99	1	2	3	4	5	7
100	1	2	3	5	7	9
101-113						6.00

RICHIE RICH MONEY WORLD
Harvey Publications: Sept, 1972 - No. 59, Sept, 1982

	GD 2.0	VG 4.0	FN 6.0	VF 8.0	VF/NM 9.0	NM- 9.2
1-(52 pg. Giant)-1st app. Mayda Munny	5	10	15	33	57	80
2-Super Richie app.	3	6	9	17	26	35
3-5	3	6	9	16	23	30
6-10: 9,10-Richie Rich mistakenly named Little Lotta on covers	2	4	6	11	16	20
11-20: 16,20-Dr. N-R-Gee	2	4	6	8	10	12
21-30	1	2	3	5	7	9
31-50	1	2	3	4	5	7
51-59						6.00
Digest 1 (2/91, $1.75)						5.00
2-8 (12/93, $1.75)						3.00

RICHIE RICH PROFITS
Harvey Publications: Oct, 1974 - No. 47, Sept, 1982

	GD 2.0	VG 4.0	FN 6.0	VF 8.0	VF/NM 9.0	NM- 9.2
1	3	6	9	19	30	40
2-5	2	4	6	13	18	22
6-10: 10-Origin of Dr. N-R-Gee	2	4	6	9	13	16
11-20: 15-Christmas-c	1	3	4	6	8	10
21-30	1	2	3	4	5	7
31-47						6.00

RICHIE RICH RELICS
Harvey Comics: Jan, 1988 - No.4, Feb, 1989 (75¢/$1.00, reprints)

	GD 2.0	VG 4.0	FN 6.0	VF 8.0	VF/NM 9.0	NM- 9.2
1-4						3.00

RICHIE RICH RICHES
Harvey Publications: July, 1972 - No. 59, Aug, 1982 (#1, 2, 41-45: 52 pgs.)

	GD 2.0	VG 4.0	FN 6.0	VF 8.0	VF/NM 9.0	NM- 9.2
1-(52 pg. Giant)-1st app. The Money Monster	5	10	15	33	57	80
2-(52 pg. Giant)	3	6	9	19	30	40
3-5	3	6	9	16	23	30
6-10: 7-1st app. Aunt Novo	2	4	6	11	16	20
11-20: 17-Super Richie app. (3/75)	2	4	6	8	10	12
21-40	1	2	3	5	6	8
41-45: 52 pg. Giants	1	3	4	6	8	10
46-59: 56-Dr. Blemish app.						6.00

RICHIE RICH: RICH RESCUE
Ape Entertainment: 2011 - No. 4, 2011 ($3.95, limited series)

	GD 2.0	VG 4.0	FN 6.0	VF 8.0	VF/NM 9.0	NM- 9.2
1-6-New short stories by various incl. Ernie Colon; Jack Lawrence-c						4.00
FCBD Edition (2011, giveaway) Flip book with Kung Fu Panda						3.00

RICHIE RICH SUCCESS STORIES
Harvey Publications: Nov, 1964 - No. 105, Sept, 1982 (#1-38: 68 pgs., 39-55, 67-90: 52 pgs.)

	GD 2.0	VG 4.0	FN 6.0	VF 8.0	VF/NM 9.0	NM- 9.2
1	16	32	48	112	249	385
2	9	18	27	57	111	165
3-5	8	16	24	51	96	140
6-10	5	10	15	35	63	90
11-20	5	10	15	31	53	75
21-30: 27-1st Penny Van Dough (8/69)	4	8	12	23	37	50
31-38: 38-Last 68 pg. Giant	3	6	9	19	30	40
39-55-(52 pgs.): 44-Super Richie app.	3	6	9	14	20	25
56-66	2	4	6	8	10	12
67-90: 52 pgs.	2	4	6	8	11	14
91-99,101-105: 91-Onion app. 101-Dr. Blemish app.						6.00
100	1	2	3	5	7	9

RICHIE RICH SUMMER BONANZA
Harvey Comics: Oct, 1991 ($1.95, one-shot, 68 pgs.)

	GD 2.0	VG 4.0	FN 6.0	VF 8.0	VF/NM 9.0	NM- 9.2
1-Richie Rich, Little Dot, Little Lotta						4.00

RICHIE RICH TREASURE CHEST DIGEST (...Magazine #3)
Harvey Publications: Apr, 1982 - No. 3, Aug, 1982 (95¢, Digest Mag.)
(#4 advertised but not publ.)

	GD 2.0	VG 4.0	FN 6.0	VF 8.0	VF/NM 9.0	NM- 9.2
1	1	3	4	6	8	10
2,3	1	2	3	4	5	7

RICHIE RICH VACATION DIGEST
Harvey Comics: Oct, 1991; Oct, 1992; Oct, 1993 ($1.75, digest-size)

	GD 2.0	VG 4.0	FN 6.0	VF 8.0	VF/NM 9.0	NM- 9.2
1-(10/91), 1-(10/92), 1-(10/93)						4.00

RICHIE RICH VACATIONS DIGEST
Harvey Publ.: 11/77; No. 2, 10/78 - No. 7, 10/81; No. 8, 8/82; No. 9, 10/82 (Digest, 132 pgs.)

Rick and Morty #1 © Cartoon Network

The Rider #2 © AJAX

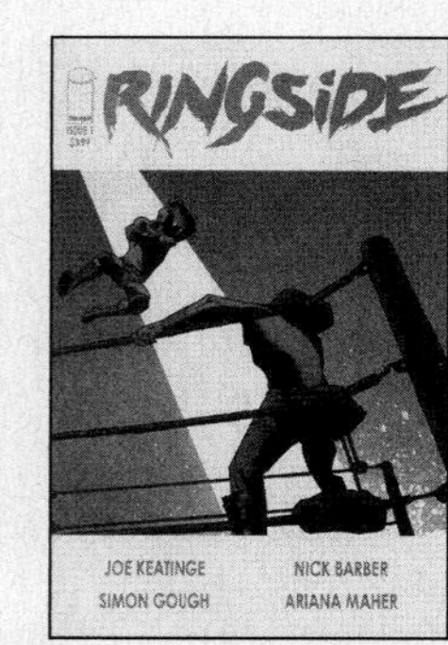

Ringside #1 © Keatinge & Barber

	GD 2.0	VG 4.0	FN 6.0	VF 8.0	VF/NM 9.0	NM- 9.2
1-Reprints	2	4	6	9	12	15
2-6	1	2	3	5	7	9
7-9						6.00

RICHIE RICH VAULT OF MYSTERY
Harvey Publications: Nov, 1974 - No. 47, Sept, 1982

	GD 2.0	VG 4.0	FN 6.0	VF 8.0	VF/NM 9.0	NM- 9.2
1	3	6	9	19	30	40
2-5: 5-The Condor app.	2	4	6	13	18	22
6-10	2	4	6	9	13	16
11-20	1	3	4	6	8	10
21-30	1	2	3	4	5	7
31-47						6.00

RICHIE RICH ZILLIONZ
Harvey Publ.: Oct, 1976 - No. 33, Sept, 1982 (#1-4: 68 pgs.; #5-18: 52 pgs.)

	GD 2.0	VG 4.0	FN 6.0	VF 8.0	VF/NM 9.0	NM- 9.2
1	3	6	9	17	26	35
2-4: 4-Last 68 pg. Giant	2	4	6	11	16	20
5-10	2	4	6	8	10	12
11-18: 18-Last 52 pg. Giant	1	2	3	5	6	8
19-33						6.00

RICH JOHNSTON'S... (Parody of the Avengers movie characters)
BOOM! Studios: Apr, 2012 ($3.99, series of one-shots)

	GD 2.0	VG 4.0	FN 6.0	VF 8.0	VF/NM 9.0	NM- 9.2
... Captain American Idol 1 - Rich Johnston-s/Chris Haley-a						4.00
... Iron Muslim 1 - Rich Johnston-s/Bryan Turner-a; Demon in a Bottle cover swipe						4.00
... Scienthorlogy 1 - Rich Johnston-s/Michael Netzer-a						4.00
... The Avengefuls 1 - Rich Johnston-s/Joshua Covey; two printings						4.00

RICK AND MORTY (Based on the Adult Swim animated series)
Oni Press: Apr, 2015 - Present ($3.99)

	GD 2.0	VG 4.0	FN 6.0	VF 8.0	VF/NM 9.0	NM- 9.2
1-Zac Gorman-s/CJ Cannon-a; multiple covers	5	10	15	31	53	75
2,3	2	4	6	9	12	15
4-23						4.00

RICK AND MORTY: LIL' POOPY SUPERSTAR (Adult Swim)
Oni Press: Jul, 2016 - No. 5, Nov, 2016 ($3.99, limited series)

	GD 2.0	VG 4.0	FN 6.0	VF 8.0	VF/NM 9.0	NM- 9.2
1-5-Sarah Graley-s/a; multiple covers						20.00

RICKY
Standard Comics (Visual Editions): No. 5, Sept, 1953

	GD 2.0	VG 4.0	FN 6.0	VF 8.0	VF/NM 9.0	NM- 9.2
5-Teenage humor	8	16	24	42	54	65

RICKY NELSON (TV)(See Sweethearts V2#42)
Dell Publishing Co.: No. 956, Dec, 1958 - No. 1192, June, 1961 (All photo-c)

	GD 2.0	VG 4.0	FN 6.0	VF 8.0	VF/NM 9.0	NM- 9.2
Four Color 956,998	15	30	45	100	220	340
Four Color 1115,1192: 1192-Manning-a	12	24	36	80	173	265

RIDE, THE (Also see Gun Candy flip-book)
Image Comics: June, 2004 - No. 2, July, 2004 ($2.95, B&W, anthology)

	GD 2.0	VG 4.0	FN 6.0	VF 8.0	VF/NM 9.0	NM- 9.2
1,2: Hughes-c/Wagner-s. 1-Hamner & Stelfreeze-a. 2-Jeanty & Pearson-a						3.00
... Die Valkyrie 1-3 (6/07 - No. 3, 2/08, $2.99) Stelfreeze-a/Wagner-s/Pearson-c						3.00
... Foreign Parts 1 (1/05, $2.95) Dixon-s/Haynes-a; Marz-s/Brunner-a; Pearson-c						3.00
... Halloween Special: The Key to Survival (10/07, $3.50) Tomm Coker-s/a						3.50
... Savannah 1 (4/07, $4.99) s/a by students of Savannah College of Art						5.00
... 2 For the Road 1 (10/04, $2.95) Dixon-s/Hamner & Gregory-a/Johnson-c						3.00
Vol. 1 TPB (2005, $9.99) r/#1,2, Foreign Parts, 2 For the Road; Chaykin intro.						10.00
Vol. 2 TPB (2005, $15.99) r/Gun Candy #1,2 & Die Valkyrie #1-3; sketch pages						16.00

RIDER, THE (Frontier Trail #6; also see Blazing Sixguns I.W. Reprint #10, 11)
Ajax/Farrell Publ. (Four Star Comic Corp.): Mar, 1957 - No. 5, 1958

	GD 2.0	VG 4.0	FN 6.0	VF 8.0	VF/NM 9.0	NM- 9.2
1-Swift Arrow, Lone Rider begin	13	26	39	72	101	130
2-5	8	16	24	42	54	65

RIDERS OF THE PURPLE SAGE (See Zane Grey & Four Color #372)

RIFLEMAN, THE (TV)
Dell Publ. Co./Gold Key No. 13 on: No. 1009, 7-9/59 - No. 12, 7-9/62; No. 13, 11/62 - No. 20, 10/64

	GD 2.0	VG 4.0	FN 6.0	VF 8.0	VF/NM 9.0	NM- 9.2
Four Color 1009 (#1)	20	40	60	138	307	475
2 (1-3/60)	10	20	30	65	135	200
3-Toth-a (4 pgs.); variant edition has back-c with "Something Special" comic strip	10	20	30	65	135	200
4-9: 6-Toth-a (4 pgs.)	9	18	27	59	117	175
10-Classic-c	21	42	63	147	324	500
11-20	7	14	21	46	86	125

NOTE: ***Warren Tufts** a-2-9. All have Chuck Connors & Johnny Crawford photo-c. Photo back c-13-15.*

RIFTWAR
Marvel Comics: July, 2009 - No. 5, Dec, 2009 ($3.99, limited series)

	GD 2.0	VG 4.0	FN 6.0	VF 8.0	VF/NM 9.0	NM- 9.2
1-5-Adaptation of Raymond E. Feist novel; Glass-s/Stegman-a						4.00

RIMA, THE JUNGLE GIRL
National Periodical Publications: Apr-May, 1974 - No. 7, Apr-May, 1975

	GD 2.0	VG 4.0	FN 6.0	VF 8.0	VF/NM 9.0	NM- 9.2
1-Origin, part 1 (#1-5: 20¢; 6,7: 25¢)	2	4	6	13	18	22
2-7: 2-4-Origin, parts 2-4. 7-Origin & only app. Space Marshal	2	3	4	6	8	10

NOTE: ***Kubert** c-1-7. **Nino** a-1-7. **Redondo** a-1-7.*

RING OF BRIGHT WATER (See Movie Classics)

RING OF THE NIBELUNG, THE
DC Comics: 1989 - No. 4, 1990 ($4.95, squarebound, 52 pgs., mature readers)

	GD 2.0	VG 4.0	FN 6.0	VF 8.0	VF/NM 9.0	NM- 9.2
1-4: Adapts Wagner cycle of operas, Gil Kane-c/a						5.00

RING OF THE NIBELUNG, THE
Dark Horse Comics: Feb, 2000 - Sept, 2001 ($2.95/$2.99/$5.99, limited series)

	GD 2.0	VG 4.0	FN 6.0	VF 8.0	VF/NM 9.0	NM- 9.2
Vol. 1 (The Rhinegold) 1-4: Adapts Wagner; P. Craig Russell-s/a						3.00
Vol. 2,3: Vol. 2 (The Valkyrie) 1-3: 1-(8/00). Vol. 3 (Siegfried) 1-3: 1-(12/00)						3.00
Vol. 4 (The Twilight of the Gods) 1-3: 1-(6/01)						3.00
4-(9/01, $5.99, 64 pgs.) Conclusion with sketch pages						6.00

RINGO KID, THE (2nd Series)
Marvel Comics Group: Jan, 1970 - No. 23, Nov, 1973; No. 24, Nov, 1975 - No. 30, Nov, 1976

	GD 2.0	VG 4.0	FN 6.0	VF 8.0	VF/NM 9.0	NM- 9.2
1-Williamson-a r-from #10, 1956.	3	6	9	19	30	40
2-11: 2-Severin-c. 11-Last 15¢ issue	2	4	6	11	16	20
12 (52 pg. Giant)	3	6	9	15	22	28
13-20: 13-Wildey-r. 20-Williamson-r/#1	2	4	6	9	13	16
21-30	2	4	6	8	10	12
27,28-(30¢-c variant, limited distribution)(5,7/76)	11	22	33	76	163	250

RINGO KID WESTERN, THE (1st Series) (See Wild Western & Western Trails)
Atlas Comics (HPC)/Marvel Comics: Aug, 1954 - No. 21, Sept, 1957

	GD 2.0	VG 4.0	FN 6.0	VF 8.0	VF/NM 9.0	NM- 9.2
1-Origin; The Ringo Kid begins	36	72	108	216	351	485
2-Black Rider app.; origin/1st app. Ringo's Horse Arab	18	36	54	107	169	230
3-5	14	28	42	82	121	160
6-8-Severin-a(3) each	15	30	45	84	127	170
9,11,12,14-21: 12-Orlando-a (4 pgs.)	13	26	39	72	101	130
10,13-Williamson-a (4 pgs.)	14	28	42	76	108	140

NOTE: ***Berg** a-8. **Maneely** a-1-5, 15, 16(text illos only), 17(4), 18, 20, 21; c-1-6, 8, 13, 15-18, 20. **J. Severin** c-10, 11. **Sinnott** a-1. **Wildey** a-16-18.*

RINGSIDE
Image Comics: Nov, 2015 - Present ($3.99)

	GD 2.0	VG 4.0	FN 6.0	VF 8.0	VF/NM 9.0	NM- 9.2
1-8-Keatinge-s/Barber-a						4.00

RINSE, THE
BOOM! Studios: Sept, 2011 - No. 4, Dec, 2011 ($1.00/$3.99)

	GD 2.0	VG 4.0	FN 6.0	VF 8.0	VF/NM 9.0	NM- 9.2
1-($1.00)-Phillips-s/Laming-a						3.00
2-4-($3.99)						4.00

RIN TIN TIN (See March of Comics #163,180,195)

RIN TIN TIN (TV) (...& Rusty #21 on; see Western Roundup under Dell Giants)
Dell Publishing Co./Gold Key: Nov, 1952 - No. 38, May-July, 1961; Nov, 1963 (All Photo-c)

	GD 2.0	VG 4.0	FN 6.0	VF 8.0	VF/NM 9.0	NM- 9.2
Four Color 434 (#1)	14	28	42	97	214	330
Four Color 476,523	9	18	27	57	111	165
4(3-5/54)-10	6	12	18	40	73	105
11-17,19,20	6	12	18	37	66	95
18-(4-5/57) 1st app. of Rusty and the Cavalry of Fort Apache; photo-c	7	14	21	46	86	125
21-38: 36-Toth-a (4 pgs.)	5	10	15	31	53	75
... & Rusty 1 (11/63-Gold Key)	5	10	15	33	57	80

RIO (Also see Eclipse Monthly)
Comico: June, 1987 ($8.95, 64 pgs.)

	GD 2.0	VG 4.0	FN 6.0	VF 8.0	VF/NM 9.0	NM- 9.2
1-Wildey-c/a						9.00

RIO AT BAY
Dark Horse Comics: July, 1992 - No. 2, Aug, 1992 ($2.95, limited series)

	GD 2.0	VG 4.0	FN 6.0	VF 8.0	VF/NM 9.0	NM- 9.2
1,2-Wildey-c/a						3.00

RIO BRAVO (Movie) (See 4-Color #1018)
Dell Publishing Co.: June, 1959

	GD 2.0	VG 4.0	FN 6.0	VF 8.0	VF/NM 9.0	NM- 9.2
Four Color 1018-Toth-a; John Wayne, Dean Martin, & Ricky Nelson photo-c.	24	48	72	168	372	575

RIO CONCHOS (See Movie Comics)

RIOT (Satire)

Riot #6 © MAR

Rip Hunter Time Master #8 © DC

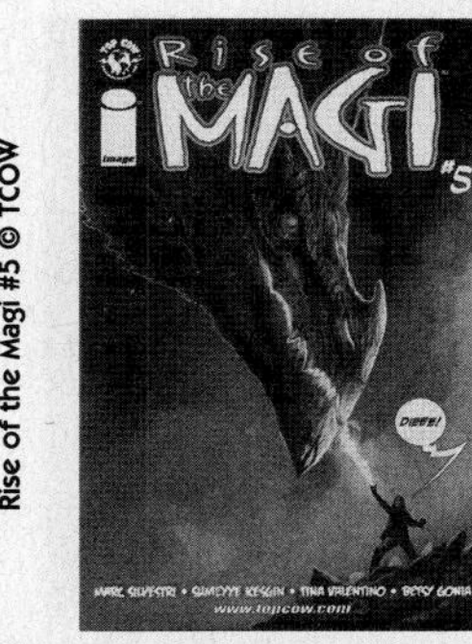

Rise of the Magi #5 © TCOW

Atlas Comics (ACI No. 1-5/WPI No. 6): Apr, 1954 - No. 3, Aug, 1954; No. 4, Feb, 1956 - No. 6, June, 1956

	GD 2.0	VG 4.0	FN 6.0	VF 8.0	VF/NM 9.0	NM- 9.2
1-Russ Heath-a	42	84	126	265	445	625
2-Li'l Abner satire by Post	29	58	87	170	278	385
3-Last precode (8/54)	25	50	75	150	245	340
4-Infinity-c; Marilyn Monroe "7 Year Itch" movie satire; Mad Rip-off ads	32	64	96	190	310	430
5-Marilyn Monroe, John Wayne parody; part photo-c	33	66	99	194	317	440
6-Lorna of the Jungle satire by Everett; Dennis the Menace satire-c/story; part photo-c	25	50	75	150	245	340

NOTE: ***Berg** a-3. **Burgos** c-1, 2. **Colan** a-1. **Everett** a-4, 6. **Heath** a-1. **Maneely** a-1, 2, 4-6; c-3, 4, 6. **Post** a-1-4. **Reinman** a-2. **Severin** a-4-6.*

RIOT GEAR
Triumphant Comics: Sept, 1993 - No. 11, July, 1994 ($2.50, serially numbered)

	GD 2.0	VG 4.0	FN 6.0	VF 8.0	VF/NM 9.0	NM- 9.2
1-11: 1-2nd app. Riot Gear. 2-1st app. Rabin. 3,4-Triumphant Unleashed x-over. 3-1st app. Surzar. 4-Death of Captain Tich						3.00
Violent Past 1,2: 1-(2/94, $2.50)						3.00

R.I.P.
TSR, Inc.: 1990 - No. 8, 1991 ($2.95, 44 pgs.)

	GD 2.0	VG 4.0	FN 6.0	VF 8.0	VF/NM 9.0	NM- 9.2
1-8-Based on TSR game						4.00

RIPCLAW (See Cyberforce)
Image Comics (Top Cow Prod.): Apr, 1995 - No. 3, June, 1995 (Limited series)

	GD 2.0	VG 4.0	FN 6.0	VF 8.0	VF/NM 9.0	NM- 9.2
1/2-Gold, 1/2-San Diego ed., 1/2-Chicago ed.	1	3	4	6	8	10
1-3: Brandon Peterson-a(p)						3.00
Special 1 (10/95, $2.50)						3.00

RIPCLAW
Image Comics (Top Cow Prod.): V2#1, Dec, 1995 - No. 6, June, 1996 ($2.50)

	GD 2.0	VG 4.0	FN 6.0	VF 8.0	VF/NM 9.0	NM- 9.2
V2#1-6: 5-Medieval Spawn/Witchblade Preview						3.00
...: Pilot Season 1 (2007, $2.99) Jason Aaron-s/Jorge Lucas-a/Tony Moore-c						3.00

RIPCORD (TV)
Dell Publishing Co.: Mar-May, 1962

	GD 2.0	VG 4.0	FN 6.0	VF 8.0	VF/NM 9.0	NM- 9.2
Four Color 1294	6	12	18	40	73	105

R.I.P.D.
Dark Horse Comics: Oct, 1999 - No. 4, Jan, 2000 ($2.95, limited series)

	GD 2.0	VG 4.0	FN 6.0	VF 8.0	VF/NM 9.0	NM- 9.2
1-4						3.00
TPB (2003, $12.95) r/#1-4						13.00

R.I.P.D.: CITY OF THE DAMNED
Dark Horse Comics: Nov, 2012 - No. 4, Mar, 2013 ($3.50, limited series)

	GD 2.0	VG 4.0	FN 6.0	VF 8.0	VF/NM 9.0	NM- 9.2
1-4-Barlow-s/Parker-a/Wilkins-c						3.50

RIP HUNTER TIME MASTER (See Showcase #20, 21, 25, 26 & Time Masters)
National Periodical Publications: Mar-Apr, 1961 - No. 29, Nov-Dec, 1965

	GD 2.0	VG 4.0	FN 6.0	VF 8.0	VF/NM 9.0	NM- 9.2
1-(3-4/61)	57	114	171	456	1028	1600
2	25	50	75	175	388	600
3-5: 5-Last 10¢ issue	15	30	45	105	232	360
6,7-Toth-a in each	10	20	30	68	144	220
8-15	8	16	24	54	102	150
16-19	6	12	18	41	76	110
20-Hitler-c/s	8	16	24	51	96	140
21-29: 29-Gil Kane-c	6	12	18	37	66	95

RIP IN TIME (Also see Teenage Mutant Ninja Turtles #5-7)
Fantagor Press: Aug, 1986 - No.5, 1987 ($1.50, B&W)

	GD 2.0	VG 4.0	FN 6.0	VF 8.0	VF/NM 9.0	NM- 9.2
1-5: Corben-c/a in all						4.00

RIP KIRBY (Also see Harvey Comics Hits #57, & Street Comix)
David McKay Publications: 1948

	GD 2.0	VG 4.0	FN 6.0	VF 8.0	VF/NM 9.0	NM- 9.2
Feature Books 51,54: Raymond-c; 51-Origin	36	72	108	216	351	485

RIPLEY'S BELIEVE IT OR NOT! (See Ace Comics, All-American Comics, Mystery Comics Digest #1, 4, 7, 10, 13, 16, 19, 22, 25)

RIPLEY'S BELIEVE IT OR NOT!
Harvey Publications: Sept, 1953 - No. 4, March, 1954

	GD 2.0	VG 4.0	FN 6.0	VF 8.0	VF/NM 9.0	NM- 9.2
1-Powell-a	14	28	42	76	108	140
2-4	10	20	30	54	72	90

RIPLEY'S BELIEVE IT OR NOT! (Continuation of Ripleys'...True Ghost Stories & Ripley's...True War Stories)
Gold Key: No. 4, April, 1967 - No. 94, Feb, 1980

	GD 2.0	VG 4.0	FN 6.0	VF 8.0	VF/NM 9.0	NM- 9.2
4-Shrunken head photo-c; McWilliams-a	4	8	12	23	37	50
5-Subtitled "True War Stories"; Evans-a; 1st Jeff Jones-a in comics? (2 pgs.)	4	8	12	23	37	50
6-10: 6-McWilliams-a. 10-Evans-a(2)	3	6	9	19	30	40
11-20: 15-Evans-a	3	6	9	16	23	30
21-30	2	4	6	13	18	22
31-38,40-60	2	4	6	9	13	16
39-Crandall-a	2	4	6	10	14	18
61-73	1	3	4	6	8	10
74,77-83-(52 pgs.)	2	4	6	9	13	16
75,76,84-94	1	2	3	5	6	8
Story Digest Mag. 1(6/70)-4-3/4x6-1/2", 148pp.	5	10	15	31	53	75

NOTE: ***Evanish** art by **Luiz Dominguez** #22-25, 27, 30, 31, 40. **Jeff Jones** a-5(2 pgs.). **McWilliams** a-65, 66, 70, 89. **Orlando** a-8. **Sparling** c-68. Reprints-74, 77-84, 87 (part); 91, 93 (all). **Williamson, Wood** a-80r/#1.*

RIPLEY'S BELIEVE IT OR NOT!
Dark Horse Comics: May, 2002 - No. 3, Oct, 2002 ($2.99, B&W, unfinished limited series)

	GD 2.0	VG 4.0	FN 6.0	VF 8.0	VF/NM 9.0	NM- 9.2
1-3-Nord-c/a. 1-Stories of Amelia Earhart & D.B. Cooper						3.00

RIPLEY'S BELIEVE IT OR NOT! TRUE GHOST STORIES (Along with Ripley's...True War Stories, the three issues together precede the 1967 series that starts its numbering with #4) (Also see Dan Curtis)
Gold Key: June, 1965 - No. 2, Oct, 1966

	GD 2.0	VG 4.0	FN 6.0	VF 8.0	VF/NM 9.0	NM- 9.2
1-Williamson, Wood & Evans-a; photo-c	7	14	21	44	82	120
2-Orlando, McWilliams-a; photo-c	4	8	12	27	44	60
Mini-Comic 1(1976-3-1/4x6-1/2")	2	4	6	8	11	14
11186(1977)-Golden Press; ($1.95, 224 pgs.)-All-r	4	8	12	23	37	50
11401(3/79)-Golden Press; ($1.00, 96 pgs.)-All-r	3	6	9	15	21	26

RIPLEY'S BELIEVE IT OR NOT! TRUE WAR STORIES (Along with Ripley's...True Ghost Stories, the three issues together precede the 1967 series that starts its numbering with #4)
Gold Key: Nov, 1965 (Aug, 1965 in indicia)

	GD 2.0	VG 4.0	FN 6.0	VF 8.0	VF/NM 9.0	NM- 9.2
1-No Williamson-a	4	8	12	27	44	60

RIPLEY'S BELIEVE IT OR NOT! TRUE WEIRD
Ripley Enterprises: June, 1966 - No. 2, Aug, 1966 (B&W Magazine)

	GD 2.0	VG 4.0	FN 6.0	VF 8.0	VF/NM 9.0	NM- 9.2
1,2-Comic stories & text	3	6	9	17	26	35

RISE OF APOCALYPSE
Marvel Comics: Oct, 1996 - No. 4, Jan, 1997 ($1.95, limited series)

	GD 2.0	VG 4.0	FN 6.0	VF 8.0	VF/NM 9.0	NM- 9.2
1-Adam Pollina-c/a in all	1	3	4	6	8	10
2-4						5.00

RISE OF THE BLACK FLAME
Dark Horse Comics: Sept, 2016 - No. 5, Jan, 2017 ($3.99, limited series)

	GD 2.0	VG 4.0	FN 6.0	VF 8.0	VF/NM 9.0	NM- 9.2
1-5-Mignola & Roberson-s/Mitten-a/Laurence Campbell-c						4.00

RISE OF THE MAGI
Image Comics (Top Cow): No. 0, May, 2014 - No. 5 ($3.50)

	GD 2.0	VG 4.0	FN 6.0	VF 8.0	VF/NM 9.0	NM- 9.2
0 (5/14, Free Comic Book Day giveaway) Silvestri-s/c; bonus character & concept art						3.00
1-5: 1-(6/14) Silvestri-s/Kesgin-a; four covers						3.50

RISING STARS
Image Comics (Top Cow): Mar, 1999 - No. 24, Mar, 2005 ($2.50/$2.99)

	GD 2.0	VG 4.0	FN 6.0	VF 8.0	VF/NM 9.0	NM- 9.2
Preview-(3/99, $5.00) Straczynski-s						6.00
0-(6/00, $2.50) Gary Frank-a/c						3.00
1/2-(8/01, $2.95) Anderson-c; art & sketch pages by Zanier						3.00
1-Four covers; Keu Cha-c/a						5.00
1-($10.00) Gold Editions-four covers						10.00
1-($50.00) Holofoil-c						50.00
2-7: 5-7-Zanier & Lashley-a(p)						4.00
8-23: 8-13-Zanier & Lashley-a(p). 14-Immonen-a. 15-Flip book B&W preview of Universe. 15-23-Brent Anderson-a						3.00
24-($3.99) Series finale; Anderson-a/c						4.00
Born In Fire TPB (11/00, $19.95) r/#1-8; foreword by Neil Gaiman						20.00
Power TPB (2002, $19.95) r/#9-16						20.00
Prelude-(10/00, $2.95) Cha-a/Lashley-c						3.00
...: Visitations (2002, $8.99) r/#0, 1/2, Preview; new Anderson-c; cover gallery						9.00
Vol. 3: Fire and Ash TPB (2005, $19.99) r/#17-24; design pages & cover gallery						20.00
Vol. 4 TPB (2006, $19.99) r/Rising Stars Bright #1-3 and Voices of the Dead #1-6						20.00
Vol. 5 TPB (2007, $16.99) r/Rising Stars: Untouchable #1-5 and ...: Visitations						17.00
Wizard #0-(3/99) Wizard supplement; Straczynski-s						3.00
Wizard #1/2						5.00

RISING STARS BRIGHT
Image Comics (Top Cow): Mar, 2003 - No. 3, May, 2003 ($2.99, limited series)

	GD 2.0	VG 4.0	FN 6.0	VF 8.0	VF/NM 9.0	NM- 9.2
1-3-Avery-s/Jurgens & Gorder-a/Beck-c						3.00

RISING STARS: UNTOUCHABLE

Riverdale One-Shot © ACP

Robin #21 © DC

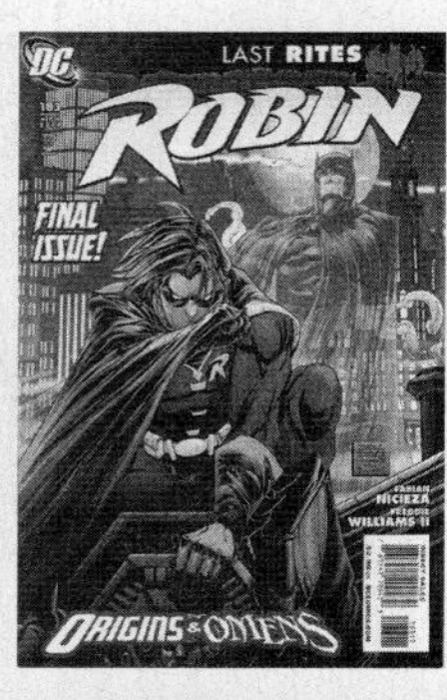

Robin #183 © DC

GD 2.0 VG 4.0 FN 6.0 VF 8.0 VF/NM 9.0 NM- 9.2

Image Comics (Top Cow): Mar, 2006 - No. 5, July, 2006 ($2.99, limited series)
1-5-Avery-s/Anderson-a 3.00

RISING STARS: VOICES OF THE DEAD
Image Comics (Top Cow): June, 2005 - No. 6, Dec, 2005 ($2.99, limited series)
1-6-Avery-s/Staz Johnson-a 3.00

RIVERDALE (Based on the 2017 TV series)
Archie Comic Publications: Apr, 2017 - Present ($3.99)
... One-Shot (4/17, $4.99) Short story prologues to the TV series; multiple covers 4.00

RIVERDALE HIGH (Archie's... #7,8)
Archie Comics: Aug, 1990 - No. 8, Oct, 1991 ($1.00, bi-monthly)
1 4.00
2-8 3.00

RIVER FEUD (See Zane Grey & Four Color #484)

RIVETS
Dell Publishing Co.: No. 518, Nov, 1953
Four Color 518 5 10 15 30 50 70

RIVETS (A dog)
Argo Publ.: Jan, 1956 - No. 3, May, 1956
1-Reprints Sunday & daily newspaper strips 6 12 18 31 38 45
2,3 5 10 15 22 26 30

ROACHMILL
Blackthorne Publ.: Dec, 1986 - No. 6, Oct, 1987 ($1.75, B&W)
1-6 3.00

ROACHMILL
Dark Horse Comics: May, 1988 - No. 10, Dec, 1990 ($1.75, B&W)
1-10: 10-Contains trading cards 3.00

ROAD RUNNER (See Beep Beep, the...)

ROAD TO OZ (Adaptation of the L. Frank Baum book)
Marvel Comics: Nov, 2012 - No. 6, May, 2013 ($3.99, limited series)
1-6-Eric Shanower-s/Skottie Young-a/c 4.00

ROAD TO PERDITION (Inspired the 2002 Tom Hanks/Paul Newman movie)
(Also see On the Road to Perdition)
DC Comics/Paradox Press: 1998, 2002 ($13.95, B&W paperback graphic novel)
nn-(1st printing) Max Allan Collins-s/Richard Piers Rayner-a 30.00
2nd & 3rd printings (2002, $13.95) 14.00
Movie photo cover edition (2002) 14.00

ROADTRIP
Oni Press: Aug, 2000 ($2.95, B&W, one-shot)
1-Reprints Judd Winick's back-up stories from Oni Double Feature #9,10 3.00

ROADWAYS
Cult Press: May, 1994 ($2.75, B&W, limited series)
1 3.00

ROARIN' RICK'S RARE BIT FIENDS
King Hell Press: July, 1994 - No. 21, Aug, 1996 ($2.95, B&W, mature)
1-21: Rick Veitch-c/a/scripts in all. 20-(5/96). 21-(8/96)-Reads Subtleman #1 on cover 3.00
Rabid Eye: The Dream Art of Rick Veitch ($14.95, B&W, TPB)-r/#1-8 & the appendix from #12 15.00
Pocket Universe (6/96, $14.95, B&W, TPB)-Reprints 15.00

ROBERT E. HOWARD'S CONAN THE BARBARIAN
Marvel Comics: 1983 ($2.50, 68 pgs., Baxter paper)
1-r/Savage Tales #2,3 by Smith, c-r/Conan #21 by Smith. 5.00

ROBERT LOUIS STEVENSON'S KIDNAPPED (See Kidnapped)

ROBIN (See Aurora, Birds of Prey, Detective Comics #38, New Teen Titans, Robin II, Robin III, Robin 3000, Star Spangled Comics #65, Teen Titans & Young Justice)

ROBIN (See Batman #457)
DC Comics: Jan, 1991 - No. 5, May, 1991 ($1.00, limited series)
1-Free poster by N. Adams; Bolland-c on all 6.00
1-2nd & 3rd printings (without poster) 3.00
2-5 4.00
2-2nd printing 3.00
Annual 1,2 (1992-93, $2.50, 68 pgs.): 1-Grant/Wagner scripts; Sam Kieth-c. 2-Intro Razorsharp; Jim Balent-c(p) 4.00

ROBIN (See Detective #668) (Also see Red Robin)
DC Comics: Nov, 1993 - No. 183, Apr, 2009 ($1.50/$1.95/$1.99/$2.25/$2.50/$2.99)
1-($2.95)-Collector's edition w/foil embossed-c; 1st app. Robin's car, The Redbird; Azrael as Batman app. 6.00
1-Newsstand ed. 3.00
0,2-49,51-66-Regular editions: 3-5-The Spoiler app. 6-The Huntress-c/story cont'd from Showcase '94 #5. 7-Knightquest: The Conclusion w/new Batman (Azrael) vs. Bruce Wayne. 8-KnightsEnd Pt. 5. 9-KnightsEnd Aftermath; Batman-c & app. 10-(9/94)-Zero Hour. 0-(10/94). 11-(11/94). 25-Green Arrow-c/app. 26-Batman app. 27-Contagion Pt. 3; Catwoman-c/app; Penguin & Azrael app. 28-Contagion Pt. 11. 29-Penguin app. 31-Wildcat-c/app. 32-Legacy Pt. 3. 33-Legacy Pt. 7. 35-Final Night. 46-Genesis. 52,53-Cataclysm pt. 7, conclusion. 55-Green Arrow app. 62-64-Flash-c/app. 3.50
14 ($2.50)-Embossed-c; Troika Pt. 4 4.00
50-($2.95)-Lady Shiva & King Snake app. 4.00
67-74,76-78: 67-72-No Man's Land 3.00
75-($2.95) 4.00
79-97: 79-Begin $2.25-c; Green Arrow app. 86-Pander Bros.-a 3.00
98,99-Bruce Wayne: Murderer x-over pt. 6, 11 3.00
100-($3.50) Last Dixon-s 4.00
101-147: 101-Young Justice x-over. 106-Kevin Lau-c. 121,122-Willingham-s/Mays-a. 125-Tim Drake quits. 126-Spoiler becomes the new Robin. 129-131-War Games. 132-Robin moves to Bludhaven, Batgirl app. 138-Begin $2.50-c. 139-McDaniel-a begins. 146-147-Teen Titans app. 3.00
148-174: 148-One Year Later; new costume. 150-Begin $2.99-c. 152,153-Boomerang app. 168,169-Resurrection of Ra's al Ghul x-over. 174 Spoiler unmasked 3.00
175-183: 175,176-Batman R.I.P. x-over. 180-Robin vs. Red Robin 3.00
#1,000,000 (11/98) 853rd Century x-over 3.00
Annual 3-5: 3-(1994, $2.95)-Elseworlds story. 4-(1995, $2.95)-Year One story. 5-(1996, $2.95)-Legends of the Dead Earth story 4.00
Annual 6 (1997, $3.95)-Pulp Heroes story. 4.00
Annual 7 (12/07, $3.99)-Pearson-c/a; prelude to Resurrection of Ra's al Ghul x-over 4.00
.../Argent 1 (2/98, $1.95) Argent (Teen Titans) app. 3.00
.../Batgirl: Fresh Blood TPB (2005, $12.99) r/#132,133 & Batgirl #58,59 13.00
...: Days of Fire and Madness (2006, $12.99, TPB) r/#140-145 13.00
...Eighty-Page Giant 1 (9/00, $5.95) Chuck Dixon's/Diego Barreto-a 6.00
...: Flying Solo (2000, $12.95, TPB) r/#1-6, Showcase '94 #5,6 13.00
...Plus 1 (12/96, $2.95) Impulse-c/app.; Waid-s 4.00
...Plus 2 (12/97, $2.95) Fang (Scare Tactics) app. 4.00
...: Search For a Hero (2009, $19.99, TPB) r/#175-183; cover gallery 20.00
.../Spoiler Special 1 (8/08, $3.99) Follows Spoiler's return in Robin #174; Dixon-s 4.00
...: Teenage Wasteland (2007, $17.99, TPB) r/#154-162 18.00
...: The Big Leagues (2008, $12.99, TPB) r/#163-167 13.00
...: Unmasked (2004, $12.95, TPB) r/#121-125; Pearson-c 13.00
...: Violent Tendencies (2008, $17.99, TPB) r/#170-174 & Robin/Spoiler Special 1 18.00
...: Wanted (2007, $12.99, TPB) r/#148-153 13.00

ROBIN: A HERO REBORN
DC Comics: 1991 ($4.95, squarebound, trade paperback)
nn-r/Batman #455-457 & Robin #1-5; Bolland-c 2 4 6 8 10 12

ROBIN HOOD (See The Advs. of..., Brave and the Bold, Classic Comics #7, Classics Giveaways (12/44), Four Color #413, 669, King Classics, Movie Comics & Power Record Comics) (...& His Merry Men, The Illustrated Story of...)

ROBIN HOOD (Disney)
Dell Publishing Co.: No. 413, Aug, 1952; No. 669, Dec, 1955
Four Color 413-(1st Disney movie Four Color book)(8/52)-Photo-c 9 18 27 60 120 180
Four Color 669 (12/55)-Reprints #413 plus photo-c 5 10 15 35 63 90

ROBIN HOOD (Adventures of... #6-8)
Magazine Enterprises (Sussex Pub. Co.): No. 52, Nov, 1955 - No. 5, Mar, 1957
52 (#1)-Origin Robin Hood & Sir Gallant of the Round Table 15 30 45 85 130 175
53 (#2), 3-5 12 24 36 67 94 120
I.W. Reprint #1,2,9: 1-r/#3. 2-r/#4. 9-r/#52 (1963) 2 4 6 9 13 16
Super Reprint #10,15: 10-r/#53. 15-r/#5 2 4 6 9 13 16
NOTE: *Bolle a-in all; c-52.*

ROBIN HOOD (Not Disney)
Dell Publishing Co.: May-July, 1963 (one-shot)
1 3 6 9 16 23 30

ROBIN HOOD (Disney) (Also see Best of Walt Disney)
Western Publishing Co.: 1973 ($1.50, 8-1/2x11", 52 pgs., cardboard-c)
96151- "Robin Hood", based on movie, 96152- "The Mystery of Sherwood Forest", 96153- "In King Richard's Service", 96154- "The Wizard's Ring" each.... 3 6 9 15 22 28

Robin Hood Tales #2 © QUA

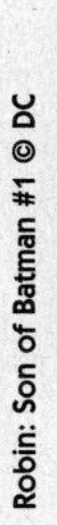

Robin: Son of Batman #1 © DC

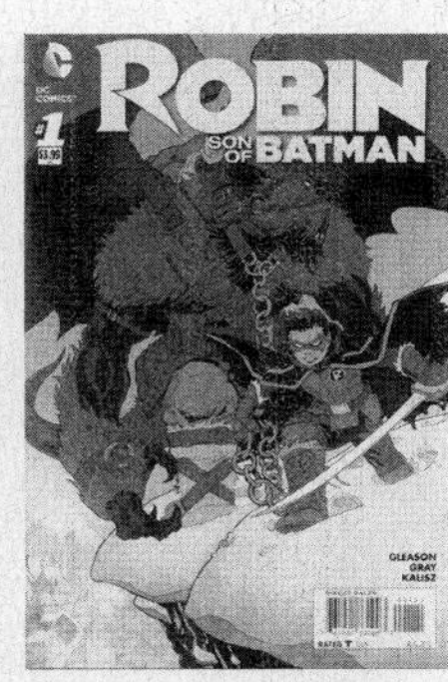

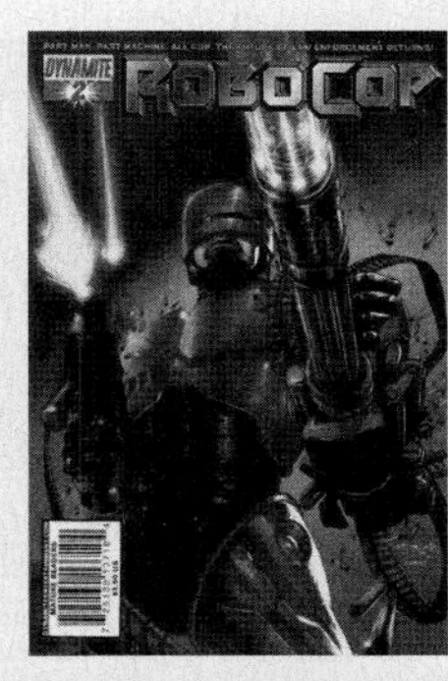

Robocop (2010 series) #2 © Orion Picts.

	GD 2.0	VG 4.0	FN 6.0	VF 8.0	VF/NM 9.0	NM- 9.2

ROBIN HOOD
Eclipse Comics: July, 1991 - No. 3, Dec, 1991 ($2.50, limited series)

1-3: Timothy Truman layouts 3.00

ROBIN HOOD AND HIS MERRY MEN (Formerly Danger & Adventure)
Charlton Comics: No. 28, Apr, 1956 - No. 38, Aug, 1958

	GD	VG	FN	VF	VF/NM	NM-
28	10	20	30	54	72	90
29-37	8	16	24	42	54	65
38-Ditko-a (5 pgs.); Rocke-c	14	28	42	76	108	140

ROBIN HOOD TALES (Published by National Periodical #7 on)
Quality Comics Group (Comic Magazines): Feb, 1956 - No. 6, Nov-Dec, 1956

	GD	VG	FN	VF	VF/NM	NM-
1-All have Baker/Cuidera-c	32	64	96	188	307	425
2-6-Matt Baker-a	30	60	90	177	289	400

ROBIN HOOD TALES (Cont'd from Quality series)(See Brave & the Bold #5)
National Periodical Publ.: No. 7, Jan-Feb, 1957 - No. 14, Mar-Apr, 1958

	GD	VG	FN	VF	VF/NM	NM-
7-All have Andru/Esposito-c	36	72	108	211	343	475
8-14	30	60	90	177	289	400

ROBIN RISES: OMEGA (See Batman & Robin #33-37)
DC Comics: Sept, 2014; Feb, 2015 ($4.99, one-shots)

Alpha 1 (2/15)-Tomasi-s/Andy Kubert-a/c; Damien returns; Talia app. 5.00
Omega 1 (9/14)-Tomasi-s/Andy Kubert-a/c; Ra's al Ghul and Justice League app. 5.00

ROBINSON CRUSOE (See King Classics & Power Record Comics)
Dell Publishing Co.: Nov-Jan, 1963-64

	GD	VG	FN	VF	VF/NM	NM-
1	3	6	9	15	21	26

ROBIN: SON OF BATMAN (Damian Wayne)
DC Comics: Aug, 2015 - No. 13, Aug, 2016 ($3.99)

1-13: 1-Gleason-s/a. 4-Deathstroke app. 5-Damian vs. Talia. 7-"Robin War" tie-in 4.00

ROBIN II (The Joker's Wild)
DC Comics: Oct, 1991 - No. 4, Dec, 1991 ($1.50, mini-series)

1-(Direct sales, $1.50)-With 4 diff.-c; same hologram on each 5.00
1-(Newsstand, $1.00)-No hologram; 1 version 3.00
1-Collector's set ($10.00)-Contains all 5 versions bagged with hologram trading card inside 18.00
2-(Direct sales, $1.50)-With 3 different-c 4.00
2-4-(Newsstand, $1.00)-1 version of each 3.00
2-Collector's set ($8.00)-Contains all 4 versions bagged with hologram trading card inside 12.00
3-(Direct sale, $1.50)-With 2 different-c 4.00
3-Collector's set ($6.00)-Contains all 3 versions bagged with hologram trading card inside 10.00
4-(Direct sales, $1.50)-Only one version 4.00
4-Collector's set ($4.00)-Contains both versions bagged with Bat-Signal hologram trading card 6.00
Multi-pack (All four issues w/hologram sticker) 14.00
Deluxe Complete Set ($30.00)-Contains all 14 versions of #1-4 plus a new hologram trading card; numbered & limited to 25,000; comes with slipcase & 2 acid free backing boards 45.00

ROBIN III: CRY OF THE HUNTRESS
DC Comics: Dec, 1992 - No. 6, Mar, 1993 (Limited series)

1-6 ($2.50, collector's ed.)-Polybagged w/movement enhanced-c plus mini-poster of newsstand-c by Zeck 4.00
1-6 ($1.25, newsstand ed.): All have Zeck-c 3.00

ROBIN 3000
DC Comics (Elseworlds): 1992 - No. 2, 1992 ($4.95, mini-series, 52 pgs.)

1,2-Foil logo; Russell-c/a 6.00

ROBIN WAR (Crossover with Grayson, Robin: Son of Batman, and We Are Robin)
DC Comics: Feb, 2016 - No. 2, Mar, 2016 ($4.99)

1,2-Tom King-s; art by various; The Court of Owls app. 5.00

ROBIN: YEAR ONE
DC Comics: 2000 - No. 4, 2001 ($4.95, square-bound, limited series)

1-4: Earliest days of Robin's career; Javier Pulido-c/a. 2,4-Two-Face app. 6.00
TPB (2002, 2008, $14.95/$14.99, 2 printings) r/#1-4 15.00

ROBOCOP
Marvel Comics: Oct, 1987 ($2.00, B&W, magazine, one-shot)

	GD	VG	FN	VF	VF/NM	NM-
1-Movie adaptation	1	3	4	6	8	10

ROBOCOP (Also see Dark Horse Comics)
Marvel Comics: Mar, 1990 - No. 23, Jan, 1992 ($1.50)

	GD	VG	FN	VF	VF/NM	NM-
1-Based on movie	1	3	4	6	8	10
2-23						3.00
nn (7/90, $4.95, 52 pgs.)-r/B&W magazine in color; adapts 1st movie						5.00

ROBOCOP
Dynamite Entertainment: 2010 - No. 6, 2010 ($3.50, limited series)

1-6-Follows the events of the first film; Neves-a 3.50

ROBOCOP
BOOM! Studios: Jul, 2014 - No. 12, Jun, 2015 ($3.99)

1-12: 1-8-Williamson-s/Magno-a. 1-Multiple covers. 9,10-Aragon-a 4.00

ROBOCOP (FRANK MILLER'S...)
Avatar Press: July, 2003 - No. 9, Jan, 2006 ($3.50/$3.99, limited series)

1-9-Frank Miller-s/Juan Ryp-a. 1-Three covers by Miller, Ryp, and Barrows. 2-Two covers 4.00
Free Comic Book Day Edition (4/03) Previews Robocop & Stargate SG•1; Busch-c 3.00

ROBOCOP (Tie-ins to the 2014 movie)
BOOM! Studios: Feb, 2014 ($3.99)

...: Beta (2/14) Brisson-s/Laiso-a 4.00
...: Hominem Ex Machina (2/14) Moreci-s/Copland-a 4.00
...: Memento Mori (2/14) Barbiere-s/Vieira-a 4.00
...: To Live and Die in Detroit (2/14) Joe Harris-s/Piotr Kowalski-a 4.00

ROBOCOP: LAST STAND
BOOM! Studios: Aug, 2013 - No. 8, Mar, 2014 ($3.99, limited series)

1-8: 1-Miller & Grant-s/Oztekin-a 4.00

ROBOCOP: MORTAL COILS
Dark Horse Comics: Sept, 1993 - No. 4, Dec, 1993 ($2.50, limited series)

1-4: 1,2-Cago painted-c 3.00

ROBOCOP: PRIME SUSPECT
Dark Horse Comics: Oct, 1992 - No. 4, Jan, 1993 ($2.50, limited series)

1-4: 1,3-Nelson painted-c. 2,4-Bolton painted-c 3.00

ROBOCOP: ROAD TRIP
Dynamite Entertainment: 2012 - No. 4, 2012 ($3.99, limited series)

1-4-De Zarate-a 4.00

ROBOCOP: ROULETTE
Dark Horse Comics: Dec, 1993 - No. 4, 1994 ($2.50, limited series)

1-4: 1,3-Nelson painted-c. 2,4-Bolton painted-c 3.00

ROBOCOP 2
Marvel Comics: Aug, 1990 ($2.25, B&W, magazine, 68 pgs.)

1-Adapts movie sequel scripted by Frank Miller; Bagley-a 4.00

ROBOCOP 2
Marvel Comics: Aug, 1990; Late Aug, 1990 - #3, Late Sept, 1990 ($1.00, limited series)

nn-(8/90, $4.95, 68 pgs., color)-Same contents as B&W magazine 5.00
1: #1-3 reprint no number issue 3.00
2,3: 2-Guice-c(i) 3.00

ROBOCOP 3
Dark Horse Comics: July, 1993 - No. 3, Nov, 1993 ($2.50, limited series)

1-3: Nelson painted-c; Nguyen-a(p) 3.00

ROBOCOP VERSUS THE TERMINATOR
Dark Horse Comics: Sept, 1992 - No. 4, 1992 (Dec.) ($2.50, limited series)

1-4: Miller scripts & Simonson-c/a in all 4.00
1-Platinum Edition 10.00
NOTE: *All contain a different Robocop cardboard cut-out stand-up.*

ROBO DOJO
DC Comics (WildStorm): Apr, 2002 - No. 6, Sept, 2002 ($2.95, limited series)

1-6-Wolfman-s 3.00

ROBO-HUNTER (Also see Sam Slade...)
Eagle Comics: Apr, 1984 - No. 5, 1984 ($1.00)

1-5-2000 A.D. 4.00

R.O.B.O.T. BATTALION 2050
Eclipse Comics: Mar, 1988 ($2.00, B&W, one-shot)

1 3.00

ROBOT COMICS
Renegade Press: No. 0, June, 1987 ($2.00, B&W, one-shot)

0-Bob Burden story & art 3.00

ROBOTECH

Robotech: The Macross Saga #12 © Comico

The Rock #1 © WWF Ent.

Rocket Comics; Ignite © DH

	GD 2.0	VG 4.0	FN 6.0	VF 8.0	VF/NM 9.0	NM- 9.2

Antarctic Press: Mar, 1997 - No. 11, Nov, 1998 ($2.95)

1-11, Annual 1 (4/98, $2.95) 4.00
...Class Reunion (12/98, $3.95, B&W) 4.00
...Escape (5/98, $2.95, B&W), ...Final Fire (12/98, $2.95, B&W) 4.00

ROBOTECH
DC Comics (WildStorm): No. 0, Feb, 2003 - No. 6, Jul, 2003 ($2.50/$2.95, limited series)

0-Tommy Yune-s; art by Jim Lee, Garza, Bermejo and others; pin-up pages by various 3.00
1-6 ($2.95)-Long Vo-a 3.00
...: From the Stars (2003, $9.95, digest-size) r/#0-6 & Sourcebook 10.00
... Sourcebook (3/03, $2.95) pin-ups and info on characters and mecha; art by various 3.00

ROBOTECH: COVERT-OPS
Antarctic Press: Aug, 1998 - No. 2, Sept, 1998 ($2.95, B&W, limited series)

1,2-Gregory Lane-s/a 4.00

ROBOTECH DEFENDERS
DC Comics: Mar, 1985 - No. 2, Apr, 1985 (Mini-series)

1,2 4.00

ROBOTECH IN 3-D (TV)
Comico: Aug, 1987 ($2.50)

1-Steacy painted-c 5.00

ROBOTECH: INVASION
DC Comics (WildStorm): Feb, 2004 - No. 5, July, 2004 ($2.95, limited series)

1-5-Faerber & Yune-s/Miyazawa & Dogan-a 3.00

ROBOTECH: LOVE AND WAR
DC Comics (WildStorm): Aug, 2003 - No. 6, Jan, 2004 ($2.95, limited series)

1-6-Long Vo & Charles Park-a/Faerber & Yune-s. 2-Variant-c by Warren 3.00

ROBOTECH MASTERS (TV)
Comico: July, 1985 - No. 23, Apr, 1988 ($1.50)

1 6.00
2-23 4.00

ROBOTECH: PRELUDE TO THE SHADOW CHRONICLES
DC Comics (WildStorm): Dec, 2005 - No. 5, Mar, 2006 ($3.50, limited series)

1-5-Yune-s/Dogan & Udon Studios-a 3.50
TPB (2010, $17.99) r/#1-5; production art 18.00

ROBOTECH: SENTINELS - RUBICON
Antarctic Press: July, 1998 ($2.95, B&W)

1 4.00

ROBOTECH SPECIAL
Comico: May, 1988 ($2.50, one-shot, 44 pgs.)

1-Steacy wraparound-c; partial photo-c 5.00

ROBOTECH THE GRAPHIC NOVEL
Comico: Aug, 1986 ($5.95, 8-1/2x11", 52 pgs.)

1-Origin SDF-1; intro T.R. Edwards, Steacy-c/a 15.00
1-Second printing (12/86) 10.00

ROBOTECH: THE MACROSS SAGA (TV)(Formerly Macross)
Comico: No. 2, Feb, 1985 - No. 36, Feb, 1989 ($1.50)

2 1 2 3 5 6 8
3-10 5.00
11-36: 12,17-Ken Steacy painted-c. 26-Begin $1.75-c. 35,36-($1.95) 4.00
Volume 1-4 TPB (WildStorm, 2003, $14.95, 5-3/4" x 8-1/4")1-Reprints #2-6 & Macross #1. 2- r/#7-12. 3-r/#13-18. 4-r/#19-24 15.00

ROBOTECH: THE NEW GENERATION
Comico: July, 1985 - No. 25, July, 1988

1 6.00
2-25 4.00

ROBOTECH: VERMILION
Antarctic Press: Mar, 1997 - No. 4, ($2.95, B&W, limited series)

1-4 4.00

ROBOTECH / VOLTRON
Dynamite Entertainment: 2013 - No. 5, 2014 ($3.99, limited series)

1-5-Tommy Yune-s 4.00

ROBOTECH: WINGS OF GIBRALTAR
Antarctic Press: Aug, 1998 - No. 2, Sept, 1998 ($2.95, B&W, limited series)

1,2-Lee Duhig-s/a 4.00

ROBOTIX
Marvel Comics: Feb, 1986 (75¢, one-shot)

1-Based on toy 4.00

ROBOTMEN OF THE LOST PLANET (Also see Space Thrillers)
Avon Periodicals: 1952 (Also see Strange Worlds #19)

1-McCann-a (3 pgs.); Fawcette-a 161 322 483 1030 1765 2500

ROB ROY
Dell Publishing Co.: 1954 (Disney-Movie)

Four Color 544-Manning-a, photo-c 7 14 21 49 92 135

ROCK, THE (WWF Wrestling)
Chaos! Comics: June, 2001 ($2.99, one-shot)

1-Photo-c; Grant-s/Neves-a 4.00

ROCK & ROLL HIGH SCHOOL
Roger Corman's Cosmic Comics: Oct, 1995 ($2.50)

1-Bob Fingerman scripts 3.00

ROCK AND ROLLO (Formerly TV Teens)
Charlton Comics: V2#14, Oct, 1957 - No. 19, Sept, 1958

V2#14-19 6 12 18 31 38 45

ROCK COMICS
Landgraphic Publ.: Jul/Aug, 1979 ($1.25, tabloid size, 28 pgs.)

1-N. Adams-c; Thor(not Marvel's) story by Adams 3 6 9 14 20 25

ROCKET COMICS
Hillman Periodicals: Mar, 1940 - No. 3, May, 1940

1-Rocket Riley, Red Roberts the Electro Man (origin), The Phantom Ranger, The Steel Shark, The Defender, Buzzard Barnes and his Sky Devils, Lefty Larson, & The Defender, the Man with a Thousand Faces begin (1st app. of each); all have Rocket Riley-c 300 600 900 1920 3310 4700
2,3 181 362 543 1158 1979 2800

ROCKET COMICS: IGNITE
Dark Horse Comics: Apr, 2003 (Free Comic Book Day giveaway)

1-Previews Dark Horse series Syn, Lone, and Go Boy 7 3.00

ROCKETEER, THE (See Eclipse Graphic Album Series, Pacific Presents & Starslayer)

ROCKETEER ADVENTURE MAGAZINE, THE
Comico/Dark Horse Comics No. 3: July, 1988 ($2.00); No. 2, July, 1989 ($2.75); No. 3, Jan, 1995 ($2.95)

1-(7/88, $2.00)-Dave Stevens-c/a in all; Kaluta back-up-a; 1st app. Jonas (character based on The Shadow) 2 4 6 8 10 12
2-(7/89, $2.75)-Stevens/Dorman painted-c 1 3 4 6 8 10
3-(1/95, $2.95)-Includes pinups by Stevens, Gulacy, Plunkett, & Mignola 5.00
Volume 2-(9/96, $9.95, magazine size TPB)-Reprints #1-3 10.00

ROCKETEER ADVENTURES
IDW Publishing: May, 2011 - No. 4, Aug, 2011 ($3.99, limited series)

1-4-Anthology of new stories by various; covers by Alex Ross and Dave Stevens 4.00

ROCKETEER ADVENTURES VOLUME 2
IDW Publishing: Mar, 2012 - No. 4, Jun, 2012 ($3.99, limited series)

1-4-Anthology by various; covers by Darwyn Cooke and Stevens. 1-Sakai-a. 4-Simonson & Byrne-a 4.00

ROCKETEER AT WAR, THE
IDW Publishing: Dec, 2015 - No. 4, Apr, 2016 ($4.99, limited series)

1-4-Guggenheim-s; covers by Bullock & Bradshaw. 1,2-Bullock-a. 3,4-J. Bone-a 5.00

ROCKETEER: CARGO OF DOOM
IDW Publishing: Aug, 2012 - No. 4, Nov, 2012 ($3.99, limited series)

1-4-Waid-s/Samnee-a/c; variant-c by Stevens on all 4.00

ROCKETEER: HOLLYWOOD HORROR
IDW Publishing: Feb, 2013 - No. 4, May, 2013 ($3.99, limited series)

1-4-Langridge-s/Bone-a/Simonson-c; variant-c on all 4.00

ROCKETEER JETPACK TREASURY EDITION
IDW Publishing: Nov, 2011 ($9.99, oversized 13" x 9-3/4" format)

1-Recolored r/Starslayer #1-3, Pacific Presents #1,2 & Rocketeer Special Edition 10.00

ROCKETEER SPECIAL EDITION, THE
Eclipse Comics: Nov, 1984 ($1.50, Baxter paper)(Chapter 5 of Rocketeer serial)

1-Stevens-c/a; Kaluta back-c; pin-ups inside 2 4 6 11 16 20
NOTE: *Originally intended to be published in Pacific Presents.*

Rocket Girl #5 © Montclare & Reeder

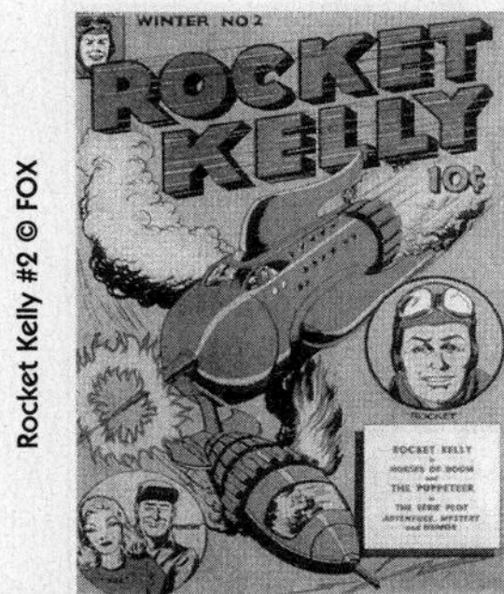

Rocket Kelly #2 © FOX

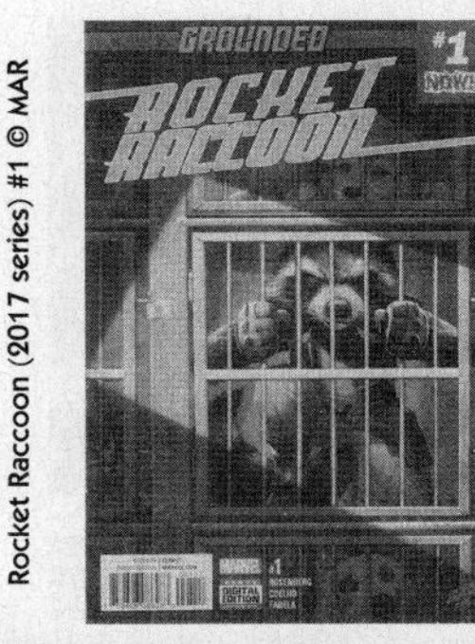

Rocket Raccoon (2017 series) #1 © MAR

	GD 2.0	VG 4.0	FN 6.0	VF 8.0	VF/NM 9.0	NM- 9.2

ROCKETEER, THE: THE COMPLETE ADVENTURES
IDW Publishing: Oct, 2009 ($29.99/$75.00, hardcover)
HC-Reprints of Dave Stevens' Rocketeer stories in Starslayer #1-3, Pacific Presents #1,2, Rocketeer Special Edition and Rocketeer Adventure Magazine #1-3; all re-colored 30.00
... Deluxe Edition ($75.00, 8"x12" slipcased HC) larger size reprints of HC content plus 100 bonus pages of sketch art, layouts, design work; intro. by Thomas Jane 110.00
... Deluxe Edition 2nd printing ($75.00, oversized slipcased HC) 75.00

ROCKETEER, THE: THE OFFICIAL MOVIE ADAPTATION
W. D. Publications (Disney): 1991
nn-($5.95, 68 pgs.)-Squarebound deluxe edition 6.00
nn-($2.95, 68 pgs.)-Stapled regular edition 4.00
3-D Comic Book (1991, $7.98, 52 pgs.) 8.00

ROCKETEER/THE SPIRIT: PULP FRICTION
IDW Publishing: Jul, 2013 - No. 4, Dec, 2013 ($3.99, limited series)
1-4: 1-Waid-s/Paul Smith-a; covers by Smith & Darwyn Cooke. 2-Wallace-a. 3,4-Bone-a 4.00

ROCKET GIRL
Image Comics: Oct, 2013 - Present ($3.50/$3.99)
1-7-Brandon Montclare-a/Amy Reeder-a/c. 6-Begin $3.99 4.00

ROCKET KELLY (See The Bouncer, Green Mask #10); becomes Li'l Pan #6)
Fox Feature Syndicate: 1944; Fall, 1945 - No. 5, Oct-Nov, 1946
nn (1944), 1 (Fall, 1945) 41 82 123 256 428 600
2-The Puppeteer app. (costumed hero) 29 58 87 172 281 390
3-5: 5-(#5 on cover, #4 inside) 26 52 78 154 252 350

ROCKETMAN (Strange Fantasy #2 on) (See Hello Pal & Scoop Comics)
Ajax/Farrell Publications: June, 1952 (Strange Stories of the Future)
1-Rocketman & Cosmo 45 90 135 284 480 675

ROCKET RACCOON (Also see Marvel Preview #7 and Incredible Hulk #271)
Marvel Comics: May, 1985 - No. 4, Aug, 1985 (color, limited series)
1-Mignola-a/Mantlo-s in all 4 8 12 28 47 65
2-4 2 4 6 11 16 20
...: Tales From Half-World 1 (10/13, $7.99) r/#1-4; new cover by McNiven 8.00

ROCKET RACCOON (Guardians of the Galaxy)
Marvel Comics: Sept, 2014 - No. 11, Jul, 2015 ($3.99)
1-Skottie Young-s/a; Groot app. 5.00
2-11-Skottie Young-s. 7,8-Andrade-a 4.00
Free Comic Book Day 2014 (5/14, giveaway) Archer-a; Groot and Wal-rus app. 3.00

ROCKET RACCOON (Guardians of the Galaxy)
Marvel Comics: Feb, 2017 - Present ($3.99)
1-3-Rosenberg-s/Coelho-a. 1-Johnny Storm app. 2,3-Kraven app. 5.00

ROCKET RACCOON & GROOT (Guardians of the Galaxy)
Marvel Comics: Mar, 2016 - No. 10, Nov, 2016 ($3.99)
1-10: 1-6-Skottie Young-s. 1-3-Filipe Andrade-a. 8-10-Gwenpool app. 4.00

ROCKET SHIP X
Fox Features Syndicate: September, 1951; 1952
1 64 128 192 406 696 985
1952 (nn, nd, no publ.)-Edited 1951-c (exist?) 39 78 117 231 378 525

ROCKET TO ADVENTURE LAND (See Pixie Puzzle...)

ROCKET TO THE MOON
Avon Periodicals: 1951
nn-Orlando-c/a; adapts Otis Adelbert Kline's "Maza of the Moon"
161 322 483 1030 1765 2500

ROCK FANTASY COMICS
Rock Fantasy Comics: Dec, 1989 - No. 16?, 1991 ($2.25/$3.00, B&W)(No cover price)
1-Pink Floyd part 1 5.00
1-2nd printing ($3.00-c) 3.00
2,3: 2-Rolling Stones #1. 3-Led Zeppelin #1 4.00
2,3: 2nd printings ($3.00-c, 1/90 & 2/90) 3.00
4-Stevie Nicks Not published
5-Monstrosities of Rock #1; photo back-c 4.00
5-2nd printing ($3.00, 3/90 indicia, 2/90-c) 3.00
6-9,11-15,17,18: 6-Guns n' Roses #1 (1st & 2nd printings, 3/90)-Begin $3.00-c. 7-Sex Pistols #1. 8-Alice Cooper; not published. 9-Van Halen #1; photo back-c. 11-Jimi Hendrix #1; wraparound-c 3.00
10-Kiss #1; photo back-c 2 4 6 8 10 12
16-($5.00, 68 pgs.)-The Great Gig in the Sky(Floyd) 5.00

ROCK HAPPENING (See Bunny and Harvey Pop Comics:...)

ROCK N' ROLL COMICS
DC Comics: Dec./Jan 1956 (ashcan)
nn-Ashcan comic, not distributed to newsstands, only for in house use (no known sales)

ROCK N' ROLL COMICS
Revolutionary Comics: Jun, 1989 - No. 65 ($1.50/$1.95/$2.50, B&W/col. #15 on)
1-Guns N' Roses 1 3 4 6 8 10
1-2nd thru 7th printings. 7th printing (full color w/new-c/a) 3.00
2-Metallica 1 3 4 6 8 10
2-2nd thru 6th printings (6th in color) 3.00
3-Bon Jovi (no reprints) 1 2 3 5 6 8
4-8,10-65: 4-Motley Crue(2nd printing only, 1st destroyed). 5-Def Leppard (2 printings). 6-Rolling Stones(4 printings). 7-The Who (3 printings). 8-Skid Row; not published. 10-Warrant/Whitesnake(2 printings; 1st has 2 diff.-c). 11-Aerosmith (2 printings?). 12-New Kids on the Block(2 printings). 12-3rd printing; rewritten & titled NKOTB Hate Book. 13-Led Zeppelin. 14-Sex Pistols. 15-Poison; 1st color issue. 16-Van Halen. 17-Madonna. 18-Alice Cooper. 19-Public Enemy/2 Live Crew. 20-Queensryche/Tesla. 21-Prince? 22-AC/DC; begin $2.50-c. 23-Living Colour. 26-Michael Jackson. 29-Ozzy. 45,46-Grateful Dead. 49-Rush. 50,51-Bob Dylan. 56-David Bowie 5.00
9-Kiss 2 4 6 8 10 12
9-2nd & 3rd printings 3.00
NOTE: *Most issues were reprinted except #3. Later reprints are in color. #8 was not released.*

ROCKO'S MODERN LIFE (TV)
Marvel Comics: June, 1994 - No. 7, Dec, 1994 ($1.95) (Nickelodeon cartoon)
1-7 3.00

ROCKSTARS
Image Comics: Dec, 2016 - Present ($3.99)
1-3-Joe Harris-s/Megan Hutchison-a 4.00

ROCKY AND BULLWINKLE (TV)
IDW Publishing: Mar, 2014 - No. 4, Jun, 2014 ($3.99)
1-4-Evanier-s/Langridge-a; bonus Dudley Do-Right short story in each; two covers 4.00

ROCKY AND HIS FIENDISH FRIENDS (TV)(Bullwinkle)
Gold Key: Oct, 1962 - No. 5, Sept, 1963 (Jay Ward)
1 (25¢, 80 pgs.) 13 26 39 86 188 290
2,3 (25¢, 80 pgs.) 9 18 27 62 126 190
4,5 (Regular size, 12¢) 7 14 21 46 86 125

ROCKY AND HIS FRIENDS (See Kite Fun Book & March of Comics #216 in the Promotional Comics section)

ROCKY AND HIS FRIENDS (TV)
Dell Publishing Co.: No. 1128, 8-10/60 - No.1311,1962 (Jay Ward)
Four Color 1128 (#1) (8-10/60) 25 50 75 175 388 600
Four Color 1152 (12-2/61), 1166, 1208, 1275, 1311('62)
16 32 48 107 236 365

ROCKY HORROR PICTURE SHOW THE COMIC BOOK, THE
Caliber Press: Jul, 1990 - No. 3, Jan, 1991 ($2.95, mini-series, 52 pgs.)
1-3: 1-Adapts cult film plus photos, etc., 1-2nd printing
1 2 3 5 6 8
...Collection ($4.95) 2 4 6 8 10 12

ROCKY JONES SPACE RANGER (See Space Adventures #15-18)

ROCKY JORDEN PRIVATE EYE (See Private Eye)

ROCKY LANE WESTERN (Allan Rocky Lane starred in Republic movies & TV for a short time as Allan Lane, Red Ryder & Rocky Lane) (See Black Jack Fawcett Movie Comics, Motion Picture Comics & Six-Gun Heroes)
Fawcett Publications/Charlton No. 56 on: May, 1949 - No. 87, Nov, 1959
1 (36 pgs.)-Rocky, his stallion Black Jack, & Slim Pickens begin; photo-c begin, end #57; photo back-c 55 110 165 352 601 850
2 (36 pgs.)-Last photo back-c 22 44 66 132 216 300
3-5 (52 pgs.): 4-Captain Tootsie by Beck 17 34 51 98 154 210
6,10 (36 pgs.): 10-Complete western novelette "Badman's Reward"
14 28 42 76 108 140
7-9 (52 pgs.) 14 28 42 82 121 160
11-13,15-17,19,20 (52 pgs.): 15-Black Jack's Hitching Post begins, ends #25. 20-Last Slim Pickens 12 24 36 67 94 120
14,18 (36 pgs.) 10 20 30 58 79 100
21,23,24 (52 pgs.): 21-Dee Dickens begins, ends #55,57,65-68
10 20 30 58 79 100
22,25-28,30 (36 pgs. begin) 10 20 30 54 72 90
29-Classic complete novel "The Land of Missing Men" with hidden land of ancient temple ruins (r-in #65) 14 28 42 76 108 140

Rocky Lane Western #3 © FAW

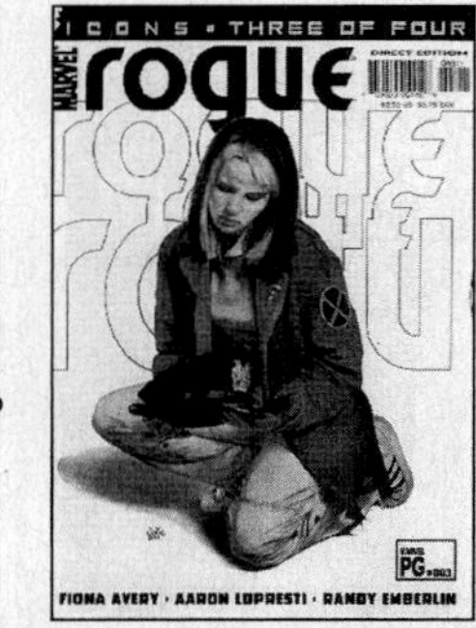

Rogue V2 #3 © MAR

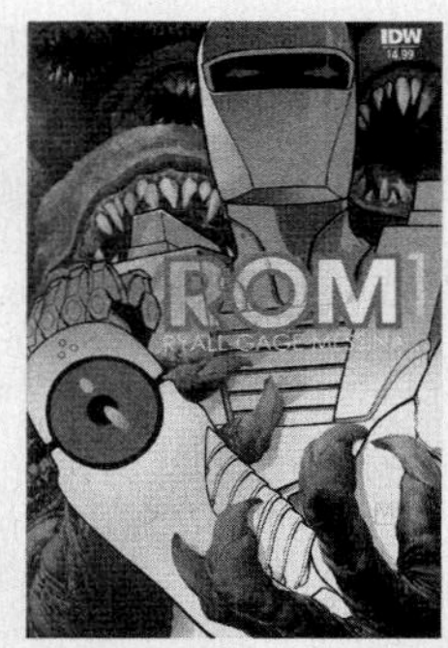

Rom (2016 series) #1 © Hasbro

	GD 2.0	VG 4.0	FN 6.0	VF 8.0	VF/NM 9.0	NM- 9.2
31-40	9	18	27	52	69	85
41-54	9	18	27	47	61	75
55-Last Fawcett issue (1/54)	9	18	27	52	69	85
56-1st Charlton issue (2/54)-Photo-c	14	28	42	82	121	160
57,60-Photo-c	10	20	30	54	72	90
58,59,61-64,66-78,80-86: 59-61-Young Falcon app. 64-Slim Pickens app. 66-68: Reprints #30,31,32	8	16	24	44	57	70
65-r/#29, "The Land of Missing Men"	9	18	27	50	65	80
79-Giant Edition (68 pgs.)	10	20	30	58	79	100
87-Last issue	9	18	27	52	69	85

NOTE: *Complete novels in #10, 14, 18, 22, 25, 30-32, 36, 38, 39, 49. Captain Tootsie in #4, 12, 20. Big Bow and Little Arrow in #11, 28, 63. Black Jack's Hitching Post in #15-25, 64, 73.*

ROCKY LANE WESTERN
AC Comics: 1989 ($2.50, B&W, one-shot?)

1-Photo-c; Giordano reprints 4.00
Annual 1 (1991, $2.95, B&W, 44 pgs.)-photo front/back & inside-c; reprints 4.00

ROD CAMERON WESTERN (Movie star)
Fawcett Publications: Feb, 1950 - No. 20, Apr, 1953

	GD	VG	FN	VF	VF/NM	NM-
1-Rod Cameron, his horse War Paint, & Sam The Sheriff begin; photo front/back-c begin	30	60	90	177	289	400
2	15	30	45	86	133	180
3-Novel length story "The Mystery of the Seven Cities of Cibola"	14	28	42	82	121	160
4-10: 9-Last photo back-c	12	24	36	69	97	125
11-19	10	20	30	58	79	100
20-Last issue & photo-c	11	22	33	62	86	110

NOTE: *Novel length stories in No. 1-8, 12-14.*

RODEO RYAN (See A-1 Comics #8)

ROGAN GOSH
DC Comics (Vertigo): 1994 ($6.95, one-shot)

nn-Peter Milligan scripts 7.00

ROGER DODGER (Also in Exciting Comics #57 on)
Standard Comics: No. 5, Aug, 1952

	GD	VG	FN	VF	VF/NM	NM-
5-Teen-age	8	16	24	40	50	60

ROGER RABBIT (Also see Marvel Graphic Novel)
Disney Comics: June, 1990 - No. 18, Nov, 1991 ($1.50)

1-18-All new stories 3.00

	GD	VG	FN	VF	VF/NM	NM-
In 3-D 1 (1992, $2.50)-Sold at Wal-Mart?; w/glasses	1	2	3	5	6	8

ROGER RABBIT'S TOONTOWN
Disney Comics: Aug, 1991 - No. 5, Dec, 1991 ($1.50)

1-5 3.00

ROGER ZELAZNY'S AMBER: THE GUNS OF AVALON
DC Comics: 1996 - No. 3, 1996 ($6.95, limited series)

1-3: Based on novel 7.00

ROG 2000
Pacific Comics: June, 1982 ($2.95, 44 pgs., B&W, one-shot, magazine)

	GD	VG	FN	VF	VF/NM	NM-
nn-Byrne-c/a (r)	2	4	6	8	10	12
2nd printing (7/82)	1	2	3	4	5	7

ROG 2000
Fantagraphics Books: 1987 - No. 2, 1987 ($2.00, limited series)

1,2-Byrne-r 3.00

ROGUE (From X-Men)
Marvel Comics: Jan, 1995 - No. 4, Apr, 1995 ($2.95, limited series)

1-4: 1-Gold foil logo 4.00
TPB-($12.95) r/#1-4 13.00

ROGUE (Volume 2)
Marvel Comics: Sept, 2001 - No. 4, Dec, 2001 ($2.50, limited series)

1-4-Julie Bell painted-c/Lopresti-a; Rogue's early days with X-Men 3.00

ROGUE (From X-Men)
Marvel Comics: Sept, 2004 - No. 12, Aug, 2005 ($2.99)

1-12: 1-Richards-a. 4-Gambit app. 11-Sunfire dies, Rogue absorbs his powers 3.00
...: Going Rogue TPB (2005, $14.99) r/#1-6 15.00
...: Forget-Me-Not TPB (2006, $14.99) r/#7-12 15.00

ROGUE ANGEL: TELLER OF TALL TALES (Based on the Alex Archer novels)
IDW Publishing: Feb, 2008 - No. 5, Jun, 2008 ($3.99)

1-5-Annja Creed adventures; Barbara-Kesel-s/Renae De Liz-a 4.00

ROGUES GALLERY
DC Comics: 1996 ($3.50, one-shot)

1-Pinups of DC villains by various artists 4.00

ROGUE TROOPER
IDW Publishing: Feb, 2014 - No. 4, May, 2014 ($3.99)

1-4-Ruckley-s/Ponticelli-a/Fabry-c 4.00

ROGUE TROOPER CLASSICS
IDW Publishing: May, 2014 - No. 8, Dec, 2014 ($3.99)

1-8-Newly colored reprints of strips from 2000 AD magazine. 1-4-Gibbons-a 4.00

ROGUES, THE (VILLAINS) (See The Flash)
DC Comics: Feb, 1998 ($1.95, one-shot)

1-Augustyn-s/Pearson-c 3.00

ROKKIN
DC Comics (WildStorm): Sept, 2006 - No. 6, Feb, 2007 ($2.99, limited series)

1-6-Hartnell-s/Bradshaw-a 3.00

ROLLING STONES: VOODOO LOUNGE
Marvel Comics: 1995 ($6.95, Prestige format, one-shot)

nn-Dave McKean-script/design/art 7.00

ROLY POLY COMIC BOOK
Green Publishing Co.: 1945 - No. 15, 1946 (MLJ reprints)

	GD	VG	FN	VF	VF/NM	NM-
1-(No number on cover or indicia, "1945 issue" on cover) Red Rube & Steel Sterling begin; Sahle-c	36	72	108	216	351	485
6-The Blue Circle & The Steel Fist app.	24	48	72	142	234	325
10-Origin Red Rube retold; Steel Sterling story (Zip #41)	28	56	84	165	270	375
11,12: The Black Hood app. in both	26	52	78	154	252	350
14-Classic decapitation-c; the Black Hood app.	290	580	870	1856	3178	4500
15-The Blue Circle & The Steel Fist app.; cover exact swipe from Fox Blue Beetle #1	36	72	108	216	351	485

ROM (Based on the Parker Brothers toy)
Marvel Comics Group: Dec, 1979 - No. 75, Feb, 1986

	GD	VG	FN	VF	VF/NM	NM-
1-Origin/1st app.	5	10	15	31	53	75
2-16,19-23,28-30: 5-Dr. Strange. 13-Saga of the Space Knights begins. 19-X-Men cameo. 23-Powerman & Iron Fist app.	1	2	3	5	6	8
17,18-X-Men app.	2	4	6	9	12	15
24-27: 24-F.F. cameo; Skrulls, Nova & The New Champions app. 25-Double size. 26,27-Galactus app.	1	2	3	5	7	9
31-49,51-60: 31,32-Brotherhood of Evil Mutants app. 32-X-Men cameo. 34,35-Sub-Mariner app. 41,42-Dr. Strange app. 56,57-Alpha Flight app. 58,59-Ant-Man app.						6.00
50-Skrulls app. (52 pgs.) Pin-ups by Konkle, Austin	1	2	3	4	5	7
61-74: 65-West Coast Avengers & Beta Ray Bill app. 65,66-X-Men app.						6.00
75-Last issue	2	4	6	9	12	15
Annual 1-4: (1982-85, 52 pgs.)						6.00

NOTE: **Austin** *c-3i, 18i, 61i.* **Byrne** *a-74i; c-56, 57, 74.* **Ditko** *a-59-75p, Annual 4.* **Golden** *c-7-12, 19.* **Guice** *a-61i; c-55, 58, 60p, 70p.* **Layton** *a-59i, 72i; c-15, 59i, 69.* **Miller** *c-2p?, 3p, 17p, 18p.* **Russell** *a(i)-64, 65, 67, 69, 71, 75; c-64, 65i, 66, 71i, 75.* **Severin** *c-41p.* **Sienkiewicz** *a-53i; c-46, 47, 52-54, 68, 71p, Annual 2.* **Simonson** *c-18.* **P. Smith** *c-59p.* **Starlin** *c-67.* **Zeck** *c-50.*

ROM (Based on the Parker Brothers toy)
IDW Publishing: Jul, 2016 - Present ($4.99/$3.99)

1-($4.99) Ryall & Gage-s/Messina-a 5.00
2-6-($3.99) 2-4-Revolution tie-in. 2-G.I. Joe app. 5-Transformers app. 4.00
Annual 2017 (1/17, $7.99) Origin of Rom; Ryall & Gage-s/Messina-a 8.00
FCBD 2016 Edition #0 - (5/16, giveaway) Prelude to series; Action Man flip book 3.00
...: Revolution (9/16, $3.99) Revolution x-over; Ryall-s/Gage-a; multiple covers 4.00

ROMANCE (See True Stories of...)

ROMANCE AND CONFESSION STORIES (See Giant Comics Edition)
St. John Publishing Co.: No date (1949) (25¢, 100 pgs.)

	GD	VG	FN	VF	VF/NM	NM-
1-Baker-c/a; remaindered St. John love comics	90	180	270	576	988	1400

ROMANCE DIARY
Marvel Comics (CDS)(CLDS): Dec, 1949 - No. 2, Mar, 1950

	GD	VG	FN	VF	VF/NM	NM-
1,2-Photo-c	19	38	57	111	176	240

ROMANCE OF FLYING, THE
David McKay Publications: 1942

	GD	VG	FN	VF	VF/NM	NM-
Feature Books 33 (nn)-WW II photos	16	32	48	94	147	200

ROMANCES OF MOLLY MANTON (See Molly Manton)

ROMANCES OF NURSE HELEN GRANT, THE

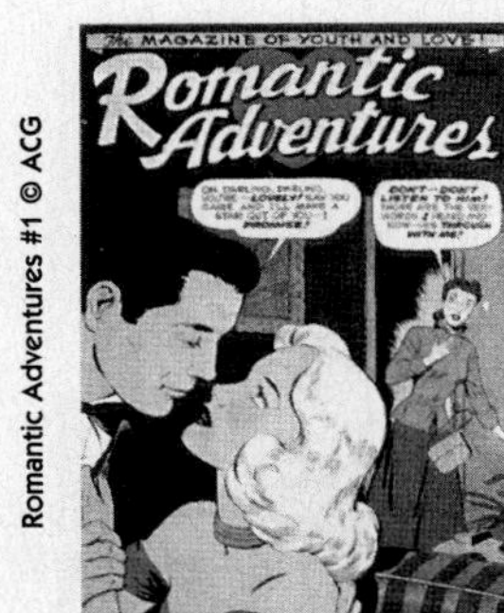

Romantic Adventures #1 © ACG

Romantic Hearts #7 © Story

Romantic Story #11 © FAW

	GD 2.0	VG 4.0	FN 6.0	VF 8.0	VF/NM 9.0	NM- 9.2
Atlas Comics (VPI): Aug, 1957						
1	13	26	39	72	101	130
ROMANCES OF THE WEST (Becomes Romantic Affairs #3?)						
Marvel Comics (SPC): Nov, 1949 - No. 2, Mar, 1950 (52 pgs.)						
1-Movie photo-c of Yvonne DeCarlo & Howard Duff (Calamity Jane & Sam Bass)	26	52	78	154	252	350
2-Photo-c	16	32	48	94	147	200
ROMANCE STORIES OF TRUE LOVE (Formerly True Love Problems & Advice Illustrated)						
Harvey Publications: No. 45, 5/57 - No. 50, 3/58; No. 51, 9/58 - No. 52, 11/58						
45-51: 45,46,48-50-Powell-a	6	12	18	31	38	45
52-Matt Baker-a	9	18	27	47	61	75
ROMANCE TALES (Formerly Western Winners #6?)						
Marvel Comics (CDS): No. 7, Oct, 1949 - No. 9, April, 1950 (7-9: photo-c)						
7	18	36	54	105	165	225
8,9: 8-Everett-a	14	28	42	76	108	140
ROMANCE TRAIL						
National Periodical Publications: July-Aug, 1949 - No. 6, May-June, 1950 (All photo-c & 52 pgs.)						
1-Kinstler, Toth-a; Jimmy Wakely photo-c	57	114	171	362	619	875
2-Kinstler-a; Jim Bannon photo-c	32	64	96	188	307	425
3-Tex Williams photo-c; Kinstler, Toth-a	34	68	102	199	325	450
4-Jim Bannon as Red Ryder photo-c; Toth-a	24	48	72	144	237	330
5,6: Photo-c on both. 5-Kinstler-a	22	44	66	132	216	300
ROMAN HOLIDAYS, THE (TV)						
Gold Key: Feb, 1973 - No. 4, Nov, 1973 (Hanna-Barbera)						
1	4	8	12	27	44	60
2-4	3	6	9	17	26	35
ROMANTIC ADVENTURES (My... #49-67, covers only)						
American Comics Group (B&I Publ. Co.): Mar-Apr, 1949 - No. 67, July, 1956 (Becomes My... #68 on)						
1	22	44	66	132	216	300
2	14	28	42	80	115	150
3-10	11	22	33	62	86	110
11-20 (4/52)	10	20	30	56	76	95
21-45,51,52: 52-Last Pre-code (2/55)	9	18	27	52	69	85
46-49-3-D effect-c/stories (TrueVision)	15	30	45	83	124	165
50-Classic cover/story "Love of A Lunatic"	53	106	159	334	567	800
53-67	9	18	27	47	61	75
NOTE: *#1-23, 52 pgs.* ***Shelly*** *a-40. Whitney c/art in many issues.*						
ROMANTIC AFFAIRS (Formerly Molly Manton's Romances #2 and/or Romances of the West #2 and/or Our Love #2?)						
Marvel Comics (SPC): No. 3, Mar, 1950						
3-Photo-c from Molly Manton's Romances #2	14	28	42	76	108	140
ROMANTIC CONFESSIONS						
Hillman Periodicals: Oct, 1949 - V3#1, Apr-May, 1953						
V1#1-McWilliams-a	21	42	63	124	202	280
2-Briefer-a; negligee panels	14	28	42	76	108	140
3-12	12	24	36	67	94	120
V2#1,2,4-8,10-12: 2-McWilliams-a	11	22	33	62	86	110
3-Krigstein-a	12	24	36	69	97	125
9-One pg. Frazetta ad	11	22	33	62	86	110
V3#1	11	22	33	60	83	105
ROMANTIC HEARTS						
Story Comics/Master/Merit Pubs.: Mar, 1951 - No. 10, Oct, 1952; July, 1953 - No. 12, July, 1955						
1(3/51) (1st Series)	18	36	54	107	169	230
2	11	22	33	64	90	115
3-10: Cameron-a	11	22	33	60	83	105
1(7/53) (2nd Series)-Some say #11 on-c	14	28	42	78	112	145
2	10	20	30	58	79	100
3-12	10	20	30	54	72	90
ROMANTIC LOVE						
Avon Periodicals/Realistic (No #14-19): 9-10/49 - #3, 1-2/50; #4, 2-3/51 - #13, 10/52; #20, 3-4/54 - #23, 9-10/54						
1-c-/Avon paperback #252	40	80	120	246	411	575
2-5: 3-c-/paperback Novel Library #12. 4-c-/paperback Diversey Prize Novel #5. 5-c-/paperback Novel Library #34	25	50	75	150	245	340
6- "Thrill Crazy" marijuana story; c-/Avon paperback #207; Kinstler-a	37	74	111	222	361	500
7,8: 8-Astarita-a(2)	24	48	72	142	234	325
9-c-/paperback Novel Library #41; Kinstler-a; headlights-c	37	74	111	222	361	500
10-12: 10-c-/Avon paperback #212. 11-c-/paperback Novel Library #17; Kinstler-a. 12-c-/paperback Novel Library #13	26	52	78	154	252	350
13,21-23: 22,23-Kinstler-c	24	48	72	142	234	325
20-Kinstler-c/a	25	50	75	147	241	335
nn(1-3/53)(Realistic-r)	16	32	48	94	147	200
NOTE: ***Astarita*** *a-7, 10, 11, 21. Painted c-1-3, 5, 7-11, 13. Photo c-4, 6.*						
ROMANTIC LOVE						
Quality Comics Group: 1963-1964						
I.W. Reprint #2,3,8,11: 2-r/Romantic Love #2	2	4	6	11	16	20
ROMANTIC MARRIAGE (Cinderella Love #25 on)						
Ziff-Davis/St. John No. 18 on (#1-8: 52 pgs.): #1-3 (1950, no months); #4, 5-6/51 - #17, 9/52; #18, 9/53 - #24, 9/54						
1-Photo-c; Cary Grant/Betsy Drake photo back-c.	27	54	81	158	259	360
2-Painted-c; Anderson-a (also #15)	18	36	54	105	165	225
3-9: 3,4,8,9-Painted-c; 5-7-Photo-c	16	32	48	94	147	200
10-Unusual format; front-c is a painted-c; back-c is a photo-c complete with logo, price, etc.	26	52	78	154	252	350
11-17 13-Photo-c. 15-Signed story by Anderson. 17-(9/52)-Last Z-D issue	15	30	45	85	130	175
18-22: 20-Photo-c	15	30	45	85	130	175
23-Baker-c; all stories are reprinted from #15	37	74	111	222	361	500
24-Baker-c	65	130	195	416	708	1000
ROMANTIC PICTURE NOVELETTES						
Magazine Enterprises: 1946						
1-Mary Worth-r; Creig Flessel-c	17	34	51	98	154	210
ROMANTIC SECRETS (Becomes Time For Love)						
Fawcett/Charlton Comics No. 5 (10/55) on: Sept, 1949 - No. 39, 4/53; No. 5, 10/55 - No. 52, 11/64 (#1-39: photo-c)						
1-(52 pg. issues begin, end #?)	18	36	54	103	162	220
2,3	11	22	33	62	86	110
4,9-Evans-a	12	24	36	67	94	120
5-8,10(9/50)	9	18	27	52	69	85
11-23	9	18	27	47	61	75
24-Evans-a	9	18	27	52	69	85
25-39('53)	8	16	24	44	57	70
5 (Charlton, 2nd Series)(10/55, formerly Negro Romances #4)	10	20	30	58	79	100
6-10	8	16	24	44	57	70
11-20	4	8	12	22	35	48
21-35	3	6	9	19	30	40
36-52('64)	3	6	9	16	23	30
NOTE: ***Bailey*** *a-20.* ***Powell*** *a(1st series)-5, 7, 10, 12, 16, 17, 20, 26, 29, 33, 34, 36, 37.* ***Sekowsky*** *a-26.* ***Swayze*** *a(1st series)-16, 18, 19, 23, 26-28, 31, 32, 39.*						
ROMANTIC STORY (Cowboy Love #28 on)						
Fawcett/Charlton Comics No. 23 on: 11/49 - #22, Sum, 1953; #23, 5/54 - #27, 12/54; #28, 8/55 - #130, 11/73						
1-Photo-c begin, end #24; 52 pgs. begins	18	36	54	103	162	220
2	11	22	33	62	86	110
3-5	10	20	30	54	72	90
6-14	9	18	27	50	65	80
15-Evans-a	10	20	30	54	72	90
16-22(Sum, '53; last Fawcett issue). 21-Toth-a?	8	16	24	42	54	65
23-39: 26,29-Wood swipes	7	14	21	37	46	55
40-(100 pgs.)	11	22	33	64	90	115
41-50	3	6	9	20	31	42
51-80: 57-Hypo needle story	3	6	9	16	23	30
81-99	2	4	6	10	14	18
100	2	4	6	13	28	22
101-130: 120-Bobby Sherman pin-up	2	4	6	9	12	15
NOTE: ***Jim Aparo*** *a-94.* ***Powell*** *a-7, 8, 16, 20, 30.* ***Marcus Swayze*** *a-2, 12, 20, 32.*						
ROMANTIC THRILLS (See Fox Giants)						
ROMANTIC WESTERN						
Fawcett Publications: Winter, 1949 - No. 3, June, 1950 (All Photo-c)						
1	22	44	66	128	209	290
2-(Spr/50)-Williamson, McWilliams-a	20	40	60	114	182	250
3	15	30	45	85	130	175

Romulus #1 © Hill & TCOW

Roswell: Little Green Man #6 © Bongo

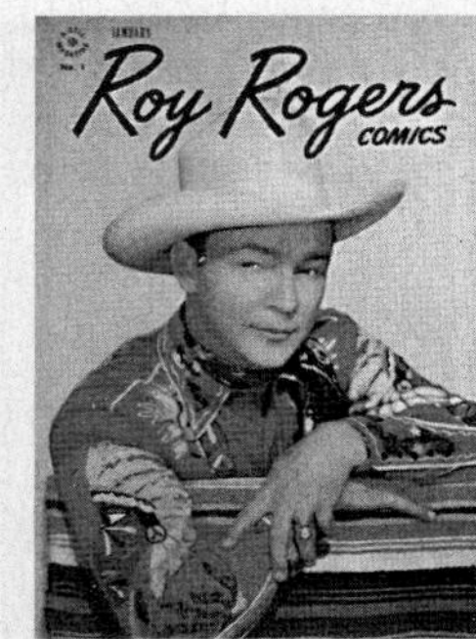

Roy Rogers Comics #1 © DELL

ROMEO TUBBS (...That Lovable Teenager; formerly My Secret Life)
Fox Feature Syndicate/Green Publ. Co. No. 27: No. 26, 5/50 - No. 28, 7/50; No. 1, 1950; No. 27, 12/52

	GD 2.0	VG 4.0	FN 6.0	VF 8.0	VF/NM 9.0	NM- 9.2
26-Teen-age	13	26	39	74	105	135
28 (7/50)	11	22	33	64	90	115
27 (12/52)-Contains Pedro on inside; Wood-a (exist?)	15	30	45	90	140	190

ROMULUS
Image Comics: Oct, 2016 - Present ($3.99)

	GD 2.0	VG 4.0	FN 6.0	VF 8.0	VF/NM 9.0	NM- 9.2
1-3-Bryan Hill-s/Nelson Blake II-a						4.00

RONALD McDONALD (TV)
Charlton Press: Sept, 1970 - No. 4, March, 1971

	GD 2.0	VG 4.0	FN 6.0	VF 8.0	VF/NM 9.0	NM- 9.2
1-Bill Yates-a in all	7	14	21	48	89	130
2-4: 2 & 3 both dated Jan, 1971	5	10	15	30	50	70
V2#1-4-Special reprint for McDonald systems; new cover art on each; "Not for resale" on cover	5	10	15	34	60	85

RONIN
DC Comics: July, 1983 - No. 6, Aug, 1984 ($2.50, limited series, 52 pgs.)

	GD 2.0	VG 4.0	FN 6.0	VF 8.0	VF/NM 9.0	NM- 9.2
1-5-Frank Miller-c/a/scripts in all	2	4	6	8	11	14
6-Scarcer; has fold-out poster.	2	4	6	10	14	18
Trade paperback (1987, $12.95)-Reprints #1-6						18.00

RONNA
Knight Press: Apr, 1997 ($2.95, B&W, one-shot)

	GD 2.0	VG 4.0	FN 6.0	VF 8.0	VF/NM 9.0	NM- 9.2
1-Beau Smith-s						3.00

ROOK (See Eerie Magazine & Warren Presents: The Rook)
Warren Publications: Oct, 1979 - No. 14, April, 1982 (B&W magazine)

	GD 2.0	VG 4.0	FN 6.0	VF 8.0	VF/NM 9.0	NM- 9.2
1-Nino-a/Corben-c; with 8 pg. color insert	3	6	9	16	23	30
2-4,6,7: 2-Voltar by Alcala begins. 3,4-Toth-a	2	4	6	9	13	16
5,8-14: 11-Zorro-s. 12-14-Eagle by Severin	2	4	6	9	13	16

ROOK
Harris Comics: No. 0, Jun, 1995 - No. 4, 1995 ($2.95)

	GD 2.0	VG 4.0	FN 6.0	VF 8.0	VF/NM 9.0	NM- 9.2
0-4: 0-short stories (3) w/preview. 4-Brereton-c.						3.00

ROOK, THE
Dark Horse Comics: Oct, 2015 - No. 4, Jan, 2016 ($3.99)

	GD 2.0	VG 4.0	FN 6.0	VF 8.0	VF/NM 9.0	NM- 9.2
1-4-Steven Grant-s/Paul Gulacy-a/c						4.00

ROOKIE COP (Formerly Crime and Justice?)
Charlton Comics: No. 27, Nov, 1955 - No. 33, Aug, 1957

	GD 2.0	VG 4.0	FN 6.0	VF 8.0	VF/NM 9.0	NM- 9.2
27	9	18	27	47	61	75
28-33	6	12	18	31	38	45

ROOM 222 (TV)
Dell Publishing Co.: Jan, 1970; No. 2, May, 1970 - No. 4, Jan, 1971

	GD 2.0	VG 4.0	FN 6.0	VF 8.0	VF/NM 9.0	NM- 9.2
1	5	10	15	31	53	75
2-4-Photo-c. 3-Marijuana story. 4 r/#1	3	6	9	21	34	45

ROOTIE KAZOOTIE (TV)(See 3-D-ell)
Dell Publishing Co.: No. 415, Aug, 1952 - No. 6, Oct-Dec, 1954

	GD 2.0	VG 4.0	FN 6.0	VF 8.0	VF/NM 9.0	NM- 9.2
Four Color 415 (#1)	9	18	27	59	117	175
Four Color 459,502(#2,3), 4(4-6/54)-6	6	12	18	41	76	110

ROOTS OF THE SWAMP THING
DC Comics: July, 1986 - No.5, Nov, 1986 ($2.00, Baxter paper, 52 pgs.)

	GD 2.0	VG 4.0	FN 6.0	VF 8.0	VF/NM 9.0	NM- 9.2
1-5: r/Swamp Thing #1-10 by Wrightson & House of Mystery-r. 1-new Wrightson-c (2-5 reprinted covers).						5.00

ROSE (See Bone)
Cartoon Books: Nov, 2000 - No. 3, Feb, 2002 ($5.95, lim. series, square-bound)

	GD 2.0	VG 4.0	FN 6.0	VF 8.0	VF/NM 9.0	NM- 9.2
1-3-Prequel to Bone; Jeff Smith-s/Charles Vess painted-a/c						6.00
HC (2001, $29.95) r/#1-3; new Vess cover painting						30.00
SC (2002, $19.95) r/#1-3; new Vess cover painting						20.00
1-($6.00)-Blood & Glory Edition						6.00

ROSE AND THORN
DC Comics: Feb, 2004 - No. 6, July, 2004 ($2.95, limited series)

	GD 2.0	VG 4.0	FN 6.0	VF 8.0	VF/NM 9.0	NM- 9.2
1-6-Simone-s/Melo-a/Hughes-c						3.00

ROSWELL: LITTLE GREEN MAN (See Simpsons Comics #19-22)
Bongo Comics: 1996 - No. 6 ($2.95, quarterly)

	GD 2.0	VG 4.0	FN 6.0	VF 8.0	VF/NM 9.0	NM- 9.2
1-6						4.00
...Walks Among Us ('97, $12.95, TPB) r/ #1-3 & Simpsons flip books						13.00

ROUGH RIDERS
AfterShock Comics: Apr, 2016 - No. 7, Nov, 2016 ($3.99)

	GD 2.0	VG 4.0	FN 6.0	VF 8.0	VF/NM 9.0	NM- 9.2
1-7: 1-Teddy Roosevelt, Annie Oakley, Houdini, Jack Johnson, Thomas Edison team						4.00
... Nation 1 (11/16, $3.99) Dossier of other Rough Rider teams; art by various						4.00

ROUGH RIDERS: RIDERS ON THE STORM
AfterShock Comics: Feb, 2017 - Present ($3.99)

	GD 2.0	VG 4.0	FN 6.0	VF 8.0	VF/NM 9.0	NM- 9.2
1-Glass-s/Olliffe-a; Monk Eastman joins team						4.00

ROUND TABLE OF AMERICA: PERSONALITY CRISIS (See Big Bang Comics)
Image Comics: Aug, 2005 ($3.50, one-shot)

	GD 2.0	VG 4.0	FN 6.0	VF 8.0	VF/NM 9.0	NM- 9.2
1-Carlos Rodriguez-a/Pedro Angosto-s						3.50

ROUNDUP (...Western Crime Stories)
D. S. Publishing Co.: July-Aug, 1948 - No. 5, Mar-Apr, 1949 (All 52 pgs.)

	GD 2.0	VG 4.0	FN 6.0	VF 8.0	VF/NM 9.0	NM- 9.2
1-Kiefer-a	19	38	57	111	176	240
2-5: 2-Marijuana drug mention story	15	30	45	83	124	165

ROUTE 666
CrossGeneration Comics: July, 2002 - No. 22, Jun, 2004 ($2.95)

	GD 2.0	VG 4.0	FN 6.0	VF 8.0	VF/NM 9.0	NM- 9.2
1-22-Bedard-s/Moline-a in most. 5-Richards-a. 15-McCrea-a						3.00

ROWANS RUIN
BOOM! Studios: Oct, 2015 - No. 4, Jan, 2016 ($3.99, limited series)

	GD 2.0	VG 4.0	FN 6.0	VF 8.0	VF/NM 9.0	NM- 9.2
1-4-Mike Carey-s/Mike Perkins-a. 1-Multiple covers						4.00

ROYAL ROY
Marvel Comics (Star Comics): May, 1985 - No.6, Mar, 1986 (Children's book)

	GD 2.0	VG 4.0	FN 6.0	VF 8.0	VF/NM 9.0	NM- 9.2
1-6						4.00

ROYALS, THE: MASTERS OF WAR
DC Comics (Vertigo): Apr, 2014 - No. 6, Sept, 2014 ($2.99, limited series)

	GD 2.0	VG 4.0	FN 6.0	VF 8.0	VF/NM 9.0	NM- 9.2
1-6-Rob Williams-s/Simon Coleby-a/c; super-powered Royal families during WWII						3.00

ROY CAMPANELLA, BASEBALL HERO
Fawcett Publications: 1950 (Brooklyn Dodgers)

	GD 2.0	VG 4.0	FN 6.0	VF 8.0	VF/NM 9.0	NM- 9.2
nn-Photo-c; life story	62	124	186	394	677	960

ROY ROGERS (See March of Comics #17, 35, 47, 62, 68, 73, 77, 86, 91, 100, 105, 116, 121, 131, 136, 146, 151, 161, 167, 176, 191, 206, 221, 236, 250)

ROY ROGERS AND TRIGGER
Gold Key: Apr, 1967

	GD 2.0	VG 4.0	FN 6.0	VF 8.0	VF/NM 9.0	NM- 9.2
1-Photo-c; reprints	4	8	12	27	44	60

ROY ROGERS ANNUAL
Wilson Publ. Co., Toronto/Dell: 1947 ("Giant Edition" on-c)(132 pgs., 50¢)

nn-Seven known copies. Front and back cover art are from Roy Rogers #2. Stories reprinted from Roy Rogers #2, Four Color #137 and Four Color #153. (A copy in VG/FN was sold in 1986 for $400, in 1996 for $1200 & in 2000 for $1500; a FN+ sold for $1,650; a GD sold for $448 in 2008, a FN sold for $717 in 2009 and a FR sold for $156 in 2015.)

ROY ROGERS COMICS (See Western Roundup under Dell Giants)
Dell Publishing Co.: No. 38, 4/44 - No. 177, 12/47 (#38-166: 52 pgs.)

	GD 2.0	VG 4.0	FN 6.0	VF 8.0	VF/NM 9.0	NM- 9.2
Four Color 38 (1944)-49 pg. story; photo front/back-c on all 4-Color issues (1st western comic with photo-c)	152	304	456	1254	2827	4400
Four Color 63 (1945)-Color photos on all four-c	38	76	114	285	641	1000
Four Color 86,95 (1945)	28	56	84	202	451	700
Four Color 109 (1946)	21	42	63	147	324	500
Four Color 117,124,137,144	17	34	51	117	259	400
Four Color 153,160,166: 166-48 pg. story	15	30	45	105	233	360
Four Color 177 (36 pgs.)-32 pg. story	15	30	45	100	220	340
HC (Dark Horse Books, 8/08, $49.95) r/Four Color #38,63,86,95,109; Roy Rogers Jr intro.						50.00

ROY ROGERS COMICS (...& Trigger #92(8/55)-on)(Roy starred in Republic movies, radio & TV) (Singing cowboy) (Also see Dale Evans, It Really Happened #8, Queen of the West Dale Evans, & Roy Rogers' Trigger)
Dell Publishing Co.: Jan, 1948 - No. 145, Sept-Oct, 1961 (#1-19: 36 pgs.)

	GD 2.0	VG 4.0	FN 6.0	VF 8.0	VF/NM 9.0	NM- 9.2
1-Roy, his horse Trigger, & Chuck Wagon Charley's Tales begin; photo-c begin, end #145	59	118	177	472	1061	1650
2	20	40	60	138	307	475
3-5	14	28	42	96	211	325
6-10	12	24	36	80	173	265
11-19: 19-Chuckwagon Charley's Tales ends	10	20	30	68	144	220
20 (52 pgs.)-Trigger feature begins, ends #46	10	20	30	69	147	225
21-30 (52 pgs.)	9	18	27	60	120	180
31-46 (52 pgs.): 37-X-Mas-c	8	16	24	51	96	140
47-56 (36 pgs.): 47-Chuck Wagon Charley's Tales returns, ends #133. 49-X-mas-c. 55-Last photo back-c	6	12	18	40	73	105

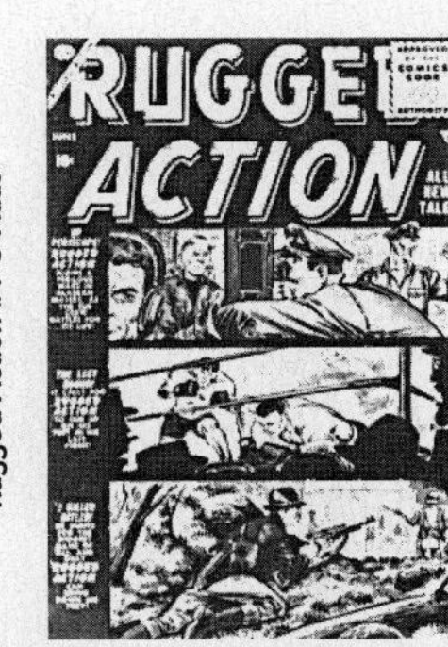

Rugged Action #4 © Atlas

Rumble #8 © Arcudi & Harren

Runaways (2008 series) #10 © MAR

	GD 2.0	VG 4.0	FN 6.0	VF 8.0	VF/NM 9.0	NM- 9.2
57 (52 pgs.)-Heroin drug propaganda story	6	12	18	41	76	110
58-70 (52 pgs.): 58-Heroin drug use/dealing story. 61-X-Mas-c	6	12	18	40	73	105
71-80 (52 pgs.): 73-X-Mas-c	5	10	15	35	63	90
81-91 (36 pgs. #81-on): 85-X-Mas-c	5	10	15	34	60	85
92-99,101-110,112-118: 92-Title changed to Roy Rogers and Trigger (8/55)	5	10	15	33	57	80
100-Trigger feature returns, ends #131	6	12	18	37	66	95
111,119-124-Toth-a	6	12	18	38	69	100
125-131: 125-Toth-a (1 pg.)	5	10	15	31	53	75
132-144-Manning-a. 132-1st Dale Evans-sty by Russ Manning. 138,144-Dale Evans featured	5	10	15	34	60	85
145-Last issue	6	12	18	40	73	105

NOTE: ***Buscema** a-74-108(2 stories each). **Manning** a-123, 124, 132-144. **Marsh** a-110. Photo back-c No. 1-9, 11-35, 38-55.*

ROY ROGERS' TRIGGER
Dell Publishing Co.: No. 329, May, 1951 - No. 17, June-Aug, 1955

	GD	VG	FN	VF	VF/NM	NM-
Four Color 329 (#1)-Painted-c	14	28	42	94	207	320
2 (9-11/51)-Photo-c	10	20	30	64	132	200
3-5: 3-Painted-c begin, end #17, most by S. Savitt	6	12	18	38	69	100
6-17: Title merges with Roy Rogers after #17	5	10	15	31	53	75

ROY ROGERS WESTERN CLASSICS
AC Comics: 1989 -No. 4 ($2.95/$3.95, 44pgs.) (24 pgs. color, 16 pgs. B&W)

1-4: 1-Dale Evans-r by Manning, Trigger-r by Buscema; photo covers & interior photos by Roy & Dale. 2-Buscema-r (3); photo-c & B&W photos inside. 3-Dale Evans-r by Manning; Trigger-r by Buscema plus other Buscema-r; photo-c 4.00

RUDOLPH, THE RED-NOSED REINDEER
National Per. Publ.: 1950 - No. 13, Winter, 1962-63 (Issues are not numbered)

	GD	VG	FN	VF	VF/NM	NM-
1950 issue (#1); Grossman-c/a in all	29	58	87	170	278	385
1951-53 issues (3 total)	18	36	54	103	162	220
1954/55, 55/56, 56/57	16	32	48	94	147	200
1957/58, 58/59, 59/60, 60/61, 61/62	9	18	27	61	123	185
1962/63 (rare)(84 pgs.)(shows "Annual" in indicia)	17	34	51	117	259	400

NOTE: *13 total issues published. Has games & puzzles also.*

RUDOLPH, THE RED-NOSED REINDEER (Also see Limited Collectors' Edition C-20, C-24, C-33, C-42, C-50; and All-New Collectors' Edition C-53 & C-60)
National Per. Publ.: Christmas 1972 (Treasury-size)

	GD	VG	FN	VF	VF/NM	NM-
nn-Precursor to Limited Collectors' Edition title (scarce) (implied to be Lim. Coll .Ed. C-20)	19	38	57	131	291	450

RUFF AND REDDY (TV)
Dell Publ. Co.: No. 937, 9/58 - No. 12, 1-3/62 (Hanna-Barbera)(#9 on: 15¢)

	GD	VG	FN	VF	VF/NM	NM-
Four Color 937(#1)(1st Hanna-Barbera comic book)	10	20	30	67	141	215
Four Color 981,1038	7	14	21	44	82	120
4(1-3/60)-12: 8-Last 10¢ issue	6	12	18	38	69	100

RUGGED ACTION (Strange Stories of Suspense #5 on)
Atlas Comics (CSI): Dec, 1954 - No. 4, June, 1955

	GD	VG	FN	VF	VF/NM	NM-
1-Brodsky-c	16	32	48	94	147	200
2-4: 2-Last precode (2/55)	13	26	39	72	101	130

NOTE: ***Ayers** a-2, 3. **Maneely** c-2, 3. **Severin** a-2.*

RUINS
Marvel Comics (Alterniverse): July, 1995 - No. 2, Sept, 1995 ($5.00, painted, limited series)

1,2: Phil Sheldon from Marvels; Warren Ellis scripts; acetate-c 6.00
Reprint (2009, $4.99) r/#1,2; cover gallery 5.00

RULAH JUNGLE GODDESS (Formerly Zoot; I Loved #28 on) (Also see All Top Comics & Terrors of the Jungle)
Fox Features Syndicate: No. 17, Aug, 1948 - No. 27, June, 1949

	GD	VG	FN	VF	VF/NM	NM-
17	142	284	426	909	1555	2200
18-Classic girl-fight interior splash	87	174	261	553	952	1350
19,20	81	162	243	518	884	1250
21-Used in **SOTI**, pg. 388,389	84	168	252	538	919	1300
22-Used in **SOTI**, pg. 22,23	82	164	246	528	902	1275
23-27	61	122	183	390	670	950

NOTE: ***Kamen** c-17-19, 21, 22.*

RUNAWAY, THE (See Movie Classics)

RUNAWAYS
Marvel Comics: July, 2003 - No. 18, Nov, 2004 ($2.95/$2.25/$2.99)

1-($2.95) Vaughan-s/Alphona-a/Jo Chen-c 4.00
2-9-($2.50) 3.00
10-18-($2.99) 11,12-Miyazawa-a; Cloak and Dagger app. 16-The mole revealed 3.00
Hardcover (2005, $34.99) oversized r/#1-18; proposal & sketch pages; Vaughan intro. 35.00
Marvel Age Runaways Vol. 1: Pride and Joy (2004, $7.99, digest size) r/#1-6 8.00
...Vol. 2: Teenage Wasteland (2004, $7.99, digest size) r/#7-12 8.00
...Vol. 3: The Good Die Young (2004, $7.99, digest size) r/#13-18 8.00

RUNAWAYS (Also see X-Men/Runaways 2006 FCBD Edition in the Promotional Section)
Marvel Comics: Apr, 2005 - No. 30, Aug, 2008 ($2.99)

1-24: 1-6-Vaughan-s/Alphona-a/Jo Chen-c. 7,8-Miyazawa-a/Bachalo-c. 11-Spider-Man app. 12-New Avengers app. 18-Gert killed 3.00
25-30-Joss Whedon-s/Michael Ryan-a. 25-Punisher app. 3.00
...: Dead End Kids HC (2008, $19.99) r/#25-30 20.00
... Saga (2007, $3.99) re-caps the 2 series thru #24; 4 new pages w/Ramos-a; Ramos-c 4.00
Hardcover (2006, $24.99) oversized r/#1-12 & X-Men/Runaways; script & sketch pages 25.00
Hardcover Vol. 3 (2007, $24.99) oversized r/#13-24; sketch pages 25.00
...Vol. 4: True Believers (2006, $7.99, digest size) r/#1-6 8.00
...Vol. 5: Escape To New York (2006, $7.99, digest size) r/#7-12 8.00
...Vol. 6: Parental Guidance (2006, $7.99, digest size) r/#13-18 8.00

RUNAWAYS (3rd series)
Marvel Comics: Oct, 2008 - No. 14, Nov, 2009 ($2.99/$3.99)

1-9,11-14: 1-6-Terry Moore-s/Humberto Ramos-a/c. 7-9-Miyazawa-a 3.00
10-($3.99) Wolverine & the X-Men app.; Yost & Asmus-s; Pichelli & Rios-a; Lafuente-c 4.00

RUNAWAYS (Secret Wars Battleworld tie-in)
Marvel Comics: Aug, 2015 - No. 4, Nov, 2015 ($3.99, limited series)

1-4-Noelle Stevenson-s/Sanford Greene-a 4.00

RUN BABY RUN
Logos International: 1974 (39¢, Christian religious)

	GD	VG	FN	VF	VF/NM	NM-
nn-By Tony Tallarico from Nicky Cruz's book	2	4	6	11	16	20

RUN, BUDDY, RUN (TV)
Gold Key: June, 1967 (Photo-c)

	GD	VG	FN	VF	VF/NM	NM-
1 (10204-706)	3	6	9	17	26	35

RUNE (See Curse of Rune, Sludge & all other Ultraverse titles for previews)
Malibu Comics (Ultraverse): 1994 - No. 9, Apr, 1995 ($1.95)

	GD	VG	FN	VF	VF/NM	NM-
0-Obtained by sending coupons from 11 comics; came w/Solution #0, poster, temporary tattoo, card	1	2	3	5	6	8

1,2,4-9: 1-Barry Windsor-Smith-c/a/stories begin, ends #6. 5-1st app. of Gemini. 6-Prime & Mantra app. 3.00
1-(1/94)-"Ashcan" edition flip book w/Wrath #1 3.00
1-Ultra 5000 Limited silver foil edition 6.00
3-(3/94, $3.50, 68 pgs.)-Flip book w/Ultraverse Premiere #1 4.00
Giant Size 1 ($2.50, 44 pgs.)-B.Smith story & art. 4.00

RUNE (2nd Series)(Formerly Curse of Rune)(See Ultraverse Unlimited #1)
Malibu Comics (Ultraverse): Infinity, Sept, 1995 - V2#7, Apr, 1996 ($1.50)

Infinity, V2#1-7: Infinity-Black September tie-in; black-c & painted-c exist. 1,3-7-Marvel's Adam Warlock app; regular & painted-c exist. 2-Flip book w/ "Phoenix Resurrection" Pt. 6 3.00
...Vs. Venom 1 (12/95, $3.95) 4.00

RUNE: HEARTS OF DARKNESS
Malibu Comics (Ultraverse): Sept, 1996 - No. 3, Nov, 1996 ($1.50, lim. series)

1-3: Moench scripts & Kyle Hotz-c/a; flip books w/6 pg. Rune story by the Pander Bros. 3.00

RUNE/SILVER SURFER
Marvel Comics/Malibu Comics (Ultraverse): Apr, 1995 ($5.95/$2.95, one-shot)

1 ($5.95, direct market)-BWS-c 6.00
1 ($2.95, newstand)-BWS-c 3.00
1-Collector's limited edition 6.00

RUNLOVEKILL
Image Comics: Apr, 2015 - No. 8 ($2.99, limited series)

1-4: 1-Tsuei-s/Canete-a 3.00

RUSE (Also see Archard's Agents)
CrossGeneration Comics: Nov, 2001 - No. 26, Jan, 2004 ($2.95)

1-Waid-s/Guice & Perkins-a 5.00
2-26: 6-Jeff Johnson-a. 11,15-Paul Ryan-a. 12-Last Waid-s 3.00
Enter the Detective Vol. 1 TPB (2002, $15.95) r/#1-6; Guice-c 16.00
...: The Silent Partner Vol. 2 (3/03, $15.95, TPB) r/#7-12 16.00
...: Criminal Intent Vol. 3 ('03, $15.95, TPB) r/#13-18 16.00
Traveler 1,2 ($9.95): Digest-size editions of the TPBs 10.00

RUSE
Marvel Comics: May, 2011 - No. 4 ($2.99, limited series)

1-4-Waid-s/Guice-c. 1,3,4-Pierfederici-a 3.00

Rusty Comics #12 © MAR

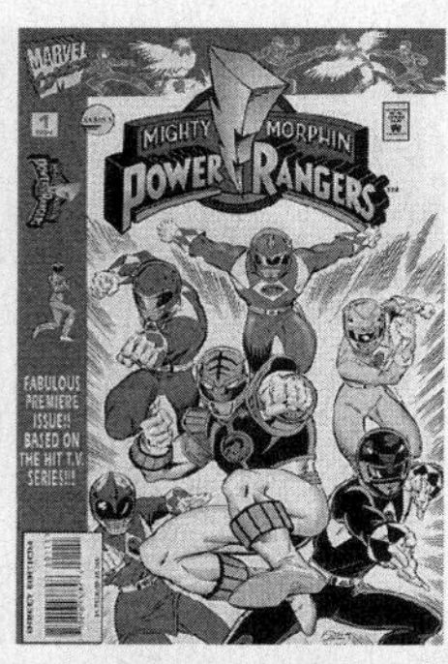

Saban's Mighty Morphin Power Rangers #1 © Saban

Sabrina #32 © ACP

GD 2.0 | VG 4.0 | FN 6.0 | VF 8.0 | VF/NM 9.0 | NM- 9.2

RUSH CITY
DC Comics: Sept, 2006 - No. 6, May, 2007 ($2.99, limited series)
1-6: 1-Dixon-s/Green-a/Jock-c. 2,3-Black Canary app. 3.00

RUSTLERS, THE (See Zane Grey Four Color 532)

RUSTY, BOY DETECTIVE
Good Comics/Lev Gleason: Mar-April, 1955 - No. 5, Nov, 1955
1-Bob Wood, Carl Hubbell-a begins 9 18 27 50 65 80
2-5 7 14 21 35 43 50

RUSTY COMICS (Formerly Kid Movie Comics; Rusty and Her Family #21, 22; The Kelleys #23 on; see Millie The Model)
Marvel Comics (HPC): No. 12, Apr, 1947 - No. 22, Sept, 1949
12-Mitzi app. 29 58 87 170 278 385
13 17 34 51 98 154 210
14-Wolverton's Powerhouse Pepper (4 pgs.) plus Kurtzman's "Hey Look" 26 52 78 154 252 350
15-17-Kurtzman's "Hey Look" 20 40 60 114 182 250
18,19 15 30 45 90 140 190
20-Kurtzman-a (5 pgs.) 20 40 60 117 189 260
21,22-Kurtzman-a (17 & 22 pgs.) 25 50 75 147 241 335

RUSTY DUGAN (See Holyoke One-Shot #2)

RUSTY RILEY
Dell Publishing Co.: No. 418, Aug, 1952 - No. 554, April, 1954 (Frank Godwin strip reprints)
Four Color 418 (...a Boy, a Horse, and a Dog #1) 6 12 18 38 69 100
Four Color 451(2/53), 486 ('53), 554 4 8 12 28 47 65

RUULE
Beckett Comics: Dec, 2003 - No. 5, Apr, 2004 ($2.99)
1-5-David Mack-c/Mike Hawthorne-a 3.00

RUULE: KISS & TELL
Beckett Comics: Jun, 2004 - No. 8 ($1.99)
1-8: 1-Amano-s/c; Rousseau-a. 4-Maleev-c 3.00
TPB (2005, $19.99) r/#1-8 20.00

RYDER OF THE STORM
Radical Comics: Oct, 2010 - No. 3, Apr, 2011 ($4.99, limited series)
1-3-David Hine-s/Wayne Nichols-a 5.00

SAARI ("The Jungle Goddess")
P. L. Publishing Co.: November, 1951
1 52 104 156 329 557 785

SABAN POWERHOUSE (TV)
Acclaim Books: 1997 ($4.50, digest size)
1,2-Power Rangers, BeetleBorgs, and others 4.50

SABAN PRESENTS POWER RANGERS TURBO VS. BEETLEBORGS METALLIX (TV)
Acclaim Books: 1997 ($4.50, digest size, one-shot)
nn 4.50

SABAN'S MIGHTY MORPHIN POWER RANGERS
Hamilton Comics: Dec, 1994 - No. 6, May, 1995 ($1.95, limited series)
1-6: 1-w/bound-in Power Ranger Barcode Card 4.00

SABAN'S MIGHTY MORPHIN POWER RANGERS (TV)
Marvel Comics: 1995 - No. 8, 1996 ($1.75)
1-8 4.00

SABLE (Formerly Jon Sable, Freelance; also see Mike Grell's...)
First Comics: Mar, 1988 - No. 27, May, 1990 ($1.75/$1.95)
1-27: 10-Begin $1.95-c 3.00

SABLE & FORTUNE (Also see Silver Sable and the Wild Pack)
Marvel Comics: Mar, 2006 - No. 4, June, 2006 ($2.99, limited series)
1-4-John Burns-a/Brendan Cahill-s 3.00

SABRE (See Eclipse Graphic Album Series)
Eclipse Comics: Aug, 1982 - No. 14, Aug, 1985 (Baxter paper #4 on)
1-14: 1-Sabre & Morrigan Tales begin. 4-6-Incredible Seven origin 3.00

SABRETOOTH (See Iron Fist, Power Man, X-Factor #10 & X-Men)
Marvel Comics: Aug, 1993 - No. 4, Nov, 1993 ($2.95, lim. series, coated paper)
1-4: 1-Die-cut-c. 3-Wolverine app. 5.00
...Special 1 "In the Red Zone" (1995, $4.95) Chromium wraparound-c 6.00
V2 #1 (1/98, $5.95, one-shot) Wildchild app. 6.00
Trade paperback (12/94, $12.95) r/#1-4 13.00

SABRETOOTH
Marvel Comics: Dec, 2004 - No. 4, Feb, 2005 ($2.99, limited series)
1-4-Sears-a. 3,4-Wendigo app. 3.00
...: Open Season TPB (2005, $9.99) r/#1-4 10.00

SABRETOOTH AND MYSTIQUE (See Mystique and Sabretooth)

SABRETOOTH CLASSIC
Marvel Comics: May, 1994 - No. 15, July, 1995 ($1.50)
1-15: 1-3-r/Power Man & Iron Fist #66,78,84. 4-r/Spec. S-M #116. 9-Uncanny X-Men #212, 10-r/Uncanny X-Men #213. 11-r/ Daredevil #238. 12-r/Classic X-Men #10 3.00

SABRETOOTH: MARY SHELLEY OVERDRIVE
Marvel Comics: Aug, 2002 - No. 4, Nov, 2002 ($2.99, limited series)
1-4-Jolley-s; Harris-c 3.00

SABRINA (Volume 2) (Based on animated series)
Archie Publications: Jan, 2000 - No. 104, Sept, 2009 ($1.79/$1.99/$2.19/$2.25/$2.50)
1-Teen-age Witch magically reverted to 12 years old 1 3 4 6 8 10
2-10: 4-Begin $1.99-c 4.00
11-104: 38-Sabrina aged back to 16 years old. 39-Begin $2.19-c. 58-Manga-style begins; Tania Del Rio-a. 67-Josie and the Pussycats app. 101-Young Salem; begin $2.50-c 3.00

SABRINA'S CHRISTMAS MAGIC (See Archie Giant Series Magazine #196, 207, 220, 231, 243, 455, 467, 479, 491, 503, 515)

SABRINA'S HALLOWEEN SPOOOKTACULAR
Archie Publications: 1993 - 1995 ($2.00, 52 pgs.)
1-Neon orange ink-c; bound-in poster 1 3 4 6 8 10
2,3-Titled "Sabrina's Holiday Spectacular" 6.00

SABRINA, THE TEEN-AGE WITCH (TV)(See Archie Giant Series, Archie's Madhouse 22, Archie's TV..., Chilling Advs. In Sorcery, Little Archie #59)
Archie Publications: April, 1971 - No. 77, Jan, 1983 (52 pg.Giants No. 1-17)
1-52 pgs. begin, end #17 13 26 39 89 195 300
2-Archie's group x-over 8 16 24 54 102 150
3-5: 3,4-Archie's Group x-over 5 10 15 35 63 90
6-10 5 10 15 31 53 75
11-17(2/74) 4 8 12 25 40 55
18-30 3 6 9 18 28 38
31-40(8/77) 3 6 9 14 20 26
41-60(6/80) 2 4 6 10 14 18
61-70 2 4 6 8 11 14
71-76-low print run 2 4 6 11 16 20
77-Last issue; low print run 3 6 9 14 20 26

SABRINA, THE TEEN-AGE WITCH
Archie Publications: 1996 ($1.50, 32 pgs., one-shot)
1-Updated origin 1 3 4 6 8 10

SABRINA, THE TEEN-AGE WITCH (Continues in Sabrina, Vol. 2)
Archie Publications: May, 1997 - No. 32, Dec, 1999 ($1.50/$1.75/$1.79)
1-Photo-c with Melissa Joan Hart 1 3 4 6 8 10
2-10: 9-Begin $1.75-c 6.00
11-20 5.00
21-32: 24-Begin $1.79-c. 28-Sonic the Hedgehog-c/app. 4.00

SABU, "ELEPHANT BOY" (Movie; formerly My Secret Story)
Fox Features Syndicate: No. 30, June, 1950 - No. 2, Aug, 1950
30(#1)-Wood-a; photo-c from movie 27 54 81 158 259 360
2-Photo-c from movie; Kamen-a 20 40 60 114 182 250

SACHS & VIOLENS
Marvel Comics (Epic Comics): Nov, 1993 - No. 4, July, 1994 ($2.25, limited series, mature)
1-($2.75)-Embossed-c w/bound-in trading card 3.00
1-($3.50)-Platinum edition (1 for each 10 ordered) 4.00
2-4: Perez-c/a; bound-in trading card: 2-(5/94) 3.00
TPB (DC, 2006, $14.99) r/series; intro. by Peter David; creator bios. 15.00

SACRAMENTS, THE
Catechetical Guild Educational Society: Oct, 1955 (35¢)
30304 6 12 18 31 38 45

SACRED AND THE PROFANE, THE (See Eclipse Graphic Album Series #9 & Epic Illustrated #20)

SADDLE JUSTICE (Happy Houlihans #1,2) (Saddle Romances #9 on)
E. C. Comics: No. 3, Spring, 1948 - No. 8, Sept-Oct, 1949
3-The 1st E.C. by Bill Gaines to break away from M. C. Gaines' old Educational Comics format. Craig, Feldstein, H. C. Kiefer, & Stan Asch-a; mentioned in Love and Death

Saddle Justice #7 © WMG

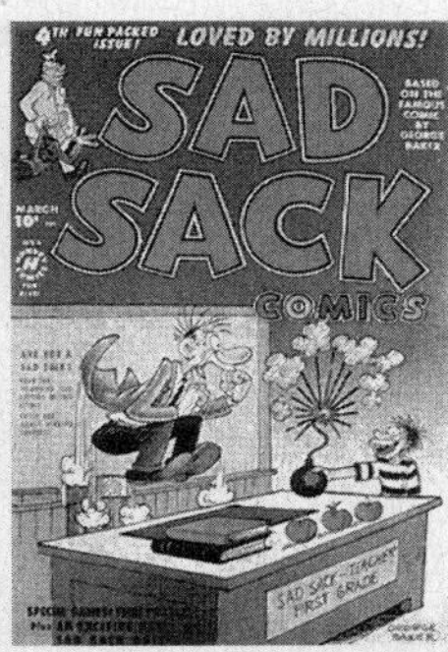

Sad Sack Comics #4 © HARV

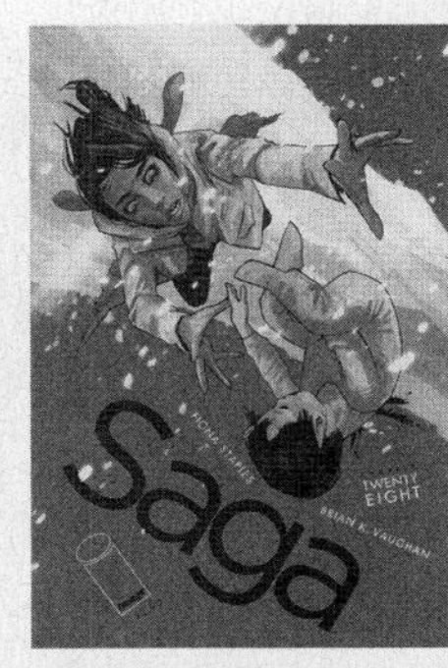

Saga #28 © Vaughan & Staples

	GD 2.0	VG 4.0	FN 6.0	VF 8.0	VF/NM 9.0	NM- 9.2
	63	126	189	403	689	975
4-1st Graham Ingels-a for E.C.	54	108	162	343	574	825
5-8-Ingels-a in all	51	102	153	318	539	760

NOTE: *Craig* and *Feldstein* art in most issues. Canadian reprints known; see Table of Contents. *Craig* c-3, 4. *Ingels* c-5-8. #4 contains a biography of *Craig*.

SADDLE ROMANCES (Saddle Justice #3-8; Weird Science #12 on)
E. C. Comics: No. 9, Nov-Dec, 1949 - No. 11, Mar-Apr, 1950

	GD 2.0	VG 4.0	FN 6.0	VF 8.0	VF/NM 9.0	NM- 9.2
9,11: 9-Ingels-c/a. 11-Ingels-a; Feldstein-c	54	108	162	340	575	810
10-Wally Wood's 1st work at E. C.; Ingels-a; Feldstein-c	54	108	162	346	591	835

NOTE: Canadian reprints known; see Table of Contents. *Wood/Harrison* a-10, 11.

SADIE SACK (See Harvey Hits #93)

SAD SACK AND THE SARGE
Harvey Publications: Sept, 1957 - No. 155, June, 1982

	GD 2.0	VG 4.0	FN 6.0	VF 8.0	VF/NM 9.0	NM- 9.2
1	12	24	36	79	170	260
2	7	14	21	46	86	125
3-10	5	10	15	35	63	90
11-20	5	10	15	30	50	70
21-30	3	6	9	19	30	40
31-50	3	6	9	14	20	25
51-70	2	4	6	9	13	16
71-90,97-99	1	3	4	6	8	10
91-96: All 52 pg. Giants	2	4	6	9	13	16
100	2	4	6	8	10	12
101-120	1	2	3	4	5	7
121-155						5.00

NOTE: *George Baker* covers on numerous issues.

SAD SACK COMICS (See Harvey Collector's Comics #16, Little Sad Sack, Tastee Freez Comics #4 & True Comics #55 for 1st app.)
Harvey Publications/Lorne-Harvey Publications (Recollections) #288 On: Sept, 1949 - No. 287, Oct, 1982; No. 288, 1992 - No. 291, 1993

	GD 2.0	VG 4.0	FN 6.0	VF 8.0	VF/NM 9.0	NM- 9.2
1-Infinity-c; Little Dot begins (1st app.); civilian issues begin, end #21; based on comic strip (first app. in True Comics #55)	136	272	408	1088	2444	3800
2-Flying Fool by Powell	31	62	93	223	499	775
3	17	34	51	117	259	400
4-10	12	24	36	79	170	260
11-21	8	16	24	54	102	150
22-("Back In The Army Again" on covers #22-36); "The Specialist" story about Sad Sack's return to Army	9	18	27	59	117	175
23-30	5	10	15	34	60	85
31-50	4	8	12	28	47	65
51-80,100: 62-"The Specialist" reprinted	3	6	9	21	33	45
81-99	3	6	9	16	23	30
101-140	3	6	9	14	19	24
141-170,200	2	4	6	11	16	20
171-199	2	4	6	9	13	16
201-207: 207-Last 12¢ issue	2	4	6	8	11	14
208-222	1	3	4	6	8	10
223-228 (25¢ Giants, 52 pgs.)	2	4	6	8	11	14
229-250	1	3	4	6	8	10
251-285						6.00
286,287-Limited distribution	1	2	3	5	7	9
288,289 ($2.75, 1992): 289-50th anniversary issue						6.00
290,291 ($1.00, 1993, B&W)						3.00
3-D 1 (1/54, 25¢)-Came with 2 pairs of glasses; titled "Harvey 3-D Hits"	14	28	42	93	204	315
...At Home for the Holidays 1 (1993, no-c price)-Publ. by Lorne-Harvey' X-Mas issue						4.00

NOTE: *The Sad Sack Comics comic book was a spin-off from a Sunday Newspaper strip launched through John Wheeler's Bell Syndicate. The previous Sunday page and the first 21 comics depicted the Sad Sack in civvies. Unpopularity caused the Sunday page to be discontinued in the early '50s. Meanwhile Sad Sack returned to the Army, by popular demand, in issue No. 22, remaining there ever since. Incidentally, relatively few of the first 21 issues were ever collected and remain scarce due to this.* ***George Baker*** *covers on numerous issues.*

SAD SACK FUN AROUND THE WORLD
Harvey Publications: 1974 (no month)

	GD 2.0	VG 4.0	FN 6.0	VF 8.0	VF/NM 9.0	NM- 9.2
1-About Great Britain	2	4	6	11	16	20

SAD SACK GOES HOME
Harvey Publications: 1951 (16 pgs. in color, no cover price)

	GD 2.0	VG 4.0	FN 6.0	VF 8.0	VF/NM 9.0	NM- 9.2
nn-By George Baker	5	10	15	31	53	75

SAD SACK LAUGH SPECIAL
Harvey Publications: Winter, 1958-59 - No. 93, Feb, 1977 (#1-9: 84 pgs.; #10-60: 68 pgs.; #61-76: 52 pgs.)

	GD 2.0	VG 4.0	FN 6.0	VF 8.0	VF/NM 9.0	NM- 9.2
1-Giant 25¢ issues begin	9	18	27	60	120	180
2	5	10	15	35	63	90
3-10	5	10	15	30	50	70
11-30	4	8	12	25	40	55
31-60: 31-Hi-Fi Tweeter app. 60-Last 68 pg. Giant	3	6	9	16	23	30
61-76-(All 52 pg. issues)	2	4	6	10	14	18
77-93	1	2	3	5	6	8

SAD SACK NAVY, GOBS 'N' GALS
Harvey Publications: Aug, 1972 - No. 8, Oct, 1973

	GD 2.0	VG 4.0	FN 6.0	VF 8.0	VF/NM 9.0	NM- 9.2
1: 52 pg. Giant	3	6	9	16	23	30
2-8	2	4	6	9	12	15

SAD SACK'S ARMY LIFE (See Harvey Hits #8, 17, 22, 28, 32, 39, 43, 47, 51, 55, 58, 61, 64, 67, 70)

SAD SACK'S ARMY LIFE (...Parade #1-57, ...Today #58 on)
Harvey Publications: Oct, 1963 - No. 60, Nov, 1975; No. 61, May, 1976

	GD 2.0	VG 4.0	FN 6.0	VF 8.0	VF/NM 9.0	NM- 9.2
1-(68 pg. issues begin)	7	14	21	44	82	120
2-10	4	8	12	27	44	60
11-20	3	6	9	19	30	40
21-34: Last 68 pg. issue	3	6	9	16	23	30
35-51: All 52 pgs.	2	4	6	10	14	18
52-61	1	3	4	6	8	10

SAD SACK'S FUNNY FRIENDS (See Harvey Hits #75)
Harvey Publications: Dec, 1955 - No. 75, Oct, 1969

	GD 2.0	VG 4.0	FN 6.0	VF 8.0	VF/NM 9.0	NM- 9.2
1	9	18	27	60	120	180
2-10	5	10	15	35	63	90
11-20	4	8	12	23	37	50
21-30	3	6	9	17	26	35
31-50	3	6	9	14	20	25
51-75	2	4	6	9	13	16

SAD SACK'S MUTTSY (See Harvey Hits #74, 77, 80, 82, 84, 87, 89, 92, 96, 99, 102, 105, 108, 111, 113, 115, 117, 119, 121)

SAD SACK USA (...Vacation #8)
Harvey Publications: Nov, 1972 - No. 7, Nov, 1973; No. 8, Oct, 1974

	GD 2.0	VG 4.0	FN 6.0	VF 8.0	VF/NM 9.0	NM- 9.2
1	3	6	9	14	20	25
2-8	2	4	6	8	10	12

SAD SACK WITH SARGE & SADIE
Harvey Publications: Sept, 1972 - No. 8, Nov, 1973

	GD 2.0	VG 4.0	FN 6.0	VF 8.0	VF/NM 9.0	NM- 9.2
1-(52 pg. Giant)	3	6	9	14	20	25
2-8	2	4	6	8	10	12

SAD SAD SACK WORLD
Harvey Publ.: Oct, 1964 - No. 46, Dec, 1973 (#1-31: 68 pgs.; #32-38: 52 pgs.)

	GD 2.0	VG 4.0	FN 6.0	VF 8.0	VF/NM 9.0	NM- 9.2
1	6	12	18	41	76	110
2-10	4	8	12	25	40	55
11-20	3	6	9	19	30	40
21-31: 31-Last 68 pg. issue	3	6	9	16	23	30
32-39-(All 52 pgs)	2	4	6	10	14	18
40-46	1	3	4	6	8	10

SAFEST PLACE IN THE WORLD, THE
Dark Horse Comics: 1993 ($2.50, one-shot)

	GD 2.0	VG 4.0	FN 6.0	VF 8.0	VF/NM 9.0	NM- 9.2
1-Steve Ditko-c/a/scripts						4.00

SAFETY-BELT MAN
Sirius Entertainment: June, 1994 - No. 6, 1995 ($2.50, B&W)

	GD 2.0	VG 4.0	FN 6.0	VF 8.0	VF/NM 9.0	NM- 9.2
1-6: 1-Horan-s/Dark One-a/Sprouse-c. 2,3-Warren-c. 4-Linsner back-up story. 5,6-Crilley-a						3.00

SAFETY-BELT MAN ALL HELL
Sirius Entertainment: June, 1996 - No. 6, Mar, 1997 ($2.95, color)

	GD 2.0	VG 4.0	FN 6.0	VF 8.0	VF/NM 9.0	NM- 9.2
1-6-Horan-s/Fillbach Bros.-a						3.00

SAGA
Image Comics: Mar, 2012 - Present ($2.99)

	GD 2.0	VG 4.0	FN 6.0	VF 8.0	VF/NM 9.0	NM- 9.2
1-Brian K. Vaughan-s/Fiona Staples-a/c; 1st app. Alana, Marko, Hazel, The Will, and Lying Cat	8	16	24	54	102	150
1-Second printing	2	4	6	13	18	22
2-1st app. The Stalk	3	6	9	17	26	35
3-5: 3-1st app. Izabel	3	6	9	14	20	25
6,7,9-12						6.00
8-1st app. Gwendolyn	2	4	6	11	16	20
13-42: 19-Intro. Ginny. 24-Lying Cat returns. 25,37-Wraparound-c						4.00

SAGA OF BIG RED, THE
Omaha World-Herald: Sept, 1976 ($1.25) (In color)

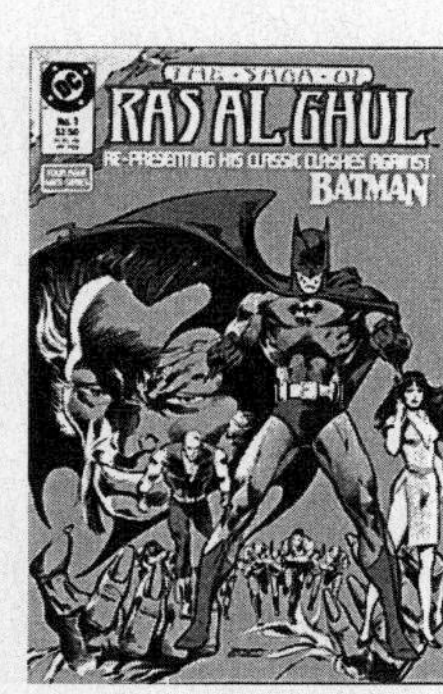

Saga of Ra's al Ghul #1 © DC

The Saint #4 © AVON

Samson #13 © AJAX

GD VG FN VF VF/NM NM-
2.0 4.0 6.0 8.0 9.0 9.2

nn-by Win Mumma; story of the Nebraska Cornhuskers (sports) 6.00

SAGA OF CRYSTAR, CRYSTAL WARRIOR, THE
Marvel Comics: May, 1983 - No. 11, Feb, 1985 (Remco toy tie-in)
1,6: 1-(Baxter paper). 6-Nightcrawler app; Golden-c 5.00
2-5,7-11: 3-Dr. Strange app. 3-11-Golden-c (painted-4,5). 11-Alpha Flight app. 4.00

SAGA OF RA'S AL GHUL, THE
DC Comics: Jan, 1988 - No. 4, Apr, 1988 ($2.50, limited series)
1-4-r/N. Adams Batman 6.00

SAGA OF SABAN'S MIGHTY MORPHIN POWER RANGERS (Also see Saban's Mighty Morphin Power Rangers)
Hamilton Comics: 1995 - No. 4, 1995 ($1.95, limited series)
1-4 4.00

SAGA OF SEVEN SUNS, THE : VEILED ALLIANCES
DC Comics (WildStorm): 2004 ($24.95, hardcover graphic novel with dustjacket)
HC-Kevin J. Anderson-s/Robert Teranishi-a 25.00
SC-(2004, $17.95) 18.00

SAGA OF THE ORIGINAL HUMAN TORCH
Marvel Comics: Apr, 1990 - No. 4, July, 1990 ($1.50, limited series)
1-4: 1-Origin; Buckler-c/a(p). 3-Hitler-c 4.00

SAGA OF THE SUB-MARINER, THE
Marvel Comics: Nov, 1988 - No. 12, Oct, 1989 ($1.25/$1.50 #5 on, maxi-series)
1-12: 9-Original X-Men app. 4.00

SAGA OF THE SWAMP THING, THE (See Swamp Thing)

SAILOR MOON (Manga)
Mixx Entertainment Inc.: 1998 - Present ($2.95)
1 3 6 9 14 20 25
1-(San Diego edition) 3 6 9 16 23 30
2-5 2 4 6 9 12 15
6-10 1 3 4 6 8 10
11-25 1 2 3 4 5 7
26-35 5.00
... Rini's Moon Stick 1 15.00

SAILOR ON THE SEA OF FATE (See First Comics Graphic Novel #11)

SAILOR SWEENEY (Navy Action #1-11, 15 on)
Atlas Comics (CDS): No. 12, July, 1956 - No. 14, Nov, 1956
12-14: 12-Shores-a. 13,14-Severin-c 20 40 60 114 182 250

SAINT, THE (Also see Movie Comics(DC) #2 & Silver Streak #18)
Avon Periodicals: Aug, 1947 - No. 12, Mar, 1952
1-Kamen bondage-c/a 116 232 348 742 1271 1800
2 52 104 156 328 552 775
3,5 45 90 135 284 480 675
4-Lingerie panels, black background, Good Girl art-c
53 106 159 334 567 800
6-Miss Fury app. by Tarpe Mills (14 pgs.) 71 142 213 454 777 1100
7-c-/Avon paperback #118 39 78 117 240 395 550
8,9(12/50): Saint strip-r in #8-12; 9-Kinstler-c 37 74 111 222 361 500
10-Wood-a, 1 pg; c-/Avon paperback #289 37 74 111 222 361 500
11 32 64 96 188 307 425
12-c-/Avon paperback #123 34 68 102 199 325 450
NOTE: *Lucky Dale, Girl Detective in #1,2,4,6.* ***Hollingsworth*** *a-4, 6. Painted-c 7, 8, 10-12.*

SAINT ANGEL
Image Comics: Mar, 2000 - No. 4, Mar, 2001 ($2.95/$3.95)
0-Altstaetter & Napton-s/Altstaetter-a 3.00
1-4-($3.95) Flip book w/Deity. 1-(6/00). 2-(10/00) 4.00

ST. GEORGE
Marvel Comics (Epic Comics): June, 1988 - No.8, Oct, 1989 ($1.25,/$1.50)
1-8: Sienkiewicz-c. 3-begin $1.50-c 3.00

SAINT GERMAINE
Caliber Comics: 1997 - No. 8, 1998 ($2.95)
1-8: 1,5-Alternate covers 3.00

ST. SWITHIN'S DAY
Trident Comics: Apr, 1990 ($2.50, one-shot)
1-Grant Morrison scripts 3.00

ST. SWITHIN'S DAY
Oni Press: Mar, 1998 ($2.95, B&W, one-shot)

GD VG FN VF VF/NM NM-
2.0 4.0 6.0 8.0 9.0 9.2

1-Grant Morrison-s/Paul Grist-a 3.00

SALOMÉ (See Night Music #6)

SALVATION RUN
DC Comics: Jan, 2008 - No. 7, Jul, 2008 ($2.99/$3.50, limited series)
1-6-DC villains banished to an alien planet; Willingham-s/Chen-a/c. 1-Var-c by Corroney 3.00
7-($3.50) Luthor cover by Chen 3.50
7-($3.50) Variant Joker cover by Neal Adams 3 6 9 19 30 40

SAM AND MAX, FREELANCE POLICE SPECIAL
Fishwrap Prod./Comico: 1987 ($1.75, B&W); Jan, 1989 ($2.75, 44 pgs.)
1 ($1.75, B&W, Fishwrap) 4.00
2 ($2.75, color, Comico) 4.00

SAM AND TWITCH (See Spawn and Case Files:...)
Image Comics (Todd McFarlane Prod.): Aug, 1999 - No. 26, Feb, 2004 ($2.50)
1-26: 1-19-Bendis-s. 1-14-Medina-a. 15-19-Maleev-a. 20-24-McFarlane-s/Maleev-a 3.00
Book One: Udaku (2000, $21.95, TPB) B&W reprint of #1-8 22.00
...: The Brian Michael Bendis Collection Vol. 1 (2/06, $24.95) r/#1-9 in color; sketch pages 25.00
...: The Brian Michael Bendis Collection Vol. 2 (6/07, $24.95) r/#10-19; cover gallery 25.00

SAM AND TWITCH: THE WRITER
Image Comics (Todd McFarlane Prod.): May, 2010 - No. 4, Jun, 2010 ($2.99)
1-4-Blengino-s/Erbetta-a/c 3.00

SAM HILL PRIVATE EYE
Close-Up (Archie): 1950 - No. 7, 1951
1 20 40 60 117 189 260
2 13 26 39 72 101 130
3-7 10 20 30 56 76 95

SAMSON (1st Series) (Captain Aero #7 on; see Big 3 Comics)
Fox Features Syndicate: Fall, 1940 - No. 6, Sept, 1941 (See Fantastic Comics)
1-Samson begins, ends #6; Powell-a, signed 'Rensie;' Wing Turner by Tuska app; Fine-c?
194 388 582 1242 2121 3000
2-Dr. Fung by Powell; Fine-c? 87 174 261 553 952 1350
3-Navy Jones app.; Joe Simon-c 66 132 198 419 722 1025
4-Yarko the Great, Master Magician begins 58 116 174 371 636 900
5,6: 6-Origin The Topper 50 100 150 315 533 750

SAMSON (2nd Series) (Formerly Fantastic Comics #10, 11)
Ajax/Farrell Publications (Four Star): No. 12, April, 1955 - No. 14, Aug, 1955
12-Wonder Boy 32 64 96 188 307 425
13,14: 13-Wonder Boy, Rocket Man 28 56 84 165 270 375

SAMSON (See Mighty Samson)

SAMSON & DELILAH (See A Spectacular Feature Magazine)

SAMUEL BRONSTON'S CIRCUS WORLD (See Circus World under Movie Classics)

SAMURAI (Also see Eclipse Graphic Album Series #14)
Aircel Publications: 1985 - No. 23, 1987 ($1.70, B&W)
1, 14-16-Dale Keown-a 4.00
1-(reprinted),2-12,17-23: 2 (reprinted issue exists) 3.00
13-Dale Keown's 1st published artwork (1987) 6.00

SAMURAI
Warp Graphics: May, 1997 ($2.95, B&W)
1 3.00

SAMURAI: BROTHERS IN ARMS
Titan Comics: Oct, 2016 - Present ($3.99)
1-6-Genet-a/DiGiorgio-s; English version of French comic 4.00

SAMURAI CAT
Marvel Comics (Epic Comics): June, 1991 - No. 3, Sept, 1991 ($2.25, limited series)
1-3: 3-Darth Vader-c/story parody 3.00

SAMURAI: HEAVEN & EARTH
Dark Horse Comics: Dec, 2004 - No. 5, Dec, 2005 ($2.99)
1-5-Luke Ross-a/Ron Marz-s 3.00
TPB (4/06, $14.95) r/#1-5; sketch pages and cover and pin-up gallery 15.00

SAMURAI: HEAVEN & EARTH (Volume 2)
Dark Horse Comics: Nov, 2006 - No. 5, June, 2007 ($2.99)
1-5-Luke Ross-a/Ron Marz-s 3.00
TPB (10/07, $14.95) r/#1-5; sketch pages and cover and pin-up gallery 15.00

SAMURAI JACK (TV)
IDW Publishing: Oct, 2013 - No. 20, May, 2015 ($3.99)

Samurai Jack (2013 series) #15 © CN

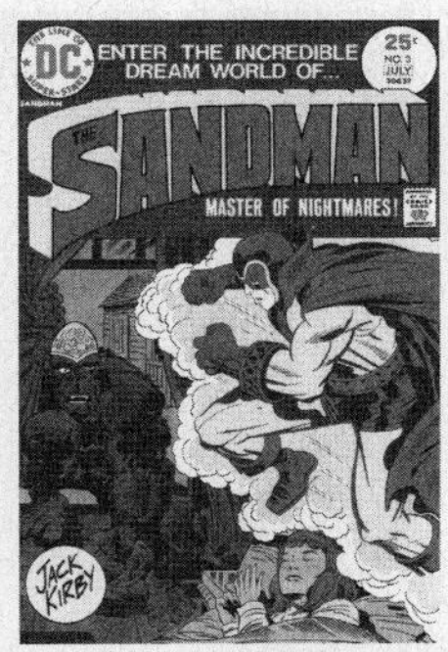

The Sandman #3 © DC

Sandman: Overture #4 © DC

GD VG FN VF VF/NM NM-
2.0 4.0 6.0 8.0 9.0 9.2

1-20: 1-5-Jim Zub-s/Andy Suriano-a; multiple covers on each 4.00
... Special - Director's Cut (2/14, $7.99) Reprints '02 DC issue; commentary by Bill Wray 8.00

SAMURAI JACK SPECIAL (TV)
DC Comics: Sept, 2002 ($3.95, one-shot)

1-Adaptation of pilot episode with origin story; Tartakovsky-s/Naylor & Wray-a 4.00

SAMURAI: LEGEND
Marvel Comics (Soleil): 2008 - No. 4, 2009 ($5.99)

1-4-Genet-a/DiGiorgio-s; English version of French comic; preview of other titles 6.00

SAMUREE
Continuity Comics: May, 1987 - No. 9, Jan, 1991

1-9 3.00

SAMUREE
Continuity Comics: V2#1, May, 1993 - V2#4, Jan,1994 ($2.50)

V2#1-4-Embossed-c: 2,4-Adams plot, Nebres-i. 3-Nino-c(i) 3.00

SAMUREE
Acclaim Comics (Windjammer): Oct, 1995 - No. 2, Nov,1995 ($2.50, lim. series)

1,2 3.00

SAN DIEGO COMIC CON COMICS
Dark Horse Comics: 1992 - No.4, 1995 (B&W, promo comic for the San Diego Comic Con)

1-(1992)-Includes various characters published from Dark Horse including Concrete, The Mask, RoboCop and others; 1st app. of Sprint from John Byrne's Next Men; art by Quesada, Byrne, Rude, Burden, Moebius & others; pin-ups by Rude, Dorkin, Allred & others; Chadwick-c 2 4 6 8 10 12
2-(1993)-Intro of Legend imprint; 1st app. of John Byrne's Danger Unlimited, Mike Mignola's Hellboy (also see John Byrne's Next Men #21), Art Adams' Monkeyman & O'Brien; contains stories featuring Concrete, Sin City, Martha Washington & others; Grendel, Madman, & Big Guy pin-ups; Don Martin-c 6 12 18 40 73 105
3-(1994)-Contains stories featuring Barb Wire, The Mask, The Dirty Pair, & Grendel by Matt Wagner; contains pin-ups of Ghost, Predator & Rascals In Paradise; The Mask-c 1 2 3 5 6 8
4-(1995)-Contains Sin City story by Miller (3pg.), Star Wars, The Mask, Tarzan, Foot Soldiers; Sin City & Star Wars flip-c 1 2 3 5 6 8

SANDMAN, THE (1st Series) (Also see Adventure Comics #40, New York World's Fair & World's Finest #3)
National Periodical Publ.: Winter, 1974; No. 2, Apr-May, 1975 - No. 6, Dec-Jan, 1975-76

1-1st app. Bronze Age Sandman by Simon & Kirby (last S&K collaboration) 6 12 18 41 76 110
2-6: 6-Kirby/Wood-c/a 3 6 9 21 33 45
The Sandman By Joe Simon & Jack Kirby HC (2009, $39.99, d.j.) r/Sandman app. from World's Finest #6,7, Adventure Comics #72-102 and Sandman #1; Morrow intro. 40.00
NOTE: ***Kirby** a-1p, 4-6p; c-1-5, 6p.*

SANDMAN (2nd Series) (See Books of Magic, Vertigo Jam & Vertigo Preview)
DC Comics (Vertigo imprint #47 on): Jan, 1989 - No. 75, Mar, 1996 ($1.50-$2.50, mature)

1 ($2.00, 52 pgs.)-1st app. Modern Age Sandman (Morpheus); Neil Gaiman scripts begin; Sam Kieth-a(p) in #1-5; Wesley Dodds (G.A. Sandman) cameo. 6 12 18 37 66 95
2-Cain & Abel app. (from HOM & HOS) 3 6 9 16 23 30
3,5: 3-John Constantine app. 2 4 6 13 18 22
4-1st app. Lucifer Morningstar; The Demon app. 4 8 12 25 40 55
6,7 2 4 6 8 11 14
8-Death-c/story (1st app.)-Regular ed. has Jeanette Kahn publishorial & American Cancer Society ad w/no indicia on inside front-c 4 8 12 25 40 55
8-Limited ed. (600+ copies?); has Karen Berger editorial and next issue teaser on inside covers (has indicia) 17 34 51 117 259 400
9-14: 10-Has explaination about #8 mixup; has bound-in Shocker movie poster. 14-(52 pgs.)-Bound-in Nightbreed fold-out 2 4 6 8 10 12
15-20: 16-Photo-c. 17,18-Kelley Jones-a. 19-Vess-a 1 2 3 5 6 8
18-Error version w/1st 3 panels on pg. 1 in blue ink 5 10 15 30 50 70
19-Error version w/pages 18 & 20 facing each other 2 4 6 9 12 15
21,23-27: Seasons of Mist storyline. 22-World Without End preview. 24-Kelley Jones/Russell-a 6.00
22-1st Daniel (Later becomes new Sandman) 2 4 6 9 12 15
28-30 5.00
31-49,51-74: 36-(52 pgs.). 41,44-48-Metallic ink on-c. 48-Cerebus appears as a doll. 54-Re-intro Prez; Death app.; Belushi, Nixon & Wildcat cameos. 57-Metallic ink on c. 65-w/bound-in trading card. 69-Death of Sandman. 70-73-Zulli-a. 74-Jon J. Muth-a. 4.00
50-($2.95, 52 pgs.)-Black-c w/metallic ink by McKean; Russell-a; McFarlane pin-up 5.00
50-($2.95)-Signed & limited (5,000) Treasury Edition with sketch of Neil Gaiman 2 4 6 9 12 15
50-Platinum 20.00
75-($3.95)-Vess-a. 5.00
Special 1 (1991, $3.50, 68 pgs.)-Glow-in-the-dark-c 5.00
Absolute Sandman Special Edition #1 (2006, 50¢) sampling from HC; recolored r/#1 3.00
Absolute Sandman Volume One (2006, $99.00, slipcased hardcover) recolored r/#1-20; Gaiman's original proposal; script and pencils from #19; character sketch gallery 100.00
Absolute Sandman Volume Two (2007, $99.00, slipcased hardcover) recolored r/#21-39; r/A Gallery of Dreams one-shot; bonus stories, scripts and pencil art 100.00
Absolute Sandman Volume Three (2008, $99.00, slipcased hardcover) recolored r/#40-56; & Special #1; bonus galleries, scripts and pencil art; Jill Thompson intro. 100.00
Absolute Sandman Volume Four (2008, $99.00, slipcased hardcover) recolored r/#57-75; scripts & sketch pages for #57 & 75; gallery of Dreaming memorabilia; Berger intro. 100.00
...: A Gallery of Dreams ($2.95)-Intro by N. Gaiman 4.00
...: Preludes & Nocturnes ($29.95, HC)-r/#1-8. 30.00
...: The Doll's House (1990, $29.95, HC)-r/#8-16. 30.00
...: Dream Country ($29.95, HC)-r/#17-20. 30.00
...: Season of Mists ($29.95, Leatherbound HC)-r/#21-28. 50.00
...: A Game of You ($29.95, HC)-r/32-37, ...: Fables and Reflections ($29.95, HC)-r/Vertigo Preview #1, Sandman Special #1, #29-31, #38-40 & #50. ...: Brief Lives ($29.95, HC)-r/#41-49. ...: World's End ($29.95, HC)-r/#51-56 30.00
...: The Kindly Ones (1996, $34.95, HC)-r/#57-69 & Vertigo Jam #1 35.00
...: The Wake ($29.95, HC)-r/#70-75. 30.00
NOTE: *A new set of hardcover printings with new covers was introduced in 1998-99. Multiple printings exist of softcover collections. Recolored (from the Absolute HC) softcover editions were released in 2010. **Bachalo** a-12; **Kelley Jones** a-17, 18, 22, 23, 26, 27. **Vess** a-19, 75.*

SANDMAN: ENDLESS NIGHTS
DC Comics (Vertigo): 2003 ($24.95, hardcover, with dust jacket)

HC-Neil Gaiman stories of Morpheus and the Endless illustrated by Fabry, Manara, Prado, Quitely, Russell, Sienkiewicz, and Storey; McKean-c 25.00
...Special (11/03, $2.95) Previews hardcover; Dream story w/Prado-a; McKean-c 4.00
SC (2004, $17.95) 18.00

SANDMAN MIDNIGHT THEATRE
DC Comics (Vertigo): Sept, 1995 ($6.95, squarebound, one-shot)

nn-Modern Age Sandman (Morpheus) meets G.A. Sandman; Gaiman & Wagner story; McKean-c; Kristiansen-a 7.00

SANDMAN MYSTERY THEATRE (Also see Sandman (2nd Series) #1)
DC Comics (Vertigo): Apr, 1993 - No. 70, Feb, 1999 ($1.95/$2.25/$2.50)

1-G.A. Sandman advs. begin; Matt Wagner scripts begin 5.00
2-49: 5-Neon ink logo. 29-32-Hourman app. 38-Ted Knight (G.A. Starman) app. 42-Jim Corrigan (Spectre) app. 45-48-Blackhawk app. 3.00
50-($3.50, 48 pgs.) w/bonus story of S.A. Sandman, Torres-a 4.00
51-70 3.00
Annual 1 (10/94, $3.95, 68 pgs.)-Alex Ross, Bolton & others-a 5.00
...: Dr. Death and the Night of the Butcher (2007, $19.99) r/#21-28 20.00
...: The Blackhawk and The Return of the Scarlet Ghost (2010, $19.99) r/#45-52 20.00
...: The Face and the Brute (2004, $19.95) r/#5-12 20.00
...: The Hourman and The Python (2008, $19.99) r/#29-36 20.00
...: The Mist and The Phantom of the Fair (2009, $19.99) r/#37-44 20.00
...: The Scorpion (2006, $12.99) r/#17-20 13.00
...: The Tarantula (1995, $14.95) r/#1-4 15.00
...: The Vamp (2005, $12.99) r/#13-16 13.00

SANDMAN MYSTERY THEATRE (2nd Series)
DC Comics (Vertigo): Feb, 2007 - No. 5, Jun, 2007 ($2.99, limited series)

1-5-Wesley Dodds and Dian in 1997; Rieber-s/Nguyen-a 3.00

SANDMAN: OVERTURE
DC Comics (Vertigo): Dec, 2013 - No. 6, Nov, 2015 ($4.99/$3.99, limited series)

1-($4.99) Prelude to Sandman #1 ('89); Gaiman-s/JH Williams III-a/c; var-c by McKean 5.00
2-6-($3.99) Gaiman-s/JH Williams III-a/c 4.00
... Special Edition 1 (1/14, $5.99) B&W version of #1 with creator interviews; bonus info 6.00
... Special Edition 2-6 ($4.99) B&W versions with creator interviews; bonus info. 6-(12/15) 5.00

SANDMAN PRESENTS...
DC Comics (Vertigo)

Taller Tales TPB (2003, $19.95) r/S.P: The Thessaliad #1-4; Merv Pumpkinhead, Agent...; The Dreaming #55; S.P. Everything You Always...; new McKean-c; intro by Willingham 20.00

SANDMAN PRESENTS: BAST
DC Comics (Vertigo): Mar, 2003 - No. 3, May, 2003 ($2.95, limited series)

1-3-Kiernan-s/Bennett-a/McKean-c 3.00

SANDMAN PRESENTS: DEADBOY DETECTIVES (See Sandman #21-28)
DC Comics (Vertigo): Aug, 2001 - No. 4, Nov, 2001 ($2.50, limited series)

1-4:Talbot-a/McKean-c/Brubaker-s 3.00

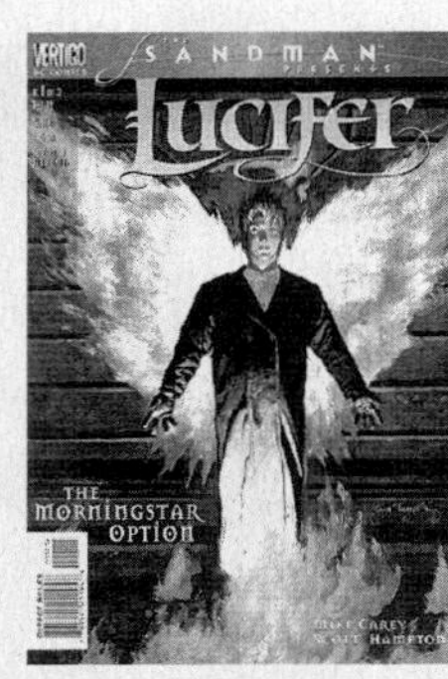

Sandman Presents: Lucifer #1 © DC

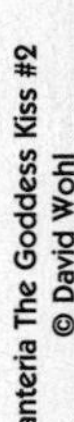
Santeria The Goddess Kiss #2 © David Wohl

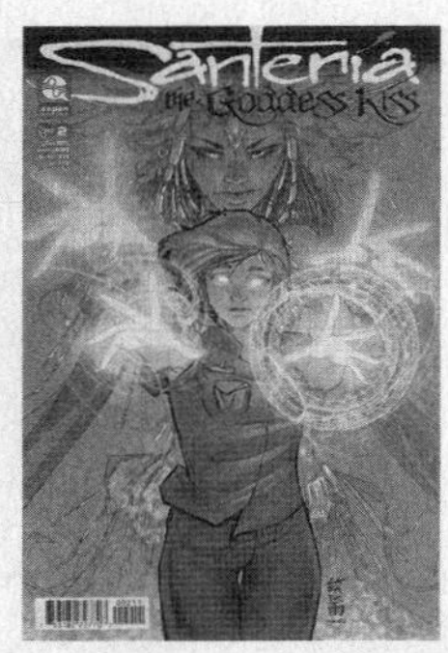

Saucer Country #6 © Cornell & Kelly

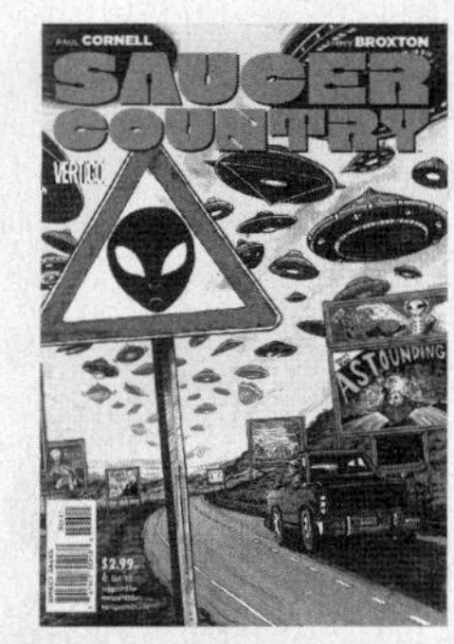

	GD 2.0	VG 4.0	FN 6.0	VF 8.0	VF/NM 9.0	NM- 9.2
TPB (2008, $12.99) r/#1-4						13.00

SANDMAN PRESENTS: EVERYTHING YOU ALWAYS WANTED TO KNOW ABOUT DREAMS...BUT WERE AFRAID TO ASK
DC Comics (Vertigo): Jul, 2001 ($3.95, one-shot)

	GD 2.0	VG 4.0	FN 6.0	VF 8.0	VF/NM 9.0	NM- 9.2
1-Short stories by Willingham; art by various; McKean-c						4.00

SANDMAN PRESENTS: LOVE STREET
DC Comics (Vertigo): Jul, 1999 - No. 3, Sept, 1999 ($2.95, limited series)

	GD 2.0	VG 4.0	FN 6.0	VF 8.0	VF/NM 9.0	NM- 9.2
1-3: Teenage Hellblazer in 1968 London; Zulli-a						3.00

SANDMAN PRESENTS: LUCIFER
DC Comics (Vertigo): Mar, 1999 - No. 3, May, 1999 ($2.95, limited series)

	GD 2.0	VG 4.0	FN 6.0	VF 8.0	VF/NM 9.0	NM- 9.2
1-Scott Hampton painted-c/a in all	1	2	3	5	6	8
2,3						4.00

SANDMAN PRESENTS: PETREFAX
DC Comics (Vertigo): Mar, 2000 - No. 4, Jun, 2000 ($2.95, limited series)

	GD 2.0	VG 4.0	FN 6.0	VF 8.0	VF/NM 9.0	NM- 9.2
1-4-Carey-s/Leialoha-a						3.00

SANDMAN PRESENTS: THE CORINTHIAN
DC Comics (Vertigo): Dec, 2001 - No. 3, Feb, 2002 ($2.95, limited series)

	GD 2.0	VG 4.0	FN 6.0	VF 8.0	VF/NM 9.0	NM- 9.2
1-3-Macan-s/Zezelj-a/McKean-c						3.00

SANDMAN PRESENTS, THE: THE FURIES
DC Comics (Vertigo): 2002 ($24.95, one-shot)

	GD 2.0	VG 4.0	FN 6.0	VF 8.0	VF/NM 9.0	NM- 9.2
Hardcover-Mike Carey-s/John Bolton-painted art; Lyta Hall's reunion with Daniel						30.00
Softcover-(2003, $17.95)						18.00

SANDMAN PRESENTS, THE: THESSALY: WITCH FOR HIRE
DC Comics (Vertigo): Apr, 2004 - No. 4, July, 2004 ($2.95, limited series)

	GD 2.0	VG 4.0	FN 6.0	VF 8.0	VF/NM 9.0	NM- 9.2
1-4-Willingham-s/McManus-a/McPherson-c						3.00
TPB-(2005, $12.99) r/#1-4						13.00

SANDMAN PRESENTS, THE: THE THESSALIAD
DC Comics (Vertigo): Mar, 2002 - No. 4, Jun, 2002 ($2.95, limited series)

	GD 2.0	VG 4.0	FN 6.0	VF 8.0	VF/NM 9.0	NM- 9.2
1-4-Willingham-s/McManus-a/McKean-c						3.00

SANDMAN, THE: THE DREAM HUNTERS
DC Comics (Vertigo): Oct, 1999 ($29.95/$19.95, one-shot graphic novel)

	GD 2.0	VG 4.0	FN 6.0	VF 8.0	VF/NM 9.0	NM- 9.2
Hardcover-Neil Gaiman-s/Yoshitaka Amano-painted art						30.00
Softcover-(2000, $19.95) new Amano-c						20.00

SANDMAN, THE: THE DREAM HUNTERS
DC Comics (Vertigo): Jan, 2009 - No. 4, Apr, 2009 ($2.99, limited series)

	GD 2.0	VG 4.0	FN 6.0	VF 8.0	VF/NM 9.0	NM- 9.2
1-4-Adaptation of the Gaiman/Amano GN by P. Craig Russell-s/a; 2 covers on each						3.00
HC (2009, $24.99) afterwords by Gaiman, Russell, Berger; cover gallery & sketch art						25.00
SC (2010, $19.99) afterwords by Gaiman, Russell, Berger; cover gallery & sketch art						20.00

SANDS OF THE SOUTH PACIFIC
Toby Press: Jan, 1953

	GD 2.0	VG 4.0	FN 6.0	VF 8.0	VF/NM 9.0	NM- 9.2
1	22	44	66	132	216	300

SANTA AND HIS REINDEER (See March of Comics #166)

SANTA AND THE ANGEL (See Dell Junior Treasury #7)
Dell Publishing Co.: Dec, 1949 (Combined w/Santa at the Zoo) (Gollub-a condensed from FC#128)

	GD 2.0	VG 4.0	FN 6.0	VF 8.0	VF/NM 9.0	NM- 9.2
Four Color 259	6	12	18	38	69	100

SANTA AT THE ZOO (See Santa And The Angel)

SANTA CLAUS AROUND THE WORLD (See March of Comics #241 in Promotional Comics section)

SANTA CLAUS CONQUERS THE MARTIANS (See Movie Classics)

SANTA CLAUS FUNNIES (Also see Dell Giants)
Dell Publishing Co.: Dec?, 1942 - No. 1274, Dec, 1961

	GD 2.0	VG 4.0	FN 6.0	VF 8.0	VF/NM 9.0	NM- 9.2
nn(#1)(1942)-Kelly-a	35	70	105	252	564	875
2(12/43)-Kelly-a	23	46	69	161	356	550
Four Color 61(1944)-Kelly-a	21	42	63	150	330	510
Four Color 91(1945)-Kelly-a	16	32	48	110	243	375
Four Color 128('46),175('47)-Kelly-a	13	26	39	91	201	310
Four Color 205,254-Kelly-a	12	24	36	82	179	275
Four Color 302,361,525,607,666,756,867	8	16	24	51	96	140
Four Color 958,1063,1154,1274	6	12	18	41	76	110

NOTE: *Most issues contain only one Kelly story.*

SANTA CLAUS PARADE
Ziff-Davis (Approved Comics)/St. John Publishing Co.: 1951; No. 2, Dec, 1952; No. 3, Jan, 1955 (25¢)

	GD 2.0	VG 4.0	FN 6.0	VF 8.0	VF/NM 9.0	NM- 9.2
nn(1951-Ziff-Davis)-116 pgs. (Xmas Special 1,2)	34	68	102	206	336	465
2(12/52-Ziff-Davis)-100 pgs.; Dave Berg-a	27	54	81	160	263	365
V1#3(1/55-St. John)-100 pgs.; reprints-c/#1	21	42	63	122	199	275

SANTA CLAUS' WORKSHOP (See March of Comics #50,168 in Promotional Comics section)

SANTA IS COMING (See March of Comics #197 in Promotional Comics section)

SANTA IS HERE (See March of Comics #49 in Promotional Comics section)

SANTA'S BUSY CORNER (See March of Comics #31 in Promotional Comics section)

SANTA'S CANDY KITCHEN (See March of Comics #14 in Promotional Comics section)

SANTA'S CHRISTMAS BOOK (See March of Comics #123 in Promotional Comics section)

SANTA'S CHRISTMAS COMICS
Standard Comics (Best Books): Dec, 1952 (100 pgs.)

	GD 2.0	VG 4.0	FN 6.0	VF 8.0	VF/NM 9.0	NM- 9.2
nn-Supermouse, Dizzy Duck, Happy Rabbit, etc.	22	44	66	132	216	300

SANTA'S CHRISTMAS LIST (See March of Comics #255 in Promotional Comics section)

SANTA'S HELPERS (See March of Comics #64, 106, 198 in Promotional Comics section)

SANTA'S LITTLE HELPERS (See March of Comics #270 in Promotional Comics section)

SANTA'S SHOW (See March of Comics #311 in Promotional Comics section)

SANTA'S SLEIGH (See March of Comics #298 in Promotional Comics section)

SANTA'S SURPRISE (See March of Comics #13 in Promotional Comics section)

SANTA'S TINKER TOTS
Charlton Comics: 1958

	GD 2.0	VG 4.0	FN 6.0	VF 8.0	VF/NM 9.0	NM- 9.2
1-Based on "The Tinker Tots Keep Christmas"	5	10	15	33	57	80

SANTA'S TOYLAND (See March of Comics #242 in Promotional Comics section)

SANTA'S TOYS (See March of Comics #12 in Promotional Comics section)

SANTA'S VISIT (See March of Comics #283 in Promotional Comics section)

SANTA THE BARBARIAN
Maximum Press: Dec, 1996 ($2.99, one-shot)

	GD 2.0	VG 4.0	FN 6.0	VF 8.0	VF/NM 9.0	NM- 9.2
1-Fraga/Mhan-s/a						3.00

SANTERIA: THE GODDESS KISS
Aspen MLT: Mar, 2016 - No. 4 ($3.99, limited series)

	GD 2.0	VG 4.0	FN 6.0	VF 8.0	VF/NM 9.0	NM- 9.2
1-3-Wohl-s/Cafaro-a						4.00

SANTIAGO (Movie)
Dell Publishing Co.: Sept, 1956 (Alan Ladd photo-c)

	GD 2.0	VG 4.0	FN 6.0	VF 8.0	VF/NM 9.0	NM- 9.2
Four Color 723-Kinstler-a	8	16	24	54	102	150

SARGE SNORKEL (Beetle Bailey)
Charlton Comics: Oct, 1973 - No. 17, Dec, 1976

	GD 2.0	VG 4.0	FN 6.0	VF 8.0	VF/NM 9.0	NM- 9.2
1	2	4	6	11	16	20
2-10	2	4	6	8	10	12
11-17	1	2	3	5	7	9

SARGE STEEL (Becomes Secret Agent #9 on; also see Judomaster)
Charlton Comics: Dec, 1964 - No. 8, Mar-Apr, 1966 (All 12¢ issues)

	GD 2.0	VG 4.0	FN 6.0	VF 8.0	VF/NM 9.0	NM- 9.2
1-Origin & 1st app.	4	8	12	23	37	50
2-5,7,8	3	6	9	16	23	30
6-2nd app. Judomaster	3	6	9	19	30	40

SATAN'S SIX
Topps Comics (Kirbyverse): Apr, 1993 - No. 4, July, 1993 ($2.95, lim. series)

	GD 2.0	VG 4.0	FN 6.0	VF 8.0	VF/NM 9.0	NM- 9.2
1-4: 1-Polybagged w/Kirbychrome trading card; Kirby/McFarlane-c plus 8 pgs. Kirby-a(p); has coupon for Kirbychrome ed. of Secret City Saga #0. 2-4-Polybagged w/3 cards. 4-Teenagents preview						4.00

NOTE: ***Ditko** a-1. **Miller** a-1.*

SATAN'S SIX: HELLSPAWN
Topps Comics (Kirbyverse): June, 1994 - No. 3, July, 1994 ($2.50, limited series)

	GD 2.0	VG 4.0	FN 6.0	VF 8.0	VF/NM 9.0	NM- 9.2
1-3: 1-(6/94)-Indicia incorrectly shows "Vol 1 #2". 2-(6/94)						3.00

SATELLITE FALLING
IDW Publishing: May, 2016 - Present ($3.99)

	GD 2.0	VG 4.0	FN 6.0	VF 8.0	VF/NM 9.0	NM- 9.2
1-3-Steve Horton-s/Stephen Thompson-a						4.00

SATELLITE SAM
Image Comics: Jul, 2013 - No. 15, Jul, 2015 ($3.50, B&W, mature)

	GD 2.0	VG 4.0	FN 6.0	VF 8.0	VF/NM 9.0	NM- 9.2
1-15-Matt Fraction-s/Howard Chaykin-a/c						3.50

SAUCER COUNTRY
DC Comics (Vertigo): May, 2012 - No. 14, Jun, 2013 ($2.99)

	GD 2.0	VG 4.0	FN 6.0	VF 8.0	VF/NM 9.0	NM- 9.2
1-14: 1-Cornell-s/Kelly-a. 6-Broxton-a. 11-Colak-a						3.00

SAURIANS: UNNATURAL SELECTION (See Sigil)

Savage #1 © VAL

Savage Dragon #179 © Erik Larsen

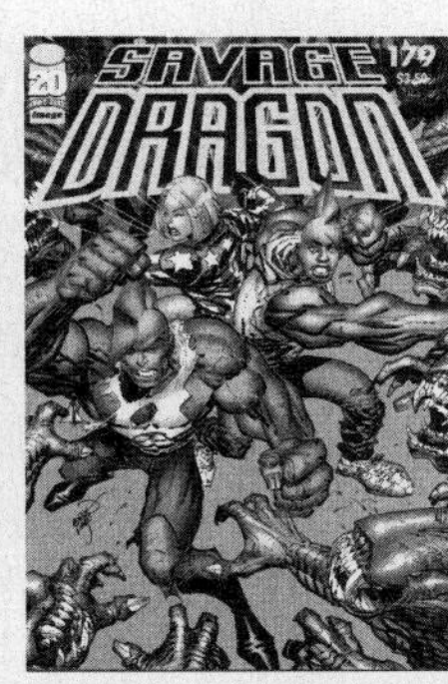

Savage Hulk #6 © MAR

GD VG FN VF VF/NM NM-
2.0 4.0 6.0 8.0 9.0 9.2

CrossGeneration Comics: Feb, 2002 - No. 2, Mar, 2002 ($2.95, limited series)
1,2-Waid-s/DiVito-a 3.00

SAVAGE
Image Comics (Shadowline): Oct, 2008 - No. 4, Jan, 2009 ($3.50, limited series)
1-4-Mayhew-c/a; Niles and Frank-s 3.50

SAVAGE
Valiant Entertainment: Nov, 2016 - No. 4 ($3.99, limited series)
1-4-B. Clay Moore-s/Larosa & Henry-a 4.00

SAVAGE AXE OF ARES
Marvel Comics: June, 2010 ($3.99, B&W, one-shot)
1-B&W short stories by Hurwitz, Palo, McKeever, Swierczynski, Manco and others 4.00

SAVAGE COMBAT TALES
Atlas/Seaboard Publ.: Feb, 1975 - No. 3, July, 1975
1,3: 1-Sgt. Stryker's Death Squad begins (origin); Goodwin-s
2 4 6 9 13 16
2-Toth-a; only app. War Hawk; Goodwin-s 2 4 6 10 14 18
NOTE: *Buckler c-3. McWilliams a-1-3; c-1. Sparling a-1, 3.*

SAVAGE DRAGON, THE (See Megaton #3 & 4)
Image Comics (Highbrow Entertainment): July, 1992 - No. 3, Dec, 1992 ($1.95, lim. series)
1-Erik Larsen-c/a/scripts & bound-in poster in all; 4 cover color variations w/4 different posters; 1st Highbrow Entertainment title 5.00
2-Intro SuperPatriot-c/story (10/92) 4.00
3-Contains coupon for Image Comics #0 4.00
3-With coupon missing 2.00
...Vs. Savage Megaton Man 1 (3/93, $1.95)-Larsen & Simpson-c/a. 4.00
TPB-('93, $9.95) r/#1-3 10.00

SAVAGE DRAGON, THE
Image Comics (Highbrow Entertainment): June, 1993 - Present ($1.95/$2.50/$2.99/$3.50)
1-Erik Larsen-c/a/scripts 5.00
2-($2.95, 52 pgs.)-Teenage Mutant Ninja Turtles-c/story; flip book features Vanguard #0 (See Megaton for 1st app.); 1st app. Supreme 4.00
3-30: 3-7: Erik Larsen-c/a/scripts. 3-Mighty Man back-up story w/Austin-a(i). 4-Flip book w/Ricochet. 5-Mighty Man flip-c & back-up plus poster. 6-Jae Lee poster. 7-Vanguard poster. 8-Deadly Duo poster by Larsen. 13A (10/94)-Jim Lee-c/a; 1st app. Max Cash (Condition Red). 13B (6/95)-Larsen story. 15-Dragon poster by Larsen. 22-TMNT-c/a; Bisley pin-up. 27-"Wondercon Exclusive" new-c. 28-Maxx-c/app. 29-Wildstar-c/app. 30-Spawn app. 3.50
25 ($3.95)-variant-c exists. 4.00
31-49,51-71: 31-God vs. The Devil; alternate version exists w/o expletives (has "God Is Good" inside Image logo) 33-Birth of Dragon/Rapture's baby. 34,35-Hellboy-c/app. 51-Origin of She-Dragon. 70-Ann Stevens killed 3.50
50-($5.95, 100 pgs.) Kaboom and Mighty Man app.; Matsuda back-c; pin-ups by McFarlane, Simonson, Capullo and others 6.00
72-74: 72-Begin $2.95-c 3.50
75-($5.95) 6.00
76-99,101-106,108-114,116-124,126-127,129-131,133-136,138: 76-New direction starts. 83,84-Madman-c/app. 84-Atomics app. 97-Dragon returns home; Mighty Man app. 134-Bomb Queen app. 3.50
100-($8.95) Larsen-s/a; inked by various incl. Sienkiewicz, Timm, Austin, Simonson, Royer; plus pin-ups by Timm, Silvestri, Miller, Cho, Art Adams, Pacheco 9.00
107-($3.95) Firebreather, Invincible, Major Damage-c/app.; flip book w/Major Damage 4.00
115-($7.95, 100 pgs.) Wraparound-c; Freak Force app.; Larsen & Englert-a 8.00
125-($4.99, 64 pgs.) new story, The Fly, & various Mr. Glum reprints 5.00
128-Wesley and the villains from Wanted app.; J.G. Jones-c 4.00
132-($6.99, 80 pgs.) new story with Larsen-a; back-up story with Fosco-a 7.00
137-(8/08) Madman and Amazing Joy Buzzards-c/app. 5.00
137-(8/08) Variant cover with Barack Obama endorsed by Savage Dragon; yellow bkgrd
7 14 21 46 86 125
137-(8/08) 2nd printing of variant cover with Barack Obama and red background
1 3 4 6 8 10
137-3rd & 4th printings: 3rd-Blue background. 4th-Purple background 6.00
139-144,146-149,151-174,176-183: 139-Start $3.50-c; Invincible app. 140,141-Witchblade, Spawn app. 148-Also a FCBD edition.155-160-Dragon War. 160-163-Flip book 3.50
145-Obama-c/app. 1 2 3 5 6 8
150-($5.99, 100 pgs.) back up r/Daredevil's origin from Daredevil #18 (1943) 6.00
175-($3.99, 48 pgs.) Darklord app.; Vanguard back-c and back-up story 4.00
184-199,201-221 ($3.99) 184,186-188-The Claw app. 190-Regular & digest-size versions. 209-Malcolm's wedding. 217-Spawn app. 4.00
200-(12/14, $8.99, 100 pgs., squarebound) Back-up story w/Trimpe-a; Burnhum-a 9.00
#0-(7/06, $1.95) reprints origin story from 2005 Image Comics Hardcover 3.50

GD VG FN VF VF/NM NM-
2.0 4.0 6.0 8.0 9.0 9.2

...Archives Vol. 1 (12/06, $19.99) B&W rep. 1st mini-series #1-3 & #1-21 20.00
...Archives Vol. 2 (2007, $19.99) B&W rep. #22-50; roster pages of Dragon's fellow cops 20.00
...Companion (7/02, $2.95) guide to issues #1-100, character backgrounds 3.50
...Endgame (2/04, $15.95, TPB) r/#47-52 16.00
The Fallen (11/97, $12.95, TPB) r/#7-11, ...Possessed (9/98, $12.95, TPB) r/#12-16, ...Revenge (1998, $12.95, TPB) r/#17-21 13.00
...Gang War (4/00, $16.95, TPB) r/#22-26 17.00
.../Hellboy (10/02, $5.95) r/#34 & #35; Mignola-c 6.00
Image Firsts: Savage Dragon #1 (4/10, $1.00) reprints #1 3.00
... Legacy FCBD 1 (5/15, giveaway) Story later re-worked for issue #211 3.00
...Team-Ups (10/98, $19.95, TPB) r/team-ups 20.00
...: Terminated HC (2/03, $28.95) r/#34-40 & #1/2 29.00
...: This Savage World HC (2002, $24.95) r/#76-81; intro. by Larsen 25.00
...: This Savage World SC (2003, $15.95) r/#76-81; intro. by Larsen 16.00
...: Worlds at War SC (2004, $16.95) r/#41-46; intro. by Larsen; sketch pages 17.00

SAVAGE DRAGON ARCHIVES (Also see Dragon Archives, The)

SAVAGE DRAGONBERT: FULL FRONTAL NERDITY
Image Comics: Oct, 2002 ($5.95, B&W, one-shot)
1-Reprints of the Savage Dragon/Dilbert spoof strips 6.00

SAVAGE DRAGON/DESTROYER DUCK, THE
Image Comics/ Highbrow Entertainment: Nov, 1996 ($3.95, one-shot)
1 4.00

SAVAGE DRAGON: GOD WAR
Image Comics: July, 2004 - No. 4, Oct, 2005 ($2.95, limited series)
1-4-Kirkman-s/Englert-a 3.50

SAVAGE DRAGON/MARSHALL LAW
Image Comics: July, 1997 - No. 2, Aug, 1997 ($2.95, B&W, limited series)
1,2-Pat Mills-s, Kevin O'Neill-a 3.50

SAVAGE DRAGON: SEX & VIOLENCE
Image Comics: Aug, 1997 - No. 2, Sept, 1997 ($2.50, limited series)
1,2-T&M Bierbaum-s, Mays, Lupka, Adam Hughes-a 3.50

SAVAGE DRAGON/TEENAGE MUTANT NINJA TURTLES CROSSOVER
Mirage Studios: Sept, 1993 ($2.75, one-shot)
1-Erik Larsen-c(i) only 4.00

SAVAGE DRAGON: THE RED HORIZON
Image Comics/ Highbrow Entertainment: Feb, 1997 - No. 3 ($2.50, lim. series)
1-3 3.50

SAVAGE FISTS OF KUNG FU
Marvel Comics Group: 1975 (Marvel Treasury)
1-Iron Fist, Shang Chi, Sons of Tiger; Adams, Starlin-a
3 6 9 17 26 35

SAVAGE HAWKMAN, THE (DC New 52)
DC Comics: Nov, 2011 - No. 20, Jun, 2013 ($2.99)
1-20: 1-Tony Daniel-s/Philip Tan-a/c; Carter Hall bonds with the Nth metal 3.00
#0-(11/12, $2.99) Origin story of Katar Hol on Thanagar; Bennett-a/c 3.00

SAVAGE HULK, THE (Also see Incredible Hulk)
Marvel Comics: Jan, 1996 ($6.95, one-shot)
1-Bisley-c; David, Lobdell, Wagner, Loeb, Gibbons, Messner-Loebs scripts; McKone, Kieth, Ramos & Sale-a 7.00

SAVAGE HULK
Marvel Comics: Aug, 2014 - No. 6, Jan, 2015 ($3.99, limited series)
1-6: 1-4-Alan Davis-s/a; follows story from X-Men #66 ('70) Silver Age X-Men & The Leader app. 2-Abomination app. 5,6-Bechko-s/Hardman-a; Dr. Strange app. 4.00

SAVAGE RAIDS OF GERONIMO (See Geronimo #4)

SAVAGE RANGE (See Luke Short, Four Color 807)

SAVAGE RED SONJA: QUEEN OF THE FROZEN WASTES
Dynamite Entertainment: 2006 - No. 4, 2006 ($3.50, limited series)
1-4: 1-Three covers by Cho, Texeira & Homs; Cho & Murray-s/Homs-a 3.50
TPB (2007, $14.99) r/series; cover gallery and sketch pages 15.00

SAVAGE RETURN OF DRACULA
Marvel Comics: 1992 ($2.00, 52 pgs.)
1-r/Tomb of Dracula #1,2 by Gene Colan 4.00

SAVAGE SHE-HULK, THE (See The Avengers, Marvel Graphic Novel #18 & The Sensational She-Hulk)

Savage She-Hulk #25 © MAR

Savage Sword of Conan #192 © CPI

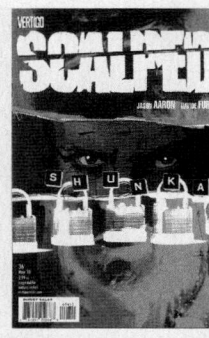

Scalped #36 © Aaron & Milosevic

Marvel Comics Group: Feb, 1980 - No. 25, Feb, 1982

	GD 2.0	VG 4.0	FN 6.0	VF 8.0	VF/NM 9.0	NM- 9.2
1-Origin & 1st app. She-Hulk	4	8	12	28	47	65
2-5,25: 25-(52 pgs.)	1	3	4	6	8	10
6-24: 6-She-Hulk vs. Iron Man. 8-Vs. Man-Thing						6.00

NOTE: ***Austin*** *a-25i; c-23i-25i.* ***J. Buscema*** *a-1p; c-1, 2p.* ***Golden*** *c-8-11.*

SAVAGE SHE-HULK (Titled All New Savage She Hulk for #3,4)
Marvel Comics: Jun, 2009 - No. 4, Sept, 2009 ($3.99, limited series)

	GD 2.0	VG 4.0	FN 6.0	VF 8.0	VF/NM 9.0	NM- 9.2
1-4-Lyra, daughter of the Hulk; She-Hulk & Dark Avengers app. 2-Campbell-c						4.00

SAVAGE SKULLKICKERS (See Skullkickers #20)

SAVAGE SWORD (ROBERT E. HOWARD'S...)
Dark Horse Comics: Dec, 2010 - Present ($7.99, squarebound)

	GD 2.0	VG 4.0	FN 6.0	VF 8.0	VF/NM 9.0	NM- 9.2
1-9-Short stories by various incl. Roy Thomas, Barry-Windsor-Smith; Conan app.						8.00

SAVAGE SWORD OF CONAN (The... #41 on; ...The Barbarian #175 on)
Marvel Comics Group: Aug, 1974 - No. 235, July, 1995 ($1.00/$1.25/$2.25, B&W magazine, mature)

	GD 2.0	VG 4.0	FN 6.0	VF 8.0	VF/NM 9.0	NM- 9.2
1-Smith-r; J. Buscema/N. Adams/Krenkel-a; origin Blackmark by Gil Kane (part 1, ends #3); Blackmark's 1st app. in magazine form-r/from paperback) & Red Sonja (3rd app.)	9	18	27	62	126	190
2-Neal Adams-c; Chaykin/N. Adams-a	5	10	15	34	60	85
3-Severin/B. Smith-a; N. Adams-a	4	8	12	27	44	60
4-Neal Adams/Kane-a(r)	3	6	9	21	33	45
5-10: 5-Jeff Jones frontispiece (r)	3	6	9	17	26	35
11-20	2	4	6	13	18	22
21-30	2	4	6	10	14	18
31-50: 34-3 pg. preview of Conan newspaper strip. 35-Cover similar to Savage Tales #1. 45-Red Sonja returns; begin $1.25-c	2	4	6	8	11	14
51-99: 63-Toth frontispiece. 65-Kane-a w/Chaykin/Miller/Simonson/Sherman finishes. 70-Article on movie. 83-Red Sonja-r by Neal Adams from #1	1	2	3	5	7	9
100	1	3	4	6	8	10
101-176: 163-Begin $2.25-c. 169-King Kull story. 171-Soloman Kane by Williamson (i). 172-Red Sonja story						6.00
177-199: 179,187,192-Red Sonja app. 190-193-4 part King Kull story. 196-King Kull story						5.00
200-220: 200-New Buscema-a; Robert E. Howard app. with Conan in story. 202-King Kull story. 204-60th anniversary (1932-92). 211-Rafael Kayanan's 1st Conan-a. 214-Sequel to Red Nails by Howard						6.00
221-230	2	4	6	8	10	12
231-234	2	4	6	11	16	20
235-Last issue	4	8	12	27	44	60
Special 1(1975, B&W)-B. Smith-r/Conan #10,13	3	6	9	16	24	32
Volume 1 TPB (Dark Horse Books, 12/07, $17.95, B&W) r/#1-10 and selected stories from Savage Tales #1-5 with covers						18.00
Volume 2 TPB (Dark Horse Books, 3/08, $17.95, B&W) r/#11-24						18.00
Volume 3 TPB (Dark Horse Books, 5/08, $19.95, B&W) r/#25-36 and selected pin-ups						20.00
Volume 4 TPB (Dark Horse Books, 9/08, $19.95, B&W) r/#37-48 and selected pin-ups						20.00
Volume 5 TPB (Dark Horse Books, 2/09, $19.95, B&W) r/#49-60 and selected pin-ups						20.00

NOTE: ***N. Adams*** *a-14p, 60, 83p(r).* ***Alcala*** *a-2 ,4, 7, 12, 15-20, 23, 24, 28, 59, 67, 69, 75, 76i, 80i, 82i, 83i, 89, 180i, 184i, 187i, 189i, 216p.* ***Austin*** *a-78i.* ***Boris*** *painted c-1, 4, 5, 7, 9, 10, 12, 15.* ***Brunner*** *a-30; c-8, 30.* ***Buscema*** *a-1-5, 7, 10-12, 15-24, 26-28, 31, 32, 36-43, 45, 47-58p, 60-67p, 70, 71-74p, 76-81p, 87-96p, 98, 99-101p, 190-204p; painted c-40.* ***Chaykin*** *c-31.* ***Chiodo*** *painted c-71, 76, 79, 81, 84, 85, 178.* ***Conrad*** *c-215, 217.* ***Corben*** *a-4, 16, 29.* ***Finlay*** *a-16.* ***Golden*** *a-98, 101; c-98, 101, 105, 106, 117, 124, 150.* ***Kaluta*** *a-11, 18; c-3, 91, 93.* ***Gil Kane*** *a-2, 3, 8, 13r, 29, 47, 64, 65, 67, 85p, 86p.* ***Rafael Kayanan*** *a-211-213, 215, 217.* ***Krenkel*** *a-9, 11, 14, 16, 24.* ***Morrow*** *a-7.* ***Nebres*** *a-93i, 101i, 107, 114.* ***Newton*** *a-6.* ***Nino*** *c/a-6.* ***Redondo*** *painted c-48-50, 52, 56, 57, 85i, 90, 96i.* ***Marie & John Severin*** *a-Special 1.* ***Simonson*** *a-7, 8, 12, 15-17.* ***Barry Smith*** *a-7, 16, 24, 82r, Special 1r.* ***Starlin*** *c-26.* ***Toth*** *a-64.* ***Williamson*** *a(i)-162, 171, 186. No. 8 , 10 & 16 contain a Robert E. Howard Conan adaptation.*

SAVAGE TALES (...Featuring Conan #4 on)(Magazine)
Marvel Comics Group: May, 1971; No. 2, 10/73; No. 3, 2/74 - No. 12, Summer, 1975 (B&W)

	GD 2.0	VG 4.0	FN 6.0	VF 8.0	VF/NM 9.0	NM- 9.2
1-Origin/1st app. The Man-Thing by Morrow; Conan the Barbarian by Barry Smith (1st Conan x-over outside his own title); Femizons by Romita-r/in #3; Ka-Zar story by Buscema	17	34	51	117	259	400
2-B. Smith, Brunner, Morrow, Williamson-a; Wrightson King Kull reprint/ Creatures on the Loose #10	5	10	15	35	63	90
3-B. Smith, Brunner, Steranko, Williamson-a	5	10	15	30	50	70
4,5-N. Adams-c; last Conan (Smith-r/#4) plus Kane/N. Adams-a. 5-Brak the Barbarian begins, ends #8	4	8	12	27	44	60
6-Ka-Zar begins; Williamson-r; N. Adams-c	3	6	9	19	30	40
7-N. Adams-i	3	6	9	15	22	28
8,9,11: 8-Shanna, the She-Devil app. thru #10; Williamson-r	3	6	9	14	20	26
10-Neal Adams-a(i), Williamson-r	3	6	9	15	22	28
...Featuring Ka-Zar Annual 1 (Summer, '75, B&W)(#12 on inside)-Ka-Zar origin by Gil Kane; B. Smith-r/Astonishing Tales	3	6	9	16	24	32

NOTE: ***Boris*** *c-7, 10.* ***Buscema*** *a-5r, 6p, 8p; c-2.* ***Colan*** *a-1p.* ***Fabian*** *c-8.* ***Golden*** *a-1, 4; c-1.* ***Heath*** *a-10p, 11p.* ***Kaluta*** *c-9.* ***Maneely*** *r-2, 4(The Crusader in both).* ***Morrow*** *a-1, 2, Annual 1.* ***Reese*** *a-2.* ***Severin*** *a-1-7.* ***Starlin*** *a-5. Robert E. Howard adaptations-1-4.*

SAVAGE TALES (Volume 2)
Marvel Comics Group: Oct, 1985 - No. 8, Dec, 1986 ($1.50, B&W, magazine, mature)

	GD 2.0	VG 4.0	FN 6.0	VF 8.0	VF/NM 9.0	NM- 9.2
1-1st app. The Nam; Golden, Morrow-a (indicia incorrectly lists this as Volume 1)						6.00
2-8: 2,7-Morrow-a. 4-2nd Nam story; Golden-a						4.00

SAVAGE TALES
Dynamite Entertainment: 2007 - No. 10, 2008 ($4.99)

	GD 2.0	VG 4.0	FN 6.0	VF 8.0	VF/NM 9.0	NM- 9.2
1-10: 1-Anthology; Red Sonja app.; three covers						5.00

SAVAGE THINGS
DC Comics (Vertigo): May, 2017 - Present ($3.99)

	GD 2.0	VG 4.0	FN 6.0	VF 8.0	VF/NM 9.0	NM- 9.2
1-Justin Jordan-s/Ibrahim Moustafa-a/J.P. Leon-c						4.00

SAVAGE WOLVERINE
Marvel Comics: Mar, 2013 - No. 23, Nov, 2014 ($3.99)

	GD 2.0	VG 4.0	FN 6.0	VF 8.0	VF/NM 9.0	NM- 9.2
1-5-Frank Cho-s/a/c; Shanna & Amadeus Cho app.						4.00
1-Variant-c by Skottie Young						8.00
6-23: 6-8-Wells-s/Madureira-a/c; Elektra, Kingpin & Spider-Man app. 9-11-Jock-s/a. 14-17-Isanove-s/a. 19-Simone-s. 21,22-WWI; Quinones-a/Nowlan-c						4.00

SAVANT GARDE (Also see WildC.A.T.S...)
Image Comics/WildStorm Productions: Mar, 1997 - No. 7, Sept, 1997 ($2.50)

	GD 2.0	VG 4.0	FN 6.0	VF 8.0	VF/NM 9.0	NM- 9.2
1-7						3.00

SAVED BY THE BELL (TV)
Harvey Comics: Mar, 1992 - No. 5, May, 1993 ($1.25, limited series)

	GD 2.0	VG 4.0	FN 6.0	VF 8.0	VF/NM 9.0	NM- 9.2
1-5, Holiday Special (3/92), Special 1 (9/92, $1.50)-photo-c, Summer Break 1 (10/92)						3.00

SAVIOR
Image Comics/Todd McFarlane Productions: Apr, 2015 - No. 8, Nov, 2015 ($2.99)

	GD 2.0	VG 4.0	FN 6.0	VF 8.0	VF/NM 9.0	NM- 9.2
1-8-Todd McFarlane & Brian Holguin-s/Clayton Crain-a/c						3.00

SAW: REBIRTH (Based on 2004 movie Saw)
IDW Publ.: Oct, 2005 ($3.99, one-shot)

	GD 2.0	VG 4.0	FN 6.0	VF 8.0	VF/NM 9.0	NM- 9.2
1-Guedes-a						4.00

SCALPED
DC Comics (Vertigo): Mar, 2007 - No. 60, Oct, 2012 ($2.99, limited series)

	GD 2.0	VG 4.0	FN 6.0	VF 8.0	VF/NM 9.0	NM- 9.2
1-Aaron-s/Guera-a/Jock-c	4	8	12	27	44	60
1-Special Edition (7/10, $1.00) r/#1 with "What's Next?" cover frame						3.00
2-5	1	2	3	5	6	8
6-20: 12-Leon-a						4.00
21-60: 50-Bonus pin-ups by various						3.00
...: Casino Blood TPB (2008, $14.99) r/#6-11; intro. by Garth Ennis						15.00
...: Dead Mothers TPB (2008, $17.99) r/#12-18						18.00
...: High Lonesome TPB (2009, $14.99) r/#25-29; intro. by Jason Starr						15.00
...: Indian Country TPB (2007, $9.99) r/#1-5; intro. by Brian K. Vaughan						10.00
...: Rez Blues (2011, $17.99) r/#35-42						18.00
...: The Gnawing (2010, $14.99) r/#30-34; intro. by Matt Fraction						15.00
...: The Gravel in Your Guts (2009, $14.99) r/#19-24; intro. by Ed Brubaker						15.00

SCAMP (Walt Disney)(See Walt Disney's Comics & Stories #204)
Dell Publ. Co./Gold Key: No. 703, 5/56 - No. 1204, 8-10/61; 11/67 - No. 45, 1/79

	GD 2.0	VG 4.0	FN 6.0	VF 8.0	VF/NM 9.0	NM- 9.2
Four Color 703(#1)	8	16	24	56	108	160
Four Color 777,806('57),833	6	12	18	40	73	105
5(3-5/58)-10(6-8/59)	5	10	15	31	53	75
11-16(12-2/60-61), Four Color 1204(1961)	4	8	12	27	44	60
1(12/67-Gold Key)-Reprints begin	4	8	12	25	40	55
2(3/69)-10	2	4	6	13	18	22
11-20	2	4	6	8	11	14
21-45	1	2	3	4	5	7

NOTE: *New stories-#20(in part), 22-25, 27, 29-31, 34, 36-40, 42-45. New covers-#11, 12, 14, 15, 17-25, 27, 29-31, 34, 36-38.*

SCARAB
DC Comics (Vertigo): Nov, 1993 - No. 8, June, 1994 ($1.95, limited series)

	GD 2.0	VG 4.0	FN 6.0	VF 8.0	VF/NM 9.0	NM- 9.2
1-8-Glenn Fabry painted-c: 1-Silver ink-c. 2-Phantom Stranger app.						3.00

SCARECROW OF ROMNEY MARSH, THE (See W. Disney Showcase #53)
Gold Key: April, 1964 - No. 3, Oct, 1965 (Disney TV Show)

	GD 2.0	VG 4.0	FN 6.0	VF 8.0	VF/NM 9.0	NM- 9.2
10112-404 (#1)	5	10	15	35	63	90
2,3	4	8	12	27	44	60

SCARECROW (VILLAINS) (See Batman)
DC Comics: Feb, 1998 ($1.95, one-shot)

	GD 2.0	VG 4.0	FN 6.0	VF 8.0	VF/NM 9.0	NM- 9.2
1-Fegredo-a/Milligan-s/Pearson-c						3.00

Scarlet #1 © Jinxworld

Scarlett Couture #4 © Des Taylor

Science Comics #6 © FOX

	GD 2.0	VG 4.0	FN 6.0	VF 8.0	VF/NM 9.0	NM- 9.2

SCARE TACTICS
DC Comics: Dec, 1996 - No. 12, Mar, 1998 ($2.25)
1-12: 1-1st app. 3.00

SCAR FACE (See The Crusaders)

SCARFACE: SCARRED FOR LIFE (Based on the 1983 movie)
IDW Publishing: Dec, 2006 - No. 5, Apr, 2007 ($3.99, limited series)
1-5-Tony Montana survives his shooting; Layman-s/Crosland-a 4.00
Scarface: Devil in Disguise (7/07 - No. 4, 10/07, $3.99) Alberto Dose-a 4.00

SCARLET
Marvel Comics (ICON): July, 2010 - Present ($3.95)
1-10-Bendis-s/Maleev-a. 1-Second printing exists. 8-(5/16) 4.00
1-5-Variant covers. 1-Deodato & Lafuente. 2-Oeming & Mack. 3,4-Oeming. 5-Bendis 6.00

SCARLET O'NEIL (See Harvey Comics Hits #59 & Invisible...)

SCARLET SPIDER
Marvel Comics: Nov, 1995 - No. 2, Jan, 1996 ($1.95, limited series)
1,2: Replaces Spider-Man title 3.00

SCARLET SPIDER
Marvel Comics: Mar, 2012 - No. 25, Feb, 2014 ($3.99/$2.99)
1-Kaine following "Spider Island"; Yost-s/Stegman-a; 2 covers by Stegman 4.00
2-12, 12.1, 13-24-($2.99) 10,11-Carnage & Venom app. 17-19-Wolverine app. 3.00
25-($3.99) Last issue; Yost-s/Baldeon-a 4.00

SCARLET SPIDERS (Tie-in for Spider-Verse in Amazing Spider-Man [2014] #9-15)
Marvel Comics: Jan, 2015 - No. 3, Mar, 2015 ($3.99, limited series)
1-3-Kaine, Ben Reilly and Jessica Drew app.; Costa-s/Diaz-a 4.00

SCARLET SPIDER UNLIMITED
Marvel Comics: Nov, 1995 ($3.95, one-shot)
1-Replaces Spider-Man Unlimited title 4.00

SCARLETT COUTURE
Titan Comics: May, 2015 - No. 4, Aug, 2015 ($3.99)
1-4-Des Taylor-s/a 4.00

SCARLET WITCH (See Avengers #16, Vision &... & X-Men #4)
Marvel Comics: Jan, 1994 - No. 4, Apr, 1994 ($1.75, limited series)
1-4 3.00

SCARLET WITCH
Marvel Comics: Feb, 2016 - No. 15, Apr, 2017 ($3.99)
1-15: 1-3: 1-Robinson-s/Del Rey-a; Agatha Harkness app. 3-Dillon-a. 7-Wu-a. 9-Civil War II tie-in; Quicksilver app.; Joelle Jones-a 4.00

SCARY GODMOTHER (Hardcover story books)
Sirius: 1997 - 2002 ($19.95, HC with dust jackets, one-shots)
Volume 1 (9/97) Jill Thompson-s/a; first app. of Scary Godmother 20.00
Vol. 2 - The Revenge of Jimmy (9/98, $19.95) 20.00
Vol. 3 - The Mystery Date (10/99, $19.95) 20.00
Vol. 4 - The Boo Flu (9/02, $19.95) 20.00

SCARY GODMOTHER
Sirius: 2001 - No. 6, 2002 ($2.95, B&W, limited series)
1-6-Jill Thompson-s/a 3.00
...: Activity Book (12/00, $2.95, B&W) Jill Thompson-s/a 3.00
...: Bloody Valentine Special (2/98, $3.95, B&W) Jill Thompson-s/a; pin-ups by Ross, Mignola, Russell 4.00
...: Ghoul's Out For Summer (2002,$14.95, B&W) r/#1-6 15.00
...: Holiday Spooktakular (11/98, $2.95, B&W) Jill Thompson-s/a; pin-ups by Brereton, LaBan, Dorkin, Fingerman 3.00

SCARY GODMOTHER: WILD ABOUT HARRY
Sirius: 2000 - No. 3 ($2.95, B&W, limited series)
1-3-Jill Thompson-s/a 3.00
TPB (2001, $9.95) r/series 10.00

SCARY TALES
Charlton Comics: 8/75 - #9, 1/77; #10, 9/77 - #20, 6/79; #21, 8/80 - #46, 10/84

	GD	VG	FN	VF	VF/NM	NM-
1-Origin/1st app. Countess Von Bludd, not in #2	3	6	9	21	33	45
2,4,6,9,10: 4,9-Sutton-c/a. 4-Man-Thing copy	2	4	6	11	16	20
3-Sutton painted-c; Ditko-a	3	6	9	14	20	25
5,11-Ditko-c/a.	3	6	9	16	23	30
7,8-Ditko-a	2	4	6	13	18	22
12,15,16,19,21,39-Ditko-a	2	4	6	11	16	20
13,17,20	2	4	6	9	12	15
14,18,30,32-Ditko-c/a	3	6	9	14	20	25
22-29,33-37,39,40: 37,38,40-New-a. 39-All Ditko reprints and cover	2	4	6	8	10	12
31,38: 31-Newton-c/a. 38-Mr. Jigsaw app.	2	4	6	8	10	12
41-45-New-a. 41-Ditko-a(3). 42-45-(Low print)	2	4	6	9	12	15
46-Reprints (Low print)	2	4	6	11	16	20
1(Modern Comics reprint, 1977)	1	3	4	6	8	10

NOTE: ***Adkins** a-31i; c-31i. **Ditko** a-3, 5, 7, 8(2), 11, 12, 14-16r, 18(3)r, 19r, 21r, 30r, 32, 39r, 41(3); c-5, 11, 14, 18, 30, 32. **Newton** a-31p; c-31p. **Powell** a-18r. **Staton** a-1(2 pgs.), 4, 20r; c-1, 20. **Sutton** a-4, 9; c-4, 9. **Zeck** a-9.*

SCATTERBRAIN
Dark Horse Comics: Jun, 1998 - No. 4, Sept, 1998 ($2.95, limited series)
1-4-Humor anthology by Aragonés, Dorkin, Stevens and others 3.00

SCAVENGERS
Quality Comics: Feb, 1988 - No. 14, 1989 ($1.25/$1.50)
1-14: 9-13-Guice-c 3.00

SCAVENGERS
Triumphant Comics: 1993(nd, July) - No. 11, May, 1994 ($2.50, serially numbered)
1-9,0,10,11: 5,6-Triumphant Unleashed x-over. 9-(3/94). 0-Retail ed. (3/94, $2.50, 36 pgs.). 0-Giveaway edition (3/94, 20 pgs.). 0-Coupon redemption edition. 10-(4/94) 3.00

SCENE OF THE CRIME (Also see Vertigo: Winter's Edge #2)
DC Comics (Vertigo): May, 1999 - No. 4, Aug, 1999 ($2.50, limited series)
1-4-Brubaker-s/Lark-a 3.00
...: A Little Piece of Goodnight TPB ('00, $12.95) r/#1-4; Winter's Edge #2 13.00

SCHOOL DAY ROMANCES (...of Teen-Agers #4; Popular Teen-Agers #5 on)
Star Publications: Nov-Dec, 1949 - No. 4, May-June, 1950 (Teenage)

	GD	VG	FN	VF	VF/NM	NM-
1-Toni Gayle (later Toni Gay), Ginger Snapp, Midge Martin & Eve Adams begin	37	74	111	222	361	500
2,3: 3-Jane Powell photo on-c & true life story	28	56	84	165	270	375
4-Ronald Reagan photo on-c; L.B. Cole-c	39	78	117	231	378	525

NOTE: *All have **L. B. Cole** covers.*

SCHWINN BICYCLE BOOK (...Bike Thrills, 1959)
Schwinn Bicycle Co.: 1949; 1952; 1959 (10¢)

	GD	VG	FN	VF	VF/NM	NM-
1949	6	12	18	28	34	40
1952-Believe It or Not facts; comic format; 36 pgs.	5	10	14	20	24	28
1959	3	6	8	11	13	15

SCIENCE COMICS (1st Series)
Fox Features Syndicate: Feb, 1940 - No. 8, Sept, 1940

	GD	VG	FN	VF	VF/NM	NM-
1-Origin Dynamo (1st app., called Electro in #1), The Eagle (1st app.), & Navy Jones; Marga, The Panther Woman (1st app.), Cosmic Carson & Perisphere Payne, Dr. Doom begin; bondage/hypo-c; Electro-c	622	1244	1866	4541	8021	11,500
2-Classic Lou Fine Dynamo-c	371	742	1113	2600	4550	6500
3-Classic Lou Fine Dynamo-c	314	624	942	2198	3849	5500
4-Kirby-a; Cosmic Carson-c by Joe Simon	314	624	942	2198	3849	5500
5-8: 5,8-Eagle-c. 6,7-Dynamo-c	194	388	582	1242	2121	3000

NOTE: *Cosmic Carson by **Tuska**-#1-3; by **Kirby**-#4. **Lou Fine** c-1-3 only.*

SCIENCE COMICS (2nd Series)
Humor Publications (Ace Magazines?): Jan, 1946 - No. 5, 1946

	GD	VG	FN	VF	VF/NM	NM-
1-Palais-c/a in #1-3; A-Bomb-c	24	48	72	144	237	330
2	14	28	42	82	121	160
3-Feldstein-a (6 pgs.); Palais-c	18	36	54	107	169	230
4,5: 4-Palais-c	12	24	36	67	94	120

SCIENCE COMICS
Ziff-Davis Publ. Co.: May, 1947 (8 pgs. in color)

	GD	VG	FN	VF	VF/NM	NM-
nn-Could be ordered by mail for 10¢; like the nn Amazing Adventures (1950) & Boy Cowboy (1950); used to test the market	47	94	141	296	498	700

SCIENCE COMICS (True Science Illustrated)
Export Publication Ent., Toronto, Canada: Mar, 1951 (Distr. in U.S. by Kable News Co.)

	GD	VG	FN	VF	VF/NM	NM-
1-Science Adventure stories plus some true science features; man on moon story	16	32	48	94	147	200

SCIENCE DOG SPECIAL (Also see Invincible)
Image Comics: Aug, 2010; No. 2, May, 2011 ($3.50)
1,2: 1-Kirkman-s/Walker-a/c; leads into Invincible #75 3.50

SCIENCE FICTION SPACE ADVENTURES (See Space Adventures)

SCION (Also see CrossGen Chronicles)
CrossGeneration Comics: July, 2000 - No. 43, Apr, 2004 ($2.95)
1-43: 1-Marz-s/Cheung-a 3.00

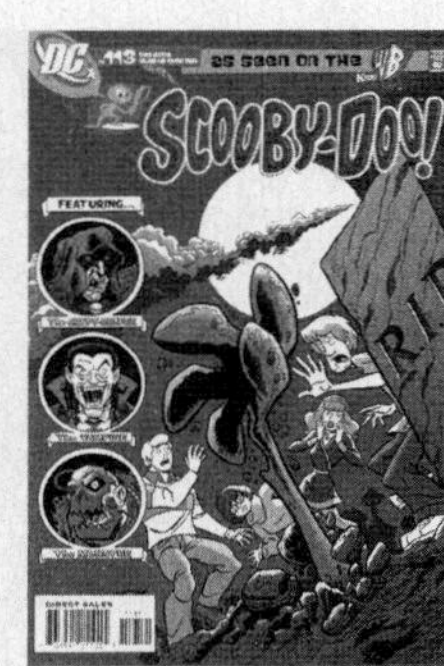

Scooby-Doo #113 © H-B

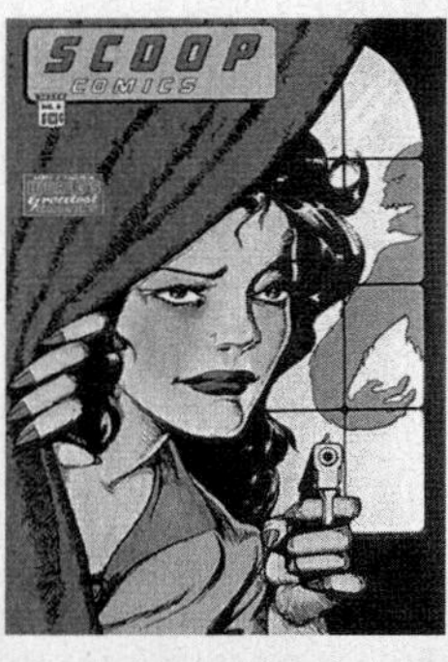
Scoop Comics #8 © CHES

Scott Pilgrim Vol. 1 © Bryan Lee O'Malley

SCI-SPY
DC Comics (Vertigo): Apr, 2002 - No. 6, Sept, 2002 ($2.50, limited series)

	GD 2.0	VG 4.0	FN 6.0	VF 8.0	VF/NM 9.0	NM- 9.2
1-6-Moench-s/Gulacy-c/a						3.00

SCI-TECH
DC Comics (WildStorm): Sept, 1999 - No. 4, Dec, 1999 ($2.50, limited series)

	GD 2.0	VG 4.0	FN 6.0	VF 8.0	VF/NM 9.0	NM- 9.2
1-4-Benes-a/Choi & Peterson-s						3.00

SCOOBY APOCALYPSE (Scooby Doo)
DC Comics: Jul, 2016 - Present ($3.99)

	GD 2.0	VG 4.0	FN 6.0	VF 8.0	VF/NM 9.0	NM- 9.2
1-10: 1-Giffen & DeMatteis-s/Porter-a; covers by Jim Lee and various; team's 1st meeting 4-Intro. Scrappy-Doo. 6-Velma's origin. 7-Eaglesham-a. 9-Scrappy-Doo back-up						4.00
.../Hanna-Barbera Halloween Comics Fest Special Edition 1 (12/16, giveaway) previews Scooby Apocalypse, Future Quest, The Flintstones, and Wacky Races						3.00

SCOOBY DOO (TV)(...Where are you? #1-16,26; ...Mystery Comics #17-25, 27 on)
(See March Of Comics #356, 368, 382, 391 in the Promotional Comics section)
Gold Key: Mar, 1970 - No. 30, Feb, 1975 (Hanna-Barbera)

	GD 2.0	VG 4.0	FN 6.0	VF 8.0	VF/NM 9.0	NM- 9.2
1	100	200	300	800	1400	2000
2-5	15	30	45	105	233	360
6-10	10	20	30	69	147	225
11-20: 11-Tufts-a	8	16	24	51	96	140
21-30: 28-Whitman edition	6	12	18	41	76	110

SCOOBY DOO (TV)
Charlton Comics: Apr, 1975 - No. 11, Dec, 1976 (Hanna-Barbera)

	GD 2.0	VG 4.0	FN 6.0	VF 8.0	VF/NM 9.0	NM- 9.2
1	10	20	30	64	132	200
2-5	6	12	18	41	76	110
6-11	5	10	15	34	60	85
nn-(1976, digest, 68 pgs., B&W)	4	8	12	28	47	65

SCOOBY-DOO (TV)(Newsstand sales only) (See Dynamutt & Laff-A-Lympics)
Marvel Comics Group: Oct, 1977 - No. 9, Feb, 1979 (Hanna-Barbera)

	GD 2.0	VG 4.0	FN 6.0	VF 8.0	VF/NM 9.0	NM- 9.2
1-Dyno-Mutt begins	5	10	15	33	57	80
1-(35¢-c variant, limited distribution)(10/77)	10	20	30	69	147	225
2-5	3	6	9	19	30	40
6-9	3	6	9	21	33	45

SCOOBY-DOO (TV)
Harvey Comics: Sept, 1992 - No. 3, May, 1993 ($1.25)

	GD 2.0	VG 4.0	FN 6.0	VF 8.0	VF/NM 9.0	NM- 9.2
V2#1-3: 3-(Low print and scarce)	2	4	6	10	14	18
Big Book 1,2 (11/92, 4/93, $1.95, 52 pgs.)	2	4	6	8	10	12
Giant Size 1,2 (10/92, 3/93, $2.25, 68 pgs.)	2	4	6	8	10	12

SCOOBY DOO (TV)
Archie Comics: Oct, 1995 -No. 21, June, 1997 ($1.50)

	GD 2.0	VG 4.0	FN 6.0	VF 8.0	VF/NM 9.0	NM- 9.2
1	2	4	6	11	16	20
2-21: 12-Cover by Scooby Doo creative designer Iwao Takamoto						6.00

SCOOBY DOO (TV)
DC Comics: Aug, 1997 - No. 159, Oct, 2010 ($1.75/$1.95/$1.99/$2.25/$2.50/$2.99)

	GD 2.0	VG 4.0	FN 6.0	VF 8.0	VF/NM 9.0	NM- 9.2
1	1	3	4	6	8	10
2-10: 5-Begin-$1.95-c						5.00
11-45: 14-Begin $1.99-c						4.00
46-89,91-157: 63-Begin $2.25-c. 75-With 2 Garbage Pail Kids stickers. 100-Wray-c						3.00
90,158,159: 90-($2.95) Bonus stories. 158,159-($2.99-c)						4.00
...Spooky Spectacular 1 (10/99, $3.95) Comic Convention story						4.00
...Spooky Spectacular 2000 (10/00, $3.95)						4.00
...Spooky Summer Special 2001 (8/01, $3.95) Staton-a						4.00
...Super Scarefest (8/02, $3.95) r/#20,25,30-32						4.00

SCOOBY-DOO TEAM-UP (TV)
DC Comics: Jan, 2014 - Present ($2.99)

	GD 2.0	VG 4.0	FN 6.0	VF 8.0	VF/NM 9.0	NM- 9.2
1-11,13-20,22,23: 1-Batman & Robin app.; Man-Bat app. 2-Ace the Bat-Hound app. 3-Bat-Mite app. 4-Teen Titans Go! 6-Super Friends & Legion of Doom app. 7-Flintstones. 8-Jetsons. 10-Jonny Quest. 13-Spectre, Deadman & Phantom Stranger						3.00
12-Harley Quinn, Poison Ivy, Catwoman & Batgirl app.						5.00
21-Harley Quinn, Joker, Batman, Robin & Batgirl app.						3.00
... FCBD Special Edition 1 (6/15, giveaway) flipbook with Teen Titans Go!						3.00
... Halloween Special Edition (12/14, giveaway) r/#1						3.00

SCOOBY-DOO: WHERE ARE YOU? (TV)
DC Comics: Nov, 2010 - Present ($2.99)

	GD 2.0	VG 4.0	FN 6.0	VF 8.0	VF/NM 9.0	NM- 9.2
1-78: 32-KISS spoof						3.00

SCOOP COMICS (Becomes Yankee Comics #4-7, a digest sized cartoon book; then after #8 it becomes Snap #9)
Harry 'A' Chesler (Holyoke): November, 1941 - No. 3, Mar, 1943; No. 8, 1944

	GD 2.0	VG 4.0	FN 6.0	VF 8.0	VF/NM 9.0	NM- 9.2
1-Intro. Rocketman & Rocketgirl & begins; origin The Master Key & begins; Dan Hastings begins; Charles Sultan-c/a	155	310	465	992	1696	2400
2-Rocket Boy begins; injury to eye story (reprinted in Spotlight #3); classic-c	258	516	774	1651	2826	4000
3-Injury to eye story-r from #2; Rocket Boy	90	180	270	576	988	1400
8-Formerly Yankee Comics; becomes Snap	57	114	171	362	619	875

SCOOTER (See Swing With...)

SCOOTER COMICS
Rucker Publ. Ltd. (Canadian): Apr, 1946

	GD 2.0	VG 4.0	FN 6.0	VF 8.0	VF/NM 9.0	NM- 9.2
1-Teen-age/funny animal	20	40	60	114	182	250

SCOOTER GIRL
Oni Press: May, 2003 - No. 6, Feb, 2004 ($2.99, B&W, limited series)

	GD 2.0	VG 4.0	FN 6.0	VF 8.0	VF/NM 9.0	NM- 9.2
1-6-Chynna Clugston-Major-s/a						3.00
TPB (5/04, $14.95, digest size) r/series; sketch pages						15.00

SCORPION
Atlas/Seaboard Publ.: Feb, 1975 - No. 3, July, 1975

	GD 2.0	VG 4.0	FN 6.0	VF 8.0	VF/NM 9.0	NM- 9.2
1-Intro.; bondage-c by Chaykin	3	6	9	14	19	24
2-Chaykin-a w/Wrightson, Kaluta, Simonson assists(p)	3	6	9	14	19	24
3-Jim Craig-c/a	2	4	6	11	16	20

NOTE: *Chaykin a-1, 2; c-1. Colon c-2. Craig c/a-3.*

SCORPION KING, THE (Movie)
Dark Horse Comics: March, 2002 - No. 2, Apr, 2002 ($2.99, limited series)

	GD 2.0	VG 4.0	FN 6.0	VF 8.0	VF/NM 9.0	NM- 9.2
1,2-Photo-c of the Rock; Richards-a						3.00

SCORPIO ROSE
Eclipse Comics: Jan, 1983 - No. 2, Oct, 1983 ($1.25, Baxter paper)

	GD 2.0	VG 4.0	FN 6.0	VF 8.0	VF/NM 9.0	NM- 9.2
1,2: Dr. Orient back-up story begins. 2-origin.						4.00

SCOTLAND YARD (Inspector Farnsworth of)(Texas Rangers in Action #5 on?)
Charlton Comics Group: June, 1955 - No. 4, Mar, 1956

	GD 2.0	VG 4.0	FN 6.0	VF 8.0	VF/NM 9.0	NM- 9.2
1-Tothish-a	14	28	42	80	115	150
2-4: 2-Tothish-a	10	20	30	54	72	90

SCOTT PILGRIM, ... (Inspired the 2010 movie)
Oni Press: Jul, 2004 - Vol. 6, Jul, 2010 ($11.99, B&W, 7-1/2" x 5", multiple printings exist)

	GD 2.0	VG 4.0	FN 6.0	VF 8.0	VF/NM 9.0	NM- 9.2
Scott Pilgrim's Precious Little Life (Vol. 1) Bryan Lee O'Malley-s/a in all						12.00
Scott Pilgrim Vs. The World (Vol. 2), S.P. & The Infinite Sadness (Vol. 3), S.P. Gets it Together (Vol. 4), S.P. Vs. The Universe (Vol. 5), Scott Pilgrim's Finest Hour (Vol. 6) each						12.00
Free Scott Pilgrim #1 (Free Comic Book Day Edition, 2006)						15.00
Full-Colour Odds & Ends 2008						12.00

SCOURGE, THE
Aspen MLT: No. 0, Aug, 2010 - No. 6, Dec, 2011 ($2.50/$2.99)

	GD 2.0	VG 4.0	FN 6.0	VF 8.0	VF/NM 9.0	NM- 9.2
0-($2.50) Lobdell-s/Battle-a; multiple covers						3.00
1-6-($2.99) Lobdell-s/Battle-a; multiple covers						3.00

SCOURGE OF THE GODS
Marvel Comics (Soleil): 2009 - No. 3, 2009 ($5.99, limited series)

	GD 2.0	VG 4.0	FN 6.0	VF 8.0	VF/NM 9.0	NM- 9.2
1-3-Mangin-s/Gajic-a; English version of French comic						6.00
...: The Fall 1-3 (2009 - No. 3, 2009)						6.00

SCOUT (See Eclipse Graphic Album #16, New America & Swords of Texas)
(Becomes Scout: War Shaman)
Eclipse Comics: Dec, 1985 - No. 24, Oct, 1987($1.75/$1.25, Baxter paper)

	GD 2.0	VG 4.0	FN 6.0	VF 8.0	VF/NM 9.0	NM- 9.2
1-15,17,18,20-24: 19-Airboy preview. 10-Bissette-a. 11-Monday, the Eliminator begins. 15-Swords of Texas						3.00
16,19: 16-Scout 3-D Special ($2.50), 16-Scout 2-D Limited Edition, 19-contains flexidisk ($2.50)						4.00
...Handbook 1 (8/87, $1.75, B&W)						3.00
Mount Fire (1989, $14.95, TPB) r/#8-14						15.00

SCOUT: WAR SHAMAN (Formerly Scout)
Eclipse Comics: Mar, 1988 - No. 16, Dec, 1989 ($1.95)

	GD 2.0	VG 4.0	FN 6.0	VF 8.0	VF/NM 9.0	NM- 9.2
1-16						3.00

SCRATCH
DC Comics: Aug, 2004 - No. 5, Dec, 2004 ($2.50, limited series)

	GD 2.0	VG 4.0	FN 6.0	VF 8.0	VF/NM 9.0	NM- 9.2
1-5-Sam Kieth-s/a/c; Batman app.						3.00

SCREAM (...Comics) (Andy Comics #20 on)
Humor Publications/Current Books(Ace Magazines): Autumn, 1944 - No. 19, Apr, 1948

	GD 2.0	VG 4.0	FN 6.0	VF 8.0	VF/NM 9.0	NM- 9.2
1-Teenage humor	19	38	57	111	176	240
2	12	24	36	67	94	120
3-16: 11-Racist humor (Indians). 16-Intro. Lily-Belle	10	20	30	58	79	100
17,19	10	20	30	54	72	90

Scream Comics #14 © ACE

Scud: the Disposable Assassin #21 © Rob Schrab

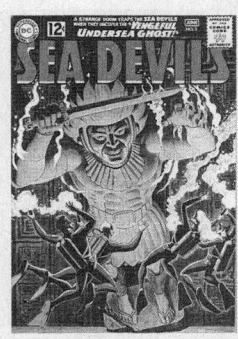

Sea Devils #5 © DC

GD VG FN VF VF/NM NM-
2.0 4.0 6.0 8.0 9.0 9.2

18-Hypo needle story 10 20 30 58 79 100

SCREAM (Magazine)
Skywald Publ. Corp.: Aug, 1973 - No. 11, Feb, 1975 (68 pgs., B&W) (Painted-c on all)

1-Nosferatu-c/1st app. (series thru #11); Morrow-a. Cthulhu/Necronomicon-s
7 14 21 49 92 135
2,3: 2-(10/73) Lady Satan 1st app. & series begins; Edgar Allan Poe adaptations begin (thru #11); Phantom of the Opera-s. 3-(12/73) Origin Lady Satan
5 10 15 33 57 80
4-1st Cannibal Werewolf and 1st Lunatic Mummy 4 8 12 28 50 70
5,7,8: 5,7-Frankenstein app. 8-Buckler-a; Werewolf-s; Slither-Slime Man-s
4 8 12 28 50 70
6, 9,10: 6-(6/74) Saga of The Victims/ I Am Horror, classic GGA Hewetson series begins (thru #11); Frankenstein 2073-s. 9-Severed head-c; Marcos-a. 9,10-Werewolf-s. 10-Dracula-c/s 5 10 15 31 53 75
11- (1975 Winter Special) "Mr. Poe and the Raven" story
5 10 15 33 57 80

NOTE: ***Buckler** a-8. **Hewetson** s-1-11. **Marcos** a-9. **Miralles** c-2. **Morrow** a-1. **Poe** s-2-11. **Segrelles** a-7; c-1.*

SCREEN CARTOONS
DC Comics: Dec, 1944 (cover only ashcan)

nn-Ashcan comic, not distributed to newsstands, only for in house use. Covers were produced, but not the rest of the book. A copy sold in 2006 for $400 and in 2008 for $500.

SCREEN COMICS
DC Comics: Dec, 1944 (cover only ashcan)

nn-Ashcan comic, not distributed to newsstands, only for in house use. Covers were produced, but not the rest of the book. A copy sold in 2006 for $400, in 2008 for $500 and in 2013 for $500.

SCREEN FABLES
DC Comics: Dec, 1944 (cover only ashcan)

nn-Ashcan comic, not distributed to newsstands, only for in house use. Covers were produced, but not the rest of the book. A copy sold in 2006 for $400 and in 2008 for $500.

SCREEN FUNNIES
DC Comics: Dec, 1944 (cover only ashcan)

nn-Ashcan comic, not distributed to newsstands, only for in house use. Covers were produced, but not the rest of the book. A copy sold in 2006 for $400 and in 2008 for $500.

SCREEN GEMS
DC Comics: Dec, 1944 (cover only ashcan)

nn-Ashcan comic, not distributed to newsstands, only for in house use. Covers were produced, but not the rest of the book. A copy sold in 2010 for $891 and a VF copy sold for $775.

SCREWBALL SQUIRREL
Dark Horse Comics: July, 1995 - No. 3, Sept, 1995 ($2.50, limited series)

1-3: Characters created by Tex Avery 3.00

SCRIBBLENAUTS UNMASKED: A CRISIS OF IMAGINATION (Based on the video game)
DC Comics: Mar, 2014 - No. 7, Sept, 2014 ($2.99)

1-7: 1-The Bat Family, the Joker and Phantom Stranger app. 3-The Anti-Monitor app. 3.00

SCRIBBLY (See All-American Comics, Buzzy, The Funnies, Leave It To Binky & Popular Comics)
National Periodical Publ.: 8-9/48 - No. 13, 8-9/50; No. 14, 10-11/51 - No. 15, 12-1/51-52

1-Sheldon Mayer-c/a in all; 52 pgs. begin 87 174 261 553 952 1350
2 55 110 165 352 601 850
3-5 45 90 135 284 480 675
6-10 36 72 108 216 351 485
11-15: 13-Last 52 pgs. 31 62 93 184 300 415

SCUD: TALES FROM THE VENDING MACHINE
Fireman Press: 1998 - No. 5 ($2.50, B&W)

1-5: 1-Kaniuga-a. 2-Ruben Martinez-a 3.00

SCUD: THE DISPOSABLE ASSASSIN
Fireman Press: Feb, 1994 - No. 20, 1997 ($2.95, B&W)
Image Comics: No. 21, Feb, 2008 - No. 24, May, 2008 ($3.50, B&W)

1 4 8 12 28 47 65
1-2nd printing in color 5.00
2 2 4 6 9 12 15
3 6.00
4-20 3.00
21-24: 21-(2/08, $3.50) Ashley Wood-c. 22-Mahfood-c 3.50
Heavy 3PO ($12.95, TPB) r/#1-4 13.00
Programmed For Damage ($14.95, TPB) r/#5-9 15.00
Solid Gold Bomb ($17.95, TPB) r/#10-15 18.00

SEA DEVILS (See Limited Collectors' Edition #39,45, & Showcase #27-29)
National Periodical Publications: Sept-Oct, 1961 - No. 35, May-June, 1967

GD VG FN VF VF/NM NM-
2.0 4.0 6.0 8.0 9.0 9.2

1-(9-10/61) 57 114 171 456 1028 1600
2-Last 10¢ issue; grey-tone-c 27 54 81 194 435 675
3-Begin 12¢ issues thru #35; grey-tone-c 18 36 54 124 275 425
4,5-Grey-tone-c 15 30 45 105 233 360
6-10 10 20 30 69 147 225
11,12,14-20: 12-Grey-tone-c 8 16 24 54 102 150
13-Kubert, Colan-a; Joe Kubert app. in story 8 16 24 55 105 155
21-35: 22-Intro. International Sea Devils; origin & 1st app. Capt. X & Man Fish. 33,35-Grey-tone-c 6 12 18 40 73 105

NOTE: ***Heath** a-Showcase 27-29, 1-10; c-Showcase 27-29, 1-10, 14-16. **Moldoff** a-16i.*

SEA DEVILS (See Tangent Comics/ Sea Devils)

SEADRAGON (Also see the Epsilion Wave)
Elite Comics: May, 1986 - No. 8, 1987 ($1.75)

1-8: 1-1st & 2nd printings exist 3.00

SEAGUY
DC Comics (Vertigo): July, 2004 - No. 3, Sept, 2004 ($2.95, limited series)

1-3-Grant Morrison-s/Cameron Stewart-a/c 3.00
TPB (2005, $9.95) r/#1-3 10.00

SEAGUY: THE SLAVES OF MICKEY EYE
DC Comics (Vertigo): Jun, 2009 - No. 3, Aug, 2009 ($3.99, limited series)

1-3-Grant Morrison-s/Cameron Stewart-a/c 4.00

SEA HOUND, THE (Captain Silver's Log Of The...)
Avon Periodicals: 1945 (no month) - No. 2, Sept-Oct, 1945

nn (#1)-29 pg. novel length sty-"The Esmeralda's Treasure"
18 36 54 105 165 225
2 13 26 39 74 105 135

SEA HOUND, THE (Radio)
Capt. Silver Syndicate: No. 3, July, 1949 - No. 4, Sept, 1949

3,4 10 20 30 54 72 90

SEA HUNT (TV)
Dell Publishing Co.: No. 928, 8/58 - No. 1041, 10-12/59; No. 4, 1-3/60 - No. 13, 4-6/62 (All have Lloyd Bridges photo-c)

Four Color 928(#1) 10 20 30 66 138 210
Four Color 994(#2), 4-13: Manning-a #4-6,8-11,13 7 14 21 48 89 130
Four Color 1041(#3)-Toth-a 7 14 21 48 89 130

SEA OF RED
Image Comics: Mar, 2005 - No. 13, Nov, 2006 ($2.95/$2.99/$3.50)

1-12-Vampirates at sea; Remender & Dwyer-s/Dwyer & Sam-a 3.00
13-($3.50) 3.50
Vol. 1: No Grave But The Sea (9/05, $8.95) r/#1-4 9.00
Vol. 2: No Quarter (2006, $11.99) r/#5-8 12.00
Vol. 3: The Deadlights (2006, $14.99) r/#9-13 15.00

SEAQUEST (TV)
Nemesis Comics: Mar, 1994 ($2.25)

1-Has 2 diff-c stocks (slick & cardboard); Alcala-i 3.00

SEARCHERS, THE (Movie)
Dell Publishing Co.: No. 709, 1956

Four Color 709-John Wayne photo-c 23 46 69 161 356 550

SEARCHERS, THE
Caliber Comics: 1996 - No. 4, 1996 ($2.95, B&W)

1-4 3.00

SEARCHERS, THE : APOSTLE OF MERCY
Caliber Comics: 1997 - No. 2, 1997 ($2.95/$3.95, B&W)

1-($2.95) 3.00
2-($3.95) 4.00

SEARCH FOR LOVE
American Comics Group: Feb-Mar, 1950 - No. 2, Apr-May, 1950 (52 pgs.)

1 14 28 42 82 121 160
2 10 20 30 56 76 95

SEARS (See Merry Christmas From...)

SEASON'S GREETINGS
Hallmark (King Features): 1935 (6-1/4x5-1/4", 24 pgs. in color)

nn-Cover features Mickey Mouse, Popeye, Jiggs & Skippy. "The Night Before Christmas" told one panel per page, each panel by a famous artist featuring their character. Art by Alex Raymond, Gottfredson, Swinnerton, Segar, Chic Young, Milt Gross, Sullivan (Messmer),

Secret Avengers (2013 series) #12 © MAR

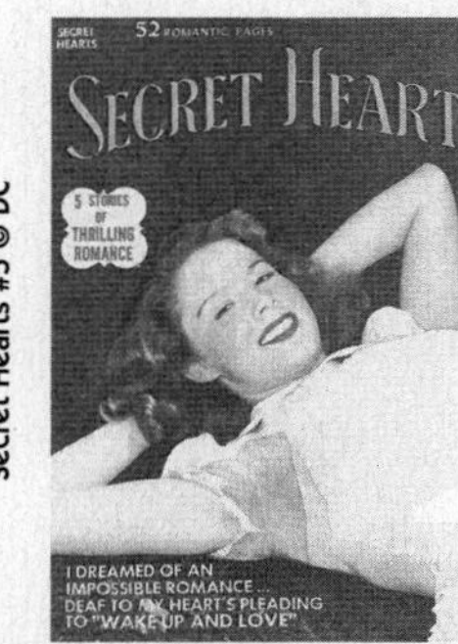

Secret Hearts #5 © DC

Secret Invasion: Dark Reign #1 © MAR

GD VG FN VF VF/NM NM-
2.0 4.0 6.0 8.0 9.0 9.2

Herriman, McManus, Percy Crosby & others (22 artists in all)
Estimated value... 950.00

SEBASTIAN O
DC Comics (Vertigo): May, 1993 - No. 3, July, 1993 ($1.95, limited series)

1-3-Grant Morrison scripts; Steve Yeowell-a 3.00
TPB (2004, $9.95) r/#1-3; intro. chronology by Morrison 10.00

SECOND LIFE OF DOCTOR MIRAGE, THE (See Shadowman #16)
Valiant: Nov, 1993 - No. 18, May, 1995 ($2.50)

1-18: 1-With bound-in poster. 5-Shadowman x-over. 7-Bound-in trading card 3.00
1-Gold ink logo edition; no price on-c 6.00

SECOND SIGHT
AfterShock Comics: Feb, 2016 - Present ($3.99)

1-6-David Hine-s/Alberto Ponticelli-a 4.00

SECRET AGENT (Formerly Sarge Steel)
Charlton Comics: V2#9, Oct, 1966; V2#10, Oct, 1967

V2#9-Sarge Steel part-r begins 3 6 9 16 24 32
10-Tiffany Sinn, CIA app. (from Career Girl Romances #39); Aparo-a
3 6 9 14 19 24

SECRET AGENT (TV) (See Four Color #1231)
Gold Key: Nov, 1966; No. 2, Jan, 1968

1-John Drake photo-c 7 14 21 49 92 135
2-Photo-c 5 10 15 35 63 90

SECRET AGENT X-9 (See Flash Gordon #4 by King)
David McKay Publ.: 1934 (Book 1: 84 pgs.; Book 2: 124 pgs.) (8x7-1/2")

Book 1-Contains reprints of the first 13 weeks of the strip by Alex Raymond; complete except for 2 dailies 47 94 141 296 498 700
Book 2-Contains reprints immediately following contents of Book 1, for 20 weeks by Alex Raymond; complete except for two dailies. Note: Raymond mis-dated the last five strips from 6/34, and while the dating sequence is confusing, the continuity is correct
40 80 120 246 411 575

SECRET AGENT X-9 (See Magic Comics)
Dell Publishing Co.: Dec, 1937 (Not by Raymond)

Feature Books 8 50 100 150 315 533 750

SECRET AGENT Z-2 (See Holyoke One-Shot No. 7)

SECRET AVENGERS (The Heroic Age)
Marvel Comics: Jul, 2010 - No. 37, Mar, 2013 ($3.99)

1-Bendis-s/Deodato-a/Djurdjevic-c; Steve Rogers assembles covert squad 4.00
1-Variant-c by Yardin 6.00
2-12: 2-Two covers. 2-4-Deodato-a. 5-Nick Fury app.; Aja-a 4.00
12.1 ($2.99) Spencer-s/Eaton-a/Deodato-c 3.00
13-21: 13-15-Fear Itself tie-in; Granov-c. 15-Aftermath of Bucky's demise. 16-21-Ellis-s 4.00
21.2-($2.99) Remender-s/Zircher-a; intro. new Masters of Evil 3.00
22-37: 22-25-Remender-s/Hardman-a/Art Adams-c. 23-Venom joins. 26-28-A vs. X 4.00

SECRET AVENGERS (Marvel NOW!)
Marvel Comics: Apr, 2013 - No. 16, Apr, 2014 ($3.99)

1-16: 1-5-Spencer-s/Luke Ross-a/Coker-c; Agent Coulson app. 5,7-Hulk app. 7,9-Guice-a 9,16-Winter Soldier app. 4.00

SECRET AVENGERS (All-New Marvel NOW!)
Marvel Comics: May, 2014 - No. 15, Jun, 2015 ($3.99)

1-15: 1-Ales Kot-s/Michael Walsh-a; M.O.D.O.K. app. 7-Deadpool app. 4.00

SECRET CITY SAGA (See Jack Kirby's Secret City Saga)

SECRET DEFENDERS (Also see The Defenders & Fantastic Four #374)
Marvel Comics: Mar, 1993 - No. 25, Mar, 1995 ($1.75/$1.95)

1-($2.50)-Red foil stamped-c; Dr. Strange, Nomad, Wolverine, Spider Woman & Darkhawk begin 4.00
2-11,13-24: 9-New team w/Silver Surfer, Thunderstrike, Dr. Strange & War Machine. 13-Thanos replaces Dr. Strange as leader; leads into Cosmic Powers limited series; 14-Dr. Druid. 15-Bound in card sheet. 15-17-Deadpool app. 18-Giant Man & Iron Fist app. 3.00
12,25: 12-($2.50)-Prismatic foil-c. 25 ($2.50, 52 pgs.) 4.00

SECRET DIARY OF EERIE ADVENTURES
Avon Periodicals: 1953 (25¢ giant, 100 pgs., one-shot)

nn-(Rare)-Kubert-a; Hollingsworth-c; Sid Check back-c
300 600 900 2010 3505 5000

SECRET FILES & ORIGINS GUIDE TO THE DC UNIVERSE
DC Comics: Mar, 2000; Feb, 2002 ($6.95/$4.95)

2000 (3/00, $6.95)-Overview of DC characters; profile pages by various 7.00
2001-2002 (2/02, $4.95) Olivetti-c 5.00

SECRET FILES PRESIDENT LUTHOR
DC Comics: Mar, 2001 ($4.95, one-shot)

1-Short stories & profile pages by various; Harris-c 5.00

SECRET HEARTS
National Periodical Publications (Beverly)(Arleigh No. 50-113):
9-10/49 - No. 6, 7-8/50; No. 7, 12-1/51-52 - No. 153, 7/71

1-Kinstler-a; photo-c begin, end #6 63 126 189 403 689 975
2-Toth-a (1 pg.); Kinstler-a 34 68 102 204 332 460
3,6 (1950) 31 62 96 182 296 410
4,5-Toth-a 31 62 93 186 303 420
7(12-1/51-52) (Rare) 42 84 126 267 451 635
8-10 (1952) 23 46 69 136 223 310
11-20 18 36 54 105 165 225
21-26: 26-Last precode (2-3/55) 15 30 45 90 140 190
27-40 7 14 21 49 92 135
41-50 6 12 18 40 73 105
51-60 5 10 15 35 63 90
61-75,100: 75-Last 10¢ issue 5 10 15 31 53 75
76-99,101-109: 83,88-Each has panel which inspired a famous Roy Lichtenstein painting
4 8 12 23 37 50
110- "Reach for Happiness" serial begins, ends #138 4 8 12 25 40 55
111-119,121-126: 114-Colan-a/c 3 6 9 17 26 35
120,134-Neal Adams-c 4 8 12 25 40 55
127 (4/68)-Beatles cameo 4 8 12 27 44 60
128-133,135-142: 141,142- "20 Miles to Heartbreak", Chapter 2 & 3 (see Young Love for Chapters 1 & 4); Toth, Colletta-a 3 6 9 16 24 32
143-148,150-152: 144-Morrow-a 3 6 9 14 20 26
149,153: 149-Toth-a. 153-Kirby-i 3 6 9 15 22 28

SECRET HISTORY OF THE AUTHORITY: HAWKSMOOR
DC Comics (WildStorm): May, 2008 - No. 6, Oct, 2008 ($2.99, limited series)

1-6-Costa-s/Staples-a/Hamner-c 3.00
TPB (2009, $19.99) r/#1-6 20.00

SECRET IDENTITIES
Image Comics: Feb, 2015 - No. 7, Sept, 2015 ($3.50/$3.99)

1-6-Faerber & Joines-s/Kyriazis-a 3.50
7-($3.99) 4.00

SECRET INVASION (Also see Mighty Avengers, New Avengers, and Skrulls!)
Marvel Comics: June, 2008 - No. 8, Jan, 2009 ($3.99, limited series)

1-Skrull invasion; Bendis-s/Yu-a/Dell'Otto-c 4.00
1-Variant cover with blank area for sketches 4.00
1-McNiven variant-c 12.00
1-Yu variant-c 30.00
1-2nd printing with old Avengers variant-c by Yu 4.00
1 Director's Cut (2008, $4.99) r/#1 with script; concept and promo art; cover gallery 5.00
2-8-Dell'Otto-c. 8-Wasp killed 4.00
2-4-McNiven variant-c. 2-Avengers. 3-Nick Fury. 4-Tony Stark, Spider-Woman, Black Widow 6.00
2-8-Yu variant-c. 2-Hawkeye & Mockingbird. 3-Spider-Woman. 4-Nick Fury 10.00
5-Rubi variant-c 5.00
6-Cho Spider-Woman variant-c 8.00
...:Aftermath: Beta Ray Bill - The Green of Eden (6/09, $3.99) Brereton-a 4.00
...: Chronicles 1,2 (4/09,6/09, $5.99) reprints from New Avengers & Illuminati issues 6.00
... Dark Reign (2/09, $3.99) villain meeting after #8; previews new series; Maleev-a/c 4.00
... Dark Reign (2/09, $3.99) Variant Green Goblin cover by Bryan Hitch 8.00
... Requiem (2009, $3.99) Hank Pym becomes The Wasp; r/TTA #44 & Avengers #215 4.00
... Saga (2008, giveaway) history of the Skrulls told through reprint panels and text 3.00
...: The Infiltration TPB (2008, $19.99) r/FF #2; New Avengers #31,32,38,39; New Avengers: Illuminati #1,5; Mighty Avengers #7; and Avengers: The Initiative Annual #1 20.00
...: War of Kings (2/09, $3.99) Black Bolt and the Inhumans; Pelletier & Dazo-a 4.00
...: Who Do You Trust? (8/08, $3.99) short tie-in stories by various; Jimenez-c 4.00

SECRET INVASION: AMAZING SPIDER-MAN
Marvel Comics: Oct, 2008 - No. 3, Dec, 2008 ($2.99, limited series)

1-3-Jackpot battles a Super-Skrull; Santucci-a. 2-Menace app. 3.00

SECRET INVASION: FANTASTIC FOUR
Marvel Comics: July, 2008 - No. 3, Sept, 2008 ($2.99, limited series)

1-3-Skrulls and Lyja invade; Kitson-a/Davis-c 3.00
1-Variant Skrull cover by McKone 5.00

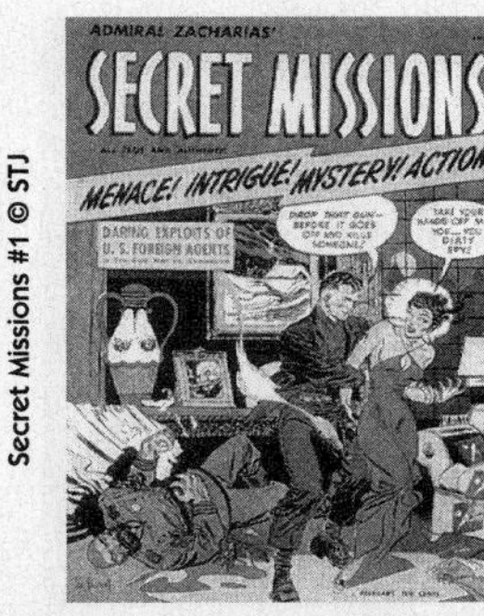

Secret Missions #1 © STJ

Secret Origins (2014 series) #4 © DC

Secret Romance #32 © CC

	GD 2.0	VG 4.0	FN 6.0	VF 8.0	VF/NM 9.0	NM- 9.2

SECRET INVASION: FRONT LINE
Marvel Comics: Sept, 2008 - No. 5, Jan, 2009 ($2.99, limited series)

1-5-Ben Urich covering the Skrull invasion; Reed-s/Castiello-a 3.00

SECRET INVASION: INHUMANS
Marvel Comics: Oct, 2008 - No. 4, Jan, 2009 ($2.99, limited series)

1-4-Raney-a/Sejic-c/Pokasky-s; search for Black Bolt 3.00

SECRET INVASION: RUNAWAYS/YOUNG AVENGERS (Follows Runaways #30)
Marvel Comics: Aug, 2008 - No. 3, Nov, 2008 ($2.99, limited series)

1-3-Miyazawa-a/Ryan-c 3.00

SECRET INVASION: THOR
Marvel Comics: Oct, 2008 - No. 3, Dec, 2008 ($2.99, limited series)

1-3-Fraction-s/Braithwaite-a; Skrulls invade Asgard; Beta Ray Bill app. 3.00
1-2nd printing with Beta Ray Bill cover 3.00

SECRET INVASION: X-MEN
Marvel Comics: Oct, 2008 - No. 4, Jan, 2009 ($2.99, limited series)

1-4-Carey-s/Nord-a/Dodson-c; Skrulls invade San Francisco 3.00
1-2nd printing with variant Nord-c 3.00

SECRET ISLAND OF OZ, THE (See First Comics Graphic Novel)

SECRET LOVE (See Fox Giants & Sinister House of...)

SECRET LOVE
Ajax-Farrell/Four Star Comic Corp. No. 2 on: 12/55 - No. 3, 8/56; 4/57 - No. 5, 2/58; No. 6, 6/58

1(12/55-Ajax, 1st series) 13 26 39 74 105 135
2,3 10 20 30 54 72 90
1(4/57-Ajax, 2nd series) 11 22 33 62 86 110
2-6: 5-Bakerish-a 9 18 27 47 61 75

SECRET LOVES
Comic Magazines/Quality Comics Group: Nov, 1949 - No. 6, Sept, 1950

1-Ward-c 31 62 93 182 296 410
2-Ward-c 24 48 72 144 237 330
3-Crandall-a 16 32 48 94 147 200
4,6 14 28 42 82 121 160
5-Suggestive art "Boom Town Babe"; photo-c 20 40 60 114 182 250

SECRET LOVE STORIES (See Fox Giants)

SECRET MISSIONS (Admiral Zacharia's...)
St. John Publishing Co.: February, 1950

1-Joe Kubert-c; stories of U.S. foreign agents 21 42 63 124 202 280

SECRET MYSTERIES (Formerly Crime Mysteries & Crime Smashers)
Ribage/Merit Publications No. 17 on: No. 16, Nov, 1954 - No. 19, July, 1955

16-Horror, Palais-a; Myron Fass-c 37 74 111 222 361 500
17-19-Horror. 17-Fass-c; mis-dated 3/54? 29 58 87 170 278 385

SECRET ORIGINS (1st Series) (See 80 Page Giant #8)
National Periodical Publications: Aug-Oct, 1961 (Annual) (Reprints)

1-Origin Adam Strange (Showcase #17), Green Lantern (Green Lantern #1), Challengers (partial-r/Showcase #6, 6 pgs. Kirby-a), J'onn J'onzz (Det. #225), The Flash (Showcase #4), Green Arrow (1 pg. text), Superman-Batman team (World's Finest #94), Wonder Woman (Wonder Woman #105) 43 86 129 318 722 1125
Replica Edition (1998, $4.95) r/entire book and house ads 5.00
Even More Secret Origins (2003, $6.95) reprints origins of Hawkman, Eclipso, Kid Flash, Blackhawks, Green Lantern's oath, and Jimmy Olsen-Robin team in 80 pg. Giant style 7.00

SECRET ORIGINS (2nd Series)
National Periodical Publications: Feb-Mar, 1973 - No. 6, Jan-Feb, 1974; No. 7, Oct-Nov, 1974 (All 20¢ issues) (All origin reprints)

1-Superman(r/1 pg. origin/Action #1, 1st time since G.A.), Batman(Detective #33), Ghost(Flash #88), The Flash(Showcase #4) 5 10 15 33 57 80
2-7: 2-Green Lantern & The Atom(Showcase #22 & 34), Supergirl(Action #252). 3-Wonder Woman (W.W. #1), Wildcat (Sensation #1). 4-Vigilante (Action #42) by Meskin, Kid Eternity(Hit #25). 5-The Spectre by Baily (More Fun #52,53). 6-Blackhawk(Military #1) & Legion of Super-Heroes(Superboy #147). 7-Robin (Detective #38), Aquaman (More Fun #73) 3 6 9 19 30 40

NOTE: *Infantino a-1. Kane a-2. Kubert a-1.*

SECRET ORIGINS (3rd Series)
DC Comics: Apr, 1986 - No. 50, Aug, 1990 (All origins)(52 pgs. #6 on)(#27 on: $1.50)

1-Origin Superman 1 2 3 5 6 8
2-6: 2-Blue Beetle. 3-Shazam. 4-Firestorm. 5-Crimson Avenger. 6-Halo/G.A. Batman 4.00
7-9,11,12,15-20,22-26: 7-Green Lantern (Guy Gardner)/G.A. Sandman. 8-Shadow Lass/Doll Man. 9-G.A. Flash/Skyman.11-G.A. Hawkman/Power Girl. 12-Challengers of Unknown/ G.A. Fury (2nd modern app.). 15-Spectre/Deadman. 16-G.A. Hourman/Warlord. 17-Adam Strange story by Carmine Infantino; Dr. Occult. 18-G.A. Gr. Lantern/The Creeper. 19-Uncle Sam/The Guardian. 20-Batgirl/G.A. Dr. Mid-Nite. 22-Manhunters. 23-Floronic Man/Guardians of the Universe. 24-Blue Devil/Dr. Fate. 25-LSH/Atom. 26-Black Lightning/Miss America 4.00
10-Phantom Stranger w/Alan Moore scripts; Legends spin-off 4.00
13-Origin Nightwing; Johnny Thunder app. 4.00
14-Suicide Squad; Legends spin-off 1 2 3 5 6 8
21-Jonah Hex/Black Condor 4.00
27-30,36-38,40-49: 27-Zatara/Zatanna. 28-Midnight/Nightshade. 29-Power of the Atom/Mr. America; new 3 pg. Red Tornado story by Mayer (last app. of Scribbly, 8/88). 30-Plastic Man/Elongated Man. 36-Poison Ivy by Neil Gaiman & Mark Buckingham/Green Lantern. 37-Legion Of Substitute Heroes/Doctor Light. 38-Green Arrow/Speedy; Grell scripts. 40-All Ape issue. 41-Rogues Gallery of Flash. 42-Phantom Girl/GrimGhost. 43-Original Hawk & Dove/Cave Carson/Chris KL-99. 44-Batman app.; story based on Det. #40. 45-Blackhawk/ El Diablo. 46-JLA/LSH/New Titans. 47-LSH. 48-Ambush Bug/Stanley & His Monster/Rex the Wonder Dog/Trigger Twins. 49-Newsboy Legion/Silent Knight/Bouncing Boy 3.00
31-35,39: 31-JSA. 32-JLA. 33-35-JLI. 39-Animal Man-c/story continued in Animal Man #10; Grant Morrison scripts; Batman app. 3.00
50-($3.95, 100 pgs.)-Batman & Robin in text, Flash of Two Worlds, Johnny Thunder, Dolphin, Black Canary & Space Museum 5.00
Annual 1 (8/87)-Capt. Comet/Doom Patrol 4.00
Annual 2 ('88, $2.00)-Origin Flash II & Flash III 4.00
Annual 3 ('89, $2.95, 84 pgs.)-Teen Titans; 1st app. new Flamebird who replaces original Bat-Girl 4.00
Special 1 (10/89, $2.00)-Batman villains: Penguin, Riddler, & Two-Face; Bolland-c; Sam Kieth-a; Neil Gaiman scripts(2) 5.00

NOTE: ***Art Adams** a-33i(part). **M. Anderson** 8, 19, 21, 25i; c-19(part). **Aparo** c/a-10. **Bissette** c-23. **Bolland** c-7. **Byrne** c/a-Annual 1. **Colan** c/a-5p. **Forte** a-37. **Giffen** a-18p, 44p, 48. **Infantino** a-17, 50p. **Kaluta** c-39. **Gil Kane** a-2, 28; c-2p. **Kirby** c-19(part). **Erik Larsen** a-13. **Mayer** a-29. **Morrow** a-21. **Orlando** a-10. **Perez** a-50i, Annual 3i; c- Annual 3. **Rogers** a-6p. **Russell** a-27i. **Simonson** c-22. **Staton** a-36, 50p. **Steacy** a-35. **Tuska** a-4p, 9p.*

SECRET ORIGINS (4th Series)(DC New 52)
DC Comics: Jun, 2014 - No. 11, May, 2015 ($4.99)

1-3,5-9,11: 1-Origin Superman, Robin. 2-Batman. 6-Wonder Woman 5.00
4-Harley Quinn 2 4 6 8 10 12
10-Batgirl; Stewart & Fletcher-s/Koh-a; Firestorm & Poison Ivy 6.00

SECRET ORIGINS 80 PAGE GIANT (Young Justice)
DC Comics: Dec, 1998 ($4.95, one-shot)

1-Origin-s of Young Justice members; Ramos-a (Impulse) 5.00

SECRET ORIGINS FEATURING THE JLA
DC Comics: 1999 ($14.95, TPB)

1-Reprints recent origin-s of JLA members; Cassaday-c 15.00

SECRET ORIGINS OF SUPER-HEROES (See DC Special Series #10, 19)

SECRET ORIGINS OF SUPER-VILLAINS 80 PAGE GIANT
DC Comics: Dec, 1999 ($4.95, one-shot)

1-Origin-s of Sinestro, Amazo and others; Gibbons-c 5.00

SECRET ORIGINS OF THE WORLD'S GREATEST SUPER-HEROES
DC Comics: 1989 ($4.95, 148 pgs.)

nn-Reprints Superman, JLA origins; new Batman origin-s; Bolland-c 1 2 3 4 5 7

SECRET ROMANCE
Charlton Comics: Oct, 1968 - No. 41, Nov, 1976; No. 42, Mar, 1979 - No. 48, Feb, 1980

1-Begin 12¢ issues, ends #? 3 6 9 17 26 35
2-10: 9-Reese-a 2 4 6 11 16 20
11-16,18,19,21-30 2 4 6 9 13 16
17,20: 17-Susan Dey poster. 20-David Cassidy pin-up 2 4 6 11 16 20
31-48 2 4 6 8 10 12

NOTE: *Beyond the Stars app.-No. 9, 11, 12, 14.*

SECRET ROMANCES (Exciting Love Stories)
Superior Publications Ltd.: Apr, 1951 - No. 27, July, 1955

1 20 40 60 120 195 270
2 14 28 42 82 121 160
3-10 13 26 39 72 101 130
11-13,15-18,20-27 11 22 33 64 90 115
14,19-Lingerie panels 12 24 36 67 94 120

SECRET SERVICE (See Kent Blake of the...)

SECRET SERVICE
Marvel Comics (Icon): Jun, 2012 - No. 6, Jun, 2013 ($2.99/$4.99, limited series)

Secret Six (2008 series) #1© DC

Secret Society of Super-Villains #1 © DC

Secret War #3 © MAR

	GD 2.0	VG 4.0	FN 6.0	VF 8.0	VF/NM 9.0	NM- 9.2
1-5-Mark Millar-s/Dave Gibbons-a/c						3.00
6-($4.99)						5.00

SECRET SIX (See Action Comics Weekly)
National Periodical Publications: Apr-May, 1968 - No. 7, Apr-May, 1969 (12¢)

	GD 2.0	VG 4.0	FN 6.0	VF 8.0	VF/NM 9.0	NM- 9.2
1-Origin/1st app.	5	10	15	35	63	90
2-7	3	6	9	21	33	45

SECRET SIX (See Tangent Comics/ Secret Six)

SECRET SIX (See Villains United)
DC Comics: Jul, 2006 - No. 6, Jan, 2007 ($2.99, limited series)

	GD 2.0	VG 4.0	FN 6.0	VF 8.0	VF/NM 9.0	NM- 9.2
1-6-Gail Simone-s/Brad Walker-a. 4-Doom Patrol app.						3.00
...: Six Degrees of Devastation TPB (2007, $14.99) r/#1-6						15.00

SECRET SIX
DC Comics: Nov, 2008 - No. 36, Oct, 2011 ($2.99)

	GD 2.0	VG 4.0	FN 6.0	VF 8.0	VF/NM 9.0	NM- 9.2
1-36: 1-Gail Simone-s/Nicola Scott-a. 2-Batman app. 8-Rodriguez-a. 11-13-Wonder Woman & Artemis app. 16-Black Alice app. 17,18-Blackest Night						3.00
...: Cats in the Cradle TPB (2011, $14.99) r/#19-24						15.00
...: Danse Macabre TPB (2010, $14.99) r/#15-18 & Suicide Squad #67 (Blackest Night)						15.00
...: Depths TPB (2010, $14.99) r/#8-14						15.00
...: The Reptile Brain TPB (2011, $14.99) r/#25-29						15.00
...: Unhinged TPB (2009, $14.99) r/#1-7; intro. by Paul Cornell						15.00

SECRET SIX
DC Comics: Feb, 2015 - No. 14, Jul, 2016 ($2.99)

	GD 2.0	VG 4.0	FN 6.0	VF 8.0	VF/NM 9.0	NM- 9.2
1-14: 1,2-Simone-s/Lashley-a; Catman & Black Alice app. 10-Superman app. 12-14-Shiva app.; Elongated Man returns						3.00

SECRET SOCIETY OF SUPER-VILLAINS
National Per. Publ./DC Comics: May-June, 1976 - No. 15, June-July, 1978

	GD 2.0	VG 4.0	FN 6.0	VF 8.0	VF/NM 9.0	NM- 9.2
1-Origin; JLA cameo & Capt. Cold app.	3	6	9	14	19	24
2-5,15: 2-Re-intro/origin Capt. Comet; Green Lantern x-over. 5-Green Lantern, Hawkman x-over; Darkseid app. 15-G.A. Atom, Dr. Midnite, & JSA app.	2	4	6	8	11	14
6-14: 9,10-Creeper x-over. 11-Capt. Comet; Orlando-i	2	3	4	6	8	10

SECRET SOCIETY OF SUPER-VILLAINS SPECIAL (See DC Special Series #6)

SECRETS OF HAUNTED HOUSE
National Periodical Publications/DC Comics: 4-5/75 - #5, 12-1/75-76; #6, 6-7/77 - #14, 10-11/78; #15, 8/79 - #46, 3/82

	GD 2.0	VG 4.0	FN 6.0	VF 8.0	VF/NM 9.0	NM- 9.2
1	5	10	15	34	60	85
2-4	3	6	9	19	30	40
5-Wrightson-c	4	8	12	23	37	50
6-14	2	4	6	11	16	20
15-30	2	4	6	8	11	14
31,44: 31-(12/80) Mr. E series begins (1st app.), ends #41. 44-Wrightson-c	2	4	6	9	13	16
32-(1/81) Origin of Mr. E	2	4	6	8	11	14
33-43,45,46: 34,35-Frankenstein Monster app.	1	3	4	6	8	10

NOTE: ***Aparo*** *c-7.* ***Aragones*** *a-1.* ***B. Bailey*** *a-8.* ***Bissette*** *a-46.* ***Buckler*** *c-32-40p.* ***Ditko*** *a-9, 12, 41, 45.* ***Golden*** *a-10.* ***Howard*** *a-13i.* ***Kaluta*** *c-8, 10, 11, 14, 16, 29.* ***Kubert*** *c-41, 42.* ***Sheldon Mayer*** *a-43p.* ***McWilliams*** *a-35.* ***Nasser*** *a-24.* ***Newton*** *a-30p.* ***Nino*** *a-1, 13, 19.* ***Orlando*** *c-13, 30, 43, 45i.* ***N. Redondo*** *a-4, 5, 29.* ***Rogers*** *c-26.* ***Spiegle*** *a-31-41.* ***Wrightson*** *c-5, 44.*

SECRETS OF HAUNTED HOUSE SPECIAL (See DC Special Series #12)

SECRETS OF LIFE (Movie)
Dell Publishing Co.: 1956 (Disney)

	GD 2.0	VG 4.0	FN 6.0	VF 8.0	VF/NM 9.0	NM- 9.2
Four Color 749-Photo-c	5	10	15	31	53	75

SECRETS OF LOVE (See Popular Teen-Agers...)

SECRETS OF LOVE AND MARRIAGE
Charlton Comics: V2#1, Aug, 1956 - V2#25, June, 1961

	GD 2.0	VG 4.0	FN 6.0	VF 8.0	VF/NM 9.0	NM- 9.2
V2#1-Matt Baker-c?	6	12	18	40	73	105
V2#2-6	4	8	12	23	37	50
V2#7-9-(All 68 pgs.)	5	10	15	35	63	90
10-25	3	6	9	19	30	40

SECRETS OF MAGIC (See Wisco)

SECRETS OF SINISTER HOUSE (Sinister House of Secret Love #1-4)
National Periodical Publ.: No. 5, June-July, 1972 - No. 18, June-July, 1974

	GD 2.0	VG 4.0	FN 6.0	VF 8.0	VF/NM 9.0	NM- 9.2
5-(52 pgs.).	65	10	15	35	63	90
6-9: 7-Redondo-a	4	8	12	23	37	50
10-Neal Adams-a(i)	4	8	12	25	40	55
11-18: 15-Redondo-a. 17-Barry-a; early Chaykin 1 pg. strip	3	6	9	16	23	30

NOTE: ***Alcala*** *a-6, 13, 14.* ***Glanzman*** *a-7.* ***Kaluta*** *c-6, 7.* ***Nino*** *a-8, 11-13. Ambrose Bierce adapt.-#14.*

SECRETS OF THE LEGION OF SUPER-HEROES
DC Comics: Jan, 1981 - No. 3, Mar, 1981 (Limited series)

	GD 2.0	VG 4.0	FN 6.0	VF 8.0	VF/NM 9.0	NM- 9.2
1-3: 1-Origin of the Legion. 2-Retells origins of Brainiac 5, Shrinking Violet, Sun-Boy, Bouncing Boy, Ultra-Boy, Matter-Eater Lad, Mon-El, Karate Kid & Dream Girl						5.00

SECRETS OF TRUE LOVE
St. John Publishing Co.: Feb, 1958

	GD 2.0	VG 4.0	FN 6.0	VF 8.0	VF/NM 9.0	NM- 9.2
1-Matt Baker-c	24	48	72	140	230	320

SECRETS OF YOUNG BRIDES
Charlton Comics: No. 5, Sept, 1957 - No. 44, Oct, 1964; July, 1975 - No. 9, Nov, 1976

	GD 2.0	VG 4.0	FN 6.0	VF 8.0	VF/NM 9.0	NM- 9.2
5	5	10	15	33	57	80
6-10: 8-Negligee panel	4	8	12	23	37	50
11-20	3	6	9	21	33	45
21-30: Last 10¢ issue?	3	6	9	19	30	40
31-44(10/64)	3	6	9	15	22	28
1-(2nd series) (7/75)	3	6	9	16	23	30
2-9	2	4	6	9	12	15

SECRET SQUIRREL (TV)(See Kite Fun Book)
Gold Key: Oct, 1966 (12¢) (Hanna-Barbera)

	GD 2.0	VG 4.0	FN 6.0	VF 8.0	VF/NM 9.0	NM- 9.2
1-1st Secret Squirrel and Morocco Mole, Squiddly Diddly, Winsome Witch	9	18	27	61	123	185

SECRET STORY ROMANCES (Becomes True Tales of Love)
Atlas Comics (TCI): Nov, 1953 - No. 21, Mar, 1956

	GD 2.0	VG 4.0	FN 6.0	VF 8.0	VF/NM 9.0	NM- 9.2
1-Everett-a; Jay Scott Pike-c	22	44	66	132	216	300
2	14	28	42	80	115	150
3-11: 11-Last pre-code (2/55)	13	26	39	74	105	135
12-21	11	22	33	62	86	110

NOTE: ***Colletta*** *a-10, 14, 15, 17, 21; c-10, 14, 17.*

SECRET VOICE, THE (See Great American Comics Presents...)

SECRET WAR
Marvel Comics: Apr, 2004 - No. 5, Dec, 2005 ($3.99, limited series)

	GD 2.0	VG 4.0	FN 6.0	VF 8.0	VF/NM 9.0	NM- 9.2
1-Bendis-s/Dell'Otto painted-a/c;						5.00
1-2nd printing with gold logo on white cover and full-color Spider-Man						4.00
1-3rd printing with white cover and B&W sketched Spider-Man						4.00
2-Wolverine-c; intro. Daisy Johnson (Quake)						12.00
2-2nd printing with white cover and B&W sketched Wolverine						12.00
3-5: 3-Capt. America-c. 4-Black Widow-c. 5-Daredevil-c						4.00
... : From the Files of Nick Fury (2005, $3.99) Fury's journal entries; profiles of characters						4.00
HC (2005, $29.99, dust jacket) r/#1-5 & ...From the Files of Nick Fury; additional art						30.00
SC (2006, $24.99) r/#1-5 & ...From the Files of Nick Fury; additional art						25.00

SECRET WARRIORS (Also see 2009 Dark Reign titles)
Marvel Comics: Apr, 2009 - No. 28, Sept, 2011 ($3.99/$2.99)

	GD 2.0	VG 4.0	FN 6.0	VF 8.0	VF/NM 9.0	NM- 9.2
1-Bendis & Hickman-s/Caselli-a/Cheung-c; Nick Fury app.; Hydra dossier; sketch pages						4.00
2-24,26-28-($2.99) 8-Dark Avengers app. 17-19-Howling Commandos return						3.00
25-($3.99) Baron Strucker app.; Vitti-a						4.00

SECRET WARS
Marvel Comics: 2014 (Giveaway)

	GD 2.0	VG 4.0	FN 6.0	VF 8.0	VF/NM 9.0	NM- 9.2
... No. 1 Halloween Comic Fest 2014 - Reprints Marvel Super Heroes Secret Wars #1						3.00

SECRET WARS (See Free Comic Book Day 2015 for prelude)
Marvel Comics: Jul, 2015 - No. 9, Mar, 2016 ($4.99/$3.99, limited series, originally planned as 8 issues)

	GD 2.0	VG 4.0	FN 6.0	VF 8.0	VF/NM 9.0	NM- 9.2
1,2-($4.99) Hickman-s/Ribic-a; end of the Marvel 616 and Ultimate universes						5.00
3-8-($3.99): 3-Miles Morales app.						4.00
9-($4.99) End of Battleworld, beginning of the Prime Earth						5.00
...: Agents of Atlas (12/15, $4.99) Taylor-s/Pugh-a/Kirk-c; Baron Zemo app.						5.00
...: Official Guide to the Marvel Multiverse 1 (12/15, $4.99) Handbook-style info on characters, events and realities tied-in with the Secret Wars series						5.00
...: Secret Love 1 (10/15, $4.99) Romance stories by various; Ms. Marvel, Squirrel Girl, Daredevil, Ghost Rider, Iron Fist & Misty Knight app.; 2 covers						5.00
..., Too 1 (1/16, $4.99) Humor short stories by various incl. Powell, Guillory, Leth						5.00

SECRET WARS: BATTLEWORLD
Marvel Comics: Jul, 2015 - No. 4, Oct, 2015 ($3.99, limited series)

	GD 2.0	VG 4.0	FN 6.0	VF 8.0	VF/NM 9.0	NM- 9.2
1-4-Short stories by various. 2-Howard the Duck app. 4-Silver Surfer app.; Francavilla-c						4.00

SECRET WARS: JOURNAL
Marvel Comics: Jul, 2015 - No. 5, Nov, 2015 ($3.99, limited series)

	GD 2.0	VG 4.0	FN 6.0	VF 8.0	VF/NM 9.0	NM- 9.2
1-5-Short stories by various. 1-Leads into Siege #1. 3-Isanove-a. 4-Lashley-a						4.00

SECRET WARS 2099
Marvel Comics: Jul, 2015 - No. 5, Nov, 2015 ($3.99, limited series)

Secret Weapons #6 © Voyager Comm.

Seekers into the Mystery #12 © DeMatteis

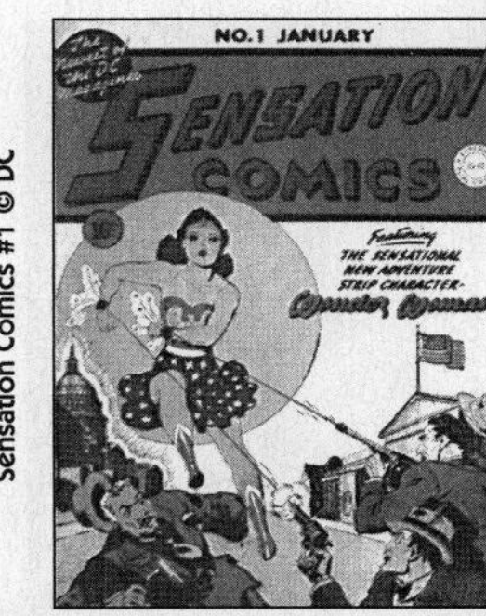

Sensation Comics #1 © DC

GD 2.0 | VG 4.0 | FN 6.0 | VF 8.0 | VF/NM 9.0 | NM- 9.2

1-5-Peter David-s/Will Sliney-a; Avengers vs. Defenders; Baron Mordo app. 4.00

SECRET WARS II (Also see Marvel Super Heroes...)
Marvel Comics Group: July, 1985 - No. 9, Mar, 1986 (Maxi-series)

1,9: 9-(52 pgs.) X-Men app., Spider-Man app. 6.00
2-8: 2,8-X-Men app. 5-1st app. Boom Boom. 5,8-Spider-Man app. 4.00

SECRET WEAPONS
Valiant: Sept, 1993 - No. 21, May, 1995 ($2.25)

1-10,12-21: 3-Reese-a(i). 5-Ninjak app. 9-Bound-in trading card. 12-Bloodshot app. 3.00
11-(Sept. on envelope, Aug on-c, $2.50)-Enclosed in manilla envelope; Bloodshot app; intro new team. 5.00

SECTAURS
Marvel Comics: June, 1985 - No. 8, Sept, 1986 (75¢) (Based on Coleco Toys)

1-8, 1-Giveaway; same-c with "Coleco 1985 Toy Fair Collectors' Edition" 4.00

SECTION ZERO
Image Comics (Gorilla): June, 2000 - No. 3, Sept, 2000 ($2.50)

1-3-Kesel-s/Grummett-a 3.00

SEDUCTION OF THE INNOCENT (Also see New York State Joint Legislative Committee to Study...)
Rinehart & Co., Inc., N. Y.: 1953, 1954 (400 pgs.) (Hardback, $4.00)(Written by Fredric Wertham, M.D.)(Also printed in Canada by Clarke, Irwin & Co. Ltd.)

(1st Version)-with bibliographical note intact (pages 399 & 400)(several copies got out before the comic publishers forced the removal of this page) 217 434 651 933 1117 1300
Dust jacket only 43 86 129 271 461 650
(1st Version)-without bibliographical note 108 216 324 464 557 650
Dust jacket only 24 48 72 140 230 320
(2nd Version)-Published in England by Rinehart, 1954, 399 pgs. has bibliographical page; "Second print" listed on inside flap of the dust jacket; publication page has no "R" colophon; unlike 1st version 19 38 57 109 172 235
1972 r-/of 2nd version; 400 pgs. w/bibliography page; Kennikat Press 6 12 18 42 79 115
2004 r/with new intro. by Wertham scholar James E. Reibman, 424 pgs; 6" x 9"; limited to 220 copies 6 12 18 42 79 115

NOTE: *Material from this book appeared in the November, 1953 (Vol.70, pp50-53,214) issue of the* ***Ladies' Home Journal*** *under the title "What Parents Don't Know About Comic Books". With the release of this book, Dr. Wertham reveals seven years of research attempting to link juvenile delinquency to comic books. Many illustrations showing excessive violence, sex, sadism, and torture are shown. This book was used at the Kefauver Senate hearings which led to the Comics Code Authority. Because of the influence this book had on the comic industry and the collector's interest in it, we feel this listing is justified. Modern printings exist in limited editions. Also see* ***Parade of Pleasure.***

SEDUCTION OF THE INNOCENT! (Also see Halloween Horror)
Eclipse Comics: Nov, 1985 - 3-D#2, Apr, 1986 ($1.75)

1-6: Double listed under cover title from #7 on 5.00
3-D 1 (10/85, $2.25, 36 pgs.)-contains unpublished Advs. Into Darkness #15 (pre-code); Dave Stevens-c 2 4 6 9 12 15
2-D 1 (100 copy limited signed & #ed edition)(B&W) 4 8 12 23 37 50
3-D 2 (4/86)-Baker, Toth, Wrightson-c 1 2 3 5 6 8
2-D 2 (100 copy limited signed & #ed edition)(B&W) 3 6 9 16 23 30

NOTE: ***Anderson*** *r-2, 3.* ***Crandall*** *c/a(r)-1.* ***Meskin*** *c/a(r)-3, 3-D 1.* ***Moreira*** *r-2.* ***Toth*** *a-1-6r; c-4r.* ***Tuska*** *r-6.*

SEDUCTION OF THE INNOCENT
Dynamite Entertainment: 2015 - No. 4, 2016 ($3.99, limited series)

1-4-Ande Parks-s/Esteve Polls-a/Francesco Francavilla-c 4.00

SEEKERS INTO THE MYSTERY
DC Comics (Vertigo): Jan, 1996 - No. 15, Apr, 1997 ($2.50)

1-14: J.M. DeMatteis scripts in all. 1-4-Glenn Barr-a. 5,10-Muth-c/a. 6-9-Zulli-c/a. 11-14-Bolton-c; Jill Thompson-a 3.00
15-($2.95)-Muth-c/a 3.00

SEEKER 3000 (See Marvel Premiere #41)
Marvel Comics: Jun, 1998 - No. 4, Sept, 1998 ($2.99/$2.50, limited series)

1-($2.99)-Set 25 years after 1st app.; wraparound-c 4.00
2-4-($2.50) 3.00
...Premiere 1 (6/98, $1.50) Reprints 1st app. from Marvel Premiere #41; wraparound-c 3.00

SELECT DETECTIVE (Exciting New Mystery Cases)
D. S. Publishing Co.: Aug-Sept, 1948 - No. 3, Dec-Jan, 1948-49

1-Matt Baker-a 36 72 108 211 343 475
2-Baker, McWilliams-a 22 44 66 132 216 300
3 18 36 54 103 162 220

SEMPER FI (Tales of the Marine Corp)
Marvel Comics: Dec, 1988- No.9, Aug, 1989 (75¢)

1-9: Severin-c/a 4.00

SENSATIONAL POLICE CASES (Becomes Captain Steve Savage, 2nd Series)
Avon Periodicals: 1952; No. 2, 1954 - No. 4, July-Aug, 1954

nn-(1952, 25¢, 100 pgs.)-Kubert-a?; Check, Larsen, Lawrence & McCann-a; Kinstler-c 50 100 150 315 533 750
2-4: 2-Kirbyish-a (3-4/54). 4-Reprint/Saint #5 20 40 60 114 182 250
I.W. Reprint #5-(1963?, nd)-Reprints Prison Break #5(1952-Realistic); Infantino-a 3 6 9 16 23 30

SENSATIONAL SHE-HULK, THE (She-Hulk #21-23) (See Savage She-Hulk)
Marvel Comics: V2#1, 5/89 - No. 60, Feb, 1994 ($1.50/$1.75, deluxe format)

V2#1-Byrne-c/a(p)/scripts begin, end #8 2 4 6 10 14 18
2,3,5-8: 3-Spider-Man app. 4.00
4,14-17,21-23: 4-Reintro G.A. Blonde Phantom. 14-17-Howard the Duck app. 21-23-Return of the Blonde Phantom. 22-All Winners Squad app. 4.00
9-13,18-20,24-49,51-60: 25-Thor app. 26-Excalibur app.; Guice-c. 29-Wolverine app. (3 pgs.). 30-Hobgoblin-c & cameo. 31-Byrne-c/a/scripts begin again. 35-Last $1.50-c. 37-Wolverine/Punisher/Spidey-c, but no app. 39-Thing app. 56-War Zone app.; Hulk cameo. 57-Vs. Hulk-c/story. 58-Electro-c/story. 59-Jack O'Lantern app. 3.00
50-($2.95, 52 pgs.)-Embossed green foil-c; Byrne app.; last Byrne-c/a; Austin, Chaykin, Simonson-a; Miller-a(2 pgs.) 5.00

NOTE: ***Dale Keown*** *a(p)-13, 15-22.*

SENSATIONAL SHE-HULK IN CEREMONY, THE
Marvel Comics: 1989 - No. 2, 1989 ($3.95, squarebound, 52 pgs.)

nn-Part 1, nn-Part 2 6.00

SENSATIONAL SPIDER-MAN
Marvel Comics: Apr, 1989 ($5.95, squarebound, 80 pgs.)

1-r/Amazing Spider-Man Annual #14,15 by Miller & Annual #8 by Kirby & Ditko 6.00

SENSATIONAL SPIDER-MAN, THE
Marvel Comics: Jan, 1996 - No. 33, Nov, 1998 ($1.95/$1.99)

0 ($4.95)-Lenticular-c; Jurgens-a/scripts 1 2 3 5 6 8
1 5.00
1-($2.95) variant-c; polybagged w/cassette 3 6 9 21 33 45
2-5: 2-Kaine & Rhino app. 3-Giant-Man app. 4.00
6-18: 9-Onslaught tie-in; revealed that Peter & Mary Jane's unborn baby is a girl. 11-Revelations. 13-15-Ka-Zar app. 14,15-Hulk app. 3.00
19-24: Living Pharoah app. 22,23-Dr. Strange app. 3.00
25-($2.99) Spiderhunt pt. 1; Normie Osborne kidnapped 4.00
25-Variant-c 1 2 3 5 6 8
26-33: 26-Nauck-a. 27-Double-c with "The Sensational Hornet #1"; Vulture app. 28-Hornet vs. Vulture. 29,30-Black Cat-c/app. 33-Last issue; Gathering of Five concludes 3.00
33.1, 33.2 (10/12, $2.99) DeFalco-s/Barberi-a/Bianchi-c 3.00
#(-1) Flashback(7/97) Dezago-s/Wieringo-a 3.00
'96 Annual ($2.95) 4.00

SENSATIONAL SPIDER-MAN, THE (Previously Marvel Knights Spider-Man #1-22)
Marvel Comics: No. 23, Apr, 2006 - No. 41, Dec, 2007 ($2.99)

23-40: 23-25-Aguirre-Sacasa-s/Medina-a. 23-Wraparound-c. 24,34,37-Black Cat app. 26-New costume. 28-Unmasked; Dr. Octopus app.; Crain-a. 35-Black costume resumes 3.00
41-($3.99) One More Day pt. 3; Straczynski-s/Quesada-a/c 4.00
... Annual 1 (2007, $3.99) Flashbacks of Peter & MJ's relationship; Larroca-a/Fraction-s 4.00
... Feral HC (2006, $19.99, dustjacket) r/#23-27; sketch pages 20.00
Civil War: Peter Parker, Spider-Man TPB (2007, $17.99) r/#28-34; Crain cover concepts 18.00

SENSATION COMICS (Sensation Mystery #110 on)
National Per. Publ./All-American: Jan, 1942 - No. 109, May-June, 1952

1-Origin Mr. Terrific (1st app.), Wildcat (1st app.), The Gay Ghost, & Little Boy Blue; Wonder Woman (cont'd from All Star #8), The Black Pirate begin; intro. Justice & Fair Play Club 6000 12,000 18,000 40,000 70,000 100,000

1-Reprint, Oversize 13-1/2x10". WARNING: This comic is an exact duplicate reprint of the original except for its size. DC published it in 1974 with a second cover titling it as a Famous First Edition. There have been many reported cases of the outer cover being removed and the interior sold as the original edition. The reprint with the new outer cover removed is practically worthless. See Famous First Edition for value.

2-Etta Candy begins 595 1190 1785 4350 7675 11,000
3-W. Woman gets secretary's job 371 742 1113 2600 4550 6500
4-1st app. Stretch Skinner in Wildcat 297 594 891 1901 3251 4600
5-Intro. Justin, Black Pirate's son 245 490 735 1568 2684 3800
6-Origin/1st app. Wonder Woman's magic lasso 371 742 1113 2600 4550 6500
7-10 194 388 582 1242 2121 3000
11,12,14-20 135 270 405 864 1482 2100
13-Hitler, Tojo, Mussolini-c (as bowling pins) 300 600 900 2010 3505 5000
21-30: 22-Cheetah app. 103 206 309 659 1130 1600
31-33 84 168 252 538 919 1300

Sensation Comics Featuring Wonder Woman #2 © DC

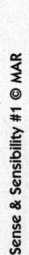

Sense & Sensibility #1 © MAR

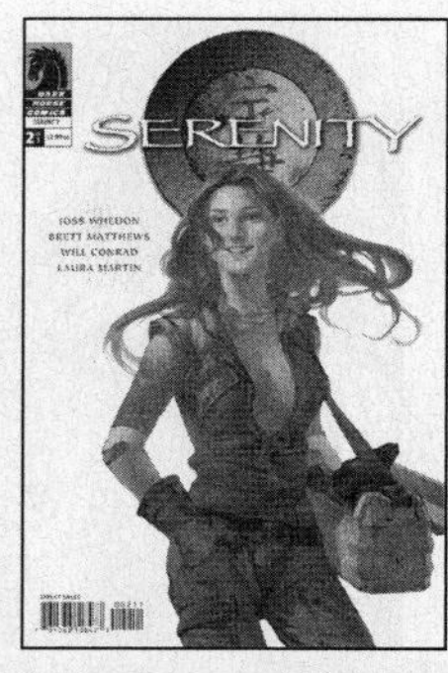

Serenity #2 © Universal

	GD 2.0	VG 4.0	FN 6.0	VF 8.0	VF/NM 9.0	NM- 9.2
34-Sargon, the Sorcerer begins (10/44), ends #36; begins again #52	87	174	261	553	952	1350
35-40: 36-2nd app. Giganta/1st cover; Cheetah app. 38-Christmas-c	81	162	243	518	884	1250
41-50: 43-The Whip app.	74	148	222	470	810	1150
51-60: 51-Last Black Pirate. 56,57-Sargon by Kubert	71	142	213	454	777	1100
61-67,70-80: 63-Last Mr. Terrific. 66-Wildcat by Kubert	65	130	195	416	708	1000
68-Origin & 1st app. Huntress (8/47)	103	206	309	659	1130	1600
69-2nd app. Huntress	71	142	213	454	777	1100
81-Used in **SOTI**, pg. 33,34; Krigstein-a	74	148	222	470	810	1150
82-93: 83-Last Sargon. 86-The Atom app. 90-Last Wildcat. 91-Streak begins by Alex Toth. 92-Toth-a (2 pgs.)	71	142	213	454	777	1100
94-1st all girl issue	116	232	348	742	1271	1800
95-99,101-106: 95-Unmasking of Wonder Woman-c/story. 99-1st app. Astra, Girl of the Future, ends #106. 103-Robot-c. 105-Last 52 pgs. 106-Wonder Woman ends	97	194	291	621	1061	1500
100-(11-12/50)	119	238	357	762	1306	1850
107-(Scarce, 1-2/52)-1st mystery issue; Johnny Peril by Toth(p), 8 pgs. & begins; continues from Danger Trail #5 (3-4/51)(see Comic Cavalcade #15 for 1st app.)	97	194	291	621	1061	1500
108-(Scarce)-Johnny Peril by Toth(p)	87	174	261	553	952	1350
109-(Scarce)-Johnny Peril by Toth(p)	94	188	282	597	1024	1450

NOTE: ***Krigstein** a-(Wildcat)-81, 83, 84. **Moldoff** Black Pirate-1-25; Black Pirate not in 34-36, 43-48. **Oskner** c(i)-89-91, 94-106. Wonder Woman by **H. G. Peter**, all issues except #8, 17-19, 21; c-4-7, 9-18, 20-88, 92, 93. **Toth** a-91, 98; c-107. Wonder Woman c-1-106.*

SENSATION COMICS (Also see All Star Comics 1999 crossover titles)
DC Comics: May, 1999 ($1.99, one-shot)

1-Golden Age Wonder Woman and Hawkgirl; Robinson-s 3.00

SENSATION COMICS FEATURING WONDER WOMAN
DC Comics: Oct, 2014 - No. 17, Feb, 2016 ($3.99, printing of digital-first comics)

1-17-Short story anthology. 1-Simone-s/Van Sciver-a. 2-Gene Ha-c. 5-Darkseid app. 8-Noelle Stevenson-a; Jae Lee-c. 10-Francavilla-c. 12-Poison Ivy app. 13-Superwoman app. 15-Garcia-López-a; Cheetah app.; McNeil-s/a. 16-Scott Hampton-a; Harley Quinn app. 4.00

SENSATION MYSTERY (Formerly Sensation Comics #1-109)
National Periodical Publ.: No. 110, July-Aug, 1952 - No. 116, July-Aug, 1953

	GD	VG	FN	VF	VF/NM	NM-
110-Johnny Peril continues	58	116	174	371	636	900
111-116-Johnny Peril in all. 116-M. Anderson-a	58	116	174	371	636	900

NOTE: ***M. Anderson** c-110. **Colan** a-114p. **Giunta** a-112. **G. Kane** c(p)-108, 109, 111-115.*

SENSE & SENSABILITY
Marvel Comics: July, 2010 - No. 5, Nov, 2010 ($3.99, limited series)

1-5-Adaptation of the Jane Austen novel; Nancy Butler-s/Sonny Liew-a/c 4.00

SENSUOUS STREAKER
Marvel Publ.: 1974 (B&W magazine, 68pgs.)

	GD	VG	FN	VF	VF/NM	NM-
1	4	8	12	27	44	60

SENTENCES: THE LIFE OF M.F. GRIMM
DC Comics (Vertigo): 2007 ($19.99, B&W graphic novel)

HC-Autobiography of Percy Carey (M.F. Grimm); Ronald Wimberly-a 20.00
SC (2008, $14.99) 15.00

SENTINEL
Marvel Comics: June, 2003 - No. 12, April, 2004 ($2.99/$2.50)

1-Sean McKeever-s/Udon Studios-a 3.00
2-12 3.00
Marvel Age Sentinel Vol. 1: Salvage (2004, $7.99, digest size) r/#1-6 8.00
Vol. 2: No Hero (2004, $7.99, digest size) r/#7-12; sketch pages 8.00

SENTINEL (2nd series)
Marvel Comics: Jan, 2006 - No. 5, May, 2006 ($2.99, limited series)

1-5-Sean McKeever-s/Joe Vriens-a 3.00
Vol. 3: Past Imperfect (2006, $7.99, digest size) r/#1-5 8.00

SENTINELS OF JUSTICE, THE (See Americomics & Captain Paragon &...)

SENTINEL SQUAD O*N*E
Marvel Comics: Mar, 2006 - No. 5, July, 2006 ($2.99, limited series)

1-5-Lopresti-a/Layman-s 3.00
Decimation: Sentinel Squad O*N*E (2006, $13.99, TPB) r/series; sketch pg. by Califore 14.00

SENTRY (Also see New Avengers and Siege)
Marvel Comics: Sept, 2000 - No. 5, Jan, 2001 ($2.99, limited series)

1-5-Paul Jenkins-s/Jae Lee-a. 3-Spider-Man-c/app. 4-X-Men, FF app. 3.00
.../Fantastic Four (2/01, $2.99) Continues story from #5; Winslade-a 3.00
.../Hulk (2/01, $2.99) Sienkiewicz-c/a 3.00
.../Spider-Man (2/01, $2.99) back story of the Sentry; Leonardi-a 3.00
.../The Void (2/01, $2.99) Conclusion of story; Jae Lee-a 3.00
.../X-Men (2/01, $2.99) Sentry and Archangel; Texeira-a 3.00
TPB (10/01, $24.95) r/#1-5 & all one-shots; Stan Lee interview 25.00
TPB (2nd edition, 2005, $24.99) 25.00

SENTRY (Follows return in New Avengers #10)
Marvel Comics: Nov, 2005 - No. 8, Jun, 2006 ($2.99, limited series)

1-8-Paul Jenkins-s/John Romita Jr.-a. 1-New Avengers app. 3-Hulk app. 3.00
1-(Rough Cut) (12/05, $3.99) Romita sketch art and Jenkins script; cover sketches 4.00
...: Fallen Sun (7/10, $3.99) Siege epilogue; Jenkins-s/Raney-a/Yu-c 4.00
...: Reborn TPB (2006, $21.99) r/#1-8 22.00

SENTRY SPECIAL
Innovation Publishing: 1991 ($2.75, one-shot)(Hero Alliance spin-off)

1-Lost in Space preview (3 pgs.) 3.00

SERENITY (Based on 2005 movie Serenity and 2003 TV series Firefly)
Dark Horse Comics: July, 2005 - No. 3, Sept, 2005 ($2.99, limited series)

1-3: Whedon & Matthews-s/Conrad-a. Three covers for each issue by various 4.00
...: Float Out (6/10, $3.50) Story of Wash; Patton Oswalt-s; covers by Jo Chen & Stockton 3.50
...: One For One (9/10, $1.00) reprints #1, Cassaday-c with red cover frame 3.00
...: Those Left Behind HC (11/07, $19.95, dustjacket) r/series; intro. by Nathan Fillion; pre-production art for the movie; Hughes-c 20.00
...: Those Left Behind TPB (1/06, $9.95) r/series; intro. by Nathan Fillion; Hughes-c 10.00

SERENITY BETTER DAYS (Firefly)
Dark Horse Comics: Mar, 2008 - No. 3, May, 2008 ($2.99, limited series)

1-3: Whedon & Matthews-s/Conrad-a; Adam Hughes-c 3.00

SERENITY: FIREFLY CLASS 03-K64 - LEAVES ON THE WIND (Follows movie)
Dark Horse Comics: Jan, 2014 - No. 6, Jun, 2014 ($3.50, limited series)

1-6: Zack Whedon-s/Georges Jeanty-a; covers by Dos Santos & Jeanty 3.50

SERENITY: FIREFLY CLASS 03-K64 - NO POWER IN THE 'VERSE (Follows movie)
Dark Horse Comics: Oct, 2016 - Present ($3.99, limited series)

1-5: Chris Roberson-s/Georges Jeanty-a; covers by Dos Santos & Jeanty 4.00

SERGEANT BARNEY BARKER (Becomes G. I. Tales #4 on)
Atlas Comics (MCI): Aug, 1956 - No. 3, Dec, 1956

	GD	VG	FN	VF	VF/NM	NM-
1-Severin-c/a(4)	22	44	66	132	216	300
2,3: 2-Severin-c/a(4). 3-Severin-c/a(5)	15	30	45	85	130	175

SERGEANT BILKO (Phil Silvers Starring as...) (TV)
National Periodical Publications: May-June, 1957 - No. 18, Mar-Apr, 1960

	GD	VG	FN	VF	VF/NM	NM-
1-All have Bob Oskner-c	60	120	180	381	653	925
2	32	64	96	188	307	425
3-5	26	52	78	154	252	350
6-18: 11,12,15,17-Photo-c	21	42	63	124	202	280

SGT. BILKO'S PVT. DOBERMAN (TV)
National Periodical Publications: June-July, 1958 - No. 11, Feb-Mar, 1960

	GD	VG	FN	VF	VF/NM	NM-
1-Bob Oskner c-1-4,7,11	22	44	66	154	340	525
2	12	24	36	79	170	260
3-5: 5-Photo-c	19	18	27	60	120	180
6-11: 6,9-Photo-c	7	14	21	44	82	120

SGT. DICK CARTER OF THE U.S. BORDER PATROL (See Holyoke One-Shot)

SGT. FURY (& His Howling Commandos)(See Fury & Special Marvel Edition)
Marvel Comics Group (BPC earlier issues): May, 1963 - No. 167, Dec, 1981

	GD	VG	FN	VF	VF/NM	NM-
1-1st app. Sgt. Nick Fury (becomes agent of Shield in Strange Tales #135); Kirby/Ayers-c/a; 1st Dum-Dum Dugan & the Howlers	417	834	1251	3545	8023	12,500
2-Kirby-a	58	116	174	464	1045	1625
3-5: 3-Reed Richards x-over. 4-Death of Junior Juniper. 5-1st Baron Strucker app.; Kirby-a	30	60	90	219	490	760
6-10: 8-Baron Zemo, 1st Percival Pinkerton app. 9-Hitler-c & app. 10-1st app. Capt. Savage (the Skipper)(9/64)	16	32	48	110	243	375
11,12,14-20: 14-1st Blitz Squad. 18-Death of Pamela Hawley	9	18	27	61	123	185
13-Captain America & Bucky app.(12/64); 2nd solo Capt. America x-over outside The Avengers; Kirby-a	41	82	123	303	689	1075
13-2nd printing (1994)	2	4	6	9	12	15
21-24,26,28-30	6	12	18	40	73	105
25,27: 25-Red Skull app. 27-1st app. Eric Koenig; origin Fury's eye patch	6	12	18	41	76	110

Sgt. Fury #153 © MAR

Sgt. Rock: The Lost Battalion #5 © DC

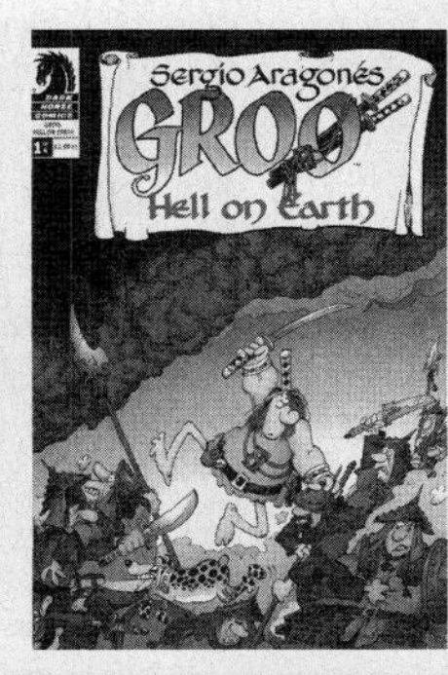

Sergio Aragonés Groo: Hell on Earth #1 © Sergio Aragonés

GD VG FN VF VF/NM NM-
2.0 4.0 6.0 8.0 9.0 9.2

31-33,35-50: 35-Eric Koenig joins Howlers. 43-Bob Hope, Glen Miller app. 44-Flashback on Howlers' 1st mission 4 8 12 27 44 60
34-Origin Howling Commandos 4 8 12 28 47 65
51-60 4 8 12 23 37 50
61-67: 64-Capt. Savage & Raiders x-over; peace symbol-c. 67-Last 12¢ issue; flag-c 3 6 9 19 30 40
68-80: 76-Fury's Father app. in WWI story 3 6 9 16 24 32
81-91: 91-Last 15¢ issue 3 6 9 14 20 26
92-(52 pgs.) 3 6 9 16 24 32
93-99: 98-Deadly Dozen x-over 3 6 9 14 19 24
100-Capt. America, Fantastic 4 cameos; Stan Lee, Martin Goodman & others app. 3 6 9 16 24 32
101-120: 101-Origin retold 2 4 6 10 14 18
121-130: 121-123-r/#19-21 2 4 6 8 11 14
131-167: 167-Reprints (from 1963) 2 4 6 8 10 12
133,134-(30¢-c variants, limited dist.)(5,7/76) 6 12 18 38 69 100
141,142-(35¢-c variants, limited dist.)(7,9/77) 10 20 30 64 132 200
Annual 1(1965, 25¢, 72 pgs.)-r/#4,5 & new-a 13 26 39 89 195 300
Special 2(1966) 6 12 18 40 73 105
Special 3(1967) All new material 5 10 15 30 50 70
Special 4(1968) 3 6 9 21 33 45
Special 5-7(1969-11/71) 3 6 9 17 26 35

NOTE: ***Ayers*** *a-8, Annual 1.* ***Ditko*** *a-15i.* ***Gil Kane*** *c-37, 96.* ***Kirby*** *a-1-7, 13p, 167p(r). Special 5; c-1-8, 10-20, 25, 167p.* ***Severin*** *a-44-46, 48, 162, 164; inks-49-79, Special 4, 6; c-4i, 5, 6, 44, 46, 110, 149i, 155i, 162-166.* ***Sutton*** *a-57p. Reprints in #80, 82, 85, 87, 89, 91, 93, 95, 99, 101, 103, 105, 107, 109, 111, 121-123, 145-155, 167.*

SGT. FURY AND HIS HOWLING COMMANDOS
Marvel Comics: July, 2009 ($3.99, one-shot)

1-John Paul Leon-a/c; WWII tale set in 1942; Baron Strucker app. 4.00

SGT. FURY AND HIS HOWLING DEFENDERS (See The Defenders #147)

SERGEANT PRESTON OF THE YUKON (TV)
Dell Publishing Co.: No. 344, Aug, 1951 - No. 29, Nov-Jan, 1958-59

Four Color 344(#1)-Sergeant Preston & his dog Yukon King begin; painted-c begin, end #18 12 24 36 81 176 270
Four Color 373,397,419('52) 8 16 24 54 102 150
5(11-1/52-53)-10(2-4/54): 6-Bondage-c. 5 10 15 35 63 90
11,12,14-17 5 10 15 33 57 80
13-Origin Sgt. Preston 5 10 15 35 63 90
18-Origin Yukon King; last painted-c 5 10 15 35 63 90
19-29: All photo-c 6 12 18 41 76 110

SGT. ROCK (Formerly Our Army at War; see Brave & the Bold #52 & Showcase #45)
National Periodical Publications/DC Comics: No. 302, Mar, 1977 - No. 422, July, 1988

302 4 8 12 28 47 65
303-310 3 6 9 16 23 30
311-320: 318-Reprints 2 4 6 10 16 20
321-350 2 4 6 8 11 14
329-Whitman variant 3 6 9 14 19 24
351-399,401-421: 412-Mlle Marie & Haunted Tank 1 2 3 5 7 9
400-(6/85) Anniversary issue 2 4 6 8 11 14
422-1st Joe, Adam, Andy Kubert-a team; last issue 2 4 6 10 14 18
Annual 2-4: 2(1982)-Formerly Sgt. Rock's Prize Battle Tales #1. 3(1983). 4(1984) 2 4 6 8 10 12

NOTE: ***Estrada*** *a-322, 327, 331, 336, 337, 341, 342i.* ***Glanzman*** *a-384, 421.* ***Kubert*** *a-302, 303, 305r, 306, 328, 351, 356, 368, 373, 422; c-317, 318r, 319-323, 325-333-on, Annual 2, 3.* ***Severin*** *a-347.* ***Spiegle*** *a-382, Annual 2, 3.* ***Thorne*** *a-384.* ***Toth*** *a-385r.* ***Wildey*** *a-307, 311, 313, 314.*

SGT. ROCK: BETWEEN HELL AND A HARD PLACE
DC Comics (Vertigo): 2003 ($24.95, hardcover one-shot)

HC-Joe Kubert-a/c; Brian Azzarello-s 25.00
SC (2004, $17.95) 18.00

SGT. ROCK'S COMBAT TALES
DC Comics: 2005 ($9.99, digest)

Vol. 1-Reprints early app. in Our Army at War, G.I. Combat, Star Spangled War Stories 10.00

SGT. ROCK SPECIAL (Sgt. Rock #14 on; see DC Special Series #3)
DC Comics: Oct, 1988 - No. 21, Feb, 1992; No. 1, 1992; No. 2, 1994 ($2.00, quarterly/monthly, 52 pgs)

1-Reprint begin 2 4 6 8 11 14
2-21: All-r; 5-r/early Sgt. Rock/Our Army at War #81. 7-Tomahawk-r by Thorne. 9-Enemy Ace-r by Kubert. 10-All Rock issue. 11-r/1st Haunted Tank story. 12-All Kubert issue; begins monthly. 13-Dinosaur story by Heath(r). 14-Enemy Ace-r (22 pgs.) by Adams/Kubert. 15-Enemy Ace (22 pgs.) by Kubert. 16-Iron Major-c/story. 16,17-Enemy Ace-r. 19-r/Batman/Sgt. Rock team-up/B&B #108 by Aparo 1 2 3 5 6 8

GD VG FN VF VF/NM NM-
2.0 4.0 6.0 8.0 9.0 9.2

1 (1992, $2.95, 68 pgs.)-Simonson-c; unpubbed Kubert-a; Glanzman, Russell, Pratt, & Wagner-a 6.00
2 (1994, $2.95) Brereton painted-c 4.00

NOTE: ***Neal Adams*** *r-1, 8, 14p.* ***Chaykin*** *a-2; r-3, 9(2pgs.); c-3.* ***Drucker*** *r-6.* ***Glanzman*** *r-20.* ***Golden*** *a-1.* ***Heath*** *a-2; r-5, 9-13, 16, 19, 21.* ***Krigstein*** *r-4, 8.* ***Kubert*** *r-1-17, 20, 21; c-1p, 2, 8, 14-21.* ***Miller*** *r-6p.* ***Severin*** *r-3, 6, 10.* ***Simonson*** *r-2, 4; c-4.* ***Thorne*** *r-7.* ***Toth*** *r-2, 8, 11.* ***Wood*** *r-4.*

SGT. ROCK SPECTACULAR (See DC Special Series #13)

SGT. ROCK'S PRIZE BATTLE TALES (Becomes Sgt. Rock Annual #2 on; see DC Special Series #18 & 80 Page Giant #7)
National Periodical Publications: Winter, 1964 (Giant - 80 pgs., one-shot)

1-Kubert, Heath-r; new Kubert-c 33 66 99 238 532 825
... Replica Edition (2000, $5.95) Reprints entire issue 6.00

SGT. ROCK: THE LOST BATTALION
DC Comics: Jan, 2009 - No. 6, Jun, 2009 ($2.99, limited series)

1-6-Billy Tucci-s/a. 1-Tucci & Sparacio-c 3.00
HC (2009, $24.99, d.j.) r/#1-6; production art; cover art gallery 25.00
SC (2010, $17.99) r/#1-6; production art; cover art gallery 18.00

SGT. ROCK: THE PROPHECY
DC Comics: Mar, 2006 - No. 6, Aug, 2006 ($2.99, limited series)

1-6-Joe Kubert-s/a/c. 1-Variant covers by Andy and Adam Kubert 3.00
TPB (2007, $17.99) r/#1-6 18.00

SGT. STRYKER'S DEATH SQUAD (See Savage Combat Tales)

SERGIO ARAGONÉS' ACTIONS SPEAK
Dark Horse Comics: Jan, 2001 - No. 6, Jun, 2001 ($2.99, B&W, limited series)

1-6-Aragonés-c/a; wordless one-page cartoons 3.00

SERGIO ARAGONÉS' BLAIR WHICH?
Dark Horse Comics: Dec, 1999 ($2.95, B&W, one-shot)

nn-Aragonés-c/a; Evanier-s. Parody of "Blair Witch Project" movie 3.00

SERGIO ARAGONÉS' BOOGEYMAN
Dark Horse Comics: June, 1998 - No. 4, Sept, 1998 ($2.95, B&W, lim. series)

1-4-Aragonés-c/a 3.00

SERGIO ARAGONÉS DESTROYS DC
DC Comics: June, 1996 ($3.50, one-shot)

1-DC Superhero parody book; Aragonés-c/a; Evanier scripts 4.00

SERGIO ARAGONÉS' DIA DE LOS MUERTOS
Dark Horse Comics: Oct, 1998 ($2.95, one-shot)

1-Aragonés-c/a; Evanier scripts 3.00

SERGIO ARAGONÉS FUNNIES
Bongo Comics: 2011 - Present ($3.50)

1-12-Color and B&W humor strips by Aragonés 3.50

SERGIO ARAGONÉS' GROO & RUFFERTO
Dark Horse Comics: Dec, 1998 - No. 4, Mar, 1999 ($2.95, lim. series)

1-3-Aragonés-c/a 3.00

SERGIO ARAGONÉS' GROO: DEATH AND TAXES
Dark Horse Comics: Dec, 2001 - No. 4, Apr, 2002 ($2.99, lim. series)

1-4-Aragonés-c/a; Evanier-s 3.00

SERGIO ARAGONÉS' GROO: HELL ON EARTH
Dark Horse Comics: Nov, 2007 - No. 4, Apr, 2008 ($2.99, lim. series)

1-4-Aragonés-c/a; Evanier-s 3.00

SERGIO ARAGONÉS' GROO: MIGHTIER THAN THE SWORD
Dark Horse Comics: Jan, 2000 - No. 4, Apr, 2000 ($2.95, lim. series)

1-4-Aragonés-c/a; Evanier-s 3.00

SERGIO ARAGONÉS' GROO: THE HOGS OF HORDER
Dark Horse Comics: Oct, 2009 - No. 4, Mar, 2010 ($3.99, lim. series)

1-4-Aragonés-c/a; Evanier-s 4.00

SERGIO ARAGONÉS' GROO THE WANDERER (See Groo...)

SERGIO ARAGONÉS' GROO: 25TH ANNIVERSARY SPECIAL
Dark Horse Comics: Aug, 2007 ($5.99, one-shot)

nn-Aragonés-c/a; Evanier scripts; wraparound cover 6.00

SERGIO ARAGONÉS' LOUDER THAN WORDS
Dark Horse Comics: July, 1997 - No. 6, Dec, 1997 ($2.95, B&W, limited series)

1-6-Aragonés-c/a 3.00

SERGIO ARAGONÉS MASSACRES MARVEL

Seven Seas Comics #3 © UPF

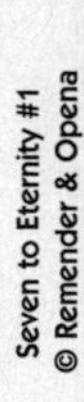
Seven to Eternity #1 © Remender & Opena

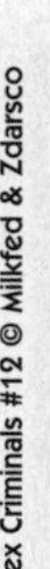
Sex Criminals #12 © Milkfed & Zdarsco

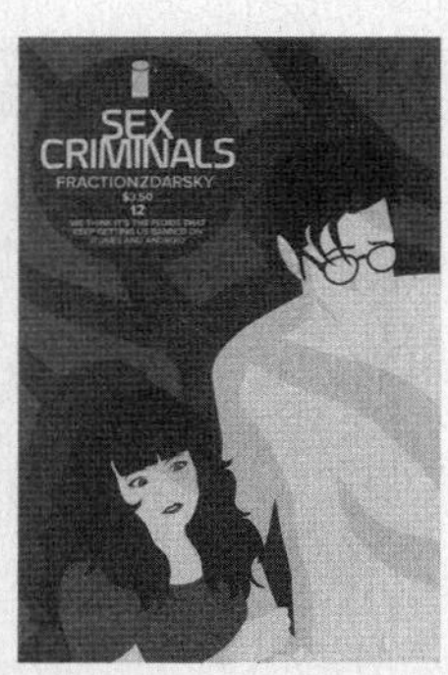

	GD	VG	FN	VF	VF/NM	NM-
	2.0	4.0	6.0	8.0	9.0	9.2

Marvel Comics: June, 1996 ($3.50, one-shot)
1-Marvel Superhero parody book; Aragonés-c/a; Evanier scripts 4.00

SERGIO ARAGONÉS STOMPS STAR WARS
Marvel Comics: Jan, 2000 ($2.95, one-shot)
1-Star Wars parody; Aragonés-c/a; Evanier scripts 3.00

SESAME STREET
Ape Entertainment: 2013 ($3.99)
1-Short stories by various; multiple covers 4.00
Free Comic Book Day edition (2013) Flip book with Strawberry Shortcake 3.00

SEVEN
Intrinsic Comics: July, 2007 ($3.00)
1-Jim Shooter-s/Paul Creddick-a 3.00

SEVEN BLOCK
Marvel Comics (Epic Comics): 1990 ($4.50, one-shot, 52 pgs.)
1-Dixon-s/Zaffino-a 6.00
nn-(IDW Publ., 2004, $5.99) reprints #1 6.00

SEVEN BROTHERS (John Woo's...)
Virgin Comics: Oct, 2006 - No. 5, Feb, 2007 ($2.99)
1-5-Garth Ennis-s/Jeevan Kang-a. 1-Two covers by Amano & Horn. 2-Kang var-c 3.00
TPB (6/07, $14.99) r/#1-5; cover gallery, deleted scenes and concept art 15.00
Volume 2 (9/07 - No. 5, 2/08) 1-Edison George-a. 4,5-David Mack-c 3.00

SEVEN DEAD MEN (See Complete Mystery #1)

SEVEN DWARFS (Also see Snow White)
Dell Publishing Co.: No. 227, 1949 (Disney-Movie)
Four Color 227 9 18 27 62 126 190

SEVEN MILES A SECOND
DC Comics (Vertigo Verité): 1996 ($7.95, one-shot)
nn-Wojnarowicz-s/Romberg-a 8.00

SEVEN-PER-CENT SOLUTION
IDW Publishing: Aug, 2015 - No. 5 ($3.99)
1-4-Sherlock Holmes/Sigmund Freud team-up; David & Scott Tipton-s/Joseph-a/Jones-c 4.00

SEVEN SAMUROID, THE (See Image Graphic Novel)

SEVEN SEAS COMICS
Universal Phoenix Features/Leader No. 6: Apr, 1946 - No. 6, 1947(no month)
1-South Sea Girl by Matt Baker, Capt. Cutlass begin; Tugboat Tessie by Baker app.
94 188 282 602 1026 1450
2-Swashbuckler-c 71 142 213 454 777 1100
3,5: 3-Six pg. Feldstein-a 129 258 387 826 1413 2000
4-Classic Baker-c 400 800 1200 2800 4900 7000
6-Baker Good Girl-c 161 322 483 1030 1765 2500
NOTE: *Baker a-1-6; c-3-6.*

SEVEN SOLDIERS OF VICTORY (Book-ends for seven related mini-series)
DC Comics: No. 0, Apr, 2005; No. 1; Dec, 2006 ($2.95/$3.99)
0-Grant Morrison-s/J.H. Williams-a 3.00
1-($3.99) Series conclusion; Grant Morrison-s/J.H. Williams-a 4.00
... Volume One (2006, $14.99) r/#0, Shining Knight #1,2; Zatanna #1,2; Guardian #1,2; and Klarion the Witch Boy #1; intro. by Morrison; character design sketches 15.00
... Volume Two (2006, $14.99) r/Shining Knight #3,4; Zatanna #3; Guardian #3,4; and Klarion the Witch Boy #2,3 15.00
... Volume Three ('06, $14.99) r/Zatanna #4; Mister Miracle #1,2; Bulleteer #1,2; Frankenstein #1 and Klarion the Witch Boy #4; 15.00
... Volume Four ('07, $14.99) r/Mister Miracle #3,4; Bulleteer #3,4; Frankenstein #2-4 and Seven Soldiers of Victory #1; script pages 15.00

SEVEN SOLDIERS: BULLETEER
DC Comics: Jan, 2006 - No. 4, May, 2006 ($2.99, limited series)
1-4-Grant Morrison-s/Yanick Paquette-a/c 3.00

SEVEN SOLDIERS: FRANKENSTEIN
DC Comics: Jan, 2006 - No. 4, May, 2006 ($2.99, limited series)
1-4-Grant Morrison-s/Doug Mahnke-a/c 3.00

SEVEN SOLDIERS: GUARDIAN
DC Comics: May, 2005 - No. 4, Nov, 2005 ($2.99, limited series)
1-4-Grant Morrison-s/Cameron Stewart-a; Newsboy Army app. 3.00

SEVEN SOLDIERS: KLARION THE WITCH BOY
DC Comics: June, 2005 - No. 4, Dec, 2005 ($2.99, limited series)
1-4-Grant Morrison-s/Frazer Irving-a 3.00

SEVEN SOLDIERS: MISTER MIRACLE
DC Comics: Nov, 2005 - No. 4, May, 2006 ($2.99, limited series)
1-4: 1-Grant Morrison-s/Pasqual Ferry-a/c. 3,4-Freddie Williams II-a/c 3.00

SEVEN SOLDIERS: SHINING KNIGHT
DC Comics: May, 2005 - No. 4, Oct, 2005 ($2.99, limited series)
1-4-Grant Morrison-s/Simone Bianchi-a 3.00

SEVEN SOLDIERS: ZATANNA
DC Comics: June, 2005 - No. 4, Dec, 2005 ($2.99, limited series)
1-4-Grant Morrison-s/Ryan Sook-a 3.00

1776 (See Charlton Classic Library)

7TH SWORD, THE
IDW Publishing (Darby Pop): Apr, 2014 - Present ($3.99)
1-6: 1-John Raffo-s/Nelson Blake II-a. 3-6-Nur Iman-a 4.00

7TH VOYAGE OF SINBAD, THE (Movie)
Dell Publishing Co.: Sept, 1958 (photo-c)
Four Color 944-Buscema-a 11 22 33 73 157 240

SEVEN TO ETERNITY
Image Comics: Sept, 2016 -Present ($3.99)
1-Rick Remender-s/Jerome Opeña-a 40.00
2 10.00
3,4 4.00

77 SUNSET STRIP (TV)
Dell Publ. Co./Gold Key: No. 1066, Jan-Mar, 1960 - No. 2, Feb, 1963 (All photo-c)
Four Color 1066-Toth-a 9 18 27 61 123 185
Four Color 1106,1159-Toth-a 7 14 21 49 92 135
Four Color 1211,1263,1291, 01-742-209(7-9/62)-Manning-a in all
7 14 21 46 86 125
1,2: Manning-a. 1(11/62-G.K.) 7 14 21 46 86 125

77TH BENGAL LANCERS, THE (TV)
Dell Publishing Co.: May, 1957
Four Color 791-Photo-c 6 12 18 41 76 110

SEVERED
Image Comics: Aug, 2011 - No. 7, Feb, 2012 ($2.99)
1-7-Scott Snyder & Scott Tuft-s/Attila Futaki-a/c 3.00

SEX
Image Comics: Mar, 2013 - Present ($2.99/$3.99)
1-26-Joe Casey-s/Piotr Kowalski-a/c 3.00
27-34-($3.99) 4.00

SEX CRIMINALS
Image Comics: Sept, 2013 - Present ($3.50/$3.99)
1-Matt Fraction-s/Chip Zdarsky-a/c 3 6 9 14 20 25
1-Variant-c by Shimizu 2 4 6 12 17 20
2 1 3 4 6 8 10
3-10 5.00
11-16 4.00
11-16-($4.69) Variant cover in pink polybag 5.00

SEYMOUR, MY SON (See More Seymour)
Archie Publications (Radio Comics): Sept, 1963
1-DeCarlo-c/a 4 8 12 28 47 65

SHADE, THE (See Starman)
DC Comics: Apr, 1997 - No. 4, July, 1997 ($2.25, limited series)
1-4-Robinson-s/Harris-c: 1-Gene Ha-a. 2-Williams/Gray-a 3-Blevins-a. 4-Zulli-a 3.00

SHADE, THE (From Starman)
DC Comics: Dec, 2011 - No. 12, Nov, 2012 ($2.99, limited series)
1-12: 1-Robinson-s/Hamner-a/Harris-c; Deathstroke app. 4-Cooke-a. 8-Thompson-a 12-Origin of the Shade; Gene Ha-a 3.00
1-12-Variant covers. 1-3-Hamner. 4-Darwyn Cooke. 5-7-Pulido. 11-Irving 4.00

SHADE, THE CHANGING GIRL
DC Comics (Young Animal): Dec, 2016 - Present ($3.99)
1-6: 1-Castellucci-s/Zarcone-a; intro. Megan Boyer/Loma Shade. 4-Element Girl back-up 4.00

SHADE, THE CHANGING MAN (See Cancelled Comic Cavalcade)
National Per. Publ./DC Comics: June-July, 1977 - No. 8, Aug-Sept, 1978

Shade, the Changing Man #57 © DC

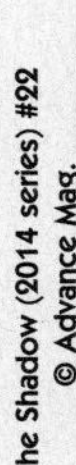

The Shadow (2014 series) #22 © Advance Mag.

Shadow Comics #1 © Conde Nast

	GD 2.0	VG 4.0	FN 6.0	VF 8.0	VF/NM 9.0	NM- 9.2
1-1st app. Shade; Ditko-c/a in all	2	4	6	11	16	20
2-8	2	3	4	6	8	10

SHADE, THE CHANGING MAN (2nd series) (Also see Suicide Squad #16)
DC Comics (Vertigo imprint #33 on): July, 1990 - No. 70, Apr, 1996 ($1.50-$2.25, mature)

1-($2.50, 52 pgs.)-Peter Milligan scripts in all 4.00
2-41,45-49,51-59: 6-Preview of World Without End. 17-Begin $1.75-c. 33-Metallic ink on-c. 41-Begin $1.95-c 3.00
42-44-John Constantine app. 3.50
50-($2.95, 52 pgs.) 4.00
60-70: 60-begin $2.25-c 3.00
...: Edge of Vision TPB (2009, $19.99) r/#7-13 20.00
...: Scream Time TPB (2010, $19.99) r/#14-19 20.00
...: The American Scream TPB (2003, 2009, $17.95/$17.99) r/#1-6 18.00
NOTE: *Bachalo a-1-9, 11-13, 15-21, 23-26, 33-39, 42-45, 47, 49, 50; c-30, 33-41.*

SHADO: SONG OF THE DRAGON (See Green Arrow #63-66)
DC Comics: 1992 - No. 4, 1992 ($4.95, limited series, 52 pgs.)

Book One - Four: Grell scripts; Morrow-a(i) 6.00

SHADOW, THE (See Batman #253, 259 & Marvel Graphic Novel #35)

SHADOW, THE (Pulp, radio)
Archie Comics (Radio Comics): Aug, 1964 - No. 8, Sept, 1965 (All 12¢)

	GD	VG	FN	VF	VF/NM	NM-
1-Jerrry Siegel scripts in all; Shadow-c.	8	16	24	55	105	155
2-8: 2-App. in super-hero costume on-c only; Reinman-a(backup). 3-Superhero begins; Reinman-a (book-length novel). 3,4,6,7-The Fly 1 pg. strips. 4-8-Reinman-a. 5-8-Siegel scripts. 7-Shield app.	5	10	15	33	57	80

SHADOW, THE
National Periodical Publications: Oct-Nov, 1973 - No. 12, Aug-Sept, 1975

	GD	VG	FN	VF	VF/NM	NM-
1-Kaluta-a begins	6	12	18	38	69	100
2	3	6	9	21	33	45
3-Kaluta/Wrightson-a	4	8	12	23	37	50
4,6-Kaluta-a ends. 4-Chaykin, Wrightson part-i	3	6	9	18	28	38
5,7-12: 11-The Avenger (pulp character) x-over	2	4	6	13	18	22

NOTE: *Craig a-10. Cruz a-10-12. Kaluta a-1, 2, 3p, 4, 6; c-1-4, 6, 10-12. Kubert c-9. Robbins a-5, 7-9; c-5, 7, 8.*

SHADOW, THE
DC Comics: May, 1986 - No. 4, Aug, 1986 (limited series)

1-4: Howard Chaykin art in all 4.00
Blood & Judgement ($12.95)-r/1-4 13.00

SHADOW, THE
DC Comics: Aug, 1987 - No. 19, Jan, 1989 ($1.50)

1-19: Andrew Helfer scripts in all. 4.00
Annual 1,2 (12/87, '88,)-2-The Shadow dies; origin retold (story inspired by the movie "Citizen Kane"). 5.00
NOTE: *Kyle Baker a-7i, 8-19, Annual 2. Chaykin c-Annual 1. Helfer scripts in all. Orlando a-Annual 1. Rogers c/a-7. Sienkiewicz c/a-1-6.*

SHADOW, THE (Movie)
Dark Horse Comics: June, 1994 - No. 2, July, 1994 ($2.50, limited series)

1,2-Adaptation from Universal Pictures film 4.00
NOTE: *Kaluta c/a-1, 2.*

SHADOW, THE
Dynamite Entertainment: 2012 - No. 25, 2014 ($3.99)

1-25: 1-Ennis-s/Campbell-a; multiple covers on all. 7-10-Gischler-s 4.00
#0-(2014, $3.99) Cullen Bunn-s/Colton Worley-a/Gabriel Hardman-c 4.00
#100-(2014, $7.99, squarebound) Short stories by various incl. Francavilla, Chaykin, Wagner, Uslan; 2 covers by Wagner & Hack 8.00
Annual 1 (2012, $4.99) Sniegoski-s/Calero-a/Alex Ross-c 5.00
Annual 2013 ($4.99) Parks-s/Evely-a/Worley-c 5.00
One Shot 2014: Agents of the Shadow ($7.99, squarebound) Robert Hack-c 8.00
... Over Innsmouth (2014, $4.99) Ron Marz-s/Ivan Rodriguez-a 5.00
Special 1 (2012, $4.99) Beatty-s/Cliquet-a/Alex Ross-c 5.00
Special 2014: Death Factory ($7.99, squarebound) Phil Hester-s/c; Ivan Rodriguez-a 8.00

SHADOW, THE (Volume 2)
Dynamite Entertainment: 2014 - No. 5, 2015 ($1.00/$3.99)

1-($1.00) Bunn-s/Timpano-a/Guice-c 3.00
2-5-($3.99) Bunn-s/Timpano-a/Guice-c 4.00

SHADOW AND DOC SAVAGE, THE
Dark Horse Comics: July, 1995 - No. 2, Aug, 1995 ($2.95, limited series)

1,2 4.00

SHADOW AND THE MYSTERIOUS 3, THE
Dark Horse Comics: Sept, 1994 ($2.95, one-shot)

1-Kaluta co-scripts. 4.00
NOTE: *Stevens c-1.*

SHADOW CABINET (See Heroes)
DC Comics (Milestone): No. 0, Jan, 1994 - No. 17, Oct, 1995 ($1.75/$2.50)

0-(1/94, $2.50, 52 pgs.)-Silver ink-c; Simonson-c 4.00
1-17: 1-(6/94) Byrne-c 3.00

SHADOW COMICS (Pulp, radio)
Street & Smith Publications: Mar, 1940 - V9#5, Aug-Sept, 1949
NOTE: *The Shadow first appeared on radio in 1929 and was featured in pulps beginning in April, 1931, written by Walter Gibson. The early covers of this series were reprinted from the pulp covers.*

	GD 2.0	VG 4.0	FN 6.0	VF 8.0	VF/NM 9.0	NM- 9.2
V1#1-Shadow, Doc Savage, Bill Barnes, Nick Carter (radio), Frank Merriwell, Iron Munro, the Astonishing Man begin	541	1082	1623	3950	6975	10,000
2-The Avenger begins, ends #6; Capt. Fury only app.	226	452	678	1446	2473	3500
3(nn-5/40)-Norgil the Magician app.; cover is exact swipe of Shadow pulp from 1/33	161	322	483	1030	1765	2500
4-The Three Musketeers begins, ends #8; classic painted decapitation-c	155	310	465	992	1696	2400
5-Doc Savage ends	119	238	357	762	1306	1850
6,8,9: 9-Norgil the Magician app.	97	194	291	621	1061	1500
7-Origin/1st app. The Hooded Wasp & Wasplet (11/40); series ends V3#8; Hooded Wasp/Wasplet app. on-c thru #9	102	204	306	648	1112	1575
10-Origin The Iron Ghost, ends #11; The Dead End Kids begins, ends #14	95	190	285	603	1039	1475
11-Origin Hooded Wasp & Wasplet retold	95	190	285	603	1039	1475
12-Dead End Kids app.	89	178	267	565	970	1375
V2#1(11/41, Vol.II#2 in indicia) Dead End Kids -s	87	174	261	553	952	1350
2-(Rare, 1/42, Vol.II#3 in indicia) Giant ant-c	194	388	582	1242	2121	3000
3-Origin & 1st app. Supersnipe (3/42); series begins; Little Nemo story (Vol.II#4 in indicia)	139	278	417	883	1517	2150
4,5: 4,8-Little Nemo story	81	162	243	518	884	1250
6-9: 6-Blackstone the Magician story	77	154	231	493	847	1200
10,12: 10-Supersnipe app.' Skull-c	74	148	222	470	810	1150
11-Classic Devil Kyoti World War 2 sunburst-c	95	190	285	603	1039	1475
V3#1,2,5,7-12: 10-Doc Savage begins, not in V5#5, V6#10-12, V8#4	71	142	213	454	777	1100
3-1st Monstrodamus-c/sty	100	200	300	635	1093	1550
4-2nd Monstrodamus; classic-c of giant salamander getting shot in the head	107	214	321	680	1165	1650
6-Classic underwater-c	110	220	330	704	1202	1700
V4#1,3-12	50	100	150	315	533	750
2-Classic severed head-c	142	284	426	909	1555	2200
V5#1-12: 1-(4/45). 12-(3/46)	47	94	141	296	498	700
V6#1-11: 9-Intro. Shadow, Jr. (12/46)	43	86	129	271	461	650
12-Powell-c/a; atom bomb panels	47	94	141	246	498	700
V7#1,2,5,7-9,12: 2,5-Shadow, Jr. app.; Powell-a	41	82	123	256	428	600
3,6,11-Powell-c/a	47	94	141	296	498	700
4-Powell-c/a; Atom bomb panels	48	96	144	302	514	725
10(1/48)-Flying Saucer-c/story (2nd of this theme; see The Spirit 9/28/47); Powell-c/a	68	136	204	435	743	1050
V8#1,2,4-12-Powell-a.	47	94	141	296	498	700
3-Powell Spider-c/a	48	96	144	302	514	725
V9#1,5-Powell-a	45	90	135	284	480	675
2-4-Powell-c/a	47	94	141	296	498	700

NOTE: *Binder c-V3#1. Powell art in most issues beginning V6#12. Painted c-1-6.*

SHADOWDRAGON
DC Comics: 1995 ($3.50, annual)

Annual 1-Year One story 4.00

SHADOW EMPIRES: FAITH CONQUERS
Dark Horse Comics: Aug, 1994 - No. 4, Nov, 1994 ($2.95, limited series)

1-4 3.00

SHADOW GLASS, THE
Dark Horse Comics: Mar, 2016 - Present ($3.99)

1-3-Aly Fell-s/a 4.00

SHADOW/GREEN HORNET: DARK NIGHTS (Pulp characters)
Dynamite Entertainment: 2013 - No. 5, 2013 ($3.99)

1-5-Lamont Cranston & Britt Reid team-up in 1939; Uslan-s; multiple covers on each 4.00

SHADOWHAWK (See Images of Shadowhawk, New Shadowhawk, Shadowhawk II, Shadowhawk III & Youngblood #2)
Image Comics (Shadowline Ink): Aug, 1992 - No. 4, Mar, 1993; No. 12, Aug, 1994 - No. 18, May, 1995 ($1.95/$2.50)

Shadowhawk V3 #5 © Jim Valentino

Shadowland #1 © MAR

Shadowman #40 © Voyager Comm.

GD VG FN VF VF/NM NM-
2.0 4.0 6.0 8.0 9.0 9.2

1-($2.50)-Embossed silver foil stamped-c; Valentino/Liefeld-c; Valentino-c/a/scripts in all; has coupon for Image #0; 1st Shadowline Ink title 5.00
1-With coupon missing 2.00
1-($1.95)-Newsstand version w/o foil stamp 3.00
2-13,0,1418: 2-Shadowhawk poster w/McFarlane-i; brief Spawn app.; wraparound-c w/silver ink highlights. 3-($2.50)-Glow-in-the-dark-c. 4-Savage Dragon-c/story; Valentino/Larsen-c. 5-11-(See Shadowhawk II and III). 12-Cont'd from Shadowhawk III; pull-out poster by Texeira.13-w/ShadowBone poster; WildC.A.T.s app. 0 (10/94)-Liefeld c/a/story; ShadowBart poster. 14-(10/94, $2.50)-The Others app. 16-Supreme app. 17-Spawn app.; story cont'd from Badrock & Co. #6. 18-Shadowhawk dies; Savage Dragon & Brigade app. 3.00
Special 1(12/94, $3.50, 52 pgs.)-Silver Age Shadowhawk flip book 4.00
Gallery (4/94, $1.95) 3.00
Out of the Shadows ($19.95)-r/Youngblood #2, Shadowhawk #1-4, Image Zero #0, Operation: Urban Storm (Never published) 20.00
.../Vampirella (2/95, $4.95)-Pt.2 of x-over (See Vampirella/Shadowhawk for Pt. 1) 5.00

NOTE: *Shadowhawk was originally a four issue limited series. The story continued in Shadowhawk II, Shadowhawk III & then became Shadowhawk again with issue #12.*

SHADOWHAWK II (Follows Shadowhawk #4)
Image Comics (Shadowline Ink): V2#1, May, 1993 - V2#3, Aug, 1993 ($3.50/$1.95/$2.95, limited series)

V2#1 ($3.50)-Cont'd from Shadowhawk #4; die-cut mirricard-c 4.00
2 ($1.95)-Foil embossed logo; reveals identity; gold-c variant exists 4.00
3 ($2.95)-Pop-up-c w/Pact ashcan insert 4.00

SHADOWHAWK III (Follows Shadowhawk II #3)
Image Comics (Shadowline Ink): V3#1, Nov, 1993 - V3#4, Mar, 1994 ($1.95, limited series);

V3#1-4: 1-Cont'd from Shadowhawk II; intro Valentine; gold foil & red foil stamped-c variations. 2-(52 pgs.)-Shadowhawk contracts HIV virus; U.S. Male by M. Anderson (p) in free 16 pg.insert. 4-Continues in Shadowhawk #12 4.00

SHADOWHAWK (Volume 2) (Also see New Man #4)
Image Comics: May, 2005 - No. 15, Sept, 2006 ($2.99/$3.50)

1-4-Eddie Collins as Shadowhawk; Rodriguez-a; Valentino-co-plotter 3.50
5-15-($3.50) 5-Cover swipe of Superman Vs. Spider-Man treasury edition 3.50
...One Shot #1 (7/06, $1.99) r/Return of Shadowhawk 3.00
Return of Shadowhawk (12/04, $2.99) Valentino-s/a/c; Eddie Collins origin retold 3.00

SHADOWHAWK (Volume 3)
Image Comics: May, 2010 - No. 5, Dec, 2010 ($3.50)

1-5-Rodríguez-a. 1-Back-up with Valentino-a/Niles-s 3.50

SHADOWHAWKS OF LEGEND
Image Comics (Shadowline Ink): Nov, 1995 ($4.95, one-shot)

nn-Stories of past Shadowhawks by Kurt Busiek, Beau Smith & Alan Moore 5.00

SHADOW, THE: HELL'S HEAT WAVE (Movie, pulp, radio)
Dark Horse Comics: Apr, 1995 - No. 3, June, 1995 ($2.95, limited series)

1-3: Kaluta story 4.00

SHADOW HUNTER (Jenna Jameson's...)
Virgin Comics: No. 0, Dec, 2007 - No. 3 ($2.99)

0-Preview issue; creator interviews; gallery of covers for upcoming issues; Greg Horn-c 3.00
1-3: 1-Two covers by Horn & Land; Jameson & Christina Z-s/Singh-a. 2-Three covers 3.00

SHADOWHUNT SPECIAL
Image Comics (Extreme Studios): Apr, 1996 ($2.50)

1-Retells origin of past Shadowhawks; Valentino script; Chapel app. 3.00

SHADOW, THE: IN THE COILS OF THE LEVIATHAN (Movie, pulp, radio)
Dark Horse Comics: Oct, 1993 - No. 4, Apr, 1994 ($2.95, limited series)

1-4-Kaluta-c & co-scripter 4.00
Trade paperback (10/94, $13.95)-r/1-4 14.00

SHADOWLAND (Also see Daredevil #508-512 & Black Panther: The Man Without Fear #513)
Marvel Comics: Sept, 2010 - No. 5, Jan, 2011 ($3.99, limited series)

1-5: 1-Diggle-s/Tan-a; Bullseye killed; Cassaday-c. 2-Ghost Rider app. 4.00
1-Variant-c by Tan 6.00
...: After the Fall 1 (2/11, $3.99) Finch-c; Black Panther app. 4.00
...: Bullseye 1 (10/10, $3.99) Chen-a; Bullseye's funeral 4.00
...: Elektra 1 (11/10, $3.99) Wells-s/Rios-a/Takeda-c 4.00
...: Ghost Rider 1 (11/10, $3.99) Williams-s/Crain-a/c 4.00
...: Spider-Man 1 (12/10, $3.99) Shang-Chi & Mr. Negative app.; Siqueira-a 4.00

SHADOWLAND: BLOOD IN THE STREETS (Leads into Heroes For Hire)
Marvel Comics: Oct, 2010 - No. 4, Jan, 2011 ($3.99, limited series)

1-4-Johnston-s/Alves-a; Misty Knight, Silver Sable, Paladin, Shroud app. 4.00

SHADOWLAND: DAUGHTERS OF THE SHADOW

GD VG FN VF VF/NM NM-
2.0 4.0 6.0 8.0 9.0 9.2

Marvel Comics: Oct, 2010 - No. 3, Dec, 2010 ($3.99, limited series)

1-3-Henderson-s/Rodriguez-a; Colleen Wing app. 3-Preview of Black Panther #513 4.00

SHADOWLAND: MOON KNIGHT
Marvel Comics: Oct, 2010 - No. 3, Dec, 2010 ($3.99, limited series)

1-3-Hurwitz-s/Dazo-a 4.00

SHADOWLAND: POWER MAN
Marvel Comics: Oct, 2010 - No. 4, Jan, 2011 ($3.99, limited series)

1-4-Van Lente-s/Asrar-a. 1-New Power Man debut; Iron Fist app. 4.00

SHADOWLINE SAGA: CRITICAL MASS, A
Marvel Comics (Epic): Jan, 1990 - No. 7, July, 1990 ($4.95, lim. series, 68 pgs)

1-6: Dr. Zero, Powerline, St. George 5.00
7 ($5.95, 84 pgs.)-Morrow-a, Williamson-c(i) 6.00

SHADOWMAN (See X-O Manowar #4)
Valiant/Acclaim Comics (Valiant): May, 1992 - No. 43, Dec, 1995 ($2.50)

1-Partial origin 3 6 9 14 20 25
2-5: 3-1st app. Sousa the Soul Eater 5.00
6,7,9-42: 15-Minor Turok app. 16-1st app. Dr. Mirage (8/93). 17,18-Archer & Armstrong x-over. 19-Aerosmith-c/story. 23-Dr. Mirage x-over. 24-(4/94). 25-Bound-in trading card. 29-Chaos Effect. 4.00
8-1st app. Master Darque 1 3 4 6 8 10
43-Shadowman jumps to his death 1 2 3 5 6 8
0-($2.50, 4/94)-Regular edition 6.00
0-($3.50)-Wraparound chromium-c edition 1 2 3 5 6 8
0-Gold 20.00
Yearbook 1 (12/94, $3.95) 5.00

SHADOWMAN (Volume 2)
Acclaim Comics (Valiant Heroes): Mar, 1997 - No. 20 ($2.50, mature)

1-1st app. Zero; Garth Ennis scripts begin, end #4 1 2 3 5 6 8
2-20: 2-Zero becomes new Shadowman. 4-Origin; Jack Boniface (original Shadowman) rises from the grave. 5-Jamie Delano scripts begin. 9-Copycat-c 3.00
1-Variant painted cover 1 2 3 5 6 8
#0 Gold 5.00

SHADOWMAN (Volume 3)
Acclaim Comics: July, 1999 - No. 5, Nov, 1999 ($3.95/$2.50)

1-($3.95)-Abnett & Lanning-s/Broome & Benjamin-a 1 2 3 5 6 8
2-5-($2.50): 3,4-Flip book with Unity 2000 3.00

SHADOWMAN
Valiant Entertainment: Nov, 2012 - No. 16, Mar, 2014 ($3.99)

1-Jordan-s/Zircher-a; two covers by Zircher (regular & pullbox) 5.00
1-Variant-c by Dave Johnson 8.00
1-Variant-c by Bill Sienkiewicz 20.00
2-16: 2-6-Jordan-s/Zircher-a 4.00
2-4-Pullbox variants 6.00
5-16-Pullbox variants 4.00
11-Variant-c with detachable Halloween mask 4.00
13X-(10/13, bagged with Bleeding Cool Magazine #7) prelude to #13; Milligan-s 3.00
#0-(5/13, $3.99) Origin of Master Darque 4.00

SHADOWMAN END TIMES
Valiant Entertainment: Apr, 2014 - No. 3, Jun, 2014 ($3.99, limited series)

1-3-Milligan-s/De Landro-a 4.00

SHADOWMASTERS
Marvel Comics: Oct, 1989 - No.4, Jan, 1990 ($3.95, squarebound, 52 pgs.)

1-4: Heath-a(i). 1-Jim Lee-c; story cont'd from Punisher 4.00

SHADOW, THE: MIDNIGHT IN MOSCOW (Pulp character)
Dynamite Entertainment: 2014 - No. 6, 2014 ($3.99, limited series)

1-6:-Howard Chaykin-s/a/c 4.00

SHADOW NOW, THE (Pulp character)
Dynamite Entertainment: 2013 - No. 6, 2014 ($3.99, limited series)

1-6: 1-David Liss-s/ColtonWorley-a; The Shadow in present day New York 4.00

SHADOW OF THE BATMAN
DC Comics: Dec, 1985 - No. 5, Apr, 1986 ($1.75, limited series)

1-Detective-r (all have wraparound-c) 1 2 3 5 6 8
2,3,5: 3-Penguin-c & cameo. 5-Clayface app. 6.00
4-Joker-c/story 1 2 3 4 5 7

NOTE: ***Austin** a(new)-2i, 3i; r-2-4i. **Rogers** a(new)-1, 2p, 3p, 4, 5; r-1-5p; c-1-5. **Simonson** a-1r.*

SHADOW ON THE TRAIL (See Zane Grey & Four Color #604)

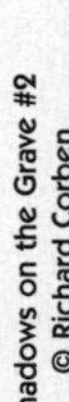

Shadows on the Grave #2 © Richard Corben

Shaft #6 © Ernest Tidyman

Shanna, the She-Devil #2 © MAR

GD VG FN VF VF/NM NM-
2.0 4.0 6.0 8.0 9.0 9.2

SHADOWPACT (See Day of Vengeance)
DC Comics: Jul, 2006 - No. 25, Jul, 2008 ($2.99)
1-25: 1-Bill Willingham-s; Detective Chimp, Ragman, Blue Devil, Nightshade, Enchantress and Nightmaster app. 1-Superman app. 13-Zauriel app.; S. Hampton-a 3.00
...: Cursed TPB (2007, $14.99) r/#4,9-13 15.00
...: Darkness and Light TPB (2008, $14.99) r/#14-19 15.00
...: The Burning Age TPB (2008, $17.99) r/#20-25 18.00
...: The Pentacle Plot TPB (2007, $14.99) r/#1-3,5-8 15.00

SHADOW PLAY (Tales of the Supernatural)
Whitman Publications: June, 1982
1-Painted-c 1 2 3 5 6 8

SHADOWPLAY
IDW Publ.: Sept, 2005 - No. 4, Dec, 2005 ($3.99)
1-4-Benson-s/Templesmith-a; Christina Z-s/Wood-a; 2 covers by Templesmith & Wood 4.00
TPB (3/06, $17.99) r/series; flip book format 18.00

SHADOW REAVERS
Black Bull Ent.: Oct, 2001 - No. 5, Mar, 2002 ($2.99)
1-5-Nelson-a; two covers for each issue 3.00
Limited Preview Edition (5/01, no cover price) 3.00

SHADOW RIDERS
Marvel Comics UK, Ltd.: June, 1993 - No. 4, Sept, 1993 ($1.75, limited series)
1-($2.50)-Embossed-c; Cable-c/story 4.00
2-4-Cable app. 2-Ghost Rider app. 3.00

SHADOWS
Image Comics: Feb, 2003 - No. 4, Nov, 2003 ($2.95)
1-4-Jade Dodge-s/Matt Camp-a/c 3.00

SHADOWS & LIGHT
Marvel Comics: Feb, 1998 - No. 3, July, 1998 ($2.99, B&W, quarterly)
1-3: 1-B&W anthology of Marvel characters; Black Widow art by Gene Ha, Hulk by Wrightson, Iron Man by Ditko & Daredevil by Stelfreeze; Stelfreeze painted-c. 2-Weeks, Sharp, Starlin, Thompson-a. 3-Buscema, Grindberg, Giffen, Layton-a 3.00

SHADOW'S FALL
DC Comics (Vertigo): Nov, 1994 - No. 6, Apr, 1995 ($2.95, limited series)
1-6: Van Fleet-c/a in all. 3.00

SHADOWS FROM BEYOND (Formerly Unusual Tales)
Charlton Comics: V2#50, October, 1966
V2#50-Ditko-c 4 8 12 28 47 65

SHADOWS ON THE GRAVE
Dark Horse Comics: Dec, 2016 - No. 8 ($3.99, B&W, limited series)
1,2-Horror story anthology; Richard Corben-s/a/c 4.00

SHADOW STATE
Broadway Comics: Dec, 1995 - No. 5, Apr, 1996 ($2.50)
1-5: 1,2-Fatale back-up story; Cockrum-a(p) 3.00
Preview Edition 1,2 (10-11/95, $2.50, B&W) 3.00

SHADOW STRIKES!, THE (Pulp, radio)
DC Comics: Sept, 1989 - No.31, May, 1992 ($1.75)
1-4,7-31: 31-Mignola-c 4.00
5,6-Doc Savage x-over 5.00
Annual 1 (1989, $3.50, 68 pgs.)-Spiegle a; Kaluta-c 5.00

SHADOW, THE : THE DEATH OF MARGO LANE (Pulp characters)
Dynamite Entertainment: 2016 - Present ($3.99)
1-4-Matt Wagner-s/a/c. 4-The Red Empress app. 4.00

SHADOW WALK
Legendary Comics: Nov, 2013 ($24.99, graphic novel)
HC - Mark Waid-s/Shane Davis-a 25.00

SHADOW WAR OF HAWKMAN
DC Comics: May, 1985 - No. 4, Aug, 1985 (limited series)
1-4 4.00

SHADOW, THE: YEAR ONE
Dynamite Entertainment: 2012 - No. 10, 2014 ($3.99)
1-9: 1-Matt Wagner-s/Wilfredo Torres-a; multiple covers 4.00
10-($4.99) 5.00

SHAFT (Based on the movie character)
Dynamite Entertainment: 2014 - No. 6, 2015 ($3.99, limited series)

GD VG FN VF VF/NM NM-
2.0 4.0 6.0 8.0 9.0 9.2

1-6-David F. Walker-s/Bilquis Evely-a; multiple covers on each 4.00

SHAFT: IMITATION OF LIFE (Based on the movie character)
Dynamite Entertainment: 2016 - No. 4, 2016 ($3.99, limited series)
1-4-David F. Walker-s/Dietrich Smith-a/Matthew Clark-c 4.00

SHAGGY DOG & THE ABSENT-MINDED PROFESSOR (See Movie Comics & Walt Disney Showcase #46)(Disney-Movie)
Dell Publ. Co.: No. 985, Apr-Jun, 1959; No. 1199, Apr, 1961; Aug, 1967
Four Color 985 7 14 21 44 82 120
Four Color 1199 (4/61) Movie, photo-c; variant "Double Feature" edition; has a "Fabulous Formula" strip on back-c 7 14 21 44 82 120
Four Color 1199-(8/67) Movie, photo-c 7 14 21 44 82 120

SHAHRAZAD
Big Dog Ink: No. 0, Apr, 2013 - No. 5, Apr, 2014 ($1.99/$3.99)
0-($1.99) Hutchison-s/Krome-a; multiple covers 3.00
1-3 ($3.99) Hutchison & Castor-s/Krome-a; multiple covers on each 4.00

SHAHRAZAD
Aspen MLT: Apr, 2015 - No. 5, Aug, 2015 ($2.99/$3.99)
1,2-($2.99) Remastered reprints of 2013 series; multiple covers on each 3.00
3-5-($3.99) Hutchison & Castor-s/Krome-a; multiple covers on each 4.00

SHALOMAN (Jewish-themed stories and history)
Al Wiesner/ Mark 1 Comics: 1988 - 2012 (B&W)
V1#1-Al Wiesner-s/a in all 5.00
2-9 3.00
V2 #1(The New Adventures)-4,6-10, V3 (The Legend of...) #1-12 3.00
V2 #5 (Color)-Shows Vol 2, No. 4 in indicia 3.00
V4 (The Saga of ...) #1(2004), 2-8: 8-Chanukah & The Holocaust 3.00
...: The Sequel (2010) "11-9", ...: The Sequel 2 (2011) Genesis #2 Jews in Space 3.00
...: The Sequel 3 (2012) Purim and the X-Suit 3.00
The Saga of Shaloman (20th Anniversary Edition) TPB (10/08, $15.99) r/V4 #1-8 16.00

SHAMAN'S TEARS (Also see Maggie the Cat)
Image Comics (Creative Fire Studio): 5/93 - No. 2, 8/93; No. 3, 11/94 - No. 0, 1/96 ($2.50/$1.95)
0-2: 0-(DEC-c, 1/96)-Last Issue. 1-(5/93)-Embossed red foil-c; Grell-c/a & scripts in all. 2-Cover unfolds into poster (8/93-c, 7/93 inside) 4.00
3-12: 3-Begin $1.95-c. 5-Re-intro Jon Sable. 12-Re-intro Maggie the Cat (1 pg.) 3.00

SHAME ITSELF
Marvel Comics: Jan, 2012 ($3.99, one-shot)
1-Spoof of "Fear Itself" x-over event; short stories by various incl. Cenac & Kupperman 4.00

SHANG-CHI: MASTER OF KUNG-FU ("Master of Kung Fu" on cover for #1&2)
Marvel Comics: Nov, 2002 - No. 6, Apr, 2003 ($2.99, limited series)
1-6-Moench-s/Gulacy-c/a 3.00
...One-Shot 1 (11/09, $3.99, B&W) Deadpool app. 4.00
... Vol. 1: The Hellfire Apocalypse TPB (2003, $14.99) r/#1-6 15.00

SHANNA, THE SHE-DEVIL (See Savage Tales #8)
Marvel Comics Group: Dec, 1972 - No. 5, Aug, 1973 (All are 20¢ issues)
1-1st app. Shanna; Steranko-c; Tuska-a(p) 5 10 15 34 60 85
2-Steranko-c; heroin drug story 3 6 9 21 33 45
3-5 3 6 9 14 20 25

SHANNA, THE SHE-DEVIL
Marvel Comics: Apr, 2005 - No. 7, Oct, 2005 ($3.50, limited series)
1-7-Reintro of Shanna; Frank Cho-s/a/c in all 3.50
HC (2005, $24.99, dust jacket) r/#1-7 25.00
SC (2006, $16.99) r/#1-7 17.00

SHANNA, THE SHE-DEVIL: SURVIVAL OF THE FITTEST
Marvel Comics: Oct, 2007 - No. 4, Jan, 2008 ($2.99, limited series)
1-4-Khari Evans-a/c; Gray & Palmiotti-s 3.00
SC (2008, $10.99) r/#1-4 11.00

SHAOLIN COWBOY
Burlyman Entertainment: Dec, 2004 - No. 7, May, 2007 ($3.50)
1-7-Geof Darrow-s/a. 3-Moebius-c 3.50

SHAOLIN COWBOY
Dark Horse Comics: Oct, 2013 - No. 4, Feb, 2014 ($3.99)
1-4-Geof Darrow-s/a. 1-Variant-c by Simonson 4.00

SHAPER
Dark Horse Comics: Mar, 2015 - No. 5, Jul, 2015 ($3.99)

Shazam! #11 © DC

Sheena, Queen of the Jungle #8 © FH

She-Hulk (2005 series) #26 © MAR

GD VG FN VF VF/NM NM-
2.0 4.0 6.0 8.0 9.0 9.2

1-5: 1-Heisserer-s/Massafera-a. 2-5-Continuado-a 4.00

SHARK FIGHTERS, THE (Movie)
Dell Publishing Co.: Jan, 1957

Four Color 762-Buscema-a; photo-c 7 14 21 49 92 125

SHARK-MAN
Thrill House/Image Comics: Jul, 2006; Jul, 2007; Jan, 2008 - No. 3, Jun, 2008 ($3.99/$3.50)

1,2: 1-(Thrill House, 7/06, $3.99)-Steve Pugh-s/a. 2-(Image Comics, 7/07) 4.00
1-3: 1-(Image, 1/08, $3.50) reprints Thrill House #1 3.50

SHARKY
Image Comics: Feb, 1998 - No. 4, 1998 ($2.50, bi-monthly)

1-4: 1-Mask app.; Elliot-s/a. Horley painted-c. 3-Three covers by Horley, Bisley, & Horley/Elliot. 4-Two covers (swipe of Avengers #4 and wraparound) 3.00
1-($2.95) "$1,000,000" variant 3.00
2-($2.50) Savage Dragon variant-c 3.00

SHARP COMICS (Slightly large size)
H. C. Blackerby: Winter, 1945-46 - V1#2, Spring, 1946 (52 pgs.)

V1#1-Origin Dick Royce Planetarian 50 100 150 315 533 750
2-Origin The Pioneer; Michael Morgan, Dick Royce, Sir Gallagher, Planetarian, Steve Hagen, Weeny and Pop app. 50 100 150 315 533 750

SHARPY FOX (See Comic Capers & Funny Frolics)
I. W. Enterprises/Super Comics: 1958; 1963

1,2-I.W. Reprint (1958): 2-r/Kiddie Kapers #1 2 4 6 8 11 14
14-Super Reprint (1963) 2 4 6 8 10 12

SHATTER (See Jon Sable #25-30)
First Comics: June, 1985; Dec, 1985 - No. 14, Apr, 1988. ($1.75, Baxter paper/deluxe paper)

1 (6/85)-1st computer generated-a in a comic book (1st printing) 4.00
1-(2nd print.); 1(12/85)-14: computer generated-a & lettering in all 3.00
Special 1 (1988) 3.00

SHATTERED IMAGE
Image Comics (WildStorm Productions): Aug, 1996 - No. 4, Dec, 1996 ($2.50, lim. series)

1-4: 1st Image company-wide x-over; Kurt Busiek scripts in all. 1-Tony Daniel-c/a(p). 2-Alex Ross-c/swipe (Kingdom Come) by Ryan Benjamin & Travis Charest 3.00

SHAUN OF THE DEAD (Movie)
IDW Publishing: June, 2005 - No. 4, Sept, 2005 ($3.99, limited series)

1-4-Adaptation of 2004 movie; Zach Howard-a 4.00
TPB (12/05, $17.99) r/series; sketch pages and cover gallery 18.00

SHAZAM (See Billy Batson and the Magic of Shazam!, Giant Comics to Color, Limited Collectors' Edition, Power Of Shazam! and Trials of Shazam!)

SHAZAM! (TV)(See World's Finest #253 for story from unpublished #36)
National Periodical Publ./DC Comics: Feb, 1973 - No. 35, May-June, 1978

1-1st revival of original Captain Marvel since G.A. (origin retold), by C.C. Beck; Mary Marvel & Captain Marvel Jr. app.; Superman-c 7 14 21 46 86 125
2-5: 2-Infinity photo-c.; re-intro Mr. Mind & Tawny. 3-Capt. Marvel-r. (10/46). 4-Origin retold; Capt. Marvel-r. (1949). 5-Capt. Marvel Jr. origin retold; Capt. Marvel-r. (1948, 7 pgs.) 3 6 9 18 28 38
6,7,9-11: 6-photo-c; Capt. Marvel-r (1950, 6 pgs.). 9-Mr. Mind app. 10-Last C.C. Beck issue. 11-Schaffenberger-a begins. 3 6 9 15 22 28
8-(100 pgs.) 8-r/1st Black Adam app. from Marvel Family #1; r/Capt. Marvel Jr. by Raboy; origin/C.M. #80; origin Mary Marvel/C.M.A. #18; origin Mr. Tawny/C.M.A. #79 6 12 18 38 69 100
12-17-(All 100 pgs.). 15-vs. Lex Luthor & Mr. Mind 5 10 15 30 50 70
18-24,26,27,29,30: 21-24-All reprints. 26-Sivana app. (10/76). 27-Kid Eternity teams up w/Capt. Marvel. 30-1st DC app. 3 Lt. Marvels 3 6 9 14 20 25
25-1st app. Isis 6 12 18 42 79 115
28-(3-4/77) 1st Bronze Age app. of Black Adam 15 30 45 103 227 350
31-35: 31-1st DC app. Minuteman. 34-Origin Capt. Nazi & Capt. Marvel Jr. retold 3 6 9 16 23 30
...: The Greatest Stories Ever Told TPB (2008, $24.99) reprints; Alex Ross-c 25.00

NOTE: *Reprints in #1-8, 10, 12-17, 21-24.* ***Beck*** *a-1-10, 12-17r, 21-24r; c-1, 3-9.* ***Nasser*** *c-35p.* ***Newton*** *a-35p.* ***Raboy*** *a-5r, 8r, 17r.* ***Schaffenberger*** *a-11, 14-20, 25, 26, 27p, 28, 29-31p, 33i, 35i; c-20, 22, 23, 25, 26i, 27i, 28-33.*

SHAZAM!
DC Comics: March, 2011 ($2.99, one-shot)

1-Richards-a/Chiang-c; Blaze app.; story continues in Titans #32 3.00

SHAZAM! AND THE SHAZAM FAMILY! ANNUAL
DC Comics: 2002 ($5.95, squarebound, one-shot)

1-Reprints Golden Age stories including 1st Mary Marvel and 1st Black Adam 1 3 4 6 8 10

GD VG FN VF VF/NM NM-
2.0 4.0 6.0 8.0 9.0 9.2

SHAZAM!: POWER OF HOPE
DC Comics: Nov, 2000 ($9.95, treasury size, one-shot)

nn-Painted art by Alex Ross; story by Alex Ross and Paul Dini 10.00

SHAZAM!: THE MONSTER SOCIETY OF EVIL
DC Comics: 2007 - No. 4, 2007 ($5.99, square-bound, limited series)

1-4: Jeff Smith-s/a/c in all. 1-Retelling of origin. 2-Mary Marvel & Dr. Sivana app. 6.00
HC (2007, $29.99, over-sized with dust jacket that unfolds to a poster) r/#1-4; Alex Ross intro.; Smith afterword; sketch pages, script pages and production notes 30.00
SC (2009, $19.99) r/#1-4; Alex Ross intro. 20.00

SHAZAM: THE NEW BEGINNING
DC Comics: Apr, 1987 - No. 4, July, 1987 (Legends spin-off) (Limited series)

1-4: 1-New origin & 1st modern app. Captain Marvel; Marvel Family cameo. 2-4-Sivana & Black Adam app. 4.00

SHEA THEATRE COMICS
Shea Theatre: No date (1940's) (32 pgs.)

nn-Contains Rocket Comics; MLJ cover in one color 15 30 45 85 130 175

SHE-BAT (See Murcielaga, She-Bat & Valeria the She-Bat)

SHE-DRAGON (See Savage Dragon #117)
Image Comics: July, 2006 ($5.99, one-shot)

nn- She-Dragon in Dimension-X; origin retold; Franchesco-a/Larsen-s; sketch pages 6.00

SHEENA (Movie)
Marvel Comics: Dec, 1984 - No. 2, Feb, 1985 (limited series)

1,2-r/Marvel Comics Super Special #34; Tanya Roberts movie 4.00

SHEENA, QUEEN OF THE JUNGLE (See Jerry Iger's Classic..., Jumbo Comics, & 3-D Sheena)
Fiction House Magazines: Spr, 1942; No. 2, Wint, 1942-43; No. 3, Spr, 1943; No. 4, Fall, 1948; No. 5, Sum, 1949; No. 6, Spr, 1950; No. 7-10, 1950(nd); No. 11, Spr, 1951 - No. 18, Wint, 1952-53 (#1-3: 68 pgs.; #4-7: 52 pgs.)

1-Sheena begins 300 600 900 1950 3375 4800
2 (Winter, 1942-43) 161 322 483 1030 1765 2500
3 (Spring, 1943) Classic Giant Ape-c 161 322 483 1030 1765 2500
4,5 (Fall, 1948, Sum, 1949): 4-New logo; cover swipe from Jumbo #20 60 120 180 381 653 925
6,7 (Spring, 1950, 1950) 48 96 144 302 514 725
8-10(1950 - Win/50, 36 pgs.) 42 84 126 267 451 635
11-17: 15-Cover swipe from Jumbo #43 40 80 120 244 402 560
18-Used in **POP**, pg. 98 41 82 123 260 435 610
I.W. Reprint #9-r/#18; c-r/White Princess #3 4 8 12 28 44 60

NOTE: ***Baker*** *c-5-10?* ***Whitman*** *c-11-18(most).* ***Zolnerowich*** *c-1-3.*

SHEENA, QUEEN OF THE JUNGLE
Devil's Due Publishing: Mar, 2007; Jun, 2007 - No. 5, Jan, 2008 (99¢/$3.50)

1-5: 1-Rodi-s/Merhoff-a; 5 covers 3.50
... 99¢ Special (3/07) Revival of the character; Rodi-s/Cummings-a; sketch pages; history 3.00
...: Dark Rising (10/08 - No. 3, 12/08) 1-3 3.50
... Trail of the Mapinguari (4/08, $5.50) Two covers 5.50

SHEENA 3-D SPECIAL (Also see Blackthorne 3-D Series #1)
Eclipse Comics: Jan, 1985 ($2.00)

1-Dave Stevens-c 2 4 6 9 12 15

SHE-HULK (Also see The Savage She-Hulk & The Sensational She-Hulk)
Marvel Comics: May, 2004 - No. 12, Apr, 2005 ($2.99)

1-Bobillo-a/Slott-s/Granov-c; Avengers app. 5.00
2-4-Bobillo-a/Slott-s/Granov-c. 4-Spider-Man-c/app. 3.00
5-12: Mayhew-c. 9-12-Pelletier-a. 10-Origin of Titania 3.00
Vol. 1: Single Green Female TPB (2004, $14.99) r/#1-6 15.00
Vol. 2: Superhuman Law TPB (2005, $14.99) r/#7-12 15.00

SHE-HULK (2nd series)
Marvel Comics: Dec, 2005 - No. 38, Apr, 2009 ($2.99)

1-Bobillo-a/Slott-s/Horn-c; New Avengers app. 5.00
2,4-7,9-24: 2-Hawkeye-c/app. 9-Jen marries John Jameson. 12-Thanos app. 16-Wolverine app. 3.00
3-($3.99) 100th She-Hulk issue; new story w/art by various incl. Bobillo, Conner, Mayhew & Powell; r/Savage She-Hulk #1 and r/Sensational She-Hulk #1 4.00
8-Civil War 15.00
8-2nd printing with variant Bobillo-c 3.00
25-($3.99) Intro. the Behemoth; Juggernaut cameo; Handbook bio pages of She-Hulk 4.00
26-37: 27-Iron Man app. 30-Hercules app. 31-X-Factor app. 32,33-Secret Invasion 3.00
38-($3.99) Thundra, Valkyrie and Invisible Woman app. 4.00

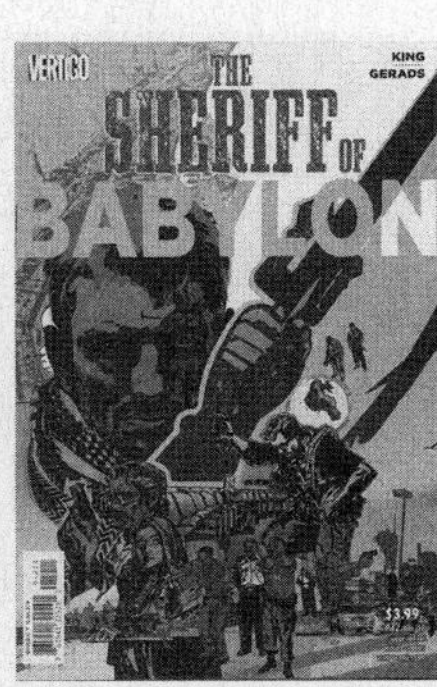

Sheriff of Babylon #12 © King & Gerads

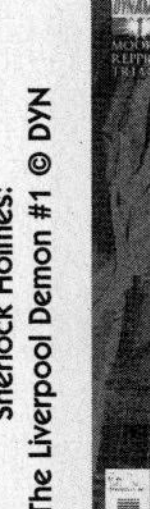
Sherlock Holmes: The Liverpool Demon #1 © DYN

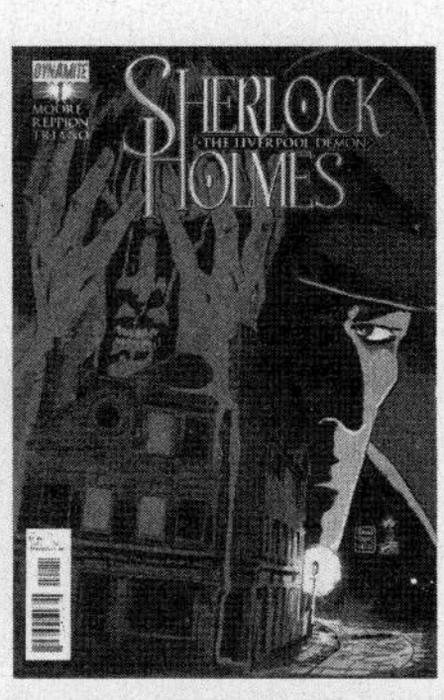

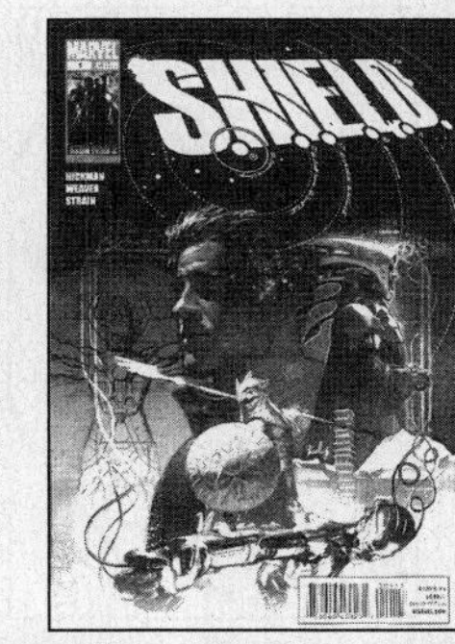

S.H.I.E.L.D. (2010 series) #1 © MAR

GD 2.0 | VG 4.0 | FN 6.0 | VF 8.0 | VF/NM 9.0 | NM- 9.2

...: Cosmic Collision 1 (2/09, $3.99) Lady Liberators app.; David-s/Asrar-a/Sejic-c 4.00
... Sensational 1 (5/10, $4.99) 30th Anniversary celebration; Stan Lee app.; Frank-c 5.00
Vol. 3: Time Trials (2006, $14.99) r/#1-5; Bobillo sketch page 15.00
Vol. 4: Laws of Attraction (2007, $19.99) r/#6-12; Paul Smith sketch page 20.00
Vol. 5: Planet Without a Hulk (2007, $19.99) r/#14-21; Slott's original series pitch 20.00
...: Jaded HC (2008, $19.99) r/#22-27; cover gallery 20.00

SHE-HULK (3rd series)
Marvel Comics: Apr, 2014 - No. 12, Apr, 2015 ($2.99)
1-12: 1-4-Soule-s/Pulido-a/Wada-c. 1-Tony Stark app. 2-Hellcat app. 3.00

SHE-HULKS
Marvel Comics: Jan, 2011 - No. 4, Apr, 2011 ($3.99/$2.99, limited series)
1-($3.99) She-Hulk & Lyra team-up; Stegman-a/McGuinness-c; character profile pages 4.00
2-4-($2.99) McGuinness-c 3.00

SHELTERED
Image Comics: Jul, 2013 - No. 15, Mar, 2015 ($2.99)
1-15-Brisson-s/Christmas-a 3.00

SHERIFF BOB DIXON'S CHUCK WAGON (TV) (See Wild Bill Hickok #22)
Avon Periodicals: Nov, 1950
1-Kinstler-c/a(3) 15 30 45 88 137 185

SHERIFF OF BABYLON, THE
DC Comics (Vertigo): Feb, 2016 - Present ($3.99)
1-12-Tom King-s/Mitch Gerads-a/John Paul Leon-c 4.00

SHERIFF OF TOMBSTONE
Charlton Comics: Nov, 1958 - No. 17, Sept, 1961
V1#1-Giordano-c; Severin-a 6 12 18 41 66 90
2 4 8 12 22 34 45
3-10 3 6 9 17 25 32
11-17 3 6 9 14 20 25

SHERLOCK: A STUDY IN PINK (Adaptation of episode from the BBC TV series)
Titan Comics: Jul, 2016 - No. 6, Dec, 2016 ($4.99/$3.99, B&W, reads back to front, right to left)
1-English version of original Japanese manga; art by Jay.; multiple covers 5.00
2-6-($3.99) 4.00

SHERLOCK HOLMES (See Classic Comics #33, Marvel Preview, New Adventures of..., & Spectacular Stories)

SHERLOCK HOLMES (All New Baffling Adventures of...)(Young Eagle #3 on?)
Charlton Comics: Oct, 1955 - No. 2, Mar, 1956
1-Dr. Neff, Ghost Breaker app. 40 80 120 246 411 575
2 36 72 108 211 343 475

SHERLOCK HOLMES (Also see The Joker)
National Periodical Publications: Sept-Oct, 1975
1-Cruz-a; Simonson-c 3 6 9 16 23 30

SHERLOCK HOLMES
Dynamite Entertainment: 2009 - No. 5, 2009 ($3.50, limited series)
1-5-Cassaday-c/Moore & Reppion-s/Aaron Campbell-a 3.50

SHERLOCK HOLMES: MORIARTY LIVES
Dynamite Entertainment: 2014 - No. 5, 2014 ($3.99, limited series)
1-5-Liss-s/Indro-a/Francavilla-c 4.00

SHERLOCK HOLMES: THE LIVERPOOL DEMON
Dynamite Entertainment: 2012 - No. 5, 2013 ($3.99, limited series)
1-5-Moore & Reppion-s/Triano-a/Francavilla-c 4.00

SHERLOCK HOLMES VS. HARRY HOUDINI
Dynamite Entertainment: 2014 - No. 5, 2015 ($3.99, limited series)
1-5-Del Col & McCreery-s/Furuzono-a; multiple covers on each 4.00

SHERLOCK HOLMES: YEAR ONE
Dynamite Entertainment: 2011 - No. 6, 2011 ($3.99, limited series)
1-6-Beatty-s; multiple covers on each 4.00

SHERLOCK: THE BLIND BANKER (Adaptation of episode from the BBC TV series)
Titan Comics: Feb, 2017 - No. 6, ($4.99/$3.99, B&W, reads back to front, right to left)
1,2-English version of original Japanese manga; art by Jay.; multiple covers 5.00

SHERRY THE SHOWGIRL (Showgirls #4)
Atlas Comics: July, 1956 - No. 3, Dec, 1956; No. 5, Apr, 1957 - No. 7, Aug, 1957
1-Dan DeCarlo-c/a in all 65 130 195 416 708 1000
2 26 52 78 154 252 350
3,5-7 22 44 66 132 216 300

SHE'S JOSIE (See Josie)

SHEVA'S WAR
DC Comics (Helix): Oct, 1998 - No. 5, Feb, 1999 ($2.95, mini-series)
1-5-Christopher Moeller-s/painted-a/c 3.00

SHI (one-shots and TPBs)
Crusade Comics
...: Akai (2001, $2.99)-Intro. Victoria Cross; Tucci-a/c; J.C. Vaughn-s 3.00
...: Akai Victoria Cross Ed. ($5.95, edition of 2000) variant Tucci-c 6.00
...: C.G.I. (2001, $4.99) preview of unpublished series 5.00
.../ Cyblade: The Battle for the Independents (9/95, $2.95) Tucci-c; Hellboy, Bone app. 3.00
.../ Cyblade: The Battle for the Independents (9/95, $2.95) Silvestri variant-c 3.00
.../ Daredevil: Honor Thy Mother (1/97, $2.95) Flip book 3.00
...: Judgment Night (200, $3.99) Wolverine app.; Battlebook card and pages; Tucci-a 4.00
...: Kaidan (10/96, $2.95) Two covers; Tucci-c; Jae Lee wraparound-c 3.00
...: Masquerade (3/98, $3.50) Painted art by Lago, Texeira, and others 3.50
...: Nightstalkers (9/97, $3.50) Painted art by Val Mayerik 3.50
...: Rekishi (1/97, $2.95) Character bios and story summaries of Shi: The Way of the Warrior told in Detective Joe Labianca's point of view; Christopher Golden script; Tucci-c; J.G. Jones-a; flip book w/Shi: East Wind Rain preview 3.00
...: The Art of War Tourbook (1998, $4.95) Blank cover for sketches; early Tucci-a inside 5.00
.../ Vampirella (10/97, $2.95) Ellis-s/Lau-a 3.00
... Vs. Tomoe (8/96, $3.95) Tucci-a/scripts; wraparound foil-c 4.00
... Vs. Tomoe (6/96, $5.00. B&W)-Preview Ed.; sold at San Diego Comic Con 5.00
The Definitive Shi Vol. 1 (2006-2007, $24.99, TPB) B&W r/Way of the Warrior, Tomoe, Rekishi, and Senryaku series; cover gallery with sketches; Tucci & Sparacio-c 25.00

SHI: BLACK, WHITE AND RED
Crusade Comics: Mar, 1998 - No. 2, May, 1998 ($2.95, B&W&Red, mini-series)
1,2-J.G. Jones-painted art 3.00
...- Year of the Dragon Collected Edition (2000, $5.95) r/#1&2 6.00

SHIDIMA
Image Comics: Jan, 2001 - No. 7, Nov, 2002 ($2.95, limited series)
1-7-Prequel to Warlands 3.00
#0-(10/01, $2.25) Short story and sketch pages 3.00

SHI: EAST WIND RAIN
Crusade Comics: Nov, 1997 - No. 2, Feb, 1998 ($3.50, limited series)
1,2-Shi at WW2 Pearl Harbor 3.50

S.H.I.E.L.D. (Nick Fury & His Agents of...) (Also see Nick Fury)
Marvel Comics Group: Feb, 1973 - No. 5, Oct, 1973 (All 20¢ issues)
1-All contain reprint stories from Strange Tales #146-155; new Steranko-c
3 6 9 19 30 40
2-New Steranko flag-c 3 6 9 14 20 25
3-5: 3-Kirby/Steranko-c(r). 4-Steranko-c(r) 2 4 6 9 12 15
NOTE: *Buscema* a-3p(r). *Kirby* layouts 1-5; c-3 (w/*Steranko*). *Steranko* a-3r, 4r(2).

S.H.I.E.L.D.
Marvel Comics: Jun, 2010 - No. 6, Apr, 2011; Aug, 2011 - No. 4, Feb, 2012 ($3.99/$2.99)
1-($3.99) Leonardo DaVinci app.; Weaver-a/Hickman-s/Parel-c; 4 printings 4.00
1-Variant-c by Weaver 6.00
1-Director's Cut (9/10, $4.99) r/#1 with character sketch-a and bios; design-a 5.00
2-6-($2.99) 2-Three printings. 3-Galactus app. 3.00
Infinity (6/11, $4.99) DaVinci, Nostradamus, Newton & Tesla app.; Parel-c 5.00
1 (2nd series) (8/11, $3.99) Weaver-a/Hickman-s/Parel-c; profile pgs of main characters 4.00
2-4-($2.99) 3.00
... Origins (1/14, $7.99) r/Battle Scars #6, Secret Avengers #1, Strange Tales #135 8.00

S.H.I.E.L.D. (Based on the TV series)
Marvel Comics: Feb, 2015 - No. 12, Jan, 2016 ($4.99/$3.99)
1-($4.99) Waid-s/Pacheco-a/Tedesco-c; Avengers app. 5.00
2-8-($3.99) 2-Ms. Marvel (Kamala Khan) app.; Ramos-a. 3-Spider-Man app.; Davis-a 4.00
9-($5.99) 50th Anniversary issue; Howling Commandos app.; r/Strange Tales #135 6.00
10-12: 10-Howard the Duck app. 11-Dominic Fortune app.; Chaykin-a 4.00

SHIELD, THE (Becomes Shield-Steel Sterling #3; #1 titled Lancelot Strong; also see Advs. of the Fly, Double Life of Private Strong, Fly Man, Mighty Comics, The Mighty Crusaders, The Original... & Pep Comics #1)
Archie Enterprises, Inc.: June, 1983 - No. 2, Aug, 1983
1,2: Steel Sterling app. 1-Weiss-c/a. 2-Kanigher-s/Buckler-c/Nebres-a 5.00
America's 1st Patriotic Comic Book Hero, The Shield (2002, $12.95, TPB) r/Pep Comics #1-5, Shield-Wizard Comics #1; foreward by Robert M. Overstreet 13.00

SHIELD, THE (Archie Ent. character) (Continued from The Red Circle)
DC Comics: Nov, 2009 - No. 10, Aug, 2010 ($3.99)

Shi: Heaven & Earth #2 © Billy Tucci

Shipwreck #1 © Warren Ellis

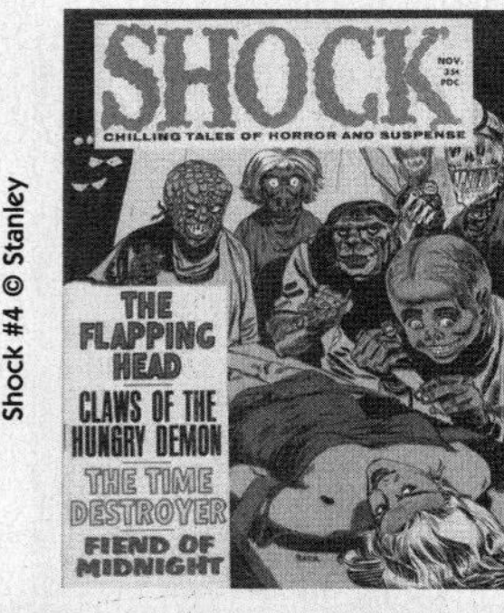

Shock #4 © Stanley

GD VG FN VF VF/NM NM-
2.0 4.0 6.0 8.0 9.0 9.2

1-10: 1-Magog app.; Inferno back-up feature thru #6; Green Arrow app. 2,3-Grodd app. 7-10-The Fox back-up feature; Oeming-a 4.00
...: Kicking Down the Door TPB ('10, $19.99) r/#1-6, Red Circle: The Web & RC: The Shield 20.00

SHIELD, THE
Archie Comic Publications: Dec, 2015 - No. 4, Jan, 2017 ($3.99)
1-4-Christopher & Wendig-s/Drew Johnson-a; a new Shield recruited; multiple covers 4.00

SHIELD, THE: SPOTLIGHT (TV)
IDW Publishing: Jan, 2004 - No. 5, May, 2004 ($3.99)
1-5-Jeff Marriote-s/Jean Diaz-a/Tommy Lee Edwards-c 4.00
TPB (7/04, $19.99) r/#1-5; Michael Chiklis photo-c 20.00

SHIELD-STEEL STERLING (Formerly The Shield)
Archie Enterprises, Inc.: No. 3, Dec, 1983 (Becomes Steel Sterling No. 4)
3-Nino-a; Steel Sterling by Kanigher & Barreto 5.00

SHIELD WIZARD COMICS (Also see Pep Comics & Top-Notch Comics)
MLJ Magazines: Summer, 1940 - No. 13, Spring, 1944
1-(V1#5 on inside)-Origin The Shield by Irving Novick & The Wizard by Ed Ashe, Jr; Flag-c
450 900 1350 3300 6650 10,000
2-(Winter/40)-Origin The Shield retold; Wizard's sidekick, Roy the Super Boy begins (see Top-Notch #8 for 1st app.) 290 580 870 1856 3178 4500
3,4 194 388 582 1242 2121 3000
5-Dusty, the Boy Detective begins; Nazi bondage-c 168 336 504 1075 1838 2600
6,7: 6-Roy the Super Boy app. 7-Shield dons new costume (Summer, 1942); S & K-c?
161 322 483 1030 1765 2500
8-Nazi bondage-c; Hitler photo on-c 213 426 639 1363 2332 3300
9-Japanese WWII bondage-c 155 310 465 992 1696 2400
10-Nazi swastica-c 161 322 483 1030 1765 2500
11,12 123 246 369 787 1344 1900
13-Japanese WWII bondage/torture-c (scarce) 181 362 543 1158 1979 2800
NOTE: *Bob Montana c-13. Novick c-1,3-6,8-11. Harry Sahle c-12.*

SHI: FAN EDITIONS
Crusade Comics: 1997
1-3-Two covers polybagged in FAN #19-21 3.00
1-3-Gold editions 4.00

SHI: HEAVEN AND EARTH
Crusade Comics: June, 1997 - No. 4, Apr, 1998 ($2.95)
1-4 3.00
4-($4.95) Pencil-c variant 5.00
Rising Sun Edition-signed by Tucci in FanClub Starter Pack 4.00
"Tora No Shi" variant-c 3.00

SHI: JU-NEN
Dark Horse Comics: July, 2004 - No. 4, May, 2005 ($2.99, mini-series)
1-4-Tucci-a/Tucci & Vaughn-s; origin retold 3.00
TPB (2/06, $12.95) r/#1-4; Tucci and Sparacio-c 13.00

SHINING KNIGHT (See Adventure Comics #66)

SHINKU
Image Comics: Jun, 2011 - No. 5, Oct, 2012 ($2.99)
1-5-Marz-s/Moder-a 3.00

SHINOBI (Based on Sega video game)
Dark Horse Comics: Aug, 2002 ($2.99, one-shot)
1-Medina-a/c 3.00

SHIP AHOY
Spotlight Publishers: Nov, 1944 (52 pgs.)
1-L. B. Cole-c 21 42 63 122 199 275

SHIP OF FOOLS
Image Comics: Aug, 1997 - No. 3 ($2.95, B&W)
0-3-Glass-s/Oeming-a 3.00

SHI: POISONED PARADISE
Avatar Press: July, 2002 - No. 2, Aug, 2002 ($3.50, limited series)
1,2-Vaughn and Tucci-s/Waller-a; 1-Four covers 3.50

SHIPWRECK
AfterShock Comics: Oct, 2016 - Present ($3.99)
1-3-Warren Ellis-s/Phil Hester-a 3.00

SHIPWRECKED! (Disney-Movie)
Disney Comics: 1990 ($5.95, graphic novel, 68 pgs.)
nn-adaptation; Spiegle-a 6.00

SHI: SEMPO
Avatar Press: Aug, 2003 - No. 2, ($3.50, B&W, limited series)
1,2-Vaughn and Tucci-s/Alves-a; 1-Four covers 3.50

SHI: SENRYAKU
Crusade Comics: Aug, 1995 - No. 3, Nov, 1995 ($2.95, limited series)
1-3: 1-Tucci-c; Quesada, Darrow, Sim, Lee, Smith-a. 2-Tucci-c; Silvestri, Balent, Perez, Mack-a. 3-Jusko-c; Hughes, Ramos, Bell, Moore-a 3.00
1-variant-c (no logo) 4.00
Hardcover ($24.95)-r/#1-3; Frazetta-c. 25.00
Trade Paperback ($13.95)-r/#1-3; Frazetta-c. 14.00

SHI: THE ILLUSTRATED WARRIOR
Crusade Comics: 2002 - No. 7, 2003 ($2.99, B&W)
1-7-Story text with Tucci full page art 3.00

SHI: THE SERIES
Crusade Comics: Aug, 1997 - No. 13 ($2.95, color #1-10, B&W #11)
1-10 3.00
11-13: 11-B&W. 12-Color; Lau-a 3.00
#0 Convention Edition 5.00

SHI: THE WAY OF THE WARRIOR
Crusade Comics: Mar, 1994 - No. 12, Apr, 1997 ($2.50/$2.95)
1/2 4.00
1 2 4 6 8 10 12
1-Commemorative ed., B&W, new-c; given out at 1994 San Diego Comic Con
2 4 6 10 14 18
1-Fan appreciation edition -r/#1 3.00
1-Fan appreciation edition (variant) 6.00
1- 10th Anniversary Edition (2004, $2.99) 3.00
2 5.00
2-Commemorative edition (3,000) 2 4 6 9 13 16
2-Fan appreciation edition -r/#2 3.00
3 4.00
4-7: 4-Silvestri poster. 7-Tomoe app. 3.00
5,6: 5-Silvestri variant-c. 6-Tomoe #1 variant-c 3.50
5-Gold edition 12.00
6,8-12: 6-Fan appreciation edition 3.00
8-Combo Gold edition 6.00
8-Signed Edition-(5000) 4.00
Trade paperback (1995, $12.95)-r/#1-4 15.00
Trade paperback (1995, $14.95)-r/#1-4 revised; Julie Bell-c 15.00

SHI: YEAR OF THE DRAGON
Crusade Comics: 2000 - No. 3, 2000 ($2.99, limited series)
1-3: 1-Two covers; Tucci-a/c; flashback to teen-aged Ana 3.00

SHMOO (See Al Capp's... & Washable Jones &...)

SHOCK (Magazine)
Stanley Publ.: May, 1969 - V3#4, Sept, 1971 (B&W reprints from horror comics, including some pre-code) (No V2#1,3)
V1#1-Cover-r/Weird Tales of the Future #7 by Bernard Baily; r/Weird Chills #1
7 14 21 48 89 130
2-Wolverton-r/Weird Mysteries 5; r-Weird Mysteries #7 used in **SOTI**; cover reprints cover to Weird Chills #1 5 10 15 35 63 90
3,5,6 4 8 12 28 47 65
4-Harrison/Williamson-r/Forbid. Worlds #6 5 10 15 30 50 70
V2#2(5/70), V1#8(7/70), V2#4(9/70)-6(1/71), V3#1-4: V2#4-Cover swipe from Weird Mysteries #6 4 8 12 27 44 60
NOTE: *Disbrow r-V2#4; Bondage c-V1#4, V2#6, V3#1.*

SHOCK DETECTIVE CASES (Formerly Crime Fighting Detective)
(Becomes Spook Detective Cases No. 22)
Star Publications: No. 20, Sept, 1952 - No. 21, Nov, 1952
20,21-L.B. Cole-c; based on true crime cases 29 58 87 170 278 385
NOTE: *Palais a-20. No. 21-Fox-r.*

SHOCK ILLUSTRATED (...Adult Crime Stories; Magazine format)
E. C. Comics: Sept-Oct, 1955 - No. 3, Spring, 1956 (Adult Entertainment on-c #1,2)(All 25¢)
1-All by Kamen; drugs, prostitution, wife swapping 22 44 66 132 216 300
2-Williamson-a redrawn from Crime SuspenStories #13 plus Ingels, Crandall, Evans & part Torres-i; painted-c 21 42 63 122 199 275
3-Only 100 known copies bound & given away at E.C. office; Crandall, Evans-a; painted-c; shows May, 1956 on-c 148 296 444 947 1624 2300

SHOCKING MYSTERY CASES (Formerly Thrilling Crime Cases)

Shock SuspenStories #6 © WMG

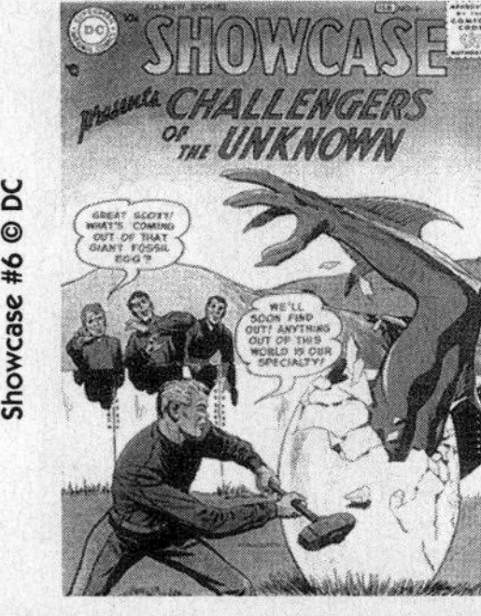

Showcase #6 © DC

Showcase #48 © DC

	GD 2.0	VG 4.0	FN 6.0	VF 8.0	VF/NM 9.0	NM- 9.2

Star Publications: No. 50, Sept, 1952 - No. 60, Oct, 1954 (All crime reprints?)
50-Disbrow "Frankenstein" story 54 108 162 343 574 825
51-Disbrow-a 37 74 111 222 361 500
52-60: 56-Drug use story 36 72 108 211 343 475
NOTE: *L. B. Cole covers on all; a-60(2 pgs.).* ***Hollingsworth*** *a-52.* ***Morisi*** *a-55.*

SHOCKING TALES DIGEST MAGAZINE
Harvey Publications: Oct, 1981 (95¢)
1-1957-58-r; Powell, Kirby, Nostrand-a 2 4 6 9 13 16

SHOCK ROCKETS
Image Comics (Gorilla): Apr, 2000 - No. 6, Oct, 2000 ($2.50)
1-6-Busiek-s/Immonen & Grawbadger-a. 6-Flip book w/Superstar preview 3.00
...: We Have Ignition TPB (Dark Horse, 8/04, $14.95, 6" x 9") r/#1-6 15.00

SHOCK SUSPENSTORIES (Also see EC Archives • Shock SuspenStories)
E. C. Comics: Feb-Mar, 1952 - No. 18, Dec-Jan, 1954-55
1-Classic Feldstein electrocution-c 120 240 360 960 1530 2100
2 53 106 159 424 675 925
3,4: 3-Classic decapitation splash. 4-Used in **SOTI**, pg. 387,388
44 88 132 352 564 775
5-Hanging-c 54 108 162 432 691 950
6-Classic hooded vigilante bondage-c 114 228 342 912 1456 2000
7-Classic face melting-c 69 138 207 552 876 1200
8-Williamson-a 43 86 129 344 547 750
9-11: 9-Injury to eye panel. 10-Junkie story 36 72 108 288 457 625
12- "The Monkey" classic junkie cover/story; anti-drug propaganda issue
57 114 171 456 728 1000
13-Frazetta's only solo story for E.C., 7 pgs, draws himself as main male character
51 102 153 408 654 900
14-Used in Senate Investigation hearings 33 66 99 264 420 575
15-Used in 1954 Reader's Digest article, "For the Kiddies to Read"
30 60 90 240 383 525
16-18: 16- "Red Dupe" editorial; rape story 29 58 87 232 366 500
NOTE: ***Ray Bradbury*** *adaptations-1, 7, 9.* ***Craig*** *a-11; c-11.* ***Crandall*** *a-9-13, 15-18.* ***Davis*** *a-1-5.* ***Evans*** *a-7, 8, 14-18; c-16-18.* ***Feldstein*** *c-1, 7-9, 12.* ***Ingels*** *a-1, 2, 6.* ***Kamen*** *a-in all; c-10, 13, 15.* ***Krigstein*** *a-14, 18.* ***Orlando*** *a-1, 3-7, 9, 10, 12, 16, 17.* ***Wood*** *a-2-15; c-2-6, 14.*

SHOCK SUSPENSTORIES (Also see EC Archives • Shock SuspenStories)
Russ Cochran/Gemstone Publishing: Sept, 1992 - No. 18, Dec, 1996 ($1.50/$2.00/$2.50, quarterly)
1-18: 1-3: Reprints with original-c. 17-r/HOF #17 4.00

SHOGUN WARRIORS
Marvel Comics Group: Feb, 1979 - No. 20, Sept, 1980 (Based on Mattel toys of the classic Japanese animation characters) (1-3: 35¢; 4-19: 40¢; 20: 50¢)
1-Raydeen, Combatra, & Dangard Ace begin; Trimpe-a
2 4 6 10 14 18
2-20: 2-Lord Maurkon & Elementals of Evil app.; Rok-Korr app. 6-Shogun vs. Shogun. 7,8-Cerberus. 9-Starchild. 11-Austin-c. 12-Simonson-c. 14-16-Doctor Demonicus. 17-Juggernaut. 19,20-FF x-over 2 3 4 6 8 10

SHOOK UP (Magazine) (Satire)
Dodsworth Publ. Co.: Nov, 1958
V1#1 4 8 12 28 44 60

SHORT RIBS
Dell Publishing Co.: No. 1333, Apr - June, 1962
Four Color 1333 5 10 15 35 63 90

SHORTSTOP SQUAD (Baseball)
Ultimate Sports Ent. Inc.: 1999 ($3.95, one-shot)
1-Ripken Jr., Larkin, Jeter, Rodriguez app.; Edwards-c/a 4.00

SHORT STORY COMICS (See Hello Pal,...)

SHORTY SHINER (The Five-Foot Fighter in the Ten Gallon Hat)
Dandy Magazine (Charles Biro): June, 1956 - No. 3, Oct, 1956
1 8 16 24 40 50 60
2,3 6 12 18 28 34 40

SHOTGUN SLADE (TV)
Dell Publishing Co.: No. 1111, July-Sept, 1960
Four Color 1111-Photo-c 6 12 18 37 66 95

SHOWCASE (See Cancelled Comic Cavalcade & New Talent...)
National Per. Publ./DC Comics: 3-4/56 - No. 93, 9/70; No. 94, 8-9/77 - No. 104, 9/78
1-Fire Fighters; w/Fireman Farrell 300 600 900 2550 5775 9000
2-Kings of the Wild; Kubert-a (animal stories) 121 242 363 968 2184 3400
3-The Frogmen by Russ Heath; Heath greytone-c (early DC example, 7-8/56)
107 214 321 856 1928 3000
4-Origin/1st app. The Flash (1st DC Silver Age hero, Sept-Oct, 1956); Kanigher-s; Infantino & Kubert-c/a; 1st app. Iris West and The Turtle; r/in Secret Origins #1 ('61 & '73); Flash shown reading G.A. Flash Comics #13; back-up story w/Broome-s/Infantino & Kubert-a
6000 12,000 24,000 54,000 92,000 130,000
5-Manhunters; Meskin-a 95 190 285 760 1705 2650
6-Origin/1st app. Challengers of the Unknown by Kirby, partly r/in Secret Origins #1 & Challengers #64,65 (1st S.A. hero team & 1st original concept S.A. series)(1-2/57)
333 666 1000 2664 6332 10,000
7-Challengers of the Unknown by Kirby (2nd app.) reprinted in Challengers of the Unknown #75 152 304 456 1254 2827 4400
8-The Flash (5-6/57, 2nd app.); origin & 1st app. Captain Cold
840 1680 2520 7600 14,300 21,000
9-Lois Lane (Pre-#1, 7-8/57) (1st Showcase character to win own series)
Superman app. on-c 660 1320 1980 5280 9640 14,000
10-Lois Lane; Jor-El cameo; Superman app. on-c 220 440 660 1815 4108 6400
11-Challengers of the Unknown by Kirby (3rd) 141 284 423 1142 2571 4000
12-Challengers of the Unknown by Kirby (4th) 141 284 423 1142 2571 4000
13-The Flash (3rd app.); origin Mr. Element 343 686 1029 2916 6608 10,300
14-The Flash (4th app.); origin Dr. Alchemy, former Mr. Element (rare in NM)
360 720 1080 3060 6930 10,800
15-Space Ranger (7-8/58, 1st app., also see My Greatest Adventure #22)
166 332 498 1370 3085 4800
16-Space Ranger (9-10/58, 2nd app.) 88 176 264 704 1577 2450
17-(11-12/58)-Adventures on Other Worlds; origin/1st app. Adam Strange by Gardner Fox & Mike Sekowsky 317 634 951 2695 6098 9500
18-Adventures on Other Worlds (2nd A. Strange) 93 186 279 744 1672 2600
19-Adam Strange; 1st Adam Strange logo 100 200 300 800 1800 2800
20-Rip Hunter; origin & 1st app. (5-6/59); Moreira-a 136 272 408 1088 2444 3800
21-Rip Hunter (7-8/59, 2nd app.); Sekowsky-c/a 54 108 162 432 966 1500
22-Origin & 1st app. Silver Age Green Lantern by Gil Kane and John Broome (9-10/59); reprinted in Secret Origins #2 900 1800 3600 11,000 24,500 38,000
23-Green Lantern (11-12/59, 2nd app.); nuclear explosion-c
197 394 591 1625 3663 5700
24-Green Lantern (1-2/60, 3rd app.) 162 324 486 1337 3019 4700
25,26-Rip Hunter by Kubert. 25-Grey tone-c 44 88 132 326 738 1150
27-Sea Devils (7-8/60, 1st app.); Heath-c/a; Grey tone-c
77 154 231 616 1383 2150
28-Sea Devils (9-10/60, 2nd app.); Heath-c/a; Grey tone-c
38 76 114 285 641 1000
29-Sea Devils; Heath-c/a; grey tone c-27-29 41 82 123 304 690 1075
30-Origin Silver Age Aquaman (1-2/61) (see Adventure #260 for 1st S.A. origin)
190 380 570 1568 3534 5500
31-Aquaman 50 100 150 400 900 1400
32,33-Aquaman 40 80 120 296 673 1050
34-Origin & 1st app. Silver Age Atom by Gil Kane & Murphy Anderson (9-10/61); reprinted in Secret Origins #2 155 310 465 1279 2890 4500
35-The Atom by Gil Kane (2nd); last 10¢ issue 50 100 150 400 900 1400
36-The Atom by Gil Kane (1-2/62, 3rd app.) 40 80 120 296 673 1050
37-Metal Men (3-4/62, 1st app.) 96 192 288 768 1734 2700
38-Metal Men (5-6/62, 2nd app.) 30 60 90 219 490 760
39-Metal Men (7-8/62, 3rd app.) 23 46 69 164 362 560
40-Metal Men (9-10/62, 4th app.) 21 42 63 147 324 500
41,42-Tommy Tomorrow (parts 1 & 2). 42-Origin 13 26 39 91 201 310
43-Dr. No (James Bond); Nodel-a; originally published as British Classics Illustrated #158A & as #6 in a European Detective series, all with diff. painted-c. This Showcase #43 version is actually censored, deleting all racial skin color and dialogue thought to be racially demeaning (1st DC S.A. movie adaptation)(based on Ian Fleming novel & movie)
51 102 153 408 929 1450
44-Tommy Tomorrow 10 20 30 66 138 210
45-Sgt. Rock (7-8/63); pre-dates B&B #52; origin retold; Heath-c
33 66 99 238 532 825
46,47-Tommy Tomorrow 9 18 27 61 123 185
48,49-Cave Carson (3rd tryout series; see B&B) 8 16 24 54 102 150
50,51-I Spy (Danger Trail-r by Infantino), King Farady story (#50 has new 4 pg. story)
7 14 21 48 89 130
52-Cave Carson 7 14 21 49 92 135
53,54-G.I. Joe (11-12/64, 1-2/65); Heath-a 10 20 30 66 138 210
55-Dr. Fate & Hourman (3-4/65); origin of each in text; 1st solo app. G.A. Green Lantern in Silver Age (pre-dates Gr. Lantern #40); 1st S.A. app. Solomon Grundy
27 54 81 194 435 675
56-Dr. Fate & Hourman 12 24 36 84 185 285
57-Enemy Ace by Kubert (7-8/65, 4th app. after Our Army at War #155)

Showcase #96 © DC

Showcase '93 #9 © DC

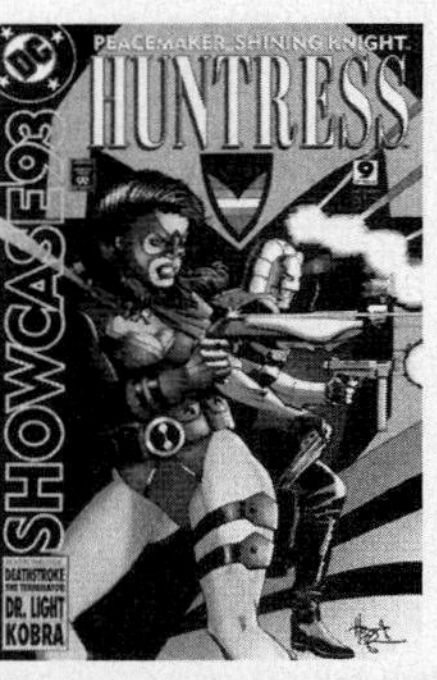

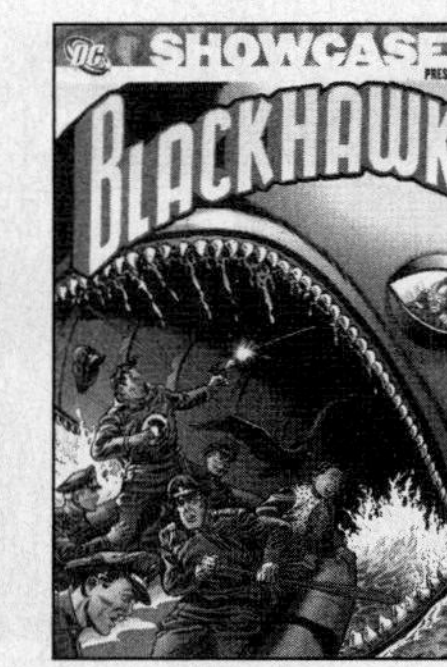

Showcase Presents Blackhawk Vol. 1 © DC

	GD 2.0	VG 4.0	FN 6.0	VF 8.0	VF/NM 9.0	NM- 9.2
	19	38	57	131	291	450
58-Enemy Ace by Kubert (5th app.)	16	32	48	107	236	365
59-Teen Titans (11-12/65, 3rd app.)	16	32	48	110	243	375
60-1st S. A. app. The Spectre; Anderson-a (1-2/66); origin in text	24	48	72	168	372	575
61-The Spectre by Anderson (2nd app.)	12	24	36	82	179	275
62-Origin & 1st app. Inferior Five (5-6/66)	8	16	24	56	108	160
63,65-Inferior Five. 63-Hulk parody. 65-X-Men parody (11-12/66)	6	12	18	37	66	95
64-The Spectre by Anderson (5th app.)	12	24	36	80	173	265
66,67-B'wana Beast	5	10	15	35	63	90
68-Maniaks (1st app., spoof of The Monkees)	5	10	15	35	63	90
69,71-Maniaks. 71-Woody Allen-c/app.	5	10	15	34	60	85
70-Binky (9-10/67)-Tryout issue; 1950's Leave It To Binky reprints with art changes	6	12	18	37	66	95
72-Top Gun (Johnny Thunder-r)-Toth-a	5	10	15	31	53	75
73-Origin/1st app. Creeper; Ditko-c/a (3-4/68)	10	20	30	69	147	225
74-Intro/1st app. Anthro; Post-c/a (5/68)	7	14	21	49	92	135
75-Origin/1st app. Hawk & the Dove; Ditko-c/a	10	20	30	64	132	200
76-1st app. Bat Lash (8/68)	7	14	21	49	92	135
77-1st app. Angel & The Ape (9/68)	6	12	18	41	76	110
78-1st app. Jonny Double (11/68)	5	10	15	30	50	70
79-1st app. Dolphin (12/68); Aqualad origin-r	6	12	18	37	66	95
80-1st S.A. app. Phantom Stranger (1/69); Neal Adams-c	11	22	33	73	157	240
81-Windy & Willy; r/Many Loves of Dobie Gillis #26 with art changes	5	10	15	34	60	85
82-1st app. Nightmaster (5/69) by Grandenetti & Giordano; Kubert-c	6	12	18	41	76	110
83,84-Nightmaster by Wrightson w/Jones/Kaluta ink assist in each; Kubert-c. 83-Last 12¢ issue 84-Origin retold; begin 15¢	6	12	18	41	76	110
85-87-Firehair; Kubert-a	3	6	9	16	23	30
88-90-Jason's Quest: 90-Manhunter 2070 app.	3	6	9	14	20	25
91-93-Manhunter 2070: 92-Origin. 93-(9/70) Last 15¢ issue	3	6	9	14	20	25
94-Intro/origin new Doom Patrol & Robotman(8-9/77)	3	6	9	14	20	25
95,96-The Doom Patrol. 95-Origin Celsius	2	3	4	6	8	10
97-Power Girl; origin; JSA cameos	3	6	9	21	33	45
98,99-Power Girl; origin in #98; JSA cameos	2	4	6	11	16	20
100-(52 pgs.)-Most Showcase characters featured	2	4	6	11	16	20
101-103-Hawkman; Adam Strange x-over	2	3	4	6	8	10
104-(52 pgs.)-O.S.S. Spies at War	2	3	4	6	8	10

NOTE: ***Anderson*** *a-22-24i, 34-36i, 55, 56, 60, 61, 64, 101-103i; c-50i, 51i, 55, 56, 60, 61, 64.* ***Aparo*** *c-94-96.* ***Boring*** *c-10.* ***Estrada*** *a-104.* ***Fraden*** *c(p)-30, 31, 33.* ***Heath*** *c-3, 27-29.* ***Infantino*** *c/a(p)-4, 8, 13, 14; c-50p, 51p.* ***Gil Kane*** *a-22-24p, 34-36p; c-17-19, 22-24p(w/Giella), 31.* ***Kane/Anderson*** *c-34-36.* ***Kirby*** *c-11, 12.* ***Kirby/Stein*** *c-6, 7.* ***Kubert*** *a-2, 4i, 25, 26, 45, 53, 54, 72; c-25, 26, 53, 54, 57, 58, 82-87, 101-104; c-2, 4i.* ***Moreira*** *c-5.* ***Orlando*** *a-62p, 63p, 97i; c-62, 63, 97i.* ***Sekowsky*** *a-65p.* ***Sparling*** *a-78.* ***Staton*** *a-94, 95-99p, 100; c-97-100p.*

SHOWCASE '93
DC Comics: Jan, 1993 - No. 12, Dec, 1993 ($1.95, limited series, 52 pgs.)

1-12: 1-Begin 4 part Catwoman story & 6 part Blue Devil story; begin Cyborg story; Art Adams/Austin-c. 3-Flash by Charest (p). 6-Azrael in Bat-costume (2 pgs.). 7,8-Knightfall parts 13 & 14. 6-10-Deathstroke app. (6,10-cameo). 9,10-Austin-i. 10-Azrael as Batman in new costume app.; Gulacy-c. 11-Perez-c. 12-Creeper app.; Alan Grant scripts 4.00

NOTE: ***Chaykin*** *c-9.* ***Fabry*** *c-8.* ***Giffen*** *a-12.* ***Golden*** *c-3.* ***Zeck*** *c-6.*

SHOWCASE '94
DC Comics: Jan, 1994 - No. 12, Dec, 1994 ($1.95, limited series, 52 pgs.)

1-12: 1,2-Joker & Gunfire stories. 1-New Gods. 4-Riddler story. 5-Huntress-c/story w/app. new Batman. 6-Huntress-c/story w/app. Robin; Atom story. 7-Penguin story by Peter David, P. Craig Russell, & Michael T. Gilbert; Penguin-c by Jae Lee. 8,9-Scarface origin story by Alan Grant, John Wagner,& Teddy Kristiansen; Prelude to Zero Hour. 10-Zero Hour tie-in story. 11-Man-Bat. 4.00

NOTE: ***Alan Grant*** *scripts-3, 4.* ***Kelley Jones*** *c-12.* ***Mignola*** *c-3.* ***Nebres*** *a(i)-2.* ***Quesada*** *c-10.* ***Russell*** *a-7p.* ***Simonson*** *c-5.*

SHOWCASE '95
DC Comics: Jan, 1995 - No. 12, Dec, 1995 ($2.50/$2.95, limited series)

1-4-Supergirl story. 3-Eradicator-c.; The Question story. 4-Thorn c/story 4.00
5-12: 5-Thorn-c/story; begin $2.95-c. 8-Spectre story. 12-The Shade story by James Robinson & Wade Von Grawbadger; Maitresse story by Claremont & Alan Davis 4.00

SHOWCASE '96
DC Comics: Jan, 1996 - No. 12, Dec, 1996 ($2.95, limited series)

1-12: 1-Steve Geppi cameo. 3-Black Canary & Lois Lane-c/story; Deadman story by Jamie Delano & Wade Von Grawbadger, Gary Frank-c. 4-Firebrand & Guardian-c/story; The Shade & Dr. Fate "Times Past" story by James Robinson & Matt Smith begins, ends #5. 6-Superboy-c/app.; Atom app.; Capt. Marvel (Mary Marvel)-c/app. 8-Supergirl by David & Dodson. 11-Scare Tactics app. 11,12-Legion of Super-Heroes vs. Brainiac. 12-Jesse Quick app. 4.00

GD VG FN VF VF/NM NM- 2.0 4.0 6.0 8.0 9.0 9.2

SHOWCASE PRESENTS... (B&W archive reprints of DC Silver Age stories)
DC Comics: 2005 - 2011 ($9.99/$16.99/$17.99/$19.99, B&W, over 500 pgs., squarebound)

Adam Strange Vol. 1 (2007, $16.99) r/Showcase #17-19 & Mystery in Space #53-84 17.00
Ambush Bug (2009, $16.99) r/first app. in DC Comics Presents #52 other early app. 17.00
Aquaman Vol. 1 (2007, $16.99) r/Aquaman #1-6 & other early app. 17.00
Aquaman Vol. 2 (2008, $16.99) r/Aquaman #7-23 & other early app. 17.00
Aquaman Vol. 3 (2009, $16.99) r/Aquaman #24-39 & other early app. 17.00
The Atom Vol. 1 (2007, $16.99) r/Showcase #34-36 & The Atom #1-17 17.00
The Atom Vol. 2 (2008, $16.99) r/The Atom #18-38 17.00
Batgirl Vol. 1 (2007, $16.99) r/early apps. from Detective #359 (1967) thru 1975 17.00
Bat Lash Vol. 1 (2009, $9.99) r/#1-7, Showcase #76, DC Special Series #16, and Jonah Hex #49,51,52 10.00
Batman Vol. 1 (2006, $16.99) r/"new look" from Detective #327-342, Batman #164-174 17.00
Batman Vol. 2 (2007, $16.99) r/"new look" from Detective #343-358, Batman #175-188 17.00
Batman Vol. 3 (2008, $16.99) r/"new look" from Detective #359-375, Batman #189, 190-192,194-197,199-202 17.00
Batman and the Outsiders Vol. 1 (2007, $16.99) r/#1-19, Annual #1; Brave and the Bold #200; and New Teen Titans #37 17.00
Blackhawk Vol. 1 (2008, $16.99) r/#108-127 17.00
Booster Gold Vol. 1 (2008, $16.99) r/#1-25 & Action Comics #594 17.00
The Brave and the Bold Batman Team-ups Vol. 1 (2007, $16.99) r/#59,64,67-71,74-87 17.00
The Brave and the Bold Batman Team-ups Vol. 2 (2007, $16.99) r/#88-108 17.00
The Brave and the Bold Batman Team-ups Vol. 3 (2008, $16.99) r/#109-134 17.00
Challengers of the Unknown Vol. 1 (2006, $16.99) r/#1-17 & Showcase #6,7,11,12 17.00
Challengers of the Unknown Vol. 2 (2008, $16.99) r/#18-37 17.00
DC Comics Presents: The Superman Team-ups Vol. 1 (2009, $17.99) r/#1-26 18.00
Dial H For Hero ('10, $9.99) r/early apps. in House of Mystery #156-173 10.00
Doc Savage ('11, $19.99) r/Doc Savage #1-8 (1975-77 Marvel B&W magazine) 20.00
The Doom Patrol Vol. 1 (2009, $16.99) r/#86-101 and My Greatest Adventure #80-85 17.00
The Doom Patrol Vol. 2 (2010, $19.99) r/#102-121 20.00
The Elongated Man Vol. 1 ('06, $16.99) r/early apps. in Flash & Detective ('60-'68) 17.00
Eclipso Vol. 1 (2009, $9.99) r/stories from House of Secrets #61-80 10.00
Enemy Ace Vol. 1 (2008, $16.99) r/Our Army at War #151 & other early app. 17.00
The Flash Vol. 1 (2007, $16.99) r/Flash Comics #104 (last G.A. issue), Showcase #4,8,13,14 & The Flash #105-119 17.00
The Flash Vol. 2 (2008, $16.99) r/The Flash #120-140 17.00
The Flash Vol. 3 (2009, $16.99) r/The Flash #141-161 17.00
The Flash, The Trial of ... (2011, $19.99) r/The Flash #323-327,329-336,340-350 20.00
The Great Disaster Featuring The Atomic Knights and Hercules Vol. 1 (2007, $16.99) 17.00
Green Arrow Vol. 1 (2006, $16.99) r/Adventure #250-269, Brave and the Bold #50,71,85; Justice League of America #4; World's Finest #95-134,136,138,140 17.00
Green Lantern Vol. 1 (2005, $9.99) r/Showcase #22-24 & Green Lantern #1-17 20.00
Green Lantern Vol. 1 (2010, $19.99) r/Showcase #22-24 & Green Lantern #1-17 20.00
Green Lantern Vol. 2 (2007, $16.99) r/Green Lantern #18-38 17.00
Green Lantern Vol. 3 (2008, $16.99) r/Green Lantern #39-59 17.00
Green Lantern Vol. 4 (2009, $16.99) r/Green Lantern #60-75 17.00
Green Lantern Vol. 5 (2011, $19.99) r/Green Lantern #76-87,89 and back up stories from Flash #217-246 20.00
Haunted Tank Vol. 1 ('06, $16.99) r/G.I. Combat #87-119, Brave & The Bold #52 and Our Army at War #155; Russ Heath-c 17.00
Haunted Tank Vol. 2 ('08, $16.99) r/G.I. Combat #120-156 17.00
Hawkman Vol. 1 ('07, $16.99) r/Brave & The Bold #34-36,42-44, Mystery in Space #87-90, Hawkman #1-11, and The Atom #7 17.00
Hawkman Vol. 2 ('08, $16.99) r/Brave & The Bold #70, Hawkman #12-27, The Atom #31, & The Atom and Hawkman #39-45 17.00
The House of Mystery Vol. 1 ('06, $16.99) r/House of Mystery #174-194 ('68-'71) 17.00
The House of Mystery Vol. 2 ('07, $16.99) r/House of Mystery #195-211 ('71-'73) 17.00
The House of Mystery Vol. 3 ('09, $16.99) r/House of Mystery #212-226 ('73-'74) 17.00
The House of Secrets Vol. 1 ('08, $16.99) r/House of Secrets #81-98 ('69-'72) 17.00
The House of Secrets Vol. 2 ('09, $17.99) r/House of Secrets #99-119 ('72-'74) 18.00
Jonah Hex Vol. 1 (2005, $16.99) r/All Star Western #10-12, Weird Western Tales #13,14, 16-33; plus the complete adventures of Outlaw from All Star Western #2-8 17.00
Justice League of America Vol. 1 ('05, $16.99) r/Brave & the Bold #28-30, J.L. of A. #1-16 and Mystery in Space #75 17.00
Justice League of America Vol. 2 ('07, $16.99) r/Justice League of America #17-36 17.00
Justice League of America Vol. 3 ('07, $16.99) r/Justice League of America #37-60 17.00
Justice League of America Vol. 4 ('09, $16.99) r/Justice League of America #61-83 17.00
Justice League of America Vol. 5 ('11, $19.99) r/Justice League of America #84-106 20.00
Legion of Super-Heroes Vol. 1 ('07, $16.99) r/Adventure #247 & early app. thru 1964 17.00
Legion of Super-Heroes Vol. 2 ('08, $16.99) r/app. in Adventure & Superboy 1964-66 17.00
Legion of Super-Heroes Vol. 3 ('09, $16.99) r/Adventure #349-368 & S.P. Jimmy Olsen #106 17.00

Showcase Presents Superman Family Vol. 3 © DC

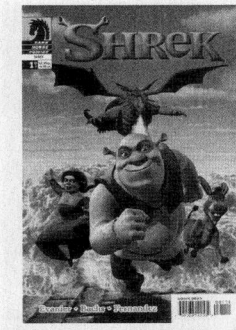

Shrek #1 © Dreamworks

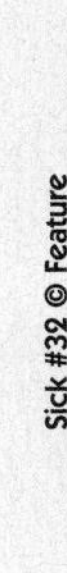
Sick #32 © Feature

GD 2.0 | VG 4.0 | FN 6.0 | VF 8.0 | VF/NM 9.0 | NM- 9.2

Legion of Super-Heroes Vol. 4 ('10, $19.99) r/app. in Adv., Action & Superboy 1968-72 20.00
Martian Manhunter Vol. 1 (2007, $16.99) r/Detective #225-304 & Batman #78 (prototype) 17.00
Martian Manhunter Vol. 2 ('09, $16.99) r/Detective #305-326 & House of Myst. #143-173 17.00
Metal Men Vol. 1 (2007, $16.99) r/#1-16; Brave & Bold #55, Showcase #37-40 17.00
Metamorpho Vol. 1 ('05, $16.99) r/Brave&Bold #57,58,66,68; Metamorpho #1-17;JLA #42 17.00
Our Army at War Vol. 1 ('10, $19.99) r/#1-20 20.00
Phantom Stranger Vol. 1 (2006, $16.99) r/#1-21 (2nd series) & Showcase #80 17.00
Phantom Stranger Vol. 2 (2008, $16.99) r/#22-41 and various 1970-1978 appearances 17.00
Robin The Boy Wonder Vol. 1 (2007, $16.99) r/back-ups from Batman, Detective, WF 17.00
Secrets of Sinister House ('10, $17.99) r/#5-18 and Sinister House of Secret Love #1-4 18.00
Sgt. Rock Vol. 1 ('07, $16.99) r/G.I. Combat #68, Our Army at War #81-117 17.00
Sgt. Rock Vol. 2 ('08, $16.99) r/Our Army at War #118-148 17.00
Sgt. Rock Vol. 3 ('10, $19.99) r/Our Army at War #149-163,165-172,174-176,178-180 20.00
Shazam! Vol. 1 ('06, $16.99) r/#1-33 17.00
Strange Adventures Vol. 1 ('08, $16.99) r/#54-73 17.00
Supergirl Vol. 1 ('07, $16.99) r/prototype from Superman #123 (8/58); 1st app. Action #252 (5/59) and early appearances thru Nov. 1961 17.00
Supergirl Vol. 2 ('08, $16.99) r/appearances in Action Comics #283-321 (1961-1965) 17.00
Superman Vol. 1 ('05, $9.99) r/Action #241-257 & Superman #122-134 (1958-59) 20.00
Superman Vol. 1 ('10, $19.99) r/Action #241-257 & Superman #122-134 (1958-59) 20.00
Superman Vol. 2 ('06, $16.99) r/Action #258-275 & Superman #134-145 (1959-61) 17.00
Superman Vol. 3 ('07, $16.99) r/Action #279-292 & Superman #146-156 & Annual #3,4 17.00
Superman Vol. 4 ('08, $16.99) r/Action #293-309 & Superman #157-166 (1962-64) 17.00
Superman Family Vol. 1 ('06, $16.99) Superman's Pal, Jimmy Olsen #1-22; Showcase #9 and Superman #22 17.00
Superman Family Vol. 2 ('08, $16.99) Superman's Pal, Jimmy Olsen #23-34; Showcase #10 and Superman's Girl Friend, Lois Lane #1-7 17.00
Superman Family Vol. 3 ('09, $16.99) Superman's Pal, Jimmy Olsen #35-44 and Superman's Girl Friend, Lois Lane #8-16 17.00
Teen Titans Vol. 1 ('06, $16.99) r/#1-18; Brave & the Bold #54,60; Showcase #59 17.00
Teen Titans Vol. 2 ('07, $16.99) r/#19-37, World's Finest #205 and Brave & Bold #83,94 17.00
The Unknown Soldier Vol. 1 ('06, $16.99) r/Star Spangled War Stories #158-188 17.00
The War That Time Forgot Vol. 1 ('07, $16.99) r/S.S.W.S. #90,92,94-125,127,128 17.00
Warlord Vol. 1 ('09, $16.99) r/#1-28 and debut in 1st Issue Special #1 17.00
The Witching Hour Vol. 1 ('11, $19.99) r/#1-19 20.00
Wonder Woman Vol. 1 ('07, $16.99) r/#98-117 17.00
Wonder Woman Vol. 2 ('08, $16.99) r/#118-137 17.00
World's Finest Vol. 1 ('07, $16.99) r/#71-111 & Superman #76 17.00
World's Finest Vol. 2 ('08, $16.99) r/#112-145 17.00
World's Finest Vol. 3 ('10, $17.99) r/#146-160,162-169,171-173 ('64-'68) 18.00

SHOWGIRLS (Formerly Sherry the Showgirl #3)
Atlas Comics (MPC No. 2): No. 4, 2/57; June, 1957 - No. 2, Aug, 1957

	GD	VG	FN	VF	VF/NM	NM-
4-(2/57) Dan DeCarlo-c/a begins	22	44	66	132	216	300
1-(6/57) Millie, Sherry, Chili, Pearl & Hazel begin	37	74	111	222	361	500
2	22	44	66	132	216	300

SHREK (Movie)
Dark Horse Comics: Sept, 2003 - No. 3, Dec, 2003 ($2.99, limited series)

1-3-Takes place after 1st movie; Evanier-s/Bachs-a; CGI cover 4.00

SHREK (Movie)
Ape Entertainment: 2010 - No. 4, 2011 ($3.95, limited series)

1-3-Short stories by various 4.00

SHROUD, THE (See Super-Villain Team-Up #5)
Marvel Comics: Mar, 1994 - No. 4, June, 1994 ($1.75, mini-series)

1-4: 1,2,4-Spider-Man & Scorpion app. 3.00

SHROUD OF MYSTERY
Whitman Publications: June, 1982

	GD	VG	FN	VF	VF/NM	NM-
1	1	2	3	4	5	7

SHRUGGED
Aspen MLT, Inc.: No. 0, June, 2006 - No. 8, Feb, 2009 ($2.50/$2.99)

0-($2.50) Turner & Mastromauro-s/Gunnell-a; intro. story and character profiles 3.00
1-8-($2.99) 1-Six covers. 2-Three covers 3.00
... : Beginnings (5/06, $1.99) Prequel intro. to Ange and Dev; Gunnell-a; development art 3.00
Volume 2 (3/13, $1.00) 1-Marks & Gunnell-a; multiple covers 3.00
V2 #2-4-($3.99) Mastromauro-s/Marks-a 4.00

SHUTTER
Image Comics: Apr, 2014 - Present ($3.50/$3.99)

1-11-Keatinge-s/Del Duca-a 3.50
12-27-($3.99) 4.00

SHUT UP AND DIE
Image Comics/Halloween: 1998 - No. 3, 1998 ($2.95,B&W, bi-monthly)

1-3: Hudnall-s 3.00

SICK (Sick Special #131) (Magazine) (Satire)
Feature Publ./Headline Publ./Crestwood Publ. Co./Hewfred Publ./ Pyramid Comm./Charlton Publ. No. 109 (4/76) on: Aug, 1960 - No. 134, Fall, 1980

	GD	VG	FN	VF	VF/NM	NM-
V1#1-Jack Paar photo on-c; Torres-a; Untouchables-s; Ben Hur movie photo-s	14	28	42	96	211	325
2-Torres-a; Elvis app.; Lenny Bruce app.	9	18	27	61	123	185
3-5-Torres-a in all. 3-Khruschev-c; Hitler-s. 4-Newhart-s; Castro-s; John Wayne. 5-JFK/Castro-c; Elvis pin-up; Hitler.	8	16	24	55	105	155
6-Photo-s of Ricky Nelson & Marilyn Monroe; JFK	9	18	27	57	111	165
V2#1,2,4-8 (#7,8,10-14): 1-(#7) Hitler-s; Brando photo-s. 2-(#8) Dick Clark-s. 4-(#10) Untouchables-c; Candid Camera-s. 5-(#11) Nixon-c; Lone Ranger-s; JFK-s. 6-(#12) Beatnik-c/s. 8-(#14) Liz Taylor pin-up, JFK-s; Dobie Gillis-s; Sinatra & Dean Martin photo-s	8	16	24	51	96	140
3-(#9) Marilyn Monroe/JFK-c; Kingston Trio-s	8	16	24	55	105	155
V3#1-7(#15-21): 1-(#15) JFK app.; Liz Tayor/Richard Burton-s. 2-(#16) Ben Casey/ Frankenstein-c/s; Hitler photo-s. 5-(#19) Nixon back-c/s; Sinatra photo-s. 6-(#20) 1st Huckleberry Fink-c	5	10	15	33	57	80
8-(#22) Cassius Clay vs. Liston-s; 1st Civil War Blackouts-/Pvt. Bo Reargard w/ Jack Davis-a	5	10	15	35	63	90
V4#1-5 (#23-27): Civil War Blackouts-/Pvt. Bo Reargard w/ Jack Davis-a in all. 1-(#23) Smokey Bear-c; Tarzan-s. 2-(#24) Goldwater & Paar-s; Castro-s. 3-(#25) Frankenstein-c; Cleopatra/Liz Taylor-s; Steve Reeves photo-s. 4-(#26) James Bond-s; Hitler-s. 5-(#27) Taylor/Burton pin-up; Sinatra, Martin, Andress, Ekberg photo-s	4	8	12	27	44	60
28,31,36,39: 31-Pink Panther movie photo-s; Burke's Law-s. 39-Westerns; Elizabeth Montgomery photo-s; Beat mag-s	4	8	12	23	37	50
29,34,37,38: 29-Beatles-c by Jack Davis. 34-Two pg. Beatles-s & photo pin-up. 37-Playboy parody issue. 38-Addams Family-s	4	8	12	27	44	60
30,32,35,40: 30-Beatles photo pin-up; James Bond photo-s. 32-Ian Fleming-s; LBJ-s; Tarzan-s. 35-Beatles cameo; Three Stooges parody. 40-Tarzan-s; Crosby/Hope-s; Beatles parody	4	8	12	28	47	65
33-Ringo Starr photo-c & spoof on "A Hard Day's Night"; inside-c has Beatles photos	5	10	15	35	63	90
41,50,51,53,54,60: 41-Sports Illustrated parody-c/s. 50-Mod issue; flip-c w/1967 calendar w/Bob Taylor-a. 51-Get Smart-s. 53-Beatles cameo; nudity panels. 54-Monkees-c. 60-TV Daniel Boone-s	3	6	9	19	30	40
42-Fighting American-c revised from Simon/Kirby-c; "Good girl" art by Sparling; profile on Bob Powell; superhero parodies	5	10	15	33	57	80
43-49,52,55-59: 43-Sneaker set begins by Sparling. 45-Has #44 on-c & #45 on inside; TV Westerns-s; Beatles cameo. 46-Hell's Angels-s; NY Mets-s. 47-UFO/Space-c. 49-Men's Adventure mag. parody issue; nudity. 52-LBJ-s. 55-Underground culture special. 56-Alfred E. Neuman-c; inventors issue. 58-Hippie issue-c/s. 59-Hippie-s	3	6	9	16	24	32
61-64,66-69,71,73,75-80: 63-Tiny Tim-c & poster; Monkees-s. 64-Flip-c. 66-Flip-c; Mod Squad-s. 69-Beatles cameo; Peter Sellers photo-s. 71-Flip-c; Clint Eastwood-s. 76-Nixon-s; Marcus Welby-s. 78-Ma Barker-s; Courtship of Eddie's Father-s; Abbie Hoffman-s	3	6	9	15	22	28
65,70,74: 65-Cassius Clay/Brando/J. Wayne-c; Johnny Carson-s. 70-(9/69) John & Yoko-c, 1/2 pg. story. 74-Clay, Agnew, Namath & others as superheroes-c/s; Easy Rider-s; Ghost and Mrs. Muir-s	3	6	9	16	24	32
72-(84 pgs.) Xmas issue w/2 pg. slick color poster; Tarzan-s; 2 pg. Superman & superheroes-s	3	6	9	21	33	45
81-85,87-95,98,99: 81-(2/71) Woody Allen photo-s. 85 Monster Mag. parody-s; Nixon-s w/Ringo & John cameo. 88-Klute photo-s; Nixon paper dolls page. 92-Lily Tomlin; Archie Bunker pin-up. 93-Woody Allen	2	4	6	13	18	22
86,96,97,100: 86-John & Yoko, Tiny Tim-c; Love Story movie photo-s. 96-Kung Fu-c; Mummy-s, Dracula & Frankenstein app. 97-Superman-s; 1974 Calendar; Charlie Brown & Snoopy pin-up. 100-Serpico-s; Cosell-s; Jacques Cousteau-s	3	6	9	14	19	24
101-103,105-114,116,119,120: 101-Three Musketeers-s; Dick Tracy-s. 102-Young Frankenstein-s. 103-Kojak-s; Evel Knievel-s. 105-Towering Inferno-s; Peanuts/Snoopy-s. 106-Cher-c/s. 10 7-Jaws-c/s. 108-Pink Panther-c/s; Archie-s. 109-Adam & Eve-s(nudity). 110-Welcome Back Kotter-s. 111-Sonny & Cher-s. 112-King Kong-c/s. 120-Star Trek-s	2	4	6	9	13	16
104,115,117,118: 104-Muhammad Ali-c/s. 115-Charlie's Angels-s. 117-Bionic Woman & Six Million $ Man-c/s; Cher D'Flower begins by Sparling (nudity). 118-Star Wars-s; Popeye-s	2	4	6	11	16	20
121-125,128-130: 122-Darth Vader-s. 123-Jaws II-s. 128-Superman-c/movie parody. 130-Alien movie-s	2	4	6	10	14	18

126,127: 126-(68 pgs.) Battlestar Galactica-c/s; Star Wars-s; Wonder Woman-s.

Sidekick #10 © Studio JMS

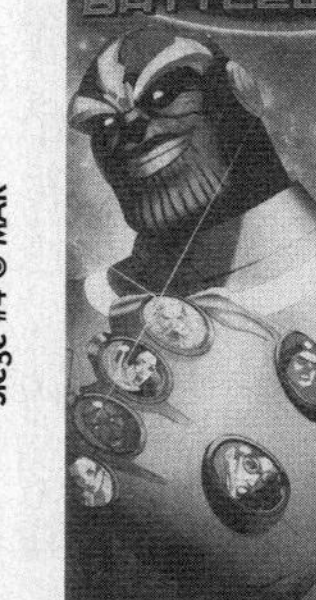

Siege #4 © MAR

Silk #5 © MAR

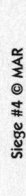

	GD 2.0	VG 4.0	FN 6.0	VF 8.0	VF/NM 9.0	NM- 9.2
127-Mork & Mindy-s; Lord of the Rings-s	2	4	6	13	18	22
131-(1980 Special) Star Wars/Star Trek/Flash Gordon wraparound-c/s; Superman parody; Battlestar Galactica-s	3	6	9	14	19	24
132,133: 132-1980 Election-c/s; Apocalypse Now-s. 133-Star Trek-s; Chips-s; Superheroes page	2	4	6	13	18	22
134 (scarce)(68 pg. Giant)-Star Wars-c; Alien-s; WKRP-s; Mork & Mindy-s; Taxi-s; MASH-s	4	8	12	19	30	40
Annual 1- Birthday Annual (1966)-3 pg. Huckleberry Fink fold out	4	8	12	23	37	50
Annual 2- 7th Annual Yearbook (1967)-Davis-c, 2 pg. glossy poster insert	4	8	12	23	37	50
Annual 3 (1968) "Big Sick Laff-in" on-c (84 pgs.)-w/psychedelic posters; Frankenstein poster	3	6	9	17	26	35
Annual 1969 "Great Big Fat Annual Sick", 1969 "9th Year Annual Sick", 1970, 1971	3	6	9	16	24	32
Annual 12,13-(1972,1973, 84 pgs.) 13-Monster-c	3	6	9	16	24	32
Annual 14,15-(1974,1975, 84 pgs.) 14-Hitler photo-s	3	6	9	16	24	32
Annual 2-4 (1980)	2	4	6	9	13	16
Special 1 (1980) Buck Rogers-c/s; MASH-s	3	6	9	14	19	24
Special 2 (1980) Wraparound Star Wars:Empire Strikes Back-c; Charlie's Angels/Farrah-s; Rocky-s; plus reprints	3	6	9	14	19	24
Yearbook 15(1975, 84 pgs.) Paul Revere-c	3	6	9	16	23	30

*NOTE: **Davis** a-42, 87; c-22, 23, 25, 29, 31, 32. **Powell** a-7, 31, 57. **Simon** a-1-3, 10, 41, 42, 87, 99; c-1, 47, 57, 59, 69, 91, 95-97, 99, 100, 102, 107, 112. **Torres** a-1-3, 29, 31, 47, 49. **Tuska** a-14, 41-43. Civil War Blackouts-23, 24. #42 has biography of Bob Powell.*

SIDEKICK (Paul Jenkins'...)
Image Comics (Desperado): June, 2006 - No. 5, May, 2007 ($3.50, limited series)
1-5-Paul Jenkins-s/Chris Moreno-a 3.50
... Super Summer Sidekick Spectacular 1 (7/07, $2.99) 3.50
... Super Summer Sidekick Spectacular 2 (9/07, $3.50) 3.50

SIDEKICK
Image Comics (Joe's Comics): Aug, 2013 - No. 12, Dec, 2015 ($2.99)
1-7,9-12: 1-Straczynski-a/Mandrake-a; intro. The Cowl and Flyboy; 6 covers. 4-6-Two covers 3.00
8-($3.99) Chrome-c 4.00

SIDEKICKS
Fanboy Ent., Inc.: Jun, 2000 - No. 3, Apr, 2001 ($2.75, B&W, lim. series)
1-3-J.Torres-s/Takesi Miyazawa-a. 3-Variant-c by Wieringo 3.00
...: Super Fun Summer Special (Oni Press, 7/03, $2.99) art by various incl. Wieringo 3.00
...: The Substitute (Oni Press, 7/02, $2.95) 3.00
...: The Transfer Student TPB (Oni Press, 6/02, $8.95, 9" x 6") r/#1-3 9.00
...: The Transfer Student TPB 2nd Ed. (10/03, $11.95, 9" x 6") r/#1-3; The Substitute 12.00

SIDESHOW
Avon Periodicals: 1949 (one-shot)

	GD	VG	FN	VF	VF/NM	NM-
1-(Rare)-Similar to Bachelor's Diary	116	232	348	742	1271	1800

SIEGE
Marvel Comics: Mar, 2010 - No. 4, Jun, 2010 ($3.99, limited series)
1-4-Asgard is invaded; Bendis-s/Coipel-a. 4-End of The Sentry 4.00
1-4-Variant covers by Dell'Otto 8.00
...: Captain America (6/10, $2.99) Gage-s/Dallocchio-a/Djurdjevic-c; both Caps app. 4.00
...: Loki (6/10, $2.99) Gillen-s/McKelvie-a/Djurdjevic-c; Hela & Mephisto app. 4.00
...: Secret Warriors (6/10, $2.99) Hickman-s/Vitti-a/Djurdjevic-c; Phobos attacks 4.00
...: Spider-Man (6/10, $2.99) Reed-s/Santucci-a/Djurdjevic-c; Venom & Ms. Marvel app. 4.00
...: Storming Asgard - Heroes & Villains (3/10, $3.99) Dossiers on participants; Land-c 4.00
...: The Cabal (2/10, $3.99) series prelude; Bendis-s/Lark-a; covers by Finch & Davis 4.00
...: Young Avengers (6/10, $2.99) McKeever-s/Asrar-a/Djurdjevic-c; Wrecking Crew app. 4.00

SIEGE (Secret Wars tie-in) (Continued from Secret Wars: Journal #1)
Marvel Comics: Sept, 2015 - No. 4, Dec, 2015 ($3.99, limited series)
1-4-Gillen-s/Andrade-a; Abigail Brand, Kate Bishop & Ms. America app. 4.00

SIEGE: EMBEDDED
Marvel Comics: Mar, 2010 - No. 4, Jul, 2010 ($3.99, limited series)
1-4-Reed-s/Samnee-a/Granov-c; Ben Urich & Volstagg cover the invasion 4.00

SIEGEL AND SHUSTER: DATELINE 1930s
Eclipse Comics: Nov, 1984 - No. 2, Sept, 1985 ($1.50/$1.75, Baxter paper #1)
1,2: 1-Unpublished samples of strips from the '30s; includes 'Interplanetary Police'; Shuster-c. 2 ($1.75, B&W)-unpublished strips; Shuster-c 4.00

SIF (See Thor titles)
Marvel Comics: Jun, 2010 ($3.99, one shot)
1-Deconnick-s/Stegman-a/Foreman-c; Beta Ray Bill app. 4.00

SIGIL (Also see CrossGen Chronicles)
CrossGeneration Comics: Jul, 2000 - No. 43, Jan, 2004 ($2.95)
1-43: 1-Barbara Kesel-s/Ben & Ray Lai-a. 12-Waid-s begin. 21-Chuck Dixon-s begin 3.00

SIGIL
Marvel Comics: May, 2011 - No. 4, Aug, 2011 ($2.99)
1-4-Carey-s/Kirk-a 3.00
1-Variant-c by McGuinness 5.00

SIGMA
Image Comics (WildStorm): March, 1996 - No. 3, June, 1996 ($2.50, limited series)
1-3: 1-"Fire From Heaven" prelude #2; Coker-a. 2-"Fire From Heaven" pt. 6. 3-"Fire From Heaven" pt. 14. 3.00

SILENT DRAGON
DC Comics (WildStorm): Sept, 2005 - No. 6, Feb, 2006 ($2.99, limited series)
1-6-Tokyo 2066 A.D.; Leinil Yu-a/c; Andy Diggle-s 3.00
TPB (2006, $19.99) r/series; sketch page 20.00

SILENT HILL: DEAD/ALIVE
IDW Publishing: Dec, 2005 - No. 5, Apr, 2006 ($3.99, limited series)
1-5-Stakal-a/Ciencin-s. 1-Four covers. 2-5-Two covers 4.00

SILENT HILL DOWNPOUR: ANNE'S STORY
IDW Publishing: Aug, 2014 - No. 4, Nov, 2014 ($3.99, limited series)
1-4-Tom Waltz-s/Tristan Jones-a; two covers on each 4.00

SILENT HILL: DYING INSIDE
IDW Publishing: Feb, 2004 - No. 5, June, 2004 ($3.99, limited series)
1-5-Based on the Konami computer game. 1-Templesmith-a; Ashley Wood-c 4.00
...: Paint It Black (2/05, $7.49) Ciencin-s/Thomas-a 7.50
...: The Grinning Man 5/05, $7.49) Ciencin-s/Stakal-a 7.50
TPB (8/04, $19.99) r/#1-5; Ashley Wood-c 20.00

SILENT HILL: PAST LIFE
IDW Publishing: Oct, 2010 - No. 4, Jan, 2011 ($3.99, limited series)
1-4-Waltz-s; two covers on each 4.00

SILENT HILL: SINNER'S REWARD
IDW Publishing: Feb, 2008 - No. 4, Apr, 2008 ($3.99, limited series)
1-4-Waltz-s/Stamb-a 4.00

SILENT INVASION, THE
Rengade Press: Apr, 1986 - No.12, Mar, 1988 ($1.70/$2.00, B&W)
1-12-UFO sightings of the '50's 3.00
Book 1- reprints ($7.95) 8.00

SILENT MOBIUS
Viz Select Comics: 1991 - No. 5, 1992 ($4.95, color, squarebound, 44 pgs.)
1-5: Japanese stories translated to English 5.00

SILENT SCREAMERS (Based on the Aztech Toys figures)
Image Comics: Oct, 2000 ($4.95)
Nosferatu Issue - Alex Ross front & back-c 5.00

SILENT WAR
Marvel Comics: Mar, 2007 - No. 6, Aug, 2007 ($2.99, limited series)
1-6-Inhumans, Black Bolt and Fantastic Four app.; Hine-s/Irving-a/Watson-c 3.00
TPB (2007, $14.99) r/series 15.00

SILK (See Amazing Spider-Man 2014 series #1 & #4 for debut)
Marvel Comics: Apr, 2015 - No. 7, Nov, 2015 ($3.99)

	GD	VG	FN	VF	VF/NM	NM-
1-Robbie Thompson-s/Stacey Lee-a/Dave Johnson-c; Spider-Man app.	1	2	3	5	6	8

2-7: 3-6-Black Cat app. 4-Fantastic Four app. 7-Secret Wars tie-in 4.00

SILK (Spider-Man)
Marvel Comics: Jan, 2016 - Present ($3.99)
1-18: 1-Robbie Thompson-s/Stacey Lee-a; Black Cat & Mockingbird app. 4,5-Fish-a. 7,8-"Spider-Women" tie-in; Spider-Woman & Spider-Gwen app. 14-17-Clone Conspiracy 4.00

SILKE
Dark Horse Comics: Jan, 2001 - No. 4, Sept, 2001 ($2.95)
1-4-Tony Daniel-s/a 3.00

SILKEN GHOST
CrossGen Comics: June, 2003 - No. 5, Oct, 2003 ($2.95, limited series)
1-5-Dixon-s/Rosado-a 3.00
Traveler Vol. 1 (2003, $9.95) digest-sized reprint #1-5 10.00

Silver Age #1 © DC

Silver Kid Western #2 © Stanmor

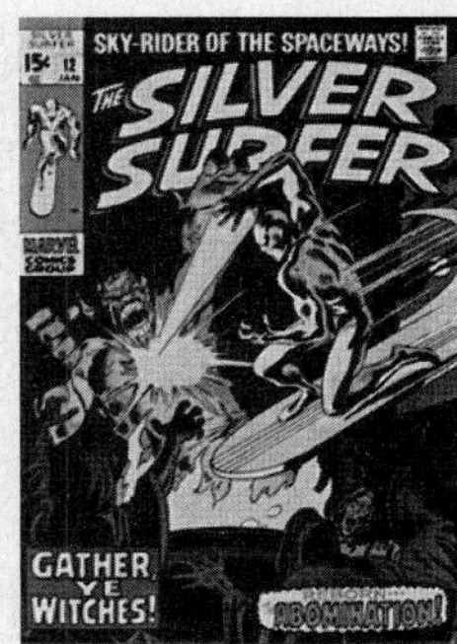

Silver Surfer #12 © MAR

GD 2.0 | VG 4.0 | FN 6.0 | VF 8.0 | VF/NM 9.0 | NM- 9.2

SILLY PILLY (See Frank Luther's...)

SILLY SYMPHONIES (See Dell Giants)

SILLY TUNES
Timely Comics: Fall, 1945 - No. 7, June, 1947

1-Silly Seal, Ziggy Pig begin 31 62 93 186 303 420
2-(2/46) 18 36 54 103 162 220
3-7: 6-New logo 15 30 45 88 137 185

SILVER (See Lone Ranger's Famous Horse...)

SILVER AGE
DC Comics: July, 2000 ($3.95, limited series)

1-Waid-s/Dodson-a; "Silver Age" style x-over; JLA & villains switch bodies 4.00
...: Challengers of the Unknown ($2.50) Joe Kubert-c; vs. Chronos 3.00
...: Dial H For Hero ($2.50) Jim Mooney-c; vs. Martian Manhunter 3.00
...: Doom Patrol ($2.50) Ramona Fradon-c/Peyer-s 3.00
...: Flash ($2.50) Carmine Infantino-c; Kid Flash and Elongated Man app. 3.00
...: Green Lantern ($2.50) Gil Kane-c/Busiek-s/Anderson-a; vs. Sinestro 3.00
...: Justice League of America ($2.50) Ty Templeton-c 3.00
...: Showcase ($2.50) Dick Giordano-c/a; Batgirl, Adam Strange app. 3.00
... Secret Files ($4.95) Intro. Agamemno; short stories & profile pages 5.00
...: Teen Titans ($2.50) Nick Cardy-c; vs. Penguin, Mr. Element, Black Manta 3.00
...: The Brave and the Bold ($2.50) Jim Aparo-c; Batman & Metal Men 3.00
... 80-Page Giant ($5.95) Conclusion of x-over; "lost" Silver Age stories 6.00

SILVERBACK
Comico: 1989 - No. 3, 1990 ($2.50, color, limited series, mature readers)

1-3: Character from Grendel: Matt Wagner-a 3.00

SILVERBLADE
DC Comics: Sept, 1987 - No. 12, Sept, 1988

1-12: Colan-c/a in all 4.00

SILVERHAWKS
Star Comics/Marvel Comics #6: Aug, 1987 - No. 6, June, 1988 ($1.00)

1-6 4.00

SILVERHEELS
Pacific Comics: Dec, 1983 - No. 3, May, 1984 ($1.50)

1-3 4.00

SILVER KID WESTERN
Key/Stanmor Publications: Oct, 1954 - No. 5, July, 1955

1 10 20 30 54 72 90
2 6 12 18 31 38 45
3-5 6 12 18 28 34 40
I.W. Reprint #1,2-Severin-c: 1-r/#? 2-r/#1 2 4 6 8 11 14

SILVER SABLE AND THE WILD PACK (See Amazing Spider-Man #265 and Sable & Fortune)
Marvel Comics: June, 1992 - No. 35, Apr, 1995 ($1.25/$1.50

1-($2.00)-Embossed & foil stamped-c; Spider-Man app. 4.00
2-24,26-35: 4,5-Dr. Doom-c/story. 6,7-Deathlok-c/story. 9-Origin Silver Sable. 10-Punisher-c/s. 15-Capt. America-c/s. 16,17-Intruders app. 18,19-Venom-c/s. 19-Siege of Darkness x-over. 23-Daredevil (in new costume) & Deadpool app. 24-Bound-in card sheet. Li'l Sylvie backup story 3.00
25-($2.00, 52 pgs.)-Li'l Sylvie backup story 4.00

SILVER STAR (Also see Jack Kirby's...)
Pacific Comics: Feb, 1983 - No. 6, Jan, 1984 ($1.00)

1-6: 1-1st app. Last of the Viking Heroes. 1-5-Kirby-c/a. 2-Ditko-a 5.00
...: Graphite Edition TPB (TwoMorrows Publ., 3/06, $19.95) r/series in B&W including Kirby's original pencils; sketch pages; original screenplay 20.00
Jack Kirby's Silver Star, Volume 1 HC (Image Comics, 2007, $34.99) r/series in color; sketch pages; original screenplay 35.00

SILVER STREAK COMICS (Crime Does Not Pay #22 on)
Your Guide Publs. No. 1-7/New Friday Publs. No. 8-17/Comic House Publ./ Newsbook Publ.: Dec, 1939 - No. 21, May, 1942; No. 23, 1946; nn, Feb, 1946
(Silver logo-#1-5)

1-(Scarce)-Intro the Claw by Cole (r-in Daredevil #21), Red Reeves Boy Magician (ends #2), Captain Fearless (ends #2), The Wasp (ends #2), Mister Midnight (ends #2) begin; Spirit Man only app. Calling The Duke begins (ends #2). Barry Lane only app. Silver Metallic-c begin, end #5; Claw-c 1,2,6-8 1000 2000 3000 7600 14,550 21,500
2-The Claw ends (by Cole); makes pact w/Hitler; Simon-c/a (The Claw); ad for Marvel Mystery Comics #2 (12/39). Lance Hale begins (receives super powers). Solar Patrol app. 432 864 1296 3154 5577 8000
3-1st app. & origin Silver Streak (2nd with Lightning speed); Dickie Dean the Boy Inventor, Lance Hale, Ace Powers (ends #6), Bill Wayne The Texas Terror (ends #6) & The Planet Patrol (ends #6) begin. Detective Snoop, Sergeant Drake only app. 400 800 1200 2800 4900 7000
4-Sky Wolf begins (ends #6); Silver Streak by Jack Cole (new costume); 1st app. Jackie, Lance Hale's sidekick. Lance Hale gains immortality 181 362 543 1158 1979 2800
5-Cole c/a(2); back-c ad for Claw app. in #6 213 426 639 1363 2332 3300
6-(Scarce, 9/40)-Origin & 1st app. Daredevil (blue & yellow costume) by Jack Binder; The Claw returns as the Green Claw; classic Cole Claw-c 2000 4000 6000 14,000 25,000 36,000
7-Claw vs. Daredevil serial begins c/sty, ends #11. Daredevil new costume-blue & red by Jack Cole & 3 other Cole stories (38 pgs.). Origin Whiz, S. S.'s Falcon 2nd app. Daredevil & 1st Daredevil-c (by Cole). Cloud Curtis, Presto Martin begins. Dynamo Hill & Zongar The Miracleman only app. 854 1708 2562 6234 11,017 15,800
8-Classic Claw vs. Daredevil by Cole c/sty; last Cole Silver streak. Dan Dearborn begins (ends #12). Secret Agent X-101 begins, (ends #9) 676 1352 2028 4935 8718 12,500
9-Claw vs. Daredevil by Cole. Silver Streak-c by Bob Wood 252 504 756 1613 2757 3900
10-Origin & 1st app. Captain Battle (5/41) by Binder; Claw vs. Daredevil by Cole; Silver Streak/robot-c by Bob Wood 210 420 630 1334 2292 3250
11-Intro./origin Mercury by Bob Wood, Silver Streak's sidekick; conclusion Claw vs. Daredevil by Rico; in 'Presto Martin,' 2nd pg., newspaper says 'Roussos does it again' 171 342 513 1086 1868 2650
12-Daredevil-c by Rico; Lance Hale finds lost valley w/cave men, battles dinosaurs, sabre-toothed cats; his last app. 145 290 435 921 1586 2250
13-Origin Thun-Dohr. Bingham Boys app. 139 278 417 883 1517 2150
14-Classic Nazi skull men-c 226 452 678 1446 2473 3500
15-Classic Mummy horror-c 206 412 618 1318 2259 3200
16-Hitler-c 271 542 813 1734 2967 4200
17-Last Daredevil issue. 135 270 405 864 1482 2100
18-The Saint begins (2/42, 1st app.) by Leslie Charteris (see Movie Comics #2 by DC); The Saint-c 129 258 387 826 1413 2000
19,20 (1942)-Ned of the Navy app. 20-Last Captain Battle, Dickie Dean & Cloud Curtis; Red Reed, Alonzo Appleseed only app.; Wolverton's Scoop Scuttle app. 63 126 189 403 689 975
21-Hitler app. in strip on cover; Wolverton's Scoop Scuttle app. 77 154 231 493 847 1200
23(1946(An Atomic Comic)-Reprints; bondage-c 90 180 270 576 988 1400
nn(2/46)(Newsbook Publ.)-R-/S.S. story from #4-7 plus 2 Captain Fearless stories, all in color; Dick Briefer bondage/torture-c w/torture meter (scarce) 226 452 678 1446 2473 3500

NOTE: **Jack Binder** *a-8-12, 15; c-3, 4, 13-15, 17.* **Dick Briefer** *a-9-20.* **Jack Cole** *a-(Claw)-#2, 3, 6-10. (Daredevil)-#6-10, (Dickie Dean)-#3-10, (Pirate Prince)-#7, (Silver Streak)-#4-8, nn; c-5 (Silver Streak), 6 (Claw), 7, 8 (Daredevil).* **Bill Everett** *Red Reed begins #20.* **Fred Guardineer** *a-#8-12.* **Don Rico** *a-11-17 (Daredevil), 15, 19 (Silver Streak); c-11, 12, 16.* **Joe Simon** *a-2 (Solar Patrol), 3 (Silver Streak); c-2.* **Basil Wolverton** *a-20.* **Bob Wood** *a-8-15 (Presto Martin), 9 (Silver Streak); c-9, 10. Captain Battle c-11, 13-15, 17. Claw c-#1, 2, 6-8. Daredevil c-7, 8, 12. Dickie Dean c-19. Ned of the Navy c-20 (war). The Saint c-18. Silver Streak c-5, 10, 16, 23.*

SILVER STREAK COMICS (Homage with Golden Age size and Golden Age art styles)
Image Comics: No. 24, Dec, 2009 ($3.99, one-shot)

24-New Daredevil, Claw, Silver Streak & Captain Battle stories; Larsen, Grist, Gilbert-a 5.00

SILVER SURFER (See Fantastic Four, Fantasy Masterpieces V2#1, Fireside Book Series, Marvel Graphic Novel, Marvel Presents #8, Marvel's Greatest Comics & Tales To Astonish #92)

SILVER SURFER, THE (Also see Essential Silver Surfer)
Marvel Comics Group: Aug, 1968 - No. 18, Sept, 1970; June, 1982

1-More detailed origin by John Buscema (p); The Watcher back-up stories begin (origin), end #7; (No. 1-7: 25¢, 68 pgs.) 59 118 177 472 1061 1650
2-1st app. Badoon 19 38 57 131 291 450
3-1st app. Mephisto 20 40 60 138 307 475
4-Lower distribution; Thor & Loki app. 44 88 132 326 738 1150
5-7-Last giant size. 5-The Stranger app.; Fantastic Four app. 6-Brunner inks. 7-(8/69)-Early cameo Frankenstein's monster (see X-Men #40) 12 24 36 84 185 285
8-10: 8-18-(15¢ issues) 10 20 30 68 144 220
11-13,15-18: 15-Silver Surfer vs. Human Torch; Fantastic Four app. 17-Nick Fury app. 18-Vs. The Inhumans; Kirby-a; Trimpe-c 10 20 30 64 132 200
14-Spider-Man x-over 15 30 45 105 233 360
... Omnibus Vol. 1 Hardcover (2007, $74.99, dustjacket) r/#1-18 re-colored with original letter pages, Fantastic Four Annual #5 & Not Brand Echh #13; Lee and Buscema bios 75.00
V2#1 (6/82, 52 pgs.)-Byrne-c/a 2 4 6 9 12 15

NOTE: **Adkins** *a-8-15i.* **Brunner** *a-6i.* **J. Buscema** *a-1-17p.* **Colan** *a-1-3p.* **Reinman** *a-1-4i. #1-14 were reprinted in Fantasy Masterpieces V2#1-14.*

SILVER SURFER (Volume 3) (See Marvel Graphic Novel #38)
Marvel Comics Group: V3#1, July, 1987 - No. 146, Nov, 1998

1-Double-size ($1.25)-Englehart & Rogers-s/a begins; vs. the Champion; Fantastic Four app.

Silver Surfer #50 © MAR

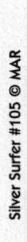

Silver Surfer #105 © MAR

Silver Surfer #140 © MAR

GD VG FN VF VF/NM NM-
2.0 4.0 6.0 8.0 9.0 9.2

w/She-Hulk; Nova (Frankie Raye) & Galactus app; Surfers exile on Earth ends
2 4 6 8 10 12
2-9: 2-Surfer returns to Zenn-La; Shalla-Bal app. as Empress of Zenn-La; Skrulls app.; Surfer story next in West Coat Avengers Annual #2 and Avengers Annual #16. 3-Collector & Champion app.; Surfer vs. the Runner; re-intro Mantis (not seen since 1975). 4-Elders of the Universe app.; Collector, Champion, Runner, Gardener, Contemplator, Grandmaster & Possessor; 1st app. of Astronomer, Obliterator & Trader; Ego revealed as an Elder; origin Mantis. 5-vs. the Obliterator. 6-Origin of the Obliterator. 7-Supreme Intelligence & the Elders app. 8-Supreme Intelligence app.; Surfer gains the Soul Gem. 9-Elders vs. Galactus; six Soul Gems app. 6.00
10-Galactus absorbs the Elders; Eternity app. 1 3 4 6 8 9
11-14: 11-1st app. Reptyl, Clumsy Foulup & the fake Surfer; Nova (Frankie Raye) app. 12-Death of fake Contemplator; Reptyl & Nova (Frankie Raye) app. 13-Ronan the Accuser vs. Surfer and Nova (Frankie Raye); fake Surfer app.; last Rogers-a. 14-Origin & death of the fake Surfer; Ronan app.; Nova (Frankie Raye) app.; story continues in Surfer Ann. #1 5.00
15,16: 15-Ron Lim-c/a begin (9/88); Soul Gems app.; Reed, Sue and Franklin of the Fantastic Four app.; Galactus & Nova (Frankie Raye), Elders of the Universe app.: Astronomer, Possessor & Trader. 16-Astromoner, Trader & In-Betweener app.; brief x-over w/Fantastic Four #319 6.00
17,18: 17-Elders of the Universe, In-Betweener, Death & Galactus app. 18-Galactus vs. the In-Betweener; Elders of the Universe, the Soul Gems & Lord Order & Master Chaos app.
1 2 3 5 6 7
19,20-Firelord & Starfox app. 5.00
21-24,26-30,32,33,39-43: 21-vs. the Obliterator. 22-Ego the Living Planet app. 26-Super-Skrull app. 27-Stranger & Super-Skrull app. 28-Death of Super-Skrull; Reptyl app. 29-Midnight Sun app; death of Reptyl. 30-Midnight Sun & the Stranger app. 32,33-Jim Valentino-s; 33-Impossible Man app. 39-Alan Grant scripts. 40-43-Surfer in Dynamo City 4.00
25,31-($1.50, 52 pgs.) 25-New Kree/Skrull war; Badoon app; Skrulls regain their shape-shifting ability. 31-Conclusion of Kree/Skrull war; Stranger & the Living Tribunal app. 5.00
34-Thanos returns (cameo); Starlin scripts begin; Death app.
3 6 9 14 20 25
35-38: 35-1st full Thanos in Silver Surfer (3/90); reintro Drax the Destroyer on last pg. (cameo). 36-Recaps history of Thanos, Captain Marvel & Warlock app. in recap. 37-Full reintro Drax the Destroyer; Drax-c. 38-Silver Surfer battles Thanos; Nebula app; Thanos story continues in Thanos Quest #1-2 1 3 4 6 8 10
44-Classic Thanos-c; 1st app. of the Infinity Gauntlet; Thanos defeats the Surfer & Drax; Mephisto cameo 4 8 12 27 44 60
45-Thanos-c; Mephisto app.; origin of the Infinity Gems
3 6 9 14 20 25
46-Return of Adam Warlock (2/91); reintro Gamora & Pip the Troll (within Soul World)
2 4 6 11 16 20
47-49: 47-Warlock vs. Drax. 48-Galactus app; last Starlin scripts (also #50). 49-Thanos & Mephisto app.; Ron Marz scripts begin 1 3 4 6 8 10
50-($1.50, 52 pgs.)-Embossed & silver foil-c; Silver Surfer has brief battle w/Thanos; story cont'd in Infinity Gauntlet #1; extended origin flashback to the Silver Surfer's life on Zenn-La 2 4 6 9 12 15
50-2nd & 3rd printings 5.00
51-59-Infinity Gauntlet x-overs; 51-Galactus and Nova (Frankie Raye) app. 52-Firelord vs. Drax; continued in Infinity Gauntlet #2. 53-Death of Clumsy Foulup. 54-vs the Rhino; Hulk cameo. 55,56-Thanos kills everyone (Surfer dream sequence); Warlock app; continued in Infinity Gauntlet #4. 57-x-over w/Infinity Gauntlet #4. 58-Defenders app. (dream sequence); Warlock app. 59-Warlock, Dr. Strange, Dr. Doom, Thor, Firelord, Drax & Thanos app; concluded in Infinity Gauntlet #6 5.00
60-69,71-73: 60-vs. Midnight Sun; Warlock & Dr. Strange cameo; Black Bolt, Gorgon & Karnak of the Inhumans app. 61-Collector app. 63-Captain Marvel app. 64-Collector app. 65-Reptyl returns. 66-Mistress Love & Master Hate app. 67-69-Infinity War x-overs. 67-Continued from Infinity War #1; x-over w/Dr. Strange #42; Nebula, Galactus, Nova (Frankie Raye) & Dr. Strange app; Magus cameo; continued in Infinity War #2. 68,69-Galactus, Nova & Dr. Strange app. 69-Magus cameo; continues in Infinity War #3. 71-Herald Ordeal Pt. 2; Nebula, Firelord & Galactus app; Surfer vs. Morg. 72-Herald Ordeal Pt. 3; 1st app. Cyborg Nebula (as seen in the GOTG movie); Firelord, Nova, Galactus & Morg app. 73-Herald Ordeal Pt. 4; reintro Gabriel the Airwalker; Firelord, Galactus, Nova, Morg app; Terrax cameo 3.00
70,74: Herald Ordeal Pts.1,5. 70-1st app. Morg (becomes the new Herald of Galactus), Nova released of her duties; Nebula app. 74-Terrax, Firelord, Airwalker, Nova, Nebula app. 4.00
75-($2.50, 52 pgs.)-Embossed foil-c; Lim-c/a; Herald Ordeal Pt. 6; Surfer, Firelord, Airwalker, Terrax & Nova vs. Morg; death of Nova; Morg stripped of the power cosmic; Firelord & Airwalker resume Herald duties 4.00
76-81,83-87,90-97: 76-Origin Jack of Hearts retold; Galactus, Airwalker, Firelord & Nebula app.; Morg cameo. 77-Jack of Hearts & Nebula app; return of Morg. 78-New Jack of Hearts costume; Nebula, Morg & Galactus app. 79-Captain Atlas & Dr. Minerva app.; Morg vs. Terrax; Gladiator & Beta Ray Bill cameo. 80-1st app. Ganymede (named in issue #81); Morg vs. Terrax. 81-1st cameo app. Tyrant; Morg, Terrax, Gladiator, Beta Ray Bill cameos. 83-85-Infinity Crusade x-overs. 83-Surfer vs. Firelord; x-over w/Infinity Crusade #3; Thanos cameo; cont'd in Infinity Crusade #4. 84-Thanos app. 85-Wonder Man & Storm vs. Surfer; concluded in Infinity Crusade #6. 86-Blood & Thunder Pt. 2; cont'd from Thor #468; Surfer & Beta Ray Bill vs. insane Thor; Pip the Troll & Warlock cameo; cont'd in Warlock Chronicles #6. 87-Blood & Thunder Pt. 6; cont'd from Thor #469; Dr. Strange, Warlock & the Infinity Watch app; cont'd in Warlock Chronicles #7. 89-Colleen Doran-a(p). 90-Legacy (son of Capt. Marvel) app. 92-Marvel Masterprints card insert; last Lim-a. 93-Fantastic Four app; Thing, Human Torch & Ant-Man (Scott Lang); Spider-Man cameo. 94-Fantastic Four & Warlock and the Infinity Watch app. 95-Fantastic Four app.; Hulk cameo. 97-Terrax app; Champion cameo 3.00

GD VG FN VF VF/NM NM-
2.0 4.0 6.0 8.0 9.0 9.2

82-($1.75. 52 pgs.)-Surfer, Morg, Terrax, Gladiator, Beta Ray Bill, Jack of Hearts & Ganymede vs. Tyrant; Galactus app. 4.00
88,99: 88-Blood & Thunder Pt. 10-cont'd from Thor #470; Thanos vs. insane Thor; Dr. Strange, Warlock & the Infinity Watch app; cont'd in Warlock Chronicles #8; 'Kay-bee Toys' coupon insert for Ghost Rider 'Hot Pursuit' comic; 7-pg. Punisher 'Suicide Run' advertisement; 7-pg. 'Juice' magazine insert featuring interviews with the New Warriors. 99-Mephisto cameo 4.00
98-vs. Champion; Drax & Thanos app. 5.00
100-($2.25, 52 pgs.)-Wraparound-c; vs. Mephisto 6.00
100-($3.95, 52 pgs.)-Enhanced-silver holofoil-c 4.00
101-108,110: 101-Tyrant cameo; Surfer returns to Zenn-La; Shalla-Bal app. 102-Galactus & Morg app; Tyrant cameo; last Marz script. 104-Morg app. Galactus, Morg & Legacy app; Surfer vs. Super-Skrull; 4-pg Rune/Silver Surfer preview. 106-Galactus, Morg & Tyrant app. 108-Tyrant vs. Galactus; Morg & Legacy app. 110-Legacy & Nebula app; John Buscema-a. 4.00
109-Tyrant vs. Galactus; Legacy app.; Morg no longer Herald. 5.00
111-121: 111-New direction; Pérez scripts begin. 112-1st app. Uni-Lord. 114-Watcher app. 120-vs. Uni-Lord. 121-End of the Uni-Lord saga; Beta Ray Bill & Quasar cameo 4.00
122-Legacy & Beta Ray Bill app. 5.00
123-124,126-127,129-130: 123-1st Dematteis script; Surfer returns to Earth; Alicia Masters app. 124-Kymaera (Namorita) app. 126-Dr. Strange app. 127-Alicia Masters & the Puppet Master app. 130-Surfer learns that Zenn-La has been destroyed; Galactus app. 4.00
125 ($2.95)-Wraparound-c; vs. Hulk-c/app. 5.00
128-Spider-Man & Daredevil-c/app. 1 3 4 6 8 10
131-134: 131-Galactus app. 133-Puppet Master app. 134-Scrier & The Other app. 4.00
135-140: 135-Agatha Harkness, Scrier & the Thing app. 136,137-Scrier & Mephisto app. 138-Thing app. 140-Jon J. Muth-a begins 6.00
141-144: 143,144-Psycho-Man app. 1 2 3 4 6 7
145-Alicia Masters; Surfer returns to Earth 1 2 3 4 6 8
146-Firelord app; last issue. 2 4 6 9 12 15
#(-1) Flashback (7/97)-Stan Lee app; 1st app. The Other; Galactus app. 3.00
Annual 1 (1988, $1.75)-Evolutionary War Pt. 3; continued from Punisher Annual #1; 1st Ron Lim-a on Silver Surfer (20 pg. back-up story & pin-ups); Eternals app. Surfer & Super-Skrull team-up; Mantis app.; story continues in West Coast Avengers #37; Evolutionary War continues in New Mutants Annual #4 5.00
Annual 2 (1989, $2.00)-Atlantis Attacks Pt. 1; Ghaur the Deviant app; Dr. Strange cameo; story continues in Iron Man Annual #10 4.00
Annual 3-6: 3-(1990, $2.00)-Lifeform Pt. 4; continued from Punisher Annual #3. 4-(1991, $2.00)-The Korvac Quest Pt. 3; continued from Thor Annual #16; 3-pg. origin story; Silver Surfer battles the Guardians of the Galaxy (30th Century version); continued in Guardians of the Galaxy Annual #1. 5-(1992, $2.25)- Return of the Defenders Pt. 3; continued from Namor the Sub-Mariner Annual #2; Hulk & Dr. Strange app.; continued in Dr. Strange Annual #2; Nebula app. in Firelord & Starfox back-up story. 6-(1993, $2.95)-Polybagged w/trading card; 1st app. Legacy; card is by Lim/Austin; Surfer & Legacy vs. Ronan the Accuser; Terrax, Jack of Hearts & Ganymede back up features 3.00
Annual 7-(1994, $2.95)-Morg resumes being Herald to Galactus; Firelord leaves; Legacy app. in back-up 4.00
Annual '97-($2.99)-Scrier app. Annual '98-($2.99)..& Thor; vs. Millennius; Avengers app. 4.00
...Dangerous Artifacts-(1996, 48 pgs.)-Marz scripts w/Claudio Castellini-a; Galactus & Thanos app; 1st app. White Raven 1 2 3 5 6 8
Graphic Novel (1988, HC, $14.95)-Judgment Day; Lee-s/Buscema-a; Galactus vs. Mephisto 30.00
Graphic Novel (1988, SC, $10.95)-Judgment Day; Jusko-c 20.00
Graphic Novel (1990, HC, $16.95)-The Enslavers; Stan Lee-s & Pollard-a; non-canon Marvel universe story 25.00
Graphic Novel (1991, SC, $12.95)-Homecoming; Starlin-a; death of Shalla-Bal 15.00
Inner Demons TPB (4/98, $3.50)r/#123,125,126 5.00
...: Rebirth of Thanos TPB (2006, $24.99) r/#34-38, Thanos Quest #1,2; Logan's Run #6 25.00
...: The First Coming of Galactus nn (11/92, $5.95, 68 pgs.)-Reprints Fantastic Four #48-50 with new Lim-c 6.00
Wizard 1/2 2 4 6 9 12 15

NOTE: *Austin c(i)-7, 8, 71, 73, 74, 76, 79.* ***Cowan*** *a-143,146.* ***Cully Hamner*** *a-83p.* ***Ron Lim*** *a(p)-15-31, 33-38, 40-55, (56, 57-part-p), 60-65, 73-82, Annual 2, 4; c(p)-15-31, 32-38, 40-84, 86-92, Annual 2, 4-6.* ***Muth*** *c/a-140-142,144,145.* ***M. Rogers*** *a-1-10, 12, 19, 21; c-1-9, 11, 12, 21.*

Silver Surfer (2016 series) #3 © MAR

Simpsons Comics #218 © Bongo

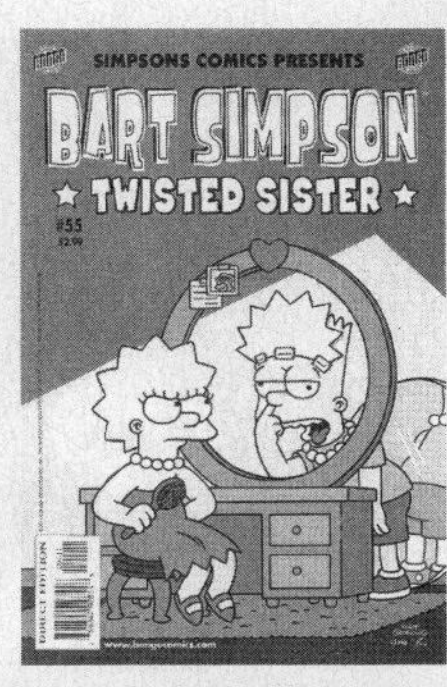

Simpsons Comics Presents Bart Simpson #55 © Bongo

GD 2.0 | VG 4.0 | FN 6.0 | VF 8.0 | VF/NM 9.0 | NM- 9.2

SILVER SURFER (Volume 4)
Marvel Comics: Sept, 2003 - No. 14, Dec, 2004 ($2.25/$2.99)
1-6: 1-Milx-a; Jusko-c. 2-Jae Lee-c 3.00
7-14-($2.99) 3.00
...Vol. 1: Communion (2004, $14.99) r/#1-6 15.00

SILVER SURFER (Volume 5)
Marvel Comics: Apr, 2011 - No. 5, Aug, 2011 ($2.99, limited series)
1-5-Pagulayan-c. 1-Segovia-a. 4,5-Fantastic Four app. 3.00

SILVER SURFER (6th series)
Marvel Comics: May, 2014 - No. 15, Jan, 2016 ($3.99)
1-10: 1-Dan Slott-s/Michael Allred-a/c. 3-Guardians of the Galaxy app. 8-10-Galactus app. 4.00
11-($4.99) Story runs upside down on top or bottom halves of the pages 5.00
12-15: 13-15-Secret Wars tie-in 4.00

SILVER SURFER (7th series)
Marvel Comics: Mar, 2016 - Present ($3.99)
1-5,7,8-Slott-s/Allred-a. 1-4-The Thing app. 3-50th Anniversary issue; Shalla Bal app. 4.00
6-(10/16, $4.99) 200th issue; Spider-Man app.; cover gallery 5.00

SILVER SURFER, THE
Marvel Comics (Epic): Dec, 1988 - No. 2, Jan, 1989 ($1.00, lim. series)
1-By Stan Lee scripts & Moebius-c/a 1 2 3 5 6 8
2 5.00
HC (1988, $19.95, dust jacket) r/#1,2; "Making Of" text section and sketch pages 30.00
... By Stan Lee & Moebius (3/13, $7.99) r/#1&2; bonus production diary from Moebius 8.00
...: Parable ('98, $5.99) r/#1&2 6.00

SILVER SURFER: IN THY NAME
Marvel Comics: Jan, 2008 - No. 4, Apr, 2008 ($2.99, limited series)
1-4-Spurrier-s/Huat-a. 1-Turner-c. 2-Dell'Otto-c. 3-Paul Pope-c. 4-Galactus app. 3.00

SILVER SURFER: LOFTIER THAN MORTALS
Marvel Comics: Oct, 1999 - No. 2, Oct, 1999 ($2.50, limited series)
1,2-Remix of Fantastic Four #57-60; Velluto-a 3.00

SILVER SURFER: REQUIEM
Marvel Comics: July, 2007 - No. 4, Oct, 2007 ($3.99, limited series)
1-4-Straczynski-s/Ribic-a. 1-Origin retold; Fantastic Four app. 4.00
HC (2007, $19.99) r/#1-4, Ribic cover sketches 20.00

SILVER SURFER/SUPERMAN
Marvel Comics: 1996 ($5.95,one-shot)
1-Perez-s/Lim-c/a(p) 6.00

SILVER SURFER VS. DRACULA
Marvel Comics: Feb, 1994 ($1.75, one-shot)
1-r/Tomb of Dracula #50; Everett Vampire-r/Venus #19; Howard the Duck back-up by Brunner; Lim-c(p) 4.00

SILVER SURFER/WARLOCK: RESURRECTION
Marvel Comics: Mar, 1993 - No. 4, June, 1993 ($2.50, limited series)
1-4-Starlin-c/a & scripts. 1-Surfer joins Warlock & the Infinity Watch to rescue Shalla-Bal; story continued from the 'Homecoming' GN. 2-Death app.; Mephisto cameo. 3-Surfer vs. Mephisto. 4-Warlock vs. Mephisto; Shalla-Bal revived. 4.00

SILVER SURFER/WEAPON ZERO
Marvel Comics: Apr, 1997 ($2.95, one-shot)
1-"Devil's Reign" pt. 8 3.00

SILVERTIP (Max Brand)
Dell Publishing Co.: No. 491, Aug, 1953 - No. 898, May, 1958
Four Color 491 (#1); all painted-c 8 16 24 52 99 145
Four Color 572,608,637,667,731,789,898-Kinstler-a 5 10 15 34 60 85
Four Color 835 5 10 15 34 60 85

SIMON DARK
DC Comics: Dec, 2007 - No. 18, May, 2009 ($2.99)
1-Intro. Simon Dark; Steve Niles-s/Scott Hampton-a/c 4.00
1-Second printing with full face variant cover 3.00
2-18 3.00
...: Ashes TPB (2009, $17.99) r/#7-12 18.00
...: The Game of Life TPB (2009, $17.99) r/#13-18 18.00
...: What Simon Does TPB (2008, $14.99) r/#1-6 18.00

SIMPSONS COMICS (See Bartman, Futurama, Itchy & Scratchy & Radioactive Man)
Bongo Comics Group: 1993 - Present ($1.95/$2.50/$2.99)
1-($2.25)-FF#1-c swipe; pull-out poster; flip book 3 6 9 14 20 25
2-5: 2-Patty & Selma flip-c/sty. 3-Krusty, Agent of K.L.O.W.N. flip-c/story. 4-Infinity-c; flip-c of Busman #1; w/trading card. 5-Wraparound-c w/trading card 1 2 3 5 6 8
6-40: All Flip books. 6-w/Chief Wiggum's "Crime Comics". 7-w/"McBain Comics". 8-w/"Edna, Queen of the Congo". 9-w/"Barney Gumble". 10-w/"Apu". 11-w/"Homer". 12-w/"White Knuckled War Stories". 13-w/"Jimbo Jones' Wedgie Comics". 14-w/"Grampa". 15-w/"Itchy & Scratchy". 16-w/"Bongo Grab Bag". 17-w/"Headlight Comics". 18-w/"Milhouse". 19,20-w/"Roswell." 21,22-w/"Roswell". 23-w/"Hellfire Comics". 24-w/"Lil' Homey". 36-39-Flip book w/Radioactive Man 5.00
41-49,51-99: 43-Flip book w/Poochie. 52-Dini-s. 77-Dixon-s. 85-Begin $2.99-c 4.00
50-($5.95) Wraparound-c; 80 pgs.; square-bound 1 2 3 5 6 8
100-($6.99) 100 pgs.; square-bound; clip issue of past highlights 1 2 3 5 6 8
101-182,184-199,201-224: 102-Barks Ducks homage. 117-Hank Scorpio app. 122-Archie spoof. 132-Movie poster enclosed. 132-133-Two-parter. 144-Flying Hellfish flashback. 150-w/Poster. 163-Aragonés-s/a. 218-Guardians of the Galaxy spoof 3.00
183-Archie Comics #1 cover swipe; Archie homage with Stan Goldberg-a 3.00
200-(2013, $4.99) Wraparound-c; short stories incl. Dorkin-s/a; Matt Groening cameo 5.00
225-237-($3.99) 225-Bonus back-up 1970s Eddie & Lou story. 237-Bartman app. 4.00
... A Go-Go (1999, $11.95)-r/#32-35; ...Big Bonanza (1998, $11.95)-r/#28-31, ...Extravaganza (1994, $10.00)-r/#1-4; infinity-c, ...On Parade (1998, $11.95)-r/#24-27, ...Simpsorama (1996, $10.95)-r/#11-14 12.00
Simpsons Classics 1-30 (2004-Present, $3.99, magazine-size, quarterly) reprints 4.00
Simpsons Comics Barn Burner ('04, $14.95) r/#57-61,63 15.00
Simpsons Comics Beach Blanket Bongo ('07, $14.95) r/#71-75,77 15.00
Simpsons Comics Belly Buster ('04, $14.95) r/#49,51,53-56 15.00
Simpsons Comics Hit the Road! ('08, $15.95) r/#85,86,88,89,90 16.00
Simpsons Comics Jam-Packed Jamboree ('06, $14.95) r/#64-69 15.00
Simpsons Comics Madness ('03, $14.95) r/#43-48 15.00
Simpsons Comics Royale ('01, $14.95) r/various Bongo issues 15.00
Simpsons Comics Treasure Trove 1-4 ('08-'09, $3.99, 6" x 8") r/various Bongo issues 4.00
Simpsons Summer Shindig ('07-'15, $4.99) 1-9-Anthology. 1-Batman/Ripken insert 5.00
Simpsons Winter Wing Ding ('06-'14, $4.99) 1-10-Holiday anthology. 1-Dini-s 5.00

SIMPSONS COMICS AND STORIES
Welsh Publishing Group: 1993 ($2.95, one-shot)
1-(Direct Sale)-Polybagged w/Bartman poster 3 6 9 14 20 25
1-(Newsstand Edition)-Without poster 6.00

SIMPSONS COMICS PRESENTS BART SIMPSON
Bongo Comics Group: 2000 - No. 100, 2016 ($2.50/$2.99)
1-99: 7-9-Dan DeCarlo-layouts. 13-Begin $2.99-c. 17,37-Bartman app. 50-Aragonés-s/a 3.00
100-($4.99) 100-year old Bart, Mrs. Krabappel, Fruit Bat Man app. 5.00
The Big Book of Bart Simpson TPB (2002, $12.95) r/#1-4 15.00
The Big Bad Book of Bart Simpson TPB (2003, $12.95) r/#5-8 15.00
The Big Bratty Book of Bart Simpson TPB (2004, $12.95) r/#9-12 15.00
The Big Beefy Book of Bart Simpson TPB (2005, $13.95) r/#13-16 15.00
The Big Bouncy Book of Bart Simpson TPB (2006, $13.95) r/#17-20 15.00
The Big Beastly Book of Bart Simpson TPB (2007, $14.95) r/#21-24 15.00
The Big Brilliant Book of Bart Simpson TPB (2008, $14.95) r/#25-28 15.00

SIMPSONS FUTURAMA CROSSOVER CRISIS II (TV) (Also see Futurama/Simpsons Infinitely Secret Crossover Crisis)
Bongo Comics: 2005 - No. 2, 2005 ($3.00, limited series)
1,2-The Professor brings the Simpsons' Springfield crew to the 31st century 3.00

SIMPSONS ILLUSTRATED (TV)
Bongo Comics: 2012 - Present ($3.99, quarterly)
1-20-Reprints 4.00
21-27-($4.99) 25-All-monster issue 5.00

SIMPSONS ONE-SHOT WONDERS (TV)
Bongo Comics: 2012 - 2014 ($2.99/$3.99)
...: Bart Simpson's Pal Milhouse 1 - Short stories; centerfold with decal 3.00
...: Duffman 1 ($3.99) - Green Lantern spoof; centerfold with die-cut Duffman mask 4.00
...: Grampa 1 ($3.99) - "Choose Your Adventure" format; wraparound-c 4.00
...: Jimbo 1 ($3.99) - Short stories; centerfold with die-cut skull sticker 4.00
...: Kang & Kodos 1 ($3.99) - Short stories; centerfold with bumper stickers 4.00
...: Li'l Homer 1 - Short stories of Homer's childhood; centerfold with cut-outs 3.00
...: Lisa 1 ($3.99) - Short stories by Matsumoto and others; sticker page centerfold 4.00
...: Maggie 1 - Short stories by Aragonés and others; paperdoll centerfold; Aragonés-c 3.00
...: McBain 1 ($3.99) - Entire issue unfolds for a poster on the back 4.00
...: Mr. Burns 1 ($3.99) - Short stories incl. Richie Rich spoof; Fruit Bat Man mask 4.00
...: Professor Frink 1 ($3.99) - Short stories; 3-D glasses insert; 3-D story and back-c 4.00
...: Ralph Wiggums Comics 1 - Short stories by Aragonés and others 3.00

Sin City: A Dame to Kill For #1 © Frank Miller

Sinestro #15 © DC

Sins of Youth: JLA Jr. #1 © DC

	GD 2.0	VG 4.0	FN 6.0	VF 8.0	VF/NM 9.0	NM- 9.2

SIMPSONS SUPER SPECTACULAR (TV)
Bongo Comics: 2006 - Present ($2.99)

1-16: 2-Bartman, Stretch Dude and The Cupcake Kid team up; back-up story Brereton-a. 5-Fradon-a on Metamorpho spoof. 8-Spirit spoof. 9,10,14-16-Radioactive Man app. 3.00

SINBAD, JR (TV Cartoon)
Dell Publishing Co.: Sept-Nov, 1965 - No. 3, May, 1966

	GD	VG	FN	VF	VF/NM	NM-
1	4	8	12	23	37	50
2,3	3	6	9	17	26	35

SIN BOLDLY
Image Comics: Dec, 2013 ($3.50, B&W, one-shot)

1-J.M. Linsner-s/a/c; short stories with Sinful Suzi and Obsidian Stone 3.50

SIN CITY (See Dark Horse Presents, A Decade of Dark Horse, & San Diego Comic Con Comics #2,4)
Dark Horse Comics (Legend)

TPB ($15.00) Reprints early DHP stories 15.00
Booze, Broads & Bullets TPB ($15.00) 15.00
Frank Miller's Sin City: One For One (8/10, $1.00) reprints debut story from DHP #51 3.00

SIN CITY (FRANK MILLER'S...) (Reissued TPBs to coincide with the April 2005 movie)
Dark Horse Books: Feb, 2005 ($17.00/$19.00, 6" x 9" format with new Miller covers)

Volume 1: The Hard Goodbye ($17.00) reprints stories from Dark Horse Presents #51-62 and DHP Fifth Anniv. Special; covers and publicity pieces 17.00
Volume 2: A Dame to Kill For ($17.00) r/Sin City: A Dame to Kill For #1-6 17.00
Volume 3: The Big Fat Kill ($17.00) r/Sin City: The Big Fat Kill #1-5; pin-up gallery 17.00
Volume 4: That Yellow Bastard ($19.00) r/Sin City: That Yellow Bastard #1-6; pin-up gallery by Mike Allred, Kyle Baker, Jeff Smith and Bruce Timm; cover gallery 19.00
Volume 5: Family Values ($12.00) r/Sin City: Family Values GN 12.00
Volume 6: Booze, Broads & Bullets ($15.00) r/Sin City: The Babe Wore Red and Other Stories; Silent Night; story from A Decade of Dark Horse; Lost Lonely & Lethal; Sex & Violence; and Just Another Saturday Night 15.00
Volume 7: Hell and Back ($28.00) r/Sin City: Hell and Back #1-9; pin-up gallery 28.00

SIN CITY: A DAME TO KILL FOR
Dark Horse Comics (Legend): Nov, 1993 - No. 6, May, 1994 ($2.95, B&W, limited series)

1-6: Frank Miller-c/a & story in all. 1-1st app. Dwight. 6.00
Limited Edition Hardcover 85.00
Hardcover 25.00
TPB ($15.00) 15.00

SIN CITY: FAMILY VALUES
Dark Horse Comics (Legend): Oct, 1997 ($10.00, B&W, squarebound, one-shot)

nn-Miller-c/a & story 10.00
Limited Edition Hardcover 75.00

SIN CITY: HELL AND BACK
Dark Horse (Maverick): Jul, 1999 - No. 9 ($2.95/$4.95, B&W, limited series)

1-8-Miller-c/a & story. 7-Color 4.00
9-($4.95) 6.00

SIN CITY: JUST ANOTHER SATURDAY NIGHT
Dark Horse Comics (Legend): Aug, 1997 (Wizard 1/2 offer, B&W, one-shot)

	GD	VG	FN	VF	VF/NM	NM-
1/2-Miller-c/a & story	1	2	3	5	6	8
nn (10/98, $2.50) r/#1/2						4.00

SIN CITY: LOST, LONELY & LETHAL
Dark Horse Comics (Legend): Dec, 1996 ($2.95, B&W and blue, one-shot)

nn-Miller-c/s/a; w/pin-ups 5.00

SIN CITY: SEX AND VIOLENCE
Dark Horse Comics (Legend): Mar, 1997 ($2.95, B&W and blue, one-shot)

nn-Miller-c/a & story 5.00

SIN CITY: SILENT NIGHT
Dark Horse Comics (Legend): Dec, 1995 ($2.95, B&W, one-shot)

1-Miller-c/a & story; Marv app. 6.00

SIN CITY: THAT YELLOW BASTARD (Second Ed. TPB listed under Sin City (Frank Miller's...)
Dark Horse Comics (Legend): Feb, 1996 - No. 6, July, 1996 ($2.95/$3.50, B&W and yellow, limited series)

1-5: Miller-c/a & story in all. 1-1st app. Hartigan. 6.00
6-($3.50) Error & corrected 6.00
Limited Edition Hardcover 25.00
TPB ($15.00) 15.00

SIN CITY: THE BABE WORE RED AND OTHER STORIES
Dark Horse Comics (Legend): Nov, 1994 ($2.95, B&W and red, one-shot)

1-r/serial run in Previews as well as other stories; Miller-c/a & scripts; Dwight app. 6.00

SIN CITY: THE BIG FAT KILL (Second Edition TPB listed under Sin City (Frank Miller's...)
Dark Horse Comics (Legend): Nov, 1994 - No. 5, Mar, 1995 ($2.95, B&W, limited series)

1-5-Miller story & art in all; Dwight app. 6.00
Hardcover 25.00
TPB ($15.00) 15.00

SIN CITY: THE FRANK MILLER LIBRARY
Dark Horse Books: Set 1, Nov, 2005; Set 2, Mar, 2006 ($150, slipcased hardcover, 8" x 12")

Set 1 - Individual hardcovers for Volume 1: The Hard Goodbye, Volume 2: A Dame to Kill For, Volume 3: The Big Fat Kill, Volume 4: That Yellow Bastard; new red foil stamped covers; slipcase box is black with red foil graphics 150.00
Set 2 - Individual hardcovers for Volume 5: Family Values, Volume 6: Booze, Broads & Bullets, Volume 7: Hell and Back, new red foil stamped covers; The Art of Sin City red hardcover; slipcase box is black with red foil graphics 150.00

SINDBAD (See Capt. Sindbad under Movie Comics, and Fantastic Voyages of Sindbad)

SINERGY
Image Comics (Shadowline): Nov, 2014 - No. 5, Mar, 2015 ($3.50)

1-5: 1-Oeming & Soma-s/Oeming-a/c 3.50

SINESTRO
DC Comics: Jun, 2014 - No. 23, Jul, 2016 ($2.99)

1-23: 1-Bunn-s/Eaglesham-a; Lyssa Drak & Arkillo app. 6-8-Godhead x-over; New Gods app. 7-Van Sciver-a. 9-11-Mongul app. 15-Lobo app. 16-20-Black Adam app. 17-20-Wonder Woman app. 19,20-Harley Quinn & Superman app. 3.00
Annual 1 (6/15, $4.99) Bunn-s/Eaglesham-c; art by various 5.00
...: Futures End 1 (11/14, $2.99, regular-c) Five years later; Bunn-s/Lima-a/Nowlan-c 3.00
...: Futures End 1 (11/14, $3.99, 3-D cover) 4.00

SINGING GUNS (See Fawcett Movie Comics)

SINGLE SERIES (Comics on Parade #30 on)(Also see John Hix...)
United Features Syndicate: 1938 - No. 28, 1942 (All 68 pgs.)

Note: See Individual Alphabetical Listings for prices

1-Captain and the Kids (#1)
2-Broncho Bill (1939) (#1)
3-Ella Cinders (1939)
4-Li'l Abner (1939) (#1)
5-Fritzi Ritz (#1)
6-Jim Hardy by Dick Moores (#1)
7-Frankie Doodle
8-Peter Pat (On sale 7/14/39)
9-Strange As It Seems
10-Little Mary Mixup
11-Mr. and Mrs. Beans
12-Joe Jinks
13-Looy Dot Dope
14-Billy Make Believe
15-How It Began (1939)
16-Illustrated Gags (1940)-Has ad for Captain and the Kids #1 reprint listed below
17-Danny Dingle
18-Li'l Abner (#2 on-c)
19-Broncho Bill (#2 on-c)
20-Tarzan by Hal Foster
21-Ella Cinders (#2 on-c; on sale 3/19/40)
22-Iron Vic
23-Tailspin Tommy by Hal Forrest (#1)
24-Alice in Wonderland (#1)
25-Abbie and Slats
26-Little Mary Mixup (#2 on-c, 1940)
27-Jim Hardy by Dick Moores (1942)
28-Ella Cinders & Abbie and Slats (1942)
1-Captain and the Kids (1939 reprint)-2nd Edition
1-Fritzi Ritz (1939 reprint)-2nd ed.

NOTE: *Some issues given away at the 1939-40 New York World's Fair (#6).*

SINISTER DEXTER
IDW Publishing: Dec, 2013 - No. 7, Jun, 2014 ($3.99)

1-7: 1-Dan Abnett-s/Andy Clarke-a; two covers by Clarke and Fuso 4.00

SINISTER HOUSE OF SECRET LOVE, THE (Becomes Secrets of Sinister House No. 5 on)
National Periodical Publ.: Oct-Nov, 1971 - No. 4, Apr-May, 1972

	GD	VG	FN	VF	VF/NM	NM-
1 (All 52 pgs.) -Grey-tone-c	13	26	39	91	201	310
2,4	7	14	21	48	89	130
3-Toth-a; Grey-tone-c	8	16	24	51	96	140

SINS OF YOUTH... (Also see Young Justice: Sins of Youth)
DC Comics: May 2000 ($4.95/$2.50, limited crossover series)

Secret Files 1 ($4.95) Short stories and profile pages; Nauck-c 5.00
...Aquaboy/Lagoon Man; Batboy and Robin; JLA Jr.; Kid Flash/Impulse; Starwoman and the JSA, Superman, Jr./Superboy, Sr.; The Secret/ Deadboy, Wonder Girls ($2.50-c) Old and young heroes switch ages 3.00

SIP KIDS (Strangers in Paradise)
Abstract Studio: 2014 - No. 4, 2015 ($4.99, color)

1-4-Strangers in Paradise characters as young kids; Terry Moore-s/a/c 5.00

SIR CHARLES BARKLEY AND THE REFEREE MURDERS
Hamilton Comics: 1993 ($9.95, 8-1/2" x 11", 52 pgs.)

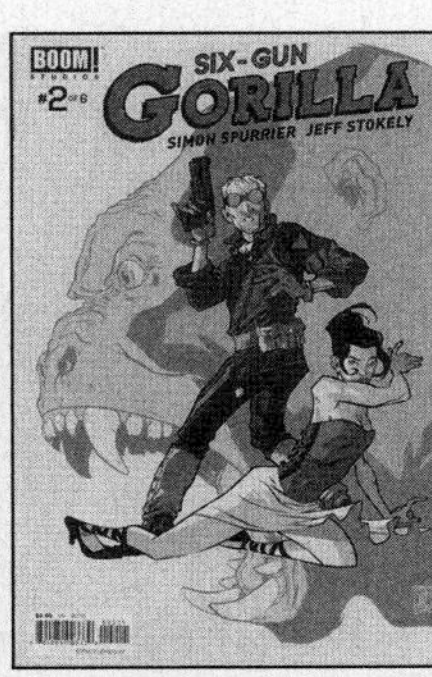

Six-Gun Gorilla #2 © BOOM

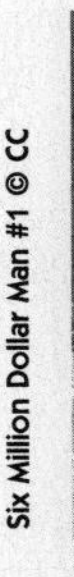
Six Million Dollar Man #1 © CC

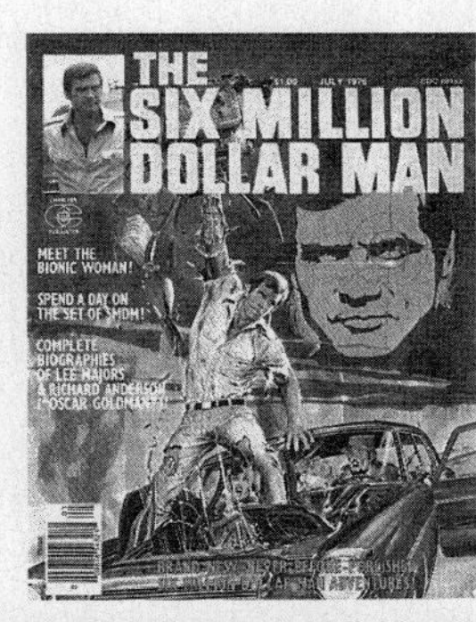

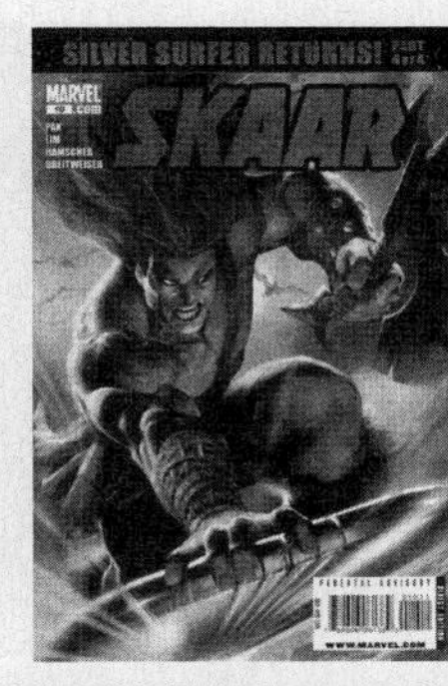

Skaar: Son of Hulk #10 © MAR

	GD 2.0	VG 4.0	FN 6.0	VF 8.0	VF/NM 9.0	NM- 9.2

nn-Photo-c; Sports fantasy comic book fiction (uses real names of NBA superstars). Script by Alan Dean Foster, art by Joe Staton. Comes with bound-in sheet of 35 gummed "Moods of Charles Barkley" stamps. Photo/story on Barkley 2 4 6 9 12 15
Special Edition of 100 copies for charity signed on an affixed book plate by Barkley, Foster & Staton 175.00
Ashcan edition given away to dealers, distributors & promoters (low distribution). Four pages in color, balance of story in b&w 2 4 6 9 12 15

SIR EDWARD GREY, WITCHFINDER: IN THE SERVICE OF ANGELS (From Hellboy)
Dark Horse Comics: July, 2009 - No. 5, Nov, 2009 ($2.99, limited series)
1-5-Mignola-s/c; Stenbeck-a 3.00

SIR EDWARD GREY, WITCHFINDER: THE MYSTERIES OF UNLAND (From Hellboy)
Dark Horse Comics: Jun, 2014 - No. 5, Oct, 2014 ($3.50, limited series)
1-5-Newman & McHugh-s/Crook-a/Tedesco-c 3.50

SIREN (Also see Eliminator & Ultraforce)
Malibu Comics (Ultraverse): Sept, 1995 - No. 3, Dec, 1995 ($1.50)
Infinity, 1-3: Infinity-Black-c & painted-c exists. 1-Regular-c & painted-c; War Machine app. 2-Flip book w/Phoenix Resurrection Pt. 3 3.00
Special 1-(2/96, $1.95, 28 pgs.)-Origin Siren; Marvel Comic's Juggernaut-c/app. 3.00

SIRENS (See George Pérez's Sirens)

SIR LANCELOT (TV)
Dell Publishing Co.: No. 606, Dec, 1954 - No. 775, Mar, 1957
Four Color 606 (not TV) 6 12 18 42 79 115
Four Color 775(...and Brian)-Buscema-a; photo-c 9 18 27 59 117 175

SIR WALTER RALEIGH (Movie)
Dell Publishing Co.: May, 1955 (Based on movie "The Virgin Queen")
Four Color 644-Photo-c 6 12 18 42 79 115

SISTERHOOD OF STEEL (See Eclipse Graphic Adventure Novel #13)
Marvel Comics (Epic Comics): Dec, 1984 -No. 8, Feb, 1986 ($1.50, Baxter paper, mature)
1-8 4.00

SITUATION, THE (TV's Jersey Shore)
Wizard World: July, 2012 (no cover price)
1-Jenkins-s/Caldwell-a; two covers by Horn & Caldwell 3.00

6 BLACK HORSES (See Movie Classics)

SIX FROM SIRIUS
Marvel Comics (Epic Comics): July, 1984 - No. 4, Oct, 1984 ($1.50, limited series, mature)
1-4: Moench scripts; Gulacy-c/a in all 4.00

SIX FROM SIRIUS II
Marvel Comics (Epic Comics): Feb, 1986 - No. 4, May, 1986 ($1.50, limited series, mature)
1-4: Moench scripts; Gulacy-c/a in all 4.00

SIX-GUN GORILLA
BOOM! Studios: Jun, 2013 - No. 6, Nov, 2013 ($3.99, limited series)
1-6: 1-Spurrier-s/Stokely-a 4.00

SIX-GUN HEROES
Fawcett Publications: March, 1950 - No. 23, Nov, 1953 (Photo-c #1-23)
1-Rocky Lane, Hopalong Cassidy, Smiley Burnette begin (same date as Smiley Burnette #1)
31 62 93 186 303 420
2 16 32 48 94 147 200
3-5: 5-Lash LaRue begins 14 28 42 76 108 140
6-15 11 22 33 62 86 110
16-22: 17-Last Smiley Burnette. 18-Monte Hale begins
10 20 30 54 72 90
23-Last Fawcett issue 10 20 30 58 79 100
NOTE: *Hopalong Cassidy photo c-1-3. Monte Hale photo c-18. Rocky Lane photo c-4, 5, 7, 9, 11, 13, 15, 17, 20, 21, 23. Lash LaRue photo c-6, 8, 10, 12, 14, 16, 19, 22.*

SIX-GUN HEROES (Cont'd from Fawcett; Gunmasters #84 on) (See Blue Bird)
Charlton Comics: No. 24, Jan, 1954 - No. 83, Mar-Apr, 1965 (All Vol. 4)
24-Lash LaRue, Hopalong Cassidy, Rocky Lane & Tex Ritter begin; photo-c
14 28 42 80 115 150
25 10 20 30 54 72 90
26-30: 26-Rod Cameron story. 28-Tom Mix begins? 9 18 27 47 61 75
31-40: 38-40-Jingles & Wild Bill Hickok (TV) 8 16 24 42 54 65
41-46,48,50: 41-43-Wild Bill Hickok (TV) 8 16 24 40 50 60
47-Williamson-a, 2 pgs; Torres-a 8 16 24 42 54 65
49-Williamson-a (5 pgs.) 9 18 27 50 65 80
51-56,58-60: 58-Gunmaster app. 3 6 9 19 30 40
57-Origin & 1st app. Gunmaster 4 8 12 25 40 55
61,63-70 3 6 9 16 23 30
62-Origin Gunmaster 3 6 9 19 30 40
71-75,77,78,80-83 2 4 6 13 18 22
76,79: 76-Gunmaster begins. 79-1st app. & origin of Bullet, the Gun-Boy
3 6 9 14 19 24

SIXGUN RANCH (See Luke Short & Four Color #580)

SIX GUNS
Marvel Comics: Jan, 2012 - No. 5, Apr, 2012 ($2.99, limited series)
1-5-Diggle-s/Gianfelice-a; Tarantula and Tex Dawson app. 3.00

SIX-GUN WESTERN
Atlas Comics (CDS): Jan, 1957 - No. 4, July, 1957
1-Crandall-a; two Williamson text illos 21 42 63 126 206 285
2,3-Williamson-a in both 15 30 45 88 137 185
4-Woodbridge-a 13 26 39 72 101 130
NOTE: *Ayers a-2, 3. Maneely a-1; c-2, 3. Orlando a-2. Pakula a-2. Powell a-3. Romita a-1, 4. Severin c-1, 4. Shores a-2.*

SIX MILLION DOLLAR MAN, THE (TV) (Also see The Bionic Man)
Charlton Comics: 6/76 - No. 4, 12/76; No. 5, 10/77; No. 6, 2/78 - No. 9, 6/78
1-Staton-c/a; Lee Majors photo on-c 3 6 9 17 26 35
2-Neal Adams-c; Staton-a 3 6 9 14 20 25
3-9 2 4 6 13 18 22

SIX MILLION DOLLAR MAN, THE (TV)(Magazine)
Charlton Comics: July, 1976 - No. 7, Nov, 1977 (B&W)
1-Neal Adams-c/a 3 6 9 21 33 45
2-Neal Adams-c 3 6 9 16 23 30
3-N. Adams part inks; Chaykin-a 3 6 9 14 19 24
4-7 2 4 6 11 16 20

SIX MILLION DOLLAR MAN, THE: FALL OF MAN (TV)
Dynamite Entertainment: 2016 - No. 5, 2016 ($3.99)
1-5: 1-Van Jensen-s/Ron Salas-a; three covers 4.00

SIX MILLION DOLLAR MAN, THE: SEASON 6 (TV)
Dynamite Entertainment: 2014 - No. 6, 2014 ($3.99)
1-Jim Kuhoric-s/Juan Antonio Ramirez-a; covers by Alex Ross & Ken Haeser & photo-c 4.00
2-6-Two covers by Ross & Haeser on each. 2-Maskatron returns 4.00

SIXPACK AND DOGWELDER: HARD TRAVELIN' HEROZ (See All-Star Section Eight)
DC Comics: Oct, 2016 - No. 6, Mar, 2017 ($3.99, limited series)
1-6-Ennis-s/Braun-a/Dillon-c. 1-Power Girl, Catwoman, & Starfire app. 2-6-Constantine app. 2-The Spectre app. 4.00

SIX STRING SAMURAI
Awesome-Hyperwerks: Sept, 1998 ($2.95)
1-Stinsman & Fraga-a 3.00

1602 WITCH HUNTER ANGELA (Secret Wars tie-in)
Marvel Comics: Aug, 2015 - No. 4, Dec, 2015 ($3.99, limited series)
1-4-Marguerite Bennett-s; Hans & Sauvage-a; The Enchantress app. 4.00

67 SECONDS
Marvel Comics (Epic Comics): 1992 ($15.95, 54 pgs., graphic novel)
nn-James Robinson scripts; Steve Yeowell-c/a 2 4 6 11 14 18

SKAAR: KING OF THE SAVAGE LAND
Marvel Comics: Jun, 2011 - No. 5 ($2.99, limited series)
1-5-Shanna & Ka-Zar app.; Ching-a. 1-Komarck-c. 2-McGuinness-c 3.00

SKAAR: SON OF HULK (Title continues in Son of Hulk #13)(Also see World War Hulk x-over)
Marvel Comics: Aug, 2008 - No. 12, Aug, 2009 ($2.99)
1-Garney-a/Pak-s; 2 covers by Pagulayan and Julie Bell; origin 4.00
1-Second printing - 2 covers by Garney and Hulk movie image 3.00
1-Third printing - Garney sketch variant-c 3.00
2-12: 2-6-Back-up story with Guice-a. 7-12-Silver Surfer app. 3.00
Planet Skaar Prologue 1 (7/09, $3.99) Panosian-a; Fantastic Four & She-Hulk app. 4.00
... Presents - Savage World of Sakaar (11/08, $3.99) Pak-s/art by various; Garney-c 4.00

SKATEMAN
Pacific Comics: Nov, 1983 (Baxter paper, one-shot)
1-Adams-c/a 4.00

SKELETON HAND (...In Secrets of the Supernatural)
American Comics Gr. (B&M Dist. Co.): Sept-Oct, 1952 - No. 6, Jul-Aug, 1953
1 61 122 183 390 670 950
2 39 78 117 240 395 550

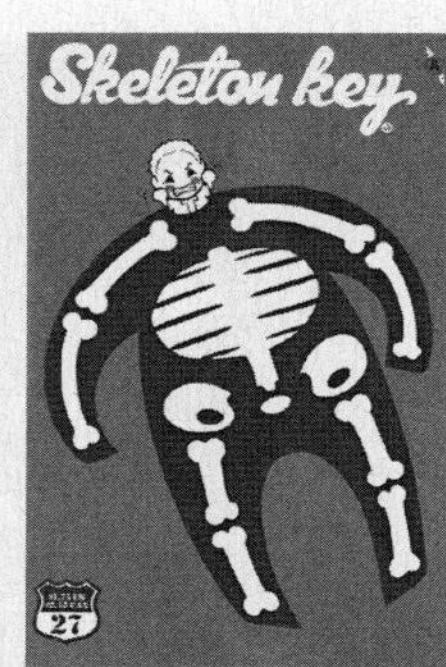

Skeleton Key #27 © Amaze Ink

Skullkickers #31 © Jim Zub

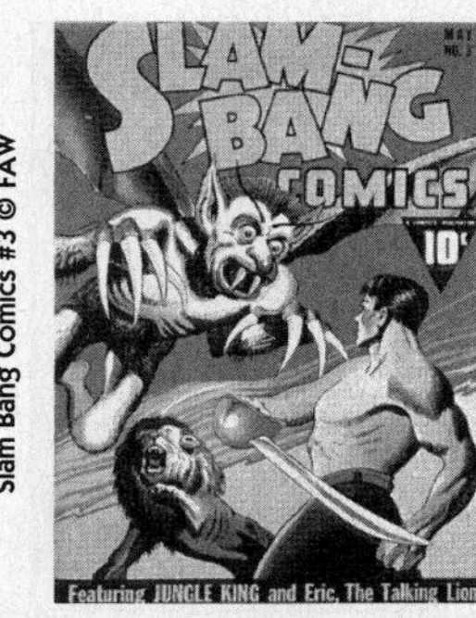

Slam Bang Comics #3 © FAW

	GD 2.0	VG 4.0	FN 6.0	VF 8.0	VF/NM 9.0	NM- 9.2
3-6	34	68	102	199	325	450

SKELETON KEY
Amaze Ink: July, 1995 - No. 30, Jan, 1998 ($1.25/$1.50/$1.75, B&W)

1-30 3.00
Special #1 (2/98, $4.95) Unpublished short stories 5.00
Sugar Kat Special (10/98, $2.95) Halloween stories 3.00
Beyond The Threshold TPB (6/96. $11.95)-r/#1-6 12.00
Cats and Dogs TPB ($12.95)-r/#25-30 13.00
The Celestial Calendar TPB ($19.95)-r/#7-18 20.00
Telling Tales TPB ($12.95)-r/#19-24 13.00

SKELETON KEY (Volume 2)
Amaze Ink: 1999 - No. 4, 1999 ($2.95, B&W)

1-4-Andrew Watson-s/a 3.00

SKELETON WARRIORS
Marvel Comics: Apr, 1995 - No. 4, July, 1995 ($1.50)

1-4: Based on animated series. 3.00

SKIN GRAFT: THE ADVENTURES OF A TATTOOED MAN
DC Comics (Vertigo): July, 1993 - No. 4, Oct, 1993 ($2.50, lim. series, mature)

1-4 3.00

SKINWALKER
Oni Press: May, 2002 - No. 4, Sept, 2002 ($2.95, limited series)

1-4-Hurtt & Dela Cruz-a; Talon-c 3.00
1-(5/05) Free Comic Book Day Edition 3.00

SKI PARTY (See Movie Classics)

SKREEMER
DC Comics: May, 1989 - No. 6, Oct, 1989 ($2.00, limited series, mature)

1-6: Contains graphic violence; Milligan-s 3.00
TPB (2002, $19.95) r/#1-6 20.00

SKRULL KILL KREW
Marvel Comics: Sept, 1995 - No. 5, Dec, 1995 ($2.95, limited series)

1-5: Grant Morrison & Mark Millar scripts; Steve Yeowell-a. 2,3-Cap America app. 5.00
TPB (2006, $16.99) r/#1-5 17.00

SKRULL KILL KREW
Marvel Comics: Jun, 2009 - No. 5, Dec, 2009 ($3.99, limited series)

1-5-Felber-s/Robinson-a 4.00

SKRULLS! (Tie-in to Secret Invasion crossover)
Marvel Comics: 2008 ($4.99, one-shot)

1-Skrull history, profiles of Skrulls, their allies & foes; checklist of appearances; Horn-c 5.00

SKRULLS VS. POWER PACK (Tie-in to Secret Invasion crossover)
Marvel Comics: Sept, 2008 - No. 4 ($2.99, limited series)

1-4-Van Lente-s/Hamscher-a; Franklin Richards app. 3.00

SKUL, THE
Virtual Comics (Byron Preiss Multimedia): Oct, 1996 - No. 3, Dec, 1996 ($2.50, lim. series)

1-3: Ron Lim & Jimmy Palmiotti-a 3.00

SKULL & BONES
DC Comics: 1992 - No. 3, 1992 ($4.95, limited series, 52 pgs.)

Book 1-3: 1-1st app. 5.00

SKULLKICKERS
Image Comics: Sept, 2010 - No. 33, Jul, 2015; No. 100, Aug, 2015 ($2.99/$3.50)

1-Jim Zubkavich-s/Edwin Huang-a; two covers 4.00
1-(2nd & 3rd printings), 2-18 3.00
24-29,31-33: 24-($3.50) "Before Watchmen" cover swipe (no issues #34-99) 3.50
30-($3.99) Multi-dimensional variant Skullkickers 4.00
#100 ($3.99, 8/15) Last issue; conclusion of Infinite Icons of the Endless Epic 4.00
All-New Secret Skullkickers 1 (6/13, $3.50) issue #22; cover swipe of X-Men #125 ('79) 3.50
Dark Skullkickers Dark 1 (7/13, $3.50) issue #23; cover swipe of Green Lantern #85 ('71) 3.50
Savage Skullkickers 1 (3/13, $3.50) issue #20; cover swipe of Savage Wolverine #1 3.50
The Mighty Skullkickers 1 (4/13, $3.50) issue #21; cover swipe of Thor #337 3.50
Uncanny Skullkickers 1 (2/13, $3.50) issue #19 3.50

SKULL, THE SLAYER
Marvel Comics Group: Aug, 1975 - No. 8, Nov, 1976 (20¢/25¢)

	GD	VG	FN	VF	VF/NM	NM-
1-Origin & 1st app.; Gil Kane-c	3	6	9	14	20	25
2-8: 2-Gil Kane-c. 5,6-(Regular 25¢-c). 8-Kirby-c	2	4	6	8	10	12
5,6-(30¢-c variants, limited distribution)(5,7/76)	3	6	9	19	30	40

SKY BLAZERS (CBS Radio)
Hawley Publications: Sept, 1940 - No. 2, Nov, 1940

	GD	VG	FN	VF	VF/NM	NM-
1-Sky Pirates, Ace Archer, Flying Aces begin	77	154	231	493	847	1200
2-WWII air battle grey-tone-c	41	82	123	250	418	585

SKYBOURNE
BOOM! Studios: Sept, 2016 - No. 5 ($3.99)

1-3-Frank Cho-s/a 4.00

SKY DOLL
Marvel Comics (Soleil): 2008 - No. 3, 2008 ($5.99, mature)

1-3-Barbucci & Canepa-s/a; English version of French comic; preview of other titles 6.00
...: Doll's Factory 1,2 (2009 - No. 2, 2009, $5.99) Barbucci & Canepa-s/a 6.00
...: Lacrima Christi 1,2 (9/10 - No. 2, 10/10, $5.99) Barbucci & Canepa and others-s/a 6.00
...: Space Ship 1,2 (7/10 - No. 2, 8/10, $5.99) Barbucci & Canepa and others-s/a 6.00

SKYE RUNNER
DC Comics (WildStorm): June, 2006 - No. 6, Mar, 2007 ($2.99)

1-6: 1-Three covers; Warner-s/Garza-a. 2-Three covers, incl. Campbell 3.00

SKYLANDERS (Based on the Activision video game)
IDW Publishing: No. 0, Jul, 2014 - No. 12, Aug, 2015 ($3.99)

0-(no cover price) Lord Kaos app.; Bowden-a; character bios 3.00
1-12: 1-Marz & Rodriguez-s/Baldeón-a 4.00
... Superchargers 1-6 (10/15 - No. 6, 3/16, $3.99) Marz & Rodriguez-s 4.00

SKYMAN (See Big Shot Comics & Sparky Watts)
Columbia Comics Gr.: Fall?, 1941 - No. 2, Fall?, 1942; No. 3, 1948 - No. 4, 1948

	GD	VG	FN	VF	VF/NM	NM-
1-Origin Skyman, The Face, Sparky Watts app.; Whitney-c/a; 3rd story-r from Big Shot #1; Whitney c-1-4	129	258	387	826	1413	2000
2 (1942)-Yankee Doodle	69	138	207	442	759	1075
3,4 (1948)	41	82	123	256	428	600

SKYMAN (Also see Captain Midnight 2013 series #4)
Dark Horse Comics: Jan, 2014 - No. 4, Apr, 2014 ($2.99)

1-4: 1-Fialkov-s/Garcia-a; origin of a new Skyman. 3,4-Captain Midnight app. 3.00
... One-Shot (11/14, $2.99) Garcia-a 3.00

SKYPILOT
Ziff-Davis Publ. Co.: No. 10, 1950(nd) - No. 11, Apr-May, 1951

	GD	VG	FN	VF	VF/NM	NM-
10,11-Frank Borth-a; Saunders painted-c	16	32	48	94	147	200

SKY RANGER (See Johnny Law...)

SKYROCKET
Harry 'A' Chesler: 1944

	GD	VG	FN	VF	VF/NM	NM-
nn-Alias the Dragon, Dr. Vampire, Skyrocket & The Desperado app.; WWII Japan zero-c	50	100	150	315	533	750

SKY SHERIFF (Breeze Lawson...) (Also see Exposed & Outlaws)
D. S. Publishing Co.: Summer, 1948

	GD	VG	FN	VF	VF/NM	NM-
1-Edmond Good-c/a	15	30	45	84	127	170

SKY WOLF (Also see Airboy)
Eclipse Comics: Mar, 1988 - No. 3, Oct, 1988 ($1.25/$1.50/$1.95, lim. series)

1-3 3.00

SLAINE, THE BERSERKER (Slaine the King #21 on)
Quality: July, 1987 - No. 28, 1989 ($1.25/$1.50)

1-28 3.00

SLAINE, THE HORNED GOD
Fleetway: 1998 - No. 3 ($6.99)

1-3-Reprints series from 2000 A.D.; Bisley-a 7.00

SLAM!
BOOM! Studios (Boom! Box): Nov, 2016 - Present ($3.99)

1-4-Roller derby; Pamela Ribon-s/Veronica Fish-a 4.00

SLAM BANG COMICS (Western Desperado #8)
Fawcett Publications: Mar, 1940 - No. 7, Sept, 1940 (Combined with Master Comics #7)

	GD	VG	FN	VF	VF/NM	NM-
1-Diamond Jack, Mark Swift & The Time Retarder, Lee Granger, Jungle King begin & continue in Master	258	516	774	1651	2826	4000
2	113	226	339	718	1234	1750
3-Classic monster-c (scarce)	300	600	900	2070	3635	5200
4-7: 6-Intro Zoro, the Mystery Man (also in #7)	90	180	270	576	988	1400

Ashcan (1940) Not distributed to newsstands, only for in house use. A copy sold in 2006 for $4,500.

SLAPSTICK
Marvel Comics: Nov, 1992 - No. 4, Feb, 1993 ($1.25, limited series)

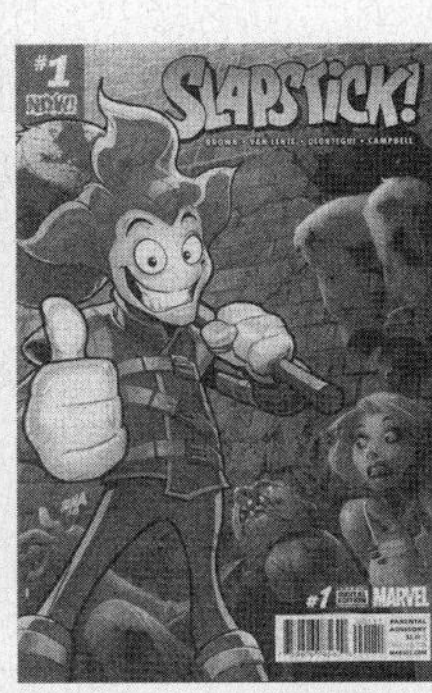

Slapstick (2017 series) #1 © MAR

Sleeper #1 © WSP

Sleepwalker #28 © MAR

GD VG FN VF VF/NM NM-
2.0 4.0 6.0 8.0 9.0 9.2

1-4: Fry/Austin-c/a. 4-Ghost Rider, D.D., F.F. app. 3.00

SLAPSTICK
Marvel Comics: Feb, 2017 - Present ($3.99)

1-4-Brown & Van Lente-s/Olortegui-a 4.00

SLAPSTICK COMICS
Comic Magazines Distributors: nd (1946?) (36 pgs.)

nn-Firetop feature; Post-a(2); Munson Paddock-c 34 68 102 204 332 460

SLASH & BURN
DC Comics (Vertigo): Jan, 2016 - No. 6, Jun, 2016 ($3.99/$4.99)

1-5-Si Spencer-s/Max Dunbar-a 4.00
6-($4.99) 5.00

SLASH-D DOUBLECROSS
St. John Publishing Co.: 1950 (Pocket-size, 132 pgs.)

nn-Western comics 22 44 66 132 216 300

SLAUGHTERMAN
Comico: Feb, 1983 - No. 2, 1983 ($1.50, B&W)

1,2 4.00

SLAVE GIRL COMICS (See Malu... & White Princess of the Jungle #2)
Avon Periodicals/Eternity Comics (1989): Feb, 1949 - No. 2, 1949 (52 pgs.); Mar, 1989 (B&W, 44 pgs)

1-Larsen-c/a 135 270 405 864 1482 2100
2-Larsen-a (no month listed) 116 232 348 742 1271 1800
1-(3/89, $2.25, B&W, 44 pgs.)-r/#1 5.00

SLAVE LABOR STORIES
SLG Publishing: May, 2003 (Giveaway, B&W)

1-Free Comic Book Day Edition; short stories by various; Dorkin Milk & Cheese-c 3.00

SLAYER: REPENTLESS (Based on the band Slayer)
Dark Horse Comics: Jan, 2017 - No. 3 ($4.99, limited series)

1-Jon Schnepp-s/Guiu Villanova-a/Glenn Fabry-c; Slayer app. 5.00

SLEDGE HAMMER (TV)
Marvel Comics: Feb, 1988 - No. 2, Mar,1988 ($1.00, limited series)

1,2 3.00

SLEDGEHAMMER 44
Dark Horse Comics: Mar, 2013 - No. 2, Apr, 2013 ($3.50, limited series)

1,2-Mignola & Arcudi-s/Latour-a; Mignola-c 3.50

SLEDGEHAMMER 44: THE LIGHTNING WAR
Dark Horse Comics: Nov, 2013 - No. 3, Jan, 2014 ($3.50, limited series)

1-3-Mignola & Arcudi-s/Laurence Campbell-a. 1-Mignola-c. 2,3-Campbell-c 3.50

SLEEPER
DC Comics (WildStorm): Mar, 2003 - No. 12, Mar, 2004 ($2.95)

1-12-Brubaker-s/Phillips-c/a. 3-Back-up preview of The Authority: High Stakes pt. 2 3.00
...: All False Moves TPB (2004, $17.95) r/#7-12 18.00
...: Out in the Cold TPB (2004, $17.95) r/#1-6 18.00

SLEEPER: SEASON TWO
DC Comics (WildStorm): Aug, 2004 - No. 12, July, 2005 ($2.95/$2.99)

1-12-Brubaker-s/Phillips-c/a. 3.00
TPB (2009, $24.99) r/#1-12 25.00
...: A Crooked Line TPB (2005, $17.99) r/#1-6 18.00
...: The Long Way Home TPB (2005, $14.99) r/#7-12 15.00

SLEEPING BEAUTY (See Dell Giants & Movie Comics)
Dell Publishing Co.: No. 973, May, 1959 - No. 984, June, 1959 (Disney)

Four Color 973 (...and the Prince) 10 20 30 66 138 210
Four Color 984 (...Fairy Godmother's) 8 16 24 56 108 160

SLEEPWALKER
Marvel Comics: June, 1991 - No. 33, Feb, 1994 ($1.00/$1.25)

1-1st app. Sleepwalker 4.00
2-33: 4-Williamson-i. 5-Spider-Man-c/stor. 7-Infinity Gauntlet x-over. 8-Vs. Deathlok-c/story. 11-Ghost Rider-c/story. 12-Quesada-c/a(p) 14-Intro Spectra. 15-F.F.-c/story. 17-Darkhawk & Spider-Man x-over. 18-Infinity War x-over; Quesada/Williamson-c. 21,22-Hobgoblin app. 19-($2.00)-Die-cut Sleepwalker mask-c 3.00
25-($2.95, 52 pgs.)-Holo-grafx foil-c; origin 4.00
Holiday Special 1 (1/93, $2.00, 52 pgs.)-Quesada-c(p) 4.00

SLEEPWALKING
Hall of Heroes: Jan, 1996 ($2.50, B&W)

1-Kelley Jones-c 3.00

SLEEPY HOLLOW (Movie Adaption)
DC Comics (Vertigo): 2000 ($7.95, one-shot)

1-Kelley Jones-a/Seagle-s 8.00

SLEEPY HOLLOW (Based on the Fox TV show)
BOOM! Studios: Oct, 2014 - No. 4, Jan, 2015 ($3.99, limited series)

1-4-Marguerite Bennett-s/Jorge Coelho-a/Phil Noto-c 4.00
...: Origins 1 (4/15, $4.99) Mike Johnson-s/Matias Bergara-a; Quinones-c 5.00
...: Providence 1-4 (8/15 - No. 4 11/15, $3.99) Carrasco-s/Santos-a 4.00

SLEEZE BROTHERS, THE
Marvel Comics (Epic Comics): Aug, 1989 - No. 6, Jan, 1990 ($1.75, mature)

1-6: 4-6 (9/89 - 11/89 indicia dates) 3.00
nn-(1991, $3.95, 52 pgs.) 4.00

SLICK CHICK COMICS
Leader Enterprises: 1947(nd) - No. 3, 1947(nd)

1-Teenage humor 21 42 63 122 199 275
2,3 15 30 45 85 130 175

SLIDERS (TV)
Acclaim Comics (Armada): June, 1996 - No. 2, July, 1996 ($2.50, lim. series)

1,2: D.G. Chichester scripts; Dick Giordano-a. 3.00

SLIDERS: DARKEST HOUR (TV)
Acclaim Comics (Armada): Oct, 1996 - No. 3, Dec, 1996 ($2.50, limited series)

1-3 3.00

SLIDERS SPECIAL
Acclaim Comics (Armada): Nov, 1996 - No 3, Mar, 1997 ($3.95, limited series)

1-3: 1-Narcotica-Jerry O'Connell-s. 2-Blood and Splendor. 3-Deadly Secrets 4.00

SLIDERS: ULTIMATUM (TV)
Acclaim Comics (Armada): Sept, 1996 - No. 2, Sept, 1996 ($2.50, lim. series)

1,2 3.00

SLIMER! (TV cartoon) (Also see the Real Ghostbusters)
Now Comics: 1989 - No. 19, Nov, 1990 ($1.75)

1-19: Based on animated cartoon 4.00

SLIM MORGAN (See Wisco)

SLINGERS (See Spider-Man: Identity Crisis issues)
Marvel Comics: Dec, 1998 - No. 12, Nov, 1999 ($2.99/$1.99)

0-(Wizard #88 supplement) Prelude story 3.00
1-($2.99) Four editions w/different covers for each hero, 16 pages common to all, the other pages from each hero's perspective 4.00
2-12: 2-Two-c. 12-Saltares-a 3.00

SLITHISS ATTACKS! (Also see Very Weird Tales)
Oceanspray Comics Group: Dec, 2001 – No. 4, Aug, 2004 ($3.00/$4.00)

1-($3.00) Origin and 1st app. of the monster Slithiss; 1st app. Overconfident Man 15.00
2-($4.00) 2nd app. Overconfident Man; "Chris Lamo" Newport, OR murder parody 12.00
3-($3.00) Rutland Vermont Halloween x-over; 3rd app. Overconfident Man 12.00
4-($3.00) 4th app. Overconfident Man 10.00
Special Edition 1($20.00) reprints #1-2 without letter column 20.00
Special Edition 1($20.00) second printing 20.00

NOTE: *Created in prevention classes taught by Jon McClure at the Oceanspray Family Center in Newport, OR and paid for by the Housing Authority of Lincoln County, all books are b&w with color covers. Bob Overstreet and other comics' professionals wrote letters of encouragement that were published in issues #2-4. Issues #1-2 penciled and inked by various artists; #3-4 penciled by James Gilmer. All comics feature characters created by students, signed and numbered by Jon McClure. Issue #1 had a 200 issue print run, while issues #2-4 have print runs of 100 each. Special Edition #1 had a print run of 26 issues, while the second printing had a 10 issue print run. Ties in with live action movie Face Eater released in 2007 and card game FaceEater released in 2010.*

SLUDGE
Malibu Comics (Ultraverse): Oct, 1993 - No. 12, Dec, 1994 ($2.50/$1.95)

1-($2.50, 48 pgs.)-Intro/1st app. Sludge; Rune flip-c/story Pt. 1 (1st app., 3 pgs.) by Barry Smith; The Night Man app. (3 pg. preview); The Mighty Magnor 1 pg strip begins by Aragonés (cont. in other titles) 4.00
1-Ultra 5000 Limited silver foil 8.00
2-11: 3-Break-Thru x-over. 4-2 pg. Mantra origin. 8-Bloodstorm app. 3.00
12 ($3.50)-Ultraverse Premiere #8 flip book; Alex Ross poster 4.00
...:Red Xmas (12/94, $2.50, 44 pgs.) 4.00

SLUGGER (Little Wise Guys Starring...)(Also see Daredevil Comics)
Lev Gleason Publications: April, 1956

1-Biro-c 8 16 24 40 50 60

Smallville: Alien #1 © DC

Smash Comics #6 © QUA

Smilin' Jack #2 © DELL

GD VG FN VF VF/NM NM-
2.0 4.0 6.0 8.0 9.0 9.2

SMALLVILLE (Based on TV series)
DC Comics: May, 2003 - No. 11, Jan, 2005 ($3.50/$3.95, bi-monthly)

1-6-Photo-c. 1-Plunkett-a; interviews with cast; season 1 episode guide begins 4.00
7-11-($3.95) 7-Chloe Chronicles begin; season 2 episode guide begins 4.00
Vol. 1 TPB (2004, $9.95) r/#1-4 & Smallville: The Comic; photo-c 10.00

SMALLVILLE: ALIEN (Based on TV series)
DC Comics: Feb, 2014 - No. 4, May, 2014 ($3.99, printings of previously released digital comics)

1-4: 1-The Monitor lands on Earth; Staggs-a. 2-4-Batman app. 4.00

SMALLVILLE: CHAOS (Based on TV series)(Season 11)
DC Comics: Oct, 2014 - No. 4, Jan, 2015 ($3.99, printings of previously released digital comics)

1-4: 1-Eclipso app.; Padilla-a. 3-Darkseid app. 3,4-Supergirl & Superboy app. 4.00

SMALLVILLE: LANTERN (Based on TV series)
DC Comics: Jun, 2014 - No. 4, Sept, 2014 ($3.99, printings of previously released digital comics)

1-4: 1-Kal-El joins the Green Lantern Corps; Takara-a. 2-4-Parallax app. 4.00

SMALLVILLE SEASON 11 (Based on TV series)
DC Comics: Jul, 2012 - No. 19, Jan, 2014 ($3.99, printings of previously released digital comics)

1-19: 1-Two covers by Gary Frank & Cat Staggs; Pere Perez-a. 5-8-Batman app. 13-15-Legion app. 15-Doomsday app. 16-19-Diana of Themyscira app. 4.00
... Special 1 (7/13, $4.99) Batman, Nightwing and Martian Manhunter app. 5.00
... Special 2 (9/13, $4.99) Lana Lang and John Corben app. 5.00
... Special 3 (12/13, $4.99) Spotlight on Luthor and Tess; Lobel-a 5.00
... Special 4 (3/14, $4.99) Superboy, Jay Garrick, Blue Beetle, Wonder Twins app. 5.00
... Special 5 (9/14, $4.99) Zatanna and John Constantine app. 5.00

SMALLVILLE SEASON 11: CONTINUITY (Based on TV series)
DC Comics: Feb, 2015 - No. 4, May, 2015 ($3.99, printings of previously released digital comics)

1-4-The Crisis vs. the Monitors; Legion of Super-Heroes app.; Guara-a 4.00

SMALLVILLE: THE COMIC (Based on TV series)
DC Comics: Nov, 2002 ($3.95, 64 pages, one-shot)

1-Photo-c; art by Martinez and Leon; interviews with cast; season 2 preview 5.00

SMASH COMICS (Becomes Lady Luck #86 on)
Quality Comics Group: Aug, 1939 - No. 85, Oct, 1949

Issue	GD 2.0	VG 4.0	FN 6.0	VF 8.0	VF/NM 9.0	NM- 9.2
1-Origin Hugh Hazard & His Iron Man, Bozo the Robot, Espionage, Starring Black X by Eisner, & Hooded Justice (Invisible Justice #2 on); Chic Carter & Wings Wendall begin; 1st Robot on the cover of a comic book (Bozo)	331	662	993	2317	4059	5800
2-The Lone Star Rider app; Invisible Hood gains power of invisibility; bondage/torture-c	145	290	435	921	1586	2250
3-Captain Cook & Eisner's John Law begin	86	172	258	546	936	1325
4,5: 4-Flash Fulton begins	81	162	243	518	884	1250
6-12: 12-One pg. Fine-a	77	154	231	493	847	1200
13-Magno begins (8/40); last Eisner issue; The Ray app. in full page ad; The Purple Trio begins	79	158	237	502	864	1225
14-Intro. The Ray (9/40) by Lou Fine & others	303	606	909	2121	3711	5300
15-1st Ray-c, 2nd app.	158	316	474	1003	1727	2450
16-The Scarlet Seal begins	129	258	387	826	1413	2000
17-Wun Cloo becomes plastic super-hero by Jack Cole (9-months before Plastic Man); Ray-c	139	278	417	883	1517	2150
18-Midnight by Jack Cole begins (origin & 1st app., 1/41)	174	348	522	1114	1907	2700
19-22: Last Ray by Fine; The Jester begins-#22. 19,21-Ray-c	92	184	276	584	1005	1425
23,24: 23-Ray-c. 24-The Sword app.; last Chic Carter; Wings Wendall dons new costume #24,25	77	154	231	493	847	1200
25-Origin/1st app. Wildfire; Rookie Rankin begins; Ray-c	79	158	237	502	864	1225
26-30: 28-Midnight-c begin, end #85	65	130	195	416	708	1000
31,32,34: The Ray by Rudy Palais; also #33	60	120	180	381	653	925
33-Origin The Marksman	63	126	189	403	689	975
35-37	50	100	150	315	533	750
38-The Yankee Eagle begins; last Midnight by Jack Cole; classic-c by Cole	102	204	306	653	1114	1575
39,40-Last Ray issue	50	100	150	315	533	750
41,44-50	41	82	123	256	428	600
42-Lady Luck begins by Klaus Nordling	135	270	405	864	1482	2100
43-Lady Luck-c (1st & only in Smash)	90	180	270	576	988	1400
51-60	32	64	96	188	307	425
61-70	24	48	72	142	234	325
71-85: 79-Midnight battles the Men from Mars-c/s	21	42	63	122	199	275

NOTE: ***Al Bryant*** *c-54, 63-68.* ***Cole*** *a-17-38, 68, 69, 72, 73, 78, 80, 83, 85; c-38, 60-62, 69-84.* ***Crandall*** *a-(Ray)-23-29, 35-38; c-36, 39, 40, 42-44, 46.* ***Fine*** *a(Ray)-14, 15, 16(w/****Tuska****), 17-22.* ***Fox*** *c-24-35.* ***Fuje*** *Ray-30.* ***Gil Fox*** *a-6-7, 9, 11-13.* ***Guardineer*** *a-(The Marksman)-39-?, 49, 52.* ***Gustavson*** *a-4-7, 9, 11-13 (The Jester)-22-46; (Magno)-13-21; (Midnight)-39(Cole inks), 49, 52, 63-65.* ***Kotzky*** *a-(Espionage)-33-38; c-45, 47-53.* ***Nordling*** *a-49, 52, 63-65.* ***Powell*** *a-11, 12, (Abdul the Arab)-13-24.Black X c-2, 6, 9, 11, 13, 16. Bozo the Robot c-1, 3, 5, 8, 10, 12, 14, 18, 20, 22, 24, 26. Midnight c-28-85. The Ray c-15, 17, 19, 21, 23, 25, 27. Wings Wendall c-4, 7.*

SMASH COMICS (Also see All Star Comics 1999 crossover titles)
DC Comics: May, 1999 ($1.99, one-shot)

1-Golden Age Doctor Mid-nite and Hourman 3.00

SMASH HIT SPORTS COMICS
Essankay Publications: V2#1, Jan, 1949

Issue	GD 2.0	VG 4.0	FN 6.0	VF 8.0	VF/NM 9.0	NM- 9.2
V2#1-L.B. Cole-c/a	29	58	87	170	278	385

SMAX (Also see Top Ten)
America's Best Comics: Oct, 2003 - No. 5, May, 2004 ($2.95, limited series)

1-5-Alan Moore-s/Zander Cannon-a 3.00
... Collected Edition (2004, $19.95, HC with dustjacket) r/#1-5 20.00
... Collected Edition SC (2005, $12.99) r/#1-5 13.00

SMILE COMICS (Also see Gay Comics, Tickle, & Whee)
Modern Store Publ.: 1955 (52 pgs.; 5x7-1/4") (7¢)

Issue	GD 2.0	VG 4.0	FN 6.0	VF 8.0	VF/NM 9.0	NM- 9.2
1	8	16	24	42	54	65

SMILEY BURNETTE WESTERN (Also see Patches #8 & Six-Gun Heroes)
Fawcett Publ.: March, 1950 - No. 4, Oct, 1950 (All photo front & back-c)

Issue	GD 2.0	VG 4.0	FN 6.0	VF 8.0	VF/NM 9.0	NM- 9.2
1-Red Eagle begins	25	50	75	150	245	340
2-4	16	32	48	94	147	200

SMILEY (THE PSYCHOTIC BUTTON) (See Evil Ernie)
Chaos! Comics: July, 1998 - May, 1999 ($2.95, one-shots)

1-Ivan Reis-a 3.00
... Holiday Special (1/99), ...'s Spring Break (4/99), ...Wrestling Special (5/99) 3.00

SMILIN' JACK (See Famous Feature Stories and Popular Comics) (Also see Super Book of Comics #1&2 and Super-Book of Comics #7&19 in the Promotional Comics section)
Dell Publishing Co.: No. 5, 1940 - No. 8, Oct-Dec, 1949

Issue	GD 2.0	VG 4.0	FN 6.0	VF 8.0	VF/NM 9.0	NM- 9.2
Four Color 5	84	168	252	538	919	1300
Four Color 10 (1940)	69	138	207	442	759	1075
Large Feature Comic 12,14,25 (1941)	65	130	195	416	708	1000
Four Color 4 (1942)	38	76	114	281	628	975
Four Color 14 (1943)	30	60	90	216	483	750
Four Color 36,58 (1943-44)	21	42	63	147	324	500
Four Color 80 (1945)	13	26	39	89	195	300
Four Color 149 (1947)	9	18	27	62	126	190
1 (1-3/48)	10	20	30	68	144	220
2	6	12	18	38	69	100
3-8 (10-12/49)	5	10	15	33	57	80

SMILING SPOOK SPUNKY (See Spunky)

SMITTY (See Popular Comics, Super Book #2, 4 & Super Comics)
Dell Publishing Co.: No. 11, 1940 - No. 7, Aug-Oct, 1949; No. 909, Apr, 1958

Issue	GD 2.0	VG 4.0	FN 6.0	VF 8.0	VF/NM 9.0	NM- 9.2
Four Color 11 (1940)	53	106	159	334	567	800
Large Feature Comic 26 (1941)	40	80	120	246	411	575
Four Color 6 (1942)	22	44	66	154	340	525
Four Color 32 (1943)	15	30	45	100	220	340
Four Color 65 (1945)	12	24	36	82	179	275
Four Color 99 (1946)	10	20	30	66	138	210
Four Color 138 (1947)	9	18	27	59	117	175
1 (2-4/48)	9	18	27	57	111	165
2-(5-7/48)	5	10	15	31	53	75
3,4: 3-(8-10/48), 4-(11-1/48-49)	4	8	12	27	44	60
5-7, Four Color 909 (4/58)	4	8	12	23	37	50

SMOKEY BEAR (TV) (See March Of Comics #234, 362, 372, 383, 407)
Gold Key: Feb, 1970 - No. 13, Mar, 1973

Issue	GD 2.0	VG 4.0	FN 6.0	VF 8.0	VF/NM 9.0	NM- 9.2
1	3	6	9	18	28	38
2-5	2	4	6	10	14	18
6-13	2	4	6	8	10	12

SMOKEY STOVER (See Popular Comics, Super Book #5,17,29 & Super Comics)
Dell Publishing Co.: No. 7, 1942 - No. 827, Aug, 1957

Issue	GD 2.0	VG 4.0	FN 6.0	VF 8.0	VF/NM 9.0	NM- 9.2
Four Color 7 (1942)-Reprints	24	48	72	170	378	585
Four Color 35 (1943)	14	28	42	96	211	325
Four Color 64 (1944)	12	24	36	79	170	260
Four Color 229 (1949)	6	12	18	40	73	105
Four Color 730,827	5	10	15	33	57	80

SMOKEY THE BEAR (See Forest Fire for 1st app.)
Dell Publ. Co.: No. 653, 10/55 - No. 1214, 8/61 (See March of Comics #234)

Snakes on a Plane #1 © New Line

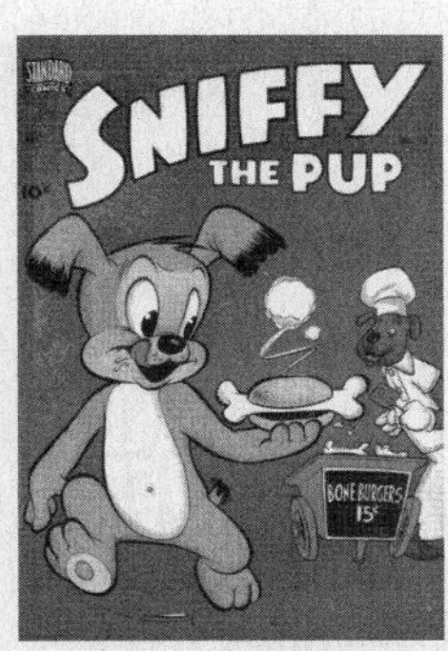

Sniffy the Pup #13 © STD

Sojourn #6 © CRO

	GD 2.0	VG 4.0	FN 6.0	VF 8.0	VF/NM 9.0	NM- 9.2
Four Color 653 (#1)	10	20	30	64	132	200
Four Color 708,754,818,932	6	12	18	40	73	105
Four Color 1016,1119,1214	5	10	15	31	53	75

SMOKY (See Movie Classics)

SMOSH
Dynamite Entertainment: 2016 - No. 6, 2016 ($3.99)

1-6: 1-3-McDermott-s/Viglino-a; back-up with Yale Stewart-s/a. 4-Boxman origin 4.00

SMURFS (TV)
Marvel Comics: 1982 (Dec) - No. 3, 1983

1-3 2 4 6 11 16 20
...Treasury Edition 1 (64 pgs.)-r/#1-3 3 6 9 17 26 35

SNAFU (Magazine)
Atlas Comics (RCM): Nov, 1955 - V2#2, Mar, 1956 (B&W)

V1#1-Heath/Severin-a; Everett, Maneely-a 16 32 48 94 147 200
V2#1,2-Severin-a 14 28 42 76 108 140

SNAGGLEPUSS (TV)(See Hanna-Barbera Band Wagon, Quick Draw McGraw #5 & Spotlight #4)
Gold Key: Oct, 1962 - No. 4, Sept, 1963 (Hanna-Barbera)

1 7 14 21 49 92 135
2-4 6 12 18 37 66 95

SNAKE EYES (G.I. Joe)
Devil's Due Publ.: Aug, 2005 - No. 6, Jan, 2006 ($2.95)

1-6-Santalucia-a 3.00
...: Declassified TPB (4/06, $18.95) r/series; source guide 19.00

SNAKE EYES (... and Storm Shadow #13-on)(Cont. from G.I. Joe: Snake Eyes, Volume 2 #7)
IDW Publishing: No. 8, Dec, 2011 - Present ($3.99)

8-21: 13-Title change to Snake Eyes and Storm Shadow 4.00

SNAKE PLISSKEN CHRONICLES, (John Carpenter's...)
Hurricane Entertainment: June, 2003 - No. 4 ($2.99)

Preview Issue (8/02, no cover price) B&W preview; John Carpenter interview 3.00
1-4: 1-Three covers; Rodriguez-a 3.00

SNAKES AND LADDERS
Eddie Campbell Comics: 2001 ($5.95, B&W, one-shot)

nn-Alan Moore-s/Eddie Campbell-a 6.00

SNAKES ON A PLANE (Adaptation of the 2006 movie)
Virgin Comics: Oct, 2006 - No. 2, Nov, 2006 ($2.99, limited series)

1,2: 1-Dixon-s/Purcell-a. JG Jones and photo-c. 2-Klebs, Jr.-a; Moore & photo-c 3.00

SNAKE WOMAN (Shekhar Kapur's...)
Virgin Comics: July, 2006 - No. 10, Apr, 2007 ($2.99)

1-10: 1-6-Michael Gaydos-a/Zeb Wells-s. 1-Two covers by Gaydos & Singh 3.00
#0 (5/07, 99¢) origin of the Snake Goddess; background info; Gaydos-a/c 3.00
... Curse of the 68 (3/08 - No. 4, 5/08, $2.99) 1-4: 1-Ingale-a. 2-Manu-a 3.00
... Tale of the Snake Charmer 1-6 (6/07-12/07, $2.99) Vivek Shinde-a 3.00
... Vol. 1 TPB (6/07, $14.99) r/#1-5; Gaydos sketch pages; creator commentary 15.00
... Vol. 2 TPB (9/07, $14.99) r/#6-10; Cebulski intro. 15.00

SNAP (Formerly Scoop #8; becomes Jest #10,11 & Komik Pages #10)
Harry 'A' Chesler: No. 9, 1944

9-Manhunter, The Voice; WWII gag-c 30 60 90 177 289 400

SNAPPY COMICS
Cima Publ. Co. (Prize Publ.): 1945

1-Airmale app.; 9 pg. Sorcerer's Apprentice adapt; Kiefer-a
36 72 108 211 343 475

SNAPSHOT
Image Comics: Feb, 2013 - No. 4, May, 2013 ($2.99, B&W, limited series)

1-4-Andy Diggle-s/Jock-a/c 3.00

SNARKED
Boom Entertainment (Kaboom!): No. 0, Aug, 2011 - No. 12, Sept, 2012 ($1.00/$3.99)

0-($1.00) Roger Langridge-s/a; sketch gallery, bonus content and games 3.00
1-12: 1-($3.99) Covers by Langridge & Samnee 4.00

SNARKY PARKER (See Life With...)

SNIFFY THE PUP
Standard Publ. (Animated Cartoons): No. 5, Nov, 1949 - No. 18, Sept, 1953

5-Two Frazetta text illos 14 28 42 80 115 150
6-10 9 18 27 47 61 75
11-18 8 16 24 40 50 60

SNOOPER AND BLABBER DETECTIVES (TV) (See Whitman Comic Books)
Gold Key: Nov, 1962 - No. 3, May, 1963 (Hanna-Barbera)

1 6 12 18 41 76 110
2,3 5 10 15 33 57 80

SNOTGIRL
Image Comics: Jul, 2016 - Present ($2.99)

1-5-Bryan O'Malley-s/Leslie Hung-a; two covers by O'Malley & Hung on each 3.00

SNOW BLIND
BOOM! Studios: Dec, 2015 - No. 4, Mar, 2016 ($3.99)

1-4-Ollie Masters-s/Tyler Jenkins-a 4.00

SNOWFALL
Image Comics: Feb, 2016 - Present ($3.99)

1-8-Joe Harris-s/Martín Morazzo-a 4.00

SNOW WHITE (See Christmas With... (in Promotional Comics section), Mickey Mouse Magazine, Movie Comics & Seven Dwarfs)
Dell Publishing Co.: No. 49, July, 1944 - No. 382, Mar, 1952 (Disney-Movie)

Four Color 49 (...& the Seven Dwarfs) 47 94 141 367 821 1275
Four Color 382 (1952)-origin; partial reprint of Four Color 49
10 20 30 64 132 200

SNOW WHITE
Marvel Comics: Jan, 1995 ($1.95, one-shot)

1-r/1937 Sunday newspaper pages 3.00

SNOW WHITE AND THE SEVEN DWARFS
Whitman Publications: April, 1982 (60¢)

nn-r/Four Color 49 1 3 4 6 8 10

SNOW WHITE AND THE SEVEN DWARFS GOLDEN ANNIVERSARY
Gladstone: Fall, 1987 ($2.95, magazine size, 52 pgs.)

1-Contains poster 2 4 6 9 13 16

SOAP OPERA LOVE
Charlton Comics: Feb, 1983 - No. 3, June, 1983

1-3-Low print run 3 6 9 19 30 40

SOAP OPERA ROMANCES
Charlton Comics: July, 1982 - No. 5, March, 1983

1-5-Nurse Betsy Crane-r; low print run 3 6 9 19 30 40

SOCK MONKEY
Dark Horse Comics: Sept, 1998 - No. 2, Oct, 1998 ($2.95/$2.99, B&W)

1,2-Tony Millionaire-s/a 4.00
Vol. 2 -(Tony Millionaire's Sock Monkey) July, 1999 - No. 2, Aug, 1999
1,2 3.00
Vol. 3 -(Tony Millionaire's Sock Monkey) Nov, 2000 - No. 2, Dec, 2000
1,2 3.00
Vol. 4 -(Tony Millionaire's Sock Monkey) May, 2003 - No. 2, Aug, 2003
1,2 3.00
...The Inches Incident (Sept, 2006 - No. 4, Apr, 2007) 1-4-Tony Millionaire-s/a 3.00

SOJOURN
White Cliffs Publ. Co.: Sept, 1977 - No. 2, 1978 ($1.50, B&W & color, tabloid size)

1,2: 1-Tor by Kubert, Eagle by Severin, E. V. Race, Private Investigator by Doug Wildey, T. C. Mars by Aragonés begin plus other strips 2 4 6 8 10 12
NOTE: Most copies came folded. Unfolded copies are worth 50% more.

SOJOURN
CrossGeneration Comics: July, 2001 - No. 34, May, 2004 ($2.95)

Prequel -Ron Marz-s/Greg Land-c/a; preview pages 3.00
1-Ron Marz-s/Greg Land-c/a in most 6.00
2,3 5.00
4-24: 7-Immonen-a. 12-Brigman-a. 17-Lopresti-a. 21-Luke Ross-a 3.00
25-34: 25-$1.00-c. 34-Cariello-a 3.00
...: From the Ashes TPB (2001, $19.95) r/#1-6; Land painted-c 20.00
...: The Dragon's Tale TPB (2002, $15.95) r/#7-12; Jusko painted-c 16.00
...: The Warrior's Tale TPB (2003, $15.95) r/#13-18 16.00
Vol. 4: The Thief's Tale (2003, $15.95) r/#19-24 16.00
Vol. 5: The Sorcerer's Tale (Checker Book Publ.,2007, $17.95) r/#25-30 18.00
Vol. 6: The Berzerker's Tale (Checker Book Publ.,2007, $17.95) r/#31-34, Prequel 18.00
Traveler Vol.1,2 ($9.95) digest-sized reprints of TPBs 10.00

SOLAR (...Man of the Atom) (Also see Doctor Solar)
Valiant/Acclaim Comics (Valiant): Sept, 1991 - No. 60, Apr, 1996 ($1.75-$2.50, 44 pgs.)

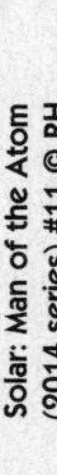
Solar: Man of the Atom (2014 series) #11 © RH

Soldier Zero #8 © BOOM

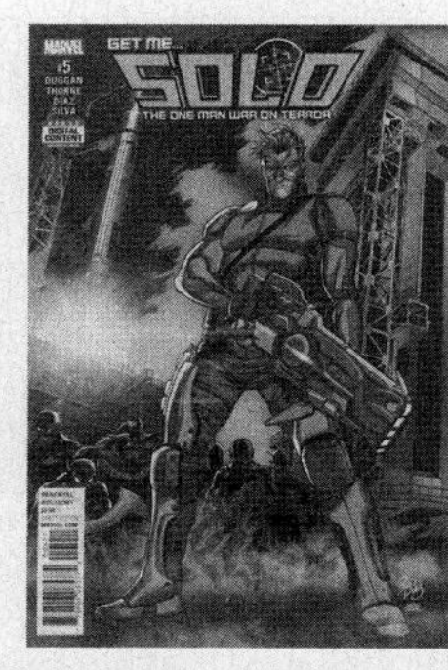

Solo (2016 series) #5 © MAR

GD VG FN VF VF/NM NM-
2.0 4.0 6.0 8.0 9.0 9.2

1-Layton-a(i) on Solar; Barry Windsor-Smith-c/a 2 4 6 10 14 18
2,4-9: 2-Layton-a(i) on Solar, B. Smith-a. 7-vs. X-O Armor
1 2 3 5 6 8
3-1st app. Harada (11/91); intro. Harbinger 3 6 9 17 26 35
10-(6/92, $3.95)-1st app. Eternal Warrior (6 pgs.); black embossed-c; origin & 1st app. Geoff McHenry (Geomancer) 3 6 9 19 30 40
10-($3.95)-2nd printing 6.00
11-15: 11-1st full app. Eternal Warrior. 12,13-Unity x-overs. 14-1st app. Fred Bender (becomes Dr. Eclipse). 15-2nd Dr. Eclipse 5.00
16-60: 17-X-O Manowar app. 23-Solar splits. 29-1st Valiant Vision book. 33-Valiant Vision; bound-in trading card. 38-Chaos Effect Epsilon Pt.1. 46-52-Dan Jurgens-a(p)/scripts w/Giordano-i. 53,54-Jurgens scripts only. 60-Giffen scripts; Jeff Johnson-a(p) 4.00
0-($9.95, trade paperback)-r/Alpha and Omega origin story; polybagged w/poster 12.00
...: Second Death (1994, $9.95)-r/issues #1-4. 10.00

NOTE: *#1-10 all have free 8 pg. insert "Alpha and Omega" which is a 10 chapter Solar origin story. All 10 centerfolds can pieced together to show climax of story.* ***Ditko*** *a-11p, 14p.* ***Giordano*** *a-46, 47, 48, 49, 50, 51, 52i.* ***Johnson*** *a-60p.* ***Jurgens*** *a-46, 47, 48, 49, 50 , 51, 52p.* ***Layton*** *a-1-3i; c-2i, 11i, 17i, 25i.* ***Miller*** *c-12.* ***Quesada*** *c-17p, 20-23p, 29p.* ***Simonson*** *c-13.* ***B. Smith*** *a-1-10; c-1, 3, 5, 7, 19i.* ***Thibert*** *c-22i, 23i.*

SOLARMAN (See Pendulum Ill. Originals)
Marvel Comics: Jan, 1989 - No. 2, May, 1990 ($1.00, limited series)

1,2 3.00

SOLAR, MAN OF THE ATOM (Man of the Atom on cover)
Acclaim Comics (Valiant Heroes): Vol. 2, May, 1997 ($3.95, one-shot, 46 pgs) (1st Valiant Heroes Special Event)

Vol. 2-Reintro Solar; Ninjak cameo; Warren Ellis scripts; Darick Robertson-a 4.00

SOLAR: MAN OF THE ATOM
Dynamite Entertainment: 2014 - No. 12, 2015 ($3.99)

1-12: 1-Barbiere-s/Bennett-a; 5 covers. 3-Female Solar in costume. 5-White costume 4.00

SOLAR, MAN OF THE ATOM: HELL ON EARTH
Acclaim Comics (Valiant Heroes): Jan, 1998 - No. 4 ($2.50, limited series)

1-4-Priest-s/ Zircher-a(p) 3.00

SOLAR, MAN OF THE ATOM: REVELATIONS
Acclaim Comics (Valiant Heroes): Nov, 1997 ($3.95, one-shot, 46 pgs.)

1-Krueger-s/ Zircher-a(p) 4.00

SOLDIER & MARINE COMICS (Fightin' Army #16 on)
Charlton Comics (Toby Press of Conn. V1#11): No. 11, Dec, 1954 - No. 15, Aug, 1955; V2#9, Dec, 1956

V1#11 (12/54)-Bob Powell-a 11 22 33 60 83 105
V1#12(2/55)-15: 12-Photo-c. 14-Photo-c; Colan-a 8 16 24 42 54 65
V2#9(Formerly Never Again; Jerry Drummer V2#10 on)
7 14 21 37 46 55

SOLDIER COMICS
Fawcett Publications: Jan, 1952 - No. 11, Sept, 1953

1 14 28 42 80 115 150
2 9 18 27 47 61 75
3-5: 4-What Happened in Taewah 8 16 24 44 57 70
6-11: 8-Illo. in **POP** 8 16 24 42 54 65

SOLDIERS OF FORTUNE
American Comics Group (Creston Publ. Corp.): Mar-Apr, 1951 - No. 13, Feb-Mar, 1953

1-Capt. Crossbones by Shelly, Ace Carter, Lance Larson begin
24 48 72 142 234 325
2-(52 pgs.) 14 28 42 82 121 160
3-10: 6-Bondage-c 13 26 39 72 101 130
11-13 (War format) 9 18 27 52 69 85

NOTE: ***Shelly*** *a-1-3, 5.* ***Whitney*** *a-6, 8-11, 13; c-1-3, 5, 6.*

SOLDIERS OF FREEDOM
Americomics: 1987 - No. 2, 1987 ($1.75)

1,2 3.00

SOLDIER X (Continued from Cable)
Marvel Comics: Sept, 2002 - No. 12, Aug, 2003 ($2.99/$2.25)

1,10,11,12-($2.99) 1-Kordey-a/Macan-s. 10-Bollers-s/Ranson-a 3.00
2-9-($2.25) 3.00

SOLDIER ZERO (From Stan Lee)
BOOM! Studios: Oct, 2010 - No. 12, Sept, 2011 ($3.99)

1-12: 1-4-Cornell-s/Pina-a 4.00

SOLITAIRE (Also See Prime V2#6-8)
Malibu Comics (Ultraverse): Nov, 1993 - No. 12, Dec, 1994 ($1.95)

GD VG FN VF VF/NM NM-
2.0 4.0 6.0 8.0 9.0 9.2

1-($2.50)-Collector's edition bagged w/playing card 4.00
1-12: 1-Regular edition w/o playing card. 2,4-Break-Thru x-over. 3-2 pg. origin The Night Man. 4-Gatefold-c. 5-Two pg. origin the Strangers 3.00

SOLO
Marvel Comics: Sept, 1994 - No. 4, Dec, 1994 ($1.75, limited series)

1-4: Spider-Man app. 3.00

SOLO (Movie)
Dark Horse Comics: July, 1996 - No. 2, Aug, 1996 ($2.50, limited series)

1,2: Adaptation of film; photo-c 3.00

SOLO (Anthology showcasing individual artists)
DC Comics: Dec, 2004 - No. 12, Oct, 2006 ($4.95/$4.99)

1-11: 1-Tim Sale-a; stories by Sale and various. 2-Richard Corben-a; stories by Corben and Arcudi. 3-Paul Pope. 4-Howard Chaykin. 5-Darwyn Cooke. 6-Jordi Bernet. 7-Michael Allred; Teen Titans & Doom Patrol app. 8-Teddy Kristiansen. 9-Scott Hampton. 10-Damion Scott. 11-Sergio Aragonés. 12-Brendan McCarthy 5.00

SOLO
Marvel Comics: Dec, 2016 - Present ($3.99)

1-5: 1-Thorne & Duggan-s/Diaz-a; Dum Dum Dugan app. 4.00

SOLO AVENGERS (Becomes Avenger Spotlight #21 on)
Marvel Comics: Dec, 1987 - No. 20, July, 1989 (75¢/$1.00)

1-Jim Lee-a on back-up story 1 2 3 5 6 8
2-20: 11-Intro Bobcat 4.00

SOLOMON AND SHEBA (Movie)
Dell Publishing Co.: No. 1070, Jan-Mar, 1960

Four Color 1070-Sekowsky-a; photo-c 8 16 24 55 105 155

SOLOMON GRUNDY
DC Comics: May, 2009 - No. 7, Nov, 2009 ($2.99)

1-7-Scott Kolins-s/a. 2-Bizarro app. 7-Blackest Night prelude 3.00
TPB (2010, $19.99) r/#1-7 20.00

SOLOMON KANE (Based on the Robert E. Howard character. Also see Blackthorne 3-D Series #60 & Marvel Premiere)
Marvel Comics: Sept, 1985 - No. 6, July, 1986 (Limited series)

1-Double size 5.00
2-6: 3-6-Williamson-a(i) 4.00

SOLOMON KANE
Dark Horse Comics: Sept, 2008 - No. 5, Feb, 2009 ($2.99)

1-5: 1-Two covers by Cassaday and Joe Kubert; Guevara-a 3.00
...: Death's Black Riders 1-4 (1/10 - No. 4, 6/10, $3.50) Robertson-c 3.50
...: Red Shadows 1-4 (4/11 - No. 4, 7/11, $3.50) Bruce Jones-s/Rahsan Ekedal-a; two covers by Davis & Manchess on each 3.50

SOLUS
CG Entertainment, Inc.: Apr, 2003 - No. 8, Jan, 2004 ($2.95)

1-8: 1-4,6,7-George Pérez-a/c; Barbara Kesel-s. 5-Ryan-a. 8-Kirk-a 3.00
Vol. 1: Genesis (1/04, $15.95) r/#1-6 16.00

SOLUTION, THE
Malibu Comics (Ultraverse): Sept, 1993 - No. 17, Feb, 1995 ($1.95)

1,3-15: 1-Intro Meathook, Deathdance, Black Tiger, Tech. 4-Break-Thru x-over; gatefold-c. 5-2 pg. origin The Strangers. 11-Brereton-c 3.00
1-($2.50)-Newsstand ed. polybagged w/trading card 4.00
1-Ultra 5000 Limited silver foil 8.00
0-Obtained w/Rune #0 by sending coupons from 11 comics 5.00
2-($2.50, 48 pgs.)-Rune flip-c/story by B. Smith; The Mighty Magnor 1 pg. strip by Aragonés 4.00
16 ($3.50)-Flip-c Ultraverse Premiere #10 4.00
17 ($2.50) 3.00

SOMERSET HOLMES (See Eclipse Graphic Novel Series)
Pacific Comics/ Eclipse Comics No. 5, 6: Sept, 1983 - No. 6, Dec, 1984 ($1.50, Baxter paper)

1-6: 1-Brent Anderson-c/a. Cliff Hanger by Williamson in all 4.00

SONG OF THE SOUTH (See Brer Rabbit)

SONIC & KNUCKLES
Archie Comics: Aug, 1995 ($2.00)

1 1 3 4 6 8 10

SONIC BOOM
Archie Comic Publications: Dec, 2014 - No. 11, Oct, 2015 ($3.99)

Sonic Super Digest #15 © SEGA

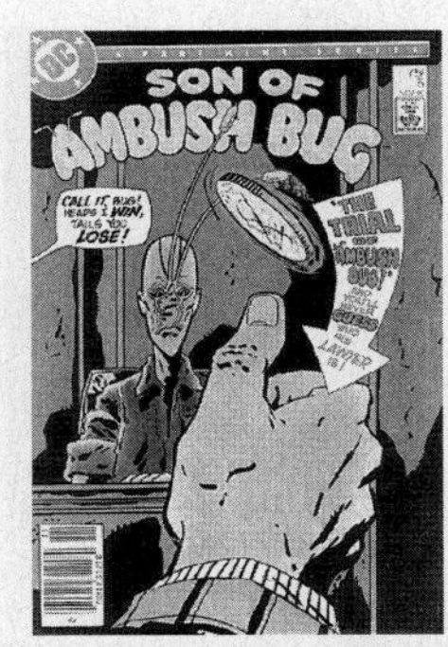

Son of Ambush Bug #5 © DC

Sons of Anarchy #1 © 20th Century Fox

GD 2.0 | VG 4.0 | FN 6.0 | VF 8.0 | VF/NM 9.0 | NM- 9.2

1-11: 1-Regular-c and 4 interlocking variant covers. 2-7,11-Two covers on each. 8-10-"Worlds Unite" Sonic/Mega Man x-over; 3 covers 4.00

SONIC COMIC ORIGINS AND MEGA MAN X
Archie Comic Publications: Jun/Jul 2014 (giveaway)
... Free Comic Book Day Edition - Flipbook; Freedom Fighters app. 3.00

SONIC DISRUPTORS
DC Comics: Dec, 1987 - No. 7, July, 1988 ($1.75, unfinished limited series)
1-7 3.00

SONIC MEGA DRIVE
Archie Comic Publications: Aug, 2016 ($3.99, limited series)
1-25th Anniversary celebration; Flynn-s/Hesse-a 4.00
... - The Next Level (12/16, $4.99) Flynn-s/Hesse-a; Metal Sonic app. 5.00

SONIC'S FRIENDLY NEMESIS KNUCKLES
Archie Publications: July, 1996 - No. 3, Sept, 1996 ($1.50, limited series)
1-3 6.00

SONIC SUPER DIGEST
Archie Publications: Dec, 2012 - Present ($3.99/$4.99)
1-7-($3.99) 4.00
8-17-($4.99) 5.00

SONIC SUPER SPECIAL
Archie Publications: 1997 - No. 15, Feb, 2001 ($2.00/$2.25/$2.29, 48 pgs)
1-3 5.00
4-6,8-15: 10-Sabrina-c/app. 15-Sin City spoof 4.00
7-(w/Image) Spawn, Maxx, Savage Dragon-c/app.; Valentino-a 4.00

SONIC THE HEDGEHOG (TV, video game)
Archie Comics: No. 0, Feb, 1993 - No. 3, May, 1993 ($1.25, mini-series)
0(2/93),1: Shaw-a(p) & covers on all 4 8 12 25 40 55
2,3 3 6 9 16 23 30
Beginnings TPB (2003, $10.95) r/#0-3 11.00
...: The Beginning TPB (2006, $10.95) r/#0-3 11.00

SONIC THE HEDGEHOG (TV, video game)
Archie Comics: July, 1993 - Present ($1.25-$2.99)
1 5 10 15 30 50 70
2,3 3 6 9 16 23 30
4-10: 8-Neon ink-c. 2 4 6 11 16 20
11-20 2 4 6 9 13 16
21-30 ($1.50): 25-Silver ink-c 2 4 6 8 10 12
31-50 1 2 3 5 6 8
51-93 4.00
94-212: 117-Begin $2.19-c. 152-Begin $2.25-c. 157-Shadow app. 198-Begin $2.50 3.00
213-249,251-263: 213-Begin $2.99-c. 248-263-Two covers 3.00
250-($3.99) Wraparound-c; part 9 of Worlds Collide x-over with Mega Man 4.00
264-274,276-290-($3.99) Two covers on most. 273,274-"Worlds Unite" Sonic/Mega Man x-over; 3 covers on each. 288-291-Genesis of a Hero 4.00
275-($4.99) "Worlds Unite" Sonic/Mega Man x-over; six covers 5.00
Free Comic Book Day Edition 1 (2007)- Leads into Sonic the Hedgehog #175 3.00
Free Comic Book Day Edition 2009 - Reprints Sonic the Hedgehog #1 from July 1993 3.00
Free Comic Book Day Edition 2010 - 2012: 2010-New story 3.00
Sonic and Mega Man: World's Collide Prelude, FCBD Edition (6-7/13) 3.00
Sonic and Mega Man: Worlds Unite FCBD Edition (6-7/15) Prelude to crossover 3.00
Sonic Sampler: Free Comic Book Day Edition (5/16) Sonic & Sonic Universe stories 3.00
Sonic: Worlds Unite Battles (9/15, $3.99) Sonic/Mega Man x-over; 3 wraparound covers 4.00
Triple Trouble Special (10/95, $2.00, 48 pgs.) 1 3 4 6 8 10

SONIC UNIVERSE (Sonic the Hedgehog)
Archie Publications: Apr, 2009 - Present ($2.50/$2.99/$3.99)
1-15 3.00
16-66: 16-Begin $2.99-c. 51-66-Two covers. 51-54-Worlds Collide 3.00
67-94-($3.99) Two covers on most. 75-"Worlds Unite" Sonic/Mega Man x-over prelude with nine covers. 76-78-"Worlds Unite" x-over; 3 covers on each. 87-90-Shattered 4.00

SONIC VS. KNUCKLES "BATTLE ROYAL" SPECIAL
Archie Publications: 1997 ($2.00, one-shot)
1 1 2 3 5 6 8

SONIC X (Sonic the Hedgehog)
Archie Publications: Nov, 2005 - No. 40, Feb, 2009 ($2.25)
1-Sam Speed app. 4.00
2-40 3.00

SON OF AMBUSH BUG (See Ambush Bug)

GD 2.0 | VG 4.0 | FN 6.0 | VF 8.0 | VF/NM 9.0 | NM- 9.2

DC Comics: July, 1986 - No. 6, Dec, 1986 (75¢)
1-6: Giffen-c/a in all. 5-Bissette-a. 4.00

SON OF BLACK BEAUTY (Also see Black Beauty)
Dell Publishing Co.: No. 510, Oct, 1953 - No. 566, June, 1954
Four Color 510, 566 5 10 15 31 53 75

SON OF FLUBBER (See Movie Comics)

SON OF HULK (Continues from Skaar: Son of Hulk #12) (See Realm of Kings)
Marvel Comics: No. 13, Sept, 2009 - No. 17, Jan, 2010 ($2.99)
13-17: 13,15-17-Galactus app. 3.00

SON OF M (Also see House of M series)
Marvel Comics: Feb, 2006 - No. 6, July, 2006 ($2.99, limited series)
1-6: 1-Powerless Quicksilver; Martinez-a. 2-Quicksilver regains powers; Inhumans app. 3.00
Decimation: Son of M (2006, $13.99, TPB) r/series; Martinez sketch pages 14.00

SON OF MERLIN
Image Comics (Top Cow): Feb, 2013 - No. 5, Jun, 2013 ($1.00/$2.99, limited series)
1-5: 1-($1.00-c); Napton-s/Zid-a; covers by Zid & Sejic. 2-($2.99) 3.00

SON OF MUTANT WORLD
Fantagor Press: 1990 - No. 5, 1990? ($2.00, bi-monthly)
1-5: 1-3: Corben-c/a. 4,5 ($1.75, B&W) 3.00

SON OF ORIGINS OF MARVEL COMICS (See Fireside Book Series)

SON OF SATAN (Also see Ghost Rider #1 & Marvel Spotlight #12)
Marvel Comics Group: Dec, 1975 - No. 8, Feb, 1977 (25¢)
1-Mooney-a; Kane-c(p), Starlin splash(p) 4 8 12 23 37 50
2,6-8: 2-Origin The Possessor. 8-Heath-a 2 4 6 11 16 20
3-5-(Regular 25¢ editions)(4-8/76): 5-Russell-p 2 4 6 11 16 20
3-5-(30¢-c variants, limited distribution) 4 8 12 23 37 50

SON OF SINBAD (Also see Abbott & Costello & Daring Adventures)
St. John Publishing Co.: Feb, 1950
1-Kubert-c/a 52 104 156 328 557 785

SON OF SUPERMAN (Elseworlds)
DC Comics: 1999 ($14.95, prestige format, one-shot)
nn-Chaykin & Tischman-s/Williams III & Gray-a 15.00

SON OF TOMAHAWK (See Tomahawk)

SON OF VULCAN (Formerly Mysteries of Unexplored Worlds #1-48; Thunderbolt V3#51 on)
Charlton Comics: V2#49, Nov, 1965 - V2#50, Jan, 1966
V2#49,50: 50-Roy Thomas scripts (1st pro work) 3 6 9 17 26 35

SONS OF ANARCHY (Based on the TV series)
BOOM! Studios: Sept, 2013 - No. 25, Sept, 2015 ($3.99, originally a 6-issue limited series)
1-24: 1-6-Christopher Golden-s/Damian Couceiro-a; multiple covers on each 4.00
25-($4.99) Last issue; Ferrier-s/Bergara-a; three covers 5.00

SONS OF ANARCHY REDWOOD ORIGINAL (TV series)
BOOM! Studios: Aug, 2016 - Present ($3.99)
1-7: 1-Prequel with 18-year-old Jax Teller. 1-4-Masters-s/Pizzari-a; multiple covers 4.00

SONS OF KATIE ELDER (See Movie Classics)

SONS OF THE DEVIL
Image Comics: May, 2015 - Present ($2.99/$3.99)
1-5: 1-Brian Buccellato-s/Toni Infante-a 3.00
6-10-($3.99) 4.00

SORCERY (See Chilling Adventures in... & Red Circle...)

SORORITY SECRETS
Toby Press: July, 1954
1 16 32 48 94 147 200

SOULFIRE (MICHAEL TURNER PRESENTS:...) (Also see Eternal Soulfire)
Aspen MLT, Inc.: No. 0, 2004 - No. 10, Jul, 2009 ($2.50/$2.99)
0-($2.50) Turner-a/c; Loeb-s; intro. to characters & development sketches 3.00
1-($2.99) Two covers 3.00
1-Diamond Previews Exclusive 5.00
2-9: 2,3-Two covers. 4-Four covers 3.00
10-($3.99) Benitez-a 4.00
... Sourcebook 1 (3/15, $4.99) Character profiles; two covers by Turner 5.00
...: The Collected Edition Vol. 1 (5/05, $6.99) r/#1,2; cover gallery 7.00
Hardcover Volume 1 (12/05, $24.99) r/#0-5 & preview from Wizard Mag.; Johns intro. 25.00

Soulfire V4 #1 © Aspen MLT

Southern Bastards #1 © Golgonooza

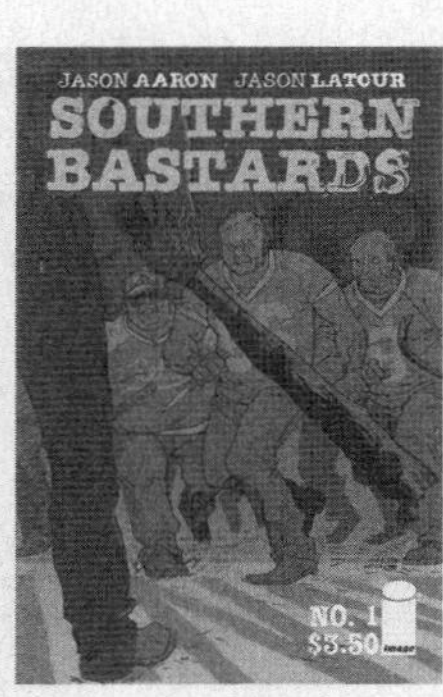

Space Adventures #12 © CC

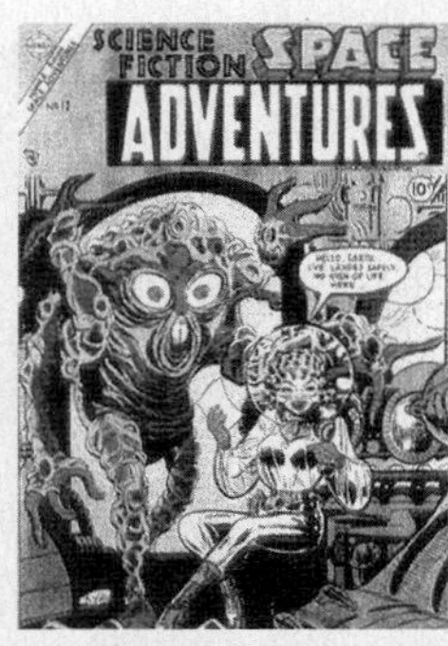

	GD 2.0	VG 4.0	FN 6.0	VF 8.0	VF/NM 9.0	NM- 9.2

SOULFIRE (MICHAEL TURNER PRESENTS:...) (Volume 2)
Aspen MLT, Inc.: No. 0, Oct, 2009 - No. 9, Jan, 2011 ($2.50/$2.99)

0-($2.50) Marcus To-a 3.00
1-9-($2.99) 1-Five covers. 9-Covers by To and Linsner 3.00

SOULFIRE (MICHAEL TURNER'S...) (Volume 3)
Aspen MLT, Inc.: No. 0, Apr, 2011 - No. 8, May, 2012 ($1.99/$2.99)

0-($1.99) Krul-s/Fabok-a; 4 covers 3.00
1-8-($2.99) 1-Four covers 3.00
... Despair (7/12, $3.99) Schwartz-s/Marks-a; 3 covers 4.00
... Faith (7/12, $3.99) McMurray-s/Oum-a; 3 covers 4.00
... Hope (7/12, $3.99) Krul-s/Varese-a; 3 covers 4.00
... Power (7/12, $3.99) Wohl-s/Randolph-a; 3 covers 4.00
... Primer (6/12, $1.00) Reprints and story summaries 3.00

SOULFIRE (MICHAEL TURNER'S...) (Volume 4)
Aspen MLT, Inc.: Aug, 2012 - No. 8, Oct, 2013 ($3.99)

1-8-Krul-s/DeBalfo-a; multiple covers on each 4.00

SOULFIRE (MICHAEL TURNER'S...) (Volume 5)
Aspen MLT, Inc.: Nov, 2013 - No. 8, Oct, 2014 ($1.00/$3.99)

1-($1.00) Krul-s/Marion-a; multiple covers 3.00
2-8-($3.99) Multiple covers on each 4.00
Annual 1 2014 (7/14, $5.99) Art by Garbowska, Hanson, Turner, Cafaro 6.00

SOULFIRE: CHAOS REIGN
Aspen MLT, Inc.: No. 0, June, 2006 - No. 3, Jan, 2007 ($2.50/$2.99)

0-($2.50) Three covers; Marcus To-a; J.T. Krul-s 3.00
1-3-($2.99) 1-Three covers 3.00
...: Beginnings (7/06, $1.99) Marcus To-a; J.T. Krul-s 3.00
...: Beginnings 1 (7/07, $1.99) Francisco Herrera-a; J.T. Krul-s 3.00

SOULFIRE: DYING OF THE LIGHT
Aspen MLT, Inc.: No. 0, 2004 - No. 5, Feb, 2006 ($2.50/$2.99)

0-($2.50) Three covers; Gunnell-a; Krul-s; back-story to the Soulfire universe 3.00
1-5-($2.99) 1-Five covers 3.00
... Vol. 1 TPB (2007, $14.99) r/#0-5; Gunnell sketch pages, cover gallery 15.00

SOULFIRE: NEW WORLD ORDER
Aspen MLT, Inc.: No. 0, Jul, 2007; May, 2009 - No. 5, Dec, 2009 ($2.50/$2.99)

0 (7/07, $2.50) Two covers; Herrera-a/Krul-s 3.00
1-5-($2.99) 1-Four covers 3.00

SOULFIRE: SHADOW MAGIC
Aspen MLT, Inc.: No. 0, Nov, 2008 - No. 5, May, 2009 ($2.50/$2.99)

0-($2.50) Two covers; Sana Takeda-a 3.00
1-5-($2.99) 1-Two covers 3.00

SOUL SAGA
Image Comics (Top Cow): Feb, 2000 - No. 5, Apr, 2001 ($2.50)

1-5: 1-Madureira-c; Platt & Batt-a 3.00

SOULSEARCHERS AND COMPANY
Claypool Comics: June, 1995 - No. 82, Jan, 2007 ($2.50, B&W)

1-10: Peter David scripts 5.00
11-25 3.00
26-82 3.00

SOULWIND
Image Comics: Mar, 1997 - No. 8 ($2.95, B&W, limited series)

1-8: 5-"The Day I Tried To Live" pt. 1 3.00
Book Five; The August Ones (Oni Press, 3/01, $8.50) 8.50
...The Kid From Planet Earth (1997, $9.95, TPB) 10.00
...The Kid From Planet Earth (Oni Press, 1/00, $8.50, TPB) 8.50
...The Day I Tried to Live (Oni Press, 4/00, $8.50, TPB) 8.50
The Complete Soulwind TPB ($29.95, 11/03, 8" x 5 1/2") r/Oni Books #1-5 30.00

SOUPY SALES COMIC BOOK (TV)(The Official...)
Archie Publications: 1965

	GD 2.0	VG 4.0	FN 6.0	VF 8.0	VF/NM 9.0	NM- 9.2
1-(Teen-age)	8	16	24	56	108	160

SOUTHERN BASTARDS
Image Comics: Apr, 2014 - Present ($3.50)

1-Jason Aaron-s/Jason Latour-a 8.00
2-16 3.50

SOUTHERN CROSS
Image Comics: Mar, 2014 - Present ($2.99/$3.99)

1-6-Becky Cloonan-s/c; Andy Belanger-a 3.00
7-11-($3.99) Cloonan-s/c; Belanger-a 4.00

SOUTHERN KNIGHTS, THE (See Crusaders #1)
Guild Publ/Fictioneer Books: No. 2, 1983 - No. 41, 1993 (B&W)

	GD 2.0	VG 4.0	FN 6.0	VF 8.0	VF/NM 9.0	NM- 9.2
2-Magazine size	1	2	3	5	6	8

3-35, 37-41 3.00
36-($3.50-c) 4.00
Dread Halloween Special 1, Primer Special 1 (Spring, 1989, $2.25) 3.00
Graphic Novels #1-4 4.00

SOVEREIGN SEVEN (Also see Showcase '95 #12)
DC Comics: July, 1995 - No. 36, July, 1998 ($1.95) (1st creator-owned mainstream DC comic)

1-1st app. Sovereign Seven (Reflex, Indigo, Cascade, Finale, Cruiser, Network & Rampart); 1st app. Maitresse; Darkseid app.; Chris Claremont-s & Dwayne Turner-c/a begins 4.00
1-Gold 8.00
1-Platinum 40.00
2-25: 2-Wolverine cameo. 4-Neil Gaiman cameo. 5,8-Batman app. 7-Ramirez cameo (from the movie Highlander). 9-Humphrey Bogart cameo from Casablanca. 10-Impulse app; Manoli Wetherell & Neal Conan cameo from Uncanny X-Men #226. 11-Robin app. 16-Final Night. 24-Superman app. 25-Power Girl app. 3.00
26-36: 26-Begin $2.25-c. 28-Impulse-c/app. 3.00
Annual 1 (1995, $3.95)-Year One story; Big Barda & Lobo app.; Jeff Johnson-c/a 4.00
Annual 2 (1996, $2.95)-Legends of the Dead Earth; Leonardi-c/a 4.00
...Plus 1(2/97, $2.95)-Legion-c/app. 4.00
TPB-($12.95) r/#1-5, Annual #1 & Showcase '95 #12 13.00

SPACE: ABOVE AND BEYOND (TV)
Topps Comics: Jan, 1996 - No. 3, Mar, 1996 ($2.95, limited series)

1-3: Adaptation of pilot episode; Steacy-c. 3.00

SPACE: ABOVE AND BEYOND--THE GAUNTLET (TV)
Topps Comics: May, 1996 -No. 2, June, 1996 ($2.95, limited series)

1,2 3.00

SPACE ACE (Also see Manhunt!)
Magazine Enterprises: No. 5, 1952

	GD 2.0	VG 4.0	FN 6.0	VF 8.0	VF/NM 9.0	NM- 9.2
5(A-1 #61)-Guardineer-a	65	130	195	416	708	1000

SPACE ACE: DEFENDER OF THE UNIVERSE (Based on the Don Bluth video game)
CrossGen Comics: Oct, 2003 - No. 6 ($2.95, limited series)

1,2-Kirkman-s/Borges-a 3.00

SPACE ACTION
Ace Magazines (Junior Books): June, 1952 - No. 3, Oct, 1952

	GD 2.0	VG 4.0	FN 6.0	VF 8.0	VF/NM 9.0	NM- 9.2
1-Cameron-a in all (1 story)	89	178	267	565	970	1375
2,3	58	116	174	371	636	900

SPACE ADVENTURES (War At Sea #22 on)
Capitol Stories/Charlton Comics: 7/52 - No. 21, 8/56; No. 23, 5/58 - No. 59, 11/64; V3#60, 10/67; V1#2, 7/68 - V1#8, 7/69; No. 9, 5/78 - No. 13, 3/79

	GD 2.0	VG 4.0	FN 6.0	VF 8.0	VF/NM 9.0	NM- 9.2
1-Fago/Morales world on fire-c	65	130	195	416	708	1000
2	31	62	93	186	303	420
3-5: 4,6-Flying saucer-c/stories	26	52	78	154	252	350
6-9: 7-Sex change story "Transformation". 8-Robot-c. 9-A-Bomb panel	24	48	72	140	230	320
10,11-Ditko-c/a. 10-Robot-c. 11-Two Ditko stories	60	120	180	385	660	935
12-Ditko-c (classic)	135	270	405	864	1482	2100
13-(Fox-r, 10-11/54); Blue Beetle-c/story	16	32	48	94	147	200
14,15,17,18: 14-Blue Beetle-c/story; Fox-r (12-1/54-55, last pre-code). 15,17,18-Rocky Jones-c/s.(TV); 15-Part photo-c	20	40	60	118	192	265
16-Krigstein-a; Rocky Jones-c/story (TV)	22	44	66	128	209	290
19	15	30	45	88	137	185
20-Reprints Fawcett's "Destination Moon"	22	44	66	132	216	300
21-(8/56) (no #22)(Becomes War At Sea)	15	30	45	88	137	185
23-(5/58; formerly Nyoka, The Jungle Girl)-Reprints Fawcett's "Destination Moon"	20	40	60	118	192	265
24,25,31,32-Ditko-a. 24-Severin-a(signed "LePoer")	20	40	60	118	192	265
26,27-Ditko-a(4) each. 26,28-Flying saucer-c	21	42	63	126	206	285
28-30	11	22	33	64	90	115
33-Origin/1st app. Capt. Atom by Ditko (3/60)	129	258	387	826	1413	2000
34-40,42-All Captain Atom by Ditko	24	48	72	142	234	325
41,43,45-59: 43-Alan Shephard strory, 2nd man in space. 45-Mercury Man app.	5	10	15	30	50	70
44-1st app. Mercury Man	5	10	15	31	53	75
V3#60(#1, 10/67)-Presents UFO origin & 1st app. Paul Mann & The Saucers From the Future	5	10	15	30	50	70

Space Comics #4 © AVON

Space Ghost (2005 series) #1 © H-B

Space Patrol #2 © Z-D

	GD 2.0	VG 4.0	FN 6.0	VF 8.0	VF/NM 9.0	NM- 9.2
2,5,6,8 (1968-69)-Ditko-a: 2-Aparo-c/a	3	6	9	19	30	40
3,4,7: 4-Aparo-c/a	3	6	9	16	23	30
9-13(1978-79)-Capt. Atom-r/Space Adventures by Ditko; 9-Reprints origin/1st app. Capt. Atom from #33						6.00

NOTE: *Aparo a-V3#60. c-V3#8. Ditko c-12, 31-42. Giordano c-3, 4, 7-9, 18p. Krigstein c-15. Shuster a-11. Issues 13 & 14 have Blue Beetle logos; #15-18 have Rocky Jones logos.*

SPACE BUSTERS
Ziff-Davis Publ. Co.: Spring, 1952 - No. 2, Fall, 1952

	GD	VG	FN	VF	VF/NM	NM-
1-Krigstein-a(3); Painted-c by Norman Saunders	88	176	264	559	960	1360
2-Kinstler-a(2 pgs.); Saunders painted-c	68	136	204	435	743	1050

NOTE: *Anderson a-2. Bondage c-2.*

SPACE CADET (See Tom Corbett,...)

SPACE CIRCUS
Dark Horse Comics: July, 2000 - No. 4, Oct, 2000 ($2.95, limited series)

1-4-Aragonés-a/Evanier-s 3.00

SPACE COMICS (Formerly Funny Tunes)
Avon Periodicals: No. 4, Mar-Apr, 1954 - No. 5, May-June, 1954

	GD	VG	FN	VF	VF/NM	NM-
4,5-Space Mouse, Peter Rabbit, Super Pup (formerly Spotty the Pup), & Merry Mouse continue from Funny Tunes	9	18	27	47	61	75
I.W. Reprint #8 (nd)-Space Mouse-r	2	4	6	8	11	14

SPACED
Anthony Smith Publ. #1,2/Unbridled Ambition/Eclipse Comics #10 on: 1982 - No. 13, 1988 ($1.25/$1.50, B&W, quarterly)

1-($1.25-c) 4.00
2-13, Special Edition (1983, Mimeo) 3.00

SPACE DETECTIVE
Avon Periodicals: July, 1951 - No. 4, July, 1952

	GD	VG	FN	VF	VF/NM	NM-
1-Rod Hathway, Space Detective begins, ends #4; Wood-c/a(3)-23 pgs.; "Opium Smugglers of Venus" drug story; Lucky Dale-r/Saint #4	142	284	426	909	1555	2200
2-Tales from the Shadow Squad story; Wood/Orlando-c; Wood inside layouts; "Slave Ship of Saturn" story	113	226	339	718	1234	1750
3,4: 3-Kinstler-c. 4-Kinstlerish-a by McCann	53	106	159	334	567	800
I.W. Reprint #1(Reprints #2), 8(Reprints cover #1 & part Famous Funnies #191)	4	8	12	23	37	50

SPACE EXPLORER (See March of Comics #202)

SPACE FAMILY ROBINSON (TV)(...Lost in Space #15-37, ...Lost in Space On Space Station One #38 on)(See Gold Key Champion)
Gold Key: Dec, 1962 - No. 36, Oct, 1969; No. 37, 10/73 - No. 54, 11/78; No. 55, 3/81 - No. 59, 5/82 (All painted covers)

	GD	VG	FN	VF	VF/NM	NM-
1-(Low distribution); Spiegle-a in all	30	60	90	216	483	750
2(3/63)-Family becomes lost in space	11	22	33	76	163	250
3-5	7	14	21	46	86	125
6-10: 6-Captain Venture back-up stories begin	6	12	18	37	66	95
11-20: 14-(10/65). 15-Title change (1/66)	4	8	12	28	47	65
21-36: 28-Last 12¢ issue. 36-Captain Venture ends	3	6	9	21	33	45
37-48: 37-Origin retold	2	4	6	10	14	18
49-59: Reprints #49,50,55-59	2	4	6	8	10	12

NOTE: *The TV show first aired on 9/15/65. Title changed after TV show debuted.*

SPACE FAMILY ROBINSON (See March of Comics #320, 328, 352, 404, 414)

SPACE GHOST (TV) (Also see Golden Comics Digest #2 & Hanna-Barbera Super TV Heroes #3-7)
Gold Key: March, 1967 (Hanna-Barbera) (TV debut was 9/10/66)

	GD	VG	FN	VF	VF/NM	NM-
1 (10199-703)-Spiegle-a	28	56	84	202	451	700

SPACE GHOST (TV cartoon)
Comico: Mar, 1987 ($3.50, deluxe format, one-shot) (Hanna-Barbera)

	GD	VG	FN	VF	VF/NM	NM-
1-Steve Rude-c/a; Evanier-s; Steacy painted-a	2	4	6	9	12	15

SPACE GHOST (TV cartoon)
DC Comics: Jan, 2005 - No. 6, June, 2005 ($2.95/$2.99, limited series)

1-6-Alex Ross-c/Ariel Olivetti-a/Joe Kelly-s; origin of Space Ghost 3.00
TPB (2005, $14.99) r/series; cover gallery 15.00

SPACE GIANTS, THE (TV cartoon)
FBN Publications: 1979 ($1.00, B&W, one-shots)

	GD	VG	FN	VF	VF/NM	NM-
1-Based on Japanese TV series	3	6	9	14	20	25

SPACEHAWK
Dark Horse Comics: 1989 - No. 3, 1990 ($2.00, B&W)

1-3-Wolverton-c/a(r) plus new stories by others. 4.00

SPACE JAM
DC Comics: 1996 ($5.95, one-shot, movie adaption)

	GD	VG	FN	VF	VF/NM	NM-
1-Wraparound photo cover of Michael Jordan	1	2	3	5	6	8

SPACE KAT-ETS (...in 3-D)
Power Publishing Co.: Dec, 1953 (25¢, came w/glasses)

	GD	VG	FN	VF	VF/NM	NM-
1	30	60	90	177	289	400

SPACEKNIGHTS
Marvel Comics: Oct, 2000 - No. 5, Feb, 2001 ($2.99, limited series)

1-5-Starlin-s/Batista-a 3.00

SPACEKNIGHTS
Marvel Comics: Dec, 2012 - No. 3, Feb, 2013 ($3.99, limited series)

1-3-Reprints the 2000-2001 series & Annihilation: Conquest Prologue 4.00

SPACEMAN (Speed Carter...)
Atlas Comics (CnPC): Sept, 1953 - No. 6, July, 1954

	GD	VG	FN	VF	VF/NM	NM-
1-Grey tone-c	100	120	300	635	1093	1550
2	54	108	162	343	574	825
3-6: 4-A-Bomb explosion-c	48	96	144	302	514	725

NOTE: *Everett c-1, 3. Heath a-1. Maneely a-1(3), 2(4), 3(3), 4-6; c-5, 6. Romita a-1. Sekowsky c-4. Sekowsky/Abel a-4(3). Tuska a-5(3).*

SPACE MAN
Dell Publ. Co.: No. 1253, 1-3/62 - No. 8, 3-5/64; No. 9, 7/72 - No. 10, 10/72

	GD	VG	FN	VF	VF/NM	NM-
Four Color 1253 (#1)(1-3/62)(15¢-c)	7	14	21	48	89	130
2,3: 2-(15¢-c). 3-(12¢-c)	4	8	12	27	44	60
4-8-(12¢-c)	3	6	9	21	33	45
9,10-(15¢-c): 9-Reprints #1253. 10-Reprints #2	2	4	6	9	12	15

SPACEMAN (From the Atomics)
Oni Press: July, 2002 ($2.95, one-shot)

1-Mike Allred-s/a; Lawrence Marvit additional art 3.00

SPACEMAN
DC Comics (Vertigo): Dec, 2011 - No. 9, Oct, 2012 ($1.00/$2.99, limited series)

1-($1.00) Azzarello-s/Risso-a/Johnson-c 4.00
2-9-($2.99) 3.00

SPACE MOUSE (Also see Funny Tunes & Space Comics)
Avon Periodicals: April, 1953 - No. 5, Apr-May, 1954

	GD	VG	FN	VF	VF/NM	NM-
1	14	28	42	76	108	140
2	8	16	24	44	57	70
3-5	8	16	24	40	50	60

SPACE MOUSE (Walter Lantz...#1; see Comic Album #17)
Dell Publishing Co./Gold Key: No. 1132, Aug-Oct, 1960 - No. 5, Nov, 1963 (Walter Lantz)

	GD	VG	FN	VF	VF/NM	NM-
Four Color 1132,1244, 1(11/62)(G.K.)	5	10	15	33	57	80
2-5	4	8	12	23	37	50

SPACE MYSTERIES
I.W. Enterprises: 1964 (Reprints)

	GD	VG	FN	VF	VF/NM	NM-
1-r/Journey Into Unknown Worlds #4 w/new-c	3	6	9	15	22	28
8,9: 9-r/Planet Comics #73	3	6	9	15	22	28

SPACE: 1999 (TV) (Also see Power Record Comics)
Charlton Comics: Nov, 1975 - No. 7, Nov, 1976

	GD	VG	FN	VF	VF/NM	NM-
1-Origin Moonbase Alpha; Staton-c/a	3	6	9	16	23	30
2,7: 2-Staton-a	2	4	6	13	18	22
3-6: All Byrne-a; c-3,5,6	3	6	9	16	23	30
nn (Charlton Press, digest, 100 pgs., B&W, no cover price) new stories & art	4	8	12	27	44	60

SPACE: 1999 (TV)(Magazine)
Charlton Comics: Nov, 1975 - No. 8, Nov, 1976 (B&W) (#7 shows #6 inside)

	GD	VG	FN	VF	VF/NM	NM-
1-Origin Moonbase Alpha; Morrow-c/a	3	6	9	15	22	28
2-8: 2,3-Morrow-c/a. 4-6-Morrow-c. 5,8-Morrow-a	2	4	6	11	16	20

SPACE PATROL (TV)
Ziff-Davis Publishing Co. (Approved Comics): Summer, 1952 - No. 2, Oct-Nov, 1952 (Painted-c by Norman Saunders)

	GD	VG	FN	VF	VF/NM	NM-
1-Krigstein-a	95	190	285	603	1039	1475
2-Krigstein-a(3)	67	134	201	426	731	1035

SPACE PIRATES (See Archie Giant Series #533)

SPACE: PUNISHER
Marvel Comics: Sept, 2012 - No. 4, Dec, 2012 ($3.99, limited series)

1-4-Outer space sci-fi pulp version of the Punisher; Tieri-s/Texeira-a/c 4.00

Space Squadron #2 © MAR

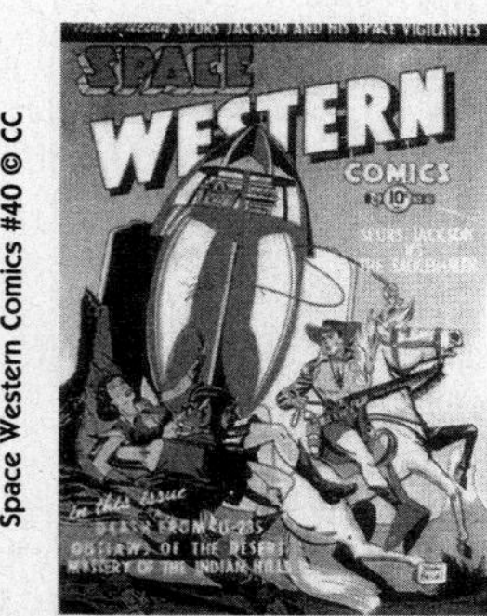

Space Western Comics #40 © CC

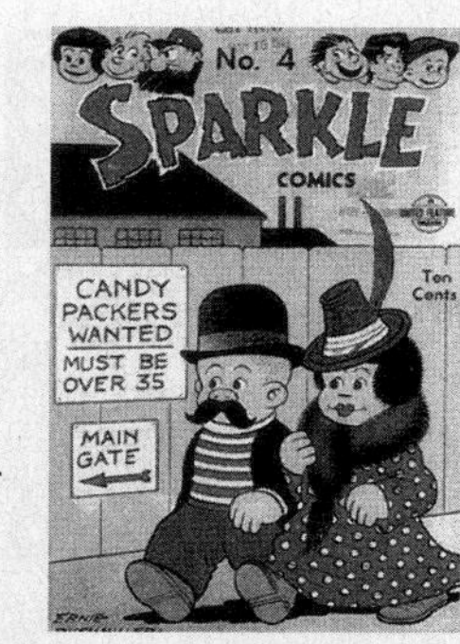

Sparkle Comics #4 © UFS

	GD 2.0	VG 4.0	FN 6.0	VF 8.0	VF/NM 9.0	NM- 9.2

SPACE RANGER (See Mystery in Space #92, Showcase #15 & Tales of the Unexpected)

SPACE SQUADRON (In the Days of the Rockets)(Becomes Space Worlds #6)
Marvel/Atlas Comics (ACI): June, 1951 - No. 5, Feb, 1952

	GD 2.0	VG 4.0	FN 6.0	VF 8.0	VF/NM 9.0	NM- 9.2
1-Space team; Brodsky c-1,5	90	180	270	576	988	1400
2: Tuska c-2-4	65	130	195	416	708	1000
3-5: 3-Capt. Jet Dixon by Tuska(3). 4-Weird advs. begin	58	116	174	371	636	900

SPACE THRILLERS
Avon Periodicals: 1954 (25¢ Giant)

	GD 2.0	VG 4.0	FN 6.0	VF 8.0	VF/NM 9.0	NM- 9.2
nn-(Scarce)-Robotmen of the Lost Planet; contains 3 rebound comics of The Saint & Strange Worlds. Contents could vary	155	310	465	992	1696	2400

SPACE TRIP TO THE MOON (See Space Adventures #23)

SPACE USAGI
Mirage Studios: June, 1992 - No. 3, 1992 ($2.00, B&W, mini-series)
V2#1, Nov, 1993 - V2#3, Jan, 1994 ($2.75)

	GD 2.0	VG 4.0	FN 6.0	VF 8.0	VF/NM 9.0	NM- 9.2
1-3: Stan Sakai-c/a/scripts, V2#1-3						3.00

SPACE USAGI
Dark Horse Comics: Jan, 1996 - No. 3, Mar, 1996 ($2.95, B&W, limited series)

	GD 2.0	VG 4.0	FN 6.0	VF 8.0	VF/NM 9.0	NM- 9.2
1-3: Stan Sakai-c/a/scripts						3.00

SPACE WAR (Fightin' Five #28 on)
Charlton Comics: Oct, 1959 - No. 27, Mar, 1964; No. 28, Mar, 1978 - No. 34, 3/79

	GD 2.0	VG 4.0	FN 6.0	VF 8.0	VF/NM 9.0	NM- 9.2
V1#1-Giordano-c begin, end #3	12	24	36	83	182	280
2,3	8	16	24	51	96	140
4-6,8,10-Ditko-c/a	12	24	36	81	176	270
7,9,11-15 (3/62): Last 10¢ issue	6	12	18	38	69	100
16 (6/62)-27 (3/64): 18,19-Robot-c	5	10	15	31	53	75
28 (3/78),29-31,33,34-Ditko-c/a(r): 30-Staton, Sutton/Wood-a. 31-Ditko-c/a(3); same-c as Strange Suspense Stories #2 (1968); atom blast-c	1	3	4	6	8	10
32-r/Charlton Premiere V2#2; Sutton-a						6.00

SPACE WARPED
Boom Entertainment (Kaboom!): Jun, 2011 - No. 6, Dec, 2011 ($3.99, limited series)

	GD 2.0	VG 4.0	FN 6.0	VF 8.0	VF/NM 9.0	NM- 9.2
1-6-Star Wars spoof; Bourhis-s/Spiessert-a						4.00

SPACE WESTERN (Formerly Cowboy Western Comics; becomes Cowboy Western Comics #46 on)
Charlton Comics (Capitol Stories): No. 40, Oct, 1952 - No. 45, Aug, 1953

	GD 2.0	VG 4.0	FN 6.0	VF 8.0	VF/NM 9.0	NM- 9.2
40-Intro Spurs Jackson & His Space Vigilantes; flying saucer story	60	120	180	381	653	925
41,43: 41-Flying saucer-c	45	90	135	284	480	675
42-Atom bomb explosion-c	48	96	144	302	514	725
44-Cowboys battle Nazis on Mars	77	154	231	493	847	1200
45-"The Valley That Time Forgot", a pre-Turok story with dinosaurs & a bow-hunting Indian; Hitler app.	52	104	156	328	552	775

SPACE WORLDS (Formerly Space Squadron #1-5)
Atlas Comics (Male): No. 6, April, 1952

	GD 2.0	VG 4.0	FN 6.0	VF 8.0	VF/NM 9.0	NM- 9.2
6-Sol Brodsky-c	53	106	159	334	567	800

SPANKY & ALFALFA & THE LITTLE RASCALS (See The Little Rascals)

SPARKIE, RADIO PIXIE (Radio)(Becomes Big Jon & Sparkie #4)
Ziff-Davis Publ. Co.: Winter, 1951 - No. 3, July-Aug, 1952 (Painted-c)(Sparkie #2,3; #1?)

	GD 2.0	VG 4.0	FN 6.0	VF 8.0	VF/NM 9.0	NM- 9.2
1-Based on children's radio program	27	54	81	158	259	360
2,3: 3-Big Jon and Sparkie on-c only	18	36	54	105	165	225

SPARKLE COMICS
United Features Synd.: Oct-Nov, 1948 - No. 33, Dec-Jan, 1953-54

	GD 2.0	VG 4.0	FN 6.0	VF 8.0	VF/NM 9.0	NM- 9.2
1-Li'l Abner, Nancy, Captain & the Kids, Ella Cinders (#1-3: 52 pgs.)	15	30	45	86	133	180
2	10	20	30	54	72	90
3-10	8	16	24	42	54	65
11-20	7	14	21	37	46	55
21-32	6	12	18	31	38	45
33-(2-3/54) 2 pgs. early Peanuts by Schulz	12	24	36	67	94	120

SPARKLE PLENTY (See Harvey Comics Library #2 & Dick Tracy)
Dell Publishing Co.: 1949

	GD 2.0	VG 4.0	FN 6.0	VF 8.0	VF/NM 9.0	NM- 9.2
Four Color 215 - Dick Tracy reprint by Gould	10	20	30	68	144	220

SPARKLER COMICS (1st series)
United Feature Comic Group: July, 1940 - No. 2, 1940

	GD 2.0	VG 4.0	FN 6.0	VF 8.0	VF/NM 9.0	NM- 9.2
1-Jim Hardy	39	78	117	240	395	550
2-Frankie Doodle	30	60	90	177	289	400

SPARKLER COMICS (2nd series)(Nancy & Sluggo #121 on)(Cover title becomes Nancy and Sluggo #101? on)
United Features Syndicate: July, 1941 - No. 120, Jan, 1955

	GD 2.0	VG 4.0	FN 6.0	VF 8.0	VF/NM 9.0	NM- 9.2
1-Origin 1st app. Sparkman; Tarzan (by Hogarth in all issues), Captain & the Kids, Ella Cinders, Danny Dingle, Dynamite Dunn, Nancy, Abbie & Slats, Broncho Bill, Frankie Doodle, begin; Spark Man c-1-9,11,12; Hap Hopper c-10,13	181	362	543	1158	1979	2800
2	60	120	180	381	653	925
3,4	45	90	135	284	480	675
5-9: 9-Spark Man's new costume	39	78	117	240	395	550
10-Spark Man's secret ID revealed	39	78	117	240	395	550
11,12-Spark Man war-c. 12-Spark Man's new costume (color change)	37	74	111	222	361	500
13-Hap Hopper war-c	31	62	93	182	296	410
14-Tarzan-c by Hogarth	61	122	183	390	670	950
15,17: 15-Capt & Kids-c. 17-Nancy & Sluggo-c	23	46	69	136	223	310
16,18-Spark Man-c. 16-Japanese WWII-c. 18-Nazi WWII-c	39	78	117	231	378	525
19-1st Race Riley and the Commandos-c/s	36	72	108	216	351	485
20-Nancy war-c	27	54	81	162	266	370
21,25,28,31,34,37-Tarzan-c by Hogarth	46	92	138	290	488	685
22-24,26,27,29,30: 22-Race Riley & the Commandos strips begin, ends #44	22	44	66	128	209	290
32,33,35,36,38,40	14	28	42	76	108	140
39-Classic Tarzan shooting an arrow into a dinosaur's eye on cover by Hogarth	77	154	231	493	847	1200
41,43,45,46,48,49	11	22	33	60	83	105
42,44,47,50-Tarzan-c (42,47,50 by Hogarth)	25	50	75	150	245	340
51,52,54-68,70: 57-Li'l Abner begins (not in #58); Fearless Fosdick app. in #58	10	20	30	58	79	100
53-Tarzan-c by Hogarth	24	48	72	144	237	330
69-Wolverton-*esque* Horror-c	12	24	36	67	94	120
71-80	9	18	27	47	61	75
81,82,84-86: 86 Last Tarzan; lingerie panels	8	16	24	40	50	60
83-Tarzan-c; Li'l Abner ends	12	24	36	69	97	125
87-96,98-99	7	14	21	37	46	55
97-Origin Casey Ruggles by Warren Tufts	8	16	24	42	54	65
100	8	16	24	42	54	65
101-107,109-112,114-119	6	12	18	31	38	45
108,113-Toth-a	7	14	21	37	46	55
120-(10-11/54) 2 pgs. early Peanuts by Schulz	10	20	30	58	79	100

SPARKLING LOVE
Avon Periodicals/Realistic (1953): June, 1950; 1953

	GD 2.0	VG 4.0	FN 6.0	VF 8.0	VF/NM 9.0	NM- 9.2
1(Avon)-Kubert-a; photo-c	36	72	108	211	343	475
nn(1953)-Reprint; Kubert-a	14	28	42	82	121	160

SPARKLING STARS
Holyoke Publishing Co.: June, 1944 - No. 33, March, 1948

	GD 2.0	VG 4.0	FN 6.0	VF 8.0	VF/NM 9.0	NM- 9.2
1-Hell's Angels, FBI, Boxie Weaver, Petey & Pop, & Ali Baba begin	21	42	63	124	202	280
2-Speed Spaulding story	14	28	42	76	108	140
3-Actual FBI case photos & war photos	11	22	33	60	83	105
4-10: 7-X-Mas-c	10	20	30	54	72	90
11-19: 13-Origin/1st app. Jungo the Man-Beast-c/s	9	18	27	50	65	80
20-Intro Fangs the Wolf Boy	10	20	30	54	72	90
21-33: 29-Bondage-c. 31-Sid Greene-a	9	18	27	47	61	75

SPARK MAN (See Sparkler Comics)
Frances M. McQueeny: 1945 (36 pgs., one-shot)

	GD 2.0	VG 4.0	FN 6.0	VF 8.0	VF/NM 9.0	NM- 9.2
1-Origin Spark Man r/Sparkler #1-3; female torture story; cover redrawn from Sparkler #1	34	68	102	199	325	450

SPARKY WATTS (Also see Big Shot Comics & Columbia Comics)
Columbia Comic Corp.: Nov?, 1942 - No. 10, 1949

	GD 2.0	VG 4.0	FN 6.0	VF 8.0	VF/NM 9.0	NM- 9.2
1(1942)-Skyman & The Face app; Hitler/Goering story/c	110	220	330	704	1202	1700
2(1943)	36	72	108	211	343	475
3(1944) "6000 Lbs. Block Buster to Bust Adolf"-c	24	48	72	142	234	325
4(1944)-Origin	20	40	60	114	182	250
5(1947)-Skyman app.; Boody Rogers-c/a	16	32	48	94	147	200
6,7,9,10: 6(1947). 9-Haunted House-c. 10(1949)	12	24	36	67	94	120
8(1948)-Surrealistic-c	14	28	42	80	115	150

NOTE: ***Boody Rogers** c-1-8.*

Spawn #6 © TMP

Spawn #252 © TMP

Spawn Kills Everyone! #1 © TMP

GD VG FN VF VF/NM NM-
2.0 4.0 6.0 8.0 9.0 9.2

GD VG FN VF VF/NM NM-
2.0 4.0 6.0 8.0 9.0 9.2

SPARTACUS (Movie)
Dell Publishing Co.: No. 1139, Nov, 1960 (Kirk Douglas photo-c)

Four Color 1139-Buscema-a 10 20 30 69 147 225

SPARTACUS (Television series)
Devil's Due Publishing: Oct, 2009 - No. 2 ($3.99)

1,2: 1-DeKnight-s. 2-Palmiotti-s 4.00

SPARTAN: WARRIOR SPIRIT (Also see WildC.A.T.S: Covert Action Teams)
Image Comics (WildStorm Productions): July, 1995 - No. 4, Nov, 1995 ($2.50, lim. series)

1-4: Kurt Busiek scripts; Mike McKone-c/a 3.00

SPARTA: USA
DC Comics (WildStorm): May, 2010 - No. 6, Oct, 2010 ($2.99, limited series)

1-6: 1-Lapham-s/Timmons-a; covers by Timmons and Lapham 3.00

SPAWN (Also see Curse of the Spawn and Sam & Twitch)
Image Comics (Todd McFarlane Prods.): May, 1992 - Present ($1.95/$2.50/$2.99)

1-1st app. Spawn; McFarlane-c/a begins; McFarlane/Steacy-c; 1st Todd McFarlane Productions title. 3 6 9 16 24 32
1-Black & white edition 10 20 30 64 132 200
2,3: 2-1st app. Violator; McFarlane/Steacy-c 2 4 6 10 14 18
4-Contains coupon for Image Comics #0 2 4 6 8 10 12
4-With coupon missing 3.00
4-Newsstand edition w/o poster or coupon 3.00
5-Cerebus cameo (1 pg.) as stuffed animal; Spawn mobile poster #1 2 4 6 8 10 12
6-8,10: 7-Spawn Mobile poster #2. 8-Alan Moore scripts; Miller poster. 10-Cerebus app.; Dave Sim scripts; 1 pg. cameo app. by Superman 6.00
9-Neil Gaiman scripts; Jim Lee poster; 1st Angela. 3 6 9 15 22 28
11-17,19,20,22-30: 11-Miller script; Darrow poster. 12-Bloodwulf poster by Liefeld. 14,15-Violator app. 16,17-Grant Morrison scripts; Capullo-c/a(p). 23,24-McFarlane-a/stories. 25-(10/94). 19-(10/94). 20-(11/94) 5.00
18-Grant Morrison script, Capullo-c/a(p); low distr. 1 3 4 6 8 10
21-low distribution 1 3 4 6 8 10
31-49: 31-1st app. The Redeemer; new costume (brief). 32-1st full app. new costume. 38-40,42,44,46,48-Tony Daniel-c/a(p). 38-1st app. Cy-Gor. 40,41-Cy-Gor & Curse app. 4.00
50-($3.95, 48 pgs.) 6.00
51-66: 52-Savage Dragon app. 56-w/ Darkchylde preview. 57-Cy-Gor-c/app. 64-Polybagged w/McFarlane Toys catalog. 65-Photo-c of movie Spawn and McFarlane 4.00
67-96: 81-Billy Kincaid returns 4.00
97-Angela-c/app. 2 4 6 8 10 12
98,99-Angela app. 6.00
100-($4.95) Angela dies; 6 total covers; the 3 variants by McFarlane, Miller, and Mignola 2 4 6 8 10 12
100-($4.95) 3 variant covers by Ross, Capullo, and Wood 1 2 3 5 6 8
101-149-($2.50) 3.00
150-($4.95) 4 covers by McFarlane, Capullo, Tan, Jim Lee 5.00
151-184: 151-($2.95) Wraparound-c by Tan. 167-Clown app. 179-Mayhew-a 3.00
185-199,201-219: 185-McFarlane & Holguin-s/Portacio-a begins. 193-Sam & Twitch app. 210-215-Michael Golden-c 3.00
200-(1/11, $3.99) 7 covers by McFarlane, Capullo, Finch, Jim Lee, Liefeld, Silvestri, Wood 4.00
220-(6/12, $3.99) 20th Anniversary issue; McFarlane-s/Kudranski-a; bonus interview, timeline and cover gallery 4.00
220: 20th Anniversary Collector's Special-(6/12, $4.99) B&W version of #220 w/bonuses 5.00
221-249: 221-231-Cover swipes of classic covers. 221-Amazing Fantasy #15. 225-Election special with 2 covers (Obama & Romney). 228-Action #1 c-swipe. 231-Spider-Man #1 ('90) c-swipe. 234-Haunt app. 3.00
250-($5.99) McFarlane-s/Kudranski-a; Al Simmons returns; multiple covers 6.00
251-270: 251-Follows Spawn Resurrection #1. 258-Erik Larsen & McFarlane-a begin. 265-Ant app. 266-Savage Dragon app. 267-270-Kudranski-a 3.00
Annual 1-Blood & Shadows ('99, $4.95) Ashley Wood-c/a; Jenkins-s 5.00
...: Architects of Fear (2/11, $6.99, squarebound GN) Briclot-a 7.00
...: Armegeddon Complete Collection TPB ('07, $29.95) r/#150-163 30.00
...: Armegeddon, Part 1 TPB (10/06, $14.99) r/#150-155 15.00
...: Armegeddon, Part 2 TPB (2/07, $15.95) r/#156-164 16.00
...Bible-(8/96, $1.95)-Character bios 4.00
Book 1 TPB($9.95) r/#1-5; Book 2-r/#6-9,11; Book 3 -r/#12-15, Book 4- r/#16-20; Book 5-r/#21-25; Book 6- r/#26-30; Book 7-r/#31-34; Book 8-r/#35-38; Book 9-r/#39-42; Book 10-r/#43-47 11.00
Book 11 TPB ($10.95) r/#48-50; Book 12-r/#51-54 11.00
... Collection Vol. 1 (10/05, $19.95) r/#1-8,11,12; intro. by Frank Miller 20.00
... Collection Vol. 2 HC (7/07, $49.95) r/#13-33 50.00
... Collection Vol. 2 SC (9/06, $29.95) r/#13-33 30.00
... Collection Vol. 3 (3/07, $29.95) r/#34-54 30.00
... Collection Vol. 4 (9/07, $29.95) r/#55-75 30.00
... Collection Vol. 5 ('08, $29.95) r/#76-95 30.00
... Collection Vol. 6 (8/08, $29.95) r/#96-116; cover gallery 30.00
Image Firsts: Spawn #1 (4/10, $1.00) reprints #1 3.00
... Godslayer Vol. 1 (9/06, $6.99) Anacleto-c/a; Holguin-s; sketch pages 7.00
... Kills Everyone! 1 (8/16, $2.99) McFarlane-s/JJ Kirby-a; mini Spawn vs. cosplayers 3.00
...: Neonoir TPB (11/08, $14.95) r/#170-175 15.00
...: New Flesh TPB ('07, $14.95) r/#166-169 15.00
... Resurrection 1 (3/15, $2.99) Follows issue #250; Jenkins-s/Jonboy-a 3.00
...Simony (5/04, $7.95) English translation of French Spawn story; Briclot-a 8.00

NOTE: *Capullo a-16p-18p; c-16p-18p.* ***Daniel*** *a-38-40, 42, 44, 46.* ***McFarlane*** *a-1-15; c-1-15p.* ***Thibert*** *a-16i(part). Posters come with issues 1, 4, 7-9, 11, 12. #25 was released before #19 & 20.*

SPAWN-BATMAN (Also see Batman/Spawn: War Devil under Batman: One-Shots)
Image Comics (Todd McFarlane Productions): 1994 ($3.95, one-shot)

1-Miller scripts; McFarlane-c/a 2 4 6 8 10 12

SPAWN: BLOOD FEUD
Image Comics (Todd McFarlane Prods.): June, 1995 - No. 4, Sept, 1995 ($2.25, lim. series)

1-4-Alan Moore scripts, Tony Daniel-a 4.00

SPAWN FAN EDITION
Image Comics (Todd McFarlane Productions): Aug, 1996 - No. 3, Oct, 1996 (Giveaway, 12 pgs.) (Polybagged w/Overstreet's FAN)

1-3: Beau Smith scripts; Brad Gorby-a(p). 1-1st app. Nordik, the Norse Hellspawn. 2-1st app. McFallon. 3-1st app. Mercy 1 2 3 5 6 8
1-3-(Gold): All retailer incentives 16.00
1-3-Variant-c 1 2 3 5 6 8
2-(Platinum)-Retailer incentive 25.00

SPAWN GODSLAYER
Image Comics (Todd McFarlane Prods.): May, 2007 - No. 8, Apr, 2008 ($2.99)

1-8: 1-Holguin-s/Tan-a/Anacleto-c 3.00

SPAWN: THE DARK AGES
Image Comics (Todd McFarlane Productions): Mar, 1999 - No. 28, Oct, 2001 ($2.50)

1-Fabry-c; Holguin-s/Sharp-a; variant-c by McFarlane 3.00
2-28 3.00

SPAWN THE IMPALER
Image Comics (Todd McFarlane Prods.): Oct, 1996 - No. 3, Dec, 1996 ($2.95, limited series)

1-3-Mike Grell scripts, painted-a 4.00

SPAWN: THE UNDEAD
Image Comics (Todd McFarlane Prod.): Jun, 1999 - No. 9, Feb, 2000 ($1.95/$2.25)

1-9-Dwayne Turner-c/a; Jenkins-s. 7-9-($2.25-c) 3.00
TPB (6/08, $24.99) r/#1-9 25.00

SPAWN/WILDC.A.T.S
Image Comics (WildStorm): Jan, 1996 - No. 4, Apr, 1996 ($2.50, lim. series)

1-4: Alan Moore scripts in all. 4.00

SPEAKER FOR THE DEAD (ORSON SCOTT CARD'S...) (Ender's Game)
Marvel Comics: Mar, 2011 - No. 5, Jul, 2011 ($3.99, limited series)

1-3-Johnston-s/Mhan-a/Camuncoli-c 4.00

SPECIAL AGENT (Steve Saunders...)(Also see True Comics #68)
Parents' Magazine Institute (Commended Comics No. 2): Dec, 1947 - No. 8, Sept, 1949 (Based on true FBI cases)

1-J. Edgar Hoover photo on-c 14 28 42 82 121 160
2 9 18 27 50 65 80
3-8 8 16 24 42 54 65

SPECIAL COLLECTORS' EDITION (See Savage Fists of Kung-Fu)

SPECIAL COMICS (Becomes Hangman #2 on)
MLJ Magazines: Winter, 1941-42

1-Origin The Boy Buddies (Shield & Wizard x-over); death of The Comet retold (see Pep #17); origin The Hangman retold; Hangman-c 400 800 1200 2800 4900 7000

SPECIAL EDITION (See Gorgo and Reptisaurus)

SPECIAL EDITION COMICS (See Promotional Section)

SPECIAL EDITION COMICS
Fawcett Publications: 1940 (August) (68 pgs., one-shot)

1-1st book devoted entirely to Captain Marvel; C.C. Beck-c/a; only app. of Captain Marvel with belt buckle; Capt. Marvel appears with button-down flap; 1st story (came out before Captain Marvel #1) 811 1622 2433 5920 10,460 15,000

NOTE: *Prices vary widely on this book. Since this book is all Captain Marvel stories, it is actually a pre-Captain*

Special Marvel Edition #1 © MAR

Spectacular Spider-Man #2 © MAR

Spectacular Spider-Man #29 © MAR

GD 2.0 | VG 4.0 | FN 6.0 | VF 8.0 | VF/NM 9.0 | NM- 9.2

Marvel #1. There is speculation that this book almost became ***Captain Marvel*** *#1. After* ***Special Edition*** *was published, there was an editor change at Fawcett. The new editor commissioned Kirby to do a nn* ***Captain Marvel*** *book early in 1941. This book was followed by a 2nd book several months later. This 2nd book was advertised as a #3 (making Special Edition the #1, & the nn issue the #2). However, the 2nd book did come out as a #2.*

SPECIAL EDITION: SPIDER-MAN VS. THE HULK (See listing under The Amazing Spider-Man)

SPECIAL EDITION X-MEN
Marvel Comics Group: Feb, 1983 ($2.00, one-shot, Baxter paper)
1-r/Giant-Size X-Men #1 plus one new story 2 4 6 11 16 20

SPECIAL FORCES
Image Comics: Oct, 2007 - No. 4, Mar, 2009 ($2.99)
1-4-Iraq war combat; Kyle Baker-s/a/c 3.00

SPECIAL MARVEL EDITION (Master of Kung Fu #17 on)
Marvel Comics Group: Jan, 1971 - No. 16, Feb, 1974 (#1-3: 25¢, 68 pgs.; #4: 52 pgs.; #5-16: 20¢, regular ed.)
1-Thor-r by Kirby; 68 pgs. 4 8 12 27 44 60
2-4: Thor-r by Kirby; 2,3-68 pg. Giant. 4-(52 pgs.) 3 6 9 16 23 30
5-14: Sgt. Fury-r; 11-r/Sgt. Fury #13 (Capt. America) 2 4 6 9 12 15
15-Master of Kung Fu (Shang-Chi) begins (1st app., 12/73); Starlin-a; origin/1st app. Nayland Smith & Dr. Petrie 13 26 39 89 195 300
16-1st app. Midnight; Starlin-a (2nd Shang-Chi) 6 12 18 41 76 110
NOTE: ***Kirby*** *c-10-14.*

SPECIAL MISSIONS (See G.I. Joe...)

SPECIAL WAR SERIES (Attack V4#3 on?)
Charlton Comics: Aug, 1965 - No. 4, Nov, 1965
V4#1-D-Day (also see D-Day listing) 4 8 12 28 47 65
2-Attack! 3 6 9 16 23 30
3-War & Attack (also see War & Attack) 3 6 9 14 20 25
4-Judomaster (intro/1st app.; see Sarge Steel) 8 16 24 56 108 160

SPECIES (Movie)
Dark Horse Comics: June, 1995 - No. 4, Sept, 1995 ($2.50, limited series)
1-4: Adaptation of film 3.00

SPECIES: HUMAN RACE (Movie)
Dark Horse Comics: Nov, 1996 - No. 4, Feb, 1997 ($2.95, limited series)
1-4 3.00

SPECTACULAR ADVENTURES (See Adventures)

SPECTACULAR FEATURE MAGAZINE, A (Formerly My Confession)
(Spectacular Features Magazine #12)
Fox Feature Syndicate: No. 11, April, 1950
11 (#1)-Samson and Delilah 27 54 81 160 263 365

SPECTACULAR FEATURES MAGAZINE (Formerly A Spectacular Feature Magazine)
Fox Feature Syndicate: No. 12, June, 1950 - No. 3, Aug, 1950
12 (#2)-Iwo Jima; photo flag-c 27 54 81 158 259 360
3-True Crime Cases From Police Files 22 44 66 128 209 290

SPECTACULAR SCARLET SPIDER
Marvel Comics: Nov, 1995 - No. 2, Dec, 1995 ($1.95, limited series)
1,2: Replaces Spectacular Spider-Man 3.00

SPECTACULAR SPIDER-GIRL
Marvel Comics: Jul, 2010 - No. 4, Oct, 2010 ($3.99, limited series)
1-4-Frenz-a; Frank Castle and the Hobgoblin app. 4.00

SPECTACULAR SPIDER-MAN, THE (See Marvel Special Edition and Marvel Treasury Edition)

SPECTACULAR SPIDER-MAN, THE (Magazine)
Marvel Comics Group: July, 1968 - No. 2, Nov, 1968 (35¢)
1-(B&W)-Romita/Mooney 52 pg. story plus updated origin story with Everett-a(i) 10 20 30 69 147 225
1-Variation w/single c-price of 40¢ 10 20 30 69 147 225
2-(Color)-Green Goblin-c & 58 pg. story; Romita painted-c (story reprinted in King Size Spider-Man #9); Romita/Mooney-a 9 18 27 61 123 185

SPECTACULAR SPIDER-MAN, THE (Peter Parker...#54-132, 134)
Marvel Comics Group: Dec, 1976 - No. 263, Nov, 1998
1-Origin recap in text; return of Tarantula 5 10 15 35 63 90
2-Kraven the Hunter app. 3 6 9 17 26 35
3-5: 3-Intro Lightmaster. 4-Vulture app. 3 6 9 14 20 25
6-8-Morbius app.; 6-r/Marvel Team-Up #3 w/Morbius 3 6 9 15 22 28
7,8-(35¢-c variants, limited distribution)(6,7/77) 7 14 21 49 92 135
9-20: 9,10-White Tiger app. 11-Last 30¢-c. 17,18-Angel & Iceman app. (from Champions); Ghost Rider cameo. 18-Gil Kane-c 2 4 6 8 11 14
9-11-(35¢-c variants, limited distribution)(8-10/77) 7 14 21 46 86 125
21,24-26: 21-Scorpion app. 26-Daredevil app. 2 3 4 6 8 10
22,23-Moon Knight app. 2 4 6 8 10 12
27-Miller's 1st art on Daredevil (2/79); also see Captain America #235 5 10 15 34 60 85
28-Miller Daredevil (p) 4 8 12 25 40 55
29-55,57,59: 33-Origin Iguana. 38-Morbius app. 1 2 3 4 5 7
56-2nd app. Jack O'Lantern (Macendale) & 1st Spidey/Jack O'Lantern battle (7/81) 1 2 3 5 6 8
58-Byrne-a(p) 1 2 3 5 6 8
60-Double size; origin retold with new facts revealed 1 2 3 5 6 8
61-63,65-68,71-74: 65-Kraven the Hunter app. 6.00
64-1st app. Cloak & Dagger (3/82) 6 12 18 38 69 100
69,70-Cloak & Dagger app. 2 4 6 8 10 12
75-Double size 1 2 3 5 6 8
76-80: 78,79-Punisher cameo 6.00
81,82-Punisher, Cloak & Dagger app. 1 3 4 6 8 10
83-Origin Punisher retold (10/83) 2 4 6 9 12 15
84,86-89,91-99: 94-96-Cloak & Dagger app. 98-Intro The Spot 6.00
85-Hobgoblin (Ned Leeds) app. (12/83); gains powers of original Green Goblin (see Amazing Spider-Man #238) 2 4 6 8 10 12
90-Spider-Man's new black costume, last panel (ties w/Amazing Spider-Man #252 & Marvel Team-Up #141 for 1st app.) 3 6 9 17 26 35
100-(3/85)-Double size 1 2 3 4 5 7
101-115,117,118,120-129: 107-110-Death of Jean DeWolff. 111-Secret Wars II tie-in. 128-Black Cat new costume 5.00
116,119-Sabretooth-c/story 2 4 6 9 12 15
130-132: 130-Hobgoblin app. 131-Six part Kraven tie-in. 132-Kraven tie-in 2 3 4 6 8 10
133-137,139,140: 140-Punisher cameo 5.00
138-1st full app. Tombstone (origin #139) 1 3 4 6 8 10
141-143-Punisher app. 1 2 3 4 5 7
144-146,148-157: 151-Tombstone returns 4.00
147-1st brief app. new Hobgoblin (Macendale), 1 page; continued in Web of Spider-Man #48 2 4 6 8 11 14
158-Spider-Man gets new powers (1st Cosmic Spidey, cont'd in Web of Spider-Man #59) 1 2 3 5 6 8
159-Cosmic Spider-Man app. 1 2 3 4 5 7
160-170: 161-163-Hobgoblin app. 168-170-Avengers x-over. 169-1st app. The Outlaws 3.00
171-188,190-199: 180-184-Green Goblin app. 197-199-Original X-Men-c/story 3.00
189-($2.95, 52 pgs.)-Silver hologram on-c; battles Green Goblin; origin Spidey retold; Vess poster w/Spidey & Hobgoblin 6.00
189-(2nd printing)-Gold hologram on-c 4.00
195-(Deluxe ed.)-Polybagged w/"Dirt" magazine #2 & Beastie Boys/Smithereens music cassette 1 3 4 6 8 10
200-($2.95)-Holo-grafx foil-c; Green Goblin-c/story 5.00
201-219,221,222,224,226-228,230-247: 212-w/card sheet. 203-Maximum Carnage x-over. 204-Begin 4 part death of Tombstone story. 207,208-The Shroud-c/story. 208-Siege of Darkness x-over (#207 is a tie-in). 209-Black Cat back-up. 215,216-Scorpion app. 217-Power & Responsibility Pt. 4. 231-Return of Kaine; Spider-Man corpse discovered. 232-New Doc Octopus app. 233-Carnage-c/app. 235-Dragon Man cameo. 236-Dragon Man-c/app; Lizard app.; Peter Parker regains powers. 238,239-Lizard app. 239-w/card insert. 240-Revelations storyline begins. 241-Flashback 3.00
213-Collectors ed. polybagged w/16 pg. preview & animation cel; foil-c; 1st meeting Spidey & Typhoid Mary 4.00
213-Version polybagged w/Gamepro #7; no-c date, price 3.00
217,219 ($2.95)-Deluxe edition foil-c: flip book 4.00
220 ($2.25, 52 pgs.)-Flip book, Mary Jane reveals pregnancy 4.00
223,229: ($2.50) 229-Spidey quits 4.00
223,225: ($2.95)-223-Die Cut-c. 225-Newsstand ed. 4.00
225,229: ($3.95) 225-Direct Market Holodisk-c (Green Goblin). 229-Acetate-c, Spidey quits 5.00
240-Variant-c 4.00
248,249,251-254,256: 249-Return of Norman Osborn 256-1st app. Prodigy 3.00
250-($3.25) Double gatefold-c 4.00
255-($2.99) Spiderhunt pt. 4 4.00
257-262: 257-Double cover with "Spectacular Prodigy #1"; battles Jack O'Lantern. 258-Spidey is cleared. 259,260-Green Goblin & Hobgoblin app. 262-Byrne-s 3.00
263-Final issue; Byrne-c; Aunt May returns 5.00
#(-1) Flashback (7/97) 3.00
1000 (6/11, $4.99) Punisher app.; Nauck & Ryan-a/Rivera-c; r/ASM #129 5.00
Annual 1 (1979)-Doc Octopus-c & 46 pg. story 2 4 6 8 11 14
Annual 2 (1980)-Origin/1st app. Rapier 1 2 3 5 6 8

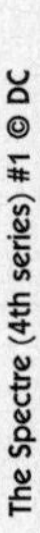
The Spectre (4th series) #1 © DC

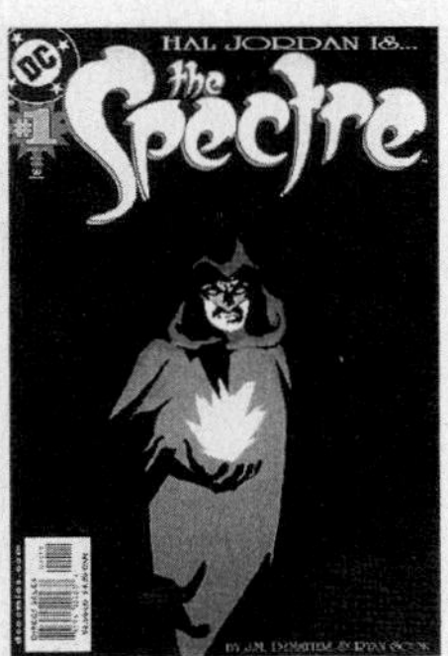

Speed Comics #3 © HARV

Speed Racer #3 © Speed Racer Ents.

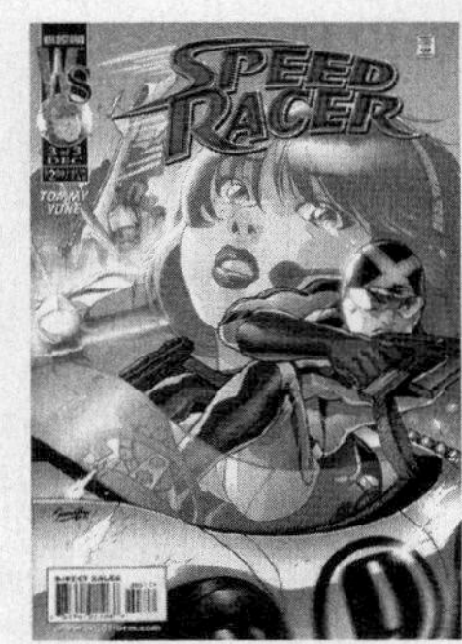

GD VG FN VF VF/NM NM-
2.0 4.0 6.0 8.0 9.0 9.2

GD VG FN VF VF/NM NM-
2.0 4.0 6.0 8.0 9.0 9.2

Annual 3-5: ('81-'83) 3-Last Man-Wolf 5.00
Annual 6-14: 8 ('88,$ 1.75)-Evolutionary War x-over; Daydreamer returns Gwen Stacy "clone" back to real self (not Gwen Stacy). 9 ('89, $2.00, 68 pgs.)-Atlantis Attacks. 10 ('90, $2.00, 68 pgs.)-McFarlane-a. 11 ('91, $2.00, 68 pgs.)-Iron Man app. 12 ('92, $2.25, 68 pgs.)-Venom solo story cont'd from Amazing Spider-Man Annual #26. 13 ('93, $2.95, 68 pgs.)-Polybagged w/trading card; John Romita, Sr. back-up-a 4.00
Special 1 (1995, $3.95)-Flip book 4.00

NOTE: ***Austin** c-21i, Annual 11i. **Buckler** a-103, 107-111, 116, 117, 119, 122, Annual 1, Annual 10; c-103, 107-111, 113, 116-119, 122, Annual 1. **Buscema** a-121. **Byrne** c(p)-17, 43, 58, 101, 102. **Giffen** a-120p. **Hembeck** c/a-86p. **Larsen** c-Annual 11p. **Miller** c-46p, 48p, 50, 51p, 52p, 54p, 55, 56p, 57, 60. **Mooney** a-7i, 11i, 21p, 23p, 25p, 26p, 29-34p, 36p, 37p, 39i, 41, 42i, 49p, 50i, 51i, 53p, 54-57i, 59-66i, 68i, 71i, 73-79i, 81-83i, 85i, 87-99i, 102i, 125p, Annual 1i, 2p. **Nasser** c-37p. **Perez** c-10. **Simonson** c-54i. **Zeck** a-22, 118, 131, 132; c-131, 132.*

SPECTACULAR SPIDER-MAN (2nd series)
Marvel Comics: Sept, 2003 - No. 27, June, 2005 ($2.25/$2.99)

1-Jenkins-s/Ramos-a/c; Venom-c/app. 4.00
2-26: 2-5-Venom app. 6-9-Dr. Octopus app. 11-13-The Lizard app. 14-Rivera painted-a. 15,16-Capt. America app. 17,18-Ramos-a. 20-Spider-Man gets organic webshooters 21,22-Caldwell-a. 23-26-Sarah & Gabriel app.; Land-c 3.00
27-($2.99) Last issue; Uncle Ben app. in flashback; Buckingham-a 4.00
... Vol. 1: The Hunger TPB (2003, $11.99) r/#1-5 12.00
... Vol. 2: Countdown TPB (2004, $11.99) r/#6-10 12.00
... Vol. 3: Here There Be Monsters TPB (2004, $9.99) r/#11-14 10.00
... Vol. 4: Disassembled TPB (2004, $14.99) r/#15-20 15.00
... Vol. 5: Sins Remembered (2005, $9.99) r/#23-26 10.00
... Vol. 6: The Final Curtain (2005, $14.99) r/#21,22,27 & Peter Parker: Spider-Man #39-41 15.00

SPECTACULAR STORIES MAGAZINE (Formerly A Star Presentation)
Fox Feature Syndicate (Hero Books): No. 4, July, 1950; No. 3, Sept, 1950

	GD 2.0	VG 4.0	FN 6.0	VF 8.0	VF/NM 9.0	NM- 9.2
4-Sherlock Holmes (true crime stories)	36	72	108	216	351	485
3-The St. Valentine's Day Massacre (true crime)	24	48	72	142	234	325

SPECTRE, THE (1st Series) (See Adventure Comics #431-440, More Fun & Showcase)
National Periodical Publ.: Nov-Dec, 1967 - No. 10, May-June, 1969 (All 12¢)

	GD 2.0	VG 4.0	FN 6.0	VF 8.0	VF/NM 9.0	NM- 9.2
1-(11-12/67)-Anderson-c/a	13	26	39	86	188	290
2-5-Neal Adams-c/a; 3-Wildcat x-over	9	18	27	57	111	165
6-8,10: 6-8-Anderson inks. 7-Hourman app.	6	12	18	41	76	110
9-Wrightson-a	7	14	21	44	82	120

SPECTRE, THE (2nd Series) (See Saga of the Swamp Thing #58, Showcase '95 #8 & Wrath of the...)
DC Comics: Apr, 1987 - No. 31, Oct, 1989 ($1.00, new format)

1-Colan-a begins 5.00
2-32: 9-Nudity panels. 10-Batman cameo. 10,11-Millennium tie-ins 3.00
Annual 1 (1988, $2.00)-Deadman app. 4.00

NOTE: ***Art Adams** c-Annual 1. **Colan** a-1-6. **Kaluta** c-1-3. **Mignola** c-7-9. **Morrow** a-9-15. **Sears** c/a-22. **Vess** c-13-15.*

SPECTRE, THE (3rd Series) (Also see Brave and the Bold #72, 75, 116, 180, 199 & Showcase '95 #8)
DC Comics: Dec, 1992 - No. 62, Feb, 1998 ($1.75/$1.95/$2.25/$2.50)

1-($1.95)-Glow-in-the-dark-c; Mandrake-a begins 5.00
2,3 4.00
4-7,9-12,14-20: 10-Kaluta-c. 11-Hildebrandt painted-c. 16-Aparo/K. Jones-a. 19-Snyder III-c. 20-Sienkiewicz-c 3.00
8,13-($2.50)-Glow-in-the-dark-c 4.00
21-62: 22-(9/94)-Superman-c & app. 23-(11/94). 43-Kent Williams-c. 44-Kaluta-c. 47-Final Night x-over. 49-Begin Bolton-c. 51-Batman-c/app. 52-Gianni-c. 54-1st app. Michael Holt (Mr. Terrific); Corben-c. 60-Harris-c 3.00
#0 (10/94) Released between #22 & #23 3.00
Annual 1 (1995, $3.95)-Year One story 4.00

NOTE: ***Bisley** c-27. **Fabry** c-2. **Kelley Jones** c-31. **Vess** c-5.*

SPECTRE, THE (4th Series) (Hal Jordan; also see Day of Judgment #5 and Legends of the DC Universe #33-36)
DC Comics: Mar, 2001 - No. 27, May, 2003 ($2.50/$2.75)

1-DeMatteis-s/Ryan Sook-c/a 4.00
2-27: 3,4-Superman & Batman-c/app. 5-Two-Face-c/app. 20-Begin $2.75-c. 21-Sinestro returns. 24-JLA app. 3.00

SPECTRE, THE (See Crisis Aftermath: The Spectre)

SPEEDBALL (See Amazing Spider-Man Annual #12, Marvel Super-Heroes & The New Warriors)
Marvel Comics: Sept, 1988(10/88-inside) - No. 11, July, 1989 (75¢)

	GD 2.0	VG 4.0	FN 6.0	VF 8.0	VF/NM 9.0	NM- 9.2
1-Ditko/Guice-a/c	1	3	4	6	8	10
2-11: Ditko/Guice-a-2-4; Ditko a-2-10; c-2-11p						4.00

SPEED BUGGY (TV)(Also see Fun-In #12, 15)
Charlton Comics: July, 1975 - No. 9, Nov, 1976 (Hanna-Barbera)

	GD 2.0	VG 4.0	FN 6.0	VF 8.0	VF/NM 9.0	NM- 9.2
1	3	6	9	15	22	28
2-9	2	4	6	10	14	18

SPEED CARTER SPACEMAN (See Spaceman)

SPEED COMICS (New Speed)(Also see Double Up)
Brookwood Publ./Speed Publ./Harvey Publications No. 14 on:
10/39 - #11, 8/40; #12, 3/41 - #44, 1-2/47 (#14-16: pocket size, 100 pgs.)

	GD 2.0	VG 4.0	FN 6.0	VF 8.0	VF/NM 9.0	NM- 9.2
1-Origin & 1st app. Shock Gibson; Ted Parrish, the Man with 1000 Faces begins; Powell-a; becomes Champion #2 on?; has earliest? full page panel in comics; classic war-c	423	846	1269	3000	5250	7500
2-Powell-a	181	362	543	1158	1979	2800
3-War-c	129	258	387	826	1413	2000
4,5: 4-Powell-a. 5-Dinosaur-c	123	246	369	787	1344	1900
6-9,11: 7-Mars Mason begins, ends #11. 9,11-War-c	116	232	348	742	1271	1800
10-Classsic Giant Moth Monster-c	142	284	426	909	1555	2200
12 (3/41; shows #11 in indicia)-The Wasp begins; Major Colt app. (Capt. Colt #12)	123	246	369	787	1344	1900
13-Intro. Captain Freedom & Young Defenders; Girl Commandos, Pat Parker (costumed heroine), War Nurse begins; Major Colt app.	135	270	405	864	1482	2100
14,15-(100 pg. pocket size, 1941): 14-2nd Harvey comic (See Pocket); Shock Gibson dons new costume; Nazi war-c. 15-Pat Parker dons costume, last in costume #23; no Girl Commandos; Nazi monsters war-c.	290	580	870	1856	3178	4500
16-(100 pg. pocket size, 1941) Cover with Hitler leading an army of Nazi ghouls to the White House	300	600	900	2010	3505	5000
17-Classic Simon & Kirby WWII Nazi bondage/torture-c; Black Cat begins (4/42, early app.; see Pocket #1); origin Black Cat-r/Pocket #1; not in #40,41	290	580	870	1856	3178	4500
18-20-S&K-c. 18-Bondage/torture-c. 19,20-Japanese war-c	226	452	678	1446	2473	3500
21-Hitler, Tojo-c; Kirby-c	300	600	900	1950	3375	4800
22-Nazi WWII-c by Kirby	181	362	543	1158	1979	2800
23-Origin Girl Commandos; war-c by Kirby	181	362	543	1158	1979	2800
24-Pat Parker team-up with Girl Commandos; Hitler, Tojo, & Mussolini-c	258	516	774	1651	2826	4000
25,27,29: 25-War-c. 27 Nazi WWII-c. 29-Nazi WWII bondage-c	168	336	504	1075	1838	2600
26-Flag-c	213	426	639	1363	2332	3300
28-Classic Nazi monster WWII-c	300	600	900	2010	3635	5200
30-Nazi WWII Death Chamber bondage-c	194	388	582	1242	2121	3000
31-Classic Schomburg Hitler & Tojo-c	314	628	942	2198	3849	5500
32-35-Schomburg-c. 32,34-Nazi war-c. 33,35-Japanese war-c	168	336	504	1075	1838	2600
36-Schomburg Japanese war-c	103	206	309	659	1130	1600
37,39-42,44: 37-Japanese war-c. 41-War-c	41	82	123	256	428	600
38-Iwo-Jima Flag-c	48	96	144	302	514	725
43-Robot-c	50	100	150	315	533	750

NOTE: ***Al Avison** c-14-16, 30, 43. **Briefer** a-6, 7. **Jon Henri** (Kirbyesque) c-17-20. **Kubert** a-37, 38, 42-44. **Kirby/Caseneuve** c-21-23. **Cecelia Munson** a-7-11(Mars Mason). **Palais** c-37, 39-42. **Powell** a-1, 2, 4-7, 28, 31, 44. **Schomburg** c-31-36. **Tuska** a-3, 6, 7. Bondage c-18, 35. Captain Freedom c-16-24, 25(part), 26-44(w/Black Cat #27, 29, 31, 32-40). Shock Gibson c-1-15.*

SPEED DEMON (Also see Marvel Versus DC #3 & DC Versus Marvel #4)
Marvel Comics (Amalgam): Apr, 1996 ($1.95, one-shot)

1 3.00

SPEED DEMONS (Formerly Frank Merriwell at Yale #1-4?; Submarine Attack #11 on)
Charlton Comics: No. 5, Feb, 1957 - No. 10, 1958

	GD 2.0	VG 4.0	FN 6.0	VF 8.0	VF/NM 9.0	NM- 9.2
5-10	7	14	21	35	43	50

SPEED FORCE (See The Flash 2nd Series #143-Cobalt Blue)
DC Comics: Nov, 1997 ($3.95, one-shot)

1-Flash & Kid Flash vs. Cobalt Blue; Waid-s/Aparo & Sienkiewicz-a; Flash family stories and pin-ups by various 4.00

SPEED RACER (Also see The New Adventures of...)
Now Comics: July, 1987 - No. 38, Nov, 1990 ($1.75)

1 4.00
2-38, 1-2nd printing 3.00
Special 1 (1988, $2.00) 4.00
Special 2 (1988, $3.50) 4.00

SPEED RACER (Also see Racer X)
DC Comics (WildStorm): Oct, 1999 - No. 3, Dec, 1999 ($2.50, limited series)

1-3-Tommy Yune-s/a; origin of Racer X; debut of the Mach 5 3.00

Spellbound #13 © Atlas

Spell on Wheels #1 © Leth & Levens

Spider-Gwen (2016 series) #3 © MAR

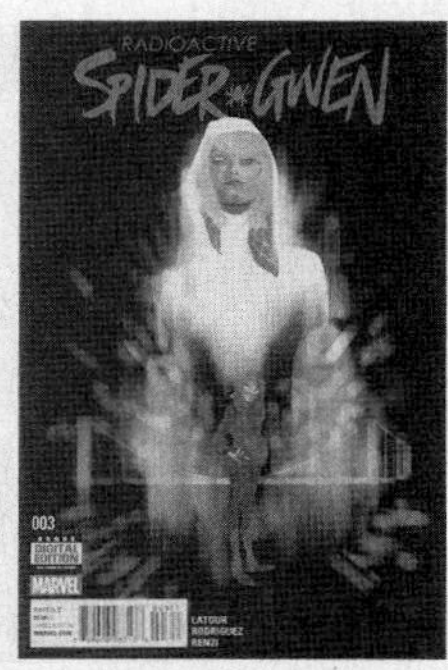

	GD 2.0	VG 4.0	FN 6.0	VF 8.0	VF/NM 9.0	NM- 9.2

...: Born To Race (2000, $9.95, TPB) r/series & conceptual art — 10.00
...: The Original Manga Vol. 1 ('00, $9.95, TPB) r/1950s B&W manga — 10.00

SPEED RACER: CHRONICLES OF THE RACER
IDW Publishing: 2007 - No. 4, Apr, 2008 ($3.99)
1-4-Multiple covers for each — 4.00

SPEED RACER FEATURING NINJA HIGH SCHOOL
Now Comics: Aug, 1993 - No. 2, 1993 ($2.50, mini-series)
1,2: 1-Polybagged w/card. 2-Exists? — 3.00

SPEED RACER: RETURN OF THE GRX
Now Comics: Mar, 1994 - No. 2, Apr, 1994 ($1.95, limited series)
1,2 — 3.00

SPEED SMITH-THE HOT ROD KING (Also see Hot Rod King)
Ziff-Davis Publishing Co.: Spring, 1952

	GD	VG	FN	VF	VF/NM	NM-
1-Saunders painted-c	25	50	75	147	241	335

SPEEDY GONZALES
Dell Publishing Co.: No. 1084, Mar, 1960

	GD	VG	FN	VF	VF/NM	NM-
Four Color 1084	6	12	18	40	73	105

SPEEDY RABBIT (See Television Puppet Show)
Realistic/I. W. Enterprises/Super Comics: nd (1953); 1963

	GD	VG	FN	VF	VF/NM	NM-
nn (1953)-Realistic Reprint?	2	4	6	11	16	20
I.W. Reprint #1 (2 versions w/diff. c/stories exist)-Peter Cottontail #?						
Super Reprint #14(1963)	2	4	6	8	11	14

SPELLBINDERS
Quality: Dec, 1986 - No. 12, Jan, 1988 ($1.25)
1-12: Nemesis the Warlock, Amadeus Wolf — 3.00

SPELLBINDERS
Marvel Comics: May, 2005 - No. 6, Oct, 2005 ($2.99, limited series)
1-6-Carey-s/Perkins-a — 3.00
...: Signs and Wonders TPB (2006, $7.99, digest) r/#1-6 — 8.00

SPELLBOUND (See The Crusaders)

SPELLBOUND (Tales to Hold You... #1, Stories to Hold You...)
Atlas Comics (ACI 1-15/Male 16-23/BPC 24-34): Mar, 1952 - #23, June, 1954; #24, Oct, 1955 - #34, June, 1957

	GD	VG	FN	VF	VF/NM	NM-
1-Horror/weird stories in all	123	246	369	787	1344	1900
2-Edgar A. Poe app.	63	126	189	403	689	975
3-Whitney-a; cannibalism story; classic Heath-c	90	180	270	576	988	1400
4,5	57	114	171	362	619	875
6-Krigstein-a	57	114	171	362	619	875
7-10: 7,8-Ayers-a	50	100	150	315	533	750
11-13,15,16,18-20	45	90	135	284	480	675
14-Ed Win-a; classic Everett-c	71	142	213	454	777	1100
17-Krigstein-a; classic Everett skeleton-c	90	180	270	576	988	1400
21-23: 23-Last precode (6/54)	39	78	117	240	395	550
24-28,30,31,34: 25-Orlando-a	32	64	96	188	307	425
29-Ditko-a (4 pgs.)	34	68	102	199	325	450
32,33-Torres-a	32	64	96	188	307	425

NOTE: ***Brodsky** a-5; c-1, 5-7, 10, 11, 13, 15, 25-27, 32. **Colan** a-17. **Everett** a-2, 5, 7, 10, 16, 28, 31; c-2, 8, 9, 14, 17-19, 28, 30. **Forgione/Abel** a-29. **Forte/Fox** a-16. **Al Hartley** a-2. **Heath** a-2, 4, 8, 9, 12, 14, 16; c-3, 4, 12, 16, 20, 21. **Infantino** a-15. **Keller** a-5. **Kida** a-2, 14. **Maneely** a-7, 14, 27; c-24, 29, 31. **Mooney** a-5, 13, 18. **Mac Pakula** a-22, 32. **Post** a-8. **Powell** a-19, 20, 32. **Robinson** a-1. **Romita** a-24, 26, 27. **R.Q. Sale** a-29. **Sekowsky** a-5. **Severin** c-29. **Sinnott** a-8, 16, 17.*

SPELLBOUND
Marvel Comics: Jan, 1988 - Apr, 1988 ($1.50, bi-weekly, Baxter paper)
1-5 — 3.00
6 ($2.25, 52 pgs.) — 4.00

SPELLJAMMER (Also see TSR Worlds Comics Annual)
DC Comics: Sept, 1990 - No. 15, Nov, 1991 ($1.75)
1-15: Based on TSR game. 11-Heck-a. — 3.00

SPELL ON WHEELS
Dark Horse Comics: Oct, 2016 - Present ($3.99)
1-5-Kate Leth-s/Megan Levens-a. 1-Ming Doyle-c — 4.00

SPENCER SPOOK (Formerly Giggle Comics)
American Comics Group: No. 100, Mar-Apr, 1955 - No. 101, May-June, 1955

	GD	VG	FN	VF	VF/NM	NM-
100,101	8	16	24	40	50	60

SPIDER, THE
Eclipse Books: 1991 - Book 3, 1991 ($4.95, 52 pgs., limited series)
Book 1-3-Truman-c/a — 5.00

SPIDER, THE
Dynamite Entertainment: 2012 - No. 18, 2014 ($3.99)
1-18: 1-Revival of the pulp character; Liss-s/Worley-a; 4 covers. 2-18-Multiple covers — 4.00
Annual 1 (2013, $4.99) Denton-s/Vitorino-a/c — 5.00

SPIDER-BOY (Also see Marvel Versus DC #3)
Marvel Comics (Amalgam): Apr, 1996 ($1.95)
1-Mike Wieringo-c/a; Karl Kesel story; 1st app. of Bizarnage, Insect Queen, Challengers of the Fantastic, Sue Storm: Agent of S.H.I.E.L. D., & King Lizard — 3.00

SPIDER-BOY TEAM-UP
Marvel Comics (Amalgam): June, 1997 ($1.95, one-shot)
1-Karl Kesel & Roger Stern-s/Jo Ladronn-a(p) — 3.00

SPIDER-GIRL (See What If... #105)
Marvel Comics: Oct, 1998 - No. 100, Sept, 2006 ($1.99/$2.25/$2.99)

	GD	VG	FN	VF	VF/NM	NM-
0-($2.99)-r/1st app. Peter Parker's daughter from What If #105; previews regular series, Avengers-Next and J2	1	2	3	4	5	7
1-DeFalco-s/Olliffe & Williamson-s	1	2	3	5	6	8
2-Two covers						4.00
3-16,18-20: 3-Fantastic Five-c/app. 10,11-Spider-Girl time-travels to meet teenaged Spider-Man						3.00
17-($2.99) Peter Parker suits up						4.00
21-24,26-49,51-59: 21-Begin $2.25-c. 31-Avengers app.						3.00
25-($2.99) Spider-Girl vs. the Savage Six						4.00
50-($3.50)						4.00
59-99-($2.99) 59-Avengers app.; Ben Parker born. 75-May in Black costume. 82-84-Venom bonds with Normie Osborn. 93-Venom-c. 95-Tony Stark app.						3.00
100-($3.99) Last issue; story plus Rogues Gallery, profile pages; r/#27,53						4.00
1999 Annual ($3.99)						4.00
...: The End! (10/10, $3.99) Frenz & Buscema-a; Mayhem app.						4.00
Wizard #1/2 (1999)						3.00
... A Fresh Start (1/99,$5.99, TPB) r/#1&2						6.00
... Presents The Buzz and Darkdevil (2007, $7.99, digest) r/mini-series						8.00

SPIDER-GIRL (Araña Corazon from Arana Heart of the Spider)
Marvel Comics: Jan, 2011 - No. 8, Sept, 2011 ($3.99/$2.99)
1-($3.99) Tobin-s/Henry-a/Kitson-c; back-up w/Haspiel-a; Fantastic Four app. — 4.00
1-Variant-c by Del Mundo — 5.00
2-8-($2.99) 2,3-Red Hulk app. 4,5-Ana Kravenoff app. 6-Hobgoblin app. 8-Powers return — 3.00

SPIDER-GWEN (See debut in Edge of Spider-Verse #2)
Marvel Comics: Apr, 2015 - No. 5, Aug, 2015 ($3.99)
1-Latour-s/Robbi Rodriguez-a/c; The Vulture app. — 6.00
2-5: 2-Spider-Ham app. 3-The Vulture & The Punisher app. — 4.00

SPIDER-GWEN
Marvel Comics: Dec, 2015 - Present ($3.99)
1-17: 1-Latour-s/Robbi Rodriguez-a; The Lizard & female Capt. America app. 7,8-"Spider-Women" tie-in; Silk & Spider-Woman app. 10-Kraven app. 16,17-Miles app.; x-over with Spider-Man #12,13 — 4.00
#0 (1/16, $4.99) Reprints #1 (4/15) plus script of Edge of Spider-Verse #2 — 5.00
Annual 1 (8/16, $4.99) Short stories; Latour-s; art by various — 5.00

SPIDER-HAM 25TH ANNIVERSARY SPECIAL
Marvel Comics: Aug, 2010 ($3.99, one-shot)
1-Jusko-c/DeFalco-s/Chabot-a; Peter Porker vs. the Swinester Six — 4.00

SPIDER ISLAND... (one-shots) (See Amazing Spider-Man #666-673)
Marvel Comics
...: Deadly Foes 1 (10/11, $4.99) Hobgoblin & Jackal stories; Caselli-c — 5.00
...: Emergence of Evil - Jackal & Hobgoblin 1 (10/11, $4.99) Hobgoblin & Jackal reprints — 5.00
...: Heroes For Hire 1 (12/11, $2.99) Misty Knight & Paladin; Hotz-a/Yardin-c — 3.00
...: I Love New York City 1 (11/11, $3.99) Short stories by various; Punisher app. — 4.00
...: Spider-Woman 1 (11/11, $2.99) Van Lente-s/Camuncoli-a; Alicia Masters app. — 3.00
... Spotlight 1 ('11, $3.99) Creator interviews and story previews — 4.00
...: The Avengers 1 (11/11, $2.99) McKone-a/Yu-c; Frog-Man app. — 3.00

SPIDER-ISLAND (Secret Wars tie-in)(Back-up MC2 Spider-Girl story in each issue)
Marvel Comics: Sept, 2015 - No. 5, Dec, 2015 ($4.99/$3.99, limited series)
1-($4.99) Gage-s/Diaz-a/Ramos-c; Venom and Werewolf By Night app. — 5.00
2-5-($3.99) Tony Stark as the Green Goblin. 3-5-Peter Parker returns — 4.00

SPIDER ISLAND: CLOAK & DAGGER (See Amazing Spider-Man #666-673)
Marvel Comics: Oct, 2011 - No. 3, Dec, 2011 ($2.99, limited series)
1-3-Spencer-s/Rios-a/Choi-c; Mr. Negative app. — 3.00

Spider-Man #44 © MAR

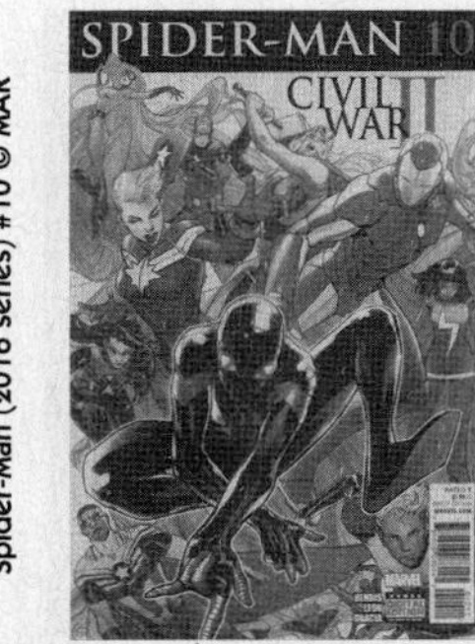

Spider-Man (2016 series) #10 © MAR

Spider-Man: Election Day HC © MAR

GD VG FN VF VF/NM NM-
2.0 4.0 6.0 8.0 9.0 9.2

SPIDER ISLAND: DEADLY HANDS OF KUNG FU (See Amazing Spider-Man #666-673)
Marvel Comics: Oct, 2011 - No. 3, Dec, 2011 ($2.99, limited series)

1-3-Johnston-s/Fiumara-a; Madame Web & Iron Fist app. 3.00

SPIDER ISLAND: THE AMAZING SPIDER-GIRL (Continued from Spider-Girl #8)
Marvel Comics: Oct, 2011 - No. 3, Dec, 2011 ($2.99, limited series)

1-3-Hobgoblin & Kingpin app.; Tobin-s/Larraz-a 3.00

SPIDER-MAN (See Amazing..., Friendly Neighborhood..., Giant-Size..., Marvel Age..., Marvel Knights..., Marvel Tales, Marvel Team-Up, Spectacular..., Spidey Super Stories, Ultimate Marvel Team-Up, Ultimate..., Venom, & Web Of...)

SPIDER-MAN (Peter Parker Spider-Man on cover but not indicia #75-on)
Marvel Comics: Aug, 1990 - No. 98, Nov, 1998 ($1.75/$1.95/ $1.99)

1-Silver edition, direct sale only (unbagged) 1 3 4 6 8 10
1-Silver bagged edition; direct sale, no price on comic, but $2.00 on plastic bag (125,000 print run) 3 6 9 14 20 25
1-Regular edition w/Spidey face in UPC area (unbagged); green-c 1 2 3 5 6 8
1-Regular bagged edition w/Spidey face in UPC area; green cover (125,000) 12.00
1-Newsstand bagged w/UPC code 8.00
1-Gold edition, 2nd printing (unbagged) with Spider-Man in box (400,000-450,000) 3 6 9 16 23 30
1-Gold 2nd printing w/UPC code; (less than 10,000 print run) intended for Wal-Mart; much scarcer than originally believed 10 20 30 66 138 210
1-Platinum ed. mailed to retailers only (10,000 print run); has new McFarlane-a & editorial material instead of ads; stiff-c, no cover price 9 18 27 61 123 185
2-10: 2-McFarlane-c/a/scripts continue. 6,7-Ghost Rider & Hobgoblin app. 8-Wolverine cameo; Wolverine storyline begins 6.00
11-25: 12-Wolverine storyline ends. 13-Spidey's black costume returns; Morbius app. 14-Morbius app. 15-Erik Larsen-c/a; Beast c/s. 16-X-Force-c/story w/Liefeld assists; continues in X-Force #4; reads sideways; last McFarlane issue. 17-Thanos-c/story; Leonardi/Williamson-c/a. 18-Ghost Rider-c/story. 18-23-Sinister Six storyline w/Erik Larsen-c/a/scripts. 19-Hulk & Hobgoblin-c & app. 20-22-Deathlok app. 22,23-Ghost Rider, Hulk, Hobgoblin app. 23-Wrap-around gatefold-c. 24-Infinity War x-over w/Demogoblin & Hobgoblin-c/story. 24-Demogoblin dons new costume & battles Hobgoblin-c/story 4.00
26-($3.50, 52 pgs.)-Silver hologram on-c w/gatefold poster by Ron Lim; origin retold 6.00
26-2nd printing; gold hologram on-c 4.00
27-45: 32-34-Punisher-c/story. 37-Maximum Carnage x-over. 39,40-Electro-c/s (cameo #38). 41-43-Iron Fist-c/stories w/Jae Lee-c/a. 42-Intro Platoon. 44-Hobgoblin app. 3.50
46-49,51-53, 55, 56,58-74,76-81: 46-Begin $1.95-c; bound-in card sheet. 51-Power & Responsibility Pt. 3. 52,53-Venom app. 60-Kaine revealed. 61-Origin Kaine. 65-Mysterio app. 66-Kaine-c/app.; Peter Parker app. 67-Carnage-c/app. 68,69-Hobgoblin-c/app. 72-Onslaught x-over; Spidey vs. Sentinels. 74-Daredevil-c/app. 77-80-Morbius-c/app. 3.00
46-($2.95)-Polybagged; silver ink-c w/16 pg. preview of cartoon series & animation style print; bound-in trading card sheet 4.00
50-($2.50)-Newsstand edition 4.00
50-($3.95)-Collectors edition w/holographic-c 5.00
51-($2.95)-Deluxe edition foil-c; flip book 4.00
54-($2.75, 52 pgs.)-Flip book 4.00
57-($2.50) 4.00
57-($2.95)-Die cut-c 5.00
65-($2.95)-Variant-c; polybagged w/cassette 4.00
75-($2.95)-Wraparound-c; Green Goblin returns; death of Ben Reilly (who was the clone) 4.00
82-97: 84-Juggernaut app. 91-Double cover with "Dusk #1"; battles the Shocker. 93-Ghost Rider app. 3.00
98-Double cover; final issue 4.00
#(-1) Flashback (7/97) 3.00
Annual '97 ($2.99), '98 ($2.99)-Devil Dinosaur-c/app. 4.00
NOTE: *Erik Larsen c/a-15, 18-23. M. Rogers/Keith Williams c/a-27, 28.*

SPIDER-MAN (Miles Morales in regular Marvel Universe)
Marvel Comics: Apr, 2016 - Present ($3.99)

1-13: 1,2-Bendis-s/Pichelli-a; Avengers & Peter Parker app. 3-Ms. Marvel app. 6-10-Civil War II tie-ins. 12,13-Crossover with Spider-Gwen #11,12 4.00

SPIDER-MAN (one-shots, hardcovers and TPBs)
...& Arana Special: The Hunter Revealed (5/06, $3.99) Del Rio-s; art by Del Rio & various 4.00
...and Batman ('95, $5.95) DeMatteis-s; Joker, Carnage app. 8.00
...and Daredevil ('84, $2.00) 1-r/Spectacular Spider-Man #26-28 by Miller 6.00
...and The Human Torch in...Bahia de Los Muertos! 1 (5/09, $3.99) Beland-s/Juan Doe-a; Diablo app.; printed in two versions (English and Spanish language) 4.00
...: Back in Black HC (2007, $34.99, dustjacket) oversized r/Amaz. S-M #539-543, Friendly Neighborhood S-M #17-23 & Annual #1; cover pencils and sketch pages 35.00
...: Back in Black SC (2008, $24.99) same contents as HC 25.00
...: Back in Black Handbook (2007, $3.99) Official Handbook format; Lopresti-c 10.00
...: Back in Quack (11/10, $3.99) Howard the Duck, Beverly and Man-Thing app. 4.00

GD VG FN VF VF/NM NM-
2.0 4.0 6.0 8.0 9.0 9.2

...: Birth of Venom TPB (2007, $29.99) r/Secret Wars #8, AS-M #252-259,298-300,315-317, AS-M Annual #25, Fantastic Four #274 and Web of Spider-Man #1 30.00
...: Brand New Day HC (2008, $24.99, dustjacket) r/Amaz. S-M #546-551, Spider-Man: Swing Shift and story from Venom Super-Special 25.00
...: Carnage nn (6/93, $6.95, TPB)-r/Amazing S-M #344,345,359-363; spot varnish-c 10.00
.../Daredevil (10/02, $2.99) Vatche Mavlian-c/a; Brett Matthews-s 3.00
...: Dead Man's Hand 1 (4/97, $2.99) 3.00
...: Death of the Stacys HC (2007, $19.99, dustjacket) r/Amazing Spider-Man #88-92 and #121,122; intro. by Gerry Conway; afterword by Romita; cover gallery incl. reprints 20.00
.../Dr. Strange: "The Way to Dusty Death" nn (1992, $6.95, 68 pgs.) 8.00
...: Election Day HC (2009, $29.99) r/#584-588; includes Barack Obama app from #583 30.00
.../Elektra '98-($2.99) vs. The Silencer 3.00
... Family (2005, $4.99, 100 pgs.) new story and reprints; Spider-Ham app. 5.00
... Fear Itself (3/09, $3.99) Spider-Man and Man-Thing; Stuart Moore-s/Joe Suitor-a 4.00
... Fear Itself Graphic Novel (2/92, $12.95) 18.00
Free Comic Book Day 2012 (Spider-Man: Season One) #1 (Giveaway) Previews the GN 3.00
Giant-Sized Spider-Man (12/98, $3.99) r/team-ups 4.00
...: Grim Hunt - The Kraven Saga (5/10, free) prelude to Grim Hunt arc; Kraven history 3.00
Holiday Special 1995 ($2.95) 4.00
...: Hot Shots nn (1/96, $2.95) fold out posters by various, inc. Vess and Ross 4.00
Identity Crisis (9/98, $19.95, TPB) 20.00
...: Kraven's Last Hunt HC (2006, $19.99) r/Amaz. S-M #293,294; Web of S-M #31,32 and Spect. S-M #131-132; intro. by DeMatteis; Zeck-a; cover pencils and interior pencils 20.00
...: Legacy of Evil 1 (6/96, $3.95) Kurt Busiek script & Mark Texeira-c/a 4.00
...Legends Vol. 1: Todd McFarlane ('03, $19.95, TPB)-r/Amaz. S-M #298-305 20.00
...Legends Vol. 2: Todd McFarlane ('03, $19.99, TPB)-r/Amaz. S-M #306-314, & Spec. Spider-Man Annual #10 20.00
...Legends Vol. 3: Todd McFarlane ('04, $24.99, TPB)-r/Amaz. S-M #315-323,325,328 25.00
...Legends Vol. 4: Spider-Man & Wolverine ('03, $13.95, TPB) r/Spider-Man & Wolverine #1-4 and Spider-Man/Daredevil #1 14.00
.../Marrow (2/01, $2.99) Garza-a 3.00
.../Mary Jane: ... You Just Hit the Jackpot TPB (2009, $24.99) early apps. & key stories 25.00
100th Anniversary Special: Spider-Man 1 (9/14, $3.99) In-Hyk Lee-a/c; Venom app. 4.00
...: One More Day HC (2008. $24.99, dustjacket) r/Amaz. S-M #544-545, Friendly N.S-M #24, Sensational S-M #41 and Marvel Spotlight: Spider-Man-One More Day 25.00
...: Origin of the Hunter (6/10, $3.99) r/Kraven apps. in ASM #15 & 34; new Mayhew-a 4.00
..., Peter Parker: Back in Black HC (2007, $34.99) oversized r/Sensational Spider-Man #35-40 & Annual #1, Spider-Man Family #1,2; Marvel Spotlight: Spider-Man and Spider-Man Back in Black Handbook; cover sketches 35.00
..., Punisher, Sabretooth: Designer Genes (1993, $8.95) 10.00
...Return of the Goblin TPB (See Peter Parker: Spider-Man)
...Revelations ('97, $14.99, TPB) r/end of Clone Saga plus 14 new pages by Romita Jr. 15.00
...: Saga of the Sandman TPB (2007, $19.99) r/1st app. Amazing S-M #4 and other app. 20.00
...: Season One HC (2012, $24.99) Origin and early days; Bunn-s/Neil Edwards-a 25.00
...: Son of the Goblin (2004, $15.99, TPB) r/AS-M#136-137,312 & Spec. S-M #189,200 16.00
... Special: Black and Blue and Read All Over 1 (11/06, $3.99) new story and r/ASM #12 4.00
Special Edition 1 (12/92-c, 11/92 inside)-The Trial of Venom; ordered thru mail with $5.00 donation or more to UNICEF; embossed metallic ink; came bagged w/bound-in poster; Daredevil app. 2 4 6 10 14 18
... Spectacular 1 (8/14, $4.99) Reprints all-ages tales; Green Goblin, Kraven app. 5.00
Super Special (7/95, $3.95)-Planet of the Symbiotes 4.00
The Best of Spider-Man Vol. 2 (2003, $29.99, HC with dust jacket) r/AS-M V2 #37-45, Peter Parker: S-M #44-47, and S-M's Tangled Web #10,11; Pearson-c 30.00
The Best of Spider-Man Vol. 3 (2004, $29.99, HC with d.j.) r/AS-M V2 #46-58, 500 30.00
The Best of Spider-Man Vol. 4 (2005, $29.99, HC with d.j.) r/#501-514; sketch pages 30.00
The Best of Spider-Man Vol. 5 (2006, $29.99, HC with d.j.) r/#515-524; sketch pages 30.00
The Complete Frank Miller Spider-Man (2002, $29.95, HC) r/Miller-s/a 30.00
The Death of Captain Stacy ($3.50) r/AS-M#88-90 5.00
The Death of Gwen Stacy ($14.95) r/AS-M#96-98,121,122 15.00
...: The Movie ($12.95) adaptation by Stan Lee-s/Alan Davis-a; plus r/Ultimate Spider-Man #8, Peter Parker #35, Tangled Web #10; photo-c 13.00
...: The Official Movie Adaptation ($5.95) Stan Lee-s/Alan Davis-a 6.00
...: The Other HC (2006, $29.99, dust jacket) r/Amazing S-M #525-528, Friendly Neighborhood S-M #1-4 and Marvel Knights S-M #19-22; gallery of variant covers 30.00
...: The Other SC (2006, $24.99) r/crossover; gallery of variant covers 25.00
...: The Other Sketchbook (2005, $2.99) sketch page preview of 2005-6 x-over 3.00
Torment TPB (5/01$15.95) r/#1-5, Spec. S-M #10 16.00
... Vs. Doctor Octopus ($17.95) reprints early battles; Sean Chen-c 18.00
... Vs. Punisher (7/00, $2.99) Michael Lopez-c/a 3.00
...Vs. Silver Sable (2006, $15.99, TPB)-r/Amazing Spider-Man #265,279-281 & Peter Parker, The Spectacular Spider-Man #128,129 16.00
...Vs. The Black Cat (2005, $14.99, TPB)-r/Amaz. S-M #194,195,204,205,226,227 15.00
...Vs. Vampires (12/10, $3.99) Blade app.; Castro-a/Grevioux-s 4.00
...Vs. Venom (1990, $8.95, TPB)-r/Amaz. S-M #300,315-317 w/new McFarlane-c 12.00

Spider-Man Adventures #6 © MAR

Spider-Man / Deadpool #5 © MAR

Spider-Man Family Featuring... #1 © MAR

	GD 2.0	VG 4.0	FN 6.0	VF 8.0	VF/NM 9.0	NM- 9.2

...Visionaries (10/01, $19.95, TPB)-r/Amaz. S-M #298-305; McFarlane-a 20.00
...Visionaries: John Romita (8/01, $19.95, TPB)-r/Amaz. S-M #39-42, 50,68,69,108,109; new Romita-c 20.00
...Visionaries: Kurt Busiek (2006, $19.99, TPB)-r/Untold Tales of Spider-Man #1-8 20.00
...Visionaries: Roger Stern (2007, $24.99, TPB)-r/Amazing Spider-Man #206 & Spectacular Spider-Man #43-52,54; Stern interview 25.00
Wizard 1/2 ($10.00) Leonardi-a; Green Goblin app. 10.00

SPIDER-MAN ADVENTURES
Marvel Comics: Dec, 1994 - No. 15, Mar, 1996 ($1.50)
1-15 ($1.50)-Based on animated series 3.00
1-($2.95)-Foil embossed-c 4.00

SPIDER-MAN AND HIS AMAZING FRIENDS (See Marvel Action Universe)
Marvel Comics Group: Dec, 1981 (one-shot)
1-Adapted from NBC TV cartoon show; Green Goblin-c/story; 1st Spidey, Firestar, Iceman team-up; Spiegle-p 4 8 12 23 37 50

SPIDER-MAN AND POWER PACK
Marvel Comics: Jan, 2007 - No. 4, Apr, 2007 ($2.99, limited series)
1-4-Sumerak-s/Gurihiru-a; Sandman app. 3,4-Venom app. 3.00
...: Big City Heroes (2007, $6.99, digest) r/#1-4 7.00

SPIDER-MAN AND THE FANTASTIC FOUR
Marvel Comics: Jun, 2007 - No. 4, Sept, 2007 ($2.99, limited series)
1-4-Mike Wieringo-a/c; Jeff Parker-s. 1,4-Impossible Man app. 3.00
...: Silver Rage TPB (2007, $10.99) r/#1-4; series outline and cover sketches 11.00

SPIDER-MAN AND THE SECRET WARS
Marvel Comics: Feb, 2010 - No. 4, May, 2010 ($2.99, limited series)
1-4-Tobin-s/Scherberger-a. 3-Black costume app. 3.00

SPIDER-MAN AND THE INCREDIBLE HULK (See listing under Amazing...)

SPIDER-MAN AND THE UNCANNY X-MEN
Marvel Comics: Mar, 1996 ($16.95, trade paperback)
nn-r/Uncanny X-Men #27, Uncanny X-men #35, Amazing Spider-Man #92, Marvel Team-Up Annual #1, Marvel Team-Up #150, & Spectacular Spider-Man #197-199 17.00

SPIDER-MAN & THE X-MEN
Marvel Comics: Feb, 2015 - No. 6, Jub, 2015 ($3.99)
1-3: Spider-Man teaching at the Jean Grey School; Kalan-s/Failla-a. 2,3-Mojo app. 4.00

SPIDER-MAN & WOLVERINE (See Spider-Man Legends Vol. 4 for TPB reprint)
Marvel Comics: Aug, 2003 - No. 4, Nov, 2003 ($2.99, limited series)
1-4-Matthews-s/Mavlian-a 3.00

SPIDER-MAN AND X-FACTOR
Marvel Comics: May, 1994 - No. 3, July, 1994 ($1.95, limited series)
1-3 3.00

SPIDER-MAN /BADROCK
Maximum Press: Mar, 1997 ($2.99, mini-series)
1A, 1B(#2)-Jurgens-s 3.00

SPIDER-MAN/BLACK CAT: THE EVIL THAT MEN DO (Also see Marvel Must Haves)
Marvel Comics: Aug, 2002 - No. 6, Mar, 2006 ($2.99, limited series)
1-6-Kevin Smith-s/Terry Dodson-c/a 3.00
HC (2006, $19.99, dust jacket) r/#1-6; script to #6 with sketches 20.00

SPIDER-MAN: BLUE
Marvel Comics: July, 2002 - No. 6, Apr, 2003 ($3.50, limited series)
1-6: Jeph Loeb-s/Tim Sale-a/c; flashback to early MJ and Gwen Stacy 3.50
HC (2003, $21.99, with dust jacket) over-sized r/#1-6; intro. by John Romita 22.00
SC (2004, $14.99) r/#1-6; cover gallery 15.00

SPIDER-MAN: BRAND NEW DAY (See Amazing Spider-Man Vol. 2)

SPIDER-MAN: BREAKOUT (See New Avengers #1)
Marvel Comics: June, 2005 - No. 5, Oct, 2005 ($2.99, limited series)
1-5-Bedard-s/Garcia-a. 1-U-Foes app. 5-New Avengers app. 3.00
TPB (2006, $13.99) r/#1-5 14.00

SPIDER-MAN: CHAPTER ONE
Marvel Comics: Dec, 1998 - No. 12, Oct, 1999 ($2.50, limited series)
1-Retelling/updating of origin; John Byrne-s/c/a 3.00
1-($6.95) DF Edition w/variant-c by Jae Lee 7.00
2-11: 2-Two covers (one is swipe of ASM #1); Fantastic Four app. 9-Daredevil. 11-Giant-Man-c/app. 3.00
12-($3.50) Battles the Sandman 4.00

	GD 2.0	VG 4.0	FN 6.0	VF 8.0	VF/NM 9.0	NM- 9.2

0-(5/99) Origins of Vulture, Lizard and Sandman 3.00

SPIDER-MAN CLASSICS
Marvel Comics: Apr, 1993 - No. 16, July, 1994 ($1.25)
1-14,16: 1-r/Amaz. Fantasy #15 & Strange Tales #115. 2-16-r/Amaz. Spider-Man #1-15. 6-Austin-c(i) 3.00
15-($2.95)-Polybagged w/16 pg. insert & animation style print; r/Amazing Spider-Man #14 (1st Green Goblin) 4.00

SPIDER-MAN COLLECTOR'S PREVIEW
Marvel Comics: Dec, 1994 ($1.50, 100 pgs., one-shot)
1-wraparound-c; no comics 4.00

SPIDER-MAN COMICS MAGAZINE
Marvel Comics Group: Jan, 1987 - No. 13, 1988 ($1.50, digest-size)
1-13-Reprints 6.00

SPIDER-MAN/DEADPOOL
Marvel Comics: Mar, 2016 - Present ($3.99)
1-14: 1-Joe Kelly-s/Ed McGuinness-a; back-up reprint of Vision #1. 6-Aukerman-s. 7-Art in 1968 Ditko-style by Koblish. 8-New black Spidey suit. 11-Penn Jillette-s 4.00
#1.MU (3/17, $4.99) Corin-s/Walker-a/Dave Johnson-c 5.00

SPIDER-MAN: DEATH AND DESTINY
Marvel Comics: Aug, 2000 - No. 3, Oct, 2000 ($2.99, limited series)
1-3-Aftermath of the death of Capt. Stacy 3.00

SPIDER-MAN/ DOCTOR OCTOPUS: OUT OF REACH
Marvel Comics: Jan, 2004 - No. 5, May, 2004 ($2.99, limited series)
1-5: 1-Keron Grant-a/Colin Mitchell-s 3.00
Marvel Age... TPB (2004, $5.99, digest size) r/#1-5 6.00

SPIDER-MAN/ DOCTOR OCTOPUS: YEAR ONE
Marvel Comics: Aug, 2004 - No. 5, Dec, 2004 ($2.99, limited series)
1-5-Kaare Andrews-a/Zeb Wells-s 3.00

SPIDER-MAN FAIRY TALES
Marvel Comics: July, 2007 - No. 4, Oct, 2007 ($2.99, limited series)
1-4: 1-Cebulski-s/Tercio-a. 2-Henrichon-a. 3-Kobayashi-a. 4-Dragotta-p/Allred-i 3.00
TPB (2007, $10.99) r/#1-4 11.00

SPIDER-MAN FAMILY (Also see Amazing Spider-Man Family)
Marvel Comics: Apr, 2007 - No. 9, Aug, 2008 ($4.99, anthology)
1-9-New tales and reprints. 1-Black costume, Sandman, Black Cat app. 4-Agents of Atlas app., Kirk-a; Puppet Master by Eliopoulos. 8-Iron Man app. 9-Hulk app. 5.00
... Featuring Spider-Clan 1 (1/07, $4.99) new Spider-Clan story; reprints w/Spider-Man 2099 and Amazing Spider-Man #252 (black costume) 5.00
... Featuring Spider-Man's Amazing Friends 1 (10/06, $4.99) new story with Iceman and Firestar; Mini Marvels w/Giarrusso-a; reprints w/Spider-Man 2099 5.00
...: Back In Black (2007, $7.99, digest) r/new content from #1-3 8.00
...: Untold Team-Ups (2008, $9.99, digest) r/new content from #4-6 10.00

SPIDER-MAN/FANTASTIC FOUR (Spider-Man and the Fantastic Four on cover)
Marvel Comics: Sept, 2010 - No. 4, Dec, 2010 ($3.99, limited series)
1-4-Gage-s/Alberti-a; Dr. Doom app. 4.00

SPIDER-MAN: FEVER
Marvel Comics: Jun, 2010 - No. 3, Aug, 2010 ($3.99, limited series)
1-3-Brendan McCarthy-s/a; Dr. Strange app. 4.00

SPIDER-MAN: FRIENDS AND ENEMIES
Marvel Comics: Jan, 1995 - No. 4, Apr, 1995 ($1.95, limited series)
1-4-Darkhawk, Nova & Speedball app. 3.00

SPIDER-MAN: FUNERAL FOR AN OCTOPUS
Marvel Comics: Mar, 1995 - No. 3, May, 1995 ($1.50, limited series)
1-3 3.00

SPIDER-MAN/ GEN 13
Marvel Comics: Nov, 1996 ($4.95, one-shot)
nn-Peter David-s/Stuart Immonen-a 5.00

SPIDER-MAN: GET KRAVEN
Marvel Comics: Aug, 2002 - No. 6, Jan, 2003 ($2.99/$2.25, limited series)
1-($2.99) McCrea-a/Quesada-c; back-up story w/Rio-a 4.00
2-6-($2.25) 2-Sub-Mariner app. 3.00

SPIDER-MAN: HOBGOBLIN LIVES
Marvel Comics: Jan, 1997 - No. 3, Mar, 1997 ($2.50, limited series)
1-3-Wraparound-c 3.00

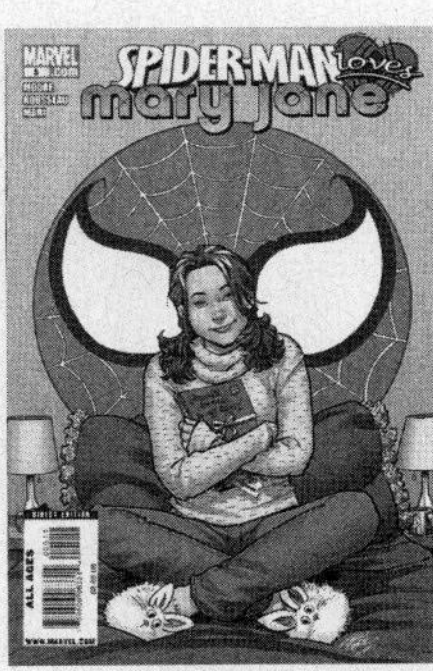

Spider-Man Loves Mary Jane Season 2 #5 © MAR

Spider-Man Noir #1 © MAR

Spider-Man Team-Up #6 © MAR

GD 2.0 | VG 4.0 | FN 6.0 | VF 8.0 | VF/NM 9.0 | NM- 9.2

TPB (1/98, $14.99) r/#1-3 plus timeline 15.00

SPIDER-MAN: HOUSE OF M (Also see House of M and related x-overs)
Marvel Comics: Aug, 2005 - No. 5, Dec, 2005 ($2.99, limited series)
1-5-Waid & Peyer-s/Larroca-a; rich and famous Peter Parker in mutant-ruled world 3.00
House of M: Spider-Man TPB (2006, $13.99) r/series 14.00

SPIDER-MAN/ HUMAN TORCH
Marvel Comics: Mar, 2005 - No. 5, July, 2005 ($2.99, limited series)
1-5-Ty Templeton-a/Dan Slott-s; team-ups from early days to the present 3.00
...: I'm With Stupid (2006, $7.99, digest) r/#1-5 8.00

SPIDER-MAN: INDIA
Marvel Comics: Jan, 2005 - No. 4, Apr, 2005 ($2.99, limited series)
1-4-Pavitr Prabhakar gains spider powers; Kang-a/Seetharaman-s 3.00

SPIDER-MAN: LEGEND OF THE SPIDER-CLAN (See Marvel Mangaverse for TPB)
Marvel Comics: Dec, 2002 - No. 5, Apr, 2003 ($2.25, limited series)
1-5-Marvel Mangaverse Spider-Man; Kaare Andrews-s/Skottie Young-c/a 3.00

SPIDER-MAN: LIFELINE
Marvel Comics: Apr, 2001 - No. 3, June, 2001 ($2.99, limited series)
1-3-Nicieza-s/Rude-c/a; The Lizard app. 3.00

SPIDER-MAN LOVES MARY JANE (Also see Mary Jane limited series)
Marvel Comics: Feb, 2006 - No. 20, Sept, 2007 ($2.99)
1-20-Mary Jane & Peter in high school; McKeever-s/Miyazawa-a/c. 5-Gwen Stacy app. 16-18,20-Firestar app. 17-Felecia Hardy app. 3.00
... Vol. 1: Super Crush (2006, $7.99, digest) r/#1-5; cover concepts page 8.00
... Vol. 2: The New Girl (2006, $7.99, digest) r/#6-10; sketch pages 8.00
... Vol. 3: My Secret Life (2007, $7.99, digest) r/#11-15; sketch pages 8.00
... Vol. 4: Still Friends (2007, $7.99, digest) r/#16-20 8.00
Hardcover Vol. 1 (2007, $24.99) oversized reprints of #1-5, Mary Jane #1-4 and Mary Jane: Homecoming #1-4; series proposals, sketch pages and covers; coloring process 25.00
Hardcover Vol. 2 (2008, $39.99) oversized reprints of #6-20, sketch & layout pages 40.00

SPIDER-MAN LOVES MARY JANE SEASON 2
Marvel Comics: Oct, 2008 - No. 5, Feb, 2009 ($2.99, limited series)
1-5-Terry Moore-s/c; Craig Rousseau-a 3.00
1-Variant-c by Alphona 8.00

SPIDER-MAN: MADE MEN
Marvel Comics: Aug, 1998 ($5.99, one-shot)
1-Spider-Man & Daredevil vs. Kingpin 6.00

SPIDER-MAN MAGAZINE
Marvel Comics: 1994 - No. 3, 1994 ($1.95, magazine)
1-3: 1-Contains 4 S-M promo cards & 4 X-Men Ultra Fleer cards; Spider-Man story by Romita, Sr.; X-Men story; puzzles & games. 2-Doc Octopus & X-Men stories 4.00

SPIDER-MAN: MAXIMUM CLONAGE
Marvel Comics: 1995 ($4.95)
Alpha #1-Acetate-c, Omega #1-Chromium-c. 6.00

SPIDER-MAN MEGAZINE
Marvel Comics: Oct, 1994 - No. 6, Mar, 1995 ($2.95, 100 pgs.)
1-6: 1-r/ASM #16,224,225, Marvel Team-Up #1 5.00

SPIDER-MAN NOIR
Marvel Comics: Dec, 2008 - No. 4, May, 2009 ($3.99, limited series)
1-4-Pulp-style Spider-Man in 1933; DiGiandomenico-a; covers by Zircher & Calero 4.00
...: Eyes Without a Face 1-4 (2/10 - No. 4, 5/10) DiGiandomenico-a; Zircher & Calero-c 4.00

SPIDER-MAN: POWER OF TERROR
Marvel Comics: Jan, 1995 - No. 4, Apr, 1995 ($1.95, limited series)
1-4-Silvermane & Deathlok app. 3.00

SPIDER-MAN/PUNISHER: FAMILY PLOT
Marvel Comics: Feb, 1996 - No. 2, Mar, 1996 ($2.95, limited series)
1,2 3.00

SPIDER-MAN: QUALITY OF LIFE
Marvel Comics: Jul, 2002 - No. 4, Oct, 2002 ($2.99, limited series)
1-4-All CGI art by Scott Sava; Rucka-s; Lizard app. 3.00
TPB (2002, $12.99) r/#1-4; a "Making of..." section detailing the CGI process 13.00

SPIDER-MAN: REDEMPTION
Marvel Comics: Sept, 1996 - No. 4, Dec, 1996 ($1.50, limited series)
1-4: DeMatteis scripts; Zeck-a 3.00

SPIDER-MAN/ RED SONJA
Marvel Comics: Oct, 2007 - No. 5, Feb, 2008 ($2.99, limited series)
1-5-Rubi-a/Oeming-s/Turner-c; Venom & Kulan Gath app. 3.00
HC (2008, $19.99, dustjacket) r/#1-5 and Marvel Team-Up #79; sketch pages 20.00

SPIDER-MAN: REIGN
Marvel Comics: Feb, 2007 - No. 4, May, 2007 ($3.99, limited series)
1-Kaare Andrews-s/a; red costume on cover 4.00
1-Variant cover with black costume 10.00
2-4 4.00
HC (2007, $19.99, dustjacket) r/#1-4; sketch pages and cover variant gallery 20.00
HC 2nd printing (2007, $19.99, dustjacket) with variant black cover 20.00
SC (2008, $14.99) r/#1-4; sketch pages and cover variant gallery 15.00

SPIDER-MAN: REVENGE OF THE GREEN GOBLIN
Marvel Comics: Oct, 2000 - No. 3, Dec, 2000 ($2.99, limited series)
1-3-Frenz & Olliffe-a; continues in AS-M #25 & PP:S-M #25 3.00

SPIDER-MAN SAGA
Marvel Comics: Nov, 1991 - No. 4, Feb, 1992 ($2.95, limited series)
1-4: Gives history of Spider-Man: text & illustrations 3.00

SPIDER-MAN 1602
Marvel Comics: Dec, 2009 - No. 5, Apr, 2010 ($3.99, limited series)
1-5- Peter Parquagh from Marvel 1602; Parker-s/Rosanas-a 4.00

SPIDER-MAN: SWEET CHARITY
Marvel Comics: Aug, 2002 ($4.95, one-shot)
1-The Scorpion-c/app.; Campbell-c/Zimmerman-s/Robertson-a 5.00

SPIDER-MAN'S TANGLED WEB (Titled **"Tangled Web"** in indicia for #1-4)
Marvel Comics: Jun, 2001 - No. 22, Mar, 2003 ($2.99)
1-3: "The Thousand" on-c; Ennis-s/McCrea-a/Fabry-c 4.00
4-"Severance Package" on-c; Rucka-s/Risso-a; Kingpin-c/app. 5.00
5,6-Flowers for Rhino; Milligan-s/Fegredo-a 3.00
7-10,12,15-20,22: 7-9-Gentlemen's Agreement; Bruce Jones-s/Lee Weeks-a. 10-Andrews-s/a. 12-Fegredo-a. 15-Paul Pope-s/a. 18-Ted McKeever-s/a. 19-Mahfood-a. 20-Haspiel-a 3.00
11,13,21-($3.50) 11-Darwyn Cooke-s/a. 13-Phillips-a. 21-Christmas-s by Cooke & Bone 4.00
14-Azzarello & Scott Levy (WWE's Raven)-s about Crusher Hogan 4.00
TPB (10/01, $15.95) r/#1-6 16.00
Volume 2 TPB (4/02, $14.95) r/#7-11 15.00
Volume 3 TPB (2002, $15.99) r/#12-17; Jason Pearson-c 16.00
Volume 4 TPB (2003, $15.99) r/#18-22; Frank Cho-c 16.00

SPIDER-MAN TEAM-UP
Marvel Comics: Dec, 1995 - No. 7, June, 1996 ($2.95)
1-7: 1-w/ X-Men. 2-w/Silver Surfer. 3-w/Fantastic Four. 4-w/Avengers. 5-Gambit & Howard the Duck-c/app. 7-Thunderbolts-c/app. 4.00
... Special 1 (5/05, $2.99) Fantastic Four app.; Todd Dezago-s/Shane Davis-a 4.00

SPIDER-MAN: THE ARACHNIS PROJECT
Marvel Comics: Aug, 1994 - No. 6, Jan, 1995 ($1.75, limited series)
1-6-Venom, Styx, Stone & Jury app. 3.00

SPIDER-MAN: THE CLONE JOURNAL
Marvel Comics: Mar, 1995 ($2.95, one-shot)
1 4.00

SPIDER-MAN: THE CLONE SAGA
Marvel Comics: Nov, 2009 - No. 6, Apr, 2010 ($3.99, limited series)
1-6-Retelling of the saga with different ending; DeFalco & Mackie-s/Nauck-a 4.00

SPIDER-MAN: THE FINAL ADVENTURE
Marvel Comics: Nov, 1995 - No. 4, Feb, 1996 ($2.95, limited series)
1-4: 1-Nicieza scripts; foil-c 3.00

SPIDER-MAN: THE JACKAL FILES
Marvel Comics: Aug, 1995 ($1.95, one-shot)
1 3.00

SPIDER-MAN: THE LOST YEARS
Marvel Comics: Aug, 1995-No. 3, Oct, 1995; No. 0, 1996 ($2.95/$3.95,lim. series)
0-(1/96, $3.95)-Reprints. 4.00
1-3-DeMatteis scripts, Romita, Jr.-c/a 3.00
NOTE: *Romita c-0i.* ***Romita, Jr.*** *a-0r, 1-3p. c-0-3p.* ***Sharp*** *a-0r.*

SPIDER-MAN: THE MANGA
Marvel Comics: Dec, 1997 - No. 31, June, 1999 ($3.99/$2.99, B&W, bi-weekly)
1-($3.99)-English translation of Japanese Spider-Man 4.00
2-31-($2.99) 3.00

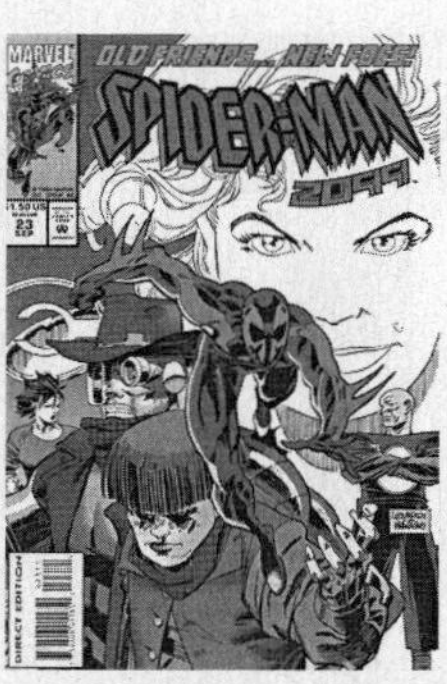

Spider-Man 2099 #23 © MAR

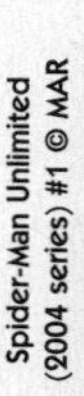
Spider-Man Unlimited (2004 series) #1 © MAR

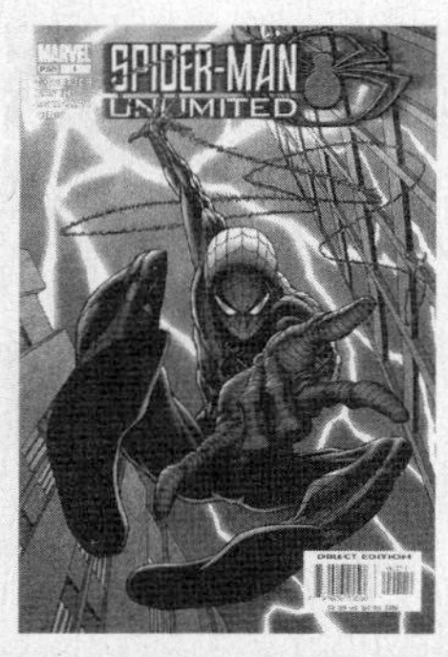

Spider-Woman #26 © MAR

GD VG FN VF VF/NM NM-
2.0 4.0 6.0 8.0 9.0 9.2

GD VG FN VF VF/NM NM-
2.0 4.0 6.0 8.0 9.0 9.2

SPIDER-MAN: THE MUTANT AGENDA
Marvel Comics: No. 0, Feb, 1994; No. 1, Mar, 1994 - No. 3, May, 1994 ($1.75, limited series)
0-(2/94, $1.25, 52 pgs.)-Crosses over w/newspaper strip; has empty pages to paste in newspaper strips; gives origin of Spidey 4.00
1-3: Beast & Hobgoblin app. 1-X-Men app. 3.00

SPIDER-MAN: THE MYSTERIO MANIFESTO (Listed as "Spider-Man and Mysterio" in indicia)
Marvel Comics: Jan, 2001 - No. 3, Mar, 2001 ($2.99, limited series)
1-3-Daredevil-c/app.; Weeks & McLeod-a 3.00

SPIDER-MAN: THE PARKER YEARS
Marvel Comics: Nov, 1995 ($2.50, one-shot)
1 3.00

SPIDER-MAN 2: THE MOVIE
Marvel Comics: Aug, 2004 ($3.50/$12.99, one-shot)
1-($3.50) Movie adaptation; Johnson, Lim & Olliffe-a 4.00
TPB-($12.99) Movie adaptation; r/Amazing Spider-Man #50, Ultimate Spider-Man #14,15 13.00

SPIDER-MAN 2099 (See Amazing Spider-Man #365)
Marvel Comics: Nov, 1992 - No. 46, Aug, 1996 ($1.25/$1.50/$1.95)
1-(stiff-c)-Red foil stamped-c; begins origin of Miguel O'Hara (Spider-Man 2099); Leonardi/Williamson-c/a begins 1 2 3 5 6 8
1-2nd printing, 2-12,14-24,26-34,39,40: 2-Origin continued, ends #3. 4-Doom 2099 app. 19-Bound-in trading cards. 3.00
13-Extra 16 pg. insert on Midnight Sons 4.00
25-($2.25, 52 pgs.)-Newsstand edition 4.00
25-($2.95, 52 pgs.)-Deluxe edition w/embossed foil-c 5.00
35-38-Venom app. 35-Variant-c. 36-Two-c; Jae Lee-a. 37,38-Two-c 5.00
41-46: 46-The Vulture app; Mike McKone-a(p) 3.00
Annual 1 (1994, $2.95, 68 pgs.) 4.00
Special 1 (1995, $3.95) 4.00
NOTE: ***Chaykin** c-37.* ***Ron Lim** a(p)-18; c(p)-13, 16, 18.* ***Kelley Jones** c/a-9.* ***Leonardi/Williamson** a-1-8, 10-13, 15-17, 19, 20, 22-25; c-1-13, 15, 17-19, 20, 22-25, 35.*

SPIDER-MAN 2099
Marvel Comics: Sept, 2014 - No. 12, Jul, 2015 ($3.99)
1-12: 1-Miguel O'Hara in 2014; Peter David-s/Will Sliney-a. 5-8-Spider-Verse tie-in 4.00

SPIDER-MAN 2099
Marvel Comics: Dec, 2015 - Present ($3.99)
1-21: 1-Miguel O'Hara still in the present; David-s/Sliney-a. 2-New costume. 13-16-Civil War II tie-ins. 14-16-Power Pack app. 17-19-Elektra app. 4.00

SPIDER-MAN 2099 MEETS SPIDER-MAN
Marvel Comics: 1995 ($5.95, one-shot)
nn-Peter David script; Leonardi/Williamson-c/a. 6.00

SPIDER-MAN UNIVERSE
Marvel Comics: Mar, 2000 - No. 7, Oct, 2000 ($4.95/$3.99, reprints)
1-5-Reprints recent issues from the various Spider-Man titles 5.00
6,7-($3.99) 4.00

SPIDER-MAN UNLIMITED
Marvel Comics: May, 1993 - No. 22, Nov, 1998 ($3.95, #1-12 were quarterly, 68 pgs.)
1-Begin Maximum Carnage storyline, ends; Carnage-c/story 5.00
2-12: 2-Venom & Carnage-c/story; Lim-c/a(p) in #2-6. 10-Vulture app. 4.00
13-22: 13-Begin $2.99-c; Scorpion-c/app. 15-Daniel-c; Puma-c/app. 19-Lizard-c/app. 20-Hannibal King and Lilith app. 21,22-Deodato-a 3.00

SPIDER-MAN UNLIMITED (Based on the TV animated series)
Marvel Comics: Dec, 1999 - No. 5, Apr, 2000 ($2.99/$1.99)
1-($2.99) Venom and Carnage app. 4.00
2-5: 2-($1.99) Green Goblin app. 3.00

SPIDER-MAN UNLIMITED (3rd series)
Marvel Comics: Mar, 2004 - No. 15, July, 2006 ($2.99)
1-16: 1-Short stories by various incl. Miyazawa & Chen-a. 2-Mays-a. 6-Allred-c. 14-Finch-c/a; Black Cat app. 3.00

SPIDER-MAN UNMASKED
Marvel Comics: Nov, 1996 ($5.95, one-shot)
nn-Art w/text 6.00

SPIDER-MAN: VENOM AGENDA
Marvel Comics: Jan, 1998 ($2.99, one-shot)
1-Hama-s/Lyle-c/a 3.00

SPIDER-MAN VS. DRACULA
Marvel Comics: Jan, 1994 ($1.75, 52 pgs., one-shot)
1-r/Giant-Size Spider-Man #1 plus new Matt Fox-a 4.00

SPIDER-MAN VS. WOLVERINE
Marvel Comics Group: Feb, 1987; V2#1, 1990 (68 pgs.)
1-Williamson-c/a(i); intro Charlemagne; death of Ned Leeds (old Hobgoblin) 3 6 9 17 26 35
V2#1 (1990, $4.95)-Reprints #1 (2/87) 6.00

SPIDER-MAN: WEB OF DOOM
Marvel Comics: Aug, 1994 - No. 3, Oct, 1994 ($1.75, limited series)
1-3 3.00

SPIDER-MAN: WITH GREAT POWER...
Marvel Comics: Mar, 2008 - No. 5, Sept, 2008 ($3.99, limited series)
1-5-Origin and early days re-told; Lapham-s/Harris-a/c 4.00

SPIDER-MAN: WITH GREAT POWER COMES GREAT RESPONSIBILITY
Marvel Comics: Jun, 2011 - No. 7, Dec, 2011 ($3.99, limited series)
1-7: Reprints of noteworthy Spider-Man stories. 1-R/Ultimate Spider-Man #33,97, and Ultimate Comics Spider-Man #1. 4-R/ Amazing Spider-Man #1,11,20 4.00

SPIDER-MAN: YEAR IN REVIEW
Marvel Comics: Feb, 2000 ($2.99)
1-Text recaps of 1999 issues 3.00

SPIDER-MEN
Marvel Comics: Aug, 2012 - No. 5, Nov, 2012 ($3.99, limited series)
1-5-Peter Parker goes to Ultimate Universe; teams with Miles Morales; Pichelli-a 4.00

SPIDER REIGN OF THE VAMPIRE KING, THE (Also see The Spider)
Eclipse Books: 1992 - No. 3, 1992 ($4.95, limited series, coated stock, 52 pgs.)
Book One - Three: Truman scripts & painted-c 5.00

SPIDER'S WEB, THE (See G-8 and His Battle Aces)

SPIDER-VERSE (See Amazing Spider-Man 2014 series #7-14)
Marvel Comics: Jan, 2015 - No. 2, Mar, 2015 ($4.99, limited series)
1,2-Short stories of alternate Spider-Men; s/a by various. 2-Anarchic Spider-Man 5.00

SPIDER-VERSE (Secret Wars tie-in)
Marvel Comics: Jul, 2015 - No. 5, Nov, 2015 ($4.99/$3.99, limited series)
1-($4.99) Costa-s/Araujo-a; Spider-Gwen, Spider-Ham & Norman Osborn app. 5.00
2-5-($3.99) Alternate Spider-Men vs. Sinister Six 4.00

SPIDER-VERSE TEAM-UP (See Amazing Spider-Man 2014 series #7-14)
Marvel Comics: Jan, 2015 - No. 3, Mar, 2015 ($3.99, limited series)
1-3-Short stories of alternate Spider-Men team-ups; s/a by various. 2-Spider-Gwen, Miles Morales and '67 animated Spider-Man app. 4.00

SPIDER-WOMAN (Also see The Avengers #240, Marvel Spotlight #32, Marvel Super Heroes Secret Wars #7, Marvel Two-In-One #29 and New Avengers)
Marvel Comics Group: April, 1978 - No. 50, June, 1983 (New logo #47 on)
1-New complete origin & mask added 3 6 9 21 33 45
2-5,7-18: 2-Excalibur app. 3,11,12-Brother Grimm app. 13,15-The Shroud-c/s. 16-Sienkiewicz-c 1 2 3 4 5 7
6,19,20,28,29,32: 6-Morgan LeFay app. 6,19,32-Werewolf by Night-c/s. 20,28,29-Spider-Man app. 32-Universal Monsters photo/Miller-c 1 2 3 5 6 8
21-27,30,31,33-36 6.00
37-1st app. Siryn of X-Force; X-Men x-over; origin retold 2 4 6 11 16 20
38-X-Men x-over 2 4 6 8 10 12
39-49: 46-Kingpin app. 49-Tigra-c/story 5.00
50-(52 pgs.)-Death of Spider-Woman; photo-c 2 4 6 9 13 16
NOTE: ***Austin** a-37i.* ***Byrne** c-26p.* ***Infantino** a-1-19.* ***Layton** c-19.* ***Miller** c-32p.*

SPIDER-WOMAN
Marvel Comics: Nov, 1993 - No. 4, Feb, 1994 ($1.75, mini-series)
V2#1-4: 1,2-Origin; U.S. Agent app. 3.00

SPIDER-WOMAN
Marvel Comics: July, 1999 - No. 18, Dec, 2000 ($2.99/$1.99/$2.25)
1-($2.99) Byrne-s/Sears-a 4.00
2-18: 2-11-($1.99). 2-Two covers. 12-Begin $2.25-c. 15-Capt. America-c/app. 3.00

SPIDER-WOMAN (Printed version of the motion comic for computers)
Marvel Comics: Nov, 2009 - No. 7, May, 2010 ($3.99/$2.99)
1-($3.99) Bendis-s/Maleev-a; covers by Maleev & Alex Ross; Jessica joins S.W.O.R.D. 4.00
2-6-($2.99) 2-4-Madame Hydra app. 6-Thunderbolts app. 3.00

Spider-Woman (2016 series) #2 © MAR

Spike #5 © 20th Century Fox

The Spirit #17 © Will Eisner

GD 2.0 VG 4.0 FN 6.0 VF 8.0 VF/NM 9.0 NM- 9.2

7-($3.99) New Avengers app. 4.00

SPIDER-WOMAN (Also see Spider-Verse event in Amazing Spider-Man 2014 series #7-14)
Marvel Comics: Jan, 2015 - No. 10, Oct, 2015 ($3.99)

1-4-Spider-Verse tie-ins; Silk app.; Hopeless-s/Land-a/c. 4-Avengers app. 4.00
5-10: 5-New costume; Javier Rodriguez-a/c. 10-Black Widow app. 4.00

SPIDER-WOMAN
Marvel Comics: Jan, 2016 - Present ($3.99)

1-16: 1-5-Hopeless-s/Javier Rodriguez-a. 4-Jessica's baby is born. 6,7-"Spider-Women x-over; Spider-Gwen & Silk app.; Joelle Jones-a. 9-11-Civil War II tie-in. 13-16-Hobgoblin app. 4.00

SPIDER-WOMAN: ORIGIN (Also see New Avengers)
Marvel Comics: Feb, 2006 - No. 5, June, 2006 ($2.99, limited series)

1-5-Bendis & Reed-s/Jonathan & Joshua Luna-a/c 3.00
1-Variant cover by Olivier Coipel 3.00
HC (2006, $19.99) r/series 20.00
SC (2007, $13.99) r/series 14.00

SPIDER-WOMEN (Crossover with Silk, Spider-Gwen and Spider-Woman)
Marvel Comics: Alpha, Jun, 2016 - Omega, Aug, 2016 ($4.99, limited series)

... Alpha 1 - Thompson-s/Del Rey-a/Putri-c; part 1 of x-over; intro. Earth-65 Cindy Moon 5.00
... Omega 1 - Hopeless-s/Leon-a/Putri-c; part 8 conclusion of x-over 5.00

SPIDEY (Spider-Man)
Marvel Comics: Feb, 2016 - No. 12, Jan, 2017 ($3.99)

1-12-High school-era Spider-Man. 1-3-Bradshaw-a. 1-Doc Ock app. 7-Black Panther app. 4.00
... No. 1 Halloween Comic Fest 2016 (12/16, giveaway) r/#1 3.00

SPIDEY SUPER STORIES (Spider-Man) (Also see Fireside Books)
Marvel/Children's TV Workshop: Oct, 1974 - No. 57, Mar, 1982 (35¢, no ads)

1-Origin (stories simplified for younger readers) 5 10 15 33 57 80
2-Kraven 3 6 9 17 26 35
3-10,15: 6-Iceman. 15-Storm-c/sty 3 6 9 14 20 26
11-14,16-20: 19,20-Kirby-c 3 6 9 14 19 24
21-30: 22-Early Ms. Marvel app. 2 4 6 13 18 22
31-53: 31-Moondragon-c/app.; Dr. Doom app. 33-Hulk. 34-Sub-Mariner. 38-F.F. 39-Thanos-c/story. 44-Vision. 45-Silver Surfer & Dr. Doom app. 2 4 6 11 16 20
54-57: 56-Battles Jack O'Lantern-c/sty (exactly one year after 1st app. in Machine Man #19) 3 6 9 14 20 26

SPIKE AND TYKE (See M.G.M.'s...)

SPIKE... (Also see Buffy the Vampire Slayer and related titles)
IDW Publ.: Aug, 2005; Jan, 2006; Apr, 2006 ($7.49, squarebound, one-shots)

...: Lost & Found (4/06, $7.49) Scott Tipton-s/Fernando Goni-a 8.00
...: Old Times (8/05, $7.49) Peter David-s/Fernando Goni-a; Cecily/Halfrek app. 8.00
...: Old Wounds (1/06, $7.49) Tipton-s/Goni-a; flashback to Black Dahlia murder case 8.00
TPB (7/06, $19.99) r/one-shots 20.00

SPIKE (Buffy the Vampire Slayer)
IDW Publ.: Oct, 2010 - No. 8, May, 2011 ($3.99, limited series)

1-8-Lynch-s; multiple covers on each. 1,2-Urru-a. 5-7-Willow app. 4.00
... 100 Page Spectacular (6/11, $7.99) reprints of four IDW Spike stories; Frison-c 8.00

SPIKE (A Dark Place) (From Buffy the Vampire Slayer)
Dark Horse Comics: Aug, 2012 - No. 5, Dec, 2012 ($2.99, limited series)

1-5-Paul Lee-a; 2 covers by Frison & Morris on each 3.00

SPIKE: AFTER THE FALL (Also see Angel: After the Fall) (Follows the last Angel TV episode)
IDW Publ.: July, 2008 - No. 4, Oct, 2008 ($3.99, limited series)

1-4-Lynch-s/Urru-a; multiple covers on each 4.00

SPIKE: ASYLUM (Buffy the Vampire Slayer)
IDW Publ.: Sept, 2006 - No. 5, Jan, 2007 ($3.99, limited series)

1-5-Lynch-s/Urru-a; multiple covers on each 4.00

SPIKE: SHADOW PUPPETS (Buffy the Vampire Slayer)
IDW Publ.: June, 2007 - No. 4, Sept, 2007 ($3.99, limited series)

1-4-Lynch-s/Urru-a; multiple covers on each 4.00

SPIKE: THE DEVIL YOU KNOW (Buffy the Vampire Slayer)
IDW Publ.: Jun, 2010 - No. 4, Sept, 2010 ($3.99, limited series)

1-4-Bill Williams-s/Chris Cross-a/Urru-c 4.00

SPIKE VS. DRACULA (Buffy the Vampire Slayer)
IDW Publ.: Feb, 2006 - No. 5, Mar, 2006 ($3.99, limited series)

1-5: 1-Peter David-s/Joe Corroney-a; Dru and Bela Lugosi app. 4.00

SPIN & MARTY (TV) (Walt Disney's)(See Walt Disney Showcase #32)
Dell Publishing Co. (Mickey Mouse Club): No. 714, June, 1956 - No. 1082, Mar-May, 1960 (All photo-c)

Four Color 714 (#1) 11 22 33 72 154 235
Four Color 767,808 (#2,3) 8 16 24 56 108 160
Four Color 826 (#4)-Annette Funicello photo-c 18 36 54 124 275 425
5(3-5/58) - 9(6-8/59) 7 14 21 44 82 120
Four Color 1026,1082 7 14 21 44 82 120

SPIN ANGELS
Marvel Comics (Soleil): 2009 - No. 4, 2009 ($5.99)

1-4-English version of French comics; Jean-Luc Sala-s/Pierre-Mony Chan-a 6.00

SPINE-TINGLING TALES (Doctor Spektor Presents...)
Gold Key: May, 1975 - No. 4, Jan, 1976 (All 25¢ issues)

1-1st Tragg-r/Mystery Comics Digest #3 2 4 6 9 13 16
2-4: 2-Origin Ra-Ka-Tep-r/Mystery Comics Digest #1; Dr. Spektor #12. 3-All Durak-r issue; 4-Baron Tibor's 1st app.-r/Mystery Comics Digest #4; painted-c 1 2 3 5 7 9

SPINWORLD
Amaze Ink (Slave Labor Graphics): July, 1997 - No. 4, Jan, 1998 ($2.95/$3.95, B&W, mini-series)

1-3-Brent Anderson-a(p) 3.00
4-($3.95) 4.00

SPIRAL ZONE
DC Comics: Feb, 1988 - No. 4, May, 1988 ($1.00, mini-series)

1-4-Based on Tonka toys 3.00

SPIRIT, THE (Newspaper comics - see Promotional Comics section)

SPIRIT, THE (1st Series)(Also see Police Comics #11 and The Best of the Spirit TPB)
Quality Comics Group (Vital): 1944 - No. 22, Aug, 1950

nn(#1)- "Wanted Dead or Alive" 142 284 426 909 1555 2200
nn(#2)- "Crime Doesn't Pay" 53 106 159 334 567 800
nn(#3)- "Murder Runs Wild" 47 94 141 296 498 700
4,5: 4-Flatfoot Burns begins, ends #22. 5-Wertham app. 39 78 117 240 395 550
6-10 36 72 108 211 343 475
11-Crandall-c 34 68 102 199 325 450
12-17-Eisner-c. 19-Honeybun app. 45 90 135 284 480 675
18,19-Strip-r by Eisner; Eisner-c 63 126 189 403 689 975
20,21-Eisner good girl covers; strip-r by Eisner 81 162 243 518 884 1250
22-Used by N.Y. Legis. Comm; classic Eisner-c 423 846 1269 3000 5250 7500
Super Reprint #11-r/Quality Spirit #19 by Eisner 3 6 9 18 27 35
Super Reprint #12-r/Spirit #17 by Fine; Sol Brodsky-c 3 6 9 18 27 35

SPIRIT, THE (2nd Series)
Fiction House Magazines: Spring, 1952 - No. 5, 1954

1-Not Eisner 53 106 159 334 567 800
2-Eisner-c/a(2) 50 100 150 315 533 750
3-Eisner/Grandenetti-c 45 90 135 284 480 675
4-Eisner/Grandenetti-c; Eisner-a 47 94 141 296 498 700
5-Eisner-c/a(4) 50 100 150 315 533 750

SPIRIT, THE
Harvey Publications: Oct, 1966 - No. 2, Mar, 1967 (Giant Size, 25¢, 68 pgs.)

1-Eisner-r plus 9 new pgs.(origin Denny Colt, Take 3, plus 2 filler pgs.) (#3 was advertised, but never published) 8 16 24 54 102 150
2-Eisner-r plus 9 new pgs.(origin of the Octopus) 7 14 21 44 82 120

SPIRIT, THE (Underground)
Kitchen Sink Enterprises (Krupp Comics): Jan, 1973 - No. 2, Sept, 1973 (Black & White)

1-New Eisner-c & 4 pgs. new Eisner-a plus-r (titled Crime Convention) 4 8 12 23 37 50
2-New Eisner-c & 4 pgs. new Eisner-a plus-r (titled Meets P'Gell) 4 8 12 25 40 55

SPIRIT, THE (Magazine)
Warren Publ. Co./Krupp Comic Works No. 17 on: 4/74 - No. 16, 10/76; No. 17, Winter, 1977 - No. 41, 6/83 (B&W w/color) (#6-14,16 are squarebound)

1-Eisner-r begin; 8 pg. color insert 6 12 18 41 76 110
2-5: 2-Powder Pouf-s; UFO-s. 4-Silk Satin-s 4 8 12 27 44 60
6-9,11-15: 7-All Ebony issue. 8-Female Foes issue. 8,12-Sand Seref-s. 9-P'Gell & Octopus-s. 12-X-Mas issue 4 8 12 25 40 55
10-Giant Summer Special ($1.50)-Origin 4 8 12 27 44 60
16-Giant Summer Special ($1.50)-Olga Bustle-c/s 4 8 12 25 40 55
17,18(8/78): 17-Lady Luck-r 3 6 9 17 26 35

The Spirit (2015 series) #7 © Will Eisner

Spitfire #1 © MAR

Spongebob Comics #43 © UPP

GD 2.0 | VG 4.0 | FN 6.0 | VF 8.0 | VF/NM 9.0 | NM- 9.2

19-21-New Eisner-a. 20,21-Wood-r (#21-r/A DP on the Moon by Wood). 20-Outer Space-r 3 6 9 17 26 35

22-41: 22,23-Wood-r (#22-r/Mission the Moon by Wood). 28-r/last story (10/5/52). 30-(7/81)-Special Spirit Jam issue w/Caniff, Corben, Bolland, Byrne, Miller, Kurtzman, Rogers, Sienkiewicz-a & 40 others. 36-Begin Spirit Section-r; r/1st story (6/2/40) in color; new Eisner-c/a(18 pgs.)($2.95). 37-r/2nd story in color plus 18 pgs. new Eisner-a. 38-41: r/3rd - 6th stories in color. 41-Lady Luck Mr. Mystic in color 3 6 9 15 22 28

Special 1(1975)-All Eisner-a (mail only, 1500 printed, full color) 13 26 39 89 195 300

NOTE: *Covers pencilled/inked by* ***Eisner*** *only #1-9,12-16; painted by Eisner & Ken Kelly #10 & 11; painted by Eisner #17-up; one color story reprinted in #1-10.* ***Austin*** *a-30i.* ***Byrne*** *a-30p.* ***Miller*** *a-30p.*

SPIRIT, THE
Kitchen Sink Enterprises: Oct, 1983 - No. 87, Jan, 1992 ($2.00, Baxter paper)

1-60: 1-Origin-r/12/23/45 Spirit Section. 2-r/ 1/20/46-2/10/46. 3-r/2/17/46-3/10/46. 4-r/3/17/46-4/7/46. 11-Last color issue. 54-r/section 2/19/50 4.00
61-87: 85-87-Reprint the Outer Space Spirit stories by Wood. 86-r/A DP on the Moon by Wood from 1952 4.00

SPIRIT, THE (Also see Batman/The Spirit in Batman one-shots)
DC Comics: Feb, 2007 - No. 32, Oct, 2009 ($2.99)

1-32: 1-6,8-12-Darwyn Cooke-s/a/c. 2-P'Gell app. 3-Origin re-told. 7-Short stories by Baker, Bernet, Palmiotti, Simonson & Sprouse; Cooke-c. 13-Short stories by various 3.00
... Femme Fatales TPB (2008, $19.99) r/1940s stories focusing on the Spirit's female adversaries like Silk Satin, P'gell, Powder Pouf and Silken Floss; Michael Uslan intro. 20.00
... Special 1 (2008, $2.99) r/stories from '47, '49, '50 newspaper strips; the Octopus app. 3.00

SPIRIT, THE (First Wave)
DC Comics: Jun, 2010 - No. 17, Oct, 2011 ($3.99/$2.99)(B&W back-up stories by various)

1-10: 1-Schultz-s/Moritat-a; covers by Ladronn and Schultz; back-up by O'Neil & Sienkiewicz. 2-Back-up by Ellison & Baker. 7-Corben-a back-up. 8-Ploog-a back-up 4.00
11-17-($2.99) 11-16-Hine-s/Moritat-a; no back-up story. 17-B&W; Bolland, Russell-a 3.00
...: Angel Smerti TPB (2011, $17.99) r/#1-7 18.00

SPIRIT, (WILL EISNER'S THE...)
Dynamite Entertainment: 2015 - No. 12, 2016 ($3.99)

1-12: 1-Wagner-s/Schkade-a; multiple covers. 2-12-Powell-c 4.00

SPIRIT, (WILL EISNER'S THE...): CORPSE MAKERS (Volume 2)
Dynamite Entertainment: 2017 - Present ($3.99)

1-Francesco Francavilla-s/a/c 4.00

SPIRIT JAM
Kitchen Sink Press: Aug, 1998 ($5.95, B&W, oversized, square-bound)

nn-Reprints Spirit (Magazine) #30 by Eisner & 50 others; and "Cerebus Vs. The Spirit" from Cerebus Jam #1 6.00

SPIRIT, THE: THE NEW ADVENTURES
Kitchen Sink Press: 1997 - No. 8, Nov, 1998 ($3.50, anthology)

1-Moore-s/Gibbons-c/a 4.00
2-8: 2-Gaiman-s/Eisner-c. 3-Moore-s/Bolland-c/Moebius back-c. 4-Allred-s/a; Busiek-s/Anderson-a. 5-Chadwick-s/c/a(p); Nyberg-i. 6-S.Hampton & Mandrake-a 3.50
Will Eisner's The Spirit Archives Volume 27 (Dark Horse, 2009, $49.95) r/#1-8 50.00

SPIRIT: THE ORIGIN YEARS
Kitchen Sink Press: May, 1992 - No. 10, Dec, 1993 ($2.95, B&W)

1-10: 1-r/sections 6/2/40(origin)-6/23/40 (all 1940s) 3.00

SPIRITMAN (Also see Three Comics)
No publisher listed: No date (1944) (10¢)(Triangle Sales Co. ad on back cover)

1-Three 16pg. Spirit sections bound together, (1944, 10¢, 52 pgs.) 30 60 90 177 289 400
2-Two Spirit sections (3/26/44, 4/2/44) bound together; by Lou Fine 26 52 78 154 252 350

SPIRIT OF THE BORDER (See Zane Grey & Four Color #197)

SPIRIT OF THE TAO
Image Comics (Top Cow): Jun, 1998 - No. 15, May, 2000 ($2.50)

Preview 5.00
1-14: 1-D-Tron-s/Tan & D-Tron-a 3.00
15-($4.95) 5.00

SPIRIT WORLD (Magazine)
Hampshire Distributors Ltd.: Fall, 1971 (B&W)

1-New Kirby-a; Neal Adams-c; poster inside 6 12 18 40 73 105
(1/2 price without poster)

SPITFIRE (Female undercover agent)
Malverne Herald (Elliot)(J. R. Mahon): No. 132, 1944 (Aug) - No. 133, 1945
Both have Classics Gift Box ads on back-c with checklist to #20

132-British spitfire WWII-c. 36 721 108 211 343 475
133-Female agent/Nazi WWII-c 97 194 291 621 1061 1500

SPITFIRE (WW2 speedster from MI:13)
Marvel Comics: Oct, 2010 ($3.99, one-shot)

1-Cornell-s/Casagrande-a; Blade app. 4.00

SPITFIRE AND THE TROUBLESHOOTERS
Marvel Comics: Oct, 1986 - No. 9, June, 1987 (Codename: Spitfire #10 on)

1-3,5-9 3.00
4-McFarlane-a 4.00

SPITFIRE COMICS (Also see Double Up) (Tied with Pocket Comics #1 for earliest Harvey)
Harvey Publications: Aug, 1941 - No. 2, Oct, 1941 (Pocket size; 100 pgs.)

1-Origin The Clown, The Fly-Man, The Spitfire & The Magician From Bagdad; British spitfire, Nazi bomber WWII-c 90 180 270 576 988 1400
2-(Rare) Fly-Man-c 84 168 252 538 919 1300

SPLITTING IMAGE
Image Comics: Mar, 1993 - No. 2, 1993 ($1.95)

1,2-Simpson-c/a; parody comic 3.00

SPONGEBOB COMICS (TV's Spongebob Squarepants)
United Plankton Pictures: 2011 - Present ($2.99)

1-51-Short stories by various. 1-Kochalka back-c. 3-Aquaman homage w/Fradon-a. 32-36-Showdown at the Shady Shoals; Mermaid Man app; Ordway-a 3.00
52-65-($3.99) 53,59,60-Chuck Dixon-s. 63,64-Mermaid Girl spotlight 4.00
Annual-Size Super-Giant Swimtacular 1 (2013, $4.99) art by Fradon, Ordway, Kochalka 5.00
Annual-Size Super-Giant Swimtacular 2 (2014, $4.99) Mermaid Man app. 5.00
Annual-Size Super-Giant Swimtacular 3 (2015, $4.99) art by Barta, Kochalka, Chabot 5.00
Annual-Size Super-Giant Swimtacular 4 (2016, $4.99) Neal Adams & others-a; Ordway-c 5.00
SpongeBob Freestyle Funnies 1 (2013, Free Comic Book Day giveaway) Short stories 3.00
SpongeBob Freestyle Funnies 2014 (Free Comic Book Day giveaway) Short stories 3.00
SpongeBob Freestyle Funnies 2015 (Free Comic Book Day giveaway) Short stories 3.00
SpongeBob Freestyle Funnies 2016 (FCBD giveaway) Short stories; Fradon-a 3.00

SPOOF
Marvel Comics Group: Oct, 1970; No. 2, Nov, 1972 - No. 5, May, 1973

1-Infinity-c; Dark Shadows-c & parody 4 8 12 25 40 55
2-5: 2-All in the Family. 3-Beatles, Osmond's, Jackson 5, David Cassidy, Nixon & Agnew-c. 5-Rod Serling, Woody Allen, Ted Kennedy-c 3 6 9 16 24 32

SPOOK (Formerly Shock Detective Cases)
Star Publications: No. 22, Jan, 1953 - No. 30, Oct, 1954

22-Sgt. Spook-r; acid in face story; hanging-c 46 92 138 290 488 685
23,25,27: 25-Jungle Lil-r. 27-Two Sgt. Spook-r 38 76 114 228 369 510
24-Used in **SOTI**, pgs. 182,183-r/Inside Crime #2; Transvestism story 39 78 117 235 385 535
26,28-30: 26-Disbrow-a. 28,29-Rulah app. 29-Jo-Jo app. 30-Disbrow-c/a(2); only Star-c 38 76 114 228 369 510

NOTE: ***L. B. Cole*** *covers-all issues except #30; a-28(1 pg.).* ***Disbrow*** *a-26(2), 28, 29(2), 30(2); No. 30 r/Blue Bolt Weird Tales #114.*

SPOOK COMICS
Baily Publications/Star: 1946

1-Mr. Lucifer story 39 78 117 231 378 525

SPOOK HOUSE
Albatross Funnybooks: 2016 - Present ($3.99)

1,2-Horror anthology by Eric Powell and others; Powell-c 4.00

SPOOKY (The Tuff Little Ghost; see Casper The Friendly Ghost)
Harvey Publications: 11/55 - 139, 11/73; No. 140, 7/74 - No. 155, 3/77; No. 156, 12/77 - No. 158, 4/78; No. 159, 9/78; No. 160, 10/79; No. 161, 9/80

	GD 2.0	VG 4.0	FN 6.0	VF 8.0	VF/NM 9.0	NM- 9.2
1-Nightmare begins (see Casper #19)	61	122	183	488	1094	1700
2	20	40	60	141	313	485
3-10(1956-57)	11	22	33	76	163	250
11-20(1957-58)	7	14	21	44	82	120
21-40(1958-59)	5	10	15	33	57	80
41-60	4	8	12	27	44	60
61-80,100	3	6	9	19	30	40
81-99	3	6	9	16	24	32
101-120	2	4	6	11	16	20
121-126,133-140	2	4	6	8	11	14
127-132: All 52 pg. Giants	2	4	6	11	16	20
141-161	1	2	3	5	7	9

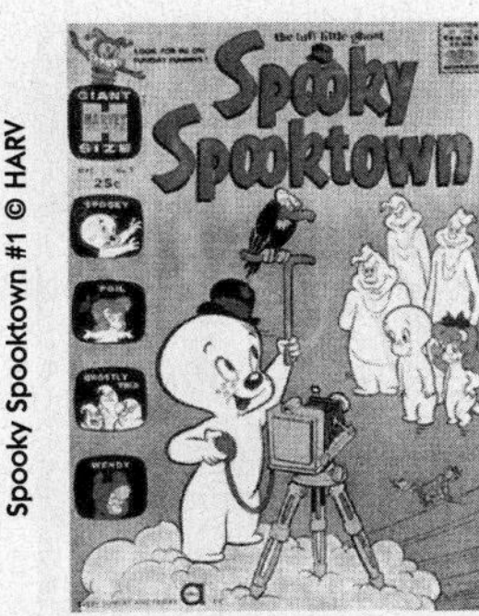

Spooky Spooktown #1 © HARV

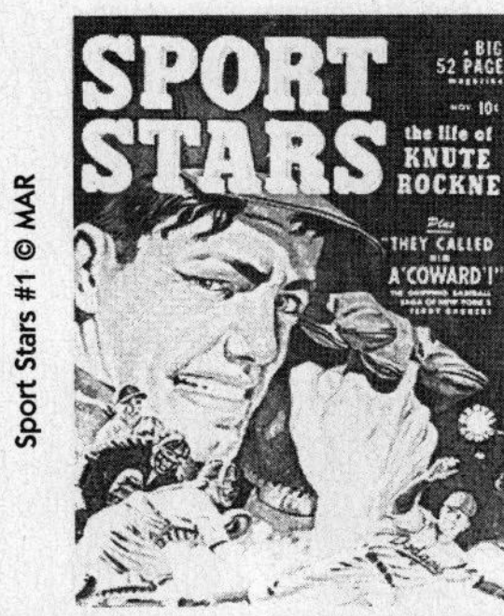

Sport Stars #1 © MAR

Spyboy / Young Justice #1 © DC & DH

	GD 2.0	VG 4.0	FN 6.0	VF 8.0	VF/NM 9.0	NM- 9.2
SPOOKY						
Harvey Comics: Nov, 1991 - No. 4, Sept, 1992 ($1.00/$1.25)						
1						4.00
2-4: 3-Begin $1.25-c						3.00
...Digest 1-3 (10/92, 6/93, 10/93, $1.75, 100 pgs.)-Casper, Wendy, etc.						4.00
SPOOKY HAUNTED HOUSE						
Harvey Publications: Oct, 1972 - No. 15, Feb, 1975						
1	3	6	9	17	26	35
2-5	2	4	6	10	14	18
6-10	2	4	6	8	10	12
11-15	1	2	3	5	7	9
SPOOKY MYSTERIES						
Your Guide Publ. Co.: No date (1946) (10¢)						
1-Mr. Spooky, Super Snooper, Pinky, Girl Detective app.	24	48	72	142	234	325
SPOOKY SPOOKTOWN						
Harvey Publ.: 9/61; No. 2, 9/62 - No. 52, 12/73; No. 53, 10/74 - No. 66, 12/76						
1-Casper, Spooky; 68 pgs. begin	14	28	42	94	207	320
2	8	16	24	54	102	150
3-5	6	12	18	38	69	100
6-10	5	10	15	31	53	75
11-20	4	8	12	23	37	50
21-39: 39-Last 68 pg. issue	3	6	9	19	30	40
40-45: All 52 pgs.	2	4	6	11	16	20
46-66: 61-Hot Stuff/Spooky team-up story	1	2	3	5	7	9
SPORT COMICS (Becomes True Sport Picture Stories #5 on)						
Street & Smith Publications: Oct, 1940 (No mo.) - No. 4, Nov, 1941						
1-Life story of Lou Gehrig	55	110	165	352	601	850
2	31	62	93	182	296	410
3,4: 4-Story of Notre Dame coach Frank Leahy	26	52	78	154	252	350
SPORT LIBRARY (See Charlton Sport Library)						
SPORTS ACTION (Formerly Sport Stars)						
Marvel/Atlas Comics (ACI No. 2,3/SAI No. 4-14): No. 2, Feb, 1950 - No. 14, Sept, 1952						
2-Powell-a; George Gipp life story	43	86	129	269	455	640
1-(nd,no price, no publ., 52pgs, #1 on-c; has same-c as #2; blank inside-c (giveaway?)	22	44	66	132	216	300
3-Everett-a	24	48	72	142	234	325
4-11,14: Weiss-a	22	44	66	128	209	290
12,13: 12-Everett-c. 13-Krigstein-a	23	46	69	136	223	310
NOTE: *Title may have changed after No. 3, to Crime Must Lose No. 4 on, due to publisher change.* ***Sol Brodsky*** *c-4-7, 13, 14.* ***Maneely*** *c-3, 8-11.*						
SPORT STARS						
Parents' Magazine Institute (Sport Stars): Feb-Mar, 1946 - No. 4, Aug-Sept, 1946 (Half comic, half photo magazine)						
1- "How Tarzan Got That Way" story of Johnny Weissmuller	40	80	120	243	402	560
2-Baseball greats	26	52	78	154	252	350
3,4	23	46	69	136	223	310
SPORT STARS (Becomes Sports Action #2 on)						
Marvel Comics (ACI): Nov, 1949 (52 pgs.)						
1-Knute Rockne; painted-c	45	90	135	284	480	675
SPORT THRILLS (Formerly Dick Cole; becomes Jungle Thrills #16)						
Star Publications: No. 11, Nov, 1950 - No. 15, Nov, 1951						
11-Dick Cole begins; Ted Williams & Ty Cobb life stories	28	56	84	165	270	375
12-Joe DiMaggio, Phil Rizzuto stories & photos on-c; L.B. Cole-c/a	22	44	66	132	216	300
13-15-All L. B. Cole-c. 13-Jackie Robinson, Pee Wee Reese stories & photo on-c. 14-Johnny Weissmuler life story	22	44	66	132	216	300
Accepted Reprint #11 (#15 on-c, nd); L.B. Cole-c	10	20	30	54	72	90
Accepted Reprint #12 (nd); L.B. Cole-c; Joe DiMaggio & Phil Rizzuto life stories-r/#12	10	20	30	54	72	90
SPOTLIGHT (TV) (newsstand sales only)						
Marvel Comics Group: Sept, 1978 - No. 4, Mar, 1979 (Hanna-Barbera)						
1-Huckleberry Hound, Yogi Bear; Shaw-a	3	6	9	19	30	40
2,4: 2-Quick Draw McGraw, Augie Doggie, Snooper & Blabber. 4-Magilla Gorilla, Snagglepuss	3	6	9	16	23	30
3-The Jetsons; Yakky Doodle	3	6	9	19	30	40

	GD 2.0	VG 4.0	FN 6.0	VF 8.0	VF/NM 9.0	NM- 9.2
SPOTLIGHT COMICS						
Country Press Inc.: Sept, 1940						
nn-Ashcan, not distributed to newsstands, only for in house use. A NM copy sold in 2009 for $1015.						
SPOTLIGHT COMICS (Becomes Red Seal Comics #14 on?)						
Harry 'A' Chesler (Our Army, Inc.): Nov, 1944, No. 2, Jan, 1945 - No. 3, 1945						
1-The Black Dwarf (cont'd in Red Seal?), The Veiled Avenger, & Barry Kuda begin; Tuska-c	135	270	405	864	1482	2100
2	69	138	207	442	759	1075
3-Injury to eye story (reprinted from Scoop #3)	73	146	219	467	796	1125
SPOTTY THE PUP (Becomes Super Pup #4, see Television Puppet Show)						
Avon Periodicals/Realistic Comics: No. 2, Oct-Nov, 1953 - No. 3, Dec-Jan, 1953-54 (Also see Funny Tunes)						
2,3	8	16	24	44	57	70
nn (1953, Realistic-r)	5	10	15	24	30	35
SPUNKY (...Junior Cowboy)(...Comics #2 on)						
Standard Comics: April, 1949 - No. 7, Nov, 1951						
1-Text illos by Frazetta	15	30	45	85	130	175
2-Text illos by Frazetta	11	22	33	60	83	105
3-7	8	16	24	44	57	70
SPUNKY THE SMILING SPOOK						
Ajax/Farrell (World Famous Comics/Four Star Comic Corp.): Aug, 1957 - No. 4, May, 1958						
1-Reprints from Frisky Fables	11	22	33	64	90	115
2-4	7	14	21	37	46	55
SPY AND COUNTERSPY (Becomes Spy Hunters #3 on)						
American Comics Group: Aug-Sept, 1949 - No. 2, Oct-Nov, 1949 (52 pgs.)						
1-Origin, 1st app. Jonathan Kent, Counterspy	30	60	90	177	289	400
2	18	36	54	103	162	220
SPYBOY						
Dark Horse Comics: Oct, 1999 - No. 17, May, 2001 ($2.50/$2.95/$2.99)						
1-17: 1-6-Peter David-s/Pop Mhan-a. 7,8-Meglia-a. 9-17-Mhan-a						3.00
13.1-13.3 (4/03-8/03, $2.99), 13.2,13.3-Mhan-a						3.00
... Special (5/02, $4.99) David-s/Mhan-a						5.00
SPYBOY: FINAL EXAM						
Dark Horse Comics: May, 2004 - No. 4, Aug, 2004 ($2.99, limited series)						
1-4-Peter David-s/Pop Mhan-a/c						3.00
TPB (2005, $12.95) r/series						13.00
SPYBOY/ YOUNG JUSTICE						
Dark Horse Comics: Feb, 2002 - No. 3, Apr, 2002 ($2.99, limited series)						
1-3: 1-Peter David-s/Todd Nauck-a/Pop Mhan-c. 2-Mhan-a						3.00
SPY CASES (Formerly The Kellys)						
Marvel/Atlas Comics (Hercules Publ.): No. 26, Sept, 1950 - No. 19, Oct, 1953						
26 (#1)	31	62	93	186	303	420
27(#2),28(#3, 2/51): 27-Everett-a; bondage-c	17	34	51	98	154	210
4(4/51) - 7,9,10: 4-Heath-a	15	30	45	88	137	185
8-A-Bomb-c/story	17	34	51	98	154	210
11-19: 10-14-War format	15	30	45	83	124	165
NOTE: ***Sol Brodsky*** *c-1-5, 8, 9, 11-14, 17, 18.* ***Maneely*** *a-8; c-7, 10.* ***Tuska*** *a-7.*						
SPY FIGHTERS						
Marvel/Atlas Comics (CSI): March, 1951 - No. 15, July, 1953 (Cases from official records)						
1-Clark Mason begins; Tuska-a; Brodsky-c	31	62	93	186	303	420
2-Tuska-a	17	34	51	98	154	210
3-13: 3-5-Brodsky-c. 7-Heath-c	15	30	45	88	137	185
14,15-Pakula-a(3), Ed Win-a. 15-Brodsky-c	15	30	45	90	140	190
SPY-HUNTERS (Formerly Spy & Counterspy)						
American Comics Group: No. 3, Dec-Jan, 1949-50 - No. 24, June-July, 1953 (#3-14: 52 pgs.)						
3-Jonathan Kent continues, ends #10	23	46	69	136	223	310
4-10: 4,8,10-Starr-a	14	28	42	80	115	150
11-15,17-22,24: 18-War-c begin. 21-War-c/stories begin	10	20	30	56	76	95
16-Williamson-a (9 pgs.)	15	30	45	88	137	185
23-Graphic torture, injury to eye panel	20	40	60	114	182	250
NOTE: ***Drucker*** *a-12.* ***Whitney*** *a-many issues; c-7, 8, 10-12, 15, 16.*						
SPYMAN (Top Secret Adventures on cover)						
Harvey Publications (Illustrated Humor): Sept, 1966 - No. 3, Feb, 1967 (12¢)						

Spy Smasher #5 © FAW

Squadron Supreme (2016 series) #9 © MAR

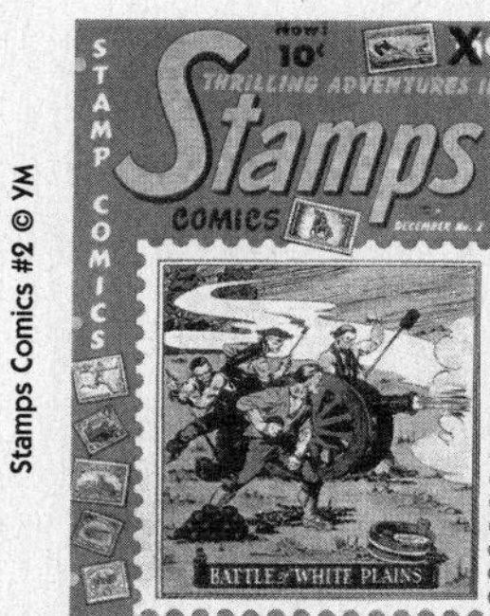

Stamps Comics #2 © YM

GD VG FN VF VF/NM NM-
2.0 4.0 6.0 8.0 9.0 9.2

1-Origin and 1st app. of Spyman. Steranko-a(p)-1st pro work; 1 pg. Neal Adams ad;
Tuska-c/a, Crandall-a(i) 6 12 18 38 69 100
2-Simon-c; Steranko-a(p) 4 8 12 27 44 60
3-Simon-c 4 8 12 25 40 55

SPY SMASHER (See Mighty Midget, Whiz & Xmas Comics) (Also see Crime Smasher)
Fawcett Publications: Fall, 1941 - No. 11, Feb, 1943

1-Spy Smasher begins; silver metallic-c 337 674 1011 2359 4130 5900
2-Raboy-c 155 310 465 992 1696 2400
3,4: 3-Bondage-c. 4-Irvin Steinberg-c 103 206 309 659 1130 1600
5-7: Raboy-a; 6-Raboy-c/a. 7-Part photo-c (movie) Japanese dragon-c
90 180 270 576 988 1400
8,11: War-c 76 152 228 486 831 1175
9-Hitler, Tojo, Mussolini-c. 139 278 417 883 3033 2150
10-Hitler-c 126 252 378 806 1378 1950

SPY THRILLERS (Police Badge No. 479 #5)
Atlas Comics (PrPI): Nov, 1954 - No. 4, May, 1955

1-Brodsky c-1,2 26 52 78 154 252 350
2-Last precode (1/55) 15 30 45 88 137 185
3,4 14 28 42 80 115 150

SQUADRON SINISTER (Secret Wars tie-in)
Marvel Comics: Aug, 2015 - No. 4, Jan, 2016 ($3.99, limited series)

1-4-Guggenheim-s/Pacheco-a/c. 1-Squadron Supreme app. 2-Frightful Four app. 4.00

SQUADRON SUPREME (Also see Marvel Graphic Novel - ...: Death of a Universe)
Marvel Comics Group: Aug, 1985 - No. 12, Aug, 1986 (Maxi-series)

1-Double size 5.00
2-12 4.00
TPB ($24.99) r/#1-12; Alex Ross painted-c; printing inks contain some of the cremated remains of late writer Mark Gruenwald 50.00
TPB-2nd printing ($24.99): Inks contain no ashes 25.00
...Death of a Universe TPB (2006, $24.99) r/Marvel Graphic Novel, Thor #280, Avengers #5,6; Avengers/Squadron Supreme Annual and Squadron Supreme: New World Order 25.00

SQUADRON SUPREME (Also see Supreme Power)
Marvel Comics: May, 2006 - No. 7, Nov, 2006 ($2.99)

1-7-Straczynski-s/Frank-a/c 3.00
Saga of Squadron Supreme (2006, $3.99) summary of Supreme Power #1-18; plus Hyperion and Nighthawk limited series; wraparound-c; preview of Squadron Supreme #1 4.00
... Vol. 1: The Pre-War Years (2006, $20.99, dustjacket) r/#1-5 & Saga of S.S. 21.00

SQUADRON SUPREME
Marvel Comics: Sept, 2008 - No. 12, Aug, 2009 ($2.99)

1-12: 1-Set 5 years after Ultimate Power; Nick Fury app.; Chaykin-s/Turini-a/Land-c 3.00

SQUADRON SUPREME
Marvel Comics: Feb, 2016 - No. 15, Mar, 2017 ($3.99)

1-15-Robinson-s; main covers by Alex Ross thru #4. 1-Kirk-a; Namor killed. 3-Avengers app. 9-12-Civil War II tie-in. 10-Thundra & Blue Marvel app. 11,12-Spider-Man app. 4.00

SQUADRON SUPREME: HYPERION VS. NIGHTHAWK
Marvel Comics: Mar, 2007 - No. 4, June, 2007 ($2.99, limited series)

1-4-Hyperion and Nighthawk in Darfur; Gulacy-a/c; Guggenheim-s 3.00
TPB (2007, $10.99) r/#1-4. 11.00

SQUADRON SUPREME: NEW WORLD ORDER
Marvel Comics: Sept, 1998 ($5.99, one-shot)

1-Wraparound-c; Kaminski-s 6.00

SQUALOR
First Comics: Dec, 1989 - Aug, 1990 ($2.75, limited series)

1-4: Sutton-a 3.00

SQUARRIORS
Devil's Due: Dec, 2014 - No. 4, Sept, 2015 ($3.99, limited series)

1-4: Maczko-s/Witter-a 4.00
Vol. 2 (5/16 - No. 4) 1-Maczko-s/Witter-a 4.00

SQUEE (Also see Johnny The Homicidal Maniac)
Slave Labor Graphics: Apr, 1997 - No. 4, May, 1998 ($2.95, B&W)

1-4: Jhonen Vasquez-s/a in all 3.00

SQUEEKS (Also see Boy Comics)
Lev Gleason Publications: Oct, 1953 - No. 5, June, 1954

1-Funny animal; Biro-c; Crimebuster's pet monkey "Squeeks" begins
10 20 30 58 79 100
2-Biro-c 7 14 21 37 46 55
3-5: 3-Biro-c 6 12 18 31 38 45

S.R. BISSETTE'S SPIDERBABY COMIX
SpiderBaby Grafix: Aug, 1996 - No. 2 ($3.95, B&W, magazine size)

Preview-(8/96, $3.95)-Graphic violence & nudity; Laurel & Hardy app. 4.00
1,2 4.00

S.R. BISSETTE'S TYRANT
SpiderBaby Grafix: Sept, 1994 - No. 4 ($2.95, B&W)

1-4 4.00

STALKER (Also see All Star Comics 1999 and crossover issues)
National Periodical Publications: June-July, 1975 - No. 4, Dec-Jan, 1975-76

1-Origin & 1st app; Ditko/Wood-c/a 2 4 6 10 14 18
2-4-Ditko/Wood-c/a 2 3 4 6 8 10

STALKERS
Marvel Comics (Epic Comics): Apr, 1990 - No. 12, Mar, 1991 ($1.50)

1-12: 1-Chadwick-c 3.00

STAMP COMICS (Stamps... on-c; Thrilling Adventures In...#8)
Youthful Magazines/Stamp Comics, Inc.: Oct, 1951 - No. 7, Oct, 1952

1-(15¢) ('Stamps' on indicia No. 1-3,5,7) 26 52 78 152 249 345
2 15 30 45 86 133 180
3-6: 3,4-Kiefer, Wildey-a 14 28 42 81 118 155
7-Roy Krenkel (4 pgs.) 17 34 51 98 154 210

NOTE: *Promotes stamp collecting; gives stories behind various commemorative stamps. No. 2, 10¢ printed over 15¢ c-price.* ***Kiefer*** *a-1-7.* ***Kirkel*** *a-1-6.* ***Napoli*** *a-2-7.* ***Palais*** *a-2-4, 7.*

STAND, THE ... (Based on the Stephen King novel)
Marvel Comics: 2008 - 2012 ($3.99, limited series)

...: American Nightmares 1-5 (5/09 - No. 5, 10/09, $3.99) Aguirre-Sacasa-s/Perkins-a 4.00
...: Captain Trips 1-5 (12/08 - No. 5, 3/09, $3.99) Aguirre-Sacasa-s/Perkins-a 4.00
...: Hardcases 1-5 (8/10 - No. 5, 1/11, $3.99) Aguirre-Sacasa-s/Perkins-a 4.00
...: No Man's Land 1-5 (4/11 - No. 5, 8/11, $3.99) Aguirre-Sacasa-s/Perkins-a 4.00
...: Soul Survivors 1-5 (12/09 - No. 5, 5/10, $3.99) Aguirre-Sacasa-s/Perkins-a 4.00
...: The Night Has Come 1-6 (10/11 - No. 6, 3/12, $3.99) Aguirre-Sacasa-s/Perkins-a 4.00

STAN LEE MEETS...
Marvel Comics: Nov, 2006 - Jan, 2007 ($3.99, series of one-shots)

Doctor Doom 1 (12/06) Lee-s/Larroca-a/c; Loeb-s/McGuinness-a; r/Fantastic Four #87 4.00
Doctor Strange 1 (11/06) Lee-s/Davis-a/c; Bendis-s/Bagley-a; r/Marvel Premiere #3 4.00
Silver Surfer 1 (1/07) Lee-s/Wieringo-a/c; Jenkins-s/Buckingham-a; r/S.S. #14 4.00
Spider-Man 1 (11/06) Lee-s/Coipel-a/c; Whedon-s/Gaydos-a; Hembeck-s/a; r/AS-M #87 4.00
The Thing 1 (12/06) Lee-s/Weeks-a/c; Thomas-s/Kolins-a; r/FF #79; FF #51 cover swipe 4.00
HC (2007, $24.99, dustjacket) r/one-shots; interviews and features 25.00

STAN LEE'S MIGHTY 7
Archie Comics (Stan Lee Comics): May, 2012 - No. 3, Sept, 2012 ($2.99, limited series)

1-3-Co-written by Stan Lee; Alex Saviuk-a; multiple covers on each 3.00

STANLEY & HIS MONSTER (Formerly The Fox & the Crow)
National Periodical Publ.: No. 109, Apr-May, 1968 - No. 112, Oct-Nov, 1968

109-112 3 6 9 21 33 45

STANLEY & HIS MONSTER
DC Comics: Feb, 1993 - No. 4, May, 1993 ($1.50, limited series)

1-4 3.00

STAN SHAW'S BEAUTY & THE BEAST
Dark Horse Comics: Nov, 1993 ($4.95, one-shot)

1 5.00

STAR
Image Comics (Highbrow Entertainment): June, 1995 - No. 4, Oct, 1995 ($2.50, lim. series)

1-4 3.00

STARBLAST
Marvel Comics: Jan, 1994 - No. 4, Apr, 1994 ($1.75, limited series)

1-($2.00, 52 pgs.)-Nova, Quasar, Black Bolt; painted-c 4.00
2-4 3.00

STAR BLAZERS
Comico: Apr, 1987 - No. 4, July, 1987 ($1.75, limited series)

1-4 3.00

STAR BLAZERS
Comico: 1989 ($1.95/$2.50, limited series)

1-5- Steacy wraparound painted-c on all 3.00

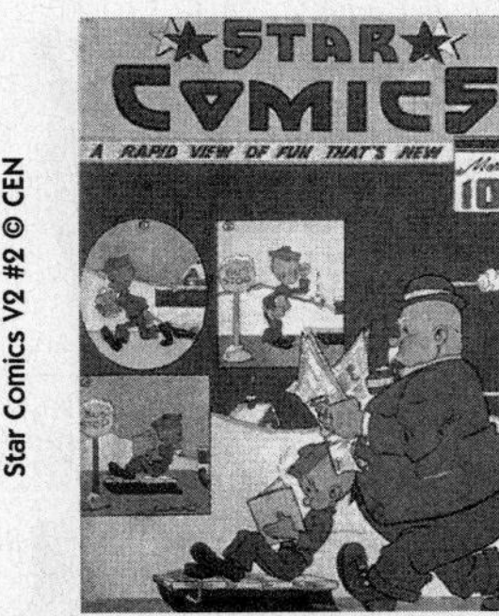

Star Comics V2 #2 © CEN

Starfire #9 © DC

Star-Lord (2016 series) #2 © MAR

GD VG FN VF VF/NM NM-
2.0 4.0 6.0 8.0 9.0 9.2

STAR BLAZERS (The Magazine of Space Battleship Yamato)
Argo Press: No. 0, Aug, 1995 - No. 3, Dec, 1995 ($2.95)

0-3 3.00

STARBORN (From Stan Lee)
BOOM! Studios: Dec, 2010 - No. 12, Nov, 2011 ($3.99)

1-12: 1-9,11-Roberson-s/Randolph-a. 1-7-Three covers on each. 10-Scalera-a 4.00

STAR BRAND
Marvel Comics (New Universe): Oct, 1986 - No. 19, May, 1989 (75¢/$1.25)

1-15: 14-begin $1.25-c 3.00
16-19-Byrne story & art; low print run 5.00
Annual 1 (10/87) 4.00
... Classic Vol. 1 TPB (2006, $19.99) r/#1-7 20.00

STARBRAND & NIGHTMASK
Marvel Comics: Feb, 2016 - No. 6, Jul, 2016 ($3.99)

1-6: 1-Weisman-s/Stanton-a; Kevin and Adam go to college; Nitro & Graviton app. 4.00

STARCHILD
Tailspin Press: 1992 - No. 12 ($2.25/$2.50, B&W)

1,2-('92),0(4/93),3-12: 0-Illos by Chadwick, Eisner, Sim, M. Wagner. 3-(7/93). 4-(11/93). 6-(2/94) 3.00

STARCHILD: MYTHOPOLIS
Image Comics: No. 0, July, 1997 - No. 4, Apr, 1998 ($2.95, B&W, limited series)

0-4-James Owen-s/a 3.00

STAR COMICS
Ultem Publ. (Harry 'A' Chesler)/Centaur Publications: Feb, 1937 - V2#7 (No. 23), Aug, 1939 (#1-6: large size)

V1#1-Dan Hastings (s/f) begins 400 800 1200 2800 4900 7000
2 226 452 678 1446 2473 3500
3-Classic Black Americana cover (rare) 423 846 1269 3000 5250 7500
4,5-Classic Winsor McCay Little Nemo-c/stories (rare) 258 516 774 1651 2826 4000
6-(9/37) 213 426 639 1363 2332 3300
7-9: 8-Severed head centerspread; Impy & Little Nemo by Winsor McCay Jr, Popeye app. by Bob Wood; Mickey Mouse & Popeye app. as toys in Santa's bag on-c; X-Mas-c 148 296 444 947 1624 2300
10 (1st Centaur; 3/38)-Impy by Winsor McCay Jr; Don Marlow by Guardineer begins 168 336 504 1075 1838 2600
11-1st Jack Cole comic-a, 1 pg. (4/38) 213 426 639 1363 2332 3300
12-15: 12-Riders of the Golden West begins; Little Nemo app. 15-Speed Silvers by Gustavson & The Last Pirate by Burgos begins 107 214 321 680 1165 1650
16 (12/38)-The Phantom Rider & his horse Thunder begins, ends V2#6 119 238 357 762 1306 1850
V2#1(#17, 2/39)-Phantom Rider-c (only non-funny-c) 142 284 426 909 1555 2200
2-7(#18-23): 2-Diana Deane by Tarpe Mills app. 3-Drama of Hollywood by Mills begins. 7-Jungle Queen app. 87 174 261 553 952 1350

NOTE: ***Biro** c-6, 9, 10. **Burgos** a-15, 16, V2#1-7. **Ken Ernst** a-10, 12, 14. **Filchock** c-15, 18, 22. **Gill Fox** c-14, 19. **Guardineer** a-6, 8-14. **Gustavson** a-13-16, V2#1-7. **Winsor McCay** c-4, 5. **Tarpe Mills** a-15, V2#1-7. **Schwab** c-20, 23. **Bob Wood** a-10, 12, 13; c-7, 8.*

STAR COMICS MAGAZINE
Marvel Comics (Star Comics): Dec, 1986 - No. 13, 1988 ($1.50, digest-size)

1,9-Spider-Man-c/s 2 4 6 8 11 14
2-8-Heathcliff, Ewoks, Top Dog, Madballs-r in #1-13 1 2 3 5 7 9
10-13 2 4 6 8 10 12

S.T.A.R. CORPS
DC Comics: Nov, 1993 - No. 6, Apr, 1994 ($1.50, limited series)

1-6: 1,2-Austin-c(i). 1-Superman app. 3.00

STARCRAFT (Based on the video game)
DC Comics (WildStorm): July, 2009 - No. 7, Jan, 2010 ($2.99)

1-7-Furman-s; two covers on each 3.00
HC (2010, $19.99, dustjacket) r/#1-7 20.00
SC (2011, $14.99) r/#1-7 15.00

STAR CROSSED
DC Comics (Helix): June, 1997 - No. 3, Aug, 1997 ($2.50, limited series)

1-3-Matt Howarth-s/a 3.00

STARDUST (See Neil Gaiman and Charles Vess' Stardust)

STARDUST KID, THE

GD VG FN VF VF/NM NM-
2.0 4.0 6.0 8.0 9.0 9.2

Image Comics/Boom! Studios #4-on: May, 2005 - No. 4 ($3.50)

1-4-J.M. DeMatteis-s/Mike Ploog-a 3.50

STAR FEATURE COMICS
I. W. Enterprises: 1963

Reprint #9-Stunt-Man Stetson-r/Feat. Comics #141 2 4 6 10 13 16

STARFIRE (Not the Teen Titans character)
National Periodical Publ./DC Comics: Aug-Sept, 1976 - No. 8, Oct-Nov, 1977

1-Origin (CCA stamp fell off cover art; so it was approved by code) 2 4 6 8 11 14
2-8 1 2 3 5 6 8

STARFIRE (Teen Titans character)(Also see Red Hood and the Outlaws)
DC Comics: Aug, 2015 - No. 12, Jul, 2016 ($2.99)

1-12: 1-Conner & Palmiotti-s/Lupacchino-a; Conner-c. 3-Intro. Atlee. 7,8-Grayson app. 9-Charretier-a begins; intro. Syl'khee 3.00

STARGATE
Dynamite Entertainment

...: Daniel Jackson 1-4 (2010 - No. 4, 2010, $3.99) Watson-a/Murray-s 4.00
...: Vala Mal Doran 1-5 (2010 - No. 5, 2010, $3.99) Razek-a/Jerwa-s 4.00

STARGATE ATLANTIS (Based on the TV series)
American Mythology Prods.: 2016 - Present ($3.99)

1-5: 1-Haynes & Vaughn-s/LaRocque-a; covers by Wheatley & LaRocque. 4,5-Gateways #1,2 on cover; Watson-a 4.00

STAR HUNTERS (See DC Super Stars #16)
National Periodical Publ./DC Comics: Oct-Nov, 1977 - No. 7, Oct-Nov, 1978

1,7: 1-Newton-a(p). 7-44 pgs. 2 4 6 8 10 12
2-6 1 2 3 4 5 7

NOTE: ***Buckler** a-4-7p; c-1-7p. **Layton** a-1-5i; c-1-6i. **Nasser** a-3p. **Sutton** a-6i.*

STARJAMMERS (See X-Men Spotlight on Starjammers)

STARJAMMERS (Also see Uncanny X-Men)
Marvel Comics: Oct, 1995 - No. 4, Jan, 1996 ($2.95, limited series)

1-4: Foil-c; Ellis scripts 4.00

STARJAMMERS
Marvel Comics: Sept, 2004 - No. 6, Jan, 2005 ($2.99, limited series)

1-6-Kevin J. Anderson-s. 1-Garza-a. 2-6-Lucas-a 3.00

STARK TERROR
Stanley Publications: Dec, 1970 - No. 5, Aug, 1971 (B&W, magazine, 52 pgs.) (1950s Horror reprints, including pre-code)

1-Bondage, torture-c 7 14 21 44 82 120
2-4 (Gillmor/Aragon-r) 4 8 12 27 44 65
5 (ACG-r) 4 8 12 25 38 55

STARLET O'HARA IN HOLLYWOOD (Teen-age) (Also see Cookie)
Standard Comics: Dec, 1948 - No. 4, Sept, 1949

1-Owen Fitzgerald-a in all 34 68 102 199 325 450
2 18 36 54 105 165 225
3,4 15 30 45 86 133 180

STARLIGHT
Image Comics: Mar, 2014 - No. 6, Oct, 2014 ($2.99)

1-5-Mark Millar-s/Goran Parlov-a. 1-Covers by Cassaday & Parlov. 2-Sienkiewicz var-c 3.00
6-($4.99) Two covers by Cassaday and Chiang 5.00

STARLORD
Marvel Comics: Dec, 1996 - No. 3, Feb, 1997 ($2.50, limited series)

1-3-Timothy Zahn-s 3.00

STAR-LORD (Guardians of the Galaxy)
Marvel Comics: Aug, 2013; 2014 ($7.99, series of reprints)

...: Annihilation - Conquest 1 (2014) r/Annihilation: Conquest - Starlord #1-4; design art 8.00
...: Tears For Heaven 1 (2014) r/Marvel Preview #18, Marvel Spotlight #6,7, and Marvel Premiere #61; bonus art; new cover by Pichelli 8.00
...: The Hollow Crown 1 (8/13) r/Marvel Preview #4,11 and Star-Lord Special Edition 8.00

STAR-LORD
Marvel Comics: Jan, 2016 - No. 8, Aug, 2016 ($3.99)

1-8: 1-Humphries-s/Garron-a; 18-year-old Peter Quill's 1st meeting with Yondu 4.00

STAR-LORD
Marvel Comics: Feb, 2017 - Present ($3.99)

1-3-Zdarsky-s/Anka-a. 1-Old Man Logan app. 3-Daredevil app. 4.00

Star-Lord & Kitty Pryde #1 © MAR

Starman (2nd series) #48 © DC

Star Ranger V2 #10 © CEN

	GD	VG	FN	VF	VF/NM	NM-
	2.0	4.0	6.0	8.0	9.0	9.2

STAR-LORD & KITTY PRYDE (Secret Wars tie-in)
Marvel Comics: Sept, 2015 - No. 3, Nov, 2015 ($3.99, limited series)
1-3-Humphries-s/Firmansyah-a; Gambit app. 4.00

STARLORD MEGAZINE
Marvel Comics: Nov, 1996 ($2.95, one-shot)
1-Reprints w/preview of new series 3.00

STAR-LORD THE SPECIAL EDITION (Also see Marvel Comics Super Special #10, Marvel Premiere & Preview & Marvel Spotlight V2#6,7)
Marvel Comics Group: Feb, 1982 (one-shot, direct sales) (1st Baxter paper comic)
1-Byrne/Austin-a; Austin-c; 8 pgs. of new-a by Golden (p); Dr. Who story by Dave Gibbons; 1st deluxe format comic 2 4 6 10 14 18

STAR MAGE
IDW Publishing: Apr, 2014 - No. 6, Sept, 2014 ($3.99, limited series)
1-6: 1-JC De La Torre-s/Ray Dillon-a. 2-6-Franco Cespedes-a 4.00

STARMAN (1st Series) (Also see Justice League & War of the Gods)
DC Comics: Oct, 1988 - No. 45, Apr, 1992 ($1.00)
1-Origin 5.00
2-25,29-45: 4-Intro The Power Elite. 9,10,34-Batman app. 14-Superman app. 17-Power Girl app. 38-War of the Gods x-over. 42-45-Eclipso-c/stories 3.00
26-1st app. David Knight (G.A.Starman's son). 5.00
27,28: 27-Starman (David Knight) app. 28-Starman disguised as Superman; leads into Superman #50 4.00

STARMAN (2nd Series) (Also see The Golden Age, Showcase 95 #12, Showcase 96 #4,5)
DC Comics: No. 0, Oct, 1994 - No. 80, Aug, 2001; No. 81, Mar, 2010 ($1.95/$2.25/$2.50)
0,1: 0-James Robinson scripts, Tony Harris-c/a(p) & Wade Von Grawbadger-a(i) begins; Sins of the Father storyline begins, ends #3; 1st app. new Starman (Jack Knight); reintro of the G.A. Mist & G.A. Shade; 1st app. Nash; David Knight dies 1 3 4 6 8 10
2-7: 2-Reintro Charity from Forbidden Tales of Dark Mansion. 3-Reintro/2nd app. "Blue" Starman (1st app. in 1st Issue Special #12); Will Payton app. (both cameos). 5-David Knight app. 6-The Shade "Times Past" story; Kristiansen-a. 7-The Black Pirate cameo 5.00
8-17: 8-Begin $2.25-c. 10-1st app. new Mist (Nash). 11-JSA "Times Past" story; Matt Smith-a. 12-16-Sins of the Child. 17-The Black Pirate app. 4.00
18-37: 18-G.A. Starman "Times Past" story; Watkiss-a. 19-David Knight app. 20-23-G.A. Sandman app. 24-26-Demon Quest; all 3 covers make-up triptych. 33-36-Batman-c/app. 37-David Knight and deceased JSA members app. 3.00
38-49,51-56: 38-Nash vs. Justice League Europe. 39,40-Crossover w/ Power of Shazam! #35,36; Bulletman app. 42-Demon-c/app. 43-JLA-c/app. 44-Phantom Lady-c/app. 46-Gene Ha-a. 51-Jor-El app. 52,53-Adam Strange-c/app. 3.00
50-($3.95) Gold foil logo on-c; Star Boy (LSH) app. 4.00
57-79: 57-62-Painted covers by Harris and Alex Ross. 72-Death of Ted Knight 3.00
80-($3.95) Final issue; cover by Harris & Robinson 4.00
81-(3/10, $2.99) Blackest Night one-shot; The Shade vs. David Knight; Harris-c 3.00
#1,000,000 (11/98) 853rd Century x-over; Snejbjerg-a 3.00
Annual 1 (1996, $3.50)-Legends of the Dead Earth story; Prince Gavyn & G.A. Starman stories; J.H. Williams III, Bret Blevins, Craig Hamilton-c/a(p) 4.00
Annual 2 (1997, $3.95)-Pulp Heroes story; 4.00
...80 Page Giant (1/99, $4.95) Harris-c 5.00
...Secret Files 1 (4/98, $4.95)-Origin stories and profile pages 5.00
...The Mist (6/98, $1.95) Girlfrenzy; Mary Marvel app. 3.00
A Starry Knight-($17.95, TPB) r/#47-53 18.00
Grand Guignol-(2004, $19.95, TPB)-r/#61-73 20.00
Infernal Devices-($17.95, TPB) r/#29-35,37,38 18.00
Night and Day-($14.95, TPB)-r/#7-10,12-16 15.00
Sins of the Father-($12.95, TPB)-r/#0-5 13.00
Sons of the Father-($14.99, TPB)-r/#75-80 15.00
Stars My Destination-(2003, $14.95, TPB)-r/#55-60 15.00
Times Past-($17.95, TPB)-r/stories of other Starmen 18.00
The Starman Omnibus Vol. One (2008, $49.99, HC with dj) r/#0,1-16; James Robinson intro. 50.00
The Starman Omnibus Vol. Two (2009, $49.99, HC with dj) r/#17-29, Annual #1, Showcase '95 #12, Showcase '96 #4,5; Harris intro.; merchandise gallery 50.00
The Starman Omnibus Vol. Three (2009, $49.99, HC with dj) r/#30-38, Annual #2, Starman Secret Files #1 and The Shade #1-4 50.00
The Starman Omnibus Vol. Four (2010, $49.99, HC with dj) r/#39-46, 80 Page Giant #1, Power of Shazam! #35,36; Starman: The Mist #1 and Batman/Hellboy/Starman #1,2 50.00
The Starman Omnibus Vol. Five (2010, $49.99, HC with dj) r/#47-60, #1,000,000; Stars and S.T.R.I.P.E. #0; All Star Comics 80 Page Giant #1; JSA: All Stars #4 50.00
The Starman Omnibus Vol. Six (2011, $49.99, HC with dj) r/#61-81, Johns intro. 50.00

STARMAN/CONGORILLA (See Justice League: Cry For Justice)
DC Comics: Mar, 2011 ($2.99, one-shot)
1-Animal Man and Rex the Wonder Dog app.; Robinson-s/Booth-a/Ha-c 3.00

STARMASTERS
Marvel Comics: Dec, 1995 - No. 3, Feb, 1996 ($1.95, limited series)
1-3-Continues in Cosmic Powers Unlimited #4 3.00

STAR PRESENTATION, A (Formerly My Secret Romance #1,2; Spectacular Stories #4 on) (Also see This Is Suspense)
Fox Features Syndicate (Hero Books): No. 3, May, 1950
3-Dr. Jekyll & Mr. Hyde by Wood & Harrison (reprinted in Startling Terror Tales #10); "The Repulsing Dwarf" by Wood; Wood-c 68 136 204 435 743 1050

STAR QUEST COMIX (Warren Presents... on cover)
Warren Publications: Oct, 1978 ($1.50, B&W magazine, 84 pgs., square-bound)
1-Corben, Maroto, Neary-a; Ken Kelly-c; Star Wars 2 4 6 9 12 15

STAR RAIDERS (See DC Graphic Novel #1)

STAR RANGER (Cowboy Comics #13 on)
Chesler Publ./Centaur Publ.: Feb, 1937 - No. 12, May, 1938 (Large size: No. 1-6)
1-(1st Western comic)-Ace & Deuce, Air Plunder; Creig Flessel-a 300 600 900 1950 3375 4800
2 142 284 426 909 1555 2200
3-6 129 258 387 826 1413 2000
7-9: 8(12/37)-Christmas-c; Air Patrol, Gold coast app.; Guardineer centerfold 103 206 309 659 1130 1600
V2#10 (1st Centaur; 3/38) 123 246 369 787 1344 1900
11,12 103 206 309 659 1130 1600
NOTE: ***J. Cole** a-10, 12; c-12. **Ken Ernst** a-11. **Gill Fox** a-8(illo), 9, 10. **Guardineer** a-1, 3, 6, 7, 8(illos), 9, 10, 12. **Gustavson** a-8-10, 12. **Fred Schwab** c-2-11. **Bob Wood** a-8-10.*

STAR RANGER FUNNIES (Formerly Cowboy Comics)
Centaur Publications: V1#15, Oct, 1938 - V2#5, Oct, 1939
V1#15-Lyin Lou, Ermine, Wild West Junior, The Law of Caribou County by Eisner, Cowboy Jake, The Plugged Dummy, Spurs by Gustavson, Red Coat, Two Buckaroos & Trouble Hunters begin 119 238 357 762 1306 1850
V2#1 (1/39) 97 194 291 621 1061 1500
2-5: 2-Night Hawk by Gustavson. 4-Kit Carson app. 82 164 246 528 902 1275
NOTE: ***Jack Cole** a-V2#1, 3; c-V2#1. **Filchock** c-V2#2, 3. **Guardineer** a-V2#3. **Gustavson** a-V2#2. **Pinajian** c/a-V2#5.*

STAR REACH (Mature content)
Star Reach Publ.: Apr, 1974 - No. 18, Oct, 1979 (B&W, #12-15 w/color)
1-(75¢, 52 pgs.) Art by Starlin, Simonson. Chaykin-c/a; origin Death. Cody Starbuck-sty 3 6 9 17 26 35
1-2nd, 3th, and 4th printings ($1.00-$1.50-c) 6.00
2-11: 2-Adams, Giordano-a; 1st Stephanie Starr-c/s. 3-1st Linda Lovecraft. 4-1st Sherlock Duck. 5-1st Gideon Faust by Chaykin. 6-Elric-c. 7-BWS-c. 9-14-Sacred & Profane-c/s by Steacy. 11-Samurai 2 4 6 8 11 14
2-2nd printing 4.00
12-15 (44 pgs.): 12-Zelazny-s. Nasser-a, Brunner-c 2 4 6 9 13 16
16-18-Magazine size: 17-Poe's Raven-c/s 2 4 6 9 13 16
NOTE: ***Adams** c-2. **Bonivert** a-17. **Brunner** a-3,5; c-3,10,12. **Chaykin** a-1,4,5; c-1(1st ed),4,5; back-c-1(2nd,3rd,4th ed). **Gene Day** a-6,8,9,11,15. **Friedrich** s-2,3,8,10. **Gasbarri** a-7. **Gilbert** a-9,12. **Giordano** a-2. **Gould** a-6. **Hirota/Mukaide** s/a-7. **Jones** c-6. **Konz** a-17. **Leialoha** a-3,4,6-i, 13,15; c-13,15. **Lyda** a-6,12-15. **Marrs** a-2-5,7,10,14,15,16,18; c-18; back-c-2. **Mukaide** a-18. **Nasser** a-12. **Nino** a-6; **Russell** a-8,10; c-8. **Dave Sim** s-7; lettering-9. **Simonson** a-1. **Skeates** a-1,2. **Starlin** a-1(x2), 2(x2); back-c-1(1st ed); c-1(2nd,3rd,4th ed). **Barry Smith** c-7. **Staton** a-5,6,7. **Steacy** a-8-14; c-9,11,14,16. **Vosburg** a-2-5,7,10. **Workman** a-2-5,8. Nudity panels in most. Wraparound-c: 3-5,7-11,13-16,18.*

STAR REACH CLASSICS
Eclipse Comics: Mar, 1984 - No. 6, Aug, 1984 ($1.50, Baxter paper)
1-6: 1-Neal Adams-r/Star Reach #1; Sim & Starlin-a 3.00

STARR FLAGG, UNDERCOVER GIRL (See Undercover...)

STARRIORS
Marvel Comics: Aug, 1984 - Feb, 1985 (Limited series) (Based on Tomy toys)
1-4 4.00

STARR THE SLAYER
Marvel Comics (MAX): Nov, 2009 - No. 4, Feb, 2010 ($3.99, limited series)
1-4- Richard Corben-c/a; Daniel Way-s 4.00

STARS AND S.T.R.I.P.E. (Also see JSA)
DC Comics: July, 1999 - No. 14, Sept, 2000 ($2.95/$2.50)
0-($2.95) 1st app. Courtney Whitmore; Moder and Weston-a; Starman app. 3.00
1-Johns and Robinson-s/Moder-a; origin new Star Spangled Kid 3.00
2-14: 4-Marvel Family app. 9-Seven Soldiers of Victory-c/app. 3.00

Starslayer #18 © FC

Star Spangled Comics #124 © DC

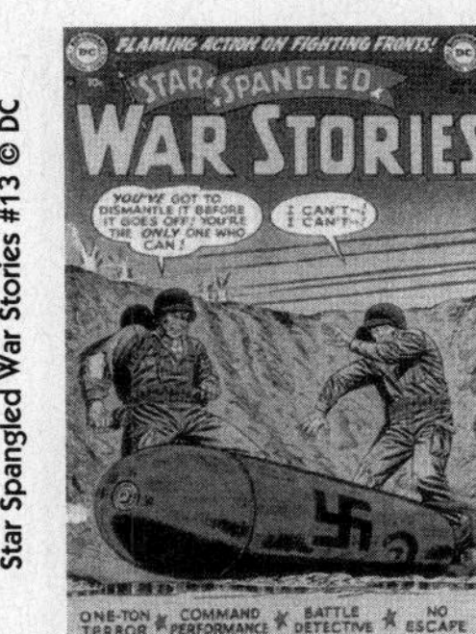

Star Spangled War Stories #13 © DC

GD VG FN VF VF/NM NM-
2.0 4.0 6.0 8.0 9.0 9.2

JSA Presents: Stars and S.T.R.I.P.E. Vol. 1 TPB (2007, $17.99) r/#1-8; Johns intro. 18.00
JSA Presents: Stars and S.T.R.I.P.E. Vol. 2 TPB (2008, $17.99) r/#0,9-14 18.00

STARS AND STRIPES COMICS
Centaur Publications: No. 2, May, 1941 - No. 6, Dec, 1941

2(#1)-The Shark, The Iron Skull, A-Man, The Amazing Man, Mighty Man, Minimidget begin; The Voice & Dash Dartwell, the Human Meteor, Reef Kinkaid app.; Gustavson Flag-c 245 490 735 1568 2684 3800
3-Origin Dr. Synthe; The Black Panther app. 155 310 465 992 1696 2400
4-Origin/1st app. The Stars and Stripes; injury to eye-c 129 258 387 826 1413 2000
5(#5 on cover & inside) 97 194 291 621 1061 1500
5(#6)-(#5 on cover, #6 on inside) 97 194 291 621 1061 1500
NOTE: ***Gustavson** c/a-3. **Myron Strauss** c-4, 5(#5), 5(#6).*

STAR SEED (Formerly Powers That Be)
Broadway Comics: No. 7, 1996 - No. 9 ($2.95)

7-9 3.00

STARSHIP TROOPERS
Dark Horse Comics: 1997 - No. 2, 1997 ($2.95, limited series)

1,2-Movie adaptation 3.00

STARSHIP TROOPERS: BRUTE CREATIONS
Dark Horse Comics: 1997 ($2.95, one-shot)

1 3.00

STARSHIP TROOPERS: DOMINANT SPECIES
Dark Horse Comics: Aug, 1998 - No. 4, Nov, 1998 ($2.95, limited series)

1-4-Strnad-s/Bolton-c 3.00

STARSHIP TROOPERS: INSECT TOUCH
Dark Horse Comics: 1997 - No. 3, 1997 ($2.95, limited series)

1-3 3.00

STAR SLAMMERS (See Marvel Graphic Novel #6)
Malibu Comics (Bravura): May, 1994 - No. 4, Aug, 1994 ($2.50, unfinished limited series)

1-4: W. Simonson-a/stories; contain Bravura stamps 3.00

STAR SLAMMERS
IDW Publishing: Mar, 2014 - No. 8, Oct, 2014 ($3.99)

1-8-Recolored reprint of 1994 series; Walt Simonson-s/a. 1-4-Two covers by Simonson 4.00

STAR SLAMMERS SPECIAL
Dark Horse Comics (Legend): June, 1996 ($2.95, one-shot)

nn-Simonson-c/a/scripts; concludes Bravura limited series. 3.00

STARSLAYER
Pacific Comics/First Comics No. 7 on: Feb, 1982 - No. 6, Apr, 1983; No. 7, Aug, 1983 - No. 34, Nov, 1985

1-Origin & 1st app.; 1 pg. Rocketeer brief app. which continues in #2 2 4 6 9 12 15
2-Origin/1st full app. the Rocketeer (4/82) by Dave Stevens (Chapter 1 of Rocketeer saga; see Pacific Presents #1,2) 3 6 9 16 23 30
3-Chapter 2 of Rocketeer saga by Stevens 2 4 6 10 14 18
4,6,7: 7-Grell-a ends 4.00
5-2nd app. Groo the Wanderer by Aragonés 2 4 6 8 10 12
8,9,11-34: 18-Starslayer meets Grimjack. 20-The Black Flame begins (9/84, 1st app.), ends #33. 27-Book length Black Flame story 3.00
10-1st app. Grimjack (11/83, ends #17) 5.00
NOTE: ***Grell** a-1-7; c-1-8. **Stevens** back c-2, 3. **Sutton** a-17p, 20-22p, 24-27p, 29-33p.*

STARSLAYER (The Director's Cut)
Acclaim Comics (Windjammer): June, 1994 - No. 8, Dec, 1995 ($2.50)

1-8: Mike Grell-c/a/scripts 3.00

STAR SPANGLED COMICS (Star Spangled War Stories #131 on)
National Periodical Publications: Oct, 1941 - No. 130, July, 1952

1-Origin/1st app. Tarantula; Captain X of the R.A.F., Star Spangled Kid (see Action #40), Armstrong of the Army begin; Robot-c 524 1048 1572 3825 6763 9700
2 194 388 582 1242 2121 3000
3-5 116 232 348 742 1271 1800
6-Last Armstrong/Army; Penniless Palmer begins 71 142 213 454 777 1100
7-(4/42)-Origin/1st app. The Guardian by S&K, & Robotman (by Paul Cassidy & created by Siegel);The Newsboy Legion (1st app.), Robotman & TNT begin; last Captain X 811 1622 2433 5920 10,460 15,000
8-Origin TNT & Dan the Dyna-Mite 252 504 756 1613 2757 3900
9,10 168 336 504 1075 1838 2600
11-17 123 246 369 787 1344 1900

GD VG FN VF VF/NM NM-
2.0 4.0 6.0 8.0 9.0 9.2

18-Origin Star Spangled Kid 155 310 465 992 1696 2400
19-Last Tarantula 123 246 369 787 1344 1900
20-Liberty Belle begins (5/43) 155 310 465 992 1696 2400
21-29-Last S&K issue; 23-Last TNT. 25-Robotman by Jimmy Thompson begins. 29-Intro Robbie the Robotdog 103 206 309 659 1130 1600
30-40: 31-S&K-c 63 126 189 403 689 975
41-51: 41,49-Kirby-c. 51-Robot-c by Kirby 57 114 171 362 619 875
52-64: 53 by S&K. 64-Last Newsboy Legion & The Guardian 52 104 156 328 552 775
65-Robin begins with c/app. (2/47); Batman cameo in 1 panel; Robin-c begins, end #95 219 438 657 1402 2401 3400
66-Batman cameo in Robin story 94 188 282 597 1024 1450
67,68,70-80: 68-Last Liberty Belle? 72-Burnley Robin-c 74 148 222 470 810 1150
69-Origin/1st app. Tomahawk by F. Ray; atom bomb story & splash (6/47); black-c (rare in high grade) 239 278 717 1530 2615 3700
81-Origin Merry, Girl of 1000 Gimmicks in Star Spangled Kid story 61 122 183 390 670 950
82,85: 82-Last Robotman? 85-Last Star Spangled Kid? 55 110 165 352 601 850
83-Tomahawk enters the lost valley, a land of dinosaurs; Capt. Compass begins, ends #130 58 116 174 371 636 900
84,87 (Rare): 87-Batman cameo in Robin 87 174 261 553 952 1350
86-Batman cameo in Robin story 62 124 186 395 678 960
88(1/49)-94: Batman-c/stories in all. 91-Federal Men begin, end #93. 94-Manhunters Around the World begin, end #121 69 138 207 442 759 1075
95-Batman story; last Robin-c 58 116 174 371 636 900
96,98-Batman cameo in Robin stories. 96-1st Tomahawk-c (also #97-121) 41 82 123 256 428 600
97,99 37 74 111 222 361 500
100 (1/50)-Pre-Bat-Hound tryout in Robin story (pre-dates Batman #92). 43 86 129 271 461 650
101-109,118,119,121: 121-Last Tomahawk-c 34 68 102 199 325 450
110,111,120-Batman cameo in Robin stories. 120-Last 52 pg. issue 34 68 102 206 336 465
112-Batman & Robin story 37 74 111 222 361 500
113-Frazetta-a (10 pgs.) 41 82 123 260 435 610
114-Retells Robin's origin (3/51); Batman & Robin story 44 88 132 277 469 660
115,117-Batman app. in Robin stories 37 74 111 218 354 490
116-Flag-c 37 74 111 218 354 490
122-(11/51)-Ghost Breaker-c/stories begin (origin/1st app.), ends #130 (Ghost Breaker covers #122-130) 54 108 162 343 574 825
123-126,128,129 37 74 111 222 361 500
127-Batman app. 39 78 117 231 378 525
130-Batman cameo in Robin story 40 80 120 244 405 565
NOTE: *Most all issues after #29 signed by Simon & Kirby are not by them. **Bill Ely** c-122-130. **Mortimer** c-65-74(most), 76-95(most). **Fred Ray** c-96-106, 109, 110, 112, 113, 115-120. **S&K** c-7-31, 33, 34, 36, 37, 39, 40, 48, 49, 50-54, 56-58. **Hal Sherman** c-1-6. **Dick Sprang** c-75.*

STAR SPANGLED COMICS (Also see All Star Comics 1999 crossover titles)
DC Comics: May, 1999 ($1.99, one-shot)

1-Golden Age Sandman and the Star Spangled Kid 3.00

STAR SPANGLED KID (See Action #40, Leading Comics & Star Spangled Comics)

STAR SPANGLED WAR STORIES
DC Comics: Aug/Sept 1952

nn - Ashcan comic, not distributed to newsstands, only for in-house use. Cover art is Western Comics #28 with interior being Western Comics #13 (a VG- copy sold for $2151 in 2012)

STAR SPANGLED WAR STORIES (Formerly Star Spangled Comics #1-130; Becomes The Unknown Soldier #205 on) (See Showcase)
National Periodical Publ.: No. 131, 8/52 - No. 133, 10/52; No. 3, 11/52 - No. 204, 2-3/77

131(#1) 194 388 582 1242 2121 3000
132 110 220 330 704 1202 1700
133-Used in **POP**, pg. 94 94 188 282 597 1024 1450
3-6: 4-Devil Dog Dugan app. 6-Evans-a 63 126 189 403 689 975
7-10 31 62 93 223 499 775
11-20 27 54 81 191 426 660
21-30: 30-Last precode (2/55) 23 46 69 164 362 560
31-33,35-40 19 38 57 133 297 460
34-Krigstein-a 20 40 60 136 303 470
41-44,46-50: 50-1st S.A. issue 18 36 54 122 271 420
45-1st DC grey tone war-c (5/56) 46 92 138 340 770 1200
51,52,54-63,65,66, 68-83 15 30 45 105 233 360
53-"Rock Sergeant," 3rd Sgt. Rock prototype; inspired "P.I. & The Sand Fleas"

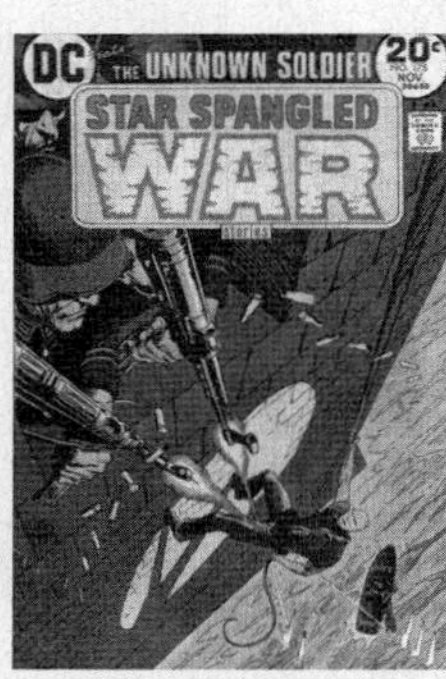

Star Spangled War Stories #175 © DC

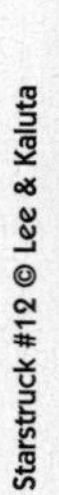

Starstruck #12 © Lee & Kaluta

Startling Comics #44 © Nedor

	GD 2.0	VG 4.0	FN 6.0	VF 8.0	VF/NM 9.0	NM- 9.2
in G.I. Combat #56 (1/57)	27	54	81	184	410	635
64-Pre-Sgt. Rock Easy Co. story (12/57)	19	38	57	133	297	460
67-Two Easy Co. stories without Sgt. Rock	20	40	60	136	303	470
84-Origin Mlle. Marie	54	108	162	432	966	1500
85-89-Mlle. Marie in all	28	56	84	202	451	700
90-1st app. "War That Time Forgot" series; dinosaur issue-c/story (4-5/60) (also see Weird War Tales #94 & #99)	86	172	258	688	1544	2400
91,93-No dinosaur stories	17	34	51	117	259	400
92-2nd dinosaur-c/s	27	54	81	194	435	675
94 (12/60)- "Ghost Ace" story; Baron Von Richter as The Enemy Ace (predates Our Army at War #151)	31	62	93	223	499	775
95-99: Dinosaur-c/s	20	40	60	138	307	475
100-Dinosaur-c/story.	21	42	63	150	330	510
101-115: All dinosaur issues. 102-Panel inspired a famous Roy Lichtenstein painting	15	30	45	105	233	360
116-125,127-133,135-137: 120-1st app. Caveboy and Dino. 137-Last dinosaur story; Heath Birdman-#129,131	13	26	39	89	195	300
126-No dinosaur story	11	22	33	73	157	240
134-Dinosaur story; Neal Adams-a	15	30	45	103	227	350
138-New Enemy Ace-c/stories begin by Joe Kubert (4-5/68), end #150 (also see Our Army at War #151 and Showcase #57)	16	32	48	112	249	385
139-Origin Enemy Ace (7/68)	10	20	30	69	147	225
140-143,145: 145-Last 12¢ issue (6-7/69)	8	16	24	54	102	150
144-Neal Adams/Kubert-a	9	18	27	58	114	170
146-Enemy Ace-c/app.	6	12	18	41	76	110
147,148-New Enemy Ace stories	7	14	21	48	89	130
149,150-Last new Enemy Ace by Kubert. Viking Prince by Kubert	7	14	21	44	82	120
151-1st solo app. Unknown Soldier (6-7/70); Enemy Ace-r begin (from Our Army at War, Showcase & SSWS); end #161	18	36	54	122	271	420
152-Reprints 2nd Enemy Ace app.	6	12	18	38	69	100
153,155-Enemy Ace reprints; early Unknown Soldier stories	5	10	15	34	60	85
154-Origin Unknown Soldier	12	24	36	84	185	285
156-1st Battle Album; Unknown Soldier story; Kubert-c/a	5	10	15	31	53	75
157-Sgt. Rock x-over in Unknown Soldier story.	4	8	12	28	47	65
158-163-(52 pgs.): New Unknown Soldier stories; Kubert-c/a. 161-Last Enemy Ace-r	4	8	12	25	40	55
164-183,200: 181-183-Enemy Ace vs. Balloon Buster serial app; Frank Thorne-a. 200-Enemy Ace back-up	3	6	9	15	22	28
184-199,201-204	2	4	6	13	18	22

NOTE: **Anderson** a-28. **Chaykin** a-167. **Drucker** a-59, 61, 64, 66, 67, 73-84. **Estrada** a-149. **John Giunta** a-72. **Glanzman** a-167, 171, 172, 174. **Heath** a-42,122, 132, 133; c-67, 122, 132-134. **Kaluta** a-197i; c-167. **G. Kane** a-169. **Kubert** a-6-163(most later issues), 200. **Maurer** a-160, 165. **Severin** a-65, 162. **S&K** c-7-31, 33, 34, 37, 40. **Simonson** a-170, 172, 174, 180. **Sutton** a-168. **Thorne** a-183. **Toth** a-164. **Wildey** a-161. Suicide Squad in 110, 116-118, 120, 121, 127.

STAR SPANGLED WAR STORIES (Featuring Mademoiselle Marie)
DC Comics: Nov, 2010 ($3.99, one-shot)

1-Mademoiselle Marie in 1944 France; Tucci-s/Justiniano-a/Bolland-c 4.00

STAR SPANGLED WAR STORIES (Featuring G.I. Zombie)
DC Comics: Sept, 2014 - No. 8, May, 2015 ($2.99)

1-8-Palmiotti & Gray-s/Scott Hampton-a. 1-6-Darwyn Cooke-c. 7-Dave Johnson-c 3.00
...: Futures End 1 (11/14, $2.99, regular-c) Five years later; Dave Johnson-c 3.00
...: Futures End 1 (11/14, $3.99, 3-D cover) 4.00

STARSTREAM (Adventures in Science Fiction)(See Questar illustrated)
Whitman/Western Publishing Co.: 1976 (79¢, 68 pgs, cardboard-c)

	GD 2.0	VG 4.0	FN 6.0	VF 8.0	VF/NM 9.0	NM- 9.2
1-4: 1-Bolle-a. 2-4-McWilliams & Bolle-a	2	4	6	10	14	18

STARSTRUCK
Marvel Comics (Epic Comics): Feb, 1985 - No. 6, Feb, 1986 ($1.50, mature)

1-6: Kaluta-a 6.00

STARSTRUCK
Dark Horse Comics: Aug, 1990 - No. 4, Nov?, 1990 ($2.95, B&W, 52pgs.)

1-3: Kaluta-r/Epic series plus new-c/a in all 4.00
4 (68 pgs.)-contains 2 trading cards 5.00
Reprint 1-13 (IDW, 8/09 - No. 13, Sept, 2010, $3.99) newly colored; Galactic Girl Guides 4.00

STAR STUDDED
Cambridge House/Superior Publishers: 1945 (25¢, 132 pgs.); 1945 (196 pgs.)

	GD 2.0	VG 4.0	FN 6.0	VF 8.0	VF/NM 9.0	NM- 9.2
nn-Captain Combat by Giunta, Ghost Woman, Commandette, & Red Rogue app.; Infantino-a	41	82	123	256	428	600
nn-The Cadet, Edison Bell, Hoot Gibson, Jungle Lil (196 pgs.); copies vary; Blue Beetle in some	43	86	129	271	461	650

STARTLING COMICS
Better Publications (Nedor): June, 1940 - No. 53, Sept, 1948

	GD 2.0	VG 4.0	FN 6.0	VF 8.0	VF/NM 9.0	NM- 9.2
1-Origin Captain Future-Man Of Tomorrow, Mystico (By Sansone), The Wonder Man; The Masked Rider & his horse Pinto begins; Masked Rider formerly in pulps; drug use story	343	686	1029	2400	4200	6000
2 -Don Davis, Espionage Ace begins	168	336	504	1075	1838	2600
3	135	270	405	864	1482	2100
4	110	220	330	704	1202	1700
5,6,9	90	180	270	576	988	1400
7,8-Nazi WWII-c	103	206	309	659	1130	1600
10-The Fighting Yank begins (9/41, origin/1st app.); Nazi WWII-c	730	1460	2190	5329	9415	13,500
11-2nd app. Fighting Yank; Nazi WWII-c	239	478	717	1530	2615	3700
12-Hitler, Tojo, Mussolini-c	297	594	891	1901	3251	4600
13-15	113	226	339	718	1234	1750
16-Origin The Four Comrades; not in #32,35	129	258	387	826	1413	2000
17-Last Masked Rider & Mystico	107	214	321	680	1165	1650
18-Pyroman begins (12/42, origin)(also see America's Best Comics #3 for 1st app., 11/42)	168	336	504	1075	1838	2600
19-Nazi WWII-c	181	362	543	1158	1979	2800
20-Classic hooded Nazi giant snake bondage/torture-c (scarce); The Oracle begins (3/43); not in issues 26,28,33,34	300	600	900	1950	3375	4800
21-Origin The Ape, Oracle's enemy; Schomburg hypo-c	161	322	483	1030	1765	2500
22-34: All have Schomburg WWII-c. 34-Origin The Scarab & only app.	135	270	405	864	1482	2100
35-Hypodermic syringe attacks Fighting Yank in drug story; Schomburg WWII-c	135	270	405	864	1482	2100
36-43: 36-Last Four Comrades. 38-Bondage/torture-c. 40-Last Capt. Future & Oracle. 41-Front Page Peggy begins; A-Bomb-c. 43-Last Pyroman	61	122	183	390	670	950
44,45: 44-Lance Lewis, Space Detective begins; Ingels-c; sci/fi-c begin. 45-Tygra begins (intro/origin, 5/47); Ingels-c/a (splash pg. & inside f/c B&W ad)	103	206	309	659	1130	1600
46-Classic Ingels-c; Ingels-a	155	310	465	992	1696	2400
47,48,50-53: 50,51-Sea-Eagle app.	116	232	348	742	1271	1800
49-Classic Schomburg Robot-c; last Fighting Yank	865	1730	2595	6315	11,158	16,000

NOTE: **Ingels** a-44, 45; c-44, 45, 46(wash). **Schomburg (Xela)** c-21-43; 47-53 (airbrush). **Tuska** c-45? Bondage c-16, 21, 37, 46-49. Captain Future c-1-9, 13, 14. Fighting Yank c-10-12, 15-17, 21, 22, 24, 26, 28, 30, 32, 34, 36, 38, 40, 42. Pyroman c-18-20, 23, 25, 27, 29, 31, 33, 35, 37, 39, 41, 43.

STARTLING STORIES: BANNER
Marvel Comics: July, 2001 - No. 4, Oct, 2001 ($2.99, limited series)

1-4-Hulk story by Azzarello; Corben-c/a 3.00
TPB (11/01, $12.95) r/1-4 13.00

STARTLING STORIES: FANTASTIC FOUR - UNSTABLE MOLECULES (See Fantastic Four - ...)

STARTLING STORIES: THE MEGALOMANIACAL SPIDER-MAN
Marvel Comics: Jun, 2002 ($2.99, one-shot)

1-Spider-Man spoof; Peter Bagge-s/a 3.00

STARTLING STORIES: THE THING
Marvel Comics: 2003 ($3.50, one-shot)

1-Zimmerman-s/Kramer-a; Inhumans and the Hulk app. 3.50

STARTLING STORIES: THE THING - NIGHT FALLS ON YANCY STREET
Marvel Comics: Jun, 2003 - No. 4, Sept, 2003 ($3.50, limited series)

1-4-Dorkin-s/Haspiel-a. 2,3-Frightful Four app. 3.50

STARTLING TERROR TALES
Star Publications: No. 10, May, 1952 - No. 14, Feb, 1953; No. 4, Apr, 1953 - No. 11, 1954

	GD 2.0	VG 4.0	FN 6.0	VF 8.0	VF/NM 9.0	NM- 9.2
10-(1st Series)-Wood/Harrison-a (r/A Star Presentation #3) Disbrow/Cole-c; becomes 4 different titles after #10; becomes Confessions of Love #11 on, The Horrors #11 on, Terrifying Tales #11 on, Terrors of the Jungle #11 on & continues w/Startling Terror #11	97	194	291	621	1061	1500
11-(8/52)-L. B. Cole Spider-c; r-Fox's "A Feature Presentation" #5 (blue-c)	300	600	900	2010	3505	5000
11-Black-c (variant; believed to be a pressrun change) (Unique)	300	600	900	2070	3635	5200
12,14	40	80	120	246	411	575
13-Jo-Jo-r; Disbrow-a	41	82	123	250	418	585
4-9,11(1953-54) (2nd Series): 11-New logo	39	78	117	231	378	525
10-Disbrow-a	41	82	123	256	428	600

NOTE: **L. B. Cole** covers-all issues. **Palais** a-V2#8r, V2#11r.

Star Trek #26 © CBS

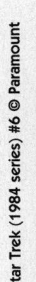

Star Trek (1984 series) #6 © Paramount

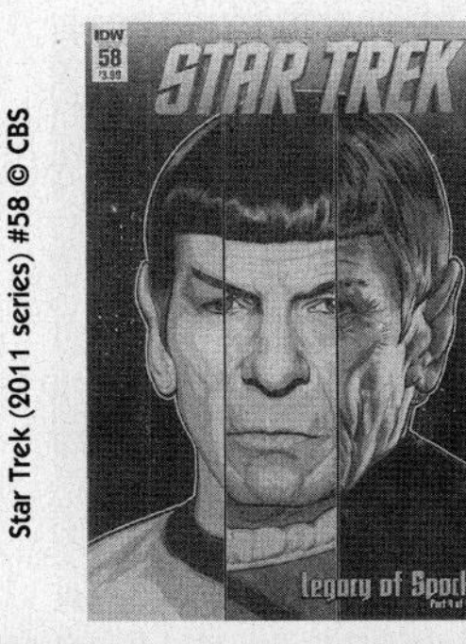

Star Trek (2011 series) #58 © CBS

STAR TREK (TV) (See Dan Curtis Giveaways, Dynabrite Comics & Power Record Comics)
Gold Key: 7/67; No. 2, 6/68; No. 3, 12/68; No. 4, 6/69 - No. 61, 3/79

	GD 2.0	VG 4.0	FN 6.0	VF 8.0	VF/NM 9.0	NM- 9.2
1-Photo-c begin, end #9; photo back-c is on all copies, no variant exists with an ad on the back-c	71	142	213	568	1284	2000
2-Regular version has an ad on back-c	24	48	72	168	372	575
2 (rare variation w/photo back-c)	38	76	114	285	641	1000
3-5-All have back-c ads	16	32	48	110	243	375
3 (rare variation w/photo back-c)	27	54	81	194	435	675
6-9	11	22	33	73	157	240
10-20	6	12	18	37	66	95
21-30	5	10	15	31	53	80
31-40	4	8	12	27	44	60
41-61: 52-Drug propaganda story	3	6	9	21	33	45
... Gold Key 100-Page Spectacular (IDW, 2/17, $7.99) r/#1,8,14; cover & pin-up gallery						8.00
...the Enterprise Logs nn (8/76)-Golden Press, ($1.95, 224 pgs.)-r/#1-8 plus 7 pgs. by McWilliams (#11185)-Photo-c	5	10	15	34	60	85
...the Enterprise Logs Vol. 2 ('76)-r/#9-17 (#11187)-Photo-c	5	10	15	31	53	75
...the Enterprise Logs Vol. 3 ('77)-r/#18-26 (#11188); McWilliams-a (4 pgs.)-Photo-c	5	10	15	31	53	75
Star Trek Vol. 4 (Winter '77)-Reprints #27,28,30-34,36,38 (#11189) plus 3 pgs. new art	5	10	15	31	53	75
... : The Key Collection (Checker Book Publ. Group, 2004, $22.95) r/#1-8						23.00
... : The Key Collection Volume 2 (Checker, 2004, $22.95) r/#9-16						23.00
... : The Key Collection Volume 3 (Checker, 2005, $22.95) r/#17-24						23.00
... : The Key Collection Volume 4 (Checker, 2005, $22.95) r/#25-33						23.00
... : The Key Collection Volume 5 (Checker, 2006, $22.95) r/#34,36,38,39,40-43						23.00

NOTE: ***McWilliams** a-38, 40-44, 46-61. #29 reprints #1; #35 reprints #4; #37 reprints #5; #45 reprints #7. The tabloids all have photo covers and blank inside covers. Painted covers #10-44, 46-59.*

STAR TREK
Marvel Comics Group: April, 1980 - No. 18, Feb, 1982

	GD 2.0	VG 4.0	FN 6.0	VF 8.0	VF/NM 9.0	NM- 9.2
1: 1-3-r/Marvel Super Special; movie adapt.	2	4	6	11	16	20
2-16: 5-Miller-c	1	3	4	6	8	10
17-Low print run	2	4	6	8	11	14
18-Last issue; low print run	2	4	6	11	16	20

NOTE: ***Austin** c-18i. **Buscema** a-13. **Gil Kane** a-15. **Nasser** c/a-7. **Simonson** c-17.*

STAR TREK (Also see Who's Who In Star Trek)
DC Comics: Feb, 1984 - No. 56, Nov, 1988 (75¢, Mando paper)

	GD 2.0	VG 4.0	FN 6.0	VF 8.0	VF/NM 9.0	NM- 9.2
1-Sutton-a(p) begins	2	4	6	8	10	12
2-5						6.00
6-10: 7-Origin Saavik						5.00
11-20: 19-Walter Koenig story						4.00
21-32						4.00
33-($1.25, 52 pgs.)-20th anniversary issue						5.00
34-49: 37-Painted-c						4.00
50-($1.50, 52 pgs.)						5.00
51-56						4.00
Annual 1-3: 1(1985). 2(1986). 3(1988, $1.50)						5.00
...: To Boldly Go TPB (Titan Books, 7/05, $19.95) r/#1-6; Koenig foreward; cast interviews						20.00
...: The Trial of James T. Kirk TPB (Titan Books, 6/06, $19.95) r/#7-12; cast interviews						20.00
...: The Return of the Worthy TPB (Titan Books, 12/06, $19.95) r/#13-18; cast interviews						20.00

NOTE: ***Morrow** a-28, 35, 36, 56. **Orlando** c-8i. **Perez** c-1-3. **Spiegle** a-19. **Starlin** c-24, 25. **Sutton** a-1-6p, 8-18p, 20-27p, 29p, 31-34p, 39-52p, 55p; c-4-6p, 8-22p, 46p.*

STAR TREK
DC Comics: Oct, 1989 - No. 80, Jan, 1996 ($1.50/$1.75/$1.95/$2.50)

	NM- 9.2
1-Capt. Kirk and crew	6.00
2,3	4.00
4-23,25-30: 10-12-The Trial of James T. Kirk. 21-Begin $1.75-c	3.00
24-($2.95, 68 pgs.)-40 pg. epic w/pin-ups	4.00
31-49,51-60	3.00
50-($3.50, 68 pgs.)-Painted-c	4.00
61-74,76-80	3.00
75 ($3.95)	4.00
Annual 1-6('90-'95, 68 pgs.): 1-Morrow-a. 3-Painted-c	4.00
Special 1-3 ('9-'95, 68 pgs.)-1-Sutton-a.	4.00
...: The Ashes of Eden (1995, $14.95, 100 pgs.)-Shatner story	18.00
...Generations (1994, $3.95, 68 pgs.)-Movie adaptation	4.00
...Generations (1994, $5.95, 68 pgs.)-Squarebound	6.00

STAR TREK...(TV)
DC Comics (WildStorm): one-shots

	NM- 9.2
All of Me (4/00, $5.95, prestige format) Lopresti-a	6.00
Enemy Unseen TPB (2001, $17.95) r/Perchance to Dream, Embrace the Wolf, The Killing Shadows; Struzan-c	18.00
Enter the Wolves (2001, $5.95) Crispin & Weinstein-s; Mota-a/c	6.00
New Frontier - Double Time (11/00, $5.95)-Captain Calhoun's USS Excalibur; Peter David-s; Stelfreeze-c	6.00
Other Realities TPB (2001, $14.95) r/All of Me, New Frontier - Double Time, and DS9-N-Vector; Van Fleet-c	15.00
Special (2001, $6.95) Stories from all 4 series by various; Van Fleet-c	7.00

STAR TREK (Further adventures of the crew from the 2009 movie)
IDW Publishing: Sept, 2011 - No. 60, Aug, 2016 ($3.99)

	NM- 9.2
1-49: 1,2-Gary Mitchell app.; Molnar-a. 11,12-Tribbles. 15,16-Mirror Universe. 21-Follows the 2013 movie; Klingons & Section 31 app. 35-40-The Q Gambit; DS9 crew app.	4.00
50-($4.99) Mirror Universe; Khan app.; bonus history of Star Trek comics, aliens	5.00
51-60: 51,52-Mirror Universe. 52-Variant Archie Comics cover. 55-58-Legacy of Spock	4.00
Annual (12/13, $7.99) "Strange New Worlds" on cover; photonovel by John Byrne	8.00
... #1: Greatest Hits (3/16, $1.00) reprints #1	3.00
... #1: Hundred Penny Press (8/13, $1.00) reprints #1	3.00
...: Flesh and Stone (7/14, $3.99) Doctors Bashir, Crusher, Pulaski, McCoy app.	4.00
...: 50th Anniversary Cover Celebration (8/16, $7.99) Gallery of IDW Star Trek covers	8.00
... Space Spanning Treasury Edition (4/13, $9.99, 13" x 8.5") Reprints #9,10,13	10.00

STAR TREK: ALIEN SPOTLIGHT
IDW Publishing: Sept, 2007 - Feb, 2008 ($3.99, series of one-shots)

	NM- 9.2
... Andorians (11/07) Storrie-s/O'Grady-a; Counselor Troi app.; two art & one photo-c	4.00
... Borg (1/08) Harris-s/Murphy-a; Janeway & Next Gen crew app.; two art & one photo-c	4.00
... Cardassians (12/09) Padilla-a; Garak & Kira app.	4.00
... The Gorn (9/07) Messina-a; Chekov app.; two art & one photo-c	4.00
... Orions (12/07) Casagrande-a; Capt. Pike app.; two art & one photo-c	4.00
... Q (8/09) Casagrande-a; takes place after Star Trek 8 movie; two art & one photo-c	4.00
... Romulans (2/08) John Byrne-s/a; Kirk era; two art & one photo-c	4.00
... Romulans (5/09) Wagner Reis-a; David Williams-c	4.00
... Tribbles (3/09) Hawthorne-a; first encounter with Klingons; one art & one photo-c	4.00
... Vulcans (10/07) Spock's early Enterprise days with Capt. Pike; two art & one photo-c	4.00

STAR TREK: ASSIGNMENT EARTH
IDW Publishing: May, 2008 - No. 5, Sept, 2008 ($3.99, limited series)

	NM- 9.2
1-5-Further adventures of Gary Seven and Roberta; John Byrne-s/a/c. 5-Nixon app.	4.00

STAR TREK: BOLDLY GO (Takes place after the 2016 movie Star Trek Beyond)
IDW Publishing: Oct, 2016 - Present ($3.99)

	NM- 9.2
1-5-The 2009 movie crew; Mike Johnson-s/Shasteen-a; The Borg app.; multiple covers	4.00

STAR TREK: BURDEN OF KNOWLEDGE
IDW Publishing: Jun, 2010 - No. 4, Sept, 2010 ($3.99, limited series)

	NM- 9.2
1-4-Original series Kirk and crew; Manfredi-a	4.00

STAR TREK: CAPTAIN'S LOG
IDW Publishing: one-shots

	NM- 9.2
...: Harriman (4/10, $3.99) Captain of the Enterprise-B following Kirk's "demise"; Currie-a	4.00
...: Jellico (10/10, $3.99) Woodward-a	4.00
...: Pike (9/10, $3.99) Events that put Pike in the chair; Woodward-a	4.00
...: Sulu (1/10, $3.99) Manfredi-a	4.00

STAR TREK: COUNTDOWN (Prequel to the 2009 movie)
IDW Publishing: Jan, 2009 - No. 4, Apr, 2009 ($3.99, limited series)

	NM- 9.2
1-4: 1-Ambassador Spock on Romulus; intro. Nero; Messina-a	4.00
Hundred Penny Press: Star Trek: Countdown #1 (4/11, $1.00) r/#1 w/new cover frame	3.00

STAR TREK: COUNTDOWN TO DARKNESS (Prequel to the 2013 movie)
IDW Publishing: Jan, 2013 - No. 4, Apr, 2013 ($3.99, limited series)

	NM- 9.2
1-4-Captain April app.; Messina-a; regular & photo covers on each	4.00

STAR TREK: CREW
IDW Publishing: Mar, 2009 - No. 5, Jul, 2009 ($3.99, limited series)

	NM- 9.2
1-5: John Byrne-s/a; Captain Pike era	4.00

STAR TREK: DEBT OF HONOR
DC Comics: 1992 ($24.95/$14.95, graphic novel)

	NM- 9.2
Hardcover ($24.95) Claremont-s/Hughes-a(p)	25.00
Softcover ($14.95)	15.00

STAR TREK: DEEP SPACE NINE (TV)
Malibu Comics: Aug, 1993 - No. 32, Jan, 1996 ($2.50)

	NM- 9.2
1-Direct Sale Edition w/line drawn-c	5.00
1-Newsstand Edition with photo-c	4.00
0-(1/95, $2.95)-Terok Nor	4.00
2-30: 2-Polybagged w/trading card. 9-4 pg. prelude to Hearts & Minds	4.00
31-($3.95)	5.00

Star Trek / Green Lantern #1 © CBS & DC

Star Trek: Infestation #1 © CBS

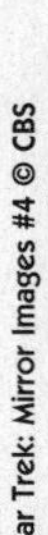

Star Trek: Mirror Images #4 © CBS

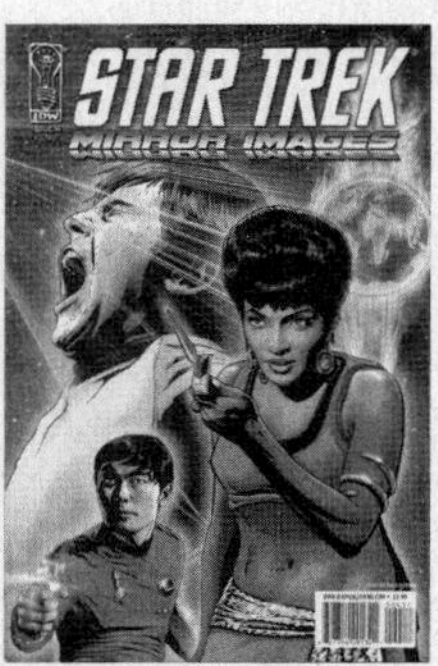

	GD 2.0	VG 4.0	FN 6.0	VF 8.0	VF/NM 9.0	NM- 9.2

32-($3.50) 5.00
Annual 1 (1/95, $3.95, 68 pgs.) 5.00
Special 1 (1995, $3.50) 5.00
Ultimate Annual 1 (12/95, $5.95) 6.00
...:Lightstorm (12/94, $3.50) 5.00

STAR TREK: DEEP SPACE NINE (TV)
Marvel Comics (Paramount Comics): Nov, 1996 - No. 15, Mar, 1998 ($1.95/$1.99)
1-15: 12,13-"Telepathy War" pt. 2,3 4.00

STAR TREK: DEEP SPACE NINE: FOOL'S GOLD
IDW Publishing: Dec, 2009 - No. 4, Mar, 2010 ($3.99)
1-4-Mantovani-a 4.00

STAR TREK: DEEP SPACE NINE -- N-VECTOR (TV)
DC Comics (WildStorm): Aug, 2000 - No. 4, Nov, 2000 ($2.50, limited series)
1-4-Cypress-a 3.00

STAR TREK DEEP SPACE NINE-THE CELEBRITY SERIES
Malibu Comics: May, 1995 ($2.95)
1-Blood and Honor; Mark Lenard script 4.00
1-Rules of Diplomacy; Aron Eisenberg script 4.00

STAR TREK: DEEP SPACE NINE HEARTS AND MINDS
Malibu Comics: June, 1994 - No. 4, Sept, 1994 ($2.50, limited series)
1-4 4.00
1-Holographic-c 5.00

STAR TREK: DEEP SPACE NINE, THE MAQUIS
Malibu Comics: Feb, 1995 - No. 3, Apr, 1995 ($2.50, limited series)
1-3-Newsstand-c, 1-Photo-c 4.00

STAR TREK: DEEP SPACE NINE/THE NEXT GENERATION
Malibu Comics: Oct, 1994 - No. 2, Nov, 1994 ($2.50, limited series)
1,2: Parts 2 & 4 of x-over with Star Trek: TNG/DS9 from DC Comics 4.00

STAR TREK: DEEP SPACE NINE WORF SPECIAL
Malibu Comics: Dec, 1995 ($3.95, one-shot)
1-Includes pinups 5.00

STAR TREK: DIVIDED WE FALL
DC Comics (WildStorm): July, 2001 - No. 4, Oct, 2001 ($2.95, limited series)
1-4: Ordover & Mack-s; Lenara Kahn, Verad and Odan app. 3.00

STAR TREK EARLY VOYAGES (TV)
Marvel Comics (Paramount Comics): Feb, 1997 - No. 17, Jun, 1998 ($2.95/$1.95/$1.99)
1-($2.95) 5.00
2-17 4.00

STAR TREK: ENTERPRISE EXPERIMENT
IDW Publishing: Apr, 2008 - No. 5, Aug, 2008 ($3.99, limited series)
1-5-Year Four story; D.C. Fontana & Derek Chester-s; Purcell-a 4.00

STAR TREK: FIRST CONTACT (Movie)
Marvel Comics (Paramount Comics): Nov, 1996 ($5.95, one-shot)
nn-Movie adaption 6.00

STAR TREK/ GREEN LANTERN (The Spectrum War)
IDW Publishing: Jul, 2015 - No. 6, Dec, 2015 ($3.99, limited series)
1-6-Crew from 2009 movie and Hal Jordan; Sinestro & Nekron app.; multiple covers 4.00

STAR TREK/ GREEN LANTERN (Stranger Worlds)
IDW Publishing: Dec, 2016 - Present ($3.99, limited series)
1-3-Sinestro & The Manhunters app.; multiple covers. 2,3-Khan app. 4.00

STAR TREK: HARLAN ELLISON'S ORIGINAL CITY ON THE EDGE OF FOREVER TELEPLAY
IDW Publishing: Jun, 2014 - No. 5, Oct, 2014 ($3.99, limited series)
1-5-Adaptation of Ellison's teleplay; J.K. Woodward-a; two covers on each 4.00

STAR TREK: INFESTATION (Crossover with G.I. Joe, Transformers & Ghostbusters)
IDW Publishing: Feb, 2011 - No. 2, Feb, 2011 ($3.99, limited series)
1,2-Zombies in the Kirk era; Maloney & Erskine-a; two covers on each 4.00

STAR TREK: KHAN
IDW Publishing: Oct, 2013 - No. 5, Feb, 2014 ($3.99, limited series)
1-5-Follows the 2013 movie; Khan's origin; Messina & Balboni-a 4.00

STAR TREK: KHAN RULING IN HELL
IDW Publishing: Oct, 2010 - No. 4, Jan, 2011 ($3.99, limited series)
1-4-Khan and the Botany Bay crew after banishment on Ceti Alpha V; Mantovani-a 4.00

STAR TREK: KLINGONS: BLOOD WILL TELL
IDW Publishing: Apr, 2007 - No. 5 ($3.99, limited series)
1-5-Star Trek TOS episodes from the Klingon viewpoint; Messina-a. 2-Tribbles 4.00
1-($4.99) Klingon Language Variant; comic with Kliingon text; English script 5.00

STAR TREK/ LEGION OF SUPER-HEROES
IDW Publishing: Oct, 2011 - No. 6, Mar, 2012 ($3.99, limited series)
1-6-Jeff Moy-a/Jimenez-c 1-Giffen var-c. 2-Lightle var-c. 3-Grell var-c. 5-Allred var-c 4.00

STAR TREK: LEONARD McCOY, FRONTIER DOCTOR
IDW Publishing: Apr, 2010 - No. 4, Jul, 2010 ($3.99, limited series)
1-4-Dr. McCoy right before Star Trek: TMP; John Byrne-s/a 4.00

STAR TREK: MANIFEST DESTINY
IDW Publishing: Apr, 2016 - No. 4, May, 2016 ($4.99/$3.99, limited series)
1-The 2009 movie crew vs. Klingons; Angel Hernandez-a 5.00
2-4-($3.99) 4.00

STAR TREK: MIRROR IMAGES
IDW Publishing: June, 2008 - No. 5, Nov, 2008 ($3.99, limited series)
1-5-Further adventures in the Mirror Universe. 3-Mirror-Picard app. 4.00

STAR TREK: MIRROR MIRROR
Marvel Comics (Paramount Comics): Feb, 1997 ($3.95, one-shot)
1-DeFalco-s 4.00

STAR TREK: MISSION'S END
IDW Publishing: Mar, 2009 - No. 5, July, 2009 ($3.99, limited series)
1-5-Kirk, Spock, Bones crew, their last mission on the pre-movie Enterprise 4.00

STAR TREK MOVIE ADAPTATION
IDW Publishing: Feb, 2010 - No. 6, Aug, 2010 ($3.99, limited series)
1-6-Adaptation of 2009 movie; Messina-a; regular & photo-c on each 4.00

STAR TREK MOVIE SPECIAL
DC Comics: 1984 (June) - No. 2, 1987 ($1.50); No. 1, 1989 ($2.00, 52 pgs)
nn-(#1)-Adapts Star Trek III; Sutton-p (68 pgs.) 5.00
2-Adapts Star Trek IV; Sutton-a; Chaykin-c. (68 pgs.) 5.00
1 (1989)-Adapts Star Trek V; painted-c 5.00

STAR TREK: NERO
IDW Publishing: Aug, 2009 - No. 4, Nov, 2009 ($3.99, limited series)
1-4-Nero's ship after the attack on the Kelvin to the arrival of Spock 4.00

STAR TREK: NEW FRONTIER
IDW Publishing: Mar, 2008 - No. 5, July, 2008 ($3.99, limited series)
1-5-Capt. Calhoun & Adm. Shelby app.; Peter David-s 4.00

STAR TREK: NEW VISIONS
IDW Publishing: May, 2014 - Present ($7.99, squarebound)
1-14-Photonovels of original crew by John Byrne. 1-Mirror Universe 8.00
... Special: More Of The Serpent Than The Dove (9/16, Humble Bundle) Gorn app. 20.00
... Special: The Cage (7/16, $7.99) 8.00

STAR TREK 100 PAGE...
IDW Publishing: Nov, 2011 - 2012 ($7.99)
...Spectacular #1 (11/11) Reprints stories of the original crew; s/a by Byrne and others 8.00
...Spectacular 2012 (2/12) Reprints; Khan, Q, Capt. Pike, the Gorn app. 8.00
...Spectacular Summer 2012 (8/12) Reprints of TNG and Voyager stories 8.00
...Spectacular Winter 2012 - Reprints; Capt. Harriman, Mirror Universe 8.00

STAR TREK: OPERATION ASSIMILATION
Marvel Comics (Paramount Comics): Dec, 1996 ($2.95, one-shot)
1 4.00

STAR TREK/PLANET OF THE APES: THE PRIMATE DIRECTIVE
IDW Publishing: Dec, 2014 - No. 5, Apr, 2015 ($3.99, limited series)
1-5-Classic crew on the Planet of the Apes; Klingons app. 2-Kirk meets Taylor 8.00

STAR TREK: ROMULANS SCHISMS
IDW Publishing: Sept, 2009 - No. 3, Nov, 2009 ($3.99, limited series)
1-3-John Byrne-s/a/c 4.00

STAR TREK: ROMULANS THE HOLLOW CROWN
IDW Publishing: Sept, 2008 - No. 2, Oct, 2008 ($3.99, limited series)
1,2-John Byrne-s/a/c 4.00

STAR TREK VI: THE UNDISCOVERED COUNTRY (Movie)
DC Comics: 1992
1-($2.95, regular edition, 68 pgs.)-Adaptation of film 5.00

STAR TREK
THE NEXT GENERATION
MICHAEL JAN FRIEDMAN and PETER KRAUSE

Star Trek: The Next Generation #20 © Paramount

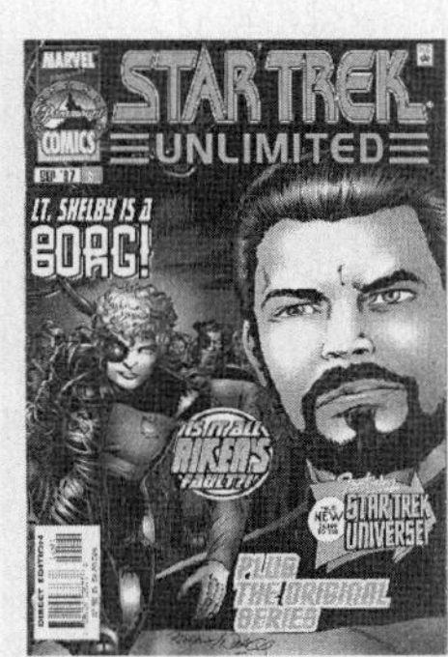

Star Trek Unlimited #5 © Paramount

Star Trek: Waypoint #1 © CBS

	GD 2.0	VG 4.0	FN 6.0	VF 8.0	VF/NM 9.0	NM- 9.2

nn-($5.95, prestige edition)-Has photos of movie not included in regular edition; painted-c by Palmer; photo back-c 1 2 3 5 6 8

STAR TREK: SPOCK: REFLECTIONS
IDW Publishing: July, 2009 - No. 4, Oct, 2009 ($3.99, limited series)
1-4-Flashbacks of Spock's childhood and career; Messina & Manfredi-a 4.00

STAR TREK: STARFLEET ACADEMY
Marvel Comics (Paramount Comics): Dec, 1996 - No. 19, Jun, 1998 ($1.95/$1.99)
1-19: Begin new series. 12-"Telepathy War" pt. 1. 18-English & Klingon editions 4.00

STAR TREK: STARFLEET ACADEMY
IDW Publishing: Dec, 2015 - No. 5, Apr, 2016 ($3.99, limited series)
1-5-Crew of the 2009 movie at the academy; Charm-a 4.00

STAR TREK: TELEPATHY WAR
Marvel Comics (Paramount Comics): Nov, 1997 ($2.99, 48 pgs., one-shot)
1-"Telepathy War" x-over pt. 6 4.00

STAR TREK - THE MODALA IMPERATIVE
DC Comics: Late July, 1991 - No. 4, Late Sept, 1991 ($1.75, limited series)
1-4 4.00
TPB ($19.95) r/series and ST:TNG - The Modala Imperative 20.00

STAR TREK: THE NEXT GENERATION (TV)
DC Comics: Feb, 1988 - No. 6, July, 1988 (limited series)
1 ($1.50, 52 pgs.)-Sienkiewicz painted-c 1 2 3 5 7 9
2-6 ($1.00) 5.00

STAR TREK: THE NEXT GENERATION (TV)
DC Comics: Oct, 1989 -No. 80, 1995 ($1.50/$1.75/$1.95)
1-Capt. Picard and crew from TV show 2 4 6 8 10 12
2,3 6.00
4-10 5.00
11-23,25-49,51-60 4.00
24,50: 24-($2.50, 52 pgs.). 50-($3.50, 68 pgs.)-Painted-c 6.00
61-74,76-80 4.00
75-($3.95, 50 pgs.) 5.00
Annual 1-6 ('90-'95, 68 pgs.) 5.00
Special 1 -3('93-'95, 68 pgs.)-1-Contains 3 stories 5.00
...-The Series Finale (1994, $3.95, 68 pgs.) 5.00

STAR TREK: THE NEXT GENERATION (TV)
DC Comics (WildStorm): one-shots
Embrace the Wolf (6/00, $5.95, prestige format) Golden & Sniegoski-s 6.00
Forgiveness (2001, $24.95, HC) David Brin-s/Scott Hampton painted-a; dust jacket-c 30.00
Forgiveness (2002, $17.95, SC) 18.00
The Gorn Crisis (1/01, $29.95, HC) Kordey painted-a/dust jacket-c 30.00
The Gorn Crisis (1/01, $17.95, SC) Kordey painted-a 18.00

STAR TREK: THE NEXT GENERATION/DEEP SPACE NINE (TV)
DC Comics: Dec, 1994 - No. 2, Jan, 1995 ($2.50, limited series)
1,2-Parts 1 & 3 of x-over with Star Trek: DS9/TNG from Malibu Comics 4.00

STAR TREK: THE NEXT GENERATION / DOCTOR WHO: ASSIMILATION[2]
IDW Publishing: May, 2012 - No. 8, Dec, 2012 ($3.99, limited series)
1-8-The Borg and Cybermen team-up; Tipton-s/Woodward-a; multiple covers on each 4.00

STAR TREK: THE NEXT GENERATION: GHOSTS
IDW Publishing: Nov, 2009 - No. 5, Mar, 2010 ($3.99)
1-5-Cannon-s/Aranda-a 4.00

STAR TREK: THE NEXT GENERATION - ILL WIND
DC Comics: Nov, 1995 - No. 4, Feb, 1996 ($2.50, limited series)
1-4: Hugh Fleming painted-c on all 4.00

STAR TREK: THE NEXT GENERATION: INTELLIGENCE GATHERING
IDW Publishing: Jan, 2008 - No. 5, May, 2008 ($3.99)
1-5-Messina-a/Scott & David Tipton-s; two covers on each 4.00

STAR TREK: THE NEXT GENERATION - PERCHANCE TO DREAM
DC Comics/WildStorm: Feb, 2000 - No. 4, May, 2000 ($2.50, limited series)
1-4-Bradstreet-c 3.00

STAR TREK: THE NEXT GENERATION - RIKER
Marvel Comics (Paramount Comics): July, 1998 ($3.50, one-shot)
1-Riker joins the Maquis 4.00

STAR TREK: THE NEXT GENERATION - SHADOWHEART
DC Comics: Dec, 1994 - No. 4, Mar, 1995 ($1.95, limited series)
1-4 4.00

STAR TREK: THE NEXT GENERATION - THE KILLING SHADOWS
DC Comics/WildStorm: Nov, 2000 - No. 4, Feb, 2001 ($2.50, limited series)
1-4-Scott Ciencin-s; Sela app. 3.00

STAR TREK: THE NEXT GENERATION: THE LAST GENERATION
IDW Publishing: Nov, 2008 - No. 5, Mar, 2009 ($3.99, limited series)
1-5-Purcell-a; alternate timeline with Klingon war; Sulu app. 4.00

STAR TREK: THE NEXT GENERATION - THE MODALA IMPERATIVE
DC Comics: Early Sept, 1991 - No. 4, Late Oct, 1991 ($1.75, limited series)
1-4 4.00

STAR TREK: THE NEXT GENERATION: THE SPACE BETWEEN
IDW Publishing: Jan, 2007 - No. 6, June, 2007 ($3.99)
1-6-Single issue stories from various seasons; photo & art covers 4.00

STAR TREK: THE WRATH OF KHAN
IDW Publishing: Jun, 2009 - No. 3, Jul, 2009 ($3.99, limited series)
1-3-Movie adaptation; Chee Yang Ong-a 4.00

STAR TREK: TNG: HIVE
IDW Publishing: Sept, 2012 - No. 4, Feb, 2013 ($3.99, limited series)
1-4-Brannon Braga-s/Joe Corroney-a; Next Generation crew vs. the Borg 4.00

STAR TREK UNLIMITED
Marvel Comics (Paramount Comics): Nov, 1996 - No. 10, July, 1998 ($2.95/$2.99)
1,2-Stories from original series and Next Generation 5.00
3-10: 3-Begin $2.99-c. 6-"Telepathy War" pt. 4. 7-Q & Trelane swap Kirk & Picard 4.00

STAR TREK UNTOLD VOYAGES
Marvel Comics (Paramount Comics): May, 1998 - No. 5, July, 1998 ($2.50)
1-5-Kirk's crew after the 1st movie 4.00

STAR TREK: VOYAGER
Marvel Comics (Paramount Comics): Nov, 1996 - No. 15, Mar, 1998 ($1.95/$1.99)
1-15: 13-"Telepathy War" pt. 5. 14-Seven of Nine joins crew 4.00

STAR TREK: VOYAGER
DC Comics/WildStorm: one-shots and trade paperbacks
- Elite Force (7/00, $5.95) The Borg app.; Abnett & Lanning-s 6.00
... Encounters With the Unknown TPB (2001, $19.95) reprints 20.00
- False Colors (1/00, $5.95) Photo-c and Jim Lee-c; Jeff Moy-a 6.00

STAR TREK: VOYAGER-- THE PLANET KILLER
DC Comics/WildStorm: Mar, 2001 - No. 3, May, 2001 ($2.95, limited series)
1-3-Voyager vs. the Planet Killer from the ST:TOS episode; Teranishi-a 3.00

STAR TREK: VOYAGER SPLASHDOWN
Marvel Comics (Paramount Comics): Apr, 1998 - No. 4, July, 1998 ($2.50, limited series)
1-4-Voyager crashes on a water planet 4.00

STAR TREK: WAYPOINT
IDW Publishing: Sept, 2016 - Present ($4.99/$3.99)
1-($4.99) Short story anthology; future Next Gen Data & Geordi; multiple covers 5.00
2,3-($3.99) 2-Gold Key style story. 3-Voyager & DS9 crews 4.00

STAR TREK/ X-MEN
Marvel Comics (Paramount Comics): Dec, 1996 ($4.99, one-shot)
1-Kirk's crew & X-Men; art by Silvestri, Tan, Winn & Finch; Lobdell-s 6.00

STAR TREK/ X-MEN: 2ND CONTACT
Marvel Comics (Paramount Comics): May, 1998 ($4.99, 64 pgs., one-shot)
1-Next Gen. crew & X-Men battle Kang, Sentinels & Borg following First Contact movie 6.00
1-Painted wraparound variant cover 6.00

STAR TREK: YEAR FOUR (Also see Star Trek: Enterprise Experiment)
IDW Publishing: July, 2007 - No. 5, Nov, 2007 ($3.99, limited series)
1-5: 1-Original series crew; Tischman-s/Conley-a; three covers on each 4.00

STARVE
Image Comics: Jun, 2015 - No. 10, Jun, 2016 ($3.99)
1-10-Brian Wood-s/Danijel Zezelj-a 4.00

STAR WARS (Movie) (See Classic..., Contemporary Motivators, Dark Horse Comics, The Droids, The Ewoks, Marvel Movie Showcase, Marvel Special Ed.)
Marvel Comics Group: July, 1977 - No. 107, Sept, 1986
1-(Regular 30¢ edition)-Price in square w/UPC code; #1-6 adapt first movie; first issue on sale before movie debuted 10 20 30 66 138 210

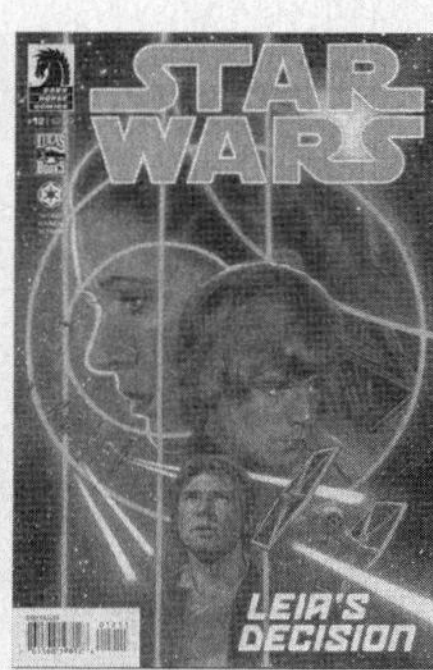

Star Wars (2013 series) #12 © Lucasfilm

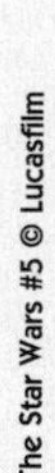
The Star Wars #5 © Lucasfilm

Star Wars: Chewbacca #1 © Lucasfilm

	GD 2.0	VG 4.0	FN 6.0	VF 8.0	VF/NM 9.0	NM- 9.2
1-(35¢-c; limited distribution - 1500 copies?)- Price in square w/UPC code (Prices vary widely on this book. In 2005 a CGC certified 9.4 sold for $6,500, a CGC certified 9.2 sold for $3,403, and a CGC certified 6.0 sold for $610)	333	666	1000	2831	6416	10,000

NOTE: *The rare 35¢ edition has the cover price in a square box, and the UPC box in the lower left hand corner has the UPC code lines running through it.*

	GD	VG	FN	VF	VF/NM	NM-
1-Reprint; has "reprint" in upper lefthand corner of cover or on inside or price and number inside a diamond with no date or UPC on cover; 30¢ and 35¢ issues published	4	8	12	28	47	65
2-9: Reprints; has "reprint" in upper lefthand corner of cover or on inside or price and number inside a diamond with no date or UPC on cover; 30¢ and 35¢ issues published	1	3	4	6	8	10
2-4-(30¢ issues). 4-Battle with Darth Vader	4	8	12	28	47	65
2-4-(35¢ with UPC code; not reprints)	54	108	162	432	966	1500
5,6: 5-Begin 35¢-c on all editions. 6-Stevens-a(i)	3	6	9	19	30	40
7-20	2	4	6	11	16	20
21-38,45-67,69,70: 50-Giant	2	4	6	8	10	12
39-41,43,44-The Empire Strikes Back-r by Al Williamson in all	2	4	6	9	12	15
42-1st Boba Fett	6	12	18	40	73	105
68-Reintro Boba Fett	4	8	12	28	47	65
71-80	2	4	6	8	11	14
81-Boba Fett app.	3	6	9	21	33	45
82-90	2	4	6	9	13	16
91,93-99: 98-Williamson-a	2	4	6	11	16	20
92,100-106: 92,100-($1.00, 52 pgs.)	3	6	9	14	20	26
107 (low dist.); Portacio-a(i)	5	10	15	35	63	90
Annual 1 (12/79, 52 pgs.)-Simonson-c	2	4	6	11	16	20
Annual 2 (11/82, 52 pgs.), 3(12/83, 52 pgs.)	2	4	6	9	12	15

... A Long Time Ago...Vol. 1 TPB (Dark Horse Comics, 6/02, $29.95) r/#1-14 30.00
... A Long Time Ago...Vol. 2 TPB (Dark Horse Comics, 7/02, $29.95) r/#15-28 30.00
... A Long Time Ago...Vol. 3 TPB (Dark Horse Comics, 11/02, $29.95) r/#39-53 30.00
... A Long Time Ago...Vol. 4 TPB (Dark Horse Comics, 1/03, $29.95) r/#54-67 & Ann. 2 30.00
... A Long Time Ago...Vol. 5 TPB (Dark Horse Comics, 3/03, $29.95) r/#68-81 & Ann. 3 30.00
... A Long Time Ago...Vol. 6 TPB (Dark Horse Comics, 5/03, $29.95) r/#82-93 30.00
... A Long Time Ago...Vol. 7 TPB (Dark Horse Comics, 6/03, $29.95) r/#96-107 30.00

Austin *a-11-15i, 21i, 38; c-12-15i, 21i.* ***Byrne*** *c-13p.* ***Chaykin*** *a-1-10p; c-1.* ***Golden*** *c/a-38.* ***Miller*** *c-47p; pin-up-43.* ***Nebres*** *c/a-Annual 2i.* ***Portacio*** *a-107i.* ***Sienkiewicz*** *c-92i, 98.* ***Simonson*** *a-16p, 49p, 51-63p, 65p, 66p; c-16, 49-51, 52p, 53-62, Annual 1.* ***Steacy*** *painted a-105i, 106i; c-105.* ***Williamson*** *a-39-44p, 50p, 98; c-39, 40, 41-44p. Painted c-81, 87, 92, 95, 98, 100, 105.*

STAR WARS (Monthly series) (Becomes Star Wars Republic #46-on)
Dark Horse Comics: Dec, 1998 - No. 45, Aug, 2005 ($2.50/$2.95/$2.99)

1-Prelude To Rebellion; Strnad-s 1 2 3 5 6 8
2-45: 2-6-Prelude To Rebellion; Strnad-s. 4-Brereton-c. 7-12-Outlander. 13,17-18-($2.95). 13-18-Emissaries to Malastare; Truman-s. 14-16-($2.50) Schultz-c. 19-22-Twilight; Duursema-a. 23-26-Infinity's End. 42-45-Rite of Passage 3.00
5,6 (Holochrome-c variants) 6.00
#0 Another Universe.com Ed.($10.00) r/serialized pages from Pizzazz Magazine; new Dorman painted-c 12.00
... A Valentine Story (2/03, $3.50) Leia & Han Solo on Hoth; Winick-s/Chadwick-a/c 3.50
...: Rite of Passage (2004, $12.95) r/#42-45 13.00
...: The Stark Hyperspace War (903, $12.95) r/#36-39 13.00

STAR WARS (Monthly series)
Dark Horse Comics: Jan, 2013 - No. 20, Aug, 2014 ($2.99)

1-Takes place after Episode IV; Brian Wood-s/Carlos D'Anda-a/Alex Ross-c 8.00
2-Ross-c 5.00
3-20: 3,4-Ross-c. 5-7-Migliari-c 3.00

STAR WARS
Dark Horse Comics (Free Comic Book Day giveaways)

...: and Captain Midnight (5/13) flip book with new Captain Midnight story & Avatar 3.00
...: Clone Wars #0 (5/09) flip book with short stories of Usagi Yojimbo, Emily the Strange 3.00
...: Clone Wars Adventures (7/04) based on Cartoon Network series; Fillbach Bros. -a 3.00
...: FCBD 2005 Special (5/05) Anakin & Obi-Wan during Clone Wars 3.00
...: FCBD 2006 Special (5/06) Clone Wars story; flip book with Conan FCBD Special 3.00
...: Tales - A Jedi's Weapon (5/02, 16 pgs.) Anakin Skywalker Episode 2 photo-c 3.00
Free Comic Book Day and Star Wars: The Clone Wars (5/11) flip book with Avatar: The Last Airbender 3.00

STAR WARS (Also see Darth Vader and Star Wars: Vader Down)
Marvel Comics: Mar, 2015 - Present ($4.99/$3.99)

1-($4.99) Takes place after Episode IV; Aaron-s/Cassaday-a; multiple covers 5.00
2-6-($3.99) Darth Vader app.; Cassaday-a. 4-6-Boba Fett app. 6-Intro Sana Solo 4.00
7-24,26-29: 7-Bianchi-a; Obi-Wan flashback. 8-12-Immonen-a. 13,14-Vader Down pts. 3,5; Deodato-a. 15,20-Obi-Wan flashback; Mayhew-a. 16-19-Yu-a. 26-29-Yoda app. 4.00
25-($4.99) Darth Vader app.; Molina-a; back-up Droids story by Eliopoulos 5.00
Annual 1 (2/16, $4.99) Gillen-s/Unzueta-a/Cassaday-c; Emperor Palpatine app. 5.00
Annual 2 (1/17, $4.99) Kelly Thompson-s/Emilio Laiso-a; intro. Pash Davane 5.00
... Special: C-3PO 1 (6/16, $4.99) Robinson-s/Harris-a/c; story of C-3PO's red arm 5.00

STAR WARS, THE
Dark Horse Comics: Sept, 2013 - No. 8, May, 2014 ($3.99)

1-8-Adaptation of George Lucas' original rough-draft screenplay; Mayhew-a/Runge-c 4.00
#0-(1/14, $3.99) Design work of characters, settings, vehicles 4.00

STAR WARS: AGENT OF THE EMPIRE - HARD TARGETS
Dark Horse Comics: Oct, 2012 - No. 5, Feb, 2013 ($2.99, limited series)

1-5: 1-Ostrander-s/Fabbri-a; Boba Fett app. 3.00

STAR WARS: AGENT OF THE EMPIRE - IRON ECLIPSE
Dark Horse Comics: Dec, 2011 - No. 5, Apr, 2012 ($3.50, limited series)

1-5: 1-Ostrander-s/Roux-a; Han Solo & Chewbacca app. 3.50

STAR WARS: A NEW HOPE - THE SPECIAL EDITION
Dark Horse Comics: Jan, 1997 - No. 4, Apr, 1997 ($2.95, limited series)

1-4-Dorman-c 4.00

STAR WARS: BLOOD TIES - BOBA FETT IS DEAD
Dark Horse Comics: Apr, 2012 - No. 4, Jul, 2012 ($3.50, limited series)

1-4-Scalf painted-a/c 3.50

STAR WARS: BLOOD TIES: JANGO AND BOBA FETT
Dark Horse Comics: Aug, 2010 - No. 4, Nov, 2010 ($3.50, limited series)

1-4-Scalf painted-a/c 3.50

STAR WARS: BOBA FETT
Dark Horse Comics: Dec, 1995 - No. 3, Aug, 1997 ($3.95) (Originally intended as a one-shot)

1-Kennedy-c/a 1 2 3 5 6 8
2,3 5.00
Death, Lies, & Treachery TPB (1/98, $12.95) r/#1-3 13.00
... - Agent of Doom (11/00, $2.99) Ostrander-s/Cam Kennedy-a 3.00
... - Overkill (3/06, $2.99) Hughes-c/Andrews-s/Velasco-a 3.00
Twin Engines of Destruction (1/97, $2.95) 4.00

STAR WARS: BOBA FETT: ENEMY OF THE EMPIRE
Dark Horse Comics: Jan, 1999 - No. 4, Apr, 1999 ($2.95, limited series)

1-4-Recalls 1st meeting of Fett and Vader 4.00

STAR WARS: CHEWBACCA
Dark Horse Comics: Jan, 2000 - No. 4, Apr, 2000 ($2.95, limited series)

1-4-Macan-s/art by various incl. Anderson, Kordey, Gibbons; Phillips-c 3.00

STAR WARS: CLONE WARS ADVENTURES
Dark Horse Comics: 2004 - No. 10, 2007 ($6.95, digest-sized)

1-10-Short stories inspired by Clone Wars animated series 7.00

STAR WARS: CRIMSON EMPIRE
Dark Horse Comics: Dec, 1997 - No. 6, May, 1998 ($2.95, limited series)

1-Richardson-s/Gulacy-a 1 2 3 4 5 7
2-6 5.00

STAR WARS: CRIMSON EMPIRE II: COUNCIL OF BLOOD
Dark Horse Comics: Nov, 1998 - No. 6, Apr, 1999 ($2.95, limited series)

1-6-Richardson & Stradley-s/Gulacy-a 4.00

STAR WARS: CRIMSON EMPIRE III: EMPIRE LOST
Dark Horse Comics: Oct, 2011 - No. 6, Apr, 2012 ($3.50, limited series)

1-6: 1-Richardson-s/Gulacy-a/Dorman-c 3.50

STAR WARS: DARK EMPIRE
Dark Horse Comics: Dec, 1991 - No. 6, Oct, 1992 ($2.95, limited series)

Preview-(99¢) 4.00
1-All have Dorman painted-c 1 3 4 6 8 10
1-3-2nd printing 4.00
2-Low print run 2 4 6 8 10 12
3 6.00
4-6 4.00
Gold Embossed Set (#1-6)-With gold embossed foil logo (price is for set) 60.00
Platinum Embossed Set (#1-6) 90.00
Trade paperback (4/93, 16.95) 17.00
Dark Empire 1 - TPB 3rd printing (2003, $16.95) 17.00
Ltd. Ed. Hardcover ($99.95) Signed & numbered 100.00

STAR WARS: DARK EMPIRE II
Dark Horse Comics: Dec, 1994 - No. 6, May, 1995 ($2.95, limited series)

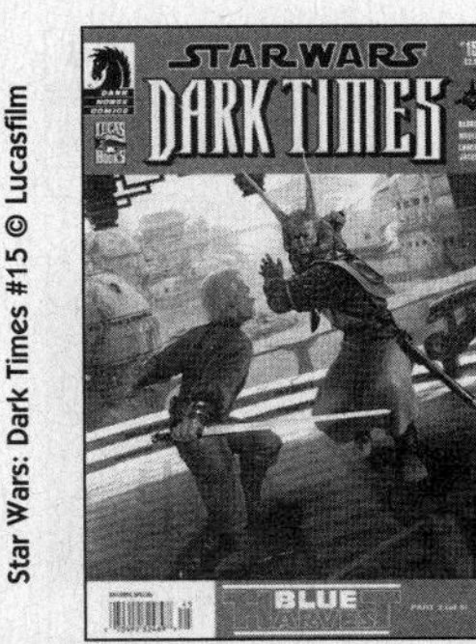
Star Wars: Dark Times #15 © Lucasfilm

Star Wars: Empire #7 © Lucasfilm

Star Wars: Infinities - The Empire Strikes Back #4 © Lucasfilm

	GD	VG	FN	VF	VF/NM	NM-
	2.0	4.0	6.0	8.0	9.0	9.2

1-Dave Dorman painted-c 5.00
2-6: Dorman-c in all. 4.00
Platinum Embossed Set (#1-6) 35.00
Trade paperback ($17.95) 18.00
TPB Second Edition (9/06, $19.95) r/#1-6 and Star Wars: Empire's End #1,2 20.00

STAR WARS: DARK FORCE RISING
Dark Horse Comics: May, 1997 - No. 6, Oct, 1997 ($2.95, limited series)
1-6 4.00
TPB (2/98, $17.95) r/#1-6 18.00

STAR WARS: DARK TIMES (Continued from Star Wars Republic #84)(Continues in Star Wars: Rebellion #15)
Dark Horse Comics: Oct, 2006 - No. 17, Jun, 2010 ($2.99)
1-17-Nineteen years before Episode IV; Doug Wheatley-a. 11-Celeste Morne awakens
13-17-Blue Harvest 3.00
#0-(7/09, $2.99) Prologue to Blue Harvest 3.00
... Volume 1: The Path To Nowhere (1/08, $17.95, TPB) r/#1-5 18.00

STAR WARS: DARK TIMES - A SPARK REMAINS
Dark Horse Comics: Jul, 2013 - No. 5, Dec, 2013 ($3.50, limited series)
1-5-Stradley-s/Wheatley-a; Darth Vader app. 3.50

STAR WARS: DARK TIMES - FIRE CARRIER
Dark Horse Comics: Feb, 2013 - No. 5, Jun, 2013 ($2.99, limited series)
1-5-Stradley-s/Guzman-a; Darth Vader app. 3.00

STAR WARS: DARK TIMES - OUT OF THE WILDERNESS
Dark Horse Comics: Aug, 2011 - No. 5, Apr, 2012 ($2.99, limited series)
1-5-Doug Wheatley-a 3.00

STAR WARS: DARTH MAUL
Dark Horse Comics: Sept, 2000 - No. 4, Dec, 2000 ($2.95, limited series)
1-4-Photo-c and Struzan painted-c; takes place 6 months before Ep. 1 3.00

STAR WARS: DARTH MAUL - DEATH SENTENCE
Dark Horse Comics: Jul, 2012 - No. 4, Oct, 2012 ($2.99, limited series)
1-4-Tom Taylor-s/Bruno Redondo-a/Dave Dorman-c 3.00

STAR WARS: DARTH MAUL - SON OF DATHOMIR
Dark Horse Comics: May, 2014 - No. 4, Aug, 2014 ($3.50, limited series)
1-4-Barlow-s/Frigeri-a/Scalf-c 3.50

STAR WARS: DARTH VADER AND THE CRY OF SHADOWS
Dark Horse Comics: Dec, 2013 - No. 5, Apr, 2014 ($3.50, limited series)
1-5-Siedell-s/Guzman-a/Massaferra-c 3.50

STAR WARS: DARTH VADER AND THE GHOST PRISON
Dark Horse Comics: May, 2012 - No. 5, Sept, 2012 ($3.50, limited series)
1-5-Blackman-s/Alessio-a/Wilkins-c. 1-Variant-c by Sanda 3.50

STAR WARS: DARTH VADER AND THE LOST COMMAND
Dark Horse Comics: Jan, 2011 - No. 5, May, 2011 ($3.50, limited series)
1-5-Blackman-s/Leonardi-a/Sanda-c. 1-Variant-c by Wheatley 3.50

STAR WARS: DARTH VADER AND THE NINTH ASSASSIN
Dark Horse Comics: Apr, 2013 - No. 5, Aug, 2013 ($3.50, limited series)
1-5-Siedell-s. 1,2,4-Thompson-a. 3,5-Fernandez-a 3.50

STAR WARS: DAWN OF THE JEDI
Dark Horse Comics: No. 0, Feb, 2012 - Present ($3.50)
0-Guide to the worlds, characters, sites, vehicles; Migliari-c 3.50
... - Force Storm (2/12 - No. 5, 6/12, $3.50) 1-5-Ostrander-s/Duursema-a/c 3.50
... - Force War (11/13 - No. 5, 3/14, $3.50) 1-5-Ostrander-s/Duursema-a/c 3.50
... - Prisoner of Bogan (11/12 - No. 5, 5/13, $2.99) 1-5-Ostrander-s/Duursema-a/c 3.00

STAR WARS: DROIDS (See Dark Horse Comics #17-19)
Dark Horse Comics: Apr, 1994 - #6, Sept, 1994; V2#1, Apr, 1995 - V2#8, Dec, 1995 ($2.50, limited series)
1-($2.95)-Embossed-c 5.00
2-6, Special 1 (1/95, $2.50), V2#1-8 4.00
Star Wars Omnibus: Droids One TPB (6/08, $24.95) r/#1-6, Special 1, V2#1-8, Star Wars: The Protocol Offensive and "Artoo's Day Out" story from Star Wars Galaxy Magazine #1 25.00

STAR WARS: EMPIRE
Dark Horse Comics: Sept, 2002 - No. 40, Feb, 2006 ($2.99)
1-40: 1-Benjamin-a; takes place weeks before SW: A New Hope. 7,28-Boba Fett-c. 14-Vader after the destruction of the Death Star. 15-Death of Biggs; Wheatley-a 3.00
... Volume 1 (2003, $12.95, TPB) r/#1-4 13.00
... Volume 2 (2004, $17.95, TPB) r/#8-12,15 18.00
... Volume 3: The Imperial Perspective (2004, $17.95, TPB) r/#13,14,16-19 18.00
... Volume 4: The Heart of the Rebellion (2005, $17.95, TPB) r/#5,6,20-22 & Star Wars: A Valentine Story 18.00
... Volume 5 (2006, $14.95, TPB) r/#23-27 15.00
... Volume 6: In the Shadows of Their Fathers (10/06, $17.95, TPB) r/#29-34 18.00
... Volume 7: The Wrong Side of the War (1/07, $17.95, TPB) r/#34-40 18.00

STAR WARS: EMPIRE'S END
Dark Horse Comics: Oct, 1995 - No. 2, Nov, 1995 ($2.95, limited series)
1,2-Dorman-c 4.00

STAR WARS: EPISODE 1 THE PHANTOM MENACE
Dark Horse Comics: May, 1999 - No. 4 ($2.95, movie adaptation)
1-4-Regular and photo-c; Damaggio & Williamson-a 4.00
TPB ($12.95) r/#1-4 13.00
...Anakin Skywalker-Photo-c & Bradstreet-c, ...Obi-Wan Kenobi-Photo-c & Egeland-c, ...Queen Amidala-Photo-c & Bradstreet-c, ...Qui-Gon Jinn-Photo-c & Bradstreet-c 4.00
Gold foil covers; Wizard 1/2 10.00

STAR WARS: EPISODE II - ATTACK OF THE CLONES
Dark Horse Comics: Apr, 2002 - No. 4, May, 2002 ($3.99, movie adaptation)
1-4-Regular and photo-c; Duursema-a 4.00
TPB ($17.95) r/#1-4; Struzan-c 18.00

STAR WARS: EPISODE III - REVENGE OF THE SITH
Dark Horse Comics: May, 2005 - No. 4, May, 2005 ($2.99, movie adaptation)
1-4-Wheatley-a/Dorman-c 3.00
TPB ($12.95) r/#1-4; Dorman-c 13.00

STAR WARS: GENERAL GRIEVOUS
Dark Horse Comics: Mar, 2005 - No. 4, June, 2005 ($2.99, limited series)
1-4-Leonardi-a/Dixon-s 3.00
TPB (2005, $12.95) r/#1-4 13.00

STAR WARS HANDBOOK
Dark Horse Comics: July, 1998 - Mar, 2000 ($2.95, one-shots)
...X-Wing Rogue Squadron (7/98)-Guidebook to characters and spacecraft 4.00
...Crimson Empire (7/99) Dorman-c 4.00
...Dark Empire (3/00) Dorman-c 4.00

STAR WARS: HEIR TO THE EMPIRE
Dark Horse Comics: Oct, 1995 - No.6, Apr, 1996 ($2.95, limited series)
1-6: Adaptation of Zahn novel 4.00

STAR WARS: INFINITIES - A NEW HOPE
Dark Horse Comics: May, 2001 - No. 4, Oct, 2001 ($2.99, limited series)
1-4: "What If..." the Death Star wasn't destroyed in Episode 4 3.00
TPB (2002, $12.95) r/ #1-4 13.00

STAR WARS: INFINITIES - THE EMPIRE STRIKES BACK
Dark Horse Comics: July, 2002 - No. 4, Oct, 2002 ($2.99, limited series)
1-4: "What If..." Luke died on the ice planet Hoth; Bachalo-c 3.00
TPB (2/03, $12.95) r/ #1-4 13.00

STAR WARS: INFINITIES - RETURN OF THE JEDI
Dark Horse Comics: Nov, 2003 - No. 4, Mar, 2004 ($2.99, limited series)
1-4:"What If..." ; Benjamin-a 3.00

STAR WARS: INVASION
Dark Horse Comics: July, 2009 - No. 5, Nov, 2009 ($2.99)
1-5-Jo Chen-c 3.00
#0-(10/09, $3.50) Dorman-c; Han Solo and Chewbacca app. 3.50
... - Rescues 1-6 (5/10 - No. 6, 12/10) Chen-c 3.00
... - Revelations 1-5 (7/11 - No. 5, 11/11, $3.50) Luke Skywalker app.; Scalf-c 3.50

STAR WARS: JABBA THE HUTT
Dark Horse Comics: Apr, 1995 ($2.50, one-shots)
nn, ...The Betrayal, ...The Dynasty Trap, ...The Hunger of Princess Nampi 4.00

STAR WARS: JANGO FETT - OPEN SEASONS
Dark Horse Comics: Apr, 2002 - No. 4, July, 2002 ($2.99, limited series)
1-4: 1-Bachs & Fernandez-a 3.00

STAR WARS: JEDI
Dark Horse Comics: Feb, 2003 - Jun, 2004 ($4.99, one-shots)
... - Aayla Secura (8/03) Ostrander-s/Duursema-a 5.00
... - Count Dooku (11/03) Duursema-a 5.00
... - Mace Windu (2/03) Duursema-a 5.00

Star Wars: Legacy #39 © Lucasfilm

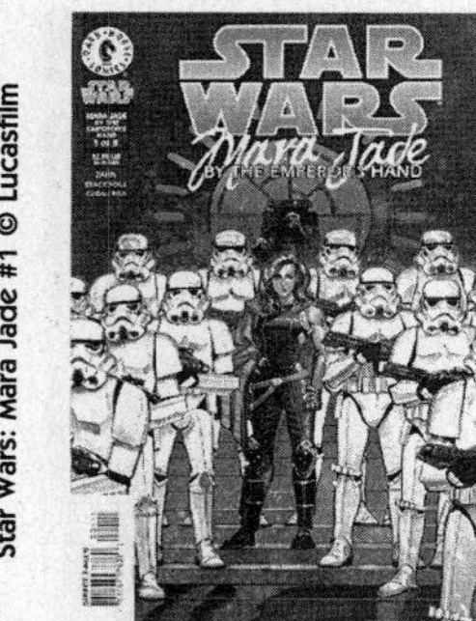

Star Wars: Mara Jade #1 © Lucasfilm

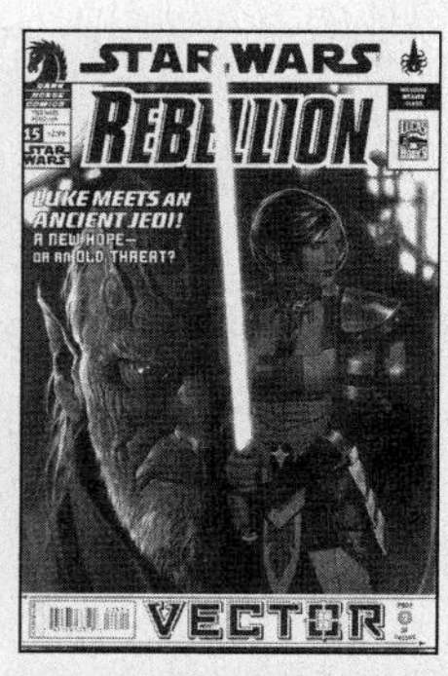

Star Wars: Rebellion #15 © Lucasfilm

GD	VG	FN	VF	VF/NM	NM-
2.0	4.0	6.0	8.0	9.0	9.2

... - Shaak Ti (5/03) Ostrander-s/Duursema-a 5.00
... - Yoda (6/04) Barlow-s/Hoon-a 5.00

STAR WARS: JEDI ACADEMY - LEVIATHAN
Dark Horse Comics: Oct, 1998 - No. 4, Jan, 1999 ($2.95, limited series)
1-4: 1-Lago-c. 2-4-Chadwick-c 4.00

STAR WARS: JEDI COUNCIL: ACTS OF WAR
Dark Horse Comics: Jun, 2000 - No. 4, Sept, 2000 ($2.95, limited series)
1-4-Stradley-s; set one year before Episode 1 3.00

STAR WARS: JEDI QUEST
Dark Horse Comics: Sept, 2001 - No. 4, Dec, 2001 ($2.99, limited series)
1-4-Anakin's Jedi training; Windham-s/Mhan-a 3.00

STAR WARS: JEDI - THE DARK SIDE
Dark Horse Comics: May, 2011 - No. 5, Sept, 2011 ($2.99, limited series)
1-5: 1-Qui-Gon Jinn 21 years befor Episode 1; Asrar-a 3.00

STAR WARS: JEDI VS. SITH
Dark Horse Comics: Apr, 2001 - No. 6, Sept, 2001 ($2.99, limited series)
1-6: Macan-s/Bachs-a/Robinson-c 3.00

STAR WARS: KNIGHT ERRANT
Dark Horse Comics: Oct, 2010 - No. 5, Feb, 2011 ($2.99)
1-5: 1-John Jackson Miller-s/Federico Dallocchio-a 3.00
... - Deluge 1-5 (8/11 - No. 5 12/11, $3.50) 1-Miller-s/Rodriguez-a/Quinones-c 3.50
... - Escape 1-5 (6/12 - No. 5 10/12, $3.50) 1-Miller-s/Castiello-a/Carré-c 3.50

STAR WARS: KNIGHTS OF THE OLD REPUBLIC
Dark Horse Comics: Jan, 2006 - No. 50, Feb, 2010 ($2.99)
1-50-Takes place 3,964 years before Episode IV. 1-6-Brian Ching-a/Travis Charest-c 3.00
... Handbook (11/07, $2.99) profiles of characters, ships, locales 3.00
.../Rebellion #0 (3/06, 25¢) flip book preview of both series 3.00
... - War 1-5 (1/12 - No. 5, 5/12, $3.50) J.J. Miller-s/Mutti-a 3.50
... Vol. 1 Commencement TPB (11/06, $18.95) r/#0-6 19.00
... Vol. 2 Flashpoint TPB (5/07, $18.95) r/#17-12 19.00
... Vol. 3 Days of Fear, Nights of Anger TPB (1/08, $18.95) r/#13-18 19.00

STAR WARS: LEGACY
Dark Horse Comics: No. 0, June, 2006 - No. 50, Aug, 2010 ($2.99)
Volume 2, Mar, 2013 - No. 18, Aug, 2014 ($2.99)
0-(25¢) Dossier of characters, settings, ships and weapons; Duursema-c 3.00
0 1/2-(1/08, $2.99) Updated dossier of characters, settings, ships, and history 3.00
1-50: 1-Takes place 130 years after Episode IV; Hughes-c/Duursema-a. 4-Duursema-c
7,39-Luke Skywalker on-c. 16-Obi-Wan Kenobi app. 50-Wraparound-c 3.00
...: Broken Vol. 1 TPB (4/07, $17.95) r/#1-3,5,6 18.00
...: One for One (9/10, $1.00) reprints #1 with red cover frame 3.00
... Volume Two 1 (3/13 - No. 18, 8/14, $2.99) 1-18: 1-Bechko-s/Hardman-a/Wilkins-c 3.00
... War 1-6 (12/10 - No. 6, 5/11, $3.50) 1-Ostrander-s/Duursema-a; Darth Krayt app. 3.50

STAR WARS: LOST TRIBE OF THE SITH - SPIRAL
Dark Horse Comics: Aug, 2012 - No. 5, Dec, 2012 ($2.99, limited series)
1-5-J.J. Miller-s/Mutti-a/Renaud-c 3.00

STAR WARS: MARA JADE
Dark Horse Comics: Aug, 1998 - No. 6, Jan, 1999 ($2.95, limited series)
1-6-Ezquerra-a 4.00

STAR WARS: OBSESSION (Clone Wars)
Dark Horse Comics: Nov, 2004 - No. 5, Apr, 2005 ($2.99, limited series)
1-5-Blackman-s/Ching-a/c; Anakin & Obi-Wan 5 months before Episode III 3.00
...: Clone Wars Vol. 7 (2005, $17.95) r/#1-5 and 2005 Free Comic Book Day edition 18.00

STAR WARS: PURGE
Dark Horse Comics: Dec, 2005 ($2.99, one-shot)
nn-Vader vs. remaining Jedi one month after Episode III; Hughes-c/Wheatley-a 5.00
... - Seconds To Die (11/09, $3.50) Vader app.; Charest-c/Ostrander-s 3.50
... - The Hidden Blade (4/10, $3.50) Vader app.; Scalf-c/a; Blackman-s 3.50
... - The Tyrant's Fist 1,2 (12/12 - No, 2, 1/13, $3.50) Vader app.; Freed-s/Dan Scott-c 3.50

STAR WARS: QUI-GON & OBI-WAN - LAST STAND ON ORD MANTELL
Dark Horse Comics: Dec, 2000 - No. 3, Mar, 2001 ($2.99, limited series)
1-3: 1-Three covers (photo, Tony Daniel, Bachs) Windham-s 3.00

STAR WARS: QUI-GON & OBI-WAN - THE AURORIENT EXPRESS
Dark Horse Comics: Feb, 2002 - No. 2, Mar, 2002 ($2.99, limited series)
1,2-Six years prior to Phantom Menace; Marangon-a 3.00

STAR WARS: REBEL HEIST
Dark Horse Comics: Apr, 2014 - No. 4, Jul, 2014 ($3.50)
1-4-Kindt-s/Castiello-a; two covers by Kindt and Adam Hughes on each 3.50

STAR WARS: REBELLION (Also see Star Wars: Knights of the Old Republic flip book)
Dark Horse Comics: Apr, 2006 - No. 16, Aug, 2008 ($2.99)
1-16-Takes place 9 months after Episode IV; Luke Skywalker app. 1-Badeaux-a/c 3.00
Vol. 1 TPB (2/07, $14.95) r/#0 (flip book) & #1-5 15.00

STAR WARS: REPUBLIC (Formerly Star Wars monthly series)
Dark Horse Comics: No. 46, Sept, 2002 - No. 83, Feb, 2006 ($2.99)
46-83-Events of the Clone Wars 3.00
...: Clone Wars Vol. 1 (2003, $14.95) r/#46-50 15.00
...: Clone Wars Vol. 2 (2003, $14.95) r/#51-53 & Star Wars: Jedi - Shaak Ti 15.00
...: Clone Wars Vol. 3 (2004, $14.95) r/#55-59 15.00
...: Clone Wars Vol. 4 (2004, $16.95) r/#54, 63 & Star Wars: Jedi - Aayla Secura & Dooku 17.00
...: Clone Wars Vol. 5 (2004, $17.95) r/#60-62, 64 & Star Wars: Jedi - Yoda 18.00
...: Clone Wars Vol. 6 (2005, $17.95) r/#65-71 18.00
(Clone Wars Vol. 7 - see Star Wars: Obsession)
...: Clone Wars Vol. 8 (2006, $17.95) r/#72-78 18.00
...: Clone Wars Vol. 9 (2006, $17.95) r/#79-83 & Star Wars: Purge 18.00
...: Honor and Duty TPB (5/06, $12.95) r/#46-48,78 13.00

STAR WARS: RETURN OF THE JEDI (Movie)
Marvel Comics Group: Oct, 1983 - No. 4, Jan, 1984 (limited series)

	GD	VG	FN	VF	VF/NM	NM-
1-Williamson-p in all; r/Marvel Super Special #27	2	4	6	11	16	20
2-4-Continues r/Marvel Super Special #27	2	4	6	9	12	15
Oversized issue (1983, $2.95, 10-3/4x8-1/4", 68 pgs., cardboard-c)-r/#1-4	2	4	6	10	13	16

STAR WARS: RIVER OF CHAOS
Dark Horse Comics: June, 1995 - No. 4, Sept, 1995 ($2.95, limited series)
1-4: Louise Simonson scripts 4.00

STAR WARS: SHADOWS OF THE EMPIRE
Dark Horse Comics: May, 1996 - No. 6, Oct, 1996 ($2.95, limited series)
1-6: Story details events between The Empire Strikes Back & Return of the Jedi; Russell-a(i). 4.00

STAR WARS: SHADOWS OF THE EMPIRE - EVOLUTION
Dark Horse Comics: Feb, 1998 - No. 5, June, 1998 ($2.95, limited series)
1-5: Perry-s/Fegredo-c. 4.00

STAR WARS: SHADOW STALKER
Dark Horse Comics: Sept, 1997 ($2.95, one-shot)
nn-Windham-a. 4.00

STAR WARS: SPLINTER OF THE MIND'S EYE
Dark Horse Comics: Dec, 1995 - No. 4, June, 1996 ($2.50, limited series)
1-4: Adaption of Alan Dean Foster novel 4.00

STAR WARS: STARFIGHTER
Dark Horse Comics: Jan, 2002 - No. 3, March, 2002 ($2.99, limited series)
1-3-Williams & Gray-c 3.00

STAR WARS: TAG & BINK ARE DEAD
Dark Horse Comics: Oct, 2001 - No. 2, Nov, 2001($2.99, limited series)
1,2-Rubio-s 3.00
Star Wars: Tag & Bink Were Here TPB (11/06, $14.95) r/both SW: Tag & Bink series 15.00

STAR WARS: TAG & BINK II
Dark Horse Comics: Mar, 2006 - No. 2, Apr, 2006($2.99, limited series)
1-Tag & Bink invade Return of the Jedi; Rubio-s. 2-Tag & Bink as Jedi younglings
during Ep II 3.00

STAR WARS TALES
Dark Horse Comics: Sept, 1999 - No. 24, Jun, 2005 ($4.95/$5.95/$5.99, anthology)
1-4-Short stories by various 6.00
5-24 ($5.95/$5.99-c) Art and photo-c on each 6.00
Volume 1-6 ($19.95) 1-(1/02) r/#1-4. 2-('02) r/#5-8. 3-(1/03) r/#9-12. 4-(1/04) r/#13-16
5-(1/05) r/#17-20; introduction pages from #1-20. 6-(1/06) r/#21-24 20.00

STAR WARS: TALES FROM MOS EISLEY
Dark Horse Comics: Mar, 1996 ($2.95, one-shot)
nn-Bret Blevins-a. 4.00

STAR WARS: TALES OF THE JEDI (See Dark Horse Comics #7)
Dark Horse Comics: Oct, 1993 - No. 5, Feb, 1994 ($2.50, limited series)
1-5: All have Dave Dorman painted-c. 3-r/Dark Horse Comics #7-9 w/new coloring & some
panels redrawn 5.00

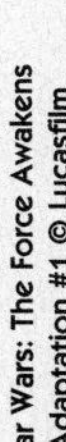
Star Wars: The Force Awakens Adaptation #1 © Lucasfilm

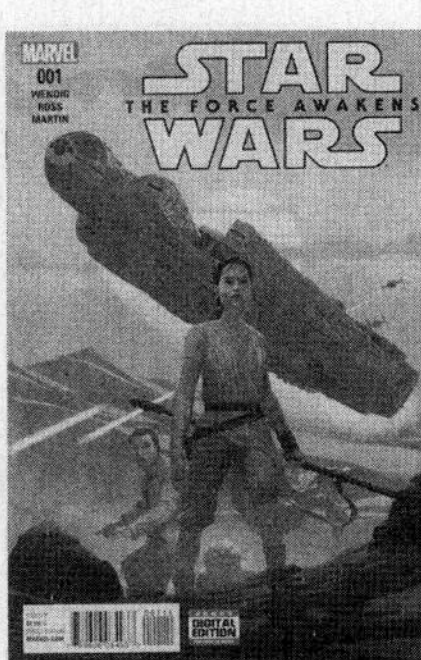

Star Wars: Vader's Quest #1 © Lucasfilm

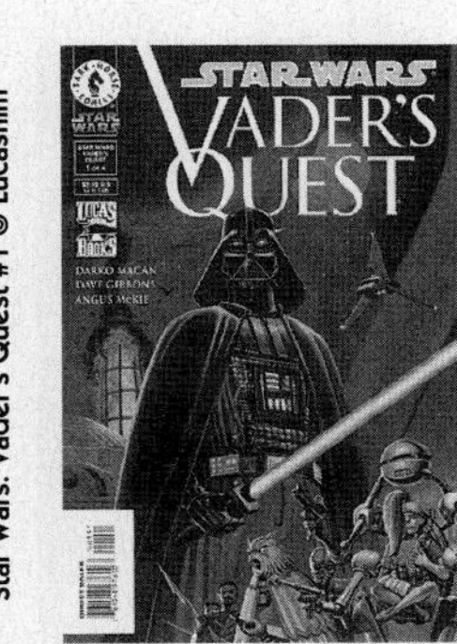

Steampunk #6 © Kelly & Bachalo

GD 2.0 | VG 4.0 | FN 6.0 | VF 8.0 | VF/NM 9.0 | NM- 9.2

GD 2.0 | VG 4.0 | FN 6.0 | VF 8.0 | VF/NM 9.0 | NM- 9.2

1-5-Gold foil embossed logo; limited # printed-7500 (set) 50.00
Star Wars Omnibus: Tales of the Jedi Volume One TPB (11/07, $24.95) r/#1-5, ... - The Golden Age of the Sith #0-5 and ... - The Fall of the Sith Empire #1-5 25.00

STAR WARS: TALES OF THE JEDI-DARK LORDS OF THE SITH
Dark Horse Comics: Oct, 1994 - No. 6, Mar, 1995 ($2.50, limited series)
1-6: 1-Polybagged w/trading card 4.00

STAR WARS: TALES OF THE JEDI-REDEMPTION
Dark Horse Comics: July, 1998 - No. 5, Nov, 1998 ($2.95, limited series)
1-5: 1-Kevin J. Anderson-s/Kordey-c 4.00

STAR WARS: TALES OF THE JEDI-THE FALL OF THE SITH EMPIRE
Dark Horse Comics: June, 1997 - No. 5, Oct, 1997 ($2.95, limited series)
1-5 4.00

STAR WARS: TALES OF THE JEDI-THE FREEDON NADD UPRISING
Dark Horse Comics: Aug, 1994 - No. 2, Nov, 1994 ($2.50, limited series)
1,2 4.00

STAR WARS: TALES OF THE JEDI-THE GOLDEN AGE OF THE SITH
Dark Horse Comics: July, 1996 - No. 5, Feb, 1997 (99¢/$2.95, limited series)
0-(99¢)-Anderson-s 3.00
1-5-Anderson-s 4.00

STAR WARS: TALES OF THE JEDI-THE SITH WAR
Dark Horse Comics: Aug, 1995 - No. 6, Jan, 1996 ($2.50, limited series)
1-6: Anderson scripts 4.00

STAR WARS: THE BOUNTY HUNTERS
Dark Horse Comics: July, 1999 - Oct, 1999 ($2.95, one-shots)
...Aurra Sing (7/99), ...Kenix Kil (10/99), ...Scoundrel's Wages (8/99) Lando Calrissian app. 4.00

STAR WARS: THE CLONE WARS (Based on the Cartoon Network series)
Dark Horse Comics: Sept, 2008 - No. 12, Jan, 2010 ($2.99)
1-12: 1-6-Gilroy-s/Hepburn-a/Filoni-c 3.00

STAR WARS: THE FORCE AWAKENS ADAPTATION (Episode VII movie)
Marvel Comics: Aug, 2016 - No. 6, Jan, 2017 ($4.99, limited series)
1-6: 1-Chuck Wendig-s/Luke Ross-a/Esad Ribic-c. 3-Marc Laming-a 5.00

STAR WARS: THE FORCE UNLEASHED (Based on the LucasArts video game)
Dark Horse Comics: Aug, 2008 ($15.95, one-shot graphic novel)
GN-Intro. Starkiller, Vader's apprentice; takes place 2 years before Battle of Yavin 16.00

STAR WARS: THE JABBA TAPE
Dark Horse Comics: Dec, 1998 ($2.95, one-shot)
nn-Wagner-s/Plunkett-a 4.00

STAR WARS: THE LAST COMMAND
Dark Horse Comics: Nov, 1997 - No. 6, July, 1998 ($2.95, limited series)
1-6: Based on the Timothy Zaun novel 4.00

STAR WARS: THE OLD REPUBLIC (Based on the video game)
Dark Horse Comics: July, 2010 - No. 6, Dec, 2010 ($2.99, limited series)
1-3 (Threat of Peace)-Chestny-s/Sanchez-a. 1-Two covers 3.00
4-6 (Blood of the Empire)-Freed-s/Dave Ross-a 3.00

STAR WARS: THE OLD REPUBLIC - THE LOST SUNS (Based on the video game)
Dark Horse Comics: Jun, 2011 - No. 5, Oct, 2011 ($3.50, limited series)
1-5-Freed-s/Carré-c/Freeman-a 3.50

STAR WARS: THE PROTOCOL OFFENSIVE
Dark Horse Comics: Sept, 1997 ($4.95, one-shot)
nn-Anthony Daniels & Ryder Windham-s 5.00

STAR WARS: UNDERWORLD - THE YAVIN VASSILIKA
Dark Horse Comics: Dec, 2000 - No. 5, June, 2001 ($2.99, limited series)
1-5-(Photo and Robinson covers) 3.00

STAR WARS: UNION
Dark Horse Comics: Nov, 1999 - No. 4, Feb, 2000 ($2.95, limited series)
1-4-Wedding of Luke and Mara Jade; Teranishi-a/Stackpole-s 4.00

STAR WARS: VADER DOWN
Marvel Comics: Jan, 2016 ($4.99, one-shot)
1-Part 1 of x-over with Star Wars (2015) #13,14 and Darth Vader #13-15; Deodato-a 5.00

STAR WARS: VADER'S QUEST
Dark Horse Comics: Feb, 1999 - No. 4, May, 1999 ($2.95, limited series)
1-4-Follows destruction of 1st Death Star; Gibbons-a 4.00

STAR WARS: VISIONARIES
Dark Horse Comics: Apr, 2005 ($17.95, TPB)
nn-Short stories from the concept artists for Revenge of the Sith movie 18.00

STAR WARS: X-WING ROGUE SQUADRON (Star Wars: X-Wing Rogue Squadron-The Phantom Affair #5-8 appears on cover only)
Dark Horse Comics: July, 1995 - No. 35, Nov, 1998 ($2.95)
1/2 8.00
1-24,26-35: 1-4-Baron scripts. 5-20-Stackpole scripts 4.00
25-($3.95) 5.00
The Phantom Affair TPB ($12.95) r/#5-8 13.00

STAR WARS: X-WING ROGUE SQUADRON: ROGUE LEADER
Dark Horse Comics: Sept, 2005 - No. 3, Nov, 2005 ($2.99)
1-3-Takes place one week after the Batttle of Endor 3.00

STATIC (See Charlton Action: Featuring "Static")

STATIC (See Heroes)
DC Comics (Milestone): June, 1993 - No. 45, Mar, 1997 ($1.50/$1.75/$2.50)
1-($2.95)-Collector's Edition; polybagged w/poster & trading card & backing board (direct sales only) 4.00
1-Platinum Edition with red background cover 6.00
1-13,15-24,26-45: 2-Origin. 8-Shadow War; Simonson silver ink-c. 27-Kent Williams-c 3.00
14-($2.50, 52 pgs.)-Worlds Collide Pt. 14 4.00
25 ($3.95) 4.00
...: Trial by Fire (2000, $9.95) r/#1-4; Leon-c 10.00

STATIC SHOCK (DC New 52)
DC Comics: Nov, 2011 - No. 8, Jun, 2012 ($2.99)
1-8: 1-McDaniel & Rozum-s/McDaniel-a/c. 6-Hardware & Technique app. 8-Origin retold 3.00

STATIC SHOCK!: REBIRTH OF THE COOL (TV)
DC Comics: Jan, 2001 - No. 4, Sept, 2001 ($2.50, limited series)
1-4: McDuffie-s/Leon-c/a 3.00

STATIC SHOCK SPECIAL
DC Comics: Aug, 2011 ($2.99, one-shot)
1-Cowan-a/Williams III-c; pin-ups by various; tribute to Dwayne McDuffie 3.00

STATIC-X
Chaos! Comics: Aug, 2002 ($5.99)
1-Polybagged with music CD; metal band as super-heroes; Pulido-s 6.00

STEALTH (Pilot Season: ...)
Image Comics (Top Cow): May, 2010 ($2.99)
1-Kirkman-s/Mitchell-a/Silvestri-c 3.00

STEAM MAN, THE
Dark Horse Comics: Oct, 2015 - No. 5, Feb, 2016 ($3.99)
1-5-Kowalski-a; Steam robot and crew in 1899 4.00

STEAMPUNK
DC/WildStorm (Cliffhanger): Apr, 2000 - No. 12, Aug, 2002 ($2.50/$3.50)
Catechism (1/00) Prologue -Kelly-s/Bachalo-a 3.00
1-4,6-11: 4-Four covers by Bachalo, Madureira, Ramos, Campbell 3.00
5,12-($3.50) 4.00
...: Drama Obscura ('03, $14.95) r/#6-12 15.00
...: Manimatron ('01, $14.95) r/#1-5, Catechism, Idiosincratica 15.00

STEAMPUNK BATTLESTAR GALACTICA 1880 (See Battlestar Galactica 1880)

STEED AND MRS. PEEL (TV)(Also see The Avengers)
Eclipse Books/ ACME Press: 1990 - No. 3, 1991 ($4.95, limited series)
Books One - Three: Grant Morrison scripts/Ian Gibson-a 5.00
1-6: 1-(BOOM! Studios, 1/12 - No. 6, 6/12, $3.99) r/Books One - Three 4.00

STEED AND MRS. PEEL (TV)(The Avengers)
BOOM! Studios: No. 0, Aug, 2012 - No. 11, Jul, 2013 ($3.99)
0-11: 0-Mark Waid-s/Steve Bryant-a; eight covers. 1-3-Sliney-a; five covers 4.00

STEED AND MRS. PEEL: WE'RE NEEDED (TV)(The Avengers)
BOOM! Studios: Jul, 2014 - No. 3, Sept, 2014 ($3.99)(Issue #1 says "1 of 6")
1-3-Edginton-s/Cosentino-a. 1-Two covers 4.00

STEEL (Also see JLA)
DC Comics: Feb, 1994 - No. 52, July, 1998 ($1.50/$1.95/$2.50)
1-8,0,9-52: 1-From Reign of the Supermen storyline. 6,7-Worlds Collide Pt. 5 &12. 8-(9/94). 0-(10/94). 9-(11/94). 46-Superboy-c/app. 50-Millennium Giants x-over 3.00
1-(3/11, $2.99, one-shot) Benes-a/Garner-c; Reign of Doomsday x-over 4.00

Steve Canyon Comics #5 © HARV

Steven Universe #7 © Cartoon Network

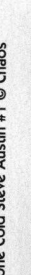

Stone Cold Steve Austin #1 © Chaos

	GD 2.0	VG 4.0	FN 6.0	VF 8.0	VF/NM 9.0	NM- 9.2

Annual 1 (1994, $2.95)-Elseworlds story 4.00
Annual 2 (1995, $3.95)-Year One story 4.00
...Forging of a Hero TPB (1997, $19.95) reprints early app. 20.00

STEEL: THE OFFICIAL COMIC ADAPTION OF THE WARNER BROS. MOTION PICTURE
DC Comics: 1997 ($4.95, Prestige format, one-shot)
nn-Movie adaption; Bogdanove & Giordano-a 5.00

STEELGRIP STARKEY
Marvel Comics (Epic): June, 1986 - No. 6, July, 1987 ($1.50, lim. series, Baxter paper)
1-6 3.00

STEEL STERLING (Formerly Shield-Steel Sterling; see Blue Ribbon, Jackpot, Mighty Comics, Mighty Crusaders, Roly Poly & Zip Comics)
Archie Enterprises, Inc.: No. 4, Jan, 1984 - No. 7, July, 1984
4-7: 4-6-Kanigher-s; Barreto-a. 5,6-Infantino-a. 6-McWilliams-a 5.00

STEEL, THE INDESTRUCTIBLE MAN (See All-Star Squadron #8 and J.L. of A. Annual #2)
DC Comics: Mar, 1978 - No. 5, Oct-Nov, 1978

	GD	VG	FN	VF	VF/NM	NM-
1	2	4	6	8	11	14
2-5: 5-44 pgs.	1	2	3	4	6	8

STEELTOWN ROCKERS
Marvel Comics: Apr, 1990 - No. 6, Sept, 1990 ($1.00, limited series)
1-6: Small town teens form rock band 3.00

STEPHEN COLBERT'S TEK JANSEN (From the animated shorts on The Colbert Report)
Oni Press: July, 2007 - No. 5, Jan, 2009 ($3.99, limited series)
1-Chantier-a/Layman & Peyer-s; back-up story by Massey-s/Rodriguez-a; Chantier-c 4.00
1-Variant-c by John Cassaday 6.00
1-Second printing with flip book of Cassaday & Chantier covers 4.00
2-5: 2-(6/08) Flip book with covers by Rodriguez & Wagner. 3-Flip-c by Darwyn Cooke 4.00

STEPHEN KING'S N. THE COMIC SERIES
Marvel Comics: May, 2010 - No. 4, Aug, 2010 ($3.99, limited series)
1-4-Guggenheim-s/Maleev-a/c 4.00

STEVE AUSTIN (See Stone Cold Steve Austin)

STEVE CANYON (See Harvey Comics Hits #52)
Dell Publishing Co.: No. 519, 11/53 - No. No. 1033, 9/59 (All Milton Caniff-a except #519, 939, 1033)

	GD	VG	FN	VF	VF/NM	NM-
Four Color 519 (1, '53)	8	16	24	54	102	150
Four Color 578 (8/54), 641 (7/55), 737 (10/56), 804 (5/57), 939 (10/58), 1033 (9/59) (photo-c)	5	10	15	35	63	90

STEVE CANYON
Grosset & Dunlap: 1959 (6-3/4x9", 96 pgs., B&W, no text, hardcover)

	GD	VG	FN	VF	VF/NM	NM-
100100-Reprints 2 stories from strip (1953, 1957)	6	12	18	31	38	45
100100 (softcover edition)	5	10	15	24	30	35

STEVE CANYON COMICS
Harvey Publ.: Feb, 1948 - No. 6, Dec, 1948 (Strip reprints, No. 4,5: 52pgs.)

	GD	VG	FN	VF	VF/NM	NM-
1-Origin; has biography of Milton Caniff; Powell-a, 2 pgs.; Caniff-a	20	40	60	120	195	270
2-Caniff, Powell-a in #2-6	14	28	42	80	115	150
3-6: 6-Intro Madame Lynx-c/story	14	28	42	76	108	140

STEVE CANYON IN 3-D
Kitchen Sink Press: June, 1986 ($2.25, one-shot)
1-Contains unpublished story from 1954 5.00

STEVE DITKO'S STRANGE AVENGING TALES
Fantagraphics Books: Feb, 1997 ($2.95, B&W)
1-Ditko-c/s/a 5.00

STEVE DONOVAN, WESTERN MARSHAL (TV)
Dell Publishing Co.: No. 675, Feb, 1956 - No. 880, Feb, 1958 (All photo-c)

	GD	VG	FN	VF	VF/NM	NM-
Four Color 675-Kinstler-a	7	14	21	48	89	130
Four Color 768-Kinstler-a	6	12	18	38	69	100
Four Color 880	5	10	15	31	53	75

STEVEN UNIVERSE (TV)
BOOM! Studios (kaBOOM): Aug, 2014 - No. 8, Mar, 2015 ($3.99)
1-8: 1-Four covers; Uncle Grandpa preview. 2-8-Three covers 4.00
...: Greg Universe Special 1 (4/15, $4.99) Short stories by various; two covers 5.00
...: 2016 Special 1 (12/16, $7.99) Short donut-themed stories by various; two covers 8.00

STEVEN UNIVERSE (Ongoing)(TV)
BOOM! Studios (kaBOOM): Feb, 2017 - Present ($3.99)
1-Four covers; Lapis & Peridot app. 4.00

STEVEN UNIVERSE AND THE CRYSTAL GEMS (TV)
BOOM! Studios (kaBOOM): Mar, 2016 - No. 4, Jun, 2016 ($3.99)
1-4-Fenton-s/Garland-a; multiple covers on each. 1-Preview of Over the Garden Wall 4.00

STEVE ROGERS: SUPER-SOLDIER (Captain America - The Heroic Age)
Marvel Comics: Sept, 2010 - No. 4, Dec, 2010 ($3.99, limited series)
1-4-Brubaker-s/Eaglesham-a/Pacheco-c. 1-Back-up rep. of origin from CA #1 ('41) 4.00
Annual 1 (6/11, $3.99) Continued from Uncanny X-Men Annual #3; Roberson-a 4.00

STEVE ROPER
Famous Funnies: Apr, 1948 - No. 5, Dec, 1948

	GD	VG	FN	VF	VF/NM	NM-
1-Contains 1944 daily newspaper-r	13	26	39	72	101	130
2	9	18	27	47	61	75
3-5	8	16	24	40	50	60

STEVE SAUNDERS SPECIAL AGENT (See Special Agent)

STEVE SAVAGE (See Captain...)

STEVE ZODIAC & THE FIRE BALL XL-5 (TV)
Gold Key: Jan, 1964

	GD	VG	FN	VF	VF/NM	NM-
10108-401 (#1)	7	14	21	44	82	120

STEVIE (Mazie's boy friend)(Also see Flat-Top, Mazie & Mortie)
Mazie (Magazine Publ.): Nov, 1952 - No. 6, Apr, 1954

	GD	VG	FN	VF	VF/NM	NM-
1-Teenage humor; Stevie, Mortie & Mazie begin	10	20	30	58	79	100
2-6	7	14	21	35	43	50

STEVIE MAZIE'S BOY FRIEND (See Harvey Hits #5)

STEWART THE RAT (See Eclipse Graphic Album Series)

ST. GEORGE (See listing under Saint...)

STIG'S INFERNO
Vortex/Eclipse: 1985 - No. 7, Mar, 1987 ($1.95, B&W)
1-7 ($1.95) 3.00
Graphic Album (1988, $6.95, B&W, 100 pgs.) 7.00

STING OF THE GREEN HORNET (See The Green Hornet)
Now Comics: June, 1992 - No. 4, 1992 ($2.50, limited series)
1-4: Butler-c/a 3.00
1-4 ($2.75)-Collectors Ed.; polybagged w/poster 4.00

STOKER'S DRACULA (Reprints unfinished Dracula story from 1974-75 with new ending)
Marvel Comics: 2004 - No. 4, May, 2005 ($3.99, B&W)
1-4: 1-Reprints from Dracula Lives! #5-8; Roy Thomas-s/Dick Giordano-a. 2-R/#10,11 & Legion of Monsters #1. 3,4-New story/artwork to finish story. 4-Giordano afterword 4.00
HC (2005, $24.99) r/#1-4; foreward by Thomas; Giordano afterword; bonus art & covers 25.00

STONE
Avalon Studios: Aug, 1998 - No. 4, Apr, 1999 ($2.50, limited series)
1-4-Portacio-a/Haberlin-s 3.00
1-Alternate-c 5.00
2-($14.95) DF Stonechrome Edition 15.00

STONE (Volume 2)
Avalon Studios: Aug, 1999 - No. 4, May, 2000 ($2.50)
1-4-Portacio-a/Haberlin-s 3.00
1-Chrome-c 5.00

STONE COLD STEVE AUSTIN (WWF Wrestling)
Chaos! Comics: Oct, 1999 - No. 4, Feb, 2000 ($2.95)
1-4-Reg. & photo-c; Steven Grant-s 3.00
1-Premium Ed. ($10.00) 10.00
Preview ($5.00) 5.00

STONE PROTECTORS
Harvey Pubications: May, 1994 - No. 3, Sept, 1994
nn (1993, giveaway)(limited distribution, scarce) 6.00
1-3-Ace Novelty action figures 4.00

STONEY BURKE (TV Western)
Dell Publishing Co.: June-Aug, 1963 - No. 2, Sept-Nov, 1963

	GD	VG	FN	VF	VF/NM	NM-
1,2-Jack Lord photo-c on both	3	6	9	16	24	32

STONY CRAIG
Pentagon Publishing Co.: 1946 (No #)
nn-Reprints Bell Syndicate's "Sgt. Stony Craig" newspaper strips

Storming Paradise #1 © Dixon & Guice

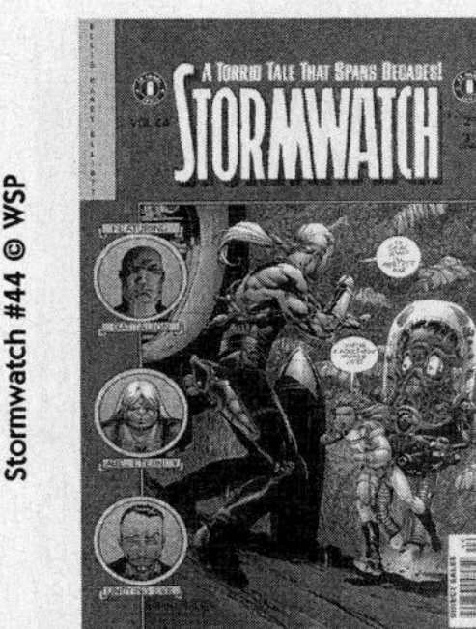

Stormwatch #44 © WSP

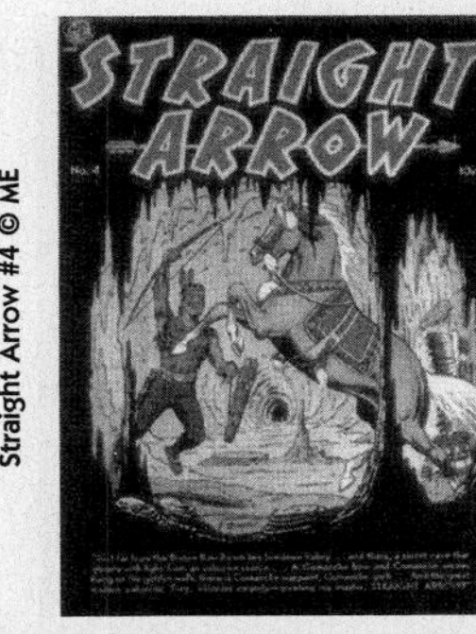

Straight Arrow #4 © ME

GD VG FN VF VF/NM NM-
2.0 4.0 6.0 8.0 9.0 9.2

8 16 24 40 50 60

STORIES BY FAMOUS AUTHORS ILLUSTRATED (Fast Fiction #1-5)
Seaboard Publ./Famous Authors Ill.: No. 6, Aug, 1950 - No. 13, Mar, 1951
1-Scarlet Pimpernel-Baroness Orczy 27 54 81 160 263 365
2-Capt. Blood-Raphael Sabatini 26 52 78 154 252 350
3-She, by Haggard 30 60 90 177 289 400
4-The 39 Steps-John Buchan 18 36 54 107 169 230
5-Beau Geste-P. C. Wren 18 36 54 107 169 230
NOTE: *The above five issues are exact reprints of Fast Fiction #1-5 except for the title change and new Kiefer covers on #1 and 2. Kiefer c(r)-3-5. The above 5 issues were released before Famous Authors #6.*
6-Macbeth, by Shakespeare; Kiefer art (8/50); used in **SOTI**, pg. 22,143;
Kiefer-c; 36 pgs. 24 48 72 142 234 325
7-The Window; Kiefer-c/a; 52 pgs. 18 36 54 107 169 230
8-Hamlet, by Shakespeare; Kiefer-c/a; 36 pgs. 21 42 63 126 206 285
9,10: 9-Nicholas Nickleby, by Dickens; G. Schrotter-a; 52 pgs. 10-Romeo & Juliet,
by Shakespeare; Kiefer-c/a; 36 pgs. 18 36 54 107 169 230
11-13: 11-Ben-Hur; Schrotter-a; 52 pgs. 12-La Svengali; Schrotter-a; 36 pgs.
13-Scaramouche; Kiefer-c/a; 36 pgs. 18 36 54 103 162 220
NOTE: *Artwork was prepared/advertised for #14, The Red Badge Of Courage. Gilberton bought out Famous Authors, Ltd. and used that story as C.I. #98. Famous Authors, Ltd. then published the Classics Junior series. The Famous Authors titles were published as part of the regular Classics Ill. Series in Brazil starting in 1952.*

STORIES FROM THE TWILIGHT ZONE
Skylark Pub: Mar, 1979, 68 pgs. (B&W comic digest, 5-1/4x7-5/8")
15405-2: Pfevfer-a, 56 pgs, new comics 3 6 9 17 26 35

STORIES OF ROMANCE (Formerly Meet Miss Bliss)
Atlas Comics (LMC): No. 5, Mar, 1956 - No. 13, Aug, 1957
5-Baker-a? 16 32 48 94 147 200
6-10,12,13 12 24 36 67 94 120
11-Baker, Romita-a; Colletta-c/a 16 32 48 94 147 200
NOTE: ***Ann Brewster** a-13. **Colletta** a-9(2), 11; c-5, 11.*

STORM (X-Men)
Marvel Comics: Feb, 1996 - No. 4, May, 1996 ($2.95, limited series)
1-4-Foil-c; Dodson-a(p); Ellis-s: 2-4-Callisto app. 4.00

STORM (X-Men)
Marvel Comics: Apr, 2006 - No. 6, Sept, 2006 ($2.99, limited series)
1-6: Ororo and T'Challa meet as teens; Eric Jerome Dickey-s 3.00
HC (2007, $19.99, dustjacket) r/#1-6 20.00
SC (2008, $14.99) r/#1-6 15.00

STORM (X-Men)
Marvel Comics: Sept, 2014 - No. 11, Jul, 2015 ($3.99)
1-11: 1-Greg Pak-s/Victor Ibañez-a. 9-Gambit app. 4.00

STORMBREAKER: THE SAGA OF BETA RAY BILL (Also see Thor)
Marvel Comics: Mar, 2005 - No. 6, Aug, 2005 ($2.99, limited series)
1-6-Oeming & Berman-s/DiVito-a; Galactus app. 6-Spider-Man app. 3.00
TPB (2006, $16.99) r/#1-6 17.00

STORMING PARADISE
DC Comics (WildStorm): Sept, 2008 - No. 6, Aug, 2009 ($2.99, limited series)
1-6-WWII invasion of Japan; Dixon-s/Guice-a/c 3.00
TPB (2009, $19.99) r/#1-6 20.00

STORM SHADOW (G.I. Joe character)
Devil's Due Publishing: May, 2007 - No. 7, Nov, 2007 ($3.50)
1-7-Larry Hama-s 3.50

STORMWATCH (Also see The Authority)
Image Comics (WildStorm Prod.): May, 1993 - No. 50, Jul, 1997 ($1.95/$2.50)
1-8,0,9-36: 1-Intro StormWatch (Battalion, Diva, Winter, Fuji, & Hellstrike); 1st app. Weatherman; Jim Lee-c & part scripts; Lee plots in all. 1-Gold edition.1-3-Includes coupon for limited edition StormWatch trading card #00 by Lee. 3-1st brief app. Backlash. 0-($2.50)-Polybagged w/card; 1st full app. Backlash. 9-(4/94, $2.50)-Intro Defile. 10-(6/94),11,12-Both (8/94). 13,14-(9/94). 15-(10/94). 21-Reads #1 on-c. 22-Direct Market; Wildstorm Rising Pt. 9, bound-in card. 23-Spartan joins team. 25-(6/94, June 1995 on-c, $2.50). 35-Fire From Heaven Pt. 5. 36-Fire From Heaven Pt. 12 3.00
10-Alternate Portacio-c, see Deathblow #5 3.00
22-($1.95)-Newsstand, Wildstorm Rising Pt. 9 3.00
37-(7/96, $3.50, 38 pgs.)-Weatherman forms new team; 1st app. Jenny Sparks, Jack Hawksmoor & Rose Tattoo; Warren Ellis scripts begin; Justice League #1-c/swipe 4.00
38-49: 44-Three covers. 3.00
50-($4.50) 4.50
Special 1 ,2(1/94, 5/95, $3.50, 52 pgs.) 4.00
Sourcebook 1 (1/94, $2.50) 3.00

GD VG FN VF VF/NM NM-
2.0 4.0 6.0 8.0 9.0 9.2

STORMWATCH (Also see The Authority)
Image Comics (WildStorm): Oct, 1997 - No. 11, Sept, 1998 ($2.50)
1-Ellis-s/Jimenez-a(p); two covers by Bennett 3.00
1-($3.50)-Voyager Pack bagged w/Gen 13 preview 4.00
2-4: 4-1st app. Midnighter and Apollo 3.00
5-11: 7,8-Freefall app. 9-Gen13 & DV8 app. 3.00
A Finer World ('99, $14.95, TPB) r/V2 #4-9 15.00
Change or Die ('99, $14.95, TPB) r/V1 #48-50 & V2 #1-3 15.00
Final Orbit ('01, $9.95, TPB) r/V2 #10,11 & WildC.A.T.S./Aliens; Hitch-c 10.00

STORMWATCH (DC New 52)
DC Comics: Nov, 2011 - No. 30, Jun, 2014 ($2.99)
1-Cornell-s/Sepulveda-a; Martian Manhunter app.; blue bkgrd cover 4.00
1-(2nd printing, cover has red bkgrd), 2-8: 7,8-Jenkins-s. 12-Martian Manhunter leaves 3.00
13-30: 13,14-Etrigan returns. 18-Team re-booted; Starlin-s/c. 20-Lobo origin 3.00
#0-(11/12, $2.99) Flashback to Demon Knights; Milligan-s/Conrad-a 3.00

STORMWATCH: P.H.D. (Post Human Division)
DC Comics (WildStorm): Jan, 2007 - No. 24, Jan, 2010 ($2.99)
1-24: 1-Two covers by Mahnke & Hairsine; Gage-s/Mahnke-a. 2-Var-c by Dell'Otto 3.00
...: Armageddon 1 (2/08, $2.99) Gage-s/Fernández-a/McKone-c 3.00
TPB (2007, $17.99) r/#1-4,6,7 & story from Worldstorm #1 18.00
... Book Two TPB (2008, $17.99) r/#5,8-12; sketch pages and concept art 18.00
... Book Three TPB (2009, $17.99) r/#13-19 18.00

STORMWATCH: TEAM ACHILLES
DC Comics (WildStorm): Sept, 2002 - No. 23, Aug, 2004 ($2.95)
1-8: 1-Two covers by Portacio; Portacio-a/Wright-s. 5,6-The Authority app. 3.00
9-23: 9-Back-up preview of The Authority: High Stakes pt. 1 3.00
TPB (2003, $14.95) r/Wizard Preview and #1-6; Portacio art pages 15.00
Book 2 (2004, $14.95) r/#7-11 & short story from Eye of the Storm Annual 15.00

STORMY (Disney) (Movie)
Dell Publishing Co.: No. 537, Feb, 1954
Four Color 537 (...the Thoroughbred)-on top 2/3 of each page; Pluto story on bottom 1/3
5 10 15 33 57 80

STORY OF JESUS (See Classics Illustrated Special Issue)

STORY OF MANKIND, THE (Movie)
Dell Publishing Co.: No. 851, Jan, 1958
Four Color 851-Vincent Price/Hedy Lamarr photo-c 7 14 21 44 82 120

STORY OF MARTHA WAYNE, THE
Argo Publ.: April, 1956
1-Newspaper strip-r 6 12 18 31 38 45

STORY OF RUTH, THE
Dell Publishing Co.: No. 1144, Nov-Jan, 1961 (Movie)
Four Color 1144-Photo-c 8 16 24 54 102 150

STORY OF THE COMMANDOS, THE (Combined Operations)
Long Island Independent: 1943 (15¢, B&W, 68 pgs.) (Distr. by Gilberton)
nn-All text (no comics); photos & illustrations; ad for Classic Comics on back cover (Rare)
41 82 123 256 428 600

STORY OF THE GLOOMY BUNNY, THE (See March of Comics #9)

STORYTELLER, THE: GIANTS (Also see Jim Henson's The Storyteller)
BOOM! Studios (Archaia): Dec, 2016 - No. 4 ($3.99, limited series)
1-3: 1-Conor Nolan-s/a. 2-Brandon Dayton-s/a. 3-Jared Cullum-s/a 4.00

STRAIGHT ARROW (Radio)(See Best of the West & Great Western)
Magazine Enterprises: Feb-Mar, 1950 - No. 55, Mar, 1956 (All 36 pgs.)
1-Straight Arrow (alias Steve Adams) & his palomino Fury begin; 1st mention of Sundown Valley & the Secret Cave 47 94 141 296 498 700
2-Red Hawk begins (1st app?) by Powell (origin), ends #55
23 46 69 136 223 310
3-Frazetta-c 31 62 93 182 296 410
4,5: 4-Secret Cave-c 21 42 63 122 199 275
6-10 17 34 51 100 158 215
11-Classic story "The Valley of Time", with an ancient civilization made of gold
22 44 66 128 209 290
12-19 14 28 42 82 121 160
20-Origin Straight Arrow's Shield 16 32 48 92 144 195
21-Origin Fury 19 38 57 109 172 235
22-Frazetta-c 25 50 75 147 241 335
23,25-30: 25-Secret Cave-c. 28-Red Hawk meets The Vikings
11 22 33 62 86 110

The Strain: The Fall #5 © GDT

Strange Adventures #78 © DC

Strange Adventures #216 © DC

GD VG FN VF VF/NM NM-
2.0 4.0 6.0 8.0 9.0 9.2

24-Classic story "The Dragons of Doom!" with prehistoric pteradactyls
14 28 42 82 121 160
31-38: 36-Red Hawk drug story by Powell 10 20 30 54 72 90
39-Classic story "The Canyon Beast", with a dinosaur egg hatching a Tyranosaurus Rex
14 28 42 76 108 140
40-Classic story "Secret of The Spanish Specters", with Conquistadors' lost treasure
11 22 33 64 90 115
41,42,44-54: 45-Secret Cave-c 9 18 27 50 65 80
43-Intro & 1st app. Blaze, S. Arrow's Warrior dog 10 20 30 58 79 100
55-Last issue 11 22 33 62 86 110

NOTE: ***Fred Meagher** a 1-55; c-1, 2, 4-21, 23-55. **Powell** a 2-55. **Whitney** a-1. Many issues advertise the radio premiums associated with Straight Arrow.*

STRAIGHT ARROW'S FURY (Also see A-1 Comics)
Magazine Enterprises: No. 119, 1954 (one-shot)

A-1 119-Origin; Fred Meagher-c/a 15 30 45 85 130 175

STRAIN, THE (Adaptation of novels by Guillermo del Toro and Chuck Hogan)
Dark Horse Comics: Dec, 2011 - No. 11, Feb, 2013 ($1.00/$3.50)

1-($1.00) Lapham, Hogan & del Toro-s/Huddleston-a/c; variant-c by Morris 3.50
2-11-($3.50) Lapham-s/Huddleston-a/c 3.50

STRAIN, THE: MISTER QUINLAN - VAMPIRE HUNTER
Dark Horse Comics: Sept, 2016 - Present ($3.99)

1-5: 1-Lapham, Hogan & del Toro-s/Salazar-a; origin of Mister Quinlan in ancient Rome 4.00

STRAIN, THE: THE FALL (Guillermo del Toro and Chuck Hogan)
Dark Horse Comics: Jul, 2013 - No. 9, Mar, 2014 ($3.99)

1-9-Lapham, Hogan & del Toro-s/Huddleston-a/Gist-c 4.00

STRAIN, THE: THE NIGHT ETERNAL (Guillermo del Toro and Chuck Hogan)
Dark Horse Comics: Aug, 2014 - No. 12, Aug, 2015 ($3.99)

1-12-Lapham, Hogan & del Toro-s/Huddleston-a/Gist-c 4.00

STRANGE (Tales You'll Never Forget)
Ajax-Farrell Publ. (Four Star Comic Corp.): March, 1957 - No. 6, May, 1958

1 27 54 81 158 259 360
2-Censored r/Haunted Thrills 15 30 45 86 133 180
3-6 14 28 42 76 108 140

STRANGE (Dr. Strange)
Marvel Comics (Marvel Knghts): Nov, 2004 - No. 6, July, 2005 ($3.50)

1-6-Straczynski & Barnes-s/Peterson-a; Dr. Strange's origin retold 3.50
...: Beginnings and Endings TPB (2006, $17.99) r/#1-6 18.00

STRANGE (Dr. Strange)
Marvel Comics: Jan, 2010 - No. 4, Apr, 2010 ($3.99, limited series)

1-4-Waid-s/Rios-a/Coker-c 4.00

STRANGE ADVENTURES
DC Comics: July/Aug 1950

nn - Ashcan comic, not distributed to newsstands, only for in-house use. Cover art is All Star Comics #47 with interior being Detective Comics #140. A second example has the interior of Detective Comics #146. A third example has an unidentified issue of Detective Comics as the interior. This is the only ashcan with multiple interiors. A FN+ copy sold for $1,000 in 2007.

STRANGE ADVENTURES
National Periodical Publ.: Aug-Sept, 1950 - No. 244, Oct-Nov, 1973 (No. 1-12: 52 pgs.)

1-Adaptation of "Destination Moon"; preview of movie w/photo-c from movie (also see Fawcett Movie Comic #2); adapt. of Edmond Hamilton's "Chris KL-99" in #1-3; Darwin Jones begins 179 358 537 1477 3339 5200
2 77 154 231 616 1383 2150
3,4 54 108 162 432 966 1500
5-8,10: 7-Origin Kris KL-99 46 92 138 359 805 1250
9-(6/51)-Origin/1st app. Captain Comet (c/story) 102 204 306 816 2241 2850
11-20: 12,13,17,18-Toth-a. 14-Robot-c 31 62 93 223 504 785
21-30: 28-Atomic explosion panel. 30-Robot-c 29 58 87 209 467 725
31,34-38 27 54 81 194 435 675
32,33-Krigstein-a 29 58 87 196 441 685
39-Ill. in **SOTI** "Treating police contemptuously" (top right)
31 62 93 223 499 775
40-49-Last Capt. Comet; not in 45,47,48 27 54 81 191 426 660
50-53-Last precode issue (2/55) 23 46 69 161 356 550
54-70 19 38 57 131 291 450
71-79,81-99 15 30 45 103 227 350
80-Grey-tone-c 21 42 63 147 324 500
100 16 32 48 108 239 370
101-110: 104-Space Museum begins by Sekowsky 12 24 36 81 176 270

GD VG FN VF VF/NM NM-
2.0 4.0 6.0 8.0 9.0 9.2

111-116,118,119: 114-Star Hawkins begins, ends #185; Heath-a in Wood E.C. style
12 24 36 79 170 260
117-(6/60)-Origin/1st app. Atomic Knights. 46 92 138 350 788 1225
120-2nd app. Atomic Knights 21 42 63 147 324 500
121,122,125,127,128,130,131,133,134: 134-Last 10¢ issue
10 20 30 69 147 225
123,126-3rd & 4th app. Atomic Knights 13 26 39 89 195 300
124-Intro/origin Faceless Creature 13 26 39 91 201 310
129,132,135,138,141,147-Atomic Knights app. 11 22 33 76 163 250
136,137,139,140,143,145,146,148,149,151,152,154,155,157-159: 136-Robot cover. 159-Star Rovers app.; Gil Kane/Anderson-a. 9 18 27 59 117 175
142-2nd app. Faceless Creature 10 20 30 64 132 200
144-Only Atomic Knights-c (by M. Anderson) 12 24 36 80 173 265
150,153,156,160: Atomic Knights in each. 150-Greytone-c. 153-(6/63)-3rd app. Faceless Creature; atomic explosion-c. 160-Last Atomic Knights
9 18 27 62 126 190
161-179: 161-Last Space Museum. 163-Star Rovers app. 170-Infinity-c. 177-Intro/origin Immortal Man 7 14 21 46 86 125
180-Origin/1st app. Animal Man 38 76 114 285 641 1000
181-183,185,186,188,189 6 12 18 37 66 95
184-2nd app. Animal Man by Gil Kane 10 20 30 64 132 200
187-Intro/origin The Enchantress 28 56 84 202 451 700
190-1st app. Animal Man in costume 12 24 36 84 185 285
191-194,196-200,202-204 5 10 15 34 60 85
195-1st full app. Animal Man 8 16 24 51 96 140
201-Last Animal Man; 2nd full app. 6 12 18 41 76 110
205-(10/67)-Intro/origin Deadman by Infantino & begin series, ends #216
46 92 138 359 805 1250
206-Neal Adams-a begins 12 24 36 84 185 285
207-210 10 20 30 64 132 200
211-216: 211-Space Museum-r. 216-(1-2/69)-Deadman story finally concludes in Brave & the Bold #86 (10-11/69); secret message panel by Neal Adams (pg. 13); tribute to Steranko
9 18 27 57 111 165
217-r/origin & 1st app. Adam Strange from Showcase #17, begin-r; Atomic Knights-r begin
3 6 9 16 23 30
218-221,223-225: 218-Last 12¢ issue. 225-Last 15¢ issue
3 6 9 14 20 26
222-New Adam Strange story; Kane/Anderson-a 3 6 9 20 31 42
226,227,230-236-(68-52 pgs.): 226, 227-New Adam Strange text story w/illos by Anderson (8,6 pgs.) 231-Last Atomic Knights-r. 235-JLA-c/s 3 6 9 14 20 26
228,229 (68 pgs.) 3 6 9 16 24 32
237-243 2 4 6 10 14 18
244-Last issue 2 4 6 11 16 20

NOTE: ***Neal Adams** a-206-216; c-207-218, 228, 235. **Anderson** a-8-52, 94, 96, 99, 115, 117, 119-163, 217r, 218r, 222, 223-225r, 226, 229r, 242i(r); c-18, 19, 21, 23, 24, 27, 30, 32-44(most); c/r-157i, 190i, 217-224, 228-231, 233, 235-239, 241-243. **Ditko** a-188, 189. **Drucker** a-42, 43, 45. **Elias** a-212. **Finlay** a-2, 3, 6, 7, 210r, 229r. **Giunta** a-237r. **Heath** a-116. **Infantino** a-10-101, 106-151, 154, 157-163, 180, 190, 218-221r, 223-244p(r); c-50; c(r)-190p, 197, 199-211, 218-221, 223-244. **Kaluta** c-238, 240. **Gil Kane** a-8-116, 124, 125, 130, 138, 146-157, 173-186, 204r, 222r, 227-231r; c(p)-11-17, 25, 154, 157. **Kubert** a-55(2 pgs.), 226; c-219, 220, 225-227, 232, 234. **Moreira** c-26, 28, 29, 71. **Morrow** c-230. **Mortimer** c-8. **Powell** a-4. **Sekowsky** a-71p, 97-162p, 217p(r), 218p(r); c-206, 217-219r. **Simon & Kirby** a-2r (2 pgs) **Sparling** a-201. **Toth** a-8, 12, 13, 17-19. **Wood** a-154i. Atomic Knights in #117, 120, 123, 126, 129, 132, 135, 138, 141, 144, 147, 150, 153, 156, 160. Atomic Knights reprints by **Anderson** in 217-221, 223-231. Chris KL99 in 1-3, 5, 7, 9, 11, 15. Capt. Comet covers-9-14, 17-19, 24, 26, 27, 32-44.*

STRANGE ADVENTURES
DC Comics (Vertigo): Nov, 1999 - No. 4, Feb, 2000 ($2.50, limited series)

1-4: 1-Bolland-c; art by Bolland, Gibbons, Quitely 3.00

STRANGE ADVENTURES
DC Comics: May, 2009 - No. 8, Dec, 2009 ($3.99, limited series)

1-8: 1-Starlin-s in all; Adam Strange, Capt. Comet, Bizarro & Prince Gavyn app. 4.00
TPB (2010, $19.99) r/#1-8; cover gallery 20.00

STRANGE ADVENTURES
DC Comics (Vertigo): Jul, 2011 ($7.99, one-shot)

1-Short story anthology; s/a by Azzarello, Risso, Milligan and others; Paul Pope-c 8.00

STRANGE ADVENTURES MAGAZINE
CJH Publications: Dec, 1936 (10¢)

1-Flash Gordon, The Master of Mars, text stories w/some full pg. panels of art by Fred Meagher (a FN+ copy sold for $1075 in 2012)

STRANGE AS IT SEEMS (See Famous Funnies-A Carnival of Comics, Feature Funnies #1, The John Hix Scrap Book & Peanuts)

STRANGE AS IT SEEMS
United Features Syndicate: 1939

Single Series 9, 1, 2 34 68 102 206 336 465

Strange Confessions #2 © Z-D

Strange Mysteries #10 © SUPR

Strangers in Paradise #4 © Terry Moore

GD VG FN VF VF/NM NM-
2.0 4.0 6.0 8.0 9.0 9.2

GD VG FN VF VF/NM NM-
2.0 4.0 6.0 8.0 9.0 9.2

STRANGE ATTRACTORS
RetroGraphix: 1993 - No. 15, Feb, 1997 ($2.50, B&W)
1-15: 1-(5/93), 2-(8/93), 3-(11/93), 4-(2/94) 3.00
Volume One-($14.95, trade paperback)-r/#1-7 15.00

STRANGE ATTRACTORS: MOON FEVER
Caliber Comics: Feb, 1997 - No. 3, June, 1997 ($2.95, B&W, mini-series)
1-3 3.00

STRANGE COMBAT TALES
Marvel Comics (Epic Comics): Oct, 1993 - No. 4, Jan, 1994 ($2.50, limited series)
1-4 3.00

STRANGE CONFESSIONS
Ziff-Davis Publ. Co.: Jan-Mar (Spring on-c), 1952 - No. 4, Fall, 1952 (All have photo-c)
1(Scarce)-Kinstler-a 65 130 195 416 708 1000
2(Scarce, 7-8/52) 48 96 144 302 514 725
3(Scarce, 9-10/52)-#3 on-c, #2 on inside; Reformatory girl story; photo-c
47 94 141 296 498 700
4(Scarce) 45 90 135 284 480 675

STRANGE DAYS
Eclipse Comics: Oct, 1984 - No. 3, Apr, 1985 ($1.75, Baxter paper)
1-3: Freakwave, Johnny Nemo, & Paradax from Vanguard Illustrated; nudity, violence & strong language 4.00

STRANGE DAYS (Movie)
Marvel Comics: Dec, 1995 ($5.95, squarebound, one-shot)
1-Adaptation of film 6.00

STRANGE FANTASY (Eerie Tales of Suspense!)(Formerly Rocketman #1)
Ajax-Farrell: Aug, 1952 - No. 14, Oct-Nov, 1954
2(#1, 8/52)-Jungle Princess story; Kamenish-a; reprinted from Ellery Queen #1
68 136 204 435 743 1050
2(10/52)-No Black Cat or Rulah; Bakerish, Kamenish-a; hypo/meathook-c
58 116 174 371 636 900
3-Rulah story, called Pulah 47 94 141 296 498 700
4-Rocket Man app. (2/53) 43 86 129 271 461 650
5,6,8,10,12,14 39 78 117 240 395 550
7-Madam Satan/Slave story 45 90 135 284 480 675
9(w/Black Cat), 9(w/Boy's Ranch; S&K-a), 9(w/War)(A rebinding of Harvey interiors; not publ. by Ajax) 41 82 123 256 428 600
9-Regular issue; Steve Ditko's 3rd published work (tied with Captain 3D)
71 142 213 454 777 1100
11-Jungle story 43 86 129 271 461 650
13-Bondage-c; Rulah (Kolah) story 43 86 129 271 461 650

STRANGE FRUIT
BOOM! Studios: Jul, 2015 - No. 4 ($3.99, limited series)
1-3-J.G. Jones-a; Jones & Mark Waid-s 4.00

STRANGE GALAXY
Eerie Publications: V1#8, Feb, 1971 - No. 11, Aug, 1971 (B&W, magazine)
V1#8-Reprints-c/Fantastic V19#3 (2/70) (a pulp) 3 6 9 21 33 45
9-11 3 6 9 17 26 35

STRANGE GIRL
Image Comics: June, 2005 - No. 18, Sept, 2007 ($2.95/$2.99/$3.50)
1-12: 1-Rick Remender-s/Eric Nguyen-a 3.50
13-18-($3.50) 3.50
... Vol. 1: Girl Afraid TPB (2005, $12.99) r/#1-4; sketch pages and pin-ups 13.00

STRANGE JOURNEY
America's Best (Steinway Publ.) (Ajax/Farrell): Sept, 1957 - No. 4, Jun, 1958 (Farrell reprints)
1-The Phantom Express 21 42 63 122 199 275
2-4: 2-Flying saucer-c. 3-Titanic-c 15 30 45 88 137 185

STRANGE LOVE (See Fox Giants)

STRANGE MYSTERIES
Superior/Dynamic Publications: Sept, 1951 - No. 21, Jan, 1955
1-Kamenish-a & horror stories begin 77 154 231 493 847 1200
2 45 90 135 284 480 675
3-5 42 84 126 265 445 625
6-8 39 78 117 240 395 550
9-Bondage 3-D effect-c 48 96 144 302 514 725
10-Used in **SOTI**, pg. 181 41 82 123 256 428 600
11-18: 13-Eyeball-c 34 68 102 199 325 450
19-r/Journey Into Fear #1; cover is a splash from one story; Baker-r(2)
34 68 102 206 336 465
20,21-Reprints; 20-r/#1 with new-c (The Devil) 26 52 78 154 252 350

STRANGE MYSTERIES
I. W. Enterprises/Super Comics: 1963 - 1964
I.W. Reprint #9; Rulah-r/Spook #28; Disbrow-a 3 6 9 19 30 40
Super Reprint #10-12,15-17(1963-64): 10,11-r/Strange #2,1. 12-r/Tales of Horror #5 (3/53) less-c. 15-r/Dark Mysteries #23. 16-r/The Dead Who Walk. 17-r/Dark Mysteries #22
3 6 9 19 30 40
Super Reprint #18-r/Witchcraft #1; Kubert-a 3 6 9 19 30 40

STRANGE PLANETS
I. W. Enterprises/Super Comics: 1958; 1963-64
I.W. Reprint #1(nd)-Reprints E. C. Incredible S/F #30 plus-c/Strange Worlds #3
5 10 15 34 60 85
I.W. Reprint #9-Orlando/Wood-r/Strange Worlds #4; cover-r from Flying Saucers #1
6 12 18 41 76 110
Super Reprint #10-Wood-r (22 pg.) from Space Detective #1; cover-r/Attack on Planet Mars
6 12 18 41 76 110
Super Reprint #11-Wood-r (25 pg.) from An Earthman on Venus
7 14 21 46 86 125
Super Reprint #12-Orlando-r/Rocket to the Moon 6 12 18 41 76 110
Super Reprint #15-Reprints Journey Into Unknown Worlds #8; Heath, Colan-r
4 8 12 27 44 60
Super Reprint #16-Reprints Avon's Strange Worlds #6; Kinstler, Check-a
4 8 12 28 47 65
Super Reprint #18-r/Great Exploits #1 (Daring Adventures #6); Space Busters, Explorer Joe, The Son of Robin Hood; Krigstein-a 4 8 12 23 37 50

STRANGERS
Image Comics: Mar, 2003 - No. 6, Sept, 2003 ($2.95)
1-6-Randy & Jean-Marc Lofficier-s; two covers. 2-Nexus back-up story 3.00

STRANGERS, THE
Malibu Comics (Ultraverse): June, 1993 - No. 24, May, 1995 ($1.95/$2.50)
1-4,6-12,14-20: 1-1st app. The Strangers; has coupon for Ultraverse Premiere #0; 1st app. the Night Man (not in costume). 2-Polybagged w/trading card. 7-Break-Thru x-over. 8-2 pg. origin Solution. 12-Silver foil logo; wraparound-c. 17-Rafferty app. 3.00
1-With coupon missing 2.00
1-Full cover holographic edition, 1st of kind w/Hardcase #1 & Prime #1
1 2 3 5 6 8
1-Ultra 5000 limited silver foil 6.00
4-($2.50)-Variant Newsstand edition bagged w/card 4.00
5-($2.50, 52 pgs.)-Rune flip-c/story by B. Smith (3 pgs.); The Mighty Magnor 1 pg. strip by Aragones; 3-pg. Night Man preview 4.00
13-($3.50, 68 pgs.)-Mantra app.; flip book w/Ultraverse Premiere #4 4.00
21-24 ($2.50) 3.00
...:The Pilgrim Conundrum Saga (1/95, $3.95, 68pgs.) 4.00

STRANGERS IN PARADISE (Also see SIP Kids)
Antarctic Press: Nov, 1993 - No. 3, Feb, 1994 ($2.75, B&W, limited series)
1 8 16 24 56 108 160
1-2nd/3rd prints 1 3 4 6 8 10
2 (2300 printed) 4 8 12 27 44 60
3 3 6 9 16 23 30
Trade paperback (Antarctic Press, $6.95)-Red -c (5000 print run) 10.00
Trade paperback (Abstract Studios, $6.95)-Red-c (2000 print run) 15.00
Trade paperback (Abstract Studios, $6.95, 1st-4th printing)-Blue- 7.00
Hardcover ('98, $29.95) includes first draft pages 30.00
Gold Reprint Series ($2.75) 1-3-r/#1-3 3.00

STRANGERS IN PARADISE
Abstract Studios: Sept, 1994 - No. 14, July, 1996 ($2.75, B&W)
1 2 4 6 9 13 16
1,3- 2nd printings 4.00
2,3: 2-Color dream sequence 1 2 3 5 6 8
4-10 4.00
4-6-2nd printings 3.00
11-14: 14-The Letters of Molly & Poo 4.00
Gold Reprint Series ($2.75) 1-13-r/#1-13 3.00
I Dream Of You ($16.95, TPB) r/#1-9 17.00
It's a Good Life ($8.95, TPB) r/#10-13 9.00

STRANGERS IN PARADISE (Volume Three)
Homage Comics #1-8/Abstract Studios #9-on: Oct, 1996 - No. 90, May, 2007 ($2.75-$2.99, color #1-5, B&W #6-on)

Strangers in Paradise V3 #44 © Terry Moore

Strange Suspense Stories #3 © FAW

Strange Tales #15 © MAR

	GD 2.0	VG 4.0	FN 6.0	VF 8.0	VF/NM 9.0	NM- 9.2
1-Terry Moore-c/s/a in all; dream seq. by Jim Lee-a						5.00
1-Jim Lee variant-c	1	2	3	6	7	8
2-5						4.00
6-16: 6-Return to B&W. 13-15-High school flashback. 16-Xena Warrior Princess parody; two covers						3.00
17-89: 33-Color issue. 46-Molly Lane. 49-Molly & Poo. 86-David dies						3.00
90-Last issue; 3 covers of Katchoo, Francine and David forming a triptych						3.00
...Lyrics and Poems (2/99)						3.00
...Source Book (2003, $2.95) Background on characters & story arcs, checklists						3.00
Brave New World ('02, $8.95, TPB) r/#44,45,47,48						9.00
Child of Rage ($15.95, TPB) r/#31-38						16.00
David's Story (6/04, $8.95, TPB) r/#61-63						9.00
Ever After ('07, $15.95, TPB) r/#83-90						16.00
Flower to Flame ('03, $15.95, TPB) r/#55-60						16.00
Heart in Hand ('03, $12.95, TPB) r/#50-54						13.00
High School ('98, $8.95, TPB) r/#13-16						9.00
Immortal Enemies ('98, $14.95, TPB) r/#6-12						15.00
Love & Lies (2006, $14.95, TPB)r/#77-82						15.00
Love Me Tender ($12.95, TPB) r/#1-5 in B&W w/ color Lee seq.						13.00
Molly & Poo (2005, $8.95, TPB)r/#46,49,73						9.00
My Other Life ($14.95, TPB) r/#25-30						15.00
Pocket Book 1-5 ($17.95, 5 1/2" x 8", TPB) 1-r/Vol.1 & 2. 2-r/#1-17 in B&W. 3-r/#18-24,26-32,34-38. 4-r/#41-45,47,48,50-60. 5-r/#46,49,61-76						18.00
Sanctuary ($15.95, TPB) r/#17-24						16.00
Tattoo ($14.95, TPB) r/#70-76; sketch pages and fan tattoo photos						15.00
Tomorrow Now (11/04, $14.95, TPB) r/#64-69						15.00
Tropic of Desire ($12.95, TPB) r/#39-43						13.00
The Complete... : Volume 3 Part 1 HC ($49.95) r/#1-12						50.00
The Complete... : Volume 3 Part 2 HC ($49.95) r/#13-15,17-25						50.00
The Complete... : Volume 3 Part 3 HC ('01, $49.95) r/#26-38						50.00
The Complete... : Volume 3 Part 4 HC ('02, $39.95) r/#39-46,49						40.00
The Complete... : Volume 3 Part 5 HC ('03, $49.95) r/#47,48,50-57						50.00
The Complete... : Volume 3 Part 6 HC ('04, $49.95) r/#58-69						50.00
The Complete... : Volume 3 Part 7 HC ('06, $49.95) r/#70-80						50.00

STRANGE SPORTS STORIES (See Brave & the Bold #45-49, DC Special, and DC Super Stars #10)
National Periodical Publications: Sept-Oct, 1973 - No. 6, July-Aug, 1974

	GD 2.0	VG 4.0	FN 6.0	VF 8.0	VF/NM 9.0	NM- 9.2
1-Devil-c	3	6	9	16	23	30
2-6: 2-Swan/Anderson-a	2	4	6	9	13	16

STRANGE SPORTS STORIES
DC Comics (Vertigo): May, 2015 - No. 4, Aug, 2015 ($4.99, limited series)

	GD 2.0	VG 4.0	FN 6.0	VF 8.0	VF/NM 9.0	NM- 9.2
1-4-Anthology of short stories by various. 1-Paul Pope-c. 4-Pope-s/a						5.00

STRANGE STORIES FROM ANOTHER WORLD (Unknown World #1)
Fawcett Publications: No. 2, Aug, 1952 - No. 5, Feb, 1953

	GD 2.0	VG 4.0	FN 6.0	VF 8.0	VF/NM 9.0	NM- 9.2
2-Saunders painted-c	50	100	150	315	533	750
3-5-Saunders painted-c	40	80	120	246	411	575

STRANGE STORIES OF SUSPENSE (Rugged Action #1-4)
Atlas Comics (CSI): No. 5, Oct, 1955 - No. 16, Aug, 1957

	GD 2.0	VG 4.0	FN 6.0	VF 8.0	VF/NM 9.0	NM- 9.2
5(#1)	50	100	150	315	533	750
6,7,9	34	68	102	199	325	450
8-Morrow/Williamson-a; Pakula-a	36	72	108	211	343	475
10-Crandall, Torres, Meskin-a	34	68	102	204	332	460
11-13: 12-Torres, Pakula-a. 13-E.C. art swipes	30	60	90	177	289	400
14-16: 14-Williamson/Mayo-a. 15-Krigstein-a. 16-Fox, Powell-a	32	64	96	188	307	425

NOTE: ***Everett** a-6, 7, 13; c-8, 9, 11-14. **Forte** a-12, 16. **Heath** a-5. **Maneely** c-5. **Morisi** a-11. **Morrow** a-13. **Powell** a-8. **Sale** a-11. **Severin** c-7. **Wildey** a-14.*

STRANGE STORY (Also see Front Page)
Harvey Publications: June-July, 1946 (52 pgs.)

	GD 2.0	VG 4.0	FN 6.0	VF 8.0	VF/NM 9.0	NM- 9.2
1-The Man in Black Called Fate by Powell	39	78	117	240	395	550

STRANGE SUSPENSE STORIES (Lawbreakers Suspense Stories #10-15; This Is Suspense #23-26; Captain Atom V1#78 on)
Fawcett Publications/Charlton Comics No. 16 on: 6/52 - No. 5, 2/53; No. 16, 1/54 - No. 22, 11/54; No. 27, 10/55 - No. 77, 10/65; V3#1, 10/67 - V1#9, 9/69

	GD 2.0	VG 4.0	FN 6.0	VF 8.0	VF/NM 9.0	NM- 9.2
1-(Fawcett)-Powell, Sekowsky-a	90	180	270	576	988	1400
2-George Evans horror story	50	100	150	315	533	750
3-5 (2/53)-George Evans horror stories	41	82	123	256	428	600
16(1-2/54)-Formerly Lawbreakers S.S.	34	68	102	199	325	450
17	27	54	81	158	259	360
18-E.C. swipe/HOF 7; Ditko-c/a(2)	49	98	147	309	522	735
19-Ditko electric chair-c; Ditko-a	77	154	231	493	847	1200
20-Ditko-c/a(2)	41	82	123	260	435	610
21-Shuster-a; a woman dangling over an alligator pit while a madman smashes her fingers with a hammer	40	80	120	246	411	575
22(11/54)-Ditko-c, Shuster-a; last pre-code issue; becomes This Is Suspense	39	78	117	231	378	525
27(10/55)-(Formerly This Is Suspense #26)	15	30	45	88	137	185
28-30,38	13	26	39	72	101	130
31-33,35,37,40-Ditko-c/a(2-3 each)	21	42	63	126	206	285
34-Story of ruthless business man, Wm. B. Gaines; Ditko-c/a	47	94	141	296	498	700
36-(15¢, 68 pgs.); Ditko-a(4)	26	52	78	154	252	350
39,41,52,53-Ditko-a	19	38	57	111	176	240
42-44,46,49,54-60	5	10	15	34	60	85
45,47,48,50,51-Ditko-c/a	12	24	36	80	173	265
61-74: 72-Has panel which inspired a famous Roy Lichtenstein painting	4	8	12	28	47	65
75(6/65)-Reprints origin/1st app. Captain Atom by Ditko from Space Advs. #33; r/Severin-a/Space Advs. #24 (75-77: 12¢ issues)	10	20	30	66	138	210
76,77-Captain Atom-r by Ditko/Space Advs.	6	12	18	37	66	95
V3#1(10/67): 12¢ issues begin	3	6	9	19	30	40
V1#2-Ditko-c/a; atom bomb-c	3	6	9	19	30	40
V1#3-9: 3-8-All 12¢ issues. 9-15¢ issue	2	4	6	13	18	22

NOTE: ***Alascia** a-19. **Aparo** a-60, V3#1, 2, 4; c-V1#4, 8, 9. **Baily** a-1-3; c-2, 5. **Evans** c-3, 4. **Giordano** c-16, 17p, 24p, 25p. **Montes/Bache** c-66. **Powell** a-4. **Shuster** a-19, 21. **Marcus Swayze** a-27.*

STRANGE TALENT OF LUTHER STRODE, THE (Also see The Legend of Luther Strode)
Image Comics: Oct, 2011 - No. 6, Mar, 2012 ($2.99, limited series)

	GD 2.0	VG 4.0	FN 6.0	VF 8.0	VF/NM 9.0	NM- 9.2
1-6: Justin Jordan-s/Tradd Moore-a						3.00

STRANGE TALES (...Featuring Warlock #178-181; Doctor Strange #169 on)
Atlas (CCPC #1-67/ZPC #68-79/VPI #80-85)/Marvel #86(7/61) on:
June, 1951 - No. 168, May, 1968; No. 169, Sept, 1973 - No. 188, Nov, 1976

	GD 2.0	VG 4.0	FN 6.0	VF 8.0	VF/NM 9.0	NM- 9.2
1-Horror/weird stories begin	595	1190	1785	4350	7675	11,000
2	194	388	582	1242	2121	3000
3,5: 3-Atom bomb panels	148	296	444	947	1624	2300
4-Cosmic eyeball story "The Evil Eye"	155	310	465	992	1696	2400
6-9: 6-Heath-c/a. 7-Colan-a	124	248	372	787	1356	1925
10-Krigstein-a	126	252	378	806	1378	1950
11-14,16-20	100	200	300	635	1093	1550
15-Krigstein-a; detached head-c	102	204	306	648	1112	1575
21,23-27,29-34: 27-Atom bomb panels. 33-Davis-a. 34-Last pre-code issue (2/55)	86	172	258	546	936	1325
22-Krigstein, Forte/Fox-a	87	174	261	553	952	1350
28-Jack Katz story used in Senate Investigation report, pgs. 7 & 169; classic skull-c	258	516	774	1651	2826	4000
35-41,43,44: 37-Vampire story by Colan	45	90	135	333	754	1175
42,45,59,61-Krigstein-a; #61 (2/58)	46	92	138	340	770	1200
46-57,60: 51-(10/56) 1st S.A. issue. 53,56-Crandall-a. 60-(8/57)	41	82	123	303	689	1075
58,64-Williamson-a in each, with Mayo-#58	42	84	126	311	706	1100
62,63,65,66: 62-Torres-a. 66-Crandall-a	41	82	123	303	689	1075
67-Prototype ish. (Quicksilver)	44	88	132	326	738	1150
68,71,72,74,77,80: Ditko/Kirby-a in #67-80	41	82	123	303	689	1075
69,70,73,75,76,78,79: 69-Prototype ish. (Prof. X). 70-Prototype ish. (Giant Man). 73-Prototype ish. (Ant-Man). 75-Prototype ish. (Iron Man). 76-Prototype ish. (Human Torch). 78-Prototype ish. (Ant-Man). 79-Prototype ish. (Dr. Strange) (12/60)	45	90	135	333	754	1175
81-83,85-88,90,91-Ditko/Kirby-a in all: 86-Robot-c. 90-(11/61)-Atom bomb blast panel	38	76	114	281	628	975
84-Prototype ish. (Magneto)(5/61); has powers like Magneto of X-Men, but two years earlier; Ditko/Kirby-a	46	92	138	340	770	1200
89-1st app. Fin Fang Foom (10/61) by Kirby	207	414	621	1708	3854	6000
92-Prototype ish. (Ancient One & Ant-Man); last 10¢ issue	38	76	114	285	641	1000
93,95,96,98-100: Kirby-a	34	68	102	245	548	850
94-Creature similar to The Thing; Kirby-a	38	76	114	285	641	1000
97-1st app. of an Aunt May & Uncle Ben by Ditko (6/62), before Amazing Fantasy #15; (see Tales Of Suspense #7); Kirby-a	114	228	342	912	2056	3200
101-Human Torch begins by Kirby (10/62); origin recap Fantastic Four & Human Torch; Human Torch-c begin	162	324	486	1337	3019	4700
102-1st app. Wizard; robot-c	44	88	132	326	738	1150
103-105: 104-1st app. Trapster. 105-2nd Wizard	38	76	114	285	641	1000
106,108,109: 106-Fantastic Four guests (3/63)	31	62	93	223	499	775
107-(4/63)-Human Torch/Sub-Mariner battle; 4th S.A. Sub-Mariner app. & 1st x-over outside of Fantastic Four	50	100	150	384	867	1350

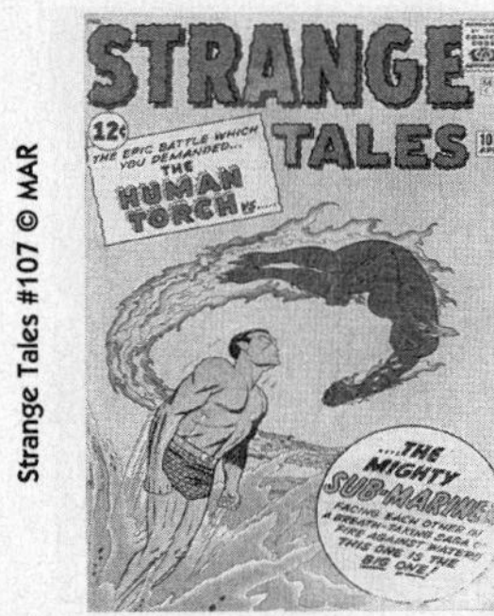

Strange Tales #107 © MAR

Strange Terrors #3 © STJ

Strange Worlds #7 © AVON

	GD 2.0	VG 4.0	FN 6.0	VF 8.0	VF/NM 9.0	NM- 9.2
110-(7/63)-Intro Doctor Strange, Ancient One & Wong by Ditko	600	1200	2400	5600	11,800	18,000
111-2nd Dr. Strange; intro. Baron Mordo	57	114	171	456	1028	1600
112-1st Eel	27	54	81	189	420	650
113-Origin/1st app. Plantman	26	52	78	182	404	625
114-Acrobat disguised as Captain America, 1st app. since the G.A.; intro. & 1st app. Victoria Bentley; 3rd Dr. Strange app. & begin series (11/63)	46	92	138	340	770	1200
115-Origin Dr. Strange; Human Torch vs. Sandman (Spidey villain; 2nd app. & brief origin); early Spider-Man x-over, 12/63	79	158	237	632	1416	2200
116-(1/64)-Human Torch battles The Thing; 1st Thing x-over	22	44	66	154	340	525
117,118,120: 120-1st Iceman x-over (from X-Men)	15	30	45	105	233	360
119-Spider-Man x-over (2 panel cameo)	17	34	51	119	265	410
121,122,124,127-134: Thing/Torch team-up in 121-134. 128-Quicksilver & Scarlet Witch app. (1/65). 130-The Beatles cameo. 134-Last Human Torch; The Watcher-c/story; Wood-a(i)	12	24	36	82	179	275
123-1st app. The Beetle (see Amazing Spider-Man #21 for next app.); 1st Thor x-over (8/64); Loki app.	15	30	45	100	220	340
125-Torch & Thing battle Sub-Mariner (10/64)	16	32	48	107	236	365
126-Intro Clea and Dormammu (cont'd in #127)	43	86	129	318	722	1125
135-Col. (formerly Sgt.) Nick Fury becomes Nick Fury Agent of Shield (origin/1st app.) by Kirby (8/65); series begins	37	74	111	274	612	950
136-140: 138-Intro Eternity	8	16	24	51	96	140
141-147,149: 145-Begins alternating-c features w/Nick Fury (odd #'s) & Dr. Strange (even #'s). 146-Last Ditko Dr. Strange who is in consecutive stories since #113; only full Ditko Dr. Strange-c this title. 147-Dr. Strange (by Everett #147-152) continues thru #168, then Dr. Strange #169	6	12	18	40	73	105
148-Origin Ancient One	8	16	24	51	96	140
150(11/66)-John Buscema's 1st work at Marvel	6	12	18	42	79	115
151-Kirby/Steranko-c/a; 1st Marvel work by Steranko	9	18	27	59	117	175
152,153-Kirby/Steranko-a	7	14	21	44	82	120
154-158-Steranko-a/script	7	14	21	44	82	120
159-Origin Nick Fury retold; Intro Val; Captain America-c/story; Steranko-a	9	18	27	58	114	170
160-162-Steranko-a/scripts; Capt. America app.	7	14	21	44	82	120
163-166,168-Steranko-a(p). 168-Last Nick Fury (gets own book next month) & last Dr. Strange who also gets own book	6	12	18	42	79	115
167-Steranko pen/script; classic flag-c	9	18	27	57	111	165
169-1st app. Brother Voodoo(origin in #169,170) & begin series, ends #173	13	26	39	89	195	300
170-174: 174-Origin Golem	3	6	9	16	23	30
175-177: 177-Brunner-c	3	6	9	14	20	25
178-(2/75)-Warlock by Starlin begins; origin Warlock & Him retold; 1st app. Magus; Starlin-c/a/scripts in #178-181 (all before Warlock #9)	8	16	24	54	102	150
179-Intro/1st app. Pip the Troll; Warlock app.	5	10	15	31	53	75
180-(6/75) Intro. Gamora (Guardians of the Galaxy) (5 panels); Warlock by Starlin	9	18	27	61	123	185
181-(8/75)-Warlock story continued in Warlock #9; 1st full app. of Gamora	4	8	12	27	44	60
182-188: 185,186-(Regular 25¢ editions)	2	4	6	8	10	12
185,186-(30¢-c variants, limited distribution)(5,7/76)	3	6	9	19	30	40
Annual 1(1962)-Reprints from Strange Tales #73,76,78, Tales of Suspense #7,9, Tales to Astonish #1,6,7, & Journey Into Mystery #53,55,59; (1st Marvel annual)	63	126	189	504	1127	1750
Annual 2(7/63)-Reprints from Strange Tales #67, Strange Worlds (Atlas) #1-3, World of Fantasy #16; new Human Torch vs. Spider-Man story by Kirby/Ditko (1st Spidey x-over; 4th app.); Kirby-c	93	186	279	744	1672	2700

NOTE: ***Briefer** a-17. **Burgos** a-123p. **J. Buscema** a-174p. **Colan** a-7, 11, 20, 37, 53, 169-173p, 188p. **Davis** c-71. **Ditko** a-46, 50, 67-122, 123-125p, 126-146, 175r, 182-188r; c-51, 93, 115, 121, 146. **Everett** a-4, 21, 40-42, 73, 147-152, 164i; c-8, 10, 11, 13, 15, 24, 45, 49-54, 56, 58, 60, 61, 63, 148, 150, 152, 158i. **Forte** a-27, 43, 50, 53, 54, 60. **Heath** a-2, 6; c-6, 18-20. **Kamen** a-45. **G. Kane** c-170-173, 182p. **Kirby** Human Torch-101-105, 108, 109, 114, 120; Nick Fury-135p, 141-143p; (Layouts)-135-153; other **Kirby** a-67-100p; c-68-70, 72-74, 76-92, 94, 95, 101-114, 116-123, 125-130, 132-135, 136p, 138-145, 147, 149, 151p. **Kirby/Ayers** c-101-106, 108-110. **Kirby/Ditko** a-80, 88, 121; c-75, 93, 97, 100, 139. **Lawrence** a-29. **Leiber/ Fox** a-110-113. **Maneely** a-3, 7, 37, 42; c-33, 40. **Moldoff** a-20. **Mooney** a-174i. **Morisi** a-53, 56. **Morrow** a-54. **Orlando** a-41, 44, 46, 49, 52. **Powell** a-42, 44, 49, 54, 130-134p; c-131p. **Reinman** a-11, 50, 74, 88, 91, 95, 104, 106, 112i, 124-127i. **Robinson** a-17. **Romita** c-169. **Roussos** c-201i. **R.Q. Sale** a-56; c-16. **Sekowski** a-3, 11. **Severin** a(i)-136-138; c-137. **Starlin** a-178, 179, 180p, 181p; c-178-180, 181p. **Steranko** a-151-161, 162-168p; c-151i, 153, 155, 157, 159, 161, 163, 165, 167. **Torres** a-53, 62. **Tuska** a-14, 166p. **Whitney** a-149. **Wildey** a-42, 56. **Woodbridge** a-59. Fantastic Four cameos #101-134. Jack Katz app.-26.*

STRANGE TALES
Marvel Comics Group: Apr, 1987 - No. 19, Oct, 1988

V2#1-19						4.00

STRANGE TALES
Marvel Comics: Nov, 1994 ($6.95, one-shot)

V3#1-acetate-c	1	2	3	5	6	8

STRANGE TALES (Anthology; continues stories from Man-Thing #8 and Werewolf By Night #6)
Marvel Comics: Sept, 1998 - No. 2, Oct, 1998 ($4.99)

1,2: 1-Silver Surfer app. 2-Two covers						5.00

STRANGE TALES (Humor anthology)
Marvel Comics: Nov, 2009 - No. 3, Jan, 2010 ($4.99, limited series)

1-3: 1-Paul Pope, Kochalka, Bagge and others-s/a. 2-Bagge-c/a. 3-Sakai-c/a						5.00

STRANGE TALES II (Humor anthology)
Marvel Comics: Dec, 2010 - No. 3, Feb, 2011 ($4.99, limited series)

1-3: 2-Jaime Hernandez-c. 3-Terry Moore-s/a; Pekar-s/Templeton-a						5.00

STRANGE TALES: DARK CORNERS
Marvel Comics: May, 1998 ($3.99, one-shot)

1-Anthology; stories by Baron & Maleev, McGregor & Dringenberg, DeMatteis & Badger; Estes painted-c						4.00

STRANGE TALES OF THE UNUSUAL
Atlas Comics (ACI No. 1-4/WPI No. 5-11): Dec, 1955 - No. 11, Aug, 1957

	GD 2.0	VG 4.0	FN 6.0	VF 8.0	VF/NM 9.0	NM- 9.2
1-Powell-a	53	106	159	334	567	800
2	34	68	102	206	336	465
3-Williamson-a (4 pgs.)	36	72	108	211	343	475
4,6,8,11: 4-UFO-c	27	54	81	160	263	365
5-Crandall, Ditko-a	32	64	96	188	307	425
7,9: 7-Kirby, Orlando-a. 9-Krigstein-a	29	58	87	172	281	390
10-Torres, Morrow-a	27	54	81	160	263	365

NOTE: ***Baily** a-6. **Brodsky** c-2-4. **Everett** a-2, 6; c-6, 9, 11. **Heck** a-1. **Maneely** c-1. **Orlando** a-7. **Pakula** a-10. **Romita** a-1. **R.Q. Sale** a-3. **Wildey** a-3.*

STRANGE TERRORS
St. John Publishing Co.: June, 1952 - No. 7, Mar, 1953

	GD 2.0	VG 4.0	FN 6.0	VF 8.0	VF/NM 9.0	NM- 9.2
1-Bondage-c; Zombies spelled Zoombies on-c; Fine-*esque* -a	77	154	231	493	847	1200
2	40	80	120	244	402	560
3-Kubert-a; painted-c	47	94	141	296	498	700
4-Kubert-a (reprinted in Mystery Tales #18); Ekgren painted-c; Fine-*esque* -a; Jerry Iger caricature	74	148	222	470	810	1150
5-Kubert-a; painted-c	47	94	141	296	498	700
6-Giant (25¢, 100 pgs.)(1/53); Tyler classic bondage/skull-c	68	136	204	435	743	1050
7-Giant (25¢, 100 pgs.); Kubert-c/a	63	126	189	403	689	975

NOTE: ***Cameron** a-6, 7. **Morisi** a-6.*

STRANGE WORLD OF YOUR DREAMS
Prize Publications: Aug, 1952 - No. 4, Jan-Feb, 1953

	GD 2.0	VG 4.0	FN 6.0	VF 8.0	VF/NM 9.0	NM- 9.2
1-Simon & Kirby-a	68	136	204	435	743	1050
2,3-Simon & Kirby-c/a. 2-Meskin-a	52	104	156	328	552	775
4-S&K-c; Meskin-a	42	84	126	265	445	625

STRANGE WORLDS (#18 continued from Avon's Eerie #1-17)
Avon Periodicals: 11/50 - No. 9, 11/52; No. 18, 10-11/54 - No. 22, 9-10/55 (No #11-17)

	GD 2.0	VG 4.0	FN 6.0	VF 8.0	VF/NM 9.0	NM- 9.2
1-Kenton of the Star Patrol by Kubert (r/Eerie #1 from 1947); Crom the Barbarian by John Giunta	165	330	495	1048	1799	2550
2-Wood-a; Crom the Barbarian by Giunta; Dara of the Vikings app.; used in **SOTI**, pg. 112; injury to eye panel	148	296	444	947	1624	2300
3-Wood/Orlando-a (Kenton), Wood/Williamson/Frazetta/Krenkel/Orlando-a (7 pgs.); Malu Slave Girl Princess app.; Kinstler-c	258	516	774	1651	2826	4000
4-Wood-c/a (Kenton); Orlando-a; origin The Enchanted Daggar; Sultan-a; classic cover	200	400	600	1280	2190	3100
5-Orlando/Wood-a (Kenton); Wood-c	110	220	330	704	1202	1700
6-Kinstler-a(2); Orlando/Wood-c; Check-a	61	122	183	390	670	950
7-Fawcette & Becker/Alascia-a	53	106	159	334	567	800
8-Kubert, Kinstler, Hollingsworth & Lazarus-a; Lazarus Robot-c	53	106	159	334	567	800
9-Kinstler, Fawcette, Alascia, Kubert-a	50	100	150	315	533	750
18-(Formerly Eerie #17)-Reprints "Attack on Planet Mars" by Kubert	37	74	111	222	361	500
19-r/Avon's "Robotmen of the Lost Planet"; last pre-code issue; Robot-c	37	74	111	222	361	500
20-War-c/story; Wood-c(r)/U.S. Paratroops #1	12	24	36	67	94	120
21,22-War-c/stories. 22-New logo	10	20	30	58	79	100
I.W. Reprint #5-Kinstler-a(r)/Avon's #9	4	8	12	24	37	50

STRANGE WORLDS

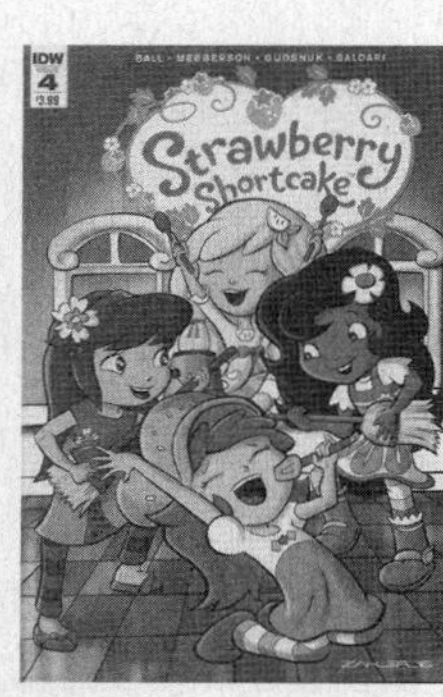

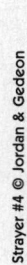

Strawberry Shortcake #4 © Shortcake I.P.

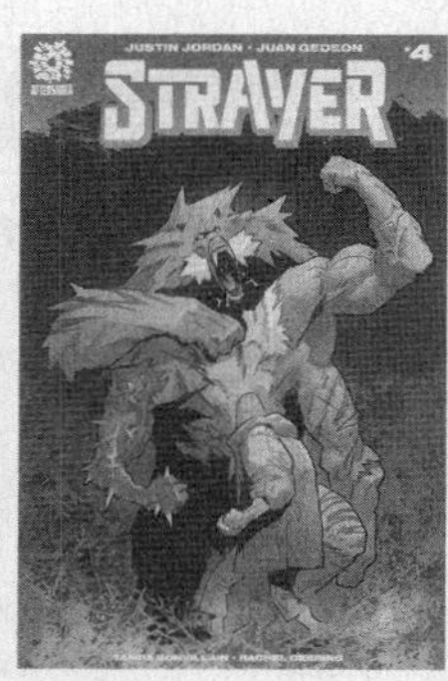

Strayer #4 © Jordan & Gedeon

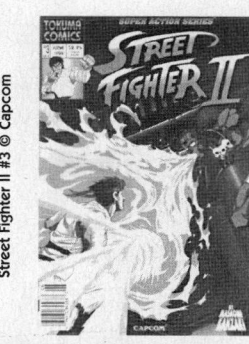

Street Fighter II #3 © Capcom

	GD 2.0	VG 4.0	FN 6.0	VF 8.0	VF/NM 9.0	NM- 9.2

Marvel Comics (MPI No. 1,2/Male No. 3,5): Dec, 1958 - No. 5, Aug, 1959

	GD 2.0	VG 4.0	FN 6.0	VF 8.0	VF/NM 9.0	NM- 9.2
1-Kirby & Ditko-a; flying saucer issue	116	232	348	742	1271	1800
2-Ditko-c/a	61	122	183	390	670	950
3-Kirby-a(2)	55	110	165	352	601	850
4-Williamson-a	50	100	150	315	533	750
5-Ditko-a	47	94	141	296	498	700

NOTE: *Buscema a-3, 4. Ditko a-1-5; c-2.. Heck a-2. Kirby a-1, 3. Kirby/Brodsky c-1, 3-5.*

STRAWBERRY SHORTCAKE
Marvel Comics (Star Comics): Jun, 1985 - No. 6, Feb, 1986 (Children's comic)

1-6: Howie Post-a 2 4 6 8 10 12

STRAWBERRY SHORTCAKE
Ape Entertainment: 2011 - No. 4, 2011 ($3.95, limited series)

1-4: 1-Scratch 'n' sniff cover 4.00
Volume 2 (2012, $3.99) 1,2 4.00

STRAWBERRY SHORTCAKE
IDW Publishing: Apr, 2016 - No. 8, Nov, 2016 ($3.99)

1-8: Multiple covers on each. 1-Georgia Ball-a/Amy Mebberson-a 4.00

STRAY
DC Comics (Homage Comics): 2001 ($5.95, prestige format, one-shot)

1-Pollina-c/a; Lobdell & Palmiotti-s 6.00

STRAY
Dark Horse Comics: 2004 (8 1/2"x 5 1/2", Diamond Comic Dist. Halloween giveaway)

nn-Reprint from The Dark Horse Book of Hauntings; Evan Dorkin-s/Jill Thompson-a 3.00

STRAY BULLETS
El Capitan Books/Image Comics: 1995 - No. 41, Mar, 2014 ($2.95/$3.50, B&W, mature)

1-David Lapham-c/a/scripts 2 4 6 8 10 12
2,3 6.00
4-8 4.00
9-21,31,32-($2.95) 3.50
22-30,33-41-($3.50) 22-Includes preview to Murder Me Dead. 40-(10/05). 41-(3/14) 3.50
Free Comic Book Day giveaway (5/02) Reprints #2 with "Free Comic Book Day" banner on-c; flip book with The Matrix (printing of internet comic) 3.00
Innocence of Nihilism Volume 1 HC ($29.95, hardcover) r/#1-7 30.00
Somewhere Out West Volume 2 HC ($34.95, hardcover) r/#8-14 35.00
Other People Volume 3 HC ($34.95, hardcover) r/#15-22 35.00
Volume 1-3 TPB ($11.95, softcover) 1-r/#1-4. 2-r/#5-8. 3-r/ #9-12 12.00
Volume 4-7 TPB ($14.95) 4- r/#13-16. 5- r/#17-20. 6- r/#21-24. 7-r/#25-28 15.00

NOTE: *Multiple printings of most issues exist & are worth cover price.*

STRAY BULLETS: KILLERS
Image Comics (El Capitan Books): Mar, 2014 - No. 8, Oct, 2014 ($3.50, B&W)

1-8-David Lapham-c/a/scripts; set in 1978 3.50

STRAY BULLETS: SUNSHINE AND ROSES
Image Comics (El Capitan Books): Feb, 2015 - Present ($3.50/$3.99, B&W)

1-10-David Lapham-c/a/scripts; set in 1979 Baltimore 3.50
11-21-($3.99) 20-Amy Racecar app. 4.00

STRAYER
AfterShock Comics: Jan, 2016 - Present ($3.99)

1-5-Justin Jordan-s/Juan Gedeon-a 4.00

STRAY TOASTERS
Marvel Comics (Epic Comics): Jan, 1988 - No. 4, April, 1989 ($3.50, squarebound, limited series)

1-4: Sienkiewicz-c/a/scripts 4.00

STREET COMIX
Street Enterprises/King Features: 1973 (50¢, B&W, 36 pgs.)(20,000 print run)

1-Rip Kirby 2 4 6 8 11 14
2-Flash Gordon 2 4 6 10 14 18

STREETFIGHTER
Ocean Comics: Aug, 1986 - No. 4, Spr, 1987 ($1.75, limited series)

1-4: 2-Origin begins 3.00

STREET FIGHTER
Malibu Comics: Sept, 1993 - No. 3, Nov, 1993 ($2.95)

1-3: 3-Includes poster; Ferret x-over 3.00

STREET FIGHTER
Image Comics: Sept, 2003 - No. 14, Feb, 2005 ($2.95)

1-Back-up story w/Madureira-a; covers by Madureira and Tsang 3.00
2-6,8-14: 2-Two covers by Campbell and Warren; back-up story w/Warren-a 3.00
7-($4.50) Larocca-c 4.50
... Vol. 1 (3/04, $9.99, digest-size) r/main stories from #1-6 10.00

STREET FIGHTER: THE BATTLE FOR SHADALOO
DC Comics/CAP Co. Ltd.: 1995 ($3.95, one-shot)

1-Polybagged w/trading card & Tattoo 4.00

STREET FIGHTER II
Tokuma Comics (Viz): Apr, 1994 - No. 8, Nov, 1994 ($2.95, limited series)

1-8 3.00

STREET FIGHTER II
UDON Comics: No. 0, Oct, 2005 - No. 6, Nov, 2006 ($1.99/$3.95/$2.95)

0-(10/05, $1.99) prelude to series; Alvin Lee-a 3.00
1-($3.95) Two covers by Alvin Lee & Ed McGuinness 4.00
2-6-($2.95) 3.00
... Legends 1 (8/06, $3.95) Spotlight on Sakura; two covers 4.00

STREET FIGHTER X G.I. JOE
IDW Publishing: Feb, 2016 - No. 6, Jul, 2016 ($4.99)

1-Sitterson-s/Laiso-a; multiple covers; Destro, Snake Eyes, Baroness, Ryu app. 5.00
2-6-($3.99) Multiple covers on each 4.00

STREET SHARKS
Archie Publications: Jan, 1996 - No. 3, Mar, 1996 ($1.50, limited series)

1-3 3.00

STREET SHARKS
Archie Publications: May, 1996 - No. 6 ($1.50)

1-6 3.00

STRICTLY PRIVATE (You're in the Army Now)
Eastern Color Printing Co.: July, 1942 (#1 on sale 6/15/42)

1,2: Private Peter Plink. 2-Says 128 pgs. on-c 32 64 96 188 307 425

STRIKE!
Eclipse Comics: Aug, 1987 - No. 6, Jan, 1988 ($1.75)

1-6, ...Vs. Sgt. Strike Special 1 (5/88, $1.95) 3.00

STRIKEBACK! (The Hunt For Nikita)
Malibu Comics (Bravura): Oct, 1994 - No. 3, Jan, 1995 ($2.95, unfinished limited series)

1-3: Jonathon Peterson script, Kevin Maguire-c/a 3.00
1-Gold foil embossed-c 5.00

STRIKEBACK!
Image Comics (WildStorm Productions): Jan, 1996 - No. 5, May, 1996 ($2.50, lim. series)

1-5: Reprints original Bravura series w/additional story & art by Kevin Maguire & Jonathon Peterson; new Maguire-c in all. 4,5-New story & art 3.00

STRIKEFORCE: AMERICA
Comico: Dec, 1995 ($2.95)

V2#1-Polybagged w/gaming card; S. Clark-a(p) 3.00

STRIKEFORCE: MORITURI
Marvel Comics Group: Dec, 1986 - No. 31, July, 1989

1,13: 13-Double size 4.00
2-12,14-31: 14-Williamson-i. 25-Heath-c 3.00
... – We Who Are About To Die 1 (3/12, $0.99) r/#1 with profile pages and cover gallery 3.00

STRIKEFORCE MORITURI: ELECTRIC UNDERTOW
Marvel Comics: Dec, 1989 - No. 5, Mar, 1990 ($3.95, 52 pgs., limited series)

1-5 Squarebound 4.00

STRONG GUY REBORN (See X-Factor)
Marvel Comics: Sept, 1997 ($2.99, one-shot)

1-Dezago-s/Andy Smith, Art Thibert-a 3.00

STRONG MAN (Also see Complimentary Comics & Power of...)
Magazine Enterprises: Mar-Apr, 1955 - No. 4, Sept-Oct, 1955

1(A-1 #130)-Powell-c/a 23 46 69 136 223 310
2-4: (A-1 #132,134,139)-Powell-a. 2-Powell-c 18 36 54 105 165 225

STRONTIUM DOG
Eagle Comics: Dec, 1985 - No. 4, Mar, 1986 ($1.25, limited series)

1-4, Special 1: 4-Moore script. Special 1 (1986)-Moore script 4.00

STRYFE'S STRIKE FILE
Marvel Comics: Jan, 1993 ($1.75, one-shot, no ads)

1-Stroman, Capullo, Andy Kubert, Brandon Peterson-a; silver metallic ink-c;

Stupid Comics #1 © Jim Mahfood

Sub-Mariner (2007 series) #1 © MAR

Sub-Mariner Comics #18 © MAR

GD 2.0 VG 4.0 FN 6.0 VF 8.0 VF/NM 9.0 NM- 9.2

X-Men tie-in to X-Cutioner's Song 4.00
1-Gold metallic ink 2nd printing 3.00

STRYKEFORCE
Image Comics (Top Cow): May, 2004 - No. 5, Oct, 2004 ($2.99)
1-5-Faerber-s/Kirkham-a. 4,5-Preview of HumanKind 3.00
Vol. 1 TPB (2005, $16.99) r/#1-5 & Codename: Strykeforce #0-3; sketch pages 17.00

STUMBO THE GIANT (See Harvey Hits #49,54,57,60,63,66,69,72,78,88 & Hot Stuff #2)

STUMBO TINYTOWN
Harvey Publications: Oct, 1963 - No. 13, Nov, 1966 (All 25¢ giants)
1-Stumbo, Hot Stuff & others begin 13 26 39 86 188 290
2 8 16 24 52 99 145
3-5 6 12 18 38 69 100
6-13 5 10 15 33 57 80

STUNT DAWGS
Harvey Comics: Mar, 1993 ($1.25, one-shot)
1 3.00

STUNTMAN COMICS (Also see Thrills Of Tomorrow)
Harvey Publ.: Apr-May, 1946 - No. 2, June-July, 1946; No. 3, Oct-Nov, 1946
1-Origin Stuntman by S&K reprinted in Black Cat #9; S&K-c
123 246 369 787 1344 1900
2-S&K-c/a; The Duke of Broadway story 68 136 204 435 743 1050
3-Small size (5-1/2x8-1/2"; B&W; 32 pgs.); distributed to mail subscribers only; S&K-a; Kid Adonis by S&K reprinted in Green Hornet #37
123 246 369 787 1344 1900
(Also see All-New #15, Boy Explorers #2, Flash Gordon #5 & Thrills of Tomorrow)

STUPID COMICS (Also see 40 oz. Collected)
Oni Press/Image Comics: July, 2000; Sept, 2002 - Present ($2.95, B&W)
1-(Oni Press, 7/00) Jim Mahfood 1 page satire strips reprinted from JAVA magazine 3.00
1-3-(Image Comics, 9/02; 10/03) Jim Mahfood 1 page and 2 page satire strips 3.00
TPB (4/06, $12.99) r/#1(Oni) and #1-3(Image); Phoenix New Times strips 13.00

STUPID HEROES
Mirage Studios: Sept, 1993 - No. 3, Dec, 1994 ($2.75, unfinished limited series)
1-3-Laird-c/a & scripts; 2 trading cards bound in 3.00

STUPID, STUPID RAT TAILS (See Bone)
Cartoon Books: Dec, 1999 - No. 3, Feb, 2000 ($2.95, limited series)
1-3-Jeff Smith-a/Tom Sniegoski-s 3.00

SUBMARINE ATTACK (Formerly Speed Demons)
Charlton Comics: No. 11, May, 1958 - No. 54, Feb-Mar, 1966
11 4 8 12 27 44 60
12-20: 16-Atomic bomb panels 3 6 9 19 30 40
21-30 3 6 9 17 26 35
31-54: 43-Cuban missile crisis story. 47-Atomic bomb panels
3 6 9 15 22 28
NOTE: *Glanzman c/a-25.* ***Montes/Bache** a-38, 40, 41.*

SUB-MARINER (See All-Select, All-Winners, Blonde Phantom, Daring, The Defenders, Fantastic Four #4, Human Torch, The Invaders, Iron Man &..., Marvel Mystery, Marvel Spotlight #27, Men's Adventures, Motion Picture Funnies Weekly, Namora, Namor, The..., Prince Namor, The Sub-Mariner, Saga Of The..., Tales to Astonish #70 & 2nd series, USA & Young Men)

SUB-MARINER, THE (2nd Series)(Sub-Mariner #31 on)
Marvel Comics Group: May, 1968 - No. 72, Sept, 1974 (No. 43: 52 pgs.)
1-Origin Sub-Mariner; story continued from Iron Man & Sub-Mariner #1
23 46 69 161 356 550
2-Triton app. 10 20 30 64 132 200
3-5: 5-1st Tiger Shark (9/68) 7 14 21 46 86 125
6,7,9,10: 6-Tiger Shark-c & 2nd app., cont'd from #5. 7-Photo-c. (1968).
9-1st app. Serpent Crown (origin in #10 & 12) 5 10 15 33 57 80
8-Sub-Mariner vs. Thing 10 20 30 64 132 200
8-2nd printing (1994) 2 4 6 9 12 15
11-13,15: 15-Last 12¢ issue 4 8 12 28 47 65
14-Sub-Mariner vs. G.A. Toro, who assumes identity of G. A. Human Torch; death of Toro (1st modern app. & only app. Toro, 6/69) 6 12 18 37 66 95
16-20: 19-1st Sting Ray (11/69); Stan Lee, Romita, Heck, Thomas, Everett & Kirby cameos. 20-Dr. Doom app. 3 6 9 21 33 45
21,23-33,37-39,41,42: 25-Origin Atlantis. 30-Capt. Marvel x-over. 37-Death of Lady Dorma. 38-Origin retold. 42-Last 15¢ issue. 3 6 9 16 24 32
22,40: 22-Dr. Strange x-over. 40-Spider-Man x-over 3 6 9 17 26 35
34-Prelude (w/#35) to 1st Defenders story; Hulk & Silver Surfer x-over
10 20 30 64 132 200
35-Namor/Hulk/Silver Surfer team-up to battle The Avengers-c/story (3/71); hints at teaming up again 6 12 18 41 76 110
36-Wrightson-a(i) 3 6 9 19 30 40
43-King Size Special (52 pgs.) 3 6 9 20 31 42
44,45-Sub-Mariner vs. Human Torch 3 6 9 18 28 38
46-49,56,62,64-72: 47,48-Dr. Doom app. 49-Cosmic Cube story. 62-1st Tales of Atlantis, ends #66. 64-Hitler cameo. 67-New costume; F.F. x-over. 69-Spider-Man x-over (6 panels)
2 4 6 9 13 16
50-1st app. Nita, Namor's niece (later Namorita in New Warriors)
2 4 6 11 16 20
51-55,57,58,60,61,63-Everett issues: 57-Venus app. (1st since 4/52); anti-Vietnam War panels. 61-Last artwork by Everett; 1st 4 pgs. completed by Mortimer; pgs. 5-20 by Mooney
2 4 6 10 14 18
59-1st battle with Thor; Everett-a 4 8 12 23 37 50
Special 1 (1/71)-r/Tales to Astonish #70-73 3 6 9 20 31 42
Special 2 (1/72)-(52 pgs.)-r/T.T.A. #74-76; Everett-a 3 6 9 16 24 32
NOTE: ***Bolle** a-67i.* ***Buscema** a(p)-1-8, 20, 24.* ***Colan** a(p)-10, 11, 40, 43, 46-49, Special 1, 2; c(p)-10, 11, 40.* ***Craig** a-17i, 19-23i.* ***Everett** a-45r, 50-55, 57, 58, 59-61(plot), 63(plot); c-47, 48i, 55, 57, 58-59i, 61, Spec. 2.* ***G. Kane** c(p)-42-52, 58, 66, 70, 71.* ***Mooney** a-24i, 25i, 32-35i, 39i, 42i, 44i, 45i, 60i, 61i, 65p, 66p, 68i.* ***John Severin** c/a-38i.* ***Marie Severin** c-a 14p.* ***Starlin** c-59p.* ***Tuska** a-41p, 42p, 69-71p.* ***Wrightson** a-36i. #53, 54-r/stories Sub-Mariner Comics #41 & 39.*

SUB-MARINER (The Initiative, follows Civil War series)
Marvel Comics: Aug, 2007 - No. 6, Jan, 2008 ($2.99, limited series)
1-6: 1-Turner-c/Briones-a/Cherniss & Johnson-s; Iron Man app. 3-Yu-c; Venom app. 3.00
...: Revolution TPB (2008, $14.99) r/#1-6 15.00

SUB-MARINER COMICS (1st Series) (The Sub-Mariner #1, 2, 33-42)(Official True Crime Cases #24 on; Amazing Mysteries #32 on; Best Love #33 on)
Timely/Marvel Comics (TCI 1-7/SePI 8/MPI 9-32/Atlas Comics (CCC 33-42)): Spring, 1941 - No. 23, Sum, 1947; No. 24, Wint, 1947 - No. 31, 4/49; No. 32, 7/49; No. 33, 4/54 - No. 42, 10/55
1-The Sub-Mariner by Everett & The Angel begin: Nazi WWII-c
2750 5500 8250 20,500 50,250 80,000
2-Everett-a; Nazi WWII-c 703 1406 2109 5132 9066 13,000
3-Churchill assassination-c; 40 pg. S-M story 622 1244 1866 4541 8021 11,500
4-Everett-a, 40 pgs.; 1 pg. Wolverton-a; Nazi WWII-c
449 898 1347 3278 5789 8300
5-Gabrielle/Klein-c; Japanese WWII-c 389 778 1167 2723 4762 6800
6-8,10-Japanese WWII-c 371 742 1113 2600 4550 6500
9-Classic Japanese WWII flag-c (Spr. 1943); Wolverton-a, 3 pgs.
389 778 1167 2723 4762 6800
11-Classic Schomburg-c 459 918 1377 3350 5925 8500
12,14-Nazi WWII-c 303 606 909 2121 3711 5300
13-Classic Schomburg hooded Japanese WWII bondage-c
371 742 1113 2600 4550 6500
15-Schomburg Japanese WWII-c 300 600 900 2070 3635 5200
16,17-Japanese WWII-c 290 580 870 1856 3178 4500
18-20 239 478 717 1530 2615 3700
21-Last Angel; Everett-a 152 304 456 965 1658 2350
22-Young Allies app. 152 304 456 965 1658 2350
23-The Human Torch, Namora x-over (Sum/47); 2nd app. Namora after Marvel Mystery #82 187 374 561 1197 2049 2900
24-Namora x-over (3rd app.) 187 374 561 1197 2049 2900
25-The Blonde Phantom begins (Spr/48), ends No. 31; Kurtzman-a; Namora x-over; last quarterly issue 174 348 522 1114 1907 2700
26,27: 26-Namora c/app. 161 322 483 1030 1765 2500
28-Namora cover; Everett-a 194 388 582 1242 2121 3000
29-31 (4/49): 29-The Human Torch app. 31-Capt. America app.
181 362 543 1158 1979 2800
32 (7/49, Scarce)-Origin Sub-Mariner 400 800 1200 2800 4900 7000
33 (4/54)-Origin Sub-Mariner; The Human Torch app.; Namora x-over in Sub-Mariner #33-42
135 270 405 864 1482 2100
34,35-Human Torch in ea. 34-Namora bondage-c 107 214 321 680 1165 1650
36,37,39-41: 36,39-41-Namora app. 105 210 315 667 1146 1625
38-Origin Sub-Mariner's wings; Namora app.; last pre-code (2/55)
110 220 330 704 1202 1700
42-Last issue 116 232 348 742 1271 1800
NOTE: *Angel by* ***Gustavson**-#1, 8.* ***Brodsky** c-34-36, 42.* ***Everett** a-1-4, 22-24, 26-42; c-32, 33, 40.* ***Maneely** a-38; c-37, 39-41.* ***Rico** c-27-31.* ***Schomburg** c-1-4, 6, 8-18, 20.* ***Sekowsky** c-24, 25, 26(w/**Rico**).* ***Shores** c-21-23, 38. Bondage c-13, 22, 24, 25, 34.*

SUB-MARINER COMICS 70th ANNIVERARY SPECIAL
Marvel Comics: June, 2009 ($3.99, one-shot)
1-New WWII story, Breitweiser-a; Williamson-a; r/debut app. from Marvel Comics #1 5.00

SUB-MARINER: THE DEPTHS
Marvel Comics: Nov, 2008 - No. 5, May, 2009 ($3.99, limited series)

Sugar & Spike #7 © DC

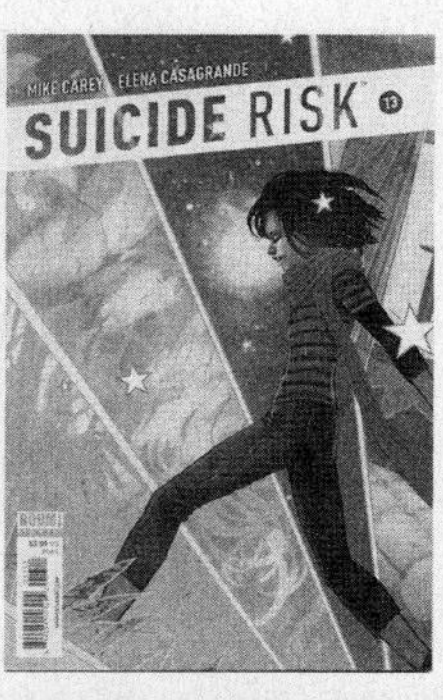

Suicide Risk #13 © BOOM & Carey

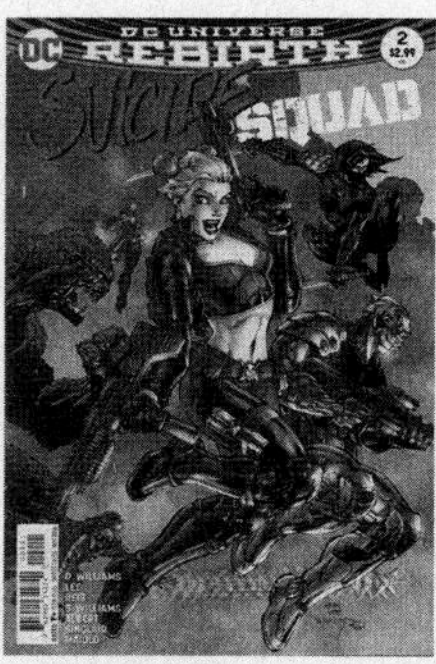

Suicide Squad (2016 series) #2 © DC

GD 2.0 | VG 4.0 | FN 6.0 | VF 8.0 | VF/NM 9.0 | NM- 9.2

1-5-Peter Milligan-s/Esad Ribic-a/c 4.00

SUBSPECIES
Eternity Comics: May, 1991 - No. 4, Aug, 1991 ($2.50, limited series)
1-4: New stories based on horror movie 3.00

SUBTLE VIOLENTS
CFD Productions: 1991 ($2.50, B&W, mature)
1-Linsner-c & story 1 3 4 8 10 12
San Diego Limited Edition 4 8 12 23 37 50

SUE & SALLY SMITH (Formerly My Secret Life)
Charlton Comics: V2#48, Nov, 1962 - No. 54, Nov, 1963 (Flying Nurses)
V2#48-2nd app. 3 6 9 16 24 32
49-54 2 4 6 13 18 22

SUGAR & SPIKE (Also see The Best of DC, DC Silver Age Classics and Legends of Tomorrow)
National Periodical Publications: Apr-May, 1956 - No. 98, Oct-Nov, 1971
1 (Scarce) 432 864 1296 3154 5577 8000
2 152 304 456 965 1658 2350
3-5: 3-Letter column begins 84 168 252 538 919 1300
6-10 50 100 150 315 533 750
11-20 39 78 117 231 378 525
21-29: 26-Christmas-c 26 52 78 154 252 350
30-Scribbly & Scribbly, Jr. x-over 27 54 81 158 259 360
31-40 20 40 60 117 189 260
41-60 8 16 24 54 102 150
61-80: 69-1st app. Tornado-Tot-c/story. 72-Origin & 1st app. Bernie the Brain 6 12 18 42 79 115
81-84,86-93,95: 84-Bernie the Brain apps. as Superman in 1 panel (9/69) 5 10 15 34 60 85
85 (68 pgs.)-r/#72 6 12 18 37 66 95
94-1st app. Raymond, African-American child 6 12 18 37 66 95
96 (68 pgs.) 6 12 18 40 73 105
97,98 (52 pgs.) 6 12 18 37 66 95
No. 1 Replica Edition (2002, $2.95) reprint of #1 4.00
NOTE: *All written and drawn by **Sheldon Mayer.** Issues with Paper Doll pages cut or missing are common.*

SUGAR BOWL COMICS (Teen-age)
Famous Funnies: May, 1948 - No. 5, Jan, 1949
1-Toth-c/a 15 30 45 84 127 170
2,4,5 9 18 27 50 65 80
3-Toth-a 10 20 30 56 76 95

SUGARFOOT (TV)
Dell Publishing Co.: No. 907, May, 1958 - No. 1209, Oct-Dec, 1961
Four Color 907 (#1)-Toth-a, photo-c 10 20 30 67 141 215
Four Color 992 (5-7/59), Toth-a, photo-c 9 18 27 63 129 195
Four Color 1059 (11-1/60), 1098 (5-7/60), 1147 (11-1/61), 1209-all photo-c. 1059,1098,1147-all have variant edition, back-c comic strip 7 14 21 49 92 135

SUGARSHOCK (Also see MySpace Dark Horse Presents)
Dark Horse Comics: Oct, 2009 ($3.50, one-shot)
1-Joss Whedon-s/Fabio Moon-a/c; story from online comic; Moon sketch pgs. 3.50

SUICIDE RISK
BOOM! Studios: May, 2013 - No. 25, May, 2015 ($3.99)
1-25: 1-Carey-s/Casagrande-a. 5-Joëlle Jones-a. 10-Coelho-a 4.00

SUICIDERS
DC Comics (Vertigo): Apr, 2015 - No. 6, Nov, 2015 ($3.99)
1-6-Lee Bermejo-s/a/c 4.00

SUICIDERS: KINGS OF HELL.A.
DC Comics (Vertigo): May, 2016 - No. 6 ($3.99)
1-6-Lee Bermejo-s/c. 1-5-Alessandro Vitti-a. 6-Gerardo Zaffino-a; Bermejo-a (2 pgs.) 4.00

SUICIDE SQUAD (See Brave & the Bold, Doom Patrol & Suicide Squad Spec., Legends #3 & note under Star Spangled War stories)
DC Comics: May, 1987 - No. 66, June, 1992; No. 67, Mar, 2010 (Direct sales only #32 on)
1-Chaykin-c 5 10 15 31 53 75
2-10: 9-Millennium x-over. 10-Batman-c/story 6.00
11-22,24-47,50-66: 13-JLI app. (Batman). 16-Re-intro Shade The Changing Man. 27-34,36,37-Snyder-a. 38- Origin Bronze Tiger. 40-43-"The Phoenix Gambit" Batman storyline. 40-Free Batman/Suicide Squad poster 4.00
23-1st Oracle 3 6 9 19 30 40
48-Joker/Batgirl-c/s 3 6 9 19 30 40
49-Joker/Batgirl-c/s 2 4 6 10 14 18
67-(3/10, $2.99) Blackest Night one-shot; Fiddler rises as a Black Lantern; Califore-a 4.00
Annual 1 (1988, $1.50)-Manhunter x-over 5.00
...: Trial By Fire TPB (2011, $19.99) r/#1-8 & Secret Origins #14 20.00

SUICIDE SQUAD (2nd series)
DC Comics: Nov, 2001 - No. 12, Oct, 2002 ($2.50)
1-Giffen-s/Medina-a; Sgt. Rock app. 5.00
2-9: 4-Heath-a 4.00
10-12-Suicide Squad vs. Antiphon: 10-J. Severin-a. 12-JSA app. 1 3 4 6 8 10

SUICIDE SQUAD (3rd series)
DC Comics: Nov, 2007 - No. 8, Jun, 2008 ($2.99, limited series)
1-8-Ostrander-s/Pina-a/Snyder III-c 4.00
...: From the Ashes TPB (2008, $19.99) r/#1-8 20.00

SUICIDE SQUAD (DC New 52)(Also see New Suicide Squad)
DC Comics: Nov, 2011 - No. 30, Jul, 2014 ($2.99)
1-Harley Quinn, Deadshot, King Shark, El Diablo, Voltaic, Black Spider team up 5 10 15 30 50 70
1-(2nd printing) 2 4 6 13 28 22
1 Special Edition (5/16, FCBD giveaway) 3.00
2-5 1 2 3 5 6 8
6-Origin Harley Quinn part 1 3 6 9 17 26 35
6,7-(2nd printing) 1 2 3 5 6 8
7-Origin Harley Quinn part 2 3 6 9 14 20 25
8-13,16-20,22-30: 19-Unknown Soldier joins. 24-29-Forever Evil tie-in. 24-Omac returns 4.00
14,15-Death of the Family tie-in; Joker app. 5.00
14-Variant die-cut Joker mask-c; Death of the Family tie-in 6.00
21-Harley Quinn-c/s 1 3 4 6 8 10
30-($3.99) Forever Evil tie-in; Coelho-a/Mahnke-c 4.00
#0 (11/12, $2.99) Amanda Waller pre-Suicide Squad; Dagnino-a 5.00
...: Amanda Waller (5/14, $4.99) Jim Zub-s/Coelho-a 5.00

SUICIDE SQUAD (DC Rebirth)
DC Comics: Oct, 2016 - Present ($2.99)
1-Harley Quinn, Deadshot, Killer Croc, Katana, Boomerang team up; Jim Lee-a; back-up origin of Deadshot retold; Fabok-a 3.00
2-7: 2,3-Zod app. 2-Back-up Boomerang origin w/Reis-a. 3-Back-up Katana origin 3.00
8-12: 8-Killer Frost joins; Justice League vs. Suicide Squad prelude; Lee-a. 9,10-JL vs. SS tie-ins. 11,12-Romita Jr.-a 3.00
...: Rebirth (10/16, $2.99) Rick Flag joins; Harley Quinn, Deadshot, Boomerang app. 3.00
... Special: War Crimes 1 (10/16, $4.99) Ostrander-s/Gus Vazquez-a; Shado app. 5.00

SUICIDE SQUAD MOST WANTED: DEADSHOT & KATANA
DC Comics: Mar, 2016 - No. 6, Aug, 2016 ($4.99, limited series)
1-6-Deadshot by Buccellato-s/Bogdanovic-a; Katana by Barr-s/Neves-a; Nord-c 5.00

SUICIDE SQUAD MOST WANTED: EL DIABLO & BOOMERANG (Title changes to Suicide Squad Most Wanted: El Diablo & Amanda Waller for #5,6)
DC Comics: Oct, 2016 - No. 6, Mar, 2017 ($4.99, limited series)
1-4-El Diablo by Nitz-s/Richards-a; Boomerang by Moreci-s/Bazaldua-a; Huddleston-c 5.00
5,6-Amanda Waller by Ayala-s/Merhoff-a; El Diablo by Nitz-s/Richards-a 5.00

SUMMER FUN (See Dell Giants)

SUMMER FUN (Formerly Li'l Genius; Holiday Surprise #55)
Charlton Comics: No. 54, Oct, 1966 (Giant)
54 3 6 9 21 33 45

SUMMER FUN (Walt Disney's...)
Disney Comics: Summer, 1991 ($2.95, annual, 68 pgs.)
1-D. Duck, M. Mouse, Brer Rabbit, Chip 'n' Dale & Pluto, Li'l Bad Wolf, Super Goof, Scamp stories 4.00

SUMMER LOVE (Formerly Brides in Love?)
Charlton Comics: V2#46, Oct, 1965; V2#47, Oct, 1966; V2#48, Nov, 1968
V2#46-Beatles-c & 8 pg. story 11 22 33 76 163 250
47-(68 pgs.) Beatles-c & 12 pg. story 9 18 27 61 123 185
48 3 6 9 15 22 28

SUMMER MAGIC (See Movie Comics)

SUNDANCE (See Hotel Deparee...)

SUNDANCE KID (Also see Blazing Six-Guns)
Skywald Publications: June, 1971 - No. 3, Sept, 1971 (52 pgs.)(Pre-code reprints & new-s)
1-Durango Kid; Two Kirby Bullseye-r 3 6 9 16 23 30
2,3: 2-Swift Arrow, Durango Kid, Bullseye by S&K; Meskin plus 1 pg. origin.

Sun Girl #2 © MAR

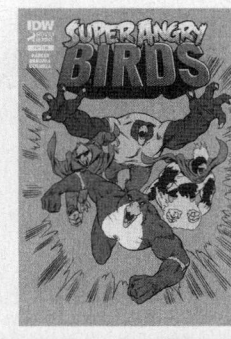

Super Angry Birds #4 © Rovio

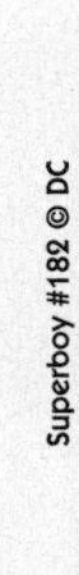

Superboy #182 © DC

	GD 2.0	VG 4.0	FN 6.0	VF 8.0	VF/NM 9.0	NM- 9.2
3-Durango Kid, Billy the Kid, Red Hawk-r	2	4	6	11	16	20
SUNDAY PIX (Christian religious)						
David C. Cook Pub/USA Weekly Newsprint Color Comics: V1#1, Mar,1949 - V16#26, July 19, 1964 (7x10", 12 pgs., mail subscription only)						
V1#1	8	16	24	42	54	65
V1#2-up	6	12	18	27	33	38
V2#1-52 (1950)	5	10	15	23	28	32
V3-V6 (1951-1953)	4	9	13	18	22	26
V7-V11#1-7,23-52 (1954-1959)	2	4	6	13	18	22
V11#8-22 (2/22-5/31/59) H.G. Wells First Men in the Moon serial	3	6	9	14	19	24
V12#1-19,21-52; V13-V15#1,2,9-52; V16#1-26(7/19/64)	2	4	6	10	14	18
V12#20 (5/15/60) 2 page interview with Peanuts' Charles Schulz	4	8	12	23	37	50
V15#3-8 (2/24/63) John Glenn, Christian astronaut	3	6	9	16	23	30
SUN DEVILS						
DC Comics: July, 1984 - No. 12, June, 1985 ($1.25, maxi series)						
1-12: 6-Death of Sun Devil						4.00
SUNDIATA: A LEGEND OF AFRICA						
NBM Publishing Inc.: 2002 ($15.95, hardcover with dustjacket)						
nn-Will Eisner-s/a; adaptation of an African folk tale						16.00
SUNDOWNERS						
Dark Horse Comics: Aug, 2014 - No. 6, Jan, 2015 ($3.50)						
1-6: 1-Tim Seeley-s/Jim Terry-a						3.50
SUN FUN KOMIKS						
Sun Publications: 1939 (15¢, B&W & red)						
1-Satire on comics (rare); 1st Hitler app. in comics?	568	1136	1704	4146	7323	10,500
NOTE: *Hitler, Stalin and Mussolini featured gag in 1-page story written in Hebrew and English. Nazi swastika and Nazi flag app. in a different 1-page "Gussie the Gob" story.*						
SUNFIRE & BIG HERO SIX (See Alpha Flight)						
Marvel Comics: Sept, 1998 - No. 3, Nov, 1998 ($2.50, limited series)						
1-Lobdell-s	4	8	12	27	44	60
2,3	2	4	6	11	16	20
SUN GIRL (See The Human Torch & Marvel Mystery Comics #88)						
Marvel Comics (CCC): Aug, 1948 - No. 3, Dec, 1948						
1-Sun Girl begins; Miss America app.	245	490	735	1568	2684	3800
2,3: 2-The Blonde Phantom begins	161	322	483	1030	1765	2500
SUNNY, AMERICA'S SWEETHEART (Formerly Cosmo Cat #1-10)						
Fox Features Syndicate: No. 11, Dec, 1947 - No. 14, June, 1948						
11-Feldstein-c/a	145	290	435	921	1586	2250
12-14: 12,13-Feldstein-a; 13,14-Lingerie panels. 13-L.B. Cole-a	97	194	291	621	1061	1500
I.W. Reprint #8-Feldstein-a; r/Fox issue	10	20	30	73	129	185
SUN-RUNNERS (Also see Tales of the...)						
Pacific Comics/Eclipse Comics/Amazing Comics: 2/84 - No. 3, 5/84; No. 4, 11/84 - No. 7, 1986 (Baxter paper)						
1-7: P. Smith-a in #2-4						4.00
Christmas Special 1 (1987, $1.95)-By Amazing						4.00
SUNSET CARSON (Also see Cowboy Western)						
Charlton Comics: Feb, 1951 - No. 4, 1951 (No month) (Photo-c on each)						
1-Photo/retouched-c (Scarce, all issues)	58	116	174	371	636	900
2-Kit Carson story; adapts "Kansas Raiders" w/Brian Donlevy, Audie Murphy & Margaret Chapman	41	82	123	256	428	600
3,4	34	68	102	199	325	450
SUNSET PASS (See Zane Grey & 4-Color #230)						
SUPER ANGRY BIRDS (Based on Rovio videogame Angry Birds)						
IDW Publishing: Sept, 2015 - No. 4, Dec, 2015 ($3.99, limited series)						
1-4: 1-The Eagle's Eye - Jeff Parker-s/Ron Randall-a; two covers						4.00
SUPER ANIMALS PRESENTS PIDGY & THE MAGIC GLASSES						
Star Publications: Dec, 1953 (25¢, came w/glasses)						
1-(3-D Comics)-L. B. Cole-c	40	80	120	246	411	575
SUPER BAD JAMES DYNOMITE						
5-D Comics: Dec, 2005 - No. 5, Feb, 2007 ($3.99)						
1-5-Created by the Wayans brothers						4.00

	GD 2.0	VG 4.0	FN 6.0	VF 8.0	VF/NM 9.0	NM- 9.2
SUPERBOY						
DC Comics: Jan, 1942						
nn-Ashcan comic, not distributed to newsstands, only for in house use. Covers were produced, but not the rest of the book. A CGC certified 9.2 copy sold in 2003 for $6,600.						
SUPERBOY (See Adventure, Aurora, DC Comics Presents, DC 100 Page Super Spectacular #15, DC Super Stars, 80 Page Giant #10, More Fun Comics, The New Advs. of... & Superman Family #191, Young Justice)						
SUPERBOY (1st Series)(...& the Legion of Super-Heroes with #231) (Becomes The Legion of Super-Heroes No. 259 on)						
National Periodical Publ./DC Comics: Mar-Apr, 1949 - No. 258, Dec, 1979 (#1-16: 52 pgs.)						
1-Superman cover; intro in More Fun #101 (1-2/45)	1000	2000	3000	7400	13,200	19,000
2-Used in **SOTI**, pg. 35-36,226	265	530	795	1694	2897	4100
3	194	388	582	1242	2121	3000
4,5: 5-1st pre-Supergirl tryout (c/story, 11-12/49)	142	284	426	909	1555	2200
6-9: 8-1st Superbaby	123	246	369	787	1344	1900
10-1st app. Lana Lang	142	284	426	909	1555	2200
11-15: 11-2nd Lana Lang app.; 1st Lana cover	90	180	270	576	988	1400
16-20: 20-2nd Jor-El cover	63	126	189	403	689	975
21-26,28-30: 21-Lana Lang app.	54	108	162	343	574	825
27-Low distribution	55	110	165	352	601	850
31-38: 38-Last pre-code issue (1/55)	47	94	141	296	498	700
39-48,50 (7/56)	42	84	126	265	445	625
49 (6/56)-1st app. Metallo (this one's Jor-El's robot)	71	142	213	454	777	1100
51-60: 51-Krypto app. 52-1st S.A. issue. 56-Krypto-c	34	68	102	199	325	450
61-67	28	56	84	165	270	375
68-Origin/1st app. original Bizarro (10-11/58)	206	412	618	1318	2259	3200
69-77,79: 76-1st Supermonkey	24	48	72	142	234	325
78-Origin Mr. Mxyzptlk & Superboy's costume	34	68	102	199	325	450
80-1st meeting Superboy/Supergirl (4/60)	36	72	108	211	343	475
81,83-85,87,88: 83-Origin/1st app. Kryptonite Kid	13	26	39	86	188	290
82-1st Bizarro Krypto	15	30	45	103	227	350
86-(1/61)-4th Legion app; Intro Pete Ross	24	48	72	170	378	585
89-(6/61)-1st app. Mon -El; 2nd Phantom Zone	34	68	102	245	548	850
90-92: 90-Pete Ross learns Superboy's I.D. 92-Last 10¢ issue	11	22	33	76	163	250
93-10th Legion app.(12/61); Chameleon Boy app.	12	24	36	79	170	260
94-97,99: 94-1st app. Superboy Revenge Squad	10	20	30	68	144	220
98-(7/62) Legion app; origin & 1st app. Ultra Boy; Pete Ross joins Legion	14	28	42	94	207	320
100-(10/62)-Ultra Boy app; 1st app. Phantom Zone villains, Dr. Xadu & Erndine. 2 pg. map of Krypton; origin Superboy retold; r-cover of Superman #1	17	34	51	117	259	400
101-120: 104-Origin Phantom Zone. 115-Atomic bomb-c. 117-Legion app.	9	18	27	57	111	165
121-128: 124-(10/65)-1st app. Insect Queen (Lana Lang). 125-Legion cameo. 126-Origin Krypto the Super Dog retold with new facts	7	14	21	49	92	135
129-(80-pg. Giant G-22)-Reprints origin Mon-El	9	18	27	57	111	165
130-137,139,140: 131-Legion statues cameo in Dog Legionnaires story. 132-1st app. Supremo. 133-Superboy meets Robin	6	12	18	41	76	110
138 (80-pg. Giant G-35)	7	14	21	46	86	125
141-146,148-155,157: 145-Superboy's parents regain their youth. 148-Legion app. 157-Last 12¢ issue	5	10	15	35	63	90
147(6/68)-Giant G-47; 1st origin of L.S.H. (Saturn Girl, Lightning Lad, Cosmic Boy); origin Legion of Super-Pets-r/Adv. #293	6	12	18	41	76	110
147 Replica Edition (2003, $6.95) reprints entire issue; cover recreation by Ordway						7.00
156-(Giant G-59)	6	12	18	38	69	100
158-164,166-171,175: 171-1st app. Aquaboy	3	6	9	18	28	38
165,174 (Giant G-71,G-83): 165-r/1st app. Krypto the Superdog from Adventure Comics #210	5	10	15	34	60	85
172,173,176-Legion app.: 172-1st app. & origin Yango (The Super Ape). 176-Partial photo-c; last 15¢ issue	3	6	9	19	30	40
177-184,186,187 (All 52 pgs.): 182-All new origin of the classic World's Finest team (Superman & Batman) as teenagers (2/72, 22pgs). 184-Origin Dial H for Hero-r	3	6	9	20	31	42
185-Also listed as DC 100 Pg. Super Spectacular #12; Legion-c/story; Teen Titans, Kid Eternity(r/Hit #46), Star Spangled Kid-r(S.S. #55)	7	14	21	46	86	125
188-190,192,194,196: 188-Origin Karkan. 196-Last Superboy solo story	3	6	9	14	19	24
191,193,195: 191-Origin Sunboy retold; Legion app. 193-Chameleon Boy & Shrinking Violet get new costumes. 195-1st app. Erg-1/Wildfire; Phantom Girl gets new costume	3	6	9	14	20	26
197-Legion series begins; Lightning Lad's new costume						

Superboy #209 © DC

Superboy (3rd series) #62 © DC

Super Comics #10 © DELL

GD VG FN VF VF/NM NM-
2.0 4.0 6.0 8.0 9.0 9.2

4 8 12 23 37 50
198,199: 198-Element Lad & Princess Projectra get new costumes
3 6 9 14 20 26
200-Bouncing Boy & Duo Damsel marry; J'onn J'onzz cameo
3 6 9 16 23 30
201,204,206,207,209: 201-Re-intro Erg-1 as Wildfire. 204-Supergirl resigns from Legion. 206-Ferro Lad & Invisible Kid app. 209-Karate Kid gets new costume
2 4 6 11 16 20
202,205-(100 pgs.): 202-Light Lass gets new costume; Mike Grell's 1st comic work-i (5-6/74)
4 8 12 28 47 65
203-Invisible Kid killed by Validus 3 6 9 15 22 28
208,210: 208-(68 pgs.). 208-Legion of Super-Villains app. 210-Origin Karate Kid
3 6 9 14 20 26
211-220: 212-Matter-Eater Lad resigns. 216-1st app. Tyroc, who joins the Legion in #218
2 4 6 9 13 16
221-230,246-249: 226-Intro. Dawnstar. 228-Death of Chemical King
2 4 6 8 10 12
231-245: (Giants). 240-Origin Dawnstar. 242-(52 pgs.). 243-Legion of Substitute Heroes app. 243-245-(44 pgs.). 2 4 6 9 13 16
244,245-(Whitman variants; low print run, no issue# shown on cover)
3 6 9 14 20 26
246-248-(Whitman variants; low ...) 2 4 6 11 16 20
250-258: 253-Intro Blok. 257-Return of Bouncing Boy & Duo Damsel by Ditko
2 3 4 6 8 10
251-258-(Whitman variants; low print run) 2 4 6 10 14 18
Annual 1 (Sum/64, 84 pgs.)-Origin Krypto-r 15 30 45 103 227 350
Spectacular 1 (1980, Giant)-1st comic distributed only through comic stores; mostly-r
2 4 6 8 10 12
...: The Greatest Team-Up Stories Ever Told TPB (2010, $19.99) r/team-ups with Robin, Supergirl, young versions of Aquaman, Green Arrow, Bruce Wayne; Davis-c 20.00

NOTE: ***Neal Adams** c-143, 145, 146, 148-155, 157-161, 163, 164, 166-168, 172, 173, 175, 176, 178. **M. Anderson** a-178,179, 245i. **Ditko** a-257p. **Grell** a-202i, 203-219, 220-224p, 235p; c-207-232, 235, 236p, 237, 239p, 240p, 243p, 246, 258. **Nasser** a(p)-222, 225, 226, 230, 231, 233, 236. **Simonson** a-237p. **Starlin** a(p)-239, 250, 251; c-238. **Staton** a-227p, 243-249p, 252-258p; c-247-251p. **Swan/Moldoff** c-109. **Tuska** a-172, 173, 176, 183, 235p. **Wood** inks-153-155, 157-161. Legion app.-172, 173, 176, 177, 183, 184, 188, 190, 191, 193, 195, 197-258.*

SUPERBOY (TV)(2nd Series)(The Adventures of...#19 on)
DC Comics: Feb, 1990 - No. 22, Dec, 1991 ($1.00/$1.25)

1-Photo-c from TV show; Mooney-a(p) 4.00
2-22: Mooney-a in 2-8,18-20; 8-Bizarro-c/story; Arthur Adams-a(i). 9-12,14-17-Swan-a 3.00
...Special 1 (1992, $1.75) Swan-a 4.00

SUPERBOY (3rd Series)
DC Comics: Feb, 1994 - No. 100, Jul, 2002 ($1.50/$1.95/$1.99/$2.25)

1-Metropolis Kid from Reign of the Supermen 4.00
2-8,0,9-24,26-76: 6,7-Worlds Collide Pts. 3 & 8. 8-(9/94)-Zero Hour x-over. 0-(10/94). 9-(11/94)-King Shark app. 21-Legion app. 28-Supergirl-c/app. 33-Final Night. 38-41-"Meltdown". 45-Legion-c/app. 47-Green Lantern-c/app. 50-Last Boy on Earth begins. 60-Crosses Hypertime. 68-Demon-c/app. 3.00
25-($2.95)-New Gods & Female Furies app.; w/pin-ups 4.00
77-99: 77-Begin $2.25-c. 79-Superboy's powers return. 80,81-Titans app. 83-New costume. 85-Batgirl app. 90,91-Our Worlds at War x-over 3.00
100-($3.50) Sienkiewicz-c; Grummett & McCrea-a; Superman cameo 4.00
#1,000,000 (11/98) 853rd Century x-over 3.00
Annual 1 (1994, $2.95, 68 pgs.)-Elseworlds story, Pt. 2 of The Super Seven (see Adventures Of Superman Annual #6) 4.00
Annual 2 (1995, $3.95)-Year One story 4.00
Annual 3 (1996, $2.95)-Legends of the Dead Earth 4.00
Annual 4 (1997, $3.95)-Pulp Heroes story 4.00
...Plus 1 (Jan, 1997, $2.95) w/Capt. Marvel Jr. 4.00
...Plus 2 (Fall, 1997, $2.95) w/Slither (Scare Tactics) 4.00
.../Risk Double-Shot 1 (Feb, 1998, $1.95) w/Risk (Teen Titans) 3.00

SUPERBOY (4th Series)
DC Comics: Jan, 2011 - No. 11, Early Oct, 2011 ($2.99)

1-11: 1-Lemire-s/Gallo-a/Albuquerque-c; Parasite & Poison Ivy app. 2,3-Noto-c 3.00
1-5: 1-Variant-c by Cassaday. 2-March-var-c. 3-Nguyen var-c. 4-Lau var-c. 5-Manapul 4.00

SUPERBOY (DC New 52)
DC Comics: Nov, 2011 - No. 34, Oct, 2014 ($2.99)

1-34: 1-New origin; Lobdell-s/Silva-a/Canete-c; Caitlin Fairchild app. 6-Supergirl app. 8-Grunge, Beast Boy & Terra app. 9-"The Culling" x-over cont. from Teen Titans Annual #1; Teen Titans and the Legion app. 14-17-H'El on Earth tie-in; Batman app. 3.00
#0-(11/12, $2.99) Origin of Kryptonian clones; Silva-a 3.00
Annual 1 (3/13, $4.99) H'El on Earth tie-in between Superboy #16 & Superman #16 5.00
...: Futures End 1 (11/14, $2.99, regular-c) Five years later, Freefall app.; Caldwell-a 3.00
...: Futures End 1 (11/14, $3.99, 3-D cover) 4.00

SUPERBOY AND THE LEGION OF SUPER-HEROES
DC Comics: 2011 ($14.99, TPB)

SC-Reprints stories from Adventure Comics #515-520 15.00

SUPERBOY & THE RAVERS
DC Comics: Sept, 1996 - No. 19, March, 1998 ($1.95)

1-19: 4-Adam Strange app. 7-Impulse-c/app. 9-Superman-c/app. 3.00

SUPERBOY COMICS
DC Comics: Jan. 1942

nn - Ashcan comic, not distributed to newsstands, only for in-house use. Cover art is Detective Comics #57 with interior being Action Comics #38. A CGC certified 9.2 copy sold for $6,600 in 2003 and for $15,750 in 2008.

SUPERBOY/ROBIN: WORLD'S FINEST THREE
DC Comics: 1996 - No. 2, 1996 ($4.95, squarebound, limited series)

1,2: Superboy & Robin vs. Metallo & Poison Ivy; Karl Kesel & Chuck Dixon scripts; Tom Grummett-c(p)/a(p) 5.00

SUPERBOY'S LEGION (Elseworlds)
DC Comics: 2001 - No. 2, 2001 ($5.95, squarebound, limited series)

1,2-31st century Superboy forms Legion; Farmer-s/i; Davis-a(p)/c 6.00

SUPERBOY: THE BOY OF STEEL
DC Comics: 2010 ($19.99, hardcover with dustjacket)

HC-Reprints stories from Adventure Comics #0-3,5,6 & Superman Secret Files 2009 20.00
SC-(2011, $14,99) Same contents as HC 15.00

SUPER BRAT (Li'l Genius #6 on)
Toby Press: Jan, 1954 - No. 4, July, 1954

1 10 20 30 58 79 100
2-4: 4-Li'l Teevy by Mel Lazarus 7 14 21 35 43 50
I.W. Reprint #1,2,3,7,8('58): 1-r/#1 2 4 6 8 11 14
I.W. (Super) Reprint #10('63) 2 4 6 8 10 12

SUPERCAR (TV)
Gold Key: Nov, 1962 - No. 4, Aug, 1963 (All painted-c)

1 10 20 30 69 147 225
2,3 6 12 18 41 76 110
4-Last issue 7 14 21 46 86 125

SUPER CAT (Formerly Frisky Animals; also see Animal Crackers)
Star Publications #56-58/Ajax/Farrell Publ. (Four Star Comic Corp.):
No. 56, Nov, 1953 - No. 58, May, 1954; Aug, 1957 - No. 4, May, 1958

56-58-L.B. Cole-c on all 20 40 60 114 182 250
1(1957-Ajax)- "The Adventures of..." c-only 10 20 30 54 72 90
2-4 7 14 21 35 43 50

SUPER CIRCUS (TV)
Cross Publishing Co.: Jan, 1951 - No. 5, Sept, 1951 (Mary Hartline)

1-(52 pgs.)-Cast photos on-c 18 36 54 105 165 225
2-Cast photos on-c 11 22 33 62 86 110
3-5 10 20 30 54 72 90

SUPER CIRCUS (TV)
Dell Publ. Co.: No. 542, Mar, 1954 - No. 694, Mar, 1956 (Mary Hartline)

Four Color 542: Mary Hartline photo-c 7 14 21 46 86 125
Four Color 592,694: Mary Hartline photo-c 6 12 18 37 66 95

SUPER COMICS
Dell Publishing Co.: May, 1938 - No. 121, Feb-Mar, 1949

1-Terry & The Pirates, The Gumps, Dick Tracy, Little Orphan Annie, Little Joe, Gasoline Alley, Smilin' Jack, Smokey Stover, Smitty, Tiny Tim, Moon Mullins, Harold Teen, Winnie Winkle begin 232 464 696 1485 2543 3600
2 84 168 252 538 919 1300
3 74 148 222 470 810 1150
4,5: 4-Dick Tracy-c; also #8-10,17,26(part),31 58 116 174 371 636 900
6-10 47 94 141 296 498 700
11-20: 20-Smilin' Jack-c (also #29,32) 39 78 117 240 395 550
21-29: 21-Magic Morro begins (origin & 1st app., 2/40). 22,27-Ken Ernst-c (also #25?); Magic Morro c-22,25,27,34 34 68 102 199 325 450
30- "Sea Hawk" movie adaptation-c/story with Errol Flynn
35 70 105 208 339 470
31-40: 34-Ken Ernst-c 28 56 84 165 270 375
41-50: 41-Intro Lightning Jim. 43-Terry & The Pirates ends
23 46 69 138 227 315

Super Dinosaur #1 © Kirkman & Howard

Super Friends (2008 series) #1 © DC

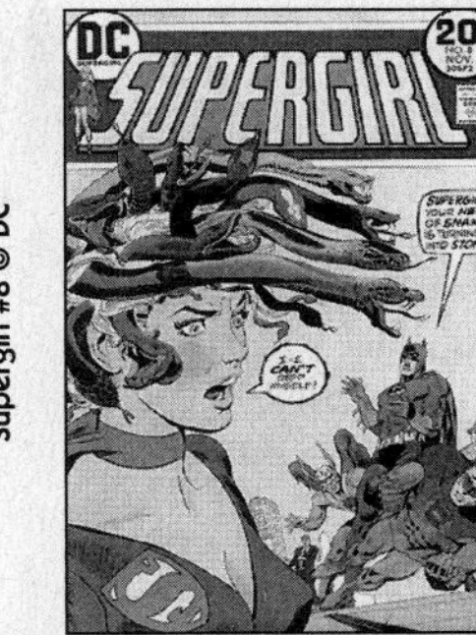

Supergirl #8 © DC

	GD 2.0	VG 4.0	FN 6.0	VF 8.0	VF/NM 9.0	NM- 9.2
51-60	19	38	57	109	172	235
61-70: 62-Flag-c. 65-Brenda Starr-r begin? 67-X-Mas-c	17	34	51	98	154	210
71-80	14	28	42	80	115	150
81-99	13	26	39	74	105	135
100	14	28	42	78	112	145
101-115-Last Dick Tracy (moves to own title)	10	20	30	56	76	95
116-121: 116,118-All Smokey Stover. 117-All Gasoline Alley. 119-121-Terry & The Pirates app. in all	9	18	27	50	65	80

SUPER COPS, THE
Red Circle Productions (Archie): July, 1974 (one-shot)

	GD 2.0	VG 4.0	FN 6.0	VF 8.0	VF/NM 9.0	NM- 9.2
1-Morrow-c/a; art by Pino, Hack, Thorne	2	4	6	8	11	14

SUPER COPS
Now Comics: Sept, 1990 - No. 4, Dec?, 1990 ($1.75)

	GD 2.0	VG 4.0	FN 6.0	VF 8.0	VF/NM 9.0	NM- 9.2
1-($2.75, 52 pgs.)-Dave Dorman painted-c (both printings)						4.00
2-4						3.00

SUPER CRACKED (See Cracked)

SUPERCROOKS
Marvel Comics (Icon): May, 2012 - No. 4, Aug, 2012 ($2.99/$4.99)

	GD 2.0	VG 4.0	FN 6.0	VF 8.0	VF/NM 9.0	NM- 9.2
1-3-($2.99) Millar-s/Yu-a. 1-Covers by Yu & Gibbons. 2-Covers by Yu & Hitch						3.00
4-($4.99) Bonus preview of Jupiter's Children (later re-titled Jupiter's Legacy)						5.00

SUPER DC GIANT (25-50¢, all 68-52 pg. Giants)
National Per. Publ.: No. 13, 9-10/70 - No. 26, 7-8/71; V3#27, Summer, 1976 (No #1-12)

	GD 2.0	VG 4.0	FN 6.0	VF 8.0	VF/NM 9.0	NM- 9.2
S-13-Binky	10	20	30	64	132	200
S-14-Top Guns of the West; Kubert-c; Trigger Twins, Johnny Thunder, Wyoming Kid-r; Moreira-r (9-10/70)	5	10	15	33	57	80
S-15-Western Comics; Kubert-c; Pow Wow Smith, Vigilante, Buffalo Bill-r; new Gil Kane-a (9-10/70)	5	10	15	33	57	80
S-16-Best of the Brave & the Bold; Batman-r & Metamorpho origin-r from Brave & the Bold; Spectre pin-up.	4	8	12	27	44	60
S-17-Love 1970 (scarce)	23	46	69	161	356	550
S-18-Three Mouseketeers; Dizzy Dog, Doodles Duck, Bo Bunny-r; Sheldon Mayer-a	9	18	27	57	111	165
S-19-Jerry Lewis; Neal Adams pin-up	9	18	27	59	117	175
S-20-House of Mystery; N. Adams-c; Kirby-r(3)	7	14	21	44	82	120
S-21-Love 1971 (scarce)	27	54	81	194	435	675
S-22-Top Guns of the West; Kubert-c	4	8	12	25	40	55
S-23-The Unexpected	4	8	12	28	47	65
S-24-Supergirl	4	8	12	25	40	55
S-25-Challengers of the Unknown; all Kirby/Wood-r	4	8	12	22	35	48
S-26-Aquaman (1971)-r/S.A. Aquaman origin story from Showcase #30	4	8	12	27	44	60
27-Strange Flying Saucers Adventures (Sum, 1976)	3	6	9	18	28	38

NOTE: ***Sid Greene** r-27p(2), **Heath** r-27. **G. Kane** a-14r(2), 15, 27r(p). **Kubert** r-16.*

SUPER DINOSAUR
Image Comics: Apr, 2011 - Present ($2.99)

	GD 2.0	VG 4.0	FN 6.0	VF 8.0	VF/NM 9.0	NM- 9.2
1-23: 1-Robert Kirkman-s/Jason Howard-a; origin story and character profiles						3.00
... Origin Special #1 FCBD Edition (5/11, giveaway) r/#1						3.00

SUPER-DOOPER COMICS
Able Mfg. Co./Harvey: 1946 - No. 7, May, 1946; No. 8, 1946 (10¢, 32 pgs., paper-c)

	GD 2.0	VG 4.0	FN 6.0	VF 8.0	VF/NM 9.0	NM- 9.2
1-The Clock, Gangbuster app. (scarce)	90	180	270	576	988	1400
2	20	40	60	114	182	250
3-6	18	36	54	105	165	225
7,8-Shock Gibson. 7-Where's Theres A Will by Ed Wheelan, Steve Case Crime Rover, Penny & Ullysses Jr. 8-Sam Hill app.	21	42	63	122	199	275

SUPER DUCK COMICS (The Cockeyed Wonder) (See Jolly Jingles)
MLJ Mag. No. 1-4(9/45)/Close-Up No. 5 on (Archie): Fall, 1944 - No. 94, Dec, 1960 (Also see Laugh #24)(#1-5 are quarterly)

	GD 2.0	VG 4.0	FN 6.0	VF 8.0	VF/NM 9.0	NM- 9.2
1-Origin; Hitler & Hirohito-c	129	258	387	826	1413	2000
2-Bill Vigoda-c	36	72	108	211	343	475
3-5: 4-20-Al Fagaly-c (most)	22	44	66	128	209	290
6-10	15	30	45	86	133	180
11-20(6/48)	12	24	36	67	94	120
21,23-40 (10/51)	10	20	30	58	79	100
22-Used in **SOTI**, pg. 35,307,308	12	24	36	69	97	125
41-60 (2/55)	9	18	27	50	65	80
61-94	8	16	24	40	50	60

SUPER DUPER (Formerly Pocket Comics #1-4?)
Harvey Publications: No. 5, 1941 - No. 11, 1941

	GD 2.0	VG 4.0	FN 6.0	VF 8.0	VF/NM 9.0	NM- 9.2
5-Captain Freedom & Shock Gibson app.	68	136	204	435	743	1050
8,11	47	94	141	296	498	700

SUPER DUPER COMICS (Formerly Latest Comics?)
F. E. Howard Publ.: No. 3, May-June, 1947

	GD 2.0	VG 4.0	FN 6.0	VF 8.0	VF/NM 9.0	NM- 9.2
3-1st app. Mr. Monster	61	122	183	390	670	950

SUPER FRIENDS (TV) (Also see Best of DC & Limited Collectors' Edition)
National Periodical Publications/DC Comics: Nov, 1976 - No. 47, Aug, 1981 (#14 is 44 pgs.)

	GD 2.0	VG 4.0	FN 6.0	VF 8.0	VF/NM 9.0	NM- 9.2
1-Superman, Batman, Robin, Wonder Woman, Aquaman, Atom, Wendy, Marvin & Wonder Dog begin (1st Super Friends)	5	10	15	35	63	90
2-Penguin-c/sty	3	6	9	16	23	30
3-5	3	6	9	14	20	26
6,8-10,14: 8-1st app. Jack O'Lantern. 9-1st app. Icemaiden. 14-Origin Wonder Twins	2	4	6	13	18	22
7-1st app. Wonder Twins & The Seraph	5	10	15	33	57	80
11-13,15-30: 13-1st app. Dr. Mist. 25-1st app. Fire as Green Fury. 28-Bizarro app.	2	4	6	9	13	16
13-16,20-23,25,32-(Whitman variants; low print run, no issue# on cover)	2	4	6	11	16	20
31,47: 31-Black Orchid app. 47-Origin Fire & Green Fury	2	4	6	10	14	18
32-46: 36,43-Plastic Man app.	2	4	6	8	11	14
TBP (2001, $14.95) r/#1,6-9,14,21,27 & Limited Collectors' Edition C-41; Alex Ross-c						15.00
...: Truth, Justice and Peace TPB (2003, $14.95) r/#10,12,13,25,28,29,31,36,37						15.00

NOTE: ***Estrada** a-1p, 2p. **Orlando** a-1p. **Staton** a-43, 45.*

SUPER FRIENDS (All ages stories with puzzles and games)(Based on Mattel toy line)
DC Comics: May, 2008 - No. 29, Sept, 2010 ($2.25/$2.99)

	GD 2.0	VG 4.0	FN 6.0	VF 8.0	VF/NM 9.0	NM- 9.2
1-29-Superman, Batman, Wonder Woman, Aquaman, Flash & Green Lantern. 29-Begin $2.99-c; Bat-Mite & Mr. Mxyzptlk app.						3.00
...: Calling All Super Friends TPB (2009, $12.99) r/#8-14; puzzles and games						13.00
...: For Justice TPB (2009, $12.99) r/#1-7; puzzles and games						13.00
...: Head of the Class TPB (2010, $12.99) r/#15-21; puzzles and games						13.00
...: Mystery in Space TPB (2011, $12.99) r/#22-28; puzzles and games						13.00

SUPER FUN
Gillmor Magazines: Jan, 1956 (By A.W. Nugent)

	GD 2.0	VG 4.0	FN 6.0	VF 8.0	VF/NM 9.0	NM- 9.2
1-Comics, puzzles, cut-outs by A.W. Nugent	9	18	27	47	61	75

SUPER FUNNIES (...Western Funnies #3,4)
Superior Comics Publishers Ltd. (Canada): Dec, 1953 - No. 4, Sept, 1954

	GD 2.0	VG 4.0	FN 6.0	VF 8.0	VF/NM 9.0	NM- 9.2
1-(3-D, 10¢)-...Presents Dopey Duck; make your own 3-D glasses cut-out inside front-c; did not come w/glasses	39	78	117	231	378	525
2-Horror & crime satire	15	30	45	86	133	180
3-Phantom Ranger-c/s; Geronimo, Billy the Kid app.	10	20	30	56	76	95
4-Phantom Ranger-c/story	10	20	30	56	76	95

SUPERGIRL
DC Comics: Feb. 1944

nn - Ashcan comic, not distributed to newsstands, only for in-house use. Cover art is Boy Commandos #1 with interior being Action Comics #80. A copy sold for $15,750 in 2008.

SUPERGIRL (See Action, Adventure #281, Brave & the Bold, Crisis on Infinite Earths #7, Daring New Advs. of..., Super DC Giant, Superman Family, & Super-Team Family)

SUPERGIRL
National Periodical Publ.: Nov, 1972 - No. 9, Dec-Jan, 1973-74; No. 10, Sept-Oct, 1974 (1st solo title)(20¢)

	GD 2.0	VG 4.0	FN 6.0	VF 8.0	VF/NM 9.0	NM- 9.2
1-Zatanna back-up stories begin, end #5	8	16	24	56	108	160
2-4,6,7,9	4	8	12	25	40	55
5,8,10: 5-Zatanna origin-r. 8-JLA x-over; Batman cameo. 10-Prez	4	8	12	27	44	60

NOTE: *Zatanna in #1-5, 7(Guest); Prez app. in #10. #1-10 are 20¢ issues.*

SUPERGIRL (Formerly Daring New Adventures of...)
DC Comics: No. 14, Dec, 1983 - No. 23, Sept, 1984

	GD 2.0	VG 4.0	FN 6.0	VF 8.0	VF/NM 9.0	NM- 9.2
14-23: 16-Ambush Bug app. 20-JLA & New Teen Titans app.						4.00
...Movie Special (1985)-Adapts movie; Morrow-a; photo back-c						4.00

SUPERGIRL
DC Comics: Feb, 1994 - No. 4, May, 1994 ($1.50, limited series)

	GD 2.0	VG 4.0	FN 6.0	VF 8.0	VF/NM 9.0	NM- 9.2
1-4: Guice-a(i)						4.00

SUPERGIRL (See Showcase '96 #8)
DC Comics: Sept, 1996 - No. 80, May, 2003 ($1.95/$1.99/$2.25/$2.50)

	GD 2.0	VG 4.0	FN 6.0	VF 8.0	VF/NM 9.0	NM- 9.2
1-Peter David scripts & Gary Frank-c/a	1	3	4	6	8	10
1-2nd printing						3.00
2,4-9: 4-Gorilla Grodd-c/app. 6-Superman-c/app. 9-Last Frank-a						4.00

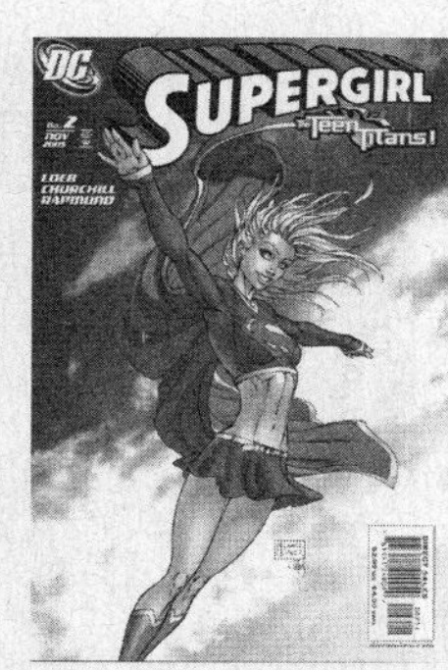

Supergirl (2005 series) #2 © DC

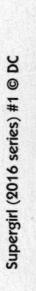

Supergirl (2016 series) #1 © DC

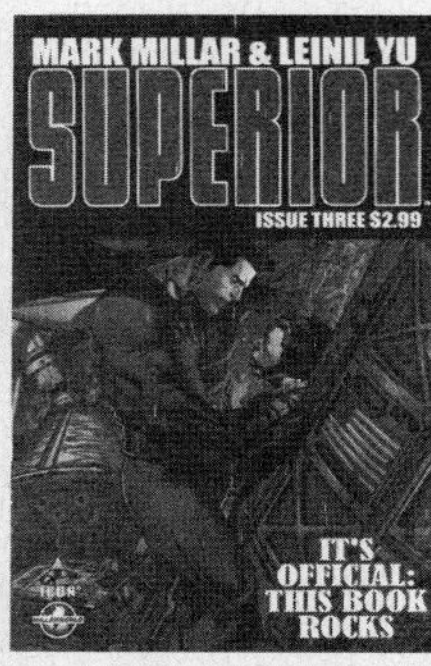

Superior #3 © MillarWorld & Yu

GD 2.0 VG 4.0 FN 6.0 VF 8.0 VF/NM 9.0 NM- 9.2

GD 2.0 VG 4.0 FN 6.0 VF 8.0 VF/NM 9.0 NM- 9.2

3-Final Night, Gorilla Grodd app. 5.00
10-19: 14-Genesis x-over. 16-Power Girl app. 3.50
20-35: 20-Millennium Giants x-over; Superman app. 23-Steel-c/app. 24-Resurrection Man x-over. 25-Comet ID revealed; begin $1.99-c 3.00
36-46: 36,37-Young Justice x-over 3.00
47-49,51-74: 47-Begin $2.25-c. 51-Adopts costume from animated series. 54-Green Lantern app. 59-61-Our Worlds at War x-over. 62-Two-Face-c/app. 66,67-Demon-c/app. 68-74-Mary Marvel app. 70-Nauck-a. 73-Begin $2.50-c 3.00
50-($3.95) Supergirl's final battle with the Carnivore 4.00
75-80: 75-Re-intro. Kara Zor-El; cover swipe of Action Comics #252 by Haynes; Benes-a. 78-Spectre app. 80-Last issue; Romita-c 3.00
#1,000,000 (11/98) 853rd Century x-over 3.00
Annual 1 (1996, $2.95)-Legends of the Dead Earth 4.00
Annual 2 (1997, $3.95)-Pulp Heroes; LSH app.; Chiodo-c 4.00
...: Many Happy Returns TPB (2003, $14.95) r/#75-80; intro. by Peter David 15.00
...Plus (2/97, $2.95) Capt.(Mary) Marvel-c/app.; David-s/Frank-a 4.00
.../Prysm Double-Shot 1 (Feb, 1998, $1.95) w/Prysm (Teen Titans) 3.00
...: Wings (2001, $5.95) Elseworlds; DeMatteis-s/Tolagson-a 6.00
TPB-('98, $14.95) r/Showcase '96 #8 & Supergirl #1-9 15.00

SUPERGIRL (See Superman/Batman #8 & #19)
DC Comics: No. 0, Oct, 2005 - No. 67, Oct, 2011 ($2.99)

0-Reprints Superman/Batman #19 with white variant of that cover 3.00
1-Loeb-s/Churchill-a; two covers by Churchill & Turner; Power Girl app. 5.00
1-2nd printing with B&W sketch variant of Turner-c 3.00
1-3rd printing with variant-c homage to Action Comics #252 by Churchill 3.00
2-4: 2-Teen Titans app. 3-Outsiders app.; covers by Turner & Churchill 3.00
5-($3.99) Supergirl vs. Supergirl; Churchill & Turner-c 4.00
6-49: 6-9-One Year Later; Power Girl app. 11-Intro. Powerboy. 12-Terra debut; Conner-a 20-Amazons Attack x-over. 21,22-Karate Kid app. 28-31-Resurrection Man app. 35,36-New Krypton x-over; Argo City story re-told; Superwoman app. 35-Ross-c. 36-Zor-El dies 3.00
50-($4.99) Lana Lang Insect Queen app.; Superwoman returns; back-up story co-written by Helen Slater with Chiang-a; Turner-c 5.00
50-Variant cover by Middleton 6.00
51-67: 51-52-New Krypton. 52-Brainiac 5 app. 53-57-Bizarro-Girl app. 55-63-Reeder-c 3.00
58-DC 75th Anniversary variant cover by Conner 6.00
Annual 1 (11/09, $3.99) Origin of Superwoman 4.00
Annual 2 (12/10, $4.99) Silver Age Legion of Super-Heroes app.; Reeder-c 5.00
...: Beyond Good and Evil TPB (2008, $17.99) r/#23-27 and Action Comics #850 18.00
...: Bizarrogirl TPB (2011, $19.99) r/#53-59 & Annual #2 20.00
...: Candor TPB (2007, $14.99) r/#6-9; and pages from JSA Classified #2, Superman #223, Superman/Batman #27 and JLA #122,123 15.00
...: Death & The Family TPB (2010, $17.99) r/#48-50 & Annual #1 18.00
...: Friends & Fugitives TPB (2010, $17.99) r/#43,45-47; Action Comics #881,882 18.00
...: Identity TPB (2007, $19.99) r/#10-16 and story from DCU Infinite Holiday Special 20.00
...: Power TPB (2006, $14.99) r/#1-5 and Superman/Batman #19; variant-c gallery 15.00
...: Way of the World TPB (2009, $17.99) r/#28-33 18.00
...: Who is Superwoman TPB (2009, $17.99) r/#34,37-42 18.00

SUPERGIRL (DC New 52)
DC Comics: Nov, 2011 - No. 40, May, 2015 ($2.99)

1-New origin; Green & Johnson-s/Asrar-a/c; Superman app. 4.00
2-40: 2,3-Superman app. 8-Pérez-a. 14-17-H'El on Earth tie-in. 17-Wonder Woman app. 19,20-Power Girl app. 19-Power Girl gets classic costume. 23,24-Cyborg Superman app. 26-28-Lobo app. 28-33-Kara joins Red Lanterns. 33-Gen13 app. 36-40-Maxima app. 3.00
#0-(11/12, $2.99) Kara's escape from Krypton 3.00
...: Futures End 1 (11/14, $2.99, regular-c) Five years later; Cyborg Superman app. 3.00
...: Futures End 1 (11/14, $3.99, 3-D cover) 4.00
... Special Edition 1 (12/15, $1.00) reprints #1 with Supergirl TV banner at top of cover 3.00

SUPERGIRL (DC Rebirth)
DC Comics: Nov, 2016 - Present ($2.99)

1-6-Orlando-s/Ching-a; Cyborg Superman app. 3.00
...: Rebirth 1 (10/16, $2.99) Orlando-s/Lupacchino-a; gets the Kara Danvers identity 3.00

SUPERGIRL AND THE LEGION OF SUPER-HEROES (Continues from Legion of Super-Heroes #15, Apr, 2006)(Continues as Legion of Super-Heroes #37)
DC Comics: No. 16, May, 2006 - No. 36, Jan, 2008 ($2.99)

16-Supergirl appears in the 31st century 4.00
16-2nd printing 3.00
17-36: 23-Mon-El cameo. 24,25-Mon-El returns 3.00
...: Adult Education TPB (2007, $14.99) r/#20-25 & LSH #6,9,13-15 15.00
...: Dominator War TPB (2007, $14.99) r/#26-30 15.00
...: Strange Visitor From Another Century TPB (2006, $14.99) r/#16-19 & LSH #11,12,15 15.00
...: The Quest For Cosmic Boy TPB (2008, $14.99) r/#31-36 15.00

SUPERGIRL: BEING SUPER
DC Comics: Feb, 2017 - No. 4 ($5.99, limited series)

1,2-Mariko Tamaki-s/Joëlle Jones-a 6.00

SUPERGIRL: COSMIC ADVENTURES IN THE 8TH GRADE (Cartoony all-ages title)
DC Comics: Feb, 2008 - No. 6, Jul, 2009 ($2.50, limited series)

1-6: 1-Supergirl lands on Earth; Eric Jones-a. 5,6-Comet & Streaky app. 3.00
TPB (2009, $12.99) r/#1-6; sketch art 13.00

SUPERGIRL/LEX LUTHOR SPECIAL (Supergirl and Team Luthor on-c)
DC Comics: 1993 ($2.50, 68 pgs., one-shot)

1-Pin-ups by Byrne & Thibert 4.00

SUPERGOD (Warren Ellis'...)
Avatar Press: Oct, 2009 - No. 5, Nov, 2010 ($3.99, limited series)

1-5-Warren Ellis-s/Garrie Gastony-a; multiple covers on each 4.00

SUPER GOOF (Walt Disney) (See Dynabrite & The Phantom Blot)
Gold Key No. 1-57/Whitman No. 58 on: Oct, 1965 - No. 74, July, 1984

	GD 2.0	VG 4.0	FN 6.0	VF 8.0	VF/NM 9.0	NM- 9.2
1	4	8	12	27	44	60
2-5	3	6	9	16	23	30
6-10	3	6	9	14	19	24
11-20	2	4	6	8	11	14
21-30	1	3	4	6	8	10
31-50	1	2	3	4	5	7
51-57						6.00
58,59 (Whitman)	1	2	3	5	6	8
60(8/80), 62(11/80) 3-pack only (scarce)	5	10	15	35	63	90
61(9-10/80) 3-pack only (rare)	8	16	24	54	102	150
63-66('81)	1	2	3	5	6	8
63 (1/81, 40¢-c) Cover price error variant (scarce)	2	4	6	11	16	20
67-69: 67(2/82), 68(2-3/82), 69(3/82)						6.00
70-74 (#90180 on-c; pre-pack, nd, nd code): 70(5/83), 71(8/83), 72(5/84), 73(6/84), 74(7/84)	3	6	9	15	22	28

NOTE: *Reprints in #16, 24, 28, 29, 37, 38, 43, 45, 46, 54(1/2), 56-58, 65(1/2), 72(r-#2).*

SUPER GREEN BERET (Tod Holton...)
Lightning Comics (Milson Publ. Co.): Apr, 1967 - No. 2, Jun, 1967

	GD 2.0	VG 4.0	FN 6.0	VF 8.0	VF/NM 9.0	NM- 9.2
1-(25¢, 68 pgs)	5	10	15	30	50	70
2-(25¢, 68 pgs)	3	6	9	21	33	45

SUPER HEROES (See Giant-Size... & Marvel...)

SUPER HEROES
Dell Publishing Co.: Jan, 1967 - No. 4, June, 1967

	GD 2.0	VG 4.0	FN 6.0	VF 8.0	VF/NM 9.0	NM- 9.2
1-Origin & 1st app. Fab 4	4	8	12	23	37	50
2-4	3	6	9	16	24	32

SUPER-HEROES BATTLE SUPER-GORILLAS (See DC Special #16)
National Periodical Publications: Winter, 1976 (52 pgs., all reprints, one-shot)

	GD 2.0	VG 4.0	FN 6.0	VF 8.0	VF/NM 9.0	NM- 9.2
1-Superman, Batman, Flash stories; Infantino-a(p)	2	4	6	11	16	20

SUPER HEROES VERSUS SUPER VILLAINS
Archie Publications (Radio Comics): July, 1966 (no month given)(68 pgs.)

	GD 2.0	VG 4.0	FN 6.0	VF 8.0	VF/NM 9.0	NM- 9.2
1-Flyman, Black Hood, Web, Shield-r; Reinman-a	6	12	18	37	66	95

SUPER HERO SQUAD (See Marvel Super Hero Squad)

SUPERHERO WOMEN, THE - FEATURING THE FABULOUS FEMALES OF MARVEL COMICS (See Fireside Book Series)

SUPERICHIE (Formerly Super Richie)
Harvey Publications: No. 5, Oct, 1976 - No. 18, Jan, 1979 (52 pgs. giants)

	GD 2.0	VG 4.0	FN 6.0	VF 8.0	VF/NM 9.0	NM- 9.2
5-Origin/1st app. new costumes for Rippy & Crashman	2	4	6	9	13	16
6-18	2	4	6	8	10	12

SUPERIOR
Marvel Comics (ICON): Dec, 2010 - No. 7, Mar, 2012 ($2.99/$4.99)

1-6-Mark Millar-s/Leinil Yu-a. 1-1st & 2nd printings 3.00
7-($4.99) Bonus preview of Supercrooks #1 5.00
... World Record Special 1 (12/11, $2.99, B&W) Comic created in less than 12 hours 3.00

SUPERIOR CARNAGE
Marvel Comics: Sept, 2013 - No. 5, Jan, 2014 ($3.99)

1-5: 1-Shinick-s/Segovia-a; covers by Crain & Checchetto. 2-5-Superior Spider-Man app. 4.00
Annual 1 (4/14, $4.99) Bunn-s/Jacinto & Henderson-a; follows #5; Kasady in prison 5.00

SUPERIOR FOES OF SPIDER-MAN (Superior Spider-Man)
Marvel Comics: Sept, 2013 - No. 17, Jan, 2015 ($3.99)

1-17: 1-Boomerang, Shocker, Overdrive, Speed Demon & Beetle team; Spencer-s 4.00

Superior Spider-Man #31 © MAR

Super Magician Comics #12 © CN

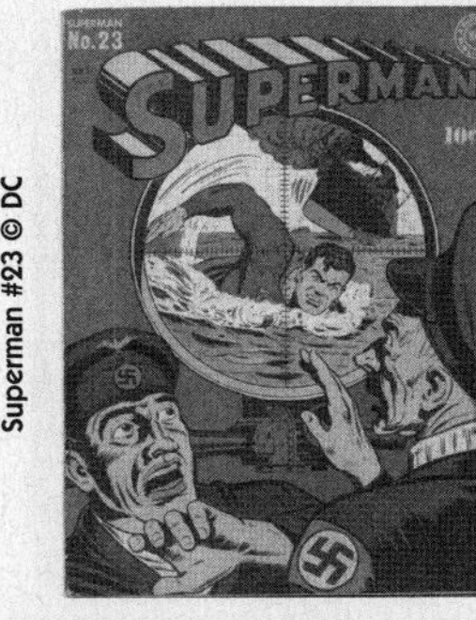

Superman #23 © DC

GD VG FN VF VF/NM NM-
2.0 4.0 6.0 8.0 9.0 9.2

SUPERIOR IRON MAN (Follows events of the Avengers & X-Men: Axis series)
Marvel Comics: Jan, 2015 - No. 9, Aug, 2015 ($3.99)

1-9: 1-Tom Taylor-s/Yildiray Cinar-a. 1-4-Daredevil app. 4.00

SUPERIOR SPIDER-MAN (Follows Amazing Spider-Man #700)
Marvel Comics: Mar, 2013 - No. 31, Jun, 2014; No. 32, Oct, 2014 - No. 33, Nov, 2014 ($3.99)

1-Doc Ock as Spider-Man; new Sinister Six app.; Slott-s/Stegman-a 8.00
1-Variant baby-c by Skottie Young 10.00
2-6: 4,5-Camuncoli-a. 4-Green Goblin cameo. 6-Ramos-a 5.00
6AU (5/13, $3.99) Alternate timeline Age of Ultron tie-in; Gage-s/Soy-a 4.00
7-24: 7,8-Ramos-a; Avengers app. 9-Peter's memories removed. 14-New costume. 17-19-Spider-Man 2099 app. 20-Black Cat app. 22-24-Venom app. 4.00
25-($4.99) Superior Venom vs. the Avengers; Ramos-a 5.00
26-30: 27-Goblin Nation begins. 29-Spider-Man 2099 app. 4.00
31-($5.99) Goblin Nation finale; covers by Camuncoli & Campbell; Silver Surfer bonus 6.00
32,33-($4.99) Edge of Spider-Verse tie-ins; takes place during issue #19 5.00
Annual 1 (1/14, $4.99) Blackout app.; Gage-s/Rodriguez-a 5.00
Annual 2 (5/14, $4.99) Leads into Superior Spider-Man #30; Gage-s/Rodriguez-a 5.00

SUPERIOR SPIDER-MAN TEAM UP
Marvel Comics: Sept, 2013 - No. 12, Jun, 2014 ($3.99)

1-10: 1-Avengers app. 8-Namor app. 9,10-Daredevil & The Punisher app. 4.00
... Special 1 (12/13, $4.99) Hulk & the original X-Men app.; Dialynas-a/Lozano-c 5.00

SUPERIOR STORIES
Nesbit Publishers, Inc.: May-June, 1955 - No. 4, Nov-Dec, 1955

1-The Invisible Man by H.G. Wells 23 46 69 136 223 310
2-4: 2-The Pirate of the Gulf by J.H. Ingrahams. 3-Wreck of the Grosvenor by William Clark Russell. 4-The Texas Rangers by O'Henry 11 22 33 62 86 110
NOTE: ***Morisi** c/a in all. Kiwanis stories in #3 & 4. #4 has photo of Gene Autry on-c.*

SUPER MAGIC (Super Magician Comics #2 on)
Street & Smith Publications: May, 1941

V1#1-Blackstone the Magician-c/story; origin/1st app. Rex King (Black Fury); Charles Sultan-c; Blackstone-c begin 200 400 600 1280 2190 3100

SUPER MAGICIAN COMICS (Super Magic #1)
Street & Smith Publications: No. 2, Sept, 1941 - V5#8, Feb-Mar, 1947

V1#2-Blackstone the Magician continues; Rex King, Man of Adventure app. 77 154 231 493 847 1200
3-Tao-Anwar, Boy Magician begins 48 96 144 302 514 725
4-7,9-12: 4-Origin Transo. 11-Supersnipe app. 43 86 129 271 461 650
8-Abbott & Costello story (1st app?, 11/42) 47 94 141 296 498 700
V2#1-The Shadow app. 44 88 132 277 469 660
2-12: 5-Origin Tigerman. 8-Red Dragon begins 27 54 81 158 259 360
V3#1-12: 5-Origin Mr. Twilight 25 50 75 150 245 340
V4#1-4,6-12: 11-Nigel Elliman Ace of Magic begins (3/46) 21 42 63 122 199 275
5-KKK-c/sty 37 74 111 222 361 500
V5#1-6 20 40 60 118 192 265
7,8-Red Dragon by Edd Cartier-c/a 39 78 117 240 395 550
NOTE: ***Jack Binder** c-1-14(most). Red Dragon c-V5#7, 8.*

SUPERMAN (See Action Comics, Advs. of..., All-New Coll. Ed., All-Star Comics, Best of DC, Brave & the Bold, Cosmic Odyssey, DC Comics Presents, Heroes Against Hunger, JLA, The Kents, Krypton Chronicles, Limited Coll. Ed., Man of Steel, Phantom Zone, Power Record Comics, Special Edition, Steel, Super Friends, Superman: The Man of Steel, Superman: The Man of Tomorrow, Taylor's Christmas Tabloid, Three-Dimension Advs., World of Krypton, World Of Metropolis, World Of Smallville & World's Finest)

SUPERMAN (Becomes Adventures of...#424 on)
National Periodical Publ./DC Comics: Summer, 1939 - No. 423, Sept, 1986
(#1-5 are quarterly)

1(nn)-1st four Action stories reprinted; origin Superman by Siegel & Shuster; has a new 2 pg. origin plus 4 pgs. omitted in Action story; see The Comics Magazine #1 & More Fun #14-17 for Superman prototype app.; cover r/splash page from Action #10; 1st pin-up Superman on back-c - 1st pin-up in comics 80,000 160,000 320,000 600,000 900,000 1,200,000
1-Reprint, Oversize 13-1/2x10". **WARNING**: This comic is an exact duplicate reprint of the original except for its size. DC published it in 1978 with a second cover titling it as a Famous First Edition. There have been many reported cases of the outer cover being removed and the interior sold as the original edition. The reprint with the new outer cover removed is practically worthless. See Famous First Edition for value.
2-All daily strip-r; full pg. ad for N.Y. World's Fair 2800 5600 8400 21,000 44,000 67,000
3-2nd story-r from Action #5; 3rd story-r from Action #6 1500 3000 4500 11,000 22,500 36,000
4-2nd mention of Daily Planet (Spr/40); also see Action #23; 2nd & 3rd app. Luthor (red-headed; also see Action #23); first issue of title to feature original stories 865 1730 2595 6315 11,158 16,000
5-4th Luthor app. (grey hair) 703 1406 2109 5132 9066 13,000
6,7: 6-1st splash pg. in a Superman comic. 7-1st Perry White? (11-12/40) 486 972 1458 3550 6275 9000
8-10: 10-5th app. Luthor (1st bald Luthor, 5-6/41) 432 864 1296 3154 5577 8000
11-13,15: 13-Jimmy Olsen & Luthor app. 343 686 1029 2400 4200 6000
14-Patriotic Shield-c classic by Fred Ray 975 1950 2919 7100 12,550 18,000
16,19,20: 16-1st Lois Lane-c this title (5-6/42); 2nd Lois-c after Action #29 300 600 900 2010 3505 5000
17-Hitler, Hirohito-c 865 1730 2595 6315 11,158 16,000
18-Classic WWII-c 314 628 942 2198 3849 5500
21,22,25: 25-Clark Kent's only military service; Fred Ray's only super-hero story 206 412 618 1318 2259 3200
23-Classic periscope-c 303 606 909 2121 3711 5300
24-Classic Jack Burnley flag-c 423 846 1269 3000 5250 7500
26-Classic war-c 331 662 993 2317 4059 5800
27-29: 27,29-Lois Lane-c. 28-Lois Lane Girl Reporter series begins, ends #40,42 174 348 522 1114 1907 2700
28-Overseas edition for Armed Forces; same as reg. #28 174 348 522 1114 1907 2700
30-Origin & 1st app. Mr. Mxyztplk (9-10/44)(pronounced "Mix-it-plk") in comic books; name later became Mxyzptlk ("Mix-yez-pit-l-ick"); the character was inspired by a combination of the name of Al Capp's Joe Blyfstyk (the little man with the black cloud over his head) & the devilish antics of Bugs Bunny; he first app. in newspapers 3/7/44; Superman flies for the first time 300 600 900 2010 3505 5000
31-40: 33-(3-4/45)-3rd app. Mxyztplk. 35,36-Lois Lane-c. 38-Atomic bomb story (1-2/46); delayed because of gov't censorship; Superman shown reading Batman #32 on cover. 40-Mxyztplk-c 135 270 405 864 1482 2100
41-50: 42-Lois Lane-c. 45-Lois Lane as Superwoman (see Action #60 for 1st app.). 46-(5-6/47)-1st app. Superboy this title? 48-1st time Superman travels thru time 116 232 348 742 1271 1800
51,52: 51-Lois Lane-c 110 220 330 704 1202 1700
53-Third telling of Superman origin; 10th anniversary issue ('48); classic origin-c by Boring 360 720 1080 2520 4410 6300
54,56-60: 57-Lois Lane as Superwoman-c. 58-Intro Tiny Trix. 59-Early use of heat vision (possibly first time) 110 220 330 704 1202 1700
55-Used in **SOTI**, pg. 33 111 222 333 705 1215 1725
61-Origin Superman retold; origin Green Kryptonite (1st Kryptonite story); Superman returns to Krypton for 1st time & sees his parents for 1st time since infancy, discovers he's not an Earth man 187 374 561 1197 2049 2900
62-70: 62-Orson Welles-c/story. 65-1st Krypton Foes: Mala, Kizo, & U-Ban. 66-2nd Superbaby story. 67-Perry Como-c/story. 68-1st Luthor-c this title (see Action Comics) 108 216 324 686 1181 1675
71-75: 74-2nd Luthor-c this title. 75-Some have #74 on-c 105 210 315 667 1146 1625
76-Batman x-over; Superman & Batman learn each other's I.D. for the 1st time (5-6/52) (also see World's Finest #71) 343 686 1029 2400 4200 6000
77-81: 78-Last 52 pg. issue; 1st meeting of Lois Lane & Lana Lang. 81-Used in **POP**, pg. 88. 81-"Superwoman From Space" story 92 184 276 584 1005 1425
82-87,89,90: 89-1st Curt Swan-c in title 86 172 258 546 936 1325
88-Prankster, Toyman & Luthor team-up 89 178 267 565 970 1375
91-95: 95-Last precode issue (2/55) 77 154 231 493 847 1200
96-99: 96-Mr. Mxyztplk-c/story 71 142 213 454 777 1100
100 (9-10/55)-Shows cover to #1 on-c 258 516 774 1651 2826 4000
101-105,107-110: 109-1st S.A. issue 52 104 156 328 689 1050
106 (7/56)-Retells origin 53 106 159 334 717 1100
111-120 47 94 141 296 623 950
121,122,124-127,129: 127-Origin/1st app. Titano. 129-Intro/origin Lori Lemaris, The Mermaid 41 82 123 256 541 825
123-Pre-Supergirl tryout-c/story (8/58). 150 300 600 1400 3200 5000
128-(4/59)-Red Kryptonite used. Bruce Wayne x-over who protects Superman's i.d. (3rd story) 42 84 126 265 558 850
130-(7/59)-2nd app, Krypto, the Superdog with Superman (see Sup.'s Pal Jimmy Olsen #29) (all other previous app. w/Superboy) 43 86 129 271 573 875
131-139: 135-2nd Lori Lemaris app. 139-Lori Lemaris app.; 34 68 102 199 412 625
140-1st Blue Kryptonite & Bizarro Supergirl; origin Bizarro Jr. #1 34 68 102 206 421 635
141-145,148: 142-2nd Batman x-over 29 58 87 170 360 550
146-(7/61)-Superman's life story; back-up hints at Earth II. Classic-c 39 78 117 235 530 825
147(8/61)-7th Legion app; 1st app. Legion of Super-Villains; 1st app. Adult Legion; swipes-c to Adv. #247 36 72 108 216 446 675
149(11/61)-8th Legion app. (cameo); "The Death of Superman" imaginary story; last 10¢ issue 36 72 108 216 446 675
150,151,153,154,157,159,160: 157-Gold Kryptonite used (see Adv. #299); Mon -El app.; Lightning Lad cameo (11/62) 13 26 39 89 195 300

Superman #208 © DC

Superman #349 © DC

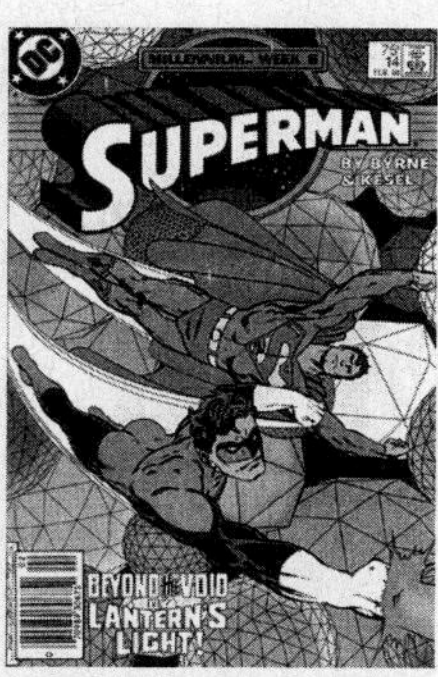

Superman (2nd series) #14 © DC

	GD 2.0	VG 4.0	FN 6.0	VF 8.0	VF/NM 9.0	NM- 9.2

152,155,156,158,162: 152(4/62)-15th Legion app. 155-(8/62)-Legion app; Lightning Man & Cosmic Man, & Adult Legion app. 156,162-Legion app. 158-1st app. Superman as Nightwing & Jimmy Olsen as Flamebird & Nor-Kann of Kandor (12/62) 13 26 39 91 201 310
161-1st told death of Ma and Pa Kent 14 28 42 94 207 320
161-2nd printing (1987, $1.25)-New DC logo; sold thru So Much Fun Toy Stores (cover title: Superman Classic) 4.00
163-166,168-180: 166-XMas-c. 168-All Luthor issue; JFK tribute/memorial. 169-Bizarro Invasion of Earth-c/story; last Sally Selwyn. 170-Pres. Kennedy story is finally published after delay from #168 due to assassination. 172,173-Legion cameos. 174-Super-Mxyzptlk; Bizarro app. 176-Legion of Super-Pets 10 20 30 69 147 225
167-New origin Brainiac, text reference of Brainiac 5 descending from adopted human son Brainiac II; intro Tharla (later Luthor's wife) 12 24 36 84 185 285
181,182,184-186,188-192,194-196,198,200: 181-1st 2465 story/series. 182-1st S.A. app. of The Toyman (1/66). 189-Origin/destruction of Krypton II. 8 16 24 56 108 160
183 (Giant G-18) 11 22 33 73 157 240
187,193,197 (Giants G-23,G-31,G-36) 9 18 27 59 117 175
199-1st Superman/Flash race (8/67): also see Flash #175 & World's Finest #198,199 (r-in Limited Coll. Ed. C-48) 36 72 108 259 580 900
201,203-206,208-211,213-216: 213-Brainiac-5 app. 216-Last 12¢ issue 6 12 18 37 66 95
202 (80-pg. Giant G-42)-All Bizarro issue 6 12 18 41 76 110
207,212,217 (Giants G-48,G-54,G-60): 207-30th anniversary Superman (6/68) 6 12 18 41 76 110
218-221,223-226,228-231 5 10 15 33 57 80
222,239(Giants, G-66,G-84) 6 12 18 38 69 100
227,232(Giants, G-72,G-78)-All Krypton issues 6 12 18 38 69 100
233-2nd app. Morgan Edge; Clark Kent switches from newspaper reporter to TV newscaster; all Kryptonite on Earth destroyed; classic Neal Adams-c; 1st Fabulous World of Krypton story; Superman pin-up by Swan 13 26 39 89 195 300
234-238 5 10 15 31 53 75
240-Kaluta-a; last 15¢ issue 4 8 12 27 44 60
241-244 (All 52 pgs.): 241-New Wonder Woman app. 243-G.A.-r/#38 4 8 12 28 47 65
245-Also listed as DC 100 Pg. Super Spectacular #7; Air Wave, Kid Eternity, Hawkman-r; Atom-r/Atom #3 9 18 27 60 120 180
246-248,250,251,253 (All 52 pgs.): 246-G.A.-r/#40. 248-World of Krypton story. 251-G.A.-r/#45. 253-Finlay-a, 2 pgs., G.A.-r/#1 4 8 12 28 47 65
249,254-Neal Adams-a. 249-(52 pgs.); 1st app. Terra-Man (Swan-a) & origin-s by Dick Dillin (p) & Neal Adams (inks) 5 10 15 35 63 90
252-Also listed as DC 100 Pg. Super Spectacular #13; Ray(r/Smash #17), Black Condor, (r/Crack #18), Hawkman(r/Flash #24); Starman-r/Adv. #67; Dr. Fate & Spectre-r/More Fun #57; N. Adams-c 10 20 30 66 138 210
255-271,273-277,279-283: 263-Photo-c. 264-1st app. Steve Lombard. 276-Intro Capt. Thunder. 279-Batman, Batgirl app. 282-Luthor battlesuit 3 6 9 14 19 24
272,278,284-All 100 pgs. G.A.-r in all. 272-r/2nd app. Mr. Mxyztplk from Action #80 5 10 15 30 50 70
285-299: 289-Partial photo-c. 292-Origin Lex Luthor retold 2 4 6 9 13 16
300-(6/76) Superman in the year 2001 3 6 9 19 30 40
301-316,318-350: 301,320-Solomon Grundy app. 323-Intro. Atomic Skull. 327-329-(44 pgs.). 327-Kobra app. 330-More facts revealed about I.D. 331,332-1st/2nd app. Master Jailer. 335-Mxyzptlk marries Ms. Bgbznz. 336-Rose & Thorn app. 338-(8/79) 40th Anniv. issue; the bottled city of Kandor enlarged. 344-Frankenstein & Dracula app. 1 3 4 6 8 10
317-Classic Neal Adams kryptonite cover 3 6 9 16 23 30
321-323,325-327,329-332,335-345,348,350 (Whitman variants; low print run; no issue # on cover) 2 4 6 9 13 16
351-399: 353-Brief origin. 354,355,357-Superman 2020 stories (354-Debut of Superman III). 356-World of Krypton story (also #360,367,375). 366-Fan letter by Todd McFarlane. 369-Christmas-c. 372-Superman 2021 story. 376-Free 6 pg. preview Daring New Advs. of Supergirl. 377-Terra-Man-c/app.; free 16 pg. preview Masters of the Universe 379-Bizarro World app. 1 2 3 4 5 7
400 (10/84, $1.50, 68 pgs.)-Many top artists featured; Chaykin painted cover, Miller back-c; Steranko-s/a (10 pages) 1 3 4 6 8 10
401-422: 405-Super-Batman story. 408-Nuclear Holocaust-c/story. 411-Special Julius Schwartz tribute issue. 414,415-Crisis x-over. 422-Horror-c by Bolland 6.00
409-(7/85) Variant-c with Superman/Superhombre logo (no reported sales)
423-Alan Moore scripts; Curt Swan-a/George Pérez-a(i); "Whatever Happened to the Man of Tomorrow?" story, cont'd in Action #583 2 4 6 8 10 12
Annual 1 (10/60, 84 pgs.)-Reprints 1st Supergirl story/Action #252; r/Lois Lane #1; Krypto-r (1st Silver Age DC annual) 82 164 246 656 1478 2300
Annual 2 (Win, 1960-61)-Super-villain issue; Brainiac, Titano, Metallo, Bizarro origin-r 35 70 105 252 564 875
Annual 3 (Sum, 1961)-Strange Lives of Superman 23 46 69 164 362 560
Annual 4(Win, 1961-62)-11th Legion app; 1st Legion origins (text & pictures); advs. in time, space & on alien worlds 20 40 60 135 300 465
Annual 5 (Sum, 1962)-All Krypton issue 16 32 48 112 249 385
Annual 6 (Win, 1962-63)-Legion-r/Adv. #247 14 28 42 97 214 330
Annual 7 (Sum, 1963)-Silver Anniversary Issue; origin-r/Superman-Batman team/Adv. #275; cover gallery of famous issues 11 22 33 76 163 250
Annual 8 (Win, 1963-64)-All origins issue 10 20 30 69 147 225
Annual 9 (8/64)-Was advertised but came out as 80 Page Giant #1 instead
Annual 9 (1983)-Toth/Austin-a 1 2 3 4 5 7
Annuals 10,12: 10(1984, $1.25)-M. Anderson-i. 12(1986)-Bolland-c 6.00
Annual 11 (1985) "For the Man Who Has Everything" story; Alan Moore-s/Dave Gibbons-a; Mongul and the Black Mercy app.; Wonder Woman, Batman & Robin app. (adapted for a Justice League Unlimited animated episode 4 8 12 23 37 50
Special 1-3 ('83-'85): 1-G. Kane-c/a; contains German-r 6.00
The Amazing World of Superman "Official Metropolis Edition" (1973, $2.00, treasury-size)-Origin retold; Wood-r(i) from Superboy #153,161; poster incl. (half price if poster missing) 4 8 12 27 44 60
11195 (2/79, $1.95, 224 pgs.)-Golden Press 4 8 12 23 37 50

NOTE: ***N. Adams** a-249i, 254p; c-204-206, 210, 212-215, 219, 231i, 233-237, 240-243, 249-252, 254, 263, 307, 308, 313, 314, 317. **Adkins** a-323i. **Austin** c-368i. **Wayne Boring** art-late 1940's to early 1960's. **Buckler** a(p)-352, 363, 364, 369; c(p)-324-327, 356, 363, 368, 369, 373, 376, 378. **Burnley** a-252r; c-19-25, 30, 33, 34, 35p, 38p, 39p, 45p. **Fine** a-252r. **Kaluta** a-400. **Gil Kane** a-272r, 367, 372, 375, Special 2; c-374p, 375p, 377, 381, 382, 384-390, 392, Annual 9, Special 2. **Joe Kubert** c-216. **Morrow** a-238. **Mortimer** a-250r. **Perez** c-364p. **Fred Ray** a-25; c-6, 8-18. **Starlin** c-355. **Staton** a-354i, 355i. **Swan/Moldoff** c-149. **Williamson** a(i)-408-410, 412-416; c-408i, 409i. **Wrightson** a-400, 416.*

SUPERMAN (2nd Series) (Title continues numbering from Adventures of Superman #649)
DC Comics: Jan, 1987 - No. 226, Apr, 2006; No. 650, May, 2006 - No. 714, Oct, 2011

0-(10/94) Zero Hour; released between #93 & #94 3.00
1-Byrne-c/a begins; intro new Metallo 1 3 4 6 8 10
2-8,10: 3-Legends x-over; Darkseid-c & app. 7-Origin/1st app. Rampage. 8-Legion app. 4.00
9-Joker-c 5.00
11-15,17-20,22-49,51,52,54-56,58-67: 11-1st new Mr. Mxyzptlk. 12-Lori Lemaris revived. 13-1st app. new Toyman. 13,14-Millennium x-over. 20-Doom Patrol app.; Supergirl cameo. 31-Mr. Mxyzptlk app. 37-Newsboy Legion app. 41-Lobo app. 44-Batman storyline, part 1. 45-Free extra 8 pgs. 54-Newsboy Legion story. 63-Aquaman x-over. 67-Last $1.00-c 3.00
16,21: 16-1st app. new Supergirl (4/88). 21-Supergirl-c/story; 1st app. Matrix who becomes new Supergirl 4.00
50-($1.50, 52 pgs.)-Clark Kent proposes to Lois 5.00
50-2nd printing 4.00
53-Clark reveals i.d. to Lois (Cont'd from Action #662) 4.00
53-2nd printing 3.00
57-($1.75, 52 pgs.) 4.00
68-72: 65,66,68-Deathstroke-c/stories. 70-Superman & Robin team-up 3.00
73-Doomsday cameo 6.00
74-Doomsday Pt. 2 (Cont'd from Justice League #69); Superman battles Doomsday 1 2 3 5 6 8
73,74-2nd printings 3.00
75-($2.50)-Collector's Ed.; Doomsday Pt. 6; Superman dies; polybagged w/poster of funeral, obituary from Daily Planet, postage stamp & armband premiums (direct sales only) 3 6 9 16 23 30
75-Direct sales copy (no upc code, 1st print) 1 3 4 6 8 10
75-Direct sales copy (no upc code, 2nd-4th prints) 4.00
75-Newsstand copy w/upc code 1 3 4 6 8 10
75-Platinum Edition; given away to retailers 6 12 18 37 66 95
76,77-Funeral For a Friend parts 4 & 8 4.00
78-($1.95)-Collector's Edition with die-cut outer-c & mini poster; Doomsday cameo 4.00
78-($1.50)-Newsstand Edition w/poster and different-c; Doomsday-c & cameo 3.00
79-81,83-89: 83-Funeral for a Friend epilogue; new Batman (Azrael) cameo. 87,88-Bizarro-c/story 3.00
82-($3.50)-Collector's Edition w/all chromium-c; real Superman revealed; Green Lantern x-over from G.L. #46; no ads 6.00
82-($2.00, 44 pgs.)-Regular Edition w/different-c 4.00
90-99: 93-(9/94)-Zero Hour. 94-(11/94). 95-Atom app. 96-Brainiac returns 3.00
100-Death of Clark Kent foil-c 4.00
100-Newsstand 3.00
101-122: 101-Begin $1.95-c; Black Adam app. 105-Green Lantern app. 110-Plastic Man-c/app. 114-Brainiac app; Dwyer-c. 115-Lois leaves Metropolis. 116-(10/96)-1st app. Teen Titans by Jurgens & Perez in 8 pg. preview. 117-Final Night. 118-Wonder Woman app. 119-Legion app. 122-New powers 3.00
123-Collector's Edition w/glow in the dark-c, new costume 6.00
123-Standard ed., new costume 4.00
124-149: 128-Cyborg-c/app. 131-Birth of Lena Luthor. 132-Superman Red/Superman Blue. 134-Millennium Giants. 136,137-Superman 2999. 139-Starlin-a. 140-Grindberg-a 3.00

Superman (2nd series) #205 © DC

Superman (2011 series) #49 © DC

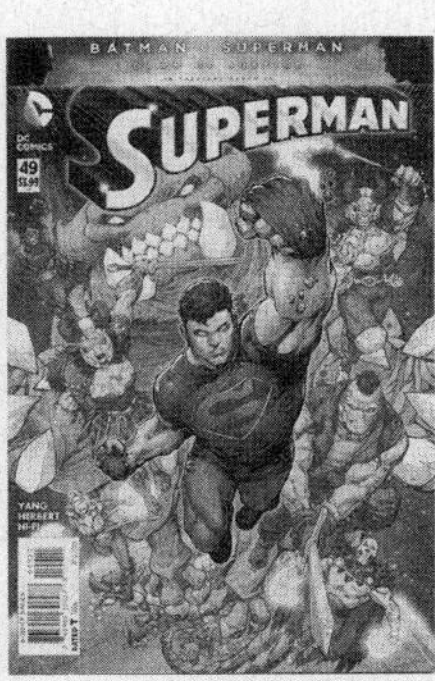

Superman (2016 series) #6 © DC

150-($2.95) Standard Ed.; Brainiac 2.0 app.; Jurgens-s 4.00
150-($3.95) Collector's Ed. w/holo-foil enhanced variant-c 5.00
151-158: 151-Loeb-s begins; Daily Planet reopens 3.00
159-174: 159-$2.25-c begin. 161-Joker-c/app. 162-Aquaman-c/app. 163-Young Justice app. 165-JLA app.; Ramos; Madureira, Liefeld, A. Adams, Wieringo, Churchill-a. 166-Collector's and reg. editions. 167-Return to Krypton. 168-Batman-c/app.(cont'd in Detective #756). 171-173-Our Worlds at War. 173-Sienkiewicz-a (2 pgs.). 174-Adopts black & red "S" logo 3.00
175-($3.50) Joker: Last Laugh x-over; Doomsday-c/app. 4.00
176-189,191-199: 176,180-Churchill-a. 180-Dracula app. 181-Bizarro-c/app. 184-Return to Krypton II. 189-Van Fleet-c. 192,193,195,197-199-New Supergirl app. 3.00
190-($2.25) Regular edition 3.00
190-($3.95) Double-Feature Issue; included reprint of Superman: The 10¢ Adventure 4.00
200-($3.50) Gene Ha-c/art by various; preview art by Yu & Bermejo 4.00
201-Mr Majestic-c/app.; cover swipe of Action #1 3.00
202,203-Godfall parts 3,6; Turner-c; Caldwell-a(p). 203-Jim Lee sketch pages 3.00
204-Jim Lee-c/a begins; Azzarello-s 3.00
204-Diamond Retailer Summit edition with sketch-c 5 10 15 31 53 75
205-214: 205-Two covers by Jim Lee and Michael Turner. 208-JLA app. 211-Battles Wonder Woman 3.00
215-($2.99) Conclusion to Azzarello/Lee arc 4.00
216-218,220-226: 216-Captain Marvel app. 221-Bizarro & Zoom app. 226-Earth-2 Superman story; Chaykin,Sale, Benes, Ordway-a 3.00
219-Omac/Sacrifice pt. 1; JLA app. 4.00
219-2nd printing with red background variant-c 3.00
(Title continues numbering from Adventures of Superman #649)
650-(5/06) One Year Later; Clark powerless after Infinite Crisis 4.00
651-665,667-669,671-674.676-680: 652-Begin $2.99-c. 654-658,662-664,667-Pacheco-a. 665-Origin of Jimmy Olsen. 671-673-Insect Queen. 676-680-Ross-c 3.00
666, 670,675-($3.99) 666-Simonson-a. 670-The Third Kryptonian. 675-Ross-c 4.00
681-699: 681-683-New Krypton x-over; Ross-c. 685-Mon-El freed from Phantom Zone. 694-Mon-El new costume. 698,699-Last Stand of New Krypton x-over 3.00
700-(8/10, $4.99) Cover by Gary Frank; Robinson-s; Straczynski-s begin 5.00
700-Variant-c by Risso 8.00
701-714: 701-"Grounded" begins; Straczynski-s/Cassaday-c. 704,706-Wilson-s 3.00
701-DC 75th Variant-c by Cassaday (Superman #1 swipe) 8.00
#1,000,000 (11/98) 853rd Century x-over; Gene Ha-c 3.00
Annual 1,2: 1 (1987)-No Byrne-a. 2 (1988)-Byrne-a; Newsboy Legion; Guardian returns 4.00
Annual 3-6 ('91-'94 68 pgs.): 1-Armageddon 2001 x-over; Batman app.; Austin-c(i) & part inks. 4-Eclipso app. 6-Elseworlds sty 4.00
Annual 3-2nd & 3rd printings; 3rd has silver ink 4.00
Annual 7 (1995, $3.95, 69 pgs.)-Year One story 4.00
Annual 8 (1996, $2.95)-Legends of the Dead Earth story 4.00
Annual 9 (1997, $3.95)-Pulp Heroes story 4.00
Annual 10 (1998, $2.95)-Ghosts; Wrightson-c 4.00
Annual 11 (1999, $2.95)-JLApe; Art Adams-c 4.00
Annual 12 (2000, $3.50)-Planet DC 4.00
Annual 13 (1/08, $3.99) Finale of Camelot Falls 4.00
Annual 14 (10/09, $3.99) Origin of Mon-El re-told; Pina-a/Guedes-c 4.00
...: 80 Page Giant (2/99, $4.95) Jurgens-c 6.00
...: 80 Page Giant 1 (5/10, $5.99) Lopresti-c; short stories by various 6.00
...: 80 Page Giant 2 (6/99, $4.95) Harris-c 6.00
...: 80 Page Giant 3 (11/00, $5.95) Nowlan-c; art by various 6.00
...: 80 Page Giant 2011 (4/11, $5.99) Nguyen-c; art by various; Bizarros app. 6.00
Special 1 (1992, $3.50, 68 pgs.)-Simonson-c/a 6.00

SUPERMAN (DC New 52)
DC Comics: Nov, 2011 - No. 52, Jul, 2016 ($2.99/$3.99)

1-Pérez-s/c; Merino-a 2 4 6 10 14 18
1-Variant-c by Jim Lee 18.00
2-23: 3-6-Nicola Scott-a. 6-Supergirl app. 13-Clark quits job. 14-17-H'El on Earth x-over with Superboy & Supergirl. 17-H'El on Earth conclusion. 19,20-Orion app. 3.00
23.1, 23.2, 23.3, 23.4 (11/13, $2.99, regular covers) 3.00
23.1 (11/13, $3.99, 3-D cover) "Bizarro #1" on cover; Fisch-s/Kuder-c/Jeff Johnson-a 5.00
23.2 (11/13, $3.99, 3-D cover) "Brainiac #1" on cover; origin; Bedard-s/Alixe-a 5.00
23.3 (11/13, $3.99, 3-D cover) "H'El #1" on cover; Jor-El app.; Lobdell-s/Jurgens-a 5.00
23.4 (11/13, $3.99, 3-D cover) "Parasite #1" on cover; origin; Kuder-s/a 5.00
24-31: 25-Krypton Returns pt. 4. 26,27-Parasite app. 28,29-Starfire app. 3.00
32-($3.99) Romita Jr.-a/Johns-s begin; intro. Ulysses; wraparound-c by Romita Jr. 4.00
33-49: 33-39-Romita Jr.-a/Johns-s. 41-Yang-s begin. 45-48-Porter-a. 49-Vandal Savage 4.00
50-($4.99) Conclusion vs. Vandal Savage; Romita Jr. -c 5.00
51,52-Final Days of Superman x-over. 52-Superman dies; pre-Flashpoint Superman app. 4.00
#0-(11/12, $2.99) Jor-El & Lara flashback on Krypton; Rocafort-a/c 3.00
Annual 1 (10/12, $4.99) Alixe-a/Rocafort-c; Helspont app. 5.00
Annual 2 (9/13, $4.99) Jurgens-a/Andy Kubert-c; Brainiac app. 5.00
Annual 3 (2/16, $4.99) Origin/history of Vandal Savage; art by Sienkiewicz & others 5.00
... By Geoff Johns and John Romita Jr. Director's Cut 1 (11/14, $4.99) r/#32 B&W pencil art and full script 5.00
...: Futures End 1 (11/14, $2.99, regular-c) Five years later; Jurgens-s/Weeks-a 3.00
...: Futures End 1 (11/14, $3.99, 3-D cover) 4.00

SUPERMAN (DC Rebirth)
DC Comics: Aug, 2016 - Present ($2.99)

1-18-Tomasi & Gleason-s. 2-The Eradicator returns. 8,9-Dinosaur Island. 10,11-Batman & Robin (Damian) app. 14-16-Multiplicity; alternate Earth Supermans & Capt. Carrot app. 3.00
Annual 1 (1/17, $4.99) Swamp Thing app.; Tomasi & Gleason-s/Jimenez-a 5.00
...: Rebirth (8/16, $2.99) Pre-52 Superman and Lana Lang app.; Tomasi-s/Mahnke-a 3.00

SUPERMAN (Hardcovers and Trade Paperbacks)
... and the Legion of Super-Heroes HC (2008, $24.99) r/Action Comics #858-863, covers and variants; intro. by Giffen; Gary Frank design sketch pages 25.00
... and the Legion of Super-Heroes SC (2009, $14.99) same contents as HC 15.00
...: Back in Action TPB (2007, $14.99) r/Action Comics #841-843 and DC Comics Presents #4,17,24; commentary by Busiek 15.00
.../Batman: Saga of the Super Sons TPB (2007, $19.99) r/Super Sons stories from '70s World's Finest #215,216,221,222,224,228,230,231,233,242,263 & Elseworlds 80-Page Giant 20.00
...: Brainiac HC (2009, $19.99, dustjacket) r/Action Comics #866-870 & Superman: New Krypton Special #1 20.00
...: Brainiac SC (2010, $12.99) r/Action #866-870 & Superman: New Krypton Spec. #1 13.00
...: Camelot Falls HC (2007, $19.99, dustjacket) r/Superman #654-658 20.00
...: Camelot Falls SC (2008, $12.99) r/Superman #654-658 13.00
...: Camelot Falls Vol. 2 HC (2008, $19.99, dj) r/Superman #662-664,667 & Ann. #13 20.00
...: Camelot Falls Vol. 2 The Weight of the World SC (2008, $12.99) r/Superman #662-664,667 & Ann. #13 13.00
...: Chronicles Vol. 1 ('06, $14.99, TPB) r/early Superman app. in Action Comics #1-13, New York World's Fair 1939 and Superman #1 15.00
...: Chronicles Vol. 2 ('07, $14.99, TPB) r/early Superman app. in Action Comics #14-20 and Superman #2,3 15.00
...: Chronicles Vol. 3 ('07, $14.99, TPB) r/early Superman app. in Action Comics #21-25, Superman #3,4 and New York World's Fair 1940 15.00
...: Chronicles Vol. 4 ('08, $14.99, TPB) r/early Superman app. in Action Comics #26-31, Superman #6,7 15.00
...: Chronicles Vol. 5 ('08, $14.99, TPB) r/early Superman app. in Action Comics #32-36, Superman #8,9 and World's Best Comics #1 15.00
...: Chronicles Vol. 6 ('09, $14.99, TPB) r/early Superman app. in Action Comics #37-40, Superman #10,11 and World's Finest Comics #2,3 15.00
...: Chronicles Vol. 7 ('09, $14.99, TPB) r/early Superman app. in Action Comics #41-43, Superman #12,13 and World's Finest Comics #4 15.00
...: Chronicles Vol. 8 ('10, $14.99, TPB) r/early Superman app. in Action Comics #44-47, and Superman #14,15 15.00
...: Chronicles Vol. 9 ('11, $17.99, TPB) r/early Superman app. in Action Comics #48-52, and Superman #16,17 and World's Finest Comics #6 18.00
...: Codename: Patriot HC ('10, $24.99, d.j.) r/partial New Krypton storyline 25.00
...: Codename: Patriot SC ('11, $14.99) r/partial New Krypton storyline 15.00
...: Critical Condition ('03, $14.95, TPB) r/2000 Kryptonite poisoning storyline 15.00
.../ Doomsday: The Collection Edition (2006, $19.99) r/Superman/Doomsday: Hunter/Prey #1-3, Doomsday Ann. #1, Superman: The Doomsday Wars #1-3, Advs. of Superman #594 and Superman #175; intro. by Dan Jurgens 20.00
...: Daily Planet (2006, $19.99, TPB)-Reprints stories of Daily Planet staff 20.00
... Earth One HC (2010, $19.99)-Updated re-imagining of Superman's debut in Metropolis; Straczynski-s/Shane Davis-a; sketch pages by Davis 20.00
... Earth One Volume Two HC (2012, $22.99)-Straczynski-s/Davis-a; sketch pages 23.00
... Earth One Volume Three HC (2014, $22.99)-Straczynski-s/Syaf-a; sketch pages 23.00
...: Emperor Joker TPB (2007, $14.99) reprints 2000 x-over from Superman titles 15.00
...: Endgame (2000, $14.95, TPB)-Reprints Y2K and Brainiac story line 15.00
...: Ending Battle (2009, $14.99, TPB) r/crossover of Superman titles from 2002 15.00
...: Eradication! The Origin of the Eradicator (1996, $12.95, TPB) 13.00
...: Escape From Bizarro World HC (2008, $24.99, dustjacket) r/Action #855-857; early apps. in Superman #140, DC Comics Presents #71 and Man of Steel #5; Vaughan intro. 25.00
...: Escape From Bizarro World SC (2009, $14.99) same contents as hardcover 15.00
...: Exile (1998, $14.95, TPB)-Reprints space exile following execution of Kryptonian criminals; 1st Eradicator 15.00
...: For Tomorrow Volume 1 HC (2005, $24.99, dustjacket) r/#204-209; intro by Azzarello; new cover and sketch section by Lee 25.00
...: For Tomorrow Volume 1 SC (2005, $14.99) r/#204-209; foil-stamped S emblem-c 15.00
...: For Tomorrow Volume 2 HC (2005, $24.99, dustjacket) r/#210-215; afterword and sketch section by Lee; new Lee-c with foil-stamped S emblem 25.00
...: For Tomorrow Volume 2 SC (2005, $14.99) r/#210-215; foil-stamped S emblem-c 15.00
...: Godfall HC (2004, $19.95, dustjacket) r/Action #812-813, Advs. of Superman #625-626, Superman #202-203; Caldwell sketch pages; Turner cover gallery; new Turner-c 20.00

Superman: The Third Kryptonian SC © DC

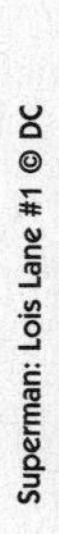

Superman: Lois Lane #1 © DC

Superman/Thundercats #1 © DC/WB/Ted Wolf

GD VG FN VF VF/NM NM-
2.0 4.0 6.0 8.0 9.0 9.2

...: Godfall SC (2004, $9.99) r/Action #812-813, Advs. of Superman #625-626, Superman #202-203; Caldwell sketch pages; Turner cover gallery; new Turner-c 10.00
...: Infinite Crisis TPB (2006, $12.99) r/Infinite Crisis #5, I.C. Secret Files and Origins 2006, Action Comics #836, Superman #226 and Advs. of Superman #649 13.00
... In the Forties ('05, $19.99, TPB) Intro. by Bob Hughes 20.00
... In the Fifties ('02, $19.95, TPB) Intro. by Mark Waid 20.00
... In the Sixties ('01, $19.95, TPB) Intro. by Mark Waid 20.00
... In the Seventies ('00, $19.95, TPB) Intro. by Christopher Reeve 20.00
... In the Eighties ('06, $19.99, TPB) Intro. by Jerry Ordway 20.00
... In the Name of Gog ('05, $17.99, TPB) r/Action Comics #820-825 18.00
... Kryptonite HC ('08, $24.99) r/Superman Confidential #1-5,11; Darwyn Cooke intro. 25.00
...: Last Son HC (2008, $19.99) r/Action Comics #844-846,851 and Annual #11; sketch pages and variant covers; Marc McClure intro. 20.00
... Mon-El HC ('10, $24.99) r/Superman #684-690, Action #874 & Annual #1, Superman: Secret Files 2009 #1 25.00
... Mon-El SC ('11, $17.99) r/Superman #684-690, Action #874 & Annual #1, Superman: Secret Files 2009 #1 18.00
... Mon-El - Man of Valor HC ('10, $24.99) r/Superman #692-697 & Annual #14, Adventure #11, Superman: Secret Files 2009 #1 25.00
... : New Krypton Vol. 1 HC ('09, $24.99, d.j.) r/Superman #681, Action #871 & one-shots 25.00
... : New Krypton Vol. 1 SC ('10, $17.99) r/Superman #681, Action #871 & one-shots 18.00
... : New Krypton Vol. 2 HC ('09, $24.99, d.j.) r/Superman #682,683, Action #872,873 & Supergirl #35,36; gallery of covers and variants 25.00
... : New Krypton Vol. 2 SC ('10, $17.99) same contents as HC 18.00
... : New Krypton Vol. 3 HC ('10, $24.99, d.j.) r/Superman: World of New Krypton #1-5 & Action Comics Annual #10; gallery of covers and variants 25.00
... : New Krypton Vol. 3 SC ('11, $17.99) same contents as HC 18.00
... : New Krypton Vol. 4 HC ('10, $24.99, d.j.) r/Superman: World of New Krypton #6-12; gallery of covers and variants; sketch and design art 25.00
... : New Krypton Vol. 4 SC ('11, $17.99) same contents as HC 18.00
... : Nightwing and Flamebird HC ('10, $24.99, d.j.) r/Action #875-879 & Annual #12 25.00
... : Nightwing and Flamebird SC ('10, $17.99) r/Action #875-879 & Annual #12 18.00
... : Nightwing and Flamebird Vol. 2 HC ('10, $24.99, d.j.) r/Action #883-889, Superman #696 & Adventure Comics #8-10 25.00
... No Limits ('00, $14.95, TPB) Reprints early 2000 stories 15.00
...: Our Worlds at War Book 1 ('02, $19.95, TPB) r/1st half of x-over 20.00
...: Our Worlds at War Book 2 ('02, $19.95, TPB) r/2nd half of x-over 20.00
...: Our Worlds at War - The Complete Collection ('06, $24.99, TPB) r/entire x-over 25.00
...: Past and Future (2008, $19.99, TPB) r/time travel stories 1947-1983 20.00
...: President Lex TPB (2003, $17.95) r/Luthor's run for the White House; Harris-c 18.00
...: Redemption TPB (2007, $12.99) r/Superman #659,666 & Action Comics #848,849 13.00
...: Return to Krypton (2004, $17.95, TPB) r/2001-2002 x-over 18.00
...: Sacrifice (2005, $14.99, TPB) prelude x-over to Infinite Crisis; r/Superman #218-220, Advs. of Superman #642,643; Action #829, Wonder Woman #219,220 15.00
...: Shadows Linger (2008, $14.99, TPB) r/Superman #671-675 15.00
... : Strange Attractors (2006, $14.99, TPB) r/Action Comics #827,828,830-835 15.00
... : Tales From the Phantom Zone ('09, $19.99, TPB) r/Phantom Zone stories 1961-68 20.00
...: That Healing Touch TPB (2005, $14.99) r/Advs. of Superman #633-638 & Superman Secret Files 2004 15.00
...: The Adventures of Nightwing and Flamebird TPB (2009, $19.99)-reprints appearances in Superman Family #173,183-194 20.00
...: The Black Ring Volume One HC (2011, $19.99, d.j.) r/Action Comics #890-895 20.00
The Bottle City of Kandor TPB (2007, $14.99)-Reprints 1st app. in Action #242 and other stories; Nightwing and Flamebird app. 15.00
The Coming of Atlas HC (2009, $19.99, dustjacket)-r/Superman #677-680 & Atlas' debut from First Issue Special #1 (1975); intro by James Robinson 20.00
The Coming of Atlas SC (2010, $14.99) same contents as HC 15.00
The Death of Clark Kent (1997, $19.95, TPB)-Reprints Man of Steel #43 (1 page), Superman #99 (1 page),#100-102, Action #709 (1 page), #710,711, Advs. of Superman #523-525, Superman:The Man of Tomorrow #1 20.00
The Death of Superman (1993, $4.95, TPB)-Reprints Man of Steel #17-19, Superman #73-75, Advs. of Superman #496,497, Action #683,684, & Justice League #69
2 4 6 9 12 15
The Death of Superman, 2nd & 3rd printings 1 3 4 6 8 10
The Death of Superman Platinum Edition 25.00
...: The Greatest Stories Ever Told ('04, $19.95, TPB) Ross-c, Uslan intro. 20.00
...: The Greatest Stories Ever Told Vol. 2 ('06, $19.99, TPB) Ross-c, Greenberger intro. 20.00
...: The Journey ('06, $14.99, TPB) r/Action Comics #831 & Superman #217,221-225 15.00
...: The Man of Steel Vol. 2 ('03, $19.95, TPB) r/Superman #1-3, Action #584-586, Advs. of Superman #424-426 & Who's Who Update '87 20.00
...: The Man of Steel Vol. 3 ('04, $19.95, TPB) r/Superman #4-6, Action #587-589, Advs. of Superman #427-429; intro. by Ordway; new Ordway-c 20.00
...: The Man of Steel Vol. 4 ('05, $19.99, TPB) r/Superman #7,8; Action #590,591; Advs. of Superman #430,431; Legion of Super-Heroes #37,38; new Ordway-c 20.00
...: The Man of Steel Vol. 5 ('06, $19.99, TPB) r/Superman #9-11, Action #592-593, Advs. of Superman #432-435; intro. by Mike Carlin; new Ordway-c 20.00
...: The Man of Steel Vol. 6 ('08, $19.99, TPB) r/Superman #12 & Ann. #1, Action #594-595 & Ann. #1, Advs. of Superman Ann.#1; Booster Gold #23; new Ordway-c 20.00
The Third Kryptonian ('08, $14.99, TPB) r/Action #847, Superman #668-670 & Ann. #13 15.00
The Trial of Superman ('97, $14.95, TPB) reprints story arc 15.00
The World of Krypton ('08, $14.99, TPB) r/World of Krypton Vol. 2 #1-4 and various tales of Krypton and its history; Kupperberg intro. 15.00
The Wrath of Gog ('05, $14.99, TPB) reprints Action Comics #812-819 15.00
...: They Saved Luthor's Brain ('00, $14.95) r/ "death" and return of Luthor 15.00
...: 3-2-1 Action! ('08, $14.99) Jimmy Olsen super-powered stories; Steve Rude-c 15.00
...: 'Til Death Do Us Part ('01, $17.95) reprints; Mahnke-c 18.00
...: Time and Time Again (1994, $7.50, TPB)-Reprints 10.00
...: Transformed ('98, $12.95, TPB) r/post Final Night powerless Superman to Electric Superman 13.00
...: Unconventional Warfare (2005, $14.95, TPB) r/Adventures of Superman #625-632 and pages from Superman Secret Files 2004 15.00
...: Up, Up and Away! (2006, $14.99, TPB) r/Superman #650-653 and Action #837-840 15.00
... Vs. Brainiac (2008, $19.99, TPB) reprints 1st meeting in Action #242 and other duels 20.00
... Vs. Lex Luthor (2006, $19.99, TPB) reprints 1st meeting in Action #23 and 11 other classic duels 1940-2001 20.00
... Vs. The Flash (2005, $19.99, TPB) reprints their races from Superman #199, Flash #175, World's Finest #198, DC Comics Presents #1&2, Advs. of Superman #463 & DC First: Flash/Superman; new Alex Ross-c 20.00
... Vs. The Revenge Squad (1999, $12.95, TPB) 13.00
...: Whatever Happened to the Man of Tomorrow? TPB (1/97, $5.99) r/Superman #423 & Action Comics #583, intro. by Paul Kupperberg 8.00
...: Whatever Happened to the Man of Tomorrow? Deluxe Edition HC (2009, $24.99, d.j.) r/Superman #423, Action #583, DC Comics Presents #85, Superman Ann #11 25.00
...: Whatever Happened to the Man of Tomorrow? SC (2010, $14.99) r/same as HC 15.00

NOTE: ***Austin*** *a(i)-1-3.* ***Byrne*** *a-1-16p, 17, 19-21p, 22; c-1-17, 20-22; scripts-1-22.* ***Guice*** *c/a-64.* ***Kirby*** *c-37p.* ***Joe Quesada*** *c-Annual 4.* ***Russell*** *c/a-23i.* ***Simonson*** *c-69i. #19-21 2nd printings sold in multi-packs.*

SUPERMAN (one-shots)

Daily News Magazine Presents DC Comics' Superman nn-(1987, 8 pgs.)-Supplement to New York Daily News; Perez-c/a 5.00
...: A Nation Divided (1999, $4.95)-Elseworlds Civil War story 5.00
... & Savage Dragon: Chicago (2002, $5.95) Larsen-a; Ross-c 6.00
... & Savage Dragon: Metropolis (11/99, $4.95) Bogdanove-a 5.00
...: At Earth's End (1995, $4.95)-Elseworlds story 5.00
...Beyond #0 (10/11, $3.99) The Batman Beyond future; Frenz-a/Nguyen-c 4.00
...: Blood of My Ancestors (2003, $6.95)-Gil Kane & John Buscema-a 7.00
...: Distant Fires (1998, $5.95)-Elseworlds; Chaykin-s 6.00
...: Emperor Joker (10/00, $3.50)-Follows Action #769 4.00
...: End of the Century (2/00, $24.95, HC)-Immonen-s/a 25.00
...: End of the Century (2003, $17.95, SC)-Immonen-s/a 18.00
... For Earth (1991, $4.95, 52 pgs, printed on recycled paper)-Ordway wraparound-c 6.00
...IV Movie Special (1987, $2.00)-Movie adaptation; Heck-a 4.00
...Gallery, The 1 (1993, $2.95)-Poster-a 3.00
..., Inc. (1999, $6.95)-Elseworlds Clark as a sports hero; Garcia-Lopez-a 7.00
...: Infinite City HC (2005, $24.99, dustjacket) Mike Kennedy-s/Carlos Meglia-a 25.00
...: Infinite City SC (2006, $17.99) Mike Kennedy-s/Carlos Meglia-a 18.00
...: Kal (1995, $5.95)-Elseworlds story 6.00
...: Lex 2000 (1/01, $3.50) Election night for the Luthor Presidency 4.00
...: Lois Lane 1 (4/14, $4.99) Marguerite Bennett-s; Rocafort-c 5.00
...: Monster (1999, $5.95)-Elseworlds story; Anthony Williams-a 6.00
... Movie Special-(9/83)-Adaptation of Superman III; other versions exist with store logos on bottom 1/3 of-c 4.00
...: New Krypton Special 1-(12/08, $3.99) Funeral of Pa Kent; newly enlarged Kandor 4.00
...: Our Worlds at War Secret Files 1-(8/01, $5.95)-Stories & profile pages 6.00
... Plus 1(2/97, $2.95)-Legion of Super-Heroes-c/app. 4.00
...'s Metropolis-(1996, $5.95, prestige format)-Elseworlds; McKeever-c/a 6.00
...: Speeding Bullets-(1993, $4.95, 52 pgs.)-Elseworlds 6.00
.../Spider-Man-(1995, $3.95)-r/DC and Marvel Presents... 4.00
... 10-Cent Adventure 1 (3/02, 10¢) McDaniel-a; intro. Cir-El Supergirl 3.00
...: The Earth Stealers 1-(1988, $2.95, 52 pgs, prestige format) Byrne script; painted-c 6.00
...: The Earth Stealers 1-2nd printing 4.00
...: The Legacy of Superman #1 (3/93, $2.50, 68 pgs.)-Art Adams-c; Simonson-a 6.00
...: The Last God of Krypton ('99,$4.95) Hildebrandt Bros.-a/Simonson-s 5.00
...: The Last Son of Krypton FCBD Special Edition (7/13) r/Action #844; Jim Lee-c 3.00
...: The Odyssey ('99, $4.95) Clark Kent's post-Smallville journey 5.00
...: 3-D (12/98, $3.95)-with glasses 4.00
.../Thundercats (1/04, $5.95) Winick-s/Garza-a; two covers by Garza & McGuinness 6.00
.../Through the Ages (2006, $3.99) r/Action #1, Superman ('87) #7; origins and pin-ups 4.00
.../Toyman-(1996, $1.95) 3.00

Superman Adventures #51 © DC

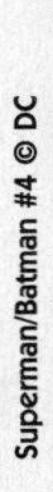

Superman/Batman #4 © DC

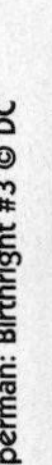

Superman: Birthright #3 © DC

	GD	VG	FN	VF	VF/NM	NM-
	2.0	4.0	6.0	8.0	9.0	9.2

...: True Brit (2004, $24.95, HC w/dust jacket) Elseworlds; Kal-El's rocket lands in England; co-written by John Cleese and Kim Howard Johnson; John Byrne-a 25.00
...: True Brit (2005, $17.99, TPB) Elseworlds; Kal-El's rocket lands in England 18.00
...: Under A Yellow Sun (1994, $5.95, 68 pgs.)-A Novel by Clark Kent; embossed-c 6.00
... Vs. Darkseid: Apokolips Now! 1 (3/03, $2.95) McKone-a; Kara (Supergirl #75) app. 4.00
...: War of the Worlds (1999, $5.95)-Battles Martians 6.00
...: Where is thy Sting? (2001, $6.95)-McCormack-Sharp-c/a 7.00
...: Y2K (2/00, $4.95)-1st Brainiac 13 app.; Guice-c/a 5.00

SUPERMAN ADVENTURES, THE (Based on animated series)
DC Comics: Oct, 1996 - No. 66, Apr, 2002 ($1.75/$1.95/$1.99)

1-Rick Burchett-c/a begins; Paul Dini script; Lex Luthor app.; 1st app. Mercy Graves in comics; silver ink, wraparound-c 4.00
2-20,22: 2-McCloud scripts begin; Metallo-c/app. 3-Brainiac-c/app. 5-1st app. Livewire in comics. 6-Mxyzptlk-c/app. 3.00
21-($3.95) 1st animated Supergirl 5.00
23-66: 23-Begin $1.99-c; Livewire app. 25-Batgirl-c/app. 28-Manley-a. 54-Retells Superman #233 "Kryptonite Nevermore" 58-Ross-c 3.00
Annual 1 (1997, $3.95)-Zatanna and Bruce Wayne app. 4.00
Special 1 (2/98, $2.95) Superman vs. Lobo 4.00
TPB (1998, $7.95) r/#1-6 8.00
... Vol 1: Up, Up and Away (2004, $6.95, digest) r/#16,19,22-24; Amancio-a 7.00
... Vol 2: The Never-Ending Battle (2004, $6.95) r/#25-29 7.00
... Vol 3: Last Son of Krypton (2006, $6.99) r/#30-34 7.00
... Vol 4: The Man of Steel (2006, $6.99) r/#35-39 7.00

SUPERMAN ALIENS 2: GOD WAR (Also see Superman Vs. Aliens)
DC Comics/Dark Horse Comics: May, 2002 - No. 4, Nov, 2002 ($2.99, limited series)

1-4-Bogdanove & Nowlan-a; Darkseid & New Gods app. 3.00
TPB (6/03, $12.95) r/#1-4 13.00

SUPERMAN: AMERICAN ALIEN
DC Comics: Jan, 2016 - No. 7, Jul, 2016 ($3.99, limited series)

1-7-Flashbacks to Clark Kent's upbringing; Max Landis-s in all. 1-Dragotta-a. 4-Jae Lee-a; Batman app. 7-Lobo app.; Jock-a 4.00

SUPERMAN & BATMAN: GENERATIONS (Elseworlds)
DC Comics: 1999 - No. 4, 1999 ($4.95, limited series)

1-4-Superman & Batman team-up from 1939 to the future; Byrne-c/s/a 5.00
TPB (2000, $14.95) r/series 15.00

SUPERMAN & BATMAN: GENERATIONS II (Elseworlds)
DC Comics: 2001 - No. 4, 2001 ($5.95, limited series)

1-4-Superman, Batman & others team-up from 1942-future; Byrne-c/s/a 6.00
TPB (2003, $19.95) r/series 20.00

SUPERMAN & BATMAN: GENERATIONS III (Elseworlds)
DC Comics: Mar, 2003 - No. 12, Feb, 2004 ($2.95, limited series)

1-12-Superman & Batman through the centuries; Byrne-c/s/a 3.00

SUPERMAN & BATMAN VS. ALIENS AND PREDATOR
DC Comics: 2007 - No. 2, 2007 ($5.99, squarebound, limited series)

1,2-Schultz-s/Olivetti-a 6.00
TPB (2007, $12.99) r/#1,2; pencil breakdown pages 13.00

SUPERMAN AND BATMAN VS. VAMPIRES AND WEREWOLVES
DC Comics: Early Dec, 2008 - No. 6, Late Feb, 2009 ($2.99, limited series)

1-6-Van Hook-s/Mandrake-a/c. 1-Wonder Woman app. 5-Demon-c/app. 3.00
TPB (2009, $14.99) r/#1-6; intro. by John Landis 15.00

SUPERMAN & BATMAN: WORLD'S FUNNEST (Elseworlds)
DC Comics: 2000 ($6.95, square-bound, one-shot)

nn-Mr. Mxyzptlk and Bat-Mite destroy each DC Universe; Dorkin-s; art by various incl. Ross, Timm, Miller, Allred, Moldoff, Gibbons, Cho, Jimenez 7.00

SUPERMAN & BUGS BUNNY
DC Comics: Jul, 2000 - No. 4, Oct, 2000 ($2.50, limited series)

1-4-JLA & Looney Tunes characters meet 3.00

SUPERMAN/BATMAN
DC Comics: Oct, 2003 - No. 87, Oct, 2011 ($2.95/$2.99)

1-Two covers (Superman or Batman in foreground) Loeb-s/McGuinness-a; Metallo app.

	1	2	3	5	6	8
1-2nd printing (Batman cover)						3.00
1-3rd printing; new McGuinness cover						3.00
1-Diamond/Alliance Retailer Summit Edition-variant	7	14	21	46	86	125
1-(6/06, Free Comic Book Day giveaway) reprints #1						3.00
2-6: 2,5-Future Superman app. 6-Luthor in battlesuit						3.00

	GD	VG	FN	VF	VF/NM	NM-
	2.0	4.0	6.0	8.0	9.0	9.2

7-Pat Lee-c/a; Superboy & Robin app. 3.00
8-Michael Turner-c/a; intro. new Kara Zor-El 5.00
8-Second printing with sketch cover 3.00
8-Third printing with new Turner cover 3.00
9-13-Michael Turner-c/a; Wonder Woman app. 10,13-Variant-c by Jim Lee 3.00
14-25: 14-18-Pacheco-a; Lightning Lord, Saturn Queen & Cosmic King app. 19-Supergirl app.; leads into Supergirl #1. 21-25-Bizarro app. 25-Superman & Batman covers; 2nd printing with white bkgrd cover 3.00
26-($3.99) Sam Loeb tribute issue; 2 covers by Turner; story & art by 26 various; back-up by Loeb & Sale 5.00
27-49: 27-Flashback to Earth-2 Power Girl & Huntress; Maguire-a. 34-36-Metal Men app. 3.00
50-($3.99) Thomas Wayne meets Jor-El; Justice League app. 4.00
51-74: 51,52-Mr. Mxyzptlk app. 66,67-Blackest Night; Man-Bat and Bizarro app. 3.00
75-($4.99) Quitely-c; Legion of Super-Heroes app.; Ordway-a; 2-pg. features by various 5.00
76-87: 76-Aftermath of Batman's "death". 77-Supergirl/Damian team-up 3.00
Annual #1 (12/06, $3.99) Re-imaging of 1st meeting from World's Finest #71 4.00
Annual #2 (5/08, $3.99) Kolins-a; re-imaging of Superman as Supernova story 4.00
Annual #3 (3/09, $3.99) Composite Superman-c by Wrightson; Batista-a 4.00
Annual #4 (8/10, $4.99) Batman Beyond; Levitz-s/Guedes-a/Lau-c 8.00
Annual #5 (6/11, $4.99) Reign of Doomsday x-over, Cyborg Superman app.; Sepulveda-a 5.00
...Absolute Power HC (2005, $19.99) r/#14-18 20.00
...Absolute Power SC (2006, $12.99) r/#14-18 13.00
..."Batman V Superman: Dawn of Justice Day" Special Edition 1 (4/16, free) r/#1 3.00
...Big Noise SC (2010, $14.99) r/#64,68-71 15.00
...Enemies Among Us SC (2009, $12.99) r/#28-33 13.00
...Finest Worlds SC (2010, $14.99) r/#50-56 15.00
...Night and Day HC (2010, $19.99) r/#60-63,65-67 20.00
...Public Enemies HC (2004, $19.95) r/#1-6 & Secret Files 2003; sketch art pages 20.00
...Public Enemies SC (2005, $12.99) r/#1-6 & Secret Files 2003; sketch art pages 15.00
...Public Enemies SC (2009, $14.99) r/#1-6 & Secret Files 2003; sketch art pages 15.00
...Secret Files 2003 (11/03, $4.95) Reis-a; pin-ups by various; Loeb/Sale short-s 5.00
... : Supergirl HC (2004, $19.95) r/#8-13; intro by Loeb, cover gallery, sketch pages 20.00
... : Supergirl SC (2005, $12.99) r/#8-13; intro by Loeb, cover gallery, sketch pages 13.00
... : The Search For Kryptonite HC (2008, $19.99) r/#44-49; Davis sketch pages 20.00
... : The Search For Kryptonite SC (2009, $12.99) r/#44-49; Davis sketch pages 13.00
... : Torment HC (2008, $19.99) r/#37-42; cover gallery, Nguyen sketch pages 20.00
... : Vengeance HC (2006, $19.99) r/#20-25; sketch pages 20.00
... : Vengeance SC (2008, $12.99) r/#20-25; sketch pages 13.00
... : Worship SC (2011, $17.99) r/#72-75 & Annual #4 18.00

SUPERMAN/BATMAN: ALTERNATE HISTORIES
DC Comics: 1996 ($14.95, trade paperback)

nn-Reprints Detective Comics Annual #7, Action Comics Annual #6, Steel Annual #1, Legends of the Dark Knight Annual #4 15.00

SUPERMAN: BIRTHRIGHT
DC Comics: Sept, 2003 - No. 12, Sept, 2004 ($2.95, limited series)

1-12-Waid-s/Leinil Yu-a; retelling of origin and early Superman years 3.00
HC (2004, $29.95, dustjacket) r/series; cover gallery; Waid proposal with Yu concept art 30.00
SC (2005, $19.99) r/series; cover gallery; Waid proposal with Yu concept art 20.00

SUPERMAN COMICS
DC Comics: 1939

nn - Ashcan comic, not distributed to newsstands, only for in-house use. Cover art is Action Comics #7 with interior being Action Comics #8. A CGC certified 9.0 copy sold for $37,375 in 2005 and for $90,000 in 2007.

SUPERMAN CONFIDENTIAL (See Superman Hardcovers and TPBs listings for reprint)
DC Comics: Jan, 2007 - No. 14, Jun, 2008 ($2.99)

1-14: 1-5,9-Darwyn Cooke-s/Tim Sale-a/c; origin of Kryptonite re-told. 8-10-New Gods and Darkside app. 3.00
...: Kryptonite TPB (2009, $14.99) r/#1-5,11; intro. by Darwyn Cooke; Tim Sale sketch-a 15.00

SUPERMAN: DAY OF DOOM
DC Comics: Jan, 2003 - No. 4, Feb, 2003 ($2.95, weekly limited series)

1-4-Jurgens-s/Jurgens & Sienkiewicz-a 3.00
TPB (2003, $9.95) r/#1-4 10.00

SUPERMAN DOOMED (DC New 52) (See Action Comics #31-34 and Superman/Wonder Woman)
DC Comics: Jul, 2014 - No. 2, Nov, 2014 ($4.99, bookends for crossover)

1,2: 1-Lashley-a; Wonder Woman & Steel app. 2-Superman vs. Brainiac 6.00

SUPERMAN/DOOMSDAY: HUNTER/PREY
DC Comics: 1994 - No. 3, 1994 ($4.95, limited series, 52 pgs.)

1-3 6.00

SUPERMAN FAMILY, THE (Formerly Superman's Pal Jimmy Olsen)

Superman For All Seasons #4 © DC

Superman: Lois and Clark #1 © DC

Superman: Red Son #1 © DC

National Per. Publ./DC Comics: No. 164, Apr-May, 1974 - No. 222, Sept, 1982

	GD 2.0	VG 4.0	FN 6.0	VF 8.0	VF/NM 9.0	NM- 9.2
164-(100 pgs.) Jimmy Olsen, Supergirl, Lois Lane begin	4	8	12	28	47	65
165-169 (100 pgs.)	3	6	9	18	28	38
170-176 (68 pgs.)	3	6	9	14	19	24
177-190 (52 pgs.): 177-181-52 pgs. 182-Marshall Rogers-a; $1.00 issues begin; Krypto begins, ends #192. 183-Nightwing-Flamebird begins, ends #194. 189-Brainiac 5, Mon -El app.	2	4	6	9	13	16
191-193,195-199: 191-Superboy begins, ends #198	2	3	4	6	8	10
194,200: 194-Rogers-a. 200-Book length sty	2	4	6	8	10	12
201-210,212-222	1	2	3	5	6	8
211-Earth II Batman & Catwoman marry	2	4	6	8	11	14

NOTE: ***N. Adams** c-182-185. **Anderson** a-186i. **Buckler** c(p)-190, 191, 209, 210, 215, 217, 220. **Jones** a-191-193. **Gil Kane** c(p)-221, 222. **Mortimer** a(p)-191-193, 199, 201-222. **Orlando** a(i)-186, 187. **Rogers** a-182, 194. **Staton** a-191-194, 196p. **Tuska** a(p)-203, 207-209.*

SUPERMAN FAMILY ADVENTURES
DC Comics: Jul, 2012 - No. 12, Jun, 2013 ($2.99)

1-12-Young-reader stories, games and DC Nation character profiles; Baltazar-a 3.00

SUPERMAN/FANTASTIC FOUR
DC Comics/Marvel Comics: 1999 ($9.95, tabloid size, one-shot)

1-Battle Galactus and the Cyborg; wraparound-c by Alex Ross and Dan Jurgens; Jurgens-s/a; Thibert-a 10.00

SUPERMAN FOR ALL SEASONS
DC Comics: 1998 - No, 4, 1998 ($4.95, limited series, prestige format)

1-Loeb-s/Sale-a/c; Superman's first year in Metropolis 6.00
2-4 5.00
Hardcover (1999, $24.95) r/#1-4 25.00

SUPERMAN FOR EARTH (See Superman one-shots)

SUPERMAN FOREVER
DC Comics: Jun, 1998 ($5.95, one-shot)

1-($5.95)-Collector's Edition with a 7-image lenticular-c by Alex Ross; Superman returns to normal; s/a by various 7.00
1-($4.95) Standard Edition with single image Ross-c 5.00

SUPERMAN/GEN13
DC Comics (WildStorm): Jun, 2000 - No. 3, Aug, 2000 ($2.50, limited series)

1-3-Hughes-s/ Bermejo-a; Campbell variant-c for each 3.00
TPB (2001, $9.95) new Bermejo-c; cover gallery 10.00

SUPERMAN: KING OF THE WORLD
DC Comics: June, 1999 ($3.95/$4.95, one-shot)

1-($3.95) Regular Ed. 4.00
1-($4.95) Collectors' Ed. with gold foil enhanced-c 5.00

SUPERMAN: LAST SON OF EARTH
DC Comics: 2000 - No. 2, 2000 ($5.95, limited series, prestige format)

1,2-Elseworlds; baby Clark rockets to Krypton; Gerber-s/Wheatley-a 6.00

SUPERMAN: LAST STAND OF NEW KRYPTON
DC Comics: May, 2010 - No. 3, Late June, 2010 ($3.99, limited series)

1-3-Robinson & Gates-s/Woods-a. 2-Pérez-c. 3-Sook-c 4.00
HC (2010, $24.99, DJ) r/#1,2, Adventure Comics #8,9, Supergirl #51 & Superman #698 25.00
Vol. 2 HC (2010, $19.99, DJ) r/#3, Adventure #10,11, Supergirl #52 & Superman #699 20.00

SUPERMAN: LAST STAND ON KRYPTON
DC Comics: 2003 ($6.95, one-shot, prestige format)

1-Sequel to Superman: Last Son of Earth; Gerber-s/Wheatley-a 7.00

SUPERMAN: LOIS & CLARK (See Convergence Superman #1 & 2)
DC Comics: Dec, 2015 - No. 8, Jul, 2016 ($3.99)

1-8: 1-Pre-Flashpoint Superman & Lois on New 52 Earth; Jurgens-s/Weeks-a 4.00

SUPERMAN: LOIS LANE (Girlfrenzy)
DC Comics: Jun, 1998 ($1.95, one shot)

1-Connor & Palmiotti-a 3.00

SUPERMAN/MADMAN HULLABALOO!
Dark Horse Comics: June, 1997 - No. 3, Aug, 1997 ($2.95, limited series)

1-3-Mike Allred-c/s/a 3.00
TPB (1997, $8.95) 9.00

SUPERMAN: METROPOLIS
DC Comics: Apr, 2003 - No. 12, Mar, 2004 ($2.95, limited series)

1-12-Focus on Jimmy Olsen; Austen-s. 1-6-Zezelj-a. 7-12-Kristiansen-a. 8,9-Creeper app. 3.00

SUPERMAN METROPOLIS SECRET FILES
DC Comics: Jun, 2000 ($4.95, one shot)

1-Short stories, pin-ups and profile pages; Hitch and Neary-c 5.00

SUPERMAN: PEACE ON EARTH
DC Comics: Jan, 1999 ($9.95, Treasury-sized, one-shot)

1-Alex Ross painted-c/a; Paul Dini-s 12.00

SUPERMAN: RED SON
DC Comics: 2003 - No. 3, 2003 ($5.95, limited series, prestige format)

1-Elseworlds; Superman's rocket lands in Russia; Mark Millar-s/Dave Johnson-c/a 10.00
2,3 6.00
TPB (2004, $17.95) r/#1-3; intro. by Tom DeSanto; sketch pages 18.00
... - The Deluxe Edition HC (2009, $24.99, d.j.) r/#1-3; sketch art by various 25.00

SUPERMAN RED/ SUPERMAN BLUE
DC Comics: Feb, 1998 ($4.95, one shot)

1-Polybagged w/3-D glasses and reprint of Superman 3-D (1955); Jurgens-plot/3-D cover; script and art by various 5.00
1-($3.95)-Standard Ed.; comic only, non 3-D cover 4.00

SUPERMAN RETURNS... (2006 movie)
DC Comics: Aug, 2006 ($3.99, movie tie-in stories by Singer, Dougherty and Harris)

Prequel 1 - Krypton to Earth; Olivetti-a/Hughes-c; retells Jor-El's story 6.00
Prequel 2 - Ma Kent; Kerschl-a/Hughes-c; Ma Kent during Clark childhood and absence 4.00
Prequel 3 - Lex Luthor; Leonardi-a/Hughes-c; Luthor's 5 years in prison 4.00
Prequel 4 - Lois Lane; Dias-a/Hughes-c; Lois during Superman's absence 4.00
The Movie and Other Tales of the Man of Steel (2006, $12.99, TPB) adaptation; origin from Amazing World of Superman; Action #810, Superman #185; Advs. of Superman #575 13.00
The Official Movie Adaptation (2006, $6.99) Pasko-s/Haley-a; photo-c 7.00
...: The Prequels TPB (2006, $12.99) r/the 4 prequels 13.00

SUPERMAN: SAVE THE PLANET
DC Comics: Oct, 1998 ($2.95, one-shot)

1-($2.95) Regular Ed.; Luthor buys the Daily Planet 3.00
1-($3.95) Collector's Ed. with acetate cover 4.00

SUPERMAN SCRAPBOOK (Has blank pages; contains no comics)

SUPERMAN: SECRET FILES
DC Comics: Jan, 1998; May 1999 ($4.95)

1,2: 1-Retold origin story, "lost" pages & pin-ups 5.00
... & Origins 2004 (8/04) pin-ups by Lee, Turner and others 5.00
... & Origins 2005 (1/06) short stories and pin-ups by various 5.00
... 2009 (10/09, $4.99) short stories and pin-ups about New Krypton x-over 5.00

SUPERMAN: SECRET IDENTITY
DC Comics: 2004 - No. 4, 2004 ($5.95, squarebound, limited series)

1-4-Busiek-s/Immonen-a/c 6.00

SUPERMAN: SECRET ORIGIN
DC Comics: Nov, 2009 - No. 6, Oct, 2010 ($3.99, limited series)

1-6-Geoff Johns-s/Gary Frank-a/c; origin mythos re-told. 2-Legion app. 5-Metallo app. 4.00
1-6-Variant covers by Frank 6.00
HC (2011, $29.99) r/#1-6; intro. by David Goyer; variant covers 30.00

SUPERMAN'S GIRLFRIEND LOIS LANE (See Action Comics #1, 80 Page Giant #3, 14, Lois Lane, Showcase #9, 10, Superman #28 & Superman Family)

SUPERMAN'S GIRLFRIEND LOIS LANE (See Showcase #9,10)
National Periodical Publ.: Mar-Apr, 1958 - No. 136, Jan-Feb, 1974; No. 137, Sept-Oct, 1974

	GD 2.0	VG 4.0	FN 6.0	VF 8.0	VF/NM 9.0	NM- 9.2
1-(3-4/58)	300	600	1200	3300	7900	12,500
2	100	200	300	800	1800	2800
3	66	132	198	528	1189	1850
4,5	47	94	141	364	820	1275
6,7	37	74	111	274	612	950
8-10: 9-Pat Boone-c/story	32	64	96	230	515	800
11-13,15-19: 12-(10/59)-Aquaman app. 17-(5/60) 2nd app. Brainiac.	19	38	57	131	291	450
14-Supergirl x-over; Batman app. on-c only	20	40	60	138	307	475
20-Supergirl-c/sty	19	38	57	133	297	460
21-28: 23-1st app. Lena Thorul, Lex Luthor's sister; 1st Lois as Elastic Lass. 27-Bizarro-c/story	14	28	42	96	211	325
29-Aquaman, Batman, Green Arrow cover app. and cameo; last 10¢ issue	15	30	45	105	233	360
30-32,34-46,48,49	9	18	27	59	117	175
33(5/62)-Mon -El app.	9	18	27	61	123	185
47-Legion app.	9	18	27	61	123	185

50(7/64)-Triplicate Girl, Phantom Girl & Shrinking Violet app.

Superman's Girlfriend Lois Lane #104 © DC

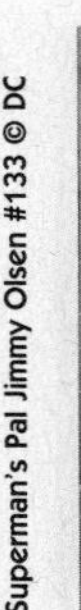

Superman's Pal Jimmy Olsen #133 © DC

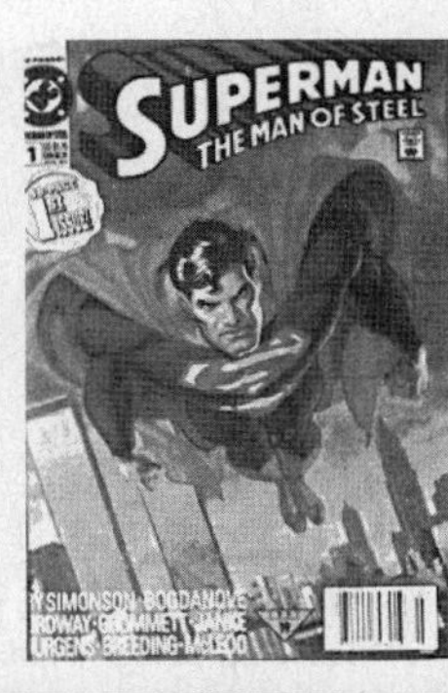

Superman: The Man of Steel #1 © DC

	GD 2.0	VG 4.0	FN 6.0	VF 8.0	VF/NM 9.0	NM- 9.2

	9	18	27	61	123	185
51-55,57-67,69: 59-Jor -El app.; Batman back-up sty	7	14	21	44	82	120
56-Saturn Girl app.	7	14	21	46	86	125
68-(Giant G-26)	8	16	24	54	102	150
70-Penguin & Catwoman app. (1st S.A. Catwoman, 11/66; also see Detective #369 for 3rd app.); Batman & Robin cameo	26	52	78	182	404	625
71-Batman & Robin cameo (3 panels); Catwoman story cont'd from #70 (2nd app.); see Detective #369 for 3rd app	10	20	30	69	147	225
72,73,75,76,78	5	10	15	34	60	85
74-1st Bizarro Flash (5/67); JLA cameo	5	10	15	35	63	90
77-(Giant G-39)	6	12	18	42	79	115
79-Neal Adams-c or c(i) begin, end #95,108	5	10	15	35	63	90
80-85,87,88,90-92: 92-Last 12¢ issue	4	8	12	28	47	65
86,95 (Giants G-51,G-63)-Both have Neal Adams-c	6	12	18	37	66	95
89,93: 89-Batman x-over; all N. Adams-c. 93-Wonder Woman-c/story	5	10	15	30	50	70
94,96-99,101-103,107-110	4	8	12	23	37	50
100	4	8	12	25	40	55
104-(Giant G-75)	5	10	15	34	60	85
105-Origin/1st app. The Rose & the Thorn.	5	10	15	34	60	85
106-"I Am Curious (Black)" story; Lois changes her skin color to black (11/70)	9	18	27	61	123	185
111-Justice League-c/s; Morrow-a; last 15¢ issue	4	8	12	25	40	55
112,114-123 (52 pgs.): 122-G.A. Lois Lane-r/Superman #30. 123-G.A. Batman-r/Batman #35 (w/Catwoman)	4	8	12	23	37	50
113-(Giant G-87) Kubert-a (previously unpublished G.A. story)(scarce in NM)	6	12	18	37	66	95
124-135: 130-Last Rose & the Thorn. 132-New Zatanna story	3	6	9	16	23	30
136,137: 136-Wonder Woman x-over	3	6	9	17	26	35
Annual 1(Sum, 1962)-r/L. Lane #12; Aquaman app.	18	36	54	128	284	440
Annual 2(Sum, 1963)	13	26	39	89	195	300

NOTE: *Buckler a-117-121p. Curt Swan or Kurt Schaffenberger a-1-81(most); c(p)-1-15.*

SUPERMAN/SHAZAM: FIRST THUNDER
DC Comics: Nov, 2005 - No. 4, Feb, 2006 ($3.50, limited series)

1-4-Retells first meeting; Winick-s/Middleton-a. Dr. Sivana app. 3.50

SUPERMAN: SILVER BANSHEE
DC Comics: Dec, 1998 - No. 2, Jan, 1999 ($2.25, mini-series)

1,2-Brereton-s/c; Chin-a 3.00

SUPERMAN'S NEMESIS: LEX LUTHOR
DC Comics: Mar, 1999 - No. 4, Jun, 1999 ($2.50, mini-series)

1-4-Semeiks-a 3.00

SUPERMAN'S PAL JIMMY OLSEN (Superman Family #164 on)
(See Action Comics #6 for 1st app. & 80 Page Giant)
National Periodical Publ.: Sept-Oct, 1954 - No. 163, Feb-Mar, 1974 (Fourth World #133-148)

	GD	VG	FN	VF	VF/NM	NM-
1	500	1000	1750	5000	11,000	17,000
2	166	332	498	1370	3085	4800
3-Last pre-code issue	100	200	300	800	1800	2800
4,5	64	128	192	512	1156	1800
6-10	44	88	132	326	738	1150
11-20: 15-1st S.A. issue	32	64	96	230	515	800
21-28,30	21	42	63	147	324	500
29-(6/58) 1st app. Krypto with Superman	22	44	66	155	345	535
31-Origin & 1st app. Elastic Lad (Jimmy Olsen)	19	38	57	133	297	460
32-40: 33-One pg. biography of Jack Larson (TV Jimmy Olsen). 36-Intro Lucy Lane. 37-2nd app. Elastic Lad & 1st cover app.	13	26	39	89	195	300
41-50: 41-1st J.O. Robot. 48-Intro/origin Superman Emergency Squad	10	20	30	66	138	210
51-56: 56-Last 10¢ issue	8	16	24	54	102	150
57-62,64-70: 57-Olsen marries Supergirl. 62-Mon-El & Elastic Lad app. but not as Legionnaires. 70-Element Boy (Lad) app.	6	12	18	40	73	105
63(9/62)-Legion of Super-Villains app.	6	12	18	41	76	110
71,74,75,78,80-84,86,89,90: 86-Jimmy Olsen Robot becomes Congorilla	5	10	15	33	57	80
72,73,76,77,79,85,87,88: 72(10/63)-Legion app; Elastic Lad (Olsen) joins. 73-Ultra Boy app. 76,85-Legion app. 76-Legion app. 77-Olsen with Colossal Boy's powers & costume; origin Titano retold. 79-(9/64)-Titled The Red-headed Beatle of 1000 B.C. 85-Legion app. 87-Legion of Super-Villains app. 88-Star Boy app.	5	10	15	34	60	85
91-94,96-98	4	8	12	28	47	65
95 (Giant G-25)	6	12	18	40	73	105
99-Olsen w/powers & costumes of Lightning Lad, Sun Boy & Element Lad	5	10	15	30	50	70
100-Legion cameo	5	10	15	31	53	75
101-103,105-112,114-120: 106-Legion app. 110-Infinity-c. 117-Batman & Legion cameo. 120-Last 12¢ issue	4	8	12	23	37	50
104 (Giant G-38)	5	10	15	34	60	85
113,122,131,140 (Giants G-50,G-62,G-74,G-86)	5	10	15	31	53	75
121,123-130,132	3	6	9	21	33	45
133-(10/70)-Jack Kirby story & art begins; re-intro Newsboy Legion; 1st app. Morgan Edge	6	12	18	40	73	105
134-1st app. Darkseid (1 panel, 12/70)	50	100	150	350	575	800
135-2nd app. Darkseid (1 pg. cameo; see New Gods & Forever People); G.A. Guardian app.	8	16	24	56	108	160
136-139: 136-Origin new Guardian. 138-Partial photo-c. 139-Last 15¢ issue	4	8	12	23	37	50
141-150: (25¢,52 pgs.). 141-Photo-c with Don Rickles; Newsboy Legion-r by S&K begin; full pg. self-portrait of Jack Kirby; Don Rickles cameo. 149,150-G.A. Plastic Man-r in both; 150-Newsboy Legion app.	3	6	9	21	33	45
151-163	3	6	9	16	23	30

... Special 1 (12/08, $4.99) New Krypton tie-in; The Guardian and Dubbilex app. 5.00
... Special 2 (10/09, $4.99) New Krypton tie-in; Mon-El app.; Chang-a 5.00
Superman: The Amazing Transformations of Jimmy Olsen TPB (2007, $14.99) reprints Olsen's transformations into Wolf-Man, Elastic Lad, Turtle Boy and others; new Bolland-c 15.00

NOTE: *Issues #141-148 contain* ***Simon & Kirby*** *Newsboy Legion reprints from Star Spangled #7, 8, 9, 10, 11, 12, 13, 14 in that order.* ***N. Adams*** *c-109-112, 115, 117, 118, 120, 121, 132, 134-136, 147, 148.* ***Kirby*** *a-133-139p, 141-148p; c-133, 137, 139, 142, 145p.* ***Kirby/N. Adams*** *c-137, 138, 141-144, 146.* ***Curt Swan*** *c-1-14(most)., 140.*

SUPERMAN SPECTACULAR (Also see DC Special Series #5)
DC Comics: 1982 (Magazine size, 52 pgs., square binding)

1-Saga of Superman Red/ Superman Blue; Luthor and Terra-Man app.; Gonzales & Colletta-a 1 3 4 6 8 10

SUPERMAN: STRENGTH
DC Comics: 2005 - No. 3, 2005 ($5.95, limited series)

1-3: Alex Ross-c/Scott McCloud-s/Aluir Amancio-a 6.00

SUPERMAN / SUPERGIRL: MAELSTROM
DC Comics: Early Jan, 2009 - No. 5, Mar, 2009 ($2.99, limited series)

1-5: Palmiotti & Gray-s/Noto-c/a; Darkseid app. 3.00
TPB (2009, $12.99) r/#1-5 13.00

SUPERMAN / SUPERHOMBRE
DC Comics: Apr, 1945

nn - Ashcan comic, not distributed to newsstands, only for in-house use (no known sales)

SUPERMAN / TARZAN: SONS OF THE JUNGLE
Dark Horse Comics: Oct, 2001 - No. 3, May, 2002 ($2.99, limited series)

1-3-Elseworlds; Kal-El lands in the jungle; Dixon-s/Meglia-a/Ramos-c 3.00

SUPERMAN: THE COMING OF THE SUPERMEN
DC Comics: Apr, 2016 - No. 6, Sept, 2016 ($3.99, limited series)

1-6: 1-Neal Adams-s/a/c in all; Kalibak app. 3,4-Orion app. 3-6-Darkseid app. 4.00

SUPERMAN: THE DARK SIDE
DC Comics: 1998 - No. 3, 1998 ($4.95, squarebound, mini-series)

1-3: Elseworlds; Kal-El lands on Apokolips 5.00

SUPERMAN: THE DOOMSDAY WARS
DC Comics: 1998 - No. 3, 1999 ($4.95, squarebound, mini-series)

1-3: Superman & JLA vs. Doomsday; Jurgens-s/a(p) 5.00

SUPERMAN: THE KANSAS SIGHTING
DC Comics: 2003 - No. 2, 2003 ($6.95, squarebound, mini-series)

1,2-DeMatteis-s/Tolagson-a 7.00

SUPERMAN: THE LAST FAMILY OF KRYPTON
DC Comics: Oct, 2010 - No. 3, Dec, 2010 ($4.99, limited series)

1-3-Elseworlds; the El family lands on Earth; Bates-s/Arlem-a/Massafera-c 5.00

SUPERMAN: THE MAN OF STEEL (Also see Man of Steel, The)
DC Comics: July, 1991 - No. 134, Mar, 2003 ($1.00/$1.25/$1.50/$1.95/$2.25)

0-(10/94) Zero Hour; released between #37 & #38 3.00
1-($1.75, 52 pgs.)-Painted-c 5.00
2-16: 3-War of the Gods x-over. 5-Reads sideways. 10-Last $1.00-c. 14-Superman & Robin team-up 3.00

	GD	VG	FN	VF	VF/NM	NM-
17-1st brief app. Doomsday	4	8	12	25	40	55
17-(2nd printing)	3	6	9	17	26	35
18-1st full app. Doomsday	3	6	9	17	26	35
18-(2nd-4th printings)	2	4	6	11	16	20
18-(5th printing)	4	8	12	23	37	50

Superman: The Man of Steel #112 © DC

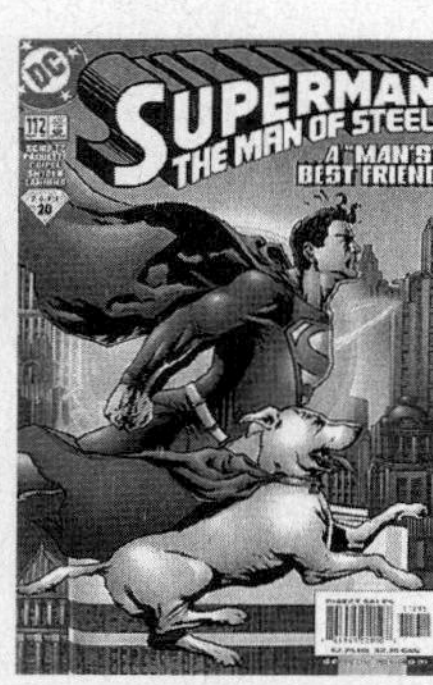

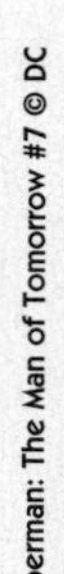
Superman: The Man of Tomorrow #7 © DC

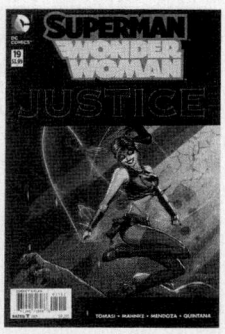

Superman/Wonder Woman #19 © DC

GD 2.0 | VG 4.0 | FN 6.0 | VF 8.0 | VF/NM 9.0 | NM- 9.2

19-Doomsday battle issue (c/story) 2 4 6 8 10 12
19-(2nd & 3rd printings) 3 6 9 16 23 30
20-22: 20,21-Funeral for a Friend. 22-($1.95)-Collector's Edition w/die-cut outer-c & bound-in poster; Steel-c/story 5.00
22-($1.50)-Newsstand Ed. w/poster & different-c 4.00
23-49,51-99: 30-Regular edition. 32-Bizarro-c/story. 35,36-Worlds Collide Pt. 1 & 10. 37-(9/94)-Zero Hour x-over. 38-(11/94). 48-Aquaman app. 54-Spectre-c/app; Lex Luthor app. 56-Mxyzptlk-c/app. 57-G.A. Flash app. 58-Supergirl app. 59-Parasite-c/app.; Steel app. 60-Reintro Bottled City of Kandor. 62-Final Night. 64-New Gods app. 67-New powers. 75-"Death" of Mxyzptlk. 78,79-Millennium Giants. 80-Golden Age style. 92-JLA app. 98-Metal Men app. 3.00
30-($2.50)-Collector's Edition; polybagged with Superman & Lobo vinyl clings that stick to wraparound-c; Lobo-c/story 4.00
50 ($2.95)-The Trial of Superman 4.00
100-($2.99) New Fortress of Solitude revealed 3.00
100-($3.99) Special edition with fold out cardboard-c 4.00
101,102-101-Batman app. 3.00
103-133: 103-Begin $2.25. 105-Batman-c/app. 111-Return to Krypton. 115-117-Our Worlds at War. 117-Maxima killed. 121-Royal Flush Gang app. 128-Return to Krypton II. 3.00
134-($2.75) Last issue; Steel app.; Bogdanove-c 3.00
#1,000,000 (11/98) 853rd Century x-over; Gene Ha-c 3.00
Annual 1-5 ('92-'96,68 pgs.): 1-Eclipso app.; Joe Quesada-c(p). 2-Intro Edge. 3 -Elseworlds; Mignola-c; Batman app. 4-Year One story. 5-Legends of the Dead Earth story 4.00
Annual 6 (1997, $3.95)-Pulp Heroes story 4.00
...Gallery (1995, $3.50) Pin-ups by various 4.00

SUPERMAN: THE MAN OF TOMORROW
DC Comics: 1995 - No. 15, Fall, 1999 ($1.95-$2.95, quarterly)

1-15: 1-Lex Luthor app. 3-Lex Luthor-c/app; Joker app. 4-Shazam! app. 5-Wedding of Lex Luthor. 10-Maxima-c/app. 13-JLA-c/app. 3.00
#1,000,000 (11/98) 853rd Century x-over; Gene Ha-c 3.00

SUPERMAN: THE SECRET YEARS
DC Comics: Feb, 1985 - No. 4, May, 1985 (limited series)

1-4-Miller-c on all 4.00

SUPERMAN: THE WEDDING ALBUM
DC Comics: Dec, 1996 ($4.95, 96 pgs, one-shot)

1-Standard Edition-Story & art by past and present Superman creators; gatefold back-c. Byrne-c 5.00
1-Collector's Edition-Embossed cardstock variant-c w/ metallic silver ink and matte and gloss varnishes 8.00
Retailer Rep. Program Edition (#'d to 250, signed by Bob Rozakis on back-c) 55.00
TPB ('97, $14.95) r/Wedding and honeymoon stories 15.00

SUPERMAN 3-D (See Three-Dimension Adventures)

SUPERMAN-TIM (See Promotional Comics section)

SUPERMAN UNCHAINED (DC New 52)
DC Comics: Aug, 2013 - No. 9, Jan, 2015 ($4.99/$3.99)

1-($4.99) Snyder-s/Jim Lee-a/c; back-up with Nguyen-a; bonus creator interviews 5.00
1-Director's Cut (9/13, $5.99) Lee's pencil art and Scott Snyder's scripts; cover gallery 6.00
2-8-($3.99) 2,6,7-Batman app. 4.00
9-($4.99) Wraparound-c by Jim Lee 5.00

SUPERMAN VILLAINS SECRET FILES
DC Comics: Jun, 1998 ($4.95, one shot)

1-Origin stories, "lost" pages & pin-ups 5.00

SUPERMAN VS. ALIENS (Also see Superman Aliens 2: God War)
DC Comics/Dark Horse Comics: July, 1995 - No. 3, Sept, 1995 ($4.95, limited series)

1-3: Jurgens/Nowlan-a 5.00

SUPERMAN VS. MUHAMMAD ALI (See All-New Collectors' Edition C-56 for original 1978 printing)
DC Comics: 2010

... Deluxe Edition (2010, $19.99, HC w/dustjacket) recolored reprint in comic size; new intro. by Neal Adams; afterword by Jenette Kahn; sketch pages, key to cover celebs 20.00
... Facsimile Edition (2010, $39.99, HC no dustjacket) recolored reprint in original Treasury size; new intro. by Neal Adams; key to cover celebs 40.00

SUPERMAN VS. PREDATOR
DC Comics/Dark Horse Comics: 2000 - No. 3, 2000 ($4.95, limited series)

1-3-Micheline-s/Maleev-a 5.00
TPB (2001, $14.95) r/series 15.00

SUPERMAN VS. THE AMAZING SPIDER-MAN (Also see Marvel Treasury Edition No. 28)
National Periodical Publications/Marvel Comics Group: 1976
($2.00, Treasury sized, 100 pgs.)

1-Superman and Spider-Man battle Lex Luthor and Dr. Octopus; Andru/Giordano-a; 1st Marvel/DC x-over. 8 16 24 56 108 160
1-2nd printing; 2000 numbered copies signed by Stan Lee on front cover & sold through mail 16 32 48 110 243 375
nn-(1995, $5.95)-r/#1 2 4 6 11 16 20

SUPERMAN VS. THE TERMINATOR: DEATH TO THE FUTURE
Dark Horse/DC Comics: Dec, 1999 - No. 4, Mar, 2000 ($2.95, limited series)

1-4-Grant-s/Pugh-a/c: Steel and Supergirl app. 3.00

SUPERMAN: WAR OF THE SUPERMEN
DC Comics: No. 0, Jun, 2010 - No. 4, Jul, 2010 ($2.99, limited series)

0-Free Comic Book Day issue; Barrows-c 3.00
1-4: 1-New Krypton destroyed 3.00
HC (2011, $19.99) r/#0-4 & Superman #700 20.00

SUPERMAN/WONDER WOMAN (DC New 52)
DC Comics: Dec, 2013 - No. 29, Jul, 2016 ($3.99)

1-Soule-s/Daniel-a; wraparound gatefold-c; Doomsday app. 4.00
2-29: 2-6-Zod app. 4-6-Faora app. 7-Doomsday app. 8-12-Doomed x-over. 14-17-Magog app. 18,19-Suicide Squad app. 26,27-Vandal Savage app. 28,29-Supergirl app. 4.00
Annual 1 (9/14, $4.99) Doomsday Superman vs. Cyborg Superman 5.00
Annual 2 (2/16, $4.99) Short stories by various; Paquette-c 5.00
...: Futures End 1 (11/14, $2.99, regular-c) Cont'd from Wonder Woman: FE #1 3.00
...: Futures End 1 (11/14, $3.99, 3-D cover) 4.00

SUPERMAN/WONDER WOMAN: WHOM GODS DESTROY
DC Comics: 1997 ($4.95, prestige format, limited series)

1-4-Elseworlds; Claremont-s 5.00

SUPERMAN WORKBOOK
National Periodical Publ./Juvenile Group Foundation: 1945 (B&W, reprints, 68 pgs)

nn-Cover-r/Superman #14 239 478 717 1530 2615 3700

SUPERMAN: WORLD OF NEW KRYPTON
DC Comics: May, 2009 - No. 12,Apr, 2010 ($2.99, limited series)

1-12: Robinson & Rucka-s/Woods-a; Frank-c and variant for each. 4-Green Lantern app. 3.00

SUPER MARIO BROS. (Also see Adventures of the..., Blip, Gameboy, and Nintendo Comics System)
Valiant Comics: 1990 - No. 6, 1991 ($1.95, slick-c) V2#1, 1991 - No. 5, 1991

1-Wildman-a 2 4 6 13 18 22
2-6, V2#1-5-($1.50) 1 3 4 6 8 10
Special Edition 1 (1990, $1.95)-Wildman-a 1 3 4 6 8 10

SUPER MARKET COMICS
Fawcett Publications: No date (1950s)

nn - Ashcan comic, not distributed to newsstands, only for in-house use (no known sales)

SUPER MARKET VARIETIES
Fawcett Publications: No date (1950s)

nn - Ashcan comic, not distributed to newsstands, only for in-house use (no known sales)

SUPERMEN OF AMERICA
DC Comics: Mar, 1999 ($3.95/$4.95, one-shot)

1-($3.95) Regular Ed.; Immonen-s/art by various 4.00
1-($4.95) Collectors' Ed. with membership kit 5.00

SUPERMEN OF AMERICA (Mini-series)
DC Comics: Mar, 2000 - No. 6, Aug, 2000 ($2.50)

1-6-Nicieza-s/Braithwaite-a 3.00

SUPERMOUSE (...the Big Cheese; see Coo Coo Comics)
Standard Comics/Pines No. 35 on (Literary Ent.): Dec, 1948 - No. 34, Sept, 1955; No. 35, Apr, 1956 - No. 45, Fall, 1958

1-Frazetta text illos (3) 39 78 117 231 378 525
2-Frazetta text illos 17 34 51 98 154 210
3,5,6-Text illos by Frazetta in all 14 28 42 82 121 160
4-Two pg. text illos by Frazetta 15 30 45 84 127 170
7-10 10 20 30 54 72 90
11-20: 13-Racist humor (Indians) 8 16 24 44 57 70
21-45 7 14 21 37 46 55
1-Summer Holiday issue (Summer, 1957, 25¢, 100 pgs.)-Pines 14 28 42 82 121 160
2-Giant Summer issue (Summer, 1958, 25¢, 100 pgs.)-Pines; has games, puzzles & stories 11 22 33 60 83 105

SUPER-MYSTERY COMICS
Ace Magazines (Periodical House): July, 1940 - V8#6, July, 1949

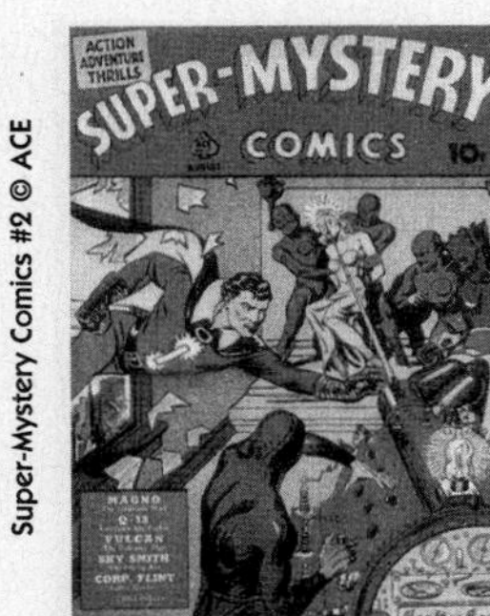
Super-Mystery Comics #2 © ACE

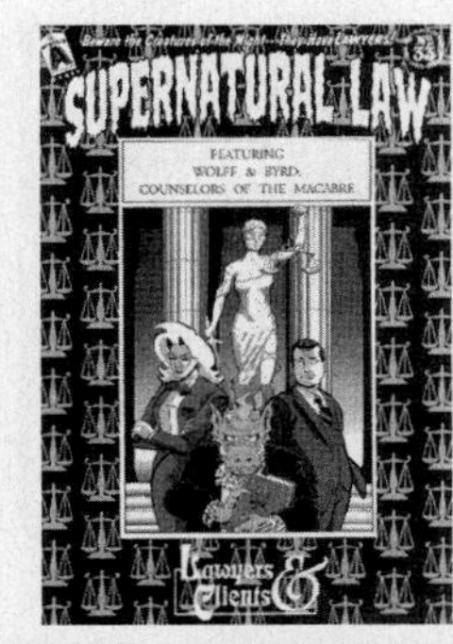
Supernatural Law #33 © Batton Lash

Super Powers (2017 series) #1 © DC

	GD 2.0	VG 4.0	FN 6.0	VF 8.0	VF/NM 9.0	NM- 9.2
V1#1-Magno, the Magnetic Man & Vulcan begins (1st app.); Q-13, Corp. Flint, & Sky Smith begin	389	778	1167	2723	4762	6800
2	194	388	582	1242	2121	3000
3-The Black Spider begins (1st app.)	155	310	465	992	1696	2400
4-Origin Davy	110	220	330	704	1202	1700
5-Intro. The Clown & begin series (12/40)	116	232	348	742	1271	1800
6(2/41)	94	188	282	597	1024	1450
V2#1(4/41)-Origin Buckskin	90	180	270	576	988	1400
2-6(2/42): 6-Vulcan begins again; bondage/torture-c	84	168	252	538	919	1300
V3#1(4/42),2: 1-Black Ace begins	90	180	270	576	988	1400
3-Intro. The Lancer; Dr. Nemesis & The Sword begin; Kurtzman-c/a(2) (Mr. Risk & Paul Revere Jr.); Robot-c	135	270	405	864	1482	2100
4-Kurtzman-c/a; classic-c	155	310	465	992	1696	2400
5-Kurtzman-a(2); L.B. Cole-a; Mr. Risk app.	97	194	291	621	1061	1500
6(10/43)-Mr. Risk app.; Kurtzman's Paul Revere Jr.; L.B. Cole-a	84	168	252	538	919	1300
V4#1(1/44)-L.B. Cole-a	58	116	174	371	636	900
2-6(4/45): 2,5,6-Mr. Risk app.	50	100	150	315	533	750
V5#1(7/45)-6	47	94	141	296	498	700
V6#1,2,4,5,6: 4-Last Magno. Mr. Risk app. in #2,4-6. 6-New logo	43	86	129	271	461	650
3-Torture c-story	161	322	483	1030	1765	2500
V7#1-6, V8#1-4,6	41	82	123	256	428	600
V8#5-Meskin, Tuska, Sid Greene-a	41	82	123	260	435	610

NOTE: *Sid Greene a-V7#4. Mooney c-V1#5, 6, V2#1-6. Palais a-V5#3, 4; c-V4#6-V5#4, V6#2, V8#4. Bondage c-V2#5, 6, V3#2, 5. Magno c-V1#1-V3#6, V4#2-V5#5, V6#2. The Sword c-V4#1, 6(w/Magno).*

SUPERNATURAL (Volume 4) (Based on the CW television series)
DC Comics: Dec, 2011 - No. 6, May, 2012 ($2.99, limited series)

1-6: 1-Sam in Scotland; Brian Wood-s/Grant Bond-a 3.00

SUPERNATURAL: BEGINNING'S END (Based on the CW television series)
DC Comics (WildStorm): Mar, 2010 - No. 6, Aug, 2010 ($2.99, limited series)

1-6-Prequel to the series; Dabb & Loflin-s/Olmos-a. 1-Olmos and photo-c 3.00
TPB (2010, $14.99) r/#1-6; character sketch pages 15.00

SUPERNATURAL FREAK MACHINE: A CAL MCDONALD MYSTERY
IDW Publishing: Mar, 2005 - No. 3 ($3.99)

1-3-Steve Niles-s/Kelley Jones-a 4.00

SUPERNATURAL LAW (Formerly Wolff & Byrd, Counselors of the Macabre)
Exhibit A Press: No. 24, Oct, 1999 - Present ($2.50/$2.95/$3.50, B&W)

24-35-Batton Lash-s/a. 29-Marie Severin-c. 33-Cerebus spoof 3.00
36-40-($2.95). 37-Frank Cho pin-up and story panels 3.00
(#41) ...First Amendment Issue (2005, $3.50) anti-censorship story; CBLDF info 3.50
(#42) With a Silver Bullet (2006, $3.50) new stories and pin-ups 3.50
(#43) At the Box Office (2006, $3.50) new stories and pin-ups 3.50
(#44) Wolff & Byrd: The Movie (2007, $3.50) new stories and pin-ups 3.50
45-($3.50) Toxic Avenger and Lloyd Kaufman app. 3.50
#1 (2005, $2.95) r/Wolff & Byrd with redrawn and re-toned art; relettered 3.00

SUPERNATURAL LAW SECRETARY MAVIS
Exhibit A Press: 2001 - No. 5 ($2.95/$3.50, B&W)

1-3: 3-DeCarlo-c 3.00
4,5-($3.50) Jaime Hernandez-c 3.50

SUPERNATURAL: ORIGINS (Based on the CW television series)
DC Comics (WildStorm): July, 2007 - No. 6, Dec, 2007 ($2.99, limited series)

1-6: 1-Bradstreet-c; Johnson-s/Smith-a; back-up w/Johns-s/Hester-a 3.00
TPB (2008, $14.99) r/#1-6; sketch pages 15.00

SUPERNATURAL: RISING SON (Based on the CW television series)
DC Comics (WildStorm): Jun, 2008 - No. 6, Nov, 2008 ($2.99, limited series)

1-6-Johnson & Dessertine-s/Olmos-a. 1-Oliver-c 3.00
1-Variant-c by Nguyen 6.00
TPB (2009, $14.99) r/#1-6 15.00

SUPERNATURALS
Marvel Comics: Dec, 1998 - No. 4, Dec, 1998 ($3.99, weekly limited series)

1-4-Pulido-s/Balent-c; bound-in Halloween masks 4.00
1-4-With bound-in Ghost Rider mask (1 in 10) 4.00
... Preview Tour Book (10/98, $2.99) Reis-c 4.00

SUPERNATURAL THRILLERS
Marvel Comics Group: Dec, 1972 - No. 6, Nov, 1973; No. 7, Jun, 1974 - No. 15, Oct, 1975

	GD 2.0	VG 4.0	FN 6.0	VF 8.0	VF/NM 9.0	NM- 9.2
1-It!; Sturgeon adap. (see Astonishing Tales #21)	3	6	9	21	33	45
2-4,6: 2-The Invisible Man; H.G. Wells adapt. 3-The Valley of the Worm; R.E. Howard adapt. 4-Dr. Jekyll & Mr. Hyde; R.L. Stevenson adapt.. 6-The Headless Horseman; last 20¢ issue	3	6	9	14	20	25
5-1st app. The Living Mummy	6	12	18	40	73	105
7-15: 7-The Living Mummy begins	3	6	9	17	26	35

NOTE: *Brunner c-11. Buckler a-5p. Ditko a-8r, 9r. G. Kane a-3p; c-3, 9p, 15p. Mayerik a-2p, 7, 8, 9p, 10p, 11. McWilliams a-14i. Mortimer a-4. Steranko c-1, 2. Sutton a-15. Tuska a-6p.*

SUPERPATRIOT (Also see Freak Force & Savage Dragon #2)
Image Comics (Highbrow Entertainment): July, 1993 - No. 4, Dec, 1993 ($1.95, lim. series)

1-4: Dave Johnson-c/a; Larsen scripts; Giffen plots 3.00

SUPERPATRIOT: AMERICA'S FIGHTING FORCE
Image Comics: July, 2002 - No. 4, Oct, 2002 ($2.95, limited series)

1-4-Cory Walker-a/c; Savage Dragon app. 3.00

SUPERPATRIOT: LIBERTY & JUSTICE
Image Comics (Highbrow Entertainment): July, 1995 - No. 4, Oct, 1995 ($2.50, lim. series)

1-4: Dave Johnson-c/a. 1-1st app. Liberty & Justice 3.00
TPB (2002, $12.95) r/#1-4; new cover by Dave Johnson; sketch pages 13.00

SUPERPATRIOT: WAR ON TERROR
Image Comics: July, 2004 - No. 4, May, 2007 ($2.95/$2.99, limited series)

1-4-Kirkman-s/Su-a 3.00

SUPER POWERS (1st Series)
DC Comics: July, 1984 - No. 5, Nov, 1984

1-5: 1-Joker/Penguin-c/story; Batman app.; all Kirby-c. 5-Kirby c/a 6.00

SUPER POWERS (2nd Series)
DC Comics: Sept, 1985 - No. 6, Feb, 1986

1-6: Kirby-c/a; Capt. Marvel & Firestorm join; Batman cameo; Darkseid storyline in all. 4-Batman cameo. 5,6-Batman app. 5.00

SUPER POWERS (3rd Series)
DC Comics: Sept, 1986 - No. 4, Dec, 1986

1-4: 1-Cyborg joins; 1st app. Samurai from Super Friends TV show. 1-4-Batman cameos; Darkseid storyline in #1-4 4.00

SUPER POWERS (All ages series)
DC Comics: Jan, 2017 - No. 6 ($2.99)

1-5-Franco & Baltazar-s/Baltazar-a/c; Superman, Batman & Wonder Woman vs. Brainiac 3.00

SUPER PUP (Formerly Spotty The Pup) (See Space Comics)
Avon Periodicals: No. 4, Mar-Apr, 1954 - No. 5, 1954

	GD 2.0	VG 4.0	FN 6.0	VF 8.0	VF/NM 9.0	NM- 9.2
4,5: 4-Atom bomb-c. 5-Robot-c	9	18	27	47	61	75

SUPER RABBIT (See All Surprise, Animated Movie Tunes, Comedy Comics, Comic Capers, Ideal Comics, It's A Duck's Life, Movie Tunes & Wisco)
Timely Comics (CmPl): Fall, 1944 - No. 14, Nov, 1948

	GD 2.0	VG 4.0	FN 6.0	VF 8.0	VF/NM 9.0	NM- 9.2
1-Hitler & Hirohito-c; war effort paper recycling PSA by S&K; Ziggy Pig & Silly Seal begin	252	504	756	1613	2757	3900
2	48	96	144	302	514	725
3-5	32	64	96	192	314	435
6-Origin	34	68	102	199	325	450
7-10: 9-Infinity-c	21	42	63	126	206	285
11-Kurtzman's "Hey Look"	22	44	66	132	216	300
12-14	21	42	63	126	206	285
I.W. Reprint #1,2('58),7,10('63): 1-r/#13. 2-r/#10.	3	6	9	14	20	25

SUPER RICHIE (Superichie #5 on) (See Richie Rich Millions #68)
Harvey Publications: Sept, 1975 - No. 4, Mar, 1976 (All 52 pg. Giants)

	GD 2.0	VG 4.0	FN 6.0	VF 8.0	VF/NM 9.0	NM- 9.2
1	3	6	9	16	23	30
2-4	2	4	6	11	16	20

SUPER SECRET CRISIS WAR! (Crossover of Cartoon Network characters)
IDW Publishing: Jun, 2014 - No. 6, Nov, 2014 ($3.99, limited series)

1-6-Powerpuff Girls, Samurai Jack, Dexter, Ben 10 vs. Aku, Mojo Jojo, Mandark 4.00
... Codename: Kids Next Door One-Shot (11/14 $3.99) 3 covers; Jampole-a 4.00
... Cow and Chicken One-Shot (10/14 $3.99) 3 covers; Jim Zub-s 4.00
... Foster's Home For Imaginary Friends One-Shot (9/14 $3.99) 3 covers; Ganucheau-a 4.00
... Johnny Bravo One-Shot (7/14 $3.99) 3 covers; Erica Henderson-a 4.00
... The Grimm Adventures of Billy and Mandy One-Shot (7/14 $3.99) 3 covers; Leth-s 4.00

SUPER SLUGGERS (Baseball)
Ultimate Sports Ent. Inc.: 1999 ($3.95, one-shot)

1-Bonds, Piazza, Caminiti, Griffey Jr. app.; Martinbrough-c/a 4.00

SUPERSNIPE COMICS (Formerly Army & Navy #1-5)
Street & Smith Publications: V1#6, Oct, 1942 - V5#1, Aug-Sept, 1949
(See Shadow Comics V2#3)

Super Sons #1 © DC

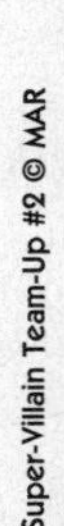

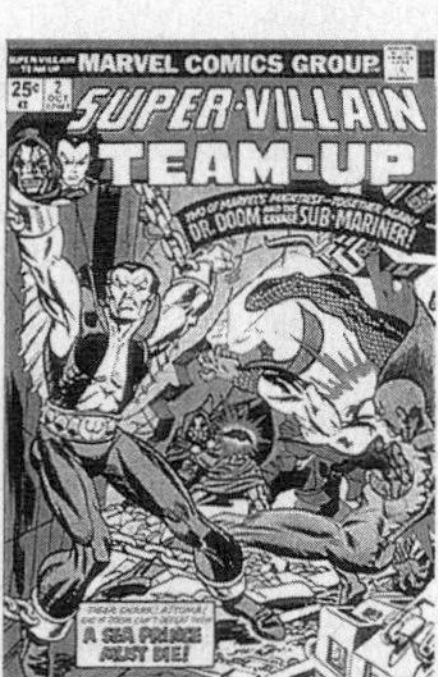

Super-Villain Team-Up #2 © MAR

Superzero #6 © Paperfilms

GD 2.0 | VG 4.0 | FN 6.0 | VF 8.0 | VF/NM 9.0 | NM- 9.2

GD 2.0 | VG 4.0 | FN 6.0 | VF 8.0 | VF/NM 9.0 | NM- 9.2

V1#6-Rex King - Man of Adventure (costumed hero, see Super Magic/Magician) by Jack Binder begins; Supersnipe by George Marcoux continues from Army & Navy #5; Bill Ward-a 77 154 231 493 847 1200
7,10-12: 10,11-Little Nemo app. 47 94 141 296 498 700
8-Hitler, Tojo, Mussolini in Hell with Devil-c 226 452 678 1446 2473 3500
9-Doc Savage x-over in Supersnipe; Hitler-c 213 426 639 1363 2332 3300
V2 #1: Both V2#1(2/44) & V2#2(4/44) have V2#1 on outside-c; Huck Finn by Clare Dwiggins begins, ends V3#5 (rare) 57 114 171 362 619 875
V2#2 (4/44) has V2#1 on outside-c; classic shark-c 43 86 129 271 461 650
3-12: 12-Statue of Liberty-c 22 44 66 132 216 300
V3#1-12: 8-Bobby Crusoe by Dwiggins begins, ends V3#12. 9-X-Mas-c 20 40 60 114 182 250
V4#1-12, V5#1: V4#10-X-Mas-c 16 32 48 94 147 200
NOTE: *George Marcoux c-V1#6-V3#4. Doc Savage app. in some issues.*

SUPER SOLDIER (See Marvel Versus DC #3)
DC Comics (Amalgam): Apr, 1996 ($1.95, one-shot)
1-Mark Waid script & Dave Gibbons-c/a. 3.00

SUPER SOLDIER: MAN OF WAR
DC Comics (Amalgam): June, 1997 ($1.95, one-shot)
1-Waid & Gibbons-s/Gibbons & Palmiotti-c/a. 3.00

SUPER SOLDIERS
Marvel Comics UK: Apr, 1993 - No. 8, Nov, 1993 ($1.75)
1-($2.50)-Embossed silver foil logo 4.00
2-8: 5-Capt. America app. 6-Origin; Nick Fury app.; neon ink-c 3.00

SUPER SONS
DC Comics: Apr, 2017 - Present ($2.99)
1-Damian Wayne (Robin) & Jon Kent (Superboy) team-up; Tomasi-s/Jimenez-a 3.00

SUPERSPOOK (Formerly Frisky Animals on Parade)
Ajax/Farrell Publications: No. 4, June, 1958
4 8 16 24 44 57 70

SUPER SPY (See Wham Comics)
Centaur Publications: Oct, 1940 - No. 2, Nov, 1940 (Reprints)
1-Origin The Sparkler 90 180 270 576 988 1400
2-The Inner Circle, Dean Denton, Tim Blain, The Drew Ghost, The Night Hawk by Gustavson, & S.S. Swanson by Glanz app. 57 114 171 362 619 875

SUPERSTAR: AS SEEN ON TV
Image Comics (Gorilla): 2001 ($5.95)
1-Busiek-s/Immonen-a 6.00

SUPER STAR HOLIDAY SPECIAL (See DC Special Series #21)

SUPER-TEAM FAMILY
National Periodical Publ./DC Comics: Oct-Nov, 1975 - No. 15, Mar-Apr, 1978
1-Reprints by Neal Adams & Kane/Wood; 68 pgs. begin, ends #4. New Gods app. 3 6 9 16 23 30
2,3: New stories 3 6 9 14 20 25
4-7: Reprints. 4-G.A. JSA-r & Superman/Batman/Robin-r from World's Finest. 5-52 pgs. begin 2 4 6 10 14 18
8-14: 8-10-New Challengers of the Unknown stories. 9-Kirby-a. 11-14: New stories 3 6 9 14 19 24
15-New Gods app. New stories 3 6 9 14 20 26
NOTE: ***Neal Adams** r-1-3. **Brunner** c-3. **Buckler** c-8p. **Tuska** a-7r. **Wood** a-1i(r), 3.*

SUPER TV HEROES (See Hanna-Barbera...)

SUPER-VILLAIN CLASSICS
Marvel Comics Group: May, 1983
1-Galactus -The Origin; Kirby-a 2 4 6 8 10 12

SUPER-VILLAIN TEAM-UP (See Fantastic Four #6 & Giant-Size...)
Marvel Comics Group: 8/75 - No. 14, 10/77; No. 15, 11/78; No. 16, 5/79; No. 17, 6/80
1-Continued from Giant-Size Super-Villain Team-Up #2; Sub-Mariner & Dr. Doom begin, end #10 4 8 12 28 47 65
2-5: 5-1st app. The Shroud 3 6 9 14 19 24
5-(30¢-c variant, limited distribution)(4/76) 4 8 12 27 44 60
6,7-(25¢ editions) 6-(6/76)-F.F., Shroud app. 7-Origin Shroud 2 4 6 8 11 14
6,7-(30¢-c, limited distribution)(6,8/76) 4 8 12 25 40 55
8,9,11-17: 9-Avengers app. 11-15-Dr. Doom & Red Skull app. 2 4 6 8 11 14
10-Classic Dr. Doom, Red Skull, Captain America battle-c 2 4 6 10 14 18
12-14-(35¢-c variants, limited distribution)(6,8,10/77) 10 20 30 64 132 200
NOTE: ***Buckler** c-4p, 5p, 7p. **Buscema** c-1. **Byrne/Austin** c-14. **Evans** a-1p, 3p. **Everett** a-1p. **Giffen** a-8p, 13p; c-13p. **Kane** c-2p, 9p. **Mooney** a-4i. **Starlin** c-6. **Tuska** r-1p, 15p. **Wood** r-15p.*

SUPER-VILLAIN TEAM-UP/ MODOK'S 11
Marvel Comics: Sept, 2007 - No. 5, Jan, 2008 ($2.99, limited series)
1-5: 1-MODOK's origin re-told; Portela-a/Powell-c; Purple Man & Mentallo app. 3.00
... TPB (2008, $13.99) r/#1-5 14.00

SUPER WESTERN COMICS (Also see Buffalo Bill)
Youthful Magazines: Aug, 1950 (One shot)
1-Buffalo Bill begins; Wyatt Earp, Calamity Jane & Sam Slade app; Powell-c/a 15 30 45 90 140 190

SUPER WESTERN FUNNIES (See Super Funnies)

SUPERWOMAN
DC Comics: Jan 1942
nn - Ashcan comic, not distributed to newsstands, only for in-house use. Cover art is More Fun Comics #73 with interior being Action Comics #38 (no known sales)

SUPERWOMAN (DC Rebirth)
DC Comics: Oct, 2016 - Present ($2.99)
1-7: 1-Phil Jimenez-s/a; Lois and Lana with powers. 2-7-Lena Luthor app. 3.00

SUPERWORLD COMICS
Hugo Gernsback (Komos Publ.): Apr, 1940 - No. 3, Aug, 1940 (68 pgs.)
1-Origin & 1st app. Hip Knox, Super Hypnotist; Mitey Powers & Buzz Allen, the Invisible Avenger, Little Nemo begin; cover by Frank R. Paul (all have sci/fi-c) (Scarce) 865 1730 2595 6315 13,158 20,000
2-Marvo 1-2 Go+, the Super Boy of the Year 2680 (1st app.); Paul-c (Scarce) 578 1156 1734 4219 7460 10,700
3 (Scarce) 459 918 1377 3350 5925 8500

SUPERZERO
AfterShock Comics: Dec, 2015 - Present ($3.99)
1-6-Conner & Palmiotti-s/De Latorre-a. 1-Covers by Conner, Cooke & Hester 4.00

SUPER ZOMBIES
Dynamite Entertainment: 2009 - No. 5, 2009 ($3.50)
1-5-Mel Rubi-a; Guggenheim & Gonzales-s; two covers for each by Rubi & Neves 3.50

SUPREME (Becomes ...The New Adventures #43-48)(See Youngblood #3)
(Also see Bloodwulf Special, Legend of Supreme, & Trencher #3)
Image Comics (Extreme Studios)/ Awesome Entertainment #49 on:
V2#1, Nov, 1992 - V2#42, Sept, 1996; V3#49 - No. 56, Feb, 1998
V2#1-Liefeld-a(i) & scripts; embossed foil logo 4.00
1-Gold Edition 1 2 3 5 6 8
2-(3/93)-Liefeld co-plots & inks; 1st app. Grizlock 3.00
3-42: 3-Intro Bloodstrike; 1st app. Khrome. 5-1st app. Thor. 6-1st brief app. The Starguard. 7-1st full app. The Starguard. 10-Black and White Pt 1 (1st app.) by Art Thibert (2 pgs. ea. installment). 25-(5/94)-Platt-c. 11-Coupon #4 for Extreme Prejudice #0; Black and White Pt. 7 by Thibert. 12-(4/94)-Platt-c. 13,14-(6/94). 15 (7/94). 16 (7/94)-Stormwatch app. 18-Kid Supreme Sneak Preview; Pitt app.19,20-Polybagged w/trading card. 20-1st app. Woden & Loki (as a dog); Overtkill app. 21-1st app. Loki (in true form). 21-23-Poly-bagged trading card. 32-Lady Supreme cameo. 33-Origin & 1st full app. of Lady Supreme (Probe from the Starguard); Babewatch! tie-in. 37-Intro Loki; Fraga-c. 40-Retells Supreme's past advs. 41-Alan Moore scripts begin; Supreme revised; intro The Supremacy; Jerry Ordway-c (Joe Bennett variant-c exists). 42-New origin w/Rick Veitch-a; intro Radar, The Hound Supreme & The League of Infinity 3.00
28-Variant-c by Quesada & Palmiotti 3.00
(#43-48-**See Supreme: The New Adventures**)
V3#49,51: 49-Begin $2.99-c 3.00
50-($3.95)-Double sized, 2 covers, pin-up gallery 4.00
52a,52b-($3.50) 4.00
53-56: 53-Sprouse-a begins. 56-McGuinness-c 3.00
Annual 1-(1995, $2.95) 4.00
...: Supreme Sacrifice (3/06, $3.99) Flip book with Suprema; Kirkman-s/Malin-a 4.00
...: The Return TPB (Checker Book Publ., 2003, $24.95) r/#53-56 & Supreme; The Return #1-6; Ross-c; additional sketch pages by Ross 25.00
...: The Story of the Year TPB (Checker Book Publ., 2002, $26.95) r/#41-52; Ross-c 27.00
NOTE: ***Rob Liefeld** a(i)-1, 2; co-plots-2-4; scripts-1, 5, 6. **Ordway** c-41. **Platt** c-12, 25. **Thibert** c(i)-7-9.*

SUPREME
Image Comics: No. 63, Apr, 2012 - Present ($2.99)
63-66: 63-Moore-s; two covers by Larsen & Hamscher 3.00
67,68-($3.99) 67-Omni-Man app. 4.00

Supreme: The Return #1 © Awesome

Surgeon X #33 © Wowbagger Prods.

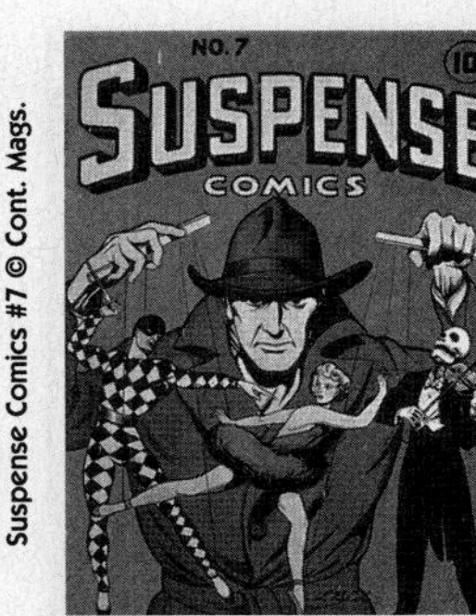

Suspense Comics #7 © Cont. Mags.

	GD 2.0	VG 4.0	FN 6.0	VF 8.0	VF/NM 9.0	NM- 9.2

GD VG FN VF VF/NM NM- 2.0 4.0 6.0 8.0 9.0 9.2

SUPREME BLUE ROSE
Image Comics: Jul, 2014 - No. 7, Mar, 2015 ($2.99)

1-7-Warren Ellis-s/Tula Lotay-a						3.00

SUPREME: GLORY DAYS
Image Comics (Extreme Studios): Oct, 1994 - No. 2, Dec, 1994 ($2.95/$2.50, limited series)

1,2: 2-Diehard, Roman, Superpatriot, & Glory app.						3.00

SUPREME POWER (Also see Squadron Supreme 2006 series)
Marvel Comics (MAX): Oct, 2003 - No. 18, Oct, 2005 ($2.99)

1-($2.99) Straczynski-s/Frank-a; Frank-c						3.00
1-($4.99) Special Edition with variant Quesada-c; includes r/early Squadron Supreme apps.						5.00
2-18: 4-Intro. Nighthawk. 6-The Blur debuts. 10-Princess Zarda returns. 17-Hyperion revealed as alien. 18-Continues in mini-series						3.00
... MGC #1 (7/11, $1.00) r/#1 with "Marvel's Greatest Comics" banner on cover						3.00
Vol. 1: Contact TPB (2004, $14.99) r/#1-6						15.00
Vol. 2: Powers & Principalities TPB (2004, $14.99) r/#7-12						15.00
Vol. 3: High Command TPB (2005, $14.99) r/#13-18						15.00
Vol. 1 HC (2005, $29.99, 7 1/2" x 11" with dustjacket) r/#1-12; Avengers #85 & 86, Straczynski intro., Frank cover sketches and character design pages						30.00
Vol. 2 HC (2006, $29.99, 7 1/2" x 11" with dustjacket) r/#13-18; ...: Hyperion #1-5; character design pages						30.00

SUPREME POWER
Marvel Comics (MAX): Aug, 2011 - No. 4, Nov, 2011 ($3.99, limited series)

1-4-Higgins-s/Garcia-a/Fiumara-c; Doctor Spectrum app.						4.00

SUPREME POWER: HYPERION
Marvel Comics (MAX): Nov, 2005 - No. 5, Mar, 2006 ($2.99, limited series)

1-5: 1-Straczynski-s/Jurgens-a/Dodson-c						3.00
TPB (2006, $14.99) r/#1-5						15.00

SUPREME POWER: NIGHTHAWK
Marvel Comics (MAX): Nov, 2005 - No. 6, Apr, 2006 ($2.99, limited series)

1-6-Daniel Way-s/Steve Dillon-a; origin of Whiteface						3.00
TPB (2006, $16.99) r/#1-6; cover concept art						17.00

SUPREME: THE NEW ADVENTURES (Formerly Supreme)
Maximum Press: V3#43, Oct, 1996 - V3#48, May, 1997 ($2.50)

V3#43-48: 43-Alan Moore scripts begin; Joe Bennett-a; Rick Veitch-a (8 pgs.); Dan Jurgens-a (1 pg.); intro Citadel Supreme & Suprematons; 1st Allied Supermen of America						3.00

SUPREME: THE RETURN
Awesome Entertainment: May, 1999 - No. 6, June, 2000 ($2.99)

1-6: Alan Moore-s. 1,2-Sprouse & Gordon-a/c. 2,4-Liefeld-c. 6-Kirby app.						3.00

SUPURBIA (GRACE RANDOLPH'S...)
BOOM! Studios: Mar, 2012 - No. 4, Jun, 2012 ($3.99, limited series)

1-4-Grace Randolph-s/Dauterman-a. 1-Garza-c						4.00

SUPURBIA (GRACE RANDOLPH'S...)(Volume 2)
BOOM! Studios: Nov, 2012 - No. 12, Oct, 2013 ($3.99, limited series)

1-12-Grace Randolph-s/Dauterman-a; multiple covers on #1-5						4.00

SURE-FIRE COMICS (Lightning Comics #4 on)
Ace Magazines: June, 1940 - No. 4, Oct, 1940 (Two No. 3's)

V1#1-Origin Flash Lightning & begins; X-The Phantom Fed, Ace McCoy, Buck Steele, Marvo the Magician, The Raven, Whiz Wilson (Time Traveler) begin (all 1st app.); Flash Lightning c-1-4	219	438	657	1402	2401	3400
2	116	232	348	742	1271	1800
3(9/40), 3(#4)(10/40)-nn on-c, #3 on inside	97	194	291	621	1061	1500

SURFACE TENSION
Titan Comics: Jun, 2015 - No. 5, Oct, 2015 ($3.99, limited series)

1-5-Jay Gunn-s/a. 1,2-Two covers						4.00

SURF 'N' WHEELS
Charlton Comics: Nov, 1969 - No. 6, Sept, 1970

1	3	6	9	19	30	40
2-6	3	6	9	14	19	24

SURGE
Eclipse Comics: July, 1984 - No. 4, Jan, 1985 ($1.50, lim. series, Baxter paper)

1-4-Ties into DNAgents series						3.00

SURGEON X
Image Comics: Sept, 2016 - No. 6, Feb, 2017 ($3.99)

1-6: 1-Sara Kenney-s/John Watkiss-a/c. 6-Watkiss & Pleece-a						4.00

SURPRISE ADVENTURES (Formerly Tormented)
Sterling Comic Group: No. 3, Mar, 1955 - No. 5, July, 1955

3-5: 3,5-Sekowsky-a	11	22	33	60	83	105

SURVIVE (Follows Cataclysm: The Ultimates Last Stand)
Marvel Comics: May, 2014 ($3.99, one-shot)

1-Bendis-s/Quinones-a; the new Ultimates team is formed						4.00

SURVIVORS' CLUB
DC Comics (Vertigo): Dec, 2015 - No. 9, Aug, 2016 ($3.99)

1-9-Beukes & Halvorsen-s/Ryan Kelly-a/Sienkiewicz-c						4.00

SUSIE Q. SMITH
Dell Publishing Co.: No. 323, Mar, 1951 - No. 553, Apr, 1954

Four Color 323 (#1)	6	12	18	37	66	95
Four Color 377, 453 (2/53), 553	5	10	15	30	50	70

SUSPENSE (Radio/TV issues #1-11; Real Life Tales of... #1-4) (Amazing Detective Cases #3 on?)
Marvel/Atlas Comics (CnPC No. 1-10/BFP No. 11-29): Dec, 1949 - No. 29, Apr, 1953 (#1-8, 17-23: 52 pgs.)

1-Powell-a; Peter Lorre, Sidney Greenstreet photo-c from Hammett's "The Verdict"	97	194	291	621	1061	1500
2-Crime stories; Dennis O'Keefe & Gale Storm photo-c from Universal movie "Abandoned"	42	84	126	265	445	625
3-Change to horror	53	106	159	334	567	800
4,7-10: 7-Dracula-sty	42	84	126	265	445	625
5-Krigstein, Tuska, Everett-a	43	86	129	271	461	650
6-Tuska, Everett, Morisi-a	42	84	126	267	451	635
11-13,15-17,19,20	39	78	117	231	378	525
14-Clasic Heath Hypo-c; A-Bomb panels	48	96	144	302	514	725
18,22-Krigstein-a	39	78	117	236	388	540
21,23,24,26-29: 24-Tuska-a	36	72	108	211	343	475
25-Electric chair-c/story	42	84	126	265	445	625

NOTE: ***Ayers** a-20. **Briefer** a-5, 7, 27. **Brodsky** c-4, 6-9, 11, 16, 17, 25. **Colan** a-8(2), 9. **Everett** a-5, 6(2), 19, 23, 28; c-21-23, 26. **Fuje** a-29. **Heath** a-5, 6, 8, 10, 12, 14; c-14, 19, 24. **Maneely** a-12, 23, 24, 28, 29; c-5, 6p, 10, 13, 15, 18. **Mooney** a-24, 28. **Morisi** a-6, 12. **Palais** a-10. **Rico** a-7-9. **Robinson** a-29. **Romita** a-20(2), 25. **Sekowsky** a-11, 13, 14. **Sinnott** a-23, 25. **Tuska** a-5, 6(2), 12; c-12. **Whitney** a-15, 16, 22. **Ed Win** a-27.*

SUSPENSE COMICS
Continental Magazines: Dec, 1943 - No. 12, Sept, 1946

1-The Grey Mask begins; bondage/torture-c; L. B. Cole-a (7 pgs.)	568	1136	1704	4146	7323	10,500
2-Intro. The Mask; Rico, Giunta, L. B. Cole-a (7 pgs.)	300	600	900	1920	3310	4700
3-L.B. Cole-a; classic Schomburg-c (Scarce)	7500	15,000	22,500	45,000	77,500	110,000
4-L. B. Cole-c begin	290	580	870	1856	3178	4500
5,6	239	478	717	1530	2615	3700
7,9,10,12: 9-L.B. Cole eyeball-c	181	362	543	1158	1979	2800
8-Classic L. B. Cole spider-c	459	918	1377	3350	5925	8500
11-Classic Devil-c	371	742	1113	2600	4550	6500

NOTE: ***L. B. Cole** c-4-12. **Fuje** a-8. **Larsen** a-11. **Palais** a-10, 11. Bondage c-1, 3, 4.*

SUSPENSE DETECTIVE
Fawcett Publications: June, 1952 - No. 5, Mar, 1953

1-Evans-a (11 pgs); Baily-c/a	45	90	135	284	480	675
2-Evans-a (10 pgs.)	27	54	81	160	263	365
3-5	23	46	69	136	223	310

NOTE: ***Baily** a-4, 5; c-1-3. **Sekowsky** a-2, 4, 5; c-5.*

SUSPENSE STORIES (See Strange Suspense Stories)

SUSSEX VAMPIRE, THE (Sherlock Holmes)
Caliber Comics: 1996 ($2.95, 32 pgs., B&W, one-shot)

nn-Adapts Sir Arthur Conan Doyle's story; Warren Ellis scripts						3.00

SUZIE COMICS (Formerly Laugh Comix; see Laugh Comics, Liberty Comics #10, Pep Comics & Top-Notch Comics #28)
Close-Up No. 49,50/MLJ Mag./Archie No. 51 on: No. 49, Spring, 1945 - No. 100, Aug, 1954

49-Ginger begins	47	94	141	296	498	700
50-55: 54-Transvestism story. 55-Woggon-a	30	60	90	177	289	400
56-Katy Keene begins by Woggon	31	62	93	182	296	410
57-65	20	40	60	114	182	250
66-80	16	32	48	94	147	200
81-87,89-99	15	30	45	85	130	175
88,100: 88-Used in **POP**, pgs. 76,77; Bill Woggon draws himself in story. 100-Last Katy Keene	16	32	48	94	147	200

NOTE: ***Al Fagaly** c-49-67. Katy Keene app. in 53-82, 85-100.*

SWAMP FOX, THE (TV, Disney)(See Walt Disney Presents #2)

Swamp Thing #16 © DC

Swamp Thing (2016 series) #1 © DC

Sweeney #5 © STD

Dell Publishing Co.: No. 1179, Dec, 1960

	GD 2.0	VG 4.0	FN 6.0	VF 8.0	VF/NM 9.0	NM- 9.2
Four Color 1179-Leslie Nielsen photo-c	8	16	24	51	96	140

SWAMP THING (See Brave & the Bold, Challengers of the Unknown #82, DC Comics Presents #8 & 85, DC Special Series #2, 14, 17, 20, House of Secrets #92, Limited Collectors' Edition C-59, & Roots of the...)

SWAMP THING
National Per. Publ./DC Comics: Oct-Nov, 1972 - No. 24, Aug-Sept, 1976

	GD 2.0	VG 4.0	FN 6.0	VF 8.0	VF/NM 9.0	NM- 9.2
1-Wrightson-c/a begins; origin	16	32	48	112	249	385
2-1st brief app. Patchwork Man (1 panel)	8	16	24	54	102	150
3-1st full app. Patchwork Man (see House of Secrets #140)	6	12	18	40	73	105
4-6,	5	10	15	34	60	85
7-Batman-c/story	6	12	18	37	66	95
8-10: 10-Last Wrightson issue	5	10	15	31	53	75
11-20: 11-19-Redondo-a. 13-Origin retold (1 pg.)	3	6	9	18	28	38
21-24: 23,24-Swamp Thing reverts back to Dr. Holland. 23-New logo	3	6	9	18	28	38
Secret of the Swamp Thing (2005, $9.99, digest) r/#1-10						10.00

NOTE: ***J. Jones** a-9i(assist). **Kaluta** a-9i. **Redondo** c-12-19, 21. **Wrightson** issues (#1-10) reprinted in DC Special Series #2, 14, 17, 20 & Roots of the Swamp Thing.*

SWAMP THING (Saga Of The... #1-38,42-45) (See Essential Vertigo:...)
DC Comics (Vertigo imprint #129 on): May, 1982 - No. 171, Oct, 1996 (Direct sales #65 on)

	GD 2.0	VG 4.0	FN 6.0	VF 8.0	VF/NM 9.0	NM- 9.2
1-Origin retold; Phantom Stranger series begins; ends #13; Yeates-c/a begins	2	4	6	8	10	12
2-15: 2-Photo-c from movie. 13-Last Yeates-a						4.00
16-19: Bissette-a.						5.00
20-1st Alan Moore issue	3	6	9	19	30	40
21-New origin	3	6	9	16	24	32
21 Special Editon (5/09, $1.00) reprint with "After Watchmen" cover frame						3.00
22,23	2	4	6	9	12	15
24-JLA x-over; last Yeates-c.	2	4	6	9	13	16
25-John Constantine 1-panel cameo	3	6	9	21	33	45
26-30	1	2	3	5	6	8
31-33,35,36: 33-r/1st app. from House of Secrets #92						6.00
34-Classic-c	2	4	6	8	10	12
37-1st app. John Constantine (Hellblazer) (6/85)	8	16	24	51	96	140
38-40: John Constantine app.	2	4	6	8	11	14
41-52,54-64: 44-Batman cameo. 44-51-John Constantine app. 46-Crisis x-over; Batman cameo. 49-Spectre app. 50-($1.25, 52 pgs.)-Deadman, Dr. Fate, Demon. 52-Arkham Asylum-c/story; Joker-c/cameo. 58-Spectre preview. 64-Last Moore issue						4.00
53-($1.25, 52 pgs.)-Arkham Asylum; Batman-c/story						5.00
65-83,85-99,101-124,126-149,151-153: 65-Direct sales only begins. 66-Batman & Arkham Asylum story. 70,76-John Constantine x-over; 76-X-over w/Hellblazer #9. 79-Superman-c/story. 85-Jonah Hex app. 102-Preview of World Without End. 116-Photo-c. 129-Metallic ink on-c. 140-Millar scripts begin, end #171						3.00
84-Sandman (Morpheus) cameo.						4.00
100,125,150: 100 ($2.50, 52 pgs.). 125-($2.95, 52 pgs.)-20th anniversary issue. 150 (52 pgs.)-Anniversary issue						4.00
154-171: 154-$2.25-c begins. 165-Curt Swan-a(p). 166,169,171-John Constantine & Phantom Stranger app. 168-Arcane returns						3.00
Annual 1,3-6('82-91): 1-Movie Adaptation; painted-c. 3-New format; Bolland-c. 4-Batman-c/story. 5-Batman cameo; re-intro Brother Power (Geek),1st app. since 1968						4.00
Annual 2 (1985)-Moore scripts; Bissette-a(p); Deadman, Spectre app.						7.00
Annual 7(1993, $3.95)-Children's Crusade						4.00
...A Murder of Crows (2001, $19.95)-r/#43-50; Moore-s						20.00
...: Earth To Earth (2002, $17.95)-r/#51-56; Batman app.						18.00
...: Infernal Triangles (2006, $19.99, TPB) r/#77-81 & Annual #3; cover gallery						20.00
...Love and Death (1990, $17.95)-r/#28-34 & Annual #2; Totleben painted-c						18.00
...: Regenesis (2004, $17.95, TPB) r/#65-70; Veitch-s						18.00
...: Reunion (2003, $19.95, TPB) r/#57-64; Moore-s						20.00
...: Roots (1998, $7.95) Jon J Muth-s/painted-a/c						8.00
Saga of the Swamp Thing ('87, '89)-r/#21-27 (1st & 2nd print)						15.00
Saga of the Swamp Thing Book One HC (2009, $24.99, d.j.) r/#20-27; Wein intro.						25.00
Saga of the Swamp Thing Book Two HC (2009, $24.99, d.j.) r/#28-34 & Annual #2						25.00
Saga of the Swamp Thing Book Three HC (2010, $24.99, d.j.) r/#35-42; Bissette intro.						25.00
Saga of the Swamp Thing Book Four HC (2010, $24.99, d.j.) r/#43-50; Gaiman foreword						25.00
Saga of the Swamp Thing Book Five HC (2011, $24.99, d.j.) r/#51-56; Bissette intro.						25.00
...: Spontaneous Generation (2005, $19.99) r/#71-76						20.00
...: The Curse (2000, $19.95, TPB) r/#35-42; Bisley-c						20.00

NOTE: ***Bissette** a(p)-16-19, 21-27, 29, 30, 34-36, 39-42, 44, 46, 50, 64; c-17i, 24-32p, 35-37p, 40p, 44p, 46-50p, 51-58, 61, 62, 63p. **Kaluta** c/a-74. **Spiegle** a-1-3, 6. **Sutton** a-98p. **Totleben** a(i)-10, 16-27, 29, 31, 34-40, 42, 44, 46, 48, 50, 53, 55i; c-25-32i, 33, 35-40i, 42i, 44i, 46-50i, 53, 55i, 59p, 64, 65, 68, 73, 76, 80, 82, 84, 89, 91-100, Annual 4, 5. **Vess** painted c-121, 129-139, Annual 7. **Williamson** 86i. **Wrightson** a-18i(r), 33r. John Constantine appears in #37-40, 44-51, 65-67, 70-77, 80-90, 99, 114, 115, 130, 134-138.*

SWAMP THING
DC Comics (Vertigo): May, 2000 - No. 20, Dec, 2001 ($2.50)

	GD 2.0	VG 4.0	FN 6.0	VF 8.0	VF/NM 9.0	NM- 9.2
1-3-Tefé Holland's return; Vaughan-s/Petersen-a; Hale painted-c.						4.00
4-20: 7-9-Bisley-c. 10-John Constantine-c/app. 10-12-Fabry-c. 13-15-Mack-c 18-Swamp Thing app.						3.00
Preview-16 pg. flip book w/Lucifer Preview						3.00

SWAMP THING
DC Comics (Vertigo): May, 2004 - No. 29, Sept, 2006 ($2.95/$2.99)

	GD 2.0	VG 4.0	FN 6.0	VF 8.0	VF/NM 9.0	NM- 9.2
1-29: 1-Diggle-s/Breccia-a; Constantine app. 2-6-Sargon app. 7,8,20-Corben-c/a. 21-29-Eric Powell-c						3.00
...: Bad Seed (2004, $9.95) r/#1-6						10.00
...: Healing the Breach (2006, $17.99) r/#15-20						18.00
...: Love in Vain (2005, $14.99) r/#9-14						15.00

SWAMP THING (DC New 52)
DC Comics: Nov, 2011 - No. 40, May, 2015 ($2.99)

	GD 2.0	VG 4.0	FN 6.0	VF 8.0	VF/NM 9.0	NM- 9.2
1-Snyder-s/Paquette-a; Superman app.						8.00
1-(2nd & 3rd printing)						3.00
2-18: 2-Abigail Arcane returns. 7-Holland transforms. 10-Francavilla-a; Anton Arcane returns. 12-X-over with Animal Man #12. 13-Poison Ivy & Deadman app.; leads into Annual #1						3.00
19-23: 19-Soule-s/Kano-a begin. 19,20-Superman app. 22,23-Constantine app.						3.00
23.1 (11/13, $2.99, regular cover)						3.00
23.1 (11/13, $3.99, 3-D cover) "Arcane #1" on cover; Soule-s/Saiz-a/c; origin of Arcane						5.00
24-39: 24-Leads into Annual #2. 26-Woodrue's origin; Animal Man app. 32-Aquaman app. 39-Constantine app.						3.00
40-($3.99)						4.00
#0-(11/12, $2.99) Kano-a; Arcane app.; Swamp Thing origin re-told						3.00
Annual #1 (12/12, $4.99) Flashback to 1st meeting of Alec & Abby; Cloonan-a						5.00
Annual #2 (12/13, $4.99) Soule-s/Pina-a						5.00
Annual #3 (12/14, $4.99) Soule-s/Pina-a: Etrigan app.						5.00
...: Futures End 1 (11/14, $2.99, regular-c) Five years later; Soule-s/Saiz-a; Arcane app.						3.00
...: Futures End 1 (11/14, $3.99, 3-D cover)						4.00

SWAMP THING
DC Comics: Mar, 2016 - No. 6, Aug, 2016 ($2.99)

	GD 2.0	VG 4.0	FN 6.0	VF 8.0	VF/NM 9.0	NM- 9.2
1-6-Len Wein-s/Kelley Jones-a. 1,2-Phantom Stranger app. 2-Matt Cable returns. 3,4,6-Zatanna app.						3.00

SWAT MALONE (America's Home Run King)
Swat Malone Enterprises: Sept, 1955

	GD 2.0	VG 4.0	FN 6.0	VF 8.0	VF/NM 9.0	NM- 9.2
V1#1-Hy Fleishman-a	11	22	33	62	86	110

SWEATSHOP
DC Comics: Jun, 2003 - No. 6, Nov, 2003 ($2.95)

	GD 2.0	VG 4.0	FN 6.0	VF 8.0	VF/NM 9.0	NM- 9.2
1-6-Peter Bagge-s/a; Destefano-a						3.00

SWEENEY (Formerly Buz Sawyer)
Standard Comics: No. 4, June, 1949 - No. 5, Sept, 1949

	GD 2.0	VG 4.0	FN 6.0	VF 8.0	VF/NM 9.0	NM- 9.2
4,5: 5-Crane-a	9	18	27	50	65	80

SWEE'PEA (Also see Popeye #46)
Dell Publishing Co.: No. 219, Mar, 1949

	GD 2.0	VG 4.0	FN 6.0	VF 8.0	VF/NM 9.0	NM- 9.2
Four Color 219	9	18	27	57	111	165

SWEET CHILDE
Advantage Graphics Press: 1995 - No. 2, 1995 ($2.95, B&W, mature)

	GD 2.0	VG 4.0	FN 6.0	VF 8.0	VF/NM 9.0	NM- 9.2
1,2						3.00

SWEETHEART DIARY (Cynthia Doyle #66-on)
Fawcett Publications/Charlton Comics No. 32 on: Wint, 1949; #2, Spr, 1950; #3, 6/50 - #5, 10/50; #6, 1951(nd); #7, 9/51 - #14, 1/53; #32, 10/55; #33, 4/56 - #65, 8/62 (#1-14: photo-c)

	GD 2.0	VG 4.0	FN 6.0	VF 8.0	VF/NM 9.0	NM- 9.2
1	20	40	60	120	195	270
2	13	26	39	74	105	135
3,4-Wood-a	15	30	45	90	140	190
5-10: 8-Bailey-a	10	20	30	56	76	95
11-14: 13-Swayze-a. 14-Last Fawcett issue	9	18	27	47	61	75
32 (10/55; 1st Charlton issue)(Formerly Cowboy Love #31)	9	18	27	52	69	85
33-40: 34-Swayze-a	7	14	21	35	43	50
41-(68 pgs.)	8	16	24	40	50	60
42-60	3	6	9	19	30	40
61-65	3	6	9	17	26	35

SWEETHEARTS (Formerly Captain Midnight)
Fawcett Publications/Charlton No. 122 on: #68, 10/48 - #121, 5/53; #122, 3/54; V2#23, 5/54 - #137, 12/73

Sweethearts #119 © FAW

Switch #4 © TCOW

The Sword #9 © Luna Bros.

	GD 2.0	VG 4.0	FN 6.0	VF 8.0	VF/NM 9.0	NM- 9.2
68-Photo-c begin	18	36	54	107	169	230
69,70	11	22	33	62	86	110
71-80	9	18	27	52	69	85
81-84,86-93,95-99,105	9	18	27	47	61	75
85,94,103,110,117-George Evans-a	10	20	30	54	72	90
100	9	18	27	52	69	85
101,107-Powell-a	9	18	27	50	65	80
102,104,106,108,109,112-116,118	8	16	24	44	57	70
111-1 pg. Ronald Reagan biography	10	20	30	56	76	95
119-Marilyn Monroe & Richard Widmark photo-c (1/54?); also appears in story; part Wood-a	90	180	270	576	988	1400
120-Atom Bomb story	12	24	36	67	94	120
121-Liz Taylor/Fernanado Lamas photo-c	36	72	108	211	343	475
122-(1st Charlton? 3/54)-Marijuana story	13	26	39	72	101	130
V2#23 (5/54)-28: 28-Last precode issue (2/55)	8	16	24	42	54	65
29-39,41,43,45,47-50	4	8	12	25	40	55
40-Photo-c; Tommy Sands story	4	8	12	27	44	60
42-Ricky Nelson photo-c/story	7	14	21	49	92	135
44-Pat Boone photo-c/story	4	8	12	27	44	60
46-Jimmy Rodgers photo-c/story	4	8	12	27	44	60
51-60	3	6	9	21	33	45
61-80,100	3	6	9	18	28	38
81-99	3	6	9	16	24	32
101-110	2	4	6	13	18	22
111-120,122-124,126-137	2	4	6	10	14	18
121,125-David Cassidy pin-ups	2	4	6	13	18	22

NOTE: *Photo c-68-121(Fawcett), 40, 42, 46(Charlton).* **Swayze** *a(Fawcett)-70-118(most).*

SWEETHEART SCANDALS (See Fox Giants)

SWEETIE PIE
Dell Publishing Co.: No. 1185, May-July, 1961 - No. 1241, Nov-Jan, 1961/62

	GD 2.0	VG 4.0	FN 6.0	VF 8.0	VF/NM 9.0	NM- 9.2
Four Color 1185 (#1)	5	10	15	34	60	85
Four Color 1241	4	8	12	28	47	65

SWEETIE PIE
Ajax-Farrell/Pines (Literary Ent.): Dec, 1955 - No. 15, Fall, 1957

	GD 2.0	VG 4.0	FN 6.0	VF 8.0	VF/NM 9.0	NM- 9.2
1-By Nadine Seltzer	10	20	30	54	72	90
2 (5/56; last Ajax?)	7	14	21	35	43	50
3-15	6	12	18	28	34	40

SWEET LOVE
Home Comics (Harvey): Sept, 1949 - No. 5, May, 1950 (All photo-c)

	GD 2.0	VG 4.0	FN 6.0	VF 8.0	VF/NM 9.0	NM- 9.2
1	10	20	30	58	79	100
2	7	14	21	37	46	55
3,4: 3-Powell-a	6	12	18	31	38	45
5-Kamen, Powell-a	9	18	27	47	61	75

SWEET ROMANCE
Charlton Comics: Oct, 1968

	GD 2.0	VG 4.0	FN 6.0	VF 8.0	VF/NM 9.0	NM- 9.2
1	3	6	9	14	20	25

SWEET SIXTEEN (...Comics and Stories for Girls)
Parents' Magazine Institute: Aug-Sept, 1946 - No. 13, Jan, 1948 (All have movie stars photos on covers)

	GD 2.0	VG 4.0	FN 6.0	VF 8.0	VF/NM 9.0	NM- 9.2
1-Van Johnson's life story; Dorothy Dare, Queen of Hollywood Stunt Artists begins (in all issues); part photo-c	28	56	84	165	270	375
2-Jane Powell, Roddy McDowall "Holiday in Mexico" photo on-c; Alan Ladd story	18	36	54	105	165	225
3,5,6,8-11: 5-Ann Francis photo on-c; Gregory Peck story. 6-Dick Haymes story. 8-Shirley Jones photo on-c. 10-Jean Simmons photo on-c; James Stewart story	15	30	45	83	124	165
4-Elizabeth Taylor photo on-c	34	68	102	199	325	450
7-Ronald Reagan's life story	27	54	81	158	259	360
12-Bob Cummings, Vic Damone story	15	30	45	85	130	175
13-Robert Mitchum's life story	15	30	45	86	133	180

SWEET XVI
Marvel Comics: May, 1991 - No. 5, Sept, 1991 ($1.00)

	GD 2.0	VG 4.0	FN 6.0	VF 8.0	VF/NM 9.0	NM- 9.2
1-5: Barbara Slate story & art						4.00

SWEET TOOTH
DC Comics (Vertigo): Nov, 2009 - No. 40, Feb, 2013 ($1.00/$2.99)

	GD 2.0	VG 4.0	FN 6.0	VF 8.0	VF/NM 9.0	NM- 9.2
1-($1.00) Jeff Lemire-s/a						3.00
2-39-($2.99) 18,33-Printed sideways. 26-28-Kindt-a						3.00
40-($4.99) Final issue; two covers by Lemire and Truman						5.00
...: Animal Armies TPB (2011, $14.99) r/#12-17						15.00
...: In Captivity TPB (2010, $12.99) r/#6-11						13.00
...: Out of the Deep Woods TPB (2010, $9.99) r/#1-5						10.00

SWIFT ARROW (Also see Lone Rider & The Rider)
Ajax/Farrell Publications: Feb-Mar, 1954 - No. 5, Oct-Nov, 1954; Apr, 1957 - No. 3, Sept, 1957

	GD 2.0	VG 4.0	FN 6.0	VF 8.0	VF/NM 9.0	NM- 9.2
1(1954) (1st Series)	16	32	48	92	144	195
2	10	20	30	56	76	95
3-5: 5-Lone Rider story	9	18	27	50	65	80
1 (2nd Series) (Swift Arrow's Gunfighters #4)	9	18	27	50	65	80
2,3: 2-Lone Rider begins	8	16	24	40	50	60

SWIFT ARROW'S GUNFIGHTERS (Formerly Swift Arrow)
Ajax/Farrell Publ. (Four Star Comic Corp.): No. 4, Nov, 1957

	GD 2.0	VG 4.0	FN 6.0	VF 8.0	VF/NM 9.0	NM- 9.2
4	8	16	24	40	50	60

SWING WITH SCOOTER
National Periodical Publ.: June-July, 1966 - No. 35, Aug-Sept, 1971; No. 36, Oct-Nov, 1972

	GD 2.0	VG 4.0	FN 6.0	VF 8.0	VF/NM 9.0	NM- 9.2
1	9	18	27	58	114	170
2,6-10: 9-Alfred E. Newman swipe in last panel	5	10	15	33	57	80
3-5: 3-Batman cameo on-c. 4-Batman cameo inside. 5-JLA cameo	5	10	15	34	60	85
11-13,15-19: 18-Wildcat of JSA 1pg. text. 19-Last 12¢-c	3	6	9	20	31	42
14-Alfred E. Neuman cameo	3	6	9	21	33	45
20 (68 pgs.)	5	10	15	30	50	70
21-23,25-31	3	6	9	17	26	35
24-Frankenstein-c.	3	6	9	21	33	45
32-34 (68 pgs.). 32-Batman cameo. 33-Interview with David Cassidy. 34-Interview with Rick Ely (The Rebels)	4	8	12	28	47	65
35-(52 pgs.). 1 pg. app. Clark Kent and 4 full pgs. of Superman	6	12	18	42	79	115
36-Bat-signal refererence to Batman	3	6	9	21	33	45

NOTE: ***Aragonés*** a-13 (1pg.), 18(1pg.), 30(2pgs.) ***Orlando*** *a-1-11; c-1-11, 13. #20, 33, 34: 68 pgs.; #35: 52 pgs.*

SWISS FAMILY ROBINSON (Walt Disney's..; see King Classics & Movie Comics)
Dell Publishing Co.: No. 1156, Dec, 1960

	GD 2.0	VG 4.0	FN 6.0	VF 8.0	VF/NM 9.0	NM- 9.2
Four Color 1156-Movie-photo-c	7	14	21	46	86	125

SWITCH (Also see Witchblade titles)
Image Comics: Oct, 2015 - Present ($3.99)

	GD 2.0	VG 4.0	FN 6.0	VF 8.0	VF/NM 9.0	NM- 9.2
1-4-Stjepan Sejic-s/a; 3 covers on each						4.00

S.W.O.R.D. (Sentient World Observation and Response Department)
Marvel Comics: Jan, 2010 - No. 5, May, 2010 ($3.99/$2.99)

	GD 2.0	VG 4.0	FN 6.0	VF 8.0	VF/NM 9.0	NM- 9.2
1-($3.99) Cassaday-c/Gillen-s/Sanders-a; Commander Brand & Henry Gyrich app.						4.00
2-5-($2.99): 2,3-Cassaday-c. 4,5-Del Mundo-c						3.00

SWORD, THE
Image Comics: Oct, 2007 - No. 24, May, 2010 ($2.99/$4.99)

	GD 2.0	VG 4.0	FN 6.0	VF 8.0	VF/NM 9.0	NM- 9.2
1-Luna Brothers-s/a						4.00
1-(2nd printing)						3.00
2-23: 12-Zakros killed						3.00
24-($4.99) Final issue						5.00

SWORD & THE DRAGON, THE
Dell Publishing Co.: No. 1118, June, 1960

	GD 2.0	VG 4.0	FN 6.0	VF 8.0	VF/NM 9.0	NM- 9.2
Four Color 1118-Movie, photo-c	7	14	21	48	89	130

SWORD & THE ROSE, THE (Disney)
Dell Publishing Co.: No. 505, Oct, 1953 - No. 682, Feb, 1956

	GD 2.0	VG 4.0	FN 6.0	VF 8.0	VF/NM 9.0	NM- 9.2
Four Color 505-Movie, photo-c	8	16	24	52	99	145
Four Color 682-When Knighthood Was in Flower-Movie, reprint of #505; Renamed the Sword & the Rose for the novel; photo-c	6	12	18	40	73	105

SWORD IN THE STONE, THE (See March of Comics #258 & Movie Comics & Wart and the Wizard)

SWORD OF DAMOCLES
Image Comics (WildStorm Productions): Mar, 1996 - No. 2, Apr, 1996 ($2.50, limited series)

	GD 2.0	VG 4.0	FN 6.0	VF 8.0	VF/NM 9.0	NM- 9.2
1,2: Warren Ellis scripts. 1-Prelude to "Fire From Heaven" x-over; 1st app. Sword						3.00

SWORD OF DRACULA
Image Comics: Oct, 2003 - No. 6, Sept, 2004 ($2.95, B&W, limited series)

	GD 2.0	VG 4.0	FN 6.0	VF 8.0	VF/NM 9.0	NM- 9.2
1-6-Tony Harris-c. 1,2-Greg Scott-a						3.00
TPB (IDW, 2/05, $14.99) r/series						15.00

SWORD OF RED SONJA: DOOM OF THE GODS
Dynamite Entertainment: 2007 - No. 4, 2007 ($3.50, limited series)

	GD 2.0	VG 4.0	FN 6.0	VF 8.0	VF/NM 9.0	NM- 9.2
1-4-Lui Antonio-a; multiple covers on each						3.50

SWORD OF SORCERY

Swords of Sorrow #5 © DYN

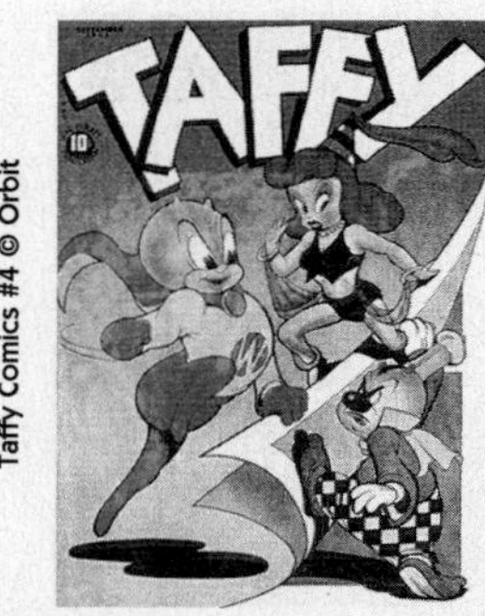

Taffy Comics #4 © Orbit

Takion #2 © DC

	GD	VG	FN	VF	VF/NM	NM-
	2.0	4.0	6.0	8.0	9.0	9.2

National Periodical Publications: Feb-Mar, 1973 - No. 5, Nov-Dec, 1973 (20¢)

1-Leiber Fafhrd & The Grey Mouser; Chaykin/Neal Adams (Crusty Bunkers) art; Kaluta-c	3	6	9	16	23	30
2,3: 2-Wrightson-c(i); Adams-a(i). 3-Wrightson-i(5 pgs.)	2	4	6	9	13	16
4,5: 5-Starlin-a(p); Conan cameo	2	4	6	8	10	12

NOTE: ***Chaykin** a-1-4p; c-2p, 3-5. **Kaluta** a-3i. **Simonson** a-3i, 4i, 5p; c-5.*

SWORD OF SORCERY (DC New 52)
DC Comics: No. 0, Nov, 2012 - No. 8, Jun, 2013 ($3.99)

0-8: 0-Origin of Amethyst retold; Lopresti-a; Beowulf back-up; Saiz-a. 4-Stalker back-up 4.00

SWORD OF THE ATOM
DC Comics: Sept, 1983 - No. 4, Dec, 1983 (Limited series)

1-4: Gil Kane-c/a in all 4.00
Special 1-3('84, '85, '88): 1,2-Kane-c/a each 4.00
TPB (2007, $19.99) r/#1-4 and Special #1-3 20.00

SWORDS OF SORROW
Dynamite Entertainment: 2015 - No. 6, 2015 ($3.99, limited series with tie-in series)

1-6-Simone-s/Davila-a; crossover of Vampirella, Red Sonja, Dejah Thoris, Lady Zorro and other female Dynamite characters; multiple covers on each 4.00
...: Black Sparrow & Lady Zorro Special 1 ($3.99, one-shot) Schultz-s/Zamora-a 4.00
...: Chaos! Prequel 1 ($3.99, one-shot) Mairghread Scott-s/Mirka Andolfo-a 4.00
...: Dejah Thoris & Irene Adler 1-3 ($3.99, lim. series) Leah Moore-s/Francesco Manna-a 4.00
...: Masquerade & Kato 1 ($3.99, one-shot) G. Willow Wilson & Erica Schultz-s 4.00
...: Miss Fury & Lady Rawhide 1 ($3.99, one-shot) Mikki Kendall-s/Ronilson Freire-a 4.00
...: Pantha & Jane Porter ($3.99, one-shot) Emma Beeby-s/Rod Rodolfo-a 4.00
...: Red Sonja & Jungle Girl 1-3 ($3.99, lim. series) Bennett-s/Andolfo-a/Anacleto-c 4.00
...: Vampirella & Jennifer Blood 1-4 ($3.99, lim. series) Nancy Collins-s/Dave Acosta-a 4.00

SWORDS OF TEXAS (See Scout #15)
Eclipse Comics: Oct, 1987 - No. 4, Jan, 1988 ($1.75, color, Baxter paper)

1-4: Scout app. 3.00

SWORDS OF THE SWASHBUCKLERS (See Marvel Graphic Novel)
Marvel Comics (Epic Comics): May, 1985 - No. 12, Jun, 1987 ($1.50; mature)

1-12-Butch Guice-c/a (cont'd from Marvel G.N.) 3.00

SWORN TO PROTECT
Marvel Comics: Sept, 1995 ($1.95) (Based on card game)

nn-Overpower Game Guide; Jubilee story 3.00

SYMMETRY
Image Comics (Top Cow): Dec, 2015 - No. 8, Oct, 2016 ($3.99)

1-8-Hawkins-s/Ienco-a 4.00

SYN
Dark Horse Comics: Aug, 2003 - No. 5, Feb, 2004 ($2.99, limited series)

1-5-Giffen-s/Titus-a 3.00

SYPHONS
Now Comics: V2#1, May, 1994 - V2#3, 1994 ($2.50, limited series)

V2#1-3: 1-Stardancer, Knightfire, Raze & Brigade begin 3.00
TPB (9/04, $15.95) B&W reprints #1-3; intro. by Tony Caputo 16.00

SYSTEM, THE
DC Comics (Vertigo Verite): May, 1996 - No. 3, July, 1996 ($2.95, lim. series)

1-3: Kuper-c/a 3.00
TPB (1997, $12.95) r/#1-3 13.00

TAFFY COMICS (Also see Dotty Dripple)
Rural Home/Orbit Publ.: Mar-Apr, 1945 - No. 12, 1948

1-L.B. Cole-c; origin & 1st app. of Wiggles The Wonderworm plus 7 chapter WWII funny animal adventures	63	126	189	403	689	975
2-L.B. Cole-c with funny animal Hitler; Wiggles-c/stories in #1-4	45	90	135	284	480	675
3,4,6-12: 6-Perry Como-c/story. 7-Duke Ellington, 2 pgs. 8-Glenn Ford-c/story. 9-Lon McCallister part photo-c & story. 10-Mort Leav-c. 11-Mickey Rooney-c/story	15	30	45	88	137	185
5-L.B. Cole-c; Van Johnson-c/story	22	44	66	128	209	290

TAILGUNNER JO
DC Comics: Sept, 1988 - No. 6, Jan, 1989 ($1.25)

1-6 3.00

TAILS
Archie Publications: Dec, 1995 - No. 3, Feb, 1996 ($1.50, limited series)

1-3: Based on Sonic, the Hedgehog video game 6.00

TAILS OF THE PET AVENGERS (Also see Lockjaw and the Pet Avengers)
Marvel Comics: Apr, 2010 ($3.99, one-shot)

1-Lockjaw, Frog Thor, Zabu, Lockheed and Redwing in short solo stories by various 4.00
...: The Dogs of Summer (9/10, $3.99) Eliopolous-s; see Avengers vs. the Pet Avengers 4.00

TAILSPIN
Spotlight Publishers: November, 1944

nn-Firebird app.; L.B. Cole-c	34	68	102	199	325	450

TAILSPIN TOMMY (Also see Popular Comics)
United Features Syndicate/Service Publ. Co.: 1940; 1946

Single Series 23(1940)	41	82	123	256	428	600
1-Best Seller (nd, 1946)-Service Publ. Co.	19	38	57	109	172	235

TAKIO
Marvel Comics (Icon): 2011; May, 2012 - No. 4 ($3.95/$9.95)

HC (2011, $9.95) Bendis-s/Oeming-a/c; Oeming sketch pages 10.00
1-4: 1-(5/12, $3.95) Bendis-s/Oeming-a/c 4.00

TAKION
DC Comics: June, 1996 - No. 7, Dec, 1996 ($1.75)

1-7: Lopresti-c/a(p). 1-Origin; Green Lantern app. 6-Final Night x-over 3.00

TALENT SHOWCASE (See New Talent Showcase)

TALE OF ONE BAD RAT, THE
Dark Horse Comics: Oct, 1994 - No. 4, Jan, 1995 ($2.95, limited series)

1-4: Bryan Talbot-c/a/scripts 3.00
HC ($69.95, signed and numbered) R/#1-4 70.00

TALES CALCULATED TO DRIVE YOU BATS
Archie Publications: Nov, 1961 - No. 7, Nov, 1962; 1966 (Satire)

1-Only 10¢ issue; has cut-out Werewolf mask (price includes mask)	15	30	45	103	227	350
2-Begin 12¢ issues	9	18	27	58	114	170
3-6: 3-UFO cover	7	14	21	49	92	135
7-Storyline change	7	14	21	46	86	125
1(1966, 25¢, 44 pg. Giant)-r/#1; UFO cover	7	14	21	44	82	120

TALES CALCULATED TO DRIVE YOU MAD
E.C. Publications: Summer, 1997 - No. 8, Winter, 1999 ($3.99/$4.99, satire)

1-6-Full color reprints of Mad: 1-(#1-3), 2-(#4-6), 3-(#7-9), 4-(#10-12) 5-(#13-15), 6-(#16-18) 6.00
7,8-($4.99-c): 7-(#19-21), 8-(#22,23) 6.00

TALES FROM RIVERDALE DIGEST
Archie Publ.: June, 2005 - No. 39, Oct, 2010 ($2.39/$2.49/$2.69, digest-size)

1-39: 1-Sabrina and Josie & the Pussycats app. 11-Begin $2.49-c. 34-Begin $2.69 3.00

TALES FROM THE AGE OF APOCALYPSE
Marvel Comics: 1996 ($5.95, prestige format, one-shots)

1, ...: Sinister Bloodlines (1997, $5.95) 6.00

TALES FROM THE BOG
Aberration Press: Nov, 1995 - No. 7, Nov, 1997 ($2.95/$3.95, B&W)

1-7 4.00
Alternate #1 (Director's Cut) (1998, $2.95) 3.00

TALES FROM THE BULLY PULPIT
Image Comics: Aug, 2004 ($6.95, square-bound)

1-Teddy Roosevelt and Edison's ghost with a time machine; Cereno-s/MacDonald-a 7.00

TALES FROM THE CLERKS (See Jay and Silent Bob, Clerks and Oni Double Feature)
Graphitti Designs, Inc.: 2006 ($29.95, TPB)

nn-Reprints all the Kevin Smith Clerks and Jay and Silent Bob stories; new Clerks II story with Mahfood-a; cover gallery, sketch pages, Mallrats credits covers; Smith intro. 30.00

TALES FROM THE CON
Image Comics: May, 2014 ($3.50, one-shot)

...: Year 1 - Brad Guigar-s/Chris Giarrusso-a/c; comic convention humor strips 3.50

TALES FROM THE CRYPT (Formerly The Crypt Of Terror; see Three Dimensional...) (Also see EC Archives • Tales From the Crypt)
E.C. Comics: No. 20, Oct-Nov, 1950 - No. 46, Feb-Mar, 1955

20-See Crime Patrol #15 for 1st Crypt Keeper	137	274	411	1096	1748	2400
21-Kurtzman-r/Haunt of Fear #15(#1)	111	222	333	888	1419	1950
22-Moon Girl costume at costume party, one panel	89	178	267	712	1131	1550
23-25: 23-"Reflection of Death" adapted for 1972 TFTC film. 24-E. A. Poe adaptation	73	146	219	584	930	1275

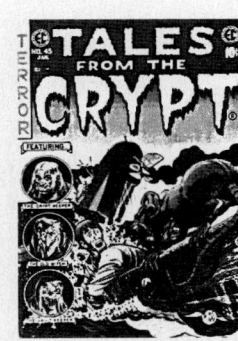

Tales From the Crypt #45 © WMG

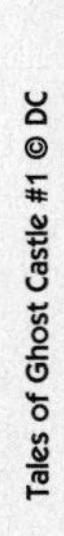
Tales of Ghost Castle #1 © DC

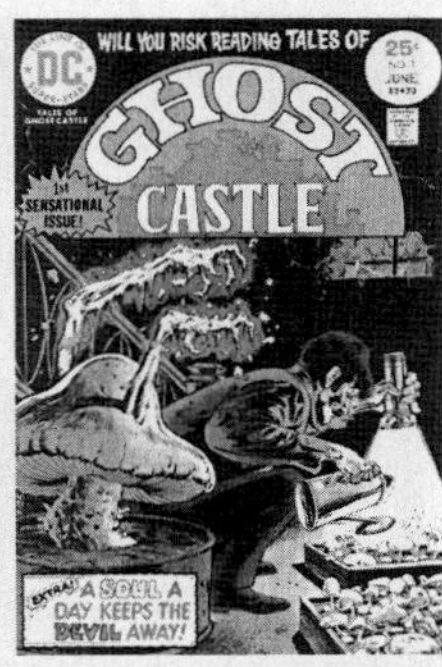

Tales of Suspense #2 © MAR

GD 2.0 | VG 4.0 | FN 6.0 | VF 8.0 | VF/NM 9.0 | NM- 9.2

26-30: 26-Wood's 2nd EC-c 60 120 180 480 765 1050
31-Williamson-a(1st at E.C.); B&W and color illos. in **POP**; Kamen draws himself, Gaines & Feldstein; Ingels, Craig & Davis draw themselves in his story
61 122 183 488 782 1075
32,35-39: 38-Censored-c 54 108 162 432 691 950
33-Origin The Crypt Keeper 71 142 213 568 909 1250
34-Used in **POP**, pg. 83; lingerie panels 54 108 162 432 691 950
40-Used in Senate hearings & in Hartford Courant anti-comics editorials-1954
53 106 159 424 675 925
41-45: 45-2 pgs. showing E.C. staff; anti-censorship editorial of upcoming Senate hearings
51 102 153 408 654 900
46-Low distribution; pre-advertised cover for unpublished 4th horror title "Crypt of Terror" used on this book; "Blind Alleys" adapted for 1972 TFTC film; classic werewolf-c by Davis
60 120 180 480 765 1050

NOTE: ***Ray Bradbury** adaptations-34, 36. **Craig** a-20, 22-24; c-20. **Crandall** a-38, 44. **Davis** a-24-46; c-29-46. **Elder** a-37, 38. **Evans** a-32-34, 36, 40, 41, 43, 46. **Feldstein** a-20-23; c-21-25, 28. Ingels a-in all. **Kamen** a-20, 22, 25, 27-31, 33-36, 39, 41-45. **Krigstein** a-40, 42, 45. **Kurtzman** a-21. **Orlando** a-27-30, 35, 37, 39, 41-45. **Wood** a-21, 24, 25; c-26, 27. Canadian reprints known; see Table of Contents.*

TALES FROM THE CRYPT (Magazine)
Eerie Publications: No. 10, July, 1968 (35¢, B&W)
10-Contains Farrell reprints from 1950s 5 10 15 35 63 90

TALES FROM THE CRYPT
Gladstone Publishing: July, 1990 - No. 6, May, 1991 ($1.95/$2.00, 68 pgs.)
1-r/TFTC #33 & Crime S.S. #17; Davis-c(r) 5.00
2-6: 2,3,5,6-Davis-c(r). 4-Begin $2.00-c; Craig-c(r) 5.00

TALES FROM THE CRYPT
Extra-Large Comics (Russ Cochran)/Gemstone Publishing: Jul, 1991 - No. 6 ($3.95, 10 1/4 x13 1/4", 68 pgs.)
1-6: 1-Davis-c(r); Craig back-c(r); E.C. reprints. 2-6 ($2.00, comic sized) 5.00

TALES FROM THE CRYPT
Russ Cochran: Sept, 1991 - No. 7, July, 1992 ($2.00, 64 pgs.)
1-7 5.00

TALES FROM THE CRYPT (Also see EC Archives • Tales From the Crypt)
Russ Cochran/Gemstone: Sept, 1992 - No. 30, Dec, 1999 ($1.50, quarterly)
1-4-r/Crypt of Terror #17-19, TFTC #20 w/original-c 4.00
5-30: 5-15 ($2.00)-r/TFTC #21-23 w/original-c. 16-30 ($2.50) 4.00
Annual 1-6('93-'99) 1-r/#1-5. 2- r/#6-10. 3- r/#11-15. 4- r/#16-20. 5-r/#21-25. 6- r/#26-30 14.00

TALES FROM THE DARKSIDE
IDW Publishing: Jun, 2016 - No. 4, Sept, 2016 ($3.99, limited series)
1-4-Joe Hill-s/Gabriel Rodriguez-a. 1-Five covers. 2-4-Two covers 4.00

TALES FROM THE GREAT BOOK
Famous Funnies: Feb, 1955 - No. 4, Jan, 1956 (Religious themes)
1-Story of Samson; John Lehti-a in all 9 18 27 52 69 85
2-4: 2-Joshua. 3-Joash the Boy King. 4-David 7 14 21 37 46 55

TALES FROM THE HEART OF AFRICA (The Temporary Natives)
Marvel Comics (Epic Comics): Aug, 1990 ($3.95, 52 pgs.)
1 4.00

TALES FROM THE TOMB (Also see Dell Giants)
Dell Publishing Co.: Oct, 1962 (25¢ giant)
1(02-810-210)-All stories written by John Stanley 13 26 39 89 195 300

TALES FROM THE TOMB (Magazine)
Eerie Publications: V1#6, July, 1969 - V7#3, 1975 (52 pgs.)
V1#6 8 16 24 51 96 140
V1#7,8 6 12 18 38 69 100
V2#1-6: 4-LSD story-r/Weird V3#5. 6-Rulah-r 5 10 15 34 60 85
V3#1-Rulah-r 5 10 15 34 60 85
2-6('71),V4#1-5('72),V5#1-6('73),V6#1-6('74),V7#1-3('75)
5 10 15 31 53 75

TALES OF ASGARD
Marvel Comics Group: Oct, 1968 (25¢, 68 pgs.); Feb, 1984 ($1.25, 52 pgs.)
1-Reprints Tales of Asgard (Thor) back-up stories from Journey into Mystery #97-106; new Kirby-c; Kirby-a 6 12 18 37 66 95
V2#1 (2/84)-Thor-r; Simonson-c 5.00

TALES OF ARMY OF DARKNESS
Dynamite Entertainment: 2006 ($5.95, one-shot)
1-Short stories by Kuhoric, Kirkman, Bradshaw, Sablik, Ottley, Acs, O'Hare and others 6.00

TALES OF EVIL
Atlas/Seaboard Publ.: Feb, 1975 - No. 3, July, 1975 (All 25¢ issues)
1-3: 1-Werewolf w/Sekowsky-a. 2-Intro. The Bog Beast; Sparling-a. 3-Origin The Man-Monster; Buckler-a(p) 2 4 6 11 16 20

NOTE: *Grandenetti a-1, 2. **Lieber** c-1. **Sekowsky** a-1. **Sutton** a-2. **Thorne** c-2.*

TALES OF GHOST CASTLE
National Periodical Publications: May-June, 1975 - No. 3, Sept-Oct, 1975 (All 25¢ issues)
1-Redondo-a; 1st app. Lucien the Librarian from Sandman (1989 series)
3 6 9 17 26 35
2,3: 2-Nino-a. 3-Redondo-a. 2 4 6 10 14 18

TALES OF G.I. JOE
Marvel Comics: Jan, 1988 - No. 15, Mar, 1989
1 ($2.25, 52 pgs.) 4.00
2-15 ($1.50): 1-15-r/G.I. Joe #1-15 3.00

TALES OF HONOR (Based on the David Weber novels)
Image Comics (Top Cow): Mar, 2014 - No. 5, Oct, 2015 ($2.99)
1-5: 1-Matt Hawkins-s/Jung-Geun Yoon-a. 2-5-Sang-il Jeong-a 3.00

TALES OF HONOR VOLUME 2 (Bred to Kill on cover)
Image Comics (Top Cow): No. 0, May, 2015 - No. 4, Dec, 2015 ($3.99)
0-Free Comic Book Day giveaway; Hawkins-s/Linda Sejic-a 3.00
1-4-Hawkins-s/Linda Sejic-a 4.00

TALES OF HORROR
Toby Press/Minoan Publ. Corp.: June, 1952 - No. 13, Oct, 1954
1-"This is Terror-Man" 48 96 144 302 514 725
2-Torture scenes 39 78 117 231 378 525
3-11,13: 9-11-Reprints Purple Claw #1-3 28 56 84 165 270 375
12-Myron Fass-c/a; torture scenes 30 60 90 177 289 400

NOTE: ***Andru** a-5. **Baily** a-5. **Myron Fass** a-2, 3, 12; c-1-3, 12. **Hollingsworth** a-2. **Sparling** a-6, 9; c-9.*

TALES OF JUSTICE
Atlas Comics(MjMC No. 53-66/Male No. 67): No. 53, May, 1955 - No. 67, Aug, 1957
53 18 36 54 105 165 225
54-57: 54-Powell-a 13 26 39 74 105 135
58,59-Krigstein-a 14 28 42 80 115 150
60-63,65: 60-Powell-a 12 24 36 67 94 120
64,66,67: 64,67-Crandall-a. 66-Torres, Orlando-a 12 24 36 69 97 125

NOTE: ***Everett** a-53, 60. **Orlando** a-65, 66. **Severin** a-64; c-58, 60, 65. **Wildey** a-64, 67.*

TALES OF LEONARDO BLIND SIGHT (See Tales of the TMNT Vol. 2 #5)
Mirage Publishing: June, 2006 - No. 4, Sept, 2006 ($3.25, B&W, limited series)
1-4-Jim Lawson-s/a 3.25

TALES OF SUSPENSE (Becomes Captain America #100 on)
Atlas (WPI No. 1,2/Male No. 3-12/VPI No. 13-18)/Marvel No. 19 on: Jan, 1959 - No. 99, Mar, 1968
1-Williamson-a (5 pgs.); Heck-c; #1-4 have sci/fi-c 350 700 1050 2975 6738 10,500
2-Ditko robot-c 111 222 333 888 1994 3100
3-Flying saucer-c/story 100 200 300 800 1800 2800
4-Williamson-a (4 pgs.); Kirby/Everett-c/a 93 186 279 744 1672 2600
5-Kirby monster-c begin 75 150 225 600 1350 2100
6,8,10 57 114 171 456 1028 1600
7-Prototype ish. (Lava Man); 1 panel app. Aunt May (see Str. Tales #97)
59 118 177 472 1061 1650
9-Prototype ish. (Iron Man) 58 116 174 464 1045 1625
11,12,15,17-19: 12-Crandall-a. 46 92 138 359 805 1250
13-Elektro-c/story 46 92 138 368 834 1300
14-Intro/1st app. Colossus-c/sty 56 112 168 448 999 1550
16-1st Metallo-c/story (4/61, Iron Man prototype) 50 100 150 390 870 1350
20-Colossus-c/story (2nd app.) 49 98 147 382 854 1325
21-25: 25-Last 10¢ issue 38 76 114 285 641 1000
26,27,29,30,31,33,34,36-38: 33-(9/62)-Hulk 1st x-over cameo (picture on wall)
36 72 108 259 580 900
28-Prototype ish. (Stone Men) 38 76 114 281 628 975
31-Prototype ish. (Doctor Doom) 38 76 114 285 641 1000
32-Prototype ish. (Dr. Strange)(8/62)-Sazzik The Sorcerer app.; "The Man and the Beehive" story, 1 month before TTA #35 (2nd Antman), came out after "The Man in the Ant Hill" in TTA #27 (1/62) (1st Antman)-Characters from both stories were tested to see which got best fan response 52 104 156 416 933 1450
35-Prototype issue (The Watcher) 37 74 111 274 612 950
39 (3/63)-Origin/1st app. Iron Man & begin series; 1st Iron Man story has Kirby layouts
1700 3400 5950 12,000 30,000 48,000
40-2nd app. Iron Man (in new armor) 200 400 600 1650 3725 5800
41-3rd app. Iron Man; Dr. Strange (villain) app. 125 250 375 1000 2250 3500

Tales of Suspense #74 © MAR

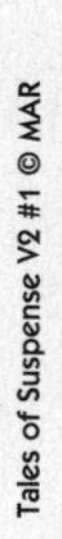
Tales of Suspense V2 #1 © MAR

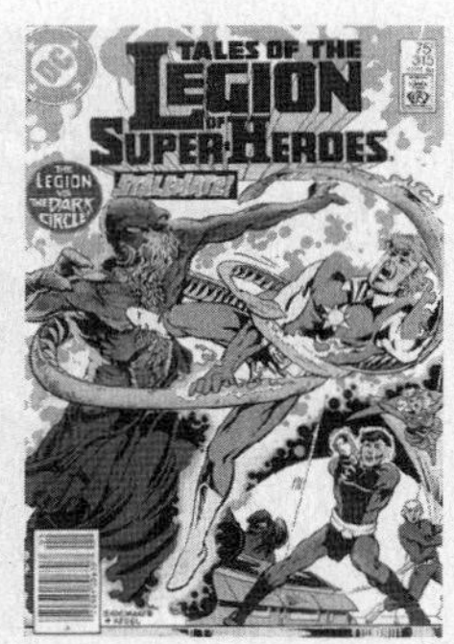

Tales of the LSH #315 © DC

GD 2.0 | VG 4.0 | FN 6.0 | VF 8.0 | VF/NM 9.0 | NM- 9.2

42-45: 45-Intro. & 1st app. Happy & Pepper 86 172 258 688 1544 2400
46,47: 46-1st app. Crimson Dynamo 59 118 177 472 1061 1650
48-New Iron Man armor by Ditko 66 132 198 528 1189 1850
49-1st X-Men x-over (same date as X-Men #3, 1/64); also 1st Avengers x-over (w/o Captain America); 1st Tales of the Watcher back-up story & begins (2nd app. Watcher; see F.F. #13) 84 168 252 672 1511 2350
50-1st app. Mandarin 57 114 171 456 1028 1600
51-1st Scarecrow 32 64 96 230 515 800
52-1st app. The Black Widow (4/64) 107 214 321 856 1928 3000
53-Origin The Watcher; 2nd Black Widow app. 35 70 105 252 564 875
54,55-2nd & 3rd Mandarin app. 26 52 78 182 404 625
56-1st app. Unicorn 27 54 81 189 420 650
57-Origin/1st app. Hawkeye (9/64) 96 192 288 768 1734 2700
58-Captain America battles Iron Man (10/64)-Classic-c; 2nd Kraven app. (Cap's 1st app. in this title) 53 106 159 424 950 1475
59-Iron Man plus Captain America double feature begins (11/64); 1st S.A. Captain America solo story; intro Jarvis, Avenger's butler; classic-c 42 84 126 311 706 1100
60-2nd app. Hawkeye (#64 is 3rd app.) 27 54 81 189 420 650
61,62,64: 62-Origin Mandarin (2/65) 15 30 45 105 233 360
63-1st Silver Age origin Captain America (3/65) 29 58 87 209 467 725
65-G.A. Red Skull in WWII stories(also in #66);-1st Silver-Age Red Skull (5/65). 26 52 78 182 404 625
66-Origin Red Skull 17 34 51 117 259 400
67,68,70: 70-Begin alternating-c features w/Capt. America (even #'s) & Iron Man (odd #'s) 9 18 27 61 123 185
69-1st app. Titanium Man 10 20 30 66 138 210
71-74,78: 78-Col. Nick Fury app. 7 14 21 46 86 125
75-1st app. Agent 13 later named Sharon Carter; intro Batroc 14 28 42 94 207 320
76-2nd app. Batroc & 1st cover app. 8 16 24 52 99 145
77-1st app. Peggy Carter (unnamed) in WW2 flashback (see Captain America #161 & 162) 7 14 21 46 86 125
79-Begin 3 part Iron Man Sub-Mariner battle story; Sub-Mariner-c & cameo; 1st app. Cosmic Cube; 1st modern Red Skull 9 18 27 57 111 165
80-Iron Man battles Sub-Mariner story cont'd in Tales to Astonish #82; classic Red Skull-c 9 18 27 58 114 170
81-93,95,96: 82-Intro the Adaptoid by Kirby (also in #83,84). 88-Mole Man app. in Iron Man story. 92-1st Nick Fury x-over (cameo, as Agent of S.H.I.E.L.D., 8/67). 95-Capt. America's i.d. revealed 6 12 18 40 73 105
94-Intro Modok 10 20 30 66 138 210
97-1st Whiplash 9 18 27 57 111 165
98-Black Panther-c/s; 1st brief app. new Zemo (son?); #99 is 1st full app. 9 18 27 60 120 180
99-Captain America story cont'd in Captain America #100; Iron Man story cont'd in Iron Man & Sub-Mariner #1 8 16 24 51 96 140
Onmibus (See Iron Man Omnibus for reprints of #39-83)
NOTE: **Abel** *a-73-81i(as Gary Michaels),* **J. Buscema** *a-1; c-3.* **Colan** *a-39, 73-99p; c(p)-73, 75, 77, 79, 81, 83, 85-87, 89, 91, 93, 95, 97, 99.* **Crandall** *a-12.* **Davis** *a-38.* **Ditko** *a-1-15, 17-44, 46, 47-49p; c-2, 10i, 13i, 23i.* **Kirby/Ditko** *a-7; c-10, 13, 22, 28, 34.* **Everett** *a-8.* **Forte** *a-5, 9.* **Giacoia** *a-82.* **Heath** *a-2, 10.* **Gil Kane** *a-88p, 89-91; c-88, 89-91p.* **Kirby** *a(p)-2-4, 6-35, 40, 41, 43, 59-75, 77-86, 92-99; layouts-69-75, 77; c(p)4-28(most), 29-56, 58-72, 74, 76, 78, 80, 82, 84, 86, 92, 94, 96, 98.* **Leiber/Fox** *a-42, 43, 45, 51.* **Reinman** *a-13, 26, 44i, 49i, 52i, 53i.* **Tuska** *a-58, 70-74.* **Wood** *c/a-71i.*

TALES OF SUSPENSE
Marvel Comics: V2#1, Jan, 1995 ($6.95, one-shot)
V2#1-James Robinson script; acetate-c. 1 2 3 5 6 8

TALES OF SUSPENSE: CAPTAIN AMERICA & IRON MAN #1 COMMEMORATIVE EDITION
Marvel Comics: 2004 ($3.99, one-shot)
nn-Reprints Captain America (2004) #1 and Iron Man (2004) #1 5.00

TALES OF SWORD & SORCERY (See Dagar)

TALES OF TELLOS (See Tellos)
Image Comics: Oct, 2004 - No. 3, ($3.50, anthology)
1-3: 1-Dezago-s; art by Yates & Rousseau; Wieringo-c. 3-Porter-a 3.50

TALES OF TERROR
Toby Press Publications: 1952 (no month)
1-Fawcette-c; Ravielli-a 37 74 111 222 361 500
NOTE: *This title was cancelled due to similarity to the E.C. title.*

TALES OF TERROR (See Movie Classics)

TALES OF TERROR (Magazine)
Eerie Publications: Summer, 1964
1 6 12 18 41 76 110

TALES OF TERROR

GD 2.0 | VG 4.0 | FN 6.0 | VF 8.0 | VF/NM 9.0 | NM- 9.2

Eclipse Comics: July, 1985 - No. 13, July, 1987 ($2.00, Baxter paper, mature)
1-13: 5-1st Lee Weeks-a. 7-Sam Kieth-a. 10-Snyder-a. 12-Vampire story 4.00

TALES OF TERROR (IDW's...)
IDW Publishing: Sept, 2004 ($16.99, hardcover)
1-Anthology of short graphic stories and text stories; incl. 30 Days of Night 17.00

TALES OF TERROR ANNUAL
E.C. Comics: 1951 - No. 3, 1953 (25¢, 132 pgs., 16 stories each)
nn(1951)(Scarce)-Feldstein infinity-c 1300 2600 3900 10,400 - -
2(1952)-Feldstein-c 303 606 909 1939 3320 4700
3(1953)-Feldstein bondage/torture-c 245 490 735 1568 2684 3800
NOTE: *No. 1 contains three horror and one science fiction comic which came out in 1950. No. 2 contains a horror, crime, and science fiction book which generally had cover dates in 1951, and No. 3 had horror, crime, and shock books that generally appeared in 1952. All E.C. annuals contain four complete books that did not sell on the stands which were rebound in the annual format, minus the covers, and sold from the E.C. office and on the stands in key cities. The contents of each annual may vary in the same year. Crypt Keeper, Vault Keeper, Old Witch app. on all-c.*

TALES OF TERROR ILLUSTRATED (See Terror Illustrated)

TALES OF TEXAS JOHN SLAUGHTER (See Walt Disney Presents, 4-Color #997)

TALES OF THE BEANWORLD
Beanworld Press/Eclipse Comics: Feb, 1985 - No. 19, 1991; No. 20, 1993 - No. 21, 1993 ($1.50/$2.00, B&W)
1-21 3.00

TALES OF THE BIZARRO WORLD
DC Comics: 2000 ($14.95, TPB)
nn-Reprints early Bizarro stories; new Jaime Hernandez-c 15.00

TALES OF THE DARKNESS
Image Comics (Top Cow): Apr, 1998 - No. 4, Dec, 1998 ($2.95)
1-4: 1,2-Portacio-c/a(p). 3,4-Lansing & Nocon-a(p) 3.00
1-American Entertainment Ed. 3.00
#1/2 (1/01, $2.95) 3.00

TALES OF THE DRAGON GUARD (English version of French comic title)
Marvel Comics (Soleil): Apr, 2010 - No. 3, Jun, 2010 ($5.99, limited series)
1-3: 1-Ange-s/Varanda-a. 2-Briones-a. 3-Guinebaud-a 6.00
...: Into the Veil 1-3 (11/10 - No. 3, 1/11) 1-Briones-a. 2-Paty-a. 3-Sieurac-a 6.00

TALES OF THE GREEN BERET
Dell Publishing Co.: Jan, 1967 - No. 5, Oct, 1969
1-Glanzman-a in 1-4 & 5r 3 6 9 19 30 40
2-5: 5-Reprints #1 3 6 9 16 23 30

TALES OF THE GREEN HORNET
Now Comics: Sept, 1990 - No. 2, 1990; V2#1, Jan, 1992 - No.4, Apr, 1992; V3#1, Sept, 1992 - No. 3, Nov, 1992
1,2 3.00
V2#1-4 ($1.95) 3.00
V3#1 ($2.75)-Polybagged w/hologram trading card 4.00
V3#2,3 ($2.50) 3.00

TALES OF THE GREEN LANTERN CORPS (See Green Lantern #107)
DC Comics: May, 1981 - No. 3, July, 1981 (Limited series)
1-Origin of G.L. & the Guardians 2 4 6 10 14 18
2 2 4 6 8 10 12
3 1 3 4 6 8 10
Annual 1 (1/85)-Gil Kane-c/a 1 2 3 5 6 8
TPB (2009, $19.99) r/#1-3 & stories from G.L. #148-151-154,161,162,164-167 ('82-'83) 20.00
Volume 2 TPB (2010, $19.99) r/Annual #1 and stories from G.L. ('83-'85) 20.00
Volume 3 TPB (2010, $19.99) r/Green Lantern #201-206 ('86) 20.00

TALES OF THE INVISIBLE SCARLET O'NEIL (See Harvey Comics Hits #59)

TALES OF THE KILLERS (Magazine)
World Famous Periodicals: V1#10, Dec, 1970 - V1#11, Feb, 1971 (B&W, 52 pg)
V1#10-One pg. Frazetta; r/Crime Does Not Pay 5 10 15 30 50 70
11-similar-c to Crime Does Not Pay #47; contains r/Crime Does Not Pay 4 8 12 27 44 60

TALES OF THE LEGION (Formerly Legion of Super-Heroes)
DC Comics: No. 314, Aug, 1984 - No. 354, Dec, 1987
314-354: 326-r-begin 4.00
Annual 4,5 (1986, 1987)-Formerly LSH Annual 5.00

TALES OF THE MARINES (Formerly Devil-Dog Dugan #1-3)
Atlas Comics (OPI): No. 4, Feb, 1957 (Marines At War #5 on)
4-Powell-a; Severin-c 15 30 45 85 130 175

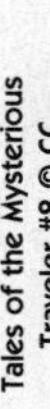
Tales of the Mysterious Traveler #8 © CC

Tales of the Teen Titans #91 © DC

Tales of the Unexpected #43 © DC

TALES OF THE MARVELS
Marvel Comics: 1995/1996 (all acetate, painted-c)

	GD 2.0	VG 4.0	FN 6.0	VF 8.0	VF/NM 9.0	NM- 9.2
...Blockbuster 1 (1995, $5.95, one-shot), ...Inner Demons 1 (1996, $5.95, one shot), ...Wonder Years 1,2 (1995, $4.95, limited series)						6.00

TALES OF THE MARVEL UNIVERSE
Marvel Comics: Feb, 1997 ($2.95, one-shot)

	GD 2.0	VG 4.0	FN 6.0	VF 8.0	VF/NM 9.0	NM- 9.2
1-Anthology; wraparound-c; Thunderbolts, Ka-Zar app.						4.00

TALES OF THE MYSTERIOUS TRAVELER (See Mysterious...)
Charlton Comics: Aug, 1956 - No. 13, June, 1959; V2#14, Oct, 1985 - No. 15, Dec, 1985

	GD 2.0	VG 4.0	FN 6.0	VF 8.0	VF/NM 9.0	NM- 9.2
1-No Ditko-a; Giordano/Alascia-c	50	100	150	315	533	750
2-Ditko-a(1)	41	82	123	256	428	600
3-Ditko-c/a(1)	42	84	126	265	445	625
4-7-Ditko-c/a(3-4 stories each)	48	96	144	302	514	725
8,9-Ditko-a(1-3 each). 8-Rocke-c	41	82	123	250	418	585
10,11-Ditko-c/a(3-4 each)	44	88	132	277	469	660
12	18	36	54	105	165	225
13-Baker-a (r?)	19	38	57	111	176	240
V2#14,15 (1985)-Ditko-c/a-low print run	2	3	4	6	8	10

TALES OF THE NEW GODS
DC Comics: 2008 ($19.99, TPB)

	GD 2.0	VG 4.0	FN 6.0	VF 8.0	VF/NM 9.0	NM- 9.2
SC-Reprints from Jack Kirby's Fourth World, Orion and Mister Miracle Special; includes previously unpublished story by Millar-s/Ditko-a						20.00

TALES OF THE NEW TEEN TITANS
DC Comics: June, 1982 - No. 4, Sept, 1982 (Limited series)

	GD 2.0	VG 4.0	FN 6.0	VF 8.0	VF/NM 9.0	NM- 9.2
1	2	4	6	11	16	20
2-4	1	3	4	6	8	10

TALES OF THE PONY EXPRESS (TV)
Dell Publishing Co.: No. 829, Aug, 1957 - No. 942, Oct, 1958

	GD 2.0	VG 4.0	FN 6.0	VF 8.0	VF/NM 9.0	NM- 9.2
Four Color 829 (#1) -Painted-c	5	10	15	35	63	90
Four Color 942-Title -Pony Express	5	10	15	31	53	75

TALES OF THE REALM
CrossGen Comics/MVCreations #4-on: Oct, 2003 - No. 5, May, 2004 ($2.95, limited series)

	GD 2.0	VG 4.0	FN 6.0	VF 8.0	VF/NM 9.0	NM- 9.2
1-5-Robert Kirkman-s/Matt Tyree-a						3.00
Volume 1 HC (8/04, $39.95, dust jacket) r/#1-5; sketch pages and concept art						40.00

TALES OF THE SINESTRO CORPS (See Green Lantern and Green Lantern Corps x-over)
DC Comics: Nov, 2007 - Jan, 2008 ($2.99/$3.99, one-shots)

	GD 2.0	VG 4.0	FN 6.0	VF 8.0	VF/NM 9.0	NM- 9.2
...: Cyborg-Superman (12/07, $2.99) Burnett-s/Blaine-a/VanSciver-c; JLA app.						3.00
...: Ion (1/08, $2.99) Marz-s/Lacombe-a/Benes-c; Sodam Yat app.						3.00
...: Parallax (11/07, $2.99) Marz-s/Melo-a; Kyle Rayner vs. Parallax						3.00
...: Superman-Prime (12/07, $3.99) Johns-s/VanSciver-c; origin re-told w/Ordway-a						4.00

TALES OF THE TEENAGE MUTANT NINJA TURTLES (See Teenage Mutant...)
Mirage Studios: May, 1987 - No. 7, Aug (Apr-c), 1989 (B&W, $1.50)

	GD 2.0	VG 4.0	FN 6.0	VF 8.0	VF/NM 9.0	NM- 9.2
1	2	4	6	10	14	18
2-Title merges w/Teenage Mutant Ninja...	1	2	3	5	6	8

TALES OF THE TEEN TITANS (Formerly The New Teen Titans)
DC Comics: No. 41, Apr, 1984 - No. 91, July, 1988 (75¢)

	GD 2.0	VG 4.0	FN 6.0	VF 8.0	VF/NM 9.0	NM- 9.2
41,45-49: 46-Aqualad & Aquagirl join						4.00
42,43: The Judas Contract parts 1&2 with Deathstroke the Terminator; concludes with part 4 in Annual #3.						6.00
44-Dick Grayson becomes Nightwing (3rd to be Nightwing) & joins Titans; Judas Contract part 3; Jericho (Deathstroke's son) joins; origin Deathstroke	5	10	15	33	57	80
50-Double size; app. Betty Kane (Bat-Girl) out of costume						6.00
51,52,56-91: 52-1st brief app. Azrael (not same as newer character). 56-Intro Jinx. 57-Neutron app. 59-r/DC Comics Presents #26. 60-91-r/New Teen Titans Baxter series. 68-B. Smith-c. 70-Origin Kole						3.00
53-55: 53-1st full app. Azrael; Deathstroke cameo. 54,55-Deathstroke-c/stories						4.00
Annual 3(1984, $1.25)-Part 4 of The Judas Contract; Deathstroke-c/story; Death of Terra; indicia says Teen Titans Annual; previous annuals listed as New Teen Titans Annual #1,2	1	3	4	6	8	10
Annual 4-(1986, $1.25)						4.00

TALES OF THE TEXAS RANGERS (See Jace Pearson...)

TALES OF THE THING (Fantastic Four)
Marvel Comics: May, 2005 - No. 3, July, 2005 ($2.50, limited series)

	GD 2.0	VG 4.0	FN 6.0	VF 8.0	VF/NM 9.0	NM- 9.2
1-3-Dr. Strange app; Randy Green-c						3.00

TALES OF THE TMNT (Also see Teenage Mutant Ninja Turtles)
Mirage Studios: Jan, 2004 - Present ($2.95/$3.25, B&W)

	GD 2.0	VG 4.0	FN 6.0	VF 8.0	VF/NM 9.0	NM- 9.2
1-7: 1-Brizuela-a						5.00
8-70: 8-Begin $3.25-c. 47-Origin of the Super Turtles						4.00

TALES OF THE UNEXPECTED (Becomes The Unexpected #105 on)(See Adventure #75, Super DC Giant)
National Periodical Publications: Feb-Mar, 1956 - No. 104, Dec-Jan, 1967-68

	GD 2.0	VG 4.0	FN 6.0	VF 8.0	VF/NM 9.0	NM- 9.2
1	125	250	375	1000	2250	3500
2	46	92	138	359	805	1250
3-5	35	70	105	252	564	875
6-10: 6-1st Silver Age issue	27	54	81	194	435	675
11,14,19,20	20	40	60	141	313	485
12,13,16,18,21-24: All have Kirby-a. 16-Characters named 'Thor' (with a magic hammer) and Loki by Kirby (8/57, characters do not look like Marvel's Thor & Loki)	23	46	69	164	362	560
15,17-Grey tone-c; Kirby-a	27	54	81	184	410	635
25-30	17	34	51	119	265	410
31-39	15	30	45	105	233	360
40-Space Ranger begins (8/59, 3rd ap.), ends #82	121	242	363	968	2184	3400
41,42-Space Ranger stories	41	82	123	303	689	1075
43-1st Space Ranger-c this title; grey tone-c	71	142	213	568	1284	2000
44-46	30	60	90	216	483	750
47-50	25	50	75	175	388	600
51-60: 54-Dinosaur-c/story	21	42	63	147	324	500
61-67: 67-Last 10¢ issue	17	34	51	117	259	400
68-82: 82-Last Space Ranger	10	20	30	66	138	210
83-90,92-99	6	12	18	40	73	105
91,100: 91-1st Automan (also in #94,97)	6	12	18	41	76	110
101-104	6	12	18	37	66	95

NOTE: ***Neal Adams** c-104. **Anderson** a-50. **Brown** a-50-82(Space Ranger); c-19, 40, & many Space Ranger-c. **Cameron** a-24, 27, 29; c-24. **Heath** a-49. **Bob Kane** a-24, 48. **Kirby** a-12, 13, 15-18, 21-24; c-13, 18, 22. **Meskin** a-15, 18, 26, 27, 35, 66. **Moreira** a-16, 20, 29, 38, 44, 62, 71; c-38. **Roussos** c-10. **Wildey** a-31.*

TALES OF THE UNEXPECTED (See Crisis Aftermath: The Spectre)
DC Comics: Dec, 2006 - No. 8, Jul, 2007 ($3.99, limited series)

	GD 2.0	VG 4.0	FN 6.0	VF 8.0	VF/NM 9.0	NM- 9.2
1-8-The Spectre, Lapham-s/Battle-a; Dr. 13, Azzarello-s/Chiang-a. 4-Wrightson-c						4.00
1-Variant Spectre cover by Neal Adams						5.00
The Spectre: Tales of the Unexpected TPB (2007, $14.99) r/#4-8						15.00

TALES OF THE VAMPIRES (Also see Buffy the Vampire Slayer and related titles)
Dark Horse Comics: 2003 - No. 5, Apr, 2004 ($2.99, limited series)

	GD 2.0	VG 4.0	FN 6.0	VF 8.0	VF/NM 9.0	NM- 9.2
1-Short stories by Joss Whedon and others. 1-Totleben-c. 3-Powell-c. 4-Edlund-c						3.00
TPB (11/04, $15.95) r/#1-5; afterword by Marv Wolfman						16.00

TALES OF THE WEST (See 3-D...)

TALES OF THE WITCHBLADE
Image Comics (Top Cow Productions): Nov, 1996 - No. 9 ($2.95)

	GD 2.0	VG 4.0	FN 6.0	VF 8.0	VF/NM 9.0	NM- 9.2
1/2	1	2	3	5	7	9
1/2 Gold	2	4	6	9	12	15
1-Daniel-c/a(p)	1	3	4	6	8	10
1-Variant-c by Turner	2	4	6	9	12	15
1-Platinum Edition	3	6	9	16	23	30
2,3						6.00
4-6: 6-Green-c						5.00
7-9: 9-Lara Croft-c						4.00
7-Variant-c by Turner	1	2	3	5	6	8
Witchblade: Distinctions (4/01, $14.95, TPB) r/#1-6; Green-c						15.00

TALES OF THE WITCHBLADE COLLECTED EDITION
Image Comics (Top Cow): May, 1998 - No. 2 ($4.95/$5.95, square-bound)

	GD 2.0	VG 4.0	FN 6.0	VF 8.0	VF/NM 9.0	NM- 9.2
1,2: 1-r/#1,2. 2-($5.95) r/#3,4						6.00

TALES OF THE WIZARD OF OZ (See Wizard of OZ, 4-Color #1308)

TALES OF THE ZOMBIE (Magazine)
Marvel Comics Group: Aug, 1973 - No. 10, Mar, 1975 (75¢, B&W)

	GD 2.0	VG 4.0	FN 6.0	VF 8.0	VF/NM 9.0	NM- 9.2
V1#1-Reprint/Menace #5; origin Simon Garth	5	10	15	34	60	85
2,3: 2-2nd app. of Brother Voodoo; Everett biog. & memorial	4	8	12	25	40	55
V2#1(#4)-Photos & text of James Bond movie "Live & Let Die"	3	6	9	20	31	42
5-10: 8-Kaluta-a	3	6	9	18	28	38
Annual 1(Summer,'75)(#11)-B&W; Everett, Buscema-a	3	6	9	20	31	42

NOTE: *Brother Voodoo app. 2, 5, 6, 10. **Alcala** a-7-9. **Boris** c-1-4. **Colan** a-2r, 6. **Heath** a-5r. **Reese** a-2. **Tuska** a-2r.*

TALES OF VOODOO
Eerie Publications: V1#11, Nov, 1968 - V7#6, Nov, 1974 (Magazine)

Tales of Wells Fargo FC #968 © DELL

Tales to Astonish #93 © MAR

Tangent Comics/The Batman #1 © DC

	GD 2.0	VG 4.0	FN 6.0	VF 8.0	VF/NM 9.0	NM- 9.2
V1#11	7	14	21	48	89	130
V2#1(3/69)-V2#4(9/69)	5	10	15	33	57	80
V3#1-6('70): 4- "Claws of the Cat" redrawn from Climax #1	4	8	12	28	47	65
V4#1-6('71), V5#1-7('72), V6#1-6('73), V7#1-6('74)	4	8	12	28	47	65
Annual 1	5	10	15	30	50	70

NOTE: *Bondage-c-V1#10, V2#4, V3#4.*

TALES OF WELLS FARGO (TV)(See Western Roundup under Dell Giants)
Dell Publishing Co.: No. 876, Feb, 1958 - No. 1215, Oct-Dec, 1961

	GD 2.0	VG 4.0	FN 6.0	VF 8.0	VF/NM 9.0	NM- 9.2
Four Color 876 (#1)-Photo-c	8	16	24	52	99	145
Four Color 968 (2/59), 1023, 1075 (3/60), 1113 (7-9/60)-All photo-c. 1075,1113-Both have variant edition, back-c comic strip	7	14	21	48	89	130
Four Color 1167 (3-5/61), 1215-Photo-c	7	14	21	44	82	120

TALESPIN (Also see Cartoon Tales & Disney's Talespin Limited Series)
Disney Comics: June, 1991 - No. 7, Dec, 1991 ($1.50)

	GD 2.0	VG 4.0	FN 6.0	VF 8.0	VF/NM 9.0	NM- 9.2
1-7						3.00

TALES TO ASTONISH (Becomes The Incredible Hulk #102 on)
Atlas (MAP No. 1/ZPC No. 2-14/VPI No. 15-21/Marvel No. 22 on: Jan, 1959 - No. 101, Mar, 1968

	GD 2.0	VG 4.0	FN 6.0	VF 8.0	VF/NM 9.0	NM- 9.2
1-Jack Davis-a; monster-c.	367	734	1101	3120	7060	11,000
2-Ditko flying saucer-c (Martians); #2-4 have sci/fi-c.	111	222	333	888	1994	3100
3,4	93	186	279	744	1672	2600
5-Prototype issue (Stone Men); Williamson-a (4 pgs.); Kirby monster-c begin	79	158	237	632	1416	2200
6-Prototype issue (Stone Men)	59	118	177	472	1061	1650
7-Prototype issue (Toad Men)	59	118	177	472	1061	1650
8-10	57	114	171	456	1028	1600
11,12,14,17-20	46	92	138	359	805	1250
13-(11/60) 1st app. Groot (Guardians of the Galaxy) by Kirby-cvr/sty; swipes story from Menace #8	550	1100	1650	4000	6000	8000
15-Prototype issue (Electro)	46	92	138	368	834	1300
16-Prototype issue (Stone Men) named "Thorr"	46	92	138	368	834	1300
21-(7/61)-Hulk prototype	50	100	150	390	870	1350
22-26,28-31,33,34	36	72	108	266	596	925
27-1st Ant-Man app. (1/62); last 10¢ issue (see Strange Tales #73,78 & Tales of Suspense #32)	900	1800	3600	11,000	28,000	45,000
32-Sandman prototype	38	76	114	281	628	975
35-(9/62)-2nd app. Ant-Man, 1st in costume; begin series & Ant-Man-c	290	580	870	2500	6250	10,000
36-3rd app. Ant-Man	91	182	273	728	1639	2550
37,39,40	51	102	153	398	887	1375
38-1st app. Egghead	53	106	159	413	932	1450
41-43	44	88	132	326	738	1150
44-Origin & 1st app. The Wasp (6/63)	175	350	700	1500	2550	3600
45-47	29	58	87	209	467	725
48-Origin & 1st app. The Porcupine	30	60	90	216	483	750
49-Ant-Man becomes Giant Man (11/63)	50	100	150	400	900	1400
50,51,53-56,58: 50-Origin/1st app. Human Top (alias Whirlwind). 58-Origin Colossus	19	38	57	131	291	450
52-Origin/1st app. Black Knight (2/64)	23	46	69	161	356	550
57-Early Spider-Man app. (7/64)	37	74	111	274	612	950
59-Giant Man vs. Hulk feature story (9/64); Hulk's 1st app. this title; 1st mention that anger triggers his transformation	36	72	108	259	580	900
60-Giant Man & Hulk double feature begins	27	54	81	189	420	650
61,64-69: 61-All Ditko issue; 1st app. of Glenn Talbot; 1st mailbag. 65-New Giant Man costume. 68-New Human Top costume. 69-Last Giant Man	13	26	39	89	195	300
62-1st app./origin The Leader; new Wasp costume; Hulk pin-up page missing from many copies	20	40	60	138	307	475
63-Origin Leader continues	15	30	45	100	220	340
70-Sub-Mariner & Incredible Hulk begins (8/65)	14	28	42	96	211	325
71-81: 72-Begin alternating-c features w/Sub-Mariner (even #'s) & Hulk (odd #'s). 79-Hulk vs. Hercules-c/story. 81-1st app. Boomerang	7	14	21	44	82	120
82-Iron Man battles Sub-Mariner (1st Iron Man x-over outside The Avengers & TOS); story cont'd from Tales of Suspense #80	8	16	24	54	102	150
83-89,94-99: 97-X-Men cameo (brief)	6	12	18	37	66	95
90-1st app. The Abomination	8	16	24	56	108	160
91-The Abomination debut continues & 1st cover	8	16	24	56	108	160
92-1st Silver Surfer x-over (outside of Fantastic Four, 6/67); 1 panel cameo only	7	14	21	48	89	130
93-Hulk battles Silver Surfer-c/story (1st full x-over)	19	38	57	131	291	450
100-Hulk battles Sub-Mariner full-length story	7	14	21	48	89	130
101-Hulk story cont'd in Incredible Hulk #102; Sub-Mariner story continued in Iron Man & Sub-Mariner #1	8	16	24	54	102	150

NOTE: ***Ayers** c(i)-9-12, 16, 18, 19. **Berg** a-1. **Burgos** a-62-64p. **Buscema** a-85-87p. **Colan** a(p)-70-76, 78-82, 84, 85, 101; c(p)-71-76, 78, 80, 82, 84, 86, 88, 90. **Ditko** a-1, 3-48, 50i, 60-67p; c-2, 7i, 8i, 14i, 17i. **Everett** a-78, 79i, 80-84, 85-90i, 94i, 95, 96; c(i)-79-81, 83, 86, 88. **Forte** a-6. **Kane** a-76, 88-91; c-89, 91. **Kirby** a(p)-1, 5-34-40, 44, 49-51, 68-70, 82, 83; layouts-71-84; c(p)-1, 3-48, 50-70, 72, 73, 75, 77, 78, 79, 81, 85, 90. **Kirby/Ditko** a-7, 8, 12, 13, 50; c-7, 8, 10, 13. **Leiber/Fox** a-47, 48, 50, 51. **Powell** a-65-69p, 73, 74. **Reinman** a-6, 36, 45, 46, 54i, 56-60i.*

TALES TO ASTONISH (2nd Series)
Marvel Comics Group: Dec, 1979 - No. 14, Jan, 1981

	GD 2.0	VG 4.0	FN 6.0	VF 8.0	VF/NM 9.0	NM- 9.2
V1#1-Reprints Sub-Mariner #1 by Buscema	2	4	6	10	14	18
2-14: Reprints Sub-Mariner #2-14	1	3	4	6	8	10

TALES TO ASTONISH
Marvel Comics: V3#1, Oct, 1994 ($6.95, one-shot)

	GD 2.0	VG 4.0	FN 6.0	VF 8.0	VF/NM 9.0	NM- 9.2
V3#1-Peter David scripts; acetate, painted-c						7.00

TALES TO HOLD YOU SPELLBOUND (See Spellbound)

TALES TO OFFEND
Dark Horse Comics: July, 1997 ($2.95, one-shot)

	GD 2.0	VG 4.0	FN 6.0	VF 8.0	VF/NM 9.0	NM- 9.2
1-Frank Miller-s/a, EC-style cover						4.00

TALES TOO TERRIBLE TO TELL (Becomes Terrology #10, 11)
New England Comics: Wint, 1989-90 - No. 11, Nov-Dec.1993 ($2.95/$3.50, B&W with card-stock covers)

	GD 2.0	VG 4.0	FN 6.0	VF 8.0	VF/NM 9.0	NM- 9.2
1-($2.95) Reprints of non-EC pre-code horror; EC-style cover by Bissette						5.00
1-($3.50, 5-6/93) Second printing with alternate cover not by Bissette						4.00
2-8-($3.50) Story reprints, history of the pre-code titles and creators; cover galleries (B&W) inside & on back-c (color)						4.00
9-11-($2.95) 10,11-"Terrology" on cover						4.00

TALKING KOMICS
Belda Record & Publ. Co.: 1947 (20 pgs, slick-c)

	GD 2.0	VG 4.0	FN 6.0	VF 8.0	VF/NM 9.0	NM- 9.2
Each comic contained a record that followed the story - much like the Golden Record sets. Known titles: Chirpy Cricket, Lonesome Octopus, Sleepy Santa, Grumpy Shark, Flying Turtle, Happy Grasshopper with records...	3	6	9	17	26	35

TALLY-HO COMICS
Swappers Quarterly (Baily Publ. Co.): Dec, 1944

	GD 2.0	VG 4.0	FN 6.0	VF 8.0	VF/NM 9.0	NM- 9.2
nn-Frazetta's 1st work as Giunta's assistant; Man in Black horror story; violence; Giunta-c	57	114	171	362	619	875

TALULLAH (See Comic Books Series I)

TALON (From Batman Court of Owls crossover)
DC Comics: No. 0, Nov, 2012 - No. 17, May, 2014 ($2.99)

	GD 2.0	VG 4.0	FN 6.0	VF 8.0	VF/NM 9.0	NM- 9.2
0-17: 0-Origin of Calvin Rose; March-a. 7-11-Bane app.						3.00

TAMMY, TELL ME TRUE
Dell Publishing Co.: No. 1233, 1961

	GD 2.0	VG 4.0	FN 6.0	VF 8.0	VF/NM 9.0	NM- 9.2
Four Color 1233-Movie	6	12	18	38	69	100

TANGENT COMICS

	GD 2.0	VG 4.0	FN 6.0	VF 8.0	VF/NM 9.0	NM- 9.2
.../ THE ATOM, DC Comics: Dec, 1997 ($2.95, one-shot)						
1-Dan Jurgens-s/Jurgens & Paul Ryan-a						3.00
.../ THE BATMAN, DC Comics: Sept, 1998 ($1.95, one-shot)						
1-Dan Jurgens-s/Klaus Janson-a						3.00
.../ DOOM PATROL, DC Comics: Dec, 1997 ($2.95, one-shot)						
1- Dan Jurgens-s/Sean Chen & Kevin Conrad-a						3.00
.../ THE FLASH, DC Comics: Dec, 1997 ($2.95, one-shot)						
1-Todd Dezago-s/Gary Frank & Cam Smith-a						3.00
.../ GREEN LANTERN, DC Comics: Dec, '97 ($2.95, one-shot)						
1-James Robinson-s/J.H. Williams III & Mick Gray-a						3.00
.../ JLA, DC Comics: Sept, 1998 ($1.95, one-shot)						
1-Dan Jurgens-s/Banks & Rapmund-a						3.00
.../ THE JOKER, DC Comics: Dec, 1997 ($2.95, one-shot)						
1-Karl Kesel-s/Matt Haley & Tom Simmons-a						3.00
.../ THE JOKER'S WILD, DC Comics: Sept, 1998 ($1.95, one-shot)						
1-Kesel & Simmons-s/Phillips & Rodriguez-a						3.00
.../ METAL MEN, DC Comics: Dec, 1997 ($2.95, one-shot)						
1-Ron Marz-s/Mike McKone & Mark McKenna-a						3.00
.../ NIGHTWING, DC Comics: Dec, 1997 ($2.95, one-shot)						
1-John Ostrander-s/Jan Duursema-a						3.00
.../ NIGHTWING: NIGHTFORCE, DC Comics: Sept, 1998 ($1.95, one-shot)						
1-John Ostrander-s/Jan Duursema-a						3.00

Tank Girl 2 #2 © DH

Target Comics #11 © NP

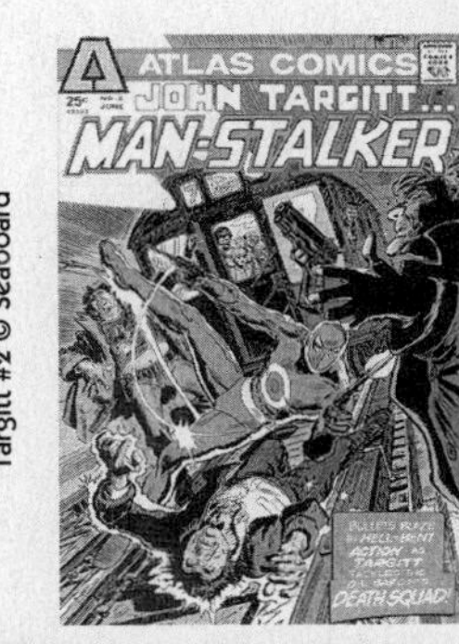

Targitt #2 © Seaboard

GD 2.0 | VG 4.0 | FN 6.0 | VF 8.0 | VF/NM 9.0 | NM- 9.2

.../ POWERGIRL, DC Comics: Sept, 1998 ($1.95, one-shot)
1-Marz-s/Abell & Vines-a 3.00

.../ SEA DEVILS, DC Comics: Dec, 1997 ($2.95, one-shot)
1-Kurt Busiek-s/Vince Giarrano & Tom Palmer-a 3.00

.../ SECRET SIX, DC Comics: Dec, 1997 ($2.95, one-shot)
1-Chuck Dixon-s/Tom Grummett & Lary Stucker-a 3.00

.../ THE SUPERMAN, DC Comics: Sept, 1998 ($1.95, one-shot)
1-Millar-s/Guice-a 3.00

.../ TALES OF THE GREEN LANTERN, DC Comics: Sept, 1998 ($1.95, one-shot)
1-Story & art by various 3.00

.../ THE TRIALS OF THE FLASH, DC Comics: Sept, 1998 ($1.95, one-shot)
1-Dezago-s/Pelletier & Lanning-a 3.00

.../ WONDER WOMAN DC Comics: Sept, 1998 ($1.95, one-shot),
1-Peter David-s/Unzueta & Mendoza-a 3.00
... Volume One TPB (2007, $19.99) r/The Atom, Metal Men, Green Lantern, The Flash, Sea Devils one-shots; intro and new cover by Jurgens 20.00
... Volume Two TPB (2008, $19.99) r/Batman, Doom Patrol, Joker, Nightwing and Secret Six one-shots; new cover by Jurgens 20.00
... Volume Three TPB (2008, $19.99) r/The Superman, Wonder Woman, Nightwing: Nightforce, The Joker's Wild, The Trials of the Flash, Tales of the Green Lantern, Powergirl, and JLA one-shots; new cover by Jurgens 20.00

TANGENT: SUPERMAN'S REIGN
DC Comics: May, 2008 - No. 12, Apr, 2009 ($2.99, limited series)
1-12-Jurgens-s; Flash & Green Lantern app.; back-up histories of Tangent heroes 3.00
Volume 1 TPB (2009, $19.99) r/#1-6 & Justice League of America #16 20.00
Volume 2 TPB (2009, $19.99) r/#7-12 20.00

TANGLED WEB (See Spider-Man's Tangled Web)

TANK GIRL
Dark Horse Comics: May, 1991 - No. 4, Aug, 1991 ($2.25, B&W, mini-series)
1-Contains Dark Horse trading cards 6.00
2-4 4.00
...: Dark Nuggets (Image Comics, 12/09, $3.99) Martin-s/Dayglo-a 4.00
...: Dirty Helmets (Image Comics, 4/10, $3.99) Martin-s/Dayglo-a 4.00
...: Hairy Heroes (Image Comics, 8/10, $3.99) Martin-s/Dayglo-a 4.00

TANK GIRL: APOCALYPSE
DC Comics: Nov, 1995 - No. 4, Feb, 1996 ($2.25, limited series)
1-4 4.00

TANK GIRL: MOVIE ADAPTATION
DC Comics: 1995 ($5.95, 68 pgs., one-shot)
nn-Peter Milligan scripts 6.00

TANK GIRL: TANK GIRL GOLD
Titan Comics: Sept, 2016 - No. 4, Mar, 2017 ($3.99, limited series)
1-4: Alan Martin-s/Brett Parson-a. 2-MAD spoof 4.00

TANK GIRL: THE GIFTING
IDW Publishing: May, 2007 - No. 4, Aug, 2007 ($3.99, limited series)
1-4: 1-Ashley Wood-a/c; Alan Martin-s; 3 covers 4.00

TANK GIRL: THE ODYSSEY
DC Comics: May, 1995 - No.4, Oct, 1995 ($2.25, limited series)
1-4: Peter Milligan scripts; Hewlett-a 4.00

TANK GIRL: THE ROYAL ESCAPE
IDW Publishing: Mar, 2010 - No. 4, Jun, 2010 ($3.99, limited series)
1-4: Alan Martin-s/Rufus Dayglo-a/c 4.00

TANK GIRL: 21ST CENTURY TANK GIRL
Titan Comics: Jul, 2015 - No. 3, Sept, 2015 ($3.99, limited series)
1-3: Alan Martin-s; art by Hewlett, Bond, Mahfood, Parson & others 4.00

TANK GIRL 2
Dark Horse Comics: June, 1993 - No. 4, Sept, 1993 ($2.50, lim. series, mature)
1-4: Jamie Hewlett & Alan Martin-s/a 4.00
TPB (2/95, $17.95) r/#1-4 18.00

TANK GIRL: TWO GIRLS, ONE TANK
Titan Comics: Jun, 2016 - No. 4, Sept, 2016 ($3.99, limited series)
1-4: Alan Martin-s/Brett Parson-a 4.00

TAPPAN'S BURRO (See Zane Grey & 4-Color #449)

TAPPING THE VEIN (Clive Barker's...)

Eclipse Comics: 1989 - No. 5, 1992 ($6.95, squarebound, mature, 68 pgs.)
Book 1-5: 1-Russell-a, Bolton-c. 2-Bolton-a. 4-Die-cut-c 7.00
TPB (2002, $24.95, Checker Book Publ. Group) r/#1-5 25.00

TARANTULA (See Weird Suspense)

TARGET: AIRBOY
Eclipse Comics: Mar, 1988 ($1.95)
1 3.00

TARGET COMICS (...Western Romances #106 on)
Funnies, Inc./Novelty Publications/Star Publ.: Feb, 1940 - V10#3 (#105), Aug-Sept, 1949

	GD 2.0	VG 4.0	FN 6.0	VF 8.0	VF/NM 9.0	NM- 9.2
V1#1-Origin & 1st app. Manowar, The White Streak by Burgos, & Bulls-Eye Bill by Everett; City Editor (ends #5), High Grass Twins by Jack Cole (ends #4), T-Men by Joe Simon (ends #9), Rip Rory (ends #4), Fantastic Feature Films by Tarpe Mills (ends #39), & Calling 2-R (ends #14) begin; marijuana use story	459	918	1377	3350	5925	8500
2-Everett-c/a	245	490	735	1568	2684	3800
3,4-Everett, Jack Cole-a	161	322	483	1030	1765	2500
5-Origin The White Streak in text; Space Hawk by Wolverton begins (6/40) (see Blue Bolt & Circus)	459	918	1377	3350	5925	8500
6-The Chameleon by Everett begins (7/40, 1st app.); White Streak origin cont'd. in text; early mention of comic collecting in letter column; 1st letter column in comics? (7/40)	245	490	735	1568	2684	3800
7-Wolverton Spacehawk-c/story (scarce)	1250	2500	3750	9200	17,100	25,000
8-Classic sci-fi cover (scarce)	343	686	1029	2400	4200	6000
9-White Streak-c	174	348	522	1114	1907	2700
10-Intro/1st app. The Target (11/40); Simon-c; Spacehawk-s; text piece by Wolverton	300	600	900	1920	3310	4700
11-Origin The Target & The Targeteers	187	374	561	1197	2049	2900
12-(1/41) Target & The Targeteers-c	142	284	426	909	1555	2200
V2#1-Target by Bob Wood; Uncle Sam flag-c	100	200	300	635	1093	1550
2-Ten part Treasure Island serial begins; Harold Delay-a; reprinted in Catholic Comics V3#1-10 (see Key Comics #5)	68	136	204	435	743	1050
3-5: 4-Kit Carter, The Cadet begins	65	130	195	416	708	1000
6-9: Red Seal with White Streak in #6-10	61	122	183	390	670	950
10-Classic-c	113	226	339	718	1234	1750
11,12: 12-10-part Last of the Mohicans serial begins; Delay-a	58	116	174	371	636	900
V3#1-3,5-7,9,10: 10-Last Wolverton issue	47	94	141	296	498	700
4-V for Victory-c	73	146	219	467	796	1125
8-Hitler, Tojo, Flag-c; 6-part Gulliver Travels serial begins; Delay-a.	97	194	291	621	1061	1500
11,12	21	42	63	122	199	275
V4#1-4,7-12: 8-X-Mas-c	15	30	45	86	133	180
5-Classic Statue of Liberty-c	24	48	72	142	234	325
6-Targetoons by Wolverton	19	38	57	111	176	240
V5#1-8	14	28	42	80	115	150
V6#1-4,6-10	14	28	42	76	108	140
5-Classic Tojo hanging/Buy War Bonds WWII-c	81	162	243	518	884	1250
V7#1-12	12	24	36	67	94	120
V8#1,3-5,8,9,11,12	11	22	33	60	83	105
2,6,7-Krigstein-a	12	24	36	67	94	120
10-L.B. Cole-c	25	50	75	150	245	340
V9#1,4,6,8,10-L.B. Cole-c	25	50	75	150	245	340
2,3,5,7,9,11, V10#1	11	22	33	60	83	105
12-Classic L.B. Cole-c	39	48	117	231	378	525
V10#2,3-L.B. Cole-c	25	50	75	150	245	340

NOTE: ***Certa*** *c-V8#9, 11, 12, V9#5, 9, 11, V10#1.* ***Jack Cole*** *a-1-8.* ***Everett*** *a-1-9; c(signed Blake)-1, 2.* ***Al Fago*** *c-V6#8.* ***Sid Greene*** *c-V2#9, 12, V3#3.* ***Walter Johnson*** *c-V5#6, V6#4.* ***Tarpe Mills*** *a-1-4, 6, 8, 11, V3#1.* ***Rico*** *a-V7#4, 10, V8#5, 6, V9#3; c-V7#6, 8, 10, V8#2, 4, 6, 7.* ***Simon*** *a-1, 2.* ***Bob Wood*** *c-V2#2, 3, 5, 6.*

TARGET: THE CORRUPTORS (TV)
Dell Publishing Co.: No. 1306, Mar-May, 1962 - No. 3, Oct-Dec, 1962
(All have photo-c)

	GD 2.0	VG 4.0	FN 6.0	VF 8.0	VF/NM 9.0	NM- 9.2
Four Color 1306(#1), #2,3	5	10	15	33	57	80

TARGET WESTERN ROMANCES (Formerly Target Comics; becomes Flaming Western Romances #3)
Star Publications: No. 106, Oct-Nov, 1949 - No. 107, Dec-Jan, 1949-50

	GD 2.0	VG 4.0	FN 6.0	VF 8.0	VF/NM 9.0	NM- 9.2
106(#1)-Silhouette nudity panel; L.B. Cole-c	25	50	75	150	245	340
107(#2)-L.B. Cole-c; lingerie panels	22	44	66	132	216	300

TARGITT
Atlas/Seaboard Publ.: March, 1975 - No. 3, July, 1975

	GD 2.0	VG 4.0	FN 6.0	VF 8.0	VF/NM 9.0	NM- 9.2
1-3: 1-Origin; Nostrand-a in all. 2-1st in costume. 3-Becomes Man-Stalker	2	4	6	10	14	18

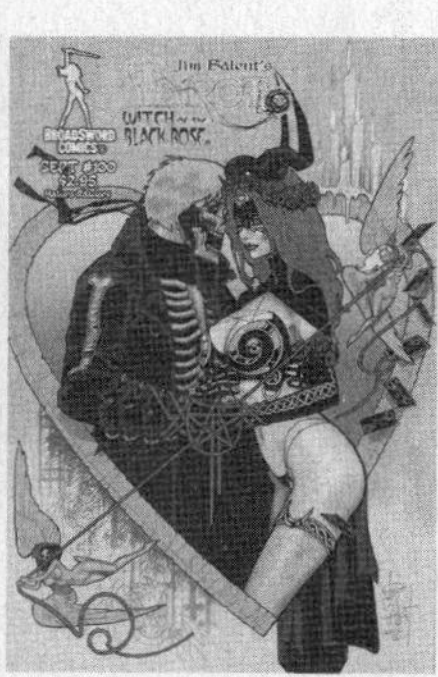

Tarot: Witch of the Black Rose #100 © Jim Balent

Tarzan #7 © ERB

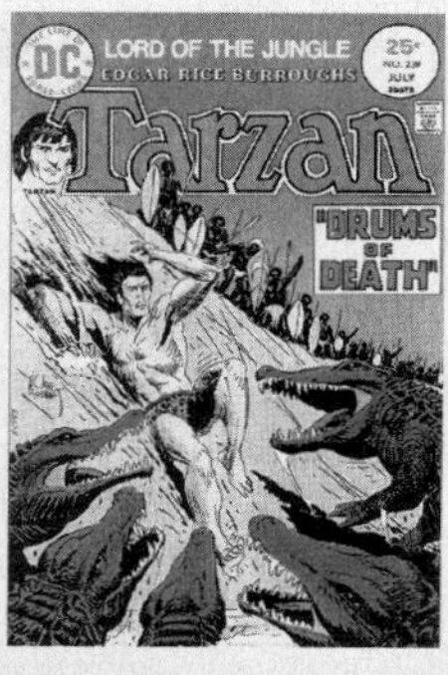

Tarzan #239 © ERB

TAROT: WITCH OF THE BLACK ROSE
Broadsword Comics: Mar, 2000 - Present ($2.95, mature)

	GD 2.0	VG 4.0	FN 6.0	VF 8.0	VF/NM 9.0	NM- 9.2
1-Jim Balent-s/c/a; at least two covers on all issues	4	8	12	25	40	55
1-Second printing (10/00)						6.00
2	2	4	6	13	18	22
3-20	1	2	3	5	6	8
21-40						5.00
41-102: 84-The Krampus app. 90-Crossover with School Bites characters						3.00

TARZAN (See Aurora, Comics on Parade, Crackajack, DC 100-Page Super Spec., Edgar Rice Burroughs'..., Famous Feature Stories #1, Golden Comics Digest #4, 9, Jeep Comics, Jungle Tales of..., Limited Collectors' Edition, Popular, Sparkler, Sport Stars #1, Tip Top & Top Comics)

TARZAN
Dell Publishing Co./United Features Synd.: No. 5, 1939 - No. 161, Aug, 1947

	GD 2.0	VG 4.0	FN 6.0	VF 8.0	VF/NM 9.0	NM- 9.2
Large Feature Comic 5('39)-(Scarce)-By Hal Foster; reprints 1st dailies from 1929	239	478	717	1530	2615	3700
Single Series 20('40)-By Hal Foster	174	348	522	1114	1907	2700
Four Color 134(2/47)-Marsh-c/a	56	112	168	448	999	1550
Four Color 161(8/47)-Marsh-c/a	46	92	138	340	770	1200

TARZAN (...of the Apes #138 on)
Dell Publishing Co./Gold Key No. 132 on: 1-2/48 - No. 131, 7-8/62; No. 132, 11/62 - No. 206, 2/72

	GD 2.0	VG 4.0	FN 6.0	VF 8.0	VF/NM 9.0	NM- 9.2
1-Jesse Marsh-a begins	98	196	294	784	1767	2750
2	43	86	129	318	722	1125
3-5	31	62	93	223	499	775
6-10: 6-1st Tantor the Elephant. 7-1st Valley of the Monsters	26	52	78	182	404	625
11-15: 11-Two Against the Jungle begins, ends #24. 13-Lex Barker photo-c begin	19	38	57	131	291	450
16-20	15	30	45	105	233	360
21-24,26-30	13	26	39	86	188	290
25-1st "Brothers of the Spear" episode; series ends #156,160,161,196-206	14	28	42	96	211	325
31-40	10	20	30	66	138	210
41-54: Last Barker photo-c	8	16	24	56	108	160
55-60: 56-Eight pg. Boy story	7	14	21	49	92	135
61,62,64-70	6	12	18	41	76	110
63-Two Tarzan stories, 1 by Manning	6	12	18	42	79	115
71-79	6	12	18	37	66	95
80-99: 80-Gordon Scott photo-c begin	5	10	15	34	60	85
100	6	12	18	37	66	95
101-109	5	10	15	33	57	80
110 (Scarce)-Last photo-c	6	12	18	37	66	95
111-120	5	10	15	31	53	75
121-131: Last Dell issue	5	10	15	30	50	70
132-1st Gold Key issue	5	10	15	31	53	75
133-138,140-154	4	8	12	25	40	55
139-(12/63)-1st app. Korak (Boy); leaves Tarzan & gets own book (1/64)	6	12	18	40	73	105
155-Origin Tarzan; text article on Tarzana, CA	5	10	15	30	50	70
156-161: 157-Banlu, Dog of the Arande begins, ends #159, 195. 169-Leopard Girl app.	3	6	9	21	33	45
162,165,168,171 (TV)-Ron Ely photo covers	4	8	12	22	35	48
163,164,166,167,169,170: 169-Leopard Girl app.	3	6	9	20	31	42
172-199,201-206: 178-Tarzan origin-r/#155; Leopard Girl app., also in #179, 190-193	3	6	9	18	28	38
200	3	6	9	21	33	45
Story Digest 1-(6/70, G.K., 148pp.)(scarce)	6	12	18	41	76	110

NOTE: *#162, 165, 168, 171 are TV issues. #1-153 all have* ***Marsh*** *art on Tarzan. #154-161, 163, 164, 166, 167, 172-177 all have* ***Manning*** *art on Tarzan. #178, 202 have* ***Manning*** *Tarzan reprints. No "Brothers of the Spear" in #1-24, 157-159, 162-195. #39-126, 128-156 all have* ***Russ Manning*** *art on "Brothers of the Spear". #196-201, 203-205 all have* ***Manning*** *B.O.T.S. reprints; #25-38, 127 all have Jesse* ***Marsh*** *art on B.O.T.S. #206 has a Marsh B.O.T.S. reprint.* ***Gollub*** *c-8-12.* ***Marsh*** *c-1-7.* ***Doug Wildey*** *a-162, 179-187. Many issues have front and back photo covers.*

TARZAN (Continuation of Gold Key series)
National Periodical Publications: No. 207, Apr, 1972 - No. 258, Feb, 1977

	GD 2.0	VG 4.0	FN 6.0	VF 8.0	VF/NM 9.0	NM- 9.2
207-Origin Tarzan by Joe Kubert, part 1; John Carter begins (origin); 52 pg. issues thru #209	5	10	15	35	63	90
208,209-(52 pgs.): 208-210-Parts 2-4 of origin. 209-Last John Carter	3	6	9	21	33	45
210-220: 210-Kubert-a. 211-Hogarth, Kubert-a. 212-214: Adaptations from "Jungle Tales of Tarzan". 213-Beyond the Farthest Star begins, ends #218. 215-218,224,225-All by Kubert. 215-part Foster-r. 219-223: Adapts "The Return of Tarzan" by Kubert	3	6	9	14	20	25
221-229: 221-223-Continues adaptation of "The Return of Tarzan". 226-Manning-a	2	4	6	10	14	18
230-DC 100 Page Super Spectacular; Kubert, Kaluta-a(p); Korak begins, ends #234; Carson of Venus app.	4	8	12	25	40	55
231-235-New Kubert-a.: 231-234-(All 100 pgs.)-Adapts "Tarzan and the Lion Man"; Rex, the Wonder Dog r-#232, 233. 235-(100 pgs.)-Last Kubert issue.	4	8	12	23	37	50
236,237,239-258: 240-243 adapts "Tarzan & the Castaways". 250-256 adapts "Tarzan the Untamed." 252,253-r/#213	2	4	6	8	10	12
238-(68 pgs.)	2	4	6	13	18	22
Digest 1-(Fall, 1972, 50¢, 164 pgs.)(DC)-Digest size; Kubert-c; Manning-a	4	8	12	25	40	55
Edgar Rice Burroughs' Tarzan The Joe Kubert Years - Volume One HC (Dark Horse Books, 10/05, $49.95, dust jacket) recolored r/#207-214; intro. by Joe Kubert						50.00
Edgar Rice Burroughs' Tarzan The Joe Kubert Years - Volume Two HC (Dark Horse Books, 2/06, $49.95, dust jacket) recolored r/#215-224; intro. by Joe Kubert						50.00
Edgar Rice Burroughs' Tarzan The Joe Kubert Years - Volume Three HC (Dark Horse Books, 6/06, $49.95, dust jacket) recolored r/#225,227-235; Kubert intro. and sketch pages						50.00

NOTE: ***Anderson*** *a-207, 209, 217, 218.* ***Chaykin*** *a-216.* ***Finlay*** *a(r)-212.* ***Foster*** *strip-r #207-209, 211, 212, 221.* ***Heath*** *a-230i.* ***G. Kane*** *a(r)-232p, 233p.* ***Kubert*** *a-207-225, 227-235, 257r, 258r; c-207-249, 253.* ***Lopez*** *a-250-255p; c-250p, 251, 252, 254.* ***Manning*** *strip-r 230-235, 238.* ***Morrow*** *a-208.* ***Nino*** *a-231-234.* ***Sparling*** *a-230, 231.* ***Starr*** *a-233r.*

TARZAN (Lord of the Jungle)
Marvel Comics Group: June, 1977 - No. 29, Oct, 1979

	GD 2.0	VG 4.0	FN 6.0	VF 8.0	VF/NM 9.0	NM- 9.2
1-New adaptions of Burroughs stories; Buscema-a	2	4	6	11	16	20
1-(35¢-c variant, limited distribution)(6/77)	5	10	15	33	57	80
2-29: 2-Origin by John Buscema. 9-Young Tarzan. 12-14-Jungle Tales of Tarzan. 25-29-New stories	1	2	3	5	6	8
2-5-(35¢-c variants, limited distribution)(7-10/77)	4	8	12	23	37	50
Annual 1-3: 1-(1977). 2-(1978). 3-(1979)	1	3	4	6	8	10

NOTE: ***N. Adams*** *c-11i, 12i.* ***Alcala*** *a-9i, 10i; c-8i, 9i.* ***Buckler*** *c-25-27p, Annual 3p.* ***John Buscema*** *a-1-3, 4-18p, Annual 1; c-1-7, 8p, 9p, 10, 11p, 12p, 13, 14-19p, 21p, 22, 23p, 24p, 28p, Annual 1.* ***Mooney*** *a-22i.* ***Nebres*** *a-22i.* ***Russell*** *a-29i.*

TARZAN
Dark Horse Comics: July, 1996 - No. 20, Mar, 1998 ($2.95)

	GD 2.0	VG 4.0	FN 6.0	VF 8.0	VF/NM 9.0	NM- 9.2
1-20: 1-6-Suydam-c						3.00

TARZAN / CARSON OF VENUS
Dark Horse Comics: May, 1998 - No. 4, Aug, 1998 ($2.95, limited series)

	GD 2.0	VG 4.0	FN 6.0	VF 8.0	VF/NM 9.0	NM- 9.2
1-4-Darko Macan-s/Igor Korday-a						3.00

TARZAN FAMILY, THE (Formerly Korak, Son of Tarzan)
National Periodical Publications: No. 60, Nov-Dec, 1975 - No. 66, Nov-Dec, 1976

	GD 2.0	VG 4.0	FN 6.0	VF 8.0	VF/NM 9.0	NM- 9.2
60-62-(68 pgs.): 60-Korak begins; Kaluta-r	2	4	6	11	16	20
63-66 (52 pgs.)	2	4	6	9	12	15

NOTE: *Carson of Venus-r 60-65. New John Carter-62-64, 65r, 66r. New Korak-60-66. Pellucidar feature-66. Foster strip r-60(9/4/32-10/16/32), 62(6/29/32-7/31/32), 63(10/11/31-12/13/31).* ***Kaluta*** *Carson of Venus-60-65.* ***Kubert*** *a-61, 64; c-60-64.* ***Manning*** *strip-r 60-62, 64.* ***Morrow*** *a-66r.*

TARZAN/JOHN CARTER: WARLORDS OF MARS
Dark Horse Comics: Jan, 1996 - No. 4, June, 1996 ($2.50, limited series)

	GD 2.0	VG 4.0	FN 6.0	VF 8.0	VF/NM 9.0	NM- 9.2
1-4: Bruce Jones scripts in all. 1,2,4-Bret Blevins-c/a. 2-(4/96)-Indicia reads #3						3.00

TARZAN KING OF THE JUNGLE (See Dell Giant #37, 51)

TARZAN, LORD OF THE JUNGLE
Gold Key: Sept, 1965 (Giant) (25¢, soft paper-c)

	GD 2.0	VG 4.0	FN 6.0	VF 8.0	VF/NM 9.0	NM- 9.2
1-Marsh-r	7	14	21	48	89	130

TARZAN: LOVE, LIES AND THE LOST CITY (See Tarzan the Warrior)
Malibu Comics: Aug. 10, 1992 - No. 3, Sept, 1992 ($2.50, limited series)

	GD 2.0	VG 4.0	FN 6.0	VF 8.0	VF/NM 9.0	NM- 9.2
1-($3.95, 68 pgs.)-Flip book format; Simonson & Wagner scripts						4.00
2,3-No Simonson or Wagner scripts						3.00

TARZAN MARCH OF COMICS (See March of Comics #82, 98, 114, 125, 144, 155, 172, 185, 204, 223, 240, 252, 262, 272, 286, 300, 332, 342, 354, 366)

TARZAN OF THE APES
Metropolitan Newspaper Service: 1934? (Hardcover, 4x12", 68 pgs.)

	GD 2.0	VG 4.0	FN 6.0	VF 8.0	VF/NM 9.0	NM- 9.2
1-Strip reprints	25	50	75	150	245	340

TARZAN OF THE APES
Marvel Comics Group: July, 1984 - No. 2, Aug, 1984 (Movie adaptation)

	GD 2.0	VG 4.0	FN 6.0	VF 8.0	VF/NM 9.0	NM- 9.2
1,2: Origin-r/Marvel Super Spec.						4.00

TARZAN ON THE PLANET OF THE APES
Dark Horse Comics: Sept, 2016 - No. 5, Jan, 2017 ($3.99, limited series)

	GD 2.0	VG 4.0	FN 6.0	VF 8.0	VF/NM 9.0	NM- 9.2
1-5-Seeley & Walker-s/Dagnino-a. 1-Cornelius & Zira adopt young Tarzan on Earth						4.00

TARZAN'S JUNGLE ANNUAL (See Dell Giants)

Taskmaster #1 © MAR

Team America #8 © MAR

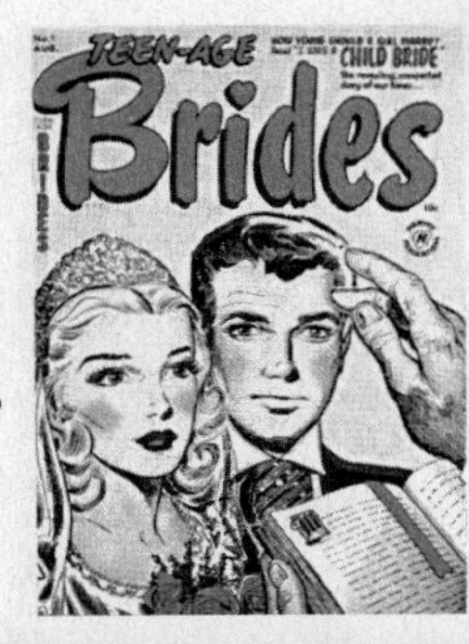

Teen-Age Brides #1 © HARV

GD 2.0 | VG 4.0 | FN 6.0 | VF 8.0 | VF/NM 9.0 | NM- 9.2

GD 2.0 | VG 4.0 | FN 6.0 | VF 8.0 | VF/NM 9.0 | NM- 9.2

TARZAN'S JUNGLE WORLD (See Dell Giant #25)

TARZAN: THE BECKONING
Malibu Comics: 1992 - No. 7, 1993 ($2.50, limited series)
1-7 3.00

TARZAN: THE LOST ADVENTURE (See Edgar Rice Burroughs' ...)

TARZAN-THE RIVERS OF BLOOD
Dark Horse Comics: Nov, 1999 - No. 8 ($2.95, limited series)
1-4: Korday-c/a 3.00

TARZAN THE SAVAGE HEART
Dark Horse Comics: Apr, 1999 - No. 4, July, 1999 ($2.95, limited series)
1-4: Grell-c/a 3.00

TARZAN THE WARRIOR (Also see Tarzan: Love, Lies and the Lost City)
Malibu Comics: Mar, 19, 1992 - No. 5, 1992 ($2.50, limited series)
1-5: 1-Bisley painted pack-c (flip book format-c) 3.00
1-2nd printing w/o flip-c by Bisley 3.00

TARZAN VS. PREDATOR AT THE EARTH'S CORE
Dark Horse Comics: Jan, 1996 - No. 4, June, 1996 ($2.50, limited series)
1-4: Lee Weeks-c/a; Walt Simonson scripts 3.00

TASKMASTER
Marvel Comics: Apr, 2002 - No. 4, July, 2002 ($2.99, limited series)
1-4-Udon Studio-s/a. 1-Iron Man app. 3.00

TASKMASTER
Marvel Comics: Nov, 2010 - No. 4, ($3.99, limited series)
1-4-Van Lente-s/Palo-a; Hydra & A.I.M. app. 4.00

TASMANIAN DEVIL & HIS TASTY FRIENDS
Gold Key: Nov, 1962 (12¢)
1-Bugs Bunny, Elmer Fudd, Sylvester, Yosemite Sam, Road Runner & Wile E. Coyote x-over
15 30 45 105 233 360

TATTERED BANNERS
DC Comics (Vertigo): Nov, 1998 - No. 4, Feb, 1999 ($2.95, limited series)
1-4-Grant & Giffen-s/McMahon-a 3.00

TATTERED MAN
Image Comics: May 2011 ($4.99, one-shot)
1-Justin Gray & Jimmy Palmiotti-s/Norberto Fernandez-a; covers by Fernandez & Conner 5.00

TEAM AMERICA (See Captain America #269)
Marvel Comics Group: June, 1982 - No. 12, May, 1983
1,12: 1-Origin; Ideal Toy motorcycle characters. 12-Double size 5.00
2-11: 9-Iron Man app. 11-Ghost Rider app. 4.00
NOTE: *There are 16 pg. variants known for most issues, possibly all. The only ad is on the inside front cover.*

TEAM HELIX
Marvel Comics: Jan, 1993 - No. 4, Apr, 1993 ($1.75, limited series)
1-4: Teen Super Group. 1,2-Wolverine app. 3.00

TEAM ONE: STORMWATCH (Also see StormWatch)
Image Comics (WildStorm Productions): June, 1995 - No. 2, Aug, 1995 ($2.50, lim. series)
1,2: Steven T. Seagle scripts 3.00

TEAM ONE: WILDC.A.T.S (Also see WildC.A.T.S)
Image Comics (WildStorm Productions): July, 1995 - No. 2, Aug, 1995 ($2.50, lim. series)
1,2: James Robinson scripts 3.00

TEAM 7
Image Comics (WildStorm): Oct, 1994 - No.4, Feb, 1995 ($2.50, limited series)
1-4: Dixon scripts in all, 1-Portacio variant-c 3.00

TEAM 7 (DC New 52)
DC Comics: No. 0, Nov, 2012 - No. 8, Jul, 2013 ($2.99)
0-8: 0-Merino-a/Lashley-c; Slade Wilson, John Lynch, Grifter and others assemble team. 3,4-Eclipso returns. 7-Pandora & Majestic app. 3.00

TEAM 7-DEAD RECKONING
Image Comics (WildStorm): Jan, 1996 - No. 4, Apr, 1996 ($2.50, limited series)
1-4: Dixon scripts in all 3.00

TEAM 7-OBJECTIVE HELL
Image Comics (WildStorm): May, 1995 - No. 3, July, 1995 ($1.95/$2.50, limited series)
1-($1.95)-Newstand; Dixon scripts in all; Barry Smith-c 3.00
1-3: 1-($2.50)-Direct Market; Barry Smith-c, bound-in card 3.00

TEAM SUPERMAN
DC Comics: July, 1999 ($2.95, one-shot)
1-Jeanty-a/Stelfreeze-c 3.00
...Secret Files 1 (5/98, $4.95)Origin-s and pin-ups of Superboy, Supergirl and Steel 5.00

TEAM TITANS (See Deathstroke & New Titans Annual #7)
DC Comics: Sept, 1992 - No. 24, Sept, 1994 ($1.75/$1.95)
1-Five different #1s exist w/origins in 1st half & the same 2nd story in each: Kilowat, Mirage, Nightrider w/Netzer/Pérez-a, Redwing, & Terra w/part Pérez-p; Total Chaos Pt. 3 4.00
2-24: 2-Total Chaos Pt 6. 11-Metallik app. 24-Zero Hour x-over 3.00
Annual 1,2 ('93, '94, $3.50, 68 pgs.): 2-Elseworlds tory 4.00

TEAM X/TEAM 7
Marvel Comics: Nov, 1996 ($4.95, one-shot)
1 5.00

TEAM X 2000
Marvel Comics: Feb, 1999 ($3.50, one-shot)
1-Kevin Lau-a; Bishop vs. Shi'ar Empire 4.00

TEAM YANKEE
First Comics: Jan, 1989 - No. 6, Feb, 1989 ($1.95, weekly limited series)
1-6 3.00

TEAM YOUNGBLOOD (Also see Youngblood)
Image Comics (Extreme Studios): Sept, 1993 - No. 22, Sept, 1995 ($1.95/$2.50)
1-22: 1-9-Liefeld scripts in all: 1,2,4-6,8-Thibert-c(i). 1-1st app. Dutch & Masada. 3-Spawn cameo. 5-1st app. Lynx. 7,8-Coupons 1 & 4 for Extreme Prejudice #0; Black and White Pt. 4 & 8 by Thibert. 8-Coupon #4 for E. P. #0. 9-Liefeld wraparound-c &(p)/a(p) on Pt. I. 16,17-Bagged w/trading card. 21-Angela & Glory-app. 3.00

TEAM ZERO
DC Comics (WildStorm Productions): Feb, 2006 - No. 6, Jul, 2006 ($2.99, limited series)
1-6-Dixon-s/Mahnke-a 3.00
TPB (2008, $17.99) r/#1-6 18.00

TECH JACKET
Image Comics: Nov, 2002 - No. 6, Apr, 2003 ($2.95)
1-6-Kirkman-s/Su-a 3.00
Vol. 1: Lost and Found TPB (7/03, $12.95, 7-3/4" x 5-1/4") B&W r/#1-6; Valentino intro. 13.00

TECH JACKET (2nd series)
Image Comics: Jul, 2014 - No. 12, Dec, 2015 ($2.99)
1-12-Keatinge-s/Randolph-a 3.00

TEDDY ROOSEVELT & HIS ROUGH RIDERS (See Real Heroes #1)
Avon Periodicals: 1950

	GD	VG	FN	VF	VF/NM	NM-
1-Kinstler-c; Palais-a; Flag-c	20	40	60	114	182	250

TEDDY ROOSEVELT ROUGH RIDER (See Battlefield #22 & Classics Illustrated Special Issue)

TED MCKEEVER'S METROPOL (See Transit)
Marvel Comics (Epic Comics): Mar, 1991 - No. 12, Mar, 1992 ($2.95, limited series)
V1#1-12: Ted McKeever-c/a/scripts 4.00

TED MCKEEVER'S METROPOL A.D.
Marvel Comics (Epic Comics): Oct, 1992 - No. 3, Dec, 1992 ($3.50, limited series)
V2#1-3: Ted McKeever-c/a/scripts 4.00

TEENA
Magazine Enterprises/Standard Comics No. 20 on: No. 11, 1948 - No. 15, 1948; No. 20, Aug, 1949 - No. 22, Oct, 1950

	GD	VG	FN	VF	VF/NM	NM-
A-1 #11-Teen-age; Ogden Whitney-c	14	28	42	80	115	150
A-1 #12, 15	12	24	36	67	94	120
20-22 (Standard)	10	20	30	54	72	90

TEEN-AGE BRIDES (True Bride's Experiences #8 on)
Harvey/Home Comics: Aug, 1953 - No. 7, Aug, 1954

	GD	VG	FN	VF	VF/NM	NM-
1-Powell-a	11	22	33	62	86	110
2-Powell-a	8	16	24	44	57	70
3-7: 3,6-Powell-a	8	16	24	40	50	60

TEEN-AGE CONFESSIONS (See Teen Confessions)

TEEN-AGE CONFIDENTIAL CONFESSIONS
Charlton Comics: July, 1960 - No. 22, 1964

	GD	VG	FN	VF	VF/NM	NM-
1	4	8	12	23	37	50
2-10	3	6	9	16	23	30
11-22	2	4	6	13	18	22

TEEN-AGE DIARY SECRETS (Formerly Blue Ribbon Comics; becomes Diary Secrets #10 on)

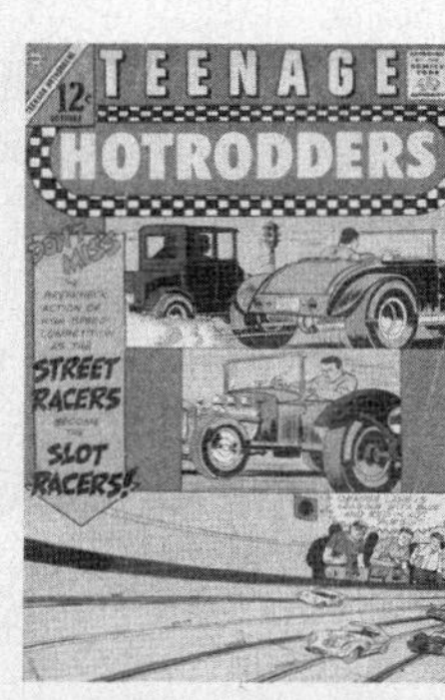

Teenage Hotrodders #20 © CC

Teenage Mutant Ninja Turtles #22 © Mirage

Teenage Mutant Ninja Turtles (2011 series) #65 © Mirage

St. John Publishing Co.: No. 4, 9/49; nn (#5), 9/49 - No. 7, 11/49; No. 8, 2/50; No. 9, 8/50

	GD 2.0	VG 4.0	FN 6.0	VF 8.0	VF/NM 9.0	NM- 9.2
4(9/49)-Oversized; part mag., part comic	53	106	159	334	567	800
nn(#5)(no indicia)-Oversized, all comics; contains sty "I Gave Boys the Green Light."	53	106	159	334	567	800
6,8: (Reg. size) -Photo-c; Baker-a(2-3) in each	57	114	171	362	619	875
7-Digest size (Pocket Comics); Baker-a(5); same contents as #9; diff.-c	77	154	231	493	847	1200
9-Digest size (Pocket Comics); Baker-a(5); same contents as #7; diff.-c by Baker	129	258	387	826	1413	2000

TEEN-AGE DOPE SLAVES (See Harvey Comics Library #1)

TEENAGE HOTRODDERS (Top Eliminator #25 on; see Blue Bird)
Charlton Comics: Apr, 1963 - No. 24, July, 1967

	GD 2.0	VG 4.0	FN 6.0	VF 8.0	VF/NM 9.0	NM- 9.2
1	5	10	15	33	57	80
2-10	3	6	9	19	30	40
11-24	3	6	9	16	24	32

TEEN-AGE LOVE (See Fox Giants)

TEEN-AGE LOVE (Formerly Intimate)
Charlton Comics: V2#4, July, 1958 - No. 96, Dec, 1973

	GD 2.0	VG 4.0	FN 6.0	VF 8.0	VF/NM 9.0	NM- 9.2
V2#4	4	8	12	27	44	60
5-9	3	6	9	19	30	40
10(9/59)-20	3	6	9	16	24	32
21-35	3	6	9	15	22	28
36-70	2	4	6	13	18	22
71-79,81,82,85-87,90-96: 61&62-Jonnie Love begins (origin)	2	4	6	10	14	18
80,84,88-David Cassidy pin-ups	3	6	9	14	19	24
83,89: 83-Bobby Sherman pin-up. 89-Danny Bonaduce pin-up	2	4	6	13	18	22

TEENAGE MUTANT NINJA TURTLES (Also see Anything Goes, Donatello, First Comics Graphic Novel, Gobbledygook, Grimjack #26, Leonardo, Michaelangelo, Raphael & Tales Of The...)
Mirage Studios: 1984 - No. 62, Aug, 1993 ($1.50/$1.75, B&W; all 44-52 pgs.)

	GD 2.0	VG 4.0	FN 6.0	VF 8.0	VF/NM 9.0	NM- 9.2
1-1st printing (3000 copies)-Origin and 1st app. of the Turtles and Splinter. Only printing to have ad for Gobbledygook #1 & 2; Shredder app. (#1-4: 7-1/2x11")	500	1000	1500	2500	3500	4500
1-2nd printing (6/84)(6,000 copies)	23	46	69	161	356	550
1-3rd printing (2/85)(36,000 copies)	11	22	33	76	163	250
1-4th printing, new-c (50,000 copies)	3	6	9	19	30	40
1-5th printing, new-c (8/88-c, 11/88 inside)	3	6	9	17	26	35
1-Counterfeit. **Note**: Most counterfeit copies have a half inch wide white streak or scratch marks across the center of back cover. Black part of cover is a bluish black instead of a deep black. Inside paper is very white & inside cover is bright white (no value)						
2-1st printing (1984; 15,000 copies)	12	24	36	79	170	260
2-2nd printing	3	6	9	19	30	40
2-3rd printing; new Corben-c/a (2/85)	2	4	6	9	12	15
2-Counterfeit with glossy cover stock (no value).						
3-1st printing (1985, 44 pgs.)	9	18	27	57	111	165
3-Variant, 500 copies, cover printed at different plant, has 'Laird's Photo' in white rather than light blue	33	64	96	230	515	800
3-2nd printing; contains new back-up story	2	4	6	9	12	15
4-1st printing (1985, 44 pgs.)	6	12	18	40	73	105
4-2nd printing (5/87) all have manufacturing error	9	18	27	59	117	175
5-Fugitoid begins, ends #7; 1st full color-c (1985)	4	8	12	28	47	65
5-2nd printing (11/87)	2	4	6	9	12	15
6-1st printing (1986)	3	6	9	17	26	35
6-2nd printing (4/88-c, 5/88 inside)						6.00
7-4 pg. Eastman/Corben color insert; 1st color TMNT (1986, $1.75-c); Bade Biker back-up story	2	4	6	13	18	22
7-2nd printing (1/89) w/o color insert						6.00
8-Cerebus-c/story with Dave Sim-a (1986)	2	4	6	11	16	20
9,10: 9-(9/86)-Rip In Time by Corben	2	4	6	8	10	12
11-15	1	3	4	6	8	10
16-18: 18-Mark Bode'-a	1	2	3	5	6	8
18-2nd printing ($2.25, color, 44 pgs.)-New-c						5.00
19-34: 19-Begin $1.75-c. 24-26-Veitch-c/a.						6.00
32-2nd printing ($2.75, 52 pgs., full color)						5.00
35-49,51: 35-Begin $2.00-c.						5.00
50-Features pin-ups by Larsen, McFarlane, Simonson, etc.	1	2	3	5	6	8
52-62: 52-Begin $2.25-c						5.00
nn (1990, $5.95, B&W)-Movie adaptation						6.00
Book 1,2($1.50, B&W): 2-Corben-c						6.00
...Christmas Special 1 (12/90, $1.75, B&W, 52 pgs.)-Cover title: Michaelangelo Christmas Special; r/Michaelangelo one-shot plus new Raphael story	1	3	4	6	8	10
... Color Special (11/09, $3.25) full color reprint of #1	1	3	4	6	8	10
...Special (The Maltese Turtle) nn (1/93, $2.95, color, 44 pgs.)						6.00
...Special: "Times" Pipeline nn (9/92, $2.95, color, 44 pgs.)-Mark Bode-c/a						6.00
Hardcover ($100)-r/#1-10 plus one-shots w/dust jackets - limited to 1000 w/letter of authenticity						150.00
Softcover ($40)-r/#1-10						45.00

TEENAGE MUTANT NINJA TURTLES
Mirage Studios: V2#1, Oct, 1993 - V2#13, Oct, 1995 ($2.75)

	GD 2.0	VG 4.0	FN 6.0	VF 8.0	VF/NM 9.0	NM- 9.2
V2#1-Wraparound-c	2	4	6	8	10	12
2-13						4.00

TEENAGE MUTANT NINJA TURTLES
Image Comics (Highbrow Ent.): June, 1996 - No. 23, Oct, 1999 ($1.95-$2.95)

	GD 2.0	VG 4.0	FN 6.0	VF 8.0	VF/NM 9.0	NM- 9.2
1-Erik Larsen-c(i)	2	4	6	8	10	12
2-23: 2-8-Erik Larsen-c(i) on all. 10-Savage Dragon-c/app.						4.00

TEENAGE MUTANT NINJA TURTLES
Mirage Publishing: V4#1, Dec, 2001 - No. 28 ($2.95, B&W)

	GD 2.0	VG 4.0	FN 6.0	VF 8.0	VF/NM 9.0	NM- 9.2
V4#1-9,11-28-Laird-s/a(i)/Lawson-a(p).						3.00
10-($3.95) Splinter dies						4.00

TEENAGE MUTANT NINJA TURTLES
Dreamwave Productions: June 2003 - No. 7 ($2.95, color)

	GD 2.0	VG 4.0	FN 6.0	VF 8.0	VF/NM 9.0	NM- 9.2
1-7-Animated style; Peter David-s/Lesean-a						3.00
Vol. 1 TPB (2003, $9.95) r/#1-4; cover gallery and sketch pages						10.00

TEENAGE MUTANT NINJA TURTLES
IDW Publishing: Aug, 2011 - Present ($3.99)

	GD 2.0	VG 4.0	FN 6.0	VF 8.0	VF/NM 9.0	NM- 9.2
1-Kevin Eastman-s & layouts; four covers by Duncan (each turtle); origin flashback	2	4	6	8	10	12
1-Variant-c by Eastman	3	6	9	16	23	30
1-Halloween Edition (10/12, no cover price) Reprints #1						4.00
2-43,45-49,51-67-Multiple variant covers on each						4.00
44-Donatello killed						10.00
50-(9/15, $7.99) Multiple variant covers; Turtles & Splinter vs. Shredder; Santolouco-a						8.00
Annual 2012 (10/12, $8.99) Eastman-s/a; wraparound-c						9.00
Annual 2014 (8/14, $7.99) Eastman-s/a; Renet app.						8.00
...: Deviations (3/16, $4.99) What If... the Turtles joined Shredder; Waltz-s/Howard-a						5.00
... FCBD (3/15, giveaway) Santolouco-a						3.00
Greatest Hits - Teenage Mutant Ninja Turtles #1 (2/16, $1.00) r/#1						3.00
... Kevin Eastman Cover Gallery (12/13, $3.99) Collection of recent Eastman covers						4.00
... Microseries 1-8 (11/11 - No. 8, 9/12) 1-Raphael. 2-Michelangelo. 3-Donatello. 4-Leonardo. 5-Splinter. 6-Casey Jones. 7-April. 8-Fugitoid						4.00
...100 Page Spectacular (4/12, $7.99) r/TMNT Adventures (1988) mini-series #1-3						8.00
... 30th Anniversary Special (5/14, $7.99) History and reprints from all eras; pin-ups by various; multiple covers						8.00
... Villains Microseries 1-8 (4/13 - No. 8, 11/13, $3.99) 1-Krang. 2-Baxter. 8-Shredder						4.00

TEENAGE MUTANT NINJA TURTLES (Adventures)
Archie Publications: Jan, 1996 - No. 3, Mar, 1996 ($1.50, limited series)

	GD 2.0	VG 4.0	FN 6.0	VF 8.0	VF/NM 9.0	NM- 9.2
1	2	4	6	11	16	20
2,3						5.00

TEENAGE MUTANT NINJA TURTLES ADVENTURES (TV)
Archie Comics: Oct, 1988 - No. 3, Dec, 1988; Mar, 1989 - No. 72, Oct, 1995 ($1.00-$1.75)

	GD 2.0	VG 4.0	FN 6.0	VF 8.0	VF/NM 9.0	NM- 9.2
1-Adapts TV cartoon; not by Eastman/Laird	3	6	9	14	20	25
2,3 (Mini-series)	1	2	3	5	6	8
1 (2nd on-going series)	2	4	6	8	10	12
1-2nd printing						5.00
2-18,20-30: 5-Begins original stories not based on TV. 14-Simpson-a(p). 22-Colan-c/a						5.00
2-11: 2nd printings						4.00
19,20,51-54: 19-1st Mighty Mutanimals (also in #20, 51-54	2	4	6	9	12	15
31-49						5.00
50-Poster by Eastman/Laird	1	2	3	5	7	9
55-60	1	2	3	4	5	7
61-70: 62-w/poster	2	3	4	6	8	10
71	2	4	6	8	10	12
72- Last issue	2	4	6	9	13	16
nn (1990, $2.50)-Movie adaptation						5.00

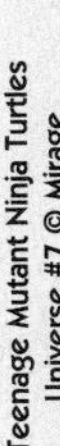
Teenage Mutant Ninja Turtles Universe #7 © Mirage

Teen-Age Romances #14 © STJ

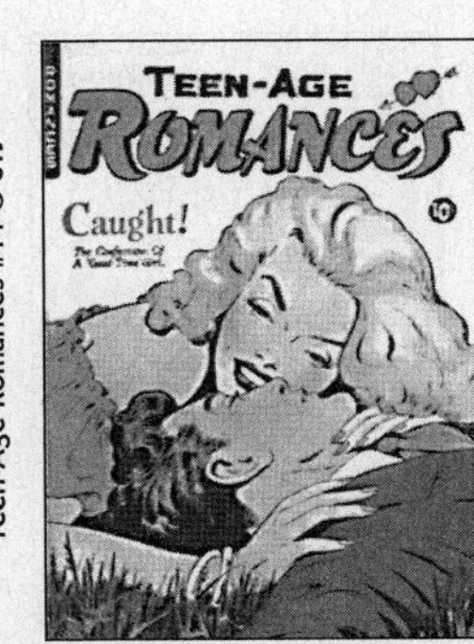

Teen Confessions #20 © CC

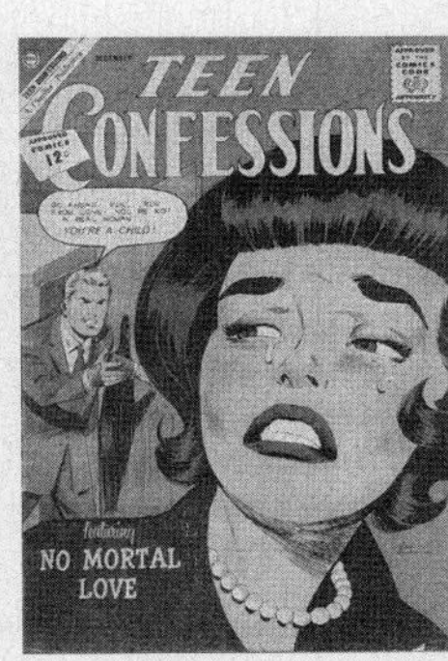

	GD 2.0	VG 4.0	FN 6.0	VF 8.0	VF/NM 9.0	NM- 9.2

nn (Spring, 1991, $2.50, 68 pgs.)-(Meet Archie) 5.00
nn (Sum, 1991, $2.50, 68 pgs.)-(Movie II)-Adapts movie sequel 5.00
...Meet the Conservation Corps 1 (1992, $2.50, 68 pgs.) 4.00
...III The Movie: The Turtles are Back...In Time (1993, $2.50, 68 pgs.) 5.00
Special 1,4,5 (Sum/92, Spr/93, Sum/93, 68 pgs.)-1-Bill Wray-c 4.00
Giant Size Special 6 (Fall/93, $1.95, 52 pgs.) 4.00
Special 7-10 (Win/93-Fall//94, 52 pgs.): 9-Jeff Smith-c 4.00
NOTE: *There are 2nd printings of #1-11 w/B&W inside covers. Originals are color.*

TEENAGE MUTANT NINJA TURTLES AMAZING ADVENTURES
IDW Publishing: Aug, 2015 - No. 14, Sept, 2016 ($3.99)
1-14-All-ages animated-style stories; two covers 4.00
... Carmelo Anthony Special One-Shot (5/16, $5.99) Turtles meet the NBA player 6.00

TEENAGE MUTANT NINJA TURTLES BEBOP & ROCKSTEADY DESTROY EVERYTHING
IDW Publishing: Jun, 2016 - No. 5, Jun, 2016 ($3.99, weekly limited series)
1-5-Dustin Weaver-s; art by various; interlocking covers 4.00

TEENAGE MUTANT NINJA TURTLES: CASEY AND APRIL
IDW Publishing: Jun, 2015 - No. 4, Sept, 2015 ($3.99, limited series)
1-4-Mariko Tamaki-s/Irene Koh-a; two covers on each 4.00

TEENAGE MUTANT NINJA TURTLES CLASSICS DIGEST (TV)
Archie Comics: Aug, 1993 - No. 8, Mar, 1995? ($1.75)
1-8: Reprints TMNT Advs. 4.00

TEENAGE MUTANT NINJA TURTLES COLOR CLASSICS
IDW Publishing: May, 2012 - Present ($3.99)
1-11-Colored reprints of the original 1984 B&W series 4.00
...: Donatello Micro-Series One-Shot (3/13, $3.99) r/Donatello, TMNT #1 (1986) 4.00
...: Leonardo Micro-Series One-Shot (4/13, $3.99) r/Leonardo, TMNT #1 4.00
...: Michaelangelo Micro-Series One-Shot (12/12, $3.99) r/Michaelangelo, TMNT #1 4.00
...: Raphael Micro-Series One-Shot (8/12, $3.99) r/Raphael #1 (1985) 4.00
... Volume 2 (11/13 - No. 7, 5/14, $3.99) 1-7: 1-Reprints TMNT #12 (1987) 4.00
... Volume 3 (1/15 - Present, $3.99) 1-14: 1-Reprints TMNT #48 (1992) 4.00

TEENAGE MUTANT NINJA TURTLES/FLAMING CARROT CROSSOVER
Mirage Publishing: Nov, 1993 - No. 4, Feb, 1994 ($2.75, limited series)
1-4: Bob Burden story 4.00

TEENAGE MUTANT NINJA TURTLES / GHOSTBUSTERS
IDW Publishing: Oct, 2014 - No. 4, Jan, 2015 ($3.99, limited series)
1-4-Burnham & Waltz-s/Schoening-a; multiple covers on each 4.00
... #1 Director's Cut (5/15, $5.99) r/#1 with creator commentary; bonus script pages 6.00

TEENAGE MUTANT NINJA TURTLES: MUTANIMALS
IDW Publishing: Feb, 2015 - No. 4, May, 2015 ($3.99, limited series)
1-4-Paul Allor-s/Andy Kuhn-a; two covers 4.00

TEENAGE MUTANT NINJA TURTLES NEW ANIMATED ADVENTURES
IDW Publishing: Jul, 2013 - No. 24, Jun, 2015 ($3.99)
1-24-Multiple covers on each 4.00
... Free Comic Book Day (5/13) Burnham-s/Brizuela-a 3.00

TEENAGE MUTANT NINJA TURTLES PRESENTS: APRIL O'NEIL
Archie Comics: Mar, 1993 - No. 3, June, 1993 ($1.25, limited series)
1-3 4.00

TEENAGE MUTANT NINJA TURTLES PRESENTS: DONATELLO AND LEATHERHEAD
Archie Comics: July, 1993 - No. 3, Sept, 1993 ($1.25, limited series)
1-3 4.00

TEENAGE MUTANT NINJA TURTLES PRESENTS: MERDUDE
Archie Comics: Oct, 1993 - No. 3, Dec, 1993 ($1.25, limited series)
1-3-See Mighty Mutanimals #7 for 1st app. Merdude 4.00

TEENAGE MUTANT NINJA TURTLES/SAVAGE DRAGON CROSSOVER
Mirage Studios: Aug, 1995 ($2.75, one-shot)
1 4.00

TEENAGE MUTANT NINJA TURTLES: THE SECRET HISTORY OF THE FOOT CLAN
IDW Publishing: Dec, 2012 - No. 4, Mar, 2013 ($3.99, limited series)
1-4-Santolouco-a/Santolouco & Burnham-s 4.00

TEENAGE MUTANT NINJA TURTLES: TURTLES IN TIME
IDW Publishing: Jun, 2014 - No. 4, Sept, 2014 ($3.99, limited series)
1-4: 1-Paul Allor-s/Ross Campbell-a; Renet app.; three covers. 2-4-Two covers each 4.00

TEENAGE MUTANT NINJA TURTLES UNIVERSE
IDW Publishing: Aug, 2016 - Present ($4.99)
1-7: 1-Allor-s/Couceiro-a; Eastman & Sienkiewicz-a; multiple covers on each 4.00

TEENAGE MUTANT NINJA TURTLES UTROM EMPIRE
IDW Publishing: Jan, 2014 - No. 3, Mar, 2014 ($3.99, limited series)
1-3-Paul Allor-s/Andy Kuhn-a; two covers on each 4.00

TEEN-AGE ROMANCE (Formerly My Own Romance)
Marvel Comics (ZPC): No. 77, Sept, 1960 - No. 86, Mar, 1962

	GD 2.0	VG 4.0	FN 6.0	VF 8.0	VF/NM 9.0	NM- 9.2
77-83	6	12	18	40	73	105
84-86-Kirby-c. 84-Kirby-a(2 pgs.). 85,86-(3 pgs.)	7	14	21	44	82	120

TEEN-AGE ROMANCES
St. John Publ. Co. (Approved Comics): Jan, 1949 - No. 45, Dec, 1955 (#3,7,10-18,21 are 1/2 inch taller than other issues)

	GD 2.0	VG 4.0	FN 6.0	VF 8.0	VF/NM 9.0	NM- 9.2
1-Baker-c/a(1)	107	214	321	680	1165	1650
2,3: 2-Baker-c/a. 3-Baker-c/a(3)	65	130	195	416	708	1000
4,5,7,8-Photo-c; Baker-a(2-3) each	40	80	120	246	411	575
6-Photo-c; part magazine; Baker-a (10/49)	42	84	126	265	445	625
9-Baker-c/a; Kubert-a	77	154	231	493	847	1200
10-12,20-Baker-c/a(2-3) each	71	142	213	454	777	1100
13-19,21,22-Complete issues by Baker	77	154	231	493	847	1200
23-25-Baker-c/a(2-3) each	65	130	195	416	708	1000
26,27,33,34,36,37,39,40,42: Baker-c/a. 33,40-Signed story by Estrada. 42-r/Cinderella Love #9; last pre-code (3/55)	58	116	174	371	656	900
28-30-No Baker-a	17	34	51	98	154	210
31,32-Baker-c. 31-Estrada-s	53	106	159	334	567	800
35-Baker-c/a (16 pgs.)	58	116	174	371	636	900
38-Baker-c/a; suggestive-c	97	194	291	621	1061	1500
41-Baker-c; Infantino-a(r); all stories are Ziff-Davis-r	53	106	159	334	567	800
43-45-Baker-c/a	55	110	165	352	601	850

TEEN-AGE TALK
I.W. Enterprises: 1964

	GD 2.0	VG 4.0	FN 6.0	VF 8.0	VF/NM 9.0	NM- 9.2
Reprint #1	2	4	6	10	14	18
Reprint #5,8,9: 5-r/Hector #? 9-Punch Comics #?; L.B. Cole-c reprint from School Day Romances #1	2	4	6	9	13	16

TEEN-AGE TEMPTATIONS (Going Steady #10 on)(See True Love Pictorial)
St. John Publishing Co.: Oct, 1952 - No. 9, Aug, 1954

	GD 2.0	VG 4.0	FN 6.0	VF 8.0	VF/NM 9.0	NM- 9.2
1-Baker-c/a; has story "Reform School Girl" by Estrada	135	270	405	864	1482	2100
2,4-Baker-c	77	154	231	493	847	1200
3,5-7,9-Baker-c/a	84	168	252	538	919	1300
8-Teenagers smoke reefer; Baker-c/a	97	194	291	621	1061	1500

NOTE: *Estrada a-1, 3-5.*

TEEN BEAM (Formerly Teen Beat #1)
National Periodical Publications: No. 2, Jan-Feb, 1968

	GD 2.0	VG 4.0	FN 6.0	VF 8.0	VF/NM 9.0	NM- 9.2
2-Superman cameo; Herman's Hermits, Yardbirds, Simon & Garfunkel, Lovin Spoonful, Young Rascals app.; Orlando, Drucker-a(r); Monkees photo-c;	15	30	45	105	233	360

TEEN BEAT (Becomes Teen Beam #2)
National Periodical Publications: Nov-Dec, 1967

	GD 2.0	VG 4.0	FN 6.0	VF 8.0	VF/NM 9.0	NM- 9.2
1-Photos & text only; Monkees photo-c; Beatles, Herman's Hermits, Animals, Supremes, Byrds app.	17	34	51	117	259	400

TEEN COMICS (Formerly All Teen; Journey Into Unknown Worlds #36 on)
Marvel Comics (WFP): No. 21, Apr, 1947 - No. 35, May, 1950

	GD 2.0	VG 4.0	FN 6.0	VF 8.0	VF/NM 9.0	NM- 9.2
21-Kurtzman's "Hey Look"; Patsy Walker, Cindy (1st app.?), Georgie, Margie app.; Syd Shores-a begins, end #23	30	60	90	177	289	400
22,23,25,27,29,31-35: 22-(6/47)-Becomes Hedy Devine #22 (8/47) on?	21	42	63	122	199	275
24,26,28,30-Kurtzman's "Hey Look". 30-Has anti-Wertham editorial	21	42	63	126	206	285

TEEN CONFESSIONS
Charlton Comics: Aug, 1959 - No. 97, Nov, 1976

	GD 2.0	VG 4.0	FN 6.0	VF 8.0	VF/NM 9.0	NM- 9.2
1	7	14	21	44	82	120
2	4	8	12	27	44	60
3-10	3	6	9	21	33	45
11-30	3	6	9	17	26	35
31-Beatles-c	10	20	30	66	138	210
32-36,38-55	3	6	9	15	21	26
37 (1/66)-Beatles Fan Club story; Beatles-c	10	20	30	66	138	210
56-58,60-76,78-97: 89,90-Newton-c	2	4	6	10	14	18
59-Kaluta's 1st pro work? (12/69)	3	6	9	19	30	40
77-Partridge Family poster	3	6	9	14	20	24

Teen Love Stories #1 © WP

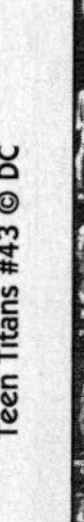

Teen Titans #43 © DC

Teen Titans (2003 series) #5 © DC

	GD	VG	FN	VF	VF/NM	NM-
	2.0	4.0	6.0	8.0	9.0	9.2

GD VG FN VF VF/NM NM-
2.0 4.0 6.0 8.0 9.0 9.2

TEEN DOG
BOOM! Entertainment (BOOM! Box): Sept, 2014 - No. 8, Apr, 2015 ($3.99)

1-8-Jake Lawrence-s/a/c; multiple covers on #1-4 4.00

TEENIE WEENIES, THE (America's Favorite Kiddie Comic)
Ziff-Davis Publishing Co.: No. 10, 1950 - No. 11, Apr-May, 1951 (Newspaper reprints)

10,11-Painted-c 20 40 60 114 182 250

TEEN-IN (Tippy Teen)
Tower Comics: Summer, 1968 - No. 4, Fall, 1969

nn(#1, Summer, 1968)(25¢) Has 3 full pg. B&W photos of Sonny & Cher, Donovan and Herman's Hermits; interviews and photos of Eric Clapton, Jim Morrison and others 9 18 27 62 126 190
nn(#2, Spring, 1969),3,4 6 12 18 37 66 95

TEEN LIFE (Formerly Young Life)
New Age/Quality Comics Group: No. 3, Winter, 1945 - No. 5, Fall, 1945 (Teenage magazine)

3-June Allyson photo on-c & story 14 28 42 80 115 150
4-Duke Ellington photo on-c & story 12 24 36 69 97 125
5-Van Johnson, Woody Herman & Jackie Robinson articles; Van Johnson & Woody Herman photos on-c 14 28 42 80 115 150

TEEN LOVE STORIES (Magazine)
Warren Publ. Co.: Sept, 1969 - No. 3, Jan, 1970 (68 pgs., photo covers, B&W)

1-Photos & articles plus 36-42 pgs. new comic stories in all; Frazetta-a 8 16 24 51 96 140
2,3: 2-Anti-marijuana story 5 10 15 34 60 85

TEEN ROMANCES
Super Comics: 1964

10,11,15-17-Reprints 2 4 6 8 11 14

TEEN SECRET DIARY (Nurse Betsy Crane #12 on)
Charlton Comics: Oct, 1959 - No. 11, June, 1961

1 5 10 15 30 50 70
2 3 6 9 20 31 42
3-11 3 6 9 17 26 35

TEEN TALK (See Teen)

TEEN TITANS (See Brave & the Bold #54,60, DC Super-Stars #1, Marvel & DC Present, New Teen Titans, New Titans, Official...Index and Showcase #59)
National Periodical Publ./DC Comics: 1-2/66 - No. 43, 1-2/73; No. 44, 11/76 - No. 53, 2/78

1-(1-2/66)-Titans join Peace Corps; Batman, Flash, Aquaman, Wonder Woman cameos 37 74 111 274 612 950
2 14 28 42 96 211 325
3-5: 4-Speedy app. 9 18 27 62 126 190
6-10: 6-Doom Patrol app.; Beast Boy x-over; readers polled on him joining Titans 7 14 21 49 92 135
11-18: 11-Speedy app. 13-X-Mas-c 6 12 18 40 73 105
19-Wood-i; Speedy begins as regular 6 12 18 41 76 110
20-22: All Neal Adams-a. 21-Hawk & Dove app.; last 12¢ issue. 22-Origin Wonder Girl 8 16 24 56 108 160
23-Wonder Girl dons new costume 5 10 15 33 57 80
24-31: 25-Flash, Aquaman, Batman, Green Arrow, Green Lantern, Superman, & Hawk & Dove guests; 1st app. Lilith who joins T.T. West in #50. 29-Hawk & Dove & Ocean Master app. 30-Aquagirl app. 31-Hawk & Dove app. 5 10 15 30 50 70
32-34,40-43: 34-Last 15¢ issue 3 6 9 19 30 40
35-39-(52 pgs.): 36,37-Superboy-r. 38-Green Arrow/Speedy-r; Aquaman/Aqualad story. 39-Hawk & Dove-r. 4 8 12 22 35 48
44-(11/76) Dr. Light app.; Mal becomes the Guardian 3 6 9 14 20 26
45,47,49,51,52 3 6 9 14 19 24
46,48: 46-Joker's daughter begins (see Batman Family). 48-Intro Bumblebee; Joker's daughter becomes Harlequin 3 6 9 21 33 45
50-1st revival original Bat-Girl; intro. Teen Titans West 3 6 9 21 33 45
53-Origin retold 3 6 9 15 22 28
... Lost Annual 1 (3/08, $4.99) Sixties-era story by Bob Haney; Jay Stephens & Mike Allred-a; President Kennedy app.; Nick Cardy-c and sketch pages 5.00

NOTE: ***Aparo** a-36. **Buckler** c-46-53. **Cardy** c-1-16. **Kane** a(p)-19, 22-24, 39r. **Tuska** a(p)-31, 36, 38, 39. DC Super-Stars #1 (3/76) was released before #44.*

TEEN TITANS (Also see Titans Beat in the Promotional Comics section)
DC Comics: Oct, 1996 - No. 24, Sept, 1998 ($1.95)

1-Dan Jurgens-c/a(p)/scripts & George Pérez-c/a(i) begin; Atom forms new team (Risk, Argent, Prysm, & Joto); 1st app. Loren Jupiter & Omen; no indicia. 1-3-Origin. 4.00
2-24: 4,5-Robin, Nightwing, Supergirl, Capt. Marvel Jr. app. 12-"Then and Now" begins w/original Teen Titans-c/app. 15-Death of Joto. 17-Capt. Marvel Jr. and Fringe join. 19-Millennium Giants x-over. 23,24-Superman app. 3.00
Annual 1 (1997, $3.95)-Pulp Heroes story 4.00

TEEN TITANS (Also see Titans/Young Justice: Graduation Day)
DC Comics: Sept, 2003 - No. 100, Late Oct, 2011 ($2.50/$2.99/$3.99)

1-McKone-c/a;Johns-s 5.00
1-Variant-c by Michael Turner 6.00
1-2nd and 3rd printings 3.00
2-Deathstroke app. 5.00
2-2nd printing 3.00
3-15: 4-Impulse becomes Kid Flash. 5-Raven returns. 6-JLA app. 4.00
16-33: 16-Titans go to 31st Century; Legion and Fatal Five app. 17-19-Future Titans app. 21-23-Dr. Light. 24,25-Outsiders #24,25 x-over. 27,28-Liefeld-a. 32,33-Infinite Crisis 3.00
34-49,51-71: 34-One Year Later begins; two covers by Daniel and Benes. 36-Begin $2.99-c. 40-Jericho returns. 42-Kid Devil origin; Snejbjerg-a. 43-Titans East. 48,49-Amazons Attack x-over; Supergirl app. 51-54-Future Titans app. 3.00
50-($3.99) Art by Pérez (4 pgs.), McKone (6 pgs.), Nauck and Green; future Titans app. 4.00
72-88: 72-Begin $3.99-c; Ravager back-up features. 77,78-Blackest Night. 83-87-Coven of Three back-up; Naifeh-a. 88-Nicola Scott-a begins 4.00
89-99-($2.99) 89-Robin (Damian) joins. 93-Solstice app. 98 Superboy-Prime returns 3.00
100-($4.99) Nicola Scott-a; pin-ups by various 5.00
Annual 1 (4/06, $4.99) Infinite Crisis x-over; Benes-c 5.00
Annual 2009 (6/09, $4.99) Deathtrap x-over prelude; McKeever-s 5.00
... And Outsiders Secret Files and Origins 2005 (10/05, $4.99) Daniel-c 5.00
...: Cold Case (2/11, $4.99) Captain Cold and the Rogues app.; Sean Murphy-a 6.00
.../Legion Special (11/04, $3.50) (cont'd from #16) Reis-a; leads into 2005 Legion of Super-Heroes series; LSH preview by Waid & Kitson 4.00
#1/2 (Wizard mail offer) origin of Ravager; Reis-a 8.00
.../Outsiders Secret Files 2003 (12/03, $5.95) Reis & Jimenez-a; pin-ups by various 6.00
...: A Kid's Game TPB (2004, $9.95) r/#1-7; Turner-c from #1; McKone sketch pages 10.00
...: Beast Boys and Girls TPB (2005, $9.99) r/#13-15 and Beast Boy #1-4 10.00
...: Changing of the Guard TPB (2009, $14.99) r/#62-69 15.00
...: Child's Play TPB (2010, $14.99) r/#71-78 15.00
...: Deathtrap TPB (2009, $14.99) r/#70, Annual #1, Titans #12,13, Vigilante #4-6 15.00
...: Family Lost TPB (2004, $9.95) r/#8-12 & #1/2 10.00
...: Life and Death TPB (2006, $14.99) r/#29-33 and pages from Infinite Crisis x-over 15.00
...: On the Clock TPB (2008, $14.99) r/#55-61 15.00
.../ Outsiders: The Death and Return of Donna Troy (2006, $14.99) r/Titans/Young Justice: Graduation Day #1-3, Teen Titans/Outsiders Secret Files 2003 and DC Special: The Return of Donna Troy #1-4; cover gallery 15.00
.../ Outsiders: The Insiders (2006, $14.99) r/Teen Titans/ #24-26 & Outsiders #24,25,28 15.00
...: Ravager - Fresh Hell TPB (2010, $14.99) r/#71-76,79-82 & Faces of Evil: Deathstroke 15.00
... Spotlight: Cyborg TPB (2009, $19.99) r/DC Special: Cyborg #1-6 20.00
... Spotlight: Raven TPB (2008, $14.99) r/DC Special: Raven #1-5 15.00
...: The Future is Now (2005, $9.99) r/#15-23 & Teen Titans/Legion Special 10.00
...: The Hunt For Raven (2011, $17.99) r/#79-87 18.00
...: Titans Around the World TPB (2007, $14.99) r/#34-41 15.00
...: Titans of Tomorrow TPB (2008, $14.99) r/#50-54 15.00

TEEN TITANS (DC New 52)
DC Comics: Nov, 2011 - No. 30, Jun, 2014 ($2.99)

1-14,17-23: 1-Lobdell-s/Booth-a/c; Red Robin assembles a team; Kid Flash, Wonder Girl app. 5-Superboy app. 9-The Culling conclusion. 13,14-Wonder Girl origin; Garza-a 3.00
15,16-"Death of the Family" tie-in. 15-Die-cut Joker mask cover. 16-Red Hood app. 5.00
23.1, 23.2 (11/13, $2.99, regular covers) 3.00
23.1 (11/13, $3.99, 3-D cover) "Trigon #1" on cover; origin; Wolfman-s/Cafu-a 5.00
23.2 (11/13, $3.99, 3-D cover) "Deathstroke #1" on cover; flashback; Deathblow app. 1 2 3 5 6 8
24-29: 24-Leads into Annual #2. 25,26-Origin of Kid Flash 3.00
30-($3.99) Last issue; origin of Skitter; Kirkham-a 4.00
#0 (11/12, $2.99) Origin of Red Robin; Kirkham-a 3.00
Annual 1 (7/12, $4.99) The Culling x-over part 1; Legion Lost members app. 5.00
Annual 2 (12/13, $4.99) Future Teen Titans; Lobdell-s/Kitson-a 5.00
Annual 3 (7/14, $4.99) Follows #30; Harvest app. 5.00
... Earth One Volume One HC (2014, $22.99) Lemire-s/Dodson-a/c; new origin story 23.00

TEEN TITANS (DC New 52)
DC Comics: Sept, 2014 - No. 24, Nov, 2016 ($2.99)

1-24: 1-Pfeifer-s/Rocafort-a/c; Manchester Black app. 5-Hepburn-a; new Power Girl app. 15-Robin War tie-in; Professor Pyg app. 18,19-Wonder Woman app. 3.00
Annual 1 (6/15, $4.99) Superboy returns; Borges & St. Claire-a; March-c 5.00
Annual 2 (8/16, $4.99) Lobdell-s/Cory Smith-a/Jonboy Meyers-c; Sister Blood app. 5.00
...: Futures End 1 (11/14, $2.99, regular-c) Five years later; Andy Smith-a 3.00
...: Futures End 1 (11/14, $3.99, 3-D cover) 4.00

TEEN TITANS (DC Rebirth)

Teen Titans Go! #36 © DC

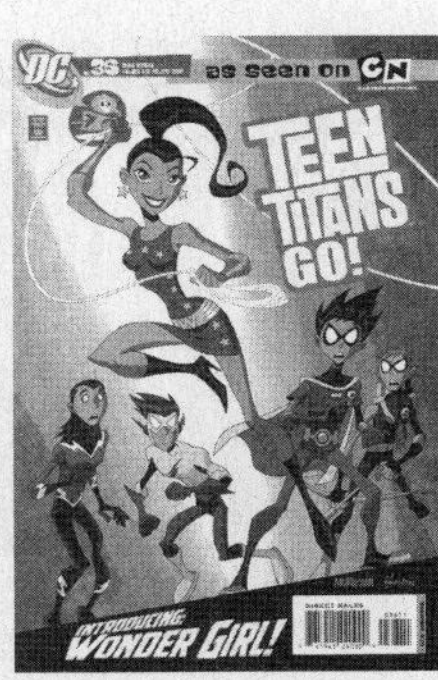

Tellos #9 © Dezago & Wieringo

Templars #5 © Ubisoft

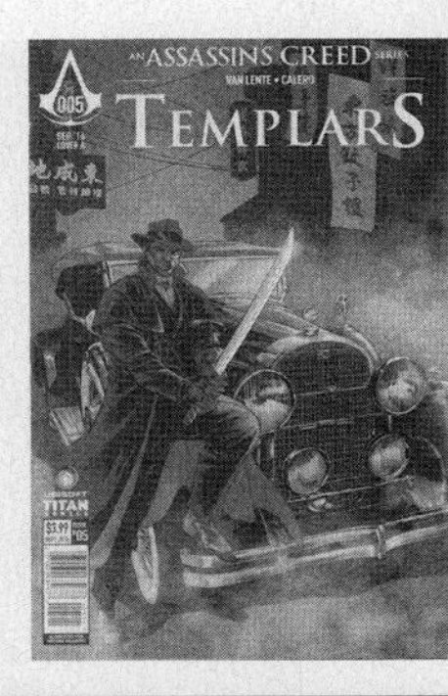

	GD 2.0	VG 4.0	FN 6.0	VF 8.0	VF/NM 9.0	NM- 9.2

DC Comics: Nov, 2016 - Present ($2.99)

1-5: 1-Percy-s/Meyers-a; Ra's al Ghul app. 2-Neves-a. 3-5-Pham-a 3.00
...: Rebirth 1 (11/16, $2.99) Meyers-a; Robin, Raven, Starfire, Beast Boy, Kid Flash app. 3.00

TEEN TITANS GO! (Based on Cartoon Network series)
DC Comics: Jan, 2004 - No. 55, Jul, 2008 ($2.25)

1-12,14-55: 1,2-Nauck-a/Bullock-c/J. Torres-s. 8-Mad Mod app. 14-Speedy-c. 28-Doom Patrol app. 31-Nightwing app. 36-Wonder Girl. 38-Mad Mod app.; Clugston-a 3.00
1-(9/04, Free Comic Book Day giveaway) r/#1; 2 bound-in Wacky Packages stickers 4.00
13-($2.95) Bonus pages with Shazam! reprint 4.00
Jam Packed Action (2005, $7.99, digest) adaptations of two TV episodes 8.00
... Vol 1: Truth, Justice, Pizza! (2004, $6.95, digest-size) r/#1-5 7.00
... Vol 2: Heroes on Patrol (2005, $6.99, digest-size) r/#6-10 7.00
... Vol 3: Bring It On! (2005, $6.99, digest-size) r/#11-15 7.00
... Vol 4: Ready For Action! (2006, $6.99, digest-size) r/#16-20 7.00
... Vol 5: On The Move! (2006, $6.99, digest-size) r/#21-25 7.00
... Titans Together TPB (2007, $12.99) r/#26-32 13.00

TEEN TITANS GO! (Based on the 2013 Cartoon Network series)
DC Comics: Feb, 2014 - Present ($2.99)

1-20: 1-Fisch-s. 2-Brotherhood of Evil app. 4-HIVE Five app. 13-Aqualad app. 3.00
... FCBD Special Edition 1 (6/14, giveaway) r/#1 3.00
... FCBD Special Edition 1 (6/15, giveaway) flipbook with Scooby-Doo! Team Up 3.00

TEEN TITANS SPOTLIGHT
DC Comics: Aug, 1986 - No. 21, Apr, 1988

1-21: 7-Guice's 1st work at DC. 14-Nightwing; Batman app. 15-Austin-c(i). 18,19-Millennium x-over. 21-($1.00-c)-Original Teen Titans; Spiegle-a 4.00
*Note: **Guice** a-7p, 8p; c-7,8. **Orlando** c/a-11p. **Perez** c-1, 17i, 19. **Sienkiewicz** c-10*

TEEN TITANS YEAR ONE
DC Comics: Mar, 2008 - No. 6, Aug, 2008 ($2.99, limited series)

1-6-The original five form a team; Wolfram-s/Kerschl-a 3.00
TPB (2008, $14.99) r/#1-6; bonus pin-up 15.00

TEEN WOLF: BITE ME (Based on the MTV series)
Image Comics (Top Cow): Sept, 2011 - No. 3, Nov, 2011 ($3.99, limited series)

1-3: 1-Tischman-s/Mooney-a/c 4.00

TEEPEE TIM (...Heap Funny Indian Boy)(Formerly Ha Ha Comics)(Also see "Cookie")
American Comics Group: No. 100, Feb-Mar, 1955 - No. 102, June-July, 1955

100-102 7 14 21 35 43 50

TEGRA JUNGLE EMPRESS (Zegra Jungle Empress #2 on)
Fox Features Syndicate: August, 1948

1-Blue Beetle, Rocket Kelly app.; used in **SOTI**, pg. 31
79 158 237 502 864 1225

TEK JANSEN (See Stephen Colbert's...)

TEKNO COMIX HANDBOOK
Tekno Comix: May, 1996 ($3.95, one-shot)

1-Guide to the Tekno Universe 4.00

TEKNOPHAGE (See Neil Gaiman's...)

TEKNOPHAGE VERSUS ZEERUS
BIG Entertainment: July, 1996 ($3.25, one-shot)

1-Paul Jenkins script 3.25

TEKWORLD (William Shatner's... on-c only)
Epic Comics (Marvel): Sept, 1992 - Aug, 1994 ($1.75)

1-Based on Shatner's novel, TekWar, set in L.A. in the year 2120 4.00
2-24 3.00

TELARA CHRONICLES (Based on the videogame Rift: Planes of Telara)
DC Comics (WildStorm): Jan, 2010; Nov, 2010 - No. 4, Feb, 2011 ($3.99, limited series)

0-(1/10, free) Preview of series 3.00
1-4-Pop Mhan-a/Drew Johnson-c 4.00
TPB (2011, $17.99) r/#0-4; background info on Telara 18.00

TELEVISION (See TV)

TELEVISION COMICS (Early TV comic)
Standard Comics (Animated Cartoons): No. 5, Feb, 1950 - No. 8, Nov, 1950

5-1st app. Willy Nilly 10 20 30 58 79 100
6-8: #6 on inside has #2 on cover 8 16 24 44 57 70

TELEVISION PUPPET SHOW (Early TV comic) (See Spotty the Pup)
Avon Periodicals: 1950 - No. 2, Nov, 1950

1-1st app. Speedy Rabbit, Spotty The Pup 22 44 66 132 216 300
2 15 30 45 88 137 185

TELEVISION TEENS MOPSY (See TV Teens)

TELL IT TO THE MARINES
Toby Press Publications: Mar, 1952 - No. 15, July, 1955

1-Lover O'Leary and His Liberty Belles (with pin-ups), ends #6; Spike & Bat begin, end #6 34 68 102 199 325 450
2-Madame Cobra-c/story 22 44 66 132 216 300
3-5 18 36 54 105 165 225
6-12,14,15: 7-9,14,15-Photo-c 15 30 45 83 124 165
13-John Wayne photo-c 20 40 60 120 195 270
I.W. Reprint #9-r/#1 above 2 4 6 11 16 20
Super Reprint #16(1964)-r/#4 above 2 4 6 8 11 14

TELLOS
Image Comics: May, 1999 - No. 10, Nov, 2000 ($2.50)

1-Dezago-s/Wieringo-a 3.00
1-Variant-c ($7.95) 8.00
2-10: 4-Four covers 3.00
...: Maiden Voyage (3/01, $5.95) Didier Crispeels-a/c 6.00
...: Sons & Moons (2002, $5.95) Nick Cardy-c 6.00
...: The Last Heist (2001, $5.95) Rousseau-a/c 6.00
Prelude ($5.00, AnotherUniverse.com) 5.00
Prologue ($3.95, Dynamic Forces) 4.00
...Collected Edition 1 (12/99, $8.95) r/#1-3 9.00
... Colossal, Vol. 1 TPB (2008, $17.99) r/#1-10, Prelude, Prologue, Scatterjack-s from Section Zero #1, cover gallery, Wieringo sketch pages; Dezago afterword 18.00
...: Kindred Spirits (2/01, $17.95) r/#6-10, Section Zero #1 (Scatterjack-s) 18.00
...: Reluctant Heroes (2/01, $17.95) r/#1-5, Prelude, Prologue; sketchbook 18.00

TELOS (See Convergence)
DC Comics: Dec, 2015 - No. 6, May, 2016 ($2.99)

1-6: 1,2-King-s/Pagulayan-a. 1-Brainiac app. 2-Arak, Son of Thunder and Validus app. 3-6-Hal Jordan Parallax app. 3.00

TEMPEST (See Aquaman, 3rd Series)
DC Comics: Nov, 1996 - No. 4, Feb, 1997 ($1.75, limited series)

1-4: Formerly Aqualad; Phil Jimenez-c/a/scripts in all 3.00

TEMPLARS (Assassin's Creed)
Titan Comics: Apr, 2016 - No. 9, Feb, 2017 ($3.99)

1-9-Black Cross; set in 1927; Van Lente-s/Calero-a 4.00

TEMPUS FUGITIVE
DC Comics: 1990 - No. 4, 1991 ($4.95, squarebound, 52 pgs.)

Book 1,2: Ken Steacy painted-c/a & scripts 6.00
Book 3,4-($5.95-c) 6.00
TPB (Dark Horse Comics, 1/97, $17.95) 18.00

TEN COMMANDMENTS (See Moses & the... and Classics Illustrated Special)

TENDER LOVE STORIES
Skywald Publ. Corp.: Feb, 1971 - No. 4, July, 1971 (Pre-code reprints and new stories)

1 (All 25¢, 52 pgs.) 6 12 18 41 76 110
2-4 5 10 15 31 53 75

TENDER ROMANCE (Ideal Romance #3 on)
Key Publications (Gilmour Magazines): Dec, 1953 - No. 2, Feb, 1954

1-Headlight & lingerie panels; B. Baily-c 27 54 81 158 259 360
2-Bernard Baily-c 15 30 45 86 133 180

TEN GRAND
Image Comics (Joe's Comics): May, 2013 - Present ($2.99)

1-12: 1-4-Straczynski-s/Templesmith-a. 1-Multiple variant covers. 2-Two covers 3.00

TENSE SUSPENSE
Fago Publications: Dec, 1958 - No. 2, Feb, 1959

1 12 24 36 69 97 125
2 9 18 27 50 65 80

TEN STORY LOVE (Formerly a pulp magazine with same title)
Ace Periodicals: V29#3, June-July, 1951 - V36#5(#209), Sept, 1956 (#3-6: 52 pgs.)

V29#3(#177)-Part comic, part text; painted-c 19 38 57 111 176 240
4-6(1/52) 12 34 36 69 97 125
V30#1(3/52)-6(1/53) 12 24 36 67 94 120
V31#1(2/53),V32#2(4/53)-6(12/53) 11 22 33 64 90 115
V33#1(1/54)-3(5#54, #195), V34#4(7/54, #196)-6(10/54, #198)
11 22 33 62 86 110

The Tenth #12 © Tony Daniel

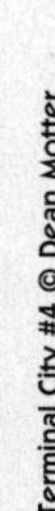

Terminal City #4 © Dean Motter

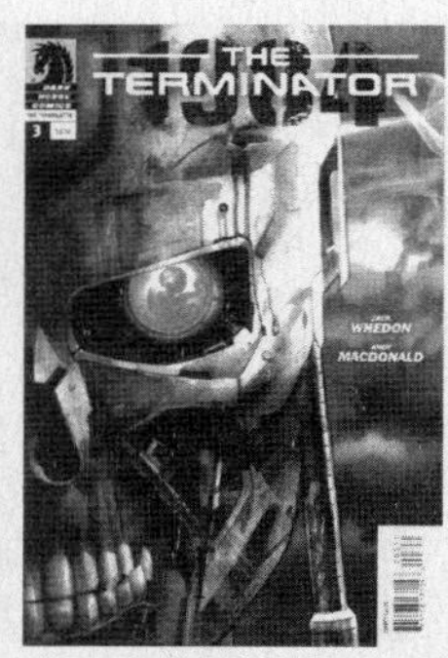

Terminator: 1984 #3 © Studio Canal

	GD 2.0	VG 4.0	FN 6.0	VF 8.0	VF/NM 9.0	NM- 9.2
V35#1(12/54, #199)-3(4/55, #201)-Last precode	11	22	33	60	83	105
V35#4-6(9/55, #201-204), V36#1(11/55, #205)-3, 5(9/56, #209)	10	20	30	58	79	100
V36#4-L.B. Cole-a	12	24	36	67	94	120

TENTH, THE
Image Comics: Jan, 1997 - No. 4, June, 1997 ($2.50, limited series)

1-4-Tony Daniel-c/a, Beau Smith-s 5.00
Abuse of Humanity TPB ($10.95) r/#1-4 12.00
Abuse of Humanity TPB (10/98, $11.95) r/#1-4 & 0(8/97) 12.00

TENTH, THE
Image Comics: Sept, 1997 - No. 14, Jan, 1999 ($2.50)

0-(8/97, $5.00) American Ent. Ed. 6.00
1-Tony Daniel-c/a, Beau Smith-s 6.00
2-9: 3,7-Variant-c 4.00
10-14 3.00
...Configuration (8/98) Re-cap and pin-ups 3.00
...Collected Edition 1 ('98, $4.95, square-bound) r/#1,2 5.00
...Special (4/00, $2.95) r/#0 and Wizard #1/2 3.00
Wizard #1/2-Daniel-s/Steve Scott-a 10.00

TENTH, THE (Volume 3) (The Black Embrace)
Image Comics: Mar, 1999 - No. 4, June, 1999 ($2.95)

1-4-Daniel-c/a 3.00
TPB (1/00, $12.95) r/#1-4 13.00

TENTH, THE (Volume 4) (Evil's Child)
Image Comics: Sept, 1999 - No. 4, Mar, 2000 ($2.95, limited series)

1-4-Daniel-c/a 3.00

TENTH, THE (Darkk Dawn)
Image Comics: July, 2005 ($4.99, one-shot)

1-Kirkham-a/Bonny-s 5.00

TENTH, THE : RESURRECTED
Dark Horse Comics: July, 2001 - No. 4, Feb, 2002 ($2.99, limited series)

1-4: 1-Two covers; Daniel-s/c; Romano-a 3.00

10th MUSE
Image Comics (TidalWave Studios): Nov, 2000 - No. 9, Jan, 2002 ($2.95)

1-Character based on wrestling's Rena Mero; regular & photo covers 3.00
2-9: 2-Photo and 2 Lashley covers; flip book Dollz preview. 5-Savage Dragon app.; 2 covers by Lashley and Larsen. 6-Tellos x-over 3.00

TEN WHO DARED (Disney)
Dell Publishing Co.: No. 1178, Dec, 1960

	GD 2.0	VG 4.0	FN 6.0	VF 8.0	VF/NM 9.0	NM- 9.2
Four Color 1178-Movie, painted-c; cast member photo on back-c	7	14	21	46	86	125

TERMINAL CITY
DC Comics (Vertigo): July, 1996 - No. 9, Mar, 1997 ($2.50, limited series)

1-9: Dean Motter scripts, 7,8-Matt Wagner-c 3.00
TPB ('97, $19.95) r/series 20.00

TERMINAL CITY: AERIAL GRAFFITI
DC Comics (Vertigo): Nov, 1997 - No. 5, Mar, 1998 ($2.50, limited series)

1-5: Dean Motter-s/Lark-a/Chiarello-c 3.00

TERMINAL HERO
Dynamite Entertainment: 2014 - No. 6, 2015 ($2.99, limited series)

1-6-Milligan-s/Kowalski-a/Jae Lee-c 3.00

TERMINATOR, THE (See Robocop vs. ... & Rust #12 for 1st app.)
Now Comics: Sept, 1988 - No. 17, 1989 ($1.75, Baxter paper)

	GD 2.0	VG 4.0	FN 6.0	VF 8.0	VF/NM 9.0	NM- 9.2
1-Based on movie	1	3	4	6	8	10

2-5 6.00
6-11,13-17 4.00
12-($2.95, 52 pgs.)-Intro. John Connor 5.00
Trade paperback (1989, $9.95) 15.00

TERMINATOR, THE
Dark Horse Comics: Aug, 1990 - No. 4, Nov, 1990 ($2.50, limited series)

1-Set 39 years later than the movie 5.00
2-4 4.00

TERMINATOR, THE
Dark Horse Comics: 1998 - No. 4, Dec, 1998 ($2.95, limited series)

1-4-Alan Grant-s/Steve Pugh-a/c 4.00
...Special (1998, $2.95) Darrow-c/Grant-s 4.00

TERMINATOR, THE: ALL MY FUTURES PAST
Now Comics: V3#1, Aug, 1990 - V3#2, Sept, 1990 ($1.75, limited series)

V3#1,2 4.00

TERMINATOR, THE: ENDGAME
Dark Horse Comics: Sept, 1992 - No. 3, Nov, 1992 ($2.50, limited series)

1-3: Guice-a(p); painted-c 4.00

TERMINATOR, THE: ENEMY OF MY ENEMY
Dark Horse Comics: Feb, 2014 - No. 6, Oct, 2014 ($3.99, limited series)

1-6-Jolley-s/Igle-a; set in 1985 4.00

TERMINATOR, THE: HUNTERS AND KILLERS
Dark Horse Comics: Mar, 1992 - No. 3, May, 1992 ($2.50, limited series)

1-3 4.00

TERMINATOR, THE: 1984
Dark Horse Comics: Sept, 2010 - No. 3, Nov, 2010 ($3.50, limited series)

1-3: Takes place during and after the 1st movie; Zack Whedon-s/Andy MacDonald-a 3.50

TERMINATOR, THE: ONE SHOT
Dark Horse Comics: July, 1991 ($5.95, 56 pgs.)

nn-Matt Wagner-a; contains stiff pop-up inside 6.00

TERMINATOR: REVOLUTION (Follows Terminator 2: Infinity series)
Dynamite Entertainment: 2008 - No. 5, 2009 ($3.50, limited series)

1-5-Furman-s/Antonio-a. 1-3-Two covers 3.50

TERMINATOR / ROBOCOP: KILL HUMAN
Dynamite Entertainment: 2011 - No. 4, 2011 ($3.99, limited series)

1-4: 1-Covers by Simonson, Lau & Feister. 2-4-Three covers on each 4.00

TERMINATOR: SALVATION MOVIE PREQUEL
IDW Publishing: Jan, 2009 - No. 4, Apr, 2009 ($3.99, limited series)

1-4: Alan Robinson-a/Dara Naraghi-s 4.00
0-Salvation Movie Preview (4/09) Mariotte-s/Figueroa-a 4.00

TERMINATOR SALVATION: THE FINAL BATTLE
Dark Horse Comics: Dec, 2013 - No. 12, Dec, 2014 ($3.99, limited series)

1-12-Straczynski-s/Woods-a 4.00

TERMINATOR, THE: SECONDARY OBJECTIVES
Dark Horse Comics: July, 1991 - No. 4, Oct, 1991 ($2.50, limited series)

1-4: Gulacy-c/a(p) in all 4.00

TERMINATOR, THE: THE BURNING EARTH
Now Comics: V2#1, Mar, 1990 - V2#5, July, 1990 ($1.75, limited series)

	GD 2.0	VG 4.0	FN 6.0	VF 8.0	VF/NM 9.0	NM- 9.2
V2#1: Alex Ross painted art (1st published work)	2	4	6	9	12	15
2-5: Ross-c/a in all	1	3	4	6	8	10

Trade paperback (1990, $9.95)-Reprints V2#1-5 18.00
Trade paperback (ibooks, 2003, $17.95)-Digitally remastered reprint 18.00

TERMINATOR, THE: THE DARK YEARS
Dark Horse Comics: Aug, 1999 - No. 4, Dec, 1999 ($2.95, limited series)

1-4-Alan Grant-s/Mel Rubi-a; Jae Lee-c 4.00

TERMINATOR, THE: THE ENEMY FROM WITHIN
Dark Horse Comics: Nov, 1991 - No. 4, Feb, 1992 ($2.50, limited series)

1-4: All have Simon Bisley painted-c 4.00

TERMINATOR, THE: 2029
Dark Horse Comics: Mar, 2010 - No. 3, May, 2010 ($3.50, limited series)

1-3: Kyle Reese before his time-jump to 1984; Zack Whedon-s/Andy MacDonald-a 3.50

TERMINATOR 2: CYBERNETIC DAWN
Malibu: Nov, 1995 - No.4, Feb, 1996; No. 0. Apr, 1996 ($2.50, lim. series)

0 (4/96, $2.95)-Erskine-c/a; flip book w/Terminator 2: Nuclear Twilight 4.00
1-4: Continuation of film. 4.00

TERMINATOR 2: INFINITY
Dynamite Entertainment: 2007 - No. 7 ($3.50)

1-7: 1-Furman-s/Raynor-a; 3 covers. 6,7-Painkiller Jane x-over 3.50

TERMINATOR 2: JUDGEMENT DAY
Marvel Comics: Early Sept, 1991 - No. 3, Early Oct, 1991 ($1.00, lim. series)

1-3: Based on movie sequel; 1-3-Same as nn issues 4.00
nn (1991, $4.95, squarebound, 68 pgs.)-Photo-c 6.00
nn (1991, $2.25, B&W, magazine, 68 pgs.) 4.00

Terra Obscura #1 © ABC

Terrors of the Jungle #9 © STAR

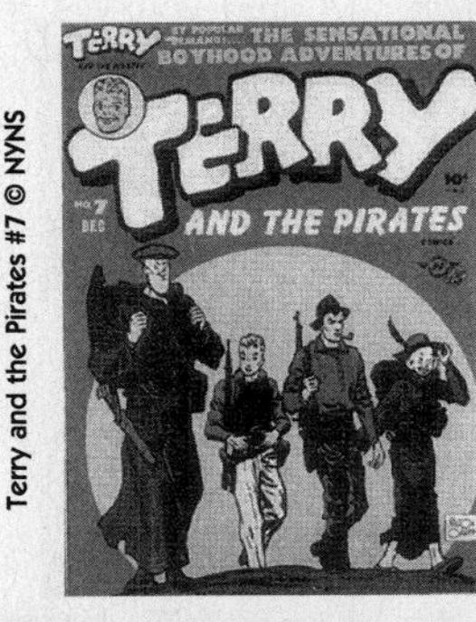

Terry and the Pirates #7 © NYNS

GD VG FN VF VF/NM NM-
2.0 4.0 6.0 8.0 9.0 9.2

TERMINATOR 2: NUCLEAR TWILIGHT
Malibu: Nov, 1995 - No.4, Feb, 1996; No. 0, Apr, 1996 ($2.50, lim. series)
0 (4/96, $2.95)-Erskine-c/a; flip book w/Terminator 2: Cybernetic Dawn 4.00
1-4:Continuation of film. 4.00

TERMINATOR 3: RISE OF THE MACHINES (... BEFORE THE RISE on cover)
Beckett Comics: July, 2003 - No. 6, Jan, 2004 ($5.95, limited series)
1-6: 1,2-Leads into movie; 2 covers on each. 3-6-Movie adaptation 6.00

TERM LIFE
Image Comics (Shadowline): Jan, 2011 ($16.99, graphic novel)
SC-Lieberman-s/Thornborrow-a/DeStefano-l 17.00

TERRA (See Supergirl {2005 series} #12)
DC Comics: Jan, 2009 - No. 4, Feb, 2009 ($2.99, limited series)
1-4-Conner-a/c. 1,2,4-Power Girl app. 2-4-Geo-Force app. 4.00
TPB (2009, $14.99) r/#1-4 & Supergirl #12 15.00

TERRAFORMERS
Wonder Color Comics: April, 1987 - No. 2, 1987 ($1.95, limited series)
1,2-Kelley Jones-a 3.00

TERRA OBSCURA (See Tom Strong)
America's Best Comics: Aug, 2003 - No. 6, Feb, 2004 ($2.95)
1-6-Alan Moore & Peter Hogan-s/Paquette-a 3.00
TPB (2004, $14.95) r/#1-6 15.00

TERRA OBSCURA VOLUME 2 (See Tom Strong)
America's Best Comics: Oct, 2004 - No. 6, May, 2005 ($2.95)
1-6-Alan Moore & Peter Hogan-s/Paquette-a; Tom Strange app. 3.00
TPB (2005, $14.99) r/#1-6 15.00

TERRARISTS
Marvel Comics (Epic): Nov, 1993 - No. 4, Feb, 1994 ($2.50, limited series)
1-4-Bound-in trading cards in all 3.00

TERRIFIC COMICS (Also see Suspense Comics)
Continental Magazines: Jan, 1944 - No. 6, Nov, 1944
1-Kid Terrific; opium story 326 652 978 2282 3991 6000
2-1st app. The Boomerang by L.B. Cole & Ed Wheelan's "Comics" McCormick, called the world's #1 comic book fan begins 290 580 870 1856 3178 4500
3-Diana becomes Boomerang's costumed aide; L.B. Cole-c
232 464 696 1485 2643 3800
4-Classic war-c (Scarce) 470 940 1410 3431 6066 8700
5-The Reckoner begins; Boomerang & Diana by L.B. Cole; Classic Schomburg bondage & hooded vigilante-c (Scarce) 1600 3200 4800 9600 19,000 33,000
6-L.B. Cole-c/a 210 420 630 1334 2567 3800
NOTE: *L.B. Cole a-1, 2(2), 3-6. Fuje a-5, 6. Rico a-2; c-1. Schomburg c-2, 5.*

TERRIFIC COMICS (Formerly Horrific; Wonder Boy #17 on)
Mystery Publ.(Comic Media)/(Ajax/Farrell): No. 14, Dec, 1954; No. 16, Mar, 1955 (No #15)
14-Art swipe/Advs. into the Unknown #37; injury-to-eye-c; pg. 2, panel 5 swiped from Phantom Stranger #4; surrealistic Palais-a; Human Cross story; classic-c
90 180 270 576 988 1400
16-Wonder Boy-c/story (last pre-code) 29 58 87 170 278 385

TERRIFYING TALES (Formerly Startling Terror Tales #10)
Star Publications: No. 11, Jan, 1953 - No. 15, Apr, 1954
11-Used in **POP**, pgs. 99,100; all Jo-Jo-r 60 120 180 381 653 925
12-Reprints Jo-Jo #19 entirely; L.B. Cole splash 54 108 162 343 574 825
13-All Rulah-r; classic devil-c 68 136 204 435 743 1050
14-All Rulah reprints 52 104 156 328 552 775
15-Rulah, Zago-r; used in **SOTI**-r/Rulah #22 50 100 150 315 533 750
NOTE: *All issues have L.B. Cole covers; bondage covers-No. 12-14.*

TERROR ILLUSTRATED (Adult Tales of...)
E.C. Comics: Nov-Dec, 1955 - No. 2, Spring (April on-c), 1956 (Magazine, 25¢)
1-Adult Entertainment on-c 25 50 75 150 245 340
2-Charles Sultan-a 18 36 54 103 162 220
NOTE: *Craig, Evans, Ingels, Orlando art in each. Crandall c-1, 2.*

TERROR INC. (See A Shadowline Saga #3)
Marvel Comics: July, 1992 - No. 13, July, 1993 ($1.75)
1-8,11-13: 6,7-Punisher-c/story. 13-Ghost Rider app. 3.00
9,10-Wolverine-c/story 4.00

TERROR INC.
Marvel Comics (MAX): Oct, 2007 - No. 5, Apr, 2008 ($3.99, limited series)
1-5: 1-Lapham-s/Zircher-a; origin of Mr. Terror retold 4.00

TERROR INC. - APOCALYPSE SOON
Marvel Comics (MAX): July, 2009 - No. 4, Sept, 2009 ($3.99, limited series)
1-4: 1-Lapham-s/Turnbull-a 4.00

TERRORS OF DRACULA (Magazine)
Modern Day Periodical/Eerie Publ.: Vol. 1 #3, May, 1979 - Vol. 3 #2, Sept, 1981 (B&W)
Vol. 1 #3 (5/79, 1st issue) 4 8 12 25 40 55
#4(8/79), #5(11/79) 3 6 9 19 30 40
Vol. 2 #1-3: 1-(2/80). 2-(5/80). 3-(8/80) 3 6 9 16 24 32
Vol. 3 #1 (5/81), #2 (9/81) 3 6 9 18 28 38

TERRORS OF THE JUNGLE (Formerly Jungle Thrills)
Star Publications: No. 17, 5/52 - No. 21, 2/53; No. 4, 4/53 - No. 10, 9/54
17-Reprints Rulah #21, used in **SOTI**; L.B. Cole bondage-c
60 120 180 381 653 925
18-Jo-Jo-r 47 94 141 296 498 700
19,20(1952)-Jo-Jo-r; Disbrow-a 43 86 129 271 461 650
21-Jungle Jo, Tangi-r; used in **POP**, pg. 100 & color illos.
47 94 141 296 498 700
4-10: All Disbrow-a. 5-Jo-Jo-r. 8-Rulah, Jo-Jo-r. 9-Jo-Jo-r; Disbrow-a; Tangi by Orlando10-Rulah-r 47 94 141 296 498 700
NOTE: *L.B. Cole c-all; bondage c-17, 19, 21, 5, 7.*

TERROR TALES (See Beware Terror Tales)

TERROR TALES (Magazine)
Eerie Publications: V1#7, 1969 - V6#6, Dec, 1974; V7#1, Apr, 1976 - V10, 1979? (V1-V6: 52 pgs.; V7 on: 68 pgs.)
V1#7 7 14 21 49 92 135
V1#8-11('69): 9-Bondage-c 5 10 15 33 57 80
V2#1-6('70), V3#1-6('71), V4#1-7('72), V5#1-6('73), V6#1-6('74), V7#1,4('76) (no V7#2), V8#1-3('77) 5 10 15 30 50 70
V7#3-(7/76) LSD story-r/Weird V3#5 5 10 15 30 50 70
V9#2-4, V10#1(1/79) 5 10 15 31 53 75

TERROR TITANS
DC Comics: Dec, 2008 - No. 6, May, 2009 ($2.99, limited series)
1-6: 1-Ravager and Clock King at the Dark Side Club; Bennett-a. 3-Static app. 3.00
TPB (2009, $17.99) r/#1-6 18.00

TERRY AND THE PIRATES (See Famous Feature Stories, Merry Christmas From Sears Toyland, Popular Comics, Super Book #3,5,9,16,28, & Super Comics)

TERRY AND THE PIRATES
Dell Publishing Co.: 1939 - 1953 (By Milton Caniff)
Large Feature Comic 2(1939) 103 206 309 659 1130 1600
Large Feature Comic 6(1938)-r/1936 dailies 81 162 243 518 884 1250
Four Color 9(1940) 77 154 231 493 847 1200
Large Feature Comic 27('41), 6('42) 65 130 195 416 708 1000
Four Color 44('43) 31 62 93 223 499 775
Four Color 101('45) 20 40 60 135 300 465
Family Album(1942) 20 40 60 118 192 265

TERRY AND THE PIRATES (Formerly Boy Explorers; Long John Silver & the Pirates #30 on) (Daily strip-r) (Two #26's)
Harvey Publications/Charlton No. 26-28: No. 3, 4/47 - No. 26, 4/51; No. 26, 6/55 - No. 28, 10/55
3(#1)-Boy Explorers by S&K; Terry & the Pirates begin by Caniff; 1st app. The Dragon Lady 40 80 120 244 402 560
4-S&K Boy Explorers 22 44 66 132 216 300
5-11: 11-Man in Black app. by Powell 13 26 39 72 101 130
12-20: 16-Girl threatened with red hot poker 10 20 30 56 76 95
21-26(4/51)-Last Caniff issue & last pre-code issue 10 20 30 54 72 90
26-28('55)(Formerly This Is Suspense)-No Caniff-a 9 18 27 47 61 75
NOTE: *Powell a (Tommy Tween)-5-10, 12, 14; 15-17(1/2 to 2 pgs. each).*

TERRY BEARS COMICS (TerryToons, The... #4)
St. John Publishing Co.: June, 1952 - No. 3, Mar, 1953
1-By Paul Terry 12 24 36 67 94 120
2,3 8 16 24 42 54 65

TERRY-TOONS ALBUM (See Giant Comics Edition)

TERRY-TOONS COMICS (1st Series) (Becomes Paul Terry's Comics #85 on; later issues titled "Paul Terry's...")
Timely/Marvel No. 1-59 (8/47)(Becomes Best Western No. 58 on?, Marvel)/ St. John No. 60 (9/47) on: Oct, 1942 - No. 86, May, 1951
1 (Scarce)-Features characters that 1st app. on movie screen; Gandy Goose & Sourpuss begin; war-c; Gandy Goose c-1-37 258 516 774 1651 2826 4000

Tessie the Typist #11 © MAR

The Texan #4 © STJ

Tex Ritter Western #1 © FAW

	GD 2.0	VG 4.0	FN 6.0	VF 8.0	VF/NM 9.0	NM- 9.2
2	90	180	270	576	988	1400
3-5	60	120	180	381	653	925
6,8-10: 9,10-World War II gag-c	45	90	135	284	480	675
7-Hitler, Hirohito, Mussolini-c	219	438	657	1402	2401	3400
11-20	32	64	96	192	314	435
21-37	23	46	69	136	223	310
38-Mighty Mouse begins (1st app., 11/45); Mighty Mouse-c begin, end #86; Gandy, Sourpuss welcome Mighty Mouse on-c	213	426	639	1363	2332	3300
39-2nd app. Mighty Mouse	64	128	192	406	696	985
40-49: 43-Infinity-c	36	72	108	216	351	485
50-1st app. Heckle & Jeckle (11/46)	61	122	183	390	670	950
51-60: 55-Infinity-c. 60-(9/47)-Atomic explosion panel; 1st St. John issue	20	40	60	114	182	250
61-86: 85,86-Same book as Paul Terry's Comics #85,86 with only a title change; published at same time?	15	30	45	88	137	185

TERRY-TOONS COMICS (2nd Series)
St. John Publishing Co./Pines: June, 1952 - No. 9, Nov, 1953; 1957; 1958

	GD 2.0	VG 4.0	FN 6.0	VF 8.0	VF/NM 9.0	NM- 9.2
1-Gandy Goose & Sourpuss begin by Paul Terry	18	36	54	105	165	225
2	10	20	30	56	76	95
3-9	9	18	27	52	69	85
Giant Summer Fun Book 101,102-(Sum, 1957, Sum, 1958, 25¢, Pines)(TV) CBS Television Presents...; Tom Terrific, Mighty Mouse, Heckle & Jeckle Gandy Goose app.	14	28	42	80	115	150

TERRYTOONS, THE TERRY BEARS (Formerly Terry Bears Comics)
Pines Comics: No. 4, Summer, 1958 (CBS Television Presents...)

	GD 2.0	VG 4.0	FN 6.0	VF 8.0	VF/NM 9.0	NM- 9.2
4	8	16	24	42	54	65

TESSIE THE TYPIST (Tiny Tessie #24; see Comedy Comics, Gay Comics & Joker Comics)
Timely/Marvel Comics (20CC): Summer, 1944 - No. 23, Aug, 1949

	GD 2.0	VG 4.0	FN 6.0	VF 8.0	VF/NM 9.0	NM- 9.2
1-Doc Rockblock & others by Wolverton	168	336	504	1075	1838	2600
2-Wolverton's Powerhouse Pepper	61	122	183	390	670	950
3-(3/45)-No Wolverton	37	74	111	222	361	500
4,5,7,8-Wolverton-a. 4-(Fall/45)	41	82	123	256	428	600
6-Kurtzman's "Hey Look", 2 pgs. Wolverton-a	41	82	123	256	428	600
9-Wolverton's Powerhouse Pepper (8 pgs.) & 1 pg. Kurtzman's "Hey Look"	42	84	126	267	451	635
10-Wolverton's Powerhouse Pepper (4 pgs.)	41	82	123	256	428	600
11-Wolverton's Powerhouse Pepper (8 pgs.)	42	84	126	267	451	635
12-Wolverton's Powerhouse Pepper (4 pgs.) & 1 pg. Kurtzman's "Hey Look"	41	82	123	256	428	600
13-Wolverton's Powerhouse Pepper (4 pgs.)	41	82	123	256	428	600
14,15: 14-Wolverton's Dr. Whackyhack (1 pg.); 1-1/2 pgs. Kurtzman's "Hey Look". 15-Kurtzman's "Hey Look" (3 pgs.) & 3 pgs. Giggles 'n' Grins	34	68	102	199	325	450
16-18-Kurtzman's "Hey Look" (?, 2 & 1 pg.)	27	54	81	158	259	360
19-Annie Oakley story (8 pgs.)	21	42	63	122	199	275
20-23: 20-Anti-Wertham editorial (2/49)	20	40	60	117	189	260

NOTE: *Lana app.-21. Millie The Model app.-13, 15, 17, 21. Rusty app.-10, 11, 13, 15, 17.*

TESTAMENT
DC Comics (Vertigo): Feb, 2006 - No. 22, Mar, 2008 ($2.99)

	GD 2.0	VG 4.0	FN 6.0	VF 8.0	VF/NM 9.0	NM- 9.2
1-22: 1-5-Rushkoff-s/Sharp-a. 6,7-Gross & Erskine-a						3.00

TEXAN, THE (Fightin' Marines #15 on; Fightin' Texan #16 on)
St. John Publishing Co.: Aug, 1948 - No. 15, Oct, 1951

	GD 2.0	VG 4.0	FN 6.0	VF 8.0	VF/NM 9.0	NM- 9.2
1-Buckskin Belle	19	38	57	111	176	240
2	12	24	36	67	94	120
3,10: 10-Oversized issue	13	26	39	72	101	130
4,5,7,15-Baker-c/a	30	60	90	177	289	400
6,9-Baker-c	24	48	72	142	234	325
8,11,13,14-Baker-c/a(2-3) each	34	68	102	199	325	450
12-All Matt Baker-c/a; Peyote story	39	78	117	231	378	525

NOTE: ***Matt Baker** c-4-9, 11-15. **Larsen** a-4-6, 8-10, 15. **Tuska** a-1, 2, 7-9.*

TEXAN, THE (TV)
Dell Publishing Co.: No. 1027, Sept-Nov, 1959 - No. 1096, May-July, 1960

	GD 2.0	VG 4.0	FN 6.0	VF 8.0	VF/NM 9.0	NM- 9.2
Four Color 1027 (#1)-Photo-c	7	14	21	49	92	135
Four Color 1096-Rory Calhoun photo-c	7	14	21	44	82	120

TEXAS CHAINSAW MASSACRE
DC Comics (WildStorm): Jan, 2007 - No. 6, Jun, 2007 ($2.99, limited series)

	GD 2.0	VG 4.0	FN 6.0	VF 8.0	VF/NM 9.0	NM- 9.2
1-6: 1-Two covers by Bermejo & Bradstreet; Abnett & Lanning-s						3.00
...: About a Boy #1 (9/07, $2.99) Abnett & Lanning-s/Gomez-a/Robertson-c						3.00
...: Book Two TPB (2009, $14.99) r/one shots & New Line Cinema's Tales of Horror story						15.00
...: By Himself #1 (10/07, $2.99) Abnett & Lanning-s/Craig-a/Robertson-c						3.00
...: Cut! #1 (8/07, $2.99) Pfeiffer-s/Raffaele-a/Robertson-c						3.00
...: Raising Cain 1-3 (7/08 - No. 3, 9/08, $3.50) Bruce Jones-s/Chris Gugliotti-a						3.50

TEXAS JOHN SLAUGHTER (See Walt Disney Presents, 4-Color #997, 1181 & #2)

TEXAS KID (See Two-Gun Western, Wild Western)
Marvel/Atlas Comics (LMC): Jan, 1951 - No. 10, July, 1952

	GD 2.0	VG 4.0	FN 6.0	VF 8.0	VF/NM 9.0	NM- 9.2
1-Origin; Texas Kid (alias Lance Temple) & his horse Thunder begin; Tuska-a	28	56	84	168	274	380
2	15	30	45	84	127	170
3-10	12	24	36	69	97	125

NOTE: ***Maneely** a-1-4; c-1, 3, 5-10.*

TEXAS RANGERS, THE (See Jace Pearson of... and Superior Stories #4)

TEXAS RANGERS IN ACTION (Formerly Captain Gallant or Scotland Yard?)
Charlton Comics: No. 5, Jul, 1956 - No. 79, Aug, 1970 (See Blue Bird Comics)

	GD 2.0	VG 4.0	FN 6.0	VF 8.0	VF/NM 9.0	NM- 9.2
5	8	16	24	44	57	70
6,7,9,10	6	12	18	28	34	40
8-Ditko-a (signed)	10	20	30	54	72	90
11-(68 pg. Giant) Williamson-a (5&8 pgs.); Torres/Williamson-a (5 pgs.)	10	20	30	54	72	90
12-(68 pg. Giant, 6/58)	6	12	18	28	34	40
13-Williamson-a (5 pgs); Torres, Morisi-a	8	16	24	42	54	65
14-20	5	10	15	23	28	32
21-30	3	6	9	15	22	28
31-59: 32-Both 10¢-c & 15¢-c exist	2	4	6	13	18	22
60-Riley's Rangers begin	3	6	9	14	19	24
61-65,68-70	2	4	6	8	11	14
66,67: 66-1st app. The Man Called Loco. 67-Origin	2	4	6	9	13	16
71-79: 77-(4/70) Ditko-c & a (8 pgs.)	1	3	4	6	8	10
76 (Modern Comics-r, 1977)						6.00

TEXAS SLIM (See A-1 Comics)

TEX DAWSON, GUN-SLINGER (Gunslinger #2 on)
Marvel Comics Group: Jan, 1973 (20¢)(Also see Western Kid, 1st series)

	GD 2.0	VG 4.0	FN 6.0	VF 8.0	VF/NM 9.0	NM- 9.2
1-Steranko-c; Williamson-r (4 pgs.); Tex Dawson-r by Romita(3) from 1955; Tuska-r	3	6	9	17	26	35

TEX FARNUM (See Wisco)

TEX FARRELL (...Pride of the Wild West)
D. S. Publishing Co.: Mar-Apr, 1948

	GD 2.0	VG 4.0	FN 6.0	VF 8.0	VF/NM 9.0	NM- 9.2
1-Tex Farrell & his horse Lightning; Shelly-c	15	30	45	88	137	185

TEX GRANGER (Formerly Calling All Boys; see True Comics)
Parents' Magazine Inst./Commended: No. 18, Jun, 1948 - No. 24, Sept, 1949

	GD 2.0	VG 4.0	FN 6.0	VF 8.0	VF/NM 9.0	NM- 9.2
18-Tex Granger & his horse Bullet begin	12	24	36	69	97	125
19	10	20	30	54	72	90
20-24: 22-Wild Bill Hickok story. 23-Vs. Billy the Kid; Tim Holt app.	8	16	24	44	57	70

TEX MORGAN (See Blaze Carson and Wild Western)
Marvel Comics (CCC): Aug, 1948 - No. 9, Feb, 1950

	GD 2.0	VG 4.0	FN 6.0	VF 8.0	VF/NM 9.0	NM- 9.2
1-Tex Morgan, his horse Lightning & sidekick Lobo begin	28	56	84	165	270	375
2	18	36	54	105	165	225
3-6: 3,4-Arizona Annie app. 5-Blaze Carson app.	14	28	42	76	108	140
7-9: All photo-c. 7-Captain Tootsie by Beck. 8-18 pg. story "The Terror of Rimrock Valley"; Diablo app.	18	36	54	105	165	225

NOTE: *Tex Taylor app. 2-6, 7, 9. **Brodsky** c-6. **Syd Shores** c-2, 5.*

TEX RITTER WESTERN (Movie star; singing cowboy; see Six-Gun Heroes and Western Hero)
Fawcett No. 1-20 (1/54)/Charlton No. 21 on: Oct, 1950 - No. 46, May, 1959 (Photo-c: 1-21)

	GD 2.0	VG 4.0	FN 6.0	VF 8.0	VF/NM 9.0	NM- 9.2
1-Tex Ritter, his stallion White Flash & dog Fury begin; photo front/back-c begin	43	86	129	271	461	650
2	21	42	63	124	202	280
3-5: 5-Last photo back-c	16	32	48	94	147	200
6-10	14	28	42	80	115	150
11-19	10	20	30	58	79	100
20-Last Fawcett issue (1/54)	11	22	33	62	86	110
21-1st Charlton issue; photo-c (3/54)	14	28	42	80	115	150
22-B&W photo back-c begin, end #32	9	18	27	52	69	85
23-30: 23-25-Young Falcon app.	9	18	27	47	61	75
31-38,40-45	8	16	24	42	54	65
39-Williamson-a; Whitman-c (1/58)	9	18	27	47	61	75
46-Last issue	8	16	24	44	57	70

TEX TAYLOR (...The Fighting Cowboy on-c #1, 2)(See Blaze Carson, Kid Colt, Tex Morgan,

Thanos (2016 series) #1 © MAR

That Wilkin Boy #1 © ACP

The Thing! #12 © CC

	GD 2.0	VG 4.0	FN 6.0	VF 8.0	VF/NM 9.0	NM- 9.2

Wild West, Wild Western, & Wisco)
Marvel Comics (HPC): Sept, 1948 - No. 9, March, 1950

1-Tex Taylor & his horse Fury begin; Blaze Carson app.	30	60	90	177	289	400
2-Blaze Carson app.	15	30	45	90	140	190
3-Arizona Annie app.	15	30	45	83	124	165
4-6: All photo-c; Blaze Carson app. 4-Anti-Wertham editorial	16	32	48	94	147	200
7-9: 7-Photo-c;18 pg. Movie-Length Thriller "Trapped in Time's Lost Land!" with sabretoothed tigers, dinosaurs; Diablo app. 8-Photo-c; 18 pg. Movie-Length Thriller "The Mystery of Devil-Tree Plateau!" with dwarf horses, dwarf people & a lost miniature Inca type village; Diablo app. 9-Photo-c; 18 pg. Movie-Length Thriller "Guns Along the Border!" Captain Tootsie by Schreiber; Nimo the Mountain Lion app.; Heth-a	19	38	57	111	176	240

NOTE: *Syd Shores c-1-3.*

THANE OF BAGARTH (Also see Hercules, 1967 series)
Charlton Comics: No. 24, Oct, 1985 - No. 25, Dec, 1985

24,25-Low print run 6.00

THANOS
Marvel Comics: Dec, 2003 - No. 12, Sept, 2004 ($2.99)

1-12: 1-6-Starlin-s/a(p)/Milgrom-i; Galactus app. 7-12-Giffen-s/Lim-a 5.00
Annual 1 (7/14, $4.99) Starlin-s/Lim-a/Keown-c 5.00
...: The Final Threat (11/12, $4.99) r/Avengers Ann. #7 & Marvel Two-In-One Ann. #2 5.00
Vol. 4: Epiphany TPB (2004, $14.99) r/#1-6 15.00
Vol. 5: Samaritan TPB (2004, $14.99) r/#7-12 15.00

THANOS
Marvel Comics: Jan, 2017 - Present ($3.99)

1-4-Lemire-s/Deodato-a; Starfox and Thane app. 2-Nebula app. 3-Imperial Guard app. 4.00

THANOS: A GOD UP THERE LISTENING
Marvel Comics: Dec, 2014 - No. 4, Dec, 2014 ($3.99, weekly limited series)

1-4-Thane and Ego The Living Planet app. 4.00

THANOS IMPERATIVE, THE
Marvel Comics: Aug, 2010 - No. 6, Jan, 2011 ($3.99, limited series)

1-6-Abnett & Lanning-s/Sepulveda-a; Vision and Silver Surfer app. 4.00
...: Devastation (3/11, $3.99) Sepulveda-a; leads into The Annihilators #1 4.00
...: Ignition (7/10, $3.99) Walker-a; prequel to series 4.00
Thanos Sourcebook (8/10, $3.99) profiles/history of Thanos and Nova Corps members 4.00

THANOS QUEST, THE (See Capt. Marvel #25, Infinity Gauntlet, Iron Man #55, Logan's Run, Marvel Feature #12, Marvel Universe: The End, Silver Surfer #34 & Warlock #9)
Marvel Comics: 1990 - No. 2, 1990 ($4.95, squarebound, 52 pgs.)

1,2-Both have Starlin scripts & covers (both printings)	3	6	9	16	24	32
1-(3/2000, $3.99) r/material from #1&2						5.00
1-(11/12, $7,99) r/#1&2, new cover by Andy Park						8.00

THANOS: THE INFINITY FINALE (Conclusion to The Infinity Entity series)
Marvel Comics: 2016 ($24.99, HC original graphic novel)

HC - Jim Starlin-s/Ron Lim-a; Adam Warlock & Annihilus app. 25.00

THANOS: THE INFINITY REVELATION (Prelude to The Infinity Entity series)
Marvel Comics: 2014 ($24.99, HC original graphic novel)

HC - Jim Starlin-s/a; Adam Warlock & Silver Surfer app. 25.00

THANOS: A GOD UP THERE LISTENING
Marvel Comics: Dec, 2014 - No. 4, Dec, 2014 ($3.99, weekly limited series)

1-4-Thane and Ego The Living Planet app. 4.00

THANOS VS. HULK
Marvel Comics: Feb, 2015 - No. 4, May, 2015 ($3.99, limited series)

1-4-Jim Starlin-s/a/c; Annihilus, Pip the Troll and Iron Man app. 4.00

THAT DARN CAT (See Movie Comics & Walt Disney Showcase #19)

THAT'S MY POP! GOES NUTS FOR FAIR
Bystander Press: 1939 (76 pgs., B&W)

nn-by Milt Gross	36	72	108	211	343	475

THAT WILKIN BOY (Meet Bingo...)
Archie Publications: Jan, 1969 - No. 52, Oct, 1982

1-1st app. Bingo's Band, Samantha & Tough Teddy	4	8	12	27	44	60
2-5	3	6	9	16	23	30
6-11	2	4	6	13	18	22
12-26-Giants. 12-No # on-c	3	6	9	14	20	26
27-40(1/77)	2	4	6	8	10	12
41-49	1	2	3	4	5	7
50-52 (low print)	2	4	6	8	10	12

THB
Horse Press: Oct, 1994 - 2002 ($5.50/$2.50/$2.95, B&W)

1 ($5.50) Paul Pope-s/a in all	3	6	9	17	26	35
1 (2nd Printing)-r/#1 w/new material						5.00
2 ($2.50)	2	4	6	10	14	18
3-5	1	2	3	5	6	8
69 (1995, no price, low distribution, 12 pgs.)-story reprinted in #1 (2nd Printing)						3.00
Giant THB-($4.95)						5.00
Giant THB 1 V2-(2003, $6.95)						7.00
...M3/THB: Mars' Mightiest Mek #1 (2000, $3.95)						4.00
...6A: Mek-Power #1, 6B: Mek-Power #2, 6C: Mek-Power #3 (2000, $3.95)						4.00
... 6D: Mek-Power #4 (2002, $4.95)						5.00

T.H.E. CAT (TV)
Dell Publishing Co.: Mar, 1967 - No. 4, Oct, 1967 (All have photo-c)

1	3	6	9	21	33	45
2-4	3	6	9	16	24	32

THERE'S A NEW WORLD COMING
Spire Christian Comics/Fleming H. Revell Co.: 1973 (35/49¢)

nn	2	4	6	10	14	18

THEY ALL KISSED THE BRIDE (See Cinema Comics Herald)

THEY'RE NOT LIKE US
Image Comics: Dec, 2014 - No. 12, Mar, 2016 ($2.99)

1-14-Stephenson-s/Gane-a/c 3.00

THIEF OF BAGHDAD
Dell Publishing Co.: No. 1229, Oct-Dec, 1961 (one-shot)

Four Color 1229-Movie, Crandall/Evans-a, photo-c	6	12	18	41	76	110

THIEF OF THIEVES
Image Comics: Feb, 2012 - Present ($2.99)

1-Kirkman & Spencer-s/Martinbrough-a/c 60.00
1-Second printing 8.00
2 25.00
3,4 15.00
5-37: 8-13-Asmus-s 3.00

THIMK (Magazine) (Satire)
Counterpoint: May, 1958 - No. 6, May, 1959

1	10	20	30	58	79	100
2-6	8	16	24	40	50	60

THING!, THE (Blue Beetle #18 on)
Song Hits No. 1,2/Capitol Stories/Charlton: Feb, 1952 - No. 17, Nov, 1954

1-Weird/horror stories in all; shrunken head-c	116	232	348	742	1271	1800
2,3	71	142	213	454	777	1100
4,6,8,10: 6-Classic decapitation story	65	130	195	416	708	1000
5-Severed head-c; headlights	71	142	213	454	777	1100
7-Injury to eye-c & inside panel	84	168	252	538	919	1300
9-Used in **SOTI**, pg. 388 & illo "Stomping on the face is a form of brutality which modern children learn early"	103	206	309	659	1130	1600
11-Necronomicon story; Hansel & Gretel parody; Injury-to-eye panel; Check-a	77	154	231	493	847	1200
12-1st published Ditko-c; "Cinderella" parody; lingerie panels. Ditko-a	145	290	435	921	1586	2250
13,15-Ditko-c/a(3 & 5)	126	252	378	806	1378	1950
14-Extreme violence/torture; Rumpelstiltskin story; Ditko-c/a(4)	129	258	387	826	1413	2000
16-Injury to eye panel	37	74	111	222	361	500
17-Ditko-c; classic parody "Through the Looking Glass"; Powell-r/Beware Terror Tales #1 & recolored	94	188	282	597	1024	1450

NOTE: *Excessive violence, severed heads, injury to eye are common No. 5 on.* ***Al Fago*** *c-4.* ***Forgione*** *c-1i, 2, 6, 8, 9. All* ***Ditko*** *issues #14, 15.* ***Giordano*** *a-6.*

THING, THE (See Fantastic Four, Marvel Fanfare, Marvel Feature #11,12, Marvel Two-In-One and Startling Stories:...- Night Falls on Yancy Street)
Marvel Comics Group: July, 1983 - No. 36, June, 1986

1-Life story of Ben Grimm; Byrne scripts begin	3	6	9	16	23	30
2-5: 5-Spider-Man, She-Hulk and Wonder-Man app.						6.00
6-10: 7-1st app. Goody Two-Shoes. 8-She-Hulk app. 10-Secret Wars tie-in						5.00
11-36						4.00

NOTE: ***Byrne*** *a-2i, 7; c-1, 7, 36i; scripts-1-13, 19-22.* ***Sienkiewicz*** *c-13i.*

The Thing #1 © MAR

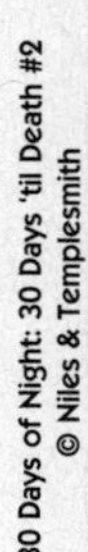

30 Days of Night: 30 Days 'til Death #2 © Niles & Templesmith

This Magazine is Haunted #10 © FAW

	GD 2.0	VG 4.0	FN 6.0	VF 8.0	VF/NM 9.0	NM- 9.2

THING, THE (Fantastic Four)
Marvel Comics: Jan, 2006 - No. 8, Aug, 2006 ($2.99)

1-8: 1-DiVito-a/Slott-s. 4-Lockjaw app. 6-Spider-Man app. 8-Super-Hero poker game 3.00
...: Idol of Millions TPB (2006, $20.99) r/#1-8; Divito sketch page 21.00

THING & SHE-HULK: THE LONG NIGHT (Fantastic Four)
Marvel Comics: May, 2002 ($2.99, one-shot)

1-Hitch-c/a(pg. 1-25); Reis-a(pg. 26-39); Dezago-s 3.00

THING, THE (From Another World)
Dark Horse Comics: 1991 - No. 2, 1992 ($2.95, mini-series, stiff-c)

1,2-Based on Universal movie; painted-c/a 5.00

THING, THE: FREAKSHOW (Fantastic Four)
Marvel Comics: Aug, 2002 - No. 4, Nov, 2002 ($2.99, limited series)

1-4-Geoff Johns-s/Scott Kolins-a 3.00
TPB (2005, $17.99) r/#1-4 & Thing & She-Hulk: The Long Night one-shot 18.00

THING FROM ANOTHER WORLD: CLIMATE OF FEAR, THE
Dark Horse Comics: July, 1992 - No. 4, Dec, 1992 ($2.50, mini-series)

1-4: Painted-c 4.00

THING FROM ANOTHER WORLD: ETERNAL VOWS
Dark Horse Comics: Dec, 1993 - No. 4, 1994 ($2.50, mini-series)

1-4-Gulacy-c/a 4.00

THINK TANK (Also see Eden's Fall)
Image Comics (Top Cow): Aug, 2012 - No. 12, Feb, 2014 ($3.99)

1-12-Hawkins-s/Ekedal-a 4.00

THINK TANK: ANIMAL
Image Comics (Top Cow): Mar, 2017 - Present ($3.99)

1-Hawkins-s/Ekedal-a 4.00

THINK TANK: CREATIVE DESTRUCTION
Image Comics (Top Cow): Apr, 2016 - No. 4, Jul, 2016 ($3.99)

1-4-Hawkins-s/Ekedal-a 4.00

THIRTEEN (...Going on 18)
Dell Publishing Co.: 11-1/61-62 - No. 25, 12/67; No. 26, 7/69 - No. 29, 1/71

	GD 2.0	VG 4.0	FN 6.0	VF 8.0	VF/NM 9.0	NM- 9.2
1	5	10	15	35	63	90
2-10	4	8	12	28	47	65
11-25	4	8	12	23	37	50
26-29-r	3	6	9	17	26	35

NOTE: *John Stanley script-No. 3-29; art?*

13: ASSASSIN
TSR, Inc.: 1990 - No. 8, 1991 ($2.95, 44 pgs.)

1-8: Agent 13; Alcala-a(i); Springer back-up-a 4.00

13th ARTIFACT, THE
Image Comics (Top Cow): Mar, 2016 ($3.99, one-shot)

1-Amit Chauhan-s/Eli Powell-a 4.00

13th SON, THE
Dark Horse Comics: Nov, 2005 - No. 4, Feb, 2006 ($2.99, limited series)

1-4-Kelley Jones-s/a/c 3.00

30 DAYS OF NIGHT
Idea + Design Works: June, 2002 - No. 3, Oct, 2002 ($3.99, limited series)

1-Vampires in Alaska; Steve Niles-s/Ben Templesmith-a/Ashley Wood-c 60.00
1-2nd printing 10.00
2 24.00
3 12.00
Annual 2004 (1/04, $4.99) Niles-s/art by Templesmith and others 5.00
Annual 2005 (12/05, $7.49) Niles-s/art by Nat Jones 7.50
... 5th Anniversary (10/07 - No. 3, $2.99) reprints original series 3.00
... Sourcebook (10/07, $7.49) Illustrated guide to the 30 Days world 7.50
... Three Tales TPB (7/06, $19.99) r/Annual 2005, ...: Dead Space #1-3, and short story from Tales of Terror (IDW's...) 20.00
Hundred Penny Press: 30 Days of Night #1 (5/11, $1.00) r/#1 3.00
TPB (2003, $17.99) r/#1-3, foreward by Clive Barker; script for #1 18.00
The Complete 30 Days of Night (2004, $75.00, oversized hardcover with slipcase) r/#1-3; prequel; script pages for #1-3; original cover and promotional materials 75.00

30 DAYS OF NIGHT
IDW Publishing: July, 2004 (Free Comic Book Day edition)

Previews CSI: Bad Rap; The Shield: Spotlight; 24: One Shot; and 30 Days of Night 3.00

30 DAYS OF NIGHT (Ongoing series)
IDW Publishing: Oct, 2011 - No. 12, Nov, 2012 ($3.99)

1-12: 1-4-Niles-s/Kieth-a; covers by Kieth and Furno. 5-12-Niles-s 4.00

30 DAYS OF NIGHT: BEYOND BARROW
IDW Publishing: Sept, 2007 - No. 3, Dec, 2007 ($3.99, limited series)

1-3-Niles-s/Sienkiewicz-a/c 4.00

30 DAYS OF NIGHT: BLOODSUCKER TALES
IDW Publishing: Oct, 2004 - No. 8, May, 2005 ($3.99, limited series)

1-8-Niles-s/Chamberlain-a; Fraction-s/Templesmith-a/c 4.00
HC (8/05, $49.99) r/#1-8; cover gallery 50.00
SC (8/05, $24.99) r/#1-8; cover gallery 25.00

30 DAYS OF NIGHT: DEAD SPACE
IDW Publishing: Jan, 2006 - No. 3, Mar, 2006 ($3.99, limited series)

1-3-Niles and Wickline-s/Milx-a/c 4.00

30 DAYS OF NIGHT: EBEN & STELLA
IDW Publishing: May, 2007 - No. 3, July, 2007 ($3.99, limited series)

1-3-Niles and DeConnick-s/Randall-a/c 4.00

30 DAYS OF NIGHT: NIGHT, AGAIN
IDW Publishing: May, 2011 - No. 4, Aug, 2011 ($3.99, limited series)

1-4-Lansdale-s/Kieth-a/c 4.00

30 DAYS OF NIGHT: RED SNOW
IDW Publishing: Aug, 2007 - No. 3, Oct, 2007 ($3.99, limited series)

1-3-Ben Templesmith-s/a/c 4.00

30 DAYS OF NIGHT: RETURN TO BARROW
IDW Publishing: Mar, 2004 - No. 6, Aug, 2004 ($3.99, limited series)

1-6-Steve Niles-s/Ben Templesmith-a/c 4.00
TPB (2004, $19.99) r/#1-6; cover gallery 20.00

30 DAYS OF NIGHT: SPREADING THE DISEASE
IDW Publishing: Dec, 2006 - No. 5, Apr, 2007 ($3.99, limited series)

1-5: 1-Wickline-s/Sanchez-a. 3-5-Sandoval-a 4.00

30 DAYS OF NIGHT: 30 DAYS 'TIL DEATH
IDW Publishing: Dec, 2008 - No. 4, Mar, 2009 ($3.99, limited series)

1-4-David Lapham-s/a; covers by Lapham and Templesmith 4.00

THIRTY SECONDS OVER TOKYO (See American Library)

THIS DAMNED BAND
Dark Horse Comics: Aug, 2016 - No. 6, Jan, 2016 ($3.99, limited series)

1-6-Paul Cornell-s/Tony Parker-a 4.00

THIS IS SUSPENSE! (Formerly Strange Suspense Stories; Strange Suspense Stories #27 on)
Charlton Comics: No. 23, Feb, 1955 - No. 26, Aug, 1955

	GD 2.0	VG 4.0	FN 6.0	VF 8.0	VF/NM 9.0	NM- 9.2
23-Wood-a(r)/A Star Presentation #3 "Dr. Jekyll & Mr. Hyde"; last pre-code issue	24	48	72	140	230	320
24-Censored Fawcett-r; Evans-a (r/Suspense Detective #1)	14	28	42	80	115	150
25,26: 26-Marcus Swayze-a	10	20	30	56	76	95

THIS IS THE PAYOFF (See Pay-Off)

THIS IS WAR
Standard Comics: No. 5, July, 1952 - No. 9, May, 1953

	GD 2.0	VG 4.0	FN 6.0	VF 8.0	VF/NM 9.0	NM- 9.2
5-Toth-a	17	34	51	98	154	210
6,9-Toth-a	14	28	42	76	108	140
7,8: 8-Ross Andru-c	11	22	33	60	83	105

THIS IS YOUR LIFE, DONALD DUCK (See Donald Duck..., Four Color #1109)

THIS MAGAZINE IS CRAZY (Crazy #? on)
Charlton Publ. (Humor Magazines): V3#2, July, 1957 - V4#8, Feb, 1959 (25¢, magazine, 68 pgs.)

	GD 2.0	VG 4.0	FN 6.0	VF 8.0	VF/NM 9.0	NM- 9.2
V3#2-V4#7: V4#5-Russian Sputnik-c parody	11	22	33	60	83	105
V4#8-Davis-a (8 pgs.)	11	22	33	64	90	115

THIS MAGAZINE IS HAUNTED (Danger and Adventure #22 on)
Fawcett Publications/Charlton No. 15(2/54) on: Oct, 1951 - No. 14, 12/53; No. 15, 2/54 - V3#21, Nov, 1954

	GD 2.0	VG 4.0	FN 6.0	VF 8.0	VF/NM 9.0	NM- 9.2
1-Evans-a; Dr. Death as host begins	77	154	231	493	847	1200
2,5-Evans-a	50	100	150	315	533	750
3,4: 3-Vampire-c/story	40	80	120	246	411	575
6-9,12	36	72	108	211	343	475
10-Severed head-c	71	142	213	454	777	1100
11-Classic skeleton-c	39	78	117	231	378	525

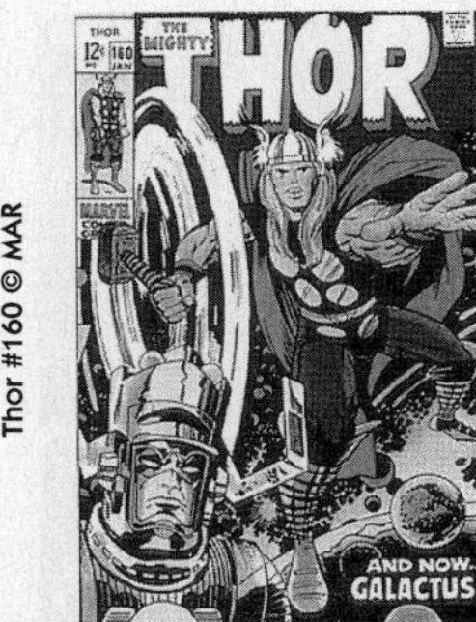

Thor #160 © MAR

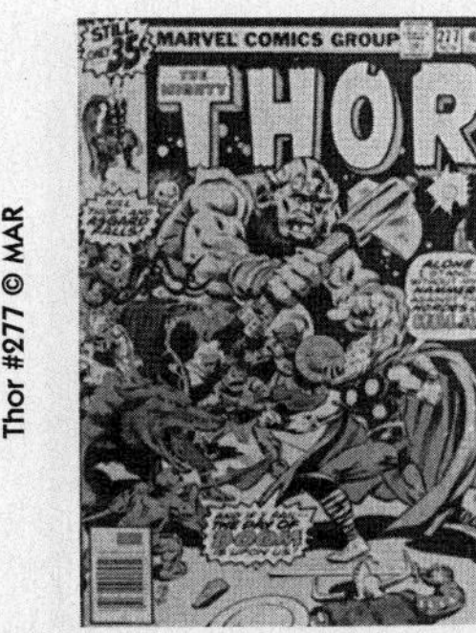

Thor #277 © MAR

Thor #366 © MAR

GD VG FN VF VF/NM NM-
2.0 4.0 6.0 8.0 9.0 9.2

13-Severed head-c/story 65 130 195 416 708 1000
14-Classic burning skull-c 50 100 150 315 533 750
15,20: 15-Dick Giordano-c. 20-Cover is swiped from panel in The Thing #16 27 54 81 160 263 365
16,19-Ditko-c. 19-Injury-to-eye panel; story-r/#1 48 96 144 302 514 725
17-Ditko-c/a(4); blood drainage story 60 120 180 381 653 925
18-Ditko-c/a(1 story); E.C. swipe/Haunt of Fear #5; injury-to-eye panel; reprints "Caretaker of the Dead" from Beware Terror Tales & recolored 52 104 156 322 549 775
21-Ditko-c, Evans-r/This Magazine Is Haunted #1 42 84 126 265 445 625

NOTE: ***Baily** a-1, 3, 4, 21r/#1. **Moldoff** c/a-1-13. **Powell** a-3-5, 11, 12, 17. **Shuster** a-18-20. Issues 19-21 have reprints which have been recolored from This Magazine is Haunted #1.*

THIS MAGAZINE IS HAUNTED (2nd Series) (Formerly Zaza the Mystic; Outer Space #17 on)
Charlton Comics: V2#12, July, 1957 - V2#16, May, 1958

V2#12-14-Ditko-c/a in all 47 94 141 296 498 700
15-No Ditko-c/a 18 36 54 105 165 225
16-Ditko-a(4). 36 72 108 211 343 475

THIS MAGAZINE IS WILD (See Wild)

THIS WAS YOUR LIFE (Religious)
Jack T. Chick Publ.: 1964 (3 1/2 x 5 1/2", 40 pgs., B&W and red)

nn, Another version (5x2 3/4", 26 pgs.) 2 4 6 10 14 18

THOR (See Avengers #1, Giant-Size..., Marvel Collectors Item Classics, Marvel Graphic Novel #33, Marvel Preview, Marvel Spectacular, Marvel Treasury Edition, Special Marvel Edition & Tales of Asgard)

THOR (Journey Into Mystery #1-125, 503-on)(The Mighty Thor #413-490)
Marvel Comics Group: No. 126, Mar, 1966 - No. 502, Sept, 1996

126-Thor continues (#125-130 Thor vs. Hercules); Tales of Asgard back-up stories continue through issue #145 35 70 105 252 564 875
127-130: 127-1st app. Pluto. 129-1st Ares Olympian God of War & Tana Nile of the Rigillian Colonizers 10 20 30 66 138 210
131,135,137-140: 135-Origin of the High Evolutionary. 137-1st Ulik the Troll. 138-139-Thor vs. Ulik. 140-Kang app; 1st Growing Man 9 18 27 57 111 165
132-1st app. Ego the Living Planet 10 20 30 64 132 200
133-Thor vs. Ego 10 20 30 69 147 225
134-Intro High Evolutionary and Man-Beast 10 20 30 66 138 210
136-(1/67) Re-intro. Sif 9 18 27 60 120 180
141-145: 142-Thor vs. Super-Skrull. 143,144-Thor vs. the Enchanters 7 14 21 49 92 135
146,147: 146-Inhumans origin; begin (early app.) in back-up stories, end #152 (see Fantastic Four #45 for 1st app.). 147-Origin continues 8 16 24 54 102 150
148,149-Origin Black Bolt in each. 148-1st app. Wrecker. 149-Origin Medusa, Crystal, Maximus, Gorgon, Karnak 9 18 27 59 117 175
150-152: Inhumans app. 150-Hela app. 151,152-Destroyer and Ulik app. 8 16 24 52 99 145
153-157,159: 154-1st Mangog. 155-157-Thor vs Mangog. 159-Origin Dr. Blake (Thor) concl. 6 12 18 42 79 115
158-Origin-r/#83; origin Dr. Blake 9 18 27 57 111 165
160-162-Galactus app. 7 14 21 46 86 125
163,164-2nd & 3th brief app. Warlock (Him) 5 10 15 35 63 90
165-1st full app. Warlock (Him) (6/69, see Fantastic Four #67); last 12¢ issue; Kirby-a 38 76 114 285 641 1000
166-2nd full app. Warlock (Him); battles Thor; see Marvel Premiere #1 10 20 30 69 147 225
167,170-179: 170-1st Thermal Man. 171-Thor vs. the Wrecker. 173-Circus of Crime app. 174-1st Crypto-Man. 176-177-Surtur app. 178-1st Buscema-a on Thor; vs the Abomination. 179-Last Kirby issue 5 10 15 34 60 85
168,169-Origin Galactus; Kirby-a 8 16 24 52 99 145
180,181-Neal Adams-a; Mephisto & Loki app. 6 12 18 37 66 95
182,183-Thor vs. Doctor Doom. 182-Buscema-a begins (11/70) 5 10 15 34 60 85
184-192: 184-1st Infinity & the Silent One. 187-Thor vs Odin. 188-Origin of Infinity. 189,190-Thor vs. Hela. 191-1st Durok the Demolisher. 192-Last 15¢ issue; Thor vs. Durok 4 8 12 27 44 60
193-(25¢, 52 pgs.); Silver Surfer x-over; Thor vs. Durok; last Stan Lee story as regular writer 11 22 33 72 154 235
194-199: 194-Gerry Conway stories begin (ends #238). 195-Mangog returns. 196-198-Thor vs. Mangog. 199-1st Ego-Prime; Pluto app. 4 8 12 23 37 50
200-Special Ragnarok issue by Stan Lee 4 8 12 28 47 65
201-206,208-220,222-224; 201-Pluto & Hela app; origin of Ego-Prime. 202-vs Ego-Prime. 203-1st Young Gods. 204-Thor exiled on Earth; Mephisto app. 205-vs Mephisto; Hitler app. 206-vs. the Absorbing Man. 208-1st Mercurio the 4th Dimensional Man. 210-211-vs. Ulik. 214-Mercurio the 4-D Man app; 1st Xorr the God-Jewel. 215-Origin of Xorr; Mecurio the 4-D Man app. 216-Xorr & Mecurio app. 217-Thor vs Odin-c. 218-220-Saga of the Black Stars. 222,223-vs Pluto. 224-The Destroyer app. 3 6 9 14 20 25
207-Rutland, Vermont Halloween x-over; leads into Avengers/Defenders war 3 6 9 19 30 40
221-Thor vs. Hercules; Hercules guest stars through issue #232,234-239 3 6 9 16 23 30
225-Intro. Firelord 6 12 18 41 76 110
226-Galactus and Firelord app. 3 6 9 14 20 25
227-231: 227-228-Thor, Firelord & Galactus vs Ego the Living Planet 2 4 6 10 14 18
232,233: 232-Firelord app. 233-Numerous guest stars; Asgard invades Earth 3 6 9 14 20 25
234-245: 234-Iron Man & Firelord app. 235-1st Kamo Tharnn, Elder of the Universe. 236-Thor vs. Absorbing Man. 237-239-Thor vs. Ulik. 240-1st Egyptian Gods; Osiris & Horus; 1st Seth-Egyptian God of Death. 241-Thor vs. Seth. 242-Len Wein scripts begin; ends #271. 242-245-Thor vs. Time-Twisters; Zarko the Tomorrow Man app. 2 4 6 10 14 18
246-250-(Regular 25¢ editions)(4-8/76): 246-247-Firelord app. 249-250-Thor vs. Mangog 2 4 6 10 14 18
246-250-(30¢-c variants, limited distribution) 4 8 12 27 44 60
251-280: 251-Thor vs. Hela. 252,253-Thor vs. Ulik. 255-Re-intro Stone Men of Saturn. 257-259-Thor vs. Grey Gargoyle. 260-Thor vs. Enchantress & Executioner. 261-272-Simonson-a. 264-266-Thor vs. Loki. 265,266-The Destroyer app. 269-Thor vs. Stilt-Man. 270-Thor vs. Blastaar. 271-Iron Man x-over. 272-Roy Thomas scripts begin. 274-Death of Balder the Brave. 276-Thor vs. Red Norvell Thor. 280-Thor vs. Hyperion 1 3 4 6 8 10
260-264-(35¢-c variants, limited distribution)(6-10/77) 8 16 24 51 96 140
281-299: 281-Space Phantom app. 282-Immortus app. 283,284-Celestials app. 284-286-Eternals app. 287-288-Thor vs. the Forgotten one. 291,292-Asgard vs Olympus. 292-1st Eye of Odin (as sentient being). 294-Origin Asgard & Odin 1 2 3 5 6 8
300-(12/80)-End of Asgard; origin of Odin & The Destroyer; double-size 2 4 6 8 10 12
301-Numerous pantheons (skyfathers) app. 1 2 3 5 6 8
302-304 5.00
305-306: 305-Airwalker app. 306-Firelord 1 2 3 5 6 8
307-331,334-336: 310-Thor vs. Mephisto. 314-Moondragon and Drax app. 315,316-Bi-Beast & Man-Beast app. 316-Iron Man x-over. 325-Mephisto app. 331-1st Crusader 5.00
332,333-Dracula app. 1 2 3 5 6 8
337-Simonson-c/a begins, ends #382; 1st app. of Beta Ray Bill who becomes the new Thor; intro Lorelei 3 6 9 21 33 45
338-Beta Ray Bill vs. Thor 2 4 6 9 12 15
339,340: 339-Beta Ray Bill gains Thor's powers. 340-Donald Blake returns as Thor 6.00
341-343,345-373,375-381,383,386: 341-Clark Kent & Lois Lane cameo. 345-349-Malekith the Accursed app. 350-352-Avengers app. 353-'Death' of Odin. 356-Hercules app. 363-Secret Wars II crossover. 364-366-Thor as a frog. 367-Malekith app. 373-X-Factor tie-in. 383-Secret Wars flashback 4.00
344-(6/84) 1st app. of Malekith the Accursed (Ruler of the Dark Elves)(villain in the 2013 movie Thor: The Dark World); Simonson-c/a 2 4 6 9 12 15
374-Mutant Massacre; X-Factor app. 5.00
382-($1.25)-Anniversary issue; last Simonson-a 6.00
384-Intro. Thor of the 26th century (Dargo Ktor) 6.00
385-Thor vs. Hulk by Stan Lee and Erik Larsen 6.00
387,388,390-399: Thor vs. the Celestials. 390-Avengers app.; Captain America lifts Mjolnir. 391-Spider-Man x-over; 1st Eric Masterson. 393-395-Daredevil app. 395-Intro. Earth Force. 396-399-Black Knight app. 4.00
389- 'Alone against the Celestials' climax 5.00
400-($1.75, 68 pgs.)-Origin Loki 6.00
401-410: 404,405-Annihilus app. 409-410-Dr. Doom app. 4.00
411-Intro New Warriors (appear in costume in last panel); Juggernaut-c/story 2 4 6 13 18 22
412-1st full app. New Warriors (Marvel Boy, Kid Nova, Namorita, Night Thrasher, Firestar & Speedball) 3 6 9 14 20 25
413-426: 413-Dr. Strange app. 419-425-Black Galaxy saga; origin Celestials 4.00
427-428-Excalibur app. 428-Ghost Rider app. 5.00
429-431: 429-Thor vs Juggernaut; Ghost Rider app. 430-Ghost Rider app. 3.00
432-(52 pgs.) Thor's 350th issue (vs. Loki) reprints origin and 1st app. from Journey into Mystery #83 4.00
433-449,451-467: 433-Intro. Eric Masterson as Thor. 434,435-Annihilus app. 437-Quasar app.; Tales of Asgard back-up stories begin. 438-441-Thor War; Beta Ray Bill app. 443-Dr. Strange & Silver Surfer x-over; last $1.00-c. 445,446-Operation Galactic Storm. 445-Thor vs. Gladiator. 448-Spider-Man app. 451,452-Bloodaxe app. 457-Original Thor returns. 458-Thor vs. Thor. 459-Intro Thunderstrike. 460-Starlin scripts begin. 461-Thor vs. Beta Ray Bill. 463-467-Infinity Crusade x-over. 466-Drax app. 3.00
450-($2.50, 68 pgs.)-Flip-book format; r/story JIM #85 (1st Loki) plus-c plus a gallery of

Thor V2 #3 © MAR

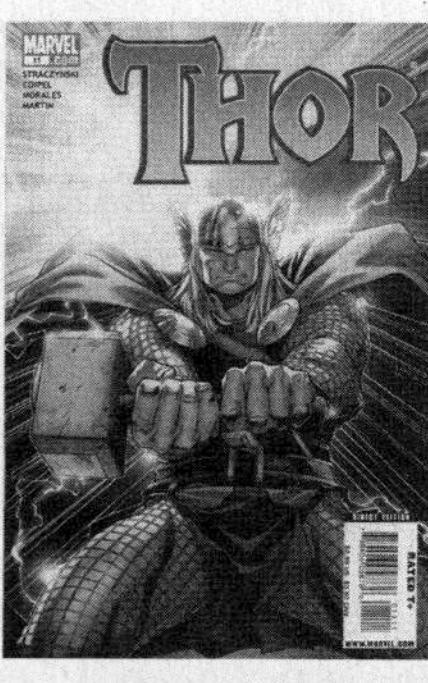

Thor (2007 series) #1 © MAR

Thor (2014 series) #8 © MAR

GD VG FN VF VF/NM NM-
2.0 4.0 6.0 8.0 9.0 9.2

past-c; gatefold-c 4.00
468,469-Blood and Thunder x-over. 468-Thor vs. Silver Surfer. 469-Infinity Watch app. 5.00
470,471-Blood and Thunder x-over. 470-Thanos and the Infinity Watch app. 471-Blood and Thunder story conclusion; Infinity Watch and Silver Surfer app. 6.00
472-474: 472-Intro the Godlings. 474-Begin $1.50-c; bound-in trading cards 3.00
475 ($2.00, 52 pgs.)-Regular edition; High Evolutionary and Man-Beast app. 4.00
475 ($2.50, 52 pgs.)-Collectors edition w/foil embossed-c 5.00
476-481: 476-Destroyer app. 477-Thunderstrike app. 478-Return of Red Norvell Thor. 479-Detailed Origin of Thor 3.00
482 ($2.95, 84 pgs.)-400th Thor issue 5.00
483,486,487,488: 486-Kurse app. 4.00
484,485,490: 484-War Machine app. 485-Thing app. 490-Absorbing Man app.; Buscema-a 5.00
489-Hulk app. 6.00
491-Warren Ellis scripts begins, ends #494; Worldengine pt.1; Deodato-c/a begins 6.00
492-494: Worldengine pt. 2-4. 492-Reintro The Enchantress; Beta Ray Bill dies 5.00
495-499: 495-Messner-Loebs scripts begin; Isherwood-c/a. 496-Captain America app. 3.00
500 ($2.50)-Double-size; wraparound-c; Deodato-c/a; Dr. Strange app. 5.00
501-Reintro Red Norvell 4.00
502-(9/96) Onslaught tie-in; Red Norvell, Jane Foster & Hela app. 5.00
NOTE: *Numbering continues with Journey Into Mystery #503 (11/96)*
600-up (See Thor 2007 series)
Special 2(9/66)-(See Journey Into Mystery for 1st annual) Destroyer app.
9 18 27 61 123 185
Special 2 (2nd printing, 1994) 2 4 6 8 10 12
King Size Special 3 (1/71) 4 8 12 23 37 50
Special 4 (12/71)-r/Thor #131,132 & JIM #113 3 6 9 19 30 40
Annual 5 (11/76)-Asgard vs Olympus; Hercules app. 2 4 6 11 16 20
Annual 6 (10/77)-Guardians of the Galaxy app. 4 8 12 25 40 55
Annual 7,8: 7 (1978)-Eternals app. 8 (1979)-Thor vs. Zeus-c/story
2 4 6 8 10 12
Annual 9-13: 9 ('81)-Dormammu app. 10 ('82)-1st Demogorge-the God Eater. 11 ('83)-Origin of Thor expanded. 12 ('84)-Intro Vidar (Thor's brother). 13 ('85)-Mephisto app. 6.00
Annual 14-19 ('86-'94, 68 pgs.): 14-Atlantis Attacks. 15 ('90)-Terminus factor Pt. 3. 16-3 pg. origin; Guardians of the Galaxy x-over. 17 ('92)-Citizen Kang Pt. 2. 18-Polybagged w/card; intro the Flame. 19 ('94) vs. Pluto 4.00
...Alone Against the Celestials nn (6/92, $5.95)-r/Thor #387-389 6.00
...Legends Vol. 2: Walter Simonson Book 2 TPB (2003, $24.99) r/#349-355,357-359 25.00
...Legends Vol. 3: Walter Simonson Book 3 TPB (2004, $24.99) r/#360-369 25.00
...: The Eternals Saga TPB (2006, $24.99) r/#283-291 & Annual #7; profile pages 25.00
...: The Eternals Saga Vol. 2 TPB ('07, $24.99) r/#292-301; Thomas & Gruenwald essays 25.00
... Visionaries: Mike Deodato Jr. TPB (2004, $19.99) r/#491-494,498-500 20.00
... Visionaries: Walter Simonson (Vol. 1) TPB (5/01, $24.95) r/#337-348 25.00
... Visionaries: Walter Simonson Vol. 4 TPB (2007, $24.99) r/#371-373 & Balder the Brave #1-4 25.00
... Visionaries: Walter Simonson Vol. 5 TPB (2008, $24.95) r/#375-382 25.00
...: Worldengine (8/96, $9.95)-r/#491-494; Deodato-c/a; story & new intermission by Warren Ellis 10.00
NOTE: ***Neal Adams** a-180,181; c-179-181. **Austin** a-342i, 346i; c-312i. **Buscema** a(p)-178, 182-213, 215-226, 231-238, 241-253, 254r, 256-259, 272-278, 283-285, 370, Annual 6, 8, 11i; c(p)-175, 178, 182-196, 198-200, 202-204, 206, 211, 212, 215, 219, 221, 226, 256, 259, 261, 262, 272-278, 283, 289, 370, Annual 6. **Everett** a(i)-143, 170-175; c(i)-171, 172, 174, 176, 241. **Gil Kane** a-318p; c(p)-201, 205, 207-210, 216, 220, 222, 223, 231, 233-240, 242, 243, 318. **Kirby** a(p)-126-177, 179, 194r, 254r; c(p)-126-169, 171-174, 176, 177, 249-253, 255, 257, 258, Annual 5, Special 2-4. **Mooney** a(i)-201, 204, 214-216, 218, 322i, 324i, 325i, 327i. **Sienkiewicz** c-332, 333, 335. **Simonson** a-260-271p, 337-354, 357-367, 380, Annual 7p; c-260, 263-271, 337-355, 357-369, 371, 373-382, Annual 7. **Starlin** c-213.*

THOR (Volume 2)
Marvel Comics: July, 1998 - No. 85, Dec, 2004 ($2.99/$1.99/$2.25)

1-($2.99)-Follows Heroes Return; Jurgens-s/Romita Jr. & Janson-a; wraparound-c; battles the Destroyer 6.00
1-Variant-c 1 2 3 5 6 8
1-Rough Cut-($2.99) Features original script and pencil pages 3.00
1-Sketch cover 28.00
2-($1.99) Two covers; Avengers app. 4.00
3-11,13-23: 3-Assumes Jake Olson ID. 4-Namor-c/app. 8-Spider-Man-c/app. 14-Iron Man c/app. 17-Juggernaut-c 3.00
12-($2.99) Wraparound-c; Hercules appears 4.00
12-($10.00) Variant-c by Jusko 10.00
24,26-31,33,34: 24-Begin $2.25-c. 26-Mignola-c/Larsen-a. 29-Andy Kubert-a. 30-Maximum Security x-over; Beta Ray Bill-c/app. 33-Intro. Thor Girl 3.00
25-($2.99) Regular edition 4.00
25-($3.99) Gold foil enhanced cover 5.00
32-($3.50, 100 pgs.) new story plus reprints w/Kirby-a; Simonson-a 5.00
35-($2.99) Thor battles The Gladiator; Andy Kubert-a 4.00
36-49,51-61: 37-Starlin-a. 38,39-BWS-c. 38-42-Immonen-a. 40-Odin killed. 41-Orbik-c. 44-'Nuff Said silent issue. 51-Spider-Man app. 57-Art by various. 58-Davis-a; x-over with Iron Man #64. 60-Brereton-c 3.00
50-($4.95) Raney-c/a; back-ups w/Nuckols-a & Armenta-s/Bennett-a 5.00
62-84: 62-Begin $2.99-c. 64-Loki-c/app. 80-Oeming-s begins; Avengers app. 3.00
85-Last issue; Thor dies; Oeming-s/DiVito-a/Epting-c 4.00
...1999 Annual ($3.50) Jurgens-s/a(p) 4.00
...2000 Annual ($3.50) Jurgens-s/Ordway-a(p); back-up stories 4.00
...2001 Annual ($3.50) Jurgens-s/Grummett-a(p); Lightle-c 4.00
...Across All Worlds (9/01, $19.95, TPB) r/#28-35 20.00
Avengers Disassembled: Thor TPB (2004, $16.99) r/#80-85; afterword by Oeming 17.00
...Resurrection ($5.99, TPB) r/#1,2 6.00
...: The Dark Gods (7/00, $15.95, TPB) r/#9-13 16.00
...Vol. 1: The Death of Odin (7/02, $12.99, TPB) r/#39-44 13.00
...Vol. 2: Lord of Asgard (9/02, $15.99, TPB) r/#45-50 16.00
...Vol. 3: Gods on Earth (2003, $21.99, TPB) r/#51-58, Avengers #63, Iron Man #64, Marvel Double-Shot #1; Beck-c 22.00
...Vol. 4: Spiral (2003, $19.99, TPB) r/#59-67; Brereton-c 20.00
...Vol. 5: The Reigning (2004, $17.99, TPB) r/#68-74 18.00
...Vol. 6: Gods and Men (2004, $13.99, TPB) r/#75-79 14.00

GD VG FN VF VF/NM NM-
2.0 4.0 6.0 8.0 9.0 9.2

THOR (Also see Fantastic Four #538)(Resumes original numbering with #600)
Marvel Comics: Sept, 2007 - No. 12, Mar, 2009; No. 600, Apr, 2009 - No. 621, May, 2011 ($2.99/$3.99) (Continues numbering as Journey Into Mystery #622) (Also see Mighty Thor #1)

1-Straczynski-s/Coipel-a/c 4.00
1-Variant-c by Michael Turner 5.00
1-Zombie variant-c by Suydam 5.00
1-Non-zombie variant-c by Suydam 5.00
1-"Marvel's Greatest Comics" edition (5/10, $1.00) r/#1 3.00
2-12: 2-Two covers by Dell'Otto and Coipel. 3-Iron Man app.; McGuinness var-c. 4-Bermejo var-c. 5-Campbell var-c. 6-Art Adams var-c. 7,8-Djurdjevic-a/c; Coipel var-c 3.00
2-Second printing with wraparound-c 3.00
7-"Marvel's Greatest Comics" edition (6/11, $1.00) r/#7 3.00

(After #12 [Mar, 2009] numbering reverted back to original Journey Into Mystery/Thor numbering with #600, Apr, 2009)

600 (4/09, $4.99) Two wraparound-c by Coipel & Djurdjevic; Coipel, Djurdjevic & Aja-a; r/Tales of Asgard from Journey Into Mystery #106,107,112,113,115; Kirby-a 5.00
601-603,611-621-($3.99) 601-603-Djurdjevic-a. 602-Sif returns. 617-Loki returns 4.00
604-610-($2.99) Tan-a. 607-609-Siege x-over. 610-Braithwaite-a; Ragnarok app. 3.00
620.1 (5/11, $2.99) Brooks-a; Grey Gargoyle app. 3.00
Annual 1 (11/09, $3.99) Suayan, Grindberg, Gaudiano-a; Djurdjevic-c 4.00
...: Ages of Thunder (6/08, $3.99) Fraction-s/Zircher-a/Djurdjevic-c 4.00
... & Hercules: Encyclopædia Mythologica (2009, $4.99) profile pages of the Pantheons 5.00
... Asgard's Avenger 1 (6/11, $4.99) profile pages of Thor characters 5.00
... Crown of Fools 1 (12/13, $3.99) Di Vito & Simonson-a 4.00
... Giant-Size Finale 1 (1/01, $3.99) Dr. Doom app.; r/origin from JIM #83 4.00
... God-Size Special (2/09, $3.99) story of Skurge the Executioner re-told; art by Brereton, Braithwaite, Allred and Sepulveda; plus reprint of Thor #362 (1985) 4.00
... Goes Hollywood 1 ('11, $3.99) Collection of movie-themed variant Thor covers 4.00
...: Man of War (1/09, $3.99) Fraction-s/Mann & Zircher-a/Djurdjevic-c 4.00
...: Reign of Blood (8/08, $3.99) Fraction-s/Evans & Zircher-a/Djurdjevic-c 4.00
...: Spotlight (5/11, $3.99) movie photo-c; movie preview; creator interviews 4.00
...: The Rage of Thor (10/10, $3.99) Milligan-s/Suayan-c/a 4.00
...: The Trial of Thor (8/09, $3.99) Milligan-s/Nord-c/a 4.00
...: Truth of History (12/08, $3.99) Thor and crew in ancient Egypt; Alan Davis-s/a/c 4.00
...: Whosoever Wields This Hammer 1 (6/11, $4.99) recolored r/J.I.M. #83,84,88 5.00
...: Wolves of the North (2/11, $3.99) Carey-s/Perkins-a 4.00
... By J. Michael Straczynski Vol. 1 HC (2008, $19.99) r/#1-6; variant cover gallery 20.00

THOR (Female Thor)
Marvel Comics: Dec, 2014 - No. 8, Jul, 2015 ($3.99)

1-Aaron-s/Dauterman-a/c; Thor, Odin and Malekith app. 10.00
2-8 2-4-Malekith app. 4-Thor vs. Thor. 5-Molina-a. 8-Identity revealed 4.00
Annual 1 (4/15, $4.99) Female Thor, King Thor stories; Young Thor by CM Punk-s 5.00

THOR ADAPTATION (MARVEL'S...)
Marvel Comics: Mar, 2012 - No. 2, Apr, 2012 ($2.99, limited series)

1,2-Adaptation of 2012 movie; Gage-s/Medina-a; photo-c 3.00

THOR AND THE WARRIORS FOUR
Marvel Comics: Jun, 2010 - No. 4, Sept, 2010 ($2.99, limited series)

1-4-Thor and Power Pack team-up; Gurihiru-a; back-up with Coover-s/a 3.00

THOR: BLOOD OATH
Marvel Comics: Nov, 2005 - No. 6, Feb, 2006 ($2.99, limited series)

1-6-Oeming-s/Kolins-a/c 3.00
HC (2006, $19.99, dust jacket) r/series; afterword by Oeming 20.00
SC (2006, $14.99) r/series; afterword by Oeming 15.00

Thor: God of Thunder #25 © MAR

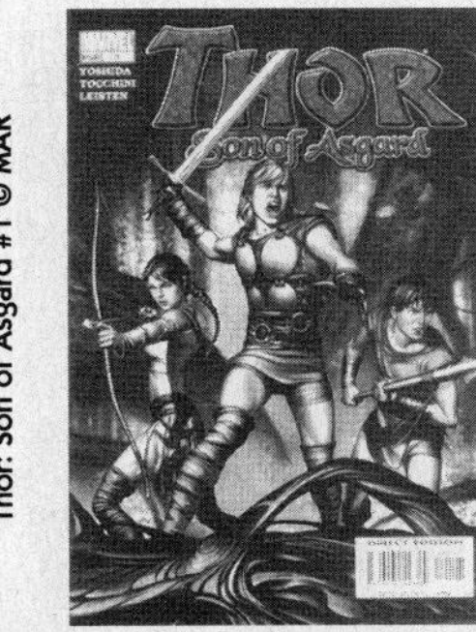

Thor: Son of Asgard #1 © MAR

3-D Batman 1953 © DC

GD VG FN VF VF/NM NM-
2.0 4.0 6.0 8.0 9.0 9.2

THOR CORPS
Marvel Comics: Sept, 1993 - No. 4, Jan, 1994 ($1.75, limited series)
1-4: 1-Invaders cameo. 2-Invaders app. 3-Spider-Man 2099, Rawhide Kid, Two-Gun Kid & Kid Colt app. 4-Painted-c 3.00

THOR: FIRST THUNDER
Marvel Comics: Nov, 2010 - No. 5, Mar, 2011 ($3.99, limited series)
1-5: 1-Huat-a; new retelling of origin; reprint of debut in JIM #83 4.00

THOR: FOR ASGARD
Marvel Comics: Nov, 2010 - No. 6, Apr, 2011 ($3.99, limited series)
1-6-Bianchi-a/c. 1-Frost Giants app. 4.00

THOR: GOD OF THUNDER (Marvel NOW!)
Marvel Comics: Jan, 2013 - No. 25, Nov, 2014 ($3.99)
1-24: 1-5-Aaron-s/Ribic-a. 6-Guice-a. 13-17-Malekith app. 19-23-Galactus app. 21-1st app. S.H.I.E.L.D. Agent Roz Solomon 4.00
25-($4.99) Art by Guera, Bisley, and Ribic; Malekith app.; new female Thor cameo 5.00

THOR: GODSTORM
Marvel Comics: Nov, 2001 - No. 3, Jan, 2002 ($3.50, limited series)
1-3-Steve Rude-c/a; Busiek-s. 1-Avengers app. 4.00

THOR: HEAVEN & EARTH
Marvel Comics: Sept, 2011 - No. 4, Nov, 2011 ($2.99, limited series)
1-4: 1-Jenkins-s/Olivetti-a/c; Loki app. 2-Texeira-a/c. 3-Alixe-a. 4-Medina-a 3.00

THORION OF THE NEW ASGODS
Marvel Comics (Amalgam): June, 1997 ($1.95, one-shot)
1-Keith Giffen-s/John Romita Jr.-c/a 3.00

THORS (Secret Wars Battleworld tie-in)
Marvel Comics: Aug, 2015 - No. 4, Jan, 2016 ($3.99, limited series)
1-4: Police squad of Thors on Doomworld; Aaron-s/Sprouse-a. 2,3-Sudzuka-a 4.00

THOR: SON OF ASGARD
Marvel Comics: May, 2004 - No. 12, Mar, 2005 ($2.99, limited series)
1-12: Teenaged Thor, Sif, and Balder; Tocchini-a. 1-6-Granov-c. 7-12-Jo Chen-c 3.00
... Vol. 1: The Warriors Teen (2004, $7.99, digest) r/#1-6 8.00
... Vol. 2: Worthy (2005, $7.99, digest) r/#7-12 8.00

THOR: TALES OF ASGARD BY STAN LEE & JACK KIRBY
Marvel Comics: 2009 - No. 6, 2009 ($3.99, limited series)
1-6-Reprints back-up stories from Journey Into Mystery #97-120; new covers by Coipel 4.00

THOR: THE DEVIANTS SAGA
Marvel Comics: Jan, 2012 - No. 5, May, 2012 ($3.99, limited series)
1-5-Rodi-s/Segovia-a; Ereshkigal app. 4.00

THOR: THE DARK WORLD PRELUDE (MARVEL'S...)
Marvel Comics: Aug, 2013 - No. 2, Aug, 2013 ($2.99, limited series)
1,2-Prelude to 2013 movie; Eaton-a; photo-c 3.00

THOR: THE LEGEND
Marvel Comics: Sept, 1996 ($3.95, one-shot)
nn-Tribute issue 4.00

THOR THE MIGHTY AVENGER
Marvel Comics: Sept, 2010 - No. 8, Mar, 2011 ($2.99, limited series)
1-8-Re-imagining of Thor's origin; Langridge-s/Samnee-a. 1-Mr. Hyde app. 3.00
Free Comic Book Day 2011 (giveaway) Captain America app. 3.00

THOR: VIKINGS
Marvel Comics (MAX): Sept, 2003 - No. 5, Jan, 2004 ($3.50, limited series)
1-5-Garth Ennis-s/Glenn Fabry-a/c 3.50
TPB (2004, $13.99) r/series 14.00

THOSE MAGNIFICENT MEN IN THEIR FLYING MACHINES (See Movie Comics)

THRAX
Event Comics: Nov, 1996 ($2.95, one-shot)
1 3.00

THREE
Image Comics: Oct, 2013 - No. 5, Feb, 2014 ($2.99)
1-5-Spartans 100 years after the Battle of Thermopylae; Ryan Kelly-a/Kieron Gillen-s 3.00

THREE CABALLEROS (Walt Disney's...)
Dell Publishing Co.: No. 71, 1945
Four Color 71-by Walt Kelly, c/a 59 118 177 472 1061 1650

THREE CHIPMUNKS, THE (TV) (Also see Alvin)
Dell Publishing Co.: No. 1042, Oct-Dec, 1959
Four Color 1042 (#1)-(Alvin, Simon & Theodore) 9 18 27 60 120 180

THREE COMICS (Also see Spiritman)
The Penny King Co.: 1944 (10¢, 52 pgs.) (2 different covers exist)
1,3,4-Lady Luck, Mr. Mystic, The Spirit app. (3 Spirit sections bound together); Lou Fine-a 30 60 90 177 289 400
NOTE: *No. 1 contains Spirit Sections 4/9/44 - 4/23/44, and No. 4 is also from 4/44.*

3-D (NOTE: The prices of all the 3-D comics listed include glasses. Deduct 40-50 percent if glasses are missing, and reduce slightly if glasses are loose.)

3-D ACTION
Atlas Comics (ACI): Jan, 1954 (Oversized, 15¢)(2 pairs of glasses included)
1-Battle Brady; Sol Brodsky-c 48 96 144 302 514 725

3-D ALIEN TERROR
Eclipse Comics: June, 1986 ($2.50)
1-Old Witch, Crypt-Keeper, Vault Keeper cameo; Morrow, John Pound-a, Yeates-c 6.00
...in 2-D: 100 copies signed, numbered(B&W) 3 6 9 14 20 25

3-D ANIMAL FUN (See Animal Fun)

THREE DAYS IN EUROPE
Oni Press: Nov, 2002 - No. 5, Apr, 2003 ($2.95, B&W, limited series)
1-5-Johnston-s/Hawthorne-a 3.00
TPB (11/03, $14.95, digest-sized) r/#1-5 15.00

3-D BATMAN (Also see Batman 3-D)
National Periodical Publications: 1953 (Reprinted in 1966)
1953-(25¢)-Reprints Batman #42 & 48 (Penguin-c/story); Tommy Tomorrow story; came with pair of 3-D Bat glasses 103 206 309 659 1130 1600
1966-Reprints 1953 issue; new cover by Infantino/Anderson; has inside-c photos of Batman & Robin from TV show (50¢) 19 38 57 131 291 450

3-D CIRCUS
Fiction House Magazines (Real Adventures Publ.): 1953 (25¢, w/glasses)
1 28 56 84 165 270 375

3-D COMICS (See Mighty Mouse, Tor and Western Fighters)

3-D DOLLY
Harvey Publications: December, 1953 (25¢, came with 2 pairs of glasses)
1-Richie Rich story redrawn from his 1st app. in Little Dot #1; shows cover in 3-D on inside 47 94 141 296 498 700

3-D-ELL
Dell Publishing Co.: No. 1, 1953; No. 3, 1953 (3-D comics) (25¢, came w/glasses)
1-Rootie Kazootie (#2 does not exist) 30 60 90 177 289 400
3-Flukey Luke 28 56 84 165 270 375

3 DEVILS
IDW Publishing: Mar, 2016 - No. 4, Jun, 2016 ($3.99, limited series)
1-4-Bo Hampton-s/a/c 4.00

3-D EXOTIC BEAUTIES
The 3-D Zone: Nov, 1990 ($2.95, 28 pgs.)
1-L.B. Cole-c 1 2 3 5 7 9

3-D FEATURES PRESENTS JET PUP
Dimensions Publications: Oct-Dec (Winter on-c), 1953 (25¢, came w/glasses)
1-Irving Spector-a(2) 30 60 90 177 289 400

3-D FUNNY MOVIES
Comic Media: 1953 (25¢, came w/glasses)
1-Bugsey Bear & Paddy Pelican 34 68 102 199 325 450

THREE-DIMENSION ADVENTURES (Superman)
National Periodical Publications: 1953 (25¢, large size, came w/glasses)
nn-Origin Superman (new art) 103 206 309 659 1130 1600

THREE DIMENSIONAL ALIEN WORLDS (See Alien Worlds)
Pacific Comics: July, 1984 (1st Ray Zone 3-D book)(one-shot)
1-Bolton-a(p); Stevens-a(i); Art Adams 1st published-a(p) 6.00

THREE DIMENSIONAL DNAGENTS (See New DNAgents)

THREE DIMENSIONAL E. C. CLASSICS (Three Dimensional Tales From the Crypt No. 2)
E. C. Comics: Spring, 1954 (Prices include glasses; came with 2 pair)
1-Stories by Wood (Mad #3), Krigstein (W.S. #7), Evans (F.C. #13), & Ingels (CSS #5); Kurtzman-c (rare in high grade due to unstable paper)

3 Geeks: Slab Madness! #2 © Rich Koslowski

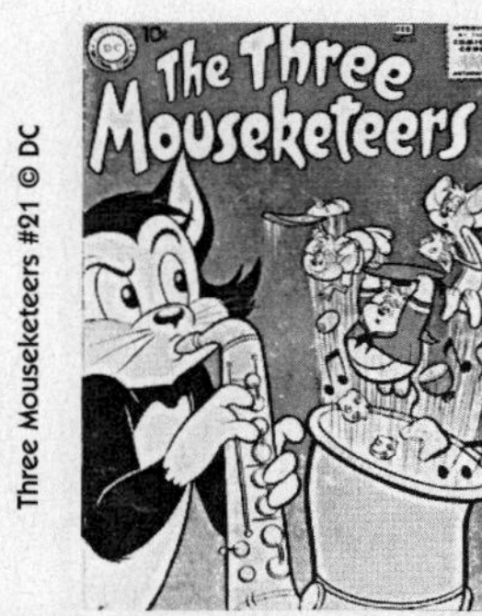

Three Mouseketeers #21 © DC

Three Stooges #39 © DELL

	GD 2.0	VG 4.0	FN 6.0	VF 8.0	VF/NM 9.0	NM- 9.2
	105	210	315	667	1146	1625

NOTE: *Stories redrawn to 3-D format. Original stories not necessarily by artists listed. CSS: Crime SuspenStories; F.C.: Frontline Combat; W.S.: Weird Science.*

THREE DIMENSIONAL TALES FROM THE CRYPT (Formerly Three Dimensional E. C. Classics)(Cover title: ...From the Crypt of Terror)
E. C. Comics: No. 2, Spring, 1954 (Prices include glasses; came with 2 pair)

	GD	VG	FN	VF	VF/NM	NM-
2-Davis (TFTC #25), Elder (VOH #14), Craig (TFTC #24), & Orlando (TFTC #22) stories; Feldstein-c (rare in high grade)	103	206	309	659	1130	1600

NOTE: *Stories redrawn to 3-D format. Original stories not necessarily by artists listed. TFTC: Tales From the Crypt; VOH: Vault of Horror.*

3-D LOVE
Steriographic Publ. (Mikeross Publ.): Dec, 1953 (25¢, came w/glasses)

	GD	VG	FN	VF	VF/NM	NM-
1	34	68	102	199	325	450

3-D NOODNICK (See Noodnick)

3-D ROMANCE
Steriographic Publ. (Mikeross Publ.): Jan, 1954 (25¢, came w/glasses)

	GD	VG	FN	VF	VF/NM	NM-
1	34	68	102	199	325	450

3-D SHEENA, JUNGLE QUEEN (Also see Sheena 3-D)
Fiction House Magazines: 1953 (25¢, came w/glasses)

	GD	VG	FN	VF	VF/NM	NM-
1-Maurice Whitman-c	69	138	207	442	759	1075

3-D SUBSTANCE
The 3-D Zone: July, 1990 ($2.95, 28 pgs.)

	GD	VG	FN	VF	VF/NM	NM-
1-Ditko-c/a(r)						5.00

3-D TALES OF THE WEST
Atlas Comics (CPS): Jan, 1954 (Oversized) (15¢, came with 2 pair of glasses)

	GD	VG	FN	VF	VF/NM	NM-
1 (3-D)-Sol Brodsky-c	47	94	141	296	498	700

3-D THREE STOOGES (Also see Three Stooges)
Eclipse Comics: Sept, 1986 - No. 2, Nov, 1986; No. 3, Oct, 1987; No. 4, 1989 ($2.50)

	GD	VG	FN	VF	VF/NM	NM-
1-4: 3-Maurer-r. 4-r-/"Three Missing Links"						5.00
1-3 (2-D)						5.00

3-D WHACK (See Whack)

3-D ZONE, THE
The 3-D Zone (Renegade Press)/Ray Zone: Feb, 1987 - No. 20, 1989 ($2.50)

	GD	VG	FN	VF	VF/NM	NM-
1,3,4,7-9,11,12,14,15,17,19,20: 1-r/A Star Presentation. 3-Picture Scope Jungle Advs. 4-Electric Fear. 7-Hollywood 3-D Jayne Mansfield photo-c. 8-High Seas 3-D, 9-Redmask-r. 11-Danse Macabre; Matt Fox c/a(r). 12-3-D Presidents. 14-Tyranostar. 15-3-Dementia Comics; Kurtzman-c, Kubert, Maurer-a. 17-Thrilling Love. 19-Cracked Classics. 20-Commander Battle and His Atomic Submarine	1	2	3	5	6	8
2,5,6,10,13,18: 2-Wolverton-r. 5-Krazy Kat-r. 6-Ratfink. 10-Jet 3-D; Powell & Williamson-r. 13-Flash Gordon. 18-Spacehawk; Wolverton-r	1	3	4	6	8	10
16-Space Vixens; Dave Stevens-c/a	3	6	9	21	33	45

NOTE: ***Davis** r-19. **Ditko** r-19. **Elder** r-19. **Everett** r-19. **Feldstein** r-17. **Frazetta** r-17. **Heath** r-19. **Kamen** r-17. **Severin** r-19. **Ward** r-17,19. **Wolverton** r-2,18,19. **Wood** r-1,17. Photo c-12*

3 GEEKS, THE (Also see Geeksville)
3 Finger Prints: 1996 - No. 11, Jun, 1999 (B&W)

	GD	VG	FN	VF	VF/NM	NM-
1,2 -Rich Koslowski-s/a in all	1	2	3	5	6	8
1-(2nd printing)						3.00
3-7, 9-11						3.00
8-(48 pgs.)						4.00
10-Variant-c						3.50
...48 Page Super-Sized Summer Spectacular (7/04, $4.95)						5.00
...Full Circle (7/03, $4.95) Origin story of the 3 Geeks; "Buck Rodinski" app.						5.00
How to Pick Up Girls If You're a Comic Book Geek (color)(7/97)						4.00
When the Hammer Fallls TPB (2001, $14.95) r/#8-11						15.00

3 GEEKS: SLAB MADNESS!
3 Finger Prints: Sept, 2008 - No. 3, Mar, 2009 ($2.99, B&W, limited series)

	GD	VG	FN	VF	VF/NM	NM-
1-3-Rich Koslowski-s/a; intro. The Cee-Gee-Cee						3.00

3 GUNS
BOOM! Studios: Aug, 2013 - No. 6, Jan, 2014 ($3.99)

	GD	VG	FN	VF	VF/NM	NM-
1-6-Steven Grant-s/Emilio Laiso-a						4.00

300 (Adapted for 2007 movie)
Dark Horse Comics: May, 1998 - No. 5, Sept, 1998 ($2.95/$3.95, limited series)

	GD	VG	FN	VF	VF/NM	NM-
1-Frank Miller-s/c/a; Spartans vs. Persians war	3	6	9	14	20	25
1-Second printing						5.00
2-4	2	4	6	8	10	12
5-($3.95-c)	2	4	6	8	10	12
HC ($30.00) -oversized reprint of series						30.00

3 LITTLE KITTENS
BroadSword Comics: Aug, 2002 - No. 3, Dec, 2002 ($2.95, limited series)

	GD	VG	FN	VF	VF/NM	NM-
1-3-Jim Balent-s/a; two covers						3.00

3 LITTLE PIGS (Disney)(...and the Wonderful Magic Lamp)
Dell Publishing Co.: No. 218, Mar, 1949

	GD	VG	FN	VF	VF/NM	NM-
Four Color 218 (#1)	10	20	30	66	138	210

3 LITTLE PIGS, THE (See Walt Disney Showcase #15 & 21)
Gold Key: May, 1964; No. 2, Sept, 1968 (Walt Disney)

	GD	VG	FN	VF	VF/NM	NM-
1-Reprints Four Color #218	3	6	9	19	30	40
2	3	6	9	15	21	26

THREE MOUSEKETEERS, THE (1st Series)(See Funny Stuff #1)
National Per. Publ.: 3-4/56 - No. 24, 9-10/59; No. 25, 8-9/60 - No. 26, 10-12/60

	GD	VG	FN	VF	VF/NM	NM-
1	23	46	69	164	362	560
2	11	22	33	73	157	240
3-5,7,9,10	8	16	24	56	108	160
6,8-Grey tone-c	10	20	30	66	138	210
11-26: 24-Cover says 11/59, inside says 9-10/59	7	14	21	49	92	135

NOTE: ***Rube Grossman** a-1-26. **Sheldon Mayer** a-1-8; c-1-7.*

THREE MOUSEKETEERS, THE (2nd Series) (See Super DC Giant)
National Periodical Publications: May-June, 1970 - No. 7, May-June, 1971 (#5-7: 68 pgs.)

	GD	VG	FN	VF	VF/NM	NM-
1-Mayer-r in all	6	12	18	40	73	105
2-4: 4-Doodles Duck begins (1st app.)	4	8	12	25	40	55
5-7:(68 pgs.). 5-Dodo & the Frog, Bo Bunny begin	5	10	15	31	53	75

THREE MUSKETEERS, THE (Also see Disney's The Three Musketeers)
Gemstone Publishing: 2004 ($3.95, squarebound, one-shot)

	GD	VG	FN	VF	VF/NM	NM-
nn-Adaptation of the 2004 DVD movie; Petrossi-c/a						4.00

THREE NURSES (Confidential Diary #12-17; Career Girl Romances #24 on)
Charlton Comics: V3#18, May, 1963 - V3#23, Mar, 1964

	GD	VG	FN	VF	VF/NM	NM-
V3#18-23	3	6	9	19	30	40

THREE RASCALS
I. W. Enterprises: 1958; 1963

	GD	VG	FN	VF	VF/NM	NM-
I.W. Reprint #1,2,10: 1-(Says Super Comics on inside)-(M.E.'s Clubhouse Rascals) DeCarlo-a. #2-(1958). 10-(1963)-r/#1	2	4	6	8	11	14

THREE RING COMICS
Spotlight Publishers: March, 1945

	GD	VG	FN	VF	VF/NM	NM-
1-Funny animal	20	40	60	114	182	250

THREE RING COMICS (Also see Captain Wizard & Meteor Comics)
Century Publications: April, 1946

	GD	VG	FN	VF	VF/NM	NM-
1-Prankster-c; Captain Wizard, Impossible Man, Race Wilkins, King O'Leary, & Dr. Mercy app.	39	78	117	240	395	550

THREE ROCKETEERS (See Blast-Off)

THREE STOOGES (See Comic Album #18, Top Comics, The Little Stooges, March of Comics #232, 248, 268, 280, 292, 304, 316, 336, 373, Movie Classics & Comics & 3-D Three Stooges)

THREE STOOGES
Jubilee No. 1/St. John No. 1 (9/53) on: Feb, 1949 - No. 2, May, 1949; Sept, 1953 - No. 7, Oct, 1954

	GD	VG	FN	VF	VF/NM	NM-
1-(Scarce, 1949)-Kubert-a; infinity-c	155	310	465	992	1696	2400
2-(Scarce)-Kubert, Maurer-a	97	194	291	621	1061	1500
1(9/53)-Hollywood Stunt Girl by Kubert (7 pgs.)	81	162	243	518	884	1250
2(3-D, 10/53, 25¢)-Came w/glasses; Stunt Girl story by Kubert	41	82	123	256	428	600
3(3-D, 10/53, 25¢)-Came w/glasses; has 3-D-c	39	78	117	240	395	550
4(3/54)-7(10/54): 4-1st app. Li'l Stooge?	39	78	117	240	395	550

NOTE: *All issues have **Kubert-Maurer** art & **Maurer** covers. 6, 7-Partial photo-c.*

THREE STOOGES
Dell Publishing Co./Gold Key No. 10 (10/62) on: No. 1043, Oct-Dec, 1959 - No. 55, June, 1972

	GD	VG	FN	VF	VF/NM	NM-
Four Color 1043 (#1)	22	44	66	155	345	535
Four Color 1078,1127,1170,1187	11	22	33	73	157	240
6(9-11/61) - 10: 6-Professor Putter begins; ends #16	9	18	27	58	114	170
11-14,16,18-20	7	14	21	48	89	130
15-Go Around the World in a Daze (movie scenes)	8	16	24	51	96	140
17-The Little Monsters begin (5/64)(1st app.?)	8	16	24	51	96	140
21,23-30	6	12	18	38	69	100
22-Movie scenes from "The Outlaws Is Coming"	6	12	18	41	76	110

Threshold #6 © DC

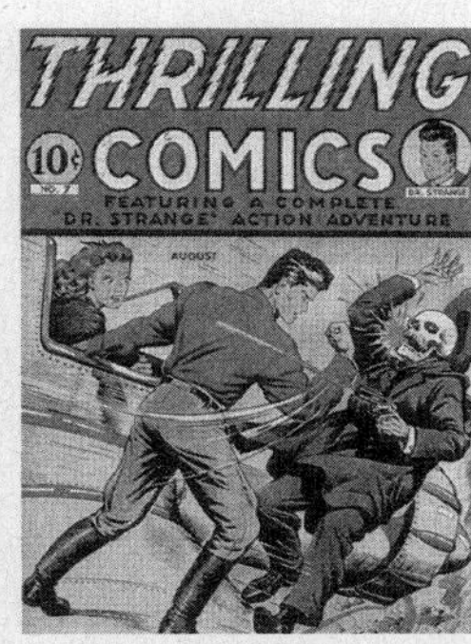

Thrilling Comics #7 © BP

Thrilling Crime Cases #49 © STAR

	GD 2.0	VG 4.0	FN 6.0	VF 8.0	VF/NM 9.0	NM- 9.2
31-55	5	10	15	31	53	75
NOTE: *All Four Colors, 6-50, 52-55 have photo-c.*						
THREE STOOGES IN 3-D, THE						
Eternity Comics: 1991 ($3.95, high quality paper, w/glasses)						
1-Reprints Three Stooges by Gold Key; photo-c						5.00
THREE STOOGES						
American Mythology Prods.: 2016 - Present (series of one-shots)						
...: Curse of the Frankenstooge (2016, $4.99) New stories and reprint from #24; 5 covers						5.00
...: Halloween Hullabaloo (2016, giveaway) New stories by various; Ropp-c						3.00
...: Merry Stoogemas (2016, $3.99) New stories and reprint from #7; 5 covers						4.00
...: Red, White, & Stooge (2016, $3.99) New story and reprint from #44; 4 covers						4.00
...: Stooge-A-Palooza 1 (2016, $4.99) New stories and reprint from FC #1170; 3 covers						5.00
...: The Boys are Back (2016, $3.99) New stories and reprint from FC #1170; 4 covers						4.00
3 WORLDS OF GULLIVER						
Dell Publishing Co.: No. 1158, July, 1961 (2 issues exist with diff. covers)						
Four Color 1158-Movie, photo-c	6	12	18	42	79	115
THRESHOLD						
DC Comics: Mar, 2013 - No. 8 ($3.99)						
1-8-Anthology. 1-5-Back-up Larfleeze stories. 5,6-Brainiac app.						4.00
THRILL COMICS (See Flash Comics, Fawcett)						
THRILLER						
DC Comics: Nov, 1983 - No. 12, Nov, 1984 ($1.25, Baxter paper)						
1-12: 1-Intro Seven Seconds; Von Eeden-c/a begins. 2-Origin. 5,6-Elvis satire						4.00
THRILLING ADVENTURE HOUR PRESENTS:...						
Image Comics: ($3.50)						
... Beyond Belief 1-3 (4/15 - No. 3, 3/16) Acker & Blacker-s/Hester-a						3.50
... Sparks Nevada: Marshal on Mars 1-4 (2/15 - No. 4, 7/15) Acker & Blacker-s/Bone-a						3.50
THRILLING ADVENTURES IN STAMPS COMICS (Formerly Stamp Comics)						
Stamp Comics, Inc. (Very Rare): V1#8, Jan, 1953 (25¢, 100 pgs.)						
V1#8-Harrison, Wildey, Kiefer, Napoli-a	75	150	225	476	818	1160
THRILLING ADVENTURE STORIES (See Tigerman)						
Atlas/Seaboard Publ.: Feb, 1975 - No. 2, Aug, 1975 (B&W, 68 pgs.)						
1-Tigerman, Kromag the Killer begin; Heath, Thorne-a; Doc Savage movie photos of Ron Ely	3	6	9	17	26	35
2-Heath, Toth, Severin, Simonson-a; Adams-c	4	8	12	23	37	50
THRILLING COMICS						
Better Publ./Nedor/Standard Comics: Feb, 1940 - No. 80, April, 1951						
1-Origin & 1st app. Dr. Strange (37 pgs.), ends #?; Nickie Norton of the Secret Service begins	389	778	1167	2723	4762	6800
2-The Rio Kid, The Woman in Red, Pinocchio begins	206	412	618	1318	2259	3200
3-The Ghost & Lone Eagle begin	168	336	504	1075	1838	2600
4-6,8,9: 5-Dr. Strange changed to Doc Strange	155	310	465	992	1696	2400
7-Classic-c	213	426	639	1363	2332	3300
10-1st WWII-c (Nazi)(11/40)	161	322	483	1030	1765	2500
11-18,20: 17-WWII-Nazi-c	142	284	426	909	1555	2200
19-Origin & 1st app. The American Crusader (8/41), ends #39,41; Schomburg Nazi WWII-c	194	388	582	1242	2121	3000
21-26,28-30: 24-Intro. Mike, Doc Strange's sidekick (1/42). 29-Last Rio Kid	110	220	330	704	1202	1700
27-Robot-c	135	270	405	864	1482	2100
31-35,37,39,40	90	180	270	576	988	1400
36-Commando Cubs begin (7/43, 1st app.)	103	206	309	659	1130	1600
38-Classic Nazi bondage-c	206	412	618	1318	2259	3200
41-Classic Hitler & Mussolini WWII-c	411	822	1233	2877	5039	7200
42-Classic Schomburg Japanese WWII-c	129	258	387	826	1413	2000
43,46-51: 51(12/45)-Last WWII-c (Japanese)	77	154	231	493	847	1200
44-Hitler WWII-c by Schomburg	314	628	942	2198	3849	5500
45-Hitler pict. on-c	107	214	321	680	1165	1650
52-Classic Schomburg hooded bondage-c; the Ghost ends	87	174	261	553	952	1350
53,54: 53-The Phantom Detective begins. The Cavalier app. in both; no Commando Cubs in either	55	110	165	352	601	850
55-The Lone Eagle ends	45	90	135	284	480	675
56 (10/46)-Princess Pantha begins (not on-c), 1st app.	61	122	183	390	670	950
57-Doc Strange-c; 2nd Princess Pantha	53	106	159	334	567	800
58-66: All Princess Pantha jungle-c, w/Doc Strange #59, his last-c. 61-Ingels-a; The Lone Eagle app. 65-Last Phantom Detective & Commando Cubs. 66-Frazetta text illo	52	104	156	328	552	775
67,70,71-Last jungle-c; Frazetta-a(5-7 pgs.) in each	55	110	165	352	601	850
68,69-Frazetta-a(2), 8 & 6 pgs.; 9 & 7 pgs.	58	116	174	371	636	900
72,73: 72-Buck Ranger, Cowboy Detective c/stys begin (western theme), end #80; Frazetta-a(5-7 ps.) in each	41	82	123	250	418	585
74-Last Princess Pantha; Tara app.	30	60	90	177	289	400
75-78: 75-All western format begins	16	32	48	94	147	200
79-Krigstein-a	17	34	51	98	154	210
80-Severin & Elder, Celardo, Moreira-a	17	34	51	98	154	210
NOTE: *Bondage c-5, 9, 13, 20, 22, 27-30, 38, 41, 52, 54, 70.* **Kinstler** *a-45.* **Leo Morey** *a-7.* **Schomburg** *(sometimes signed as* **Xela***) c-7, 9-19, 36-80 (airbrush 62-71).* **Tuska** *a-62, 63. Woman in Red not in #19, 23, 31-33, 39-45. No. 45 exists as a Canadian reprint but numbered #48. No. 72 exists as a Canadian reprint with no* **Frazetta** *story. American Crusader c-20-24. Buck Ranger c-72-80. Commando Cubs c-37, 39, 41, 43, 45, 47, 49, 51. Doc Strange c-1-19, 25-36, 38, 40, 42, 44, 46, 48, 50, 52-57, 59. Princess Pantha c-58, 60-71.*						
THRILLING COMICS (Also see All Star Comics 1999 crossover titles)						
DC Comics: May, 1999 ($1.99, one-shot)						
1-Golden Age Hawkman and Wildcat; Russ Heath-a						3.00
THRILLING CRIME CASES (Formerly 4Most; becomes Shocking Mystery Cases #50 on)						
Star Publications: No. 41, June-July, 1950 - No. 49, July, 1952						
41	36	72	108	211	343	475
42-45: 42-L. B. Cole-c/a (1); Chameleon story (Fox-r)	32	64	96	188	307	425
46-48: 47-Used in **POP**, pg. 84	31	62	93	182	296	410
49-(7/52)-Classic L. B. Cole-c	119	238	357	762	1306	1850
NOTE: **L. B. Cole** *c-all; a-43p, 45p, 46p, 49(2 pgs.).* **Disbrow** *a-48.* **Hollingsworth** *a-48.*						
THRILLING ROMANCES						
Standard Comics: No. 5, Dec, 1949 - No. 26, June, 1954						
5	21	42	63	122	199	275
6,8	14	28	42	78	112	145
7-Severin/Elder-a (7 pgs.)	15	30	45	84	127	170
9,10-Severin/Elder-a; photo-c	14	28	42	82	121	160
11,14-21,26: 14-Gene Tierney & Danny Kaye photo-c from movie "On the Riviera". 15-Tony Martin/Janet Leigh photo-c	13	26	39	74	105	135
12-Wood-a (2 pgs.); Tyrone Power/ Susan Hayward photo-c	15	30	45	85	130	175
13-Severin-a	14	28	42	78	112	145
22-25-Toth-a	14	28	42	82	121	160
NOTE: *All photo-c.* **Celardo** *a-9, 16.* **Colletta** *a-23, 24(2).* **Toth** *text illos-19.* **Tuska** *a-9.*						
THRILLING SCIENCE TALES						
AC Comics: 1989 - No. 2 ($3.50, 2/3 color, 52 pgs.)						
1,2: 1-r/Bob Colt #6(saucer); Frazetta, Guardineer (Space Ace), Wood, Krenkel, Orlando, WIlliamson-r; Kaluta-c. 2-Capt. Video-r by Evans, Capt. Science-r by Wood, Star Pirate-r by Whitman & Mysta of the Moon-r by Moreira						4.00
THRILLING TRUE STORY OF THE BASEBALL...						
Fawcett Publications: 1952 (Photo-c, each)						
...Giants-photo-c; has Willie Mays rookie photo-biography; Willie Mays, Eddie Stanky & others photos on-c	68	136	204	432	746	1060
...Yankees-photo-c; Yogi Berra, Joe DiMaggio, Mickey Mantle & others photos on-c	66	132	198	419	722	1025
THRILLING WONDER TALES						
AC Comics : 1991 ($2.95, B&W)						
1-Includes a Bob Powell Thun'da story						3.00
THRILLKILLER						
DC Comics : Jan, 1997 - No. 3, Mar, 1997($2.50, limited series)						
1-3-Elseworlds Robin & Batgirl; Chaykin-s/Brereton-c/a						3.00
...'62 ('98, $4.95, one-shot) Sequel; Chaykin-s/Brereton-c/a						5.00
TPB-(See Batman: Thrillkiller)						
THRILLOGY						
Pacific Comics: Jan, 1984 (One-shot, color)						
1-Conrad-c/a						4.00
THRILL-O-RAMA						
Harvey Publications (Fun Films): Oct, 1965 - No. 3, Dec, 1966						
1-Fate (Man in Black) by Powell app.; Doug Wildey-a(2); Simon-c	5	10	15	31	53	75
2-Pirana begins (see Phantom #46); Williamson 2 pgs.; Fate (Man in Black) app.; Tuska/Simon-c	3	6	9	21	33	45
3-Fate (Man in Black) app.; Sparling-c	3	6	9	18	28	38
THRILLS OF TOMORROW (Formerly Tomb of Terror)						

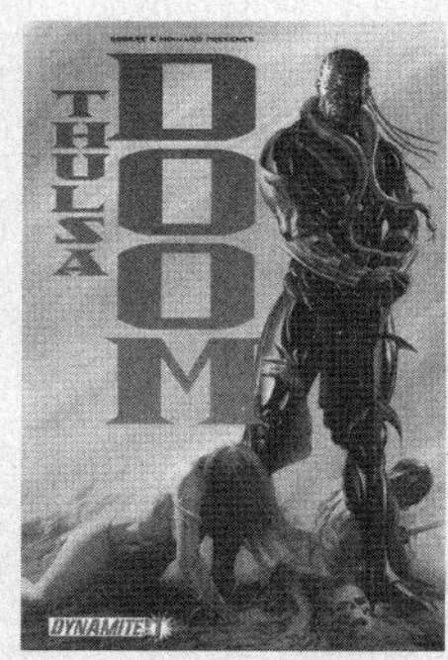

Thulsa Doom #1 © TD Corp.

Thunder Agents #17 © TC

Thunderbolts #11 © MAR

	GD 2.0	VG 4.0	FN 6.0	VF 8.0	VF/NM 9.0	NM- 9.2

Harvey Publications: No. 17, Oct, 1954 - No. 20, April, 1955

17-Powell-a (horror); r/Witches Tales #7 — 15 30 45 88 137 185
18-Powell-a (horror); r/Tomb of Terror #1 — 14 28 42 82 121 160
19,20-Stuntman-c/stories by S&K (r/from Stuntman #1 & 2); 19 has origin & is last pre-code (2/55) — 31 62 93 182 296 410

NOTE: *Kirby c-19, 20. Palais a-17. Simon c-18?*

THROBBING LOVE (See Fox Giants)

THROUGH GATES OF SPLENDOR
Spire Christian Comics (Flemming H. Revell Co.): 1973, 1974 (36 pages) (39-49 cents)

nn-1973 Edition — 3 6 9 14 19 24
nn-1974 Edition — 2 4 6 9 13 16

THULSA DOOM (Robert E. Howard character)
Dynamite Entertainment: 2009 - No. 4, 2009 ($3.50, limited series)

1-4-Alex Ross-c/Lui Antonio-a — 3.50

THUMPER (Disney)
Dell Publishing Co.: No, 19, 1942 - No. 243, Sept, 1949

Four Color 19-Walt Disney's...Meets the Seven Dwarfs; reprinted in Silly Symphonies — 44 88 132 326 738 1150
Four Color 243-...Follows His Nose — 11 22 33 72 154 235

THUN'DA (...King of the Congo)
Magazine Enterprises: 1952 - No. 6, 1953

1(A-1 #47)-Origin; Frazetta c/a; only comic done entirely by Frazetta; all Thun'da stories, no Cave Girl — 219 438 657 1402 2401 3400
2(A-1 #56)-Powell-c/a begins, ends #6; Intro/1st app. Cave Girl in filler strip (also app. in 3-6) — 31 62 93 182 296 410
3(A-1 #73), 4(A-1 #78) — 21 42 63 124 202 280
5(A-1 #83), 6(A-1 #86) — 20 40 60 120 195 270

THUN'DA
Dynamite Entertainment: 2012 - No. 5, 2012 ($3.99, limited series)

1-5-Napton-s/Richards-a/Jae Lee-c. 1-4-Bonus reprints of Thun'da #1 (1952) Frazetta-a — 4.00

THUN'DA TALES (See Frank Frazetta's...)

THUNDER AGENTS (See Dynamo, Noman & Tales Of Thunder)
Tower Comics: 11/65 - No. 17, 12/67; No. 18, 9/68, No. 19, 11/68, No. 20, 11/69 (No. 1-16: 68 pgs.; No. 17 on: 52 pgs.)(All are 25¢)

1-Origin & 1st app. Dynamo, Noman, Menthor, & The Thunder Squad; 1st app. The Iron Maiden — 17 34 51 119 265 410
2-Death of Egghead; A-bomb blast panel — 9 18 27 61 123 185
3-5: 4-Guy Gilbert becomes Lightning who joins Thunder Squad; Iron Maiden app. — 7 14 21 49 92 135
6-10: 7-Death of Menthor. 8-Origin & 1st app. The Raven — 6 12 18 38 69 100
11-15: 13-Undersea Agent app.; no Raven story — 5 10 15 35 63 90
16-19 — 5 10 15 34 60 85
20-Special Collectors Edition; all reprints — 4 8 12 27 44 60
...Archives Vol. 1 (DC Comics, 2003, $49.95, HC) r/#1-4, restored and recolored — 50.00
...Archives Vol. 2 (DC Comics, 2003, $49.95, HC) r/#5-7, Dynamo #1 — 50.00
...Archives Vol. 3 (DC Comics, 2003, $49.95, HC) r/#8-10, Dynamo #2 — 50.00
...Archives Vol. 4 (DC Comics, 2004, $49.95, HC) r/#11, Noman #1,2 & Dynamo #3 — 50.00

NOTE: *Crandall a-1, 4p, 5p, 18, 20r; c-18. Ditko a-6, 7p, 12p, 13?, 14p, 16, 18. Giunta a-6. Kane a-1, 5p, 6p?, 14, 16p; c-14, 15. Reinman a-13. Sekowsky a-6. Tuska a-1p, 7, 8, 10, 13-17, 19. Whitney a-9p, 10, 13, 15, 17, 18; c-17. Wood a-1-11, 15(w/Ditko-12, 18), (inks-#9, 13, 14, 16, 17), 19i, 20r; c-1-8, 9i, 10-13(#10 w/Williamson(p)), 16.*

T.H.U.N.D.E.R. AGENTS (See Blue Ribbon Comics, Hall of Fame Featuring the..., JCP Features & Wally Wood's...)
JC Comics (Archie Publications): May, 1983 - No. 2, Jan, 1984

1,2: 1-New Manna/Blyberg-c/a. 2-Blyberg-c — 6.00

T.H.U.N.D.E.R. AGENTS
DC Comics: Jan, 2011 - No. 10, Oct, 2011 ($3.99/$2.99)

1-3-($3.99): 1-Spencer-s/Cafu-a/Quitely-c. 3-Chaykin-a (5 pgs.) — 4.00
4-10-($2.99): 4-Pérez-a (5 pgs.). 7-10-Grell & Dragotta-a — 3.00
1-Variant-c by Darwyn Cooke — 8.00

T.H.U.N.D.E.R. AGENTS
DC Comics: Jan, 2012 - No. 6, Jun, 2012 ($2.99, limited series)

1-6-Spencer-s/Craig-a. 1-Andy Kubert-c. 3-Craig & Simonson-a — 3.00

T.H.U.N.D.E.R. AGENTS
IDW Publishing: Aug, 2013 - No. 8, Apr, 2014 ($3.99)

1-8: 1-4-Hester-s/Di Vito-a. 1-Four interlocking covers by Di Vito. 5-8-Roger Robinson-a — 4.00

THUNDER BIRDS (See Cinema Comics Herald)

THUNDERBOLT (See The Atomic...)

THUNDERBOLT (Peter Cannon...; see Crisis on Infinite Earths, Peter Cannon, Captain Atom and Judomaster)
Charlton Comics: Jan, 1966; No. 51, Mar-Apr, 1966 - No. 60, Nov, 1967

1-Origin & 1st app. Thunderbolt — 4 8 12 27 44 60
51-(Formerly Son of Vulcan #50) — 3 6 9 19 30 40
52-Judomaster story — 3 6 9 16 23 30
53-Captain Atom story, 2 pgs. — 3 6 9 16 23 30
54-59: 54-Sentinels begin. 59-Last Thunderbolt & Sentinels (back-up story) — 3 6 9 14 19 24
60-Prankster only app. — 3 6 9 15 21 26
57,58 ('77)-Modern Comics-r — 6.00

NOTE: *Aparo a-60. Morisi a-1, 51-56, 58; c-1, 51-56, 58, 59.*

THUNDERBOLT JAXON (Revival of 1940s British comics character)
DC Comics (WildStorm): Apr, 2006 - No. 5, Sept, 2006 ($2.99, limited series)

1-5-Dave Gibbons-s/John Higgins-a — 3.00
TPB (2007, $19.99) r/#1-5; intro. by Gibbons; cover gallery — 20.00

THUNDERBOLTS (Title re-named Dark Avengers with #175)(Also see New Thunderbolts and Incredible Hulk #449)
Marvel Comics: Apr, 1997 - No. 81, Sept, 2003; No. 100, May, 2006 - No. 174, Jul, 2012 ($1.95-$2.99)

1-($2.99)-Busiek-s/Bagley-c/a — 2 4 6 8 10 12
1-2nd printing; new cover colors — 3.00
2-4: 2-Two covers. 4-Intro. Jolt — 6.00
5-11: 9-Avengers app. — 3.50
12-($2.99)-Avengers and Fantastic Four-c/app. — 4.00
13-24: 14-Thunderbolts return to Earth. 21-Hawkeye app. — 3.00
25-($2.99) Wraparound-c — 4.00
26-38: 26-Manco-a — 3.00
39-($2.99) 100 Page Monster; Iron Man reprints — 4.00
40-49: 40-Begin $2.25-c; Sandman-c/app. 44-Avengers app. 47-Captain Marvel app. 49-Zircher-a — 3.00
50-($2.99) Last Bagley-a; Captain America becomes leader — 4.00
51-74,76,77,80,81: 51,52-Zircher-a; Dr. Doom app. 80,81-Spider-Man app. — 3.00
75-($3.50) Hawkeye leaves the team; Garcia-a — 4.00
78,79-($2.99-c) Velasco-a begins — 3.00
(See New Thunderbolts for #82-99)
100 (5/06, $3.99) resumes from New Thunderbolts #18; back-up origin stories — 4.00
101-109: 103-105-Civil War x-over — 3.00
110-New team begins including Bullseye, Venom and Norman Osborn; Ellis-s/Deodato-a — 5.00
111-136,138-149: 111-121-Ellis-s/Deodato-a. 112-Stan Lee cameo. 123-125-Secret Invasion x-over. 128-Dark Reign begins. 130,131-X-over with Deadpool #8,9. 141-143-Siege — 3.00
137-(12/09, $3.99) Iron Fist and Luke Cage app. — 4.00
150-(1/11, $4.99) Thunderbolts vs. Avengers; r/#1; storyline synopses of #1-150 — 5.00
151-158,160-163, 163.1, 164-174-($2.99) 151-153-Land-c. 155-Satana joins. 158-162-Fear Itself tie-in. 163-165-Thunderbolts in WWII; Invaders app. — 3.00
159-($4.99) Fear Itelf tie-in; Juggernaut app.; short stories of escape from The Raft — 5.00
Annual '97 ($2.99)-Wraparound-c — 4.00
Annual 2000 ($3.50) Breyfogle-a — 4.00
...: Breaking Point (1/08, $2.99, one-shot) Gage-s/Denham-a/Djurdjevic-c — 3.00
... By Warren Ellis Vol. 1 HC (2007, $24.99, dustjacket) r/#150-154, ...: Desperate Measures and stories from Civil War: Choosing Sides and The Initiative — 25.00
... By Warren Ellis Vol. 1: Faith in Monsters SC (2008, $19.99) same contents as HC — 20.00
Civil War: Thunderbolts TPB (2007, $13.99) r/#101-105 — 14.00
...: Desperate Measures (9/07, $2.99, one-shot) Jenkins-s/Steve Lieber-a — 3.00
...: Distant Rumblings (#-1) (7/97, $1.95) Busiek-s — 5.00
First Strikes (1997, $4.99,TPB) r/#1,2 — 5.00
...: From the Marvel Vault (6/11, $3.99) Jack Monroe app.; Nicieza-s/Aucoin-a — 4.00
...: Guardian Protocols (2007, $10.99) r/#106-109 — 11.00
...: International Incident (4/08, $2.99, one-shot) Gage-s/Oliver-a/Djurdjevic-c — 3.00
...: Life Sentences (7/01, $3.50) Adlard-a — 4.00
...: Marvel's Most Wanted TPB ('98, $16.99) r/origin stories of original Masters of Evil — 17.00
...: Reason in Madness (7/08, $2.99, one-shot) Gage-s/Oliver-a/Djurdjevic-c — 3.00
Wizard #0 (bagged with Wizard #89) — 3.00

THUNDERBOLTS (Marvel NOW!)
Marvel Comics: Feb, 2013 - No. 32, Dec, 2014 ($2.99)

1-32: 1-Punisher, Red Hulk, Elektra, Venom & Deadpool team; Dillon-a. 7-11-Noto-a. 14-18-Infinity tie-ins; Soule-s/Palo-a. 20-Ghost Rider joins — 3.00
Annual 1 (2/14, $4.99) Dr. Strange & Elsa Bloodstone app.; Lolli-a — 5.00

THUNDERBOLTS

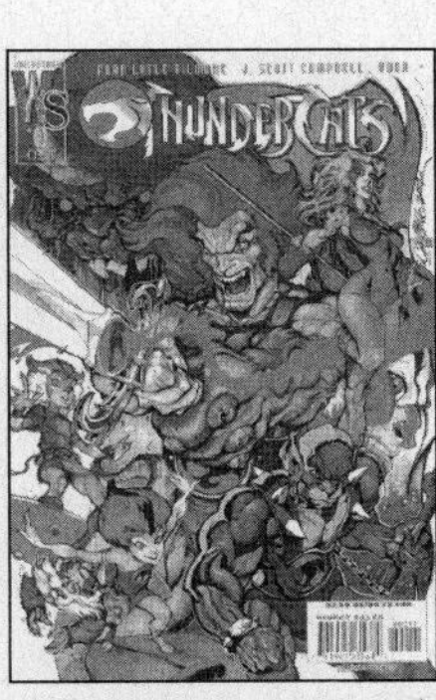

Thundercats #0 © WB & Ted Wolf

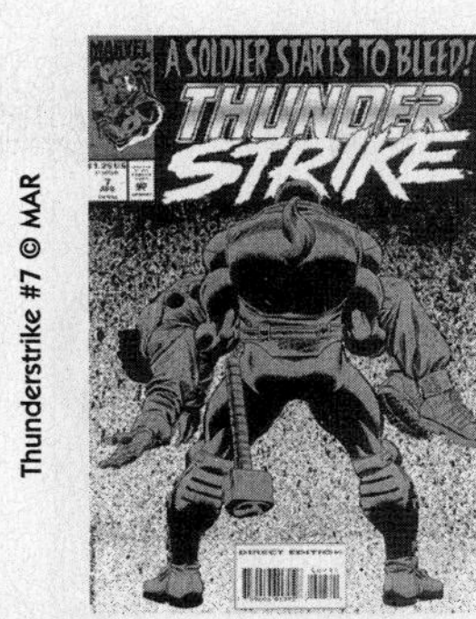

Thunderstrike #7 © MAR

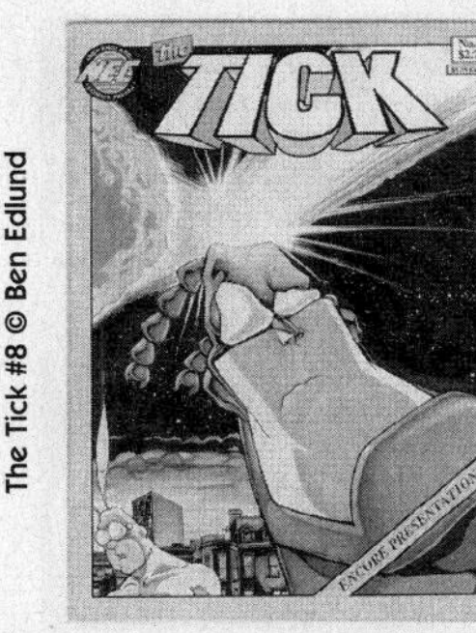

The Tick #8 © Ben Edlund

	GD	VG	FN	VF	VF/NM	NM-
	2.0	4.0	6.0	8.0	9.0	9.2

Marvel Comics: Jul, 2016 - Present ($3.99)

1-9: 1-Bucky Barnes leads the team of Kobik, Atlas, Fixer, Moonstone, & Mach-X. 4-Squadron Supreme app. 5-Spider-Man (Miles) app. 4.00
10-($4.99) 20th Anniversary Special; prologue by Busiek-s/Bagley-a; Jolt returns 5.00

THUNDERBOLTS PRESENTS: ZEMO - BORN BETTER
Marvel Comics: Apr, 2007 - No. 4, July, 2007 ($2.99, limited series)

1-4-History of Baron Zemo; Nicieza-s/Grummett-a/c 3.00
TPB (2007, $10.99) r/#1-4 11.00

THUNDERBUNNY (See Blue Ribbon Comics #13, Charlton Bullseye & Pep Comics #393)
Red Circle Comics: Jan, 1984 (Direct sale only)
WaRP Graphics: Second series No. 1, 1985 - No. 6, 1985
Apple Comics: No. 7, 1986 - No. 12, 1987

1-Humor/parody; origin Thunderbunny; 2 page pin-up by Anderson 5.00
(2nd series) 1,2-Magazine size 4.00
3-12-Comic size 4.00

THUNDERCATS (TV)
Marvel Comics (Star Comics)/Marvel #22 on: Dec, 1985 - No. 24, June, 1988 (75¢)

1-Mooney-c/a begins 2 4 6 13 18 22
2-20: 2-(65¢ & 75¢ cover exists). 12-Begin $1.00-c. 18-20-Williamson-i 1 2 3 5 7 9
21-24: 23-Williamson-c(i) 1 3 4 6 8 10

THUNDERCATS (TV)
DC Comics (WildStorm): No. 0, Oct, 2002 - No. 5, Feb, 2003 ($2.50/$2.95, limited series)

0-($2.50) J. Scott Campbell-c/a 3.00
1-5-($2.95) 1-McGuinness-a/c; variant cover by Art Adams; rebirth of Mumm-Ra 3.00
.../ Battle of the Planets (7/03, $4.95) Kaare Andrews-s/a; 2 covers by Campbell & Ross 5.00
...: Origins-Heroes & Villains (2/04, $3.50) short stories by various 3.50
...Reclaiming Thundera TPB (2003, $12.95) r/#0-5 13.00
... Sourcebook (1/03, $2.95) pin-ups and info on characters; art by various; A. Adams-c 3.00

THUNDERCATS: DOGS OF WAR
DC Comics (WildStorm): Aug, 2003 - No. 5, Dec, 2003 ($2.95, limited series)

1-5: 1-Two covers by Booth & Pearson; Booth-a/Layman-s. 2-4-Two covers 3.00
TPB (2004, $14.95) r/#1-5 15.00

THUNDERCATS: ENEMY'S PRIDE
DC Comics (WildStorm): Aug, 2004 - No. 5 ($2.95, limited series)

1-5-Vriens-a/Layman-s 3.00
TPB (2005, $14.99) r/#1-5 15.00

THUNDERCATS: HAMMERHAND'S REVENGE
DC Comics (WildStorm): Dec, 2003 - No. 5, Apr, 2004 ($2.95, limited series)

1-5-Avery-s/D'Anda-a. 2-Variant-c by Warren 3.00
TPB (2004, $14.95) r/#1-5 15.00

THUNDERCATS: THE RETURN
DC Comics (WildStorm): Apr, 2003 - No. 5, Aug, 2003 ($2.95, limited series)

1-5: 1-Two covers by Benes & Cassaday; Gilmore-s 3.00
TPB (2004, $12.95) r/series 13.00

THUNDER MOUNTAIN (See Zane Grey, Four Color #246)

THUNDERSTRIKE (See Thor #459)
Marvel Comics: June, 1993 - No. 24, July, 1995 ($1.25)

1-($2.95, 52 pgs.)-Holo-grafx lightning patterned foil-c; Bloodaxe returns 4.00
2-24: 2-Juggernaut-c/s. 4-Capt. America app. 4-6-Spider-Man app. 8-bound-in trading card sheet. 18-Bloodaxe app. 24-Death of Thunderstrike 3.00
Marvel Double Feature...Thunderstrike/Code Blue #13 ($2.50)-Same as Thunderstrike #13 w/Code Blue flip book 4.00

THUNDERSTRIKE
Marvel Comics: Jan, 2011 - No. 5, Jun, 2011 ($3.99, limited series)

1-5-DeFalco-s/Frenz-a. 1-Back-up origin retold; Nauck-a 4.00

TICK, THE (Also see The Chroma-Tick)
New England Comics Press: Jun, 1988 - No. 12, May, 1993
($1.75/$1.95/$2.25; B&W, over-sized)

Special Edition 1-1st comic book app. serially numbered & limited to 5,000 copies 6 12 18 38 69 100
Special Edition 1-(5/96, $5.95)-Double-c; foil-c; serially numbered (5,001 thru 14,000) & limited to 9,000 copies 2 4 6 11 16 20
Special Edition 2-Serially numbered and limited to 3000 copies 5 10 15 30 50 70
Special Edition 2-(8/96, $5.95)-Double-c; foil-c; serially numbered (5,001 thru 14,000) & limited to 9,000 copies 1 2 3 5 6 8
1-Regular Edition 1st printing; reprints Special Ed. 1 w/minor changes 4 8 12 25 40 55
1-2nd printing 6.00
1-3rd-5th printing 4.00
2-Reprints Special Ed. 2 w/minor changes 2 4 6 13 18 22
2-8-All reprints 4.00
3-5: 4-1st app. Paul the Samurai 1 3 4 6 8 10
6,8 ($2.25) 6.00
7-1st app. Man-Eating Cow 1 2 3 5 6 8
8-Variant with no logo, price, issue number or company logos. 3 6 9 14 20 25
9-12 ($2.75) 5.00
12-Special Edition; card-stock, virgin foil-c; numbered edition 2 4 6 13 18 22
100: The Tick Meets Invincible (6/12, $6.99) Invincible travels to Tick's universe 7.00
101: The Tick Meets Madman (11/12, $6.99) Bonus publishing history of the Tick 7.00
Pseudo-Tick #13 (11/00, $3.50) Continues story from #12 (1993) 5.00
Promo Sampler-(1990)-Tick-c/story 1 2 3 5 6 8

TICK, THE (One shots)

... Big Back to School Special 1-(10/98, $3.50, B&W) Tick & Arthur undercover in H.S. 4.00
... Big Cruise Ship Vacation Special 1-(9/00, $3.50, B&W) 4.00
... Big Father's Day Special 1-(6/00, $3.50, B&W) 4.00
... Big Halloween Special 1-(10/99, $3.50, B&W) 4.00
... Big Halloween Special 2000 (10/00, $3.50) 4.00
... Big Halloween Special 2001 (9/01, $3.95) 4.00
... Big Mother's Day Special 1-(4/00, $3.50, B&W) 4.00
... Big Red-N-Green Christmas Spectacle 1-(12/01, $3.95) 4.00
... Big Romantic Adventure 1-(2/98, $2.95, B&W) Candy box-c with candy map on back 4.00
... Big Summer Annual 1-(7/99, $3.50, B&W) Chainsaw Vigilante vs. Barry 4.00
... Big Summer Fun Special 1-(8/98, $3.50, B&W) Tick and Arthur at summer camp 4.00
... Big Tax Time Terror 1-(4/00, $3.50, B&W) 4.00
... Big Year 2000 Spectacle 1-(3/00, $3.50, B&W) 4.00
... Incredible Internet Comic 1-(7/01, $3.95, color) r/New England Comics website story 4.00
FCBD Special Edition (5/10) - reprints debut from 1988; Ben Edlund-s/a 3.00
Free Comic Book Day 2013 (6/13) - New stories; McClelland-s/Redhead-a 3.00
Free Comic Book Day 2014 (6/14) - New stories; McClelland-s/Redhead-a 3.00
Free Comic Book Day 2015 (6/15) - New stories; McClelland-s/Redhead-a 3.00
Free Comic Book Day 2016 (6/16) - New stories; McClelland-s/Redhead-a; Nichols-a 3.00
Introducing the Tick 1-(4/02, $3.95, color) summary of Tick's life and adventures 4.00
The Tick's Back #0 -(8/97, $2.95, B&W) 4.00
The Tick's Comic Con Extravaganza -(6/07, $3.95, color) Wang-c 4.00
The Tick's 20th Anniversary Special Edition #1 (5/07, $5.95) short stories by various; history of the character; creator profiles; 2 covers by Suydam & Bisley 6.00

--MASSIVE SUMMER DOUBLE SPECTACLE

1,2-(7,8/00, $3.50, B&W) 4.00

TICK & ARTIE

1-(6/02, $3.50, color) prints strips from Internet comic 4.00
2-(10/02, $3.95) 4.00

TICK AND ARTHUR, THE
New England Comics: Feb, 1999 - No. 6 ($3.50, B&W)

1-6-Sean Wang-s/a 4.00

TICK BIG BLUE DESTINY, THE
New England Comics: Oct, 1997 - No. 9 ($2.95)

1-4: 1-"Keen" Ed. 2-Two covers 4.00
1-($4.95) "Wicked Keen" Ed. w/die cut-c 5.00
5-($3.50) 4.00
6-Luny Bin Trilogy Preview #0 (7/98, $1.50) 4.00
7-9: 7-Luny Bin Trilogy begins 4.00

TICK BIG BLUE YULE LOG SPECIAL, THE
New England Comics: Dec, 1997; 1999 ($2.95, B&W)

1-"Jolly" and "Traditional" covers; flip book w/"Arthur Teaches the Tick About Hanukkah" 4.00
...1999 ($3.50) 4.00
Tick Big Yule Log Special 2001-(12/00, $3.50, B&W) 4.00

TICK, THE : CIRCUS MAXIMUS
New England Comics: Mar, 2000 - No. 4, Jun, 2000 ($3.50, B&W)

1-4-Encyclopedia of characters from Tick comics 4.00
Giant No. 1 (8/03, $14.95) r/#1-4, Redux 15.00
Redux No. 1 (4/01, $3.50) 4.00

TICK, THE - COLOR

The Tick Karma Tornado #5 © Ben Edlund

Tigra #1 © MAR

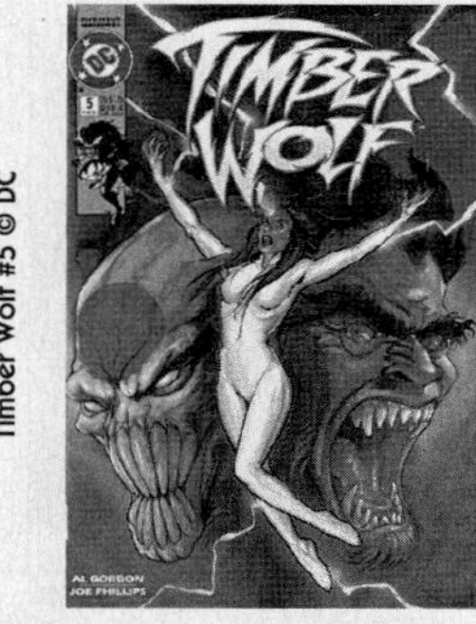

Timber Wolf #5 © DC

	GD 2.0	VG 4.0	FN 6.0	VF 8.0	VF/NM 9.0	NM- 9.2

New England Comics: Jan, 2001 - No. 6 ($3.95)
1-6: 1-Marc Sandroni-a 4.00

TICK, THE : DAYS OF DRAMA
New England Comics: July, 2005 - No. 6, June, 2006 ($4.95/$3.95, limited series)
1-($4.95) Dave Garcia-a; has a mini-comic attached to cover 5.00
2-6-($3.95) 4.00

TICK, THE - HEROES OF THE CITY
New England Comics: Feb, 1999 - No. 6 ($3.50, B&W)
1-6-Short stories by various 4.00

TICK KARMA TORNADO (The...)
New England Comics Press: Oct, 1993 - No. 9, Mar, 1995 ($2.75, B&W)
1-($3.25) 5.00
2-9: 2-$2.75-c begins 4.00

TICK NEW SERIES (The...)
New England Comics: Dec, 2009 - No. 8 ($4.95)
1-8 5.00

TICK'S BIG XMAS TRILOGY, THE
New England Comics: Dec, 2002 - No. 3, Dec, 2002 ($3.95, limited series)
1-3 4.00

TICK'S GOLDEN AGE COMIC, THE
New England Comics: May, 2002 - No. 3, Feb, 2003 ($4.95, Golden Age size)
1-3-Facsimile 1940s-style Tick issue; 2 covers 5.00
Giant Edition TPB (9/03, $12.95) r/#1-3 13.00

TICK'S GIANT CIRCUS OF THE MIGHTY, THE
New England Comics: Summer, 1992 - No. 3, Fall, 1993 ($2.75, B&W, magazine size)
1-(A-O). 2-(P-Z). 3-1993 Update 5.00

TICKLE COMICS (Also see Gay, Smile, & Whee Comics)
Modern Store Publ.: 1955 (7¢, 5x7-1/4", 52 pgs)
1 8 16 24 40 50 60

TICK TOCK TALES
Magazine Enterprises: Jan, 1946 - V3#33, Jan-Feb, 1951
1-Koko & Kola begin 21 42 63 124 202 280
2 14 28 42 76 108 140
3-10 12 24 36 69 97 125
11-33: 19-Flag-c. 23-Muggsy Mouse, The Pixies & Tom-Tom the Jungle Boy app.
24-X-mas-c. 25-The Pixies & Tom-Tom app. 11 22 33 62 86 110

TIGER (Also see Comics Reading Libraries in the Promotional Comics section)
Charlton Press (King Features): Mar, 1970 - No. 6, Jan, 1971 (15¢)
1 3 6 9 14 19 24
2-6: 3-Ad for life-size inflatable doll 2 4 6 8 11 14

TIGER BOY (See Unearthly Spectaculars)

TIGER GIRL
Gold Key: Sept, 1968 (15¢)
1(10227-809)-Sparling-c/a; Jerry Siegel scripts; advertising on back-c
4 8 12 25 40 55
1-Variant edition with pin-up on back cover 5 10 15 31 53 75

TIGERMAN (Also see Thrilling Adventure Stories)
Seaboard Periodicals (Atlas): Apr, 1975 - No. 3, Sept, 1975 (All 25¢ issues)
1-3: 1-Origin; Colan-c. 2,3-Ditko-p in each 2 4 6 11 16 20

TIGER WALKS, A (See Movie Comics)

TIGRA (The Avengers)
Marvel Comics: May, 2002 - No. 4, Aug, 2002 ($2.99, limited series)
1-4-Christina Z-s/Deodato-c/a 3.00

TIGRESS, THE
Hero Graphics: Aug, 1992 - No. 6?, June, 1993 ($3.95/$2.95, B&W)
1,6: 1-Tigress vs. Flare. 6-44 pgs. 4.00
2-5: 2-$2.95-c begins 3.00

TILLIE THE TOILER (See Comic Monthly)
Dell Publishing Co.: No. 15, 1941 - No. 237, July, 1949
Four Color 15(1941) 55 110 165 352 601 850
Large Feature Comic 30(1941) 39 78 117 231 378 525
Four Color 8(1942) 24 48 72 168 372 575
Four Color 22(1943) 17 34 51 117 259 400
Four Color 55(1944), 89(1945) 12 24 36 84 185 285
Four Color 106('45),132('46): 132-New stories begin 10 20 30 64 132 200
Four Color 150,176,184 9 18 27 60 120 180
Four Color 195,213,237 8 16 24 51 96 140

TIMBER WOLF (See Action Comics #372, & Legion of Super-Heroes)
DC Comics: Nov, 1992 - No. 5, Mar, 1993 ($1.25, limited series)
1-5 3.00

TIME BANDITS
Marvel Comics Group: Feb, 1982 (one-shot, Giant)
1-Movie adaptation 4.00

TIME BEAVERS (See First Comics Graphic Novel #2)

TIME BOMB
Radical Comics: Jul, 2010 - No. 3, Dec, 2010 ($4.99, limited series)
1-3-Palmiotti & Gray-s/Gulacy-a/c 5.00

TIMECOP (Movie)
Dark Horse Comics: Sept, 1994 - No. 2, Nov, 1994 ($2.50, limited series)
1,2-Adaptation of film 3.00

TIME FOR LOVE (Formerly Romantic Secrets)
Charlton Comics: V2#53, Oct, 1966; Oct, 1967 - No. 47, May, 1976
V2#53(10/66) Herman-s Hermits app. 3 6 9 19 30 40
1-(10/67) 3 6 9 21 33 45
2-(12/67) -10 3 6 9 15 21 26
11,12,14-20 2 4 6 11 16 20
13-(11/69) Ditko-a (7 pgs.) 3 6 9 16 23 30
21-27 2 4 6 9 13 16
28,29,31: 28-Shirley Jones poster. 29-Bobby Sherman pin-up. 31-Bobby Sherman pin-up
2 4 6 11 16 20
30-(10/72)-David Cassidy full page poster 3 6 9 16 24 32
32-47 2 4 6 8 11 14

TIMELESS TOPIX (See Topix)

TIMELY COMICS... (Reprints of recent Marvel issues)
Marvel Comics: Aug, 2016 ($3.00)
...: All-New, All-Different Avengers (8/16) r/#1-3; Alex Ross-c 3.00
...: All-New Inhumans (8/16) r/#1-3; Caselli-c 3.00
...: Carnage (8/16) r/#1-3; Del Mundo-c 3.00
...: Daredevil (8/16) r/#1-3; Garney-c 3.00
...: Doctor Strange (8/16) r/#1-3; Bachalo-c 3.00
...: Drax (8/16) r/#1-3; Hepburn-c 3.00
...: Invincible Iron Man (8/16) r/#1-3; Marquez-c 3.00
...: Moon Girl and Devil Dinosaur (8/16) r/#1-3; Reeder-c 3.00
...: New Avengers (8/16) r/#1-3; Sandoval-c 3.00
...: Scarlet Witch (8/16) r/#1-3; Aja-c 3.00
...: Squadron Supreme (8/16) r/#1-3; Alex Ross-c 3.00
...: The Totally Awesome Hulk (8/16) r/#1-3; Cho-c 3.00
...: Ultimates (8/16) r/#1-3; Rocafort-c 3.00
...: Uncanny Inhumans (8/16) r/#1-3; McNiven-c 3.00
...: Venom: Space Knight (8/16) r/#1-3; Olivetti-c 3.00
...: Web Warriors (8/16) r/#1-3; Tedesco-c 3.00

TIMELY PRESENTS: ALL WINNERS
Marvel Comics: Dec, 1999 ($3.99)
1-Reprints All Winners Comics #19 (Fall 1946); new Lago-c 5.00

TIMELY PRESENTS: HUMAN TORCH
Marvel Comics: Feb, 1999 ($3.99)
1-Reprints Human Torch Comics #5 (Fall 1941); new Lago-c 5.00

TIME MACHINE, THE
Dell Publishing Co.: No. 1085, Mar, 1960 (H.G. Wells)
Four Color 1085-Movie, Alex Toth-a; Rod Taylor photo-c
12 24 36 82 179 275

TIME MASTERS
DC Comics: Feb, 1990 - No. 8, Sept, 1990 ($1.75, mini-series)
1-8: New Rip Hunter series. 5-Cave Carson, Viking Prince app. 6-Dr. Fate app. 3.00
TPB (2008, $19.99) r/#1-8 and Secret Origins #43; intro. by Geoff Johns 20.00

TIME MASTERS: VANISHING POINT (Tie-in to Batman: The Return of Bruce Wayne)
DC Comics: Sept, 2010 - No. 6, Feb, 2011 ($3.99, limited series)
1-6-Jurgens-s/a/c; Rip Hunter, Superman, Green Lantern & Booster Gold app. 4.00
TPB (2011, $14.99) r/#1-6 15.00

Timewalker #14 © VAL

Tim Holt #21 © ME

Tiny Tim FC #235 © News Synd.

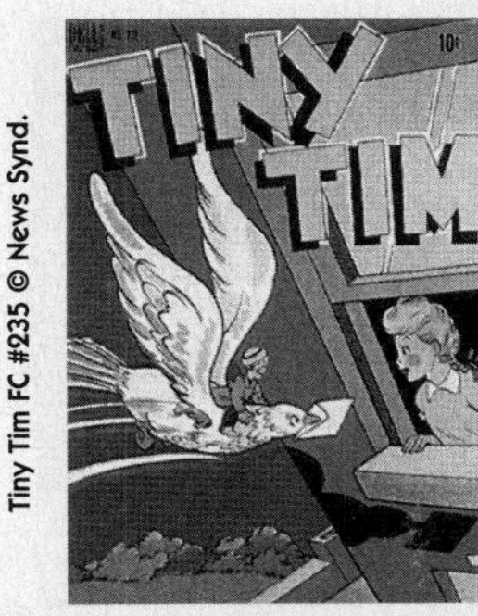

	GD 2.0	VG 4.0	FN 6.0	VF 8.0	VF/NM 9.0	NM- 9.2

TIMESLIP COLLECTION
Marvel Comics: Nov, 1998 ($2.99, one-shot)
1-Pin-ups reprinted from Marvel Vision magazine 3.00

TIMESLIP SPECIAL (The Coming of the Avengers)
Marvel Comics: Oct, 1998 ($5.99, one-shot)
1-Alternate world Avengers vs. Odin 6.00

TIMESTORM 2009/2099
Marvel Comics: June, 2009 - No. 4, Oct, 2009 ($3.99, limited series)
1-4-Punisher 2099 transports Spider-Man to 2099; Wolverine app.; Battle-a 4.00
...: Spider-Man One Shot (8/09, $3.99) Reed-s/Craig-a/Renaud-c 4.00
...: X-Men One Shot (8/09, $3.99) Reed-s/Irving-a/Renaud-c 4.00

TIME TO RUN (Based on 1973 Billy Graham movie)
Spire Christian Comics (Fleming H. Revell Co.): 1975 (39¢)
nn-By Al Hartley 2 4 6 13 18 22

TIME TUNNEL, THE (TV)
Gold Key: Feb, 1967 - No. 2, July, 1967 (12¢)
1-Photo back-c on both issues 6 12 18 40 73 105
2 5 10 15 31 53 75

TIME TWISTERS
Quality Comics: Sept, 1987 - No. 21, 1989 ($1.25/$1.50)
1-21: Alan Moore scripts in 1-4, 6-9, 14 (2 pg.). 14-Bolland-a (2 pg.). 15,16-Guice-c 4.00

TIME 2: THE EPIPHANY (See First Comics Graphic Novel #9)

TIMEWALKER (Also see Archer & Armstrong)
Valiant: Jan, 1994 - No. 15, Oct, 1995 ($2.50)
1-15,0(3/96): 2-"JAN" on-c, February, 1995 in indicia. 3.00
Yearbook 1 (5/95, $2.95) 3.00

TIME WARP (See The Unexpected #210)
DC Comics, Inc.: Oct-Nov, 1979 - No. 5, June-July, 1980 ($1.00, 68 pgs.)
1 2 4 6 11 16 20
2-5 2 4 6 8 11 14
NOTE: ***Aparo** a-1. **Buckler** a-1p. **Chaykin** a-2. **Ditko** a-1-4. **Kaluta** c-1-5. **G. Kane** a-2. **Nasser** a-4. **Newton** a-1-5p. **Orlando** a-2. **Sutton** a-1-3.*

TIME WARP
DC Comics (Vertigo): May, 2013 ($7.99, one-shot)
1-Short story anthology by various incl. Lindelof, Simone; covers by Risso & Jae Lee 8.00

TIME WARRIORS: THE BEGINNING
Fantasy General Comics: 1986 (Aug) - No. 2, 1986? ($1.50)
1,2-Alpha Track/Skellon Empire 3.00

TIM HOLT (Movie star) (Becomes Red Mask #42 on; also see Crack Western #72, & Great Western)
Magazine Enterprises: 1948 - No. 41, April-May, 1954 (All 36 pgs.)
1-(A-1 #14)-Line drawn-c w/Tim Holt photo on-c; Tim Holt, His horse Lightning & sidekick Chito begin 53 106 159 334 567 800
2-(A-1 #17)(9-10/48)-Photo-c begin, end #18 27 54 81 158 259 360
3-(A-1 #19)-Photo back-c 20 40 60 117 189 260
4(1-2/49),5: 5-Photo front/back-c 15 30 45 85 130 175
6-(5/49)-1st app. The Calico Kid (alias Rex Fury), his horse Ebony & Sidekick Sing-Song (begin series); photo back-c 23 46 69 136 223 310
7-10: 7-Calico Kid by Ayers. 8-Calico Kid by Guardineer (r-in/Great Western #10). 9-Map of Tim's Home Range 15 30 45 83 124 165
11-The Calico Kid becomes The Ghost Rider (origin & 1st app.) by Dick Ayers (r-in/Great Western I.W. #8); his horse Spectre & sidekick Sing-Song begin series 58 116 174 371 636 900
12-16,18-Last photo-c 13 26 39 74 105 135
17-Frazetta Ghost Rider-c 45 90 135 284 480 675
19,22,24: 19-Last Tim Holt-c; Bolle line-drawn-c begin; Tim Holt photo on covers #19-28, 30-41. 22-interior photo-c 11 22 33 62 86 110
20-Tim Holt becomes Redmask (origin); begin series; Redmask-c #20-on 15 30 45 88 137 185
21-Frazetta Ghost Rider/Redmask-c 38 76 114 228 369 510
23-Frazetta Redmask-c 29 58 87 170 278 385
25-1st app. Black Phantom 19 38 57 109 172 235
26-30: 28-Wild Bill Hickok, Bat Masterson team up with Redmask. 29-B&W photo-c 10 20 30 58 79 100
31-33-Ghost Rider ends 10 20 30 54 72 90
34-Tales of the Ghost Rider begins (horror)-Classic "The Flower Women" & "Hard Boiled Harry!" 14 28 42 82 121 160
35-Last Tales of the Ghost Rider 11 22 33 62 86 110
36-The Ghost Rider returns, ends #41; liquid hallucinogenic drug story 14 28 42 76 108 140
37-Ghost Rider classic "To Touch Is to Die!", about Inca treasure 14 28 42 76 108 140
38-The Black Phantom begins (not in #39); classic Ghost Rider "The Phantom Guns of Feather Gap!" 14 28 42 76 108 140
39-41: All 3-D effect c/stories 14 28 42 81 118 155
NOTE: ***Dick Ayers** a-7, 9-41. **Bolle** a-1-41; c-19, 20, 22, 24-28, 30-41.*

TIM McCOY (Formerly Zoo Funnies; Pictorial Love Stories #22 on)
Charlton Comics: No. 16, Oct, 1948 - No. 21, Aug, 1949 (Western Movie Stories)
16-John Wayne, Montgomery Clift app. in "Red River"; photo back-c 34 68 102 199 325 450
17-21: 17-Allan "Rocky" Lane guest stars. 18-Rod Cameron guest stars. 19-Whip Wilson, Andy Clyde guest star; Jesse James story. 20-Jimmy Wakely guest stars. 21-Johnny Mack Brown guest stars 24 48 72 142 234 325

TIMMY
Dell Publishing Co.: No. 715, Aug, 1956 - No. 1022, Aug-Oct, 1959
Four Color 715 (#1) 5 10 15 35 63 90
Four Color 823 (8/57), 923 (8/58), 1022 5 10 15 31 53 75

TIMMY THE TIMID GHOST (Formerly Win-A-Prize?; see Blue Bird)
Charlton Comics: No. 3, 2/56 - No. 44, 10/64; No. 45, 9/66; 10/67 - No. 23, 7/71; V4#24, 9/85 - No. 26, 1/86
3(1956) (1st Series) 14 28 42 76 108 140
4,5 8 16 24 44 57 70
6-10 3 6 9 19 30 40
11,12(4/58,10/58)-(100 pgs.) 6 12 18 37 66 95
13-20 3 6 9 17 26 35
21-45(1966): 27-Nazi story 3 6 9 14 19 24
1(10/67, 2nd series) 3 6 9 15 22 28
2-10 2 4 6 10 14 18
11-23: 23 (7/71) 1 3 4 8 10 12
24-26 (1985-86): Fago-r (low print run) 6.00

TIM TYLER (See Harvey Comics Hits #54)

TIM TYLER (Also see Comics Reading Libraries in the Promotional Comics section)
Better Publications: 1942
1 15 30 45 88 137 185

TIM TYLER COWBOY
Standard Comics (King Features Synd.): No. 11, Nov, 1948 - No. 18, Aug, 1950
11-By Lyman Young 9 18 27 52 69 85
12-18: 13-15-Full length western adventures 7 14 21 37 46 55

TINKER BELL (Disney, TV)(See Walt Disney Showcase #37)
Dell Publishing Co.: No. 896, Mar, 1958 - No. 982, Apr-June, 1959
Four Color 896 (#1)-The Adventures of... 9 18 27 57 111 165
Four Color 982-The New Advs. of... 8 16 24 52 99 145

TINY FOLKS FUNNIES
Dell Publishing Co.: No. 60, 1944
Four Color 60 14 28 42 94 207 329

TINY TESSIE (Tessie #1-23; Real Experiences #25)
Marvel Comics (20CC): No. 24, Oct, 1949 (52 pgs.)
24 18 36 54 105 165 225

TINY TIM (Also see Super Comics)
Dell Publishing Co.: No. 4, 1941 - No. 235, July, 1949
Large Feature Comic 4('41) 45 90 135 284 480 675
Four Color 20(1941) 41 82 123 250 418 585
Four Color 42(1943) 16 32 48 110 243 375
Four Color 235 6 12 18 41 76 110

TINY TITANS (Teen Titans)
DC Comics: Apr, 2008 - No. 50, May, 2012 ($2.25/$2.50/$2.99)
1-29-All ages stories of Teen Titans in Elementary school; Baltazar & Franco-s/a 3.00
1-(6/08, Free Comic Book Day giveaway) r/#1; Baltazar & Franco-s/a 3.00
30-50: 30-Begin $2.99-c. 37-Marvel Family app. 44-Doom Patrol app. 3.00

TINY TITANS / LITTLE ARCHIE (Teen Titans) (Digest-size reprint in World of Archie Double Digest Magazine #5)
DC Comics: Dec, 2010 - No. 3, Feb, 2011 ($2.99, limited series)
1-3-Character crossover; Baltazar & Franco-s/a. 2-Josie and the Pussycats app. 3.00

TINY TITANS: RETURN TO THE TREEHOUSE

Tiny Tot Comics #6 © EC

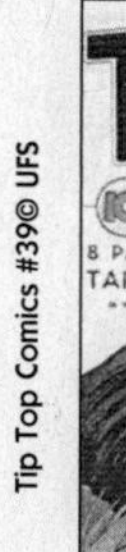

Tip Top Comics #39© UFS

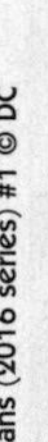

Titans (2016 series) #1 © DC

DC Comics: Aug, 2014 - No. 6, Jan, 2015 ($2.99, limited series)

	GD 2.0	VG 4.0	FN 6.0	VF 8.0	VF/NM 9.0	NM- 9.2
1-6-Baltazar & Franco-s/a. 1-Brainiac app. 3-Marvel Family app.						3.00

TINY TOT COMICS
E. C. Comics: Mar, 1946 - No. 10, Nov-Dec, 1947 (For younger readers)

	GD 2.0	VG 4.0	FN 6.0	VF 8.0	VF/NM 9.0	NM- 9.2
1(nn)-52 pg. issues begin, end #4	45	90	135	284	480	675
2 (5/46)	27	54	81	160	263	365
3-10: 10-Christmas-c	25	50	75	150	245	340

TINY TOT FUNNIES (Formerly Family Funnies; becomes Junior Funnies)
Harvey Publ. (King Features Synd.): No. 9, June, 1951

	GD 2.0	VG 4.0	FN 6.0	VF 8.0	VF/NM 9.0	NM- 9.2
9-Flash Gordon, Mandrake, Dagwood, Daisy, etc.	8	16	24	42	54	65

TINY TOTS COMICS
Dell Publishing Co.: 1943 (Not reprints)

	GD 2.0	VG 4.0	FN 6.0	VF 8.0	VF/NM 9.0	NM- 9.2
1-Kelly-a(2); fairy tales	39	78	117	240	395	550

TIPPY & CAP STUBBS (See Popular Comics)
Dell Publishing Co.: No. 210, Jan, 1949 - No. 242, Aug, 1949

	GD 2.0	VG 4.0	FN 6.0	VF 8.0	VF/NM 9.0	NM- 9.2
Four Color 210 (#1)	6	12	18	42	79	115
Four Color 242	5	10	15	31	53	75

TIPPY'S FRIENDS GO-GO & ANIMAL
Tower Comics: July, 1966 - No. 15, Oct, 1969 (25¢)

	GD 2.0	VG 4.0	FN 6.0	VF 8.0	VF/NM 9.0	NM- 9.2
1	9	18	27	61	123	185
2-5,7,9-15: 12-15 titled "Tippy's Friend Go-Go"	5	10	15	35	63	90
6-The Monkees photo-c	8	16	24	54	102	150
8-Beatles app. on front/back-c	10	20	30	66	138	210

TIPPY TEEN (See Vicki)
Tower Comics: Nov, 1965 - No. 25, Oct, 1969 (25¢)

	GD 2.0	VG 4.0	FN 6.0	VF 8.0	VF/NM 9.0	NM- 9.2
1	10	20	30	68	144	220
2-4,6-10	6	12	18	40	73	105
5-1 pg. Beatles pin-up	7	14	21	44	82	120
11-20: 16-Twiggy photo-c	6	12	18	37	66	95
21-25	5	10	15	34	60	85
Special Collectors' Editions nn-(1969, 25¢)	6	12	18	37	66	95

TIPPY TERRY
Super/I. W. Enterprises: 1963

	GD 2.0	VG 4.0	FN 6.0	VF 8.0	VF/NM 9.0	NM- 9.2
Super Reprint #14('63)-r/Little Groucho #1	2	4	6	8	10	12
I.W. Reprint #1 (nd)-r/Little Groucho #1	2	4	6	8	10	12

TIP TOP COMICS
United Features #1-188/St. John #189-210/Dell Publishing Co. #211 on:
4/36 - No. 210, 1957; No. 211, 11-1/57-58 - No. 225, 5-7/61

	GD 2.0	VG 4.0	FN 6.0	VF 8.0	VF/NM 9.0	NM- 9.2
1-Tarzan by Hal Foster, Li'l Abner, Broncho Bill, Fritzi Ritz, Ella Cinders, Capt. & The Kids begin; strip-r (1st comic book app. of each)	900	1800	2700	5400	9450	13,500
2-Tarzan-c (6/36)	194	388	582	1242	2121	3000
3-Tarzan-c (7/36)	177	354	531	1124	1937	2750
4-(8/36)	97	194	291	621	1061	1500
5-8,10: 7-Photo & biography of Edgar Rice Burroughs. 8-Christmas-c	69	138	207	442	759	1075
9-Tarzan-c (1/37)	90	180	270	576	988	1400
11,13,16,18-Tarzan-c: 11-Has Tarzan pin-up	69	138	207	442	759	1075
12,14,15,17,19,20: 20-Christmas-c	51	102	153	318	539	760
21,24,27,30-(10/38)-Tarzan-c	55	110	165	352	601	850
22,23,25,26,28,29	39	78	117	234	385	535
31,35,38,40	36	72	108	216	351	485
32,36-Tarzan-c: 32-1st published Jack Davis-a (cartoon). 36-Kurtzman panel (1st published comic work)	57	114	171	362	619	875
33,34,37,39-Tarzan-c	53	106	159	334	567	800
41-Reprints 1st Tarzan Sunday; Tarzan-c	57	114	171	362	619	875
42,44,46,48,49	31	62	93	182	296	410
43,45,47,50,52-Tarzan-c. 43-Mort Walker panel	40	80	120	246	411	575
51,53	29	58	87	170	278	385
54-Origin Mirror Man & Triple Terror, also featured on cover	37	74	111	218	354	490
55,56,58: Last Tarzan by Foster	24	48	72	142	234	325
57,59-62-Tarzan by Hogarth	31	62	93	182	296	410
63-80: 65,67-70,72-74,77,78-No Tarzan	15	30	45	88	137	185
81-90	14	28	42	80	115	150
91-99	13	26	39	72	101	130
100	14	28	42	76	108	140
101-140: 110-Gordo story. 111-Li'l Abner app. 118, 132-No Tarzan. 137-Sadie Hawkins Day story	10	20	30	54	72	90
141-170: 145,151-Gordo stories. 153-Fritzi Ritz lingerie panels. 157-Last Li'l Abner; lingerie panels	8	16	24	44	57	70
171,172,174-183: 171-Tarzan reprints by B. Lubbers begin; end #188	9	18	27	47	61	75
173-Peanuts by Schulz	28	56	84	165	270	375
184-Peanuts app.	19	38	57	109	172	235
185-188-Peanuts stories with Charlie Brown & Snoopy on the covers	110	220	330	700	1125	1550
189,191-225-Peanuts apps.(4 pg. to 8 pg stories) in most						
Issues with Peanuts	12	24	36	67	94	120
Issues without Peanuts	8	16	24	40	50	60
190-Peanuts with Charlie Brown & Snoopy partial-c (comic strip at bottom of cover)	27	54	81	158	259	360
Bound Volumes (Very Rare) sold at 1939 World's Fair; bound by publisher in pictorial comic boards (also see Comics on Parade)						
Bound issues 1-12 (Rare)	371	742	1113	2600	4550	6500
Bound issues 13-24	181	362	543	1158	1979	2800
Bound issues 25-36	155	310	465	992	1696	2400

NOTE: *Tarzan by* ***Foster****-#1-40, 44-50; by* ***Rex Maxon****-#41-43; by* ***Burne Hogarth****-#57, 59, 62.*

TIP TOPPER COMICS
United Features Syndicate: Oct-Nov, 1949 - No. 28, 1954

	GD 2.0	VG 4.0	FN 6.0	VF 8.0	VF/NM 9.0	NM- 9.2
1-Li'l Abner, Abbie & Slats	14	28	42	82	121	160
2	9	18	27	52	69	85
3-5: 5-Fearless Fosdick app.	9	18	27	47	61	75
6-10: 6-Fearless Fosdick app.	8	16	24	42	54	65
11-16	7	14	21	37	46	55
17(6-7/52) (2nd app. of Peanuts by Schulz in comics?) (see United Comics #22 for 5-6/52 app.)	26	52	78	154	252	350
18-26,28: 18-24,26,28-Early Peanuts (2 pgs.). 25-Early Peanuts (3 pgs.) 26,28-Twin Earths	15	30	45	83	124	165
27-Twin Earths	8	16	24	44	57	70

NOTE: *Many lingerie panels in Fritzi Ritz stories.*

TITAN A.E.
Dark Horse Comics: May, 2000 - No. 3, July, 2000 ($2.95, limited series)

	GD 2.0	VG 4.0	FN 6.0	VF 8.0	VF/NM 9.0	NM- 9.2
1-3-Movie prequel; Al Rio-a						3.00

TITANS (Also see Teen Titans, New Teen Titans and New Titans)
DC Comics: Mar, 1999 - No. 50, Apr, 2003 ($2.50/$2.75)

	GD 2.0	VG 4.0	FN 6.0	VF 8.0	VF/NM 9.0	NM- 9.2
1-Titans re-form; Grayson-s; 2 covers						4.00
2-11,13-24,26-50: 2-Superman-c/app. 9,10,21,22-Deathstroke app. 24-Titans from "Kingdom Come" app. 32-36-Asamiya-c. 44-Begin $2.75-c						3.00
12-($3.50, 48 pages)						4.00
25-($3.95) Titans from "Kingdom Come" app.; Wolfman & Faerber-s; art by Pérez, Cardy, Grumment, Jimenez, Dodson, Pelletier						4.00
Annual 1 ('00, $3.50) Planet DC; intro Bushido						4.00
... East Special 1 (1/08, $3.99) Winick-s/Churchill-a; continues in Titans #1 (2008)						4.00
...Secret Files 1,2 (3/99, 10/00; $4.95) Profile pages & short stories						5.00

TITANS (Also see Teen Titans)
DC Comics: Jun, 2008 - No. 38, Oct, 2011 ($3.50/$2.99)

	GD 2.0	VG 4.0	FN 6.0	VF 8.0	VF/NM 9.0	NM- 9.2
1-($3.50) Titans re-form again; Winick-s/Churchill-a; covers by Churchill & Van Sciver						4.00
2-38: 2-4-Trigon returns. 6-10-Jericho app. 24-Deathstroke & Luthor app.						3.00
Annual 1 (9/11, $4.99) Justice League app.; Jericho returns; Richards-a						5.00
...: Villains For Hire Special 1 (7/10, $4.99) Deathstroke's team; Atom (Ryan Choi) killed						5.00
...: Fractured TPB (2010, $17.99) r/#14,16-22						18.00
...: Lockdown TPB (2009, $14.99) r/#7-11						15.00
...: Old Friends HC (2008, $24.99) r/#1-6 & Titans East Special						25.00
...: Villains For Hire TPB (2011, $14.99) r/#24-27 & Villains For Hire Special 1						15.00

TITANS (DC Rebirth)(Follows Titans Hunt series)
DC Comics: Aug, 2016 - Present ($2.99)

	GD 2.0	VG 4.0	FN 6.0	VF 8.0	VF/NM 9.0	NM- 9.2
1-8: 1-Abnett-s/Booth-a; Abra Kadabra returns. 7-Superman app.						3.00
...: Rebirth 1 (8/16, $2.99) Abnett-s/Booth-a; Wally West reunites with the Titans						3.00

TITANS HUNT (Also see DC Universe: Rebirth)
DC Comics: Dec, 2015 - No. 8, Jun, 2016 ($3.99, limited series)

	GD 2.0	VG 4.0	FN 6.0	VF 8.0	VF/NM 9.0	NM- 9.2
1-7: 1-Abnett-s/Siqueira-a; 1970s-era Titans app. incl. Lilith & Gnarrk. 2,4-Segovia-a						4.00
8-Titans vs. Mr. Twister						4.00

TITANS/ LEGION OF SUPER-HEROES: UNIVERSE ABLAZE
DC Comics: 2000 - No. 4, 2000 ($4.95, prestige format, limited series)

	GD 2.0	VG 4.0	FN 6.0	VF 8.0	VF/NM 9.0	NM- 9.2
1-4-Jurgens-s/a; P. Jimenez-a; teams battle Universo						5.00

TITAN SPECIAL
Dark Horse Comics: June, 1994 ($3.95, one-shot)

	GD 2.0	VG 4.0	FN 6.0	VF 8.0	VF/NM 9.0	NM- 9.2
1-($3.95, 52 pgs.)						4.00

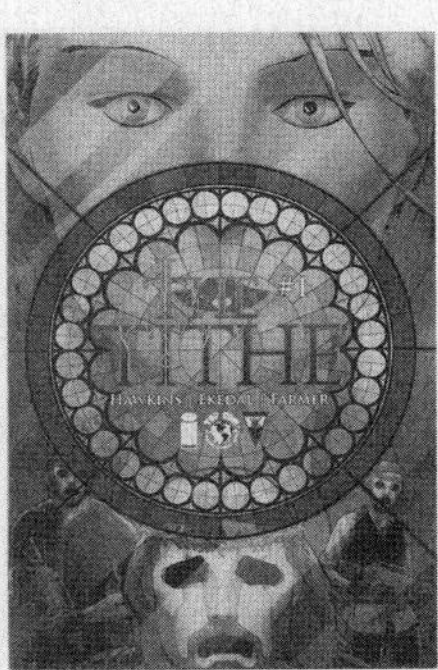

The Tithe #1 © Hawkins & Ekedal

Tokyo Ghost #3 © Remender & Murphy

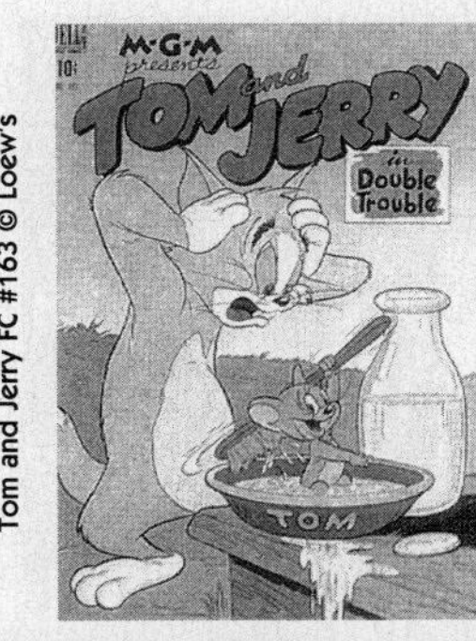

Tom and Jerry FC #163 © Loew's

TITANS: SCISSORS, PAPER, STONE
DC Comics: 1997 ($4.95, one-shot)

	GD 2.0	VG 4.0	FN 6.0	VF 8.0	VF/NM 9.0	NM- 9.2
1-Manga style Elseworlds; Adam Warren-s/a(p)						5.00

TITANS SELL-OUT SPECIAL
DC Comics: Nov, 1992 ($3.50, 52 pgs., one-shot)

	GD 2.0	VG 4.0	FN 6.0	VF 8.0	VF/NM 9.0	NM- 9.2
1-Fold-out Nightwing poster; 1st Teeny Titans						4.00

TITANS/ YOUNG JUSTICE: GRADUATION DAY
DC Comics: Early July, 2003 - No. 3, Aug, 2003 ($2.50, limited series)

	GD 2.0	VG 4.0	FN 6.0	VF 8.0	VF/NM 9.0	NM- 9.2
1,2-Winick-s/Garza-a; leads into Teen Titans and The Outsiders series. 2-Lilith dies						3.00
3-Death of Donna Troy (Wonder Girl)						3.00
TPB (2003, $6.95) r/#1-3; plus previews of Teen Titans and The Outsiders series						7.00

TITHE, THE (Also see Eden's Fall)
Image Comics (Top Cow): Apr, 2015 - No. 8 ($3.99, limited series)

	GD 2.0	VG 4.0	FN 6.0	VF 8.0	VF/NM 9.0	NM- 9.2
1-7-Hawkins-s/Ekedal-a; multiple covers on each. 5-7-Sevy-a						4.00

T-MAN (Also see Police Comics #103)
Quality Comics Group: Sept, 1951 - No. 38, Dec, 1956

	GD 2.0	VG 4.0	FN 6.0	VF 8.0	VF/NM 9.0	NM- 9.2
1-Pete Trask, T-Man begins; Jack Cole-a	50	100	150	315	533	750
2-Crandall-c	28	56	84	165	270	375
3,7,8: All Crandall-c	25	50	75	150	245	340
4,5-Crandall-c/a each	27	54	81	158	259	360
6-"The Man Who Could Be Hitler" c/story; Crandall-c.	39	78	117	231	378	525
9,10-Crandall-c	22	44	66	132	216	300
11-Used in **POP**, pg. 95 & color illo.	20	40	60	114	182	250
12,13,15-19,22-26: 23-H-Bomb panel. 24-Last pre-code issue (4/55). 25-Not Crandall-a	15	30	45	90	140	190
14-Hitler-c	30	60	90	177	289	400
20-H-Bomb explosion-c/story	20	40	60	114	182	250
21- "The Return of Mussolini" c/story	20	40	60	114	182	250
27-33,35-38	15	30	45	84	127	170
34-Hitler-c	27	54	81	158	259	360

NOTE: *Anti-communist stories common.* ***Crandall*** *c-2-10p.* ***Cuidera*** *c(i)-1-38. Bondage c-15.*

TMNT... (Also see Teenage Mutant Ninja Turtles and related titles)
Mirage Publishing: March 2007 ($3.25/$4.95, B&W, one-shots)

	GD 2.0	VG 4.0	FN 6.0	VF 8.0	VF/NM 9.0	NM- 9.2
...: Raphael Movie Prequel 1; ...: Michelangelo Movie Prequel 2; ...: Donatello Movie Prequel 3; ...: April Movie Prequel 4; ...: Leonardo Movie Prequel 5; back-story for movie						3.25
...: The Official Movie Adaptation ($4.95) adapts 2007 movie; Munroe-c						5.00

TMNT MUTANT UNIVERSE SOURCEBOOK
Archie Comics: 1992 - No. 3, 1992? ($1.95, 52 pgs.)(Lists characters from A-Z)

	GD 2.0	VG 4.0	FN 6.0	VF 8.0	VF/NM 9.0	NM- 9.2
1-3: 3-New characters; fold-out poster						5.00

TNT COMICS
Charles Publishing Co.: Feb, 1946 (36 pgs.)

	GD 2.0	VG 4.0	FN 6.0	VF 8.0	VF/NM 9.0	NM- 9.2
1-Yellowjacket app.	37	74	111	222	361	500

TOBY TYLER (Disney, see Movie Comics)
Dell Publishing Co.: No. 1092, Apr-June, 1960

	GD 2.0	VG 4.0	FN 6.0	VF 8.0	VF/NM 9.0	NM- 9.2
Four Color 1092-Movie, photo-c	6	12	18	38	69	100

TODAY'S BRIDES
Ajax/Farrell Publishing Co.: Nov, 1955; No. 2, Feb, 1956; No. 3, Sept, 1956; No. 4, Nov, 1956

	GD 2.0	VG 4.0	FN 6.0	VF 8.0	VF/NM 9.0	NM- 9.2
1	12	24	36	67	94	120
2-4	9	18	27	50	65	80

TODAY'S ROMANCE
Standard Comics: No. 5, March, 1952 - No. 8, Sept, 1952 (All photo-c?)

	GD 2.0	VG 4.0	FN 6.0	VF 8.0	VF/NM 9.0	NM- 9.2
5-Photo-c	14	28	42	81	118	155
6-Photo-c; Toth-a	14	28	42	82	121	160
7,8	12	24	36	67	94	120

TODD, THE UGLIEST KID ON EARTH
Image Comics: Jan, 2013 - No. 8, Jan, 2014 ($2.99)

	GD 2.0	VG 4.0	FN 6.0	VF 8.0	VF/NM 9.0	NM- 9.2
1-8-Perker-a/Kristensen-s						3.00

TOE TAGS FEATURING GEORGE A. ROMERO
DC Comics: Dec, 2004 - No. 6, May, 2005 ($2.95/$2.99)

	GD 2.0	VG 4.0	FN 6.0	VF 8.0	VF/NM 9.0	NM- 9.2
1-6-Zombie story by George Romero; Wrightson-c/Castillo-a						3.00

TOIL AND TROUBLE
BOOM! Studios (Archaia): Sept, 2015 - No. 6 ($3.99)

	GD 2.0	VG 4.0	FN 6.0	VF 8.0	VF/NM 9.0	NM- 9.2
1-6-Mairghread Scott-s/Kelly & Nicole Matthews-a						4.00

TOKA (Jungle King)
Dell Publishing Co.: Aug-Oct, 1964 - No. 10, Jan, 1967 (Painted-c #1,2)

	GD 2.0	VG 4.0	FN 6.0	VF 8.0	VF/NM 9.0	NM- 9.2
1	4	8	12	28	47	65
2	3	6	9	17	26	35
3-10	3	6	9	15	22	28

TOKYO GHOST
Image Comics: Sept, 2015 - No. 10, Aug, 2016 ($3.99)

	GD 2.0	VG 4.0	FN 6.0	VF 8.0	VF/NM 9.0	NM- 9.2
1-10-Rick Remender-s/Sean Murphy-a						4.00

TOKYO STORM WARNING (See Red/Tokyo Storm Warning for TPB)
DC Comics (Cliffhanger): Aug, 2003 - No. 3, Dec, 2003 ($2.95, limited series)

	GD 2.0	VG 4.0	FN 6.0	VF 8.0	VF/NM 9.0	NM- 9.2
1-3-Warren Ellis-s/James Raiz-a						3.00

TOMAHAWK (Son of... on-c of #131-140; see Star Spangled Comics #69 & World's Finest Comics #65)
National Periodical Publications: Sept-Oct, 1950 - No. 140, May-June, 1972

	GD 2.0	VG 4.0	FN 6.0	VF 8.0	VF/NM 9.0	NM- 9.2
1-Tomahawk & boy sidekick Dan Hunter begin by Fred Ray	187	374	561	1197	2049	2900
2-Frazetta/Williamson-a (4 pgs.)	68	136	204	435	743	1050
3-5	41	82	123	256	428	600
6-10: 7-Last 52 pg. issue	36	72	108	211	343	475
11-20	24	48	72	142	234	325
21-27,30: 30-Last precode (2/55)	21	42	63	126	206	285
28-1st app. Lord Shilling (arch-foe)	22	44	66	132	216	300
29-Frazetta-r/Jimmy Wakely #3 (3 pgs.)	26	52	78	154	252	350
31-40	18	36	54	107	169	230
41-50	10	20	30	64	132	200
51-56,58-60	9	18	27	58	114	170
57-Frazetta-r/Jimmy Wakely #6 (3 pgs.)	10	20	30	64	132	200
61-77: 77-Last 10¢ issue	8	16	24	54	102	150
78-85: 81-1st app. Miss Liberty. 83-Origin Tomahawk's Rangers	7	14	21	46	86	125
86-99: 96-Origin/1st app. The Hood, alias Lady Shilling	5	10	15	35	63	90
100	6	12	18	37	66	95
101-110: 107-Origin/1st app. Thunder-Man	5	10	15	30	50	70
111-115,120,122: 122-Last 12¢ issue	4	8	12	28	47	65
116-1st Neal Adams cover	21	42	63	147	324	500
117-119,121,123-130-Neal Adams-c. 118-Origin of the Rangers	6	12	18	38	69	100
131-Frazetta-r/Jimmy Wakely #7 (3 pgs.); origin Firehair retold	3	6	9	21	33	45
132-135: 135-Last 15¢ issue	3	6	9	16	24	32
136-138,140 (52 pg. Giants)	3	6	9	19	30	40
139-Frazetta-r/Star Spangled #113	3	6	9	21	33	45

NOTE: ***Fred Ray*** *c-1, 2, 8, 11, 30, 34, 35, 40-43, 45, 46, 82. Firehair by* ***Kubert****-131-134, 136.* ***Maurer*** *a-138.* ***Severin*** *a-135.* ***Starr*** *a-5.* ***Thorne*** *a-137, 140.*

TOM AND JERRY (See Comic Album #4, 8, 12, Dell Giant #21, Dell Giants, Golden Comics Digest #1, 5, 8, 13, 15, 18, 22, 25, 28, 35, Kite fun Book & March of Comics #21, 46, 61, 70, 88, 103, 119, 128, 145, 154, 173, 190, 207, 224, 281, 295, 305, 321,333, 345, 361, 365, 388, 400, 444, 451, 463, 480)

TOM AND JERRY (...Comics, early issues) (M.G.M.)
(Formerly Our Gang No. 1-59) (See Dell Giants for annuals)
Dell Publishing Co./Gold Key No. 213-327/Whitman No. 328 on: No. 193, 6/48; No. 60, 7/49 - No. 212, 7-9/62; No. 213, 11/62 - No. 291, 2/75; No. 292, 3/77 - No. 342, 5/82 - No. 344, 6/84

	GD 2.0	VG 4.0	FN 6.0	VF 8.0	VF/NM 9.0	NM- 9.2
Four Color 193 (#1)-Titled "M.G.M. Presents..."	23	46	69	164	362	560
60-Barney Bear, Benny Burro cont. from Our Gang; Droopy begins	11	22	33	76	163	250
61	9	18	27	60	120	180
62-70: 66-X-Mas-c	7	14	21	49	92	135
71-80: 77,90-X-Mas-c. 79-Spike & Tyke begin	6	12	18	40	73	105
81-99	5	10	15	35	63	90
100	6	12	18	37	66	95
101-120	5	10	15	31	53	75
121-140: 126-X-Mas-c	4	8	12	28	47	65
141-160	4	8	12	25	40	55
161-200	4	8	12	23	37	50
201-212(7-9/62)(Last Dell issue)	3	6	9	21	33	45
213,214-(84 pgs.)-Titled "...Funhouse"	5	10	15	35	63	90
215-240: 215-Titled "...Funhouse"	3	6	9	16	24	32
241-270	2	4	6	11	16	20
271-300: 286- "Tom & Jerry"	2	4	6	8	11	14
301-327 (Gold Key)	1	3	4	6	8	10
328,329 (Whitman)	2	4	6	8	11	14
330(8/80),331(10/80), 332-(3-pack only)	4	8	12	27	44	60

Tomb of Dracula #11 © MAR

Tomb of Terror #9 © HARV

Tomb Raider #11 © Square Enix

GD VG FN VF VF/NM NM-
2.0 4.0 6.0 8.0 9.0 9.2

333-341: 339(2/82), 340(2-3/82), 341(4/82) 2 4 6 8 10 12
342-344 (All #90058, no date, date code, 3-pack): 342(6/83), 343(8/83), 344(6/84)
3 6 9 16 24 32
Mouse From T.R.A.P. 1(7/66)-Giant, G. K. 4 8 12 28 47 65
Summer Fun 1(7/67, 68 pgs.)(Gold Key)-Reprints Barks' Droopy from Summer Fun #1
4 8 12 28 47 65
NOTE: *#60-87, 98-121, 268, 277, 289, 302 are 52 pgs.. Reprints-#225, 241, 245, 247, 252, 254, 266, 268, 270, 292-327, 329-342, 344.*

TOM & JERRY
Harvey Comics: Sept, 1991 - No. 18, Aug, 1994 ($1.25)
1-18: 1-Tom & Jerry, Barney Bear-r by Carl Barks 3.00
50th Anniversary Special 1 (10/91, $2.50, 68 pgs.)-Benny the Lonesome Burro-r by Barks (story/a)/Our Gang #9 4.00

TOMB OF DARKNESS (Formerly Beware)
Marvel Comics Group: No. 9, July, 1974 - No. 23, Nov, 1976
9 4 8 12 23 37 50
10-23: 11,16,18-21-Kirby-a. 15,19-Ditko-r. 17-Woodbridge-r/Astonishing #62; Powell-r. 20-Everett Venus-r/Venus #19. 23-Everett-r 3 6 9 16 23 30
20,21-(30¢-c variants, limited distribution)(5,7/76) 8 16 24 51 96 140

TOMB OF DRACULA (See Giant-Size Dracula, Dracula Lives, Nightstalkers, Power Record Comics & Requiem for Dracula)
Marvel Comics Group: Apr, 1972 - No. 70, Aug, 1979
1-1st app. Dracula & Frank Drake; Colan-p in all; Neal Adams-c
15 30 45 105 233 360
2 8 16 24 51 96 140
3-6: 3-Intro. Dr. Rachel Van Helsing & Inspector Chelm. 6-Neal Adams-c
6 12 18 40 73 105
7-9 5 10 15 35 63 90
10-1st app. Blade the Vampire Slayer (who app. in 1998, 2002 and 2004 movies)
26 52 78 182 404 625
11,14-16,20: 5 10 15 30 50 70
12-2nd app. Blade; Brunner-c(p) 8 16 24 54 102 150
13-Origin Blade 9 18 27 61 123 185
17,19: 17-Blade bitten by Dracula. 19-Blade discovers he is immune to vampire's bite. 1st mention of Blade having vampire blood in him 6 12 18 38 69 100
18-Two-part x-over cont'd in Werewolf by Night #15 5 10 15 35 63 90
21,24-Blade app. 5 10 15 30 50 70
22,23,26,27,29 3 6 9 19 30 40
25-1st app. & origin Hannibal King 4 8 12 27 44 60
25-2nd printing (1994) 2 4 6 8 10 12
28-Blade app. on-c & inside as an illusion 4 8 12 27 44 60
30,41,42,44,45-Blade app. 45-Intro. Deacon Frost, the vampire who bit Blade's mother
4 8 12 25 40 55
31-40 3 6 9 17 26 35
43-Blade-c by Wrightson 4 8 12 28 47 65
43-45-(30¢-c variants, limited distribution) 7 14 21 44 82 120
46,47-(Regular 25¢ editions)(4-8/76) 3 6 9 14 20 25
46,47-(30¢-c variants, limited distribution) 5 10 15 35 63 90
48,49,51-57,59,60: 57,59,60-(30¢-c) 3 6 9 14 20 25
50-Silver Surfer app. 4 8 12 23 37 50
57,59,60-(35¢-c variants)(6-9/77) 10 20 30 64 132 200
58-All Blade issue (Regular 30¢ edition) 4 8 12 28 47 65
58-(35¢-c variant)(7/77) 11 22 33 76 163 250
61-69 3 6 9 14 20 25
70-Double size 4 8 12 23 37 50
NOTE: ***N. Adams** c-1, 6. **Colan** a-1-70p; c(p)-8, 38-42, 44-56, 58-70. **Wrightson** c-43.*

TOMB OF DRACULA, THE (Magazine)
Marvel Comics Group: Oct, 1979 - No. 6, Aug, 1980 (B&W)
1,3: 1-Colan-a; features on movies "Dracula" and "Love at First Bite" w/photos. 3-Good girl cover-a; Miller-a (2 pg. sketch) 2 4 6 11 16 20
2,6: 2-Ditko-a (36 pgs.); Nosferatu movie feature. 6-Lilith story w/Sienkiewicz-a
2 4 6 8 11 14
4,5: Stephen King interview 2 4 6 13 18 22
NOTE: ***Buscema** a-4p, 5p. **Chaykin** c-5, 6. **Colan** a(p)-1, 3-6. **Miller** a-3. **Romita** a-2p.*

TOMB OF DRACULA
Marvel Comics (Epic Comics): 1991 - No. 4, 1992 ($4.95, 52 pgs., squarebound, mini-series)
Book 1-4: Colan/Williamson-a; Colan painted-c 5.00

TOMB OF DRACULA
Marvel Comics: Dec, 2004 - No. 4, Mar, 2005 ($2.99, limited series)
1-4-Blade app.; Tolagson-a/Sienkiewicz-c 3.00

TOMB OF DRACULA PRESENTS: THRONE OF BLOOD
Marvel Comics: Jun, 2011 ($3.99, one-shot)
1-Story of Raizo Kodo in 1585 Japan; Parlov-a; Hitch-c 4.00

TOMB OF LEGEIA (See Movie Classics)

TOMB OF TERROR (Thrills of Tomorrow #17 on)
Harvey Publications: June, 1952 - No. 16, July, 1954
1 54 108 162 343 574 825
2 39 78 117 231 378 525
3-Bondage-c; atomic disaster story 39 78 117 235 385 535
4-12: 4-Heart ripped out. 8-12-Nostrand-a 37 74 111 222 361 500
13-Special S/F issue (1/54) White letter shadow-c 47 94 141 296 498 700
13-Logo variant-c (striped letter shadow) 53 106 159 334 567 800
14-Classic S/F-c; Check-a 68 136 204 435 743 1050
15-S/F issue; c-shows face exploding 245 490 735 1568 2684 3800
16-Special S/F issue; horror-c; Nostrand-a 47 94 141 296 498 700
NOTE: ***Edd Cartier** a-13? **Elias** c-2, 5-16. **Kremer** a-1, 7; c-1. **Nostrand** a-8-12, 15r 16. **Palais** a-2, 3, 5-7. **Powell** a-1, 3, 5, 9-16. **Sparling** a-12, 13, 15.*

TOMB OF TERROR
Marvel Comics: Dec, 2010 ($3.99, B&W, one-shot)
1-Short stories of Man-Thing, Son of Satan, Werewolf By Night & The Living Mummy 4.00

TOMB RAIDER (Also see Lara Croft And The Frozen Omen)
Dark Horse Comics: Feb, 2014 - No. 18, Jul, 2015 ($3.50/$3.99)
1-18: 1-6-Gail Simone-s/Nicolás Daniel Selma-a. 13-Begin $3.99-c 4.00

TOMB RAIDER
Dark Horse Comics: Feb, 2016 - No. 12, Jan, 2017 ($3.99)
1-12-Mariko Tamaki-s/Phillip Sevy-a 4.00

TOMB RAIDER (one-shots)
Image Comics (Top Cow Prod.)
...: Arabian Nights (8/04, $5.99) Avery-s/Tan-a/c 6.00
... Cover Gallery 2006 (4/06, $2.99) artist galleries and series gallery; pin-ups 3.00
.../The Darkness Special 1 (2001, TopCowStore.com)-Wohl-s/Tan-a 3.00
Epiphany 1 (8/03, $4.99)-Jurgens-s/Banks-a/Haley-c; preview of Witchblade Animated 5.00
Takeover 1 (1/04, $2.99)-Benefiel-a/Daniel-c 3.00
... Vs. The Wolf-Men: Monster War 2005 (7/05, $2.99) 2nd part of Monster War x-over 3.00
.../Witchblade/Magdalena/Vampirella #1 (8/05, $2.99, B&W) three covers; Chin-a 3.00

TOMB RAIDER: JOURNEYS
Image Comics (Top Cow Prod.): Jan, 2002 - No. 12, May, 2003 ($2.50/$2.99)
1-12: 1-Avery-s/Drew Johnson-a. 1-Two covers by Johnson & Hughes 3.00

TOMB RAIDER: THE GREATEST TREASURE OF ALL
Image Comics (Top Cow Prod.): 2002; Oct, 2005 ($6.99)
Prelude (2002, 16 pgs., no cover price) Jusko-c/a 3.00
1-(10/05, $6.99) Jusko-a/Jurgens-s; sketch pages, reference photos, art in progress 7.00

TOMB RAIDER: THE SERIES (Also see Witchblade/Tomb Raider)
Image Comics (Top Cow Prod.): Dec, 1999 - No. 50, Mar, 2005 ($2.50/$2.99)
1-Jurgens-s/Park-a; 3 covers by Park, Finch, Turner 5.00
2-24,26-29,31-50: 21-Black-c w/foil. 31-Mhan-a. 37-Flip book preview of Stryke Force 3.00
25-Michael Turner-c/a; Witchblade app.; Endgame x-over with Witchblade #60 & Evo #1 4.00
30-($4.99) Tony Daniel-a 5.00
#0 (6/01, $2.50) Avery-s/Ching-a/c 3.00
#1/2 (10/01, $2.95) Early days of Lara Croft; Jurgens-s/Lopez-a 3.00
...: Chasing Shangri-La (2002, $12.95, TPB) r/#11-15 13.00
Free Comic Book Day giveaway - (5/02) r/#1 with "Free Comic Book Day" banner on-c 3.00
... Gallery (12/00, $2.95) Pin-ups & previous covers by various 3.00
... Magazine (6/01, $4.95) Hughes-c; r/#1,2; Jurgens interview 5.00
...: Mystic Artifacts (2001, $14.95, TPB) r/#5-10 15.00
...: Saga of the Medusa Mask (9/00, $9.95, TPB) r/#1-4; new Park-c 10.00
... Vol. 1 Compendium (11/06, $59.99) r/#1-50; variant covers and pin-up art 60.00

TOMB RAIDER/WITCHBLADE SPECIAL (Also see Witchblade/Tomb Raider)
Top Cow Prod.: Dec, 1997 (mail-in offer, one-shot)
1-Turner-s/a(p); green background cover 1 3 4 6 8 10
1-Variant-c with orange sun background 1 3 4 6 8 10
1-Variant-c with black sides 1 3 4 6 8 10
1-Revisited (12/98, $2.95) reprints #1, Turner-c 3.00
...: Trouble Seekers TPB (2002, $7.95) rep. T.R./W & W/T.R. & W/T.R. 1/2; new Turner-c 8.00

TOMBSTONE TERRITORY
Dell Publishing Co.: No. 1123, Aug, 1960
Four Color 1123 7 14 21 49 92 135

Tom Mix Western #8 © FAW

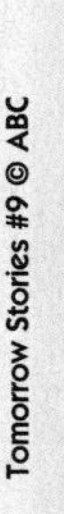
Tomorrow Stories #9 © ABC

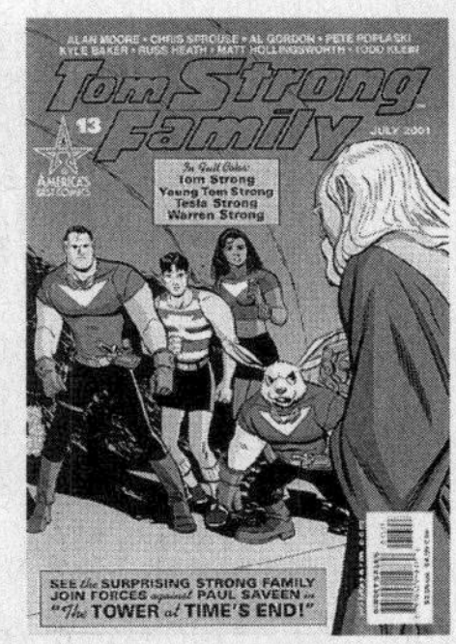

Tom Strong #13 © ABC

	GD 2.0	VG 4.0	FN 6.0	VF 8.0	VF/NM 9.0	NM- 9.2

TOM CAT (Formerly Bo; Atom The Cat #9 on)
Charlton Comics: No. 4, Apr, 1956 - No. 8, July, 1957

	GD	VG	FN	VF	VF/NM	NM-
4-Al Fago-c/a	8	16	24	44	57	70
5-8	6	12	18	31	38	45

TOM CLANCY'S SPLINTER CELL: ECHOES
Dynamite Entertainment: 2014 - No. 4, 2014 ($3.99)

	GD	VG	FN	VF	VF/NM	NM-
1-4-Nathan Edmonson-s/Marc Laming-a						4.00

TOM CORBETT, SPACE CADET (TV)
Dell Publishing Co.: No. 378, Jan-Feb, 1952 - No. 11, Sept-Nov, 1954 (All painted covers)

	GD	VG	FN	VF	VF/NM	NM-
Four Color 378 (#1)-McWilliams-a	16	32	48	110	243	375
Four Color 400,421-McWilliams-a	10	20	30	64	132	200
4(11-1/53) - 11	7	14	21	46	86	125

TOM CORBETT SPACE CADET (See March of Comics #102)

TOM CORBETT SPACE CADET (TV)
Prize Publications: V2#1, May-June, 1955 - V2#3, Sept-Oct, 1955

	GD	VG	FN	VF	VF/NM	NM-
V2#1-Robot-c	34	68	102	204	332	460
2,3-Meskin-c	25	50	75	150	245	340

TOM, DICK & HARRIET (See Gold Key Spotlight)

TOM LANDRY AND THE DALLAS COWBOYS
Spire Christian Comics/Fleming H. Revell Co.: 1973 (35/49¢)

	GD	VG	FN	VF	VF/NM	NM-
nn-35¢ edition	3	6	9	16	23	30
nn-49¢ edition	2	4	6	10	16	20

TOM MIX WESTERN (Movie, radio star) (Also see The Comics, Crackajack Funnies, Master Comics, 100 Pages Of Comics, Popular Comics, Real Western Hero, Six Gun Heroes, Western Hero & XMas Comics)
Fawcett Publications: Jan, 1948 - No. 61, May, 1953 (1-17: 52 pgs.)

	GD	VG	FN	VF	VF/NM	NM-
1 (Photo-c, 52 pgs.)-Tom Mix & his horse Tony begin; Tumbleweed Jr. begins, ends #52,54,55	53	106	159	334	567	800
2 (Photo-c)	25	50	75	150	245	340
3-5 (Painted/photo-c): 5-Billy the Kid & Oscar app.	19	38	57	111	176	240
6-8: 6,7 (Painted/photo-c). 8-Kinstler tempera-c	16	32	48	94	147	200
9,10 (Paint/photo-c) 9-Used in **SOTI**, pgs. 323-325	15	30	45	90	140	190
11-Kinstler oil-c	14	28	42	82	121	160
12 (Painted/photo-c)	14	28	42	78	112	145
13-17 (Painted-c, 52 pgs.)	14	28	42	78	112	145
18,22 (Painted-c, 36 pgs.)	12	24	36	69	97	125
19 (Photo-c, 52 pgs.)	13	26	39	74	105	135
20,21,23 (Painted-c, 52 pgs.)	12	24	36	69	97	125
24,25,27-29 (52 pgs.): 24-Photo-c begin, end #61. 29-Slim Pickens app.	11	22	33	60	83	105
26,30 (36 pgs.)	10	20	30	56	76	95
31-33,35-37,39,40,42 (52 pgs.): 39-Red Eagle app.	10	20	30	56	76	95
34,38 (36 pgs. begin)	9	18	27	52	69	85
41,43-60: 57-(9/52)-Dope smuggling story	8	16	24	40	50	60
61-Last issue	9	18	27	47	61	75

NOTE: *Photo-c from 1930s Tom Mix movies (he died in 1940). Many issues contain ads for Tom Mix, Rocky Lane, Space Patrol and other premiums. Captain Tootsie by* **C.C. Beck** *in #6-11, 20.*

TOM MIX WESTERN
AC Comics: 1988 - No. 2, 1989? ($2.95, B&W w/16 pgs. color, 44 pgs.)

	GD	VG	FN	VF	VF/NM	NM-
1-Tom Mix-r/Master #124,128,131,102 plus Billy the Kid-r by Severin; photo front/back/inside-c						4.00
2-($2.50, B&W)-Gabby Hayes-r; photo covers						4.00
...Holiday Album 1 (1990, $3.50, B&W, one-shot, 44 pgs.)-Contains photos & 1950s Tom Mix-r; photo inside-c						4.00

TOMMY OF THE BIG TOP (Thrilling Circus Adventures)
King Features Synd./Standard Comics: No. 10, Sep, 1948 - No. 12, Mar, 1949

	GD	VG	FN	VF	VF/NM	NM-
10-By John Lehti	12	24	36	67	94	120
11,12	9	18	27	50	65	80

TOMMY TOMORROW (See Action Comics #127, Real Fact #6, Showcase #41,42,44,46,47 & World's Finest #102)

TOMOE (Also see Shi: The Way Of the Warrior #6)
Crusade Comics: July, 1995 - No. 3, June, 1996($2.95)

	GD	VG	FN	VF	VF/NM	NM-
0-3: 2-B&W Dogs o' War preview. 3-B&W Demon Gun preview						3.00
0 (3/96, $2.95)-variant-c.						3.00
0-Commemorative edition (5,000)	2	4	6	8	10	12
1-Commemorative edition (5,000)	2	4	6	9	12	15
1-($2.95)-FAN Appreciation edition						3.00
TPB (1997, $14.95) r/#0-3						15.00

TOMOE: UNFORGETTABLE FIRE
Crusade Comics: June, 1997 ($2.95, one-shot)

	GD	VG	FN	VF	VF/NM	NM-
1-Prequel to Shi: The Series						3.00

TOMOE-WITCHBLADE/FIRE SERMON
Crusade Comics: Sept, 1996 ($3.95, one-shot)

	GD	VG	FN	VF	VF/NM	NM-
1-Tucci-c						5.00
1-($9.95)-Avalon Ed. w/gold foil-c						10.00

TOMOE-WITCHBLADE/MANGA SHI PREVIEW EDITION
Crusade Comics: July, 1996 ($5.00, B&W)

	GD	VG	FN	VF	VF/NM	NM-
nn-San Diego Preview Edition						5.00

TOMORROW KNIGHTS
Marvel Comics (Epic Comics): June, 1990 - No. 6, Mar, 1991 ($1.50)

	GD	VG	FN	VF	VF/NM	NM-
1-($1.95, 52 pgs.)						4.00
2-6						3.00

TOMORROW STORIES
America's Best Comics: Oct, 1999 - No. 12, Aug, 2002 ($3.50/$2.95)

	GD	VG	FN	VF	VF/NM	NM-
1-Two covers by Ross and Nowlan; Moore-s						4.00
2-12-($2.95) 6-1st app. Splash Brannigan						3.00
... Special (1/06, $6.99) Nowlan-c; Moore-s; Greyshirt tribute to Will Eisner						7.00
... Special 2 (5/06, $6.99) Gene Ha-c; Moore-s; Promethea app.						7.00
Book 1 Hardcover (2002, $24.95) r/#1-6						25.00
Book 1 TPB (2003, $17.95) r/#1-6						18.00
Book 2 Hardcover (2004, $24.95) r/#7-12						25.00
Book 2 TPB (2005, $17.99) r/#7-12						18.00

TOM SAWYER (See Adventures of... & Famous Stories)

TOM SKINNER-UP FROM HARLEM (See Up From Harlem)

TOM STRONG (Also see Many Worlds of Tesla Strong)
America's Best Comics: June, 1999 - No. 36, May, 2006 ($3.50/$2.95/$2.99)

	GD	VG	FN	VF	VF/NM	NM-
1-Two covers by Ross and Sprouse; Moore-s/Sprouse-a						4.00
1-Special Edition (9/09, $1.00) reprint with "After Watchmen" cover frame						3.00
2-36: 4-Art Adams-a (8 pgs.) 13-Fawcett homage w/art by Sprouse, Baker, Heath 20-Origin of Tom Stone. 22-Ordway-a. 31,32-Moorcock-s						3.00
...: Book One HC ('00, $24.95) r/#1-7, cover gallery and sketchbook						25.00
...: Book One TPB ('01, $14.95) r/#1-7, cover gallery and sketchbook						15.00
...: Book Two HC ('02, $24.95) r/#8-14, sketchbook						25.00
...: Book Two TPB ('03, $14.95) r/#8-14, sketchbook						15.00
...: Book Three HC ('04, $24.95) r/#15-19, sketchbook						25.00
...: Book Three TPB ('04, $17.95) r/#15-19, sketchbook						18.00
...: Book Four HC ('04, $24.95) r/#20-25, sketch pages						25.00
...: Book Four TPB ('05, $17.99) r/#20-25, sketch pages						18.00
...: Book Five HC ('05, $24.99) r/#26-30, sketch pages						25.00
...: Book Five TPB ('06, $17.99) r/#26-30, sketch pages						18.00
...: Book Six HC ('06, $24.99) r/#31-36						25.00
...: Book Six TPB ('08, $17.99) r/#31-36						18.00
...: The Deluxe Edition Book One (2009, $39.99, d.j.) r/#1-12; Moore intro.; sketch-a						40.00
...: The Deluxe Edition Book Two (2010, $39.99, d.j.) r/#13-24; sketch-a						40.00

TOM STRONG AND THE PLANET OF PERIL
DC Comics (Vertigo): Sept, 2013 - No. 6, Feb, 2014 ($2.99, limited series)

	GD	VG	FN	VF	VF/NM	NM-
1-6-Hogan-s/Sprouse-a/c. 2-Travel to Terra Obscura						3.00

TOM STRONG AND THE ROBOTS OF DOOM
DC Comics (WildStorm): Aug, 2010 - No. 6, Jan, 2011 ($3.99, limited series)

	GD	VG	FN	VF	VF/NM	NM-
1-6-Hogan-s/Sprouse-a. 1-Covers by Sprouse & Williams						4.00
TPB (2011, $17.99) r/#1-6						18.00

TOM STRONG'S TERRIFIC TALES
America's Best Comics: Jan, 2002 - No. 12 ($3.50/$2.95)

	GD	VG	FN	VF	VF/NM	NM-
1-Short stories; Moore-s; art by Adams, Rivoche, Hernandez, Weiss						3.50
2-12-($2.95) 2-Adams, Ordway, Weiss-a; Adams-c. 4-Rivoche-a. 5-Pearson, Aragonés-a 11-Timm-a						3.00
...: Book One HC ('04, $24.95) r/#1-6, cover gallery and sketch pages						25.00
...: Book One SC ('05, $17.99) r/#1-6, cover gallery and sketch pages						18.00
...: Book Two HC ('05, $24.95) r/#7-12, covers						25.00

TOM TERRIFIC! (TV)(See Mighty Mouse Fun Club Magazine #1)
Pines Comics (Paul Terry): Summer, 1957 - No. 6, Fall, 1958
(See Terry Toons Giant Summer Fun Book)

	GD	VG	FN	VF	VF/NM	NM-
1-1st app.?; CBS Television Presents...	21	42	63	126	206	285
2-6-(scarce)	16	32	48	94	147	200

TOM THUMB

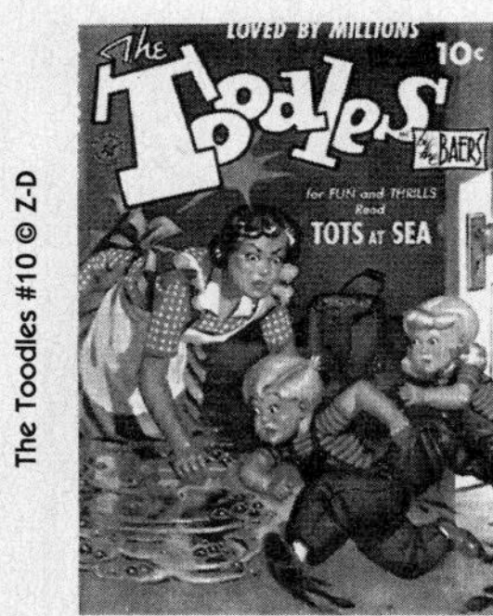

The Toodles #10 © Z-D

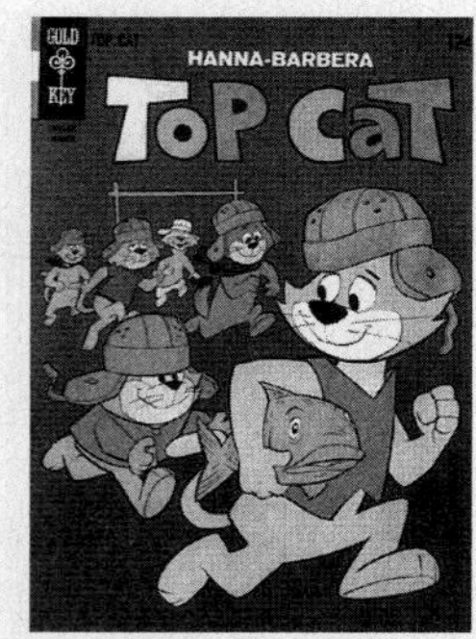

Top Cat #17 © H-B

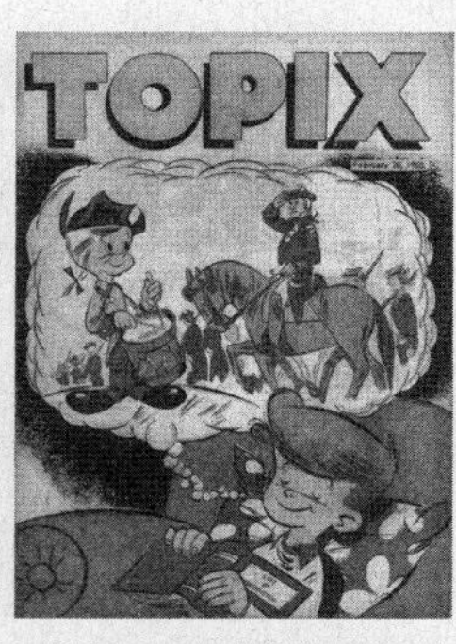

Topix V8 #19 © CG

GD 2.0 | VG 4.0 | FN 6.0 | VF 8.0 | VF/NM 9.0 | NM- 9.2

Dell Publishing Co.: No. 972, Jan, 1959
Four Color 972-Movie, George Pal 8 16 24 52 99 145

TOM-TOM, THE JUNGLE BOY (See A-1 Comics & Tick Tock Tales)
Magazine Enterprises: 1947 - No. 3, 1947; Nov, 1957 - No. 3, Mar, 1958
1-Funny animal 14 28 42 76 108 140
2,3(1947): 3-Christmas issue 9 18 27 52 69 85
Tom-Tom & Itchi the Monk 1(11/57) - 3(3/58) 6 12 18 28 34 40
I.W. Reprint No. 1,2,8,10: 1,2,8-r/Koko & Kola #? 2 4 6 8 10 12

TONGUE LASH
Dark Horse Comics: Aug, 1996 - No. 2, Sept, 1996 ($2.95, lim. series, mature)
1,2: Taylor-c/a 3.00

TONGUE LASH II
Dark Horse Comics: Feb, 1999 - No. 2, Mar, 1999 ($2.95, lim. series, mature)
1,2: Taylor-c/a 3.00

TONKA (Disney)
Dell Publishing Co.: No. 966, Jan, 1959
Four Color 966-Movie (Starring Sal Mineo)-photo-c 8 16 24 54 102 150

TONTO (See The Lone Ranger's Companion...)

TONY TRENT (The Face #1,2)
Big Shot/Columbia Comics Group: No. 3, 1948 - No. 4, 1949
3,4: 3-The Face app. by Mart Bailey 19 38 57 111 176 240

TOODLES, THE (The Toodle Twins with #1)
Ziff-Davis (Approved Comics)/Argo: No. 10, July-Aug, 1951; Mar, 1956 (Newspaper-r)
10-Painted-c, some newspaper-r by The Baers 14 28 42 82 121 160
...Twins 1(Argo, 3/56)-Reprints by The Baers 8 16 24 42 54 65

TOO MUCH COFFEE MAN
Adhesive Comics: July, 1993 - No. 10, Dec, 2000 ($2.50, B&W)
1-Shannon Wheeler story & art 2 4 6 9 12 15
2,3 1 2 3 5 7 9
4,5 6.00
6-10 4.00
Full Color Special-nn($2.95),2-(7/97, $3.95) 4.00

TOO MUCH COFFEE MAN SPECIAL
Dark Horse Comics: July, 1997 ($2.95, B&W)
nn-Reprints Dark Horse Presents #92-95 4.00

TOO MUCH HOPELESS SAVAGES
Oni Press: June, 2003 - No. 4, Apr, 2004 ($2.99, B&W, limited series)
1-4-Van Meter-s/Norrie-a 3.00
TPB (8/04, $11.95, digest-size) r/series 12.00

TOOTH & CLAW (See Autumnlands: Tooth & Claw)

TOOTS AND CASPER
Dell Publishing Co.: No. 5, 1942
Large Feature Comic 5 22 44 66 132 216 300

TOP ADVENTURE COMICS
I. W. Enterprises: 1964 (Reprints)
1-r/High Adv. (Explorer Joe #2); Krigstein-r 2 4 6 11 16 20
2-Black Dwarf-r/Red Seal #22; Kinstler-c 2 4 6 13 18 22

TOP CAT (TV) (Hanna-Barbera)(See Kite Fun Book)
Dell Publ.Co./Gold Key No. 4 on: 12-2/61-62 - No. 3, 6-8/62; No. 4, 10/62 - No. 31, 9/70
1 (TV show debuted 9/27/61) 13 26 39 89 195 300
2-Augie Doggie back-ups in #1-4 7 14 21 48 89 130
3-5: 3-Last 15¢ issue. 4-Begin 12¢ issues; Yakky Doodle app. in 1 pg. strip.
5-Touché Turtle app. 6 12 18 37 66 95
6-10 5 10 15 30 50 70
11-20 4 8 12 23 37 50
21-31-Reprints 3 6 9 18 28 38

TOP CAT (TV) (Hanna-Barbera)(See TV Stars #4)
Charlton Comics: Nov, 1970 - No. 20, Nov, 1973
1 6 12 18 38 69 100
2-10 3 6 9 19 30 40
11-20 3 6 9 16 24 32
NOTE: *#8 (1/72) went on sale late in 1972 between #14 and #15 with the 1/73 issues.*

TOP COMICS
K. K. Publications/Gold Key: July, 1967 (All reprints)
nn-The Gnome-Mobile (Disney-movie) 2 4 6 13 18 22
1-Beagle Boys (#7), Beep Beep the Road Runner (#5), Bugs Bunny, Chip 'n' Dale, Daffy Duck (#50), Flipper, Huey, Dewey & Louie, Junior Woodchucks, Lassie, The Little Monsters (#71), Moby Duck, Porky Pig (has Gold Key label - says Top Comics on inside), Scamp, Super Goof, Tom & Jerry, Top Cat (#21), Tweety & Sylvester (#7), Walt Disney C&S (#322), Woody Woodpecker known issues; each character given own book 2 4 6 9 13 16
1-Donald Duck (not Barks), Mickey Mouse 2 4 6 13 18 22
1-Flintstones 3 6 9 21 33 45
1-Huckleberry Hound, Yogi Bear (#30) 3 6 9 14 19 24
1-The Jetsons 4 8 12 28 47 65
1-Tarzan of the Apes (#169) 3 6 9 15 22 28
1-Three Stooges (#35) 3 6 9 17 26 35
1-Uncle Scrooge (#70) 3 6 9 16 23 30
1-Zorro (r/G.K. Zorro #7 w/Toth-a; says 2nd printing) 3 6 9 14 19 24
2-Bugs Bunny, Daffy Duck, Mickey Mouse (#114), Porky Pig, Super Goof, Tom & Jerry, Tweety & Sylvester, Walt Disney's C&S (r/#325), Woody Woodpecker 2 4 6 9 12 15
2-Donald Duck (not Barks), Three Stooges, Uncle Scrooge (#71)-Barks-c, Yogi Bear (#30), Zorro (r/#8; Toth-a) 2 4 6 11 16 20
2-Snow White & 7 Dwarfs(6/67)(1944-r) 2 4 6 10 14 18
3-Donald Duck 2 4 6 11 16 20
3-Uncle Scrooge (#72) 2 4 6 13 18 22
3,4-The Flintstones 3 6 9 21 33 45
3,4: 3-Mickey Mouse (r/#115), Tom & Jerry, Woody Woodpecker, Yogi Bear.
4-Mickey Mouse, Woody Woodpecker 2 4 6 9 12 15
NOTE: *Each book in this series is identical to its counterpart except for cover, and came out at same time. The number in parentheses is the original issue it contains.*

TOP COW (Company one-shots)
Image Comics (Top Cow Productions)
... Book of Revelations (7/03, $3.99)-Pin-ups and info; art by various; Gossett-c 4.00
... Convention Sketchbook 2004 (4/04, $3.00, B&W) art by various 3.00
... Holiday Special Vol. 1 (12/10, $12.99) Flip book with Jingle Belle 13.00
... Preview Book 2005 (3/05, 99¢) Preview pages of Tomb Raider, Darkness, Rising Stars 3.00
... Productions, Inc./Ballistic Studios Swimsuit Special (5/95, $2.95) 3.00
...'s Best of: Dave Finch Vol. 1 TPB (8/06, $19.99) r/issues of Cyberforce, Aphrodite IX, Ascension and The Darkness; art & cover gallery 20.00
...'s Best of: Michael Turner Vol. 1 TPB (12/05, $24.99) r/Witchblade #1,10,12,18,19,25 & Witchblade/Tomb Raider chapters 1&3; Tomb Raider #25; art & cover gallery 25.00
... Secrets: Special Winter Lingerie Edition 1 (1/96, $2.95) Pin-ups 3.00
... 2001 Preview (no cover price) Preview pages of Tomb Raider; Jusko-a; flip cover & pages of Inferno 3.00

TOP COW CLASSICS IN BLACK AND WHITE
Image Comics (Top Cow): Feb, 2000 - Present ($2.95, B&W reprints)
...: Aphrodite IX #1(9/00) B&W reprint 3.00
...: Ascension #1(4/00) B&W reprint plus time-line of series 3.00
...: Battle of the Planets #1(1/03) B&W reprint plus script and cover gallery 3.00
...: Darkness #1(3/00) B&W reprint plus time-line of series 3.00
...: Fathom #1(5/00) B&W reprint 3.00
...: Magdalena #1(10/02) B&W reprint plus time-line of series 3.00
...: Midnight Nation #1(9/00) B&W preview 3.00
...: Rising Stars #1(7/00) B&W reprint plus cover gallery 3.00
...: Tomb Raider #1(12/00) B&W reprint plus back-story 3.00
...: Witchblade #1(2/00) B&W reprint plus back-story 3.00
...: Witchblade #25(5/01) B&W reprint plus interview with Wohl & Haberlin 3.00

TOP DETECTIVE COMICS
I. W. Enterprises: 1964 (Reprints)
9-r/Young King Cole #14; Dr. Drew (not Grandenetti) 2 4 6 10 14 18

TOP DOG (See Star Comics Magazine, 75¢)
Star Comics (Marvel): Apr, 1985 - No. 14, June, 1987 (Children's book)
1-14: 10-Peter Parker & J. Jonah Jameson cameo 5.00

TOP ELIMINATOR (Teenage Hotrodders #1-24; Drag 'n' Wheels #30 on)
Charlton Comics: No. 25, Sept, 1967 - No. 29, July, 1968
25-29 3 6 9 16 23 30

TOP FLIGHT COMICS: Four Star Publ.: 1947 (Advertised, not published)

TOP FLIGHT COMICS
St. John Publishing Co.: July, 1949
1(7/49, St. John)-Hector the Inspector; funny animal 11 22 33 60 83 105

TOP GUN (See Luke Short, 4-Color #927 & Showcase #72)

TOP GUNS OF THE WEST (See Super DC Giant)

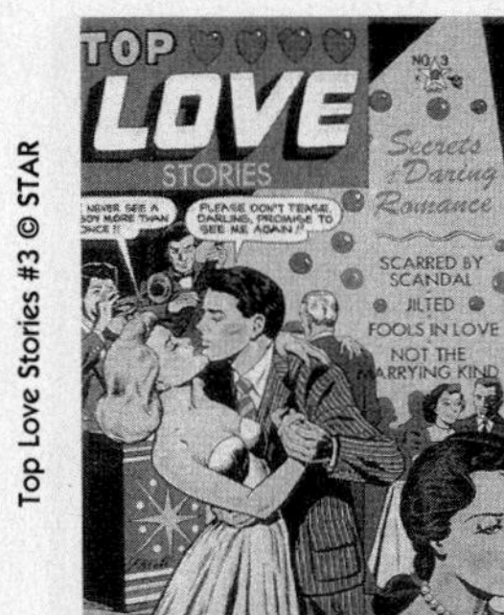

Top Love Stories #3 © STAR

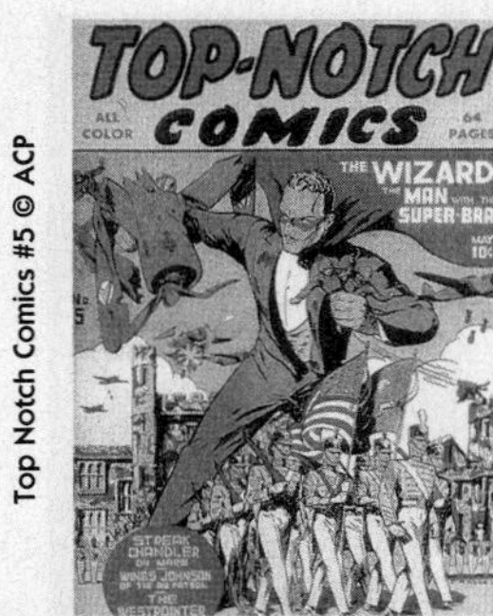

Top Notch Comics #5 © ACP

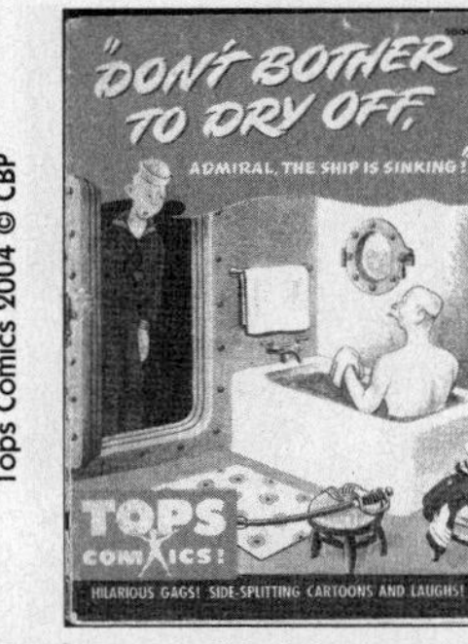

Tops Comics 2004 © CBP

TOPIX (...Comics) (Timeless Topix-early issues) (Also see Men of Battle, Men of Courage & Treasure Chest)(V1-V5#1,V7 on-paper-c)
Catechetical Guild Educational Society: 11/42 - V10#15, 1/28/52 (Weekly - later issues)

	GD 2.0	VG 4.0	FN 6.0	VF 8.0	VF/NM 9.0	NM- 9.2
V1#1(8 pgs.,8x11")	24	48	72	140	230	320
2,3(8 pgs.,8x11")	14	28	42	80	115	150
4-8(16 pgs.,8x11")	11	22	33	64	90	115
V2#1-10(16 pgs.,8x11"): V2#8-Pope Pius XII	10	20	30	56	76	95
V3#1-10(16 pgs.,8x11"): V3#1-(9/44)	10	20	30	54	72	90
V4#1-10: V4#1-(9/45)	9	18	27	47	61	75
V5#1(10/46,52 pgs.,2(11/46),no #3),4(1/47)-9(6/47),10(7/47), no #13,4(10/47), 14(11/47),15(12/47)	8	16	24	40	50	60
11(8/47),12(9/47)-Life of Christ editions	10	20	30	54	72	90
V6#4(1/48),5(2/48),7(3/48),8(4/48),9(5/48),10(6/48),11(7/48)-14 (no #1-3,6)	7	14	21	35	43	50
V7#1(9/1/48)-20(6/15/49), 36 pgs.	6	12	18	29	36	42
V8#1(9/19/49)-3,5-11,13-30(5/15/50) 30-Hitler app.	6	12	18	28	34	40
4-Dagwood Splits the Atom(10/10/49)-Magazine format	8	16	24	42	54	65
12-Ingels-a	10	20	30	54	72	90
V9#1(9/25/50)-11,13-30(5/14/51)	6	12	18	27	33	38
12-Special 36 pg. Xmas issue, text illos format	6	12	18	28	34	40
V10#1(10/1/51)-15: 14-Hollingsworth-a	6	12	18	27	33	38

TOP JUNGLE COMICS
I. W. Enterprises: 1964 (Reprint)

	GD 2.0	VG 4.0	FN 6.0	VF 8.0	VF/NM 9.0	NM- 9.2
1(nd)-Reprints White Princess of the Jungle #3, minus cover; Kintsler-a	3	6	9	16	23	30

TOP LOVE STORIES (Formerly Gasoline Alley #2)
Star Publications: No. 3, 5/51 - No. 19, 3/54

	GD 2.0	VG 4.0	FN 6.0	VF 8.0	VF/NM 9.0	NM- 9.2
3(#1)	25	50	75	150	245	340
4,5,7-9: 8-Wood story	20	40	60	120	195	270
6-Wood-a	26	52	78	154	252	350
10-16,18,19-Disbrow-a	20	40	60	120	195	270
17-Wood art (Fox-r)	21	42	63	124	202	280

NOTE: *All have* **L. B. Cole** *covers.*

TOP-NOTCH COMICS (...Laugh #28-45; Laugh Comix #46 on)
MLJ Magazines: Dec, 1939 - No. 45, June, 1944

	GD 2.0	VG 4.0	FN 6.0	VF 8.0	VF/NM 9.0	NM- 9.2
1-Origin/1st app. The Wizard; Kardak the Mystic Magician, Swift of the Secret Service (ends #3), Air Patrol, The Westpointer, Manhunters (by J. Cole), Mystic (ends #2) & Scott Rand (ends #3) begin; Wizard covers begin, end #8	530	1060	1590	3869	6835	9800
2-(1/40)-Dick Storm (ends #8), Stacy Knight M.D. (ends #4) begin; Jack Cole-a; 1st app. Nazis swastika on-c	271	542	813	1734	2967	4200
3-Bob Phantom, Scott Rand on Mars begin; J. Cole-a	187	374	561	1197	2049	2900
4-Origin/1st app. Streak Chandler on Mars; Moore of the Mounted only app.; J. Cole-a	161	322	483	1030	1765	2500
5-Flag-c; origin/1st app. Galahad; Shanghai Sheridan begins (ends #8); Shield cameo; Novick-a; classic-c	194	388	582	1242	2121	3000
6-Meskin-a	123	246	369	787	1344	1900
7-The Shield x-over in Wizard; The Wizard dons new costume	152	304	456	965	1658	2350
8-Origin/1st app. The Firefly & Roy, the Super Boy (9/40, 2nd costumed boy hero after Robin?; also see Toro in Human Torch #1 (Fall/40)	158	316	474	1003	1727	2450
9-Origin & 1st app. The Black Hood; 1st Black Hood-c & logo (10/40); Fran Frazier begins (Scarce)	649	1298	1947	4738	8369	12,000
10-2nd app. Black Hood	226	452	678	1446	2476	3500
11-3rd Black Hood	155	310	465	992	1696	2400
12-15	129	258	387	826	1413	2000
16-18,20	119	238	357	762	1306	1850
19-Classic bondage-c	129	258	387	826	1413	2000
21-30: 23-26-Roy app. 24-No Wizard. 25-Last Bob Phantom. 27-Last Firefly; Nazi war-c. 28-Suzie, Pokey Oakey begin. 29-Last Kardak	90	180	270	576	988	1400
31-44: 33-Dotty & Ditto by Woggon begins (2/43, 1st app.). 44-Black Hood series ends	47	94	141	296	498	700
45-Last issue	52	104	156	328	552	775

NOTE: **J. Binder** *a-1-3.* **Meskin** *a-2, 3, 6, 15.* **Bob Montana** *a-30; c-28-31.* **Harry Sahle** *c-42-45.* **Woggon** *a-33-40, 42. Bondage c-17, 19. Black Hood also appeared on radio in 1944.Black Hood app. on c-9-34, 41-44. Roy the Super Boy app. on c-8, 9, 11-27. The Wizard app. on c-1-8, 11-13, 15-22, 24, 25, 27. Pokey Oakey app. on c-28-43. Suzie app. on c-44-on.*

TOPPER & NEIL (TV)
Dell Publishing Co.: No. 859, Nov, 1957

	GD 2.0	VG 4.0	FN 6.0	VF 8.0	VF/NM 9.0	NM- 9.2
Four Color 859	5	10	15	34	60	85

TOPPS COMICS: Four Star Publications: 1947 (Advertised, not published)

TOPS
July, 1949 - No. 2, Sept, 1949 (25¢, 10-1/4x13-1/4", 68 pgs.)
Tops Magazine, Inc. (Lev Gleason): (Large size-magazine format; for the adult reader)

	GD 2.0	VG 4.0	FN 6.0	VF 8.0	VF/NM 9.0	NM- 9.2
1 (Rare)-Story by Dashiell Hammett; Crandall/Lubbers, Tuska, Dan Barry, Fuje-a; Biro painted-c	290	580	870	1856	3178	4500
2 (Rare)-Crandall/Lubbers, Biro, Kida, Fuje, Guardineer-a	245	490	735	1568	2684	3800

TOPS COMICS
Consolidated Book Publishers: 1944 (10¢, 132 pgs.)

	GD 2.0	VG 4.0	FN 6.0	VF 8.0	VF/NM 9.0	NM- 9.2
2000-(Color-c, inside in red shade & some in full color)-Ace Kelly by Rick Yager, Black Orchid, Don on the Farm, Dinky Dinkerton (Rare)	43	86	129	271	461	650

NOTE: *This book is printed in such a way that when the staple is removed, the strips on the left side of the book correspond with the same strips on the right side. Therefore, if strips are removed from the book, each strip can be folded into a complete comic section of its own.*

TOPS COMICS (See Tops in Humor)
Consolidated Book (Lev Gleason): 1944 (7-1/4x5", 32 pgs.)

	GD 2.0	VG 4.0	FN 6.0	VF 8.0	VF/NM 9.0	NM- 9.2
2001-The Jack of Spades (costumed hero)	26	52	78	154	252	350
2002-Rip Raider	18	36	54	105	165	225
2003-Red Birch (gag cartoons)	10	20	30	56	76	95
2004-Gag cartoons	18	36	54	105	165	225

TOP SECRET
Hillman Publ.: Jan, 1952

	GD 2.0	VG 4.0	FN 6.0	VF 8.0	VF/NM 9.0	NM- 9.2
1	24	48	72	140	230	320

TOP SECRET ADVENTURES (See Spyman)

TOP SECRETS (...of the F.B.I.)
Street & Smith Publications: Nov, 1947 - No. 10, July-Aug, 1949

	GD 2.0	VG 4.0	FN 6.0	VF 8.0	VF/NM 9.0	NM- 9.2
1-Powell-c/a	36	72	108	211	343	475
2-Powell-c/a	25	50	75	147	241	335
3-6,8,10-Powell-a	22	44	66	132	216	300
9-Powell-c/a	23	46	69	136	223	310
7-Used in **SOTI**, pg. 90 & illo. "How to hurt people"; used by N.Y. Legis. Comm.; Powell-c/a	34	68	102	206	336	465

NOTE: **Powell** *c-1-3, 5-10.*

TOPS IN ADVENTURE
Ziff-Davis Publishing Co.: Fall, 1952 (25¢, 132 pgs.)

	GD 2.0	VG 4.0	FN 6.0	VF 8.0	VF/NM 9.0	NM- 9.2
1-Crusader from Mars, The Hawk, Football Thrills, He-Man; Powell-a; painted-c	50	100	150	315	533	750

TOPS IN HUMOR (See Tops Comics?)
Consolidated Book Publ. (Lev Gleason)/Wise Publs.: 1944 (7-1/4x5", #2 digest size)

	GD 2.0	VG 4.0	FN 6.0	VF 8.0	VF/NM 9.0	NM- 9.2
2001(#1)-Origin The Jack of Spades, Ace Kelly by Rick Yager, Black Orchid (female crime fighter) app.	26	52	78	154	252	350
2-Wise Publs.; WWII serviceman humor	15	30	45	90	140	190

TOP SPOT COMICS
Top Spot Publ. Co.: 1945

	GD 2.0	VG 4.0	FN 6.0	VF 8.0	VF/NM 9.0	NM- 9.2
1-The Menace, Duke of Darkness app.	39	78	117	240	395	550

TOPSY-TURVY (Teenage)
R. B. Leffingwell Publ.: Apr, 1945

	GD 2.0	VG 4.0	FN 6.0	VF 8.0	VF/NM 9.0	NM- 9.2
1-1st app. Cookie	22	44	66	132	216	300

TOP TEN
America's Best Comics: Sept, 1999 - No. 12, Oct, 2001 ($3.50/$2.95)

	GD 2.0	VG 4.0	FN 6.0	VF 8.0	VF/NM 9.0	NM- 9.2
1-Two covers by Ross and Ha/Cannon; Alan Moore-s/Gene Ha-a						3.50
2-11-($2.95)						3.00
12-($3.50)						3.50
Hardcover ('00, $24.95) Dust jacket with Gene Ha-a; r/#1-7						25.00
Softcover ('00, $14.95) new Gene Ha-c; r/#1-7						15.00
Book 2 HC ('02, $24.95) Dust jacket with Gene Ha-a; r/#8-12						25.00
Book 2 SC ('03, $14.95) new Gene Ha-c; r/#8-12						15.00
...: The Forty-Niners HC (2005, $24.99, dust jacket) prequel set in 1949; Moore-s/Ha-a						25.00

TOP TEN: BEYOND THE FARTHEST PRECINCT
America's Best Comics: Oct, 2005 - No. 5, Feb, 2006 ($2.99, limited series)

	GD 2.0	VG 4.0	FN 6.0	VF 8.0	VF/NM 9.0	NM- 9.2
1-5-Jerry Ordway-a/Paul DiFilippo-s						3.00
TPB (2006, $14.99) r/series; cover sketch pages						15.00

TOP TEN SEASON TWO
America's Best Comics: Dec, 2008 - No. 4, Mar, 2009 ($2.99, limited series)

The Torch #2 © MAR

Total Eclipse #3 © ECL

Totally Awesome Hulk #8 © MAR

GD 2.0 | VG 4.0 | FN 6.0 | VF 8.0 | VF/NM 9.0 | NM- 9.2

1-4-Cannon-s/Ha-a 3.00
... Special (5/09, $2.99) Cannon-s/Daxiong-a/Ha-c 3.00

TOR (Prehistoric Life on Earth) (Formerly One Million Years Ago)
St. John Publ. Co.: No. 2, Oct, 1953; No. 3, May, 1954 - No. 5, Oct, 1954

3-D 2(10/53)-Kubert-c/a 15 30 45 84 127 170
3-D 2(10/53)-Oversized, otherwise same contents 14 28 42 78 112 145
3-D 2(11/53)-Kubert-c/a; has 3-D cover 14 28 42 78 112 145
3-5-Kubert-c/a: 3-Danny Dreams by Toth; Kubert 1 pg. story (w/self portrait) 15 30 45 84 127 170

NOTE: *The two October 3-D's have same contents and* **Powell** *art; the October & November issues are titled 3-D Comics. All 3-D issues are 25¢ and came with 3-D glasses.*

TOR (See Sojourn)
National Periodical Publications: May-June, 1975 - No. 6, Mar-Apr, 1976

1-New origin by Kubert 2 4 6 11 16 20
2-6: 2-Origin-r/St. John #1 1 2 3 5 6 8

NOTE: ***Kubert** a-1, 2-6r; c-1-6.* ***Toth** a(p)-3r.*

TOR (3-D)
Eclipse Comics: July, 1986 - No. 2, Aug, 1987 ($2.50)

1,2: 1-r/One Million Years Ago. 2-r/Tor 3-D #2 5.00
...2-D: 1,2-Limited signed & numbered editions 2 4 6 11 16 20

TOR
Marvel Comics (Epic Comics/Heavy Hitters): June, 1993 - No. 4, 1993 ($5.95, lim. series)

1-4: Joe Kubert-c/a/scripts 6.00

TOR (Joe Kubert's...)
DC Comics: Jul, 2008 - No. 6, Dec, 2008 ($2.99, limited series)

1-6-New story; Joe Kubert-c/a/scripts 3.00
...: A Prehistoric Odyssey HC (2009, $24.99, DJ) r/#1-6; Roy Thomas intro.; sketch-a 25.00
...: A Prehistoric Odyssey SC (2010, $14.99) r/#1-6; Roy Thomas intro.; sketch-a 15.00

TOR BY JOE KUBERT
DC Comics: 2001 - 2003 ($49.95, hardcovers with dust jacket)

Volume 1 (2001) r/One Million Years Ago #1 & 3-D Comics #1&2 in flat color; script pages, sketch pages, proposals for TV and newspapers strips; intro. by Roy Thomas 50.00
Volume 2 (2002) r/Tor (St. John) #3-5; Danny Dreams; portfolio section 50.00
Volume 3 (2003) r/Tor (DC '75) #1; (Marvel '93) #1-4; portfolio section 50.00

TORCH, THE
Marvel Comics (with Dynamite Ent.): Nov, 2009 - No. 8, Jul, 2010 ($3.99, limited series)

1-8-Thinker resurrects the Golden Age Human Torch; Toro app; Alex Ross-c on all; Berkenkotter-a. 3-5-Namor app. 4.00

TORCH OF LIBERTY SPECIAL
Dark Horse Comics (Legend): Jan, 1995 ($2.50, one-shot)

1-Byrne scripts 3.00

TORCHWOOD (Based on the BBC TV series)
Titan Comics: Sept, 2010 - No. 6, Jan, 2011 ($3.99)

1-6: 1-Barrowman-s/Edwards-a; Churchill & photo-c. 2-Art by Yeowell & Grist 4.00

TORCHWOOD (Based on the BBC TV series)
Titan Comics: Aug, 2016 - No. 4, Jan, 2017 ($3.99)

1-4-John & Carole Barrowman-s/Fuso & Qualano-a; multiple covers 4.00

TORCHY (...Blonde Bombshell) (See Dollman, Military, & Modern)
Quality Comics Group: Nov, 1949 - No. 6, Sept, 1950

1-Bill Ward-c, Gil Fox-a 206 412 618 1318 2259 3200
2,3-Fox-c/a 82 164 246 528 902 1275
4-Fox-c/a(3), Ward-a (9 pgs.) 103 206 309 659 1130 1600
5,6-Ward-c/a, 9 pgs; Fox-a(3) each 113 226 339 718 1234 1750
Super Reprint #16(1964)-r/#4 with new-c 7 14 21 49 92 135

TO RIVERDALE AND BACK AGAIN (Archie Comics Presents...)
Archie Comics: 1990 ($2.50, 68 pgs.)

nn-Byrne-c, Colan-a(p); adapts NBC TV movie 5.00

TORMENTED, THE (Becomes Surprise Adventures #3 on)
Sterling Comics: July, 1954 - No. 2, Sept, 1954

1,2: Weird/Horror stories 37 74 111 222 361 500

TORNADO TOM (See Mighty Midget Comics)

TORSO (See Jinx: Torso)

TOTAL ECLIPSE
Eclipse Comics: May, 1988 - No. 5, Apr, 1989 ($3.95, 52 pgs., deluxe size)

Book 1-5: 3-Intro/1st app. new Black Terror. 4-Many copies have upside down pages and are mis-cut 5.00

TOTAL ECLIPSE
Image Comics: July, 1998 (one-shot)

1-McFarlane-c; Eclipse Comics character pin-ups by Image artists 3.00

TOTAL ECLIPSE: THE SERAPHIM OBJECTIVE
Eclipse Comics: Nov, 1988 ($1.95, one-shot, Baxter paper)

1-Airboy, Valkyrie, The Heap app. 3.00

TOTAL JUSTICE
DC Comics: Oct, 1996 - No. 3, Nov, 1996 ($2.25, bi-weekly limited series) (Based on toyline)

1-3 3.00

TOTAL RECALL (Movie)
DC Comics: 1990 ($2.95, 68 pgs., movie adaptation, one-shot)

1-Arnold Schwarzenegger photo-c 4.00

TOTALLY AWESOME HULK, THE (Amadeus Cho as The Hulk)
Marvel Comics: Feb, 2016 - Present ($4.99/$3.99)

1-($4.99) Frank Cho-a/Greg Pak-s; She-Hulk and Spider-Man (Miles) app. 5.00
2-16-($3.99) 2,3-Fin Fang Foom and Lady Hellbender app. 5,6-Mike Choi-a. 7,8-Alan Davis-a. 9-11-Civil War II tie-in. 9-Del Mundo-a. 10-12-Black Panther app. 13-15-Jeremy Lin app. 4.00
#1.MU (5/17, $4.99) Monsters Unleashed tie-in; art by Templeton, Ortiz, Lindsay 5.00

TOTAL RECALL (Continuation of movie)
Dynamite Entertainment: 2011 - No. 4, 2011 ($3.99, limited series)

1-4-Quaid and Melina on Mars following the movie; Razek-a/Robertson-c 4.00

TOTAL WAR (M.A.R.S. Patrol #3 on)
Gold Key: July, 1965 - No. 2, Oct, 1965 (Painted-c)

1-Wood-a in both issues 6 12 18 38 69 100
2 5 10 15 31 53 75

TOTEMS (Vertigo V2K)
DC Comics (Vertigo): Feb, 2000 ($5.95, one-shot)

1-Swamp Thing, Animal Man, Zatanna, Shade app.; Fegredo-c 6.00

TO THE HEART OF THE STORM
Kitchen Sink Press: 1991 (B&W, graphic novel)

Softcover-Will Eisner-s/a/c 20.00
Hardcover ($24.95) 30.00
TPB-(DC Comics, 9/00, $14.95) reprints 1991 edition 15.00

TO THE LAST MAN (See Zane Grey Four Color #616)

TOUCH OF SILVER, A
Image Comics: Jan, 1997 - No. 6, Nov, 1997 ($2.95, B&W, bi-monthly)

1-6-Valentino-s/a; photo-c: 5-color pgs. w/Round Table 3.00
TPB ($12.95) r/#1-6 13.00

TOUGH KID SQUAD COMICS
Timely Comics (TCI): Mar, 1942

1-(Scarce)-Origin & 1st app.The Human Top & The Tough Kid Squad; The Flying Flame app. 920 1840 2760 6700 12,600 18,500

TOWER OF SHADOWS (Creatures on the Loose #10 on)
Marvel Comics Group: Sept, 1969 - No. 9, Jan, 1971

1-Romita-c, classic Steranko-a; Craig-a(p) 8 16 24 51 96 140
2,3: 2-Neal Adams-a. 3-Barry Smith, Tuska-a 5 10 15 30 50 70
4,6: 4-Marie Severin-c. 6-Wood-a 4 8 12 27 44 60
5-B. Smith-a(p), Wood-a; Wood draws himself (1st pg., 1st panel) 4 8 12 28 47 65
7-9: 7-B. Smith-a(p), Wood-a. 8-Wood-a; Wrightson-c. 9-Wrightson-c; Roy Thomas app. 5 10 15 30 50 70
Special 1(12/71, 52 pgs.)-Neal Adams-a; Romita-c 4 8 12 27 44 60

NOTE: ***J. Buscema** a-1p, 2p, Special 1r.* ***Colan** a-3p, 6p, Special 1.* ***J. Craig** a(r)-1p.* ***Ditko** a-6, 8, 9r, Special 1.* ***Everett** a-9(i)r; c-5i.* ***Kirby** a-9(p)r.* ***Severin** c-5p, 6.* ***Steranko** a-1p.* ***Tuska** a-3.* ***Wood** a-5-8. Issues 1-9 contain new stories with some pre-Marvel age reprints in 6-9.* ***H. P. Lovecraft** adaptation-9.*

TOXIC AVENGER (Movie)
Marvel Comics: Apr, 1991 - No. 11, Feb, 1992 ($1.50)

1-11: Based on movie character. 3,10-Photo-c 3.00

TOXIC CRUSADERS (TV)
Marvel Comics: May, 1992 - No. 8, Dec, 1992 ($1.25)

1-8: 1-3,8-Sam Kieth-c; based on USA Network cartoon 3.00

TOXIN (Son of Carnage)
Marvel Comics: June, 2005 - No. 6, Nov, 2005 ($2.99, limited series)

Toy Story #4 © DIS/Pixar

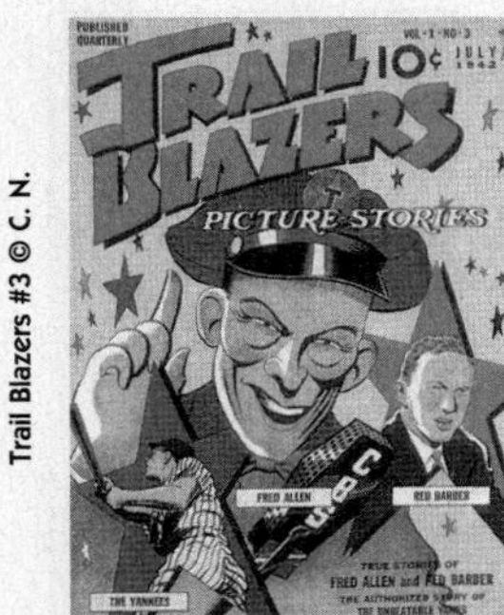

Trail Blazers #3 © C. N.

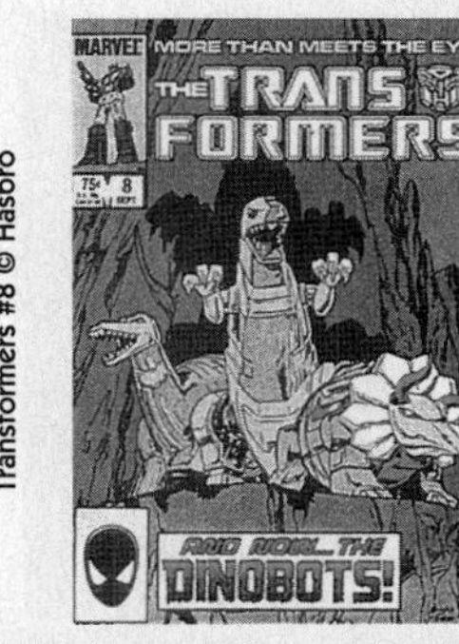

Transformers #8 © Hasbro

GD 2.0 | VG 4.0 | FN 6.0 | VF 8.0 | VF/NM 9.0 | NM- 9.2

1-6-Milligan-s/Robertson-a; Spider-Man app. 3.00
...: The Devil You Know TPB (2006, $17.99) r/#1-6 18.00

TOYBOY
Continuity Comics: Oct, 1986 - No. 7, Mar, 1989 ($2.00, Baxter paper)
1-7 3.00
*NOTE: **N. Adams** a-1; c-1, 2,5. **Golden** a-7p; c-6,7. **Nebres** a(i)-1,2.*

TOYLAND COMICS
Fiction House Magazines: Jan, 1947 - No. 2, Mar, 1947; No. 3, July, 1947
1-Wizard of the Moon begins 30 60 90 177 289 400
2,3-Bob Lubbers-c. 3-Tuska-a 17 34 51 100 158 215
NOTE: *All above contain strips by **Al Walker.***

TOY STORY (Disney/Pixar movies)
BOOM! Entertainment (BOOM! KIDS): No. 0, Nov, 2009 - No. 7, Sept, 2010 ($2.99)
0-7: 0,1-Three covers. 2-7-Two covers 3.00
Free Comic Book Day Edition (5/10, giveaway) r/#0 The Return of Buzz Lightyear 3.00
...: The Return of Buzz Lightyear (10/10, Halloween giveaway, 8-1/2" x 5-1/4") 3.00

TOY STORY (Disney/Pixar movies)
Marvel Comics: May, 2012 - No. 4, 2012 ($2.99, limited series)
1-4: 1-Master Woody. 2-A Scary Night. 3-To The Attic. 4-Water Rescue 3.00

TOY STORY: MYSTERIOUS STRANGER (Disney/Pixar movies)
BOOM! Entertainment (BOOM! KIDS): May, 2009 - No. 4, July, 2009 ($2.99)
1-4-Jolley-s/Moreno-a. 1-Three covers. 2-4-Two covers 3.00

TOY STORY: TALES FROM THE TOY CHEST (Disney/Pixar movies)
BOOM! Entertainment (BOOM! KIDS): July, 2010 - No. 4, Oct, 2010 ($2.99)
1-4-Snider-s/Luthi-a. 1-Two covers. 2-4-One cover 3.00

TOY TOWN COMICS
Toytown/Orbit Publ./B. Antin/Swapper Quarterly: 1945 - No. 7, May, 1947
1-Mertie Mouse; L. B. Cole-c/a; funny animal 39 78 117 240 395 550
2-L. B. Cole-a 22 44 66 132 216 300
3-7-L. B. Cole-a. 5-Wiggles the Wonderworm-c 20 40 60 114 182 250

TRACKER
Image Comics (Top Cow): Nov, 2009 - No. 5, Sept, 2010 ($2.99/$3.99)
1,2-Lincoln-s/Tsai-a. 1-Two covers 3.00
3-5-($3.99) 4.00

TRAGG AND THE SKY GODS (See Gold Key Spotlight, Mystery Comics Digest #3,9 & Spine Tingling Tales)
Gold Key/Whitman No. 9: June, 1975 - No. 8, Feb, 1977; No. 9, May, 1982 (Painted-c #3-8)
1-Origin 3 6 9 14 19 24
2-8: 4-Sabre-Fang app. 8-Ostellon app. 2 4 6 8 11 14
9-(Whitman, 5/82) r/#1 1 2 3 5 7 9
NOTE: ***Santos** a-1, 2, 9r; c-3-7. **Spiegel** a-3-8.*

TRAILBLAZER
Image Comics: June 2011 ($5.99, one shot, graphic novel)
nn-Gray & Palmiotti-s/Daly-a; covers by Johnson and Conner 6.00

TRAIL BLAZERS (Red Dragon #5 on)
Street & Smith Publications: 1941; No. 2, Apr, 1942 - No. 4, Oct, 1942
(True stories of American heroes)
1-Life story of Jack Dempsey & Wright Brothers 39 78 117 235 385 535
2-Brooklyn Dodgers-c/story; Ben Franklin story 22 44 66 132 216 300
3,4: 3-Fred Allen, Red Barber, Yankees stories 20 40 60 117 189 260

TRAIL COLT (Also see Extra Comics, Manhunt! & Undercover Girl)
Magazine Enterprises: 1949 - No. 2, 1949
nn(A-1 #24)-7 pg. Frazetta-a r-in Manhunt #13; Undercover Girl app.; The Red Fox by L. B. Cole; Ingels-c; Whitney-a (Scarce) 39 78 117 240 395 550
2(A-1 #26)-Undercover Girl; Ingels-c; L. B. Cole-a (6 pgs.) 31 62 93 182 296 410

TRAIN CALLED LOVE, A
Dynamite Entertainment: 2015 - No. 10, 2016 ($3.99)
1-9-Garth Ennis-s/Mark Dos Santos-a 4.00
10-($5.99) Last issue 6.00

TRANSFORMERS, THE (TV)(See G.I. Joe and...)
(Continues in Transformers: Regeneration)
Marvel Comics Group: Sept, 1984 - No. 80, July, 1991 (75¢/$1.00)
1-Based on Hasbro Toys 7 14 21 46 86 125
1-2nd & 3rd printing 2 4 6 11 16 20
2-5: 2-Golden-c. 3-(1/85) Spider-Man (black costume)-c/app. 4-Texeira-c; brief app. of Dinobots 3 6 9 14 20 25
2-10: 2nd & 3rd prints 4.00
6,7,9: 6-1st Josie Beller. 9-Circuit Breaker 1st full app. 2 4 6 8 11 14
8-Dinobots 1st full app. 3 6 9 16 24 32
10-Intro. Constructicons 2 4 6 11 16 20
11,14: 11-1st app. Jetfire. 14-Jetfire becomes an Autobot; 1st app. of Grapple, Hoist, Smokescreen, Skids, and Tracks 2 4 6 8 10 12
12,13,15,17,18,20-24,26-49: 17-1st app. of Blaster, Powerglide, Cosmos, Seaspray, Warpath, Beachcomber, Preceptor, Straxus, Kickback, Bombshell, Shrapnel, Dirge, and Ramjet. 21-1st app. of Aerialbots; 1st Slingshot; Circuit Breaker app. 22-Retells origin of Circuit Breaker, 1st Stunticons. 23-Battle at Statue of Liberty. 24-1st app. Protectobots, Combaticons; Optimus Prime killed. 26-Intro The Mechanic, Prime's Funeral. 27-Grimlock named new Autobot leader. 28-The Mechanic app. 29-Intro Scraplets, 1st app. of Triple Changers 1 2 3 5 6 8
16-Plight of the Bumblebee 2 4 6 9 12 15
19-1st Omega Supreme 1 3 4 6 8 10
25-1st Predacons 2 4 6 8 10 12
50-60: 53-Jim Lee-c. 54-Intro Micromasters. 60-Brief 1st app. of Primus 2 4 6 8 10 12
61-70: 61-Origin of Cybertron and the Transformers, Unicron app.; app. of Primus, creator of the Transformers. 62-66 Matrix Quest 5-part series. 67-Jim Lee-c 2 4 6 10 14 18
71-77: 75-($1.50, 52 pgs.) (Low print run) 3 6 9 17 26 35
78,79 (Low print run) 4 8 12 23 37 50
80-Last issue 5 10 15 31 53 75
*NOTE: Second and third printings of most early issues (1-9?) exist and are worth less than originals. Was originally planned as a four issue mini-series. **Wrightson** a-64i(4 pgs.).*

TRANSFORMERS
IDW Publishing: No. 0, Oct, 2005 (99¢, one-shot)
0-Prelude to Transformers: Infiltration series; Furman-s/Su-a; 4 covers 3.00

TRANSFORMERS
IDW Publishing: Nov, 2009 - No. 31, Dec, 2011 ($3.99)
1-31: Multple covers on each, 21-Chaos arc begins 4.00
...: Continuum (11/09, $3.99) Plot synopses of recent Transformers storylines 4.00
...: Death of Optimus Prime (12/11, $3.99) Roche-a 4.00
Hundred Penny Press: Transformers Classics #1 (6/11, $1.00) r/#1 (1984 Marvel series) 3.00
Hundred Penny Press (3/14, $1.00) r/#1 (1984 Marvel series) 3.00

TRANSFORMERS (See Transformers: Robots in Disguise for #1-34)
IDW Publishing: No. 34, Nov, 2014 - No. 57, Sept, 2016 ($3.99)
35-49: 39-42-Combiner Wars x-over 4.00
50-($7.99, squarebound) Barber-s/Griffith-a 8.00
51-57: 51-55-All Hail Optimus. 56-Revolution tie-in 4.00
...: Deviations (3/16, $4.99) What If... Optimus Prime never died; Easton-s; 2 covers 5.00
... Holiday Special (12/15, $5.99) Covers by Coller & Garbowska 6.00
...: Revolution 1 (10/16, $3.99) Revolution tie-in; Barber-s/Griffith-a; multiple covers 4.00
...: Titans Return (7/16, $4.99) Road to Revolution; Ramondelli-a 5.00

TRANSFORMERS (Free Comic Book Day Editions)
Dreamwave Productions/IDW Publishing
... Animated (IDW, 5/08) Free Comic Book Day Edition; from the Cartoon Network series 3.00
... Armada (Dreamwave Prods., 5/03) Free Comic Book Day Edition 3.00
.../Beast Wars Special (IDW, 2006) Free Comic Book Day Edition; flip book 3.00
.../G.I. Joe (IDW, 2009) Free Comic Book Day Edition; flip book 3.00
... Movie Prequel (IDW, 5/07) Free Comic Book Day Edition; Figueroa-c 3.00

TRANSFORMERS: ALL HAIL MEGATRON
IDW Publishing: Jul, 2008 - No. 16, Oct, 2009 ($3.99, limited series)
1-16: 1-8,10-12-McCarthy-s/Guidi-a; 2 covers 4.00

TRANSFORMERS: ALLIANCE (Prequel to 2009 Transformers 2 movie)
IDW Publishing: Dec, 2008 - No. 4, Mar, 2009 ($3.99, limited series)
1-4-Milne-a; 2 covers 4.00

TRANSFORMERS ANIMATED: THE ARRIVAL
IDW Publishing: Sept, 2008 - No. 5, Dec, 2008 ($3.99, limited series)
1-5-Brizuela-a; 2 covers 4.00

TRANSFORMERS ARMADA (Continues as Transformers Energon with #19)
Dreamwave Productions: July, 2002 - No. 18, Dec, 2003 ($2.95)
1-Sarracini-s/Raiz-a; wraparound gatefold-c 5.00
2-18 4.00
Vol. 1 TPB (2003, $13.95) r/#1-5 14.00
Vol. 2 TPB (2003, $15.95) r/#6-11 16.00

Transformers/G.I. Joe #3 © Hasbro

Transformers: Lost Light #1 © Hasbro

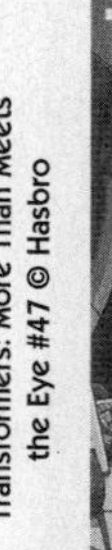
Transformers: More Than Meets the Eye #47 © Hasbro

	GD 2.0	VG 4.0	FN 6.0	VF 8.0	VF/NM 9.0	NM- 9.2

TRANSFORMERS ARMADA: MORE THAN MEETS THE EYE
Dreamwave Productions: Mar, 2004 - No. 3, May, 2004 ($4.95, limited series)
1-3-Pin-ups with tech info; art by Pat Lee & various 5.00

TRANSFORMERS, BEAST WARS: THE ASCENDING
IDW Publishing: Aug, 2007 - No. 4, Nov, 2007 ($3.99, limited series)
1-4-Furman-s/Figueroa-a; multiple covers on all 4.00

TRANSFORMERS, BEAST WARS: THE GATHERING
IDW Publishing: Feb, 2006 - No. 4, May, 2006 ($2.99, limited series)
1-4-Furman-s/Figueroa-a; multiple covers on all 4.00
TPB (8/06, $17.99) r/series; sketch pages & gallery of covers and variants 18.00

TRANSFORMERS: BUMBLEBEE
IDW Publishing: Dec, 2009 - No. 4, Mar, 2010 ($3.99, limited series)
1-4: Zander Cannon-s; multiple covers on all 4.00

TRANSFORMERS COMICS MAGAZINE (Digest)
Marvel Comics: Jan, 1987 - No. 10, July, 1988

	GD	VG	FN	VF	VF/NM	NM-
1,2-Spider-Man-c/s	2	4	6	10	14	18
3-10	2	4	6	8	10	12

TRANSFORMERS: DARK CYBERTRON
IDW Publishing: Nov, 2013 ($3.99)
1-Part 1 of a 12-part crossover with Transformers: More Than Meets the Eye #23-27 and Transformers: Robots in Disguise #23-27; multiple covers 4.00
1-Deluxe Edition ($7.99, squarebound) r/#1 with bonus script and B&W art pages 8.00
... Finale (3/14, $3.99) Three covers 4.00

TRANSFORMERS: DARK OF THE MOON MOVIE ADAPTATION (2011 movie)
IDW Publishing: Jun, 2011 - No. 4, Jun, 2011 ($3.99, weekly limited series)
1-4-Barber-s/Jimenez-a 4.00

TRANSFORMERS: DEFIANCE (Prequel to 2009 Transformers 2 movie)
IDW Publishing: Jan, 2009 - No. 4, Apr, 2009 ($3.99, limited series)
1-4-Mowry-s; 2 covers 4.00

TRANSFORMERS: DEVASTATION
IDW Publishing: Sept, 2007 - No. 6, Feb, 2008 ($3.99, limited series)
1-6-Furman-s/Su-a; multiple covers on all 4.00

TRANSFORMERS: DRIFT
IDW Publishing: Sept, 2010 - No. 4, Oct, 2010 ($3.99, limited series)
1-4-McCarthy-s/Milne-a; multiple covers on all 4.00

TRANSFORMERS: DRIFT – EMPIRE OF STONE
IDW Publishing: Nov, 2014 - No. 4, Feb, 2015 ($3.99, limited series)
1-4-McCarthy-s/Guidi & Ferreira-a; multiple covers on all 4.00

TRANSFORMERS ENERGON (Continued from Transformers Armada #18)
Dreamwave Productions: No. 19, Jan, 2004 - No. 30, Dec, 2004 ($2.95)
19-30-Furman-s 4.00

TRANSFORMERS: ESCALATION
IDW Publishing: Nov, 2006 - No. 6, Apr, 2007 ($3.99, limited series)
1-6-Furman-s/Su-a; multiple covers 4.00

TRANSFORMERS: EVOLUTIONS - HEARTS OF STEEL
IDW Publishing: June, 2006 - No. 4, Sept, 2006 ($2.99, limited series)
1-4-Bumblebee meets John Henry in 1880s railroad times 4.00

TRANSFORMERS: FOUNDATION (Prequel to 2011 Transformers: Dark of the Moon movie)
IDW Publishing: Feb, 2011 - No. 4, May, 2011 ($3.99, limited series)
1-4-Barber-s/Griffith-a; 2 covers 4.00

TRANSFORMERS: GENERATION 1
Dreamwave Productions: Apr, 2002 - No. 6, Oct, 2002 ($2.95)
Preview- 6 pg. story; robot sketch pages; Pat Lee-a 3.00
1-Pat Lee-a; 2 wraparound covers by Lee 5.00
2-6: 2-Optimus Prime reactivated; 2 covers by Pat Lee 4.00
...Vol. 1 HC (2003, $49.95) r/#1-6; black hardcover with red foil lettering and art 50.00
...Vol. 1 TPB (2002, $17.95) r/#1-6 plus six page preview; 8 pg. preview of future issues 18.00

TRANSFORMERS: GENERATION 1 (Volume 2)
Dreamwave Productions: Apr, 2003 - No. 6, Sept, 2003 ($2.95)
1-6: 1-Pat Lee-a; 2 wraparound gatefold covers by Lee 4.00
1-($5.95) Chrome wraparound variant-c 6.00
...Vol. 2 TPB (IDW Publ., 3/06, $19.99) r/#1-6 plus cover gallery 20.00

TRANSFORMERS: GENERATION 1 (Volume 3)
Dreamwave Productions: No. 0, Dec, 2003 - Present ($2.95)
0-10: 0-Pat Lee-a. 1-Figueroa-a; wrapaound-c 4.00

TRANSFORMERS: GENERATION 2
Marvel Comics: Nov, 1993 - No. 12, Oct, 1994 ($1.75)

	GD	VG	FN	VF	VF/NM	NM-
1-($2.95, 68 pgs.)-Collector's ed. w/bi-fold metallic-c	2	4	6	8	10	12
1-11: 1-Newsstand edition (68 pgs.). 2-G.I. Joe app., Snake-Eyes, Scarlett, Cobra Commander app. 5-Red Alert killed, Optimus Prime gives Grimlock leadership of Autobots. 6-G.I. Joe app.	1	2	3	4	5	7
12-($2.25, 52 pgs.)	1	3	4	6	8	10

TRANSFORMERS: GENERATIONS
IDW Publishing: Mar, 2006 - No. 12, Mar, 2007 ($1.99/$2.49/$3.99)
1,2: 1-R/Transformers #7 (1985); preview of Transformers, Beast Wars. 2-R/#13 4.00
3-10-($2.49) 3-R/Transformers #14 (1986). 4-6-Reprint #16-18. 7-R/#24 4.00
11,12-($3.99) 4.00
Volume 1 (12/06, $19.99) r/#1-6; cover gallery 20.00

TRANSFORMERS/G.I. JOE
Dreamwave Productions: Aug, 2003 - No. 6, Mar, 2004 ($2.95/$5.25)
1-Art & gatefold wraparound-c by Jae Lee; Ney Rieber-s; variant-c by Pat Lee 4.00
1-($5.95) Holofoil wraparound-c by Norton 6.00
2-6-Jae Lee-a/c 4.00
TPB (8/04, $17.95) r/#1-6; cover gallery and sketch pages 18.00

TRANSFORMERS/G.I. JOE: DIVIDED FRONT
Dreamwave Productions: Oct, 2004 ($2.95)
1-Art & gatefold wraparound-c by Pat Lee 4.00

TRANSFORMERS: HEADMASTERS
Marvel Comics Group: July, 1987 - No. 4, Jan, 1988 ($1.00, limited series)

	GD	VG	FN	VF	VF/NM	NM-
1-Springer, Akin, Garvey-a	1	2	3	5	6	8

2-4-Springer-c on all 6.00

TRANSFORMERS: HEART OF DARKNESS
IDW Publishing: Mar, 2011 - No. 4, Jun, 2011 ($3.99, limited series)
1-4-Abnett & Lanning-s/Farinas-a 4.00

TRANSFORMERS: INFESTATION (Crossover with Star Trek, Ghostbusters & G.I. Joe)
IDW Publishing: Feb, 2011 - No. 2, Feb, 2011 ($3.99, limited series)
1,2-Abnett & Lanning-s/Roche-a; covers by Roche & Snyder III 4.00

TRANSFORMERS: INFILTRATION
IDW Publishing: Jan, 2006 - No. 6, June, 2006 ($2.99, limited series)
1-6-Furman-s/Su-a; multiple covers on all 4.00
... Cover Gallery (8/06, $5.99) 6.00

TRANSFORMERS: IRONHIDE
IDW Publishing: May, 2010 - No. 4, Aug, 2010 ($3.99, limited series)
1-4: Mike Costa-s; multiple covers on all 4.00

TRANSFORMERS: LAST STAND OF THE WRECKERS
IDW Publishing: Jan, 2010 - No. 5, May, 2010 ($3.99, limited series)
1-5-Nick Roche-s/a; two covers 4.00

TRANSFORMERS: LOST LIGHT
IDW Publishing: Dec, 2016 - Present ($3.99)
1,2-James Roberts-s/Jack Lawrence-a; multiple covers on each 4.00

TRANSFORMERS: MAXIMUM DINOBOTS
IDW Publishing: Dec, 2008 - No. 5, Apr, 2009 ($3.99, limited series)
1-5-Furman-s/Roche-a; 2 covers for each 4.00

TRANSFORMERS: MEGATRON ORIGIN
IDW Publishing: May, 2007 - No. 4, Sept, 2008 ($3.99, limited series)
1-4-Alex Milne-a; 2 covers 4.00

TRANSFORMERS: MICROMASTERS
Dreamwave Productions: June, 2004 - No. 4 ($2.95, limited series)
1-4-Ruffolo-a; Pat Lee-c 4.00

TRANSFORMERS: MONSTROSITY
IDW Publishing: Jun, 2013 - No. 4, Sept, 2013 ($3.99)
1-4: 1-Three covers; Ramondelli-a 4.00

TRANSFORMERS: MORE THAN MEETS THE EYE
Dreamwave Productions: Apr, 2003 - No. 8, Nov, 2003 ($5.25)
1-8-Pin-ups with tech info on Autobots and Decepticons; art by Pat Lee & various 5.25
Vol. 1,2 (2004, $24.95, TPB) 1-r/#1-4. 2-r/#5-8 25.00

Transformers: Nefarious #5 © Hasbro

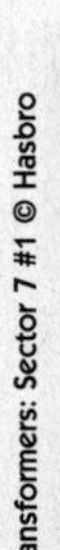

Transformers: Sector 7 #1 © Hasbro

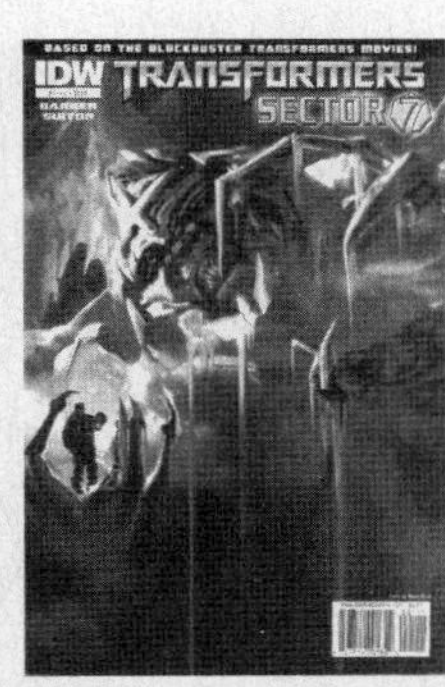

Transformers: Till All are One #2 © Hasbro

GD VG FN VF VF/NM NM-
2.0 4.0 6.0 8.0 9.0 9.2

TRANSFORMERS: MORE THAN MEETS THE EYE
IDW Publishing: Jan, 2012 - No. 57, Sept, 2016 ($3.99)

1-49: 1-Five covers; Roche-a. 2-Three covers; Milne-a. 23-27-Dark Cybertron x-over. 26-1st app. of Windblade 4.00
50-(2/16, $7.99) "The Dying of the Light" begins; five covers 8.00
51-57: 51-55-The Dying of the Light. 56,57-Titans Return 4.00
Annual 2012 (8/12, $7.99) Salgado & Cabaltierra-a; three covers 8.00
...: Revolution 1 (11/16, $3.99) Revolution tie-in; Roche-s/Roberts-a; multiple covers 4.00

TRANSFORMERS: MOVIE ADAPTATION (For the 2007 live action movie)
IDW Publishing: June, 2007 - No. 4, June, 2007 ($3.99, weekly limited series)

1-4: Wraparound covers on each; Milne-a 4.00

TRANSFORMERS: MOVIE PREQUEL (For the 2007 live action movie)
IDW Publishing: Feb, 2007 - No. 4, May, 2007 ($3.99, limited series)

1-4: 1-Origin of the Transformers on Cybertron; multiple covers on each 4.00
Special (6/08, $3.99) 2 covers 4.00
TPB (6/07, $19.99) r/series; gallery of covers and variants 20.00

TRANSFORMERS: NEFARIOUS (Sequel to Transformers: Revenge of the Fallen movie)
IDW Publishing: Mar, 2010 - No. 6, Aug, 2010 ($3.99, limited series)

1-6: Furman-s; multiple covers on all 4.00

TRANSFORMERS: PRIMACY
IDW Publishing: Aug, 2014 - No. 4, Nov, 2014 ($3.99, limited series)

1-4-Metzen & Dille-s/Ramondelli-a; Omega Supreme app.; multiple covers on each 4.00

TRANSFORMERS: PRIME
IDW Publishing: Jan, 2011 - No. 4, Jan, 2011 ($3.99, weekly limited series)

1-4: 1-Mike Johnson-s/E.J. Su-a 4.00

TRANSFORMERS PRIME: BEAST HUNTERS
IDW Publishing: May, 2013 - No. 8, Dec, 2013($3.99, limited series)

1-8-Agustin Padilla-a 4.00

TRANSFORMERS PRIME: RAGE OF THE DINOBOTS
IDW Publishing: Nov, 2012 - No. 4, Feb, 2013 ($3.99, limited series)

1-4: 1-Mike Johnson-s/Agustin Padilla-a 4.00

TRANSFORMERS: PUNISHMENT
IDW Publishing: Jan, 2015 ($5.99, squarebound, one-shot)

1-Windblade app.; Barber-s/Ramondelli-a 6.00

TRANSFORMERS: REDEMPTION
IDW Publishing: Oct, 2015 ($7.99, squarebound, one-shot)

1-Dinobots app.; John Barber-s/Livio Ramondelli-a 8.00

TRANSFORMERS: REGENERATION ONE (Continues story from Transformers #80 (1991))
IDW Publishing: No. 80.5, May, 2012 - No. 100, Mar, 2014 ($3.99)

80.5 (5/12, Free Comic Book Day giveaway) Furman-s/Wildman-a 3.00
81-99 ($3.99) 81-92-Furman-s/Wildman-a; multiple covers on all 4.00
100-($5.99) Six covers; Furman-s/Wildman, Senior & Guidi-a; bonus cover gallery 6.00
#0 (9/13, $3.99) Hot Rod in the timestream; various artists; 4 covers 4.00
... 100-Page Spectacular (7/12, $7.99) Reprints Transformers #76-80 (1991) 8.00

TRANSFORMERS: REVENGE OF THE FALLEN OFFICIAL MOVIE ADAPTATION
(For the 2009 live action movie sequel)
IDW Publishing: May, 2009 - No. 4, June, 2009 ($3.99, weekly limited series)

1-4: Furman-s; 2 covers on each 4.00

TRANSFORMERS: RISING STORM (Prequel to 2011 Transformers: Dark of the Moon movie)
IDW Publishing: Feb, 2011 - No. 4, May, 2011 ($3.99, limited series)

1-3-Barber-s/Magno-a; 2 covers 4.00

TRANSFORMERS: ROBOTS IN DISGUISE (Re-titled Transformers #35-on)
IDW Publishing: Jan, 2012 - No. 34, Oct, 2014 ($3.99)

1-34: 1-Five covers; Griffith-a. 2-27-Three covers. 23-27-Dark Cybertron x-over 4.00

TRANSFORMERS: ROBOTS IN DISGUISE (Based on the animated series)
IDW Publishing: No. 0, May, 2015 - Present ($3.99)

0-Free Comic Book Day Edition; Barber-s/Tramontano-a; Bumblebee & Strongarm app. 3.00
1-5: 1-Georgia Ball-s/Priscilla Tramontano-a 4.00

TRANSFORMERS: SAGA OF THE ALLSPARK (From the 2007 live action movie)
IDW Publishing: Jul, 2008 - No. 4, Oct, 2008 ($3.99, limited series)

1-4-Launch of the Allspark into outer space; Furman-s/Roche-c 4.00

TRANSFORMERS: SECTOR 7 (From the 2007 live action movie)
IDW Publishing: Sept, 2010 - No. 5, Jan, 2011 ($3.99, limited series)

GD VG FN VF VF/NM NM-
2.0 4.0 6.0 8.0 9.0 9.2

1-5-Barber-s 4.00

TRANSFORMERS: SINS OF THE WRECKERS
IDW Publishing: Nov, 2015 - No. 5, May, 2016 ($3.99, limited series)

1-5-Roche-s/Burcham-a 4.00

TRANSFORMERS: SPOTLIGHT
IDW Publishing: Sept, 2006 - Present ($3.99, multiple covers on each)

... Arcee (2/08); ... Blaster (1/08); ... Blurr (11/08); ... Bumblebee (3/13); ... Cliffjumper (6/09); ... Cyclonus (6/08); ...Doubledealer (8/08); ...Drift (4/09); ...Galvatron (7/07);...Grimlock (3/08); ...Hardhead (7/08); ... Hoist (5/13); ... Hot Rod (11/06); ... Jazz (3/09); ... Kup (4/07); ... Megatron (2/13); ... Metroplex (7/09); ... Mirage (3/08); ... Nightbeat (10/06); ... Orion Pax (12/12); ... Prowl (4/10);... Ramjet (11/07); ... Shockwave (9/06); ... Sideswipe (9/08); ... Sixshot (12/06); ... Soundwave (3/07); Thundercracker (1/13); ... Trailcutter (4/13); ... Ultra Magnus (1/07) 4.00
... Optimus Prime: 3-D (11/08, $5.99, with glasses) Furman-s/Figueroa-a 6.00

TRANSFORMERS: STORMBRINGER
IDW Publishing: Jul, 2006 - No. 4, Oct, 2006 ($2.99, limited series)

1-4-Furman-s/Figueroa-a; multiple covers on all 4.00
TPB (2/07, $17.99) r/series; cover gallery and sketch pages 18.00

TRANSFORMERS SUMMER SPECIAL
Dreamwave Productions: May, 2004 ($4.95)

1-Pat Lee-a; Figueroa-a 5.00

TRANSFORMERS: TALES OF THE FALLEN
IDW Publishing: Aug, 2009 - No. 6 ($3.99, limited series)

1-6: 2,4-Furman-s mulitple covers on all 4.00

TRANSFORMERS: TARGET 2006
IDW Publishing: Apr, 2007 - No. 5, Aug, 2007 ($3.99, limited series)

1-5-Reprints from 1980s series; multiple covers on all 4.00

TRANSFORMERS: THE ANIMATED MOVIE
IDW Publishing: Oct, 2006 - No. 4, Jan, 2007 ($3.99, limited series)

1-4-Adapts animated movie; Don Figueroa-a 4.00

TRANSFORMERS, THE MOVIE
Marvel Comics Group: Dec, 1986 - No. 3, Feb, 1987 (75¢, limited series)

1-3-Adapts animated movie 2 4 6 8 10 12

TRANSFORMERS: THE REIGN OF STARSCREAM
IDW Publishing: Apr, 2008 - No. 5, Aug, 2008 ($3.99, limited series)

1-5-Continuation of the 2007 movie; Milne-a; multiple covers 4.00

TRANSFORMERS: THE WAR WITHIN
Dreamwave Productions: Oct, 2002 - No. 6, Mar, 2003 ($2.95)

1-6-Furman-s/Figueroa-a. 1-Wraparound gatefold-c 4.00
TPB (2003, $15.95) r/#1-6; plus cover gallery 16.00

TRANSFORMERS: TILL ALL ARE ONE
IDW Publishing: Jun, 2016 - Present ($3.99)

1-6-Road to Revolution; Mairghread Scott-s; multiple covers on all 4.00
...: Revolution 1 (10/16, $3.99) Revolution tie-in; Windblade app.; multiple covers 4.00

TRANSFORMERS UNIVERSE
Marvel Comics Group: Dec, 1986 - No. 4, Mar, 1987 ($1.25, limited series)

1-4-A guide to all characters 1 3 4 6 8 10
TPB-r/#1-4 15.00

TRANSFORMERS VS. G.I. JOE
IDW Publishing: No. 0, May, 2014 - No. 13, Jun, 2016 ($3.99)

Free Comic Book Day #0 (5/14, giveaway) Tom Scioli-a; Scioli & John Barber-s 3.00
1-12-Tom Scioli-a; Scioli & John Barber-s; multiple covers on each; creator commentary 4.00
13-($7.99, squarebound) Last issue; bonus commentary; 3 covers 8.00

TRANSFORMERS WAR WITHIN: THE AGE OF WRATH
Dreamwave Productions: Sept, 2004 - No. 6 ($2.95, limited series)

1-3-Furman-s/Ng-a 4.00

TRANSFORMERS WAR WITHIN: THE DARK AGES
Dreamwave Productions: Oct, 2003 - No. 6 ($2.95)

1-6: 1-Furman-s/Wildman-a; two covers by Pat Lee & Figueroa 4.00
TPB (2004, $17.95) r/#1-6; plus cover gallery and design sketches 18.00

TRANSFORMERS: WINDBLADE (See Transformers More Than Meets the Eye #26)
IDW Publishing: Apr, 2014 - No. 4, Jul, 2014 ($3.99, limited series)

1-4-Mairghread Scott-s/Sarah Stone-a; three covers on each 4.00
Vol. 2 (3/15 - No. 7, 9/15, $3.99) 1-7-Scott-s; multiple covers on each. 1-Stone-a 4.00

Transmetropolitan #14 © Ellis & Robertson

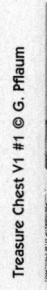

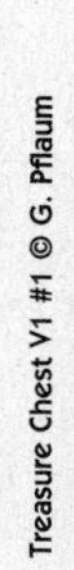
Treasure Chest V1 #1 © G. Pflaum

Treasure Comics #9 © PRIZE

GD 2.0 VG 4.0 FN 6.0 VF 8.0 VF/NM 9.0 NM- 9.2

TRANSFUSION
IDW Publishing: Oct, 2012 - No. 3, Feb, 2013 ($3.99, limited series)
1-3-Vampires vs. Robots; Niles-s/Menton3-a 4.00

TRANSIT
Vortex Publ.: March, 1987 - No. 5, Nov, 1987 (B&W)
1-5-Ted McKeever-s/a 1 2 3 5 6 8

TRANSLUCID
BOOM! Studios: Apr, 2014 - No. 6, Sept, 2014 ($3.99)
1-6-Sanchez & Echert-s/Bayliss-a; multiple covers on each 4.00

TRANSMETROPOLITAN
DC Comics (Helix/Vertigo): Sept, 1997 - No. 60, Nov, 2002 ($2.50)
1-Warren Ellis-s/Darick Robertson-a(p) 4 8 12 27 44 60
1-Special Edition (5/09, $1.00) r/#1 with "After Watchmen" cover frame 3.00
2,3 1 3 4 6 8 10
4-8 5.00
9-60: 15-Jae Lee-c. 25-27-Jim Lee-c. 37-39-Bradstreet-c 3.00
Back on the Street ('97, $7.95) r/#1-3 10.00
Back on the Street ('09, $14.99) r/#1-6; intro. by Garth Ennis 15.00
Dirge ('03/'10, $14.95/$14.99) r/#43-48 15.00
Filth of the City ('01, $5.95) Spider's columns with pin-up art by various 6.00
Gouge Away ('02/'09, $14.95/$14.99) r/#31-36 15.00
I Hate It Here ('00, $5.95) Spider's columns with pin-up art by various 6.00
Lonely City ('01/'09, $14.95/$14.99) r/#25-30; intro. by Patrick Stewart 15.00
Lust For Life ('98, $14.95) r/#4-12 20.00
Lust For Life ('09, $14.99) r/#7-12 15.00
One More Time ('04, $14.95) r/#55-60 15.00
One More Time ('11, $19.99) r/#55-60 & Filth of the City & I Hate It Here one-shots 20.00
Spider's Thrash ('02/'10, $14.95/$14.99) r/#37-42; intro. by Darren Aronofsky 15.00
Tales of Human Waste ('04, $9.95) r/Filth of the City, I Hate It Here & story from Vertigo Winter's Edge 2 10.00
The Cure ('03/'11, $14.95/$14.99) r/#49-54 15.00
The New Scum ('00, $12.95) r/#19-24 & Vertigo: Winter's Edge #3 15.00
The New Scum ('09, $14.99) r/#19-24 & Vertigo: Winter's Edge #3 15.00
Year of the Bastard ('99, $12.95)('09, $12.99) r/#13-18 13.00

TRANSMUTATION OF IKE GARUDA, THE
Marvel Comics (Epic Comics): July, 1991 - No. 2, 1991 ($3.95, 52 pgs.)
1,2 4.00

TRAPPED!
Periodical House Magazines (Ace): Oct, 1954 - No. 4, April, 1955
1 (All reprints) 10 20 30 54 72 90
2-4: 4-r/Men Against Crime #4 in its entirety 7 14 21 35 43 50
NOTE: *Colan a-1, 4. Sekowsky a-1.*

TRASH
Trash Publ. Co.: Mar, 1978 - No. 4, Oct, 1978 (B&W, magazine, 52 pgs.)
1,2: 1-Star Wars parody. 2-UFO-c 2 4 6 10 14 18
3-Parodies of KISS, the Beatles, and monsters 3 6 9 14 19 24
4-(84 pgs.)-Parodies of Happy Days, Rocky movies 3 6 9 14 20 26

TRAVELER, THE (Developed by Stan Lee)
BOOM! Studios: Nov, 2010 - No. 12, Oct, 2011 ($3.99)
1-12-Waid-s/Hardin-a; three covers on each 4.00

TRAVELS OF JAIMIE McPHEETERS, THE (TV)
Gold Key: Dec, 1963
1-Kurt Russell photo on-c plus photo back-c 4 8 12 25 40 55

TREASURE CHEST (Catholic Guild; also see Topix)
George A. Pflaum: 3/12/46 - V27#8, July, 1972 (Educational comics) (Not published during Summer)
V1#1 30 60 90 177 289 400
2-6 (5/21/46): 5-Dr. Styx app. by Baily 14 28 42 80 115 150
V2#1-20 (9/3/46-5/27/47) 11 22 33 60 83 105
V3#1-5,7-20 (1st slick cover) 10 20 30 54 72 90
V3#6-Jules Verne's "Voyage to the Moon" 12 24 36 67 94 120
V4#1-20 (9/9/48-5/31/49) 9 18 27 47 61 75
V5#1-20 (9/6/49-5/31/50) 8 16 24 44 57 70
V6#1-20 (9/14/50-5/31/51) 8 16 24 42 54 65
V7#1-20 (9/13/51-6/5/52) 8 16 24 40 50 60
V8#1-20 (9/11/52-6/4/53) 7 14 21 37 46 55
V9#1-20 ('53-'54), V10#1-20 ('54-'55) 7 14 21 35 43 50
V11('55-'56), V12('56-'57) 6 12 18 29 36 42
V13#1,3-5,7,9-20-V17#1 ('57-'63) 6 12 18 27 33 38
V13#2,6,8-Ingels-a 5 10 15 35 63 90
V17#2- "This Godless Communism" series begins(not in odd #'d issues); cover shows hammer & sickle over Statue of Liberty; 8 pg. Crandall-a of family life under communism (9/28/61) 16 32 48 112 249 385
V17#3,5,7,9,11,13,15,17,19 3 6 9 16 24 32
V17#4,6,14- "This Godless Communism" stories 12 24 36 84 185 285
V17#8-Shows red octopus encompassing Earth, firing squad; 8 pgs. Crandall-a (12/21/61) 15 30 45 105 233 360
V17#10- "This Godless Communism" - how Stalin came to power, part I; Crandall-a 13 26 39 91 201 310
V17#12-Stalin in WWII, forced labor, death by exhaustion; Crandall-a 13 26 39 91 201 310
V17#16-Kruschev takes over; de-Stalinization 13 26 39 91 201 310
V17#18-Kruschev's control; murder of revolters, brainwash, space race by Crandall 13 26 39 91 201 310
V17#20-End of series; Kruschev-people are puppets, firing squads hammer & sickle over Statue of Liberty, snake around communist manifesto by Crandall 16 32 48 112 249 385
V18#1,3,4,6-10,12-20, V19#11-20, V20#1-20(1964-65): V20#6-JFK photo-c & story. V20#16-Babe Ruth-c & story by Sinnott 3 6 9 16 23 30
V18#2-Kruschev on-c (9/27/62) 3 6 9 19 30 40
V18#5- "What About Red China?" - describes how communists took over China 9 18 27 58 99 140
V18#11-Crandall draws himself & 13 other artists on cover (1/31/63) 3 6 9 20 30 40
V19#1-10- "Red Victim" anti-communist series in all 8 16 24 51 96 140
V21, V22 #1-16,18-20,V23-V25(1965-70)-(two V24#5's 11/7/68 & 11/21/68) (no V24#6): 3 6 9 14 19 24
V22#17-Flying saucer wraparound-c 3 6 9 16 24 32
V26, V27#1-8 (V26,27-68 pgs.) 3 6 9 15 22 28
Summer Edition V1#1-6('66), V2#1-6('67) 3 6 9 16 23 30
NOTE: *Anderson a-V18#13. Borth a-V7#10-19 (serial), V8#8-17 (serial), V9#1-10 (serial), V13#2, 6, 11, V14-V25 (except V22#1-3, 11-13), Summer Ed. V1#3-6. Crandall a-V16#7, 9, 12, 14, 16-18, 20; V17#1, 2, 4-6, 10, 12, 14, 16-18, 20; V18#1, 2, 3(2 pg.), 7, 9-20; V19#4, 11, 13, 16, 19, 20; V20#1, 2, 4, 6, 8-10, 12, 14-16, 18, 20; V21#1-5, 8-11, 13, 16-18; V22#3, 7, 9-11, 14; V23#3, 6, 9, 16, 18; V24#7, 8, 10, 13, 16; V25#8, 16; V27#1-7r, 8r(2 pg.), Summer Ed. V1#3-5, V2#3; c-V16#7, V18#2(part), 7, 11, V19#4, 19, 20, V20#15, V21#5, 9, V22#3, 7, 9, 11, V23#9, 16, V24#13, 16, V25#8, Summer Ed. V1#2 (back c-V1#2-5). Powell a-V10#11. V19#11, 15, V10#13, V13#6, 8 all have wraparound covers.*

TREASURE CHEST OF THE WORLD'S BEST COMICS
Superior, Toronto, Canada: 1945 (500 pgs., hard-c)
Contains Blue Beetle, Captain Combat, John Wayne, Dynamic Man, Nemo, Li'l Abner; contents can vary - represents random binding of extra books; Captain America on-c 142 284 426 909 1555 2200

TREASURE COMICS
Prize Publications? (no publisher listed): No date (1943) (50¢, 324 pgs., cardboard-c)
1-(Rare)-Contains rebound Prize Comics #7-11 from 1942 (blank inside-c) 371 742 1113 2600 4550 6500

TREASURE COMICS
Prize Publ. (American Boys' Comics): June-July, 1945 - No. 12, Fall, 1947
1-Paul Bunyan & Marco Polo begin; Highwayman & Carrot Topp only app.; Kiefer-a 53 106 159 334 567 800
2-Arabian Knight, Gorilla King, Dr. Styx begin 32 64 96 188 307 425
3,4,9,12: 9-Kiefer-a 25 50 75 150 245 340
5-Marco Polo-c; Krigstein-a 32 64 96 190 310 430
6,11-Krigstein-a; 11-Krigstein-c 31 62 93 186 303 420
7,8-Frazetta-a (5 pgs. each). 7-Capt. Kidd Jr. app. 41 82 123 260 435 610
10-Simon & Kirby-c/a 38 76 114 228 369 510
NOTE: *Barry a-9-11; c-12. Kiefer a-3, 5, 7; c-2, 6, 7. Roussos a-11.*

TREASURE ISLAND (See Classics Illustrated #64, Doc Savage Comics #1, King Classics, Movie Classics & Movie Comics)
Dell Publishing Co.: No. 624, Apr, 1955 (Disney)
Four Color 624-Movie, photo-c 7 14 21 48 89 130

TREASURY OF COMICS
St. John Publishing Co.: 1947; No. 2, July, 1947 - No. 4, Sept, 1947; No. 5, Jan, 1948
nn(#1)-Abbie an' Slats (nn on-c, #1 on inside) 14 28 42 82 121 160
2-Jim Hardy Comics; featuring Windy & Paddles 11 22 33 64 90 115
3-Bill Bumlin 10 20 30 56 76 95
4-Abbie an' Slats 11 22 33 64 90 115
5-Jim Hardy Comics #1 11 22 33 64 90 115

TREASURY OF COMICS
St. John Publishing Co.: Mar, 1948 - No. 5, 1948 (Reg. size); 1948-1950

Treehouse of Horror #22 © Bongo

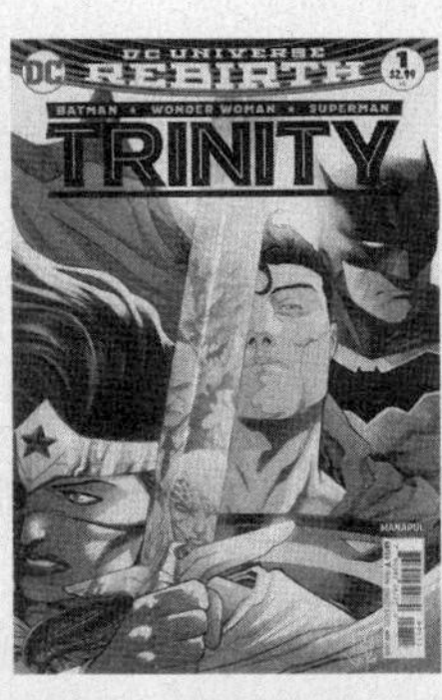

Trinity (2016 series) #1 © DC

Triple Helix #1 © John Byrne

	GD 2.0	VG 4.0	FN 6.0	VF 8.0	VF/NM 9.0	NM- 9.2
(Over 500 pgs., $1.00)						
1	20	40	60	114	182	250
2(#2 on-c, #1 on inside)	12	24	36	69	97	125
3-5	10	20	30	58	79	100
1-(1948, 500 pgs., hard-c)-Abbie & Slats, Abbott & Costello, Casper, Little Annie Rooney, Little Audrey, Jim Hardy, Ella Cinders (16 books bound together) (Rare)	206	412	618	1318	2259	3200
1(1949, 500 pgs.)-Same format as above	161	322	483	1030	1765	2500
1(1950, 500 pgs.)-Same format as above; different-c; (also see Little Audrey Yearbook) (Rare)	161	322	483	1030	1765	2500

TREASURY OF DOGS, A (See Dell Giants)

TREASURY OF HORSES, A (See Dell Giants)

TREEHOUSE OF HORROR (Bart Simpson's...)
Bongo Comics: 1995 - Present ($2.95/$2.50/$3.50/$4.50/$4.99, annual)

1-(1995, $2.95)-Groening-c; Allred, Robinson & Smith stories 2 4 6 11 16 20
2-(1996, $2.50)-Stories by Dini & Bagge; infinity-c by Groening 5.00
3-(1997, $2.50)-Dorkin-s/Groening-c 5.00
4-(1998, $2.50)-Lash & Dixon-s/Groening-c 5.00
5-(1999, $3.50)-Thompson-s; Shaw & Aragonés-s/a; TenNapel-s/a 5.00
6-(2000, $4.50)-Mahfood-s/a; DeCarlo-a; Morse-s/a; Kuper-s/a 5.00
7-(2001, $4.50)-Hamill-s/Morrison-a; Ennis-s/McCrea-a; Sakai-s/a; Nixey-s/a; Brereton back-c 5.00
8-(2002, $3.50)-Templeton, Shaw, Barta, Simone, Thompson-s/a 5.00
9-(2003, $4.99)-Lord of the Rings-Brereton-a; Dini, Naifeh, Millidge, Boothby, Noto-s/a 5.00
10-(2004, $4.99)-Monsters of Rock w/Alice Cooper, Gene Simmons, Rob Zombie and Pat Boone; art by Rodriguez, Morrison, Morse, Templeton 5.00
11-(2005, $4.99)-EC style w/art by John Severin, Angelo Torres & Al Williamson and flip book with Dracula by Wolfman/Colan and Squish Thing by Wein/Wrightson 5.00
12-(2006, $4.99)-Terry Moore, Kyle Baker, Eric Powell-s/a 5.00
13-(2007, $4.99)-Oswalt, Posehn, Lennon-s; Guerra, Austin, Barta, Rodriguez-a 5.00
14-(2008, $4.99)-s/a by Niles & Fabry; Boothby & Matsumoto; Gilbert Hernandez 5.00
15-(2009, $4.99)-s/a by Jeffrey Brown, Tim Hensley, Ben Jones and others 5.00
16-(2010, $4.99)-s/a by Kelley Jones, Evan Dorkin and others; Mars Attacks homage 5.00
17-(2011, $4.99)-s/a by Gene Ha, Jane Wiedlin and others; Nosferatu homage 5.00
18-(2012, $4.99)-s/a by Jim Valentino, Phil Noto and others; Rosemary's Baby spoof 5.00
19-(2013, $4.99)-s/a by Len Wein, Dan Brereton and others; Cthulhu spoof 5.00
20-(2014, $4.99)-All Zombie issue, including The Walking Ned 5.00
21-(2015, $4.99)-Gremlins & Metropolis spoofs 5.00
22-(2016, $4.99)-Ghostbusters & Gossamer spoofs 5.00

TREES
Image Comics: May, 2014 - Present ($2.99)

1-14-Warren Ellis-s/Jason Howard-a 3.00

TREKKER (See Dark Horse Presents #6)
Dark Horse Comics: May, 1987 - No. 6, Mar, 1988 ($1.50, B&W)

1-6: Sci/Fi stories 3.00
Color Special 1 (1989, $2.95, 52 pgs.) 4.00
Collection ($5.95, B&W) 6.00
Special 1 (6/99, $2.95, color) 3.00

TRENCHCOAT BRIGADE, THE
DC Comics (Vertigo): Mar, 1999 - No. 4, Jun, 1999 ($2.50, limited series)

1-4: Hellblazer, Phantom Stranger, Mister E, Dr. Occult app. 3.00

TRENCHER (See Blackball Comics)
Image Comics: May, 1993 - No. 4, Oct, 1993 ($1.95, unfinished limited series)

1-4: Keith Giffen-c/a/scripts. 3-Supreme-c/story 3.00

TRIALS OF SHAZAM!
DC Comics: Oct, 2006 - No. 12, May, 2008 ($2.99)

1-12: 1-8-Winick-s/Porter-a. 9-11-Cascioli-a. 10-Shadowpact app. 12-JLA app. 3.00
... Volume 1 TPB (2007, $14.99) r/#1-6 and story from DCU Brave New World #1 15.00
... Volume 2 TPB (2008, $14.99) r/#7-12 15.00

TRIB COMIC BOOK, THE
Winnipeg Tribune: Sept. 24, 1977 - Vol. 4, #36, 1980 (8-1/2"x11", 24 pgs., weekly) (155 total issues)

	GD	VG	FN	VF	VF/NM	NM-
V1# 1-Color pages (Sunday strips)-Spiderman, Asterix, Disney's Scamp, Wizard of Id, Doonesbury, Inside Woody Allen, Mary Worth, & others (similar to Spirit sections)	2	4	6	10	14	18
V1#2-15, V2#1-52, V3#1-52, V4#1-33	1	3	4	6	8	10
V4#34-36 (not distributed)	2	4	6	11	16	20

NOTE: *All issues have Spider-Man. Later issues contain Star Trek and Star Wars. 20 strips in ea. The first newspaper to put Sunday pages into a comic book format.*

TRIBE (See WildC.A.T.S #4)
Image Comics/Axis Comics No. 2 on: Apr, 1993; No. 2, Sept, 1993 - No. 3, 1994 ($2.50/$1.95)

1-By Johnson & Stroman; gold foil & embossed on black-c 4.00
1-($2.50)-Ivory Edition; gold foil & embossed on white-c; available only through the creators 4.00
2,3: 2-1st Axis Comics issue. 3-Savage Dragon app. 3.00

TRIBUTE TO STEVEN HUGHES, A
Chaos! Comics: Sept, 2000 ($6.95)

1-Lady Death & Evil Ernie pin-ups by various artists; testimonials 7.00

TRICK 'R TREAT
DC Comics (WildStorm): 2009 ($19.95,SC)

nn-Short Halloween-themed story anthology; Andreyko-s; art by Huddleston & others 20.00

TRIGGER (See Roy Rogers'...)

TRIGGER
DC Comics (Vertigo): Feb, 2005 - No. 8, Sept, 2005 ($2.95/$2.99)

1-8-Jason Hall-s/John Watkiss-a/c 3.00

TRIGGER TWINS
National Periodical Publications: Mar-Apr, 1973 (20¢, one-shot)

1-Trigger Twins & Pow Wow Smith-r/All-Star Western #94,103 & Western Comics #81; Infantino-r(p) 2 4 6 13 18 22

TRILLIUM
DC Comics (Vertigo): Oct, 2013 - No. 8, Jun, 2014 ($2.99)

1-8-Jeff Lemire-s/a. 1-Flip-book 3.00

TRINITY (See DC Universe: Trinity)

TRINITY
DC Comics: Aug, 2008 - No. 52, July, 2009 ($2.99, weekly series)

1-52-Superman, Batman & Wonder Woman star; Busiek-s/Bagley-a. 52-Wraparound-c 3.00
Vol. 1 TPB (2009, $29.99) r/#1-17 30.00
Vol. 2 TPB (2009, $29.99) r/#18-35 30.00
Vol. 3 TPB (2009, $29.99) r/#36-52 30.00

TRINITY (DC Rebirth)
DC Comics: Nov, 2016 - Present ($2.99)

1-6: 1-Superman, Batman & Wonder Woman; Manapul-s/a. 3-Mann-a. 4-6-Mongul app. 3.00

TRINITY ANGELS
Acclaim Comics (Valiant Heroes): July, 1997 - No. 12, June, 1998 ($2.50)

1-12-Maguire-s/a(p):4-Copycat-c 3.00

TRINITY: BLOOD ON THE SANDS
Image Comics (Top Cow): July, 2009 ($2.99, one-shot)

1-Witchblade, The Darkness and Angelus in the 14th century Arabian desert 3.00

TRINITY OF SIN (DC New 52)
DC Comics: Dec, 2014 - No. 6, May, 2015 ($2.99)

1-6-Pandora, The Question and Phantom Stranger; Guichet-a 3.00

TRINITY OF SIN: PANDORA (DC New 52)
DC Comics: Aug, 2013 - No. 14, Oct, 2014 ($2.99)

1-14: 1-Fawkes-s; origin re-told. 1-3-Trinity War tie-ins. 4-9-Forever Evil tie-ins 3.00
...: Futures End 1 (11/14, $2.99, regular-c) Five years later; Pandora vs. 7 Deadly Sins 3.00
...: Futures End 1 (11/14, $3.99, 3-D cover) 4.00

TRINITY OF SIN: THE PHANTOM STRANGER (See Phantom Stranger 2012 series)

TRIO (Continues in Triple Helix #1)
IDW Publishing: May, 2012 - No. 4, Aug, 2012 ($3.99, limited series)

1-4-John Byrne-s/a/c 4.00

TRIPLE GIANT COMICS (See Archie All-Star Specials under Archie Comics)

TRIPLE HELIX (Also see Trio)
IDW Publishing: Oct, 2013 - No. 4, Jan, 2014 ($3.99, limited series)

1-4-John Byrne-s/a/c; The Trio app. 4.00

TRIPLE THREAT
Special Action/Holyoke/Gerona Publ.: Winter, 1945

1-Duke of Darkness, King O'Leary 37 74 111 222 361 500

TRISH OUT OF WATER
Aspen MLT: Oct, 2013 - No. 5, Mar, 2014 ($1.00/$3.99)

Triumph #2 © DC

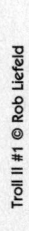

Troll II #1 © Rob Liefeld

True Believers #1 © MAR

GD 2.0 | VG 4.0 | FN 6.0 | VF 8.0 | VF/NM 9.0 | NM- 9.2

1-($1.00) Vince Hernandez-s/Giuseppe Cafaro-a; multiple covers 3.00
2-5-($3.99) Multiple covers on each 4.00

TRIUMPH (Also see JLA #28-30, Justice League Task Force & Zero Hour)
DC Comics: June, 1995 - No. 4, Sept, 1995 ($1.75, limited series)
1-4: 3-Hourman, JLA app. 3.00

TRIUMPHANT UNLEASHED
Triumphant Comics: No. 0, Nov, 1993 - No. 1, Nov, 1993 ($2.50, lim. series)
0-Serially numbered, 0-Red logo, 0-White logo (no cover price; giveaway), 1-Cover is negative & reverse of #0-c 3.00

TROJAN WAR (Adaptation of Trojan war histories from ancient Greek and Roman sources)
Marvel Comics: July, 2009 - No. 5, Nov, 2009 ($3.99, limited series)
1-5-Roy Thomas-s/Miguel Sepulveda-a/Dennis Calero-c 4.00

TROLL (Also see Brigade)
Image Comics (Extreme Studios): Dec, 1993 ($2.50, one-shot, 44 pgs.)
1-1st app. Troll; Liefeld scripts; Matsuda-c/a(p) 4.00
Halloween Special (1994, $2.95)-Maxx app. 4.00
...Once A Hero (8/94, $2.50) 4.00

TROLLORDS
Tru Studios/Comico V2#1 on: 2/86 - No. 15, 1988; V2#1, 11/88 - V2#4, 1989 (1-15: $1.50, B&W)
1-First printing 5.00
1-Second printing, 2-15: 6-Christmas issue; silver logo 3.00
V2#1-4 ($1.75, color, Comico) 3.00
Special 1 ($1.75, 2/87, color)-Jerry's Big Fun Bk. 3.00

TROLLORDS
Apple Comics: July, 1989 - No. 6, 1990 ($2.25, B&W, limited series)
1-6: 1-"The Big Batman Movie Parody" 3.00

TROLL PATROL
Harvey Comics: Jan, 1993 ($1.95, 52 pgs.)
1 4.00

TROLL II (Also see Brigade)
Image Comics (Extreme Studios): July, 1994 ($3.95, one-shot)
1 4.00

TRON (Based on the video game and film)
Slave Labor Graphics: Apr, 2006 - No. 6 ($3.50/$3.95)
1-4: 1-DeMartinis-a/Walker & Jones-s 4.00
5,6-($3.95) 4.00

TRON: BETRAYAL
Marvel Comics: Nov, 2010 - No. 2, Dec, 2010 ($3.99, limited series)
1,2-Prequel to Tron Legacy movie; Larroca-c 4.00

TRON: ORIGINAL MOVIE ADAPTATION
Marvel Comics: Jan, 2011 - No. 2, Feb, 2011 ($3.99, limited series)
1,2-Peter David-s/Mirco Pierfederici-a/Greg Land-c 4.00

TROUBLE
Marvel Comics (Epic): Sept, 2003 - No. 5, Jan, 2004 ($2.99, limited series)
1-5-Photo-c; Richard and Ben meet Mary and May; Millar-s/Dodson-a 3.00
1-2nd printing with variant Frank Cho-c 5.00

TROUBLED SOULS
Fleetway: 1990 ($9.95, trade paperback)
nn-Garth Ennis scripts & John McCrea painted-c/a. 10.00

TROUBLEMAKERS
Acclaim Comics (Valiant Heroes): Apr, 1997 - No. 19, June, 1998 ($2.50)
1-19: Fabian Nicieza scripts in all. 1-1st app. XL, Rebound & Blur; 2 covers. 8-Copycat-c. 12-Shooting of Parker 3.00

TROUBLE SHOOTERS, THE (TV)
Dell Publishing Co.: No. 1108, Jun-Aug, 1960
Four Color 1108-Keenan Wynn photo-c 6 12 18 37 66 95

TROUBLE WITH GIRLS, THE
Malibu Comics (Eternity Comics) #7-14/Comico V2#1-4/Eternity V2#5 on: 8/87 - #14, 1988; V2#1, 2/89 - V2#23, 1991? ($1.95, B&W/color)
1-14 ($1.95, B&W, Eternity)-Gerard Jones scripts & Tim Hamilton-c/a in all 3.00
V2#1-23-Jones scripts, Hamilton-c/a. 3.00
Annual 1 (1988, $2.95) 4.00
Christmas Special 1 (12/91, $2.95, B&W, Eternity)-Jones scripts, Hamilton-c/a 4.00
Graphic Novel 1,2 (7/88, B&W)-r/#1-3 & #4-6 8.00

TROUBLE WITH GIRLS, THE: NIGHT OF THE LIZARD
Marvel Comics (Epic Comics/Heavy Hitters): 1993 - No. 4, 1993 ($2.50/$1.95, lim. series)
1-Embossed-c; Gerard Jones scripts & Bret Blevins-c/a in all 4.00
2-4: 2-Begin $1.95-c. 3.00

TRUE ADVENTURES (Formerly True Western)(Men's Adventures #4 on)
Marvel Comics (CCC): No. 3, May, 1950 (52 pgs.)
3-Powell, Sekowsky-a; Brodsky-c 22 44 66 132 216 300

TRUE ANIMAL PICTURE STORIES
True Comics Press: Winter, 1947 - No. 2, Spring-Summer, 1947
1 13 26 39 72 101 130
2 11 22 33 62 86 110

TRUE AVIATION PICTURE STORIES (Becomes Aviation Adventures & Model Building #16 on)
Parents' Mag. Institute: 1942; No. 2, Jan-Feb, 1943 - No. 15, Sept-Oct, 1946
1-(#1 & 2 titled ...Aviation Comics Digest)(not digest size) 16 32 48 94 147 200
2 11 22 33 60 83 105
3-14: 3-10-Plane photos on-c. 11,13-Photo-c 10 20 30 54 72 90
15-(Titled "True Aviation Adventures & Model Building") 9 18 27 50 65 80

TRUE BELIEVERS
Marvel Comics: Sept, 2008 - No. 5, Jan, 2009 ($2.99, limited series)
1-5-Cary Bates-s/Paul Gulacy-a. 1,2-Reed Richards app. 3-Luke Cage app. 3.00

TRUE BELIEVERS...
Marvel Comics: Jun, 2015 - Present ($1.00, series of one-shot reprints)
...: Age of Apocalypse 1 - Reprints X-Men: Alpha #1; Cruz & Epting-a; wraparound-c 3.00
...: Age of Ultron 1 - Reprints Age of Ultron #1; Bendis-s/Hitch-a 3.00
...: All-New, All-Different Avengers - Cyclone 1 - Reprints issue #4; Waid-s/Asrar-a 3.00
...: All-New Wolverine 1 - Reprints issue #1; Taylor-s/Lopez-a 3.00
...: Amazing Spider-Man - The Dark Kingdom 1 - Reprints Amazing Spider-Man #6 3.00
...: Armor Wars 1 - Reprints Iron Man #225; Michelinie-s/Bright & Layton-a 3.00
...: Black Widow 1 - Reprints Black Widow #1 (2014); Edmondson-s/Noto-a 3.00
...: Captain Marvel 1 - Reprints Captain Marvel #1 (2014); DeConnick-s/Lopez-a 3.00
...: Chewbacca 1 - Reprints Chewbacca #1; Duggan-s/Noto-a 3.00
...: Civil War 1 - Reprints Civil War #1; Millar-s/McNiven-a 3.00
...: Daredevil - Practice to Deceive 1 - Reprints Daredevil #6 (2016); Soule-s/Buffagni-a 3.00
...: Darth Vader 1 - Reprints Darth Vader #1; Gillen-s/Larroca-a 3.00
...: Deadpool 1 - Reprints 1st app. from New Mutants #98 (1991); Liefeld-a 3.00
...: Deadpool - Deadpool vs. Sabretooth 1 - Reprints Deadpool #8 (2016) 3.00
...: Deadpool Origins 1 - Reprints Wolverine Origins #25; Dillon-a 3.00
...: Deadpool The Musical 1 - Reprints Deadpool #49.1; McCrea-a 3.00
...: Deadpool Variants 1 - Gallery of variant covers 3.00
...: Detective Deadpool 1 - Reprints Cable & Deadpool #13; Nicieza-s/Zircher-a 3.00
...: Doctor Strange - The Last Days of Magic 1 - Reprints Doctor Strange #6 (2015) 3.00
...: Droids 1 - Reprints Droids #1; Star Wars C-3PO & R2-D2 app.; John Romita-a 3.00
...: Evil Deadpool 1 - Reprints Deadpool #45; Espin-a 3.00
...: Extraordinary X-Men - The Burning Man 1 - Reprints issue #6; Ibañez-a 3.00
...: Guardians of the Galaxy - Galaxy's Most Wanted 1 - Reprints GOTG #6 (2015) 3.00
...: House of M 1 - Reprints House of M #1; Bendis-s/Coipel-a 3.00
...: Infinity Gauntlet 1 - Reprints Infinity Gauntlet #1; Starlin-s/Pérez-a 3.00
...: Invincible Iron Man - The War Machines 1 - Reprints Invincible Iron Man #6 3.00
...: Kanan 1 - Reprints Kanan #1; Star Wars; Weisman-s/Larraz-a 3.00
...: Lando 1 - Reprints Lando #1; Star Wars; Soule-s/Maleev-a 3.00
...: Marvel Zombies 1 - Reprints Marvel Zombies #1; Bendis-s/Phillips-a 3.00
...: Mighty Thor - The Strongest Viking There Is 1 - Reprints Mighty Thor #6 3.00
...: Miles Morales 1 - Reprints Ultimate Comics Spider-Man #1; Bendis-s/Pichelli-a 3.00
...: Ms. Marvel 1 - Reprints Ms. Marvel #1 (2014); Wilson-s/Alphona-a 3.00
...: Old Man Logan 1 - Reprints Wolverine #66 (2008); Millar-s/McNiven-a; wraparound-c 3.00
...: Planet Hulk 1 - Reprints Incredible Hulk #92 (2006); Pak-s/Pagulayan-a 3.00
...: Princess Leia 1 - Reprints Princess Leia #1; Waid-s/Dodson-a 3.00
...: Shattered Empire 1 - Reprints Journey to Star Wars: The Force Awakens – Shattered Empire #1; Rucka-s/Checchetto-a 3.00
...: She-Hulk 1 - Reprints She-Hulk #1 (2014); Soule-s/Pulido-a 3.00
...: Silk 1 - Reprints Silk #1 (2015); Thompson-a/Stacey Lee-a; Spider-Man app. 3.00
...: Spider-Gwen 1 - Reprints Spider-Gwen #1 (2015); Latour-s/Robbi Rodriguez-a 3.00
...: Spider-Woman 1 - Reprints Spider-Woman #5 (2015); Hopeless-s/Javier Rodriguez-a 3.00
...: Star Wars 1 - Reprints Star Wars #1 (2015); Aaron-s/Cassaday-a 3.00
...: Star Wars Classic 1 - Reprints Star Wars #1 (1977); Roy Thomas-s/Howard Chaykin-a 3.00
...: Star Wars Covers 1 - Gallery of variant covers for Star Wars #1 (2015) 3.00
...: Vader Down 1 - Reprints Star Wars: Vader Down #1; Aaron-s/Deodato-a 3.00

True Blood #1 © HBO

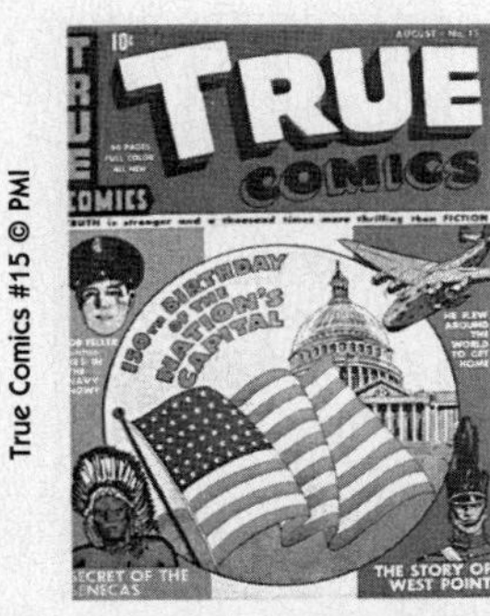

True Comics #15 © PMI

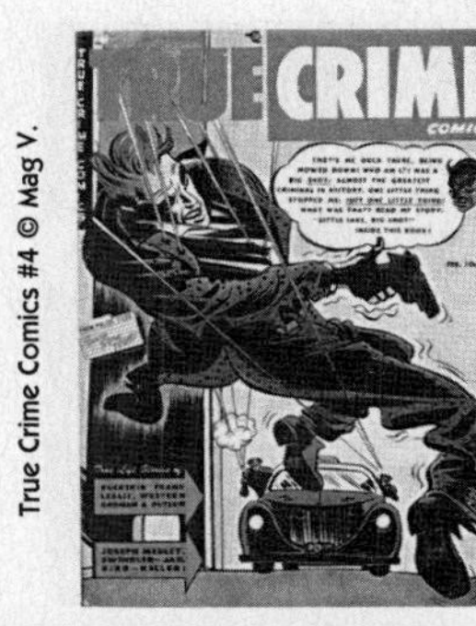

True Crime Comics #4 © Mag V.

GD 2.0 | VG 4.0 | FN 6.0 | VF 8.0 | VF/NM 9.0 | NM- 9.2

...: The Groovy Deadpool 1 - Reprints Deadpool #13 (2013) 1970s art style 3.00
...: The Meaty Deadpool 1 - Reprints Deadpool #11 (2008) Bullseye (as Hawkeye) app. 3.00
...: The Unbeatable Squirrel Girl 1 - Reprints The Unbeatable Squirrel Girl #1 (2015) 3.00
...: The Wedding of Deadpool 1 - Reprints Deadpool #27 (2013) wraparound-c 3.00
...: Thor 1 - Reprints Thor #1 (2014); debut of female Thor; Aaron-s/Dauterman-a 3.00
...: Uncanny Avengers - The Bagalia Job 1 - Reprints Uncanny Avengers #5 3.00
...: Uncanny Deadpool 1 - Reprints Cable & Deadpool #38; Nicieza-s/Brown-a 3.00
...: Wolverine 1 - Reprints #1 (1982) Claremont-s/Miller-a 3.00
...: Wolverine and the X-Men 1 - Reprints #1; Aaron-s/Bachalo-a 3.00
...: Wolverine - Enemy of the State 1 - Reprints Wolverine #20 (2003); Millar-s/Romita Jr.-a 3.00
...: Wolverine - Old Man Logan 1 - Reprints Old Man Logan #1; Bendis-s/Sorrentino-a 3.00
...: Wolverine - Origin 1 - Reprints Wolverine: The Origin #1; Andy Kubert-a 3.00
...: Wolverine - Save the Tiger 1 - Reprints Marvel Comics Presents #1-3; Buscema-a 3.00
...: Wolverine vs. Hulk 1 - Reprints Incredible Hulk #181; Wein-s/Trimpe-a 3.00
...: Wolverine - Weapon X 1 - Reprints Marvel Comics Presents #72-74 3.00
...: Wolverine - X-23 1 - Reprints X-23 #1; Craig Kyle-s/Billy Tan-a 3.00

TRUE BLOOD (Based on the HBO vampire series)
IDW Publishing: Aug, 2010 - No. 6, Dec, 2010 ($3.99)

1-Messina-a; 4 covers by Messina, Campbell, Currie and Corroney 5.00
2-6-Multiple covers on each 4.00
...: Legacy Edition (1/11, $4.99) r/#1, cover gallery; full script 5.00

TRUE BLOOD (2nd series)(Based on the HBO vampire series)
IDW Publishing: May, 2012 - No. 14, Jun, 2013 ($3.99)

1-14-Gaydos-a in most; 2 covers (photo & Bradstreet-c) on each. 5-Manfredi-a 4.00

TRUE BLOOD: TAINTED LOVE (Based on the HBO vampire series)
IDW Publishing: Feb, 2011 - No. 6, Jul, 2011 ($3.99, limited series)

1-4: 1,2,4,5-Corroney-a; multiple covers. 3-Molnar-a 4.00
... Legacy Edition 1 (7/11, $4.99) r/#1 with full script and cover gallery 5.00

TRUE BLOOD: THE FRENCH QUARTER (Based on the HBO vampire series)
IDW Publishing: Aug, 2011 - No. 6, Jan, 2012 ($3.99, limited series)

1-6-Huehner & Tischman-s; multiple covers. 3-Molnar-a 4.00

TRUE BLOOD: THE GREAT REVELATION (Prequel to the 2008 HBO vampire series)
HBO/Top Cow: July, 2008 (no cover price, one shot continued on HBO website)

1-David Wohl-s/Jason Badower-a/c 4.00

TRUE BRIDE'S EXPERIENCES (Formerly Teen-Age Brides)
(True Bride-To-Be Romances No. 17 on)
True Love (Harvey Publications): No. 8, Oct, 1954 - No. 16, Feb, 1956

8-"I Married a Farmer" 9 18 27 52 69 85
9,10: 10-Last pre-code (2/55) 7 14 21 37 46 55
11-15 6 12 18 31 38 45
16-Last issue 7 14 21 37 46 55

NOTE: ***Powell** a-8-10, 12, 13.*

TRUE BRIDE-TO-BE ROMANCES (Formerly True Bride's Experiences)
Home Comics/True Love (Harvey): No. 17, Apr, 1956 - No. 30, Nov, 1958

17-S&K-c, Powell-a 10 20 30 56 76 95
18-20,22,25-28,30 6 12 18 31 38 45
21,23,24,29-Powell-a. 29-Baker-a (1 pg.) 7 14 21 35 43 50

TRUE COMICS (Also see Outstanding American War Heroes)
True Comics/Parents' Magazine Press: April, 1941 - No. 84, Aug, 1950

1-Marathon run story; life story Winston Churchill 34 68 102 204 332 460
2-Red Cross story; Everett-a 16 32 48 94 147 200
3-Baseball Hall of Fame story; Chiang Kai-Shek-c/s 18 36 54 105 165 225
4,5: 4-Story of American flag "Old Glory". 5-Life story of Joe Louis
14 28 42 82 121 160
6-Baseball World Series story 16 32 48 94 147 200
7-10: 7-Buffalo Bill story. 10,11-Teddy Roosevelt 12 24 36 67 94 120
11-14,16,18-20: 11-Thomas Edison, Douglas MacArthur stories. 13-Harry Houdini story. 14-Charlie McCarthy story. 18-Story of America begins, ends #26. 19-Eisenhower-c/s
10 20 30 58 79 100
15-Flag-c; Bob Feller story 11 22 33 62 86 110
17-Brooklyn Dodgers story 12 24 36 69 97 125
21-30: 24-Marco Polo story. 28-Origin of Uncle Sam. 29-Beethoven story. 30-Cooper Brothers baseball story 9 18 27 50 65 80
31-Red Grange "Galloping Ghost" story 8 16 24 42 54 65
32-46: 33-Origin/1st app. Steve Saunders, Special Agent of the FBI, series begins. 35-Mark Twain story. 38-General Bradley-c/s. 39-FDR story. 44-Truman story. 46-George Gershwin story 8 16 24 40 50 60
47-Atomic bomb issue (c/story, 3/46) 10 20 30 58 79 100
48-(4/46) "Hero Without a Gun" Desmond Doss story; inspired 2016 movie Hacksaw Ridge
9 18 27 47 61 75
49-54,56-65: 49-1st app. Secret Warriors. 53-Bobby Riggs story. 58-Jim Jeffries (boxer) story; Harry Houdini story. 59-Bob Hope story; pirates-c/s. 60-Speedway Speed Demon-c/story.
7 14 21 37 46 55
55-(12/46)-1st app. Sad Sack by Baker (1/2 pg.) 26 52 78 154 252 350
66-Will Rogers-c/story 8 16 24 40 50 60
67-1st oversized issue (12/47); Steve Saunders, Special Agent begins
9 18 27 47 61 75
68-70,74-77,79: 68-70,74-77-Features Steve Sanders True FBI advs. 68-Oversized; Admiral Byrd-c/s. 69-Jack Benny story. 74-Amos 'n' Andy story
7 14 21 37 46 55
71-Joe DiMaggio-c/story. 9 18 27 52 69 85
72-Jackie Robinson story; True FBI advs. 8 16 24 44 57 70
73-Walt Disney's life story 9 18 27 52 69 85
78-Stan Musial-c/story; True FBI advs. 8 16 24 44 57 70
80-84 (Scarce)-All distr. to subscribers through mail only; paper-c. 80-Rocket trip to the moon story. 81-Red Grange story. 84-Wyatt Earp app. (1st app. in comics?); Rube Marquard story
18 36 54 107 169 230
(Prices vary widely on issues 80-84)

NOTE: ***Bob Kane** a-7. **Palais** a-80. **Powell** c/a-80. #80-84 have soft covers and combined with Tex Granger, Jack Armstrong, and Calling All Kids. #68-78 featured true FBI adventures.*

TRUE COMICS AND ADVENTURE STORIES
Parents' Magazine Institute: 1965 (Giant) (25¢)

1,2: 1-Fighting Hero of Viet Nam; LBJ on-c 3 6 9 17 26 35

TRUE COMPLETE MYSTERY (Formerly Complete Mystery)
Marvel Comics (PrPI): No. 5, Apr, 1949 - No. 8, Oct, 1949

5-Criminal career of Rico Mancini 30 60 90 177 289 400
6-8: 6-8-Photo-c 21 42 63 126 206 285

TRUE CONFIDENCES
Fawcett Publications: 1949 (Fall) - No. 4, June, 1950 (All photo-c)

1-Has ad for Fawcett Love Adventures #1, but publ. as Love Memoirs #1 as Marvel published the title first; Swayze-a 18 36 54 105 165 225
2-4: 3-Swayze-a. 4-Powell-a 12 24 36 67 94 120

TRUE CRIME CASES (...From Official Police Files)
St. John Publishing Co.: 1944 (25¢, 100 pg. Giant)

nn-Matt Baker-c 71 142 213 454 777 1100

TRUE CRIME COMICS (Also see Complete Book of...)
Magazine Village: No. 2, May, 1947; No. 3, July-Aug, 1948 - No. 6, June-July, 1949; V2#1, Aug-Sept, 1949 (52 pgs.)

2-Jack Cole-c/a; used in **SOTI**, pgs. 81,82 plus illo. "A sample of the injury-to-eye motif" & illo. "Dragging living people to death"; used in **POP**, pg. 105; "Murder, Morphine and Me" classic drug propaganda story used by N.Y. Legis. Comm.
232 464 696 1485 2543 3600
3-Classic Cole-c/a; drug story with hypo, opium den & with drawing addict
161 322 483 1030 1765 2500
4-Jack Cole-c/a; c-taken from a story panel in #3 (r-(2) **SOTI** & **POP** stories/#2?) 113 226 339 718 1234 1750
5-Jack Cole-c, Marijuana racket story (Canadian ed. w/cover similar to #3 exists w/out drug story) 77 154 231 493 847 1200
6-Not a reprint, original story (Canadian ed. reprints #4 w/different coloring on-c)
65 130 195 416 708 1000
V2#1-Used in **SOTI**, pgs. 81,82 & illo. "Dragging living people to death"; Toth, Wood (3 pgs.), Roussos-a; Cole-r from #2 110 220 330 704 1202 1700

NOTE: *V2#1 was reprinted in Canada as V2#9 (12/49); same-c & contents minus Wood-a.*

TRUE FAITH
Fleetway: 1990 ($9.95, graphic novel)

nn-Garth Ennis scripts 2 4 6 12 16 20
Reprinted by DC/Vertigo ('97, $12.95) 13.00

TRUE GHOST STORIES (See Ripley's...)

TRUE LIFE ROMANCES (...Romance on cover)
Ajax/Farrell Publications: Dec, 1955 - No. 3, Aug, 1956

1 14 28 42 80 115 150
2 10 20 30 54 72 90
3-Disbrow-a 10 20 30 58 79 100

TRUE LIFE SECRETS
Romantic Love Stories/Charlton: Mar-April, 1951 - No. 28, Sept, 1955; No. 29, Jan, 1956

1-Photo-c begin, end #3? 20 40 60 114 182 250
2 12 24 36 69 97 125
3-11,13-19: 11 22 33 60 83 105

True Love Pictorial #4 © STJ

True Sport Picture Storeis V3 #11 © SS

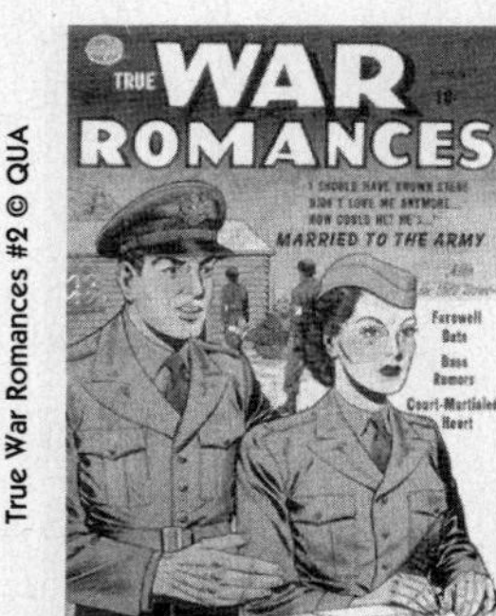

True War Romances #2 © QUA

	GD 2.0	VG 4.0	FN 6.0	VF 8.0	VF/NM 9.0	NM- 9.2
12-"I Was An Escort Girl" story	14	28	42	80	115	150
20-22,24-29: 25-Last precode (3/55)	10	20	30	54	72	90
23-Classic-c	20	40	60	117	189	260

TRUE LIFE TALES (Formerly Mitzi's Romances #8?)
Marvel Comics (CCC): No. 8, Oct, 1949 - No. 2, Jan, 1950 (52 pgs.)

	GD	VG	FN	VF	VF/NM	NM-
8(#1, 10/49), 2-Both have photo-c	14	28	42	82	121	160

TRUE LIVES OF THE FABULOUS KILLJOYS
Dark Horse Comics: Jun, 2013 - No. 6, Jan, 2014 ($3.99)

1-6-Gerald Way & Shaun Simon-s/Becky Cloonan-a; covers by Cloonan & Bá 4.00

TRUE LOVE
Eclipse Comics: Jan, 1986 - No. 2, Jan, 1986 ($2.00, Baxter paper)

	GD	VG	FN	VF	VF/NM	NM-
1-Love stories reprinted from pre-code Standard Comics; Toth-a(p); Dave Stevens-c	1	3	4	6	8	10
2-Toth-a; Mayo-a						4.00

TRUE LOVE CONFESSIONS
Premier Magazines: May, 1954 - No. 11, Jan, 1956

	GD	VG	FN	VF	VF/NM	NM-
1-Marijuana story	20	40	60	114	.182	250
2	12	24	36	69	97	125
3-11	11	22	33	62	86	110

TRUE LOVE PICTORIAL
St. John Publishing Co.: Dec, 1952 - No. 11, Aug, 1954

	GD	VG	FN	VF	VF/NM	NM-
1-Only photo-c	34	68	102	199	325	450
2-Baker-c/a	77	154	231	493	847	1200
3-5(All 25¢, 100 pgs.): 4-Signed story by Estrada. 5-(4/53)-Formerly Teen-Age Temptations; Kubert-a in #3; Baker-c/a in #3-5	116	232	348	742	1271	1800
6,7: Baker-c/a; signed stories by Estrada	68	136	204	435	743	1050
8,10,11-Baker-c/a	68	136	204	435	743	1050
9-Baker-c	61	122	183	390	670	950

TRUE LOVE PROBLEMS AND ADVICE ILLUSTRATED (Becomes Romance Stories of True Love No. 45 on)
McCombs/Harvey Publ./Home Comics: June, 1949 - No. 6, Apr, 1950; No. 7, Jan, 1951 - No. 44, Mar, 1957

	GD	VG	FN	VF	VF/NM	NM-
V1#1	15	30	45	86	133	180
2-Elias-c	10	20	30	54	72	90
3-10: 3,4,7-9-Elias-c	8	16	24	42	54	65
11-13,15-23,25-31: 31-Last pre-code (1/55)	7	14	21	35	43	50
14,24-Rape scene	7	14	21	37	46	55
32-37,39-44	6	12	18	29	36	42
38-S&K-c	9	18	27	52	69	85

NOTE: *Powell a-1, 2, 7-14, 17-25, 28, 29, 33, 40, 41. #3 has True Love... on inside.*

TRUE MOVIE AND TELEVISION (Part teenage magazine)
Toby Press: Aug, 1950 - No. 3, Nov, 1950; No. 4, Mar, 1951 (52 pgs.)(1-3: 10¢)

	GD	VG	FN	VF	VF/NM	NM-
1-Elizabeth Taylor photo-c; Gene Autry, Shirley Temple app.	68	136	204	435	743	1050
2-(9/50)-Janet Leigh/Liz Taylor/Ava Gardner & others photo-c; Frazetta John Wayne illo from J.Wayne Adv. Comics #2 (4/50)	50	100	150	315	533	750
3-June Allyson photo-c; Montgomery Cliff, Esther Williams, Andrews Sisters app; Li'l Abner featured; Sadie Hawkins' Day	34	68	102	199	325	450
4-Jane Powell photo-c (15¢)	21	42	63	126	206	285

NOTE: *16 pgs. in color, rest movie material in black & white.*

TRUE SECRETS (Formerly Our Love?)
Marvel (IPS)/Atlas Comics (MPI) #4 on: No. 3, Mar, 1950; No. 4, Feb, 1951 - No. 40, Sept, 1956

	GD	VG	FN	VF	VF/NM	NM-
3 (52 pgs.)(IPS one-shot)`	20	40	60	117	189	260
4,5,7-10	14	28	42	80	115	150
6,22-Everett-a	15	30	45	85	130	175
11-20	13	26	39	72	101	130
21,23-28: 24-Colletta-c. 28-Last pre-code (2/55)	12	24	36	67	94	120
29-40: 34,36-Colletta-a	11	22	33	62	86	110

TRUE SPORT PICTURE STORIES (Formerly Sport Comics)
Street & Smith Publications: V1#5, Feb, 1942 - V5#2, July-Aug, 1949

	GD	VG	FN	VF	VF/NM	NM-
V1#5-Joe DiMaggio-c/story	37	74	111	218	354	490
6-12 (1942-43): 12-Jack Dempsey story	21	42	63	122	199	275
V2#1-12 (1943-45): 7-Stan Musial-c/story; photo story of the New York Yankees	20	40	60	115	185	255
V3#1-12 (1946-47): 7-Joe DiMaggio, Stan Musial, Bob Feller & others back from the armed service story. 8-Billy Conn vs. Joe Louis-c/story	19	38	57	111	176	240
V4#1-12 (1947-49), V5#1,2: v4#8-Joe Louis on-c	18	36	54	105	165	225

NOTE: ***Powell** a-V3#10, V4#1-4, 6-8, 10-12; V5#1, 2; c-V3#10-12, V4#2-7, 9-12. **Ravielli** c-V5#2.*

TRUE STORIES OF ROMANCE
Fawcett Publications: Jan, 1950 - No. 3, May, 1950 (All photo-c)

	GD	VG	FN	VF	VF/NM	NM-
1	15	30	45	84	127	170
2,3: 3-Marcus Swayze-a	11	22	33	62	86	110

TRUE STORY OF JESSE JAMES, THE (See Jesse James, Four Color 757)

TRUE SWEETHEART SECRETS
Fawcett Publs.: 5/50; No. 2, 7/50; No. 3, 1951(nd); No. 4, 9/51 - No. 11, 1/53 (All photo-c)

	GD	VG	FN	VF	VF/NM	NM-
1-Photo-c; Debbie Reynolds?	17	34	51	98	154	210
2-Wood-a (11 pgs.)	20	40	60	114	182	250
3-11: 4,5-Powell-a. 8-Marcus Swayze-a. 11-Evans-a	13	26	39	72	101	130

TRUE TALES OF LOVE (Formerly Secret Story Romances)
Atlas Comics (TCI): No. 22, April, 1956 - No. 31, Sept, 1957

	GD	VG	FN	VF	VF/NM	NM-
22	14	28	42	80	115	150
23-24,26-31-Colletta-a in most:	10	20	30	58	79	100
25-Everett-a; Colletta-a	11	22	33	62	86	110

TRUE TALES OF ROMANCE
Fawcett Publications: No. 4, June, 1950

	GD	VG	FN	VF	VF/NM	NM-
4-Photo-c	11	22	33	62	86	110

TRUE 3-D
Harvey Publications: Dec, 1953 - No. 2, Feb, 1954 (25¢)(Both came with 2 pair of glasses)

	GD	VG	FN	VF	VF/NM	NM-
1-Nostrand, Powell-a	5	10	15	35	55	75
2-Powell-a	6	12	18	37	59	80

NOTE: *Many copies of #1 surfaced in 1984.*

TRUE-TO-LIFE ROMANCES (Formerly Guns Against Gangsters)
Star Publ.: #8, 11-12/49; #9, 1-2/50; #3, 4/50 - #5, 9/50; #6, 1/51 - #23, 10/54

	GD	VG	FN	VF	VF/NM	NM-
8(#1, 1949)	32	64	96	188	307	425
9(#2),4-10	22	44	66	132	216	300
3-Janet Leigh/Glenn Ford photo on-c plus true life story of each	24	48	72	140	230	320
11,22,23	20	40	60	120	195	270
12-14,17-21-Disbrow-a	21	42	63	126	206	285
15,16-Wood & Disbrow-a in each	24	48	72	140	230	320

NOTE: ***Kamen** a-13. **Kamen/Feldstein** a-14. All have **L.B. Cole** covers.*

TRUE WAR EXPERIENCES
Harvey Publications: Aug, 1952 - No. 4, Dec, 1952

	GD	VG	FN	VF	VF/NM	NM-
1-Korean War	8	16	24	56	93	130
2-4	5	10	15	32	51	70

TRUE WAR ROMANCES (Becomes Exotic Romances #22 on)
Quality Comics Group: Sept, 1952 - No. 21, June, 1955

	GD	VG	FN	VF	VF/NM	NM-
1-Photo-c	17	34	51	98	154	210
2-(10/52)	11	22	33	60	83	105
3-10: 3-(12/52). 8,9-Whitney-a	10	20	30	56	76	95
11-21: 20-Last precode (4/55). 14-Whitney-a	9	18	27	52	69	85

TRUE WAR STORIES (See Ripley's...)

TRUE WESTERN (True Adventures #3)
Marvel Comics (MMC): Dec, 1949 - No. 2, March, 1950

	GD	VG	FN	VF	VF/NM	NM-
1-Photo-c; Billy The Kid story	17	34	51	98	154	210
2-Alan Ladd photo-c	20	40	60	114	182	250

TRUMP
HMH Publishing Co.: Jan, 1957 - No. 2, Mar, 1957 (50¢, magazine)

	GD	VG	FN	VF	VF/NM	NM-
1-Harvey Kurtzman satire	26	52	78	154	252	350
2-Harvey Kurtzman satire	20	40	60	118	192	265

NOTE: ***Davis, Elder, Heath, Jaffee** art-#1,2; **Wood** a-1. Article by Mel Brooks in #2.*

TRUMPETS WEST (See Luke Short, Four Color #875)

TRUTH ABOUT CRIME (See Fox Giants)

TRUTH ABOUT MOTHER GOOSE (See Mother Goose, Four Color #862)

TRUTH BEHIND THE TRIAL OF CARDINAL MINDSZENTY, THE (See Cardinal Mindszenty in the Promotional Comics section))

TRUTHFUL LOVE (Formerly Youthful Love)
Youthful Magazines: No. 2, July, 1950

	GD	VG	FN	VF	VF/NM	NM-
2-Ingrid Bergman's true life story	14	28	42	82	121	160

TRUTH RED, WHITE & BLACK
Marvel Comics: Jan, 2003 - No. 6 ($3.50, limited series)

1-Kyle Baker-a/Robert Morales-s; the testing of Captain America's super-soldier serum 3.50

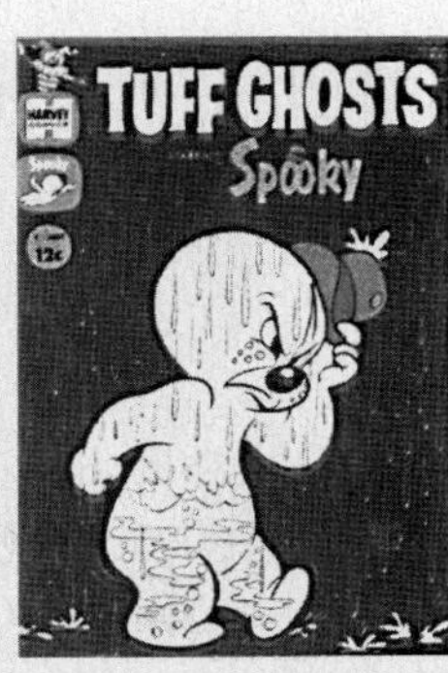

Tuff Ghosts Starring Spooky #1 © HARV

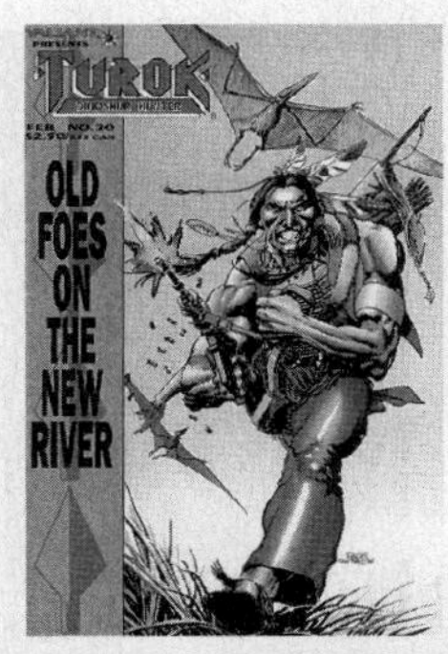

Turok, Dinosaur Hunter #20 © ACC

Turok, Son of Stone #1 © RH

	GD 2.0	VG 4.0	FN 6.0	VF 8.0	VF/NM 9.0	NM- 9.2
2-7: 3-Isaiah Bradley 1st dons the Captain America costume						3.50
TPB (2004, $17.99) r/series						18.00

TRY-OUT WINNER BOOK
Marvel Comics: Mar, 1988

	GD 2.0	VG 4.0	FN 6.0	VF 8.0	VF/NM 9.0	NM- 9.2
1-Spider-Man vs. Doc Octopus						5.00

TSR WORLD (...Annual on cover only)
DC Comics: 1990 ($3.95, 84 pgs.)

	GD 2.0	VG 4.0	FN 6.0	VF 8.0	VF/NM 9.0	NM- 9.2
1-Advanced D&D, ForgottenRealms, Dragonlance & 1st app. Spelljammer						4.00

TSUNAMI GIRL
Image Comics: 1999 - No. 3, 1999 ($2.95)

	GD 2.0	VG 4.0	FN 6.0	VF 8.0	VF/NM 9.0	NM- 9.2
1-3-Sorayama-c/Paniccia-s/a						3.00

TUBBY (See Marge's...)

TUFF GHOSTS STARRING SPOOKY
Harvey Publications: July, 1962 - No. 39, Nov, 1970; No. 40, Sept, 1971 - No. 43, Oct, 1972

	GD 2.0	VG 4.0	FN 6.0	VF 8.0	VF/NM 9.0	NM- 9.2
1-12¢ issues begin	11	22	33	73	157	240
2-5	6	12	18	38	69	100
6-10	5	10	15	30	50	70
11-20	4	8	12	23	37	50
21-30: 29-Hot Stuff/Spooky team-up story	3	6	9	16	23	30
31-39,43	2	4	6	13	18	22
40-42: 52 pg. Giants	3	6	9	14	20	25

TUFFY
Standard Comics: No. 5, July, 1949 - No. 9, Oct, 1950

	GD 2.0	VG 4.0	FN 6.0	VF 8.0	VF/NM 9.0	NM- 9.2
5-All by Sid Hoff	9	18	27	50	65	80
6-9	7	14	21	35	43	50

TUFFY TURTLE
I. W. Enterprises: No date

	GD 2.0	VG 4.0	FN 6.0	VF 8.0	VF/NM 9.0	NM- 9.2
1-Reprint	2	4	6	8	11	14

TUG & BUSTER
Art & Soul Comics: Nov, 1995 - No. 7, Feb, 1998 ($2.95, B&W, bi-monthly)

	GD 2.0	VG 4.0	FN 6.0	VF 8.0	VF/NM 9.0	NM- 9.2
1-7: Marc Hempel-c/a/scripts						3.00
1-(Image Comics, 8/98, $2.95, B&W)						3.00

TUKI
Cartoon Books: Jul, 2014 - Present ($3.99)

	GD 2.0	VG 4.0	FN 6.0	VF 8.0	VF/NM 9.0	NM- 9.2
1-4-Jeff Smith-s/a/c; story reads sideways						4.00

TURF
Image Comics: Apr, 2010 - No. 2 ($2.99, limited series)

	GD 2.0	VG 4.0	FN 6.0	VF 8.0	VF/NM 9.0	NM- 9.2
1,2-Jonathan Ross-s/Tommy Lee Edwards-a						3.00

TUROK
Acclaim Comics: Mar, 1998 - No. 4, Jun, 1998 ($2.50)

	GD 2.0	VG 4.0	FN 6.0	VF 8.0	VF/NM 9.0	NM- 9.2
1-4-Nicieza-s/Kayanan-a						3.00
..., Child of Blood 1 (1/98, $3.95) Nicieza-s/Kayanan-a						4.00
... Evolution 1 (8/02, $2.50) Nicieza-s/Kayanan-a						3.00
..., Redpath 1 (10/97, $3.95) Nicieza-s/Kayanan-a						4.00
... / Shadowman 1 (2/99, $3.95) Priest-s/Broome & Jimenez-a						4.00
...: Spring Break in the Lost Land 1 (7/97, $3.95) Nicieza-s/Kayanan-a						4.00
...: Tales of the Lost Land 1 (4/98, $3.95)						4.00
...: The Empty Souls 1 (4/97, $3.95) Nicieza-s/Kayanan-a; variant-c						4.00

TUROK, DINOSAUR HUNTER (See Magnus Robot Fighter #12 & Archer & Armstrong #2)
Valiant/Acclaim Comics: June, 1993 - No. 47, Aug, 1996 ($2.50)

	GD 2.0	VG 4.0	FN 6.0	VF 8.0	VF/NM 9.0	NM- 9.2
1-($3.50)-Chromium & foil-c						4.00
1-Gold foil-c variant						15.00
0, 2-47: 4-Andar app. 5-Death of Andar. 7-9-Truman/Glanzman-a. 11-Bound-in trading card. 16-Chaos Effect						3.00
Yearbook 1 (1994, $3.95, 52 pgs.)						4.00

TUROK: DINOSAUR HUNTER
Dynamite Entertainment: 2014 - No. 12, 2015 ($3.99)

	GD 2.0	VG 4.0	FN 6.0	VF 8.0	VF/NM 9.0	NM- 9.2
1-12: 1-5-New version; Greg Pak-s/Mirko Colak-a; Sears-c. 6-8-Miyazawa-a						4.00
1-12-Variant-c by Jae Lee						4.00

TUROK, SON OF STONE (See Dan Curtis, Golden Comics Digest #31, Space Western #45 & March of Comics #378, 399, 408)
Dell Publ. Co. #1-29(9/62)/Gold Key #30(12/62)-85(7/73)/Gold Key or Whitman #86(9/73)-125(1/80)/Whitman #126(3/81) on: No. 596, 12/54 - No. 29, 9/62; No. 30, 12/62 - No. 91, 7/74; No. 92, 9/74 - No. 125, 1/80; No. 126, 3/81 - No. 130, 4/82

	GD 2.0	VG 4.0	FN 6.0	VF 8.0	VF/NM 9.0	NM- 9.2
Four Color 596 (12/54)(#1)-1st app./origin Turok & Andar; dinosaur-c. Created by Matthew H. Murphy; written by Alberto Giolitti	79	158	237	632	1416	2200
Four Color 656 (10/55)(#2)-1st mention of Lanok	34	68	102	245	548	850
3(3-5/56)-5: 3-Cave men	21	42	63	147	324	500
6-10: 8-Dinosaur of the deep; Turok enters Lost Valley; series begins. 9-Paul S. Newman-s (most issues thru end)	15	30	45	103	227	350
11-20: 17-Prehistoric Pygmies	11	22	33	76	163	250
21-29	9	18	27	58	114	170
30-1st Gold Key. 30-33-Painted back-c.	9	18	27	59	117	175
31-Drug use story	9	18	27	58	114	170
32-40	7	14	21	46	86	125
41-50	6	12	18	37	66	95
51-57,59,60	5	10	15	34	60	85
58-Flying Saucer c/story	5	10	15	35	63	90
61-70: 62-12¢ & 15¢ covers. 63,68-Line drawn-c	5	10	15	30	50	70
71-84: 84-Origin & 1st app. Hutec	4	8	12	27	44	60
85-99: 93-r-c/#19 w/changes. 94-r-c/#28 w/changes. 97-r-c/#31 w/changes. 98-r/#58 w/o spaceship & spacemen on-c. 99-r-c/#52 w/changes.	4	8	12	23	37	50
100	4	8	12	28	47	65
101-129: 114,115-(52 pgs.). 129(2/82)	4	8	12	23	37	50
130(4/82)-Last issue	5	10	15	35	63	90
Giant 1(30031-611) (11/66)-Slick-c; r/#10-12 & 16 plus cover to #11	9	18	27	63	126	190
Giant 1-Same as above but with paper-c	10	20	30	67	141	210

NOTE: *Most painted-c; line-drawn #63 & 130.* ***Alberto Gioletti*** *a-24-27, 30-119, 123; painted-c No. 30-129.* ***Sparling*** *a-117, 120-130. Reprints-#36, 54, 57, 75, 112, 114(1/3), 115(1/3), 118, 121, 125, 127(1/3), 128, 129(1/3), 130(1/3), Giant 1. Cover r-93, 94, 97-99, 126(all different from original covers.*

TUROK, SON OF STONE
Dark Horse Comics: Oct, 2010 - No. 4, Oct, 2011 ($3.50)

	GD 2.0	VG 4.0	FN 6.0	VF 8.0	VF/NM 9.0	NM- 9.2
1-4: 1-Shooter-s/Francisco-a/Swanland-c; back-up reprint of debut in Four Color 596						3.50
1-Variant-c by Francisco						3.50

TUROK THE HUNTED
Valiant/Acclaim Comics: Mar, 1995 - No. 2, Apr, 1995 ($2.50, limited series)

	GD 2.0	VG 4.0	FN 6.0	VF 8.0	VF/NM 9.0	NM- 9.2
1,2-Mike Deodato-a(p); price omitted on #1						3.00

TUROK THE HUNTED
Acclaim Comics (Valiant): Feb, 1996 - No. 2, Mar, 1996 ($2.50, limited series)

	GD 2.0	VG 4.0	FN 6.0	VF 8.0	VF/NM 9.0	NM- 9.2
1,2-Mike Grell story						3.00

TUROK, TIMEWALKER
Acclaim Comics (Valiant): Aug, 1997 - No. 2, Sept, 1997 ($2.50, limited series)

	GD 2.0	VG 4.0	FN 6.0	VF 8.0	VF/NM 9.0	NM- 9.2
1,2-Nicieza story						3.00

TUROK 2 (Magazine)
Acclaim Comics: Oct, 1998 ($4.99, magazine size)

	GD 2.0	VG 4.0	FN 6.0	VF 8.0	VF/NM 9.0	NM- 9.2
...Seeds of Evil-Nicieza-s/Broome & Benjamin-a; origin back-up story						5.00
#2 Adon's Curse -Mack painted-c/Broome & Benjamin-a; origin pt. 2						5.00

TUROK 3: SHADOW OF OBLIVION
Acclaim Comics: Sept, 2000 ($4.95, one-shot)

	GD 2.0	VG 4.0	FN 6.0	VF 8.0	VF/NM 9.0	NM- 9.2
1-Includes pin-up gallery						5.00

TURTLE SOUP
Mirage Studios: Sept, 1987 ($2.00, 76 pgs., B&W, one-shot)

	GD 2.0	VG 4.0	FN 6.0	VF 8.0	VF/NM 9.0	NM- 9.2
1-Featuring Teenage Mutant Ninja Turtles	1	2	3	5	6	8

TURTLE SOUP
Mirage Studios: Nov, 1991 - No. 4, 1992 ($2.50, limited series, coated paper)

	GD 2.0	VG 4.0	FN 6.0	VF 8.0	VF/NM 9.0	NM- 9.2
1-4: Features the Teenage Mutant Ninja Turtles						4.00

TV CASPER & COMPANY
Harvey Publications: Aug, 1963 - No. 46, April, 1974 (25¢ Giants)

	GD 2.0	VG 4.0	FN 6.0	VF 8.0	VF/NM 9.0	NM- 9.2
1- 68 pg. Giants begin; Casper, Little Audrey, Baby Huey, Herman & Catnip, Buzzy the Crow begin	10	20	30	66	138	210
2-5	6	12	18	37	66	95
6-10	4	8	12	28	47	65
11-20	4	8	12	23	37	50
21-31: 31-Last 68 pg. issue	3	6	9	17	26	35
32-46: All 52 pgs.	3	6	9	16	23	30

NOTE: *Many issues contain reprints.*

TV FUNDAY FUNNIES (See Famous TV...)

TV FUNNIES (See New Funnies)

TV FUNTIME (See Little Audrey)

TV LAUGHOUT (See Archie's...)

TV Stars #3 © H-B

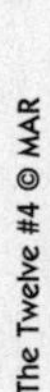

The Twelve #4 © MAR

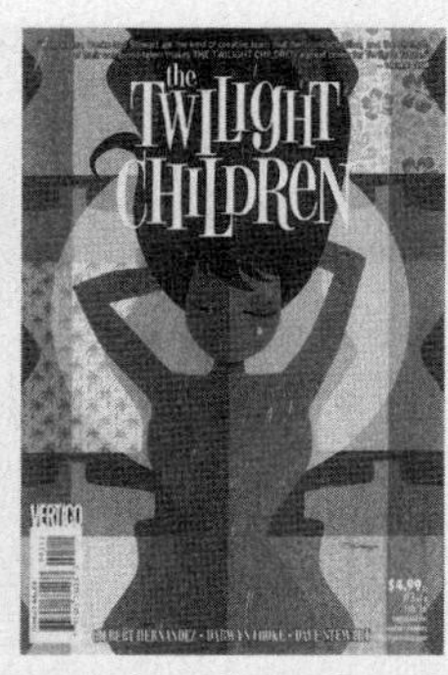

Twilight Children #3 © Hernandez & Cooke

TV SCREEN CARTOONS (Formerly Real Screen)
National Periodical Publ.: No. 129, July-Aug, 1959 - No. 138, Jan-Feb, 1961

	GD 2.0	VG 4.0	FN 6.0	VF 8.0	VF/NM 9.0	NM- 9.2
129-138 (Scarce) Fox and the Crow	6	12	18	37	66	95

TV STARS (TV) (Newsstand sales only)
Marvel Comics Group: Aug, 1978 - No. 4, Feb, 1979 (Hanna-Barbera)

	GD 2.0	VG 4.0	FN 6.0	VF 8.0	VF/NM 9.0	NM- 9.2
1-Great Grape Ape app.	3	6	9	17	26	35
2,4: 4-Top Cat app.	3	6	9	15	22	28
3-Toth-c/a; Dave Stevens inks	3	6	9	16	24	32

TV TEENS (Formerly Ozzie & Babs; Rock and Rollo #14 on)
Charlton Comics: V1#14, Feb, 1954 - V2#13, July, 1956

	GD 2.0	VG 4.0	FN 6.0	VF 8.0	VF/NM 9.0	NM- 9.2
V1#14 (#1)-Ozzie & Babs	12	24	36	67	94	120
15 (#2)	8	16	24	42	54	65
V2#3(6/54) - 6-Don Winslow	8	16	24	40	50	60
7-13-Mopsy. 8(7/55). 9-Paper dolls	7	14	21	37	46	55

TWEETY AND SYLVESTER (1st Series) (TV) (Also see Looney Tunes and Merrie Melodies)
Dell Publishing Co.: No. 406, June, 1952 - No. 37, June-Aug, 1962

	GD 2.0	VG 4.0	FN 6.0	VF 8.0	VF/NM 9.0	NM- 9.2
Four Color 406 (#1)	12	24	36	81	176	270
Four Color 489,524	7	14	21	49	92	135
4 (3-5/54) - 20	5	10	15	35	63	90
21-37	5	10	15	31	53	75

(See March of Comics #421, 433, 445, 457, 469, 481)

TWEETY AND SYLVESTER (2nd Series)(See Kite Fun Book)
Gold Key No. 1-102/Whitman No. 103 on: Nov, 1963; No. 2, Nov, 1965 - No. 121, Jun, 1984

	GD 2.0	VG 4.0	FN 6.0	VF 8.0	VF/NM 9.0	NM- 9.2
1	6	12	18	37	66	95
2-10	3	6	9	19	30	40
11-30	3	6	9	14	20	25
31-50	2	4	6	9	12	15
51-70	1	3	4	6	8	10
71-102	1	2	3	5	6	8
103,104 (Whitman)	1	3	4	6	8	10
105(9/80),106(10/80),107(12/80) 3-pack only	4	8	12	28	47	65
108-116: 113(2/82),114(2-3/82),115(3/82),116(4/82)	2	4	6	8	10	12
117-121 (All # 90094 on-c; nd, nd code): 117(6/83). 118(7/83). 119(2/84)-r(1/3). 120(5/84). 121(6/84)	3	6	9	17	26	35
Digest nn (Charlton/Xerox Pub., 1974) (low print run)	3	6	9	16	23	30
Mini Comic No. 1(1976, 3-1/4x6-1/2")	1	3	4	6	8	10

TWELVE, THE (Golden Age Timely heroes)
Marvel Comics: No. 0; 2008; No. 1, Mar, 2008 - No. 12, Jun, 2012 ($2.99, limited series)

	GD 2.0	VG 4.0	FN 6.0	VF 8.0	VF/NM 9.0	NM- 9.2
0-Rockman, Laughing Mask & Phantom Reporter intro. stories (1940s); series preview						4.00
1/2 (2008, $3.99) r/early app. of Fiery Mask, Mister E and Rockman; Weston-c						5.00
1-12-Straczynski-s/Weston-a; Timely heroes re-surface in the present						4.00
... Must Have 1 (4/12, $3.99) r/#7,8						4.00
...: Spearhead 1 (5/10, $3.99) Weston-s/a; Phantom Reporter in WW2; Invaders app.						5.00

12 O'CLOCK HIGH (TV)
Dell Publishing Co.: Jan-Mar, 1965 - No. 2, Apr-June, 1965 (Photo-c)

	GD 2.0	VG 4.0	FN 6.0	VF 8.0	VF/NM 9.0	NM- 9.2
1- Sinnott-a	5	10	15	34	60	85
2	4	8	12	28	47	65

TWELVE REASONS TO DIE
Black Mask Studios: 2013 - No. 6, 2014 ($3.50)

	GD 2.0	VG 4.0	FN 6.0	VF 8.0	VF/NM 9.0	NM- 9.2
1-6: 1-Five covers; created by Ghostface Killah						3.50

2099 A.D.
Marvel Comics: May, 1995 ($3.95, one-shot)

	GD 2.0	VG 4.0	FN 6.0	VF 8.0	VF/NM 9.0	NM- 9.2
1-Acetate-c by Quesada & Palmiotti						4.00

2099 APOCALYPSE
Marvel Comics: Dec, 1995 ($4.95, one-shot)

	GD 2.0	VG 4.0	FN 6.0	VF 8.0	VF/NM 9.0	NM- 9.2
1-Chromium wraparound-c; Ellis script						5.00

2099 GENESIS
Marvel Comics: Jan, 1996 ($4.95, one-shot)

	GD 2.0	VG 4.0	FN 6.0	VF 8.0	VF/NM 9.0	NM- 9.2
1-Chromium wraparound-c; Ellis script						5.00

2099 MANIFEST DESTINY
Marvel Comics: Mar, 1998 ($5.99, one-shot)

	GD 2.0	VG 4.0	FN 6.0	VF 8.0	VF/NM 9.0	NM- 9.2
1-Origin of Fantastic Four 2099; intro Moon Knight 2099						6.00

2099 UNLIMITED
Marvel Comics: Sept, 1993 - No. 10, 1996 ($3.95, 68 pgs.)

	GD 2.0	VG 4.0	FN 6.0	VF 8.0	VF/NM 9.0	NM- 9.2
1-10: 1-1st app. Hulk 2099 & begins. 1-3-Spider-Man 2099 app. 9-Joe Kubert-c; Len Wein & Nancy Collins scripts						4.00

2099 WORLD OF DOOM SPECIAL
Marvel Comics: May, 1995 ($2.25, one-shot)

	GD 2.0	VG 4.0	FN 6.0	VF 8.0	VF/NM 9.0	NM- 9.2
1-Doom's "Contract w/America"						3.00

2099 WORLD OF TOMORROW
Marvel Comics: Sept, 1996 - No. 8, Apr, 1997 ($2.50) (Replaces 2099 titles)

	GD 2.0	VG 4.0	FN 6.0	VF 8.0	VF/NM 9.0	NM- 9.2
1-8: 1-Wraparound-c. 2-w/bound-in card. 4,5-Phalanx						3.00

21
Image Comics (Top Cow Productions): Feb, 1996 - No. 3, Apr, 1996 ($2.50)

	GD 2.0	VG 4.0	FN 6.0	VF 8.0	VF/NM 9.0	NM- 9.2
1-3: Len Wein scripts						3.00
1-Variant-c						3.00

21 DOWN
DC Comics (WildStorm): Nov, 2002 - No. 12, Nov, 2003 ($2.95)

	GD 2.0	VG 4.0	FN 6.0	VF 8.0	VF/NM 9.0	NM- 9.2
1-12: 1-Palmiotti & Gray-s/Saiz-a/Jusko-c						3.00
...: The Conduit (2003, $19.95, TPB) r/#1-7; intro. by Garth Ennis						20.00

24 (Based on TV series)
IDW Publishing: Apr, 2014 - No. 5, Aug, 2014 ($3.99, limited series)

	GD 2.0	VG 4.0	FN 6.0	VF 8.0	VF/NM 9.0	NM- 9.2
1-5-Brisson-s/Gaydos-a; multiple covers on each						4.00

24 (Based on TV series)
IDW Publishing: July, 2004 - July, 2005 ($6.99/$7.49, square-bound, one-shots)

	GD 2.0	VG 4.0	FN 6.0	VF 8.0	VF/NM 9.0	NM- 9.2
...: Midnight Sun (7/05, $7.49) J.C. Vaughn & Mark Haynes-s; Renato Guedes-a						7.50
...: One Shot (7/04, $6.99)-Jack Bauer's first day on the job at CTU; Vaughn & Haynes-s; Guedes-a						7.50
...: Stories (1/05, $7.49) Manny Clark-a; Vaughn & Haynes-s						7.50

24: NIGHTFALL (Based on TV series)
IDW Publishing: Nov, 2006 - No. 5, Mar, 2007 ($3.99, limited series)

	GD 2.0	VG 4.0	FN 6.0	VF 8.0	VF/NM 9.0	NM- 9.2
1-5-Two years before Season One; Vaughn & Haynes-s; Diaz-a; two covers						4.00

28 DAYS LATER (Based on the 2002 movie)
Boom! Studios: July, 2009 - No. 24, Jun, 2011 ($3.99)

	GD 2.0	VG 4.0	FN 6.0	VF 8.0	VF/NM 9.0	NM- 9.2
1-24: 1-Covers by Bradstreet and Phillips						4.00

2020 VISIONS
DC Comics (Vertigo): May, 1997 - No. 12, Apr, 1998 ($2.25, limited series)

	GD 2.0	VG 4.0	FN 6.0	VF 8.0	VF/NM 9.0	NM- 9.2
1-12-Delano-s: 1-3-Quitely-a. 4-"la tormenta"-Pleece-a						3.00

20,000 LEAGUES UNDER THE SEA (Movie)(See King Classics, Movie Comics & Power Record Comics)
Dell Publishing Co.: No. 614, Feb, 1955 (Disney)

	GD 2.0	VG 4.0	FN 6.0	VF 8.0	VF/NM 9.0	NM- 9.2
Four Color 614-Movie, painted-c	8	16	24	54	102	150

TWICE TOLD TALES (See Movie Classics)

TWILIGHT
DC Comics: 1990 - No. 3, 1991 ($4.95, 52 pgs, lim. series, squarebound, mature)

	GD 2.0	VG 4.0	FN 6.0	VF 8.0	VF/NM 9.0	NM- 9.2
1-3: Tommy Tomorrow app; Chaykin scripts, Garcia-Lopez-c/a						5.00

TWILIGHT CHILDREN, THE
DC Comics (Vertigo): Dec, 2015 - No. 4, Mar, 2016 ($4.99, limited series)

	GD 2.0	VG 4.0	FN 6.0	VF 8.0	VF/NM 9.0	NM- 9.2
1-4-Gilbert Hernandez-s/Darwyn Cooke-a/c						5.00

TWILIGHT EXPERIMENT
DC Comics (WildStorm): Apr, 2004 - No. 6, Sept, 2005 ($2.95, limited series)

	GD 2.0	VG 4.0	FN 6.0	VF 8.0	VF/NM 9.0	NM- 9.2
1-6-Gray & Palmiotti-s/Santacruz-a						3.00
TPB (2011, $17.99) r/#1-6						18.00

TWILIGHT GUARDIAN (Also see Pilot Season: Twilight Guardian)
Image Comics (Top Cow): Jan, 2011 - No. 4, Apr, 2011 ($3.99, limited series)

	GD 2.0	VG 4.0	FN 6.0	VF 8.0	VF/NM 9.0	NM- 9.2
1-4-Hickman-s/Kotean-a						4.00

TWILIGHT MAN
First Publishing: June, 1989 - No. 4, Sept, 1989 ($2.75, limited series)

	GD 2.0	VG 4.0	FN 6.0	VF 8.0	VF/NM 9.0	NM- 9.2
1-4						3.00

TWILIGHT ZONE, THE (TV) (See Dan Curtis & Stories From...)
Dell Publishing Co./Gold Key/Whitman No. 92: No. 1173, 3-5/61 - No. 91, 4/79; No. 92, 5/82

	GD 2.0	VG 4.0	FN 6.0	VF 8.0	VF/NM 9.0	NM- 9.2
Four Color 1173 (#1)-Crandall-c/a	18	36	54	128	284	440
Four Color 1288-Crandall/Evans-c/a	10	20	30	69	147	225
01-860-207 (5-7/62-Dell, 15¢)	8	16	24	54	102	150
12-860-210 on-c; 01-860-210 on inside(8-10/62-Dell)-Evans-c/a (3 stories); art by Frazetta & Crandall	8	16	24	54	102	150
1(11/62-Gold Key)-Crandall/Frazetta-a (10 & 11 pgs.); Evans-a	13	26	39	89	195	300
2	7	14	21	49	92	135

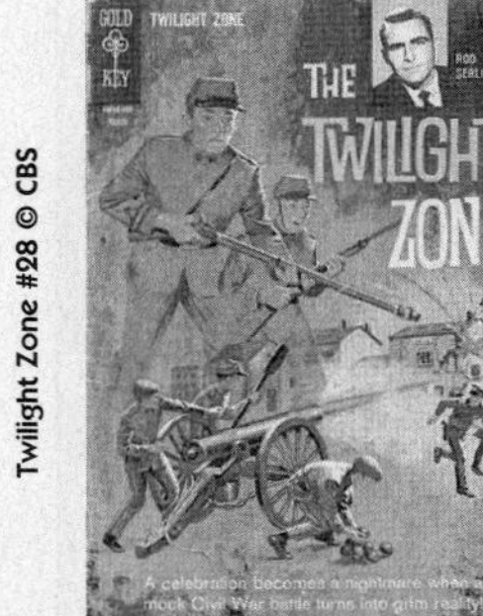

Twilight Zone #28 © CBS

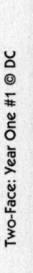

Two-Face: Year One #1 © DC

Two-Gun Kid #19 © MAR

	GD 2.0	VG 4.0	FN 6.0	VF 8.0	VF/NM 9.0	NM- 9.2
3-11: 3(11 pgs.),4(10 pgs.),9-Toth-a	6	12	18	37	66	95
12-15: 12-Williamson-a. 13,15-Crandall-a. 14-Orlando/Crandall/Torres-a	5	10	15	31	53	75
16-20	4	8	12	25	40	55
21-25: 21-Crandall-a(r). 25-Evans/Crandall-a(r); Toth-r/#4; last 12¢ issue	3	6	9	19	30	40
26,27: 26-Flying Saucer-c/story; Crandall, Evans-a(r). 27-Evans-r(2)	3	6	9	18	28	38
28-32: 32-Evans-a(r)	3	6	9	16	24	32
33-51: 43-Celardo-a. 51-Williamson-a	2	4	6	13	18	22
52-70	2	4	6	10	14	18
71-82,86-91: 71-Reprint	2	4	6	8	11	14
83-(52 pgs.)	3	6	9	14	20	25
84-(52 pgs.) Frank Miller's 1st comic book work	9	18	27	60	120	180
85-Frank Miller-a (2nd)	5	10	15	33	57	80
92-(Whitman, 5/82) Last issue; r/#1.	2	4	6	9	13	16
Mini Comic #1(1976, 3-1/4x6-1/2")	2	4	6	8	10	12

NOTE: ***Bolle** a-13(w/**McWilliams**), 50, 55, 57, 59, 77, 78, 80, 83, 84. **McWilliams** a-59, 78, 80, 82, 84. **Miller** a-84, 85. **Orlando** a-15, 19, 20, 22, 23. **Sekowsky** a-3. **Simonson** a-50, 54, 55, 83r. **Weiss** a-39, 79r(#39). (See Mystery Comics Digest 3, 6, 9, 12, 15, 18, 21, 24). Reprints-26(1/3), 71, 73, 79, 83, 84, 86, 92. Painted c-1-91.*

TWILIGHT ZONE, THE (TV)
Now Comics: Nov, 1990 ($2.95); Oct, 1991; V2#1, Nov, 1991 - No. 11, Oct, 1992 ($1.95); V3#1, 1993 - No. 4, 1993 ($2.50)

	NM-
1-(11/90, $2.95, 52 pgs.)-Direct sale edition; Neal Adams-a, Sienkiewicz-c; Harlan Ellison scripts	5.00
1-(11/90, $1.75)-Newsstand ed. w/N. Adams-c	4.00
1-Prestige Format (10/91, $4.95)-Reprints above with extra Harlan Ellison short story	5.00
1-Collector's Edition (10/91, $2.50)-Non-code approved and polybagged; reprints 11/90 issue; gold logo, 1-Reprint ($2.50)-r/direct sale 11/90 version, 1-Reprint ($2.50)-r/newsstand 11/90 version each...	4.00
V2#1-Direct sale & newsstand ed. w/different-c	3.00
V2#2-8,10-11	3.00
V2#9-($2.95)-3-D Special; polybagged w/glasses & hologram on-c	4.00
V2#9-($4.95)-Prestige Edition; contains 2 extra stories & a different hologram on-c; polybagged w/glasses	5.00
V3#1-4, Anniversary Special 1 (1992, $2.50)	3.00
Annual 1 (4/93, $2.50)-No ads	4.00
...Science Fiction Special (3/93, $3.50)	4.00

TWILIGHT ZONE, THE (TV)
Dynamite Entertainment: 2014 - No. 12, 2015 ($3.99)

	NM-
1-12-Straczynski-s/Vilanova-a/Francavilla-c	4.00
#1959 (2016, $5.99) Short stories set in 1959; Valiente & Worley-a; Lau-c	6.00
Annual 2014 ($7.99) Three short stories; Rahner-s/Valiente, Malaga, Menna-a	8.00

TWILIGHT ZONE THE SHADOW (TV)
Dynamite Entertainment: 2016 - No. 4, 2016 ($3.99, limited series)

	NM-
1-4-Avallone-s/Acosta-a/Francavilla-c; Shiwwan Khan app.	4.00

TWILIGHT ZONE, THE: SHADOW & SUBSTANCE (TV)
Dynamite Entertainment: 2015 - No. 4, 2015 ($3.99)

	NM-
1-4-Rahner-s/Menna-a; multiple covers on each	4.00

TWINKLE COMICS
Spotlight Publishers: May, 1945

	GD	VG	FN	VF	VF/NM	NM-
1	27	54	81	158	259	360

TWIST, THE
Dell Publishing Co.: July-Sept, 1962

	GD	VG	FN	VF	VF/NM	NM-
01-864-209-Painted-c	4	8	12	23	37	50

TWISTED TALES (See Eclipse Graphic Album Series #15)
Pacific Comics/Independent Comics Group (Eclipse) #9,10: 11/82 - No. 8, 5/84; No. 9, 11/84; No. 10, 12/84 (Baxter paper)

	GD	VG	FN	VF	VF/NM	NM-
1-9: 1-B. Jones/Corben-c; Alcala-a; nudity/violence in al. 2-Wrightson-c; Ploog-a						5.00
10-Wrightson painted art; Morrow-a	1	2	3	4	5	7

NOTE: ***Bolton** painted c-4, 6, 7; a-7. **Conrad** a-1, 3, 5; c-1i, 3, 5. **Guice** a-8. **Wildey** a-3.*

TWO BIT THE WACKY WOODPECKER (See Wacky...)
Toby Press: 1951 - No. 3, May, 1953

	GD	VG	FN	VF	VF/NM	NM-
1	12	24	36	69	97	125
2,3	8	16	24	40	50	60

TWO FACE: YEAR ONE
DC Comics: 2008 - No. 2, 2008 ($5.99, squarebound, limited series)

	NM-
1,2-Origin re-told; Sable-s/Saiz & Haun-a	6.00

TWO-FISTED TALES (Formerly Haunt of Fear #15-17)
(Also see EC Archives • Two-Fisted Tales)
E. C. Comics: No. 18, Nov-Dec, 1950 - No. 41, Feb-Mar, 1955

	GD 2.0	VG 4.0	FN 6.0	VF 8.0	VF/NM 9.0	NM- 9.2
18(#1)-Kurtzman-c	111	222	333	888	1419	1950
19-Kurtzman-c	74	148	222	592	946	1300
20-Kurtzman-c	51	102	153	408	654	900
21,22-Kurtzman-c	41	82	123	328	527	725
23-25-Kurtzman-c	31	62	93	248	399	550
26-29,31-Kurtzman-c. 31-Civil War issue	24	48	72	192	309	425
30-Classic Davis-c	29	58	87	232	366	500
32-34: 33- "Atom Bomb" by Wood	24	48	72	192	309	425
35-Classic Davis Civil War-c/s	30	60	90	240	383	525
36-41	19	38	57	152	246	340
Two-Fisted Annual (1952, 25¢, 132 pgs.)	119	238	357	893	1372	1850
Two-Fisted Annual (1953, 25¢, 132 pgs.)	86	172	258	645	985	1325

NOTE: ***Berg** a-29. **Colan** a-30,39p. **Craig** a-18, 19, 32. **Crandall** a-35, 36. **Davis** a-20-36, 40; c-30, 34, 35, 41, Annual 2. **Estrada** a-30. **Evans** a-34, 40, 41; c-40. **Feldstein** a-18. **Krigstein** a-41. **Kubert** a-32, 33. **Kurtzman** a-18-25; c-18-29, 31, Annual 1. **Severin** a-26, 28, 29, 31, 34-41 (No. 37-39 are all-**Severin** issues); c-36-39. **Severin/Elder** a-19-29, 31, 33, 36. **Wood** a-18-28, 30-35, 41; c-32, 33. Special issues: #26 (ChanJin Reservoir), 31 (Civil War), 35 (Civil War). Canadian reprints known; see Table of Contents. #25-Davis biog. #27-Wood biog. #28-Kurtzman biog.*

TWO-FISTED TALES
Russ Cochran/Gemstone Publishing: Oct, 1992 - No. 24, May, 1998 ($1.50/$2.00/$2.50)

	NM-
1-24: 1-4r/Two-Fisted Tales #18-21 w/original-c	4.00

TWO-GUN KID (Also see All Western Winners, Best Western, Black Rider, Blaze Carson, Kid Colt, Western Winners, Wild West, & Wild Western)
Marvel/Atlas (MCI No. 1-10/HPC No. 11-59/Marvel No. 60 on): 3/48(No mo.) - No. 10, 11/49; No. 11, 12/53 - No. 59, 4/61; No. 60, 11/62 - No. 92, 3/68; No. 93, 7/70 - No. 136, 4/77

	GD	VG	FN	VF	VF/NM	NM-
1-Two-Gun Kid & his horse Cyclone begin; The Sheriff begins	148	296	444	947	1624	2300
2	55	110	165	352	601	850
3,4: 3-Annie Oakley app.	42	84	126	265	445	625
5-Pre-Black Rider app. (Wint. 48/49); Anti-Wertham editorial (1st?)	43	86	129	271	461	650
6-10(11/49): 8-Blaze Carson app. 9-Black Rider app.	36	72	108	211	343	475
11(12/53)-Black Rider app.; 1st to have Atlas globe on-c; explains how Kid Colt became an outlaw	30	60	90	177	289	400
12-Black Rider app.	27	54	81	158	259	360
13-20: 14-Opium story	23	46	69	136	223	310
21-24,26-29	21	42	63	126	206	285
25,30: 25-Williamson-a (5 pgs.). 30-Williamson/Torres-a (4 pgs.)	22	44	66	132	216	300
31-33,35,37-40	12	24	36	79	170	260
34-Crandall-a	12	24	36	80	173	265
36,41,42,48-Origin in all	12	24	36	82	179	275
43,44,47	11	22	33	73	157	240
45,46-Davis-a	11	22	33	76	163	250
49,50,52,53-Severin-a(2/3) in each	10	20	30	70	150	230
51-Williamson-a (5 pgs.)	11	22	33	76	163	250
54,55,57,59-Severin-a(3) in each. 59-Kirby-a; last 10¢ issue (4/61)	10	20	30	70	150	230
56	10	20	30	68	144	220
58-New origin; Kirby/Ayers-c/a "The Monster of Hidden Valley" cover/story (Kirby monster-c)	27	54	81	189	420	650
60-New origin	54	108	162	432	966	1500
60-Edition w/handwritten issue number on cover	57	114	171	456	1028	1600
61,62-Kirby-a	13	26	39	89	195	300
63-74: 64-Intro. Boom-Boom	8	16	24	54	102	150
75,76-Kirby-a (reprint)	8	16	24	56	108	160
77-Kirby-a (reprint); Black Panther-esque villain	9	18	27	59	117	175
78-89	5	10	15	31	53	75
90,95-Kirby-a	5	10	15	31	53	75
91,92: 92-Last new story; last 12¢ issue	4	8	12	28	47	65
93,94,96-99	3	6	9	16	23	30
100-Last 15¢-c	3	6	9	16	24	32
101-Origin retold/#58; Kirby-a	3	6	9	16	24	32
102-120-reprints	2	4	6	11	16	20
121-136-reprints. 129-131-(Regular 25¢ editions)	2	4	6	11	16	20
129-131-(30¢-c variants, limited distribution)(4-8/76)	7	14	21	44	82	120

NOTE: ***Ayers** a-13, 24, 26, 27, 63, 66. **Davis** c-45-47. **Drucker** a-23. **Everett** a-82, 91. **Fuje** a-13. **Heath** a-3(2), 4(3), 5(2), 7; c-13, 21, 23, 53. **Keller** a-16, 19, 28, 42. **Kirby** a-54, 55, 57-62, 75-77, 90, 95, 101, 119, 120, 129; c-10, 52, 54-65, 67-72, 74-76, 116. **Maneely** a-20; c-11, 12, 16, 19, 20, 24-28, 30, 35, 41, 42, 49. **Powell** a-38, 102,*

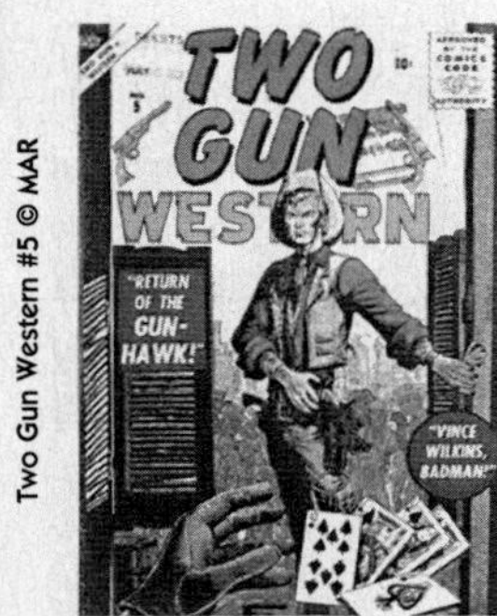

Two Gun Western #5 © MAR

Uber #19 © Avatar

Ultimate Captain America #1 © MAR

GD VG FN VF VF/NM NM-
2.0 4.0 6.0 8.0 9.0 9.2

*104. **Severin** a-9, 29, 51, 55, 57, 99r(3); c-9, 39, 51. **Shores** c-1-8, 11. **Trimpe** c-99. **Tuska** a-11, 12. **Whitney** a-87, 89-92, 98-113, 124, 129; c-87, 89, 91, 113. **Wildey** a-21. **Williamson** a-110r. Kid Colt in #13, 14, 16-21.*

TWO GUN KID: SUNSET RIDERS
Marvel Comics: Nov, 1995 - No. 2, Dec, 1995 ($6.95, squarebound, lim. series)

1,2: Fabian Nicieza scripts in all. 1-Painted-c. 7.00

TWO GUN WESTERN (1st Series) (Formerly Casey Crime Photographer #1-4? or My Love #1-4?)
Marvel/Atlas Comics (MPC): No. 5, Nov, 1950 - No. 14, June, 1952

5-The Apache Kid (Intro & origin) & his horse Nightwind begin by Buscema
32 64 96 188 307 425
6-10: 8-Kid Colt, The Texas Kid & his horse Thunder begin?
21 42 63 124 202 280
11-14: 13-Black Rider app. 15 30 45 90 140 190
NOTE: *Maneely a-6, 7, 9; c-6, 11-13. Morrow a-9. Romita a-8. Wildey a-8.*

2-GUN WESTERN (2nd Series) (Formerly Billy Buckskin #1-3; Two-Gun Western #5 on)
Atlas Comics (MgPC): No. 4, May, 1956

4-Colan, Ditko, Severin, Sinnott-a; Maneely-c 19 38 57 109 172 235

TWO-GUN WESTERN (Formerly 2-Gun Western)
Atlas Comics (MgPC): No. 5, July, 1956 - No. 12, Sept, 1957

5-Return of the Gun-Hawk-c/story; Black Rider app. 18 36 54 105 165 225
6,7 15 30 45 83 124 165
8,10,12-Crandall-a 15 30 45 85 130 175
9,11-Williamson-a in both (5 pgs. each) 15 30 45 88 137 185
NOTE: ***Ayers** a-9. **Colan** a-5. **Everett** c-12. **Forgione** a-5, 6. **Kirby** a-12. **Maneely** a-6, 8, 12; c-5, 6, 8, 11. **Morrow** a-9, 10. **Powell** a-7, 11. **Severin** c-10. **Sinnott** a-5. **Wildey** a-9.*

TWO MINUTE WARNING
Ultimate Sports Ent.: 2000 - No. 2 ($3.95, cardstock covers)

1,2-NFL players & Teddy Roosevelt battle evil 4.00

TWO MOUSEKETEERS, THE (See 4-Color #475, 603, 642 under M.G.M.'s...;

TWO ON A GUILLOTINE (See Movie Classics)

TWO-STEP
DC Comics (Cliffhanger): Dec, 2003 - No. 3, Jul, 2004 ($2.95, limited series)

1-3-Warren Ellis-s/Amanda Conner-a 3.00
TPB (2010, $19.99) r/#1-3; sketch pages; script for #1 with B&W art 20.00

2000 A.D. MONTHLY/PRESENTS (Showcase #25 on)
Eagle Comics/Quality Comics No. 5 on: 4/85 - #6, 9/85; 4/86 - #54, 1991 ($1.25-$1.50, Mando paper)

1-6,1-25:1-4 r/British series featuring Judge Dredd; Alan Moore scripts begin.
1-25 ($1.25)-Reprints from British 2000 AD 4.00
26,27/28, 29/30, 31-54: 27/28, 29/30,31-Guice-c 3.00

2001, A SPACE ODYSSEY (Movie) (See adaptation in Treasury edition)
Marvel Comics Group: Dec, 1976 - No. 10, Sept, 1977 (30¢)

1-Kirby-c/a in all 3 6 9 17 26 35
2-7,9,10 2 4 6 9 12 15
7,9,10-(35¢-c variants, limited distribution)(6-9/77) 8 16 24 54 102 150
8-Origin/1st app. Machine Man (called Mr. Machine) 5 10 15 33 57 80
8-(35¢-c variant, limited distribution)(6,8/77) 17 34 51 117 259 400
...Treasury 1 ('76, 84 pgs.)-All new Kirby-a 3 6 9 16 23 30

2001 NIGHTS
Viz Premiere Comics: 1990 - No. 10, 1991 ($3.75, B&W, lim. series, mature readers, 84 pgs.)

1-10: Japanese sci-fi. 1-Wraparound-c 5.00

2010 (Movie)
Marvel Comics Group: Apr, 1985 - No. 2, May, 1985

1,2-r/Marvel Super Special movie adaptation. 4.00

TYPHOID (Also see Daredevil)
Marvel Comics: Nov, 1995 - No. 4, Feb, 1996 ($3.95, squarebound, lim. series)

1-4: Van Fleet-c/a 4.00

ÜBER
Avatar Press: No. 0, Mar, 2013 - No. 27, Jul, 2015 ($3.99)

0-27: 0-11-Kieron Gillen-s/Caanan White-a. 12-14-Andrade-a 4.00
... FCBD 2014 (2/14, Free Comic Book Day giveaway) Text synopsis of early storyline 3.00
... Special 1 (3/14, $5.99) Andrade-a 6.00

UFO & ALIEN COMIX
Warren Publishing Co.: Jan, 1978 (B&W magazine, 84 pgs., one-shot)

nn-Toth-a, J. Severin-a(r); Pie-s 2 4 6 10 14 18

UFO & OUTER SPACE (Formerly UFO Flying Saucers)
Gold Key: No. 14, June, 1978 - No. 25, Feb, 1980 (All painted covers)

14-Reprints UFO Flying Saucers #3 1 3 4 6 8 10
15,16-Reprints 1 3 4 6 8 10
17-25: 17-20-New material. 23-McWilliams-a. 24-(3 pg.-r). 25-Reprints UFO Flying Saucers #2 w/cover 1 3 4 6 8 10

UFO ENCOUNTERS
Western Publishing Co.: May, 1978 ($1.95, 228 pgs.)

11192-Reprints UFO Flying Saucers 4 8 12 27 44 60
11404-Vol.1 (128 pgs.)-See UFO Mysteries for Vol. 2 4 8 12 23 37 50

UFO FLYING SAUCERS (UFO & Outer Space #14 on)
Gold Key: Oct, 1968 - No. 13, Jan, 1977 (No. 2 on, 36 pgs.)

1(30035-810) (68 pgs.) 5 10 15 33 57 80
2(11/70), 3(11/72), 4(11/74) 3 6 9 17 26 35
5(2/75)-13: Bolle-a #4 on 2 4 6 13 18 22

UFOLOGY
BOOM! Studios: Apr, 2015 - No. 6, Nov, 2015 ($3.99, limited series)

1-6-James Tynion IV & Noah J. Yuenkel-s/Matthew Fox-a 4.00

UFO MYSTERIES
Western Publishing Co.: 1978 ($1.00, reprints, 96 pgs.)

11400-(Vol.2)-Cont'd from UFO Encounters, pgs. 129-224
4 8 12 23 37 50

ULTIMAN GIANT ANNUAL (See Big Bang Comics)
Image Comics: Nov, 2001 ($4.95, B&W, one-shot)

1-Homage to DC 1960's annuals 5.00

ULTIMATE... (Collects 4-issue alternate titles from X-Men Age of Apocalypse crossovers)
Marvel Comics: May, 1995 ($8.95, trade paperbacks, gold foil covers)

Amazing X-Men, Astonishing X-Men, Factor-X, Gambit & the X-Ternals, Generation Next, X-Calibre, X-Man 9.00
Weapon X 10.00

ULTIMATE ADVENTURES
Marvel Comics: Nov, 2002 - No. 6, Dec, 2003 ($2.25)

1-6: 1-Intro. Hawk-Owl; Zimmerman-s/Fegredo-a. 3-Ultimates app. 3.00
One Tin Soldier TPB (2005, $12.99) r/#1-6 13.00

ULTIMATE ANNUALS
Marvel Comics: 2006; 2007 ($13.99, SC)

Vol. 1 (2006, $13.99) r/Ult. FF Ann. #1, Ult. X-Men Ann. #1, Ult S-M #1, Ultimates Ann #1 14.00
Vol. 2 (2007, $13.99) r/Ult. FF Ann. #2, Ult. X-Men Ann. #2, Ult S-M #2, Ultimates Ann #2 14.00

ULTIMATE ARMOR WARS (Follows Ultimatum x-over)
Marvel Comics: Nov, 2009 - No. 4, Apr, 2010 ($3.99, limited series)

1-4-Warren Ellis-s/Steve Kurth-a/Brandon Peterson-c. 1-Variant-c by Kurth 4.00

ULTIMATE AVENGERS (Follows Ultimatum x-over)
Marvel Comics: Oct, 2009 - No. 18 ($3.99)

1-6-Mark Millar-s/Carlos Pacheco-a/c; Red Skull app. 4.00
1-Variant Red Skull-c by Leinil Yu 8.00
7-12-(Ultimate Avengers 2 #1-6 on cover) Yu-a; Punisher joins. 10-Origin Ghost Rider 4.00
7-Variant Ghost Rider-c by Silvestri 8.00
13-18-(Ultimate Avengers 3 #1-6 on cover) Dillon-a; Blade and a new Daredevil app. 4.00

ULTIMATE AVENGERS VS. NEW ULTIMATES (Death of Spider-Man tie-in)
Marvel Comics: Apr, 2011 - No. 6, Sept, 2011 ($3.99, limited series)

1-6: 1-Millar-s/Yu-a/c; variant covers by Cho & Hitch. 3-6-Punisher app. 4.00

ULTIMATE CAPTAIN AMERICA
Marvel Comics: Mar, 2011 - No. 4, Jun, 2011 ($3.99)

1-4: 1-Aaron-s/Garney-a; 2 covers by Garney & McGuinness 4.00
Annual 1 (12/08, $3.99, one-shot) Origin of the Black Panther; Djurdjevic-a 4.00

ULTIMATE CIVIL WAR: SPIDER-HAM (See Civil War and related titles)
Marvel Comics: March, 2007 ($2.99, one-shot)

1-Spoof of Civil War series featuring Spider-Ham; art by various incl. Olivetti, Severin 3.00

ULTIMATE COMICS IRON MAN
Marvel Comics: Dec, 2012 - No. 4, Mar, 2013 ($3.99, limited series)

1-4-Edmonson-s/Buffagni-a/Stockton-c 4.00

ULTIMATE COMICS SPIDER-MAN (See Ultimate Spider-Man 2011 series)

ULTIMATE COMICS ULTIMATES (See Ultimates 2011 series)

ULTIMATE COMICS WOLVERINE

Ultimate Fantastic Four #3 © MAR

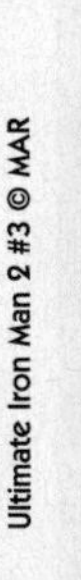

Ultimate Iron Man 2 #3 © MAR

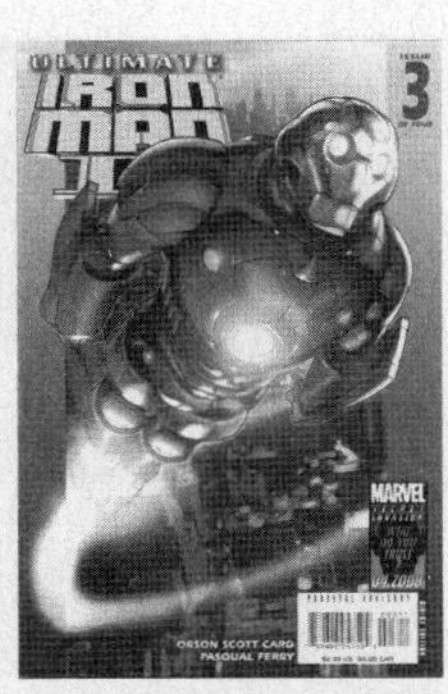

Ultimate New Ultimates #3 © MAR

GD 2.0 | VG 4.0 | FN 6.0 | VF 8.0 | VF/NM 9.0 | NM- 9.2

Marvel Comics: May, 2013 - No. 4, Jul, 2013 ($3.99, limited series)
1-4: 1-Bunn-s/Messina-a/Art Adams-c; Wolverine app. in flashback 4.00

ULTIMATE COMICS X-MEN (See Ultimate X-Men 2011 series)

ULTIMATE DAREDEVIL AND ELEKTRA
Marvel Comics: Jan, 2003 - No. 4, Mar, 2003 ($2.25, limited series)
1-4-Rucka-s/Larroca-c/a; 1st meeting of Elektra and Matt Murdock 3.00
... Vol.1 TPB (2003, $11.99) r/#1-4, Daredevil Vol. 2 #9; Larroca sketch pages 12.00

ULTIMATE DOOM (Follows Ultimate Mystery mini-series)
Marvel Comics: Feb, 2011 - No. 4, May, 2011 ($3.99, limited series)
1-4-Bendis-s/Sandoval-a; Fantastic Four, Spider-Man, Jessica Drew & Nick Fury app. 4.00

ULTIMATE ELEKTRA
Marvel Comics: Oct, 2004 - No. 5, Feb, 2005 ($2.25, limited series)
1-5-Carey-s/Larroca-c/a. 2-Bullseye app. 3.00
... : Devil's Due TPB (2005, $11.99) r/#1-5 12.00

ULTIMATE END (Secret Wars Battleworld tie-in)
Marvel Comics: Jul, 2015 - No. 5, Feb, 2016 ($3.99, limited series)
1-5-Bendis-s/Bagley-a; Spider-Man & Earth-616 Avengers & Ultimate Universe app. 4.00

ULTIMATE ENEMY (Follows Ultimatum x-over)(Leads into Ultimate Mystery)
Marvel Comics: Mar, 2010 - No. 4, July, 2010 ($3.99, limited series)
1-4-Bendis-s/Sandoval-a 1-Covers by McGuinness and Pearson 4.00

ULTIMATE EXTINCTION (See Ultimate Nightmare and Ultimate Secret limited series)
Marvel Comics: Mar, 2006 - No. 5, July, 2006 ($2.99, limited series)
1-5-The coming of Gah Lak Tus; Ellis-s/Peterson-a 3.00
TPB (2006, $12.99) r/#1-5 13.00

ULTIMATE FALLOUT (Follows Death of Spider-Man in Ultimate Spider-Man #160)
Marvel Comics: Sept, 2011 - No. 6, Oct, 2011 ($3.99, weekly limited series)
1-3,5,6: 1-Bendis-s/Bagley-a/c. 2,6-Hitch-c. 3,5-Andy Kubert-c 4.00
4-Debut of Miles Morales as the new Spider-Man; polybagged
2 4 6 11 16 20

ULTIMATE FANTASTIC FOUR (Continues in Ultimatum mini-series)
Marvel Comics: Feb, 2004 - No. 60, Apr, 2009 ($2.25/$2.50/$2.99)
1-Bendis & Millar-s/Adam Kubert-a/Hitch-c 5.00
2-20: 2-Adam Kubert-a/c; intro. Moleman 7-Ellis-s/Immonen-a begin; Dr. Doom app. 13-18-Kubert-a. 19,20-Jae Lee-a. 20-Begin $2.50-c 3.50
21-Marvel Zombies; begin Greg Land-c/a; Mark Millar-s; variant-c by Land 5.00
22-29,33-59: 24-26-Namor app. 28-President Thor. 33-38-Ferry-a. 42-46-Silver Surfer 3.00
30-32-Marvel Zombies; Millar-s/Land-a; Dr. Doom app. 5.00
30-32-Zombie variant-c by Suydam 6.00
50-White variant-c by Kirkham 5.00
60-($3.99) Ultimatum crossover; Kirkham-a 4.00
Annual 1 (10/05, $3.99) The Inhumans app.; Jae Lee-a/Mark Millar-s/Greg Land-c 4.00
Annual 2 (10/06, $3.99) Mole Man app.; Immonen & Irving-a/Carey-s 4.00
... MGC #1 (6/11, $1.00) r/#1 with "Marvel's Greatest Comics" logo on cover 3.00
.../Ult. X-Men Annual 1 (11/08, $3.99) Continued from Ult. X-Men/Ult. F.F. Annual #1 4.00
.../X-Men 1 (3/06, $2.99) Carey-s/Ferry-a; continued from Ult. X-Men/Fantastic Four #1 3.00
... Vol. 1: The Fantastic (2004, $12.99, TPB) r/#1-6; cover gallery 13.00
... Vol. 2: Doom (2004, $12.99, TPB) r/#7-12 13.00
... Vol. 3: N-Zone (2005, $12.99, TPB) r/#13-18 13.00
... Vol. 4: Inhuman (2005, $12.99, TPB) r/#19,20 & Annual #1 13.00
... Vol. 5: Crossover (2006, $12.99, TPB) r/#21-26 13.00
... Vol. 6: Frightful (2006, $14.99, TPB) r/#27-32; gallery of cover sketches & variants 15.00
... Vol. 7: God War (2007, $16.99, TPB) r/#33-38 17.00
... Vol. 8: Devils (2007, $12.99, TPB) r/#39-41 & Annual #2 13.00
... Vol. 9: Silver Surfer (2007, $13.99, TPB) r/#42-46 14.00
Volume 1 HC (2005, $29.99, 7x11", dust jacket) r/#1-12; introduction, proposals and scripts by Millar and Bendis; character design pages by Hitch 30.00
Volume 2 HC (2006, $29.99, 7x11", dust jacket) r/#13-20; Jae Lee sketch page 30.00
Volume 3 HC (2007, $29.99, 7x11", dust jacket) r/#21-32; Greg Land sketch pages 30.00
Volume 4 HC (2007, $29.99, 7x11", dust jacket) r/#33-41, Annual #2, Ultimate FF/X-Men and Ultimate X-Men/FF; character design pages 30.00
Volume 5 HC (2008, $34.99, 7x11", dust jacket) r/#42-53 35.00

ULTIMATE FF
Marvel Comics: Jun, 2014 - No. 6, Oct, 2014 ($3.99)
1-6: 1-Team of Sue Storm, Iron Man, Falcon, Machine Man. 4,5-Spider-Ham app. 4.00

ULTIMATE GALACTUS TRILOGY
Marvel Comics: 2007 ($34.99, hardcover, dustjacket)
HC-Oversized reprint of Ultimate Nightmare #1-5, Ultimate Secret #1-4, Ultimate Vision #0, and Ultimate Extinction #1-5; sketch pages and cover galery 35.00

ULTIMATE HAWKEYE (Ultimate Comics)
Marvel Comics: Oct, 2011 - No. 4, Jan, 2012 ($3.99, limited series)
1-4: 1-Hickman-s/Sandoval-a/Andrews-c; polybagged. 2-4-Hulk app. 4.00
1-Variant-c by Neal Adams 6.00
1-Variant-c by Adam Kubert 8.00

ULTIMATE HULK
Marvel Comics: Dec, 2008 ($3.99, one-shot)
Annual 1 (12/08, $3.99) Zarda battles Hulk; McGuinness & Djurdjevic-a/Loeb-s 4.00

ULTIMATE HUMAN
Marvel Comics: Mar, 2008 - No. 4, Jun, 2008 ($2.99, limited series)
1-4-Iron Man vs. The Hulk; The Leader app.; Ellis-s/Nord-a 3.00
HC (2008, $19.99) r/#1-4 20.00

ULTIMATE IRON MAN
Marvel Comics: May, 2005 - No. 5, Feb, 2006 ($2.99, limited series)
1-Origin of Iron Man; Orson Scott Card-s/Andy Kubert-a; two covers 4.00
1-2nd & 3rd printings; each with B&W variant-c 3.00
2-5-Kubert-c 3.00
Volume 1 HC (2006, $19.99, dust jacket) r/#1-5; rough cut of script for #1, cover sketches 20.00
Volume 1 SC (2006, $14.99) r/#1-5; rough cut of script for #1, cover sketches 15.00

ULTIMATE IRON MAN II
Marvel Comics: Feb, 2008 - No. 5, July, 2008 ($2.99, limited series)
1-5-Early days of the Iron Man prototype; Orson Scott Card-s/Pasqual Ferry-a/c 3.00

ULTIMATE MARVEL FLIP MAGAZINE
Marvel Comics: July, 2005 - No. 26, Aug, 2007 ($3.99/$4.99)
1-11-Reprints Ultimate Fantastic Four and Ultimate X-Men in flip format 4.00
12-26-($4.99) 5.00

ULTIMATE MARVEL MAGAZINE
Marvel Comics: Feb, 2001 - No. 11, 2002 ($3.99, magazine size)
1-11: Reprints of recent stories from the Ultimate titles plus Marvel news and features. 1-Reprints Ultimate Spider-Man #1&2. 11-Lord of the Rings-c 4.00

ULTIMATE MARVEL SAMPLER
Marvel Comics: 2007 (no cover price, limited series)
1-Previews of 2008 Ultimate Marvel story arcs; Finch-c 3.00

ULTIMATE MARVEL TEAM-UP (Spider-Man Team-up)
Marvel Comics: Apr, 2001 - No. 16, July, 2002 ($2.99/$2.25)
1-Spider-Man & Wolverine; Bendis-s in all; Matt Wagner-a/c 5.00
2,3-Hulk; Hester-a 3.50
4,5,9-16: 4,5-Iron Man; Allred-a. 9-Fantastic Four; Mahfood-a. 10-Man-Thing; Totleben-a. 11-X-Men; Clugston-Major-a. 12,13-Dr. Strange; McKeever-a.14-Black Widow; Terry Moore-a. 15,16-Shang-Chi; Mays-a 3.00
6-8-Punisher; Sienkiewicz-a. 7,8-Daredevil app. 4.00
TPB (11/01, $14.95) r/#1-5 15.00
... Ultimate Collection TPB ('06, $29.99) r/#1-16 & Ult. Spider-Man Spec.; sketch pages 30.00
HC (8/02, $39.99) r/#1-16 & Ult. Spider-Man Special; Bendis afterword 40.00
...: Vol. 2 TPB (2003, $11.99) r/#9-13; Mahfood-c 12.00
...: Vol. 3 TPB (2003, $12.99) r/#14-16 & Ultimate Spider-Man Super Special; Moore-c 13.00

ULTIMATE MYSTERY (Follows Ultimate Enemy)(Leads into Ultimate Doom)
Marvel Comics: Sept, 2010 - No. 4, Dec, 2010 ($3.99, limited series)
1-4-Bendis-s/Sandoval-a; Rick Jones returns; Captain Marvel app. 1-3-Campbell-c 4.00

ULTIMATE NEW ULTIMATES (Follows Ultimatum x-over)
Marvel Comics: May, 2010 - No. 5, Mar, 2011 ($3.99)
1-5: 1-Jeph Loeb-s/Frank Cho-a; 6-page wraparound-c by Cho; Defenders app. 4.00
1-Villains variant-c by Yu 8.00

ULTIMATE NIGHTMARE (Leads into Ultimate Secret limited series)
Marvel Comics: Oct, 2004 - No. 5, Feb, 2005 ($2.25, limited series)
1-5: Ellis-s; Ultimates, X-Men, Nick Fury app. 1,2,4,5-Hairsine-a/c. 3-Epting-a 3.00
Ultimate Galactus Book 1: Nightmare TPB (2005, $12.99) r/Ultimate Nightmare #1-5 13.00

ULTIMATE ORIGINS
Marvel Comics: Aug, 2008 - No. 5, Dec, 2008 ($2.99, limited series)
1-5-Bendis-s/Guice-a. 1-Nick Fury origin in the 1940s. 2-Capt. America origin 3.00

ULTIMATE POWER
Marvel Comics: Dec, 2006 - No. 9, Feb, 2008 ($2.99, limited series)

Ultimates (2011 series) #1 © MAR

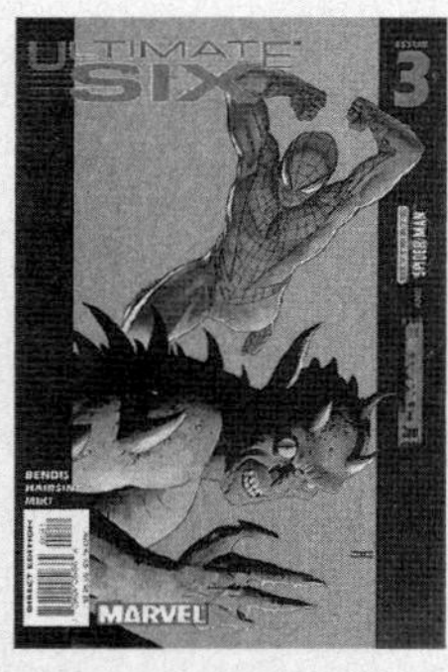

Ultimate Six #3 © MAR

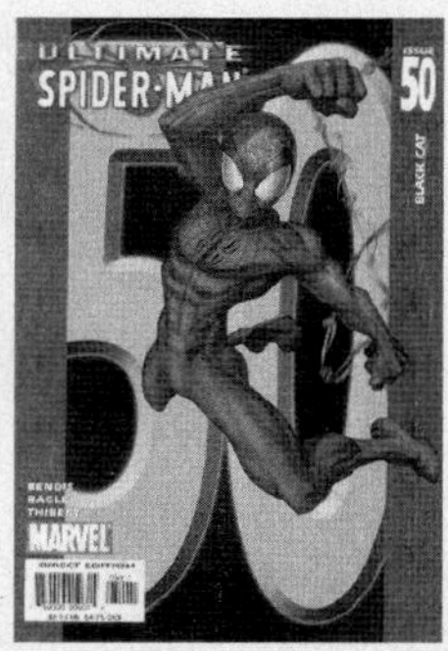

Ultimate Spider-Man #50 © MAR

GD VG FN VF VF/NM NM-
2.0 4.0 6.0 8.0 9.0 9.2

1-9: 1-Ultimate FF meets the Squadron Supreme; Bendis-s; Land-a/c. 2-Spider-Man, X-Men and the Ultimates app. 6-Doom app. 3.00
1-Variant sketch-c 5.00
1-Director's Cut (2007, $3.99) r/#1 and B&W pencil and ink pages; covers to #2,3 4.00
HC (2008, $34.99) oversized r/series; profile pages; B&W sketch art 35.00

ULTIMATES, THE (Avengers of the Ultimate line)
Marvel Comics: Mar, 2002 - No. 13, Apr, 2004 ($2.25)

1-Intro. Capt. America; Millar-s/Hitch-a & wraparound-c 6.00
2-Intro. Giant-Man and the Wasp 4.00
3-12: 3-1st Capt. America in new costume. 4-Intro. Thor. 5-Ultimates vs. The Hulk. 8-Intro. Hawkeye 3.00
13-($3.50) 4.00
... MGC #1 (5/11, $1.00) r/#1 with "Marvel's Greatest Comics" logo on cover 3.00
... Saga (2007, $3.99) Re-caps 1st 2 Ultimates series; new framing art by Charest; prelude to Ultimates 3 series; Brooks-c 4.00
... Volume 1 HC (2004, $29.99) oversized r/series; commentary pages with Millar & Hitch; cover gallery and character design pages; intro. by Joss Whedon 30.00
... Volume 1: Super-Human TPB (8/02, $12.99) r/#1-6 13.00
... Volume 2: Homeland Security TPB (2004, $17.99) r/#7-13 18.00

ULTIMATES (Ultimate Comics) (Continues in Hunger)
Marvel Comics: Oct, 2011 - No. 30, Nov, 2013 ($3.99)

1-30: 1-Hickman-s/Ribic-a/Andrews-c; polybagged. 4-Reed Richards returns 4.00
1-Variant-c by Esad Ribic 6.00
#18.1 (2/13, $2.99) Eaglesham-a; Stark gets the Iron Patriot armor 3.00
Ultimate Comics Ultimates Must Have 1 (2/12, $4.99) r/#1-3 5.00

ULTIMATES (Follows Secret War event)
Marvel Comics: Jan, 2016 - No. 12, Dec, 2016 ($3.99)

1-12: 1-Ewing-s/Rocafort-a; team of Capt. Marvel, Blue Marvel, Black Panther, Spectrum, and Ms. America; Galactus app. 5,7-11-Thanos app. 6,12-Christian Ward-a. 8-12-Civil War II tie-ins 4.00

ULTIMATES 2
Marvel Comics: Feb, 2005 - No. 13, Feb, 2007 ($2.99/$3.99)

1-Millar-s/Hitch-a; Giant-Man becomes Ant-Man 4.00
2-11: 6-Intro. The Defenders. 7-Hawkeye shot. 8-Intro The Liberators 3.00
12,13-($3.99) Wraparound-c; X-Men, Fantastic Four, Spider-Man app. 4.00
13-Variant white cover featuring The Wasp 15.00
Annual 1 (10/05, $3.99) Millar-s/Dillon-a/Hitch-c; Defenders app. 4.00
Annual 2 (10/06, $3.99) Deodato-a; flashback to WWII with Sook-a; Falcon app. 4.00
HC (2007, $34.99) oversized r/series; commentary pages with Millar & Hitch; cover gallery, sketch and script pages; intro. by Jonathan Ross 35.00
... Volume 1: Gods & Monsters TPB (2005, $15.99) r/#1-6 16.00
... Volume 2: Grand Theft America TPB (2007, $19.99) r/#7-13; cover gallery w/sketches 20.00

ULTIMATES 2
Marvel Comics: Jan, 2017 - Present ($3.99)

1-4-Ewing-s/Foreman-a; team of Capt. Marvel, Blue Marvel, Black Panther, Spectrum, and Ms. America 4.00

ULTIMATES 3
Marvel Comics: Feb, 2008 - No. 5, Nov, 2008 ($2.99)

1-Loeb-s/Madureira-a; two gatefold wraparound covers by Madureira; Scarlet Witch shot 4.00
1,2-Second printings: 1-Wraparound cover by Madureira. 2-Madureira-c 3.00
2-5: 2-Spider-Man app. 3-Wolverine app. 5-Two gatefold wraparound-c (Heroes & Ultron) 3.00
2-Variant Thor cover by Turner 8.00
3-Variant Scarlet Witch cover by Cho 8.00
4-Variant Valkyrie cover by Finch 4.00

ULTIMATE SECRET (See Ultimate Nightmare limited series)
Marvel Comics: May, 2005 - No. 4, Dec, 2005 ($2.99, limited series)

1-4-Ellis-s; Captain Marvel app. 1,2-McNiven-a. 2,3-Ultimates & FF app. 3.00
Ultimate Galactus Book 2: Secret TPB (2006, $12.99) r/#1-4 13.00

ULTIMATE SECRETS
Marvel Comics: 2008 ($3.99, one-shot)

1-Handbook-styled profiles of secondary teams and characters from Ultimate universe 4.00

ULTIMATE SIX (Reprinted in Ultimate Spider-Man Vol. 5 hardcover)
Marvel Comics: Nov, 2003 - No. 7, June, 2004 ($2.25) (See Ultimate Spider-Man for TPB)

1-The Ultimates & Spider-Man team-up; Bendis-s/Quesada & Hairsine-a; Cassaday-c 5.00
2-7-Hairsine-a; Cassaday-c 3.00

ULTIMATE SPIDER-MAN
Marvel Comics: Oct, 2000 - No. 133, June, 2009 ($2.99/$2.25/$2.99/$3.99)

GD VG FN VF VF/NM NM-
2.0 4.0 6.0 8.0 9.0 9.2

1-Bendis-s/Bagley & Thibert-a; cardstock-c; introduces revised origin and cast separate from regular Spider-continuity 6 12 18 41 76 110
1-Variant white-c (Retailer incentive) 9 18 27 62 126 190
1-Dynamic Forces Edition 5 10 15 35 63 90
1-Kay Bee Toys variant edition 2 4 6 9 12 15
2-Cover with Spider-Man on car 3 6 9 18 27 35
2-Cover with Spider-Man swinging past building 3 6 9 18 27 35
3,4: 4-Uncle Ben killed 2 4 6 10 14 18
5-7: 6,7-Green Goblin app. 2 4 6 9 12 15
8-13: 13-Reveals secret to MJ 1 3 4 6 8 10
14-21: 14-Intro. Gwen Stacy & Dr. Octopus 5.00
22-($3.50) Green Goblin returns 6.00
23-32 4.00
33-1st Ultimate Venom-c; intro. Eddie Brock 5.00
34-38-Ultimate Venom 4.00
39-49,51-59: 39-Nick Fury app. 43,44-X-Men app. 46-Prelude to Ultimate Six; Sandman app. 51-53-Elektra app. 54-59-Doctor Octopus app. 3.00
50-($2.99) Intro. Black Cat 4.00
60-Intro. Ultimate Carnage on cover 4.00
61-Intro Ben Reilly; Punisher app. 3.00
62-Gwen Stacy killed by Carnage 4.00
63-92: 63,64-Carnage app. 66,67-Wolverine app. 68,69-Johnny Storm app. 78-Begin $2.50-c. 79-Debut Moon Knight. 81-85-Black Cat app. 90-Vulture app. 91-94-Deadpool 3.00
93-99: 93-Begin $2.99-c. 95-Morbius & Blade app. 97-99-Clone Saga 3.00
100-($3.99) Wraparound-c; Clone Saga; re-cap of previous issues 4.00
101-103-Clone Saga continues; Fantastic Four app. 102-Spider-Woman origin 3.00
104-($3.99) Clone Saga concludes; Fantastic Four and Dr. Octopus app. 4.00
105-132: 106-110-Daredevil app. 111-Last Bagley art; Immonen-a (6 pgs.) 112-Immonen-a; Norman Osborn app. 118-Liz Allen ignites. 123,128-Venom app. 129-132-Ultimatum 3.00
133-($3.99) Ultimatum crossover; Spider-Woman app. 4.00
(Issues #150-up, see second series)
Annual 1 (10/05, $3.99) Kitty Pryde app.; Bendis-s/Brooks-a/Bagley-c 4.00
Annual 2 (10/06, $3.99) Punisher, Moon Knight and Daredevil app.; Bendis-s/Brooks-a 4.00
Annual 3 (12/08, $3.99) Mysterio app.; Bendis-s/Lafuente-a 4.00
Collected Edition (1/01, $3.99) r/#1-3 4.00
Free Comic Book Day giveaway (5/02) - r/#1 with "Free Comic Book Day" banner on-c 3.00
... MGC #1 (5/11, $1.00) r/#1 with "Marvel's Greatest Comics" logo on cover 3.00
...Special (7/02, $3.50) art by Bagley and various incl. Romita, Sr., Brereton, Cho, Mack, Sienkiewicz, Phillips, Pearson, Oeming, Mahfood, Russell 4.00
Ultimate Spider-Man 100 Project (2007, $10.00, SC, charity book for the HERO Initiative) collection of 100 variant covers by Romita Sr. & Jr., Cho, Bagley, Quesada and more 10.00
...: Venom HC (2007, $19.99) r/#33-39 20.00
...(Vol. 1): Power and Responsibility TPB (4/01, $14.95) r/#1-7 15.00
...(Vol. 2): Learning Curve TPB (12/01, $14.95) r/#8-13 15.00
...(Vol. 3): Double Trouble TPB (6/02, $17.95) r/#14-21 18.00
Vol. 4: Legacy TPB (2002, $14.99) r/#22-27 15.00
Vol. 5: Public Scrutiny TPB (2003, $11.99) r/#28-32 12.00
Vol. 6: Venom TPB (2003, $15.99) r/#33-39 16.00
Vol. 7: Irresponsible TPB (2003, $12.99) r/#40-45 13.00
Vol. 8: Cats & Kings TPB (2004, $17.99) r/#47-53 18.00
Vol. 9: Ultimate Six TPB (2004, $17.99) r/#46 & Ultimate Six #1-7 18.00
Vol. 10: Hollywood TPB (2004, $12.99) r/#54-59 13.00
Vol. 11: Carnage TPB (2004, $12.99) r/#60-65 13.00
Vol. 12: Superstars TPB (2005, $12.99) r/#66-71 13.00
Vol. 13: Hobgoblin TPB (2005, $15.99) r/#72-78 16.00
Vol. 14: Warriors TPB (2005, $17.99) r/#79-85 18.00
Vol. 15: Silver Sable TPB (2006, $15.99) r/#86-90 & Annual #1 16.00
Vol. 16: Deadpool TPB (2006, $19.99) r/#91-96 & Annual #2 20.00
Vol. 17: Clone Saga TPB (2007, $24.99) r/#97-105 25.00
Vol. 18: Ultimate Knights TPB (2007, $13.99) r/#106-111 14.00
Vol. 19: Death of a Goblin TPB (2008, $14.99) r/#112-117 15.00
Hardcover (3/02, $34.95, 7x11", dust jacket) r/#1-13 & Amazing Fantasy #15; sketch pages and Bill Jemas' initial plot and character outlines 35.00
Volume 2 HC (2003, $29.99, 7x11", dust jacket) r/#14-27; pin-ups & sketch pages 30.00
Volume 3 HC (2003, $29.99, 7x11", dust jacket) r/#28-39 & #1/2; script pages 30.00
Volume 4 HC (2004, $29.99, 7x11", dust jacket) r/#40-45, 47-53; sketch pages 30.00
Volume 5 HC (2004, $29.99, 7x11", dust jacket) r/#46,54-59, Ultimate Six #1-7 30.00
Volume 6 HC (2005, $29.99, 7x11", dust jacket) r/#60-71; sketch page 30.00
Volume 7 HC (2006, $29.99, 7x11", dust jacket) r/#72-85; sketch & profile pages 30.00
Volume 8 HC (2007, $29.99, 7x11", dust jacket) r/#86-96 & Annual #1&2; sketch page 30.00
Volume 9 HC (2008, $39.99, 7x11", dust jacket) r/#97-111; sketch pages 40.00
Volume 10 HC (2009, $39.99, 7x11", dust jacket) r/#112-122; sketch pages 40.00
Wizard #1/2 1 3 4 6 8 10

Ultimate Spider-Man (2009 series) #1 © MAR

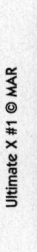

Ultimate X #1 © MAR

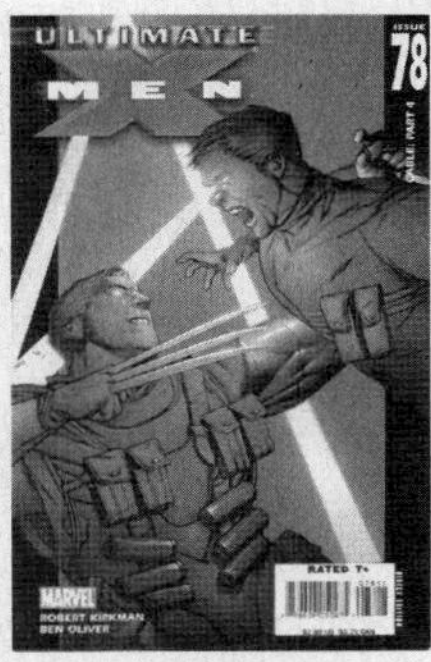

Ultimate X-Men #78 © MAR

	GD 2.0	VG 4.0	FN 6.0	VF 8.0	VF/NM 9.0	NM- 9.2

ULTIMATE SPIDER-MAN (2nd series)(Follows Ultimatum x-over)
Marvel Comics: Oct, 2009 - No. 15, Dec, 2010; No. 150, Jan, 2011 - No. 160, Aug, 2011 ($3.99)

1-15: 1-Bendis-s/Lafuente-a/c; new Mysterio. 1-Variant-c by Djurdjevic. 7,8-Miyazawa-a. 9-Spider-Woman app. 4.00
150-(1/11, $5.99) Resumes original numbering; wraparound-c by Lafuente; Bendis-s with art by Lafuente, Pichelli, Joëlle Jones, McKelvie & Young; r/Ult. S-M Special #1 6.00
150-Variant wraparound-c by Bagley 10.00
151-159: 151-154-Black Cat & Mysterio app. 157-Spider-Man shot by Punisher 4.00
153-159-Variant covers. 153-155-Pichelli. 157-McGuinness. 158-McNiven. 159-Cho 8.00
160-Black Polybagged; Bagley cover inside; Death of Spider-Man part 5 4.00
160-Red Polybagged variant; Kaluta cover inside; Death of Spider-Man part 5 20.00

ULTIMATE SPIDER-MAN (3rd series, with Miles Morales)(See Ultimate Fallout #4 for debut)
Marvel Comics: Nov, 2011 - No. 28, Dec, 2013 ($3.99)

1-Polybagged, with Kaare Andrews-c; Bendis-s/Pichelli-a; origin 6.00
1-Variant Pichelli-c with unmasked Spider-Man 4 8 12 28 47 65
1-Variant Pichelli-c with Spider-Man & city bkgrd 6 12 18 37 66 95
2-28: 4,5-Spider-Woman app. 5-Nick Fury & Ultimates app. 6-Samnee-a. 19-22-Venom War; Pichelli-a. 23-Cloak and Dagger app. 28-Leads into Cataclysm 4.00
#16.1 (12/12, $2.99) Marquez-a; Venom returns 3.00
200-(6/14, $4.99) Art by Marquez and others; 2 interlocking covers by Bagley & Marquez 5.00
Ultimate Comics Spider-Man Must Have 1 (2/12, $4.99) r/#1-3 5.00

ULTIMATE SPIDER-MAN (Based on the animated series)(See Marvel Universe...)

ULTIMATE TALES FLIP MAGAZINE
Marvel Comics: July, 2005 - No. 26, Aug, 2007 ($3.99/$4.99)

1-11-Each reprints 2 issues of Ultimate Spider-Man in flip format 4.00
12-26-($4.99) 5.00

ULTIMATE THOR
Marvel Comics: Dec, 2010 - No. 4, Apr, 2011 ($3.99, limited series)

1-4: 1-Hickman-s/Pacheco-a; two covers by Pacheco & Choi; origin story 4.00

ULTIMATE VISION
Marvel Comics: No. 0, Jan, 2007 - No. 5, Jan, 2008 ($2.99, limited series)

0-Reprints back-up serial from Ultimate Extinction and related series; pin-ups 3.00
1-5: 1-(2/07) Carey-s/Peterson-a/c 3.00
TPB (2007, $14.99) r/#0-5; design pages and cover gallery 15.00

ULTIMATE WAR
Marvel Comics: Feb, 2003 - No. 4, Apr, 2003 ($2.25, limited series)

1-4-Millar-s/Bachalo-c/a; The Ultimates vs. Ultimate X-Men 3.00
Ultimate X-Men Vol. 5: Ultimate War TPB (2003, $10.99) r/#1-4 11.00

ULTIMATE WOLVERINE VS. HULK
Marvel Comics: Feb, 2006 - No. 6, July, 2009 ($2.99, limited series)

1,2-Leinil Yu-a/c; Damon Lindelof-s. 2-(4/06) 4.00
1,2-(2009) New printings 3.00
3-6: 3-(5/09) Intro. She-Hulk. 4-Origin She-Hulk 3.00

ULTIMATE X (Follows Ultimatum x-over)
Marvel Comics: Apr, 2010 - No. 5, Aug, 2011 ($3.99)

1-5: 1-Jeph Loeb-s/Art Adams-a; two covers by Adams. 5-Hulk app. 4.00

ULTIMATE X-MEN
Marvel Comics: Feb, 2001 - No. 100, Apr, 2009 ($2.99/$2.25/$2.50)

1-Millar-s/Adam Kubert & Thibert-a; cardstock-c; introduces revised origin and cast separate from regular X-Men continuity 2 4 6 9 12 15
1-DF Edition 2 4 6 11 16 20
1-DF Sketch Cover Edition 3 6 9 14 20 25
1-Free Comic Book Day Edition (7/03) r/#1 with "Free Comic Book Day" banner on-c 3.00
2 2 4 6 9 12 15
3-6 1 3 4 6 8 10
7-10 6.00
11-24,26-33: 13-Intro. Gambit. 18,19-Bachalo-a. 23,24-Andrews-a 4.00
25-($3.50) leads into the Ultimate War mini-series; Kubert-a 5.00
34-Spider-Man-c/app.; Bendis-s begin; Finch-a 5.00
35-74: 35-Spider-Man app. 36,37-Daredevil-c/app. 40-Intro. Angel. 42-Intro. Dazzler. 44-Beast dies. 46-Intro. Mr. Sinister. 50-53-Kubert-a; Gambit app. 54-57,59-63-Immonen-a. 60-Begin $2.50-c. 61-Variant Coipel-c. 66-Kirkman-s begin. 69-Begin $2.99-c 3.00
61-Retailer Edition with variant Coipel B&W sketch-c 10.00
75-($3.99) Turner-c; intro. Cable; back-up story with Emma Frost's students 4.00
76-99: 76-Intro. Bishop. 91-Fantastic Four app. 92-96-Phoenix app. 96-Spider-Man app. 99-Ultimatum x-over 3.00
100-($3.99) Ultimatum x-over; Brooks-a 4.00
Annual 1 (10/05, $3.99) Vaughan-s/Raney-a; Gambit & Rogue in Vegas 4.00
Annual 2 (10/06, $3.99) Kirkman-s/Larroca-a; Nightcrawler & Dazzler 4.00
.../Fantastic Four 1 (2/06, $2.99) Carey-s/Ferry-a; concluded in Ult. Fantastic Four/X-Men 3.00
... MGC #1 (6/11, $1.00) r/#1 with "Marvel's Greatest Comics" logo on cover 3.00
.../Ult. Fantastic Four Ann. 1 (11/08, $3.99) Continues in Ult. F.F./Ult. X-Men Annual #1 4.00
.../Fantastic Four TPB (2006, $12.99) reprints Ult X-Men/Ult. FF x-over and Official Handbook of the Ultimate Marvel Universe #1-2 13.00
... Ultimate Collection Vol. 1 (2006, $24.99) r/#1-12 & #1/2; unused Bendis script for #1 25.00
... Ultimate Collection Vol. 2 (2007, $24.99) r/#13-25; Kubert cover sketch pages 25.00
...: (Vol. 1) The Tomorrow People TPB (7/01, $14.95) r/#1-6 15.00
...: (Vol. 2) Return to Weapon X TPB (4/02, $14.95) r/#7-12 15.00
Vol. 3: World Tour TPB (2002, $17.99) r/#13-20 18.00
Vol. 4: Hellfire and Brimstone TPB (2003, $12.99) r/#21-25 13.00
Vol. 5 (See Ultimate War)
Vol. 6: Return of the King TPB (2003, $16.99) r/#26-33 17.00
Vol. 7: Blockbuster TPB (2004, $12.99) r/#34-39 13.00
Vol. 8: New Mutants TPB (2004, $12.99) r/#40-45 13.00
Vol. 9: The Tempest TPB (2004, $10.99) r/#46-49 11.00
Vol. 10: Cry Wolf TPB (2005, $8.99) r/#50-53 9.00
Vol. 11: The Most Dangerous Game TPB (2005, $9.99) r/#54-57 10.00
Vol. 12: Hard Lessons TPB (2005, $12.99) r/#58-60 & Annual #1 13.00
Vol. 13: Magnetic North TPB (2006, $12.99) r/#61-65 13.00
Vol. 14: Phoenix? TPB (2006, $14.99) r/#66-71 15.00
Vol. 15: Magical TPB (2007, $11.99) r/#72-74 & Annual #2 12.00
Vol. 16: Cable TPB (2007, $14.99) r/#75-80; sketch pages 15.00
Vol. 17: Sentinels TPB (2008, $17.99) r/#81-88 18.00
Volume 1 HC (8/02, $34.99, 7x11", dust jacket) r/#1-12 & Giant-Size X-Men #1; sketch pages and Millar and Bendis' initial plot and character outlines 35.00
Volume 2 HC (2003, $29.99, 7x11", dust jacket) r/#13-25; script for #20 30.00
Volume 3 HC (2003, $29.99, 7x11", dust jacket) r/#26-33 & Ultimate War #1-4 30.00
Volume 4 HC (2005, $29.99, 7x11", dust jacket) r/#34-45 30.00
Volume 5 HC (2006, $29.99, 7x11", dust jacket) r/#46-57; Vaughan intro.; sketch pages 30.00
Volume 6 HC (2006, $29.99, 7x11", dust jacket) r/#58-65, Annual #1 & Wizard #1/2 30.00
Volume 7 HC (2007, $29.99, 7x11", dust jacket) r/#66-74, Annual #2 30.00
Wizard #1/2 2 4 6 9 12 15

ULTIMATE X-MEN (Ultimate Comics X-Men) (See Cataclysm)
Marvel Comics: Nov, 2011 - No. 33, Dec, 2013 ($3.99)

1-Spencer-s/Medina-a/Andrews-c; polybagged 4.00
1-Variant-c by Mark Bagley 6.00
2-33: 2-Rogue returns. 6-Prof. X returns. 21-Iron Patriot app. 4.00
#18.1 (1/13, $2.99) Andrade-a/Pichelli-c 3.00
Ultimate Comics X-Men Must Have 1 (2/12, $4.99) r/#1-3 5.00

ULTIMATUM
Marvel Comics: Jan, 2009 - No. 5, July, 2009 ($3.99, limited series)

1-5-Loeb-s/Finch-a; cover by Finch & ; Ultimate heroes vs. Magneto 4.00
1-5-Variant covers by McGuinness 8.00
5-Double gatefold variant-c by Finch 4.00
March on Ultimatum Saga ('08, giveaway) text and art panel history of Ultimate universe 3.00
...: Fantastic Four Requiem 1 (9/09,$3.99) Pokaski-s/Atkins-a; Dr. Strange app. 4.00
...: Spider-Man Requiem 1,2 (8/09, 9/09,$3.99) Bendis-s/Bagley & Immonen-a 4.00
...: X-Men Requiem 1 (9/09,$3.99) Coleite-s/Oliver-a/Brooks-c 4.00
NOTE: *Numerous variant covers and 2nd & 3rd printings exist.*

ULTRA
Image Comics: Aug, 2004 - No. 8, Mar, 2005 ($2.95, limited series)

1-8: 1-Intro. Ultra/Pearl Penalosa; Luna Brothers-s/a 3.00
Vol. 1: Seven Days TPB (4/05, $17.95) r/#1-8; sketch pages 18.00

ULTRAFORCE (1st Series) (Also see Avengers/Ultraforce #1)
Malibu Comics (Ultraverse): Aug, 1994 - No. 10, Aug, 1995 ($1.95/$2.50)

0 (9/94, $2.50)-Perez-c/a. 4.00
1-($2.50, 44 pgs.)-Bound-in trading card; team consisting of Prime, Prototype, Hardcase, Pixx, Ghoul, Contrary & Topaz; Gerard Jones scripts begin, ends #6; Pérez-c/a begins 4.00
1-Ultra 5000 Limited Silver Foil Edition 1 2 3 5 6 8
1-Holographic-c, no price 1 2 3 6 8 10
2-5: Perez-c/a in all. 2 (10/94, $1.95)-Prime quits, Strangers cameo. 3-Origin of Topaz; Prime rejoins. 5-Pixx dies. 3.00
2 ($2.50)-Florescent logo; limited edition stamp on-c 4.00
6-10: 6-Begin $2.50-c, Perez-c/a. 7-Ghoul story, Steve Erwin-a. 8-Marvel's Black Knight enters the Ultraverse (last seen in Avengers #375); Perez-c/a. 9,10-Black Knight app.; Perez-c. 10-Leads into Ultraforce/Avengers Prelude 3.00
Malibu "Ashcan ": Ultraforce #0A (6/94) 3.00
.../Avengers Prelude 1 (8/95, $2.50)-Perez-c. 3.00
.../Avengers 1 (8/95, $3.95)-Warren Ellis script; Perez-c/a; foil-c 4.00

Ultraverse Premiere #2 © MAL

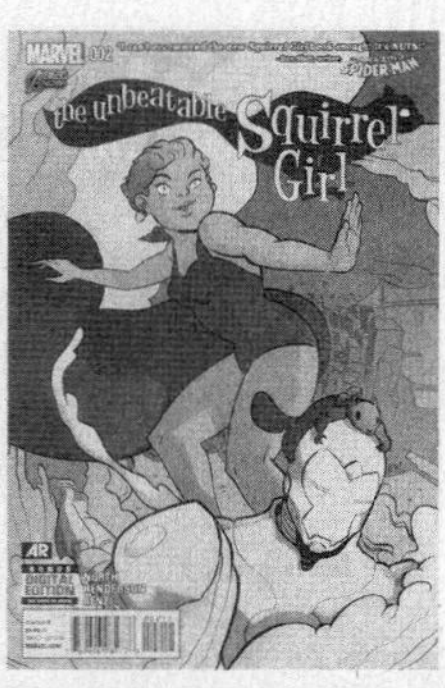

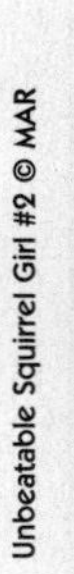
Unbeatable Squirrel Girl #2 © MAR

Uncanny Avengers (2015 series) #1 © MAR

GD	VG	FN	VF	VF/NM	NM-
2.0	4.0	6.0	8.0	9.0	9.2

GD VG FN VF VF/NM NM- 2.0 4.0 6.0 8.0 9.0 9.2

ULTRAFORCE (2nd Series)(Also see Black September)
Malibu Comics (Ultraverse): Infinity, Sept, 1995 - V2#15, Dec, 1996 ($1.50)
Infinity, V2#1-15: Infinity-Team consists of Marvel's Black Knight, Ghoul, Topaz, Prime & redesigned Prototype; Warren Ellis scripts begin, ends #3; variant-c exists. 1-1st app.Cromwell, Lament & Wreckage. 2-Contains free encore presentation of Ultraforce #1; flip book "Phoenix Resurrection" Pt. 7. 7-Darick Robertson, Jeff Johnson & others-a. 8,9-Intro. Future Ultraforce (Prime, Hellblade, Angel of Destruction, Painkiller & Whipslash); Gary Erskine-c/a. 9-Foxfire app. 10-Len Wein scripts & Deodato Studios-c/a begin. 10-Lament back-up story. 11-Ghoul back-up story by Pander Bros. 12-Ultraforce vs. Maxis (cont'd in Ultraverse Unlimited #2); Exiles & Iron Clad app. 13-Prime leaves; Hardcase returns 3.00
Infinity (2000 signed) 4.00
.../Spider-Man ($3.95)-Marv Wolfman script; Green Goblin app; 2 covers exist. 4.00

ULTRAGIRL
Marvel Comics: Nov, 1996 - No. 3 Mar, 1997($1.50, limited series)
1-3: 1-1st app. 3.00

ULTRA KLUTZ
Onward Comics: 1981; 6/86 - #27, 1/89, #28, 4/90 - #31, 1990? ($1.50/$1.75/$2.00, B&W)
1 (1981)-Re-released after 2nd #1 3.00
1-30: 1-(6/86). 27-Photo back-c 3.00
31-($2.95, 52 pgs.) 4.00

ULTRAMAN
Nemesis Comics: Mar, 1994 - No. 4, Sept, 1994 ($1.75/$1.95)
1-($2.25)-Collector's edition; foil-c; special 3/4 wraparound-c 4.00
1-($1.75)-Newsstand edition 3.00
2-4: 3-$1.95-c begins 3.00
#(-1) (3/93) 3.00

ULTRAMAN TIGA
Dark Horse Comics: Aug, 2003 - No. 10, June, 2004 ($3.99)
1-10-Khoo Fuk Lung-a/Tony Wong-s 4.00

ULTRAVERSE DOUBLE FEATURE
Malibu Comics (Ultraverse): Jan, 1995 ($3.95, one-shot, 68 pgs.)
1-Flip-c featuring Prime & Solitaire. 4.00

ULTRAVERSE ORIGINS
Malibu Comics (Ultraverse): Jan, 1994 (99¢, one-shot)
1-Gatefold-c; 2 pg. origins all characters 3.00
1-Newsstand edition; different-c, no gatefold 3.00

ULTRAVERSE PREMIERE
Malibu Comics (Ultraverse): 1994 (one-shot)
0-Ordered thru mail w/coupons 5.00

ULTRAVERSE UNLIMITED
Malibu Comics (Ultraverse): June, 1996; No. 2, Sept, 1996 ($2.50)
1,2: 1-Adam Warlock returns to the Marvel Universe; Rune-c/app. 2-Black Knight, Reaper & Sierra Blaze return to the Marvel Universe 3.00

ULTRAVERSE YEAR ONE
Malibu Comics (Ultraverse): 1994 ($4.95, one-shot)
nn-In-depth synopsis of the first year's titles & stories. 5.00

ULTRAVERSE YEAR TWO
Malibu Comics (Ultraverse): Aug, 1995 ($4.95, one-shot)
nn-In-depth synopsis of second year's titles & stories 5.00

ULTRAVERSE YEAR ZERO: THE DEATH OF THE SQUAD
Malibu Comics (Ultraverse): Apr, 1995 - No. 4, July, 1995 ($2.95, lim. series)
1-4: 3-Codename: Firearm back-up story. 3.00

ULTRON (See Age of Ultron series)
Marvel Comics: Jun, 2013 ($3.99, one-shot)
1AU-Victor Mancha from the Runaways (son of Ultron); K. Immonen-s/Pinna-a 4.00

UMBRAL
Image Comics: Nov, 2013 - Present ($2.99)
1-12-Johnston-s/Mitten-a 3.00

UMBRELLA ACADEMY (Zero Killer & Pantheon City on back-c)
Dark Horse Comics: Apr, 2007
1-Free Comic Book Day Edition - previews of the upcoming series; James Jean-c 5.00

UMBRELLA ACADEMY: APOCALYPSE SUITE
Dark Horse Comics: Sept, 2007 - No. 6, Feb, 2008 ($2.99, limited series)
1-Origin of the Umbrella Academy; Gerald Way-s/Gabriel Bá-a/James Jean-c 5.00
1-White variant-c by Bá 25.00
1-Variant-c by Gerald Way 20.00
1-2nd printing with variant-c by Bá 3.00
2-6 3.00
...: One for One (9/10, $1.00) r/#1 with red cover frame 3.00
Vol.1: Apocalypse Suite TPB (7/08, $17.95) r/#1-6, FCBD story and web shorts; design art; Grant Morrison intro.; cover gallery 18.00

UMBRELLA ACADEMY: DALLAS
Dark Horse Comics: Nov, 2008 - No. 6, May, 2009 ($2.99, limited series)
1-6-Gerald Way-s/Gabriel Bá-a/c 3.00
1-Wraparound variant-c by Jim Lee 5.00

UNBEATABLE SQUIRREL GIRL, THE
Marvel Comics: Mar, 2015 - No. 8, Oct, 2015 ($3.99)
1-8: 1-Doreen Green and Tippy-Toe at college; North-s/Henderson-a. 1-Kraven app. 3,4-Galactus app. 7-Avengers cameo. 8-Lady Thor, Odinson & Loki app. 4.00

UNBEATABLE SQUIRREL GIRL, THE
Marvel Comics: Dec, 2015 - Present ($3.99)
1-17: 1-North-s/Henderson-a. 2-Doreen goes to the 1960s; Doctor Doom app. 6-Crossover with Howard the Duck #6. 10-Mole Man app. 13,14-Scott Lang app. 16-25th Anniversary issue; origin re-told; Hulk app. 4.00
... Beats Up The Marvel Universe (2016, $24.99, HC) original graphic novel; North-s; Henderson-a; Spider-Man & Avengers app.; bonus game pages and design art 25.00
...: You Choose the Story No. 1 Halloween Comic Fest 2016 (giveaway, 12/16) r/#7 3.00

UNBELIEVABLE GWENPOOL, THE (Also see Gwenpool Special)
Marvel Comics: Jun, 2016 - Present ($3.99)
1-($4.99) Hastings-s/Gurihiru-a; MODOK app. 5.00
2-12-($3.99) 2-Thor (Jane) app. 3-Doctor Strange app. 5,6-Spider-Man (Miles) app. 4.00
#0-(7/16, $4.99) Reprints apps. in Howard the Duck #1-3 & Gwenpool Special #1 5.00

UNBIRTHDAY PARTY WITH ALICE IN WONDERLAND (See Alice In Wonderland, Four Color #341)

UNCANNY
Dynamite Entertainment: 2013 - No. 6, 2014 ($3.99)
1-6-Andy Diggle-s/Aaron Campbell-a 4.00

UNCANNY, (SEASON TWO)
Dynamite Entertainment: 2015 - No. 6, 2015 ($3.99)
1-6-Andy Diggle-s/Aaron Campbell-a 4.00

UNCANNY AVENGERS (Marvel NOW!)
Marvel Comics: Dec, 2012 - No. 25, Dec, 2014 ($3.99)
1-25: 1-Capt. America, Thor, Scarlet Witch, Wolverine, Havok & Rogue team; Remender-s/Cassaday-a; Red Skull app. 5-Coipel-a. 14-Rogue & Scarlet Witch die. 24,25-Axis 4.00
8AU-(7/13, $3.99) Age of Ultron tie-in; Adam Kubert-a 4.00
Annual 1 (6/14, $4.99) Remender-s/Renaud-a/Art Adams-c; Mojo app. 5.00

UNCANNY AVENGERS
Marvel Comics: Mar, 2015 - No. 5, Aug, 2015 ($3.99)
1-5: 1-Capt. America (Sam Wilson), Vision, Scarlet Witch, Quicksilver, Sabretooth, Rogue & Doctor Voodoo team; Remender-s/Acuna-a 4.00

UNCANNY AVENGERS
Marvel Comics: Dec, 2015 - Present ($3.99)
1-($4.99) Steve Rogers, Spider-Man, Deadpool, Human Torch, Quicksilver, Rogue, Synapse & Doctor Voodoo team; Duggan-s/Stegman-a 5.00
2-20-($3.99) 2-5-Cable app. 5,6-Pacheco-a. 7,8-Pleasant Hill Standoff tie-ins. 13,14-Civil War II tie-in. 16,17-Hulk returns 4.00
Annual 1 (1/16, $4.99) Robinson-s/Laming & Giles-a/Deodato-c; Emerald Warlock app. 5.00

UNCANNY AVENGERS: ULTRON FOREVER
Marvel Comics: Jul, 2015 ($4.99)(Continued from New Avengers: Ultron Forever)
1-Part 3 of 3-part crossover with Avengers and New Avengers; Ewing-s/Alan Davis-a; team-up of past, present and future Avengers vs. Ultron 5.00

UNCANNY INHUMANS
Marvel Comics: No. 0, Jun, 2015; No. 1, Dec, 2015 - Present ($4.99/$3.99)
0-Soule-s/McNiven-a/c; Black Bolt, Medusa & Kang the Conqueror app. 5.00
1-($4.99) Johnny Storm, Beast & Kang the Conqueror app. 5.00
2-19-($3.99) 2-4-Kang app. 5-Mad Thinker and The Leader app. 11-14-Civil War II tie-in 4.00
#1.MU (4/17, $4.99) Monsters Unleashed tie-in; Allor-s/Level-a 5.00
Annual 1 (10/16, $4.99) Soule-s/Kev Walker-a 5.00

UNCANNY ORIGINS
Marvel Comics: Sept, 1996 - No. 14, Oct, 1997 (99¢)

Uncanny Tales #14 © MAR

Uncanny X-Force #1 © MAR

Uncle Sam Quarterly #1 © QUA

GD VG FN VF VF/NM NM-
2.0 4.0 6.0 8.0 9.0 9.2

1-14: 1-Cyclops. 2-Quicksilver. 3-Archangel. 4-Firelord. 5-Hulk. 6-Beast. 7-Venom. 8-Nightcrawler. 9-Storm. 10-Black Cat. 11-Black Knight. 12-Dr. Strange. 13-Daredevil. 14-Iron Fist 3.00

UNCANNY SKULLKICKERS (See Skullkickers #19)

UNCANNY TALES
Atlas Comics (PrPl/PPI): June, 1952 - No. 56, Sept, 1957

1-Heath-a; horror/weird stories begin 135 270 405 864 1482 2100
2 66 132 198 419 722 1025
3-5 60 120 180 381 653 925
6-Wolvertonish-a by Matt Fox 61 122 183 390 670 950
7-10: 8-Atom bomb story; Tothish-a (by Sekowsky?). 9-Crandall-a 53 106 159 334 567 800
11-20: 17-Atom bomb panels; anti-communist story; Hitler story. 19-Krenkel-a. 20-Robert Q. Sale-c 43 86 129 271 461 650
21-25,27: 25-Nostrand-a? 39 78 117 240 395 550
26-Spider-Man prototype c/story 65 130 195 416 708 1000
28-Last precode issue (1/55); Kubert-a; #1-28 contain 2-3 sci/fi stories each 40 80 120 244 405 565
29-41,43-49,51: 29-Variant-c exists with Feb. blanked out and Mar. printed on. Regular version just has Mar. 30 60 90 177 289 400
42,54,56-Krigstein-a 31 62 93 182 296 410
50,53,55-Torres-a 30 60 90 177 289 400
52-Oldest Iron Man prototype (2/57) 37 74 111 222 361 500

NOTE: ***Andru** a-15, 27. **Ayers** a-14, 22, 28, 37. **Bailey** a-51. **Briefer** a-19, 20. **Brodsky** c-1, 3, 4, 6, 8, 12-16, 19. **Brodsky/Everett** c-9. **Cameron** a-47. **Colan** a-11, 16, 17, 49, 52. **Drucker** a-37, 42, 45. **Everett** a-2, 9, 12, 32, 36, 39, 48; c-7, 11, 17, 39, 41, 50, 52, 53. **Fass** a-9, 10, 15, 24. **Forte** a-18, 27, 33-35, 52, 53. **Heath** a-13, 14; c-5, 10, 18. **Keller** a-3. **Lawrence** a-14, 17, 19, 23, 27, 28, 35. **Maneely** a-4, 8, 10, 16, 29, 35; c-2, 22, 26, 33, 38. **Moldoff** a-23. **Morisi** a-48, 52. **Morrow** a-46, 51. **Orlando** a-49, 50, 53. **Powell** a-12, 18, 34, 36, 38, 43, 50, 56. **Robinson** a-3, 13. **Reinman** a-12, 36. **Romita** a-10. **Roussos** a-8. **Sale** a-34, 47, 53; c-20. **Sekowsky** a-25. **Sinnott** a-14, 15, 38, 52. **Torres** a-53. **Tothish**-a by **Andru**-27. **Wildey** a-22, 48.*

UNCANNY TALES
Marvel Comics Group: Dec, 1973 - No. 12, Oct, 1975

1-Crandall-r/Uncanny Tales #9('50s) 4 8 12 25 40 55
2-12: 7,12-Kirby-a 3 6 9 17 26 35

NOTE: ***Ditko** reprints-#4, 6-8, 10-12.*

UNCANNY X-FORCE
Marvel Comics: Dec, 2010 - No. 35, Feb, 2013 ($3.99)

1-17: 1-Wolverine, Psylocke, Archangel, Fantomex & Deadpool team; Opeña-a; Ribic-c 4.00
1-Variant-c by Clayton Crain 10.00
5.1 (5/11, $2.99) Albuquerque-a/Bianchi-c; Lady Deathstrike app. 3.00
18-Polybagged; Dark Angel Saga conclusion 4.00
19-35: 19-Grampa-c. 20-Yu-c 4.00
19.1 (3/12, $2.99) Remender-s/Tan-a; other-dimension X-Men vs. Apocalypse 3.00
...: The Apocalypse Solution 1 (5/11, $4.99) r/#1-3 5.00

UNCANNY X-FORCE (Marvel NOW!)
Marvel Comics: Mar, 2013 - No. 17, Mar, 2014 ($3.99)

1-17: 1-Storm, Psylocke, Spiral, Fantomex & Puck team; Bishop app.; Garney-a 4.00

UNCANNY X-MEN, THE (See X-Men, The, 1st series, #142-on)

UNCANNY X-MEN (2nd series) (X-Men Regenesis)
Marvel Comics: Dec, 2010 - No. 20, Dec, 2012 ($3.99)

1-10: 1-3-Gillen-s/Pacheco-a/c; Mr. Sinister app. 4-Peterson-a. 5-8-Land-a 4.00
1-Variant-c by Keown 6.00
11-20: 11-19-Avengers vs. X-Men x-over 4.00

UNCANNY X-MEN (3rd series) (Marvel NOW!)
Marvel Comics: Apr, 2013 - No. 35, Sept, 2015 ($3.99)

1-24,26-35: 1-Cyclops, Emma Frost, Magneto, Magik team; Bendis-s/Bachalo-a. 2,3-Avengers app. 5-7,10,11-Irving-a. 8,9,12,13,16,17,19,20-22,25,27-32-Bachalo-a. 12,13-Battle of the Atom. 23,24-Original Sin tie-in 4.00
25-($4.99) Original Sin tie-in 5.00
#600-(1/16, $5.99) Stories by various incl. Bendis, Pichelli, Immonen; Bachalo-c 6.00
Annual 1 (2/15, $4.99) Story of Eva Bell; Bendis-s/Sorrentino-a 5.00
Special 1 (8/14, $4.99) Death's Head & Iron Man app.; Ackins-a 5.00

UNCANNY X-MEN (4th series) (After Secret Wars)
Marvel Comics: Mar, 2016 - Present ($3.99)

1-5: 1-Bunn-s/Land-a; Magneto, Psylocke, Sabretooth, M, and Archangel team 4.00
6-($4.99) Apocalypse Wars x-over; Lashley-a 5.00
7-18: 7-10-Apocalypse Wars x-over; Lashley-a. 11-14-Land-a; Hellfire Club app. 4.00
Annual 1 (1/17, $4.99) Bunn-s/Lashley-a; Elixir returns 5.00

UNCANNY X-MEN AND THE NEW TEEN TITANS (See Marvel and DC Present...)

UNCANNY X-MEN: FIRST CLASS
Marvel Comics: Sept, 2009 - No. 8, Apr, 2010 ($2.99)

1-8: 1-The X-Men #94 (1975) team; Cruz-a; Inhumans app. 3.00
... Giant-Size Special (8/09, $3.99) short stories by various; Scottie Young-c 4.00

UNCENSORED MOUSE, THE
Eternity Comics: Apr, 1989 - No. 2, Apr, 1989 ($1.95, B&W)(Came sealed in plastic bag) (Both contain racial stereotyping & violence)

1,2-Early Gottfredson strip-r in each 2 4 6 11 16 20

NOTE: *Both issues contain unauthorized reprints. Series was cancelled. **Win Smith** r-1, 2.*

UNCHARTED (Based on the video game)
DC Comics: Jan, 2012 - No. 6, Jun, 2012 ($2.99, limited series)

1-6-Williamson-s/Sandoval-a. 1-3-Harris-c 3.00

UNCLE CHARLIE'S FABLES (Also see Adventures in Wonderland)
Lev Gleason Publ.: Jan, 1952 - No. 5, Sept, 1952 (All have Biro painted-c)

1-Peter Pester by Hy Mankin begins, ends #5. Michael the Misfit by Kida, Janice & the Lazy Giant by Maurer, Lawrence the Fortune Teller app.; has photo of Biro 17 34 51 98 154 210
2-Fuje-a; Biro photo 11 22 33 60 83 105
3-5: 5-Two Who Built a Dream, The Blacksmith & The Gypsies by Maurer, The Sleepy King by Hubbel; has photo of Biro 9 18 27 52 69 85

NOTE: ***Kida** a-1. Hubbell a-5. **Hy Mankin** a-1-5. **Norman Maurer** a-1, 5. **Dick Rockwell** a-5.*

UNCLE DONALD & HIS NEPHEWS DUDE RANCH (See Dell Giant #52)

UNCLE DONALD & HIS NEPHEWS FAMILY FUN (See Dell Giant #38)

UNCLE GRANDPA (Based on the Cartoon Network series)
BOOM! Studios (kaboom!): Oct, 2014 - No. 4, Jan, 2015 ($3.99)

1-4-Short stories and gag pages; multiple covers on each 4.00
...: Good Morning Special 1 (4/16, $4.99) Short stories and gag pages; back-c mask 5.00
...: Pizza Steve Special 1 (6/15, $4.99) Short stories and gag pages 5.00

UNCLE JOE'S FUNNIES
Centaur Publications: 1938 (B&W)

1-Games, puzzles & magic tricks, some interior art; Bill Everett-c 116 232 348 742 1271 1800

UNCLE MILTY (TV)
Victoria Publications/True Cross: Dec, 1950 - No. 4, July, 1951 (52 pgs.)(Early TV comic)

1-Milton Berle photo on-c of #1,2 54 108 162 343 574 825
2 35 70 105 208 339 470
3,4 29 58 87 172 281 390

UNCLE REMUS & HIS TALES OF BRER RABBIT (See Brer Rabbit, 4-Color #129, 208, 693)

UNCLE SAM
DC Comics (Vertigo): 1997 - No. 2, 1997 ($4.95, limited series)

1,2-Alex Ross painted c/a. Story by Ross and Steve Darnell 5.00
Hardcover (1998, $17.95) 18.00
Softcover (2000, $9.95) 10.00

UNCLE SAM AND THE FREEDOM FIGHTERS
DC Comics: Sept, 2006 - No. 8, Apr, 2007 ($2.99, limited series)

1-8-Acuña-a/c; Gray & Palmiotti-s. 3-Intro. Black Condor 3.00
TPB (2007, $14.99) r/#1-8 and story from DCU Brave New World #1 15.00

UNCLE SAM AND THE FREEDOM FIGHTERS
DC Comics: Nov, 2007 - No. 8, Jun, 2008 ($2.99, limited series)

1-8-Gray & Palmiotti-s/Arlem-a/Johnson-c 3.00
...: Brave New World TPB (2008, $14.99) r/#1-8 15.00

UNCLE SAM QUARTERLY (Blackhawk #9 on)(See Freedom Fighters)
Quality Comics Group: Autumn, 1941 - No. 8, Autumn, 1943 (see National Comics)

1-Origin Uncle Sam; Fine/Eisner-c, chapter headings, 2 pgs. by Eisner; (2 versions: dark cover, no price; light cover with price sticker); Jack Cole-a 377 754 1131 2639 4620 6600
2-Cameos by The Ray, Black Condor, Quicksilver, The Red Bee, Alias the Spider, Hercules & Neon the Unknown; Eisner, Fine-c/a 148 296 444 947 1624 2300
3-Tuska-c/a; Eisner-a(2) 113 226 339 718 1209 1750
4 110 220 330 704 1202 1700
5,7-Hitler, Mussolini & Tojo-c 148 296 444 947 1624 2300
6,8 71 142 213 454 777 1100

NOTE: ***Kotzky** (or **Tuska**) a-3-8.*

UNCLE SCROOGE (Disney) (Becomes Walt Disney's... #210 on) (See Cartoon Tales, Dell Giants #33, 55, Disney Comic Album, Donald and Scrooge, Dynabrite, Four Color #178, Gladstone Comic Album, Walt Disney's Comics & Stories #98, Walt Disney's ...)

Uncle Scrooge #12 © DIS

Uncle Scrooge (2015 series) #12 © DIS

Underdog #6 © Leonardo TTV

	GD	VG	FN	VF	VF/NM	NM-
	2.0	4.0	6.0	8.0	9.0	9.2

Dell #1-39/Gold Key #40-173/Whitman #174-209: No. 386, 3/52 - No. 39, 8-10/62; No. 40, 12/62 - No. 209, 7/84

Four Color 386(#1)-in "Only a Poor Old Man" by Carl Barks; r-in Uncle Scrooge & Donald Duck #1('65) & The Best of Walt Disney Comics ('74). The 2nd cover app. of Uncle Scrooge (see Dell Giant Vacation Parade #2 (7/51) for 1st-c) 179 358 537 1477 3739 6000
1-(1986)-Reprints F.C. #386; given away with lithograph "Dam Disaster at Money Lake" & as a subscription offer giveaway to Gladstone subscribers 3 6 9 15 20 24
Four Color 456(#2)-in "Back to the Klondike" by Carl Barks; r-in Best of U.S. & D.D. #1('66) & Gladstone C.A. #4 88 176 264 704 1702 2700
Four Color 495(#3)-r-in #105 59 118 177 472 1136 1800
4(12-2/53-54)-r-in Gladstone Comic Album #11 43 86 129 318 722 1125
5-r-in Gladstone Special #2 & Walt Disney Digest #1 36 72 108 266 596 925
6-r-in U.S. #106,165,233 & Best of U.S. & D.D. #1('66) 31 62 93 223 499 775
7-The Seven Cities of Cibola by Barks; r-in #217 & Best of D.D. & U.S. #2 ('67) 28 56 84 202 451 700
8-10: 8-r-in #111,222. 9-r-in #104,214. 10-r-in #67 25 50 75 175 388 600
11-20: 11-r-in #237. 17-r-in #215. 19-r-in Gladstone C.A. #1. 20-r-in #213 20 40 60 141 313 485
21-30: 24-X-Mas-c. 26-r-in #211 16 32 48 112 249 385
31-35,37-40: 34-r-in #228. 40-X-Mas-c 13 26 39 89 195 300
36-1st app. Magica De Spell; Number one dime 1st identified by name 15 30 45 100 220 340
41-60: 48-Magica De Spell-c/story (3/64). 49-Sci/fi-c. 51-Beagle Boys-c/story (8/64) 11 22 33 73 157 240
61-63,65,66,68-71:71-Last Barks issue w/original story (#71-he only storyboarded the script) 10 20 30 66 138 210
64-(7/66) Barks Vietnam War story "Treasure of Marco Polo" banned for reprints by Disney from 1977-1989 because of its Third World revolutionary war theme. It later appeared in the hardcover Carl Barks Library set (4/89) and Walt Disney's Uncle Scrooge Adventures #42 (1/97) 15 30 45 100 220 340
67,72,73: 67,72,73-Barks-r 9 18 27 60 120 180
74-84: 74-Barks-r(1pg.). 75-81,83-Not by Barks. 82,84-Barks-r begin 7 14 21 44 82 120
85-100 6 12 18 38 69 100
101-110 5 10 15 33 57 80
111-120 4 8 12 27 44 60
121-141,143-152,154-157 3 6 9 21 33 45
142-Reprints Four Color #456 with-c 4 8 12 22 35 48
153,158,162-164,166,168-170,178,180: No Barks 3 6 9 15 22 28
155-Whitman edition 3 6 9 17 26 35
159-160,165,167 3 6 9 16 23 30
161(r/#14), 171(r/#11), 177(r/#16),183(r/#6)-Barks-r 3 6 9 16 23 30
172(1/80),173(2/80)-Gold Key. Barks-a 3 6 9 17 26 35
174(3/80),175(4/80),176(5/80)-Whitman. Barks-a 4 8 12 22 35 48
177(6/80),178(7/80) 4 8 12 23 37 50
179(9/80)(r/#9)-(Very low distribution) 57 114 171 456 1028 1600
180(11/80),181(12/80, r/4-Color #495), pre-pack? 8 16 24 51 96 140
182-195: 182-(50¢-c). 184,185,187,188-Barks-a. 182,186,191-194-No Barks. 189(r/#5), 190(r/#4), 195(r/4-Color #386) 3 6 9 16 23 30
182(1/81, 40¢-c) Cover price error variant 4 8 12 22 35 48
196(4/82),197(5/82): 196(r/#13) 3 6 9 17 26 35
198-209 (All #90038 on-c; pre-pack; no date or date code): 198(4/83), 199(5/83), 200(6/83), 201(6/83), 202(7/83), 203(7/83), 204(8/83), 205(8/83), 206(4/84), 207(5/83), 208(6/84), 209(7/84). 198-202,204-206: No Barks. 203(r/#12), 207(r/#93,92), 208(r/U.S. #18), 209(r/U.S. #21)-Barks-r 4 8 12 25 40 55
Uncle Scrooge & Money(G.K.)-Barks-r/from WDC&S #130 (3/67) 5 10 15 31 53 75
Mini Comic #1(1976)(3-1/4x6-1/2")-r/U.S. #115; Barks-c 2 4 6 8 10 12

NOTE: ***Barks** c-Four Color 386, 456, 495, #4-37, 39, 40, 43-71.*

UNCLE SCROOGE (See Walt Disney's Uncle Scrooge for previous issues)
Boom Entertainment (BOOM! Kids): No. 384, Oct, 2009 - No. 404, Jun, 2011 ($2.99/$3.99)

384-399: 384-Magica de Spell app.; 2 covers. 392-399-Duck Tales 3.00
400-(2/11, $3.99) "Carl Barks" apps. as Scrooge story-teller; Rosa wraparound-c 4.00
400-$6.99) Deluxe Edition with Barks painted cover of Four Color #386 cover image 7.00
401-404: 401-($3.99)-Rosa-s/a 4.00
...: The Mysterious Stone Ray and Cash Flow (5/11, $6.99) reprints; Barks-s/a; Rosa-s/a 7.00

UNCLE SCROOGE
IDW Publishing: Apr, 2015 - Present ($3.99)

1-Legacy numbered #405; art by Scarpa and others; multiple covers 4.00
2-23-English translations of Dutch, Norwegian & Italian stories; multiple covers on each 4.00

UNCLE SCROOGE AND DONALD DUCK
Gold Key: June, 1965 (25¢, paper cover)

1-Reprint of Four Color #386(#1) & lead story from Four Color #29 7 14 21 46 86 125

UNCLE SCROOGE COMICS DIGEST
Gladstone Publishing: Dec, 1986 - No. 5, Aug, 1987 ($1.25, Digest-size)

1,3 1 2 3 5 6 8
2,4 6.00
5 (low print run) 1 2 3 5 7 9

UNCLE SCROOGE GOES TO DISNEYLAND (See Dell Giants)
Gladstone Publishing Ltd.: Aug, 1985 ($2.50)

1-Reprints Dell Giant w/new-c by Mel Crawford, based on old cover 2 4 6 8 10 12
...Comics Digest 1 ($1.50, digest size) 2 4 6 8 11 14

UNCLE SCROOGE IN COLOR
Gladstone Publishing: 1987 ($29.95, Hardcover, 9-1/4"X12-1/4", 96 pgs.)

nn-Reprints "Christmas on Bear Mountain" from Four Color 178 by Barks; Uncle Scrooge's Christmas Carol (published as Donald Duck & the Christmas Carol, A Little Golden Book), reproduced from the original art as adapted by Norman McGary from pencils by Barks; and Uncle Scrooge the Lemonade King, reproduced from the original art, plus Barks' original pencils 4 8 12 25 40 55
nn-Slipcase edition of 750, signed by Barks, issued at $79.95 300.00

UNCLE SCROOGE THE LEMONADE KING
Whitman Publishing Co.: 1960 (A Top Top Tales Book, 6-3/8"x7-5/8", 32 pgs.)

2465-Storybook pencilled by Carl Barks, finished art adapted by Norman McGary 33 66 99 238 532 825

UNCLE WIGGILY (See March of Comics #19) (Also see Animal Comics)
Dell Publishing Co.: No. 179, Dec, 1947 - No. 543, Mar, 1954

Four Color 179 (#1)-Walt Kelly-c 14 28 42 94 207 320
Four Color 221 (3/49)-Part Kelly-c 9 18 27 58 114 170
Four Color 276 (5/50), 320 (#1, 3/51) 7 14 21 49 92 135
Four Color 349 (9-10/51), 391 (4-5/52) 6 12 18 41 76 110
Four Color 428 (10/52), 503 (10/53), 543 5 10 15 34 63 90

UNDEAD, THE
Chaos! Comics (Black Label): Feb, 2002 ($4.99, B&W)

1-Pulido-s/Denham-a 5.00

UNDERCOVER GIRL (Starr Flagg) (See Extra Comics, Manhunt! & Trail Colt)
Magazine Enterprises: No. 5, 1952 - No. 7, 1954

5(#1)(A-1 #62)-Fallon of the F.B.I. in all 28 56 84 165 270 375
6(A-1 #98), 7(A-1 #118)-All have Starr Flagg 26 52 78 154 252 350

NOTE: ***Powell** c-6, 7. **Whitney** a-5-7.*

UNDERDOG (TV)(See Kite Fun Book, March of Comics #426, 438, 467, 479)
Charlton Comics/Gold Key: July, 1970 - No. 10, Jan, 1972; Mar, 1975 - No. 23, Feb, 1979

1 (1st series, Charlton)-1st app. Underdog 10 20 30 64 132 200
2-10 6 12 18 37 66 95
1 (2nd series, Gold Key) 6 12 18 41 76 110
2-10 4 8 12 23 37 50
11-20: 13-1st app. Shack of Solitude 3 6 9 18 28 38
21-23 3 6 9 19 30 40

UNDERDOG
Spotlight Comics: 1987 - No. 3?, 1987 ($1.50)

1-3 4.00

UNDERDOG (Volume 2)
Harvey Comics: Nov, 1993 - No. 5, July, 1994 ($2.25)

1-5 4.00
Summer Special (10/93, $2.25, 68 pgs.) 4.00

UNDERSEA AGENT
Tower Comics: Jan, 1966 - No. 6, Mar, 1967 (25¢, 68 pgs.)

1-Davy Jones, Undersea Agent begins 8 16 24 51 96 140
2-6: 2-Jones gains magnetic powers. 5-Origin & 1st app. of Merman. 6-Kane/Wood-c(r) 5 10 15 34 60 85

NOTE: ***Gil Kane** a-3-6; c-4, 5. **Moldoff** a-2i.*

UNDERSEA FIGHTING COMMANDOS (See Fighting Undersea...)
I.W. Enterprises: 1964

Underworld #2 © MAR

The Unexpected #122 © DC

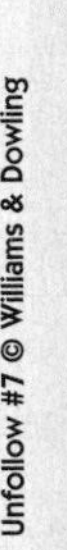

Unfollow #7 © Williams & Dowling

GD VG FN VF VF/NM NM-
2.0 4.0 6.0 8.0 9.0 9.2

I.W. Reprint #1,2('64): 1-r/#? 2-r/#1; Severin-c 2 4 6 9 13 16

UNDERTAKER (World Wrestling Federation)(Also see WWE Undertaker)
Chaos! Comics: Feb, 1999 - No. 10, Jan, 2000 ($2.50/$2.95)

Preview (2/99) 3.00
1-10: Reg. and photo covers for each. 1-(4/99) 3.00
1-($6.95) DF Ed.; Brereton painted-c 7.00
...Halloween Special (10/99, $2.95) Reg. & photo-c 3.00
Wizard #0 3.00

UNDERWATER CITY, THE
Dell Publishing Co.: No. 1328, 1961

Four Color 1328-Movie, Evans-a 6 12 18 42 79 115

UNDERWORLD (...True Crime Stories)
D. S. Publishing Co.: Feb-Mar, 1948 - No. 9, June-July, 1949 (52 pgs.)

1-Moldoff (Shelly)-c; excessive violence 50 100 150 315 533 750
2-Moldoff (Shelly)-c; Ma Barker story used in **SOTI**, pg. 95; female electrocution panel; lingerie art 44 88 132 277 469 660
3-McWilliams-c/a; extreme violence, mutilation 41 82 123 250 418 585
4-Used in Love and Death by Legman; Ingels-a 37 74 111 222 361 500
5-Ingels-a 24 48 72 142 234 325
6-9: 8-Ravielli-a. 9-R.Q. Sale-a 20 40 60 114 182 250

UNDERWORLD
DC Comics: Dec, 1987 - No. 4, Mar, 1988 ($1.00, limited series, mature)

1-4 3.00

UNDERWORLD (Movie)
IDW Publishing: Sept, 2003; Dec, 2005 ($6.99)

1-Movie adaptation; photo-c 7.00
... Evolution (12/05, $7.49) adaptation of movie sequel; Vazquez-a 7.50
TPB (7/04, $19.99) r/#1 and Underworld:Red in Tooth and Claw #1-3 20.00

UNDERWORLD
Marvel Comics: Apr, 2006 - No. 5, Aug, 2006 ($2.99, limited series)

1-5: Staz Johnson-a. 2-Spider-Man app. 3,4-Punisher app. 3.00

UNDERWORLD CRIME
Fawcett Publications: June, 1952 - No. 7, Sept, 1953

1 34 68 102 206 336 465
2 21 42 63 126 206 285
3-6 20 40 60 114 182 250
7-(9/53)-Red hot poker/bondage/torture-c 258 516 774 1651 2826 4000

UNDERWORLD: RED IN TOOTH AND CLAW (Movie)
IDW Publishing: Feb, 2004 - No. 3, Apr, 2004 ($3.99, limited series)

1-3-The early days of the Vampire and Lycan war; Postic & Marinkovich-a 4.00

UNDERWORLD: RISE OF THE LYCANS (Movie)
IDW Publishing: Nov, 2008 - No. 2, Nov, 2008 ($3.99, limited series)

1,2-Grevioux-s/Huerta-a 4.00

UNDERWORLD STORY, THE (Movie)
Avon Periodicals: 1950

nn-(Scarce)-Ravielli-c 34 68 102 199 325 450

UNDERWORLD UNLEASHED
DC Comics: Nov, 1995 - No. 3, Jan, 1996 ($2.95, limited series)

1-3: Mark Waid scripts & Howard Porter-c/a(p) 3.50
...: Abyss: Hell's Sentinel 1-($2.95)-Alan Scott, Phantom Stranger, Zatanna app. 3.00
...: Apokolips-Dark Uprising 1 ($1.95) 3.00
...: Batman-Devil's Asylum 1-($2.95)-Batman app. 3.00
...: Patterns of Fear-($2.95) 3.00
TPB (1998, $17.95) r/#1-3 & Abyss-Hell's Sentinel 18.00

UNEARTHLY SPECTACULARS
Harvey Publications: Oct, 1965 - No. 3, Mar, 1967

1-(12¢)-Tiger Boy; Simon-c 4 8 12 25 40 55
2-(25¢ giants)-Jack Q. Frost, Tiger Boy & Three Rocketeers app.; Williamson, Wood, Kane-a; r-1 story/Thrill-O-Rama #2 4 8 12 28 47 65
3-(25¢ giants)-Jack Q. Frost app.; Williamson/Crandall-a; r-from Alarming Advs. #1,1962 4 8 12 28 47 65

NOTE: ***Crandall** a-3r. **G. Kane** a-2. **Orlando** a-3. **Simon, Sparling, Wood** c-2. **Simon/Kirby** a-3r. **Torres** a-1?. **Wildey** a-1(3). **Williamson** a-2, 3r. **Wood** a-2(2).*

UNEXPECTED, THE (Formerly Tales of the...)
National Per. Publ./DC Comics: No. 105, Feb-Mar, 1968 - No. 222, May, 1982

GD VG FN VF VF/NM NM-
2.0 4.0 6.0 8.0 9.0 9.2

105-Begin 12¢ cover price 6 12 18 40 73 105
106-113: 113-Last 12¢ issue (6-7/69) 5 10 15 30 50 70
114,115,117,118,120-125 4 8 12 22 35 48
116 (36 pgs.)-Wrightson-a 4 8 12 23 37 50
119-Wrightson-a, 8pgs.(36 pgs.) 5 10 15 31 53 75
126,127,129-136-(52 pgs.) 4 8 12 22 35 48
128(52 pgs.)-Wrightson-a 5 10 15 31 53 75
137-156 3 6 9 15 22 28
157-162-(100 pgs.) 4 8 12 28 47 65
163-188: 187,188-(44 pgs.) 2 4 6 11 16 20
189,190,192-195 ($1.00, 68 pgs.): 189 on are combined with House of Secrets & The Witching Hour 2 4 6 13 18 22
191-Rogers-a(p) ($1.00, 68 pgs.) 3 6 9 14 19 24
196-222: 200-Return of Johhny Peril by Tuska. 205-213-Johnny Peril app. 210-Time Warp story. 222-Giffen-a 2 4 6 8 10 12

NOTE: ***Neal Adams** c-110, 112-115, 118, 121, 124. **J. Craig** a-195. **Ditko** a-189, 221p, 222p; c-222. **Drucker** a-107r, 132r. **Giffen** a-219, 222. **Kaluta** c-203, 212. **Kirby** a-127r, 162. **Kubert** c-204, 214-216, 219-221. **Mayer** a-217p, 220, 221p. **Moldoff** a-136r. **Moreira** a-133. **Mortimer** a-212p. **Newton** a-204p. **Orlando** a-202; c-191. **Perez** a-217p. **Redondo** a-155, 166, 195. **Reese** a-145. **Sparling** a-107, 205-209p, 212p. **Spiegle** a-217. **Starlin** c-198. **Toth** a-126r, 127r. **Tuska** a-127, 132, 134, 136, 139, 152, 180, 200p. **Wildey** a-128r, 193. **Wood** a-122i, 133i, 137i, 138i. **Wrightson** a-161r(2 pgs.). Johnny Peril in #106-114, 116, 117, 200, 205-213.*

UNEXPECTED, THE
DC Comics: Dec, 2011 ($7.99, one-shot)

1-Short horror stories by various incl. Gibbons, Thompson, Lapham, Fialkov; 2 covers 8.00

UNEXPECTED ANNUAL, THE (See DC Special Series #4)

UNFOLLOW
DC Comics (Vertigo): Jan, 2016 - Present ($3.99)

1-16: 1-Rob Williams-s/Mike Dowling-a. 6-R.M. Guéra-a. 7-Marguerite Sauvage-a 4.00
... Special Edition 1 (3/16, $4.99) r/#1&2 5.00

UNHOLY UNION
Image Comics (Top Cow): July, 2007 ($3.99, one-shot)

1-Witchblade & The Darkness meet Hulk, Ghost Rider & Doctor Strange; Silvestri-c 4.00

UNIDENTIFIED FLYING ODDBALL (See Walt Disney Showcase #52)

UNION
Image Comics (WildStorm Productions): June, 1993 - No. 0, July, 1994 ($1.95, lim. series)

0-(7/94, $2.50) 3.00
0-Alternate Portacio-c (See Deathblow #5) 5.00
1-($2.50)-Embossed foil-c; Texeira-c/a in all 4.00
1-($1.95)-Newsstand edition w/o foil-c 3.00
2-4: 4-(7/94) 3.00

UNION
Image Comics (WildStorm Prod.): Feb, 1995 - No. 9, Dec, 1995 ($2.50)

1-3,5-9: 3-Savage Dragon app. 6-Fairchild from Gen 13 app. 3.00
4-($1.95, Newsstand)-WildStorm Rising Pt. 3 3.00
4-($2.50, Direct Market)-WildStorm Rising Pt. 3, bound-in card 3.00

UNION: FINAL VENGEANCE
Image Comics (WildStorm Productions): Oct, 1997 ($2.50)

1-Golden-c/Heisler-s 3.00

UNION JACK
Marvel Comics: Dec, 1998 - No. 3, Feb, 1999 ($2.99, limited series)

1-3-Raab-s/Cassaday-s/a 3.00

UNION JACK
Marvel Comics: Nov, 2006 - No. 4, Feb, 2007 ($2.99, limited series)

1-4-Gage-s/Perkins-c/a 3.00
...: London Falling TPB (2007, $10.99) r/#1-4; Perkins sketch page 11.00

UNITED COMICS (Formerly Fritzi Ritz #7; has Fritzi Ritz logo)
United Features Syndicate: Aug, 1940; No. 8, 1950 - No. 26, Jan-Feb, 1953

1(68 pgs.)-Fritzi Ritz & Phil Fumble 28 56 84 165 270 375
8-Fritzi Ritz, Abbie & Slats 10 20 30 58 79 100
9-20: 20-Strange As It Seems; Russell Patterson Cheesecake-a 9 18 27 52 69 85
21-(3-4/52) 1 pg. early Peanuts by Schulz (1st in comics?) 58 116 174 371 636 900
22-(5-6/52) 2 pgs. early Peanuts by Schulz 41 82 123 256 428 600
23-26: 23-(7-8/52). 24-(9-10/52). 25-(11-12/52). 26-(1-2/53). All have 2 pgs. early Peanuts by Schulz 24 48 72 142 234 325

NOTE: *Abbie & Slats reprinted from Tip Top.*

UNITED NATIONS, THE (See Classics Illustrated Special Issue)

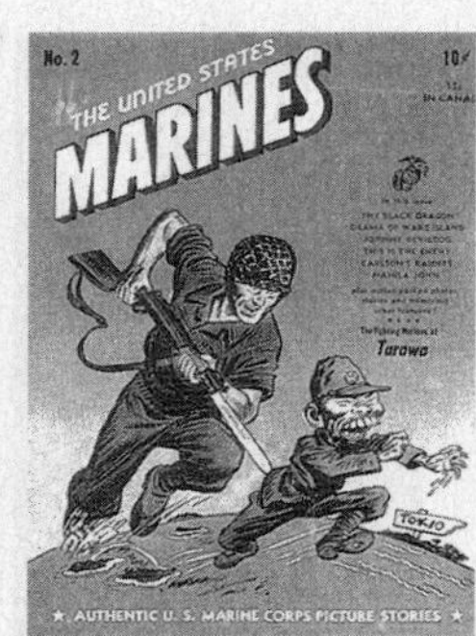

United States Marines #2 © WHW

Unity (2013 series) #25 © VAL

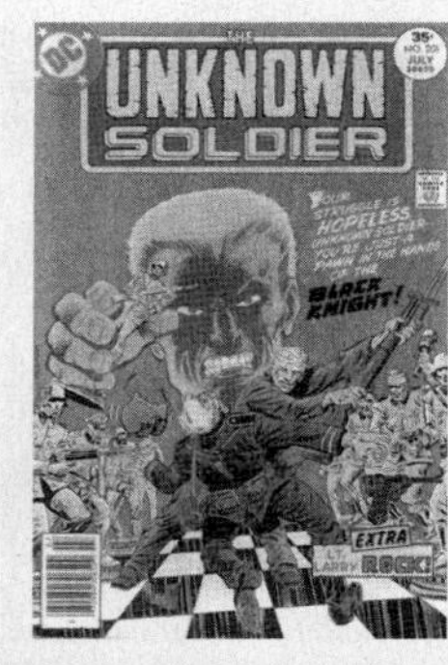

Unknown Soldier #206 © DC

	GD 2.0	VG 4.0	FN 6.0	VF 8.0	VF/NM 9.0	NM- 9.2

UNITED STATES AIR FORCE PRESENTS: THE HIDDEN CREW
U.S. Air Force: 1964 (36 pgs.)

nn-Schaffenberger-a 2 4 6 11 16 20

UNITED STATES FIGHTING AIR FORCE (Also see U.S. Fighting Air Force)
Superior Comics Ltd.: Sept, 1952 - No. 29, Oct, 1956

1 17 34 51 98 154 210
2 11 22 33 60 83 105
3-10 10 20 30 54 72 90
11-29 9 18 27 50 65 80

UNITED STATES MARINES
William H. Wise/Life's Romances Publ. Co./Magazine Ent. #5-8/Toby Press #7-11: 1943 - No. 4, 1944; No. 5, 1952 - No. 8, 1952; No. 7 - No. 11, 1953

nn-Mart Bailey-c/a; Marines in the Pacific theater 34 68 102 199 325 450
2-Bailey-a; Tojo classic-c 116 232 348 742 1271 1800
3-Classic WWII Tojo-c 103 206 309 659 1130 1600
4-WWII photos; Tony DiPreta-a; grey-tone-c 18 36 54 105 165 225
5(A-1 #55)-Bailey-a, 6(A-1 #60), 8(A-1 #72) 13 26 39 74 105 135
7(A-1 #68) Flamethrower with burning bodies-c 20 40 60 114 182 250
7-11 (Toby) 12 24 36 67 94 120
NOTE: *Powell a-5-7.*

UNITED STATES OF MURDER INC., THE
Marvel Comics (Icon): May, 2014 - No. 6, Feb, 2015 ($3.99)

1-6-Bendis-s/Oeming-a 4.00

UNITY
Valiant: No. 0, Aug, 1992 - No. 1, 1992 (Free comics w/limited dist., 20 pgs.)

0 (Blue)-Prequel to Unity x-overs in all Valiant titles; B. Smith-c/a. (Free to everyone that bought all 8 titles that month.) 5.00
0 (Red)-Same as above, but w/red logo (5,000) 4 8 12 25 40 55
1-Epilogue to Unity x-overs; B. Smith-c/a. (1 copy available for every 8 Valiant books ordered by dealers.) 5.00
1 (Gold), 1-(Platinum)-Promotional copy. 2 4 6 8 10 12
...: The Lost Chapter 1 (Yearbook) (2/95, $3.95)-"1994" in indicia 4.00

UNITY
Valiant Entertainment: Nov, 2013 - Present ($3.99)

1-24: Multiple covers on each. 1-Kindt-s/Braithwaite-a. 5,6-Cafu-a 4.00
25-($4.99) Short stories by various incl. Kindt, Asmus, Kano, Jordan, Schkade 5.00
#0 (10/14, $3.99) Kindt-s/Nord-a; the story of Unit Y in WW One 4.00

UNITY 2000 (See preludes in Shadowman #3,4 flipbooks)
Acclaim Comics: Nov, 1999 - No. 3, Jan, 2000 ($2.50, unfinished limited series planned for 6 issues)

Preview -B&W plot preview and cover art; paper cover 3.00
1-3-Starlin-a/Shooter-s 3.00

UNIVERSAL MONSTERS
Dark Horse Comics: 1993 ($4.95/$5.95, 52 pgs.)(All adapt original movies)

Creature From the Black Lagoon nn-($4.95)-Art Adams/Austin-c/a, Dracula nn-($4.95), Frankenstein nn-($3.95)-Painted-c/a, The Mummy nn-($4.95)-Painted-c
1 2 3 4 5 7
...: Cavalcade of Horror TPB (1/06, $19.95) r/one-shots; Eric Powell intro. & cover 20.00

UNIVERSAL PRESENTS DRACULA-THE MUMMY& OTHER STORIES
Dell Publishing Co.: Sept-Nov, 1963 (one-shot, 84 pgs.) (Also see Dell Giants)

02-530-311-r/Dracula 12-231-212, The Mummy 12-437-211 & part of Ghost Stories No. 1
15 30 45 100 220 340

UNIVERSAL SOLDIER (Movie)
Now Comics: Sept, 1992 - No. 3, Nov, 1992 (Limited series, polybagged, mature)

1-3 ($2.50, Direct Sales) 1-Movie adapatation; hologram on-c (all direct sales editions have painted-c) 4.00
1-3 ($1.95, Newsstand)-Rewritten & redrawn code approved version; all newsstand editions have photo-c 3.00

UNIVERSAL WAR ONE
Marvel Comics (Soleil): 2008 - No. 3, 2008 ($5.99, limited series)

1-3-Denis Bajram-s/a; English version of French comic. 1-Bajram interview 6.00
...: Revelations 1-3 (2009 - No. 3, 2009, $5.99) Bajram-s/a 6.00

UNIVERSE
Image Comics (Top Cow): Sept, 2001 - No. 8, July, 2002 ($2.50)

1-7-Jenkins-s 3.00
8-($4.95) extra short-s by Jenkins; pin-up pages 5.00

UNIVERSE X (See Earth X)
Marvel Comics: Sept, 2000 - No. 12, Sept, 2001 ($3.99/$3.50, limited series)

0-Ross-c/Braithwaite-a/Ross & Krueger-s 4.00
1-12: 5-Funeral of Captain America 4.00
... Beasts (6/00, $3.99) Yeates-a/Ross-c 4.00
... Cap (Capt. America) (2/01, $3.99) Yeates & Totleben-a/Ross-c; Cap dies 4.00
... 4 (Fantastic 4) (10/00, $3.99) Brent Anderson-a/Ross-c 4.00
... Iron Men (9/01, $3.99) Anderson-a/Ross-c; leads into #12 4.00
... Omnibus (6/01, $3.99) Ross B&W sketchbook and character bios 4.00
Sketchbook- Wizard supplement; B&W character sketches and bios 3.00
...Spidey (1/01, $3.99) Romita Sr. flashback-a/Guice-a/Ross-c 4.00
...X (11/01, $3.99) Series conclusion; Braithwaith-a/Ross wraparound-c 4.00
Volume 1 TPB (1/02, $24.95) r/#0-7 & Spidey, 4, & Cap; new Ross-c 25.00
Volume 2 TPB (6/02, $24.95) r/#8-12 &X, Beasts, Iron Men and Omnibus 25.00

UNKNOWN, THE
BOOM! Studios: May, 2009 - No. 4, Aug, 2009 ($3.99)

1-4-Mark Waid-s/Minck Oosterveer-a; two covers on each 4.00
...: The Devil Made Flesh 1-4 (9/09 - No. 4, 12/09, $3.99) Waid-s/Oosterveer-a 4.00

UNKNOWN MAN, THE (Movie)
Avon Periodicals: 1951

nn-Kinstler-c 34 68 102 199 325 450

UNKNOWN SOLDIER (Formerly Star-Spangled War Stories)
National Periodical Publications/DC Comics: No. 205, Apr-May, 1977 - No. 268, Oct, 1982 (See Our Army at War #168 for 1st app.)

205 3 6 9 17 26 35
206-210,220,221,251: 220,221 (44pgs.). 251-Enemy Ace begins
3 6 9 14 19 24
211-218,222-247,250,252-264 2 4 6 11 16 20
219-Miller-a (44 pgs.) 3 6 9 16 23 30
248,249,265-267: 248,249-Origin. 265-267-Enemy Ace vs. Balloon Buster.
2 4 6 11 16 20
268-Death of Unknown Soldier 3 6 9 19 30 40
NOTE: ***Chaykin** a-234. **Evans** a-265-267; c-235. **Kubert** c-Most. **Miller** a-219p. **Severin** a-251-253, 260, 261, 265-267. **Simonson** a-254-256. **Spiegle** a-258, 259, 262-264.*

UNKNOWN SOLDIER, THE (Also see Brave &the Bold #146)
DC Comics: Winter, 1988-'89 - No. 12, Dec, 1989 ($1.50, maxi-series, mature)

1-12: 8-Begin $1.75-c 5.00

UNKNOWN SOLDIER
DC Comics (Vertigo): Apr, 1997 - No 4, July, 1997 ($2.50, mini-series)

1-Ennis-s/Plunkett-a/Bradstreet-c in all 6.00
2-4 4.00
TPB (1998, $12.95) r/#1-4 13.00

UNKNOWN SOLDIER
DC Comics (Vertigo): Dec, 2008 - No. 25, Dec, 2010 ($2.99)

1-25: 1-Dysart-s/Ponticelli-a; intro. Lwanga Moses; two covers by Kordey and Corben. 2-20,22-25-Ponticelli-a. 21-Veitch-a 3.00
...: Beautiful World TPB (2011, $14.99) r/#21-25; Dysart afterword; sketch/design art 15.00
...: Dry Season TPB (2010, $14.99) r/#15-20; war history 15.00
...: Easy Kill TPB (2010, $17.99) r/#7-14; war history 18.00
...: Haunted House TPB (2009, $9.99) r/#1-6; glossary 10.00

UNKNOWN WORLD (Strange Stories From Another World #2 on)
Fawcett Publications: June, 1952

1-Norman Saunders painted-c 55 110 165 352 601 850

UNKNOWN WORLDS (See Journey Into...)

UNKNOWN WORLDS
American Comics Group/Best Synd. Features: Aug, 1960 - No. 57, Aug, 1967

1-Schaffenberger-c 20 40 60 138 307 475
2-Dinosaur-c/story 10 20 30 64 132 200
3-5 8 16 24 56 108 160
6-11: 9-Dinosaur-c/story. 11-Last 10¢ issue 7 14 21 46 86 125
12-19: 12-Begin 12¢ issues?; ends #57 6 12 18 37 66 95
20-Herbie cameo (12-1/62-63) 6 12 18 38 69 100
21-35: 27-Devil on-c. 31-Herbie one pagers thru #39 5 10 15 30 50 70
36- "The People vs. Hendricks" by Craig; most popular ACG story ever
5 10 15 31 53 75
37-46 4 8 12 27 44 60
47-Williamson-a r-from Adventures Into the Unknown #96, 3 pgs.; Craig-a
4 8 12 28 47 65

The Unstoppable Wasp #1 © MAR

Untamed Love #1 © QUA

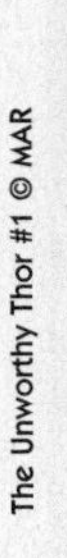
The Unworthy Thor #1 © MAR

	GD 2.0	VG 4.0	FN 6.0	VF 8.0	VF/NM 9.0	NM- 9.2
48-57: 53-Frankenstein app.	4	8	12	25	40	55

NOTE: *Ditko a-49, 50p, 54. Forte a-3, 6, 11. Landau a-56(2). Reinman a-3, 9, 13, 20, 22, 23, 36, 38, 54. Whitney c/a-most issues. John Force, Magic Agent app.-35, 36, 48, 50, 52, 54, 56.*

UNKNOWN WORLDS OF FRANK BRUNNER
Eclipse Comics: Aug, 1985 - No. 2, Aug, 1985 ($1.75)

1,2-B&W-r in color 4.00

UNKNOWN WORLDS OF SCIENCE FICTION
Marvel Comics: Jan, 1975 - No. 6, Nov, 1975; 1976 ($1.00, B&W Magazine)

	GD	VG	FN	VF	VF/NM	NM-
1-Williamson/Krenkel/Torres/Frazetta-r/Witzend #1, Neal Adams-r/Phase 1; Brunner & Kaluta-r; Freas/Romita-c	3	6	9	16	23	30
2-6: 5-Kaluta text illos	3	6	9	14	19	24
Special 1(1976,100 pgs.)-Newton painted-c	3	6	9	15	22	28

NOTE: *Brunner a-2; c-4, 6. Buscema a-Special 1p. Chaykin a-5. Colan a(p)-1, 3, 5, 6. Corben a-4. Kaluta a-2, Special 1(ext illos); c-2. Morrow a-3, 5. Nino a-3, 6, Special 1. Perez a-2, 3. Ray Bradbury interview in #1.*

UNLIMITED ACCESS (Also see Marvel Vs. DC))
Marvel Comics: Dec, 1997 - No. 4, Mar, 1998 ($2.99/$1.99, limited series)

1-Spider-Man, Wonder Woman, Green Lantern & Hulk app. 4.00
2,3-($1.99): 2-X-Men, Legion of Super-Heroes app. 3-Original Avengers vs. original Justice League 3.00
4-($2.99) Amalgam Legion vs. Darkseid & Magneto 4.00

UN-MEN, THE
DC Comics (Vertigo): Oct, 2007 - No. 13, Oct, 2008 ($2.99)

1-13-Whalen-s/Hawthorne-a/Hanuka-c 3.00
...: Children of Paradox TPB (2008, $19.99) r/#6-13 20.00
...: Get Your Freak On! TPB (2008, $9.99) r/#1-5; cover gallery 10.00

UNSANE (Formerly Mighty Bear #13, 14? or The Outlaws #10-14?)(Satire)
Star Publications: No. 15, June, 1954

	GD	VG	FN	VF	VF/NM	NM-
15-Disbrow-a(2); L. B. Cole-c	34	68	102	199	325	450

UNSEEN, THE
Visual Editions/Standard Comics: No. 5, 1952 - No. 15, July, 1954

	GD	VG	FN	VF	VF/NM	NM-
5-Horror stories in all; Toth-a	50	100	150	315	533	750
6,7,9,10-Jack Katz-a	40	80	120	246	411	575
8,11,13,14	37	74	111	222	361	500
12,15-Toth-a. 12-Tuska-a	40	80	120	246	411	575

NOTE: *Nick Cardy c-12. Fawcette a-13, 14. Sekowsky a-7, 8(2), 10, 13, 15.*

UNSTOPPABLE WASP, THE
Marvel Comics: Mar, 2017 - Present ($3.99)

1-3-Whitley-s/Charretier-a. 1-Ms. Marvel & Mockingbird app. 2,3-Moon Girl app. 4.00

UNTAMED
Marvel Comics (Epic Comics/Heavy Hitters): June, 1993 - No. 3, Aug, 1993 ($1.95, lim. series)

1-($2.50)-Embossed-c 4.00
2,3 3.00

UNTAMED LOVE (Also see Frank Frazetta's Untamed Love)
Quality Comics Group (Comic Magazines): Jan, 1950 - No. 5, Sept, 1950

	GD	VG	FN	VF	VF/NM	NM-
1-Ward-c, Gustavson-a	36	72	108	211	343	475
2,4: 2-5-Photo-c	21	42	63	122	199	275
3,5-Gustavson-a	21	42	63	126	206	285

UNTOLD LEGEND OF CAPTAIN MARVEL, THE
Marvel Comics: Apr, 1997 - No. 3, June, 1997 ($2.50, limited series)

1-3 5.00

UNTOLD LEGEND OF THE BATMAN, THE (Also see Promotional section)
DC Comics: July, 1980 - No. 3, Sept, 1980 (Limited series)

	GD	VG	FN	VF	VF/NM	NM-
1-Origin; Joker-c; Byrne's 1st work at DC	1	3	4	6	8	10
2,3						6.00

NOTE: *Aparo a-1i, 2, 3. Byrne a-1p.*

UNTOLD ORIGIN OF THE FEMFORCE, THE (Also see Femforce)
AC Comics: 1989 ($4.95, 68 pgs.)

1-Origin Femforce; Bill Black-a(i) & scripts 6.00

UNTOLD TALES OF BLACKEST NIGHT (Also see Blackest Night crossover titles)
DC Comics: Dec, 2010 ($4.99, one-shot)

1-Short stories by various incl. Johns, Benes, Booth; 2 covers by Kirkham & Van Sciver 5.00

UNTOLD TALES OF CHASTITY
Chaos! Comics: Nov, 2000 ($2.95, one-shot)

1-Origin; Steven Grant-s/Peter Vale-c/a 3.00
1-Premium Edition with glow in the dark cover 10.00

UNTOLD TALES OF LADY DEATH
Chaos! Comics: Nov, 2000 ($2.95, one-shot)

1-Origin of Lady Death; Cremator app.; Kaminski-s 3.00
1-Premium Edition with glow in the dark cover by Steven Hughes 10.00

UNTOLD TALES OF PUNISHER MAX
Marvel Comics: Aug, 2012 - No. 5, Dec, 2012 ($4.99/$3.99, limited series)

1-($4.99) Anthology; Starr-s/Boschi-a/c 5.00
2-5-($3.99) 2-Andrews-c. 3-Ribic-c. 5-Skottie Young-s/Del Mundo-c 4.00

UNTOLD TALES OF PURGATORI
Chaos! Comics: Nov, 2000 ($2.95, one-shot)

1-Purgatori in 57 B.C.; Rio-a/Grant-s 3.00
1-Premium Edition with glow in the dark cover 10.00

UNTOLD TALES OF SPIDER-MAN (Also see Amazing Fantasy #16-18)
Marvel Comics: Sept, 1995 - No. 25, Sept, 1997 (99¢)

1-Kurt Busiek scripts begin; Pat Olliffe-c/a in all (except #9). 4.00
2-22, -1(7/97), 23-25: 2-1st app. Batwing. 4-1st app. The Spacemen (Gantry, Orbit, Satellite & Vacuum). 8-1st app. The Headsman; The Enforcers (The Big Man, Montana, The Ox & Fancy Dan) app. 9-Ron Frenz-a. 10-1st app. Commanda. 16-Reintro Mary Jane Watson. 21-X-Men-c/app. 25-Green Goblin 3.00
...'96-(1996, $1.95, 46 pgs.)-Kurt Busiek scripts; Mike Allred-c/a; Kurt Busiek & Pat Olliffe app. in back-up story; contains pin-ups 4.00
...'97-(1997, $1.95)-Wraparound-c 4.00
...: Strange Encounters ('98, $5.99) Dr. Strange app. 6.00

UNTOLD TALES OF THE NEW UNIVERSE (Based on Marvel's 1986 New Universe titles)
Marvel Comics: May, 2006 ($2.99, series of one-shots)

...: D. P. 7 - Takes place between issues #4 & 5 of D. P. 7 series; Bright-a/Cebulski-s 3.00
...: Justice - Peter David-s/Carmine Di Giandomenico-a 3.00
...: Nightmask - Takes place between issues #4 & 5 of Nightmask series; The Gnome app. 3.00
...: Psi-Force - Tony Bedard-s/Russ Braun-a 3.00
...: Star Brand - Romita & Romita Jr.-c/Pulido-a 3.00
TPB (2006, $15.99) r/one-shots & stories from Amaz. Fantasy #18,19 & New Avengers #16 16.00

UNTOUCHABLES, THE (TV)
Dell Publishing Co.: No. 1237, 10-12/61 - No. 4, 8-10/62 (All have Robert Stack photo-c)

	GD	VG	FN	VF	VF/NM	NM-
Four Color 1237(#1)	17	34	51	114	252	390
Four Color 1286	12	24	36	80	173	265
01-879-207, 12-879-210(01879-210 on inside)	8	16	24	54	102	150

UNTOUCHABLES
Caliber Comics: Aug, 1997 - No. 4 ($2.95, B&W)

1-4: 1-Pruett-s; variant covers by Kaluta & Showman 3.00

UNUSUAL TALES (Blue Beetle & Shadows From Beyond #50 on)
Charlton Comics: Nov, 1955 - No. 49, Mar-Apr, 1965

	GD	VG	FN	VF	VF/NM	NM-
1	32	64	96	192	314	435
2	17	34	51	98	154	210
3-5	14	28	42	82	121	160
6-Ditko-c only	20	40	60	114	182	250
7,8-Ditko-c/a. 8-Robot-c	30	60	90	177	289	400
9-Ditko-c/a (20 pgs.)	32	64	96	192	314	435
10-Ditko-c/a(4)	34	68	102	199	325	450
11-(3/58, 68 pgs.)-Ditko-a(4)	32	64	96	192	314	435
12,14-Ditko-a	20	40	60	114	182	250
13,16-20	6	12	18	41	76	110
15-Ditko-c/a	25	50	75	150	245	340
21,24,28	5	10	15	35	63	90
22,23,25-27,29-Ditko-a	19	18	27	59	117	175
30-49	5	10	15	30	50	70

NOTE: *Colan a-11. Ditko c-22, 23, 25-27, 31(part).*

UNWORTHY THOR, THE (See Original Sin)
Marvel Comics: Jan, 2017 - Present ($3.99)

1-4-Aaron-s/Coipel-a; multiple covers; Beta Ray Bill app. 2-Thanos app. 4.00

UNWRITTEN, THE
DC Comics (Vertigo): July, 2009 - Present ($1.00/$2.99)

1-($1.00) Intro. Tommy Taylor; Mike Carey-s/Peter Gross-a; two covers (white & black) 3.00
2-16,18-31,(31.5), 32, (32.5), 33, (33.5), 34, (34.5), (35.5), 36-49-($2.99): 31.5-Art by Gross, Kaluta, Geary & Talbot. 37-Series re-cap 3.00
17-($3.99) Story printed sideways; Pick-a-Story format 4.00
35-($4.99) 5.00
50-(8/13, $4.99) Fables characters app.; Carey & Willingham-s; Gross & Buckingham-a 5.00
51-54-Fables characters app. 3.00

USA Comics #8 © MAR

Usagi Yojimbo V3 #69 © Stan Sakai

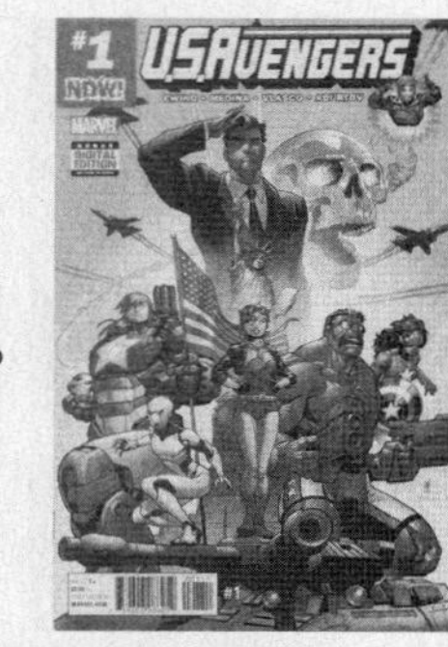

U.S.Avengers #1 © MAR

	GD 2.0	VG 4.0	FN 6.0	VF 8.0	VF/NM 9.0	NM- 9.2

...: Dead Man's Knock TPB (2011, $14.99) r/#13-18; intro. by novelist Steven Hall 15.00
...: Inside Man TPB (2010, $12.99) r/#6-12; intro. by Paul Cornell 13.00
...: Tommy Taylor and the Bogus Identity TPB (2010, $9.99) r/#1-5; sketch art; prose 10.00

UNWRITTEN, THE: APOCALYPSE
DC Comics (Vertigo): Mar, 2014 - No. 12, Mar, 2015 ($3.99)

1-11-Mike Carey-s/Peter Gross-a 4.00
12-($4.99) Mike Carey-s/Peter Gross-a 5.00

UP FROM HARLEM (Tom Skinner...)
Spire Christian Comics (Fleming H. Revell Co.): 1973 (35/49¢)

nn-(35¢ cover) 3 6 9 14 19 24
nn-(49¢ cover) 2 4 6 9 13 16

UP-TO-DATE COMICS
King Features Syndicate: No date (1938) (36 pgs.; B&W cover) (10¢)

nn-Popeye & Henry cover; The Phantom, Jungle Jim & Flash Gordon by Raymond, The Katzenjammer Kids, Curley Harper & others. Note: Variations in content exist. 32 64 96 188 307 425

UP YOUR NOSE AND OUT YOUR EAR (Satire)
Klevart Enterprises: Apr, 1972 - No. 2, June, 1972 (52 pgs., magazine)

V1#1,2 2 4 6 11 16 20

URTH 4 (Also see Earth 4)
Continuity Comics: May, 1989 - No. 4, Dec, 1990 ($2.00, deluxe format)

1-4: Ms. Mystic characters. 2-Neal Adams-c(i) 3.00

URZA-MISHRA WAR ON THE WORLD OF MAGIC THE GATHERING
Acclaim Comics (Armada): 1996 - No. 2, 1996 ($5.95, limited series)

1,2 6.00

U.S. (See Uncle Sam)

USA COMICS
Timely Comics (USA): Aug, 1941 - No. 17, Fall, 1945

1-Origin Major Liberty (called Mr. Liberty #1), Rockman by Wolverton; 1st app. The Whizzer by Avison; The Defender with sidekick Rusty & Jack Frost begin; The Young Avenger only app.; S&K-c plus 1 pg. art 1000 2000 3000 7000 12,500 20,000
2-Origin Captain Terror & The Vagabond; last Wolverton Rockman; Hitler-c 476 952 1428 3475 6138 8800
3-No Whizzer 366 732 1098 2562 4481 6400
4-Last Rockman, Major Liberty, Defender, Jack Frost, & Capt. Terror; Corporal Dix app.; "Remember Pearl Harbor" small cover logo 343 686 1029 2400 4200 6000
5-Origin American Avenger & Roko the Amazing; The Blue Blade, The Black Widow & Victory Boys, Gypo the Gypsy Giant & Hills of Horror only app.; Sergeant Dix begins; no Whizzer; Hitler, Mussolini & Tojo-c 486 972 1458 3550 6275 9000
6-Captain America (ends #17), The Destroyer, Jap Buster Johnson, Jeep Jones begin; Terror Squad only app. 838 1676 2514 6117 10,809 15,500
7-Captain Daring, Disk-Eyes the Detective by Wolverton app.; origin & only app. Marvel Boy (3/43); Secret Stamp begins; no Whizzer, Sergeant Dix; classic Schomburg-c 1100 2200 3300 8360 15,180 22,000
8-Classic Japanese WWII bondage/torture-c 757 1514 2271 5526 9763 14,000
9-Last Secret Stamp; Hitler-c; classic-c 811 1622 2433 5920 10,460 15,000
10-The Thunderbird only app.; Schomburg Japanese WWII-c 649 1298 1947 4738 8369 12,000
11-13: 11-No Jeep Jones. 13-No Whizzer; Jeep Jones ends; Schomburg Japanese WWII-c 423 846 1269 3000 5250 7500
14-17: 15-No Destroyer; Jap Buster Johnson ends 206 412 618 1318 2259 3200

NOTE: ***Brodsky** c-14. **Gabrielle** c-4. **Schomburg** c-6, 7, 10, 12, 13, 15-17. **Shores** a-1, 4; c-9, 11. **Ed Win** a-4. Cover features: 1-The Defender; 2, 3-Captain Terror; 4-Major Liberty; 5-Victory Boys; 6-17-Captain America & Bucky.*

USA COMICS 70TH ANNIVERSARY SPECIAL
Marvel Comics: Sept, 2009 ($3.99, one-shot)

1-New story of The Destroyer; Arcudi-s/Ellis-a; r/All Winners #3; two covers 5.00

U.S. AGENT (See Jeff Jordan...)

U.S. AGENT (See Captain America #354)
Marvel Comics: June, 1993 - No. 4, Sept, 1993 ($1.75, limited series)

1-4 3.00

U.S. AGENT
Marvel Comics: Aug, 2001 - No. 3, Oct, 2001 ($2.99, limited series)

1-3: Ordway-s/a(p)/c. 2,3-Captain America app. 3.00

USAGI YOJIMBO (See Albedo, Doomsday Squad #3 & Space Usagi)
Fantagraphics Books: July, 1987 - No. 38 ($2.00/$2.25, B&W)

1 3 6 9 19 30 40
1,8,10-2nd printings 3.00
2-9 6.00
10,11: 10-Leonardo app. (TMNT). 11-Aragonés-a 1 2 3 5 6 8
12-29 4.00
30-38: 30-Begin $2.25-c 5.00
Color Special 1 (11/89, $2.95, 68 pgs.)-new & r 4.00
Color Special 2 (10/91, $3.50) 4.00
Color Special #3 (10/92, $3.50)-Jeff Smith's Bone promo on inside-c 4.00
Summer Special 1 (1986, B&W, $2.75)-r/early Albedo issues 4.00

USAGI YOJIMBO
Mirage Studios: V2#1, Mar, 1993 - No. 16, 1994 ($2.75)

V2#1-16: 1-Teenage Mutant Ninja Turtles app. 3.00

USAGI YOJIMBO
Dark Horse Comics: V3#1, Apr, 1996 - Present ($2.95/$2.99/$3.50, B&W)

V3#1-99,101-116: Stan Sakai-c/a 3.00
100-(1/07, $3.50) Stan Sakai roast by various incl. Aragonés, Wagner, Miller, Geary 3.50
117-150-($3.50) 136-Variant-c. 141-"200th issue" 3.50
151-160-($3.99) 152-The River Rising 4.00
...: One For One (8/10, $1.00) Reprints #1 3.00
Color Special #4 (7/97, $2.95) "Green Persimmon" 3.00
Color Special #5: The Artist (7/14, $3.99) Bonus preview of Usagi Yojimbo: Senso 4.00
Daisho TPB ('98, $14.95) r/Mirage series #7-14 15.00
Demon Mask TPB ('01, $15.95) 16.00
Glimpses of Death TPB (7/06, $15.95) r/#76-82 16.00
Grasscutter TPB ('99, $16.95) r/#13-22 17.00
Gray Shadows TPB ('00, $14.95) r/#23-30 15.00
Seasons TPB ('99, $14.95) r/#7-12 15.00
Shades of Death TPB ('97, $14.95) r/Mirage series #1-6 15.00
The Brink of Life and Death TPB ('98, $14.95) r/Mirage series #13,15,16 & Dark Horse series #1-6 15.00
The Shrouded Moon TPB (1/03, $15.95) r/#46-52 16.00

USAGI YOJIMBO: SENSO
Dark Horse Comics: Aug, 2014 - No. 6, Jan, 2015 ($3.99, B&W)

1-6-Stan Sakai-s/c/a; Martian invasion set 20 years later; wraparound-c on each 4.00

U.S. AIR FORCE COMICS (Army Attack #38 on)
Charlton Comics: Oct, 1958 - No. 37, Mar-Apr, 1965

1 6 12 18 41 76 110
2 4 8 12 25 40 55
3-10 3 6 9 21 33 45
11-20 3 6 9 19 30 40
21-37 3 6 9 16 23 30

NOTE: ***Glanzman** c/a-9, 10, 12. **Montes/Bache** a-33.*

USA IS READY
Dell Publishing Co.: 1941 (68 pgs., one-shot)

1-War propaganda 48 96 144 302 514 725

U.S.AVENGERS
Marvel Comics: Mar, 2017 - Present ($3.99)

1-3-Ewing-s/Medina-a; team of Squirrel Girl, Cannonball, Iron Patriot, Enigma, Red Hulk 4.00

U.S. BORDER PATROL COMICS (Sgt. Dick Carter of the...) (See Holyoke One Shot)

USER
DC Comics (Vertigo): 2001 - No. 3, 2001 ($5.95, limited series)

1-3-Devin Grayson-s; Sean Phillips & John Bolton-a 6.00

U.S. FIGHTING AIR FORCE (Also see United States Fighting Air Force)
I. W. Enterprises: No date (1960s?)

1,9(nd): 1-r/United States Fighting...#?. 9-r/#1 2 4 6 8 11 14

U.S. FIGHTING MEN
Super Comics: 1963 - 1964 (Reprints)

10-r/With the U.S. Paratroops #4(Avon) 2 4 6 9 13 16
11,12,15-18: 11-r/Monty Hall #10. 12,16,17,18-r/U.S. Fighting Air Force #10,3,?&? 15-r/Man Comics #11 2 4 6 9 13 16

U.S. JONES (Also see Wonderworld Comics #28)
Fox Features Syndicate: Nov, 1941 - No. 2, Jan, 1942

1-U.S. Jones & The Topper begin; Nazi-c 213 426 639 1363 2332 3300
2-Nazi-c 194 388 582 1242 2121 3000

U.S. MARINES
Charlton Comics: Fall, 1964 (12¢, one-shot)

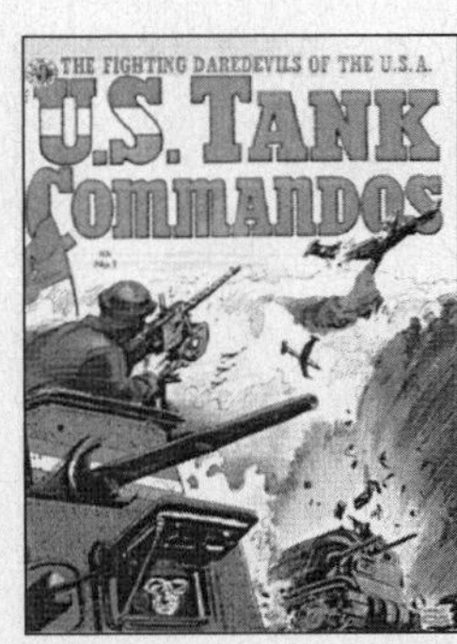

U.S. Tank Commandos #1 © AVON

Valkyrie (2010) #1 © MAR

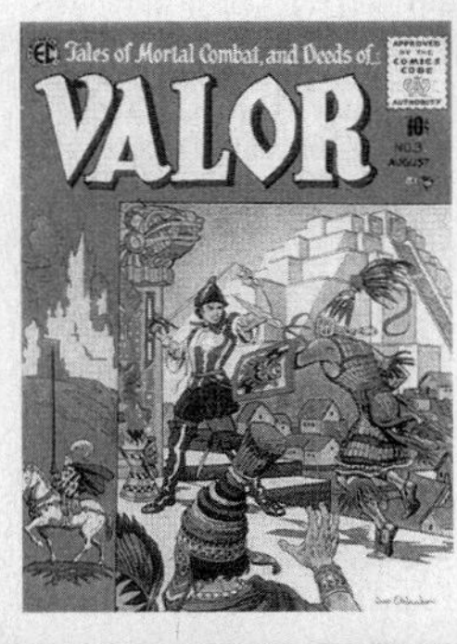

Valor #3 © WMG

GD 2.0 | VG 4.0 | FN 6.0 | VF 8.0 | VF/NM 9.0 | NM- 9.2

1-1st app. Capt. Dude; Glanzman-a 5 10 15 30 50 70

U.S. MARINES IN ACTION
Avon Periodicals: Aug, 1952 - No. 3, Dec, 1952
1-Louis Ravielli-c/a 14 28 42 80 115 150
2,3: 3-Kinstler-c 10 20 30 56 76 95

U.S. 1
Marvel Comics Group: May, 1983 - No. 12, Oct, 1984 (7,8: painted-c)
1-12: 2-Sienkiewicz-c. 3-12-Michael Golden-c 4.00

U.S. PARATROOPS (See With the...)

U.S. PARATROOPS
I. W. Enterprises: 1964?
1,8: 1-r/With the U.S. Paratroops #1; Wood-c. 8-r/With the U.S. Paratroops #6; Kinstler-c
2 4 6 9 13 16

U.S. TANK COMMANDOS
Avon Periodicals: June, 1952 - No. 4, Mar, 1953
1-Kinstler-c 14 28 42 80 115 150
2-4: Kinstler-c 10 20 30 58 79 100
I.W. Reprint #1,8: 1-r/#1. 8-r/#3 2 4 6 9 13 16
NOTE: ***Kinstler** a-I.W. #1; c-1-4, I.W. #1, 8.*

U.S. WAR MACHINE (Also see Iron Man and War Machine)
Marvel Comics (MAX): Nov, 2001 - No. 12, Jan, 2002 ($1.50, B&W, weekly limited series)
1-12-Chuck Austen-s/a/c 3.00
TPB (12/01, $14.95) r/#1-12 15.00

U.S. WAR MACHINE 2.0
Marvel Comics (MAX): Sept, 2003 - No. 3, Sept, 2003 ($2.99, weekly, limited series)
1-3-Austen-s/Christian Moore-CGI art 3.00

"V" (TV)
DC Comics: Feb, 1985 - No. 18, July, 1986
1-Based on TV movie & series (Sci/Fi) 5.00
2-18: 17,18-Denys Cowan-c/a 4.00

VACATION COMICS (Also see A-1 Comics)
Magazine Enterprises: No. 16, 1948 (one-shot)
A-1 16-The Pixies, Tom Tom, Flying Fredd & Koko & Kola
9 18 27 47 61 75

VACATION DIGEST
Harvey Comics: Sept, 1987 ($1.25, digest size)
1 1 2 3 5 6 8

VACATION IN DISNEYLAND (Also see Dell Giants)
Dell Publishing Co./Gold Key (1965): Aug-Oct, 1959; May, 1965 (Walt Disney)
Four Color 1025-Barks-a 14 28 42 93 204 315
1(30024-508)(G.K., 5/65, 25¢)-r/Dell Giant #30 & cover to #1 ('58); celebrates Disneyland's 10th anniversary 5 10 15 31 53 75

VACATION PARADE (See Dell Giants)

VALEN THE OUTCAST
BOOM! Studios: Dec, 2011 - No. 8, Jul, 2012 ($1.00/$3.99)
1-($1.00) Nelson-s/Scalera-a; eight covers 3.00
2-8-($3.99) 2-4-Six covers on each. 5-8-Five covers on each 4.00

VALERIA THE SHE BAT
Continuity Comics: May, 1993 - No. 5, Nov, 1993
1-Premium; acetate-c; N. Adams-a/scripts; given as gift to retailers
1 2 3 5 6 8
5 (11/93)-Embossed-c; N. Adams-a/scripts 3.00
NOTE: *Due to lack of continuity, #2-4 do not exist.*

VALERIA THE SHE BAT
Acclaim Comics (Windjammer): Sept, 1995 - No.2, Oct, 1995 ($2.50, limited series)
1,2 3.00

VALHALLA MAD
Image Comics: May, 2015 - No. 4, Aug, 2015 ($3.50, limited series)
1-4-Joe Casey-s/Paul Maybury-a 3.00

VALIANT, THE (Leads into Bloodshot Reborn series)
Valiant Entertainment: Dec, 2014 - No. 4, Mar, 2015 ($3.99, limited series)
1-4-Lemire & Kindt-s/Rivera-a; Eternal Warrior & Bloodshot app. 4.00

VALIANT...
Valiant Entertainment: May, 2012 - Present (giveaways)
... Comics FCBD 2012 Special 1 (5/12) Previews X-O Manowar, Harbinger and other Valiant 2012 titles; creator interviews 3.00
... FCBD 2013 Special #1 (5/13) Previews Harbinger Wars, X-O Manowar and others 3.00
... FCBD 2014 Armor Hunters Special #1 (5/14) Previews Armor Hunters and others 3.00
... FCBD 2014 Valiant Universe Handbook #1 (5/14) Character profiles 3.00
... FCBD 2015 Valiant 25th Anniversary Special (5/15) Previews Bloodshot and Ninjak 3.00
... : 4001 A.D. FCBD Special (5/16) Prelude to the 4001 A.D. series; Crain-c 3.00
... Masters: 2013 Showcase Edition #1 (5/13) Samples of hardcover volume offerings 3.00
... Universe Handbook 2015 Edition #1 (5/15, $2.99) Character profiles 3.00
... Universe Handbook 2016 Edition #1 (8/16, $2.99) Character profiles 3.00

VALKYRIE (See Airboy)
Eclipse Comics: May, 1987 - No. 3, July, 1987 ($1.75, limited series)
1-3: 2-Holly becomes new Black Angel 3.00

VALKYRIE
Marvel Comics: Jan, 1997; Nov, 2010 ($2.95/$3.99, one-shots)
1-(1/97, $2.95) w/pin-ups 3.00
1-(11/10, $3.99) Origin re-told; Winslade-a/Glass-s; Anacleto-c 4.00

VALKYRIE!
Eclipse Comics: July, 1988 - No. 3, Sept, 1988 ($1.95, limited series)
1-3 3.00

VALLEY OF THE DINOSAURS (TV)
Charlton Comics: Apr, 1975 - No. 11, Dec, 1976 (Hanna-Barbara)
1-W. Howard-i 3 6 9 14 19 24
2,4-11: 2-W. Howard-i 2 4 6 8 11 14
3-Byrne text illos (early work, 7/75) 2 4 6 10 14 18

VALLEY OF THE DINOSAURS (Volume 2)
Harvey Comics: Oct, 1993 ($1.50, giant-sized)
1-Reprints 5.00

VALLEY OF GWANGI (See Movie Classics)

VALOR
E. C. Comics: Mar-Apr, 1955 - No. 5, Nov-Dec, 1955
1-Williamson/Torres-a; Wood-c/a 31 62 93 248 392 535
2-Williamson-c/a; Wood-a 25 50 75 200 318 435
3,4: 3-Williamson, Crandall-a. 4-Wood-c 19 38 57 152 244 335
5-Wood-c/a; Williamson/Evans-a 18 36 54 144 227 310
NOTE: ***Crandall** a-3, 4. **Ingels** a-1, 2, 4, 5. **Krigstein** a-1-5. **Orlando** a-3, 4; c-3. **Wood** a-1, 2, 5; c-1, 4, 5.*

VALOR
Gemstone Publishing: Oct, 1998 - No. 5, Feb, 1999 ($2.50)
1-5-Reprints 4.00

VALOR (Also see Legion of Super-Heroes & Legionnaires)
DC Comics: Nov, 1992 - No. 23, Sept, 1994 ($1.25/$1.50)
1-22: 1-Eclipso The Darkness Within aftermath. 2-Vs. Supergirl. 4-Vs. Lobo. 12-Lobo cameo. 14-Legionnaires, JLA app. 17-Austin-c(i); death of Valor. 18-22-Build-up to Zero Hour 3.00
23-Zero Hour tie-in 3.00

VALOR THUNDERSTAR AND HIS FIREFLIES
Now Comics: Dec, 1986 ($1.50)
1-Ordway-c(p) 3.00

VAMPI (Vampirella's...)
Harris Publications (Anarchy Studios): Aug, 2000 - No. 25, Feb, 2003 ($2.95/$2.99)
Limited Edition Preview Book (5/00) Preview pages & sketchbook 3.00
1-(8/00, $2.95) Lau-a(p)/Conway-s 5.00
1-Platinum Edition 20.00
2-25: 17-Barberi-a 4.00
2-25-Deluxe Edition variants ($9.95): 4-Finch-c. 5-Wieringo-c. 6-Cha-c 10.00
...Digital 1 (11/01, $2.95) CGI art; Haberlin-s 4.00
...Digital Preview (Anarchy Studios, 7/01, $2.95) preview of CGI art 4.00
Switchblade Kiss HC (2001, $24.95) r/#1-6 25.00
Vicious Preview Ed. (Apr, 2003, $1.99) Flip book w/ Xin: Journey of the Monkey King Preview Ed. 4.00
Wizard #1/2 (mail order, $9.95) includes sketch pages 10.00

VAMPIRE BITES
Brainstorm Comics: May, 1995 - No. 2, Sept, 1996 ($2.95, B&W)
1,2:1-Color pin-up 3.00

VAMPIRE DIARIES, THE (Based on the CW television series)
DC Comics: Mar, 2014 - Present ($3.99, printings of online comics)

Vampirella #14 © WP

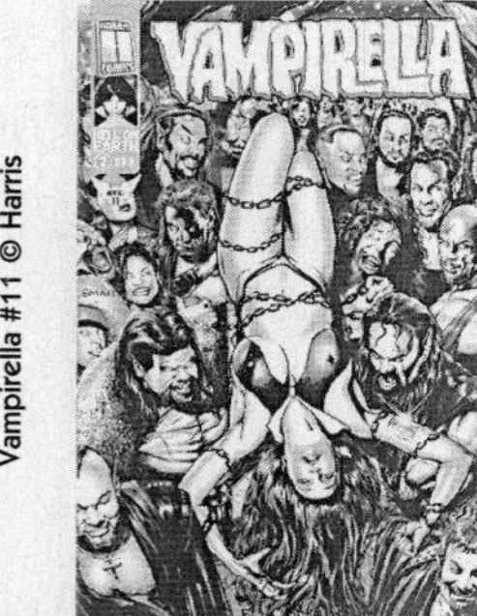

Vampirella #11 © Harris

Vampirella (2010 series) #1 © DFI

GD 2.0 | VG 4.0 | FN 6.0 | VF 8.0 | VF/NM 9.0 | NM- 9.2

1-6: 1,3-Doran-s/Shasteen-a. 5-Calero-a. 6-Doran-s/a 4.00

VAMPIRE LESTAT, THE
Innovation Publishing: Jan, 1990 - No. 12, 1991 ($2.50, painted limited series)

1-Adapts novel; Bolton painted-c on all 2 4 6 10 14 18
1-2nd printing (has UPC code, 1st prints don't) 3.00
1-3rd & 4th printings 3.00
2-1st printing 1 2 3 5 6 8
2-2nd & 3rd printings 3.00
3-5 5.00
3-6,9-2nd printings 3.00
6-12 4.00

VAMPIRELLA (Magazine)(See Warren Presents)(Also see Heidi Saha)
Warren Publishing Co./Harris Publications #113: Sept, 1969 - No. 112, Feb, 1983; No. 113, Jan, 1988? (B&W)

1-Intro. Vampirella in original costume & wings; Frazetta-c/intro. page; Adams-a; Crandall-a 46 92 138 359 805 1250
2-1st app. Vampirella's cousin Evily-c/s; 1st/only app. Draculina, Vampirella's blonde twin sister 12 24 36 79 170 260
3 (Low distribution) 25 50 75 175 388 600
4,6 8 16 24 54 102 150
5,7,9: 5,7-Frazetta-c. 9-Barry Smith-a; Boris/Wood-c 9 18 27 57 111 165
8-Vampirella begins by Tom Sutton as serious strip (early issues-gag line) 9 18 27 59 117 175
10-No Vampi story; Brunner, Adams, Wood-a 6 12 18 40 73 105
11-Origin & 1st app. Pendragon; Frazetta-c 7 14 21 46 86 125
12-Vampi by Gonzales begins 7 14 21 46 86 125
13-15: 14-1st Maroto-a; Ploog-a 6 12 18 42 79 115
16,22,25: 16-1st full Dracula-c/app. 22-Color insert preview of Maroto's Dracula. 25-Vampi on cocaine-s 6 12 18 41 76 110
17,18,20,21,23,24: 17-Tomb of the Gods begins by Maroto, ends #22. 18-22-Dracula-s 6 12 18 38 69 100
19 (1973 Annual) Creation of Vampi text bio 7 14 21 44 82 120
26,28,34,35,39,40: All have 8 pg. color inserts. 28-Board game inside covers. 34,35-1st Fleur the Witch Woman. 39,40-Color Dracula-s. 40-Wrightson bio 5 10 15 33 57 80
27 (1974 Annual) New color Vampi-s; mostly-r 6 12 18 37 66 95
29,38,45: 38-2nd Vampi as Cleopatra/Blood Red Queen of Hearts; 1st Mayo-a. 5 10 15 31 53 75
30-32: 30-Intro. Pantha; Corben-a(color). 31-Origin Luana, the Beast Girl. 32-Jones-a 5 10 15 33 57 80
33-Wrightson-a; Pantha ends 5 10 15 33 57 80
36,37: 36-1st Vampi as Cleopatra/Blood Red Queen of Hearts; issue has 8 pg. color insert. 37-(1975 Annual) 5 10 15 34 60 85
41-44,47,48: 41-Dracula-s 4 8 12 28 47 65
46-(10/75) Origin-r from Annual 1 5 10 15 30 50 70
49-1st Blind Priestess; The Blood Red Queen of Hearts storyline begins; Poe-s 4 8 12 28 47 65
50-Spirit cameo by Eisner; 40 pg. Vampi-s; Pantha & Fleur app.; Jones-a 4 8 12 28 47 65
51-53,56,57,59-62,65,66,68,75,79,80,82-86,88,89: 60-62,65,66-The Blood Red Queen of Hearts app. 60-1st Blind Priestess-c 4 8 12 23 37 50
54,55,63,81,87: 54-Vampi-s (42 pgs.); 8 pg. color Corben-a. 55-All Gonzales-a(r). 63-10 pgs. Wrightson-a 4 8 12 23 37 50
58,70,72: 58-(92 pgs.) 70-Rook app. 4 8 12 27 44 60
64,73: 64-(100 pg. Giant) All Mayo-a; 70 pg. Vampi-s. 73-69 pg. Vampi-s; Mayo-a 4 8 12 28 47 65
67,69,71,74,76-78-All Barbara Leigh photo-c 4 8 12 27 44 60
90-99: 90-Toth-a. 91-All-r; Gonzales-a. 93-Cassandra St. Knight begins, ends #103; new Pantha series begins, ends #108 4 8 12 23 37 50
100 (96 pg. r-special)-Origin reprinted from Ann. 1; mostly reprints; Vampirella appears topless in new 21 pg. story 6 12 18 41 76 110
101-104,106,107: All lower print run. 101,102-The Blood Red Queen of Hearts app. 107-All Maroto reprint-a issue 5 10 15 34 60 85
105,108-110: 108-Torpedo series by Toth begins; Vampi nudity splash page. 110-(100 pg. Summer Spectacular) 5 10 15 34 60 85
111,112: Low print run. 111-Giant Collector's Edition ($2.50) 112-(84 pgs.) last Warren issue 7 14 21 46 86 125
113 (1988)-1st Harris Issue; very low print run 23 46 69 161 356 550
Annual 1(1972)-New definitive origin of Vampirella by Gonzales; reprints by Neal Adams (from #1), Wood (from #9) 19 38 57 131 291 450
Special 1 (1977) Softcover (color, large-square bound)-Only available thru mail order 14 28 42 94 207 320
Special 1 (1977) Hardcover (color, large-square bound)-Only available through mail order (scarce)(500 produced, signed & #'d) 30 60 90 212 476 740
#1 1969 Commemorative Edition (2001, $4.95) reprints entire #1 5.00
...Crimson Chronicles Vol. 1 (2004, $19.95, TPB) reprints stories from #1-10 20.00
...Crimson Chronicles Vol. 2 (2005, $19.95, TPB) reprints stories from #11-18 20.00
...Crimson Chronicles Vol. 3 (2005, $19.95, TPB) reprints stories from #19-28 20.00
...Crimson Chronicles Vol. 4 (2006, $19.95, TPB) reprints stories from #29-41 20.00

NOTE: ***Ackerman*** *s-1-3.* ***Neal Adams*** *a-1, 10p, 19p(r/#10), 44(1 pg.), Annual 1.* ***Alcala*** *a-78, 90, 93i.* ***Bodé/Todd*** *c-3.* ***Bodé/Jones*** *c-4.* ***Boris/Wood*** *c-9.* ***Brunner*** *a-10, 12(1 pg.).* ***Corben*** *a-30, 31, 33, 36, 54; c-30, 31, 33, 54.* ***Crandall*** *a-1, 19(r/#1).* ***Frazetta*** *c-1, 5, 7, 11, 31.* ***Heath*** *a-58, 61, 67, 76-78, 83.* ***Infantino*** *a-57-62.* ***Jones*** *a-5, 9, 12, 27, 32 (color), 33(2 pg.), 34, 50i, 83r.* ***Ken Kelly*** *c-6, 38, 39, 40(back-c), 46, 70, 95.* ***Nebres*** *a-84, 88-90, 92-96.* ***Nino*** *a-59i, 61i, 67, 76, 85, 90.* ***Ploog*** *a-14.* ***Barry Smith*** *a-9.* ***Starlin*** *a-78.* ***Sutton*** *a-1-5, 7-11, Annual 1.* ***Toth*** *a-90i, 108, 110.* ***Wood*** *a-9, 10, 12, 19(r/#12), 27r, Annual 1; c-9(partial).* ***Wrightson*** *a-33(w/****Jones****), 40(Bio cameo) 63r. All reprint issues-19, 74, 83, 91, 105, 107, 109, 111. Annuals from 1973 on are included in regular numbering. Later annuals are same format as regular issues. Color inserts (8 pgs.) in 22, 25-28, 30-35, 39, 40, 45, 46, 49, 54, 55, 67, 72. 16 pg color insert in #36.*

VAMPIRELLA (Also see Cain/... & Vengeance of...)
Harris Publications: Nov, 1992 - No. 5, Nov, 1993 ($2.95)

0-Bagged 6.00
0-Gold 3 6 9 16 24 32
1-Jim Balent inks in #1-3; Adam Hughes c-1-3 2 4 6 13 18 22
1-2nd printing 5.00
1-(11/97) Commemorative Edition 4.00
2 2 4 6 9 13 16
3-5: 4-Snyder III-c. 5-Brereton painted-c 1 2 3 5 6 8
Trade paperback nn (10/93, $5.95)-r/#1-4; Jusko-c 1 3 4 6 8 10

NOTE: *Issues 1-5 contain certificates for free* ***Dave Stevens*** *Vampirella poster.*

VAMPIRELLA (THE NEW MONTHLY)
Harris Publications: Nov, 1997 - No. 26, Apr, 2000 ($2.95)

1-3-"Ascending Evil" -Morrison & Millar-s/Conner & Palmiotti-a. 1-Three covers by Quesada/Palmiotti, Conner, and Conner/Palmiotti 5.00
1-3-($9.95) Jae Lee variant covers 10.00
1-($24.95) Platinum Ed.w/Quesada-c 25.00
4-6-"Holy War"-Small & Stull-a, 4-Linsner variant-c 4.00
7-9-"Queen's Gambit"-Shi app. 7-Two covers. 8-Pantha-c/app. 4.00
7-($9.95) Conner variant-c 10.00
10-12-"Hell on Earth"; Small-a/Coney-s. 12-New costume 4.00
10-Jae Lee variant-c 1 3 4 6 8 10
13-15-"World's End" Zircher-p; Pantha back-up, Texeira-a 4.00
16,17: 16-Pantha-c;Texeira-a; Vampi back-up story. 17-(Pantha #2) 4.00
18-20-"Rebirth": Jae Lee-c on all. 18-Loeb-s/Sale-a. 19-Alan Davis-a. 20-Bruce Timm-a 4.00
18-20-($9.95) Variant covers: 18-Sale. 19-Davis. 20-Timm 12.00
21-26: 21,22-Dangerous Games; Small-a. 23-Lady Death-c/app.; Cleavenger-a. 24,25-Lau-a. 26-Lady Death & Pantha-c/app.; Cleavenger-a. 4.00
0-(1/99) also variant-c with Pantha #0; same contents 4.00
TPB ($7.50) r/#1-3 "Ascending Evil" 8.00
Ascending Evil Ashcan (8/97, $1.00) 3.00
...: Grant Morrison/Mark Millar Collection TPB (2006, $24.95) r/#1-6; interviews 25.00
Hell on Earth Ashcan (7/98, $1.00) 3.00
... Presents: Tales of Pantha TPB (2006, $19.95) r/stories from #13-17 & one-shots 20.00
The End Ashcan (3/00, $6.00) 6.00
...30th Anniversary Celebration Preview (7/99) B&W preview of #18-20 10.00

VAMPIRELLA
Harris Publications: June, 2001 - No. 22, Aug, 2003 ($2.95/$2.99)

1-Four covers (Mayhew w/foil logo, Campbell, Anacleto, Jae Lee) Mayhew-a; Mark Millar-s 5.00
2-22: 2-Two covers (Mayhew & Chiodo). 3-Timm var-c. 4-Horn var-c. 7-10-Dawn Brown-a; Pantha back-up w/Texeira-a. 15-22-Conner-c 4.00
Giant-Size Ashcan (5/01, $5.95) B&W preview art and Mayhew interview 6.00
...: Halloween Trick & Treat (10/04, $4.95) stories & art by various; three covers 5.00
... : Nowheresville Preview Edition (3/01, $2.95)- previews Mayhew art and photo models 4.00
...Nowheresville TPB (1/02, $12.95) r/#1-3 with cover gallery 13.00
... Summer Special #1 (2005, $5.95) Batman Begins photo-c and 2 variant-c 6.00
...: 2006 Halloween Special (2006, $2.95) Conner-c; Hester-s/Segovia-a; 4 covers 4.00

VAMPIRELLA
Dynamite Entertainment: 2010 - No. 38, 2014 ($3.99)

1-Four covers (Campbell, Madureira, J. Djurdjevic, Alex Ross swipe of Frazetta's #1) 4.00
1-Variant-c of blood-soaked Vampirella by Alex Ross 8.00
2-37: 2-6-Trautmann-s/Wagner Reis-a; four covers. 7-Geovani-a 4.00
38-($4.99, 40 pgs.) Pantha and Dracula app. 5.00
Annual 1 (2011, $4.99) Jerwa-s/Casalos-a; reprint with Alan Davis-a 5.00
Annual 2 (2012, $4.99) Rahner-s/Kyriazis-a; reprint with Pantha app.; Linsner-c 5.00
Annual 2013 ($4.99) Rahner-s/Valiente-a/Bolson-c 5.00

Vampirella V3 #1 © DFI

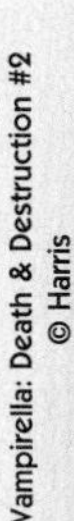

Vampirella: Death & Destruction #2 © Harris

Vampirella/Painkiller Jane #1 © Harris

	GD	VG	FN	VF	VF/NM	NM-
	2.0	4.0	6.0	8.0	9.0	9.2

...: NuBlood (2013, $4.99) Spoof of True Blood; Rahner-s/Razek-a/c; back-up w/Timm-a 5.00
... Vs. Fluffy (2012, $4.99) Spoof of Buffy the Vampire Slayer; Bradshaw-c 5.00

VAMPIRELLA (Volume 2)
Dynamite Entertainment: 2014 - No. 13, 2015 ($3.99)

1-12: Multiple covers on each. 1-Nancy Collins-s/Berkenkotter-a 4.00
13-($4.99) Lord Drago app.; Collins-s/Berkenkotter-a; 3 covers 5.00
#100 (2015, $7.99) Short stories by various incl. Tim Seeley; multiple covers 8.00
#1969 (2015, $7.99) Short stories by various incl. Hester & Worley; 2 covers 8.00
Annual 2015 ($5.99) Collins-s/Aneke-a/Anacleto-c 6.00
...: Prelude to Shadows (2014, $7.99) Collins-s/Zamora-a; r/Vampirella #13 w/new color 8.00

VAMPIRELLA (Volume 3)
Dynamite Entertainment: 2016 - No. 6, 2016 ($3.99)

1-6: Multiple covers on each. 1-Kate Leth-s/Eman Casallos-a; new costume 4.00

VAMPIRELLA (Volume 4)
Dynamite Entertainment: 2017 - Present ($3.99)

#0-(25¢) Multiple covers; Cornell-s/Broxton-a 3.00
1-($3.99) Vampirella in the far future; Cornell-s/Broxton-a 4.00

VAMPIRELLA / ALIENS
Dynamite Entertainment: 2015 - No. 6, 2016 ($3.99, limited series)

1-6-Corinna Bechko-s/Javier Garcia-Miranda-a; multiple covers on each 4.00

VAMPIRELLA & PANTHA SHOWCASE
Harris Publications: Jan, 1997 ($1.50, one-shot)

1-Millar-s/Texeira-c/a; flip book w/"Blood Lust"; Robinson-s/Jusko-c/a 4.00

VAMPIRELLA & THE BLOOD RED QUEEN OF HEARTS
Harris Publications: Sept, 1996 ($9.95, 96 pgs., B&W, squarebound, one-shot)

nn-r/Vampirella #49,60-62,65,66,101,102; John Bolton-c; Michael Bair back-c
1 3 4 6 8 10

VAMPIRELLA AND THE SCARLET LEGION
Dynamite Entertainment: 2011 - No. 5 ($3.99)

1-5: 1-Three covers (Campbell, Chen and Tucci); Malaga-a 4.00

VAMPIRELLA / ARMY OF DARKNESS
Dynamite Entertainment: 2015 - No. 4, 2015 ($3.99, limited series)

1-4-Ash meets Vampirella in 1300 AD; Mark Rahner-s/Jeff Morales-a 4.00

VAMPIRELLA: BLOODLUST
Harris Publications: July, 1997 - No. 2, Aug, 1997 ($4.95, limited series)

1,2-Robinson-s/Jusko-painted c/a 5.00

VAMPIRELLA CLASSIC
Harris Publications: Feb, 1995 - No. 5, Nov, 1995 ($2.95, limited series)

1-5: Reprints Archie Goodwin stories. 4.00

VAMPIRELLA COMICS MAGAZINE
Harris Publications: Oct, 2003 - No. 9 ($3.95/$9.95, magazine-sized)

1-9-($3.95) 1-Texiera-c; b&w and color stories, Alan Moore interview; reviews. 2-KISS interview. 4-Chiodo-c. 6-Brereton-c 4.00
1-9-($9.95) 1-Three covers (Model Photo cover, Palmiotti-c, Wheatley Frankenstein-c) 10.00

VAMPIRELLA: CROSSOVER GALLERY
Harris Publications: Sept, 1997 ($2.95, one-shot)

1-Wraparound-c by Campbell, pinups by Jae Lee, Mack, Allred, Art Adams, Quesada & Palmiotti and others 4.00

VAMPIRELLA: DEATH & DESTRUCTION
Harris Publications: July, 1996 - No. 3, Sept, 1996 ($2.95, limited series)

1-3: Amanda Conner-a(p) in all. 1-Tucci-c. 2-Hughes-c. 3-Jusko-c 4.00
1-($9.95)-Limited Edition; Beachum-c 10.00

VAMPIRELLA/DRACULA & PANTHA SHOWCASE
Harris Publications: Aug, 1997 ($1.50, one-shot)

1-Ellis, Robinson, and Moore-s; flip book w/"Pantha" 4.00

VAMPIRELLA/DRACULA: THE CENTENNIAL
Harris Publications: Oct, 1997 ($5.95, one-shot)

1-Ellis, Robinson, and Moore-s; Beachum, Frank/Smith, and Mack/Mays-a Bolton-painted-c 6.00

VAMPIRELLA: FEARY TALES
Dynamite Entertainment: 2014 - No. 5, 2015 ($3.99, limited series)

1-5: Anthology of short stories by various; multiple covers on each 4.00

VAMPIRELLA: INTIMATE VISIONS
Harris Publications: 2006 ($3.95, one-shots)

..., Amanda Conner 1 - r/Vampirella Monthly #1 with commentary; interview; 2 covers 4.00
..., Joe Jusko 1 - r/Vampirella; Blood Lust #1 with commentary; interview; 2 covers 4.00

VAMPIRELLA: JULIE STRAIN SPECIAL
Harris Publications: Sept, 2000 ($3.95, one-shot)

1-Photo-c w/yellow background; interview and photo gallery 4.00
1-Limited Edition ($9.95); cover photo w/black background 10.00

VAMPIRELLA/LADY DEATH (Also see Lady Death/Vampirella)
Harris Publications: Feb, 1999 ($3.50, one-shot)

1-Small-a/Nelson painted-c 4.00
1-Valentine Edition ($9.95); pencil-c by Small 10.00

VAMPIRELLA: LEGENDARY TALES
Harris Publications: May, 2000 - No. 2, June, 2000 ($2.95, B&W)

1,2-Reprints from magazine; Cleavenger painted-c 4.00
1,2-($9.95) Variant painted-c by Mike Mayhew 10.00

VAMPIRELLA LIVES
Harris Publications: Dec, 1996 - No. 3, Feb, 1997 ($3.50/$2.95, limited series)

1-Die cut-c; Quesada & Palmiotti-c, Ellis-s/Conner-a 5.00
1-Deluxe Ed.-photo-c 5.00
2,3-($2.95)-Two editions (1 photo-c): 3-J. Scott Campbell-c 4.00

VAMPIRELLA: MORNING IN AMERICA
Harris Publications/Dark Horse Comics: 1991 - No. 4, 1992 ($3.95, B&W, lim. series, 52 pgs.)

1,2-All have Kaluta painted-c 1 2 3 5 6 8
3,4 1 3 4 6 8 10

VAMPIRELLA OF DRAKULON
Harris Publications: Jan, 1996 - No. 5, Sept, 1996 ($2.95)

0-5: All reprints. 0-Jim Silke-c. 3-Polybagged w/card. 4-Texeira-c 4.00

VAMPIRELLA/PAINKILLER JANE
Harris Publications: May, 1998 ($3.50, one-shot)

1-Waid & Augustyn-s/Leonardi & Palmiotti-a 4.00
1-($9.95) Variant-c 10.00

VAMPIRELLA PIN-UP SPECIAL
Harris Publications: Oct, 1995 ($2.95, one-shot)

1-Hughes-c, pin-ups by various 5.00
1-Variant-c 5.00

VAMPIRELLA QUARTERLY
Harris Publications: Spring, 2007 - Summer, 2008 ($4.95/$4.99, quarterly)

Spring, 2007 - Summer, 2008-New stories and re-colored reprints; five or six covers 5.00

VAMPIRELLA: RETRO
Harris Publications: Mar, 1998 - No. 3, May, 1998 ($2.50, B&W, limited series)

1-3: Reprints; Silke painted covers 4.00

VAMPIRELLA: REVELATIONS
Harris Publications: No. 0, Oct, 2005 - No. 3, Feb, 2006 ($2.99, limited series)

0-3-Vampirella's origin retold, Lilith app.; Carey-s/Lilly-a; two covers on each 4.00
... Book 1 TPB (2006, $12.95) r/series; Carey interview, script for #1, Lilly sketch pages 13.00

VAMPIRELLA: SAD WINGS OF DESTINY
Harris Publications: Sept, 1996 ($3.95, one-shot)

1-Jusko-c 5.00

VAMPIRELLA: SECOND COMING
Harris Publications: 2009 - No. 4 ($1.99, limited series)

1-4: 1-Hester-s/Sampere-a; multiple covers on each. 3,4-Rio-a 4.00

VAMPIRELLA/SHADOWHAWK: CREATURES OF THE NIGHT (Also see Shadowhawk)
Harris Publications: 1995 ($4.95, one-shot)

1 5.00

VAMPIRELLA/SHI (See Shi/Vampirella)
Harris Publications: Oct, 1997 ($2.95, one-shot)

1-Ellis-s 4.00
1-Chromium-c 6.00

VAMPIRELLA: SILVER ANNIVERSARY COLLECTION
Harris Publications: Jan, 1997 - No. 4 Apr, 1997 ($2.50, limited series)

1-4: Two editions: Bad Girl by Beachum, Good Girl by Silke 4.00

VAMPIRELLA: SOUTHERN GOTHIC

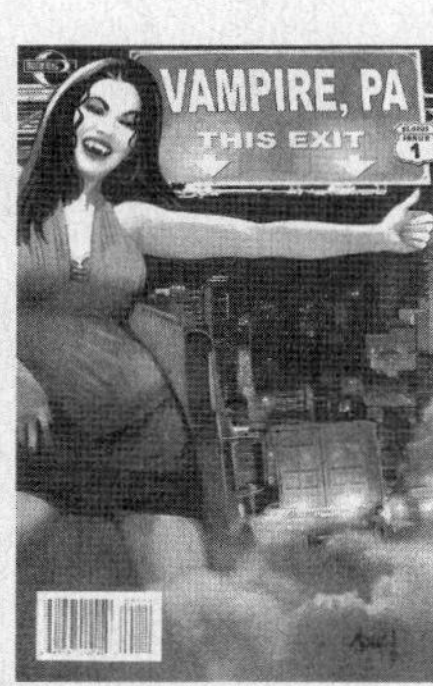

Vampire, PA #1 © Vaughn & Solof

Vampire Tales #1 © MAR

Vamps: Pumpkin Time #3 © Lee & Simpson

	GD 2.0	VG 4.0	FN 6.0	VF 8.0	VF/NM 9.0	NM- 9.2

Dynamite Entertainment: 2013 - No. 5, 2014 ($3.99)
1-5-Nate Cosby-s/José Luis-a; regular & photo-c on each 4.00

VAMPIRELLA'S SUMMER NIGHTS
Harris Publications: 1992 (one-shot)
1-Art Adams infinity cover; centerfold by Stelfreeze 2 4 6 10 14 18

VAMPIRELLA STRIKES
Harris Publications: Sept, 1995 - No. 8, Dec, 1996 ($2.95, limited series)
1-8: 1-Photo-c. 2-Deodato-c; polybagged w/card. 5-Eudaemon-c/app; wraparound-c; alternate-c exists. 6-(6/96)-Mark Millar script; Texeira-c; alternate-c exists. 7-Flip book 4.00
1-Newsstand Edition; diff. photo-c., 1-Limited Ed.; diff. photo-c 4.00
Annual 1-(12/96, $2.95) Delano-s; two covers 4.00

VAMPIRELLA STRIKES
Dynamite Entertainment: 2013 - No. 6, 2013 ($3.99)
1-6: 1-Five covers (Turner, Finch, Manara, Desjardins & photo); Desjardins-a 4.00

VAMPIRELLA THE RED ROOM
Dynamite Entertainment: 2012 - No. 4, 2012 ($3.99)
1-4-Three covers on each; Brereton-s/Diaz-a 4.00

VAMPIRELLA: 25TH ANNIVERSARY SPECIAL
Harris Publications: Oct, 1996 ($5.95, squarebound, one-shot)
nn-Reintro The Blood Red Queen of Hearts; James Robinson, Grant Morrison & Warren Ellis scripts; Mark Texeira, Michael Bair & Amanda Conner-a(p); Frank Frazetta-c 7.00
nn-($6.95)-Silver Edition 8.00

VAMPIRELLA VS. DRACULA
Dynamite Entertainment: 2012 - No. 6, 2012 ($3.99, limited series)
1-6-Harris-s/Rodriguez-a/Linsner-c 4.00

VAMPIRELLA VS. HEMORRHAGE
Harris Publications: Apr, 1997 ($3.50)
1 4.00

VAMPIRELLA VS. PANTHA
Harris Publications: Mar, 1997 ($3.50)
1-Two covers; Millar-s/Texeira-c/a 4.00

VAMPIRELLA/WETWORKS (See Wetworks/Vampirella)
Harris Publications: June, 1997 ($2.95, one-shot)
1 4.00
1-($9.95) Alternate Edition; cardstock-c 10.00

VAMPIRELLA/WITCHBLADE
Harris Publications: 2003; Oct, 2004; Oct, 2005 ($2.99, one-shots)
1-Brian Wood-s/Steve Pugh-a; 3 covers by Texeira, Conner and Pugh 4.00
...: The Feast (10/05, $2.99) Joyce Chin-a; covers by Chin, Conner, Rodriguez 4.00
...: Union of the Damned (10/04, $2.99, one-shot) Sharp-a; three covers 4.00
Trilogy TPB (2006, $12.95) r/one-shots; art gallery and gallery of multiple covers 13.00

VAMPIRE, PA
Moonstone: 2010 - No. 3, Oct, 2010 ($3.99)
1-3: 1-Intro. Vampire Hunter Dean; J.C. Vaughn-s/Brendon & Brian Fraim-a; three covers. 3-Zombie Proof back-up; Spencer-a 4.00

VAMPIRE'S CHRISTMAS, THE (Also see Dark Ivory)
Image Comics: Oct, 2003 ($5.95, over-sized graphic novel)
nn-Linsner-s/a; Dubisch-painted-a 6.00

VAMPIRES: THE MARVEL UNDEAD
Marvel Comics: Dec, 2011 ($3.99, one-shot)
1-Handbook-style profiles of vampire characters in the Marvel Universe; Seeley-c 4.00

VAMPIRE TALES
Marvel Comics Group: Aug, 1973 - No. 11, June, 1975 (75¢, B&W, magazine)

	GD	VG	FN	VF	VF/NM	NM-
1-Morbius, the Living Vampire begins by Pablo Marcos (1st solo Morbius series & 5th Morbius app.)	7	14	21	44	82	120
2-Intro. Satana; Steranko-r	6	12	18	38	69	100
3,5,6: 3-Satana app. 5-Origin Morbius. 6-1st full Lilith app. in this title (continued from Giant-Size Chillers #1)	4	8	12	28	47	65
4,7: 4-1st Lilith cameo app. on inside back-c	4	8	12	23	37	50
8-1st solo Blade story (see Tomb of Dracula)	6	12	18	38	69	100
9-Blade app.	5	10	15	30	50	70
10,11	4	8	12	23	37	50
Annual 1(10/75)-Heath-r/#9	4	8	12	23	37	50

NOTE: *Alcala a-6, 8, 9i. Boris c-4, 6. Chaykin a-7. Everett a-1r. Gulacy a-7p. Heath a-9. Infantino a-3r. Gil Kane a-4, 5r.*

	GD 2.0	VG 4.0	FN 6.0	VF 8.0	VF/NM 9.0	NM- 9.2

VAMPIRE VERSES, THE
CFD Productions: Aug, 1995 - No. 4, 1995 ($2.95, B&W, mature)
1-4 3.00

VAMPI VICIOUS
Harris Publications (Anarchy Studios): Aug, 2003 - No. 3, Nov, 2003 ($2.99)
1-3: 1-McKeever-s/Dogan-a; 3 covers by Dogan, Lau & Noto. 3-Kau-a 4.00

VAMPI VICIOUS CIRCLE
Harris Publications (Anarchy Studios): Jun, 2004 - No. 3, Sept, 2004 ($2.99/$9.95)
1-3: B. Clay Moore-s 4.00
1-3-($9.95) Limited Edition w/variant-c. 1-Noto-c. 2-Norton-c. 3-Lucas-c 10.00

VAMPI VICIOUS RAMPAGE
Harris Publications (Anarchy Studios): Feb, 2005 - No. 2, Apr, 2005 ($2.99)
1,2: Raab-s/Lau-a; two covers on each 4.00

VAMPI VS. XIN
Harris Publications (Anarchy Studios): Oct, 2004 - No. 2, Jan, 2005 ($2.99)
1,2-Faerber-s/Lau-a; two covers 4.00

VAMPS
DC Comics (Vertigo): Aug, 1994 - No. 6, Jan, 1995 ($1.95, lim. series, mature)
1-6-Bolland-c 3.00
Trade paperback ($9.95)-r/#1-6 10.00

VAMPS: HOLLYWOOD & VEIN
DC Comics (Vertigo): Feb, 1996 - No. 6, July, 1996 ($2.25, lim. series, mature)
1-6: Winslade-c 3.00

VAMPS: PUMPKIN TIME
DC Comics (Vertigo): Dec, 1998 - No. 3, Feb, 1999 ($2.50, lim. series, mature)
1-3: Quitely-c 3.00

VANDROID
Dark Horse Comics: Feb, 2014 - No. 5, Jun, 2014 ($3.99, limited series)
1-5-Tommy Lee Edwards & Noah Smith-s/Dan McDaid-a/Edwards-c 4.00

VANGUARD (...Outpost: Earth) (See Megaton)
Megaton Comics: 1987 ($1.50)
1-Erik Larsen-c(p) 4.00

VANGUARD (See Savage Dragon #2)
Image Comics (Highbrow Entertainment): Oct, 1993 - No. 6, 1994 ($1.95)
1-6: 1-Wraparound gatefold-c; Erik Larsen back-up-a; Supreme x-over. 3-(12/93)-Indicia says December 1994. 4-Berzerker back-up. 5-Angel Medina-a(p) 3.00

VANGUARD (See Savage Dragon #2)
Image Comics: Aug, 1996 - No. 4, Feb, 1997 ($2.95, B&W, limited series)
1-4 3.00

VANGUARD: ETHEREAL WARRIORS
Image Comics: Aug, 2000 ($5.95, B&W)
1-Fosco & Larsen-a 6.00

VANGUARD ILLUSTRATED
Pacific Comics: Nov, 1983 - No. 11, Oct, 1984 (Baxter paper)(Direct sales only)
1,3-6,8-11: 1-Nudity scenes 3.00
2-1st app. Stargrazers (see Legends of the Stargrazers; Dave Stevens-c 1 3 4 6 8 10
7-1st app. Mr. Monster (r-in Mr. Monster #1); nudity scenes 5.00
NOTE: *Evans a-7. Kaluta c-5, 7p. Perez a-6; c-6. Rude a-1-4; c-4. Williamson c-3.*

VANGUARD: STRANGE VISITORS
Image Comics: Oct, 1996 - No.4, Feb, 1997 ($2.95, B&W, limited series)
1-4: 3-Supreme-c/app. 3.00

VAN HELSING: FROM BENEATH THE RUE MORGUE (Based on the 2004 movie)
Dark Horse Comics: Apr, 2004 ($2.99, one-shot)
1-Hugh Jackman photo-c; Dysart-s/Alexander-a 3.00

VANITY (See Pacific Presents #3)
Pacific Comics: Jun, 1984 - No. 2, Aug, 1984 ($1.50, direct sales)
1,2: Origin 3.00

VARIETY COMICS (The Spice of Comics)
Rural Home Publ./Croyden Publ. Co.: 1944 - No. 2, 1945; No. 3, 1946
1-Origin Captain Valiant 25 50 75 150 245 340

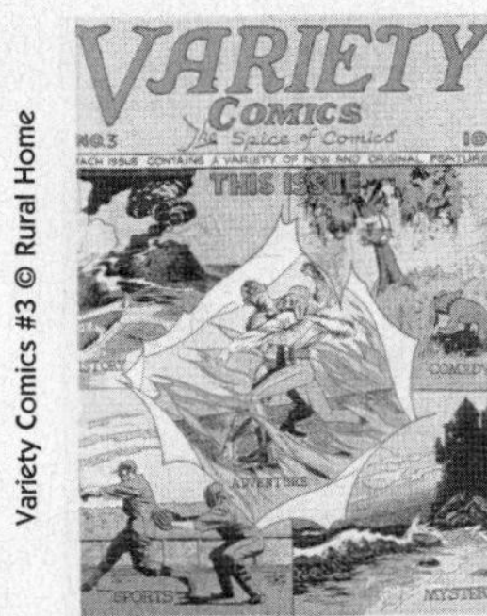

Variety Comics #3 © Rural Home

Velvet #15 © Basement & Epting

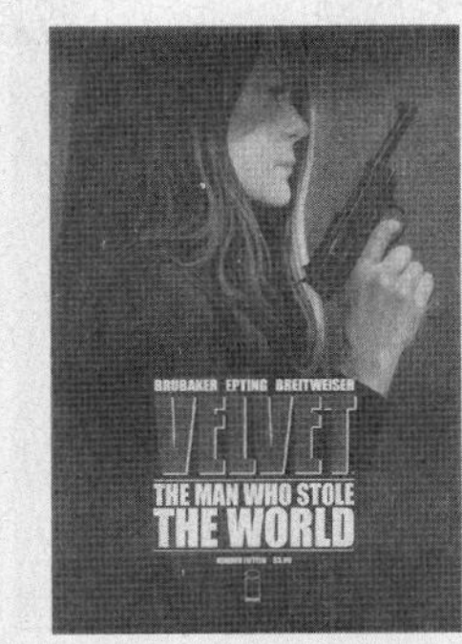

Venom (2003 series) #1 © MAR

GD VG FN VF VF/NM NM-
2.0 4.0 6.0 8.0 9.0 9.2

2-Captain Valiant 15 30 45 88 137 185
3(1946-Croyden)-Captain Valiant 14 28 42 82 121 160

VARIETY COMICS (See Fox Giants)

VARSITY
Parents' Magazine Institute: 1945

1 11 22 33 60 83 105

VAULT OF EVIL
Marvel Comics Group: Feb, 1973 - No. 23, Nov, 1975

1 (1950s reprints begin) 4 8 12 25 40 55
2-23: 3,4-Brunner-c. 11-Kirby-a 3 6 9 17 26 35

NOTE: ***Ditko** a-14r, 15r, 20-22r.* ***Drucker** a-10r(Mystic #52), 13r(Uncanny Tales #42).* ***Everett** a-11r(Menace #2), 13r(Menace #4); c-10.* ***Heath** a-5r.* ***Gil Kane** c-1, 6.* ***Kirby** a-11.* ***Krigstein** a-20r(Uncanny Tales #54).* ***Reinman** r-1.* ***Tuska** a-6r.*

VAULT OF HORROR (Formerly War Against Crime #1-11) (Also see EC Archives)
E. C. Comics: No. 12, Apr-May, 1950 - No. 40, Dec-Jan, 1954-55

12 (Scarce)-ties w/Crypt Of Terror as 1st horror comic
571 1142 1713 4568 7284 10,000
13-Morphine story 114 228 342 912 1456 2000
14 94 188 282 753 1201 1650
15- "Terror in the Swamp" is same story w/minor changes as "The Thing in the Swamp" from Haunt of Fear #15 89 178 267 712 1131 1550
16 69 138 207 552 876 1200
17-Classic werewolf-c 77 154 231 616 983 1350
18,19 56 112 168 448 712 975
20-25: 22-Frankenstein-c & adaptation. 23-Used in **POP**, pg. 84; Davis-a(2); Ingels bio. 24-Craig bio. 51 102 153 408 654 900
26-B&W & color illos in **POP** 51 102 153 408 654 900
27-29,31,33,34,36: 31-Ray Bradbury bio. 36- "Pipe Dream" classic opium addict story by Krigstein; "Twin Bill" cited in articles by T.E. Murphy, Wertham
47 94 141 376 601 825
30-Classic severed arm-c 74 148 222 592 946 1300
32-Censored-c 63 126 189 504 802 1100
35-X-Mas-c; "And All Through the House" adapted for 1972 Tales From The Crypt film
80 160 240 640 1020 1400
37-1st app. Drusilla, a Vampirella look alike; Williamson-a
57 114 171 456 728 1000
38 47 94 141 376 601 825
39-Classic Craig woman in bondage/torture-c 69 138 207 552 876 1200
40-Low distribution 51 102 153 408 654 900

NOTE: ***Craig** art in all but No. 13 & 33; c-12-40.* ***Crandall** a-33, 34, 39.* ***Davis** a-17-38.* ***Evans** a-27, 28, 30, 32, 33.* ***Feldstein** a-12-16.* ***Ingels** a-13-20, 22-40.* ***Kamen** a-15-22, 25, 29, 35.* ***Krigstein** a-36, 38-40.* ***Kurtzman** a-12, 13.* ***Orlando** a-24, 31, 40.* ***Wood** a-12-14. #22, 29 & 31 have Ray Bradbury adaptations. #16 & 17 have H. P. Lovecraft adaptations.*

VAULT OF HORROR, THE
Gladstone Publ.: Aug, 1990 - No. 6, June, 1991 ($1.95, 68 pgs.)(#4 on: $2.00)

1-Craig-c(r); all contain EC reprints 5.00
2-6: 2,4-6-Craig-c(r). 3-Ingels-c(r) 5.00

VAULT OF HORROR
Russ Cochran/Gemstone Publishing: Sept, 1991 - No. 5, May, 1992 ($2.00); Oct, 1992 - No. 29, Oct, 1999 ($1.50/$2.00/$2.50)

1-29: E.C reprints. 1-4r/VOH #12-15 w/original-c 4.00

V...-COMICS (Morse code for "V" - 3 dots, 1 dash)
Fox Features Syndicate: Jan, 1942 - No. 2, Mar-Apr, 1942

1-Origin V-Man & the Boys; The Banshee & The Black Fury, The Queen of Evil, & V-Agents begin; Nazi-c 245 490 735 1568 2684 3800
2-Nazi bondage/torture-c 232 464 696 1485 2543 3600

VECTOR
Now Comics: 1986 - No. 4, 1986? ($1.50, 1st color comic by Now Comics)

1-4: Computer-generated art 3.00

VEIL
Dark Horse Comics: Mar, 2014 - No. 5, Oct, 2014 ($3.50)

1-5-Greg Rucka-s/Toni Fejzula-a/c 3.50

VEILS
DC Comics (Vertigo): 1999 ($24.95, one-shot)

Hardcover-($24.95) Painted art and photography; McGreal-s 25.00
Softcover ($14.95) 15.00

VELOCITY (Also see Cyberforce)
Image Comics (Top Cow Productions): Nov, 1995 - No. 3, Jan, 1996 ($2.50, limited series)

GD VG FN VF VF/NM NM-
2.0 4.0 6.0 8.0 9.0 9.2

1-3: Kurt Busiek scripts in all. 2-Savage Dragon-c/app. 3.00
...: Pilot Season 1 (10/07, $2.99) Casey-s/Maguire-a 3.00
Vol. 2 #1-4 (6/10 - No. 4, 4/11, $3.99) Rocafort-a/Marz-s; multiple covers 4.00

VELVET
Image Comics: Oct, 2013 - No. 15, Jul, 2016 ($3.50/$3.99)

1-14-Brubaker-s/Epting-a/c. 5-$2.99-c 3.50
15-($3.99) 4.00

VENGEANCE
Marvel Comics: Sept, 2011 - No. 6, Feb, 2012 ($3.99, limited series)

1-6-Casey-s/Dragotta-a. 1-Magneto and Red Skull app. 4-Loki cover 4.00

VENGEANCE OF THE MOON KNIGHT
Marvel Comics: Nov, 2009 - No. 10, Sept, 2010 ($3.99/$2.99)

1,9: 1-($3.99) Hurwitz-s/Opeña-a; covers by Yu, Ross & Finch; back-up r/Moon Knight #1 ('80) 9-Spider-Man & Sandman app.; Campbell-c 4.00
2-8,10: 2-Sentry app. 5-Spider-Man app. 7,8-Deadpool app. 10-Secret Avengers app. 3.00

VENGEANCE OF VAMPIRELLA (Becomes Vampirella: Death & Destruction)
Harris Comics: Apr, 1994 - No. 25, Apr, 1996 ($2.95)

1-($3.50)-Quesada/Palmiotti "bloodfoil" wraparound-c 1 2 3 5 6 8
1-2nd printing; blue foil-c 4.00
1-Gold 20.00
2-8: 8-Polybagged w/trading card 5.00
9-25: 10-w/coupon for Hyde -25 poster. 11,19-Polybagged w/ trading card. 25-Quesada & Palmiotti red foil-c 4.00
...: Bloodshed (1995, $6.95) 7.00

VENGEANCE OF VAMPIRELLA: THE MYSTERY WALK
Harris Comics: Nov, 1995 ($2.95, one-shot)

0 4.00

VENGEANCE SQUAD
Charlton Comics: July, 1975 - No. 6, May, 1976 (#1-3 are 25¢ issues)

1-Mike Mauser, Private Eye begins by Staton 2 4 6 9 13 16
2-6: Morisi-a in all 1 2 3 5 7 9
5,6 (Modern Comics-r, 1977) 6.00

VENOM
Marvel Comics: June, 2003 - No. 18, Nov, 2004 ($2.25/$2.99)

1-15: 1-7-Herrera-a/Way-s. 6,7-Wolverine app. 8-10-Wolverine-c/app.; Kieth-c. 11-Fantastic Four app. 4.00
16-18 6.00
... Vol. 1: Shiver (2004, $13.99, TPB) r/#1-5 14.00
... Vol. 2: Run (2004, $19.99, TPB) r/#6-13 20.00
... Vol. 3: Twist (2004, $13.99, TPB) r/#14-18 14.00

VENOM (See Amazing Spider-Man #654 & 654.1)(Also see Secret Avengers)
Marvel Comics: May, 2011 - No. 42, Dec, 2013 ($3.99/$2.99)

1-Flash Thompson with the symbiote; Remender-s/Tony Moore-a/Quesada-c
2 4 6 11 16 20
2-Cover swipe of ASM #300; Kraven app. 3 6 9 14 20 25
3-12-($2.99) 3-Deodato-c. 6-8-Spider Island 4.00
13-($3.99) Circle of Four; Red Hulk, X-23, and Ghost Rider app. 4.00
13.1, 13.2, 13.3, 13.4, 14-($2.99) Circle of Four parts 2-6 3.00
15-27, 27.1, 28-42: 15-Secret Avengers app. 16,17-Toxin app. 26,27-Minimum Carnage. 38-1st app. Mania. 42-Mephisto app. 4.00
...: Flashpoint 1 (2011, $4.99) r/Amazing Spider-Man #654, 654.1 and Venom #1
2 4 6 9 12 15

VENOM
Marvel Comics: Jan, 2017 - Present ($3.99)

1-4: 1-Mike Costa-s/Gerardo Sandoval-a; intro. Lee Price; Mac Gargan app. 4.00

VENOM: LETHAL PROTECTOR
Marvel Comics: Feb, 1993 - No. 6, July, 1993 ($2.95, limited series)

1-Red holo-grafx foil-c; Bagley-c/a in all 1 3 4 6 8 10
1-Gold variant sold to retailers 4 8 12 27 44 60
1-Black-c (at least 146 copies have been authenticated by CGC since 2000)
17 34 51 117 259 400

NOTE: Counterfeit copies of the black-c exist and are valueless

2-6: Spider-Man app. in all 5.00

VENOM: SPACE KNIGHT
Marvel Comics: Jan, 2016 - No. 13, Dec, 2016 ($3.99)

1-13: 1-Robbie Thompson-s/Ariel Olivetti-a. 8-10-Jacinto-a. 11,12-Civil War II tie-in 4.00

Venture #1 © Faerber & Igle

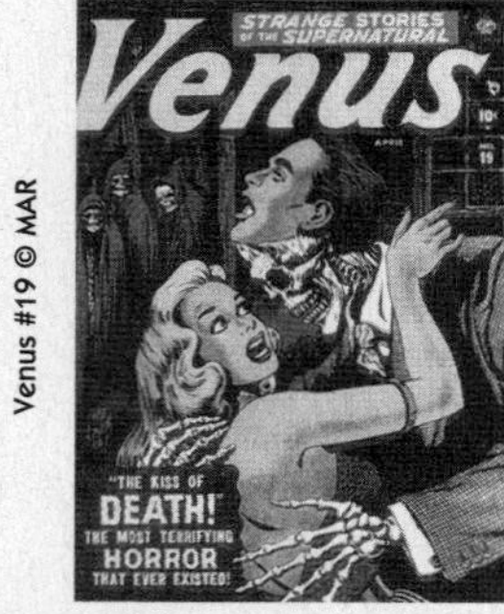

Venus #19 © MAR

Veronica #202 © ACP

GD VG FN VF VF/NM NM-
2.0 4.0 6.0 8.0 9.0 9.2

GD VG FN VF VF/NM NM-
2.0 4.0 6.0 8.0 9.0 9.2

VENOM: Marvel Comics (Also see Amazing Spider-Man #298-300)
... ALONG CAME A SPIDER, 1/96 - No. 4, 4/96 ($2.95)-Spider-Man & Carnage app. 4.00
... CARNAGE UNLEASHED, 4/95 - No. 4, 7/95 ($2.95) 4.00
... DARK ORIGIN, 10/08 - No. 5, 2/09 ($2.99) 1-5-Medina-a 4.00
... /DEADPOOL: WHAT IF?, 4/11 ($2.99) Remender-s/Moll-a/Young-c; Galactus app. 8 16 24 54 102 150
... DEATHTRAP: THE VAULT, 3/93 ($6.95) r/Avengers: Deathtrap: The Vault 7.00
... FUNERAL PYRE, 8/93- No. 3, 10/93 ($2.95)-#1-Holo-grafx foil-c; Punisher app. in all 4.00
... LICENSE TO KILL,6/97 - No. 3, 8/97 ($1.95) 5.00
... NIGHTS OF VENGEANCE, 8/94 - No. 4, 11/94 ($2.95), #1-Red foil-c 4.00
... ON TRIAL, 3/97 - No. 3, 5/97 ($1.95) 4.00
... SEED OF DARKNESS, 7/97 ($1.95) #(-1) Flashback 4.00
... SEPARATION ANXIETY,12/94- No. 4, 3/95 ($2.95) #1-Embossed-c 4.00
... SIGN OF THE BOSS,3/97 - No. 2, 10/97 ($1.99) 4.00
... SINNER TAKES ALL, 8/95 - No. 5, 10/95 ($2.95) 4.00
... SUPER SPECIAL, 8/95($3.95) #1-Flip book 5.00
... THE ENEMY WITHIN, 2/94 - No. 3, 4/94 ($2.95)-Demogoblin & Morbius app.
1-Glow-in-the-dark-c 4.00
... THE FINALE, 11/97 - No. 3, 1/98 ($1.99) 4.00
... THE HUNGER, 8/96- No. 4, 11/96 ($1.95) 4.00
... THE HUNTED, 5/96-No. 3, 7/96 ($2.95) 4.00
... THE MACE, 5/94 - No. 3, 7/94 ($2.95)-#1-Embossed-c 4.00
... THE MADNESS, 11/93- No. 3, 1/94 ($2.95)-Kelley Jones-c/a(p).
1-Embossed-c; Juggernaut app. 4.00
... TOOTH AND CLAW, 12/96 - No. 3, 2/97 ($1.95)-Wolverine-c/app. 4.00
... VS. CARNAGE, 9/04 - No. 4, 12/04 ($2.99)-Milligan-s/Crain-a; Spider-Man app. 4.00
TPB (2004, $9.99) r/#1-4 10.00

VENTURE
AC Comics (Americomics): Aug, 1986 - No. 3, 1986? ($1.75)
1-3: 1-3-Bolt. 1-Astron. 2-Femforce. 3-Fazers 3.00

VENTURE
Image Comics: Jan, 2003 - No. 4, Sept, 2003 ($2.95)
1-4-Faerber-s/Igle-a 3.00

VENUS (See Agents of Atlas, Marvel Spotlight #2 & Weird Wonder Tales)
Marvel/Atlas Comics (CMC 1-9/LCC 10-19): Aug, 1948 - No. 19, Apr, 1952 (Also see Marvel Mystery #91)
1-Venus & Hedy Devine begin; 1st app. Venus; Kurtzman's "Hey Look" 226 452 678 1446 2473 3500
2 123 246 369 787 1344 1900
3,5 81 162 243 518 884 1250
4-Kurtzman's "Hey Look" 84 168 252 538 919 1300
6-9: 6-Loki app. 7,8-Painted-c. 9-Begin 52 pgs.; book-length feature "Whom the Gods Destroy!" 71 142 213 454 777 1100
10-S/F-horror issues begin (7/50) 100 200 300 635 1093 1550
11-S/F end of the world (11/50) 116 232 348 742 1271 1800
12-Colan-a 68 136 204 435 743 1050
13-16-Venus by Everett, 2-3 stories each; covers-#13,15,16; 14-Everett part cover (Venus). 129 258 387 826 1413 2000
17-Classic Everett horror & skeleton/bondage-c (scarce) 314 628 942 2198 3849 5500
19-Classic Everett skeleton Good Girl-c 343 686 1029 2400 4200 6000
NOTE: ***Berg** s/f story-13. **Everett** c-13, 14(part; Venus only), 15-19. **Heath** s/f story-11. **Maneely** s/f story 10(3pg.), 16. **Morisi** a-19. **Syd Shores** c-6.*

VENUS
BOOM! Studios: Dec, 2015 - No. 4, Mar, 2016 ($3.99)
1-4-Loverd-s/Danlan-a 4.00

VERI BEST SURE FIRE COMICS
Holyoke Publishing Co.: No date (circa 1945) (Reprints Holyoke one-shots)
1-Captain Aero, Alias X, Miss Victory, Commandos of the Devil Dogs, Red Cross, Hammerhead Hawley, Capt. Aero's Sky Scouts, Flagman app.; same-c as Veri Best Sure Shot #1 46 92 138 290 488 685

VERI BEST SURE SHOT COMICS
Holyoke Publishing Co.: No date (circa 1945) (Reprints Holyoke one-shots)
1-Capt. Aero, Miss Victory by Quinlan, Alias X, The Red Cross, Flagman, Commandos of the Devil Dogs, Hammerhead Hawley, Capt. Aero's Sky Scouts; same-c as Veri Best Sure Fire #1 46 92 138 290 488 685

VERMILLION
DC Comics (Helix): Oct, 1996 - No. 12, Sept, 1997 ($2.25/$2.50)
1-12: 1-4: Lucius Shepard scripts. 4,12-Kaluta-c 3.00

VERONICA (Also see Archie's Girls, Betty &...)
Archie Comics: Apr, 1989 - No. 210, Feb, 2012
1-(75¢-c) 2 4 6 9 12 15
2-10: 2-(75¢-c) 5.00
11-38 4.00
39-Love Showdown pt. 4, Cheryl Blossom 6.00
40-70: 34-Neon ink-c 3.00
71-201,203-206: 134-Begin $2.19-c. 152,155-Cheryl Blossom app. 163-Begin $2.25-c 3.00
202-Intro. Kevin Keller, 1st openly gay Archie character; cover has blue background 2 4 6 9 12 15
202-Second printing; cover has black background 1 3 4 6 8 10
207-210-Kevin Keller mini-series 3.00

VERONICA'S PASSPORT DIGEST MAGAZINE (Becomes Veronica's Digest Magazine #3 on)
Archie Comics: Nov, 1992 - No. 6 ($1.50/$1.79, digest size)
1 5.00
2-6 3.00

VERONICA'S SUMMER SPECIAL (See Archie Giant Series Magazine #615, 625)

VERTICAL
DC Comics (Vertigo): 2003 ($4.95, 3-1/4" wide pages, one-shot)
1-Seagle-s/Allred & Bond-a; odd format 1/2 width pages with some 20" long spreads 5.00

VERTIGO DOUBLE SHOT
DC Comics (Vertigo): 2008 ($2.99)
1-Reprints House of Mystery (2008) #1 and Young Liars #1 in flip-book format 3.00

VERTIGO ESSENTIALS
DC Comics (Vertigo): Dec, 2013 - Feb, 2014 ($1.00, Flip book reprints with DC & Vertigo Essential Graphics novels catalog)
...: American Vampire 1 (2/14) Reprints #1; flip-c by Ryan Sook 3.00
...: Fables 1 (1/14) Reprints #1; flip-c by Ryan Sook 3.00
...: 100 Bullets 1 (2/14) Reprints #1; flip-c by Ryan Sook 3.00
...: The Sandman #1 (12/13, $1.00) Reprints Sandman #1 (1989) with flipbook 3.00
...: V For Vendetta 1 (12/13) Reprints first chapter; flip-c by Ryan Sook 3.00
...: Y: The Last Man 1 (1/14) Reprints #1; flip-c by Ryan Sook 3.00

VERTIGO: FIRST BLOOD
DC Comics (Vertigo): Feb, 2012 ($7.99, squarebound)
TPB-Reprints first issues of American Vampire, I Zombie, The Unwritten & Sweet Tooth 8.00

VERTIGO: FIRST CUT
DC Comics (Vertigo): 2008 ($4.99, TPB)
TPB-Reprints first issues of DMZ, Army@Love, Jack of Fables, Exterminators, Scalped, Crossing Midnight, and Loveless; preview of Air 5.00

VERTIGO: FIRST OFFENSES
DC Comics (Vertigo): 2005 ($4.99, TPB)
TPB-Reprints first issues of The Invisibles, Preacher, Fables, Sandman Mystery Theater, and Lucifer 5.00

VERTIGO: FIRST TASTE
DC Comics (Vertigo): 2005 ($4.99, TPB)
TPB-Reprints first issues of Y: The Last Man, 100 Bullets, Transmetropolitan, Books of Magick: Life During Wartime, Death: The High Cost of Living, and Saga of the Swamp Thing #21 (Alan Moore's first story on that title) 5.00

VERTIGO GALLERY, THE: DREAMS AND NIGHTMARES
DC Comics (Vertigo): 1995 ($3.50, one-shot)
1-Pin-ups of Vertigo characters by Sienkiewicz, Toth, Van Fleet & others; McKean-c 4.00

VERTIGO JAM
DC Comics (Vertigo): Aug, 1993 ($3.95, one-shot, 68 pgs.)(Painted-c by Fabry)
1-Sandman by Neil Gaiman, Hellblazer, Animal Man, Doom Patrol, Swamp Thing, Kid Eternity & Shade the Changing Man 5.00

VERTIGO POP! BANGKOK
DC Comics (Vertigo): July, 2003 - No. 4, Oct, 2003 ($2.95, limited series)
1-4-Camuncoli-c/a; Jonathan Vankin-s 3.00

Vertigo Winter's Edge #1 © DC

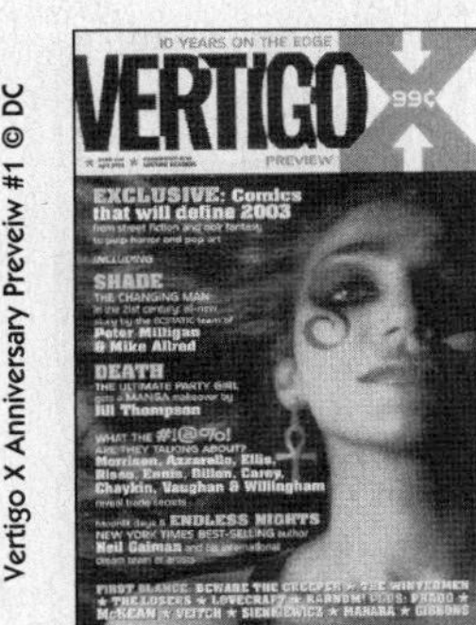

Vertigo X Anniversary Preveiw #1 © DC

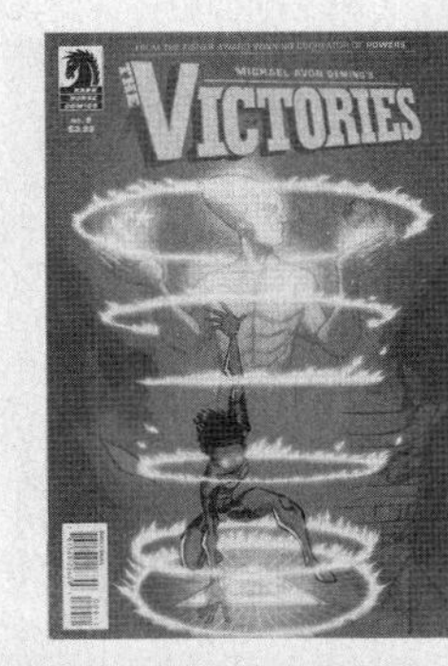

Victories V2 #9 © Oeming

GD	VG	FN	VF	VF/NM	NM-
2.0	4.0	6.0	8.0	9.0	9.2

VERTIGO POP! LONDON
DC Comics (Vertigo): Jan, 2003 - No. 4, Apr, 2003 ($2.95, limited series)
1-4-Philip Bond-c/a; Peter Milligan-s 3.00

VERTIGO POP! TOKYO
DC Comics (Vertigo): Sept, 2002 - No. 4, Dec, 2002 ($2.95, limited series)
1-4-Seth Fisher-c/a; Jonathan Vankin-s 3.00
Tokyo Days, Bangkok Nights TPB (2009, $19.99) r/#1-4 & Vertogo Pop! Bangkok #1-4 20.00

VERTIGO PREVIEW
DC Comics (Vertigo): 1992 (75¢, one-shot, 36 pgs.)
1-Vertigo previews; Sandman story by Neil Gaiman 3.00

VERTIGO QUARTERLY CMYK
DC Comics (Vertigo): Jun, 2014 - No. 4, Mar, 2015 ($7.99, limited series)
1-4-Color themed short story anthology. 1-Cyan. 2-Magenta. 3-Yellow. 4-Black 8.00

VERTIGO QUARTERLY SFX
DC Comics (Vertigo): Jun, 2015 - No. 4, Mar, 2016 ($7.99, limited series)
1-4-Sound effect-themed short story anthology. 1-"Pop!". 2-"Slam!". 3-"Krak!". 4-"Bang" 8.00

VERTIGO RAVE
DC Comics (Vertigo): Fall, 1994 (99¢, one-shot)
1-Vertigo previews 3.00

VERTIGO RESURRECTED: ...
DC Comics (Vertigo): Dec, 2010 - Present ($7.99, squarebound, reprints)
The Extremist 1 (1/11, 12/13) r/The Extremist #1-4 8.00
Finals 1 (5/11) r/Finals #1-4; Jill Thompson-a 8.00
Hellblazer 1 (2/11) r/Hellblazer #57,58,245,246 8.00
Hellblazer - Bad Blood 1 (6/11) r/Hellblazer Special: Bad Blood #1-4 8.00
Jonny Double 1 (10/11) r/Jonny Double #1-4; Azzarello-s/Risso-a 8.00
My Faith in Frankie 1 (1/12) r/My Faith in Frankie #1-4; Carey-s 8.00
Sandman Presents - Petrefax 1 (8/11) r/Sandman Presents: Petrefax #1-4 8.00
Sgt. Rock: Between Hell and a Hard Place 1,2 (1/12, 2/12) r/the 2003 HC 8.00
Shoot 1 (12/10) r/short stories by various incl. Quitely, Sale, Bolland, Risso, Jim Lee 8.00
The Eaters 1 (12/11) r/Vertigo Visions - The Eaters and other short stories 8.00
Winter's Edge 1 (2/11) r/Vertigo's Winter Edge #1-3; Bermejo-c 8.00

VERTIGO SECRET FILES
DC Comics (Vertigo): Aug, 2000 ($4.95)
...: Hellblazer 1 (8/00, $4.95) Background info and story summaries 5.00
...: Swamp Thing 1 (11/00, $4.95) Backstories and origins; Hale-c 5.00

VERTIGO VERITE: THE UNSEEN HAND
DC Comics (Vertigo): Sept, 1996 - No. 4, Dec, 1996 ($2.50, limited series)
1-4: Terry LaBan scripts in all 3.00

VERTIGO VISIONS
DC Comics (Vertigo): June, 1993 - Present (one-shots)
Dr. Occult 1 (7/94, $3.95) 4.00
Dr. Thirteen 1 (9/98, $5.95) Howarth-s 6.00
Prez 1 (7/95, $3.95) 4.00
The Geek 1 (6/93, $3.95) 4.00
The Eaters ($4.95, 1995)-Milligan story. 5.00
The Phantom Stranger 1 (10/93, $3.50) 4.00
Tomahawk 1 (7/98, $4.95) Pollack-s 5.00

VERTIGO WINTER'S EDGE
DC Comics (Vertigo): 1998, 1999 ($7.95/$6.95, square-bound, annual)
1-Winter stories by Vertigo creators; Desire story by Gaiman/Bolton; Bolland wraparound-c 8.00
2,3-($6.95)-Winter stories: 2-Allred-c. 3-Bond-c; Desire by Gaiman/Zulli 7.00

VERTIGO X ANNIVERSARY PREVIEW
DC Comics (Vertigo): 2003 (99¢, one-shot, 48 pgs.)
1-Previews of upcoming titles and interviews; Endless Nights, Shade, The Originals 4.00

VERY BEST OF DENNIS THE MENACE, THE
Fawcett Publ.: July, 1979 - No. 2, Apr, 1980 (95¢/$1.00, digest-size, 132 pgs.)
1,2-Reprints 2 4 6 8 10 12

VERY BEST OF DENNIS THE MENACE, THE
Marvel Comics Group: Apr, 1982 - No. 3, Aug, 1982 ($1.25, digest-size)
1-3: Reprints 2 3 4 6 8 10
1,2-Mistakenly printed with DC logo on cover 2 4 6 9 12 15
NOTE: *Hank Ketcham c-all. A few thousand of #1 & 2 were printed with DC emblem.*

VERY VICKY
Meet Danny Ocean: 1993? - No. 8, 1995 ($2.50, B&W)
1-8, ...: Calling All Hillbillies (1995, $2.50) 3.00

VERY WEIRD TALES (Also see Slithiss Attacks!)
Oceanspray Comics Group: Aug, 2002 - No. 2, Oct, 2002 ($4.00)
1-Mutant revenge, methamphetamine, corporate greed horror stories 3 6 9 16 23 30
2-Weird fantasy and horror stories 2 4 6 9 12 15
NOTE: *Created in prevention classes taught by Jon McClure at the Oceanspray Family Center in Newport, Oregon, and paid for by the Housing Authority of Lincoln County. All books are b&w with color covers. Issues #1-2 penciled and inked by various artists. All comics feature characters created by students and are signed and numbered by Jon McClure. Issues #1-2 have print runs of 100 each.*

VEXT
DC Comics: Mar, 1999 - No. 6, Aug, 1999 ($2.50, limited series)
1-6-Giffen-s. 1-Superman app. 3.00

V FOR VENDETTA
DC Comics: Sept, 1988 - No. 10, May, 1989 ($2.00, maxi-series)
1-Alan Moore scripts in all; David Lloyd-a 3 6 9 21 33 45
2-10 1 3 4 6 8 10
HC (1990) Limited edition 60.00
HC (2005, $29.99, dustjacket) r/series; foreward by Lloyd; promo art and sketches 30.00
Trade paperback (1990, $14.95) 20.00

VIBE (See Justice League of America's Vibe)

VIC BRIDGES FAZERS SKETCHBOOK AND FACT FILE
AC Comics: Nov, 1986 ($1.75)
1 3.00

VICE
Image Comics (Top Cow): Nov, 2005 - No. 5 ($2.99)
1-5-Coleite-s/Kirkham-a. 1-Three covers 3.00
1-Code Red Edition; variant Benitez-c 3.00

VIC FLINT(Crime Buster...)(See Authentic Police Cases #10-14 & Fugitives From Justice #2)
St. John Publ. Co.: Aug, 1948 - No. 5, Apr, 1949 (Newspaper reprints; NEA Service)
1 18 36 54 103 162 220
2 13 26 39 72 101 130
3-5 11 22 33 62 86 110

VIC FLINT (Crime Buster...)
Argo Publ.: Feb, 1956 - No. 2, May, 1956 (Newspaper reprints)
1,2 9 18 27 50 65 80

VIC JORDAN (Also see Big Shot Comics #32)
Civil Service Publ.: April, 1945
1-1944 daily newspaper-r 15 30 45 86 133 180

VICKI (Humor)
Atlas/Seaboard Publ.: Feb, 1975 - No. 4, Aug, 1975 (No. 1,2: 68 pgs.)
1,2-(68 pgs.)-Reprints Tippy Teen; Good Girl art 5 10 15 30 50 70
3,4 (Low print) 5 10 15 31 53 75

VICKI VALENTINE (...Summer Special #1)
Renegade Press: July, 1985 - No. 4, July, 1986 ($1.70, B&W)
1-4: Woggon, Rausch-a; all have paper dolls. 2-Christmas issue 3.00

VICKY
Ace Magazine: Oct, 1948 - No. 5, June, 1949
nn(10/48)-Teenage humor 12 24 36 67 94 120
4(12/48), nn(2/49), 4(4/49), 5(6/49): 5-Dotty app. 10 20 30 54 72 90

VICTORIAN UNDEAD
DC Comics (WildStorm): Jan, 2010 - No. 6, Jun, 2010 ($2.99)
1-6-Sherlock Holmes vs. Zombies; Edginton-s/Fabbri-a. 1-Two covers (Moore, Coleby) 3.00
...: Sherlock Holmes vs. Jekyll and Hyde (12/10, $4.99) Domingues-a/Van Sciver-c 5.00
...: Sherlock Holmes vs. Zombies TPB (2010, $17.99) r/#1-6; character design sketch art 18.00
... Volume 2 (1/11 - No. 5, 5/11) 1-3-($3.99) "Sherlock Holmes vs. Dracula" on-c; Fabbri-a 4.00
... Volume 2 - 4,5-($2.99) "Sherlock Holmes vs. Dracula" on-c; Fabbri-a 3.00

VICTORIES, THE
Dark Horse Comics: Aug, 2012 - No. 5, Dec, 2012 ($3.99 limited series)
1-5-Michael Avon Oeming-s/a/c 4.00
...Volume 2: Transhuman 1-15 (6/13 - No. 15, 9/14) Oeming-s/a/c. 11-15 Metahuman 4.00

VIC TORRY & HIS FLYING SAUCER (Also see Mr. Monster's...#5)
Fawcett Publications: 1950 (one-shot)

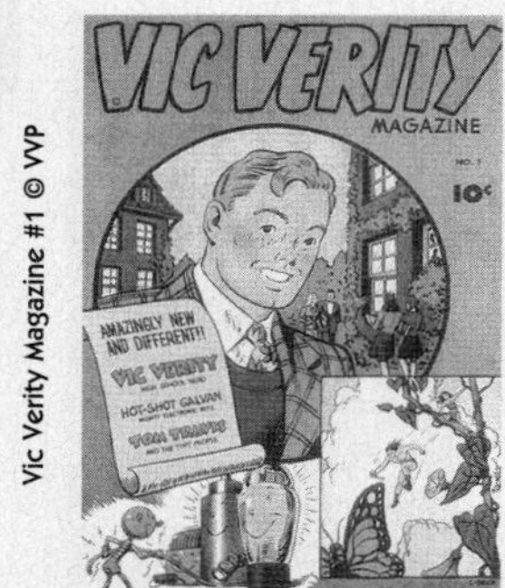

Vic Verity Magazine #1 © VVP

Vigilante #48 © DC

Violent Love #1 © Barbiere & Santos

GD 2.0 | VG 4.0 | FN 6.0 | VF 8.0 | VF/NM 9.0 | NM- 9.2

nn-Book-length saucer story by Powell; photo/painted-c 69 138 207 442 759 1075

VICTORY
Topps Comics: June, 1994 ($2.50, unfinished limited series)
1-Kurt Busiek script; Giffen-c/a; Rob Liefeld variant-c exists 3.00

VICTORY
Image Comics: May, 2003 - No. 4, Feb, 2004 ($2.95, limited series)
1-4: 1-Two covers; Francisco-a. 4-Two covers 3.00

VICTORY (Volume 2)
Image Comics: Aug, 2004 - No. 4, Jan, 2005 ($2.95, limited series)
1-4: 1-Three covers; Francisco-a 3.00

VICTORY COMICS
Hillman Periodicals: Aug, 1941 - No. 4, Dec, 1941 (#1 by Funnies, Inc.)
1-The Conqueror by Bill Everett, The Crusader, & Bomber Burns begin; Conqueror's origin in text; Everett-c 343 686 1029 2400 4200 6000
2-Everett-c/a 168 336 504 1075 1838 2600
3,4 129 258 387 826 1413 2000

VIC VERITY MAGAZINE
Vic Verity Publ: 1945; No. 2, Jan?, 1947 - No. 7, Sept, 1946 (A comic book)
1-C. C. Beck-c/a 41 82 123 256 428 600
2-Beck-c 28 56 84 165 270 375
3-7: 6-Beck-a. 7-Beck-c 26 52 78 154 252 350

VIDEO JACK
Marvel Comics (Epic Comics): Nov, 1987 - No. 6, Nov, 1988 ($1.25)
1-5 3.00
6-Neal Adams, Keith Giffen, Wrightson, others-a 5.00

VIETNAM JOURNAL
Apple Comics: Nov, 1987 - No. 16, Apr, 1991 ($1.75/$1.95, B&W)
1-16: Don Lomax-c/a/scripts in all, 1-2nd print 4.00
...: Indian Country Vol. 1 (1990, $12.95)-r/#1-4 plus one new story 13.00

VIETNAM JOURNAL: VALLEY OF DEATH
Apple Comics: June, 1994 - No. 2, Aug, 1994 ($2.75, B&W, limited series)
1,2: By Don Lomax 4.00

VIGILANTE, THE (Also see New Teen Titans #23 & Annual V2#2)
DC Comics: Oct, 1983 - No. 50, Feb, 1988 ($1.25, Baxter paper)
1-Origin 1 2 3 5 6 8
2-16,19-49: 3-Cyborg app. 4-1st app. The Exterminator; Newton-a(p). 6,7-Origin. 20,21-Nightwing app. 35-Origin Mad Bomber. 47-Batman-c/s 4.00
17,18-Alan Moore scripts 5.00
50-Ken Steacy painted-c 5.00
Annual nn, 2 ('85, '86) 5.00

VIGILANTE
DC Comics: Nov, 2005 - No. 6, Apr, 2006 ($2.99, limited series)
1-6-Bruce Jones-s. 1,2,4-6-Ben Oliver-a 3.00

VIGILANTE
DC Comics: Feb, 2009 - No. 12, Jan, 2010 ($2.99)
1-12: 1-Wolfman-s/Leonardi-a. 3-Nightwing app. 5-X-over with Titans and Teen Titans 3.00

VIGILANTE: CITY LIGHTS, PRAIRIE JUSTICE (Also see Action Comics #42, Justice League of America #78, Leading Comics & World's Finest #244)
DC Comics: Nov, 1995 - No. 4, Feb, 1996 ($2.50, limited series)
1-4: James Robinson scripts/Tony Salmons-a/Mark Chiarello-c 3.00
TPB (2009, $19.99) r/#1-4 20.00

VIGILANTE 8: SECOND OFFENSE
Chaos! Comics: Dec, 1999 ($2.95, one-shot)
1-Based on video game 3.00

VIGILANTES, THE
Dell Publishing Co.: No. 839, Sept, 1957
Four Color 839-Movie 7 14 21 44 82 120

VIGILANTE: SOUTHLAND
DC Comics: Dec, 2016 - No. 3, Feb, 2017 ($3.99, unfinished series originally set for 6 issues)
1-3-Phillips-s/Casagrande-a; intro. Donny Fairchild 4.00

VIKING PRINCE, THE
DC Comics: 2010 ($39.99, hardcover with dustjacket)

GD 2.0 | VG 4.0 | FN 6.0 | VF 8.0 | VF/NM 9.0 | NM- 9.2

HC-Recolored reprints of apps. in Brave and the Bold #1-5, 7-24 & team-up with Sgt. Rock in Our Army at War #162,163; new intro. by Joe Kubert 40.00

VIKINGS, THE (Movie)
Dell Publishing Co.: No. 910, May, 1958
Four Color 910-Buscema-a, Kirk Douglas photo-c 8 16 24 51 96 140

VIKINGS: GODHEAD (Based on the History Channel series)
Titan Comics: May, 2016 - No. 4, Sept, 2016 ($3.99)
1-4: 1-Cavan Scott-s/Staz Johnson-a; 3 covers 4.00

VIKINGS: UPRISING (Based on the History Channel series)
Titan Comics: Oct, 2016 - No. 4, Jan, 2017 ($3.99)
1-4: 1-Cavan Scott-s/Daniel Indro-a. 1-Five covers. 2-4-Three covers 4.00

VILLAINS AND VIGILANTES
Eclipse Comics: Dec, 1986 - No. 4, May, 1987 ($1.50/$1.75, limited series, Baxter paper)
1-4: Based on role-playing game. 2-4 ($1.75-c) 3.00

VILLAINS FOR HIRE
Marvel Comics: No. 0.1, Jan, 2012; No. 1, Feb, 2012 - No. 4, May, 2012 ($2.99)
0.1-Misty Knight, Silver Sable, Black Panther app.; Arlem-a 3.00
1-4-Abnett & Lanning-s/Arlem-a; Misty Knight app. 3.00

VILLAINS UNITED (Leads into Infinite Crisis)
DC Comics: July, 2005 - No. 6, Dec, 2005 ($2.95/$2.50, limited series)
1-6-Simone-s/JG Jones-c. 1-The Secret Six and the "Society" form 3.00
...: Infinite Crisis Special 1 (6/06, $4.99) Simone-s/Eaglesham-a 5.00

VILLAINY OF DOCTOR DOOM, THE
Marvel Comics: 1999 ($17.95, TPB)
nn-Reprints early battle with the Fantastic Four 18.00

VIMANARAMA
DC Comics (Vertigo): Apr, 2005 - No. 3, June, 2005 ($2.95, limited series)
1-3-Grant Morrison-s/Philip Bond-a 3.00
TPB (2005, $12.99) r/#1-3 13.00

VINTAGE MAGNUS (...Robot Fighter)
Valiant: Jan, 1992 - No. 4, Apr, 1992 ($2.25, limited series)
1-4: 1-Layton-c; r/origin from Magnus R.F. #22 3.00

VINYL UNDERGROUND
DC Comics (Vertigo): Dec, 2007 - No. 12, Nov, 2008 ($2.99)
1-12: 1-Spencer-s/Gane & Stewart-a/Phillips-c 3.00
...: Pretty Dead Things TPB ('08, $17.99) r/#6-12 18.00
...: Watching the Detectives TPB ('08, $9.99) r/#1-5; David Laphan intro. 10.00

VIOLATOR (Also see Spawn #2)
Image Comics (Todd McFarlane Prods.): May, 1994 - No. 3, Aug, 1994 ($1.95, lim. series)
1-Alan Moore scripts in all 5.00
2,3: Bart Sears-c(p)/a(p) 4.00

VIOLATOR VS. BADROCK
Image Comics (Extreme Studios): May, 1995 - No. 4, Aug, 1995 ($2.50, limited series)
1-4: Alan Moore scripts in all. 1-1st app Celestine; variant-c (3?) 3.00

VIOLENT, THE
Image Comics: Dec, 2015 - No. 5, Jul, 2016 ($2.99)
1-5-Brisson-s/Gorham-a 3.00

VIOLENT LOVE
Image Comics: Nov, 2016 - Present ($3.99)
1-4-Frank Barbiere-s/Victor Santos-a/c 4.00

VIOLENT MESSIAHS (...: Lamenting Pain on cover for #9-12, numbered as #1-4)
Image Comics: June, 2000 - No. 12 ($2.95)
1-Two covers by Travis Smith and Medina 4.00
1-Tower Records variant edition 5.00
2-8: 5-Flip book sketchbook 3.00
9-12-Lamenting Pain; 2 covers on each 3.00
...: Genesis (12/01, $5.95) r/'97 B&W issue, Wizard 1/2 prologue 6.00
...: The Book of Job TPB (7/02, $24.95) r/#1-8; Foreward by Gossett 25.00

VIP (TV)
TV Comics: 2000 ($2.95, unfinished series)
1-Based on the Pamela Lee (Anderson) TV show; photo-c 3.00

VIPER (TV)
DC Comics: Aug, 1994 - No. 4, Nov, 1994 ($1.95, limited series)

Vision (2016 series) #6 © DC

Voltron: From the Ashes #6 © WEP

Voodoo #7 © AJAX

GD 2.0 | VG 4.0 | FN 6.0 | VF 8.0 | VF/NM 9.0 | NM- 9.2

1-4-Adaptation of television show 3.00

VIRGINIAN, THE (TV)
Gold Key: June, 1963
1(10060-306)-Part photo-c of James Drury plus photo back-c
4 8 12 27 44 60

VIRTUA FIGHTER (Video Game)
Marvel Comics: Aug, 1995 (2.95, one-shot)
1-Sega Saturn game 3.00

VIRUS
Dark Horse Comics: 1993 - No. 4, 1993 ($2.50, limited series)
1-4: Ploog-c 3.00

VISION, THE
Marvel Comics: Nov, 1994 - No. 4, Feb, 1995 ($1.75, limited series)
1-4 4.00

VISION, THE (AVENGERS ICONS: ...)
Marvel Comics: Oct, 2002 - No. 4, Jan, 2003 ($2.99, limited series)
1-4-Geoff Johns-s/Ivan Reis-a 4.00
...: Yesterday and Tomorrow TPB (2005, $14.99) r/#1-4 & Avengers #57 (1st app.) 15.00

VISION (From the Avengers)
Marvel Comics: Jan, 2016 - No. 12, Dec, 2016 ($3.99)
1-12: 1-Tom King-s/Gabriel Walta-a; the Vison and his new synthezoid family 4.00

VISION AND THE SCARLET WITCH, THE (See Marvel Fanfare)
Marvel Comics Group: Nov, 1982 - No. 4, Feb, 1983 (Limited series)
1-4: 2-Nuklo & Future Man app. 5.00

VISION AND THE SCARLET WITCH, THE
Marvel Comics Group: Oct, 1985 - No. 12, Sept, 1986 (Maxi-series)
V2#1-12: 1-Origin; 1st app. in Avengers #57. 2-West Coast Avengers x-over 5.00

VISIONS
Vision Publications: 1979 - No. 5, 1983 (B&W, fanzine)
1-Flaming Carrot begins (1st app?); N. Adams-c 5 10 15 35 63 90
2-N. Adams, Rogers-a; Gulacy back-c; signed & numbered to 2000
5 10 15 30 50 70
3-Williamson-c(p); Steranko back-c 3 6 9 21 33 45
4-Flaming Carrot-c & info. 4 8 12 23 37 50
5-1 pg. Flaming Carrot 3 6 9 17 26 35
NOTE: *Eisner a-4. Miller a-4. Starlin a-3. Williamson a-5. After #4, Visions became an annual publication of The Atlanta Fantasy Fair.*

VISITOR, THE
Valiant/Acclaim Comics (Valiant): Apr, 1995 - No. 13, Nov, 1995 ($2.50)
1-13: 8-Harbinger revealed. 13-Visitor revealed to be Sting from Harbinger 3.00

VISITOR VS. THE VALIANT UNIVERSE, THE
Valiant: Feb, 1995 - No. 2, Mar, 1995 ($2.95, limited series)
1,2 3.00

VIXEN: RETURN OF THE LION (From Justice League of America)
DC Comics: Dec, 2008 - No. 5, Apr, 2009 ($2.99, limited series)
1-5-G. Willow Wilson-s/Cafu-a; Justice League app. 3.00
TPB (2009, $17.99) r/#1-5 18.00

VOGUE (Also see Youngblood)
Image Comics (Extreme Studios): Oct, 1995 - No.3, Jan, 1996 ($2.50, limited series)
1-3: 1-Liefeld-c, 1-Variant-c 3.00

VOID INDIGO (Also see Marvel Graphic Novel)
Marvel Comics (Epic Comics): 11/84 - No. 2, 3/85 ($1.50, direct sales, unfinished series, mature)
1,2: Cont'd from Marvel G.N.; graphic sex & violence 3.00

VOLCANIC REVOLVER
Oni Press: Dec, 1998 - No. 3, Mar, 1999 ($2.95, B&W, limited series)
1-3: Scott Morse-s/a 3.00
TPB (12/99, $9.95, digest size) r/#1-3 and Oni Double Feature #7 prologue 10.00

VOLTRON (TV)
Modern Publishing: 1985 - No. 3, 1985 (75¢, limited series)
1-3: Ayers-a in all 2 4 6 8 10 12

VOLTRON (Volume 1)
Dynamite Entertainment: 2011 - No. 12, 2013 ($3.99)
1-12: 1-Padilla-a; covers by Alex Ross, Sean Chen & Wagner Reis. 2-5-Two covers 4.00

VOLTRON: A LEGEND FORGED (TV)
Devils Due Publishing: Jul, 2008 - No. 5, Apr, 2009 ($3.50)
1-5-Blaylock-s/Bear-a; 4 covers 3.50

VOLTRON: DEFENDER OF THE UNIVERSE (TV)
Image Comics: No. 0, May, 2003 - No. 5, Sept, 2003 ($2.50)
0-Jolley-s/Brooks-a; character pin-ups with background info 3.00
1-5-($2.95) 1-Three covers by Norton, Brooks and Andrews; Norton-a 3.00
...: Revelations TPB (2004, $11.95, digest-sized) r/#1-5; cover gallery 12.00

VOLTRON: DEFENDER OF THE UNIVERSE (TV)
Image Comics: Jan, 2004 - No. 11, Dec, 2004 ($2.95)
1-11: 1-Jolley-s; wraparound-c 3.00

VOLTRON: FROM THE ASHES
Dynamite Entertainment: 2015 - No. 6, 2016 ($3.99)
1-6: 1-Cullen Bunn-s/Blacky Shepherd-a 4.00

VOLTRON: YEAR ONE
Dynamite Entertainment: 2012 - No. 6, 2012 ($3.99, limited series)
1-6: 1-Two covers; Brandon Thomas-s/Craig Cermak-a 4.00

VOODA (Jungle Princess) (Formerly Voodoo) (See Crown Comics)
Ajax-Farrell (Four Star Publications): No. 20, April, 1955 - No. 22, Aug, 1955
20-Baker-c/a (r/Seven Seas #6) 50 100 150 315 533 750
21,22-Baker-a plus Kamen/Baker story, Kimbo Boy of Jungle, & Baker-c(p) in all.
22-Censored Jo-Jo-r (name Powaa) 43 86 129 271 461 650
NOTE: *#20-22 each contain one heavily censored-r of South Sea Girl by **Baker** from Seven Seas Comics with name changed to Vooda. #20-r/Seven Seas #6; #21-r/#4; #22-r/#3.*

VOODOO (Weird Fantastic Tales) (Vooda #20 on)
Ajax-Farrell (Four Star Publ.): May, 1952 - No. 19, Jan-Feb, 1955
1-South Sea Girl-r by Baker 84 168 252 538 919 1300
2-Rulah story-r plus South Sea Girl from Seven Seas #2 by Baker (name changed from Alani to El'nee) 71 142 213 454 777 1100
3-Bakerish-a; man stabbed in face 57 114 171 362 619 875
4,8-Baker-r. 8-Severed head panels 57 114 171 362 619 875
5-Nazi death camp story (flaying alive) 58 116 174 371 636 900
6,7,9,10: 6-Severed head panels 50 100 150 315 533 750
11-18: 14-Zombies take over America. 15-Opium drug story-r/Ellery Queen #3.
16-Post nuclear world story.17-Electric chair panels
48 96 144 302 514 725
19-Bondage-c; Baker-r(2)/Seven Seas #5 w/minor changes & #1, heavily modified; last pre-code; contents & covers change to jungle theme
53 106 159 334 567 800
Annual 1(1952, 25¢, 100 pgs.)-Baker-a (scarce) 181 362 543 1158 1979 2800

VOODOO
Image Comics (WildStorm): Nov, 1997 - No. 4, Mar, 1998 ($2.50, lim. series)
1-4: Alan Moore-s in all; Hughes-c. 2-4-Rio-a 3.00
1-Platinum Ed 10.00
Dancing on the Dark TPB ('99, $9.95) r/#1-4 10.00
...-Zealot: Skin Trade (8/95, $4.95) 5.00

VOODOO (DC New 52) (Also see Grifter)
DC Comics: Nov, 2011 - No. 12, Oct, 2012; No. 0, Nov, 2012 ($2.99)
1-12: 1-Marz-s/Basri-a/c. 3-Green Lantern (Kyle) app. 3.00
#0 (11/12, $2.99) Origin of Voodoo; Basri-a/c 3.00

VOODOO (See Tales of...)

VOODOO CHILD (Weston Cage & Nicolas Cage's...)
Virgin Comics: July, 2007 - No. 6, Dec, 2007 ($2.99)
1-6: 1-Mike Carey-s/Dean Hyrapiet-a; covers by Hyrapiet & Templesmith 3.00
Vol. 1 TPB (1/08, $14.99) r/#1-6; variant covers; intro by Weston Cage & Nicolas Cage 15.00

VOODOOM
Oni Press: June, 2000 ($4.95, B&W)
1-Scott Morse-s/Jim Mahfood-a 5.00

VORTEX
Vortex Publs.: Nov, 1982 - No. 15, 1988 (No month) ($1.50/$1.75, B&W)
1 ($1.95)-Peter Hsu-a; Ken Steacy-c; nudity 1 2 3 5 7 9
2,12: 2-1st app. Mister X (on-c only). 12-Sam Kieth-a 6.00
3-11,13-15 3.00

VORTEX

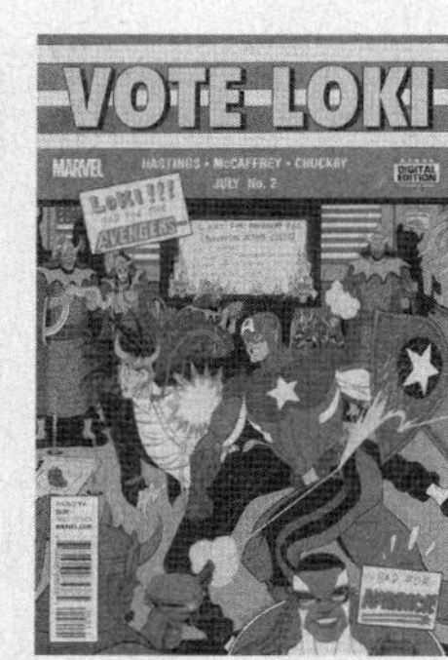

Vote Loki #2 © MAR

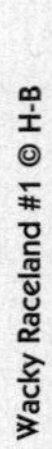

Wacky Raceland #1 © H-B

The Walking Dead #85 © Robert Kirkman

Comico: 1991 - No. 2? ($2.50, limited series)

	GD 2.0	VG 4.0	FN 6.0	VF 8.0	VF/NM 9.0	NM- 9.2
1,2: Heroes from The Elementals						3.00

VOTE LOKI
Marvel Comics: Aug, 2016 - No. 4, Nov, 2016 ($3.99, limited series)

	GD 2.0	VG 4.0	FN 6.0	VF 8.0	VF/NM 9.0	NM- 9.2
1-4: 1-Loki runs for President; Hastings-s/Foss-a. 2-McCaffrey-a						4.00

VOYAGE TO THE BOTTOM OF THE SEA (Movie, TV)
Dell Publishing Co./Gold Key: No. 1230, Sept-Nov, 1961; Dec, 1964 - #16, Apr, 1970 (Painted-c)

	GD 2.0	VG 4.0	FN 6.0	VF 8.0	VF/NM 9.0	NM- 9.2
Four Color 1230 (1961)	10	20	30	64	132	200
10133-412(#1, 12/64)(Gold Key)	7	14	21	46	86	125
2(7/65) - 5: Photo back-c, 1-5	5	10	15	31	53	75
6-14	4	8	12	27	44	60
15,16-Reprints	3	6	9	17	26	35

VOYAGE TO THE DEEP
Dell Publishing Co.: Sept-Nov, 1962 - No. 4, Nov-Jan, 1964 (Painted-c)

	GD 2.0	VG 4.0	FN 6.0	VF 8.0	VF/NM 9.0	NM- 9.2
1	5	10	15	31	53	75
2-4	4	8	12	23	37	50

V-WARS
IDW Publishing: Apr, 2014 - No. 11, Mar, 2015 ($3.99)

	GD 2.0	VG 4.0	FN 6.0	VF 8.0	VF/NM 9.0	NM- 9.2
1-11: 1-Vampire epidemic; Jonathan Maberry-s/Alan Robinson-a						4.00

WACKO
Ideal Publ. Corp.: Sept, 1980 - No. 3, Oct, 1981 (84 pgs., B&W, magazine)

	GD 2.0	VG 4.0	FN 6.0	VF 8.0	VF/NM 9.0	NM- 9.2
1-3	2	4	6	8	11	14

WACKY ADVENTURES OF CRACKY (Also see Gold Key Spotlight)
Gold Key: Dec, 1972 - No. 12, Sept, 1975

	GD 2.0	VG 4.0	FN 6.0	VF 8.0	VF/NM 9.0	NM- 9.2
1	3	6	9	14	20	26
2	2	4	6	10	14	18
3-12	2	4	6	8	10	12

(See March of Comics #405, 424, 436, 448)

WACKY DUCK (...Comics #3-6; formerly Dopey Duck; Justice Comics #7 on) (See Film Funnies)
Marvel Comics (NPP): No. 3, Fall, 1946 - No. 6, Summer, 1947; Aug, 1948 - No. 2, Oct, 1948

	GD 2.0	VG 4.0	FN 6.0	VF 8.0	VF/NM 9.0	NM- 9.2
3	32	64	96	188	307	425
4-Infinity-c	24	48	72	142	234	325
5,6(1947)-Becomes Justice comics	21	42	63	122	199	275
1(1948)	22	44	66	132	216	300
2(1948)	16	32	48	94	147	200
I.W. Reprint #1,2,7('58): 1-r/Wacky Duck #6	2	4	6	10	14	18
Super Reprint #10(I.W. on-c, Super-inside)	2	4	6	9	13	16

WACKY QUACKY (See Wisco)

WACKY RACELAND (Update of Hanna-Barbera's Wacky Races)
DC Comics: Aug, 2016 - No. 6, Jan, 2017 ($3.99)

	GD 2.0	VG 4.0	FN 6.0	VF 8.0	VF/NM 9.0	NM- 9.2
1-6: 1-Pontac-s/Manco-a; multiple covers; Penelope Pitstop & Dick Dastardly app.						4.00

WACKY RACES (TV)
Gold Key: Aug, 1969 - No. 7, Apr, 1972 (Hanna-Barbera)

	GD 2.0	VG 4.0	FN 6.0	VF 8.0	VF/NM 9.0	NM- 9.2
1	5	10	15	31	53	75
2-7	3	6	9	21	33	45

WACKY SQUIRREL (Also see Dark Horse Presents)
Dark Horse Comics: Oct, 1987 - No. 4, 1988 ($1.75, B&W)

	GD 2.0	VG 4.0	FN 6.0	VF 8.0	VF/NM 9.0	NM- 9.2
1-4: 4-Superman parody						3.00
Halloween Adventure Special 1 (1987, $2.00)						3.00
Summer Fun Special 1 (1988, $2.00)						3.00

WACKY WITCH (Also see Gold Key Spotlight)
Gold Key: March, 1971 - No. 21, Dec, 1975

	GD 2.0	VG 4.0	FN 6.0	VF 8.0	VF/NM 9.0	NM- 9.2
1	4	8	12	23	37	50
2	3	6	9	14	20	26
3-10	2	4	6	10	14	18
11-21	2	4	6	8	10	12

(See March of Comics #374, 398, 410, 422, 434, 446, 458, 470, 482)

WACKY WOODPECKER (See Two Bit the...)
I. W. Enterprises/Super Comics: 1958; 1963

	GD 2.0	VG 4.0	FN 6.0	VF 8.0	VF/NM 9.0	NM- 9.2
I.W. Reprint #1,2,7 (nd-reprints Two Bit...): 7-r/Two-Bit, the Wacky Woodpecker #1.	2	4	6	9	13	16
Super Reprint #10('63): 10-r/Two-Bit, The Wacky Woodpecker #?						

	GD 2.0	VG 4.0	FN 6.0	VF 8.0	VF/NM 9.0	NM- 9.2
	2	4	6	8	11	14

WAGON TRAIN (1st Series) (TV) (See Western Roundup under Dell Giants)
Dell Publishing Co.: No. 895, Mar, 1958 - No. 13, Apr-June, 1962 (All photo-c)

	GD 2.0	VG 4.0	FN 6.0	VF 8.0	VF/NM 9.0	NM- 9.2
Four Color 895 (#1)	9	18	27	62	126	190
Four Color 971(#2),1019(#3)	6	12	18	41	76	110
4(1-3/60),6-13	5	10	15	34	60	85
5-Toth-a	6	12	18	37	66	95

WAGON TRAIN (2nd Series)(TV)
Gold Key: Jan, 1964 - No. 4, Oct, 1964 (All front & back photo-c)

	GD 2.0	VG 4.0	FN 6.0	VF 8.0	VF/NM 9.0	NM- 9.2
1-Tufts-a in all	5	10	15	30	50	70
2-4	4	8	12	23	37	50

WAITING PLACE, THE
Slave Labor Graphics: Apr, 1997 - No. 6, Sept, 1997 ($2.95)

	GD 2.0	VG 4.0	FN 6.0	VF 8.0	VF/NM 9.0	NM- 9.2
1-6-Sean McKeever-s						3.00
Vol. 2 - 1(11/99), 2-11						3.00
12-($4.95)						5.00

WAITING ROOM WILLIE (See Sad Case of...)

WAKE, THE
DC Comics (Vertigo): Jul, 2013 - No. 10, Sept, 2014 ($2.99)

	GD 2.0	VG 4.0	FN 6.0	VF 8.0	VF/NM 9.0	NM- 9.2
1-Scott Snyder-s/Sean Murphy-a/c						5.00
1-Variant-c by Andy Kubert						8.00
1-Director's Cut (10/13, $4.99) B&W version, behind-the-scenes production content						5.00
2-10: 6-Story jumps 200 years ahead; Leeward app.						3.00
... Part One TPB (2/14, $9.99) r/#1-5						10.00

WAKE THE DEAD
IDW Publishing: Sept, 2003 - No. 5, Mar, 2004 ($3.99, limited series)

	GD 2.0	VG 4.0	FN 6.0	VF 8.0	VF/NM 9.0	NM- 9.2
1-5-Steve Niles-s/Chee-a						4.00
TPB (6/04, $19.99) r/series; intro. by Michael Dougherty; embossed die cut cover						20.00

WAKFU - SHAK SHAKA (Based on the French TV show and the Ankama game)
Titan Comics: Jan, 2016 - Present ($3.99)

	GD 2.0	VG 4.0	FN 6.0	VF 8.0	VF/NM 9.0	NM- 9.2
1-Kahel-s/Mig & Saturax-a						4.00

WALK IN (Dave Stewart's ...)
Virgin Comics: Dec, 2006 - No. 6, May, 2007 ($2.99)

	GD 2.0	VG 4.0	FN 6.0	VF 8.0	VF/NM 9.0	NM- 9.2
1-6: 1-5-Parker-s/Padlekar-a. 6-Parker-a						3.00

WALKING DEAD, THE (Inspired the 2010 AMC television series)
Image Comics: Oct, 2003 - Present ($2.95/$2.99, B&W)

	GD 2.0	VG 4.0	FN 6.0	VF 8.0	VF/NM 9.0	NM- 9.2
1-Robert Kirkman-s in all/Tony Moore-a; 1st app. Rick Grimes, Shane, Morgan & Duane	44	88	132	326	738	1150
1 Special Edition (5/08, $3.99) r/#1; Kirkman afterword; original script and proposal	3	6	9	16	23	30
2-Tony Moore-a through #6	15	30	45	103	227	350
3	9	18	27	60	120	180
4	8	16	24	51	96	140
5,6: 6-Shane killed	6	12	18	40	73	105
7-Charlie Adlard-a begins; 1st app. Tyreese	6	12	18	37	66	95
8-10	4	8	12	25	40	55
11-18,20: 13-Prison arc begins	3	6	9	16	23	30
19-1st app. Michonne	11	22	33	76	163	250
21-26,28-47,49,50: 25-Adlard covers begin. 28-Rick loses his hand. 46-Tyreese killed.	2	4	6	9	12	15
27-1st app of The Governor	8	16	24	54	102	150
48-Lori, Herschel, others killed	4	8	12	25	40	55
50-Variant wraparound superhero-style cover by Erik Larsen	5	10	15	34	60	85
51,52,54-60: 58-Morgan returns	2	4	6	8	10	12
53-1st app. Abraham & Rosita	5	10	15	31	53	75
61-Preview of Chew; 1st app. Gabriel	4	8	12	25	40	55
62,64-74: 66-Dale dies. 70-1st Douglas Monroe	1	3	4	6	8	10
63-Flip book with B&W reprint of Chew #1	3	6	9	14	20	25
75-(7/10, $3.99) Orange background-c; back-up alien/sci-fi "fantasy" in color; TV series preview with cast photos	2	4	6	9	12	15
75-Variant-c homage to issue #1	3	6	9	17	26	35
76-91: 85-Flip book w/Witch Doctor #0. 86-Flip book w/Elephantmen	1	2	3	5	6	8
92-Intro. Paul Monroe (Jesus)	5	10	15	33	57	80
93-96						6.00
97-99,101-114: 97-"Something to Fear" pt. 1. 98-Abraham killed. 107-Intro Ezekiel						4.00
100-(7/12, $3.99) 1st app. Negan; Glen killed; multiple covers by Adlard, Silvestri, Quitely,						

The Walking Dead #108 © Robert Kirkman

The Walking Dead #156 © Robert Kirkman

Wall•E #4 © DIS/Pixar

	GD 2.0	VG 4.0	FN 6.0	VF 8.0	VF/NM 9.0	NM- 9.2
McFarlane, Phillips, Hitch, & Ottley	1	3	4	6	8	10
100-Wraparound-c by Adlard						6.00
106-Variant wraparound-c by Adlard for his 100th issue	1	3	4	6	8	10
115-"All Out War" begins; 10 connecting covers by Adlard						6.00
116-126-"All Out War"						4.00
127-(5/14) Intro. Magna; bonus preview of Outcast	2	4	6	8	10	12
128-165: 132-1st Whisperers attack. 135-Intro. Lydia. 138-Intro. Alpha. 139-Michonne returns 144-Death of Ezekiel and Rosita and others. 150-Six covers. 156-Death of Alpha. 157-162-Whisperer War; 2 covers (Adlard & Art Adams). 163-(25¢-c)						4.00
... FCBD 2013 Special (5/13, giveaway) reprints bonus stories from Michonne Special and The Governor Special; new Tyreese background story						3.00
Image Firsts: The Walking Dead #1 (3/10, $1.00) reprints #1	2	4	6	10	14	18
...: Michonne Special (10/12, $2.99) Reprints debut from #19 and story from Playboy						6.00
...: Michonne Special - 2nd printing (3/13, $2.99)						3.00
... #1 Tenth Anniversary Special (10/13, $5.99) reprints #1 with color; Kirkman's original series proposal; Kirkman interview	1	3	4	6	8	10
...: The Governor Special (2/13, $2.99) Reprints debut from #27 and story from CBLDF Liberty Annual 2012						4.00
...: Tyreese Special (10/13, $2.99) Reprints debut from #7 and story from FCBD 2013						4.00
... Book 1 HC (2006, $29.99) r/#1-12; sketch pages, cover gallery; Kirkman afterword						45.00
... Book 2 HC (2006, $29.99) r/#13-24; sketch pages, cover gallery						40.00
... Book 3 HC (2007, $29.99) r/#25-36; sketch pages, cover gallery						35.00
... Book 4 HC (2008, $29.99) r/#37-48; sketch pages, cover gallery						35.00
... Book 5 HC (2010, $29.99) r/#49-60; sketch pages, cover gallery						35.00
... Book 6 HC (2010, $34.99) r/#61-72; sketch pages, cover gallery						35.00
... Book 7 HC (2011, $34.99) r/#73-84; sketch pages, cover gallery						35.00
... Book 8 HC (2012, $34.99) r/#85-96; sketch pages, cover gallery						35.00
... Book 9 HC (2013, $34.99) r/#97-108; sketch pages, cover gallery						35.00
... Book 10 HC (2014, $34.99) r/#109-120; sketch pages, cover gallery						35.00
... Book 11 HC (2015, $34.99) r/#121-132; sketch pages, cover gallery						35.00
...Vol. 1: Days Gone Bye (5/04, $9.95, TPB) r/#1-4						20.00
...Vol. 2: Miles Behind Us (10/04, $12.95, TPB) r/#7-12						18.00
...Vol. 3: Safety Behind Bars (2005, $12.95, TPB) r/#13-18						18.00
...Vol. 4: The Heart's Desire (2005, $12.99, TPB) r/#19-24						18.00
...Vol. 5: The Best Defense (2006, $12.99, TPB) r/#25-30						18.00
...Vol. 6: This Sorrowful Life (2007, $12.99, TPB) r/#31-36						15.00
...Vol. 7: The Calm Before (2007, $12.99, TPB) r/#37-42						15.00
...Vol. 8: Made to Suffer (2008, $14.99, TPB) r/#43-48						15.00
...Vol. 9: Here We Remain (2009, $14.99, TPB) r/#49-54						15.00
...Vol. 10: The Road Ahead (2009, $14.99, TPB) r/#55-60						15.00
...Vol. 11: Fear the Hunters (2010, $14.99, TPB) r/#61-66						15.00
...Vol. 12: Life Among Them (2010, $14.99, TPB) r/#67-72						15.00
...Vol. 13: Too Far Gone (2010, $14.99, TPB) r/#73-78						15.00
...Vol. 14: No Way Out (2011, $14.99, TPB) r/#79-84						15.00
...Vol. 15: We Find Ourselves (2011, $14.99, TPB) r/#85-90						15.00
...Vol. 16: A Larger World (2012, $14.99, TPB) r/#91-96						15.00
...Vol. 17: Something to Fear (2012, $14.99, TPB) r/#97-102						15.00
...Vol. 18: What Comes After (2013, $14.99, TPB) r/#103-108						15.00
...Vol. 19: March To War (2013, $14.99, TPB) r/#109-114						15.00
...Vol. 20: All Out War Part 1 (2014, $14.99, TPB) r/#115-120						15.00
...Vol. 21: All Out War Part 2 (2014, $14.99, TPB) r/#121-126						15.00
...Vol. 22: A New Beginning (2014, $14.99, TPB) r/#127-132						15.00
...Vol. 23: Whispers Into Screams (2015, $14.99, TPB) r/#133-138						15.00
...Vol. 24: Life and Death (2015, $14.99, TPB) r/#139-144						15.00
...Vol. 25: No Turning Back (2016, $14.99, TPB) r/#145-150						15.00
...Vol. 26: Call to Arms (2016, $14.99, TPB) r/#151-156						15.00
...Vol. 27: The Whisperer War (2017, $14.99, TPB) r/#157-162						15.00

WALKING DEAD SURVIVORS' GUIDE, THE
Image Comics: Apr, 2011 - No. 4 ($2.99, B&W)

	GD	VG	FN	VF	VF/NM	NM-
1,2-Alphabetical listings of character profiles, first (and last) apps. and current status	2	4	6	9	12	15
3,4	1	2	3	5	6	8

WALKING DEAD WEEKLY, THE (Reprints)
Image Comics: Jan, 2011 - No. 52, Dec, 2011 ($2.99, B&W, weekly)

	GD	VG	FN	VF	VF/NM	NM-
1-Reprints issues with original letter columns; new Kirkman afterword	3	6	9	21	33	45
1-Arizona Comic Con variant-c	3	6	9	16	23	30
2-7	2	4	6	9	12	15
8-18,20-26,28-52	1	2	3	5	6	8

	GD 2.0	VG 4.0	FN 6.0	VF 8.0	VF/NM 9.0	NM- 9.2
19-r/1st Michonne	4	8	12	25	40	55
27-r/1st app. The Governor	3	6	9	14	20	25

WALL·E (Based on the Disney/Pixar movie)
BOOM! Studios: No. 0, Nov, 2009 - No. 7, Jun, 2010 ($2.99)

	GD	VG	FN	VF	VF/NM	NM-
0-7: 0-Prequel; J. Torres-s						3.00

WALLY (Teen-age)
Gold Key: Dec, 1962 - No. 4, Sept, 1963

	GD	VG	FN	VF	VF/NM	NM-
1	3	6	9	20	31	42
2-4	3	6	9	16	24	32

WALLY THE WIZARD
Marvel Comics (Star Comics): Apr, 1985 - No. 12, Mar, 1986 (Children's comic)

	GD	VG	FN	VF	VF/NM	NM-
1-12: Bob Bolling a-1,3; c-1,9,11,12						5.00
1-Variant with "Star Chase" game on last page and inside back-c	2	4	6	9	12	15

WALLY WOOD'S T.H.U.N.D.E.R. AGENTS (See Thunder Agents)
Deluxe Comics: Nov, 1984 - No. 5, Oct, 1986 ($2.00, 52 pgs.)

	GD	VG	FN	VF	VF/NM	NM-
1-5: 5-Jerry Ordway-c/a in Wood style						6.00

NOTE: ***Anderson*** *a-2i, 3i.* ***Buckler*** *a-4.* ***Ditko*** *a-3, 4.* ***Giffen*** *a-1p-4p.* ***Perez*** *a-1p, 2, 4; c-1-4.*

WALT DISNEY CHRISTMAS PARADE (Also see Christmas Parade)
Whitman Publ. Co. (Golden Press): Wint, 1977 ($1.95, cardboard-c, 224 pgs.)

	GD	VG	FN	VF	VF/NM	NM-
11191-Barks-r/Christmas in Disneyland #1, Dell Christmas Parade #9 & Dell Giant #53	4	8	12	25	40	55

WALT DISNEY COMICS DIGEST
Gold Key: June, 1968 - No. 57, Feb, 1976 (50¢, digest size)

	GD	VG	FN	VF	VF/NM	NM-
1-Reprints Uncle Scrooge #5; 192 pgs.	6	12	18	42	79	115
2-4-Barks-r	5	10	15	31	53	75
5-Daisy Duck by Barks (8 pgs.); last published story by Barks (art only) plus 21 pg. Scrooge-r by Barks	7	14	21	44	82	120
6-13-All Barks-r	3	6	9	21	33	45
14,15	3	6	9	16	23	30
16-Reprints Donald Duck #26 by Barks	3	6	9	20	31	42
17-20-Barks-r	3	6	9	17	26	35
21-31,33,35-37-Barks-r; 24-Toth Zorro	3	6	9	16	23	30
32,41,45,47-49	2	4	6	11	16	20
34,38,39: 34-Reprints 4-Color #318. 38-Reprints Christmas in Disneyland #1. 39-Two Barks-r/WDC&S #272, 4-Color #1073 plus Toth Zorro-r	3	6	9	16	23	30
40-Mickey Mouse-r by Gottfredson	2	4	6	13	18	22
42,43-Barks-r	2	4	6	13	18	22
44-(Has Gold Key emblem, 50¢)-Reprints 1st story of 4-Color #29,256,275,282	5	10	15	30	50	70
44-Republished in 1976 by Whitman; not identical to original; a bit smaller, blank back-c, 69¢	3	6	9	16	23	30
46,50,52-Barks-r. 52-Barks-r/WDC&S #161,132	2	4	6	11	16	20
51-Reprints 4-Color #71	3	6	9	16	23	30
53-55: 53-Reprints Dell Giant #30. 54-Reprints Donald Duck Beach Party #2. 55-Reprints Dell Giant #49	2	4	6	10	14	18
56-r/Uncle Scrooge #32 (Barks)	2	4	6	13	18	22
57-r/Mickey Mouse Almanac('57) & two Barks stories	2	4	6	11	16	20

NOTE: ***Toth*** *a-52r. #1-10, 196 pgs.; #11-41, 164 pgs.; #42 on, 132 pgs. Old issues were being reprinted & distributed by Whitman in 1976.*

WALT DISNEY GIANT (Disney)
Bruce Hamilton Co. (Gladstone): Sept, 1995 - No. 7, Sept, 1996 ($2.25, bi-monthly, 48 pgs.)

	GD	VG	FN	VF	VF/NM	NM-
1-7: 1-Scrooge McDuck in "Hearts of the Yukon"; Rosa-c/a/scripts plus r/F.C. #218; Scrooge & Glittering Goldie-c. 2-Uncle Scrooge-r by Barks plus 17 pg. text story. 3-Donald the Mighty Duck; Rosa-c; Barks & Rosa-r. 4-Mickey and Goofy; new-a (story actually stars Goofy. Mickey Mouse by Caesar Ferioli; Donald Duck by Giorgio Cavazzano (1st in U.S.). 6-Uncle Scrooge & the Jr. Woodchucks; new-a and Barks-r. 7-Uncle Scrooge-r by Barks plus new-a						4.00

NOTE: *Series was initially solicited as Uncle Walt's Collectory. Issue #8 was advertised, but later cancelled.*

WALT DISNEY PAINT BOOK SERIES
Whitman Publ. Co.: No dates; circa 1975 (Beware! Has 1930s copyright dates) (79¢-c, 52 pgs. B&W, treasury-sized) (Coloring books, text stories & comics-r)

	GD	VG	FN	VF	VF/NM	NM-
#2052 (Whitman #886-r) Mickey Mouse & Donald Duck Gag Book	3	6	9	20	31	42
#2053 (Whitman #677-r)	3	6	9	20	31	42
#2054 (Whitman #670-r) Donald-c	4	8	12	22	35	48
#2055 (Whitman #627-r) Mickey-c	3	6	9	20	31	42
#2056 (Whitman #660-r) Buckey Bug-c	3	6	9	18	28	38

Walt Disney's Comics and Stories #33 © DiS

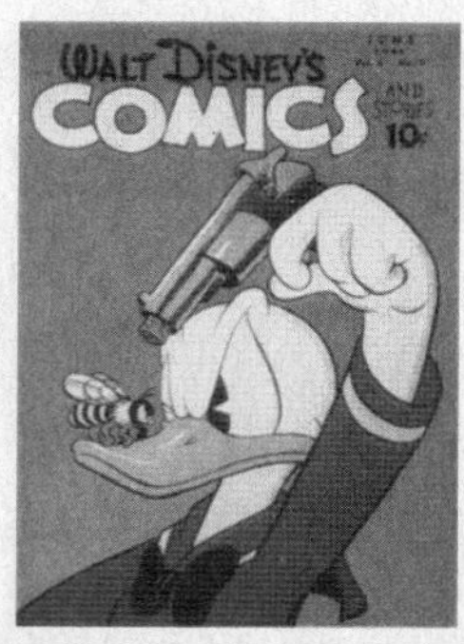

Walt Disney's Comics and Stories #69 © DiS

Walt Disney's Comics and Stories #545 © DiS

GD 2.0 | VG 4.0 | FN 6.0 | VF 8.0 | VF/NM 9.0 | NM- 9.2

#2057 (Whitman #887-r) Mickey & Donald-c 3 6 9 20 31 42

WALT DISNEY PRESENTS (TV)(Disney)
Dell Publishing Co.: No. 997, 6-8/59 - No. 6, 12-2/1960-61; No. 1181, 4-5/61 (All photo-c)

Four Color 997 (#1) 6 12 18 42 79 115
2(12-2/60)-The Swamp Fox(origin), Elfego Baca, Texas John Slaughter (Disney TV show) begin 5 10 15 30 50 70
3-6: 5-Swamp Fox by Warren Tufts 4 8 12 28 47 65
Four Color 1181-Texas John Slaughter 5 10 15 35 63 90

WALT DISNEY'S CHRISTMAS PARADE (Also see Christmas Parade)
Gladstone: Winter, 1988; No. 2, Winter, 1989 ($2.95, 100 pgs.)

1-Barks-r/painted-c 2 4 6 8 10 12
2-Barks-r 1 2 3 5 7 9

WALT DISNEY'S CHRISTMAS PARADE
Gemstone Publishing: Dec, 2003; 2004, 2005, 2006,2008 ($8.95/$9.50, prestige format)

1-4: 1-Reprints and 3 new European holiday stories. 2-All reprints. 3-Reprints and 2 new stories, 4-Reprints and 5 new stories 9.00
5-($9.50) R/Uncle Scrooge #47 and European stories 9.50

WALT DISNEY'S COMICS AND STORIES (Cont. of Mickey Mouse Magazine)
(#1-30 contain Donald Duck newspaper reprints) (Titled "Comics And Stories" #264 to #?; titled "Walt Disney's Comics And Stories" #511 on)
Dell Publishing Co./Gold Key #264-473/Whitman #474-510/Gladstone #511-547/ Disney Comics #548-585/Gladstone #586-633/Gemstone Publishing #634-698/ Boom! Kids #699-720/IDW Publishing #721-on: 10/40 - #263, 8/62; #264, 10/62 - #510, 7/84; #511, 10/86 - #633, 2/99; #634, 7/03 - #698, 11/08; #699, 10/09 - #720, 6/11; #721, 7/15 - Present

NOTE: The whole number can always be found at the bottom of the title page in the lower left-hand or right hand panel.

1(V1#1-c; V2#1-indicia)-Donald Duck strip-r by Al Taliaferro & Gottfredson's Mickey Mouse begin 2250 4500 6750 15,750 32,875 50,000
2 892 1784 2676 6512 12,256 18,000
3 389 778 1167 2723 5612 8500
4-X-Mas-c; 1st Huey, Dewey & Louie-c this title (See Mickey Mouse Magazine V4#2 for 1st-c ever) 300 600 900 1920 4460 7000
4-Special promotional, complimentary issue; cover same except one corner was blanked out & boxed in to identify the giveaway (not a paste-over). This special pressing was probably sent out to former subscribers to Mickey Mouse Mag. whose subscriptions had expired. (Very rare-5 known copies) 423 846 1269 3000 7000 11,000
5-Goofy-c 245 490 735 1568 3184 4800
6-10: 8-Only Clarabelle Cow-c. 9-Taliaferro-c (1st) 206 412 618 1318 2659 4000
11-14: 11-Huey, Dewey & Louie-c/app. 155 310 465 992 1996 3000
15-17: 15-The 3 Little Kittens (17 pgs.). 16-The 3 Little Pigs (29 pgs.); X-Mas-c. 17-The Ugly Duckling (4 pgs.) 135 270 405 864 1682 2500
18-21 119 238 357 762 1531 2300
22-30: 22-Flag-c. 24-The Flying Gauchito (1st original comic book story done for WDC&S). 27-Jose Carioca by Carl Buettner (2nd original story in WDC&S) 100 200 300 635 1293 1950
31-New Donald Duck stories by Carl Barks begin (See F.C. #9 for 1st Barks Donald Duck) 400 800 1200 2800 5250 7700
32-Barks-a 232 464 696 1485 2543 3600
33-Barks-a; Gremlins app. (Vivie Risto-s/a); infinity-c 161 322 483 1030 1765 2500
34-Gremlins by Walt Kelly begin, end #41; Barks-a 129 258 387 826 1463 2100
35,36-Barks-a 123 246 369 787 1394 2000
37-Donald Duck by Jack Hannah 71 142 213 454 852 1250
38-40-Barks-a. 39-X-Mas-c. 40,41-Gremlins by Kelly 81 162 243 518 934 1350
41-50-Barks-a. 43-Seven Dwarfs-c app. (4/44). 45-50-Nazis in Gottfredson's Mickey Mouse Stories. 46-War Bonds-c 68 136 204 435 818 1200
51-60-Barks-a. 51-X-Mas-c. 52-Li'l Bad Wolf begins, ends #203 (not in #55). 58-Kelly flag-c 32 64 96 230 515 800
61-70: Barks-a. 61-Dumbo story. 63,64-Pinocchio stories. 63-Cover swipe from New Funnies #94. 64-X-Mas-c. 65-Pluto story. 66-Infinity-c. 67,68-Mickey Mouse Sunday-r by Bill Wright 28 56 84 202 451 700
71-80: Barks-a. 75-77-Brer Rabbit stories, no Mickey Mouse. 76-X-Mas-c 25 50 75 175 388 600
81-87,89,90: Barks-a. 82-Goofy-c. 82-84-Bongo stories. 86-90-Goofy & Agnes app. 89-Chip 'n' Dale story 20 40 60 138 307 475
88-1st app. Gladstone Gander by Barks (1/48) 24 48 72 168 372 575
91-97,99: Barks-a. 95-1st WDC&S Barks-c. 96-No Mickey Mouse; Little Toot begins, ends #97. 99-X-Mas-c 18 36 54 126 281 435
98-1st Uncle Scrooge app. in WDC&S (11/48) 29 58 87 209 467 725

GD 2.0 | VG 4.0 | FN 6.0 | VF 8.0 | VF/NM 9.0 | NM- 9.2

100-(1/49)-Barks-a 21 42 63 147 324 500
101-110-Barks-a. 107-Taliaferro-c; Donald acquires super powers 16 32 48 107 236 365
111,114,117-All Barks-a 13 26 39 89 195 300
112-Drug (ether) issue (Donald Duck) 12 24 36 84 185 285
113,115,116,118-123: No Barks. 116-Dumbo x-over. 121-Grandma Duck begins, ends #168; not in #135,142,146,155 10 20 30 64 132 200
124,126-130-All Barks-a. 124-X-Mas-c 10 20 30 70 150 230
125-1st app. Junior Woodchucks (2/51); Barks-a 15 30 45 105 233 360
131,133,135-137,139-All Barks-a 10 20 30 67 141 215
132-Barks-a(2) (D. Duck & Grandma Duck) 10 20 30 69 147 225
134-Intro. & 1st app. The Beagle Boys (11/51) 20 40 60 135 300 465
138-Classic Scrooge money story 14 28 42 96 211 325
140-(5/52)-1st app. Gyro Gearloose by Barks; 2nd Barks Uncle Scrooge-c; 3rd Uncle Scrooge cover app. 20 40 60 135 300 465
141-150-All Barks-a. 143-Little Hiawatha begins, ends #151,159 9 18 27 58 114 170
151-170-All Barks-a 8 16 24 51 96 140
171-199-All Barks-a 7 14 21 46 86 125
200 7 14 21 49 92 135
201-240: All Barks-a. 204-Chip 'n' Dale & Scamp begin 6 12 18 40 73 105
241-283: Barks-a. 241-Dumbo x-over. 247-Gyro Gearloose begins, ends #274. 256-Ludwig Von Drake begins, ends #274 5 10 15 35 63 90
284,285,287,290,295,296,309-311-Not by Barks 3 6 9 19 30 40
286,288,291-294,297,298,308-All Barks stories; 293-Grandma Duck's Farm Friends. 297-Gyro Gearloose. 298-Daisy Duck's Diary-r 4 8 12 23 37 50
289-Annette-c & back-c & story; Barks-s 4 8 12 27 44 60
299-307-All contain early Barks-r (#43-117). 305-Gyro Gearloose 4 8 12 25 40 55
312-Last Barks issue with original story 4 8 12 25 40 55
313-315,317-327,329-334,336-341 3 6 9 15 22 28
316-Last issue published during life of Walt Disney 3 6 9 15 22 28
328,335,342-350-Barks-r 3 6 9 15 22 28
351-360-With posters inside; Barks reprints (2 versions of each with & without posters) 4 8 12 25 40 55
351-360-Without posters... 3 6 9 14 19 24
361-400-Barks-r 3 6 9 14 20 26
401-429-Barks-r 3 6 9 14 19 24
430,433,437,438,441,444,445,466-No Barks 2 4 6 8 11 14
431,432,434-436,439,440,442,443-Barks-r 2 4 6 10 14 18
440-Whitman edition 3 6 9 14 19 24
446-465,467-473-Barks-r 2 4 6 9 13 16
474(3/80),475-478 (Whitman) 3 6 9 14 19 24
479(8/80),481(10/80)-484(1/81) pre-pack only 5 10 15 30 50 70
480 (8-12/80)-(Very low distribution) 11 22 33 76 163 250
484 (1/81, 40¢-c) Cover price error variant (scarce) 6 12 18 38 69 100
484 (1/81) Regular 50¢ cover price; not pre-pack 3 6 9 19 30 40
485-499: 494-r/WDC&S #98 2 4 6 11 16 20
500-510 (All #90011 on-c; pre-packs): 500(4/83), 501(5/83), 502&503(7/83), 504-506(all 8/83), 507(4/84), 508(5/84), 509(6/84), 510(7/84). 506-No Barks 2 4 6 13 18 22
511-Donald Duck by Daan Jippes (1st in U.S.; in all through #518); Gyro Gearloose Barks-r begins (in most through #547); Wuzzles by Disney Studio (1st by Gladstone) 3 6 9 16 24 32
512,513 2 4 6 10 14 18
514-516,520 2 4 6 8 10 12
517-519,521,522,525,527,529,530,532-546: 518-Infinity-c. 522-r/1st app. Huey, Dewey & Louie from D. Duck Sunday. 535-546-Barks-r. 537-1st Donald Duck by William Van Horn in WDC&S. 541-545-52 pgs. 546,547-68 pgs. 546-Kelly-r. 547-Rosa-a 6.00
523,524,526,528,531,547: Rosa-s/a in all. 523-1st Rosa 10 pager 2 4 6 9 12 15
548-($1.50, 6/90)-1st Disney issue; new-a; no M. Mouse 1 2 3 4 5 7
549,551-570,572,573,577-579,581,584 ($1.50): 549-Barks-r begin, ends #585, not in #555, 556, & 564. 551-r/1 story from F.C. #29. 556,578-r/Mickey Mouse Cheerios Premium by Dick Moores. 562,563,568-570, 572, 581-Gottfredson strip-r. 570-Valentine issue; has Mickey/Minnie centerfold. 584-Taliaferro strip-r 4.00
550 ($2.25, 52 pgs.)-Donald Duck by Barks; previously printed only in The Netherlands (1st time in U.S.); r/Chip 'n Dale & Scamp from #204 5.00
571-($2.95, 68 pgs)-r/Donald Duck's Atom Bomb by Barks from 1947 Cheerios premium 6.00
574-576,580,582,583 ($2.95, 68 pgs.): 574-r/1st Pinocchio Sunday strip (1939-40). 575-Gottfredson-r, Pinocchio-r/WDC&S #64. 580-r/Donald Duck's 1st app. from Silly Symphony strip 12/16/34 by Taliaferro; Gottfredson strip-r begin; not in #584 & 600.

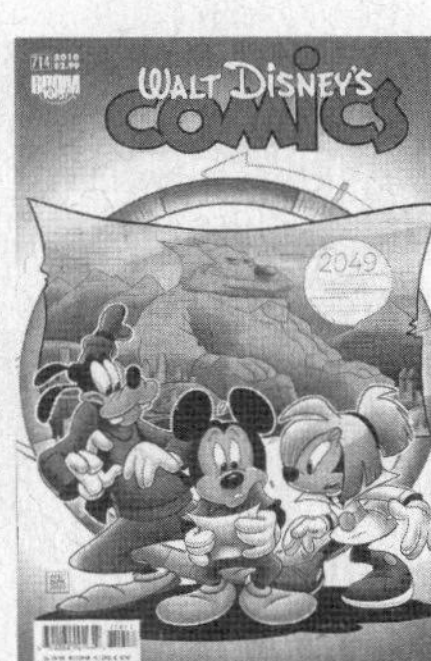

Walt Disney's Comics and Stories #714 © DiS

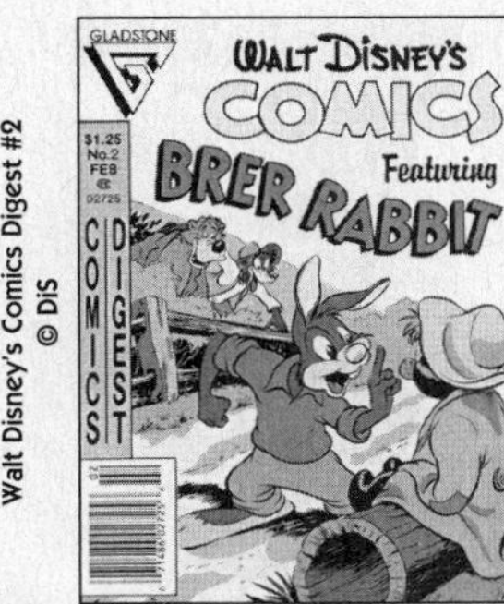

Walt Disney's Comics Digest #2 © DiS

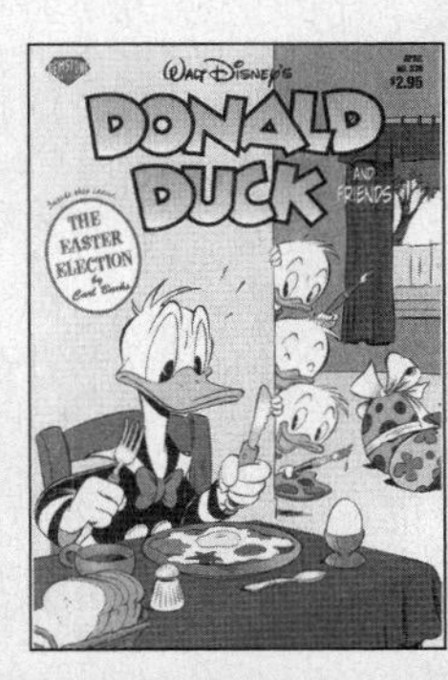

Walt Disney's Donald Duck and Friends #338 © DiS

	GD 2.0	VG 4.0	FN 6.0	VF 8.0	VF/NM 9.0	NM- 9.2

582,583-r/Mickey Mouse on Sky Island from WDC&S #1,2 5.00
585 ($2.50, 52 pgs.)-r/#140; Barks-r/WDC&S #140 5.00
586,587: 586-Gladstone issues begin again; begin $1.50-c; Gottfredson-r begins (not in #600). 587-Donald Duck by William Van Horn begins 4.00
588-597: 588,591-599-Donald Duck by William Van Horn 3.00
598,599 ($1.95, 36 pgs.): 598-r/1st drawings of Mickey Mouse by Ub Iwerks 3.00
600 ($2.95, 48 pgs.)-L.B. Cole-c(r)/WDC&S #1; Barks-r/WDC&S #32 plus Rosa, Jippes, Van Horn-r and new Rosa centerspread 4.00
601-611 ($5.95, 64 pgs., squarebound, bi-monthly): 601-Barks-c, r/Mickey Mouse V1#1, Rosa-a/scripts. 602-Rosa-c. 604-Taliaferro strip-r/1st Silly Symphony Sundays from 1932. 604,605-Jippes-a. 605-Walt Kelly-c; Gottfredson "Mickey Mouse Outwits the Phantom Blot" r/F.C. #16 6.00
612-633 ($6.95): 633-(2/99) Last Gladstone issue 7.00
634-675: 634-(7/03) First Gemstone issue; William Van Horn-c. 666-Mickey's Inferno 7.00
676-681: 676-Begin $7.50-c. 677-Bucky Bug's 75th Anniversary 7.50
682-698-($7.99) 8.00
699-714: 699-(9/09, $2.99) First BOOM! Kids issue. 700-Back-up story w/Van Horn-a 3.00
715-720: 715-(1/11, $3.99) 70th Anniverary issue; cover swipe of #1 by Van Horn; Jippes, Rosa-a. 716-Barks reprints 4.00
721-736: 721-(7/15, $3.99) First IDW issue; Italian, Dutch & classic reprints 4.00
... 75th Anniversary Special (10/15, $5.99) Classic short story reprints by various 6.00

NOTE: *(#1-38, 68 pgs.; #39-42, 60 pgs.; #43-57, 61-134, 143-168, 446, 447, 52 pgs.; #58-60, 135-142, 169-540, 36 pgs.)*

NOTE: ***Barks** art in all issues #31 on, except where noted; c-95, 96, 104, 108, 109, 130-172, 174-178, 183, 198-200, 204, 206-209, 212-216, 218, 220, 226, 228-233, 235-238, 240-243, 247, 250, 253, 256, 260, 261, 276-283, 288-292, 295-298, 301, 303, 304, 306, 307, 309, 310, 313-316, 319, 321, 322, 324, 326, 328, 329, 331, 332, 334, 341, 342, 350, 351, 527r, 530r, 540(never before published), 546r, 557-586r(most), 596p, 601p. **Kelly** a-24p, 34-41, 43; r-522-524, 546, 547, 582, 583; covers(most)-34-118, 531r, 537r, 541r-543r, 562r, 571r, 605r. Walt Disney's Comics & Stories featured Mickey Mouse serials which were in practically every issue from #1 through #394 and #511 to date. The titles of the serials, along with the issues they are in, are listed in previous editions of this price guide. **Floyd Gottfredson** Mickey Mouse serials in issues #1-14, 18-66, 69-74, 78-100, 128, 562, 563, 568-572, 582, 583, 586-599 , 601-603 , 605-present , plus "Service with a Smile" in #13; "Mickey Mouse in a Warplant" (3 pgs.), and "Pluto Catches a Nazi Spy" (4 pgs.) in #62; "Mystery Next Door", #93; "Sunken Treasure", #94; "Aunt Marissa", #95 (r in #575); "Gangland", #98 (r in #562); "Thanksgiving Dinner", #99 (r in #567); and "The Talking Dog", #100 (r in #563); "Morty's Escapade," #128. "The Brave Little Tailor", #580; "Introducing Mickey Mouse Movies ", #581; Circus Roustabout, #585; "Rumplewatt the Giant", #604. Mickey Mouse by **Paul Murry** #152-547 except 155-57 (**Dick Moore**), 327-29 (**Tony Strobl**), 348-50 (**Jack Manning**), 533 (**Bill Wright**). **Don Rosa** story/a-523, 524, 526, 528, 531, 547, 601-present. **Al Taliaferro** Silly Symphonies in #5-"Three Little Pigs"; #13-"Birds of a Feather"; #14-"The Boarding School Mystery"; #15-"Cookieland" and "Three Little Kittens"; #16-"The Practical Pig"; #17-"The Ugly Duckling"; "The Wise Little Hen" in #580; and "Ambrose the Robber Kitten"; #19-"Penguin Isle"; and "Bucky Bug" in #20-23, 25, 26, 28 (one continuous story from 1932-34; first 2 pgs. not Taliaferro). **Gottfredson** strip r-562, 563, 568-572, 581, 585, 586, 590. **Taliaferro** strip r-584, 580. **Van Horn** a-537, 545, 561, 574, 587, 588, 591-on.*

WALT DISNEY'S COMICS DIGEST
Gladstone: Dec, 1986 - No. 7, Sept, 1987

1	1	2	3	5	6	8

2-7 6.00

WALT DISNEY'S COMICS PENNY PINCHER
Gladstone: May, 1997 - No. 4, Aug, 1997 (99¢, limited series)

1-4 3.00

WALT DISNEY'S DONALD AND MICKEY (Formerly Walt Disney's Mickey and Donald)
Gladstone (Bruce Hamilton Co.): No. 19, Sept, 1993 - No. 30, 1995 ($1.50, 36 & 68 pgs.)

19,21-24,26-30: New & reprints. 19,21,23,24-Barks-r. 19,26-Murry-r. 22-Barks "Omelet" story r/WDC&S #146. 27-Mickey Mouse story by Caesar Ferioli (1st U.S work). 29-Rosa-c; Mickey Mouse story actually starring Goofy (does not include Mickey except on title page.) 4.00
20,25-($2.95, 68 pgs.): 20-Barks, Gottfredson-r 5.00
NOTE: *Donald Duck stories were all reprints.*

WALT DISNEY'S DONALD DUCK
Gemstone Publishing: 2006

... Free Comic Book Day (5/06) r/WDC&S #531; Rosa-s/a; P&S. Block-s/a; Van Horn-s/a 3.00

WALT DISNEY'S DONALD DUCK ADVENTURES (D.D. Adv. #1-3)
Gladstone: 11/87-No. 20, 4/90 (1st Series); No. 21,8/93-No. 48, 2/98(3rd Series)

1	1	2	3	5	6	8

2-r/F.C. #308 4.00
3,4,6,7,9-11,13,15-18: 3-r/F.C. #223. 4-r/F.C. #62. 9-r/F.C. #159, "Ghost of the Grotto". 11-r/F.C. #159, "Adventure Down Under." 16-r/F.C. #291; Rosa-c. 18-r/FC #318; Rosa-c 4.00
5,8: 5-Don Rosa-c/a. 8-Rosa-a 5.00
12($1.50, 52pgs)-Rosa-c/s/a; "Return to Plain Awful" story; sequel to Four Color #223 (square egg story); Barks centerfold poster 6.00
14-r/F.C. #29, "Mummy's Ring" 4.00
19($1.95, 68 pgs.)-Barks-r/F.C. #199 (1 pg.) 4.00
20($1.95, 68 pgs.)-Barks-r/F.C. #189 & cover-r; William Van Horn-a 4.00
21,22: 21-r/D.D. #46. 22-r/F.C. #282 3.00
23-25,27,29,31,32-($1.50, 36 pgs.): 21,23,29-Rosa-c. 23-Intro/1st app. Andold Wild Duck by Marco Rota. 24-Van Horn-a. 27-1st Pat Block-a, "Mystery of Widow's Gap." 31,32-Block-c 3.00
26,28($2.95, 68 pgs.): 26-Barks-r/F.C. #108, "Terror of the River". 28-Barks-r/F.C. #199, "Sheriff of Bullet Valley" 4.00
30($2.95, 68 pgs.)-r/F.C. #367, Barks' "Christmas for Shacktown" 4.00
33($1.95, 68 pgs.)-r/F.C. #408, Barks' "The Golden Helmet;"Van Horn-c 4.00
34-43: 34-Resume $1.50-c. 34,35,37-Block-a/scripts. 38-Van Horn-c/a 3.00
44-48-($1.95-c) 3.00
NOTE: ***Barks** a-1-22r, 26r, 28r, 33r, 36r; c-3r, 8r, 10r, 14r, 20r. **Block** a-27, 30, 34, 35, 37; c-27, 30-32, 34, 35, 37; c-27, 30, 31, 32, 34, 35, 37. **Rosa** a-5, 8, 12, 43; c-13, 16, 18, 21, 23, 43.*

WALT DISNEY'S DONALD DUCK ADVENTURES (2nd Series)
Disney Comics: June, 1990 - No. 38, July, 1993 ($1.50)

1-Rosa-a & scripts 5.00
2-21,23,25,27-33,35,36,38: 2-Barks-r/WDC&S #35; William Van Horn-a begins, ends #20. 9-Barks-r/F.C. #178. 9,11,14,17-No Van Horn-a. 11-Mad #1 cover parody. 14-Barks-r. 17-Barks-r. 21-r/FC #203 by Barks. 29-r/MOC #20 by Barks 3.00
22,24,26,34,37: 22-Rosa-a (10 pgs.) & scripts. 24-Rosa-a & scripts. 26-r/March of Comics #41 by Barks. 34-Rosa-c/a. 37-Rosa-a; Barks-r 4.00
NOTE: ***Barks** r-2, 4, 9(F.C. #178), 14(D.D. #45), 17, 21, 26, 27, 29 , 35, 36(D.D #60)-38. **Taliaferro** a-34r, 36r.*

WALT DISNEY'S DONALD DUCK ADVENTURES
Gemstone Publishing: May, 2003 (giveaway promoting 2003 return of Disney Comics)

...Free Comic Book Day Edition - cover logo on red background; reprints "Maharajah Donald" & "The Peaceful Hills" from March of Comics #4; Barks-s/a; Kelly original-c on back-c 3.00
...San Diego Comic-Con 2003 Edition - cover logo on gold background 3.00
...ANA World's Fair of Money Baltimore Edition - cover logo on green background 3.00
...WizardWorld Chicago 2003 Edition - cover logo on blue background 3.00

WALT DISNEY'S DONALD DUCK ADVENTURES (Take-Along Comic)
Gemstone Publishing: July, 2003 - No. 21, Nov, 2006 ($7.95, 5" x 7-1/2")

1-21-Mickey Mouse & Uncle Scrooge app. 9-Christmas-c 8.00
... , The Barks/Rosa Collection Vol. 2 (3/08, $8.99) reprints Donald Duck's Atom Bomb, Super Snooper & The Trouble With Dimes by Barks; The Duck Who Fell to Earth, Super Snooper Strikes Again & The Money Pit by Rosa 9.00
... , The Barks/Rosa Collection Vol. 3 (9/08, $8.99) r/FC #408 "The Golden Helmet" by Barks & DDA #43 "The Lost Charts of Columbus" by Rosa; cover gallery and bonus art 9.00

WALT DISNEY'S DONALD DUCK AND FRIENDS (Continues as Donald Duck and Friends)
Gemstone Publishing: No. 308, Oct, 2003 - No. 346, Dec, 2006 ($2.95)

308-346: 308-Numbering resumes from Gladstone Donald Duck series; Halloween-c. 332-Halloween-c; r/#26 by Carl Barks 3.00

WALT DISNEY'S DONALD DUCK AND MICKEY MOUSE (Formerly Walt Disney's Donald and Mickey)
Gladstone (Bruce Hamilton Company): Sept, 1995 - No. 7, Sept, 1996 ($1.50, 32 pgs.)

1-7: 1-Barks-r and new Mickey Mouse stories in all. 5,6-Mickey Mouse stories by Caesar Ferioli. 7-New Donald Duck and Mickey Mouse x-over story; Barks-r/WDC&S #51 3.00
NOTE: *Issue #8 was advertised, but cancelled.*

WALT DISNEY'S DONALD DUCK AND UNCLE SCROOGE
Gemstone Publishing: Nov, 2005 ($6.95, square-bound one-shot)

nn-New story by John Lustig and Pat Block and r/Uncle Scrooge #59 7.00

WALT DISNEY'S DONALD DUCK FAMILY
Gemstone Publishing: Jun, 2008 ($8.99, square-bound)

... The Daan Jippes Collection Vol. 1 - R/Barks-s re-drawn by Jippes for Dutch comics 9.00

WALT DISNEY'S DONALD DUCK IN THE CASE OF THE MISSING MUMMY
Gemstone Publishing: Oct, 2007 ($8.99, square-bound one-shot)

nn-New story by Shelley and Pat Block and r/Donald Duck FC #29 9.00

WALT DISNEY'S GYRO GEARLOOSE
Gemstone Publishing: May, 2008

... Free Comic Book Day (5/08) short stories by Barks, Rosa, Van Horn, Gerstein 3.00

WALT DISNEY SHOWCASE
Gold Key: Oct, 1970 - No. 54, Jan, 1980 (No. 44-48: 68pgs., 49-54: 52pgs.)

	GD 2.0	VG 4.0	FN 6.0	VF 8.0	VF/NM 9.0	NM- 9.2
1-Boatniks (Movie)-Photo-c	3	6	9	17	26	35
2-Moby Duck	3	6	9	14	19	24
3,4,7: 3-Bongo & Lumpjaw-r. 4,7-Pluto-r	2	4	6	10	14	18
5-$1,000,000 Duck (Movie)-Photo-c	3	6	9	15	22	28
6-Bedknobs & Broomsticks (Movie)	3	6	9	15	22	28
8-Daisy & Donald	2	4	6	11	16	20
9- 101 Dalmatians (cartoon feat.); r/F.C. #1183	3	6	9	16	24	32
10-Napoleon & Samantha (Movie)-Photo-c	3	6	9	15	22	28
11-Moby Duck-r	2	4	6	10	14	18

Walt Disney's Mickey Mouse and Friends #293 © DiS

Walt Disney's Pinocchio Special #1 © DiS

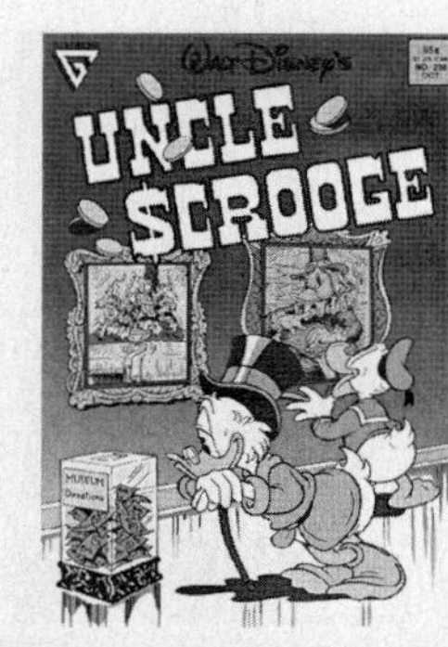

Walt Disney's Uncle Scrooge #238 © DiS

	GD 2.0	VG 4.0	FN 6.0	VF 8.0	VF/NM 9.0	NM- 9.2
12-Dumbo-r/Four Color #668	2	4	6	11	16	20
13-Pluto-r	2	4	6	10	14	18
14-World's Greatest Athlete (Movie)-Photo-c	3	6	9	15	22	28
15- 3 Little Pigs-r	2	4	6	11	16	20
16-Aristocats (cartoon feature); r/Aristocats #1	3	6	9	15	22	28
17-Mary Poppins; r/M.P. #10136-501-Photo-c	3	6	9	15	22	28
18-Gyro Gearloose; Barks-r/F.C. #1047,1184	3	6	9	17	26	35
19-That Darn Cat; r/That Darn Cat #10171-602-Hayley Mills photo-c	3	6	9	15	22	28
20,23-Pluto-r	2	4	6	11	16	20
21-Li'l Bad Wolf & The Three Little Pigs	2	4	6	10	14	18
22-Unbirthday Party with Alice in Wonderland; r/Four Color #341	3	6	9	14	19	24
24-26: 24-Herbie Rides Again (Movie); sequel to "The Love Bug"; photo-c. 25-Old Yeller (Movie); r/F.C. #869; Photo-c. 26-Lt. Robin Crusoe USN (Movie); r/Lt. Robin Crusoe USN #10191-601; photo-c	2	4	6	11	16	20
27-Island at the Top of the World (Movie)-Photo-c	3	6	9	14	19	24
28-Brer Rabbit, Bucky Bug-r/WDC&S #58	2	4	6	11	16	20
29-Escape to Witch Mountain (Movie)-Photo-c	3	6	9	14	19	24
30-Magica De Spell; Barks-r/Uncle Scrooge #36 & WDC&S #258	3	6	9	20	31	42
31-Bambi (cartoon feature); r/Four Color #186	2	4	6	13	18	22
32-Spin & Marty-r/F.C. #1026; Mickey Mouse Club (TV)-Photo-c	3	6	9	14	19	24
33-40: 33-Pluto-r/F.C. #1143. 34-Paul Revere's Ride with Johnny Tremain (TV); r/F.C. #822. 35-Goofy-r/F.C. #952. 36-Peter Pan-r/F.C. #442. 37-Tinker Bell & Jiminy Cricket-r/F.C. #982,989. 38,39-Mickey & the Sleuth, Parts 1 & 2. 40-The Rescuers (cartoon feature)	2	4	6	9	13	16
41-Herbie Goes to Monte Carlo (Movie); sequel to "Herbie Rides Again"; photo-c	2	4	6	10	14	18
42-Mickey & the Sleuth	2	4	6	9	13	16
43-Pete's Dragon (Movie)-Photo-c	2	4	6	13	18	22
44-Return From Witch Mountain (new) & In Search of the Castaways-r (Movies)-Photo-c; 68 pg. giants begin	3	6	9	14	19	24
45-The Jungle Book (Movie); r/#30033-803	3	6	9	16	24	32
46-48: 46-The Cat From Outer Space (Movie)(new), & The Shaggy Dog (Movie)-r/F.C. #985; photo-c. 47-Mickey Mouse Surprise Party-r. 48-The Wonderful Advs. of Pinocchio-r/F.C. #1203; last 68 pg. issue	2	4	6	10	14	18
49-54: 49-North Avenue Irregulars (Movie); Zorro-r/Zorro #11; 52 pgs. begin; photo-c. 50-Bedknobs & Broomsticks-r/#6; Mooncussers-r/World of Adv. #1; photo-c. 51-101 Dalmatians-r. 52-Unidentified Flying Oddball (Movie); r/Picnic Party #8; photo-c. 53-The Scarecrow-r (TV). 54-The Black Hole (Movie)-Photo-c (predates Black Hole #1)	2	4	6	9	13	16

WALT DISNEY'S MAGAZINE (TV)(Formerly Walt Disney's Mickey Mouse Club Magazine) (50¢, bi-monthly)
Western Publishing Co.: V2#4, June, 1957 - V4#6, Oct, 1959

	GD	VG	FN	VF	VF/NM	NM-
V2#4-Stories & articles on the Mouseketeers, Zorro, & Goofy and other Disney characters & people	6	12	18	38	69	100
V2#5, V2#6(10/57)	5	10	15	35	63	90
V3#1(12/57), V3#3-5	5	10	15	33	57	80
V3#2-Annette Funicello photo-c	9	18	27	63	129	195
V3#6(10/58)-TV Zorro photo-c	7	14	21	44	82	120
V4#1(12/58) - V4#2-4,6(10/59)	5	10	15	33	57	80
V4#5-Annette Funicello photo-c, w/ 2-photo articles	9	18	27	63	129	195

NOTE: *V2#4-V3#6 were 11-1/2x8-1/2", 48 pgs.; V4#1 on were 10x8", 52 pgs. (Peak circulation of 400,000).*

WALT DISNEY'S MERRY CHRISTMAS (See Dell Giant #39)

WALT DISNEY'S MICKEY AND DONALD (M & D #1,2)(Becomes Walt Disney's Donald & Mickey #19 on)
Gladstone: Mar, 1988 - No. 18, May, 1990 (95¢)

	NM-
1-Don Rosa-a; r/1949 Firestone giveaway	6.00
2-8: 3-Infinity-c. 4-8-Barks-r	4.00
9-15: 9-r/1948 Firestone giveaway; X-Mas-c	3.00
16($1.50, 52 pgs.)-r/FC #157	5.00
17-(68 pgs.) Barks M.M.-r/FC #79 plus Barks D.D.-r; Rosa-a; x-mas-c	6.00
18($1.95, 68 pgs.)-Gottfredson-r/WDC&S #13,72-74; Kelly-c(r); Barks-r	5.00

NOTE: ***Barks** reprints in 1-15, 17, 18. **Kelly** c-13r, 14 (r/Walt Disney's C&S #58), 18r.*

WALT DISNEY'S MICKEY MOUSE
Gemstone Publishing: May, 2007

... Free Comic Book Day (5/07) Floyd Gottfredson-s/a 3.00

WALT DISNEY'S MICKEY MOUSE ADVENTURES (Take-Along Comic)
Gemstone Publishing: Aug, 2004 - No. 12 ($7.95, 5" x 7-1/2")

1-12-Goofy, Donald Duck & Uncle Scrooge app. 8.00

WALT DISNEY'S MICKEY MOUSE AND BLOTMAN IN BLOTMAN RETURNS
Gemstone Publishing: Dec, 2006 ($5.99, squarebound, one-shot)

nn-Wraparound-c by Noel Van Horn; Super Goof back-up story 6.00

WALT DISNEY'S MICKEY MOUSE AND FRIENDS (See Mickey Mouse and Friends for #296)
Gemstone Publishing: No. 257, Oct, 2003 - No. 295, Dec, 2006 ($2.95)

257-295: 257-Numbering resumes from Gladstone Mickey Mouse series; Halloween-c. 285-Return of the Phantom Blot 3.00

WALT DISNEY'S MICKEY MOUSE AND UNCLE SCROOGE
Gemstone Publishing: June, 2004 (Free Comic Book Day giveaway)

nn-Flip book with r/Uncle Scrooge #15 and r/Mickey Mouse Four Color #79 (only Barks drawn Mickey Mouse story) 3.00

WALT DISNEY'S MICKEY MOUSE CLUB MAGAZINE (TV)(Becomes Walt Disney's Magazine)
Western Publishing Co.: Winter, 1956 - V2#3. Apr, 1957 (11-1/2x8-1/2", quarterly, 48 pgs.)

	GD	VG	FN	VF	VF/NM	NM-
V1#1	12	24	36	83	182	280
2-4	8	16	24	51	96	140
V2#1,2	6	12	18	41	76	110
3-Annette photo-c	11	22	33	76	163	250
Annual(1956)-Two different issues; ($1.50-Whitman); 120 pgs., cardboard covers, 11-3/4x8-3/4"; reprints	12	24	36	83	182	280
Annual(1957)-Same as above	10	20	30	69	147	225

WALT DISNEY'S MICKEY MOUSE MEETS BLOTMAN
Gemstone Publishing: Aug, 2005 ($5.99, squarebound, one-shot)

nn-Wraparound-c by Noel Van Horn; Super Goof back-up story 6.00

WALT DISNEY'S PINOCCHIO SPECIAL
Gladstone: Spring, 1990 ($1.00)

1-50th anniversary edition; Kelly-r/F.C. #92 3.00

WALT DISNEY'S SEBASTIAN
Disney Comics, Inc.: 1992

1-(36 pgs.) 3.00

WALT DISNEY'S SPRING FEVER
Gemstone Publishing: Apr, 2007; Apr, 2008 ($9.50, squarebound)

1,2: 1-New stories and reprints incl. "Mystery of the Swamp" by Carl Barks 9.50

WALT DISNEY'S THE ADVENTUROUS UNCLE SCROOGE MCDUCK
Gladstone: Jan, 1998 - No. 2, Mar, 1998 ($1.95)

1,2: 1-Barks-a(r). 2-Rosa-a(r) 3.00

WALT DISNEY'S THE JUNGLE BOOK
W.D. Publications (Disney Comics): 1990 ($5.95, graphic novel, 68 pgs.)

	NM-
nn-Movie adaptation; movie rereleased in 1990	6.00
nn-($2.95, 68 pgs.)-Comic edition; wraparound-c	4.00

WALT DISNEY'S UNCLE SCROOGE (Formerly Uncle Scrooge #1-209)
Gladstone #210-242/Disney Comics #243-280/Gladstone #281-318/Gemstone #319 on: No. 210, 10/86 - No. 242, 4/90; No. 243, 6/90 - No. 318, 2/99; No. 319, 7/03 - No. 383, 11/08

	GD	VG	FN	VF	VF/NM	NM-
210-1st Gladstone issue; r/WDC&S #134 (1st Beagle Boys)	2	4	6	9	13	16
211-218: 216-New story ("Go Slowly Sands of Time") plotted and partly scripted by Barks. 217-r/U.S. #7, "Seven Cities of Cibola"	2	4	6	9	12	15
219-"Son Of The Sun" by Rosa (his 1st pro work)	3	6	9	14	20	25
220-Don Rosa-a/scripts	1	2	3	5	6	8
221-223,225,228-234,236-240						4.00
224,226,227,235: 224-Rosa-c/a. 226,227-Rosa-a. 235-Rosa-a/scripts						5.00
241-($1.95, 68 pgs.)-Rosa finishes over Barks-r						6.00
242-($1.95, 68 pgs.)-Barks-r; Rosa-a(1 pg.)						6.00
243-249,251-260,264-275,277-280,282-284-($1.50): 243-1st by Disney Comics. 274-All Barks issue. 275-Contains centerspread by Rosa. 279-All Barks issue; Rosa-c. 283-r/WDC&S #98						3.00
250-($2.25, 52 pgs.)-Barks-r; wraparound-c						4.00
261-263,276-Don Rosa-c/a						5.00
281-Gladstone issues start again; Rosa-c						6.00
285-The Life and Times of Scrooge McDuck Pt. 1; Rosa-c/a/scripts	1	3	4	6	8	10
286-293: The Life and Times of Scrooge McDuck Pt. 2-9; Rosa-c/a/scripts. 292-Scrooge & Glittering Goldie & Goose Egg Nugget on-c						6.00
294-299, 301-308-($1.50, 32 pgs.): 294-296-The Life and Times of Scrooge McDuck Pt. 10-12. 296-Christmas-c. 297-The Life and Times of Uncle Scrooge Pt. 0; Rosa-c/a/scripts						3.00
300-($2.25, 48 pgs.)-Rosa-c; Barks-r/WDC&S #104 and U.S. #216; r/U.S. #220;						

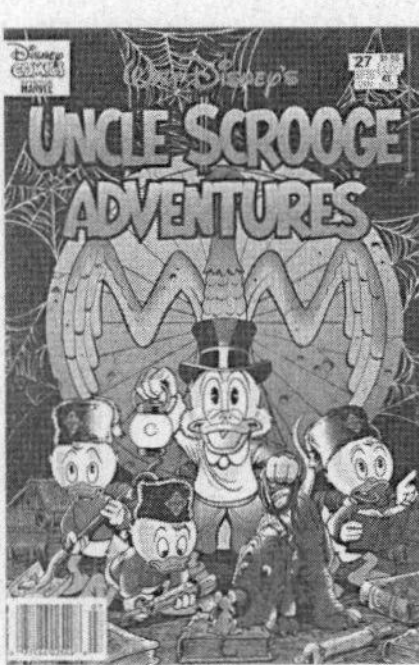

Walt Disney's Uncle Scrooge Adventures #27 © DiS

Wambi, Jungle Boy #10 © FH

Wanted Comics #28 © Toytown

GD 2.0 | VG 4.0 | FN 6.0 | VF 8.0 | VF/NM 9.0 | NM- 9.2

includes new centerfold. 4.00
309-($6.95) Low print run 3 6 9 14 20 25
310-($6.95) Low print run 4 8 12 27 44 60
311-320-($6.95) 318-(2/99) Last Gladstone issue. 319-(7/03) First Gemstone issue; The Dutchman's Secret by Don Rosa 2 4 6 8 10 12
321-360 7.00
361-366: 361-Begin $7.50-c 7.50
367-383-($7.99) 8.00
... Adventures, The Barks/Rosa Collection Vol. 1 (Gemstone, 7/07, $8.50) reprints Pygmy Indians appearances in U.S. #18 by Barks and WDC&S #633 by Rosa 8.50
Walt Disney's The Life and Times of Scrooge McDuck by Don Rosa TPB (Gemstone, 2005, $16.99) Reprints #285-296, with foreword, commentaries & sketch pages by Rosa 17.00
Walt Disney's The Life and Times of Scrooge McDuck Companion by Don Rosa TPB (Gemstone, 2006, $16.99) additional chapters, with foreword & commentaries 17.00

NOTE: ***Barks** r-210-218, 220-223, 224(2pg.), 225-234, 236-242, 245, 246, 250-253, 255, 256, 258, 261(2 pg.), 265, 267, 268, 270(2), 272-284, 299-present; c(r)-210, 212, 221, 228, 229, 232, 233, 284. scripts-287, 293. **Rosa** a-219, 220, 224, 226, 227, 235, 261-263, 268, 275-277, 285-297; c-219, 224, 231, 261-263, 276, 278-281, 285-296; scripts-219, 220, 224, 235, 261-263, 268, 276, 285-296.*

WALT DISNEY'S UNCLE SCROOGE
Gemstone Publishing

nn-(5/05, FCBD) Reprints Uncle Scrooge's debut in Four Color Comics #386; Barks-s/a 3.00
nn-(2007, 8-1/2"x 5-1/2", Halloween giveaway) Hound of the Whiskevilles; Barks-s/a 3.00

WALT DISNEY'S UNCLE SCROOGE ADVENTURES (U. Scrooge Advs. #1-3)
Gladstone Publishing: Nov, 1987 - No. 21, May, 1990; No. 22, Sept, 1993 - No. 54, Feb, 1998

1-Barks-r begin, ends #26 2 4 6 8 10 12
2-4 4.00
5,9,14: 5-Rosa-c/a; no Barks-r. 9,14-Rosa-a 5.00
6-8,10-13,15-19: 10-r/U.S. #18(all Barks) 3.00
20,21 ($1.95, 68 pgs.) 20-Rosa-c/a. 21-Rosa-a 5.00
22 ($1.50)-Rosa-c; r/U.S. #26 5.00
23-($2.95, 68 pgs.)-Vs. The Phantom Blot-r/P.B. #3; Barks-r 4.00
24-26,29,31,32,34-36: 24,25,29,31,32-Rosa-c. 25-r/U.S. #21 3.00
27-Guardians of the Lost Library - Rosa-c/a/story; origin of Junior Woodchuck Guidebook 4.00
28-($2.95, 68 pgs.)-r/U.S. #13 w/restored missing panels 4.00
30-($2.95, 68 pgs.)-r/U.S. #12; Rosa-c 4.00
33-($2.95, 64 pgs.)-New Barks story 4.00
37-54 3.00

NOTE: ***Barks** r-1-4, 6-8, 10-13, 15-21, 23, 22, 24; c(r)-15, 16, 17, 21. **Rosa** a-5, 9, 14, 20, 21, 27, 51; c-5, 13, 14, 17(finishes), 20, 22, 24, 25, 27, 28, 51; scripts-5, 9, 14, 27.*

WALT DISNEY'S UNCLE SCROOGE AND DONALD DUCK
Gladstone: Jan, 1998 - No. 2, Mar, 1998 ($1.95)

1,2: 1-Rosa-a(r) 3.00

WALT DISNEY'S UNCLE SCROOGE ADVENTURES IN COLOR
Gladstone Publ.: Dec, 1995 - Present ($8.95/$9.95, squarebound, 56 issue limited series) (Polybagged w/card) (Series chronologically reprints all the stories written & drawn by Carl Barks)

1-56: 1-(12/95)-r/FC #386. 15-(12/96)-r/US #15. 16-(12/96)-r/US #16. 18-(1/97)-r/US #18 10.00

WALT DISNEY'S VACATION PARADE
Gemstone Publishing: 2004 - No. 5, July, 2008 ($8.95/$9.95, squarebound, annual)

1-3: 1-Reprints stories from Dell Giant Comics Vacation Parade 1 (July 1950) 10.00
4,5-($9.95): 4-(5/07). 5-(7/08) 10.00

WALT DISNEY'S WHEATIES PREMIUMS (See Wheaties in the Promotional section)

WALT DISNEY'S WORLD OF THE DRAGONLORDS
Gemstone Publishing: 2005 ($12.99, squarebound, graphic novel)

SC-Uncle Scrooge, Donald & nephews app.; Byron Erickson-s/Giorgio Cavazzano-a 13.00

WALT DISNEY TREASURES - DISNEY COMICS: 75 YEARS OF INNOVATION
Gemstone Publishing: 2006 ($12.99, TPB)

SC-Reprints from 1930-2004, including debut of Mickey Mouse newspaper strip 13.00

WALT DISNEY TREASURES - UNCLE SCROOGE: A LITTLE SOMETHING SPECIAL
Gemstone Publishing: 2008 ($16.99, TPB)

SC-Uncle Scrooge classics from 1954-2006, including "The Seven Cities of Cibola" 17.00

WALT DISNEY UNCLE SCROOGE AND DONALD DUCK
Fantagraphic Books: 2014 (giveaway)

Free Comic Book Day - A Matter of Some Gravity; Don Rosa-s/a 3.00

WALTER LANTZ ANDY PANDA (Also see Andy Panda)
Gold Key: Aug, 1973 - No. 23, Jan, 1978 (Walter Lantz)

GD 2.0 | VG 4.0 | FN 6.0 | VF 8.0 | VF/NM 9.0 | NM- 9.2

1-Reprints 3 6 9 14 19 24
2-10-All reprints 2 4 6 9 12 15
11-23: 15,17-19,22-Reprints 1 2 3 5 7 9

WALT KELLY'S...
Eclipse Comics: Dec, 1987; Apr, 1988 ($1.75/$2.50, Baxter paper)

...Christmas Classics 1 (12/87)-Kelly-r/Peter Wheat & Santa Claus Funnies, ...Springtime Tales 1 (4/88, $2.50)-Kelly-r 4.00

WALTONS, THE (See Kite Fun Book)

WALT SCOTT (See Little People)

WALT SCOTT'S CHRISTMAS STORIES (See Little People, 4-Color #959, 1062)

WAMBI, JUNGLE BOY (See Jungle Comics)
Fiction House Magazines: Spr, 1942; No. 2, Win, 1942-43; No. 3, Spr, 1943; No. 4, Fall, 1948; No. 5, Sum, 1949; No. 6, Spr, 1950; No. 7-10, 1950(nd); No. 11, Spr, 1951 - No. 18, Win, 1952-53 (#1-3: 68 pgs.)

1-Wambi, the Jungle Boy begins 103 206 309 659 1130 1600
2 (1942)-Kiefer-c 43 86 129 271 461 650
3 (1943)-Kiefer-c/a 39 78 117 240 395 550
4 (1948)-Origin in text 30 60 90 177 289 400
5 (Fall, 1949, 36 pgs.)-Kiefer-c/a 21 42 63 122 199 275
6-10: 7-(52 pgs.)-New logo 17 34 51 98 154 210
11-18 14 28 42 82 121 160
I.W. Reprint #8('64)-r/#12 with new-c 3 6 9 14 20 25

NOTE: ***Alex Blum** c-8. **Kiefer** c-1-5. **Whitman** c-11-18.*

WANDERERS (See Adventure Comics #375, 376)
DC Comics: June, 1988 - No. 13, Apr, 1989 ($1.25) (Legion of Super-Heroes spin off)

1-13: 1,2-Steacy-c. 3-Legion app. 3.00

WANDERING STAR
Pen & Ink Comics/Sirius Entertainment No. 12 on: 1993 - No. 21, Mar, 1997 ($2.50/$2.75, B&W)

1-1st printing; Teri Sue Wood c/a/scripts in all 1 2 3 5 6 8
1-2nd and 3rd printings 3.00
2-1st printing. 4.00
2-21: 2-2nd printing. 12-(1/96)-1st Sirius issue 3.00
Trade paperback ($11.95)-r/1-7; 1st printing of 1000, signed and #'d 18.00
Trade paperback-2nd printing, 2000 signed 15.00
TPB Volume 2,3 (11/98, 12/98, $14.95) 2-r/#8-14, 3-r/#15-21 15.00

WANTED
Image Comics (Top Cow): Dec, 2003 - No. 6, Feb, 2004 ($2.99)

1-Three covers; Mark Millar-s/J.G. Jones-a; intro Wesley Gibson 4.00
1-4-Death Row Edition; r/#1-4 with extra sketch pages and deleted panels 3.00
2-6: 2-Cameos of DC villains. 6-Giordano-a in flashback scenes 3.00
...Dossier (5/04, $2.99) Pin-ups and character info; art by Jones, Romita Jr. & others 3.00
Image Firsts: Wanted #1 (9/10, $1.00) reprints #1 3.00
... Movie Edition Vol. 1 TPB (2008, $19.99) r/#1-6 & Dossier; movie photo-c; sketch pages & cover gallery; interviews with movie cast and director 20.00
HC (2005, $29.99) r/#1-6 & Dossier; intro by Vaughan, sketch pages & cover gallery 30.00

WANTED COMICS
Toytown Publications/Patches/Orbit Publ.: No. 9, Sept-Oct, 1947 - No. 53, April, 1953 (#9-33: 52 pgs.)

9-True crime cases; radio's Mr. D. A. app. 37 74 111 222 361 500
10,11: 10-Giunta-a; radio's Mr. D. A. app. 23 46 69 136 223 310
12-Used in **SOTI**, pg. 277 25 50 75 147 241 335
13-Heroin drug propaganda story 24 48 72 140 230 320
14-Marijuana drug mention story (2 pgs.) 21 42 63 126 206 285
15-17,19,20 19 38 57 109 172 235
18-Marijuana story, "Satan's Cigarettes"; r-in #45 & retitled 40 80 120 246 411 575
21,22: 21-Krigstein-a. 22-Extreme violence 19 38 57 109 172 235
23,25-32,34,36-38,40-44,46-48,53 16 32 48 94 147 200
24-Krigstein-a; "The Dope King", marijuana mention story 21 42 63 126 206 285
33-Spider web-c 22 44 66 132 216 300
35-Used in **SOTI**, pg. 160 21 42 63 126 206 285
39-Drug propaganda story "The Horror Weed" 29 58 87 170 278 385
45-Marijuana story from #18 20 40 60 114 182 250
49-Has unstable pink-c that fades easily; rare in mint condition 26 52 78 154 252 350
50-Has unstable pink-c like #49; surrealist-c by Buscema; horror stories 30 60 90 177 289 400

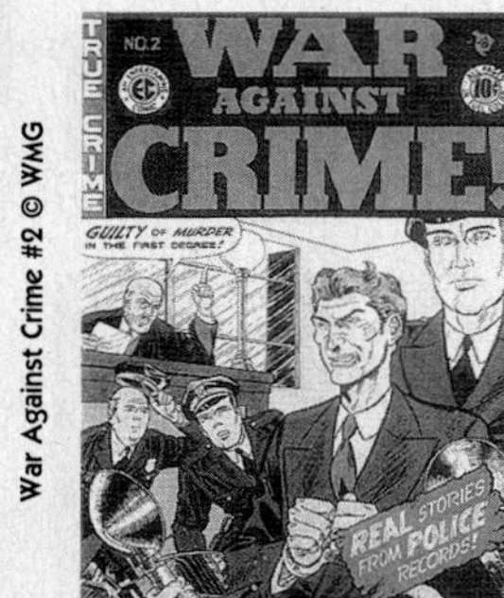

War Against Crime #2 © WMG

War Battles #4 © HARV

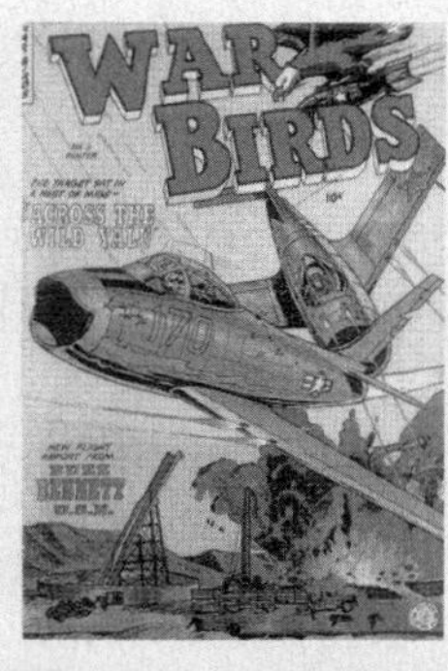

War Birds #3 © FH

	GD 2.0	VG 4.0	FN 6.0	VF 8.0	VF/NM 9.0	NM- 9.2
51- "Holiday of Horror" junkie story; drug-c	30	60	90	177	289	400
52-Classic "Cult of Killers" opium use story	41	82	123	256	428	600

NOTE: *Buscema c-50, 51. Lawrence and Leav c/a most issues. Syd Shores c/a-48; c-37. Issues 9-46 have wanted criminals with their descriptions & drawn picture on cover.*

WANTED: DEAD OR ALIVE (TV)
Dell Publishing Co.: No. 1102, May-July, 1960 - No. 1164, Mar-May, 1961

	GD 2.0	VG 4.0	FN 6.0	VF 8.0	VF/NM 9.0	NM- 9.2
Four Color 1102 (#1)-Steve McQueen photo-c	11	22	33	73	157	240
Four Color 1164-Steve McQueen photo-c	8	16	24	56	108	160

WANTED, THE WORLD'S MOST DANGEROUS VILLAINS (See DC Special)
National Periodical Publ.: July-Aug, 1972 - No. 9, Aug-Sept, 1973 (All reprints & 20¢ issues)

	GD 2.0	VG 4.0	FN 6.0	VF 8.0	VF/NM 9.0	NM- 9.2
1-Batman, Green Lantern (story r-from G.L. #1), & Green Arrow	3	6	9	21	33	45
2-Batman/Joker/Penguin-c/story r-from Batman #25; plus Flash story (r-from Flash #121)	3	6	9	16	24	32
3-9: 3-Dr. Fate(r/More Fun #65), Hawkman(r/Flash #100), & Vigilante(r/Action #69). 4-Green Lantern(r/All-American #61) & Kid Eternity(r/Kid Eternity #15). 5-Dollman/Green Lantern. 6-Burnley Starman; Wildcat/Sargon. 7-Johnny Quick(r/More Fun #76), Hawkman(r/Flash #90), Hourman by Baily(r/Adv. #72). 8-Dr. Fate/Flash(r/Flash #114). 9-S&K Sandman/Superman	3	6	9	14	20	26

NOTE: *B. Bailey a-7r. Infantino a-2r. Kane r-1, 5. Kubert r-3i, 6, 7. Meskin r-3, 7. Reinman r-4, 6.*

WAR (See Fightin' Marines #122)
Charlton Comics: Jul, 1975 - No. 9, Nov, 1976; No. 10, Sept, 1978 - No. 47, 1984

	GD 2.0	VG 4.0	FN 6.0	VF 8.0	VF/NM 9.0	NM- 9.2
1-Boyette painted-c	3	6	9	14	19	24
2-10: 3-Sutton painted-c	2	4	6	8	10	12
11-20	1	2	3	5	6	8
21-40	1	2	3	4	5	7
41,42,44-47 (lower print run): 47-Reprints	1	2	3	5	6	8
43 (2/84) (lower print run) Ditko-a (7 pgs.)	2	4	6	8	10	12
7,9 (Modern Comics-r, 1977)						6.00

WAR, THE (See The Draft & The Pitt)
Marvel Comics: 1989 - No. 4, 1990 ($3.50, squarebound, 52 pgs.)

	GD 2.0	VG 4.0	FN 6.0	VF 8.0	VF/NM 9.0	NM- 9.2
1-4: Characters from New Universe						4.00

WAR ACTION (Korean War)
Atlas Comics (CPS): April, 1952 - No. 14, June, 1953

	GD 2.0	VG 4.0	FN 6.0	VF 8.0	VF/NM 9.0	NM- 9.2
1	34	68	102	199	325	450
2-Hartley-a	18	36	54	105	165	225
3-10,14: 7-Pakula-a. 14-Colan-a	15	30	45	90	140	190
11-13-Krigstein-a. 11-Romita-a	16	32	48	94	147	200

NOTE: *Berg c-11. Brodsky a-2; c-1-4. Heath a-1; c-7, 14. Keller a-6. Maneely a-1; c-12. Sale a-7. Tuska a-2, 8.*

WAR ADVENTURES (Korean War)
Atlas Comics (HPC): Jan, 1952 - No. 13, Feb, 1953

	GD 2.0	VG 4.0	FN 6.0	VF 8.0	VF/NM 9.0	NM- 9.2
1-Tuska-a	34	68	102	199	325	450
2	18	36	54	105	165	225
3-7,9-13: 3-Pakula-a. 7-Maneely-c. 9-Romita-a	15	30	45	90	140	190
8-Krigstein-a	16	32	48	94	147	200

NOTE: *Brodsky c-1-3, 6, 8, 11, 12. Heath a-2, 5, 7, 10; c-4, 5, 9, 13. Reinman a-13. Robinson a-3; c-10.*

WAR ADVENTURES ON THE BATTLEFIELD (See Battlefield)

WAR AGAINST CRIME! (Becomes Vault of Horror #12 on)
E. C. Comics: Spring, 1948 - No. 11, Feb-Mar, 1950

	GD 2.0	VG 4.0	FN 6.0	VF 8.0	VF/NM 9.0	NM- 9.2
1-Real Stories From Police Records on-c #1-9	110	220	330	704	1202	1700
2,3	57	114	171	362	619	875
4-9	52	104	156	328	552	775
10-1st Vault Keeper app. & 1st Vault of Horror	210	420	630	1334	2292	3250
11-2nd Vault Keeper app.; 1st EC horror-c	145	290	435	921	1586	2250

NOTE: *All have Johnny Craig covers. Feldstein a-4, 7-9. Harrison/Wood a-11. Ingels a-1, 2, 8. Palais a-8. Changes to horror with #10.*

WAR AGAINST CRIME
Gemstone Publishing: Apr, 2000 - No. 11, Feb, 2001 ($2.50)

	GD 2.0	VG 4.0	FN 6.0	VF 8.0	VF/NM 9.0	NM- 9.2
1-11: E.C. reprints						4.00

WAR AND ATTACK (Also see Special War Series #3)
Charlton Comics: Fall, 1964; V2#54, June, 1966 - V2#63, Dec, 1967

	GD 2.0	VG 4.0	FN 6.0	VF 8.0	VF/NM 9.0	NM- 9.2
1-Wood-a (25 pgs.)	5	10	15	35	63	90
V2#54(6/66)-#63 (Formerly Fightin' Air Force)	3	6	9	15	22	28

NOTE: *Montes/Bache a-55, 56, 60, 63.*

WAR AT SEA (Formerly Space Adventures)
Charlton Comics: No. 22, Nov, 1957 - No. 42, June, 1961

	GD 2.0	VG 4.0	FN 6.0	VF 8.0	VF/NM 9.0	NM- 9.2
22	8	16	24	42	54	65
23-30: 26-Pearl Harbor, FDR app.	6	12	18	29	36	42
31-42: 42-Cuba's Fidel Castro story	3	6	9	18	28	38

WAR BATTLES
Harvey Publications: Feb, 1952 - No. 9, Dec, 1953

	GD 2.0	VG 4.0	FN 6.0	VF 8.0	VF/NM 9.0	NM- 9.2
1-Powell-a; Elias-c	9	18	27	63	107	150
2-Powell-a	5	10	15	34	55	75
3,4,7-9: 3,7-Powell-a	5	10	15	32	51	70
5-Flamethrower cover	14	28	42	82	121	160
6-Nostrand-a	6	12	18	39	62	85

WAR BIRDS
Fiction House Magazines: 1952(nd) - No. 3, Winter, 1952-53

	GD 2.0	VG 4.0	FN 6.0	VF 8.0	VF/NM 9.0	NM- 9.2
1	20	40	60	120	195	270
2,3	14	28	42	76	108	140

WARBLADE: ENDANGERED SPECIES (Also see WildC.A.T.S: Covert Action Teams)
Image Comics (WildStorm Productions): Jan, 1995 - No. 4, Apr, 1995 ($2.50, limited series)

	GD 2.0	VG 4.0	FN 6.0	VF 8.0	VF/NM 9.0	NM- 9.2
1-4: 1-Gatefold wraparound-c						3.00

WAR COMBAT (Becomes Combat Casey #6 on)
Atlas Comics (LBI No. 1/SAI No. 2-5): March, 1952 - No. 5, Nov, 1952

	GD 2.0	VG 4.0	FN 6.0	VF 8.0	VF/NM 9.0	NM- 9.2
1	32	64	96	188	307	425
2	17	34	51	98	154	210
3-5	15	30	45	90	140	190

NOTE: *Berg a-2, 4, 5. Brodsky c-1, 2, 4. Henkel a-5. Maneely a-1, 4; c-3. Reinman a-2. Sale a-5; c-5.*

WAR COMICS (War Stories #5 on)(See Key Ring Comics)
Dell Publishing Co.: May, 1940 (No month given) - No. 4, Sept, 1941

	GD 2.0	VG 4.0	FN 6.0	VF 8.0	VF/NM 9.0	NM- 9.2
1-Sikandur the Robot Master, Sky Hawk, Scoop Mason, War Correspondent begin; McWilliams-c; 1st war comic	110	220	330	704	1202	1700
2-Origin Greg Gilday (5/41)	41	82	123	256	428	600
3-Joan becomes Greg Gilday's aide	34	68	102	199	325	450
4-Origin Night Devils	34	68	102	206	336	465

WAR COMICS
Marvel/Atlas (USA No. 1-41/JPI No. 42-49): Dec, 1950 - No. 49, Sept, 1957

	GD 2.0	VG 4.0	FN 6.0	VF 8.0	VF/NM 9.0	NM- 9.2
1-1st Atlas War comic	43	86	129	271	461	650
2	24	48	72	142	234	325
3-10	21	42	63	122	199	275
11-Flame thrower w/burning bodies on-c	58	116	174	371	636	900
12-20: 16-Romita-a	19	38	57	111	176	240
21,23-32: 26-Valley Forge story. 32-Last pre-code issue (2/55)	18	36	54	103	162	220
22-Krigstein-a	18	36	54	107	169	230
33-37,39-42,44,45,47,48: 40-Romita-a	17	34	51	98	154	210
38-Kubert/Moskowitz-a	18	36	54	103	162	220
43,49-Torres-a. 43-Severin/Elder E.C. swipe from Two-Fisted Tales #31	18	36	54	103	162	220
46-Crandall-a	18	36	54	103	162	220

NOTE: *Ayers a-17. Berg a-13. Colan a-4, 36, 48, 49; c-17. Drucker a-37, 43, 48. Everett a-17. Heath a-6-9, 16, 19, 25, 36; c-11, 16, 19, 23, 25, 26, 29-32, 36. G. Kane a-19. Lawrence a-36. Maneely a-7, 9, 13, 14, 20, 23; c-6, 27, 37. Orlando a-42, 48. Pakula a-26, 40. Ravielli a-27. Reinman a-11, 16, 26. Robinson a-15; c-13. Severin a-26, 27; c-48. Shores a-13. Sinnott a-37.*

WAR DANCER (Also see Charlemagne, Doctor Chaos #2 & Warriors of Plasm)
Defiant: Feb, 1994 - No. 6, July, 1994 ($2.50)

	GD 2.0	VG 4.0	FN 6.0	VF 8.0	VF/NM 9.0	NM- 9.2
1-3,5,6: 1-Intro War Dancer; Weiss-c/a begins. 1-3-Weiss-a(p). 6-Pre-Schism issue						3.00
4-($3.25, 52 pgs.)-Charlemagne app.; Billy Ballistic gains quantum powers						4.00

WAR DOGS OF THE U.S. ARMY
Avon Periodicals: 1952

	GD 2.0	VG 4.0	FN 6.0	VF 8.0	VF/NM 9.0	NM- 9.2
1-Kinstler-c/a	17	34	51	98	154	210

WAREHOUSE 13 (Based on the Syfy TV series)
Dynamite Entertainment: 2011 - No. 5, 2012 ($3.99)

	GD 2.0	VG 4.0	FN 6.0	VF 8.0	VF/NM 9.0	NM- 9.2
1-5: 1-Raab & Hughes-s/Morse-a						4.00

WARFRONT
Harvey Publications: 9/51 - #35, 11/58; #36, 10/65; #39, 2/67

	GD 2.0	VG 4.0	FN 6.0	VF 8.0	VF/NM 9.0	NM- 9.2
1-Korean War	9	18	27	59	117	175
2	5	10	15	34	60	85
3-10	5	10	15	30	50	70
11,12,14,16-20	4	8	12	27	44	60
13,15,22-Nostrand-a	5	10	15	34	60	85
21,23-27,31-33,35	4	8	12	27	44	60
28-30,34-Kirby-c	5	10	15	35	63	90
36-(12/66)-Dynamite Joe begins, ends #39; Williamson-a	5	10	15	30	50	70

War Fury #3 © CM

War Heroes #10 © DELL

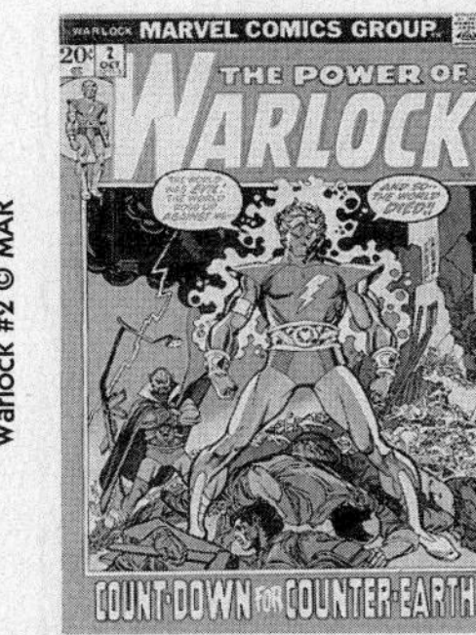

Warlock #2 © MAR

	GD 2.0	VG 4.0	FN 6.0	VF 8.0	VF/NM 9.0	NM- 9.2
37-Wood-a (17 pgs.)	5	10	15	30	50	70
38,39-Wood-a, 2-3 pgs.; Lone Tiger app.	4	8	12	27	44	60

NOTE: *Powell a-1-6, 9-11, 14, 17, 20, 23, 25-28, 30, 31, 34, 36. Powell/Nostrand a-12, 13, 15. Simon c-36?, 38.*

WAR FURY
Comic Media/Harwell (Allen Hardy Assoc.): Sept, 1952 - No. 4, Mar, 1953

	GD	VG	FN	VF	VF/NM	NM-
1-Heck-c/a in all; Palais-a; bullet hole in forehead-c; all issues are very violent; soldier using flame thrower on enemy	129	258	387	826	1413	2000
2-4: 4-Morisi-a	37	74	111	222	361	500

WAR GODS OF THE DEEP (See Movie Classics)

WARHAWKS
TSR, Inc.: 1990 - No. 10, 1991 ($2.95, 44 pgs.)

1-10-Based on TSR game, Spiegle a-1-6 — 4.00

WARHEADS
Marvel Comics UK: June, 1992 - No. 14, Aug, 1993 ($1.75)

1-Wolverine-c/story; indicia says #2 by mistake — 4.00
2-14: 2-Nick Fury app. 3-Iron Man-c/story. 4,5-X-Force. 5-Liger vs. Cable. 6,7-Death's Head II app. (#6 is cameo) — 3.00

WAR HEROES (See Marine War Heroes)

WAR HEROES
Dell Publishing Co.: 7-9/42 (no month); No. 2, 10-12/42 - No. 10, 10-12/44 (Quarterly)

	GD	VG	FN	VF	VF/NM	NM-
1-General Douglas MacArthur-c	30	60	90	177	289	400
2-James Doolittle and other officers-c	16	32	48	94	147	200
3,5: 3-Pro-Russian back-c; grey-tone-c. 5-General Patton-c	14	28	42	82	121	160
4-Disney's Gremlins app.; grey-tone-c	20	40	60	114	182	250
6-10: 6-Tothish-a by Discount. 6,9-Grey-tone-c	11	22	33	64	90	115

NOTE: *No. 1 was to be released in July, but was delayed. Painted c-4, 6-9.*

WAR HEROES
Ace Magazines: May, 1952 - No. 8, Apr, 1953

	GD	VG	FN	VF	VF/NM	NM-
1	15	30	45	85	130	175
2-Lou Cameron-a	11	22	33	60	83	105
3-8: 6,7-Cameron-a	10	20	30	54	72	90

WAR HEROES (Also see Blue Bird Comics)
Charlton Comics: Feb, 1963 - No. 27, Nov, 1967

	GD	VG	FN	VF	VF/NM	NM-
1,2: 2-John F. Kennedy story	4	8	12	25	40	55
3-10	3	6	9	17	26	35
11-26: 22-True story about plot to kill Hitler	3	6	9	14	20	26
27-1st Devils Brigade by Glanzman	3	6	9	17	26	35

NOTE: *Montes/Bache a-3-7, 21, 25, 27; c-3-7.*

WAR HEROES
Image Comics: July, 2008 - No. 6 ($2.99, limited series)

1-3-Soldiers given super powers; Mark Millar-s/Tony Harris-a/c; four covers — 3.00

WAR IS HELL
Marvel Comics Group: Jan, 1973 - No. 15, Oct, 1975

	GD	VG	FN	VF	VF/NM	NM-
1-Williamson-a(r), 5 pgs.; Ayers-a	3	6	9	17	26	35
2-8-Reprints. 6-(11/73). 7-(6/74). 7,8-Kirby-a	2	4	6	10	14	18
9-Intro Death	5	10	15	35	63	90
10-15-Death app.	3	6	9	17	26	35

NOTE: *Bolle a-3r. Powell a-1. Woodbridge a-1. Sgt. Fury reprints-7, 8.*

WAR IS HELL: THE FIRST FLIGHT OF THE PHANTOM EAGLE
Marvel Comics (MAX): May, 2008 - No. 5, Sept, 2008 ($3.99, limited series)

1-5-World War I fighter pilots; Ennis-s/Chaykin-a/Cassaday-c — 4.00

WARLANDS
Image Comics: Aug, 1999 - No. 12, Feb, 2001 ($2.50)

1-9,11,12-Pat Lee-a(p)/Adrian Tsang-s — 3.00
10-($2.95) Flip book w/Shidima preview — 4.00
... Chronicles 1,2 (2/00, 7/00; $7.95) 1-r/#1-3. 2-r/#4-6 — 8.00
...Darklyte TPB (8/01, $14.95) r/#0,1/2,1-6 w/cover gallery; new Lee-c — 15.00
...Epilogue: Three Stories (3/01, $5.95) includes r/Wizard #1/2 & AE #0 — 6.00
Another Universe #0 — 3.00
Wizard #1/2 — 5.00

WARLANDS: THE AGE OF ICE (Volume 2)
Image Comics: July, 2001 - No. 9, Nov, 2002 ($2.95)

#0-(2/02, $2.25) — 3.00
#1/2 (4/02, $2.25) — 3.00
1-9: 2-Flip book preview of Banished Knights — 3.00
TPB (2003, $15.95) r/#1-9 — 16.00

WARLANDS: DARK TIDE RISING (Volume 3)
Image Comics: Dec, 2002 - No. 6, May, 2003 ($2.95)

1-6: 1-Wraparound gatefold-c — 3.00

WARLOCK (The Power of...)(Also see Avengers Annual #7, Fantastic Four #66, 67, Incredible Hulk #178, Infinity Crusade, Infinity Gauntlet, Infinity War, Marvel Premiere #1, Marvel Two-In-One Annual #2, Silver Surfer V3#46, Strange Tales #178-181 & Thor #165)
Marvel Comics Group: Aug, 1972 - No. 8, Oct, 1973; No. 9, Oct, 1975 - No. 15, Nov, 1976

	GD	VG	FN	VF	VF/NM	NM-
1-Origin by Kane	8	16	24	56	108	160
2,3	4	8	12	28	47	65
4-8: 4-Death of Eddie Roberts	3	6	9	17	26	35
9-Starlin's 2nd Thanos saga begins, ends #15; new costume Warlock; Thanos cameo only; story cont'd from Strange Tales #178-181; Starlin-c/a in #9-15	4	8	12	28	47	65
10-Origin Thanos & Gamora; recaps events from Capt. Marvel #25-34. Thanos vs.The Magus-c/story	4	8	12	28	47	65
11-Thanos app.; Warlock dies	3	6	9	20	31	42
12-14: (Regular 25¢ edition) 14-Origin Star Thief; last 25¢ issue	3	6	9	17	26	35
12-14-(30¢-c, limited distribution)	5	10	15	30	50	70
15-Thanos-c/story	3	6	9	19	30	40

NOTE: *Buscema a-2p; c-8p. G. Kane a-1p, 3-5p; c-1p, 2, 3, 4p, 5p, 7p. Starlin a-9-14p, 15; c-9, 10, 11p, 12p, 13-15. Sutton a-1-8i.*

WARLOCK (...Special Edition on-c)
Marvel Comics Group: Dec, 1982 - No. 6, May, 1983 ($2.00, slick paper, 52 pgs.)

1-Warlock-r/Strange Tales #178-180. — 6.00
2-6: 2-r/Str. Tales #180,181 & Warlock #9. 3-r/Warlock #10-12(Thanos origin recap). 4-r/Warlock #12-15. 5-r/Warlock #15, Marvel Team-Up #55 & Avengers Ann. #7. 6-r/2nd half Avengers Annual #7 & Marvel Two-in-One Annual #2 — 5.00
Special Edition #1(12/83) — 5.00

NOTE: *Byrne a-5r. Starlin a-1-6r; c-1-6(new). Direct sale only.*

WARLOCK
Marvel Comics: V2#1, May, 1992 - No. 6, Oct, 1992 ($2.50, limited series)

V2#1-6: 1-Reprints 1982 reprint series w/Thanos — 4.00

WARLOCK
Marvel Comics: Nov, 1998 - No. 4, Feb, 1999 ($2.99, limited series)

1-4-Warlock vs. Drax — 3.00

WARLOCK (M-Tech)
Marvel Comics: Oct, 1999 - No. 9, June, 2000 ($1.99/$2.50)

1-5: 1-Quesada-c. 2-Two covers — 3.00
6-9: 6-Begin $2.50-c. 8-Avengers app. — 3.00

WARLOCK
Marvel Comics: Nov, 2004 - No. 4, Feb, 2005 ($2.99, limited series)

1-4-Adlard-a/Williams-c — 3.00

WARLOCK AND THE INFINITY WATCH (Also see Infinity Gauntlet)
Marvel Comics: Feb, 1992 - No. 42, July, 1995 ($1.75) (Sequel to Infinity Gauntlet)

1-Starlin-s begin; continued from Infinity Gauntlet #6; brief origin recap; Living Tribunal app. — 6.00
2-7: 2-1st app. Infinity Watch: Infinity Gauntlet broken up; Warlock (Soul gem), Gamora (Time gem), Drax (Power gem), Moondragon (Mind gem) & Pip (Space gem). 3,4-High Evolutionary app. 5,6-Man-Beast app. 7-Re-intro Magus (dream sequence); brief Thanos app; leads into Infinity War #1. Tom Raney-a begins — 4.00
8-10: 8-Thanos teams up w/Infinity Watch; Magus app; X-Men, Avengers, Alpha Flight & Fantastic Four cameo; leads into Infinity War #4. 9-Origin Gamora; Galactus, Eternity, Thanos & Infinity app; leads into Infinity War #5. 10-Thanos vs. his doppelganger; Magus app.; continues in Infinity War #6 — 4.00
11-22: 11-Eternity & Living Tribunal app.; origins of the Watch. 12-1st app Maxam (brief cameo); Hulk cameo. 13-Drax vs Hulk; last Raney-a. 14-1st app. Count Abyss. 15-Eternity app. 16-1st full app. Maxam; Count Abyss app. 17-Maxam joins the Watch. 18-22-Infinity Crusade tie-ins; 18-Goddess & Reed Richards app; continued in Infinity Crusade #2. 19-X-Men, Avengers, Fantastic Four, Thanos app.; continued in Infinity Crusade #3. 20-Pip becomes master of reality; Goddess app; continued in Infinity Crusade #4. 21-Drax vs. Thor; continued in Infinity Crusade #5. 22-Goddess app; continued in Infinity Crusade #6 — 4.00
23,24-Blood and Thunder Pts. 4 & 8; continued from Warlock Chronicles #6; Silver Surfer & Warlock vs. Thor; continued in Thor #469. 24-Continued from Warlock Chronicles #7; Silver Surfer app.; continued in Thor #470 — 5.00
25-($2.95, 52 pgs.)-Die-cut & embossed double-c; Blood & Thunder Pt.12; continued from Warlock Chronicles #8; Thor, Dr. Strange, Beta Ray Bill & Silver Surfer app.;

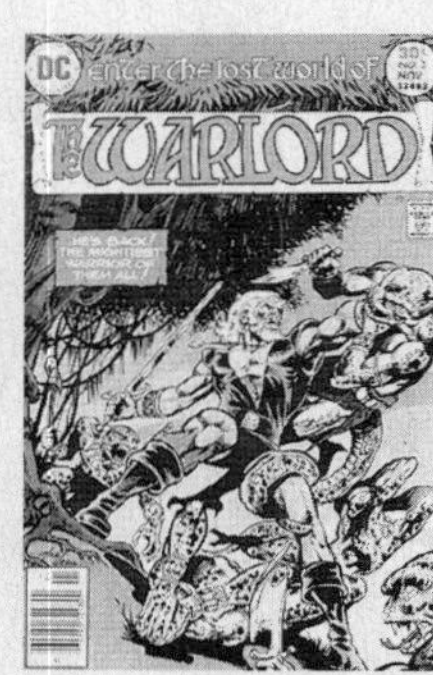

Warlord #3 © DC

Warlord of Mars #26 © DYN

War Machine (2009 series) #7 © MAR

Thanos vs. Odin 2 4 6 9 12 15
26-32: 26-Avengers & Count Abyss app. 27-vs. the Avengers. 28-Avengers, Man-Beast & Count Abyss app. 29,30-Count Abyss app. 31-Origin Count Abyss; last Starlin-s. 32-Count Abyss defeats the Watch 4.00
33-35: 33-vs. Count Abyss. 34-Mole Man app.; Tyrannus cameo. 35-Mole Man & Tyrannus app. 4.00
36-Dr. Strange app; as 'Strange' 7.00
37-39: 37-1st app. Zakaius; Firelord app. 38-1st app. Domitan; Zakaius app. 39-Zakaius, Domitan & Firelord app. 6.00
40,41: 40-Thanos app.; Gamora leaves the Watch; Maxam receives the Time gem. 41-Origin Maxam; Gamora joins Thanos 1 2 3 5 6 8
42-Last issue; the Watch breaks up; the Infinity Gems disappear (see Rune/Silver Surfer #1); Thanos app. 2 4 6 9 12 15

NOTE: ***Austin*** *c/a-1-4i, 7i.* ***Leonardi*** *a(p)-3, 4.* ***Medina*** *c/a(p)-1, 2, 5; 6, 9, 10, 14, 15, 20.* ***Williams*** *a(i)-8, 12, 13, 16-19.*

WARLOCK CHRONICLES
Marvel Comics: June, 1993 - No. 8, Feb, 1994 ($2.00, limited series)

1-($2.95)-Holo-grafx foil & embossed-c; Starlin/Raney-s/a; Infinity Crusade tie-in; 1st app. Darklore; origin of Warlock & the Infinity Gems; cont'd in Warlock & the Infinity Watch #18 5.00
2-5-Infinity Crusade x-overs; 2-Cont'd from Infinity Crusade #2; Lord Order, Master Chaos, Eternity & Thanos app.; cont'd in Warlock & the Infinity Watch #19. 3-Cont'd from Infinity Crusade #3; Mephisto teams up w/Warlock & Thanos; cont'd in Warlock & the Infinity Watch #20. 4-Magus app.; cont'd in Warlock & the Infinity Watch #21. 5-Cont'd from Infinity Crusade #5; Goddess & Magus app.; cont'd in Warlock & the Infinity Watch #22 4.00
6-Blood & Thunder Pt. 3; cont'd from Silver Surfer #86; insane Thor cameo; brief Silver Surfer app.; cont'd in Warlock & the Infinity Watch #23 5.00
7-Blood & Thunder Pt. 7; cont'd from Silver Surfer #87; Dr. Strange, Beta Ray Bill & Silver Surfer app.; cont'd in Warlock & the Infinity Watch #24 6.00
8-Blood & Thunder Pt. 11; cont'd from Silver Surfer #88; Thanos, Silver Surfer, Dr. Strange app.; cont'd in Warlock & the Infinity Watch #25 1 2 3 5 6 8

WARLOCK 5
Aircel Pub.: 11/86 - No. 22, 5/89; V2#1, June, 1989 - V2#5, 1989 ($1.70, B&W)

1-5,7-11-Gordon Derry-s/Denis Beauvais-a thru #11. 5-Green Cyborg on-c. 5-Misnumbered as #6 (no #6); Blue Girl on-c. 3.00
12-22-Barry Blair-s/a. 18-$1.95-c begins 4.00
V2#1-5 ($2.00, B&W)-All issues by Barry Blair 3.00
Compilation 1,2: 1-r/#1-5 (1988, $5.95); 2-r/#6-9 6.00

WARLORD (See 1st Issue Special #8) (B&W reprints in Showcase Presents: Warlord)
National Periodical Publications/DC Comics #123 on: 1-2/76; No.2, 3-4/76; No.3, 10-11/76 - No. 133, Win, 1988-89

1-Story cont'd. from 1st Issue Special #8 4 8 12 23 37 50
2-Intro. Machiste 3 6 9 14 20 25
3-5 2 4 6 9 12 15
6-10: 6-Intro Mariah. 7-Origin Machiste. 9-Dons new costume 1 3 4 6 8 10
11-20: 11-Origin-r. 12-Intro Aton. 15-Tara returns; Warlord has son 6.00
21-36,40,41: 27-New facts about origin. 28-1st app. Wizard World. 32-Intro Shakira. 40-Warlord gets new costume 5.00
22-Whitman variant edition 2 4 6 13 18 22
37-39: 37,38-Origin Omac by Starlin. 38-Intro Jennifer Morgan, Warlord's daughter. 39-Omac ends. 6.00
42-48: 42-47-Omac back-up series. 48-(52 pgs.)-1st app. Arak; contains free 14 pg. Arak Son of Thunder; Claw The Unconquered app. 5.00
49-62,64-99,101-132: 49-Claw The Unconquered app. 50-Death of Aton. 51-Reprints #1. 55-Arion Lord of Atlantis begins, ends #62. 91-Origin w/new facts. 114,115-Legends x-over. 125-Death of Tara. 131-1st DC work by Rob Liefeld (9/88) 4.00
63-The Barren Earth begins; free 16pg. Masters of the Universe preview 5.00
100-($1.25, 52 pgs.) 5.00
133-($1.50, 52 pgs.) 5.00
Annual 1-6 ('82-'87): 1-Grell-c,/a(p). 6-New Gods app. 5.00
The Savage Empire TPB (1991, $19.95) r/#1-10,12 & First Issue Special #8; Grell intro. 25.00

NOTE: ***Grell*** *a-1-15, 16-50p, 51r, 52p, 59p, Annual 1p; c-1-70, 100-104, 112, 116, 117, Annual 1, 5.* ***Wayne Howard*** *a-64i.* ***Starlin*** *a-37-39p.*

WARLORD
DC Comics: Jan, 1992 - No. 6, June, 1992 ($1.75, limited series)

1-6: Grell-c & scripts in all 3.00

WARLORD
DC Comics: Apr, 2006 - No. 10, Jan, 2007 ($2.99)

1-10: 1-Bruce Jones-s/Bart Sears-a. 10-Winslade-a 3.00

WARLORD
DC Comics: Jun, 2009 - No. 16, Sept, 2010 ($2.99)

1-16: 1-Grell-s/Prado-a/Grell-c. 7-9,11,12,15,16-Grell-s/a/c. 10-Hardin-a 3.00
...: The Saga SC (2010, $17.99) r/#1-6; cover gallery 18.00

WARLORD OF MARS
Dynamite Entertainment: 2010 - No. 35, 2014 ($1.00/$3.99)

1-($1.00) John Carter on Earth; Sadowski-a; covers by Ross, Campbell, Jusko. Parrillo 3.00
2-35-($3.99) Multiple covers on each. 3-Carter arrives on Mars. 4-Dejah Thoris intro. 4.00
100-($7.99, squarebound) Short stories; art by Antonio, Malaga, Luis; multiple covers 8.00
#0 (2014, $3.99) Brady-s/Jadson-a; John Carter back on Earth 4.00
... Annual 1 (2012, $4.99) Sadowski-a/Parrillo-c 5.00

WARLORD OF MARS: DEJAH THORIS
Dynamite Entertainment: 2011 - No. 37, 2014 ($3.99/$4.99)

1-36: 1-Five covers; Nelson-s/Rafael-a. 2-5-Four covers. 6-31-Multiple covers on all 4.00
37-($4.99) Napton-s/Carita-a; Neves & Anacleto-c 5.00

WARLORD OF MARS: FALL OF BARSOOM
Dynamite Entertainment: 2011 - No. 5, 2012 ($3.99, limited series)

1-5-Napton-s/Castro-a/Jusko-c 4.00

WARLORDS (See DC Graphic Novel #2)

WARLORDS OF APPALACHIA
BOOM! Studios: Oct, 2016 - No. 4 ($3.99)

1,2-Phillip Kennedy Johnson-s/Jonas Scharf-a 4.00

WAR MACHINE (Also see Iron Man #281,282 & Marvel Comics Presents #152)
Marvel Comics: Apr, 1994 - No. 25, Apr, 1996 ($1.50)

"Ashcan" edition (nd, 75¢, B&W, 16 pgs.) 3.00
1-($2.00, 52 pgs.)-Newsstand edition; Cable app. 5.00
1-($2.95, 52 pgs.)-Collectors ed.; embossed foil-c 6.00
2-14, 16-25: 2-Bound-in trading card sheet; Cable app. 2,3-Deathlok app. 8-red logo 3.00
8-($2.95)-Polybagged w/16 pg. Marvel Action Hour preview & acetate print; yellow logo 4.00
15 ($2.50)-Flip book 4.00

WAR MACHINE (Also see Dark Reign and Secret Invasion crossovers)
Marvel Comics: Feb, 2009 - No. 12, Feb, 2010 ($2.99)

1-12: 1-5-Pak-s/Manco-a/c; cyborg Jim Rhodes. 10-12-Dark Reign 3.00
1-Variant Titanium Man cover by Deodato 6.00

WAR MAN
Marvel Comics (Epic Comics): Nov, 1993 - No. 2, Dec, 1993 ($2.50, lim. series)

1,2 3.00

WAR OF KINGS
Marvel Comics: May, 2009 - No. 6, Oct, 2009 ($3.99, limited series)

1-6-Pelletier-a/Abnett & Lanning-s; Inhumans vs. the Shi'Ar 4.00
... Saga (2009, giveaway) synopsies of stories involving Kree, Shi'Ar, Inhumans, etc. 3.00
...: Savage World of Skaar 1 (8/09, $3.99) Gorgon & Starbolt land on Sakaar 4.00
...: Who Will Rule? 1 (11/09, $3.99) Pelletier-a; profile pages 4.00

WAR OF KINGS: ASCENSION
Marvel Comics: June, 2009 - No. 4, Sept, 2009 ($3.99, limited series)

1-4-Alves-a/Abnett & Lanning-s; Darkhawk app. 4.00

WAR OF KINGS: DARKHAWK (Leads into War Of Kings: Ascension limited series)
Marvel Comics: Apr, 2009 - No. 2, May, 2009 ($3.99, limited series)

1,2-Cebulski-s/Tolibao & Dazo-a/Peterson-c; r/Darkhawk #1,2 (1991) origin 4.00

WAR OF KINGS: WARRIORS
Marvel Comics: Sept, 2009 - No. 2, Oct, 2009 ($3.99, limited series)

1,2-Prequel to x-over; Gage-s/Asrar & Magno-a 4.00

WAR OF THE GODS
DC Comics: Sept, 1991 - No. 4, Dec, 1991 ($1.75, limited series)

1-4: Perez layouts, scripts & covers. 1-Contains free mini posters (Robin, Deathstroke). 2-4-Direct sale versions include 4 pin-ups printed on cover stock plus different-c 4.00

WAR OF THE GREEN LANTERNS: AFTERMATH
DC Comics: Sept, 2011 - No. 2, Oct, 2011 ($3.99, limited series)

1,2: 1-Bedard-s/Sepulveda & Kirkham-a. 2-Getty & Smith-a 4.00

WAR OF THE UNDEAD
IDW Publishing: Jan, 2007 - No. 3, Apr, 2007 ($3.99, limited series)

1-3-Bryan Johnson-s/Walter Flanagan-a 4.00

WAR OF THE WORLDS, THE
Caliber: 1996 - No. 5 ($2.95, B&W, 32 pgs.)(Based on H. G. Wells novel)

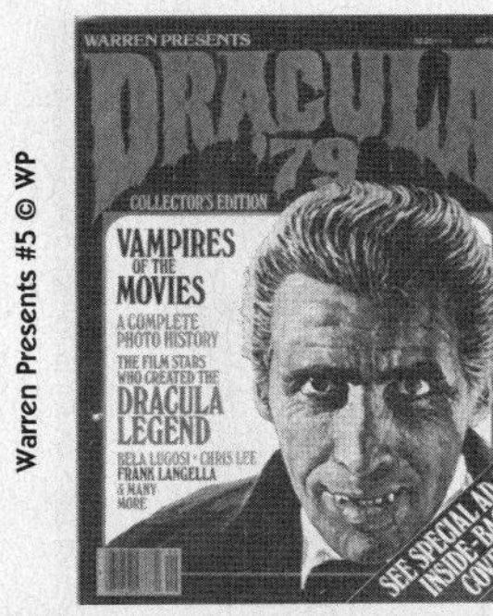

Warren Presents #5 © WP

Warriors Three #2 © MAR

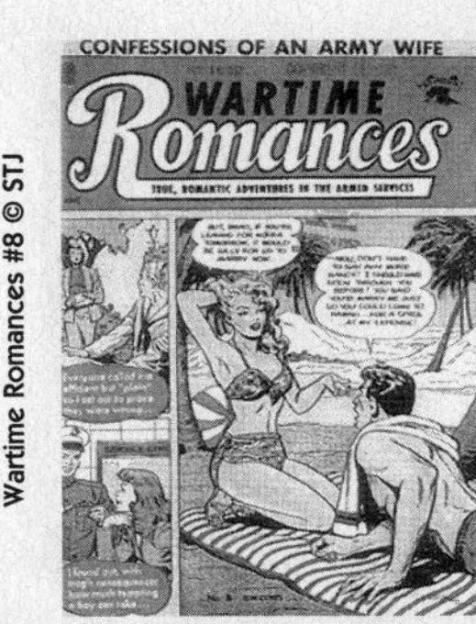

Wartime Romances #8 © STJ

GD VG FN VF VF/NM NM-
2.0 4.0 6.0 8.0 9.0 9.2

1-5: 1-Randy Zimmerman scripts begin 3.00

WARP
First Comics: Mar, 1983 - No. 19, Feb, 1985 ($1.00/$1.25, Mando paper)

1-Sargon-Mistress of War app.; Brunner-c/a thru #9 4.00
2-19: 2-Faceless Ones begin. 10-New Warp advs., & Outrider begin 3.00
Special 1-3: 1(7/83, 36 pgs.)-Origin Chaos-Prince of Madness; origin of Warp Universe begins, ends #3. 2(1/84)-Lord Cumulus vs. Sargon Mistress of War ($1.00). 3(6/84)-Chaos-Prince of Madness 3.00

WARPATH (Indians on the...)
Key Publications/Stanmor: Nov, 1954 - No. 3, Apr, 1955

1 11 22 33 62 86 110
2,3 8 16 24 40 50 60

WARPED
Empire Entertainment (Solson): Jun, 1990 - No. 2, Oct-Nov, 1990 (B&W mag)

1,2 3.00

WARP GRAPHICS ANNUAL
WaRP Graphics: Dec, 1985; 1988 ($2.50)

1-Elfquest, Blood of the Innocent, Thunderbunny & Myth Adventures 5.00
1 (1988) 4.00

WARREN PRESENTS
Warren Publications: Jan, 1979 - No. 14, Nov, 1981(B&W magazine)

1-Eerie, Creepy, & Vampirella-r; Ring of the Warlords; Merlin-s; Dax-s; Sanjulian-c
3 6 9 15 21 26
2-6(10/79): 2-The Rook. 3-Alien Invasions Comix. 4-Movie Aliens. 5-Dracula '79. 6-Strange Stories of Vampires Comix 2 4 6 9 13 16
8(10/80)-r/1st app. Pantha from Vamp. #30 2 4 6 11 16 20
9(11/80) Empire Encounters Comix 2 4 6 10 14 18
13(10/81),14(11/81):13-Sword and Sorcery Comix 3 6 9 14 19 24
(#7,10,11,12 may not exist, or may be a Special below)
Special-Alien Collectors Edition (1979) 3 6 9 14 19 24
Special-Close Encounters of the Third Kind (1978) 2 4 6 9 13 16
Special-Lord of the Rings (6/79) 3 6 9 18 28 38
Special-Meteor (1/80) 2 4 6 9 13 16
Special-Moonraker/James Bond (10/79) 2 4 6 9 13 16
Special-Star Wars (1977) 3 6 9 18 28 38

WAR REPORT
Ajax/Farrell Publications (Excellent Publ.): Sept, 1952 - No. 5, May, 1953

1 17 34 51 98 154 210
2-Flame thrower w/burning bodies on-c 24 48 72 142 234 325
3,5 11 22 33 60 83 105
4-Used in POP, pg. 94 11 22 33 64 90 115

WARRIOR (Wrestling star)
Ultimate Creations: May, 1996 - No. 4, 1997 ($2.95)

1-4: Warrior scripts; Callahan-c/a. 3-Wraparound-c. 4-Warrior #3 in indicia; pin-ups 3.00
1-Variant-c. 5.00
X-Mas (11/96, $3.50) listed as "No. 3" in indicia; pin-ups by various; Quesada-c 4.00

WARRIOR COMICS
H.C. Blackerby: 1945 (1930s DC reprints)

1-Wing Brady, The Iron Man, Mark Markon 21 42 63 126 206 285

WARRIOR OF WAVERLY STREET, THE
Dark Horse Comics: Nov, 1996 - No. 2, Dec, 1996 ($2.95, mini-series)

1,2-Darrow-c 3.00

WARRIORS
CFD Productions: 1993 (B&W, one-shot)

1-Linsner, Dark One-a 2 4 6 11 16 20

WARRIORS, THE: OFFICIAL MOVIE ADAPTATION (Based on the 1979 movie)
Dabel Brothers Publishing/Dynamite Ent.: Feb, 2009 - No. 5, 2010 ($3.99, limited series)

1-5: 1-Three covers plus wraparound photo-c; Dibari-a. 3-Eric Powell-c 4.00
...: Jailbreak 1 (7/09, $3.99) Apon & Herman-a 4.00

WARRIORS OF MARS (Also see Warlord of Mars titles)
Dynamite Entertainment: 2012 - No. 5, 2012 ($3.99, limited series)

1-5-Gullivar Jones visits Barsoom; Jusko-c 4.00

WARRIORS OF PLASM (Also see Plasm and Dogs of War #5)
Defiant: Aug, 1993 - No. 13, Aug, 1995 ($2.95/$2.50)

1-4: Shooter-scripts; Lapham-c/a: 1-1st app. Glory. 4-Bound-in fold-out poster 4.00

GD VG FN VF VF/NM NM-
2.0 4.0 6.0 8.0 9.0 9.2

5-7,10-13: 5-Begin $2.50-c. 13-Schism issue; last Defiant comic published 3.00
8,9-($2.75, 44 pgs.) 4.00
The Collected Edition (2/94, $9.95)-r/Plasm #0, WOP #1-4 & Splatterball 10.00

WARRIORS THREE (Fandral, Volstagg, and Hogun from Thor)
Marvel Comics: Jan, 2011 - No. 4, Apr, 2011 ($3.99, limited series)

1-4-Bill Willingham-s/Neil Edwards-a. 2,4-Conner-c 4.00

WAR ROMANCES (See True...)

WAR SHIPS
Dell Publishing Co.: 1942 (36 pgs.)(Similar to Large Feature Comics)

nn-Cover by McWilliams; contains photos & drawings of U.S. war ships
20 40 60 114 182 250

WAR STORIES (Formerly War Comics)
Dell Publ. Co.: No. 5, 1942(nd); No. 6, Aug-Oct, 1942 - No. 8, Feb-Apr, 1943

5-Origin The Whistler 33 66 99 194 317 440
6-8: 6-8-Night Devils app. 8-Painted-c 25 50 75 150 245 340

WAR STORIES (Korea)
Ajax/Farrell Publications (Excellent Publ.): Sept, 1952 - No. 5, May, 1953

1 17 34 51 98 154 210
2 11 22 33 60 83 105
3-5 10 20 30 54 72 90

WAR STORIES
Avatar Press: Sept, 2014 - Present ($3.99)

1-19: Garth Ennis-s in all; multiple covers on all. 1-Matt Martin-a 4.00

WAR STORIES (See Star Spangled...)

WAR STORY
DC Comics (Vertigo): Nov, 2001 - Apr, 2003 ($4.95, series of World War II one-shots)

...: Archangel (4/03) Ennis-s/Erskine-a 5.00
...: Condors (3/03) Ennis-s/Ezquerra-a 5.00
...: D-Day Dodgers (12/01) Ennis-s/Higgins-a 5.00
...: J For Jenny (2/03) Ennis-s/Lloyd-a 5.00
...: Johann's Tiger (11/01) Ennis-s/Weston-a 5.00
...: Nightingale (2/02) Ennis-s/Lloyd-a 5.00
...: Screaming Eagles (1/02) Ennis-s/Gibbons-a 5.00
...: The Reivers (1/03) Ennis-s/Kennedy-a 5.00
Vol. 1 (2004, $19.95) r/Johann's Tiger, D-Day Dodgers, Screaming Eagles, Nightingale 20.00
Vol. 2 (2006, $19.99) r/J For Jenny, The Reivers, Condors, Archangel; Ennis afterword 20.00

WARSTRIKE
Malibu Comics (Ultraverse): May, 1994 - No. 7, Nov, 1995 ($1.95)

1-7: 1-Simonson-c 3.00
1-Ultra 5000 Limited silver foil 6.00
Giant Size 1 (12/94, $2.50, 44pgs.)-Prelude to Godwheel 4.00

WART AND THE WIZARD (See The Sword & the Stone under Movie Comics)
Gold Key: Feb, 1964 (Walt Disney)(Characters from Sword in the Stone movie)

1 (10102-402) 4 8 12 27 44 60

WAR THAT TIME FORGOT, THE
DC Comics: Jul, 2008 - No. 12, Jun, 2009 ($2.99, limited series)

1-12: 1-Bruce Jones-s/Al Barrionuevo-a/Neal Adams-c; Enemy Ace app. 3.00

WARTIME ROMANCES
St. John Publishing Co.: July, 1951 - No. 18, Nov, 1953

1-All Baker-c/a 110 220 330 704 1202 1700
2-All Baker-c/a 65 130 195 416 708 1000
3,4-All Baker-c/a 61 122 183 390 670 950
5-8-Baker-c/a(2-3) each 58 116 174 371 636 900
9,11,12,16,18: Baker-c/a each. 9-Two signed stories by Estrada
54 108 162 343 574 825
10,13-15,17-Baker-c only 50 100 150 315 533 750

WAR VICTORY ADVENTURES (#1 titled War Victory Comics)
U.S. Treasury Dept./War Victory/Harvey Publ.: Sum, 1942 - No. 3, Wint, 1943-44 (5¢/10¢)

1-(5¢)(Promotion of Savings Bonds)-Featuring America's greatest comic art by top syndicated cartoonists; Blondie, Joe Palooka, Green Hornet, Dick Tracy, Superman, Gumps, etc.; (36 pgs.); all profits were contributed to U.S.O. & Army/Navy relief funds
58 116 174 371 636 900
2-(10¢) Battle of Stalingrad story; Powell-a (8/43); flag & WWII Japanese-c
90 180 270 576 988 1400
3-(10¢) Capt. Red Cross-c & text only; WWII Nazi-c; Powell-a
77 154 231 493 847 1200

Watchmen #1 © DC

Weapon X: First Class #2 © MAR

We Are Robin #4 © DC

GD VG FN VF VF/NM NM-
2.0 4.0 6.0 8.0 9.0 9.2

WAR WAGON, THE (See Movie Classics)

WAR WINGS
Charlton Comics: Oct, 1968

	GD	VG	FN	VF	VF/NM	NM-
1	3	6	9	14	20	26

WARWORLD!
Dark Horse Comics: Feb, 1989 ($1.75, B&W, one-shot)

	GD	VG	FN	VF	VF/NM	NM-
1-Gary Davis sci/fi art in Moebius style						3.00

WASHABLE JONES AND THE SHMOO (Also see Al Capp's Shmoo)
Toby Press: June, 1953

	GD	VG	FN	VF	VF/NM	NM-
1- "Super-Shmoo"	20	40	60	114	182	250

WASH TUBBS (See The Comics, Crackajack Funnies)
Dell Publishing Co.: No. 11, 1942 - No. 53, 1944

	GD	VG	FN	VF	VF/NM	NM-
Four Color 11 (#1)	26	52	78	182	404	625
Four Color 28 (1943)	17	34	51	117	259	400
Four Color 53	13	26	39	89	195	300

WASP (See Unstoppable Wasp)

WASTELAND
DC Comics: Dec, 1987 - No. 18, May, 1989 ($1.75-$2.00 #13 on, mature)

	GD	VG	FN	VF	VF/NM	NM-
1-5(4/88), 5(5/88), 6(5/88)-18: 13,15-Orlando-a						3.00

NOTE: ***Orlando** a-12, 13, 15. **Truman** a-10; c-13.*

WATCHMEN (Also see 2012-2013 Before Watchmen prequel titles)
DC Comics: Sept, 1986 - No. 12, Oct, 1987 (maxi-series)

	GD	VG	FN	VF	VF/NM	NM-
1-Alan Moore scripts & Dave Gibbons-c/a in all	4	8	12	27	44	60
1-(2009, $1.50) Second printing						3.00
2-12	2	4	6	10	14	18
Hardcover Collection-Slip-cased-r/#1-12 w/new material; produced by Graphitti Designs						100.00
HC (2008, $39.99) recolored r/#1-12; design & promotional art; Moore & Gibbons intros						40.00
Trade paperback (1987, $14.95)-r/#1-12						25.00

WATER BIRDS AND THE OLYMPIC ELK (Disney)
Dell Publishing Co.: No. 700, Apr, 1956

	GD	VG	FN	VF	VF/NM	NM-
Four Color 700-Movie	5	10	15	33	57	80

WATERWORLD: CHILDREN OF LEVIATHAN
Acclaim Comics: Aug, 1997 - No. 4, Nov, 1997 ($2.50, mini-series)

	GD	VG	FN	VF	VF/NM	NM-
1-4						3.00

WAY OF THE RAT
CrossGeneration Comics: Jun, 2002 - No. 24, June, 2004 ($2.95)

	GD	VG	FN	VF	VF/NM	NM-
1-24: 1-Dixon-s/ Jeff Johnson-a. 5-Whigham-a. 9,14-Luke Ross-a						3.00
Free Comic Book Day Special (6/03) reprints #1 w/features, interviews, CrossGen info						3.00
...: The Walls of Zhumar Vol. 1 (1/03, $15.95) r/#1-6						16.00
Vol. 2: The Dragon's Wake (2003, $15.95) r/#7-12						16.00

WAYWARD
Image Comics: Aug, 2014 - Present ($3.50)

	GD	VG	FN	VF	VF/NM	NM-
1-20: 1-Jim Zub-s/Cummings-a; multiple covers						3.50

WEAPON X
Marvel Comics: Apr, 1994 ($12.95, one-shot)

	GD	VG	FN	VF	VF/NM	NM-
nn-r/Marvel Comics Presents #72-84						13.00

WEAPON X
Marvel Comics: Mar, 1995 - No. 4, June, 1995 ($1.95)

	GD	VG	FN	VF	VF/NM	NM-
1-Age of Apocalypse						4.00
2-4						3.00

WEAPON X
Marvel Comics: Nov, 2002 - No. 28, Nov, 2004 ($2.25/$2.99)

	GD	VG	FN	VF	VF/NM	NM-
1-7: 1-Sabretooth-c/app.; Tieri-s/Jeanty-a						3.00
8-28: 8-Begin $2.99-c. 14-Invaders app. 15-Chamber joins. 16-18,21-25-Wolverine app.						3.00
Vol. 1: The Draft TPB (2003, $21.99) r/#1-5, #1/2 & The Draft one-shots						22.00
Vol. 2: The Underground TPB (2003, $19.99) r/#6-13						20.00
Wizard #1/2 (2002)						5.00

WEAPON X: DAYS OF FUTURE NOW
Marvel Comics: Sept, 2005 - No. 5, Jan, 2006 ($2.99, limited series)

	GD	VG	FN	VF	VF/NM	NM-
1-5-Tieri-s/Sears-a; Chamber, Sauron & Fantomex app.						3.00
TPB (2006, $13.99) r/#1-5						14.00

WEAPON X: FIRST CLASS
Marvel Comics: Jan, 2009 - No. 3, Mar, 2009 ($3.99, limited series)

	GD	VG	FN	VF	VF/NM	NM-
1-3:1-Sabretooth-c/app. 2-Deadpool-c/app.						4.00

WEAPON X NOIR
Marvel Comics: May, 2010 ($3.99, one-shot)

	GD	VG	FN	VF	VF/NM	NM-
1-Dennis Calero-s/a; C.P. Smith-c						4.00

WEAPON X: THE DRAFT (Leads into 2002 Weapon X series)
Marvel Comics: Oct, 2002 ($2.25, one-shots)

	GD	VG	FN	VF	VF/NM	NM-
...Kane 1- JH Williams-c/Raimondi-a						3.00
...Marrow 1- JH Williams-c/Badeaux-a						3.00
...Sauron 1- JH Williams-c/Kerschl-a; Emma Frost app.						3.00
...Wild Child 1- JH Williams-c/Van Sciver-a; Aurora (Alpha Flight) app.						3.00
...Zero 1- JH Williams-c/Plunkett-a; Wolverine app.						3.00

WEAPON ZERO
Image Comics (Top Cow Productions): No. T-4(#1), June, 1995 - No. T-0(#5), Dec, 1995 ($2.50, limited series)

	GD	VG	FN	VF	VF/NM	NM-
T-4(#1): Walt Simonson scripts in all.						5.00
T-3(#2) - T-1(#4)						4.00
T-0(#5)						3.00

WEAPON ZERO
Image Comics (Top Cow Productions): V2#1, Mar, 1996 - No. 15, Dec, 1997 ($2.50)

	GD	VG	FN	VF	VF/NM	NM-
V2#1-Walt Simonson scripts.						4.00
2-14: 8-Begin Top Cow. 10-Devil's Reign						3.00
15-($3.50) Benitez-a						4.00

WEAPON ZERO/SILVER SURFER
Image Comics/Marvel Comics: Jan, 1997 ($2.95, one-shot)

	GD	VG	FN	VF	VF/NM	NM-
1-Devil's Reign Pt. 1						3.00

WE ARE ROBIN (Also see Batman: Rebirth #1)
DC Comics: Aug, 2015 - No. 12, Jul, 2016 ($3.99)

	GD	VG	FN	VF	VF/NM	NM-
1-12: 1-Bermejo-s/c; Corona-a. 3-Batman (Gordon) app. 4-Batgirl app.; Harvey-a						4.00

WEASELGUY: ROAD TRIP
Image Comics: Sept, 1999 - No. 2 ($3.50, limited series)

	GD	VG	FN	VF	VF/NM	NM-
1,2-Steve Buccellato-s/a						3.50
1-Variant-c by Bachalo						5.00

WEASELGUY/WITCHBLADE
Hyperwerks: July, 1998 ($2.95, one-shot)

	GD	VG	FN	VF	VF/NM	NM-
1-Steve Buccellato-s/a; covers by Matsuda and Altstaetter						3.00

WEASEL PATROL SPECIAL, THE (Also see Fusion #17)
Eclipse Comics: Apr, 1989 ($2.00, B&W, one-shot)

	GD	VG	FN	VF	VF/NM	NM-
1-Funny animal						3.00

WEAVEWORLD
Marvel Comics (Epic): Dec, 1991 - No. 3, 1992 ($4.95, lim. series, 68 pgs.)

	GD	VG	FN	VF	VF/NM	NM-
1-3: Clive Barker adaptation						5.00

WEB, THE (Also see Mighty Comics & Mighty Crusaders)
DC Comics (Impact Comics): Sept, 1991 - No. 14, Oct, 1992 ($1.00)

	GD	VG	FN	VF	VF/NM	NM-
1-14: 5-The Fly x-over 9-Trading card inside						5.00
Annual 1 (1992, $2.50, 68 pgs.)-With Trading card						5.00

NOTE: ***Gil Kane** c-5, 9, 10, 12-14. **Bill Wray** a(i)-1-9, 10(part).*

WEB, THE (Continued from The Red Circle)
DC Comics: Nov, 2009 - No. 10, Aug, 2010 ($3.99)

	GD	VG	FN	VF	VF/NM	NM-
1-10: 1-Roger Robinson-a; The Hangman back-up feature. 3-Batgirl app. 5-Caldwell-a						4.00

WEB OF EVIL
Comic Magazines/Quality Comics Group: Nov, 1952 - No. 21, Dec, 1954

	GD	VG	FN	VF	VF/NM	NM-
1-Used in **SOTI**, pg. 388. Jack Cole-a; morphine use story	79	158	237	502	864	1225
2-4,6,7: 2,3-Jack Cole-a. 4,6,7-Jack Cole-c/a	46	92	138	288	487	685
5-Electrocution-c/story; Jack Cole-c/a	73	146	219	467	796	1125
8-11-Jack Cole-a	41	82	123	260	435	610
12,13,15,16,19-21	32	64	96	190	310	430
14-Part Crandall-c; Old Witch swipe	34	68	102	204	332	460
17-Opium drug propaganda story	34	68	102	199	325	450
18-Acid-in-face story	34	68	102	204	332	460

NOTE: ***Jack Cole** a(2 each)-2, 6, 8, 9. **Cuidera** c-1-21i. **Ravielli** a-13.*

WEB OF HORROR
Major Magazines: Dec, 1969 - No. 3, Apr, 1970 (Magazine)

	GD	VG	FN	VF	VF/NM	NM-
1-Jeff Jones painted-c; Wrightson-a, Kaluta-a	8	16	24	51	96	140
2-Jones painted-c; Wrightson-a(2), Kaluta-a	7	14	21	44	82	120
3-Wrightson-c/a (1st published-c); Brunner, Kaluta, Bruce Jones-a						

Web of Spider-Man #2 © MAR

Web Warriors #1 © MAR

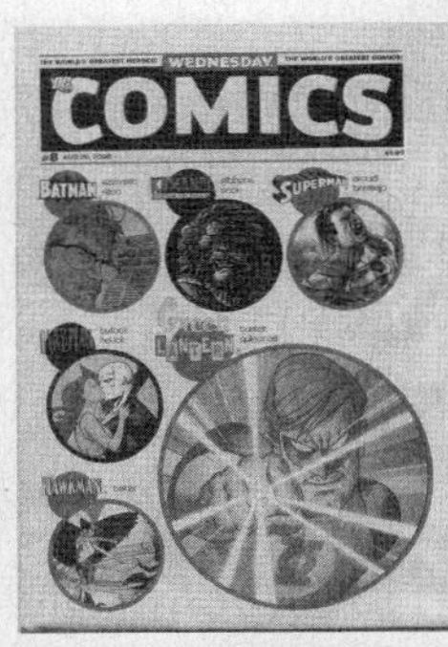
Wednesday Comics #8 © DC

	GD 2.0	VG 4.0	FN 6.0	VF 8.0	VF/NM 9.0	NM- 9.2
	8	16	24	56	108	160

WEB OF MYSTERY
Ace Magazines (A. A. Wyn): Feb, 1951 - No. 29, Sept, 1955

	GD 2.0	VG 4.0	FN 6.0	VF 8.0	VF/NM 9.0	NM- 9.2
1	68	136	204	435	743	1050
2-Bakerish-a	39	78	117	240	395	550
3-10: 4-Colan-a	37	74	111	222	361	500
11-18,20-26: 12-John Chilly's 1st cover art. 13-Surrealistic-c. 20-r/The Beyond #1	34	68	102	199	325	450
19-Reprints Challenge of the Unknown #6 used in N.Y. Legislative Committee	34	68	102	199	325	450
27-Bakerish-a(r/The Beyond #2); last pre-code ish	30	60	90	177	289	400
28,29: 28-All-r	24	48	72	142	234	325

NOTE: *This series was to appear as "Creepy Stories", but title was changed before publication.* ***Cameron*** *a-6, 8, 11-13, 17-20, 22, 24, 25, 27; c-8, 13, 17.* ***Palais*** *a-28r.* ***Sekowsky*** *a-1-3, 7, 8, 11, 14, 21, 29.* ***Tothish*** *a-by* ***Bill Discount*** *#16. 29-all-r, 19-28-partial-r.*

WEB OF SCARLET SPIDER
Marvel Comics: Oct, 1995 - No. 4, Jan, 1996 ($1.95, limited series)

	GD 2.0	VG 4.0	FN 6.0	VF 8.0	VF/NM 9.0	NM- 9.2
1-4: Replaces "Web of Spider-Man"						3.00

WEB OF SPIDER-MAN (Replaces Marvel Team-Up)
Marvel Comics Group: Apr, 1985 - No. 129, Sept, 1995

	GD 2.0	VG 4.0	FN 6.0	VF 8.0	VF/NM 9.0	NM- 9.2
1-Painted-c (5th app. black costume?)	3	6	9	15	22	28
2,3						6.00
4-8: 7-Hulk x-over; Wolverine splash						5.00
9-13: 10-Dominic Fortune guest stars; painted-c						4.00
14-17,19-28: 19-Intro Humbug & Solo						4.00
18-1st app. Venom (behind the scenes, 9/86)	2	4	6	11	16	20
29-Wolverine, new Hobgoblin (Macendale) app.	1	3	4	6	8	10
30-Origin recap The Rose & Hobgoblin I (entire book is flashback story); Punisher & Wolverine cameo						5.00
31,32-Six part Kraven storyline begins	2	4	6	9	12	15
33-35,37,39-47,49						3.00
36-1st app. Tombstone	3	6	9	16	23	30
38-Hobgoblin app.; begin $1.00-c						4.00
48-Origin Hobgoblin II(Demogoblin) cont'd from Spectacular Spider-Man #147; Kingpin app.	1	3	4	6	8	10
50-($1.50, 52 pgs.)						4.00
51-58						3.00
59-Cosmic Spidey cont'd from Spect. Spider-Man						4.00
60-89,91-99,101-106: 66,67-Green Goblin (Norman Osborn) app. as a super-hero. 69,70-Hulk x-over. 74-76-Austin-c(i). 76-Fantastic Four x-over. 78-Cloak & Dagger app. 81-Origin/1st app. Bloodshed. 84-Begin 6 part Rose & Hobgoblin II storyline; last $1.00-c. 86-Demon leaves Hobgoblin; 1st Demogoblin. 93-Gives brief history of Hobgoblin. 93,94-Hobgoblin (Macendale) Reborn-c/story, parts 1,2; MoonKnight app. 94-Venom cameo. 95-Begin 4 part x-over w/Spirits of Venom w/Ghost Rider/Blaze/Spidey vs. Venom & Demogoblin (cont'd in Ghost Rider/Blaze #5,6). 96-Spirits of Venom part 3; painted-c. 101,103-Maximum Carnage x-over. 103-Venom & Carnage app. 104-106-Nightwatch back-up stories						3.00
90-($2.95, 52 pgs.)-Polybagged w/silver hologram-c, gatefold poster showing Spider-Man & Spider-Man 2099 (Williamson-i)	1	3	4	6	8	10
90-2nd printing; gold hologram-c						4.00
100-($2.95, 52 pgs.)-Holo-grafx foil-c; intro new Spider-Armor						4.00
107-111: 107-Intro Sandstorm; Sand & Quicksand app.						3.00
112-116,121-124, 126-128: 112-Begin $1.50-c; bound-in trading card sheet. 113-Regular Ed.; Gambit & Black Cat app.						3.00
113-($2.95)-Collector's ed. polybagged w/foil-c; 16 pg. preview of Spider-Man cartoon & animation cel						4.00
117-($1.50)-Flip book; Power & Responsibility Pt.1						3.00
117-($2.95)-Collector's edition; foil-c; flip book						4.00
118-1st solo Scarlet Spider story; Venom app.	2	4	6	11	16	20
119-Regular edition						6.00
119-($6.45)-Direct market edition; polybagged w/ Marvel Milestone Amazing Spider-Man #150 & coupon for Amazing Spider-Man #396, Spider-Man #53, & Spectacular Spider-Man #219.	1	3	4	6	8	10
120 ($2.25)-Flip book w/ preview of the Ultimate Spider-Man						4.00
125 ($3.95)-Holodisk-c; Gwen Stacy clone						5.00
125,129: 125 ($2.95)-Newsstand. 129-Last issue						4.00
#129.1, #129.2 (both 10/12, $2.99) Brooklyn Avengers app.; Damion Scott-a						3.00
Annual 1 (1985)						5.00
Annual 2 (1986)-New Mutants; Art Adams-a	1	2	3	5	6	8
Annual 3-10 ('87-'94, 68 pgs.): 4-Evolutionary War x-over. 5-Atlantis Attacks; Captain Universe by Ditko (p) & Silver Sable stories; F.F. app. 6-Punisher back-up plus Capt. Universe by Ditko; G. Kane-a. 7-Origins of Hobgoblin I, Hobgoblin II, Green Goblin I & II & Venom; Larsen/Austin-c. 9-Bagged w/card						4.00
Super Special 1 (1995, $3.95)-flip book						4.00

NOTE: ***Art Adams*** *a-Annual 2.* ***Byrne*** *c-3-6.* ***Chaykin*** *c-10.* ***Mignola*** *a-Annual 2.* ***Vess*** *c-1, 8, Annual 1, 2.* ***Zeck*** *a-6i, 31, 32; c-31, 32.*

WEB OF SPIDER-MAN (Anthology)
Marvel Comics: Dec, 2009 - No. 12, Nov, 2010 ($3.99)

	GD 2.0	VG 4.0	FN 6.0	VF 8.0	VF/NM 9.0	NM- 9.2
1-12: 1-Spider-Girl app. thru #7; Ben Reilly app. 2-6-Origins of villains retold. 7-Kraven origin; Paper Doll app.; Mahfood-a. 9-11-Jackpot back-up; Takeda-a. 11,12-Black Cat app.						4.00

WEBSPINNERS: TALES OF SPIDER-MAN
Marvel Comics: Jan, 1999 - No. 18, Jun, 2000 ($2.99/$2.50)

	GD 2.0	VG 4.0	FN 6.0	VF 8.0	VF/NM 9.0	NM- 9.2
1-DeMatteis-s/Zulli-a; back-up story w/Romita Sr. art						4.00
1-($6.95) DF Edition						7.00
2,3: 2-Two covers						3.00
4-11,13-18: 4,5-Giffen-a; Silver Surfer-c/app. 7-9-Kelly-s/Sears and Smith-a. 10,11-Jenkins-s/Sean Phillips-a						3.00
12-($3.50) J.G. Jones-c/a; Jenkins-s						4.00

WEB WARRIORS
Marvel Comics: Jan, 2016 - No. 11, Nov, 2016 ($4.99/$3.99)

	GD 2.0	VG 4.0	FN 6.0	VF 8.0	VF/NM 9.0	NM- 9.2
1-($4.99) Spider-verse characters team-up; Costa-s/Baldeon-a; alternate Black Cat app.						5.00
2-11-($3.99) 2-5-Multiple Spider-Mans vs. multiple Electros						4.00

WEDDING BELLS
Quality Comics Group: Feb, 1954 - No. 19, Nov, 1956

	GD 2.0	VG 4.0	FN 6.0	VF 8.0	VF/NM 9.0	NM- 9.2
1-Whitney-a	20	40	60	114	182	250
2	13	26	39	72	101	130
3-9: 8-Last precode (4/55)	11	22	33	60	83	105
10-Ward-a (9 pgs.)	15	30	45	90	140	190
11-14,17	10	20	30	56	76	95
15-Baker-c	17	34	51	98	154	210
16-Baker-c/a	20	40	60	114	182	250
18,19-Baker-a each	14	28	42	80	115	150

WEDDING OF DRACULA
Marvel Comics: Jan, 1993 ($2.00, 52 pgs.)

	GD 2.0	VG 4.0	FN 6.0	VF 8.0	VF/NM 9.0	NM- 9.2
1-Reprints Tomb of Dracula #30,45,46						4.00

WEDNESDAY COMICS (Newspaper-style, twice folded pages on 20" x 14" newsprint)
DC Comics: Sept, 2009 - No. 12, Nov, 2009 ($3.99, weekly limited series)

	GD 2.0	VG 4.0	FN 6.0	VF 8.0	VF/NM 9.0	NM- 9.2
1-12-Superman, Batman, Kamandi, Hawkman, Deadman, Green Lantern, Flash, Teen Titans, Metamorpho, Adam Strange, Supergirl, Metal Men, Wonder Woman, The Demon with Catwoman, Sgt. Rock; s-a/ by various incl. Ryan Sook, Joe Kubert, Gaiman, Allred, Risso, Kyle Baker, Paul Pope, Conner, Simonson, Garcia-Lopez, Stelfreeze, Bermejo						4.00

WEEKENDER, THE (Illustrated...)
Rucker Pub. Co.: V1#1, Sept, 1945? - V1#4, Nov, 1945; V2#1, Jan, 1946 - V2#3, Aug, 1946 (52 pgs.)

	GD 2.0	VG 4.0	FN 6.0	VF 8.0	VF/NM 9.0	NM- 9.2
V1#1-4: 1-Same-c as Zip Comics #45, inside-c and back-c blank; Steel Sterling, Senor Banana, Red Rube and Ginger. 2-Capt. Victory on-c. 3-Super hero-c; Mr. E, Dan Hastings, Sky Chief and the Echo. 4-Same-c as Punch Comics #10 (9/44); r/Hale the Magician (7 pgs.) & r/Mr. E (8 pgs.-Lou Fine? or Gustavson?) plus 3 humor strips & many B&W photos & r/newspaper articles plus cheesecake photos of Hollywood stars	39	78	117	240	395	550
V2#1-Same-c as Dynamic Comics #11; 36 pgs. comics, 16 in newspaper format with photos; partial Dynamic Comics reprints; 4 pgs. of cels from the Disney film Pinocchio; Little Nemo story by Winsor McCay, Jr.; Jack Cole-a	55	110	165	352	601	850
V2#2,3: 2-Same-c as Dynamic Comics #9 by Raboy; Dan Hastings (Tuska), Rocket Boy, The Echo, Lucky Coyne. 3-Humor-c by Boddington?; Dynamic Man, Ima Slooth, Master Key, Dynamic Boy, Captain Glory	34	68	102	199	325	450

WEIRD
Eerie Publications: V1#10, 1/66 - V8#6, 12/74; V9#1, 1/75 - V14#3, Nov, 1981 (Magazine) (V1-V8: 52 pgs.; V9 on: 68 pgs.)

	GD 2.0	VG 4.0	FN 6.0	VF 8.0	VF/NM 9.0	NM- 9.2
V1#10(#1)-Intro. Morris the Caretaker of Weird (ends V2#10); Burgos-a	8	16	24	54	102	150
11,12	5	10	15	35	63	90
V2#1-4(10/67), V3#1(1/68), V2#6(4/68)-V2#7,9,10(12/68)	5	10	15	35	63	90
V2#8-r/Ditko's 1st story/Fantastic Fears #5	6	12	18	40	73	105
V3#1(2/69)-V3#4	5	10	15	33	57	80
V3#5(12/69)-Rulah reprint; "Rulah" changed to "Pulah", LSD story reprinted in Horror Tales V4#4, Tales From the Tomb V2#4, & 20	5	10	15	33	57	80
V4#1-6('70), V5#1-6('71), V6#1-7('72), V7#1-7('73), V8#1-3, V8#4(8/74), V8#4(10/74), (V8#5 does not exist), V8#6('74), V9#1-4(1/75-'76), V10#1-3('77), V11#1-4('78), V12#1(2/79)-V14#3(11/81)	5	10	15	31	53	75

Weird Comics #2 © FOX

Weird Fantasy #17 © WMG

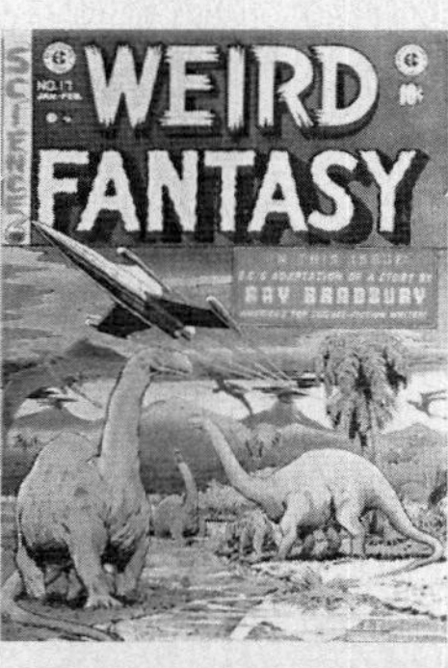

Weird Science #6 © WMG

	GD	VG	FN	VF	VF/NM	NM-
	2.0	4.0	6.0	8.0	9.0	9.2

NOTE: *There are two V8#4 issues (8/74 & 10/74). V9#4 (12/76) has a cover swipe from Horror Tales V5#1 (2/73). There are two V13#3 issues (6/80 & 9/80).*

WEIRD
DC Comics (Paradox Press): Sum, 1997 - No. 4 ($2.99, B&W, magazine)
1-4: 4-Mike Tyson-c 3.00

WEIRD, THE
DC Comics: Apr, 1988 - No. 4, July, 1988 ($1.50, limited series)
1-4: Wrightson-c/a in all 5.00

WEIRD ADVENTURES
P. L. Publishing Co. (Canada): May-June, 1951 - No. 3, Sept-Oct, 1951
1- "The She-Wolf Killer" by Matt Baker (6 pgs.) 66 132 198 419 722 1025
2-Bondage/hypodermic panel 50 100 150 315 533 750
3-Male bondage/torture-c; severed head story 43 86 129 271 461 650

WEIRD ADVENTURES
Ziff-Davis Publishing Co.: No. 10, July-Aug, 1951
10-Painted-c 42 84 126 265 445 625

WEIRD CHILLS
Key Publications: July, 1954 - No. 3, Nov, 1954
1-Wolverton-r/Weird Mysteries No. 4; blood transfusion-c by Baily
161 322 483 1030 1765 2500
2-Extremely violent injury to eye-c by Baily; Hitler story
168 336 504 1075 1838 2600
3-Bondage E.C. swipe-c by Baily 63 126 189 403 689 975

WEIRD COMICS
Fox Features Syndicate: Apr, 1940 - No. 20, Jan, 1942
1-The Birdman, Thor, God of Thunder (ends #5), The Sorceress of Zoom, Blast Bennett, Typhon, Voodoo Man, & Dr. Mortal begin; George Tuska bondage-c
811 1622 2433 5920 10,460 15,000
2-Lou Fine-c 343 686 1029 2400 4200 6000
3,4: 3-Simon-c. 4-Torture-c 271 542 813 1734 2967 4200
5-Intro. Dart & sidekick Ace (8/40) (ends #20); bondage/hypo-c
277 554 831 1759 3030 4300
6,7-Dynamite Thor app. in each. 6-Super hero covers begin
161 322 483 1030 1765 2500
8-Dynamo, the Eagle (11/40, early app.; see Science #1) & sidekick Buddy & Marga, the Panther Woman begin 168 336 504 1075 1838 2600
9,10: 10-Navy Jones app. 135 270 405 864 1482 2100
11-19: 16-Flag-c. 17-Origin The Black Rider. 123 246 369 787 1344 1900
20-Origin The Rapier; Swoop Curtis app; Churchill & Hitler-c
541 1082 1623 3950 6975 10,000
NOTE *Cover features: Sorceress of Zoom-4; Dr. Mortal-5; Dart & Ace-6-13, 15; Eagle-14, 16-20.*

WEIRD DETECTIVE
Dark Horse Comics: Jun, 2016 - No. 5, Oct, 2016 ($3.99)
1-5-Van Lente-s/Vilanova-a 4.00

WEIRD FANTASY (Formerly A Moon, A Girl, Romance; becomes Weird Science-Fantasy #23 on)
E. C. Comics: No. 13, May-June, 1950 - No. 22, Nov-Dec, 1953
13(#1) (1950) 229 458 687 1832 2916 4000
14-Necronomicon story; Cosmic Ray Bomb explosion-c/story by Feldstein; Feldstein & Gaines star 109 218 327 872 1386 1900
15,16: 16-Used in **SOTI**, pg. 144 86 172 258 688 1094 1500
17 (1951) 63 126 189 504 802 1100
6-Robot-c 57 114 171 456 728 1000
7-10 54 108 162 432 691 950
11-13 (1952): 11-Feldstein bio. 12-E.C. artists cameo; Orlando bio. 13-Anti-Wertham "Cosmic Correspondence" 44 88 132 352 564 775
14-Frazetta/Williamson(1st team-up at E.C.)/Krenkel-a (7 pgs.); Orlando draws E.C. staff
56 112 168 448 712 975
15-Williamson/Evans-a(3), 4,3,&7 pgs. 46 92 138 368 584 800
16-19-Williamson/Krenkel-a in all. 17-Feldstein dinosaur-c; classic sci-fi story "The Aliens". 18-Williamson/Feldstein-c; classic anti-prejudice story "Judgment Day". 19-Williamson bio.
43 86 129 344 547 750
20-Frazetta/Williamson-a (7 pgs.); contains house ad for original, uncensored cover to Vault of Horror #32 (meat cleaver in forehead) 47 94 141 376 601 825
21-Frazetta/Williamson-c & Williamson/Krenkel-a 74 148 222 592 946 1300
22-Bradbury adaptation 36 72 108 288 457 625
NOTE: ***Crandall** a-22. **Elder** a-17. **Feldstein** a-13(#1)-8; c-13(#1)-18 (#18 w/**Williamson**), 20. **Harrison/Wood** a-13. **Kamen** a-13(#1)-16, 18-22. **Krigstein** a-22. **Kurtzman** a-13(#1)-17(#5), 6. **Orlando** a-9-22 (2 stories in #16); c-19, 22. **Severin/Elder** a-18-21. **Wood** a-13(#1)-14, 17(2 stories ea. in #10-13). Ray Bradbury adaptations in #13,17-22. Canadian reprints exist; see Table of Contents.*

	GD	VG	FN	VF	VF/NM	NM-
	2.0	4.0	6.0	8.0	9.0	9.2

WEIRD FANTASY
Russ Cochran/Gemstone Publ.: Oct, 1992 - No. 22, Jan, 1998 ($1.50/$2.00/$2.50)
1-22: 1,2: 1,2-r/Weird Fantasy #13,14; Feldstein-c. 3-5-r/Weird Fantasy #15-17 4.00

WEIRD HORRORS (Nightmare #10 on)
St. John Publishing Co.: June, 1952 - No. 9, Oct, 1953
1-Tuska-a 76 152 228 486 831 1175
2,3: 3-Hashish story 41 82 123 256 428 600
4,5 39 78 117 231 378 525
6-Ekgren-c; atomic bomb story 84 168 252 538 919 1300
7-Ekgren-c; Kubert, Cameron-a 84 168 252 538 919 1300
8,9-Kubert-c/a 48 96 144 302 514 725
NOTE: ***Cameron** a-7, 9. **Finesque** a-1-5. **Forgione** a-6. **Morisi** a-3. Bondage c-8.*

WEIRD MYSTERIES
Gillmor Publications: Oct, 1952 - No. 12, Sept, 1954
1-Partial Wolverton-c swiped from splash page "Flight to the Future" in Weird Tales of the Future #2; "Eternity" has an Ingels swipe 148 296 444 947 1624 2300
2- "Robot Woman" by Wolverton; Bernard Baily-c reprinted in Mister Mystery #18; acid in face panel 206 412 618 1318 2259 3200
3,6: Both have decapitation-c 107 214 321 680 1165 1650
4- "The Man Who Never Smiled" (3 pgs.) by Wolverton; Classic B. Baily skull-c
432 864 1296 3154 5577 8000
5-Wolverton story "Swamp Monster" (6 pgs.). Classic exposed brain-c
757 1514 2271 5526 9763 14,000
7-Used in **SOTI**, illo "Indeed", illo "Sex and blood" 139 278 417 883 1517 2150
8-Wolverton-c panel-r/#5; used in a '54 Readers Digest anti-comics article by T. E. Murphy entitled "For the Kiddies to Read" 81 162 243 518 884 1250
9-Excessive violence, gore & torture 74 148 222 470 810 1150
10-Silhouetted nudity panel 68 136 204 435 743 1050
11,12: 12-r/Mr. Mystery #8(2), Weird Mysteries #3 & Weird Tales of the Future #6
68 136 204 435 743 1050
NOTE: ***Baily** c-2-12. Anti-Wertham column in #5. #1-12 all have 'The Ghoul Teacher' (host).*

WEIRD MYSTERIES (Magazine)
Pastime Publications: Mar-Apr, 1959 (35¢, B&W, 68 pgs.)
1-Torres-a; E. C. swipe from Tales From the Crypt #46 by Tuska "The Ragman"
14 28 42 80 115 150

WEIRD MYSTERY TALES (See DC 100 Page Super Spectacular)

WEIRD MYSTERY TALES (See Cancelled Comic Cavalcade)
National Periodical Publications: July-Aug, 1972 - No. 24, Nov, 1975
1-Kirby-a; Wrightson splash pg. 5 10 15 33 57 80
2-Titanic-c/s 3 6 9 20 31 42
3,21: 21-Wrightson-c 3 6 9 17 26 35
4-10 3 6 9 14 19 24
11-20,22-24 2 4 6 11 16 20
NOTE: ***Alcala** a-5, 10, 13, 14. **Aparo** c-4. **Bailey** a-8. **Bolle** a-8?. **Howard** a-4. **Kaluta** a-4, 24; c-1. **G. Kane** a-10. **Kirby** a-1, 2p, 3p. **Nino** a-5, 6, 9, 13, 16, 21. **Redondo** a-9, 17. **Sparling** c-6. **Starlin** a-3?, 4. **Wood** a-23.*

WEIRD ROMANCE (Seduction of the Innocent #9)
Eclipse Comics: Feb, 1988 ($2.00, B&W)
1-Pre-code horror-r; Lou Cameron-r(2) 4.00

WEIRD SCIENCE (Formerly Saddle Romances) (Becomes Weird Science-Fantasy #23 on) (Also see EC Archives • Weird Science)
E. C. Comics: No. 12, May-June, 1950 - No. 22, Nov-Dec, 1953
12(#1) (1950)-"Lost in the Microcosm" classic-c/story by Kurtzman; "Dream of Doom" stars Gaines & E.C. artists 229 458 687 1832 2916 4000
13-Flying saucers over Washington-c/story, 2 years before supposed UFO sighting
109 218 327 872 1386 1900
14-Robot, End of the World-c/story by Feldstein 100 200 300 800 1275 1750
15-War of Worlds-c/story (1950) 89 178 267 712 1131 1550
5-Atomic explosion-c 66 132 198 528 839 1150
6-8,10 57 114 171 456 728 1000
9-Wood's 1st EC-c 71 142 213 568 909 1250
11-14 (1952) 11-Kamen bio. 12-Wood bio 44 88 132 352 564 775
15-18-Williamson/Krenkel-a in each; 15-Williamson-a. 17-Used in **POP**, pgs. 81,82. 18-Bill Gaines doll app. in story 46 92 138 368 584 800
19,20-Williamson/Frazetta-a (7 pgs. each). 19-Used in **SOTI**, illo "A young girl on her wedding night stabs her sleeping husband to death with a hatpin..." 19-Bradbury bio.
57 114 171 456 728 1000
21-Williamson/Frazetta-a (6 pgs.); Wood draws E.C. staff; Gaines & Feldstein app. in story
57 114 171 456 728 1000
22-Williamson/Frazetta/Krenkel-a (8 pgs.); Wood draws himself in his story (last pg. & panel) 57 114 171 456 728 1000

Weird Science-Fantasy #28 © WMG

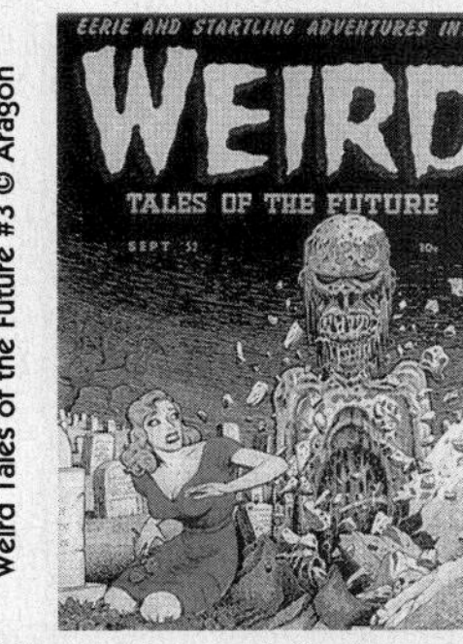

Weird Tales of the Future #3 © Aragon

Weird War Tales #28 © DC

GD 2.0 VG 4.0 FN 6.0 VF 8.0 VF/NM 9.0 NM- 9.2

NOTE: ***Elder*** *a-14, 19.* ***Evans*** *a-22.* ***Feldstein*** *a-12(#1)-8; c-12(#1)-8, 11.* ***Ingels*** *a-15.* ***Kamen*** *a-12(#1)-13, 15-18, 20, 21.* ***Kurtzman*** *a-12(#1)-7.* ***Orlando*** *a-10-22.* ***Wood*** *a-12(#1), 13(#2), 5-22 (#9, 10, 12, 13 all have 2* ***Wood*** *stories); c-9, 10, 12-22. Canadian reprints exist; see Table of Contents. Ray Bradbury adaptations in #17-22.*

WEIRD SCIENCE
Gladstone Publishing: Sept, 1990 - No. 4, Mar, 1991 ($1.95/$2.00, 68 pgs.)

1-4: Wood-c(r); all reprints in each 5.00

WEIRD SCIENCE (Also see EC Archives • Weird Science)
Russ Cochran/Gemstone Publishing: Sept, 1992 - No. 22, Dec, 1997 ($1.50/$2.00/$2.50)

1-22: 1,2: r/Weird Science #12,13 w/original-c. ,4-r/#14,15. 5-7-w/original-c 4.00

WEIRD SCIENCE-FANTASY (Formerly Weird Science & Weird Fantasy)
(Becomes Incredible Science Fiction #30)
E. C. Comics: No. 23 Mar, 1954 - No. 29, May-June, 1955 (#23,24: 15¢)

23-Williamson, Wood-a; Bradbury adaptation 41 82 123 328 527 725
24-Williamson & Wood-a; Harlan Ellison's 1st professional story, "Upheaval!", later adapted into a short story as "Mealtime", and then into a TV episode of Voyage to the Bottom of the Sea as "The Price of Doom" 41 82 123 328 527 725
25-Williamson dinosaur-c; Williamson/Torres/Krenkel-a plus Wood-a; Bradbury adaptation and fan letter; cover price back to 10¢ 47 94 141 376 601 825
26-Flying Saucer Report; Wood, Crandall-a; A-bomb panels 43 86 129 344 547 750
27-Adam Link/I Robot series begins 41 82 123 328 527 725
28-Williamson/Krenkel/Torres-a; Wood-a 42 84 126 336 536 735
29-Classic Frazetta-c; Williamson/Krenkel & Wood-a; Adam Link/I Robot series concludes; last pre-code issue; new logo 154 308 462 1232 1966 2700

NOTE: ***Crandall*** *a-26, 27, 29.* ***Evans*** *a-26.* ***Feldstein*** *c-24, 26, 28.* ***Kamen*** *a-27, 28.* ***Krigstein*** *a-23-25.* ***Orlando*** *a-in all.* ***Wood*** *a-in all; c-23, 27. The cover to #29 was originally intended for Famous Funnies #217 (Buck Rogers), but was rejected for being "too violent."*

WEIRD SCIENCE-FANTASY
Russ Cochran/Gemstone Publishing: Nov, 1992 - No. 7, May , 1994 ($1.50/$2.00/$2.50)

1-7: 1,2: r/Weird Science-Fantasy #23,24. 3-7 r/#25-29 4.00

WEIRD SCIENCE-FANTASY ANNUAL
E. C. Comics: 1952, 1953 (Sold thru the E. C. office & on the stands in some major cities) (25¢, 132 pgs.)

1952-Feldstein-c 303 606 909 1939 3320 4700
1953-Feldstein-c 171 342 513 1283 1967 2650

NOTE: *The 1952 annual contains books cover-dated in 1951 & 1952, and the 1953 annual from 1952 & 1953. Contents of each annual may vary in same year.*

WEIRD SECRET ORIGINS
DC Comics: Oct, 2004 ($5.95, square-bound, one-shot)

nn-Reprints origins of Dr. Fate, Spectre, Congorilla, Metamorpho, Animal Man & others 6.00

WEIRD SUSPENSE
Atlas/Seaboard Publ.: Feb, 1975 - No. 3, July, 1975

1-3: 1-Tarantula begins. 3-Freidrich-s 2 4 6 10 14 18

NOTE: ***Boyette*** *a-1-3.* ***Buckler*** *c-1, 3.*

WEIRD SUSPENSTORIES
Superior Comics (Canada): Oct, 1951 - No. 3, Dec, 1951; No. 3, no date (EC reprints)

1-3,3(no date)-(Rare): Reprints Crime SuspenStories #1-3, covers & contents w/Canadian ads replacing U.S. ads 950 1900 2850 - - -

NOTE: *Canada passed a law against importing crime comic books between 1949-1953, thus Crime Suspenstories became Weird Suspenstories in Canada creating a new EC title. The word "crime" was not allowed on comic books in Canada during this time.*

WEIRD TALES ILLUSTRATED
Millennium Publications: 1992 - No. 2, 1992 ($2.95, high quality paper)

1,2-Bolton painted-c. 1-Adapts E.A. Poe & Harlan Ellison stories. 2-E.A. Poe & H.P. Lovecraft adaptations 4.00
1-($4.95, 52 pgs.)-Deluxe edition w/Tim Vigil-a not in regular #1; stiff-c; Bolton painted-c 6.00

WEIRD TALES OF THE FUTURE
S.P.M. Publ. No. 1-4/Aragon Publ. No. 5-8: Mar, 1952 - No. 8, July-Aug, 1953

1-Andru-a(2); Wolverton partial-c 129 258 387 826 1413 2000
2,3-Wolverton-c/a(3) each. 2- "Jumpin Jupiter" satire by Wolverton begins, ends #5 284 568 852 1818 3109 4400
4- "Jumpin Jupiter" satire, partial Wolverton-c 158 316 474 1003 1727 2450
5-Wolverton-c/a(2); "Jumpin Jupiter" satire 284 568 852 1818 3109 4400
6-Bernard Baily-c 77 154 231 493 847 1200
7- "The Mind Movers" from the art to Wolverton's "Brain Bats of Venus" from Mr. Mystery #7 which was cut apart, pasted up, partially redrawn, and rewritten by Harry Kantor, the editor; Baily-c 174 348 522 1114 1907 2700
8-Reprints Weird Mysteries #1(10/52) minus cover; gory cover showing heart ripped out, by B. Baily 161 322 483 1030 1765 2500

WEIRD TALES OF THE MACABRE (Magazine)
Atlas/Seaboard Publ.: Jan, 1975 - No. 2, Mar, 1975 (75¢, B&W)

1-Jeff Jones painted-c; Boyette-a 4 8 12 28 47 65
2-Boris Vallejo painted-c; Severin-a 5 10 15 32 53 75

WEIRD TERROR (Also see Horrific)
Allen Hardy Associates (Comic Media): Sept, 1952 - No. 13, Sept, 1954

1- "Portrait of Death", adapted from Lovecraft's "Pickman's Model"; lingerie panels, Hitler story 71 142 213 454 777 1100
2,3: 2-Text on Marquis DeSade, Torture, Demonology, & St. Elmo's Fire. 3-Extreme violence, whipping, torture; article on sin eating, dowsing 57 114 171 362 619 875
4-Dismemberment, decapitation, article on human flesh for sale, Devil, whipping 58 116 174 371 636 900
5-Article on body snatching, mutilation; cannibalism story 53 106 159 334 567 800
6-Dismemberment, decapitation, man hit by lightning 54 108 162 343 574 825
7-Body burning in fireplace-c 58 116 174 371 636 900
8,11: 8-Decapitation story; Ambrose Bierce adapt. 11-End of the world story w/atomic blast panels; Tothish-a by Bill Discount 52 104 156 328 552 775
9,10,13: 13-Severed head panels 43 86 129 271 461 650
12-Discount-a 43 86 129 271 461 650

NOTE: ***Don Heck*** *a-most issues; c-1-13.* ***Landau*** *a-6.* ***Morisi*** *a-2-5, 7, 9, 12.* ***Palais*** *a-1, 5, 6, 8(2), 10, 12.* ***Powell*** *a-10.* ***Ravielli*** *a-11.*

WEIRD THRILLERS
Ziff-Davis Publ. Co. (Approved Comics): Sept-Oct, 1951 - No. 5, Oct-Nov, 1952 (#2-5: painted-c)

1-Rondo Hatton photo-c 107 214 321 680 1165 1650
2-Toth, Anderson, Colan-a 73 146 219 467 796 1125
3-Two Powell, Tuska-a; classic-c; Everett-a 102 204 306 648 1112 1575
4-Kubert, Tuska-a 66 132 198 419 722 1025
5-Powell-a 61 122 183 390 670 950

NOTE: ***M. Anderson*** *a-2, 3.* ***Roussos*** *a-4. #2, 3 reprinted in Nightmare #10 & 13; #4, 5 reprinted in Amazing Ghost Stories #16 & #15.*

WEIRD VAMPIRE TALES (Comic magazine)
Modern Day Periodical Pub.: V3 #1, Apr, 1979 - V5 #3, Mar, 1982 (B&W)

V3 #1 (4/79) First issue, no V1 or V2 4 8 12 25 40 55
V3 #2-4 3 6 9 19 30 40
V4 #2 (4/80), V4 #3 (7/80) (no V4 #1) 3 6 9 17 26 35
V5 #1 (1/81), V5 #2 (two issues, 4/81 & 8/81) 3 6 9 17 26 35
V5 #3 (3/82) Last issue; low print 3 6 9 21 33 45

WEIRD WAR TALES
National Periodical Publ./DC Comics: Sept-Oct, 1971 - No. 124, June, 1983 (#1-5: 52 pgs.)

1-Kubert-a in #1-4,7; c-1-7 21 42 63 147 324 500
2,3-Drucker-a: 2-Crandall-a. 3-Heath-a 10 20 30 64 132 200
4,5: 5-Toth-a; Heath-a 8 16 24 54 102 150
6,7,9,10: 6,10-Toth-a. 7-Heath-a 6 12 18 37 66 95
8-Neal Adams-c/a(i) 6 12 18 41 76 110
11-20 4 8 12 22 35 48
21-35 3 6 9 16 24 32
36-(68 pgs.)-Crandall & Kubert-r/#2; Heath-r/#3; Kubert-c 3 6 9 18 28 38
37-50: 38,39-Kubert-c 2 4 6 10 14 18
51-63: 58-Hitler-c/app. 60-Hindenburg-c/s 2 4 6 9 13 16
64-Frank Miller-a (1st DC work) 5 10 15 33 57 80
65-67,69-89,91,92: 89-Nazi Apes-c/s. 2 4 6 8 10 12
68-Frank Miller-a (2nd DC work) 3 6 9 21 33 45
90-Hitler app. 2 4 6 8 11 14
93-Intro/origin Creature Commandos 2 4 6 8 11 14
94-Return of War that Time Forgot; dinosaur-c/s 2 4 6 10 14 18
95,96,98,102-123: 98-Sphinx-c. 102-Creature Commandos battle Hitler. 110-Origin/1st app. Medusa. 123-1st app. Captain Spaceman 2 4 6 8 10 12
97,99,100,101,124: 99-War that Time Forgot. 100-Creature Commandos in War that Time Forgot. 101-Intro/origin G.I. Robot 2 4 6 8 11 14

NOTE: ***Chaykin*** *a-76, 82.* ***Ditko*** *a-95, 99, 104-106.* ***Evans*** *c-73, 74, 83, 85.* ***Kane*** *c-116, 118.* ***Kubert*** *c-55, 58, 60, 62, 72, 75-81, 87, 88, 90-96, 100, 103, 104, 106, 107.* ***Newton*** *a-122.* ***Starlin*** *c-89.* ***Sutton*** *a-91, 92, 103.* ***Creature Commandos*** *-93, 97, 100, 102, 105, 108-112, 114, 116-119, 121, 124.* ***G.I. Robot*** *- 101, 108, 111, 113, 116-118, 120, 122.* ***War That Time Forgot*** *- 94, 99, 100, 103, 106, 109, 120.*

WEIRD WAR TALES
DC Comics (Vertigo): June, 1997 - No. 4, Sept, 1997 ($2.50)

1-4-Anthology by various 3.00

Weird Western Tales #71 © DC

Weirdworld (2016 series) #1 © MAR

Wendy Parker Comics #2 © MAR

	GD 2.0	VG 4.0	FN 6.0	VF 8.0	VF/NM 9.0	NM- 9.2

WEIRD WAR TALES
DC Comics (Vertigo): April, 2000 ($4.95, one-shot)

1-Anthology by various; last Biukovic-a 5.00

WEIRD WAR TALES
DC Comics: Nov, 2010 ($3.99, one-shot)

1-Anthology by various incl. Cooke, Strnad, Pugh; Cooke-c 4.00

WEIRD WESTERN TALES (Formerly All-Star Western)
National Per. Publ./DC Comics: No. 12, June-July, 1972 - No. 70, Aug, 1980

Issue	GD	VG	FN	VF	VF/NM	NM-
12-(52 pgs.)-3rd app. Jonah Hex; Bat Lash, Pow Wow Smith reprints; El Diablo by Neal Adams/Wrightson	12	24	36	82	179	275
13-Jonah Hex-c & 4th app.; Neal Adams-a	8	16	24	56	108	160
14-Toth-a	6	12	18	41	76	110
15-Adams-c/a; no Jonah Hex	4	8	12	28	47	65
16,17,19,20	4	8	12	28	47	65
18,29: 18-1st all Jonah Hex issue (7-8/73) & begins. 29-Origin Jonah Hex; 1st full app. of Quentin Turnbull	6	12	18	37	66	95
21-28,30: Jonah Hex in all	4	8	12	23	37	50
31-38: Jonah Hex in all. 38-Last Jonah Hex	3	6	9	18	28	38
39-Origin/1st app. Scalphunter & begins	2	4	6	13	18	22
40-47,50-69: 64-Bat Lash-c/story	2	4	6	8	10	12
48,49: (44 pgs.)-1st & 2nd app. Cinnamon	2	4	6	8	11	14
70-Last issue	2	4	6	9	13	16

NOTE: *Alcala a-16, 17. Evans inks-39-48; c-39i, 40, 47. G. Kane a-15, 20. Kubert c-12, 33. Starlin c-44, 45. Wildey a-26. 48 & 49 are 44 pgs..*

WEIRD WESTERN TALES (Blackest Night crossover)
DC Comics: No. 71, March, 2010 ($2.99, one-shot)

71-Jonah Hex, Scalphunter, Super-Chief, Firehair and Bat Lash rise as Black Lanterns 3.00

WEIRD WESTERN TALES
DC Comics (Vertigo): Apr, 2001 - No. 4, Jul, 2001 ($2.50, limited series)

1-4-Anthology by various 3.00

WEIRD WONDER TALES
Marvel Comics Group: Dec, 1973 - No. 22, May, 1977

Issue	GD	VG	FN	VF	VF/NM	NM-
1-Wolverton-r/Mystic #6 (Eye of Doom)	4	8	12	24	38	55
2-10	3	6	9	17	26	35
11-22: 16-18-Venus-r by Everett from Venus #19,18 & 17. 19-22-r/Dr. Droom (re-named Dr. Druid) by Kirby. 22-New art by Byrne	3	6	9	16	23	30
15-17-(30¢-c variants, limited distribution)(4-8/76)	4	8	12	27	44	60

NOTE: *All 1950s & early 1960s reprints. Check r-1. Colan r-17. Ditko r-4, 5, 10-13, 19-21. Drucker r-12, 20. Everett r-3(Spellbound #16), 6(Astonishing #10), 9(Adv. Into Mystery #5). Heath a-13r. Heck a-1or, 14r. Gil Kane c-1, 2, 10. Kirby r-4, 6, 10, 11, 13, 15-22; c-17, 19, 20. Krigstein r-19. Kubert r-22. Maneely r-8. Mooney r-7p. Powell r-3, 7. Torres r-7. Wildey r-2, 7.*

WEIRDWORLD (Secret Wars tie-in)
Marvel Comics: Aug, 2015 - No. 5, Dec, 2015 ($3.99, limited series)

1-5-Aaron-s/Del Mundo-a; Arkon, Morgan Le Fay, and Skull the Slayer app. 4.00

WEIRDWORLD (After Secret Wars)
Marvel Comics: Feb, 2016 - No. 6, Jul, 2016 ($3.99)

1-6-Humphries-s/Del Mundo-a; Goleta the Wizardslayer & Morgan Le Fay app. 4.00

WEIRD WORLD OF JACK STAFF (See Jack Staff)
Image Comics: Feb, 2010 - No. 6, Apr, 2011 ($3.50)

1-6-Paul Grist-s/a. 2-Ian Churchill-c 3.50

WEIRD WORLDS (See Adventures Into...)

WEIRD WORLDS (Magazine)
Eerie Publications: V1#10(12/70), V2#1(2/71) - No. 4, Aug, 1971 (52 pgs.)

Issue	GD	VG	FN	VF	VF/NM	NM-
V1#10-Sci-fi/horror	5	10	15	33	57	80
V2#1-4	5	10	15	30	50	70

WEIRD WORLDS (Also see Ironwolf: Fires of the Revolution)
National Periodical Publications: Aug-Sept, 1972 - No. 9, Jan-Feb, 1974; No. 10, Oct-Nov, 1974 (All 20¢ issues)

Issue	GD	VG	FN	VF	VF/NM	NM-
1-Edgar Rice Burrough's John Carter Warlord of Mars & David Innes begin (1st DC app.); Kubert-c	3	6	9	17	26	35
2-4: 2-Infantino/Orlando-c. 3-Murphy Anderson-c. 4-Kaluta-a	2	4	6	10	14	18
5-7: .5-Kaluta-c. 7-Last John Carter.	2	4	6	8	11	14
8-10: 8-Iron Wolf begins by Chaykin (1st app.)	2	4	6	8	11	14

NOTE: *Neal Adams a-2i, 3i. John Carter by Andersonin #1-3. Chaykin c-7, 8. Kaluta a-4; c-4-6, 10. Orlando a-4i; c-2, 3, 4i. Wrightson a-2i, 4i.*

WEIRD WORLDS
DC Comics: Mar, 2011 - No. 6, Aug, 2011 ($3.99, limited series)

1-6-Short stories of Lobo, Garbage Man and Tanga; Ordway-a; Maguire-s/a; Lopresti-s/a 4.00

WELCOME BACK, KOTTER (TV) (See Limited Collectors' Edition #57 for unpublished #11)
National Periodical Publ./DC Comics: Nov, 1976 - No. 10, Mar-Apr, 1978

Issue	GD	VG	FN	VF	VF/NM	NM-
1-Sparling-a(p)	3	6	9	16	23	30
2-10: 3-Estrada-a	2	4	6	10	14	18

WELCOME SANTA (See March of Comics #63,183)

WELCOME TO HOLSOM
Gospel Publishing House: 2005 - Present (no cover price)

1-12-Craig Schutt-s/Steven Butler-a 3.00

WELCOME TO THE LITTLE SHOP OF HORRORS
Roger Corman's Cosmic Comics: May, 1995 -No. 3, July, 1995 ($2.50, limited series)

1-3 4.00

WELCOME TO TRANQUILITY
DC Comics (WildStorm): Feb, 2007 - No. 12, Jan, 2008 ($2.99)

1-12: 1-Simone-s/Googe-a; two covers by Googe and Campbell. 8-Pearson-a 3.00
...: Armageddon 1 (1/08, $2.99) Gage-s/Googe-a 3.00
...: One Foot in the Grave 1-6 (7/10 - No. 6, 2/11, $3.99) Simone-s/Domingues-a 4.00
...: One Foot in the Grave TPB (2011, $17.99) r/mini-series #1-6 18.00
... Book One TPB (2008, $19.99) r/#1-6 and variant cover gallery 20.00
... Book Two TPB (2008, $19.99) r/#7-12; sketch pages 20.00

WELLS FARGO (See Tales of...)

WENDY AND THE NEW KIDS ON THE BLOCK
Harvey Comics: Mar, 1991 - No. 3, July, 1991 ($1.25)

1-3 5.00

WENDY DIGEST
Harvey Comics: Oct, 1990 - No. 5, Mar, 1992 ($1.75, digest size)

1-5 4.00

WENDY PARKER COMICS
Atlas Comics (OMC): July, 1953 - No. 8, July, 1954

Issue	GD	VG	FN	VF	VF/NM	NM-
1	22	44	66	132	216	300
2	16	32	48	94	147	200
3-8	15	30	45	83	124	165

WENDY, THE GOOD LITTLE WITCH (TV)
Harvey Publ.: 8/60 - #82, 11/73; #83, 8/74 - #93, 4/76; #94, 9/90 - #97, 12/90

Issue	GD	VG	FN	VF	VF/NM	NM-
1-Wendy & Casper the Friendly Ghost begin	34	68	102	245	548	850
2	12	24	36	84	185	285
3-5	9	18	27	62	126	190
6-10	7	14	21	44	82	120
11-20	5	10	15	34	60	85
21-30	4	8	12	27	44	60
31-50	3	6	9	17	26	35
51-64,66-69	2	4	6	13	18	22
65 (2/71)-Wendy origin.	3	6	9	16	24	32
70-74: All 52 pg. Giants	3	6	9	16	23	30
75-93	2	4	6	9	13	16
94-97 (1990, $1.00-c): 94-Has #194 on-c						5.00

(See Casper the Friendly Ghost #20 & Harvey Hits #7, 16, 21, 23, 27, 30, 33)

WENDY THE GOOD LITTLE WITCH (2nd Series)
Harvey Comics: Apr, 1991 - No. 15, Aug, 1994 ($1.00/$1.25 #7-11/$1.50 #12-15)

1-15-Reprints Wendy & Casper stories. 12-Bunny app. 3.00

WENDY WITCH WORLD
Harvey Publications: 10/61; No. 2, 9/62 - No. 52, 12/73; No. 53, 9/74

Issue	GD	VG	FN	VF	VF/NM	NM-
1-(25¢, 68 pg. Giants begin)	12	24	36	84	185	285
2-5	7	14	21	44	82	120
6-10	5	10	15	33	57	80
11-20	4	8	12	27	44	60
21-30	3	6	9	21	33	45
31-39: 39-Last 68 pg. issue	3	6	9	16	24	32
40-45: 52 pg. issues	2	4	6	13	18	22
46-53	2	4	6	9	13	16

WEREWOLF (Super Hero) (Also see Dracula & Frankenstein)
Dell Publishing Co.: Dec, 1966 - No. 3, April, 1967

Issue	GD	VG	FN	VF	VF/NM	NM-
1-1st app.	4	8	12	23	37	50
2,3	3	6	9	16	23	30

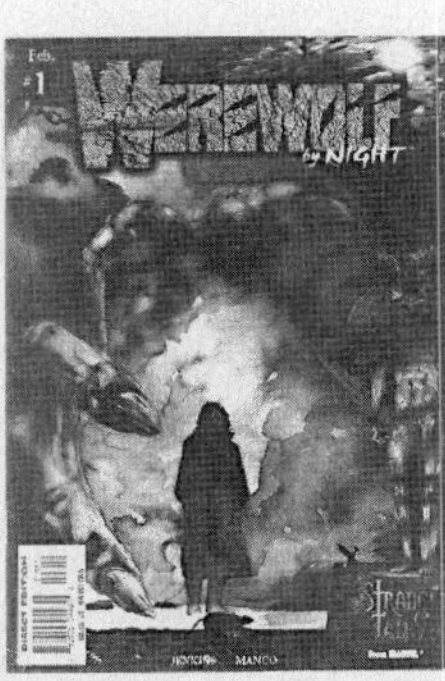

Werewolf By Night V2 #1 © MAR

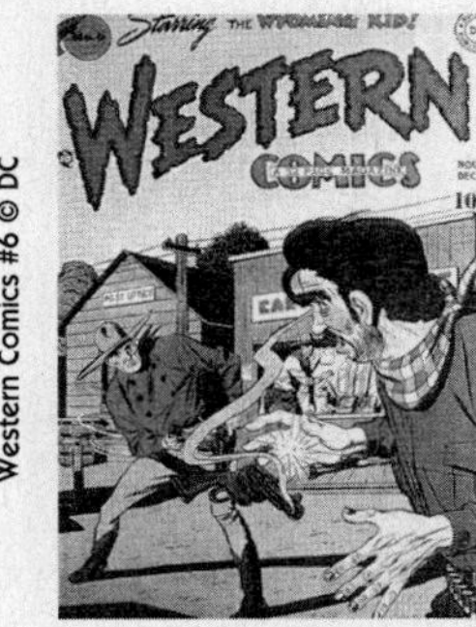

Western Comics #6 © DC

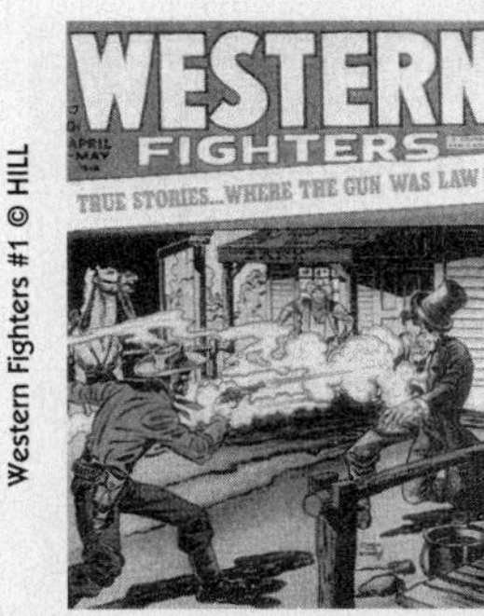

Western Fighters #1 © HILL

WEREWOLF BY NIGHT (See Giant-Size..., Marvel Spotlight #2-4 & Power Record Comics)
Marvel Comics Group: Sept, 1972 - No. 43, Mar, 1977

	GD 2.0	VG 4.0	FN 6.0	VF 8.0	VF/NM 9.0	NM- 9.2
1-Ploog-a cont'd. from Marvel Spotlight #4	12	24	36	82	179	275
2	6	12	18	40	73	105
3-5	5	10	15	31	53	75
6-10	4	8	12	25	40	55
11-14,16-20	3	6	9	18	28	38
15-New origin Werewolf; Dracula-c/story cont'd from Tomb of Dracula #18; classic Ploog-c	4	8	12	28	47	65
21-31	3	6	9	14	20	26
32-Origin & 1st app. Moon Knight (8/75)	46	92	138	359	805	1250
33-2nd app. Moon Knight	9	18	27	59	117	175
34,36,38-43	3	6	9	14	19	24
35-Starlin/Wrightson-c	3	6	9	16	23	30
37-Moon Knight app; part Wrightson-c	5	10	15	30	50	70
38,39-(30¢-c variants, limited distribution)(5,7/76)	4	8	12	27	44	60

NOTE: ***Bolle** a-6i. **G. Kane** a-11p, 12p; c-21, 22, 24-30, 34p. **Mooney** a-7i. **Ploog** 1-4p, 5, 6p, 7p, 13-16p; c-5-8, 13-16. **Reinman** a-8i. **Sutton** a(i)-9, 11, 16, 35.*

WEREWOLF BY NIGHT (Vol. 2, continues in Strange Tales #1 (9/98))
Marvel Comics Group: Feb, 1998 - No. 6, July, 1998 ($2.99)

	GD 2.0	VG 4.0	FN 6.0	VF 8.0	VF/NM 9.0	NM- 9.2
1-6-Manco-a: 2-Two covers. 6-Ghost Rider-c/app.						3.00

WEREWOLVES & VAMPIRES (Magazine)
Charlton Comics: 1962 (One Shot)

	GD 2.0	VG 4.0	FN 6.0	VF 8.0	VF/NM 9.0	NM- 9.2
1	9	18	27	58	114	170

WEREWOLVES ON THE MOON: VERSUS VAMPIRES
Dark Horse Comics: June, 2009 - No. 3 ($3.50, limited series)

	GD 2.0	VG 4.0	FN 6.0	VF 8.0	VF/NM 9.0	NM- 9.2
1,2-Dave Land-s & Fillbach Brothers-s/a						3.50

WE STAND ON GUARD
Image Comics: Jul, 2015 - No. 6, Dec, 2015 ($2.99, limited series)

	GD 2.0	VG 4.0	FN 6.0	VF 8.0	VF/NM 9.0	NM- 9.2
1-U.S. invasion of Canada; Vaughan-s/Skroce-a						5.00
2-6						3.00

WEST COAST AVENGERS
Marvel Comics Group: Sept, 1984 - No. 4, Dec, 1984 (lim. series, Mando paper)

	GD 2.0	VG 4.0	FN 6.0	VF 8.0	VF/NM 9.0	NM- 9.2
1-Origin & 1st app. W.C. Avengers (Hawkeye, Iron Man, Mockingbird & Tigra)	1	3	4	6	8	10
2-4						5.00

WEST COAST AVENGERS (Becomes Avengers West Coast #48 on)
Marvel Comics Group: Oct, 1985 - No. 47, Aug, 1989

	GD 2.0	VG 4.0	FN 6.0	VF 8.0	VF/NM 9.0	NM- 9.2
V2#1	1	2	3	5	6	8
2-41						4.00
42-47: 42-Byrne-a(p)/scripts begin. 46-Byrne-c; 1st app. Great Lakes Avengers						4.00
Annual 1-3 (1986-1988): 3-Evolutionary War app.						5.00
Annual 4 (1989, $2.00)-Atlantis Attacks; Byrne/Austin-a						5.00

WESTERN ACTION
I. W. Enterprises: No. 7, 1964

	GD 2.0	VG 4.0	FN 6.0	VF 8.0	VF/NM 9.0	NM- 9.2
7-Reprints Cow Puncher #? by Avon	2	4	6	8	11	14

WESTERN ACTION
Atlas/Seaboard Publ.: Feb, 1975

	GD 2.0	VG 4.0	FN 6.0	VF 8.0	VF/NM 9.0	NM- 9.2
1-Kid Cody by Wildey & The Comanche Kid stories; intro. The Renegade	2	4	6	11	16	20

WESTERN ACTION THRILLERS
Dell Publishers: Apr, 1937 (10¢, square binding; 100 pgs.)

	GD 2.0	VG 4.0	FN 6.0	VF 8.0	VF/NM 9.0	NM- 9.2
1-Buffalo Bill, The Texas Kid, Laramie Joe, Two-Gun Thompson, & Wild West Bill app.	129	258	387	826	1413	2000

WESTERN ADVENTURES COMICS (Western Love Trails #7 on)
Ace Magazines: Oct, 1948 - No. 6, Aug, 1949

	GD 2.0	VG 4.0	FN 6.0	VF 8.0	VF/NM 9.0	NM- 9.2
nn(#1)-Sheriff Sal, The Cross-Draw Kid, Sam Bass begin	21	42	63	126	206	285
nn(#2)(12/48)	14	28	42	76	108	140
nn(#3)(2/49)-Used in **SOTI**, pgs. 30,31	14	28	42	78	112	145
4-6	11	22	33	64	90	115

WESTERN BANDITS
Avon Periodicals: 1952 (Painted-c)

	GD 2.0	VG 4.0	FN 6.0	VF 8.0	VF/NM 9.0	NM- 9.2
1-Butch Cassidy, The Daltons by Larsen; Kinstler-a; c-part-r/paperback Avon Western Novel #1	19	38	57	111	176	240

WESTERN BANDIT TRAILS (See Approved Comics)
St. John Publishing Co.: Jan, 1949 - No. 3, July, 1949

	GD 2.0	VG 4.0	FN 6.0	VF 8.0	VF/NM 9.0	NM- 9.2
1-Tuska-a; Baker-c; Blue Monk, Ventrilo app.	34	68	102	199	325	450
2-Baker-c	28	56	84	165	270	375
3-Baker-c/a; Tuska-a	32	64	96	188	307	425

WESTERN COMICS (See Super DC Giant #15)
National Per. Publ: Jan-Feb, 1948 - No. 85, Jan-Feb, 1961 (1-27: 52pgs.)

	GD 2.0	VG 4.0	FN 6.0	VF 8.0	VF/NM 9.0	NM- 9.2
1-Wyoming Kid & his horse Racer, The Vigilante in "Jesse James Rides Again" (Meskin-a), Cowboy Marshal, Rodeo Rick begin	76	152	228	486	831	1175
2	36	72	108	211	343	475
3,4-Last Vigilante	32	64	96	188	307	425
5-Nighthawk & his horse Nightwind begin (not in #6); Captain Tootsie by Beck	27	54	81	158	259	360
6,7,9,10	21	42	63	122	199	275
8-Origin Wyoming Kid; 2 pg. pin-ups of rodeo queens	34	68	102	199	325	450
11-20	18	36	54	103	162	220
21-40: 24-Starr-a. 27-Last 52 pgs. 28-Flag-c	14	28	42	82	121	160
41,42,44-49: 49-Last precode issue (2/55)	14	28	42	80	115	150
43-Pow Wow Smith begins, ends #85	14	28	42	81	118	155
50-60	12	24	36	67	94	120
61-85-Last Wyoming Kid. 77-Origin Matt Savage Trail Boss. 82-1st app. Fleetfoot, Pow Wow's girlfriend	10	20	30	56	76	95

NOTE: ***G. Kane, Infantino** art in most. **Meskin** a-1-4. **Moreira** a-28-39. **Post** a-3-5.*

WESTERN CRIME BUSTERS
Trojan Magazines: Sept, 1950 - No. 10, Mar-Apr, 1952

	GD 2.0	VG 4.0	FN 6.0	VF 8.0	VF/NM 9.0	NM- 9.2
1-Six-Gun Smith, Wilma West, K-Bar-Kate, & Fighting Bob Dale begin; headlight-a	36	72	108	216	351	485
2	19	38	57	111	176	240
3-5: 3-Myron Fass-c	18	36	54	105	165	225
6-Wood-a	32	64	96	188	307	425
7-Six-Gun Smith by Wood	32	64	96	188	307	425
8	18	36	54	105	165	225
9-Tex Gordon & Wilma West by Wood; Lariat Lucy app.	32	64	96	188	307	425
10-Wood-a	29	58	87	172	281	390

WESTERN CRIME CASES (Formerly Indian Warriors #7,8; becomes The Outlaws #10 on)
Star Publications: No. 9, Dec, 1951

	GD 2.0	VG 4.0	FN 6.0	VF 8.0	VF/NM 9.0	NM- 9.2
9-White Rider & Super Horse; L. B. Cole-c	21	42	63	126	206	285

WESTERNER, THE (Wild Bill Pecos)
"Wanted" Comic Group/Toytown/Patches: No. 14, June, 1948 - No. 41, Dec, 1951 (#14-31: 52 pgs.)

	GD 2.0	VG 4.0	FN 6.0	VF 8.0	VF/NM 9.0	NM- 9.2
14	15	30	45	85	130	175
15-17,19-21: 19-Meskin-a	9	18	27	52	69	85
18,22-25-Krigstein-a	11	22	33	60	83	105
26(4/50)-Origin & 1st app. Calamity Kate, series ends #32; Krigstein-a	14	28	42	78	112	145
27-Krigstein-a(2)	13	26	39	74	105	135
28-41: 33-Quest app. 37-Lobo, the Wolf Boy begins	8	16	24	40	50	60

NOTE: ***Mort Lawrence** a-20-27, 29, 37, 39; c-19, 22-24, 26, 27. **Leav** c-14-18, 20, 31. **Syd Shores** a-39; c-34, 35, 37-41.*

WESTERNER, THE
Super Comics: 1964

	GD 2.0	VG 4.0	FN 6.0	VF 8.0	VF/NM 9.0	NM- 9.2
Super Reprint 15-17: 15-r/Oklahoma Kid #? 16-r/Crack West. #65; Severin-c; Crandall-r. 17-r/Blazing Western #2; Severin-c	2	4	6	8	11	14

WESTERN FIGHTERS
Hillman Periodicals/Star Publ.: Apr-May, 1948 - V4#7, Mar-Apr, 1953 (#1-V3#2: 52 pgs.)

	GD 2.0	VG 4.0	FN 6.0	VF 8.0	VF/NM 9.0	NM- 9.2
V1#1-Simon & Kirby-c	37	74	111	222	361	500
2-Not Kirby-a	14	28	42	82	121	160
3-Fuje-c	13	26	39	72	101	130
4-Krigstein, Ingels, Fuje-a	14	28	42	78	112	145
5,6,8,9,12	10	20	30	58	79	100
7,10-Krigstein-a	12	24	36	67	94	120
11-Williamson/Frazetta-a	31	62	93	182	296	410
V2#1-Krigstein-a	12	24	36	67	94	120
2-12: 4-Berg-a	9	18	27	47	61	75
V3#1-11,V4#1,4-7	8	16	24	44	57	70
12,V4#2,3-Krigstein-a	12	24	36	67	94	120
3-D 1(12/53, 25¢, Star Publ.)-Came w/glasses; L. B. Cole-c	36	72	108	216	351	485

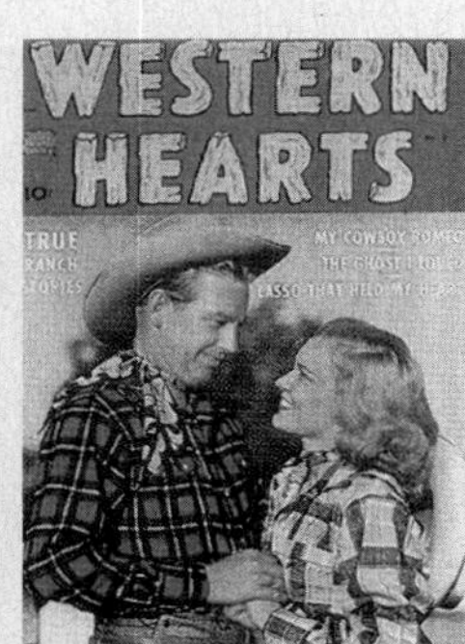

Western Hearts #3 © STD

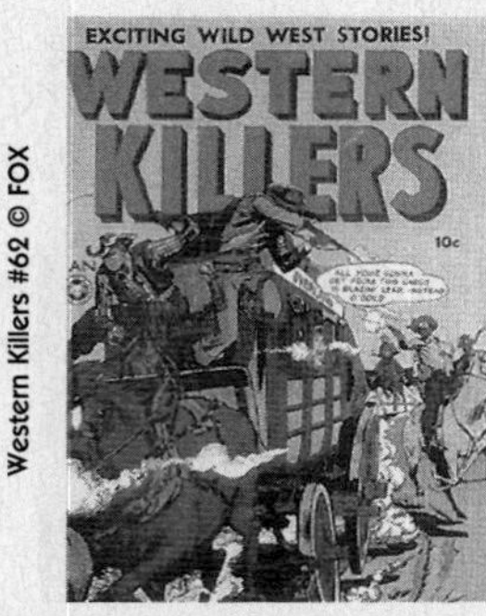

Western Killers #62 © FOX

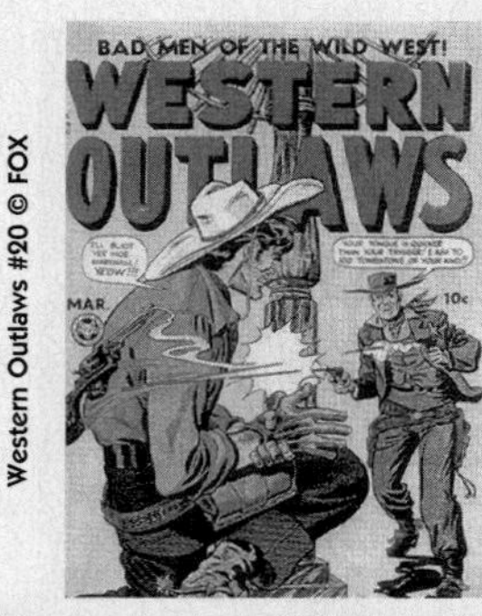

Western Outlaws #20 © FOX

NOTE: **Kinstlerish** a-V2#6, 8, 9, 12; V3#2, 5-7, 11, 12; V4#1(plus cover). **McWilliams** a-11. **Powell** a-V2#2. **Reinman** a-1-12, V4#3. **Rowich** c-5, 6i. **Starr** a-5.

WESTERN FRONTIER
P. L. Publishers: Apr-May, 1951 - No. 7, 1952

	GD 2.0	VG 4.0	FN 6.0	VF 8.0	VF/NM 9.0	NM- 9.2
1	15	30	45	84	127	170
2	9	18	27	52	69	85
3-7	8	16	24	44	57	70

WESTERN GUNFIGHTERS (1st Series) (Apache Kid #11-19)
Atlas Comics (CPS): No. 20, June, 1956 - No. 27, Aug, 1957

	GD 2.0	VG 4.0	FN 6.0	VF 8.0	VF/NM 9.0	NM- 9.2
20	15	30	45	90	140	190
21-Crandall-a	15	30	45	90	140	190
22-Wood & Powell-a	21	42	63	122	199	275
23,24: 23-Williamson-a. 24-Toth-a	15	30	45	90	140	190
25-27	13	26	39	74	105	135

NOTE: **Berg** a-20. **Colan** a-20, 26, 27. **Crandall** a-21. **Heath** a-25. **Maneely** a-24, 25; c-22, 23, 25. **Morisi** a-24. **Morrow** a-26. **Pakula** a-23. **Severin** c-20, 27. **Torres** a-26. **Woodbridge** a-27.

WESTERN GUNFIGHTERS (2nd Series)
Marvel Comics Group: Aug, 1970 - No. 33, Nov, 1975 (#1-6: 25¢, 68 pgs.)

	GD 2.0	VG 4.0	FN 6.0	VF 8.0	VF/NM 9.0	NM- 9.2
1-Ghost Rider begins; Fort Rango, Renegades & Gunhawk app.	6	12	18	38	69	100
2,3,5,6: 2-Origin Nightwind (Apache Kid's horse)	3	6	9	21	33	45
4-Barry Smith-a	4	8	12	23	37	50
7-(52 pgs) Origin Ghost Rider retold	3	6	9	19	30	40
8-13: 10-Origin Black Rider. 12-Origin Matt Slade	3	6	9	14	20	25
14-Steranko-c	3	6	9	16	24	32
15-20	2	4	6	10	14	18
21-33	2	4	6	9	13	16

NOTE: **Baker** r-2, 3. **Colan** r-2. **Drucker** r-3. **Everett** a-6i. **G. Kane** c-29, 31. **Kirby** a-1p(r), 5, 10-12; c-19, 21. **Kubert** r-2. **Maneely** r-2, 10. **Morrow** r-29. **Severin** c-10. **Shores** a-3, 4. **Barry Smith** a-4. **Steranko** c-14. **Sutton** a-1, 2i, 5, 4. **Torres** r-26('57). **Wildey** r-8, 9. **Williamson** r-2, 18. **Woodbridge** r-27('57). Renegades in #4, 5; Ghost Rider in #1-7.

WESTERN HEARTS
Standard Comics: Dec, 1949 - No. 10, Mar, 1952 (All photo-c)

	GD 2.0	VG 4.0	FN 6.0	VF 8.0	VF/NM 9.0	NM- 9.2
1-Severin-a; Whip Wilson & Reno Browne photo-c	23	46	69	136	223	310
2-Beverly Tyler & Jerome Courtland photo-c from movie "Palomino"; Williamson/Frazetta-a (2 pgs.)	23	46	69	136	223	310
3-Rex Allen photo-c	14	28	42	80	115	150
4-7,10: 4-Severin & Elder, Al Carreno-a. 5-Ray Milland & Hedy Lamarr photo-c from movie "Copper Canyon". 6-Fred MacMurray & Irene Dunn photo-c from movie "Never a Dull Moment". 7-Jock Mahoney photo-c. 10-Bill Williams & Jane Nigh photo-c	14	28	42	78	112	145
8-Randolph Scott & Janis Carter photo-c from "Santa Fe"; Severin & Elder-a	14	28	42	80	115	150
9-Whip Wilson & Reno Browne photo-c; Severin & Elder-a	15	30	45	83	124	165

WESTERN HERO (Wow Comics #1-69; Real Western Hero #70-75)
Fawcett Publications: No. 76, Mar, 1949 - No. 112, Mar, 1952

	GD 2.0	VG 4.0	FN 6.0	VF 8.0	VF/NM 9.0	NM- 9.2
76(#1, 52 pgs.)-Tom Mix, Hopalong Cassidy, Monte Hale, Gabby Hayes, Young Falcon (ends #78,80), & Big Bow and Little Arrow (ends #102,105) begin; painted-c begin	16	32	48	94	147	200
77 (52 pgs.)	11	22	33	64	90	115
78,80-82 (52 pgs.): 81-Capt. Tootsie by Beck	11	22	33	60	83	105
79,83 (36 pgs.): 83-Last painted-c	10	20	30	54	72	90
84-86,88-90 (52 pgs.): 84-Photo-c begin, end #112. 86-Last Hopalong Cassidy	10	20	30	53	76	95
87,91,95,99 (36 pgs.): 87-Bill Boyd begins, ends #95	9	18	27	50	65	80
92-94,96-98,101 (52 pgs.): 96-Tex Ritter begins. 101-Red Eagle app.	9	18	27	52	69	85
100 (52 pgs.)	10	20	30	56	76	95
102-111: 102-Begin 36 pg. issues	9	18	27	50	65	80
112-Last issue	9	18	27	52	69	85

NOTE: 1/2 to 1 pg. Rocky Lane (Carnation) in 80-83, 86, 88, 97. Photo covers feature Hopalong Cassidy #84, 86, 89; Tom Mix #85, 87, 90, 92, 94, 97; Monte Hale #88, 91, 93, 95, 98, 100, 104, 107, 110; Tex Ritter #96, 99, 101, 105, 108, 111; Gabby Hayes #103.

WESTERN KID (1st Series)
Atlas Comics (CPC): Dec, 1954 - No. 17, Aug, 1957

	GD 2.0	VG 4.0	FN 6.0	VF 8.0	VF/NM 9.0	NM- 9.2
1-Origin; The Western Kid (Tex Dawson), his stallion Whirlwind & dog Lightning begin	22	44	66	132	216	300
2 (2/55)-Last pre-code	14	28	42	80	115	150
3-8	12	24	36	69	97	125
9,10-Williamson-a in both (4 pgs. each)	13	26	39	72	101	130
11-17	11	22	33	60	83	105

NOTE: **Ayers** a-6, 7. **Heck** a-3. **Maneely** c-2-7, 10, 13-15. **Romita** a-1-17; c-1, 12. **Severin** c-11, 16, 17.

WESTERN KID, THE (2nd Series)
Marvel Comics Group: Dec, 1971 - No. 5, Aug, 1972 (All 20¢ issues)

	GD 2.0	VG 4.0	FN 6.0	VF 8.0	VF/NM 9.0	NM- 9.2
1-Reprints; Romita-c/a(3)	3	6	9	17	26	35
2,4,5: 2-Romita-a; Severin-c. 4-Everett-r	2	4	6	13	18	22
3-Williamson-a	3	6	9	14	20	26

WESTERN KILLERS
Fox Features Syndicate: nn, July?, 1948; No. 60, Sept, 1948 - No. 64, May, 1949; No. 6, July, 1949

	GD 2.0	VG 4.0	FN 6.0	VF 8.0	VF/NM 9.0	NM- 9.2
nn(#59?)(nd, F&J Trading Co.)-Range Busters; formerly Blue Beetle #57?	24	48	72	142	234	335
60 (#1, 9/48)-Extreme violence; lingerie panel	27	54	81	158	259	360
61-Jack Cole, Starr-a	21	42	63	126	206	285
62-64, 6 (#6-exist?)	20	40	60	114	182	250

WESTERN LIFE ROMANCES (My Friend Irma #3 on?)
Marvel Comics (IPP): Dec, 1949 - No. 2, Mar, 1950 (52 pgs.)

	GD 2.0	VG 4.0	FN 6.0	VF 8.0	VF/NM 9.0	NM- 9.2
1-Whip Wilson & Reno Browne photo-c	20	40	60	117	189	260
2-Audie Murphy & Gale Storm photo-c	17	34	51	98	154	210

WESTERN LOVE
Prize Publ.: July-Aug, 1949 - No. 5, Mar-Apr, 1950 (All photo-c & 52 pgs.)

	GD 2.0	VG 4.0	FN 6.0	VF 8.0	VF/NM 9.0	NM- 9.2
1-S&K-a; Randolph Scott photo-c from movie "Canadian Pacific" (see Prize Comics #76)	32	64	96	188	307	425
2,5-S&K-a: 2-Whip Wilson & Reno Browne photo-c. 5-Dale Robertson photo-c	24	48	72	142	234	325
3,4: 3-Pat Williams photo-c	15	30	45	88	137	185

NOTE: **Meskin & Severin/Elder** a-2-5.

WESTERN LOVE TRAILS (Formerly Western Adventures)
Ace Magazines (A. A. Wyn): No. 7, Nov, 1949 - No. 9, Mar, 1950

	GD 2.0	VG 4.0	FN 6.0	VF 8.0	VF/NM 9.0	NM- 9.2
7	12	24	36	67	94	120
8,9	10	20	30	54	72	90

WESTERN MARSHAL (See Steve Donovan…)
Dell Publishing Co.: No. 534, 2-4/54 - No. 640, 7/55 (Based on Ernest Haycox's "Trailtown")

	GD 2.0	VG 4.0	FN 6.0	VF 8.0	VF/NM 9.0	NM- 9.2
Four Color 534 (#1)-Kinstler-a	6	12	18	38	69	100
Four Color 591 (10/54), 613 (2/55), 640-All Kinstler-a	5	10	15	34	60	85

WESTERN OUTLAWS (Junior Comics #9-16; My Secret Life #22 on)
Fox Features Syndicate: No. 17, Sept, 1948 - No. 21, May, 1949

	GD 2.0	VG 4.0	FN 6.0	VF 8.0	VF/NM 9.0	NM- 9.2
17-Kamen-a; Iger shop-a in all; 1 pg. "Death and the Devil Pills" r-in Ghostly Weird #122	34	68	102	199	325	450
18-21	20	40	60	114	182	250

WESTERN OUTLAWS
Atlas Comics (ACI No. 1-14/WPI No. 15-21): Feb, 1954 - No. 21, Aug, 1957

	GD 2.0	VG 4.0	FN 6.0	VF 8.0	VF/NM 9.0	NM- 9.2
1-Heath, Powell-a; Maneely hanging-c	27	54	81	162	266	370
2	15	30	45	84	127	170
3-10: 7-Violent-a by R.Q. Sale	13	26	39	72	101	130
11,14-Williamson-a in both (6 pgs. each)	14	28	42	78	112	145
12,18,20,21: Severin covers	12	24	36	67	94	120
13,15: 13-Baker-a. 15-Torres-a	13	26	39	72	101	130
16-Williamson text illo	12	24	36	67	94	120
17,19-Crandall-a. 17-Williamson text illo	13	26	39	72	101	130

NOTE: **Ayers** a-7, 10, 18, 20. **Bolle** a-21. **Colan** a-5, 10, 11, 17. **Drucker** a-11. **Everett** a-9, 10. **Heath** a-1; c-3, 4, 8, 16. **Kubert** a-9p. **Maneely** a-13, 16, 17, 19; c-1, 5, 7, 9, 10, 12, 13. **Morisi** a-18. **Powell** a-3, 16. **Romita** a-7, 13. **Severin** a-8, 16, 19; c-17, 18, 20, 21. **Tuska** a-6, 15.

WESTERN OUTLAWS & SHERIFFS (Formerly Best Western)
Marvel/Atlas Comics (IPC): No. 60, Dec, 1949 - No. 73, June, 1952

	GD 2.0	VG 4.0	FN 6.0	VF 8.0	VF/NM 9.0	NM- 9.2
60 (52 pgs.) Photo-c	24	48	72	144	237	330
61-65: 61-Photo-c	19	38	57	111	176	240
66-Story contains 5 hangings	20	40	60	114	182	250
67-Cannibalism story	20	40	60	114	182	250
68-72	15	30	45	85	130	175
73-Black Rider story; Everett-c	17	34	51	98	154	210

NOTE: **Maneely** a-62, 67; c-62, 69-73. **Robinson** a-68. **Sinnott** a-70. **Tuska** a-69-71.

WESTERN PICTURE STORIES (1st Western comic)
Comics Magazine Company: Feb, 1937 - No. 4, June, 1937

	GD 2.0	VG 4.0	FN 6.0	VF 8.0	VF/NM 9.0	NM- 9.2
1-Will Eisner-a	239	478	717	1530	2615	3700
2-Will Eisner-a	123	246	369	787	1344	1900
3,4: 3-Eisner-a. 4-Caveman Cowboy story	103	206	309	659	1130	1600

WESTERN PICTURE STORIES (See Giant Comics Edition #6, 11)

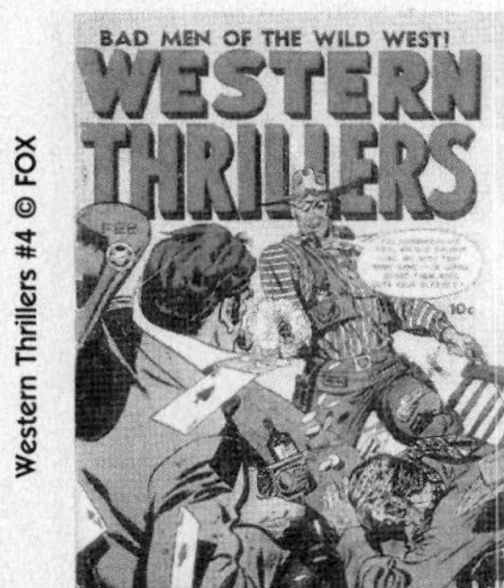

Western Thrillers #4 © FOX

Wetworks #42 © WSP

What If? #24 © MAR

GD VG FN VF VF/NM NM-
2.0 4.0 6.0 8.0 9.0 9.2

GD VG FN VF VF/NM NM-
2.0 4.0 6.0 8.0 9.0 9.2

WESTERN ROMANCES (See Target...)

WESTERN ROUGH RIDERS
Gillmor Magazines No. 1,4 (Stanmor Publ.): Nov, 1954 - No. 4, May, 1955

1 10 20 30 56 76 95
2-4 8 16 24 40 50 60

WESTERN ROUNDUP (See Dell Giants & Fox Giants)

WESTERN SERENADE
DC Comics: May/June, 1949

nn - Ashcan comic, not distributed to newsstands, only for in-house use (no known sales)

WESTERN TALES (Formerly Witches...)
Harvey Publications: No. 31, Oct, 1955 - No. 33, July-Sept, 1956

31,32-All S&K-a; Davy Crockett app. in each 15 30 45 86 133 180
33-S&K-a; Jim Bowie app. 15 30 45 84 127 170
NOTE: *#32 & 33 contain Boy's Ranch reprints. **Kirby** c-31.*

WESTERN TALES OF BLACK RIDER (Formerly Black Rider; Gunsmoke Western #32 on)
Atlas Comics (CPS): No. 28, May, 1955 - No. 31, Nov, 1955

28 (#1): The Spider (a villain) dies 22 44 66 132 216 300
29-31 16 32 48 94 147 200
NOTE: ***Lawrence** a-30. **Maneely** c-28-30. **Severin** a-28. **Shores** c-31.*

WESTERN TEAM-UP
Marvel Comics Group: Nov, 1973 (20¢)

1-Origin & 1st app. The Dakota Kid; Rawhide Kid-r; Gunsmoke Kid-r by Jack Davis
3 6 9 21 33 45

WESTERN THRILLERS (My Past Confessions #7 on)
Fox Features Syndicate/M.S. Distr. No. 52: Aug, 1948 - No. 6, June, 1949; No. 52, 1954?

1- "Velvet Rose" (Kamenish-a); "Two-Gun Sal", "Striker Sisters" (all women outlaws issue); Brodsky-c 58 116 174 371 636 900
2 26 52 78 154 252 350
3-6: 4,5-Bakerish-a; 5-Butch Cassidy app. 21 42 63 122 199 275
52-(Reprint, M.S. Dist.)-1954? No date given (becomes My Love Secret #53)
10 20 30 54 72 90

WESTERN THRILLERS (Cowboy Action #5 on)
Atlas Comics (ACI): Nov, 1954 - No. 4, Feb, 1955 (All-r/Western Outlaws & Sheriffs)

1 19 38 57 111 176 240
2-4 12 24 36 67 94 120
NOTE: ***Heath** c-3. **Maneely** a-1; c-2. **Powell** a-4. **Robinson** a-4. **Romita** c-4. **Tuska** a-2.*

WESTERN TRAILS (Ringo Kid Starring in...)
Atlas Comics (SAI): May, 1957 - No. 2, July, 1957

1-Ringo Kid app.; Severin-c 15 30 45 88 137 185
2-Severin-c 11 22 33 60 83 105
NOTE: ***Bolle** a-1, 2. **Maneely** a-1, 2. **Severin** c-1, 2.*

WESTERN TRUE CRIME (Becomes My Confessions)
Fox Features Syndicate: No. 15, Aug, 1948 - No. 6, June, 1949

15(#1)-Kamen-a; formerly Zoot #14 (5/48)? 32 64 96 188 307 425
16(#2)-Kamenish-a; headlight panels, violence 23 46 69 136 223 310
3-Kamen-a 25 50 75 147 241 335
4-6: 4-Johnny Craig-a 15 30 45 90 140 190

WESTERN WINNERS (Formerly All-Western Winners; becomes Black Rider #8 on & Romance Tales #7 on?)
Marvel Comics (CDS): No. 5, June, 1949 - No. 7, Dec, 1949

5-Two-Gun Kid, Kid Colt, Black Rider; Shores-c 32 64 96 192 314 435
6-Two-Gun Kid, Black Rider, Heath Kid Colt story; Captain Tootsie by C.C. Beck
27 54 81 158 259 360
7-Randolph Scott Photo-c w/true stories about the West
27 54 81 158 259 360

WEST OF THE PECOS (See Zane Grey, 4-Color #222)

WESTWARD HO, THE WAGONS (Disney)(Also see Classic Comics #14)
Dell Publishing Co.: No. 738, Sept, 1956 (Movie)

Four Color 738-Fess Parker photo-c 8 16 24 54 102 150

WE3
DC Comics (Vertigo): Oct, 2004 - No. 3, May, 2005 ($2.95, limited series)

1-3-Domestic animal cyborgs: Grant Morrison-s/Frank Quitely-a 3.00
TPB (2005, $12.99) r/series 13.00

WETWORKS (See WildC.A.T.S: Covert Action Teams #2)
Image Comics (WildStorm): June, 1994 - No. 43, Aug, 1998 ($1.95/$2.50)

1-"July" on-c; gatefold wraparound-c; Portacio/Williams-c/a 4.00
1-Chicago Comicon edition 6.00
1-(2/98, $4.95) "3-D Edition" w/glasses 5.00
2-4 3.00
2-Alternate Portacio-c, see Deathblow #5 6.00
5-7,9-24: 5-($2.50). 13-Portacio-c. 16,17-Fire From Heaven Pts. 4 & 11 3.00
8 ($1.95)-Newstand, Wildstorm Rising Pt. 7 3.00
8 ($2.50)-Direct Market, Wildstorm Rising Pt. 7 3.00
25-($3.95) 4.00
26-43: 32-Variant-c by Pat Lee & Charest. 39,40-Stormwatch app. 42-Gen 13 app. 3.00
Sourcebook 1 (10/94, $2.50)-Text & illustrations (no comics) 3.00
Voyager Pack (8/97, $3.50)- #32 w/Phantom Guard preview 4.00

WETWORKS
DC Comics (WildStorm): Nov, 2006 - No. 15, Jan, 2008 ($2.99)

1-15: 1-Carey-s/Portacio-a; two covers by Portacio and Van Sciver. 2-Golden var-c 3-Pearson var-c. 4-Powell var-c 3.00
...: Armageddon 1 (1/08, $2.99) Gage-s/Badeaux-a 3.00
... Book One (2007, $14.99) r/#1-5 and stories from Eye of the storm Annual and Coup D'Etat Afterword 15.00
... Book Two (2008, $14.99) r/#6-9,13-15 15.00
...: Mutations 1 (11/10, $3.99) Grevioux & Long-s/Gopez-a 4.00

WETWORKS/VAMPIRELLA (See Vampirella/Wetworks)
Image Comics (WildStorm Productions): July, 1997 ($2.95, one-shot)

1-Gil Kane-c 4.00

WHACK (Satire)
St. John Publishing Co. (Jubilee Publ.): Oct, 1953 - No. 3, May, 1954

1-(3-D, 25¢)-Kubert-a; Maurer-c; came w/glasses 24 48 72 142 234 325
2,3-Kubert-a in each. 2-Bing Crosby on-c; Mighty Mouse & Steve Canyon parodies. 3-Li'l Orphan Annie parody; Maurer-c 15 30 45 84 127 170

WHACKY (See Wacky)

WHA...HUH?
Marvel Comics: 2005 ($3.99, one-shot)

1-Humor spoofs of Marvel characters; Mahfood-a/c; Bendis, Stan Lee and others-s 4.00

WHAM COMICS (See Super Spy)
Centaur Publications: Nov, 1940 - No. 2, Dec, 1940

1-The Sparkler, The Phantom Rider, Craig Carter and his Magic Ring, Detecto, Copper Slug, Speed Silvers by Gustavson, Speed Centaur & Jon Linton (s/f) begin
194 388 582 1242 2121 3000
2-Origin Blue Fire & Solarman; The Buzzard app. 148 296 444 947 1624 2300

WHAM-O GIANT COMICS
Wham-O Mfg. Co. : April, 1967 (98¢, newspaper size, one-shot)(Six issue subscription was advertised)

1-Radian & Goody Bumpkin by Wood; 1 pg. Stanley-a; Fine, Tufts-a; flying saucer reports; wraparound-c 9 18 27 62 126 190

WHATEVER HAPPENED TO BARON VON SHOCK?
Image Comics: May, 2010 - Present ($3.99)

1-4-Rob Zombie-s/Donny Hadiwidjaja-a 4.00

WHAT IF? (1st Series) (What If? Featuring... #13 & #?-33) (Also see Hero Initiative)
Marvel Comics Group: Feb, 1977 - No. 47, Oct, 1984; June, 1988 (All 52 pgs.)

1-Brief origin Spider-Man, Fantastic Four 4 8 12 25 40 55
2-Origin The Hulk retold 2 4 6 10 14 18
3-5: 3-Avengers. 4-Invaders. 5-Capt. America 2 4 6 8 11 14
6-9,13,17: 7-Betty Brant as Spider-Girl. 8-Daredevil; Spidey parody. 9-Origins Venus, Marvel Boy, Human Robot, 3-D Man. 13-Conan app.; John Buscema-c/a(p). 17-Ghost Rider & Son of Satan app. 2 3 4 6 8 10
10-(8/78) What if Jane Foster was Thor 4 8 12 28 47 65
11,12,14-16: 11-Marvel Bullpen as F.F. 1 2 3 5 6 8
18-26,29: 18-Dr. Strange. 19-Spider-Man. 22-Origin Dr. Doom retold
1 2 3 4 5 7
27-X-Men app.; Miller-c 3 6 9 14 20 26
28-Daredevil by Miller; Ghost Rider app. 2 4 6 10 16 20
30-"What If...Spider-Man's Clone Had Lived?" 2 4 6 8 10 12
31-Begin $1.00-c; featuring Wolverine & the Hulk; X-Men app.; death of Hulk, Wolverine & Magneto 3 6 9 16 23 30
32-34,36-47: 32,36-Byrne-a. 34-Marvel crew each draw themselves. 37-Old X-Men & Silver Surfer app. 39-Thor battles Conan 5.00
35-What if Elektra had lived?; Miller/Austin-a. 2 4 6 8 10 12
Special 1 ($1.50, 6/88)-Iron Man, F.F., Thor app. 5.00

What If...? #85 © MAR

What If... Karen Page Had Lived? #1 © MAR

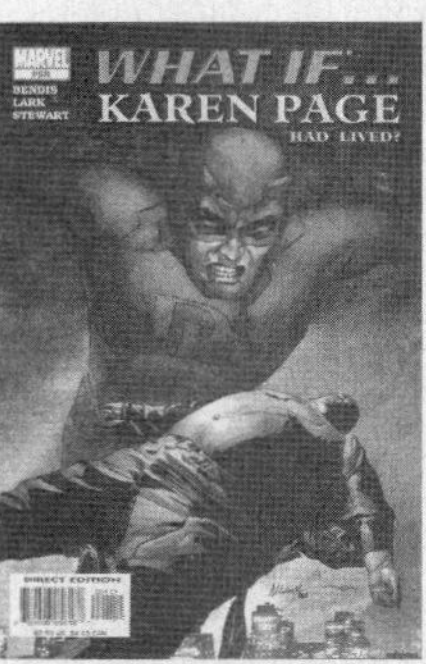

What The--?! #7 © MAR

GD 2.0 | VG 4.0 | FN 6.0 | VF 8.0 | VF/NM 9.0 | NM- 9.2

... Classic Vol. 1 TPB (2004, $24.99) r/#1-6; checklist 25.00
... Classic Vol. 2 TPB (2005, $24.99) r/#7-12 25.00
... Classic Vol. 3 TPB (2006, $24.99) r/#14,15,17-20 25.00
... Classic Vol. 4 TPB (2007, $24.99) r/#21-26; checklist of all What If? series/issues 25.00

NOTE: ***Austin*** *a-27p, 32i, 34, 35i; c-35i, 36i.* ***J. Buscema*** *a-13p, 15p; c-10, 13p, 23p.* ***Byrne*** *a-32i, 36; c-36p.* ***Colan*** *a-21p; c-17p, 18p, 21p.* ***Ditko*** *a-35, Special 1.* ***Golden*** *c-29, 40-42.* ***Guice*** *a-40p.* ***Gil Kane*** *a-3p, 24p; c(p)-2-4, 7, 8.* ***Kirby*** *a-11p; c-9p, 11p.* ***Layton*** *a-32i, 33i; c-30, 32p, 33i, 34.* ***Mignola*** *c-39i.* ***Miller*** *a-28p, 32i, 34(1), 35p; c-27, 28p.* ***Mooney*** *a-8i, 30i.* ***Perez*** *a-15p.* ***Robbins*** *a-4p.* ***Sienkiewicz*** *c-43-46.* ***Simonson*** *a-15p, 32i.* ***Starlin*** *a-32i.* ***Stevens*** *a-8, 16i(part).* ***Sutton*** *a-2i, 18p, 28.* ***Tuska*** *a-5p.* ***Weiss*** *a-37p.*

WHAT IF...? (2nd Series)
Marvel Comics: V2#1, July, 1989 - No. 114, Nov, 1998 ($1.25/$1.50)

V2#1-...The Avengers Had Lost the Evolutionary War 5.00
2-5: 2-Daredevil, Punisher app. 4.00
6-X-Men app. 5.00
7-Wolverine app.; Liefeld-c/a(1st on Wolvie?) 6.00
8,10,11,13-15,17-30: 10-Punisher app. 11-Fantastic Four app.; McFarlane-c(i).13-Prof. X; Jim Lee-c. 14-Capt. Marvel; Lim/Austin-c.15-F.F.; Capullo-c/a(p). 17-Spider-Man/Kraven. 18-F.F. 19-Vision. 20,21-Spider-Man. 22-Silver Surfer by Lim/Austin-c/a 23-X-Men. 24-Wolverine; Punisher app. 25-(52 pgs.)-Wolverine app. 26-Punisher app. 27-Namor/F.F. 28,29-Capt. America. 29-Swipes cover to Avengers #4. 30-(52 pgs.)-F.F. 4.00
9,12-X-Men 5.00
16-Wolverine battles Conan; Red Sonja app.; X-Men cameo 5.00
31-40,42-48: 31-Cosmic Spider-Man & Venom app.; Hobgoblin cameo. 32,33-Phoenix; X-Men app. 35-Fantastic Five (w/Spidey). 36-Avengers vs. Guardians of the Galaxy. 37-Wolverine; Thibert-c(i). 38-Thor; Rogers-p(part). 40-Storm; X-Men app. 42-Spider-Man. 43-Wolverine. 44-Venom/Punisher. 45-Ghost Rider. 46-Cable. 47-Magneto 3.00
41,50: 41-(52 pgs.)-Avengers vs. Galactus. 50-(52 pgs.)-Foil embossed-c; "What If Hulk Had Killed Wolverine" 1 2 3 5 6 8
49-Infinity Gauntlet w/Silver Surfer & Thanos 3 6 9 16 23 30
51-(7/93) "What If the Punisher Became Captain America" (see it happen in 2007's Punisher War Journal #6-10) 6.00
52-99,101-103: 52-Dr. Doom. 54-Death's Head. 57-Punisher as Shield. 58-"What if Punisher Had Killed Spider-Man" w/cover similar to Amazing S-M #129. 59-...Wolverine led Alpha Flight. 60-X-Men Wedding Album. 61-Bound-in card sheet. 61,86,88-Spider-Man. 74,77,81,84,85-X-Men. 76-Last app. Watcher in title. 78-Bisley-c. 80-Hulk. 87-Sabretooth. 89-Fantastic Four. 90-Cyclops & Havok. 91-The Hulk. 93-Wolverine. 94-Juggernaut. 95-Ghost Rider 3.00
100-($2.99, double-sized) Gambit and Rogue, Fantastic Four 1 2 3 5 6 8
104-Silver Surfer, Thanos vs. Impossible Man 1 2 3 5 6 8
105-Spider-Girl (Peter Parker's daughter) debut; Sienkiewicz-a; (Betty Brant also app. as a Spider-Girl in What If? (1st series) #7) 3 6 9 21 33 45
106,107,109-114: 106-Gambit. 111-Wolverine. 114-Secret Wars 3.00
108-Avengers vs. Carnage 2 4 6 9 12 15
#(-1) Flashback (7/97) 3.00

WHAT IF...? (one-shots)
Marvel Comics: Feb, 2005 ($2.99)

... Aunt May Had Died Instead of Uncle Ben? - Brubaker-s/DiVito-a/Brase-c 3.00
... Dr. Doom Had Become The Thing? - Karl Kesel-s/Paul Smith-a/c 3.00
... General Ross Had Become The Hulk? - Peter David-s/Pat Olliffe-a/Gary Frank-c 3.00
... Jessica Jones Had Joined The Avengers? - Bendis-s/Gaydos-a/McNiven-c 3.00
... Karen Page Had Lived? - Bendis-s/Lark-a/c 3.00
... Magneto and Professor X Had Formed The X-Men Together? - Claremont-s/Raney-a 3.00
What If...: Why Not? TPB (2005, $16.99) r/one-shots 17.00

WHAT IF... (one-shots)
Marvel Comics: Feb, 2006 ($2.99)

... : Captain America - Fought in the Civil War?; Bedard-s/Di Giandomenico-a 3.00
... : Daredevil - The Devil Who Dares; Daredevil in feudal Japan; Veitch-s/Edwards-a 3.00
... : Fantastic Four - Were Cosmonauts?; Marshall Rogers-a/c; Mike Carey-s 3.00
... : Submariner - Grew Up on Land?; Pak-s/Lopez-a 3.00
... : Thor - Was the Herald of Galactus?; Kirkman-s/Oeming-a/c 3.00
... : Wolverine - In the Prohibition Era; Way-s/Proctor-a/Harris-c 3.00
What If: Mirror Mirror TPB (2006, $16.99) r/one-shots; design pages and Rogers sketches 17.00

WHAT IF ?... (one-shots altering recent Marvel "event" series)
Marvel Comics: Jan, 2007 - Feb, 2007 ($3.99)

... Avengers Disassembled; Parker-s/Lopresti-a/c 4.00
... Spider-Man The Other; Peter David-s/Khoi Pham-a; Venom app. 4.00
... Wolverine Enemy of the State; Robinson-s/DiGiandomenico-a/Alexander-c 4.00
... X-Men Age of Apocalypse; Remeder-s/Wilkins-a/Djurdjevic-c 4.00
... X-Men Deadly Genesis; Hine-s/Yardin-a/c 4.00
What If?: Event Horizon TPB (2007, $16.99) r/one-shots; design pages and cover sketches 17.00

WHAT IF ?... (one-shots altering recent Marvel "event" series)

GD 2.0 | VG 4.0 | FN 6.0 | VF 8.0 | VF/NM 9.0 | NM- 9.2

Marvel Comics: Dec, 2007 - Feb, 2008 ($3.99)

... Annihilation; Nova, Iron Man, Captain America app. 2 4 6 9 12 15
... Civil War; 2 covers by Silvestri & Djurdjevic 1 2 3 5 6 8
... Planet Hulk; Pagulayan-c; Kirk, Sandoval & Hembeck-a 10.00
... Spider-Man vs. Wolverine; Romita Jr.-c; Henry-a; Nick Fury app. 6.00
... X-Men - Rise and Fall of the Shi'ar Empire; Coipel-c 4.00
What If?: Civil War TPB (2008, $16.99) r/one-shots; design pages and cover sketches 17.00

WHAT IF ?... (one-shots altering recent Marvel "event" series)
Marvel Comics: Feb, 2009 ($3.99) (Serialized back-up Runaways story in each issue)

... Fallen Son; if Iron Man had died instead of Capt. America; McGuinness-c 4.00
... House of M; if the Scarlet Witch had said "No more powers" instead; Cheung-c 4.00
... Newer Fantastic Four; team of Spider-Man, Hulk, Iron Man and Wolverine 4.00
... Secret Wars; if Doctor Doom had kept the Beyonder's power; origin re-told 4.00
... Spider-Man Back in Black; if Mary Jane had been shot instead of Aunt May 4.00

WHAT IF ?... (one-shots)
Marvel Comics: Feb, 2010 ($3.99)

... Astonishing X-Men; if Ord resurrected Jean Grey; Campbell-c 4.00
... Daredevil vs. Elektra; Kayanan-a; Klaus Janson-c swipe of Daredevil #168 4.00
... Secret Invasion; if the Skrulls succeeded; Yu-c 4.00
... Spider-Man: House of M; if Gwen Stacy survived the House of M; Dodson-c 4.00
... World War Hulk; if the heroes lost the war; Romita Jr.-c 4.00

WHAT IF ?... (one-shots) (4 part Deadpool back-up story in all but #200)
(Also see Venom/Deadpool: What If?)
Marvel Comics: Feb, 2011 ($3.99)

... #200 ($4.99) Siege on cover; if Osborn won the Siege of Asgard; Stan Lee back-up 5.00
... Dark Reign; if Norman Osborn was killed; Tanaka-a/Deodato-c 4.00
... Iron Man: Demon in an Armor; if Tony Stark became Dr. Doom; Nolan-a 4.00
... Spider-Man; if Spider-Man killed Kraven; Jimenez-c 4.00
... Wolverine: Father; if Wolverine raised Daken; Tocchini-a; Yu-a 4.00

WHAT IF ? AGE OF ULTRON
Marvel Comics: Jun, 2014 - No. 5, Jun, 2014 ($3.99, weekly limited series)

1-5: 1-Hank Pym's story. 2-Wolverine, Hulk, Spider-Man, Ghost Rider app. 4.00

WHAT IF ? AVX (Avengers vs. X-Men)
Marvel Comics: Sept, 2013 - No. 4, Sept, 2013 ($3.99, weekly limited series)

1-4-Palmiotti-s/Molina-a; Hope merges with the Phoenix force 4.00

WHAT IF ? INFINITY - ... (one-shots)
Marvel Comics: Dec, 2015 ($3.99)

... Dark Reign; if The Green Goblin stole the Infinity Gauntlet; Williamson-s/Sudzuka-a 4.00
... Guardians of the Galaxy; if The Guardians tried to free Thanos; Copland-a 4.00
... Inhumans; if Black Bolt betrayed Earth; Rossmo-a 4.00
... Thanos; if Thanos joined the Avengers; Henderson-a 4.00
... X-Men; if the X-Men were the sole survivors of Infinity; Norton-a 4.00

'WHAT'S NEW? - THE COLLECTED ADVENTURES OF PHIL & DIXIE'
Palliard Press: Oct, 1991 - No. 2, 1991 ($5.95, mostly color, sq.-bound, 52 pgs.)

1,2-By Phil Foglio 6.00

WHAT THE- -?!
Marvel Comics: Aug, 1988 - No. 26, 1993 ($1.25/$1.50/$2.50, semi-annual #5 on)

1-All contain parodies 4.00
2-24: 3-X-Men parody; Todd McFarlane-a. 5-Punisher/Wolverine parody; Jim Lee-a. 6-Punisher, Wolverine, Alpha Flight. 9-Wolverine. 16-EC back-c parody. 17-Wolverine/Punisher parody. 18-Star Trek parody w/Wolverine. 19-Punisher, Wolverine, Ghost Rider. 21-Weapon X parody. 22-Punisher/Wolverine parody 3.00
25-Summer Special 1 (1993, $2.50)-X-Men parody 4.00
26-Fall Special ($2.50, 68 pgs.)-Spider-Ham 2099-c/story; origin Silver Surfer; Hulk & Doomsday parody; indica reads "Winter Special." 4.00

NOTE: ***Austin*** *a-6i.* ***Byrne*** *a-2, 6, 10; c-2, 6-8, 10, 12, 13.* ***Golden*** *a-22.* ***Dale Keown*** *a-8p(8 pgs.).* ***McFarlane*** *a-3.* ***Rogers*** *c-15i, 16p.* ***Severin*** *a-2.* ***Staton*** *a-21p.* ***Williamson*** *a-2i.*

WHEDON THREE WAY, THE
Dark Horse Comics: Sept, 2014 ($1.00, one-shot)

1-Reprints Buffy Season 10 #1, Angel & Faith Season 10 #1, Serenity: Leaves #1 3.00

WHEE COMICS (Also see Gay, Smile & Tickle Comics)
Modern Store Publications: 1955 (7¢, 5x7-1/4", 52 pgs.)

1-Funny animal 8 16 24 40 50 60

WHEEDIES (See Panic #11 -EC Comics)

WHEELIE AND THE CHOPPER BUNCH (TV)
Charlton Comics: July, 1975 - No. 7, July, 1976 (Hanna-Barbera)

Where Monsters Dwell (2015 series) #5 © MAR

Whisper #1 © Grant & Larson

White Princess of the Jungle #1 © AVON

GD VG FN VF VF/NM NM-
2.0 4.0 6.0 8.0 9.0 9.2

1-3: 1-Byrne text illo (see Nightmare for 1st art); Staton-a. 2-Byrne-a.
2,3-Mike Zeck text illos. 3-Staton-a; Byrne-c/a 3 6 9 17 26 35
4-7-Staton-a 2 4 6 12 16 20

WHEN KNIGHTHOOD WAS IN FLOWER (See The Sword & the Rose, 4-Color #505, 682)

WHEN SCHOOL IS OUT (See Wisco in Promotional Comics section)

WHERE CREATURES ROAM
Marvel Comics Group: July, 1970 - No. 8, Sept, 1971

1-Kirby/Ayers-c/a(r) 5 10 15 33 57 80
2-8: 2-5,7,8-Kirby-c/a(r). 6-Kirby-a(r) 4 8 12 22 35 48
NOTE: *Ditko r-1-6, 7. Heck r-2, 5. All contain pre super-hero reprints.*

WHERE IN THE WORLD IS CARMEN SANDIEGO (TV)
DC Comics: June, 1996 - No. 4, Dec, 1996 ($1.75)

1-4: Adaptation of TV show 3.00

WHERE MONSTERS DWELL
Marvel Comics Group: Jan, 1970 - No. 38, Oct, 1975

1-Kirby/Ditko-r; all contain pre super-hero-r 5 10 15 34 60 85
2-5,7-10: 4-Crandall-a(r) 4 8 12 23 37 50
6-(11/70) Reprints Groot's 1st app. in Tales to Astonish #13
4 8 12 24 44 60
11,13-20: 11-Last 15¢ issue. 18,20-Starlin-c 3 6 9 19 30 40
12-Giant issue (52 pgs.) 4 8 12 25 40 55
21-Reprints 1st Fin Fang Foom app. 3 6 9 21 33 45
22-37 3 6 9 16 24 32
38-Williamson-r/World of Suspense #3 3 6 9 17 26 35
NOTE: *Colan r-12. Ditko a(r)-4, 6, 8, 10, 12, 17-19, 23-25, 37. Kirby r-1-3, 5-16, 18-27, 30-32, 34-36, 38; c-12? Reinman a-3r, 4r, 12r. Severin c-15.*

WHERE MONSTERS DWELL (Secret Wars tie-in)
Marvel Comics: Jul, 2015 - No. 5, Dec, 2015 ($3.99, limited series)

1-5-Garth Ennis-s/Russ Braun-a/Frank Cho-c; The Phantom Eagle app. 4.00

WHERE'S HUDDLES? (TV) (See Fun-In #9)
Gold Key: Jan, 1971 - No. 3, Dec, 1971 (Hanna-Barbera)

1 3 6 9 18 28 38
2,3: 3-r/most #1 2 4 6 11 16 20

WHIP WILSON (Movie star) (Formerly Rex Hart; Gunhawk #12 on; see Western Hearts, Western Life Romances, Western Love)
Marvel Comics: No. 9, April, 1950 - No. 11, Sept, 1950 (#9,10: 52 pgs.)

9-Photo-c; Whip Wilson & his horse Bullet begin; origin Bullet; issue #23 listed on splash page; cover changed to #9 49 98 147 309 522 735
10,11: Both have photo-c. 11-36 pgs. 28 56 84 168 274 380
I.W. Reprint #1(1964)-Kinstler-c; r-Marvel #11 3 6 9 15 22 28

WHIRLWIND COMICS (Also see Cyclone Comics)
Nita Publication: June, 1940 - No. 3, Sept, 1940

1-Origin & 1st app. Cyclone; Cyclone-c 300 600 900 2010 3505 5000
2,3: Cyclone-c 161 322 483 1030 1765 2500

WHIRLYBIRDS (TV)
Dell Publishing Co.: No. 1124, Aug, 1960 - No. 1216, Oct-Dec, 1961

Four Color 1124 (#1)-Photo-c 7 14 21 49 92 135
Four Color 1216-Photo-c 7 14 21 46 86 125

WHISKEY DICKEL, INTERNATIONAL COWGIRL
Image Comics: Aug, 2003 ($12.95, softcover, B&W)

nn-Mark Ricketts-s/Mike Hawthorne-a; pin-up by various incl. Oeming, Thompson, Mack 13.00

WHISPER (Female Ninja)
Capital Comics: Dec, 1983 - No. 2, 1984 ($1.75, Baxter paper)

1,2: 1-Origin; Golden-c, Special (11/85, $2.50) 4.00

WHISPER (Vol. 2)
First Comics: Jun, 1986 - No. 37, June, 1990 ($1.25/$1.75/$1.95)

1-37 3.00

WHISPER
Boom! Studios: Nov, 2006 ($3.99)

1-Grant-s/Dzialowski-a 4.00

WHISPERS
Image Comics: Jan, 2012 - No. 6, Oct, 2013 ($2.99)

1-6-Joshua Luna-s/a 3.00

WHITE CHIEF OF THE PAWNEE INDIANS
Avon Periodicals: 1951

nn-Kit West app.; Kinstler-c 18 36 54 107 169 230

WHITE EAGLE INDIAN CHIEF (See Indian Chief)

WHITE FANG
Disney Comics: 1990 ($5.95, 68 pgs.)

nn-Graphic novel adapting new Disney movie 6.00

WHITE INDIAN
Magazine Enterprises: No. 11, July, 1953 - No. 15, 1954

11(A-1 94), 12(A-1 101), 13(A-1 104)-Frazetta-r(Dan Brand) in all from Durango Kid.
11-Powell-c 20 40 60 114 182 250
14(A-1 117), 15(A-1 135)-Check-a; Torres-a-#15 14 28 42 76 108 140
NOTE: *#11 contains reprints from Durango Kid #1-4; #12 from #5, 9, 10, 11; #13 from #7, 12, 13, 16. #14 & 15 contain all new stories.*

WHITEOUT (Also see Queen & Country)
Oni Press: July, 1998 - No. 4, Nov, 1998 ($2.95, B&W, limited series)

1-4: 1-Matt Wagner-c. 2-Mignola-c. 3-Gibbons-c 3.00
TPB (5/99, $10.95) r/#1-4; Miller-c 11.00

WHITEOUT: MELT
Oni Press: Sept, 1999 - No. 4, Feb, 2000 ($2.95, B&W, limited series)

1-4-Greg Rucka-s/Steve Lieber-a 3.00
Whiteout: Melt, The Definitive Edition TPB (9/07, $13.95) r/#1-4; Rucka afterword 14.00

WHITE PRINCESS OF THE JUNGLE (Also see Jungle Adventures & Top Jungle Comics)
Avon Periodicals: July, 1951 - No. 5, Nov, 1952

1-Origin of White Princess (Taanda) & Capt'n Courage (r); Kinstler-c
68 136 204 435 743 1050
2-Reprints origin of Malu, Slave Girl Princess from Avon's Slave Girl Comics #1 w/Malu changed to Zora; Kinstler-c/a(2) 46 92 138 290 488 685
3-Origin Blue Gorilla; Kinstler-c/a 41 82 123 260 435 610
4-Jack Barnum, White Hunter app.; r/Sheena #9 39 78 117 235 385 535
5-Blue Gorilla by McCann?; Kinstler inside-c; Fawcette/Alascia-a(3)
40 80 120 244 402 560

WHITE RIDER AND SUPER HORSE (Formerly Humdinger V2#2; Indian Warriors #7 on; also see Blue Bolt #1, 4Most & Western Crime Cases)
Novelty-Star Publications/Accepted Publ.: No. 4, 9/50 - No. 6, 3/51

4-6-Adapts "The Last of the Mohicans". 4(#1)-(9/50)-Says #11 on inside
16 32 48 94 147 200
Accepted Reprint #5(r/#5),6 (nd); L.B. Cole-c 9 18 27 50 65 80
NOTE: *All have L. B. Cole covers.*

WHITE SUITS, THE
Dark Horse Comics: Feb, 2014 - No. 4, Jul, 2014 ($3.99, limited series)

1-4-Barbiere-s/Cypress-a 4.00

WHITE TIGER
Marvel Comics: Jan, 2007 - No. 6, Nov, 2007 ($2.99, limited series)

1-6: 1-David Mack-c; Pierce & Liebe-s/Briones-a; Spider-Man & Black Widow app. 3.00
...: A Hero's Compulsion SC (2007,$14.99) r/#1-6; re-cap art and profile page 15.00

WHITE WILDERNESS (Disney)
Dell Publishing Co.: No. 943, Oct, 1958

Four Color 943-Movie 6 12 18 37 66 95

WHITMAN COMIC BOOK, A
Whitman Publishing Co.: Sept., 1962 (136 pgs.; 7-3/4x5-3/4; hardcover) (B&W)

1-3,5,7: 1-Yogi Bear. 2-Huckleberry Hound. 3-Mr. Jinks and Pixie & Dixie. 5-Augie Doggie & Loopy de Loop. 7-Bugs Bunny-r from #47,51,53,54 & 55
6 12 18 38 69 100
4,6: 4-The Flintstones. 6-Snooper & Blabber Fearless Detectives/Quick Draw McGraw of the Wild West 6 12 18 41 76 110
8-Donald Duck-reprints most of WDC&S #209-213. Includes 5 Barks stories, 1 complete Mickey Mouse serial by Paul Murry & 1 Mickey Mouse serial missing the 1st episode
7 14 21 46 86 125
NOTE: *Hanna-Barbera #1-6(TV), reprints of British tabloid comics. Dell reprints-#7,8.*

WHIZ COMICS (Formerly Flash & Thrill Comics #1)(See 5 Cent Comics)
Fawcett Publications: No. 2, Feb, 1940 - No. 155, June, 1953

1-(nn on cover, #2 inside)-Origin & 1st newsstand app. Captain Marvel (formerly Captain Thunder) by C. C. Beck (created by Bill Parker), Spy Smasher, Golden Arrow, Ibis the Invincible, Dan Dare, Scoop Smith, Sivana, & Lance O'Casey begin
20,000 40,000 60,000 120,000 180,000 240,000
(The only Mint copy sold in 1995 for $176,000 cash)
1-Reprint, oversize 13-1/2x10". **WARNING**: This comic is an exact duplicate reprint (except for dropping "Gangway for Captain Marvel" from-c) of the original except for its size. DC published it in 1974 with a second cover

Whiz Comics #44 © FAW

Whodunnit? #1 © ECL

The Wicked + The Divine #12 © Gillen & McKelvie

titling it as a Famous First Edition. There have been many reported cases of the outer cover being removed and the interior sold as the original edition. The reprint with the new outer cover removed is practically worthless. See Famous First Edition for value.

2-(3/40, nn on cover, #3 inside); cover to Flash #1 redrawn, pg. 12, panel 4; Spy Smasher reveals I.D. to Eve 757 1514 2271 5526 9763 14,000
3-(4/40, #3 on-c, #4 inside)-1st app. Beautia 459 918 1377 3350 5925 8500
4-(5/40, #4 on cover, #5 inside)-Brief origin Capt. Marvel retold 383 766 1149 2681 4691 6700
5-Captain Marvel wears button-down flap on splash page only 326 652 978 2282 3991 5700
6-10: 7-Dr. Voodoo begins (by Raboy-#9-22) 258 516 774 1651 2826 4000
11-14: 12-Capt. Marvel does not wear cape 181 362 543 1158 1979 2800
15-Origin Sivana; Dr. Voodoo by Raboy 187 374 561 1197 2049 2900
16-18-Spy Smasher battles Captain Marvel 206 412 618 1318 2259 3200
19-Classic shark-c 194 388 582 1242 2121 3000
20 116 232 348 742 1271 1800
21-(9/41)-Origin & 1st cover app. Lt. Marvels, the 1st team in Fawcett comics. In this issue, Capt. Death similar to Ditko's later Dr. Strange 119 238 357 762 1306 1850
22-24: 23-Only Dr. Voodoo by Tuska 94 188 282 597 1024 1450
25-(12/41)-Captain Nazi jumps from Master Comics #21 to take on Capt. Marvel solo after being beaten by Capt. Marvel/Bulletman team, causing the creation of Capt. Marvel Jr.; 1st app./origin of Capt. Marvel Jr. (part II of trilogy origin by CC. Beck & Mac Raboy); Captain Marvel sends Jr. back to Master #22 to aid Bulletman against Capt. Nazi; origin Old Shazam in text 568 1136 1704 4146 7323 10,500
26-30 65 130 195 416 708 1000
31,32: 32-1st app. The Trolls; Hitler/Mussolini satire by Beck 57 114 171 362 619 875
33-Spy Smasher, Captain Marvel x-over on cover and inside 74 148 222 470 810 1150
34,36-40: 37-The Trolls app. by Swayze 43 86 129 271 461 650
35-Captain Marvel & Spy Smasher-c 61 122 183 390 670 950
41-50: 42-Classic time travel-c. 43-Spy Smasher, Ibis, Golden Arrow x-over in Capt. Marvel. 44-Flag-c. 47-Origin recap (1 pg.) 39 78 117 240 395 550
51-60: 52-Capt. Marvel x-over in Ibis. 57-Spy Smasher, Golden Arrow, Ibis cameo 32 64 96 188 307 425
61-70 30 60 90 177 289 400
71,77-80 28 56 84 165 270 375
72-76-Two Captain Marvel stories in each; 76-Spy Smasher becomes Crime Smasher 28 56 84 168 274 380
81-85,87-99: 91-Infinity-c 28 56 84 165 270 375
86-Captain Marvel battles Sivana Family; robot-c 33 66 99 194 317 440
100-(8/48)-Anniversary issue 39 78 117 231 378 525
101-106: 102-Commando Yank app. 106-Bulletman app. 30 60 90 177 289 400
107-149: 107-Capitol Building photo-c. 108-Brooklyn Bridge photo-c. 112-Photo-c. 139-Infinity-c. 140-Flag-c. 142-Used in **POP**, pg. 89 31 62 93 182 296 410
150-152-(Low dist.) 39 78 117 235 385 535
153-155-(Scarce):154,155-1st/2nd Dr. Death stories 50 100 150 315 533 750

NOTE: ***C.C. Beck*** *Captain Marvel-No. 25(part).* ***Krigstein*** *Golden Arrow-No. 75, 78, 91, 95, 96, 98-100.* ***Mac Raboy*** *Dr. Voodoo-No. 9-22. Captain Marvel-No. 25(part).* ***M.Swayze*** *a-37, 38, 59; c-38.* ***Schaffenberger*** *c-138-155(most).* ***Wolverton*** *1/2 pg. "Culture Corner"-No. 65-67, 68(2 1/2 pgs), 70-85, 87-96, 98-100, 102-109, 112-121, 123, 125, 126, 128-131, 133, 134, 136, 142, 143, 146.*

WHIZ KIDS (Also see Big Bang Comics)
Image Comics: Apr, 2003 ($4.95, B&W, one-shot)
1-Galahad, Cyclone, Thunder Girl and Moray app.; Jeff Austin-a 5.00

WHOA, NELLIE (Also see Love & Rockets)
Fantagraphics Books: July, 1996 - No. 3, Sept, 1996 ($2.95, B&W, lim. series)
1-3: Jamie Hernandez-c/a/scripts 3.00

WHODUNIT
D.S. Publishing Co.: Aug-Sept, 1948 - No. 3, Dec-Jan, 1948-49 (#1,2: 52 pgs.)
1-Baker-a (7 pgs.) 32 64 96 188 307 425
2,3-Detective mysteries 15 30 45 85 130 175

WHODUNNIT?
Eclipse Comics: June, 1986 - No. 3, Apr, 1987 ($2.00, limited series)
1-3: Spiegle-a. 2-Gulacy-c 3.00

WHO FRAMED ROGER RABBIT (See Marvel Graphic Novel)

WHO IS NEXT?
Standard Comics: No. 5, Jan, 1953
5-Toth, Sekowsky, Andru-a; crime stories 47 94 141 296 498 700

WHO IS THE CROOKED MAN?
Crusade: Sept, 1996 ($3.50, B&W, 40 pgs.)
1-Intro The Martyr, Scarlet 7 & Garrison 4.00

WHO'S MINDING THE MINT? (See Movie Classics)

WHO'S WHO IN STAR TREK
DC Comics: Mar, 1987 - #2, Apr, 1987 ($1.50, limited series)
1,2 6.00

NOTE: ***Byrne*** *a-1, 2.* ***Chaykin*** *c-1, 2.* ***Morrow*** *a-1, 2.* ***McFarlane*** *a-2.* ***Perez*** *a-1, 2.* ***Sutton*** *a-1, 2.*

WHO'S WHO IN THE LEGION OF SUPER-HEROES
DC Comics: Apr, 1987 - No. 7, Nov, 1988 ($1.25, limited series)
1-7 4.00

WHO'S WHO: THE DEFINITIVE DIRECTORY OF THE DC UNIVERSE
DC Comics: Mar, 1985 - No. 26, Apr, 1987 (Maxi-series, no ads)
1-DC heroes from A-Z 4.00
2-26: All have 1-2 pgs-a by most DC artists 4.00

NOTE: ***Art Adams*** *a-4, 11, 18, 20.* ***Anderson*** *a-1-5, 7-12, 14, 15, 19, 21, 23-25.* ***Aparo*** *a-2, 3, 9, 10, 12, 13, 14, 15, 17, 18, 21, 23.* ***Byrne*** *a-4, 7, 14, 16, 18i, 19, 22i, 24; c-22.* ***Cowan*** *a-3-5, 8, 10-13, 16-18, 22-25.* ***Ditko*** *a-19-22.* ***Evans*** *a-20.* ***Giffen*** *a-1, 3,-6, 8, 13, 15, 17, 18, 23.* ***Grell*** *a-6, 9, 14, 20, 23, 25, 26.* ***Infantino*** *a-1-10, 12, 15, 17-22, 24, 25.* ***Kaluta*** *a-14, 21.* ***Gil Kane*** *a-1-11, 13, 14, 16, 19, 21-23, 25.* ***Kirby*** *a-2-6, 8-18, 20, 22, 25.* ***Kubert*** *a-2, 3, 7-11, 19, 20, 25.* ***Erik Larsen*** *a-24.* ***McFarlane*** *a-10-12, 17, 19, 25, 26.* ***Morrow*** *a-4, 7, 25, 26.* ***Orlando*** *a-1, 4, 10, 11, 21i.* ***Perez*** *a-1-5, 8-19, 22-26; c-1-4, 13-18.* ***Rogers*** *a-1, 2, 5-7, 11, 12, 15, 24.* ***Starlin*** *a-13, 14, 16.* ***Stevens*** *a-4, 7, 18.*

WHO'S WHO UPDATE '87
DC Comics: Aug, 1987 - No. 5, Dec, 1987 ($1.25, limited series)
1-5: Contains art by most DC artists 4.00

NOTE: ***Giffen*** *a-1.* ***McFarlane*** *a-1-4; c-4.* ***Perez*** *a-1-4.*

WHO'S WHO UPDATE '88
DC Comics: Aug, 1988 - No. 4, Nov, 1988 ($1.25, limited series)
1-4: Contains art by most DC artists 4.00

NOTE: ***Giffen*** *a-1.* ***Erik Larsen*** *a-1.*

WICKED, THE
Avalon Studios: Dec, 1999 - No. 7, Aug, 2000 ($2.95)
Preview-(7/99, $5.00, B&W) 5.00
1-7-Anacleto-c/Martinez-a 3.00
...: Medusa's Tale (11/00, $3.95, one shot) story plus pin-up gallery 4.00
...: Vol. 1: Omnibus (2003, $19.95) r/#0-8; Drew-c 20.00

WICKED + THE DIVINE, THE
Image Comics: Jun, 2014 - Present ($3.50/$3.99)
1-25: 1-Gillen-s/McKelvie-a. 12-Kate Brown-a. 13-Lotay-a. 15-Hans-a. 23-Wada-a 3.50
26-($3.99) 4.00
1831 One-Shot (9/16, $3.99) Set in 1831; Stephanie Hans-a 4.00

WIDOWMAKER
Marvel Comics: Feb, 2011 - No. 4, Apr, 2011 ($3.99, limited series)
1-4-Black Widow, Hawkeye & Mockingbird app. 1,2-Jae Lee-c. 3,4-Noto-c 4.00

WIDOW WARRIORS
Dynamite Entertainment: 2010 - No. 4, 2010 ($3.99, limited series)
1-4-Pat Lee-a/c 4.00

WILBUR COMICS (Teen-age) (Also see Laugh Comics, Laugh Comix, Liberty Comics #10 & Zip Comics)
MLJ Magazines/Archie Publ. No. 8, Spring, 1946 on: Sum', 1944 - No. 87, 11/59; No. 88, 9/63; No. 89, 10/64; No. 90, 10/65 (No. 1-46: 52 pgs.) (#1-11 are quarterly)
1 69 138 207 442 759 1075
2(Fall, 1944) 37 74 111 222 361 500
3,4(Wint, '44-45; Spr, '45) 26 52 78 154 252 350
5-1st app. Katy Keene (Sum, '45) & begin series; Wilbur story same as Archie story in Archie #1 except Wilbur replaces Archie 155 310 465 992 1696 2400
6-10: 10-(Fall, 1946) 30 60 90 177 289 400
11-20 17 34 51 98 154 210
21-30: 30-(4/50) 12 24 36 69 97 125
31-50 10 20 30 54 72 90
51-70 9 18 27 47 61 75
71-90: 88-Last 10¢ issue (9/63) 4 8 12 27 44 60

NOTE: *Katy Keene in No. 5-56, 58-61, 63-69.* ***Al Fagaly*** *c-6-9, 12-24 at least.* ***Vigoda*** *c-2.*

WILD
Atlas Comics (IPC): Feb, 1954 - No. 5, Aug, 1954
1 36 72 108 211 343 475
2 20 40 60 117 189 260
3-5 18 36 54 107 169 230

NOTE: ***Berg*** *a-5; c-4.* ***Burgos*** *c-3.* ***Colan*** *a-4.* ***Everett*** *a-1-3.* ***Heath*** *a-2, 3, 5.* ***Maneely*** *a-1-3, 5; c-1, 5.* ***Post*** *a-2,*

Will Bill Hickok #1 © AVON

WildC.A.T.s #16 © WSP

Wildcats V5 #23 © WSP

	GD 2.0	VG 4.0	FN 6.0	VF 8.0	VF/NM 9.0	NM- 9.2

5. Ed Win a-1, 3.

WILD! (This Magazine Is...) (Satire)
Dell Publishing Co.: Jan, 1968 - No. 3, 1968 (35¢, magazine, 52 pgs.)

	GD	VG	FN	VF	VF/NM	NM-
1-3: Hogan's Heroes, The Rat Patrol & Mission Impossible TV spoofs	3	6	9	16	23	30

WILD ANIMALS
Pacific Comics: Dec, 1982 ($1.00, one-shot, direct sales)

	GD	VG	FN	VF	VF/NM	NM-
1-Funny animal; Sergio Aragonés-a; Shaw-c/a						4.00

WILD BILL ELLIOTT (Also see Western Roundup under Dell Giants)
Dell Publishing Co.: No. 278, 5/50 - No. 643, 7/55 (No #11,12) (All photo-c)

	GD	VG	FN	VF	VF/NM	NM-
Four Color 278 (#1, 52pgs.)-Titled "Bill Elliott"; Bill & his horse Stormy begin; photo front/back-c begin	12	24	36	79	170	260
2 (11/50), 3 (52 pgs.)	7	14	21	44	82	120
4-10 (10-12/52)	5	10	15	35	63	90
Four Color 472 (6/53), 520(12/53)-Last photo back-c	5	10	15	5	63	90
13 (4-6/54) - 17 (4-6/55)	5	10	15	30	50	70
Four Color 643 (7/55)	5	10	15	33	57	80

WILD BILL HICKOK (Also see Blazing Sixguns)
Avon Periodicals: Sept-Oct, 1949 - No. 28, May-June, 1956

	GD	VG	FN	VF	VF/NM	NM-
1-Ingels-c	28	56	84	165	270	375
2-Painted-c; Kit West app.	15	30	45	85	130	175
3-5-Painted-c (4-Cover by Howard Winfield)	12	24	36	69	97	125
6-10,12: 8-10-Painted-c. 12-Kinsler-c?	12	24	36	67	94	120
11,13,14-Kinstler-c/a (#11-c & inside-f/c art only)	13	26	39	72	101	130
15,17,18,20: 18-Kit West story. 20-Kit West by Larsen	11	22	33	60	83	105
16-Kamen-a; r-3 stories/King of the Badmen of Deadwood	11	22	33	62	86	110
19-Meskin-a	11	22	33	60	83	105
21-Reprints 2 stories/Chief Crazy Horse	10	20	30	58	79	100
22-McCann-a?; r/Sheriff Bob Dixon's...	10	20	30	58	79	100
23-27: 23-Kinstler-c. 24-27-Kinstler-c/a(r) (24,25-r?)	10	20	30	58	79	100
28-Kinstler-c/a (new); r-/Last of the Comanches	11	22	33	60	83	105
I.W. Reprint #1-r/#2; Kinstler-c	2	4	6	9	13	16
Super Reprint #10-12: 10-r/#18. 11-r/#?. 12-r/#8	2	4	6	9	13	16

NOTE: *#23, 25 contain numerous editing deletions in both art and script due to code.* ***Kinstler*** *c-6, 7, 11-14, 17, 18, 20-22, 24-28.* ***Howard Larsen*** *a-1, 2, 4, 5, 6(3), 7-9, 11, 12, 17, 18, 20-24, 26.* ***Meskin*** *a-7.* ***Reinman*** *a-6, 17.*

WILD BILL HICKOK AND JINGLES (TV)(Formerly Cowboy Western) (Also see Blue Bird)
Charlton Comics: No. 68, Aug, 1958 - No. 75, Dec, 1959

	GD	VG	FN	VF	VF/NM	NM-
68,69-Williamson-a (all are 10¢ issues)	11	22	33	60	83	105
70-Two pgs. Williamson-a	8	16	24	42	54	65
71-75 (#76, exist?)	6	12	18	28	34	40

WILD BILL PECOS WESTERN (Also see The Westerner)
AC Comics: 1989 ($3.50, 1/2 color, 1/2 B&W, 52 pgs.)

	GD	VG	FN	VF	VF/NM	NM-
1-Syd Shores-c/a(r)/Westerner; photo back-c						4.00

WILD BOY OF THE CONGO (Also see Approved Comics)
Ziff-Davis No. 10-12,4-8/St. John No. 9,11 on: No. 10, 2-3/51 - No. 12, 8-9/51; No. 4, 10-11/51 - No. 9, 10/53; No. 11-#15,6/55 (No #10, 1953)

	GD	VG	FN	VF	VF/NM	NM-
10(#1)(2-3/51)-Origin; bondage-c by Saunders (painted); used in **SOTI**, pg. 189; painted-c begin thru #9 (except #7)	32	64	96	188	307	425
11(4-5/51),12(8-9/51)-Norman Saunders painted-c	17	34	51	98	154	210
4(10-11/51)-Saunders painted bondage-c	16	32	48	94	147	200
5(Winter,'51)-Saunders painted-c	15	30	45	85	130	175
6,8,9(10/53): Painted-c. 6-Saunders-c	15	30	45	85	130	175
7(8-9/52)-Kinstler-a	16	32	48	94	147	200
11-13-Baker-c. 11-r/#7 w/new Baker-c; Kinstler-a (2 pgs.)	19	38	57	111	176	240
14(4/55)-Baker-c; r-#12('51)	19	38	57	111	176	240
15(6/55)	14	28	42	80	115	150

WILDCAT (See Sensation Comics #1)

WILDC.A.T.S ADVENTURES (TV cartoon)
Image Comics (WildStorm): Sept, 1994 - No. 10, June, 1995 ($1.95/$2.50)

	GD	VG	FN	VF	VF/NM	NM-
1-10						3.00
Sourcebook 1 (1/95, $2.95)						3.00

WILDC.A.T.S: COVERT ACTION TEAMS (Also see Alan Moore's... for TPB reprints)
Image Comics (WildStorm Productions): Aug, 1992 - No. 4, Mar, 1993; No. 5, Nov, 1993 - No. 50, June, 1998 ($1.95/$2.50)

	NM-
1-1st app; Jim Lee/Williams-c/a & Lee scripts begin; contains 2 trading cards (Two diff versions of cards inside); 1st WildStorm Productions title	5.00
1-All gold foil signed edition	20.00
1-All gold foil unsigned edition	10.00
1-Newsstand edition w/o cards	3.00
1-"3-D Special"(8/97, $4.95) w/3-D glasses; variant-c by Jim Lee.	5.00
2-($2.50)-Prism foil stamped-c; contains coupon for Image Comics #0 & 4 pg. preview to Portacio's Wetworks (back-up)	5.00
2-With coupon missing	2.00
2-Direct sale misprint w/o foil-c	5.00
2-Newsstand ed., no prism or coupon	3.00
3-Lee/Liefeld-c (1/93-c, 12/92 inside)	4.00
4-($2.50)-Polybagged w/Topps trading card; 1st app. Tribe by Johnson & Stroman; Youngblood cameo	4.00
4-Variant w/red card	6.00
5-7-Jim Lee/Williams-c/a; Lee script	3.00
8-X-Men's Jean Grey & Scott Summers cameo	4.00
9-12: 10-1st app. Huntsman & Soldier; Claremont scripts begin, ends #13. 11-1st app. Savant, Tapestry & Mr. Majestic.	3.00
11-Alternate Portacio-c, see Deathblow #5	5.00
13-19,21-24: 15-James Robinson scripts begin, ends #20. 15,16-Black Razor story. 21-Alan Moore scripts begin, end #34; intro Tao & Ladytron; new WildC.A.T.S team forms (Mr. Majestic, Savant, Condition Red (Max Cash), Tao & Ladytron). 22-Maguire-a	3.00
20-($2.50)-Direct Market, WildStorm Rising Pt. 2 w/bound-in card	4.00
20-($1.95)-Newsstand, WildStorm Rising Part 2	3.00
25-($4.95)-Alan Moore script; wraparound foil-c.	5.00
26-49: 29-(5/96)-Fire From Heaven Pt 7; reads Apr on-c. 30-(6/96)-Fire From Heaven Pt. 13; Spartan revealed to have transplanted personality of John Colt (from Team One: WildC.A.T.S). 31-(9/96)-Grifter rejoins team; Ladytron dies	3.00
40-($3.50)Voyager Pack bagged w/Divine Right preview	5.00
50-($3.50) Stories by Robinson/Lee, Choi & Peterson/Benes, and Moore/Charest; Charest sketchbook; Lee wraparound-c	4.00
50-Chromium cover	6.00
Annual 1 (2/98, $2.95) Robinson-s	4.00
Compendium (1993, $9.95)-r/#1-4; bagged w/#0	15.00
Sourcebook 1 (9/93, $2.50)-Foil embossed-c	3.00
Sourcebook 1-($1.95)-Newsstand ed. w/o foil embossed-c	3.00
Sourcebook 2 (11/94, $2.50)-wraparound-c	3.00
Special 1 (11/93, $3.50, 52 pgs.)-1st Travis Charest WildC.A.T.S-a	4.00
...A Gathering of Eagles (5/97, $9.95, TPB) r/#10-12	10.00
.../ Cyberforce: Killer Instinct TPB (2004, $14.95) r/#5-7 & Cyberforce V2 #1-3	15.00
...Gang War ('98, $16.95, TPB) r/#28-34	17.00
...Homecoming (8/98, $19.95, TPB) r/#21-27	20.00
James Robinson's Complete Wildc.a.t.s TPB (2009, $24.99) r/#15-20,50; Annual 1, WildStorm Rising #1, Team One Wildc.a.t.s #1,2; cover and pin-up gallery	25.00

WILDCATS (3rd series)
DC Comics (WildStorm): Mar, 1999 - No. 28, Dec, 2001 ($2.50)

	NM-
1-Charest-a; six covers by Lee, Adams, Bisley, Campbell, Madureira and Ramos; Lobdell-s	4.00
1-($6.95) DF Edition; variant cover by Ramos	7.00
2-28: 2-Voodoo cover. 3-Bachalo variant-c. 5-Hitch-a/variant-c. 7-Meglia-a. 8-Phillips-a begins. 17-J.G. Jones-c. 18,19-Jim Lee-c. 20,21-Dillon-a	3.00
Annual 2000 (12/00, $3.50) Bermejo-a; Devil's Night x-over	4.00
...: Battery Park ('03, $17.95, TPB) r/#20-28; Phillips-c	18.00
... Ladytron (10/00, $5.95) Origin; Casey-s/Canete-a	6.00
... Mosaic (2/00, $3.95) Tuska-a (10 pg. back-up story)	4.00
...: Serial Boxes ('01, $14.95, TPB) r/#14-19; Phillips-c	15.00
...: Street Smart ('03, $24.95, HC) r/#1-6; Charest-c	25.00
...: Street Smart ('02, $14.95, SC) r/#1-6; Charest-c	15.00
...: Vicious Circles ('00, $14.95, TPB) r/#8-13; Phillips-c	15.00

WILDCATS (Volume 4)
DC Comics (WildStorm): Dec, 2006 ($2.99)

	NM-
1-Grant Morrison-s/Jim Lee-a; Jim Lee-c	3.00
1-Variant-c by Todd McFarlane/Jim Lee	6.00
...: Armageddon 1 (2/08, $2.99) Gage-s/Caldwell-a	3.00

WILDCATS (Volume 5) (World's End on cover for #1,2)
DC Comics (WildStorm): Sept, 2008 - No. 30, Feb, 2011 ($2.99)

	NM-
1-30: 1-Christos Gage-s/Neil Googe-a. 5-Woods-a	3.00
...: Family Secrets TPB (2010, $17.99) r/#8-12	18.00
...: World's End TPB (2009, $17.99) r/#1-7	18.00

WILDC.A.T.S/ ALIENS

Wildcore #1 © Aegis

Wild Girl #1 © DC

Wildstorm Revelations #5 © WSP

	GD 2.0	VG 4.0	FN 6.0	VF 8.0	VF/NM 9.0	NM- 9.2

Image Comics/Dark Horse: Aug, 1998 ($4.95, one-shot)

1-Ellis-s/Sprouse-a/c; Aliens invade Skywatch; Stormwatch app.; death of Winter; destruction of Skywatch	1	2	3	5	6	8
1-Variant-c by Gil Kane	1	3	4	6	8	10

WILDCATS: NEMESIS
DC Comics (WildStorm): Nov, 2005 - No. 9, July, 2006 ($2.99, limited series)
1-9: 1-Robbie Morrison-s/Talent Caldwell & Horacio Domingues-a/Caldwell-c 3.00
TPB (2006, $19.99) r/#1-9; cover gallery 20.00

WILDC.A.T.S: SAVANT GARDE FAN EDITION
Image Comics/WildStorm Productions: Feb, 1997 - No. 3, Apr, 1997 (Giveaway, 8 pgs.) (Polybagged w/Overstreet's FAN)
1-3: Barbara Kesel-s/Christian Uche-a(p) 3.00
1-3-(Gold): All retailer incentives 10.00

WILDC.A.T.S TRILOGY
Image Comics (WildStorm Productions): June, 1993 - No. 3, Dec, 1993 ($1.95, lim. series)
1-($2.50)-1st app. Gen 13 (Fairchild, Burnout, Grunge, Freefall) Multi-color foil-c; Jae Lee-c/a in all 5.00
1-($1.95)-Newsstand ed. w/o foil-c 3.00
2,3-($1.95)-Jae Lee-c/a 3.00

WILDCATS VERSION 3.0
DC Comics (WildStorm): Oct, 2002 - No. 24, Oct, 2004 ($2.95)
1-24: 1-Casey-s/Nguyen-a; two covers by Nguyen and Rian Hughes and Nguyen. 8-Back-up preview of The Authority: High Stakes pt. 3 3.00
...: Brand Building TPB (2003, $14.95) r/#1-6 15.00
...: Full Disclosure TPB (2004, $14.95) r/#7-12 15.00
...: Year One TPB (2010, $24.99) r/#1-12 25.00
...: Year Two TPB (2011, $24.99) r/#13-24 25.00

WILDC.A.T.S/ X-MEN: THE GOLDEN AGE (See also X-Men/WildC.A.T.S.: The Dark Age)
Image Comics (WildStorm Productions): Feb, 1997 ($4.50, one-shot)
1-Lobdell-s/Charest-a; Two covers (Charest, Jim Lee) 5.00
1-"3-D" Edition ($6.50) w/glasses 7.00

WILDC.A.T.S/ X-MEN: THE MODERN AGE
Image Comics (WildStorm Productions): Aug, 1997 ($4.50, one-shot)
1-Robinson-s/Hughes-a; Two covers (Hughes, Paul Smith) 5.00
1-"3-D" Edition ($6.50) w/glasses 7.00

WILDC.A.T.S/ X-MEN: THE SILVER AGE
Image Comics (WildStorm Productions): June, 1997 ($4.50, one-shot)
1-Lobdell-s/Jim Lee-a; Two covers(Neal Adams, Jim Lee) 5.00
1-"3-D" Edition ($6.50) w/glasses 7.00

WILDCORE
Image Comics (WildStorm Prods.): Nov, 1997 - No. 10, Dec, 1998 ($2.50)
1-10: 1-Two covers (Booth/McWeeney, Charest) 3.00
1-($3.50)-Voyager Pack w/DV8 preview 4.00
1-Chromium-c 5.00

WILD DOG
DC Comics: Sept, 1987 - No. 4, Dec, 1987 (75¢, limited series)
1-4 3.00
Special 1 (1989, $2.50, 52 pgs.) 4.00

WILDERNESS TREK (See Zane Grey, Four Color 333)

WILDFIRE (See Zane Grey, FourColor 433)

WILDFIRE
Image Comics (Top Cow): Jun, 2014 - No. 4, Oct, 2014 ($3.99, limited series)
1-4-Matt Hawkins-s/Linda Sejic-a 4.00

WILD FRONTIER (Cheyenne Kid #8 on)
Charlton Comics: Oct, 1955 - No. 7, Apr, 1957

1-Davy Crockett	10	20	30	54	72	90
2-6-Davy Crockett in all	7	14	21	37	46	55
7-Origin & 1st app. Cheyenne Kid	9	18	27	47	61	75

WILD GIRL
DC Comics (WildStorm): Jan, 2005 - No. 6, Jun, 2005 ($2.95/$2.99)
1-6-Leah Moore & John Reppion-s/Shawn McManus-a/c 3.00

WILDGUARD: CASTING CALL
Image Comics: Sept, 2003 - No. 6, Feb, 2004 ($2.95)
1-6: 1-Nauck-s/a; two covers by Nauck and McGuinness. 2-Wieringo var-c. 6-Noto var-c 3.00
... Vol. 1: Casting Call (1/05, $17.95, TPB) r/#1-6; cover gallery; Todd Nauck bio 18.00
Wildguard: Fire Power 1 (12/04, $3.50) Nauck-a; two covers 3.50
Wildguard: Fool's Gold (7/05 - No. 2, 7/05, $3.50) 1,2-Todd Nauck-s/a 3.50
Wildguard: Insider (5/08 - No. 3, 7/08, $3.50) 1-3-Todd Nauck-s/a 3.50

WILD'S END
BOOM! Studios: Sept, 2014 - No. 6, Feb, 2015 ($3.99, limited series)
1-6-Dan Abnett-s/I.N.J. Culbard-a/c 4.00

WILD'S END: THE ENEMY WITHIN
BOOM! Studios: Sept, 2015 - No. 6, Feb, 2016 ($3.99, limited series)
1-6-Dan Abnett-s/I.N.J. Culbard-a/c 4.00

WILDSIDERZ
DC Comics (WildStorm): No. 0, Aug, 2005 - No. 2, Jan, 2006 ($1.99/$3.50)
0-(8/05, $1.99) Series preview & character profiles; J. Scott Campbell-a 3.00
1,2: 1-(10/05, $3.50) J. Scott Campbell-s/a; Andy Hartnell-s 3.50

WILDSTAR (Also see The Dragon & The Savage Dragon)
Image Comics (Highbrow Entertainment): Sept, 1995 - No. 3, Jan, 1996 ($2.50, lim. series)
1-3: Al Gordon scripts; Jerry Ordway-c/a 3.00

WILDSTAR: SKY ZERO
Image Comics (Highbrow Entertainment): Mar, 1993 - No. 4, Nov, 1993 ($1.95, lim. series)
1-4: 1-($2.50)-Embossed-c w/silver ink; Ordway-c/a in all 3.00
1-($1.95)-Newsstand ed. w/silver ink-c, not embossed 3.00
1-Gold variant 6.00

WILD STARS
Collector's Edition/Little Rocket Productions: Summer, 1984 - Present (B&W)
Vol. 1 #1 (Summer 1984, $1.50) 5.00
Vol. 2 #1 (Winter 1988, $1.95) Foil-c; die-cut front & back-c 5.00
Vol. 3: #1-6-Brunner-c; Tierney-s. 1,2-Brewer-a. 3-6-Simons-a 3.00
7-($5.95) Simons-a 6.00
TPB (2004, $17.95) r/Vol. 1-3 18.00

WILDSTORM
Image Comics/DC Comics (WildStorm Publishing): 1994 - Present (one-shots, TPBs)
... After the Fall TPB (2009, $19.99) r/back-up stories from Wildcats V5 #1-11, The Authority V5 #1-11; Gen 13 V4 #21-28, and Stormwatch: PHD #13-20 20.00
...Annual 2000 (12/00, $3.50) Devil's Night x-over; Moy-a 4.00
...: Armageddon TPB (2008, $17.99) r/Armageddon one-shots in Midnighter, Welcome To Tranquility, Wetworks, Gen13, Stormwatch PHD, and Wildcats titles 18.00
...Chamber of Horrors (10/95, $3.50)-Bisley-c 4.00
...Fine Arts: Spotlight on Gen13 (2/08, $3.50) art and covers with commentary 3.50
...Fine Arts: Spotlight on Jim Lee (2/07, $3.50) art and covers by Lee with commentary 3.50
...Fine Arts: Spotlight on J. Scott Campbell (5/07, $3.50) art and covers with commentary 3.50
...Fine Arts: Spotlight on The Authority (1/08, $3.50) art and covers with commentary 3.50
...Fine Arts: Spotlight on WildCATs (3/08, $3.50) art and covers with commentary 3.50
...Fine Arts: The Gallery Collection (12/98, $19.95) Lee-c 20.00
...Halloween 1 (10/97, $2.50) Warner-c 3.00
...Rarities 1(12/94, $4.95, 52 pgs.)-r/Gen 13 1/2 & other stories 5.00
...Summer Special 1 (2001, $5.95) Short stories by various; Hughes-c 6.00
...Swimsuit Special 1 (12/94, $2.95), ...Swimsuit Special 2 (1995, $2.50) 3.00
...Swimsuit Special '97 #1 (7/97, $2.50) 3.00
...Thunderbook 1 (10/00, $6.95) Short stories by various incl. Hughes, Moy 7.00
...Ultimate Sports 1 (8/97, $2.50) 3.00
...Universe Sourcebook (5/95, $2.50) 3.00
...Universe 2008 Convention Exclusive ('08, no cover price) preview of World's End x-over 3.00

WILDSTORM!
Image Comics (WildStorm): Aug, 1995 - No. 4, Nov, 1995 ($2.50, B&W/color, anthology)
1-4: 1-Simonson-a 3.00

WILD STORM, THE
DC Comics (WildStorm): Apr, 2017 - Present ($3.99)
1-Warren Ellis-s/Jon Davis-Hunt-a; Zealot and the Engineer app. 4.00

WILDSTORM PRESENTS: ...
DC Comics (WildStorm): Jan, 2011 - Present ($7.99, squarebound, reprints)
1-(1/11) r/short stories by various incl. Pearson, Conner, Corben, Jeanty, Mahnke 8.00
Planetary: Lost Worlds (2/11) r/Planetary/Authority & Planetary/JLA: Terra Occulta 8.00

WILDSTORM REVELATIONS
DC Comics (WildStorm): Mar, 2008 - No. 6, May, 2008 ($2.99, limited series)
1-6-Beatty & Gage-s/Craig-a. 2-The Authority app. 3.00
TPB (2008, $17.99) r/#1-6; cover sketches 18.00

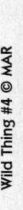

Wild Thing #4 © MAR

Wild Western Action #1 © Skywald

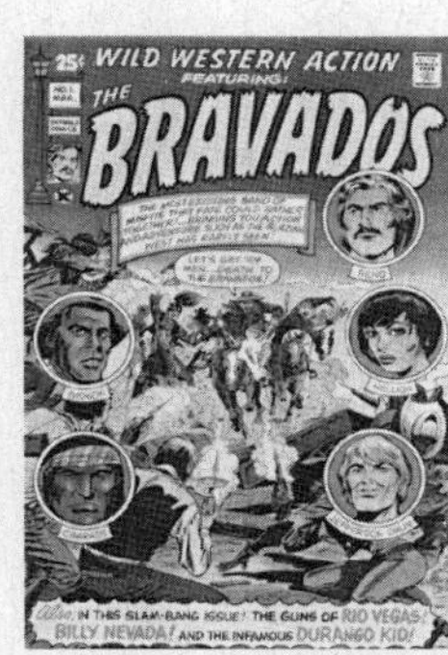

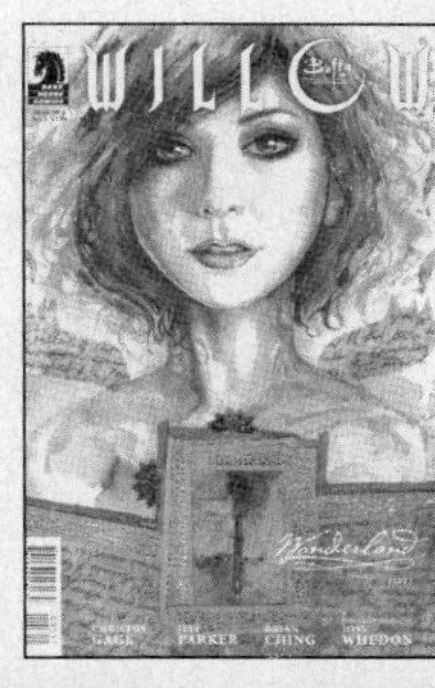

Willow #5 © 20th Century Fox

WILDSTORM RISING
Image Comics (WildStorm Publishing): May, 1995 - No.2, June, 1995 ($1.95/$2.50)

	GD 2.0	VG 4.0	FN 6.0	VF 8.0	VF/NM 9.0	NM- 9.2
1-($2.50)-Direct Market, WildStorm Rising Pt. 1 w/bound-in card						3.00
1-($1.95)-Newstand, WildStorm Rising Pt. 1						3.00
2-($2.50)-Direct Market, WildStorm Rising Pt. 10 w/bound-in card; continues in WildC.A.T.S #21.						3.00
2-($1.95)-Newstand, WildStorm Rising Pt. 10						3.00
Trade paperback (1996, $19.95)-Collects x-over; B. Smith-c						20.00

WILDSTORM SPOTLIGHT
Image Comics (WildStorm Publishing): Feb, 1997 - No. 4 ($2.50)

	GD 2.0	VG 4.0	FN 6.0	VF 8.0	VF/NM 9.0	NM- 9.2
1-4: 1-Alan Moore-s						3.00

WILDSTORM UNIVERSE '97
Image Comics (WildStorm Publishing): Dec, 1996 - No. 3 ($2.50, limited series)

	GD 2.0	VG 4.0	FN 6.0	VF 8.0	VF/NM 9.0	NM- 9.2
1-3: 1-Wraparound-c. 3-Gary Frank-c						3.00

WILDTHING
Marvel Comics UK: Apr, 1993 - No. 7, Oct, 1993 ($1.75)

	GD 2.0	VG 4.0	FN 6.0	VF 8.0	VF/NM 9.0	NM- 9.2
1-($2.50)-Embossed-c; Venom & Carnage cameo						4.00
2-7: 2-Spider-Man & Venom. 6-Mysterio app.						3.00

WILD THING (Wolverine's daughter in the M2 universe)
Marvel Comics: Oct, 1999 - No. 5, Feb, 2000 ($1.99)

	GD 2.0	VG 4.0	FN 6.0	VF 8.0	VF/NM 9.0	NM- 9.2
1-5: 1-Lim-a in all. 2-Two covers						3.00
Wizard #0 supplement; battles the Hulk						3.00
Spider-Girl Presents Wild Thing. Crash Course (2007, $7.99, digest) r/#0-5						8.00

WILDTIMES
DC Comics (WildStorm Productions): Aug, 1999 ($2.50, one-shots)

	GD 2.0	VG 4.0	FN 6.0	VF 8.0	VF/NM 9.0	NM- 9.2
...Deathblow #1 -set in 1899; Edwards-a; Jonah Hex app., ...DV8 #1 -set in 1944; Altieri-s/p; Sgt. Rock app., ...Gen13 #1 -set in 1969; Casey-s/Johnson-a; Teen Titans app., ...Grifter #1 -set in 1923; Paul Smith-a, ...Wetworks #1 -Waid-s/Lopresti-a; Superman app.						3.00
...WildC.A.T.s #0 -Wizard supplement; Charest-c						3.00

WILD WEST (Wild Western #3 on)
Marvel Comics (WFP): Spring, 1948 - No. 2, July, 1948

	GD 2.0	VG 4.0	FN 6.0	VF 8.0	VF/NM 9.0	NM- 9.2
1-Two-Gun Kid, Arizona Annie, & Tex Taylor begin; Shores-c	37	74	111	222	361	500
2-Captain Tootsie by Beck; Shores-c	24	48	72	142	234	325

WILD WEST (Black Fury #1-57)
Charlton Comics: V2#58, Nov, 1966

	GD 2.0	VG 4.0	FN 6.0	VF 8.0	VF/NM 9.0	NM- 9.2
V2#58	2	4	6	11	16	20

WILD WEST C.O.W.-BOYS OF MOO MESA (TV)
Archie Comics: Dec, 1992 - No. 3, Feb, 1993 (limited series)
V2#1, Mar, 1993 - No. 3, July, 1993 ($1.25)

	GD 2.0	VG 4.0	FN 6.0	VF 8.0	VF/NM 9.0	NM- 9.2
1-3,V2#1-3						3.00

WILD WESTERN (Formerly Wild West #1,2)
Marvel/Atlas (WFP): No. 3, 9/48 - No. 57, 9/57 (3-11: 52 pgs, 12-on: 36 pgs)

	GD 2.0	VG 4.0	FN 6.0	VF 8.0	VF/NM 9.0	NM- 9.2
3(#1)-Tex Morgan begins; Two-Gun Kid, Tex Taylor, & Arizona Annie continue from Wild West	30	60	90	177	289	400
4-Last Arizona Annie; Captain Tootsie by Beck; Kid Colt app.	21	42	63	126	206	285
5-2nd app. Black Rider (1/49); Blaze Carson, Captain Tootsie (by Beck) app.	26	52	78	154	252	350
6-8: 6-Blaze Carson app; anti-Wertham editorial	17	34	51	98	154	210
9-Photo-c; Black Rider app., also in #11-19	20	40	60	120	195	270
10-Charles Starrett photo-c	24	48	72	140	230	320
11-(Last 52 pg. issue) The Prairie Kid app.	18	36	54	103	162	220
12-14,16-19: All Black Rider-c/stories. 12-14-The Prairie Kid & his horse Fury app.	20	40	60	117	189	260
15-Red Larabee, Gunhawk (origin), his horse Blaze, & Apache Kid begin, end #22; Black Rider-c/story	20	40	60	120	195	270
20-30: 20-Kid Colt-c begin. 24-Has 2 Kid Colt stories. 26-1st app. The Ringo Kid? (2/53); 4 pg. story. 30-Katz-a	14	28	42	82	121	160
31-40	11	22	33	67	94	120
41-47,49-51,53,57	11	22	33	60	83	105
48-Williamson/Torres-a (4 pgs); Drucker-a	13	26	39	72	101	130
52-Crandall-a	13	26	39	72	101	130
54,55-Williamson-a in both (5 & 4 pgs.), #54 with Mayo plus 2 text illos	13	26	39	72	101	130
56-Baker-a?	11	22	33	60	83	105

NOTE: *Annie Oakley in #46, 47. Apache Kid in #15-22, 39. Arizona Kid in #21, 23. Arrowhead in #34-39. Black Rider in #5, 8-19, 33-44. Fighting Texan in #17. Kid Colt in #4-6, 8-11, 20-47, 51, 52, 54-56. Outlaw Kid in #43. Red Hawkins in #13, 14. Ringo Kid in #26, 39, 41, 43, 44, 46, 47, 50-56. Tex Morgan in #3, 4, 6, 9, 11. Tex Taylor in #3-6, 9, 11. Texas Kid in #23-25. Two-Gun Kid in #3-6, 8, 9, 11, 12, 33-39, 41. Wyatt Earp in #47.* ***Ayers*** *a-41, 42, 53, 54.* ***Berg*** *a-26; c-24.* ***Colan*** *a-49.* ***Forte*** *a-28, 30.* ***Al Hartley*** *a-16, 51.* ***Heath*** *a-4, 5, 8; c-34, 44.* ***Keller*** *a-24, 26(2), 29-40, 44-46, 48, 51, 52.* ***Maneely*** *a-10, 12, 15, 16, 28, 35, 38, 40-45; c-18-22, 33, 35, 36, 38-42, 45, 51, 53, 54, 56, 57.* ***Morisi*** *a-23, 52.* ***Pakula*** *a-42, 52.* ***Powell*** *a-51.* ***Romita*** *a-24(2).* ***Severin*** *a-46, 47; c-48.* ***Shores*** *a-3, 5, 30, 31, 33, 35, 36, 38, 41; c-3-5.* ***Sinnott*** *a-34-39.* ***Wildey*** *a-43. Bondage c-19.*

WILD WESTERN ACTION (Also see The Bravados)
Skywald Publ. Corp.: Mar, 1971 - No. 3, June, 1971 (25¢, reprints, 52 pgs.)

	GD 2.0	VG 4.0	FN 6.0	VF 8.0	VF/NM 9.0	NM- 9.2
1-Durango Kid, Straight Arrow-r; with all references to "Straight" in story relettered to "Swift"; Bravados begin; Shores-a (new)	3	6	9	16	24	32
2,3: 2-Billy Nevada, Durango Kid. 3-Red Mask, Durango Kid	2	4	6	13	18	22

WILD WESTERN ROUNDUP
Red Top/Decker Publications/I. W. Enterprises: Oct, 1957; 1960-'61

	GD 2.0	VG 4.0	FN 6.0	VF 8.0	VF/NM 9.0	NM- 9.2
1(1957)-Kid Cowboy-r	5	10	15	22	26	30
I.W. Reprint #1('60-61)-r/#1 by Red Top	2	4	6	8	11	14

WILD WEST RODEO
Star Publications: 1953 (15¢)

	GD 2.0	VG 4.0	FN 6.0	VF 8.0	VF/NM 9.0	NM- 9.2
1-A comic book coloring book with regular full color cover & B&W inside	9	18	27	52	69	85

WILD WILD WEST, THE (TV)
Gold Key: June, 1966 - No. 7, Oct, 1969 (All have Robert Conrad photo-c)

	GD 2.0	VG 4.0	FN 6.0	VF 8.0	VF/NM 9.0	NM- 9.2
1-McWilliams-a	10	20	30	67	141	215
1-Variant edition with photo back-c (scarce)	11	22	33	73	157	240
2-Robert Conrad photo-c; McWilliams-a	8	16	24	51	96	140
2-Variant edition with Conrad photo back-c (scarce)	8	16	24	56	108	160
3-7	6	12	18	42	79	115
3-Variant edition with photo back-c (scarce)	8	16	24	51	96	140

WILD, WILD WEST, THE (TV)
Millennium Publications: Oct, 1990 - No. 4, Jan?, 1991 ($2.95, limited series)

	GD 2.0	VG 4.0	FN 6.0	VF 8.0	VF/NM 9.0	NM- 9.2
1-4-Based on TV show						3.00

WILKIN BOY (See That...)

WILL EISNER READER
Kitchen Sink Press: 1991 ($9.95, B&W, 8 1/2" x 11", TPB)

	GD 2.0	VG 4.0	FN 6.0	VF 8.0	VF/NM 9.0	NM- 9.2
nn-Reprints stories from Will Eisner's Quarterly; Eisner-s/a/c						15.00
nn-(DC Comics, 10/00, $9.95)						10.00

WILL EISNER'S JOHN LAW: ANGELS AND ASHES, DEVILS AND DUST
IDW Publ.: Apr, 2006 - No. 4 ($3.99, B&W, limited series)

	GD 2.0	VG 4.0	FN 6.0	VF 8.0	VF/NM 9.0	NM- 9.2
1-New stories with Will Eisner's characters; Gary Chaloner-s/a						4.00

WILLIE COMICS (Formerly Ideal #1-4; Crime Cases #24 on; Li'l Willie #20 & 21)
(See Gay Comics, Laugh, Millie The Model & Wisco)
Marvel Comics (MgPC): #5, Fall, 1946 - #19, 4/49; #22, 1/50 - #23, 5/50 (No #20 & 21)

	GD 2.0	VG 4.0	FN 6.0	VF 8.0	VF/NM 9.0	NM- 9.2
5(#1)-George, Margie, Nellie the Nurse & Willie begin	39	78	117	231	378	525
6,8,9	21	42	63	124	202	280
7(1),10,11-Kurtzman's "Hey Look"	22	44	66	128	209	290
12,14-18,22,23	20	40	60	117	189	260
13,19-Kurtzman's "Hey Look" (#19-last by Kurtzman?)	20	40	60	120	195	270

NOTE: *Cindy app. in #17. Jeanie app. in #17. Little Lizzie app. in #22.*

WILLIE MAYS (See The Amazing...)

WILLIE THE PENGUIN
Standard Comics: Apr, 1951 - No. 6, Apr, 1952

	GD 2.0	VG 4.0	FN 6.0	VF 8.0	VF/NM 9.0	NM- 9.2
1-Funny animal	11	22	33	62	86	110
2-6	7	14	21	37	46	55

WILLIE THE WISE-GUY (Also see Cartoon Kids)
Atlas Comics (NPP): Sept, 1957

	GD 2.0	VG 4.0	FN 6.0	VF 8.0	VF/NM 9.0	NM- 9.2
1-Kida, Maneely-a	15	30	45	85	130	175

WILLOW
Marvel Comics: Aug, 1988 - No. 3, Oct, 1988 ($1.00)

	GD 2.0	VG 4.0	FN 6.0	VF 8.0	VF/NM 9.0	NM- 9.2
1-3-R/Marvel Graphic Novel #36 (movie adaptation)						4.00

WILLOW (From Buffy the Vampire Slayer)
Dark Horse Comics: Nov, 2012 - No. 5, Mar, 2013 ($2.99, limited series)

	GD 2.0	VG 4.0	FN 6.0	VF 8.0	VF/NM 9.0	NM- 9.2
1-5-Jeff Parker-s/Brian Ching-a; covers by David Mack & Megan Lara; Aluwyn app.						3.00

WILL ROGERS WESTERN (Formerly My Great Love #1-4; see Blazing & True Comics #66)

Wings Comics #43 © FH

Winnie-The-Pooh #8 © DIS

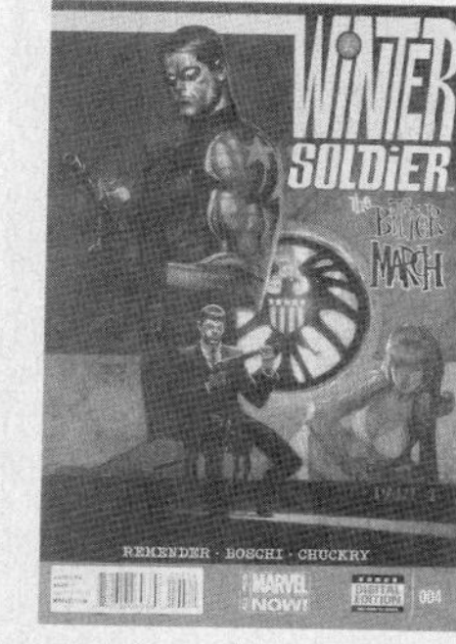

Winter Soldier #4 © MAR

GD 2.0 | VG 4.0 | FN 6.0 | VF 8.0 | VF/NM 9.0 | NM- 9.2

Fox Features Syndicate: No. 5, June, 1950 - No. 2, Aug, 1950
5(#1) Photo-c 31 62 93 186 303 420
2: Photo-c 26 52 78 154 252 350

WILL TO POWER (Also see Comic's Greatest World)
Dark Horse Comics: June, 1994 - No. 12, Aug, 1994 ($1.00, weekly limited series, 20 pgs.)
1-12: 12-Vortex kills Titan. 3.00
NOTE: ***Mignola** c-10-12. **Sears** c-1-3.*

WILL-YUM!
Dell Publishing Co.: No. 676, Feb, 1956 - No. 902, May, 1958
Four Color 676 (#1), 765 (1/57), 902 4 8 12 28 47 65

WIN A PRIZE COMICS (Timmy The Timid Ghost #3 on?)
Charlton Comics: Feb, 1955 - No. 2, Apr, 1955
V1#1-S&K-a; Poe adapt; E.C. War swipe 67 134 201 426 731 1035
2-S&K-a 48 96 144 302 514 725

WINDY & WILLY (Also see Showcase #81)
National Periodical Publications: May-June, 1969 - No. 4, Nov-Dec, 1969
1- r/Dobie Gillis with some art changes begin 5 10 15 31 53 75
2-4 3 6 9 21 33 45

WINGS COMICS
Fiction House Mag.: 9/40 - No. 109, 9/49; No. 110, Wint, 1949-50; No. 111, Spring, 1950; No. 112, 1950(nd); No. 113 - No. 115, 1950(nd); No. 116, 1952(nd); No. 117, Fall, 1952 - No. 122, Wint, 1953-54; No. 123 - No. 124, 1954(nd)
1-Skull Squad, Clipper Kirk, Suicide Smith, Jane Martin, War Nurse, Phantom Falcons, Greasemonkey Griffin, Parachute Patrol & Powder Burns begin; grey-tone-c 300 600 900 1920 3310 4700
2 126 252 378 806 1378 1950
3-5 86 172 258 546 936 1325
6-10: 8-Indicia shows #7 (#8 on cover) 66 132 198 419 722 1025
11-15 61 122 183 390 670 950
16-Origin & 1st app. Captain Wings & begin series 66 132 198 419 722 1025
17-20: 20-(4/42) 1st Japanese WWII-c 54 108 162 343 574 825
21-25,27-30 49 98 147 309 522 735
26-1st Good Girl WWII-c for this title 71 142 213 454 777 1100
31-34,36-40 41 82 123 256 428 600
35-Classic Nazi WWII-c 47 94 141 296 498 700
41-50 36 72 108 211 343 475
51-60: 60-Last Skull Squad 32 64 96 192 314 435
61-67: 66-Ghost Patrol begins (becomes Ghost Squadron #71 on), ends #112? 30 60 90 177 289 400
68,69: 68-Clipper Kirk becomes The Phantom Falcon-origin, Part 1; part 2 in #69 30 60 90 177 289 400
70-72: 70-1st app. The Phantom Falcon in costume, origin-Part 3; Capt. Wings battles Col. Kamikaze in all 29 58 87 170 278 385
73-88,92,93,95-99: 80-Phantom Falcon by Larsen. 99-King of the Congo begins? 29 58 87 170 278 385
89-91,94-Classic Good Girl covers 77 154 231 493 847 1200
100-(12/48) 30 60 90 177 289 400
101-124: 111-Last Jane Martin. 112-Flying Saucer-c (1950). 115-Used in **POP**, pg. 89. 121-Atomic Explosion-c. 122-Korean War 21 42 63 126 206 285
NOTE: *World War II covers (Nazi or Japanese) on #1-17, 19-67. Bondage covers are common. Captain Wings battles Sky Hag-#75, 76; ...Mr. Atlantis-#85-92; ...Mr. Pupin(Red Agent)-#98-103. Capt. Wings by **Elias**-#52-64, 68, 69; by **Lubbers**-#29-32, 70-111; by **Renee**-#33-46. **Evans** a-85-106, 108-111(Jane Martin); text illos-72-84. **Larsen** a-52, 59, 64, 73-77. Jane Martin by **Fran Hopper**-#68-84; Suicide Smith by **John Celardo**-#72, 74, 76, 80-104; by **Hollingsworth**-#68-70, 105-109, 111; Ghost Squadron by **Astarita**-#67-79; by **Maurice Whitman**-#80-111. King of the Congo by **Moreira**-#99, 100. Skull Squad by **M. Baker**-#52-60; Clipper Kirk by **Baker**-#60, 61; by **Colan**-#53; by **Ingels**-(some issues?). Phantom Falcon by **Larsen**-#73-84. **Elias** c-58-72. **Fawcette** c-3-12, 16, 17, 19, 22-33. **Lubbers** c-74-109. **Tuska** a-5. **Whitman** c-110-124. **Zolnerwich** c-15, 21.*

WINGS OF THE EAGLES, THE
Dell Publishing Co.: No. 790, Apr, 1957 (10¢ & 15¢ editions exist)
Four Color 790-Movie; John Wayne photo-c; Toth-a 12 24 36 83 182 280

WINKY DINK (Adventures of...)
Pines Comics: No. 75, Mar, 1957 (one-shot)
75-Marv Levy-c/a 7 14 21 35 43 50

WINKY DINK (TV)
Dell Publishing Co.: No. 663, Nov, 1955
Four Color 663 (#1) 8 16 24 51 96 140

WINNIE-THE-POOH (Also see Dynabrite Comics)
Gold Key No. 1-17/Whitman No. 18 on: January, 1977 - No. 33, July, 1984
(Walt Disney) (Winnie-The-Pooh began as Edward Bear in 1926 by Milne)
1-New art 4 8 12 25 40 55
2-5: 5-New material 2 4 6 13 18 22
6-17: 12-up-New material 2 4 6 9 13 16
18,19(Whitman) 2 4 6 13 18 22
20,21('80) pre-pack only 4 8 12 28 47 65
22('80) (scarcer) pre-pack only 5 10 15 34 60 85
23-28: 27(2/82), 28(4/82) 3 6 9 14 19 24
29-33 (#90299 on-c, no date or date code; pre-pack): 29(4/82), 30(5/83), 31(8/83), 32(4/84), 33(7/84) 3 6 9 20 31 42

WINNIE WINKLE (See Popular Comics & Super Comics)
Dell Publishing Co.: 1941 - No. 7, Sept-Nov, 1949
Large Feature Comic 2 (1941) 32 64 96 188 307 425
Four Color 94 (1945) 12 24 36 79 170 260
Four Color 174 8 16 24 54 102 150
1(3-5/48)-Contains daily & Sunday newspaper-r from 1939-1941 8 16 24 51 96 140
2 (6-8/48) 5 10 15 33 57 80
3-7 4 8 12 27 44 60

WINTER MEN, THE
DC Comics (WildStorm): Oct, 2005 - No. 5, Nov, 2006 ($2.99, limited series)
1-5-Brett Lewis-s/John Paul Leon-a 3.00
... Winter Special (2/09, $3.99) Lewis-s/Leon-a 4.00
TPB (2010, $19.99) r/#1-5 & Winter Special; original proposal, development & sketch-a 20.00

WINTER SOLDIER (See Captain America 2005 series)
Marvel Comics: Apr, 2012 - No. 19, Aug, 2013 ($2.99)
1-19: 1-Black Widow app.; Brubaker-s/Guice-a/Bermejo-c. 3-5-Dr. Doom app. 3.00

WINTER SOLDIER: THE BITTER MARCH
Marvel Comics: Apr, 2014 - No. 5, Sept, 2014 ($3.99, limited series)
1-5: 1-Remender-s/Boschi-a/Robinson-c; set in 1966; Nick Fury app. 4.00

WINTER SOLDIER: WINTER KILLS
Marvel Comics: Feb, 2007 ($3.99, one-shot)
1-Flashback to Christmas Eve 1944; Toro & Sub-Mariner app.; Brubaker-s/Weeks-a 5.00

WINTERWORLD
Eclipse Comics: Sept, 1987 - No. 3, Mar, 1988 ($1.75, limited series)
1-3 3.00

WINTERWORLD
IDW Publishing: Jun, 2014 - No. 7, Jan, 2015 ($3.99)
1-7: 1-Chuck Dixon-s/Butch Guice-a; three covers. 5-7-Giorello-a 4.00
#0-(3/15, $3.99) Origin of Wynn; Dixon-s/Edwards-a; covers by Edwards & Guice 4.00

WINTERWORLD: FROZEN FLEET
IDW Publishing: May, 2015 - No. 3, Jul, 2015 ($3.99, limited series)
1-3: 1-Chuck Dixon-s/Esteve Polls-a; three covers. 2,3-Two covers 4.00

WISDOM
Marvel Comics (MAX): Jan, 2007 - No. 6, July, 2007 ($3.99, limited series)
1-6: 1-Hairsine-a/c; Cornell-s. 3-6-Manuel Garcia-a 4.00
...: Rudiments of Wisdom TPB (2007, $21.99) r/#1-6; series pitch and sketch page 22.00

WISE GUYS (See Harvey...)

WISE LITTLE HEN, THE
David McKay Publ./Whitman: 1934 ,1935(48 pgs.); 1937 (Story book)
nn-(1934 edition w/dust jacket)(48 pgs. with color, 8-3/4x9-3/4") -Debut of Donald Duck (see Advs. of Mickey Mouse); Donald app. on cover with Wise Little Hen & Practical Pig; painted cover; same artist as the B&W's from Silly Symphony Cartoon, The Wise Little Hen (1934) (McKay)
Book w/dust jacket 265 530 795 1694 2897 4100
Dust jacket only 63 126 189 403 689 975
nn-(1935 edition w/dust jacket), same as 1934 ed. 152 304 456 965 1658 2350
888 (1937)(9-1/2x13", 12 pgs.)(Whitman) Donald Duck app. 39 78 117 231 378 525

WISE SON: THE WHITE WOLF
DC Comics (Milestone): Nov, 1996 - No. 4, Feb, 1997 ($2.50, limited series)
1-4: Ho Che Anderson-c/a 3.00

WIT AND WISDOM OF WATERGATE (Humor magazine)
Marvel Comics: 1973, 76 pgs., squarebound
1-Low print run 5 10 15 31 53 75

WITCHBLADE (Also see Cyblade/Shi, Tales Of The..., & Top Cow Classics)

Witchblade #26 © TCOW

Witchblade: Animated #1 © TCOW

Witchblade/Wolverine #1 © TCOW & MAR

Image Comics (Top Cow Productions): Nov, 1995 - No. 185, Nov, 2015 ($2.50/$2.99)

	GD 2.0	VG 4.0	FN 6.0	VF 8.0	VF/NM 9.0	NM- 9.2
0	1	2	3	5	6	8
1/2-Mike Turner/Marc Silvestri-c.	3	6	9	19	30	40
1/2 Gold Ed., 1/2 Chromium-c	3	6	9	19	30	40
1/2-(Vol. 2, 11/02, $2.99) Wohl-s/Ching-a/c						3.00
1-Mike Turner-a(p)	4	8	12	19	30	40
1,2-American Ent. Encore Ed.	1	2	3	4	5	7
2,3	2	4	6	11	16	20
4,5	2	4	6	8	10	12
6-9: 8-Wraparound-c. 9-Tony Daniel-a(p)	1	2	3	5	6	8
9-Sunset variant-c	2	4	6	8	10	12
9-DF variant-c	2	4	6	9	12	15
10-Flip book w/Darkness #0, 1st app. the Darkness	1	3	4	6	8	10
10-Variant-c	2	4	6	8	10	12
10-Gold logo	3	6	9	14	20	25
10-($3.95) Dynamic Forces alternate-c	1	2	3	5	6	8
11-15						5.00
16-19: 18,19-"Family Ties" Darkness x-over pt. 1,4						4.00
18-Face to face variant-c, 18-American Ent. Ed., 19-AE Gold Ed.	1	2	3	5	6	8
20-25: 24-Pearson, Green-a. 25-($2.95) Turner-a(p)						4.00
25 (Prism variant)						25.00
25 (Special)						10.00
26-39: 26-Green-a begins						3.00
27 (Variant)						6.00
40-49,51-53: 40-Begin Jenkins & Veitch-s/Keu Cha-a. 47-Zulli-c/a						3.00
40-Pittsburgh Convention Preview edition; B&W preview of #40						3.00
49-Gold logo						5.00
50-($4.95) Darkness app.; Ching-a; B&W preview of Universe						5.00
54-59: 54-Black outer-c with gold foil logo; Wohl-s/Manapul-a						3.00
60-74,76-91,93-99: 60-($2.99) Endgame x-over with Tomb Raider #25 & Evo #1. 64,65-Magdalena app. 71-Kirk-a. 77,81-85-Land-c. 80-Four covers. 87-Bachalo-a						3.00
75-($4.99) Manapul-a						5.00
92-($4.99) Origin of the Witchblade; art by various incl. Bachalo, Perez, Linsner, Cooke						5.00
100-($4.99) Five covers incl. Turner, Silvestri, Linsner; art by various; Jake dies						5.00
101-124,126-143: 103-Danielle Baptiste gets the Witchblade; Linsner variant-c. 116-124,140,141-Sejic-a. 126-128-War of the Witchblades. 134-136-Aphrodite IV app. 139-Gaydos-a. 143-Matt Dow Smith-a						3.00
125-($3.99) War of the Witchblades begins; 3 covers; Sejic-a						4.00
144-($4.99) Origin retold; wraparound-c; Sejic-a; back-up w/Sablik-s; pin-up gallery						5.00
145-149-($3.99) Sejic-a/c. 149-Angelus app.						4.00
150-($4.99) Four covers; last Marz-s; Sejic-a; cover gallery & series timeline						5.00
151-174-($2.99) Altered reality after Artifacts #13; Seeley-s; multiple covers						3.00
175-($5.99) Three covers; Marz-s; Laura Braga-a; Temple of Shadows back-up						6.00
176-184-($3.99) 180-Hine-s/Rearte-a						4.00
185-($5.99)-Last issue; Marz & Hawkins-s; art by various; bonus preview of Switch #1						6.00
... and Tomb Raider (4/05, $2.99) Jae Lee-c; art by Lee and Texiera						3.00
...: Animated (8/03, $2.99) Magdalena & Darkness app.; Dini-s/Bone, Bullock, Cooke-a/c						3.00
... Annual 2009 (4/09, $3.99) Basaldua-a						4.00
... Annual #1 (12/10, $4.99) the Witchblade in Stalingrad 1942, Shasteen-a; Haley-a						5.00
...: Art of the Witchblade (7/06, $2.99) pin-ups by various incl. Turner, Land, Linsner						3.00
...: Bearers of the Blade (7/06, $2.99) pin-up/profiles of bearers of the Witchblade						3.00
...: Blood Oath (8/04, $4.99) Sara teams with Phenix & Sibilla; Roux-a						5.00
...: Blood Relations TPB (2003, $12.99) r/#54-58						13.00
... Case Files 1 (10/14, $3.99) Character profiles and story summaries						4.00
... Compendium Vol. 1 (2006, $59.99) r/#1-50; gallery of variant covers and art						60.00
... Compendium Vol. 2 (2007, $59.99) r/#51-100; gallery of variant covers and art						60.00
... Cover Gallery Vol. 1 (12/05, $2.99) intro. by Stan Lee						3.00
.../Darkchylde (7/00, $2.50) Green-s/a(p)						3.00
.../Dark Minds (6/04, $9.99) new story plus r/Dark Minds/Witchblade #1						10.00
.../Darkness: Family Ties Collected Edition (10/98, $9.95) r/#18,19 and Darkness #9,10						10.00
.../Darkness Special (12/99, $3.95) Green-c/a						4.00
... Day of the Outlaws (4/13, $3.99) Fialkov-s/Blake-a; Witchblade in 1878 Colorado						4.00
...: Demon 1 (2003, $6.99) Mark Millar-s/Jae Lee-c/a						7.00
.../Devi (4/08, $3.99) Basaldua-a/Land-c; continues in Devi/Witchblade						4.00
...: Distinctions (See Tales of the Witchblade)						
...: Due Process (8/10, $3.99) Alina Urusov-a/c; Phil Smith-s						4.00
.../Elektra (3/97, $2.95) Devil's Reign Pt. 6						4.00
... Gallery (11/00, $2.95) Profile pages and pin-ups by various; Turner-c						3.00
Image Firsts: Witchblade #1 (4/10, $1.00) reprints #1						3.00
Infinity (5/99, $3.50) Lobdell-s/Pollina-c/a						4.00
.../Lady Death (11/01, $4.95) Manapul-c/a						5.00
...: Prevailing TPB (2000, $14.95) r/#20-25; new Turner-c						15.00
...: Revelations TPB (2000, $24.95) r/#9-17; new Turner-c						25.00
.../The Punisher (6/07, $3.99) Marz-s/Melo-a/Linsner-c						4.00
.../Tomb Raider #1/2 (7/00, $2.95) Covers by Turner and Cha						4.00
... Unbalanced Pieces FCBD Edition (5/12, giveaway) Christopher-c						3.00
...: Vol. 1 TPB (1/08, $4.99) r/#80-85; Marz intro.; cover gallery						5.00
...: Vol. 2 TPB (2/08, $14.99) r/#86-92; cover gallery						15.00
...: Vol. 3 TPB (3/08, $14.99) r/#93-100; Edginton intro.; cover gallery						15.00
... vs. Frankenstein: Monster War 2005 (8/05, $2.99) pt. 3 of x-over						3.00
...: Witch Hunt Vol. 1 TPB (2/06, $14.99) r/#80-85; Marz intro.; Choi afterward; cover gallery						15.00
Wizard #500						10.00
.../Wolverine (6/04, $2.99) Basaldua-c/a; Claremont-s						3.00

WITCHBLADE/ALIENS/THE DARKNESS/PREDATOR
Dark Horse Comics/Top Cow Productions: Nov, 2000 ($2.99)

	GD 2.0	VG 4.0	FN 6.0	VF 8.0	VF/NM 9.0	NM- 9.2
1-3-Mel Rubi-a						4.00

WITCHBLADE COLLECTED EDITION
Image Comics (Top Cow Productions): July, 1996 - No. 8 ($4.95/$6.95, squarebound, limited series)

	GD 2.0	VG 4.0	FN 6.0	VF 8.0	VF/NM 9.0	NM- 9.2
1-7-($4.95): Two issues reprinted in each						5.00
8-($6.95) r/#15-17						7.00
...Slipcase (10/96, $10.95)-Packaged w/ Coll. Ed. #1-4						11.00

WITCHBLADE: DEMON REBORN
Dynamite Entertainment: 2012 - No. 4, 2012 ($3.99, limited series)

	GD 2.0	VG 4.0	FN 6.0	VF 8.0	VF/NM 9.0	NM- 9.2
1-4-Ande Parks-s/Jose Luis-a; covers by Calero & Jae Lee						4.00

WITCHBLADE: DESTINY'S CHILD
Image Comics (Top Cow): Jun, 2000 - No. 3, Sept, 2000 ($2.95, limited series)

	GD 2.0	VG 4.0	FN 6.0	VF 8.0	VF/NM 9.0	NM- 9.2
1-3: 1-Boller-a/Keu Cha-c						3.00

WITCHBLADE: MANGA (Takeru Manga)
Image Comics (Top Cow): Feb, 2007 - No. 12, Mar, 2008 ($2.99/$3.99)

	GD 2.0	VG 4.0	FN 6.0	VF 8.0	VF/NM 9.0	NM- 9.2
1-4-Colored reprints of Japanese Witchblade manga. 1-Three covers. 2-Two covers						3.00
5-12-($3.99)						4.00

WITCHBLADE: OBAKEMONO
Image Comics (Top Cow Productions): 2002 ($9.95, one-shot graphic novel)

	GD 2.0	VG 4.0	FN 6.0	VF 8.0	VF/NM 9.0	NM- 9.2
1-Fiona Avery-s/Billy Tan-a; forward by Straczynski						10.00

WITCHBLADE/ RED SONJA
Dynamite Ent./Top Cow: 2012 - No. 5, 2012 ($3.99, limited series)

	GD 2.0	VG 4.0	FN 6.0	VF 8.0	VF/NM 9.0	NM- 9.2
1-5-Doug Wagner-s/Cezar Razek-a/Alé Garza-c						4.00

WITCHBLADE: SHADES OF GRAY
Dynamite Ent./Top Cow: 2007 - No. 4, 2007 ($3.50, lim. series)

	GD 2.0	VG 4.0	FN 6.0	VF 8.0	VF/NM 9.0	NM- 9.2
1,2: 1-Sara Pezzini meets Dorian Gray; Segovia-a; multiple covers						3.50

WITCHBLADE/ TOMB RAIDER SPECIAL (Also see Tomb Raider/...)
Image Comics (Top Cow Productions): Dec, 1998 ($2.95)

	GD 2.0	VG 4.0	FN 6.0	VF 8.0	VF/NM 9.0	NM- 9.2
1-Based on video game character; Turner-a(p)						4.00
1-Silvestri variant-c						6.00
1-Turner bikini variant-c						10.00
1-Prism-c						12.00
Wizard 1/2 -Turner-s						10.00

WITCHCRAFT (See Strange Mysteries, Super Reprint #18)
Avon Periodicals: Mar-Apr, 1952 - No. 6, Mar, 1953

	GD 2.0	VG 4.0	FN 6.0	VF 8.0	VF/NM 9.0	NM- 9.2
1-Kubert-a; 1 pg. Check-a	89	178	267	565	970	1375
2-Kubert & Check-a; classic skull-c	84	168	252	538	919	1300
3,6: 3-Lawrence-a; Kinstler inside-c	53	106	159	334	567	800
4-People cooked alive c/story	81	162	243	518	884	1250
5-Kelly Freas painted-c	87	174	261	553	952	1350

NOTE: ***Hollingsworth** a-4-6; c-4, 6. **McCann** a-3?*

WITCHCRAFT
DC Comics (Vertigo): June, 1994 - No. 3, Aug, 1994 ($2.95, limited series)

	GD 2.0	VG 4.0	FN 6.0	VF 8.0	VF/NM 9.0	NM- 9.2
1-3: James Robinson scripts & Kaluta-c in all						4.00
1-Platinum Edition						15.00
Trade paperback-(1996, $14.95)-r/#1-3; Kaluta-c						15.00

WITCHCRAFT: LA TERREUR
DC Comics (Vertigo): Apr, 1998 - No. 3, Jun, 1998 ($2.50, limited series)

	GD 2.0	VG 4.0	FN 6.0	VF 8.0	VF/NM 9.0	NM- 9.2
1-3: Robinson-s/Zulli & Locke-a; interlocking cover images						3.00

WITCH DOCTOR (See Walking Dead #85 flip book for preview)
Image Comics: Jun, 2011 - No. 4, Nov, 2011 ($2.99, limited series)

	GD 2.0	VG 4.0	FN 6.0	VF 8.0	VF/NM 9.0	NM- 9.2
1-4-Seifert-s/Ketner-a/c						3.00

Witches Tales #3 © HARV

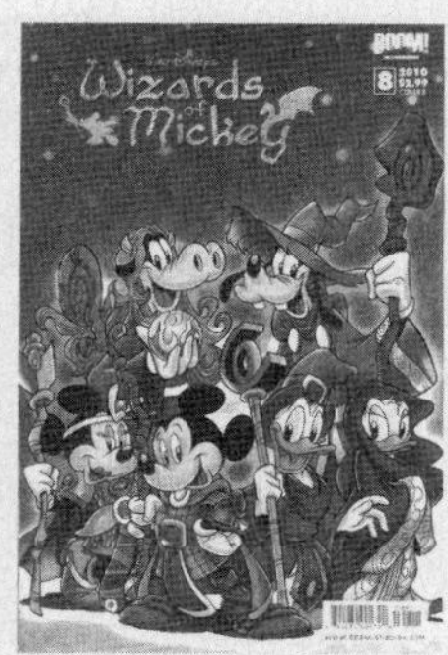

	GD 2.0	VG 4.0	FN 6.0	VF 8.0	VF/NM 9.0	NM- 9.2
...: Mal Practice 1-6 (11/12 - No. 6, 4/13, $2.99) Seifert-s/Ketner-a/c						3.00
...: The Resuscitation (12/11, $2.99) Seifert-s/Ketner-a/c						3.00

WITCHER, THE
Dark Horse Comics: Mar, 2014 - No. 5, Jul, 2014 ($3.99, limited series)

1-5-Tobin-s/Querio-a 4.00

WITCHER, THE: FOX CHILDREN
Dark Horse Comics: Apr, 2015 - No. 5, Aug, 2015 ($3.99, limited series)

1-5-Tobin-s/Querio-a 4.00

WITCHES
Marvel Comics: Aug, 2004 - No. 4, Sept, 2004 ($2.99, limited series)

1-4: 1,2-Deodato, Jr-a; Dr. Strange app. 3,4-Conrad-a 3.00
... Vol. 1: The Gathering (2004, $9.99) r/series 10.00

WITCHES TALES (Witches Western Tales #29,30)
Witches Tales/Harvey Publications: Jan, 1951 - No. 28, Dec, 1954 (date misprinted as 4/55)

	GD	VG	FN	VF	VF/NM	NM-
1-Powell-a (1 pg.)	66	132	198	419	722	1025
2-Eye injury panel	39	78	117	240	395	550
3-7,9,10	34	68	102	199	325	450
8-Eye injury panels	37	74	111	218	354	490
11-13,15,16: 12-Acid in face story	31	62	93	186	303	420
14,17-Powell/Nostrand-a. 17-Atomic disaster story	33	66	99	194	317	440
18-Nostrand-a; E.C. swipe/Shock S.S.	33	66	99	194	317	440
19-Nostrand-a; E.C. swipe/ "Glutton"; Devil-c	39	78	117	240	395	550
20-24-Nostrand-a. 21-E.C. swipe; rape story. 23-Wood E.C. swipes/Two-Fisted Tales #34	33	66	99	194	317	440
25-Nostrand-a; E.C. swipe/Mad Barber; decapitation-c	116	232	348	742	1271	1800
26-28: 27-r/#6 with diff.-c. 28-r/#8 with diff.-c	21	42	63	126	206	285

NOTE: ***Check** a-24. **Elias** c-8, 10, 16-27. **Kremer** a-18; c-25. **Nostrand** a-17-25; 14, 17(w/Powell). **Palais** a-1, 2, 4(2), 5(2), 7-9, 12, 14, 15, 17. **Powell** a-3-7, 10, 11, 19-27. Bondage-c 1, 3, 5, 6, 8, 9.*

WITCHES TALES (Magazine)
Eerie Publications: V1#7, July, 1969 - V7#1, Feb, 1975 (B&W, 52 pgs.)

	GD	VG	FN	VF	VF/NM	NM-
V1#7(7/69)	7	14	21	46	86	125
V1#8(9/69), 9(11/69)	6	12	18	37	66	95
V2#1-6('70), V3#1-6('71)	5	10	15	31	53	75
V4#1-6('72), V5#1-6('73), V6#1-6('74), V7#1	4	8	12	28	47	65

NOTE: *Ajax/Farrell reprints in early issues.*

WITCHES' WESTERN TALES (Formerly Witches Tales)(Western Tales #31 on)
Harvey Publications: No. 29, Feb, 1955 - No. 30, Apr, 1955

	GD	VG	FN	VF	VF/NM	NM-
29,30-Featuring Clay Duncan & Boys' Ranch; S&K-r/from Boys' Ranch including-c. 29-Last pre-code	15	30	45	86	133	180

WITCHFINDER, THE
Image Comics (Liar): Sept, 1999 - No. 3, Jan, 2000 ($2.95)

1-3-Romano-a/Sharon & Matthew Scott-plot 3.00

WITCHFINDER: CITY OF THE DEAD
Dark Horse Comics: Aug, 2016 - No. 5, Dec, 2016 ($3.99, limited series)

1-5-Mignola & Roberson-s/Stenbeck-a/Tedesco-c 4.00

WITCHFINDER: LOST AND GONE FOREVER
Dark Horse Comics: Feb, 2011 - No. 5, Jun, 2011 ($3.50, limited series)

1-5-John Severin-a; Mignola & Arcudi-s. 1-Two covers by Mignola & Severin 3.50

WITCH HUNTER
Malibu Comics (Ultraverse): Apr, 1996 ($2.50, one-shot)

1 3.00

WITCHING, THE
DC Comics (Vertigo): Aug, 2004 - No. 10, May, 2005 ($2.95/$2.99)

1-10-Vankin-s/Gallagher-a/McPherson-c. 1,2-Lucifer app. 3.00

WITCHING HOUR ("The ..." in later issues)
National Periodical Publ./DC Comics: Feb-Mar, 1969 - No. 85, Oct, 1978

	GD	VG	FN	VF	VF/NM	NM-
1-Toth-a, plus Neal Adams-a (2 pgs.)	13	26	39	89	195	300
2,6: 6-Toth-a	6	12	18	42	79	115
3,5-Wrightson-a; Toth-p. 3-Last 12¢ issue	7	14	21	46	86	125
4,12-Toth-a	5	10	15	31	53	75
7-11-Adams-c; Toth-a in all. 8-Adams-a	6	12	18	41	76	110
13-Neal Adams-c/a, 2pgs.	6	12	18	42	79	115
14-Williamson/Garzon, Jones-a; N. Adams-c	7	14	21	44	82	120
15	3	6	9	19	30	40
16-21-(52 pg. Giants)	4	8	12	23	37	50
22-37,39,40	3	6	9	14	19	24
38-(100 pgs.)	5	10	15	31	53	75
41-60	2	4	6	10	14	18
61-83,85	2	4	6	8	11	14
84-(44 pgs.)	2	4	6	9	13	16

NOTE: *Combined with The Unexpected with #189. **Neal Adams** c-7-11, 13, 14. **Alcala** a-24, 27, 33, 41, 43. **Anderson** a-9, 38. **Cardy** c-4, 5. **Kaluta** a-7. **Kane** a-12p. **Morrow** a-10, 13, 15, 16. **Nino** a-31, 40, 45, 47. **Redondo** a-20, 23, 24, 34, 65; c-53. **Reese** a-23. **Sparling** a-1. **Toth** a-1, 3-12, 38r. **Tuska** a-11, 12. **Wood** a-15.*

WITCHING HOUR, THE
DC Comics (Vertigo): 1999 - No. 3, 2000 ($5.95, limited series)

1-3-Bachalo & Thibert-c/a; Loeb & Bachalo-s 6.00
Hardcover (2000, $29.95) r/#1-3; embossed cover 30.00
Softcover (2003, $19.95), (2009, $19.99) r/#1-3 20.00

WITCHING HOUR, THE
DC Comics (Vertigo): Dec, 2013 ($7.99, one-shot)

1-Short story anthology by various incl. DeConnick, Doyle, Buckingham; Frison-c 8.00

WITHIN OUR REACH
Star Reach Productions: 1991 ($7.95, 84 pgs.)

nn-Spider-Man, Concrete by Chadwick, Gift of the Magi by Russell; Christmas stories; Chadwick-c; Spidey back-c 8.00

WITH THE MARINES ON THE BATTLEFRONTS OF THE WORLD
Toby Press: 1953 (no month) - No. 2, Mar, 1954 (Photo covers)

	GD	VG	FN	VF	VF/NM	NM-
1-John Wayne story	31	62	93	186	303	420
2-Monty Hall in #1,2	11	22	33	64	90	115

WITH THE U.S. PARATROOPS BEHIND ENEMY LINES (Also see U.S. Paratroops...; #2-6 titled U.S. Paratroops...)
Avon Periodicals: 1951 - No. 6, Dec, 1952

	GD	VG	FN	VF	VF/NM	NM-
1-Wood-c & inside f/c	20	40	60	120	195	270
2-Kinstler-c & inside f/c only	13	26	39	74	105	135
3-6: 6-Kinstler-c & inside f/c only	12	24	36	67	94	120

NOTE: ***Kinstler** c-2, 4-6.*

WITNESS, THE (Also see Amazing Mysteries, Captain America #71, Ideal #4, Marvel Mystery #92 & Mystic #7)
Marvel Comics (MjMe): Sept, 1948

	GD	VG	FN	VF	VF/NM	NM-
1(Scarce)-Rico-c?	300	600	900	2010	3505	5000

WITTY COMICS
Irwin H. Rubin Publ./Chicago Nite Life News No. 2: 1945 - No. 2, 1945

	GD	VG	FN	VF	VF/NM	NM-
1-The Pioneer, Junior Patrol; Japanese war-c	36	72	108	216	351	485
2-The Pioneer, Junior Patrol	16	32	48	94	147	200

WIZARD OF FOURTH STREET, THE
Dark Horse Comics: Dec, 1987 - No. 2, 1988 ($1.75, B&W, limited series)

1,2: Adapts novel by S/F author Simon Hawke 3.00

WIZARD OF OZ (See Classics Illustrated Jr. 535, Dell Jr. Treasury No. 5, First Comics Graphic Novel, Marvelous..., & Marvel Treasury of Oz)
Dell Publishing Co.: No. 1308, Mar-May, 1962 (TV)

	GD	VG	FN	VF	VF/NM	NM-
Four Color 1308	11	22	33	73	157	240

WIZARDS OF MICKEY (Mickey Mouse)
BOOM! Studios: Jan, 2010 - No. 8, Aug, 2010 ($2.99)

1-8: 1,2-Ambrosio-s; 3 covers on each. 3-8-Two covers 3.00

WIZARD'S TALE, THE
Image Comics (Homage Comics): 1997 ($19.95, squarebound, one-shot)

nn-Kurt Busiek-s/David Wenzel-painted-a/c 20.00

WOLF & RED
Dark Horse Comics: Apr, 1995 - No. 3, June, 1995 ($2.50, limited series)

1-3: Characters created by Tex Avery 3.00

WOLF COP
Dynamite Entertainment: 2016 - No. 3, 2016 ($3.99)

1-3-Max Marks-s/Arcana Studios-a 4.00

WOLFF & BYRD, COUNSELORS OF THE MACABRE (Becomes Supernatural Law with issue #24)
Exhibit A Press: May, 1994 - No. 23, Aug, 1999 ($2.50, B&W)

1-23-Batton Lash-s/a 3.00

WOLF GAL (See Al Capp's...)

WOLFMAN, THE (See Movie Classics)

Wolverine #124 © MAR

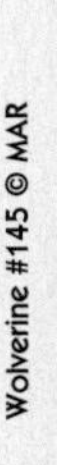
Wolverine #145 © MAR

Wolverine (2003 series) #51 © MAR

	GD 2.0	VG 4.0	FN 6.0	VF 8.0	VF/NM 9.0	NM- 9.2

WOLF MOON
DC Comics (Vertigo): Feb, 2015 - No. 6, Jul, 2015 ($3.99, limited series)

1-6-Bunn-s/Haun-a. 1-Covers by Jae Lee and Jeremy Haun 4.00

WOLFPACK
Marvel Comics: Feb, 1988 ($7.95); Aug, 1988 - No. 12, July, 1989 (Lim. series)

1-(2/88) 1st app./origin (Marvel Graphic Novel #31) 2 4 6 8 10 12
1-12: 1-(8/88) Hama-s 4.00

WOLVERINE (See Alpha Flight, Daredevil #196, 249, Ghost Rider; Wolverine; Punisher, Havok &..., Incredible Hulk #180, Incredible Hulk &..., Kitty Pryde And..., Marvel Comics Presents, New Avengers, Power Pack, Punisher and..., Rampaging ..., Spider-Man vs... & X-Men #94)

WOLVERINE (See Incredible Hulk #180 for 1st app.)
Marvel Comics Group: Sept, 1982 - No. 4, Dec, 1982 (limited series)

1-Frank Miller-c/a(p) in all; Claremont-s 5 10 15 35 63 90
2-4 4 8 12 27 44 60
... By Claremont & Miller HC (2006, $19.99) r/#1-4 & Uncanny X-Men #172-173 20.00
TPB 1(7/87, $4.95)-Reprints #1-4 with new Miller-c 2 4 6 11 16 20
TPB nn (2nd printing, $9.95)-r/#1-4 2 4 6 8 10 12

WOLVERINE
Marvel Comics: Nov, 1988 - No. 189, June, 2003 ($1.50/$1.75/$1.95/$1.99/$2.25)

1 4 8 12 27 44 60
2 3 6 9 14 20 25
3-5: 4-BWS back-c 2 4 6 9 13 16
6,7,9: 6-McFarlane back-c. 7-Hulk app. 1 3 4 6 8 10
8-Classic Grey Hulk-c; Hulk app. 3 6 9 16 23 30
10-1st battle with Sabretooth (before Wolverine had his claws)
3 6 9 19 30 40
11-16: 11-New costume 1 2 3 5 6 8
17-20: 17-Byrne-c/a(p) begins, ends #23 1 2 3 4 5 7
21-30: 24,25,27-Jim Lee-c. 26-Begin $1.75-c 5.00
31-40,44,47 4.00
41-Sabretooth claims to be Wolverine's father; Cable cameo
1 3 4 6 8 10
41-Gold 2nd printing ($1.75) 2 4 6 8 10 12
42-Sabretooth, Cable & Nick Fury app.; Sabretooth proven not to be Wolverine's father
1 3 4 6 8 10
42-Gold ink 2nd printing ($1.75) 1 3 4 6 8 10
43-Sabretooth cameo (2 panels); saga ends 5.00
45,46-Sabretooth-c/stories 5.00
48,49,51-Sabretooth app. 48-Begin 3 part Weapon X sequel. 51-Sabretooth-c & app. 5.00
50-(64 pgs.)-Die cut-c; Wolverine back to old yellow costume; Forge, Cyclops, Jubilee, Jean Grey & Nick Fury app. 1 2 3 5 6 8
52-74,76-80: 54-Shatterstar (from X-Force) app. 55-Gambit, Jubilee, Sunfire-c/story. 55-57,73-Gambit app. 57-Mariko Yashida dies (Late 7/92). 58,59-Terror, Inc. x-over. 60-64-Sabretooth storyline (60,62,64-c) 4.00
75-($3.95, 68 pgs.)-Wolverine hologram on-c 6.00
81-84,86: 81-bound-in card sheet 4.00
85-($2.50)-Newsstand edition 4.00
85-($3.50)-Collectors edition 5.00
87-90 ($1.95)-Deluxe edition 4.00
87-90 ($1.50)-Regular edition 3.00
91-99,101-114: 91-Return from "Age of Apocalypse," 93-Juggernaut app. 94-Gen X app. 101-104-Elektra app. 104-Origin of Onslaught. 105-Onslaught x-over. 110-Shaman-c/app. 114-Alternate-c 3.00
100 ($3.95)-Hologram-c; Wolverine loses humanity 2 4 6 8 10 12
100 ($2.95)-Regular-c. 5.00
102.5 (1996 Wizard mail-away)-Deadpool app.; Vallejo-c/Buckingham-a 100.00
115-124: 115- Operation Zero Tolerance 3.00
125-($2.99) Wraparound-c; Viper secret 4.00
125-($6.95) Jae Lee variant-c 8.00
126-144: 126,127-Sabretooth-c/app. 128-Sabretooth & Shadowcat app.; Platt-a. 129-Wendigo-c/app. 131-Initial printing contained lettering error. 133-Begin Larsen-s/ Matsuda-a. 138-Galactus-c/app. 139-Cable app.; Yu-a. 142,143-Alpha Flight app. 3.00
145-($2.99) 25th Anniversary issue; Hulk and Sabretooth app. 4.00
145-($3.99) Foil enhanced cover (also see Promotional section for Nabisco mail-in ed.) 5.00
146,147-Apocalypse: The Twelve; Angel-c/app. 1 2 3 5 6 8
148,149: 149-Nova-c/app. 3.00
150-($2.99) Steve Skroce-s/a 4.00
151-153,156-174,176-182,184-189: 151-Begin $2.25-c. 156-Churchill-a. 159-Chen-a begins. 160-Sabretooth app. 163-Texeira-a(p). 167-BWS-c. 172,173-Alpha Flight app. 176-Colossus app. 185,186-Punisher app. 3.00
154,155-Deadpool app.; Liefeld-s/a. 2 4 6 11 16 20

	GD 2.0	VG 4.0	FN 6.0	VF 8.0	VF/NM 9.0	NM- 9.2

175,183-($3.50) 175-Sabretooth app. 4.00
#(-1) Flashback (7/97) Logan meets Col. Fury; Nord-a 3.00
Annual nn (1990, $4.50, squarebound, 52 pgs.)-The Jungle Adventure; Simonson scripts; Mignola-c/a 6.00
Annual 2 (12/90, $4.95, squarebound, 52 pgs.)-Bloodlust 6.00
Annual nn (#3, 8/91, $5.95, 68 pgs.)-Rahne of Terror; Cable & The New Mutants app.; Andy Kubert-c/a (2nd print exists) 6.00
Annual '95 (1995, $3.95) 4.00
Annual '96 (1996, $2.95)- Wraparound-c; Silver Samurai, Yukio, and Red Ronin app. 4.00
Annual '97 ($2.99) - Wraparound-c 4.00
Annual 1999, 2000 ($3.50) : 1999-Deadpool app. 4.00
Annual 2001 ($2.99) - Tieri-s; JH Williams-c 4.00
...Battles The Incredible Hulk nn (1989, $4.95, squarebound, 52 pg.) r/Incr. Hulk #180,181
2 4 6 8 10 12
Best of Wolverine Vol. 1 HC (2004, $29.99) oversized reprints of Hulk #181, mini-series #1-4, Capt. America Ann, #8, Uncanny X-Men #205 & Marvel Comics Presents #72-84 30.00
...Black Rio (11/98, $5.99)-Casey-s/Oscar Jimenez-a 6.00
...Blood Debt TPB (7/01, $12.95)-r/#150-153; Skroce-c 13.00
...Blood Hungry nn (1993, $6.95, 68 pgs.)-Kieth-r/Marvel Comics Presents #85-92 w/ new Kieth-c 7.00
...: Bloody Choices nn (1993, $7.95, 68 pgs.)-r/Graphic Novel; Nick Fury app. 8.00
... Cable Guts and Glory (10/99, $5.99) Platt-a 6.00
... Classic Vol. 1 TPB (2005, $12.99) r/#1-5 15.00
... Classic Vol. 2 TPB (2005, $12.99) r/#6-10 15.00
... Classic Vol. 3 TPB (2006, $14.99) r/#11-16; The Gehenna Stone Affair 15.00
... Classic Vol. 4 TPB (2006, $14.99) r/#17-23 15.00
... Classic Vol. 5 TPB (2007, $14.99) r/#24-30 15.00
.../Deadpool: Weapon X TPB (7/02, $21.99)-r/#162-166 & Deadpool #57-60 22.00
... Doombringer (11/97, $5.99)-Silver Samurai-c/app. 6.00
... Evilution (9/94, $5.95) 6.00
...: Global Jeopardy 1 (12/93, $2.95, one-shot)-Embossed-c; Sub-Mariner, Zabu, Ka-Zar, Shanna & Wolverine app.; produced in cooperation with World Wildlife Fund 5.00
...:Inner Fury nn (1992, $5.95, 52 pgs.)-Sienkiewicz-c/a 6.00
...: Judgment Night (2000, $3.99) Shi app.; Battlebook 4.00
...: Killing (9/93)-Kent Williams-a 6.00
...: Knight of Terra (1995, $6.95)-Ostrander script 7.00
... Legends Vol. 2: Meltdown (2003, $19.99) r/Havok & Wolverine: Meltdown #1-4 20.00
... Legends Vol. 3 (2003, $12.99) r/#181-186 13.00
... Legends Vol. 4,5: 4-(See Wolverine: Xisle). 5-(See Wolverine: Snikt!)
... Legends Vol. 6: Marc Silvestri Book 1 (2004, $19.99) r/#31-34, 41-42, 48-50 20.00
.../ Nick Fury: The Scorpio Connection Hardcover (1989, $16.95) 25.00
.../ Nick Fury: The Scorpio Connection Softcover(1990, $12.95) 15.00
...: Not Dead Yet (12/98, $14.95, TPB)-r/#119-122 15.00
...: Save The Tiger 1 (7/92, $2.95, 84 pgs.)-Reprints Wolverine stories from Marvel Comics Presents #1-10 w/new Kieth-c 4.00
...Scorpio Rising ($5.95, prestige format, one-shot) 6.00
.../Shi: Dark Night of Judgment (Crusade Comics, 2000, $2.99) Tucci-a 4.00
...Triumphs And Tragedies-(1995, $16.95, trade paperback)-r/Uncanny X-Men #109,172,173, Wolverine limited series #4, & Wolverine #41,42,75 17.00
...Typhoid's Kiss (6/94, $6.95)-r/Wolverine stories from Marvel Comics Presents #109-116 7.00
...Vs. Spider-Man 1 (3/95, $2.50) -r/Marvel Comics Presents #48-50 5.00
.../Witchblade 1 (3/97, $2.95) Devil's Reign Pt. 5 4.00
Wizard #1/2 (1997) Joe Phillips-a(p) 10.00

NOTE: ***Austin*** *c-3i.* ***Bolton*** *c(back)-5.* ***Buscema*** *a-1-16,25,27p; c-1-10.* ***Byrne*** *a-17-22p, 23; c-1(back), 17-22, 23p.* ***Colan*** *a-24.* ***Andy Kubert*** *c/a-51.* ***Jim Lee*** *c-24, 25, 27.* ***Silvestri*** *a(p)-31-43, 45, 46, 48-50, 52, 53, 55-57; c-31-42p, 43, 45p, 46p, 48, 49p, 50p, 52p, 53p, 55-57p.* ***Stroman*** *a-44p; c-60p.* ***Williamson*** *a-1i, 3-8i; c(i)-1, 3-6.*

WOLVERINE (Volume 3) (Titled Dark Wolverine from #75-90)(See Daken: Dark Wolverine)
Marvel Comics: July, 2003 - No. 90, Oct, 2010 ($2.25/$2.50/$2.99)

1-Rucka-s/Robertson-a 5.00
2-19: 6-Nightcrawler app. 13-16-Sabretooth app. 3.00
20-Millar-s/Romita, Jr.-a begin, Elektra app. 4.00
20-B&W variant-c 1 3 4 6 8 10
21-39: 21-Elektra-c/app. 23,24-Daredevil app. 26-28-Land-c. 29-Quesada-c; begin $2.50-c. 33-35-House of M. 36,37-Decimation. 36-Quesada-c. 39-Winter Soldier app. 3.00
40,43-48: 40-Begin $2.99-c; Winter Soldier app.; Texeira-a. 43-46-Civil War; Ramos-a. 45-Sub-Mariner app. 3.00
41,49-($3.99) 41-C.P. Smith-a/Stuart Moore-s 4.00
42-Civil War 5.00
50-($3.99) Sabretooth app.; Bianchi-a/c & Loeb-s begin; wraparound-c; McGuinness-a 4.00
50-($3.99) Variant Edition; uncolored art and cover; Bianchi pencil art page 4.00
51-55-(Regular and variant uncolored editions) Bianchi-a/Loeb-s; Sabretooth app. 3.00
55-EC-style variant-c by Greg Land 5.00
56-($3.99) Howard Chaykin-a/c 4.00
57-65: 57-61-Suydam Zombie-c; Chaykin-a. 62-65-Mystique app. 3.00

Wolverine (2010 series) #1 © MAR

Wolverine and Jubilee #1 © MAR

Wolverine: First Class #21 © MAR

	GD 2.0	VG 4.0	FN 6.0	VF 8.0	VF/NM 9.0	NM- 9.2

66-Old Man Logan begins; Millar-s/McNiven-a; McNiven wraparound-c
3 6 9 17 26 35
66-Variant-c by Michael Turner 5 10 15 33 57 80
66-Variant sketch-c by Michael Turner 100.00
66-2nd printing with McNiven variant-c of Logan and Hulk gang member
3 6 9 16 23 30
66-(5/10, $1.00) Reprint with "Marvel's Greatest Comics" on cover 3.00
67-72-Old Man Logan (concludes in Wolverine: Old Man Logan Giant-Sized Special).
67-Intro. Ashley, Spider-Man's granddaughter. 72-Red Skull app.
1 3 4 6 8 10
73,74-Andy Kubert-a 4.00
75-($3.99) Dark Reign, Daken as Wolverine on Osborn's team; Camuncoli-a 5.00
76-90: 76-86-Multiple covers for each. 76-Dark Reign; Yu-c. 82-84-Siege. 88,89-Franken-Castle x-over; Punisher app. 3.00
#900 (7/10, $4.99) Short stories by various incl. Finch, Rivera, Segovia, McGuinness 5.00
Annual 1 (12/07, $3.99) Hurwitz-s/Frusin-a 4.00
Annual 2 (11/08, $3.99) Swierczynski-s/Deodato-a/c 4.00
...: Blood & Sorrow TPB (2007, $13.99) r/#41,49, stories from Giant-Size Wolverine #1 and X-Men Unlimited #12 14.00
...: Chop Shop 1 (1/09, $2.99) Benson-s/Boschi-a/Hanuka-c 3.00
Civil War: Wolverine TPB (2007, $17.99) r/#42-48; gallery of B&W cover inks 18.00
... Dangerous Games 1 (8/08, $3.99) Spurrier-s/Oliver-a; Remender-s/Opena-a 4.00
...Enemy of the State HC Vol. 1 (2005, $19.99) r/#20-25; Ennis intro.; variant covers 20.00
...Enemy of the State HC Vol. 2 (2005, $19.99) r/#26-32 20.00
...Enemy of the State SC Vol. 1 (2005, $14.99) r/#20-25; Ennis intro.; variant covers 15.00
...Enemy of the State SC Vol. 2 (2006, $16.99) r/#26-32 17.00
...Enemy of the State - The Complete Edition (2006, $34.99) r/#20-32; Ennis intro.; sketch pages, variant covers and pin-up art 35.00
...: Evolution SC (2008, $14.99) r/#50-55 15.00
...: Flies to a Spider (2/09, $3.99) Bradstreet-c/Hurwitz-s/Opena-a 4.00
...: Killing Made Simple (10/08, $3.99) Yost-s/Turnbull-a 4.00
...: Enemy of the State MGC #20 (7/11, $1.00) r/#20 with "Marvel's Greatest Comics" logo 3.00
...: Japan's Most Wanted HC (2014, $34.99) printing of material that debuted online 35.00
...: Mr. X (5/10, $3.99) Tieri-s/Diaz-a/Mattina-c 4.00
...: Old Man Logan Giant-Sized Special (11/09, $4.99) Continued from #72; cover gallery 5.00
...Origins & Endings HC (2006, $19.99) r/#36-40 20.00
...Origins & Endings SC (2006, $13.99) r/#36-40 14.00
...: Origin of an X-Man Free Comic Book Day 2009 (5/09) Gurihiru-a/McGuinness-c 3.00
...: Revolver (8/09, $3.99) Gischler-s/Pastoras-a 4.00
... Saga (2009, giveaway) history of the character in text and comic panels 3.00
...: Saudade (2008, $4.99) English adaptation of Wolverine story from French comic 5.00
...: Savage (4/10, $3.99) J. Scott Campbell-c; The Lizard app. 4.00
...Special: Firebreak (2/08, $3.99) Carey-s/Kolins-a; Lolos-a 4.00
...: Switchback 1 (3/09, $3.99) short stories; art by Pastoras & Doe 4.00
...: The Amazing Immortal Man & Other Bloody Tales (7/08, $3.99) Lapham short stories 4.00
...: The Anniversary (6/09, $3.99) Mariko flashback short stories; art by various 4.00
...: The Death of Wolverine HC (2008, $19.99) r/#56-61 20.00
...: The Road to Hell (11/10, $3.99) Previews new Wolverine titles and Generation Hope 4.00
...: Under the Boardwalk (2/10, $3.99) Coker-a 4.00
...Vol. 1: The Brotherhood (2003, $12.99) r/#1-6 13.00
...Vol. 2: Coyote Crossing (2004, $11.99) r/#7-11 12.00
... Weapon X Files (2009, $4.99) Handbook-style pages of Wolverine characters 5.00
...: Wendigo! 1 (3/10, $3.99) Gulacy-a; back-up with Thor 4.00

WOLVERINE (Volume 4) (Also see Savage Wolverine)
Marvel Comics: Nov, 2010 - No. 20, Feb, 2012; No. 300, Mar, 2012 - No. 317, Feb, 2013 ($3.99/$4.99)

1-5-Jae Lee-c/Guedes-a; Wolverine Goes to Hell. 1-Back-up with Silver Samurai 4.00
5.1-(4/11, $2.99) Aaron-s/Palo-a/Rivera-c 3.00
6-20: 6-Jae Lee-c/Acuña-a; X-Men & Magneto app. 20-Kingpin & Sabretooth app. 4.00
300-(3/12, $4.99) Adam Kubert-c; Sabretooth & new Silver Samurai app. 5.00
301-308,310-317: 301-304-Aaron-s. 302-Art Adams-c. 310-313-Bianchi-a/c 4.00
309-($4.99) Elixir with X-Force; Albuquerque-a; Ribic-c 5.00
#1000 (4/11, $4.99) Short stories by various incl. Palmiotti, Green, Luke Ross; Segovia-c 5.00
Annual 1 (10/12, $4.99) Alan Davis-s/a/c; the Clan Destine app. (see Daredevil Ann. #1) 5.00
...: Debt of Death 1 (11/11, $3.99) Lapham-s/Aja-a/c; Nick Fury app. 4.00
.../Deadpool: The Decoy 1 (9/11, $3.99) prints online story from Marvel.com; Young-c 4.00

WOLVERINE (5th series)
Marvel Comics: May, 2013 - No. 13, Mar, 2014 ($3.99)

1-13: 1-4-Cornell-s/Alan Davis-a/c; Nick Fury II app. 5-7-Pierfederici-a. 8-13-Killable 4.00
... In the Flesh (9/13, $3.99) Cosentino-s/Talajic-a 4.00

WOLVERINE (6th series)
Marvel Comics: Apr, 2014 - No. 12, Oct, 2014 ($3.99)

1-11: 1-Cornell-s/Stegman-a. 2-Superior Spider-Man app. 8,9-Iron Fist app. 4.00
12-($5.99) "1 Month To Die"; Cornell-s/Woods-a; Thor & Sabretooth app. 6.00
Annual 1 (10/14, $4.99) Jubilee app; Nguyen-c/Kalan-s/Marks-a 5.00

WOLVERINE & BLACK CAT: CLAWS 2 (See Claws for 1st series)
Marvel Comics: Aug, 2011 - No. 3, Nov, 2011 ($3.99, limited series)

1-3-Linsner-a/c; Palmiotti & Gray-s; Killraven app. 4.00

WOLVERINE AND JUBILEE
Marvel Comics: Mar, 2011 - No. 4, Jun, 2011 ($2.99, limited series)

1-4: 1-Vampire Jubilee; Kathryn Immonen-s/Phil Noto-a; Coipel-c 3.00

WOLVERINE AND POWER PACK
Marvel Comics: Jan, 2009 - No. 4, Apr, 2009 ($2.99, limited series)

1-4-Sumerak-s. 1,2-GuriHiru-a. 1-Sauron app. 3-Meet Wolverine as a child; Koblish-a 3.00

WOLVERINE AND THE PUNISHER: DAMAGING EVIDENCE
Marvel Comics: Oct, 1993 - No. 3, Dec, 1993 ($2.00, limited series)

1-3: 2,3-Indicia says "The Punisher and Wolverine..." 4.00

WOLVERINE & THE X-MEN (Regenesis)(See X-Men: Schism)
Marvel Comics: Dec, 2011 - No. 42, Apr, 2014 ($3.99)

1-8: 1-3-Aaron-s/Bachalo-a/c. 3-Sabretooth app. 4-Bradshaw-a; Deathlok app. 4.00
9-27: 9-16,18-Avengers vs. X-Men tie-in. 17-Allred-a 4.00
27AU (6/13, $3.99) Age of Ultron tie-in; continues in Age of Ultron #6 4.00
28-41: 30-35-Hellfire Saga. 36,37-Battle of the Atom 4.00
42-($4.99) Cover swipe of X-Men #141 (1981) Graduation Day 5.00
Annual 1 (1/14, $4.99) Aaron-s/Bradshaw-a; Gladiator app. 5.00

WOLVERINE & THE X-MEN (2nd series)
Marvel Comics: May, 2014 - No. 12, Jan, 2015 ($3.99)

1-9,11,12: 1-Latour-s/Asrar-a; Fantomex app. 7-Daredevil app. 11-Spider-Man app. 4.00
10-($4.99) Follows Wolverine's death; art by various incl. Anka, Bertram, Rugg, Shalvey 5.00

WOLVERINE AND THE X-MEN: ALPHA & OMEGA
Marvel Comics: Dec, 2011 - No. 5, Jul, 2012 ($3.99, limited series)

1-5-Brooks-c/Boschi & Brooks-a; Quentin Quire vs. Wolverine 4.00

WOLVERINE/CAPTAIN AMERICA
Marvel Comics: Apr, 2004 - No. 4, Apr, 2004 ($2.99, limited series)

1-4-Derenick-a/c 3.00

WOLVERINE: DAYS OF FUTURE PAST
Marvel Comics: Dec, 1997 - No. 3, Feb, 1998 ($2.50, limited series)

1-3: J.F. Moore-s/Bennett-a 4.00

WOLVERINE/DOOP (Also see X-Force and X-Statix)(Reprinted in X-Statix Vol. 2)
Marvel Comics: July, 2003 - No. 2, July, 2003 ($2.99, limited series)

1,2-Peter Milligan-s/Darwyn Cooke & J. Bone-a 3.00

WOLVERINE: FIRST CLASS
Marvel Comics: May, 2008 - No. 21, Jan, 2010 ($2.99)

1-21: 1-Wolverine and Kitty Pryde's first mission; DiVito-a. 2,9-Sabretooth app. 3.00

WOLVERINE/GAMBIT: VICTIMS
Marvel Comics: Sept, 1995 - No. 4, Dec, 1995 ($2.95, limited series)

1-4: Jeph Loeb scripts & Tim Sale-a; foil-c 5.00

WOLVERINE/HERCULES: MYTHS, MONSTERS & MUTANTS
Marvel Comics: May, 2011 - No. 4, Aug, 2011 ($2.99, limited series)

1-4-Tieri-s/Santacruz-a/Jusko-c 3.00

WOLVERINE/HULK
Marvel Comics: Apr, 2002 - No. 4, July, 2002 ($3.50, limited series)

1-4-Sam Kieth-s/a/c 4.00
Wolverine Legends Vol. 1: Wolverine/Hulk (2003, $9.99, TPB) r/#1-4 10.00

WOLVERINE: MANIFEST DESTINY
Marvel Comics: Dec, 2008 - No. 4, Mar, 2009 ($2.99, limited series)

1-4-Aaron-s/Segovia-a 3.00

WOLVERINE MAX
Marvel Comics: Dec, 2012 - No. 15, Mar, 2014 ($3.99)

1-15: 1-5-Starr-s/Boschi-a/Jock-c; Victor Creed app. 4.00

WOLVERINE: NETSUKE
Marvel Comics: Nov, 2002 - No. 4, Feb, 2003 ($3.99, limited series)

1-4-George Pratt-s/painted-a 4.00

WOLVERINE: NOIR (1930s Pulp-style)

Wolverine: Origins #26 © MAR

Wolverines #13 © MAR

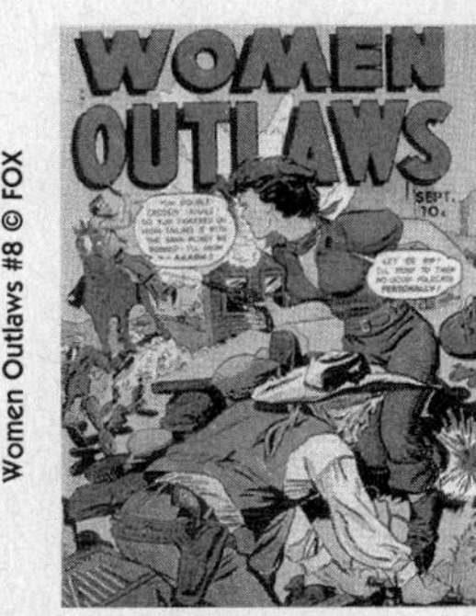

Women Outlaws #8 © FOX

GD VG FN VF VF/NM NM-
2.0 4.0 6.0 8.0 9.0 9.2

Marvel Comics: Apr, 2009 - No. 4, Sept, 2009 ($3.99, limited series)
1-4-C.P. Smith-a/Stuart Moore; covers by Smith & Calero; alternate Logan as detective 4.00

WOLVERINE: ORIGINS
Marvel Comics: June, 2006 - No. 50, Sept, 2010 ($2.99)
1-15: 1-Daniel Way-s/Steve Dillon-a/Quesada-c 3.00
1-10-Variant covers. 1-Turner. 2-Quesada & Hitch. 3-Bianchi. 4-Dell'Otto. 7-Deodato 4.00
16-($3.99) Captain America WW2 app.; preview of Wolverine #56; r/X-Men #268 4.00
16-Variant-c by McGuinness 4.00
17-24: 17-20-Capt. America & Bucky app. 21-24-Deadpool app.; Bianchi-c 3.00
25-($3.99) Deadpool app.; Bianchi-c; r/Deadpool's 1st app. in New Mutants #98 5.00
26-49: 26-Origin of Dakan; Way-s/Segovia-a/Land-c. 28-Hulk & Wendigo app. 3.00
50-($3.99) Last issue; Nick Fury app. 4.00
Annual 1 (9/07, $3.99) Way-s/Andrews-a; flashback to 1932 4.00
... Vol. 1 - Born in Blood HC (2006, $19.99, dustjacket) r/#1-5; variant covers 20.00
... Vol. 1 - Born in Blood SC (2007, $13.99) r/#1-5; variant covers 14.00
... Vol. 2 - Savior HC (2007, $19.99, dustjacket) r/#6-10; variant covers 20.00
... Vol. 2 - Savior SC (2007, $13.99) r/#6-10; variant covers 14.00
... Vol. 3 - Swift & Terrible HC (2007, $19.99, dustjacket) r/#11-15 20.00
... Vol. 3 - Swift & Terrible SC (2007, $13.99) r/#11-15 14.00
... Vol. 4 - Our War HC (2008, $19.99, dustjacket) r/#16-20 & Annual #1 20.00
... Vol. 4 - Our War SC (2008, $14.99) r/#16-20 & Annual #1 15.00

WOLVERINE/PUNISHER
Marvel Comics: May, 2004 - No. 5, Sept, 2004 ($2.99, limited series)
1-5: Milligan-s/Weeks-a 3.00
... Vol. 1 TPB (2004, $13.99) r/series 14.00

WOLVERINE, PUNISHER & GHOST RIDER: OFFICIAL INDEX TO THE MARVEL UNIVERSE
Marvel Comics: Oct, 2011 - No. 8, May, 2012 ($3.99)
1-8-Each issue has chronological synopsies, creator credits, character lists for 30-40 issues of their own titles and headlining mini-series 4.00

WOLVERINE/PUNISHER REVELATIONS (Marvel Knights)
Marvel Comics: Jun, 1999 - No. 4, Sept, 1999 ($2.95, limited series)
1-4: Pat Lee-a(p) 4.00
...: Revelation (4/00, $14.95, TPB) r/#1-4 15.00

WOLVERINES (Follows Death of Wolverine)
Marvel Comics: Mar, 2015 - No. 20, Aug, 2015 ($3.99, weekly series)
1-20: 1-Soule-s/Bradshaw-a; Sabretooth, Daken, Mystique, X-23 app. 13-Deadpool app. 4.00

WOLVERINE SAGA
Marvel Comics: Sept, 1989 - No. 4, Mid-Dec, 1989 ($3.95, lim. series, 52 pgs.)
1-Gives history; Liefeld/Austin-c (front & back) 6.00
2-4: 2-Romita, Jr./Austin-c. 4-Kaluta-c 6.00

WOLVERINE: SNIKT!
Marvel Comics: July, 2003 - No. 5, Nov, 2003 ($2.99, limited series)
1-5-Manga-style; Tsutomu Nihei-s/a 3.00
Wolverine Legends Vol. 5: Snikt! TPB (2003, $13.99) r/#1-5 14.00

WOLVERINE: SOULTAKER
Marvel Comics: May, 2005 - No. 5, Aug, 2005 ($2.99, limited series)
1-5-Yoshida-s/Nagasawa-a/Terada-c; Yukio app. 3.00
TPB (2005, $13.99) r/#1-5 14.00

WOLVERINE: THE BEST THERE IS
Marvel Comics: Feb, 2011 - No. 12, Jan, 2012 ($3.99)
1-12: 1,2-Huston-s/Ryp-a; covers by Hitch and Djurdjevic. 3-12-Hitch-c 4.00
... - Contagion 1 (6/11, $4.99) r/#1-3, cover gallery 5.00

WOLVERINE: THE END
Marvel Comics: Jan, 2004 - No. 6, Dec, 2004 ($2.99, limited series)
1-5-Jenkins-s/Castellini-a 3.00
1-Wizard World Texas variant-c 20.00
TPB (2005, $14.99) r/#1-5 15.00

WOLVERINE: THE ORIGIN
Marvel Comics: Nov, 2001 - No. 6, July, 2002 ($3.50, limited series)
1-Origin of Logan; Jenkins-s/Andy Kubert-a; Quesada-c 35.00
1-DF edition 25.00
2 10.00
3-6 6.00
HC (3/02, $34.95, 11" x 7-1/2") r/#1-6; dust jacket; sketch pages and treatments 35.00
HC (2006, $19.99) r/#1-6; dust jacket; sketch pages and treatments 20.00
SC (2002, $14.95) r/#1-6; afterwords by Jemas and Quesada 15.00

GD VG FN VF VF/NM NM-
2.0 4.0 6.0 8.0 9.0 9.2

WOLVERINE WEAPON X
Marvel Comics: June, 2009 - No. 16, Oct, 2010 ($3.99)
1-16: 1-5,11-Aaron-s/Garney-a. 1-Four covers. 2,3-Two covers. 11-15-Deathlok app. 4.00

WOLVERINE: XISLE
Marvel Comics: June, 2003 - No. 5, June, 2003 ($2.50, weekly limited series)
1-5-Bruce Jones-s/Jorge Lucas-a 3.00
Wolverine Legends Vol. 4 TPB (2003, $13.99) r/ #1-5 14.00

WOMANTHOLOGY: SPACE
IDW Publishing: Sept, 2012 - No. 5, Feb, 2013 ($3.99)
1-5-Anthology of short stories by women creators 4.00

WOMEN IN LOVE (A Feature Presentation #5)
Fox Features Synd./Hero Books: Aug, 1949 - No. 4, Feb, 1950
1 41 82 123 256 428 600
2-Kamen/Feldstein-c 37 74 111 222 361 500
3 26 52 78 154 252 350
4-Wood-a 32 64 96 188 307 425

WOMEN IN LOVE (Thrilling Romances for Adults)
Ziff-Davis Publishing Co.: Winter, 1952 (25¢, 100 pgs.)
nn-(Scarce)-Kinstler-a; painted-c 81 162 243 518 884 1250

WOMEN OF MARVEL
Marvel Comics: 2006, 2007 ($24.99, TPB)
SC-Reprints 1st apps. of Dazzler, Ms. Marvel, Shanna, The Cat plus notable stories of other female Marvel characters; Mayhew-c 25.00
Vol. 2 (2007) More stories of female Marvel characters; Mayhew-c; cover process art 25.00

WOMEN OF MARVEL
Marvel Comics: Jan, 2011 - No. 2, Feb, 2011 ($3.99, limited series)
1,2-Short stories of female Marvel characters. 1-Pichelli-c. 2-Land-c 4.00

WOMEN OUTLAWS (My Love Memories #9 on)(Also see Red Circle)
Fox Features Syndicate: July, 1948 - No. 8, Sept, 1949
1-Used in **SOTI**, illo "Giving children an image of American womanhood"; negligee panels 90 180 270 576 988 1400
2,3: 3-Kamenish-a 66 132 198 419 722 1025
4-8 53 106 159 334 567 800
nn(nd)-Contains Cody of the Pony Express; same cover as #7 27 54 81 158 259 360

WOMEN TO LOVE
Realistic: No date (1953)
nn-(Scarce)-Reprints Complete Romance #1; c-/Avon paperback #165 41 82 123 256 428 600

WONDER BOY (Formerly Terrific Comics) (See Blue Bolt, Bomber Comics & Samson)
Ajax/Farrell Publ.: No. 17, May, 1955 - No. 18, July, 1955 (Code approved)
17-Phantom Lady app. Bakerish-c/a 50 100 150 315 533 750
18-Phantom Lady app. 41 82 123 256 428 600
NOTE: *Phantom Lady not by Matt Baker.*

WONDER COMICS (Wonderworld #3 on)
Fox Features Syndicate: May, 1939 - No. 2, June, 1939 (68 pgs.)
1-(Scarce)-Wonder Man only app. by Will Eisner; Dr. Fung (by Powell), K-5 begins; Bob Kane-a; Eisner-c 2400 4800 7200 17,000 29,500 42,000
2-(Scarce)-Yarko the Great, Master Magician (see Samson) by Eisner begins; 'Spark' Stevens by Bob Kane, Patty O'Day, Tex Mason app. Lou Fine's 1st-c; Fine-a (2 pgs.); Yarko-c (Wonder Man-c #1) 757 1514 2271 5526 9763 14,000

WONDER COMICS
Great/Nedor/Better Publications: May, 1944 - No. 20, Oct, 1948
1-The Grim Reaper & Spectro, the Mind Reader begin; Hitler/Hirohito bondage-c 343 686 1029 2400 4200 6000
2-Origin The Grim Reaper; Super Sleuths begin, end #8,17; Schomburg Nazi WWII-c 181 362 543 1158 1979 2800
3-5: All Schomburg Nazi WWII-c. 3-Indicia reads "Vol. 1, #2" 168 336 504 1075 1838 2600
6-Japanese WWII Flag-c 116 232 348 742 1271 1800
7-10: 8-Last Spectro. 9-Wonderman begins 84 168 252 538 919 1300
11-13: 11-Dick Devens, King of Futuria begins, ends #14. 11,12-Ingels-c & splash pg. 12-Bondage/headlight-c by Ingels 103 206 309 659 1130 1600
14-Classic Schomburg sci-fi good girl bondage-c 129 258 387 826 1413 2000
15-Tara begins (origin), ends #20; classic Schomburg bondage/torture-c 226 452 678 1446 2473 3500

Wonder Comics #17 © BP

Wonderful Wizard of Oz #7 © MAR

Wonder Woman #6 © DC

GD VG FN VF VF/NM NM-
2.0 4.0 6.0 8.0 9.0 9.2

16,18: 16-Spectro app.; last Grim Reaper. 18-The Silver Knight begins
76 152 228 486 831 1175
17-Wonderman with Frazetta panels; Jill Trent with all Frazetta inks
79 158 237 502 864 1225
19-Frazetta panels 79 158 237 502 864 1225
20-Most of Silver Knight by Frazetta 100 200 300 635 1093 1550
NOTE: ***Ingels** c-11, 12. **Roussos** a-19. **Schomburg (Xela)** c-1-10; (airbrush)-13-20. Bondage c-12, 13, 15. Cover features: Grim Reaper #1-8; Wonder Man #9-15; Tara #16-20.*

WONDER DUCK (See Wisco)
Marvel Comics (CDS): Sept, 1949 - No. 3, Mar, 1950
1-Funny animal 21 42 63 126 206 285
2,3 15 30 45 84 127 170

WONDERFUL ADVENTURES OF PINOCCHIO, THE (See Movie Comics & Walt Disney Showcase #48)
Whitman Publishing Co.: April, 1982 (Walt Disney)
nn-(#3 Continuation of Movie Comics?); r/FC #92 6.00

WONDERFUL WIZARD OF OZ (Adaptation of the original 1900 L. Frank Baum book)
(Also see the sequels Marvelous Land of Oz, Ozma of Oz, and Dorothy & The Wizard in Oz)
Marvel Comics: Feb, 2009 - No. 8, Sept, 2009 ($3.99, limited series)
1-8-Eric Shanower-a/Skottie Young-a/c 4.00
1-Variant Good Witch & Dorothy wraparound cover by J. Scott Campbell 8.00
1-Variant Scarecrow & Dorothy cover by Eric Shanower 10.00
1-(4/10, $1.00) Reprint with "Marvel's Greatest Comics" on cover 3.00
... Sketchbook (2008, giveaway) Young character design sketches; Shanower intro. 3.00
HC (2009, $29.99, dustjacket) r/#1-8; Shanower intro.; cover gallery; sketch art 30.00

WONDERFUL WORLD FOR BOYS AND GIRLS
DC Comics: May, 1964
nn - Ashcan comic, not distributed to newsstands, only for in-house use (no known sales)

WONDERFUL WORLD OF DISNEY, THE (Walt Disney)
Whitman Publishing Co.: 1978 (Digest, 116 pgs.)
1-Barks-a (reprints) 3 6 9 16 23 30
2 (no date) 2 4 6 11 16 20

WONDERFUL WORLD OF THE BROTHERS GRIMM (See Movie Comics)

WONDER GIRL (Cassandra Sandsmark from Teen Titans)
DC Comics: Nov, 2007 - No. 6, Apr, 2008 ($2.99, limited series)
1-6-Torres-s/Greene-a; Hercules app. 2-6-Female Furies app. 5,6-Wonder Woman app. 3.00
Teen Titans Spotlight: Wonder Girl TPB (2008, $17.99) r/#1-6 18.00
1-(3/11, $2.99, one-shot) Nicola Scott-c; intro. Solstice 3.00

WONDERLAND (See Grimm Fairy Tales Presents Wonderland)

WONDERLAND COMICS
Feature Publications/Prize: Summer, 1945 - No. 9, Feb-Mar, 1947
1-Alex in Wonderland begins; Howard Post-c 34 68 102 199 325 450
2-Howard Post-c/a(2) 18 36 54 105 165 225
3-9: 3,4-Post-c 16 32 48 94 147 200

WONDER MAN (See The Avengers #9, 151)
Marvel Comics Group: Mar, 1986 ($1.25, one-shot, 52 pgs.)
1 5.00

WONDER MAN
Marvel Comics Group: Sept, 1991 - No. 29, Jan, 1994 ($1.00)
1-29: 1-Free fold out poster by Johnson/Austin. 1-3-Johnson/Austin-c/a.
2-Avengers West Coast x-over. 4 Austin-c(i) 3.00
Annual 1 (1992, $2.25)-Immonen-a (10 pgs.) 4.00
Annual 2 (1993, $2.95)-Bagged w/trading card 4.00

WONDER MAN
Marvel Comics: Feb, 2007 - No. 5, June, 2007 ($2.99, limited series)
1-5: 1-Peter David-s/Andrew Currie-a; Beast app. 4-Nauck-a 3.00
...: My Fair Super Hero TPB (2007, $13.99) r/#1-5; Currie sketch page 14.00

WONDERS OF ALADDIN, THE
Dell Publishing Co.: No. 1255, Feb-Apr, 1962
Four Color 1255-Movie 6 12 18 40 73 105

WONDER WOMAN (See Adventure Comics #459, All-Star Comics, Brave & the Bold, DC Comics Presents, JLA, Justice League of America, Legend of..., Power Record Comics, Sensation Comics, Super Friends and World's Finest Comics #244)

WONDER WOMAN
DC Comics: Jan 1942
1-Ashcan comic, not distributed to newsstands, only for in-house use. Cover art is Sensation Comics #1 with interior being Sensation Comics #2. A CGC certified 8.5 copy sold for $17,250 in 2002.

WONDER WOMAN
National Periodical Publications/All-American Publ./DC Comics:
Summer, 1942 - No. 329, Feb, 1986
1-Origin Wonder Woman retold (more detailed than All Star #8); H. G. Peter-c/a begins
7500 15,000 22,500 50,000 87,500 125,000
1-Reprint, Oversize 13-1/2x10". **WARNING:** This comic is an exact reprint of the original except for its size. DC published it in 1974 with a second cover titling it as a Famous First Edition. There have been many reported cases of the outer cover being removed and the interior sold as the original edition. The reprint with the new outer cover removed is practically worthless. See Famous First Edition for value.
2-Origin/1st app. Mars; Duke of Deception app. 568 1136 1704 4146 7323 10,500
3 331 663 993 2317 4059 5800
4,5: 5-1st Dr. Psycho app. 290 580 870 1856 3178 4500
6-1st Cheetah app. 541 1082 1623 3950 6975 10,000
7-Wonder Woman for President-c/sty 568 1136 1704 4146 7323 10,500
8,9: 9-1st app. Giganta (Sum/44) 219 438 657 1402 2401 3400
10-Invasion from Saturn classic sci-fi-c/s 226 452 678 1446 2473 3500
11-20 129 258 387 826 1413 2000
21-30: 23-Story from Wonder Woman's childhood. 28-Cheetah and Giganta-c/app.
110 220 330 704 1202 1700
31-33,35-40: 38-Last H.G. Peter-c 100 200 300 635 1093 1550
34-Robot-c 103 206 309 659 1130 1600
41-44,46-48 94 188 282 597 1024 1450
45-Origin retold 194 388 582 1242 2121 3000
49-Used in **SOTI**, pgs. 234,236; last 52 pg. issue 97 194 291 621 1061 1500
50-(44 pgs.)-Used in **POP**, pg. 97 97 194 291 621 1061 1500
51-60: 60-New logo 90 180 270 576 988 1400
61-72: 62-Origin of W.W. i.d. 64-Story about 3-D movies. 70-1st Angle Man
app. 72-Last pre-code (2/55) 87 174 261 553 952 1350
73-90: 80-Origin The Invisible Plane. 89-Flying saucer-c/story
77 154 231 493 847 1200
91-94,96,97: 97-Last H. G. Peter-a 65 130 195 416 708 1000
95-A-Bomb-c 69 138 207 442 759 1075
98-(5/58) 1st Silver Age Wonder Woman; new origin & new art team (Andru & Esposito)
begin; Kanigher-s; 1st meets Steve Trevor 300 600 900 2010 3505 5000
99-New origin continues; origin Diana Prince i.d. 71 142 213 454 777 1100
100-(8/58) 69 138 207 442 759 1075
101-104,106,108-110 48 96 144 302 514 725
105-(Scarce, 4/59)-Wonder Woman's origin (part 3); she appears as a girl (no costume yet)
(called Wonder Girl - see DC Super-Stars #1) 245 490 735 1568 2684 3800
107-1st advs. of Wonder Girl; 1st Merboy; tells how Wonder Woman won her costume
55 110 165 352 601 850
111-120 37 74 111 222 361 500
121-126: 121-1st app. Wonder Woman Family. 122-1st app. Wonder Tot. 124-Wonder Woman
Family app. 126-Last 10¢ issue 30 60 90 177 289 400
127-130: 128-Origin The Invisible Plane retold. 129-3rd app. Wonder Woman Family
(#133 is 4th app.) 13 26 39 89 195 300
131-150: 132-Flying saucer-c 11 22 33 73 157 240
151-155,157,158,161-170 (1967): 151-Wonder Girl solo issue.
9 18 27 57 111 165
156-(8/65)-Early mention of a comic book shop & comic collecting; mentions DCs selling
for $100 a copy 9 18 27 60 120 180
159-Origin retold (1/66); 1st S.A. origin? 10 20 30 68 144 220
160-1st S.A. Cheetah app. 9 18 27 57 111 165
171-176 7 14 21 44 82 120
177-W. Woman/Supergirl battle 8 16 24 56 108 160
178-(10/68) 1st new Wonder Woman on-c only; appears in old costume w/powers inside
9 18 27 61 123 185
179-Classic-c; wears no costume to issue #203 9 18 27 57 111 165
180-195: 180-Death of Steve Trevor. 182-Last 12¢ issue. 195-Wood inks
5 10 15 33 57 80
196 (52 pgs.)-Origin-r/All Star #8 (6 out of 9 pgs.) 5 10 15 35 63 90
197,198 (52 pgs.)-Reprints 5 10 15 34 60 85
199-Jeff Jones painted-c; 52 pgs. 8 16 24 56 108 160
200 (5-6/72)-Jeff Jones-c; 52 pgs. 8 16 24 56 108 160
201,202-Catwoman app. 202-Fafhrd & The Grey Mouser debut.
4 8 12 28 47 65
203,205-210,212: 212-The Cavalier app. 3 6 9 18 28 38
204-(2/73) Return to old costume; death of I Ching; intro. Nubia
4 8 12 28 47 65
211,214-(100 pgs.) 7 14 21 44 82 120
213,215,216,218-220: 220-N. Adams assist 3 6 9 16 24 32

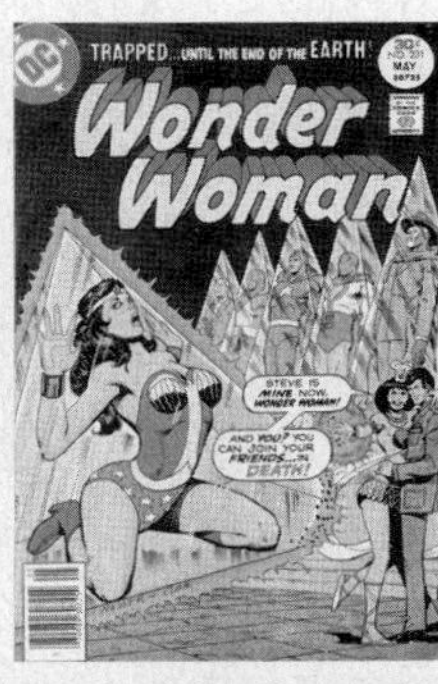

Wonder Woman #231 © DC

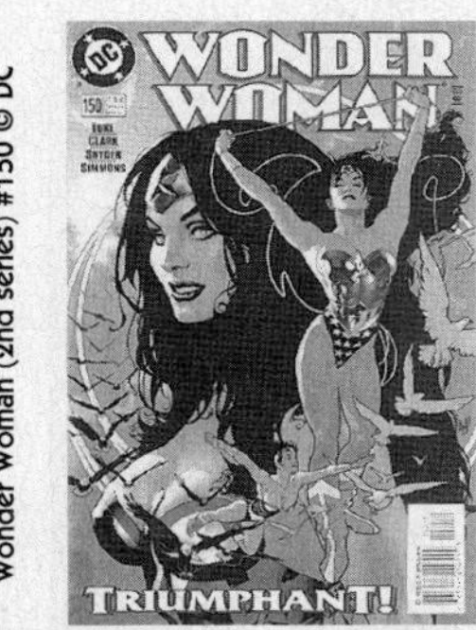

Wonder Woman (2nd series) #150 © DC

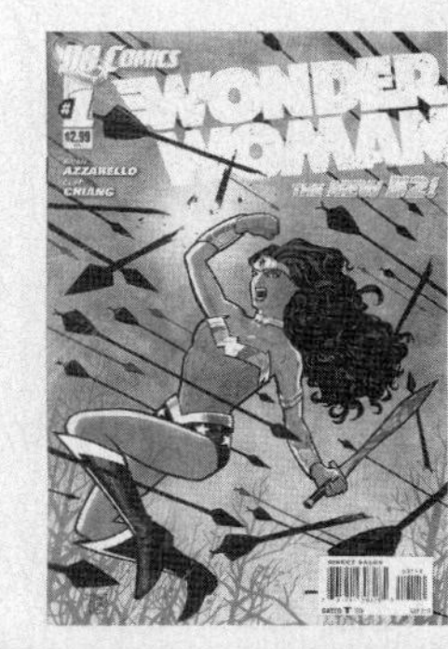

Wonder Woman (2011 series) #1 © DC

GD VG FN VF VF/NM NM-
2.0 4.0 6.0 8.0 9.0 9.2

217: (68 pgs.) 3 6 9 21 33 45
221,222,224-227,229,230,233-236,238-240: 227-Judy Garland tribute
2 4 6 10 14 18
223,228,231,232,237,241,248: 223-Steve Trevor revived as Steve Howard & learns W.W.'s I.D. 228-Both Wonder Women team up & new World War II stories begin, end #243. 231,232: JSA app. 237-Origin retold. 240-G.A. Flash app. 241-Intro Bouncer; Spectre app. 248-Steve Trevor Howard dies (44 pgs.) 2 4 6 11 16 20
242-246,252-266,269,270: 243-Both W. Women team-up again. 269-Last Wood a(i) for DC? (7/80) 2 3 4 6 8 10
247,249,250,271: 247,249 (44 pgs.). 249-Hawkgirl app. 250-Origin/1st app. Orana, the new Wonder Woman. 271-Huntress & 3rd Life of Steve Trevor begin
2 4 6 8 10 12
250-252,255-262,264-(Whitman variants, low print run, no issue # on cover)
2 4 6 13 18 22
251-Orana dies 2 4 6 11 16 20
267,268-Re-intro Animal Man (5/80 & 6/80) 2 4 6 8 10 12
272-280,284-286,289,290,294-299,301-325 6.00
281-283: Joker-c/stories in Huntress back-ups 2 3 4 6 8 10
287,288,291-293: 287-New Teen Titans x-over. 288-New costume & logo. 291-293-Three part epic with Super-Heroines 1 2 3 4 5 7
300-($1.50, 76 pgs.)-Anniv. issue; Giffen-a; New Teen Titans, Bronze Age Sandman, JLA & G.A. Wonder Woman app.; 1st app. Lyta Trevor who becomes Fury in All-Star Squadron #25; G.A. Wonder Woman & Steve Trevor revealed as married
1 2 3 5 7 9
326-328 1 2 3 4 5 7
329 (Double size)-S.A. W.W. & Steve Trevor wed 2 4 6 9 13 16
...: Chronicles Vol. 1 TPB (2010, $17.99) reprints debut in All Star Comics #8, apps. in Sensation Comics #1-9 and Wonder Woman #1 18.00
Diana Prince: Wonder Woman Vol. 1 TPB (2008, $19.99) r/#178-183 20.00
Diana Prince: Wonder Woman Vol. 2 TPB (2008, $19.99) r/#185-189, Brave and the Bold #87, and Superman's Girl Friend, Lois Lane #93 20.00
Diana Prince: Wonder Woman Vol. 3 TPB ('08, $19.99) r/#190-198, World's Finest #204 20.00
Diana Prince: Wonder Woman Vol. 4 TPB ('09, $19.99) r/#199-204, Brave & Bold #105 20.00
...: The Greatest Stories Ever Told TPB (2007, $19.99) intro. by Lynda Carter; Ross-c 20.00

NOTE: ***Andru/Esposito** c-66-160(most). **Buckler** a-300. **Colan** a-288-305p; c-288-290p. **Giffen** a-300p. **Grell** c-217. **Kaluta** c-297. **Gil Kane** c-294p, 303-305, 307, 312, 314. **Miller** c-298p. **Morrow** c-233. **Nasser** a-232p; c-231p, 232p. **Bob Oskner** c(i)-39-65(most). **Perez** c-283p, 284p. **Spiegle** a-312. **Staton** a(p)-241, 271-287, 289, 290, 294-299; c(p)-241, 245, 246. Huntress back-up stories 271-287, 289, 290, 294-299, 301-321.*

WONDER WOMAN
DC Comics: Feb, 1987 - No. 226, Apr, 2006 (75¢/$1.00/$1.25/$1.95/$1.99/$2.25/$2.50)

0-(10/94) Zero Hour; released between #90 & #91 5.00
1-New origin; Perez-c/a begins 3 6 9 14 20 25
2-5 6.00
6-20: 9-Origin Cheetah. 12,13-Millennium x-over. 18,26-Free 16 pg. story 5.00
21-49: 24-Last Perez-a; scripts continue thru #62 4.00
50-($1.50, 52 pgs.)-New Titans, Justice League 5.00
51-62: Perez scripts. 60-Vs. Lobo; last Perez-c. 62-Last $1.00-c 4.00
63-New direction & Bolland-c begin; Deathstroke story continued from W. W. Special #1 5.00
64-84 4.00
85-1st Deodato-a; ends #100 3 5 7 10 12 14
86-88: 88-Superman-c & app. 6.00
89-97: 90-(9/94)-1st Artemis. 91-(11/94). 93-Hawkman app. 96-Joker-c 5.00
98,99 4.00
100 ($2.95, Newsstand)-Death of Artemis; Bolland-c ends. 4.00
100 ($3.95, Direct Market)-Death of Artemis; foil-c. 6.00
101-119, 121-125: 101-Begin $1.95-c; Byrne-c/a/scripts begin. 101-104-Darkseid app. 105-Phantom Stranger cameo. 106-108-Phantom Stranger & Demon app. 107,108-Arion app. 111-1st app. new Wonder Girl. 111,112-Vs. Doomsday. 112-Superman app. 113-Wonder Girl-c/app; Sugar & Spike app. 3.00
120 ($2.95)-Perez-c 4.00
126-149: 128-Hippolyta becomes new W.W. 130-133-Flash (Jay Garrick) & JSA app. 136-Diana returns to W.W. role; last Byrne issue. 137-Priest-s. 139-Luke-s/Paquette-a begin; Hughes-c thru #146 3.00
150-($2.95) Hughes-c/Clark-a; Zauriel app. 4.00
151-158-Hughes-c. 153-Superboy app. 3.00
159-163: 159-Begin $2.25-c. 160,161-Clayface app. 162,163-Aquaman app. 3.00
164-171: Phil Jimenez-s/a begin; Hughes-c; Batman app. 168,169-Pérez co-plot 169-Wraparound-c.170-Lois Lane-c/app. 3.00
172-Our Worlds at War; Hippolyta killed 4.00
173,174: 173-Our Worlds at War; Darkseid app. 174-Every DC heroine app. 3.00
175-($3.50) Joker: Last Laugh; JLA app.; Jim Lee-c 4.00
176-199: 177-Paradise Island returns. 179-Jimenez-c. 184,185-Hippolyta-c/app.; Hughes-c 186-Cheetah app. 189-Simonson-s/Ordway-a begin. 190-Diana's new look. 195-Rucka-s/Drew Johnson-a begin. 197-Flash-c/app. 198,199-Noto-c 3.00

GD VG FN VF VF/NM NM-
2.0 4.0 6.0 8.0 9.0 9.2

200-($3.95) back-up stories in 1940s and 1960s styles; pin-ups by various 4.00
201-218,220-225: 203,204-Batman-c/app. 204-Matt Wagner-c. 212-JLA app. 214-Flash app. 215-Morales-a begins. 218-Begin $2.50-c. 220-Batman app. 3.00
219-Omac tie-in/Sacrifice pt. 4; Wonder Woman kills Max Lord; Superman app. 4.00
219-(2nd printing) Altered cover with red background 3.00
226-Last issue; flashbacks to meetings with Superman; Rucka-s/Richards-a 4.00
#1,000,000 (11/98) 853rd Century x-over; Deodato-c 3.00
Annual 1,2: 1 ('88, $1.50)-Art Adams-a. 2 ('89, $2.00, 68 pgs.)-All women artists issue; Perez-c(i)/a. 4.00
Annual 3 (1992, $2.50, 68 pgs.)-Quesada-c(p) 4.00
Annual 4 (1995, $3.50)-Year One 4.00
Annual 5 (1996, $2.95)-Legends of the Dead Earth story; Byrne scripts; Cockrum-a 4.00
Annual 6 (1997, $3.95)-Pulp Heroes 4.00
Annual 7,8 ('98,'99, $2.95)-7-Ghosts; Wrightson-c. 8-JLApe, A.Adams-c 4.00
...: Beauty and the Beasts TPB (2005, $19.95) r/#15-19 & Action Comics #600 20.00
...: Bitter Rivals TPB (2004, $13.95) r/#200-205; Jones-c 14.00
...: Challenge of the Gods TPB ('04, $19.95) r/#8-14; Pérez-s/a 20.00
...: Destiny Calling TPB (2006, $19.99) r/#20-24 & Annual #1; Pérez-c & pin-up gallery 20.00
...Donna Troy (6/98, $1.95) Girlfrenzy; Jimenez-a 3.00
...: Down To Earth TPB (2004, $14.95) r/#195-200; Greg Land-c 15.00
... 80-Page Giant 1 (2002, $4.95) reprints in format of 1960s' 80-Page Giants 5.00
...: Eyes of the Gorgon TPB ('05, $19.99) r/#206-213 20.00
Gallery (1996, $3.50)-Bolland-c; pin-ups by various 4.00
...: Gods and Mortals TPB ('04, $19.95) r/#1-7; Pérez-a 20.00
...: Gods of Gotham TPB ('01, $5.95) r/#164-167; Jimenez-s/a 6.00
...: Land of the Dead TPB ('06, $12.99) r/#214-217 & Flash #219 13.00
Lifelines TPB ('98, $9.95) r/#106-112; Byrne-c/a 10.00
...: Mission's End TPB ('06, $19.99) r/#218-226; cover gallery 20.00
...: Our Worlds at War (10/01, $2.95) History of the Amazons; Jae Lee-c 3.00
...: Paradise Found TPB ('03, $14.95) r/#171-177, Secret Files #3; Jimenez-s/a 15.00
...: Paradise Lost TPB ('02, $14.95) r/#164-170; Jimenez-s/a 15.00
Plus 1 (1/97, $2.95)-Jesse Quick-c/app. 4.00
Second Genesis TPB (1997, $9.95)-r/#101-105 10.00
Secret Files 1-3 (3/98, 7/99, 5/02; $4.95) 5.00
Special 1 (1992, $1.75, 52 pgs.)-Deathstroke-c/story continued in Wonder Woman #63 5.00
...: The Blue Amazon (2003, $6.95) Elseworlds; McKeever-a 7.00
The Challenge Of Artemis TPB (1996, $9.95)-r/#94-100; Deodato-c/a 10.00
...: The Once and Future Story (1998, $4.95) Trina Robbins-s/Doran & Guice-a 5.00

NOTE: ***Art Adams** a-Annual 1. **Byrne** c/a 101-107. **Bolton** a-Annual 1. **Deodato** a-85-100. **Perez** a-Annual 1; c-Annual 1(i). **Quesada** c(p)-Annual 3.*

WONDER WOMAN (Also see Amazons Attack mini-series)
DC Comics: Aug, 2006 - No. 44, Jul, 2010; No. 600, Aug, 2010 - No. 614, Oct, 2011 ($2.99)

1-Donna Troy as Wonder Woman after Infinite Crisis; Heinberg-s/Dodson-a/c 3.00
1-Variant-c by Adam Kubert 6.00
2-44: 2-4-Giganta & Hercules app. 6-Jodi Picoult-s begins. 8-Hippolyta returns. 9-12-Amazons Attack tie-in; JLA app. 14-17-Simone-s/Dodson-a/c. 20-23-Stalker app. 26-33-Rise of the Olympian. 40,41-Power Girl app. 3.00
14-DC Nation Convention giveaway edition 6.00
(Title re-numbered after #44, July 2010 to cumilative numbering of #600)
600-(8/10, $4.99) Short stories and pin-ups by various incl. Pérez, Conner, Kramer, Jim Lee; intro. by Lynda Carter; debut of new costume; cover by Pérez 5.00
600-Variant cover by Adam Hughes 8.00
600-2nd printing with new costume cover by Don Kramer 5.00
601-614: 601-606-Kramer-a; two covers by Kramer and Garner. 608-Borges-a 3.00
... Annual 1 (11/07, $3.99) Story cont'd from #4; Heinberg-s/Dodson-a/c; back-up Frank-a 4.00
...: Contagion SC (2010, $14.99) r/#40-44 15.00
...: Ends of the Earth HC (2009, $24.99) r/#20-25 25.00
...: Ends of the Earth SC (2010, $14.99) r/#20-25 15.00
...: Love and Murder HC (2007, $19.99) r/#6-10 20.00
...: Odyssey Volume One HC (2011, $22.99) r/#600-606; afterwords by Jim Lee & JMS 23.00
...: Rise of the Olympian HC (2009, $24.99) r/#26-33 & pages from DC Universe #0 25.00
...: Rise of the Olympian SC (2009, $14.99) r/#26-33 & pages from DC Universe #0 15.00
...: The Circle HC (2008, $24.99) r/#14-19; Mercedes Lackey intro.; Dodson sketch pages 25.00
...: The Circle SC (2009, $14.99) r/#14-19; Mercedes Lackey intro.; Dodson sketch pages 15.00
...: Warkiller SC (2010, $14.99) r/#34-39 15.00
...: Who is Wonder Woman? HC (2007, $19.99) r/#1-4 & Annual #1; Vaughan intro. 20.00
...: Who is Wonder Woman? SC (2009, $14.99) r/#1-4 & Annual #1; Vaughan intro. 15.00

WONDER WOMAN (DC New 52)
DC Comics: Nov, 2011 - No. 52, Jul, 2016 ($2.99/$3.99)

1-Azzarello-s/Chiang-a/c 2 4 6 9 12 15
2-23: 2-4-Azzarello-s/Chiang-a/c. 5,6,9,10,13,14,17-Akins-a. 14-19,21-23-Orion app. 3.00
23.1, 23.2 (11/13, $2.99, regular covers) 3.00
23.1 (11/13, $3.99, 3-D cover) "Cheetah #1" on cover; origin; Ostrander-s/Ibanez-a 5.00

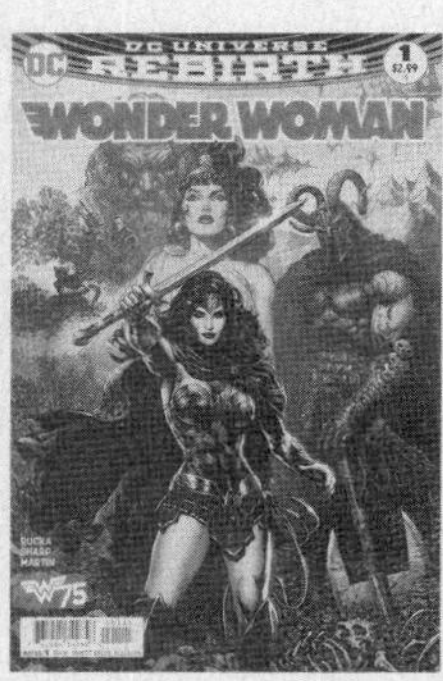

Wonder Woman (2016 series) #1 © DC

The Woods #21 © James Tynion IV

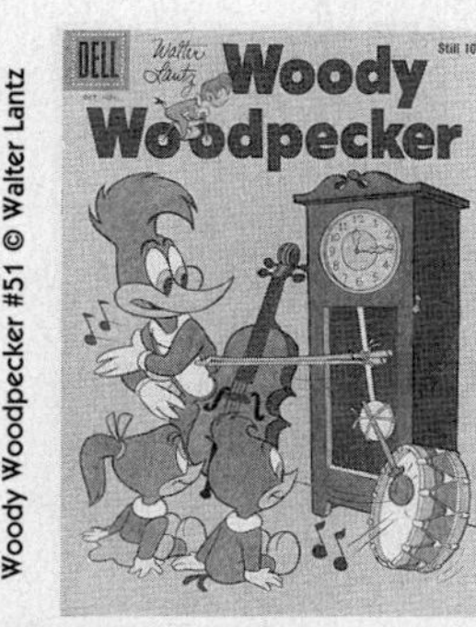

Woody Woodpecker #51 © Walter Lantz

	GD 2.0	VG 4.0	FN 6.0	VF 8.0	VF/NM 9.0	NM- 9.2

23.2 (11/13, $3.99, 3-D cover) "First Born #1" on cover; origin; Azzarello-s/Aco-a 5.00
24-35: 25-Orion app. 29-Diana becomes God of War. 35-Last Azzarello-s/Chiang-a/c 3.00
36-40: 36-Meredith Finch-s/David Finch-a begins. 37-Donna Troy returns 3.00
41-49,51,52: 41-New costume; begin $3.99-c. 43-Churchill-a 4.00
50-($4.99) Finch & Desjardins-a; Ares app.; back-up Donna Troy story 5.00
#0 (11/12, $2.99) 12 year-old Princess Diana's training; Azzarello-s/Chiang-a/c 3.00
Annual 1 (8/15, $4.99) Concludes "War Torn" arc from #36-40; David Finch-a 5.00
...: Futures End 1 (11/14, $2.99, regular-c) Five years later; Soule-s/Morales-a 3.00
...: Futures End 1 (11/14, $3.99, 3-D cover) 4.00

WONDER WOMAN (DC Rebirth)
DC Comics: Aug, 2016 - Present ($2.99)

1-17: 1,3,5,7-Rucka-s/Sharp-a; Cheetah app. 2,4,6,10,12,14-Year One; Nicola Scott-a 3.00
...: Rebirth 1 (8/16, $2.99) Rucka-s; multiples origins; new costume 3.00
... 75th Anniversary Special 1 (12/16, $7.99) short stories and pin-ups by various incl. Sharp, Moon, Bolland, DeLiz, Frison, Albuquerque, Larson, Jimenez, Sauvage; Jim Lee-c 8.00

WONDER WOMAN: AMAZONIA
DC Comics: 1997 ($7.95, Graphic Album format, one shot)

1-Elseworlds; Messner-Loebs-s/Winslade-a 8.00

WONDER WOMAN: EARTH ONE
DC Comics: 2016 ($22.99, HC Graphic Novel)

Volume 1 - Grant Morrison-s/Yanick Paquette-a; alternate retelling of origin; bonus art 23.00

WONDER WOMAN '77
DC Comics: Jun, 2015 - Present ($7.99, square-bound, printing of digital-first stories)

1-4-Stories based on the Lynda Carter series. 1-Covers by Nicola Scott & Phil Jimenez; Dr. Psycho app.; bonus sketch design art; afterword by Mangels. 2-(11/15) Scott-c; The Cheetah, Celsia & Solomon Grundy app. 3-Clayface app. 8.00

WONDER WOMAN '77 MEETS THE BIONIC WOMAN (TV)
Dynamite Entertainment: 2016 - Present ($3.99, limited series)

1,2-Andy Mangels-s/Judit Tondora-a; multiple covers 4.00

WONDER WOMAN SPECTACULAR (See DC Special Series #9)

WONDER WOMAN: SPIRIT OF TRUTH
DC Comics: Nov, 2001 ($9.95, treasury size, one-shot)

nn-Painted art by Alex Ross; story by Alex Ross and Paul Dini 10.00

WONDER WOMAN: THE HIKETEIA
DC Comics: 2002 ($24.95, hardcover, one-shot)

nn-Wonder Woman battles Batman; Greg Rucka-s/J.G. Jones-a 25.00
Softcover (2003, $17.95) 18.00

WONDER WOMAN: THE TRUE AMAZON
DC Comics: 2016 ($22.99, HC Graphic Novel)

HC-Retelling of childhood & origin; Jill Thompson-s/painted-a; bonus design pages 23.00

WONDERWORLD COMICS (Formerly Wonder Comics)
Fox Features Syndicate: No. 3, July, 1939 - No. 33, Jan, 1942

	GD	VG	FN	VF	VF/NM	NM-
3-Intro The Flame by Fine; Dr. Fung (Powell-a), K-51 (Powell-a?), & Yarko the Great, Master Magician (Eisner-a) continues; Eisner/Fine-c	975	1950	2919	7100	12,550	18,000
4-Lou Fine-c	400	800	1200	2800	4900	7000
5,6,9,10: Lou Fine-c	290	580	870	1856	3178	4500
7-Classic Lou Fine-c	649	1298	1947	4738	8369	12,000
8-Classic Lou Fine-c	432	864	1296	3154	5577	8000
11-Origin The Flame	239	478	717	1530	2615	3700
12-15:13-Dr. Fung ends; last Fine-c(p)	194	388	582	1242	2121	3000
16-20	135	270	405	864	1482	2100
21-Origin The Black Lion & Cub	129	258	387	826	1413	2000
22-27: 22,25-Dr. Fung app.	110	220	330	704	1202	1700
28-Origin & 1st app. U.S. Jones (8/41); Lu-Nar, the Moon Man begins	161	322	483	1030	1765	2500
29,31,33	97	194	291	621	1061	1500
30-Intro & Origin Flame Girl	135	270	405	864	1482	2100
32-Hitler-c	290	580	870	1856	3178	4500

NOTE: *Spies at War by* ***Eisner*** *in #13, 17. Yarko by* ***Eisner*** *in #3-11.* ***Eisner*** *text illos-3.* ***Lou Fine*** *a-3-11; c-3-13, 15(i); text illos-4.* ***Nordling*** *a-4-14.* ***Powell*** *a-3-12.* ***Tuska*** *a-5-9. Bondage-c 14, 15, 28, 31, 32. Cover features: The Flame-#3, 5-31; U.S. Jones-#32, 33.*

WONDERWORLDS
Innovation Publishing: 1992 ($3.50, squarebound, 100 pgs.)

1-Rebound super-hero comics, contents may vary; Hero Alliance, Terraformers, etc. 5.00

WOODS, THE
BOOM! Studios: May, 2014 - Present ($3.99)

1-30: 1-Tynion-s/Dialynas-a; multiple covers 4.00

WOODSY OWL (See March of Comics #395)
Gold Key: Nov, 1973 - No. 10, Feb, 1976 (Some Whitman printings exist)

	GD	VG	FN	VF	VF/NM	NM-
1	2	4	6	13	18	22
1-Whitman variant	3	6	9	14	20	25
2-10	2	4	6	8	10	12

WOODY WOODPECKER (Walter Lantz... #73 on?)(See Dell Giants for annuals)
(Also see The Funnies, Jolly Jingles, Kite Fun Book, New Funnies)
Dell Publishing Co./Gold Key No. 73-187/Whitman No. 188 on:
No. 169, 10/47 - No. 72, 5-7/62; No. 73, 10/62 - No. 201, 3/84 (nn 192)

	GD	VG	FN	VF	VF/NM	NM-
Four Color 169(#1)-Drug turns Woody into a Mr. Hyde	18	36	54	128	284	440
Four Color 188	11	22	33	73	157	240
Four Color 202,232,249,264,288	8	16	24	56	108	160
Four Color 305,336,350	6	12	18	41	76	110
Four Color 364,374,390,405,416,431('52)	6	12	18	37	66	95
16 (12-1/52-53) - 30('55)	4	8	12	27	44	60
31-50	3	6	9	21	33	45
51-72 (Last Dell)	3	6	9	17	26	35
73-75 (Giants, 84 pgs., Gold Key)	5	10	15	30	50	70
76-80	3	6	9	15	22	28
81-103: 103-Last 12¢ issue	3	6	9	14	19	24
104-120	2	4	6	11	16	20
121-140	2	4	6	9	12	15
141-160: 141-UFO-c	1	3	4	6	8	10
161-187	1	2	3	5	7	9
188,189 (Whitman)	2	4	6	9	13	16
190(9/80),191(11/80)-pre-pack only	6	12	18	38	69	100
(No #192)						
193-197: 196(2/82), 197(4/82)	2	4	6	11	16	20
198-201 (All #90062 on-c, no date or date code, pre-pack): 198(6/83), 199(7/83), 200(8/83), 201(3/84)	3	6	9	16	24	32
Christmas Parade 1(11/68-Giant)(G.K.)	4	8	12	25	40	55
Summer Fun 1(6/66-G.K.)(84 pgs.)	4	8	12	28	47	65
nn (1971, 60¢, 100 pgs. digest) B&W one page gags	3	6	9	16	24	32

NOTE: *15¢ Canadian editions of the 12¢ issues exist. Reprints-No. 92, 102, 103, 105, 106, 124, 125, 152, 153, 157, 162, 165, 194(1/3)-200(1/3).*

WOODY WOODPECKER (See Comic Album #5,9,13, Dell Giant #24, 40, 54, Dell Giants, The Funnies, Golden Comics Digest #1, 3, 5, 8, 15, 16, 20, 24, 32, 37, 44, March of Comics #16, 34, 85, 93, 109, 124, 139, 158, 177, 184, 203, 222, 239, 249, 261, 420, 454, 466, 478, New Funnies & Super Book #12, 24)

WOODY WOODPECKER
Harvey Comics: Sept, 1991 - No. 15, Aug, 1994 ($1.25)

1-15: 1-r/W.W. #53 4.00
50th Anniversary Special 1 (10/91, $2.50, 68 pgs.) 5.00

WOODY WOODPECKER AND FRIENDS
Harvey Comics: Dec, 1991 - No. 4, 1992 ($1.25)

1-4 4.00

WOOL (Hugh Howey's...)
Cryptozoic Entertainment: Jul, 2014 - No. 6, Nov, 2014 ($3.99)

1-6-Palmiotti & Gray-s/Broxton-a/Darwyn Cooke-c 4.00

WORD WARRIORS (Also see Quest for Dreams Lost)
Literacy Volunteers of Chicago: 1987 ($1.50, B&W)(Proceeds donated to help literacy)

1-Jon Sable by Grell, Ms. Tree, Streetwolf; Chaykin-c 3.00

WORLD AROUND US, THE (Illustrated Story of...)
Gilberton Publishers (Classics Illustrated): Sep, 1958 -No. 36, Oct, 1961 (25¢)

	GD	VG	FN	VF	VF/NM	NM-
1-Dogs; Evans-a	9	18	27	52	69	85
2-4: 2-Indians; Check-a. 3-Horses; L. B. Cole-c. 4-Railroads; L. B. Cole-a (5 pgs.)	9	18	27	47	61	75
5-Space; Ingels-a	10	20	30	56	76	95
6-The F.B.I.; Disbrow, Evans, Ingels-a	10	20	30	56	76	95
7-Pirates; Disbrow, Ingels, Kinstler-a	9	18	27	52	69	85
8-Flight; Evans, Ingels, Crandall-a	9	18	27	52	69	85
9-Army; Disbrow, Ingels, Orlando-a	9	18	27	47	61	75
10-13: 10-Navy; Disbrow, Kinstler-a. 11-Marine Corps. 12-Coast Guard; Ingels-a (9 pgs.). 13-Air Force; L.B. Cole-c	9	18	27	47	61	75
14-French Revolution; Crandall, Evans, Kinstler-a	10	20	30	56	76	95
15-Prehistoric Animals; Al Williamson-a, 6 & 10 pgs. plus Morrow-a	10	20	30	58	79	100

16-18: 16-Crusades; Kinstler-a. 17-Festivals; Evans, Crandall-a. 18-Great Scientists;

The World Below #3 © Paul Chadwick

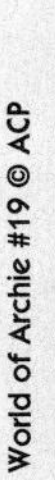
World of Archie #19 © ACP

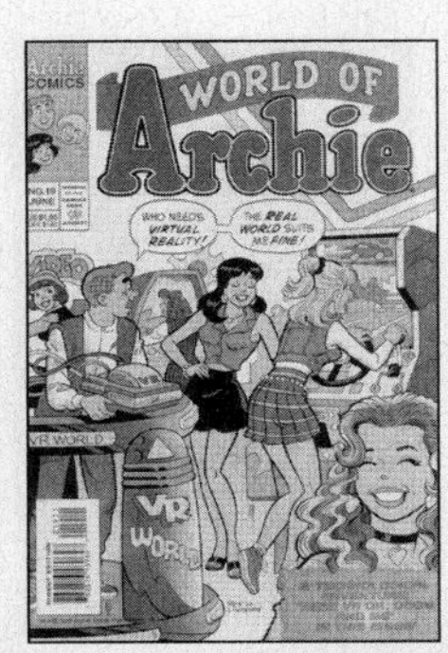

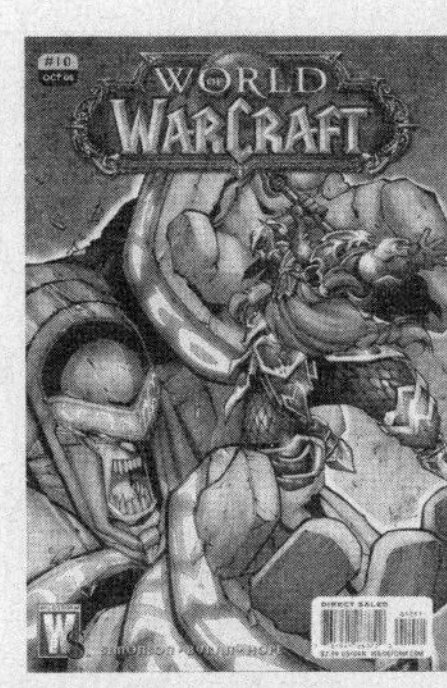
World of Warcraft #10 © Blizzard

	GD 2.0	VG 4.0	FN 6.0	VF 8.0	VF/NM 9.0	NM- 9.2
Crandall, Evans, Torres, Williamson, Morrow-a	9	18	27	52	69	85
19-Jungle; Crandall, Williamson, Morrow-a	10	20	30	58	79	100
20-Communications; Crandall, Evans, Torres-a	10	20	30	56	76	95
21-American Presidents; Crandall/Evans, Morrow-a	10	20	30	56	76	95
22-Boating; Morrow-a	8	16	24	44	57	70
23-Great Explorers; Crandall, Evans-a	9	18	27	52	69	85
24-Ghosts; Morrow, Evans-a	10	20	30	56	76	95
25-Magic; Evans, Morrow-a	10	20	30	56	76	95
26-The Civil War	11	22	33	62	86	110
27-Mountains (High Advs.); Crandall/Evans, Morrow, Torres-a	9	18	27	52	69	85
28-Whaling; Crandall, Evans, Morrow, Torres, Wildey-a; L.B. Cole-c	9	18	27	52	69	85
29-Vikings; Crandall, Evans, Torres, Morrow-a	10	20	30	58	79	100
30-Undersea Adventure; Crandall/Evans, Kirby, Morrow, Torres-a	10	20	30	56	76	95
31-Hunting; Crandall/Evans, Ingels, Kinstler, Kirby-a	9	18	27	52	69	85
32,33: 32-For Gold & Glory; Morrow, Kirby, Crandall, Evans-a. 33-Famous Teens; Torres, Crandall, Evans-a	9	18	27	52	69	85
34-36: 34-Fishing; Crandall/Evans-a. 35-Spies; Kirby, Morrow?, Evans-a. 36-Fight for Life (Medicine); Kirby-a	9	18	27	52	69	85

NOTE: See Classics Illustrated Special Edition. Another *World Around Us* issue entitled *The Sea* had been prepared in 1962 but was never published in the U.S. It was published in the British/European *World Around Us* series. Those series then continued with seven additional WAU titles not in the U.S. series.

WORLD BELOW, THE
Dark Horse Comics: Mar, 1999 - No. 4, Jun, 1999 ($2.50, limited series)

	NM- 9.2
1-4-Paul Chadwick-s/c/a	3.00
TPB (1/07, $12.95) r/#1-4; intro. by Chadwick; gallery of sketches and covers	13.00

WORLD BELOW, THE: DEEPER AND STRANGER
Dark Horse Comics: Dec, 1999 - No. 4, Mar, 2000 ($2.95, B&W)

	NM- 9.2
1-4-Paul Chadwick-s/c/a	3.00

WORLD FAMOUS HEROES MAGAZINE
Comic Corp. of America (Centaur): Oct, 1941 - No. 4, Apr, 1942 (comic book)

	GD 2.0	VG 4.0	FN 6.0	VF 8.0	VF/NM 9.0	NM- 9.2
1-Gustavson-c; Lubbers, Glanzman-a; Davy Crockett, Paul Revere, Lewis & Clark, John Paul Jones stories; Flag-c	116	232	348	742	1271	1800
2-Lou Gehrig life story; Lubbers-a	57	114	171	362	619	875
3,4-Lubbers-a. 4-Wild Bill Hickok story; 2 pg. Marlene Dietrich story	54	108	162	343	574	825

WORLD FAMOUS STORIES
Croyden Publishers: 1945

	GD 2.0	VG 4.0	FN 6.0	VF 8.0	VF/NM 9.0	NM- 9.2
1-Ali Baba, Hansel & Gretel, Rip Van Winkle, Mid-Summer Night's Dream	14	28	42	76	108	140

WORLD IS HIS PARISH, THE
George A. Pflaum: 1953 (15¢)

	GD 2.0	VG 4.0	FN 6.0	VF 8.0	VF/NM 9.0	NM- 9.2
nn-The story of Pope Pius XII	6	12	18	31	38	45

WORLD OF ADVENTURE (Walt Disney's...)(TV)
Gold Key: Apr, 1963 - No. 3, Oct, 1963 (12¢)

	GD 2.0	VG 4.0	FN 6.0	VF 8.0	VF/NM 9.0	NM- 9.2
1-Disney TV characters; Savage Sam, Johnny Shiloh, Capt. Nemo, The Mooncussers	3	6	9	20	31	42
2,3	3	6	9	15	21	26

WORLD OF ARCHIE, THE (See Archie Giant Series Mag. #148, 151, 156, 160, 165, 171, 177, 182, 188, 193, 200, 208, 213, 225, 232, 237, 244, 249, 456, 461, 468, 473, 480, 485, 492, 497, 504, 509, 516, 521, 532, 543, 554, 565, 574, 587, 599, 612, 627)

WORLD OF ARCHIE
Archie Comics: Aug, 1992 - No. 22 ($1.25/$1.50)

	NM- 9.2
1	4.00
2-15: 9-Neon ink-c	3.00
16-22	3.00

WORLD OF ARCHIE DOUBLE DIGEST MAGAZINE (World of Archie Comics Digest #41-on)
Archie Comics: Dec, 2010 - Present ($3.99/$4.99/$6.99)

	NM- 9.2
1-29,31-37,39,40: 5-r/Tiny Titans/Little Archie #1-3 with sketch-a. 17-Archie babies	4.00
30-($5.99) Double Double Digest	6.00
38-$4.99-c	5.00
41,46,51,55,60,63-($6.99) 41-World of Archie Double Double Digest. 46-Jumbo Digest	7.00
42-45,47-50,52,54,57,58,61,64,65-($4.99) Titled World of Archie Comics Digest	5.00
53,56,59,62,66-($5.99): 56-Winter Annual. 59-Summer Annual	6.00
World of Archie Digest, Free Comic Book Day Edition (6-7/13, giveaway) Reprints	3.00

WORLD OF FANTASY
Atlas Comics (CPC No. 1-15/ZPC No. 16-19): May, 1956 - No. 19, Aug, 1959

	GD 2.0	VG 4.0	FN 6.0	VF 8.0	VF/NM 9.0	NM- 9.2
1	74	148	222	470	810	1150
2-Williamson-a (4 pgs.)	41	82	123	256	428	600
3-Sid Check, Roussos-a	39	78	117	240	395	550
4-7	36	72	108	211	343	475
8-Matt Fox, Orlando, Berg-a	37	74	111	222	361	500
9-Krigstein-a	36	72	108	211	343	475
10-15: 10-Colan-a. 11-Torres-a	32	64	96	188	307	425
16-Williamson-a (4 pgs.); Ditko, Kirby-a	46	92	138	290	488	685
17-19-Ditko, Kirby-a	46	92	138	290	488	685

NOTE: ***Ayers** a-3. **B. Baily** a-4. **Berg** a-5, 6, 8. **Brodsky** c-3. **Check** a-3. **Ditko** a-17, 19. **Everett** a-2; c-4-7, 9, 12, 13. **Forte** a-4, 8. **Infantino** a-14. **Kirby** c-15, 17-19. **Krigstein** a-9. **Maneely** c-2, 14. **Mooney** a-14. **Morrow** a-7. **Orlando** a-8, 13, 14. **Pakula** a-9. **Powell** a-4, 6. **Reinman** a-8, 10. **R.Q. Sale** a-3, 7, 9, 10. **Severin** c-1.*

WORLD OF GIANT COMICS, THE (See Archie All-Star Specials under Archie Comics)

WORLD OF GINGER FOX, THE (Also see Ginger Fox)
Comico: Nov, 1986 ($6.95, 8 1/2 x 11", 68 pgs., mature)

	NM- 9.2
Graphic Novel ($6.95)	10.00
Hardcover ($27.95)	30.00

WORLD OF JUGHEAD, THE (See Archie Giant Series Mag. #9, 14, 19, 24, 30, 136, 143, 149, 152, 157, 161, 166, 172, 178, 183, 189, 194, 202, 209, 215, 227, 233, 239, 245, 251, 457, 463, 469, 475, 481, 487, 493, 499, 505, 511, 517, 523, 531, 542, 553, 564, 577, 590, 602)

WORLD OF KRYPTON, THE (World of...#3) (See Superman #248)
DC Comics, Inc.: 7/79 - No. 3, 9/79; 12/87 - No. 4, 3/88 (Both are lim. series)

	GD 2.0	VG 4.0	FN 6.0	VF 8.0	VF/NM 9.0	NM- 9.2
1-3 (1979, 40¢; 1st comic book mini-series): 1-Jor-El marries Lara. 3-Baby Superman sent to Earth; Krypton explodes; Mon-el app.	1	2	3	5	6	8
1-4 (75¢)-Byrne scripts; Byrne/Simonson-c						4.00

WORLD OF METROPOLIS, THE
DC Comics: Aug, 1988 - No. 4, July, 1988 ($1.00, limited series)

	NM- 9.2
1-4: Byrne scripts	4.00

WORLD OF MYSTERY
Atlas Comics (GPI): June, 1956 - No. 7, July, 1957

	GD 2.0	VG 4.0	FN 6.0	VF 8.0	VF/NM 9.0	NM- 9.2
1-Torres, Orlando-a; Powell-a?	55	110	165	352	601	850
2-Woodish-a	25	50	75	150	245	340
3-Torres, Davis, Ditko-a	29	58	87	172	281	390
4-Pakula, Powell-a	29	58	87	172	281	390
5,7: 5-Orlando-a	24	48	72	142	234	325
6-Williamson/Mayo-a (4 pgs.); Ditko-a; Colan-a; Crandall text illo	29	58	87	172	281	390

NOTE: ***Ayers** a-4. **Brodsky** c-2, 5, 6. **Colan** a-6, 7. **Everett** c-1, 3. **Pakula** a-4, 6. **Romita** a-2. **Severin** c-7.*

WORLD OF SMALLVILLE
DC Comics: Apr, 1988 - No. 4, July, 1988 (75¢, limited series)

	NM- 9.2
1-4: Byrne scripts	4.00

WORLD OF SUSPENSE
Atlas News Co.: Apr, 1956 - No. 8, July, 1957

	GD 2.0	VG 4.0	FN 6.0	VF 8.0	VF/NM 9.0	NM- 9.2
1	50	100	150	315	533	750
2-Ditko-a (4 pgs.)	29	58	87	170	278	385
3,7-Williamson-a in both (4 pgs.); #7-with Mayo	28	56	84	165	270	375
4-6,8	24	48	72	140	230	320

NOTE: ***Berg** a-6. **Cameron** a-2. **Ditko** a-2. **Drucker** a-1. **Everett** a-1, 5; c-6. **Heck** a-5. **Maneely** a-1; c-1-3. **Orlando** a-5. **Powell** a-6. **Reinman** a-4. **Roussos** a-6. **Sale** a-4. **Shores** a-1.*

WORLD OF TANKS
Dark Horse Comics: Aug, 2016 - No. 5, Feb, 2017 ($3.99)

	NM- 9.2
1-5-Ennis-s/Ezquerra-a; set in 1944 Normandy	4.00

WORLD OF WARCRAFT (Based on the Blizzard Entertainment video game)
DC Comics (WildStorm): Jan, 2008 - No. 25, Jan, 2010 ($2.99)

	NM- 9.2
1-Walt Simonson-s/Lullabi-a; cover by Samwise Didier	8.00
1-Variant cover by Jim Lee	12.00
1,2-Second printing with Jim Lee sketch cover	5.00
2-Two covers by Jim Lee and Samwise Didier	5.00
3-24: 3-14-Two covers on each	3.00
25-($3.99) Walt & Louise Simonson-s	4.00
... Special 1 (2/10, $3.99) Costa-s/Mhan-a/c	4.00
... Book One HC (2008, $19.99, dustjacket) r/#1-7; intro. by Chris Metzen of Blizzard	20.00
... Book One SC (2009, $14.99) r/#1-7; intro. by Chris Metzen of Blizzard	15.00
... Book Two HC (2009, $19.99, dustjacket) r/#8-14	20.00
... Book Two SC (2010, $14.99) r/#8-14	15.00
... Book Three HC (2010, $19.99, dustjacket) r/#15-21	20.00
... Book Three SC (2011, $17.99) r/#15-21	18.00

WORLD OF WARCRAFT: ASHBRINGER
DC Comics (WildStorm): Nov, 2008 - No. 4, Feb, 2009 ($3.99)

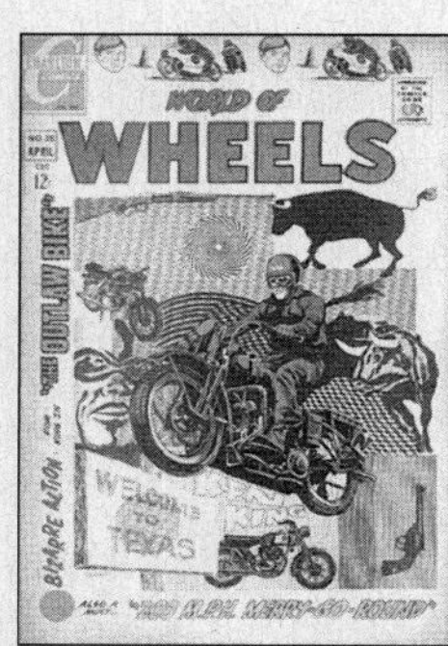

World of Wheels #25 © CC

Worlds' Finest #19 © DC

World's Finest Comics #90 © DC

GD VG FN VF VF/NM NM-
2.0 4.0 6.0 8.0 9.0 9.2

GD VG FN VF VF/NM NM-
2.0 4.0 6.0 8.0 9.0 9.2

1-4-Neilson-s/Lullabi & Washington-a; 2 covers by Robinson & Lullabi 4.00
TPB (2010, $14.99) r/#1-4 15.00

WORLD OF WARCRAFT: CURSE OF THE WORGEN
DC Comics (WildStorm #1,2): Jan, 2011 - No. 5, May, 2011 ($3.99/$2.99)

1,2-($3.99) Neilson & Waugh-s/Lullabi & Washington-a; Polidora-c 4.00
3-5-($2.99) 3.00

WORLD OF WHEELS (Formerly Dragstrip Hotrodders)
Charlton Comics: No. 17, Oct, 1967 - No. 32, June, 1970

17-20-Features Ken King 3 6 9 17 26 35
21-32-Features Ken King 3 6 9 15 22 28
Modern Comics Reprint 23(1978) 6.00

WORLD OF WOOD
Eclipse Comics: 1986 - No. 4, 1987; No. 5, 2/89 ($1.75, limited series)

1,2: 1-Dave Stevens-c. 2-Wood/Stevens-c 1 3 4 6 8 10
3-5: 5-($2.00, B&W)-r/Avon's Flying Saucers 5.00

WORLD'S BEST COMICS
DC Comics: Feb 1940

nn - Ashcan comic, not distributed to newsstands, only for in-house use. Cover art is Action Comics #29 with interior being Action Comics #24. One copy sold for $21,000 in 2000.

WORLD'S BEST COMICS (World's Finest Comics #2 on)
National Per. Publications (100 pgs.): Spring, 1941 (Cardboard-c)(DC's 6th annual format comic)

1-The Batman, Superman, Crimson Avenger, Johnny Thunder, The King, Young Dr. Davis, Zatara, Lando, Man of Magic, & Red, White & Blue begin; Superman, Batman & Robin covers begin (inside-c is blank); Fred Ray-c; 15¢ cover price
1550 3100 4650 11,000 19,000 27,000

WORLD'S BEST COMICS: GOLDEN AGE SAMPLER
DC Comics: 2003 (99¢, one-shot, samples from DC Archive editions)

1-Golden Age reprints from Superman #6, Batman #5, Sensation #11, Police #11 3.00

WORLD'S BEST COMICS: SILVER AGE SAMPLER
DC Comics: 2004 (99¢, one-shot, samples from DC Archive editions)

1-Silver Age reprints from Justice League #4, Adventure #247, Our Army at War #81 3.00

WORLDS BEYOND (Stories of Weird Adventure)(Worlds of Fear #2 on)
Fawcett Publications: Nov, 1951

1-Powell, Bailey-a; Moldoff-c 58 116 174 371 636 900

WORLDS COLLIDE
DC Comics: July, 1994 ($2.50, one-shot)

1-($2.50, 52 pgs.)-Milestone & Superman titles x-over 4.00
1-($3.95, 52 pgs.)-Polybagged w/vinyl clings 5.00

WORLD'S FAIR COMICS (See New York...)

WORLD'S FINEST (Also see Legends of The World's Finest)
DC Comics: 1990 - No. 3, 1990 ($3.95, squarebound, limited series, 52 pgs.)

1-3: Batman & Superman team-up against The Joker and Lex Luthor; Dave Gibbons scripts & Steve Rude-c/a. 2,3-Joker/Luthor painted-c by Steve Rude 5.00
TPB-(1992, $19.95) r/#1-3; Gibbons intro. 20.00
...: The Deluxe Edition HC (2008, $29.99) r/#1-3; Gibbons intro. from 1992; Gibbons story outline and sketches; Rude sketch pages and notes 30.00

WORLD'S FINEST
DC Comics: Dec, 2009 - No. 4, Mar, 2010 ($2.99, limited series)

1-4: Gates-s/two covers by Noto on each. 3-Supergirl/Batgirl team up. 4-Noto-a 3.00
TPB (2010, $14.99) r/#1-4, Action Comics #865 & DC Comics Presents #31 15.00

WORLDS' FINEST (Also see Earth 2 series)
DC Comics: Jul, 2012 - No. 32, May, 2015 ($2.99)

1-32: 1-Huntress and Power Girl; Levitz-s/art by Pérez & Maguire. 6,7-Damian app. 19-Huntress meets Batman. 20,21-X-over with Batman/Superman #8,9. 25-Return to Earth-2. 27-29-Secret History of Earth 2. 32-Death of Lois 3.00
1-Variant-c by Maguire 5.00
#0-(11/12, $2.99) Flashback to Robin's and Supergirl's training 3.00
Annual 1 (3/14, $4.99) Earth 2 flashback; Wonder Woman & Fury app. 5.00
...: Futures End 1 (11/14, $2.99, regular-c) Five years later; Cinar-a; Deathstroke app. 3.00
...: Futures End 1 (11/14, $3.99, 3-D cover) 4.00

WORLD'S FINEST COMICS (Formerly World's Best Comics #1)
National Periodical Publ./DC Comics: No. 2, Sum, 1941 - No. 323, Jan, 1986 (#1-17 have cardboard covers) (#2-9 have 100 pgs.)

2 (100 pgs.)-Superman, Batman & Robin covers continue from World's Best; (cover price 15¢ #2-70) 423 846 1269 3000 5250 7500
3-The Sandman begins; last Johnny Thunder; origin & 1st app. The Scarecrow
389 778 1167 2723 4762 6800
4-Hop Harrigan app.; last Young Dr. Davis 258 516 774 1651 2826 4000
5-Intro. TNT & Dan the Dyna-Mite; last King & Crimson Avenger
258 516 774 1651 2826 4000
6-Star Spangled Kid begins (Sum/42); Aquaman app.; S&K Sandman with Sandy in new costume begins, ends #7 194 388 582 1242 2121 3000
7-Green Arrow begins (Fall/42); last Lando & Red, White & Blue; S&K art
206 412 618 1318 2259 3200
8-Boy Commandos begin (by Simon(p) #12); last The King; includes "Minute Man Answers the Call" promo 181 362 543 1158 1979 2800
9-Batman cameo in Star Spangled Kid; S&K-a; last 100 pg. issue; Hitler, Mussolini, Tojo-c 252 504 756 1613 2757 3900
10-S&K-a; 76 pg. issues begin 168 336 504 1075 1838 2600
11-17: 17-Last cardboard cover issue 158 316 474 1003 1727 2450
18-20: 18-Paper covers begin; last Star Spangled Kid. 19-Joker story. 20-Last quarterly issue
155 310 465 992 1696 2400
21-30: 21-Begin bi-monthly. 30-Johnny Everyman app.
107 214 321 680 1165 1650
31-40: 33-35-Tomahawk app. 35-Penguin app. 103 206 309 659 1130 1600
41-43,45-50: 41-Boy Commandos end. 42-The Wyoming Kid begins (9-10/49), ends #63. 43-Full Steam Foley begins, ends #48. 48-Last square binding. 49-Tom Sparks, Boy Inventor begins; robot-c 100 200 300 635 1093 1550
44-Used in SOTI, ref. to Batman & Robin being gay, and a cop being shot in the face
110 220 330 704 1202 1700
51-60: 51-Zatara ends. 54-Last 76 pg. issue. 59-Manhunters Around the World begins (7-8/52), ends #62 97 194 291 621 1061 1500
61-64: 61-Joker story. 63-Capt. Compass app. 94 188 282 597 1024 1450
65-Origin Superman; Tomahawk begins (7-8/53), ends #101
129 258 387 826 1413 2000
66-70-(15¢ issues, scarce)-Last 15¢, 68pg. issue 100 200 300 635 1093 1550
71-(10¢ issue, scarce)-Superman & Batman begin as team (7-8/54); were in separate stories until now; Superman & Batman exchange identities; 10¢ issues begin
300 600 900 1950 3375 4800
72,73-(10¢ issue, scarce) 129 258 387 826 1413 2000
74-Last pre-code issue 94 188 282 597 1024 1450
75-(1st code approved, 3-4/55) 90 180 270 576 988 1400
76-80: 77-Superman loses powers & Batman obtains them
68 136 204 435 743 1050
81-87,89: 84-1st S.A. issue. 89-2nd Batmen of All Nations (aka Club of Heroes)
32 64 96 230 515 800
88-1st Joker/Luthor team-up 57 114 171 362 619 875
90-Batwoman's 1st app. in World's Finest (10/57, 3rd app. anywhere) plus-c app.
65 130 195 416 708 1000
91-93,95-99: 96-99-Kirby Green Arrow. 99-Robot-c 25 50 75 175 388 600
94-Origin Superman/Batman team retold 59 118 177 472 1061 1650
100 (3/59) 36 72 108 259 580 900
101-110: 102-Tommy Tomorrow begins, ends #124 15 30 45 105 233 360
111-121: 111-1st app. The Clock King. 113-Intro. Miss Arrowette in Green Arrow; 1st Bat-Mite/Mr. Mxyzptlk team-up (11/60). 117-Batwoman-c. 121-Last 10¢ issue
12 24 36 79 170 260
122-128: 123-2nd Bat-Mite/Mr. Mxyzptlk team-up (2/62). 125-Aquaman begins (5/62), ends #139 (Aquaman #1 is dated 1-2/62) 10 20 30 64 132 200
129-Joker/Luthor team-up-c/story 11 22 33 77 166 250
130-142: 135-Last Dick Sprang story. 140-Last Green Arrow. 142-Origin The Composite Superman (villain); Legion app. 8 16 24 51 96 140
143-150: 143-1st Mailbag. 144-Clayface/Brainiac team-up. 148-Clayface/Luthor team-up; last Clayface until Action #443 6 12 18 42 79 115
151-153,155,157-160: 157-2nd Super Sons story; last app. Kathy Kane (Bat-Woman) until Batman Family #10; 1st Bat-Mite Jr. 5 10 15 35 63 90
154-1st Super Sons story; last Bat-Woman in costume until Batman Family #10.
6 12 18 41 76 110
156-1st Bizarro Batman; Joker-c/story 11 22 33 76 163 250
161,170 (80-Pg. Giants G-28,G-40) 6 12 18 40 73 105
162-165,167,168,171,172: 168,172-Adult Legion app.
5 10 15 31 53 75
166-Joker-c/story 6 12 18 38 69 100
169-3rd app. new Batgirl(9/67)(cover and 1 panel cameo); 3rd Bat-Mite/Mr. Mxyzptlk team-up 8 16 24 54 102 150
173-('68)-1st S.A. app. Two-Face as Batman becomes Two-Face in story
8 16 24 56 108 160
174-Adams-c 5 10 15 33 57 80
175,176-Neal Adams-c/a; both reprint J'onn J'onzz origin/Detective #225,226

World's Finest Comics #253 © DC

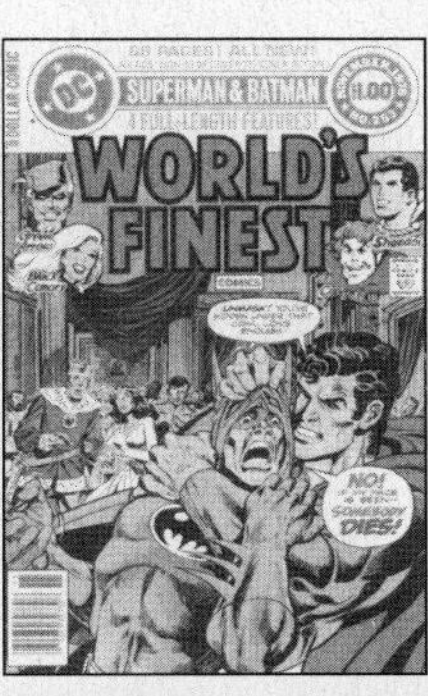

Worlds of Aspen 2010 © Aspen MLT

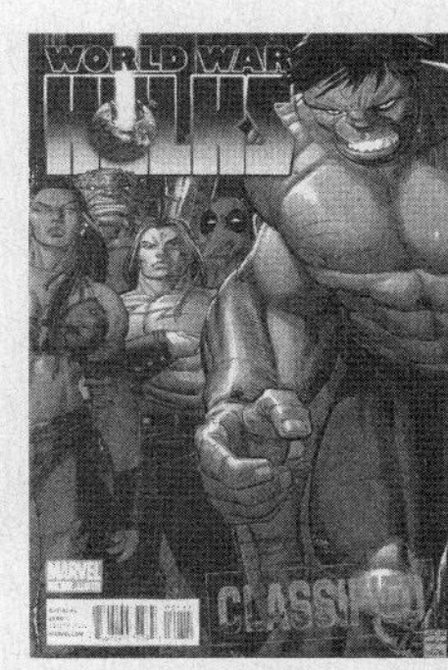

World War Hulks #1 © MAR

GD 2.0 | VG 4.0 | FN 6.0 | VF 8.0 | VF/NM 9.0 | NM- 9.2

6 12 18 37 66 95
177-Joker/Luthor team-up-c/story 6 12 18 37 66 95
178-(9/68) Intro. of Super Nova (revived in "52" weekly series); Adams-c
6 12 18 37 66 95
179-(80 Page Giant G-52) -Adams-c; r/#94 6 12 18 37 66 95
180,182,183,185,186: Adams-c on all. 182-Silent Knight-r/Brave & Bold #6.
185-Last 12¢ issue. 186-Johnny Quick-r 4 8 12 27 44 60
181,184,187: 187-Green Arrow origin-r by Kirby (Adv. #256)
4 8 12 23 37 50
188,197:(Giants G-64,G-76; 64 pages) 5 10 15 34 60 85
189-196: 190-193-Robin-r 3 6 9 20 31 42
198,199-3rd Superman/Flash race (see Flash #175 & Superman #199).
199-Adams-c 10 20 30 64 132 200
200-Adams-c 4 8 12 25 40 55
201-203: 203-Last 15¢ issue. 3 6 9 18 38 38
204,205-(52 pgs.) Adams-c: 204-Wonder Woman app. 205-Shining Knight-r
(6 pgs.) by Frazetta/Adv. #153; Teen Titans x-over 3 6 9 21 33 45
206 (Giant G-88, 64 pgs.) 5 10 15 30 50 70
207,212-(52 pgs.) 3 6 9 20 31 42
208-211(25¢-c) Adams-c: 208-(52 pgs.) Origin Robotman-r/Det. #138.
209-211-(52 pgs.) 3 6 9 21 33 45
213,214,216-222,229: 217-Metamorpho begins, ends #220; Batman/Superman team-ups
resume. 229-r/origin Superman-Batman team 2 4 6 13 18 22
215-(12/72-1/73) Intro. Batman Jr. & Superman Jr. (see Superman/Batman: Saga of the Super
Sons TPB for all the Super Sons stories) 3 6 9 18 28 38
223-228-(100 pgs.). 223-N. Adams-r. 223-Deadman origin. 226-N. Adams, S&K, Toth-r;
Manhunter part origin-r/Det. #225,226. 227-Deadman app.
5 10 15 30 50 70
230-(68 pgs.) 3 6 9 17 26 35
231-243: 231, 233, 238, 242-Super Sons 2 4 6 9 13 16
244-246-Adams-c: 244-$1.00, 84 pg. issues begin; Green Arrow, Black Canary,
Wonder Woman, Vigilante begin; 246-Death of Stuff in Vigilante; origin Vigilante retold
3 6 9 14 20 26
247-252 (84 pgs.): 248-Last Vigilante. 249-The Creeper begins by Ditko, 84 pgs. 250-The
Creeper origin retold by Ditko. 251-1st app. Count Vertigo. 252-Last 84 pg. issue
2 4 6 13 18 22
253-257,259-265: 253-Capt. Marvel begins; 68 pgs. begin, end #265. 255-Last Creeper.
256-Hawkman begins. 257-Black Lightning begins. 263-Super Sons. 264-Clay Face app.
2 4 6 8 11 14
258-Adams-c 2 4 6 10 14 18
266-270,272-282-(52 pgs.). 267-Challengers of the Unknown app.; 3 Lt. Marvels return.
268-Capt. Marvel Jr. origin retold. 274-Zatanna begins. 279, 280-Capt. Marvel Jr. &
Kid Eternity learn they are brothers 1 3 4 6 8 10
271-(52pgs.) Origin Superman/Batman team retold 2 4 6 8 10 12
283-299: 284-Legion app. 1 2 3 4 5 7
300-($1.25, 52pgs.)-Justice League of America, New Teen Titans & The Outsiders app.;
Perez-a (4 pgs.) 1 2 3 5 7 9
301-322: 304-Origin Null and Void. 309,319-Free 16 pg. story in each
(309-Flash Force 2000, 319-Mask preview) 5.00
323-Last issue 6.00

NOTE: ***Neal Adams** a-230ir; c-174-176, 178-180, 182, 183, 185, 186, 199-205, 208-211, 244-246, 258. **Austin** a-244-246i. **Burnley** a-8, 10; c-7-9, 11-14, 15p?, 16-18p, 20-31p. **Colan** a-274p, 297, 299. **Ditko** a-249-255. **Giffen** a-322; c-284p, 322. **G. Kane** a-38, 174r, 282, 283; c-281, 282, 289. **Kirby** a-187. **Kubert** Zatara-40-44. **Miller** c-285p. **Mooney** c-134. **Morrow** a-245-248. **Mortimer** c-16-21, 26-71. **Nasser** a(p)-244-246, 259, 260. **Newton** a-253-281p. **Orlando** a-224r. **Perez** a-300i; c-271, 276, 277p, 278p. **Fred Ray** c-1-5. **Fred Ray/Robinson** c-13-16. **Robinson** a-5, 6, 9-11, 13?, 14-16; c-6. **Rogers** a-259p. **Roussos** a-212r. **Simonson** c-291. **Spiegle** a-275-278, 284. **Staton** a-262p, 273p. **Swan/Moldoff** c-126. **Swan/Mortimer** c-79-82. **Toth** a-228r. **Tuska** a-230r, 250p, 252p, 254p, 257p, 283p, 284p, 308p. Boy Commandos by **Infantino** #39-41.*

WORLD'S FINEST COMICS DIGEST (See DC Special Series #23)

WORLD'S FINEST: OUR WORLDS AT WAR
DC Comics: Oct, 2001 ($2.95, one-shot)
1-Concludes the Our Worlds at War x-over; Jae Lee-c; art by various 3.00

WORLD'S GREATEST ATHLETE (See Walt Disney Showcase #14)

WORLD'S GREATEST SONGS
Atlas Comics (Male): Sept, 1954
1-(Scarce)-Heath & Harry Anderson-a; Eddie Fisher life story plus-c; gives lyrics to
Frank Sinatra song "Young at Heart" 47 94 141 296 498 700

WORLD'S GREATEST STORIES
Jubilee Publications: Jan, 1949 - No. 2, May, 1949
1-Alice in Wonderland; Lewis Carroll adapt. 32 64 96 188 307 425
2-Pinocchio 30 60 90 177 289 400

WORLDS OF ASPEN
Aspen MLT, Inc.: 2006 - Present (Free Comic Book Day giveaways)
...: FCBD 2006, 2007, #3, #4 Editions; Fathom, Soulfire, Shrugged short stories; Turner-c 3.00
... 2010 (5/10) Previews Fathom, Mindfield, Soulfire, Executive Assistant: Iris and Dellec 3.00
... 2011 (5/11) Previews Fathom, Soulfire, Charismagic, Lady Mechanika & others 3.00
... 2012 (5/12) Previews Fathom, Homecoming, Idolized, Shrugged & others 3.00
... 2013 (5/13) Flip book; previews Fathom, Zoohunters & others 3.00
... 2014 (5/14) Flip book; previews Damsels in Excess & Zoohunters; pin-ups 3.00
... 2015 (5/15) Flip book; previews Eternal Soulfire & Fathom Blue; pin-ups 3.00
... 2016 (5/16) Prelude to Aspen Universe: Revelations; character profile pages 3.00

WORLDS OF FEAR (Stories of Weird Adventure)(Formerly Worlds Beyond #1)
Fawcett Publications: V1#2, Jan, 1952 - V2#10, June, 1953
V1#2 54 108 162 343 574 825
3-Evans-a 45 90 135 284 480 675
4-6(9/52) 40 80 120 246 411 575
V2#7,8 39 78 117 240 395 550
9-Classic drowning-c (4/53) 41 82 123 256 428 600
10-Saunders painted-c; man with no eyes surrounded by eyeballs-c plus
eyes ripped out story 181 362 543 1158 1979 2800

NOTE: ***Moldoff** c-2-8. **Powell** a-2, 4, 5. **Sekowsky** a-4, 5.*

WORLDSTORM
DC Comics (WildStorm): Nov, 2006 (Dec on cover) - No. 2, May, 2007 ($2.99)
1,2-Previews and pin-ups for re-launched WildStorm titles.1-Art Adams-c 3.00

WORLDS UNKNOWN
Marvel Comics Group: May, 1973 - No. 8, Aug, 1974
1-r/from Astonishing #54; Torres, Reese-a 3 6 9 17 26 35
2-8 2 4 6 13 18 22

NOTE: ***Adkins/Mooney** a-5. **Buscema** c/a-4p. **W. Howard** c/a-3i. **Kane** a(p)-1,2; c(p)-5, 6, 8. **Sutton** a-2. **Tuska** a(p)-7, 8; c-7p. No. 7, 8 has Golden Voyage of Sinbad movie adaptation.*

WORLD WAR HULK (See Incredible Hulk #106)
Marvel Comics: Aug, 2007 - No. 5, Jan, 2008 ($3.99, limited series)
1-Hulk returns to Earth; Iron Man and Avengers app.; Romita Jr.-a/Pak-s/Finch-c 4.00
1-Variant cover by Romita Jr. 6.00
2-5: 2-Hulk battles The Avengers and FF; Finch-c. 3,4-Dr. Strange app. 5-Sentry app. 4.00
2-5-Variant cover by Romita Jr. 6.00
...: Aftersmash 1 (1/08, $3.99) Sandoval-a/Land-c; Hercules, Iron Man app. 4.00
...: Gamma Files (2007, $3.99) profile pages of Hulk characters 4.00
...Prologue: World Breaker 1 (7/07, one-shot) Rio, Weeks, Phillips, Miyazawa-a 4.00
TPB (2008, $19.99) r/#1-5 20.00

WORLD WAR HULK AFTERSMASH: DAMAGE CONTROL
Marvel Comics: Mar, 2008 - No. 3, May, 2008 ($2.99, limited series)
1-3-The clean-up; McDuffie-s. 2-Romita- Jr.-c. 3-Romita Sr.-c 3.00

WORLD WAR HULK AFTERSMASH: WARBOUND
Marvel Comics: Feb, 2008 - No. 5, Jun, 2008 ($2.99, limited series)
1-5-Kirk & Sandoval-a/Cheung-c 3.00

WORLD WAR HULK: FRONT LINE (See Incredible Hulk #106)
Marvel Comics: Aug, 2007 - No. 6, Dec, 2007 ($2.99, limited series)
1-6-Ben Urich & Sally Floyd report World War Hulk; Jenkins-s/Bachs-a 3.00
TPB (2008, $16.99) r/#1-5 & WWH Prologue: World Breaker 17.00

WORLD WAR HULK: GAMMA CORPS
Marvel Comics: Sept, 2007 - No. 4, Jan, 2008 ($2.99, limited series)
1-4-Tieri-s/Ferreira-a/Roux-c 3.00
TPB (2008, $10.99) r/#1-4 11.00

WORLD WAR HULKS
Marvel Comics: Jun, 2010; Sept, 2010 ($3.99, one-shot & limited series)
1-Short stories by various; Deadpool app.; Romita Jr.-c 4.00
...: Spider-Man vs. Thor 1,2 (9/10 - No. 2, 9/10) Gillen-s/Molina-a 4.00
...: Wolverine vs. Captain America 1,2 (9/10 - No. 2, 9/10) "Capt America vs Wolv." on-c 4.00

WORLD WAR HULK: X-MEN (See New Avengers: Illuminati and Incredible Hulk #92)
Marvel Comics: Aug, 2007 - No. 3, Oct, 2007 ($2.99, limited series)
1-3-Gage-s/DiVito-a/McGuinness-c; Hulk invades the Xavier Institute 3.00
TPB (2008, $24.99) r/#1-3, Avengers: The Initiative #4-5, Irredeemable Ant-Man #10,
Iron Man #19-20, and Ghost Rider #12-13 25.00

WORLD WAR STORIES
Dell Publishing Co.: Apr-June, 1965 - No. 3, Dec, 1965
1-Glanzman-a in all 4 8 12 25 40 55
2,3 3 6 9 16 24 32

World War X #3 © Snejbjerg & Frissen

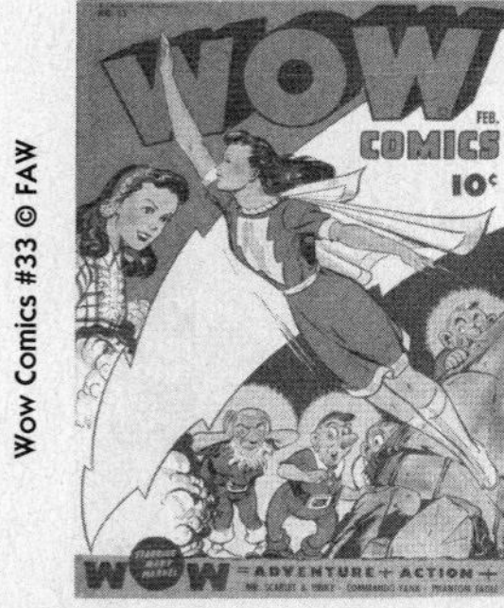

Wow Comics #33 © FAW

Wraith #5 © IDW

GD 2.0 | VG 4.0 | FN 6.0 | VF 8.0 | VF/NM 9.0 | NM- 9.2

WORLD WAR II (See Classics Illustrated Special Issue)

WORLD WAR III
Ace Periodicals: Mar, 1953 - No. 2, May, 1953

1-(Scarce)-Atomic bomb blast-c; Cameron-a 161 322 483 1030 1765 2500
2-Used in **POP**, pg. 78 & B&W & color illos; Cameron-a
81 162 243 518 884 1250

WORLD WAR X
Titan Comics: Jan, 2017 - Present ($3.99, English version of French comic series)

1-3-Jerry Frissen-s/Peter Snejbjerg-a; multiple covers on each 4.00

WORLD WITHOUT END
DC Comics: 1990 - No. 6, 1991 ($2.50, limited series, mature, stiff-c)

1-6: Horror/fantasy; all painted-c/a 3.00

WORLD WRESTLING FEDERATION BATTLEMANIA
Valiant: 1991 - No. 5?, 1991 ($2.50, magazine size, 68 pgs.)

1-5: 5-Includes 2 free pull-out posters 4.00

WORST FROM MAD, THE (Annual)
E. C. Comics: 1958 - No. 12, 1969 (Each annual cover is reprinted from the cover of the Mad issues being reprinted)(Value is 1/2 if bonus is missing)

nn(1958)-Bonus; record labels & travel stickers; 1st Mad annual; r/Mad #29-34
43 86 129 271 461 650
2(1959)-Bonus is small 33 1/3 rpm record entitled "Meet the Staff of Mad"; r/Mad #35-40
42 84 126 265 445 625
3(1960)-Has 20x30" campaign poster "Alfred E. Neuman for President"; r/Mad #41-46
15 30 45 103 227 350
4(1961)-Sunday comics section; r/Mad #47-54 14 28 42 97 214 330
5(1962)-Has 33-1/3 record; r/Mad #55-62 20 40 60 138 307 475
6(1963)-Has 33-1/3 record; r/Mad #63-70 20 40 60 138 307 475
7(1964)-Mad protest signs; r/Mad #71-76 9 18 27 61 123 185
8(1965)-Build a Mad Zeppelin 10 20 30 66 138 210
9(1966)-33-1/3 rpm record; Beatles on-c 14 28 42 94 207 320
10(1967)-Mad bumper sticker 6 12 18 40 73 105
11(1968)-Mad cover window stickers 6 12 18 37 66 95
12(1969)-Mad picture postcards; Orlando-a 6 12 18 37 66 95
NOTE: *Covers: **Bob Clarke-#8. Mingo**-#7, 9-12.*

WOTALIFE COMICS (Formerly Nutty Life #2; Phantom Lady #13 on)
Fox Features Syndicate/Norlen Mag.: No. 3, Aug-Sept, 1946 - No. 12, July, 1947; 1959

3-Cosmo Cat, Li'l Pan, others begin 14 28 42 80 115 150
4-12-Cosmo Cat, Li'l Pan in all 10 20 30 58 79 100
1(1959-Norlen)-Atomic Rabbit, Atomic Mouse; reprints cover to #6; reprints entire book?
8 16 24 40 50 60

WOTALIFE COMICS
Green Publications: 1959 - No. 5, 1959

1-Funny animal; Li'l Pan & Tamale app. 7 14 21 35 43 50
2-5 5 10 15 22 26 30

WOW COMICS ("Wow, What A Magazine!" on cover of first issue)
Henle Publishing Co.: July, 1936 - No. 4, Nov, 1936 (52 pgs., magazine size)

1-Buck Jones in "The Phantom Rider" (1st app. in comics), Fu Manchu; Capt. Scott Dalton begins; Will Eisner-a (1st in comics); Baily-a(1); Briefer-c
411 822 1233 2877 5039 7200
2-Ken Maynard, Fu Manchu, Popeye by Segar plus article on Popeye; Eisner-a
297 594 891 1901 3251 4600
3-Eisner-c/a(3); Popeye by Segar, Fu Manchu, Hiram Hick by Bob Kane, Space Limited app.; Jimmy Dempsey talks about Popeye's punch; Bob Ripley Believe it or Not begins; Briefer-a
284 568 852 1818 3109 4400
4-Flash Gordon by Raymond, Mandrake, Popeye by Segar, Tillie The Toiler, Fu Manchu, Hiram Hick by Bob Kane; Eisner-a(3); Briefer-c/a
300 600 900 2070 3635 5200

WOW COMICS (Real Western Hero #70 on)(See XMas Comics)
Fawcett Publ.: Winter, 1940-41; No. 2, Summer, 1941 - No. 69, Fall, 1948

nn(#1)-Origin Mr. Scarlet by S&K; Atom Blake, Boy Wizard, Jim Dolan, & Rick O'Shay begin; Diamond Jack, The White Rajah, & Shipwreck Roberts, only app.; 1st mention of Gotham City in comics; the cover was printed on unstable paper stock and is rarely found in fine or mint condition; blank inside-c; bondage-c by Beck
1350 2700 4050 10,400 18,700 27,000
2 (Scarce)-The Hunchback begins 177 354 531 1124 1937 2750
3 (Fall, 1941) 107 214 321 680 1165 1650
4-Origin & 1st app. Pinky 108 216 324 686 1181 1675
5 65 130 195 416 708 1000
6-Origin & 1st app. The Phantom Eagle (7/15/42); Commando Yank begins
65 130 195 416 708 1000
7,8 57 114 171 362 619 875
9-(1/6/43)-Capt. Marvel, Capt. Marvel Jr., Shazam app.; Scarlet & Pinky x-over; Mary Marvel-c/stories begin 290 580 870 1856 3178 4500
10-Swayze-c/a on Mary Marvel 74 148 222 470 810 1150
11-17,19,20: 15-Flag-c 55 110 165 352 601 850
18-1st app. Uncle Marvel (10/43); infinity-c 58 116 174 371 636 900
21-30: 23-Robot-c. 28-Pinky x-over in Mary Marvel 39 78 117 235 385 535
31-40: 32-68-Phantom Eagle by Swayze 28 56 84 165 270 375
41-50 25 50 75 150 245 340
51-58: Last Mary Marvel 22 44 66 132 216 300
59-69: 59-Ozzie (teenage) begins. 62-Flying Saucer gag-c (1/48). 65-69-Tom Mix stories (cont'd in Real Western Hero) 20 40 60 114 182 250
NOTE: *Cover features: Mr. Scarlet-#1-5; Commando Yank-#6, 7, (w/Mr. Scarlet #8); Mary Marvel-#9-56, (w/Commando Yank-#46-50), (w/Mr. Scarlet & Commando Yank-#51), (w/Mr. Scarlet & Pinky #53), (w/Phantom Eagle #54, 56), (w/Commando Yank & Phantom Eagle #58); Ozzie-#59-69.*

WRAITH (Prequel to the novel NOS4A2)
IDW Publishing: Nov, 2013 (incorrect Nov, 2012 in indicia) - No. 7, May, 2014 ($3.99)

1-7: Joe Hill-s/C.P. Wilson III-a. 5-(incorrect #4 in indicia) 4.00
1-Director's Cut (7/14, $4.99) Includes full script 5.00

WRAITHBORN
DC Comics (WildStorm): Nov, 2005 - No. 6, July, 2006 ($2.99, limited series)

1-6-Marcia Chen & Joe Benitez-s/a 3.00
TPB (2007, $19.99) r/series; sketch pages and unused cover sketches 20.00

WRAITHBORN REDUX
Benitez Productions: Feb, 2016 - No. 6, Aug, 2016 ($3.99)

1-6-Remastered printing of the 2005 series; Chen & Benitez-s/a; multiple covers 4.00
... HCF 2016 #1 (10/16, Halloween giveaway) r/#1 3.00

WRATH (Also see Prototype #4)
Malibu Comics: Jan, 1994 - No. 9, Nov, 1995 ($1.95)

1-9: 2-Mantra x-over. 3-Intro/1st app. Slayer. 4,5-Freex app. 8-Mantra & Warstrike app. 9-Prime app. 3.00
1-Ultra 5000 Limited silver foil 6.00
Giant Size 1 (2.50, 44 pgs.) 4.00

WRATH OF THE ETERNAL WARRIOR
Valiant Entertainment: Nov, 2015 - No. 14, Dec, 2016 ($3.99)

1-14: 1-Venditti-s/Allén-a 4.00

WRATH OF THE SPECTRE, THE
DC Comics: May, 1988 - No. 4, Aug, 1988 ($2.50, limited series)

1-3: Aparo-r/Adventure #431-440 5.00
4-Three scripts intended for Adventure #441-on, but not drawn by Aparo until 1988
1 2 3 5 6 8
TPB (2005, $19.99) r/series; Peter Sanderson intro. 20.00

WRECK OF GROSVENOR (See Superior Stories #3)

WRETCH, THE
Caliber: 1996 ($2.95, B&W)

1-Phillip Hester-a/scripts 3.00

WRETCH, THE
Amaze Ink: 1997 - No. 4, 1998 ($2.95, B&W)

1-4-Phillip Hester-a/scripts 3.00
... Vol. 1: Everyday Doomsday (4/03, $13.95) 14.00

WRINGLE WRANGLE (Disney)
Dell Publishing Co.: No. 821, July, 1957

Four Color 821-Based on movie "Westward Ho, the Wagons"; Marsh-a; Fess Parker photo-c
7 14 21 46 86 125

WULF
Ardden Entertainment: Mar, 2011 - No. 6, Sept, 2012 ($2.99)

1-6-Steve Niles-s/Nat Jones-a/c; Lomax app. 3-6-Iron Jaw app. 3.00

WULF THE BARBARIAN
Atlas/Seaboard Publ.: Feb, 1975 - No. 4, Sept, 1975

1,2: 1-Origin; Janson-a. 2-Intro. Berithe the Swordswoman; Janson-a w/Neal Adams, Wood, Reese-a assists 2 4 6 11 16 20
3,4: 3-Skeates-s. 4-Friedrich-s 2 4 6 9 13 16

WWE (WWE Wrestling)
BOOM! Studios: Jan, 2017 - Present ($3.99)

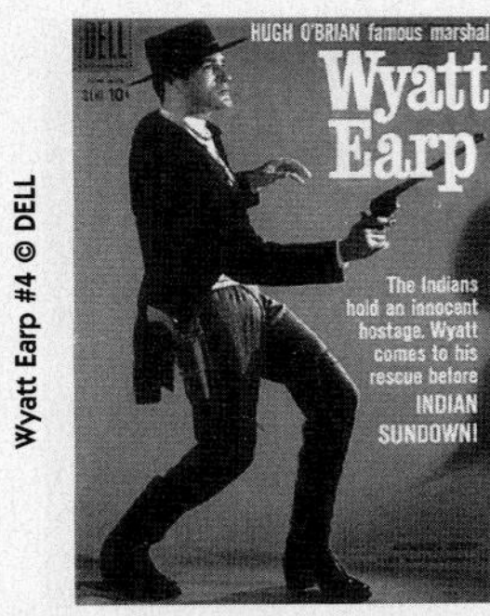

Wyatt Earp #4 © DELL

Wynonna Earp (2016 series) #2 © Beau Smith

X-Club #1 © MAR

	GD 2.0	VG 4.0	FN 6.0	VF 8.0	VF/NM 9.0	NM- 9.2

1,2-Seth Rollins & Triple H app.; Serg Acuña-a; multiple covers. 1-Back-up w/Guillory-a 4.00
...Then. Now. Forever. 1 (11/16, $3.99) Short stories by various; multiple covers 4.00

WWE HEROES (WWE Wrestling) (#7 titled WWE Undertaker)
Titan Comics: Apr, 2010 - No. 8 ($3.99)

1-6: 1-Two covers by Andy Smith and Liam Sharp. 5-Covers by Smith and Mayhew 4.00
7,8-"Undertaker" on cover; Rey Mysterio app. 4.00

WWE SUPERSTARS (WWE Wrestling)
Papercutz (Super Genius): Dec, 2013 - No. 12, Feb, 2015 ($2.99/$3.99)

1-($2.99)-Mick Foley-s; John Cena, Randy Orton & CM Punk app. 3.00
2-12: 2-($3.99) Mick Foley-s. 9-Hulk Hogan cover by Jusko 4.00

WYATT EARP
Atlas Comics/Marvel No. 23 on (IPC): Nov, 1955 - #29, Jun, 1960; #30, Oct, 1972 - #34, Jun, 1973

	GD 2.0	VG 4.0	FN 6.0	VF 8.0	VF/NM 9.0	NM- 9.2
1	24	48	72	144	237	330
2-Williamson-a (4 pgs.)	15	30	45	83	124	165
3-6,8-11: 3-Black Bart app. 8-Wild Bill Hickok app.	12	24	36	69	97	125
7,12-Williamson-a, 4 pgs. ea.; #12 with Mayo	13	26	39	74	105	135
13-20: 17-1st app. Wyatt's deputy, Grizzly Grant	11	22	33	62	86	110
21-Davis-c	10	20	30	58	79	100
22-24,26-29: 22-Ringo Kid app. 23-Kid From Texas app. 29-Last 10¢ issue	9	18	27	52	69	85
25-Davis-a	10	20	30	54	72	90
30-Williamson-r (1972)	2	4	6	13	18	22
31-34-Reprints. 32-Torres-a(r)	2	4	6	9	13	16

NOTE: *Ayers a-8, 10(2), 16(4), 17, 20(4), 26(5), 27(3), 29(3). Berg a-9. Everett c-6. Kirby c-22, 24-26, 29. Maneely a-1; c-1-4, 8, 12, 17, 20. Maurer a-2(2), 3(4), 4(4), 8(4). Severin a-4, 9(4), 10; c-2, 9, 10, 14. Wildey a-5, 17, 24, 27, 28.*

WYATT EARP (TV) (Hugh O'Brian Famous Marshal)
Dell Publishing Co.: No. 860, Nov, 1957 - No. 13, Dec-Feb, 1960-61 (Hugh O'Brian photo-c)

	GD 2.0	VG 4.0	FN 6.0	VF 8.0	VF/NM 9.0	NM- 9.2
Four Color 860 (#1)-Manning-a	9	18	27	59	117	175
Four Color 890,921(6/58)-All Manning-a	6	12	18	42	79	115
4 (9-11/58) - 12-Manning-a. 4-Variant edition exists with back-c comic strip; Russ Manning-a. 5-Photo back-c	5	10	15	33	57	80
13-Toth-a	5	10	15	34	60	85

WYATT EARP FRONTIER MARSHAL (Formerly Range Busters) (Also see Blue Bird)
Charlton Comics: No. 12, Jan, 1956 - No. 72, Dec, 1967

	GD 2.0	VG 4.0	FN 6.0	VF 8.0	VF/NM 9.0	NM- 9.2
12	9	18	27	47	61	75
13-19	6	12	18	31	38	45
20-(68 pgs.)-Williamson-a(4), 8,5,5,& 7 pgs.	10	20	30	54	72	90
21-(100 pgs.) Mastroserio, Maneely, Severin-a (signed LePoer)	5	10	15	30	50	70
22-30	3	6	9	16	23	30
31-50	2	4	6	12	16	20
51-72 (1967)	2	4	6	9	11	14

WYNONNA EARP
Image Comics (WildStorm Productions): Dec, 1996 - No. 5, Apr, 1997 ($2.50)

1-5-Beau Smith-s/Chin-a 3.00

WYNONNA EARP
IDW Publishing: Feb, 2016 - No. 8, Sept, 2016 ($3.99)

1-8: 1-Beau Smith-s/Lora Innes-a; multiple covers; bonus look at the SyFy TV series 4.00

WYNONNA EARP: HOME ON THE STRANGE
IDW Publishing: Dec, 2003 - No. 3, Feb, 2004 ($3.99)

1-3-Beau Smith-s/Ferreira-a 4.00

WYNONNA EARP LEGENDS: DOC HOLLIDAY
IDW Publishing: Nov, 2016 - No. 2, Dec, 2016 ($3.99)

1,2: 1-Beau Smith & Tim Rozon-s/Chris Evenhuis-a; multiple covers; 4.00

WYNONNA EARP: THE YETI WARS
IDW Publishing: May, 2011 - No. 4, Aug, 2011 ($3.99)

1-4-Beau Smith-s/Enrique Villagran-a 4.00

WYRMS
Marvel Comics (Dabel Brothers): Feb, 2007 - No. 6, Jan, 2008 ($2.99)

1-6-Orson Scott Card & Jake Black-s. 1-3-Batista-a 3.00
TPB (2008, $14.99) r/#1-6 15.00

WYTCHES
Image Comics: Oct, 2014 - No. 6, May, 2015 ($2.99/$3.99)

1-Scott Snyder-s/Jock-a 5.00
2-5 3.00
6-($3.99) Bonus production art and Snyder afterword 4.00
Image Firsts: Wytches (12/14, $1.00) r/#1 3.00

X (Comics' Greatest World: X #1 only) (Also see Comics' Greatest World & Dark Horse Comics #8)
Dark Horse Comics: Feb, 1994 - No. 25, Apr, 1996 ($2.00/$2.50)

1-25: 3-Pit Bulls x-over. 8-Ghost-c & app. 18-Miller-c.; Predator app. 19-22-Miller-c. 3.00
Hero Illustrated Special #1,2 (1994, $1.00, 20 pgs.) 3.00
One Shot to the Head (1994, $2.50, 36 pgs.)-Miller-c. 3.00
NOTE: *Miller c-18-22. Quesada c-6. Russell a-6.*

X (Comics' Greatest World)
Dark Horse Comics: No. 0, Apr, 2013 - No. 24, Apr, 2015 ($2.99)

0-24: 0-Swierczynski-s/Eric Nguyen-a. 13,14-Atkins-a 3.00
One For One (1/14, $1.00) r/#1 3.00

XANADU COLOR SPECIAL
Eclipse Comics: Dec, 1988 ($2.00, one-shot)

1-Continued from Thoughts & Images 3.00

XAVIER INSTITUTE ALUMNI YEARBOOK (See X-Men titles)
Marvel Comics: Dec, 1996 ($5.95, square-bound, one-shot)

1-Text w/art by various 6.00

X-BABIES
Marvel Comics: Dec, 2009 - No. 4, Mar, 2010 ($3.99, limited series)

1-4-Schigiel-s/Chabot-a; Skottie Young-c 4.00
...: Murderama (8/98, $2.95) J.J. Kirby-a 4.00
...: Reborn (1/00, $3.50) J.J. Kirby-a 4.00

X-CALIBRE
Marvel Comics: Mar, 1995 - No. 4, July, 1995 ($1.95, limited series)

1-4-Age of Apocalypse 3.00

X-CAMPUS
Marvel Comics: July, 2010 - No. 4, Nov, 2010 ($4.99, limited series)

1-4-Alternate version of X-Men; stories by European creators; Nauck-c 5.00

X-CLUB
Marvel Comics: Feb, 2012 - No. 5, Jun, 2012 ($2.99, limited series)

1-5-X-Men scientist team; Dr. Nemesis & Danger app. 1-Bradshaw-c. 2-5-Esquejo-c 3.00

XENA (TV)
Dynamite Entertainment: 2006 - 2007 ($3.50)

1-4-Three covers on each; Neves-a/Layman-s 3.50
Vol. 2 #1-4-(Dark Xena) Four covers; Salonga-a/Layman-s 3.50
Annual 1 (2007, $4.95) Three covers; Salonga-a/Champagne-s 5.00
... Vol. 2: Dark Xena TPB (2007, $14.99) r/Vol. 2 #1-4; variant cover gallery 15.00

XENA / ARMY OF DARKNESS: WHAT...AGAIN?!
Dynamite Entertainment: 2008 - No. 4, 2009 ($3.50, limited series)

1-4-Xena, Gabrielle, & Autolycus team up with Ash; Montenegro-a; two covers on each 3.50

XENA: WARRIOR PRINCESS (TV)
Topps Comics: Aug, 1997 - No. 0, Oct, 1997 ($2.95)

	GD 2.0	VG 4.0	FN 6.0	VF 8.0	VF/NM 9.0	NM- 9.2
1-Two stories by various; J. Scott Campbell-c	1	3	4	6	8	10
1,2-Photo-c	1	3	4	6	8	10
2-Stevens-c	1	3	4	6	8	10
0-(10/97)-Lopresti-c, 0-(10/97)-Photo-c	1	2	3	5	6	8

...First Appearance Collection ('97, $9.95) r/Hercules the Legendary Journeys #3-5 and 5-page story from TV Guide 10.00

XENA: WARRIOR PRINCESS (TV)
Dark Horse Comics: Sept, 1999 - No. 14, Oct, 2000 ($2.95/$2.99)

1-14: 1-Mignola-c and photo-c. 2,3-Bradstreet-c & photo-c 3.50

XENA: WARRIOR PRINCESS (Volume 2) (TV)
Dynamite Entertainment: 2016 - No. 6, 2016 ($3.99)

1-6: 1-Valentine-s/Medel-a; main covers by Land & Frison 4.00

XENA: WARRIOR PRINCESS AND THE ORIGINAL OLYMPICS (TV)
Topps Comics: Jun, 1998 - No. 3, Aug, 1998 ($2.95, limited series)

1-3-Regular and Photo-c; Lim-a/T&M Bierbaum-s 3.50

XENA: WARRIOR PRINCESS-BLOODLINES (TV)
Topps Comics: May, 1998 - No. 2, June, 1998 ($2.95, limited series)

1,2-Lopresti-s/c/a. 2-Reg. and photo-c 3.50
1-Bath photo-c, 1-American Ent. Ed. 4.50

XENA: WARRIOR PRINCESS / JOXER: WARRIOR PRINCE (TV)

Xero #8 © DC

X-Factor #125 © MAR

X-51 #1 © MAR

GD VG FN VF VF/NM NM-
2.0 4.0 6.0 8.0 9.0 9.2

Topps Comics: Nov, 1997 - No. 3, Jan, 1998 ($2.95, limited series)
1-3-Regular and Photo-c; Lim-a/T&M Bierbaum-s 3.50

XENA: WARRIOR PRINCESS-THE DRAGON'S TEETH (TV)
Topps Comics: Dec, 1997 - No. 3, Feb, 1998 ($2.95, limited series)
1-3-Regular and Photo-c; Teranishi-a/Thomas-s 3.50

XENA: WARRIOR PRINCESS-THE ORPHEUS TRILOGY (TV)
Topps Comics: Mar, 1998 - No. 3, May, 1998 ($2.95, limited series)
1-3-Regular and Photo-c; Teranishi-a/T&M Bierbaum-s 3.50

XENA: WARRIOR PRINCESS VS. CALLISTO (TV)
Topps Comics: Feb, 1998 - No. 3, Apr, 1998 ($2.95, limited series)
1-3-Regular and Photo-c; Morgan-a/Thomas-s 3.50

XENOBROOD
DC Comics: No. 0, Oct, 1994 - No. 6, Apr, 1995 ($1.50, limited series)
0-6: 0-Indicia says "Xenobroods" 3.00

XENON
Eclipse Comics: Dec, 1987 - No. 23, Nov. 1, 1988 ($1.50, B&W, bi-weekly)
1-23 3.00

XENOZOIC TALES (Also see Cadillacs & Dinosaurs, Death Rattle #8)
Kitchen Sink Press: Feb, 1986 - No. 14, Oct, 1996
1-Mark Schultz-s/a in all 2 4 6 9 12 15
1(2nd printing)(1/89) 4.00
2-14 6.00
Volume 1 ($14.95) r/#1-6 & Death Rattle #8 15.00
Volume 2 (5/03, $14.95, TPB) B&W r/#7-14; intro by Frank Cho 15.00

XENYA
Sanctuary Press: Apr, 1994 - No. 3 ($2.95)
1-3: 1-Hildebrandt-c; intro Xenya 3.00

XERO
DC Comics: May, 1997 - No. 12, Apr, 1998 ($1.75)
1-7 3.00
8-12 3.00

X-FACTOR (Also see The Avengers #263, Fantastic Four #286 and Mutant X)
Marvel Comics Group: Feb, 1986 - No. 149, Sept, 1998
1-($1.25, 52 pgs)-Story recaps 1st app. from Avengers #263; story cont'd from F.F. #286; return of original X-Men (now X-Factor); Guice/Layton-a; Baby Nathan app. (2nd after X-Men #201) 2 4 6 10 14 18
2-4 6.00
5-1st brief app. Apocalypse (1 page) 3 6 9 16 24 32
6-1st full app. Apocalypse 6 12 18 37 66 95
7-10: 10-Sabretooth app. (11/86, 3 pgs.) cont'd in X-Men #212; 1st app. in an X-Men comic book 5.00
11-18,20-22: 13-Baby Nathan app. in flashback. 14-Cyclops vs. The Master Mold. 15-Intro wingless Angel 4.00
19-Apocalypse-c/app. 2 4 6 9 12 15
23-1st brief app. Archangel (2 pages) 2 4 6 8 10 12
24-1st full app. Archangel (now in Uncanny X-Men); Fall Of The Mutants begins; origin Apocalypse 4 8 12 23 37 50
25,26: Fall Of The Mutants; 26-New outfits 6.00
27-37,39,41-49,51-59,63-70,72-83,87-91,93-99,101: 35-Origin Cyclops. 51-53-Sabretooth app. 52-Liefeld-c(p). 54-Intro Crimson; Silvestri-c/a(p). 63-Portacio/Thibert-c/a(p) begins, ends #69. 65-68-Lee co-plots. 65-The Apocalypse Files begins, ends #68. 66,67-Baby Nathan app. 67-Inhumans app. 68-Baby Nathan is sent into future to save his life. 69,70-X-Men(w/Wolverine) x-over. 77-Cannonball (of X-Force) app. 87-Quesada-c/a(p) in monthly comic begins,ends #92. 88-1st app. Random 3.00
38,50,60-62,71,75: 38,50-(52 pgs.): 50-Liefeld/McFarlane-c. 60-X-Tinction Agenda x-over; New Mutants (w/Cable) x-over in #60-62; Wolverine in #62. 61,62-X-Tinction Agenda. 62-Jim Lee-c. 71-New team begins (Havok, Polaris, Strong Guy, Wolfsbane & Madrox); Stroman-c/a begins. 75-(52 pgs.) 4.00
40-Rob Liefeld-c/a (4/89, 1st at Marvel?) 5.00
60,71-2nd printings. 60-Gold ink 2nd printing. 71-2nd printing ($1.25) 3.00
84-86 -Jae Lee a(p); 85,86-Jae Lee-c. Polybagged with trading card in each; X-Cutioner's Song x-overs. 4.00
92-($3.50, 68 pgs.)-Wraparound-c by Quesada w/Havok hologram on-c; begin X-Men 30th anniversary issues; Quesada-a. 6.00
92-2nd printing 4.00
100-($2.95, 52 pgs.)-Embossed foil-c; Multiple Man dies. 6.00
100-($1.75, 52 pgs.)-Regular edition 4.00
102-105,107: 102-bound-in card sheet 3.00
106-($2.00)-Newsstand edition 3.00
106-($2.95)-Collectors edition 4.00
108-124,126-148: 112-Return from Age of Apocalypse. 115-card insert. 119-123-Sabretooth app. 123-Hound app. 124-w/Onslaught Update. 126-Onslaught x-over; Beast vs. Dark Beast. 128-w/card insert; return of Multiple Man. 130-Assassination of Grayson Creed. 146,148-Moder-a 3.00
125-($2.95)-"Onslaught"; Post app.; return of Havok 4.00
149-Last issue 5.00
#(-1) Flashback (7/97) Matsuda-a 3.00
Annual 1-9: 1-(10/86-'94, 68 pgs.) 3-Evolutionary War x-over. 4-Atlantis Attacks; Byrne/Simonson-a;Byrne-c. 5-Fantastic Four, New Mutants x-over; Keown 2 pg. pin-up. 6-New Warriors app.; 5th app. X-Force cont'd from X-Men Annual #15. 7-1st Quesada-a(p) on X-Factor plus-c(p). 8-Bagged w/trading card. 9-Austin-a(i) 4.00
...Prisoner of Love (1990, $4.95, 52 pgs.)-Starlin scripts; Guice-a 5.00
... Visionaries: Peter David Vol. 1 TPB (2005, $15.99) r/#71-75 16.00
... Visionaries: Peter David Vol. 2 TPB (2007, $15.99) r/#76-78 & Incr. Hulk #390-392 16.00
... Visionaries: Peter David Vol. 3 TPB (2007, $15.99) r/#79-83 & Annual #7 16.00
NOTE: ***Art Adams** a-41p, 42p. **Buckler** a-50p. **Liefeld** a-40; c-40, 50i, 52p. **McFarlane** c-50i. **Mignola** c-70. **Brandon Peterson** a-78p(part). **Whilce Portacio** c/a(p)-63-69. **Quesada** a(p)-87-92, Annual 7. c(p)-78, 79, 82, Annual 7. **Simonson** c/a-10, 11, 13-15, 17-19, 21, 23-31, 33, 34, 36-39; c-12, 16. **Paul Smith** a-44-48; c-43. **Stroman** a(p)-71-75, 77, 78(part), 80, 81; c(p)-71-77, 80, 81, 84. **Zeck** c-2.*

X-FACTOR (Volume 2)
Marvel Comics: June, 2002 - No. 4, Oct, 2002 ($2.50)
1-4: Jensen-s/Ranson-a. 1-Phillips-c. 2,3-Edwards-c 3.00

X-FACTOR (Volume 3) (Also see All-New X-Factor)
Marvel Comics: Jan, 2006 - No. 262, Nov, 2013 ($2.99)
1-24: 1-Peter David-s/Ryan Sook-a. 8,9-Civil War. 21-24-Endangered Species back-up 3.00
25-49: 25-27-Messiah Complex x-over; Finch-c. 26-2nd printing with new Eaton-c 3.00
50-(12/09, $3.99) Madrox in the future; DeLandro-a/Yardin-c 4.00
200-(2/10, $4.99) Resumes original series numbering; 3 covers; Fantastic Four app. 5.00
201-224,224.1, 225-262 ($2.99) 201,202-Dr. Doom & Fant. Four app. 211,212-Thor app. 230-Wolverine app.; Havok & Polaris return 3.00
... Special: Layla Miller (10/08, $3.99) David-s/DeLandro-a 4.00
...: The Quick and the Dead (7/08, $2.99) Raimondi-a; Quicksilver regains powers 3.00
...: The Longest Night HC (2006, $19.99, dust jacket) r/#1-6; sketch pages by Sook 20.00
...: The Longest Night SC (2007, $14.99) r/#1-6; sketch pages by Sook 15.00
...: Life and Death Matters HC (2007, $19.99, dust jacket) r/#7-12 20.00
...: Life and Death Matters SC (2007, $14.99) r/#7-12 15.00
...: The Many Lives of Madrox SC (2007, $14.99) r/#13-17 15.00
...: Heart of Ice HC (2007, $19.99, dust jacket) r/#18-24 20.00
...: Heart of Ice SC (2008, $17.99, dust jacket) r/#18-24 18.00

X-FACTOR FOREVER
Marvel Comics: May, 2010 - No. 5, Sept, 2010 ($3.99, limited series)
1-5-Louise Simonson-s/Dan Panosian-a; back-up origin of Apocalypse 4.00

X-51 (Machine Man)
Marvel Comics: Sept, 1999 - No. 12, Jul, 2000 ($1.99/$2.50)
1-7: 1-Joe Bennett-a. 2-Two covers 3.00
8-12: 8-Begin $2.50-c 3.00
Wizard #0 3.00

X-FILES, THE (TV)
Topps Comics: Jan, 1995 - No. 41, July, 1998 ($2.50)
-2(9/96)-Black-c; r/X-Files Magazine #1&2 5.00
-1(9/96)-Silver-c; r/Hero Illustrated Giveaway 5.00
0-($3.95)-Adapts pilot episode 4.00
0-"Mulder" variant-c 1 2 3 5 6 8
0-"Scully" variant-c 1 2 3 5 6 8
1/2-W/certificate 1 2 3 5 6 8
1-New stories based on the TV show; direct market & newsstand editions; Miran Kim-c on all 3 6 9 14 20 25
2 1 2 3 6 8 10
3,4 6.00
5-10: 6-Begin $2.95-c 5.00
11-41: 21-W/bound-in card. 40,41-Reg. & photo-c 4.00
Annual 1,2 ($3.95) 4.00
Afterflight TPB ($5.95) Art by Thompson, Saviuk, Kim 6.00
Classics #1: Hundred Penny Press Edition (12/13 $1.00) r/#1 3.00
Collection 1 TPB ($19.95)-r/#1-6. 20.00
Collection 2 TPB ($19.95)-r/#7-12, Annual #1. 20.00
...Fight the Future ('98, $5.95) Movie adaptation 6.00
Hero Illustrated Giveaway (3/95) 1 2 3 5 6 8

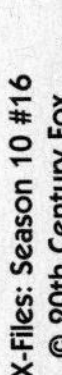
X-Files: Season 10 #16 © 20th Century Fox

X-Force #59 © MAR

X-Force (2008 series) #9 © MAR

GD	VG	FN	VF	VF/NM	NM-
2.0	4.0	6.0	8.0	9.0	9.2

GD VG FN VF VF/NM NM-
2.0 4.0 6.0 8.0 9.0 9.2

Special Edition 1-5 ($3.95/$4.95)-r/#1-3, 4-6, 7-9, 10-12, 13, Annual 1 5.00
Star Wars Galaxy Magazine Giveaway (B&W) 1 3 4 6 8 10
Trade paperback ($19.95) 20.00
Volume 1 TPB (Checker Books, 2005, $19.95) r/#13-17, #0, Season One: Squeeze 20.00
Volume 2 TPB (Checker Books, 2005, $19.95) r/#18-24, #1/2, Comics Digest #1 20.00
Volume 3 TPB (Checker Books, 2006, $19.95) r/#23-26, Fire, Ice, Hero III. Giveaway 20.00

X-FILES, THE (TV)
DC Comics (WildStorm): No. 0, Sept, 2008 - No. 6, Jun, 2009 ($3.99/$3.50)

0-($3.99) Spotnitz-s/Denham-a; photo-c 4.00
1-6-($3.50) 1-Spotnitz-s/Denham-a; 2 covers. 4-Wolfman-s 3.50
TPB (2009, $19.99) r/#0-6 20.00

X-FILES, THE (TV)
IDW Publishing: Apr, 2016 - Present ($3.99)

1-11: 1-Joe Harris-s/Matthew Dow Smith-a 4.00
... Annual 2014 (4/14, $7.99) Back-up story with Dave Sim-s/Currie-a; 2 covers 8.00
... Annual 2016 (7/16, $7.99) Greg Scott-a; Valenzuela & photo-c 8.00
...: Art Gallery (5/14, $3.99) Gallery of sketch card art by various incl. Kim & Staggs 4.00
...: Deviations (3/16, $4.99) What If... young Fox Mulder was abducted by aliens 5.00
...: Deviations 2017 (3/17, $4.99) Samantha Mulder and Scully team; Califano-a 5.00
... X-Mas Special (12/14, $7.99) Joe Harris-s/Matt Smith-a; Kesel-s/Southworth-a 8.00
... X-Mas Special 2016 (12/16, $7.99) Joe Harris-s/Wayne Nichols-a 8.00

X-FILES COMICS DIGEST, THE
Topps Comics: Dec, 1995 - No. 3 ($3.50, quarterly, digest-size)

1-3: 1,2: New X-Files stories w/Ray Bradbury Comics-r. 1-Reg. & photo-c 4.00
NOTE: *Adlard a-1, 2. **Jack Davis** a-2r. **Russell** a-1r.*

X-FILES, THE: CONSPIRACY
IDW Publishing: Jan, 2014 - No. 2, Mar, 2014 ($3.99, limited series)

1,2-Bookends for 6-part Lone Gunmen series; Crilley-s/Stanisci-a; Kim & Corroney-c 4.00
X-Files/Ghostbusters: Conspiracy (1/14, $3.99) Part 2; Navarro-a 4.00
X-Files/Teenage Mutant Ninja Turtles: Conspiracy (2/14, $3.99) Part 3; Walsh-a 4.00
X-Files/Transformers: Conspiracy (2/14, $3.99) Part 4; Verma-a 4.00
X-Files/The Crow: Conspiracy (3/14, $3.99) Part 5; Malhotra-a 4.00

X-FILES, THE: GROUND ZERO (TV)
Topps Comics: Nov, 1997 - No. 4, March, 1998 ($2.95, limited series)

1-4-Adaptation of the Kevin J. Anderson novel 4.00

X-FILES, THE: ORIGINS (TV)
IDW Publishing: Aug, 2016 - No. 4, Nov, 2016 ($4.99)

1-4-Flipbooks with teenage Mulder and Scully 5.00

X-FILES, THE: SEASON ONE (TV)
Topps Comics: July, 1997 - July, 1998 ($4.95, adaptations of TV episodes)

1,2,Squeeze, Conduit, Ice, Space, Fire, Beyond the Sea, Shadows 5.00

X-FILES, THE: SEASON 10 (TV)
IDW Publishing: Jun, 2013 - No. 25, Jun, 2015 ($3.99)

1-25: 1-5-Co-written by Chris Carter; multiple covers on each. 6,7-Flukeman returns. 17-Frank Black app. 18-Doggett & Reyes app. 4.00
... #1: IDW's Greatest Hits (4/16, $1.00) r/#1 3.00

X-FILES, THE: SEASON 11 (TV)
IDW Publishing: Aug, 2015 - No. 8, Mar, 2016 ($3.99)

1-8: 1-Joe Harris-s/Matthew Smith-a 4.00

X-FILES, THE / 30 DAYS OF NIGHT
DC Comics (WildStorm)/IDW: Sept, 2010 - No. 6, Feb, 2011 ($3.99, limited series)

1-6-Steve Niles & Adam Jones-s/Tom Mandrake-a. 1-Three covers 4.00
TPB (2011, $17.99) r/#1-6; cover gallery 18.00

X-FILES, THE: YEAR ZERO (TV)
IDW Publishing: Jul, 2014 - No. 5, Nov, 2014 ($3.99)

1-5: 1-Karl Kesel-s; Greg Scott & Vic Malhotra-a; flashback to 1946 4.00

X-FORCE (Becomes X-Statix) (Also see The New Mutants #100)
Marvel Comics: Aug, 1991 - No. 129, Aug, 2002 ($1.00-$2.25)

1-($1.50, 52 pgs.)-Polybagged with 1 of 5 diff. Marvel Universe trading cards inside (1 each); 6th app. of X-Force; Liefeld-c/a begins 6.00
1-1st printing with Cable trading card inside 1 2 3 5 6 8
1-1st printing with Deadpool trading card inside 1 3 4 6 8 10
1-2nd printing; metallic ink-c (no bag or card) 4.00
2-Deadpool-c/story (2nd app.) 2 4 6 10 14 18
3,4: 3-New Brotherhood of Evil Mutants app. 4-Spider-Man x-over; cont'd from Spider-Man #16; reads sideways 4.00
5-10: 6-Last $1.00-c. 7,9-Weapon X back-ups. 8-Intro The Wild Pack (Cable, Kane, Domino, Hammer, G.W. Bridge, & Grizzly); Liefeld-c/a (4); Mignola-a. 10-Weapon X full-length story (part 3). 4.00
11-1st Weapon Prime; Deadpool-c/story (3rd app.) 2 4 6 11 16 20
12-14,20-22,24,26-33 3.00
15-Cable leaves X-Force; Deadpool-c/app. 2 4 6 9 12 15
16-18-Polybagged w/trading card in each; X-Cutioner's Song x-overs 4.00
19-1st Copycat 2 4 6 9 12 15
23-Deadpool-c/app. 6.00
25-($3.50, 52 pgs.)-Wraparound-c w/Cable hologram on-c; Cable returns 5.00
34-37,39-45: 34-bound-in card sheet 3.00
38,40-43: 38-($2.00)-Newsstand edition. 40-43 ($1.95)-Deluxe edition 3.00
38-($2.95)-Collectors edition (prismatic) 5.00
44-49,51-67: 44-Return from Age of Apocalypse. 45-Sabretooth app. 49-Sebastian Shaw app. 52-Blob app., Onslaught cameo. 55-Vs. S.H.I.E.L.D. 56-Deadpool app. 57-Mr. Sinister & X-Man-c/app. 57,58-Onslaught x-over. 59-W/card insert; return of Longshot. 60-Dr. Strange 3.00
50 ($3.95)-Gatefold wrap-around foil-c 4.00
50 ($3.95)-Liefeld variant-c 5.00
68-74: 68-Operation Zero Tolerance 3.00
75,100-($2.99): 75-Cannonball-c/app. 4.00
76-99,101,102: 81-Pollina poster. 95-Magneto-c. 102-Ellis-s/Portacio-a 3.00
103-115: 103-Begin $2.25-c; Portacio-a thru #106. 115-Death of old team 3.00
116-New team debuts; Allred-c/a; Milligan-s; no Comics Code stamp on-c 4.00
117-129: 117-Intro. Mr. Sensitive. 120-Wolverine-c/app. 123-'Nuff Said issue. 124-Darwyn Cooke-a/c. 128-Death of U-Go Girl. 129-Fegredo-a 3.00
#(-1) Flashback (7/97) story of John Proudstar; Pollina-a 3.00
Annual 1-3 ('92-'94, 68 pgs.) 1-1st Greg Capullo-a(p) on X-Force. 2-Polybagged w/trading card; intro X-Treme & Neurtap 4.00
...And Cable '95 (12/95, $3.95)-Impossible Man app. 4.00
...And Cable '96, ...'97 ('96, 7/97) -'96-Wraparound-c 4.00
...And Spider-Man: Sabotage nn (11/92, $6.95)-Reprints X-Force #3,4 & Spider-Man #16 7.00
.../ Champions '98 ($3.50) 4.00
Annual 99 ($3.50) 4.00
...: Famous, Mutant & Mortal HC (2003, $29.99) oversized r/#116-129; foreward by Milligan; gallery of covers and pin-ups; script for #123 30.00
...New Beginnings TPB (10/01, $14.95) r/#116-120 15.00
...Rough Cut ($2.99) Pencil pages and script for #102 3.00
...Youngblood (8/96, $4.95)-Platt-c 5.00
NOTE: ***Capullo** a(p)-15-25, Annual 1; c(p)-14-27. **Rob Liefeld** a-1-7, 9p; c-1-9, 11p; plots-1-12. **Mignola** a-8p.*

X-FORCE
Marvel Comics: Oct, 2004 - No. 6, Mar, 2005 ($2.99, limited series)

1-6-Liefeld-c/a; Nicieza-s. 5,6-Wolverine & The Thing app. 3.00
X-Force & Cable Vol. 1: The Legend Returns (2005, $14.99) r/#1-6 15.00

X-FORCE (Also see Uncanny X-Force)
Marvel Comics: Apr, 2008 - No. 28, Sept, 2010 ($2.99)

1-Crain-a; Wolverine & X-23 app.; two covers (regular and bloody) by Crain on #1-5 4.00
2-21,23-28: 2,3-Bastion app. 4-6-Archangel app. 7-10-Choi-a. 9-11-Ghost Rider app. 26-28-Second Coming x-over; Granov-c. 26-Nightcrawler killed 3.00
22-($3.99) Necrosha x-over; Crain-a 4.00
...: Angels and Demons MGC #1 (5/11, $1.00) r/#1 with "Marvel's Greatest Comics" on-c 3.00
... Annual 1 (2/10, $3.99) Kirkman-s/Pearson-a/c; Deadpool back-up w/Barberi-a 4.00
... /Cable: Messiah War 1 (5/09, $3.99) Choi-a; covers by Andrews and Choi 4.00
... Special: Ain't No Dog (8/08, $3.99) Huston-s/Palo-a; Dell'Edera-a; Hitch-c 4.00

X-FORCE
Marvel Comics: Apr, 2014 - No. 15, Apr, 2015 ($3.99)

1-15: 1-Team of Cable, Fantomex, Psylocke & Marrow; Rock-He Kim-a. 4-6-Molina-a 4.00

X-FORCE MEGAZINE
Marvel Comics: Nov, 1996 ($3.95, one-shot)

1-Reprints 4.00

X-FORCE: SEX AND VIOLENCE
Marvel Comics: Sept, 2010 - No. 3, Nov, 2010 ($3.99, limited series)

1-3-Dell'Otto-a/Kyle & Yost-s; Domino & Wolverine vs. The Hand & The Assassins Guild 4.00

X-FORCE: SHATTERSTAR
Marvel Comics: Apr, 2005 - No. 4, July, 2005 ($2.99, limited series)

1-4-Liefeld-c/s; Michaels-a 3.00
TPB (2005, $15.99) r/#1-4 & New Mutants #99,100 16.00

X-INFERNUS
Marvel Comics: Feb, 2009 - No. 4, May, 2009 ($3.99, limited series)

Xmas Comics #1 © FAW

X-Men #35 © MAR

X-Men #125 © MAR

GD 2.0 | VG 4.0 | FN 6.0 | VF 8.0 | VF/NM 9.0 | NM- 9.2

1-4-Illyana Rasputin in Limbo; Cebulski-s/Camuncoli-a/Finch-c 4.00

XIN: JOURNEY OF THE MONKEY KING
Anarchy Studios: May, 2003 - No. 3, July, 2003 ($2.99)

Preview Edition (Apr, 2003, $1.99) Flip book w/ Vampi Vicious Preview Edition 3.00
1-3-Kevin Lau-a. 1-Three covers by Lau, Park and Nauck. 2-Three covers 3.00

XIN: LEGEND OF THE MONKEY KING
Anarchy Studios: Nov, 2002 - No. 3, Jan, 2003 ($2.99)

Preview Edition (Summer 2002, Diamond Dateline supplement) 3.00
1-3-Kevin Lau-a. 1-Two covers by Lau & Madureira. 2-Two covers by Lau & Oeming 3.00
TPB (10/03, $12.95) r/#1-3; cover gallery and sketch pages 13.00

X-MAN (Also see X-Men Omega & X-Men Prime)
Marvel Comics: Mar, 1995 - No. 75, May, 2001 ($1.95/$1.99/$2.25)

1-Age of Apocalypse 5.00
1-2nd print 3.00
2-4,25: 25-($2.99)-Wraparound-c 4.00
5-24, 26-28: 5-Post Age of Apocalypse stories begin. 5-7-Madelyne Pryor app. 10-Professor X app. 12-vs. Excalibur. 13-Marauders, Cable app. 14-Vs. Cable; Onslaught app. 15-17-Vs. Holocaust. 17-w/Onslaught Update. 18-Onslaught x-over; X-Force-c/app; Marauders app. 19-Onslaught x-over. 20-Abomination-c/app.; w/card insert. 23-Bishop app. 24-Spider-Man, Morbius-c/app. 27-Re-appearance of Aurora(Alpha Flight) 3.00
29-49,51-62: 29-Operation Zero Tolerance. 37,38-Spider-Man-c/app. 56-Spider-Man app. 3.00
50-($2.99) Crossover with Generation X #50 4.00
63-74: 63-Ellis & Grant-s/Olivetti-a begins. 64-Begin $2.25-c 3.00
75 ($2.99) Final issue; Alcatena-a 4.00
#(-1) Flashback (7/97) 3.00
...'96, ...'97-($2.95)-Wraparound-c; '96-Age of Apocalypse 4.00
...: All Saints' Day ('97, $5.99) Dodson-a 6.00
.../Hulk '98 ($2.99) Wraparound-c; Thanos app. 4.00

XMAS COMICS
Fawcett Publications: 12?/1941 - No. 2, 12?/1942; (50¢, 324 pgs.)
No. 7, 12?/1947 (25¢, 132 pgs.)(#3-6 do not exist for this series, see 1949-1952 series)

1-Contains Whiz #21, Capt. Marvel #3, Bulletman #2, Wow #3, & Master #18; front & back-c by Raboy. Not rebound, remaindered comics; printed at same time as originals 476 952 1428 3475 6138 8800
2-Capt. Marvel, Bulletman, Spy Smasher 213 426 639 1363 2332 3300
7-Funny animals (Hoppy, Billy the Kid & Oscar) 84 168 252 538 919 1300

XMAS COMICS
Fawcett Publications: No. 4, Dec, 1949 - No. 7, Dec, 1952 (50¢, 196 pgs.)

4-Contains Whiz, Master, Tom Mix, Captain Marvel, Nyoka, Capt. Video, Bob Colt, Monte Hale, Hot Rod Comics, & Battle Stories. Not rebound, remaindered comics; printed at the same time as originals. Title logo and Santa's suit on cover are topped by red felt 113 226 339 718 1234 1750
5-7: 5-Green felt tree on-c. 6-Cover has red felt like #4. 7-Bill Boyd app.; stocking on cover is made of green felt (novelty cover) 90 18 270 576 988 1400

X-MEN, THE (See Adventures of Cyclops and Phoenix, Amazing Adventures, Archangel, Brotherhood, Capt. America #172, Classic X-Men, Exiles, Further Adventures of Cyclops & Phoenix, Gambit, Giant-Size..., Heroes For Hope..., Kitty Pryde & Wolverine, Marvel & DC Present, Marvel Collector's Edition:..., Marvel Fanfare, Marvel Graphic Novel, Marvel Super Heroes, Marvel Team-Up, Marvel Triple Action, The Marvel X-Men Collection, New Mutants, Nightcrawler, Official Marvel Index To..., Rogue, Special Edition..., Ultimate..., Uncanny..., Wolverine, X-Factor, X-Force, X-Terminators)

X-MEN, THE (1st series)(Becomes Uncanny X-Men at #142)(The X-Men #1-93; X-Men #94-141) (The Uncanny X-Men on-c only #114-141)
Marvel Comics Group: Sept, 1963 - No. 66, Mar, 1970; No. 67, Dec, 1970 - No. 141, Jan, 1981; Uncanny X-Men No. 142, Feb, 1981 - No. 544, Dec, 2011

1-Origin/1st app. X-Men (Angel, Beast, Cyclops, Iceman & Marvel Girl); 1st app. Magneto & Professor X 1250 2500 4375 11,500 26,750 48,000
2-1st app. The Vanisher 159 318 477 1312 2956 4600
3-1st app. The Blob (1/64) 100 200 300 800 1800 2800
4-1st Quicksilver & Scarlet Witch & Brotherhood of the Evil Mutants (3/64); 1st app. Toad; 2nd app. Magneto 190 380 570 1568 3534 5500
5-Magneto & Evil Mutants-c/story 68 136 204 544 1222 1900
6,7: 6-Sub-Mariner app. 7-Magneto app. 52 104 156 416 921 1425
8,9,11: 8-1st Unus the Untouchable. 9-Early Avengers app. (1/65); 1st Lucifer. 11-1st app. The Stranger. 44 88 132 326 738 1150
10-1st S.A. app. Ka-Zar & Zabu the sabertooth (3/65) 45 90 135 333 754 1175
12-Origin Prof. X; Origin/1st app. Juggernaut 54 108 162 432 966 1500
13-Juggernaut and Human Torch app. 32 64 96 230 515 800
14,15: 14-1st app. Sentinels. 15-Origin Beast 31 62 93 223 499 775
16-20: 19-1st app. The Mimic (4/66) 19 38 57 131 291 450
21-27,29,30: 27-Re-enter The Mimic (r-in #75); Spider-Man cameo

GD 2.0 | VG 4.0 | FN 6.0 | VF 8.0 | VF/NM 9.0 | NM- 9.2

13 26 39 89 195 300
28-1st app. The Banshee (1/67)(r-in #76) 22 44 66 154 340 525
28-2nd printing (1994) 2 4 6 9 12 15
31-34,36,37,39: 34-Adkins-c/a. 39-New costumes 10 20 30 69 147 225
35-Spider-Man x-over (8/67)(r-in #83); 1st app. Changeling 24 48 72 168 372 575
38,40: 38-Origins of the X-Men series begins, ends #57. 40-(1/68) 1st app. Frankenstein's monster at Marvel 11 22 33 73 157 240
41-48: 42-Death of Prof. X (Changeling disguised as). 44-1st S.A. app. G.A. Red Raven. 10 20 30 64 132 200
49-Steranko-c; 1st Polaris 12 24 36 82 179 275
50,51-Steranko-c/a 10 20 30 68 144 220
52 9 18 27 61 123 185
53-Barry Smith-c/a (his 1st comic book work) 10 20 30 66 138 210
54,55-B. Smith-c. 54-1st app. Alex Summers who later becomes Havok. 55-Summers discovers he has mutant powers 10 20 30 67 141 215
56,57,59-63,65-Neal Adams-a(p). 56-Intro Havok w/o costume. 60-1st Sauron. 65-Return of Professor X. 11 22 33 73 157 240
58-1st app. Havok in costume; N. Adams-a(p) 14 28 42 94 207 320
62,63-2nd printings (1994) 2 4 6 8 10 12
64-1st app. Sunfire 10 20 30 69 147 225
66-Last new story w/original X-Men; battles Hulk 11 22 33 76 163 250
67-70: 67-Reprints begin, end #93. 67-70: (52 pgs.) 9 18 27 59 117 175
71-93: 71-Last 15¢ issue. 72: (52 pgs.). 73-86-r/#25-38 w/new-c. 83-Spider-Man-c/story. 87-93-r/#39-45 with covers 8 16 24 51 96 140
94 (8/75)-New X-Men begin (see Giant-Size X-Men for 1st app.); Colossus, Nightcrawler, Thunderbird, Storm, Wolverine, & Banshee join; Angel, Marvel Girl & Iceman resign 70 140 210 500 950 1400
95-Death of Thunderbird 15 30 45 105 233 360
96,97 10 20 30 64 132 200
98,99-(Regular 25¢ edition)(4,6/76) 9 18 27 63 129 195
98,99-(30¢-c variants, limited distribution) 23 46 69 161 356 550
100-Old vs. New X-Men; part origin Phoenix; last 25¢ issue (8/76) 10 20 30 70 150 230
100-(30¢-c variant, limited distribution) 27 54 81 189 420 650
101-Phoenix origin concludes 14 28 42 96 211 325
102-104: 102-Origin Storm. 104-1st brief app. Starjammers; Magneto-c/story 7 14 21 49 92 135
105-107-(Regular 30¢ editions). 106-(8/77)Old vs. New X-Men. 107-1st full app. Starjammers; last 30¢ issue 7 14 21 46 86 125
105-107-(35¢-c variants, limited distribution) 32 64 96 230 515 800
108-Byrne-a begins (see Marvel Team-Up #53) 7 14 21 49 92 135
109-1st app. Weapon Alpha (becomes Vindicator) 7 14 21 46 86 125
110,111: 110-Phoenix joins 6 12 18 38 69 100
112-116 6 12 18 38 69 100
117-119: 117-Origin Professor X 5 10 15 34 60 85
120-1st app. Alpha Flight, story line begins (4/79); 1st app. Vindicator (formerly Weapon Alpha); last 35¢ issue 7 14 21 46 86 125
121-1st full Alpha Flight story 6 12 18 42 79 115
122-128: 123-Spider-Man x-over. 124-Colossus becomes Proletarian 5 10 15 31 53 75
129-Intro Kitty Pryde (1/80); last Banshee; Dark Phoenix saga begins; intro. Emma Frost (White Queen) 8 16 24 56 108 160
130-1st app. The Dazzler by Byrne (2/80) 6 12 18 37 66 95
131-135: 131-Dazzler app.; 1st White Queen-c. 133-1st Wolverine solo-c. 134-Phoenix becomes Dark Phoenix 5 10 15 31 53 75
136,138: 138-History of the X-Men recounted; Dazzler app.; Cyclops leaves 4 8 12 28 47 65
137-Giant; death of Phoenix 6 12 18 38 69 100
139-Alpha Flight app.; Kitty Pryde joins; new costume for Wolverine 5 10 15 31 53 75
140-Alpha Flight app. 5 10 15 31 53 75
141-"Days of Future Past" part 1; intro Future X-Men & The New Brotherhood of Evil Mutants; 1st app. Rachel (Phoenix II); Death of alt. future Franklin Richards 7 14 21 46 86 125

X-MEN: Titled THE UNCANNY X-MEN No. 142, Feb, 1981 - No. 544, Dec, 2011

142-"Days of Future Past" part 2; Rachel app.; deaths of alt. future Wolverine, Storm & Colossus 6 12 18 37 66 95
143-Last Byrne issue 4 8 12 23 37 50
144-150: 144-Man-Thing app. 145-Old X-Men app. 148-1st app. Caliban; Spider-Woman, Dazzler app. 150-Double size 2 4 6 9 13 16
151-157,159-161,163,164: 161-Origin Magneto. 163-Origin Binary. 164-1st app. Binary as Carol Danvers 2 4 6 8 10 12

Uncanny X-Men #308 © MAR

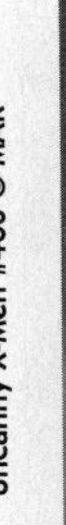

	GD 2.0	VG 4.0	FN 6.0	VF 8.0	VF/NM 9.0	NM- 9.2
158-1st app. Rogue in X-Men (6/82, see Avengers Annual #10)	3	6	9	16	24	32
162-Wolverine solo story	2	4	6	10	14	18
165-Paul Smith-c/a begins, ends #175	2	4	6	8	11	14
166-170: 166-Double size; Paul Smith-a. 167-New Mutants app. (3/83); same date as New Mutants #1; 1st meeting w/X-Men; ties into N.M. #3,4; Starjammers app.; contains skin "Tattooz" decals. 168-1st brief app. Madelyne Pryor (last page) in X-Men (see Avengers Annual #10)	2	3	4	6	8	10
171-Rogue joins X-Men; Simonson-c/a	2	4	6	13	18	22
172-174: 172,173-Two part Wolverine solo story. 173-Two cover variations, blue & black. 174-Phoenix cameo	1	3	4	6	8	10
175-(52 pgs.)-Anniversary issue; Phoenix returns	2	4	6	8	10	12
176-185,187-192,194-199: 181-Sunfire app. 182-Rogue solo story. 184-1st app. Forge (8/84). 190,191-Spider-Man & Avengers x-over. 195-Power Pack x-over	1	2	3	5	7	9
186,193: 186-Double-size; Barry Smith/Austin-a. 193-Double size; 100th app. New X-Men; 1st app. Warpath in costume (see New Mutants #16)	1	3	4	6	8	10
200-(12/85, $1.25, 52 pgs.)	2	4	6	8	10	12
201-(1/86)-1st app. Cable? (as baby Nathan; see X-Factor #1); 1st Whilce Portacio-c/a(i) on X-Men (guest artist)	3	6	9	19	30	40
202-204,206-209: 204-Nightcrawler solo story; 2nd Portacio-a(i) on X-Men. 207-Wolverine/Phoenix story	1	2	3	5	7	9
205-Wolverine solo story by Barry Smith	2	4	6	9	13	16
210,211-Mutant Massacre begins	3	6	9	14	19	24
212,213-Wolverine vs. Sabretooth (Mutant Mass.)	3	6	9	15	22	28
214-220,223,224: 219-Havok joins (7/87); brief app. Sabretooth.	1	2	3	5	6	8
221-1st app. Mr. Sinister	3	6	9	19	30	40
222-Wolverine battles Sabretooth-c/story	3	6	9	14	20	26
225-242: 225-227: Fall Of The Mutants. 226-Double size. 240-Sabretooth app. 242-Double size, X-Factor app., Inferno tie-in	1	2	3	5	6	8
243,245-247: 245-Rob Liefeld-a(p)	1	2	3	5	6	8
244-1st app. Jubilee	3	6	9	21	33	45
248-1st Jim Lee art on X-Men (1989)	3	6	9	14	20	25
248-2nd printing (1992, $1.25)	1	3	4	6	8	10
249-252: 252-Lee-c	1	2	3	4	5	7
253-255: 253-All new X-Men begin. 254-Lee-c	1	2	3	4	5	7
256-Betsy Braddock (Psylocke) 1st app. as purple-haired Asian in ninja costume; Jim Lee-c/a	2	4	6	11	16	20
257-Jim Lee-c/a; Psylocke as Lady Mandarin	1	3	4	6	8	10
258-Wolverine solo story; Lee-c/a	1	3	4	6	8	10
259-Silvestri-c/a; no Lee-a	1	2	3	4	5	7
260-265-No Lee-a. 260,261,264-Lee-c	1	2	3	4	5	7
266-(8/90) 1st full app. Gambit (see Annual #14)-No Lee-a	7	14	21	46	86	125
267-Jim Lee-c/a resumes; 2nd full Gambit app.	2	4	6	10	14	18
268-Capt. America, Black Widow & Wolverine team-up; Lee-c/a	2	4	6	11	16	20
268,270: 268-2nd printing. 270-Gold 2nd printing	1	3	4	6	8	10
269,273,274: 269-Lee-a. 273-New Mutants (Cable) & X-Factor x-over; Golden, Byrne & Lee part pencils	1	2	3	4	5	7
270-X-Tinction Agenda begins	1	2	3	5	6	8
271,272-X-Tinction Agenda	1	2	3	5	6	8
275-(52 pgs.)-Tri-fold-c by Jim Lee (p); Prof. X	1	2	3	5	6	8
275-Gold 2nd printing						5.00
276-280: 277-Last Lee-c/a. 280-X-Factor x-over						6.00
281-(10/91)-New team begins (Storm, Archangel, Colossus, Iceman & Marvel Girl); Whilce Portacio-c/a begins; Byrne scripts begin; wraparound-c (white logo)	1	2	3	5	6	8
281-2nd printing with red metallic ink logo w/o UPC box ($1.00-c); does not say 2nd printing inside						5.00
282-1st brief app. Bishop (cover & 1 page)	2	4	6	13	18	22
282-Gold ink 2nd printing ($1.00-c)	1	2	3	5	6	8
283-1st full app. Bishop (12/91)	2	4	6	8	10	12
284-299: 284-Last $1.00-c. 286,287-Lee plots. 287-Bishop joins team. 288-Lee/Portacio plots. 290-Last Portacio-c/a. 294-Peterson-a(p) begins (#292 is 1st Peterson-c). 294-296 ($1.00)-Bagged w/trading card in each; X-Cutioner's Song x-overs; Peterson/Austin-c/a on all						4.00
297-Gold Edition	12	24	36	79	170	260
300-($3.95, 68 pgs.)-Holo-grafx foil-c; Magneto app.						6.00
301-303,305-309,311						3.00
303,307-Gold Edition	4	8	12	27	44	60
304-($3.95, 68 pgs.)-Wraparound-c with Magneto hologram on-c; 30th anniversary issue; Jae Lee-a (4 pgs.)						6.00
310-($1.95)-Bound-in trading card sheet						3.00
312-$1.50-c begins; bound-in card sheet; 1st Madureira						4.00
313-321: 318-1st app. Generation X						3.00
316,317-($2.95)-Foil enhanced editions						4.00
318-321-($1.95)-Deluxe editions						4.00
322-Onslaught						5.00
323,324,326-346: 323-Return from Age of Apocalypse. 328-Sabretooth-c. 329,330-Dr. Strange app. 331-White Queen-c/app. 334-Juggernaut app.; w/Onslaught Update. 335-Onslaught, Avengers, Apocalypse, & X-Man app. 336-Onslaught. 338-Archangel's wings return to normal. 339-Havok vs. Cyclops; Spider-Man app. 341-Gladiator-c/app. 342-Deathbird cameo; two covers. 343,344-Phalanx						3.00
325-($3.95)-Anniversary issue; gatefold-c						5.00
342-Variant-c	2	4	6	8	10	12
347-349:347-Begin $1.99-c. 349-"Operation Zero Tolerance"						3.00
350-Newsstand version	2	4	6	9	12	15
350-($3.99, 48 pgs.) Prismatic etched foil gatefold wraparound-c; Trial of Gambit; Seagle-s begin	2	4	6	10	14	18
351-359: 353-Bachalo-a begins. 354-Regular-c. 355-Alpha Flight-c/app. 356-Original X-Men-c						3.00
354-Dark Phoenix variant-c	1	3	4	6	8	10
360-($2.99) 35th Anniv. issue; Pacheco-c						4.00
360-($3.99) Etched Holo-foil enhanced-c						5.00
360-($6.95) DF Edition with Jae Lee variant-c	1	3	4	6	8	10
361-374,378,379: 361-Gambit returns; Skroce-a. 362-Hunt for Xavier pt. 1; Bachelo-a. 364-Yu-a. 366-Magneto-c. 369-Juggernaut-c						3.00
375-($2.99) Autopsy of Wolverine						5.00
376,377-Apocalypse: The Twelve	1	2	3	5	6	8
380-($2.99) Polybagged with X-Men Revolution Genesis Edition preview						4.00
381,382,384-389,391-393: 381-Begin $2.25-c; Claremont-s. 387-Maximum Security						3.00
383-($2.99)						4.00
390-Colossus dies to cure the Legacy Virus	2	4	6	8	10	12
394-New look X-Men begins; Casey-s/Churchill-c/a						4.00
395-399-Poptopia. 398-Phillips & Wood-a						3.00
400-($3.50) Art by Ashley Wood, Eddie Campbell, Hamner, Phillips, Pulido and Matt Smith; wraparound-c by Wood						5.00
401-415: 401-'Nuff Said issue; Garney-a. 404,405,407-409,413-415-Phillips-a						3.00
416-421: 416-Asamiya-a begins. 421-Garney-a						3.00
422-($3.50) Alpha Flight app.; Garney-a						4.00
423-(25¢-c) Holy War pt. 1; Garney-a/Philip Tan-c						3.00
424-449,452-454: 425,426,429,430-Tan-a. 428-Birth of Nightcrawler. 437-Larroca-a begins. 444-New team, new costumes; Claremont-s/Davis-a begins. 448,449-Coipel-a						3.00
450-X-23 app.; Davis-a	1	2	3	5	6	8
451-X-23 app.; Davis-a	2	4	6	8	10	12
455-459-X-23 app.; Davis-a						5.00
460-471: 460-Begin $2.50-c; Raney-a. 462-465-House of M. 464-468-Bachalo-a						3.00
472-499: 472-Begin $2.99-c; Bachalo-a. 475-Wraparound-c. 492-494-Messiah Complex						3.00
500-($3.99) X-Men new HQ in San Francisco; Magneto app.; Land & Dodson-a; wraparound covers by Alex Ross and Greg Land						6.00
500-Classic X-Men Dynamic Forces variant-c by Ross						8.00
500-X-Men variant-c by Michael Turner	4	8	12	22	32	40
500-X-Men sketch variant-c by Michael Turner	11	22	33	76	163	250
500-X-Women variant-c by Dodson	3	6	9	14	20	25
500-X-Women sketch variant-c by Dodson	10	20	30	64	132	200
501-511,515-521,523-525: 501-Brubaker & Fraction-s/Land-a. 523-525-Second Coming						3.00
512-514,522-($3.99). 513,514-Utopia x-over. 522-Kitty Pryde returns to Earth; Portacio-a						4.00
526-543-($3.99) 526-The Heroic Age; aftermath of Second Coming. 530-534-Land-a 540-543-Fear Itself tie-in, Juggernaut attacks; Land-a. 542-Colossus becomes the Juggernaut						4.00
534.1 (6/11, $2.99) Pacheco-a/c						3.00
544-(12/11, $3.99) Final issue; Land-a/c; Mr. Sinister app.	1	3	4	6	8	10
#(-1) Flashback (7/97) Ladronn-c/Hitch & Neary-a						3.00
Special 1(12/70)-Kirby-c/a; origin The Stranger	10	20	30	66	138	210
Special 2(11/71, 52 pgs.)	8	16	24	51	96	140
Annual 3(1979, 52 pgs.)-New story; Miller/Austin-c; Wolverine still in old yellow costume	5	10	15	30	48	65
Annual 4(1980, 52 pgs.)-Dr. Strange guest stars	3	6	9	14	20	25
Annual 5(1981, 52 pgs.)	2	4	6	8	10	12
Annual 6-8('82-'84 52 pgs.)-6-Dracula app.	1	2	3	5	6	8
Annual 9,10('85, '86)-9-New Mutants x-over cont'd from New Mutants Special Ed. #1; Art Adams-a. 10-Art Adams-a	2	4	6	8	10	12
Annual 11-13:('87-'89, 68 pgs.): 12-Evolutionary War; A.Adams-a(p). 13-Atlantis Attacks						5.00
Annual 14(1990, $2.00, 68 pgs.)-1st app. Gambit (minor app., 5 pgs.); Fantastic Four, New Mutants (Cable) & X-Factor x-over; Art Adams-c/a(p)						

X-Men (2nd series) #46 © MAR

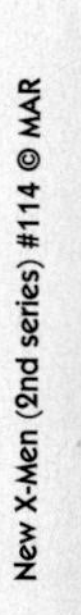

New X-Men (2nd series) #114 © MAR

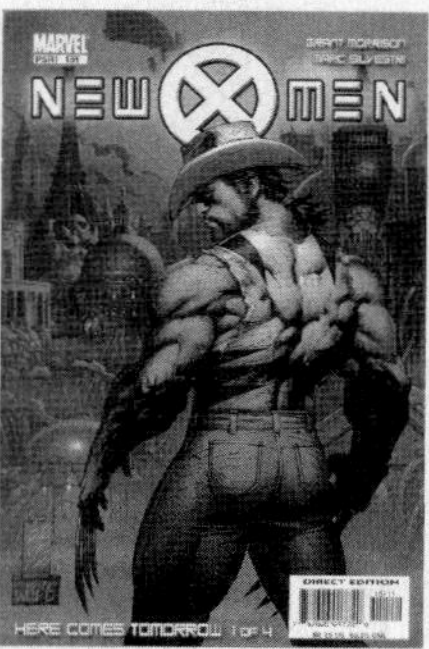

New X-Men (2nd series) #151 © MAR

GD 2.0 | VG 4.0 | FN 6.0 | VF 8.0 | VF/NM 9.0 | NM- 9.2

3 6 9 19 30 40
Annual 15 (1991, $2.00, 68 pgs.)-4 pg. origin; New Mutants x-over; 4 pg. Wolverine solo back-up story; 4th app. X-Force cont'd from New Warriors Annual #1 5.00
Annual 16-18 ('92-'94, 68 pgs.)-16-Jae Lee-c/a(p). 17-Bagged w/card 4.00
Annual '95-(11/95, $3.95)-Wraparound-c 4.00
Annual '96,'97-Wraparound-c 4.00
.../Fantastic Four Annual '98 ($2.99) Casey-s 4.00
Annual '99 ($3.50) Jubilee app. 4.00
Annual 2000 ($3.50) Cable app.; Ribic-a 4.00
Annual 2001 ($3.50, printed wide-ways) Ashley Wood-c/a; Casey-s 4.00
Annual (Vol. 2) #1 (8/06, $3.99) Storm & Black Panther wedding prelude 4.00
Annual (Vol. 2) #2 (3/09, $3.99) Dark Reign; flashback to Sub-Mariner/Emma Frost 4.00
Annual (Vol. 2) #3 (5/11, $3.99) Escape From the Negative Zone; Bradshaw-a 4.00
....At The State Fair of Texas (1983, 36 pgs., one-shot); Supplement to the Dallas Times Herald 2 4 6 9 12 15
...: The Dark Phoenix Saga TPB 1st printing (1984, $12.95) 40.00
...: The Dark Phoenix Saga TPB 2nd-5th printings 25.00
...: The Dark Phoenix Saga TPB 6th-10th printings 20.00
... Days of Future Past TPB (2004, $19.99) r/#138-143 & Annual #4 20.00
... Eve of Destruction TPB (2005, $14.99) r/#391-393 & X-Men #111-113; Churchill-c 15.00
...:Dream's End (2004, $17.99)-r/Death of Colossus story arc from Uncanny X-Men #388-390, Cable #87, Bishop #16 and X-Men #108,110; debut pages from Giant-Size X-Men #1 18.00
... From The Ashes TPB (1990, $14.95) r/#168-176 15.00
... Future History - The Messiah War Sourcebook (2009, $3.99) Cable's files on X-Men 4.00
...: God Loves, Man Kills ($6.95)-r/Marvel Graphic Novel #5 7.00
...: God Loves, Man Kills - Special Edition (2003, $4.99)-reprint with new Hughes-c 5.00
...: God Loves, Man Kills HC (2007, $19.99) reprint with Claremont & Anderson interviews; original artist Neal Adams' six sketch pages and interview 20.00
...: Hope (5/10, $2.99) Collects Cable and Hope back-ups; Dillon-a 3.00
House of M: Uncanny X-Men TPB (2006, $13.99) r/#462-465 and selections from Secrets Of The House of M one-shot 14.00
...In The Days of Future Past TPB (1989, $3.95, 52 pgs.) 10.00
...: No More Humans HC (2014, $24.99) Carey-s/Larroca-a 25.00
...Old Soldiers TPB (2004, $19.99) r/#213,215 & Ann. #11; New Mutants Ann. #2&3 20.00
...Poptopia TPB (10/01, $15.95) r/#394-399 16.00
...: Rise & Fall of the Shi'Ar Empire HC (2007, $34.99, dustjacket) r/#475-486; bonus art 35.00
...: Rise & Fall of the Shi'Ar Empire SC (2008, $29.99) r/#475-486; bonus art 30.00
...: Season One HC (2012, $24.99) Origin re-told; Hopeless-s/McKelvie-a 25.00
...: Sword of the Braddocks (5/09, $3.99) Psylocke vs. Slaymaster; Claremont-s 4.00
...: The Complete Onslaught Epic Book 1 TPB (2007, $29.99) r/X-Men #53-54, Uncanny X-Men #334-335, Fantastic Four #414-415, Avengers #400-401, Onslaught: X-Men, Cable #34 and Incredible Hulk #444 30.00
...: The Complete Onslaught Epic Book 2 TPB ('08, $29.99) r/Excalibur #100, Wolverine #104, X-Factor #125-126, Amazing Spider-Man #415, Green Goblin #12, Spider-Man #72, Punisher #11, X-Man #18 & X-Force #57 30.00
...: The Extremists TPB (2007, $13.99) r/#487-491 14.00
...: The Heroic Age (9/10, $3.99) Beast, Steve Rogers and Princess Powerful app. 4.00
Uncanny X-Men Omnibus Vol. 1 HC (2006, $99.99, dust jacket) r/Giant-Size X-Men #1, (Uncanny) X-Men #94-131 & Annual #3; cover gallery, promo and sketch art 140.00
Vignettes TPB (9/01, $17.95) r/Claremont & Bolton Classic X-Men #1-13 18.00
Vignettes Vol. 2 TPB (2005, $17.99) r/Claremont & Bolton Classic X-Men #14-25 18.00
... Vol. 1: Hope TPB (2003, $12.99) r/#410-415; Harris-c 13.00
... Vol. 2: Dominant Species TPB (2003, $11.99) r/#416-420; Asamiya-c 12.00
... Vol. 3: Holy War TPB (2003, $17.99) r/#421-427 18.00
... Vol. 4: The Draco TPB (2004, $15.99) r/#428-434 16.00
... Vol. 5: She Lies with Angels TPB (2004, $11.99) r/#437-441 12.00
... Vol. 6: Bright New Mourning TPB (2004, $14.99) r/#435,436,442,443 & (New) X-Men #155,156; Larroca sketch covers 15.00
...Vs. Apocalypse Vol. 1: The Twelve TPB (2008, $29.99) r/#376-377, Cable #73-76, X-Men #96,97 and Wolverine #145-147 30.00
... - The New Age Vol. 1: The End of History (2004, $12.99) r/#444-449 13.00
... - The New Age Vol. 2: The Cruelest Cut (2005, $11.99) r/#450-454 12.00
... - The New Age Vol. 3: On Ice (2006, $15.99) r/#455-461 16.00
... - The New Age Vol. 4: End of Greys (2006, $14.99) r/#466-471 15.00
... - The New Age Vol. 5: First Foursaken (2006, $11.99) r/#472-474 & Annual #1 12.00

NOTE: **Art Adams** *a-Annual 9, 10p, 12p, 14p; c-218p.* **Neal Adams** *a-56-63p, 65p; c-56-63.* **Adkins** *a-34, 35p; c-31, 34, 35.* **Austin** *a-108i, 109i, 111-117i, 119-143i, 186i, 204i, 228i, 294-297i, Annual 3i, 7i, 9i, 13; c-109-111i, 114-122i, 123, 124-141i, 142, 143, 196i, 204i, 228i, 294-297i, Annual 3i.* **J. Buscema** *c-42, 43, 45.* **Buscema/Tuska** *a-45.* **Byrne** *a(p)-108, 109, 111-143, 273; c(p)-113-116, 127, 129, 131-141.* **Capullo** *c-14.* **Ditko** *r-86, 89-91, 93.* **Everett** *c-73.* **Golden** *a-273, Annual 7p.* **Guice** *a-216p, 217p.* **G. Kane** *c(p)-33, 74-76, 79, 80, 94, 95.* **Kirby** *a(p)-1-17 (#12-17, 67r-layouts); c(p)-1-17, 25, 30 (18, 26-parts).* **Layton** *a-105i; c-112i, 113i.* **Jim Lee** *a(p)-248, 256-258, 267-277; c(p)-252, 254, 256-261, 264, 267, 268 ,270, 275-277, 286.* **Perez** *a-Annual 3p; c(p)-112, 128, Annual 3.* **Peterson** *a(p)-294-300, 304(part); c(p)-294-299.* **Whilce Portacio** *a(p)-281-286, 289, 290; a(i)-267; c-281-285p, 289p, 290; c(i)-267.* **Romita, Jr.** *a-300; c-300.* **Roussos** *a-84i.* **Simonson** *a-171p; c-171, 217.* **B. Smith** *a-53, 186p, 198p, 205, 214; c-53-55, 186p, 198, 205, 212, 214, 216.* **Paul Smith** *a(p)-165-170, 172-175, 278; c-165-170, 172-175, 278.* **Sparling** *a-78p.* **Steranko** *a-50p, 51p; c-49-51.* **Sutton** *a-106i.* **Art Thibert** *a(i)-281-286; c(i)-281, 282, 284, 285.* **Toth** *a-12p, 67p(r).* **Tuska** *a-40-42i, 43-46p, 88i(r); c-39-41, 77p, 78p.* **Williamson** *a-202i, 203i, 211i; c-202i, 203i, 206i.* **Wood** *c-14i.*

UNCANNY X-MEN AND THE NEW TEEN TITANS (See Marvel and DC Present...)

X-MEN (2nd Series)(Titled New X-Men with #114) (Titled X-Men Legacy with #210)
Marvel Comics: Oct, 1991 - No. 275, Dec, 2012 ($1.00-$2.99)

1 a-d (four different covers, $1.50, 52 pgs.)-Jim Lee-c/a begins, ends #11; new team begins (Cyclops, Beast, Wolverine, Gambit, Psylocke & Rogue); new Uncanny X-Men & Magneto app.; 6.00
1 e ($3.95)-Double gate-fold-c consisting of all four covers from 1a-d by Jim Lee; contains all pin-ups from #1a-d plus inside-c foldout poster; no ads; printed on coated stock 1 2 3 5 6 8
1-20th Anniversary Edition-(12/11, $3.99) r/#1 with double gatefold-c; Jim Lee pin-ups 5.00
2-7: 4-Wolverine back to old yellow costume (same date as Wolverine #50); last $1.00-c. 5-Byrne scripts. 6-Sabretooth-c/story 5.00
8-10: 8-Gambit vs. Bishop-c/story; last Lee-a; Ghost Rider cameo cont'd in Ghost Rider #26. 9-Wolverine vs. Ghost Rider; cont'd/G.R. #26. 10-Return of Longshot 5.00
11-13,17-24,26-29,31: 12,13-Art Thibert-c/a. 28,29-Sabretooth app. 4.00
11-Silver ink 2nd printing; came with X-Men board game 2 4 6 9 12 15
14-16-($1.50)-Polybagged with trading card in each; X-Cutioner's Song x-overs; 14-Andy Kubert-c/a begins 5.00
25-($3.50, 52 pgs.)-Wraparound-c with Gambit hologram on-c; Professor X erases Magneto's mind 2 4 6 10 14 18
25-30th anniversary issue w/B&W-c with Magneto in color & Magneto hologram & no price on-c 4 8 12 23 37 50
25-Gold 50.00
30-($1.95)-Wedding issue w/bound-in trading card sheet 5.00
32-37: 32-Begin $1.50-c; bound-in card sheet. 33-Gambit & Sabretooth-c/story 4.00
36,37-($2.95)-Collectors editions (foil-c) 5.00
38-44,46-49,51-65: 42,43- Paul Smith-a. 46,49,53-56-Onslaught app. 51-Waid scripts begin, end #56. 54-(Reg. edition)-Onslaught revealed as Professor X. 55,56-Onslaught x-over; Avengers, FF & Sentinels app. 56-Dr. Doom app. 57-Xavier taken into custody; Byrne-c/swipe (X-Men,1st Series #138). 59-Hercules-c/app. 61-Juggernaut-c/app. 62-Re-intro. Shang Chi; two covers. 63-Kingpin cameo. 64- Kingpin app. 4.00
45-($3.95)-Annual issue; gatefold-c 6.00
50-($2.95)-Vs. Onslaught, wraparound-c. 6.00
50-($3.95)-Vs. Onslaught, wraparound foil-c. 6.00
50-($2.95)-Variant gold-c. 4 8 12 23 37 50
50-($2.95)-Variant silver-c. 2 4 6 9 12 15
54-(Limited edition)-Embossed variant-c; Onslaught revealed as Professor X 3 6 9 19 30 40
66-69,71-74,76-79: 66-Operation Zero Tolerance. 76-Origin of Maggott 3.00
70-($2.99, 48 pgs.)-Joe Kelly's-s begin, new members join 4.00
75-($2.99, 48 pgs.) vs. N'Garai; wraparound-c 4.00
80-($3.99) 35th Anniv. issue; holo-foil-c 5.00
80-($2.99) Regular-c 4.00
80-($6.95) Dynamic Forces Ed.; Quesada-c 7.00
81-93,95,98,99: 82-Hunt for Xavier pt. 2. 85-Davis-a. 86-Origin of Joseph. 87-Magneto War ends. 88-Juggernaut app. 3.00
94-($2.99) Contains preview of X-Men: Hidden Years 4.00
96,97-Apocalypse: The Twelve 1 2 3 5 6 8
100-($2.99) Art Adams-c; begin Claremont-s/Yu-a 4.00
100-DF alternate-c 1 3 4 6 8 10
101-105,107,108,110-114: 101-Begin $2.25-c. 107-Maximum Security x-over; Bishop-c/app. 108-Moira MacTaggart dies; Senator Kelly shot. 111-Magneto-c. 112,113-Eve of Destruction 3.00
106-($2.99) X-Men battle Domina 4.00
109-($3.50, 100 pgs.) new and reprinted Christmas-themed stories 5.00
114-(7/01) Title change to "New X-Men," Morrison-s/Quitely-c/a begins 4.00
114-(8/10, $1.00) "Marvel's Greatest Comics" reprint 3.00
115-Two covers (Quitely & BWS) 4.00
116-125,127,129-149: 116-Emma Frost joins. 117,118-Van Sciver-a. 121,122,135-Quitely-a. 127-Leon & Sienkiewicz-a. 132,139-141-Jimenez-a. 136-138-Quitely-a. 142-Sabretooth app.; Bachalo-c/a thru #145. 146-Magneto returns; Jimenez-a 3.00
126-($3.25) Quitely-a; defeat of Cassanova 4.00
128-1st app. Fantomex; Kordey-a 3 6 9 17 26 35
150-($3.50) Jean Grey dies again; last Jimenez-a 4.00
151-156: 151-154-Silvestri-c/a 3.00
157-169: 157-X-Men Reload begins 3.00
170-184: 171- Begin $2.50-c. 175,176-Crossover with Black Panther #8,9. 181-184-Apocalypse returns 3.00
185-199,201-229,231-249,251-261: 185-Begin $2.99-c. 188-190,192-194,197-199-Bachalo-a. 195,196,201-203-Ramos-a. 201-204-Endangered Species back-up. 205-207-Messiah

X-Men (2nd series) #238 © MAR

X-Men (2010 series) #1 © MAR

X-Men/Alpha Flight #1 © MAR

GD VG FN VF VF/NM NM-
2.0 4.0 6.0 8.0 9.0 9.2

Complex x-over. 208-Romita Jr.-a. 210-Starts X-Men: Legacy. 228,229-Acuña-a.
235-237-Second Coming x-over. 238-The Heroic Age. 245-Age of X begins 3.00
200-($3.99) Two wraparound covers by Bachalo & Finch; Bachalo & Ramos-a 4.00
230-($3.99) Acuña-a; Rogue vs. Emplate 4.00
250-($4.99) Suayan-c/Pham-a; back-up r/New Mutants #27 5.00
261.1-(3/12, $2.99) The N'Garai app.; Brooks-c 3.00
262-275-Brooks-c. 266-270-Avengers vs. X-Men tie-in 3.00
#(-1) Flashback (7/97); origin of Magneto 3.00
Annual 1-3 ('92-'94, $2.25-$2.95, 68 pgs.) 1-Lee-c & layouts; #2-Bagged w/card 4.00
Special '95 ($3.95) 4.00
... '96,...'97-Wraparound-c 4.00
.../ Dr. Doom '98 Annual ($2.99) Lopresti-a 4.00
... Annual '99 ($3.50) Adam Kubert-c 4.00
Annual 2000 ($3.50) Art Adams-c/Claremont-s/Eaton-a 4.00
...2001 Annual ($3.50) Morrison-s/Yu-a; issue printed sideways 4.00
...2007 Annual #1 (3/07, $3.99) Casey-s/Brooks-a; Cable and Mystique app. 4.00
...Legacy Annual 1 (11/09, $3.99) Acuña-a; Emplate returns 4.00
Animation Special Graphic Novel (12/90, $10.95) adapts animated series 12.00
Ashcan #1 (1994, 75¢) Introduces new team members 3.00
... Archives Sketchbook (12/00, $2.99) Early B&W character design sketches by various incl. Lee, Davis, Yu, Pacheco, BWS, Art Adams, Liefeld 3.00
...: Bizarre Love Triangle TPB (2005, $9.99)-r/X-Men #171-174 10.00
.../ Black Panther TPB (2006, $11.99)-r/X-Men #175,176 & Black Panther (2005) #8,9 12.00
...: Blinded By the Light (2007, $14.99)-r/X-Men #200-204 15.00
...: Blind Science (7/10, $3.99) Second Coming x-over; Parel-c 4.00
...: Blood of Apocalypse (2006, $17.99)-r/X-Men #182-187 18.00
...: Day of the Atom (2005, $19.99)-r/X-Men #157-165 20.00
Decimation: X-Men - The Day After TPB (2006, $15.99) r/#177-181 & Decimation: House of M - The Day After 16.00
...: Declassified (10/00, $3.50) Profile pin-ups by various; Jae Lee-c 4.00
...: Earth's Mutant Heroes (7/11, $4.99) Handbook-style profiles of mutants 5.00
...: Endangered Species (8/07, $3.99) prologue to 17-part back-up series in X-Men titles 4.00
...: Endangered Species HC (2008, $24.99, d.j.) over-sized r/prologue and 17-part series 25.00
...: Evolutions 1 (12/11, $3.99) Collection of variant covers from May 2011 Marvel titles 4.00
...: Fatal Attractions ('94, $17.95)-r/x-Factor #92, X-Force #25, Uncanny X-Men #304, X-Men #25, Wolverine #75, & Excalibur #71 18.00
...: Golgotha (2005, $12.99)-r/X-Men #166-170 13.00
... Millennial Visions (8/00, $3.99) Various artists interpret future X-Men 4.00
... Millennial Visions 2 (1/02, $3.50) Various artists interpret future X-Men 4.00
...: Mutant Genesis (2006, $19.99)-r/X-Men #1-7; sketch pages and extra art 20.00
New X-Men: E is for Extinction TPB (11/01, $12.95) r/#114-117 13.00
New X-Men: Imperial TPB (7/02, $19.99) r/#118-126; Quitely-c 20.00
New X-Men: New Worlds TPB (2002, $14.99) r/#127-133; Quitely-c 15.00
New X-Men: Riot at Xavier's TPB (2003, $11.99) r/#134-138; Quitely-c 12.00
New X-Men: Vol. 5: Assault on Weapon Plus TPB (2003, $14.99) r/#139-145 15.00
New X-Men: Vol. 6: Planet X TPB (2004, $12.99) r/#146-150 13.00
New X-Men: Vol. 7: Here Comes Tomorrow TPB (2004, $10.99) r/#151-154 11.00
New X-Men: Volume 1 HC (2002, $29.99) oversized r/#114-126 & 2001 Annual 30.00
New X-Men: Volume 2 HC (2003, $29.99) oversized r/#127-141; sketch & script pages 30.00
New X-Men: Volume 3 HC (2004, $29.99) oversized r/#142-154; sketch & script pages 30.00
New X-Men Omnibus HC (2006, $99.99) oversized r/#114-154 & Annual 2001; Morrison's original pitch; sketch & script pages; variant covers & promo art; Carey intro. 140.00
...: Odd Men Out (2008, $3.99) Two unpublished stories with Dave Cockrum-a 4.00
... Original Sin 1 (12/08, $3.99) Wolverine and Daken; Deodato & Eaton-a 4.00
... Origin: Colossus (7/08, $3.99) Yost-s/Hairsine-a; Piotr Rasputin before joining X-Men 4.00
... Phoenix Force Handbook (9/10, $4.99) bios of those related to the Phoenix; Raney-c 5.00
...: Pixies and Demons Director's Cut (2008, $3.99) r/FCBD 2008 story with script 4.00
... Pizza Hut Mini-comics-(See Marvel Collector's Edition: X-Men in Promotional Comics section)
... Premium Edition #1 (1993)-Cover says "Toys 'R' Us Limited Edition X-Men" 3.00
...: Rarities (1995, $5.95)-Reprints 6.00
...: Return of Magik Must Have (2008, $3.99) r/X-Men Unlimited #14, New X-Men #37 and X-Men: Divided We Stand #2; Coipel-c 4.00
...: Road Trippin' ('99, $24.95, TPB) r/X-Men road trips 25.00
...: Supernovas ('07, $34.99, oversized HC w/d.j.) r/X-Men 188-199 & Annual #1 35.00
...: Supernovas ('08, $29.99, SC) r/X-Men 188-199 & Annual #1 30.00
...: The Coming of Bishop ('95, $12.95)-r/Uncanny X-Men #282-285, 287,288 13.00
...: The Magneto War (3/99, $2.99) Davis-a 4.00
...: The Rise of Apocalypse ('98, $16.99)-r/Rise Of Apocalypse #1-4, X-Factor #5,6 17.00
... Visionaries: Chris Claremont ('98, $24.95)-r/Claremont-s; art by Byrne, BWS, Jim Lee 25.00
... Visionaries: Jim Lee ('02, $29.99)-r/Jim Lee-a from various issues between Uncanny X-Men #248 & 286; r/Classic X-Men #39 and X-Men Annual #1 30.00
... Visionaries: Joe Madureira (7/00, $17.95)-r/Uncanny X-Men #325,326,329,330,341-343; new Madureira-c 18.00
... Vs. Hulk (3/09, $3.99) Claremont-s/Raapack-a; r/X-Men #66 4.00

...: Zero Tolerance ('00, $24.95, TPB) r/crossover series 25.00
NOTE: ***Jim Lee** a-1-11p; c-1-6p, 7, 8, 9p, 10, 11p.* ***Art Thibert** a-6-9i, 12, 13; c-6i, 12, 13.*

X-MEN (3rd series)
Marvel Comics: Sept, 2010 - No. 41, Apr, 2013 ($3.99)

1-41: 1-6-"Curse of the Mutants" x-over; Medina-a. 7-10-Spider-Man app.; Bachalo-a. 12-Continued from X-Men Giant-Size #1. 16-19-FF & Skull the Slayer app. 20-23-War Machine app. 16-Deadpool app. 28-FF & Spider-Man app. 38,39-Domino & Daredevil team-up 4.00
15.1 ($2.99) Pearson-c/Conrad-a; Ghost Rider app. 3.00
...: Curse of the Mutants - Blade 1 (10/10, $3.99) Tim Green-a 4.00
...: Curse of the Mutants - Smoke and Blood 1 (11/10, $3.99) Crain-c 4.00
...: Curse of the Mutants Spotlight 1 (1/11, $3.99) creator profiles and interviews 4.00
...: Curse of the Mutants - Storm and Gambit 1 (11/10, $3.99) Bachalo-a; 2 covers 4.00
...: Curse of the Mutants - X-Men vs. Vampires 1,2 (11/10 - No. 2, 12/10, $3.99) Bradshaw-c 4.00
... Giant-Size 1 (7/11, $4.99) Medina & Talajic-a; cover swipe of Giant-Size X-Men #1 5.00
...: Regenesis 1 (12/11, $3.99) Splits X-Men into 2 teams; Tan-a/Bachalo-c 4.00
... Spotlight 1 (7/11, $3.99) Character profiles and creator interviews 4.00
...: With Great Power 1 (2011, $4.99) r/#7-9 5.00

X-MEN (4th series)
Marvel Comics: Jul, 2013 - No. 26, Jun, 2015 ($3.99)

1-26: 1-All-female team; Brian Wood-s/Olivier Coipel-a. 5,6-Battle of the Atom 4.00
100th Anniversary Special: X-Men (9/14, $3.99) Takes place in 2061; Furth-s/Masters-a 4.00

X-MEN (Free Comic Book Day giveaways)
Marvel Comics: 2006; May, 2008

FCBD 2008 Edition #1-(5/08) Features Pixie; Carey-s/Land-a/c 3.00
.../Runaways: FCBD 2006 Edition; new x-over story; Mighty Avengers preview; Chen-c 3.00

X-MEN ADVENTURES (TV)
Marvel Comics: Nov, 1992 - No. 15, Jan, 1994 ($1.25)(Based on animated series)

1,15: 1-Wolverine, Cyclops, Jubilee, Rogue, Gambit. 15-($1.75, 52 pgs.) 4.00
2-14: 3-Magneto-c/story. 6-Sabretooth-c/story. 7-Cable-c/story. 10-Archangel guest star. 11-Cable-c/story. 3.00

X-MEN ADVENTURES II (TV)
Marvel Comics: Feb, 1994 - No. 13, Feb, 1995 ($1.25/$1.50)(Based on 2nd TV season)

1-13: 4-Bound-in trading card sheet. 5-Alpha Flight app. 3.00
...Captive Hearts/Slave Island (TPB, $4.95)-r/X-Men Adventures #5-8 5.00
...The Irresistible Force, The Muir Island Saga (5.95, 10/94, TPB) r/X-Men Advs. #9-12 6.00

X-MEN ADVENTURES III (TV)(See Adventures of the X-Men)
Marvel Comics: Mar, 1995 - No. 13, Mar, 1996 ($1.50) (Based on 3rd TV season)

1-13 3.00

X-MEN: AGE OF APOCALYPSE
Marvel Comics: May, 2005 - No. 6, June, 2005 ($2.99, weekly limited series)

1-6-Bachalo-c/a; Yoshida-s; follows events in the "Age of Apocalypse" storyline 4.00
... One Shot (5/05, $3.99) prequel to series; Hitch wraparound-c; pin-ups by various 4.00
X-Men: The New Age of Apocalypse TPB (2005, $20.99) r/#1-6 & one-shot 21.00

X-MEN ALPHA
Marvel Comics: 1994 ($3.95, one-shot)

nn-Age of Apocalypse; wraparound chromium-c 1 3 4 6 8 10
nn ($49.95)-Gold logo 55.00

X-MEN/ALPHA FLIGHT
Marvel Comics Group: Dec, 1985 - No. 2, Dec, 1985 ($1.50, limited series)

1,2: 1-Intro The Berserkers; Paul Smith-a 5.00

X-MEN/ALPHA FLIGHT
Marvel Comics Group: May, 1998 - No. 2, June, 1998 ($2.99, limited series)

1,2-Flashback to early meeting; Raab-s/Cassaday-s/a 3.00

X-MEN AND POWER PACK
Marvel Comics: Dec, 2005 - No. 4, Mar, 2006 ($2.99, limited series)

1-4-Sumerak-s/Gurihiru-a. 1-Wolverine & Sabretooth app. 3.00
...: The Power of X (2006, $6.99, digest size) r/#1-4 7.00

X-MEN AND THE MICRONAUTS, THE
Marvel Comics Group: Jan, 1984 - No. 4, Apr, 1984 (Limited series)

1-4: Guice-c/a(p) in all 5.00

X-MEN: APOCALYPSE/DRACULA
Marvel Comics: Apr, 2006 - No. 4, July, 2006 ($2.99, limited series)

1-4-Tieri-s/Henry-a/Jae Lee-c 3.00
TPB (2006, $10.99) r/series; cover gallery 11.00

X-Men: Emperor Vulcan #4 © MAR

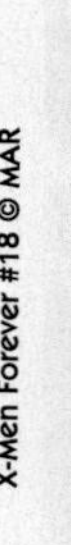

X-Men Forever #18 © MAR

X-Men: Hidden Years #8 © MAR

	GD 2.0	VG 4.0	FN 6.0	VF 8.0	VF/NM 9.0	NM- 9.2

X-MEN ARCHIVES
Marvel Comics: Jan, 1995 - No. 4, Apr, 1995 ($2.25, limited series)
1-4: Reprints Legion stories from New Mutants. 4-Magneto app. 3.00

X-MEN ARCHIVES FEATURING CAPTAIN BRITAIN
Marvel Comics: July, 1995 - No. 7, 1996 ($2.95, limited series)
1-7: Reprints early Capt. Britain stories 3.00

X-MEN: BATTLE OF THE ATOM
Marvel Comics: Nov, 2013 - No. 2, Dec, 2013 ($3.99, bookends for X-Men title crossover)
1,2: 1-Bendis-s/Cho-a/Art Adams-c; bonus pin-ups of the various X-teams 4.00

X-MEN BLACK SUN (See Black Sun:...)

X-MEN BOOKS OF ASKANI
Marvel Comics: 1995 ($2.95, one-shot)
1-Painted pin-ups w/text 3.00

X-MEN: CHILDREN OF THE ATOM
Marvel Comics: Nov, 1999 - No. 6 ($2.99, limited series)
1-6-Casey-s; X-Men before issue #1. 1-3-Rude-c/a. 4-Paul Smith-a/Rude-c. 5,6-Essad Ribic-c/a 3.00
TPB (11/01, $16.95) r/series; sketch pages; Casey intro. 17.00

X-MEN CHRONICLES
Marvel Comics: Mar, 1995 - No. 2, June, 1995 ($3.95, limited series)
1,2: Age of Apocalypse x-over. 1-wraparound-c 5.00

X-MEN: CLANDESTINE
Marvel Comics: Oct, 1996 - No. 2, Nov, 1996 ($2.95, limited series, 48 pgs.)
1,2: Alan Davis-c(p)/a(p)/scripts & Mark Farmer-c(i)/a(i) in all; wraparound-c 4.00

X-MEN CLASSIC (Formerly Classic X-Men)
Marvel Comics: No. 46, Apr, 1990 - No. 110, Aug, 1995 ($1.25/$1.50)
46-110: Reprints from X-Men. 54-(52 pgs.). 57,60-63,65-Russell-c(i); 62-r/X-Men #158(Rogue). 66-r/#162(Wolverine). 69-Begins-r of Paul Smith issues (#165 on). 70,79,90,97(52 pgs.). 70-r/X-Men #166. 90-r/#186. 100-($1.50). 104-r/X-Men #200 3.00

X-MEN CLASSICS
Marvel Comics Group: Dec, 1983 - No. 3, Feb, 1984 ($2.00, Baxter paper)
1-3: X-Men-r by Neal Adams 6.00
NOTE: *Zeck c-1-3.*

X-MEN: COLOSSUS BLOODLIINE
Marvel Comics: Nov, 2005 - No. 5, Mar, 2006 ($2.99, limited series)
1-5-Colossus returns to Russia; David Hine-s/Jorge Lucas-a; Bachalo-c 3.00
TPB (2006, $13.99) r/#1-5 14.00

X-MEN: DEADLY GENESIS (See Uncanny X-Men #475)
Marvel Comics: Jan, 2006 - No. 6, July, 2006 ($3.99/$3.50, limited series)
1-($3.99) Silvestri-c swipe of Giant-Size X-Men #1; Hairsine-a/Brubaker-s 4.00
2-6-($3.50) 2-Silvestri-c; Banshee killed. 4-Intro Kid Vulcan 3.50
HC (2006, $24.99, dust jacket) r/#1-6 25.00
SC (2006, $19.99) r/#1-6 20.00

X-MEN: DIE BY THE SWORD
Marvel Comics: Dec, 2007 - No. 5, Feb, 2008 ($2.99, limited series)
1-5-Excalibur and The Exiles app.; Claremont-s/Santacruz-a 3.00
TPB (2008, $13.99) r/#1-5; handbook pages of Merlyn, Roma and Saturne 14.00

X-MEN: DIVIDED WE STAND
Marvel Comics: June, 2008 - No. 2, July, 2008 ($3.99, limited series)
1,2-Short stories by various; Peterson-c 4.00

X-MEN: EARTHFALL
Marvel Comics: Sept, 1996 ($2.95, one-shot)
1-r/Uncanny X-Men #232-234; wraparound-c 4.00

X-MEN: EMPEROR VULCAN
Marvel Comics: Nov, 2007 - No. 5, Mar, 2008 ($2.99, limited series)
1-5: 1-Starjammers app.; Yost-s/Diaz-a/Tan-c 3.00
TPB (2008, $13.99) r/#1-5 14.00

X-MEN: EVOLUTION (Based on the animated series)
Marvel Comics: Feb, 2002 - No. 9, Sept, 2002 ($2.25)
1-9: 1-8-Grayson-s/Udon-a. 9-Farber-s/J.J.Kirby-a 3.00
TPB (7/02, $8.99) r/#1-4 9.00
Vol. 2 TPB (2003, $11.99) r/#5-9; Asamiya-c 12.00

X-MEN FAIRY TALES
Marvel Comics: July, 2006 - No. 4, Oct, 2006 ($2.99, limited series)
1-4-Re-imagining of classic stories; Cebulski-s. 2-Baker-a. 3-Sienkiewicz-a. 4-Kobayashi-a 3.00
TPB (2006, $10.99) r/#1-4 11.00

X-MEN/ FANTASTIC FOUR
Marvel Comics: Feb, 2005 - No. 5, June, 2005 ($3.50, limited series)
1-5-Pat Lee-a/c; Yoshida-s; the Brood app. 3.50
HC (2005, $19.99, 7 1/2" x 11", dustjacket) oversized r/#1-5; cover gallery 20.00

X-MEN FIRST CLASS
Marvel Comics: Nov, 2006 - No. 8, Jun, 2007 ($2.99, limited series)
1-8-Xavier's first class of X-Men; Cruz-a/Parker-s. 5-Thor app. 7-Scarlet Witch app. 3.00
... Special 1 (7/07, $3.99) Nowlan-c; Nowlan, Paul Smith, Coover, Dragotta & Allred-a 4.00
... - Tomorrow's Brightest HC (2007, $24.99, d.j) r/#1-8; cover & character design art 25.00
... - Tomorrow's Brightest SC (2007, $19.99) r/#1-8; cover & character design art 20.00

X-MEN FIRST CLASS (2nd series)
Marvel Comics: Aug, 2007 - No. 16, Nov, 2008 ($2.99)
1-16: 1-Cruz-a/Parker-s; Fantastic Four app. 8-Man-Thing app. 10-Romita Jr.-c 3.00
... Giant-Size Special 1 (12/08, $3.99) 5 new short stories; Haspiel-a; r/X-Men #40 4.00
... - Mutant Mayhem TPB (2008, $13.99) r/#1-5 & X-Men First Class Special 14.00

X-MEN FIRST CLASS FINALS
Marvel Comics: Apr, 2009 - No. 4, July, 2009 ($3.99, limited series)
1-4-Cruz-a/Parker-s. 1-3-Coover-a 4.00

X-MEN FIRSTS
Marvel Comics: Feb, 1996 ($4.95, one-shot)
1-r/Avengers Annual #10, Uncanny X-Men #266, #221; Incredible Hulk #181 5.00

X-MEN FOREVER
Marvel Comics: Jan, 2001 - No. 6, June, 2001 ($3.50, limited series)
1-6-Jean Grey, Iceman, Mystique, Toad, Juggernaut app.; Maguire-a 4.00

X-MEN FOREVER
Marvel Comics: Aug, 2009 - No. 24, July, 2010 ($3.99)
1-24: 1-Claremont-s/Grummett-a/c. 7-Nick Fury app. 4.00
... Alpha 1 (2009, $4.99) r/X-Men (1991) #1-3; 8 page preview of X-Men Forever #1 5.00
... Annual 1 (6/10, $4.99) Wolverine & Jean Grey romance; Sana Takeda-a/c 5.00
... Giant-Size 1 (7/10, $3.99) Grell-a/c; Lilandra & Gladiator app.; r/(Uncanny)X-Men #108 4.00

X-MEN FOREVER 2
Marvel Comics: Aug, 2010 - No. 16, Mar, 2011 ($3.99)
1-16: 1-Claremont-s/Grummett-a/c. 2,3-Spider-Man app. 9,10-Grell-a 4.00

X-MEN: GOLD
Marvel Comics: Jan, 2014 ($5.99, one-shot)
1-50th Anniversary anthology; short stories by various incl. Stan Lee, Simonson, Claremont, Thomas, Olliffe, Wein, Molina, McLeod, Larroca; Coipel-c 6.00

X-MEN: HELLBOUND
Marvel Comics: July, 2010 - No. 3, Sept, 2010 ($3.99, limited series)
1-3-Second Coming x-over; Tolibao-a/Djurdjevic-c; Majik rescued from Limbo 4.00

X-MEN: HELLFIRE CLUB
Marvel Comics: Jan, 2000 - No. 4, Apr, 2000 ($2.50, limited series)
1-4-Origin of the Hellfire Club 3.00

X-MEN: HIDDEN YEARS
Marvel Comics: Dec, 1999 - No. 22, Sept. 2001 ($3.50/$2.50)
1-New adventures from pre-#94 era; Byrne-s/a(p) 4.00
2-4,6-11,13-22-($2.50): 2-Two covers. 3-Ka-Zar app. 8,9-FF-c/app. 3.00
5-($2.75) 3.00
12-($3.50) Magneto-c/app. 4.00

X-MEN: KING BREAKER
Marvel Comics: Feb, 2009 - No. 4, May, 2009 ($3.99, limited series)
1-4-Emperor Vulcan and a Shi'ar invasion; Havok, Rachel Grey and Polaris app. 4.00

X-MEN: KITTY PRYDE - SHADOW & FLAME
Marvel Comics: Aug, 2005 - No. 5, Dec, 2005 ($2.99, limited series)
1-5-Akira Yoshida-s/Paul Smith-a/c; Kitty & Lockheed go to Japan 3.00
TPB (2006, $14.99) r/#1-5 15.00

X-MEN LEGACY (See X-Men 2nd series)

X-MEN LEGACY (Marvel NOW!)
Marvel Comics: Jan, 2013 - No. 24, Apr, 2014; No. 300, May, 2014 ($2.99)
1-24: 1-Legion (Professor X's son); Spurrier-s/Huat-a. 2-X-Men app. 5,6-Molina-a 3.00

X-Men '92 #6 © MAR

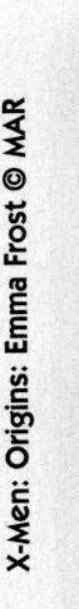

X-Men: Origins: Emma Frost © MAR

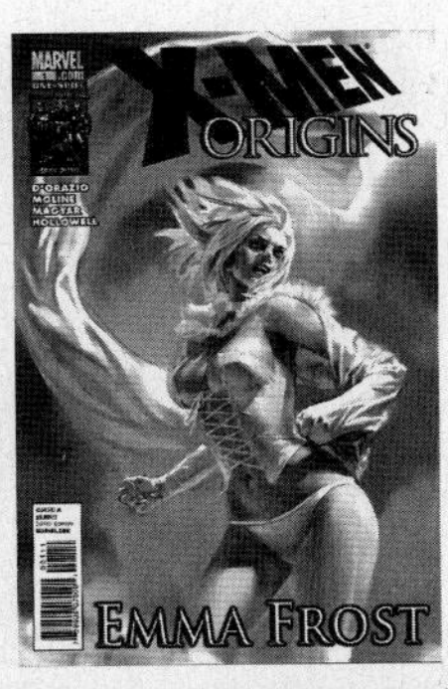

X-Men: Ronin #1 © MAR

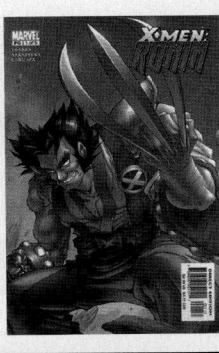

GD 2.0 | VG 4.0 | FN 6.0 | VF 8.0 | VF/NM 9.0 | NM- 9.2

300-(5/14, $4.99) Spurrier, Carey & Gage-s/Huat, Kurth & Sandoval-a; Mann-c 5.00

X-MEN: LIBERATORS
Marvel Comics: Nov, 1998 - No. 4, Feb, 1999 ($2.99, limited series)

1-4-Wolverine, Nightcrawler & Colossus; P. Jimenez 4.00

X-MEN LOST TALES
Marvel Comics: 1997 ($2.99)

1,2-r/Classic X-Men back-up stories 4.00

X-MEN: MAGNETO TESTAMENT
Marvel Comics: Nov, 2008 - No. 5, Mar, 2009 ($3.99, limited series)

1-5-Max Eisenhardt in 1930s Nazi-occupied Poland; Pak-s/DiGiandomenico-a. 5-Back-up story of artist Dina Babbitt with Neal Adams-a 4.00

X-MEN: MANIFEST DESTINY
Marvel Comics: Nov, 2008 - No. 5, Mar, 2009 ($3.99, limited series)

1-5-Short stories of X-Men re-location to San Francisco; s/a by various 4.00
... Nightcrawler 1 (5/09, $3.99) Molina & Syaf-a; Mephisto app. 4.00

X-MEN: MESSIAH COMPLEX
Marvel Comics: Dec, 2007 ($3.99)

1-Part 1 of x-over with X-Men, Uncanny X-Men, X-Factor and New X-Men; 2 covers 4.00
... - Mutant Files (2007, $3.99) Handbook pages of x-over participants; Kolins-c 4.00
HC (2008, $39.99, oversized) r/#1, Uncanny X-Men #492-494, X-Men #205-207, New X-Men #44-46 and X-Factor #25-27 40.00

X-MEN '92 (Secret Wars tie-in)
Marvel Comics: Aug, 2015 - No. 4, Nov, 2015 ($4.99, limited series)

1-4-Koblish-a; Cassandra Nova app. 2-4-X-Force app. 4-Apocalypse cameo 5.00

X-MEN '92 (Follows Secret Wars)
Marvel Comics: May, 2016 - Present ($3.99)

1-10: 1-Firmansyah-a; Omega Red & Alpha Red app. 2-U-Go Girl joins. 3,4-Dracula app. 9,10-New Mutants app. 4.00

X-MEN NOIR
Marvel Comics: Nov, 2008 - No. 4, May, 2009 ($3.99, limited series)

1-4-Pulp-style story set in 1930s NY; Van Lente-s/Calero-a 4.00
...: Mark of Cain (2/10 - No. 4, 5/10, $3.99) Van Lente-s/Calero-a 4.00

X-MEN OMEGA
Marvel Comics: June, 1995 ($3.95, one-shot)

nn-Age of Apocalyse finale 1 3 4 6 8 10
nn-($49.95)-Gold edition 55.00

X-MEN: ORIGINS
Marvel Comics: Oct, 2008 - Sept, 2010 ($3.99, series of one-shots)

...: Beast (11/08) High school years; Carey-s; painted-a/c by Woodward 5.00
...: Cyclops (3/10) Magneto app.; Delperdang-a/Granov-c 1 2 3 5 6 8
...: Deadpool (9/10) Fernandez-a/Swierczynski-s 4 8 12 23 37 50
...: Emma Frost (7/10) Moline-a; r/excerpt from 1st app. in Uncanny X-Men #129 5.00
...: Gambit (8/09) Mr. Sinister, Sabretooth and the Marauders app.; Yardin-a 2 4 6 11 16 20
...: Iceman (1/10) Noto-a 5.00
...: Jean Grey (10/08) Childhood & early X-days; McKeever-s; Mayhew painted-a/c 5.00
...: Nightcrawler (5/10) Cary Nord-a; r/excerpt from 1st app. in Giant-Size X-Men #1 5.00
...: Sabretooth (4/09) Childhood and early meetings with Wolverine; Panosian-a/c 1 2 3 5 6 8
...: Wolverine (6/09) Pre-X-Men days and first meeting with Xavier; Texeira-a/c 5.00

X-MEN: PHOENIX
Marvel Comics: Dec, 1999 - No. 3, Mar, 2000 ($2.50, limited series)

1-3: 1-Apocalypse app. 4.00

X-MEN: PHOENIX - ENDSONG
Marvel Comics: Mar, 2005 - No. 5, June, 2005 ($2.99, limited series)

1-5-The Phoenix Force returns to Earth; Greg Land-c/a; Greg Pak-s 3.00
HC (2005, $19.99, dust jacket) r/#1-5; Land sketch pages 20.00
SC (2006, $14.99) 15.00

X-MEN: PHOENIX - LEGACY OF FIRE
Marvel Comics: July, 2003 - No. 3, Sep, 2003 ($2.99, limited series)

1-3-Manga-style; Ryan Kinnard-s/a/c; intro page art by Adam Warren 3.00

X-MEN: PHOENIX - WARSONG
Marvel Comics: Nov, 2006 - No. 5, Mar, 2007 ($2.99, limited series)

1-5-Tyler Kirkham-a/Greg Pak-s/Marc Silvestri-c 3.00
HC (2007, $19.99, dustjacket) r/#1-5; variant cover gallery and Handbook pages 20.00
SC (2007, $14.99) r/#1-5; variant cover gallery and Handbook pages 15.00

X-MEN: PIXIE STRIKES BACK
Marvel Comics: Apr, 2010 - No. 4, July, 2010 ($3.99, limited series)

1-4-Kathryn Immonen-s/Sara Pichelli-a/Stuart Immonen-c 4.00

X-MEN: PRELUDE TO SCHISM
Marvel Comics: Jul, 2011 - No. 4, Aug, 2011 ($2.99, limited series)

1-4-Jenkins-s/Camuncoli-c. 1-De La Torre-a. 2-Magneto childhood. 3-Conrad-a 3.00

X-MEN PRIME
Marvel Comics: July, 1995 ($4.95, one-shot)

nn-Post Age of Apocalyse begins 1 3 4 6 8 10

X-MEN RARITIES
Marvel Comics: 1995 ($5.95, one-shot)

nn-Reprints hard-to-find stories 6.00

X-MEN ROAD TO ONSLAUGHT
Marvel Comics: Oct, 1996 ($2.50, one-shot)

nn-Retells Onslaught Saga 3.00

X-MEN: RONIN
Marvel Comics: May, 2003 - No. 5, July, 2003 ($2.99, limited series)

1-5-Manga-style X-Men; Torres-s/Nakatsuka-a 3.00

X-MEN: SCHISM
Marvel Comics: Sept, 2011 - No. 5, Dec, 2011 ($4.99/$3.99, limited series)

1-($4.99) Aaron-s/Pacheco-a/c 5.00
2-5-($3.99) 2-Cho-a/c. 3-Acuña-a/c. 4-Alan Davis-a/c. 5-Adam Kubert-a 4.00

X-MEN: SEARCH FOR CYCLOPS
Marvel Comics: Oct, 2000 - No. 4, Mar, 2001 ($2.99, limited series)

1-4-Two covers (Raney, Pollina); Raney-a 4.00

X-MEN: SECOND COMING
Marvel Comics: May, 2010 - No. 2, Sept, 2010 ($3.99)

1-Cable & Hope return to the present; Bastion app.; Finch-a; covers by Granov & Finch 4.00
2-Conclusion to x-over; covers by Granov & Finch 4.00
...: Prepare (4/10, free) previews x-over; short story w/Immonen-a; cover sketch art 3.00

X-MEN / SPIDER-MAN ("X-Men and Spider-Man" on cover)
Marvel Comics: Jan, 2009 - No. 4, Apr, 2009 ($3.99, limited series)

1-4: 1-Team-up from pre-blue Beast days; Kraven app.; Gage-s/Alberti-a 4.00

X-MEN SPOTLIGHT ON... STARJAMMERS (Also see X-Men #104)
Marvel Comics: 1990 - No. 2, 1990 ($4.50, 52 pgs.)

1,2: Features Starjammers 5.00

X-MEN SURVIVAL GUIDE TO THE MANSION
Marvel Comics: Aug, 1993 ($6.95, spiralbound)

1 7.00

X-MEN: THE COMPLETE AGE OF APOCALYPSE EPIC
Marvel Comics: 2005 - Vol. 4, 2006 ($29.99, TPB)

Book 1-4: Chronological reprintings of the crossover 30.00

X-MEN: THE EARLY YEARS
Marvel Comics: May, 1994 - No. 17, Sept, 1995 ($1.50/$2.50)

1-16: r/X-Men #1-8 w/new-c 3.00
17-$2.50-c; r/X-Men #17,18 4.00

X-MEN: THE END
Marvel Comics: Oct, 2004 - No. 6, Feb, 2005 ($2.99, limited series)

1-6-Claremont-s/Chen-a/Land-c 3.00
... Book One: Dreamers and Demons TPB (2005, $14.99) r/#1-6 15.00

X-MEN: THE END - HEROES AND MARTYRS (Volume 2)
Marvel Comics: May, 2005 - No. 6, Oct, 2005 ($2.99, limited series)

1-6-Claremont-s/Chen-a/Land-c; continued from X-Men: The End 3.00
... Vol. 2 TPB (2006, $14.99) r/#1-6 15.00

X-MEN: THE END (MEN & X-MEN) (Volume 3)
Marvel Comics: Mar, 2006 - No. 6, Aug, 2006 ($2.99, limited series)

1-6-Claremont-s/Chen-a. 1-Land-c. 2-6-Gene Ha-c 3.00
... Vol. 3 TPB (2006, $14.99) r/#1-6 15.00

X-MEN: THE MANGA

X-Men 2099 #35 © MAR

X-Men Unlimited #9 © MAR

X-O Manowar #34 © VAL

GD 2.0 | VG 4.0 | FN 6.0 | VF 8.0 | VF/NM 9.0 | NM- 9.2

Marvel Comics: Mar, 1998 - No. 26, June, 1999 ($2.99, B&W)
1-26-English version of Japanese X-Men comics: 23,24-Randy Green-c 4.00

X-MEN: THE MOVIE
Marvel Comics: Aug, 2000; Sept, 2000
Adaptation (9/00, $5.95) Macchio-s/Williams & Lanning-a 6.00
Adaptation TPB (9/00, $14.95) Movie adaptation and key reprints of main characters; four photo covers (movie X, Magneto, Rogue, Wolverine) 15.00
Prequel: Magneto (8/00, $5.95) Texeira & Palmiotti-a; art & photo covers 6.00
Prequel: Rogue (8/00, $5.95) Evans & Nikolakakis-a; art & photo covers 6.00
Prequel: Wolverine (8/00, $5.95) Waller & McKenna-a; art & photo covers 6.00
TPB X-Men: Beginnings (8/00, $14.95) reprints 3 prequels w/photo-c 15.00

X-MEN 2: THE MOVIE
Marvel Comics: 2003
Adaptation (6/03, $3.50) Movie adaptation; photo-c; Austen-s/Zircher-a 4.00
Adaptation TPB (2003, $12.99) Movie adaptation & r/Prequels Nightcrawler & Wolverine 13.00
Prequel: Nightcrawler (5/03, $3.50) Kerschl-a; photo cover 4.00
Prequel: Wolverine (5/03, $3.50) Mandrake-a; photo cover; Sabretooth app. 4.00

X-MEN: THE 198 (See House of M)
Marvel Comics: Mar, 2006 - No. 5, July, 2006 ($2.99, limited series)
1-5-Hine-s/Muniz-a 3.00
... Files (2006, $3.99) profiles of the 198 mutants who kept their powers after House of M 4.00
Decimation: The 198 (2006, $15.99, TPB) r/#1-5 & X-Men: The 198 Files 16.00

X-MEN: THE TIMES AND LIFE OF LUCAS BISHOP
Marvel Comics: Apr, 2009 - No. 3, June, 2009 ($3.99, limited series)
1-3-Swierczynski-s/Stroman-a. 1-Bishop's birth and childhood 4.00

X-MEN: THE ULTRA COLLECTION
Marvel Comics: Dec, 1994 - No. 5, Apr, 1995 ($2.95, limited series)
1-5: Pin-ups; no scripts 3.00

X-MEN: THE WEDDING ALBUM
Marvel Comics: 1994 ($2.95, magazine size, one-shot)
1-Wedding of Scott Summers & Jean Grey 4.00

X-MEN: TO SERVE AND PROTECT
Marvel Comics: Jan, 2011 - No. 4, Apr, 2011 ($3.99, limited series)
1-4-Short story anthology by various.1-Bradshaw-c. 2-Camuncoli-c 4.00

X-MEN TRUE FRIENDS
Marvel Comics: Sept, 1999 - No. 3, Nov, 1999 ($2.99, limited series)
1-3-Claremont-s/Leonardi-a 4.00

X-MEN 2099 (Also see 2099: World of Tomorrow)
Marvel Comics: Oct, 1993 - No. 35, Aug, 1996 ($1.25/$1.50/$1.95)
1-($1.75)-Foil-c; Ron Lim/Adam Kubert-a begins 4.00
1-2nd printing ($1.75) 3.00
1-Gold edition (15,000 made); sold thru Diamond for $19.40 20.00
2-24,26-35: 3-Death of Tina; Lim-c/a(p) in #1-8. 8-Bound-in trading card sheet. 35-Nostromo (from X-Nation) app; storyline cont'd in 2099: World of Tomorrow 3.00
25-($2.50)-Double sized 4.00
Special 1 ($3.95) 4.00
...: Oasis ($5.95, one-shot) -Hildebrandt Bros.-c/a 6.00

X-MEN ULTRA III PREVIEW
Marvel Comics: 1995 ($2.95)
nn-Kubert-a 3.00

X-MEN UNIVERSE
Marvel Comics: Dec, 1999 - No. 15, Feb, 2001 ($4.99/$3.99)
1-8-Reprints stories from recent X-Men titles 5.00
9-15-($3.99) 4.00

X-MEN UNIVERSE: PAST, PRESENT AND FUTURE
Marvel Comics: Feb, 1999 ($2.99, one-shot)
1-Previews 1999 X-Men events; background info 3.00

X-MEN UNLIMITED
Marvel Comics: 1993 - No. 50, Sept, 2003 ($3.95/$2.99, 68 pgs.)
1-Chris Bachalo-c/a; Quesada-a. 6.00
2-11: 2-Origin of Magneto script. 3-Sabretooth-c/story. 10-Dark Beast vs. Beast; Mark Waid script. 11-Magneto & Rogue 5.00
12-33: 12-Begin $2.99-c; Onslaught x-over; Juggernaut-c/app. 19-Caliafore-a. 20-Generation X app. 27-Origin Thunderbird. 29-Maximum Security x-over; Bishop-c/app. 30-Mahfood-a. 31-Stelfreeze-c/a. 32-Dazzler; Thompson-c/a 33-Kaluta-c 4.00

GD 2.0 | VG 4.0 | FN 6.0 | VF 8.0 | VF/NM 9.0 | NM- 9.2

34-37,39,40-42-($3.50) 34-Von Eeden-a. 35-Finch, Conner, Maguire-a. 36-Chiodo-c/a; Larroca, Totleben-a. 39-Bachalo-c; Pearson-a. 41-Bachalo-c; X-Statix app. 4.00
38-($2.25) Kitty Pryde; Robertson-a 3.00
43-50-($2.50) 43-Sienkiewicz-c/a; Paul Smith-a. 45-Noto-c. 46-Bisley-a. 47-Warren-s/Mays-a. 48-Wolverine story w/Isanove painted-a 3.00
X-Men Legends Vol. 4: Hated and Feared TPB (2003, $19.99) r/stories by various 20.00
NOTE: ***Bachalo** c/a-1. **Quesada** a-1. **Waid** scripts-10*

X-MEN UNLIMITED
Marvel Comics: Apr, 2004 - No. 14, Jun, 2006 ($2.99)
1-14: 1-6-Pat Lee-c; short stories by various. 2-District X preview; Granov-a 3.00

X-MEN VS. AGENTS OF ATLAS
Marvel Comics: Dec, 2009 - No. 2, Jan, 2010 ($3.99, limited series)
1,2-Pagulayan-a. 1-McGuinness-c. 2-Granov-c 4.00

X-MEN VS. DRACULA
Marvel Comics: Dec, 1993 ($1.75)
1-r/X-Men Annual #6; Austin-c(i) 4.00

X-MEN VS. THE AVENGERS, THE
Marvel Comics Group: Apr, 1987 - No. 4, July, 1987 ($1.50, limited series, Baxter paper)
1-Silvestri-a/c 1 2 3 5 6 8
2-4: 2,3-Silvestri-a/c. 4-Pollard-a/c 5.00

X-MEN VS. THE BROOD, THE
Marvel Comics Group: Sept, 1996 - No. 2, Oct, 1996 ($2.95, limited series)
1,2-Wraparound-c; Ostrander-s/Hitch-a(p) 4.00
TPB('97, $16.99) reprints X-Men/Brood: Day of Wrath #1,2 & Uncanny X-Men #232-234 17.00

X-MEN VISIONARIES
Marvel Comics: 1995,1996,2000 (trade paperbacks)
nn-($8.95) Reprints X-Men stories; Adam & Andy Kubert-a 9.00
...2: The Neal Adams Collection (1996) r/X-Men #56-63,65 30.00
...2: The Neal Adams Col. (2nd printing, 2000, $24.95) new Adams-c 25.00

X-MEN/WILDC.A.T.S.: THE DARK AGE (See also WildC.A.T.S./X-Men...)
Marvel Comics: 1998 ($4.50, one-shot)
1-Two covers (Broome & Golden); Ellis-s 5.00

X-MEN: WORLDS APART
Marvel Comics: Dec, 2008 - No. 4, Mar, 2009 ($3.99, limited series)
1-4-Storm and the Black Panther vs. the Shadow King. 1-Campbell-c 4.00

X-MEN: WORST X-MAN EVER
Marvel Comics: Apr, 2016 - No. 5, Aug, 2016 ($3.99, limited series)
1-5: 1-Intro. Bailey Hoskins; Max Bemis-s/Michael Walsh-a. 3,4-Magneto app. 4.00

X-NATION 2099
Marvel Comics: Mar, 1996 - No. 6, Aug, 1996 ($1.95)
1-($3.95)-Humberto Ramos-a(p); wraparound, foil-c 5.00
2-6: 2,3-Ramos-a. 4-Exodus-c/app. 6-Reed Richards app 3.00

X NECROSIA
Marvel Comics: Dec, 2009 ($3.99)
1-Beginning of X-Force/X-Men/New Mutants x-over; Crain-a; Selene returns 4.00
...: The Gathering (2/10, $3.99) Wither, Blink, Senyaka, Mortis & Eliphas short stories 4.00

X-O MANOWAR (1st Series)
Valiant/Acclaim Comics (Valiant) No. 43 on: Feb, 1992 - No. 68, Sept, 1996 ($1.95/$2.25/$2.50, high quality)
0-(8/93, $3.50)-Wraparound embossed chromium-c by Quesada; Solar app.; origin Aric (X-O Manowar) 5.00
0-Gold variant 2 4 6 11 16 20
1-Intro/1st app. & partial origin of Aric (X-O Manowar); Barry Smith/Layton-a; Shooter & Englehart-s 3 6 9 16 23 30
2,3: 2-B. Smith/Layton-c. 3-Layton-c(i) 1 3 4 6 8 10
4-1st app. Shadowman; Harbinger app. 3 6 9 19 30 40
5,6: 5-B. Smith-c. 6-Begin $2.25-c; Ditko-a(p) 1 2 3 5 6 8
7-15: 7,8-Unity x-overs. 7-Miller-c. 8-Simonson-c. 12-1st app. Randy Calder. 14,15-Turok-c/stories 4.00
15-Hot pink logo variant; came with Ultra Pro Rigid Comic Sleeves box; no price on-c 1 2 3 5 6 8
16-24,26-43: 20-Serial number contest insert. 27-29-Turok x-over. 28-Bound-in trading card. 30-1st app. new "good skin"; Solar app. 33-Chaos Effect Delta Pt. 3. 42-Shadowman app.; includes X-O Manowar Birthquake! Prequel 3.00
25-($3.50)-Has 16 pg. Armorines #0 bound-in w/origin 4.00
44-66: 44-Begin $2.50-c. 50-X, 50-O, 51, 52, 63-Bart Sears-c/a/scripts.

X-O Manowar (2012 series) #15 © VAL

X-Statix #2 © MAR

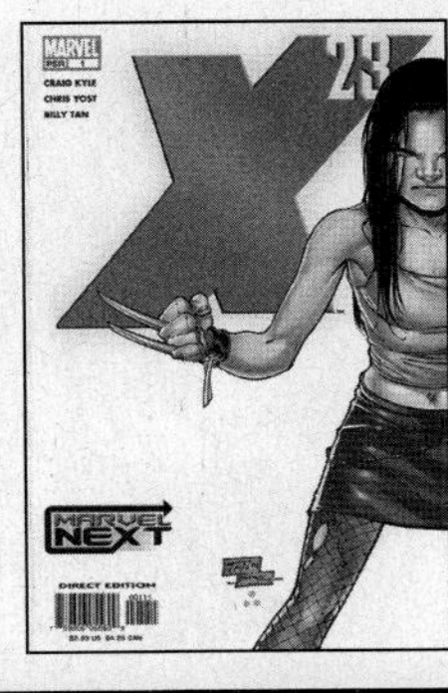

X-23 #1 © MAR

	GD 2.0	VG 4.0	FN 6.0	VF 8.0	VF/NM 9.0	NM- 9.2

67 1 2 3 5 6 8
68-Revealed that Aric's past stories were premonitions of his future 2 4 6 10 14 18
...: Birth HC (2008, $24.95) recolored reprints #0-6; script and breakdowns for #0; cover gallery; new "The Rise of Lydia" story by Layton and Leeke 25.00
Trade paperback nn (1993, $9.95)-Polybagged with copy of X-O Database #1 inside 15.00
Yearbook 1 (4/95, $2.95) 4.00
NOTE: *Layton a-1i, 2i(part); c-1, 2i, 3i, 6i, 21i.* ***Reese*** *a-4i(part); c-26i.*

X-O MANOWAR (2nd Series)(Also see Iron Man/X-O Manowar: Heavy Metal)
Acclaim Comics (Valiant Heroes): V2#1, Oct, 1996 - No. 21, Jun, 1998 ($2.50)
V2#1-21: 1-Mark Waid & Brian Augustyn scripts begin; 1st app. Donavon Wylie; Rand Banion dies; painted variant-c exists. 2-Donavon Wylie becomes new X-O Manowar. 7-9-Augustyn-s. 10-Copycat-c 3.00

X-O MANOWAR (3rd series)
Valiant Entertainment: May, 2012 - No. 50, Sept, 2016 ($3.99)
1-Robert Venditti-s/Cary Nord-a/Esad Ribic-c; origin re-told 4.00
1-Pullbox variant-c by Nord 5.00
1-Variant-c by David Aja 10.00
1-QR Voice variant-c by Jelena Kevic-Djurdjevic 20.00
2-24: 2-Origin continues. 2,3-Kevic-Djurdjevic-c. 5-8-Ninjak app.; Garbett-a. 9,10-Hairsine-a 11-14-Planet Death; Nord-a. 19-21-Unity tie-in 4.00
2-5,8-14-Pullbox variant covers. 2-Lozzi. 3-Suayan. 4-Kramer. 5-Tan. 14-Eight-bit art 5.00
25-($4.99) Hitch-a; Armor Hunters app., Owly & Wormy short story by Runton 5.00
26-37,39-49: 26-29-Armor Hunters tie-in. 30-32-Armorines app. 34-37-Dead Hand. 47-49-Polybagged with micro-print 4.00
38-(7/15, $4.99) Wedding of Aric and Saana; Doctor Mirage app.; flashbacks 5.00
50-(9/16, $4.99) Polybagged; wraparound-c by 50 artists; art by various 5.00
#0 (10/14, $3.99) Flashback to Aric before his kidnapping; Clay Mann-a 4.00
Annual 2016 #1 (5/16, $5.99) Art by JG Jones, Perez, McKone, Gorham, De La Torre 6.00
...: Commander Trill #0 (12/15, $3.99) Origin of Trill; Venditti-s/Portela-a 4.00
...: Valiant 25th Anniversary Special (6/15, $3.99) Origin of Shanhara; Venditti-s/Cafu-a 4.00

X-O MANOWAR FAN EDITION
Acclaim Comics (Valiant Heroes): Feb, 1997 (Overstreet's FAN giveaway)
1-Reintro the Armorines & the Hard Corps; 1st app. Citadel; Augustyn scripts; McKone-c/a 4.00

X-O MANOWAR/IRON MAN: IN HEAVY METAL (See Iron Man/X-O Manowar: Heavy Metal)
Acclaim Comics (Valiant Heroes): Sept, 1996 ($2.50, one-shot)
(1st Marvel/Valiant x-over)
1-Pt 1 of X-O Manowar/Iron Man x-over; Arnim Zola app.; Nicieza scripts; Andy Smith-a 5.00

XOMBI
DC Comics (Milestone): Jan, 1994 - No. 21, Feb, 1996 ($1.75/$2.50)
0-($1.95)-Shadow War x-over; Simonson silver ink varnish-c 3.00
1-21: 1-John Byrne-c 3.00
1-Platinum 8.00

XOMBI
DC Comics: May, 2011 - No. 6, Oct, 2011 ($2.99)
1-6-Rozum-s/Irving-a/c 3.00

X-PATROL
Marvel Comics (Amalgam): Apr, 1996 ($1.95, one-shot)
1-Cruz-a(p) 3.00

XSE
Marvel Comics: Nov, 1996 - No. 4, Feb, 1997 ($1.95, limited series)
1-4: 1-Bishop & Shard app. 3.00
1-Variant-c 4.00

X-STATIX
Marvel Comics: Sept, 2002 - No. 26, Oct, 2004 ($2.99/$2.25)
1-($2.99) Allred-a/c; intro. Venus Dee Milo; back-up w/Cooke-a 4.00
2-9-($2.25) 4-Quitely-c. 5-Pope-c/a 3.00
10-26: 10-Begin $2.99-c; Bond-a; U-Go Girl flashback. 13,14-Spider-Man app. 21-25-Avengers app. 26-Team dies 3.00
... Vol. 1: Good Omens TPB (2003, $11.99) r/#1-5 12.00
... Vol. 2: Good Guys & Bad Guys TPB (2003, $15.99) r/#6-10 & Wolverine/Doop #1&2 16.00
... Vol. 3: Back From the Dead TPB (2004, $19.99) r/#11-18 20.00
... Vol. 4: X-Statix Vs. the Avengers TPB (2004, $19.99) r/#19-26; pin-ups 20.00

X-STATIX PRESENTS: DEAD GIRL
Marvel Comics: Mar, 2006 - No. 5, July, 2006 ($2.99, limited series)
1-5-Dr. Strange, Dead Girl, Miss America, Tike app. Milligan-s/Dragotta & Allred-a 3.00

TPB (2006, $13.99) r/series 14.00

X-TERMINATION (Crossover with Astonishing X-Men and X-Treme X-Men)
Marvel Comics: May, 2013 - No. 2, Jun, 2013 ($3.99)
1,2-Lapham-s/David Lopez-a 4.00

X-TERMINATORS
Marvel Comics: Oct, 1988 - No. 4, Jan, 1989 ($1.00, limited series)
1-1st app.; X-Men/X-Factor tie-in; Williamson-i 5.00
2-4 4.00

X, THE MAN WITH THE X-RAY EYES (See Movie Comics)

X-TINCTION AGENDA (Secret Wars tie-in)
Marvel Comics: Aug, 2015 - No. 4, Nov, 2015 ($3.99, limited series)
1-4-Guggenheim-s/Di Giandomenico-a; Havok & Wolfsbane app. 4.00

X-TREME X-MEN (Also see Mekanix)
Marvel Comics: July, 2001 - No. 46, Jun, 2004 ($2.99/$3.50)
1-Claremont-s/Larroca-c/a 4.00
2-24: 2-Two covers (Larroca & Pacheco); Psylocke killed 3.00
25-35, 40-46: 25-30-God Loves, Man Kills II; Stryker app.; Kordey-a 3.00
36-39-($3.50) 3.50
Annual 2001 ($4.95) issue opens longways 5.00
... Vol. 1: Destiny TPB (2002, $19.95) r/#1-9 20.00
... Vol. 2: Invasion TPB (2003, $19.99) r/#10-18 20.00
... Vol. 3: Schism TPB (2003, $16.99) r/#19-23; X-Treme X-Posé #1&2 17.00
... Vol. 4: Mekanix TPB (2003, $16.99) r/Mekanix #1-6 17.00
... Vol. 5: God Loves Man Kills TPB (2003, $19.99) r/#25-30 20.00
... Vol. 6: Intifada TPB (2004, $16.99) r/#24,31-35 17.00
... Vol. 7: Storm the Arena TPB (2004, $16.99) r/#36-39 17.00
... Vol. 8: Prisoner of Fire TPB (2004, $19.99) r/#40-46 and Annual 2001 20.00

X-TREME X-MEN
Marvel Comics: Sept, 2012 - No. 13, Jun, 2013 ($2.99)
1-13: 1-Pak-s/Segovia-a; Dazzler with alternate reality Wolverine, Nightcrawler, Emma 3.00
7.1-(2/12) Cyclops & The Brood app. 3.00

X-TREME X-MEN: SAVAGE LAND
Marvel Comics: Nov, 2001 - No. 4, Feb, 2002 ($2.99, limited series)
1-4-Claremont-s/Sharpe-c/a; Beast app. 3.00

X-TREME X-POSE
Marvel Comics: Jan, 2003 - No. 2, Feb, 2003 ($2.99, limited series)
1,2-Claremont-s/Ranson-a/Migliari-c 3.00

X-23 (See debut in NYX #3)(See NYX X-23 HC for reprint)
Marvel Comics: Mar, 2005 - No. 6, July, 2005 ($2.99, limited series)
1-Origin of the Wolverine clone girl; Tan-a 2 4 6 9 12 15
1-Variant Billy Tan-c with red background 2 4 6 11 16 20
2-6-Origin continues 5.00
2-Variant B&W sketch-c 1 3 4 6 8 10
One shot 1 (5/10, $3.99) Urasov-c/Liu-s; Wolverine & Jubilee app. 2 4 6 11 16 20
...: Innocence Lost MGC 1 (5/11, $1.00) r/#1 with "Marvel's Greatest Comics" cover logo 3.00
...: Innocence Lost TPB (2006, $15.99) r/#1-6 20.00

X-23
Marvel Comics: Nov, 2010 - No. 21, May, 2012 ($3.99/$2.99)
1-Marjorie Liu-s/Will Conrad-a; origin retold; Luo-c 3 6 9 14 20 25
1-Djurdjevic variant-c 3 6 9 14 20 25
1-Dell'Otto variant-c 21 42 63 147 324 500
2-Luo-c 1 3 4 6 8 10
2-Mayhew variant-c 6 12 18 33 69 100
3-21: 3,10-12,17-19-Takeda-a. 8,9-Daken app. 13-16-Spider-Man app.; Noto-a. 20-Jubilee app.; Noto-a. 21-Silent issue; Noto-a 4.00

X-23: TARGET X
Marvel Comics: Feb, 2007 - No. 6, July, 2007 ($2.99, limited series)
1-Kyle & Yost-s/Choi & Oback-a 2 4 6 9 12 15
2-6: 6-Gallery of variant covers and sketches 6.00
TPB (2007, $15.99) r/#1-6; gallery of variant covers and sketches 16.00

X-UNIVERSE
Marvel Comics: May, 1995 - No. 2, June, 1995 ($3.50, limited series)
1,2: Age of Apocalypse 5.00

X-VENTURE (Super Heroes)
Victory Magazines Corp.: July, 1947 - No. 2, Nov, 1947

X-Women #1 © MAR

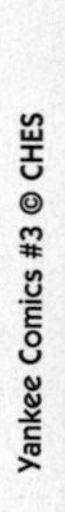

Yankee Comics #3 © CHES

Years of Future Past #4 © MAR

	GD 2.0	VG 4.0	FN 6.0	VF 8.0	VF/NM 9.0	NM- 9.2

1-Atom Wizard, Mystery Shadow, Lester Trumble begin 116 232 348 742 1271 1800
2 57 114 171 362 619 875

X-WOMEN
Marvel Comics: 2010 ($4.99, one-shot)
1-Milo Manara-a/Chris Claremont-s; a female X-Men adventure; Quesada afterword 5.00

XYR (See Eclipse Graphic Album Series #21)

YAK YAK
Dell Publishing Co.: No. 1186, May-July, 1961 - No. 1348, Apr-June, 1962
Four Color 1186 (#1)- Jack Davis-c/a; 2 versions, one minus 3 pgs. 8 16 24 54 102 150
Four Color 1348 (#2)-Davis c/a 7 14 21 46 86 125

YAKKY DOODLE & CHOPPER (TV) (See Dell Giant #44)
Gold Key: Dec, 1962 (Hanna-Barbera)
1 6 12 18 42 79 115

YANG (See House of Yang)
Charlton Comics: Nov, 1973 - No. 13, May, 1976; V14#15, Sept, 1985 - No. 17, Jan, 1986 (No V14#14, series resumes with #15)
1-Origin; Sattler-a begins; slavery-s 2 4 6 11 16 20
2-13(1976) 1 2 3 6 9 10
15-17(1986): 15-Reprints #1 (Low print run) 6.00
3,10,11(Modern Comics-r, 1977) 6.00

YANKEE COMICS
Harry 'A' Chesler: Sept, 1941 - No. 7, 1942?
1-Origin The Echo, The Enchanted Dagger, Yankee Doodle Jones, The Firebrand, & The Scarlet Sentry; Black Satan app.; Yankee Doodle Jones app. on all covers 226 452 678 1446 2473 3500
2-Origin Johnny Rebel; Major Victory app.; Barry Kuda begins 103 206 309 659 1130 1600
3,4: 4-(3/42) 77 154 231 493 847 1200
4 (nd, 1940s; 7-1/4x5", 68 pgs, distr. to the service)-Foxy Grandpa, Tom, Dick & Harry, Impy, Ace & Deuce, Dot & Dash, Ima Slooth by Jack Cole (Remington Morse publ.) 19 38 57 109 172 235
5-7 (nd; 10¢, 7-1/4x5", 68 pgs.)(Remington Morse publ.)-urges readers to send their copies to servicemen. 15 30 45 88 137 185

YANKEE DOODLE THE SPIRIT OF LIBERTY
Spire Publications: 1984 (no price, 36 pgs)
nn-Al Hartley-s/c/a 2 4 6 9 13 16

YANKS IN BATTLE
Quality Comics Group: Sept, 1956 - No. 4, Dec, 1956
1-Cuidera-c(i) 14 28 42 76 108 140
2-4: Cuidera-c(i) 9 18 27 47 61 75

YARDBIRDS, THE (G. I. Joe's Sidekicks)
Ziff-Davis Publishing Co.: Summer, 1952
1-By Bob Oskner 16 32 48 94 147 200

YARNS OF YELLOWSTONE
World Color Press: 1972 (50¢, 36 pgs.)
nn-Illustrated by Bill Chapman 2 4 6 9 12 15

YEAH!
DC Comics (Homage): Oct, 1999 - No. 9, Jun, 2000 ($2.95)
1-Bagge-s/Hernandez-a 3.00
2-9: 2-Editorial page contains adult language 3.00

YEAR OF MARVELS, A
Marvel Comics: ($4.99)
...: The Amazing (6/16) Spider-Man vs. The Vulture; Ant-Man 5.00
...: The Incredible (8/16) Spider-Man & D-Man story; Wolverine (X-23) & She-Hulk story 5.00
...: The Unbeatable (12/16) Nick Fury story; Rocket Raccoon & Tippy-Toe story 5.00
...: The Uncanny (2/17) Hawkeye (Kate Bishop) story; Punisher story 5.00
...: The Unstoppable (10/16) Nova & Iron Man story; Winter Soldier story 5.00

YEARS OF FUTURE PAST (Secret Wars Battleworld tie-in)
Marvel Comics: Aug, 2015 - No. 5, Nov, 2015 ($4.99/$3.99, limited series)
1-($4.99) Bennett-s/Norton-a; Art Adams-c; Kitty Pryde, Wolverine, Colossus app. 5.00
2-5-($3.99) Storm, Magneto, Mystique, Blob, Sentinels app. 4.00

YELLOW CLAW (Also see Giant Size Master of Kung Fu)
Atlas Comics (MjMC): Oct, 1956 - No. 4, Apr, 1957

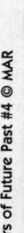

	GD 2.0	VG 4.0	FN 6.0	VF 8.0	VF/NM 9.0	NM- 9.2

1-Origin by Joe Maneely 148 296 444 947 1624 2300
2-Kirby-a 116 232 348 742 1271 1800
3,4-Kirby-a; 4-Kirby/Severin-a 110 220 330 704 1202 1700
NOTE: ***Everett** c-3. **Maneely** c-1. **Reinman** a-2i, 3. **Severin** c-2, 4.*

YELLOWJACKET COMICS (Jack in the Box #11 on)(See TNT Comics)
E. Levy/Frank Comunale/Charlton: Sept, 1944 - No. 10, June, 1946
1-Intro & origin Yellowjacket; Diana, the Huntress begins; E.A. Poe's "The Black Cat" adaptation 68 136 204 435 743 1050
2-Yellowjacket-c begin, end #10 45 90 135 284 480 675
3,5 43 86 129 271 461 650
4-E.A. Poe's "Fall of the House Of Usher" adaptation; Palais-a 45 90 135 284 480 675
6 41 82 123 256 428 600
7-Classic skull-c; Toth-a (1 pg. gag feature) 65 130 195 416 708 1000
8-10: 1,3,4,6-10-Have stories narrated by old witch in "Tales of Terror" (1st horror series?) 40 80 120 246 411 575

YELLOWSTONE KELLY (Movie)
Dell Publishing Co.: No. 1056, Nov-Jan, 1959/60
Four Color 1056-Clint Walker photo-c 5 10 15 35 63 90

YELLOW SUBMARINE (See Movie Comics)

YEAR ONE: BATMAN/RA'S AL GHUL
DC Comics: 2005 - No. 2, 2005 ($5.99, squarebound, limited series)
1-Devin Grayson-s/Paul Gulacy-a 6.00
TPB (2006, $9.99) r/#1,2 10.00

YEAR ONE: BATMAN SCARECROW
DC Comics: 2005 - No. 2, 2005 ($5.99, squarebound, limited series)
1-Scarecrow's origin; Bruce Jones-s/Sean Murphy-a 6.00

YOGA HOSERS: A SUNDANCE SUPER SPECIAL
Dynamite Entertainment: 2016 ($10.00, one-shot)
1-Prologue to the Kevin Smith movie; Smith-s/Jeff Quigley-a 10.00

YOGI BEAR (See Dell Giant #41, Golden Comics Digest, Kite Fun Book, March of Comics #253, 265, 279, 291, 309, 319, 337, 344, Movie Comics under "Hey There It's..." & Whitman Comic Books)

YOGI BEAR (TV) (Hanna-Barbera) (See Four Color #990)
Dell Publishing Co./Gold Key No. 10 on: No. 1067, 12-2/59-60 - No. 9, 7-9/62; No. 10, 10/62 - No. 42, 10/70
Four Color 1067 (#1)-TV show debuted 1/30/61 12 24 36 82 179 275
Four Color 1104,1162 (5-7/61) 8 16 24 54 102 150
4(8-9/61) - 6(12-1/61-62) 5 10 15 33 57 80
Four Color 1271(11/61) 6 12 18 40 73 105
Four Color 1349(1/62)-Photo-c 8 16 24 54 102 150
7(2-3/62) - 9(7-9/62)-Last Dell 5 10 15 33 57 80
10(10/62-G.K.), 11(1/63)-titled "Yogi Bear Jellystone Jollies" (80 pgs.); 11-X-Mas-c 6 12 18 41 76 110
12(4/63), 14-20 4 8 12 28 47 65
13(7/63, 68 pgs.)-Surprise Party 6 12 18 40 73 105
21-30 3 6 9 19 30 40
31-42 3 6 9 16 24 32

YOGI BEAR (TV)
Charlton Comics: Nov, 1970 - No. 35, Jan, 1976 (Hanna-Barbera)
1 5 10 15 31 53 75
2-6,8-10 3 6 9 16 24 32
7-Summer Fun (Giant, 52 pgs.) 4 8 12 27 44 60
11-20 3 6 9 15 22 28
21-35: 28-31-partial-r 2 4 6 11 16 20
Digest (nn, 1972, 75¢-c, B&W, 100 pgs.) (scarce) 3 6 9 18 28 38

YOGI BEAR (TV)(See The Flintstones, 3rd series & Spotlight #1)
Marvel Comics Group: Nov, 1977 - No. 9, Mar, 1979 (Hanna-Barbera)
1,7-9: 1-Flintstones begin (Newsstand sales only) 3 6 9 16 23 30
2-6 2 4 6 11 16 20

YOGI BEAR (TV)
Harvey Comics: Sept, 1992 - No. 6, Mar, 1994 ($1.25/$1.50) (Hanna-Barbera)
V2#1-6 3.00
...Big Book V2#1,2 ($1.95, 52 pgs): 1-(11/92). 2-(3/93) 4.00
...Giant Size V2#1,2 ($2.25, 68 pgs.): 1-(10/92). 2-(4/93) 4.00

YOGI BEAR (TV)
Archie Publ.: May, 1997
1 3.00

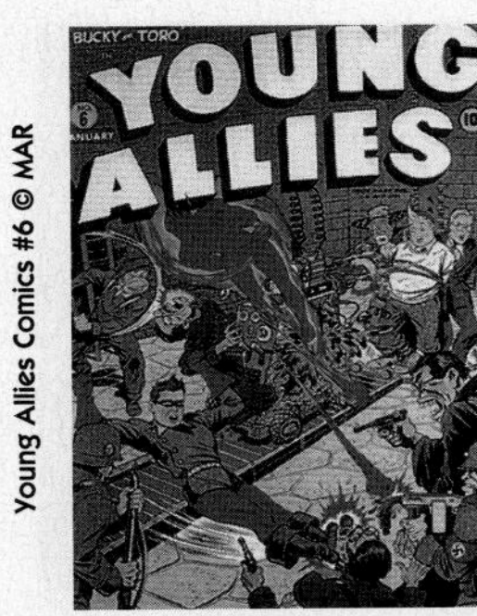

Young Allies Comics #6 © MAR

Young Avengers #1 © MAR

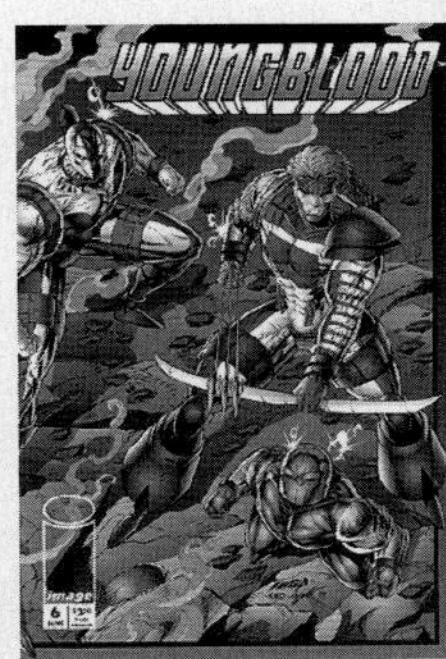

Youngblood #6 © Awesome Ent.

YOGI BEAR'S EASTER PARADE (See The Funtastic World of Hanna-Barbera #2)

YOGI BERRA (Baseball hero)
Fawcett Publications: 1951 (Yankee catcher)

	GD 2.0	VG 4.0	FN 6.0	VF 8.0	VF/NM 9.0	NM- 9.2
nn-Photo-c (scarce)	76	152	228	486	831	1175

YOSEMITE SAM (...& Bugs Bunny) (TV)
Gold Key/Whitman: Dec, 1970 - No. 81, Feb, 1984

	GD 2.0	VG 4.0	FN 6.0	VF 8.0	VF/NM 9.0	NM- 9.2
1	5	10	15	31	53	75
2-10	3	6	9	16	23	30
11-20	2	4	6	11	16	20
21-30	2	4	6	9	13	16
31-50	2	4	6	8	10	12
51-65 (Gold Key)	1	2	3	5	7	9
66,67 (Whitman)	2	4	6	8	10	12
68(9/80), 69(10/80), 70(12/80) 3-pack only	5	10	15	30	50	70
71-78: 76(2/82), 77(3/82), 78(4/82)	2	4	6	9	13	16
79-81 (All #90263 on-c, no date or date code; 3-pack): 79(7/83). 80(8/83). 81(2/84)-(1/3-r)	3	6	9	16	24	32

(See March of Comics #363, 380, 392)

YOSSEL
DC Comics: 2003/2011 ($14.99, B&W graphic novel)

SC-Joe Kubert-s/a/c; Nazi-occupied Poland during World War II 15.00

YOUNG ALLIES
Marvel Comics: Aug, 2010 - No. 6, Jan, 2011 ($3.99/$2.99)

1-($3.99) Wraparound-c; Nomad, Araña, Firestar, Gravity, Toro team-up; origin pages 5.00
2-6-($2.99) 2-Lafuente-c/McKeever-s/Baldeon-a. 6-Miyazawa-c; Emma Frost app. 4.00

YOUNG ALLIES COMICS (All-Winners #21; see Kid Komics #2)
Timely Comics (USA 1-7/NPI 8,9/YAI 10-20): Sum, 1941 - No. 20, Oct, 1946

	GD 2.0	VG 4.0	FN 6.0	VF 8.0	VF/NM 9.0	NM- 9.2
1-Origin/1st app. The Young Allies (Bucky, Toro, others); 1st meeting of Captain America & Human Torch; Red Skull-c & app.; S&K-c/splash; Hitler-c; Note: the cover was altered after its preview in Human Torch #5. Stalin was shown with Hitler but was removed due to Russia becoming an ally	1300	2600	3900	9100	16,250	26,000
2-(Winter, 1941)-Captain America & Human Torch app.; Simon & Kirby-c	432	864	1296	3154	5577	8000
3-Remember Pearl Harbor issue (Spring, 1942); Stan Lee scripts; Vs. Japanese-c/full-length story; Captain America & Human Torch app.; Father Time story by Alderman	400	800	1200	2800	4900	7000
4-The Vagabond & Red Skull, Capt. America, Human Torch app. Classic Red Skull-c	514	1028	1542	3750	6625	9500
5-Captain America & Human Torch app.	258	516	774	1651	2826	4000
6,7: 6-Japanese/Nazi war-c	194	388	582	1242	2121	3000
8-Classic Schomburg WWII Japanese bondage-c	213	426	639	1363	2332	3300
9-Hitler, Tojo, Mussolini-c.	300	600	900	2010	3505	5000
10-Classic Schomburg Hooded Villain bondage-c; origin Tommy Tyme & Clock of Ages; ends #19	174	348	522	1114	1907	2700
11-16: 12-Classic decapitation story; Japanese war-c. 16-Last Schomburg WWII-c	155	310	465	992	1696	2400
17-20	119	238	357	762	1306	1850

NOTE: *Brodsky c-15. Ferstadt a-3. Gabriele a-3; c-3, 4. S&K c-1, 2. Schomburg c-5-13, 16-19. Shores c-20.*

YOUNG ALLIES 70TH ANNIVERSARY SPECIAL
Marvel Comics: Aug, 2009 ($3.99, one-shot)

1-Bucky & Young Allies app.; Stern-s/Rivera-a; Terry Vance rep. from Marvel Myst. #14 5.00

YOUNG ALL-STARS
DC Comics: June, 1987 - No. 31, Nov, 1989 ($1.00, deluxe format)

1-31: 1-1st app. Iron Munro & The Flying Fox. 8,9-Millennium tie-ins 4.00
Annual 1 (1988, $2.00) 4.00

YOUNG AVENGERS
Marvel Comics: Apr, 2005 - No. 12, Aug, 2006 ($2.99)

1-Intro. Iron Lad, Patriot, Hulkling, Asgardian; Heinberg-s/Cheung-a 5.00
1-Director's Cut (2005, $3.99) r/#1 plus character sketches; original script 4.00
2-12: 3-6-Kang app. 7-DiVito-a. 9-Skrulls app. 3.00
... Special 1 (2/06, $3.99) origins of the heroes; art by various incl. Neal Adams, Jae Lee, Bill Sienkiewicz, Gene Ha, Michael Gaydos and Pasqual Ferry 4.00
... Vol. 1: Sidekicks HC (2005, $19.99, dustjacket) r/#1-6; character design sketches 20.00
... Vol. 1: Sidekicks TPB (2006, $14.99) r/#1-6; character design sketches 15.00
... Vol. 2: Family Matters HC (2006, $22.99, dustjacket) r/#7-12 & YA Special #1 23.00
... Vol. 2: Family Matters SC (2007, $17.99) r/#7-12 & YA Special #1 18.00
HC (2008, $29.99, d.j.) oversized reprint of #1-12 and Special #1; script & sketch pages 30.00

YOUNG AVENGERS (Marvel NOW!)
Marvel Comics: Mar, 2013 - No. 15, Mar, 2014 ($2.99)

1-15: 1-Loki assembles team; Marvel Boy, Miss America app.; Gillen-s/McKelvie-a/c. 11-Loki ages back to adult. 14,15-Multiple artists 3.00
1-Variant-c by Bryan Lee O'Malley 6.00
1-Variant-c by Skottie Young 6.00

YOUNG AVENGERS PRESENTS
Marvel Comics: Mar, 2008 - No. 6, Aug, 2008 ($2.99, limited series)

1-6: 1-Patriot; Bucky app. 2-Hulkling; Captain Marvel app. 3-Wiccan & Speed. 4-Vision. 5-Stature. 6-Hawkeye; Clint Barton app.; Alan Davis-a 3.00

YOUNGBLOOD (See Brigade #4, Megaton Explosion & Team Youngblood)
Image Comics (Extreme Studios): Apr, 1992 - No. 4, Feb, 1993 ($2.50, lim. series); No. 5-(Flip book w/Brigade #4); No. 6, June, 1994 - No. 10, Dec, 1994 ($1.95/$2.50)

1-Liefeld-c/a/scripts in all; flip book format with 2 trading cards; 1st Image/Extreme Studios title. 5.00
1,2-2nd printing 3.00
2-(JUN-c, July 1992 indicia)-1st app. Shadowhawk in solo back-up story; 2 trading cards inside; flip book format; 1st app. Prophet, Kirby, Berzerkers, Darkthorn 4.00
3,0,4,5: 3-(OCT-c, August 1992 indicia)-Contains 2 trading cards inside (flip book); 1st app. Supreme in back-up story; 1st app. Showdown. 0-(12/92, $1.95)-Contains 2 trading cards; 2 cover variations exist, green or beige logo; w/Image #0 coupon. 4-(2/93)-Glow-in-the-dark cover w/2 trading cards; 2nd app. Dale Keown's The Pitt; Bloodstrike app. 5-Flip book w/Brigade #4 3.00
6-($3.50, 52 pgs.)-Wraparound-c 4.00
7-10: 7, 8-Liefeld-c(p)/a(p)/story. 8,9-(9/94) 9-Valentino story & art 3.00
Battlezone 1 (May-c, 4/93 inside, $1.95)-Arsenal book; Liefeld-c(p) 3.00
Battlezone 2 (7/94, $2.95)-Wraparound-c 4.00
Image Firsts: Youngblood #1 (3/10, $1.00) reprints #1 3.00
...Super Special (Winter '97, $2.99) Sprouse -a 4.00
Yearbook 1 (7/93, $2.50)-Fold out panel; 1st app. Tyrax & Kanan 4.00
Vol. 1 HC (2008, $34.99) oversized r/#1-5, recolored and remastered; sketch art and cover gallery; Mark Millar intro. 35.00
TPB (1996, $16.95)-r/Team Youngblood #8-10 & Youngblood #6-8,10 17.00

YOUNGBLOOD
Image Comics (Extreme Studios)/Maximum Press No. 14: V2#1, Sept, 1995 - No. 14, Dec, 1996 ($2.50)

V2#1-10,14: Roger Cruz-a in all. 4-Extreme Destroyer Pt. 4 w/gaming card. 5-Variant-c exists. 6-Angela & Glory. 7-Shadowhunt Pt. 3; Shadowhawk app. 8,10-Thor (from Supreme) app. 10-(7/96). 14-(12/96)-1st Maximum Press issue 3.00

YOUNGBLOOD (Volume 3)
Awesome/ Awesome-Hyperwerks #2: Feb, 1998 - No. 2, Aug, 1998 ($2.50)

1-Alan Moore-s/Skroce & Stucker-a; 12 diff. covers 3.00
2-(8/98) Skroce & Liefeld covers 3.00
...Imperial 1 (Arcade Comics, 6/04, $2.99) Kirkman-sMychaels-a 3.00

YOUNGBLOOD (Volume 4)
Image Comics: Jan, 2008 - No. 9, Sept, 2009; No. 71, May, 2012 - Present ($2.99/$3.99)

1-7-Casey-s/Donovan-a; two covers by Donovan & Liefeld on each 3.00
8-Obama flip cover by Liefeld; Obama app. in story 3.00
9-(9/09, $3.99) Obama flip cover by Liefeld; Free Agent rejoins; Obama app. in story 4.00
71-74: 71-(5/12, $2.99) Liefeld & Malin-a; three covers 3.00
75-(1/13, $4.99) Five covers; Malin-a 5.00
76-78-($3.99) Malin-a 4.00

YOUNGBLOOD: STRIKEFILE
Image Comics (Extreme Studios): Apr, 1993 - No. 11, Feb, 1995 ($1.95/$2.50/$2.95)

1-10: 1-($1.95)-Flip book w/Jae Lee-c/a & Liefeld-c/a in #1-3; 1st app. The Allies,Giger, & Glory. 3-Thibert-i asisst. 4-Liefeld-c(p); no Lee-a. 5-Liefeld-c(p). 8-Platt-c 3.00

NOTE: *Youngblood: Strikefile began as a four issue limited series.*

YOUNGBLOOD/X-FORCE
Image Comics (Extreme Studios): July, 1996 ($4.95, one-shot)

1-Cruz-a(p); two covers exist 5.00

YOUNG BRIDES (True Love Secrets)
Feature/Prize Publ.: Sept-Oct, 1952 - No. 30, Nov-Dec, 1956 (Photo-c: V1 #1-6, V2 #1,2)

	GD 2.0	VG 4.0	FN 6.0	VF 8.0	VF/NM 9.0	NM- 9.2
V1#1-Simon & Kirby-a	45	90	135	284	480	675
2-S&K-a	26	52	78	154	252	350
3-6-S&K-a	22	44	66	132	216	300
V2#1-7,10-12 (#7-18)-S&K-a	21	42	63	122	199	275
8,9-No S&K-a	12	24	36	69	97	125
V3#1-3(#19-21)-Last precode (3-4/55)	11	22	33	64	90	115
4,6(#22,24), V4#1,3(#25,27)	11	22	33	60	83	105

Young Hearts #2 © MAR

Young Justice (2011 series) #2 © DC

Young Love #2 © PRIZE

	GD 2.0	VG 4.0	FN 6.0	VF 8.0	VF/NM 9.0	NM- 9.2
V3#5(#23)-Meskin-c	11	22	33	62	86	110
V4#2(#26)-All S&K issue	20	40	60	117	189	260
V4#4(#28)-S&K-a	17	34	51	98	154	210
V4#5,6(#29,30)	11	22	33	64	90	115

YOUNG DR. MASTERS (See The Adventures of Young Dr. Masters)

YOUNG DOCTORS, THE
Charlton Comics: Jan, 1963 - No. 6, Nov, 1963

	GD 2.0	VG 4.0	FN 6.0	VF 8.0	VF/NM 9.0	NM- 9.2
V1#1	3	6	9	20	31	42
2-6	3	6	9	14	19	24

YOUNG EAGLE
Fawcett Publications/Charlton: 12/50 - No. 10, 6/52; No. 3, 7/56 - No. 5, 4/57 (Photo-c: 1-10)

	GD 2.0	VG 4.0	FN 6.0	VF 8.0	VF/NM 9.0	NM- 9.2
1-Intro Young Eagle	18	36	54	103	162	220
2-Complete picture novelette "The Mystery of Thunder Canyon"	10	20	30	58	79	100
3-9	9	18	27	50	65	80
10-Origin Thunder, Young Eagle's Horse	8	16	24	44	57	70
3-5(Charlton)-Formerly Sherlock Holmes?	7	14	21	35	43	50

YOUNG GUNS SKETCHBOOK
Marvel Comics: Feb, 2005 ($3.99, one-shot)

	GD 2.0	VG 4.0	FN 6.0	VF 8.0	VF/NM 9.0	NM- 9.2
1-Sketch pages from 2005 Marvel projects by Coipel, Granov, McNiven, Land & others						4.00

YOUNG HEARTS
Marvel Comics (SPC): Nov, 1949 - No. 2, Feb, 1950

	GD 2.0	VG 4.0	FN 6.0	VF 8.0	VF/NM 9.0	NM- 9.2
1-Photo-c	20	40	60	117	189	260
2-Colleen Townsend photo-c from movie	14	28	42	82	121	160

YOUNG HEARTS IN LOVE
Super Comics: 1964

	GD 2.0	VG 4.0	FN 6.0	VF 8.0	VF/NM 9.0	NM- 9.2
17,18: 17-r/Young Love V5#6 (4-5/62)	2	4	6	9	13	16

YOUNG HEROES (Formerly Forbidden Worlds #34)
American Comics Group (Titan): No. 35, Feb-Mar, 1955 - No. 37, Jun-Jul, 1955

	GD 2.0	VG 4.0	FN 6.0	VF 8.0	VF/NM 9.0	NM- 9.2
35-37-Frontier Scout	10	20	30	54	72	90

YOUNG HEROES IN LOVE
DC Comics: June, 1997 - No. 17; #1,000,000, Nov, 1998 ($1.75/$1.95/$2.50)

	GD 2.0	VG 4.0	FN 6.0	VF 8.0	VF/NM 9.0	NM- 9.2
1-1st app. Young Heroes; Madan-a						4.00
2-17: 3-Superman-c/app. 7-Begin $1.95-c						3.00
#1,000,000 (11/98, $2.50) 853 Century x-over						3.00

YOUNG INDIANA JONES CHRONICLES, THE
Dark Horse Comics: Feb, 1992 - No. 12, Feb, 1993 ($2.50)

	GD 2.0	VG 4.0	FN 6.0	VF 8.0	VF/NM 9.0	NM- 9.2
1-12: Dan Barry scripts in all						3.00

NOTE: ***Dan Barry** a(p)-1, 2, 5, 6, 10; c-1-10. **Morrow** a-3, 4, 5p, 6p. **Springer** a-1i, 2i.*

YOUNG INDIANA JONES CHRONICLES, THE
Hollywood Comics (Disney): 1992 ($3.95, squarebound, 68 pgs.)

	GD 2.0	VG 4.0	FN 6.0	VF 8.0	VF/NM 9.0	NM- 9.2
1-3: 1-r/YIJC #1,2 by D. Horse. 2-r/#3,4. 3-r/#5,6						4.00

YOUNG JUSTICE (Also see Teen Titans, Titans/Young Justice and DC Comics Presents: ...)
DC Comics: Sept, 1998 - No. 55, May, 2003 ($2.50/$2.75)

	GD 2.0	VG 4.0	FN 6.0	VF 8.0	VF/NM 9.0	NM- 9.2
1-Robin, Superboy & Impulse team-up; David-s/Nauck-a						4.00
2,3: 3-Mxyzptlk app.						3.00
4-20: 4-Wonder Girl, Arrowette and the Secret join. 6-JLA app. 13-Supergirl x-over. 20-Sins of Youth aftermath						3.00
21-49: 25-Empress ID revealed. 28,29-Forever People app. 32-Empress origin. 35,36-Our Worlds at War x-over. 38-Joker: Last Laugh. 41-The Ray joins. 42-Spectre-c/app. 44,45-World Without YJ x-over pt. 1,5; Ramos-c. 48-Begin $2.75-c						3.00
50-($3.95) Wonder Twins, CM3 and other various DC teen heroes app.						4.00
51-55: 53,54-Darkseid app. 55-Last issue; leads into Titans/Young Justice mini-series						3.00
#1,000,000 (11/98) 853 Century x-over						3.00
...: A League of Their Own (2000, $14.95, TPB) r/#1-7, Secret Files #1						15.00
...: 80-Page Giant (5/99, $4.95) Ramos-c; stories and art by various						5.00
...: In No Man's Land (7/99, $3.95) McDaniel-c						4.00
...: Our Worlds at War (8/01, $2.95) Jae Lee-c; Linear Men app.						3.00
...: Secret Files (1/99, $4.95) Origin-s & pin-ups						5.00
...: The Secret (6/98, $1.95) Girlfrenzy; Nauck-a						3.00

YOUNG JUSTICE (Based on the 2011 Cartoon Network series)
DC Comics: No. 0, Mar, 2011 - No. 25, Apr, 2013 ($2.99)

	GD 2.0	VG 4.0	FN 6.0	VF 8.0	VF/NM 9.0	NM- 9.2
0-19: 1-Miss Martian joins; Joker app. 2-Joker-c/app. 5-Kid Flash & Aqualad origins						3.00
20-25: 20-(11/12) Starts Invasion; 5 years later						3.00
FCBD 2011 Young Justice Batman BB Super Sampler (7/11) Flash app.						3.00

YOUNG JUSTICE: SINS OF YOUTH (Also see Sins of Youth x-over issues and Sins of Youth: Secret Files)
DC Comics: May, 2000 - No. 2, May, 2000 ($3.95, limited series)

	GD 2.0	VG 4.0	FN 6.0	VF 8.0	VF/NM 9.0	NM- 9.2
1,2-Young Justice, JLA & JSA swap ages; David-s/Nauck-a						4.00
TPB (2000, $19.95) r/#1,2 & all x-over issues						20.00

YOUNG KING COLE (...Detective Tales)(Becomes Criminals on the Run)
Premium Group/Novelty Press: Fall, 1945 - V3#12, July, 1948

	GD 2.0	VG 4.0	FN 6.0	VF 8.0	VF/NM 9.0	NM- 9.2
V1#1-Toni Gayle begins	37	74	111	222	361	500
2	18	36	54	103	162	220
3-4	16	32	48	94	147	200
V2#1-7(8-9/46-7/47): 6,7-Certa-c	14	28	42	76	108	140
V3#1,3-6,8,9,12: 3-Certa-c. 5-McWilliams-c/a. 8,9-Harmon-c	13	26	39	74	105	135
2-L.B. Cole-a; Certa-c	18	36	54	103	162	220
7-L.B. Cole-c/a	22	44	66	132	216	300
10,11-L.B. Cole-c	20	40	60	114	182	350

YOUNG LAWYERS, THE (TV)
Dell Publishing Co.: Jan, 1971 - No. 2, Apr, 1971 (photo-c)

	GD 2.0	VG 4.0	FN 6.0	VF 8.0	VF/NM 9.0	NM- 9.2
1	3	6	9	16	23	30
2	2	4	6	11	16	20

YOUNG LIARS (David Lapham's...)(See Vertigo Double Shot for reprint of #1)
DC Comics (Vertigo): May, 2008 - No. 18, Oct, 2009 ($2.99)

	GD 2.0	VG 4.0	FN 6.0	VF 8.0	VF/NM 9.0	NM- 9.2
1-18: 1-Intro. Sadie Dawkins; David Lapham-s/a/c in all						3.00
...: Daydream Believer TPB (2008, $9.99) r/#1-6; Gerald Way intro.						10.00
...: Maestro TPB (2009, $14.99) r/#7-12; Peter Milligan intro.						15.00
...: Rock Life TPB (2010, $14.99) r/#13-18; Brian Azzarello intro.						15.00

YOUNG LIFE (Teen Life #3 on)
New Age Publ./Quality Comics Group: Summer, 1945 - No. 2, Fall, 1945

	GD 2.0	VG 4.0	FN 6.0	VF 8.0	VF/NM 9.0	NM- 9.2
1-Skip Homeier, Louis Prima stories	19	38	57	111	176	240
2-Frank Sinatra photo on-c plus story	21	42	63	122	199	275

YOUNG LOVE (Sister title to Young Romance)
Prize(Feature)Publ.(Crestwood): 2-3/49 - No. 73, 12-1/56-57; V3#5, 2-3/60 - V7#1, 6-7/63

	GD 2.0	VG 4.0	FN 6.0	VF 8.0	VF/NM 9.0	NM- 9.2
V1#1-S&K-c/a(2)	68	136	204	435	743	1050
2-Photo-c begin; S&K-a	36	72	108	211	343	475
3-S&K-a	24	48	72	140	230	320
4-6-Minor S&K-a	17	34	51	100	158	215
V2#1(#7)-S&K-a(2)	23	46	69	136	223	310
2-5(#8-11)-Minor S&K-a	15	30	45	85	130	175
6,8(#12,14)-S&K-c only. 14-S&K 1 pg. art	18	36	54	105	165	225
7,9-12(#13,15-18)-S&K-c/a	23	46	69	136	223	310
V3#1-4(#19-22)-S&K-c/a	21	42	63	122	199	275
5-7,9-12(#23-25,27-30)-Photo-c resume; S&K-a	17	34	51	100	158	215
8(#26)-No S&K-a	11	22	33	62	86	110
V4#1,6(#31,36)-S&K-a	15	30	45	90	140	190
2-5,7-12(#32-35,37-42)-Minor S&K-a	14	28	42	80	115	150
V5#1-12(#43-54), V6#3,7,9(#57,61,63)-Last precode	10	20	30	58	79	100
V6#1,2,4-6,8(#55,56,58-60,62) S&K-a	12	24	36	67	94	120
V6#10-12(#64-66)	5	10	15	34	60	85
V7#1-7(#67-73)	5	10	15	31	53	75
V3#5(2-3/60),6(4-5/60)(Formerly All For Love)	4	8	12	28	47	65
V4#1(6-7/60)-6(4-5/61)	4	8	12	27	44	60
V5#1(6-7/61)-6(4-5/62)	4	8	12	27	44	60
V6#1(6-7/62)-6(4-5/63), V7#1	4	8	12	25	40	55

NOTE: ***Meskin** a-14(2), 27, 42. **Powell** a-V4#6. **Severin/Elder** a-V1#3. S&K art not in #53, 57, 61, 63-65. Photo-c most V1 #1-6, V2 #3, V3#5-V5#11.*

YOUNG LOVE
National Periodical Publ.(Arleigh Publ. Corp #49-61)/DC Comics:
#39, 9-10/63 - #120, Wint./75-76; #121, 10/76 - #126, 7/77

	GD 2.0	VG 4.0	FN 6.0	VF 8.0	VF/NM 9.0	NM- 9.2
39	6	12	18	37	66	95
40-50	4	8	12	28	47	65
51-68,70	4	8	12	25	40	55
69-(68 pg. Giant)(8-9/68)	6	12	18	38	69	100
71,72,75-77,80	3	6	9	20	31	42
73,74,78,79-Toth-a	3	6	9	21	33	45
81-99: 88-96-(52 pg. Giants)	3	6	9	19	30	40
100	3	6	9	20	31	42
101-106,115-120	3	6	9	16	24	32
107 (100 pgs.)	7	14	21	49	92	135
108-114 (100 pgs.)	7	14	21	44	82	120
121-126 (52 pgs.)	4	8	12	26	41	55

NOTE: ***Bolle** a-117. **Colan** a-107r. **Nasser** a-123, 124. **Orlando** a-122. **Simonson** c-125. **Toth** a-73, 78, 79, 122-*

Young Men #25 © MAR

Young Romance #201 © DC

Youthful Romances #18 © Ribage

	GD 2.0	VG 4.0	FN 6.0	VF 8.0	VF/NM 9.0	NM- 9.2

125r. **Wood** a-109r(4 pgs.).

YOUNG LOVER ROMANCES (Formerly & becomes Great Lover...)
Toby Press: No. 4, June, 1952 - No. 5, Aug, 1952

4,5-Photo-c 12 24 36 69 97 125

YOUNG LOVERS (My Secret Life #19 on)(Formerly Brenda Starr?)
Charlton Comics: No. 16, July, 1956 - No. 18, May, 1957

16,17('56): 16-Marcus Swayze-a 13 26 39 74 105 135
18-Elvis Presley picture-c, text story (biography)(Scarce) 90 180 270 576 988 1400

YOUNG MARRIAGE
Fawcett Publications: June, 1950

1-Powell-a; photo-c 15 30 45 83 124 165

YOUNG MEN (Formerly Cowboy Romances)(...on the Battlefield #12-20(4/53); ...In Action #21)
Marvel/Atlas Comics (IPC): No. 4, 6/50 - No. 11, 10/51; No. 12, 12/51 - No. 28, 6/54

4-(52 pgs.) 26 52 78 154 252 350
5-11 17 34 51 98 154 210
12-23: 12-20-War format. 21-23-Hot Rod issues starring Flash Foster 18 36 54 105 165 225
24-(12/53)-Origin Captain America, Human Torch, & Sub-Mariner which are revived thru #28; Red Skull app. 371 742 1113 2600 4550 6500
25-28: 25-Romita-c/a (see Men's Advs.). 27-Death of Golden Age Red Skull 161 322 483 1030 1765 2500
25-2nd printing (1994) 2 4 6 8 10 12

NOTE: **Berg** a-7, 14, 17, 18, 20; c-17? **Brodsky** c-4-9, 13, 14, 16, 17, 21-25. **Burgos** c-26-28. **Colan** a-14, 15, 20. **Everett** a-18-20. **Heath** a-13, 14. **Maneely** c-10-12, 15. **Pakula** a-14, 15. **Robinson** c-18. Captain America by **Romita**-#24?, 25, 26?, 27, 28. Human Torch by **Burgos**-#25, 27, 28. Sub-Mariner by **Everett**-#24-28.

YOUNG REBELS, THE (TV)
Dell Publishing Co.: Jan, 1971

1-Photo-c 3 6 9 14 19 24

YOUNG ROMANCE COMICS (The 1st romance comic)
Prize/Headline (Feature Publ.) (Crestwood): Sept-Oct, 1947 - V16#4, June-July, 1963 (#1-33: 52 pgs.)

V1#1-S&K-c/a(2) 81 162 243 518 884 1250
2-S&K-c/a(2-3) 41 82 123 256 428 600
3-6-S&K-c/a(2-3) each 37 74 111 222 361 500
V2#1-6(#7-12)-S&K-c/a(2-3) each 32 64 96 192 314 435
V3#1-3(#13-15): V3#1-Photo-c begin; S&K-a 21 42 63 122 199 275
4-12(#16-24)-Photo-c; S&K-a 21 42 63 122 199 275
V4#1-11(#25-35)-S&K-a 20 40 60 117 189 260
12(#36)-S&K, Toth-a 21 42 63 122 199 275
V5#1-12(#37-48), V6#4-12(#52-60)-S&K-a 20 40 60 117 189 260
V6#1-3(#49-51)-No S&K-a 11 22 33 64 90 115
V7#1-11(#61-71)-S&K-a in most 15 30 45 90 140 190
V7#12(#72), V8#1-3(#73-75)-Last precode (12-1/54-55)-No S&K-a 10 20 30 58 79 100
V8#4(#76, 4-5/55), 5(#77)-No S&K-a 10 20 30 54 72 90
V8#6-8(#78-80, 12-1/55-56)-S&K-a 14 28 42 80 115 150
V9#3,5,6(#81, 2-3/56, 83,84)-S&K-a 14 28 42 80 115 150
4, V10#1(#82,85)-All S&K-a 15 30 45 83 124 165
V10#2-6(#86-90, 10-11/57)-S&K-a 8 16 24 54 102 150
V11#1,2,5,6(#91,92,95,96)-S&K-a 8 16 24 54 102 150
3,4(#93,94), V12#2,4,5(#98,100,101)-No S&K 5 10 15 31 57 80
V12#1,3,6(#97,99,102)-S&K-a 8 16 24 54 102 150
V13#1(#103)-Powell-a; S&K's last-a for Crestwood 8 16 24 54 102 150
2,4-6(#104-108) 5 10 15 30 50 70
V13#3(#105, 4-5/60)-Elvis Presley-c app. only 8 16 24 55 105 155
V14#1-6, V15#1-6, V16#1-4(#109-124) 4 8 12 28 47 65

NOTE: **Meskin** a-16, 24(2), 33, 47, 50. **Robinson/Meskin** a-6. **Leonard Starr** a-11. Photo c-13-32, 34-65. Issues 1-3 say "Designed for the More **Adult** Readers of **Comics**" on cover.

YOUNG ROMANCE COMICS (Continued from Prize series)
National Periodical Publ.(Arleigh Publ. Corp. No. 127): No. 125, Aug-Sept, 1963 - No. 208, Nov-Dec, 1975

125 7 14 21 46 86 125
126-140 5 10 15 30 50 70
141-153,156-162,165-169 4 8 12 23 37 50
154-Neal Adams-c 5 10 15 31 53 75
155-1st publ. Aragonés-s (no art) 5 10 15 30 50 70
163,164-Toth-a 4 8 12 27 44 60
170-172 (68 pg. Giants): 170-Michell from Young Love ends; Lily Martin, the Swinger begins 5 10 15 30 50 70
173-183 (52 pgs.) 4 8 12 23 37 50
184-196 3 6 9 17 26 35
197-204-(100 pgs.) 7 14 21 44 82 120
205-208 3 6 9 16 24 32

YOUNG ROMANCE: THE NEW 52 VALENTINE'S DAY SPECIAL
DC Comics: Apr, 2013 ($7.99, one-shot)

1-Short stories by various; Superman/Wonder Woman-c by Rocafort; bonus valentines 8.00

YOUNG X-MEN
Marvel Comics: May, 2008 - No. 12, May, 2009 ($2.99)

1-12: 1-Cyclops forms new team; Guggenheim-s/Paquette-a/Dodson-c. 11,12-Acuña-a 3.00

YOUR DREAMS (See Strange World of...)

YOUR HIGHNESS
Dark Horse Comics: 2011 ($7.99, one-shot)

nn-Prequel to 2011 movie; Danny McBride & Jeff Fradley-s/Phillips-a/c 8.00

YOUR UNITED STATES
Lloyd Jacquet Studios: 1946

nn-Used in **SOTI**, pg. 309,310; Sid Greene-a 27 54 81 158 259 360

YOUTHFUL HEARTS (Daring Confessions #4 on)
Youthful Magazines: May, 1952 - No. 3, Sept, 1952

1-"Monkey on Her Back" swipes E.C. drug story/Shock SuspenStories #12; Frankie Laine photo on-c; Doug Wildey-a in al 39 78 117 240 395 550
2,3: 2-Vic Damone photo on-c. 3-Johnny Raye photo on-c 23 46 69 136 223 310

YOUTHFUL LOVE (Truthful Love #2)
Youthful Magazines: May, 1950

1 27 52 78 154 252 350

YOUTHFUL ROMANCES
Pix-Parade #1-14/Ribage #15 on: 8-9/49 - No. 5, 4/50; No. 6, 2/51; No. 7, 5/51 - #14, 10/52; #15, 1/53 - #18, 7/53; No. 5, 9/53 - No. 9, 8/54

1-(1st series)-Titled Youthful Love-Romances 36 72 108 211 341 465
2-Walter Johnson c-1-4 21 42 63 122 194 270
3-5 18 36 54 103 162 220
6,7,9-14(10/52, Pix-Parade; becomes Daring Love #15). 10(1/52)-Mel Torme photo-c/story. 12-Tony Bennett photo-c, 8pg. story & text bio.13-Richard Hayes (singer) photo-c/story; Bob & Ray photo/text story. 16 32 48 94 147 200
8-Frank Sinatra photo/text story; Wood-c/a 25 50 75 150 241 330
15-18 (Ribage)-All have photos on-c. 15-Spike Jones photo-c/story. 16-Tony Bavaar photo-c 15 30 45 90 140 190
5(9/53, Ribage)-Les Paul & Mary Ford photo-c/story; Charlton Heston photo/text story 15 30 45 86 133 180
6-9: 6-Bobby Wayne (singer) photo-c/story; Debbie Reynolds photo/text story. 7(2/54)-Tony Martin photo-c/story; Cyd Charise photo/text story. 8(5/54)-Gordon McCrae photo-c/story. (8/54)-Ralph Flanagan (band leader) photo-c/story; Audrey Hepburn photo/text story 14 28 42 84 127 170

YTHAQ: NO ESCAPE
Marvel Comics (Soleil): 2009 - No. 3, 2009 ($5.99, limited series)

1-3-English language version of French comic; Arleston-s/Floch-a 6.00

YTHAQ: THE FORSAKEN WORLD
Marvel Comics (Soleil): 2008 - No. 3, 2009 ($5.99, limited series)

1-3-English language version of French comic; Arleston-s/Floch-a 6.00

Y: THE LAST MAN
DC Comics (Vertigo): Sept, 2002 - No. 60, Mar, 2008 ($2.95/$2.99)

1-Intro. Yorick Brown; Brian K. Vaughan-s/Pia Guerra-a/J.G. Jones-c 8 16 24 56 108 160
2 3 6 9 16 24 32
3-5 1 2 3 5 6 8
6-10 5.00
11-59: 16,17-Chadwick-a. 21,22-Parlov-a. 32,39-41,48,53,54-Sudzuka-a. 3.00
60-($4.99) Final issue; sixty years in the future 6.00
... Double Feature Edition (2002, $5.95) r/#1,2 1 2 3 5 6 8
... Special Edition (2009, $1.00) r/#1, "After Watchmen" trade dress on cover 3.00
... - Cycles TPB (2003, $12.95) r/#6-10; sketch pages by Guerra 13.00
... - Girl on Girl TPB (2005, $12.99) r/#32-36 13.00
... - Kimono Dragons TPB (2006, $14.99) r/#43-48 15.00
... - Motherland TPB (2007, $14.99) r/#49-54 15.00
... - One Small Step TPB (2004, $12.95) r/#11-17 13.00
... - Paper Dolls TPB (2006, $14.99) r/#37-42 15.00

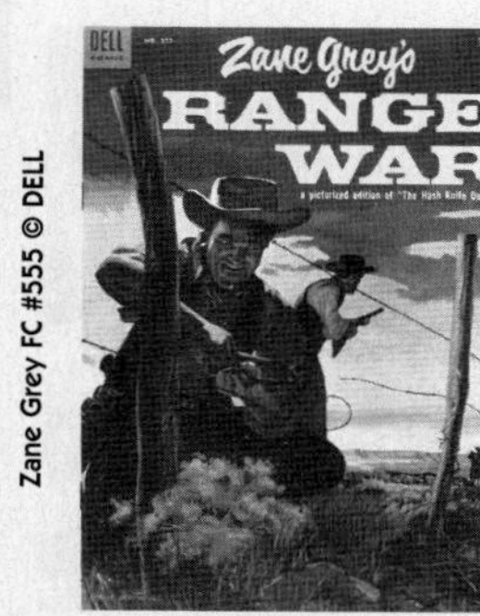

Zane Grey FC #555 © DELL

Zatanna (2010 series) #7 © DC

Zen Intergalactic Ninja #6 © S&C

	GD 2.0	VG 4.0	FN 6.0	VF 8.0	VF/NM 9.0	NM- 9.2
... - Ring of Truth TPB (2005, $14.99) r/#24-31						15.00
... - Safeword TPB (2004, $12.95) r/#18-23						13.00
... - Unmanned TPB (2002, $12.95) r/#1-5						15.00
... - Whys and Wherefores TPB (2008, $14.99) r/#55-60						15.00
... - The Deluxe Edition Book One HC (2008, $29.99, dustjacket) oversized r/#1-10; Guerra sketch pages						30.00
... - The Deluxe Edition Book Two HC (2009, $29.99, dustjacket) oversized r/#11-23; full script to #18						30.00
... - The Deluxe Edition Book Three HC (2010, $29.99, dustjacket) oversized r/#24-36; full script to #36						30.00
... - The Deluxe Edition Book Four HC (2010, $29.99, dustjacket) oversized r/#37-48; full script to #42						30.00
... - The Deluxe Edition Book Five HC (2011, $29.99, dustjacket) oversized r/#49-60; full script to #60						30.00

Y2K: THE COMIC
New England Comics Press: Oct, 1999 ($3.95, one-shot)

	GD	VG	FN	VF	VF/NM	NM-
1-Y2K scenarios and survival tips						4.00

YUPPIES FROM HELL (Also see Son of...)
Marvel Comics: 1989 ($2.95, B&W, one-shot, direct sales, 52 pgs.)

	GD	VG	FN	VF	VF/NM	NM-
1-Satire						4.00

ZAGO (..., Jungle Prince) (My Story #5 on)
Fox Features Syndicate: Sept, 1948 - No. 4, Mar, 1949

	GD	VG	FN	VF	VF/NM	NM-
1-Blue Beetle app.; partial-r/Atomic #4 (Toni Luck)	73	146	219	467	796	1125
2,3-Kamen-a	58	116	174	371	636	900
4-Baker-c	52	104	156	328	552	775

ZANE GREY'S STORIES OF THE WEST
Dell Publishing Co./Gold Key 11/64: No. 197, 9/48 - No. 996, 5-7/59; 11/64 (All painted-c)

	GD	VG	FN	VF	VF/NM	NM-
Four Color 197(#1)(9/48)	11	22	33	73	157	240
Four Color 222,230,236('49)	7	14	21	46	86	125
Four Color 246,255,270,301,314,333,346	5	10	15	35	63	90
Four Color 357,372,395,412,433,449,467,484	5	10	15	33	57	80
Four Color 511-Kinstler-a; Kubert-a	5	10	15	35	63	90
Four Color 532,555,583,604,616,632(5/55)	5	10	15	33	57	80
27(9-11/55) - 39(9-11/58)	4	8	12	28	47	65
Four Color 996(5-7/59)	5	10	15	33	57	80
10131-411-(11/64-G.K.)-Nevada; r/4-Color #996	3	6	9	21	33	45

ZANY (Magazine)(Satire)(See Frantic & Ratfink)
Candor Publ. Co.: Sept, 1958 - No. 4, May, 1959

	GD	VG	FN	VF	VF/NM	NM-
1-Bill Everett-c	15	30	45	84	127	170
2-4: 4-Everett-c	10	20	30	58	79	100

ZATANNA (See Adv. Comics #413, JLA #161, Supergirl #1, World's Finest Comics #274)
DC Comics: July, 1993 - No. 4, Oct, 1993 ($1.95, limited series)

	GD	VG	FN	VF	VF/NM	NM-
1-4						6.00
...: Everyday Magic (2003, $5.95, one-shot) Dini-s/Mays-a/Bolland-c; Constantine app.	3	6	9	19	30	40
Special 1(1987, $2.00)-Gray Morrow-c/a	1	3	4	6	8	10

ZATANNA
DC Comics: Jul, 2010 - No. 16, Oct, 2011 ($2.99)

	GD	VG	FN	VF	VF/NM	NM-
1-Dini-s/Roux-a/c	1	2	3	4	6	8
1-Variant-c by Bolland	3	6	9	14	20	25
2-6-Variant-c by Bolland	2	4	6	9	12	15
2-10,12: 4,5,7-Hardin-a. 7-Beechen-s. 8-Chang-a						5.00
11,13,14-Hughes-c	2	4	6	9	12	15
15-Hughes-c	3	6	9	14	20	25
16-Hughes-c	4	8	12	23	37	50
...: The Mistress of Magic TPB (2011, $17.99) r/#1-6; variant cover gallery						18.00

ZAZA, THE MYSTIC (Formerly Charlie Chan; This Magazine Is Haunted V2#12 on)
Charlton Comics: No. 10, Apr, 1956 - No. 11, Sept, 1956

	GD	VG	FN	VF	VF/NM	NM-
10,11	14	28	42	76	108	140

ZEALOT (Also see WildC.A.T.S: Covert Action Teams)
Image Comics: Aug, 1995 - No. 3, Nov, 1995 ($2.50, limited series)

	GD	VG	FN	VF	VF/NM	NM-
1-3						3.00

ZEGRA (Jungle Empress) (Formerly Tegra)(My Love Life #6 on)
Fox Features Syndicate: No. 2, Oct, 1948 - No. 5, April, 1949

	GD	VG	FN	VF	VF/NM	NM-
2	73	146	219	467	796	1125
3-5	54	108	162	346	591	835

ZEN INTERGALACTIC NINJA
No Publisher: 1987 -1993 ($1.75/$2.00, B&W)

	GD	VG	FN	VF	VF/NM	NM-
1	2	4	6	10	14	18
2-6: Copyright-Stern & Cote	1	3	4	6	8	10
V2#1-4-($2.00)						3.00
V3#1-5-($2.95)						3.00
... :Christmas Special 1 (1992, $2.95)						3.00
... :Earth Day Special 1 (1993, $2.95)						3.00

ZEN (Intergalactic Ninja)
Zen Comics Publishing: No. 0, Apr, 2003 - No. 4, Aug, 2003 ($2.95)

	GD	VG	FN	VF	VF/NM	NM-
0-4-Bill Maus-a/Steve Stern-s. 0-Wraparound-c						3.00

ZEN, INTERGALACTIC NINJA (mini-series)
Zen Comics/Archie Comics: Sept, 1992 - No. 3, 1992 ($1.25)(Formerly a B&W comic by Zen Comics)

	GD	VG	FN	VF	VF/NM	NM-
1-3: 1-Origin Zen; contains mini-poster						3.00

ZEN INTERGALACTIC NINJA
Entity Comics: No. 0, June-July, 1993 - No. 3, 1994 ($2.95, B&W, limited series)

	GD	VG	FN	VF	VF/NM	NM-
0-Gold foil stamped-c; photo-c of Zen model						3.00
1-3: Gold foil stamped-c; Bill Maus-c/a						3.00
0-(1993, $3.50, color)-Chromium-c by Jae Lee						4.00
...Sourcebook 1-(1993, $3.50)						4.00
...Sourcebook '94-(1994, $3.50)						4.00

ZEN INTERGALACTIC NINJA: APRIL FOOL'S SPECIAL
Parody Press: 1994 ($2.50, B&W)

	GD	VG	FN	VF	VF/NM	NM-
1-w/flip story of Renn Intergalactic Chihuahua						3.00

ZEN INTERGALACTIC NINJA COLOR
Entity Comics: 1994 - No. 7, 1995 ($2.25)

	GD	VG	FN	VF	VF/NM	NM-
1-($3.95)-Chromium die cut-c						4.00
1, 0-($2.25)-Newsstand; Jae Lee-c; r/...All New Color Special #0						3.00
2-($2.50)-Flip book						3.00
2-($3.50)-Flip book, polybagged w/chromium trading card						4.00
3-7						3.00
Summer Special (1994, $2.95)						3.00
Yearbook: Hazardous Duty 1 (1995)						3.00
Zen-isms 1 (1995, 2.95)						3.00
Ashcan-Tour of the Universe-(no price) w/flip cover						3.00

ZEN INTERGALACTIC NINJA COMMEMORATIVE EDITION
Zen Comics Publishing: 1997 ($5.95, color)

	GD	VG	FN	VF	VF/NM	NM-
1-Stern-s/Cote-a						6.00

ZEN INTERGALACTIC NINJA: HARD BOUNTY
1First Comics: 2015 - No. 6 ($3.99, limited series)

	GD	VG	FN	VF	VF/NM	NM-
1-Stern-s/Mychaels-a						4.00

ZEN INTERGALACTIC NINJA MILESTONE
Entity Comics: 1994 - No. 3, 1994 ($2.95, limited series)

	GD	VG	FN	VF	VF/NM	NM-
1-3: Gold foil logo; r/Defend the Earth						3.00

ZEN INTERGALATIC NINJA SPRING SPECTACULAR
Entity Comics: 1994 ($2.95, B&W, one-shot)

	GD	VG	FN	VF	VF/NM	NM-
1-Gold foil logo						3.00

ZEN INTERGALACTIC NINJA STARQUEST
Entity Comics: 1994 - No. 6, 1995 ($2.95, B&W)

	GD	VG	FN	VF	VF/NM	NM-
1-6: Gold foil logo						3.00

ZEN, INTERGALACTIC NINJA: THE HUNTED
Entity Comics: 1993 - No. 3, 1994 ($2.95, B&W, limited series)

	GD	VG	FN	VF	VF/NM	NM-
1-3: Newsstand Edition; foil logo						3.00
1-($3.50)-Polybagged w/chromium card by Kieth; foil logo						4.00

ZERO GIRL
DC Comics (Homage): Feb, 2001 - No. 5, Jun, 2001 ($2.95, limited series)

	GD	VG	FN	VF	VF/NM	NM-
1-5-Sam Kieth-s/a						3.00
TPB (2001, $14.95) r/#1-5; intro. by Alan Moore						15.00

ZERO GIRL: FULL CIRCLE
DC Comics (Homage): Jan, 2003 - No. 5, May, 2003 ($2.95, limited series)

	GD	VG	FN	VF	VF/NM	NM-
1-5-Sam Kieth-s/a						3.00
TPB (2003, $17.95) r/#1-5						18.00

ZERO HOUR: CRISIS IN TIME (Also see Showcase '94 #8-10)
DC Comics: No. 4(#1), Sept, 1994 - No. 0(#5), Oct, 1994 ($1.50, limited series)

Zero Zero #24 © Fantagraphics

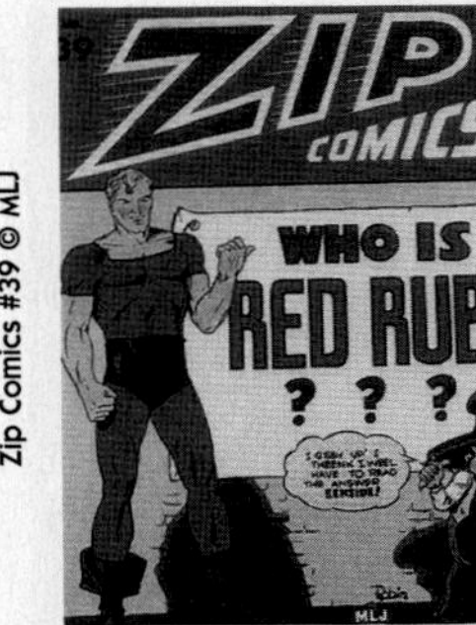

Zip Comics #39 © MLJ

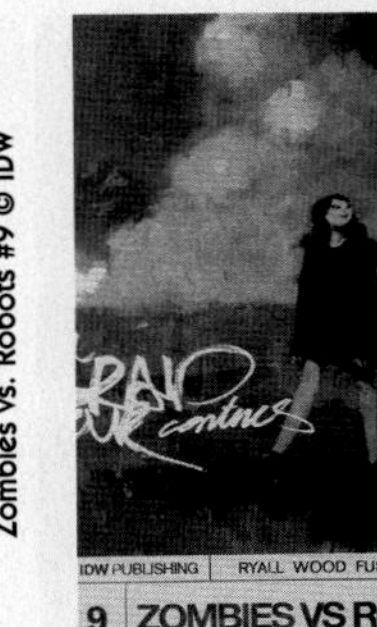

Zombies vs. Robots #9 © IDW

	GD 2.0	VG 4.0	FN 6.0	VF 8.0	VF/NM 9.0	NM- 9.2
4(#1)-0(#5)						4.00
"Ashcan"-(1994, free, B&W, 8 pgs.) several versions exist						3.00
TPB ('94, $9.95)						10.00

ZERO KILLER
Dark Horse Comics: Jul, 2007 - No.6, Oct, 2009 ($2.99)

1-6-Arvid Nelson-s/Matt Camp-a 3.00

ZERO PATROL, THE
Continuity Comics: Nov, 1984 - No. 2 ($1.50); 1987 - No. 5, May, 1989 ($2.00)

1,2: Neal Adams-c/a; Megalith begins 4.00
1-5 (#1,2-reprints above, 1987) 3.00

ZERO TOLERANCE
First Comics: Oct, 1990 - No. 4, Jan, 1991 ($2.25, limited series)

1-4: Tim Vigil-c/a(p) (his 1st color limited series) 3.00

ZERO ZERO
Fantagraphics: Mar, 1995 - No. 27 ($3.95/$4.95, B&W, anthology, mature)

1-7,9-15,17-25 5.00
8,16,26,27: 26-($4.95) Bagge-c 6.00

ZIGGY PIG-SILLY SEAL COMICS (See Animal Fun, Animated Movie-Tunes, Comic Capers, Krazy Komics, Silly Tunes & Super Rabbit)
Timely Comics (CmPL): Fall, 1944 - No. 4, Summer, 1945; No. 5, Summer, 1946; No. 6, Sept, 1946

	GD 2.0	VG 4.0	FN 6.0	VF 8.0	VF/NM 9.0	NM- 9.2
1-Vs. the Japanese	39	79	117	235	385	535
2-(Spring, 1945)	24	48	72	142	234	325
3-5	20	40	60	114	182	250
6-Infinity-c	21	42	63	122	199	275
I.W. Reprint #1(1958)-r/Krazy Komics	2	4	6	10	14	18
I.W. Reprint #2,7,8	2	4	6	10	14	18

ZIP COMICS
MLJ Magazines: Feb, 1940 - No. 47, Summer, 1944 (#1-7?: 68 pgs.)

	GD 2.0	VG 4.0	FN 6.0	VF 8.0	VF/NM 9.0	NM- 9.2
1-Origin Kalathar the Giant Man, The Scarlet Avenger, & Steel Sterling; Mr. Satan (by Edd Ashe), Nevada Jones (masked hero) & Zambini, the Miracle Man, War Eagle, Captain Valor begins	459	918	1377	3350	5925	8500
2-Nevada Jones adds mask & horse Blaze	271	542	813	1734	2967	4200
3-Biro robot-c	297	594	891	1901	3251	4600
4,5-Biro WWII-c	194	388	582	1242	2121	3000
6-8-Biro-c	187	374	561	1197	2049	2900
9-Last Kalathar & Mr. Satan; classic-c	232	464	696	1485	2543	3600
10-Inferno, the Flame Breather begins, ends #13	200	400	600	1280	2190	3100
11-Inferno without costume	148	296	444	947	1624	2300
12-Biro bondage/torture-c with dwarf ghouls	174	348	522	1114	1907	2700
13-Electrocution-c	194	388	582	1242	2121	3000
14-Biro bondage/torture guillotine-c	161	322	483	1030	1765	2500
15-Classic spider-c	194	388	582	1242	2121	3000
16-Female hanging execution-c by Biro (Rare)	194	388	582	1242	2121	3000
17-Last Scarlet Avenger; women in bondage being cooked alive-c by Biro	219	438	657	1402	2401	3400
18-Wilbur begins (9/41, 1st app.); sci-fi-c	213	426	639	1363	2332	3300
19	161	322	483	1030	1765	2500
20-Origin & 1st app. Black Jack (11/41); Hitler-c	290	580	870	1856	3178	4500
21-Sinister Nazi using lethal chemical weapons on the General-c	168	336	504	1075	1838	2600
22-Classic Nazi Grim Reaper w/sickle, V for Victory-c	423	846	1269	3000	5250	7500
23-Nazi WWII-c	135	270	405	864	1482	2100
24,25: 25-Last Nevada Jones	123	246	369	787	1344	1900
26-Classic Nazi/Japanese "Remember Pearl Harbor!" WWII cover; Black Witch begins; last Captain Valor (scarce)	258	516	774	1651	2826	4000
27-Intro. Web (7/42) plus-c app.; Japanese WWII-c	271	542	813	1734	2967	4200
28-Origin Web; classic Baron Gastapo Nazi WWII-c	239	478	717	1530	2615	3700
29-The Hyena app. (scarce); Nazi WWII-c	200	400	600	1280	2190	3100
30-WWII-c	155	310	465	992	1696	2400
31,35-WWII-c. 35-Last Zambini, Black Jack	135	270	405	864	1482	2100
32-Classic skeleton Nazi WWII-c	206	412	618	1318	2259	3200
33-Japanese war-c showing nurses bound, blindfolded, lined up at a firing squad	155	310	465	992	1696	2400
34-Japanese WWII bondage & hanging-c; 1st Applejack app.	194	388	582	1242	2121	3000
36-38: 38-Last Web issue	61	122	183	390	670	950
39-Red Rube begins (origin, 8/43)	63	126	189	403	689	975
40-43	54	108	162	343	574	825
44-46: WWII covers. 45-Wilbur ends	63	126	189	405	689	975
47-Last issue; scarce	65	130	195	416	708	1000

NOTE: *Biro a-5, 9, 17; c-3-17.* ***Meskin*** *a-1-3, 5-7, 9, 10, 12, 13, 15, 16 at least.* ***Montana*** *c-29, 30, 32-35.* ***Novick*** *c-18-28, 31.* ***Sahle*** *c-37, 38, 40-46. Bondage c-8, 9, 33, 34. Cover features: Steel Sterling-1-43, 47; (w/Blackjack-20-27 & Web-27-35), 28-39; (w/Red Rube-40-43); Red Rube-44-47.*

ZIP-JET (Hero)
St. John Publishing Co.: Feb, 1953 - No. 2, Apr-May, 1953

	GD 2.0	VG 4.0	FN 6.0	VF 8.0	VF/NM 9.0	NM- 9.2
1-Rocketman-r from Punch Comics; #1-c from splash in Punch #10	97	194	291	621	1061	1500
2	55	110	165	352	601	850

ZIPPY THE CHIMP (CBS TV Presents...)
Pines (Literary Ent.): No. 50, March, 1957; No. 51, Aug, 1957

	GD 2.0	VG 4.0	FN 6.0	VF 8.0	VF/NM 9.0	NM- 9.2
50,51	8	16	24	40	50	60

ZODIAC STARFORCE
Dark Horse Comics: Aug, 2015 - No. 4, Feb, 2016 ($3.99, limited series)

1-4-Kevin Panetta-s/Paulina Ganucheau-a. 2-Wada-c. 4-Babs Tarr-c 4.00

ZODY, THE MOD ROB
Gold Key: July, 1970

	GD 2.0	VG 4.0	FN 6.0	VF 8.0	VF/NM 9.0	NM- 9.2
1	3	6	9	16	23	30

ZOMBIE
Marvel Comics: Nov, 2006 - No. 4, Feb, 2007 ($3.99, limited series)

1-4-Kyle Hotz-a/c; Mike Raicht-s 4.00
TPB (2007, $13.99) r/#1-4 14.00
...: Simon Garth (1/08 - No. 4, 4/08) Hotz-s/a/c 4.00

ZOMBIE BOY
Timbuktu Graphics/Antarctic Press: Mar, 1988 - Nov, 1996 ($1.50/$2.50/$2.95, B&W)

1-Mark Stokes-s/a 3.00
...'s Hoodoo Tales (11/89, $1.50) 3.00
... Rises Again (1/94, $2.50) r/#1 and Hoodoo Tales 3.00
1-(Antarctic Press, 11/96, $2.95) new story 3.00

ZOMBIE KING
Image Comics: No. 0, June, 2005 ($2.95, B&W, one-shot)

0-Frank Cho-s/a 5.00

ZOMBIE PROOF
Moonstone: 2007 - Present ($3.50)

1-3: 1-J.C. Vaughn-s/Vincent Spencer-a; two covers by Spencer and Neil Vokes 4.00
1-Baltimore Comic-Con 2007 variant-c by Vokes (ltd. ed. of 500) 6.00
2-Big Apple 2008 Convention Edition; Tucci-c (ltd. ed. of 250) 6.00
3-Convention Edition; Beck-c (ltd. ed. of 100) 6.00
...: Zombie Zoo #1 Virginia Comicon Exclusive Edition (2012, ed. of 150) 10.00
...: Zombie Zoo - WVPOP Exclusive Edition (2012) 10.00

ZOMBIES CHRISTMAS CAROL (See Marvel Zombies Christmas Carol)

ZOMBIES!: ECLIPSE OF THE UNDEAD
IDW Publ.: Nov, 2006 - No. 4, Feb, 2007 ($3.99, limited series)

1-4-Torres-s/Herrera-a; two covers 4.00

ZOMBIES!: FEAST
IDW Publ.: May, 2006 - No. 5, Oct, 2006 ($3.99, limited series)

1-5: 1-Chris Bolton-a/Shane McCarthy-s. 3-Lorenzana-a 4.00

ZOMBIES!: HUNTERS
IDW Publ.: May, 2008 ($3.99)

1-Don Figueroa-a/c; Dara Naraghi-s 4.00

ZOMBIES VS. ROBOTS
IDW Publ.: Oct, 2006 - No. 2, Dec, 2006 ($3.99, limited series)

1-Chris Ryall-s/Ashley Wood-a; two covers by Wood 15.00
2 10.00

ZOMBIES VS. ROBOTS
IDW Publ.: Jan, 2015 - No. 10, Oct, 2015 ($3.99/$4.99)

1-8-Short stories by Chris Ryall-s/Ashley Wood-a and others 4.00
9,10-($4.99) Two covers on each 5.00

ZOMBIES VS. ROBOTS AVENTURE
IDW Publ.: Feb, 2010 - No. 4, May, 2010 ($3.99, limited series)

1-4-Short stories; Ryall-s; art by Matthews III, McCaffrey, & Hernandez; Wood-c 4.00

ZOMBIES VS. ROBOTS: UNDERCITY

Zoohunters #3 © Aspen MLT

Zoot #7 © FOX

Zot! #25 © Scott McCloud

GD 2.0 | VG 4.0 | FN 6.0 | VF 8.0 | VF/NM 9.0 | NM- 9.2

IDW Publ.: Apr, 2011 - No. 3, Jun, 2011 ($3.99, limited series)
1-3-Chris Ryall-s/Mark Torres; two covers on each by Torres and Garry Brown 4.00

ZOMBIES VS. ROBOTS VS. AMAZONS
IDW Publ.: Sept, 2007 - No. 3, Feb, 2008 ($3.99, limited series)
1-3-Chris Ryall-s/Ashley Wood-a; two covers by Wood on each 5.00

ZOMBIE TALES THE SERIES
BOOM! Studios: Apr, 2008 - No. 12, Mar, 2009 ($3.99)
1-Niles-s; Lansdale-s/Barreto-a; two covers on each 4.00

ZOMBIE WAR
IDW Publishing: Oct, 2013 - No. 2, Nov, 2013 ($3.99, limited series)
1,2-Kevin Eastman & Tom Skulan-s/Eastman & Eric Talbot-a; 2 covers on each 4.00

ZOMBIE WORLD (one-shots)
Dark Horse Comics
... :Eat Your Heart Out (4/98, $2.95) Kelley Jones-c/s/a 3.00
... :Home For The Holidays (12/97, $2.95) 3.00

ZOMBIE WORLD: CHAMPION OF THE WORMS
Dark Horse Comics: Sept, 1997 - No. 3, Nov, 1997 ($2.95, limited series)
1-3-Mignola & McEown-c/s/a 3.00

ZOMBIE WORLD: DEAD END
Dark Horse Comics: Jan, 1998 - No. 2, Feb, 1998 ($2.95, limited series)
1,2-Stephen Blue-c/s/a 3.00

ZOMBIE WORLD: TREE OF DEATH
Dark Horse Comics: Jun, 1999 - No. 4, Oct, 1999 ($2.95, limited series)
1-4-Mills-s/Deadstock-a 3.00

ZOMBIE WORLD: WINTER'S DREGS
Dark Horse Comics: May, 1998 - No. 4, Aug, 1998 ($2.95, limited series)
1-4-Fingerman-s/Edwards-a 3.00

ZOO ANIMALS
Star Publications: No. 8, 1954 (15¢, 36 pgs.)
8-(B&W for coloring) 8 16 24 44 57 70

ZOO FUNNIES (Tim McCoy #16 on)
Charlton Comics/Children Comics Publ.: Nov, 1945 - No. 15, 1947
101(#1)(11/45, 1st Charlton comic book)-Funny animal; Al Fago-c
21 42 63 126 206 285
2(12/45, 52 pgs.) Classic-c 15 30 45 83 124 165
3-5 11 22 33 62 86 110
6-15: 8-Diana the Huntress app. 9 18 27 52 69 85

ZOO FUNNIES (Becomes Nyoka, The Jungle Girl #14 on?)
Capitol Stories/Charlton Comics: July, 1953 - No. 13, Sept, 1955; Dec, 1984
1-1st app.? Timothy The Ghost; Fago-c/a 12 24 36 69 97 125
2 8 16 24 42 54 65
3-7 7 14 21 37 46 55
8-13-Nyoka app. 9 18 27 52 69 85
1(1984) (Low print run) 1 2 3 4 5 7

ZOOHUNTERS, THE
Aspen MLT: Nov, 2014 - Present ($3.99)
1-3-Peter Stiegerwald-s/a; five covers on each 4.00

ZOONIVERSE
Eclipse Comics: 8/86 - No. 6, 6/87 ($1.25/$1.75, limited series, Mando paper)
1-6 3.00

ZOO PARADE (TV)
Dell Publishing Co.: #662, 1955 (Marlin Perkins)
Four Color 662 5 10 15 33 57 80

ZOOM COMICS
Carlton Publishing Co.: Dec, 1945 (one-shot)
nn-Dr. Mercy, Satannas, from Red Band Comics; Capt. Milksop origin retold
42 84 126 265 445 625

ZOOT (Rulah Jungle Goddess #17 on)
Fox Features Syndicate: nd (1946) - No. 16, July, 1948 (Two #13s & 14s)
nn-Funny animal only 27 54 81 158 259 360
2-The Jaguar app. 21 42 63 124 202 280
3(Fall, 1946) - 6-Funny animals & teen-age 15 30 45 83 124 165
7-(6/47)-Rulah, Jungle Goddess (origin/1st app.) 129 258 387 826 1413 2000
8-10 77 154 231 493 847 1200

GD 2.0 | VG 4.0 | FN 6.0 | VF 8.0 | VF/NM 9.0 | NM- 9.2

11-Kamen bondage-c 94 188 282 597 1024 1450
12-Injury-to-eye panels, torture scene 65 130 195 416 708 1000
13(2/48) 60 120 190 381 653 925
14(3/48)-Used in **SOTI**, pg. 104, "One picture showing a girl nailed by her wrists to trees with blood flowing from the wounds, might be taken straight from an ill. ed. of the Marquis deSade" 86 172 258 546 936 1325
13(4/48),14(5/48)-Western True Crime #15 on? 58 116 174 371 636 900
15,16 58 116 174 371 636 900

ZORRO (Walt Disney with #882)(TV)(See Eclipse Graphic Album)
Dell Publishing Co.: May, 1949 - No. 15, Sept-Nov, 1961 (Photo-c 882 on)
(Zorro first appeared in a pulp story Aug 19, 1919)
Four Color 228 (#1) 18 36 54 126 281 435
Four Color 425,617,732 10 20 30 69 147 225
Four Color 497,538,574-Kinstler-a 11 22 33 73 157 240
Four Color 882-Photo-c begin;1st TV Disney; Toth-a 13 26 39 89 195 300
Four Color 920,933,960,976-Toth-a in all 10 20 30 66 138 210
Four Color 1003('59)-Toth-a 10 20 30 66 138 210
Four Color 1037-Annette Funicello photo-c 12 24 36 81 176 270
8(12-2/59-60) 7 14 21 48 89 130
9-Toth-a 8 16 24 51 96 140
10,11,13-15-Last photo-c 7 14 21 46 86 125
12-Toth-a; last 10¢ issue 8 16 24 51 96 140
NOTE: *Warren Tufts a-4-Color 1037, 8, 9, 10, 13.*

ZORRO (Walt Disney)(TV)
Gold Key: Jan, 1966 - No. 9, Mar, 1968 (All photo-c)
1-Toth-a 7 14 21 44 82 120
2,4,5,7-9-Toth-a. 5-r/F.C. #1003 by Toth 4 8 12 28 47 65
3,6-Tufts-a 4 8 12 27 44 60
NOTE: *#1-9 are reprinted from Dell issues.* ***Tufts*** *a-3, 4. #1-r/F.C. #882. #2-r/F.C. #960. #3-r/#12-c & #8 inside. #4-r/#9-c & insides. #6-r/#11(all); #7-r/#14-c. #8-r/F.C. #933 inside & back-c & #976-c. #9-r/F.C. #920.*

ZORRO (TV)
Marvel Comics: Dec, 1990 - No. 12, Nov, 1991 ($1.00)
1-12: Based on TV show. 12-Toth-c 3.00

ZORRO (Also see Mask of Zorro)
Topps Comics: Nov, 1993 - No. 11, Nov, 1994 ($2.50/$2.95)
0-(11/93, $1.00, 20 pgs.)-Painted-c; collector's ed. 3.00
1,4,6-9,11: 1-Miller-c. 4-Mike Grell-c. 6-Mignola-c. 7-Lady Rawhide-c by Gulacy. 8-Perez-c. 10-Julie Bell-c. 11-Lady Rawhide-c 3.00
2-Lady Rawhide-app. (not in costume) 5.00
3-1st app. Lady Rawhide in costume, 3-Lady Rawhide-c by Adam Hughes
1 2 3 5 6 8
5-Lady Rawhide app. 4.00
10-($2.95)-Lady Rawhide-c/app. 4.00
The Lady Wears Red (12/98, $12.95, TPB) r/#1-3 13.00
Zorro's Renegades (2/99, $14.95, TPB) r/#4-8 15.00

ZORRO
Dynamite Entertainment: 2008 - No. 20, 2010 ($3.50)
1-Origin retold; Wagner-s; three covers 3.50
2-20-Two covers on all 3.50

ZORRO MATANZAS
Dynamite Entertainment: 2010 - No. 4, 2010 ($3.99)
1-4-Mayhew-a/McGregor-s 4.00

ZORRO RIDES AGAIN
Dynamite Entertainment: 2011 - No. 12, 2012 ($3.99)
1-12: 1-6-Wagner-s/Polls-a. 7-12-Snyder III-a. 10-Lady Zorro on cover 4.00

ZOT!
Eclipse Comics: 4/84 - No. 10, 7/85; No. 11, 1/87 - No. 36 7/91 ($1.50, Baxter-p)
1 5.00
2,3 4.00
4-10: 4-Origin. 10-Last color issue 3.00
10 1/2 (6/86, 25¢, Not Available Comics) Ashcan; art by Feazell & Scott McCloud 4.00
11-14,15-35-($2.00-c) B&W issues 3.00
14 1/2 (Adventures of Zot! in Dimension 10 1/2)(7/87) Antisocialman app. 3.00
36-($2.95-c) B&W 5.00
... The Complete Black and White Collection TPB (2008, $24.95) r/#11-36 with commentary, interviews and bonus artwork 25.00

Z-2 COMICS (Secret Agent...)(See Holyoke One-Shot #7)
ZULU (See Movie Classics)

COSMIC COMICS!
LAS VEGAS, NV

BUSINESS CARD ADS

To have your ads seen here in future editions, contact our Advertising Dept.
Gemstone Publishing, Inc.
1940 Greenspring Dr., Suite I-L
Timonium, MD 21093
or e-mail **feedback@gemstonepub.com.**

ALWAYS BUYING COMICS .COM

Dan Gallo
Vintage Comic Books - Original Comic Art

(954) 547-9063
dgallo1291@aol.com
e-Bay ID: dgallo1291

Top Five Selection on the Web!

Strict, consistent grading.
NEW COLLECTIONS in the House!
EASY-TO-USE, secure WEBSITE!
FREE SHIPPING w/ $75 order!
info@houseofcomics.com Call us at (510) 847-3376
www.HouseofComics.com

BUYING AND SELLING COMICS FOR 30 YEARS!
WORLDWIDE COMICS
ALWAYS BUYING!
CALL US TODAY!
SENIOR OVERSTREET ADVISOR
wwcomics.com
STEPHEN RITTER • stephen@wwcomics.com
Tel: (830) 368-4103 • 29369 Raintree Ridge, Fair Oaks Ranch, TX 78015 (San Antonio Area)
COMICS GUARANTY, LLC Charter Member Dealer

Get the MAX in CASH TODAY!!!

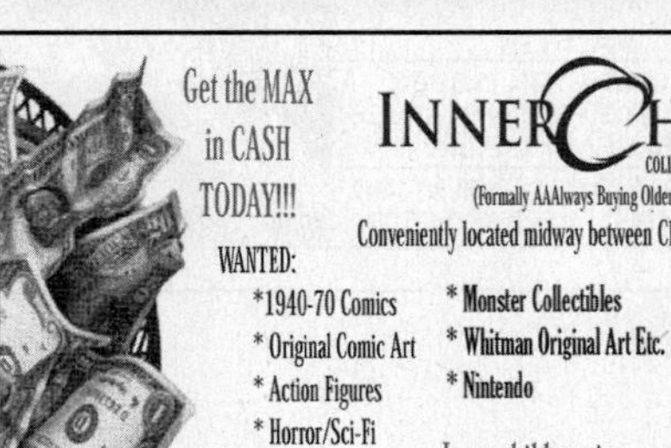

5921 6th Avenue A Kenosha, WI. 53140 (262)-653-0400 (312)-269-0189

1 East Dayton Street
West Alexandria, OH 45381
(937) 839 - 7068
WWW.JIMDANCOMICS.COM

Check out our website for information on our quarterly COMIC & TOY SHOW!

Outer Limits
Comic Books & Collectables
Buy • Sell • Trade

Open Wednesday - Saturday

Rod Matlack
427 S. Santa Fe Avenue
Pueblo, CO 81003
Pueblo'sOuterLimits *1000's of $1.00 Comics* **719.583.2750**

BUSINESS CARD ADS

BATMAN
WONDER WOMAN
COLLECTORS

E-mail: batt90@aol.com
wwali@aol.com

COLLECTORS
P.O. Box 604925
Flushing, NY 11360-4925

COMIC BOOK WORLD, INC.
EST. 1981

OVER 100,000 BACK ISSUES IN STOCK EVERY SINGLE DAY!
7130 TURFWAY ROAD
FLORENCE, KY 41042
859 • 371 • 9562
WWW.COMICBOOKWORLD.COM

COMIC BOOK WORLD, INC.
EST. 1981

THE BEST COMIC BOOK STORE IN LOUISVILLE!
6905 SHEPHERDSVILLE ROAD
LOUISVILLE, KY 40219
502 • 964 • 5500
WWW.COMICBOOKWORLD.COM

JOHN ZAWADZKI

COMIC BOOKS & COLLECTABLES
BUY & SELL

ebay id: JZ98 **716.479.7618**
JZAWADZKI@roadrunner.com

30% OFF ALL COMIC BOOKS WITH MEMBERSHIP

BEST COMICS
INTERNATIONAL
(Est.1991)

TOMMY MALETTA

•COMIC BOOKS•BACK ISSUES
•GRAPHIC NOVELS•TOYS•STATUES
•SPORTS MEMORABILIA

1300 JERICHO TURNPIKE NEW HYDE PARK, NY 11040
Phone: 516-328-1900 WWW.BESTCOMICS.COM

---

www.comics-4-kids.org comics4kids@aim.com

Comics4Kids INC gives comics to kids for free to improve literacy and encourage imagination!! We are a Seattle based 501 (c) 3 charity. All donations are tax deductible to the fullest extent of Law!

Office of the President
Dale Moore (206) 327-7436

What's In Your Collection?

myslabbedcomics.com

andrew@myslabbedcomics.com

Selling - Buying - Consign

Andrew Cretella
andrew@gacollectibles.com

GA COLLECTIBLES
www.gacollectibles.com

PO Box 2123
Woburn, MA 01888
978-265-9850

Comics, Original Art, Pulps, Paperbacks
CGC Signature Series

To have your ads seen here in future editions, contact our Advertising Dept.
Gemstone Publishing, Inc.
1940 Greenspring Dr., Suite I-L
Timonium, MD 21093
or e-mail **feedback@gemstonepub.com.**

DIRECTORY LISTINGS

(PAID ADVERTISING - STORE LISTINGS)

You can have your store listed here for very reasonable rates. Send for details for next year's Guide. The following list of stores have paid to be included in this list. We cannot assume any responsibility in your dealings with these shops. This list is provided for your information only. When planning trips, it would be advisable to make appointments in advance. Remember, to get your shop included in the next edition, contact us for rates.

Gemstone Publishing, Inc.
1940 Greenspring Dr., Suite I-L
Timonium, MD 21093
E-MAIL: feedback@gemstonepub.com

Items stocked by these shops are noted at the end of each listing and are coded as follows:

(a) Golden Age Comics
(b) Silver Age Comics
(c) Bronze Age Comics
(d) New Comics & Magazines
(e) Back Issue magazines
(f) Comic Supplies
(g) Collectible Card Games
(h) Role Playing Games
(i) Gaming Supplies
(j) Manga
(k) Anime
(l) Underground Comics
(m) Original Comic Art
(n) Pulps
(o) Big Little Books
(p) Books - Used
(q) Books - New
(r) Comic Related Posters
(s) Movie Posters
(t) Trading Cards
(u) Statues/Mini-busts, etc.
(v) Premiums (Rings, Decoders)
(w) Action Figures
(x) Other Toys
(y) Records/CDs
(z) DVDs/VHS
(1) Doctor Who Items
(2) Simpsons Items
(3) Star Trek Items
(4) Star Wars Items
(5) HeroClix

ARIZONA

Fantastic Worlds
9393 N. 90th Street
Suite 119
Scottsdale, AZ 85258
PH: (480) 256-1454
Johns
@fantasticworldscomics.com
fantasticworldscomics.com
(a-f,m-q,u,x,3,4)

CALIFORNIA

Sterling Silver Comics
2210 Pickwick Drive
Camarillo, CA 93010
PH: (805) 484-4708
mike@sterlingsilvercomics.com
www.sterlingsilvercomics.com
(a-f,j,l,t,w,1,4)

Legacy Comics and Cards
123 W. Wilson Ave.
Glendale, CA 91203
PH: (818) 247-8803
FAX: (818) 247-8801
LegacyComics@hotmail.com
LegacyComics.com
(a-d,f-j,l,r,t,u,w,4,5)

Terry's Comics
P.O. Box 2065
Orange, CA 92859
PH: (714) 288-8993
FAX: (714) 288-8992
info@TerrysComics.com
www.TerrysComics.com
(a-f,l-p,r,s)

ArchAngels
4629 Cass Street #9
Pacific Beach, CA 92109
PH: (310) 480-8105
rhughes@archangels.com
www.archangels.com

Captain Nemo Games and Comics
565 Higuera St.
San Luis Obispo, CA 93401
PH: (805) 543-NEMO (6366)
CaptainNemo@CaptainNemo.biz
(a-k,r,u,w-z,3-5)

CPRS (Condition Potential Realization Service)
596 E. El Camino Real
Sunnyvale, CA 94087
PH: (408) 315-1965
FAX: (408) 732-7131
phil@comic-press.com
www.comic-press.com

COLORADO

RTS Unlimited, Inc.
P. O. Box 150412
Lakewood, CO 80215-0412
PH: (303) 403-1840
FAX: (303) 403-1837
RTSUnlimitedinc@gmail.com
www.RTSUnlimited.com
(a,b,c,e,f,m,s)

Outer Limits Comic Books & Collectables
427 S. Santa Fe Ave.
Pueblo, CO 81003
PH: (719) 583-2750
(a-f,i,m,y)

FLORIDA

Phil's Comic Shoppe
6512 West Atlantic Blvd.
Margate, FL 33063
PH: (954) 977-6947
philscomix@att.net
eBay id: philscomicshop
(a-f,m,t,w)

Comic Book Certification Service (CBCS)
2400 31st Street South
St. Petersburg, FL 33712
PH: (727) 803-6822
PH: (844) 870-CBCS
www.CBCScomics.com

Classic Collectible Services
P.O. Box 4738
Sarasota, FL 34230
PH: (855) CCS-1711
CCSpaper.com

CGC
P.O. Box 4738
Sarasota, FL 34230
PH: (877) NM-COMIC
FAX: (941) 360-2558
www.CGCcomics.com

Culture and Thrills Collectibles Gallery
5205 N. Florida Ave.
Tampa, FL 33603
PH: (813) 237-5400
davidt@cultureandthrills.com
www.dtacollectibles.com
(a,b,c,e,f,l,m-x,3,4)

David T. Alexander Collectibles
P.O. Box 273086
Tampa, FL 33618
PH: (813) 968-1805
davidt@cultureandthrills.com
www.dtacollectibles.com
(a-c,e,l-o,r-t,v,x,3,4)

Pedigree Comics, Inc.
12541 Equine Lane
Wellington, FL 33414
PH/FAX: (561) 422-1120
CELL: (561) 596-9111
E-Mail: DougSchmell
@pedigreecomics.com
www.pedigreecomics.com

GEORGIA

Mountain Man Comics
771-B East Main Street
Blue Ridge, GA 30513
PH: (706) 946-4400
info@mountainmancomics.com
mountainmancomics.com

HAWAII

Maui Comics & Collectibles
333 Dairy Road; Unit 102
Kahului, HI 96732
PH: (808) 868-0219
CEL: (808) 298-5261
MauiComicsandCollectibles
@gmail.com
(a-m,w-y)

ILLINOIS

Yesterday
1143 W. Addison St.
Chicago, IL 60613
PH: (773) 248-8087
(a-c,e,f,l,n-p,r-t,v,x-z,1,3,4)

Comics4Less
Chicago, IL
PH: (888) 88-COMIC
oldcomics@yahoo.com
www.Comics4Less.com

Mellow Blue Planet
2212 5th Ave.
Rock Island, IL 61201
PH: (309) 788-1653
mellowblueplanet@hotmail.com
www.mellowblueplanet.com
(a-f,i,j,l,o,q-u,w,x,1-5)

Aw Yeah Comics!
4933 Oakton St.
Skokie, IL 60077
PH: (847) 423-2916
www.awyeahcomics.com

INDIANA

Comics Ina Flash
P.O. Box 3611
Evansville, IN 47735-3611
PH/FAX: (812) 401-6127
comicflash@aol.com
www.comicsinaflash.com

Aw Yeah Comics!
107 North High St.
Muncie, IN 47305
PH: (765) 282-5297
www.awyeahcomics.com

KENTUCKY

Dale Roberts Comics
P.O. Box 707
Calvert City, KY 42029
PH: (270) 556-2988
Dale@DaleRobertsComics.com
www.DaleRobertsComics.com

Comic Book World, Inc.
7130 Turfway Rd.
Florence, KY 41042
PH: (859) 371-9562
FAX: (859) 371-6925
mark@comicbookworld.com
www.comicbookworld.com
(a-j,l-r,t,u,w,1,3-5)

Comic Book World, Inc.
6905 Shepherdsville Rd.
Louisville, KY 40219
PH/FAX: (502) 964-5500
doug@comicbookworld.com
www.comicbookworld.com
(a-j,l-u,w,x,5)

Leroy Harper
P.O. Box 212
West Paducah, KY 42086
PH: (270) 748-9364
LHCOMICS@hotmail.com

LOUISIANA

Excalibur Comics, Cards & Games
937 E. 70th Street
Shreveport, LA 71106
PH: (318) 868-4389
FAX: (318) 868-4369
excaliburccg@gmail.com
www.excaliburccg.com
(a-j,t,u,w,x,1,3-5)

MAINE

Top Shelf Comics
115 Main St.; 1st Floor
Bangor, ME 04401
PH: (207) 947-4939
topshelf@tcomics.com
www.tcomics.com
(a-f)

MARYLAND

E. Gerber
1720 Belmont Ave.; Suite C
Baltimore, MD 21244

Esquire Comics.com
Mark S. Zaid, ESQ.
P.O. Box 3422492
Bethesda, MD 20827
PH: (202) 498-0011
esquirecomics@aol.com
www.esquirecomics.com
(b-k,r,u,w,4,5)

Alternate Worlds
10854 York Road
Cockeysville, MD 21030
PH: (410) 666-3290
AltWorldStore@comcast.net
www.Alternateworlds.biz
(b-j,q,r,u,w,x,1-5)

Basement Comics
2113 Columbia Park Drive
Suite 2A
Edgewood, MD 21040
PH: (443) 831-2761
basmntcomx@aol.com
(a,b,c,e,l,m,n,o,r,s,4)

Reece's Rare Comics
11028 Graymarsh Pl.
Ijamsville, MD 21754
PH: (240) 575-8600
greg@gregreececomics.com
www.gregreececomics.com
(a,b,c,e,f)

Cards Comics and Collectibles
100 A Chartley Drive
Reisterstown, MD 21136
PH: (410) 526-7410
FAX: (410) 526-4006
cardscomicscollectibles
@yahoo.com
www.cardscomicscollectibles.
com
(a-d,f,g,j,t,w,5)

Diamond Comic Distributors
10150 York Road, Suite 300
Hunt Valley, MD 21030
PH: (443) 318-8001

Diamond International Galleries
1940 Greenspring Dr., Suite I-L
Timonium, MD 21093
Contact: pokevin@
DiamondGalleries.com
www.DiamondGalleries.com

MASSACHUSETTS

New England Comics
716A Crescent St.
Brockton, MA 02302
PH/FAX: (508) 559-5068
support@newenglandcomics.
com
www.newenglandcomics.com
(a-k,r,t,u,w,x,z,1-5)

New England Comics
316 Harvard St.
Coolidge Corner
Brookline, MA 02446
PH/FAX: (617) 566-0115
support@newenglandcomics.
com
www.newenglandcomics.com
(a-k,r,t,u,w,x,z,1-5)

New England Comics
14A Eliot St.
Harvard Square
Cambridge, MA 02138
PH/FAX: (617) 354-5352
support@newenglandcomics.
com
www.newenglandcomics.com
(a-k,r,t,u,w,x,z,1-5)

Gary Dolgoff Comics
116 Pleasant St.
Easthampton, MA 01027
PH: (413) 529-0326
FAX: (413) 529-9824
gary@gdcomics.com
www.gdcomics.com

SuperworldComics.com
456 Main St., Suite F
Holden, MA 01520
PH: (508) 829-2259
PH: (508) UB-WACKY
Ted@Superworldcomics.com
www.Superworldcomics.com
(a-c,m)

New England Comics
95 Pleasant St.
Malden, MA 02148
PH/FAX: (781) 322-2404
support@newenglandcomics.
com
www.newenglandcomics.com
(a-k,r,t,u,w,x,z,1-5)

New England Comics
2184 Acushnet Ave.
New Bedford, MA 02745
PH/FAX: (508) 995-2693
support@newenglandcomics.
com
www.newenglandcomics.com
(a-k,r,t,u,w,x,z,1-5)

New England Comics
732 Washington St.
Norwood, MA 02062
PH/FAX: (781) 769-4552
support@newenglandcomics.
com
www.newenglandcomics.com
(a-k,r,t,u,w,x,z,1-5)

New England Comics
1511 Hancock St.
Quincy, MA 02169
PH/FAX: (617) 770-1848
support@newenglandcomics.
com
www.newenglandcomics.com
(a-k,r,t,u,w,x,z,1-5)

New England Comics
We Buy Old Comics
Top Dollar Paid
Quincy, MA 02169
PH: (617) 770-1848
support@newenglandcomics.
com
www.newenglandcomics.com
(a,b,c)

Bill Cole Enterprises Inc.
P.O. Box 60
Randolph, MA 02368-0060
PH: (781) 986-2653
FAX: (781) 986-2656
sales@bcemylar.com
www.bcemylar.com

The Outer Limits
437 Moody Street
Waltham, MA 02453
PH: (781) 891-0444
AskOuterLimits@aol.com
www.eOuterLimits.com
(a-p,r-z,1-5)

MICHIGAN

Comix Corner
32032 Utica Rd.
Fraser, MI 48026
PH: (586) 296-2758
(b,c,d,f,u,w,x,5)

Harley Yee Comics
P.O. Box 51758
Livonia, MI 48151-5758
PH: (800) 731-1029
FAX: (734) 421-7928
HarleyComx@aol.com
www.HarleyYeeComics.com

Comix Corner
861 E. Auburn Rd.
Rochester Hills, MI 48307
PH: (248) 852-3356
(b,c,d,f,u,w,x,5)

NEBRASKA

Robert Beerbohm Comic Art
P.O. Box 507
Fremont, NE 68026
PH: (402) 919-9393
BeerbohmRL@gmail.com
www.BLBcomics.com
(a,b,c,e,l-o,r)

NEVADA

Redbeard's Book Den
P.O. Box 217
Crystal Bay, NV 89402
PH: (775) 831-4848
FAX: (775) 831-4483
www.redbeardsbookden.com
(a,b,c,l,o,p)

Cactus Comics
2655 Windmill Parkway
Henderson, NV 89074
PH: (702) 270-3232
Best Cactus@aol.com
We're on Facebook
(a-l,r-x,3,5)

Cosmic Comics!
3830 E. Flamingo Rd.
Suite F-2
Las Vegas, NV 89121
PH: (702) 451-6611
info@CosmicComicsLV.com
www.CosmicComicsLV.com
(a-l,n,o,r,t-x,5)

Torpedo Comics
7300 Arroyo Crossing Pkwy
Suite 105
Las Vegas, NV 89113
PH: (702) 444-4432
TorpedoComics@gmail.com

NEW HAMPSHIRE

Rare Books & Comics
James F. Payette
P.O. Box 750
Bethlehem, NH 03574
PH: (603) 869-2097
FAX: (603) 869-3475
JimPayette@msn.com
www.JamesPayetteComics.com
(a,b,c,e,n,o,p)

NEW JERSEY

Nationwide Comics
Buying All 10¢ & 12¢
original priced comics
Derek Woywood
Clementon, NJ 08021
PH: (856) 217-5737 or
Hotline: (800) 938-0325
FAX: (714) 288-8992
dwoywood@yahoo.com
www.philadelphiacomic-con.com
(a,b,d-h,m,n,q)

Zapp Comics
700 Tennent Road
Manalapan, NJ 07726
PH: (732) 617-1333
Ben@zappcomics.com
www.zappcomics.com
(a-d,f,g,j,t,2-5)

Zapp Comics
574 Valley Road
Wayne, NJ 07470
PH: (973) 628-4500
ben@zappcomics.com
www.zappcomics.com
(a-g,j,l,t,u,w,x,2,4,5)

JHV Associates
(By Appointment Only)
P. O. Box 317
Woodbury Heights, NJ 08097
PH: (856) 845-4010
FAX: (856) 845-3977
JHVassoc@hotmail.com
(a,b,n,s)

NEW YORK

Pinocchio Collectibles
1814 McDonald Ave.
(off Ave. P)
Brooklyn, NY 11223
PH: (718) 645-2573
a19gaba@aol.com
(b-d,f,i,w,x)

HighGradeComics.com
17 Bethany Drive
Commack, NY 11725
PH: (631) 543-1917
FAX: (631) 864-1921
BobStorms@HighGradeComics.com
www.HighGradeComics.com
(a,b,c,e)

Aw Yeah Comics!
313 Halstead Ave.
Harrison, NY 10528
www.awyeahcomics.com

Best Comics
1300 Jericho Turnpike
New Hyde Park, NY 11040
PH: (516) 328-1900
FAX: (516) 328-1909
TommyBest@aol.com
www.bestcomics.com
(a,b,d,f,m,t,u,w,3,4)

ComicConnect.com
36 West 37th St.; 6th Floor
New York, NY 10018
PH: (212) 895-3999
FAX: (212) 260-4304
support@comicconnect.com
www.comicconnect.com
(a,b,c,m,n,s,v)

Metropolis Collectibles
36 West 37th St.; 6th Floor
New York, NY 10018
PH: (800) 229-6387
FAX: (212) 260-4304
E-Mail: buying@metropoliscomics.com
www.metropoliscomics.com

Bags Unlimited
P7 Canal St.
Rochester, NY 14608
PH: (800) 767-2247
FAX: (585) 328-8526
Email: customercare@BagsUnlimited.com
www.BagsUnlimited.com
(f)

Dave and Adam's
55 Oriskany Dr.
Tonawanda, NY 14150
PH: (888) 440-9787
FAX: (716) 838-9896
service@dacardworld.com
www.dacardworld.com
(a-i,m,r,t,w,x,1-5)

Dave and Adam's
2217 Sheridan Dr.
Tonawanda, NY 14223
PH: (716) 837-4920
sheridan-store@dacardworld.com
www.dacwstore.com
(a-c,f-i,m,t,w,x,1-5)

Dan Gallo
Westchester County, NY
PH: (954) 547-9063
DGallo1291@aol.com
eBay ID: DGallo1291
(a,b,c,m)

Dave and Adam's
8075 Sheridan Dr.
Williamsville, NY 14221
PH: (716) 626-0000
Transit-store@dacardworld.com
www.dacwstore.com
(a-d,f-i,m,r,t,w,x,1-5)

NORTH CAROLINA

Heroes Aren't Hard to Find
1957 E 7th St.
Charlotte, NC 28204
PH: (704) 375-7462
FAX: (704) 375-7464
www.heroesonline.com

NORTH DAKOTA

Tom's Coin, Stamp, Gem, Baseball & Comic Shop
2 First St. SW
Minot, ND 58701
PH: (701) 852-4522
tomscoin@minot.com
www.tomscoins.com
(a-z,1-4)

OHIO

Comics and Friends, LLC
7850 Mentor Ave.
Suite 1054
Mentor, OH 44096
PH: (440) 255-4242
comics.and.friends.store@gmail.com
www.comicsandfriends.com
(a-g,i,j,l,m,n,r,t,u,w-z,1-5)

Parker's Records & Comics
1222 Suite C Rt. 28
Milford, OH 45150
PH/FAX: (513) 575-3665
dkparker39@fuse.net
www.parkersrc.com
(a-f,h,i,y)

New Dimension Comics
Ohio Valley Mall
67800 Mall Ring Rd Unit 875
Saint Clairsville, OH 43950
PH: (740) 695-1020
ohiovalley@ndcomics.com
www.ndcomics.com

World's Greatest Comics
5992 Westerville Rd.
Westerville, OH 43081
PH: (614) 891-3000
worldsgreatestcomics@gmail.com
www.wgcomics.com
(a-f,u,w,x)

OKLAHOMA

All Star Comics
6900 N. May Ave.
Ste. 10-A
Oklahoma City, OK 73116
PH: (405) 842-7800
AllStarComicsOKC@gmail.com
AllStarComicsOKC.com

Want List Comics
(Appointment Only)
P.O. Box 701932
Tulsa, OK 74170
PH: (918) 299-0440
E-Mail: wlc777@cox.net
(a,b,c,m,n,o,s,t,x,3)

OREGON

Future Dreams
1847 East Burnside St.
Suite 116
Portland, OR 97214-1587
PH: (503) 231-8311
fdb@hevanet.com
www.futuredreamsbooks.com
(a-g,i,j,l-n,p-u,w,x,3,4)

PENNSYLVANIA

New Dimension Comics
108 South Main Street
Butler, PA 16001
PH: (724) 282-5283
butler@ndcomics.com
www.ndcomics.com
(a-l,n,o,r,t,u,w,x,1-5)

New Dimension Comics
Piazza Plaza
20550 Route 19 (Perry Hwy.)
Cranberry Township, PA
16066
PH: (724) 776-0433
cranberry@ndcomics.com
www.ndcomics.com
(a-l,n,o,r,t,u,w,x,1-5)

New Dimension Comics
Megastore
516 Lawrence Ave.
Ellwood City, PA 16117
PH: (724) 758-2324
ec@ndcomics.com
www.ndcomics.com
(a-l,n,o,r,t,u,w,x,1-5)

Eide's Entertainment, LLC
1121 Penn Ave.
Pittsburgh, PA 15222
PH: (412) 261-0900
eBay: stores.eBay.com/eides-entertainment-comics
eides@eides.com
www.eides.com
(a-z,1-5)

New Dimension Comics
Pittsburgh Mills
590 Pittsburgh Mill Circle
Tarentum, PA 15084
PH: (724) 758-1560
mills@ndcomics.com
www.ndcomics.com
(a-l,n,o,r,t,u,w,x,1-5)

New Dimension Comics
Pittsburgh Century III Mall
3075 Clairton Rd. #940
West Mifflin, PA 15213
PH: (412) 655-8661
century3@ndcomics.com
www.ndcomics.com
(a-l,n,o,r,t,u,w,x,1-5)

Hake's Americana & Collectibles
P.O. Box 12001
York, PA 17402
PH: (866) 404-9800
www.hakes.com

SOUTH DAKOTA

Top Notch Comics
P.O. Box 229
Yankton, SD 57078
PH: (605) 660-3135
topnotch@iw.net

TEXAS

Comic Heaven
P.O. Box 900
Big Sandy, TX 75755
PH: (903) 636-5555
www.comicheaven.net

Heritage Auction Galleries
3500 Maple Avenue
17th Floor
Dallas, TX 75219-3941
PH: (800) 872-6467
www.HA.com

Worldwide Comics
29369 Raintree Ridge
Fair Oaks Ranch, TX 78015
PH: (830) 368-4103
stephen@wwcomics.com
wwcomics.com

William Hughes' Vintage Collectables
P.O. Box 270244
Flower Mound, TX 75027
PH: (972) 539-9190
PH: (973) 432-4070
Whughes199@yahoo.com
www.VintageCollectables.net

Monster's Lair Comics
2416 19th Street
Lubbock, TX 79401
PH: (806) 701-5800

Excalibur Comics, Cards & Games
2811 N. State Line Avenue
Texarkana, TX 75503
PH: (903) 792-5767
excalicom1@aol.com
www.excaliburccg.com
(a-i,t,u,w,x,3-5)

WASHINGTON

Mill Geek Comics
17928 Bothell Everett Highway
Unit B and C
Bothell, WA 98012
PH: (425) 415-6666
millgeekcomics@gmail.com
www.millgeekcomics.com
(a-d,f-i,1,3,4)

Pristine Comics
2008 South 314th Street
Federal Way, WA 98003
PH: (253) 941-1986
www.PristineComics.com

Comics4Kids Inc.
5009 50th Ave. SW
Seattle, WA 98136-1017
PH: (206) 327-7436
comics4kids@aim.com
www.comics4kidsinc.org
(a,b,c,w,5)

WISCONSIN

Inner Child Collectibles and Comics
5921 Sixth Avenue "A"
Kenosha, WI 53140
PH: (262) 653-0400
StevenKahn@sbcglobal.net
innerchildcomics.com
(a-f,l-p,r,s,u-x,1-4)

Jef Hinds Comics
P.O. Box 44803
Madison, WI 53744-4803
PH: (608) 345-8750
jhcomics@jhcomics.com
www.jhcomics.com
(a-c,e,m-o,s,w)

CANADA

BRITISH COLUMBIA

Rare Golden Age Comics
Vancouver, BC
raregoldenage@hotmail.com
www.RareGoldenAge.com
(a,b,c,e,m,n,o,s,2)

MANITOBA

Doug Sulipa's Comic World
Box 21986
Steinbach, MB., R5G 1B5
PH: (204) 346-3674
FAX: (204) 346-1632
dsulipa@gmail.com
www.dougcomicworld.com
(a-e,h,l,n-t,y,z,3,4)

ONTARIO

Big B Comics
1045 Upper James St.
Hamilton, ON L9C 3A6
PH: (905) 318-9636
mailbox@bigbcomics.com
www.bigbcomics.com
(a-g,i,j,l,m,u-x,1-5)

Leisure Park Entertainment
378 Moffatt Pond Crt
Ottawa, ON K2J 0C7
PH: (613) 440-7675
admin@LeisureParkEnt.ca
www.LeisureParkEnt.ca
(u,w-z,1-5)

Pendragon Comics & Books
3759 Lakeshore Boulevard West
Toronto, ON M8W 1R1
PH: (416) 253-6974
pendragoncomics@rogers.com
www.pendragoncomics.com
(a-g,l,n-p,u)

QUEBEC

Heroes Comics
1166 Curé Labelle
Laval, QC H7V 2V5
PH: (450) 686-9155
FAX: (450) 686-2097
info@heroscomics.ca
www.heroscomics.ca
(a-d,f-i,t-x,1-5)

INTERNET

ComicLink Auctions & Exchange
PH: (617) 517-0062
buysell@ComicLink.com
www.ComicLink.com

MyComicShop.com
PH: (817) 860-7827
buytrade@mycomicshop.com
www.mycomicshop.com

Sell My Comic Books
PH: (514) 803-0635
ash@SellMyComicBooks.com
www.SellMyComicBooks.com

Sharp Comics
PH: (410) 848-0275
Sales@SharpComics.com
www.SharpComics.com

Items stocked by these shops are noted at the end of each listing and are coded as follows:

(a) Golden Age Comics
(b) Silver Age Comics
(c) Bronze Age Comics
(d) New Comics & Magazines
(e) Back Issue magazines
(f) Comic Supplies
(g) Collectible Card Games
(h) Role Playing Games
(i) Gaming Supplies
(j) Manga
(k) Anime
(l) Underground Comics
(m) Original Comic Art
(n) Pulps
(o) Big Little Books
(p) Books - Used
(q) Books - New
(r) Comic Related Posters
(s) Movie Posters
(t) Trading Cards
(u) Statues/Mini-busts, etc.
(v) Premiums (Rings, Decoders)
(w) Action Figures
(x) Other Toys
(y) Records/CDs
(z) DVDs/VHS
(1) Doctor Who Items
(2) Simpsons Items
(3) Star Trek Items
(4) Star Wars Items
(5) HeroClix

GLOSSARY

a - Story art; **a(i)** - Story art inks; **a(p)** - Story art pencils; **a(r)** - Story art reprint.

ADULT MATERIAL - Contains story and/or art for "mature" readers. Re: sex, violence, strong language.

ADZINE - A magazine primarily devoted to the advertising of comic books and collectibles as its first publishing priority as opposed to written articles.

ALLENTOWN COLLECTION - A collection discovered in 1987-88 just outside Allentown, Pennsylvania. The Allentown collection consisted of 135 Golden Age comics, characterized by high grade and superior paper quality.

ANNUAL - (1) A book that is published yearly; (2) Can also refer to some square bound comics.

ARRIVAL DATE - The date written (often in pencil) or stamped on the cover of comics by either the local wholesaler, newsstand owner, or distributor. The date precedes the cover date by approximately 15 to 75 days, and may vary considerably from one locale to another or from one year to another.

ASHCAN - A publisher's in-house facsimile of a proposed new title. Most ashcans have black and white covers stapled to an existing coverless comic on the inside; other ashcans are totally black and white. In modern parlance, it can also refer to promotional or sold comics, often smaller than standard comic size and usually in black and white, released by publishers to advertise the forthcoming arrival of a new title or story.

ATOM AGE - Comics published from 1946-1956.

B&W - Black and white art.

BACK-UP FEATURE - A story or character that usually appears after the main feature in a comic book; often not featured on the cover.

BAD GIRL ART - A term popularized in the early '90s to describe an attitude as well as a style of art that portrays women in a sexual and often action-oriented way.

BAXTER PAPER - A high quality, heavy, white paper used in the printing of some comics.

BC - Abbreviation for Back Cover.

BI-MONTHLY - Published every two months.

BI-WEEKLY - Published every two weeks.

BONDAGE COVER - Usually denotes a female in bondage.

BOUND COPY - A comic that has been bound into a book. The process requires that the spine be trimmed and sometimes sewn into a book-like binding.

BRITISH ISSUE - A comic printed for distribution in Great Britain; these copies sometimes have the price listed in pence or pounds instead of cents or dollars.

BRITTLENESS - A severe condition of paper deterioration where paper loses its flexibility and thus chips and/or flakes easily.

BRONZE AGE - Comics published from 1970 to 1984.

BROWNING - (1) The aging of paper characterized by the ever-increasing level of oxidation characterized by darkening; (2) The level of paper deterioration one step more severe than tanning and one step before brittleness.

c - Cover art; **c(i)** - Cover inks; **c(p)** - Cover pencils; **c(r)** - Cover reprint.

CAMEO - The brief appearance of one character in the strip of another.

CANADIAN ISSUE - A comic printed for distribution in Canada; these copies sometimes have no advertising.

CCA - Abbreviation for **Comics Code Authority**.

CCA SEAL - An emblem that was placed on the cover of all CCA approved comics beginning in April-May, 1955.

CENTER CREASE - See Subscription Copy.

CENTERFOLD or CENTER SPREAD - The two folded pages in the center of a comic book at the terminal end of the staples.

CERTIFIED GRADING - A process provided by a professional grading service that certifies a given grade for a comic and seals the book in a protective **Slab**.

CF - Abbreviation for Centerfold.

CFO - Abbreviation for Centerfold Out.

CGC - Abbreviation for the certified comic book grading company, Comics Guaranty, LLC.

CIRCULATION COPY - See Subscription Copy.

CIRCULATION FOLD - See Subscription Fold.

CLASSIC COVER - A cover considered by collectors to be highly desirable because of its subject matter, artwork, historical importance, etc.

CLEANING - A process in which dirt and dust is removed.

COLOR TOUCH - A restoration process by which colored ink is used to hide color flecks, color flakes, and larger areas of missing color. Short for Color Touch-Up.

COLORIST - An artist who paints the color guides for comics. Many modern colorists use computer technology.

COMIC BOOK DEALER - (1) A seller of comic books; (2) One who makes a living buying and selling comic books.
COMIC BOOK REPAIR - When a tear, loose staple or centerfold has been mended without changing or adding to the original finish of the book. Repair may involve tape, glue or nylon gossamer, and is easily detected; it is considered a defect.
COMICS CODE AUTHORITY - A voluntary organization comprised of comic book publishers formed in 1954 to review (and possibly censor) comic books before they were printed and distributed. The emblem of the CCA is a white stamp in the upper right hand corner of comics dated after February 1955. The term "post-Code" refers to the time after this practice started, or approximately 1955 to the present.
COMPLETE RUN - All issues of a given title.
CON - A convention or public gathering of fans.
CONDITION - The state of preservation of a comic book, often inaccurately used interchangeably with Grade.
CONSERVATION - The European Confederation of Conservator-Restorers' Organizations (ECCO) in its professional guidelines, defines conservation as follows: "Conservation consists mainly of direct action carried out on cultural heritage with the aim of stabilizing condition and retarding further deterioration."
COPPER AGE - Comics published from 1984 to 1992.
COSMIC AEROPLANE COLLECTION - A collection from Salt Lake City, Utah discovered by Cosmic Aeroplane Books, characterized by the moderate to high grade copies of 1930s-40s comics with pencil check marks in the margins of inside pages. It is thought that these comics were kept by a commercial illustration school and the check marks were placed beside panels that instructors wanted students to draw.
COSTUMED HERO - A costumed crime fighter with "developed" human powers instead of super powers.
COUPON CUT or COUPON MISSING - A coupon has been neatly removed with scissors or razor blade from the interior or exterior of the comic as opposed to having been ripped out.
COVER GLOSS - The reflective quality of the cover inks.
COVER TRIMMED - Cover has been reduced in size by neatly cutting away rough or damaged edges.
COVERLESS - A comic with no cover attached. There is a niche demand for coverless comics, particularly in the case of hard-to-find key books otherwise impossible to locate intact.
C/P - Abbreviation for **Cleaned and Pressed**. See **Cleaning**.
CREASE - A fold which causes ink removal, usually resulting in a white line. See **Reading Crease**.
CROSSOVER - A story where one character appears prominently in the story of another character. See **X-Over**.
CVR - Abbreviation for Cover.
DEALER - See **Comic Book Dealer**.
DEACIDIFICATION - Several different processes that reduce acidity in paper.
DEBUT - The first time that a character appears anywhere.
DEFECT - Any fault or flaw that detracts from perfection.
DENVER COLLECTION - A collection consisting primarily of early 1940s high grade number one issues bought at auction in Pennsylvania by a Denver, Colorado dealer.
DIE-CUT COVER - A comic book cover with areas or edges precut by a printer to a special shape or to create a desired effect.
DISTRIBUTOR STRIPES - Color brushed or sprayed on the edges of comic book stacks by the distributor/wholesaler to code them for expedient exchange at the sales racks. Typical colors are red, orange, yellow, green, blue, and purple. Distributor stripes are not a defect.
DOUBLE - A duplicate copy of the same comic book.
DOUBLE COVER - When two covers are stapled to the comic interior instead of the usual one; the exterior cover often protects the interior cover from wear and damage. This is considered a desirable situation by some collectors and may increase collector value; this is not considered a defect.
DRUG PROPAGANDA STORY - A comic that makes an editorial stand about drug use.
DRUG USE STORY - A comic that shows the actual use of drugs: needle use, tripping, harmful effects, etc.
DRY CLEANING - A process in which dirt and dust is removed.
DUOTONE - Printed with black and one other color of ink. This process was common in comics printed in the 1930s.
DUST SHADOW - Darker, usually linear area at the edge of some comics stored in stacks. Some portion of the cover was not covered by the comic immediately above it and it was exposed to settling dust particles. Also see **Oxidation Shadow** and **Sun Shadow**.
EDGAR CHURCH COLLECTION - See **Mile High Collection**.
EMBOSSED COVER - A comic book cover with a pattern, shape or image pressed into the cover from

the inside, creating a raised area.
ENCAPSULATION - Refers to the process of sealing certified comics in a protective plastic enclosure. Also see **Slabbing**.
EYE APPEAL - A term which refers to the overall look of a comic book when held at approximately arm's length. A comic may have nice eye appeal yet still possess defects which reduce grade.
FANZINE - An amateur fan publication.
FC - Abbreviation for Front Cover.
FILE COPY - A high grade comic originating from the publisher's file; contrary to what some might believe, not all file copies are in Gem Mint condition. An arrival date on the cover of a comic does not indicate that it is a file copy, though a copyright date may.
FIRST APPEARANCE - See **Debut**.
FLASHBACK - When a previous story is recalled.
FOIL COVER - A comic book cover that has had a thin metallic foil hot stamped on it. Many of these "gimmick" covers date from the early '90s, and might include chromium, prism and hologram covers as well.
FOUR COLOR - Series of comics produced by Dell, characterized by hundreds of different features; named after the four color process of printing. See **One Shot**.
FOUR COLOR PROCESS - The process of printing with the three primary colors (red, yellow, and blue) plus black.
FUMETTI - Illustration system in which individual frames of a film are colored and used for individual panels to make a comic book story. The most famous example is DC's *Movie Comics* #1-6 from 1939.
GATEFOLD COVER - A double-width fold-out cover.
GENRE - Categories of comic book subject matter; e.g. Science Fiction, Super-Hero, Romance, Funny Animal, Teenage Humor, Crime, War, Western, Mystery, Horror, etc.
GIVEAWAY - Type of comic book intended to be given away as a premium or promotional device instead of being sold.
GLASSES ATTACHED - In 3-D comics, the special blue and red cellophane and cardboard glasses are still attached to the comic.
GLASSES DETACHED - In 3-D comics, the special blue and red cellophane and cardboard glasses are not still attached to the comic; obviously less desirable than Glasses Attached.
GOLDEN AGE - Comics published from 1938 (*Action Comics* #1) to 1945.
GOOD GIRL ART - Refers to a style of art, usually from the 1930s-50s, that portrays women in a sexually implicit way.
GREY-TONE COVER - A cover art style in which pencil or charcoal underlies the normal line drawing, used to enhance the effects of light and shadow, thus producing a richer quality. These covers, prized by most collectors, are sometimes referred to as **Painted Covers** but are not actually painted.
HC - Abbreviation for Hardcover.
HEADLIGHTS - Forward illumation devices installed on all automobiles and many other vehicles... OK, OK, it's a euphemism for a comic book cover prominently featuring a woman's breasts in a provocative way. Also see **Bondage Cover** for another collecting euphemism that has long since outlived its appropriateness in these politically correct times.
HOT STAMPING - The process of pressing foil, prism paper and/or inks on cover stock.
HRN - Abbreviation for Highest Reorder Number. This refers to a method used by collectors of Gilberton's *Classic Comics* and *Classics Illustrated* series to distinguish first editions from later printings.
ILLO - Abbreviation for Illustration.
IMPAINT - Another term for **Color Touch**.
INDICIA - Publishing and title information usually located at the bottom of the first page or the bottom of the inside front cover. In some pre-1938 comics and many modern comics, it is located on internal pages.
INFINITY COVER - Shows a scene that repeats itself to infinity.
INKER - Artist that does the inking.
INTRO - Same as **Debut**.
INVESTMENT GRADE COPY - (1) Comic of sufficiently high grade and demand to be viewed by collectors as instantly liquid should the need arise to sell; (2) A comic in VF or better condition; (3) A comic purchased primarily to realize a profit.
ISSUE NUMBER - The actual edition number of a given title.
ISH - Short for Issue.
JLA - Abbreviation for Justice League of America.
JSA - Abbreviation for Justice Society of America.
KEY, KEY BOOK or KEY ISSUE - An issue that contains a first appearance, origin, or other historically or artistically important feature considered especially desirable by collectors.
LAMONT LARSON - Pedigreed collection of high grade 1940s comics with the initials or name of its original owner, Lamont Larson.
LENTICULAR COVERS or "FLICKER" COVERS - A comic book cover overlayed with a ridged plastic sheet such that the special artwork underneath appears to move when the cover is tilted at different angles perpendicular to the ridges.
LETTER COL or LETTER COLUMN - A feature in a comic book that

prints and sometimes responds to letters written by its readers.

LINE DRAWN COVER - A cover published in the traditional way where pencil sketches are over-drawn with india ink and then colored. See also **Grey-Tone Cover**, **Photo Cover**, and **Painted Cover**.

LOGO - The title of a strip or comic book as it appears on the cover or title page.

LSH - Abbreviation for Legion of Super-Heroes.

MAGIC LIGHTNING COLLECTION - A collection of high grade 1950s comics from the San Francisco area.

MARVEL CHIPPING - A bindery (trimming/cutting) defect that results in a series of chips and tears at the top, bottom, and right edges of the cover, caused when the cutting blade of an industrial paper trimmer becomes dull. It was dubbed Marvel Chipping because it can be found quite often on Marvel comics from the late '50s and early '60s but can also occur with any company's comic books from the late 1940s through the middle 1960s.

MILE HIGH COLLECTION - High grade collection of over 22,000 comics discovered in Denver, Colorado in 1977, originally owned by Mr. Edgar Church. Comics from this collection are now famous for extremely white pages, fresh smell, and beautiful cover ink reflectivity.

MODERN AGE - A catch-all term applied to comics published since 1992.

MYLAR™ - An inert, very hard, space-age plastic used to make high quality protective bags and sleeves for comic book storage. "Mylar" is a trademark of the DuPont Co.

ND - Abbreviation for **No Date**.

NN - Abbreviation for **No Number**.

NO DATE - When there is no date given on the cover or indicia page.

NO NUMBER - No issue number is given on the cover or indicia page; these are usually first issues or one-shots.

N.Y. LEGIS. COMM. - New York Legislative Committee to Study the Publication of Comics (1951).

ONE-SHOT - When only one issue is published of a title, or when a series is published where each issue is a different title (e.g. Dell's *Four Color Comics*).

ORIGIN - When the story of a character's creation is given.

over guide - When a comic book is priced at a value over *Guide* list.

OXIDATION SHADOW - Darker, usually linear area at the edge of some comics stored in stacks. Some portion of the cover was not covered by the comic immediately above it, and it was exposed to the air. Also see **Dust Shadow** and **Sun Shadow**.

p - Art pencils.

PAINTED COVER - (1) Cover taken from an actual painting instead of a line drawing; (2) Inaccurate name for a grey-toned cover.

PANELOLOGIST - One who researches comic books and/or comic strips.

PANNAPICTAGRAPHIST - One possible term for someone who collects comic books; can you figure out why it hasn't exactly taken off in common parlance?

PAPER COVER - Comic book cover made from the same newsprint as the interior pages. These books are extremely rare in high grade.

PARADE OF PLEASURE - A book about the censorship of comics.

PB - Abbreviation for Paperback.

PEDIGREE - A book from a famous and usually high grade collection - e.g. Allentown, Lamont Larson, Edgar Church/Mile High, Denver, San Francisco, Cosmic Aeroplane, etc. Beware of non-pedigree collections being promoted as pedigree books; only outstanding high grade collections similar to those listed qualify.

PENCILER - Artist that does the pencils...you're figuring out some of these definitions without us by now, aren't you?

PERFECT BINDING - Pages are glued to the cover as opposed to being stapled to the cover, resulting in a flat binded side. Also known as **Square Back or Square Bound**.

PG - Abbreviation for Page.

PHOTO COVER - Comic book cover featuring a photographic image instead of a line drawing or painting.

PIECE REPLACEMENT - A process by which pieces are added to replace areas of missing paper.

PIONEER AGE - Comics published from the 1500s to 1828.

PLATINUM AGE - Comics published from 1883 to 1938.

POLYPROPYLENE - A type of plastic used in the manufacture of comic book bags; now considered harmful to paper and not recommended for long term storage of comics.

POP - Abbreviation for the anti-comic book volume, *Parade of Pleasure*.

POST-CODE - Describes comics published after February 1955 and usually displaying the CCA stamp in the upper right-hand corner.

POUGHKEEPSIE - Refers to a large collection of Dell Comics file copies believed to have originated from the warehouse of Western Publishing in Poughkeepsie, NY.

PP - Abbreviation for Pages.

PRE-CODE - Describes comics published before the **Comics Code Authority** seal began appearing on covers in 1955.

PRE-HERO DC - A term used to describe *More Fun* #1-51

(pre-Spectre), *Adventure* #1-39 (pre-Sandman), and *Detective* #1-26 (pre-Batman). The term is actually inaccurate because technically there were "heroes" in the above books.

PRE-HERO MARVEL - A term used to describe *Strange Tales* #1-100 (pre-Human Torch), *Journey Into Mystery* #1-82 (pre-Thor), *Tales To Astonish* #1-35 (pre-Ant-Man), and *Tales Of Suspense* #1-38 (pre-Iron Man).

PRESERVATION - Another term for **Conservation**.

PRESSING - A term used to describe a variety of processes or procedures, professional and amateur, under which an issue is pressed to eliminate wrinkles, bends, dimples and/or other perceived defects and thus improve its appearance. Some types of pressing involve disassembling the book and performing other work on it prior to its pressing and reassembly. Some methods are generally easily discerned by professionals and amateurs. Other types of pressing, however, can pose difficulty for even experienced professionals to detect. In all cases, readers are cautioned that unintended damage can occur in some instances. Related defects will diminish an issue's grade correspondingly rather than improve it.

PROVENANCE - When the owner of a book is known and is stated for the purpose of authenticating and documenting the history of the book. Example: A book from the Stan Lee or Forrest Ackerman collection would be an example of a value-adding provenance.

PULP - Cheaply produced magazine made from low grade newsprint. The term comes from the wood pulp that was used in the paper manufacturing process.

QUARTERLY - Published every three months (four times a year).

R - Abbreviation for Reprint.

RARE - 10-20 copies estimated to exist.

RAT CHEW - Damage caused by the gnawing of rats and mice.

RBCC - Abbreviation for Rockets Blast Comic Collector, one of the first and most prominent adzines instrumental in developing the early comic book market.

READING COPY - A comic that is in FAIR to GOOD condition and is often used for research; the condition has been sufficiently reduced to the point where general handling will not degrade it further.

READING CREASE - Book-length, vertical front cover crease at staples, caused by bending the cover over the staples. Square-bounds receive these creases just by opening the cover too far to the left.

REILLY, TOM - A large high grade collection of 1939-1945 comics with 5000+ books.

REINFORCEMENT - A process by which a weak or split page or cover is reinforced with adhesive and reinforcement paper.

REPRINT COMICS - In earlier decades, comic books that contained newspaper strip reprints; modern reprint comics usually contain stories originally featured in older comic books.

RESTORATION - Any attempt, whether professional or amateur, to enhance the appearance of an aging or damaged comic book using additive procedures. These procedures may include any or all of the following techniques: recoloring, adding missing paper, trimming, re-glossing, reinforcement, glue, etc. Amateur work can lower the value of a book, and even professional restoration has now gained a negative aura in the modern marketplace from some quarters. In all cases a restored book can never be worth the same as an unrestored book in the same condition. There is no consensus on the inclusion of pressing, non-aqueous cleaning, tape removal and in some cases staple replacement in this definition. Until such time as there is consensus, we encourage continued debate and interaction among all interested parties and reflection upon the standards in other hobbies and art forms.

REVIVAL - An issue that begins republishing a comic book character after a period of dormancy.

ROCKFORD - A high grade collection of 1940s comics with 2000+ books from Rockford, IL.

ROLLED SPINE - A condition where the left edge of a comic book curves toward the front or back; a defect caused by folding back each page as the comic was read.

ROUND BOUND - Standard saddle stitch binding typical of most comics.

RUN - A group of comics of one title where most or all of the issues are present. See **Complete Run**.

S&K - Abbreviation for the legendary creative team of Joe Simon and Jack Kirby, creators of Marvel Comics' Captain America.

SADDLE STITCH - The staple binding of magazines and comic books.

san francisco collection - (see **Reilly, Tom**)

SCARCE - 20-100 copies estimated to exist.

SEDUCTION OF THE INNOCENT - An inflammatory book written by Dr. Frederic Wertham and published in 1953; Wertham asserted that comics were responsible for rampant juvenile deliquency in American youth.

SET - (1) A complete run of a given title; (2) A grouping of comics for sale.

SEMI-MONTHLY - Published twice a month, but not necessarily **Bi-Weekly**.
SEWN SPINE - A comic with many spine perforations where binders' thread held it into a bound volume. This is considered a defect.
SF - Abbreviation for Science Fiction (the other commonly used term, "sci-fi," is often considered derogatory or indicative of more "low-brow" rather than "literary" science fiction, i.e. "sci-fi television."
SILVER AGE - Comics published from 1956 to 1970.
SILVER PROOF - A black and white actual size print on thick glossy paper hand-painted by an artist to indicate colors to the engraver.
SLAB - Colloquial term for the plastic enclosure used by grading certification companies to seal in certified comics.
SLABBING - Colloquial term for the process of encapsulating certified comics in a plastic enclosure.
SOTI - Abbreviation for **Seduction of the Innocent**.
SPINE - The left-hand edge of the comic that has been folded and stapled.
SPINE ROLL - A condition where the left edge of the comic book curves toward the front or back, caused by folding back each page as the comic was read.
SPINE SPLIT SEALED - A process by which a spine split is sealed using an adhesive.
SPLASH PAGE - A **Splash Panel** that takes up the entire page.
SPLASH PANEL - (1) The first panel of a comic book story, usually larger than other panels and usually containing the title and credits of the story; (2) An oversized interior panel.
SQUARE BACK or SQUARE BOUND - See **Perfect Binding**.
STORE STAMP - Store name (and sometimes address and telephone number) stamped in ink via rubber stamp and stamp pad.
SUBSCRIPTION COPY - A comic sent through the mail directly from the publisher or publisher's agent. Most are folded in half, causing a subscription crease or fold running down the center of the comic from top to bottom; this is considered a defect.
SUBSCRIPTION CREASE - See **Subscription Copy**.
SUBSCRIPTION FOLD - See **Subscription Copy**. Differs from a **Subscription Crease** in that no ink is missing as a result of the fold.
SUN SHADOW - Darker, usually linear area at the edge of some comics stored in stacks. Some portion of the cover was not covered by the comic immediately above it, and it suffered prolonged exposure to light. A serious defect, unlike a **Dust Shadow**, which can sometimes be removed. Also see **Oxidation Shadow**.
SUPER-HERO - A costumed crime fighter with powers beyond those of mortal man.
SUPER-VILLAIN - A costumed criminal with powers beyond those of mortal man; the antithesis of **Super-Hero**.
SWIPE - A panel, sequence, or story obviously borrowed from previously published material.
TEAR SEALS - A process by which a tear is sealed using an adhesive.
TEXT ILLO. - A drawing or small panel in a text story that almost never has a dialogue balloon.
TEXT PAGE - A page with no panels or drawings.
TEXT STORY - A story with few if any illustrations commonly used as filler material during the first three decades of comics.
3-D COMIC - Comic art that is drawn and printed in two color layers, producing a 3-D effect when viewed through special glasses.
3-D EFFECT COMIC - Comic art that is drawn to appear as if in 3-D but isn't.
TITLE - The name of the comic book.
TITLE PAGE - First page of a story showing the title of the story and possibly the creative credits and indicia.
TRIMMED - (1) A bindery process which separates top, right, and bottom of pages and cuts comic books to the proper size; (2) A repair process in which defects along the edges of a comic book are removed with the use of scissors, razor blades, and/or paper cutters. Comic books which have been repaired in this fashion are considered defectives.
TTA - Abbreviation for *Tales to Astonish*.
UK - Abbreviation for British edition (United Kingdom).
UNDER GUIDE - When a comic book is priced at a value less than Guide list.
UPGRADE - To obtain another copy of the same comic book in a higher grade.
VARIANT COVER - A different cover image used on the same issue.
VERY RARE - 1 to 10 copies estimated to exist.
VICTORIAN AGE - Comics published from 1828 to 1883.
WANT LIST - A listing of comics needed by a collector, or a list of comics that a collector is interested in purchasing.
WAREHOUSE COPY - Originating from a publisher's warehouse; similar to file copy.
WHITE MOUNTAIN COLLECTION - A collection of high grade 1950s and 1960s comics which originated in New England.
X-OVER - Short for **Crossover**.
ZINE - Short for **Fanzine**.

ADVENTURE COMICS #73
April 1942. CGC 9.2. Rockford copy.
Highest Graded. 1st app. Manhunter. © DC

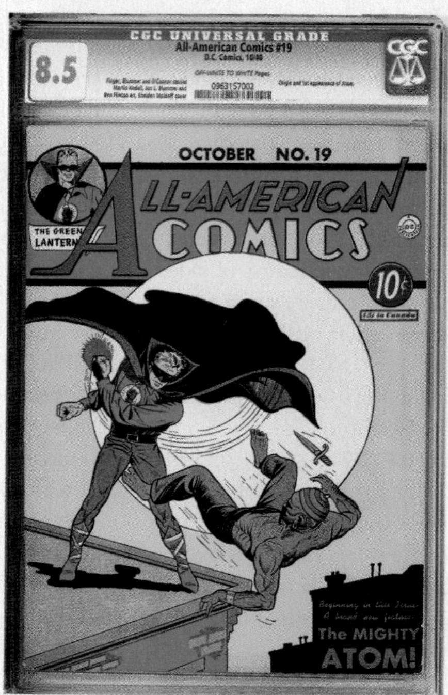

ALL-AMERICAN COMICS #19
October 1940. CGC 8.5.
Highest Graded. 1st app. The Atom. © DC

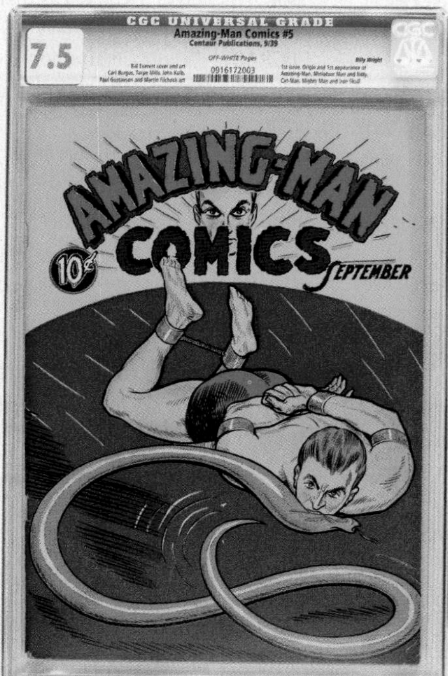

AMAZING-MAN COMICS #5
September 1939. CGC 7.5. Billy Wright.
2nd highest graded. © CEN

GREEN HORNET COMICS #24
May 1945. CGC 9.4. Mile High.
Highest graded, next highest is a 7.0. © HARV

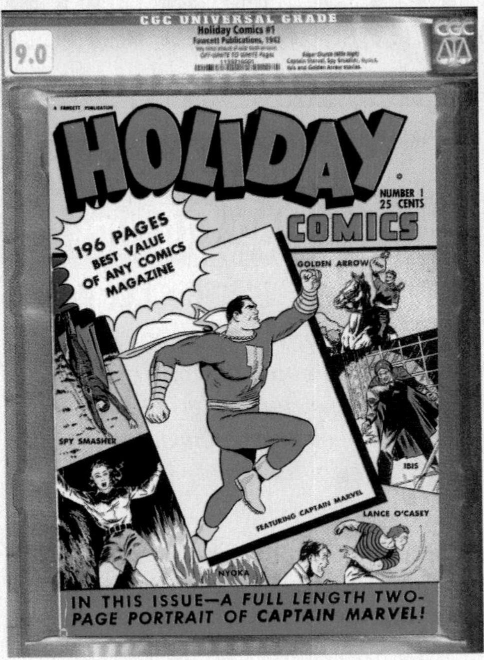

HOLIDAY COMICS #1
1942. CGC 9.0. Mile High. Highest graded, next highest is a 7.0. © FAW

SHEENA, QUEEN OF THE JUNGLE #3
Spring 1943. CGC 9.4. Mile High. Highest Graded. © FH

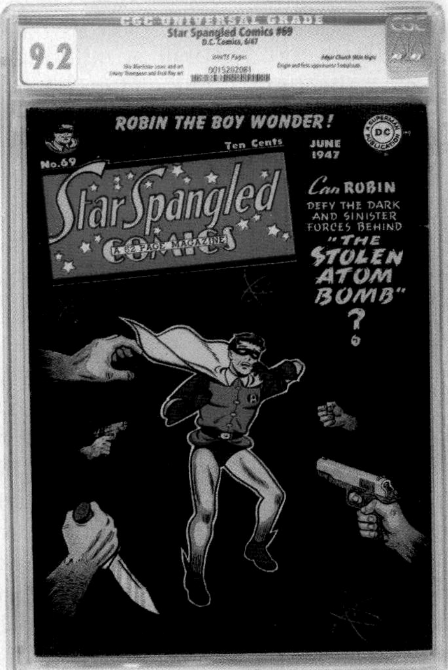

STAR SPANGLED COMICS #69
June 1947. CGC 9.2. Mile High. Highest Graded. 1st app. Tomahawk. © DC

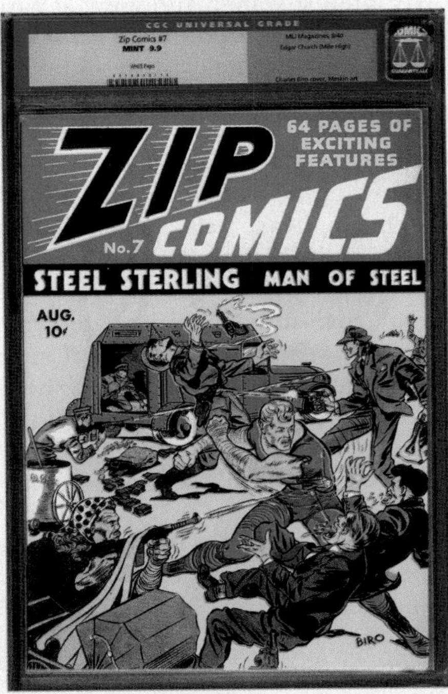

ZIP COMICS #7
August 1940. CGC 9.9. Mile High. Earliest Golden Age book graded 9.9. © MLJ

FINDING HIS INNER CHILD

DR. STEVEN KAHN ON BEING A CUSTODIAN OF POP CULTURE

By J.C. Vaughn

Talking comics, sports cards, action figures or just about any other aspect of popular culture with Dr. Steven Kahn, one runs the risk of getting lost in the conversation, overwhelmed by the sheer enthusiasm that the formal oral surgeon possesses for the material and freely shares.

While Steven Kahn wasn't able to collect much as child, he did collect DC comics in the 1950s and read his sister's Little Lulu books. At that point, though, he said he didn't realize the bigger world of other comics – such as the Golden Age – that he had missed.

His interest waned and grew at various times. As Kahn started dental school, Jack Kirby and Jim Steranko were hitting their strides at Marvel, and he dove into comics. After he started his residency, by necessity collecting took a back seat.

Following his residency and a journey through Southeast Asia, he had a major, diverse reawakening of his collecting appetites, including Coromandel screens, oriental art, and many related areas. During the years he ran the oral surgery clinic at the University of Illinois, he kept collecting and had to find places to store his goods.

This would be a recurring theme for him.

His re-entry into pop culture collecting began with sports cards, specifically Star basketball cards in the early 1990s. Before that bubble burst, many thought they would fund their futures with sports cards, comics, and all sorts of collectibles. Speculation was rampant.

When that bubble burst as bubbles do, Kahn found there was a saving grace for him among the ruins of many manufacturers: he loved what he was collecting.

"If it was worth a fraction of what I thought, so be it. I encourage all of my radio listeners and customers at the store the same thing. Collect what you love and you will never lose. So I wasn't going to cash it all in and become a millionaire from my collecting. I enjoyed it when I was accumulating and the joy is in the journey after all, isn't it?" he asked rhetorically.

"Rhetorically" because he had found *his* answer.

By the middle '90s comic books had once again taken center stage for him. He was still a popular, practicing oral surgeon, but he had so many comics he was having trouble storing them.

"I probably would have been content continuing to find more storage facilities were it not for my wife's foresight. I was getting near retirement from my Oral Surgery practice and she has always believed in the adage that man is not meant to retire to his home, he needs to find something that fills his passions. And that will keep the marriage healthy," he said. That consideration and then-recent, multiple floods at his storage areas with significant losses prompted him to purchase a warehouse. He settled on the historic district in downtown Kenosha, Wisconsin.

"I opened the store on weekends for the last two years of my practice, and we are now closing in on our fifth year in business and have gradually expanded our hours," he said. As the business has expended, he's never given up hope of landing that big, amazing, high-grade collection, but his perspective is informed by time, which in turn has propelled his eagerness to engage others who might identify with his enthusiasm.

"At the store, I wanted to create an environment of nostalgia and fun. It is so satisfying to have people and families go through the store and rekindle long lost and fond childhood memories. A not insignificant part of my inventory in the store is not for sale. It comes from my personal collection and I want to share it with others," he said.

"I realized a long time ago that we are only renting this stuff. None of it goes with us when we go to wherever we all ultimately go. I have had experiences in the last several years that have put it all into a little sharper perspective. There were three collections that I was involved with that ultimately got away. Each of the owners had something in common. They all thought they would never lose control of their collections. One thing that they also had in common was that they didn't want their collections 'blown up' and scattered," he said. "And yet that is what happened to each of them. They passed away and their collections fell into the hands of disinterested relatives who couldn't have cared less about where the collections landed. They then went to the lawyers and finally to the auction houses."

Kahn said that would be the lasting piece of advice he would want to directly pass on to Overstreet readers: "Many of you have spent a lifetime of love putting together your collections. Please take the time to figure out what you want to ultimately do with it and plan it out in detail. It will be a freeing experience, I can assure you. And it will remove a burden from your children or relatives."

Part of his original plans in opening his store was to pare down his collection. That hasn't exactly happened. He hasn't stopped dreaming yet either.

"I hope I am around for a while yet and able to keep this going. Long term, the dream would be to find the right building and open a pop culture museum. Not for profit, just for the nostalgia of it all," he said.

For our full interview with Dr. Steven Kahn, read The Best of Comic Book Marketplace, *due out in Fall 2017 from Gemstone Publishing. Dr. Kahn's son, Deniz, is a highly respected authority on collecting video games and is featured in* The Overstreet Guide To Collecting Video Games.

CBCS: An Interview with Steve Borock

By J.C. Vaughn & Carrie Wood

His enthusiasm for comic books made Steve Borock an intriguing figure even before his tenure as the first President and Primary Grader for CGC and Senior Consignment Director for Heritage Auctions. He was profiled as a collector and was noted for his knowledge of stories, creators and the industry's history in addition to his attention to the physical details of comics.

Now as President and Primary Grader of Comic Book Certification Service (CBCS) he continues to put his passions to good use, not only at his new company, now entering its third year, but also as a board member of the Hero Initiative, the 501 (c)(3) charity that aids comic book creators in need, and as the auctioneer for the New York Comic Con and C2E2 fundraiser comic art auctions for St. Jude Children's Hospital.

Borock has also participated as an advisor for many years to The Overstreet Comic Book Price Guide, The Overstreet Guide to Grading Comics, *and* The Overstreet Guide to Collecting Comic and Animation Art.

Overstreet: Independent third-party grading of comics is such a part of the industry or hobby now that it's difficult for many to remember how it was initially perceived when it was first introduced. What do you remember about the period in which it started?

Steve Borock (SB): The fact is that the majority of people who expressed an opinion thought it wouldn't work, and they weren't shy about saying so. There were some early proponents, of course, but they were vastly outnumbered. That said, the need for independent grading had become very apparent to a core group. The market was largely stagnant. Key dealers with keen eyes for grading and sterling reputations, enjoyed the trust of their peers, but there was no mechanism for others to build up to that level of consumer or peer confidence.

Internet sales, largely through eBay, opened a whole new frontier, but they also came with a significant number of disputes about the grades. The lack of independent, verifiable grades was an impediment to a larger, healthier market.

Overstreet: What sort of turning points do you remember in its evolution?

SB: After slow going at first, certification saw its first real victory in an auction staged by Greg Manning Auctions. Watchers were surprised by the prices realized. After that, through 2003-2004, the industry saw a dramatic increase in the number of certified comics available at conventions and from dealers.

Since then, we've seen the evolution of the business, an increase in high end liquidity, and a substantial increase in consumer confidence in the comics they're buying in person, online or from catalogs. It's no longer only confined by having to know the dealer in question very well. Instead, the consumer can focus on the critical factors: "Is this the comic I'm looking for, is it in the grade I want and is this the price I am willing to pay?" Between 1999, when I helped start CGC and their grading standards, and 2008, when I left, we saw the attitude of the marketplace entirely shift on the subject of certification.

Overstreet: What brought you back to grading?

SB: When I left grading to work as the Senior Consignment Director at Heritage, I really thought that was it. In the end, though, there's something very compelling about this challenge. Even with all our experience and transparency, we are still the "new kids on the block." We had to do something better just to get in the door. Again, I wouldn't be doing this if I didn't think we had something great to offer the hobby I love.

And speaking of experience, over the last year people have come to know our staff and, I'm pleased to say, that West Stephan, Tim Bildhauser, Daniel Ertle, Joshua St. Amand, Steve Ricketts, Sarah Daly, Jim Noble, and Paul Figura, among others, are on board. Between just me and these few hobbyists, we have about a combined 300 years of grading, pedigree knowledge, and restoration detection experience from buying and selling as well as "professional" grading. We have all been collecting and reading comic books for many more years than that, but I wanted to put a practical number of years for experience. Once again, it goes back to transparency.

CBCS believes that our graders should have experience in the market place as that's how you truly learn to grade, learning and refining what hobbyists expect a grade should be when buying and selling. As many will tell you, grading is an art, not just a science. The overall look of an unrestored comic must really be factored into the grade, not just the "technical" aspects.

All of us at CBCS think that most things are better when there's competition. Consumers benefit from having selections to make. There is much competition in the card, paper money, and coin hobbies, why shouldn't our hobby have their choice of real certification companies as well?

Overstreet: What sort of reactions did you hear when you announced CBCS?

SB: It was overwhelmingly positive. Even people who said they would take a "wait and see" approach mentioned they would be very happy to submit once we were established and accepted by the collecting community. To me, it's clear that the collecting community has spoken by buying and selling CBCS-certified comic books. Even eBay has added a CBCS search since there are so many of our books on there.

Overstreet: What are some of the reactions you've received so far?

SB: Most have been very positive, I am very happy to say. I get emails, posts and PMs on Facebook and the CBCS forums that many collectors will only use CBCS. It is very humbling.

Overstreet: What, if anything, has worked out differently from how you thought it would in regards to the process of starting CBCS and getting it up and running?

SB: First of all, we never expected to be swamped with comic submission from the start. That was a great thing - unexpected, but great! Because of that influx of books, even though we had the core team set in place, we needed to hire more people quickly. That is not an easy thing to do, especially for grading and restoration detection. That said, even filling other positions was easier, but not easy as we at CBCS want to hire collectors with a true passion for our hobby. As of this interview, we are now up to 34 employees and still looking to hire.

Another thing that we did not envision from the beginning was our Original Art tier. We at CBCS thought that it was silly that when you got your favorite artist to do a sketch on a "sketch" cover comic that people would say "Great piece! Too bad it's not a 9.8." That's crazy! Original art is original art. Now, hobbyists have a choice, they can choose to have a numerical grade on the CBCS label or just a label that states Original Art and who the artist is. Many collectors have taken to it and are loving it, so are many artists. As an original art collector myself, if I was allowed to submit to CBCS, this is the choice I would make. I do not care about the grade of the book, only the art on it.

Overstreet: What do you think the presence of CBCS in the marketplace has done for buyers and sellers?

SB: It's done a great thing by giving the buyers and sellers a choice. It has also forced our esteemed competitor to make some changes, and that is great for our hobby. Imagine, if you will, that Ford was still the only company making cars. We would be paying $50K for that car and getting eight miles a gallon. Competition is great for the hobby!

Overstreet: What are some of your high profile and/or record-setting sales?

SB: I don't pay attention to the market, as I need to stay impartial, but I know we have set record prices on some very high profile books. I was told we set huge records with CBCS-graded comics from the "Mr. Majik Woo" collection at Heritage Auctions as well as setting records on both the *Suspense Comics* #3 from the Edgar Church/Mile High and the San Francisco pedigree collections, and ComicConnect has had record sales of CBCS graded comics, including an *Amazing Fantasy* #15 in 9.0. CBCS also graded a *Marvel Comics* #1. This was an unknown copy, and the owner thought CBCS would be the best company to have it certified. I have also been told by ComicLink that we are setting new record prices every auction.

Overstreet: We've already mentioned it a few times, but over the years, transparency is a theme you've come back to repeatedly in our conversations. What are some of the ways you've implemented it at CBCS?

SB: We feel that transparency is the key to helping the collecting community buy and sell comics. This goes for all buyers and sellers, whether in high profile, public transactions or discreet, private deals. Full-time retailers, weekend show dealers, any seller of comic books benefits when consumer confidence is legitimately high. Likewise, any buyer who can make a purchase with confidence adds to the collective faith in the market. Toward that end, we published our "grading guideline" on our website. We offer scheduled tours of our facility, so that our clients can see where their comics are graded and how they are safely stored, as well as seeing the flow and professionalism of the certification process. As I said when we started, it's our belief that once someone has paid CBCS to certify his or her comic, it is only fair that a submitter should know how our grading team factored in the defects that resulted in the given grade.

Overstreet: It took a while, but now you've launched CBCS forums online. They will have been online only a few months when this book comes out. What are your hopes for them?

SB: As always, I hope to bring our great community together. I live for this hobby and want all to feel welcome. I love the fact the new collectors can learn from the veteran collectors and CBCS graders on our forum. I was blown away that the day we launched the forums we had 400 members! I have no clue how many we have now, but I am having a blast talking comics and other things on there. We also have our Facebook group, the CBCS Comic Collectors Club, which can be found at facebook.com/groups/cbcscomics.

Overstreet: When you launched CBCS, you said that based on experience you wanted to do some things differently. What were those things and have you succeeded thus far in doing them differently?

SB: Free grading notes have been a game changer for certification. We put each invoice and corresponding comic number on the front label, so that if you see a CBCS comic for sale online, you can look up the notes on our website to see why CBCS graded the comic the way we did. What's really cool is that we also put a QR code on the back of the CBCS label. If a collector or seller is at a convention or store, all they have to do is use their smart phone, with a free QR reader download, and the grading notes will pop up on their phone.

The CBCS Verified Signature Program (VSP) has been a huge success. There are so many un-witnessed signatures out there, and many collectors want them authenticated. We came up with a way to do this by working with an independent, professional company called Comic

Signature Authentication (CSA). We send CSA a digital photo of the autograph and then their professional signature evaluators go through their process which includes Characteristic Signature Mapping (CSM), a 28-point verification system. CSM is really is state-of-the-art. Once we get confirmation that the signature has passed CSA's very high standards, we put on that it was signed by the professional on the CBCS label. It's great to see signatures by great creators from our hobby, particularly those who have passed away, in a CBCS holder and certified as genuine. Of course it's not only for creators who have passed. Additionally, with VSP, we're able to certify comics signed by celebrities since CSA can authenticate those as well.

Another thing we have done is made a crystal clear, safe holder that does not "dull" or "filmy" the look of a comic book. We also put the top label on the inside of the holder, so that it does not get dirty, can't be removed, and will not come off the holder from too much handling. I hear that our esteemed competition has already followed us on this. That's great for everybody! The interior sleeve we use is made of virgin PETG and does not need to be changed out after many years because it is archival safe material that lets the comic "breathe."

Grade screening has become big, as there is no minimum submission and submitters may designate a different grade for each individual book sent in. The two-day Modern tier has also been huge. Many collectors and sellers have been using that for "hot" modern variants, so that they can get them to market quickly and affordably. The reactions to our online submission form have been solid, as expected. Most folks seem to love our no-fee, easy-to-use, online submission experience.

Overstreet: CBCS is part of the convention circuit. What services does the company offer onsite, and how has it been fine-tuned since you started up?

SB: It has only been "fine-tuned" by the fact that we are better at receiving the books quicker and have added more "witnesses" to go with a collector to have their book signed or sketched, so that we know for a fact that the signature or art is real. We have started doing "on-site" grading and it seems to be a big hit with both the buyers and sellers.

Overstreet: Are there other things you are doing – or not doing – to bolster consumer confidence?

SB: In addition to our interactions with our customers, we believe it's also very important how we conduct ourselves when it comes to potential conflicts of interest. Neither CBCS employees – full or part time – nor any of their family members are allowed to buy and sell CBCS-certified comics or submit comic books for CBCS grading.

Now, of course, just about everyone at CBCS loves comics. They wouldn't be here otherwise, but if our grades are going to be perceived in a light that is beneficial to everyone, the trust factor has to be there. This is one way we will work to cultivate it. A CBCS employee who collects comics should not have any need to have a comic certified, as they should be able to purchase a comic for their personal collection using their knowledge of comics or having one of our graders to look that book over for them. Full or part time, they are not allowed to sell ungraded comic books through auction houses or any anonymous sources.

CBCS pre-graders, senior graders and management are not allowed to accept gifts of any kind, including food, drink or entertainment, from any CBCS submitter or potential submitter. These CBCS employees must pay their own way, at all times, during conventions for items not reimbursed to them by CBCS.

Overstreet: What are your current goals for future growth?

SB: We are looking into grading and restoration seminars and panels at conventions. Some would not only be CBCS graders, as I would also like to include other seasoned hobbyists to join the panels and share as well. This hobby is about all of us, not just CBCS. There are some special projects coming in the near future, but I will save talking about them until next year's *Overstreet Price Guide*.

CBCS

CBCS INTRODUCED CLARITY COMIC BOOK CERTIFICATIO

Record Sale Price! $262,900

The Strange Story of Israel Waldman and the I.W./Super Comics Mystery

by Jon Martin McClure with research assistant Jacob Balcom

I.W. Enterprises was founded in 1958 (named for the company's owner, Israel Waldman) and published comics from 1958-1959 and 1963-1964. As of 1963, the company used the name "Super Comics" and changed its cover logo to match. Replacing the usual Comics Code Authority seal of approval, a little box reads, "A Top Quality Comic," which appeared on all 1958-1959 I.W. reprints, while 1963-1964 issues have a "Super Comics" seal of quality. The 1958-1959 I.W. books reprinted original covers with minor art changes, and primarily with random contents. Covers were sometimes used multiple times on the same title, and many books have contents that do not match the original cover, Type 9a Variants. One title, *Pee-Wee Pixies* (1958-1959, 1963) has three total issues (#1, 8, 10), with the same cover. The 1963-1964 Super Comics have new covers.

Waldman's NewYork-based company allegedly acquired printing plates from Eastern Color, primarily from defunct publishers who owed Eastern money. Waldman approached Quality Publications, too: "Al Grenet (editor at Quality) remembers when (Everett Arnold, aka "Busy Arnold," publisher of Quality) sold what art had remained to a guy who was going into the comic book business. The guy took all the original artwork." (*The Quality Companion*, 2011, p. 31.) That "guy" was Israel Waldman. The Quality reprints from I.W./Super comics are *Buccaneer* #1, 8, *Buccaneers* #12, *Candy* #12, 16-17, *Doll Man* #11, 15, 17, *Hollywood Secrets of Romance* #9, *Intimate Confessions* #12, *Love and Marriage* #17, *Plastic Man* #11, 16, 18, *Spirit* #11-12, *Star Feature* #9, *Torchy* #16, and *Westerner* #16. In 1974, DC comics had problems with copyrights on some Quality and Fawcett material "...as well as the problem of just physically laying our hands on some of it..." (Archie Goodwin, *Detective Comics* #440(4-5/74), p. 26.) As Waldman was in possession of most or all of the surviving Quality artwork, finding it would have been difficult indeed! "Busy Arnold" had the habit of destroying artwork, possibly for fear the artists might try to sell their own work, so Waldman could only have acquired what remained after the storm. "Creig Flessel (co-creator of the Sandman)... once visited Quality and witnessed "Busy Arnold" cutting up art and throwing it in a bin. Flessel looked to Jack Cole (creator of Plastic Man), who shrugged his shoulders as if to say, "Nothing I can do about it." "There are no public records of DC renewing original Quality Publications. This is the reason why original printed Quality Comics have "lapsed" into the public domain and are sometimes retouched and repackaged by independent publishers." (*The Quality Companion,* 2011, pp. 18, 33.) Copyrights are public record, and DC didn't have one.

Pee-Wee Pixies #8

"Waldman probably never obtained the necessary copyrights for these reprintings, which included former Quality Comics titles such as *Plastic Man* or *Doll Man* that DC had acquired rights to as well as several issues of Will Eisner's *The Spirit*. It appears that he was rarely, if ever, challenged by the actual copyright holders. Perhaps this is because his titles never appeared on the newsstands or spinner racks..." (*Horror Comics in Black and White, A History and Catalog, 1964-2004*, 2013, p. 162.) There was no legitimate reason for issues of *Plastic Man, Doll Man* and *The Spirit* to have been published by Super Comics in 1963-1964... or was there? *Plastic Man, Doll Man* and *The Spirit* stories were in limbo at the time Waldman reprinted them, well before DC published *Plastic Man* #1(11-12/66). Waldman paid "Busy Arnold" to get the surviving artwork and plates; it's not like he climbed in a window at Quality at midnight with a flashlight and a Santa sack to obtain them. Having bought out Quality, he was within his rights to publish *Plastic Man, Doll Man* and *The Spirit*, or any of the other Quality books he obtained, since the only value he was purchasing was the ability to reprint old comic books.

Waldman's business strategy was direct and effective: he would buy out printing plates and original art from defunct comics publishers, sometimes gaining possession of material from companies still in business, probably by accident. "Israel and Sol [Brodsky] bought tons of original artwork from bankrupt companies—some from Fawcett, some from Fiction House, wherever they found a warehouse of the stuff, and they'd buy it for a penny on the dollar, a penny a page, 20¢ a page..." (Mike Esposito, *Alter Ego* #54, 2005, pp. 17-18). Waldman successfully avoided one risk that every other publisher had to endure: he accepted no returns (*Andru & Esposito*, 2006, p. 74.) Unlike other I.W. issues, *My Secret Marriage* #9(1958) notes in the indicia, "Reprinted by Eastern Color." The indicia of all I.W. books reads, "Reproduction in part or whole is prohibited," which is ironic because Waldman was able to obtain and reprint material from 37 companies including Timely and EC, the latter two definitely without any legal right or permission. Waldman probably acquired such forbidden fruit along with legitimate books, all of which ended up getting reprinted; the swiped EC comic was *Incredible Science Fiction* #30(7-8/55), reprinted in I.W.'s *Strange Planets* #1(1964), including the letter column, a delightful accident.

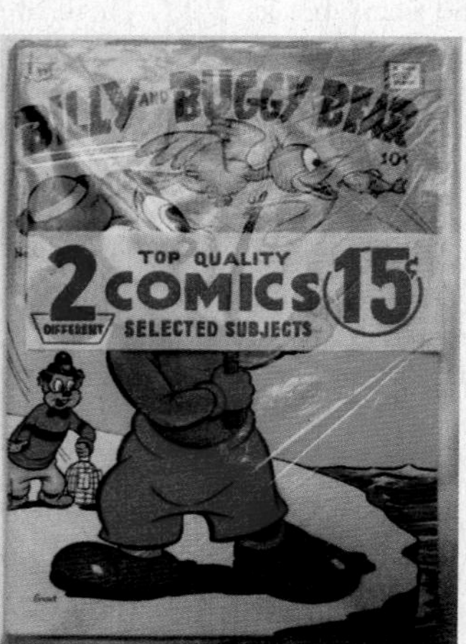

Joe Simon paints a fascinating picture of the elusive Waldman and their meeting: "I took a quick turn in Waldman's building, then climbed the black iron steps to the third floor [and] found myself in a small, caged cubicle facing another door, this one huge, iron, intimidating. A very loud buzzer startled me. There was a bell which I rang. I could see the door snap from its lock. A tinny voice from an unseen sound system... requested that I state my name and business, [then] directed me to enter.

"Mr Waldman introduced himself. He leaned over a well scratched wooden desk with peeling varnish [that was] holding neat stacks of yellowing artwork that must have been recently retrieved from warehouses. More stacks of dusty art work and engravers' proofs lined the floors. There were love comics, superhero comics, even Will Eisner's wonderful Spirit. Mr. Waldman sat down and gestured at the other chair in the room. He smiled cordially, for the first and last time. A slim man in his early forties, he was tie-less, his shirtsleeves rolled up below the elbow, his hands smudged with the dust of the old artwork."

Joe Simon describes Israel Waldman as cordial but "...all business. He took the comic books out of the envelope I shoved at him: *Bullseye, Foxhole, In Love, Police Trap*. He rifled through a few pages of each, [and] set them down next to [his] checkbook. I was disappointed that he hadn't read a story or two." Simon told Waldman, "We need to keep the copyrights." Normally this sort of deal would include legal documents and agreements, "...but Waldman didn't have the time or the inclination to mess around with such trifles." Waldman reportedly said, "So keep them. What do I need with copyrights?" (The Comic Book Makers, 1990, p. 165.)

No I.W. or Super Comics were cover dated because they were designed to have an indefinite shelf life. Waldman was the first publisher to sell comics in plastic bags, in sets of two for fifteen cents, an innovation. The pair of 15 cent bagged sets I've seen contain *Super Rabbit* #1 with *Wacky Woodpecker* #1, and *Billy and Buggy Bear* #1 with *Sharpy Fox* #1. The bag says, "2 different top quality comics," and "selected subjects," so other categories such as superhero or horror would likely have been paired as well. One collector online claims to own two 2-packs and to have previously owned a 4-pack, which had the titles of the four comics inside printed on the header of the bag, and claims to have never seen a 3-pack. Some claim to remember seeing three packs of 12 cent books in the 1963-1964 Super Comics era, but I have found no evidence as of yet, no plastic bags. "They (Super Comics) often appeared in plastic bags at a cut rate (three for 25 cents) in places where comics were not usually sold—variety stores, five-and-dime stores, small grocery stores, etc." (*The Comic Book in America*, 1989, page 129.) I'm inclined to believe that there are three and four packs out there, and that surviving examples will probably eventually surface, although such hopes and pursuits are reminiscent of monster hunting. Major publishers like Charlton, D.C., Gold Key, Marvel and others would later follow the practice of selling bagged comics in the 1960s and 1970s, in discounted groups of two to four comics per bag, and in Gold Key's case, ten in a box. (For more information on bagged and boxed groups, check out my article "The Whitman Mystery" in *Comic Book Marketplace* #85-86, Gemstone Publications, 2001.) Wholesaling bagged comics to discount retail and grocery stores put Waldman's products in a different category, that of toys and novelties. Keeping I.W./Super Comics under the radar was a cunning strategy that kept Waldman out of the clutches of the Comics Code Authority, a problem that would have increased expenses, to say nothing of publishing delays and potential legal problems. Professionals including Abel, Andru, Colletta, Esposito, Severin, Simon and others, created covers for the reprints and the unpublished stories, including issues of *Danger* (1963-1964), *Daring Adventures* (1958, 1963-1964), and *Fantastic Adventures* (1963-1964).

"At the end of 1945, publisher C.H. Albrecht had an idea for Atlas Comics, featuring a superhero named after Charles Atlas, but Albrecht wasn't able to bring it to fruition. On the Pulp Artist website, historian David Saunders shows a striking Atlas Comics unpublished cover with its leopard skin-patterned logo to complement the body builder's briefs. The cover strongly resembles *Action Comics* #1(6/38), where Superman lifts a car. The inside cover proof, which has a March 1946 date, shows a letter from the "editor"—Charles Atlas himself! "Welcome to ATLAS COMICS—to a brand new, sparkling comic book that's DIFFERENT... I want you to feel that I'm YOUR friend—that your problems are mine." The stories had been unearthed and printed in I.W. Publishing/Super Comics' *Daring Adventures* #18 (1964). In *Daring Adventures* #18, the scavenger publisher commissioned a new cover and dropped Charles Atlas' letter, which would have linked the body-builder to the comic book." (*Super Weird Heroes,* 2016, pp. 12-13.) Waldman's comic book business was a low budget act by design, and *Daring Adventures* #18 would not exist without Waldman's penchant for digging through dusty old printing plates—it would be lost in time. The fact that Waldman published unseen stories and art in several issues brings collecting I.W./Super Comics to a higher level.

Based on my experience hunting I.W./Super Comics I believe about 5 percent of them are rare, and possibly the rarest of all is *Full of Fun* #8(1959); about 10 percent of them are scarce, while roughly 25 percent are uncommon, and approximately 60 percent are easily obtained. Consider *Human Fly* #1(1958), a book with Blue Beetle and other reprints where the Human Fly never makes an appearance! Waldman preferred turning a profit to fruitless perfectionism; apparently he thought the book would sell better with the title *Human Fly* than *Blue Beetle*. The randomness of the issue numbers is in fact not; they are all numbered based on the sequence of the printings instead of by title. I.W. Enterprises issues #1-6 were printed in 1958, and issues #7-9 were printed in 1959. Super Comics issues #10-11 were published in 1963, and although some #12s are dated 1963, others are dated 1964, an error fixed part way through the printing process. Because print runs are the issue numbers, we know all #12s were printed in 1964. No #13 exists, possibly to evade the karmic fate inherent in many comic book horror stories. Issues #14-18 were published in 1964. Some of the I.W./Super Comics are type 9a variants, defined as unlicensed after-market reprints that have the same title, cover and issue number as the original with only minor cover changes and new ads, but with different contents, such as U.S. Paratroopers #1(1958). Type 9b variants are defined as simultaneously published unlicensed after-market reprints with the same title and issue number as another book with the same title and issue number, but with different covers, ads and contents. *Speedy Rabbit* #1 is a good example of 9b variants; *Little Eva* #10(1963) is another. No "regular edition" can be identified and so both issues are considered variants; assigning numbers 1 and 1a is arbitrary but suffices for cataloging. The following list of 332 I.W./Super Comics includes the original titles, issue numbers, dates of publication and publishers:

Algie (1964) #15; *Algie* #3(4/54)(Timor), *Apache* (1958) #1; *Apache* #1(1951)(Fiction House), *Avenger* (1959) #9, *Avenger* #1(2-3/55)(Magazine Ent., ME hereafter), *Battle Stories* (1963-1964) #10-12, 15-18; #10: *U.S. Tank Commandos* #2(8/52)(Avon), #11: *U.S. Paratroops Behind Enemy Lines* #5(10/52) (Avon), #12: *Tell it to the Marines* #8(7/54)(Toby), #15: *American Air Forces* #7(8/52)(ME), #16: *Men in Action* #3(9/57)(Ajax/Farrell), #17: *With the Marines on the Battlefronts of the World* #2(3/54)(Toby), #18: *U.S. Fighting Air Force* #28(9/56)(Superior), *Billy and Buggy Bear* (1958-1959, 1963) #1, 7, 10; #1: *All Surprise* #8(Fall 1945)(Timely), #7: *All Surprise* #8(Fall 1945)(Timely), #10: *Monkeyshines Comics* #27(7/49)(Ace), *Black Knight* (1963) #11; *Black Knight* #1(5/53)(Toby), *Blazing Six-Guns* (1958-1959, 1963-1964) #1, 8-12, 15-18; #1: *Western Killers* #62(1/49)(Fox) with the cover of *Blazing Sixguns* #1(12/52)(Avon), #8: *Blazing Western* #4(7/54)

(Timor) with the cover to *Kit Carson* #3(12/51) (Avon), #9: *Blazing Western* #1(1/54)(Timor) with the cover to *Dalton Boys* #1(1951)(Avon), #10: *Rider* #2(6/57)(Farrell), #11: *Rider* #1(3/57)(Farrell), #12: *Bull's Eye* #3(12-1/54-55)(Mainline), #15: *Silver Kid Western* #2(12/54)(Key), #16: *Buffalo Bill* #9(12/51) (Youthful), #17: *Western True Crime* #5(4/49)(Fox), #18: *Straight Arrow* #54(2/56)(ME), *Brain* (1958-1959, 1963-1964) #1-4 , 8-10, 14, 18; (all ME), #1: *Brain* #1(9/56) #2: *Brain* #2(4/57), #3: *Brain* #3(8/57), #4: *Brain* 4(10/57), #8: *Brain* #5(11/57), #9: *Brain* #7(3/58), #10: *Brain* #4(10/57), #14: *Brain* #3(8/57), *Brain* #18: *Brain* #1(9/56), *Buccaneer* (1958-1959, 1963) #1, 8; #1: *Buccaneers* #20(3/50)(Quality), #8: *Buccaneers* #23(9/50) (Quality), *Buccaneers* #12, *Buccaneers* #21(5/50) (Quality), *Buster Bear* (1959, 1963) #9-10, both *Frisky Fables* v3 #6(9/47)(Novelty), *Candy* (1964) #12, 16-17; #12: *Candy* #17(8/50)(Quality), #16: *Candy* #8(2/49)(Quality), #17: *Candy* #14(2/50) (Quality), *Casper Cat* (1958-1959, 1964) #1, 7, 14; all three reprint *Dopey Duck* #2(4/46)(Timely), *Cosmo Cat* (1958) #1, *Cosmo Cat* #7(7/47)(Fox), *Cowboys'n" Injuns* (1958-1959, 1963) #1, 7, 10; all three reprint *Tick Tock Tales* #31(7-8/51)(ME), *Danger* (1963-1964) #10-12, 15-18; #10: *Great Comics* #1(Novak) (1945), #11: *Johnny Danger* #1(8/54)(Toby), #12: *Red Seal* #14(10/45)(Chesler), #15: *Spy Cases* #26(9/50)(Timely), #16: *Yankee Comics* #5(Chesler) contains material from an unpublished issue, #17: *Scoop* #8(1944)(Chesler), #18: *Guns Against Gangsters* #5(5-6/49)(Novelty), *Danger is our Business* (1958) #9, *Danger is our Business* #1(12/53)(Toby), *Daring Adventures* (1959, 1963-1964) #9-12, 15-18; #9: *Blue Bolt* #115(10/52)(Star), #10: *Dynamic* #24(3/48)(Superior), #11: *Dynamic* #16(10/45)(Chesler), #12: *Phantom Lady* #14(10/47) (Fox), #15: *Hooded Menace* #1(1951)(Avon), #16: *Dynamic* #1(12/41)(Chesler), *Dynamic* #3(2/42) (Chesler), *Dynamic* #12(11/44)(Chesler) and *Punch Comics* #1(11/41)(Chesler), #17: *Green Lama* #3(3/45)(Spark), #18: intended for *Atlas Comics* #1, an unpublished issue, *Dr. Fu Manchu*(1958) #1, *Mask of Dr. Fu Manchu* #1(1951)(Avon), *Dogface Dooley* (1958, 1964) #1, *Dogface Dooley* #2(1951) (ME), *Doll Man*(1963-1964) #11, 15, 17; #11: *Doll Man* #20(1/49)(Quality), #15: *Doll Man* #23(7/49) (Quality), #17: *Doll Man* #28(5/50)(Quality), *Dream of Love* (1958-1959) #1-2, 8-9; #1: *Dream Book of Love* #1(6-7/54)(ME), #2: *Great Lover Romances* #10(6/53)(Toby), #8: *Great Lover Romances* #2(1951)(Toby), #9: *Great Lover Romances* #3(3/52) (Toby), *Dynamic Adventures* (1959) #8-9; #8: *Fight* #53(12/47)(Fiction House), #9: *Escape From Devil's Island* #1(1952)(Avon), *Dynamic Comics* (1958) #1, *Dynamic* #23(11/47)(Chesler) with the cover flipped, from *Sensational Police Cases* #3(5-6/54) (Avon), *Eerie* (1958-1959) #1, 8-9; #1: *Spook* #1(1946) (Baily) with the cover to *Strange Worlds* #6(2/52) (Avon), #8: *Ghost* #10(Spring 1954)(Fiction House) with the cover of *Eerie* #12(8/53)(Avon), #9: *Tales of Terror* #1(1952)(Toby) with the cover of *Eerie* #2(8-9/51)(Toby), *Eerie Tales* (1963-1964) #10-12, 15; #10: *Spook* #27(1/54)(Star), #11: *Purple Claw* #3(5/53)(Toby), #12: *Eerie* #1(5-6/51)(Avon), #15: *Blue Bolt Weird Tales* #113(5/52)(Star), *Famous Funnies* (1964) #15, 17-18; #15: *Super Cat* #4(5/58) (Farrell), #17: *Double Trouble* #1(11/57)(St. John), #18: *Super Pup* #5(7/54)(Avon), *Fantastic Adventures* (1963-1964) #10-12, 15-18; #10: *He-Man* #2(7/54)(Toby), #11: *Blue Bolt Weird Tales* #118(4/53)(Star), #12: unpublished material from *Chesler,* #15: *Spook* #23(3/53)(Star), #16: *Dark Shadows* #2(1/58)(Steinway), #17: *Seven Seas* #6(1947)(Leader), #18: *Superior Stories* #1(5-6/55) (Nesbit), *Fantastic Tales* (1958) #1, *City of the Living Dead* #1(1952)(Avon), *Fighting Daniel Boone* (1958) #1, *Fighting Daniel Boone* #1(1953)(Avon), *Firehair* (1959) #8, *Rangers* #57(2/51)(Fiction House) with the cover of *Fighting Indians of the Wild West* #2(11/52)(Avon), *Foxhole* (1963-1964) #11-12, 15-18; #11: *Foxhole* #1(10/54)(Mainline), #12: *Foxhole* #2(12/54)(Mainline), #15: *United States Marines* #5(1952)(ME), #16: *United States Marines* #8(1952) (ME), #17: *Tell it to the Marines* #13(3/55)(Toby), #18: *Foxhole* #3(2/55)(Mainline), *Frontier Romances* (1958) #1, 9; #1: *Frontier Romances* #1(11-12/49) (Avon), #9: *Cowgirl Romances* #5(6/51)(Fiction House) with cover to *Wild Bill Hickok* #13(11/52) (Avon), *Full of Fun* (1958) #8, from undetermined source, most likely unpublished *Bernard Baily Studio* material from the mid-1940s, *Great Action Comics* (1958) #1, 8-9; #1: *Gold Meda*l #1(1945) (Cambridge), #8: *Phantom Lady* #15(12/47)(Fox), #9: *Phantom Lady* #23(4/49)(Fox), *Great Western* (1958) #1-2, 8-9; #1: *Straight Arrow* #36(5-6/54) (ME), #2: *Straight Arrow* #42(2/55)(ME), #8: *Tim Holt* #11(11/49)(ME) with the cover to *Fighting Indians of the Wild West Annual* #1(1952)(Avon), #9: *Straight Arrow* #48(8/55)(ME) with the cover to *Kit Carson* #5(11-12/54)(Avon), *Gunfighters* (1963-64) #11-12, 15-16, 18; #11: *Billy the Kid Adventure Magazine* #24(8-9/54)(Toby), #12: *Gunsmoke Trail* #2(8/57)(Farrell), #15: *Straight Arrow* #42(2/55) (ME), #16: *Billy the Kid Adventure Magazine* #27(2-3/55)(Toby), #18: *The Rider* #3(8/57)(Farrell), *Hollywood Secrets of Romance* (1958) #9, *Hollywood Secrets* #2(1/50)(Quality), *Human Fly* (1958, 1963) #1, 10; #1: *Blue Beetle* #44(9-10/46)(Fox), #10: *Blue Beetle* #46(7/47)(Fox), *Indian Braves* (1958) #1,

Indian Braves #4(9/51)(Ace), *Indians of the Wild West* (1958) #9, *Indians* #11(4/52)(Fiction House), *Intimate Confessions* (1958, 1963-1964) #9-10, 12, 18; #9: *Intimate Confessions* #2(9-10/51)(Avon), #10: *Intimate Confessions* #6(6/52)(Avon), #12: *Love Confessions* #2(12/49)(Quality), #18: *Dream Book of Romance* #8(9-10/54)(ME), *Jet Power* (1958) #1-2; #1: *Jet Powers* #1(1/51), #2: *Jet Powers* #2(4-6/51) (ME), *Jungle Adventures* (1963-1964) #10, 12, 15, 17-18; #10: *Zoot Comics* #13b(4/48)(Fox), *Terrors of the Jungle* #4(4/53)(Star), #12: *Zoot* #14(3/48)(Fox), #15: *Jungle* #152(8/52)(Fiction House), #17: *Jo-Jo* #22(12/48)(Fox), #18: *White Princess of the Jungle* #1(7/51)(Avon), *Jungle Comics* (1959) #9, *Jungle Comics* #151(7/52)(Fiction House) and *Terrors of the Jungle* #8(3/54)(Star), *Ka'a'nga (*1958-1959) #1, 8; #1: *Ka'a'nga* #18(Winter 1953/1954)(Fiction House), #8: *Ka'a'nga* #10(Winter 1951/1952) (Fiction House), *Kat Karson* (1958) #1, *Cowboys 'n' Injuns* #3(1947)(ME), *Kid Koko* (1958) #1-2; #1: *Koko and Kola* #4(4/47)(ME), #2: *Koko and Kola* #3(3/47)(ME), *Kiddie Kapers* (1963-1964) #10, 14-15, 17; #10: *Animal Adventures* #1(12/53), #14: *Animal Adventures* #1(12/53)(Timor), #15: *Animal Adventures* #2(2/54)(Timor), #17: *Cowboys & Injuns* #7(1951)(ME), *Kit Carson* (1963) #10, *Kit Carson* #1(1950)(Avon), *Krazy Krow* (1958-1959) #1, 2, 7: #1: *Krazy Krow* #3(Winter 1945-1946)(Timely), #2: *Krazy Krow* #1(Summer 1945)(Timely), #7: *Krazy Krow* #3(Winter 1945-1946)((Timely), *Leo the Lion* (1958) #1: *Adventures of Patorzu nn*(Winter 1946) (Green) contains *Animal Crackers* reprints, *Atomic Rabbit* #7(6/57)(Charlton), *Little Eva* (1958-1959, 1963-1964) #1-4, 6-10, 12, 14, 16, 18, pub'd by St. John, (SJ); #1: *Little Eva* #12(10/53)(SJ), #2: *Little Eva* 13(11/53)(SJ) and #29(9/56)(SJ), #3: *Little Eva* #24(4/56)(SJ), #4: *Little Eva* #15(3/54)(SJ), #6: *Little Eva* #14(1/54)(SJ), *Little Eva* #30(10/56)(SJ), #7: *Little Eva* #16(5/54)(SJ), #8: *Little Eva* #1(5/52)(SJ), #9: *Little Eva* #2(7/52)(SJ), #10: *Little Eva* #3(9/52) (SJ), #10a: *Little Eva* #14(1/54)(SJ) *Little Eva* #30(10/56)(SJ), #12: *Little Eva* #5(12/52)(SJ), #14: *Little Eva* #3(9/52)(SJ), #16: *Little Eva* #8(6/53)(SJ), *Little Ike* #3(8/53)(SJ), #18: *Little Eva* #9(7/53)(SJ), *Little Spunky* (1958) #1, *Frisky Fables v3* #8(11/47) (Novelty), *Love and Marriage (*1958-1959, 1963-1964) #2, 8, 11, 12, 15, 17; #2: *Love and Marriage* #1(3/52)(Superior), #8: *Love and Marriage* #3(7/52) (Superior), #10: *Love and Marriage* #4(9/52) (Superior), #11: *Love and Marriage* #11(11/53(Superior), #12: *My Secret Marriage* #4(11/53)(Superior), #15: *My Secret Marriage* #7(5/54)(Superior), #17: *Heart Throbs* #3(11/49) (Quality), *Malu in the Land of Adventure* (1958) #1, *Slave Girl Comics* #1(2/49)(Avon), *Man o' Mars* (1958) #1, *Man o' Mars* #1(4/53)(Fiction House), *Marmaduke Monk* (1958, 1964) #1, 14; #1: *Monkeyshines Comics* #13(2/47)(Ace), #14: *Monkeyshines Comics* #13(2/47)(Ace), *Marty Mouse* (1958) #1, *Monkeyshines Comics* #27(7/49)(Ace), *Master Detective* (1964) #17, *Criminals on the Run* v2 #2(9/48)(Novelty), *Meet Merton* (1959, 1963-1964) #9, 11, 18; #9: *Meet Merton* #1(12/53)(Toby), #11 *Meet Merton* #4(6/54)(Toby), #18: *Meet Merton* #3(4/54)(Toby), *Mighty Atom* (1958) #1, *Mighty Atom and the Pixies* #6(10/49)(ME), *Muggsy Mouse* (1958, 1964) #1-2, 14; #1: *Muggsy Mouse* #3(8-9/51) (Magazine Ent., ME hereafter), #2: *Muggsy Mouse* #4(1953)(ME), #14: *Muggsy Mouse* #3(8-9/51)(ME), *Muggy-Doo, Boy Cat* (1964) #12, 16; #12: *Muggy-Do, Boy Cat* #4(1/54)(Stanhall), #16: *Muggy-Do, Boy Cat* #1(7/53)(Stanhall), *My Secret Marriage (*1959) #9, *My Secret Marriage* #2(7/53)(Superior), *Mystery Tales* (1964) #16-18; #16: *Tales of Horror* #2(9/52) (Toby), #17: *Eerie* #14(1-2/54)(Avon), #18: *Strange Terrors* #4(11/52)(St. John), *Pee-Wee Pixies* (1958-1959, 1963) #1, 8, 10; #1: *Pixies* #3(Summer 1947) (ME), #8: *Pixies* #4(Fall 1947)(ME), #10: *Pixies* #4(Fall 1947)(ME), *Pinky the Egghead* (1958, 1964) #1-2, 14; #1: *Noodnick* #3(4/54)(Comic Media), #2: *Noodnick* #4(6/54)(Comic Media), #14: *Noodnick* #4(6/54)(Comic Media), *Planet Comics* (1958-1959) #1, 8-9; #1: *Planet Comics* #70(Spring 1953)(Fiction House), #8: *Planet Comics* #72(Fall 1953)(Fiction House) with cover to *Attack on Planet Mars* #1(1951)(Avon), *Plastic Man* (1963-1964) #11, 16, 18; #11: *Plastic Man* #16(3/49)(Quality), #16: *Plastic Man* #21(1/50)(Quality), #18: *Police Comics* #95(10/49)(Quality), *Police Trap* (1963-1964) #11, 16-18; #11: *Police Trap* #3(12-1/55)(Mainline), #16: *Police Trap* #1(8-9/54)(Mainline), #17: *Justice Traps the Guilty* #83(10-11/56)(Prize), #18: *Inside Crime* #3(7/50)(Fox), *Purple Claw* (1959) #8, *Purple Claw* #1(1/53)(Toby), *Realistic Romances* (1958-1959) #1, 8-9; #1: *Realistic Romances* #4(8/52)(Avon), #8: *Realistic Romances* #7(Avon) with the cover to *Realistic Romances* #16(6-7/54)(Avon), #9: *Complete Romance* #1(1949)(Avon) with the cover to *Intimate Secrets of Romance* #1(9/53)(Star), *Red Mask* (1958-1959) #1-2, 8; #1: *Red Mask* #52(2-3/56)(ME), #2: *Red Mask* #51(9-10/55)(ME), #8: *Red Mask* #52(2-3/56)(ME), *Robin Hood* (1958-1959, 1963-1964) #1-2, 9-10, 15; #1: *Robin Hood* #3(3/56)(ME), #2: *Robin Hood* #4(5/56)(ME), #9: *Robin Hood* #52(11/55) (ME), #10: *Robin Hood* #53(1/56)(ME), #15: *Robin Hood* #5(3/57)(ME), *Romantic Love* (1958-1959, 1963) #2-3, 8, 10-11; #2: *Romantic Love* #2(11-12/49)(Avon), #3: *Romantic Love* #3(1-2/50(Avon), #8: *Romantic Love* #4(2-3/51)(Avon) with the cover to *Realistic Romances* #17(8-9/54)(Avon), #10: *Great*

Lover Romances #6(10/52)(Toby), #11: *Great Lover Romances* #20(1/55)(Toby), *Sensational Police Cases* (1959) #5, *Prison Break* #5(10/52)(Avon), *Sharpy Fox* (1958, 1964) #1-2, 14; #1: *Ideal Comics* #3(Summer 1945)(Timely), #2: *Kiddie Kapers* #1(1945)(Kiddie Kapers Company), #14: *Ribtickler* #7(1957)(Green), *Sheena, Queen of the Jungle* (1958) #9, *Sheena, Queen of the Jungle* #17(Fall 1952)(Fiction House) with the cover to *White Princess of the Jungle* #4(8/52)(Fiction House), *Silver Kid Western* (1958) #1-2; #1: *Silver Kid Western* #2(12/54)(Stanmore), #2: *Silver Kid Western* #1(10/54)(Stanmore), *Space Comics* (1959) #8, *Space Comics* #5(5-6/54)(Avon) with the cover to *Space Comics* #4(3-4/54)(Avon), *Space Detective* (1958-1959) #1, 8; #1: *Space Detective* #2(11/51) (Avon), #8: *Famous Funnies* #191(12/50)(Eastern Color) with the cover to *Space Detective* #1(7/51) (Avon), *Space Mysteries* (1958-1959) #1, 8-9; #1: *Journey into Unknown Worlds* #4(4/51)(Atlas), #9: *Planet Comics* #73(Winter 1953)(Fiction House) with the cover to *Strange Worlds* #19(2/55)(Avon), *Speedy Rabbit* (1958, 1964) #1, 1a, 14; #1: *Peter Cottontail* #1(1/54)(Key), #1a: *Peter Cottontail* #2(3/54)(Key), #14: *Peter Cottontail* #1(1/54)(Key), *Spirit* (1963-1964) #11-12; #11: *Spirit* #19(1/50)(Quality), #12: *Spirit* #17(9/49)(Quality), *Star Feature Comics* (1958) #9, *Feature Comics* #141(12/49)(Quality), *Strange Mysteries* (1959, 1963-1964) #9-12, 15-18; #9: *Spook* #28(4/54)(Star), #10: *Strange* #2(7/57)(Ajax), #11: *Strange* #1(3/57)(Ajax), #12: *Tales of Horror* #5(3/53)(Toby) with first page uncolored, #15: *Dark Mysteries* #23(5/55)(Master), #16: *Dead Who Walk* #1(1952)(Realistic), #17: *Dark Mysteries* #22(3/55) (Master), #18: *Witchcraft* #1(3-4/52)(Avon), *Strange Planets* (1958-1959, 1963-1964) #1, 9-12, 15-16, 18; #1: *Incredible Science Fiction* #30(7-8/55)(EC) with the cover to *Strange Worlds* #3(6/51)(Avon), #9: *Strange Worlds* #4(9/51)(Avon) with the cover to *Flying Saucers* #1(1952)(Avon), #10: *Space Detective* #1(7/51)(Avon) with the cover to *Attack on Planet Mars* #1(1951)(Avon), #11: *An Earthman on Venus* #1(1951)(Avon), #12: *Rocket to the Moon* #1(1951) (Avon), #15: *Journey into Unknown Worlds* #6(8/51) (Atlas), #16: *Strange Worlds* #6(2/51)(Avon), #18: *Great Exploits* #1(1957)(Farrell), *Strange Worlds* (1959) #5, *Strange Worlds* #9(11/52)(Avon), *Sunny, America's Sweetheart* (1959) #8, *Sunny America's Sweetheart* #11(12/47)(Fox) with the cover to *Penny* #3(1948)(Avon), *Super Brat* (1958-1959, 1963) #1-3, 7-8, 10; #1: *Super Brat* #1(1/54)(Toby), #2: *Super Brat* #2(3/54)(Toby), #3: *Super Brat* #3(5/54)(Toby), #7: *Super Brat* #1(1/54)(Toby), #8: *Super Brat* #2(3/54)(Toby), #10: *Super Brat* #2(5/54)(Toby), *Super Rabbit* (1958-1959, 1963) #1-2, 7, 10; #1: *Super Rabbit* #13(9/48)(Atlas), #2: *Super Rabbit* #10(3/48)(Atlas), #7: *Super Rabbit* #13(9/48)(Atlas), *Super Rabbit* #10: *Peter Cottontail* #2(3/54)(Key), *Teen Romances* (1963-1964) #10-11, 15-17; #10: *Popular Teen-Agers* #7(4/51)(Star), #11: *Popular Teen-Agers* #17(1953)(Star), #15: *Popular Teen-Agers* #21(1954)(Star), #16: *Popular Teen-Agers* #20(1/54)(Star) #17: *Popular Teen-Agers* #11(5-6/52)(Star), *Teen-Age Talk* (1959) #5, 8-9; #5: *Oh Brother!* #5(10/53)(Stanmore), #8: *Hector* #3(3/54) (Stanhall), #9: *Punch Comics* #23(1/48)(Superior), *School Day Romances* #1(11-12/49)(Star), *Tell It to the Marines*(1958-1959, 1964) #1, 9, 16; #1: *Tell it to the Marines* #15(5/55)(Toby), #9: *Tell it to the Marines* #1(3/52)(Toby) with the cover to *U.S. Marines in Action* #1(8/52)(Avon), #16: *Tell it to the Marines* #4(9/52)(Toby), *Three Rascals* (1958, 1963) #1-2, 10; #1: *Clubhouse Rascals* #1(6/56)(ME), #2: *Clubhouse Rascals* #2(10/56)(ME), #10: *Clubhouse Rascals* #1(6/56)(ME), *Tippy Terry* (1958, 1964) #1, 14; #1: *Little Groucho* #1(2-3/55)(Reston), #14: *Little Groucho* #1(2-3/55) (Reston), *Tom-Tom the Jungle Boy* (1958-1959, 1963) #1-2, 8, 10; #1: *Tick Tock Tales* #22(10/47)(ME), #2: *Tick Tock Tales* #25(1/48)(ME), #8: *Tick Tock Tales* #22(10/47)(ME), #10: *Tick Tock Tales* #18(6/47) (ME), *Top Adventure Comics* (1958) #1-2; #1: *High Adventure* #1(10/57)(Decker), #2: *Red Seal* #22(12/47) with the cover to *Prison Break* #5(10/52) (Avon), *Top Detective Comics* (1959) #9, *Criminals on the Run* #5(2-3/49)(Novelty) with the cover to *Police Line-Up* #4(7/52)(Avon), *Top Jungle Comics* (1958) #1, *White Princess of the Jungle* #3(5/52) (Avon), *Torchy* (1964) #16, *Torchy* #4(5/50)(Quality), *Tuffy Turtle* (1958) #1, *Ribtickler* #7(3-4/47)(Green), *U.S. Fighting Air Force* (1958-1959) #1, 9; #1: *U.S. Fighting Air Force* #11(11/54)(Superior), #9: *U.S. Fighting Air Force* #1(9/52)(Superior), *U.S. Fighting Men* (1963-1964) #10-12, 15-18; #10: *U.S. Paratroopers* #4(8/52)(Avon), #11: *Tell it to the Marines* #14(5/55)(Toby), #12: *U.S. Fighting Air Force* #10(10/54)(Superior), #15: *Man Comics* #11(12/51)(Atlas), #16: *U.S. Fighting Air Force* #3(1/53)(Superior), #17: *U.S. Fighting Air Force* #19(12/55)(Superior), #18: *U.S. Fighting Air Force* #6(1/54)(Superior), *U.S. Paratroopers* (1958-1959)

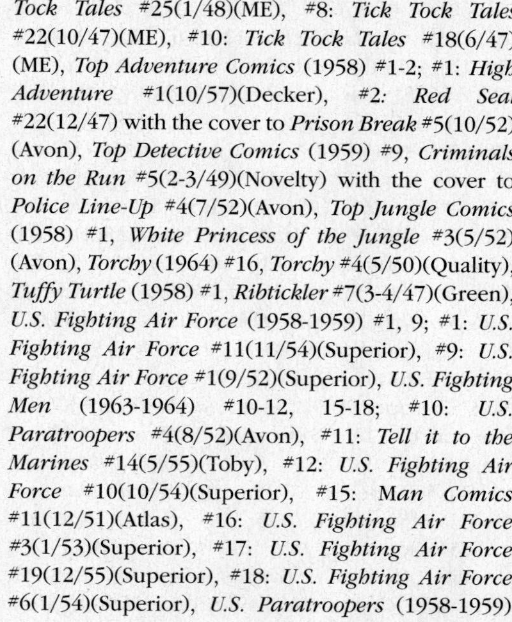

Space Mysteries #1

#1, 8; #1: *With the U.S. Paratroopers* #3(1951)(Avon) with the cover to *U.S. Paratroopers* #4(1951)(Avon), #8: *With the U.S. Paratroopers* #6(12/52)(Avon) with the cover to *With the U.S. Paratroopers* #4(8/52), *U.S. Tank Commandos* (1958-1959) #1, 8; #1: *U.S. Tank Commandos* #4(3/53)(Avon) with the cover to *U.S. Tank Commandos* #2, #8: *U.S. Tank Commandos* #3(11/52)(Avon), *Funny Tunes* #1(7/53)(Avon), *Undersea Commandos* (1958) #2, *Fighting Undersea Commandos* #2(8/52)(Avon), *Wacky Duck* (1958-1959, 1963) #1-2, 7, 10; #1: *Wacky Duck* #6(Summer 1947)(Timely), #2: *Wacky Duck* #5(Spring 1947)(Timely), #7: *Wacky Duck* #6(Summer 1947)(Timely), #10: *Wacky Duck* #5(Spring 1947)(Timely), *Wacky Woodpecker* (1958-1959, 1963) #1-2, 7, 10; #1: *Two-Bit, the Wacky Woodpecker* #3(5/53)(Toby), #2: *Two-Bit, the Wacky Woodpecker* #1(1951)(Toby), #7: *Two-Bit, the Wacky Woodpecker* #1(1951)(Toby), #10: *Two-Bit, the Wacky Woodpecker* #3(5/53)(Toby), *Wambi*(1958) #8, *Jungle Boy* #12(Summer 1951)(Fiction House) with the cover to *White Princess of the Jungle* #5(11/52)(Avon), *Western Action* (1958) #7, *Cow Puncher* #7(1949)(Avon), *Westerner* (1964) #15-17; #15: *Oklahoma Kid* #4(1/58)(Farrell), #16: *Crack Western* #65(3/50)(Quality), #17: *Blazing Western* #2(3/54)(Timor), *Whip Wilson* (1958) #1, *Whip Wilson* #11(9/50)(Atlas) with the cover to *Kit Carson* #2(8/51)(Avon), *Wild Bill Hickok* (1958, 1963-1964) #1, 10-12; #1: *Wild Bill Hickock* #2(12-1/49)(Avon) with the cover to *Wild Bill Hickok* #11(1951)(Avon), #10: *Wild Bill Hickock* #18(1954)(Avon), #11: *Wild Bill Hickock* #19(7-8/54)(Avon), #12: *Wild Bill Hickock* #8(8/51)(Avon), *Wild Western Roundup* (1958) #1, *Wild Western Roundup* #1(10/57)(Decker/Red Top), *Young Hearts in Love* (1964) #17-18; #17: *Young Love* #31(4-5/62)(Prize), #18: *Young Love* #33(8-9/62)(Prize), and *Ziggy Pig* (1958-1959) #1-2, 7-8; #1: *Krazy Komic* #17(Spring 1945)(Timely), #2: *Silly Tunes* #1(Fall 1945)(Timely), #7: *Krazy Komic* #17(Spring 1945)(Timely), #8: *Silly Tunes* #1(Fall 1945)(Timely).

For a full index of individual stories and creators in the I.W./Super Comics, go to Grand Comics Database. Issue numbers with print runs are as follows: #1 is 65 issues, #2 is 24 issues, #3 is 4 issues, #4 is two issues, #5 is three issues, #6 is one issue, #7 is 11 issues, #8 is 29 issues, #9 is 30 issues, #10 is 32 issues, #11 is 21 issues, #12 is 20 issues, (#13 is zero), #14 is 10 issues, #15 is 20 issues, #16 is 20 issues, #17 is 20 issues, and #18 is 20 issues. Comics originally published with 52 pages were edited down into 36 pages, rendering such books partial reprints but not legitimate representative copies; usually a story or two would be cut. Some issues were cannibalized from different sources and combined into one new product, such as I.W.'s *Daring Adventures* #16(1964) which reprints stories from four different Chesler comics. A handful of issues have on the cover, in place of the standard I.W. triangle symbol, what appears to be a small shield, hand drawn with the initials I.W. inside of it; *Billy and Buggy Bear* #1(1958) is one example.

Waldman may have decided to stop publishing comics with issue #9 in 1959 because of a more lucrative opportunity, or on a whim. Why did Israel Waldman disappear from the comics business for four years? Was he under duress to stop publishing? I.W./Super Comics fan Dick Sabo helped me create answers to what might have happened to cause some incredibly small print runs, and what Waldman may have been up to prior to vanishing:

Let's conjecture that in 1958 Waldman purchases 99 printing plates from Eastern Color. He takes 89 of them, divided into four stacks, to a printer. The Biggest stack of 65 is supposed to have no series repeats in it, and the stack of 24 is supposed to contain only the second copy of a series (for example, *Great Western* has an issue #1 and an issue #2). Meanwhile, Waldman has put four sets of plates in the wrong piles. The big stack has two different copies of *Speedy Rabbit* #1. The stack of 24 has three plates (*Love and Marriage, Romantic Love*, and *Undersea Commandos*) that should have been placed in the big stack. Regarding the remaining six plates, Waldman placed the third plate of *The Brain, Little Eva* and *Super Brat*, and the second plate of *Romantic Love* in the pile designated for issue #3, and the last pile #4 has *The Brain* and *Little Eva*, the only two titles to have issues #1-4. Waldman now finds three misplaced plates (*Sensational Police Cases, Strange Worlds*, and *Teen-Age Talk*). He tells the printer he has no idea if these three titles have already been printed and decides to print them as #5. Later, he finds one more issue of *Little Eva* and issue #6 is born, with issue seven showing a more normal print run of 11 issues. Waldman purchases another 91 printing plates. He decides to split the group into three parts. He takes 29 plates to the printer for issue #8, followed by 30 plates for issue #9. The last 32 plates are fated to wait indefinitely as Waldman is visited by attorneys representing Timely/Atlas/Marvel and told to cease and desist. Although cynical, it's a possibility.

Four years later Waldman purchases a warehouse with 100 printing plates. Having overcome his fear of a copyright lawsuit, assuming he was threatened to begin with, he returns to comics publishing, beginning with the 32 plates that were left out when he stopping publishing in 1959.

The printer is instructed to make some changes... #1: The I.W. triangle will be replaced by the Super Comics Seal of Quality on the cover, #2: The publisher in the indicia is changed to "published by Super Comics, Inc.," #3: The sentence, "Comics copyrighted and must not be reproduced without permission," is included in the indicia, and #4: A year of publication will be listed. Waldman hopes such tactics, combined with new covers, will keep him safe from discovery. Regardless of his attempts to distance himself, the address for Super Comics is the same as I.W. Enterprises, and the numbering continues with the release of issue #10, so Waldman wasn't actually invisible, just lurking nearby. And then there's *Pee Wee Pixies* #10, where the indicia correctly states "Super Comics" while the cover shows an incriminating I.W. symbol! A few #1 and #2 issues say "reissue" on the cover; *Apache* #1(1958) is one example, another is *Great Western* #2(1958). Waldman may have intended to put "reissue" on every cover, possibly as some kind of legal firewall, but decided against it. Waldman sold advertising in the comics, and even collected money at his office for processing Honor House products (Department I.W. in the ads), a longtime mail order toy company; his other solicitors were all over the map with products offered, and such advertisers would have led back to Waldman. He did business with Honor House from 1958-1959 and 1963-1964, and later in 1971 with Skywald color comics.

The 100 plates Waldman bought join 31 random books he has picked up from other sources, and they are divided into seven stacks. Waldman takes 21 plates to the printer for issue #11. He must have taken the printer a group of 30 and made two piles, of 10 and 20 issues respectively, for issues #12 and #14. Waldman tells the printer not to use #13 because it's unlucky, and that the other pile of ten would be for #14, and some indicia on #12 are accidentally labeled 1963 instead of 1964 before the mistake is noticed. The final issue numbers #15-18 all have twenty issue print runs. Waldman bought modern material that became *Young Hearts in Love* #18(1964), and oddities such as the unpublished Charles Atlas comic that became *Daring Adventures* #18(1964). I don't believe everything Waldman had on hand saw print, and we'll probably never know the extent of his myriad acquisitions or what became of them. The Skywald horror line later reprints material from the I.W./Super Comics inventory that was not reprinted before, so evidently there were additional books on hand. Fly by night publishers Green(1957), Literary Entertainment(1958), Norlen(1959) and Cornell[n.d.], (all of them list the same address in the indicia) released some of the same titles as I.W. did in the late 1950s, such as *Cosmo Cat*. There are too many examples of the same reprints across too many titles for it to be a coincidence. Waldman must have bought the "fly by night" inventory.

Daring Adventures #18

"[I.W./Super Comics is] ...a comic book company whose stand against the mediocre was, for its day, heroic." (*The Comics Journal* #57, 1980, p. 119.) The author of the article, T. Casey Brennan, who was a writer for Skywald, glows with enthusiasm for I.W./Super Comics, at one point giving credit to I.W. for choosing the best comics to reprint. The comics and single stories were actually random material Waldman purchased in bulk and bits. Waldman purchased comic book material that ranged from the early 1940s all the way up to Young Love #33(8-9/62), reprinted by Super Comics as *Young Hearts in Love* #18(1964), so his acquisitions continued right up to the point Super Comics hit the scene. Waldman's books were the only post-code source of crime, horror and other forbidden genres from 1958-1964, and the first exposure to Golden Age comics for many young collectors during a time when B&W photocopy reprints cost several dollars each. Pat S. Calhoun says "[Waldman is the] "...secret king of pirate reprints, [so] one feels almost guilty celebrating I.W. Comics; after all their publication protocol was not exactly legal." (*Comic Book Marketplace* #8, 1991, p. 6.) Printing rights had no influence over Waldman, so I.W./Super Comics exist as guilty pleasures. "There are questions about whether he had any actual rights to reprint them, but, legal or not, those books came out." (*Eerie Publications*, 2010, p. 74.)

One early fanzine article, "The Lowdown on I.W.," written by Vern Debes, discusses logistics related to I.W. distribution and pricing. "In New York, there is a small publishing company that publishes reprints of old pre-ban comics. This company has a unique way of distributing their wares, without the comics code seal. I.W. comics are distributing through cigar and candy distributors, who also handle old comics. They sell the comics to small markets and drug stores for 3 to 7 1/2 cents per issue. The distributors also bundle them up in boxes of 100 with other back issue comics (mainly Charlton comics) and sell them to back issue shops and second hand stores. Although marked 10 cents per issue these comics sell for 6 to 8 cents per issue…" (Character Get Together, 1964, p. 9.) So we witness part of the illicit secondary market of whole copy returns along with the oft repeated story of I.W. distribution through the eyes of a young comics fan. Debes had firsthand knowledge of the business or knew someone who did. His description of both I.W. distribution and the bundles of Charlton and other "back issue comics" returning to market are consistent with other reports, and the writer didn't realize what he was viewing. Ironically, Debes focuses entirely on I.W. at the time Super Comics were for sale! Waldman's National Distributor was Harry Williams during the Super Comics era, and Williams had already seen a courtroom prior to slinging Waldman's comics. The following lawsuits provide some insight:

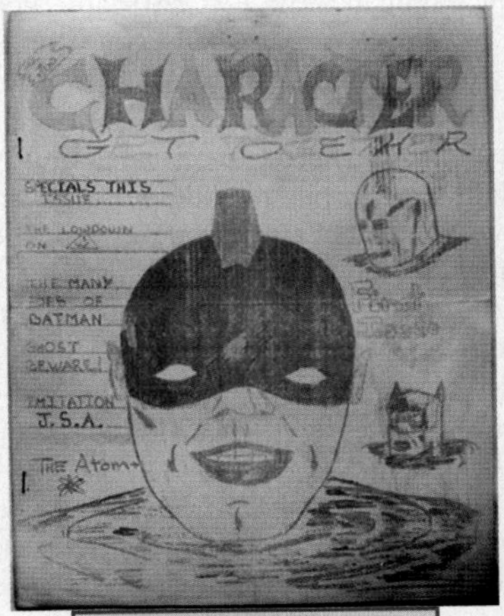

Character Get Together

Case #293 F2d 510 Independent News Co., Inc., National Periodical Publications, Inc., Superman, Inc., v. Harry Williams, United States Court of Appeals Third Circuit. Argued March 9, 1961. Decided June 6, 1961. DC sues Distributor Harry Williams over sale of coverless comics. Williams is vindicated after much ado about the responsibilities of being a second-hand periodical dealer; he purchased cover-removed comics from waste paper dealers. DC argued that having such returns on the market was an injury to them. The court found that the critical facts involved the distribution system used in marketing the comics and their theoretical destruction after going to market and being pulled. The legal bottom line is that DC had no continuing right or control over such items once sold to waste paper dealers, and that such items as coverless magazines exchange hands in the normal course of business, and that it would create an unreasonable hardship on the used book dealer to attempt to sort and separate such material.

Case #404 F2d 758 Independent News Co., Inc., National Periodical Publications, Inc., Superman, Inc., v. Harry Williams, United States Court of Appeals Third Circuit. Argued October 25, 1968. Decided December 4, 1968. National tries again. Williams wins again with an upheld decision.

Case #485 F2d 1099 (3rd Cir. 1973) Harry Williams v Independent News Co., Inc., and National Periodical Publications, Inc. Argued June 18, 1973. Decided September 11, 1973. As Amended October 23, 1973. Williams bought complete issue returns of comics books that were not purchased by the public and were removed because of shelf life and sent back through the chain of distribution: from the retailer to the wholesaler to the distributor to the publisher without any changes to the contents or covers removed. "Harry Williams' sole source of off-sale full-copy return Atlas comic books was one Israel Waldman, a middleman, who from 1959-1963 purchased off-sale full-copy return Atlas comic books from Magazine [Enterprises] and resold some of them to Williams." Waldman was supposed to have bought the comics from ME for use as "premiums" but he had in fact sold them outright. "When ME learned that Waldman was not using the comics as premiums, but rather was reselling these issues for distribution in competition with its current cover comic books, ME terminated its sale of Atlas comics to Waldman. As a result, Waldman could no longer supply Williams." Williams position is that he was put out of business illegally by Independent News Co., and that by attempting to control "…the destiny and conditions for the resale of these comics." The president of Independent insisted that they never told ME that they had to terminate Waldman, but rather that they had to "…police [the books] better, that if they wanted to continue their sales, that they had to see to it that they went through the proper channels that Mr. Waldman promised." The court found that there was no evidence that Independent and ME had anything more than an exclusive distribution arrangement, and that there was no evidence to find a conspiracy to violate the anti-trust laws. "Waldman was …restricted to the type of customers to whom he could resell these comics, [and] …Waldman's violations of this restriction led to both warnings of termination and actual termination of sales from ME to [Waldman]," referred to in the court documents as "the recalcitrant purchaser." Joe Simon recalls that "…bundles of returns… intended to be used for paper recycling purposes only… would fall into the hands of outlaw entrepreneurs and [be] sold illicitly," (*The Comic Book Makers,* 1990, p. 163).

Martin Goodman, publisher at Marvel, was slammed by the FTC in 1942 for deceptively reprinting stories as new fiction, substituting new titles for the original titles, changing the names of characters, stripping copyrights, etc. Goodman seemed to view his punishment as an inconvenience. He was forced to behave more honestly which seriously impeded his cash flow. (*The Secret History of Marvel Comics*, 2013, p. 28.) Goodman and Waldman were longtime associates, and neither of them cared about copyrights. Waldman was doing the same thing that Alan Class did in the U.K., reprinting whatever comic was on the plates he purchased. Class was another publisher with blurred ethics. Both Waldman and Class had no monthly dates on the covers or in the indicia of their books in order to extend shelf life, and both men started in 1958.

Skywald magazines came into existence in 1970 as an amalgamation of the originator's names: the name Skywald was born of Sol Brodsky and Israel Waldman. Between stints with the comics Waldman sold children's books and coloring books, including such titles as *Little Eva, Marty Mouse,* and *Wild Bill Hickok.* He knew Brodsky as a production manager with comic experience going back to the Golden Age. "With the advent of Nightmare and Psycho, Brodsky and Waldman created the first large format b&w magazines to seriously challenge Warren's horror mag... status," *(Ghastly Terror,* 1999, pp. 129-130.)

Al Hewetson, an editor and writer for Skywald Publications until its demise in 1975, claims he left Jim Warren's employment for the creative freedom Waldman embodied. Waldman ran Skywald with his son Herschel Waldman and Sol Brodsky, the latter having worked with him on I.W./Super Comics. "He once told me his philosophy of management," Hewetson quotes Waldman: "Surround yourself with extremely competent people, and leave them alone to do their job." Waldman was a smart businessman and apparently also a nice person; Pablo Marcos recounts their first meeting and Waldman's kindness as the reason he kept working with Skywald when other publishers were paying him more money. (*Skywald Horror-Mood,* 2004, pp. 68, 182.) Al Hewetson once asked Herschel Waldman for his opinion on whether Skywald books were of true value, if people would be reading the stories in 25 years. "And he took a long time to think about it, and he very simply and sadly said: "No." Much like the staff of the Marvel and EC Bullpens had nicknames for each other, so did Skywald have their own set of "office" names. Herschel Waldman's nickname was "Homicidal." Hewetson nicknamed himself "Archaic." "The only [person] associated with Skywald Horror-Mood who did not get a horror nickname was Israel Waldman, which I didn't think would be appropriate..." (Al Hewetson, *Skywald Horror-Mood*, 2004, p.16.)

Al Hewetson remembers Waldman: "Israel Waldman was over six feet tall and distinguished in appearance, sartorial, an immigrant from Portugal after the second world war, and was very much a respectful gentleman of the old school, quite conservative in how he conducted himself..." "You might think that because he had a background in republishing and discount-packaging fairly sordid reprints in the '50s and '60s, that he'd have a similar attitude to packaging the Skywald magazines, but that was not true, not at all." "He wanted only the highest quality stories and artwork and packaging. He never suggested that I cut corners and save a few bucks. He always insisted that everybody do their best work. And we did." "Mr. Waldman, who was usually around unless he was on a business trip, had many other successful publishing interests... once he came to me rather excitedly and said, 'I like this cover.' It was the "All-Ghoul issue" with a man turning into a werewolf in several stages as the cover artwork." (Psycho #15(11/73.) Waldman said, "Make all the covers like this: Monsters, monsters, and more monsters." He became passionate. "Al, put monster stories in every issue. Come up with new monster characters. The reader's love monsters, so give them monsters!" (*Comic Book Artist* #5, 2004, pp. 54-55.)

"May 28, 1972: Found some black-and-white stats of very old Waldman comics, circa early 1950s, in the artwork vaults. Asked Herschel [Waldman] if we had printed copies around and he said he didn't recall ever seeing them. Ever? I said: "Didn't your father ever bring comics home for you to read?" And he replied: "Oh, no, never. I never read comics as a kid. I don't remember wanting to read a comic. I don't think I was ever aware of what my father did for a living until I was 15 or 16. He was in business, I knew he was a publisher, but he never brought his work home or discussed it." Amazed, I asked him to recount for me the history of Waldman comics, since I didn't know myself, and he replied vaguely he'd never been inclined to ask his father and didn't really know. I asked Israel himself and he said, very simply, that he had published color comics for a while but had stopped "around the time of the Wertham trouble," but not because of Wertham directly — because the distributor was having trouble getting comics on newsstands." (Al Hewetson, *Comics Journal* #127, February 1989.)

Waldman answered Hewetson artfully, because he doesn't start publishing I.W.s until close to five years after *Seduction of the Innocent* was released, and as for Harry Williams, the unidentified distributor, Waldman purposefully did not sell his comics on the newsstands, so there was never a distribution problem. The only other thing Waldman could have been referring to is how from 1959-1963 he purchased and resold full copy return Atlas/Marvel comic books to Williams, which ended badly, as seen in the suit filed by Williams. This is where it gets murky: Why would Waldman feel a need to invent the story of his publishing past for Hewetson? My guess is, it was probably Waldman's pat answer, employed when necessary. And then there's Waldman's son Herschel who dodges Hewetson's questions with odd claims of ignorance. Herschel says he didn't recall ever seeing I.W./Super comics, yet early on in their business, "[Skywald] used a handful of Waldman's reprints for some of the interiors…" before going to all original art, (*Eerie Publications*, 2010, p. 74.) How is it that Skywald utilized some Waldman reprints yet Business Manager Herschel claims he has never seen any of them? The implausible narratives and evasiveness of father and son seem suspicious. Herschel acts as if he barely knew his father and comes off like a Lovecraft character when questioned. I believe Waldman didn't want people looking into his business so he withheld information or stretched the truth. I think it was easier and more profitable from 1959-1963 for Waldman to wholesale Williams the unsold full copy returns of Martin Goodman's Atlas/Marvels than to print his own comics, and Goodman had to know he was doing it; Waldman was buying returns directly from Atlas/Marvel. Waldman didn't disappear for four years from the comics industry, and the dates fit perfectly; he simply changed hats.

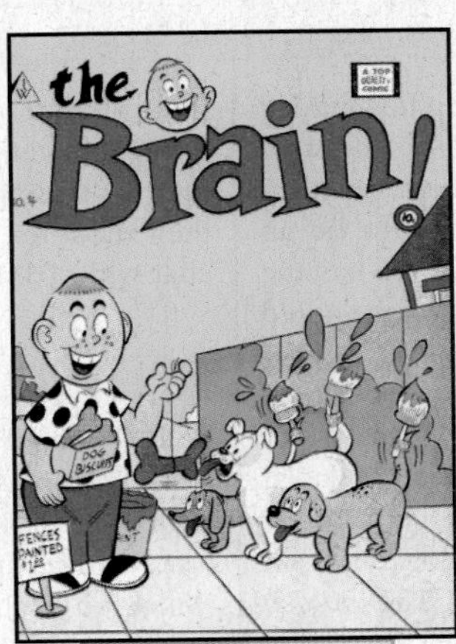

The Brain #4

Of Skywald's comic book line, *Butch Cassidy* #2-3(8, 10/71), *The Heap* #1(9/71), *Jungle Adventures* #1-3(3-6/71), *Sundance Kid* #1-3(6-9/71), *Tender Love Stories* #1, 3-4(2-7/71) and *Wild Western Action* #2(5/71) all contain I.W./Super Comics reprints. There are two examples of Timely books: *Butch Cassidy* #2(8/71) contains *Whip Wilson* #10(6/50), and *Sundance Kid* #3(9/71) contains *Black Rider* #15(7/51). Two Timely stories were reprinted in Skywald's *Wild Western Action* #2(5/71) from *Tex Taylor* #7(1948). Although it has been suggested that an old Timely horror story or two ended up in a Skywald comic, that is not the case. After reprinting books (including Timely and EC) in the 1950s and 1960s, Waldman is ultimately emboldened to put out copyrighted material again, this time on the newsstand. He competes directly with Martin Goodman and includes Goodman's copyrighted characters inside as filler. Waldman and Sol Brodsky had snatched a fair amount of talent from Goodman to work at Skywald, and Goodman noticed. "I do seem to recall hearing, during this period, that Waldman came up to the Magazine Management offices for a meeting with Goodman, and the person who told me that said that when Waldman left he looked very much crestfallen," (*Alter Ego*, July 2015, p. 5.) Perhaps he was more or less told by an angry Goodman to shut down his color line or else. Waldman was upset by this outcome and forced to leave the comic book business, although Skywald survived and profited. It seems he finally stepped out of the shadows only to be swatted back into them.

So who was Israel Waldman? Depends on who you ask. "[Israel Waldman] …was a sweet, sweet man. Mild-tempered, never got upset or irritated… he was a really nice guy." Esposito admired Waldman, adding, "Israel Waldman drove a Lincoln, and when I saw it, I decided that I would buy one." (Mike Esposito, *Alter Ego* #54, 2005, pp. 17-18.) But not everyone agrees. "I know of Izzy Waldman because he was a con man. I got a call… from an editor that he had, asking if I'd do something for him. I turned it down. I didn't want to have anything to do with him." (Tony Tallarico, *Alter Ego* #109, 2012, p. 43.) My opinion after researching Waldman is that most people who knew him liked him. The guy made his living in part by reprinting comic books and not everyone approved of his style. Today we have all 332 of the I.W./Super Comics to enjoy due to his efforts, and there is something about them, a classic innocence that appeals to me.

I.W./Super Comics are vastly undervalued and unrecognized. Some *Overstreet Price Guide* listings land under $20 in 9.2 NM-. The rarest I.W./Super Comics issues are *The Brain* #4, *Full of Fun* #8, *Kiddie Kapers* 10, 15, *Love and Marriage* #2, 12, *Romantic Love* #10, *Super Brat* #8, *Teen Romances* #10-11, and *U.S. Fighting Men* #11; such books are truly elusive, and like many rare books, may often be found only in permanent collections or at ransom prices. I.W./Super Comics are the most undervalued set of books in their age range in the history of comics. The following "money books" can be had between $25 and $100 in VG/F or so, and all have something going for them in terms of contents or general awesomeness: *Daring Adventures* #9-10,

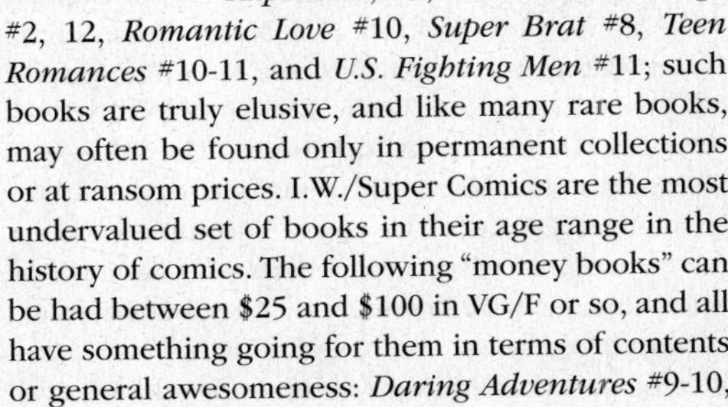

12, 16, 18, *Eerie* #1, 8-9, *Eerie Tales* #10-11,15, *Great Action Comics* #8-9, *Human Fly* #1, 10, *Indian Braves* #1, *Indians of the Wild West* #9, *Jungle Comics* #9, *Space Comics* #1, *Space Detective* #1, 8, *Space Mysteries* #1, 9, *Strange Planets* #1, 9, and *Undersea Commandos* #2. I firmly believe that the I.W./Super Comics are sleeping giants, especially high grade keys with killer covers like *Eerie* #1(1958), which arguably has the best redrawn cover. I.W./Super Comics are almost 60 years old. It's time to recognize the unique coolness of such amazing material. I believe the marketplace will embrace I.W./Super Comics once more collectors become aware of the Silver Age gems awaiting them.

So there you have it: the odd story of absconded comic book stories and the clever and unapologetic Mr. Waldman, a savvy businessman if nothing else. Except you're not off the hook yet. I've got an Earth 2 frisbee to toss your way, some real *Twilight Zone* stuff.

Brother Power the Geek #1

Behold "The thing that should not exist!" The apparent I.W./Super Comic, *Brother Power the Geek* #1 (1998) does in fact exist. I found this B&W book at a flea market two years before beginning this project, and as a longtime fan, I was excited to purchase such an enigma for a mere 50 cents! It appears to be an ashcan at 5 1/2" by 8 1/4". The front cover has the "Super Comics Seal Of Quality" over what should be the "DC Superman National Comics," the cover month October is deleted, and "A Top Quality Comic" appears over what should be the 12 cent cover price. The blue cover background has been replaced with dot matrix. The inside front cover has a Public Service ad, "Smoking is for Squares," replacing what should be a "Sales Leadership Club" ad. The indicia, utterly altered, states, "Brother Power the Geek, Vol.2, No.1, Mar. 1998. Published by Super Comics, West 47 St., New York 36, N.Y. Myron Fass, Editor. Israel Waldman, Editorial Director. No Subscriptions. SECOND CLASS POSTAGE ENTRY PENDING AT SPARTA, ILL. Copyright Joe Simon." The address is Waldman's old address. The remainder of the indicia is standard DC fare. The comic is complete except for the original ads; the page bottoms that indicate upcoming ads with statements at page bottoms such as "continued on second page following," have been deleted and drawn over. One interior ad for Revell models is replaced with a Wayne Boring "How Superman has tricked Mr. Mxyzptlk" house ad. All of the ad replacements are circa 1950s to early 1960s. Only a 1/2 page "Meet Joe Simon" feature at the end of the comic remains unscathed. Perhaps Joe Simon was selected because of his 1990 book *The Comic Book Makers* and the Waldman section therein. The inside back cover has a Public Service ad, "Countdown on Excellence," in place of the original Honor House toy ad. The back cover replaces a Hot Wheels ad with a vintage Charles Atlas ad in Spanish! Who would go to so much trouble to create such an oddity? Who was the intended audience? Some mysteries remain unsolved.

Myron Fass was in the comic industry since the 1950s but went on to be a publisher, probably best known for Eerie Publications. He exploited anything he thought he could make a dime on: celebrities, sex, violence, you name it, Myron was game. Israel Waldman often played by his own rules, realizing profits in unconventional ways. Whomever is responsible for the elaborate *Brother Power the Geek* #1 joke-zine-thing obviously saw something in common between the two men, possibly their reputations and maybe their thirst for cash. If I had to pick one of them to chat with, I'd rather have a beer with Mr. Waldman.

Jon McClure is a senior advisor to the Overstreet Comic Book Price Guide *and an award-winning historian. He has written numerous articles for Gemstone's* Comic Book Marketplace *magazine and was featured in the August 2001 issue of* Diamond Dialogue. *Jon released the feature length cult film* Face Eater *in 2007 with director Jarrod Perrot, and the card game Face Eater in 2010 with John Harris of a5, which was endorsed by Al Feldstein. For more information about I.W./Super Comics variants and many other variants, refer to Jon's article, "A History of Publisher Experimentation and Variant Comic Books," in* OPG *#40, pages 1010-1033. Please visit jonmcclurecomics.com and see Jon's ad on the following page. Jon continues to research comics and write both fiction and non-fiction. He hopes that any complaints about this longwinded article be directed at J.C. Vaughn for asking him to write it.*

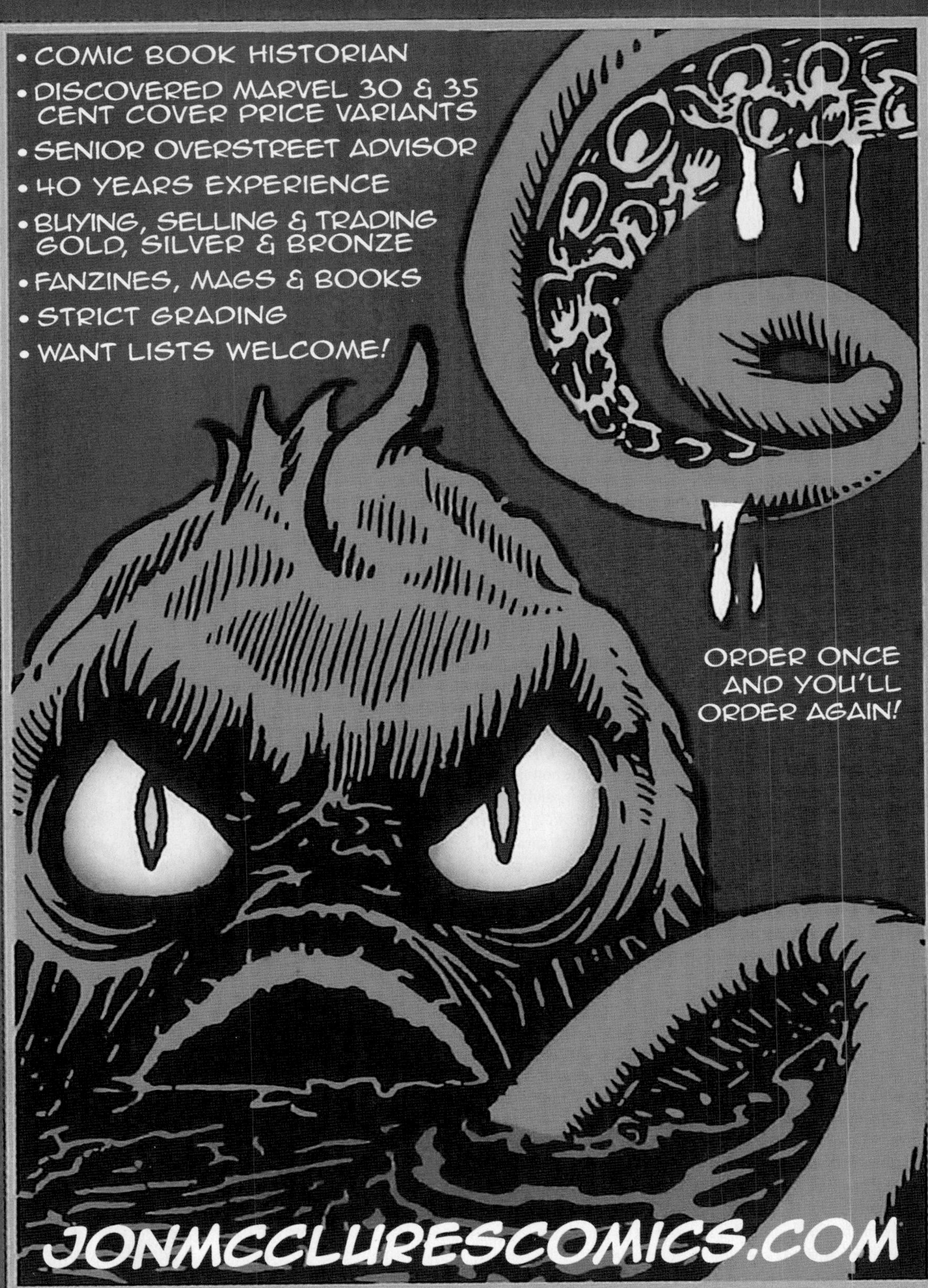
• COMIC BOOK HISTORIAN
• DISCOVERED MARVEL 30 & 35 CENT COVER PRICE VARIANTS
• SENIOR OVERSTREET ADVISOR
• 40 YEARS EXPERIENCE
• BUYING, SELLING & TRADING GOLD, SILVER & BRONZE
• FANZINES, MAGS & BOOKS
• STRICT GRADING
• WANT LISTS WELCOME!
ORDER ONCE AND YOU'LL ORDER AGAIN!
JONMCCLURESCOMICS.COM

CGC

How the Company Has Grown and How It Works

By the CGC Grading Team

The world of comic book collecting has grown and matured considerably since the 2000 introduction of CGC (Certified Guaranty Company). Before the founding of CGC comic book transactions required sellers to grade their own comic books, a practice that often lacked consistency and impartiality. They also had to check their books for restoration, which was limited to each sellers' skills at detection. During the first decades of fandom most sales took place through mail order, as well as local comic shops or the occasional convention. The advent of the internet changed all that, allowing global buying and selling, regardless of a person's location or experience. While this greatly expanded the comic book market, it also greatly increased the potential for inaccurate grading and restoration detection.

CGC was created to help bring order and stability to comic book sales, and to put an end to the risk and the chaos that accompanied online sales. CGC is the first and largest independent, impartial, third-party comic book grading service. A proven and respected commitment to integrity, accuracy, consistency and impartiality has made CGC the leader in its field, becoming a tool to help people with their buying and selling decisions. The universally accepted grading scale ensures consistency and gives both dealers and collectors a sense of dependability when making purchasing decisions. With CGC certification, a collector knows what he or she is getting based on an accurate and comprehensive description that can be found on the CGC certification label.

If you've ever wondered about how it's done, here's a look at how CGC came together and how a book is certified.

The Formation of the Company

In January of 2000, CGC was launched under the umbrella of the Certified Collectibles Group, which includes Numismatic Guaranty Corporation (NGC), the largest third-party coin grading company in the world, Numismatic Conservation Services (NCS), the leading authority in numismatic conservation, Paper Money Guaranty (PMG), the world's leading currency certification company and Classic Collectible Services (CCS), the world's premier comic book restoration, restoration removal and pressing company.

The Collectibles Group sought out talented and ethical individuals to grade comic books. Experts needed a history of comics as well as necessary skills to verify a comic book's authenticity and to detect restoration that can affect its value. To identify these individuals, many of the most respected individuals in the hobby were consulted, and, based on their recommendations a core grading team was selected.

The members of the CGC grading team come from diverse backgrounds, and many were comic book dealers at some time in their careers. Experience in the commercial sector can be an essential ingredient in becoming familiar with market standards.

When it was time to develop a uniform grading standard, the hobby's leaders were once again called upon. Everyone agreed that the *Overstreet Guide* was the foundation of this standard, but there were a number of subjective interpretations of its published definitions. It was critical to understand how these guidelines were being applied to the everyday buying and selling of comics. To accomplish this, approximately 50 of the hobby's top experts took part in an extensive grading test. Their grades were averaged and an accurate grading standard reflecting the collective experience of the hobby's most prominent individuals was thus developed. CGC now had the best standard and the best team to apply it.

With the graders in place and the grading scale established, the next step was to develop a tamper-evident holder for the long-term storage and display of certified comics. This proved to be a technical challenge. Exhaustive material tests were conducted to determine that the holders were archival safe. To create a true first line of defense, it was determined that the comic book should be sealed in a soft inner well, then sealed again inside a tamper evident hard plastic case with interlocking ridges to enable compact storage. The CGC certified grade appears on a label sealed inside the holder for an additional level of security.

Submitting Books

Comic books may be submitted for certification in two ways - they can be submitted by authorized dealers or by Collectors Society members. The Collectors Society is an online community with direct access to certification service from CGC, and submissions can be prepared using online submission forms or paper forms. Both dealers and Collectors Society members typically send their comics to CGC's offices by registered mail or through an insured express company. Submissions are also accepted at many of the Comic Cons that occur around the country throughout the year. CGC will grade on-site at selected shows.

Receiving the Books

Every day, CGC's Receiving Department opens newly arrived packages and immediately verifies that the number of books in each package matches the number shown on the submitted invoice, and checks the submission for any damage sustained in shipping. Once this is done, a more detailed comparison is made to ensure that their invoice descriptions correspond to the actual comics. This information is entered into a computer, and from this time forth, the comics will be traceable at all stages of the grading process by their invoice number and their line number within that invoice. Each book is checked to see that it is properly prepared for grading in an appropriately sized comic bag with backing board and then is labeled with a numbered barcode containing the pertinent data of invoice number and line item information for quick reading by the computer. Before any grading is performed, the book is examined by a CGC Restoration Detection Specialist. If any form of restoration work is detected, this information is entered into the computer, making it available to the grading team.

The Grading Begins

After being examined by a Restoration Detection Specialist, the book is then passed on to the graders. At this stage the comics have been properly sleeved and barcoded for grading and have been separated from their original invoice. This step is taken to ensure that graders do not know whose books they are grading, as a further guarantee of impartiality. The grading process begins by having the book's pages counted and entering into the computer any peculiarities or flaws that may affect a book's grade. Some examples of this would be "Spine Stress Lines Break Color," "Right Top Front Cover Small Crease Breaks Color," "Top Back Cover Tear with Crease" and "Staple Rusted w/Rust Stained Interior." This information is entered into the "Graders Notes" field and a grade is assigned.

When other graders examine the comic, they do not see any previous assigned grades, so as to not influence their evaluation. Graders are able to view previous Graders Notes after determining their own grade. The Grader may then add to the existing commentary if he believes more remarks are in order. The Grading Finalizer is the last person to examine the book. He makes a final restoration check before determining his own grade, at which time he reviews the grades and notes entered by the previous graders. If all grades are in agreement or are very close, he will assign the book's final grade. The book is then forwarded to the Encapsulation Department for sealing. If there is disagreement among the graders, a discussion will ensue until a final determination is made and the book forwarded.

Each comic book receives a restoration check and the results appear on the label.

CGC RESTORED GRADE
X-Men #1
Marvel Comics, 9/63
Restoration includes: color touch, pieces added, tear seals, cover cleaned, interior lightened, reinforced.
OFF-WHITE Pages

Encapsulating the Comics

After each comic has been graded and the necessary numbers and text entered into their respective data fields, all the comics on a particular invoice are taken from the Grading Department into the Encapsulation Department. Here, appropriately color-coded labels are printed bearing the proper descriptive text, including each book's grade and identification number. This is critical, as it serves to make each certified comic unique and is also a significant deterrent to counterfeiting CGC's valued product. All of the above information is duplicated in a barcode, which also appears on the comic's label.

The newly-printed labels are stacked in the same sequence as the comics to be encapsulated with them, ensuring that each book and its label match one another. The comic is now ready to be fitted inside an archival-quality interior well, which is then sealed within a transparent capsule, along with the book's color-coded label. This is accomplished through a combination of compression and ultrasonic vibration.

The Comics are Shipped

After encapsulation, all comics are set briefly to the Quality Control for inspection. Here, they are examined to make certain that their labels are correct for both the grade and its accompanying descriptive information. Quality control also inspects each book for any flaws in its holder, such as scuffs or nicks. While these are quite rare, CGC is careful to make certain that the comics it certifies are not only accurately graded, but attractively presented as well. When all the comics have been inspected, they're delivered to our Shipping Department for packaging. The comics are counted and their labels checked against the original invoice to make certain that no mistakes have occurred. A Shipping Department employee then verifies the method of transport as selected by the submitter on the invoice and prepares the comics for delivery or they are held in CGC's vault for in-person pick-up by the submitter.

No matter whether the US Postal Service or some private carrier is used, the method of packaging is essentially the same. The encapsulated comics are placed vertically inside sturdy cardboard boxes. In 2005, CGC developed a custom shipping box to enable the highest level of stability during shipping. A copy of the submitter's invoice is included before the box is sealed and heavy tape is used to prevent accidental or unauthorized opening of the box while it's in transit.

The barcode of every comic book is scanned before it is placed into its shipping box. The status of the book is changed to "shipped" in our tracking system, and we retain a record of what books were shipped in which box. This is the final crucial step of our detailed internal tracking system.

The CGC Label

Comic books certified by CGC bear color-coded labels that have different meanings. Whenever purchasing a CGC-certified comic, be certain to note not only the book's grade but also its label category. A Universal label is denoted by the color blue and indicates that a book was not found to have any qualifying defects or signs of restoration. There is one exception to this policy: At CGC's discretion, comics having a very minor amount of color touch-up may still qualify for a Universal label provided such restoration is noted underneath the assigned grade.

As its name implies, the Restored label, identified by its purple color, is used for books found to have restoration work performed on them. The grade assigned is based on the book's appearance, with the restoration noted. The Restoration scale is as follows: **Quality (Aesthetic) Scale** – (Determined by materials used and visual quality of work)

A (Excellent)

- Material used: rice paper, wheat paste, acrylic or water color, leafcasting
- Color match near perfect, no bleed through
- Piece fill seamless and correct thickness
- No fading, excessive whiteness, ripples, cockling, or ink smudges from cover or interior cleaning
- Book feels natural
- Near perfect staple alignment, or replaced exactly as they were
- Filled edges cut to look natural and even
- Cleaned staples or staples replaced with vintage staples
- Married cover/pages match in size and page quality. Professionally attached

B (Fine)

- Material used: pencil, crayon, chalk, re-glossing agent, piece fill from cadavers
- Piece fill obvious upon close inspection, obvious to the touch
- Color touch obvious upon close inspection, or done with materials listed above
- Cover cleaning resulting in slight color fading or excessively white
- Interior cleaning resulting in slight puffiness, cockling, excessively white
- Enlarged staple holes, obviously crooked staples, or backwards staple insertion
- Replaced staples not vintage
- Married cover/pages do not match in size and/or page quality. Professionally attached

C (Poor)

- Material used: glue, pen, marker, white out, white paper to fill missing pieces
- Piece fill obvious at arm's length
- Bad color matching, use of pen or marker. Bleed through evident
- Cover cleaning resulting in washed out/speckled colors, moderate cockling and/or ripples
- New staple holes created upon reinsertion, or non-comic book staples used
- Trimming of any kind
- Married cover/pages poorly attached with non-professional materials

Quantity Scale – *(Determined primarily by extent of piece fill and color touch)*

1 (Slight)

All conservation work, re-glossing, interior lightening, piece fill no more than size of two bindery chips, light color touch in small areas like spine stress, corner crease or bindery chip fill. Married cover or interior pages/wraps (if other work is present)

2 (Slight/Moderate)

Piece fill up to the ½" x ½" and/or color touch covering up to 1" x 1". Interior piece fill up to 1" x 1"

3 (Moderate)

Piece fill up to the size of 1" x 1" and/or color touch covering up to 2" x 2". Interior piece fill up to 2" x 2"

4 (Moderate/Extensive)

Piece fill up to the size of 2" x 2" and/or color touch covering up to 4" x 4". Interior piece fill up to 4" x 4"

5 (Extensive)
Any piece fill over 2” x 2” and/or color touch over 4” x 4”. Recreated interior pages or cover

Conservation Repairs

- Tear seals
- Spine split seals
- Reinforcement
- Piece reattachment
- Some cover or interior cleaning (water or solvent)
- Staples cleaned or replaced
- Some leaf casting

Materials Used for Conservation Repairs:

- Rice paper
- Wheat glue
- Vintage staples
- Archival tape

Conserved Label (Similar to the blue Universal label, but differentiated by a silver bar across the top. Conservation is noted in a similar fashion on the label as on the purple CGC Restored Label.) This label is applied to any comic book with specific repairs done to improve the structural integrity and long-term preservation. These repairs include tear seals, support, staple replacement, piece reattachment and certain kinds of cleaning.

The Qualified label is green, and this indicates that one qualifying defect is present on a book. An example of such a qualifying feature would be a missing Marvel Value Stamp that does not affect the story. While such a book technically may grade 1.5, it may appear to grade 9.6. In such instances, assigning a grade of just 1.5 does not fully represent the value of the comic to a collector. Through use of the green Qualified label, a comic buyer is able to make an informed decision as to what he is purchasing in terms of its overall desirability. Because of the complexity involved, green labels are assigned quite seldom and then only when considered absolutely necessary. In addition, comic books that have an unwitnessed signature, and therefore are not eligible for the Signature Series label (see below), get the Qualified label. This is the most common use for the Qualified label. This shows what the grade of the book would have been if the signature was not present.

CGC’s Signature Series label is yellow, and this is used when a comic book has been signed or been sketched on by a creator in the presence of a CGC representative, assuring the signature’s or sketch’s authenticity. Only books that meet CGC’s strict criteria for authenticity are eligible for the Signature Series label. In addition to the certified grade, the yellow label includes who signed it and when it was signed. If appropriate, a Signature Series label may state where a book was signed. In 2007, CGC introduced a Signature Series Restored label. Similar to the CGC Signature Series label in color, it is differentiated by a purple bar across the top. Restoration is noted in the same fashion as on the purple CGC Restored label, and, as with the regular Signature Series label, restored books must be signed in the presence of CGC representatives in order to be eligible for signature authentication.

CGC encapsulation is not limited to standard size comics. Magazines and small promotional comics are included as well.

The Evolution of CGC and CCG

In October of 2003, CGC began to certify comic book related magazines. The certification process and label system for magazines is exactly the same as for comic books. Some examples of comic book related magazines CGC certifies are *MAD Magazine*, *Vampirella*, *Creepy*, *Eerie* and *Famous Monsters of Filmland*.

More recently CGC introduced grading and encapsulation for *Sports Illustrated* and *Playboy* magazines, Movie Lobby Cards, Photographs, and Concert Posters making us the first independent, impartial, expert third-party grading service for all types of collectibles. CGC has graded over 4.1 million collectibles to date.

In a move intended to strengthen CGC’s commitment to promoting the comic collecting hobby and enhance the collecting experience, CGC’s parent company Certified Collectibles Group acquired Classics Incorporated, the world’s premier comic book restoration, restoration removal and pressing company, in 2012. Previously located in Dallas, TX, Classics Incorporated relocated to Sarasota, FL to become an independent member of the Certified Collectibles Group under the new name Classic Collectible Services (CCS). Customers who wish to send books in for pressing, restoration or restoration removal are be able to send them to CCS and have them transfer directly to CGC for grading — creating a synergistic relationship that saves customers time, shipping and insurance expenses.

For more information on comic book certification and CGC’s many services, please visit our website at www.CGCcomics.com

THE OVERSTREET HALL OF FAME

The Overstreet Hall of Fame was conceived to single out individuals who have made great contributions to the comic book arts.

This includes writers, artists, editors, publishers and others who have plied their craft in insightful and meaningful ways.

While such evaluations are inherently subjective, they also serve to aid in reflecting upon those who shaped the experience of reading comic books over the years.

This year's class of inductees begins on this next page.

THE PREVIOUS INDUCTEES

Class of 2006
Murphy Anderson
Jim Aparo
Jim Lee
Mac Raboy

Class of 2007
Dave Cockrum
Steve Ditko
Bruce Hamilton
Martin Nodell
George Pérez
Jim Shooter
Dave Stevens
Alex Toth
Michael Turner

Class of 2008
Carl Barks
Will Eisner
Al Feldstein
Harvey Kurtzman
Stan Lee
Marshall Rogers
John Romita, Sr.
John Romita, Jr.
Julius Schwartz
Mike Wieringo

Class of 2009
Neal Adams
Matt Baker
Chris Claremont
Palmer Cox
Bill Everett
Frank Frazetta
Neil Gaiman
William M. Gaines
Carmine Infantino
Jack Kirby
Joe Kubert
Paul Levitz
Russ Manning
Todd McFarlane
Don Rosa
John Severin
Joe Simon
Al Williamson

Class of 2010
Sergio Aragonés
M.C. Gaines
Archie Goodwin
Winsor McCay
Mike Mignola
Frank Miller
Robert M. Overstreet
Mike Richardson
Jerry Robinson
Joe Shuster
Jerry Siegel
Jim Steranko
Wally Wood

Class of 2011
Jack Davis
Martin Goodman
Dean Mullaney
Marie Severin
Walt Simonson
Major Malcolm Wheeler-Nicholson

Class of 2012
John Buscema
Dan DeCarlo
Jean Giraud (Moebius)
Larry Hama
Kurt Schaffenberger
Bill Sienkiewicz
Curt Swan
Roy Thomas

Class of 2013
Mark Chiarello
Mike Deodato, Jr.
Bill Finger
Jack Kamen
Bob Kane
Andy Kubert

Class of 2014
George Evans
Lou Fine
Gardner Fox
Terry Moore
Dave Sim
Jeff Smith

Class of 2015
Paul Gulacy
Don McGregor
Alex Schomburg
Mark Waid

Class of 2016
Darwyn Cooke
Russ Heath
Rob Liefeld
R.F. Outcault
Tim Truman

After inking Dave Cockrum's pencils on *Superboy* (with the Legion of Super-Heroes) #202, Mike Grell got the assignment to pencil the series beginning with #203. On the title, he developed many elements of his now-familiar style. His run on the series was followed by the marriage of Saturn Girl and Lightning Lad in the treasury-sized special *All-New Collectors' Edition* #C-55. His own creation, The Warlord, debuted in *1st Issue Special* #8 and then landed his own series beginning with *The Warlord* #1, the start of a 35-issue run as writer-artist. Grell then launched two creator-owned series, *Starslayer* (at Pacific Comics) and *Jon Sable Freelance* (at First Comics). He enjoyed another long run as writer-artist, 43 issues, on *Sable*. Following that, he undertook writing and illustrating the three-issue mini-series *Green Arrow: The Longbow Hunters*, which in turn spawned an ongoing *Green Arrow* series, which Grell wrote for 80 issues (periodically providing covers). Grell has continued to work on many characters, including revivals of *The Warlord* and *Jon Sable Freelance*.

–J.C. Vaughn

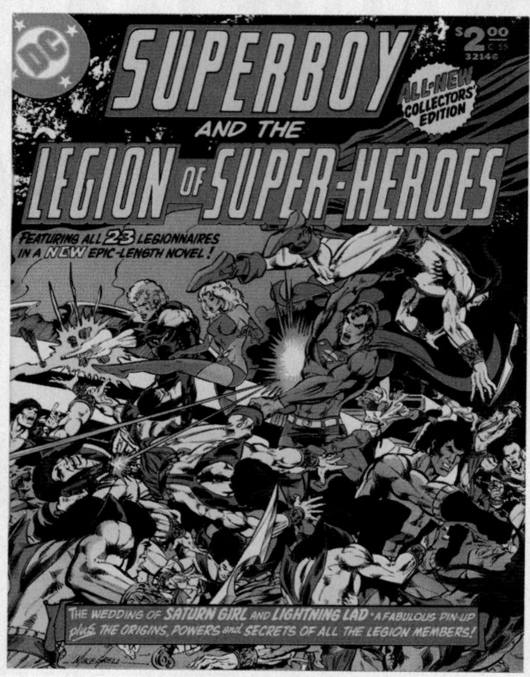

ALL-NEW COLLECTOR'S EDITION C-55
1978. © DC

GREEN ARROW #2
March 1988. © DC

GREEN ARROW: THE LONGBOW HUNTERS BOOK 3 1987. © DC

JAMES BOND: PERMISSION TO DIE #1
1989. © Mike Grell, Acme Press, Glidrose Publ. Ltd.

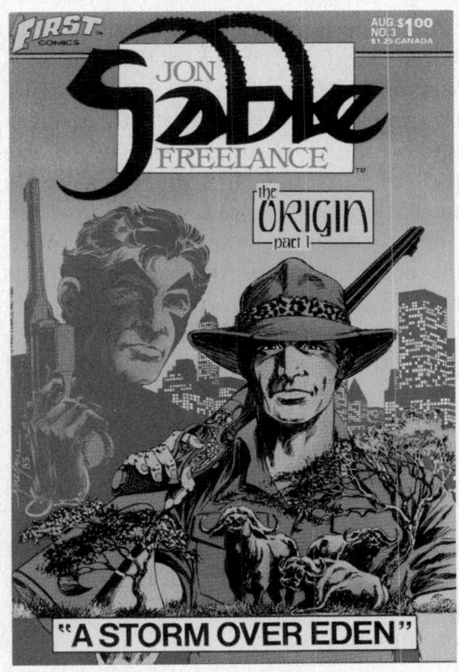

JON SABLE, FREELANCE #3
August 1983. © First Comics

STARSLAYER #5
November 1982. © Mike Grell

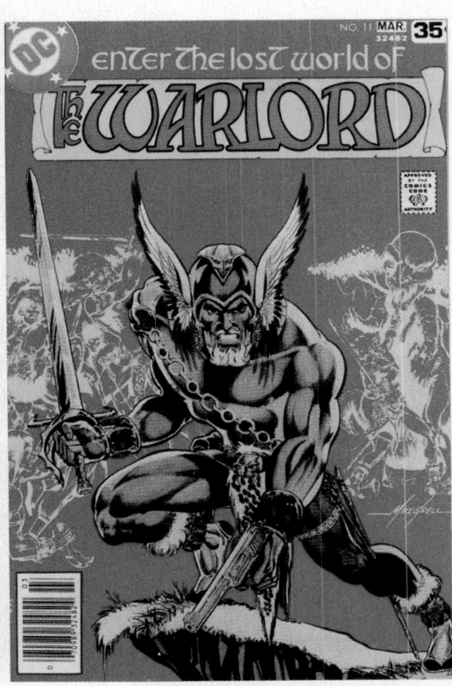

WARLORD #11
February-March 1978. © DC

HALL OF FAME

After the conclusion of World War II, Osamu Tezuka created his first manga, *Diary of Ma-Chan*, at just 17 years old. This time period in Japan featured a huge boom in manga – similar to the rapid expansion of comic books in America – and Tezuka's work contributed greatly to it. Tezuka's complete portfolio contains more than 700 volumes for more than 150,000 pages, and many of his creations have become known around the world thanks to successful anime adaptations. Though most would point to *Astro Boy* or *Black Jack* as his best work, his "life's work" was *Phoenix*, which he began in 1967 and continued working on until his death in 1989. Perhaps the most prolific manga artist of all time, Osamu Tezuka's influence can still be felt today in a number of contemporary series.

-Carrie Wood

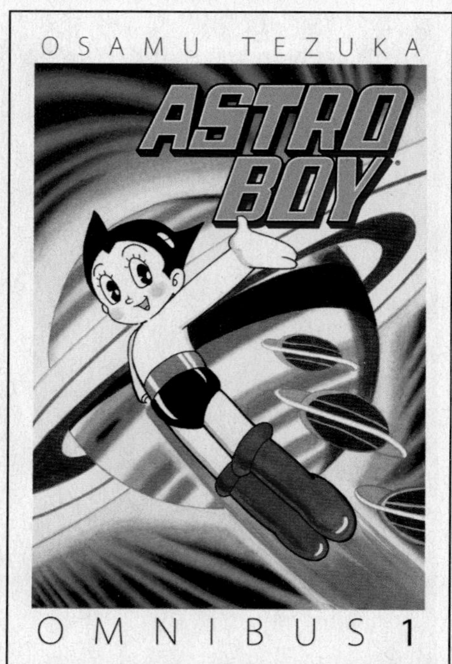

ASTRO BOY OMNIBUS VOL. 1
Dark Horse cover - 2016. Originally published 1952-1968.
© Osamu Tezuka

BLACK JACK
Japanese volume. Originally published 1973-1983.
© Vertical

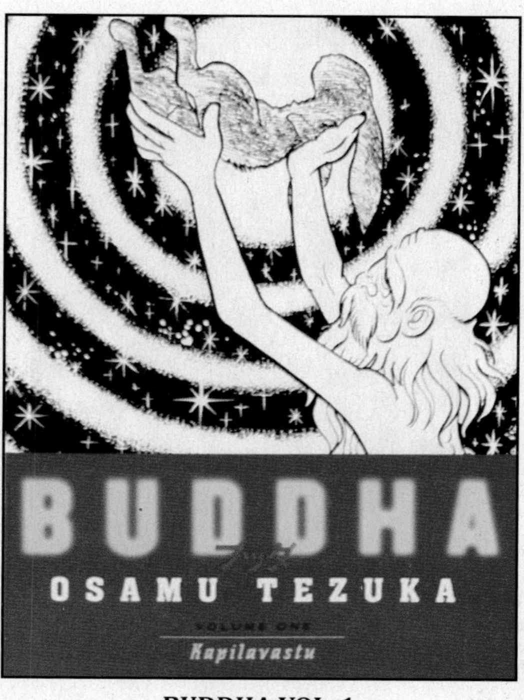

BUDDHA VOL. 1
Vertical cover - 2006. Originally published 1972-1983.
© Osamu Tezuka

DIARY OF MA CHAN
Kodansha cover. Originally published in 1946.
© Osamu Tezuka

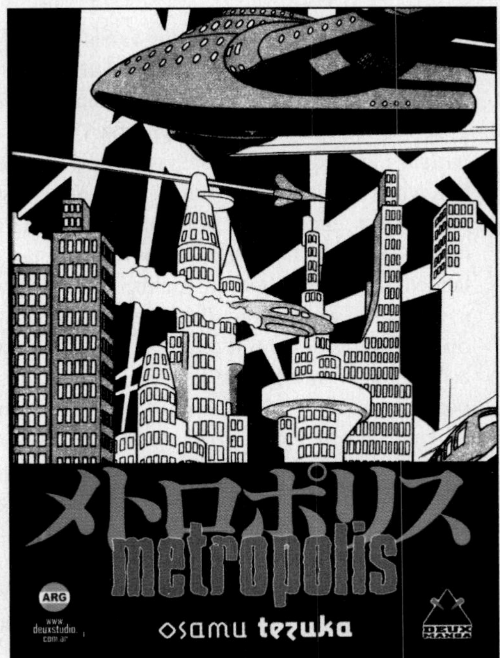

METROPOLIS
Dark Horse cover. Originally published in 1949.
© Osamu Tezuka

PHOENIX VOL. #7
Viz cover - 2006. Originally published 1967-1988.
© Osamu Tezuka

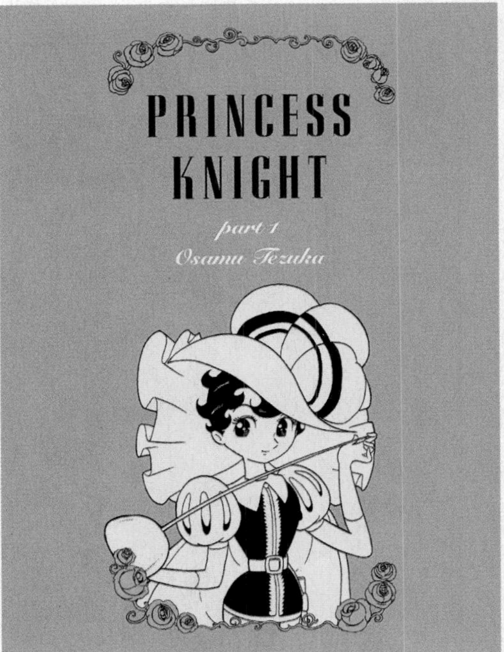

PRINCESS KNIGHT PART 1
Vertical cover - 2011. Originally published 1953-1968.
© Osamu Tezuka

Image Comics co-founder Jim Valentino first garnered attention for his work on *normalman*, which debuted as a back-up story in Dave Sim's *Cerebus*. That was followed by the launch of a 13-issue *normalman* limited series at Sim's Aardvark-Vanaheim, but when Sim and then-wife Deni Loubert split, *normalman* ended up at Loubert's Renegade Press for #9-13. From that slightly convoluted start, he landed at Marvel, where he grabbed attention with a variety of work, which included a 27-issue run on *Guardians of the Galaxy*. That series that established him with a strong fanbase and put him in position to leave Marvel to co-found Image. There he launched his creator-owned *ShadowHawk* and followed it up with the autobiographical *A Touch of Silver*. Like his earlier work, he served as its writer and artist. After serving a stint as the company's publisher and diversifying the company's line-up, he used his Shadowline imprint at Image to launch *Bomb Queen*, *After the Cape* and *Sam Noir*, among other projects.

– J.C. Vaughn

ALTERED IMAGE #1
April 1998. © Jim Valentino

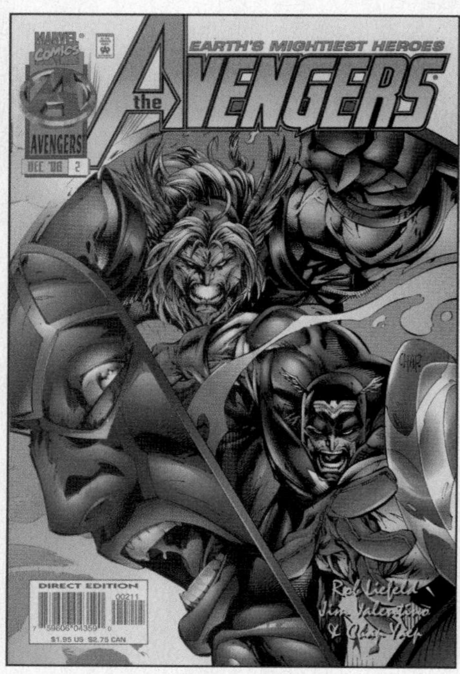

AVENGERS VOL. 2 #2
December 1996. © MAR

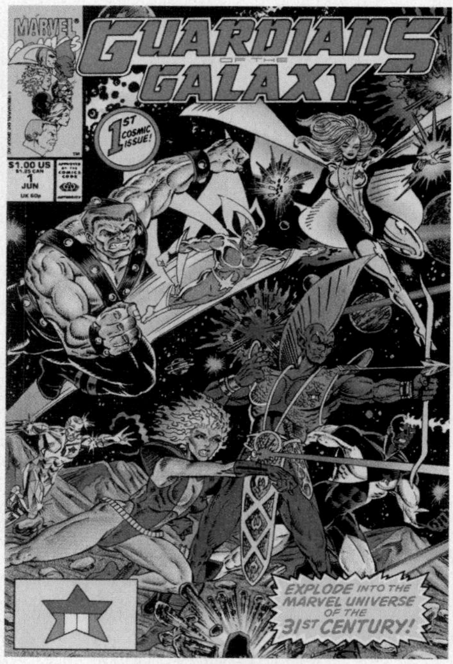

GUARDIANS OF THE GALAXY #1
June 1990. © MAR

JIM VALENTINO

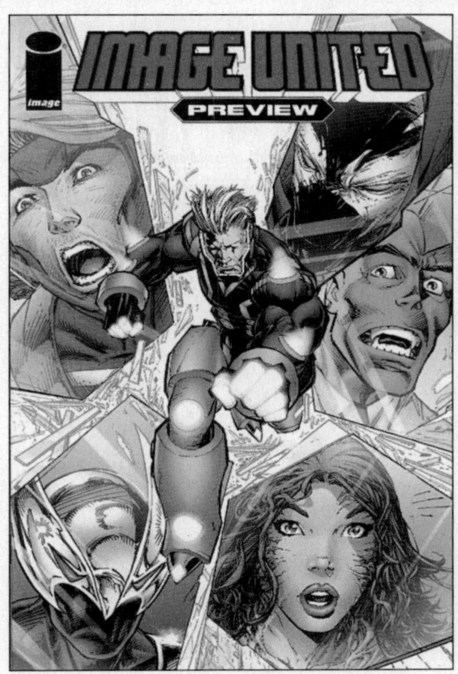

IMAGE UNITED #0 (PREVIEW)
July 2009. © Image

NORMALMAN 3-D
1986. © Jim Valentino

SHADOWHAWK #2
October 1992. © Jim Valentino

A TOUCH OF SILVER #1
January 1997. © Jim Valentino

Writer, artist, editor and publisher Mark Wheatley's creations include *Mars*, *Breathtaker*, *Prince Nightmare*, *Hammer of the Gods*, *Blood of the Innocent*, *Radical Dreamer*, *Frankenstein Mobster*, *Miles the Monster*, *The Mighty Motor-Sapiens*, *EZ Street*, *Lone Justice*, and *Titanic Tales*, among others. Often collaborating with fellow Insight Studios Group member Marc Hempel, studio founder Wheatley has also worked on are *Tarzan the Warrior*, *The Black Hood*, *The Adventures of Baron Munchausen*, *Jonny Quest*, Dr. Strange, The Flash, Argus and *The Spider*. He has won the Inkpot, Mucker, Gem, Speakeasy and Eisner awards and his projects have been nominated for the Harvey and Ignatz awards as well. His efforts have been repeatedly included in the annual Spectrum selection of fantastic art and has appeared in private gallery shows as well as the Library of Congress where several of his originals are in the LoC permanent collection. His work has also been displayed at the Norman Rockwell Museum, The Toledo Museum of Art, and The Huntington Museum of Art in Huntington, WV.

– J.C. Vaughn

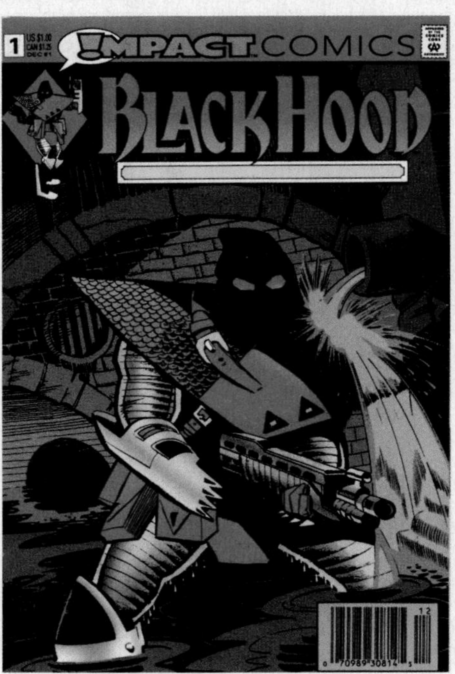

BLACK HOOD #1
December 1991. © ACP

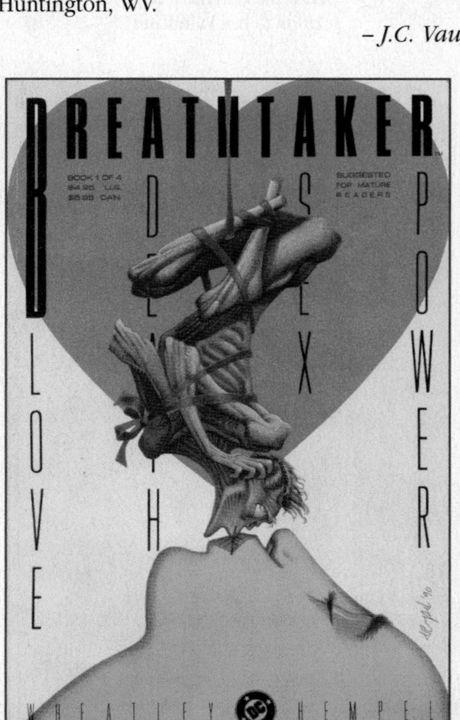

BREATHTAKER, BOOK ONE
1990. © Mark Wheatley & Marc Hempel

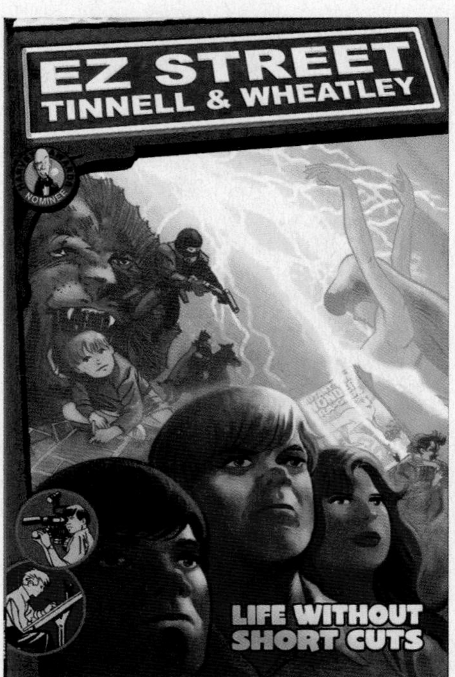

EZ STREET
2010. © Mark Wheatley & Robert Tinnell

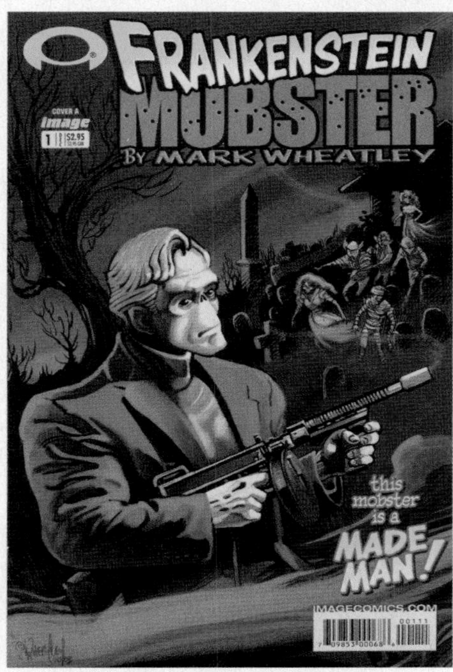

FRANKENSTEIN MOBSTER #1
December 2003. © Mark Wheatley

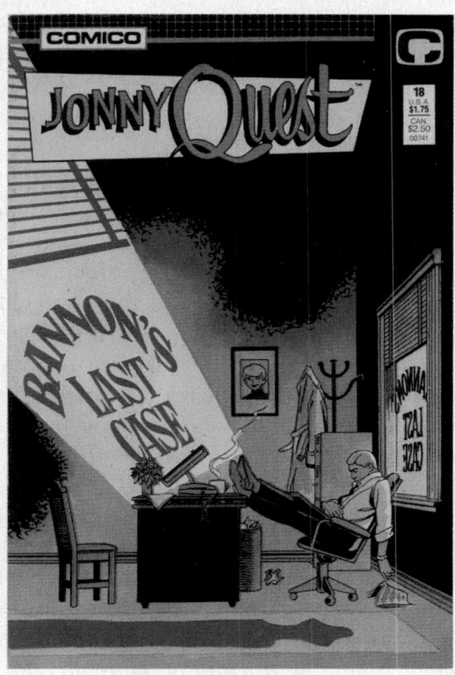

JONNY QUEST #18
November 1987. © H-B

MARS TPB
August 2005. © Mark Wheatley & Marc Hempel

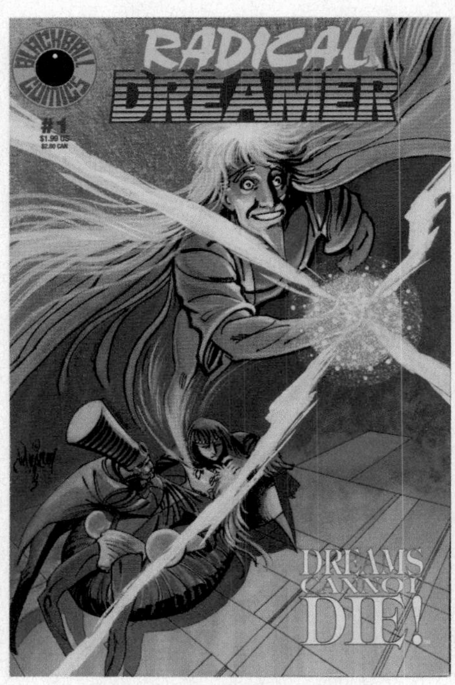

RADICAL DREAMER #1
July 1994. © Mark Wheatley

After beginning his professional career as an illustrator for *The Baltimore Sun* in 1966, Bernie Wrightson's path was altered by a meeting with Frank Frazetta. Inspired to create his own comic book stories, his first comic work appeared in *House of Mystery* #179. By 1971, after working for both DC and Marvel, he teamed with writer Len Wein to co-create Swamp Thing. He went on to produce original work and adaptations of Poe and Lovecraft for Warren Publishing and then spent seven years on the detailed pen-and-ink illustrations for an edition of Mary Shelley's *Frankenstein*. In addition to continuing comic book work over the years, he also illustrated the one-sheet and the adaptation of the Stephen King-George Romero horror film *Creepshow*, and teamed with King for *Cycle of the Werewolf* and *The Stand*, created Captain Sternn (of *Heavy Metal* fame), and provided conceptual art for such films as *Ghostbusters*, *The Faculty*, *Galaxy Quest*, *Spider-Man*, *Land of the Dead*, and *The Mist*. He passed away March 18, 2017.

–J.C. Vaughn

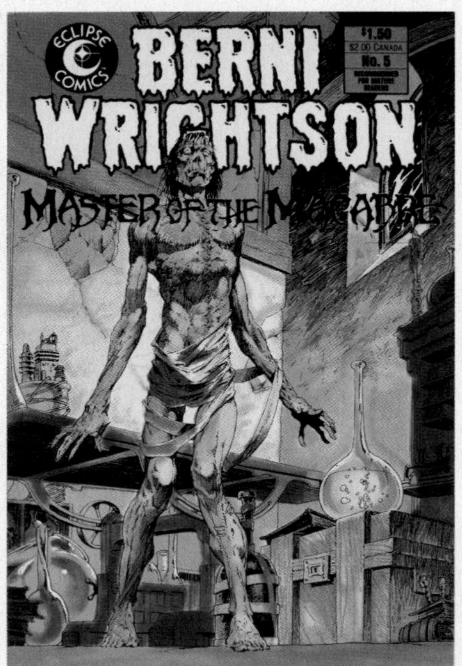

BERNI WRIGHTSON: MASTER OF THE MACABRE #5
November 1984. © Berni Wrightson & ECL

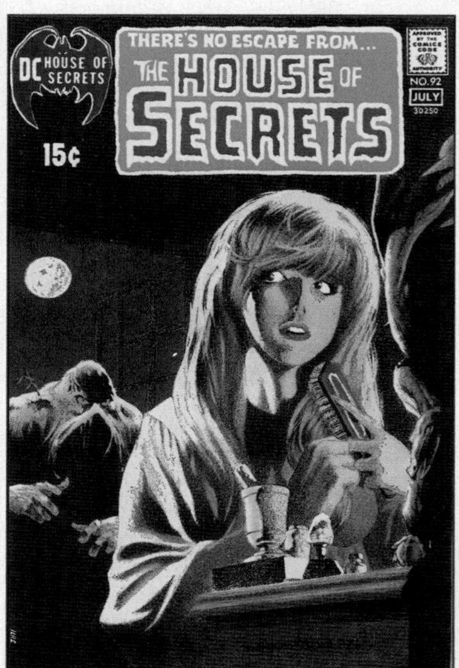

HOUSE OF SECRETS #92
June-July 1971. © DC

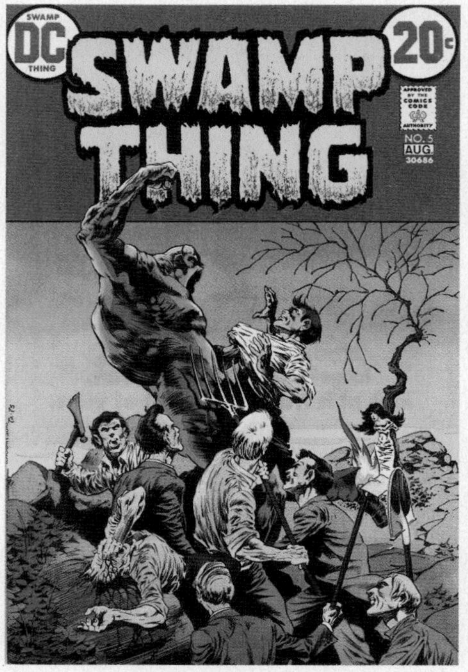

SWAMP THING #5
July-August 1973. © DC

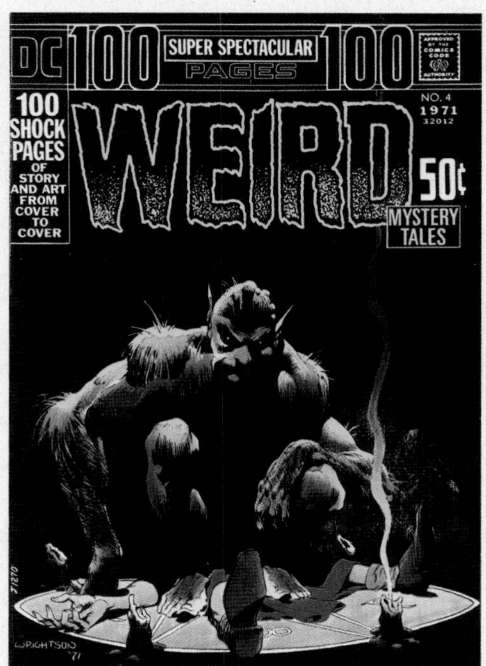

DC 100-PAGE SUPER SPECTACULAR #4
1971. © DC

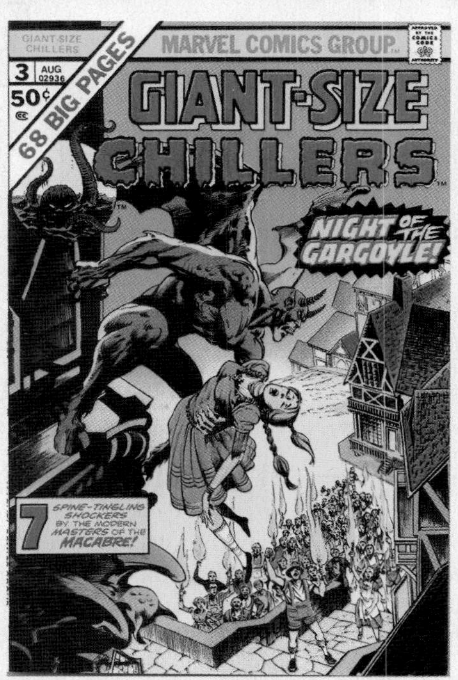

GIANT-SIZE CHILLERS #3
August 1975. © MAR

FRANKENSTEIN ART PRINT
1980s. © Bernie Wrightson

The Richard F. Outcault Legacy

by Richard D. Olson, Ph.D. & Hans K. Pedersen

While there may be debate over who created the first comic book or newspaper comic, there is no doubt that Richard F. Outcault created the first newspaper comic superstar, the Yellow Kid. Although Palmer Cox's Brownies were a popular children's fantasy feature in *St. Nicholas Magazine*, and were widely merchandised, it wasn't until the Yellow Kid took New York City by storm from 1895-1898 that a newspaper comic character not only influenced sales but was also used to merchandise everything from soap to whiskey. He first appeared in *The World* in a small black and white cartoon reprinted from *Truth* on February 17, 1895, and later in color on May 5, 1895 in a blue nightshirt; he didn't consistently appear in a yellow nightshirt until several months later.

However, as fast as the Yellow Kid's star rose, it fell, and Outcault tried to create other Sunday comics featuring children: *Kelly's Kindergarten*, *The New Bully*, and then *Pore Li'l Mose*. On May 4, 1902,

R. F. Outcault original art for the 1903 *New York Herald Sunday*, "Buster Brown and a Pair of Roller Skates."

R. F. Outcault tear sheet for the *New York Herald Sunday*, "A Summer in Rushville," which features the Yellow Kid in blackface. His nightshirt reads, "HULLY GEE. DEY DON'T RECOGNIZE ME. I AM SAFE IN DIS GUISE. SEE."

Buster Brown first appeared in the *New York Herald*. Unlike his earlier comics, which dealt with the poor children of New York City or a black boy and his adventures in the city, Buster Brown had wealthy parents and always got punished for his bad behavior. Adults favored this strip and with the technological advances in printing, Buster Brown became a national favorite. In 1904 at the St. Louis World's Fair, the Brown Shoe Company agreed to terms with Outcault to make Buster the face of their company, taking merchandising to new heights that still

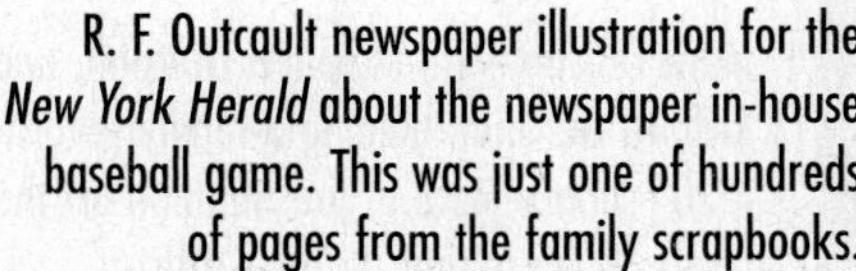
R. F. Outcault newspaper illustration for the *New York Herald* about the newspaper in-house baseball game. This was just one of hundreds of pages from the family scrapbooks.

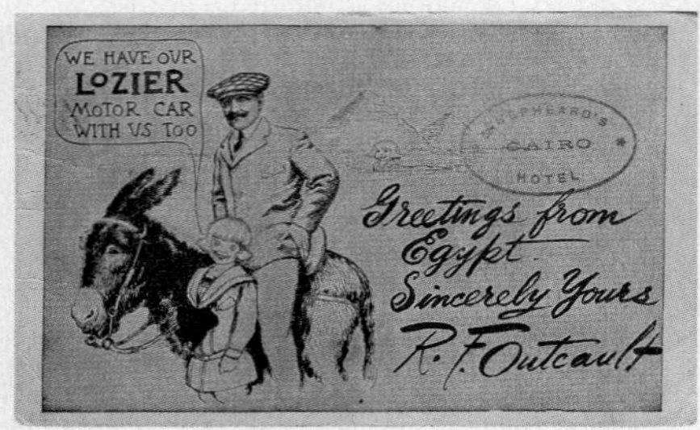

R. F. Outcault original art for the Lozier car he used in Egypt. The art is about 15″ x 12″ and was used to make the postcard, which is next to it, for the Lozier car.

continue today. Buster Brown was so popular that the strip ran until 1921, with Outcault dying in 1928 a very wealthy man.

Unlike many of his colleagues, Outcault kept a lot of his original art and some of it has passed down through four generations of the various branches of the family. After his grandson's Peter Outcault's death, his children decided to keep some of Peter's collection but sell the rest. We were very fortunate to be invited to visit them and inspect the family collection of Sunday tear sheets from 1897-1918, about 300 pieces of original art ranging from small pieces of toppers to full, hand-colored Sunday pages, a special piece of presentation art that had hung in Peter's office at his graphics arts studio, and some related material. Mark, Meloni, and Richard Outcault could not have been nicer to us, and even helped with the photography of the collection. By the time we left, we were all friends. We were able to match some of the toppers with their appropriate pages, and we plan to visit the Billy Ireland Cartoon Library and Museum at The Ohio State University and try and match the remaining toppers with their pages. It is the world's leading center for the study and preservation of the newspaper comic. You can visit their web site at cartoons.osu.edu

While it was not comic art, we were also able to look at ledgers from the Outcault Advertising Company as well as scrapbooks compiled by family over the years that contained material neither of us had ever seen before our visit.

Needless to say, we were in awe of the collection. It represented the greatest single accumulation of original R. F. Outcault art and related material that we had ever seen, and now we would like to share some of it with you.

Mark Outcault, Sr., Meloni F. Outcault, and Richard Outcault, holding a family favorite, a 20″ square piece of presentation art that always hung in their father's office.

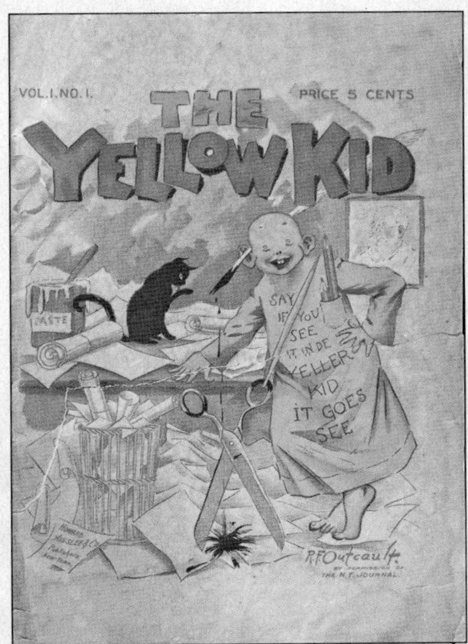

The Yellow Kid magazine, Vol. 1, No. 1, by R. F. Outcault. This magazine is illustrative of the books and magazines in the family's collection.

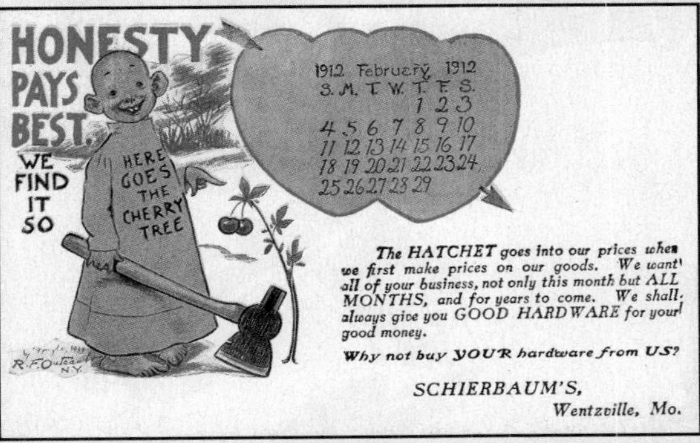

R. F. Outcault original art for the Yellow Kid calendar postcard for February, 1912, and the postcard. The same illustrations for both the Yellow Kid and the Buster Brown calendar postcards were used for several years before changing them.

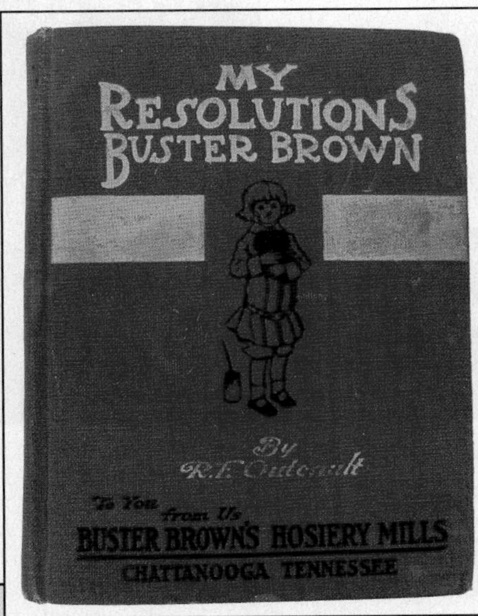

R. F. Outcault original art for a Buster Brown advertisement of his latest book, *My Resolutions, Buster Brown*. A copy of the book, which was first sold and then later given away as a premium, is shown with the ad.

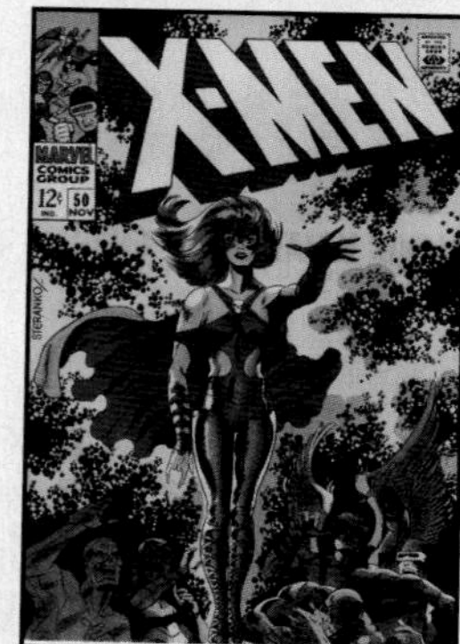

STERANKO:
THE OVERSTREET INTERVIEW

Artist Jim Steranko has worn many hats: musician, author, photographer, carnival fire-eater, publisher, male model, art director, magician, designer, historian, escape artist and comic book artist among others. Through each of his careers he seems to have made an impact. His performances inspired the character Mister Miracle, his *History of Comics* volumes have sold more than 100,000 copies each, and his concept work on *Raiders of the Lost Ark* defined the look of Indiana Jones.

It's as a comic book writer-artist that continues to bring him to the attention of collectors, dealers and collectors today. His tenures on *Nick Fury: Agent of S.H.I.E.L.D.*, *X-Men*, and *Captain America* showcased a revolutionary narrative approach to the medium. He went on to produce graphic novels such as *Red Tide* and *Outland*, among other efforts. His Batman cover for *The Overstreet Comic Book Price Guide* #47 is his first Overstreet cover, as hard as that might to believe for longtime fans of both Steranko and Overstreet.

OVERSTREET: You're known not only for an incredible design sense, but also for a profound awareness of comics history. Why is Batman compelling to you?

STERANKO: We both own the night! For some nameless psychological reason, I come alive after dark – especially creatively – and get into more trouble after the sun vanishes than I care to admit. The fact that I knew Bill Finger, Jerry Robinson, Juile Schwartz, Vin Sullivan, Dick Sprang, Mort Weisinger, Carmine Infantino, Neal Adams, Denny O'Neil, David Mazzucchelli, Andy Kubert, Darwyn Cooke, Jim Lee and others, including Bob Kane – all key figures in Batman history – may have had something to do with it, too.

But the connection is infinitely deeper. Batman is essentially a comic book version of The Shadow. I mention it because Batman co-creator, Bill Finger, confirmed to me he pirated not only The Shadow's basic elements and devices, but clipped Shadow stories and recast them for Batman. How's that for raw candor?

The Shadow is a seminal American crime-fighter, one of the most popular and influential in pop-culture history. He proliferated in magazines, hardbound books, radio, comic strips, movie serials, feature films, toys and games, and more, for decades. The character was created by Walter Gibson aka Maxwell Grant in 1931, and, of the 325 novels featuring the character, he scribed an astonishing 283. Gibson was my adopted grandfather. And Bruce Elliott, who scribed The Shadow stories in the '40s, was like my father. So, because I was a member of the family—not to mention having painted 30 Shadow book covers—they called me, "The son of the son of The Shadow."

Let's just say Batman's in my blood!

OVERSTREET: How did you develop the idea for our cover image?

STERANKO: I employed what I call the First Rule of Batman, something his creators and narrators failed to perceive in more than 70 years and thousands of adventures. Example: In 1986 or so, I was hailed by Warner Bros' to meet with the Caped Crusader's new director: Tim Burton. At the time, I was publishing the international film magazine *PREVUE*, and well aware from inside sources that he'd be calling the shots on the next Batflick. We connected at his Hollywood offices on the Warner Bros. lot. He was enthusiastic and unpretentious, looked like he was about six months overdue for a haircut, dressed in all-black thrift-shop clothes, and heavy-duty logger boots, which he kept planted flat on the seat as he perched on a chair throughout the afternoon. I expected offbeat – and got it!

It was obvious he was still doing homework on the character. No surprise, because Batman had endured a series of transformations over the years. Burton grew up with the '60's Infantino-Giella-Novick yarns, the TV series, and maybe the Adams-Aparo versions, but was more interested in the character than his illustrators. We spent the day talking about his take on the hero, until it became apparent – like all Batman editors, writers, and artists before that point – that, impossible as it sounds, he didn't know the First Rule of Batman! I enlightened him...

Batman *only* comes out at night! And my cover image reiterates that concept.

OVERSTREET: More than that, the image is a series of mysteries, one inside another.

STERANKO: The image is *an illusion*! At first glance, it's standard Batman, strictly de rigueur—the Caped Crusader over Gotham!

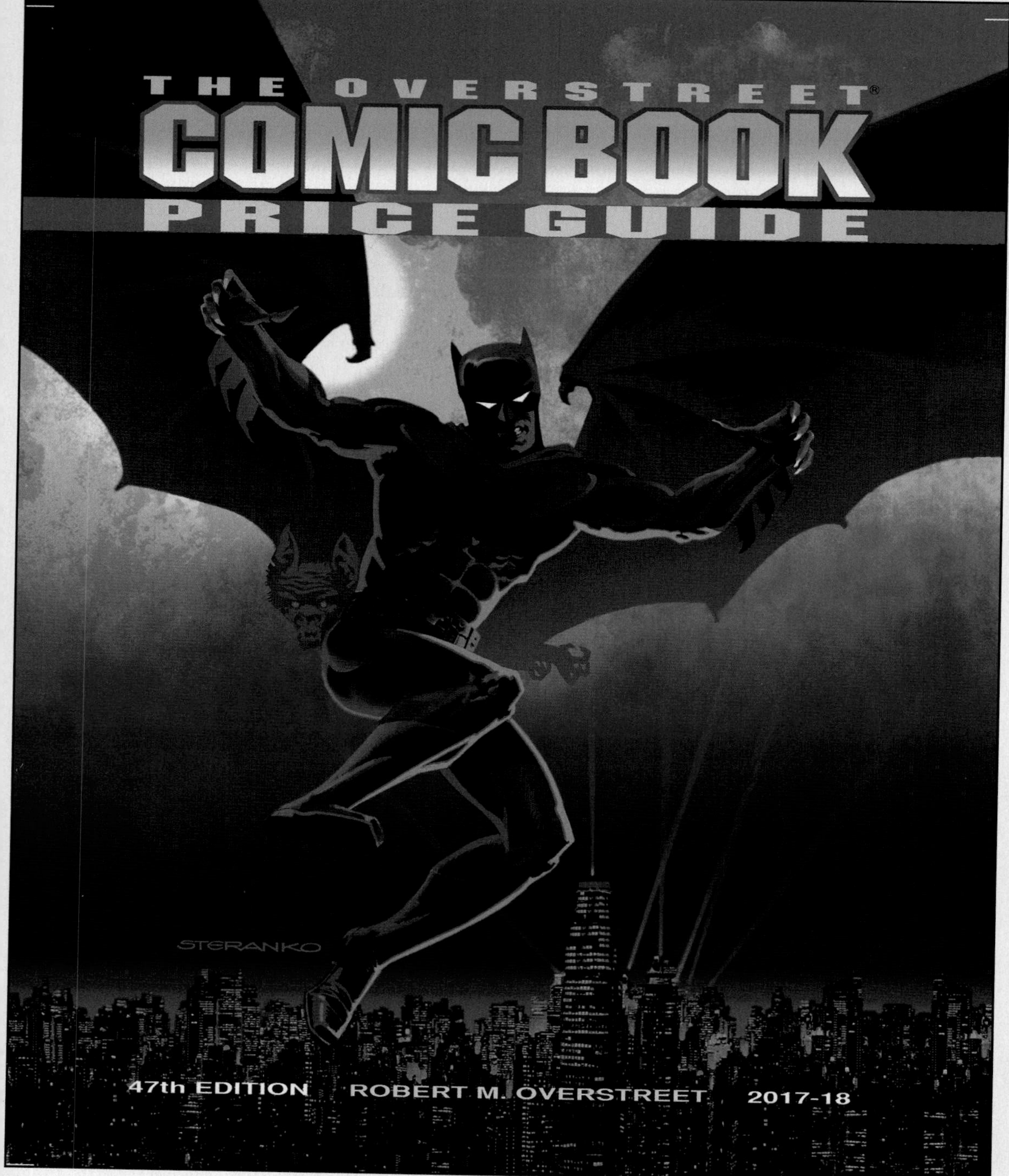

One aspect of my cover creation is to engage potential buyers interactively. To get their attention, I deliberately *violated* the standard Overstreet policy of vibrant colors, all shouting for consumer attention. Instead, I adopted a severely-limited, low-key palette, knowing the viewer would pick up the book out of curiosity – beginning the game of engagement.

At first glance, they perceive what they believe is the silhouette of a figure with a cape fluttering in the configuration of batwings. But, as they tighten their perception, they realize there is *no cape*. Instead, a massive bat seems to materialize mystically out of the costumed figure's presence – part metaphor, part riddle suggesting the character's true, ultra-paranoid persona.

That revelation begins visually with the bat's claw, then the discovery of its face, which I deliberately obscured in the silhouette edge and by utilizing low-chroma color values. Further interactive engagement materializes with additional details, such as the bat's claws replicated on the man – or is it the opposite? Additional minutiae is half-obscured, half-revealed in the shadows of the figure, suggesting more about his modus operandi: Fearsome. Unexpected. Lethal!

The twin silhouettes – oppressively jagged, but graphically stimulating – eclipse a radiant moon, and create a stark expectation regarding the action about to unfold. Burning eyes scan the scene for hidden danger or sudden death. Slowly, the viewer becomes aware of other details, including how shapes and colors have colluded to create a psychogenic illusion. Gotham below is another diversion, seemingly placid and quiet, another trick, betrayed by shifting spotlights that appear like deadly spikes, hoping to spear something or someone in their deadly sweep across the obsidian skyscape. Is one of them the Batsignal? The scene is a nightmare of harrowing duplicity and subtle shockers – all creating an *emotional bond* with the viewer.

It's a chilling, psychological process – the eyes seeing a specific image, and the mind realizing it's been tricked! Suddenly, a kind of terrifying metaphor emerges: Is the subject more man or more bat? Which is the greater reality? Welcome to the World of Batman!

OVERSTREET: Did you come up with the color scheme before or after you created the art?

STERANKO: My approach, the *mise en scene*, and color strategy was determined a long time ago, except no one knew it – until I revealed the patently obvious to Burton. Like The Shadow, Batman demands a certain ambience. I simply fulfilled that requirement.

Think about it: There have been thousands of Batman covers since his debut, almost 80 years ago. It would be natural to assume it had all been done before. No way in Hell! That's why I opted to generate a surreal image for a surreal protagonist. It's a haunting mystery, and either way, the solution is disturbing! But isn't that what Batman should always be about?

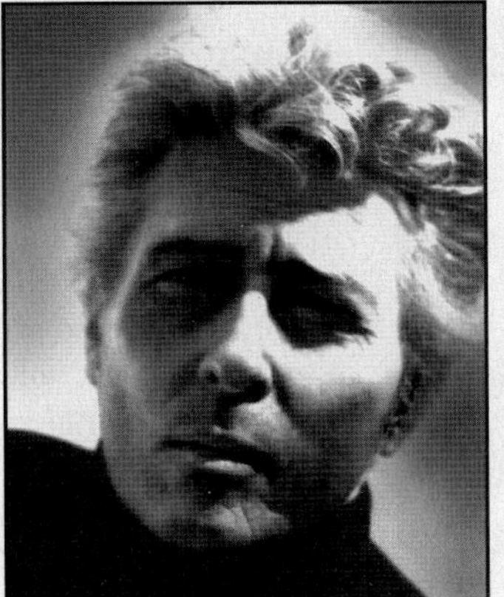

©2017 Jim Steranko

OVERSTREET: Does your Batman lean toward any particular era of the character's long history or does it exist on its own?

STERANKO: The look, the feel of my Batman represents an attempt to coalesce the past, present, and future – and create an entity as timeless as the night.

OVERSTREET: It's been said that your total body of comic book work was only 29 issues, but that they showcase large number of innovations. To what do you attribute your approach and its subsequent impact?

STERANKO: The medium got off to a wrong start by imitating newspaper strips, instead of analyzing the page-turning pamphlet process, which it was. Shockingly, even the most imaginative artists and writers never realized the handicap. Few were superb storytellers, and they inevitably focused on elements inside the panels, rather than creating effective techniques to tell stories. I've looked intensely at the form's history for decades, and discovered only a few artists who created or developed even one or two narrative innovations. Considering the latitude they embrace, I find it terminally disappointing there's been minimal progress

in the form's development. Comic books are essentially the same as they were 85 years ago.

My drawing skills are derived from comic books and strips, but my narrative technique is informed completely by film – an aspect that readers responded to immediately after experiencing my *S.H.I.E.L.D.* work. That approach set me apart from most of my peers, in addition to the fact that I was deeply entrenched in cognitive science, from my advertising background. It was a natural expression for me to create a *new, visual language* – new techniques, tropes, and transitions – to expand and enhance drama on the comic book page.

Those innovations ranged from large – a four-page, panoramic scene that climaxed a nine-month storyline – to small – an empty word balloon expressing female contempt. One innovation featured a three-page silent sequence, but, unlike previous silent sequences that were riddled with captions explaining the action, these pages had no explanatory text, *just pure silence*! Another innovation plunged Fury into an enemy maze so convoluted the reader had to navigate through each panel to get to the next, even to the point of turning the book *upside down* to do it! Some innovations were so subtle, they have yet to be discovered. But, those that were, revolutionized narrative technique, and paved the way for modern storytelling.

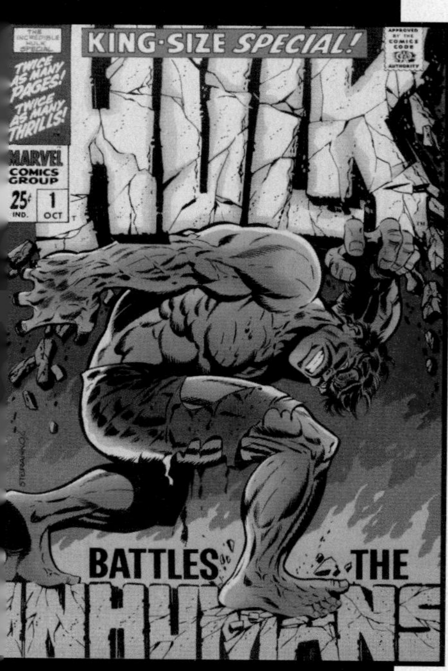

OVERSTREET: Are there other Batman projects in your future?

STERANKO: For openers, I recently sold DC 10 Batman and Superman cover images. That in mind, it's terminally paradoxical that there have been dozens of books written about Batman – none of which even remotely capture *the real story behind his creation*! They're all bogus! After 78 years, that event is still shrouded in mystery. However, with the help of the men who were there when it happened, most of whom I've known personally, I've solved that mystery. It's a fascinating convolution of events that will be revealed in a new book I currently have in production. And the Batman story is just the tip of the iceberg – or maybe I should say a pop-culture cyclone that'll blow the comic book universe to atoms! Think you can handle it?

– J.C. Vaughn

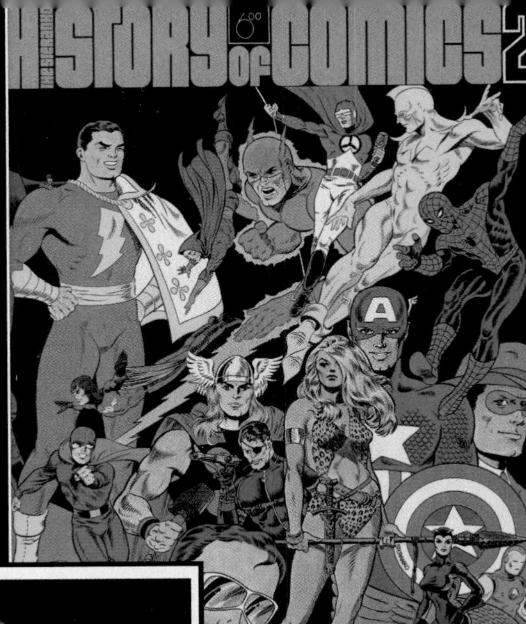

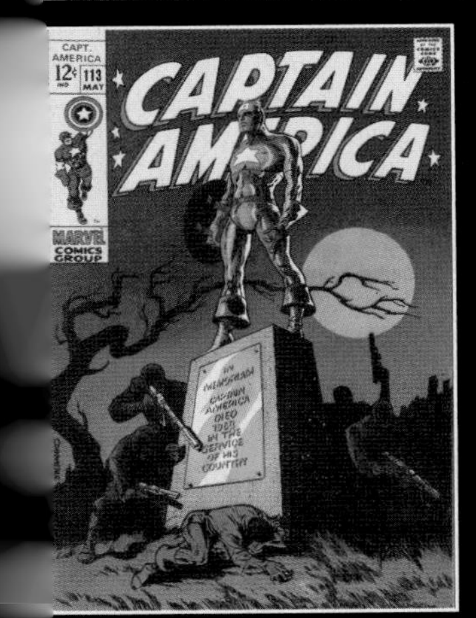

©2017 Jim Steranko

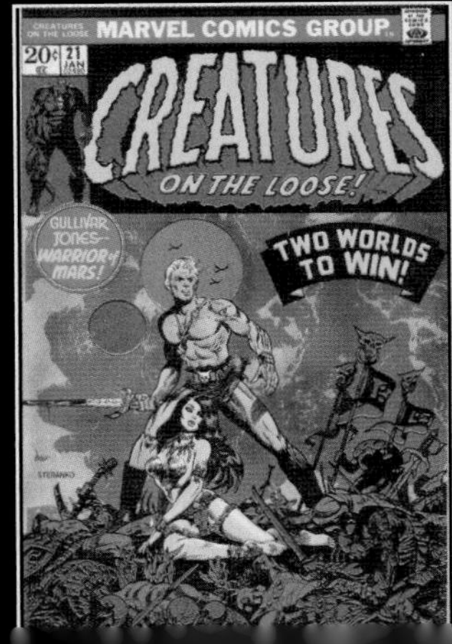

Black Canary at 70

By Amanda Sheriff

With her blond wig, fishnets, and black leather jacket, Black Canary is instantly memorable. Tough, empowering, and sexy, the DC Comics character was one of their earliest superheroines. Having debuted in *Flash Comics* #86 in August 1947, this year marks Black Canary's 70th anniversary.

Created by writer Robert Kanigher and artist Carmine Infantino, the alter ego of Black Canary was first taken by Dinah Drake, then later by Dinah Laurel Lance. Trained in martial arts, she is also an adept investigator, covert operative, gymnast, and motorcyclist.

In her second incarnation, Black Canary gained the power of the Canary Cry, sending ultrasonic vibrations that can do serious damage to both organic and inorganic material. As of the New 52, the Canary Cry also gave her the power to propel herself to fly by using the force to defy gravity.

Dinah Drake wanted to become a police officer in Gotham City, but her application was rejected. After her father passed away, Dinah used her inheritance to open a flower shop while simultaneously becoming a crime fighter. Inspired by other heroes of the time, she covered her dark hair in a blond wig and became the Black Canary.

Pretending to be a criminal, she infiltrated the darker side of Gotham. Then after revealing herself as a superheroine, she joined the Justice Society of America. Once she retired from the JSA she married detective Larry Lance and had a daughter, also named Dinah. But domestic bliss did not last, as Dinah Drake Lance died of cancer from radiation, due to a fight with the cosmic-powered villain Aquarius.

The second Black Canary, Dinah Laurel Lance, debuted in *Justice League of America* #75 in November 1969. She grew up hearing JSA members' stories about her mother's adventures as a heroine. Similar to her mom, she was a good athlete, but also had a metagene that gave her the ultrasonic Canary Cry power. In addition to knowing Judo, her "uncle" Ted Grant, a/k/a Wildcat, taught her to box. Other JSA members also taught her fighting styles and techniques.

Dinah Lance was one of the first among the second generation heroes. As Black Canary II she worked alone, as part of the Justice League of America, and was the primary Bird of Prey working for Oracle. It was also during this time that she started a relationship with Green Arrow/Oliver Queen – one of the steamiest in mainstream comics.

After Infinite Crisis, Black Canary and Lady Shiva traded places and she trained overseas while Lady Shiva became a Bird of Prey. In Vietnam she became a mentor for Sin, a young girl who was Lady Shiva's successor. She also signed on as chairwoman of the new Justice League.

During Dinah and Oliver's wedding, supervillains crashed the ceremony, since the gathering of superheroes was such an appealing target. Black Canary helped stop the attack and found that her husband was being impersonated by a shapeshifter. She killed the imposter then rescued Oliver, who was imprisoned on Themyscira.

In the New 52 she was a leader in the Birds of Prey, working with Katana, Poison Ivy, and Batgirl. She also worked with Team 7 as a covert ops agent and during that time she secretly married longtime partner, Kurt Lance.

In 2016's DC Rebirth, Dinah and Ollie rekindled their romance, and she's been regularly featured in *Green Arrow*. With the relaunch her name combined both iterations of Black Canary as Dinah Laurel Drake-Lance.

Seven decades after her debut, Black Canary is still beating the bad guys with gusto, style, and attitude. Whether solo or part of a team, undercover or in the spotlight, Dinah proves herself as a skilled heroine. It's best not to get in the way when this Canary sings.

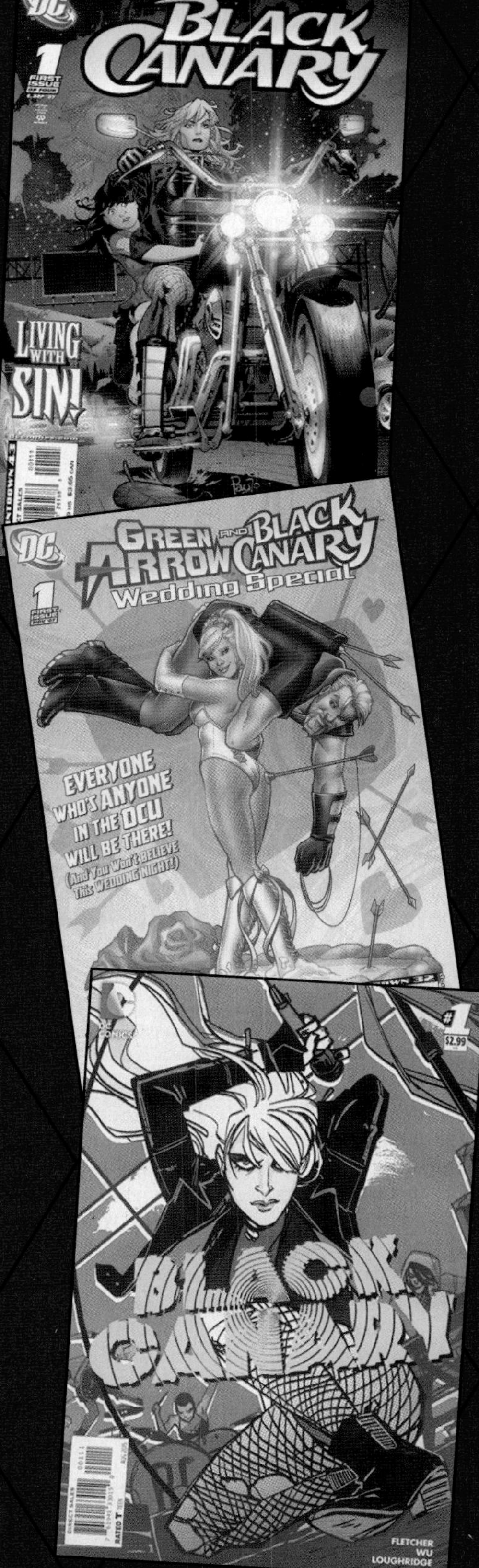

CAPTAIN MARVEL AT 50

By Carrie Wood

The "Captain Marvel" name has long been the subject of debate. Longtime DC (or Fawcett) fans might identify the moniker as the alter-ego of young Billy Batson, though Marvel fans will instead point to a superpowered alien (or, more recently, to Carol Danvers). While the magic word "Shazam!" might have its place in history, it's Marvel's own Captain Marvel that celebrates his 50th anniversary this year.

Marvel was able to publish a book under the *Captain Marvel* name due to some trademarks expiring in their favor. Fawcett Comics published their Captain Marvel comic books from 1940 to 1953 (the character later published by DC), but stopped due to a copyright lawsuit from DC Comics. After the trademark on "Captain Marvel" lapsed, Marvel Comics jumped on it, and published the first appearance of their Captain Marvel in 1967.

The character debuted in *Marvel Super-Heroes* #12 in December 1967 in a story written by Stan Lee and illustrated by Gene Colan. His backstory was given in *Captain Marvel* #1 in May 1968; a Kree named Mar-Vell, he originally came to Earth as a spy in order to decide if humans would pose a threat to the Kree Empire. The name "Captain Marvel" is assigned to him after people mishear him saying his own name. He eventually sides with humanity and is found guilty of treason against the Kree Empire, though he escapes his death sentence in a stolen rocket.

Later, he would be linked to Rick Jones, who would serve as somewhat of an alter-ego for Mar-Vell, who landed himself trapped in the Negative Zone. By using "nega-bands," Mar-Vell and Jones could switch places for a short period of time. Unfortunately, the character failed to grab audiences, and despite the changes to make him more science fiction-oriented, would end up only being published occasionally throughout the late '60s. The title was canceled with issue #21 in 1970.

However, after Mar-Vell appeared in the Kree-Skull War from '71 to '72, his series kicked back off with issue #22 in September 1972.

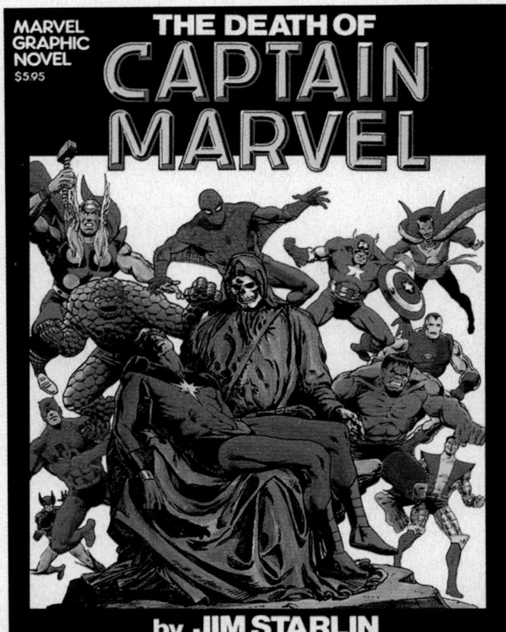

The character was revamped by Jim Starlin in issue #25, and Captain Marvel grew a stronger following because of it. Despite the start of the *Ms. Marvel* spin-off series in 1977, sales never picked up in the way that Marvel wanted them to, and the series would be canceled again in 1979. Mar-Vell's death was written by Starlin in *The Death of Captain Marvel*, which was also Marvel's first graphic novel.

The Death of Captain Marvel saw a rather definitive end for the character: Mar-Vell discovers that past exposure to "Compound 13" gas had given him cancer that will eventually kill him. As the Kree still considered him a traitor, he lacked access to their medical expertise that may have saved him. Eventually, his many allies – and even his sworn enemies, the Skrulls – pay their respects to the dying hero. As he nears death, he experiences a vision of Thanos, who has arrived to guide Mar-Vell into the afterlife, along with Mistress Death.

Mar-Vell was seen on a rare occasion in the 1990s and 2000s, when other characters (such as the Silver Surfer) find themselves in the Realm of the Dead. During *Chaos War* he, along with several other deceased Avengers, are restored to life. Unfortunately for Mar-Vell, his resurrection is short-lived, being killed once more by the Grim Reaper himself.

Though Mar-Vell might not be the most popular Captain Marvel – that likely goes to Carol Danvers, who will be the titular character in the upcoming *Captain Marvel* film – he'll always be the first. His selflessness and heroism established the standard that all other Captain Marvels have been held to, and though it's unlikely that Mar-Vell will ever be permanently restored to life, his legacy clearly lives on.

THE QUESTION CELEBRATES 50 YEARS

BY BRAELYNN BOWERSOX

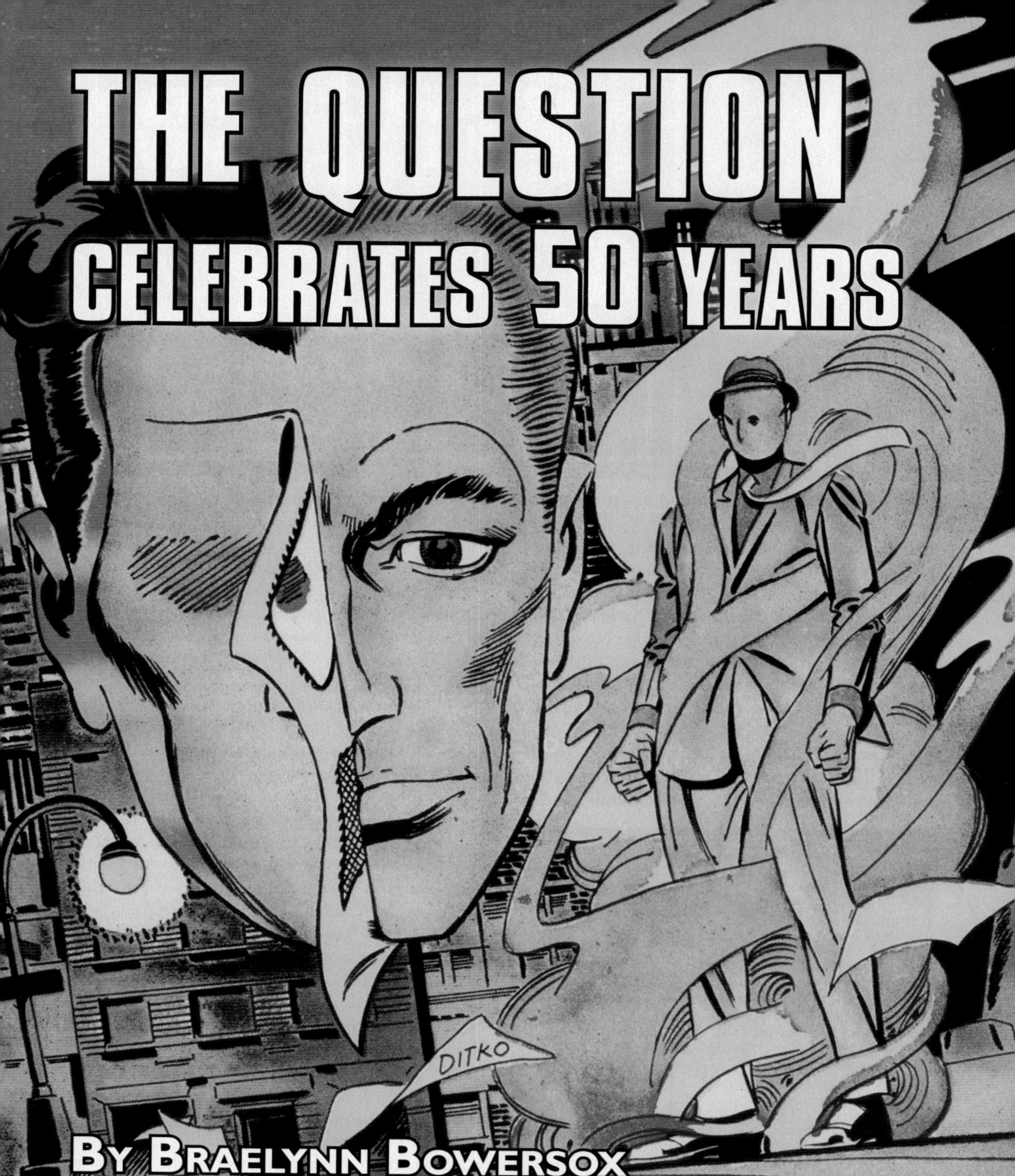

The debonaire shaman and master detective known as The Question strolled onto the comic scene 50 years ago. As the brainchild of artist-writer Steve Ditko, The Question originally debuted in Charlton Comics' *Blue Beetle* #1 in June 1967. During the 1980s, the character was acquired by DC Comics and was later incorporated into the DC proper.

The Question - real name Charles Victor Szasz, a/k/a Vic Sage - forged his legacy as a highly outspoken, aggressive investigative journalist in Hub City. Throughout his early appear-

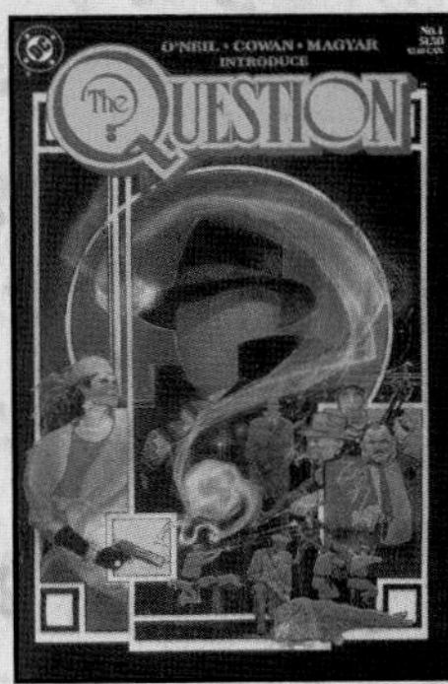

ances, there was very little backstory provided for Sage. All that was truly known of Sage was his penchant for using ruthless methods against criminals, and always espousing a firm standard of ethics. In the Charlton Comics series, Sage was most frequently opposed by Max Bine, the Banshee. He also briefly appeared alongside his fellow Charlton "Action Heroes" as part of the Sentinels of Justice.

When the Charlton Comics company was in decline in 1983, several of their characters were purchased by DC, including The Question. After briefly appearing in 1985's *Crisis on Infinite Earths* and a three-issue arc of DC's *Blue Beetle* revival, The Question was given his own solo series in 1987. This new series, which was published for 36 issues, was led by writer Dennis O'Neil and primarily drawn by Denys Cowan. Throughout this solo series, the backstory for Sage was heavily expanded upon.

Abandoned as a child, Vic Sage was raised in a Hub City orphanage. While there he gained a reputation as a defiant troublemaker, often leading to beatings by the nuns and being victimized by the other children. After aging out of the system, Sage studied journalism in college, but despite finding work as a reporter, he felt dissatisfied with his life and struggled to control his violent tendencies. Sometime later Sage met Aristotle Rodor, who helped him channel his aggression into a new, heroic persona - The Question.

Using this new alter ego, Sage was finally able to get the answers his civilian identity could not. Rather than hunting down petty perpetrators like other vigilante superheroes of that time, O'Neil's Question was primarily focused on the politics and corrupt government within Hub City. While the character maintained some similar aspects to its early incarnation, this version of Sage drifted toward a more Zen philosophy.

This iteration of The Question possessed no superhuman powers or abilities, but was exceptionally skilled in martial arts, acrobatics, and hand-to-hand combat. His genius-level intellect made him a masterful detective, and the pseudoderm mask he wore, which bonded to his skin via binary glasses, allowed him to change the color of his hair and clothing. For a brief period, Sage acquired the mystical abilities of a shaman, allowing him to communicate with the planet, and to generate illusions.

During DC's New 52 event, the character was significantly rebooted, essentially becoming an in-name-only version of Sage. Instead of being a journalist, this Sage was a corrupt, amoral bureaucrat working as a government functionary. He was later recruited from his private sector to co-run the Suicide Squad with Amanda Waller. The partnership didn't last long, and after attempting to murder Waller, Sage found himself behind bars.

Thankfully, imprisonment is only a mere inconvenience for this savvy character. The Question continues to be rebooted, revamped, and restyled into various incarnations across the comic universe. Comic writer Alan Moore even cited The Question as partial inspiration behind his Watchmen character, Rorshach, stating that he wanted to create a "quintessential Steve Ditko character."

Just think, what will Ditko's Question accomplish in another 50 years?

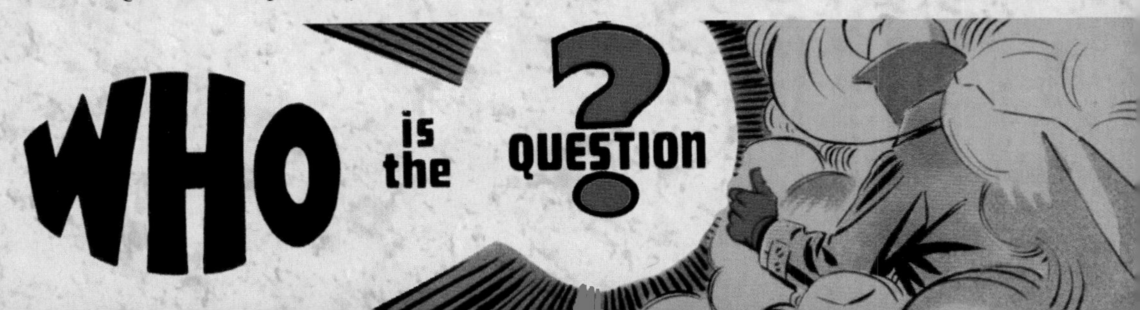

SPIDER-WOMAN AT 40

By
CARRIE WOOD

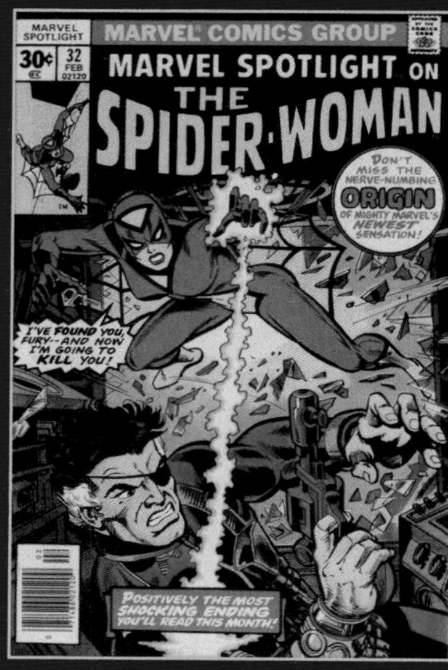

These days, the Spider-Family at Marvel Comics is immense. What started as just a high school kid being bit by a radioactive spider has expanded to include many more characters with similar powers, including some contemporary favorites like Miles Morales and Gwen Stacy. But one of the most important members of the web-slinging crew celebrates her 40th anniversary in 2017 – Jessica Drew, a/k/a Spider-Woman.

The character made her debut in *Marvel Spotlight* #32 and had been created by Archie Goodwin and Marie Severin. As for *why* she was created, Stan Lee once said that it was about the name – that he didn't want another company to have the rights to use "Spider-Woman" in a comic book. Regardless of how petty the original reason for Jessica's creation may have been, she quickly gained her own solo series (written by Marv Wolfman and illustrated by Carmine Infantino) after her debut issue sold remarkably well.

Wolfman immediately took to humanizing the character and changing her backstory; her first appearance had her as a human that had evolved from a spider, and this was deemed just slightly too ridiculous. Instead, she was given a proper human identity as Jessica Drew, and HYDRA had implanted false memories of being a spider into her. Wolfman left the series after issue #8 and was replaced by Mark Gruenwald, who put a big focus on Jessica's inner struggles as she dealt with her social awkwardness and isolation from society.

By 1979 an animated television series began airing on ABC, though the *Spider-Woman* series wildly differed from the comic books. While Marvel spent a lot of time promoting the character, sales of the books had already started to slip at this point. The show only lasted 16 episodes.

Gruenwald and Infantino left the book at issue #20, and new writer Michael Fleisher dramatically shifted the tone of the story when he came on by making her a bounty hunter. Longtime readers criticized a number of the story decisions made around this time, and by issue #32 Fleisher was replaced with Chris Claremont, who once again changed her occupation to that of a P.I.

While Claremont's run was praised, it was somewhat of a too-little-too-late situation, and like many of the other writers' turns on *Spider-Woman*, was definitely too short. Claremont left after 13 issues, and the decision was made shortly thereafter to cancel the series at issue #50. Ann Nocenti and Brian Postman were put in charge of writing and penciling the final four issues. In the last issue, Jessica Drew dies in a battle with her longtime foe Morgan le Fay, and a spell is cast to make the rest of the Marvel Universe forget she ever even existed. While it somewhat fit her origin story, it was a massive insult to the readers who had come to love the character over several years.

Fortunately, the top brass at Marvel took the fans' reaction to Jessica's death pretty seriously, and she was revived less than a year later in *The Avengers* #240-241 in 1984. However, Jessica Drew only made limited appearances throughout the late '80s and early '90s, and she was almost never in her classic costume. A backup feature in *Sensational Spider-Man Annual '96* put her back in her costume for the first time in more than 10 years, but this story is considered non-canonical.

It wouldn't be until the mid-2000s that Spider-Woman returned as a regular costumed hero in *The New Avengers* (though for a while she had been replaced by a Skrull imposter). In 2014 she played a major role in the *Spider-Verse* event, and a new solo series, written by Dennis Hopeless, began running as well. Jessica also got her first costume redesign for the first time since the 1970s in her new series, which has proven to be fairly popular.

It may have taken 40 years, but it seems that Spider-Woman is finally hitting her stride and is now more popular than ever. Regardless of where she goes next, the story that follows her is sure to be interesting for years to come.

OVERSTREET ADVISORS

DARREN ADAMS
Pristine Comics
Seattle, WA

WELDON ADAMS
Heritage Auctions
Fort Worth, TX

GRANT ADEY
Halo Certification
Brisbane, QLD, Australia

BILL ALEXANDER
Collector
Sacramento, CA

DAVID T. ALEXANDER
David Alexander Comics
Tampa, FL

TYLER ALEXANDER
David Alexander Comics
Tampa, FL

LON ALLEN
Heritage Auctions
Dallas, TX

DAVE ANDERSON
Want List Comics
Tulsa, OK

L.E. BECKER
Comic*Pop Collectibles
Wixom, MI

ROBERT BEERBOHM
Robert Beerbohm Comic Art
Fremont, NE

JON BERK
Collector
Hartford, CT

JIM BERRY
Collector
Portland, OR

JON BEVANS
Collector
Baltimore, MD

TIM BILDHAUSER
Foreign Comics Specialist
CBCS

PETER BILELIS, ESQ.
Collector
South Windsor, CT

DR. ARNOLD T. BLUMBERG
Collector
Baltimore, MD

MIKE BOLLINGER
Hake's Americana
York, PA

STEVE BOROCK
CBCS
St Petersburg, FL

SCOTT BRADEN
Comics Historian
Hanover, PA

RICHARD BROWN
Collector
Detroit, MI

SHAWN CAFFREY
Finalizer/Modern Age Specialist
CGC

MICHAEL CARBONARO
Dave & Adam's
New York

BRETT CARRERAS
VA Comicon
Richmond, VA

GARY CARTER
Collector
Coronado, CA

CHARLES CERRITO
Hotflips
Farmingdale, NY

JEFF CERRITO
Hotflips
Farmingdale, NY

JOHN CHRUSCINSKI
Tropic Comics
Lyndora, PA

PAUL CLAIRMONT
PNJ Comics
Winnipeg, MB
Canada

ART CLOOS
Collector/Historian
Flushing, NY

GARY COLABUONO
Dealer/Collector
Arlington Heights, IL

BILL COLE
Bill Cole Enterprises, Inc.
Randolph, MA

TIM COLLINS
RTS Unlimited, Inc.
Lakewood, CO

ANDREW COOKE
Writer/Director
New York City, NY

JON B. COOKE
Editor - Comic Book Artist Magazine
West Kingston, RI

JACK COPLEY
Coliseum of Comics
Florida

ASHLEY COTTER-CAIRNS
SellMyComicBooks.com
Montreal, Canada

JESSE JAMES CRISCIONE
Jesse James Comics
Glendale, AZ

FRANK CWIKLIK
Metropolis Comics
New York, NY

BROCK DICKINSON
Collector
St. Catharines, ONT Canada

PETER DIXON
Paradise Comics
Toronto, ONT Canada

GARY DOLGOFF
Gary Dolgoff Comics
Easthampton, MA

JOHN DOLMAYAN
Torpedo Comics
Las Vegas, NV

SHELTON DRUM
Heroes Aren't Hard to Find
Charlotte, NC

WALTER DURAJLIJA
Big B Comics
Hamilton, ONT
Canada

KEN DYBER
Cloud 9 Comics
Portland, OR

TOMIS ERB
Comic Verification Authority
Brooklyn, NY

DANIEL ERTLE
Modern Age Specialist
CBCS

CONRAD ESCHENBERG
Collector/Dealer
Cold Spring, NY

MICHAEL EURY
Author
Concord, NC

RICHARD EVANS
Bedrock City Comics
Houston, TX

D'ARCY FARRELL
Pendragon Comics
Toronto, ONT Canada

BILL FIDYK
Collector
Annapolis, MD

PAUL FIGURA
Quality Control Specialist
CBCS

JOSEPH FIORE
ComicWiz.com
Toronto, ONT Canada

STEPHEN FISHLER
Metropolis Collectibles, Inc.
New York, NY

DAN FOGEL
Hippy Comix, Inc.
Cleveland, OH

BRAD FOSTER
SharpComics.com
Plainfield, IL

JOHN FOSTER
South Philly Comics
Philadelphia, PA

DAN GALLO
Dealer/Comic Art Con
Westchester Co., NY

STEPHEN H. GENTNER
Golden Age Specialist
Portland, OR

JOSH GEPPI
Diamond Int. Galleries
ComicWow.com
Timonium, MD

STEVE GEPPI
Diamond Int. Galleries
Timonium, MD

DOUG GILLOCK
ComicLink
Portland, ME

MICHAEL GOLDMAN
Motor City Comics
Farmington Hills, MI

DAWN GOMEZ
Coliseum of Comics
Celebration, FL

SEAN GOODRICH
SellMyComicBooks.com
Maine, USA

KEITH GOSS
Collector
Staten Island, NY

TOM GORDON III
Collector/Dealer
Westminster, MD

JAMIE GRAHAM
Graham Crackers
Chicago, IL

DANIEL GREENHALGH
Showcase
New England
Northford, CT

ANDY GREENHAM
Forest City Coins
London, ON Canada

ERIC J. GROVES
Dealer/Collector
Oklahoma City, OK

GARY GUZZO
Atomic Studios
Boothbay Harbor, ME

JOHN HAINES
Dealer/Collector
Kirtland, OH

JIM HALPERIN
Heritage Auctions
Dallas, TX

MARK HASPEL
Finalizer/
Pedigree Specialist
CGC

JEF HINDS
Jef Hinds Comics
Madison, WI

TERRY HOKNES
Hoknes Comics
Saskatoon, SK
Canada

GREG HOLLAND, Ph.D.
Collector
Alexander, AR

JOHN HONE
Collector
Silver Spring, MD

STEVEN HOUSTON
Torpedo Comics
Las Vegas, NV

BILL HUGHES
Dealer/Collector
Flower Mound, TX

ROB HUGHES
Arch Angels
Pacific Beach, CA

JEFF ITKIN
Elite Comic Source
Portland, OR

ED JASTER
Heritage Auctions
Dallas, TX

DR. STEVEN KAHN
Inner Child Comics
& Collectibles
Kenosha, WI

NICK KATRADIS
Collector
Tenafly, NJ

DENNIS KEUM
Fantasy Comics
Goldens Bridge, NY

IVAN KOCMAREK
Comics Historian
Hamilton, ON
Canada

ROBERT KRAUSE
Primo Comics
Venice, FL

MICHAEL KRONENBERG
Historian/Designer
Chapel Hill, NC

BENJAMIN LABONOG
Collector
Burlingame, CA

BEN LICHTENSTEIN
Zapp Comics
Wayne, NJ

STEPHEN LIPSON
Comics Historian
Mississauga, ON

PAUL LITCH
Primary Grader
CGC

DOUG MABRY
The Great Escape
Madison, TN

TOMMY MALETTA
Best Comics
International
New Hyde Park, NY

JOE MANNARINO
Heritage Auctions
Ridgewood, NJ

NADIA MANNARINO
Heritage Auctions
Ridgewood, NJ

BRIAN MARCUS
Cavalier Comics
Wise, VA

WILL MASON
Dave & Adam's
New York

HARRY MATETSKY
Collector
Middletown, NJ

JON McCLURE
Comics Historian,
Writer
Portland, OR

TODD McDEVITT
New Dimension Comics
Cranberry Township,
PA

MIKE McKENZIE
Alternate Worlds
Cockeysville, MD

ANDY McMAHON
Duncanville Bookstore
Duncanville, TX

PETER MEROLO
Collector
Sedona, AZ

JOHN JACKSON MILLER
Historian, Writer
Scandinavia, WI

STEVE MORTENSEN
Miracle Comics
Santa Clara, CA

MARC NATHAN
Cards, Comics &
Collectibles
Reisterstown, MD

JOSHUA NATHANSON
ComicLink
Portland, ME

MATT NELSON
President, CCS
Sarasota, FL

TOM NELSON
Top Notch Comics
Yankton, SD

JAMIE NEWBOLD
Southern California
Comics
San Diego, CA

CHARLIE NOVINSKIE
Silver Age Specialist
Lake Havasu City, AZ

VINCE OLIVA
Grader
CGC

RICHARD OLSON
Collector/Academician
Poplarville, MS

TERRY O'NEILL
Terry's Comics
Orange, CA

MICHAEL PAVLIC
Purple Gorilla Comics
Calgary, AB Canada

JIM PAYETTE
Golden Age Specialist
Bethlehem, NH

BILL PONSETI
Fantastic Worlds Comics
Scottsdale, AZ

RON PUSSELL
Redbeard's Book Den
Crystal Bay, NV

JEFF RADER
Offbeat Archives
Comics & Collectibles
Gilroy, CA

ALEX REECE
Reece's Rare Comics
Ijamsville, MD

GREG REECE
Reece's Rare Comics
Ijamsville, MD

ROB REYNOLDS
ComicConnect
New York, NY

STEPHEN RITTER
Worldwide Comics
Fair Oaks Ranch, TX

ROBERT ROGOVIN
Four Color Comics
Scarsdale, NY

CHUCK ROZANSKI
Mile High Comics
Denver, CO

BEN SAMUELS
Collector
St. Louis, MS

BARRY SANDOVAL
Heritage Auctions
Dallas, TX

BUDDY SAUNDERS
MyComicShop.com
Arlington, TX

CONAN SAUNDERS
MyComicShop.com
Arlington, TX

MATT SCHIFFMAN
Bronze Age Specialist
Bend, OR

PHIL SCHLAEFER
CPRS/Champion Comics
Sunnyvale, CA

DOUG SCHMELL
Pedigree Comics, Inc.
Wellington, FL

BRIAN SCHUTZER
Sparkle City Comics
Neat Stuff Collectibles
North Bergen, NJ

DYLAN SCHWARTZ
DylanUniverseComics.com
Great Neck, NY

ALIKA SEKI
Maui Comics and
Collectibles
Waiehu, HI

TODD SHEFFER
Hake's Americana
York, PA

FRANK SIMMONS
Coast to Coast Comics
Rocklin, CA

DOUG SIMPSON
Paradise Comics
Toronto, ONT Canada

MARC SIMS
Big B Comics
Barrie, ONT

LAUREN SISSELMAN
Comics Journalist
Baltimore, MD

ANTHONY SNYDER
Anthony's
Comic Book Art
Leonia, NJ

MARK SQUIREK
Collector/Historian
Baltimore, MD

TONY STARKS
Silver Age Specialist
Evansville, IN

WEST STEPHAN
CBCS
St Petersburg, FL

AL STOLTZ
Basement Comics
Havre de Grace, MD

DOUG SULIPA
"Everything 1960-1996"
Manitoba, Canada

CHRIS SWARTZ
Collector
San Diego, CA

MAGGIE THOMPSON
Collector/Historian
Iola, WI

MICHAEL TIERNEY
The Comic Book
Store
Little Rock, AR

TED VAN LIEW
Superworld Comics
Worcester, MA

JOE VERENEAULT
JHV Associates
Woodbury Heights, NJ

JASON VERSAGGI
Collector
Brooklyn, NY

JOSEPH VETERI, ESQ.
Comic Art Con
Springfield, NJ

TODD WARREN
Collector
Fort Washington, PA

BOB WAYNE
Collector
Fairfield, CT

JEFF WEAVER
Victory Comics
Falls Church, VA

LON WEBB
Dark Adventure
Comics
Norcross, GA

RICK WHITELOCK
New Force Comics
Lynn Haven, FL

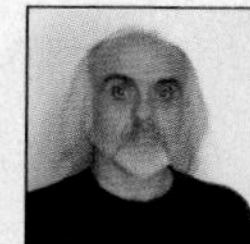

MIKE WILBUR
Diamond Int.
Galleries
Timonium, MD

ALEX WINTER
Hake's Americana
York, PA

HARLEY YEE
Dealer/Collector
Detroit, MI

MARK ZAID
EsquireComics.com
Bethesda, MD

VINCENT ZURZOLO, JR.
Metropolis
Collectibles, Inc.
New York, NY

OVERSTREET PRICE GUIDE BACK ISSUES

The Overstreet® Comic Book Price Guide has held the record for being the longest running annual comic book publication. We are now celebrating our 47th anniversary, and the demand for the Overstreet® price guides is very strong. Collectors have created a legitimate market for them, and they continue to bring record prices each year. Collectors also have a record of comic book prices going back further than any other source in comic fandom. The prices listed below are for NM condition only, with GD-25% and FN-50% of the NM value. Canadian editions exist for a couple of the early issues. Abbreviations: SC-softcover, HC-hardcover, L-leather bound.

1970
#1 White SC
$1825.00

1970
#1 Blue SC
(2nd Printing)
$1550.00

1972
#2 SC $650.00
#2 HC $1100.00

1973
#3 SC $325.00
#3 HC $950.00

1974
#4 SC $165.00
#4 HC $475.00

1975
#5 SC $155.00
#5 HC $260.00

1976
#6 SC $105.00
#6 HC $155.00

1977
#7 SC $155.00
#7 HC $230.00

1978
#8 SC $130.00
#8 HC $180.00

1979
#9 SC $130.00
#9 HC $180.00

1980
#10 SC $140.00
#10 HC $190.00

1981
#11 SC $85.00
#11 HC $115.00

1982

#12 SC $85.00
#12 HC $115.00

1983

#13 SC $85.00
#13 HC $115.00

1984

#14 SC $55.00
#14 HC $110.00
#14 L $170.00

1985

#15 SC $55.00
#15 HC $80.00
#15 L $160.00

1986

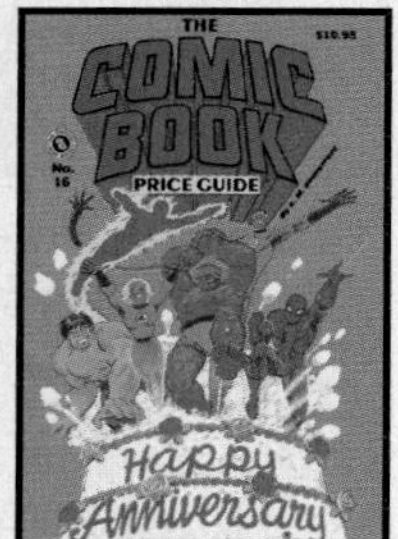

#16 SC $60.00
#16 HC $85.00
#16 L $170.00

1987

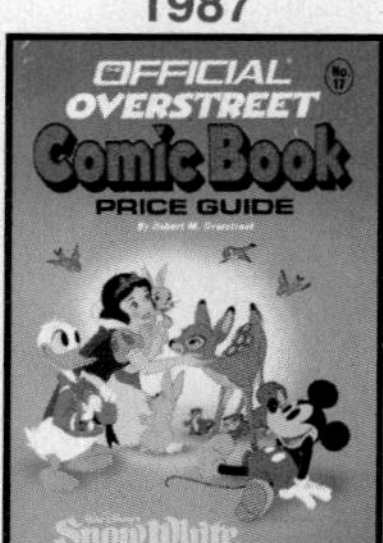

#17 SC $55.00
#17 HC $110.00
#17 L $160.00

1988

#18 SC $45.00
#18 HC $65.00
#18 L $160.00

1989

#19 SC $50.00
#19 HC $60.00
#19 L $170.00

1990

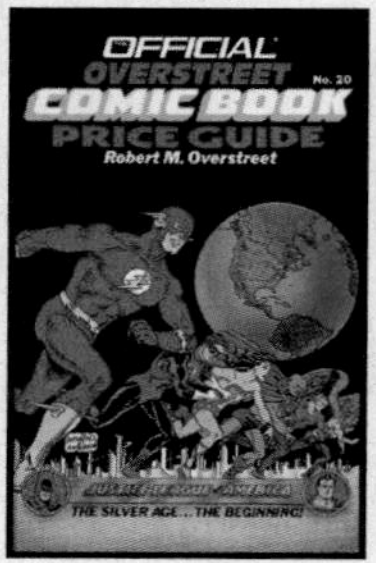

#20 SC $32.00
#20 HC $50.00
#20 L $135.00

1991

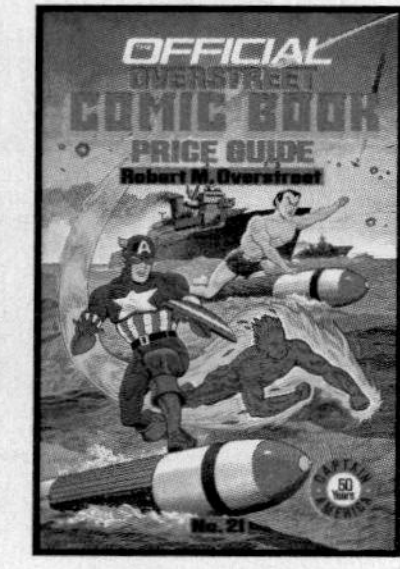

#21 SC $40.00
#21 HC $60.00
#21 L $145.00

1992

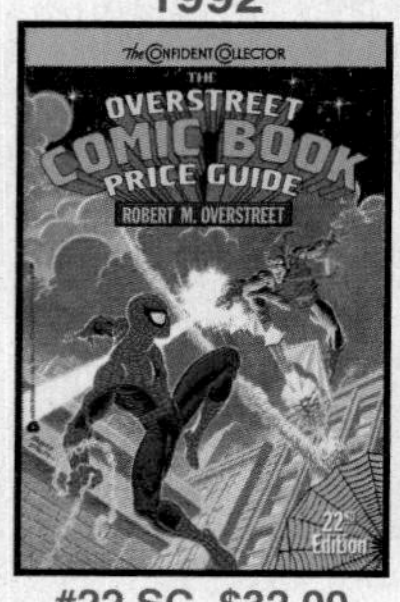

#22 SC $32.00
#22 HC $50.00

1993

#23 SC $32.00
#23 HC $50.00

1994

#24 SC $26.00
#24 HC $36.00

1995

#25 SC $26.00
#25 HC $36.00
#25 L $110.00

1996

#26 SC $20.00
#26 HC $30.00
#26 L $100.00

1997

#27 SC $22.00
#27 HC $38.00
#27 L $125.00

1997

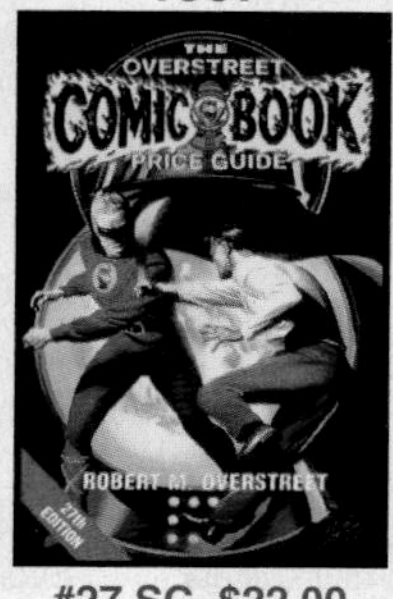

#27 SC $22.00
#27 HC $38.00
#27 L $125.00

1998

#28 SC $20.00
#28 HC $35.00

1998

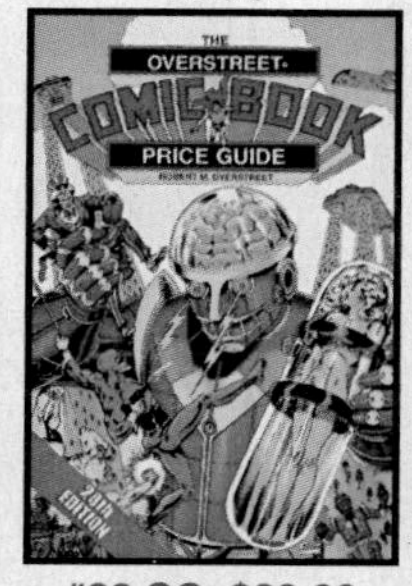

#28 SC $20.00
#28 HC $35.00

1999

#29 SC $25.00
#29 HC $40.00

1999

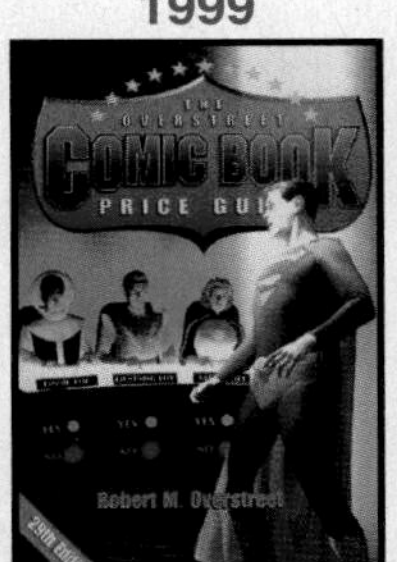

#29 SC $20.00
#29 HC $37.00

2000

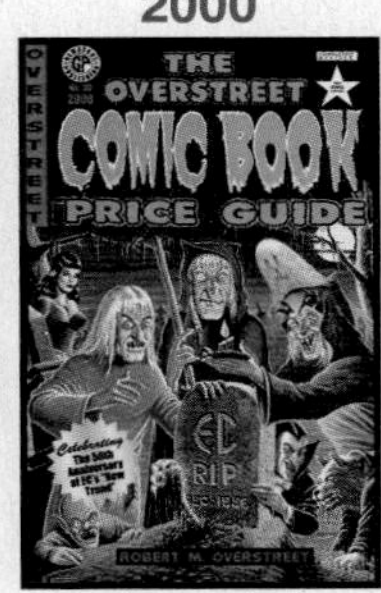

#30 SC $22.00
#30 HC $32.00

2000

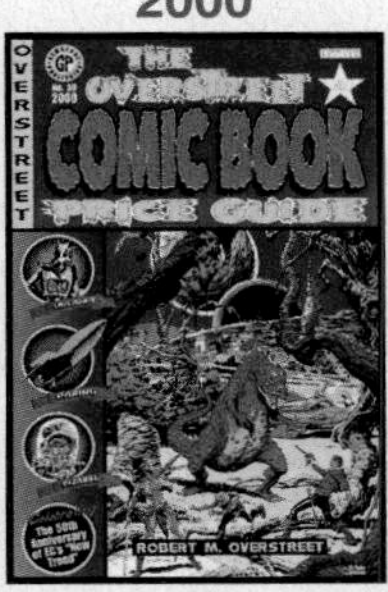

#30 SC $22.00
#30 HC $32.00

2001

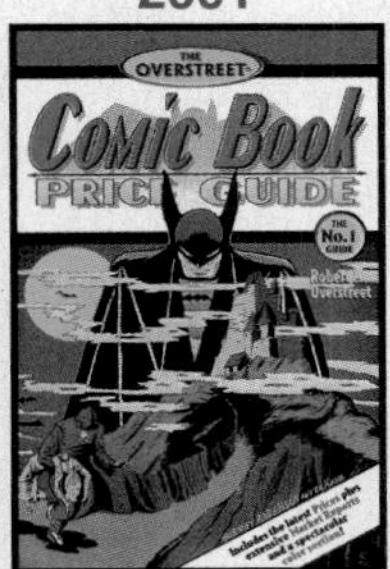

#31 SC $22.00
#31 HC $32.00

2001

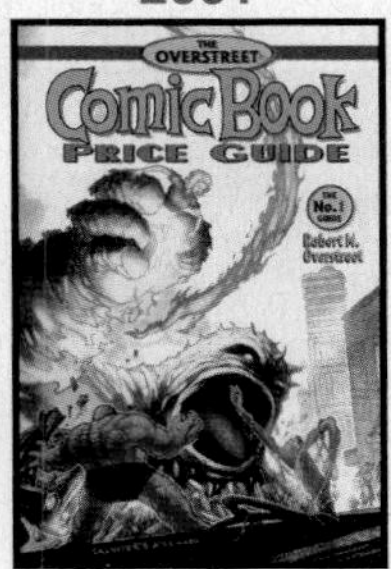

#31 SC $22.00
#31 HC $32.00

2001

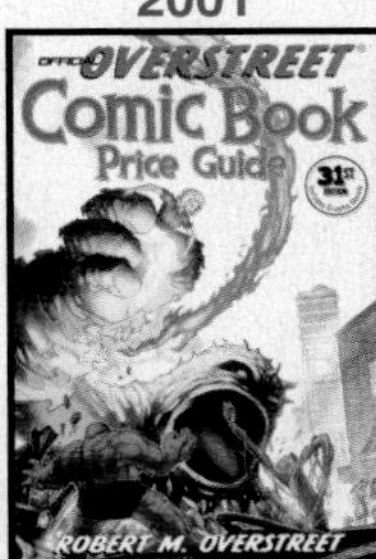

#31 Bookstore Ed.
SC only $22.00

2002

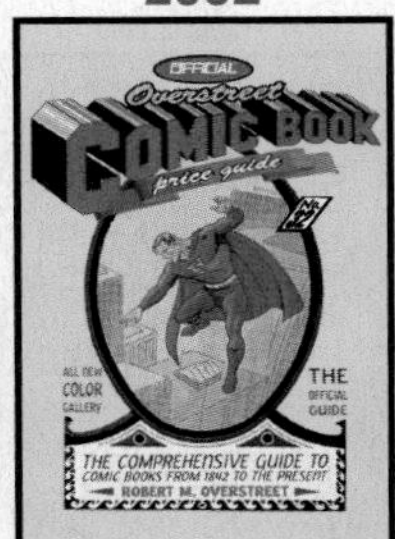

#32 SC $22.00
#32 HC $32.00

2002

#32 SC $22.00
#32 HC $32.00

2002

#32 Bookstore Ed.
SC only $22.00

2003

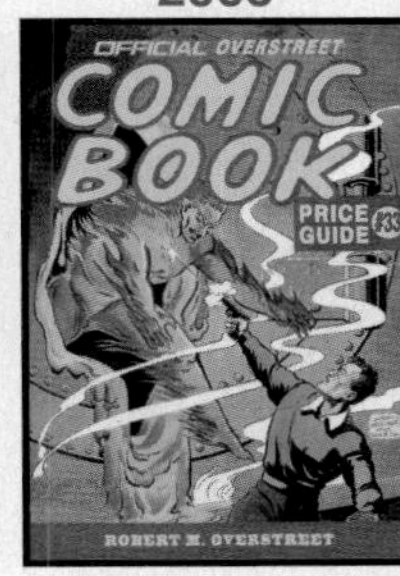

#33 SC $25.00
#33 HC $32.00

2003

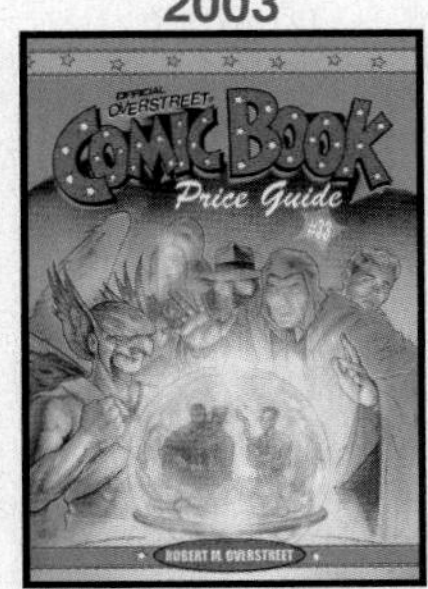

#33 SC $25.00
#33 HC $32.00

2003

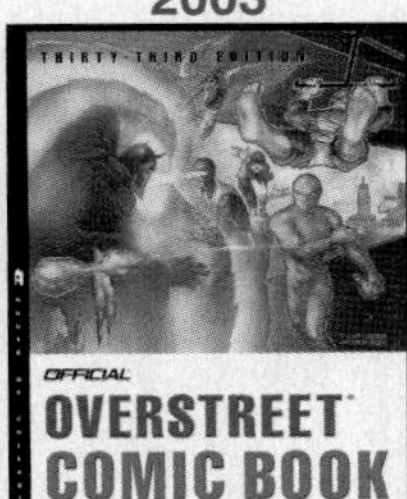

#33 Bookstore Ed.
SC only $25.00

2004

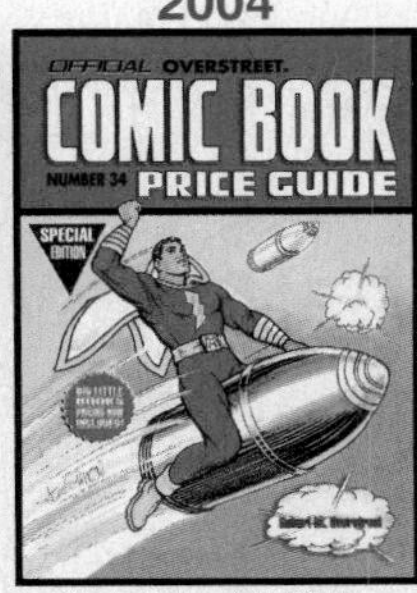

#34 SC $25.00
#34 HC $32.00

2004

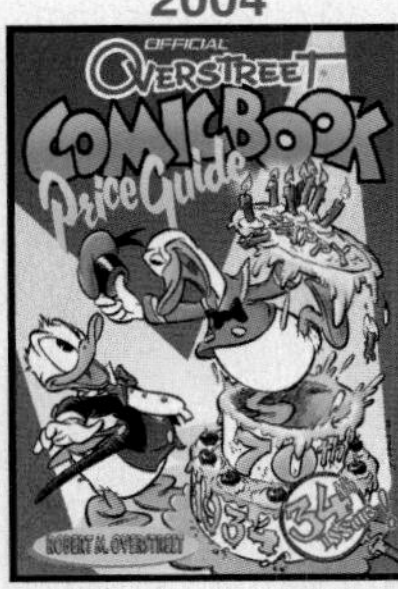

#34 SC $25.00
#34 HC $32.00

2004

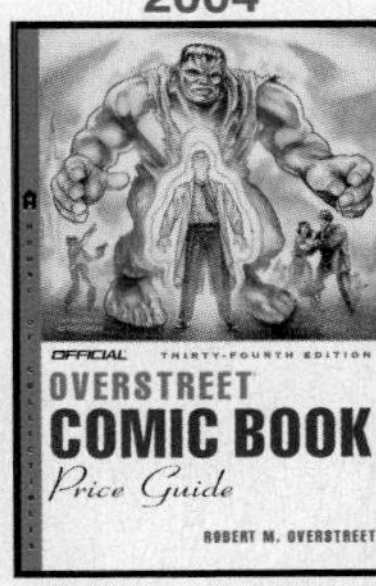

#34 Bookstore Ed.
SC only $25.00

2005

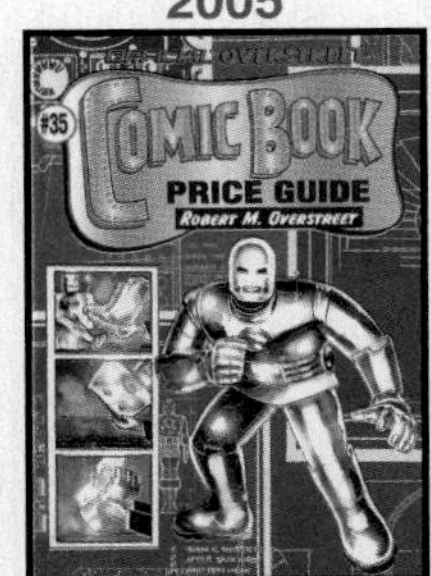

#35 SC $25.00
#35 HC $32.00

2005

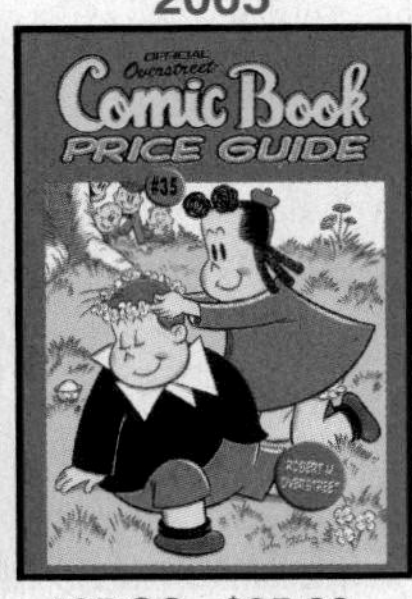

#35 SC $25.00
#35 HC $55.00

2005

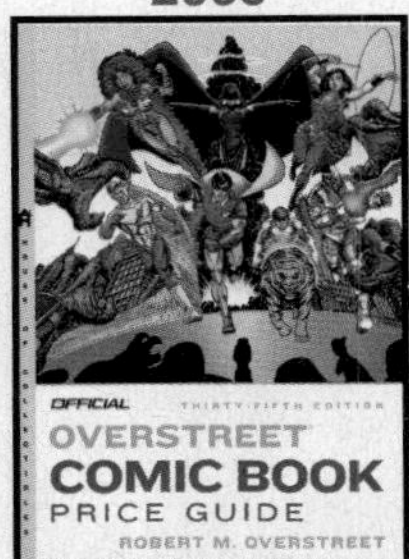

#35 Bookstore Ed.
SC only $25.00

2006

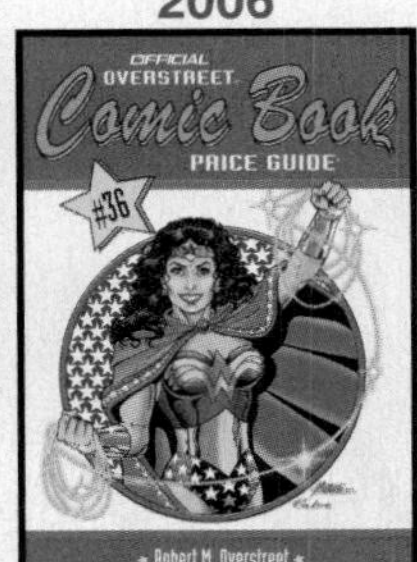

#36 SC $25.00
#36 HC $32.00

2006

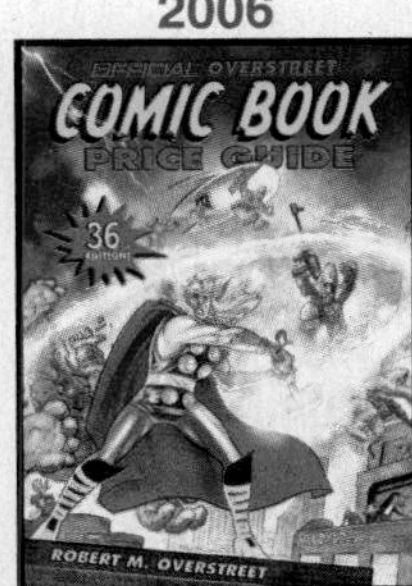

#36 SC $25.00
#36 HC $32.00

2006

#36 Bookstore Ed.
SC only $25.00

2007

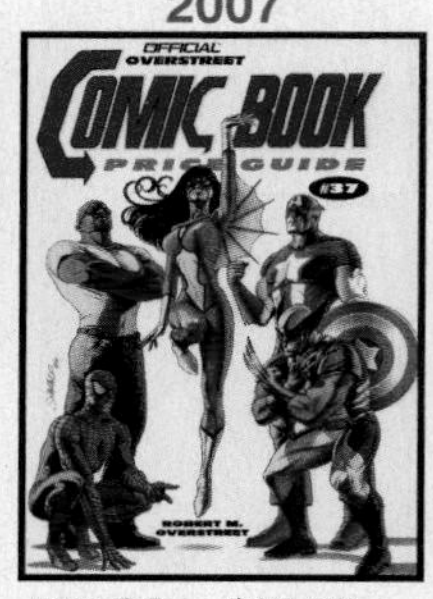

#37 SC $30.00
#37 HC $35.00

2007

#37 SC $30.00
#37 HC $35.00

2007

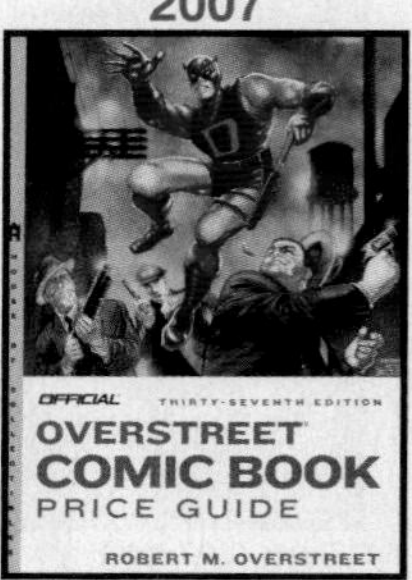

#37 Bookstore Ed.
SC only $30.00

2008

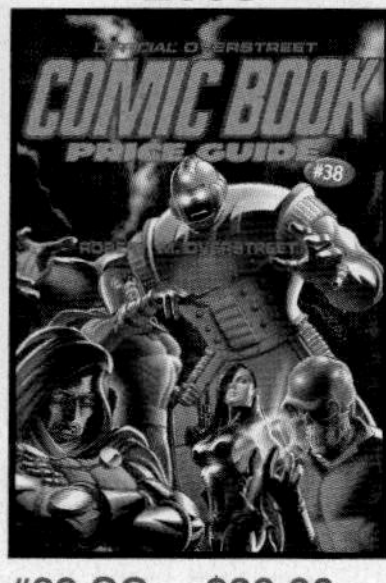

#38 SC $30.00
#38 HC $35.00

2008

#38 SC $30.00
#38 HC $35.00

2008

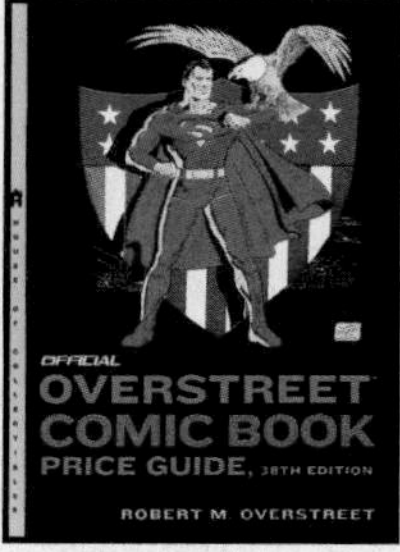

#38 Bookstore Ed.
SC only $30.00

2009

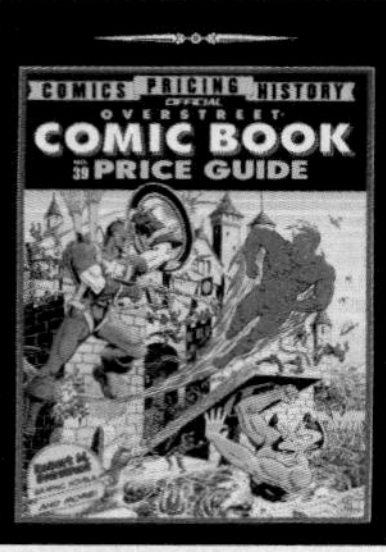

#39 SC $30.00
#39 HC $35.00

2009

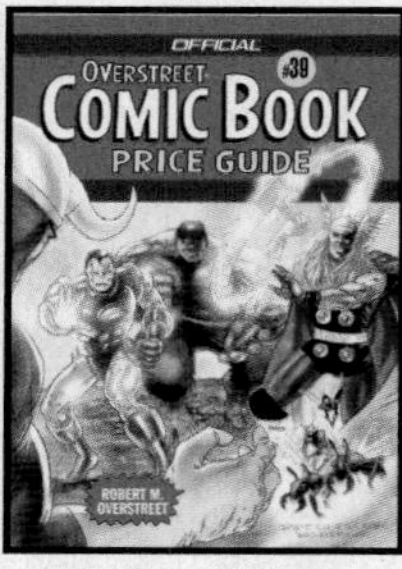

#39 SC $30.00
#39 HC $35.00

2009

#39 Bookstore Ed.
SC only $30.00

2010

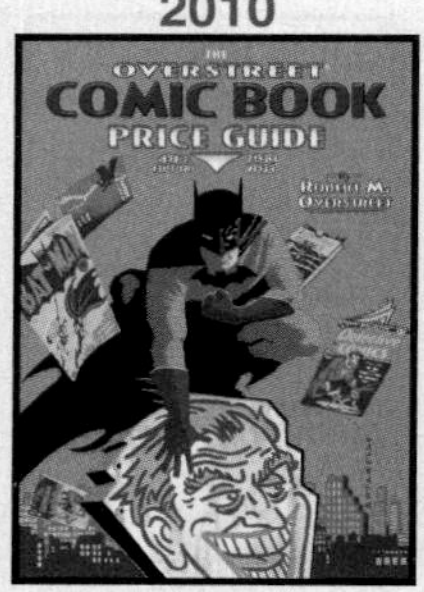

#40 SC $30.00
#40 HC $35.00

2010

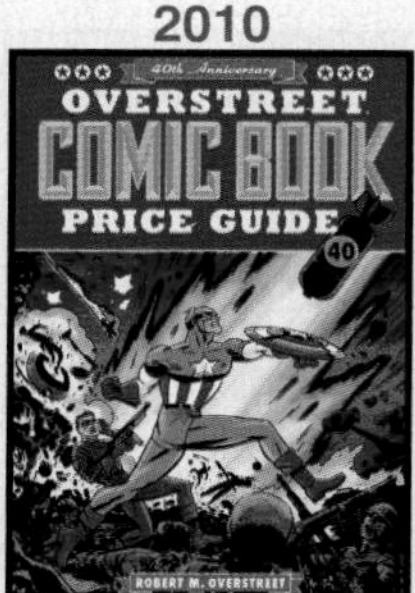

#40 SC $30.00
#40 HC $35.00

2010

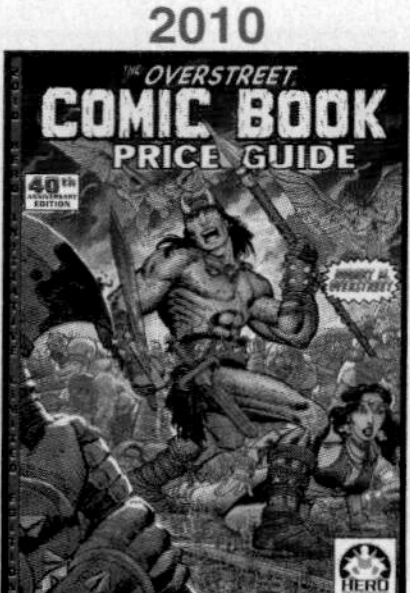

#40 HERO Initiative Ed.
HC only $35.00

2011

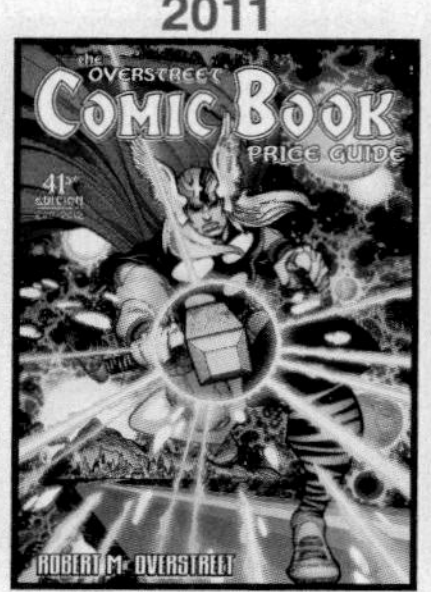

#41 SC $30.00
#41 HC $35.00

2011

#41 SC $30.00
#41 HC $35.00

2011

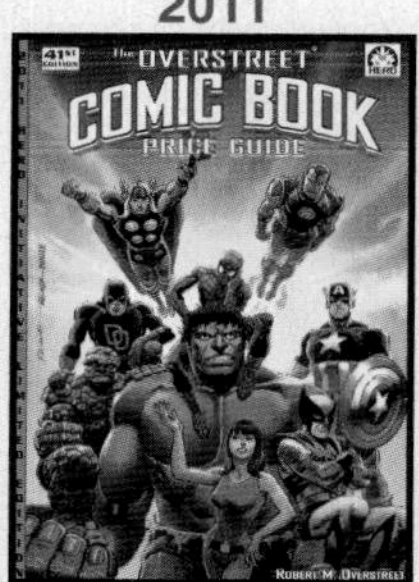

#41 HERO Initiative Ed.
HC only $35.00

2012

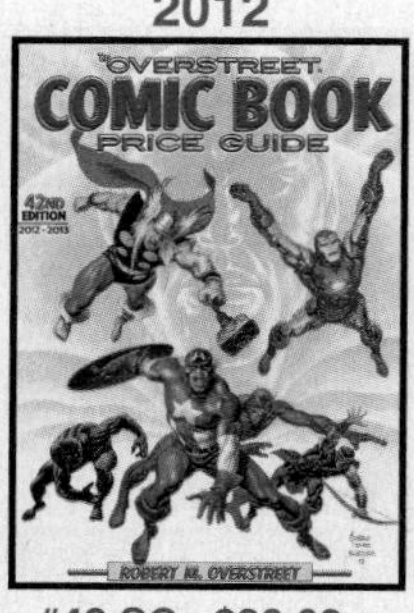

#42 SC $30.00
#42 HC $35.00

2012

#42 SC $30.00
#42 HC $35.00

2012

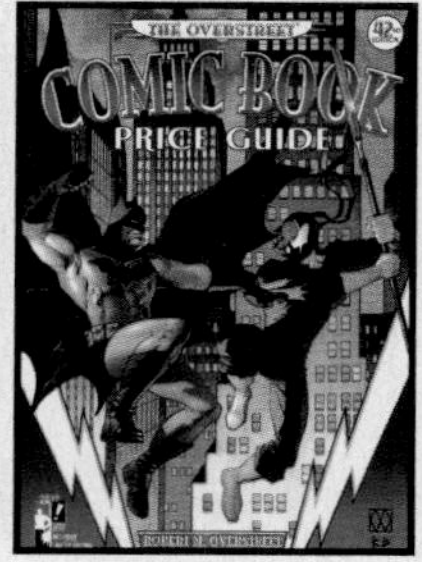

#42 HERO Initiative Ed.
HC only $35.00

2013

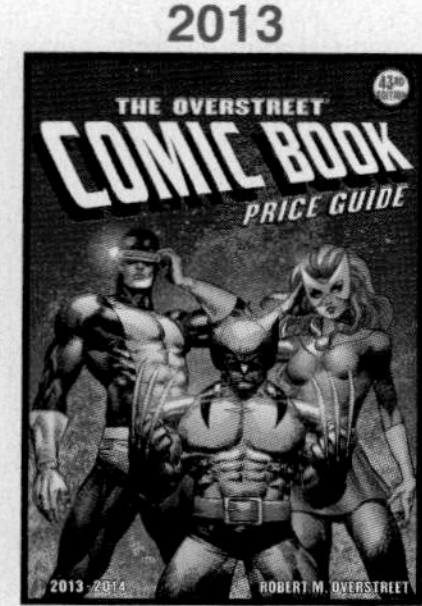

#43 SC $30.00
#43 HC $35.00

2013

#43 SC $30.00
#43 HC $35.00

2013

#43 HERO Initiative Ed.
HC only $35.00

2014

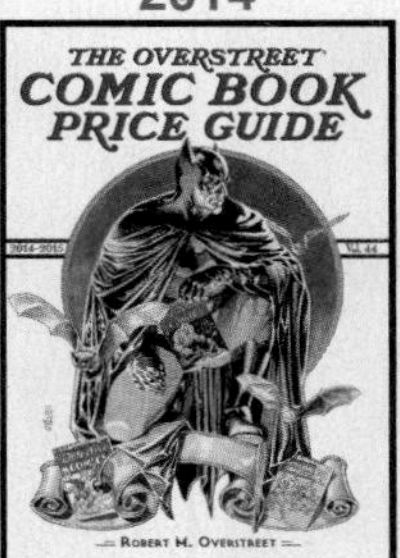

#44 SC $30.00
#44 HC $35.00

2014

#44 SC $30.00
#44 HC $35.00

2014

#44 HERO Initiative Ed.
HC only $35.00

2015

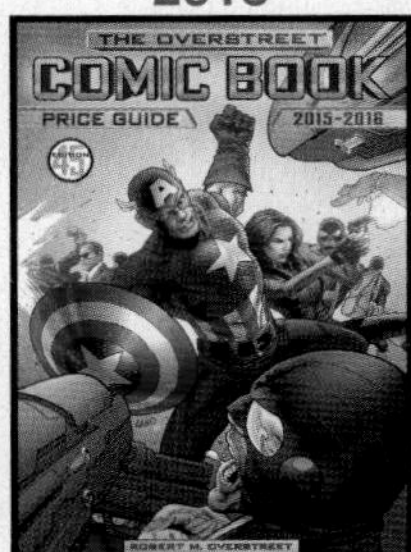

#45 SC $30.00
#45 HC $35.00

2015

#45 SC $30.00
#45 HC $35.00

2015

#45 SC $30.00
#45 HC $35.00

2015

#45 SC $30.00
#45 HC $35.00

2015

#45 HERO Initiative Ed.
HC only $35.00

2016

#46 SC $30.00
#46 HC $35.00

2016

#46 SC $30.00
#46 HC $35.00

2016

#46 SC $30.00
#46 HC $35.00

2016

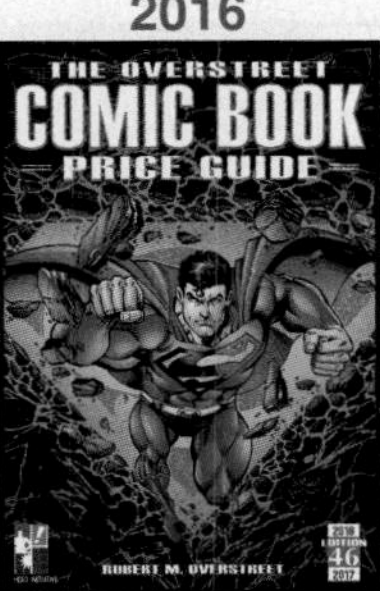

#46 HERO Initiative Ed.
HC only $35.00

BACK ISSUE GUIDES

Many (but not all!) backdate editions of *The Overstreet Comic Book Price Guide* are available for sale on the Gemstone Publishing website. All of the past editions we offer are as-new uncirculated copies (unless otherwise noted), and supplies on most are very limited.

www.gemstonepub.com

Or contact Mike Wilbur at (443) 318-8455 for more information.

2001

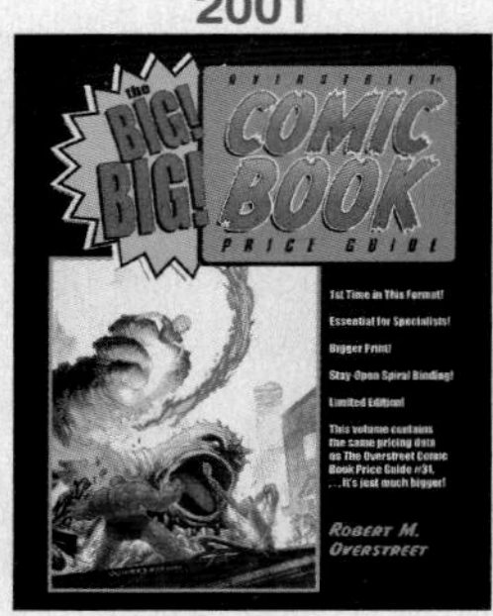

#31 Big Big CBPG
$35.00

2002

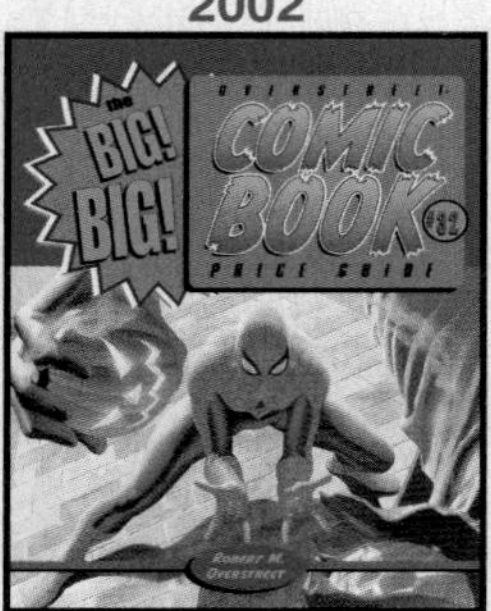

#32 Big Big CBPG
$35.00

2003

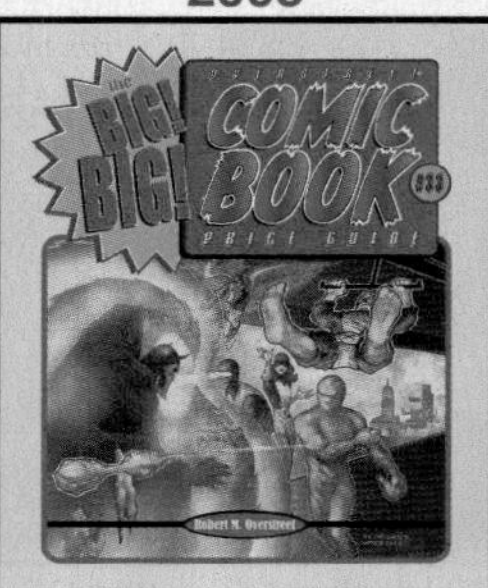

#33 Big Big CBPG
$37.00

2004

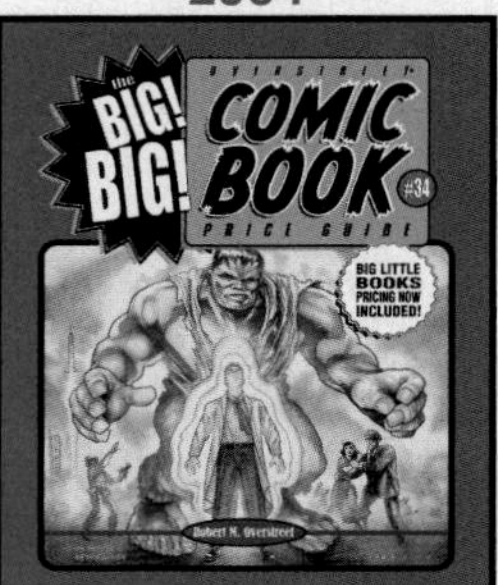

#34 Big Big CBPG
$37.00

2005

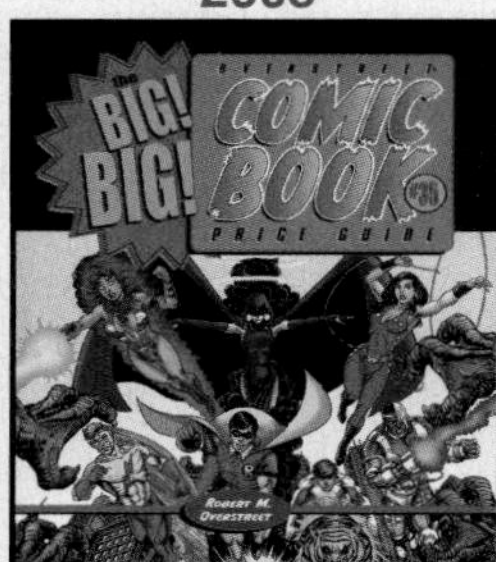

#35 Big Big CBPG
$37.00

2006

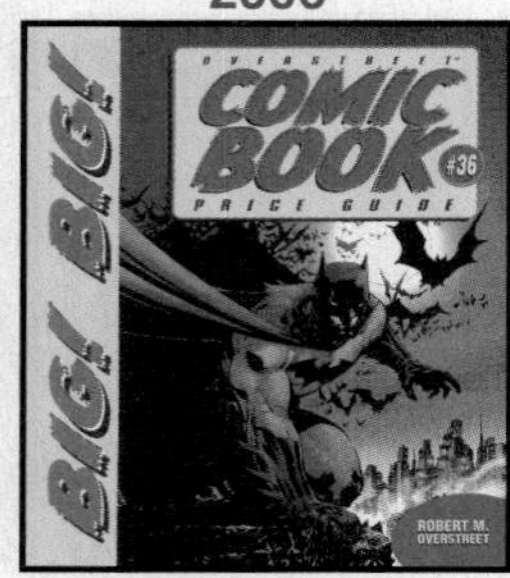

#36 Big Big CBPG
$37.00

2007

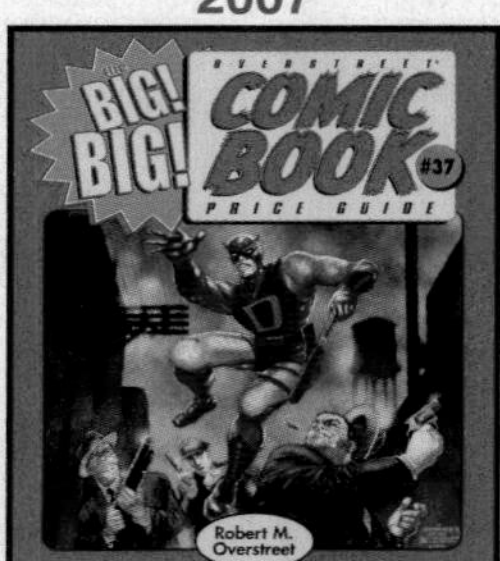

#37 Big Big CBPG
$37.00

2008

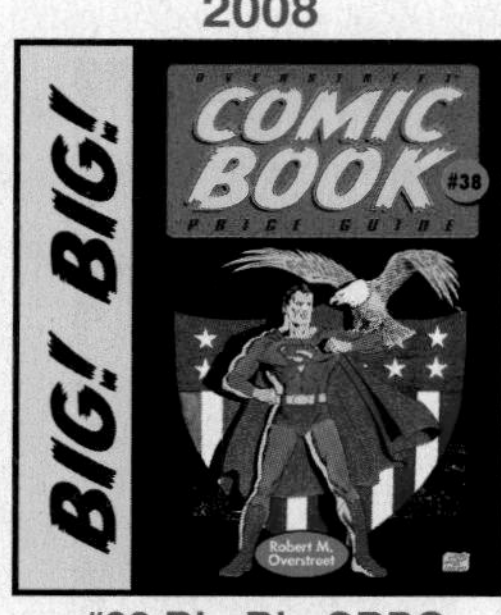

#38 Big Big CBPG
$37.00

2012

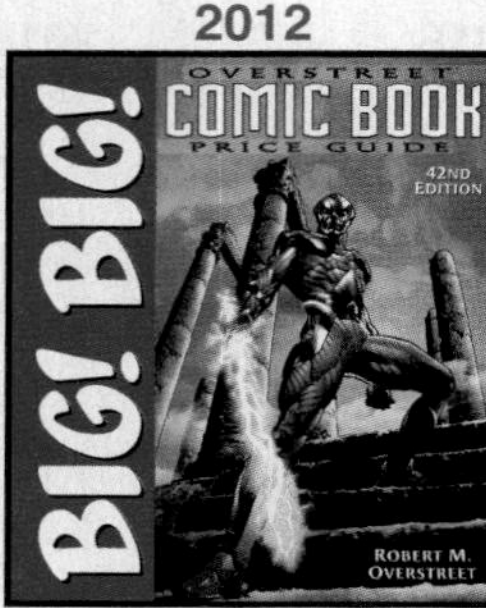

#42 Big Big CBPG
$45.00

2013

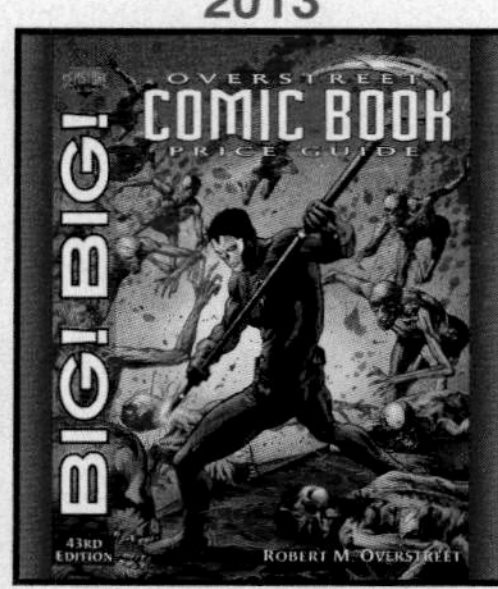

#43 Big Big CBPG
$45.00

2014

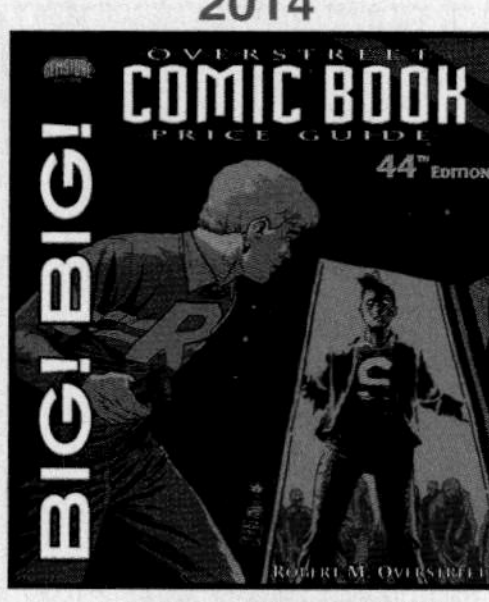

#44 Big Big CBPG
$45.00

2015

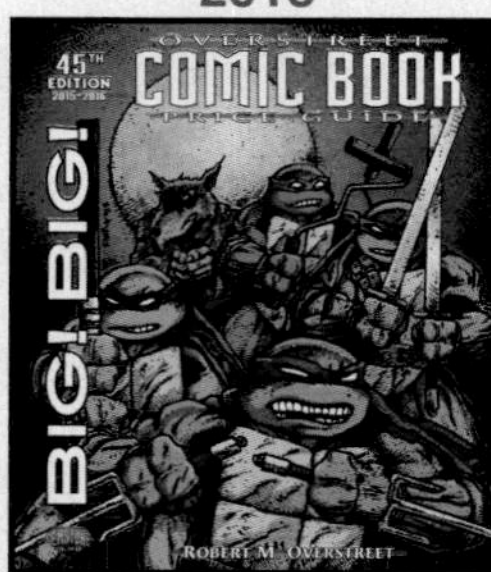

#45 Big Big CBPG
$47.50

2016

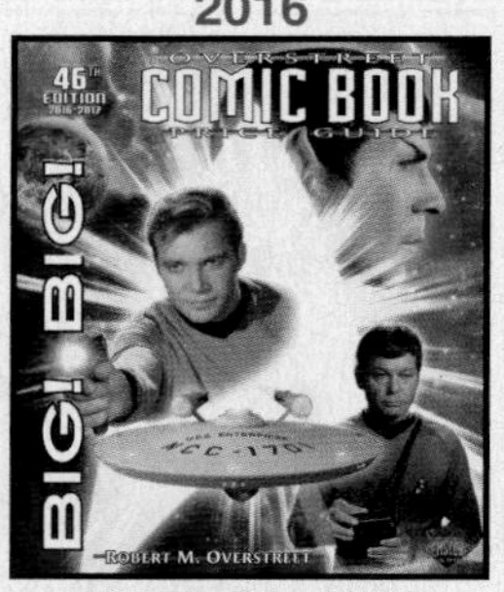

#46 Big Big CBPG
$47.50

ADVERTISERS' INDEX

A

B

C

D

E

F

G

H